A Concordance
to the plays and prefaces
# of Bernard Shaw

A Concordance
to the plays and prefaces
of Bernard Shaw

In Ten Volumes

VOLUME V

HONEST—LITTLE

Compiled by E. Dean Bevan

GALE RESEARCH COMPANY

The Book Tower · Detroit, Michigan 48226

Library of Congress Catalog Card Number 77-166191

Identification code used in this Concordance

The first 17 spaces of each line cite the source of the succeeding excerpt as follows:

The initial three or four characters identify the play or preface according to the title codes listed below.

To the right of this appears the dramatic or other division of the play. Acts are designated by roman numerals, scenes by Arabic numerals. Other dramatic divisions are designated as PROLOG, EPILOG and INTRLUD.

Prefaces are designated as PREFACE.

Page numbers are included in parentheses at the right. R indicates a Roman numeral.

For exceptions, special notations and discussions of the coding system, consult the sections *The Basic Text* (p. vi) and *The Citations* (p. x) in the Preface.

TITLE CODES

2TRU	*Too True to be Good*
3PLA	*Three Plays for Puritans* (Preface)
6CAL	*The Six of Calais*
ANNA	*Annajanska, the Bolshevik Empress*
APPL	*The Apple Cart*
ARMS	*Arms and the Man*
AUGS	*Augustus Does His Bit*
BARB	*Major Barbara*
BASH	*The Admirable Bashville*
BULL	*John Bull's Other Island*
BUOY	*Buoyant Billions*
CAND	*Candida*
CAPT	*Captain Brassbound's Conversion*
CATH	*Great Catherine*
CLEO	*Caesar and Cleopatra*
CURE	*The Music-Cure*
CYMB	*Cymbeline Refinished*
DEST	*The Man of Destiny*
DEVL	*The Devil's Disciple*
DOCT	*The Doctor's Dilemma*
FABL	*Farfetched Fables*
FANY	*Fanny's First Play*
FOUN	*The Fascinating Foundling*
GENV	*Geneva*
GETT	*Getting Married*
GLIM	*The Glimpse of Reality*
HART	*Heartbreak House*
INCA	*The Inca of Perusalem*
JITT	*Jitta's Atonement*
JOAN	*Saint Joan*
KING	*"In Good King Charles's Golden Days"*
LADY	*The Dark Lady of the Sonnets*
LIED	*How He Lied to Her Husband*
LION	*Androcles and the Lion*
METH	*Back to Methuselah* (Preface)
MILL	*The Millionairess*
MIS.	*Misalliance*
MRS	*Mrs. Warren's Profession*
MTH1	*Back to Methuselah*, Part I
MTH2	*Back to Methuselah*, Part II
MTH3	*Back to Methuselah*, Part III
MTH4	*Back to Methuselah*, Part IV
MTH5	*Back to Methuselah*, Part V
NEVR	*You Never Can Tell*
O'FL	*O'Flaherty V.C.*
OVER	*Overruled*
PHIL	*The Philanderer*
PLES	*The Four Pleasant Plays* (Preface)
POSN	*The Shewing-Up of Blanco Posnet*
PPP	*Passion, Poison, and Petrifaction*
PRES	*Press Cuttings*
PYGM	*Pygmalion*

ROCK	*On the Rocks*	TRFL	*Trifles and Tomfooleries* (Preface)
SHAK	*Shakes Versus Shav*	UNPL	*The Three Unpleasant Plays* (Preface)
SIM	*The Simpleton of the Unexpected Isles*	VWOO	*Village Wooing*
SUPR	*Man and Superman*	WIDO	*Widower's Houses*

SEQUENCE OF COMPUTER CHARACTERS

The sequence of characters below has been followed in both first- and second-field ordering (*see* Preface, p. ix):

: ? A B C D E F G H I . (J K L M N O
P Q R - ') ; S T U V W X Y Z , " !

Roman numerals are alphabetized as letters. For Arabic numerals occurring in the text, see Volume I, pp. 1-14.

GETT (299)	WHY IS THE MAN ALWAYS TO BE PUT IN THE WRONG? BE	HONEST	, EDITH. WHY WERENT YOU DRESSED? WERE YOU GOING TO
CAPT I (221)	DETERMINEDLY) AND THE SOMEONE WAS A VERRA	HONEST	, STRAIGHTFORWARD MAN, AS FAR AS I COULD JUDGE.
GETT (280)	MEN IS RIDICULOUS. SOMEBODY MUST MARRY THE PLAIN,	HONEST	, STUPID FELLOWS. HAVE YOU THOUGHT OF THAT? /LEO/
SUPR III (81)	I HAVE SEEN MEN LESS GIFTED, AND I'LL SWEAR LESS	HONEST	, SUPPING AT THE SAVOY ON FOIE GRAS AND CHAMPAGNE.
MIS. PREFACE(94)	BUT THIS OBJECTIVITY, THOUGH INTELLECTUALLY	HONEST	, TELLS THE CHILD ONLY WHAT OTHER PEOPLE BELIEVE.
BULL IV (176)	MADMAN WHO CALLS THE ASS HIS BROTHER-- AND A VERY	HONEST	, USEFUL AND FAITHFUL BROTHER TOO. THE ASS, SIR, IS
BARB PREFACE(213)	BE SACRIFICED, IS NOT TO BE POOR. " POOR BUT	HONEST	," " THE RESPECTABLE POOR," AND SUCH PHRASES ARE AS
		HONESTER	
GETT PREFACE(220)	WOULD BE FAR BETTER FOR EVERYONE, AS WELL AS FAR	HONESTER	, IF YOUNG PEOPLE WERE TAUGHT THAT WHAT THEY CALL
DOCT PREFACE(69)	ROGUES WILL HAVE A MUCH STRONGER, BECAUSE A MUCH	HONESTER	, INCENTIVE TO BE NOT ONLY GOOD CITIZENS BUT ACTIVE
		HONESTEST	
CAPT I (220)	IN THAT WAY. /DRINKWATER/ MAWT YEPPN TO THE	HONESTEST	, BEST MEANIN PUSSON, AW DO ASSURE YER, GAVNER.
		HONESTLY	
MIS. PREFACE(59)	WRITING, AND ENOUGH ARITHMETIC TO USE MONEY	HONESTLY	AND ACCURATELY, TOGETHER WITH THE RUDIMENTS OF LAW
MILL IV (205)	TO SUPPORT ME FOR A HUNDRED YEARS. I DID IT	HONESTLY	AND LEGITIMATELY. I EXPLAINED THE WAY IN WHICH IT
JOAN 6 (130)	SIMPLETONS FOR LIARS AND HYPOCRITES. THEY BELIEVE	HONESTLY	AND SINCERELY THAT THEIR DIABOLICAL INSPIRATION IS
METH PREFACE(R16)	BECAUSE THEIR EDUCATION AS SLAYERS HAS BEEN	HONESTLY	AND THOROUGHLY CARRIED OUT. ESSENTIALLY THE RULERS
POSN PREFACE(426)	IT IS NO MORE POSSIBLE FOR ME TO DO MY WORK	HONESTLY	AS A PLAYWRIGHT WITHOUT GIVING PAIN THAN IT IS FOR
CAND I (90)	MORE THAN IN THE OTHER. SO LONG AS YOU COME HERE	HONESTLY	AS A SELF-RESPECTING, THOROUGH, CONVINCED
SUPR PREFACE(R24)	THE SUN IN THE SOLAR SYSTEM: HE LOOKED FOR IT AS	HONESTLY	AS A SHEPHERD SEEKS HIS PATH IN A MIST. BUT
CAND III (132)	I HAVE NO DOUBT YOU CONDUCTED THE TRANSACTION AS	HONESTLY	AS IF YOU WERE BUYING A POUND OF CHEESE. (HE STOPS
MTH2 (64)	TO STEER IT CLEAR OF UTOPIAN ABSURDITIES. I CAN	HONESTLY	ASK FOR YOUR SUPPORT ON THE MOST ADVANCED SOCIALIST
JOAN PREFACE(5)	WOUNDS THEIR VANITY, BUT QUITE HUMBLY AND	HONESTLY	BECAUSE IT FRIGHTENS THEM. FEAR WILL DRIVE MEN TO
FABL PREFACE(74)	RECEIVE ME ON SUCH TERMS, OR INTO WHICH I COULD	HONESTLY	CONSENT TO BE RECEIVED? THERE ARE SHAW SOCIETIES;
2TRU PREFACE(14)	OF SLAVERY. 9. PEOPLE WHO THINK THEY CAN BE	HONESTLY	FREE ALL THE TIME ARE IDIOTS: PEOPLE WHO SEEK
ROCK II (240)	TO ARTHUR, YOU ARE PLEDGED NOW TO GIVE US OUR PAY	HONESTLY	FREE OF INCOME TAX AND MAKE THESE LAZY IDLE LUBBERS
MTH3 (95)	MANNED BY CHINESE, THE COUNTRY HAS BEEN WELL AND	HONESTLY	GOVERNED. WHAT MORE IS NEEDED? /BURGE-LUBIN/ WHAT
CAND I (91)	DECISION) SHAKE HANDS, BURGESS. NOW YOURE TALKING	HONESTLY	. I DONT THINK THEYLL MAKE ME A BISHOP; BUT IF THEY
GLIM (183)	A GOOD ONE OR NO: IT IS FOR ME TO EARN HIS MONEY	HONESTLY	. WHEN I SAID I SHOULD NOT LIKE TO KILL A MAN WITH
MILL I (157)	SLENDER RESOURCES AT AN APPALLING RATE, I SHOULD	HONESTLY	LIKE A FEW LESSONS FROM ALASTAIR IN THE ART OF
CATH PREFACE(155)	INSULAR THAN ANY BRITON, I WILL NOT PLEAD, AS I	HONESTLY	MIGHT, THAT THE FICTION HAS YET TO BE WRITTEN THAT
DOCT PREFACE(65)	THE WORK-DAY OF 24 HOURS, AND THE USELESSNESS OF	HONESTLY	PRESCRIBING WHAT MOST OF THE PATIENTS REALLY NEED:
CAND I SD(85)	BUT HE HAS NO SUSPICION OF THIS HIMSELF, AND	HONESTLY	REGARDS HIS COMMERCIAL PROSPERITY AS THE INEVITABLE
SUPR III (81)	THE DAUGHTERS OF THE ENGLISH PEERAGE; AND I CAN	HONESTLY	SAY THAT I WOULD HAVE SOLD THE LOT, FACES, DOWRIES,
GETT PREFACE(224)	CHANGE BOTH OF FATHERS AND MOTHERS. NOW I CANNOT	HONESTLY	SAY THAT THESE AND SIMILAR CASES HAVE CONVINCED ME
MTH2 (71)	WHAT HAS JUST PASSED I SINCERELY WISH I COULD	HONESTLY	SAY YES, BURGE. BUT IT SEEMS TO ME THAT YOU HAVE
POSN PREFACE(367)	FORM THE INTELLECTUAL FABRIC OF THE PLAY, AND MAY	HONESTLY	SEE NOTHING BUT AN ORDINARY " CHARACTER PART" IN A
NEVR II (257)	/VALENTINE/ THROWN THIS ENCHANTMENT ON ME. I'M	HONESTLY	TRYING TO BE SENSIBLE AND SCIENTIFIC AND EVERYTHING
DOCT PREFACE(35)	DOWN HIS HOUSE TO ROAST HIS PIG WAS NO DOUBT	HONESTLY	UNABLE TO CONCEIVE ANY LESS DISASTROUS WAY OF
MRS III (223)	THE OLD GIRL BACK TO TOWN SOMEHOW, PRAED. COME!	HONESTLY	, DEAR PRADDY, DO YOU LIKE SEEING THEM TOGETHER?
LIED (191)	WITHOUT CONCEALMENT OR SUBTERFUGE, FREELY AND	HONESTLY	, IN FULL HONOR AND SELF-RESPECT. /SHE/ (STARING
APPL I (208)	MAN MYSELF, THERE MAY BE SOMETHING IN THAT. BUT	HONESTLY	, MAGNUS, AS MAN TO MAN, DO YOU TELL ME YOUD RATHER
MTH3 (126)	ENOUGH TO SAY THAT I FRIGHTEN YOU. /BURGE-LUBIN/	HONESTLY	, YOU DO. AND WILL YOU THINK ME VERY RUDE IF I SAY
BUOY III (38)	NOR I WITH HIM. WE WERE BOTH SANE. YET WE CAN SAY	HONESTLY	" WHOM GOD HATH JOINED"-- /SIR F./ OH, DO PLEASE
		HONESTY	
2TRU II (56)	AND A NOTE TO SAY THAT MY FAVOR CAN BE EARNED BY	HONESTY	AND DILIGENCE, BUT NOT PURCHASED. /MEEK/ THEY WONT
3PLA PREFACE(R31)	PESSIMISM THERE IS A CHOICE BETWEEN INTELLECTUAL	HONESTY	AND DISHONESTY. HOGARTH DREW THE RAKE AND THE HARLOT
DOCT PREFACE(18)	MAY HAVE TO FOUND HIS SELF-RESPECT ON SOBRIETY,	HONESTY	AND INDUSTRY; BUT A NAPOLEON NEEDS NO SUCH PROPS FOR
FANY PROLOG (264)	OF DIVISION OF LABOR TOO FAR, THIS KEEPING OF THE	HONESTY	AND THE OTHER QUALITIES IN SEPARATE COMPARTMENTS.
BARB III (320)	HIGH EXPLOSIVES; BUT YOURE ALL READY TO HANDLE	HONESTY	AND TRUTH AND JUSTICE AND THE WHOLE DUTY OF MAN, AND
CAND III (143)	TO OFFER YOU BUT MY STRENGTH FOR YOUR DEFENCE, MY	HONESTY	FOR YOUR SURETY, MY ABILITY AND INDUSTRY FOR YOUR
HART II (116)	IS THAT THE ONLY REASON? ARE YOU QUITE SURE	HONESTY	HAS NOTHING TO DO WITH IT? /ELLIE/ OH, YOU ARE VERY
2TRU I (41)	ZOO. NO: I AM NOT GOING TO STEAL THOSE JEWELS.	HONESTY	IS THE BEST POLICY. I HAVE ANOTHER IDEA, AND A MUCH
2TRU III (91)	ME MUNIFICENTLY. HENCE MY PRESENT OPULENCE.	HONESTY	IS THE BEST POLICY-- SOMETIMES. /THE ELDER/ WORSE
3PLA PREFACE(R23)	OF SENSUOUS ECSTASY FOR INTELLECTUAL ACTIVITY AND	HONESTY	IS THE VERY DEVIL. IT HAS ALREADY BROUGHT US TO
SUPR HANDBOK(223)	SUBORDINATION AS FEAR OF THE POLICE SIMULATES	HONESTY	. DISOBEDIENCE, THE RAREST AND MOST COURAGEOUS OF
MRS PREFACE(163)	MIND! PRAY DO NOT THINK THAT I QUESTION HIS	HONESTY	. I AM QUITE SURE THAT HE SINCERELY THINKS ME A
2TRU III (93)	NO DOUBT I SHALL BE ABLE TO AFFORD THE LUXURY OF	HONESTY	. I LEARNT THAT FROM MY RELIGIOUS EDUCATION. /THE
DOCT II (128)	SIMPLER STILL IF DUBEDAT HAD SOME OF BLENKINSOP'S	HONESTY	. THE WORLD ISNT GOING TO BE MADE SIMPLE FOR YOU, MY
FABL PREFACE(76)	IF IT IS TO BE CREDITED WITH THE INTELLECTUAL	HONESTY	NECESSARY TO ITS INFLUENCE AND AUTHORITY. SHAKE THAT
BARB II SD(273)	ENOUGH TO BE CAPABLE OF ANYTHING IN REASON EXCEPT	HONESTY	OR ALTRUISTIC CONSIDERATIONS OF ANY KIND. THE WOMAN
2TRU III (111)	A THIEF WHO AT HIS FIRST GREAT THEFT HAS FOUND	HONESTY	THE BEST POLICY AND RESTORED HIS BOOTY TO ITS OWNER.
MIS. PREFACE(97)	ADMIRING IT IS LIKE GIVING A PRIZE FOR	HONESTY	TO A MAN WHO HAS NOT STOLEN YOUR WATCH BECAUSE HE
BULL PREFACE(23)	EXISTENCE OF ANY MYSTERIOUS IRISH PLUCK, IRISH	HONESTY	, IRISH BIAS ON THE PART OF PROVIDENCE, OR STERLING
MILL PREFACE(128)	TO EARN HIS OWN LIVING AS A MATTER OF ELEMENTARY	HONESTY	, OR THAT DOES NOT EXALT VAST PERSONAL RICHES AND
		HONEY	
CATH 1 (162)	THE LADY, HOLDING THE DOOR HANDLE) LITTLE DARLING	HONEY	: IS HIS HIGHNESS THE PRINCE VERY BUSY? /VARINKA/ HIS
SUPR PREFACE(R19)	OR THE CANAANITE) SMOKED OUT AND UNLOADED OF HIS	HONEY	BY BEINGS INFERIOR TO HIMSELF IN SIMPLE
SIM I (41)	ARE SWEET AND PURE. /THE DARK ONE/ " FOR HE ON	HONEY	DEW HATH FED"-- /THE FAIR ONE/ -- " AND DRUNK THE MILK
MTH1 II (30)	EVEN A BEAR WOULD NOT EAT A MAN IF IT COULD GET	HONEY	INSTEAD. /CAIN/ I DO NOT WANT TO BE A BEAR. I DO NOT
LADY (240)	SLEEP, FAIR ONE; FOR THEN YOUR WORDS DROP LIKE	HONEY	. /THE LADY/ (WITH COLD MAJESTY) KNOW YOU TO WHOM YOU
CLEO NOTES (203)	PLENTY OF HONEY TIL IT GETS THE CONSISTENCY OF	HONEY	; THEN THE BEAR'S GREASE AND MARROW TO BE MIXED (WHEN
CLEO NOTES (203)	TO BE POUNDED WHEN DRY, AND MIXED WITH PLENTY OF	HONEY	TIL IT GETS THE CONSISTENCY OF HONEY; THEN THE BEAR'S
GENV IV (120)	THEY WORK LIKE BEES AND KEEP BARELY ENOUGH OF THE	HONEY	TO KEEP THEMSELVES MISERABLY ALIVE. RUSSIA BELONGS TO
FABL IV (114)	TO LIVE ON PLANTS AND FRUITS, AND EVEN ON GRASS,	HONEY	, AND NUTS: A DIET WHICH THEY CALLED VEGETARIAN. FULL
CLEO NOTES (203)	IT THAT YOU FIRST MIXED THE SOLID POWDERS WITH	HONEY	, AND THEN ADDED THE GREASE. I EXPECT CLEOPATRA
LION PREFACE(22)	CLOTHED IN SKINS AND LIVING ON LOCUSTS AND WILD	HONEY	, PRACTISING A SAVAGE AUSTERITY. HE COURTED MARTYRDOM,
GENV I (41)	HERE YOU HAND ME A MOUTHFUL. WHAT A SCOOP FOR ME,	HONEY	! YOU ARE A PEACH. (HE KISSES HER). SOMEONE KNOCKS
		HONEYED	
BASH III (122)	LORD WORTHINGTON BY NAME, THIS MORNING CAME WITH	HONEYED	WORDS BESEECHING ME TO MOUNT HIS FOUR-IN-HAND, AND
		HONEYMOON	
PYGM EPILOG (294)	MRS EYNSFORD HILL, WOULD HAVE SPENT A PENNILESS	HONEYMOON	BUT FOR A WEDDING PRESENT OF 500 POUNDS FROM THE
DOCT II (125)	THIRTY POUNDS SAVED; AND WE SPENT IT ALL ON OUR	HONEYMOON	IN THREE WEEKS, AND A LOT MORE THAT HE BORROWED.
2TRU II (65)	I SAY IS THAT A LOVE AFFAIR SHOULD ALWAYS BE A	HONEYMOON	. AND THE ONLY WAY TO MAKE SURE OF THAT IS TO KEEP
SUPR IV (164)	TANNER) IVE COME TO SAY GOODBYE. I'M OFF FOR MY	HONEYMOON	. /MRS WHITEFIELD/ (CRYING) OH, DONT SAY THAT,
MILL I (145)	NEVER SHALL I FORGET THE DAY-- IT WAS DURING OUR	HONEYMOON	-- WHEN HIS COLDNESS INFURIATED ME TO SUCH A
GETT PREFACE(190)	OF HEALTH AND TEMPERANCE; INAUGURATED A LIFE-LONG	HONEYMOON	; AND PLACED THEIR PLEASURES ON EXACTLY THE SAME
WIDO II (28)	FOR A COUPLE OF MONTHS, IF WE CARE TO PASS OUR	HONEYMOON	THERE. (HE HANDS SARTORIUS ANOTHER LETTER). IT'S
		HONEYMOONED	
BASH III (124)	A TEARSTAINED NOTE TO TESTIFY THAT HAVING SWEETLY	HONEYMOONED	WITH ME, HE NOW COULD SAY, O DEATH, WHERE IS THY
		HONEYSUCKLE	
VWOO 2 (132)	/Z/ NO; BUT I USED TO SING A SONG CALLED THE	HONEYSUCKLE	AND THE BEE. /A/ (RESOLUTELY) GOOD MORNING. (
		HONG	
BUOY III (27)	IS NOT HOLY. WE ARE IN BELGRAVE SQUARE, NOT IN	HONG	KONG. /THE PRIEST/ SIR: IN MANY OLD ENGLISH HOUSES
		HONKING	
MILL II SD(173)	MY CHAUFFEUR COMES BACK. THE MOTOR HORN IS HEARD	HONKING	, /THE DOCTOR/ HE HAS COME BACK. /EPIFANIA/ DAMN!

2TRU II	(77)	LOOK AT THAT ELECTRIC HORN THERE. IF IT STARTS	HONKING	, LOOK OUT; FOR IT WILL MEAN THAT A BODY OF
			HONLY	
CAND I	(91)	THEYLL AVE TO GIVE YOU SOMETHINK SOMEDAY, IF IT'S	HONLY	TO STOP YOUR MOUTH. YOU AD THE RIGHT INSTINC ARTER
			HONOR	
SUPR I	(13)	DONT, TAVY: YOULL MAKE ME ILL. I AM NOT A MAN OF	HONOR	: I AM A MAN STRUCK DOWN BY A DEAD HAND. TAVY: YOU
GENV IV	(105)	AS YOU PRETEND TO BE. (TO THE JUDGE) YOUR	HONOR	: I AM SATISFIED. HE HAS ADMITTED HIS GUILT. (HE
BULL II	(114)	TO LONDON AND NEVER SEE YOU AGAIN. THATS ON MY	HONOR	: I WILL. AM I INTERFERING WITH HIM? /NORA/ (
MILL IV	(195)	BUT I WONT BE BEATEN BY A WOMAN. IT'S A POINT OF	HONOR	: OF SELF-RESPECT. /SAGAMORE/ YES; BUT HOW DO YOU
LIED	(196)	MY DREAMS. I WILL LIE AND PROTEST AND STAND ON MY	HONOR	: OH, I WILL PLAY THE GENTLEMAN, NEVER FEAR. /SHE/
BULL PREFACE	(64)	AND ITS COST, AND THAT LIFE IS WORTHLESS WITHOUT	HONOR	? IT IS TRUE THAT SIR JOHN FALSTAFF DID NOT THINK SO;
OVER	(187)	ON HIS ARM). WHAT PRETENSION HAS HE TO ANY SUCH	HONOR	? /JUNO/ I SINNED IN INTENTION. (MRS JUNO ABANDONS
O'FL	(223)	ARRA HOLD YOUR WHISHT, MOTHER. DONT YOU SEE HIS	HONOR	? /MRS O'FLAHERTY/ OH, SIR, I'M RUINED AND DESTROYED.
CAPT I	(222)	ENTHUSIASM) AN SHLL AW TEOLL YER WOT E IS, YR	HONOR	? /RANKIN/ (NOT AT ALL IMPRESSED) IF YE WILL BE SO
MIS.	(160)	POINT OF HONOR, WONT YOU? /LINA/ ONLY A POINT OF	HONOR	? /TARLETON/ (IMPULSIVELY) NO, BY GOD! A POINT OF
DOCT III	(149)	DO YOU TAKE ME FOR? HAVE YOU NO CONFIDENCE IN MY	HONOR	? /WALPOLE/ NONE WHATEVER. /LOUIS/ OH WELL, OF COURSE
NEVR IV	(305)	THAT PRIVILEGE AS COUNSEL'S FEE. MAY I HAVE THE	HONOR	? THANK YOU. (HE DANCES AWAY WITH GLORIA, AND
GENV II	(56)	SECRETARY/ I AM DESOLATE AT HAVING BROUGHT YOUR	HONOR	ALL THE WAY FROM THE HAGUE. A WORD FROM YOU WOULD HAVE
O'FL	(217)	/MRS O'FLAHERTY/ (HILARIOUSLY) LET YOUR	HONOR	ALONE FOR FINDING THE RIGHT WORD! A BIG BOSTHOON HE
MTH4 II	(192)	ARE THE LIFETIME OF A SOUL THAT NEVER LOSES ITS	HONOR	AND A BRAIN THAT NEVER LOSES ITS EAGERNESS, THEY ARE
MTH2	(41)	CONSCIENCE AT ALL. SOME ROMANTIC POINTS OF	HONOR	AND A FEW CONVENTIONS. A WORLD WITHOUT CONSCIENCE:
SUPR HANDBOK	(221)	MEN; BUT EVERY TRUE MAN HAS ONE MAIN POINT OF	HONOR	AND A FEW MINOR ONES. YOU CANNOT BELIEVE IN HONOR
METH PREFACE	(R42)	AND INTELLIGENCE, OF STRENGTH AND PURPOSE, OF	HONOR	AND ASPIRATION, TO SUCH CASUALLY PICTURESQUE CHANGES
MIS. PREFACE	(55)	PUBLICLY AS A SATISFACTION TO WHAT HE CALLED HIS	HONOR	AND AUTHORITY. I HAD INTENDED TO GIVE THE PARTICULARS
INCA	(256)	BEAUTY AND HEALTHFULNESS OF ITS CITIES, ON THE	HONOR	AND COMFORT OF ITS WORN-OUT WORKERS. THEY REFUSED; AND
DOCT PREFACE	(5)	THERE IS ANOTHER DIFFICULTY IN TRUSTING TO THE	HONOR	AND CONSCIENCE OF A DOCTOR. DOCTORS ARE JUST LIKE
DOCT PREFACE	(4)	THE HIGH CHARACTER OF A NOBLE PROFESSION AND THE	HONOR	AND CONSCIENCE OF ITS MEMBERS. I MUST REPLY THAT THE
DOCT PREFACE	(4)	THIS ARE LIVING IN A FOOL'S PARADISE. AS TO THE	HONOR	AND CONSCIENCE OF DOCTORS, THEY HAVE AS MUCH AS ANY
PHIL II	(130)	(STARTING UP) WELL, UPON MY LIFE! UPON MY	HONOR	AND CONSCIENCE! ! NOW REALLY! ! ! I SHALL GO THIS
3PLA PREFACE	(R16)	IT TO THEM, EVEN TO THE EXTENT PERMITTED BY THE	HONOR	AND CONSCIENCE OF THE BEST MANAGERS, BECAUSE A THEATRE
ANNA	(300)	THEY HAD NO IMAGINATION, NO IDEALS, NO SENSE OF	HONOR	AND DIGNITY TO SUSTAIN THEM. /THE GRAND DUCHESS/ MY
HART I	(74)	MEN'S MORAL SENSE, AND CARRIES THEM BEYOND	HONOR	AND DISHONOR. YOU KNOW THAT, DONT YOU? /LADY
FANY PREFACE	(255)	THING: PEOPLE TALKED OF RIGHT AND WRONG, OF	HONOR	AND DISHONOR, OF SIN AND GRACE, OF SALVATION AND
DOCT PREFACE	(46)	THE RIGHT TO PUT A DOG OUTSIDE THE LAWS OF	HONOR	AND FELLOWSHIP, CONCEDES TO HIM ALSO THE RIGHT TO PUT
HART I	(59)	(HOPELESSLY) NO: IT'S NO USE. I AM BOUND IN	HONOR	AND GRATITUDE. I WILL GO THROUGH WITH IT. /MRS
METH PREFACE	(R66)	MAY BE PROFESSED ATHEISTS WHO ARE ALSO MEN OF	HONOR	AND HIGH PUBLIC SPIRIT. THE OLD BELIEF THAT IT MATTERS
BARB PREFACE	(212)	DESTRUCTIVE OF OUR WILL, AND CONSEQUENTLY OF OUR	HONOR	AND MANHOOD. NOW IT IS TRUE THAT CAPTAIN WILSON'S
BULL PREFACE	(48)	HIMSELF, TO JUDGE FOR HIMSELF, TO CONSULT HIS OWN	HONOR	AND MANHOOD, TO DREAD ANY CONSEQUENCE EXCEPT THE
LIED	(201)	WITH HIS DUTY TO ME AS HOST; AND IT DID HIM	HONOR	AND ME TOO. BUT (WITH GATHERING FURY) SHE ISNT GOOD
SUPR III	(127)	AND HE CAME, SWORD IN HAND, TO VINDICATE OUTRAGED	HONOR	AND MORALITY BY MURDERING ME. /THE STATUE/ MURDERING!
SUPR IV	(149)	CARE. I AM TAKING CARE. I'M TAKING CARE OF MY	HONOR	AND MY POSITION IN ENGLISH SOCIETY. /MALONE/ (HOTLY)
MIS. PREFACE	(4)	OF INTIMIDATING PERSONS WHO HAVE PRACTICALLY NO	HONOR	AND NO CONSCIENCE, IS NOT A FACT. DEATH IS FOR MANY OF
DOCT PREFACE	(5)	JUST LIKE OTHER ENGLISHMEN: MOST OF THEM HAVE NO	HONOR	AND NO CONSCIENCE: WHAT THEY COMMONLY MISTAKE FOR
BULL PREFACE	(39)	HANDS AND SEAL OUR OWN LIPS IN THE NAME OF OUR	HONOR	AND PATRIOTISM. AS FAR AS MONEY OR COMFORT IS
CLEO IV	(189)	BREED MURDER, ALWAYS IN THE NAME OF RIGHT AND	HONOR	AND PEACE, UNTIL THE GODS ARE TIRED OF BLOOD AND
ROCK PREFACE	(163)	IN OUR COUNTRY HE WOULD ENJOY HIS GAINS IN HIGH	HONOR	AND PERSONAL SECURITY, AND THANK HIS STARS THAT HE
METH PREFACE	(R66)	OF A MAN FOR PUBLIC TRUST WAS TESTED, NOT BY HIS	HONOR	AND PUBLIC SPIRIT, BUT BY ASKING HIM WHETHER HE
METH PREFACE	(R66)	DAMN, WAS AN ERROR: FOR THE DIVINITY IS IN THE	HONOR	AND PUBLIC SPIRIT, NOT IN THE MOUTHED CREDO OR NON
DOCT PREFACE	(51)	HIM, IT IS CHILDISH FOR HIM TO STAND ON HIS	HONOR	AND REPUTATION AND HIGH CHARACTER AND THE CREDIT OF A
SUPR IV	(169)	THEM ALL. /TANNER/ YOU WOULD SELL FREEDOM AND	HONOR	AND SELF FOR HAPPINESS? /ANN/ IT WILL NOT BE ALL
MILL IV	(195)	BUT HOW DO YOU ARRIVE AT THE FIGURE? WHY IS YOUR	HONOR	AND SELF-RESPECT WORTH TWO THOUSAND FIVE HUNDRED
LIED	(191)	OR SUBTERFUGE, FREELY AND HONESTLY, IN FULL	HONOR	AND SELF-RESPECT. /SHE/ (STARING AT HIM) AND WHERE
SUPR PREFACE	(R18)	THEIR PATRIOTISM, THEIR REPUTATION, THEIR	HONOR	AND SO FORTH. ON THE WHOLE, THIS IS A SENSIBLE AND
PYGM II	SD(233)	RESERVE. HIS PRESENT POSE IS THAT OF WOUNDED	HONOR	AND STERN RESOLUTION. /DOOLITTLE/ (AT THE DOOR,
SIM PREFACE	(8)	DO IT FOR HIM. NOW OUTSIDE RUSSIA THE HEIGHT OF	HONOR	AND SUCCESS IS TO BE A GENTLEMAN OR LADY, WHICH MEANS
CAPT III	(299)	FAREWELL. /BRASSBOUND/ WITH MY HEART'S NOBLEST	HONOR	AND TRIUMPH, FAREWELL. (HE TURNS AND FLIES). /LADY
CAND III	(129)	OR EVEN A POETIC ATTITUDE. I PUT YOU ON YOUR	HONOR	AND TRUTH. NOW SAY WHATEVER YOU WANT TO. /MARCHBANKS/
CAND III	(129)	MUST SAY THAT NOW, BECAUSE YOU HAVE PUT ME ON MY	HONOR	AND TRUTH; AND I NEVER THINK OR FEEL MRS MORELL: IT IS
POSN	(453)	WORD OF A WOMAN OF BAD CHARACTER. I STAND ON THE	HONOR	AND VIRTUE OF MY AMERICAN MANHOOD. I SAY THAT SHE'S
SUPR HANDBOK	(202)	THE APPARENT ABSENCE OF ANY CONCEPTION OF MANLY	HONOR	AND VIRTUE, OF PERSONAL COURAGE AND SELF-RESPECT, IN
GETT PREFACE	(195)	REPRESENTING THE HIGHEST ATTAINABLE DEGREE OF	HONOR	AND VIRTUE, WHILST ANY CRITICISM OF OR REVOLT AGAINST
PHIL I	(82)	YOU COME AWAY IMMEDIATELY. ON MY SACRED WORD OF	HONOR	AS A GENTLEMAN-- AS AN ENGLISHMAN-- AS ANYTHING YOU
DEST	(157)	LET ME GO, EXCELLENCY. IT IS MY POINT OF	HONOR	AS AN INNKEEPER TO COME WHEN I AM CALLED. I APPEAL TO
DEST	(183)	GENERAL BONAPARTE-- WILL YOU PROMISE ME ON YOUR	HONOR	AS AN OFFICER AND A GENTLEMAN NOT TO FIGHT WITH HIM OR
DEST	(183)	ROUND THE TABLE) NOT UNTIL YOU HAVE REGAINED YOUR	HONOR	AS AN OFFICER. REMEMBER: YOU HAVE NOT CAPTURED MY
LIED	(200)	NEED TO INSULT ME LIKE THIS. I ASSURE YOU, ON MY	HONOR	AS A-- /HER HUSBAND/ (TOO ANGRY TO TOLERATE A REPLY,
JITT I	(19)	BECAUSE IT IS UNCONSCIOUS, BINDS MY SENSE OF	HONOR	AS IF HE SPARED US KNOWINGLY. /JITTA/ (CHANGING HER
LADY PREFACE	(230)	GET BATES AND WILLIAMS DRAWN WITH ALL RESPECT AND	HONOR	AS NORMAL RANK AND FILE MEN. IN JULIUS CAESAR,
JITT I	(21)	FREE IN MY CONSCIENCE, RIGHT IN MY HEART, IN ALL	HONOR	AS WELL AS IN ALL AFFECTION TO THE VERY END. (HE
O'FL	(216)	LADIES? OH, IT'S RIGHT GLAD WE ARE TO SEE YOUR	HONOR	BACK AGAIN AND LOOKING THE PICTURE OF HEALTH. /SIR
MRS III	(228)	CODE IS A SIMPLE ONE, AND, I THINK, A GOOD ONE.	HONOR	BETWEEN MAN AND MAN; FIDELITY BETWEEN MAN AND WOMAN;
GETT	(337)	EVEN FOR GEORGE? /MRS GEORGE/ THERE MUST BE	HONOR	BETWEEN ME AND GEORGE, HAPPINESS OR NO HAPPINESS. DO
DEST	(183)	TO HAVE YOUR HORSE AND PISTOLS BACK. /LIEUTENANT/	HONOR	BRIGHT? /LADY/ HONOR BRIGHT. (SHE OFFERS HER HAND).
DEST	(183)	PISTOLS BACK. /LIEUTENANT/ HONOR BRIGHT? /LADY/	HONOR	BRIGHT. (SHE OFFERS HER HAND). /LIEUTENANT/ (TAKING
ARMS II	(37)	/SERGIUS/ THAT DOESNT MATTER. YOU HAVE STAINED MY	HONOR	BY MAKING ME A PARTY TO YOUR EAVESDROPPING. AND YOU
BASH II,1,	(110)	PROFESSION. /CASHEL/ TEMPT ME NOT, WOMAN. IT IS	HONOR	CALLS. SLAVE TO THE RING I REST UNTIL THE FACE OF
GETT PREFACE	(242)	CAN OCCUR ONLY VERY EXCEPTIONALLY); AND A MAN OF	HONOR	CANNOT ADVISE A WOMAN TO DO FOR HIS SAKE WHAT HE WOULD
SUPR III	(90)	WAS MY DUTY. MY FATHER DREW ON MY ASSAILANT: HIS	HONOR	DEMANDED IT. HE FELL: THAT WAS THE REWARD OF HONOR. I
O'FL	(217)	ORDER TEA. /MRS O'FLAHERTY/ OH, WHY WOULD YOUR	HONOR	DISTURB YOURSELF? SURE I CAN TAKE THE BOY INTO THE
GETT	(321)	IT WITH YOU, REJJY. IF YOUR SENSE OF PERSONAL	HONOR	DOESNT MAKE YOU UNDERSTAND, NOTHING WILL. /SOAMES/ (
SUPR HANDBOK	(224)	GENTLEMAN IS THAT HE SACRIFICES EVERYTHING TO HIS	HONOR	EXCEPT HIS GENTILITY. A GENTLEMAN OF OUR DAYS IS ONE
LION II	(135)	EXHORT ME! REMIND ME THAT IF I RAISE MY SWORD MY	HONOR	FALLS AND MY MASTER IS CRUCIFIED AFRESH. /ANDROCLES/
BARB PREFACE	(243)	POWER WIELDED BY COWARDS AND WEAKLINGS, AND OUR	HONOR	FALSE IN ALL ITS POINTS. I AM AN ENEMY OF THE EXISTING
HART PREFACE	(28)	WHO, SOONER THAN DO HONEST WORK, WILL SELL HIS	HONOR	FOR A BOTTLE OF WINE, A VISIT TO THE THEATRE, AND AN
GETT	(335)	THAT IS ONE OF THE OVERSIGHTS OF YOUR CODE OF	HONOR	FOR HUSBANDS: THE MAN WHO CAN BULLY THEM CAN INSULT
GLIM	(177)	AN HONOR FOR THEM! BUT IT WOULD HAVE BEEN NO	HONOR	FOR ME TO DIE MERELY THAT YOU MIGHT MARRY YOUR CLOD OF
GLIM	(177)	DIE THAT THE RICH MAY LIVE. /FERRUCCIO/ WHAT AN	HONOR	FOR THEM! BUT IT WOULD HAVE BEEN NO HONOR FOR ME TO
BARB PREFACE	(217)	WEALTHY, SAYS UNDERSHAFT, IS WITH ME A POINT OF	HONOR	FOR WHICH I AM PREPARED TO KILL AT THE RISK OF MY OWN
MTH2	(50)	OUR RESCUE? WHY DID YOU LET AMERICA SNATCH THAT	HONOR	FROM ENGLAND? /BURGE/ BARNABAS: AMERICA WAS CARRIED
MTH2	(71)	CONTINUITY CAN HAVE NEITHER CONSCIENCE NOR	HONOR	FROM ONE DAY TO ANOTHER. THE RESULT IS THAT YOU HAVE
DOCT II	(128)	SCALE ALL THE FAITH HE HAS JUSTIFIED AND THE	HONOR	HE HAS CREATED. /RIDGEON/ COME COME, PADDY! NONE OF
DOCT II	(128)	SCALE ALL THE FAITH HE HAS DESTROYED AND THE	HONOR	HE HAS LOST, AND YOULL PUT INTO BLENKINSOP'S SCALE ALL
BULL III	(121)	AND PLASTERING HIM WITH COMPLIMENTS, WITH YOUR	HONOR	HERE AND YOUR HONOR THERE, WHEN ALL THE TIME THEIR
MTH1 II	(30)	WITH FINE CLOTHES, SO THAT MEN MAY GLORIFY AND	HONOR	HIM INSTEAD OF CURSING HIM AS MURDERER AND THIEF. ALL
NEVR III	(266)	YOU IN EARNEST? /VALENTINE/ (DESPERATELY) ON MY	HONOR	I AM IN EARNEST. (SHE LOOKS SEARCHINGLY AT HIM. HIS
DEST	(174)	TRYING TO ROB YOU. /LADY/ (EARNESTLY) NO: ON MY	HONOR	I ASK FOR NO LETTER OF YOURS: NOT A WORD THAT HAS BEEN
GENV III	(78)	BUT THE MONEY WAS MADE BY MY GRANDFATHER. UPON MY	HONOR	I DONT KNOW HOW I GOT LANDED WHERE I AM. I AM QUITE AN
KING I	(179)	ON OUR HOST'S VALUABLE TIME. MR NEWTON: ON MY	HONOR	I HAD NO PART IN BRINGING UPON YOU THIS INVASION OF
BARB PREFACE	(224)	OR GO TO ANOTHER PLANET. HE MUST SAVE THE WORLD'S	HONOR	IF HE IS TO SAVE HIS OWN. THIS IS WHAT ALL THE
CAND II	(107)	BUT KEEPING HER WITS ABOUT HER: HER POINT OF	HONOR	IN ENCOUNTERS WITH STRANGE YOUNG MEN) WICKED PEOPLE
MTH2	(45)	MY NIECE WOULDNT OPEN IT! THE PROPHET IS WITHOUT	HONOR	IN HIS OWN FAMILY. WELL, WHAT DO YOU THINK OF LIVING
DEST	(180)	YOU? /NAPOLEON/ YOU MUST FIND THAT MAN. YOUR	HONOR	IS AT STAKE; AND THE FATE OF THE CAMPAIGN, THE DESTINY
PRES	(157)	I KNOW WHAT YOU OFFICERS ARE. TO YOU A WOMAN'S	HONOR	IS NOTHING, AND THE IDLE PLEASURE OF THE MOMENT IS
DOCT PREFACE	(50)	OF THE PURSUIT OF KNOWLEDGE FROM THE LAWS OF	HONOR	IS THE MOST HIDEOUS CONCEIVABLE ENLARGEMENT OF
MIS. PREFACE	(62)	IS THE WORLD OF THE BOYS, WHERE THE POINT OF	HONOR	IS TO BE UNTAMEABLE, ALWAYS READY TO FIGHT, RUTHLESS
POSN PREFACE	(361)	CLASS OF LOOSE-LIVED PLAYGOERS WHOSE POINT OF	HONOR	IS TO DERIDE ALL OFFICIAL AND CONVENTIONAL SERMONS. AS

GETT PREFACE(220)	SORT SHOULD BE FOUNDED ON IT: THE REAL POINT OF	HONOR	IS TO TAKE NO CORRUPT ADVANTAGE OF IT. WHEN WE HEAR OF
JOAN 4 (101)	POLITICAL BISHOP: MY FAITH IS TO ME WHAT YOUR	HONOR	IS TO YOU; AND IF THERE BE A LOOPHOLE THROUGH WHICH
LION II (129)	/ANDROCLES/ (APOLOGETICALLY) WELL, PERHAPS	HONOR	IS TOO STRONG AN EXPRESSION. STILL, YOU KNOW, I
BULL PREFACE(64)	IS SUPPOSED TO UNDERSTAND BETTER THAN THEY THAT	HONOR	IS WORTH ITS DANGER AND ITS COST, AND THAT LIFE IS
PLES PREFACE(R15)	THE PIT. IT IS HARD FOR AN ACTOR WHOSE POINT OF	HONOR	IT IS TO BE A PERFECT GENTLEMAN, TO SYMPATHIZE WITH AN
LIED PREFACE(185)	OTHELLO'S ROMANTIC ASSUMPTIONS AND FALSE POINT OF	HONOR	.
DOCT PREFACE(49)	OF THE BEST THINGS, THAT ARE BARRED TO ALL MEN OF	HONOR	. AGAIN, HAS THE SILLIEST BURGLAR EVER PRETENDED THAT
GETT (345)	/THE BISHOP/ NOT AT ALL. I'M NOT REPUDIATING THAT	HONOR	. ALLOW ME (HE KISSES HER HAND). /MRS GEORGE/ THANK
CLEO IV (189)	SHEW THE WORLD HOW ROME AVENGES HER SONS AND HER	HONOR	. AND SO, TO THE END OF HISTORY, MURDER SHALL BREED
CAPT II (270)	LOVELINESS, YE SHALL BE LED BACK TO MOGADOR WITH	HONOR	. AND THOU, ACCURSED BRASSBOUND, SHALT GO THITHER A
MIS. (150)	AS ONE OF THE FAMILY-- IF YOU WILL DO ME THE	HONOR	. AND YOUR FRIEND TOO. WHERES YOUR FRIEND? /PERCIVAL/
DOCT PREFACE(18)	FOR MORE THAN ONE REALLY INFLEXIBLE POINT OF	HONOR	. ANDREA DEL SARTO, LIKE LOUIS DUBEDAT IN MY PLAY,
MIS. PREFACE(53)	WHICH HE HAS BEEN BROUGHT UP TO CONSULT HIS OWN	HONOR	. AS A SPORTSMAN (AND WAR IS FUNDAMENTALLY THE SPORT
MTH2 (43)	TAUGHT BOURGEOIS MANNERS AND BOURGEOIS POINTS OF	HONOR	. BOURGEOIS MANNERS MAY BE SNOBBISH MANNERS: THERE MAY
SUPR III (89)	BECAUSE HE WAS, HE SAID, DEFENDING HIS DAUGHTER'S	HONOR	. BY THIS HE MEANT THAT BECAUSE I FOOLISHLY FELL IN
MIS. (184)	TARLETON/ OH, GO ALONG WITH YOU AND YOUR WORD OF	HONOR	. DO YOU THINK I'M A FOOL? I WONDER YOU CAN LOOK THE
O'FL (217)	HOUSE). /MRS O'FLAHERTY/ SURE HE HAS THAT, YOUR	HONOR	. GOD BLESS YOUR HONOR! (THE GENERAL BEING NOW OUT
CLEO PRO2 (96)	UP HIS SPEAR) LET US RECEIVE THIS MAN WITH	HONOR	. HE BEARS EVIL TIDINGS. THE GUARDSMEN SEIZE THEIR
SUPR III (90)	DEMANDED IT. HE FELL: THAT WAS THE REWARD OF	HONOR	. I AM HERE: IN HELL, YOU TELL ME: THAT IS THE REWARD
GENV IV (108)	MR BATTLER? /BATTLER/ I ALSO THANK YOUR	HONOR	. I AM SATISFIED (HE RESUMES HIS SEAT; BUT HIS
GETT (356)	NOW, I'M NOT A MAN OF SENTIMENT, BUT A MAN OF	HONOR	. I KNOW WELL WHAT WILL HAPPEN TO ME WHEN ONCE I CROSS
BASH PREFACE(87)	ACKNOWLEDGED THE THRONE AS THE FOUNTAIN OF SOCIAL	HONOR	. I PAID PARTICULAR ATTENTION TO THE CONSTRUCTION OF
MIS. PREFACE(36)	ENJOY, AND INCULCATE THE REPAYMENT AS A POINT OF	HONOR	. IF WE DID THAT TODAY -- AND NOTHING BUT FLAT
DOCT I (100)	/BLENKINSOP/ IT'S THE FIRST TIME IVE HAD THAT	HONOR	. IN MY POOR LITTLE PRACTICE THERE ARE NO CHANCES OF
LADY PREFACE(216)	BUSINESS, AND INTO THE ARMY WITHOUT A LESSON IN	HONOR	. IT HAS BEEN SAID, WITH THE OBJECT OF PROVING
O'FL (216)	HIM. /MRS O'FLAHERTY/ AND INDEED AND I AM, YOUR	HONOR	. IT'S THE BRAVE BOY HE IS; AND WHY WOULDNT HE BE,
GENV IV (129)	TO THE LAST MOMENT; BUT WE CAN ALL WORK FOR	HONOR	. (HE GOES OUT). /SIR O./ WONDERFUL LUCK THAT MAN
CAPT I (219)	WELL, SIT YE DOON. /DRINKWATER/ AW THENK YR	HONOR	. (HE SITS DOWN ON THE SEAT UNDER THE TREE AND
DEST (153)	WELL. /GIUSEPPE/ YOUR EXCELLENCY DOES ME TOO MUCH	HONOR	. (STRETCHING HIS HAND TOWARDS THE FLASK) PERHAPS
O'FL (216)	AND LEARN BEHAVIOR WHILE I PAY MY JUTY TO HIS	HONOR	. (TO SIR PEARCE, HEARTILY) AND HOW IS YOUR HONOR'S
3PLA PREFACE(R21)	CONVENTIONS WILL BECOME THE LAWS OF PERSONAL	HONOR	. JEALOUSY, WHICH IS EITHER AN EGOTISTICAL MEANNESS OR
CAPT I (221)	ENLIGHTENMENT) AOH, NAR AW TIKES YER WIV ME, YR	HONOR	. NAH SAMMUN ES BIN A TEOLLN YOU THET KEPN BRARSBAHND
GETT (356)	/HOTCHKISS/ THEY ARE PEOPLE OF SENTIMENT, NOT OF	HONOR	. NOW, I'M NOT A MAN OF SENTIMENT, BUT A MAN OF HONOR.
O'FL (217)	RIGHT WORD! A BIG BOSTHOON HE IS INDEED, YOUR	HONOR	. OH, TO THINK OF THE TIMES AND TIMES I HAVE SAID THAT
KING I (173)	OUR FOES: THEY CARE FOR NOTHING BUT TO STEAL OUR	HONOR	. PRAY FOR ME, FRIEND FOX: I THINK YOU HAVE GOD BY THE
SUPR HANDBOK(222)	YOUR MEMORY CAN NEVER BE AS TRUSTWORTHY AS YOUR	HONOR	. PROPERTY, PROPERTY, SAID PROUDHON, IS THEFT. THIS IS
DOCT IV (167)	WORLD IS A MAN OF GENIUS WHO IS NOT ALSO A MAN OF	HONOR	. RIDGEON AND WALPOLE WHEEL THE CHAIR INTO THE RECESS.
BULL III (140)	HOME? /MATTHEW/ OH SURE IT'D BE THROUBLIN YOUR	HONOR	. /BROADBENT/ I INSIST: IT WILL GIVE ME THE GREATEST
BULL III (144)	(APPEARING IN THE SHRUBBERY) HERE I AM, YOUR	HONOR	. /BROADBENT/ GO AND CATCH THE PIG AND PUT IT INTO THE
PHIL I (82)	OATHS. I WANT YOUR PROMISE: YOUR SACRED WORD OF	HONOR	. /CHARTERIS/ CERTAINLY: ANYTHING YOU DEMAND, ON
MTH3 (110)	TIME. /BARNABAS/ OF COURSE. A SIMPLE POINT OF	HONOR	. /CONFUCIUS/ NOT AT ALL. A SIMPLE NECESSITY.
APPL II (273)	MAN, MR BOANERGES. /PLINY/ WELL, IT DOES YOU	HONOR	. /CRASSUS/ NOT ALL OF US WOULD BE CAPABLE OF A
PHIL II (98)	HELPED ME TO BEHAVE WELL MYSELF: IT HAS, ON MY	HONOR	. /CRAVEN/ YES: YOU ALWAYS BELIEVED IN HEARTH AND
GLIM (180)	TO THE NET, EXCELLENCY, WITH THANKS FOR THE	HONOR	. /GIULIA/ TO LOVE, SIGNOR. /FERRUCCIO/ TO HATE: THE
CYMB V (144)	OF ALL LIARS THAT EVER SWORE AWAY A WOMAN'S	HONOR	. /IACHIMO/ I THINK, MADAM, YOU DO FORGET THAT CHEST.
DEST (173)	ME! WHY? /LADY/ I AM GOING TO SEE YOU LOSE YOUR	HONOR	. /NAPOLEON/ HM! NOTHING WORSE THAN THAT? (HE TAKES
CAPT I (221)	HIS HEARTY SAILOR MANNER) AN WEOLLCOME, YR	HONOR	. /RANKIN/ WHO IS THIS CAPTAIN BRASSBOUND?
ANNA (298)	DOG OF A SUBALTERN, RESTORE THAT PISTOL, AND MY	HONOR	. /SCHNEIDEKIND/ (REACHING OUT WITH THE PISTOL TO THE
O'FL (205)	HEARD DISMOUNTING). /A LABORER'S VOICE/ YES, YOUR	HONOR	. /THE GENTLEMAN'S VOICE/ TAKE THIS HORSE TO THE
GENV III (70)	DO ME THE HONOR TO SHARE MY TABLE, YOUR	HONOR	. /THE JUDGE/ THANK YOU. MAY I INTRODUCE COMMISSAR
NEVR IV (303)	MR VALENTINE: I APPEAL TO YOUR SENSE OF	HONOR	. /VALENTINE/ YOURE QUITE RIGHT. IT'S PERFECT MADNESS.
NEVR IV (300)	FIRST THING I HAVE HEARD YOU SAY THAT DOES YOU	HONOR	. /VALENTINE/ STUFF! COME: SAY WHAT YOU WANT TO SAY
GENV IV (89)	YET, MR SECRETARY? /THE SECRETARY/ NONE, YOUR	HONOR	. THE PARTIES ON YOUR LEFT ARE ALL PLAINTIFFS. ON YOUR
SUPR HANDBOK(221)	REFUSE TITLES BECAUSE THEY ARE JEALOUS OF THEM.	HONOR	. THERE ARE NO PERFECTLY HONORABLE MEN; BUT EVERY TRUE
METH PREFACE(R16)	TO DO SO AS AN ARTICLE OF RELIGION AND A POINT OF	HONOR	. THOSE IN WHOM NATURAL ENLIGHTENMENT HAS REACTED
GETT (354)	IN ANYTHING BUT MY OWN WILL AND MY OWN PRIDE AND	HONOR	. YOUR FISHES AND YOUR CATECHISMS AND ALL THE REST OF
KING I (186)	BUT A WORD OF HONOR MUST BE A GENTLEMAN'S WORD OF	HONOR	; YOU, MONSIEUR, ARE A BOURGEOIS. YOU MUST SWEAR ON
O'FL (205)	WILL YOU? /A LABORER'S VOICE/ RIGHT, YOUR	HONOR	. YUP THERE. GWAN NOW, GWAN. (THE HORSE IS LED AWAY).
2TRU III (89)	CAN NOW GIVE YOU A GOOD REASON FOR BEING A MAN OF	HONOR	." HE TURNS FROM THEM AND IS RUSHING DISTRACTEDLY AWAY
GENV IV (108)	YOU FROM YOUR DREAMS. /WIDOW/ I THANK YOUR	HONOR	(SHE SITS DOWN). /JUDGE/ ARE YOU SATISFIED, MR
MIS. PREFACE(94)	THE CHILD MUST HAVE A CONSCIENCE AND A CODE OF	HONOR	(WHICH IS THE ESSENCE OF RELIGION) EVEN IF IT BE ONLY
CAPT I (220)	THROUGH HENNY LITTLE EXCURSION IN REASON. YR	HONOR	MAWT MENTION IT. /RANKIN/ I WILL CERTAINLY NOT PROPOSE
MTH2 (43)	BETTER THAN NO MANNERS. MANY BOURGEOIS POINTS OF	HONOR	MAY BE FALSE; BUT AT LEAST THEY EXIST. THE WOMEN KNOW
KING I (186)	MY WORD OF HONOR, MADAM. /LOUISE/ BUT A WORD OF	HONOR	MUST BE A GENTLEMAN'S WORD OF HONOR. YOU, MONSIEUR,
GETT PREFACE(232)	PERSON, THE DECLARATION BINDS THE PARTIES IN	HONOR	NEVER TO SEE ONE ANOTHER AGAIN UNLESS THEY CONTEMPLATE
NEVR IV (286)	MR CLANDON? /VALENTINE/ (MAKING IT A POINT OF	HONOR	NOT TO BE IMPRESSED BY HIM) DO I LOOK LIKE IT? MY
LIED (191)	ENVIRONMENT PERMITTED. WE OWE IT TO HIM IN ALL	HONOR	NOT TO LET HIM LEARN THE TRUTH FROM THE LIPS OF A
SUPR III SD(136)	BEFORE HE GETS ON HIS FEET, MAKING IT A POINT OF	HONOR	NOT TO SHEW ANY UNDUE INTEREST IN THE EXCITEMENT OF
KING II (227)	PERHAPS STAY THERE TO ALL ETERNITY. AND ON MY	HONOR	NOTHING CAME OF THAT: I NEVER TOUCHED HER. BUT SHE HAD
DOCT PREFACE(69)	PRESENTLY TAKE THE PLACE IN GENERAL INTEREST AND	HONOR	NOW OCCUPIED BY OUR MILITARY AND NAVAL FORCES. IT IS
LIED (197)	NOW I WILL NOT LIE BY HALVES. I'LL WALLOW IN THE	HONOR	OF A GENTLEMAN. /SHE/ DEAREST BOY, I KNEW YOU WOULD.
LION II (129)	MY HONOR, YOU KNOW. /THE EDITOR/ HONOR! THE	HONOR	OF A TAILOR? /ANDROCLES/ (APOLOGETICALLY) WELL,
LION II (142)	HOUR. NO: ON THE FAITH OF A CHRISTIAN AND THE	HONOR	OF A TAILOR, I ACCEPT THE LOT THAT HAS FALLEN ON ME.
NEVR IV (286)	MY NAME IS BOHUN. (GENERAL AWE). HAVE I THE	HONOR	OF ADDRESSING MRS CLANDON? (MRS CLANDON BOWS. BOHUN
DEVL III (60)	/RICHARD/ A THOUSAND PARDONS. I THOUGHT I HAD THE	HONOR	OF ADDRESSING GENTLEMANLY JOHNNY. SENSATION AMONG THE
ARMS II (36)	OUT HIS RIGHT HAND IN AFFIRMATION) NO! ON THE	HONOR	OF A-- (HE CHECKS HIMSELF; AND HIS HAND DROPS,
GENV I (42)	IS THE EMERGENCY ONE IN WHICH WE CAN HAVE THE	HONOR	OF ASSISTING YOU, MY LORD? /BISHOP/ YOUR ADVICE WOULD
WIDO I (7)	DR TRENCH. MY NAME IS SARTORIUS; AND I HAVE THE	HONOR	OF BEING KNOWN TO LADY ROXDALE, WHO IS, I BELIEVE, A
JOAN 1 (58)	ADJECTIVE BY ADJECTIVE) YOU HAVE NOT ONLY THE	HONOR	OF BEING MY STEWARD, BUT THE PRIVILEGE OF BEING THE
SUPR I (29)	VIOLET DOESNT LIKE ME. THIRD, IF I HAD THE	HONOR	OF BEING THE FATHER OF VIOLET'S CHILD, I SHOULD BOAST
CAPT NOTES (304)	TO PEOPLE TRAINED FROM INFANCY TO MAKE A POINT OF	HONOR	OF BELIEF IN ABSTRACTIONS AND INCREDIBILITIES? AND SO
KING I (176)	(HE GOES TO THE DOOR). AND NOW MAY I HAVE THE	HONOR	OF CONDUCTING YOUR GRACE TO YOUR COACH-- OR IS IT ONE
LION PREFACE(17)	DREAD OF HIDEOUS AND ETERNAL TORTURE. THE	HONOR	OF DIVINE PARENTAGE. ONE MORE TRADITION MUST BE NOTED.
MILL IV (192)	FITZFASSENDEN. THE NAME IS SO UNUSUAL. HAVE I THE	HONOR	OF ENTERTAINING THE CELEBRATED-- /ALASTAIR/ (
JITT II (34)	GRIEF? /EDITH/ (UNSYMPATHETIC) IT HAS THE	HONOR	OF FATHER'S NAME. IS THAT NOTHING? /LENKHEIM/ (
GENV IV (123)	THAT THIS WAS YOUR ATTITUDE ALSO. BUT I HAD THE	HONOR	OF INFORMING YOU EXPLICITLY-- VERY EXPLICITLY, MR
BULL PREFACE(32)	IF ONLY SO CHEAP A FLUID COULD HAVE PURCHASED THE	HONOR	OF IRELAND, HE GREATLY MISTAKES THE IRISH PROTESTANT
MIS. (178)	IT. MISS TARLETON'S CONDUCT, SINCE I HAVE HAD THE	HONOR	OF KNOWING HER, HAS BEEN, I NEED HARDLY SAY, IN EVERY
WIDO II (25)	NOT MUCH THIS MORNING, SIR. I HAVE JUST HAD THE	HONOR	OF MAKING DR TRENCH'S ACQUAINTANCE, SIR. /SARTORIUS/ (
MILL I (142)	FOR LIBEL I SHALL HAVE TO DEFEND IF YOU DO ME THE	HONOR	OF MAKING ME YOUR SOLICITOR. /EPIFANIA/ YOU ARE WRONG.
LION II (142)	(TO LAVINIA) MADAM: I AM PROUD TO HAVE THE	HONOR	OF MAKING YOUR ACQUAINTANCE. YOUR BROTHER IS THE GLORY
KING I (165)	BE ENOUGH FOR THEM, I SHOULD THINK. /NEWTON/ THE	HONOR	OF MEETING ME! DONT TALK NONSENSE. THEY ARE GREAT MEN
KING I (165)	TO MEET. /MRS BASHAM/ THOSE TWO MEN INDEED! THE	HONOR	OF MEETING YOU OUGHT TO BE ENOUGH FOR THEM, I SHOULD
MIS. (154)	TO THE PRESIDENT OF THE LEAGUE TO LET ME SAVE THE	HONOR	OF MY FAMILY. HE ARRANGED IT FOR ME. /TARLETON/ OH, I
MTH2 (50)	HUN WAS AT THE GATE. OUR COUNTRY, OUR LIVES, THE	HONOR	OF OUR WIVES AND MOTHERS AND DAUGHTERS, THE TENDER
CLEO III (157)	MY JAWS ARE? /BRITANNUS/ BUT YOUR HONOR-- THE	HONOR	OF ROME-- /CAESAR/ I DO NOT MAKE HUMAN SACRIFICES TO
GENV IV (128)	/BATTLER/ (CALLING AFTER HIM) YOU WILL HAVE THE	HONOR	OF SHARING MY LITTLE DOG'S FATE. BUT NOBODY WILL WEEP
PHIL II (122)	I WERE YOU I SHOULD INVITE THE CRAVENS TO TEA IN	HONOR	OF THE COLONEL'S ESCAPE FROM A HORRIBLE DOOM. BY THE
BARB PREFACE(240)	THE WOLVES OF PLUTOCRACY, THROWS HIMSELF ON THE	HONOR	OF THE MAN, THE MAN, NOT BEING A WOLF (NOR A LONDON
BULL II SD(107)	MAUVE OVER HER SHOULDERS, ALL VERY TRIM IN	HONOR	OF THE OCCASION. SHE LOOKS ROUND FOR LARRY; IS
METH PREFACE(R43)	BEING STONED OR CRUCIFIED AS THE DESTROYER OF THE	HONOR	OF THE RACE AND THE PURPOSE OF THE WORLD, WAS HAILED
POSN (453)	NOT HAD THE OATH, AND THAT YOU DARENT FOR THE	HONOR	OF THE TOWN GIVE HER THE OATH BECAUSE HER LIPS WOULD
CLEO PRO2 (98)	THESE ROMANS: THEY FIGHT TO WIN. THE PRIDE AND	HONOR	OF WAR ARE NOTHING TO THEM. /PERSIAN/ TELL US THE TALE
CLEO PRO2 (100)	FIELD IS FULL OF SHEEP, EXCEPT FOR THE PRIDE AND	HONOR	OF WAR, OF WHICH THESE ROMANS KNOW NOTHING. SO WE
INCA (255)	I RECOGNIZE MY PRESUMPTION IN HAVING SOUGHT THE	HONOR	OF YOUR HAND. AS YOU SAY, I CANNOT AFFORD IT.
DEST (178)	SEEM TO HAVE FORGOTTEN YOUR SOLICITUDE FOR THE	HONOR	OF YOUR OLD FRIEND. /LADY/ I DO NOT THINK SHE RUNS ANY
DOCT PREFACE(6)	IN THE LAST ANALYSIS THERE IS NO OTHER SORT OF	HONOR	OR CONSCIENCE IN EXISTENCE-- THAT THE ASSENT OF THE

BULL III (131)	THE MARROW OUT OF HER. IF WE CANT HAVE MEN OF	HONOR	OWN THE LAND, LETS HAVE MEN OF ABILITY. IF WE CANT
METH PREFACE(R15)	A SOCIETY BASED ON PROFITEERING, AND IS TAUGHT TO	HONOR	PARASITIC IDLENESS AND LUXURY, LEARNS TO SHOOT AND
BULL PREFACE(40)	EVERY IRISHMAN IS IN LANCELOT'S POSITION: HIS	HONOR	ROOTED IN DISHONOR STANDS; AND FAITH UNFAITHFUL KEEPS
LIED (196)	WISH ME TO TELL A LIE-- /SHE/ SURELY, AS A MAN OF	HONOR	-- AS A GENTLEMAN, YOU WOULDNT TELL THE TRUTH: WOULD
MIS. (184)	(GASPING) MRS TARLETON: I GIVE YOU MY WORD OF	HONOR	-- /MRS TARLETON/ OH, GO ALONG WITH YOU AND YOUR WORD
PRES (141)	MEDALS AND ORDERS AND SO FORTH. GET A GUARD OF	HONOR	-- SOMETHING SHOWY-- HORSE GUARDS OR SOMETHING OF THAT
CLEO III (157)	HOW STUBBORN MY JAWS ARE? /BRITANNUS/ BUT YOUR	HONOR	-- THE HONOR OF ROME-- /CAESAR/ I DO NOT MAKE HUMAN
ARMS III (64)	TWO MEN-- REAL MEN-- MEN OF HEART, BLOOD AND	HONOR	-- TO MAKE A GENUINE COMBAT. I COULD NO MORE FIGHT
SUPR I (5)	TO ME: " TAVY IS A GENEROUS LAD AND THE SOUL OF	HONOR	; AND WHEN I SEE HOW LITTLE CONSIDERATION OTHER MEN
BASH II,1, (105)	IMMUNITY. TO STRIKE YOU WERE AGAINST HIS CODE OF	HONOR	; BUT ME, ABOVE THE BELT, HE MAY PERFORM ON T' TH'
METH PREFACE(R67)	GOD BUT GOLDSMITH, WHO HAD WARNED THEM THAT "	HONOR	SINKS WHERE COMMERCE LONG PREVAILS." THE LIEUTENANTS
O'FL (225)	OF HIS OWN ACCORD. /MRS O'FLAHERTY/ WOULDNT YOUR	HONOR	TELL HIM THAT HIS MOTHER HAS THE FIRST CALL ON IT?
DOCT PREFACE(47)	BY COMING FORWARD TO ASSURE THE PUBLIC ON HIS	HONOR	THAT ALL EXPERIMENTS ON ANIMALS ARE COMPLETELY
O'FL (225)	THE TEA TABLE. /TERESA/ BUT AMMENT I TELLING YOUR	HONOR	THAT I NEVER SAID A WORD TO HIM? HE GAVE ME A
O'FL (216)	MARRIED TO A FINE YOUNG NOBLEMAN. OH, IT'S YOUR	HONOR	THAT IS THE LUCKY AND HAPPY FATHER! IT WILL BE BAD
O'FL (225)	A BEAUTIFUL GOLD CHAIN. HERE IT IS TO SHEW YOUR	HONOR	THAT IT'S NO LIE I'M TELLING YOU. /SIR PEARCE/ WHATS
SUPR III SD(72)	ONLY BECAUSE EVERYBODY DOES AS YOU DO, LET US	HONOR	THAT MAN AND SERIOUSLY CONSIDER THE ADVISABILITY OF
SUPR HANDBOK(204)	AND THE VIVISECTOR WHO PLEDGES HIS KNIGHTLY	HONOR	THAT NO ANIMAL OPERATED ON IN THE PHYSIOLOGICAL
GENV III (79)	MIND, SENORA, NEVER MIND. WE ARE INTERRUPTING HIS	HONOR	THE JUDGE. (TO THE JUDGE) YOU WERE ABOUT TO SAY--?
BULL III (121)	WITH COMPLIMENTS, WITH YOUR HONOR HERE AND YOUR	HONOR	THERE, WHEN ALL THE TIME THEIR FINGERS WERE ITCHING TO
DOCT PREFACE(7)	OF COURSE, IMPOSSIBLE FOR ANY MAN OF SENSE AND	HONOR	TO ASSUME DIVINE OMNISCIENCE BY ANSWERING THIS IN THE
GETT PREFACE(236)	THAT PERSONS HAVING THAT GROUND ARE BOUND IN	HONOR	TO AVAIL THEMSELVES OF IT. IT IS GENERALLY ADMITTED
SUPR III (75)	TO ALL RULES. IT IS TRUE THAT I HAVE THE	HONOR	TO BE A JEW; AND WHEN THE ZIONISTS NEED A LEADER TO
MTH2 (55)	THE LIBERAL PARTY. THE PARTY OF WHICH I HAVE THE	HONOR	TO BE LEADER. /LUBIN/ HAVE YOU NOW? THATS VERY
KING I (166)	SIR. (RISING) WILL YOUR NOBLE FRIEND DO ME THE	HONOR	TO BE SEATED IN MY HUMBLE DWELLING? CHARLES BOWS AND
JOAN 4 (97)	WHO KISSES HIS RING.) /WARWICK/ DO ME THE	HONOR	TO BE SEATED. (HE GIVES CAUCHON HIS CHAIR, PLACING IT
KING I (172)	AT THE WRONG SIDE OF MY DOOR. /NELLY/ IT IS AN	HONOR	TO BE SEEN AT YOUR DOOR, MR NEWTON. (LOOKING ROUND
INCA (256)	HIMSELF TOGETHER SUDDENLY) MADAM: I HAVE THE	HONOR	TO BE YOUR MOST OBEDIENT (HE CLICKS HIS HEELS AND
JOAN 1 (58)	I AM NOBODY, SIR, EXCEPT THAT I HAVE THE	HONOR	TO BE YOUR STEWARD. /ROBERT/ (DRIVING HIM TO THE
GLIM (179)	YOUR GRACIOUSNESS MAKES IS THAT WE SHALL HAVE THE	HONOR	TO EAT WITH YOU INSTEAD OF AFTER YOU. /FERRUCCIO/ DOG
DEST (180)	INSTRUCTIONS, EXCELLENCY, AND IS NOW DOING ME THE	HONOR	TO GAMBLE WITH ME TO PASS THE TIME. /NAPOLEON/ SEND
2TRU PREFACE(17)	SCIENTIFIC GENIUSES, WITH WHOM IT IS A POINT OF	HONOR	TO HAVE UNCONDITIONALLY OPEN MINDS EVEN ON THE MOST
SUPR I SD(16)	COSTUME OF BLACK AND VIOLET SILK WHICH DOES	HONOR	TO HER LATE FATHER AND REVEALS THE FAMILY TRADITION OF
DOCT IV SD(159)	SELL THEM TO IDLY CURIOUS PEOPLE, HAS NOTHING BUT	HONOR	TO LOSE BY INACCURACY AND UNVERACITY), HE HAS PERFORCE
HART II (102)	SH-SH-SH-SH-SH: MR MANGAN: YOU ARE BOUND IN	HONOR	TO OBLITERATE FROM YOUR MIND ALL YOU HEARD WHILE YOU
CATH 1 (164)	EDSTASTON OF THE LIGHT DRAGOONS. I HAVE THE	HONOR	TO PRESENT TO YOUR HIGHNESS THIS LETTER FROM THE
JOAN PREFACE(38)	THERE IS NOTHING FOR US BUT TO MAKE IT A POINT OF	HONOR	TO PRIVILEGE HERESY TO THE LAST BEARABLE DEGREE ON THE
PRES (165)	WITH THE HUSBAND OF MRS BANGER. I HAVE THE	HONOR	TO PROPOSE FOR YOUR HAND. /MRS FARRELL/ D'YE MEAN YOU
NEVR I (214)	BOARD THE STEAMER, THE FIRST OFFICER DID ME THE	HONOR	TO PROPOSE TO ME. /DOLLY/ NO: IT WAS TO ME. /MRS
GENV III (70)	KNOW THE JUDGE, BOSS. /THE SECRETARY/ DO ME THE	HONOR	TO SHARE MY TABLE, YOUR HONOR. /THE JUDGE/ THANK YOU.
GETT PREFACE(221)	THE CONSCIENTIOUS ONES THEREFORE FEEL BOUND IN	HONOR	TO STAND BY WHAT THEY HAVE PROMISED, ONE OF THE SUREST
KING I (165)	IS A PERSON WHOSE VISIT WILL BE COUNTED A GREAT	HONOR	TO US. BUT I MUST WARN YOU THAT JUST AS I HAVE MY
NEVR II (250)	TO PUT IT AS IF IT WAS NOT A COMPLIMENT AND AN	HONOR	TO US, MR CRAMPTON, VERY KIND INDEED. THE MORE YOU ARE
CATH 1 (170)	THE OCCASION WILL NOT ARISE. (RISING) I HAVE THE	HONOR	TO WISH YOUR HIGHNESS GOOD MORNING. /PATIOMKIN/ (
BULL III (138)	I SUPPOSE. /LARRY/ OH! THEYVE TRANSFERRED THE	HONOR	TO YOU, HAVE THEY? /BROADBENT/ (COMPLACENTLY) WELL,
SUPR III (90)	AM I HERE? I, WHO REPUDIATED ALL DUTY, TRAMPLED	HONOR	UNDERFOOT, AND LAUGHED AT JUSTICE! /THE OLD WOMAN/
SUPR HANDBOK(221)	HONOR AND A FEW MINOR ONES, YOU CANNOT BELIEVE IN	HONOR	UNTIL YOU HAVE ACHIEVED IT. BETTER KEEP YOURSELF CLEAN
SUPR III (78)	PERCENTAGE OF HIS PRINCIPAL'S RANSOM IF HE WILL	HONOR	US BY ACCEPTING IT. /STRAKER/ I SEE. JUST TO ENCOURAGE
MTH3 (105)	IN INSTINCTIVE IMITATION OF THE ARCHBISHOP)	HONOR	US BY TAKING A SEAT, O SAGE. /CONFUCIUS/ CEREMONY IS
INCA (240)	TO ASK YOU TO LET ME KNOW HOW LONG YOU INTEND TO	HONOR	US WITH YOUR PRESENCE. /THE PRINCESS/ (RISING
SUPR I (35)	TO FEEL OBLIGATIONS, TO FIND THAT VERACITY AND	HONOR	WERE NO LONGER GOODY-GOODY EXPRESSIONS IN THE MOUTHS
DEVL EPILOG (82)	THE CURIOUS PERVERSION OF THE ENGLISH SENSE OF	HONOR	WHEN THE PRIVILEGES AND PRESTIGE OF THE ARISTOCRACY
JOAN 4,SD(97)	HEAD OF THE TABLE). CAUCHON ACCEPTS THE PLACE OF	HONOR	WITH A GRAVE INCLINATION. WARWICK FETCHES THE LEATHER
NEVR I SD(202)	AGE. SUAVITY AND SELF POSSESSION ARE POINTS OF	HONOR	WITH HIM; AND THOUGH THIS, RIGHTLY CONSIDERED, IS ONLY
MIS. (154)	RISKING HIS LIFE-- OR HER LIFE. IT'S A POINT OF	HONOR	WITH US TO KEEP UP THAT TRADITION. USUALLY SEVERAL OF
GENV III (77)	FIRST. /THE WIDOW/ WHAT MATTER! IN EITHER CASE	HONOR	WOULD BE SATISFIED. /THE SECRETARY/ HONOR! THE STOCK
BULL I (77)	DESERVE IT. /TIM/ I'M SURE YOU WOULDNT; AND I	HONOR	YOU FOR IT. YOURE GOIN TO IRELAND, THEN, OUT O
BARB PREFACE(218)	THEY EVEN DEMAND ABSTRACT CONDITIONS: JUSTICE,	HONOR	, A NOBLE MORAL ATMOSPHERE, A MYSTIC NEXUS TO REPLACE
METH PREFACE(R17)	RELIGION NOR A GENERALLY RECOGNIZED POINT OF	HONOR	, AND ARE ALL AT SIXES AND SEVENS WITH THEIR VARIOUS
SUPR I (13)	YOU ARE PREJUDICED AGAINST JACK. HE IS A MAN OF	HONOR	, AND INCAPABLE OF ABUSING-- /TANNER/ DONT, TAVY:
NEVR III (268)	GOING DOWN ON HIS KNEES AND SWEARING TO LOVE,	HONOR	, AND OBEY AND SO ON. /MRS CLANDON/ EXCUSE ME: THAT
SUPR I (6)	MET ONLY ONE MAN IN THE WORLD WHO WAS THE SOUL OF	HONOR	, AND THAT WAS ROEBUCK RAMSDEN. /RAMSDEN/ OH, THAT WAS
CAPT II (269)	COME ON BEHALF OF MY MASTER THE SULTAN TO DO HIM	HONOR	, AND TO CAST DOWN HIS ENEMIES. /SIR HOWARD/ YOU ARE
CLEO III (157)	/CAESAR/ I DO NOT MAKE HUMAN SACRIFICES TO MY	HONOR	, AS YOUR DRUIDS DO. SINCE YOU WILL NOT BURN THESE, AT
SUPR III (118)	TO PREACH PRUDENCE, CAREFUL SELECTION, VIRTUE,	HONOR	, CHASTITY-- /ANA/ DON JUAN: A WORD AGAINST CHASTITY
SUPR III (119)	OF CHILDREN AND THE CLOSEST CARE OF THEM. FOR	HONOR	, CHASTITY, AND ALL THE REST OF YOUR MORAL FIGMENTS IT
GETT PREFACE(223)	ITSELF PURITY, HOME, MOTHERHOOD, RESPECTABILITY,	HONOR	, DECENCY, AND ANY OTHER FINE NAME THAT HAPPENS TO BE
SUPR III (90)	BE WELCOME IN HELL, SENORA. HELL IS THE HOME OF	HONOR	, DUTY, JUSTICE, AND THE REST OF THE SEVEN DEADLY
SUPR HANDBOK(205)	REINFORCED BY THE STRONGEST CONVENTIONS OF	HONOR	, ESPRIT DE CORPS, PUBLICITY AND RESPONSIBILITY,
WIDO I (23)	WITH AFFECTION) BLANCHE: ON MY MOST SACRED	HONOR	, FAMILY OR NO FAMILY, PROMISE OR NO PROMISE-- (THE
SUPR IV (169)	YOU. BUT I AM FIGHTING FOR MY FREEDOM, FOR MY	HONOR	, FOR MY SELF, ONE AND INDIVISIBLE. /ANN/ YOUR
3PLA PREFACE(R38)	MERE PREUX CHEVALIER, WHOSE FANATICAL PERSONAL	HONOR	, GALLANTRY, AND SELF-SACRIFICE, ARE FOUNDED ON A
BARB PREFACE(219)	IN THE WORLD, IT REPRESENTS HEALTH, STRENGTH,	HONOR	, GENEROSITY AND BEAUTY AS CONSPICUOUSLY AND
WIDO II (43)	HOUSES HAVE NO RIGHT TO THROW STONES. BUT, ON MY	HONOR	, I NEVER KNEW THAT MY HOUSE WAS A GLASS ONE UNTIL YOU
BULL II (113)	INDIFFERENCE) HAVE YOU NOW? WELL, THATS A GREAT	HONOR	, I'M SURE. /BROADBENT/ I HAVE LOOKED FORWARD TO
GETT PREFACE(252)	WHICH CONCEAL NOTHING OF SEX BUT ITS DIGNITY, ITS	HONOR	, ITS SACREDNESS, ITS RANK AS THE FIRST NECESSITY OF
SUPR HANDBOK(188)	ALL MAN'S PRESENT TRUMPERY IDEALS OF RIGHT, DUTY,	HONOR	, JUSTICE, RELIGION, EVEN DECENCY, AND ACCEPT MORAL
BARB II (291)	ME: IS THERE ANY PLACE IN YOUR RELIGION FOR	HONOR	, JUSTICE, TRUTH, LOVE, MERCY AND SO FORTH?
LADY PREFACE(207)	THAT THE DARK LADY, FAR FROM BEING A MAID OF	HONOR	, KEPT A TAVERN IN OXFORD AND WAS THE MOTHER OF
CLEO III (153)	A HUNDRED EGGS OF THE SACRED BLUE PIGEON. ON YOUR	HONOR	, LET NOT ONE OF THEM BE BROKEN. /APOLLODORUS/ ON MY
DOCT PREFACE(78)	YEARS OF THE SOUL, WHEN THE GREAT VITAL DOGMAS OF	HONOR	, LIBERTY, COURAGE, THE KINSHIP OF ALL LIFE, FAITH
KING I (186)	IT IS FOR ME ALONE. /NEWTON/ YOU HAVE MY WORD OF	HONOR	, MADAM. /LOUISE/ BUT A WORD OF HONOR MUST BE A
BULL II (116)	STONE). NO: ON MY WORD, ON MY MOST SACRED WORD OF	HONOR	, MISS REILLY, I TRIPPED OVER THAT STONE. IT WAS AN
2TRU II (64)	VERY FEW PEOPLE HAVE MORE THAN ONE POINT OF	HONOR	, MOPS. AND LOTS OF THEM HAVNT EVEN ONE. /THE
NEVR III (266)	CLANDON! /MRS CLANDON/ (RELENTLESSLY) ON YOUR	HONOR	, MR VALENTINE, ARE YOU IN EARNEST? /VALENTINE/ (
GETT (297)	YOU HAVE BEEN BEFOREHAND WITH ME. /SYKES/ ON MY	HONOR	, NO. ALL I SAID WAS THAT I DIDNT KNOW THE LAW WHEN I
BULL III (131)	ANYBODY'S BETTER THAN MATT, WHO HAS NEITHER	HONOR	, NOR ABILITY, NOR CAPITAL, NOR ANYTHING BUT MERE
GETT PREFACE(220)	HUSBAND EVER SECURED HIS DOMESTIC HAPPINESS AND	HONOR	, NOR HAS ANY WIFE EVER SECURED HERS, BY RELYING ON
DOCT PREFACE(30)	SHOULD BE FREE FROM THE RESTRAINTS OF LAW, OF	HONOR	, OF PITY, OF REMORSE, OF EVERYTHING THAT
MIS. PREFACE(55)	IN WHICH SUCH OBSCENITIES ARE MADE POINTS OF	HONOR	, OR OF INSTITUTIONS IN WHICH THEY ARE AN ACCEPTED
CLEO II (125)	ANTICIPATING A LATER STATESMAN) PEACE WITH	HONOR	, POTHINUS. /POTHINUS/ (MUTINOUSLY) CAESAR: BE
2TRU PREFACE(21)	DESTROY PEACE, JUSTICE, RELIGION, GOOD BREEDING,	HONOR	, REASONABLE FREEDOM, AND EVERYTHING THAT GOVERNMENT
LION PREFACE(93)	DRIVE OF EVOLUTION, WHICH WE CALL CONSCIENCE AND	HONOR	, SEIZES ON SUCH SLIPS, AND SHAMES US TO THE DUST FOR
BULL IV (180)	CERTAINLY JOIN IT. /KEEGAN/ YOU DO ME TOO MUCH	HONOR	, SIR. (WITH PRIESTLY HUMILITY TO LARRY) MR DOYLE: I
GETT PREFACE(194)	NATION WILL HAVE TO GO. IT IS NO USE TALKING OF	HONOR	, VIRTUE, PURITY, AND WHOLESOME, SWEET, CLEAN ENGLISH
LADY PREFACE(207)	BARD. NOW THIS, IF THE DARK LADY WAS A MAID OF	HONOR	, WAS QUITE EASY. IF SHE WERE A TAVERN LANDLADY, IT
DEVL III (51)	REPROACHFUL EARNESTNESS) RICHARD DUDGEON: ON YOUR	HONOR	, WHAT WOULD YOU HAVE DONE IN HIS PLACE? /RICHARD/
LIED (199)	TELL YOU THAT MRS BOMPAS IS A LADY OF STAINLESS	HONOR	, WHO HAS NEVER CAST AN UNWORTHY THOUGHT ON ME. THE
MIS. (160)	I SACRIFICE MY OWN. YOULL RESPECT THAT POINT OF	HONOR	, WONT YOU? /LINA/ ONLY A POINT OF HONOR? /TARLETON/
LION II (129)	BUT I MUST GO INTO THE ARENA WITH THE REST. MY	HONOR	, YOU KNOW. /THE EDITOR/ HONOR! THE HONOR OF A
INCA (257)	/THE INCA/ (CAUTIOUSLY) IN THE STRICTEST	HONOR	, YOU UNDERSTAND. /ERMYNTRUDE/ DONT BE AFRAID. I
ROCK II (269)	VERY MUCH HONORED, MR HIPNEY. /HIPNEY/ NO GREAT	HONOR	, YOUR GRACE. BUT OLD HIPNEY CAN TELL YOU SOMETHING
MIS. (185)	I APPEAL TO YOU AS A GENTLEMAN! AS A MAN OF	HONOR	! AS A MAN BOUND TO STAND BY ANOTHER MAN! YOU WERE
SUPR II (53)	REMORSEFULLY) NO, DEAR TAVY, NOT RIDICULE, ON MY	HONOR	! HOWEVER, NO MATTER, GO ON. /OCTAVIUS/ HER SENSE OF
O'FL (217)	SURE HE HAS THAT, YOUR HONOR. GOD BLESS YOUR	HONOR	! (THE GENERAL BEING NOW OUT OF HEARING, SHE TURNS
LION II (129)	WITH THE REST. MY HONOR, YOU KNOW. /THE EDITOR/	HONOR	! THE HONOR OF A TAILOR? /ANDROCLES/ (
GENV III (77)	CASE HONOR WOULD BE SATISFIED. /THE SECRETARY/	HONOR	! THE STOCK EXCUSE FOR MAKING A CORPSE. /THE

SUPR III	(98)	(AGAIN TOUCHING THE MARBLE HAND) AH, WHAT AN	HONOR	! WHAT A TRIUMPH FOR OUR CAUSE! THANK YOU, THANK
			HONORABLE	
MRS II	(199)	WARREN: DONT YOU BE ALARMED. MY INTENTIONS ARE	HONORABLE	: EVER SO HONORABLE; AND YOUR LITTLE GIRL IS JOLLY
CLEO PRO2	(96)	RISING FROM HIS KNEE) ARE EVIL TIDINGS, THEN, SO	HONORABLE	? /BELZANOR/ O BARBAROUS PERSIAN, HEAR MY
LION I	(115)	WILL YOU NOT CHOOSE RATHER A KINDLY LOVE AND AN	HONORABLE	ALLIANCE? /LAVINIA/ THEY CANNOT VIOLATE MY SOUL.
GETT PREFACE	(244)	OF HONEST POVERTY. WHEN EVERY YOUNG WOMAN HAS AN	HONORABLE	AND COMFORTABLE LIVELIHOOD OPEN TO HER ON
UNPL PREFACE	(R25)	THAT THE AVERAGE HOMEBRED ENGLISHMAN, HOWEVER	HONORABLE	AND GOODNATURED HE MAY BE IN HIS PRIVATE CAPACITY,
GETT PREFACE	(233)	AS CONCEIVED IN THE CONVENTIONAL NOVELET. WHAT AN	HONORABLE	AND SENSIBLE MAN DOES WHEN HIS HOUSEHOLD IS
WIDO I	(15)	NO. I MAY SAY THAT YOUR PROPOSAL SEEMS TO BE AN	HONORABLE	AND STRAIGHTFORWARD ONE, AND THAT IT IS VERY
POSN PREFACE	(416)	INTO TWO SECTIONS. THE FIRST SECTION CONSISTS OF	HONORABLE	AND SUCCESSFUL MANAGERS LIKE MR ALEXANDER, WHO
2TRU II	(62)	THAT THE EX-CHAPLAIN IS HER HALF STEPBROTHER THE	HONORABLE	AUBREY BAGOT, THAN CLOUDS OF WITNESSES SPRING UP
DOCT PREFACE	(74)	A LIFE SPENT IN MAKING MISTAKES IS NOT ONLY MORE	HONORABLE	BUT MORE USEFUL THAN A LIFE SPENT DOING NOTHING.
GETT PREFACE	(258)	SEXUAL RELATIONS BETWEEN MEN AND WOMEN DECENT AND	HONORABLE	BY MAKING WOMEN ECONOMICALLY INDEPENDENT OF MEN,
BULL PREFACE	(47)	FRIENDS AND RELATIVES OFFICERS WHOSE AMIABLE AND	HONORABLE	CHARACTER SEEMS TO CONTRADICT EVERYTHING I HAVE
GETT	(305)	IT IS HER RIGHT AND HER DUTY TO STAND OUT FOR	HONORABLE	CONDITIONS. IF WE CAN AGREE ON THE CONDITIONS, I
GETT	(322)	PREPARED TO DO WITHOUT ANYTHING I CANT HAVE ON	HONORABLE	CONDITIONS. /SOAMES/ (AFTER A SILENCE EXPRESSIVE
DOCT PREFACE	(49)	PRODUCED NOTHING SO IMPORTANT AS THE INNOCENT AND	HONORABLE	DISCOVERY OF RADIOGRAPHY; AND ONE OF THE REASONS
MTH3	(117)	SOMETHING UNUSUAL. /CONFUCIUS/ I NOTICE THAT THE	HONORABLE	DOMESTIC MINISTER, ON LEARNING THE ADVANCED AGE OF
BARB III	(320)	BE FACETIOUS. I PRETEND TO NOTHING MORE THAN ANY	HONORABLE	ENGLISH GENTLEMAN CLAIMS AS HIS BIRTHRIGHT (HE
LIED	(191)	AS YOU SOON WILL SEE-- THAT THIS IS THE ONLY WAY	HONORABLE	ENOUGH FOR YOUR FEET TO TREAD. LET US GO OUT
BARB PREFACE	(240)	SO MUCH OF IT FOR SIXPENCE. THAT RIGHTEOUS AND	HONORABLE	HIGH HUMAN DEED IS NOT WASTED ON EUROPE, LET US
UNPL PREFACE	(R26)	CONTRACTS, AND MRS WARREN'S PROFESSION WITH	HONORABLE	INDUSTRIES GUARDED BY A HUMANE INDUSTRIAL CODE AND
DOCT PREFACE	(49)	EVERY VIVISECTOR IS A DESERTER FROM THE ARMY OF	HONORABLE	INVESTIGATORS. BUT THE VIVISECTOR DOES NOT SEE
MTH2	(48)	I SUPPOSE I SHOULDNT SAY CHEESE IT TO A RIGHT	HONORABLE	, BUT THE STRAND, YOU KNOW! DO COME OFF IT.
PRES	(157)	LOVE-- REAL LOVE-- MAKES ALL INTENTIONS	HONORABLE	, BUT YOU COULD NEVER UNDERSTAND THAT. /MITCHENER/
MIS.	(201)	AND TAKE CARE OF HIM: THAT WOULD BE FOOLISH, BUT	HONORABLE	, I DO NOT MIND YOU, OLD PAL: YOU ARE WHAT YOU
BULL II	(115)	I AM SINCERE; AND MY INTENTIONS ARE PERFECTLY	HONORABLE	, I THINK YOU WILL ACCEPT THE FACT THAT I'M AN
GETT	(328)	THIS. I LOVE YOU. MY INTENTIONS ARE NOT	HONORABLE	. (SHE SHEWS NO DISMAY). SCREAM. RING THE BELL.
SUPR III	(124)	WOULD COUNTENANCE MY ADVANCES, PROVIDED THEY WERE	HONORABLE	, ON INQUIRING WHAT THAT PROVISO MEANT, I FOUND
PYGM II	(237)	THAT MR HIGGINS'S INTENTIONS ARE ENTIRELY	HONORABLE	. /DOOLITTLE/ COURSE THEY ARE, GOVERNOR. IF I
GENV I	(31)	YOU MY WORD THAT MY INTENTIONS ARE COMPLETELY	HONORABLE	. /SHE/ WELL, WHAT ABOUT THE PAY? AND HOW LONG
JOAN PREFACE	(4)	THE FACT THAT HE WAS AN OLD SOLDIER AND A MAN OF	HONORABLE	LIFE, AND THAT HIS ACCUSER WAS A SILLY SNOB. HE
PLES PREFACE	(R13)	RUINING THEMSELVES, THAT THEY CAN ALL POINT TO	HONORABLE	LOSSES INCURRED THROUGH AIMING " OVER THE HEADS OF
SUPR III	(121)	OF THINKING, TO BEND MAN'S MIND WHOLLY TOWARDS	HONORABLE	LOVE AS THE HIGHEST GOOD, AND TO UNDERSTAND BY
SUPR III	(121)	LOVE AS THE HIGHEST GOOD, AND TO UNDERSTAND BY	HONORABLE	LOVE ROMANCE AND BEAUTY AND HAPPINESS IN THE
AUGS	(270)	THIS WEEK, YOU WILL SEE THAT I AM ENGAGED TO THE	HONORABLE	LUCY POPHAM, YOUNGEST DAUGHTER OF -- /THE CLERK/
LIED	(191)	TO YOUR HUSBAND. WE ARE HIS GUESTS HERE: HE IS AN	HONORABLE	MAN: HE HAS BEEN KIND TO US: HE HAS PERHAPS LOVED
BULL IV	(166)	/NORA/ (SEVERELY) THEN WHY DIDNT YOU IF YOURE AN	HONORABLE	MAN? /BROADBENT/ WELL, TO TELL YOU THE TRUTH,
GETT	(304)	MARRIED? /SYKES/ WILL SOMEBODY TELL ME WHAT AN	HONORABLE	MAN AND A SINCERE ANGLICAN IS TO PROPOSE TO A
DOCT PREFACE	(48)	TURN ROUND AND ASK HOW ANY PERSON DARE SUSPECT AN	HONORABLE	MAN LIKE MYSELF OF TELLING LIES. MOST SENSIBLE AND
DOCT III	(147)	I HAVE MADE IT A RULE NOT SO TO ARGUE. NOW, AS AN	HONORABLE	MAN, HAVING MADE THAT RULE AS TO PAYING PATIENTS,
HART I	(58)	PAPA SO MUCH, AND SAW SO PLAINLY THAT HE WAS AN	HONORABLE	MAN, THAT THEY LET HIM OFF AT SIX-AND-EIGHTPENCE
DOCT III	(136)	WELL, RIDGEON, IF THIS IS WHAT YOU CALL BEING AN	HONORABLE	MAN! I SPOKE TO YOU IN CONFIDENCE. /SIR PATRICK/
WIDO II	(43)	OUR PROPERTY, AND AM MAINTAINING IT BY THE SAME	HONORABLE	MEANS. /COKANE/ (GREATLY RELIEVED) ADMIRABLE, MY
BULL PREFACE	(63)	SHOULD HAVE FACED IT AND FOUGHT IT BRAVELY BY	HONORABLE	MEANS, INSTEAD OF WILDLY LASHING AND STRANGLING A
GETT PREFACE	(246)	TO THE DOCTOR IF NOT TO THE EXECUTIONER; AND THAT	HONORABLE	MEN AND WOMEN, WHEN THEIR CIRCUMSTANCES PERMIT IT,
DOCT PREFACE	(48)	HUMANE PEOPLE WOULD, I HOPE, REPLY FLATLY THAT	HONORABLE	MEN DO NOT BEHAVE DISHONORABLY EVEN TO DOGS. THE
GETT	(290)	FALSE AT ONE TIME OR ANOTHER, AND THAT SOME VERY	HONORABLE	MEN SHOULD NEVER GO INTO ACTION AT ALL, BECAUSE
SUPR HANDBOK	(221)	JEALOUS OF THEM. HONOR. THERE ARE NO PERFECTLY	HONORABLE	MEN; BUT EVERY TRUE MAN HAS ONE MAIN POINT OF
GETT PREFACE	(228)	HOME AS THE HOLY OF HOLIES IN THE TEMPLE OF	HONORABLE	MOTHERHOOD, INNOCENT CHILDHOOD, MANLY VIRTUE, AND
ROCK I	(213)	YOURS DEVOTEDLY, BROLLY. AND WHAT HAS HIS RIGHT	HONORABLE	NIBS TO SAY TO THAT. /SIR ARTHUR/ (CONCENTRATING
PYGM EPILOG	(295)	HIGGINS DECLARED, WAS A MUCH MORE USEFUL AND	HONORABLE	OCCUPATION THAN WORKING IN THE CITY. WHEN ELIZA
GETT	(271)	MINE AS A SOLDIER? /COLLINS/ I'M SURE IT'S VERY	HONORABLE	OF YOU TO SAY SO, GENERAL. /THE GENERAL/ (
GETT	(307)	THE SITUATION. THESE LADIES NOT ONLY REFUSE OUR	HONORABLE	OFFERS, BUT AS I UNDERSTAND IT-- AND I'M SURE I
ROCK PREFACE	(165)	THE INFAMOUS CATEGORY OF INTELLIGENTSIA TO THE	HONORABLE	ONE OF " THE INTELLECTUAL PROLETARIAT." EVEN LENIN
ARMS II	(26)	BUT OF COURSE WE SAW TO IT THAT THE TREATY WAS AN	HONORABLE	ONE. IT DECLARES PEACE-- /CATHERINE/ (OUTRAGED)
HART I	(59)	DOWN AT HER) YOU KNOW, OF COURSE, THAT IT'S NOT	HONORABLE	OR GRATEFUL TO MARRY A MAN YOU DONT LOVE. DO YOU
BUOY II	(24)	PERCEIVE BY YOUR ASSURANCE THAT YOU ARE A HIGHLY	HONORABLE	PERSON AMONG YOUR OWN PEOPLE; BUT HERE YOU ARE A
MRS I	(195)	AND FLIPPANCY, AND TO WORK YOUR WAY INTO AN	HONORABLE	PROFESSION AND LIVE ON IT AND NOT UPON ME. /FRANK/
SIM I	(48)	IT. BUT WHY SHOULD SHE REJECT ME IF I MAKE HER AN	HONORABLE	PROPOSAL? /LADY FARWATERS/ BECAUSE SHE WILL
SIM I	(48)	/LADY FARWATERS/ BECAUSE SHE WILL CONSIDER YOUR	HONORABLE	PROPOSAL DISHONORABLE, MR HAMMINGTAP, UNLESS IT
MRS II	(199)	BE ALARMED. MY INTENTIONS ARE HONORABLE: EVER SO	HONORABLE	; AND YOUR LITTLE GIRL IS JOLLY WELL ABLE TO TAKE
OVER	(188)	MOMENT MY INTENTIONS WERE STRICTLY AND RESOLUTELY	HONORABLE	; THOUGH MY CONDUCT, WHICH I COULD NOT CONTROL AND
PHIL I SD	(84)	VIGILANT, IRASCIBLE EYE, PILED-UP HAIR, AND THE	HONORABLE	SERIOUSNESS WITH WHICH HE TAKES HIMSELF, GIVE HIM
BULL I	(82)	IT WAS NOT BORROWING EXACTLY. HE SHEWED A VERY	HONORABLE	SPIRIT ABOUT MONEY. I BELIEVE HE WOULD SHARE HIS
GETT	(270)	BEEN TRAINED TO DO WITHOUT WHAT I CANT HAVE ON	HONORABLE	TERMS, NO MATTER WHAT IT IS. /THE GENERAL/ I
PRES	(157)	PENNY-NOVELETTE NOTION THAT AN OFFICER IS LESS	HONORABLE	THAN A CIVILIAN IN HIS RELATIONS WITH WOMEN. WHILE
GETT	(290)	NOT USE THAT VISITING CARD. NO DOUBT IT'S AN	HONORABLE	TRAIT IN YOUR CHARACTER THAT YOU DONT WISH ANY MAN
CAND I	(92)	JAMES AND ME IS COME TO A NUNNERSTANNIN. A	HONORABLE	UNNERSTANNIN. AIN WE, JAMES? /MORELL/ (
BARB PREFACE	(236)	ORGANIZING SOCIETY SO THAT HE SHALL GET IT IN AN	HONORABLE	WAY: THEY CONCLUDE THAT HIS CHARACTER IS UNSOUND
BULL PREFACE	(44)	WAS PERFECTLY RIGHT. THAT BRUTE FORCE WAS A MORE	HONORABLE	WEAPON THAN THE POVERTY WHICH WE USED TO UNDERSELL
GETT PREFACE	(256)	TO MAKE IT NOT ONLY HARMLESS BUT COMFORTABLE,	HONORABLE	, AND USEFUL. THE COST OF DIVORCE. BUT PLEASE DO
GENV IV	(88)	YOU ARE THE FOREIGN SECRETARY, NUNKY, YOU ARE AN	HONORABLE	, BILLIKINS, AND I'M NOT EXACTLY A NOBODY. /THE
SIM PREFACE	(6)	OF THE QUESTION ALSO SEE THE THOUGHTFUL, SENTIMENTAL,	HONORABLE	, CONSCIENTIOUS PEOPLE WHO NEED NO HELL TO
PHIL III	(137)	/CHARTERIS/ I AM AFRAID YOUR INTENTIONS HAVE BEEN	HONORABLE	, JULIA. /JULIA/ YOU CAD! /CHARTERIS/ (WITH A
BARB III	(331)	I MET BARBARA I THOUGHT MYSELF IN THE MAIN AN	HONORABLE	, TRUTHFUL MAN, BECAUSE I WANTED THE APPROVAL OF
GETT PREFACE	(194)	FACT IS THAT ENGLISH HOME LIFE TODAY IS NEITHER	HONORABLE	, VIRTUOUS, WHOLESOME, SWEET, CLEAN, NOR IN ANY
			HONORABLY	
FANY III	(322)	WANTING TO KNOW WHETHER HE INTENDED TO BEHAVE	HONORABLY	? /DUVALLET/ AH, MADAM, MY DAUGHTERS ARE FRENCH
DEST	(159)	WORTHY OF HIS CONFIDENCE: I BROUGHT THEM ALL BACK	HONORABLY	. BUT WOULD YOU BELIEVE IT? WHEN I TRUSTED HIM
2TRU PREFACE	(12)	LIBERTY IF THEY ARE FORCED TO EARN THEIR LIVING	HONORABLY	. THE RETORT THAT THEY HAVE NOTHING TO LOSE BUT
GETT PREFACE	(234)	THE MARRIAGE TO BE DISSOLVED AND THE PARTIES	HONORABLY	RE-SORTED AND RECOUPLED WITHOUT DISGRACE AND
GETT	(278)	IT WOULD BE SO HORRID FOR REJJY. I OFFERED	HONORABLY	TO DO IT MYSELF, AND LET HIM DIVORCE ME; BUT HE
CLEO PRO1	(91)	TO UTTER NOTHINGNESS, HE MADE A LAST STAND TO DIE	HONORABLY	, AND DID NOT DESPAIR; FOR HE SAID, " AGAINST ME
			HONORARIUM	
DOCT PREFACE	(64)	END TO THE TRADITION THAT THE DOCTOR'S FEE IS AN	HONORARIUM	. EVEN THE MOST EMINENT PHYSICIANS, AS SUCH
			HONORARY	
GETT	(291)	HAVE BEEN FULLY APPRECIATED. I WAS MADE AN	HONORARY	MEMBER OF TWO OF THE SMARTEST CLUBS IN LONDON WHEN
			HONORED	
SUPR III	(123)	OF THE REAL PURPOSE OF MARRIAGE WILL BE	HONORED	AND ACCEPTED, WHILST THEIR ROMANTIC VOWINGS AND
ROCK PREFACE	(160)	HAD NO PLACE: ON THE CONTRARY THEY WERE HIGHLY	HONORED	AND REWARDED, AS OUR ENGLISH DOGGEREL RUNS, THE
MTH3	(114)	TO SEE YOU, MRS LUTESTRING. /CONFUCIUS/ WE ARE	HONORED	BY YOUR CELESTIAL PRESENCE. /BARNABAS/ GOOD DAY,
PYGM V	(281)	MISS YOUR WEDDING. /DOOLITTLE/ I SHOULD INDEED BE	HONORED	BY YOUR CONDESCENSION, MAAM; AND MY POOR OLD WOMAN
2TRU III	(101)	DO YOU SUPPOSE, BECAUSE THE BRIGANDAGE WHICH I AM	HONORED	FOR SUPPRESSING HAS NO EXISTENCE, THAT I HAVE NEVER
OVER PREFACE	(167)	OF THE DISTINGUISHED LADIES AND GENTLEMEN WHO	HONORED	HIM WITH THEIR PRESENCE ON THAT OCCASION, AND THEN
MILL I	(138)	DI PARERGA. /SAGAMORE/ (BOWING) OH! I AM INDEED	HONORED	. PRAY BE SEATED. /EPIFANIA/ SIT DOWN YOURSELF; AND
MILL IV	(192)	SURPRISES HIM). OH, INDEED, SIR! WE ARE	HONORED	. /ALASTAIR/ ANYTHING WRONG? /THE MANAGER/ OH NO,
FOUN	(212)	(WITH EMOTION) MY FAITHFUL MERCER. /MERCER/ MY	HONORED	MASTER. (THEY SHAKE HANDS, WEEPING). /THE LORD
PHIL II	(102)	DO YOU SEE THAT OLD MAN, GROWN GREY IN THE	HONORED	SERVICE OF HIS COUNTRY, WHOSE LAST DAYS YOU HAVE
PRES	(151)	THE VOICE OF MY OFFICER. I SHOULD FEEL PROUD AND	HONORED	TO BE ABLE TO SERVE MY COUNTRY BY OBEYING ITS
ANNA	(290)	HIS FATHER, YOUR TOILING MILLIONS WERE ONLY TOO	HONORED	TO RECEIVE THE TOES OF OUR BOOTS IN THE PROPER SPOT
ANNA	(290)	HAVE KEPT OUR PLACE FOR US AT THEIR COURTS,	HONORED	US, PROMOTED US, SHED THEIR GLORY ON US, MADE US

SUPR II (68) THE MOST OVERWHELMING CAWNFIDNCE IVE EVER BEEN HONORED WITH. TANNER RETURNS WITH STRAKER, WHO GOES TO HIS
MILL II (174) IT. /EPIFANIA/ CONSIDER IT! YOU WILL FEEL HONORED , GRATIFIED, DELIGHTED. /THE DOCTOR/ I SEE. ENORMOUS
ROCK II (269) WEVE NEVER BEEN INTRODUCED. /THE DUKE/ VERY MUCH HONORED , MR HIPNEY. /HIPNEY/ NO GREAT HONOR, YOUR GRACE.

HONORIA
MRS I (186) I HAVE. LAST MAY I SPENT SIX WEEKS IN LONDON WITH HONORIA FRASER. MAMMA THOUGHT WE WERE DOING A ROUND OF
MRS IV SD(235) ACT IV. HONORIA FRASER'S CHAMBERS IN CHANCERY LANE. AN OFFICE AT THE
MRS III (234) GOING TO? WHERE SHALL WE FIND YOU? /VIVIE/ AT HONORIA FRASER'S CHAMBERS, 67 CHANCERY LANE, FOR THE REST OF
MRS IV (236) WAS SETTLED TWENTY MINUTES AFTER I ARRIVED HERE. HONORIA HAS FOUND THE BUSINESS TOO MUCH FOR HER THIS YEAR;
MRS I (188) TO-MORROW EARNING MY OWN LIVING BY DEVILLING FOR HONORIA , BESIDES, I HAVE NO MYSTERIES TO KEEP UP; AND IT

HONORIA'S
MRS IV (236) EVER SO SERIOUSLY. /VIVIE/ VERY WELL: SIT DOWN IN HONORIA'S CHAIR AND TALK HERE. I LIKE TEN MINUTES CHAT AFTER
MRS IV SD(247) VIVIE, COMPOSED AND EXTREMELY GRAVE, SITS DOWN IN HONORIA'S CHAIR, AND WAITS FOR HER MOTHER TO SPEAK. MRS
MRS I (186) OF SIGHTSEEING TOGETHER; BUT I WAS REALLY AT HONORIA'S CHAMBERS IN CHANCERY LANE EVERY DAY, WORKING AWAY

HONORING
SUPR III SD(71) CONSCIOUS OF THEMSELVES AS PICTURESQUE SCOUNDRELS HONORING THE SIERRA BY USING IT AS AN EFFECTIVE PICTORIAL

HONORIS
FABL PREFACE(91) PERPETUAL SERENADING." WILLIAM MORRIS, EQUALLY HONORIS CAUSA, COULD NOT TOLERATE A PIANO IN HIS HOUSE. WHEN

HONOR'S
MTH3 (94) SECRETARY, AND HOLDS HIMSELF ENTIRELY AT HIS HONOR'S AUGUST DISPOSAL. /A CHINESE VOICE/ HE IS COMING.
CAPT I (218) HIMSELF DUTIFULLY TO THE INTERRUPTION). YR HONOR'S EOLTH. /RANKIN/ (RESERVEDLY) GOOD AFTERNOON, MR
O'FL (216) HE IS; AND WHY WOULDNT HE BE, BROUGHT UP ON YOUR HONOR'S ESTATE AND WITH YOU BEFORE HIS EYES FOR A PATTERN OF
O'FL (216) HONOR. (TO SIR PEARCE, HEARTILY) AND HOW IS YOUR HONOR'S GOOD SELF? AND HOW IS HER LADYSHIP AND ALL THE
CAPT I (234) SIR HOWARD AND LADY CICELY. /DRINKWATER/ YR HONOR'S SERVANT. (TO THE ITALIAN) MAWTZOW: IS LAWDSHIP SR
GENV II (61) USEFUL SAFETY VALVE. /THE SECRETARY/ I WAS ON HIS HONOR'S SIDE MYSELF ONCE, UNTIL MY OFFICIAL EXPERIENCE HERE

HONORS
DOCT I (83) WHAT DO YOU SUPPOSE I CARE ABOUT THE BIRTHDAY HONORS ? GET OUT OF THIS WITH YOUR CHATTERING. DR RIDGEON
DOCT I (83) /REDPENNY/ NO. /EMMY/ NOT SEEN THE BIRTHDAY HONORS ? /REDPENNY/ (BEGINNING TO SWEAR) WHAT THE-- /EMMY/
FABL III (109) ARE CLASSED AS A MEDIOCRITY. DID YOU PASS WITH HONORS ? /THE TOURIST/ NO. THEY WERE GROSSLY UNFAIR TO ME.
CATH 2 (175) IN ME: YOU BASK IN MY SMILES: YOU GET TITLES AND HONORS AND FAVORS FROM ME: YOU ARE DAZZLED BY MY CROWN AND
JOAN 4 (95) CRACK; AND AS HE HAS BEEN TO THE HOLY LAND TOO, HONORS ARE EASY BETWEEN US AS FAR AS THAT GOES. /THE
MIS. (185) PERCIVAL: YOURE WHITEWASHED. SO ARE YOU, PATSY. HONORS ARE EASY. LETS DROP THE SUBJECT. THE NEXT THING TO DO
LION PREFACE(47) US THAT WHEN JESUS EXPLICITLY CLAIMED DIVINE HONORS BY THE SACRAMENT OF HIS BODY AND BLOOD, SO MANY OF
MRS I (185) PRACTICAL TO CONSIDER NOT ONLY THE WORK THESE HONORS COST, BUT ALSO THE CULTURE THEY BRING. /VIVIE/
CATH 4 (191) VICTORIOUS, HAPPY AND GLORIOUS! OH, LET ETERNAL HONORS CROWN HIS NAME! VOLTAIRE THRICE WORTHY ON THE ROLLS
2TRU III (101) I, TOO, HAVE WON REAL BATTLES, AND SEEN ALL THE HONORS GO TO A BRIGADIER WHO DID NOT EVEN KNOW WHAT WAS
JOAN 5 (110) CHARLES AND MADE HIM A REAL KING; AND ALL THE HONORS HE IS HANDING OUT HAVE GONE TO THEM. THEN WHY DO THEY
FABL PREFACE(89) VALUE. UNLESS A POSTULANT FOR FIRST CLASS HONORS IN POLITICS CAN WRITE AN ESSAY SHEWING THAT HE (OR
BUOY 1 (9) BUT YOU COULD HAVE IF YOU HAD CHOSEN TO WORK FOR HONORS INSTEAD OF JOINING RATHER DISREPUTABLE CLUBS AND
GETT (310) AND I SHALL BE PROUD TO RETURN WITH MUNICIPAL HONORS . (HE STALKS OUT GALLANTLY, COLLINS RISING FOR A
2TRU III (100) /MEEK/ YOUR K. C. B., SIR. (PRESENTING A PAPER) HONORS LIST BY WIRELESS. /TALLBOYS/ (RISING JOYOUSLY TO
MTH2 (87) THERE WILL BE AN O.M. FOR SOMEBODY WHEN THE FIRST HONORS LIST COMES ROUND (BY THIS TIME HE HAS TALKED HIMSELF
MTH3 (92) TODAY TO RECEIVE THAT AMERICAN FELLOW, AND DO THE HONORS OF A RIDICULOUS CINEMA SHOW. THAT IS NOT THE BUSINESS
PYGM PREFACE(202) WRATH AND DISDAIN, HE CANNOT EXPECT THEM TO HEAP HONORS ON HIM. OF THE LATER GENERATIONS OF PHONETICIANS I
CAPT I (234) THETS WOT E IS. KEPN BRARSBAHND'S RESPECTS TO YR HONORS ; AN E AWITES YR COMMAWNDS. /RANKIN/ SHALL WE GO
MILL PREFACE(133) SCHOOL, AND UNIVERSITY WITH THE HIGHEST ACADEMIC HONORS WITHOUT KNOWING THE DIFFERENCE BETWEEN A CHANTY AND A
BASH III (125) RIGHT TO MAKE A DECLARATION WHICH FLATTERS ME AND HONORS YOUR AMBITION. PRIOR ATTACHMENT BIDS ME FIRMLY SAY
MTH4 II (189) WHEN I SAY A RECEPTION I MEAN A RECEPTION. ROYAL HONORS , MIND YOU! A SALUTE OF A HUNDRED AND ONE GUNS! THE
GENV PREFACE(20) OF THE GERMAN REALM WITH MORE THAN ROYAL HONORS , THOUGH HIS WHOLE STOCK-IN-TRADE WAS A BRAZEN VOICE

HONOUR
SHAK (139) TOWN, WHERE EVERY YEAR A FESTIVAL IS HELD TO HONOUR MY RENOWN NOT FOR AN AGE BUT FOR ALL TIME. HITHER I

HOO
CATH 4 (196) ! /THE SERGEANT/ SAINTED NICHOLAS! /VARINKA/ HOO HOO! (A STIFLED SPLUTTER OF LAUGHTER). /EDSTASTON/
PYGM I (210) TO PAY FOUR-AND-SIX A WEEK. (IN TEARS) OH, BOO-- HOO -- OO-- /THE NOTE TAKER/ LIVE WHERE YOU LIKE; BUT STOP
APPL I (239) NIGHT" -- LIKE THAT. THE OTHER WENT " BOO! HOO ! I WANT AMANDA'S TEDDY BEAR TO PLAY WITH." THEY SANG
CATH 4 (196) /THE SERGEANT/ SAINTED NICHOLAS! /VARINKA/ HOO HOO ! (A STIFLED SPLUTTER OF LAUGHTER). /EDSTASTON/

HOOCHLIPOOCHLI
BUOY II (25) BENEVOLENCE. HE THEREFORE BELIEVED NOT ONLY IN HOOCHLIPOOCHLI BUT IN POOCHLIHOOCHLI, THE GOD OF HELL, WHOM
BUOY II (24) BUT HERE HIS HOLY NAME (HE BENDS HIS NECK) IS HOOCHLIPOOCHLI . HE HAS A HUNDRED EARTHLY BRIDES; AND SHE
BUOY II (25) AND THOUGHT THEY SHEWED THE TERRIBLE GREATNESS OF HOOCHLIPOOCHLI . MY FATHER SAW THEM ALSO, BUT COULD NOT
BUOY II (26) THIRST FOR RIGHTEOUSNESS. THAT SOMETHING MUST BE HOOCHLIPOOCHLI . /HE/ WAS IT HOOCHLIPOOCHLI WHO SET YOU
BUOY II (24) WE WHITE MEN HAVE A GOD MUCH MUCH GREATER THAN HOOCHLIPOOCHLI . /THE NATIVE/ SIR: THAT MAY BE SO. BUT YOU
BUOY II (26) AND NO BENEVOLENCE. /HE/ AND CONSEQUENTLY NO HOOCHLIPOOCHLI . /THE NATIVE/ NOT AT ALL. YOU ARE THROWING
BUOY II (26) WIVES, YOU WERE HUMBUGGING ME. /THE NATIVE/ SIR: HOOCHLIPOOCHLI POSSESSES ALL OF US MORE OR LESS; AND SO
BUOY II (26) SOMETHING MUST BE HOOCHLIPOOCHLI. /HE/ WAS IT HOOCHLIPOOCHLI WHO SET YOU TALKING PIDGIN ENGLISH TO ME
FABL PREFACE(69) AS WELL AS A DIVINITY: POOCHLIHOOCHLI AS WELL AS HOOCHLIPOOCHLI , AHRIMAN AS WELL AS ORMUDZ, LUCIFER

HOOCHLIPOOCHLI'S
BUOY II (26) WHEN YOU TOLD ME THAT THE WOMAN HERE IS ONE OF HOOCHLIPOOCHLI'S MANY HUNDRED EARTHLY WIVES, YOU WERE

HOOD
MTH1 I (6) OF ALL THE CREATURES OF THE FIELD. /EVE/ YOUR HOOD IS MOST LOVELY. (SHE STROKES IT AND PETS THE SERPENT).
MTH4 III SD(201) SIZE IS NOW NATURAL. HER FACE IS HIDDEN BY HER HOOD . HE FLINCHES AS IF FROM AN ELECTRIC SHOCK; TURNS TO
MTH1 I (6) IT IS I. I HAVE COME TO SHEW YOU MY BEAUTIFUL NEW HOOD . SEE (SHE SPREADS A MAGNIFICENT AMETHYSTINE HOOD)!
MILL PREFACE(124) THAN THAT OF THE WOLF IN LITTLE RED RIDING HOOD . WE ALL LIVE IN GLASS HOUSES. IS IT WISE TO THROW
MTH1 I (7) ME OF IT? I FORGOT IT WHEN I SAW YOUR BEAUTIFUL HOOD . YOU MUST NOT REMIND ME OF UNHAPPY THINGS. /THE
INCA SD(237) APPEARANCE IN A LONG STRAIGHT WATERPROOF WITH A HOOD OVER HER HEAD GEAR. SHE COMES TO THE END OF THE TABLE
MTH1 I (6) HOOD. SEE (SHE SPREADS A MAGNIFICENT AMETHYSTINE HOOD)! /EVE/ (ADMIRING IT) OH! BUT WHO TAUGHT YOU TO
BARB PREFACE(225) PROFESSIONAL PLAYGOERS, WHO STILL WEAR THEIR TOM HOOD SHIRTS AND UNDERPAY THEIR WASHERWOMEN WITHOUT THE

HOODED
MTH4 III SD(195) CONVERSED WITH NAPOLEON, AND IS NOW DRAPED AND HOODED IN VOLUMINOUS FOLDS OF A SINGLE PIECE OF GREY-WHITE

HOODOO
DOCT PREFACE(73) THE DEVIL OF DISEASE UNLESS IT BE SOME TERRIFYING HOODOO OF TORTURES AND STINKS, THE M.O.H. WILL NO DOUBT FOR

HOODS
JOAN PREFACE(50) PLATE ARMOR OR MOVING SILENTLY IN THE FROCKS AND HOODS OF THE ORDER OF ST DOMINIC. TRAGEDY, NOT MELODRAMA.

HOODWINKED
GETT PREFACE(184) OF SOCIETY ON VARIOUS OTHER GROUNDS TO BE HOODWINKED BY THE KEEPING UP OF THE VERY THINNEST
GENV PREFACE(3) MOTOR BUS, WHICH TOWNSMEN RUN DAILY, IS GREATER. HOODWINKED HEROISM. IT WAS THIS IMPROBABILITY WHICH MADE

HOODWINKS
FANY PROLOG (261) FATHER A PICTURESQUE PANTALOON, AND THE VALET WHO HOODWINKS THE FATHER AND BRINGS ABOUT THE HAPPINESS OF THE

HOOF
MIS. (193) I REALLY CANT HAVE HIM HERE STICKING HIS CLUMSY HOOF INTO MY AFFAIRS. /LORD SUMMERHAYS/ THE QUESTION IS, MR
BULL IV (177) TO BROWSE HERE WITHOUT KNOWING THAT THE SOIL HIS HOOF TOUCHES IS HOLY GROUND. IRELAND, SIR, FOR GOOD OR EVIL,

HOOFS
SUPR PREFACE(R26) WE ARE ALL NOW UNDER WHAT BURKE CALLED " THE HOOFS OF THE SWINISH MULTITUDE." BURKE'S LANGUAGE GAVE GREAT

HOOK
DEVL II SD(28) BARS, MOVABLE IRON GRIDDLE SOCKETED TO THE HOB, HOOK ABOVE FOR ROASTING, AND BROAD FENDER, ON WHICH STAND A
CLEO III SD(155) MIDDLE TO THE BROAD COPING. A HUGE CHAIN WITH A HOOK HANGS DOWN FROM THE LIGHTHOUSE CRANE ABOVE HIS HEAD.
KING I (190) TO HIM. THE ELECTOR OF HANOVER HAS THE SAME HOOK ON TO GRANDFATHER JAMES. BOTH OF THEM ARE RANK
KING I (207) SAME. THE PROTESTANTS WILL HAVE YOU, JAMIE, BY HOOK OR CROOK: I FORESEE THAT: THEY ARE THE REAL MEN OF
JOAN PREFACE(53) INSTEAD OF BEGINNING THERE. IT WAS NECESSARY BY HOOK OR CROOK TO SHEW THE CANONIZED JOAN AS WELL AS THE
APPL I (232) THAT IS WHAT JOE ALWAYS CONTRIVES TO DO, BY HOOK OR CROOK. /PLINY/ YOU DIDNT ARRANGE IT WITH HIM, MANDY:
METH PREFACE(R75) LONG RUN. OUR STATESMEN MUST GET A RELIGION BY HOOK OR CROOK; AND AS WE ARE COMMITTED TO ADULT SUFFRAGE IT
FABL VI (127) SUCCESSES. WE HAVE TO DESTROY THE LOCUST AND THE HOOK WORM AND THE COLORADO BEETLE BECAUSE, IF WE DO NOT,

HOOKAH
ARMS III SD(66) IN THE ROOM BY TAKING THE LITTLE TABLE WITH THE HOOKAH AWAY TO THE WALL NEAR THE WINDOWS. /RAINA/ (RISING
ARMS III SD(46) WITH A NEWSPAPER IN HIS HAND AND THE TUBE OF HIS HOOKAH WITHIN EASY REACH. CATHERINE SITS AT THE STOVE, WITH

HOOKED
BULL I (77) IF MY NAME WERE BREITSTEIN, AND I HAD A HOOKED NOSE AND A HOUSE IN PARK LANE, I SHOULD CARRY A UNION

HOOKNOSE
CLEO IV (167) MYSELF SERVED AS CAESAR IS SERVED. /CHARMIAN/ OLD HOOKNOSE ! (THEY LAUGH AGAIN). /CLEOPATRA/ (REVOLTED)

HOOKNOSED
CLEO III (151) LONGINGLY AT THE PURSE-- THIS SENTINEL IS A HOOKNOSED MAN, UNLIKE HIS COMRADE, WHO IS SQUAB FACED) DO

HOOK-HIT
BASH II,2, (116) MONARCH: THIS IS CALLED THE UPPER CUT, AND THIS A HOOK-HIT OF MINE OWN INVENTION. THE HOLLOW REGION WHERE I

HOOKS
JOAN 1 (63) SERVICE, POLLY. A FRIENDLY TALK. SIT DOWN. (HE HOOKS THE STOOL FROM UNDER THE TABLE WITH HIS INSTEP).
LION II (140) THROUGH FROM THE PASSAGE AS BEFORE) ROPES AND HOOKS THERE! ROPES AND HOOKS! /THE EDITOR/ WELL, NEED YOU
LION II SD(140) TWO SLAVES IN ETRUSCAN MASKS, WITH ROPES AND DRAG HOOKS , HURRY IN. /ONE OF THE SLAVES/ HOW MANY DEAD? /THE
LION II (140) AS BEFORE) ROPES AND HOOKS THERE! ROPES AND HOOKS ! /THE EDITOR/ WELL, NEED YOU EXCITE YOURSELF ABOUT

HOOLIGAN
CAPT I (233) WHAT! THE HOOLIGAN! /RANKIN/ (PUZZLED) HOOLIGAN ? NO, MY LORD: HE IS AN ENGLISHMAN. /SIR HOWARD/
ROCK I (194) THE MOUNTED MEN CAN HAVE A FAIR WHACK AT THE HOOLIGAN FRINGE WHEN THEY GET TOO OBSTREPEROUS." /SIR
ROCK I (195) WHEN THEY GET TOO OBSTREPEROUS." /SIR ARTHUR/ HOOLIGAN FRINGE! HE GOT THAT OUT OF THE PAPERS. IT ONLY
MIS. PREFACE(69) KNOWS THAT HIS SON WILL BECOME AN ILLITERATE HOOLIGAN IF HE IS LEFT TO THE STREETS, THERE IS NO REAL
CAPT I (233) ON MERELY BECAUSE HIS MOTHER BROUGHT HIM UP AS A HOOLIGAN , I AM SURE NOBODY COULD BE NICER THAN HE WAS WHEN
ROCK II (261) SHIRTS, OR RED SHIRTS, AND GIVE ONE TO EVERY HOOLIGAN WHO IS OUT FOR ANY SORT OF MISCHIEF AND EVERY
CAPT I (227) CALLS OOLIGANISM. /SIR HOWARD/ OH! YOU WERE A HOOLIGAN , WERE YOU? /LADY CICELY/ (PUZZLED) A HOOLIGAN!
CAPT I (227) A HOOLIGAN, WERE YOU? /LADY CICELY/ (PUZZLED) A HOOLIGAN ! /DRINKWATER/ (DEPRECATINGLY) NIME GIV HUZ PORE
CAPT I (233) SAILOR! /SIR HOWARD/ (HORRIFIED) WHAT! THE HOOLIGAN ! /RANKIN/ (PUZZLED) HOOLIGAN? NO, MY LORD: HE

HOOLIGANISM
MILL PREFACE(120) WHICH THEY POOHPOOHED AS A TRANSIENT OUTBURST OF HOOLIGANISM FOMENTED BY A FEW BLOODTHIRSTY SCOUNDRELS,
SUPR PREFACE(R27) " GOVERNING CLASS" ANY MORE THAN A HEREDITARY HOOLIGANISM . WE MUST EITHER BREED POLITICAL CAPACITY OR BE
ROCK II (262) I TELL YOU, DEXY, IF YOU TRY ANY COLORED SHIRT HOOLIGANISM ON ME, I'LL BACK THE P.M. AND SHEW YOU WHAT

HOOLIGANS
GENV III (68) IMPRISONED IN CONCENTRATION CAMPS COMMANDED BY HOOLIGANS ? HAVE YOU BEEN DRIVEN OUT OF YOUR COUNTRY TO
CAPT I (234) HOWARD/ IN SHORT, WE ARE TO HAVE AN ESCORT OF HOOLIGANS COMMANDED BY A FILIBUSTER. VERY WELL, VERY WELL.

HOOLIHAN
BULL I (87) GOT TO CALL THE UNFORTUNATE ISLAND KATHLEEN NI HOOLIHAN AND PRETEND SHE'S A LITTLE OLD WOMAN. IT SAVES

HOOMAN
CAPT I (225) /DRINKWATER/ JIST THORT EED TRAH IT ORN, E DID. HOOMAN NITRE IS THE SIME EVERYWHERES. THEM EATHENS IS JAST

HOONAWTED
CAPT I (238) NAOW KEPN TO TEOLL US WOT TO DO. NAOW, LIDY: HOONAWTED WE STEND: DEEVAWDID WE FALL. /LADY CICELY/ OH, IF

HOOPS
SUPR IV SD(141) THAT THERE IS NO TENNIS NET NOR SET OF CROQUET HOOPS , BUT, ON OUR LEFT, A LITTLE IRON GARDEN TABLE WITH

HOORAY
ROCK II (281) ALL RIGHT ABOUT FLAVIA. WE MAY PUT UP THE BANNS. HOORAY ! (HE RUBS HANDS GLEEFULLY). /SIR ARTHUR/ MAY I ASK
PRES (167) GO AND TELL THE SERGEANT WHAT I THINK OF HIM. HOORAY ! (HE RUSHES OUT). /MRS FARRELL/ (GOING TO THE
BARB II (303) HAS PROMISED US FIVE THOUSAND POUNDS-- /BARBARA/ HOORAY ! /JENNY/ GLORY! /MRS BAINES/ -- IF-- /BARBARA/ "
PRES (167) RECOMMEND YOU FOR A COMMISSION. /THE ORDERLY/ HOORAY ! THE PARKINSONS O STEPNEY'LL BE PROUD TO HAVE ME

HOOSIANS
DEVL III (71) FORM THAT SQUARE THERE, WILL YOU, YOU DAMNED HOOSIANS , NO USE TALKIN GERMAN TO THEM: TALK TO THEIR TOES

HOOT
POSN PREFACE(424) SINCE HER STOOL IS A FIXTURE, SHE MAY HISS AND HOOT AND MAKE IT IMPOSSIBLE TO PROCEED WITH THE PERFORMANCE,

HOOTED
MILL I (158) OF MY BOX IN SCREAMING HYSTERICS. THE AUDIENCE HOOTED AND BOOED; BUT THEY COULD NOT MAKE THEMSELVES HEARD
UNPL PREFACE(R13) PRINCIPLE; THE ORDINARY PLAYGOING FIRST-NIGHTERS HOOTED ME FRANTICALLY ON THE SAME GROUND; I, BEING AT THAT

HOOTER
METH PREFACE(R50) BUS, AND THE AUDILE IMPRESSION PRODUCED BY ITS HOOTER . BUT IF YOU ALLOW YOURSELF TO DEFY HIM TO EXPLAIN

HOOVES
MTH1 I (6) IT. IT IS POISONING THE AIR. (HE GATHERS ITS HOOVES IN HIS HAND AND CARRIES IT AWAY IN THE DIRECTION FROM

HOP
2TRU I (47) AND ME YOU CAN JUMP OUT TO DRESS YOURSELF AND HOP IT FROM HERE. WRAP YOURSELF UP WELL: WE HAVE A CAR
PYGM I (216) OIL SHOP. LETS SEE HOW FAST YOU CAN MAKE HER HOP IT. (SHE GETS IN AND PULLS THE DOOR TO WITH A SLAM AS
KING I (210) IN CURVES LIKE THE ARCHES OF A BRIDGE, HOP, HOP, HOP . BUT WHAT DOES IT MATTER WHETHER IT FLIES STRAIGHT OR
LION II (133) AND STRANGLE HIM WITH HIS OWN NET BEFORE HE CAN HOP OFF. (TO THE RETIARIUS) YOU SEE IF I DONT. (HE GOES
KING I (210) SEA IN CURVES LIKE THE ARCHES OF A BRIDGE, HOP, HOP , HOP. BUT WHAT DOES IT MATTER WHETHER IT FLIES STRAIGHT
KING I (210) THE SEA IN CURVES LIKE THE ARCHES OF A BRIDGE, HOP , HOP, HOP. BUT WHAT DOES IT MATTER WHETHER IT FLIES
MIS. PREFACE(24) BACKWARD WHENEVER MONSIEUR DELCROZE CALLS OUT " HOP ! " OH YES: I KNOW ALL ABOUT THESE WONDERFUL SCHOOLS

HOPE
BARB III (333) KNOW WHAT MY PROFITS ARE? /CUSINS/ ENORMOUS, I HOPE : OTHERWISE I SHALL REQUIRE TWENTYFIVE PER CENT.
MTH1 II (32) THERE IS ALWAYS SOME NEW WONDER, OR SOME NEW HOPE : SOMETHING TO LIVE FOR. THEY NEVER WANT TO DIE.
SUPR III (96) ONLY THINK WHAT A RELIEF THAT IS! FOR WHAT IS HOPE ? A FORM OF MORAL RESPONSIBILITY. HERE THERE IS NO
BARB I (265) TO BARBARA) BARBARA-- I AM RIGHT THIS TIME, I HOPE ? /BARBARA/ QUITE RIGHT. (THEY SHAKE HANDS). /LADY
HART II (120) WHEN THEY ARE STRIPPED OF EVERYTHING, EVEN OF HOPE ? /ELLIE/ (GRIPPING THE HAND) IT SEEMS SO; FOR I FEEL

PHIL II	(122)	SHAKE HANDS). /PARAMORE/ THANKS, QUITE WELL, I	HOPE	? /GRACE/ QUITE, THANK YOU. YOURE LOOKING OVERWORKED.
GETT	(357)	HAVE NOTHING TO FEAR. /MRS GEORGE/ AND NOTHING TO	HOPE	? /HOTCHKISS/ SINCE YOU PUT IT IN THAT MORE THAN KIND
PHIL II	(112)	ARE YOU ILL? /CUTHBERTSON/ NO BAD NEWS, I	HOPE	? /PARAMORE/ (DESPAIRINGLY) THE WORST OF NEWS!
WIDO III	(49)	OH, PAPA, THERES NOTHING THE MATTER WITH YOU, I	HOPE	? /SARTORIUS/ THERE WILL BE: THERE MUST BE, BLANCHE,
FANY PROLOG	(263)	YOU DID NOT SAY THAT THE PLAY WAS BY HER, I	HOPE	? /SAVOYARD/ NO: THATS BEEN KEPT A DEAD SECRET. I JUST
PHIL II	(95)	HIS COAT STRAIGHT). MRS TRANFIELD QUITE WELL, I	HOPE	? /SYLVIA/ (TURNING HER HEAD INDIGNANTLY) SH-- SH--
MTH1 I	(17)	SERPENT/ YES. HOPE. HOPE. HOPE. /ADAM/ WHAT IS	HOPE	? /THE SERPENT/ AS LONG AS YOU DO NOT KNOW THE FUTURE
ROCK II	(256)	/ALOYSIA/ I HAVNT MENTIONED IT TO HIM YET. I	HOPE	ALL YOU GENTLEMEN WILL REMEMBER THAT I WAS NOT THE ONE
OVER	(194)	/JUNO/ I HOPE WE SHALL MEET VERY OFTEN. BUT I	HOPE	ALSO WE SHALL NOT DEFEND OUR CONDUCT. /MRS JUNO/ (
ROCK II	(269)	BUT THAT WAS WHEN IT WAS A DREAM AND A VISION, A	HOPE	AND A FAITH AND A PROMISE. IT LASTED UNTIL THEY DRAGGED
JOAN 6	(150)	I HEARD LAUGHTER. FORGIVE ME FOR SAYING THAT I	HOPE	AND BELIEVE IT WAS ENGLISH LAUGHTER. /THE CHAPLAIN/ (
LION PREFACE	(81)	POWER OF BRINGING TO SIMPLE PEOPLE A MESSAGE OF	HOPE	AND CONSOLATION THAT NO OTHER RELIGION OFFERS. BUT THIS
ROCK PREFACE	(188)	LOOKS FORWARD WITH HOPE. TERROR DRIVES MEN MAD:	HOPE	AND FAITH GIVE THEM DIVINE WISDOM. THE MEN WHOM YOU
MTH5	(262)	HOPE AND FAITH IN THEM, THEY ARE DOOMED. IN THAT	HOPE	AND FAITH I HAVE LET THEM LIVE FOR A MOMENT; AND IN
MTH5	(262)	STAGNATION; FOR FROM THE MOMENT I, LILITH, LOSE	HOPE	AND FAITH IN THEM, THEY ARE DOOMED. IN THAT HOPE AND
MTH5	(262)	BUT MIGHTIER CREATURES THAN THEY HAVE KILLED	HOPE	AND FAITH, AND PERISHED FROM THE EARTH; AND I MAY NOT
CAND II	(120)	THINK OF ME THEN. /MORELL/ NO EVIL, CANDIDA. I	HOPE	AND TRUST, NO EVIL. /CANDIDA/ (DUBIOUSLY) THAT WILL
CAND I	(100)	TENDERNESS) EUGENE: LISTEN TO ME. SOME DAY, I	HOPE	AND TRUST, YOU WILL BE A HAPPY MAN LIKE ME. (EUGENE
JOAN 1,SD	(60)	TO BAUDRICOURT'S PRESENCE AT LAST, AND FULL OF	HOPE	AS TO THE RESULT. HIS SCOWL DOES NOT CHECK OR FRIGHTEN
MRS I	(186)	I HOPE-- ER-- /VIVIE/ IT'S NOT SO MUCH WHAT YOU	HOPE	AS WHAT YOU BELIEVE, THAT I WANT TO KNOW. /PRAED/ WELL,
DEST	(167)	A LITTLE AWAY FROM HIM; BUT A RAY OF RALLYING	HOPE	BEAMS FROM HER EYE. HE BEGINS LIKE A MAN ENJOYING SOME
SUPR III	(96)	OVER THE GATE HERE ARE THE WORDS " LEAVE EVERY	HOPE	BEHIND, YE WHO ENTER." ONLY THINK WHAT A RELIEF THAT
GETT	(299)	AND CHINNERY ARE LIARS AND THIEVES, AND THAT I	HOPE	BY NEXT WEDNESDAY TO HAVE IN MY HANDS CONCLUSIVE
MIS.	(138)	FOR SOMETHING TO HAPPEN. THEN THERE WOULD BE	HOPE	EVEN IF NOTHING DID HAPPEN. BUT THIS ETERNAL CACKLE
BARB II	(284)	IS WIGHT? /SHIRLEY/ THIRTEEN FOUR. (BILL'S LAST	HOPE	EXPIRES). /BARBARA/ GO AND TALK TO HIM, BILL. HE'LL
BUOY II	(25)	SCIENCE AND SEVEN HUNDRED IN HISTORY YOU CANNOT	HOPE	FOR A DEGREE THERE. /THE NATIVE/ CAN IT BE TRUE THAT
METH PREFACE	(R82)	WE HAVE A GREAT RELIGIOUS MOVEMENT WE CANNOT	HOPE	FOR A GREAT ARTISTIC ONE. THE DISILLUSIONED RAPHAEL
SUPR III	(80)	CAPABLE OF SPREADING AMONG BRIGANDS, IT CAN NEVER	HOPE	FOR A POLITICAL MAJORITY. /TANNER/ BUT ARE YOUR
SUPR HANDBOK	(177)	INDIVIDUAL GREED AND FOLLY, WHAT MIGHT WE NOT	HOPE	FOR AS A MAIN PRODUCT OF HIS UNIVERSAL ASPIRATION?
OVER	(183)	DIDNT KEEP ON SAYING SO. /JUNO/ IS THERE THEN NO	HOPE	FOR ME? /MRS LUNN/ OH, YES. GREGORY HAS AN IDEA THAT
CURE	(236)	INTERFERING WITH YOUR PROFESSION? IS THERE ANY	HOPE	FOR ME? /STREGA/ (COMING AWAY FROM THE PIANO) MY
BUOY 1	(9)	SIGHT. /SON/ I HAVE. AT FIRST SIGHT THERE IS NO	HOPE	FOR OUR CIVILIZATION. BUT ONE CAN STILL MAKE MONEY IN
LADY	(245)	OF HIM. /THE DARK LADY/ MADAM: AS I LIVE AND	HOPE	FOR SALVATION-- /SHAKESPEAR/ (SARDONICALLY) HA! /THE
FANY II	(296)	I DONT CARE FOR ANYTHING ELSE. /MARGARET/ DONT	HOPE	FOR THAT, FATHER. MIND: I'LL TELL EVERYBODY. IT OUGHT
DOCT III	(151)	KEEP YOUR SPIRITS UP; KEEP THE PATIENT CHEERFUL;	HOPE	FOR THE BEST; NO TONIC LIKE A CHARMING WOMAN; NO
HART III	(129)	IN THE NIGHT THERE IS PEACE FOR THE OLD AND	HOPE	FOR THE YOUNG. /HECTOR/ IS THAT REMARK YOUR OWN?
BARB II	(310)	ME. /BARBARA/ I'LL GET YOU A JOB, PETER. THATS	HOPE	FOR YOU: THE YOUTH WILL HAVE TO BE ENOUGH FOR ME. (SHE
METH PREFACE	(R48)	HAD THROWN OVER THE GULF WHICH SEPARATES LIFE AND	HOPE	FROM DEATH AND DESPAIR. WE WERE INTELLECTUALLY
GETT PREFACE	(252)	ON HER AND DEGRADING HER UNTIL SHE HAS NOTHING TO	HOPE	FROM OUR COURTS; AND SO, WITH POLICEMEN AT EVERY
METH PREFACE	(R43)	SAVIOR, PROPHET, REDEEMER, ENLIGHTENER, RESCUER,	HOPE	GIVER, AND EPOCH MAKER; WHILST POOR LAMARCK WAS SWEPT
GENV PREFACE	(11)	THE ATOMIC BOMB HAS MADE WAR IMPOSSIBLE. THAT	HOPE	HAS OFTEN BEEN ENTERTAINED BEFORE. COLONEL ROBINSON, IN
ROCK II	(274)	HAVE HEARD WHAT HE SAID ABOUT IT. /SIR ARTHUR/ I	HOPE	HE DID NOT USE THE ADJECTIVE HIS SISTER APPLIED TO POOR
CAND III	(144)	CIRCUMSTANCES! YOU KNOW HOW STRONG HE IS (I	HOPE	HE DIDNT HURT YOU): HOW CLEVER HE IS: HOW HAPPY. (WITH
NEVR II	(249)	GUINEAS. WHAT A LESSON, SIR! /CRAMPTON/ WELL, I	HOPE	HE IS GRATEFUL TO YOU, AND RECOGNIZES WHAT HE OWES YOU.
ARMS II	(39)	ABOUT THE CHOCOLATE CREAM SOLDIER OR NOT. I HALF	HOPE	HE MAY. (SHE AGAIN TURNS AND STROLLS FLIPPANTLY AWAY
2TRU PREFACE	(26)	MR CHESTERTON HAS PUT IT IN A NUTSHELL; AND I	HOPE	HE WILL APPRECIATE THE SOUND CATHOLICISM WITH WHICH I
DEVL I	(16)	NOSE. HER HUSBAND SPEAKS. /UNCLE TITUS/ WELL, I	HOPE	HE WILL HAVE THE GRACE NOT TO COME. I HOPE SO. THE
MILL I	(162)	ALASTAIR WAS THE FIRST MAN I EVER LOVED; AND I	HOPE	HE WILL NOT BE THE LAST. BUT LEGAL DIFFICULTIES DO NOT
PPP	(201)	DYING. /PHYLLIS/ (WITH CONCERN) INDEED, SIR? I	HOPE	HE WILL NOT THINK IT UNFEELING OF ME TO APPEAR AT HIS
O'FL	(212)	IT WAS OR NOT, BETTER THAN YOU NOR ME, GENERAL. I	HOPE	HE WONT BE TOO HARD ON ME FOR IT, ANYHOW. /SIR PEARCE/
DEVL II	(31)	(SINKING ON THE SEAT AND CLASPING HER HANDS) I	HOPE	HE WONT COME! OH, I PRAY THAT HE MAY NOT COME!
NEVR II	(243)	US DARE GIVE THAT MAN AN ORDER AGAIN! /DOLLY/ I	HOPE	HE WONT MIND MY SENDING HIM FOR GINGER-BEER. /CRAMPTON/
BUOY IV	(53)	EVER COME BACK. (HE GOES OUT). /SHE/ I HALF	HOPE	HE WONT. /JUNIUS/ (COMING BACK) BY THE WAY, WHATS YOUR
HART II	(97)	TELEGRAPH TONIGHT. /MAZZINI/ I SUPPOSE SO. I DO	HOPE	HE'LL WAKE UP IN THE COURSE OF THE NIGHT. (HE GOES OUT
BARB II	(298)	WHAT MAN? /JENNY/ THE MAN THAT HIT ME. OH, I	HOPE	HE'S COMING BACK TO JOIN US. BILL WALKER, WITH FROST ON
JOAN 4	(95)	THAT IS, GOODBYE TO YOU AND ME. /THE CHAPLAIN/ I	HOPE	I AM A FAITHFUL SERVANT OF THE CHURCH; AND THERE ARE
CAND III	(140)	ANGER) EUGENE IS VERY QUICK-WITTED, JAMES. I	HOPE	I AM GOING TO LAUGH; BUT I AM NOT SURE THAT I AM NOT
MILL I	(153)	LEFT). /ADRIAN/ (SITTING DOWN) THANK YOU. I	HOPE	I AM NOT INTERRUPTING THIS LADY. /PATRICIA/ NOT AT ALL.
APPL I	(218)	(NOT ALTOGETHER DISPLEASED) WELL, SIR, I	HOPE	I AM NOT SUCH A FOOL AS SOME FOOLS THINK ME. I MAY NOT
APPL I	(215)	FACE DARKENS. /MAGNUS/ WELCOME, GENTLEMEN. I	HOPE	I AM NOT TOO EARLY. (NOTING THE PRIME MINISTER'S
BULL II	(112)	WITH YOU? /BROADBENT/ NO. IVE COME INSTEAD. I	HOPE	I AM NOT UNWELCOME. /NORA/ (DEEPLY MORTIFIED) I'M
GETT	(307)	PARDON MOST HEARTILY, LESBIA, IF I'M WRONG, AS I	HOPE	I AM-- THEY ACTUALLY CALL ON US TO ENTER INTO-- I'M
CAND III	(129)	A GLANCE. /MORELL/ (GRAVE AND SELF-CONTAINED) I	HOPE	I DONT DISTURB YOU. CANDIDA STARTS UP VIOLENTLY, BUT
ROCK I	(214)	TOO GLAD TO RISE TOO. /SIR ARTHUR/ AT LEAST I	HOPE	I HAVE CONVINCED YOU ABOUT THE WINDOWS, MR MAYOR. /THE
MTH2	(71)	OF ME. BUT WE WORKED TOGETHER FOR YEARS; AND I	HOPE	I HAVE DONE NOTHING TO JUSTIFY YOU IN THE AMAZING
CAPT I	(220)	GOOD, DO IT, GAVNER? /RANKIN/ I DONT SAY THAT. I	HOPE	I HAVE DONE SOME GOOD. THEY COME TO ME FOR MEDICINE
MTH4 I	(153)	I BEAR THEIR NAMES, BOLGE AND BLUEBIN; AND I	HOPE	I HAVE INHERITED SOMETHING OF THEIR MAJESTIC SPIRIT.
CLEO NOTES	(209)	PERSON THAN THE HISTORIAN OF THE GALLIC WARS. I	HOPE	I HAVE NOT BEEN TOO MUCH IMPOSED ON BY THE DRAMATIC
DEST	(186)	TO THE LIEUTENANT WITH SARDONIC POLITENESS) I	HOPE	I HAVE NOT BEEN MAKING YOU FEEL AMBITIOUS. /LIEUTENANT/
BULL IV	(153)	O PRETENDIN WE DONT? /BROADBENT/ (STIFFLY) I	HOPE	I HAVE SAID OR DONE NOTHING THAT CALLS FOR ANY SUCH
WIDO III	(56)	/BLANCHE/ (RISING) I BEG YOUR PARDON. I	HOPE	I HAVNT CRUSHED IT. /LICKCHEESE/ (GALLANTLY, AS HE
PHIL II	(99)	(COMING BETWEEN THEM) DO SO BY ALL MEANS. I	HOPE	I HAVNT DISTURBED YOUR CHAT BY COMING TOO SOON.
HART II	(90)	AND TURNS ON THE LIGHT). OH, MR MANGAN, SIR, I	HOPE	I HAVNT HURT YOU PLUMPING INTO YOUR LAP LIKE THAT. (
HART II	(90)	HE REMAINS QUITE INSENSIBLE) OH, MY GOOD LORD, I	HOPE	I HAVNT KILLED HIM. SIR! MR MANGAN! SIR! (SHE
CAND II	(106)	/MARCHBANKS/ (APPROACHING HER HUMBLY) I	HOPE	I HAVNT OFFENDED YOU. PERHAPS I SHOULDNT HAVE ALLUDED
LADY	(242)	US. /THE LADY/ GRAMERCY FOR YOUR SERMON, SIR. I	HOPE	I KNOW MY DUTY. /THE MAN/ THIS IS NO SERMON, BUT THE
2TRU I	(43)	BURGLAR/ (A LITTLE HURT) OH, NOT A CURATE. I	HOPE	I LOOK AT LEAST LIKE A BENEFICED CLERGYMAN. BUT IT IS
MRS III	(232)	GETTING ON FAMOUSLY WITH ME. /CROFTS/ WELL, I	HOPE	I MAY FLATTER MYSELF THAT YOU THINK BETTER OF ME THAN
JOAN EPILOG	(166)	I CAN SAY IS THAT THOUGH I DARE NOT BLESS YOU, I	HOPE	I MAY ONE DAY ENTER INTO YOUR BLESSEDNESS. MEANWHILE,
BULL II	(97)	MAN/ AN IS THAT YOURSELF, MISTHER GRASSHOPPER? I	HOPE	I SEE YOU WELL THIS FINE EVENIN. /THE GRASSHOPPER/ (
WIDO III	(54)	OF OURS. /LICKCHEESE/ AND A KIND ONE TO ME. I	HOPE	I SEE YOU WELL, MISS BLANCHE. /BLANCHE/ WHY, IT'S MR
WIDO II	(38)	/BLANCHE/ I'M SURE I HAVE NO WISH TO STAY. I	HOPE	I SHALL FIND YOU ALONE WHEN I COME BACK. (AN
GETT	(286)	SHE WANTS ME TO MEET HER IN HEAVEN. I	HOPE	I SHALL. /THE GENERAL/ WELL, I MUST SAY I HOPE NOT,
METH PREFACE	(R90)	OF THE EARLY CHRISTIANS AT ICONOGRAPHY. IN THAT	HOPE	I WITHDRAW AND RING UP THE CURTAIN.
CYMB V	(149)	THEN, FOR BY THIS GENTLEMAN'S REPORT AND MINE I	HOPE	IMPERIAL CAESAR WILL REKNIT HIS FAVOUR WITH THE RADIANT
METH PREFACE	(R13)	AWAKE FOR FIVE MINUTES OVER A BOOK? IS THERE ANY	HOPE	IN EDUCATION? THE USUAL ANSWER IS THAT WE MUST EDUCATE
BUOY PREFACE	(7)	NEWS AND POLICE NEWS TO SMILING COMEDY WITH SOME	HOPE	IN IT! I DO NOT. WHEN THEY BEGIN I SWITCH OFF THE
SUPR HANDBOK	(194)	THE WORLD PRODIGIOUSLY, BUT THERE IS NO MORE	HOPE	IN THAT IF THAN IN THE EQUALLY PLAUSIBLE ASSURANCE THAT
DEVL I	(20)	GLANCE LIGHTS ON ESSIE) PROVIDED ONLY THERE IS	HOPE	IN THE EYES OF THE CHILD. (BRISKLY) NOW THEN, LAWYER
KING I	(203)	HOW YOU LET THESE BOLD IMPIOUS FELLOWS EXTINGUISH	HOPE	IN YOU. THEIR DAY IS SHORT; BUT THE INNER LIGHT IS
MIS.	(118)	THAT EVERYBODY'S BUSINESS IS NOBODY'S BUSINESS. I	HOPE	I'M NOT A HARD MAN, NOR A NARROW MAN, NOR UNWILLING TO
WIDO I	(11)	(STUPIDLY) YES: THEY CANT BE VERY LONG NOW. I	HOPE	I'M NOT DETAINING YOU. /BLANCHE/ I THOUGHT YOU WERE
DOCT I	(94)	WALPOLE. HE'S JEALOUS. /WALPOLE/ BY THE WAY, I	HOPE	I'M NOT DISTURBING YOU TWO IN ANYTHING PRIVATE.
SUPR HANDBOK	(201)	THAT HE WILL CAST IT FOR HIS EMANCIPATORS. THE	HOPE	IS NOT FULFILLED; BUT THE LIFELONG IMPRISONMENT OF
METH PREFACE	(R18)	SERVE, NATURE WILL TRY ANOTHER EXPERIMENT. WHAT	HOPE	IS THERE THEN OF HUMAN IMPROVEMENT? ACCORDING TO THE
MTH1 I	(17)	DESTROY HOPE. /ADAM/ (ANGRILY) BE SILENT, WOMAN.	HOPE	IS WICKED. HAPPINESS IS WICKED. CERTAINTY IS BLESSED.
LADY	(247)	ME GREAT ENOUGH TO GRANT ME A BOON. /ELIZABETH/ I	HOPE	IT IS A BOON THAT MAY BE ASKED OF A VIRGIN QUEEN
MIS.	(177)	SLIGHTLY, BUT OTHERWISE MOTIONLESS. /PERCIVAL/ I	HOPE	IT IS NOT NECESSARY FOR ME TO ASSURE YOU ALL THAT THERE
BARB III	(319)	SUCCESSION TO THE GANNON BUSINESS. /STEPHEN/ I	HOPE	IT IS SETTLED THAT I REPUDIATE THE CANNON BUSINESS.
NEVR IV	(290)	DIFFERENCE IS TO BE SMOOTHED OVER AS WE ALL	HOPE	IT MAY BE, MRS CLANDON, AS A MATTER OF SOCIAL
NEVR IV	(287)	CASE WE SHALL WANT HIM. /WAITER/ (PLEADING) I	HOPE	IT MAY NOT BE NECESSARY, SIR, BUSY EVENING FOR ME, SIR,
CAND III	(138)	THE DOOR). /LEXY/ IT'S EVIDENTLY MY DUTY TO GO. I	HOPE	IT MAY NOT BE NECESSARY. GOODNIGHT, MRS MORELL. (TO
MIS.	(153)	EH? WHAT? FAMILY REASONS? /MRS TARLETON/ I	HOPE	IT WASNT TO SPITE YOUR MOTHER? /PERCIVAL/ (QUICKLY)
DOCT III	(140)	YOURE UTTERLY WRONG ON THE LEGAL POINT; AND I	HOPE	IT WILL BE A LESSON TO YOU NOT TO BE SO JOLLY COCKSURE
APPL I	(205)	I HAVE NOT FORGOTTEN KING CHARLES'S HEAD. WELL, I	HOPE	IT WILL BE SETTLED BY A LIVING PERSON AND NOT BY AN
NEVR II	(231)	SERIOUSLY. /PHILIP/ (WITH PROFOUND GRAVITY) I	HOPE	IT WILL DESERVE IT, MR M'COMAS. MY KNOWLEDGE OF HUMAN
FANY PROLOG	(272)	TAKE YOU IN TO DINNER. /FANNY/ YES, PAPA. OH, I	HOPE	IT WILL GO OFF WELL. /THE COUNT/ YES, LOVE, OF COURSE

SIM II (54) HAVE EVER ASSEMBLED IN ONE PLACE. /HYERING/ I HOPE IT WILL NEVER HAPPEN AGAIN. IF WE DONT GET RID OF THEM
FANY PROLOG (268) YOU ARE AFRAID IT WILL SHOCK YOUR FATHER. WELL, I HOPE IT WILL. AND IF HE CONSULTS ME ABOUT IT I SHALL
PYGM III (251) /FREDDY/ KILLING! /MRS EYNSFORD HILL/ I'M SURE I HOPE IT WONT TURN COLD. THERES SO MUCH INFLUENZA ABOUT. IT
FABL II (107) TALKING. /C.-IN-C./ THAT IS TRUE: IT MAY. LET US HOPE IT WONT. /OLDHAND/ HOPE WONT HELP US IF IT DOES. OUR
PRES (133) WHERE ON EARTH DID YOU GET THE DRESS? I HOPE IT'S NOT A FRENCH DRESS! /BALSQUITH/ GREAT HEAVENS,
O'FL (211) TELL IT TO YOU. /SIR PEARCE/ (STILL SULKILY) I HOPE IT'S NOTHING YOU OUGHTNT TO SAY TO ME, O'FLAHERTY.
PYGM II (230) I SHALL FEEL RESPONSIBLE FOR THAT GIRL. I HOPE IT'S UNDERSTOOD THAT NO ADVANTAGE IS TO BE TAKEN OF HER
PYGM II (218) YOU WANTED HER TO TALK INTO YOUR MACHINES. I HOPE IVE NOT DONE WRONG; BUT REALLY YOU SEE SUCH QUEER
NEVR I (216) ON THE SOFA. VALENTINE RETURNS. /VALENTINE/ I HOPE IVE NOT KEPT YOU WAITING. THAT LANDLORD OF MINE IS
MRS I (182) US? /VIVIE/ NO. /PRAED/ NOW, GOODNESS ME, I HOPE IVE NOT MISTAKEN THE DAY. THAT WOULD BE JUST LIKE ME,
MIS. (202) INDEED? I DIDNT KNOW: YOULL EXCUSE MY MISTAKE, I HOPE . BUT THE PRINCIPLE IS THE SAME. NOW I TRUST YOU WONT
MILL II (168) /ADRIAN/ (ANNOYED) I AM NOT OUT OF TEMPER, I HOPE . BUT YOU PROMISED ME A VERY SPECIAL TREAT. YOU SAID
SIM I (44) /THE CLERGYMAN/ OH, NOT AN EXPERIMENT, I HOPE . CHEMICAL EXPERIMENTS ARE BAD ENOUGH: I AM ONE MYSELF;
BARB III (326) THE TOWN. /BARBARA/ WELL? /CUSINS/ NOT A RAY OF HOPE . EVERYTHING PERFECT! WONDERFUL! REAL! IT ONLY NEEDS
CATH 1 (169) AN EPIGRAM! (GRAVELY) YOU UNDERSTAND IT, I HOPE . HAVE YOU HAD A COLLEGE EDUCATION, DARLING? I HAVE.
MTH1 I (17) HAVE YOU A REMEDY FOR IT? /THE SERPENT/ YES. HOPE . HOPE. HOPE. /ADAM/ WHAT IS HOPE? /THE SERPENT/ AS
MTH1 I (17) YOU A REMEDY FOR IT? /THE SERPENT/ YES. HOPE. HOPE . HOPE. /ADAM/ WHAT IS HOPE? /THE SERPENT/ AS LONG AS
MTH1 I (17) DOES NOT CONSOLE ME. FEAR IS STRONGER IN ME THAN HOPE . I MUST HAVE CERTAINTY. (HE RISES THREATENINGLY).
PHIL I (86) TO BE VERY CLOSE FRIENDS, AND ARE SO STILL, I HOPE . (CUTHBERTSON GOES TO CRAVEN AND PRESSES HIS HAND
GETT (274) LEAVE THIS HOUSE OR AM I? /REGINALD/ YOU ARE, I HOPE . (HE EMPHASIZES HIS INTENTION TO STAY BY SITTING
PHIL III (146) COME NOW, CHARTERIS: YOURE NOT OFFENDED, I HOPE . (WITH A CONCILIATORY OUTBURST) WELL, PERHAPS I
GENV III (86) SAY. /THE JUDGE/ YOU WILL ALL BE PRESENT, I HOPE . MAY I SUGGEST THAT YOU TELEPHONE AT ONCE TO SECURE
NEVR IV (292) TO THE WAITER) YOU DONT MIND OUR DETAINING YOU, I HOPE . MR BOHUN WISHES IT. /WAITER/ (NOW QUITE AT HIS EASE)
BUOY IV (57) FOR THE WORST. /SIR FERDINAND/ OR THE BEST, I HOPE . MY OFFER IS HARDLY A MISFORTUNE, AS I SEE IT. /OLD
ROCK I (225) SO. (WITH SUDDEN MISGIVING) YOU MEAN MY DEATH, I HOPE . NOT MY WIFE NOR ANY OF THE CHILDREN? /THE LADY/ (
JITT II (29) IT WONT UPSET OR DELAY YOUR ENGAGEMENT, I HOPE . NOT THAT I COULD BLAME YOU IF YOU BROKE IT OFF.
MRS II (212) THE SORT THE WORLD IS MOSTLY MADE OF, I SHOULD HOPE . OTHERWISE I DONT UNDERSTAND HOW IT GETS ITS BUSINESS
BARB PREFACE(227) SUCH ACTIVITY; AND WHERE THERE IS DANGER THERE IS HOPE . OUR PRESENT SECURITY IS NOTHING, AND CAN BE NOTHING,
MTH1 I (17) IT WILL NOT BE HAPPIER THAN THE PAST. THAT IS HOPE . /ADAM/ IT DOES NOT CONSOLE ME. FEAR IS STRONGER IN ME
MTH1 I (17) AWAY FROM THE SERPENT) BUT IT WILL DESTROY HOPE . /ADAM/ (ANGRILY) BE SILENT, WOMAN. HOPE IS WICKED.
MTH1 I (17) A REMEDY FOR IT? /THE SERPENT/ YES. HOPE. HOPE. HOPE . /ADAM/ WHAT IS HOPE? /THE SERPENT/ AS LONG AS YOU DO
BARB I (270) BARBARA) YOU DONT THINK I AM MOCKING, MY LOVE, I HOPE . /BARBARA/ NO, OF COURSE NOT; AND IT WOULDNT MATTER IF
DEVL III (69) OF-- GUESS WHAT. /SWINDON/ THEIR SURRENDER, I HOPE . /BURGOYNE/ NO: OUR EVACUATION OF THE TOWN. THEY OFFER
CLEO II (128) JUSTICE! /THEODOTUS/ BUT NOT ROMAN GRATITUDE, I HOPE . /CAESAR/ GRATITUDE! AM I IN YOUR DEBT FOR ANY
MTH1 II (31) DO THAN COMPLAIN? /EVE/ BECAUSE THERE IS STILL HOPE . /CAIN/ OF WHAT? /EVE/ OF THE COMING OF TRUE OF YOUR
PHIL III (144) ACCEPT GRACE'S CONGRATULATIONS AS WELL AS MINE, I HOPE . /CRAVEN/ SHE WILL, JO. (PEREMPTORILY) NOW, JULIA.
JITT III (53) AND YOU ARE GOING TO TALK TO ME SERIOUSLY, I HOPE . /FESSLER/ (SURPRISED) BUT CERTAINLY, MY DEAR MRS
MIS. (185) A LADY'S CHARACTER. YOU AGREE WITH ME, I HOPE . /GUNNER/ YES: THAT SOUNDS ALL RIGHT. /PERCIVAL/ BUT
DEVL II (46) TO HIM IN ALL KINDNESS AND CHARITY, JUDITH, I HOPE . /JUDITH/ I KISSED HIM. /ANDERSON/ WHAT! JUDITH!
CAPT I (238) MAKE AN EXCURSION. YOU DO NOT OBJECT, CICELY, I HOPE . /LADY CICELY/ OH NO. AFTER ALL, THOSE MEN MUST REALLY
DOCT I (114) IS CATCHING. YOU TAKE EVERY PRECAUTION, I HOPE . /MRS DUBEDAT/ I AM NOT LIKELY TO FORGET IT. THEY
ARMS III (57) (TO NICOLA) I AM NOT IN THE WAY OF YOUR WORK, I HOPE . /NICOLA/ (IN A SMOOTH, ELDERLY MANNER) OH NO, SIR:
GENV I (36) YOU HAVE NOTHING TO SAY AGAINST LIBERTY, I HOPE . /SHE/ I HAVE NOTHING TO SAY AGAINST ANYTHING. I AM
BUOY IV (52) THE WAY, WHERE SHALL WE LIVE? NOT IN PANAMA, I HOPE . /SHE/ NO. IN PANAMA I SHOULD BE NERVOUS ABOUT YOU
SUPR I (40) MISUNDERSTAND IT. YOU DO NOT MISUNDERSTAND IT, I HOPE . /TANNER/ MY BLOOD INTERPRETS FOR ME, ANN. POOR RICKY
SUPR I (22) I CAN BEAR YOUR BRUTALITIES BECAUSE THEY GIVE ME HOPE . /TANNER/ TAVY: THATS THE DEVILISH SIDE OF A WOMAN'S
SUPR I (31) YOU DONT MIND BEING MADE RESPONSIBLE FOR ME, I HOPE . /TANNER/ THE LATEST ADDITION TO YOUR COLLECTION OF
SIM PRO,3, (33) ARE NOT YET SUFFICIENTLY REGENERATED. BUT YOU MAY HOPE . /THE Y.W./ YOU TAKE CARE, BOY. I THINK YOUVE GOT A
WIDO II (34) NO. /BLANCHE/ PAPA HAS NOT BEEN DISAGREEABLE, I HOPE . /TRENCH/ NO: I HAVE HARDLY SPOKEN TO HIM SINCE I WAS
SIM II (77) (RISING) PROLA HAS TURNED BACK FROM THE FORLORN HOPE . /VASHTI/ PROLA IS A COWARD. SHE FEARS DEFEAT AND
MIS. (188) GOING TO DO WITH HIM. /HYPATIA/ SPANK HIM, I HOPE . SPANK HIM HARD. /LORD SUMMERHAYS/ I HOPE SO. I HOPE
ROCK PREFACE(188) GIVE WAY TO THE KINGDOM THAT LOOKS FORWARD WITH HOPE . TERROR DRIVES MEN MAD: HOPE AND FAITH GIVE THEM
APPL II (264) SIT UP WAITING FOR A MESSAGE. EARLY TOMORROW, I HOPE . THANK YOU FOR BRINGING ME THE NEWS BEFORE THE PAPERS
APPL II (271) WE CAN STILL LOOK FORWARD TO THE FUTURE WITH HOPE . THAT FUTURE HAS ITS DANGERS AND ITS DIFFICULTIES. IT
BARB II (310) OUT, AND LOST MY JOB. /SHIRLEY/ YOUVE YOUTH AN HOPE . THATS TWO BETTER THAN ME. /BARBARA/ I'LL GET YOU A
BARB III (314) THANK YOU, MY LADY. YOU WONT MIND MY ASKING, I HOPE . THE OCCASION IS IN A MANNER OF SPEAKING NEW TO ME.
VWOO 2 (127) VERY MUCH. /A/ I AM NOT INTERRUPTING YOUR WORK, I HOPE . THERE IS NOTHING SO MADDENING AS TO BE TALKED TO WHEN
PRES (140) BY THE SUBSCRIPTIONS OF THE LOCAL ASSOCIATIONS, I HOPE . THEY DONT PAY FOR THE GAS AT THE MEETINGS.
GENV PREFACE(25) NOT HUMAN ATTAINMENT BUT HUMAN POSSIBILITY AND HOPE . THEY PROVE THAT THOUGH WE IN THE MASS ARE ONLY CHILD
PYGM II (242) CALL THE LIKE OF THEM MY FRIENDS NOW, I SHOULD HOPE . THEYVE TOOK IT OUT OF ME OFTEN ENOUGH WITH THEIR
DEST (164) GOING) YOULL EXCUSE MY LEAVING YOU, GENERAL, I HOPE . VERY SORRY, I'M SURE. (HE TALKS HIMSELF OUT OF THE
HART II (89) (HUMBLY) YOU DONT DISLIKE TOUCHING ME, I HOPE . YOU NEVER TOUCHED ME BEFORE, I NOTICED. /ELLIE/ NOT
LION PREFACE(93) THE SOCRATIC MAN AND NOT IN THE WESLEYAN THAT OUR HOPE LIES NOW. THE RIGHT TO REFUSE ATONEMENT, CONSEQUENTLY,
KING I (171) IS NO WORSE THAN MARY MAGDALEN. /MRS BASHAM/ I HOPE MARY MAGDALEN MADE A GOOD END AND WAS FORGIVEN; THOUGH
JOAN EPILOG (157) THE PURE OF HEART. /JOAN/ WELL, WELL, PETER, I HOPE MEN WILL BE THE BETTER FOR REMEMBERING ME; AND THEY
WIDO II (31) YOU CAN FOR A MANSION IN PARK LANE. /TRENCH/ I HOPE MR SARTORIUS HASNT MUCH OF THAT SORT OF PROPERTY,
MRS III (223) EVER SO SORRY THEY COULDNT STOP; AND THAT YOU HOPE MRS WARREN SLEPT WELL; AND-- AND-- SAY ANY BLESSED
MRS PREFACE(176) CHEAPENING THEM FOR OTHER PURPOSES AS WELL. I HOPE MRS WARREN'S PROFESSION WILL BE PLAYED EVERYWHERE, IN
HART I (73) YOU (HE GOES OUT THROUGH THE GARDEN). /DUNN/ I HOPE NOBODY HERE BELIEVES THAT I AM A THIEF, A PIRATE, OR A
POSN PREFACE(378) THEY HAD SIMPLY BEEN THOUGHTLESS IN THE MATTER. I HOPE NOBODY WILL SUPPOSE THAT THIS IN ANY WAY EXONERATES
CLEO IV (187) THINK OF ANYONE BEING KILLED OR EVEN HURT; AND I HOPE NOTHING REALLY SERIOUS HAS-- (HER VOICE DIES AWAY
CLEO V (202) THE HEART. HE WILL RETURN SOME DAY. /CLEOPATRA/ I HOPE NOT. BUT I CANT HELP CRYING, ALL THE SAME. (SHE WAVES
HART II (96) AND COMING TO THE BACK OF THE CHAIR) OH, I HOPE NOT. DID YOU, ELLIE? /ELLIE/ (WEARILY) HE ASKED ME
BUOY 1 (15) STUFF WILL MAKE ITSELF FOR NOTHING. /FATHER/ I HOPE NOT. FOR IF EVERY MAN JACK OF US CAN BLOW THE WORLD TO
JOAN 6 (124) FRIENDLY TO YOU, MY LORD. /CAUCHON/ (STERNLY) I HOPE NOT. I AM DETERMINED THAT THE WOMAN SHALL HAVE A FAIR
GENV IV (128) BUT NOBODY WILL WEEP FOR YOU, BARDO. /BBDE/ I HOPE NOT. I DO NOT DEAL IN TEARS. (HE STRIDES OUT).
DEVL II (44) ESSIE'S SHOULDER AND TRYING TO COMFORT HER) I HOPE NOT, I HOPE NOT. PERHAPS IF YOURE VERY QUIET AND
JOAN 2 (76) TO DIE, CAPTAIN. /LA HIRE/ (CROSSING HIMSELF) I HOPE NOT. (HE BACKS OUT OF THE CONVERSATION). /BLUEBEARD/
MRS IV (242) AND PRESERVING HIS POLITENESS WITH AN EFFORT) I HOPE NOT. (MORE EMPHATICALLY) I HOPE NOT, MISS WARREN.
NEVR I (207) /DOLLY/ OR WHO HE IS. HE MAY BE ALIVE. /PHILIP/ I HOPE NOT. NO MAN ALIVE SHALL FATHER ME. /DOLLY/ HE MIGHT
DEVL II (44) SHOULDER AND TRYING TO COMFORT HER) I HOPE NOT. I HOPE NOT. PERHAPS IF YOURE VERY QUIET AND PATIENT, WE MAY BE
MIS. (144) A KID-- BEG PARDON: A CHILD. /LORD SUMMERHAYS/ I HOPE NOT. /HYPATIA/ IT'S A DIRTY JOB; BUT JOHNNY AND I WERE
PHIL I (86) (ALARMED) OH, DONT SAY THAT, MY DEAR FELLOW. I HOPE NOT. /JULIA/ (WITH ANGUISH IN HER VOICE) DADDY! (
GETT (286) GENERAL/ WELL, I MUST SAY I HOPE NOT, ALFRED. I HOPE NOT. /MRS BRIDGENORTH/ SHE SAYS SHE IS HAPPILY MARRIED,
HART II (112) BURGLAR MAY TURN UP. /MAZZINI/ OH, IMPOSSIBLE! I HOPE NOT. /RANDALL/ WHY NOT? THERE IS MORE THAN ONE BURGLAR
NEVR II (248) ON MY PATIENTS AS I PLAYED ON YOU? /CRAMPTON/ I HOPE NOT. /VALENTINE/ THE EXPLANATION IS THAT I'M STARK MAD,
NEVR II (258) YOUR EXPERIENCE ARE NOT INFALLIBLE. AT LEAST I HOPE NOT. /VALENTINE/ I MUST BELIEVE THEM, UNLESS YOU WISH
JITT III (64) IT HAD RATHER THE OPPOSITE EFFECT. /JITTA/ I HOPE NOT. TELL ME: DOES MY HUSBAND KNOW OF THIS NEW TURN?
PLES PREFACE(R18) PLAYS OF THE MODERN SCHOOL. FOR MY PART I HOPE NOT; FOR IDEALISM, WHICH IS ONLY A FLATTERING NAME FOR
GETT (286) I HOPE I SHALL. /THE GENERAL/ WELL, I MUST SAY I HOPE NOT, ALFRED. I HOPE NOT. /MRS BRIDGENORTH/ SHE SAYS SHE
NEVR II (245) ALL. /MRS CLANDON/ (WITH DEEP RESENTMENT) I HOPE NOT, FINCH. (SHE RISES: THEY ALL RISE A LITTLE). MR
HART II (113) BADLY YOU HAVE BEEN BROUGHT UP. /MAZZINI/ OH, I HOPE NOT, LADY UTTERWORD. REALLY! /LADY UTTERWORD/ I KNOW
SUPR IV (146) BE UNREASONABLE WITH HIM, MR MALONE. /MALONE/ I HOPE NOT, MISS ROBINSON; BUT AT YOUR AGE YOU MIGHT THINK
MRS IV (242) AN EFFORT) I HOPE NOT. (MORE EMPHATICALLY) I HOPE NOT, MISS WARREN. /FRANK/ (WHISTLES) WHEW! /VIVIE/
6CAL (93) SAINTS IS UPON THIS EXPEDITION. /THE PRINCE/ I HOPE NOT, SIR. I-- /THE KING/ (RAGING ON) MAY GOD WITHER
LION PREFACE(36) HIMSELF SHALL COME AFTER HIM DOES THE OLD JEWISH HOPE OF A MESSIAH BEGIN TO STIR AGAIN; AND AS JESUS BEGINS
SUPR HANDBOK(210) MAN TO WHOM HE IS ONLY AN ELDERLY STRANGER. ALL HOPE OF ADVANCE DIES IN HIS BOSOM AS HE WATCHES THEM: HE
SUPR HANDBOK(205) WE CONNIVE AT THE MOST ABOMINABLE TORTURES IN THE HOPE OF DISCOVERING SOME MAGICAL CURE FOR OUR OWN DISEASES
LION PREFACE(12) EASY FOR THE RICH. IT CUTS OFF THE POOR FROM ALL HOPE OF DIVINE FAVOR. AND THIS QUICKENS THE MORAL CRITICISM
JOAN 6 (131) WILL BE SO CRUEL THAT WE SHOULD FORFEIT OUR OWN HOPE OF DIVINE MERCY WERE THERE ONE GRAIN OF MALICE AGAINST
ROCK PREFACE(187) TO PARLEY WITH YOU AT THIS LENGTH IN THE MERCIFUL HOPE OF FINDING AN EXCUSE FOR TOLERATING YOUR BLASPHEMY AND
JITT III (53) LAST BATCH OF LETTERS THREE TIMES OVER IN THE HOPE OF FINDING SOME CLUE. BUT IT'S NO USE: THERES NOTHING.
MTH1 II (31) IS NOW A MASS OF NETTLES AND THISTLES, IN THE HOPE OF FINDING THE SERPENT TO TALK TO. BUT YOU HAVE MADE
POSN PREFACE(398) COPY. BUT IT WOULD CERTAINLY DISAPPOINT THE MAIN HOPE OF ITS ADVOCATES: THE HOPE THAT IT WOULD PROTECT AND
METH PREFACE(R11) IN PUBLIC DISCUSSIONS. IT WAS IN THE HOPE OF MAKING ME CLEAR THE MATTER UP THAT THE FABIAN
GETT PREFACE(223) LIBERALS OR CONSERVATIVES WITHOUT ANY HOPE OF SEATS IN PARLIAMENT, KNIGHTHOODS, OR POSTS IN THE
2TRU II (71) THERE IS THE SERGEANT. AND THERE IS ALWAYS THE HOPE OF SOMETHING TURNING UP AND THE SENSE OF BEING READY

MIS. PREFACE(90)	MAKE THE HISTORY OF THE PAST LIVE FOR US OR THE	HOPE	OF THE FUTURE SHINE FOR US, WHICH ALONE CAN GIVE
HART PREFACE(25)	SEEMED MAD, FUTILE, SILLY, INCOMPETENT, WITH NO	HOPE	OF VICTORY EXCEPT THE HOPE THAT THE ENEMY MIGHT BE JUST
METH PREFACE(R64)	HIM; EVERY CATHOLIC HATER OF FACTION FOUNDED A	HOPE	ON HIM; EVERY BLACKGUARD FELT JUSTIFIED BY HIM; AND
PHIL II (107)	UP EXCITEDLY) IN LOVE WITH JULIA! A RAY OF	HOPE	ON THE HORIZON! DO YOU REALLY MEAN IT? /SYLVIA/ I
BULL III (133)	DEMPSEY! HE IS DISESTABLISHED: HE HAS NOTHING TO	HOPE	OR FEAR FROM THE STATE; AND THE RESULT IS THAT HE'S THE
DOCT IV (158)	YOU ARE SO KIND, SIR RALPH. BUT DONT GIVE ME MUCH	HOPE	OR I SHALL CRY; AND LOUIS CANT BEAR THAT. /B.B./ (
KING I (202)	NONE WOULD LIVE PAST YEARS AGAIN; YET ALL	HOPE	PLEASURE IN WHAT YET REMAIN; AND FROM THE DREGS OF LIFE
HART III (147)	ARE TREMBLING. I CANT GET A SOUND. /MAZZINI/ I	HOPE	POOR MANGAN IS SAFE. /MRS HUSHABYE/ HE IS HIDING IN THE
GETT (299)	WHEN I PROPOSED TO YOU; AND NOW I CANT GO BACK. I	HOPE	PROVIDENCE WILL SPARE MY POOR MOTHER. I SAY AGAIN I'M
MRS IV (240)	I ASSURE YOU I HAVE CRIED-- I SHALL CRY AGAIN, I	HOPE	-- AT FIFTY! AT YOUR AGE, MISS WARREN, YOU WOULD NOT
DEVL I (11)	YOUR HELP. /ANDERSON/ AND WHOM TO FORGIVE, I	HOPE	-- ELI HAWKINS AND MYSELF, IF WE HAVE EVER SET UP OUR
MRS I (186)	ON WITH MY MOTHER? /PRAED/ (STARTLED) WELL, I	HOPE	-- ER-- /VIVIE/ IT'S NOT SO MUCH WHAT YOU HOPE AS WHAT
MTH4 II (189)	/THE ENVOY/ WHAT DO YOU MEAN BY SHORT WORK? I	HOPE	-- /ZOZIM/ (WITH OBVIOUSLY FEIGNED GENIALITY) OH,
PPP (200)	FROM THE BED) ANTIDOTE! /MAGNESIA/ (WITH WILD	HOPE	) ANTIDOTE! /FITZ/ IF AN ANTIDOTE WOULD NOT BE TOO
CLEO IV (190)	THE FLOOD. /CLEOPATRA/ (WITH A RAY OF CUNNING	HOPE	) BUT, CAESAR, IF YOU DO, YOU WILL PERISH YOURSELF.
LION EPILOG (152)	ROSE AND LEFT THE HOUSE, UNABLE TO ENDURE THE (I	HOPE	) VERY CLEAR AND FAIR EXPOSITION OF AUTOCRATIC
CLEO I (111)	EATS WOMEN. /CLEOPATRA/ (SPRINGING UP FULL OF	HOPE	) WHAT! /CAESAR/ (IMPRESSIVELY) BUT HE EATS GIRLS (
PHIL III (134)	RISES AND GAZES AT HIM, BREATHLESS WITH A NEW	HOPE	) YOUR GREAT GIFTS OF CHARACTER THAT ARE ONLY HALF
NEVR IV (288)	COFFEE, MISS? (HE GIVES A LITTLE GASP OF	HOPE	). CERTAINLY, MISS. THANK YOU, MISS: VERY TIMELY, MISS,
BULL IV (163)	KNOWN ME FOR 24 HOURS. I AM A REASONABLE MAN, I	HOPE	; AND I AM PREPARED TO WAIT AS LONG AS YOU LIKE.
HART II (110)	AND HAVE DONE WITH IT. I HAVE A CONSCIENCE TOO, I	HOPE	; AND I DO NOT FEEL AT ALL SURE THAT WE HAVE ANY RIGHT
BARB I (256)	BEAR AN IMMORAL MAN. I AM NOT A PHARISEE, I	HOPE	; AND I SHOULD NOT HAVE MINDED HIS MERELY DOING WRONG
BARB I (256)	THE STEVENAGES ARE AS GOOD AS THE ANTONINES, I	HOPE	; AND YOU ARE A STEVENAGE. BUT THAT WAS ANDREW ALL
PHIL III (145)	/GRACE/ NO: WE SHALL REMAIN VERY GOOD FRIENDS, I	HOPE	; BUT NOTHING WOULD INDUCE ME TO MARRY YOU. (SHE TAKES
INCA (239)	QUITE RIGHT. YOULL EXCUSE MY MENTIONING IT, I	HOPE	; BUT WHAT WAGES -- ER -- ? /ERMYNTRUDE/ THE SAME AS
LION II (132)	OF TOO MUCH SEVERITY. THESE PEOPLE HAVE NO	HOPE	; THEREFORE THEY HAVE NOTHING TO RESTRAIN THEM FROM
PHIL I (88)	ALL. /CRAVEN/ BUT, MY PRECIOUS, I MOST SINCERELY	HOPE	SHE WAS RIGHT. SHE PAID YOU THE HIGHEST COMPLIMENT.
AUGS (275)	/AUGUSTUS/ YOU NEED HAVE NO FEAR, MADAM. I	HOPE	SHE WILL COME AND TRY IT ON. FASCINATION IS A GAME THAT
BUOY IV (52)	DAMN YOU. YOU ARE STEALING MY DAUGHTER FROM ME. I	HOPE	SHE WILL SOON TIRE OF YOU AND COME BACK TO ME. (TO
2TRU II (60)	IT MUST HAVE BEEN DEAR FLORENCE DORCHESTER. I	HOPE	SHE WONT COME HERE. I WANT TO HAVE AN ABSOLUTE HOLIDAY.
MIS. (203)	IN-- I MAY SAY IN ALMOST ALL OF US. THEREFORE I	HOPE	SHE'LL STAY TO DINNER, AND NOT INSIST ON FLYING AWAY IN
MTH4 I (171)	WHEN THEY ARE THOUSANDS OF MILES APART. WE	HOPE	SHORTLY TO ORGANIZE THEIR LABOR, AND PRESS NATURAL
SUPR II (65)	(WITH STRONG SYMPTOMS OF MORAL REPUGNANCE) I	HOPE	SO. A MAN NEED BE VERY YOUNG AND PRETTY FOOLISH TOO TO
PRES (140)	WILL BE, BY THE OTHER SUBALTERNS. /MITCHENER/ I	HOPE	SO. ANYHOW, OUT HE GOES. OUT OF THE ARMY. HE OR I.
NEVR II (254)	ON HIS HAT). IS THAT YOUR LAST WORD? /GLORIA/ I	HOPE	SO. HE LOOKS STUBBORNLY AT HER FOR A MOMENT; NODS
MIS. (188)	HIM, I HOPE. SPANK HIM HARD. /LORD SUMMERHAYS/ I	HOPE	SO. I HOPE SO. TARLETON: I'M BEYOND MEASURE HUMILIATED
BULL IV (152)	GET INTO PARLIAMENT. /BROADBENT/ (DELIGHTED) I	HOPE	SO. I THINK SO. (FLUCTUATING) YOU REALLY THINK SO?
HART I (54)	HAVE SOME DELIGHTFUL TALKS WITH HIM. /MAZZINI/ I	HOPE	SO. (TO ELLIE) SO HERE YOU ARE, ELLIE, DEAR. (HE
MRS I (189)	YES: IT WILL PASS OFF PRESENTLY. /CROFTS/ I	HOPE	SO. (VIVIE REAPPEARS WITH TWO MORE CHAIRS. HE HURRIES
HART III (149)	NIGHT. /ELLIE/ (RADIANT AT THE PROSPECT) OH, I	HOPE	SO. RANDALL AT LAST SUCCEEDS IN KEEPING THE HOME FIRES
FOUN (217)	AWFULLY RIGHT ABOUT YOU. /THE LORD CHANCELLOR/ I	HOPE	SO. /ANASTASIA/ I DONT SEE THE DIFFERENCE MYSELF.
MRS IV (246)	A PLEASANT TRIP. /PRAED/ THANK YOU: THANK YOU. I	HOPE	SO. /FRANK/ (TO MRS WARREN) GOODBYE: YOUD EVER SO MUCH
GETT (311)	AGREEMENT, AS IT WERE. /EDITH/ (UNCONVINCED) I	HOPE	SO. /HOTCHKISS/ WHAT IS THE FIRST CLAUSE IN AN
DEVL I (25)	DOUBTFULLY AT JUDITH). I THINK SO. I MEAN I-- I	HOPE	SO. /RICHARD/ ESSIE: DID YOU EVER HEAR OF A PERSON
NEVR IV (304)	HAVE A GOOD DEAL MORE. /CRAMPTON/ POSSIBLY. I	HOPE	SO. /VALENTINE/ AND THE GENTLEMAN HASNT A RAP. /BOHUN/
GETT (304)	TO VISIT YOU WHEN YOU MARRY HIM? /HOTCHKISS/ I	HOPE	SO. SURELY YOURE NOT GOING TO BE VINDICTIVE, REJJY.
MIS. (188)	SPANK HIM HARD. /LORD SUMMERHAYS/ I HOPE SO. I	HOPE	SO. TARLETON: I'M BEYOND MEASURE HUMILIATED AND ANNOYED
DEVL I (16)	I HOPE HE WILL HAVE THE GRACE NOT TO COME. I	HOPE	SO. THE DUDGEONS ALL MURMUR ASSENT, EXCEPT CHRISTY, WHO
BUOY III (40)	FAMOUS NAME AND ITS ASSOCIATIONS WITH BILLIONS. I	HOPE	SO. WHAT MORE IS THERE TO BE SAID? /THE YOUTH/ WHAT
LION I (123)	PAYS ALL SCORES. /ANDROCLES/ WELL, LET US	HOPE	SO, BROTHER, FOR YOUR SAKE. YOUVE HAD A GAY TIME, HAVNT
FABL PREFACE(63)	THE TENSOR CALCULUS. I KNOW BETTER, AND CAN ONLY	HOPE	THAT A BATCH OF CHILDISH FABLES MAY STICK IN SOME HEADS
METH PREFACE(R89)	BRILLIANT WHEN I WAS IN MY PRIME. IT IS MY	HOPE	THAT A HUNDRED APTER AND MORE ELEGANT PARABLES BY
SIM II (60)	THANK YOU, DEAR VASHTI, THANK YOU. YOU GIVE ME	HOPE	THAT EVEN MAYA WILL GET TIRED OF ME SOMEDAY. /MAYA/ I
SUPR HANDBOK(201)	POOR MAN IS GIVEN A VOTE BY THE LIBERALS IN THE	HOPE	THAT HE WILL CAST IT FOR HIS EMANCIPATORS. THE HOPE IS
3PLA PREFACE(R39)	FOR ANY PUBLIC-SPIRITED CITIZEN OF THE WORLD TO	HOPE	THAT HIS REPUTATION MIGHT ENDURE; FOR THIS WOULD BE TO
PYGM EPILOG (294)	TO HIM BESIDES. HIS PROSPECTS CONSISTED OF A	HOPE	THAT IF HE KEPT UP APPEARANCES SOMEBODY WOULD DO
METH PREFACE(R72)	AND COLLIDING AND RUNNING ON THE ROCKS, IN THE	HOPE	THAT IF THEY CONTINUE TO DO THEIR WORST THEY WILL GET
POSN PREFACE(398)	DISAPPOINT THE MAIN HOPE OF ITS ADVOCATES: THE	HOPE	THAT IT WOULD PROTECT AND FOSTER THE HIGHER DRAMA. IT
JOAN 1 (65)	SNATCHING AT A DILATORY STEP WITH AN UNCONSCIOUS	HOPE	THAT JOAN WILL MAKE UP HIS MIND FOR HIM) DO YOU THINK I
ROCK PREFACE(164)	NOTHING COULD BE DONE IN THE INDUSTRIES; AND THE	HOPE	THAT PICKED MEMBERS OF THE PROLETARIAT COULD TAKE UP
PHIL II (122)	I'M OUT OF THE RUNNING. NEVERTHELESS, LIKE YOU, I	HOPE	THAT SHE MAY BE HAPPY WITH ALL MY-- WHAT DID YOU CALL
ARMS I SD(16)	THE CHEST OF DRAWERS. HE WATCHES HER WITH A VAGUE	HOPE	THAT SHE MAY HAVE SOMETHING MORE FOR HIM TO EAT. SHE
GENV PREFACE(11)	OF THEM ARE NOW CONSOLING THEMSELVES WITH THE	HOPE	THAT THE ATOMIC BOMB HAS MADE WAR IMPOSSIBLE. THAT HOPE
HART PREFACE(25)	INCOMPETENT, WITH NO HOPE OF VICTORY EXCEPT THE	HOPE	THAT THE ENEMY MIGHT BE JUST AS MAD. ONLY BY VERY
3PLA PREFACE(R40)	HIS REPUTATION MIGHT ENDURE; FOR THIS WOULD BE TO	HOPE	THAT THE FLOOD OF GENERAL ENLIGHTENMENT MAY NEVER RISE
METH PREFACE(R67)	HAD PASSED IT, ITS WILDEST OPPONENT HAD NO	HOPE	THAT THE GOVERNMENT WOULD CANCEL IT, OR SHELVE IT, OR
METH PREFACE(R27)	POSSIBILITIES TO THE EXTENT OF ENABLING US TO	HOPE	THAT THE MOST PROLONGED AND DIFFICULT OPERATIONS OF OUR
DOCT PREFACE(33)	STUPID, AND INDEED BLASPHEMOUS AND DESPAIRING, TO	HOPE	THAT THE THIRST FOR KNOWLEDGE WILL EITHER DIMINISH OR
POSN PREFACE(375)	THE MATTER WITH WHICH IT HAD TO DEAL, AND IN THE	HOPE	THAT THE TREATMENT OF SUBSEQUENT WITNESSES AND THE
GENV PREFACE(11)	THEIR OWN DISCOVERY, AND THE VANQUISHED WITH THE	HOPE	THAT THEY MAY SOON DISCOVER FOR THEMSELVES HOW TO
LION I (112)	GLADIATORS. /LAVINIA/ CAPTAIN: IS THERE NO	HOPE	THAT THIS CRUEL PERSECUTION -- /CENTURION/ (SHOCKED)
BULL PREFACE(44)	WRONG THAT HAS ROTTED HER ALMOST TO THE MARROW, I	HOPE	THAT WHEN HOME RULE IS AT LAST ACHIEVED, ONE OF OUR
SIM II (82)	THINKING TO DO. /LADY FARWATERS/ WELL, DEAR: I	HOPE	THAT WILL COUNT AS WORK. I SHALL FEEL SAFER WITH MY
PHIL II (121)	SHE MAY LIVE HAPPILY EVER AFTER. /PARAMORE/ I DO	HOPE	THAT WITH ALL MY SOUL-- (CORRECTING HIMSELF) I MEAN
PHIL II (121)	NOW IT'S A PERFECTLY DAMNABLE THING FOR YOU TO	HOPE	THAT YOUR LIVER THEORY IS TRUE, BECAUSE IT AMOUNTS TO
PHIL II (121)	LEAST YOULL ADMIT THAT IT'S AMIABLE AND HUMAN TO	HOPE	THAT YOUR THEORY ABOUT JULIA IS RIGHT, BECAUSE IT
2TRU II (55)	WELL, NEXT TIME YOU ARE SENT WITH A LETTER I	HOPE	THE BRIGANDS WILL CATCH YOU AND KEEP YOU. /MEEK/ THERE
GENV II (51)	HAVE BEEN MASSACRED. /BEGONIA/ DIRTY SWINE! I	HOPE	THE BRITISH FLEET WILL NOT LEAVE A STONE STANDING OR A
BULL IV (149)	(HE COLLECTS HIMSELF FOR A SPEECH). GENTLEMEN: I	HOPE	THE GRAVITY OF THE PERIL THROUGH WHICH WE HAVE ALL
WIDO II (44)	ARE GETTING READY FOR IT I CAN SEE BLANCHE; AND I	HOPE	THE RESULT WILL BE QUITE SATISFACTORY TO US ALL. (THE
MIS. (204)	STORM. I MUST RISK MY LIFE TOMORROW. /BENTLEY/ I	HOPE	THERE WILL BE A STORM. /LINA/ (GRASPING HIS ARM) YOU
GETT (311)	HINTS FROM IT FOR YOUR OWN CONTRACT. /EDITH/ I	HOPE	THERE WILL BE NO HINTING. LET US HAVE THE PLAIN
LIED (197)	HAVNT BEEN ABLE TO CALL ON HER THIS LAST WEEK. I	HOPE	THERES NOTHING THE MATTER WITH HER. /HER HUSBAND/
DOCT I (97)	SERUM. YOU WERE OUT, UNFORTUNATELY. /RIDGEON/ I	HOPE	THEY EXPLAINED TO YOU CAREFULLY-- /B.B./ (WAVING AWAY
BULL II (108)	NOT A BIT: WE NEVER HAVE IT AIRLIER THAN THIS. I	HOPE	THEY GAVE YOU A GOOD DINNER AT ATHENMULLET. /BROADBENT/
SIM II (58)	HIM). THERE GOES THE NOONDAY CANNON! /HYERING/ I	HOPE	THEY GOT THE MESSAGE IN TIME. THE GARDEN AND ITS
JITT II (31)	TO CALL ON THEM. I HAVE BEEN REALLY TOO ILL. I	HOPE	THEY KNOW THAT. /FESSLER/ (WITH AFFECTIONATE
BULL III (117)	FROM LONDON BY PARCEL POST. /BROADBENT/ I	HOPE	THEY MADE YOU COMFORTABLE LAST NIGHT. /HODSON/ I WAS NO
SIM PREFACE(19)	THE ROOTS OR THE CLAY OR EVEN THE LEAVES. LET US	HOPE	THEY NEVER WILL. ON THE INDIAN OCEAN, APRIL 1935. THE
CAPT I (220)	SHOULD EV IT HIN THEIR MAWNDS TO GOW. /RANKIN/ I	HOPE	THEY WONT. /DRINKWATER/ AN SOW AW DO TOO, GAVNER.
ROCK II (283)	A STAND, THE COWARDS? /LADY CHAVENDER/ INDEED I	HOPE	THEY WONT. WHAT ARE YOU THINKING OF, HILDA? /SIR
HART III (149)	/MRS HUSHABYE/ BUT WHAT A GLORIOUS EXPERIENCE! I	HOPE	THEYLL COME AGAIN TOMORROW NIGHT. /ELLIE/ (RADIANT AT
SUPR II (65)	ER-- IN VIOLET. /OCTAVIUS/ (SYMPATHETICALLY) I	HOPE	THIS IS NOT A DISAPPOINTMENT TO YOU. /HECTOR/ (
DOCT III (155)	YOU. /RIDGEON/ GOODBYE. (SHE TAKES HIS HAND). I	HOPE	THIS WILL BE A LASTING FRIENDSHIP. /MRS DUBEDAT/ IT
MTH4 II (186)	THE ORACLE AND HAD THE STRAIGHT TIP FROM HER. I	HOPE	THIS ZOZIM CHAP IS NOT GOING TO KEEP US WAITING MUCH
GENV PREFACE(20)	CHOOSE WHAT RULERS THEY PLEASE, BEFORE HE CAN	HOPE	TO BE ACCEPTED BY THEM AS A FIGURE HEAD. HITLER HAD
JITT II (41)	I GO TO WORK ON THE SCIENTIFIC PAPERS. /JITTA/ I	HOPE	TO BE ALLOWED TO GO OUT AGAIN IN A DAY OR TWO. MAY I
POSN (455)	AS I HOPE TO BE SAVED, SHERIFF-- OR RATHER AS I	HOPE	TO BE DAMNED; FOR I HAVE NO TASTE FOR PIOUS COMPANY AND
POSN (455)	BUT IF I HAD THAT HORSE I SHOULDNT BE HERE. AS I	HOPE	TO BE SAVED, SHERIFF-- OR RATHER AS I HOPE TO BE
BUOY 1 (14)	MAN THAN HIS FATHER HAD EVER BEEN OR COULD	HOPE	TO BE. THAT IS WHAT MAY HAPPEN TO ME. BUT THERE IS A
SUPR III (103)	THITHER I SHALL GO PRESENTLY, BECAUSE THERE I	HOPE	TO ESCAPE AT LAST FROM LIES AND FROM THE TEDIOUS,
MIS. PREFACE(97)	TO WHICH ALL VIRTUE IS AN ASPIRATION, AND TO	HOPE	TO FIND THIS BODY OF ART PURIFIED FROM ALL THAT IS
JITT II (31)	/JITTA/ COME AGAIN SOON, DOCTOR. /FESSLER/ I	HOPE	TO FIND YOU QUITE WELL THEN, DEAR LADY. HE KISSES HER
DOCT PREFACE(37)	METHOD CAN CUT US OFF FROM THE KNOWLEDGE WE	HOPE	TO GAIN BY IT. THE ONLY KNOWLEDGE WE LOSE BY FORBIDDING
VWOO 3 (141)	GAS-- IF THE DESTINY OF MAN HOLDS OUT NO HIGHER	HOPE	TO HIM THAN THE FINAL EXTINCTION AND ANNIHILATION OF SO
GETT (350)	HAND ALMOST AFFECTIONATELY ON HIS). SOME DAY I	HOPE	TO MAKE A FRIEND OF YOU; AND THEN WE SHALL GET ON VERY
APPL I (237)	HIS PROCESS OR WHATEVER IT MAY BE THAN HE COULD	HOPE	TO MAKE BY A LEGITIMATE USE OF IT; AND WHEN THEY HAVE

NEVR II	(255)	ENLIGHTENED MIND? /GLORIA/ (EARNESTLY) I	HOPE	TO MEET MANY SUCH PEOPLE IN ENGLAND. /VALENTINE/ (
SUPR IV	(171)	MISS WHITEFIELD. I CONGRATULATE MR TANNER; AND I	HOPE	TO MEET YOU AND HIM AS FREQUENT GUESTS AT THE ABBEY.
INCA	(241)	OF THE FIVE FIFTEEN EXPRESS, FROM WHICH YOU	HOPE	TO PICK UP SOME FAT ARMAMENTS CONTRACTOR WHO WILL DRINK
KING I	(189)	SUPPORTER OF THE EXCLUSION BILL BECAUSE I	HOPE	TO PROVE THAT THE ROMISH CHURCH IS THE LITTLE HORN OF
CAND I	(99)	HER! EUGENE: TAKE CARE. I HAVE BEEN PATIENT. I	HOPE	TO REMAIN PATIENT. BUT THERE ARE SOME THINGS I WONT
LION PREFACE	(40)	I CANNOT BELIEVE THAT A LITERARY FORGER COULD	HOPE	TO SAVE THE SITUATION BY SO OUTRAGEOUS A PRETENSION.
JOAN 1	(65)	/ROBERT/ YOU WILL REALLY GAMBLE ON A FORLORN	HOPE	TO THE TUNE OF SIXTEEN FRANCS? /POULENGEY/ IT IS NOT A
LION PREFACE	(36)	IS BAPTIZED BY HIM, NOBODY CONNECTS HIM WITH THAT	HOPE	UNTIL PETER HAS THE SUDDEN INSPIRATION WHICH PRODUCES
WIDO II	(47)	ON HER FATHER'S BREAST). /TRENCH/ (NERVOUSLY) I	HOPE	WE ARE NOT INTRUDING. /SARTORIUS/ (FORMIDABLY) DR
BARB II	(303)	ENOUGH TO KEEP THE SHELTER OPEN? /MRS BAINES/ I	HOPE	WE SHALL HAVE ENOUGH TO KEEP ALL THE SHELTERS OPEN.
OVER	(194)	IT BORES ME. BUT I DO LIKE TO BE AMUSED. /JUNO/ I	HOPE	WE SHALL MEET VERY OFTEN. BUT I HOPE ALSO WE SHALL NOT
WIDO II	(27)	WITHDRAWS. /TRENCH/ (GLANCING AT LICKCHEESE) I	HOPE	WE'RE NOT IN THE WAY. /SARTORIUS/ BY NO MEANS. SIT
MIS.	(180)	DOWN HELPLESSLY AND DIPS THE PEN IN THE INK.) I	HOPE	WHAT YOU ARE SIGNING IS NO MERE FORM OF WORDS TO YOU,
METH PREFACE	(R18)	TO THE NEO-DARWINISTS, TO THE MECHANISTS, NO	HOPE	WHATEVER, BECAUSE IMPROVEMENT CAN COME ONLY THROUGH
FABL II	(107)	IS TRUE: IT MAY. LET US HOPE IT WONT. /OLDHAND/	HOPE	WONT HELP US IF IT DOES. OUR FIRST DUTY IS AT ALL COST
SUPR I	(18)	WOMAN SHOULD BE LEFT QUITE TO HER OWN GUIDANCE. I	HOPE	YOU AGREE WITH ME, GRANNY? /TANNER/ (STARTING)
MRS I	(183)	DO YOU KNOW, YOU ARE JUST LIKE WHAT I EXPECTED. I	HOPE	YOU ARE DISPOSED TO BE FRIENDS WITH ME. /PRAED/ (AGAIN
NEVR II	(257)	HAVE SET TO WORK IN MY IMAGINATION? /GLORIA/ I	HOPE	YOU ARE NOT GOING TO BE SO FOOLISH-- SO VULGAR-- AS TO
BARB I	(261)	A SHRUG. CHARLES LOOKS PAINFULLY UNWORTHY). I	HOPE	YOU ARE NOT GOING TO OBJECT, BARBARA. /BARBARA/ I! WHY
MIS.	(156)	SHE IS ACCESSIBLE. GOOD. /LORD SUMMERHAYS/ I	HOPE	YOU ARE NOT SERIOUS. REMEMBER: YOU HAVE A FAMILY. YOU
INCA	(238)	KNOW. IT'S VERY SHARP OF YOU TO FIND THAT OUT. I	HOPE	YOU ARE NOT TOO SHARP. /ERMYNTRUDE/ A LADY'S MAID HAS
SUPR I	(18)	LEARNED TO SPEAK. /RAMSDEN/ (SARCASTICALLY) I	HOPE	YOU ARE SATISFIED, MR TANNER. GO ON, ANNIE: I QUITE
ARMS II	(27)	YOU ARE A BARBARIAN AT HEART STILL, PAUL. I	HOPE	YOU BEHAVED YOURSELF BEFORE ALL THOSE RUSSIAN OFFICERS.
ARMS III	(51)	ONE REALLY BEAUTIFUL AND NOBLE PART OF MY LIFE. I	HOPE	YOU CAN UNDERSTAND THAT. /BLUNTSCHLI/ (SCEPTICALLY)
ARMS II	(43)	IT AND SPOILT IT. (TO BLUNTSCHLI, WINNINGLY) I	HOPE	YOU DIDNT THINK THAT YOU WERE THE CHOCOLATE CREAM
CAND III	(140)	EUGENE AWAY WITHOUT DEIGNING TO LOOK AT HIM) I	HOPE	YOU DONT MEAN THAT AS A THREAT, CANDIDA. /CANDIDA/ (
MTH4 I	(172)	THEM OUT, YOU SEND A COLD SHIVER DOWN MY SPINE. I	HOPE	YOU DONT MEAN THAT YOU-- THAT YOU-- THAT YOU ASSIST
HART III	(139)	IDEALIST, HAVE SUCCEEDED BRILLIANTLY. /MAZZINI/ I	HOPE	YOU DONT MIND MY BEING LIKE THIS, MR HUSHABYE. (HE
WIDO I	(15)	I WANT TO MARRY YOUR DAUGHTER, MR SARTORIUS. I	HOPE	YOU DONT OBJECT. /SARTORIUS/ (CONDESCENDING TO
GETT	(265)	HAVE BEEN A BIT OF USE TO ME. /MRS BRIDGENORTH/ I	HOPE	YOU DONT TELL YOUR WIFE THAT YOU GO ELSEWHERE FOR
FANY II	(294)	IN WHAT OTHER PEOPLE DID TO ME. /MRS KNOX/ I	HOPE	YOU DONT THINK YOURSELF A HEROINE OF ROMANCE.
CAPT I	(220)	AW DID. /RANKIN/ (WITH SOME INDIGNATION) I	HOPE	YOU DONT THINK I MET SIR HOWRRD IN THAT WAY.
FABL I	(101)	PLEASE. I DONT CARE WHERE YOU SIT. /YOUNG MAN/ I	HOPE	YOU DONT THINK ME INTRUSIVE? /YOUNG WOMAN/ I AM NOT
MRS III	(231)	THE INTEREST ON MY CAPITAL LIKE OTHER PEOPLE: I	HOPE	YOU DONT THINK I DIRTY MY OWN HANDS WITH THE WORK.
MILL IV	(189)	/MANAGER/ (BETWEEN THEM) GOOD AFTERNOON, SIR. I	HOPE	YOU FIND EVERYTHING HERE TO YOUR LIKING. /ALASTAIR/
CAPT III	(276)	COMES IN. /SIR HOWARD/ GOOD MORNING, MR RANKIN. I	HOPE	YOU GOT HOME SAFELY FROM THE YACHT LAST NIGHT. /RANKIN/
MIS.	(202)	TO BE SURPRISED AT YOU, GOVERNOR, IS THERE? I	HOPE	YOU GOT IT AS HOT AS I DID. MIND, MISS SHEPANOSKA: IT
FANY I	(283)	YES, MADAM. /MRS GILBEY/ (RATHER SHOCKED) I	HOPE	YOU HAD NOT BEEN EXCEEDING, JUGGINS. /JUGGINS/ YES,
APPL I	(210)	NOT EVERYBODY WHO IS RECEIVED AS YOU HAVE BEEN. I	HOPE	YOU HAVE ENJOYED YOUR VISIT. /BOANERGES/ WELL, I PULLED
BULL IV	(148)	CAP WITH DIGNITY AND PLACING IT ON THE TABLE) I	HOPE	YOU HAVE NOT BEEN ANXIOUS ABOUT ME. /AUNT JUDY/ DEEDN
APPL II	(266)	PALACE. YOU WORE A MOST BECOMING COSTUME THEN. I	HOPE	YOU HAVE NOT GIVEN IT UP. /BOANERGES/ BUT THE PRINCESS
DOCT V	(171)	IS INFAMOUS THAT THEY SHOULD WRITE LIKE THAT. I	HOPE	YOU HAVE NOT SENT THEM TICKETS FOR TODAY. /THE
ROCK II	(235)	/SIR DEXTER/ (NERVOUSLY) BY THE WAY, BASHAM, I	HOPE	YOU HAVE THE UNEMPLOYED WELL IN HAND TODAY. /BASHAM/
NEVR II	(231)	EMPHATICALLY) BALD HEADED. /M'COMAS/ (NETTLED) I	HOPE	YOU INTEND TO TAKE WHAT I HAVE TO SAY SERIOUSLY.
MIS.	(158)	I DONT KNOW WHAT YOURE TALKING ABOUT; AND I ONLY	HOPE	YOU KNOW YOURSELVES. HOWEVER, YOU SHALL HAVE WHAT YOU
SUPR I	(9)	WELL, IF THESE ARE ANARCHIST MANNERS, I	HOPE	YOU LIKE THEM. AND ANNIE WITH HIM! ANNIE! A-- (HE
APPL II	(274)	THAT UNWHOLESOME CONCEALMENT WILL END. I	HOPE	YOU LOOK FORWARD TO OUR NEW FOOTING AS PLEASURABLY AS I
PHIL II	(115)	NO MORE ABOUT IT. I CONGRATULATE YOU, CRAVEN, AND	HOPE	YOU MAY LONG BE SPARED. (CRAVEN OFFERS HIS HAND). NO,
PHIL I	(87)	DONT CRY, JULIA. /CUTHBERTSON/ (HUSKILY) I	HOPE	YOU MAY LONG BE SPARED, DAN. /CRAVEN/ TO OBLIGE ME, JO,
DOCT V	(174)	AND AFFECTIONATENESS THAT ONLY ANIMALS HAVE. I	HOPE	YOU MAY NEVER FEEL WHAT I FELT WHEN I HAD TO PUT HIM
JITT III	(64)	ME-- ABOVE MY OWN MOTHER. /FESSLER/ WELL, I	HOPE	YOU MAY, DARLING. DOES THAT PLEASE YOU? JITTA COMES IN
WIDO I	(23)	THAT, BLANCHE: IT SOUNDS AS IF YOU DIDNT CARE. I	HOPE	YOU REGARD IT AS SETTLED. YOU HAVNT MADE ANY PROMISE,
BULL III	(119)	GALONG! HOW CAN YOU LIKE WHATS NOT NATURAL? I	HOPE	YOU SLEPT WELL. /NORA/ DID ANYTHING WAKE YUP WITH A
MIS.	(120)	WAS EXCEEDINGLY RUDE OF BENTLEY, MRS TARLETON. I	HOPE	YOU TOLD HIM SO. /MRS TARLETON/ OH, BLESS YOU! I DONT
LIED	(203)	OUT THREE DAYS. /SHE/ DONT BE FOOLISH, TEDDY. I	HOPE	YOU WERE NOT REALLY HURT, HENRY. (SHE FEELS THE BACK
GETT	(284)	QUITE RIGHT, DEAR: STAND UP FOR YOUR HUSBAND. I	HOPE	YOU WILL ALWAYS STAND UP FOR ALL YOUR HUSBANDS. (HE
GETT	(295)	SOCIAL INTERCOURSE. /THE GENERAL/ (MARKEDLY) I	HOPE	YOU WILL ALWAYS TELL ME THE TRUTH, MY DARLING, AT ALL
MILL I	(140)	KNOW. BUT THEY NEVER DO. /EPIFANIA/ I WILL. AND I	HOPE	YOU WILL BE HANGED FOR GIVING IT TO ME. /SAGAMORE/ I AM
SUPR I	(45)	I APOLOGIZE-- ABJECTLY APOLOGIZE. /VIOLET/ I	HOPE	YOU WILL BE MORE CAREFUL IN FUTURE ABOUT THE THINGS YOU
CLEO II	(124)	A THRONE WHEN IT IS OFFERED TO YOU. /RUFIO/ I	HOPE	YOU WILL HAVE THE GOOD SENSE TO FOLLOW YOUR OWN ADVICE
ARMS III	(71)	IS UNSPEAKABLY TAKEN ABACK). NEXT TIME, I	HOPE	YOU WILL KNOW THE DIFFERENCE BETWEEN A SCHOOLGIRL OF
NEVR I	(215)	WHO HAVE GONE THROUGH WHAT I HAVE GONE THROUGH. I	HOPE	YOU WILL NEVER BE QUALIFIED FOR SUCH CONFIDENCES.
MTH4 I	(172)	/THE ELDERLY GENTLEMAN/ (EAGERLY) NEVER. I	HOPE	YOU WILL NOT BE OFFENDED IF I SAY THAT IT WOULD BE A
GENV IV	(94)	ACCOUNT OF THEM WITH PERFECT COMPLACENCY AND-- I	HOPE	YOU WILL NOT MIND MY SAYING SO-- WITH SOME AMUSEMENT.
MTH3	(115)	DO WITH COMMON WEAKNESSES, MR CHIEF SECRETARY. I	HOPE	YOU WILL RESPECT THEM. /CONFUCIUS/ (AFTER BOWING TO
WIDO II	(44)	/SARTORIUS/ I WILL SHEW YOU YOUR ROOM, HARRY. I	HOPE	YOU WILL SOON BE PERFECTLY AT HOME IN IT. YOU ALSO, MR
PHIL II	(127)	WELL, MRS TRANFIELD, ALL I CAN SAY IS THAT I	HOPE	YOU WILL SUCCEED IN ESTABLISHING YOUR COMPLAINT, AND
CATH 1	(172)	WHO IS NOT AFRAID OF HIM. HE IS SO STRONG! I	HOPE	YOU WILL THROW HIM DOWN ON THE FLOOR MANY, MANY, MANY
PYGM III	(253)	HILL/ I DARESAY I AM VERY OLD-FASHIONED; BUT I DO	HOPE	YOU WONT BEGIN USING THAT EXPRESSION, CLARA. I HAVE GOT
HART II	(106)	ON THE TABLE AND STAGGERS ROUND TO THE CHAIR). I	HOPE	YOU WONT BELIEVE I REALLY INTENDED TO. HECTOR COMES IN.
MILL IV	(203)	ALASTAIR IS TO SEEDYSTOCKINGS. /PATRICIA/ WELL, I	HOPE	YOU WONT HAVE TO WAIT TOO LONG. /EPIFANIA/ I NEVER
DEST	(181)	AUSTRIANS FOR YOU, DESPATCHES OR NO DESPATCHES. I	HOPE	YOU WONT INSIST ON MY STARTING OFF ON A WILD GOOSE
GENV II	(54)	MY FRIEND, IT'S YOU WHO HAVE DRAGGED ME. AND I	HOPE	YOU WONT MIND MY ASKING YOU WHAT ON EARTH YOU THINK YOU
SUPR IV	(164)	YOU SHOULDNT SAY THINGS LIKE THAT, JACK. I	HOPE	YOU WONT TELL ANN THAT I HAVE BEEN SPEAKING TO YOU. I
OVER	(187)	I WONT BE BELITTLED. /MRS LUNN/ (TO MRS JUNO) I	HOPE	YOULL COME AND STAY WITH US NOW THAT YOU AND GREGORY
WIDO II	(44)	SO. WE'RE ALL IN THE SAME SWIM, IT APPEARS. I	HOPE	YOULL EXCUSE MY MAKING SUCH A FUSS. /SARTORIUS/ NOT
PHIL II	(118)	SAY ANOTHER WORD AGAINST YOUR PROFESSION. BUT I	HOPE	YOULL LET ME STICK TO THE GOOD OLDFASHIONED SHAKING-UP
PHIL II	(130)	GO THIS INSTANT. COME ON, SYLVIA. CUTHBERTSON: I	HOPE	YOULL MARK YOUR SENSE OF THIS SORT OF THING BY COMING
ARMS II	(44)	I AM SURE. (TO CATHERINE) MY FAULT, MADAM: I	HOPE	YOULL OVERLOOK IT. (HE BOWS, AND IS GOING TO THE STEPS
SUPR IV	(153)	TO THE LAWN AND RUNNING TO HECTOR'S LEFT HAND) I	HOPE	YOULL SHAKE HANDS WITH ME BEFORE YOU GO, HECTOR. I
MIS.	(113)	DECENT CHAP'S FIST, FOR INSTANCE. /BENTLEY/ I	HOPE	YOUR BEASTLY FIST MAY COME UP AGAINST A MAD BULL OR A
NEVR II	(240)	CLANDON/ (TROUBLED) I-- I DID NOT MEAN THAT. I	HOPE	YOUR HEALTH IS GOOD. /CRAMPTON/ THANK YOU. NO: IT'S NOT
APPL I	(226)	FEATURES AS BEST SHE CAN) EXCUSE ME. /CRASSUS/ I	HOPE	YOUR MAJESTY RECOGNIZES THAT KINGS ARE NOT THE ONLY
DOCT III	(138)	THE ONLY THING THAT WAS ON MY CONSCIENCE. NOW I	HOPE	YOURE ALL SATISFIED. /SIR PATRICK/ NOT QUITE, MR
FANY III	(304)	MEG, I DO FIND THAT A BIT THICK, I MUST SAY. I	HOPE	YOURE NOT IN EARNEST WHEN YOU TALK THAT WAY. /MARGARET/
PYGM II	(232)	WIPE THEM IN MY HAIR IN FUTURE. /MRS PEARCE/ I	HOPE	YOURE NOT OFFENDED, MR HIGGINS. /HIGGINS/ (SHOCKED AT
CAPT III	(278)	FROM A LAWYER'S POINT OF VIEW. /SIR HOWARD/ I	HOPE	YOURE NOT OFFENDED. /LADY CICELY/ (WITH THE UTMOST
O'FL	(216)	WEVE BROUGHT YOU BACK YOUR SON SAFE AND SOUND. I	HOPE	YOURE PROUD OF HIM. /MRS O'FLAHERTY/ AND INDEED AND I
APPL I	(231)	THE ROOM). /BALBUS/ YOUVE DONE IT NOW, MANDY. I	HOPE	YOURE PROUD OF YOURSELF. /MAGNUS/ IT IS YOU, AMANDA.
ARMS II	(42)	LONGER THE ENEMY, HAPPILY. (RATHER ANXIOUSLY) I	HOPE	YOUVE CALLED AS A FRIEND, AND NOT ABOUT HORSES OR
SUPR IV	(151)	CONTENDING FOR A PRINCIPLE. I AM A SON, AND, I	HOPE	, A DUTIFUL ONE; BUT BEFORE EVERYTHING I'M A MAHN! !
FANY PROLOG	(258)	I'M RATHER A STRANGER IN YOUR WORLD. I AM NOT, I	HOPE	, A MODERN MAN IN ANY SENSE OF THE WORD. I'M NOT REALLY
SUPR PREFACE	(R30)	VIEW AND NO MORE, NEITHER TRUE NOR FALSE, BUT, I	HOPE	, A WAY OF LOOKING AT THE SUBJECT WHICH THROWS INTO THE
MRS PREFACE	(158)	IF YOU PLEASE, UNNECESSARY. EVERYBODY WILL, I	HOPE	, ADMIT THAT THIS STATE OF THINGS IS INTOLERABLE; THAT
GETT	(287)	LEFT, AND SITTING DOWN) NOT MORE RITUALISM, I	HOPE	, ALFRED? /THE BISHOP/ OH NO. I MEAN ANCIENT ROME. (
BARB PREFACE	(230)	CONFESSION AND EXPIATION. FOR THOUGH I AM NOT, I	HOPE	, AN UNMERCIFUL PERSON, I DO NOT THINK THAT THE
PLES PREFACE	(R18)	OF THE EXISTENCE OF COURAGE, PATRIOTISM, FAITH,	HOPE	, AND CHARITY, I SAW THAT IT WAS NOT REALLY MERE MATTER
SUPR III	(96)	A FORM OF MORAL RESPONSIBILITY. HERE THERE IS NO	HOPE	, AND CONSEQUENTLY NO DUTY, NO WORK, NOTHING TO BE
ROCK II	(282)	LIKE DESPAIR; BUT IT IS REALLY THE BEGINNING OF	HOPE	, AND THE END OF HYPOCRISY. DO YOU THINK I DIDNT KNOW.
SUPR IV	(159)	MARRY YOU FOR WORLDS, TAVY. /OCTAVIUS/ I HAVE NO	HOPE	, ANN: I ACCEPT MY ILL LUCK. BUT I DONT THINK YOU QUITE
DOCT PREFACE	(37)	ONE." CRUELTY FOR ITS OWN SAKE. IT WILL NOW, I	HOPE	, BE CLEAR WHY THE ATTACK ON VIVISECTION IS NOT AN
OVER PREFACE	(168)	ALL FUTURE WRITERS OF FARCICAL COMEDY, MAY NOW, I	HOPE	, BE READ WITHOUT SHOCK. I MAY JUST ADD THAT MR
BARB PREFACE	(246)	THIS PLAY OF MINE, MAJOR BARBARA, IS, I	HOPE	, BOTH TRUE AND INSPIRED; BUT WHOEVER SAYS THAT IT ALL
FANY PROLOG	(260)	SEEM TO KNOW YOUR WAY ABOUT MUCH IN ENGLAND, I	HOPE	, BY THE WAY, THAT EVERYTHING HAS GIVEN SATISFACTION TO
WIDO I	(22)	SEE YOU AFTERWARDS. BUT IF ALL TURNS OUT AS WE	HOPE	, DR TRENCH'S BEST FRIENDS WILL THEN BE OUR BEST
MIS.	(166)	TO HIM) INDEED? AND HOW IS SHE? QUITE WELL, I	HOPE	, EH? /THE MAN/ SHE IS DEAD. DEAD, MY GOD! AND YOU
DEVL I	(14)	OF THE REMARK) YOU ARE NOT GOING TO BE SULLEN, I	HOPE	, ESSIE. /ESSIE/ NO. /JUDITH/ THATS A GOOD GIRL! (SHE

SUPR PREFACE(R12)	OWING TO YOUR UNFORTUNATE HABIT-- YOU NOW, I	HOPE	, FEEL ITS INCONVENIENCE-- OF NOT EXPLAINING YOURSELF,
METH PREFACE(R51)	GRANDCHILDREN'S TAILS TOO, AND WAITED, FULL OF	HOPE	, FOR THE BIRTH OF CURTAILED GREAT-GRANDCHILDREN. BUT
ARMS III (71)	COMPLACENTLY) I HAVE PUT EVERYTHING RIGHT, I	HOPE	, GRACIOUS YOUNG LADY. /RAINA/ (GOING TO THE TABLE TO
WIDO II (28)	TO SAY TO MY DAUGHTER, DR TRENCH: YOU WILL NOT, I	HOPE	, GRUDGE ME THE PLEASURE OF BREAKING THIS NEWS TO HER:
MIS. PREFACE(74)	HAVE DECIDEDLY THE WORST OF IT. THIS MUCH	HOPE	, HOWEVER, CAN BE EXTRACTED FROM THE PRESENT STATE OF
GENV III (69)	SENORA, NO DOUBT. WE ARE ALL GOOD CATHOLICS, I	HOPE	, IN A SENSE. YOU WILL REMEMBER THAT OUR SAVIOR WAS OF
KING I (202)	CONSIDER LIFE, 'TIS ALL A CHEAT; YET, FOOLED WITH	HOPE	, MEN FAVOR THE DECEIT; TRUST ON, AND THINK TOMORROW
JOAN 6 (130)	AGAINST YOUR NATURAL COMPASSION. YOU ARE ALL, I	HOPE	, MERCIFUL MEN: HOW ELSE COULD YOU HAVE DEVOTED YOUR
HART I (66)	HAND) VERY PLEASED. (TURNING TO ELLIE) I	HOPE	, MISS ELLIE, YOU HAVE NOT FOUND THE JOURNEY DOWN TOO
WIDO I (19)	UPON HIM). /SARTORIUS/ I DO NOT DISTURB YOU, I	HOPE	, MR COKANE. /COKANE/ BY NO MEANS. OUR FRIEND TRENCH
PPP (196)	HA, HA! NOTHING! HA, HA, HA! /ADOLPHUS/ I	HOPE	, MR FITZTOLLEMACHE, YOU ARE NOT LAUGHING AT MY
WIDO II (41)	A CONSERVATIVE, NOT A NARROW OR PREJUDICED ONE, I	HOPE	, NOR AT ALL OPPOSED TO TRUE PROGRESS. STILL, A SOUND
PHIL I (70)	WANTED TO BE IN LOVE WITH SOMEONE EVER SINCE. I	HOPE	, NOW THAT I AM IN LOVE WITH YOU, YOU WILL LIKE ME FOR
SUPR I (28)	MAY DISTORT IT TO GRATIFY YOUR MALICIOUS HUMOR. I	HOPE	, OCTAVIUS, NO SUSPICION OF ME IS POSSIBLE IN YOUR
HART II (99)	GOING TO SIT DOWN AND DIE OF A BROKEN HEART, I	HOPE	, OR BE AN OLD MAID LIVING ON A PITTANCE FROM THE SICK
MTH4 I (163)	ELDERLY GENTLEMAN/ I WAS ILLUSTRATING-- NOT, I	HOPE	, QUITE INFELICITOUSLY-- THE GREAT MARCH OF PROGRESS. I
DOCT PREFACE(48)	LIES. MOST SENSIBLE AND HUMANE PEOPLE WOULD, I	HOPE	, REPLY FLATLY THAT HONORABLE MEN DO NOT BEHAVE
MIS. (151)	ADVENTURE TO DROP OUT OF THE SKY, AND IS NOW, I	HOPE	, SATISFIED AT LAST. LORD SUMMERHAYS: A MAN KNOWN
DEVL III (60)	PERFECT POLITENESS). YOU WILL UNDERSTAND, SIR, I	HOPE	, SINCE YOU SEEM TO BE A GENTLEMAN AND A MAN OF SOME
WIDO I (19)	YOU WONT MIND MY TAKING BLANCHE IN TO DINNER, I	HOPE	, SIR? /SARTORIUS/ BY ALL MEANS, DR TRENCH. PRAY DO
PYGM II (223)	HIGGINS, THOUGH HE MAY NOT ALWAYS MEAN IT. I DO	HOPE	, SIR, YOU WONT ENCOURAGE HIM TO DO ANYTHING FOOLISH.
MIS. PREFACE(76)	MORBID RESULT OF OVER-DOMESTICATION WOULD, LET US	HOPE	, SOON DISAPPEAR WITH ITS CAUSE. MOBILIZATION. THOSE
MIS. (112)	THATS ENOUGH, THANK YOU. YOU DONT SUPPOSE, I	HOPE	, THAT I SHOULD HAVE COME DOWN IF I HAD KNOWN THAT THAT
MTH2 (73)	CERTAINLY OLDER. YOU WILL GRANT ME IN RETURN, I	HOPE	, THAT IF THE SKY FELL WE SHOULD ALL CATCH LARKS.
KING I (220)	/JAMES/ (TAKING LOUISE) YOU HAVE REMEMBERED, I	HOPE	, THAT MADAM CARWELL IS A CATHOLIC? /MRS BASHAM/ YES:
CAPT II (252)	/SIR HOWARD/ YOU KNOW ALSO, MR JOHNSON, I	HOPE	, THAT YOU CAN DEPEND ON ME. /JOHNSON/ (TURNING) ON
CAND III (136)	I AM CERTAINLY THE BIGGER OF THE TWO, AND, I	HOPE	, THE STRONGER, CANDIDA. SO YOU HAD BETTER LEAVE THE
SUPR HANDBOK(209)	IS A NATION THAT NEEDS REMAKING. OUR ONLY	HOPE	, THEN, IS IN EVOLUTION. WE MUST REPLACE THE MAN BY THE
BARB PREFACE(240)	HIGH HUMAN DEED IS NOT WASTED ON EUROPE, LET US	HOPE	, THOUGH IT BENEFITS THE FUGITIVE WOLF ONLY FOR A
PLES PREFACE(R9)	PERSON HIS OR HER OWN POINT OF VIEW, AND HAVE, I	HOPE	, TO THE FULL EXTENT OF MY UNDERSTANDING OF HIM, BEEN
METH PREFACE(R89)	WHICH ENABLES MEN TO LIVE FOR EVER. I AM NOT, I	HOPE	, UNDER MORE ILLUSION THAN IS HUMANLY INEVITABLE AS TO
MTH2 (82)	AS A SORT OF RELIGIOUS ASPIRATION AND PERSONAL	HOPE	, USING IT AT THE SAME TIME TO REMOVE THEIR PREJUDICES
BARB PREFACE(241)	A HOUSEHOLDER, USUALLY APPEALS, AND OFTEN, LET US	HOPE	, WITH SUCCESS, TO HIS CAPTOR NOT TO DELIVER HIM OVER
APPL I (210)	TODAY WITH SOME OF HIS COLLEAGUES -- INCLUDING, I	HOPE	, YOURSELF -- TO DISCUSS THE CRISIS. (TAKING ALICE'S

HOPED

ROCK II (270)	FOR ME; THOUGH THERE WAS NO MAN ALIVE THAT HAD	HOPED	AS MUCH FROM IT, NOR SPOKE DEEPER FROM HIS HEART ABOUT
CLEO IV (191)	/CAESAR/ (WITH INFINITE PRIDE) HE WHO HAS NEVER	HOPED	CAN NEVER DESPAIR. CAESAR, IN GOOD OR BAD FORTUNE,
WIDO III (62)	LICKCHEESE FORCE MY HAND. BESIDES, DR TRENCH, I	HOPED	FOR SOME TIME THAT OUR INTERESTS MIGHT BE JOINED BY
MTH5 (222)	US! PROFANED HIS ART! YOU KNOW HOW MUCH WE	HOPED	FROM THE TWELVE BUSTS HE PLACED IN THE TEMPLE TO BE
POSN (437)	I'D HAVE FORGIVEN HIM CHEERFULLY. I'M SURE I	HOPED	HE WOULD GET AWAY; FOR HE HAD TWO HOURS START OF THE
HART PREFACE(6)	NO CORRECTIVE TO THIS STATE OF THINGS COULD BE	HOPED	. IT IS SAID THAT EVERY PEOPLE HAS THE GOVERNMENT IT
LADY (243)	THIS FELLOW AT LEAST AN ESQUIRE; FOR I HAD	HOPED	THAT EVEN THE VILEST OF MY LADIES WOULD NOT HAVE
SUPR I (33)	BRUTAL, STUPID, VULGAR THINGS. I ALWAYS	HOPED	THAT IT WOULD BE SOMETHING REALLY HEROIC AT LAST. (
MTH4 I (149)	AM TO BE TREATED WITH PROPER CONSIDERATION. I HAD	HOPED	THAT MY POSITION AS A GUEST WOULD PROTECT ME FROM
BUOY III (42)	AT THE COMPANY IN DISMAY) AM I INTRUDING? I HAD	HOPED	TO FIND YOU ALONE. /SHE/ THE BUOYANTS ARE NEVER ALONE.
BASH II,1, (106)	A PRIZEFIGHTER. /CASHEL/ IT WAS MY GLORY. I HAD	HOPED	TO OFFER TO MY LADY THERE MY BELTS, MY CHAMPIONSHIPS,
BASH II,1, (110)	THEN I SHALL POSSESS TEN THOUSAND POUNDS. I HAD	HOPED	TO TEMPT THEE WITH THAT MONSTROUS SUM. /LYDIA/ THOU
BASH III (120)	SANS STAKES, SANS VICTORY, SANS EVERYTHING I HAD	HOPED	TO WIN. OH, I COULD SIT ME DOWN AND WEEP FOR
JITT II (36)	OF ALL THIS HUMBUG. I TURNED TO YOU BECAUSE I	HOPED	YOU WOULD UNDERSTAND ME, AND LET ME OPEN MY HEART TO

HOPED-FOR

DOCT PREFACE(47)	THE RABBIT ALL SUFFERED IN VAIN, AS FAR AS THE	HOPED-FOR	RESCUE OF THE RACE FROM PULMONARY CONSUMPTION IS

HOPEFUL

PLES PREFACE(R18)	AND CONVERTED MISERABLY ENSLAVED PROVINCES INTO	HOPEFUL	AND GALLANT LITTLE STATES, WILL SURVIVE THE GENERAL
SUPR HANDBOK(191)	SUCH A DEMOCRACY IS THE ONLY CHANGE THAT IS NOW	HOPEFUL	ENOUGH TO NERVE US TO THE EFFORT THAT REVOLUTION
HART PREFACE(11)	HOUSE SMITTEN; AND THE YOUNG, THE INNOCENT, THE	HOPEFUL	EXPIATED THE FOLLY AND WORTHLESSNESS OF THEIR
BARB PREFACE(219)	THE UNIVERSAL REGARD FOR MONEY IS THE ONE	HOPEFUL	FACT IN OUR CIVILIZATION, THE ONE SOUND SPOT IN OUR
METH PREFACE(R33)	AS EXCITING, AGREEABLE, ABOVE ALL AS	HOPEFUL	. LET ME THEREFORE TRY TO BRING BACK SOMETHING OF
GENV PREFACE(22)	NEWSPAPERS AND THE POLITICAL WINDBAGS AMUSED AND	HOPEFUL	. WE ARE STILL HUMBUGGING OURSELVES INTO THE BELIEF
ROCK I (215)	ARTHUR/ LET US CLOSE OUR LITTLE TALK ON A MORE	HOPEFUL	NOTE. I ASSURE YOU IT HAS BEEN INTENSELY INTERESTING
FOUN (222)	LEAST I'M A FOUNDLING. /BRABAZON/ (EXCITED AND	HOPEFUL	) A FOUNDLING? /ANASTASIA/ I HAVNT A RELATION IN
PHIL II (125)	HIS OFFER TO MARRY ME. /JULIA/ (INCREDULOUS, BUT	HOPEFUL	) YOU HAVE REFUSED! /GRACE/ YES; BECAUSE I WILL NOT
BULL PREFACE(72)	HEARD THAT CRY BEFORE, AND REGARD IT AS A VERY	HOPEFUL	SIGN THAT THEY WILL HAVE IT GLADLY ENOUGH WHEN THEY
MRS PREFACE(166)	A LONG TIME PAST WITHOUT KNOWING IT) IS FAR LESS	HOPEFUL	THAN MY OWN DETERMINATION TO ACCEPT PROBLEM AS THE
PLES PREFACE(R8)	BURNE-JONES, ON THE WHOLE, BIRMINGHAM WAS MORE	HOPEFUL	THAN THE ITALIAN CITIES; FOR THE ART IT HAD TO SHEW
GETT PREFACE(228)	AUGEAN STABLE, SO FILTHY THAT IT WOULD SEEM MORE	HOPEFUL	TO BURN IT DOWN THAN TO ATTEMPT TO SWEEP IT OUT. AND
2TRU PREFACE(20)	ROUND FOR A SAVIOR, AND WERE READY TO GIVE A	HOPEFUL	TRIAL TO ANYONE BOLD ENOUGH TO ASSUME DICTATORSHIP
DOCT PREFACE(77)	NO DOUBT, BUT SANE AND SENSIBLE, POETIC AND	HOPEFUL	, COMPARED TO THE PSEUDO SCIENCE OF THE COMMERCIAL

HOPEFULLER

BARB PREFACE(225)	ANDREW UNDERSHAFT, WILL CLEARLY LEAD TO SOMETHING	HOPEFULLER	THAN DISTRIBUTING BREAD AND TREACLE AT THE
2TRU PREFACE(7)	WERE RICH, THAT THEY MAKE THEMSELVES POORER, IF	HOPEFULLER	; BY BACKING HORSES AND BUYING SWEEPSTAKE TICKETS

HOPEFULLY

NEVR II (253)	HER FACE FOR SOME RESPONSE, AND CONTINUES LESS	HOPEFULLY	AND MORE URGENTLY) SOMEONE WHO LET YOU DO AS YOU
JOAN 6 (136)	THE CHURCH. I WILL OBEY THE CHURCH -- /CAUCHON/ (	HOPEFULLY	LEANING FORWARD) YOU WILL? /JOAN/ -- PROVIDED IT
MILL PREFACE(117)	MENTALITY OF THAT DELUDED TIME WAS STILL	HOPEFULLY	PARLIAMENTARY. DEMOCRACY WAS A DREAM, AN IDEAL.
MTH3 (112)	BUT HE DIED. /THE ARCHBISHOP/ NO. /BURGE-LUBIN/ (	HOPEFULLY	) DO YOU MEAN TO SAY HE IS STILL ALIVE? /THE
PYGM I (207)	SMALLER THAN SIXPENCE. /THE FLOWER GIRL/ (	HOPEFULLY	) I CAN GIVE YOU CHANGE FOR A TANNER, KIND LADY.
FANY III (299)	OF JILTING. IT'S NOT CORRECT IN ITSELF. /BOBBY/ (	HOPEFULLY	) I'LL TELL YOU WHAT, I'LL SAY I CANT HOLD HER TO
BULL IV (159)	REMEMBERING AND ROMANCING ABOUT THEM. /NORA/ (	HOPEFULLY	) OH! YOU DO REMEMBER THE PLACES, THEN? /LARRY/
CLEO I (111)	AS HE WISHES THEM TO APPEAR TO HIM. /CLEOPATRA/ (	HOPEFULLY	) THEN WE WILL CHEAT HIM. I WILL PUT ON
NEVR II (253)	I HAD FORGOTTEN. /CRAMPTON/ (LOOKING UP	HOPEFULLY	) WHAT WAS THAT? /GLORIA/ (MERCILESSLY) THE WHIP
PYGM III (248)	YOU TO MEET A FRIEND OF OURS. /HIGGINS/ (TURNING	HOPEFULLY	) YES, BY GEORGE! WE WANT TWO OR THREE PEOPLE.
FABL I (104)	WHICH DIDNT BELONG TO US. /YOUNG MAN/ (	HOPEFULLY	) YES, BY GEORGE! SO WE DID. /YOUNG WOMAN/ WELL,
DOCT IV (166)	HIM THAT THIS IS THE END). /MRS DUBEDAT/ (	HOPEFULLY	) YES, YES: YOU SHALL. /LOUIS/ BECAUSE I SUDDENLY
SUPR IV (153)	SOLUTION OF THE MONEY DIFFICULTY. VIOLET LOOKS UP	HOPEFULLY	). HECTOR: DONT BE RASH, MY BOY. I'M SORRY FOR
CLEO III (163)	YOU HAVE SHIPS IN THE EAST HARBOR. /BRITANNUS/ (	HOPEFULLY	, AT THE PARAPET) THE RHODIAN GALLEYS ARE STANDING

HOPELESS

PYGM IV SD(263)	THINK IT MADE ANY DIFFERENCE NOW. A PAUSE. ELIZA	HOPELESS	AND CRUSHED. HIGGINS A LITTLE UNEASY. /HIGGINS/ (
METH PREFACE(R69)	RISK, AND TO KNOW THAT A REVOLUTION ALWAYS SEEMS	HOPELESS	AND IMPOSSIBLE THE DAY BEFORE IT BREAKS OUT, AND
METH PREFACE(R69)	AND INDEED NEVER DOES BREAK OUT UNTIL IT SEEMS	HOPELESS	AND IMPOSSIBLE; FOR RULERS WHO THINK IT POSSIBLE
GETT (304)	THE RELIEF, THE NEW FACE, THE FRESH NEWS, THE	HOPELESS	ATTACHMENT: I SHALL ONLY BE THE HUSBAND. /REGINALD/
LION PREFACE(85)	TO UNREADABLENESS BECAUSE IT CONSISTS OF A	HOPELESS	ATTEMPT BY PAUL TO EVADE THE CONCLUSION THAT IF A
BULL PREFACE(68)	COURTS WERE BOYCOTTED. UPON THIS INTERESTING BUT	HOPELESS	ATTEMPT TO IGNORE BRITISH RULE THE GOVERNMENT LET
LION PREFACE(97)	AND FOURTEEN MILLIONS. THE FRENCH ARE NOT IN OUR	HOPELESS	CHRISTIAN MINORITY OF ELEVEN PER CENT; BUT THEY ARE
2TRU III SD(81)	THE DEEPEST MOURNING; AND HIS ATTITUDE IS ONE OF	HOPELESS	DEJECTION. SWEETIE, NOW FULLY AND BRILLIANTLY
FABL III (112)	YOURE QUITE RIGHT THERE; BUT I'M A DUFFER, A	HOPELESS	DUFFER. I CAN ALWAYS SEE WHAT THE OTHER FELLOWS
GETT PREFACE(232)	FROM OBSERVATION OR RECORD, THE EXPERIMENT IS A	HOPELESS	FAILURE: ONE OF THE TWO RIVALS FOR THE REALLY
LADY PREFACE(225)	HE HAS. FOR, AFTER ALL, WHAT IS THE SECRET OF THE	HOPELESS	FAILURE OF THE ACADEMIC BARDOLATERS TO GIVE US A
2TRU I (41)	US TO BE BURGLARS. OUR FIRST ATTEMPT HAS BEEN A	HOPELESS	FAILURE. LET US APOLOGIZE AND WITHDRAW. /THE NURSE/
2TRU PREFACE(18)	SEEING THAT THE CHRISTIAN SYSTEM HAS BEEN SUCH A	HOPELESS	FAILURE, DO YOU GO BACK TO IT, AND INVITE US TO GO
HART PREFACE(24)	PUBLIC SIDE OF THE WAR AN AIR OF MONSTROUS AND	HOPELESS	FARCE. THEY PROVED NOT ONLY THAT THEY WERE USELESS
DOCT PREFACE(40)	THE DOG-STARVER IS PASSED OVER AS SUCH A	HOPELESS	FOOL THAT IT IS IMPOSSIBLE TO TAKE ANY INTEREST IN

MIS. PREFACE(74)	IS THE SENSIBLE SCHEMES, UNFORTUNATELY, THAT ARE	HOPELESS	IN ENGLAND. THEREFORE I HAVE GREAT HOPES THAT MY
JITT PREFACE(3)	OF THE RUDIMENTS OF STAGE TECHNIQUE, AND HIS	HOPELESS	INCAPACITY FOR REPRESENTING HUMAN NATURE
HART PREFACE(38)	BE GUESSED BY THOSE WHO KNOW, AS HE DOES, HOW	HOPELESS	IS REMONSTRANCE, AND HOW HAPPY LINCOLN WAS IN
GENV IV (112)	BY A BOLSHEVIST? /SECRETARY/ YOU SEE HOW	HOPELESS	IT IS FOR US TO GET ANY FURTHER. YOU HAVE ONLY TO
BULL PREFACE(66)	IN THE MATTER: ANOTHER ILLUSTRATION OF HOW	HOPELESS	IT IS TO INDUCE ONE MODERN NATION, PREOCCUPIED AS
GENV II (61)	UNTIL MY OFFICIAL EXPERIENCE HERE TAUGHT ME HOW	HOPELESS	IT IS TO KNOCK SUPERNATIONALISM-- /SIR O./ SUPER
MIS. PREFACE(46)	OTHER PEOPLE. THE SIN OF ATHANASIUS. IT SEEMS	HOPELESS	. ANARCHISTS ARE TEMPTED TO PREACH A VIOLENT AND
NEVR III (279)	HAVE PERSUADED THE CHILDREN THAT HE IS NOT QUITE	HOPELESS	. DO AS YOU PLEASE. /M'COMAS/ (TAKING HER HAND AND
METH PREFACE(R86)	OF THEIR TIME: THAT IS, THEY ARE BITTER AND	HOPELESS	. IT IS NOT A QUESTION OF MERE DATES. GOETHE WAS AN
GENV IV (122)	WHAT IS SCOUNDRELISM? I GIVE YOU UP AS	HOPELESS	. MAN IS A FAILURE AS A POLITICAL ANIMAL. THE
MTH2 (41)	FRINGE WITH HER FINGERS, BUT GIVES IT UP AS	HOPELESS	. /FRANKLYN/ MR HASLAM, OUR NEW RECTOR. (TO
ROCK II SD(246)	SHRUGS HIS SHOULDERS AND INTIMATES THAT IT IS	HOPELESS	. THE DUKE RESIGNS HIMSELF TO THE EXPECTED. /SIR
JITT I (17)	/JITTA/ (RELIEVED) OH, A MAN! THE MOST	HOPELESS	MATERIALIST I KNOW IS MY HUSBAND; AND I DO NOT WANT
BULL PREFACE(52)	TWO IRISHMEN AND THREE ENGLISHMEN, HAVING MADE A	HOPELESS	MESS OF IT, AND BEING NOW IN SERIOUS DANGER, MADE
GENV III (82)	RUSSIA. /THE JUDGE/ RACE! NONSENSE! YOU ARE ALL	HOPELESS	MONGRELS PRETENDING TO BE THOROUGHBREDS. WHY NOT
GENV PREFACE(4)	CREW THE GERMAN CAPTAIN PUT TO SEA AGAIN AGAINST	HOPELESS	ODDS; SCUTTLED HIS SHIP; AND COMMITTED SUICIDE. THE
LION PREFACE(3)	GIVE CHRISTIANITY A TRIAL? THE QUESTION SEEMS A	HOPELESS	ONE AFTER 2000 YEARS OF RESOLUTE ADHERENCE TO THE
LION PREFACE(57)	FIGURES YOU FIND THAT IT BRINGS YOU BACK TO THE	HOPELESS	PLAN OF PAYING FOR A MAN'S TIME; AND YOUR
LIED (195)	MUST GET ME OUT OF IT AGAIN. /HE/ (POLITE AND	HOPELESS	) ALL I CAN SAY IS THAT I AM ENTIRELY AT YOUR
WIDO I (12)	POWER OF SPEECH). /BLANCHE/ (GIVING HIM UP AS	HOPELESS	) I DONT THINK THERES MUCH DANGER OF YOUR MAKING UP
MTH4 I (156)	RATHER THAN OF SAVAGERY. /ZOO/ (GIVING HIM UP AS	HOPELESS	) OH, DADDY, DADDY! I CAN HARDLY BELIEVE THAT YOU
JITT II (42)	WATCHING HIM. FINALLY HE GIVES THE BOOK UP AS	HOPELESS	; SHUTS UP THE PAGES; AND STARES AT THE MASS OF
BASH III (125)	TO THE BRITISH SOCIAL SCHEME, YOUR LOVE IS	HOPELESS	; STILL, YOUR SERVICES, MADE ZEALOUS BY
ROCK II (267)	BE IN RUSSIA TODAY? (HE RESUMES HIS SEAT WITH A	HOPELESS	SHRUG). /SIR ARTHUR/ IN OUR PROPER PLACE, THE
2TRU PREFACE(3)	ACTIVE MOUTH THEY HAD RECEIVED IT WAS THE MOST	HOPELESS	SORT OF SCOUNDREL: THAT IS, ONE WHOSE SCOUNDRELISM
ANNA (300)	MEAN THAT? YOU WOULD KEEP THE PEOPLE IN THEIR	HOPELESS	SQUALID MISERY? YOU WOULD FILL THOSE INFAMOUS
CAND I (95)	TEMPLES BETWEEN HIS FISTS, WITH AN EXPRESSION OF	HOPELESS	SUFFERING). /CANDIDA/ (BUSTLING HIM GOODNATUREDLY)
APPL II SD(277)	A GOOD LITTLE BOY. THE KING, WITH A GRIMACE OF	HOPELESS	TENDERNESS, ALLOWS HIMSELF TO BE LED AWAY. THE END.
SUPR III SD(87)	ORDER. SHE WANDERS AND WANDERS IN HER SLOW	HOPELESS	WAY, MUCH AS A WASP FLIES IN ITS RAPID BUSY WAY,
MIS. PREFACE(105)	RESISTANCE TO ANY ATTEMPT TO BETTER A	HOPELESS	WORLD. THE WISE MAN KNOWS THAT IMAGINATION IS NOT
PYGM EPILOG (301)	ABOUT FLOWER SHOPS. AT LAST THEY GAVE IT UP AS	HOPELESS	, AND SHOOK THE DUST OF THE SHORTHAND SCHOOLS, AND
SUPR IV (151)	LOVE SHOULD BE LOCKED UP. (HE GIVES HECTOR UP AS	HOPELESS	, AND TURNS AWAY TOWARDS THE GARDEN; BUT MALONE,
CATH 4 (192)	LIFE. DRAG HER BACK. YOU WILL BE KNOUTED . IT IS	HOPELESS	, MADEMOISELLE: YOU MUST OBEY ORDERS. GUARD THERE!
BULL PREFACE(8)	DOMINATION OF THE PRIEST IS MAKING HIS OWN LOT	HOPELESS	, NEVERTHELESS STANDS SHOULDER TO SHOULDER WITH THE

HOPELESSLY

ROCK I (231)	SYSTEM. /THE LADY/ IF A MAN IS BORN WITH A	HOPELESSLY	BAD SET OF TEETH I THINK IT IS BETTER FOR HIM,
INCA (255)	SAY, I CANNOT AFFORD IT. VICTORIOUS AS I AM, I AM	HOPELESSLY	BANKRUPT; AND THE WORST OF IT IS, I AM
GENV III (79)	AND INDUSTRIOUS THAT HIS FELLOW-COUNTRYMEN ARE	HOPELESSLY	BEATEN BY HIM IN THE COMPETITION FOR THE CONDUCT
OVER (188)	/MRS LUNN/ I REALLY DONT KNOW. I'M GETTING	HOPELESSLY	CONFUSED. /JUNO/ WHY DONT YOU LET MY WIFE SAY
OVER (195)	/GREGORY/ OH, OF COURSE: I BEG YOUR PARDON. I'M	HOPELESSLY	CONFUSED. (HE OFFERS HIS ARM TO MRS JUNO, RATHER
SIM II (75)	DECLARES THAT REPORTS OF UTTERANCES BY ANGELS ARE	HOPELESSLY	CONTRADICTORY, AND THAT ALLEGED VERBATIM REPORTS
METH PREFACE(R14)	OF THE JESUITS; SAMUEL BUTLER WAS THE PUPIL OF A	HOPELESSLY	CONVENTIONAL AND ERRONEOUS COUNTRY PARSON. BUT
MTH2 (42)	SHE BECOMES A SOCIALIST. THAT IS, SHE BECOMES	HOPELESSLY	DEMORALIZED. /CONRAD/ WELL, ARNT YOU A
ROCK II (263)	NO: THERE IS NO CLASS WAR: THE WORKING CLASS IS	HOPELESSLY	DIVIDED AGAINST ITSELF. BUT I WILL TELL YOU WHAT
FABL PREFACE(98)	PLUTOCRACY, WITH ITS INHERENT CLASS WARFARE, HAS	HOPELESSLY	FAILED TO SOLVE, WILL NOT YIELD TO THE
DOCT V (177)	MY OWN HANDS, AND KILLING YOU. /RIDGEON/ I AM SO	HOPELESSLY	IDIOTIC ABOUT YOU THAT I SHOULD NOT MIND IT A
LION PREFACE(82)	AND OCCASIONAL ILLUMINATIONS, BUT ALWAYS	HOPELESSLY	IN THE TOILS OF SIN, DEATH, AND LOGIC, WHICH HAD
LIED SD(188)	ORDINARY SOUTH KENSINGTON FEMALE OF ABOUT 37,	HOPELESSLY	INFERIOR IN PHYSICAL AND SPIRITUAL DISTINCTION TO
DEST SD(157)	REVERENCE, WITHOUT IMAGINATION, WITHOUT SENSE,	HOPELESSLY	INSUSCEPTIBLE TO THE NAPOLEONIC OR ANY OTHER
ROCK PREFACE(149)	THE LATIN RACE, AS BOTH THESE LINGUAL STOCKS ARE	HOPELESSLY	INTERBRED BY THIS TIME, SUCH A SACRIFICE TO
LION PREFACE(39)	WHOSE ACCOUNT OF CHRIST'S CAREER AND CHARACTER IS	HOPELESSLY	IRRECONCILABLE WITH MATTHEW'S. HE IS ALMOST AS
MIS. PREFACE(86)	TERM THE FAMILY IS TO CONFUSE THE QUESTION	HOPELESSLY	. THE MODERN SMALL FAMILY IS MUCH TOO STUFFY:
MILL II (177)	AND YOU THINK I AM BEATEN TOO. /THE DOCTOR/	HOPELESSLY	. YOU DO NOT KNOW WHAT HOMELESS POVERTY IS; AND
MILL PREFACE(125)	HIS VERY MIXED BLOOD (ALL OUR BLOODS TODAY ARE	HOPELESSLY	MIXED) GOT FORTIFIED SOMEWHERE IN THE PAST BY
GENV IV (98)	IMPRESSING A MODERN CROWD? AND YOUR SLOGANS ARE	HOPELESSLY	OBSOLETE. /SIR O./ I DO NOT QUITE FOLLOW. WHAT,
APPL PREFACE(188)	OF THE LABOR PARTY. A FOURTH, THE MOST	HOPELESSLY	OUT OF DATE OF THEM ALL, CONTAINS SCRAPS OF THE
MTH2 (51)	DOES IT PROVE ABOUT THEM EXCEPT THAT THEY ARE	HOPELESSLY	OUT OF DATE EVEN IN PARTY POLITICS? THAT THEY
ROCK PREFACE(148)	HAS AN IMMORTAL SOUL AND A RABBIT HAS NONE IS AS	HOPELESSLY	OUT OF DATE AS A GENTLEMAN DUELLIST PLEADING HIS
ARMS III SD(46)	DECORATED CUSHIONS. THERE IS ONE OBJECT, HOWEVER,	HOPELESSLY	OUT OF KEEPING WITH ITS SURROUNDINGS. THIS IS A
UNPL PREFACE(R7)	LONDON PLAYGOERS. TO FULFIL THIS CONDITION WAS	HOPELESSLY	OUT OF MY POWER. I HAD NO TASTE FOR WHAT IS
LION PREFACE(10)	ARE A PEOPLE APART; AND IF THEY WERE NOT	HOPELESSLY	OUTNUMBERED BY THE WORLDLY, THEY WOULD TURN THE
CAPT II (271)	DONT FIGHT. (BRASSBOUND, SEEING THAT HIS MEN ARE	HOPELESSLY	OUTNUMBERED, MAKES NO RESISTANCE. THEY ARE MADE
DEVL EPILOG (81)	WHERE, FAILING THE EXPECTED REINFORCEMENT, HE WAS	HOPELESSLY	OUTNUMBERED, AND HIS OFFICERS PICKED OFF, BOER
ROCK I (207)	HIM. /LADY CHAVENDER/ AND I MARRIED A MAN WITH A	HOPELESSLY	PARLIAMENTARY MIND; AND THAT WAS THE END OF ME.
LION PREFACE(17)	EVER SINCE COMMERCIAL CIVILIZATION PRODUCED A	HOPELESSLY	POOR CLASS CUT OFF FROM ENJOYMENT IN THIS WORLD.
MRS PREFACE(171)	IS (TO PUT IT AS POLITELY AS POSSIBLE) A	HOPELESSLY	PRIVATE PERSON. THE NOTION THAT MRS WARREN MUST
ARMS I (8)	CURLS, CLEAR QUICK EYES AND GOOD BROWS AND MOUTH,	HOPELESSLY	PROSAIC NOSE LIKE THAT OF A STRONG MINDED BABY,
MTH4 II (192)	HAS BECOME THE RIDICULOUS. (TURNING ON THE	HOPELESSLY	PUZZLED ZOZIM) " BEHOLD, THOU HAST MADE MY DAYS
MTH4 I (151)	HERE IT IS SO HARD TO FEEL SURE-- ER-- /ZOO/ (	HOPELESSLY	PUZZLED) WHAT? /THE ELDERLY GENTLEMAN/ MARRIAGE
OVER (183)	AMOROUS DEMONSTRATION). IT'S NO USE, MR JUNO: I'M	HOPELESSLY	RESPECTABLE: THE JENKINSES ALWAYS WERE. DONT YOU
HART I (59)	IF I AM TO HAVE ANYTHING TO DO WITH IT. /ELLIE/ (	HOPELESSLY	) NO: IT'S NO USE. I AM BOUND IN HONOR AND
CAND II (107)	TO COPY A PASSAGE FROM IT. /MARCHBANKS/ (	HOPELESSLY	) NOTHING THATS WORTH SAYING IS PROPER. (HE
CAPT II (262)	THATS THE IDEA, ISNT IT? /BRASSBOUND/ (	HOPELESSLY	) YOU ARE LAUGHING AT ME. /LADY CICELY/ NO:
NEVR I SD(208)	THAT YEARS OF SUCH REMONSTRANCE HAVE LEFT DOLLY	HOPELESSLY	SPOILED. GLORIA, WHO IS HARDLY PAST TWENTY, IS A
GETT PREFACE(218)	NOT HAPPEN, ARE EITHER INSINCERE, INSANE, OR	HOPELESSLY	STUPID. THERE IS SOME SENSE IN A CONTRACT TO
2TRU III (109)	HERE, FALLING, FALLING, FALLING ENDLESSLY AND	HOPELESSLY	THROUGH A VOID IN WHICH THEY CAN FIND NO FOOTING.
METH PREFACE(R50)	FOR EXISTENCE PLUS SEXUAL SELECTION FAIL AS	HOPELESSLY	TO ACCOUNT FOR DARWIN'S OWN LIFE WORK AS FOR MY
LION I (118)	A DEBAUCHEE, THE WRECK OF A GOOD-LOOKING MAN GONE	HOPELESSLY	TO THE BAD. ANDROCLES IS OVERWHELMED WITH GRIEF.
MRS PREFACE(158)	EVERY OTHER CONSIDERATION TO LOVE ARE AS	HOPELESSLY	UNHEROIC ON THE STAGE AS LUNATICS OR
MIS. PREFACE(12)	ALWAYS. MOST CHILDREN CAN BE, AND MANY ARE,	HOPELESSLY	WARPED AND WASTED BY PARENTS WHO ARE IGNORANT AND
JOAN PREFACE(55)	ME THAT MY PLAY, THOUGH A GREAT PLAY, MUST FAIL	HOPELESSLY	, BECAUSE IT DOES NOT BEGIN AT A QUARTER TO NINE
DOCT I (107)	AFFECT THE PHAGOCYTES AT ALL. HE'S ALL WRONG:	HOPELESSLY	, DANGEROUSLY WRONG. TO PUT A TUBE OF SERUM INTO

HOPELESSNESS

MTH3 (126)	BUT OUR FAULTS AND FOLLIES DROVE ME TO CYNICAL	HOPELESSNESS	. WE ALL ENDED THEN LIKE THAT. IT IS THE
INCA PREFACE(231)	PHILOSOPHY OF HISTORY, AND THE CONSEQUENT	HOPELESSNESS	OF OVERCOMING SO MAGNIFICENTLY ACCOMPLISHED AN
MIS. PREFACE(108)	HAVE ALL THE EVIL CONSEQUENCES AND ALL THE SOCIAL	HOPELESSNESS	THAT RESULT FROM TURNING A NATION OF POTENTIAL
MIS. PREFACE(23)	OF TREATING LOVE AND MATERNITY AS OBSCENE JOKES,	HOPELESSNESS	, EVASION, DERISION, COWARDICE, AND ALL THE
BULL I (86)	OH, GOOD LORD, ROSSCULLEN! THE DULLNESS! THE	HOPELESSNESS	! THE IGNORANCE! THE BIGOTRY! /BROADBENT/ (

HOPES

JITT II (44)	DID HE SAY TO YOU ABOUT THE BOOK AND ABOUT HIS	HOPES	? WHY DID YOU NEVER SAY A WORD ABOUT THEM TO ME?
FANY II (295)	THAT YOU MIGHT BE ENLIGHTENED. BUT IF ALL MY	HOPES	AND ALL MY PRAYERS ARE TO COME TO THIS, THAT YOU MIX
O'FL PREFACE(202)	OF IRISH EMIGRATION, THAT ALL AN IRISHMAN'S	HOPES	AND AMBITIONS TURN ON HIS OPPORTUNITIES OF GETTING OUT
MTH4 I (156)	VACUUM IN WHICH YOU CAN INDULGE YOUR DESIRES AND	HOPES	AND LOVES AND HATES WITHOUT ANY OBSTRUCTION FROM THE
ROCK I (208)	SEEN VISIONS AND DREAMT DREAMS. WE HAVE CHERISHED	HOPES	AND STRIVEN TOWARDS IDEALS. WE HAVE ASPIRED TO THINGS
BARB II (292)	THEIR WILL; OR THEY MISS THEIR WILL; AND THEIR	HOPES	ARE DEAD OR ARE PINED FOR STILL; BUT WHOE'ER CAN KNOW
BARB II (292)	MILLIONS FLOAT AND FLOW AND SEETHE WITH A MILLION	HOPES	AS LEAVEN; AND THEY WIN THEIR WILL; OR THEY MISS THEIR
JOAN PREFACE(17)	ASSURED HER THAT SHE WOULD BE RESCUED. HERE HER	HOPES	FLATTERED HER; BUT THEY WERE NOT UNREASONABLE: HER
DOCT PREFACE(30)	UNTIL THE AVERAGE DOCTOR EITHER DEPENDS UPON OR	HOPES	FOR AN APPOINTMENT IN THE PUBLIC HEALTH SERVICE FOR
ROCK PREFACE(182)	TRUTH IS OF THE PRESENT, NOT OF THE FUTURE. YOUR	HOPES	FOR THE FUTURE ARE NOT THE TRUTH. EVEN IN THE PRESENT
JITT II (43)	OFTEN SPOKE TO ME ABOUT THIS BOOK, AND ABOUT THE	HOPES	HE HAD BUILT ON IT. /LENKHEIM/ TO YOU! WHAT DO YOU
ROCK I (218)	THEY GOT IT. THEIR HOPES WAS IN YOU; AND YOUR	HOPES	IS IN SPANISH ONIONS. WHAT A WORLD IT IS, AINT IT,
HART PREFACE(37)	WICKED; BUT THE THEATRES MOSTLY DISAPPOINT BOTH	HOPES	. IF EVER A REVOLUTION MAKES ME DICTATOR, I SHALL
DOCT PREFACE(12)	HIS CASE AND RECEIVED DAMAGES ABOVE HIS UTMOST	HOPES	. THIS AMAZING CASE MAKES IT POSSIBLE TO SAY, WITH
PLES PREFACE(R15)	AND CASES LIKE MINE WOULD STILL LEAVE FORLORN	HOPES	LIKE THE INDEPENDENT THEATRE ITS REASON FOR EXISTING.

BARB PREFACE(227)	OF RATES, TAXES, AND RENT; NO IMPORTUNATE	HOPES	NOR EXACTING DUTIES; NOTHING BUT THE REST AND SAFETY
NEVR III (279)	OBJECTION TO THAT, I THINK. I HAVE THE GREATEST	HOPES	OF A HAPPY SETTLEMENT. GOODBYE FOR THE PRESENT. (HE
CYMB V (140)	I MUST HASTEN BACK TO LUCIUS TO BLAST HIS	HOPES	OF ANY HELP FROM YOU. WHERE, THINK YOU, IS IACHIMO?
KING II (231)	OF THE DIFFERENCE IN OUR FORTUNES! ALL YOUR	HOPES	OF BEING A KING WERE CUT OFF: YOU WERE AN EXILE, AN
SUPR III (98)	HIM HERE ORIGINALLY; AND WE HAD THE GREATEST	HOPES	OF HIM. HIS SENTIMENTS WERE IN THE BEST TASTE OF OUR
SUPR III (134)	FIRST, BEFORE HE RECOVERED HIS WITS. I HAD SOME	HOPES	OF HIM; BUT HE WAS A CONFIRMED LIFE FORCE WORSHIPPER.
BARB PREFACE(237)	AND SOOTHING AND CHEERING THE VICTIMS WITH	HOPES	OF IMMENSE AND INEXPENSIVE HAPPINESS IN ANOTHER WORLD
CURE (227)	RESIGN FROM MY CLUBS. MY MOTHER SAID THAT ALL HER	HOPES	OF MARRYING ME TO A RICH WOMAN WERE SHATTERED. AND I'D
METH PREFACE(R43)	BLACKED EVERY UPWARD AND ONWARD PATH SINCE THE	HOPES	OF MEN HAD TURNED TO SCIENCE AS THEIR TRUE SAVIOR. IT
HART PREFACE(8)	HIM A FAIRLY STRONG INTEREST IN ENCOURAGING HIS	HOPES	OF SALVATION AND ALLAYING HIS FEAR OF DAMNATION BY
2TRU I (29)	YOU OUGHT TO CHANGE THE PRESCRIPTION? I HAD SUCH	HOPES	OF THAT LAST BOTTLE; BUT YOU KNOW IT WAS AFTER THAT
METH PREFACE(R88)	BY MR ESME PERCY, WHO LED ONE OF THE FORLORN	HOPES	OF THE ADVANCED DRAMA AT THAT TIME. ALSO I SUPPLIED
SUPR PREFACE(R27)	ELEMENTS IN PRACTICAL HEREDITY HAS DEMOLISHED THE	HOPES	OF THE EDUCATIONISTS AS WELL AS THE TERRORS OF THE
PHIL II (120)	HAPPINESS TO THE HOUSEHOLD IN WHICH THE BEST	HOPES	OF YOUR LIFE ARE CENTRED. CONFOUND IT, MAN, YOULL
JOAN 4 (97)	AND -- I MUST NOT DECEIVE YOU , NOR FLATTER YOUR	HOPES	-- WE CANNOT PREVENT IT. I SUPPOSE IT WILL MAKE A
GENV III (82)	WE DESPAIR OF HUMAN NATURE, WHEREAS RUSSIA HAS	HOPES	THAT HAVE CARRIED HER THROUGH THE MOST APPALLING
MIS. PREFACE(4)	THAT HIS DEATH WILL MAKE ROOM FOR A BIRTH; AND HE	HOPES	THAT IT WILL BE A BIRTH OF SOMETHING THAT HE ASPIRED
MIS. PREFACE(74)	ARE HOPELESS IN ENGLAND. THEREFORE I HAVE GREAT	HOPES	THAT MY OWN VIEWS, THOUGH FUNDAMENTALLY SENSIBLE, CAN
JITT II (30)	IS. /LENKHEIM/ OH, JITTA IS GETTING OVER IT. SHE	HOPES	TO BE ABLE TO GET UP FOR A COUPLE OF HOURS TODAY. JUST
DEST SD(151)	MARSHAL'S BATON IN HIS KNAPSACK, BUT BECAUSE HE	HOPES	TO CARRY AT LEAST HALF A DOZEN SILVER FORKS THERE NEXT
MTH4 II (180)	A CERTAINTY IF THE FIGHTING GOES ON FOR EVER: HE	HOPES	TO ESCAPE FOR SIX MONTHS, BUT KNOWS HE CANNOT ESCAPE
ROCK I (218)	COULD MAKE OF THE VOTE WHEN THEY GOT IT. THEIR	HOPES	WAS IN YOU; AND YOUR HOPES IS IN SPANISH ONIONS. WHAT
BULL III (144)	THEIR FACES. IRELAND HAS NEVER SMILED SINCE HER	HOPES	WERE BURIED IN THE GRAVE OF GLADSTONE. /LARRY/ OH,
SUPR PREFACE(R30)	OF THE EFFICIENT ENGINEERING CLASS WHICH WILL, HE	HOPES	, FINALLY SWEEP THE JABBERERS OUT OF THE WAY OF
SUPR III (133)	AND DECREPITUDE, BROKEN NERVE AND SHATTERED	HOPES	, VAIN REGRETS FOR THAT WORST AND SILLIEST OF WASTES

HOPING

FANY II (292)	NICE AND SAILORLIKE. I WENT AND STOOD BESIDE HIM,	HOPING	HE WOULD SPEAK TO ME. /MRS KNOX/ (GASPS) MARGARET!
CLEO V (201)	SHOULDERS; BUT BRISK AND FRESH, STRONG AND YOUNG,	HOPING	IN THE MORNING, FIGHTING IN THE DAY, AND REVELLING IN
PHIL II (121)	HIMSELF) I MEAN WITH ALL MY FUNCTION OF	HOPING	. /CHARTERIS/ THEN, SINCE BOTH THEORIES ARE EQUALLY
PHIL II (121)	YOUR LIVER THEORY IS TRUE, BECAUSE IT AMOUNTS TO	HOPING	THAT CRAVEN WILL DIE AN AGONIZING DEATH. /PARAMORE/
DEVL I (23)	FORGIVENESS FOR ALL MY SINS AND MISTAKES, AND	HOPING	THAT HE WILL SO GUIDE MY SON THAT IT MAY NOT BE SAID
PHIL II (121)	ABOUT JULIA IS RIGHT, BECAUSE IT AMOUNTS TO	HOPING	THAT SHE MAY LIVE HAPPILY EVER AFTER. /PARAMORE/ I DO
MRS IV SD(248)	LOOKS FORLORNLY AT VIVIE, WHO WAITS, SECRETLY	HOPING	THAT THE COMBAT IS OVER. BUT THE CUNNING EXPRESSION
MILL PREFACE(134)	I ASKED HIM WHAT HE COULD DO WITHOUT THEM,	HOPING	TO OPEN HIS EYES TO THE FACT THAT APART FROM THE

HOPINIONS

CAND II (111)	THAT IT WAS ONY HIS OPINIONS; THOUGH, MIND YOU,	HOPINIONS	BECOMES VURRY SERIOUS THINGS WHEN PEOPLE TAKES TO
CAND I (89)	GIT ON WELL ENOUGH, SPITE OF OUR DIFFERENT	HOPINIONS	. WOY ARE YOU SO CHANGED TO ME? I GIVE YOU MY

HOPKINS

MTH2 (85)	CONVICTION) THE FUTURE DOES NOT EXIST FOR HENRY	HOPKINS	LUBIN. /LUBIN/ IF BY THE FUTURE YOU MEAN THE

HOPPED

3PLA PREFACE(R39)	SEEM PRODIGIOUSLY CLEVER TO THOSE WHO HAVE NEVER	HOPPED	HUNGRY AND CURIOUS, ACROSS THE FIELDS OF

HOPPING

MRS IV (245)	A SPARROW-- EVER SO TINY AND PRETTY A SPARROW	HOPPING	IN THE ROADWAY-- AND YOU SAW A STEAM ROLLER COMING

HOR

CAPT I (224)	IN AHR BUSINESS. ALL WE DAZ IS HESCORT, TOURIST	HOR	COMMERCIAL. COOK'S HEXCURSIONS TO THE HATLAS MAHNTNS:

HORACE

BARB II (303)	A NEW CREATION, MY DEAR. YOU HAVE HEARD OF SIR	HORACE	BODGER? /BARBARA/ BODGER! DO YOU MEAN THE
FOUN SD(209)	AT WORK. ENTER, TO HIM, THROUGH THE PUBLIC DOOR,	HORACE	BRABAZON, A SMART AND BEAUTIFUL YOUNG MAN OF
FOUN (210)	DONT YOU? /THE LORD CHANCELLOR/ YOU ARE YOUNG	HORACE	BRABAZON, ARE YOU? /BRABAZON/ I AM, MY LORD. SUCH IS
MTH2 (58)	I DONT MAKE PETS OF POETS. WHO'S YOURS? /LUBIN/	HORACE	. /SAVVY/ HORACE WHO? /LUBIN/ QUINTUS HORATIUS
O'FL (224)	WALL WHERE THE COW WALKED THROUGH IT. AND SIR	HORACE	PLUNKETT BREAKING HIS HEART ALL THE TIME TELLING THEM
MIS. (179)	BROWN. /TARLETON/ OH COME! COULDNT YOU MAKE IT	HORACE	SMITH? OR ALGERNON ROBINSON? /GUNNER/ (AGITATEDLY)
DEVL EPILOG (82)	ARISTOCRATIC COMMANDERS TO SUCCESSFUL ONES.	HORACE	WALPOLE, WHEN THE PARLIAMENTARY RECESS CAME AT A
MTH2 (58)	OF POETS. WHO'S YOURS? /LUBIN/ HORACE. /SAVVY/	HORACE	WHO? /LUBIN/ QUINTUS HORATIUS FLACCUS: THE NOBLEST

HORACE'S

MTH2 (58)	IN MUST HAVE BEEN OURSELVES. YOU MUST BE	HORACE'S	REINCARNATION. /LUBIN/ (DELIGHTED) THAT IS THE

HORATIO

FABL PREFACE(79)	. YET MORE FANATICALLY DEIFIED IN GERMANY THAN	HORATIO	BOTTOMLEY IN ENGLAND. ONE OF THE PUZZLES OF HISTORY
O'FL (210)	THAT WE SHALL NEVER BEAT THE BOSHES UNTIL WE MAKE	HORATIO	BOTTOMLEY LORD LEFTNANT OF ENGLAND. DO YOU THINK
2TRU PREFACE(24)	LIBERTY TO RETURN SUCH CANDIDATES AS THE LATE	HORATIO	BOTTOMLEY TO PARLIAMENT BY ENORMOUS MAJORITIES; BUT
FABL PREFACE(82)	WERE LORD GEORGE GORDON, TITUS OATES, AND	HORATIO	BOTTOMLEY THE PEOPLE? WERE GENERAL ROBERTS AND
LION PREFACE(56)	THE WIDOW WHO PUT HER MITE IN THE POOR-BOX, MR	HORATIO	BOTTOMLEY, SHAKESPEAR, MR JACK JOHNSON, SIR ISAAC
GENV PREFACE(15)	VOTING FOR TITUS OATES, LORD GEORGE GORDON,	HORATIO	BOTTOMLEY, NAPOLEON, OR HITLER. MY EXPERIENCE AS AN
AUGS (264)	THE GENTLEMAN I HAVE BEEN CORRESPONDING WITH: MR	HORATIO	FLOYD BEAMISH? /THE CLERK/ (RETURNING AND BOWING)
AUGS (260)	AS LORD AUGUSTUS HIGHCASTLE, AND CHARLES ROCK AS	HORATIO	FLOYD BEAMISH.
AUGS (269)	REELING AGAINST THE TABLE IN HIS HORROR) A RISE!	HORATIO	FLOYD BEAMISH: DO YOU KNOW THAT WE ARE AT WAR? /THE
AUGS (264)	NAME OF THAT SORT? /THE CLERK/ YOU MAY DROP THE	HORATIO	FLOYD. BEAMISH IS GOOD ENOUGH FOR ME. /AUGUSTUS/ IS
LADY PREFACE(224)	HER GRAVE; AND WHEN HE DISCUSSES THE SCENE WITH	HORATIO	IMMEDIATELY AFTER, HE UTTERLY FORGETS HER, THOUGH HE
SUPR PREFACE(R34)	BUT FOR HIS USEFULNESS AS A STAGE CONFIDANT, A	HORATIO	OR " CHARLES HIS FRIEND": WHAT THEY CALL ON THE
LADY PREFACE(212)	MAY PERHAPS HAVE ECHOED HAMLET'S OH GOD,	HORATIO	, WHAT A WOUNDED NAME-- THINGS STANDING THUS

HORATIOS

CATH PREFACE(156)	HAVE TO LEAVE HAMLET OUT, AND BE CONTENT WITH	HORATIOS	FOR HEROES. SOME OF THE DIFFERENCE BETWEEN
CATH PREFACE(156)	THE AUTHOR, IF THE BEST AVAILABLE ACTORS ARE ONLY	HORATIOS	, THE AUTHORS WILL HAVE TO LEAVE HAMLET OUT, AND BE

HORATIUS

MTH2 (58)	HORACE. /SAVVY/ HORACE WHO? /LUBIN/ QUINTUS	HORATIUS	FLACCUS: THE NOBLEST ROMAN OF THEM ALL, MY DEAR.

HORDER

CAPT III (288)	DOWNT LET EM BURN EM, LIDY. THEY DASSENT IF YOU	HORDER	EM NOT TO. (WITH DESPERATE ELOQUENCE) YER DUNNO WOT
CAPT II (249)	ITS ALL RIGHT, ISN'T IT? /DRINKWATER/ YUSS, AN	HORDER	HUZ ABAHT AS IF WE WAS KEB TAHTS! AN THE KEPN AFRIDE

HORDERS

CAPT II (245)	HOWARD) YUSS; AN WHAWL YOURE WITIN, YLL TIKE YOUR	HORDERS	FROM ME! SEE? /JOHNSON/ (WITH SLOW SEVERITY, TO

HORDES

DEST SD(149)	IN THE CHURCHES, BUT RUTHLESSLY DISDAINFUL OF TWO	HORDES	OF MISCHIEVOUS INSECTS WHICH ARE THE FRENCH AND

HORFF

CAND III (138)	A BOTTLE. SHE TOOK TWO GLASSES ALMOST STRAIGHT	HORFF	. /MORELL/ (ANXIOUS ABOUT HER) GO AND LOOK AFTER HER,
CAND II (116)	COME INTO MY ED ONCE OR TWYST THAT HE WAS A BIT	HORFF	'IS CHUMP! (HE CROSSES THE ROOM TO THE DOOR, LIFTING

HORFFER

CAND I (91)	THAN YOU ARE. BUT TODAY, IF HENNYONE WAS TO	HORFFER	TO BET ME A THOUSAN POUN THAT YOULL HEND BY BEIN A

HORFICER

PPP	(205)	FALL). JEST OWLD THIS LEOONATIC, WILL YOU, MISTER	HORFICER	? /THE POLICEMAN/ (DRAGGING BOTH OF THEM TO THEIR

HORIZON

CLEO I	(112)	STEAL ACROSS THE DESERT. THE MOONLIGHT WANES: THE	HORIZON	AGAIN SHOWS BLACK AGAINST THE SKY, BROKEN ONLY BY
CLEO I	SD(106)	MOON, IT RISES FULL OVER THE DESERT; AND A VAST	HORIZON	COMES INTO RELIEF, BROKEN BY A HUGE SHAPE WHICH SOON
SUPR IV	SD(141)	AT THE FOOT OF THE GARDEN AND LOOK UPHILL, OUR	HORIZON	IS THE STONE BALUSTRADE OF A FLAGGED PLATFORM ON THE
MIS. PREFACE(40)		FRACTIONS, WITH THE BLACK CLOUD OF ALGEBRA ON THE	HORIZON	, AND IF A BOY RUSHES THROUGH ALL THAT, THERE IS
NEVR I	(207)	(LIKE A CASTAWAY MARINER WHO SEES A SAIL ON THE	HORIZON	) WHAT! HAVE YOU A GRANDFATHER? /DOLLY/ ONLY ONE.
APPL II	(266)	IS RATHER A THREATENING CLOUD ON THE WESTERN	HORIZON	, MR PLINY. (TO PROTEUS) HAVE YOU HEARD THE NEWS
PHIL II	(107)	IN LOVE WITH JULIA! A RAY OF HOPE ON THE	HORIZON	! DO YOU REALLY MEAN IT? /SYLVIA/ I SHOULD THINK I

HORIZONTAL

MTH5	SD(226)	A SQUARE-FINGERED YOUTH WITH HIS FACE LAID OUT IN	HORIZONTAL	BLOCKS, AND A PERPETUAL SMILE OF EAGER BENEVOLENT
LION II	SD(143)	STRETCHES OUT HIS NOSE FORWARD AND HIS TAIL IN A	HORIZONTAL	LINE BEHIND, LIKE A POINTER, AND UTTERS AN

HORMONE

BUOY IV	(59)	DO YOU SUPPOSE THAT THERE IS NO MATHEMATICAL	HORMONE	? OUR ANATOMISTS HAVE NOT YET DISCOVERED IT; BUT IT
BUOY IV	(60)	I SHALL QUALIFY AS A DOCTOR AND LOOK FOR THAT	HORMONE	. JUNIUS COMES IN WITH THE LICENCE IN HIS HAND.
JOAN PREFACE(16)		PITUITRIN, AND INSULIN, WITH PICK-ME-UPS OF	HORMONE	STIMULANTS, THE BLOOD BEING FIRST CAREFULLY
KING PREFACE(158)		TO DISCOVER IN EITHER SEX ANY SPECIFIC ORGAN OR	HORMONE	THAT A BIOLOGIST CAN LABEL AS THE SOUL. SO WE

HORMONES

JOAN PREFACE(16)		INCORRIGIBLE IGNORAMUSES, AND THAT ST TERESA'S	HORMONES	HAD GONE ASTRAY AND LEFT HER INCURABLY
BUOY IV	(59)	GLANDS, ADRENAL GLANDS, THYROID GLANDS, POURING	HORMONES	INTO THEIR BLOOD. DO YOU SUPPOSE THAT THERE IS NO
FABL V	(120)	EXACT PRESCRIPTION OF THE NECESSARY PROTOPLASMS,	HORMONES	, VITAMINS, ENZYMES AND THE REST, WE NEVER AGREE ON

HORN

MILL II	SD(173)	WITH ME UNTIL MY CHAUFFEUR COMES BACK. THE MOTOR	HORN	IS HEARD HONKING. /THE DOCTOR/ HE HAS COME BACK.
JOAN PREFACE(12)		ONE NOW ACCEPTS. ON THE SUBJECT OF THE ELEVENTH	HORN	OF THE BEAST SEEN BY THE PROPHET DANIEL HE WAS MORE
GETT PREFACE(238)		WE SHALL HAVE TO REMAIN IMPALED ON THE OTHER	HORN	OF THE DILEMMA AND MAINTAIN MARRIAGE AS A SLAVERY. AND
KING I	(189)	TO PROVE THAT THE ROMISH CHURCH IS THE LITTLE	HORN	OF THE FOURTH BEAST MENTIONED BY THE PROPHET DANIEL.
2TRU II	SD(51)	HUT ON THE HITHER SIDE, WITH A KLAXON ELECTRIC	HORN	PROJECTING FROM A BOARD ON THE WALL, SHEWS THAT WE ARE
BARB III	(350)	RIBS WITH HER FINGER TIPS AND IMITATING A BICYCLE	HORN	) PIP! PIP! /LADY BRITOMART/ (HIGHLY INDIGNANT) HOW
2TRU II	(77)	TO RAID US AT ANY MOMENT? LOOK AT THAT ELECTRIC	HORN	THERE. IF IT STARTS HONKING, LOOK OUT; FOR IT WILL MEAN
DEVL II	(48)	FROM A LEATHER BELT WITH TWO PISTOLS, A POWDER	HORN	, AND A BAG OF BULLETS ATTACHED TO IT. SHE THROWS IT ON

HORNED

CLEO IV	SD(166)	WHITE BEARD, MOUSTACHE AND EYEBROWS TWISTED AND	HORNED	AT THE ENDS, AND A CONSCIOUSLY KEEN AND PRETENTIOUS

HORNES

BULL PREFACE(39)		HORTONS, CAMPBELLS, WALTERS, AND SILVESTER	HORNES	, WHO ARE TO BE FOUND AMONG THE ROMAN CATHOLIC LAITY

HORNETS

2TRU II	(77)	MEEK, WE MAY HAVE THEM DOWN ON US LIKE A SWARM OF	HORNETS	, I DONT LIKE THIS AT ALL. I MUST GET TO THE BOTTOM
GENV I	(46)	IN HELL. SHE ACCUSED THE SOVIETS OF BEING THE	HORNETS	PROPHESIED IN THE BOOK OF REVELATION. WE WERE ABOUT

HORNIMAN

BULL PREFACE(13)		OWED TO THE PUBLIC SPIRIT OF MISS A.E.F.	HORNIMAN	(AN ENGLISHWOMAN, OF COURSE), WHO, TWELVE YEARS
PLES PREFACE(R7)		FOR A SEASON ON THE NEW LINES BY MISS A.E.F.	HORNIMAN	, WHO HAD FAMILY REASONS FOR NOT YET APPEARING

HORNS

SUPR PREFACE(R15)		BRIMSTONE, THERE TO BE TORMENTED BY DEVILS WITH	HORNS	AND TAILS. OF THAT ANTAGONIST, AND OF THAT CONCEPTION
BULL I	SD(81)	DASHED BY THIS ANNOUNCEMENT. HE DRAWS IN HIS	HORNS	AT ONCE, AND SCOWLS SUSPICIOUSLY AT DOYLE UNDER A
SIM PREFACE(6)		OUTGROWN THE DEVIL WITH HIS BARBED TAIL AND	HORNS	JUST AS I OUTGREW THE COCK IN THE CHIMNEY. BUT WHAT OF
MTH4 II	(181)	AND BECOME A COMMON ONE. HOW AM I TO ESCAPE THE	HORNS	OF THIS TRAGIC DILEMMA? VICTORY I CAN GUARANTEE: I AM
MTH1 II	SD(20)	SHIELD; HIS CASQUE IS A TIGER'S HEAD WITH BULL'S	HORNS	; HE WEARS A SCARLET CLOAK WITH GOLD BROOCH OVER A
METH PREFACE(R56)		IN THE DEVIL AS WELL. THE PAINTED DEVIL, WITH HIS	HORNS	, HIS BARBED TAIL, AND HIS ABODE OF BURNING BRIMSTONE,

HORNSEY

FOUN	(213)	HIS TOBACCONIST, THE PARLIAMENTARY CANDIDATE FOR	HORNSEY	ALWAYS ADDRESSES ME AS A GENTLEMAN. BUT THEN HE AINT

HORNY-HANDED

ROCK PREFACE(165)		ALLOWED THEIR PARENTS TO BE DESCRIBED AS	HORNY-HANDED	CULTIVATORS OF THE SOIL. THE PRETENCE HAS NOW

HORRIBLE

FANY II	(295)	YOUR WICKEDNESS IN THE WORDS OF GRACE, IT'S TOO	HORRIBLE	: IT SOUNDS LIKE THE DEVIL MAKING FUN OF RELIGION.
BASH III	(120)	HERE. HAST THOU DONE MURDER, THEN, THAT IN SO	HORRIBLE	A GUISE THOU COMEST? /CASHEL/ MURDER! I WOULD I
OVER PREFACE(156)		WHO REGARD GALLANT ADVENTURES AS CRIMES OF SO	HORRIBLE	A NATURE THAT ONLY THE MOST DEPRAVED AND DESPERATE
JOAN 6	(139)	RESPECT, I MUST EMPHASIZE THE GRAVITY OF TWO VERY	HORRIBLE	AND BLASPHEMOUS CRIMES WHICH SHE DOES NOT DENY,
MIS. PREFACE(40)		OLDEST GRAMMAR SCHOOLS. IN OUR TIMES AN EVEN MORE	HORRIBLE	AND CYNICAL CLAIM HAS BEEN MADE FOR THE RIGHT TO
BULL PREFACE(60)		LORD DUFFERIN WAS ABOLISHING THE BASTINADO AS " A	HORRIBLE	AND INFAMOUS PUNISHMENT." IN 1906 LORD CROMER
PYGM III	(253)	FILTHY AND BEASTLY; THOUGH I DO THINK IT	HORRIBLE	AND UNLADYLIKE. BUT THIS LAST IS REALLY TOO MUCH.
MIS. PREFACE(19)		NOTHING ON EARTH INTENDED FOR INNOCENT PEOPLE SO	HORRIBLE	AS A SCHOOL. TO BEGIN WITH, IT IS A PRISON. BUT IT
MIS. PREFACE(98)		A SCHOOL BOOK; AND IT IS NOT A BAD STORY BOOK,	HORRIBLE	AS SOME OF THE STORIES ARE. THEREFORE AS BETWEEN
ROCK PREFACE(184)		IT IS CRUELTY; AND THAT CRUELTY IS WICKED AND	HORRIBLE	BECAUSE IT IS THE WEAPON WITH WHICH THE SONS OF
GENV III	(69)	YOUR SAVIOR WAS A JEW. /THE WIDOW/ OH, WHAT A	HORRIBLE	BLASPHEMY! (SHE REACHES FOR HER PISTOL). SIR
SUPR HANDBOK(184)		OF MARRIAGE, TO ABOLISH DIVORCE, TO CONFIRM THE	HORRIBLE	BOND WHICH STILL CHAINS DECENT PEOPLE TO DRUNKARDS,
BARB I	(255)	TO LET ME ALONE FOR ONCE, AND TELL ME ABOUT THIS	HORRIBLE	BUSINESS OF MY FATHER WANTING TO SET ME ASIDE FOR
MRS IV	(241)	OH, STOP, STOP: LET US HAVE NO MORE OF THAT	HORRIBLE	CANT. MR PRAED: IF THERE ARE REALLY ONLY THOSE TWO
JITT PREFACE(4)		MY PERSONAL DEBT TO HIM IS INCALCULABLE. WHEN THE	HORRIBLE	CATASTROPHE OF THE WAR HAD TORN ANGLO-GERMAN
GENV IV	(99)	OF THE COMMUNITY. IT IS A CRIME OF THE MOST	HORRIBLE	CHARACTER TO DROP A BOMB UPON A CROWDED CITY. IT IS
BASH II,2,	(114)	DESIRE MAKES POSSIBILITY ITS SLAVE. AND THEN--	HORRIBLE	CLIMAX! ALL-UNDOING SPITE! -- TH' IMPORTUNATE
CAPT III	(292)	NOW I AM HALF A MAN, AT ANY RATE. /REDBROOK/ A	HORRIBLE	COMBINATION, GOVERNOR: CHURCHWARDEN FROM THE WAIST
MILL PREFACE(128)		SINCE KARL MARX AND FRIEDRICH ENGELS EXPOSED THE	HORRIBLE	CONDITION OF THE WORKING CLASSES THAT UNDERLIES THE
CURE	SD(230)	ROLLS FROM THE SOFA AND WRITHES ON THE CARPET IN	HORRIBLE	CONTORTIONS. SHE STOPS PLAYING, AMAZED. /REGINALD/
POSN	(458)	HE'S MAKIN A COFFIN FOR IT. /BLANCO/ (WITH A	HORRIBLE	CONVULSION OF THE THROAT-- FRANTICALLY) DEAD! THE
GETT PREFACE(245)		OF MARRIAGE INVOLVES THE POSSIBILITY OF THE MOST	HORRIBLE	CRIME IMAGINABLE: THAT OF THE PERSON WHO, WHEN
JOAN 2,SD(72)		HE IS ACCUSED OF TRYING TO EXTRACT PLEASURE FROM	HORRIBLE	CRUELTIES, AND HANGED. SO FAR, HOWEVER, THERE IS NO
3PLA PREFACE(R30)		SUGGESTS AT ONCE A TRAGEDY OF CIRCE, WITH THE	HORRIBLE	DIFFERENCE THAT WHEREAS THE ANCIENT MYTH RIGHTLY
BARB III	(342)	PROCEED, EURIPIDES. /CUSINS/ YOU HAVE ME IN A	HORRIBLE	DILEMMA. I WANT BARBARA. /UNDERSHAFT/ LIKE ALL
JITT III	(62)	AFRAID THAT IF YOU FIND HER OUT, SHE WILL PROVE A	HORRIBLE	DISAPPOINTMENT TO YOU. /EDITH/ NEVER FEAR. I KNOW
CURE	(235)	DRAWS IT FROM ME. LISTEN, STREGA (SHE PLAYS A	HORRIBLE	DISCORD) I MEAN MISS THUNDRIDGE. /STREGA/ THATS
GENV I	(43)	MUST STOP THE BOLSHIES FROM DISSEMINATING THEIR	HORRIBLE	DOCTRINES IN ENGLAND. IT IS IN THE TREATIES. HE IS
UNPL PREFACE(R18)		HIM TO OPEN HIS PORTS. IN PROPORTION AS THIS	HORRIBLE	DOMESTIC INSTITUTION IS BROKEN UP BY THE ACTIVE
PHIL II	(122)	TO TEA IN HONOR OF THE COLONEL'S ESCAPE FROM A	HORRIBLE	DOOM. BY THE WAY, IF YOUVE DONE WITH THAT BRITISH
BULL II	(115)	(FEARFULLY AGITATED) BUT THIS IS SUCH A	HORRIBLE	DOUBT TO PUT INTO MY MIND-- TO-- TO-- FOR HEAVEN'S
GETT	(305)	STAND THERE AND COUNTENANCE THIS LUNACY? IS IT A	HORRIBLE	DREAM OR AM I AWAKE? IN THE NAME OF COMMON SENSE
LIED	(195)	(AGAIN COLLAPSING ON THE STOOL) THIS IS SOME	HORRIBLE	DREAM. WHAT HAS BECOME OF YOU? YOU ARE NOT MY
ROCK PREFACE(160)		LIVES OF HONEST CITIZENS IN GUARDING THEM; SETS A	HORRIBLE	EXAMPLE OF CRUELTY AND MALICIOUS INJURY; COSTS A
JOAN PREFACE(34)		NO PRE-EMINENCE IN MERE PHYSICAL PAIN: MUCH MORE	HORRIBLE	EXECUTIONS THAN THEIRS ARE ON RECORD, TO SAY
MIS.	(142)	JUST IT. I'M FED UP WITH-- /LORD SUMMERHAYS/	HORRIBLE	EXPRESSION. DONT. /HYPATIA/ OH, I DARESAY IT'S
HART I	(65)	KNOW WHY I'M TALKING TO YOU SO CALMLY. I HAVE A	HORRIBLE	FEAR THAT MY HEART IS BROKEN, BUT THAT HEARTBREAK
DEVL II	(32)	THAT, TONY, EVEN IN JEST. YOU DONT KNOW WHAT A	HORRIBLE	FEELING IT GIVES ME. /ANDERSON/ (LAUGHING) WELL,

MTH5 (261)	AMONG WHICH LIVING SKELETONS CRAWLED IN SEARCH OF	HORRIBLE	FOOD. THE PANGS OF ANOTHER BIRTH WERE ALREADY UPON
MRS IV (242)	BUT I CANT UTTER THEM: THE SHAME OF THEM IS TOO	HORRIBLE	FOR ME. (SHE BURIES HER FACE IN HER HANDS. THE TWO
MIS. PREFACE(30)	DOES HAPPEN OFTENER THAN WOULD SEEM POSSIBLE) A	HORRIBLE	FRAUD IS BEING PRACTISED ON BOTH THE MAN AND THE
ROCK PREFACE(158)	AS JOHN THE BAPTIST. BUT THE MOB WANTED THE	HORRIBLE	FUN OF SEEING SOMEBODY CRUCIFIED: AN ABOMINABLY
BARB III (324)	YOUR EXPLOSIVES-- IF YOU MURDERED DOLLY WITH YOUR	HORRIBLE	GUNS-- I COULD FORGIVE YOU IF MY FORGIVENESS WOULD
OVER (194)	ME. /JUNO/ BUT, MY PRECIOUS, THIS IS THE MOST	HORRIBLE	IMMORALITY. /MRS LUNN/ I DONT INTEND TO GIVE UP
MTH4 I (168)	IS HAPPENING TO ME. I FEEL HOT ALL OVER. I HAVE A	HORRIBLE	IMPULSE TO INJURE YOU. WHAT HAVE YOU DONE TO ME?
JOAN 4 (102)	VIEW OF WHAT WOULD OTHERWISE BE A VERY	HORRIBLE	INCIDENT? /CAUCHON/ YES: IT IS A PAINFUL DUTY:
DOCT PREFACE(39)	BRANDED AS EXCEPTIONALLY CRUEL AND AS DEVISERS OF	HORRIBLE	INSTRUMENTS OF TORTURE BY PEOPLE WHOSE MAIN NOTION
SUPR I (45)	YOU FOUND OUT THE TRUTH. BUT I WONT BEAR SUCH A	HORRIBLE	INSULT AS TO BE COMPLIMENTED BY JACK ON BEING ONE
SUPR I (11)	READS). /TANNER/ IT'S ALL MY OWN DOING: THATS THE	HORRIBLE	IRONY OF IT. HE TOLD ME ONE DAY THAT YOU WERE TO BE
MTH5 (209)	STUFF! DONT BE FRIVOLOUS. /THE YOUTH/ SOMETHING	HORRIBLE	IS HAPPENING TO YOU. YOU ARE LOSING ALL HEART, ALL
SUPR III (106)	DEATH. THESE PEOPLE: THEY LOVE IT; AND THE MORE	HORRIBLE	IT IS THE MORE THEY ENJOY IT. HELL IS A PLACE FAR
HART I (59)	NOT THAT. I THINK ALL THE PART ABOUT JEALOUSY IS	HORRIBLE	. BUT DONT YOU THINK IT MUST HAVE BEEN A WONDERFUL
SUPR III (130)	TERROR ON EARTH DID I DREAM THAT HELL WAS SO	HORRIBLE	. I LIVE, LIKE A HAIRDRESSER, IN THE CONTINUAL
PPP (197)	WORN MY NEW CLOTHES ONCE. /MAGNESIA/ IT IS TOO	HORRIBLE	. (TO FITZ) FIEND! WHAT DROVE YOU TO THIS WICKED
MTH5 (238)	SHE MEANT TO KILL HIM. /STREPHON/ THIS IS	HORRIBLE	. /THE FEMALE FIGURE/ (WRESTLING WITH PYGMALION)
BASH II,1, (100)	LANGUAGE OF A FLOWER-GIRL. /LYDIA/ TRUE. IT IS	HORRIBLE	. SAID I " SOME WET"? I MEANT, SOME DRINK. WHY DID
FANY II (292)	THINGS; AND THE POLICE CAME IN. THEN IT WAS QUITE	HORRIBLE	. THE STUDENTS FOUGHT WITH THE POLICE; AND THE
GENV I (41)	A MURDERESS. HER DEAREST FRIEND. SHE HAD TO.	HORRIBLE	. THEYVE SHOT HER HUSBAND. SHE SAYS SHE WILL SHOOT
SUPR III (87)	WALK SEEING NOTHING. I HAVE WANDERED FOR HOURS IN	HORRIBLE	LONELINESS. /DON JUAN/ (SIGHING) OH! YOU HAVE NOT
KING I (183)	POISON THE KING WE SHALL BE EXECUTED IN THE MOST	HORRIBLE	MANNER. IT MUST BE SOMETHING THAT WILL BE GOOD FOR
MILL II (167)	THAT IT'S A RIVERSIDE HOTEL. WE HAVE JUST HAD A	HORRIBLE	MEAL OF TOMATO TEA CALLED SOUP, THE REMAINS OF
MTH5 (240)	AS IT IS, HOW AM I TO KILL THEM WITHOUT MAKING A	HORRIBLE	MESS? /THE MALE FIGURE/ (POSING HEROICALLY) HA!
MILL I (143)	MY DISTRESS, MY DISGRACE, MY HUMILIATION, THE	HORRIBLE	MESS AND FAILURE I HAVE MADE OF MY LIFE. SEEM TO
GETT (289)	IF THEYD KNOWN WHAT THEY WERE DOING. IVE A	HORRIBLE	MISGIVING ABOUT THAT PAMPHLET. ALL PROGRESS MEANS
GETT (300)	AND SHE COULD NOT GET A DIVORCE FROM THAT	HORRIBLE	MURDERER. THEY WOULD NOT EVEN KEEP HIM IMPRISONED
CATH 2 (176)	LET ME DOWN. /CATHERINE/ (MEANWHILE) WHAT A	HORRIBLE	NOISE! NARYSHKIN: SEE WHAT IT IS. NARYSHKIN GOES
MIS. PREFACE(95)	BE ABLE TO EXCLUDE RELIGION FROM THEM. THE MOST	HORRIBLE	OF ALL RELIGIONS: THAT WHICH TEACHES US TO REGARD
JOAN 4 (102)	YES: IT IS A PAINFUL DUTY: EVEN, AS YOU SAY, A	HORRIBLE	ONE. BUT IN COMPARISON WITH THE HORROR OF HERESY IT
MILL II (171)	ABOUT YOU. ARE YOU IN PAIN? /EPIFANIA/ YES.	HORRIBLE	PAIN. /THE DOCTOR/ WHERE? /EPIFANIA/ DONT
ROCK PREFACE(179)	HIMSELF AS AN ACCUSED MAN THREATENED WITH A	HORRIBLE	PENALTY, INSTEAD OF A GOD GOING THROUGH AN
BUOY 1 (13)	WITHIN THE LAST THIRTY YEARS WE HAVE HAD MORE	HORRIBLE	PERSECUTIONS AND MASSACRES, MORE DIABOLICAL
BARB III (338)	COMPARISON. POVERTY BLIGHTS WHOLE CITIES; SPREADS	HORRIBLE	PESTILENCES; STRIKES DEAD THE VERY SOULS OF ALL WHO
SIM PRO,2, (27)	TOWN. /THE E.O./ DONT DECEIVE YOURSELF. IT'S A	HORRIBLE	PLACE. THE CLIMATE IS SOMETHING TERRIBLE. DO YOU
MTH5 (233)	THE POOR BEAST OF A MAN. I HADNT PROVIDED FOR HIS	HORRIBLE	PREHISTORIC METHODS OF FEEDING HIMSELF. SUPPOSE THE
SUPR II (59)	BE? AN EXQUISITE DANCE OF NYMPHS. WHAT IS IT? A	HORRIBLE	PROCESSION OF WRETCHED GIRLS, EACH IN THE CLAWS OF
BASH II,1, (110)	MOUNTAIN SHALL BE THINE THE DAY THOU QUITST THY	HORRIBLE	PROFESSION. /CASHEL/ TEMPT ME NOT, WOMAN. IT IS
MTH5 (232)	LITTLE OF WHAT HE SWALLOWED; BUT THE PROCESS LEFT	HORRIBLE	RESIDUES WHICH HE HAD NO MEANS OF GETTING RID OF.
JOAN 6 (131)	THE CRUDE HERESIES OF WHICH YOU HAVE TOLD US ARE	HORRIBLE	; BUT THEIR HORROR IS LIKE THAT OF THE BLACK DEATH:
MTH4 I (159)	OF MILES, AND BUILT MICROSCOPE TEMPLES IN WHICH	HORRIBLE	SACRIFICES WERE OFFERED. THEY EVEN GAVE THEIR OWN
LIED (193)	TO BREAK UP MY HOME AND DISGRACE ME AND MAKE A	HORRIBLE	SCANDAL IN THE PAPERS. IT'S CRUEL, UNMANLY,
JITT III (76)	REPUTATION AND MY REPUTATION. YOU PREVENTED A	HORRIBLE	SCANDAL. YOU HAVE MANAGED TO MAKE HIS WIFE AND
PHIL II (109)	FACE YOU AFTER LAST NIGHT. CAN YOU IMAGINE A MORE	HORRIBLE	SCENE? DONT YOU HATE THE VERY SIGHT OF ME AFTER
PHIL II (110)	I SEE HOW IT IS, GRACE: YOU CANT FORGET THAT	HORRIBLE	SCENE LAST NIGHT. IMAGINE HER SAYING I HAD KISSED
FOUN (210)	THE LORD CHANCELLOR. GOOD. (TO MERCER) HENCE,	HORRIBLE	SHADOW! UNREAL MOCKERY, HENCE. MY LORD, I HAVE
CAND II (106)	OF OTHERS. BUT WHEN I TRY TO ASK FOR IT, THIS	HORRIBLE	SHYNESS STRANGLES ME; AND I STAND DUMB, OR WORSE
DOCT PREFACE(72)	BY THE MYSTICAL AIR OF THE BURNING AND THE	HORRIBLE	SMELL, THAT IT EXORCISES THE DEMONS OF SMALLPOX AND
CAPT NOTES (305)	UP TO DATE. BUT TOMPKINS SOMETIMES PERPETRATED	HORRIBLE	SOLECISMS. HE WOULD PRONOUNCE FACE AS FICE,
MILL PREFACE(126)	A MAN HUNT; AND MAN HUNTING IS NOT ONLY A VERY	HORRIBLE	SPORT BUT SOCIALLY A DANGEROUS ONE, AS IT REVIVES A
KING I (198)	OLD NOLL, AND BUTCHERED IT RATHER THAN HAVE THEIR	HORRIBLE	SPORT CUT SHORT. /JAMES/ SERVE THE RASCALS RIGHT!
MILL I (146)	FOOLING; AND I DONT KNOW WHAT I WANT. THAT IS A	HORRIBLE	STATE OF MIND. I AM A WOMAN WHO MUST ALWAYS WANT
CATH 4 (193)	LIKE A BULL-DOG) DONT GO. DONT LEAVE ME IN THIS	HORRIBLE	STATE. LOOSEN ME. (THIS IS WHAT HE IS SAYING; BUT
FABL PREFACE(71)	VENTURE INTO AN INFECTED HOUSE UNLESS WE MAKE A	HORRIBLE	STINK IN IT WITH BURNING SULPHUR," I PASSED THE
ARMS III (62)	BLUNTSCHLI. IT IS HE WHO IS SPREADING THIS	HORRIBLE	STORY ABOUT ME. (SHE WALKS ABOUT EXCITEDLY).
DOCT IV (161)	I'M VERY WEAK AND TIRED. DONT PUT ON ME THE	HORRIBLE	STRAIN OF PRETENDING THAT I DONT KNOW. IVE BEEN
2TRU III (93)	THE MIRACLES OF THE PRIESTS, ITS CRUELTIES MORE	HORRIBLE	THAN ALL THE ATROCITIES OF THE INQUISITION. ITS
MIS. (143)	IT'S MORE UNBEARABLE THAN ANY POVERTY: MORE	HORRIBLE	THAN ANY REGULAR-RIGHT-DOWN WICKEDNESS. OH, HOME!
BULL IV (179)	SAVED ENGLAND FROM POVERTY AND DEGRADATION MORE	HORRIBLE	THAN WE HAVE EVER DREAMED OF? WHEN I WENT TO
NEVR I (217)	CALL HIM. /GLORIA/ PHIL: CAN YOU BELIEVE SUCH A	HORRIBLE	THING AS THAT ABOUT OUR FATHER? WHAT MOTHER SAID
NEVR II (255)	PROCEEDS, WITH ENTHUSIASM) DONT YOU THINK IT A	HORRIBLE	THING THAT A MAN AND A WOMAN CAN HARDLY KNOW ONE
CAND II (122)	HER) IT IS YOUR CRUELTY. I HATE CRUELTY. IT IS A	HORRIBLE	THING TO SEE ONE PERSON MAKE ANOTHER SUFFER.
JITT I (11)	IT WILL ONLY DISTRESS YOU. ANGINA PECTORIS IS A	HORRIBLE	THING; BUT IT PASSES OFF SOON. YOU CAN DO NOTHING,
DOCT PREFACE(38)	THE CRUELTIES OF VIVISECTION. WE ALL DO JUST AS	HORRIBLE	THINGS, WITH EVEN LESS EXCUSE. BUT IN MAKING THAT
LION II (129)	YOU MEAN SO KINDLY BY ME THAT IT SEEMS QUITE	HORRIBLE	TO DISOBLIGE YOU. IF YOU COULD ARRANGE FOR ME TO
MRS II (211)	OF ME TOMORROW MORNING. /MRS WARREN/ OH, IT'S TOO	HORRIBLE	TO HEAR YOU TALK LIKE THAT. YOU WOULDNT-- YOU
SUPR I (22)	TO EAT YOU. /OCTAVIUS/ (RISING, PETTISHLY) IT'S	HORRIBLE	TO TALK LIKE THAT ABOUT HER WHEN SHE IS UPSTAIRS
DEST SD(152)	HISTORY A HUNDRED YEARS LATER, BUT MONSTROUS AND	HORRIBLE	TO THE CONTEMPORARY NORTH ITALIAN INFANT, TO WHOM
BULL IV (155)	HEALING, AND THE WEAK IN CHARACTER ARE PUT TO THE	HORRIBLE	TORTURE OF IMPRISONMENT, NOT FOR HOURS BUT FOR
BARB III (331)	OH I SAY! ! ! /CUSINS/ WHEN I LEARNT THE	HORRIBLE	TRUTH-- /LADY BRITOMART/ WHAT DO YOU MEAN BY THE
BARB III (332)	TRUTH-- /LADY BRITOMART/ WHAT DO YOU MEAN BY THE	HORRIBLE	TRUTH, PRAY? /CUSINS/ THAT SHE WAS ENORMOUSLY
GENV III (71)	JEWS. DO YOU REALIZE THAT IF I LIVED UNDER THE	HORRIBLE	TYRANNY OF THE SOVIET I SHOULD BE SHOT? /THE JEW/
GENV IV (117)	ONLY TWO FAITHS: CATHOLICS AND HERETICS. THE	HORRIBLE	VULGARITY CALLED DEMOCRACY HAS GIVEN POLITICAL
SIM PREFACE(5)	HAS KILLED THOUSANDS OF CHILDREN IN A QUITE	HORRIBLE	WAY WHEREAS NO CHILD HAS EVER BEEN A PENNY THE
LION II (130)	BEAR TO THINK OF IT! IN THE MIDST OF HIS SIN!	HORRIBLE	, HORRIBLE! /THE EDITOR/ SERVE THE ROTTER RIGHT!
BULL I (87)	CONFIDENCE) AND ALL THE WHILE THERE GOES ON A	HORRIBLE	, SENSELESS, MISCHIEVOUS LAUGHTER. WHEN YOURE
MIS. (196)	I'M SURE THEY DONT FEEL. TARLETON: THIS IS TOO	HORRIBLE	, TOO BRUTAL. IF NEITHER OF THESE YOUNG PEOPLE HAVE
BASH II,1, (102)	/LUCIAN/ FIGHTING WITH NAKED FISTS. /LYDIA/ OH,	HORRIBLE	! I'LL HEAR NO MORE. OR STAY: HOW DID IT END? WAS
PYGM II (240)	A NEW FASHION, BY GEORGE! AND IT OUGHT TO LOOK	HORRIBLE	! /DOOLITTLE/ (WITH FATHERLY PRIDE) WELL, I NEVER
BASH II,1, (106)	NOT THEN MY MOTHER IS AN ACTRESS? /LUCIAN/ HOW	HORRIBLE	! /LYDIA/ NAY, NAY: HOW INTERESTING! /CASHEL/ A
ARMS III (63)	POOR DEVILS IN THE SAME PREDICAMENT. /RAINA/ HOW	HORRIBLE	! /SERGIUS/ AND HOW RIDICULOUS! OH, WAR! WAR!
LION II (130)	THINK OF IT! IN THE MIDST OF HIS SIN! HORRIBLE,	HORRIBLE	! /THE EDITOR/ SERVE THE ROTTER RIGHT! /THE

HORRIBLY

WIDO I (11)	NO IDEA HOW YOU WILL RECEIVE THIS: IT MUST SEEM	HORRIBLY	ABRUPT; BUT THE CIRCUMSTANCES DO NOT ADMIT OF-- THE
BARB III (346)	TEARS MEN'S BODIES TO PIECES HAS NEVER BEEN SO	HORRIBLY	ABUSED AS THE INTELLECTUAL POWER, THE IMAGINATIVE
INCA PREFACE(231)	WITH OUR HEARTS IN OUR MOUTHS. MANY WERE SO	HORRIBLY	AFRAID OF HIM THAT THEY COULD NOT FORGIVE ME FOR
GETT (335)	RESPECTS AN AVERAGE MAN, PROBABLY. HE WILL BE	HORRIBLY	AFRAID OF ME; AND IF UNDER THE STIMULUS OF YOUR
PRES (144)	MY OWN. IT SOUNDS NICER. YOU REALLY NEEDNT BE SO	HORRIBLY	AFRAID OF THE OTHER COUNTRIES. THEYRE ALL IN THE
DEST (167)	HANDS). WOULD YOU HAVE BEEN AFRAID? /LADY/ OH,	HORRIBLY	AFRAID, AGONIZINGLY AFRAID. (SHE PRESSES HER HANDS
JITT II (38)	IN THOSE WORDS: THEY ARE TOO POLITE TO SPEAK AS	HORRIBLY	AS THEY THINK; BUT I KNOW. AND MY MOTHER ENCOURAGES
SIM PREFACE(16)	GRANDFATHER'S DOG. MY GRANDFATHER WOULD HAVE BEEN	HORRIBLY	ASHAMED OF HIMSELF IF THE DOG'S DEATH HAD NOT BEEN
DEST SD(151)	ART OF WAR UNDER ORDERS FROM VIENNA, AND GETTING	HORRIBLY	BEATEN BY NAPOLEON, WHO ACTS ON HIS OWN
HART I (75)	THAT I'M A BOHEMIAN, BECAUSE WE ARE ALL SO	HORRIBLY	BOHEMIAN. BUT I'M NOT. I HATE AND LOATHE
MTH5 (211)	WHEN I SHALL NOT COME BACK AT ALL. /STREPHON/ HOW	HORRIBLY	COLD AND UNCOMFORTABLE! /THE MAIDEN/ OH, DONT TALK
GETT PREFACE(227)	LIMITED FAMILY IN ITS LITTLE BRICK BOX IS	HORRIBLY	COMPLETE, BAD MANNERS, UGLY DRESSES, AWKWARDNESS,
PHIL II (117)	SCIENCE? BETWEEN OURSELVES, YOU KNOW, IT'S	HORRIBLY	CRUEL: YOU MUST ADMIT THAT IT'S A DEUCED NASTY
FABL PREFACE(76)	THAT ALL RULERS WHO ORDER SUCH EXTERMINATION ARE	HORRIBLY	CRUEL. " BLOODY MARY" BELIEVED THAT HERETICS MUST
HART I (65)	COURAGE, HE WILL GO STRAIGHT OFF AND DO THE MOST	HORRIBLY	DANGEROUS THINGS TO CONVINCE HIMSELF THAT HE ISNT A
BARB II (304)	CYNICALLY, ASIDE TO BARBARA, HIS VOICE AND ACCENT	HORRIBLY	DEBASED) WOT PRAWCE SELVYTION NAH? /BARBARA/ STOP.
PYGM II (223)	IRRESISTIBLE. SHE'S SO DELICIOUSLY LOW-- SO	HORRIBLY	DIRTY-- /LIZA/ (PROTESTING EXTREMELY)
LIED (188)	I'M THE ONLY AURORA IN THE WORLD. AND IT'S SO	HORRIBLY	EASY TO RHYME TO IT! OH, HENRY, WHY DIDNT YOU TRY
SUPR I (24)	WOMAN, AS DANGEROUS TO HER AS SHE TO HIM, AND AS	HORRIBLY	FASCINATING. OF ALL HUMAN STRUGGLES THERE IS NONE
DEVL I (18)	TOWARDS MRS DUDGEON'S CHAIR; AND HIS LIP ROLLS UP	HORRIBLY	FROM HIS DOG TOOTH AS HE MEETS HER LOOK OF
ROCK II (267)	TO ASSERT MYSELF AND BULLY PEOPLE. THIRD, I'M SO	HORRIBLY	HARD UP FOR POCKET MONEY WITHOUT KNOWING HOW TO DO
MTH5 (231)	NO LONGER GROWING AS FLESH, BUT PROLIFERATING	HORRIBLY	IN A LOWER FORM WHICH WAS CALLED CANCER, UNTIL THE
METH PREFACE(R31)	THE NERVES, AND, POSITIVELY, HOW MISERABLY A	HORRIBLY	INJURED DOG CAN DIE, LEAVING US TO INFER THAT WE

MIS. PREFACE	(104)	THIS IS TRUE ALSO OF POPULAR RELIGION: IT IS SO	HORRIBLY	IRRELIGIOUS THAT NOBODY WITH THE SMALLEST PRETENCE
PHIL III	(137)	ROOM AT YOU. ARE YOU AFRAID OF ME? /CHARTERIS/	HORRIBLY	. (HE MOVES THE CHAIR SLOWLY, WITH GREAT
GLIM	(186)	SYMPATHY) POOR SIGNORINO! THAT MUST HAVE HURT	HORRIBLY	. /FERRUCCIO/ WHAT! YOU PITY ME FOR THE TOOTH
2TRU I	(37)	AND CLUMSY WHEN I AM SO ILL. I AM SUFFERING	HORRIBLY	. SHUT THAT WINDOW AND SWITCH OFF HALF THOSE LIGHTS
CAND II	(108)	OUT LOUD; AND THE WORLD OVERHEARS THEM. BUT IT'S	HORRIBLY	LONELY NOT TO HEAR SOMEONE ELSE TALK SOMETIMES.
HART PREFACE	(5)	SLEPT AT THE FIRST CHORD OF SCHUMANN WERE BORN,	HORRIBLY	MISPLACED, INTO THE GARDEN OF KLINGSOR; BUT
DOCT PREFACE	(53)	WHEN ALMOST EVERY FACE THEY SAW IN THE STREET WAS	HORRIBLY	PITTED WITH SMALLPOX, AND THAT ALL THIS
MTH5	(222)	IDEALLY BEAUTIFUL NYMPHS AND YOUTHS, THEY ARE	HORRIBLY	REALISTIC STUDIES OF-- BUT I REALLY CANNOT BRING MY
HART PREFACE	(18)	THAT LED TO THE WAR: THEY WENT CLEAR-SIGHTED TO A	HORRIBLY	REPUGNANT DUTY. MEN ESSENTIALLY GENTLE AND
PHIL I	(90)	YOUVE SAID GOODNIGHT TO MRS TRANFIELD. IT'D BE	HORRIBLY	RUDE. /JULIA/ YOU CAN STAY IF YOU LIKE, DADDY: I
SUPR III SD	(72)	OFFER NO SUCH POSITIONS. WE MISUSE OUR LABORERS	HORRIBLY	; AND WHEN A MAN REFUSES TO BE MISUSED, WE HAVE NO
HART II	(116)	LOTS OF MONEY: THAT IS WHY OUR SOULS ARE SO	HORRIBLY	STARVED. /CAPTAIN SHOTOVER/ MANGAN'S SOUL LIVES ON
MTH5	(244)	ARE CAPABLE OF, IT BREAKS UP AT ONCE AND BECOMES	HORRIBLY	TAINTED. /THE SHE-ANCIENT/ LET IT BE A LESSON TO
2TRU PREFACE	(19)	THE POOR WILL BE BLEST AND HAPPY, AND THE RICH	HORRIBLY	TORTURED. MATTERS AT LAST REACHED A POINT AT WHICH
SIM PREFACE	(18)	LONGER BELIEVE AND NEW STORIES WHICH ARE ONLY TOO	HORRIBLY	TRUE TO SERIOUS AND RESPONSIBLE PUBLIC TRIBUNALS.
SUPR I	(33)	WANTED TO TALK ABOUT YOURSELF. /TANNER/ AH, TRUE,	HORRIBLY	TRUE. BUT WHAT A DEVIL OF A CHILD YOU MUST HAVE
SUPR IV	(167)	/TANNER/ (SMITING HIS BROW) HOW FRIGHTFULLY,	HORRIBLY	TRUE! IT HAS BEEN STARING ME IN THE FACE ALL MY
CATH 4	(196)	FISH. SEE HOW I KISS, THOUGH IT IS ONLY MY	HORRIBLY	UGLY OLD UNCLE (SHE THROWS HER ARMS ROUND
CAND III	(127)	ME. (SHE PUTS IT DOWN). /MARCHBANKS/ IT MADE ME	HORRIBLY	UNEASY. /CANDIDA/ WHY DIDNT YOU TELL ME? I'D HAVE
DEVL II	(48)	/JUDITH/ (TURNING WITH THE PURSE IN HER HAND)	HORRIBLY	UNLIKE HIM. /ANDERSON/ (SNATCHING THE PURSE FROM
MILL PREFACE	(134)	STARVED, AND OCCASIONALLY PUT TO DEATH, SOMETIMES	HORRIBLY	, BY THE LITTLE ONES. THEIR CASE IS HELPLESS
BARB III	(327)	OF HIS BEING A CUNNING OLD RASCAL; BUT IT'S ALL	HORRIBLY	, FRIGHTFULLY, IMMORALLY, UNANSWERABLY PERFECT.
			HORRID	
JOAN 2	(85)	WOULD YOU NOT FIGHT FOR HIM? /CHARLES/ NO: A	HORRID	BOY. HE HATES ME. HE HATES EVERYBODY, SELFISH LITTLE
BASH II,1,	(100)	HOW COULD I HAVE SAID " SOME WET"? /LUCIAN/ THE	HORRID	CONVERSATION OF THIS MAN HATH NUMBED THY ONCE
2TRU I	(33)	NO: SHE GAVE THEM TO ME. THESE HUMANS ARE FULL OF	HORRID	DISEASES: THEY INFECT US POOR MICROBES WITH THEM; AND
MTH2	(56)	THEY HAD TO BE CARRIED OUT KICKING AND MAKING A	HORRID	DISTURBANCE. /CONRAD/ NO: IT WAS LATER, AT A MEETING
GETT	(278)	IN TEARS) I'M SURE I NEVER THOUGHT IT WOULD BE SO	HORRID	FOR REJJY. I OFFERED HONORABLY TO DO IT MYSELF, AND
2TRU I	(35)	AND DEATH IN MY POCKET; BUT I HAVE NOTHING BUT A	HORRID	HEADACHE. OH DEAR! OH DEAR! THE MONSTER WANDERS
OVER	(171)	TIRED AND SORRY, AS I SHOULD BE IF I WERE TO BE	HORRID	. I DONT WANT YOU TO BE TIRED AND SORRY. DO COME AND
OVER	(171)	NOT BEING HORRID, MRS JUNO. I'M NOT GOING TO BE	HORRID	. I LOVE YOU: THATS ALL. I'M EXTRAORDINARILY HAPPY.
OVER	(171)	HIS ARMS ROUND HER). /THE LADY/ DONT-- OH DONT BE	HORRID	. PLEASE, MR LUNN (SHE RISES FROM THE LOUNGE AND
OVER	(171)	AND RETREATS BEHIND IT)! PROMISE ME YOU WONT BE	HORRID	. /GREGORY LUNN/ I'M NOT BEING HORRID, MRS JUNO. I'M
OVER	(172)	SAVE THE SITUATION; AND THATS WHAT YOU CALL BEING	HORRID	. WITH A BEAUTIFUL, WITTY, KIND WOMAN, THERES NO TIME
2TRU I	(31)	DAY THAT IT STOPPED FOR FIVE MINUTES WHEN THAT	HORRID	NURSE WAS RUDE TO HER. /THE DOCTOR/ NONSENSE! SHE
BASH III	(123)	FOR NOT UNTIL THE FINAL ROUND WE REACHED THE	HORRID	SCENE. BE SILENT ALL; FOR NOW I DO APPROACH MY
2TRU III	(106)	ME, BECAUSE I SACRIFICED MYSELF TO HER. SHE WAS A	HORRID	SELFISH GIRL, ALWAYS ILL AND COMPLAINING, AND NEVER
BASH II,2,	(114)	DOOM, AND IN THE MURKY CORNERS EVER SEES TWO	HORRID	SHADOWS, DEATH AND POVERTY; IN THE WHICH ANGUISH AN
MTH1 I	(14)	TO END TODAY. YOU MUST CLEAR AWAY SOME OF THOSE	HORRID	THINGS, OR WE SHALL BE SCRATCHED AND STUNG WHENEVER
ROCK I	(205)	YOU ARE SO GOOD! /SIR ARTHUR/ NONSENSE! SUCH A	HORRID	WICKED THING TO SAY. DONT YOU KNOW, MY LOVE, THAT YOU
OVER	(171)	YOU WONT BE HORRID. /GREGORY LUNN/ I'M NOT BEING	HORRID	, MRS JUNO. I'M NOT GOING TO BE HORRID. I LOVE YOU:
BULL III	(118)	MOUTHFUL, SIR. IT TASTED OF PEAT: OH! SOMETHING	HORRID	, SIR. THE PEOPLE HERE CALL PEAT TURF. POTCHEEN AND
			HORRIDLY	
OVER	(172)	WHO FIND THEMSELVES SITUATED AS WE ARE NOW BEHAVE	HORRIDLY	? /MRS JUNO/ BECAUSE THEY CANT HELP IT IF THEY LET
MTH4 I	(161)	REMARKABLE PASSAGE ABOUT YOUR DISPOSITIONS BEING	HORRIDLY	SHAKEN BY THOUGHTS BEYOND THE REACHES OF YOUR
			HORRIFICALLY	
BULL PREFACE	(26)	AND BLESS HIS FLOCK WITH TWO FINGERS, HE BECOMES	HORRIFICALLY	INCOMPREHENSIBLE TO THE IRISH PROTESTANT
			HORRIFIED	
2TRU III	(110)	OF THE REALITY THAT WAS HIDDEN. AND THEY ARE NOT	HORRIFIED	: THEY EXULT IN HAVING FOUND US OUT: THEY EXPOSE
MIS.	(164)	THE FACE). DAMN YOU! (RECOVERING HIMSELF,	HORRIFIED	AT HIS LAPSE) I BEG YOUR PARDON; BUT SINCE WEVE
LION PREFACE	(17)	PAID FOR BY THOSE WHO ARE CONVINCED, AND WHO ARE	HORRIFIED	AT THE INDIFFERENCE OF THE IRRELIGIOUS TO THE
MTH2	(77)	OF HIS SONS INVENTED MEAT-EATING. THE OTHER WAS	HORRIFIED	AT THE INNOVATION. WITH THE FEROCITY WHICH IS
LION PREFACE	(31)	HAD TAKEN COMPLETE HOLD OF HIM. WE SHOULD FEEL	HORRIFIED	AT THE SCOURGING AND MOCKING AND CRUCIFIXION JUST
DOCT PREFACE	(45)	A LEASH OF GREYHOUNDS LOOSE ON A HARE WOULD BE	HORRIFIED	AT THE THOUGHT OF LETTING THEM LOOSE ON A HUMAN
MIS. PREFACE	(91)	REPELLED BY UGLINESS, CHILLED BY VULGARITY,	HORRIFIED	BY COARSENESS, DEEPLY AND SWEETLY MOVED BY THE
ROCK PREFACE	(156)	BOOK IN A SERIES OF COERCION ACTS THAT WOULD HAVE	HORRIFIED	DUBLIN CASTLE. IN A REALLY CIVILIZED STATE
MTH2	(42)	SAVVY'S MANNERS JAR ON ME. THEY WOULD HAVE	HORRIFIED	HER GRANDMOTHER. /CONRAD/ (OBSTINATELY) THEY ARE
MILL I	(145)	AGONY AND MY BODY WRITHING ON THE FLOOR, HE WAS	HORRIFIED	. HE SAID HE DID IT AUTOMATICALLY-- THAT HE ALWAYS
LION PREFACE	(75)	FEAR OF DEATH. THIS MUST HAVE BOTH FASCINATED AND	HORRIFIED	PAUL, OR SAUL, AS HE WAS FIRST CALLED. THE HORROR
NEVR IV	(302)	GLORIA: THE GLORIA WHO WAS SHOCKED, OFFENDED,	HORRIFIED	-- OH YES, QUITE TRULY-- WHO WAS DRIVEN ALMOST MAD
FANY II	(292)	AND WENT INTO A GREAT THEATRE. /MRS KNOX/ (	HORRIFIED	) A THEATRE! /MARGARET/ YES. LOTS OF OTHER WOMEN
JOAN 6	(141)	DEATH EASIER. IT WILL BE A CRUEL DEATH. /JOAN/ (	HORRIFIED	) BUT YOU ARE NOT GOING TO BURN ME NOW? /THE
MTH5	(211)	WELL WITHOUT TOUCHING ONE ANOTHER. /STREPHON/ (	HORRIFIED	) CHLOE! OH, THIS IS THE WORST SYMPTOM OF ALL!
BULL II	(115)	IN THE EVENING AFTER YOUR TEA. /BROADBENT/ (	HORRIFIED	) DO YOU MEAN TO SAY THAT I-- I-- I-- MY GOD!
NEVR III	(268)	HAVE TAUGHT ME-- NOTHING. GOODBYE. /VALENTINE/ (	HORRIFIED	) GOODBYE! OH, MAYNT I SEE HER BEFORE I GO? /MRS
MTH3	(99)	KNICKERS, AND SILK STOCKINGS. /BURGE-LUBIN/ (	HORRIFIED	) I BEG YOUR PARDON A THOUSAND TIMES-- (THE
GETT	(303)	THEM YOUD SEE THEM DAMNED FIRST. /THE BISHOP/ (	HORRIFIED	) NO, NO, REALLY, BOXER! YOU MUST NOT-- /THE
GETT	(349)	/LESBIA/ BOXER! /THE GENERAL/ (RISING,	HORRIFIED	) NO, NO, YOU MUST KNOW, MY DEAR LESBIA, THAT I
CLEO III	(146)	IS THE WOMAN YOUR WIFE? /APOLLODORUS/ (	HORRIFIED	) NO, NO! (CORRECTING HIMSELF POLITELY) NOT THAT
NEVR I	(210)	MAN IN A FIRST RATE POSITION. /MRS CLANDON/ (	HORRIFIED	) OH DOLLY! DOLLY! MY DEAREST: HOW CAN YOU BE SO
MTH1 I	(4)	I SHALL FORGET AND STUMBLE. /EVE/ I TOO. /ADAM/ (	HORRIFIED	) OH NO, NO. I SHOULD BE ALONE. ALONE FOR EVER.
HART II	(109)	WILL FIND IT IN THE NEAREST BANK. /THE BURGLAR/ (	HORRIFIED	) OH WHAT A THING FOR A GENTLEMAN TO PUT INTO THE
FANY II	(294)	NOT FOR THE PRAYER MEETING. /MRS KNOX/ (DEEPLY	HORRIFIED	) OH, DONT SAY SUCH A THING AS THAT. I KNOW THAT
LION I	(112)	CHRISTIANS AGAIN LAUGH HEARTILY. /CENTURION/ (	HORRIFIED	) SILENCE, I TELL YOU! KEEP SILENCE THERE. DID
CAPT II	(262)	AND BUTTONS THE LOWEST BUTTON). /LADY CICELY/ (	HORRIFIED	) STOP. NO. YOU MUST NEVER PULL A COAT AT THE
PRES	(132)	A PAIR OF FASHIONABLE TROUSERS. /MITCHENER/ (	HORRIFIED	) STOP, MADAM. WHAT ARE YOU DOING? YOU MUST NOT
ANNA	(294)	(BLAZING) ME, OR THE SOLDIER? /STRAMMFEST/ (	HORRIFIED	) THE SOLDIER, MADAM. /THE GRAND DUCHESS/ TELL HIM
NEVR II	(234)	WILLIAM! /WAITER/ COMING, SIR. /M'COMAS/ (	HORRIFIED	) THE WAITER! STOP! STOP! I WILL NOT PERMIT
PHIL I	(90)	I'M OFF. (SHE MAKES FOR THE DOOR). /CRAVEN/ (	HORRIFIED	) WHAT ARE YOU DOING, JULIA? YOU CANT GO UNTIL
CAPT I	(233)	THAT NICE TRUTHFUL SAILOR! /SIR HOWARD/ (	HORRIFIED	) WHAT! THE HOOLIGAN! /RANKIN/ (PUZZLED)
CURE	(234)	AND BACH, AND SCHUMANN, AND-- /REGINALD/ (	HORRIFIED	) YOU DONT MEAN CLASSICAL MUSIC? /STREGA/ I DO (
PYGM III	(251)	TO KILL THEM. /MRS EYNSFORD HILL/ (TO ELIZA,	HORRIFIED	) YOU SURELY DONT BELIEVE THAT YOUR AUNT WAS
PHIL II	(96)	WILL HAPPEN TO THE GUINEA PIG. (SYLVIA RISES,	HORRIFIED	). I SHALL REQUIRE A KNIFE SPECIALLY MADE TO GET
SIM II	(60)	YOU. /IDDY/ THERE NOW! I OUGHT TO BE WOUNDED AND	HORRIFIED	; BUT I'M NOT: I FEEL AS IF YOUD GIVEN ME A
GETT PREFACE	(190)	WOULD HAVE BEEN SHOCKED; BYRON WOULD HAVE BEEN	HORRIFIED	; DON JUAN WOULD HAVE FLED FROM THE CONFERENCE
LION PREFACE	(49)	AS A STILL ACTIVE GOD, SUCH WORSHIPPERS ARE MORE	HORRIFIED	THAN DON JUAN WAS WHEN THE STATUE STEPPED FROM ITS
LION PREFACE	(30)	EXACTLY WHAT HE HAS DONE (THE BLASPHEMY THAT HAS	HORRIFIED	THE HIGH PRIEST DOES NOT MOVE THE ROMAN), TRIES TO
JOAN PREFACE	(39)	IS CARRIED TO AN EXTENT THAT WOULD HAVE	HORRIFIED	THE INQUISITION AND STAGGERED ARCHBISHOP LAUD. OUR
CAND I	(92)	CANDIDA! WHY-- (HE LOOKS AT HIS WATCH, AND IS	HORRIFIED	TO FIND IT SO LATE). MY DARLING! (HURRYING TO
MIS. PREFACE	(55)	US TO A FOULNESS IN OUR STREETS WHICH WOULD HAVE	HORRIFIED	US HAD THE STREET BEEN OUR DRAWING ROOM CARPET.
POSN PREFACE	(424)	IN LONDON, MANY PEOPLE WILL BE SINCERELY	HORRIFIED	WHEN THE MIRACLE OF THE MASS IS SIMULATED ON THE
MIS. PREFACE	(42)	NIGHTS AND WAS DEVOURING IT WITH AVIDITY, SHE WAS	HORRIFIED	, AND HID IT AWAY FROM ME LEST IT SHOULD BREAK MY
NEVR III	(271)	GLORIA RAISES HER CLENCHED HANDS. /MRS CLANDON/ (	HORRIFIED	, CATCHING HER UPLIFTED ARM) GLORIA! ! MY DEAR!
FANY I	(277)	ONE MAY SAY: SAFE UNDER LOCK AND KEY. /GILBEY/ (	HORRIFIED	, PITIABLE) OH MY-- (HIS BREATH FAILS HIM). DO
			HORRIFIES	
CAND I	(99)	HIM) OH, LET US PUT ASIDE ALL THAT CANT. IT	HORRIFIES	ME WHEN I THINK OF THE DOSES OF IT SHE HAS HAD TO
			HORRIFYING	
POSN PREFACE	(399)	HIS UNCLE, SHOULD BE STRUCK OUT AS UNBEARABLY	HORRIFYING	AND IMPROPER. BUT COMPLIANCE WITH THESE
MRS PREFACE	(157)	ALL THAT, SAYS THE EXAMINER IN EFFECT, IS	HORRIFYING	, LOATHSOME. PRECISELY! WHAT DOES HE EXPECT IT TO

		HORRIFYINGLY	
MRS PREFACE(177)	EVERYWHERE TOLERATED, PLAYS WHICH HAVE AN ALMOST	HORRIFYINGLY	CONTRARY EFFECT ARE FIERCELY ATTACKED BY
		HORROCKSES	
BARB II (279)	YOUNG SOAKER OF YOUR AGE. GO AND TAKE MY JOB AT	HORROCKSES	, WHERE I WORKED FOR TEN YEAR. THEY WANT YOUNG
		HORROR	
MTH1 I (17)	SNAKE. OH NO. HOW CAN YOU EVEN THINK SUCH A	HORROR	? /ADAM/ FEAR WILL DRIVE ME TO ANYTHING. THE SERPENT
LION PREFACE(84)	POSSIBLY DETEST THEM, OR READ WITHOUT PITY AND	HORROR	A DESCRIPTION OF THEIR BEING INSULTED, TORTURED, AND
ANNA (300)	WAS IN THE MIDDLE OF THE DIRT AND UGLINESS AND	HORROR	A LITTLE PATCH OF COURT SPLENDOR IN WHICH YOU COULD
LION PREFACE(75)	PAUL, OR SAUL, AS HE WAS FIRST CALLED. THE	HORROR	ACCOUNTS FOR HIS FIERCE PERSECUTION OF THE
LION PREFACE(49)	YOU WILL PRODUCE AN EXTRAORDINARY DISMAY AND	HORROR	AMONG THE ICONOLATERS. YOU WILL HAVE MADE THE PICTURE
MTH5 (232)	GHASTLIEST CREATURE: A MORE DREADFUL MIXTURE OF	HORROR	AND ABSURDITY THAN YOU WHO HAVE NOT SEEN HIM CAN
ROCK PREFACE(180)	CAN REDEEM IT EXCEPT FOR PEOPLE WHO ENJOY	HORROR	AND CATASTROPHE FOR THEIR OWN SAKE AND HAVE NO
JITT PREFACE(5)	REALISM) IS BANISHED FROM THE THEATRE, CRUELTY,	HORROR	AND DEATH BECOME PAINLESS THERE, AND EVEN LUXURIOUS,
LION II (140)	(RUNNING IN THROUGH THE PASSAGE, SCREAMING WITH	HORROR	AND HIDING HIS EYES) ! ! ! /LAVINIA/ ANDROCLES,
METH PREFACE(R44)	LEVITY, AS IT SEEMED, WAS RECEIVED WITH	HORROR	AND INDIGNATION. THE TIDE HAS NOW TURNED; AND EVERY
MTH5 (248)	TO BE NOTHING BUT REFLEXES, YOU ARE FILLED WITH	HORROR	AND LOATHING, AND WOULD GIVE WORLDS TO BE YOUNG
ROCK II (251)	YOUR POCKETS WITH GOLD TO CONSOLE YOU FOR THE	HORROR	AND REMORSE OF YOUR DREAMS; BUT THE VENGEANCE THEY
DOCT PREFACE(19)	THAT THE EXPERTS ON WHOSE ASSURANCE WE FACE THIS	HORROR	AND SUFFER THIS MUTILATION SHOULD HAVE NO INTERESTS
BULL IV (155)	THE HARDEST TOIL IS A WELCOME REFUGE FROM THE	HORROR	AND TEDIUM OF PLEASURE, AND WHERE CHARITY AND GOOD
BULL IV (155)	SYBARITE. NOW, SIR, THERE IS ONLY ONE PLACE OF	HORROR	AND TORMENT KNOWN TO MY RELIGION; AND THAT PLACE IS
MILL PREFACE(121)	THE LIBERAL NEWSPAPERS IN EUROPE SHRIEKED WITH	HORROR	AS IF NOTHING ELSE WAS HAPPENING IN ITALY. MUSSOLINI
FABL PREFACE(69)	MURDER AND SUDDEN DEATH, WERE NOT REGARDED WITH	HORROR	AS THE WORK OF SHELLEY'S ALMIGHTY FIEND, BUT WITH AWE
CLEO V (200)	SHUDDER. BUT THIS WAS NATURAL SLAYING: I FEEL NO	HORROR	AT IT. RUFIO, SATISFIED, NODS AT CLEOPATRA, MUTELY
LION II SD(127)	WITH HIS HEAD CLUTCHED IN HIS HANDS, FULL OF	HORROR	AT THE APPROACH OF MARTYRDOM. ON THE EAST SIDE OF THE
LION EPILOG (148)	MEN WHOM THEY PERSECUTE; AND THEIR PROFESSIONS OF	HORROR	AT THE BLUNT UTTERANCE OF THEIR OWN OPINIONS ARE
BUOY 1 (13)	THE HISTORY OF THEIR OWN TIMES THEY WOULD DIE OF	HORROR	AT THEIR OWN WICKEDNESS. KARL MARX CHANGED THE MIND
METH PREFACE(R37)	TRIVIAL AND EVEN COMIC; BUT THERE IS AN ABYSS OF	HORROR	BENEATH THEM. THEY REVEAL A CONDITION SO UTTERLY
BARB III (333)	/CUSINS/ TAKE CARE! THERE IS AN ABYSS OF MORAL	HORROR	BETWEEN ME AND YOUR ACCURSED AERIAL BATTLESHIPS.
ROCK PREFACE(180)	IN CHILDHOOD; AND CHILDREN GO ON FROM HORROR TO	HORROR	BREATHLESSLY, KNOWING NOTHING OF THE CONSTITUTIONAL
LION PREFACE(86)	DOUBT THAT THEY WOULD HAVE BEEN REPUDIATED WITH	HORROR	BY JESUS? OUR OWN NOTION THAT THE MASSACRE OF ST
MIS. PREFACE(3)	GO UP FROM THE HUMAN RACE AS NO OTHER CONCEIVABLE	HORROR	COULD PROVOKE. WITH ALL OUR PERVERSE NONSENSE AS TO
SUPR III (96)	ANA. A BAD FENCER, BUT A SOUND THINKER. /ANA/ (	HORROR	CREEPING UPON HER) I BEGIN TO UNDERSTAND. THESE ARE
DEVL III (61)	BURST OUT LAUGHING. /JUDITH/ (HER DREAD AND	HORROR	DEEPENING AT EVERY ONE OF THESE JESTS AND
MTH5 SD(239)	HER AND STAGGERING) OH! A GENERAL SHRIEK OF	HORROR	ECHOES HIS EXCLAMATION. HE TURNS DEADLY PALE, AND
ROCK PREFACE(157)	PEOPLE EXTERMINATED. BUT I SHOULD RECOIL WITH	HORROR	FROM A PROPOSAL TO PUNISH THEM. LET ME ILLUSTRATE MY
DOCT PREFACE(57)	INTO THE NORTH SEA, THERE WOULD BE A SHRIEK OF	HORROR	FROM ALL OUR EXPERTS. YET IF CROMWELL HAD DONE THAT
POSN PREFACE(399)	CENSOR MIGHT, WHILST SHRINKING EVEN WITH	HORROR	FROM IBSEN'S VIEWS, PERCEIVE THAT ANY NATION WHICH
CLEO PRO2,SD(103)	ARE SLAIN AND EATEN THE NEXT DAY. A SHUDDER OF	HORROR	FROM THE WOMEN. FTATATEETA, DESPISING THEM AND
SUPR I (29)	I SHOULD HAVE PUT AWAY THE SUSPICION WITH	HORROR	IF ONLY YOU WOULD THINK AND FEEL NATURALLY ABOUT IT.
POSN (446)	MAKES FOR THE DOOR). /BLANCO/ (SEIZING HIM, WITH	HORROR	IN HIS EYES) DONT GO: DONT LEAVE ME ALONE: DO YOU
JOAN 6 (131)	OF WHICH YOU HAVE TOLD US ARE HORRIBLE; BUT THEIR	HORROR	IS LIKE THAT OF THE BLACK DEATH: THEY RAGE FOR A
LION PREFACE(3)	WHO TOOK THE PART OF ANNAS WENT HOME AND DIED OF	HORROR	. BUT RESPONSIBLE PEOPLE HAVE NEVER MADE SUCH
BULL PREFACE(50)	JUNE 1906 BY WAY OF OBJECT-LESSON. THE DENSHAWAI	HORROR	. DENSHAWAI IS A LITTLE EGYPTIAN VILLAGE IN THE NILE
JITT III SD(60)	HOW HE DIED. MRS HALDENSTEDT COVERS HER EYES IN	HORROR	. FESSLER, OPENING THE STUDY DOOR, APPEARS ON THE
DEVL II (39)	GRASP IS NOT THE HUMOR OF THE SITUATION BUT ITS	HORROR	. HE TURNS TO THE SERGEANT, WHO IS APPROACHING HIM
CAND I (98)	HIS FACE DESPERATELY WITH HIS HANDS) FULL OF	HORROR	. (THEN, DROPPING HIS HANDS, AND THRUSTING HIS FACE
ROCK PREFACE(156)	WHO WAS OFFICIALLY OBLIGED TO WITNESS IT DIED OF	HORROR	. JOAN OF ARC, FOR WEARING MEN'S CLOTHES AND BEING A
AUGS (280)	I HAVE NEVER BEEN ABLE TO THINK OF ONE WITHOUT	HORROR	. /AUGUSTUS/ YOU MEAN IT WAS A REAL GUN, AND ACTUALLY
CLEO II (129)	(TO LUCIUS SEPTIMIUS) BEGONE: YOU FILL ME WITH	HORROR	. /LUCIUS/ (COLD AND UNDAUNTED) PSHAW! YOU HAVE
SUPR II (55)	WITHOUT IT THE WORLD WOULD BE A DREAM OF SORDID	HORROR	. /TANNER/ AND THIS-- THIS IS THE MAN WHO ASKS ME TO
MTH3 (117)	COMMIT OURSELVES TO THE IMPLICATIONS OF THE WORD	HORROR	. /THE ARCHBISHOP/ BY THE WORD HORROR THE ACCOUNTANT
SIM I (45)	ARE THE BEST SORT. A STRONGMINDED BISHOP IS A	HORROR	. /THE CLERGYMAN/ I AM TOO YOUNG. /SIR CHARLES/ YOU
BARB III (343)	NATION ON EARTH; AND OUR SUCCESS IS A MORAL	HORROR	. /UNDERSHAFT/ THAT IS WHAT COMES OF YOUR GOSPEL OF
LION PREFACE(49)	TO LIFE; AND THE MOB MAY NOT BE ABLE TO BEAR THAT	HORROR	. THE ALTERNATIVE TO BARABBAS. BUT MOBS MUST BE FACED
BUOY PREFACE(3)	FAR AS ANY MORTAL CAN BELIEVE IN AN UNIMAGINABLE	HORROR	. THEY HAVE A COHORT OF SLATE WRITERS AND WRITING
MTH3 (117)	BY ADDRESSING CONFUCIUS) WELL, THIS UNNATURAL	HORROR	. WILL THAT SATISFY YOU? /CONFUCIUS/ THAT IS IN
PHIL I (79)	A-- /JULIA/-- A CRIMINAL, AN IMBECILE OR A	HORROR	. YOU SAID THAT BEFORE. (SHE SITS DOWN BESIDE HIM
FANY EPILOG (329)	NOT SURPRISED, NOT CONCERNED; THAT MY OWN	HORROR	(YES, GENTLEMEN, HORROR-- HORROR OF THE VERY SOUL)
HART PREFACE(21)	A BOMB DROPPING INTO HIS EGG-CUP, THEIR WRATH AND	HORROR	KNEW NO BOUNDS. THEY DECLARED THAT THIS WOULD PUT A
HART II (120)	WHERE IT IS. YOU HAD BETTER SEE FOR YOURSELF THE	HORROR	OF AN OLD MAN DRINKING. /ELLIE/ YOU SHALL NOT DRINK.
NEVR III (276)	OTHER HAND, MRS CLANDON, YOUR HUSBAND HAD A GREAT	HORROR	OF ANYTHING GETTING INTO THE PAPERS. THERE WAS HIS
NEVR IV (293)	AND ALL THEIR CIRCLE. THEY HAVE A GREAT	HORROR	OF ANYTHING THAT IS AT ALL-- AT ALL-- WELL-- /BOHUN/
METH PREFACE(R56)	TO DO. NEITHER CONCLUSION DELIVERED US FROM THE	HORROR	OF ATTRIBUTING THE CRUELTY OF NATURE TO THE WORKINGS
MRS PREFACE(152)	INVOLUNTARY AND FRANTIC CONFESSION OF SIN, OF A	HORROR	OF CONSCIENCE IN WHICH THE POWER OF DISTINGUISHING
SUPR III (91)	BE A REAL LADY, NOTHING IS REAL HERE. THAT IS THE	HORROR	OF DAMNATION. /THE OLD WOMAN/ OH, THIS IS ALL
DEVL III (73)	SEEM IN A HURRY, MR DUDGEON. /RICHARD/ (WITH THE	HORROR	OF DEATH UPON HIM) DO YOU THINK THIS IS A PLEASANT
MTH3 (120)	FOUND OUT IF I WENT ON DRAWING IT TOO LONG. THE	HORROR	OF FACING ANOTHER LIFETIME OF DRUDGERY, OF MISSING MY
MIS. PREFACE(39)	ONLY BEING SET AT VIRGIL, WITH THE CULMINATING	HORROR	OF GREEK AND HOMER IN RESERVE AT THE END OF THAT. I
MTH1 I (5)	WRONG. (HE SITS DOWN AGAIN, SULKILY). IT IS THE	HORROR	OF HAVING TO BE WITH MYSELF FOR EVER. I LIKE YOU; BUT
MTH1 I (5)	BUT I KNOW VERY WELL THAT WHAT YOU MEAN IS THE	HORROR	OF HAVING TO BE HERE WITH ME FOR EVER. /ADAM/ OH!
MTH1 I (5)	YOU SAY YOU ARE NOT THINKING OF ME, BUT OF THE	HORROR	OF HAVING TO BE HERE FOREVER. BUT I KNOW VERY WELL
MTH1 I (12)	AND YET NO END! IF ONLY I CAN BE RELIEVED OF THE	HORROR	OF HAVING TO ENDURE MYSELF FOR EVER! IF ONLY THE
JOAN 4 (102)	SAY, A HORRIBLE ONE. BUT IN COMPARISON WITH THE	HORROR	OF HERESY IT IS LESS THAN NOTHING. I AM NOT THINKING
JOAN PREFACE(23)	SOCIAL INSTITUTIONS OF THE MIDDLE AGES. SHE HAD A	HORROR	OF HERETICS WITHOUT SUSPECTING THAT SHE WAS HERSELF A
POSN (435)	COST SOLID MONEY, AND PRETENDING THEY DO IT IN	HORROR	OF HIS WICKEDNESS, THOUGH HALF OF THEM WOULD HAVE A
GENV IV (107)	WAKE UP WITH MY MIND CLEARER AND CLEARER, AND THE	HORROR	OF IT DEEPER AND MORE AGONIZING. /BATTLER/ (
METH PREFACE(R15)	EDUCATION. BUT MEANWHILE-- AND HERE COMES THE	HORROR	OF IT-- OUR TECHNICAL INSTRUCTION IS HONEST AND
LADY PREFACE(233)	ILLUSIONS AND IDOLATRIES, AND WITH ALL SWIFT'S	HORROR	OF ITS CRUELTY AND UNCLEANLINESS. NOW IT HAPPENS TO
DOCT PREFACE(58)	BEEN THE CASE. WE NOW KNOW THAT THE MEDIEVAL	HORROR	OF LEPROSY WAS OUT OF ALL PROPORTION TO THE DANGER OF
OVER (173)	ROUND THE CORNER. BUT WHAT IS THAT TO THE	HORROR	OF MEETING IT ON EVERY BEAUTIFUL WOMAN, AND KNOWING
MTH2 (41)	A WORLD WITHOUT CONSCIENCE: THAT IS THE	HORROR	OF OUR CONDITION. /HASLAM/ (BEAMING) SIMPLY FATUOUS.
HART PREFACE(11)	SWIFT, WHO BOTH WENT THROUGH THIS EXPERIENCE. THE	HORROR	OF PEER GYNT IN THE MADHOUSE, WHEN THE LUNATICS,
APPL I (200)	GATES, AND PORTICOED COUNTRY HOUSES. THINK OF THE	HORROR	OF THAT ISLAND TO HIM! A VOID! A PLACE WHERE HE WAS
GETT PREFACE(222)	DECENT, MUCH LESS ENNOBLING, UNTIL THIS CENTRAL	HORROR	OF THE DEPENDENCE OF WOMEN ON MEN IS DONE AWAY WITH.
LION PREFACE(7)	LYING : HE BELIEVED LITERALLY WHAT HE SAID. THE	HORROR	OF THE HIGH PRIEST WAS PERFECTLY NATURAL: HE WAS A
LION PREFACE(35)	EVERY DEVICE IS USED TO GET RID OF THE RUTHLESS	HORROR	OF THE MATTHEW CHRONICLE, AND TO RELIEVE THE STRAIN
2TRU III (110)	MAGAZINES, ARE NUDER THAN SHORN LAMBS. BUT THE	HORROR	OF THE NAKED MIND IS STILL MORE THAN WE CAN BEAR.
SUPR HANDBOK(207)	DIGNITY OF THEIR SUPERIORITY, AS A SET-OFF TO THE	HORROR	OF THE ONE AND THE LONELINESS OF THE OTHER. IX: THE
MIS. PREFACE(35)	HOLIDAY IS A GOOD WORKING DEFINITION OF HELL. THE	HORROR	OF THE PERPETUAL HOLIDAY, IT WILL BE SAID HERE THAT,
HART PREFACE(36)	THE CATHEDRAL OF RHEIMS THE WORLD RANG WITH THE	HORROR	OF THE SACRILEGE. WHEN THEY BOMBED THE LITTLE THEATRE
GETT (307)	BUT THE ONLY WORD I CAN FIND IS THE FULL	HORROR	OF THE SITUATION. THESE LADIES NOT ONLY REFUSE OUR
FANY EPILOG (329)	THAT MY OWN HORROR (YES, GENTLEMEN, HORROR--	HORROR	OF THE VERY SOUL) APPEARS UNACCOUNTABLE TO YOU,
JOAN 6 (130)	EVEN LAUDABLE; BUT IT ENDS IN SUCH A MONSTROUS	HORROR	OF UNNATURAL WICKEDNESS THAT THE MOST TENDER-HEARTED
BARB III (337)	FIRST SHOCK MATTERED COMPARED TO THE DREAD AND	HORROR	OF WAITING FOR THE SECOND? THAT IS HOW I FEEL IN
PPP (204)	HAS HAPPENED? /FITZ/ (STRIKING HIS FOREHEAD)	HORROR	ON HORROR'S HEAD! /THE LANDLORD/ WOTJEMEAN?
2TRU PREFACE(17)	PERSONAL DIRECTIONS WHICH WOULD PRODUCE GENERAL	HORROR	OR BE TAKEN AS PROOFS OF INSANITY THEIR AUTHORITY
FANY EPILOG (329)	CONCERNED; THAT MY OWN HORROR (YES, GENTLEMEN,	HORROR	-- HORROR OF THE VERY SOUL) APPEARS UNACCOUNTABLE TO
AUGS (269)	/AUGUSTUS/ (REELING AGAINST THE TABLE IN HIS	HORROR	) A RISE! HORATIO FLOYD BEAMISH: DO YOU KNOW THAT WE
DEST (168)	DESPATCHES? /LADY/ (OVERCOME BY THE IMAGINED	HORROR	) DONT ASK ME. I MUST HAVE COME. /NAPOLEON/ WHY?
GETT (341)	YOU TO FALL IN LOVE, ANTHONY. /SOAMES/ (WITH	HORROR	) I! ! /THE BISHOP/ YES, YOU! THINK OF WHAT IT
MTH1 I (16)	SHOULD NOT MAKE ME DIE. /ADAM/ (SCRAMBLING UP IN	HORROR	) MAKE YOU DIE! ! ! WHAT A FRIGHTFUL THOUGHT!
DEVL III (62)	TO BE HANGED, MR ANDERSON? /JUDITH/ (SICK WITH	HORROR	) MY GOD! /RICHARD/ (TO JUDITH) YOUR PROMISE! (TO
ANNA (297)	MUST SPEAK TO YOU ALONE. /STRAMMFEST/ (RISING IN	HORROR	) NO: THIS IS THE LAST STRAW: I CANNOT CONSENT. IT IS
LION II (128)	FOR YOU. HE'S HUNGRY. /SPINTHO/ (GROANING WITH	HORROR	) OH, LORD! CANT YOU STOP TALKING ABOUT IT? ISNT IT

CLEO II	(129)	AND SWEET MEASURE OF VENGEANCE. /CAESAR/ (WITH	HORROR	) VENGEANCE! /POTHINUS/ OUR FIRST GIFT TO YOU, AS
LION I	(123)	WOULD BE SPLENDID. /FERROVIUS/ (SPRINGING UP IN	HORROR	) WHAT! /ANDROCLES/ OH, SISTER! /FERROVIUS/
DEVL I	(20)	HIS HEAD DEPLORINGLY. THE RELATIVES FREEZE WITH	HORROR	). THATS RIGHT: PULL YOUR LONGEST FACES (HIS VOICE
PHIL II	(113)	TO THE JOURNAL WITH A GHASTLY EXPRESSION OF	HORROR	)! IF THIS IS TRUE, IT WAS ALL A MISTAKE: THERE IS
MIS. PREFACE	(74)	EXCEPT BY A PACK OF FOXHOUNDS IS REGARDED WITH	HORROR	; BUT YOU MAY AND DO KILL CHILDREN IN A HUNDRED AND
JITT I	SD(25)	REMAINS HANGING AND HIS JAW DROPS. WITH A GASP OF	HORROR	SHE REPLACES THE HEAD AND CLOSES THE OPEN MOUTH. THEN
LADY PREFACE	(221)	AND WERE EXPRESSED WITH THE REALISTIC POWER AND	HORROR	THAT MAKES HAMLET SAY THAT THE HEAVENS GOT SICK WHEN
MTH3	(117)	OF THE WORD HORROR. /THE ARCHBISHOP/ BY THE WORD	HORROR	THE ACCOUNTANT GENERAL MEANS ONLY SOMETHING UNUSUAL.
MIS. PREFACE	(11)	OF THE CHILD'S SOUL, WHICH CAN BRING NOTHING BUT	HORROR	TO ANYONE. THE MANUFACTURE OF MONSTERS. THIS INDUSTRY
ROCK PREFACE	(180)	READ IT IN CHILDHOOD; AND CHILDREN GO ON FROM	HORROR	TO HORROR BREATHLESSLY, KNOWING NOTHING OF THE
LION PREFACE	(76)	DOMINION THAT THEIR OWN COMMON NATURE BECAME A	HORROR	TO THEM, AND THE RELIGIOUS LIFE BECAME A DENIAL OF
PHIL I	(77)	TURNED OUT A DRUNKARD, A CRIMINAL, AN IMBECILE, A	HORROR	TO YOU; AND YOU COULDNT HAVE RELEASED YOURSELF. TOO
CLEO II	(138)	/THEODOTUS/ (ON THE STEPS, WITH UPLIFTED ARMS)	HORROR	UNSPEAKABLE! WOE, ALAS! HELP! /RUFIO/ WHAT NOW?
SIM PREFACE	(10)	WITH JEWS, AND BURNED BOTH. CONCEIVE, THEN, OUR	HORROR	WHEN THE INQUISITION SUDDENLY ROSE UP AGAIN IN
BARB I	(254)	THAT PEOPLE GET INTO A STATE OF DUMB HELPLESS	HORROR	WHEN THEY FIND THAT THERE ARE WICKED PEOPLE IN THE
GETT	(326)	YES. BUT THERE WAS SOMETHING WORSE. JUDGE OF MY	HORROR	WHEN, CALLING ON THE COAL MERCHANT TO MAKE A TRIFLING
MTH3	(129)	I AM GOING TO RAISE THE COUNTRY AGAINST THIS	HORROR	, AND AGAINST YOU, IF YOU SHEW THE SLIGHTEST SIGN OF
HART II	(118)	AT YOUR AGE I LOOKED FOR HARDSHIP, DANGER,	HORROR	, AND DEATH, THAT I MIGHT FEEL THE LIFE IN ME MORE
JOAN PREFACE	(33)	REMAINS THAT THE BURNING OF JOAN OF ARC WAS A	HORROR	, AND THAT A HISTORIAN WHO WOULD DEFEND IT WOULD
MTH2	(51)	IT TO BE FOUGHT AT ALL! AN ELECTION IS A MORAL	HORROR	, AS BAD AS A BATTLE EXCEPT FOR THE BLOOD: A MUD BATH
3PLA PREFACE	(R16)	HAD HE BEEN ENTHRALLED BY THE PLAY, EVEN WITH	HORROR	, INSTEAD OF HIMSELF ENTHRALLING WITH THE DREAD OF
CAND II	(114)	(REASSURED) NONSENSE, PAPA! IT'S ONLY POETIC	HORROR	, ISNT IT, EUGENE (PETTING HIM)? /BURGESS/ (
GETT PREFACE	(198)	BE A VERY GOOD THING, CHRONIC SENTIMENTALITY IS A	HORROR	, MORE DANGEROUS, BECAUSE MORE POSSIBLE, THAN THE
METH PREFACE	(R12)	GOOD-NATURED MAJORITY ARE LOOKING ON IN HELPLESS	HORROR	, OR ALLOWING THEMSELVES TO BE PERSUADED BY THE
MRS PREFACE	(160)	THE PALACE BY HIS INDIGNANT FATHER-IN-LAW. TO HIS	HORROR	, WHEN HE PROCEEDS TO CARRY OUT THIS STRATAGEM, THE
CAND II	(114)	YOU ILL, EUGENE? /MARCHBANKS/ NO: NOT ILL. ONLY	HORROR	! HORROR! HORROR! (HE BOWS HIS HEAD ON HIS
CAND II	(114)	EUGENE? /MARCHBANKS/ NO: NOT ILL. ONLY HORROR!	HORROR	! HORROR! (HE BOWS HIS HEAD ON HIS HANDS).
CAND II	(114)	/MARCHBANKS/ NO: NOT ILL. ONLY HORROR! HORROR!	HORROR	! (HE BOWS HIS HEAD ON HIS HANDS). /BURGESS/ (
DEST	(194)	THAT, HOW THEY WOULD HOLD UP THEIR HANDS IN PIOUS	HORROR	! (HE GOES TO THE INNER DOOR AND HOLDS IT OPEN,
			HORROR-STRICKEN	
PPP	SD(205)	FLUID AT THE COST OF HIS LIFE. THE OTHERS LOOK ON	HORROR-STRICKEN	AS THE THREE VICTIMS, AFTER REELING,
CAND I	(97)	OCCASIONS; BUT A CHANCE VISITOR IS. (THE HUNTED	HORROR-STRICKEN	EXPRESSION COMES OUT WITH SUDDEN VIVIDNESS
OVER	(174)	HUSBAND! WHAT DO YOU MEAN? (CLUTCHING HIM,	HORROR-STRICKEN	) DONT TELL ME HE'S DEAD. /GREGORY/ (
			HORROR'S	
PPP	(204)	/FITZ/ (STRIKING HIS FOREHEAD) HORROR ON	HORROR'S	HEAD! /THE LANDLORD/ WOTJEMEAN? /MAGNESIA/ THE
			HORRORS	
GENV I	(40)	LEAGUE OF NATIONS IF IT CANNOT PUT A STOP TO SUCH	HORRORS	? /SHE/ WELL, IT'S NOT THE LEAGUE'S BUSINESS, IS
LION I	(124)	IVE DRUNK ALL MY NERVES AWAY. I SHALL HAVE THE	HORRORS	ALL NIGHT. /ANDROCLES/ (SYMPATHETIC) OH, DONT TAKE
DOCT IV	(162)	LITTLE HELL OF CRAPE AND CRYING AND UNDERTAKER'S	HORRORS	AND WITHERING FLOWERS AND ALL THAT VULGAR RUBBISH.
GENV PREFACE	(9)	WE DISCOVERED THAT THE MANUFACTURE OF THESE NEW	HORRORS	HAD BEEN PLANNED FOR ON SUCH A SCALE THAT BUT FOR
METH PREFACE	(R57)	SELECTION: THAT IS TO SAY, OF A METHOD BY WHICH	HORRORS	HAVING EVERY APPEARANCE OF BEING ELABORATELY PLANNED
BARB PREFACE	(215)	LAY UP FOR HIMSELF, NOT TREASURES IN HEAVEN, BUT	HORRORS	IN HELL UPON EARTH. THIS BEING SO, IS IT REALLY WISE
JOAN PREFACE	(28)	AND THAT THE INQUISITION WAS A CHAMBER OF	HORRORS	INVENTED EXPRESSLY AND EXCLUSIVELY FOR SUCH
POSN	(457)	SHERIFF/ SHUT YOUR MOUTH, WILL YOU. YOUVE GOT THE	HORRORS	. (TO THE WOMAN) NOW YOU. WHO ARE YOU? AND WHAT
2TRU PREFACE	(11)	DREAM BECAUSE THEY HAVE NO EXPERIENCE OF ITS	HORRORS	. OF COURSE THE ANSWER OF OUTRAGED NATURE IS DROWNED
SIM PRO,2,	(28)	BY THEIR OWN HANDS TO ESCAPE WHAT THEY CALL THE	HORRORS	, WE DO NOT ENCOURAGE THEM TO LIVE. THE EMPIRE IS
HART II	(108)	OF WHAT IT IS FOR US TO BE DRAGGED THROUGH THE	HORRORS	OF A CRIMINAL COURT, AND HAVE ALL OUR FAMILY AFFAIRS
PLES PREFACE	(R17)	PIECES AFTER THREE DAYS UNDER FIRE, ENDING IN THE	HORRORS	OF A ROUT AND PURSUIT; HE HAS FOUND BY EXPERIENCE
ROCK PREFACE	(155)	PARENTS, AND A HIDEOUS CRIMINAL CODE. WHEN THE	HORRORS	OF ANARCHY FORCE US TO SET UP LAWS THAT FORBID US TO
GENV IV	(114)	FLANCO IS STRIVING TO SAVE HIS COUNTRY FROM THE	HORRORS	OF COMMUNISM HE HAS MY SYMPATHY. /COMMISSAR/ WHICH
MIS. PREFACE	(6)	FURIOUSLY RESISTED BY THE PARENTS, EVEN WHEN THE	HORRORS	OF FACTORY SLAVERY WERE AT THEIR WORST; AND THE
CURE	(236)	ON WHOSE INCOME I CAN LIVE WITHOUT THE SORDID	HORRORS	OF HAVING TO MAKE MONEY FOR MYSELF. I AM A POOR
BULL I	SD(75)	TO HIMSELF, AS HE IS SECRETLY PURSUED BY THE	HORRORS	OF INCIPIENT DELIRIUM TREMENS. /HAFFIGAN/ TIM
GENV PREFACE	(17)	CONCENTRATION CAMPS. THE WITNESSES DESCRIBE THE	HORRORS	OF LIFE AND DEATH IN THEM; AND THE NEWSPAPERS CLASS
PRES	(164)	HEAD. I PRECIOUS NEARLY PUNCHED SANDSTONE'S. THE	HORRORS	OF MARTIAL LAW ADMINISTERED BY MRS BANGER ARE TOO
MIS. PREFACE	(68)	AND OTHER PEOPLE MISERABLE BY THE HEATHEN	HORRORS	OF MOURNING, STAYING AWAY FROM THE THEATRE BECAUSE
MIS. PREFACE	(9)	GO. ALL THE WAYS DISCOVERED SO FAR LEAD TO THE	HORRORS	OF OUR EXISTING CIVILIZATIONS, DESCRIBED QUITE
BARB PREFACE	(241)	HIS CAPTOR NOT TO DELIVER HIM OVER TO THE USELESS	HORRORS	OF PENAL SERVITUDE. IN OTHER CASES THE LAWBREAKER
SUPR HANDBOK	(193)	ESPECIALLY THE SELF-RESPECT OF WOMEN. ADD TO THE	HORRORS	OF POPULAR LANGUAGE THE HORRORS OF POPULAR POVERTY.
SUPR HANDBOK	(193)	WOMEN. ADD TO THE HORRORS OF POPULAR LANGUAGE THE	HORRORS	OF POPULAR POVERTY. IN CROWDED POPULATIONS POVERTY
2TRU PREFACE	(3)	RICH. OUR REVOLUTIONARY WRITERS HAVE DWELT ON THE	HORRORS	OF POVERTY. OUR CONVENTIONAL AND ROMANTIC WRITERS
MTH5	(261)	COME OF THAT. AND SO MUCH CAME OF IT THAT THE	HORRORS	OF THAT TIME SEEM NOW BUT AN EVIL DREAM. THEY HAVE
2TRU PREFACE	(9)	FLED FROM FASHIONABLE SOCIETY IN LONDON TO THE	HORRORS	OF THE CRIMEAN HOSPITALS RATHER THAN BEHAVE LIKE A
MILL PREFACE	(120)	SOLDIERS, WHO, AFTER SUFFERING ALL THE	HORRORS	OF THE WAR, HAD RETURNED TO FIND THAT THE MEN WHO
FABL PREFACE	(85)	HERESY AND A MAD PARADOX. LET US SEE. WHEN THE	HORRORS	OF UNREGULATED SELFISH PRIVATE ENTERPRISE FORCED
O'FL PREFACE	(202)	A FRESH APPEAL. IRISHMEN: DO YOU WISH TO HAVE THE	HORRORS	OF WAR BROUGHT TO YOUR OWN HEARTHS AND HOMES?
UNPL PREFACE	(R25)	CHARACTER AND DESTINY, BUT WITH THOSE SOCIAL	HORRORS	WHICH ARISE FROM THE FACT THAT THE AVERAGE HOMEBRED
GETT PREFACE	(244)	BECAUSE MY MISSION IS NOT TO DEAL WITH OBVIOUS	HORRORS	, BUT TO OPEN THE EYES OF NORMAL RESPECTABLE MEN TO
2TRU PREFACE	(3)	AND ROMANTIC WRITERS HAVE IGNORED THOSE	HORRORS	, DWELLING PLEASANTLY ON THE ELEGANCES OF AN
MTH5	(245)	AFTER ALL. /MARTELLUS/ WHAT! HAVE THOSE TWO	HORRORS	, WHOSE ASHES I HAVE JUST DEPOSITED WITH PECULIAR
MTH5	(239)	SCIENCE? SERVE HIM RIGHT FOR MAKING THAT PAIR OF	HORRORS	! /THE MALE FIGURE/ (GLARING) HA! /THE FEMALE
			HORS	
SUPR PREFACE	(R23)	OF GENIUS, CHOPINS, MUSSETS AND THE LIKE, AS MERE	HORS	D'OEUVRES. I STATE THE EXTREME CASE, OF COURSE; BUT
			HORSA	
MTH4 I	(153)	WHEN TWO OF MY ANCESTORS, JOYCE BOLGE AND HENGIST	HORSA	BLUEBIN, WRESTLED WITH ONE ANOTHER FOR THE PRIME
			HORSE	
POSN	(444)	IT. NEITHER GOD NOR DEVIL TEMPTED ME TO TAKE THE	HORSE	: I TOOK IT ON MY OWN. HE HAD A CLEVERER TRICK THAN
POSN	(445)	IS THAT ANY REASON WHY STRAPPER SHOULDNT HAVE HIS	HORSE	? I TELL YOU I'M RESPONSIBLE TO HIM FOR IT. (BENDING
POSN	(441)	COMES BACK. WHAT POSSESSED YOU TO STEAL THAT	HORSE	? /BLANCO/ I DIDNT STEAL IT. I DISTRAINED ON IT FOR
POSN	(445)	THE GREAT SECRET NOW IS, WHAT DID YOU DO WITH THE	HORSE	? /BLANCO/ (STRIKING THE TABLE WITH HIS FIST) MAY MY
ARMS III	(61)	WELL SAID, SWITZER. SHALL I LEND YOU MY BEST	HORSE	? /BLUNTSCHLI/ NO: DAMN YOUR HORSE! THANK YOU ALL
JOAN 6	(138)	IN A STATE OF GRACE WHEN YOU STOLE THE BISHOP'S	HORSE	? /CAUCHON/ (RISING IN A FURY) OH, DEVIL TAKE THE
POSN	(453)	FOR YOU. /THE SHERIFF/ YOU SAY YOU SAW HIM ON MY	HORSE	? /FEEMY/ I DID. /BLANCO/ AND I ATE IT, I SUPPOSE,
POSN	(454)	DID ANYONE ELSE SEE THE PRISONER WITH THE	HORSE	? /FEEMY/ (PASSIONATELY) AINT I GOOD ENOUGH?
DEST	(183)	THE BETTER SIDE OF MY NATURE. WHAT ABOUT MY	HORSE	? /LADY/ IT IS PART OF THE BARGAIN THAT YOU ARE TO
DEST	(186)	EH, GENERAL? (TO THE LADY) I SAY: WHERES MY	HORSE	? /LADY/ SAFE AT BORGHETTO, WAITING FOR YOU,
JOAN 1	(65)	GIRL LIKE THAT DO YOU OUT OF SIXTEEN FRANCS FOR A	HORSE	? /POULENGEY/ I WILL PAY FOR THE HORSE. /ROBERT/ YOU
POSN	(449)	/THE SHERIFF/ WHATS THAT? AINT YOU GOT THE	HORSE	? /STRAPPER/ NO. HE TRADED IT BEFORE WE OVERTOOK HIM,
DEST	(158)	A HUNDRED MINUTES LATE, ON FOOT. WHERE IS YOUR	HORSE	? /THE LIEUTANANT/ (MOODILY PULLING OFF HIS GLOVES
ARMS I	(15)	AT HIS HORSE. /RAINA/ WHY SHOULD HE PULL AT HIS	HORSE	? /THE MAN/ (IMPATIENT OF SO STUPID A QUESTION) IT'S
POSN	(457)	IT. WELL, SHE CANT COME IN. WHAT WOMAN? WHAT	HORSE	? WHATS THE GOOD OF SHOVING LIKE THAT? WHO SAYS?
GETT	SD(275)	PENETRATION; SO THAT SHE IS ALWAYS ON THE HIGH	HORSE	ABOUT WORDS AND ALWAYS IN THE PERAMBULATOR ABOUT
POSN	(457)	OUT. YES IT IS, SURE. I TELL YOU IT IS. IT'S THE	HORSE	ALL RIGHT ENOUGH. ROT. GO AND LOOK. BY GUM! /THE
JOAN 1	(60)	CAPTAIN SQUIRE. CAPTAIN! YOU ARE TO GIVE ME A	HORSE	AND ARMOR AND SOME SOLDIERS, AND SEND ME TO THE
CLEO IV	(192)	MUST TAKE SHIP FOR THE WESTERN LAKE. SEE TO MY	HORSE	AND ARMOR. (BRITANNUS RUNS OUT.) WITH THE REST, I
JOAN PREFACE	(19)	HAVING A SOLDIER'S DRESS AND ARMS AND SWORD AND	HORSE	AND EQUIPMENT, AND ON TREATING HER ESCORT OF SOLDIERS
DEST	(159)	CALL THAT NOTHING. HE GAVE ME HIS PISTOLS AND HIS	HORSE	AND HIS DESPATCHES-- MOST IMPORTANT DESPATCHES-- AND
CLEO NOTES	(211)	FAIR FIGHT, BUT WITH ENCHANTED SWORD, SUPEREQUINE	HORSE	AND MAGICAL INVULNERABILITY, THE POSSESSION OF WHICH,
CYMB V	(139)	SCORE AS FROM A CATAPULT FOUR HUNDRED TONS OF	HORSE	AND MAN IN ONE ENORMOUS SHOCK HURLED ON OUR SHAKEN
LADY PREFACE	(229)	MAKING RICHARD OFFER HIS KINGDOM FOR A	HORSE	AND OTHELLO DECLARE OF CASSIO THAT " HAD ALL HIS HAIRS
DEST	(183)	IS PART OF THE BARGAIN THAT YOU ARE TO HAVE YOUR	HORSE	AND PISTOLS BACK. /LIEUTENANT/ HONOR BRIGHT? /LADY/

POSN (449)	YOU KNOW, I SUPPOSE, THAT IF YOUVE STOLE A	HORSE	AND THE JURY FIND AGAINST YOU, YOU WONT HAVE ANY TIME
SUPR HANDBOK(177)	THE CHARGER OF HENRY V TO THE BREWER'S DRAUGHT	HORSE	AND THE RACE-HORSE, ARE REAL; FOR HERE MAN HAS PLAYED
DEST (187)	EAGER ADMIRATION) THEY SAY YOU JUMPED OFF YOUR	HORSE	AND WORKED THE BIG GUNS WITH YOUR OWN HANDS, GENERAL.
JOAN 6 (138)	(RISING IN A FURY) OH, DEVIL TAKE THE BISHOP'S	HORSE	AND YOU TOO! WE ARE HERE TO TRY A CASE OF HERESY; AND
POSN (462)	FOR YOU. AS YOU ARE IN A HURRY, I'LL SELL YOU THE	HORSE	AT A REASONABLE FIGURE. NOW, BOYS, LET NOBODY GO OUT
POSN (453)	WHY SHOULD I? WE NEVER SAID A WORD ABOUT THE	HORSE	AT ALL. HOW WAS I TO KNOW WHAT IT WAS IN YOUR MIND TO
POSN (453)	NEITHER. BUT FEEMY EVANS SAW YOU PASS ON THE	HORSE	AT FOUR O'CLOCK TWENTY-FIVE MILES FROM THE SPOT WHERE
DEST (156)	THAT IS ALL. THE POSTILLION SAYS SHE LEFT A	HORSE	AT THE GOLDEN EAGLE, A CHARGER, WITH MILITARY
APPL I (214)	NOT TO MENTION THAT YOU MAY HAVE MORE THAN ONE	HORSE	AT YOUR DISPOSAL. /PROTEUS/ RIGHT YOU ARE. PERFECTLY
POSN (445)	PUT STRAPPER IN THE WAY OF GETTING HIS BROTHER'S	HORSE	BACK. /BLANCO/ NOT THEY. HANGING'S TOO BIG A TREAT FOR
MTH3 (98)	LIKE YOU. YOU ARE BETTER COMPANY THAN A DOG OR A	HORSE	BECAUSE YOU CAN SPEAK. /BURGE-LUBIN/ AM I A BARBARIAN
POSN (448)	THROW HER OUT ON THE DUMP. YOUVE GOT TO FIND THAT	HORSE	BEFORE YOU GET A ROPE ROUND MY NECK. (HE TURNS AWAY
POSN (440)	ME. THAT WAS A ROTTEN THING TO DO, BECAUSE THE	HORSE	BELONGED TO YOUR BROTHER-- OR TO THE MAN HE STOLE IT
METH PREFACE(R52)	AND DOCKED TAILS, PRACTISED BY DOG FANCIERS AND	HORSE	BREEDERS ON MANY GENERATIONS OF THE UNFORTUNATE
JOAN 5 (117)	ARMY. THE DAY AFTER SHE HAS BEEN DRAGGED FROM HER	HORSE	BY A GODDAM OR A BURGUNDIAN, AND HE IS NOT STRUCK
3PLA PREFACE(R31)	MAN AS THE YAHOO, SHOCKING HIS SUPERIOR THE	HORSE	BY HIS EVERY ACTION. STRINDBERG, THE ONLY GENUINELY
BULL III (142)	TELL A RAISONABLE LIE WHEN YOURE ABOUT IT? WHAT	HORSE	CAN GO FORTY MILE AN HOUR? /HODSON/ ORSE! WY, YOU
SUPR HANDBOK(219)	IMPARTIAL JUDGMENT AND PERFECT KNOWLEDGE. IF A	HORSE	COULD WAIT AS LONG FOR ITS SHOES AND WOULD PAY FOR
POSN (440)	BEAR TO SEE IT IN THE LIGHT. YOUR BROTHER'S	HORSE	DID THE SAME, AS ANY SENSIBLE HORSE WOULD. INSTEAD OF
DEST (187)	WON THE BATTLE OF LODI? I'LL TELL YOU. MY	HORSE	DID. /NAPOLEON/ (RISING) YOUR FOLLY IS CARRYING YOU
SUPR HANDBOK(206)	PUT HIS MASTER TO THE EXPENSE OF BUYING A NEW	HORSE	EVERY SECOND DAY; FOR YOU CANNOT WORK A HORSE TO DEATH
DOCT I (101)	PEOPLE TO ST MORITZ OR TO EGYPT, OR RECOMMEND	HORSE	EXERCISE OR MOTORING OR CHAMPAGNE JELLY OR COMPLETE
POSN (461)	VERY WELL, THEN. IN MY OPINION, TO COMMANDEER A	HORSE	FOR THE PURPOSE OF GETTING A DYING CHILD TO A DOCTOR
POSN (458)	(TO THE WOMAN) WHAT CALL HAD YOU TO TAKE THE	HORSE	FROM ELDER DANIEL'S STABLE TO FIND A DOCTOR? THERES A
POSN (438)	PLEASE GOD I'LL GET THE WHEREABOUTS OF THE	HORSE	FROM HIM IF YOULL BE SO GOOD AS TO CLEAR OUT FROM
POSN (453)	BEAR WITNESS ALL THAT I HAD A RIGHT TO TAKE A	HORSE	FROM HIM WITHOUT STEALING TO MAKE UP FOR WHAT HE
APPL I (200)	ONLY DISGUSTED HIM. HE WOULDNT LOOK AT A	HORSE	GRAZING IN A FIELD; BUT PUT SPLENDID TRAPPINGS ON IT
PRES (141)	FORTH. GET A GUARD OF HONOR-- SOMETHING SHOWY--	HORSE	GUARDS OR SOMETHING OF THAT SORT; AND CALL ON THE OLD
ROCK I (194)	HIS PAPERS). /HILDA/ TRAFALGAR SQUARE'S FULL. THE	HORSE	GUARDS PARADE IS FULL. THE MALL IS FULL ALL THE WAY
ROCK I (194)	TO THE COMMISSIONER OF WOODS AND FORESTS. THE	HORSE	GUARDS PARADE IS RESERVED FOR THE MILITARY. THE MALL
ROCK II (294)	THE SIDE GATE: AND LET THEM THROUGH INTO THE	HORSE	GUARDS PARADE. THEY ARE TRYING TO SING. /SIR ARTHUR/
POSN (453)	OF MY OWN KNOWLEDGE. I ONLY ARGUE THAT IF THE	HORSE	HAD BEEN WORTH ITS KEEP, YOU WOULDNT HAVE LENT IT TO
LADY PREFACE(220)	APPRECIATE IT, " IT IS A VICE IN HER EARS WHICH	HORSE	HAIRS, AND CATS' GUTS, AND THE VOICE OF UNPAVED EUNUCH
SIM II (84)	I FEEL LIKE THE LEADER OF A CAVALRY CHARGE WHOSE	HORSE	HAS BEEN SHOT THROUGH THE HEAD AND DROPPED DEAD UNDER
6CAL (105)	WITH HER DISTAFF. THE GREY MARE IS THE BETTER	HORSE	HERE. DO YOUR WORST, DAME: I LIKE YOUR SPUNK BETTER
POSN (463)	GAIN? OR AM I A SNIVELLING CRY-BABY THAT LET A	HORSE	HIS LIFE DEPENDED ON BE TOOK FROM HIM BY A WOMAN, AND
POSN (455)	OF GETTING IT BACK, I WOULD. BUT IF I HAD THAT	HORSE	I SHOULDNT BE HERE. AS I HOPE TO BE SAVED, SHERIFF--
FABL PREFACE(75)	EVERYWHERE. NOT EVEN ANTHROPOMORPHIC IDOLS BUT	HORSE	IDOLS, CAT IDOLS, ELEPHANT IDOLS AND WHAT NOT? THE
DEST (181)	I'LL GO AFTER HIM, GENERAL: I'LL FIND THAT	HORSE	IF IT'S ALIVE ANYWHERE IN ITALY. AND I SHANT FORGET
POSN (437)	SACK ALSO). /JESSIE/ IT CANT HAVE BEEN MUCH OF A	HORSE	IF THEY CAUGHT HIM WITH TWO HOURS START. /ELDER
JOAN 6 (128)	MAGIC WELLS. SOME OF THEM WOULD STEAL THE POPE'S	HORSE	IF THEY GOT THE CHANCE. HERESY, GENTLEMEN, HERESY IS
POSN (452)	/THE SHERIFF/ HOW DO YOU KNOW IT WAS A ROTTEN	HORSE	IF YOU DIDNT STEAL IT? /BLANCO/ I DONT KNOW OF MY OWN
POSN (451)	DONT LIKE THIS JURY, HE SHOULD HAVE STOLE A	HORSE	IN ANOTHER TOWN; FOR THIS IS ALL THE JURY HE'LL GET
DEST (158)	ON THIS SERVICE AS A HARD RIDER WITH THE FASTEST	HORSE	IN THE CAMP. YOU ARRIVE A HUNDRED MINUTES LATE, ON
SUPR I (14)	OF KEEPING A CARRIAGE, ASHAMED OF KEEPING ONE	HORSE	INSTEAD OF TWO AND A GROOM-GARDENER INSTEAD OF A
DEVL EPILOG (79)	HIMSELF FOR HIS OFFICERS WHEN HE INTRODUCED LIGHT	HORSE	INTO THE ENGLISH ARMY, HIS OPINION THAT ENGLISH
O'FL SD(205)	A NOTE OF ALARM AND FLIES AWAY. THE TRAMP OF A	HORSE	IS HEARD. /A GENTLEMAN'S VOICE/ TIM! HI! TIM! (HE
O'FL (205)	YOUR HONOR. YUP THERE. GWAN NOW. GWAN. (THE	HORSE	IS LED AWAY). GENERAL SIR PEARCE MADIGAN, AN ELDERLY
JOAN EPILOG (164)	POINT OUT ON BEHALF OF THE CHURCH THAT THE MAID'S	HORSE	IS NO GREATER OBSTRUCTION TO TRAFFIC THAN ANY OTHER
3PLA PREFACE(R9)	OF A PERSIAN CAT AND THE LABOR OF A COCKNEY CAB	HORSE	IS NOT GREATER THAN THE DIFFERENCE BETWEEN THE
SIM II (84)	AND DROPPED DEAD UNDER HIM. WELL, A DEAD HOBBY	HORSE	IS NOT THE END OF THE WORLD. REMEMBER: WE ARE IN THE
DEST (184)	COMES BACK BY THE OUTER DOOR. /GIUSEPPE/ THE	HORSE	IS READY, LIEUTENANT. /LIEUTENANT/ I'M NOT GOING JUST
POSN (461)	PROVIDED, AS IN THE PRESENT CASE, THAT THE	HORSE	IS RETURNED SAFE AND SOUND. I RULE THAT THERE HAS BEEN
POSN (461)	IF THE SHERIFF IS SATISFIED AND THE OWNER OF THE	HORSE	IS SATISFIED, THERES NO MORE TO BE SAID. I HAVE HAD TO
POSN (436)	THE SHERIFF? /BABSY/ YOU ARE. WAITLE YOUR OWN	HORSE	IS STOLEN, AND YOULL KNOW BETTER. I HAD AN UNCLE THAT
POSN (436)	/BABSY/ THERE! YOU HEAR THAT? I SAY STEALING A	HORSE	IS TEN TIMES WORSE THAN KILLING A MAN. AND IF THE
DEST (187)	WITH CONVICTION, AS HE RISES FROM THE COUCH) THAT	HORSE	IS THE TRUE CONQUEROR OF THE AUSTRIANS. /NAPOLEON/ (
DEVL II (47)	THERE THAT I'LL GIVE HIM A SILVER DOLLAR IF THE	HORSE	IS WAITING FOR ME WHEN I COME, AND THAT I AM CLOSE ON
JOAN EPILOG (164)	/JOAN/ EH! I AM GLAD THEY HAVE NOT FORGOTTEN MY	HORSE	. A VISION OF THE STATUE BEFORE RHEIMS CATHEDRAL
JOAN 6 (128)	/COURCELLES/ YES, IF IT WERE AN ORDINARY	HORSE	. BUT THE BISHOP'S HORSE! HOW CAN SHE BE ACQUITTED
POSN (436)	IN THE SAGE BRUSH BECAUSE A NEGRO STOLE HIS	HORSE	. BUT THEY CAUGHT HIM AND BURNED HIM; AND SERVE HIM
JOAN PREFACE(26)	GREY MARE IS AS LIKELY AS NOT TO BE THE BETTER	HORSE	. BUT THIS EXPLANATION DOES NOT CONVINCE ME. I CANNOT
JOAN 5 (116)	RANSOM WITH THE MAN THAT HAS POKED THEM OFF THEIR	HORSE	. CANT YOU SEE THAT ALL THE LIKE OF THAT IS GONE BY
POSN (461)	OF YOUNG STRAPPER. I AM ALSO THE OWNER OF THE	HORSE	. DOES ANY MAN SAY I AM NOT? (SILENCE). VERY WELL,
POSN (436)	AS MUCH AS STOLE A SADDLE OR BRIDLE, MUCH LESS A	HORSE	. ELDER DANIELS COMES IN. /ELDER DANIELS/ SORRY TO
POSN (458)	MY ANGEL. YOU GOT IT FROM THE MAN THAT STOLE THE	HORSE	. HE GAVE IT TO YOU BECAUSE HE WAS A SOFTY AND WENT TO
POSN (440)	HIM. WELL, YOU FOUND ME; BUT YOU DIDNT FIND THE	HORSE	. IF I HAD TOOK THE HORSE, I'D HAVE BEEN ON THE HORSE.
POSN (448)	THE INTERRUPTION)-- AND YOU FOUND A MAN WITHOUT A	HORSE	. IS A MAN ON A HORSE THE SAME AS A MAN ON FOOT?
POSN (457)	HOLD HARD, GEORGE. (AT THE DOOR) THEYVE GOT THE	HORSE	. (HE COMES IN, FOLLOWED BY WAGGONER JO, AN ELDERLY
HART I (77)	NOTHING WILL KILL ADDY: SHE IS AS STRONG AS A	HORSE	. (RELEASING HIM) NOW I AM GOING OFF TO FASCINATE
2TRU II (78)	FAR OFF? /SERGEANT FIELDING/ (INVISIBLE) FORTY	HORSE	. NINE HUNDRED YARDS, ABOUT, I MAKE IT. /MEEK/ RIFLES
POSN (459)	US A WAY OUT HERE. TWO WOMEN SAW BLANCO WITH A	HORSE	. ONE HAS A DELICACY ABOUT SAYING SO. THE OTHER WILL
POSN (437)	HAS HE DONE, MR DANIELS? /ELDER DANIELS/ STOLE A	HORSE	. /BABSY/ AND ARE WE TO BE TURNED OUT OF THE TOWN HALL
POSN (444)	MAN. IT WAS THE DEVIL TEMPTED YOU TO STEAL THE	HORSE	. /BLANCO/ NOT A BIT OF IT. NEITHER GOD NOR DEVIL
CLEO V (197)	/BRITANNUS/ CAESAR: I CLUNG TO THE TAIL OF YOUR	HORSE	. /CAESAR/ THESE ARE NOT THE DEEDS OF A SLAVE,
JOAN 6 (126)	FACT THAT THE MAID STOLE THE BISHOP OF SENLIS'S	HORSE	. /CAUCHON/ (KEEPING HIS TEMPER WITH DIFFICULTY) THIS
POSN (460)	TAKEN THE OATH. YOU SAW THE MAN THAT TOOK THE	HORSE	. /FEEMY/ I DID. AND HE WAS A LOW-DOWN ROTTEN DRUNKEN
POSN (435)	KILLING A MAN IS WORSE ANY DAY THAN STEALING A	HORSE	. /HANNAH/ (ELDERLY AND WISE) I DONT SAY IT'S RIGHT
JOAN EPILOG (164)	NO GREATER OBSTRUCTION TO TRAFFIC THAN ANY OTHER	HORSE	. /JOAN/ EH! I AM GLAD THEY HAVE NOT FORGOTTEN MY
DEST (181)	YOU FORGET, LIEUTENANT: HE HAS YOUR	HORSE	. /LIEUTENANT/ (STARTING) I FORGOT THAT. (
DEST (158)	EMOTION) YOU DONT KNOW HOW FOND I WAS OF THAT	HORSE	. /NAPOLEON/ (ANGRILY SARCASTIC) INDEED! (WITH
ARMS I (15)	HM! YOU SHOULD SEE THE POOR DEVIL PULLING AT HIS	HORSE	. /RAINA/ WHY SHOULD HE PULL AT HIS HORSE? /THE MAN/
JOAN 1 (66)	OF GOOD NEWS. /JOAN/ JACK WILL GO HALVES FOR THE	HORSE	. /ROBERT/ WELL! I (HE SITS, DEFLATED). /POULENGEY/
JOAN 1 (65)	FOR A HORSE? /POULENGEY/ I WILL PAY FOR THE	HORSE	. /ROBERT/ YOU WILL! /POULENGEY/ YES: I WILL BACK MY
POSN (455)	BETWEEN HIM AND ETERNITY, WHAT HE DONE WITH MY	HORSE	. /THE BOYS/ HEAR, HEAR! THATS RIGHT. THATS FAIR.
POSN (455)	SACRED EVEN TO THE ROTTENEST OF US, AND THAT IS A	HORSE	. /THE BOYS/ GOOD. WELL SAID, BLANCO. THATS STRAIGHT.
POSN (449)	YES, GOT EVERYTHING. /BLANCO/ EXCEPT THE	HORSE	. /THE SHERIFF/ WHATS THAT? AINT YOU GOT THE HORSE..
DEST (190)	THING AFTER I RODE AWAY ON THAT POOR LIEUTENANT'S	HORSE	. SO YOU SEE I KNOW WHATS IN THEM; AND YOU DONT.
POSN (453)	THIEF. BUT YOU HAVNT PROVED YET THAT I TOOK THE	HORSE	. STRAPPER KEMP: HAD I THE HORSE WHEN YOU TOOK ME OR
JOAN PREFACE(53)	WITH THE VICTORIOUS FRENCH LED BY JOAN ON A REAL	HORSE	. THE CORONATION WOULD ECLIPSE ALL PREVIOUS THEATRICAL
POSN (438)	AND OF COURSE HE DENIES THAT HE EVER HAD THE	HORSE	. THE SHERIFF'S BROTHER WANTED TO TIE HIM UP AND LASH
CLEO PRO2 (101)	KNOW BETTER. I WILL TAKE HER ON THE CRUPPER OF MY	HORSE	. WHEN WE SOLDIERS HAVE CARRIED HER OUT OF CAESAR'S
POSN (440)	IF I HAD TOOK THE HORSE, I'D HAVE BEEN ON THE	HORSE	. WOULD I HAVE TAKEN ALL THAT TIME TO GET TO WHERE I
DEVL I (22)	SECOND, THAT HE SHALL BE A GOOD FRIEND TO MY OLD	HORSE	JIM"-- (AGAIN SHAKING HIS HEAD) HE SHOULD HAVE
FANY PROLOG (265)	IS IT? BANNAL MAY NOT RIDE THE LITERARY HIGH	HORSE	LIKE TROTTER AND THE REST; BUT I'D TAKE HIS OPINION
SUPR HANDBOK(205)	COMPANY WHICH DISCOVERS ACTUARIALLY THAT THOUGH A	HORSE	MAY LIVE FROM 24 TO 40 YEARS, YET IT PAYS BETTER TO
POSN (453)	YOU? AND DID YOU SAY ONE WORD TO ME ABOUT THE	HORSE	NOT BELONGING TO YOU? /ELDER DANIELS/ WHY SHOULD I..
SUPR HANDBOK(178)	EATABLE APPLE; NOT FOR A SUPER-HORSE, BUT FOR A	HORSE	OF GREATER DRAUGHT OR VELOCITY. NEITHER IS IT OF ANY
HART III (131)	THIS. MY SHIP MADE A MAN OF ME; AND A SHIP IS THE	HORSE	OF THE SEA. /LADY UTTERWORD/ EXACTLY HOW HASTINGS
DOCT PREFACE(52)	CREDULOUS ABOUT THE COW, WOULD NOT HAVE THE	HORSE	ON ANY TERMS; AND TO THIS DAY THE LAW WHICH PRESCRIBES
POSN (455)	OR RUN LIKE A THIEF; AND WAS THERE ANY SIGN OF A	HORSE	ON ME OR NEAR ME? /STRAPPER/ YOU WERE LOOKING AT A
APPL I (230)	WHICH? YOU SAID THAT IF TWO MEN RODE THE SAME	HORSE	ONE OF THEM MUST RIDE BEHIND. I SAID WHICH? (
METH PREFACE(R71)	WOLVES COMBINE TO KILL A HORSE, THE DEATH OF THE	HORSE	ONLY SETS THEM FIGHTING ONE ANOTHER FOR THE CHOICEST
CAPT I (237)	WILL BE VICIOUS; SO WILL ALL THE MEN. IF EITHER	HORSE	OR MAN TRIES ANY OF HIS VICIOUSNESS ON ME, SO MUCH THE
ARMS I (14)	THE DEAD CERTAINTY THAT IF THE GUNS GO OFF NOT A	HORSE	OR MAN WILL EVER GET WITHIN FIFTY YARDS OF THE FIRE..
2TRU I (29)	BORN. /THE MONSTER/ SHE HAS THE CONSTITUTION OF A	HORSE	OR SHE'D HAVE DIED LIKE THE OTHERS. /THE ELDERLY LADY/
PRES (154)	DOWN. /MRS BANGER/ (PRODUCING AN XVIII CENTURY	HORSE	PISTOL) IS IT YOUR DUTY TO TAKE POSSESSION OF THIS

CURE	(233)	I CAN PLAY. /STREGA/ PARDON ME. I HAVE HEARD A	HORSE	PLAY THE HARMONIUM AT A MUSIC HALL. I CAN BELIEVE
GENV II	(59)	BURNT DOWN HIS RECTORY AND DUCKED HIM IN THE	HORSE	POND TO TEACH HIM A LITTLE BRITISH PATRIOTISM: HOW
2TRU III	(100)	YOU NOT BE CONTENT WITH A MOTOR CYCLE OF ORDINARY	HORSE	POWER? MUST YOU ALWAYS TRAVEL AT EIGHTY MILES AN
DEVL II	(49)	RETURNS. HE SWOOPS AT HER AT ONCE). WELL: IS THE	HORSE	READY? /ESSIE/ (BREATHLESS) IT WILL BE READY WHEN
JOAN 6	(128)	SHOCKED) MY LORD: DO YOU CALL THE BISHOP'S	HORSE	RUBBISH? /THE INQUISITOR/ (BLANDLY) MASTER DE
POSN	(448)	DRUNK TO TELL WHICH WAS THE MAN AND WHICH WAS THE	HORSE	-- /FEEMY/ (BREAKING IN) YOU LIE. I WASNT DRUNK-- AT
POSN	(437)	SACK) I AM SORRY TO SAY IT WAS THE SHERIFF'S	HORSE	-- THE ONE HE LOANED TO YOUNG STRAPPER. STRAPPER
CAPT II	(268)	RETAINER) OSMAN: BE SURE YOU CHOOSE ME A GOOD	HORSE	; AND GET A NICE STRONG CAMEL FOR MY LUGGAGE. OSMAN,
POSN	(445)	BEEN SAFE AND FIFTY MILES AWAY BY NOW WITH THAT	HORSE	; AND HERE I AM WAITING TO BE HUNG UP AND FILLED WITH
JOAN 6	(136)	WOULD NEVER HAVE PULLED ME BACKWARDS OFF MY	HORSE	; AND I SHOULD NOT HAVE BEEN HERE. /THE CHAPLAIN/ IF
CAPT III	(286)	CHIEF; BUT CAPTAIN BRASSBOUND CRUELLY SHOT HIS	HORSE	; AND THE CHIEF SHOT THE COUNT; AND THEN-- /KEARNEY/
CAPT NOTES	(302)	DESIRABLE PLACE TO LIVE IN, HE TOOK SHIP AND	HORSE	; CHANGED THE HAT FOR A TURBAN; AND MADE STRAIGHT FOR
APPL II	(264)	/THE QUEEN/ NO: IT IS NOT THE CLIMATE. IT IS THE	HORSE	SHOW. THE KING RISES VERY THOUGHTFULLY; AND VANHATTAN
PYGM II	(240)	THERE IS. WOOLLY TOWELS, THERE IS; AND A TOWEL	HORSE	SO HOT, IT BURNS YOUR FINGERS. SOFT BRUSHES TO SCRUB
POSN	(442)	PERHAPS I'D RATHER BE HANGED FOR STEALING A	HORSE	THAN LET OFF FOR A DAMNED PIECE OF SENTIMENTALITY.
BULL III	(131)	EARS) OR WORKING HIM HARDER THAN YOUD WORK A	HORSE	THAT COST YOU FIFTY GUINEAS. /DORAN/ HWAT! ! !
POSN	(458)	YOU. WHO ARE YOU? AND WHAT ARE YOU DOING WITH A	HORSE	THAT DOESNT BELONG TO YOU? /THE WOMAN/ I TOOK IT TO
DEST	(187)	WAS THE FIRST MAN TO CROSS; AND I KNOW. IT WAS MY	HORSE	THAT FOUND IT. (WITH CONVICTION, AS HE RISES FROM THE
HART II	(115)	/CAPTAIN SHOTOVER/ WHY DO HORSE-THIEVES PREFER A	HORSE	THAT IS BROKEN-IN TO ONE THAT IS WILD? /ELLIE/ (WITH
MTH3	(97)	YOUR STEADFAST REFUSAL TO BE GOVERNED AT ALL. A	HORSE	THAT KICKS EVERYONE WHO TRIES TO HARNESS AND GUIDE HIM
POSN	(440)	AND TELL THEM ABOUT YOUR BIG BROTHER'S LITTLE	HORSE	THAT SOME WICKED MAN STOLE. GO AND CRY IN YOUR MAMMY'S
POSN	(448)	YOU FOUND A MAN WITHOUT A HORSE. IS A MAN ON A	HORSE	THE SAME AS A MAN ON FOOT? YAH! TAKE YOUR WITNESS
DEVL II	(47)	TELL THEM TO SADDLE THE FASTEST AND STRONGEST	HORSE	THEY HAVE (JUDITH RISES BREATHLESS, AND STARES AT HIM
GETT PREFACE	(188)	WAS SOMETHING MORE HATEFUL TO A HUSBAND THAN A	HORSE	THIEF: TO WIT, A WIFE THIEF, AND SOMETHING MORE
POSN	(456)	NOW, ON YOUR OATH, DID YOU SEE THE PRISONER ON MY	HORSE	THIS MORNING ON THE ROAD TO PONY HARBOR? /FEEMY/ ON
POSN	(447)	/FEEMY/ THATS THE LITTLE LOT THAT WAS ON YOUR	HORSE	THIS MORNING, STRAPPER. NOT A DOUBT OF IT. /BLANCO/ (
POSN	(440)	ALL THAT TIME TO GET TO WHERE I DID IF I'D A	HORSE	TO CARRY ME? /STRAPPER/ I DONT BELIEVE YOU STARTED
SUPR HANDBOK	(206)	NEW HORSE EVERY SECOND DAY; FOR YOU CANNOT WORK A	HORSE	TO DEATH AND THEN PICK UP ANOTHER ONE FOR NOTHING, AS
POSN	(459)	WOULD NEVER HAVE BEEN SO CRUEL AS TO SEND ME THE	HORSE	TO DISAPPOINT ME LIKE THAT. /BLANCO/ JUST WHAT HE
ARMS I	SD(13)	THE MAN, ALL NERVES, SHIES LIKE A FRIGHTENED	HORSE	TO THE OTHER SIDE OF THE ROOM. /THE MAN/ (IRRITABLY)
O'FL	(205)	YOUR HONOR. /THE GENTLEMAN'S VOICE/ TAKE THIS	HORSE	TO THE STABLES, WILL YOU? /A LABORER'S VOICE/ RIGHT,
BARB II	(284)	DAN ME. (HE SITS DOWN MOODILY ON THE EDGE OF THE	HORSE	TROUGH). /SHIRLEY/ YOU AINT GOIN. I THOUGHT NOT. (HE
POSN	(452)	SON. /STRAPPER/ YOURE ACCOUNTABLE TO ME FOR THE	HORSE	UNTIL YOU CLEAR YOURSELF, ELDER: REMEMBER THAT.
POSN	(452)	MY HOUSE. EVERYBODY KNOWS THAT IN THE MORNING THE	HORSE	WAS GONE AND YOU WERE GONE. /BLANCO/ (IN A FORENSIC
POSN	(458)	WITH THE DEAD BODY ON HER LAP, STUPID-LIKE. THE	HORSE	WAS GRAZIN ON THE OTHER SIDE O THE ROAD. /THE SHERIFF/
POSN	(437)	SHOVING US OUT LIKE THAT! /HANNAH/ WHOSE	HORSE	WAS IT, MR DANIELS? /ELDER DANIELS/ (RETURNING TO
POSN	(448)	LIAR. /BLANCO/ (TO STRAPPER) SHE SAW A MAN ON A	HORSE	WHEN SHE WAS TOO DRUNK TO TELL WHICH WAS THE MAN AND
POSN	(438)	GROUP) THE STRANGE THING IS THAT HE WASNT ON THE	HORSE	WHEN THEY TOOK HIM. HE WAS WALKING; AND OF COURSE HE
POSN	(453)	THAT I TOOK THE HORSE. STRAPPER KEMP: HAD I THE	HORSE	WHEN YOU TOOK ME OR HAD I NOT? /STRAPPER/ NO, NOR YOU
APPL I	(230)	IS HELD RESPONSIBLE. A DEMAGOGUE MAY STEAL A	HORSE	WHERE A KING DARE NOT LOOK OVER A HEDGE. /LYSISTRATA/
MILL PREFACE	(119)	AND AMIABLE INTO THE BARGAIN, COULD STEAL A	HORSE	WHERE A SOCIALIST DARE NOT LOOK OVER A HEDGE. THE
JOAN 1	(61)	MYSELF. /JOAN/ (BUSILY) PLEASE DO, SQUIRE. THE	HORSE	WILL COST SIXTEEN FRANCS. IT IS A GOOD DEAL OF MONEY;
LION II	(140)	TIME I EVER HIT A MAN WAS WHEN HE LASHED AN OLD	HORSE	WITH A WHIP. IT WAS TERRIBLE: I DANCED ON HIS FACE
POSN	(435)	GOOD LOOKS) I SAY THAT A MAN THAT WOULD STEAL A	HORSE	WOULD DO ANYTHING. /LOTTIE/ (A SENTIMENTAL GIRL, NEAT
POSN	(440)	BROTHER'S HORSE DID THE SAME, AS ANY SENSIBLE	HORSE	WOULD. INSTEAD OF GOING TO LOOK FOR THE HORSE, YOU
POSN	(441)	TIL YOU CAN FIND A WITNESS THAT SAW ME WITH THAT	HORSE	YOU CANT TOUCH ME; AND YOU KNOW IT. /STRAPPER/ IS THAT
POSN	(452)	I SAY NOTHING; EXCEPT THAT IT WAS THE ROTTENEST	HORSE	YOU EVER TRIED TO SELL. /THE SHERIFF/ HOW DO YOU KNOW
APPL I	(214)	WHEN CROSSING A STREAM. /NICOBAR/ WHY NOT, IF THE	HORSE	YOU HAVE GOT IS SUBJECT TO HYSTERICS? /BOANERGES/ NOT
CAPT NOTES	(301)	MYSTERY TO A SEDENTARY PERSON LIKE MYSELF. THE	HORSE	, A DANGEROUS ANIMAL WHOM, WHEN I CANNOT AVOID, I
DEST	(159)	IT? WHEN I TRUSTED HIM WITH MY PISTOLS, AND MY	HORSE	, AND MY DESPATCHES-- /NAPOLEON/ WHAT THE DEVIL DID
BUOY II	(23)	CAN ALSO HUNT IF SOMEBODY WILL FETCH ME A SADDLED	HORSE	, AND STABLE IT FOR ME AND TAKE IT OFF MY HANDS AGAIN
JOAN 6	(128)	ALLEGES THAT SHE PAID HANDSOMELY FOR THE BISHOP'S	HORSE	, AND THAT IF HE DID NOT GET THE MONEY THE FAULT WAS
HART PREFACE	(27)	AS A YAHOO REBUKED BY THE SUPERIOR VIRTUE OF THE	HORSE	, AND WELLINGTON DECLARING THAT THE BRITISH CAN BEHAVE
POSN	(459)	THAT HE'D SWING FOR IT. AND THEN HE GAVE ME THE	HORSE	, AND WENT AWAY CRYING AND LAUGHING AND SINGING
POSN	(441)	BE HANGED BECAUSE YOUVE LOST YOUR BIG BROTHER'S	HORSE	, AND YOULL WANT TO KILL SOMEBODY TO RELIEVE YOUR
POSN	(440)	(FURIOUS) YOU JOUNCE ME ANY MORE ABOUT THAT	HORSE	, BLANCO POSNET; AND I'LL-- I'LL-- /BLANCO/ YOULL
POSN	(447)	/BLANCO/ A WOMAN! OH LORD! YOU SAW ME ON A	HORSE	, DID YOU? /FEEMY/ YES, I DID. /BLANCO/ GOT UP EARLY
SUPR HANDBOK	(210)	EXAMINATION MARKS ON A MAN AS HARNESS IS PUT ON A	HORSE	, ERMINE ON A JUDGE, PIPECLAY ON A SOLDIER, OR A WIG
POSN	(452)	AS WHAT HE SAYS ABOUT ME IS CONCERNED. AS TO THE	HORSE	, I SAY NOTHING; EXCEPT THAT IT WAS THE ROTTENEST
POSN	(440)	BUT YOU DIDNT FIND THE HORSE. IF I HAD TOOK THE	HORSE	, I'D HAVE BEEN ON THE HORSE. WOULD I HAVE TAKEN ALL
APPL I	(230)	IT FOLLOW? /PROTEUS/ IF TWO MEN RIDE THE SAME	HORSE	, ONE MUST RIDE BEHIND. /LYSISTRATA/ WHICH? /PROTEUS/
FABL PREFACE	(63)	AND THAT WHOEVER CAN ADD TWO AND TWO, BET ON A	HORSE	, OR PLAY WHIST OR BRIDGE, CAN TAKE IN THE TENSOR
POSN	(455)	THATS STRAIGHT. /BLANCO/ YOU HAVE A RIGHT TO YOUR	HORSE	, SHERIFF; AND IF I COULD PUT YOU IN THE WAY OF
METH PREFACE	(R71)	WE DO NOT YET KNOW. WHEN WOLVES COMBINE TO KILL A	HORSE	, THE DEATH OF THE HORSE ONLY SETS THEM FIGHTING ONE
DEST	(153)	GRINNING) THERE IS NOTHING BUT YOUR EXCELLENCY'S	HORSE	, THE SENTINEL, THE LADY UPSTAIRS, AND MY WIFE.
CAPT II	(251)	IT TOO, JOHNNY, DIDNT YOU? /BRASSBOUND/ TAKE	HORSE	, THEN; AND RIDE FAST TO YOUR MASTER THE SHEIKH SIDI
POSN	(447)	I STAYED UP LATE ON A SPREE. /BLANCO/ I WAS ON A	HORSE	, WAS I? /FEEMY/ YES YOU WERE; AND IF YOU DENY IT
DOCT PREFACE	(52)	WHICH HAD FORMERLY MISLED HIM TO A DISEASE OF THE	HORSE	, WHICH, PERHAPS BECAUSE WE DO NOT DRINK ITS MILK AND
SUPR HANDBOK	(206)	LIVE AND LET LIVE UP TO A CERTAIN POINT. EVEN THE	HORSE	, WITH HIS DOCKED TAIL AND BITTED JAW, FINDS HIS
POSN	(440)	HORSE WOULD. INSTEAD OF GOING TO LOOK FOR THE	HORSE	, YOU WENT LOOKING FOR ME. THAT WAS A ROTTEN THING TO
LADY PREFACE	(233)	HE WOULD HAVE SAID THAT RICHARD DIED, AND CRIED A	HORSE	! A HORSE! HE BURBAGE CRIED" WAS THE FATHER OF NINE
POSN	(461)	MAY I BE STRUCK DEAD IF I EVER SAW HIM WITH THE	HORSE	! EVERYBODY DRAWS A LONG BREATH. DEAD SILENCE.
LADY PREFACE	(233)	SAID THAT RICHARD DIED, AND CRIED A HORSE! A	HORSE	! HE BURBAGE CRIED" WAS THE FATHER OF NINE
CLEO IV	(171)	HAS BEEN JUST AS GOOD TO HIM. NAY, ASK HIS VERY	HORSE	! HIS KINDNESS IS NOT FOR ANYTHING IN ME: IT IS IN
JOAN 6	(128)	IF IT WERE AN ORDINARY HORSE. BUT THE BISHOP'S	HORSE	! HOW CAN SHE BE ACQUITTED FOR THAT? (HE SITS DOWN
BARB II	(281)	GOOD WORKER. AND SENT TO THE KNACKERS LIKE AN OLD	HORSE	! /BARBARA/ NO MATTER: IF YOU DID YOUR PART GOD WILL
POSN	(457)	PRIVATELY TO HIM). /THE BOYS/ WHAT! NO! GOT THE	HORSE	! SHERIFF'S HORSE! WHO TOOK IT, THEN? WHERE? GET
ARMS III	(61)	YOU MY BEST HORSE? /BLUNTSCHLI/ NO: DAMN YOUR	HORSE	! THANK YOU ALL THE SAME, MY DEAR FELLOW. (RAINA
POSN	(457)	/THE BOYS/ WHAT! NO! GOT THE HORSE! SHERIFF'S	HORSE	! WHO TOOK IT, THEN? WHERE? GET OUT. YES IT IS.

HORSEBACK

SUPR III	(107)	RUNS AWAY, WHEN THE OTHERS CHASE THE FUGITIVES ON	HORSEBACK	AND CUT THEM TO PIECES AS THEY FLY. AND THIS, THE
BARB PREFACE	(218)	THAT THOUGH TO ROB AND PILL WITH YOUR OWN HAND ON	HORSEBACK	AND IN STEEL COAT MAY HAVE BEEN A GOOD LIFE, TO
HART PREFACE	(24)	SORT OF COURAGE: NEITHER HEARTBREAK HOUSE NOR	HORSEBACK	HALL HAD BRED IT, MUCH LESS THE SUBURBS. WHEN
HART PREFACE	(8)	THAN FALSE DOCTRINE; BUT HEARTBREAK HOUSE AND	HORSEBACK	HALL UNFORTUNATELY SUFFERED FROM BOTH. FOR HALF A
HART PREFACE	(4)	AND THEIR LIKE, IT WAS A VERITABLE CAPUA.	HORSEBACK	HALL, BUT WHERE WERE OUR FRONT BENCHERS TO NEST IF
HART PREFACE	(28)	THEY DO NOT INCLUDE EITHER HEARTBREAK HOUSE OR	HORSEBACK	HALL. PLAGUE ON BOTH YOUR HOUSES! MEANWHILE THE
HART PREFACE	(3)	HEARTBREAK HOUSE AND	HORSEBACK	HALL, WHERE HEARTBREAK HOUSE STANDS. HEARTBREAK
HART PREFACE	(4)	HERE? THE ALTERNATIVE TO HEARTBREAK HOUSE WAS	HORSEBACK	HALL, CONSISTING OF A PRISON FOR HORSES WITH AN
GENV IV	(119)	OF THE BEGGAR ON HORSEBACK. WE TWO ARE BEGGARS ON	HORSEBACK	. FOR THE CREDIT OF LEADERSHIP LET US RIDE
BUOY III	(32)	BE RICH AND POOR. THE CHANCELLOR IS A BEGGAR ON	HORSEBACK	. HE WILL BE SENT BACK TO THE GUTTER AT THE NEXT
GENV IV	(119)	INSPIRATION AND THE MADNESS OF THE BEGGAR ON	HORSEBACK	. WE TWO ARE BEGGARS ON HORSEBACK. FOR THE CREDIT
MILL PREFACE	(127)	AN AUTOCRAT AND AT ONCE YOU HAVE THE BEGGAR ON	HORSEBACK	RIDING TO THE DEVIL. EVEN WHEN, AS THE SON OF HIS
MILL I	(139)	RUIN HIM. TO DESTROY HIM. TO MAKE HIM A BEGGAR ON	HORSEBACK	SO THAT HE MAY RIDE TO THE DEVIL. MONEY GOES TO
BULL PREFACE	(51)	YEAR BEFORE, ACCOMPANIED BY ONE OTHER OFFICER ON	HORSEBACK	, AND ALSO BY A DRAGOMAN AND AN OMBASHI, OR POLICE
CLEO PRO1	(90)	LITTLENESS, THEN THE OLD ROME, LIKE THE BEGGAR ON	HORSEBACK	, PRESUMED ON THE FAVOR OF THE GODS, AND SAID, "
ARMS III	(61)	DRILLING-GROUND ON THE KLISSOURA ROAD, ALONE, ON	HORSEBACK	, WITH MY SABRE. DO YOU UNDERSTAND? /BLUNTSCHLI/
JOAN 4	(103)	/WARWICK/ WHAT CAN YOU EXPECT? A BEGGAR ON	HORSEBACK	! HER HEAD IS TURNED. /CAUCHON/ WHO HAS TURNED

HORSEBACK'S

ARMS III	(61)	THE NEXT SENTENCE). I SHALL FIGHT YOU ON FOOT.	HORSEBACK'S	TOO DANGEROUS: I DONT WANT TO KILL YOU IF I CAN

HORSEBOYS

6CAL	(101)	MAN OF YOU, IN YOUR SHIRTS, TO MAKE MIRTH FOR MY	HORSEBOYS	AND THEIR TRULLS. /THE QUEEN/ OH NO-- /THE KING/ (

HORSEBREAKER

BASH II,1,	(108)	RELIGION IS OUTWORN, AND THAT THE PAMPA TO THE	HORSEBREAKER	OPES NEW CAREERS. BID THE PROFESSOR QUIT HIS

		HORSEBREAKERS	
HART PREFACE(5)	GARDEN OF KLINGSOR; BUT SOMETIMES ONE CAME UPON	HORSEBREAKERS	AND HEARTBREAKERS WHO COULD MAKE THE BEST OF
		HORSEBREEDER	
GLIM (182)	THE TROUBLE: MOST OF THEM ARE SCREWS. WELL, THE	HORSEBREEDER	GETS RID OF HIS SCREWS FOR WHAT THEY WILL
		HORSEDEALER	
DEVL I (18)	FOR THE SOFA). AND NOW, WHERE IS THAT UPRIGHT	HORSEDEALER	UNCLE TITUS? UNCLE TITUS: COME FORTH. (HE
DEVL I (26)	A MAN ABLE TO TAKE CARE OF HIMSELF) OR AN UPRIGHT	HORSEDEALER	! (UNCLE TITUS SNARLS AT HIM IN RAGE AND
		HORSEHAIR	
BULL III SD(117)	HAS A MAHOGANY FRAME AND IS UPHOLSTERED IN BLACK	HORSEHAIR	, LARRY RISES AND GOES OFF THROUGH THE SHRUBBERY
DEVL I SD(4)	THE DOOR AND THE CORNER, A SHAMELESSLY UGLY BLACK	HORSEHAIR	SOFA STANDS AGAINST THE WALL. AN INSPECTION OF ITS
NEVR IV SD(286)	AND OILED, AND EYEBROWS LIKE EARLY VICTORIAN	HORSEHAIR	UPHOLSTERY. PHYSICALLY AND SPIRITUALLY A COARSENED
BULL IV SD(145)	CORNER BEHIND THEM IS THE SOFA, OF MAHOGANY AND	HORSEHAIR	, MADE UP AS A BED FOR BROADBENT. AGAINST THE WALL
		HORSELAUGH	
3PLA PREFACE(R32)	COMEDY ITS CRITICISM, OR EVEN BAWDRY ITS	HORSELAUGH	AT THE EXPENSE OF SEXUAL INFATUATION, IF IT MUST;
		HORSEMAN	
CAPT III (288)	TODD, THE DEMON BARBER OF LONDON; THE SKELETON	HORSEMAN	-- /DRINKWATER/ (RUSHING FORWARD IN PAINFUL ALARM
		HORSEMEN	
CLEO II (119)	A STRANGER ONE MARK ANTONY A ROMAN CAPTAIN OF	HORSEMEN	ACROSS THE SANDS OF THE DESERT AND HE SET MY FATHER
CYMB V (140)	BID ALL MAKE FOR THE ROCKS; FOR THERE THEIR	HORSEMEN	CANNOT COME". I TOOK HIS COUNSEL; AND HERE I AM.
CLEO II (120)	TELL THE KING, ACHILLAS, HOW MANY SOLDIERS AND	HORSEMEN	FOLLOW THE ROMAN? /THEODOTUS/ LET THE KING'S
CLEO PRO2 (100)	THE ROMANS WHO HAVE NO CHARIOTS, SENT A CLOUD OF	HORSEMEN	IN PURSUIT, AND SLEW MULTITUDES. THEN OUR HIGH
CLEO II (120)	THREE THOUSAND SOLDIERS AND SCARCE A THOUSAND	HORSEMEN	. THE COURT BREAKS INTO DERISIVE LAUGHTER; AND A
CYMB V (139)	THEY SHOOT TOGETHER AND ADVANCE IN STEP: THEIR	HORSEMEN	TROT IN ORDER TO THE CHARGE AND THEN LET LOOSE TH'
CLEO II (134)	STRONG ROUND ARMS, CAME OVER THE DESERT WITH MANY	HORSEMEN	, AND SLEW MY SISTER'S HUSBAND AND GAVE MY FATHER
CLEO II (134)	HE IS A GOD. /CAESAR/ HE IS A GREAT CAPTAIN OF	HORSEMEN	, AND SWIFTER OF FOOT THAN ANY OTHER ROMAN.
		HORSEPOND	
BULL I (79)	IF WE CALL YOU A BAILIFF, THEYLL DUCK YOU IN THE	HORSEPOND	. I HAVE A SECRETARY ALREADY; AND-- /TIM/ THEN
		HORSE-DEALING	
ARMS II (31)	AND HE OWED HIS FIRST STEP TO HIS KNOWLEDGE OF	HORSE-DEALING	. (WITH MOCK ENTHUSIASM) AH, HE WAS A
		HORSE-SHOE	
LION PREFACE(55)	IS HIS. BUT THE BLACKSMITH KNOWS THAT THE	HORSE-SHOE	DOES NOT BELONG SOLELY TO HIM, BUT TO HIS
LION PREFACE(55)	HAS MADE A HORSE-SHOE, AND THAT THEREFORE THE	HORSE-SHOE	IS HIS. BUT THE BLACKSMITH KNOWS THAT THE
LION PREFACE(55)	A CHILD IT SEEMS THAT THE BLACKSMITH HAS MADE A	HORSE-SHOE	, AND THAT THEREFORE THE HORSE-SHOE IS HIS. BUT
SUPR III SD(71)	SIERRA. LOOKING AT IT FROM THE WIDE END OF THE	HORSE-SHOE	, ONE SEES, A LITTLE TO THE RIGHT, IN THE FACE OF
		HORSE-THIEF	
POSN (437)	ARE WE TO BE TURNED OUT OF THE TOWN HALL FOR A	HORSE-THIEF	? AINT A STABLE GOOD ENOUGH FOR HIS RELIGION..
POSN (451)	SAY THAT THE MAN THAT IS NOT PREJUDICED AGAINST A	HORSE-THIEF	IS NOT FIT TO SIT ON A JURY IN THIS TOWN. /THE
POSN (439)	DEVILS, MORE LIKELY, AND TOO GOOD COMPANY FOR A	HORSE-THIEF	. /ALL/ HORSE-THIEF! HORSE-THIEF!
POSN (444)	LIKE A THIEF IN THE NIGHT-- AYE, LIKE A THIEF-- A	HORSE-THIEF	-- /ELDER DANIELS/ (SHOCKED) OH! /BLANCO/ (
POSN (446)	/FEEMY/ (FOLLOWING HIM) I'LL HANG YOU, YOU DIRTY	HORSE-THIEF	; OR NOT A MAN IN THIS CAMP WILL EVER GET A WORD
POSN (438)	IT'S NOT THE LAW. /BABSY/ LAW! WHAT RIGHT HAS A	HORSE-THIEF	TO ANY LAW? LAW IS THROWN AWAY ON A BRUTE LIKE
POSN (459)	COMMIT PERJURY. ON THE OTHER HAND, WE DONT WANT A	HORSE-THIEF	TO GET OFF THROUGH A LADY'S DELICACY. /THE
		HORSE-THIEF	
POSN (440)	/STRAPPER/ THEYRE SOUND ENOUGH TO HANG A	HORSE-THIEF	, ANYHOW. /BLANCO/ ANY FOOL CAN HANG THE WISEST
POSN (439)	AND TOO GOOD COMPANY FOR A HORSE-THIEF. /ALL/	HORSE-THIEF	! HORSE-THIEF! HORSE-THIEF! /BLANCO/ DO WOMEN
POSN (439)	COMPANY FOR A HORSE-THIEF. /ALL/ HORSE-THIEF!	HORSE-THIEF	! HORSE-THIEF! /BLANCO/ DO WOMEN MAKE THE LAW
POSN (438)	DOOR. /BABSY/ (SPITTING AT HIM AS HE PASSES HER)	HORSE-THIEF	! HORSE-THIEF! /OTHERS/ YOU WILL HANG FOR IT;
POSN (439)	A HORSE-THIEF. /ALL/ HORSE-THIEF! HORSE-THIEF!	HORSE-THIEF	! /BLANCO/ DO WOMEN MAKE THE LAW HERE, OR MEN?
POSN (438)	(SPITTING AT HIM AS HE PASSES HER) HORSE-THIEF!	HORSE-THIEF	! /OTHERS/ YOU WILL HANG FOR IT; DO YOU HEAR..
		HORSE-THIEVES	
POSN (436)	THE SHERIFF--? /JESSIE/ WHO'S TAKING THE PART OF	HORSE-THIEVES	AGAINST THE SHERIFF? /BABSY/ YOU ARE. WAITLE
POSN (436)	WELL! IF PEOPLE ARE GOING TO TAKE THE PART OF	HORSE-THIEVES	AGAINST THE SHERIFF--? /JESSIE/ WHO'S TAKING
POSN (451)	/BLANCO/ WHAT IS JUSTICE? /THE SHERIFF/ HANGING	HORSE-THIEVES	IS JUSTICE; SO NOW YOU KNOW. NOW THEN: WEVE
POSN (440)	AINT HE? /STRAPPER/ YES, HE IS. HE HANGS	HORSE-THIEVES	. /BLANCO/ (WITH CALM CONVICTION) HE'S A
POSN (448)	YOURE A WORSE DANGER TO A TOWN LIKE THIS THAN TEN	HORSE-THIEVES	. /FEEMY/ MR KEMP: WILL YOU STAND BY AND HEAR
HART II (115)	WOMEN'S HUSBANDS? /CAPTAIN SHOTOVER/ WHY DO	HORSE-THIEVES	PREFER A HORSE THAT IS BROKEN-IN TO ONE THAT
		HORSE-TROUGH	
BARB II (301)	THE SOVEREIGN ON THE DRUM, AND SITS DOWN ON THE	HORSE-TROUGH	. THE COIN FASCINATES SNOBBY PRICE, WHO TAKES
BARB II SD(273)	LEADING TO THE STREET ON THEIR LEFT, WITH A STONE	HORSE-TROUGH	JUST BEYOND IT, AND, ON THE RIGHT, A PENTHOUSE
		HORSE'S	
SUPR HANDBOOK(206)	THE MAN WHO, TO HIS OWN LOSS, WILL SHORTEN HIS	HORSE'S	LIFE IN MERE STINGINESS, WE HAVE THE TRAMWAY COMPANY
CLEO NOTES (203)	BURNT, ONE PART; OF VINE RAG BURNT, ONE PART; OF	HORSE'S	TEETH BURNT, ONE PART; OF BEAR'S GREASE ONE; OF
POSN (455)	FOR PLAYING THE HARP-- I KNOW NO MORE OF THAT	HORSE'S	WHEREABOUTS THAN YOU DO YOURSELF. /STRAPPER/ WHO DID
POSN (436)	WAS BORN CROOKED BECAUSE ITS MOTHER HAD TO DO A	HORSE'S	WORK THAT WAS STOLEN. /BABSY/ THERE! YOU HEAR
		HORSES	
JOAN 3 (91)	AYE, LAD; BUT YOU CANNOT FIGHT STONE WALLS WITH	HORSES	: YOU MUST HAVE GUNS, AND MUCH BIGGER GUNS TOO.
SIM II (71)	VIALS FULL OF THE WRATH OF GOD? /JANGA/ THE FOUR	HORSES	? /KANCHIN/ THE TWO WITNESSES? /THE ANGEL/ MY GOOD
ARMS III (72)	TWENTY HORSES. /BLUNTSCHLI/ BUT WHO WANTS TWENTY	HORSES	? WE'RE NOT GOING TO KEEP A CIRCUS. /CATHERINE/ (
BARB PREFACE(238)	WOUNDING NINETYNINE. AND OF ALL THESE, THE	HORSES	ALONE ARE INNOCENT OF THE GUILT HE IS AVENGING: HAD
METH PREFACE(R29)	PEDIGREE MEN COUNTED PEDIGREE DOGS AND PEDIGREE	HORSES	AMONG THEIR MOST CHERISHED POSSESSIONS, FAR FROM
ANNA (299)	GREAT TRUTHS BEGIN AS BLASPHEMIES. ALL THE KING'S	HORSES	AND ALL THE KING'S MEN CANNOT SET UP MY FATHER'S
MILL IV (210)	SWEPT AWAY SOONER OR LATER; AND ALL THE KING'S	HORSES	AND ALL THE KING'S MEN CANNOT SET THEM UP AGAIN; BUT
BUOY III (32)	/SIR F./ DO NOT DEPEND ON THAT. ALL THE KING'S	HORSES	AND ALL THE KING'S MEN CANNOT BRING BACK THE UNEARNED
2TRU PREFACE(7)	MAKE THEMSELVES POORER, IF HOPEFULLER, BY BACKING	HORSES	AND BUYING SWEEPSTAKE TICKETS ON THE CHANCE OF
SUPR III (134)	INDISCRIMINATE CONTEMPT FOR THE HUMAN. TO A MAN,	HORSES	AND DOGS AND CATS ARE MERE SPECIES, OUTSIDE THE MORAL
CLEO NOTES (205)	SOCIALLY INCOMPATIBLE. THE SAME THING IS TRUE OF	HORSES	AND DOGS. NOW THERE IS CLEARLY ROOM FOR GREAT CHANGES
PHIL II (117)	/PARAMORE/ (TURNING ON HIM) HOW MANY CAMELS AND	HORSES	AND MEN WERE RIPPED UP IN THAT SOUDAN CAMPAIGN WHERE
MIS. PREFACE(35)	WHAT OTHER PEOPLE HAVE TO BE PAID TO DO: DRIVING	HORSES	AND MOTOR CARS; TRYING ON DRESSES AND WALKING UP AND
MIS. PREFACE(55)	WAS IMPOSED ON US AS A NECESSITY BY THE USE OF	HORSES	AND OF HUGE RETINUES; BUT FLOGGING HAS NEVER BEEN SO
MIS. PREFACE(42)	OF MINE WHO, WHEN I WAS A SMALL CHILD, UNUSED TO	HORSES	AND VERY MUCH AFRAID OF THEM, INSISTED ON PUTTING ME
DOCT I (107)	TO BE WITH THEIR POOR PATIENTS. AND I KNOW WHAT	HORSES	ARE, SIR PATRICK. I WAS BROUGHT UP IN THE COUNTRY.
BARB PREFACE(238)	HIS MARK, BUT SCATTERING THE BOWELS OF AS MANY	HORSES	AS ANY BULL IN THE ARENA, AND SLAYING TWENTYTHREE
ARMS I (15)	THE WOUNDS ARE MOSTLY BROKEN KNEES, FROM THE	HORSES	CANNONING TOGETHER. /RAINA/ UGH! BUT I DONT BELIEVE
ARMS III (72)	BLUE ENVELOPE; AND TURNS TO SERGIUS). HOW MANY	HORSES	DID YOU SAY? /SERGIUS/ TWENTY, NOBLE SWITZER.
ROCK I (217)	THAT DO HIM? /HIPNEY/ WHAT GOOD DOES BACKING	HORSES	DO HIM? WHAT GOOD DOES DRINKING DO HIM? WHAT GOOD
ARMS II (31)	EVERY INCH A SOLDIER! IF ONLY I HAD BOUGHT THE	HORSES	FOR MY REGIMENT INSTEAD OF FOOLISHLY LEADING IT INTO
CATH PREFACE(157)	TENNYSON PRODUCED A FEW GLARINGLY ARTIFICIAL HIGH	HORSES	FOR THE GREAT ACTORS OF THEIR TIME; BUT THE
POSN (452)	EVERYBODY KNOWS I BORROWED ONE OF THE SHERIFF'S	HORSES	FROM STRAPPER BECAUSE MY OWN'S GONE LAME. EVERYBODY
BARB PREFACE(237)	HAVING FOR ITS MAIN AMUSEMENT THE SPECTACLE OF	HORSES	GORED AND DISEMBOWELLED BY THE BULL, AFTER WHICH,
KING I (197)	HAD BETTER PICK ME. /CHARLES/ THERE ARE ONLY TWO	HORSES	IN THE RACE NOW: THE PROTESTANT AND THE CATHOLIC. I
MIS. PREFACE(91)	WITH LITTLE MORE CULTURE THAN THEIR DOGS AND	HORSES	. AND YOU WILL FIND POOR FAMILIES, CUT OFF BY POVERTY

KING I (207) IN IT, AND THEN TORE HIM TO PIECES WITH GALLOPING HORSES . BUT HENRY LAY DEAD ALL THE SAME. THE PROTESTANTS
ARMS III (72) NOBLE SWITZER. /BLUNTSCHLI/ I HAVE TWO HUNDRED HORSES . (THEY ARE AMAZED). HOW MANY CARRIAGES? /SERGIUS/
JOAN 6 (138) THROWN BACK BY IDIOTS WHO UNDERSTAND NOTHING BUT HORSES . (TREMBLING WITH RAGE, HE FORCES HIMSELF TO SIT
DOCT PREFACE(42) AND MUTILATE THE EARS AND TAILS OF DOGS AND HORSES . LET CRUELTY OR KINDNESS OR ANYTHING ELSE ONCE
ARMS III (72) COMFORTABLE ESTABLISHMENT. SERGIUS KEEPS TWENTY HORSES . /BLUNTSCHLI/ BUT WHO WANTS TWENTY HORSES? WE'RE
HART III (131) WITH GOOD APPETITES AND SOUND SLEEP IN IT, IS HORSES . /MRS HUSHABYE/ HORSES! WHAT RUBBISH! /LADY
ARMS II (31) EXCHANGE SINCE. HE OVER-REACHED US ABOUT THOSE HORSES . /SERGIUS/ OF COURSE HE OVER-REACHED US. HIS FATHER
POSN (452) IN LAW WE CUT OUR BROTHER OFF WHEN HE STEALS HORSES . /THE FOREMAN/ BESIDES, YOU NEEDNT HANG HIM, YOU
CAPT I (237) A DOZEN MEN, JUST AS I MAY REQUIRE A DOZEN HORSES . SOME OF THE HORSES WILL BE VICIOUS; SO WILL ALL THE
GLIM (182) ENOUGH. I LEARNT THAT WHEN I TOOK TO BREEDING HORSES . THE HORSES YOU BREED FROM THOROUGHBREDS ARE NOT ALL
HART III (131) HORSES! WHAT RUBBISH! /LADY UTTERWORD/ YES: HORSES . WHY HAVE WE NEVER BEEN ABLE TO LET THIS HOUSE?
SIM PREFACE(14) HAD NO SUCH SATISFACTION. NEITHER HAD THE TRAMWAY HORSES NOR THE SLAVES, NOR HAVE THE DISCARDED " TOO OLD AT
BULL PREFACE(12) NOT HAVE TOLERATED. THERE ARE, INDEED, A HUNDRED HORSES ON WHICH I COULD RIDE OFF IF I WISHED TO SHIRK THE
ARMS II (42) I HOPE YOUVE CALLED AS A FRIEND, AND NOT ABOUT HORSES OR PRISONERS. /CATHERINE/ OH, QUITE AS A FRIEND,
SIM PREFACE(13) THEY WOULD BE SHOT; AND IF THEY WERE CHANGED INTO HORSES OR SLAVES THEY WOULD BE WORN OUT BY OVERWORK BEFORE
CLEO NOTES (210) SO TO SPEAK, AS A LIFE-OR-DEATH COURIER KILLS HORSES -- ENABLES MEN WITH COMMON IDEAS AND SUPERSTITIONS TO
PHIL II (114) OF ALL THIS VIVISECTION. YOU GO EXPERIMENTING ON HORSES ; AND OF COURSE THE RESULT IS THAT YOU TRY TO GET ME
DOCT I (105) COME FOR YOU; AND IT'S FRIGHTENING SIR PATRICK'S HORSES ; SO COME ALONG QUICK. /WALPOLE/ (RISING) GOODBYE,
DOCT PREFACE(58) SO IS THE CONTROVERSY AS TO THE DOCKING OF HORSES ' TAILS AND THE CROPPING OF DOGS' EARS. SO IS THE
FANY III (323) WE WERE QUITE SATISFIED WHEN OUR MARSHALS HAD SIX HORSES SHOT UNDER THEM, AND OUR STUPID OLD GROGNARDS DIED
BARB PREFACE(239) ROUTINE THAT THEY CAN BE TAKEN TO SEE THE HORSES SLAUGHTERED AS HELPLESSLY AS THEY COULD NO DOUBT BE
DOCT I (107) PATRICK. HOW LONG MORE ARE YOU GOING TO KEEP THEM HORSES STANDING IN THE DRAUGHT? /SIR PATRICK/ WHATS THAT TO
FABL PREFACE(65) I HAD BEEN STRUCK BY THE FACT THAT WHEN THE HORSES STOOD ROUND TIMIDLY AT A DISTANCE, A HANDSOME AND
LADY (249) THE FEET OF THE HORSES, IF INDEED THERE BE ANY HORSES THEN, AND MEN BE STILL RIDING INSTEAD OF FLYING. NOW
JOAN 5 (116) AND HEAP ARMOR ON THEMSELVES AND ON THEIR POOR HORSES TO KEEP OUT THE ARROWS; AND WHEN THEY FALL THEY CANT
SIM PREFACE(13) FOUND THAT THE MOST PROFITABLE WAY OF EXPLOITING HORSES WAS TO WORK THEM TO DEATH IN FOUR YEARS. PLANTERS IN
APPL I (213) NOT AT SUCH A MOMENT AS THIS. DONT LET US SWOP HORSES WHEN CROSSING A STREAM. /NICOBAR/ WHY NOT, IF THE
ROCK II (237) PLATE? EVEN SPORT WILL NOT BE SAFE: OUR BREED OF HORSES WILL BE DOOMED; OUR PACKS OF HOUNDS SOLD OR
CAPT I (237) JUST AS I MAY REQUIRE A DOZEN HORSES. SOME OF THE HORSES WILL BE VICIOUS; SO WILL ALL THE MEN. IF EITHER HORSE
BASH II,1, (112) MADAM, THE COACHMAN CAN NO LONGER WAIT: THE HORSES WILL TAKE COLD. /LYDIA/ I DO BESEECH HIM A MOMENT'S
HART PREFACE(4) WAS HORSEBACK HALL, CONSISTING OF A PRISON FOR HORSES WITH AN ANNEX FOR THE LADIES AND GENTLEMEN WHO RODE
GLIM (182) I LEARNT THAT WHEN I TOOK TO BREEDING HORSES. THE HORSES YOU BREED FROM THOROUGHBREDS ARE NOT ALL WORTH THE
POSN PREFACE(384) ON THE IMMORALITY OF RIDING ASTRIDE THEIR HORSES , A PRACTICE THAT HAS SINCE ESTABLISHED ITSELF SO
JOAN 6 (128) MAID IS BROUGHT BEFORE US, OF THESE STEALINGS OF HORSES , AND DANCINGS ROUND FAIRY TREES WITH THE VILLAGE
BUOY II (23) TO TRACK GAME, TO CATCH AND BREAK-IN WILD HORSES , AND TO TACKLE NATIVES ARMED WITH POISONED ARROWS. I
KING II (233) BIRDS AND ENGLISH TREES, ENGLISH DOGS AND IRISH HORSES , ENGLISH RIVERS AND ENGLISH SHIPS; BUT ENGLISH MEN!
DEVL EPILOG (84) STORES, ARTILLERY, ARMS, AMMUNITION, CARRIAGES, HORSES , ETC., ETC., MUST BE DELIVERED TO COMMISSARIES
LADY (249) YOU AND I WILL BE DUST BENEATH THE FEET OF THE HORSES , IF INDEED THERE BE ANY HORSES THEN, AND MEN BE
DEVL EPILOG (83) ETC., THEIR PROVISIONS EXHAUSTED, THEIR MILITARY HORSES , TENTS AND BAGGAGE TAKEN OR DESTROYED, THEIR RETREAT
ROCK II (283) THE MOUNTED POLICE. /SIR ARTHUR/ THEYVE SPLENDID HORSES , THOSE FELLOWS. /HILDA/ THE PEOPLE ARE ALL RUNNING
HART III (131) AND SOUND SLEEP IN IT, IS HORSES. /MRS HUSHABYE/ HORSES ! WHAT RUBBISH! /LADY UTTERWORD/ YES: HORSES. WHY
ARMS III (73) OH, I SHALL BE ONLY TOO GLAD. TWO HUNDRED HORSES ! WHEW! /SERGIUS/ WHAT SAYS THE LADY? /RAINA/ (

HORSESHOE
CAPT II (243) PAGRI ON HIS WHITE HAT, ENTERS THROUGH THE HORSESHOE ARCH, FOLLOWED BY A COUPLE OF MEN SUPPORTING THE
CAPT II (249) SO GOOD OF YOU, MR KIDBROOK. (SHE MAKES FOR THE HORSESHOE ARCH, FOLLOWED BY REDBROOK). /DRINKWATER/ NAH,
CAPT II (242) WILL YR. WIKE AP. (HE RUSHES IN THROUGH THE HORSESHOE ARCH, HOT AND EXCITED, AND RUNS ROUND, KICKING THE
CAPT II SD(242) THIS SEAT WOULD HAVE THE CHIEF ENTRANCE, A LARGE HORSESHOE ARCH, ON HIS LEFT, AND ANOTHER SADDLE SEAT BETWEEN

HORSEWHIP
WIDO I (14) SHOULD NOT HAVE BEEN SURPRISED TO SEE HIM BRING A HORSEWHIP WITH HIM. I SHALL NOT INTRUDE ON THE PAINFUL

HORSEWOMEN
HART PREFACE(5) THE STABLES, MISERABLY DISCONTENTED; AND HARDY HORSEWOMEN WHO SLEPT AT THE FIRST CHORD OF SCHUMANN WERE

HORSHAM
MRS I (182) DOWN FROM LONDON AND THAT I WAS TO COME OVER FROM HORSHAM TO BE INTRODUCED TO YOU. /VIVIE/ (NOT AT ALL

HORTONS
BULL PREFACE(39) VOLTAIRES, THE FOXES AND PENNS, THE CLIFFORDS, HORTONS , CAMPBELLS, WALTERS, AND SILVESTER HORNES, WHO ARE

HORUS
CLEO II (135) /CLEOPATRA/ YES, I ALWAYS CALL HIM HORUS, BECAUSE HORUS IS THE MOST BEAUTIFUL OF OUR GODS. BUT I WANT TO KNOW
CLEO II (135) REAL NAME? /CLEOPATRA/ YES, I ALWAYS CALL HIM HORUS , BECAUSE HORUS IS THE MOST BEAUTIFUL OF OUR GODS. BUT

HOSE
OVER PREFACE(165) WHEN GARRICK PLAYED RICHARD III IN SLASHED TRUNK HOSE AND PLUMES, IT WAS NOT BECAUSE HE BELIEVED THAT THE

HOSEA'S
LION PREFACE(20) DOUBT LED HIM TO SEEK FOR SOME LEGEND BEARING OUT HOSEA'S " OUT OF EGYPT HAVE I CALLED MY SON," AND JEREMIAH'S

HOSKYN
BASH II,1, (99) THAT EVENTFUL NIGHT WHEN AS WE GATHERED WERE AT HOSKYN HOUSE TO HEAR A LECTURE BY HERR ABENDGASSE, HE PLACED

HOSMAN
CAPT II (266) IS THE COMMAWNDER OF THE FYTHFUL AN IS VIZZEER HOSMAN . /SIDI/ WHERE IS THE WOMAN? /OSMAN/ THE SHAMELESS

HOSPITABLE
DEVL II (36) OF COURSE, YOU HAVE REALLY BEEN SO KIND AND HOSPITABLE AND CHARMING TO ME THAT I ONLY WANT TO GO AWAY
SUPR HANDBOK(189) BUT THE ABLEST MAN IN THE COMMUNITY. BUT IN MORE HOSPITABLE CLIMATES, OR WHERE THE SOCIAL ORGANIZATION OF THE
BUOY II (18) THAT COMPLICATES MATTERS. I THOUGHT YOU WERE A HOSPITABLE FRIENDLY SAVAGE. I SEE YOU ARE A COMMERCIAL
ARMS I (20) ME IF THERE WAS ANY MISTAKE. MY FATHER IS A VERY HOSPITABLE MAN: HE KEEPS SIX HOTELS; BUT I COULDNT TRUST HIM
BULL II SD(111) WHIM TO GO OUT FOR A LATE STROLL PROVOKES NEITHER HOSPITABLE REMONSTRANCE NOR SURPRISE. INDEED AUNT JUDY WANTS
PHIL I (85) HIS FUR-COLLARED OVERCOAT. /CUTHBERTSON/ (WITH A HOSPITABLE SHOW OF DELIGHT AT FINDING VISITORS) DONT STOP,
BULL PREFACE(29) TO ANY IRISHMAN OF HIS ACQUAINTANCE, AND BE KIND, HOSPITABLE , AND SERVICEABLE IN HIS INTERCOURSE WITH

HOSPITABLY
BULL II (107) MR BROADBENT: ME SISTER JUDY. /AUNT JUDY/ (HOSPITABLY : GOING TO BROADBENT AND SHAKING HANDS HEARTILY)
MRS III (224) HAS LEFT ANY TO SHEW. /REV. S./ (MOONING HOSPITABLY AT THEM) I SHALL BE PLEASED, I'M SURE, IF SIR
MIS. SD(120) AND BUSIES HERSELF WITH HER NEEDLE. MRS TARLETON, HOSPITABLY FUSSY, GOES OVER TO HIM. /MRS TARLETON/ OH, LORD
FANY PROL,SD(266) PERCEPTION IN CHECK. THE COUNT APPROACHES THEM HOSPITABLY . /SAVOYARD/ COUNT O'DOWDA, GENTLEMEN. MR
GETT (291) SNORTING SNOB YOURSELF. /THE BISHOP/ (AMUSED BUT HOSPITABLY REMONSTRANT) MY DEAR BOXER! /HOTCHKISS/ (
DEVL II (33) NOBODY STANDS ON MUCH CEREMONY WITH US. (HOSPITABLY) COME IN. (RICHARD COMES IN CARELESSLY AND
HART I (54) BOW TO MAZZINI, WHO RETURNS IT). /MRS HUSHABYE/ (HOSPITABLY , SHAKING HANDS) HOW GOOD OF YOU TO COME, MR

HOSPITAHLITY
CAPT III (290) YOU IN THE NAME OF THE UNITED STATES FOR THE HOSPITAHLITY YOU HAVE EXTENDED TO US TODAY; AND I INVITE YOU

HOSPITAL
DOCT I (104) CASE AND A TETANUS CASE SIDE BY SIDE IN THE HOSPITAL : A BEADLE AND A CITY MISSIONARY. THINK OF WHAT
GENV IV (103) AND GREEN LIGHTS? AM I TO SLEEP IN A SMALLPOX HOSPITAL ? AM I TO CROSS THE RIVER ON A TIGHT ROPE INSTEAD
GENV IV (102) TOOK YOU OUT OF THE TRENCHES AND LANDED YOU IN A HOSPITAL BED? /BBDE/ EXTREMELY GLAD. BUT THAT WAS PART OF
PYGM V (272) WITH THE DOCTORS: USED TO SHOVE ME OUT OF THE HOSPITAL BEFORE I COULD HARDLY STAND ON MY LEGS, AND NOTHING
2TRU III (90) NURSE THAT EVER RAISED THE MORTALITY OF A HOSPITAL BY TEN PER CENT. BUT-- /SWEETIE/ OH, WHAT A LIE!
NEVR I (200) PEOPLE WHO PAY. /THE DENTIST/ (LAUGHING) OH, THE HOSPITAL DOESNT COUNT. I ONLY MEANT MY FIRST TOOTH IN

BUOY IV (54)	MY BROTHER CYRIL IS A DOCTOR, HEAD OF A MENTAL	HOSPITAL	FOR INCURABLES. HE IS THE MAN YOU SHOULD CONSULT.
DOCT I (108)	MINUTES. COME IN WITH AN URGENT CALL FROM THE	HOSPITAL	FOR ME. YOU UNDERSTAND: SHE'S TO HAVE A STRONG HINT
DOCT I SD(100)	COLLEAGUES: AS THEIR CONTEMPORARY AND OLD	HOSPITAL	FRIEND, THOUGH EVEN IN THIS HE HAS TO STRUGGLE WITH
HART PREFACE(7)	AND AT THE HOSPITAL WITH AN EPIDEMIC OF	HOSPITAL	GANGRENE, SLAUGHTERING RIGHT AND LEFT UNTIL THE
PHIL II (113)	WITH, BESIDES HAVING THE RUN OF THE LARGEST	HOSPITAL	IN ITALY. (WITH DESPERATE RESOLUTION) BUT I WONT
MILL II (171)	LANDLORD IS TAKING THE GENTLEMAN TO THE COTTAGE	HOSPITAL	IN YOUR CAR. /EPIFANIA/ IN MY CAR! I WILL NOT
SIM II (75)	ANGEL IN LEICESTER SQUARE REMOVED TO MENTAL	HOSPITAL	. CHURCH ASSEMBLY AT LAMBETH PALACE DECIDES BY A
MILL II (171)	PENNILESS MAHOMETAN REFUGEES; AND I WORK IN THE	HOSPITAL	. I CANNOT ATTEND TO YOU. /EPIFANIA/ YOU CAN ATTEND
DOCT PREFACE(75)	IN SIR ALMROTH'S FAMOUS LABORATORY IN ST MARY'S	HOSPITAL	. IT WOULD HAVE BECOME NECESSARY TO DENOUNCE
WIDO I (4)	FOUR YEARS IN THE MEDICAL SCHOOL AND WALKING THE	HOSPITAL	. (HE AGAIN BURSTS INTO SONG). /COKANE/ (RISING)
JITT II (30)	/FESSLER/ OH, GOOD. WELL, I MUST BE OFF TO THE	HOSPITAL	. (HE RISES). TELL HER I ASKED AFTER HER.
LION I (120)	AND ASKED HIS FORGIVENESS BY HIS BEDSIDE IN THE	HOSPITAL	. (PUTTING HIS HANDS ON LENTULUS'S SHOULDERS WITH
PHIL I (91)	OF THE SAME SORT? I SUPPOSE HE'S SOMETHING IN A	HOSPITAL	. /CHARTERIS/ HOSPITAL! NONSENSE! HE'S A DRAMATIC
BUOY IV (55)	BY IT? IT IS YOU WHO SHOULD GO TO THE MENTAL	HOSPITAL	. /SIR FERDINAND/ THAT ALSO IS A MATTER FOR
MILL IV (192)	AN INVALID, ONLY JUST DISCHARGED FROM THE COTTAGE	HOSPITAL	. THE EGYPTIAN DOCTOR RECOMMENDED OUR CHEF TO HIM;
DOCT III (146)	OF TONGS. LET HIM TAKE HIS LUNGS TO THE BROMPTON	HOSPITAL	. THEY WONT CURE HIM; BUT THEYLL TEACH HIM MANNERS.
MRS II (216)	THE ROUGH WITH THE SMOOTH, JUST LIKE A NURSE IN A	HOSPITAL	OR ANYONE ELSE. IT'S NOT WORK THAT ANY WOMAN WOULD
MIS. PREFACE(33)	THAN ITS PLEASURES, THAT ITS SACRIFICE IN A	HOSPITAL	OR LABORATORY EXPERIMENT MIGHT SAVE MILLIONS OF
KING PREFACE(156)	HIM TO DO, WHETHER IT WAS BUILDING GREENWICH	HOSPITAL	OR MAKING DUKES OF HIS BASTARDS, AS A HUSBAND HE
DOCT PREFACE(12)	SUCCESSFUL IF THE PATIENT CAN BE GOT OUT OF THE	HOSPITAL	OR NURSING HOME ALIVE, THOUGH THE SUBSEQUENT
SUPR HANDBOK(212)	FARM (PIOUSLY DISGUISED AS A REFORMED FOUNDLING	HOSPITAL	OR SOMETHING OF THAT SORT) MIGHT WELL, UNDER PROPER
DOCT PREFACE(46)	WITH HIMSELF. HIS FIRST EXPERIMENT WAS ON TWO	HOSPITAL	PATIENTS. ON RECEIVING A MESSAGE FROM THE HOSPITAL
FABL III (109)	SORT? /THE TOURIST/ NO. THEY OFFERED ME A JOB AS	HOSPITAL	PORTER BECAUSE I'M PHYSICALLY STRONG. HOW UTTERLY
JITT II (31)	ARE YOU? /FESSLER/ I MUST. I HAVE TO BE AT THE	HOSPITAL	; AND I AM LATE ALREADY. /JITTA/ COME AGAIN SOON,
WIDO II (32)	IT. IVE SEEN IT ALL AMONG THE OUT-PATIENTS AT THE	HOSPITAL	; AND IT USED TO MAKE MY BLOOD BOIL TO THINK THAT
MILL II (174)	DIED ON THE TABLE. THEY DIED AFTER THEY LEFT THE	HOSPITAL	; BUT AS THEY WERE CARRIED AWAY FROM THE TABLE
DOCT PREFACE(63)	IS REGARDED AS A MONSTER. EVEN IF WE MUST DISMISS	HOSPITAL	SERVICE AS REALLY VENAL, THE FACT REMAINS THAT MOST
BARB PREFACE(245)	PENALTIES, ATONEMENTS, REDEMPTIONS, SALVATIONS,	HOSPITAL	SUBSCRIPTION LISTS AND WHAT NOT, TO ENABLE US TO
DOCT I (110)	OF THE TONE OF HIS OWN VOICE) BUT I HAVE AT THE	HOSPITAL	TEN TUBERCULOUS PATIENTS WHOSE LIVES I BELIEVE I
DOCT I (112)	SIGN OF ALARM) THEYVE JUST TELEPHONED FROM THE	HOSPITAL	THAT YOURE TO COME INSTANTLY-- A PATIENT ON THE
DOCT PREFACE(46)	PATIENTS. ON RECEIVING A MESSAGE FROM THE	HOSPITAL	TO THE EFFECT THAT THESE TWO MARTYRS TO THERAPEUTIC
HART PREFACE(7)	THAT ANYONE THINKS OF TRACING TO IT, IN A	HOSPITAL	TWO GENERATIONS OF MEDICAL STUDENTS MAY TOLERATE
2TRU I (38)	AND YOUR LIKE, BECAUSE I WAS ONCE A PATIENT IN A	HOSPITAL	WHERE THE WOMEN PATIENTS WERE A ROUGH LOT, AND THE
2TRU I (38)	PATIENT/ AND DO YOU THINK I AM A POOR WOMAN IN A	HOSPITAL	WHOM YOU CAN ILLTREAT AS YOU PLEASE? DO YOU KNOW
HART PREFACE(7)	STRIKES AT THE CITY WITH A PESTILENCE AND AT THE	HOSPITAL	WITH AN EPIDEMIC OF HOSPITAL GANGRENE, SLAUGHTERING
DOCT I (83)	HADNT TIME TO COME UP ON HIS WAY TO THE	HOSPITAL	, BUT WAS DETERMINED TO BE FIRST-- COMING BACK, HE
MILL IV (195)	AND COSTS. /SAGAMORE/ AND CAB FARE TO THE COTTAGE	HOSPITAL	, I SUPPOSE. /ADRIAN/ NO! I WENT IN HER OWN CAR.
NEVR I (200)	SOMEBODY. /THE YOUNG LADY/ YES: SOMEBODY IN A	HOSPITAL	, NOT PEOPLE WHO PAY. /THE DENTIST/ (LAUGHING) OH,
LION PREFACE(54)	IN EVERY FIVE DIES IN A WORKHOUSE, A PUBLIC	HOSPITAL	, OR A MADHOUSE. IN CITIES LIKE LONDON THE
BARB PREFACE(235)	NOT BEING A MODERN TETZEL, OR THE TREASURER OF A	HOSPITAL	, REFUSES TO SELL ABSOLUTION TO BILL FOR A
MILL IV (197)	I HAD TO GIVE THEM A SUBSCRIPTION AT THE COTTAGE	HOSPITAL	, WHERE YOUR MAN TOOK ME. I HAD TO GO FROM THERE TO
PHIL I (91)	SUPPOSE HE'S SOMETHING IN A HOSPITAL. /CHARTERIS/	HOSPITAL	! NONSENSE! HE'S A DRAMATIC CRITIC. DIDNT YOU
		HOSPITALITY	
HART I (72)	HESIONE. LADY UTTERWORD IS ENTITLED NOT ONLY TO	HOSPITALITY	BUT TO CIVILIZATION. /LADY UTTERWORD/ (
HART I (45)	AND ABANDONED, TIRED AND STARVING. THIS IS OUR	HOSPITALITY	. THESE ARE OUR MANNERS. NO ROOM READY. NO HOT
ARMS I (18)	PATRONIZINGLY). NOW LISTEN. YOU MUST TRUST TO OUR	HOSPITALITY	. YOU DO NOT YET KNOW IN WHOSE HOUSE YOU ARE. I
BULL IV (150)	AND WE MUST NOT ABUSE THE WARMHEARTED IRISH	HOSPITALITY	OF MISS DOYLE BY TURNING HER SITTING ROOM INTO A
ARMS II (42)	HATLESS, RUSHES FROM THE HOUSE IN A FLUSTER OF	HOSPITALITY	, FOLLOWED BY SERGIUS). /PETKOFF/ (AS HE
DEVL II (33)	HIS COAT) I THINK, SIR, THAT SINCE YOU ACCEPT MY	HOSPITALITY	, YOU CANNOT HAVE SO BAD AN OPINION OF IT. SIT
ARMS I (20)	HAD SIMPLY THROWN YOURSELF AS A FUGITIVE ON OUR	HOSPITALITY	, YOU WOULD HAVE BEEN AS SAFE AS IN YOUR
		HOSPITAL-TURNED-OUT	
POSN (463)	OR YOU WOULDNT BE IN THIS JUMPED-UP, JERKED-OFF,	HOSPITAL-TURNED-OUT	CAMP THAT CALLS ITSELF A TOWN. I TOOK
		HOSPITALS	
2TRU III (82)	THAT IN THE WAR: PRETTY LADIES BRIGHTENING UP THE	HOSPITALS	AND LOSING THEIR SILLY HEADS, LET ALONE UPSETTING
2TRU III (94)	DO BETTER AS A SAINT. A FEW THOUSANDS TO THE	HOSPITALS	AND THE POLITICAL PARTY FUNDS WILL BUY ME A HALO
DOCT PREFACE(27)	BEYOND THEIR MEANS OR SENDING THEM TO THE PUBLIC	HOSPITALS	, WHEN IT COMES TO PROPHYLACTIC INOCULATION, THE
2TRU PREFACE(9)	SOCIETY IN LONDON TO THE HORRORS OF THE CRIMEAN	HOSPITALS	RATHER THAN BEHAVE LIKE A LADY, AND WHY MY
GETT PREFACE(213)	BEES AND POULTRY AND VILLAGE SCHOOLS AND COTTAGE	HOSPITALS	; AND I FIND MYSELF REPEATEDLY ASKING MYSELF WHY
DOCT PREFACE(68)	SUCH A SERVICE IS ORGANIZED AT PRESENT ONLY IN	HOSPITALS	; THOUGH IN LARGE TOWNS THE PRACTICE OF CALLING IN
2TRU PREFACE(9)	BETTER THE WARDS OF THE MOST TERRIBLE OF FIELD	HOSPITALS	THAN A DRAWING ROOM IN MAYFAIR: BETTER THE SOUTH
BARB III (348)	OTHER BREAD; WHEN WE TEND THE SICK, IT IS IN THE	HOSPITALS	THEY ENDOW; IF WE TURN FROM THE CHURCHES THEY
DOCT PREFACE(29)	THAT INVOLVE HIGHLY ORGANIZED LABORATORIES,	HOSPITALS	, AND PUBLIC INSTITUTIONS GENERALLY, IT UNLUCKILY
BARB I (268)	ALL THE SPARE MONEY MY TRADE RIVALS SPEND ON	HOSPITALS	, CATHEDRALS, AND OTHER RECEPTACLES FOR CONSCIENCE
DOCT PREFACE(69)	IN COMPETITION WITH EVERYBODY WHO HAS WALKED THE	HOSPITALS	, SCRAPED THROUGH THE EXAMINATIONS, AND BOUGHT A
		HOST	
FANY III SD(311)	WALL AND PLACES THEM AT THE TABLE, BETWEEN THE	HOST	AND HOSTESS. THEN HE WITHDRAWS. /MRS GILBEY/ (TO MRS
ROCK I (221)	WAIT TIL YOURE A LABOR LEADER. (HE WINKS AT HIS	HOST	AND MAKES FOR THE DOOR). /SIR ARTHUR/ HA HA! HA HA
NEVR II (238)	/PHILIP/ ALLOW ME TO DISCHARGE MY FIRST DUTY AS	HOST	BY ORDERING YOUR WINE. (HE TAKES THE WINE LIST FROM
MTH2 SD(38)	THE VISITOR IS SO VERY UNWELCOME THAT HIS	HOST	FORGETS TO RISE; AND THE TWO BROTHERS STARE AT THE
FANY III (324)	AS WE ARE, DECLARE THAT EVERY FRENCHMAN IS A	HOST	IN HIMSELF, AND THAT WHEN ONE FRENCHMAN ATTACKS THREE
KING I (200)	WOULD NOT LIKE THAT: HE KNOWS HIS DUTIES AS YOUR	HOST	. AND IF YOU WILL EXCUSE ME SAYING SO, SIR: YOU ALL
MRS III (221)	/REV. S./ NONSENSE, SIR. I AM SIR GEORGE CROFTS'	HOST	. I MUST TALK TO HIM ABOUT SOMETHING; AND HE HAS ONLY
ROCK II (272)	DOOR). /BASHAM/ GOODBYE. I WISH YOU JOY OF YOUR	HOST	. /THE DUKE/ YOU DONT APPRECIATE HIM. HE IS ABSOLUTELY
LION PREFACE(34)	WAS WITH THE ANGEL A MULTITUDE OF THE HEAVENLY	HOST	. THESE SHEPHERDS GO TO THE STABLE AND TAKE THE PLACE
MTH1 II (22)	HOST, AND EACH HOST SHALL TRY TO KILL THE OTHER	HOST	. THINK OF THAT! ALL THOSE MULTITUDES OF MEN FIGHTING,
KING I (172)	PRESENT, MISTRESS GWYNN, I THINK. MAY I MAKE OUR	HOST	KNOWN TO YOU? THE EMINENT PHILOSOPHER, MR NEWTON.
DOCT PREFACE(69)	PRIVATE ILLNESS SERVICE. TO PUT IT ANOTHER WAY, A	HOST	OF MEN AND WOMEN WHO HAVE NOW A STRONG INCENTIVE TO BE
FABL PREFACE(68)	THEIR GOD COULD NOT BE OMNIPRESENT; AND A	HOST	OF MINOR GODS SPRANG UP. THE GREEKS ADDED TO ZEUS AND
JOAN PREFACE(47)	THE INCREDIBLE SMALLNESS OF THE ATOM, AND A	HOST	OF OTHER MARVEL MONGERS WHOSE CREDULITY WOULD HAVE
GENV PREFACE(8)	TO BURY, HEAPS OF RUBBLE TO CLEAR AWAY, AND A	HOST	OF PRISONERS TO FEED, MEANWHILE THE BRITISH AND
ARMS III (72)	(SWIFTLY MAKING UP HIS MIND AND COMING TO HIS	HOST	) IN THAT CASE, MAJOR PETKOFF, I BEG TO PROPOSE
LIED (201)	BOMPAS WERE NOT CONSISTENT WITH HIS DUTY TO ME AS	HOST	; AND IT DID HIM HONOR AND ME TOO. BUT (WITH GATHERING
MTH1 II (22)	HOST AND DESIRE TO FIGHT AND KILL HOST. AND EACH	HOST	SHALL TRY TO KILL THE OTHER HOST. THINK OF THAT! ALL
CAPT III (282)	RAHNKIN! WHO IS RAHNKIN? /SIR HOWARD/ OUR	HOST	THE MISSIONARY. /KEARNEY/ (SUBSIDING UNWILLINGLY) OH!
MTH2 (54)	COMFORTABLY AND KINDLY, MUCH AS IF HE WERE THE	HOST	, AND FRANKLYN AN EMBARRASSED BUT WELCOME GUEST). I HAD
SUPR III (101)	COME HERE, THAT THE BLEST, ONCE CALLED A HEAVENLY	HOST	, ARE A CONTINUALLY DWINDLING MINORITY. THE SAINTS, THE
DEST SD(152)	LITTLE INNKEEPER OF 40. NATURALLY AN EXCELLENT	HOST	, HE IS IN THE HIGHEST SPIRITS THIS EVENING AT HIS GOOD
KING I (209)	ON THE DUKE'S LEFT). /CHARLES/ MR NEWTON IS OUR	HOST	, MR KNELLER; AND HE IS A VERY EMINENT PHILOSOPHER.
METH PREFACE(R35)	WERE IN QUESTION THERE WERE NO SCEPTICS. OUR	HOST	, SEEING THAT HIS GUESTS WOULD VANISH PRECIPITATELY IF
GETT (357)	BUT TO BETRAY A COMRADE, TO BE DISLOYAL TO A	HOST	, TO BREAK THE COVENANT OF BREAD AND SALT, IS
		HOSTAGE	
JOAN PREFACE(25)	GREEK JINGOISM AND GREEK RELIGION, WRITTEN BY A	HOSTAGE	OR A SLAVE; AND LA PUCELLE MAKES BUTLER'S THEORY
		HOSTELRY	
BASH III (127)	ADDRESS, YOU, ROBERT MELLISH, TO THE BLUE ANCHOR	HOSTELRY	ATTEND HIM; ASSUAGE HIS HURTS, AND BID BILL
		HOSTESS	
FANY PROLOG (267)	FIRST PARTY: YOUR FIRST APPEARANCE IN ENGLAND AS	HOSTESS	, BUT YOURE DOING IT BEAUTIFULLY. DONT BE AFRAID.
HART I (45)	NO ROOM READY. NO HOT WATER. NO WELCOMING	HOSTESS	, OUR VISITOR IS TO SLEEP IN THE TOOLSHED, AND TO
FANY III SD(311)	PLACES THEM AT THE TABLE, BETWEEN THE HOST AND	HOSTESS	, THEN HE WITHDRAWS. /MRS GILBEY/ (TO MRS KNOX) HOW

FOUN (221)	AGREEABLE OBJECT OF CONTEMPLATION, AND A CHARMING	HOSTESS	, WITH THAT OBJECT MAY I VENTURE TO PROPOSE A
PYGM V (270)	AS HE BECOMES CONSCIOUS THAT HE HAS FORGOTTEN HIS	HOSTESS	) ASKING YOUR PARDON, MAAM. (HE APPROACHES HER AND
PYGM III (249)	TO ELIZA TO INDICATE TO HER WHICH LADY IS HER	HOSTESS	). ELIZA, WHO IS EXQUISITELY DRESSED, PRODUCES AN
		HOSTILE	
ROCK PREFACE(174)	AND LIE AWAKE AT NIGHTS IN CONTINUAL DREAD OF	HOSTILE	AEROPLANES, THE OBVIOUS MORAL BEING THAT WHETHER WE
3PLA PREFACE(R26)	WHEN A GOOD DEAL OF THE SAME TALK, BOTH	HOSTILE	AND FRIENDLY, WAS PROVOKED BY MY LAST VOLUME OF
CAND I (101)	AT HOME, WE SIT AS IF IN CAMP, ENCOMPASSED BY A	HOSTILE	ARMY OF DOUBTS. WILL YOU PLAY THE TRAITOR AND LET
POSN PREFACE(365)	ITS OPPOSITION, ALL THESE INFLUENCES HAD CREATED	HOSTILE	BODIES BY THE OPERATION OF THE MERE IMPULSE TO
BULL PREFACE(30)	IS A SEPARATION OF THE IRISH PEOPLE INTO TWO	HOSTILE	CAMPS: ONE PROTESTANT, GENTLEMANLY, AND
ROCK PREFACE(190)	THEY WOULD HAVE BEEN WRONG IN SUPPOSING THAT A	HOSTILE	CRITIC OF THE EXISTING SOCIAL ORDER EITHER COULD OR
2TRU II (59)	CHILD. SHE IS AFRAID THAT IF I MAKE THE SLIGHTEST	HOSTILE	DEMONSTRATION THE BRIGANDS WILL CUT OFF THE GIRL'S
BULL II (99)	A CUNNING DEVELOPED BY HIS CONSTANT DREAD OF A	HOSTILE	DOMINANCE, WHICH HE HABITUALLY TRIES TO DISARM AND
LION PREFACE(24)	THE COUNTERACTING OF EVIL BY GOOD INSTEAD OF BY A	HOSTILE	EVIL, AND AN ORGANIC CONCEPTION OF SOCIETY IN WHICH
SUPR PREFACE(R34)	HERO, WHO ACTUALLY LEAVES YOU COLD AND SECRETLY	HOSTILE	. YOU SUDDENLY SEE THAT SHAKESPEAR, WITH ALL HIS
BULL IV (180)	ME. I BEG YOUR PARDON. /LARRY/ (UNIMPRESSED AND	HOSTILE	) I DIDNT STAND ON CEREMONY WITH YOU: YOU NEEDNT
WIDO III (51)	NOD AT SARTORIUS. /SARTORIUS/ (BRACING HIMSELF:	HOSTILE	) WELL? /LICKCHEESE/ QUITE WELL, SARTORIUS,
METH PREFACE(R75)	IF HE HAS LITTLE CONSCIENCE, AND INDIGNANTLY	HOSTILE	TO IT IF HE HAS A GOOD DEAL. THE SAME REVOLT AGAINST
SUPR HANDBOK(184)	SEXUAL SELECTION WITH IRRELEVANT CONDITIONS, ARE	HOSTILE	TO THE EVOLUTION OF THE SUPERMAN, IT IS EASY TO
UNPL PREFACE(R16)	OF NATURE BECOME QUITE OBSOLETE. HE WAS OPENLY	HOSTILE	TO THE NEW MOVEMENT; AND HIS EVIDENCE BEFORE THE
CLEO III SD(145)	GET BACK TO YOUR SHOP. FTATATEETA, ROUSED BY HIS	HOSTILE	TONE, STEALS TOWARDS THE EDGE OF THE QUAY WITH THE
2TRU II (77)	DONT YOU REALIZE THAT THE HILLS HERE ARE FULL OF	HOSTILE	TRIBES WHO MAY TRY TO RAID US AT ANY MOMENT? LOOK
JOAN PREFACE(19)	WAY OF TRAVELLING THROUGH A COUNTRY INFESTED WITH	HOSTILE	TROOPS AND BANDS OF MARAUDING DESERTERS FROM BOTH
		HOSTILITIES	
APPL INTR,SD(255)	LOUDLY AND REPEATEDLY. THE TWO COMBATANTS CEASE	HOSTILITIES	AND SCRAMBLE HASTILY TO THEIR FEET. /MAGNUS/
MILL PREFACE(113)	SCOUNDRELS; AND IF HE IS FORCED TO SUSPEND	HOSTILITIES	FOR A WHILE, AND DOES SO BY A TREATY WHICH
FANY III SD(307)	DUVALLET. DUVALLET ENTERS. SUDDEN CESSATION OF	HOSTILITIES	, AND DEAD SILENCE. THE COMBATANTS SEPARATE BY
		HOSTILITY	
GENV IV (97)	THE POWERS OF EUROPE ON A BASIS OF IRRECONCILABLE	HOSTILITY	BETWEEN CAMBERWELL AND PECKHAM: THAT IS OUR
LION PREFACE(102)	A CIVIL WORD; AND THEY SHEWED THEIR SENSE OF HIS	HOSTILITY	BY GETTING HIM KILLED AS SOON AS POSSIBLE. HE WAS,
JOAN 6,SD(148)	LOOK AT ONE ANOTHER FOR A MOMENT WITH UNCONCEALED	HOSTILITY	. THEN CAUCHON FOLLOWS THE INQUISITOR OUT. WARWICK
BULL PREFACE(68)	AND DRILLED AS VOLUNTEERS IN SPITE OF THE	HOSTILITY	OF THE GOVERNMENT, WHICH MEANWHILE GAVE EVERY
PLES PREFACE(R11)	I HAVE NOT BEEN DRIVEN TO THIS EXPEDIENT BY ANY	HOSTILITY	ON THE PART OF OUR MANAGERS. I WILL NOT PRETEND
PHIL II (119)	AND FLINGS HIMSELF INTO IT WITH DETERMINED	HOSTILITY	). /CHARTERIS/ (FOLLOWING HIM, TOO DEEPLY
PYGM EPILOG (298)	SUDDENLY TOOK AN INTEREST IN HER, AND REVEALED A	HOSTILITY	TO CONVENTIONAL RELIGION WHICH SHE HAD NEVER
BULL PREFACE(64)	I AM HAMPERED, AS AN IRISHMAN, BY MY IMPLACABLE	HOSTILITY	TO ENGLISH DOMINATION. MISTRUSTING MY OWN
DOCT PREFACE(62)	HAS MADE IT IMPOSSIBLE FOR ME TO SHARE THAT	HOSTILITY	TO THE DOCTOR AS A MAN WHICH EXISTS AND IS GROWING
BULL PREFACE(26)	RESERVES ALL THE CLASS RANCOR, THE POLITICAL	HOSTILITY	, THE RELIGIOUS BIGOTRY, AND THE BAD BLOOD
		HOST'S	
KING I (167)	YOU I HAVE NO BUSINESS HERE EXCEPT TO WASTE OUR	HOST'S	INVALUABLE TIME AND TO IMPROVE MY OWN, IF HE WILL BE
FANY PROLOG (257)	THANKS. (THEY SIT. SAVOYARD, LOOKING AT HIS	HOST'S	OBSOLETE COSTUME, CONTINUES) I HAD NO IDEA YOU WERE
KING I (179)	ARE MAKING A MOST UNWARRANTABLE INTRUSION ON OUR	HOST'S	VALUABLE TIME. MR NEWTON: ON MY HONOR I HAD NO PART
		HOSTS	
KING PREFACE(158)	SO WE CHRISTEN IT THE HOLY GHOST OR THE LORD OF	HOSTS	AND DECHRISTEN IT AS A LIFE FORCE OR ELAN VITAL. AS
MTH1 II (22)	THOUSAND TREES. I WILL DIVIDE THEM INTO TWO GREAT	HOSTS	. ONE OF THEM I WILL LEAD; AND THE OTHER WILL BE LED
BULL PREFACE(10)	EVER AGAIN BE TO THE ENGLISH FLEET. THE LORD OF	HOSTS	MAY NOT BE QUITE THE SORT OF POWER THAT PHILIP OF
SUPR III (97)	ME ILL SPOKEN OF; AND YET, BELIEVE ME, I HAVE	HOSTS	OF FRIENDS THERE. /ANA/ YES: YOU REIGN IN THEIR
POSN (446)	ME. BUT BACK DOWN I NEVER WILL, NOT IF ALL THE	HOSTS	OF HEAVEN COME TO SNIVEL AT ME IN WHITE SURPLICES AND
FABL PREFACE(74)	THAT IS FOR THE MOMENT ESTABLISHED. THERE ARE	HOSTS	OF SUCH CREEDLESS VOTERS, ACTING STRONGLY AS A
BULL PREFACE(10)	IMPERIALIST DOES NOT BELIEVE IN THE LORD OF	HOSTS	; BUT THE ARMADA WAS DEFEATED FOR ALL THAT, THOUGH
BULL PREFACE(9)	ARMADA. SPAIN RECKONED WITHOUT THE LORD OF	HOSTS	, WHO SCATTERED THAT INVINCIBLE ARMADA FOR LITTLE
		HOT	
MTH1 II (25)	TASTE LIFE WITHOUT MAKING IT BITTER AND BOILING	HOT	: YOU CANNOT LOVE LUA UNTIL HER FACE IS PAINTED, NOR
JOAN 5 (114)	TELL YOU: THAT YOU MUST STRIKE WHILE THE IRON IS	HOT	? I TELL YOU WE MUST MAKE A DASH AT COMPIEGNE AND
APPL PREFACE(179)	THAT I AM TOO POLITE TO CALL DEMOS A WINDBAG OR A	HOT	AIR MERCHANT; BUT I AM GOING TO ASK YOU TO BEGIN OUR
APPL PREFACE(179)	IT FIRST AS A BIG BALLOON, FILLED WITH GAS OR	HOT	AIR, AND SENT UP SO THAT YOU SHALL BE KEPT LOOKING UP AT
GENV PREFACE(9)	STIFLED BY HAVING NOTHING TO BREATHE BUT WHITE	HOT	AIR, AND THEN BURNT TO CINDERS AND BURIED UNDER THE
ROCK II (282)	HAD NOT HAD YOU HERE TO REMIND ME THAT IT WAS ALL	HOT	AIR, I COULDNT HELP KNOWING AS WELL AS ANY OF THOSE
MTH4 I (168)	VERY DISAGREEABLE IS HAPPENING TO ME. I FEEL	HOT	ALL OVER. I HAVE A HORRIBLE IMPULSE TO INJURE YOU. WHAT
INCA (242)	BEDROOMS -- /THE MANAGER/ THERE ARE BASINS WITH	HOT	AND COLD TAPS. /ERMYNTRUDE/ (SCORNFULLY) YES: THERE
PYGM II (240)	/LIZA/ I TELL YOU, IT'S EASY TO CLEAN UP HERE.	HOT	AND COLD WATER ON TAP, JUST AS MUCH AS YOU LIKE, THERE
CAPT II (242)	AP. (HE RUSHES IN THROUGH THE HORSESHOE ARCH,	HOT	AND EXCITED, AND RUNS ROUND, KICKING THE SLEEPERS). NAH
MIS. (202)	AT YOU, GOVERNOR, IS THERE? I HOPE YOU GOT IT AS	HOT	AS I DID. MIND, MISS SHEPANOSKA: IT WASNT LOST ON ME.
GLIM (174)	THE LONGER SHE WILL SUFFER. SO LET HER HAVE IT AS	HOT	AS POSSIBLE. (THE GIRL RECOILS). DO NOT LET GO MY HAND:
JOAN 5 (114)	/DUNOIS/ IF OUR CANNON BALLS WERE ALL AS	HOT	AS YOUR HEAD, AND WE HAD ENOUGH OF THEM, WE SHOULD
LION II (135)	RUNS THROUGH MY VEINS: I FEEL MY BLOOD SURGE UP	HOT	BEHIND MY EYES: I MUST CHARGE: I MUST STRIKE: I MUST
SUPR III (108)	BATTLE ALL YOU NEED TO MAKE YOU FIGHT IS A LITTLE	HOT	BLOOD AND THE KNOWLEDGE THAT IT'S MORE DANGEROUS TO LOSE
DEVL II (47)	FLESHY PURSES UNDER HIS EYES BECOME INJECTED WITH	HOT	BLOOD; THE MAN OF PEACE VANISHES, TRANSFIGURED INTO A
BASH PREFACE(90)	PASSIONATE AND RICHLY COLORED STYLE IT SOLD LIKE	HOT	CAKES. I MUST MAKE A PERSONAL CONFESSION IN THIS MATTER.
GETT PREFACE(204)	FOR EXAMPLE, IT IS THE WILL OF THE PEOPLE ON A	HOT	DAY THAT THE MEANS OF RELIEF FROM THE EFFECTS OF THE
CAPT III (272)	EXACTLY AS SHE MIGHT BE IN SURREY ON A VERY	HOT	DAY). SIT YE DOON, LEDDY CEECILY. /LADY CICELY/ (
DOCT PREFACE(59)	FOUND THE EFFECT EXACTLY THE SAME, AND THAT ANY	HOT	DRINK WOULD HAVE DONE AS WELL. BIOMETRIKA, ANOTHER
6CAL (95)	NOT BRING A BRAZIER AND SOME CUSHIONS, AND A	HOT	DRINK-- A POSSET-- /THE QUEEN/ (CURTSEYING) SIR:
VWOO 1 (121)	WHEN YOU GET A HOLIDAY YOU GO OFF IN A CROWDED	HOT	EXCURSION TRAIN TO THE SEASIDE AND MAKE YOURSELF TIRED
DEVL II (48)	HE SNATCHES UP HAT AND CLOAK, AND PUTS BOTH ON IN	HOT	HASTE) NOW LISTEN, YOU. IF YOU CAN GET A WORD WITH HIM
BARB III (329)	I CHUCKED IT AWAY. /BILTON/ THE TOP OF IT WAS RED	HOT	INSIDE, SIR. /LOMAX/ WELL, SUPPOSE IT WAS! I DIDN'T
LION II (140)	THE WHIP). IF THAT WILL NOT MOVE THEM, BRING THE	HOT	IRONS. THE MAN IS LIKE A MOUNTAIN. (HE RETURNS ANGRILY
CYMB V (146)	WHOLE WORLD SHALL NOT SAVE HIM. /BELARIUS/ NOT SO	HOT	. FIRST PAY ME FOR THE NURSING OF THY SONS; AND LET IT
PYGM II (231)	HAS JUST USED IT HERSELF BECAUSE THE BATH WAS TOO	HOT	. IT BEGINS WITH THE SAME LETTER AS BATH. SHE KNOWS NO
GLIM (184)	SIGNOR. THE BLOOD FLOWS FREEST WHEN IT IS	HOT	. /FERRUCCIO/ SHE DEVIL! LISTEN TO ME, GIULIETTA--
GLIM (176)	TRICK. I SHOULD HAVE KILLED YOU WHEN MY BLOOD WAS	HOT	. /SQUARCIO/ WILL YOUR EXCELLENCY PLEASE TO STEP IN? MY
MIS. (186)	STARTLES AND ALMOST CHOKES HIM). IT'S RATHER	HOT	. /TARLETON/ DO YOU GOOD. DONT BE AFRAID OF IT. /MRS
DEVL III (54)	STORE BY THE GOODNESS THAT ONLY COMES OUT RED	HOT	. WHAT I DID LAST NIGHT, I DID IN COLD BLOOD, CARING NOT
DOCT PREFACE(42)	JACKETS; OR AS FANCIERS BLIND SINGING BIRDS WITH	HOT	NEEDLES, AND MUTILATE THE EARS AND TAILS OF DOGS AND
CYMB V (149)	WHEN YOU ARRIVED JUST NOW I, AS YOU SAW, WAS	HOT	ON KILLING HIM. LET HIM BEAR WITNESS THAT I DREW ON HIM
6CAL (94)	MAN, WOMAN, AND CHILD TORN TO PIECES WITH RED	HOT	PINCERS FOR IT. /THE PRINCE/ TRULY, DEAR SIR, YOU HAVE
JOAN EPILOG (155)	MUD AND BLOOD. UP THE LADDERS WITH THE STONES AND	HOT	PITCH RAINING DOWN. LIKE YOU. /JOAN/ NO! DID MAKE A MAN
NEVR II SD(241)	BAD HABIT! THE COOK, FOLLOWED BY A WAITER WITH	HOT	PLATES, BRINGS IN THE FISH FROM THE KITCHEN TO THE
BUOY IV (55)	THE CHILDREN ARE BORN, AND THEN DROPS THEM LIKE	HOT	POTATOES. MONEY GUARANTEES COMFORT AND WHAT YOU CALL
MTH2 (44)	IN THE COALITION. OF COURSE, HE DROPPED ME LIKE A	HOT	POTATO. /CONRAD/ WELL, NOW THAT THE COALITION HAS
CLEO PRO2 (99)	DID WE LEARN? EVEN THAT CAESAR IS COMING ALSO IN	HOT	PURSUIT OF HIS FOE, AND THAT PTOLEMY HAS SLAIN POMPEY,
LION II SD(144)	DOWN AGAIN ON THE OTHER SIDE, WITH THE LION IN	HOT	PURSUIT. ANDROCLES RUSHES AFTER THE LION; OVERTAKES HIM
MIS. (177)	SEEN DARTING ACROSS THE GARDEN WITH PERCIVAL IN	HOT	PURSUIT. IMMEDIATELY AFTERWARDS SHE APPEARS AGAIN, AND
JOAN 5 (114)	I SAY TOO. WE SHALL GO THROUGH THEM LIKE A RED	HOT	SHOT THROUGH A POUND OF BUTTER. WHAT DO YOU SAY,
2TRU I (36)	DO YOU THINK IT WOULD BE WELL TO HAVE ANOTHER	HOT	WATER BOTTLE AGAINST HER ARM UNTIL IT IS QUITE WARM
VWOO 3 (141)	DROPS; PEPPER AND MUSTARD; COSY COMFORTERS AND	HOT	WATER BOTTLES. THROUGH THE WINDOW I DELIGHT MY EYES WITH
NEVR I (223)	TO KNOW YOUR FAMILY, MR CRAMPTON. (HE POURS SOME	HOT	WATER INTO THE TUMBLER). /CRAMPTON/ SORRY I CANT
SUPR IV (168)	DEPEND ON? /TANNER/ NO: A THOUSAND TIMES NO:	HOT	WATER IS THE REVOLUTIONIST'S ELEMENT. YOU CLEAN MEN AS
CAND III SD(137)	COMES IN WITH GLASSES, LEMONS, AND A JUG OF	HOT	WATER ON A TRAY. /CANDIDA/ WHO WILL HAVE SOME LEMONADE?
INCA (242)	IN THE ROOMS IS COMFORTABLY WARM, AND HAVE	HOT	WATER PUT IN ALL THE BEDROOMS -- /THE MANAGER/ THERE ARE
MRS PREFACE(151)	SOCIAL INSTITUTIONS KEPT ME SO CONTINUALLY IN	HOT	WATER THAT THE ADDITION OF ANOTHER JUGFUL OF BOILING
DOCT PREFACE(59)	HAD TRIED THE CONTROL EXPERIMENT OF TAKING THE	HOT	WATER WITHOUT THE MUMMY, YOU MIGHT HAVE FOUND THE EFFECT

SUPR IV	(168)	DRESS AND ARE INSULTED AND GET INTO ALL SORTS OF	HOT	WATER, AND THEN THEIR HUSBANDS GET DRAGGED IN TOO, AND
HART I	(45)	THESE ARE OUR MANNERS, NO ROOM READY. NO	HOT	WATER. NO WELCOMING HOSTESS. OUR VISITOR IS TO SLEEP IN
NEVR I	SD(223)	MINE AS HERS. THE PARLORMAID BRINGS IN A JUG OF	HOT	WATER. /VALENTINE/ THANK YOU. (SHE GIVES HIM THE JUG
NEVR I	(223)	DROPS THE FORCEPS WITH A CLINK INTO THE	HOT	WATER), YOU NEEDNT WARM THAT THING TO USE ON ME. I'M NOT
PPP	(201)	(GIVING HER THE BUST); DISSOLVE IT IN A JUG OF	HOT	WATER; AND BRING IT BACK INSTANTLY. MR BASTABLE'S LIFE
6CAL	(100)	WILL YOU AND YOUR FRIENDS PARTAKE OF SOME CUPS OF	HOT	WINE IN MY PAVILION? YOU SHALL BE FURNISHED WITH GOWNS.
6CAL	(100)	WITH GOWNS. /THE KING/ (CHOKING WITH WRATH)	HOT	W--! /EUSTACHE/ ALAS, MADAM, WHEN THE KING HAS ENDED
NEVR IV	(288)	YOU, MAAM? /MRS CLANDON/ ER-- OH YES: IT'S SO	HOT	, I THINK WE MIGHT HAVE A JUG OF CLARET CUP. /WAITER/ (
2TRU II	(57)	(GIVING HIM HER FINGER TIPS) HOW DO, COLONEL?	HOT	, ISNT IT? (HER DIALECT IS NOW A SPIRITED AMALGAMATION
PYGM II	(240)	IS. WOOLLY TOWELS, THERE IS; AND A TOWEL HORSE SO	HOT	, IT BURNS YOUR FINGERS. SOFT BRUSHES TO SCRUB YOURSELF,

HOTCHKISS

GETT	SD(327)	GOES INTO THE STUDY. MRS GEORGE STROLLS ACROSS TO	HOTCHKISS	AND CONTEMPLATES HIM CURIOUSLY. /HOTCHKISS/
GETT	(300)	TAKES IT TO THE BISHOP; THEN SITS DOWN BETWEEN	HOTCHKISS	AND HER MOTHER). /THE BISHOP/ (READING THE TITLE)
GETT	SD(352)	THROUGH THE TOWER). MRS GEORGE, LEFT ALONE WITH	HOTCHKISS	AND SOAMES, SUDDENLY PUTS HER HANDS ON SOAMES'S
GETT	SD(308)	SOMETHING CLEVER! CAN I BE MISTAKEN IN HIM?	HOTCHKISS	COMES BACK WITH A BLOTTER AND SOME PAPER. HE TAKES
GETT	SD(289)	EDITH SHOULD BE ONE OF THE COMBATANTS! ST JOHN	HOTCHKISS	COMES INTO THE TOWER USHERED BY COLLINS. HE IS A
GETT	SD(344)	THE STUDY DOOR AND CRIES) YES: COME IN, COME IN.	HOTCHKISS	COMES SOFTLY IN FROM THE STUDY. /HOTCHKISS/ WILL
GETT	SD(338)	/THE BISHOP/ I CAN QUITE BELIEVE IT, SINJON.	HOTCHKISS	GOES INTO THE STUDY. /THE BISHOP/ (TURNING TO MRS
GETT	SD(308)	MATERIALS, BISHOP? /THE BISHOP/ DO, SINJON.	HOTCHKISS	GOES INTO THE LIBRARY. /COLLINS/ IF I MIGHT POINT
GETT	(299)	ANSWER YES OR NO WITHOUT SPOILING IT AND SETTING	HOTCHKISS	HERE GRINNING LIKE A CHESHIRE CAT? IF SHE PUTS ON
GETT	(309)	IT BY SOME VERY STYLISH GENTLEMAN-- PERHAPS MR	HOTCHKISS	HERE WOULD BE GOOD ENOUGH TO TAKE IT-- AND SHE'LL
GETT	(289)	AS HE STRONGLY DISAPPROVES OF THE PART PLAYED BY	HOTCHKISS	IN REGINALD'S DOMESTIC AFFAIRS). /THE BISHOP/ ALL
GETT	(324)	BRIDGENORTH/ (INTRODUCING HOTCHKISS) MR ST JOHN	HOTCHKISS	, HOTCHKISS, STILL FAR ALOOF BY THE STUDY DOOR,
GETT	(289)	IN VAIN TO SNUB HIM. /COLLINS/ (ANNOUNCING) MR	HOTCHKISS	. (HE WITHDRAWS). /HOTCHKISS/ (CLAPPING REGINALD
GETT	(351)	IS, OR EVER HAS BEEN, ANYTHING BETWEEN ME AND MR	HOTCHKISS	. /COLLINS/ BLESS YOU, MAAM! ONE COULD ALWAYS SEE
GETT	(296)	(GRAVELY) THERE IS SUCH A THING AS DELICACY, MR	HOTCHKISS	. /HOTCHKISS/ THERE IS SUCH A THING AS CURIOSITY,
GETT	(310)	BE GOOD ENOUGH TO GIVE ME THAT RING, MR	HOTCHKISS	. /HOTCHKISS/ WITH PLEASURE. (HE HANDS IT TO
GETT	(303)	HE SHOULD HAVE KICKED YOU OUT OF THE HOUSE, MR	HOTCHKISS	. /REGINALD/ (RISING) HOW COULD I KICK HIM OUT OF
GETT	(281)	PUT-UP JOB. SHE WANTS TO MARRY SOME FELLOW NAMED	HOTCHKISS	. /REGINALD/ A FELLOW WITH A FACE LIKE-- /LEO/ YOU
GETT	(299)	BETTER-- /REGINALD/ (VIOLENTLY) NOW LOOK HERE,	HOTCHKISS	, WHO ASKED YOU TO CUT IN? IS YOUR NAME EDITH?
GETT	(279)	ME. /MRS BRIDGENORTH/ I SHALL SEND A NOTE TO MR	HOTCHKISS	NOT TO COME. /LEO/ (WEEPING AGAIN) OH, ALICE! (
GETT	SD(332)	GOES HALF WAY TO THE GARDEN DOOR TO SPEAK TO HIM.	HOTCHKISS	POSTS HIMSELF ON THE HEARTH. /MRS GEORGE/ WHERE
GETT	(349)	THE OAK CHEST AND SEATS HIM THERE. HE CHUCKLES.	HOTCHKISS	RESUMES HIS SEAT, BROODING). /THE BISHOP/ ALL THE
GETT	(349)	GORELL BARNES THAT I HAVE CHANGED MY MIND. (TO	HOTCHKISS	) I MIGHT HAVE KNOWN THAT YOU WERE TOO CLEVER TO
GETT	(324)	HAS, HAVNT YOU? /MRS BRIDGENORTH/ (INTRODUCING	HOTCHKISS	) MR ST JOHN HOTCHKISS. HOTCHKISS, STILL FAR ALOOF
GETT	(305)	DOORWAY) IVE BEEN THINKING. /THE BISHOP/ (TO	HOTCHKISS	) NOTHING LIKE MAKING PEOPLE THINK: IS THERE,
GETT	(310)	BISHOP/ (TAKING OFF HIS RING AND HANDING IT TO	HOTCHKISS	) OBLIGE ME BY UNDERTAKING THE MISSION.
GETT	(298)	I SHALL NOT TAKE AN ACTION, CECIL. /EDITH/ TO	HOTCHKISS	) SORRY; BUT YOU ARE OLD ENOUGH TO KNOW BETTER. (
GETT	(353)	(LEAVING SOAMES AND GOING A STEP OR TWO NEARER	HOTCHKISS	) WHY ARNT YOU LIKE HIM, SONNY? WHY DO YOU HANG
GETT	(351)	THE TOWER, FOLLOWED BY SYKES). /REGINALD/ (TO	HOTCHKISS	) YOUVE ALWAYS TALKED A PRECIOUS LOT ABOUT
GETT	(314)	OAK CHEST, AND PERCHES HERSELF ON IT CLOSE BESIDE	HOTCHKISS	). /REGINALD/ (WATCHING THEM SOURLY) YOU DO IT
GETT	(327)	INTO THE STUDY). /SYKES/ (LOOKS IRRESOLUTELY AT	HOTCHKISS	)--? /HOTCHKISS/ TOO LATE: YOU CANT SAVE ME NOW,
GETT	(290)	THE NAME. I'LL NOT REFUSE YOUR ACQUAINTANCE, MR	HOTCHKISS	; PARTLY BECAUSE YOURE MY BROTHER'S GUEST, AND
GETT	SD(347)	END OF THE TABLE AND GOES ON WITH HIS WORK.	HOTCHKISS	SITS DOWN IN THE NEXT CHAIR ROUND THE TABLE
GETT	(294)	STEADY. (REGINALD SUBSIDES INTO HIS CHAIR.	HOTCHKISS	SITS ON HIS RIGHT, APPEASING HIM). /THE BISHOP/
GETT	(348)	(BREAKING LOOSE FROM HER AND STUMPING OFF PAST	HOTCHKISS	TOWARDS THE HEARTH) NO, I'M DASHED IF I'LL BE
GETT	(348)	MY FACE? (HE SEEMS ON THE POINT OF ASSAULTING	HOTCHKISS	WHEN LEO GETS BETWEEN THEM AND DRAWS REGINALD AWAY
GETT	(304)	YOU? HOW IS IT THAT WE ALWAYS GET TALKING ABOUT	HOTCHKISS	WHEN OUR BUSINESS IS ABOUT EDITH? (HE FUMES UP
GETT	(320)	FOR MY LOOKING AFTER REJJY. (SHE LEAVES	HOTCHKISS	, AND GOES BACK TO HER CHAIR AT THE END OF THE
GETT	SD(324)	AS FAR AS SOAMES'S CHAIR WHEN MRS GEORGE APPEARS.	HOTCHKISS	, APPARENTLY RECOGNIZING HER, RECOILS IN
GETT	(354)	NOT PRESUME TO ACCUSE ME OF UNBELIEF. AND DO YOU,	HOTCHKISS	, NOT DESPISE THIS WOMAN'S SOUL BECAUSE SHE SPEAKS
GETT	(278)	SERPENT? /LEO/ HE ISNT. /REGINALD/ SINJON	HOTCHKISS	, OF COURSE. /MRS BRIDGENORTH/ SINJON HOTCHKISS!
GETT	(338)	YOUR FRIENDS. CAN WE HELP YOU? /MRS GEORGE/ (TO	HOTCHKISS	, POINTING TO THE STUDY) GO IN THERE, YOU. YOURE
GETT	SD(324)	(INTRODUCING HOTCHKISS) MR ST JOHN HOTCHKISS.	HOTCHKISS	, STILL FAR ALOOF BY THE STUDY DOOR, BOWS. /MRS
GETT	(289)	GENERAL). /THE GENERAL/ (READING) " MR ST JOHN	HOTCHKISS	, THE CELEBRATED COWARD, LATE LIEUTENANT IN THE
GETT	(301)	I SAID YES; AND I MEAN YES. THERE WAS ONE NIGHT,	HOTCHKISS	, WHEN I JOLLY NEARLY SHOT YOU AND LEO AND
GETT	SD(338)	TO THE FIREPLACE; SEIZES THE POKER; AND MAKES FOR	HOTCHKISS	, WHO FLIES TO THE STUDY DOOR. THE BISHOP ENTERS
GETT	(326)	ARE AWAY, SOAMES? /SOAMES/ YES, CERTAINLY. (TO	HOTCHKISS	, WHO IS IN HIS WAY) EXCUSE ME. THE BISHOP AND
GETT	SD(326)	BISHOP AND SOAMES GO INTO THE STUDY, DISTURBING	HOTCHKISS	, WHO, PLUNGED IN A STRANGE REVERIE, HAS FORGOTTEN
GETT	(300)	TO MURDER SOMEBODY, UNCLE REJJY? /REGINALD/ (AT	HOTCHKISS	, WITH INTENSE EXPRESSION) YES. /LEO/ REJJY!
GETT	(278)	HOTCHKISS, OF COURSE. /MRS BRIDGENORTH/ SINJON	HOTCHKISS	! WHY, HE'S COMING TO THE WEDDING! /REGINALD/

HOTCHKISS'S

GETT	SD(358)	GENTLEMEN: WAY FOR THE MAYORESS. MRS GEORGE TAKES	HOTCHKISS'S	ARM, AND GOES OUT, PRECEDED BY THE BEADLE.
GETT	SD(306)	A LITTLE PUZZLED, COMES FORWARD AFFABLY TO	HOTCHKISS'S	LEFT. /HOTCHKISS/ (RISING, IMPRESSED BY THE

HOTE

WIDO I	SD(3)	A WOODEN ANNEXE WITH AN ENTRANCE MARKED TABLE D'	HOTE	. A WAITER IS IN ATTENDANCE. A COUPLE OF ENGLISH

HOTEL

NEVR I	(202)	OH, DO, MR VALENTINE. /PHILIP/ AT THE MARINE	HOTEL	: HALF PAST ONE. /THE YOUNG LADY/ WE SHALL BE ABLE TO
MILL IV	(189)	WELL, WHAT MORE COULD ANYONE ASK BUT A NICE	HOTEL	? ALL THE HOUSEKEEPING DONE FOR US; NO TROUBLE WITH
BULL II	(108)	THE WAY, HADNT I BETTER SEE ABOUT A ROOM AT THE	HOTEL	? (THEY STARE AT HIM). /CORNELIUS/ THE HOTEL!
BULL II	(108)	/CORNELIUS/ THE HOTEL! /FATHER DEMPSEY/ HWAT	HOTEL	? /AUNT JUDY/ INDEEDN YOURE NOT GOIN TO A HOTEL.
BULL IV	(173)	WILL DOOLAN HELP YOU TO GET A LICENSE FOR YOUR	HOTEL	? /BROADBENT/ MY DEAR SIR: TO ALL INTENTS AND
JITT III	(67)	THERE TO CLOSE HIS EYES, LIKE A CHAMBERMAID IN A	HOTEL	? /JITTA/ SHE DID NOT CLOSE HIS EYES. SHE STOLE AWAY
NEVR III	(279)	TO SETTLE THE DIFFICULTY? HERE? IN THIS	HOTEL	? TONIGHT? WHAT DO YOU SAY? /MRS CLANDON/ BUT WHERE
BULL IV	(168)	GOLF LINKS, FRIDAY TO TUESDAY, RAILWAY TICKET AND	HOTEL	ALL INCLUSIVE. I TELL YOU, NORA, I'M GOING TO DEVELOP
BULL IV	(168)	THIS VIEW. THIS WOULD BE A JOLLY GOOD PLACE FOR A	HOTEL	AND A GOLF LINKS. FRIDAY TO TUESDAY, RAILWAY TICKET
MRS III	(230)	SUCH THINGS IN SOCIETY. ONCE LET OUT THE WORD	HOTEL	AND EVERYBODY SAYS YOU KEEP A PUBLIC-HOUSE. YOU
ARMS II	(31)	OF COURSE HE OVER-REACHED US. HIS FATHER WAS A	HOTEL	AND LIVERY STABLE KEEPER; AND HE OWED HIS FIRST STEP
MIS. PREFACE	(77)	OF THE IDLE RICH, WANDERING FROM HOTEL TO	HOTEL	AND NEVER REALLY LIVING ANYWHERE, YET I SHOULD NO MORE
NEVR III	SD(261)	WITH A MAROON CLOTH ON WHICH OPULENTLY BOUND	HOTEL	AND RAILWAY GUIDES ARE DISPLAYED. A VISITOR ENTERING
MILL IV	(196)	HAVE ALLOWED MY HUSBAND TO BRING A WOMAN TO MY	HOTEL	AND REGISTER HER IN MY NAME. YOU ARE FIRED. (SHE IS
SUPR IV	(144)	MESSAGE? /STRAKER/ YES, MISS. I TOOK IT TO THE	HOTEL	AND SENT IT UP, EXPECTING TO SEE YOUNG MR MALONE. THEN
DOCT II	SD(119)	NATURE! REFINED-- BLENKINSOP COMES FROM THE	HOTEL	AND TAKES THE EMPTY CHAIR NEXT RIDGEON. /BLENKINSOP/
MILL IV	(205)	NOT ALLAH HIMSELF CAN DO THAT. BUT I CAME TO THIS	HOTEL	AS A SCULLERY MAID: THE MOST INCOMPETENT SCULLERY MAID
INCA	(241)	THE MILLIONAIRES OF AMERICA. WHEN I EXPOSE YOUR	HOTEL	AS THE SECOND-RATE LITTLE HOLE IT IS, NOT A SOUL ABOVE
NEVR I	(216)	WAIT TO SEE HIM NOW: I HAVE AN APPOINTMENT AT THE	HOTEL	AT A QUARTER TO ONE WITH AN OLD FRIEND WHOM I HAVE NOT
WIDO I	SD(3)	ACT I. IN THE GARDEN RESTAURANT OF A	HOTEL	AT REMAGEN ON THE RHINE, ON A FINE AFTERNOON IN AUGUST
BULL IV	(177)	THE ATTITUDE OF THE PRIEST REBUKING SIN) WHEN THE	HOTEL	BECOMES INSOLVENT (BROADBENT TAKES HIS CIGAR OUT OF
GETT	(277)	HIS WIFE'S NAME? HOW WOULD YOU LIKE TO GO INTO A	HOTEL	BEFORE ALL THE WAITERS AND PEOPLE WITH-- WITH THAT ON
SUPR IV	(154)	GIVE ME THE REMITTANCE. HE WILL WANT IT FOR HIS	HOTEL	BILL. I'LL SEE WHETHER I CAN INDUCE HIM TO ACCEPT IT.
SUPR III	(84)	ANY CASUAL WORDS CAN. (HE PRODUCES A PACKET OF	HOTEL	BILLS SCRAWLED WITH MANUSCRIPT, AND KNEELS AT THE FIRE
PYGM EPILOG	(302)	WAS THE COLONEL'S; AND HE AND HIGGINS PAID THE	HOTEL	BILLS. MR F. HILL, FLORIST AND GREENGROCER (THEY SOON
GETT	(277)	AFTER DINNER. I HAD TO PUT HER DOWN IN THE	HOTEL	BOOK AS MRS REGINALD BRIDGENORTH: LEO'S NAME! DO YOU
AUGS	(278)	CLERK/ NO. I COME BECAUSE THE WAITER FROM THE	HOTEL	BROUGHT THIS PAPER. YOU LEFT IT ON THE COFFEE-ROOM
GENV III	SD(86)	HASTILY AND DISAPPEAR IN THE DIRECTION OF THE	HOTEL	BUREAU. /THE SECRETARY/ YOU REALLY THINK THE DICTATORS
NEVR II	SD(245)	SHEPHERDS HIS ASSISTANT ALONG WITH HIM INTO THE	HOTEL	BY THE KITCHEN ENTRANCE, LEAVING THE LUNCHEON PARTY TO
2TRU II	(65)	COUNTESS, BUT I'M ONLY A HOTEL CHAMBERMAID; AND A	HOTEL	CHAMBERMAID GETS SO USED TO NEW FACES THAT AT LAST
2TRU III	(98)	LOVE. WITH THAT THING. AND THOUGH I WAS NEVER A	HOTEL	CHAMBERMAID I GOT TIRED OF HIM SOONER THAN SWEETIE
2TRU II	(65)	IF I WERE A REAL COUNTESS, BUT I'M ONLY A	HOTEL	CHAMBERMAID; AND A HOTEL CHAMBERMAID GETS SO USED TO
SUPR I	SD(3)	METHODS, OR BY THE ENTERPRISE OF THE RAILWAY AND	HOTEL	COMPANIES WHICH SELL YOU A SATURDAY TO MONDAY OF LIFE
APPL II	(276)	MEN ALL OVER THE WORLD ARE AS MUCH ALIKE AS	HOTEL	DINNERS. IT'S NO USE PRETENDING THAT THE AMERICA OF
NEVR II	(233)	A WORD). COME, DOLLY. (AS SHE GOES TO THE	HOTEL	DOOR, THE WAITER COMES OUT WITH A TRAY OF PLATES, ETC.
CURE	SD(225)	MAN OF 22, IS PROSTRATE ON A SOFA IN A LARGE	HOTEL	DRAWING ROOM, CRYING CONVULSIVELY. HIS DOCTOR IS

BULL IV (177)	DO IF HE WERE ALIVE NOW. YOU MAY EVEN BUILD THE	HOTEL	EFFICIENTLY IF YOU CAN FIND ENOUGH EFFICIENT MASONS,
NEVR II (237)	SIR. NAME OF M'COMAS, SIR. (HE GOES TOWARDS THE	HOTEL	ENTRANCE WITH THE COAT AND STICK, HAPPILY UNCONSCIOUS
NEVR II (240)	SOB) LOOK AT ME! /PHILIP/ SH! (POINTING TO THE	HOTEL	ENTRANCE, WHERE THE WAITER HAS JUST APPEARED) ORDER
BULL IV (178)	FINALLY PROFIT VERY EFFICIENTLY BY GETTING THAT	HOTEL	FOR A FEW SHILLINGS IN THE POUND. (MORE AND MORE
NEVR II SD(225)	OF THE ORDINARY ESPLANADE PATTERN. ACCESS TO THE	HOTEL	FOR VISITORS IS BY AN ENTRANCE IN THE MIDDLE OF ITS
HART PREFACE(21)	GENTLEMAN AT BREAKFAST IN A WEEK-END MARINE	HOTEL	HAD BEEN INTERRUPTED BY A BOMB DROPPING INTO HIS
ARMS III (69)	IVE MET IN BULGARIA. I'LL MAKE HIM MANAGER OF A	HOTEL	IF HE CAN SPEAK FRENCH AND GERMAN. /LOUKA/ (SUDDENLY
MILL IV (197)	AS YOU OR I. /EPIFANIA/ I WILL SET FIRE TO THE	HOTEL	IF NECESSARY. (SHE SEES ADRIAN). HALLO! WHAT IS
MILL IV (193)	FUSS, DARLING. WEVE A PERFECT RIGHT TO BE IN HER	HOTEL	IF WE PAY OUR WAY JUST LIKE ANYBODY ELSE. /ALASTAIR/
GENV PREFACE(19)	OF THE OLD SILENT FILMS, DRIVING TO HER	HOTEL	IN A TAXI. FOR A MOMENT HITLER MAY HAVE FANCIED THAT A
BULL II (108)	WHY, THE DRIVER TOLD ME THERE WAS THE FINEST	HOTEL	IN IRELAND HERE. (THEY REGARD HIM JOYLESSLY). /AUNT
BULL II (108)	THE LEAST. /FATHER DEMPSEY/ MAN ALIVE! THERES NO	HOTEL	IN ROSSCULLEN. /BROADBENT/ NO HOTEL! WHY, THE DRIVER
MIS. (127)	I WAS YOUNG. THEN I PICKED IT UP ONE EVENING IN A	HOTEL	IN SUNDERLAND WHEN I HAD LEFT ALL MY PAPERS IN THE
BULL II (108)	SO MUCH TROUBLE UNNECESSARILY. I SHANT MIND THE	HOTEL	IN THE LEAST. /FATHER DEMPSEY/ MAN ALIVE! THERES NO
WIDO I SD(3)	GARDEN TO THE RIVERSIDE IS SEEN ON THE RIGHT. THE	HOTEL	IS ON THE LEFT. IT HAS A WOODEN ANNEXE WITH AN
DOCT II SD(115)	SCHUTZMACHER AND WALPOLE. THE ENTRANCE TO THE	HOTEL	IS ON THEIR RIGHT, BEHIND B.B. THE FIVE MEN ARE
NEVR II (250)	I HAVE ALWAYS SAID THAT THE GREAT ADVANTAGE OF A	HOTEL	IS THAT IT'S A REFUGE FROM HOME LIFE, SIR. /CRAMPTON/
BULL IV (181)	COME ALONG AND HELP ME TO CHOOSE THE SITE FOR THE	HOTEL	.
DOCT II SD(130)	STRIKES THE BELL AS SIR PATRICK MAKES FOR THE	HOTEL	. A WAITER COMES. /RIDGEON/ (TO THE WAITER) MY BILL,
NEVR II SD(225)	TWO AT EACH SIDE AND ONE AT THE END NEXT THE	HOTEL	, AGAINST THE PARAPET ANOTHER TABLE IS PREPARED AS A
NEVR III SD(261)	ACT III. THE CLANDONS' SITTING ROOM IN THE	HOTEL	, AN EXPENSIVE APARTMENT ON THE GROUND FLOOR, WITH A
MILL IV (189)	NOR TAXES. I HAVE NEVER HAD ANY PEACE EXCEPT IN A	HOTEL	. BUT PERHAPS A MAN DOESNT FEEL THAT WAY. THE MANAGER
FANY III (326)	MYSELF TO AN OLD BUTLER OF OURS WHO KEPT A	HOTEL	. HE TAUGHT ME MY PRESENT BUSINESS, AND GOT ME A PLACE
GENV I (43)	THIS GENTLEMAN'S ACQUAINTANCE LAST NIGHT AT MY	HOTEL	. HIS INTEREST IN THE CHURCH OF ENGLAND KEPT US UP
SUPR III (84)	IN TEN YEARS I SHOULD HAVE OWNED A FIRST-CLASS	HOTEL	. I MET HER; AND-- YOU SEE! -- I AM A BRIGAND, AN
WIDO I (4)	TRIUMPHANTLY) HERE, HARRY, HERE: AT THIS	HOTEL	. I RECOGNIZED THE FATHER'S UMBRELLA IN THE HALL.
DOCT II (124)	/THE MAID/ I BEG PARDON, SIR. IT'S NOT ABOUT THE	HOTEL	. I'M NOT ALLOWED TO BE ON THE TERRACE; AND I SHOULD
NEVR II SD(225)	ACT II. ON THE TERRACE AT THE MARINE	HOTEL	. IT IS A SQUARE FLAGGED PLATFORM, GLARING IN THE SUN,
OVER SD(171)	IN A RETIRED CORNER OF THE LOUNGE OF A SEASIDE	HOTEL	. IT IS A SUMMER NIGHT: THE FRENCH WINDOW BEHIND THEM
SUPR III (138)	STUPID ABOUT NAMES. /MENDOZA/ IT WAS AT THE SAVOY	HOTEL	. (TO HECTOR) YOU, SIR, USED TO COME WITH THIS LADY (
NEVR II SD(239)	IN ITSELF. MRS CLANDON AND GLORIA COME FROM THE	HOTEL	. MRS CLANDON ADVANCES WITH COURAGEOUS SELF-POSSESSION
NEVR II (235)	(M'COMAS SHAKES HIM OFF AND MARCHES INTO THE	HOTEL	. PHIL FOLLOWS WITH UNRUFFLED COMPOSURE). /DOLLY/ (
HART I (52)	WRETCH. (RISING ANGRILY) I'LL GO STRAIGHT TO A	HOTEL	. /MRS HUSHABYE/ (SEIZING HER BY THE SHOULDERS) MY
SUPR IV (165)	INDEED. DONT CRY, DEAR: I'M ONLY GOING TO THE	HOTEL	. /MRS WHITEFIELD/ BUT GOING IN THAT DRESS, WITH YOUR
MILL IV (191)	AND THE NEXT THE PROPRIETRESS OF A FIRST CLASS	HOTEL	. /PATRICIA/ AND ARE THE OLD PEOPLE SATISFIED AND
MILL IV (189)	THIS IS WHAT HOME OUGHT TO BE, THOUGH IT'S ONLY A	HOTEL	. /PATRICIA/ WELL, WHAT MORE COULD ANYONE ASK BUT A
INCA (240)	TIME TO FIND A PROPER APARTMENT IN A RESPECTABLE	HOTEL	. /THE MANAGER/ I DO NOT UNDERSTAND. /ERMYNTRUDE/ YOU
MRS III (230)	HARD IT IS TO FIND A REALLY COMFORTABLE PRIVATE	HOTEL	. /VIVIE/ (SICKENED, AVERTING HER FACE) YES: GO ON.
NEVR II SD(254)	AS IF HE AGREED TO THAT; AND GOES INTO THE	HOTEL	. SHE LOOKS AT HIM WITH EQUAL STEADINESS UNTIL HE
PYGM V (274)	AND BEING AFRAID TO, AND PARTLY IN THE CARLTON	HOTEL	. SHE TOLD ME OF THE BRUTAL WAY YOU TWO TREATED HER.
BUOY 1 (11)	OF OUR PRESENT FORTUNE, BEGAN AS A PORTER IN A	HOTEL	. THANKS TO HIS ABILITY AND THE SOCIAL SYSTEM THAT
MILL IV SD(188)	THE CARDINAL'S HAT, A VERY ATTRACTIVE RIVERSIDE	HOTEL	. THE LONG TABLES ARE GONE, REPLACED BY SEVERAL
WIDO I (5)	OF MIND! (HE STROLLS WITH HIM TOWARDS THE	HOTEL	. THE WAITER COMES OUT WITH THE BEER). KELLNER:
WIDO I (12)	DROWNED BY THE CLANGOR OF A BELL FROM WITHIN THE	HOTEL	. THE WAITER APPEARS ON THE STEPS, RINGING IT. COKANE
WIDO I SD(3)	A COUPLE OF ENGLISH TOURISTS COME OUT OF THE	HOTEL	. THE YOUNGER, DR HARRY TRENCH, IS ABOUT 24, STOUTLY
DOCT PREFACE(16)	BY RUNNING WHAT IS THE MOST EXPENSIVE KIND OF	HOTEL	. THESE GAINS ARE SO GREAT THAT THEY UNDO MUCH OF THE
DOCT II SD(126)	AND EXCUSE THE LIBERTY. SHE GOES INTO THE	HOTEL	. THEY WATCH HER IN SILENCE. /RIDGEON/ (WHEN SHE IS
CURE (225)	IS NOTHING BUT NERVES. REMEMBER THAT YOURE IN A	HOTEL	. THEYLL PUT YOU OUT IF YOU MAKE A ROW. /REGINALD/ (
MILL II (166)	OLD INN TRYING TO PRETEND THAT IT'S A RIVERSIDE	HOTEL	. WE HAVE JUST HAD A HORRIBLE MEAL OF TOMATO TEA
NEVR II (258)	THIS PLACE? IT'S NOT HEAVEN: IT'S THE MARINE	HOTEL	. WHATS THE TIME? IT'S NOT ETERNITY: IT'S ABOUT HALF
BULL II (108)	HOTEL? /AUNT JUDY/ INDEEDN YOURE NOT GOIN TO A	HOTEL	. YOULL STAY WITH US. I'D HAVE PUT YOU INTO LARRY'S
BARB PREFACE(224)	CHEAPENED BY PROSTITUTION AS UNSCRUPULOUSLY AS A	HOTEL	KEEPER TRADES IN WAITERS' LABOR CHEAPENED BY TIPS, OR
2TRU III (96)	STEAMBOAT COMPANIES, RAILWAYS, MOTOR CAR PEOPLE,	HOTEL	KEEPERS, DRESSMAKERS, SERVANTS, ALL TRYING TO GET MY
ROCK II (263)	THEYRE EMPTIED AGAIN BY WEST END TRADESMEN AND	HOTEL	KEEPERS, FASHIONABLE DOCTORS AND LAWYERS AND PARSONS
GETT PREFACE(227)	MENTION THE CLUBS); WHERE THERE IS TRAVELLING AND	HOTEL	LIFE; AND WHERE THE MEN ARE BROUGHT UP, NOT IN THE
ANNA (297)	WAS MINE? /STRAMMFEST/ A WAITER AT THE POTTERDAM	HOTEL	LOOKED AT THE OFFICER'S PASSPORT WHEN HE WAS IN HIS
MILL IV (205)	NO TUPPENCE-HAPENY AN HOUR HERE. /THE DOCTOR/ THE	HOTEL	LOOKS WELL IN PHOTOGRAPHS; AND THE WAGES YOU PAY WOULD
MILL IV SD(188)	ALL THE APPURTENANCES OF A BRAND NEW FIRST CLASS	HOTEL	LOUNGE ARE IN EVIDENCE. ALASTAIR, IN BOATING FLANNELS,
DOCT II SD(124)	HONEST ENGLISHMEN WITH HONEST JEWS. ONE OF THE	HOTEL	MAIDS, A PRETTY, FAIR-HAIRED WOMAN OF ABOUT 25, COMES
MILL I (159)	MONTHS HARD LABOR, TO INDUCE ANOTHER FRIEND OR	HOTEL	MANAGER TO CASH ANOTHER CHEQUE FOR YOU FOR TWO HUNDRED
MILL I (159)	AT THE BANK. YOU MUST THEN INDUCE A FRIEND OR A	HOTEL	MANAGER TO CASH ANOTHER CHEQUE FOR ONE HUNDRED POUNDS
JITT I SD(9)	THAN HER FACE. SHE IS WELL DRESSED, LIKE A	HOTEL	MANAGERESS. SHE OPENS THE DOOR, LETTING IN SOME
INCA SD(236)	PRINCESS, HATTED AND GLOVED, IS USHERED IN BY THE	HOTEL	MANAGER, SPRUCE AND ARTIFICIALLY BLAND BY PROFESSIONAL
APPL I (239)	PLAY WITH." THEY SANG IT UNDER THE WINDOWS OF HIS	HOTEL	NEXT TIME HE CAME. HE CANCELLED HIS MEETING AND LEFT.
NEVR II SD(225)	LUNCHEON TABLE WITH HIS BACK TO THE SEA, HAS THE	HOTEL	ON HIS RIGHT, AND ON HIS LEFT, IN THE CORNER NEAREST
NEVR II (226)	WILL SAY, " REMEMBER, WILLIAM: WE CAME TO THIS	HOTEL	ON YOUR ACCOUNT, HAVING HEARD WHAT A PERFECT WAITER
SUPR IV (144)	IT'S ALL RIGHT AND HE'LL COME WITH ME. SO AS THE	HOTEL	PEOPLE SAID HE WAS MR ECTOR MALONE, I FETCHED HIM. AND
MILL IV SD(189)	MAN, SMARTLY DRESSED, ENTERS. HE CARRIES THE	HOTEL	REGISTER, WHICH HE OPENS AND PLACES ON THE NEWSPAPER
NEVR II (235)	SEIZING M'COMAS'S ARM AND LEADING HIM TOWARDS THE	HOTEL	) FINCH: COME AND WASH YOUR HANDS. /M'COMAS/ I AM
DOCT PREFACE(27)	(EXCEPT AS A PRETEXT FOR KEEPING AN ORDINARY	HOTEL	) TWO YEARS HENCE. IN A POOR PRACTICE THE DOCTOR MUST
NEVR II (240)	(SHE GOES TO THE END OF THE TABLE NEAREST THE	HOTEL	). FERGUS: WILL YOU TAKE THE HEAD OF THE TABLE,
DOCT II (127)	I'M COMING. (WALPOLE AND BLENKINSOP GO INTO THE	HOTEL	). GOODNIGHT, MY DEAR RIDGEON (SHAKING HANDS
WIDO I (14)	YOU. (SARTORIUS APPEARS ON THE THRESHOLD OF THE	HOTEL	). HERE IS MY FRIEND SARTORIUS, COMING, NO DOUBT, TO
NEVR II (227)	MAAM. THANK YOU, MAAM. (HE WITHDRAWS INTO THE	HOTEL	). MRS CLANDON COMES FORWARD LOOKING FOR HER VISITOR,
WIDO I (7)	MORE CUPS. /WAITER/ YES, ZARE. (HE GOES INTO THE	HOTEL	). /BLANCHE/ DO YOU TAKE SUGAR, MR COKANE? /COKANE/
NEVR II (250)	TELL, SIR: YOU NEVER CAN TELL. (HE GOES INTO THE	HOTEL	). /CRAMPTON/ (HIS EYES SHINING HARDLY AS HE PROPS
NEVR II (238)	MISS. (HE TAKES THE STICK AND COAT INTO THE	HOTEL	). /M'COMAS/ (HAVING STARED CRAMPTON OUT OF
NEVR II (241)	MR CRAMPTON LIKES HERE, SIR. (HE GOES INTO THE	HOTEL	). /PHILIP/ (LOOKING GRAVELY AT HIS FATHER) YOU
WIDO I (12)	LADIES AND ZHENTELLMENN. (HE GOES INTO THE	HOTEL	). /SARTORIUS/ (GRAVELY) I INTENDED YOU TO ACCOMPANY
WIDO I (18)	AND BLANCHE, READY FOR DINNER, COME FROM THE	HOTEL	). /TRENCH/ SH! HERE THEY COME. GET THE LETTER
DOCT II (119)	I COULD OVERTAKE HIM-- (HE RUSHES INTO THE	HOTEL	). /WALPOLE/ (CALLING AFTER HIM) HE'S IN THE MOTOR,
WIDO I (6)	OUT HERE. /WAITER/ YES, ZARE. (HE GOES INTO THE	HOTEL	). THE GENTLEMAN SELECTS A SMALL COIN FROM HIS HANDFUL
DOCT II (127)	GOODNIGHT. (HE GOODNIGHTS HIMSELF INTO THE	HOTEL	). THE OTHERS HAVE MEANWHILE GONE WITHOUT CEREMONY.
NEVR II (234)	WILL BE HERE IMMEDIATELY. (SHE GOES INTO THE	HOTEL	). THE WAITER TAKES HIS TRAY TO THE SERVICE TABLE.
NEVR II (236)	YOU MAY DEPEND ON ME, MISS. (SHE GOES INTO THE	HOTEL	). VALENTINE COMES LIGHTLY UP THE STEPS FROM THE
DOCT II (127)	OH, THEYLL GIVE ME SOME BROWN PAPER IN THE	HOTEL	; AND A FEW THICKNESSES OF BROWN PAPER ACROSS THE
WIDO I (17)	TO AN UNDERSTANDING WITH YOU. (HE GOES INTO THE	HOTEL	; AND COKANE, WHO HAS BEEN HANGING ABOUT
NEVR II SD(225)	NOON, IS TOASTING HIS PROTENDED INSTEPS. AT THE	HOTEL	SIDE OF THE TERRACE, THERE IS A GARDEN SEAT OF THE
AUGS (273)	SHOT AS A TRAITOR IN THE COURTYARD OF THE RITZ	HOTEL	SIMPLY BECAUSE I HAVE GERMAN BROTHERS-IN-LAW. (WITH
INCA SD(236)	THE PLAY. A	HOTEL	SITTING ROOM. A TABLE IN THE CENTRE. ON IT A
JITT I SD(9)	IN HOTELS, BUT THE PLACE IS NOT QUITE LIKE A	HOTEL	SITTING ROOM; BECAUSE THERE IS VERY LITTLE FURNITURE:
CAPT I (226)	ON YOU, MR RANKIN; BUT IN THE ABSENCE OF A	HOTEL	THERE SEEMS TO BE NO ALTERNATIVE. /LADY CICELY/ (
SUPR IV (144)	AND HE AINT YOU, NOT BY A LONG CHALK. AT THE	HOTEL	THEY TOLD ME THAT YOUR NAME IS ECTOR MALONE-- /MALONE/
NEVR IV (285)	RAILINGS UNTIL MISS CLANDON DISAPPEARED INTO THE	HOTEL	THROUGH THE WINDOW. /GLORIA/ SO IT HAS COME TO THIS.
MILL III (186)	WEEK. I SHALL TAKE A JOB AS SCULLERY MAID AT A	HOTEL	TO FILL UP MY TIME. BUT FIRST I MUST GO ROUND TO THE
MIS. PREFACE(77)	VAGABONDAGE OF THE IDLE RICH, WANDERING FROM	HOTEL	TO HOTEL AND NEVER REALLY LIVING ANYWHERE, YET I
MILL IV (191)	WOMAN, SIR, THAT IF SHE TOLD ME TO BURN DOWN THE	HOTEL	TONIGHT I'D DO IT WITHOUT A MOMENT'S HESITATION. WHEN
MIS. PREFACE(24)	ADVOCATED OR HOW HE DID IT THAN THE MANAGER OF A	HOTEL	WHICH BEGAN AS A HYDROPATHIC HAS OF THE WATER CURE. OR
BARB PREFACE(234)	SARDONIC SMILE BY REFUSING TO STAY IN THE SAME	HOTEL	WITH A RUSSIAN MAN OF GENIUS WHO HAS CHANGED WIVES
INCA (241)	OVER FOR EVERYTHING BECAUSE HE IS IN THE SAME	HOTEL	WITH HER HIGHNESS, AND CAN BOAST OF HAVING TURNED HER
WIDO I SD(13)	BLANCHE SILENTLY TAKES HIS ARM AND GOES INTO THE	HOTEL	WITH HIM. COKANE, HARDLY LESS MOMENTOUS THAN SARTORIUS
SUPR IV (165)	PUTTING HER ARM ROUND HER) LET ME TAKE YOU TO THE	HOTEL	WITH ME: THE DRIVE WILL DO YOU GOOD. COME IN AND GET A
SUPR IV (153)	COME, MRS MALONE: YOUVE GOT TO MOVE TO THE	HOTEL	WITH ME, AND TAKE YOUR PROPER PLACE BEFORE THE WORLD.
NEVR II (241)	IN THE FILIAL LINE. (THE WAITER RETURNS FROM THE	HOTEL	WITH THE DRINKS). WILLIAM: COME AND RESTORE GOOD
ANNA (297)	/STRAMMFEST/ WHEN THE WAITER RETURNED TO THE	HOTEL	WITH THE POLICE THE OFFICER HAD VANISHED; AND YOU WERE
NEVR I (203)	QUITE IMPOSSIBLE FOR ME TO LUNCH AT THE MARINE	HOTEL	WITH TWO PERFECT STRANGERS. /THE YOUNG LADY/ (
NEVR II (233)	NO BRAVADO. (GLORIA WINCES, AND GOES INTO THE	HOTEL	WITHOUT A WORD). COME, DOLLY. (AS SHE GOES TO THE

DOCT II SD(118) HURTS ME. GOODNIGHT. LOUIS GOES OUT THROUGH THE HOTEL WITHOUT NOTICING SCHUTZMACHER. MRS DUBEDAT HESITATES,
MILL IV SD(189) A MAN DOESNT FEEL THAT WAY. THE MANAGER OF THE HOTEL , A YOUNG MAN, SMARTLY DRESSED, ENTERS. HE CARRIES THE
MILL IV (207) IN ARREAR WITH MY BILL FOR MY DAILY BREAD IN YOUR HOTEL , AND AM EXPECTING EVERY DAY TO BE TOLD BY YOUR
2TRU PREFACE(5) SILLY. THE VULGAR PUB MAY BE IN FACT A PALACE HOTEL , AND THE PINTS OF BEER OR GLASSES OF WHISKY AN
BULL IV (172) YOU WILL COMFORT ME WITH THE BUSTLE OF A GREAT HOTEL , AND THE SIGHT OF THE LITTLE CHILDREN CARRYING THE
WIDO I (5) CAN GO AND HAVE A WASH. (HE TURNS TO GO INTO THE HOTEL , BUT STOPS IN CONSTERNATION, SEEING SOME PEOPLE
WIDO I (3) EYES. /COKANE/ (ON THE THRESHOLD OF THE HOTEL , CALLING PEREMPTORILY TO THE WAITER) TWO BEERS FOR US
DEST (169) NOT HAVE THE COURAGE TO ASK TO SEE YOU AT YOUR HOTEL , EVEN. MY COURAGE IS MERE SLAVISHNESS: IT IS OF NO
WIDO I (3) HAVE SECURED THE ROOM WITH THE BEST VIEW IN THE HOTEL , HARRY, THANKS TO MY TACT. WE'LL LEAVE IN THE
DOCT III (139) GOOD, THAT, FOR A STILL-ROOM MAID AT A SEASIDE HOTEL , I THINK. WHAT HAVE YOU FELLOWS DONE FOR HER TO
BULL IV (171) KEEGAN. /BROADBENT/ NOTHING PAYS LIKE A GOLFING HOTEL , IF YOU HOLD THE LAND INSTEAD OF THE SHARES, AND IF
DOCT II SD(117) COME: NOW I KNOW. LOUIS DUBEDAT COMES FROM THE HOTEL , IN HIS OVERCOAT, HIS THROAT WRAPPED IN A SHAWL. HE
NEVR II SD(246) DO NOT NOTICE THE RETURN OF THE WAITER FROM THE HOTEL , LADEN WITH CRAMPTON'S COAT, VALENTINE'S STICK, A
NEVR II (243) ANY TURN FOR REAL WORK, SIR. (HE GOES INTO THE HOTEL , LEAVING THE COMPANY SOMEWHAT OVERWHELMED BY HIS
DOCT II SD(124) FAIR-HAIRED WOMAN OF ABOUT 25, COMES FROM THE HOTEL , RATHER FURTIVELY. SHE ACCOSTS RIDGEON. /THE MAID/ I
WIDO I (4) NEGLIGE WAS QUITE EN REGLE; BUT HERE, IN THIS HOTEL , SOME OF THEM ARE SURE TO DRESS FOR DINNER; AND YOU
MILL IV (192) IF IT WERE NOT THAT THE PROPRIETRESS OF THIS HOTEL , THE LADY I TOLD YOU OF, IS A MRS FITZFASSENDEN.
NEVR II (238) (HE TAKES UP VALENTINE'S STICK AND MAKES FOR THE HOTEL , THROWING THE COAT ACROSS HIS ARM.) M'COMAS TURNS THE
OVER (176) WHAT! MAKE A SCANDAL IN THE FACE OF THE WHOLE HOTEL ! CERTAINLY NOT, DONT BE A FOOL. /GREGORY/ YES; BUT I
BULL II (108) THE HOTEL? (THEY STARE AT HIM). /CORNELIUS/ THE HOTEL ! /FATHER DEMPSEY/ HWAT HOTEL? /AUNT JUDY/ INDEEDN
BULL II (108) THERES NO HOTEL IN ROSSCULLEN. /BROADBENT/ NO HOTEL ! WHY, THE DRIVER TOLD ME THERE WAS THE FINEST HOTEL

HOTEL-MANAGER
INCA (232) PLAYFAIR AS THE WAITER, ALFRED DRAYTON AS THE HOTEL-MANAGER , C. WORDLEY HULSE AS THE ARCHDEACON, AND

HOTELS
ARMS III (55) WITH THEM ALL? /RAINA/ (TIMIDLY) NINE THOUSAND HOTELS ? /BLUNTSCHLI/ HOTELS! NONSENSE. IF YOU ONLY KNEW!
2TRU PREFACE(11) COME HOME TO THE RICH TOURISTS IN THE PALACE HOTELS AND LUXURY LINERS JUST AS THEY DO TO THE TRAMPS ON
SHAK (141) (HEADLESS) I WILL RETURN TO STRATFORD: THE HOTELS ARE CHEAPER THERE. (HE PICKS UP HIS HEAD, AND GOES
BULL II SD(111) SERVICE AND THAT OF THE SOUTH AND EAST COAST HOTELS AT WHICH HE SPENDS HIS FRIDAYS-TO-TUESDAYS WHEN HE IS
ARMS III (55) FOR HOME IN AN HOUR. HE HAS LEFT A LOT OF BIG HOTELS BEHIND HIM TO BE LOOKED AFTER. (HE TAKES UP A FAT
MILL II (167) WILL WHISK YOU OUT TO ONE OF A DOZEN FIRST RATE HOTELS IN LOVELY SCENERY. AND YET YOU CHOOSE THIS FILTHY OLD
BULL IV (173) /KEEGAN/ YOU CANNOT BUILD YOUR GOLF LINKS AND HOTELS IN THE AIR. FOR THAT YOU MUST OWN OUR LAND. AND HOW
JITT I SD(9) APHRODISIAC CHARACTER CONSIDERED DE RIGUEUR IN HOTELS . BUT THE PLACE IS NOT QUITE LIKE A HOTEL SITTING
2TRU PREFACE(11) YOU NEED ANYTHING OR NOT. COME TO OUR PALACE HOTELS . COME ROUND THE WORLD IN OUR LINERS. COME AND WALLOW
MTH4 I (146) YOU CAN TRAVEL COMFORTABLY. WHERE THERE ARE GOOD HOTELS . EXCUSE ME; BUT, THOUGH YOU SAY YOU ARE NINETY-FOUR,
DOCT I (114) TO FORGET IT. THEY TREAT US LIKE LEPERS AT THE HOTELS . /EMMY/ (AT THE DOOR) WELL, DEARY: HAVE YOU GOT
MIS SD(109) LUXURY IS FOUNDED ON THE LOUNGES OF WEEK-END HOTELS . THE ARCH IS NOT QUITE IN THE CENTRE OF THE WALL.
SIM II (79) A MEETING OF THE CHAMBER. MAYFAIR A DESERT: SIX HOTELS LEFT WITHOUT A SINGLE GUEST. FRESH DISAPPEARANCES.
MTH4 I (154) A MAN UTTERLY WEARY OF THE WEEK-END RIVERSIDE HOTELS OF THE EUPHRATES, THE MINSTRELS AND PIERROTS ON THE
VWOO 1 (121) A WALKING TOUR, SPENDING THE NIGHTS IN THE BEST HOTELS ; BUT I CHOSE THE SHIP BECAUSE IT'S MORE DRESSY AND
ARMS I (20) MY FATHER IS A VERY HOSPITABLE MAN: HE KEEPS SIX HOTELS ; BUT I COULDNT TRUST HIM AS FAR AS THAT. WHAT ABOUT
BULL IV (179) /KEEGAN/ WHICH IS THE MAKING OF GOLF LINKS AND HOTELS TO BRING IDLERS TO A COUNTRY WHICH WORKERS HAVE LEFT
INCA (240) GAVE UP THEIR DOCTORS, BUT KEPT THEIR WEEK-END HOTELS , CLOSING EVERY CAREER TO ME EXCEPT THE CAREER OF A
MIS. (146) NOT ABOUT HIMSELF OR THEMSELVES. THEYRE ABOUT HOTELS , SCENERY, ABOUT THE WEATHER, ABOUT GETTING WET AND
ARMS III (55) (TIMIDLY) NINE THOUSAND HOTELS? /BLUNTSCHLI/ HOTELS ! NONSENSE. IF YOU ONLY KNEW! OH, IT'S TOO

HOTHEADED
ROCK PREFACE(175) EVERYWHERE, AND MUST BE MET, NOT WITH RIDICULOUS HOTHEADED ATTACKS ON GERMANY, ITALY, AND RUSSIA, BUT BY A
JOAN 6 (149) CHAPLAIN/ I DID NOT KNOW WHAT I WAS DOING. I AM A HOTHEADED FOOL; AND I SHALL BE DAMNED TO ALL ETERNITY FOR

HOTHOUSE
GETT PREFACE(227) SENSITIVE CHILD THE EFFECT OF BEING FORCED IN A HOTHOUSE ATMOSPHERE OF UNNATURAL AFFECTION MAY BE

HOTLY
CATH 1 (164) THROWS THE LETTER ASIDE. EDSTASTON ADDS HOTLY) ALSO SOME CIVILITY, IF YOU PLEASE. /PATIOMKIN/ (
WIDO I (13) ADVANTAGE OF THAT UNPROTECTED GIRL. /TRENCH/ (HOTLY) COKANE! /COKANE/ (INEXORABLE) HER FATHER SEEMS TO
BARB II (281) (GUESSING) I KNOW. SECULARIST? /SHIRLEY/ (HOTLY) DID I OFFER TO DENY IT? /BARBARA/ WHY SHOULD YOU..
MRS III (226) BUT SHE'S A BAD LOT, A VERY BAD LOT. /VIVIE/ (HOTLY) FRANK--! (HE STANDS HIS GROUND. SHE TURNS AWAY AND
MTH2 (64) LEVEL, THAN ANY DUKE OR ANY ARCHBISHOP. /BURGE/ (HOTLY) I DENY IT. YOU THINK I HAVE NEVER BEEN POOR. YOU
SUPR I (14) RAMSDEN: I BEGIN TO PITY YOU. /RAMSDEN/ (HOTLY) I DONT WANT TO KNOW HOW YOU FEEL TOWARDS ME, MR
ROCK I (211) YOU SERIOUSLY IN THAT GET-UP? /OXFORD YOUTH/ (HOTLY) I SHALL WEAR WHAT I DAMN WELL PLEASE. I-- /ALOYSIA/
2TRU I (46) MARRIED. AT LEAST SO SHE TELLS ME. /THE NURSE/ (HOTLY) I TELL YOU WHAT IS TRUE. (TO THE PATIENT) POPSY AND
ROCK II (249) TO HELL WITH YOUR FILTHY LIBERTY! /BLEE/ (HOTLY) I-- /THE MAYOR/ ORDER! ORDER! DONT ARGUE WITH HIM,
PHIL II (118) MACHINE GUNS AGAINST NAKED SPEARMEN. /CRAVEN/ (HOTLY) NAKED SPEARMEN CAN KILL, PARAMORE. I RISKED MY LIFE:
CAND I (87) JAMES? AND YOU SO PARTICLAR, TOO! /MORELL/ (HOTLY) NO, SIR: IT'S NOT BECOMING LANGUAGE FOR A CLERGYMAN.
WIDO II (37) THAN SHUFFLING AS YOU HAVE DONE. /TRENCH/ (HOTLY) SHUFFLING! IF I'D THOUGHT YOU CAPABLE OF TURNING ON
BULL I (92) THAT THERES SOMETHING BEHIND ALL THIS. /DOYLE/ (HOTLY) WHAT IS THERE BEHIND IT? DO YOU THINK I'M
SIM PRO,1, (21) ON THE CHANCE OF GETTING ROUND ME. /WILKS/ (HOTLY) YOULL EITHER TAKE THAT BACK OR PROVE IT. /THE E.O./
SUPR IV (149) AND MY POSITION IN ENGLISH SOCIETY. /MALONE/ (HOTLY) YOUR POSITION HAS BEEN GOT BY MY MONEY: DO YOU KNOW
NEVR IV (291) WRONG WITH MISS CLANDON'S DRESS? /CRAMPTON/ (HOTLY TO VALENTINE) MY OPINION IS AS GOOD AS YOURS. /GLORIA/
CLEO PRO2 (98) ALWAYS GOOD TO THEIR POOR RELATIONS. /BELZANOR/ (HOTLY , TO THE PERSIAN) MAN TO MAN, ARE WE WORSE THAN THE

HOT-HEADED
DOCT PREFACE(49) ONLY INSISTS THAT THE REAL POINT IS WHETHER SOME HOT-HEADED ANTI-VIVISECTIONIST IS A LIAR (WHICH HE PROVES

HOT-WATER
MIS. SD(109) GARDEN, WITH A COUPLE OF STEPS TO SURMOUNT THE HOT-WATER PIPES WHICH SKIRT THE GLASS. AT INTERVALS ROUND

HOTSPOT
ROCK II (238) A NEW VISITOR. /HILDA/ ADMIRAL SIR BEMROSE HOTSPOT . (SHE GOES OUT). SIR BEMROSE IS A HALFWITTED
ROCK II (254) EMBRACES IT WITH THE STURDY ARMS OF SIR BEMROSE HOTSPOT . THE POLICE ARE ENTHUSIASTIC. THE ARMY WILL BE WITH

HOTSPUR
LADY PREFACE(230) GUILDENSTERN, OSRIC, THE FOP WHO ANNOYED HOTSPUR , AND A DOZEN PASSAGES CONCERNING SUCH PEOPLE! IF

HOTTENTOT
PYGM III (257) /HIGGINS/ CONTINENTAL DIALECTS, AFRICAN DIALECTS, HOTTENTOT /PICKERING/ HALLS; AND IT'S ALL THE SAME TO HER:

HOTTER
METH PREFACE(R76) AS LIKELY TO JUMP BACK AGAIN, NOW THAT WE FEEL HOTTER THAN EVER. HISTORY RECORDS VERY LITTLE IN THE WAY OF

HOTTEST
LION PREFACE(66) TO JUDGE ANGELO, AND WHY SWIFT RESERVED THE HOTTEST CORNER OF HIS HELL FOR JUDGES. ALSO, OF COURSE, WHY
DOCT PREFACE(59) OF THE DUST OF A DEAD EGYPTIAN IN A PINT OF THE HOTTEST WATER YOU COULD BEAR TO DRINK; AND IT DID YOU A

HOULD
BULL III (134) HE'S CORNY DOYLE'S SON? /DORAN/ (BRUTALLY) ARRA HOULD YOUR WHISHT: WHO'S GOIN TO SEND HIM INTO PARLIAMENT..

HOULDIN
BULL IV (149) KILT! IT'S A MERCY DHERES TWO BONES OF YOU LEFT HOULDIN TOGETHER. HOW DIJJESCAPE AT ALL AT ALL? WELL, I

HOUND
CATH 1 (163) HIM BY THE THROAT) WHAT DO YOU MEAN BY THIS, YOU HOUND ? DO YOU WANT FIVE THOUSAND BLOWS OF THE STICK?
BARB PREFACE(239) AT AN ENGLISH PRINCESS! MONSTROUS! HIDEOUS! HOUND DOWN THE WRETCH TO HIS DOOM; AND OBSERVE, PLEASE, THAT
DEST (161) COAXING FAWNING WAYS, THE MEAN EFFEMINATE LITTLE HOUND . (LOWERING HIS VOICE WITH THRILLING INTENSITY) BUT
6CAL (97) EDWARD WITH THEM. /THE KING/ ON YOUR KNEES, HOUND . /PETER/ I AM A GOOD DOG, BUT NOT OF YOUR KENNEL,

6CAL	(100)	ON HIS FIVE COLLEAGUES. /THE KING/ NO: LET THAT	HOUND	LIE. HANGING IS TOO GOOD FOR HIM. THE QUEEN HURRIES IN
POSN	(460)	I DID. AND HE WAS A LOW-DOWN ROTTEN DRUNKEN LYING	HOUND	THAT WOULD GO FURTHER TO HURT A WOMAN ANY DAY THAN TO
GLIM	(175)	TO A JELLY. COME OUT, DOG, SWINE, ANIMAL, MANGY	HOUND	, LOUSY-- (SQUARCIO COMES OUT, SWORD IN HAND). DO YOU
LADY	(243)	/THE DARK LADY/ WE SHALL SEE THAT, FALSE LYING	HOUND	, YOU AND YOUR FILTHY TRULL. (WITH TWO VIGOROUS
LION I	(124)	HIM AGAIN) PRAY THIS INSTANT, YOU DOG, YOU ROTTEN	HOUND	, YOU SLIMY SNAKE, YOU BEASTLY GOAT, OR -- /SPINTHO/
MTH1 II	(33)	HE MIGHT HAVE PUT THE HURDLE BACK, LAZY	HOUND	! (HE REPLACES THE HURDLE ACROSS THE PASSAGE). /EVE/

HOUNDED

AUGS	(276)	KNEW THAT I HAD SAID IT, I SHOULD BE AT ONCE	HOUNDED	DOWN AS A PRO-GERMAN. /THE LADY/ I WILL BE SILENT AS
JOAN PREFACE	(13)	BY A SUPERSTITIOUS RABBLE OF MEDIEVAL PRIESTS	HOUNDED	ON BY A CORRUPT POLITICAL BISHOP, IT MUST BE ASSUMED
APPL I	(238)	BUT IF I ATTEMPT TO FIGHT THEM I SHALL BE	HOUNDED	OUT OF PUBLIC LIFE, AND THEY WILL SHOVE MOULDY MIKE

HOUNDS

ROCK PREFACE	(147)	CRUEL STEEL TRAPS, AGONIZING POISONS, OR PACKS OF	HOUNDS	AS METHODS OF EXTERMINATION. KILLING CAN BE CRUELLY
MILL PREFACE	(130)	SUCH PRODUCTS MORE EASILY THAN WITH A PACK OF	HOUNDS	. OUR PUBLIC SCHOOL AND UNIVERSITY EDUCATION EQUIPS
PHIL II	(118)	MY LIVER: A CLINKING RUN ACROSS COUNTRY WITH THE	HOUNDS	. /PARAMORE/ (WITH BITTER IRONY) ISNT THAT RATHER
6CAL	(95)	BASE RASCALS OF BURGESSES: THESE HUCKSTERING	HOUNDS	OF MERCHANTS WHO HAVE MADE THIS PORT OF CALAIS A NEST
ROCK PREFACE	(166)	WHEN ALL WESTERN EUROPE SET ON HIM LIKE A PACK OF	HOUNDS	ON A FOX. BUT AS ALL THE SOLDIERS WERE PEASANTS, AND
SUPR HANDBOK	(186)	BY REGARDING MANKIND AS A TROUBLESOME PACK OF	HOUNDS	ONLY WORTH KEEPING FOR THE SPORT OF HUNTING WITH
ROCK II	(237)	OUR BREED OF HORSES WILL BE DOOMED; OUR PACKS OF	HOUNDS	SOLD OR SLAUGHTERED; AND OUR MASTERS OF HOUNDS WILL
ROCK II	(237)	OF HOUNDS SOLD OR SLAUGHTERED; AND OUR MASTERS OF	HOUNDS	WILL BE CADDIES ON MOTOR BICYCLES. THAT IS TO BE

HOUNSLOW

PYGM II	(233)	GOVERNOR. /HIGGINS/ (TO PICKERING) BROUGHT UP IN	HOUNSLOW	. MOTHER WELSH, I SHOULD THINK. (DOOLITTLE OPENS

HOUR

FANY II	(285)	HOURS. /MRS KNOX/ WHAT BRINGS YOU HOME AT THIS	HOUR	? HAVE YOU HEARD ANYTHING? /KNOX/ NO. HAVE YOU? /MRS
PHIL I	(89)	TO ME. BUT YOU CAN JOIN US. /CHARTERIS/ WHAT	HOUR	? /CUTHBERTSON/ ANY TIME AFTER TWELVE. (TO CRAVEN)
PHIL I	(74)	TO BREATHE). WHO THE DEUCE IS CALLING AT THIS	HOUR	? /GRACE/ I CANT IMAGINE. (THEY LISTEN GUILTILY. THE
BULL III	(142)	YOURE ABOUT IT? WHAT HORSE CAN GO FORTY MILE AN	HOUR	? /HODSON/ ORSE! WY, YOU SILLY AOWL ROTTER, IT'S NOT
2TRU III	(100)	POWER? MUST YOU ALWAYS TRAVEL AT EIGHTY MILES AN	HOUR	? /MEEK/ I HAVE GOOD NEWS FOR YOU, COLONEL; AND GOOD
MIS. PREFACE	(36)	THE WORKING FOLK. THEREFORE, IF FOR ONLY HALF AN	HOUR	A DAY, A CHILD SHOULD DO SOMETHING SERVICEABLE TO THE
FANY PROLOG	(266)	AT NINE. I HAVE HAD TO PUT FORWARD THE DINNER	HOUR	A LITTLE. MAY I SHEW YOU TO YOUR ROOMS? (HE GOES OUT,
MILL III	(180)	A WOMAN LOOKING FOR WORK AT TUPPENCE HAPENY AN	HOUR	AFFORD A WEST END SHOE LIKE THAT? I ASSURE YOU WE DONT
NEVR II SD	(225)	THE SUN, WHICH, IN AUGUST AND AT LESS THAN AN	HOUR	AFTER NOON, IS TOASTING HIS PROTENDED INSTEPS. AT THE
POSN	(441)	FOR YOUR FOOLERY NOW; FOR YOULL BE A DEAD MAN AN	HOUR	AFTER THE SHERIFF COMES BACK. WHAT POSSESSED YOU TO
HART III	(138)	THIS IS SOME ENIGMA. /ELLIE/ ONLY HALF AN	HOUR	AGO I BECAME CAPTAIN SHOTOVER'S WHITE WIFE. /MRS
VWOO 2	(132)	NOT A BARGAIN. WHEN I ENTERED THIS SHOP HALF AN	HOUR	AGO I HAD NOT THE FAINTEST NOTION OF BUYING A VILLAGE
PHIL III	(136)	WAR. WE SHOULD HAVE BEEN HERE QUARTER OF AN	HOUR	AGO ONLY FOR HIS NONSENSE. /CHARTERIS/ (STILL
CLEO III	(156)	RISK. I SHOULD NOT HAVE COME TO EGYPT. /RUFIO/ AN	HOUR	AGO YOU WERE ALL FOR VICTORY. /CAESAR/ (
CAND I	(104)	THE HAPPIEST OF MORTALS. /MORELL/ SO WAS I-- AN	HOUR	AGO.
CLEO IV	(187)	TO POTHINUS? I SET HIM FREE, HERE, NOT HALF AN	HOUR	AGO. DID THEY NOT PASS HIM OUT? /LUCIUS/ AY, THROUGH
NEVR IV	(285)	OH, HE'LL COME ALL RIGHT ENOUGH: THAT WAS HALF AN	HOUR	AGO. I DIDNT LIKE TO BORROW FIVE SHILLINGS FROM HIM AND
CAND III	(127)	I FINISHED THE POEM ABOUT THE ANGEL QUARTER OF AN	HOUR	AGO. IVE READ YOU SEVERAL THINGS SINCE. /CANDIDA/ (
CLEO II	(140)	IS BRITANNUS ASLEEP? I SENT HIM FOR MY ARMOR AN	HOUR	AGO. (CALLING) BRITANNICUS, THOU BRITISH ISLANDER.
2TRU I	(28)	IS: THEY TOOK IT FROM UNDER HER TONGUE HALF AN	HOUR	AGO. (SCRUTINIZING THE TABLE AND DISCOVERING THE
CAND I	(81)	YOU SHOULD HAVE BEEN OFF ON YOUR ROUNDS HALF AN	HOUR	AGO. /LEXY/ (PERPLEXED) IS SHE IN EARNEST, MORELL?
SUPR I	(43)	/TANNER/ I WANTED TO SEND FOR THAT CAB HALF AN	HOUR	AGO. /MISS RAMSDEN/ I AM GLAD SHE UNDERSTANDS THE
PYGM V	(274)	BUT I THINK YOU MIGHT HAVE TOLD US THIS HALF AN	HOUR	AGO. /MRS HIGGINS/ ELIZA CAME TO ME THIS MORNING. SHE
SIM PRO,3,	(35)	THAT YOU WERE QUITE RIGHT TO OBJECT TO ME HALF AN	HOUR	AGO. YOUR OFFENSIVE PERSONAL REMARKS WERE FULLY
MIS.	(174)	SAYS SHE HEARD YOU CALLING ME A QUARTER OF AN	HOUR	AGO; AND THAT YOUR VOICE SOUNDED AS IF YOU WERE ILL. (
2TRU II	(73)	MOPS: YOURE HYSTERICAL. YOU FELT SPLENDID AN	HOUR	AGO; AND YOU WILL FEEL SPLENDID AGAIN AN HOUR FROM NOW.
WIDO II	(36)	THATS ALL. /BLANCHE/ YOU HAD NO OBJECTION HALF AN	HOUR	AGO, WHEN YOU MET ME IN THE HALL, AND SHEWED ME ALL THE
JOAN PREFACE	(52)	KNIGHTS OF THE BLUE PENCIL, HAVING SAVED AN	HOUR	AND A HALF BY DISEMBOWELLING THE PLAY, WOULD AT ONCE
MRS IV	(244)	HIS MONEY AGAIN). I MADE ALL THAT YESTERDAY IN AN	HOUR	AND A HALF. BUT I MADE IT IN A HIGHLY SPECULATIVE
HART I	(77)	YOUR LIFE? /CAPTAIN SHOTOVER/ NINETY MINUTES. AN	HOUR	AND A HALF. (HE GOES INTO THE PANTRY). HECTOR, LEFT
2TRU III	(111)	AND PREACH AND PREACH NO MATTER HOW LATE THE	HOUR	AND HOW SHORT THE DAY, NO MATTER WHETHER I HAVE NOTHING
SUPR II	(56)	INCHES OF DUST ALL OVER HIM, AT SIXTY MILES AN	HOUR	AND THE RISK OF HIS LIFE AND MINE. EXCEPT, OF COURSE,
CAND I	(94)	COME ALONG: YOU CAN SPARE US QUARTER OF AN	HOUR	AT ALL EVENTS. THIS IS MY FATHER-IN-LAW. MR BURGESS--
O'FL	(227)	OF THE NOISE AND WANTED TO HAVE A PEACEFUL	HOUR	AT HOME. WELL: THEM TWO HAS TAUGHT ME A LESSON. THIS
APPL II	(271)	MORE TO BE SAID. /AMANDA/ THAT MEANS ANOTHER HALF	HOUR	AT LEAST. /BOANERGES/ WOMAN: THIS IS NOT THE MOMENT FOR
MILL IV	(189)	CONQUEROR. CARDINAL WOLSEY STOPPED ONCE FOR AN	HOUR	AT THE PIG AND WHISTLE WHEN HIS MULE CAST A SHOE AND
SUPR II	(55)	/STRAKER/ PARIS TO BISKRA AT FORTY MILE AN	HOUR	AVERAGE, NOT COUNTIN THE MEDITERRANEAN. /TANNER/ HOW
MRS IV	(237)	BROTHER AND SISTER. IT'S EXACTLY WHAT I FELT AN	HOUR	BEFORE CROFTS MADE HIS REVELATION. IN SHORT, DEAR VIV,
DOCT I	(102)	A POUND OF RIPE GREENGAGES EVERY DAY HALF AN	HOUR	BEFORE LUNCH, I'M SURE YOUD FIND A BENEFIT. THEYRE VERY
DOCT I	(103)	INJECT IT THREE TIMES A DAY QUARTER OF AN	HOUR	BEFORE MEALS; AND WHAT IS THE RESULT? THE PHAGOCYTES
DOCT I	(98)	OF THEM: SECOND, INJECT THEM A QUARTER OF AN	HOUR	BEFORE MEALS, THREE TIMES A DAY. /RIDGEON/ (APPALLED)
BULL II	(107)	BEEN HERE BEFORE ME. HE STARTED IN OUR MOTOR AN	HOUR	BEFORE MR DOYLE ARRIVED, TO MEET US AT ATHENMULLET,
BULL I	(81)	(POCKETING IT) THANK YOU, I'LL BE THERE HALF AN	HOUR	BEFORE THE THRAIN STARTS. (LARRY IS HEARD AT THE
CLEO PRO2	(100)	TO CAESAR; FOR HIS ADVANCE GUARD IS SCARCE AN	HOUR	BEHIND ME; AND NOT AN EGYPTIAN WARRIOR IS LEFT STANDING
DEVL I SD	(3)	ACT I. AT THE MOST WRETCHED	HOUR	BETWEEN A BLACK NIGHT AND A WINTRY MORNING IN THE YEAR
ROCK I	(218)	THUMBS IN YOUR WAISTCOAT HOLES AND WAIT HALF AN	HOUR	BETWEEN EVERY SENTENCE TO THINK OF WHAT TO SAY NEXT;
DEST	(168)	THAT LETTER IN YOUR HAND, KNOWING THAT WHEN THE	HOUR	CAME, YOUR FEAR HAD TIGHTENED, NOT YOUR HEART, BUT YOUR
BASH I	(96)	SHALL TWADDLE ABOUT HIS DUTY. MELLISH: AT NO	HOUR	CAN I REGARD THEE WHOLLY WITHOUT LOATHING; BUT WHEN
GETT PREFACE	(207)	OF MARRIAGE CANNOT BE PUT OFF FOR EVER. WHEN ITS	HOUR	COMES, WHAT ARE THE POINTS THE CABINET WILL HAVE TO
JOAN EPIL,SD	(167)	INTO A WHITE RADIANCE DESCENDING ON JOAN. THE	HOUR	CONTINUES TO STRIKE. /JOAN/ O GOD THAT MADEST THIS
CAPT III	(289)	LIKE TO BEHAVE YOURSELF VERY NICELY INDEED. WHAT	HOUR	DID YOU SAY WE WERE TO LUNCH AT, CAPTAIN KEARNEY?
GLIM	(186)	ARE. A PRIEST SAID TO ME ONCE, " IN YOUR LAST	HOUR	EVERYTHING WILL FALL AWAY FROM YOU EXCEPT YOUR
MRS III	(220)	(LOOKING AT HIS WATCH) HALF-PAST ELEVEN. NICE	HOUR	FOR A RECTOR TO COME DOWN TO BREAKFAST! /REV. S./ DONT
GENV I	(43)	OF ENGLAND KEPT US UP TALKING LONG AFTER MY USUAL	HOUR	FOR RETIREMENT. (SHAKING HIS HAND WARMLY) HOW DO YOU
MILL III	(182)	NATURAL WAGE? /THE MAN/ TUPPENCE HAPENY AN	HOUR	FOR TWELVE HOURS A DAY. /EPIFANIA/ SLAVERY! /THE
PYGM II	(221)	OF MINE GETS FRENCH LESSONS FOR EIGHTEENPENCE AN	HOUR	FROM A REAL FRENCH GENTLEMAN. WELL, YOU WOULDNT HAVE
MILL III	(184)	OH NO: THAT WOULDNT BE RIGHT. HE HIRES IT BY THE	HOUR	FROM BOLTON'S. /EPIFANIA/ IS THE DRIVER ALWAYS THE SAME
MRS IV	(239)	IN HIS HIGH SPIRITS JARS ON HER). I START IN AN	HOUR	FROM HOLBORN VIADUCT. I WISH I COULD PERSUADE YOU TO
2TRU II	(73)	AN HOUR AGO; AND YOU WILL FEEL SPLENDID AGAIN AN	HOUR	FROM NOW. YOU WILL ALWAYS FEEL SPLENDID IF YOU KEEP
3PLA PREFACE	(R22)	GALLANTRY. THE SQUIRE WHO HAS NEVER SPARED AN	HOUR	FROM THE HUNTING FIELD TO DO A LITTLE PUBLIC WORK ON A
DEVL I	(26)	THREATENINGLY ON HIM) HAVE A CARE, YOU. IN AN	HOUR	FROM THIS THERE WILL BE NO LAW HERE BUT MARTIAL LAW. I
ROCK PREFACE	(165)	BACK INTO HIS FARM AND TOLD TO CARRY ON UNTIL HIS	HOUR	HAD COME; AND A PLEASANT CONVENTION WAS ESTABLISHED
CLEO IV	(192)	AWAY, BRITANNUS: TELL PETRONIUS THAT WITHIN AN	HOUR	HALF OUR FORCES MUST TAKE SHIP FOR THE WESTERN LAKE.
LION II	(133)	/CAESAR/ (TURNING AT THE DOOR OF THE BOX) THE	HOUR	HAS COME, FERROVIUS. I SHALL GO INTO MY BOX AND SEE YOU
BUOY IV	(48)	AND MY SPECULATIONS TURN OUT WELL WHEN I SPEND AN	HOUR	HERE AND JUST EMPTY MY MIND. /PRIEST/ WHEN THE MIND IS
MILL IV	(205)	NOW ITS OWNER; AND THERE IS NO TUPPENCE-HAPENY AN	HOUR	HERE. /THE DOCTOR/ THE HOTEL LOOKS WELL IN PHOTOGRAPHS;
ARMS I	(17)	I KNOW HOW GOOD YOUVE BEEN TO ME: TO MY LAST	HOUR	I SHALL REMEMBER THOSE THREE CHOCOLATE CREAMS. IT WAS
MTH5	(229)	I SHALL NOT DETAIN YOU TWO MINUTES. /ALL/ HALF AN	HOUR	IF YOU LIKE. PLEASE GO ON, PYGMALION. (THEY RUSH HIM
SUPR III	(112)	REFUTING YOU. LET US GO ON FOR ANOTHER	HOUR	IF YOU LIKE. /DON JUAN/ GOOD: LET US. /THE STATUE/ NOT
BULL II	(102)	BROAD IRISH VERNACULAR OF HIS SPEECH TO PATSY) AN	HOUR	IF YOU LIKE, MISS REILLY: YOURE ALWAYS WELCOME. SHALL
MIS.	(184)	ON WITH MY DAUGHTER BEFORE YOUD BEEN HALF AN	HOUR	IN MY HOUSE. FIE, FOR SHAME! /PERCIVAL/ LORD
MIS. PREFACE	(69)	HIS CONDITION THAT HE IS NOT PREPARED TO SPEND AN	HOUR	IN REMEDYING IT. THE COSTER MAY RESENT THE INQUIRY
BASH I	(98)	BEAUTIFUL AGAIN. (THE CASTLE CLOCK STRIKES THE	HOUR	IN THE DISTANCE.) HARK! HARK! HARK! HARK! HARK!
LADY	(245)	HAVE YET TO DEMAND WHAT YOUR BUSINESS IS AT THIS	HOUR	IN THIS PLACE, AND HOW YOU COME TO BE SO CONCERNED WITH
DEVL I	(23)	THAN TO OTHERS IN THE PERPLEXITY OF MY LAST	HOUR	IN THIS STRANGE PLACE." /ANDERSON/ AMEN. /THE UNCLES
ROCK I	(222)	THAT IF YOU WILL TALK TO EVERYBODY FOR HALF AN	HOUR	INSTEAD OF LETTING ME GET RID OF THEM FOR YOU IN TWO
BULL I	(78)	NO: IT'S NEAR HITCHIN. IF YOU CAN SPARE HALF AN	HOUR	I'LL GO INTO IT WITH YOU. /TIM/ I TELL YOU HWAT. GIMME
SUPR I	(30)	PEOPLE'S NECESSITIES. THE NEED OF THE PRESENT	HOUR	IS A HAPPY MOTHER AND A HEALTHY BABY. BEND YOUR
PPP	(198)	(IN A BROKEN VOICE) FAREWELL, MAGNESIA: MY LAST	HOUR	IS AT HAND. FAREWELL, FAREWELL, FAREWELL! /MAGNESIA/
SHAK	(139)	THOU SHAMELESS FRAUD. FOR ONE OR BOTH OF US THE	HOUR	IS COME. PUT UP YOUR HANDS. /SHAV/ COME ON. THEY SPAR.
JITT III	(57)	/AGNES/ WHAT COMFORT IS THERE IN THAT? ONE	HOUR	IS ENOUGH FOR A MAN. THEN HE CAN SIT ALONE AT HIS DESK,

GETT (286)	(RISING) NOT DRESSED! DOES SHE KNOW WHAT	HOUR	IT IS? /LESBIA/ SHE HAS LOCKED HERSELF INTO HER ROOM,
CATH 1 (171)	ME ONLY HALF AN HOUR TO-- /PATIOMKIN/ IN HALF AN	HOUR	IT WILL BE TOO LATE FOR THE PETIT LEVER. COME ALONG.
MIS. (137)	CHILDREN! THREE OR FOUR TIMES IN THE LAST HALF	HOUR	IVE BEEN ON THE POINT OF SCREAMING. /LORD SUMMERHAYS/
KING I (200)	OF ALE ARE ENOUGH FOR ME OR FOR ANY MAN AT THIS	HOUR	. ALL THE REST COME BACK EXCEPT MRS BASHAM, BARBARA,
CLEO PRO1 (89)	AND SET, AND THE MOON CHANGE HER SHAPE AND HER	HOUR	. AS THEY WERE SO YE ARE; AND YET NOT SO GREAT; FOR THE
SUPR III (74)	BY THUNDER: YOUR LAST POINT OF ORDER TOOK HALF AN	HOUR	. BESIDES, ANARCHISTS DONT BELIEVE IN ORDER. /THE
2TRU PREFACE(8)	IN THE CALCUTTA OR IRISH SWEEPS. TRYING IT FOR AN	HOUR	. BESIDES, EVEN QUITE POOR PEOPLE SAVE UP FOR HOLIDAYS
BARB PREFACE(224)	CLERGYMAN HAS, LIKE BARBARA, A VERY BAD QUARTER	HOUR	. BUT HE CANNOT HELP HIMSELF BY REFUSING TO ACCEPT
SUPR II (60)	TO ALGIERS AND TO BISKRA, AT SIXTY MILES AN	HOUR	. COME RIGHT DOWN TO THE CAPE IF YOU LIKE. THAT WILL BE
SIM II (54)	BELFAST HAS ANNOUNCED FIRING PRACTICE AT THE SAME	HOUR	. DO YOU SEE THAT SLOOP THAT CAME IN LAST NIGHT? /SIR
BUOY III (46)	PEACE. IT HAS BEEN TERRIBLY PROFANED FOR THE LAST	HOUR	. FATHER BUOYANT WILL BE HERE PRESENTLY FOR HIS REST,
ARMS III (55)	YES: I SHALL HAVE TO START FOR HOME IN AN	HOUR	. HE HAS LEFT A LOT OF BIG HOTELS BEHIND HIM TO BE
CAPT II (256)	SHEIKH SIDI EL ASSIF. HE WILL BE HERE WITHIN AN	HOUR	. HE IS A JUDGE, LIKE YOURSELF. YOU CAN TALK LAW TO
PYGM EPILOG (299)	CUSTOM STALE HIS INFINITE VARIETY IN HALF AN	HOUR	. HIS PLEASANT NEATNESS AND COMPACTNESS, HIS SMALL
SUPR II (58)	AND I COMMIT YOU TO TAVY'S CARE FOR THE NEXT	HOUR	. I AM OFF FOR A TURN IN THE CAR. /ANN/ NO, JACK. I
SUPR III (118)	OF CORAL AND IVORY, DESERTED ME IN THAT SUPREME	HOUR	. I REMEMBERED THEM AND DESPERATELY STROVE TO RECOVER
VWOO 1 (115)	THE STEWARD WILL BE ROUND WITH SOUP IN HALF AN	HOUR	. I THOUGHT WE SHOULD HAVE TO WAIT AN HOUR. /A/ I NEVER
PHIL II (109)	OLD GIRL. IVE BEEN WAITING FOR YOU THIS LAST	HOUR	. I'M STARVING. /GRACE/ ALL RIGHT, DEAR. (TO
POSN PREFACE(382)	OF MAKING THE TRAIN TRAVEL AT SIXTY MILES AN	HOUR	. IT IS IMMORALITY, NOT MORALITY, THAT NEEDS
PYGM V (271)	TWO CONVERSATIONS WITH YOU, AT HALF-A-CROWN AN	HOUR	. IVE NEVER SEEN YOU SINCE. /DOOLITTLE/ OH! DRUNK! AM
CAND I (103)	I TOLD YOU YOU MUSNT. IT WILL BE READY IN HALF AN	HOUR	. (SHE PUTS A FINAL TOUCH TO THE BOW. HE KISSES HER
2TRU II (73)	A HIDING THAT WILL KEEP YOU SCREAMING FOR HALF AN	HOUR	. (SWEETIE SUBSIDES). I WANT TO BEAT SOMEBODY: I WANT
NEVR III (265)	HIS CONSCIENCE PRESAGING A BAD QUARTER OF AN	HOUR	. MRS CLANDON TAKES PHIL'S CHAIR, AND SEATS HERSELF
LION II (142)	/ANDROCLES/ NO: I SHOULD NEVER HAVE ANOTHER HAPPY	HOUR	. NO: ON THE FAITH OF A CHRISTIAN AND THE HONOR OF A
PHIL I (81)	AS SOMETHING MORE THAN THE AMUSEMENT OF AN IDLE	HOUR	. OH, LEONARD, LEONARD, YOUVE NEVER GIVEN ME A CHANCE:
DEVL III (58)	BEEN WAITING YOUR CONVENIENCE FOR FULLY HALF AN	HOUR	. PERFECTLY READY, SIR. /BURGOYNE/ (BLANDLY) SO AM I.
GETT PREFACE(230)	WITH A CHANGE OF PARTNERS EVERY DAY OR EVERY	HOUR	. PHYSICALLY THERE IS NOTHING TO DISTINGUISH HUMAN
VWOO 1 (115)	HALF AN HOUR, I THOUGHT WE SHOULD HAVE TO WAIT AN	HOUR	. /A/ I NEVER TAKE IT. IT INTERRUPTS MY WORK. /Z/ WHY
PHIL II (128)	JUST. BE REASONABLE, CRAVEN: GIVE HIM HALF AN	HOUR	. /CUTHBERTSON/ (STERNLY) WHAT DO YOU MEAN BY THIS,
MILL IV (206)	A DAY FOR HER AT MOST: NOT EVEN ONE PIASTRE AN	HOUR	. /EPIFANIA/ THAT COMES OF MARRYING AN INCOMPETENT
MILL IV (205)	THE WOMEN STILL SLAVE FOR HIM AT ONE PIASTRE AN	HOUR	. /EPIFANIA/ YOU CANNOT CHANGE THE MARKET PRICE OF
SUPR IV (153)	THE GARDEN FOR ME? I'LL JOIN YOU IN HALF AN	HOUR	. /HECTOR/ VERY WELL. YOULL DINE WITH US, DAD, WONT
JITT II (44)	GO BACK TO BED. /LENKHEIM/ YOU HAVNT BEEN UP AN	HOUR	. /JITTA/ BUT I AM DEAD TIRED. /LENKHEIM/ YOU CANT BE
PHIL I (82)	BEEN ON THE POINT OF SWEARING FOR THE LAST HALF	HOUR	. /JULIA/ (DESPAIRINGLY) YOU ARE ONLY MAKING FUN OF
DEST (183)	SIGNAL; AND HE WILL BE HERE IN QUARTER OF AN	HOUR	. /LIEUTENANT/ HE'S NOT FAR OFF, THEN. /LADY/ NO: QUITE
GENV IV (114)	YET, MR SECRETARY. WE HAVE BEEN HERE LESS THAN AN	HOUR	. /SECRETARY/ IT SEEMS TO ME TWENTY YEARS. /JUDGE/ I AM
DEVL III (50)	THE COURT SITS. /RICHARD/ BUT IT HAS STRUCK THE	HOUR	. /SERGEANT/ SO IT HAS, SIR; BUT THERE'S A DELAY.
MTH3 (119)	WOMAN THAN WITH A MAYFLY THAT LIVES ONLY AN	HOUR	. /THE ARCHBISHOP/ WHAT SET YOU THINKING OF IT FIRST..
DOCT V (171)	THE PRIVATE VIEW WILL BEGIN IN LESS THAN HALF AN	HOUR	. /THE SECRETARY/ I THINK I'D BETTER RUN OVER TO THE
KING II (234)	TO THAT WHEN THE HOUR STRIKES FOR ME: THE LAST	HOUR	. SO MY VERY BELOVEDEST WILL DIE HAPPY; AND THAT IS ALL
ROCK PREFACE(169)	IT ENRICHES US BY INCREASING THE PRODUCT PER	HOUR	. SOME OF US WOULD LIKE TO TAKE THINGS EASY AND RETIRE
HART III (130)	AND I TELL YOU, ALF, THERE IS NO TRAIN AT THIS	HOUR	. THE LAST IS NINE FORTYFIVE. /MANGAN/ BUT A GOODS
BASH III (120)	THESE FISTS HAVE POUNDED BY SHREWSB'RY CLOCK AN	HOUR	. THIS BRUISED GRASS AND CAKED MUD ADHERING TO MY FORM
VWOO 3 (133)	SLAVING YET. YOU HAVE BEEN AT IT FOR HALF AN	HOUR	. WHATEVER ON EARTH ARE YOU WORKING AT SO HARD? /A/ I
2TRU I (36)	RECOMMENDED. I CANT GET A NEW NURSE AT THIS	HOUR	. WONT YOU TRY, FOR MY SAKE, TO PUT UP WITH HER UNTIL
HART III (145)	SPLENDID! AND YOU HAVNT HAD A DROP FOR AN	HOUR	. YOU SEE YOU DONT NEED IT: YOUR OWN SPIRIT IS NOT
FANY III (306)	I'LL JUST TROT OFF AND COME BACK IN HALF AN	HOUR	. YOU TWO CAN MAKE IT UP TOGETHER. I'M REALLY NOT FIT
VWOO 1 (115)	HALF PAST TEN. /A/ THE CLOCKS WERE PUT ON HALF AN	HOUR	LAST NIGHT. WE ARE GOING EAST. /Z/ I ALWAYS THINK IT
KING II (225)	I TOLD THE SAME ONE TWICE OVER WITHIN AN	HOUR	LAST TUESDAY. THIS MORNING BARBARA CALLED ME AN OLD
FANY II (287)	MANY A GIRL OUT OF THE SHOP FOR BEING HALF AN	HOUR	LATE AT NIGHT; AND HERES MY OWN DAUGHTER GONE FOR A
ARMS II SD(26)	HIS COFFEE). CATHERINE, WHO, HAVING AT THIS EARLY	HOUR	MADE ONLY A VERY PERFUNCTORY TOILET, WEARS A BULGARIAN
BARB II (280)	LIKE ME, FILLIN YOURSELF WITH GIN AT THIS	HOUR	O THE MORNIN! /BILL/ AW'M NAO GIN DRINKER, YOU OALD
JOAN PREFACE(54)	AFTER ARRIVING AS LATE AS (OR LATER THAN) THE	HOUR	OF BEGINNING CAN POSSIBLY BE MADE FOR THEM. THUS FROM
MTH5 (213)	CHLOE. IS THERE ANY SIGN OF THE ANCIENT YET? THE	HOUR	OF BIRTH IS OVERDUE. THE BABY IS KICKING LIKE MAD. SHE
CLEO V (196)	SHOUTING. /CAESAR/ I SEE MY SHIP AWAITS ME. THE	HOUR	OF CAESAR'S FAREWELL TO EGYPT HAS ARRIVED. AND NOW,
CAND I (82)	MAN FEELS THAT HE MUST PAY HEAVEN FOR EVERY	HOUR	OF HAPPINESS WITH A GOOD SPELL OF HARD UNSELFISH WORK
CAPT II (252)	IS ALL. JOHNSON: GIVE HIM A DOLLAR; AND NOTE THE	HOUR	OF HIS GOING, THAT HIS MASTER MAY KNOW HOW FAST HE
PHIL III (133)	NATURE ONE UNSELFISH SPOT. HE WOULD NOT SPEND ONE	HOUR	OF HIS REAL LIFE WITH-- (A SOB CHOKES HER: SHE RISES
SUPR I SD(3)	DETERMINATE MOUTH DISARMED AND REFINED SINCE THE	HOUR	OF HIS SUCCESS BY THE WITHDRAWAL OF OPPOSITION AND THE
BARB PREFACE(245)	THAT IT, AT LEAST, IS IRREVOCABLE-- AS IF ONE	HOUR	OF IMPRISONMENT WERE NOT AS IRREVOCABLE AS ANY
VWOO 1 (122)	/A/ I AM NOT TRAINED TO MANUAL WORK. HALF AN	HOUR	OF IT WOULD MAKE ME WISH MYSELF DEAD, AND FIVE MINUTES
LADY (241)	MANNER OF LOVELINESS IN IT. GRUDGE ME NOT A SHORT	HOUR	OF ITS MUSIC. /THE LADY/ SIR: YOU ARE OVERBOLD. SEASON
JOAN 5 (115)	BY MY OWN WITS; AND I TELL YOU THAT YOUR LITTLE	HOUR	OF MIRACLES IS OVER, AND THAT FROM THIS TIME ON HE WHO
MILL IV (204)	CERTIFICATE. I LEARNED IN THE FIRST HALF	HOUR	OF MY SEARCH FOR EMPLOYMENT THAT THE LIVING WAGE FOR A
BULL PREFACE(51)	OBTAINED NO REDRESS: THE LAW FAILED THEM IN THEIR	HOUR	OF NEED. SO ONE LEADING FAMILY OF PIGEON FARMERS,
LADY PREFACE(213)	A FAINTHEARTED FRIEND WHO WAS FAILING HIM IN HIS	HOUR	OF NEED, AND LEFT THE ROOM IN ANGER. HARRIS'S
CLEO V (195)	OF THE ROARING OF THE SOLDIERS! AFTER HALF AN	HOUR	OF THE ENTHUSIASM OF AN ARMY, ONE FEELS THE NEED OF A
ROCK PREFACE(182)	STRIKES. /PILATE/ VERY PRETTY, MY FRIEND; BUT THE	HOUR	OF THE GODS IS NOW AND ALWAYS; AND ALL THE WORLD KNOWS
MTH5 (261)	ALL THAT THEY HAVE DONE SEEMS BUT THE FIRST	HOUR	OF THE INFINITE WORK OF CREATION. YET I WILL NOT
SIM PRO,1, (22)	NEXT BOAT, MY LADY. /THE Y.W./ (UNMOVED) AT THIS	HOUR	OF THE MORNING TOO! DONT YOU KNOW YOU SHOULDNT? /THE
MTH5 (261)	AND THEIR LIFE DOES NOT FAIL THEM EVEN IN THE	HOUR	OF THEIR DESTRUCTION. THEIR BREASTS ARE WITHOUT MILK:
HART PREFACE(24)	MOST OF THE MEN OF ACTION, OCCUPIED TO THE LAST	HOUR	OF THEIR TIME WITH URGENT PRACTICAL WORK, HAD TO LEAVE
DEVL III (76)	HIMSELF THE DEVIL'S DISCIPLE; BUT WHEN THE	HOUR	OF TRIAL CAME TO HIM, HE FOUND THAT IT WAS HIS DESTINY
DEVL III (77)	MINISTER OF THE GOSPEL OF PEACE; BUT WHEN THE	HOUR	OF TRIAL CAME TO ME, I FOUND THAT IT WAS MY DESTINY TO
LION EPILOG (149)	BLACK COATS AND SAY QUITE SIMPLY, " I FIND IN THE	HOUR	OF TRIAL THAT THE SERMON ON THE MOUNT IS TOSH, AND THAT
DEVL III (76)	(BETWEEN JUDITH AND RICHARD) SIR: IT IS IN THE	HOUR	OF TRIAL THAT A MAN FINDS HIS TRUE PROFESSION. THIS
LION II (135)	/LAVINIA/ YOU WILL FIND YOUR REAL FAITH IN THE	HOUR	OF TRIAL. /FERROVIUS/ THAT IS WHAT I FEAR. I KNOW THAT
6CAL (102)	IN YOUR HAND TO DO AS YOU WILL WITH IN THIS YOUR	HOUR	OF VICTORY: IT IS AS IF YOU WERE GOD HIMSELF. YOU SAID
MTH5 (220)	YOU CALLING A CHILD? I AM FULLY QUARTER OF AN	HOUR	OLD. (SHE SITS DOWN ON THE CURVED BENCH NEAR STREPHON
MTH2 (40)	STICK IT OR CHUCK IT-- JUST LIKE THAT-- FOR AN	HOUR	ON END IN THE SPRING. I WISH MY FATHER HAD FOUND SOME
METH PREFACE(R50)	ENOUGH. YOU MAY ALSO DEFY HIM TO ACT FOR A SINGLE	HOUR	ON THE ASSUMPTION THAT HE MAY SAFELY CROSS OXFORD
BARB III (337)	ALL? SCRAP IT. SCRAP IT WITHOUT WASTING ANOTHER	HOUR	OR ANOTHER POUND ON IT. WELL, YOU HAVE MADE FOR
GETT PREFACE(200)	HABITUALLY WALK AT THE RATE OF FIVE MILES AN	HOUR	OR CARRY A HUNDREDWEIGHT CONTINUALLY ON THEIR BACKS.
LION PREFACE(56)	BUT TO PAY A WORKER BY LABOR TIME: SO MUCH AN	HOUR	OR DAY OR WEEK OR YEAR. BUT HOW MUCH? WHEN THAT
JOAN PREFACE(48)	AND DEATH AT THE STAKE WERE A MATTER OF HALF AN	HOUR	OR SO. NEITHER DO I CLAIM MORE FOR MY DRAMATIZATIONS OF
SUPR IV (144)	WOULD HAVE GUESSED IN THE COURSE OF ANOTHER	HOUR	OR SO. /STRAKER/ (COOLLY DEFIANT) NO, NOT IN ANOTHER
SUPR II (50)	YOU? /TANNER/ OH, ABOUT THREE QUARTERS OF AN	HOUR	OR SO. /THE CHAUFFEUR/ (REMONSTRATING) NOW, NOW, MR
ARMS II (32)	MANNERS. SHE VERY MODESTLY ENTERTAINED HIM FOR AN	HOUR	OR SO, AND THEN CALLED IN HER MOTHER LEST HER CONDUCT
JITT III (57)	ALL THE TIME HE IS THINKING OF HER, LIVING THE	HOUR	OVER AGAIN, AND LOOKING FORWARD TO THE NEXT ONE, RIGHT
CLEO PRO2 (103)	SOLDIER, THAT THE QUEEN HAS BEEN MISSING SINCE AN	HOUR	PAST SUNDOWN. /BELZANOR/ (FURIOUSLY) HAG: YOU HAVE
GETT (306)	YOU, MY LORD; BUT THE CHURCH HAS BEEN FULL THIS	HOUR	PAST; AND THE ORGANIST HAS PLAYED ALL THE WEDDING MUSIC
SUPR II (56)	RIGHT, HENRY, ALL RIGHT. WE'LL GO OUT FOR HALF AN	HOUR	PRESENTLY. /STRAKER/ (IN DISGUST) ARF AN AHR! (HE
HART II (92)	TO FIGHT WITH WOMEN AND GIRLS OVER A HALFPENNY AN	HOUR	RUTHLESSLY! A CAPTAIN OF INDUSTRY, I THINK YOU CALL
ROCK I (222)	TO LET THAT RIDICULOUS OLD MAN TALK TO YOU FOR AN	HOUR	--! (SHE SITS DOWN ANGRILY). /SIR ARTHUR/ NONSENSE!
MIS. (200)	THAN TO BE MADE LOVE TO. I HAVE NOT BEEN HERE AN	HOUR	; AND ALREADY EVERYBODY MAKES LOVE TO ME AS IF BECAUSE
SUPR II (49)	BEEN TOLD THAT THIS CAR IS CAPABLE OF 84 MILES AN	HOUR	; AND I ALREADY KNOW WHAT YOU ARE CAPABLE OF WHEN THERE
GLIM (187)	YOUR RELIGION." BUT I HAVE LIVED THROUGH MY LAST	HOUR	; AND MY RELIGION WAS THE FIRST THING THAT FELL AWAY
CAND I (88)	BY MACHINERY. NOT A MAN 'AS LESS THAN SIXPENCE A	HOUR	; AND THE SKILLED ANDS GITS THE TRADE UNION RATE. (
NEVR I (212)	CHILDREN; IN WHICH NO ROOM IS PRIVATE AND NO	HOUR	SACRED; IN WHICH DUTY, OBEDIENCE, AFFECTION, HOME,
ARMS II SD(28)	THE STING OF THE PETTY DISILLUSIONS WHICH EVERY	HOUR	SPENT AMONG MEN BRINGS TO HIS SENSITIVE OBSERVATION, HE
KING II (234)	DIE A PROTESTANT. YOU MUST SEE TO THAT WHEN THE	HOUR	STRIKES FOR ME: THE LAST HOUR. SO MY VERY BELOVEDEST
ROCK PREFACE(182)	SHALL PREVAIL OVER THE PEACE OF ROME WHEN GOD'S	HOUR	STRIKES. /PILATE/ VERY PRETTY, MY FRIEND; BUT THE HOUR
CURE (228)	DO THE TRICK, I EXPECT. IF YOU FIND AFTER HALF AN	HOUR	THAT IT HAS ONLY EXCITED YOU, TAKE ANOTHER. I'LL LEAVE
GETT PREFACE(191)	MANY BLANKETS SHOULD BE ON THE BED, AND AT WHAT	HOUR	THEY SHOULD GO TO BED AND GET UP SO AS TO AVOID
JOAN EPILOG (164)	AND TWENTY. /DUNOIS/ (RAISING JOAN) HALF AN	HOUR	TO BURN YOU, DEAR SAINT; AND FOUR CENTURIES TO FIND OUT
KING I (161)	/MRS BASHAM/ ROWLEY? I DONT KNOW HIM. THIS IS NO	HOUR	TO CALL ON MR NEWTON. /THE MAID/ NO INDEED, MAAM. AND
BULL PREFACE(55)	THE GALLOWS, AND HAD TO LEAVE HIM HANGING HALF AN	HOUR	TO MAKE SURE WORK AND GIVE HIS FAMILY PLENTY OF TIME TO

DOCT I (89)	IT TO HIM) READ THAT THE NEXT TIME YOU HAVE AN	HOUR	TO SPARE; AND YOULL FIND OUT WHY. /SIR PATRICK/ (
MILL IV (205)	THE COMPASSIONATE. HAD YOU ADDED A FARTHING AN	HOUR	TO THE WAGES OF THOSE SWEATED WOMEN, THAT WICKED
CATH 1 (171)	ON. /EDSTASTON/ BUT IT WILL TAKE ME ONLY HALF AN	HOUR	TO-- /PATIOMKIN/ IN HALF AN HOUR IT WILL BE TOO LATE
APPL PREFACE(189)	PAPER IT IS POSSIBLE TO DISCOVER WITHIN HALF AN	HOUR	WHAT IS WRONG WITH HIM PHYSICALLY. WHAT I AM WAITING
LADY (250)	ON HIS ROUND). AND NOW, SIR, WE ARE UPON THE	HOUR	WHEN IT BETTER BESEEMS A VIRGIN QUEEN TO BE ABED THAN
CAND III (145)	NO LONGER A BOY'S-- IN THE WORDS) I KNOW THE	HOUR	WHEN IT STRIKES. I AM IMPATIENT TO DO WHAT MUST BE
SUPR III (120)	WELL, DID YOU EVER OPEN THE SPINET FROM THE	HOUR	WHEN THE CHURCH UNITED HIM TO YOU? /ANA/ YOU ARE A
MILL I (151)	THEY CAN MAKE A MAN OR WOMAN HAPPY FOR HALF AN	HOUR	WHEN THEY ARE PLEASED WITH THEMSELVES AND DISPOSED TO
BUOY III (27)	SUCH BURDENS. HE COMES HERE AND SITS FOR HALF AN	HOUR	WHILE I GO THROUGH MY ACT OF WORSHIP, OF WHICH HE DOES
HART PREFACE(28)	A BOTTLE OF WINE, A VISIT TO THE THEATRE, AND AN	HOUR	WITH A STRANGE WOMAN, ALL OBTAINED BY PASSING A
AUGS (272)	LEARNING WHAT I HAD DONE, AND CONVERSING FOR AN	HOUR	WITH ME ON EUROPEAN POLITICS AND MILITARY STRATEGY,
BULL PREFACE(56)	AS HE WAS HANGING FOR FULLY QUARTER OF AN	HOUR	WITHOUT ANY FLOGGING TO AMUSE HIS FELLOW VILLAGERS AND
MRS II (212)	SAYS) WELL, THAT IS ENOUGH FOR TONIGHT. AT WHAT	HOUR	WOULD YOU LIKE BREAKFAST? IS HALF-PAST EIGHT TOO EARLY
2TRU PREFACE(8)	IDLE AND RICH, IF NOT FOR LIFE, AT LEAST FOR AN	HOUR	, AN AFTERNOON, OR EVEN A WEEK. AND FOR THE POOR THESE
CAPT III (284)	THE CADI STIMULATED HIMSELF TO SOME TEN KNOTS AN	HOUR	, AND LODGED YOU AND YOUR MEN IN MOGADOR JAIL AT MY
SUPR IV (144)	HE CAN DRIVE A MOTOR CAR AT SEVENTY MILES AN	HOUR	, AND MEND IT WHEN IT BREAKS DOWN. WE ARE DEPENDENT ON
GETT PREFACE(183)	FREE TO SIP EVERY FLOWER AND CHANGE EVERY	HOUR	, AS THEIR FANCY MAY DICTATE, IN SPITE OF THE LEGAL
DEVL I (12)	DUDGEON/ WHAT DOES SHE WANT TROUBLING ME AT THIS	HOUR	, BEFORE I AM PROPERLY DRESSED TO RECEIVE PEOPLE?
DOCT III (136)	WE SHALL MAKE OURSELVES AT HOME FOR HALF AN	HOUR	, DUBEDAT. DONT BE ALARMED: YOURE A MOST FASCINATING
APPL I (241)	THIS EVENING TO CONSIDER MY DECISION. AT THAT	HOUR	, IF I CAN FIND NO OTHER WAY OUT, I WILL SIGN WITHOUT
MRS IV (252)	THIS TIME FORTH, SO HELP ME HEAVEN IN MY LAST	HOUR	, I'LL DO WRONG AND NOTHING BUT WRONG. AND I'LL PROSPER
GETT PREFACE(200)	THE SUMMIT OF MONT BLANC AND STAY THERE FOR AN	HOUR	, IT IS POSSIBLE FOR THEM TO LIVE THERE. CHILDREN ARE
ARMS I (4)	HE SENDS ME THE NEWS. SERGIUS IS THE HERO OF THE	HOUR	, THE IDOL OF THE REGIMENT. /RAINA/ TELL ME, TELL ME.
MRS I (188)	HOW DO, MATER? MR PRAED'S BEEN HERE THIS HALF	HOUR	, WAITING FOR YOU. /MRS WARREN/ WELL, IF YOUVE BEEN
JOAN 5 (110)	THEY WILL SAY " I-AM-THY-HELP." BUT IT IS AT THE	HOUR	, WHEN THE GREAT BELL GOES AFTER "
PYGM IV (262)	WAS WORSE: SITTING GORGING THERE FOR OVER AN	HOUR	, WITH NOBODY BUT A DAMNED FOOL OF A FASHIONABLE WOMAN
ROCK PREFACE(173)	PLATOON TO PLATOON SAYING SO JUST BEFORE ZERO	HOUR	, WITH OR WITHOUT THE ADDITION " SIRS, YE ARE BRETHREN:
JOAN 6 (142)	BE PRAISED THAT HE HAS SAVED YOU AT THE ELEVENTH	HOUR	! (HE HURRIES TO THE VACANT SEAT AT THE SCRIBES'
GETT (296)	/LEO/ BUT SHE MUST COME AND DRESS. LOOK AT THE	HOUR	! /MRS BRIDGENORTH/ COME, LEO DEAR. (LEO FOLLOWS HER
ARMS III (51)	IT WAS SOMETHING I PROBABLY DID EVERY DAY! EVERY	HOUR	! THAT IS HOW MEN THINK OF WOMEN. (SHE PACES THE
		HOURLY	
BASH II.1, (112)	AND WHEN HE WILL: OBSEQUIOUS TRAMS AWAIT HIM	HOURLY	: SUBTERRANEAN TUBES WITH TIRELESS COURSERS WHISK HIM
BARB III (346)	WHAT IS ALL HUMAN CONDUCT BUT THE DAILY AND	HOURLY	SALE OF OUR SOULS FOR TRIFLES? WHAT I AM NOW SELLING
		HOUR-GLASS	
DOCT III SD(131)	LAY FIGURE, IN A CARDINAL'S ROBE AND HAT, WITH AN	HOUR-GLASS	IN ONE HAND AND A SCYTHE SLUNG ON ITS BACK,
DOCT IV SD(156)	THE WALL. CARDINAL DEATH, HOLDING HIS SCYTHE AND	HOUR-GLASS	LIKE A SCEPTRE AND GLOBE, SITS ON THE THRONE, ON
LION PREFACE(46)	THAT THE EARTH IS CYLINDRICAL, OR ANNULAR, OR	HOUR-GLASS	SHAPED, AND HE IS LOST. THE THING HE BELIEVES MAY
		HOUR'S	
MTH1 II (21)	HIM A DAY'S GLORIOUS HEALTH-GIVING SPORT AND AN	HOUR'S	AMUSING PLAY WITH THE FIRE. YOU LEARNT NOTHING FROM
SUPR I (13)	OF HAPPINESS. IF IT WERE ONLY THE FIRST HALF	HOUR'S	HAPPINESS, TAVY, I WOULD BUY IT FOR YOU WITH MY LAST
DOCT I (85)	TO MONDAY, I'LL TAKE YOU DOWN IN MY MOTOR AT AN	HOUR'S	NOTICE. /RIDGEON/ JUST ROLLING IN MONEY! I WISH YOU
2TRU II (55)	IT DONE SO YOUR LIFE WOULD NOT BE WORTH HALF AN	HOUR'S	PURCHASE. /MEEK/ NO, SIR. AM I TO FILE THE LETTER AND
APPL INTRLUD(252)	TO ENJOY TALKING TO YOU LIKE THIS WHEN I NEED AN	HOUR'S	RESPITE FROM ROYALTY: WHEN MY STUPID WIFE HAS BEEN
DOCT PREFACE(64)	HE WILL BE CALLED UP BEFORE HE HAS SNATCHED AN	HOUR'S	SLEEP. TO THE STRAIN OF SUCH INHUMAN CONDITIONS MUST
3PLA PREFACE(R22)	FEELING, WOULD PRODUCE NOTHING WORSE THAN AN	HOUR'S	SOON-FORGOTTEN FUSS. MEN WILL BE SLAIN NEEDLESSLY ON
		HOURS	
BARB III (344)	GET UP AT FIVE. MY HOURS ARE HEALTHY, RATIONAL	HOURS	: ELEVEN TO FIVE. /UNDERSHAFT/ COME WHEN YOU PLEASE:
MTH3 (125)	ON EARTH TO LIVE IN THAN ENGLAND OUT OF OFFICE	HOURS	? AND TO WHOM DO WE OWE THAT? TO OURSELVES, NOT TO
JITT I (16)	ARE YOU CONTENT WITH THESE HEARTBREAKING STOLEN	HOURS	? I'D RISK YOU BECOMING A COMMONPLACE: I WANT YOU TO
HART II (91)	TO MAZZINI) YOU SAY HE IS ALL RIGHT FOR EIGHTEEN	HOURS	? /MAZZINI/ WELL, I WAS ASLEEP FOR EIGHTEEN HOURS.
POSN (453)	HARBOR, DID YOU WALK TWENTY-FIVE MILES IN THREE	HOURS	? THAT SO, FEEMY? EH? /FEEMY/ THATS SO. AT FOUR I
ROCK II (248)	MY LIBERTY-- /BARKING/ LIBERTY TO WORK FOURTEEN	HOURS	A DAY AND BRING UP THREE CHILDREN ON THIRTYFOUR
MIS. PREFACE(36)	EVERYBODY WORKED STRENUOUSLY FOR TWENTY-FOUR	HOURS	A DAY AND NEVER GOT ANYTHING TO EAT. ONCE REALIZE THAT
WIDO III (57)	ME WHEN SHE STOOD AT HER WASH-TUB FOR THIRTEEN	HOURS	A DAY AND THOUGHT HERSELF RICH WHEN SHE MADE FIFTEEN
MRS I (185)	IT MEANS GRIND, GRIND, GRIND FOR SIX TO EIGHT	HOURS	A DAY AT MATHEMATICS, AND NOTHING BUT MATHEMATICS. I'M
HART II (122)	HE HAS THE GIFT OF BEING ABLE TO WORK SIXTEEN	HOURS	A DAY AT THE DULLEST DETAIL, AND ACTUALLY LIKES IT.
MRS II (214)	ONE OF THEM WORKED IN A WHITELEAD FACTORY TWELVE	HOURS	A DAY FOR NINE SHILLINGS A WEEK UNTIL SHE DIED OF LEAD
APPL INTRLUD(248)	UP IN THE MORNING AT FOUR AND WORKING SIXTEEN	HOURS	A DAY FOR THIRTY YEARS, LIKE CORAL INSECTS, MAKE THEM
GETT PREFACE(254)	TAKE THE CHILD OUT OF THE PARENTS' HANDS SEVERAL	HOURS	A DAY IN THE STILL MORE SACRED NAME OF COMPULSORY
MIS. PREFACE(38)	LIVING WITH INFANTS TOILING IN A FACTORY FOR TEN	HOURS	A DAY OR BOYS DRUDGING FROM NINE TO SIX UNDER GAS
MRS II (214)	I WENT TO THE BAR AT WATERLOO STATION: FOURTEEN	HOURS	A DAY SERVING DRINKS AND WASHING GLASSES FOR FOUR
BARB II (276)	FOR IT? HOLY GOD! IVE WORKED TEN TO TWELVE	HOURS	A DAY SINCE I WAS THIRTEEN, AND PAID MY WAY ALL
GETT (311)	CAPABLE OF STICKING TO HIS DESK FOR SIXTEEN	HOURS	A DAY, BUT THE RESULT OF HAVING BISHOPS OF THIS SORT
DEST (193)	WORK UNDER THE LASH IN HIS FACTORIES FOR SIXTEEN	HOURS	A DAY. HE MAKES TWO REVOLUTIONS, AND THEN DECLARES WAR
CURE (237)	THE WEARY HOURS WHEN I PRACTISED SCALES FOR EIGHT	HOURS	A DAY, IT HAS PURSUED ME THROUGH THE APPLAUSE OF
MILL III (182)	/THE MAN/ TUPPENCE HAPENY AN HOUR FOR TWELVE	HOURS	A DAY. /EPIFANIA/ SLAVERY! /THE WOMAN/ OH NO, MAAM:
JOAN PREFACE(48)	USE I HAVE HAD TO CONDENSE INTO THREE AND A HALF	HOURS	A SERIES OF EVENTS WHICH IN THEIR HISTORICAL HAPPENING
MIS. PREFACE(16)	AND SO FORTH REALLY COME TO IN PRACTICE. HOW MANY	HOURS	A WEEK OF THE TIME WHEN HIS CHILDREN ARE OUT OF BED
POSN (441)	/STRAPPER/ I DONT BELIEVE YOU STARTED NOT FOR TWO	HOURS	AFTER YOU SAY YOU DID. /BLANCO/ WHO CARES WHAT YOU
CAND III (142)	EUGENE WAS RIGHT. AS YOU TOLD ME A FEW	HOURS	AFTER, HE IS ALWAYS RIGHT. HE SAID NOTHING THAT YOU
ARMS I (13)	INSTEAD; AND I FINISHED THE LAST CAKE OF THAT	HOURS	AGO. /RAINA/ (OUTRAGED IN HER MOST CHERISHED IDEALS
JITT III (55)	HAVE BEEN FOR MONTHS PAST, WHILE MY HUSBAND SPENT	HOURS	AND HOURS AND HOURS IN HIS STUDY, WRITING, WRITING,
JITT III (55)	FOR MONTHS PAST, WHILE MY HUSBAND SPENT HOURS AND	HOURS	AND HOURS IN HIS STUDY, WRITING, WRITING, WRITING,
GENV II (51)	SECRETARY/ THEY HAVE. FORTUNATELY IT WAS AFTER	HOURS	AND THE STAFF HAD GONE HOME, OTHERWISE THEY WOULD
BARB III (344)	ITS OWN DYNAMITE BEFORE I WILL GET UP AT FIVE. MY	HOURS	ARE HEALTHY, RATIONAL HOURS: ELEVEN TO FIVE.
GETT PREFACE(218)	WHO DISLIKE ONE ANOTHER FURIOUSLY FOR SEVERAL	HOURS	AT A TIME; THERE ARE COUPLES WHO DISLIKE ONE ANOTHER
MIS. PREFACE(40)	AN EXCUSE FOR KEEPING THE CHILD SLAVING FOR TEN	HOURS	AT PHYSICAL EXERCISES ON THE GROUND THAT IT IS NOT YET
JOAN PREFACE(55)	STAND IN QUEUES OUTSIDE THE THEATRE DOORS FOR	HOURS	BEFOREHAND IN BITINGLY COLD WEATHER TO SECURE A SEAT.
MTH1 I (5)	EXIST ALWAYS AND FOR EVER. YOU SOMETIMES SIT FOR	HOURS	BROODING AND SILENT, HATING ME IN YOUR HEART. WHEN I
BULL IV (155)	TO THE HORRIBLE TORTURE OF IMPRISONMENT, NOT FOR	HOURS	BUT FOR YEARS, IN THE NAME OF JUSTICE. IT IS A PLACE
FABL V (118)	FIGURES. THEY COULD NOT CHANGE THEIR WORKING	HOURS	BY THE SUN OFTENER THAN TWICE A YEAR; AND IT TOOK ONE
BULL PREFACE(63)	OCCUPATION. THE HOUSE OF COMMONS HAD TWENTY-FOUR	HOURS	CLEAR NOTICE, WITH THE TELEGRAPH UNDER THE HAND OF SIR
2TRU PREFACE(14)	OF THE COMPULSION TO WORK LASTS ONLY AS MANY	HOURS	DAILY AS SUFFICE TO DISCHARGE THE ECONOMIC DUTIES OF
FABL V (118)	SIXTHS BEARABLY IN TUNE. THEY WASTED MILLIONS OF	HOURS	EVERY DAY BECAUSE THEY COULD NOT OR WOULD NOT DO THE
GENV IV (110)	/BBDE/ HE PRACTISES THAT TERRIBLE EXPRESSION FOR	HOURS	EVERY DAY BEFORE THE LOOKING GLASS; BUT IT IS NOT A
GETT PREFACE(199)	THE ORDINARY CITIZEN'S ATTENTION TO A COUPLE OF	HOURS	EVERY SEVENTH DAY, AND LET HIM ALONE ON WEEK-DAYS, IF
HART I (63)	THATS ALL, REALLY. /MRS HUSHABYE/ IT MAKES THE	HOURS	GO FAST, DOESNT IT? NO TEDIOUS WAITING TO GO TO SLEEP
DEVL I (9)	THE QUESTION). /ANDERSON/ YES. IN HIS LAST	HOURS	HE CHANGED HIS MIND. /MRS DUDGEON/ (WHITE WITH
HART II (114)	SHOTOVER/ IVE STOOD ON THE BRIDGE FOR EIGHTEEN	HOURS	IN A TYPHOON. LIFE HERE IS STORMIER; BUT I CAN STAND
JOAN PREFACE(52)	THE PLAY, WOULD AT ONCE PROCEED TO WASTE TWO	HOURS	IN BUILDING ELABORATE SCENERY, HAVING REAL WATER IN
JITT III (55)	PAST, WHILE MY HUSBAND SPENT HOURS AND HOURS AND	HOURS	IN HIS STUDY, WRITING, WRITING, WRITING, USING UP
SUPR III (87)	WHICH I WALK SEEING NOTHING. I HAVE WANDERED FOR	HOURS	IN HORRIBLE LONELINESS. /DON JUAN/ (SIGHING) OH! YOU
MIS. PREFACE(36)	FACTORY IS NOT CAUSED BY LIGHTER TASKS OR SHORTER	HOURS	IN THE FACTORY, NOR ALTOGETHER BY THE TEMPTATION OF
MIS. PREFACE(42)	IS SO COMMON IN COUNTRY HOUSES THAT YOU MAY SPEND	HOURS	IN THEM LISTENING TO STORIES OF BROKEN COLLAR BONES,
JITT I (16)	SIGHING BLISSFULLY) THE HAPPINESS OF THESE STOLEN	HOURS	IS SO DELICIOUS THAT IT MAKES UP TO ME FOR EVERYTHING
2TRU PREFACE(11)	CAN SATISFY WITHOUT SATIATING FOR MORE THAN A FEW	HOURS	IS THE NEED FOR FOOD AND DRINK AND SLEEP. SO FROM ONE
UNPL PREFACE(R26)	A WOMAN WHO SELLS THE USE OF HER PERSON FOR A FEW	HOURS	IS TOO VENIAL TO BE WORTH MENTIONING; FOR RICH MEN
HART PREFACE(29)	OUT, ITS WATERLOOS LASTED MONTHS INSTEAD OF	HOURS	. BUT THERE WOULD HAVE BEEN NOTHING SURPRISING IN ITS
GENV PREFACE(7)	OFF BUT NOT THREE YEARS OFF, MUCH LESS THREE	HOURS	. HAD MARX AND ENGELS BEEN CONTEMPORARIES OF
SUPR III (79)	TOMORROW. IN FACT, YOU HAVE ARRIVED OUT OF OFFICE	HOURS	. HOWEVER, IF YOU WOULD PREFER TO SETTLE THE QUESTION
BULL IV (163)	YOU FOR AN ANSWER BEFORE YOU HAVE KNOWN ME FOR 24	HOURS	. I AM A REASONABLE MAN, I HOPE; AND I AM PREPARED TO
CURE (232)	ENGAGED ME TO COME TO THIS ROOM AND PLAY FOR TWO	HOURS	. I NEVER BREAK AN ENGAGEMENT, ESPECIALLY A TWO
MRS IV (235)	/FRANK/ WAITING TO SEE YOU. IVE BEEN HERE FOR	HOURS	. IS THIS THE WAY YOU ATTEND TO YOUR BUSINESS? (HE

JOAN 5 (109)	HER) COME COME! IT WILL BE OVER IN A COUPLE OF	HOURS	. IT'S BETTER THAN THE BRIDGE AT ORLEANS: EH? /JOAN/
ARMS II (34)	IF YOU ARE AWAY FIVE MINUTES, IT WILL SEEM FIVE	HOURS	. (RAINA RUNS TO THE TOP OF THE STEPS, AND TURNS
GENV PREFACE(3)	A DISTANCE OF 30 MILES, LONDON BURNING FOR THREE	HOURS	. NEXT MORNING I READ IN THE NEWSPAPERS THAT A BOMB
BULL III (123)	HARDLY HAVE KNOWN HER FOR MORE THAN A COUPLE OF	HOURS	. /BROADBENT/ I AM AFRAID IT WAS HARDLY A COUPLE OF
KING I (167)	MY HOUSEKEEPER, AND THE FAITHFUL GUARDIAN OF MY	HOURS	. /CHARLES/ YOUR SERVANT, MISTRESS BASHAM. /FOX/ GOD
HART II (91)	HOURS? /MAZZINI/ WELL, I WAS ASLEEP FOR EIGHTEEN	HOURS	. /MRS HUSHABYE/ WERE YOU ANY THE WORSE FOR IT?
HART I (82)	NEITHER HAVE I. AND IT IS DARK: IT MUST BE ALL	HOURS	. /MRS HUSHABYE/ OH, GUINNESS WILL PRODUCE SOME SORT
FANY II SD(285)	TO SEE HER HUSBAND AT HOME DURING BUSINESS	HOURS	. /MRS KNOX/ WHAT BRINGS YOU HOME AT THIS HOUR? HAVE
MTH4 II (176)	IN THEIR PRESENCE IN LESS THAN THREE	HOURS	. /NAPOLEON/ YOU CAN KEEP THIS IDLE FABLE OF
ARMS I (17)	SLEEPY AS I HAVNT CLOSED MY EYES FOR FORTY-EIGHT	HOURS	. /RAINA/ (AT HER WIT'S END) BUT WHAT AM I TO DO WITH
JOAN 4,SD(94)	TURNING OVER THE LEAVES OF AN ILLUMINATED BOOK OF	HOURS	. THE NOBLEMAN IS ENJOYING HIMSELF: THE CHAPLAIN IS
HART II (91)	TO WAKE ME UP AFTER I HAD SLEPT EIGHTEEN	HOURS	. THEY HAD TO CARRY ME UPSTAIRS; AND AS THE POOR
KING I (164)	HUNDRED AND TEN THOUSAND TWO HUNDRED AND FORTY	HOURS	. TWELVE MILLION SIX HUNDRED AND FOURTEEN THOUSAND,
2TRU I (33)	DOSED HER SO THAT SHE WONT SPEAK AGAIN FOR TEN	HOURS	. YOU WILL OVERDO THAT SOME DAY. /THE DOCTOR/
CYMB FORWORD(134)	ROMANTIC MELANCHOLY, STOOD DUMB ON THE STAGE FOR	HOURS	(AS IT SEEMED) WHILST THE OTHERS TOILED THROUGH A
2TRU PREFACE(14)	THE ECONOMIC DUTIES OF THE CITIZEN, THE REMAINING	HOURS	(OVER AND ABOVE THOSE NEEDED FOR FEEDING, SLEEPING,
MILL II (175)	OSTRICH. I HAVE A CLOCKWORK INSIDE. I SLEEP EIGHT	HOURS	LIKE A LOG. WHEN I WANT ANYTHING I LOSE MY HEAD SO
JOAN PREFACE(55)	MY BREAD. I DO NOT GIVE THEM PERFORMANCES TWELVE	HOURS	LONG, BECAUSE CIRCUMSTANCES DO NOT AT PRESENT MAKE
MIS. PREFACE(107)	LIFE ARE ORGANIZED SEPARATELY FROM THE ACTIVE	HOURS	OF ADULT LIFE, SO THAT ADULTS CAN ENJOY THE SOCIETY OF
LION PREFACE(57)	MANY MINUTES OF A BOOKMAKER'S TIME ARE WORTH TWO	HOURS	OF AN ASTRONOMER'S? VITAL DISTRIBUTION. IN THE END
MIS. PREFACE(107)	INCULCATED. WHAT IS MORE, UNTIL THE ACTIVE	HOURS	OF CHILD LIFE ARE ORGANIZED SEPARATELY FROM THE ACTIVE
BULL I (91)	GREEN; AND I WANT TO BRING GALWAY WITHIN 3	HOURS	OF COLCHESTER AND 24 OF NEW YORK. I WANT IRELAND TO BE
MIS. (171)	LIFE IS? I SPEND MY DAYS FROM NINE TO SIX-- NINE	HOURS	OF DAYLIGHT AND FRESH AIR-- IN A STUFFY LITTLE DEN
POSN (439)	UP AND TIDYING HIMSELF)-- OH WOMAN, IN OUR	HOURS	OF EASE, UNCERTAIN, COY, AND HARD TO PLEASE-- IS MY
PHIL I (78)	WHICH TAUGHT ME A GREAT DEAL, AND BROUGHT ME SOME	HOURS	OF EXQUISITE HAPPINESS. /JULIA/ LEONARD: YOU CONFESS
NEVR I (223)	TO HIS LAST FARTHING, AND IS WITHIN TWENTY FOUR	HOURS	OF HAVING HIS FURNITURE DISTRAINED UPON BY HIS
BULL I (85)	EMIGRANT " SITTING ON THE STILE, MARY," OR THREE	HOURS	OF IRISH PATRIOTISM IN BERMONDSEY OR THE SCOTLAND
JOAN PREFACE(54)	AND THAT TO ASK PEOPLE TO ENDURE MORE THAN TWO	HOURS	OF IT (WITH TWO LONG INTERVALS OF RELIEF) IS AN
DOCT PREFACE(17)	TO INFECTION, AND HAS TO FACE ALL WEATHERS AT ALL	HOURS	OF THE NIGHT AND DAY, OFTEN NOT ENJOYING A COMPLETE
GETT PREFACE(190)	AND NATURAL TO THEM THAT OUT OF EVERY TWENTY-FOUR	HOURS	OF THEIR LIVES THEY SHOULD PASS EIGHT SHUT UP IN ONE
DOCT PREFACE(14)	BUT THE PATIENT PAYS FOR THE ANESTHESIA WITH	HOURS	OF WRETCHED SICKNESS; AND WHEN THAT IS OVER THERE IS
BULL IV (172)	THE CONQUERING ENGLISHMAN, SIR. WITHIN 24	HOURS	OF YOUR ARRIVAL YOU HAVE CARRIED OFF OUR ONLY HEIRESS,
MIS. (192)	THE QUESTION THAT MEN AND WOMEN WILL SPEND	HOURS	OVER WITHOUT COMPLAINING. THE QUESTION THAT OCCUPIES
JOAN PREFACE(55)	CLASSICAL LIMIT OF THREE AND A HALF	HOURS	PRACTICALLY CONTINUOUS PLAYING, BARRING THE ONE
LION PREFACE(99)	ON ASSUMPTIONS WHICH WOULD IN TWENTY-FOUR	HOURS	PROVOKE THE VILLAGE AT ITS GATES TO INSURRECTION. THAT
PHIL I (79)	SOLEMN PROMISES NOT TO DO IT AGAIN; OF SPENDING	HOURS	-- AYE, DAYS! PIECING TOGETHER THE CONTENTS OF MY
DOCT PREFACE(16)	A SURGEON TO EARN SIMILAR SUMS IN A COUPLE OF	HOURS	; AND IF THE SURGEON ALSO KEEPS A NURSING HOME, HE
HART I (45)	HERE. HER LUGGAGE IS LEFT ON THE STEPS FOR	HOURS	; AND SHE HERSELF IS DEPOSITED IN THE POOP AND
JOAN PREFACE(54)	BEEN CUT DOWN TO TEN MINUTES AND PLAYS TO TWO	HOURS	; AND, EVEN AT THAT, CONGREGATIONS SIT LONGING FOR THE
GENV III (80)	COULD HOLD THE HOUSE OF COMMONS SPELLBOUND FOR	HOURS	; BUT MOST UNSAFE. MERE ENTERTAINERS. /BEGONIA/ MY
BARB PREFACE(220)	FOUR MEN THREE SHILLINGS EACH FOR TEN OR TWELVE	HOURS	' DRUDGERY AND ONE MAN A THOUSAND POUNDS FOR NOTHING.
JOAN PREFACE(54)	AND INSISTS SO EFFECTIVELY ON A CERTAIN NUMBER OF	HOURS	' ENTERTAINMENT THAT TOURING MANAGERS ARE SOMETIMES
2TRU PREFACE(4)	EVENING OFF IS REALLY OFF: IN THOSE HARD EARNED	HOURS	SHE CEASES TO BE A HOUSEMAID AND CAN BE HERSELF; BUT
MTH5 (257)	JEALOUS OF YOU. THAT LOOKS LIKE THE END. TWO	HOURS	SLEEP IS ENOUGH FOR ME. I AM AFRAID I AM BEGINNING TO
ROCK I (203)	DISTURB YOUR FATHER, THOUGH HE HAS HAD HARDLY SIX	HOURS	SLEEP THIS WEEK, AND WAS UP ALL NIGHT. I AM SO SORRY,
POSN (437)	SURE I HOPED HE WOULD GET AWAY; FOR HE HAD TWO	HOURS	START OF THE VIGILANCE COMMITTEE. BUT THEY CAUGHT HIM.
POSN (437)	BEEN MUCH OF A HORSE IF THEY CAUGHT HIM WITH TWO	HOURS	START. /ELDER DANIELS/ (COMING BACK TO THE CENTRE OF
MTH5 (210)	MAKING A BUSINESS OF SITTING TOGETHER AT FIXED	HOURS	TO ABSORB OUR NOURISHMENT; TAKING LITTLE POISONS WITH
ANNA (292)	OF THE PANDEROBAJENSKY HUSSARS. I GIVE YOU TWELVE	HOURS	TO CATCH HIM OR . . . WHATS THAT YOU SAY ABOUT THE
ANNA (299)	ORDERS ME TO OFFER ALL THE NEUTRAL COUNTRIES 48	HOURS	TO CHOOSE BETWEEN ADOPTING HIS VIEWS ON THE SINGLE TAX
DEVL III (69)	EVACUATION OF THE TOWN. THEY OFFER US JUST SIX	HOURS	TO CLEAR OUT. /SWINDON/ WHAT MONSTROUS IMPUDENCE!
GETT PREFACE(191)	WORK A DAY AND TOOK FROM SEVEN TO NINE OFFICE	HOURS	TO DO IT IN. AND THEY WERE NO GOOD FOR ANY MORTAL
BULL PREFACE(55)	THE LOCAL PAPERS DESCRIBED IT), THUS HAVING TWO	HOURS	TO KILL AS WELL AS FOUR MEN, THEY KEPT THE
JITT II (30)	SHE HOPES TO BE ABLE TO GET UP FOR A COUPLE OF	HOURS	TODAY. JUST IN A DRESSING-GOWN, YOU KNOW, TO SIT ABOUT
CURE (237)	MY DREAM. IT HAS CONSOLED ME THROUGH THE WEARY	HOURS	WHEN I PRACTISED SCALES FOR EIGHT HOURS A DAY. IT HAS
KING I (204)	PART: I HAD TO STAND MUM ON THE STAGE FOR	HOURS	WHILE THE OTHERS WERE SPOUTING. MR DRYDEN DOES NOT
MIS. PREFACE(89)	A FRONT BENCH POLITICIAN SAYING NOTHING FOR TWO	HOURS	WHILST HIS UNFORTUNATE COUNTRY IS PERISHING THROUGH
MIS. PREFACE(105)	A MEANS OF PLEASING HIMSELF AND BEGUILING TEDIOUS	HOURS	WITH ROMANCES AND FAIRY TALES AND FOOLS' PARADISES (A
GETT PREFACE(191)	WALKS, AND THE REST OF IT. THEY DID LESS THAN TWO	HOURS	WORK A DAY AND TOOK FROM SEVEN TO NINE OFFICE HOURS TO
BUOY 1 (15)	EASY FOR US TO SUPPORT OURSELVES AS WELL BY TWO	HOURS	WORK AS NOW BY TWO YEARS, WE SHALL MOVE MOUNTAINS AND
MRS IV (236)	CANT AFFORD IT. I SHALL PUT IN ANOTHER SIX	HOURS	WORK BEFORE I GO TO BED. /FRANK/ CANT AFFORD IT, CANT
CAND II (112)	DINNER, JAMES? /MORELL/ NOT FOR A COUPLE OF	HOURS	YET. /BURGESS/ (WITH PLAINTIVE RESIGNATION) GIMME A
CLEO PRO2 (103)	AND THEIR WIVES BECOME MOTHERS IN THREE	HOURS	, AND ARE SLAIN AND EATEN THE NEXT DAY. A SHUDDER OF
DOCT PREFACE(65)	TYRANNY OF IGNORANT PATIENTS, THE WORK-DAY OF 24	HOURS	, AND THE USELESSNESS OF HONESTLY PRESCRIBING WHAT
FABL PREFACE(80)	DIFFERENT RITUALS MUST BE PERFORMED AT DIFFERENT	HOURS	, AS THEY ARE AT THE ALBERT HALL IN LONDON, THE USHER
CAND III (128)	YOUVE BEEN READING TO ME FOR MORE THAN TWO	HOURS	, EVER SINCE JAMES WENT OUT. I WANT TO TALK.
MIS. PREFACE(32)	SCHOOL KEPT THE CHILDREN QUIET DURING MY WORKING	HOURS	, I DID NOT FOR THE SAKE OF MY OWN PERSONAL
ROCK I (229)	OVERBURDENED, OVERDRIVEN MAN, SUFFERING FROM LATE	HOURS	, IRREGULAR SNATCHED MEALS, NO TIME FOR DIGESTION NOR
PHIL III (139)	ABUSED ME TO YOUR HEART'S CONTENT FOR A COUPLE OF	HOURS	, THEN THE REACTION WOULD COME; AND YOU WOULD AT LAST
LION PROLOG (107)	TO SIT AND TALK TO THOSE DUMB BRUTE BEASTS FOR	HOURS	, WHEN YOU HADNT A WORD FOR ME. /ANDROCLES/ THEY NEVER
		HOUSE	
HART (1)	HEARTBREAK	HOUSE	: A FANTASIA IN THE RUSSIAN MANNER ON ENGLISH THEMES.
MIS. (129)	NATURAL CHAP. HE KEPT A TAME PHILOSOPHER IN THE	HOUSE	: A SORT OF COLERIDGE OR HERBERT SPENCER KIND OF CARD.
APPL I (203)	OH, SIT DOWN, MAN, SIT DOWN. YOURE IN YOUR OWN	HOUSE	: CEREMONY CUTS NO ICE WITH ME. /MAGNUS/ (GRATEFULLY)
JITT III (65)	WHETHER HE WILL EVER COME BACK. THIS IS A MARKED	HOUSE	: EVERYBODY DESERTS IT. WHO KNOWS HOW SOON I SHALL BE
HART III (142)	THINGS. /ELLIE/ YOUR HOUSE IS NOT HEARTBREAK	HOUSE	: IS IT, LADY UTTERWORD? /HECTOR/ YET SHE BREAKS
HART III (140)	FOR YOUR HOUSE? /CAPTAIN SHOTOVER/ IT IS NOT MY	HOUSE	: IT IS ONLY MY KENNEL. /HECTOR/ WE HAVE BEEN TOO LONG
HART II (105)	AWAY, BOSS MANGAN? /MANGAN/ TO HELL OUT OF THIS	HOUSE	: LET THAT BE ENOUGH FOR YOU AND ALL HERE. /CAPTAIN
HART I (46)	HUSHABYE, WHO INVITED YOU HERE. I KEEP THIS	HOUSE	: SHE UPSETS IT. I DESIRE TO ATTAIN THE SEVENTH DEGREE
SUPR HANDBOK(225)	MODERATE DRINKERS BOTH, IN A MODERATELY HEALTHY	HOUSE	: THAT IS THE TRUE MIDDLE CLASS UNIT. THE UNCONSCIOUS
HART I (77)	BEEN TO THE GRAVEL PIT. DONT DROP IT ABOUT THE	HOUSE	: THERES A DEAR. (SHE GOES INTO THE GARDEN, WHERE THE
HART III (140)	HAVE BEEN TOO LONG HERE. WE DO NOT LIVE IN THIS	HOUSE	: WE HAUNT IT. /LADY UTTERWORD/ (HEART TORN) IT IS
ARMS I SD(9)	THEM ANGRILY FROM WITHIN THIS IS MAJOR PETKOFF'S	HOUSE	: YOU CANT COME IN HERE; BUT A RENEWAL OF THE CLAMOR,
BUOY IV (50)	DADDY, BUT YOU WILL KNOW YOUR NATURAL PLACE IN MY	HOUSE	: YOU HAVE ALWAYS KNOWN IT IN YOUR OWN. I CAN TRUST
HART I (51)	CAN CHILDREN BE EXPECTED TO BE YOUTHFUL IN THIS	HOUSE	? ALMOST BEFORE WE COULD SPEAK WE WERE FILLED WITH
HART III (131)	HORSES. WHY HAVE WE NEVER BEEN ABLE TO LET THIS	HOUSE	? BECAUSE THERE ARE NO PROPER STABLES. GO ANYWHERE IN
SHAK (141)	COMPLETE. COULDST THOU HAVE WRITTEN HEARTBREAK	HOUSE	? BEHOLD MY LEAR. A TRANSPARENCY IS SUDDENLY LIT UP,
GENV IV (91)	HOW CAN I BE ANYTHING ELSE? HOW DO YOU BUILD A	HOUSE	? BY FIRST MAKING GOOD SOUND BRICKS. YOU CANT BUILD
GETT (304)	(RISING) HOW COULD I KICK HIM OUT OF THE	HOUSE	? HE'S STRONGER THAN ME: HE COULD HAVE KICKED ME OUT
DOCT III (143)	ANY MORE CIVILITIES TO ADDRESS TO ME IN MY OWN	HOUSE	? I SHOULD LIKE TO GET THEM OVER BEFORE MY WIFE COMES
HART III (136)	/MANGAN/ SHAME! WHAT SHAME IS THERE IN THIS	HOUSE	? LET'S ALL STRIP STARK NAKED. WE MAY AS WELL DO THE
O'FL (226)	DID YOU HEAR ME ORDERING YOU TO GO INTO THE	HOUSE	? MRS O'FLAHERTY! (LOUDER) MRS O'FLAHERTY! ! WILL
BUOY II (18)	YOU DO NOT LOOK MARRIED. HAVE YOU ANY MILK IN THE	HOUSE	? OR A HUNK OF BREAD AND AN ONION? /SHE/ NOT FOR
HART III (140)	/HECTOR/ DO YOU ACCEPT THAT NAME FOR YOUR	HOUSE	? /CAPTAIN SHOTOVER/ IT IS NOT MY HOUSE: IT IS ONLY
BARB I (261)	ADOLPHUS, TO INVITE MY OWN HUSBAND TO MY OWN	HOUSE	? /CUSINS/ (GALLANTLY) YOU HAVE MY UNHESITATING
HART I (74)	GOT ROUND HIM BEFORE YOU WERE TEN MINUTES IN THE	HOUSE	? /ELLIE/ I DID. /MRS HUSHABYE/ YOU LITTLE DEVIL! (
GETT (335)	/MRS GEORGE/ SUPPOSE HE KICKS YOU OUT OF THE	HOUSE	? /HOTCHKISS/ HOW CAN HE? IVE FOUGHT SEVEN DUELS
HART III (130)	NUMSKULL. /CAPTAIN SHOTOVER/ WHATS WRONG WITH MY	HOUSE	? /LADY UTTERWORD/ JUST WHAT IS WRONG WITH A SHIP,
PRES (147)	WELL AS THEY FITTED GENERAL BLAKE AT THE MANSION	HOUSE	? /MITCHENER/ THEY DIDNT FIT HIM. HE LOOKED A
NEVR II (235)	I DONT KNOW. FINCH: DOES HE KEEP A PUBLIC	HOUSE	? /M'COMAS/ (RISING, SCANDALIZED) NO, NO, NO. YOUR
DEST (189)	MEAN GO ALONE? IN THE DARK? WITH A WITCH IN THE	HOUSE	? /NAPOLEON/ PSHA! YOURE A POLTROON. (TO THE
SIM I (38)	AND ADMIRATION) OH DEAR! IS THIS THE LADY OF THE	HOUSE	? /PROLA/ (COMING PAST PRA TO THE CLERGYMAN) WHO IS
WIDO III (58)	FRIENDS WITH HIM. /BLANCHE/ AND TO ASK HIM TO THE	HOUSE	? /SARTORIUS/ ONLY ON BUSINESS. YOU NEED NOT MEET HIM
SIM II (73)	THERE ANY WAY OF GETTING OUT ON THE ROOF OF THIS	HOUSE	? /SIR CHARLES/ (RISING) CERTAINLY: IT IS A FLAT
MIS. (157)	/LORD SUMMERHAYS/ WELL, IS THERE A BIBLE IN THE	HOUSE	? /TARLETON/ STACKS OF EM. THERES THE FAMILY BIBLE,
HART II (108)	TO BE INHOSPITABLE; BUT WILL YOU KINDLY LEAVE THE	HOUSE	? /THE BURGLAR/ RIGHT. I'LL GO TO THE POLICE STATION

GENV I	(33)	/SHE/ BURGLARY! DID THEY BREAK INTO YOUR	HOUSE	? /THE JEW/ I CANNOT SPEAK OF IT. EVERYTHING I
ROCK I	(198)	SHALL I BE ANY BETTER AT HOME HERE LEADING THE	HOUSE	? SITTING UP ALL NIGHT IN BAD AIR LISTENING TO FOOLS
BULL II	(106)	JUDY/ AH THEN, HOW COULD YOU STAY AT A PUBLIC	HOUSE	? THEYD HAVE NO PLACE TO PUT YOU EVEN IF IT WAS A
GETT	(351)	AND UPSET WHEN THERES NOBODY TO LIVEN UP THE	HOUSE	A BIT. /HOTCHKISS/ I'LL DO MY BEST. /REGINALD/ (
CAPT I	(224)	OF LUXURIOUS IDLENESS): I HAVE BROUGHT TO YOUR	HOUSE	A CHRISTIAN DOG AND HIS WOMAN. /DRINKWATER/ THERES
JITT III	(60)	DID YOUR DUTY: NOBODY CAN BLAME YOU. BUT WAS HIS	HOUSE	A HOME FOR HIM, AS HIS HEART MADE IT A HOME FOR ME?
MIS.	(151)	DISTINCTION VANISHES. I'M PROUD TO RECEIVE IN MY	HOUSE	A LADY OF EVIDENT REFINEMENT AND DISTINCTION. ALLOW ME
HART II	(104)	YOU ARE GOING TO COME RELIGION OVER ME. IN THIS	HOUSE	A MAN'S MIND MIGHT AS WELL BE A FOOTBALL. I'M GOING. (
SIM II	(67)	WE HAVE IMAGINATIONS. /KANCHIN/ WE HAVE MADE THIS	HOUSE	A TEMPLE. /JANGA/ WE HAVE MADE PROLA ITS GODDESS.
DOCT III	(133)	ENOUGH TO WORK STEADILY, I'D MAKE MY DARLING'S	HOUSE	A TEMPLE, AND HER SHRINE A CHAPEL MORE BEAUTIFUL THAN
GETT	(352)	GEORGE LIKES YOUR CONVERSATION YOULL FIND THEIR	HOUSE	A VERY PLEASANT ONE: LIVELIER THAN MR REGINALD'S WAS.
DEST	(156)	BE SWEARING, FUMING, THREATENING, PULLING THE	HOUSE	ABOUT OUR EARS. /NAPOLEON/ GIUSEPPE: YOUR FLATTERIES
MTH1 II	SD(20)	IN MESOPOTAMIA. CLOSE AT HAND THE END OF A LOG	HOUSE	ABUTS ON A KITCHEN GARDEN. ADAM IS DIGGING IN THE
SUPR IV	(172)	AT MY EXPENSE. WE PROPOSE TO FURNISH OUR OWN	HOUSE	ACCORDING TO OUR OWN TASTE; AND I HEREBY GIVE NOTICE
FANY III	(315)	SHE DOES NOW; AND I SHALL HAVE A COMPANION IN THE	HOUSE	AFTER ALL THESE LONELY YEARS. /KNOX/ (BEGINNING TO
LIED	(189)	BE A LAW AGAINST A MAN'S SISTER EVER ENTERING HIS	HOUSE	AFTER HE'S MARRIED. I'M AS CERTAIN AS THAT I'M SITTING
MTH2	(60)	THERE IS OF OUR FINDING YOU BESIDE US IN THE	HOUSE	AFTER THE NEXT ELECTION. /FRANKLYN/ WHEN I SPEAK OF
HART II	(88)	LIKE; BUT, IF YOU DO, YOULL NEVER ENTER HESIONE'S	HOUSE	AGAIN: I WILL TAKE CARE OF THAT. /MANGAN/ (GASPING)
WIDO III	(64)	HERE. YOU HAVE HAD THE MEANNESS TO COME INTO THIS	HOUSE	AGAIN. (HE FLUSHES AND RETREATS A STEP. SHE FOLLOWS
JITT III	(77)	SPEAK TO YOU NOR CROSS THE THRESHOLD OF YOUR	HOUSE	AGAIN. /LENKHEIM/ (MORE AMUSED THAN EVER) EXCEPT WHEN
HART I	(47)	SHE MARRIED HIM, AND WILL NEVER SET FOOT IN THIS	HOUSE	AGAIN. /NURSE GUINNESS/ (CARRYING THE TABLE, WITH THE
DEVL II	SD(28)	DUDGEONS; BUT IT IS SO PLAIN ITSELF THAT A MODERN	HOUSE	AGENT WOULD LET BOTH AT ABOUT THE SAME RENT. THE CHIEF
MTH2	(76)	LEASE FOR EVER, HE TOOK CARE TO MAKE IT WHAT THE	HOUSE	AGENTS CALL A HIGHLY DESIRABLE COUNTRY RESIDENCE. BUT
BULL PREFACE	(63)	THE DENSHAWAI EXECUTIONS, BUT APPEALED TO THE	HOUSE	ALMOST PASSIONATELY NOT TO CRITICIZE OR REPUDIATE
BULL III	(139)	BE THEM WHEN THEY PUT A GUN IN THE THATCH OF HIS	HOUSE	AN THEN WENT AND FOUND IT THERE, BAD CESS TO THEM!
BUOY 1	(15)	A SHILLING BUY ENOUGH CHEMICAL SALTS TO BLOW THIS	HOUSE	AND ALL ITS INHABITANTS TO SMITHEREENS. A GLASS
FANY II	(295)	BEEN SET FREE FROM THIS SILLY LITTLE HOLE OF A	HOUSE	AND ALL ITS PRETENCES. I KNOW NOW THAT I AM STRONGER
CAPT II	(268)	(IMPRESSIVELY) BRASSBOUND: I AM IN MINE OWN	HOUSE	AND AMID MINE OWN PEOPLE. I AM THE SULTAN HERE.
PYGM II	(234)	YOUR DAUGHTER HAD THE AUDACITY TO COME TO MY	HOUSE	AND ASK ME TO TEACH HER HOW TO SPEAK PROPERLY SO THAT
JITT PREFACE	(3)	UNKNOWN TO ME WHEN HE APPEARED ONE DAY AT MY	HOUSE	AND ASKED TO SEE ME WITH A VIEW TO HIS BECOMING MY
SUPR PREFACE	(R15)	AND BECOME DONA JUANA, BREAKING OUT OF THE DOLL'S	HOUSE	AND ASSERTING HERSELF AS AN INDIVIDUAL INSTEAD OF A
KING I	(189)	I DO NOT. /CHARLES/ MR NEWTON: WE ARE IN YOUR	HOUSE	AND AT YOUR ORDERS. WILL YOU ALLOW MY BROTHER AND
GETT	(356)	WHEN ONCE I CROSS THE THRESHOLD OF YOUR HUSBAND'S	HOUSE	AND BREAK BREAD WITH HIM. THIS MARRIAGE BOND WHICH I
ROCK I	(194)	THE MALL IS FULL ALL THE WAY DOWN TO MARLBOROUGH	HOUSE	AND BUCKINGHAM PALACE. /SIR ARTHUR/ THEY HAVE NO RIGHT
SIM I	(38)	/PRA/ YOU WERE THEIR-- ! (HE TURNS TO THE	HOUSE	AND CALLS) PROLA. PROLA. /PROLA'S VOICE/ YES. WHAT IS
LION II	(142)	YOU ARE ALL FREE. PRAY GO INTO THE FRONT OF THE	HOUSE	AND ENJOY THE SPECTACLE TO WHICH YOUR BROTHER HAS SO
BULL IV	(170)	WILL FIND YOUR WORK CUT OUT FOR YOU KEEPING TOM'S	HOUSE	AND ENTERTAINING TOM'S FRIENDS AND GETTING TOM INTO
SUPR II	(58)	YOU ABOUT RHODA. RICKY: WILL YOU GO BACK TO THE	HOUSE	AND ENTERTAIN YOUR AMERICAN FRIEND. HE'S RATHER ON
GENV PREFACE	(8)	THEY WERE DESTROYING GERMAN CITIES, AND HAVING TO	HOUSE	AND FEED THEIR SURVIVING INHABITANTS AFTER WRECKING
GETT	(269)	IS A GREAT LOUT OF A MAN SMOKING ALL OVER MY	HOUSE	AND GOING TO SLEEP IN HIS CHAIR AFTER DINNER, AND
LION PROLOG	(106)	PEOPLE DO, INSTEAD OF HAVING US HUNTED OUT OF	HOUSE	AND HOME FOR BEING DIRTY DISREPUTABLE BLASPHEMING
BULL I	(84)	MORTGAGE AND TURNING POOR NICK LESTRANGE OUT OF	HOUSE	AND HOME HAS RATHER TAKEN ME ABACK; FOR I LIKED THE
JOAN PREFACE	(42)	BEEN SLAUGHTERED, STARVED TO DEATH, BURNT OUT OF	HOUSE	AND HOME, AND WHAT NOT THAT PERSECUTION AND TERROR
HART PREFACE	(3)	HEARTBREAK	HOUSE	AND HORSEBACK HALL. WHERE HEARTBREAK HOUSE STANDS.
HART PREFACE	(8)	ARE WORSE THAN FALSE DOCTRINE; BUT HEARTBREAK	HOUSE	AND HORSEBACK HALL UNFORTUNATELY SUFFERED FROM BOTH.
6CAL	(101)	BEEN OBEDIENT. BY GOD, I WILL BE MASTER IN MY OWN	HOUSE	AND KING IN MY OWN CAMP. TAKE THESE FELLOWS OUT AND
HART III	SD(148)	IT'S MAGNIFICENT. THEY ALL TURN AWAY FROM THE	HOUSE	AND LOOK UP, LISTENING. /HECTOR/ (GRAVELY) MISS DUNN:
HART II	(92)	JUST BECAUSE HE WILL KEEP HER IN AN EXPENSIVE	HOUSE	AND MAKE HER WEAR DIAMONDS TO SHEW HOW RICH HE IS?
PLES PREFACE	(R14)	SUCCESS, HE COULD TRANSFER IT TO HIS FASHIONABLE	HOUSE	AND MAKE THE MOST OF IT THERE. SUCH MANAGERSHIP WOULD
BARB II	(291)	GARRISON. IT PICKS THE WASTER OUT OF THE PUBLIC	HOUSE	AND MAKES A MAN OF HIM: IT FINDS A WORM WRIGGLING IN A
OVER PREFACE	(161)	STRANGLE HER LIKE OTHELLO, OR TURN HER OUT OF THE	HOUSE	AND NEVER SEE HER OR ALLOW HER TO SEE HER CHILDREN
BASH III	(121)	IMAGE OF DIVINITY? I LOATHE THEE. HENCE FROM MY	HOUSE	AND NEVER SEE ME MORE. /CASHEL/ I GO. THE MEANEST LAD
MIS.	(187)	ME AGAIN: IF YOU SAY ANOTHER WORD, I'LL LEAVE THE	HOUSE	AND NOT ENTER IT UNTIL YOU LEAVE IT. /JOHNNY/ PUT THAT
KING I	(176)	CHAIR). /NELL/ AFTER ALL, DEAR, IT'S MR NEWTON'S	HOUSE	AND NOT OURS. HE WAS IN THE ACT OF PUTTING ME OUT WHEN
MRS IV	(248)	IN EUROPE AT YOUR FEET; IT MEANS A LOVELY	HOUSE	AND PLENTY OF SERVANTS; IT MEANS THE CHOICEST OF
MIS. PREFACE	(15)	IS NEVERTHELESS TO PACK THEM ALL INTO THE SAME	HOUSE	AND PRETEND THAT THEY ARE HAPPY, AND THAT THIS
GETT PREFACE	(233)	SAME WAY. IF A ROMANTIC YOUNG LADY CAME INTO HER	HOUSE	AND PROPOSED TO ADORE HER HUSBAND ON A TOLERATED
ARMS II	(28)	MAJOR SERGIUS SARANOFF! (HE GOES INTO THE	HOUSE	AND RETURNS PRESENTLY WITH A THIRD CHAIR, WHICH HE
MIS.	(168)	WORD TO SAY AGAINST HER, TAKE YOURSELF OUT OF MY	HOUSE	AND SAY IT ELSEWHERE. /THE MAN/ WHAT SORT OF A JOKER
ROCK I	(207)	THAT YOU HAVE SACRIFICED YOURSELF TO KEEPING MY	HOUSE	AND SEWING ON MY BUTTONS; AND I AM NOT UNGRATEFUL. I
MIS.	(175)	(TO GUNNER) I'LL TEACH YOU TO COME INTO MY	HOUSE	AND SHOOT MY HUSBAND. /GUNNER/ TEACH AWAY. I NEVER
BUOY II	(19)	WHERE YOU ARE NOT WANTED. (SHE GOES INTO THE	HOUSE	AND SLAMS THE DOOR). AN ELDERLY NATIVE ARRIVES WITH A
BUOY II	(23)	YOU ARE AN INFERNAL NUISANCE (SHE GOES INTO THE	HOUSE	AND SLAMS THE DOOR), THE NATIVE RETURNS WITH ANOTHER
BULL PREFACE	(49)	ALL THE CIVIL EMPLOYEES ON HIS ESTATE AND IN HIS	HOUSE	AND STABLES WITHOUT THE AID OF A MUTINY ACT, WILL
ARMS II	(30)	/RAINA/ (SUDDENLY COMING ROUND THE CORNER OF THE	HOUSE	AND STANDING AT THE TOP OF THE STEPS IN THE PATH)
BARB PREFACE	(214)	PRECISELY PARALLEL CASE OF A MAN BREAKING INTO MY	HOUSE	AND STEALING MY WIFE'S DIAMONDS I AM EXPECTED AS A
SUPR II	(49)	OF IT, EH? /TANNER/ I MAY AS WELL WALK TO THE	HOUSE	AND STRETCH MY LEGS AND CALM MY NERVES A LITTLE. (
HART III	(147)	IS THE HAND OF GOD. /HECTOR/ (RETURNING FROM THE	HOUSE	AND STRIDING ACROSS TO HIS FORMER PLACE) THERE IS NOT
APPL PREFACE	(181)	HEADS THEY ARE AS LIKELY AS NOT TO BURN THE WRONG	HOUSE	AND TEAR THE WRONG MAN TO PIECES. WHEN WE HAVE WHAT IS
HART III	(147)	IT'S MR HUSHABYE TURNING ON ALL THE LIGHTS IN THE	HOUSE	AND TEARING DOWN THE CURTAINS. /RANDALL/ (RUSHING IN
KING I	(178)	I WILL CONTINUE TO TESTIFY AGAINST THE STEEPLE	HOUSE	AND THE BRAZEN CLANGOR OF ITS BELFRIES. /MRS BASHAM/
MRS III	SD(220)	AN UNFENCED PINE WOOD. ON THE LAWN, BETWEEN THE	HOUSE	AND THE DRIVE, IS A CLIPPED YEW TREE, WITH A GARDEN
CAPT NOTES	(301)	HOW MEN AND CITIES ARE CONCEIVED IN THE COUNTING	HOUSE	AND THE VOLUNTEER CORPS. HE IS, I UNDERSTAND, A
ROCK II	(281)	NO MORE CHILDREN. FREE TO GIVE UP LIVING IN A BIG	HOUSE	AND TO SPEND THE REMAINDER OF OUR LIVES AS WE PLEASE.
SIM II	SD(69)	/VASHTI/ IT'S SWOOPING DOWN. IDDY COMES FROM THE	HOUSE	AND TROTS DOWN THE STEPS WITH A FIELD GLASS IN HIS
KING I	(162)	OF A MAN THAT WOULD CALL A CHURCH A STEEPLE	HOUSE	AND WALK INTO IT WITHOUT TAKING OFF HIS HAT? GO THIS
BUOY II	(22)	NOT NATURAL. IN NATIVE LIFE THE WOMAN KEEPS THE	HOUSE	AND WORKS THERE: THE MAN KEEPS THE WOMAN AND RESTS
BUOY II	SD(18)	IN PYJAMA SLACKS AND A PULLOVER, COMES OUT OF THE	HOUSE	AND, FROM THE TOP OF THE STEPS, PROCEEDS TO MAKE THE
FANY PROLOG	(270)	NOT PLAYS. I CANT CONSENT TO REMAIN IN THIS	HOUSE	ANOTHER MINUTE IF ANYTHING REMOTELY RESEMBLING THEM IS
DEVL I	SD(4)	TO THE DEDUCTIVE OBSERVER THAT THE MEN OF THE	HOUSE	ARE ALL AWAY, AS THERE ARE NO HATS OR COATS ON THEM.
HART II	(123)	OTHELLO. /RANDALL/ SOME OF YOUR GAMES IN THIS	HOUSE	ARE DAMNED ANNOYING, LET ME TELL YOU. /HECTOR/ YES: I
DOCT V	(174)	TO ME NOW. /JENNIFER/ THE ANIMALS IN SIR RALPH'S	HOUSE	ARE LIKE SPOILED CHILDREN. WHEN MR WALPOLE HAD TO TAKE
HART III	(148)	MISS DUNN: YOU CAN DO NO GOOD HERE. WE OF THIS	HOUSE	ARE ONLY MOTHS FLYING INTO THE CANDLE. YOU HAD BETTER
HART II	(125)	GOOD ARE YOU? YOU ARE AS MUCH TROUBLE IN THE	HOUSE	AS A CHILD OF THREE. YOU COULDNT LIVE WITHOUT YOUR
GETT PREFACE	(232)	PARTY MAY ACCEPT THE SITUATION AND REMAIN IN THE	HOUSE	AS A FRIEND TO SAVE APPEARANCES, OR FOR THE SAKE OF
2TRU II	(78)	/THE PATIENT/ ONE HAS SO MUCH MORE CONTROL OF THE	HOUSE	AS A SERVANT THAN AS A MISTRESS NOWADAYS, COLONEL.
GETT PREFACE	(227)	AND AS FRANKLY, KINDLY, AND EASILY IN A STRANGE	HOUSE	AS AT HOME. IN THE MIDDLE CLASSES, WHERE THE
ARMS II	SD(43)	STEPS, PETKOFF FOLLOWING), RAINA COMES FROM THE	HOUSE	AS BLUNTSCHLI PUTS HIS FOOT ON THE FIRST STEP. /RAINA/
BULL PREFACE	(59)	IT. ON THE SCAFFOLD, DARWEESH TURNED TO HIS	HOUSE	AS HE STOOD ON THE TRAP, AND EXCLAIMED " MAY GOD
HART III	(140)	LIKE A FOOL, THOUGH I'M AS GOOD A MAN IN THIS	HOUSE	AS IN THE CITY. /ELLIE/ (MUSICALLY) YES: THIS SILLY
DEVL II	SD(28)	IN SHORT, THAT LIFE IS AS EASY AT THE MINISTER'S	HOUSE	AS IT IS HARD AT THE FARM. THIS IS TRUE; BUT TO
CAPT I	(235)	PAIN) KEPN BRARSBAHND. (HE GETS AS FAR FROM THE	HOUSE	AS POSSIBLE, ON RANKIN'S LEFT. RANKIN RISES TO RECEIVE
ROCK I	(231)	THE CABINET. FINALLY THE LEADERSHIP OF THE	HOUSE	AS PRIME MINISTER. INTELLECT, INTELLECT, ALL THE TIME.
DEVL I	SD(21)	PRESENTLY WITH A JUG AND GOING OUT OF THE	HOUSE	AS QUIETLY AS POSSIBLE. /HAWKINS/ THE WILL IS NOT
GETT	(304)	LIKE A MUSHROOM. I WAS AS GLAD TO HAVE HIM IN THE	HOUSE	AS SHE WAS: HE AMUSED ME. AND WE WERE A COUPLE OF
MIS.	(197)	SELFISH, DIRTY-MINDED. YOU CAN CLEAR OUT OF MY	HOUSE	AS SOON AS YOU CAN COAX HIM TO TAKE YOU; AND THE
GETT	(330)	BACHELOR; AND I FELT QUITE HAPPY AT THEIR	HOUSE	AS THEIR FRIEND. LEO WAS AN AMUSING LITTLE DEVIL; BUT
HART I	(81)	ON 500 POUNDS. /MRS HUSHABYE/ NOT KEEPING OPEN	HOUSE	AS WE DO HERE, DADDIEST. /CAPTAIN SHOTOVER/ ONLY 500
ARMS II	(41)	AM VERY GLAD TO SEE YOU; BUT YOU MUST LEAVE THIS	HOUSE	AT ONCE. (HE RAISES HIS EYEBROWS). MY HUSBAND HAS
HART I	(55)	I WAS. /ELLIE/ (WITH DIGNITY) I WILL LEAVE YOUR	HOUSE	AT ONCE. (SHE TURNS TO THE DOOR). /MRS HUSHABYE/ IF
WIDO II	(28)	FELLOW FOR HIS AGE YOU EVER MET. HE OFFERS US HIS	HOUSE	AT ST ANDREWS FOR A COUPLE OF MONTHS, IF WE CARE TO
DEVL I	(22)	GO ON, SIR. /HAWKINS/ " I GIVE AND BEQUEATH MY	HOUSE	AT WEBSTERBRIDGE WITH THE LAND BELONGING TO IT AND ALL
KING I	(172)	PRIESTS, NOT ALLOWED TO MARRY. /NEWTON/ IS MY	HOUSE	BEAUTIFULLY KEPT? I HAVE NEVER NOTICED IT. THIS IS
PYGM EPILOG	(291)	BEST ART OF HER TIME TO ENABLE HER TO MAKE HER	HOUSE	BEAUTIFUL, SHE SETS A STANDARD FOR HIM AGAINST WHICH
WIDO II	(28)	OCCASIONALLY WHEN SHE WISHES TO READ. I CHOSE THE	HOUSE	BECAUSE IT IS ON GRAVEL. THE DEATH-RATE IS VERY LOW.
SIM II	(65)	UM. CARRY ON, DARLING. /IDDY/ PROLA CAN RULE THIS	HOUSE	BECAUSE SHE KNOWS WHAT IS HAPPENING IN IT. BUT HOW IS
GENV II	(63)	I GET INTO THE HOUSE; AND I SHALL GET INTO THE	HOUSE	BECAUSE THERE ARE LOTS OF PEOPLE IN CAMBERWELL WHO

CAND I (102)	IDEAS AGAINST THEM. YOU ARE DRIVING ME OUT OF THE	HOUSE	BECAUSE YOU DARENT LET HER CHOOSE BETWEEN YOUR IDEAS
JITT III (78)	MY PROMISE TO YOU, AND WALK STRAIGHT OUT OF YOUR	HOUSE	BEFORE ALL THE WORLD. /LENKHEIM/ THAT WILL ONLY MAKE
GETT (324)	LIFE, THEN? /MRS GEORGE/ NOT ALL. WE REACHED THE	HOUSE	BEFORE HE BROUGHT IT UP TO THE PRESENT DAY. BUT ENOUGH
MIS. (112)	A GIRL SHOULD KNOW WHAT A MAN IS LIKE IN THE	HOUSE	BEFORE SHE MARRIES HIM. THATS BEEN GOING ON FOR TWO
KING I (175)	WAS YOU WOULD BE ONLY TOO MUCH AT HOME IN IT. THE	HOUSE	BEING WHAT IT IS YOU ARE OUT OF PLACE IN IT. YOU GO OR
WIDO III (56)	DOCTOR. YOU NEVER BIN HERE BEFORE; BUT I KNOW THE	HOUSE	BETTER THAN MY OWN. /BLANCHE/ HERE THEY ARE. DONT SAY
GETT SD(259)	TO SHEW HOW MUCH MATERIAL THEY COULD LAVISH ON A	HOUSE	BUILT FOR THE GLORY OF GOD, INSTEAD OF KEEPING A
GETT SD(259)	AND RESPECTABLE IN A NORMAN FORTRESS. IT IS A	HOUSE	BUILT TO LAST FOR EVER. THE WALLS AND BEAMS ARE BIG
UNPL PREFACE(R12)	BLOW WAS STRUCK BY THE PRODUCTION OF A DOLL'S	HOUSE	BY CHARLES CHARRINGTON AND JANET ACHURCH. WHILST THEY
SUPR PREFACE(R9)	IN THE CRITICISM OF THE THEATRE AND THE OPERA	HOUSE	BY MAKING IT THE PRETEXT FOR A PROPAGANDA OF OUR OWN
MILL I (149)	WHERE COULD I GO TO WHEN YOU DROVE ME OUT OF THE	HOUSE	BY YOUR TANTRUMS? /EPIFANIA/ (MOST UNEXPECTEDLY
LION PROLOG (107)	ADDICTED TO ANIMALS. HOW IS ANY WOMAN TO KEEP HER	HOUSE	CLEAN WHEN YOU BRING IN EVERY STRAY CAT AND LOST CUR
DEVL II SD(28)	AND STORAGE, NOT FOR ORNAMENT; AND THE MINISTER'S	HOUSE	COAT HANGS ON A PEG FROM ITS DOOR, SHEWING THAT HE IS
DOCT PREFACE(15)	TURNS THE KITCHEN INTO A LABORATORY AND ENGINE	HOUSE	COMBINED, MANAGE, WHEN THEY ARE SENT OUT INTO THE
SUPR PREFACE(R39)	MERRY FROM TIME TO TIME, YOU WILL FIND THAT YOUR	HOUSE	CONTAINS A GREAT QUANTITY OF HIGHLY SUSCEPTIBLE COPPER
CAPT NOTES (301)	AND DEYS WHO PUT HIM, TOO, IN PRISON. THE SHOCKED	HOUSE	DEMANDED THAT HE SHOULD WITHDRAW HIS CRUEL WORD. " I
GLIM (183)	EATS AND IS USELESS, AND MAKES AN HONEST MAN'S	HOUSE	DIRTY. (HE RISES). COME, SANDRO, AND HELP ME TO CLEAN
SUPR HANDBOK(177)	APPLE TO THE PIPPIN, FROM THE WOLF AND FOX TO THE	HOUSE	DOG, FROM THE CHARGER OF HENRY V TO THE BREWER'S
DEVL I (13)	NICE MANNERS, THAT! (SOMEONE KNOCKS AT THE	HOUSE	DOOR: SHE TURNS AND CRIES INHOSPITABLY) COME IN. (
MTH3 (118)	IN A BLACK DRESS AND WHITE APRON, WHO OPENED THE	HOUSE	DOOR WHEN PEOPLE KNOCKED OR RANG, AND WAS EITHER YOUR
BULL III (139)	I UNDERSTAND, SIR. /CORNELIUS/ (APPEARING AT THE	HOUSE	DOOR WITH MATT) PATSY'LL DRIVE THE PIG OVER THIS
ARMS II (25)	/NICOLA/ IT'S COMING, SIR. (HE GOES TO THE	HOUSE	DOOR, LOUKA, WITH FRESH COFFEE, A CLEAN CUP, AND A
ARMS II (27)	THAN BEFORE) NICOLA! /NICOLA/ (APPEARING AT THE	HOUSE	DOOR) YES, SIR. /PETKOFF/ ARE YOU DEAF? DONT YOU HEAR
CAPT I (233)	(HE CLAPS HIS HANDS. AN ARAB BOY APPEARS AT THE	HOUSE	DOOR). MULEY: IS SAILOR MAN HERE? (MULEY NODS). TELL
DEVL I (15)	HAVE COME. /CHRISTY/ GOOD MORNING. (HE OPENS THE	HOUSE	DOOR). THE MORNING IS NOW FAIRLY BRIGHT AND WARM; AND
ARMS I SD(9)	THE PURSUERS IN THE STREET BATTER AT THE	HOUSE	DOOR, SHOUTING OPEN THE DOOR! OPEN THE DOOR! WAKE
DEVL I (16)	IN A MOMENT. ARE WE ALL HERE? /CHRISTY/ (AT THE	HOUSE	DOOR, WHICH HE HAS JUST SHUT) ALL EXCEPT DICK. THE
MILL II (172)	NOT YOURS. /THE DOCTOR/ YOU WOULD SCREAM THE	HOUSE	DOWN IF YOUR WRIST WERE SPRAINED. YOU ARE SHAMMING--
MIS. (174)	YOU HEAR WHAT MRS TARLETON SAYS. WELL, IN THIS	HOUSE	EVERYBODY DOES WHAT SHE SAYS OR OUT THEY GO. /GUNNER/
KING I (205)	THEM DO IT WHEN THEY WILL NOT ENTER A MEETING	HOUSE	FOR A PENNY IN THE PLATE TO HEAR THE WORDS OF GOD
GETT (263)	OLD BORE, ALICE; BUT WHEN I COME TO THIS	HOUSE	FOR A WEDDING-- TO THESE SCENES-- TO-- TO--
MRS II (215)	PROFIT! " LIZ WAS SAVING MONEY THEN TO TAKE A	HOUSE	FOR HERSELF IN BRUSSELS; AND SHE THOUGHT WE TWO COULD
SUPR IV (147)	CANNOT ANY WELL BRED WOMAN KEEP SUCH A	HOUSE	FOR HIM? /MALONE/ NO: SHE MUST BE BORN TO IT.
JITT III (59)	I DONT SAY I WASNT. BUT SHE HADNT TO KEEP THE	HOUSE	FOR HIM. SHE HAD NOTHING TO DO BUT PLEASE HIM, AND IF
BULL II (106)	THERE; AN TAKE FATHER DEMPSEY'S HAMPER TO HIS	HOUSE	FOR HIM; N THEN COME BACK FOR THE REST. /FATHER
BARB II (305)	ARE YOU GOING TO MAKE OUR SHELTER ANOTHER TIED	HOUSE	FOR HIM, AND ASK ME TO KEEP IT? /BILL/ ROTTEN DRANKEN
BULL IV (171)	BACK HERE AN LIVE ON IT. AN IF I HAVE TO KEEP HIS	HOUSE	FOR HIM, AT ALL EVENTS I CAN KEEP YOU OUT OF IT; FOR
JITT III (60)	OH, I KNOW VERY WELL HOW TIDY YOU KEPT HIS	HOUSE	FOR HIM, JUST AS I KEEP MY ROOM. YOU DID YOUR DUTY:
DEVL I (11)	HERE. DOES HE EXPECT US TO LEAVE HIS FATHER'S	HOUSE	FOR HIS CONVENIENCE? LET THEM ALL COME, AND COME
HART II (111)	DIAMONDS? /GUINNESS/ WHAT DID YOU BREAK INTO THE	HOUSE	FOR IF YOURE NO BURGLAR? /RANDALL/ MISTOOK THE HOUSE
HART I (82)	SHOTOVER/ (WEIRDLY CHANTING) I BUILDED A	HOUSE	FOR MY DAUGHTERS, AND OPENED THE DOORS THEREOF, THAT
SHAK (142)	(RAISING HIS HAND AND INTONING) I BUILDED A	HOUSE	FOR MY DAUGHTERS AND OPENED THE DOORS THEREOF THAT MEN
GETT (315)	THE MAN MUST BE CLEARED COMPLETELY OUT OF THE	HOUSE	FOR TWO YEARS ON EACH OCCASION. AT SUCH TIMES HE IS
HART I (54)	OF HER TO COME AND ATTRACT YOUNG PEOPLE TO THE	HOUSE	FOR US. /MAZZINI/ (SMILING) I'M AFRAID ELLIE IS NOT
BUOY III (39)	OF US TWO IS THE REASONABLE ONE? WHO KEEPS THE	HOUSE	FOR YOU? WHO LOOKS AFTER YOUR CLOTHES? WHO SEES THAT
HART II (111)	FOR IF YOURE NO BURGLAR? /RANDALL/ MISTOOK THE	HOUSE	FOR YOUR OWN AND CAME IN BY THE WRONG WINDOW, EH?
BULL PREFACE(41)	THE IRISH COAST BY THE ENGLISH GUNS OF THE PIGEON	HOUSE	FORT, ONLY A QUAINT LITTLE OFFSHOOT OF ENGLISH
GETT PREFACE(188)	NAMELY, ONE WHO WOULD STEAL HER HUSBAND'S	HOUSE	FROM OVER HER HEAD, AND LEAVE HER DESTITUTE AND
HART PREFACE(41)	THAT IS WHY I HAD TO WITHHOLD HEARTBREAK	HOUSE	FROM THE FOOTLIGHTS DURING THE WAR; FOR THE GERMANS
GENV I (30)	ROOM ON THE THIRD FLOOR OF A TUMBLEDOWN OLD	HOUSE	FULL OF RATS. AND AS TO MY SALARY I SHOULD BE ASHAMED
BARB II (302)	WITH APPROVAL OF THEIR METHOD) AND THE MANSION	HOUSE	FUND WENT UP NEXT DAY FROM THIRTY THOUSAND POUNDS TO
FANY EPILOG (331)	TO EXAMINE THEM, JUST TO SET ALL THE FOOLS IN THE	HOUSE	GIGGLING. THEN WHAT DOES IT ALL COME TO? AN ATTEMPT
HART PREFACE(17)	THAT VERY NEARLY CAME TRUE; FOR WHEN NEARLY EVERY	HOUSE	HAD A SLAUGHTERED SON TO MOURN, WE SHOULD ALL HAVE
JITT III (71)	HALF SITTING AGAINST ITS EDGE) YES: I KNOW. THIS	HOUSE	HAS BEEN A SORT OF MADHOUSE SINCE MY FATHER DIED. WE
POSN PREFACE(405)	LASTS ONLY A YEAR, AND NEED NOT BE RENEWED IF HIS	HOUSE	HAS BEEN CONDUCTED IN A DISORDERLY MANNER IN THE
HART PREFACE(30)	HAS THROWN ME BACK ON THIS EXPEDIENT. HEARTBREAK	HOUSE	HAS NOT YET REACHED THE STAGE. I HAVE WITHHELD IT
HART II (124)	/HECTOR/ (RISING) SOMETHING IN THE AIR OF THE	HOUSE	HAS UPSET YOU. IT OFTEN DOES HAVE THAT EFFECT. (HE
SUPR III (105)	THE PEASANTS OF TEN THOUSAND YEARS AGO; AND THE	HOUSE	HE LIVES IN HAS NOT ALTERED AS MUCH IN A THOUSAND
JITT II (46)	YEARS. /LENKHEIM/ LOVE! LOVE IN THE SORT OF	HOUSE	HE WAS FOUND DEAD IN! /JITTA/ LOVE WHEREVER WE WERE.
SUPR III SD(72)	COMPELLING THE GUARDIANS TO FEED, CLOTHE, AND	HOUSE	HIM BETTER THAN HE COULD FEED, CLOTHE, AND HOUSE
SUPR III SD(72)	HOUSE HIM BETTER THAN HE COULD FEED, CLOTHE, AND	HOUSE	HIMSELF WITHOUT GREAT EXERTION. WHEN A MAN WHO IS BORN
HART II (118)	CAN HYPNOTIZE YOU. YOU ARE THE ONLY PERSON IN THE	HOUSE	I CAN SAY WHAT I LIKE TO. I KNOW YOU ARE FOND OF ME.
HART III (140)	YOU GO AGAIN. EVER SINCE I CAME INTO THIS SILLY	HOUSE	I HAVE BEEN MADE TO LOOK LIKE A FOOL, THOUGH I'M AS
HART II (110)	CAPTAIN SHOTOVER, EVER SINCE I CAME INTO THIS	HOUSE	I HAVE DONE HARDLY ANYTHING ELSE BUT ASSURE YOU THAT I
FANY III (325)	WANT NO MORE OF IT. WOULD YOU INVITE THEM TO YOUR	HOUSE	IF HE MARRIED HER? /MRS KNOX/ HE OUGHT TO MARRY HER
ROCK II (271)	/BASHAM/ I WONDER SHOULD I FIND ANY BOMBS IN YOUR	HOUSE	IF I SEARCHED IT. /HIPNEY/ YOU WOULD IF YOU PUT THEM
ROCK I (200)	/HILDA/ OH, WHAT IS THE USE OF LEADING THE	HOUSE	IF IT NEVER GOES ANYWHERE? IT JUST BREAKS MY HEART TO
PHIL I (75)	YOU REALLY CANNOT STAY IN MRS TRANFIELD'S	HOUSE	IF SHE OBJECTS. SHE CAN RING THE BELL AND HAVE US BOTH
ROCK II (270)	RESPONSIBLE TO NOBODY, TO TURN YOU OUT OF YOUR	HOUSE	IF YOU DONT PAY HIM FOR THE RIGHT TO EXIST ON THE
KING I (222)	MUCH? WE SHALL NEVER GET THESE PEOPLE OUT OF THE	HOUSE	IF-- (THEY PASS OUT OF HEARING). THERE IS PEACE IN
GETT PREFACE(197)	AS AN OXFORD COLLEGE SURPASSES AN EIGHT-ROOMED	HOUSE	IN A CHEAP STREET. TEN CHILDREN, WITH THE NECESSARY
SIM II SD(59)	SILENCE HIM, O YE STARS. IDDY COMES FROM THE	HOUSE	IN A CONDITION OF LAZY SELF-COMPLACENCE. HE IS
ARMS II (42)	HER THE CARD, PETKOFF, HATLESS, RUSHES FROM THE	HOUSE	IN A FLUSTER OF HOSPITALITY, FOLLOWED BY SERGIUS).
BARB III (339)	BUT BY THIRTYEIGHT SHILLINGS A WEEK, A SOUND	HOUSE	IN A HANDSOME STREET, AND A PERMANENT JOB. IN THREE
O'FL SD(205)	AT THE DOOR OF AN IRISH COUNTRY	HOUSE	IN A PARK. FINE SUMMER WEATHER: THE SUMMER OF 1915.
WIDO III SD(49)	ACT III. THE DRAWING-ROOM IN SARTORIUS'S	HOUSE	IN BEDFORD SQUARE, LONDON. WINTER EVENING: FIRE
LION PREFACE(20)	NAMED JOSEPH, WHO WAS RICH ENOUGH TO LIVE IN A	HOUSE	IN BETHLEHEM TO WHICH KINGS COULD BRING GIFTS OF GOLD
MRS II (215)	AS HER PARTNER. WHY SHOULDNT I HAVE DONE IT? THE	HOUSE	IN BRUSSELS WAS REAL HIGH CLASS: A MUCH BETTER PLACE
FANY I SD(273)	THE PLAY. IN THE DINING ROOM OF A	HOUSE	IN DENMARK HILL, AN ELDERLY LADY SITS AT BREAKFAST
SUPR IV (172)	FISH SLICES, THE COPIES OF PATMORE'S ANGEL IN THE	HOUSE	IN EXTRA MOROCCO, AND THE OTHER ARTICLES YOU ARE
APPL PREFACE(195)	IMMEDIATE NECESSITY FOR A NEW CENTRAL CLEARING	HOUSE	IN FARRINGDON MARKET, CONNECTED WITH THE EXISTING
HART II (94)	ELLIE MAKE HIM JUMP, THOUGH, WHEN SHE TAKES HIS	HOUSE	IN HAND! /MRS HUSHABYE/ THEN THE CREATURE IS A FRAUD
MRS III (223)	OF THE CLERGYMAN, WHO COMES OUT OF THE	HOUSE	IN HASTE AND DISMAY). /REV. S./ FRANK: MRS WARREN AND
SUPR I (11)	EXPECT THE PEOPLE WHO WERE GLAD TO COME TO THE	HOUSE	IN HER FATHER'S TIME TO TROUBLE MUCH ABOUT HER NOW.
DOCT PREFACE(68)	SHOULD NONE THE LESS WELCOME HIM AND SET ITS	HOUSE	IN ORDER FOR THE SOCIAL CHANGE WHICH WILL FINALLY BE
BULL I (77)	WERE BREITSTEIN, AND I HAD A HOOKED NOSE AND A	HOUSE	IN PARK LANE, I SHOULD CARRY A UNION JACK HANDKERCHIEF
FABL II (107)	DEAD BEFORE THEY STINK US OUT. WE MUST MAKE EVERY	HOUSE	IN THE COUNTRY GAS-PROOF, AND RIGIDLY ENFORCE THE
SUPR PREFACE(R37)	VERY DEVOUT METHODIST, MOVED FROM COLCHESTER TO A	HOUSE	IN THE NEIGHBORHOOD OF THE CITY ROAD, IN LONDON,
BARB III (350)	WHAT DO YOU WANT, BARBARA? /BARBARA/ I WANT A	HOUSE	IN THE VILLAGE TO LIVE IN WITH DOLLY. (DRAGGING AT
SUPR HANDBOK(208)	NATURAL AND ARTIFICIAL SANITATION (THE OLDEST	HOUSE	IN THE WORLD, UNEARTHED THE OTHER DAY IN CRETE, HAS
BARB III (340)	SYSTEM. BUT HUDDLE THEM TOGETHER IN A CERTAIN	HOUSE	IN WESTMINSTER; AND LET THEM GO THROUGH CERTAIN
CAND I (96)	OF A POET TO KNOW THE STATE A WOMAN FINDS HER	HOUSE	IN WHEN SHE'S BEEN AWAY FOR THREE WEEKS. GIVE ME MY
HART PREFACE(3)	NOT WASTE ANY SYMPATHY ON IT: IT WAS TO HIM THE	HOUSE	IN WHICH EUROPE WAS STIFLING ITS SOUL; AND HE KNEW
2TRU III (111)	OUT OF MY HANDS. THE WAR HAS BEEN A FIERY FORCING	HOUSE	IN WHICH WE HAVE GROWN WITH A RUSH LIKE FLOWERS IN A
BARB I SD(249)	IN THE LIBRARY IN LADY BRITOMART UNDERSHAFT'S	HOUSE	IN WILTON CRESCENT. A LARGE AND COMFORTABLE SETTEE IS
BARB I SD(249)	THE UNIVERSE EXACTLY AS IF IT WERE A LARGE	HOUSE	IN WILTON CRESCENT, THOUGH HANDLING HER CORNER OF IT
SIM II (76)	IRRESPONSIBLE PERSONS, DECLARED THAT THE MANSION	HOUSE	INCIDENT WAS QUITE INCOMPREHENSIBLE TO HIM, AS HE
GENV III (69)	YOU ARE MAKING SPEECHES OUTSIDE YOUR PARLIAMENT	HOUSE	INSTEAD OF INSIDE IT. BUT TO ME THE PERSECUTION IS A
JOAN PREFACE(26)	COMBINE BAYARD WITH ESTHER SUMMERSON FROM BLEAK	HOUSE	INTO AN UNIMPEACHABLE AMERICAN SCHOOL TEACHER IN
2TRU PREFACE(21)	WALKS OVER IT; FOR HE MAY NOT KICK ME OUT OF MY	HOUSE	INTO THE STREET WITH HIS BOOTS; BUT HE MAY DO SO WITH
O'FL (225)	DIRTY DRISCOLL; AND IF I SEE YOU NEXT OR NIGH MY	HOUSE	I'LL PUT YOU IN THE DITCH WITH A FLEA IN YOUR EAR:
PYGM V (272)	UNLESS THEY LOOKS AFTER ME TWICE A DAY. IN THE	HOUSE	I'M NOT LET DO A HAND'S TURN FOR MYSELF: SOMEBODY ELSE
MILL IV (191)	FOR MY PARENTS, WITH NO PROSPECTS. NOW THE	HOUSE	IS A CREDIT TO THE NEIGHBORHOOD AND GIVES MORE
HART I SD(44)	AN OBSERVATORY. BETWEEN THE OBSERVATORY AND THE	HOUSE	IS A FLAGSTAFF ON A LITTLE ESPLANADE, WITH A HAMMOCK
OVER (182)	AND I'M SO TIRED OF THE SUBJECT! OUR	HOUSE	IS ALWAYS FULL OF WOMEN WHO ARE IN LOVE WITH MY
DEVL I (13)	DUDGEON/ (STIFFLY) THANK YOU, MRS ANDERSON, MY	HOUSE	IS ALWAYS READY FOR ANYONE TO COME INTO. /MRS
KING I (193)	DUTCH BILLY IS NOT AFRAID OF HIM. AND BILLY'S	HOUSE	IS BUILT, NOT ON A ROCK, NOT EVEN ON THE SANDS, BUT IN

CAND III	(144)	IN ONE. ASK PROSSY AND MARIA HOW TROUBLESOME THE	HOUSE	IS EVEN WHEN WE HAVE NO VISITORS TO HELP US TO SLICE
HART I	(45)	/NURSE GUINNESS/ YOULL GET USED TO IT, MISS: THIS	HOUSE	IS FULL OF SURPRISES FOR THEM THAT DONT KNOW OUR WAYS.
DEVL I	(26)	THAT OATH MADE A MAN OF ME. FROM THIS DAY THIS	HOUSE	IS HIS HOME; AND NO CHILD SHALL CRY IN IT: THIS HEARTH
MRS III	(222)	(CHANGING THE SUBJECT) WELL, I MUST SAY YOUR	HOUSE	IS IN A CHARMING SPOT HERE. REALLY MOST CHARMING.
MIS.	(112)	YOU THAT EXCEPT HYPATIA, NOT ONE PERSON IN THIS	HOUSE	IS IN FAVOR OF HER MARRYING YOU; AND I DONT BELIEVE
MIS.	SD(109)	DEAL OF MONEY OUT OF TARLETON'S UNDERWEAR. THE	HOUSE	IS IN SURREY, ON THE SLOPE OF HINDHEAD; AND JOHNNY,
DEVL II	SD(28)	ACT II. MINISTER ANDERSON'S	HOUSE	IS IN THE MAIN STREET OF WEBSTERBRIDGE, NOT FAR FROM
CAPT I	SD(217)	SEAT IN THE SHADE OF A TAMARISK TREE. THE	HOUSE	IS IN THE SOUTH WEST CORNER OF THE GARDEN, AND THE
KING I	(194)	WHO AM CALLED A KING, CANNOT GET RID OF HIM. THIS	HOUSE	IS ISAAC NEWTON'S; AND HE CAN ORDER YOU OUT AND THROW
KING I	(187)	THE PHILOSOPHER. I AM ALSO AN ENGLISHMAN; AND MY	HOUSE	IS MY CASTLE. AT LEAST IT WAS UNTIL THIS MORNING. WHEN
MIS.	(156)	/TARLETON/ WELL, IS SHE? A WOMAN I BRING INTO MY	HOUSE	IS MY GUEST. A WOMAN YOU BRING INTO MY HOUSE IS MY
MIS.	(156)	MY HOUSE IS MY GUEST. A WOMAN YOU BRING INTO MY	HOUSE	IS MY GUEST. BUT A WOMAN WHO DROPS BANG DOWN OUT OF
BULL IV	SD(145)	SIDEBOARD. A DOOR LEADING TO THE INTERIOR OF THE	HOUSE	IS NEAR THE FIREPLACE, BEHIND AUNT JUDY. THERE ARE
2TRU	PREFACE(10)	CRITICISM WHICH DISCOVERS THAT THE GREAT COUNTRY	HOUSE	IS NOT BUILT ON THE ETERNAL ROCK BUT ON THE SANDY
HART III	(142)	IT BY DOING THESE RIDICULOUS THINGS. /ELLIE/ YOUR	HOUSE	IS NOT HEARTBREAK HOUSE: IS IT, LADY UTTERWORD?
HART	PREFACE(3)	HALL. WHERE HEARTBREAK HOUSE STANDS. HEARTBREAK	HOUSE	IS NOT MERELY THE NAME OF THE PLAY WHICH FOLLOWS THIS
SIM I	SD(36)	BUT AT PRESENT SHIPLESS. THE WESTERN FACE OF THE	HOUSE	IS REACHED BY A TERRACE AND A FLIGHT OF STEPS. THE
ARMS II	SD(23)	THEM FROM WITHIN THE GARDEN, THE SIDE OF THE	HOUSE	IS SEEN ON THE LEFT, WITH A GARDEN DOOR REACHED BY A
KING I	(221)	COMES LAST. THE MISTRESS OF THIS AND EVERY OTHER	HOUSE	IS SHE WHO COOKS THE DINNER. (HE GOES OUT). /MRS
MIS.	(162)	IT, WHAT SORT OF GIRL ARE YOU? WHAT SORT OF	HOUSE	IS THIS? MUST I THROW ALL GOOD MANNERS TO THE WINDS?
KING I	(189)	HAVE THIS ROOM TO OURSELVES AWHILE? /NEWTON/ MY	HOUSE	IS YOURS, SIR. I AM A RESOLUTE SUPPORTER OF THE
HART III	(142)	/HECTOR/ YET SHE BREAKS HEARTS, EASY AS HER	HOUSE	IS. THAT POOR DEVIL UPSTAIRS WITH HIS FLUTE HOWLS WHEN
NEVR I	(202)	ONLY BEEN HERE SIX WEEKS AND HE'S A BACHELOR THE	HOUSE	ISNT HIS AND THE FURNITURE IS THE LANDLORD'S BUT THE
DOCT III	(134)	I'LL BE FRANK WITH YOU. WHATS THE MATTER IN THIS	HOUSE	ISNT LUNGS BUT BILLS. IT DOESNT MATTER ABOUT ME; BUT
HART II	(99)	/MRS HUSHABYE/ POOH! YOULL GET OVER IT. YOUR	HOUSE	ISNT RUINED. /ELLIE/ OF COURSE I SHALL GET OVER IT.
HART	PREFACE(9)	THE UNCULTURED WORLD OUTSIDE. BUT BEING AN IDLE	HOUSE	IT WAS A HYPOCHONDRIACAL HOUSE, ALWAYS RUNNING AFTER
MIS.	(174)	KNEW WHAT GOES ON IN THIS SO-CALLED RESPECTABLE	HOUSE	IT WOULD BE PUT A STOP TO. THESE ARE THE MORALS OF OUR
HART II	(110)	LORD, WHAT HAVE I DONE? DONT TELL ME IT'S YOUR	HOUSE	IVE BROKEN INTO, CAPTAIN SHOTOVER. THE CAPTAIN SEIZES
CAPT III	SD(272)	WALLS OF THE LARGEST ROOM IN LESLIE RANKIN'S	HOUSE	. A CLEAN COOL ROOM, WITH THE TABLE (A CHRISTIAN
KING I	(174)	YOU ARE AN UNINVITED GUEST. /BARBARA/ A PRETTY	HOUSE	. A PRETTY PHILOSOPHER. A HOUSE KEPT FOR YOU TO MEET
CAPT I	SD(235)	WITH DARK SOUTHERN EYES AND HAIR COMES FROM THE	HOUSE	. AGE ABOUT 36. HANDSOME FEATURES, BUT JOYLESS; DARK
KING I	(171)	TOLD SO. BUT I SHOULD NOT HAVE ASKED HER INTO MY	HOUSE	. AND AT LEAST SHE WAS NOT ON THE STAGE. (SHE RETIRES
HART I	(57)	WE ALL GOT NEW CLOTHES AND MOVED INTO ANOTHER	HOUSE	. AND I WENT TO ANOTHER SCHOOL FOR TWO YEARS. /MRS
SUPR I	(26)	AGAIN I'LL TAKE YOU AT YOUR WORD AND LEAVE YOUR	HOUSE	. ANN: WHERE IS VIOLET NOW? /ANN/ WHY? ARE YOU GOING
MTH1 II	(26)	BECAUSE I WOULD NOT HAVE SUCH WRETCHES IN MY	HOUSE	. BECAUSE I HATE CREATURES WITH TWO HEADS, OR WITH
ROCK I	(199)	/SIR ARTHUR/ NO. NO POLYGAMISTS AT THE CHURCH	HOUSE	. BESIDES, EVERYBODY KNOWS THAT THE FAMILY MEANS THE
HART I	SD(43)	TO THE OPEN SEA, BUT TO THE ENTRANCE HALL OF THE	HOUSE	. BETWEEN THIS DOOR AND THE STERN GALLERY ARE
GETT	(316)	OWN SEPARATE HOUSE, OR MY OWN SEPARATE PART OF A	HOUSE	. BOXER SMOKES: I CANT ENDURE TOBACCO. BOXER BELIEVES
MIS.	PREFACE(65)	WITHOUT EXHAUSTING THE INDULGENCE OF THE COUNTRY	HOUSE	. BUT LET HIM DARE TO BE " DISRESPECTFUL" AND HE IS A
POSN	PREFACE(398)	GHOSTS, IS FAR LESS SUBVERSIVE THAN A DOLL'S	HOUSE	. BUT THE LORD CHAMBERLAIN DOES NOT MEDDLE WITH SUCH
DOCT	PREFACE(3)	ALSO BE NECESSARY TO HANG A MAN OR PULL DOWN A	HOUSE	. BUT WE TAKE GOOD CARE NOT TO MAKE THE HANGMAN AND
ARMS II	(41)	(VEHEMENTLY) BE QUICK! (LOUKA RUNS INTO THE	HOUSE	. CATHERINE SNATCHES HER APRON OFF AND THROWS IT
FANY II	(287)	STOPPED. WE SHALL HAVE A CROWD ROUND THE	HOUSE	. DO DO SOMETHING TO STOP HIM. KNOX RETURNS WITH A
CAND I	(101)	IN HER HEART." /MORELL/ (WRATHFULLY) LEAVE MY	HOUSE	. DO YOU HEAR? (HE ADVANCES ON HIM THREATENINGLY).
BULL III	SD(125)	BARNEY DORAN, AND MATTHEW HAFFIGAN COME FROM THE	HOUSE	. DORAN IS A STOUT BODIED, SHORT ARMED, ROUNDHEADED,
BASH II,1,SD(99)		ACT II. SCENE 1. LONDON. A ROOM IN LYDIA'S	HOUSE	. ENTER LYDIA AND LUCIAN. /LYDIA/ WELCOME, DEAR
MIS.	PREFACE(27)	DISSENTS FROM HIS VIEWS TO BE BROUGHT INTO HIS	HOUSE	. EVEN AT HIS CLUB HE RESENTS SEEING IT, AND EXCLUDES
POSN	(452)	ARRIVED IN THE TOWN YESTERDAY AND PUT UP IN MY	HOUSE	. EVERYBODY KNOWS THAT IN THE MORNING THE HORSE WAS
MIS	(184)	MY DAUGHTER BEFORE YOUD BEEN HALF AN HOUR IN MY	HOUSE	. FIE, FOR SHAME! /PERCIVAL/ LORD SUMMERHAYS: I
MRS III	(224)	STAND IN THE MIDDLE OF THE GARDEN LOOKING AT THE	HOUSE	. FRANK, IN AN ECSTASY OF DISSIMULATION, TURNS GAILY
ARMS II	(40)	HE KNOWS WHO YOU ARE: HE SAID THE LADY OF THE	HOUSE	. HE GAVE ME THIS LITTLE TICKET FOR YOU. (SHE TAKES A
NEVR I	SD(218)	A COAT FOR A SHIPYARD RATHER THAN A COUNTING	HOUSE	. HE HAS TAKEN A FANCY TO VALENTINE, WHO CARES NOTHING
VWOO 1	(120)	ME. SHE WANTED ME TO BE A PARLORMAID IN A GREAT	HOUSE	. HE WANTED ME TO BE A TELEPHONE OPERATOR. HE SAID
BUOY III	(41)	MAN HAS COME. /SHE/ HERE! ! ! /NATIVE/ IN THIS	HOUSE	. HE WILL NOT BE DENIED. HE HAS DIVINE GUIDANCE. HE
SIM II	(82)	/PRA/ I KNOW. I AM PART OF THE FURNITURE OF YOUR	HOUSE	. I AM A MATTER OF COURSE. BUT WAS I ALWAYS THAT? WAS
MIS.	(201)	MY LIVING. I AM A FREE WOMAN: I LIVE IN MY OWN	HOUSE	. I AM A WOMAN OF THE WORLD: I HAVE THOUSANDS OF
HART II	(121)	/HECTOR/ YOU ARE IN WHAT IS SUPPOSED TO BE MY	HOUSE	. I AM AT YOUR DISPOSAL. HECTOR SITS DOWN IN THE
HART I	(51)	BEAUTY! NOVELTY! THEY ARE BADLY WANTED IN THIS	HOUSE	. I AM EXCESSIVELY OLD. HESIONE IS ONLY MODERATELY
KING I	(201)	ME THAT THE PLAYHOUSE IS AS DIVINE AS MY MEETING	HOUSE	. I FIND YOUR COMPANY AGREEABLE TO ME, BUT VERY
MIS.	(189)	AND ANNOYED BY MY SON'S BEHAVIOR IN YOUR	HOUSE	. I HAD BETTER TAKE HIM HOME. /TARLETON/ NOT AT ALL:
HART I	(49)	I HAVE ALWAYS BEEN THE MISTRESS OF GOVERNMENT	HOUSE	. I HAVE BEEN SO HAPPY: I HAD FORGOTTEN THAT PEOPLE
ARMS III	(73)	TWO LIVERY STABLES, A TEA GARDENS, AND A PRIVATE	HOUSE	. I HAVE FOUR MEDALS FOR DISTINGUISHED SERVICES; I
LIED	(199)	RORY AND I WILL BE PROUD TO HAVE YOU ABOUT THE	HOUSE	. I HAVE HEARD FAR THINNER STORIES FROM MUCH OLDER
2TRU	PREFACE(5)	IN FOR A DRINK. THE OLD SOLDIER AND THE PUBLIC	HOUSE	. I HAVE NEVER FORGOTTEN THAT SOLDIER, BECAUSE HIS
HART I	(70)	SAID SHE'D MARRY ANYBODY TO GET AWAY FROM THIS	HOUSE	. I SHOULD NOT HAVE RECOGNIZED YOU: YOUR HEAD IS NO
DOCT I	(93)	YOUR CHEQUE AND ROLLED UP YOUR BAG AND LEFT THE	HOUSE	. I TELL YOU, COLLY, CHLOROFORM HAS DONE A LOT OF
MTH2	(54)	THE PLEASURE OF MEETING YOU ONCE AT THE MANSION	HOUSE	. I THINK IT WAS TO CELEBRATE THE CONCLUSION OF THE
HART III	(131)	THE FLUTE; BUT I NEVER LET HIM BRING IT INTO MY	HOUSE	. IF HE WOULD ONLY-- (SHE IS INTERRUPTED BY THE
ROCK I	(197)	A RARE LOT OF GASBAGS UNDER YOUR THUMB IN THE	HOUSE	. IF YOU COULD SEND HALF A DOZEN OF THEM DOWN TO THE
CAND I	(103)	A SNIVELLING LITTLE WHELP AND PUT ME OUT OF THE	HOUSE	. IF YOU DONT TELL HER, I WILL: I'LL WRITE IT TO HER.
BULL IV	SD(145)	ACT IV. THE PARLOR IN CORNELIUS DOYLE'S	HOUSE	. IT COMMUNICATES WITH THE GARDEN BY A HALF GLAZED
ARMS II	SD(23)	OF MARCH, 1886. IN THE GARDEN OF MAJOR PETKOFF'S	HOUSE	. IT IS A FINE SPRING MORNING: THE GARDEN LOOKS FRESH
DOCT	PREFACE(15)	BETTER FOOD, AND A BETTER DRAINED AND VENTILATED	HOUSE	. IT IS KINDER TO GIVE HIM A BOTTLE OF SOMETHING
HART I	(57)	HE HAD NEVER EVEN SEEN ME! HE NEVER CAME TO OUR	HOUSE	. IT WAS ABSOLUTELY DISINTERESTED. PURE GENEROSITY.
JITT III	(57)	WOMAN TO MEET HIM IN SUCH A ROOM IN SUCH A	HOUSE	. IT WAS FIT NEITHER FOR HIM NOR FOR HER. /LENKHEIM/ (
WIDO II	(28)	AUNT MARIA WANTS BLANCHE TO BE MARRIED FROM HER	HOUSE	. (HE HANDS SARTORIUS A LETTER). /SARTORIUS/ AUNT
DEVL II	(48)	MONEY, MONEY: I WANT MONEY-- ALL THE MONEY IN THE	HOUSE	. (HE STOOPS OVER THE OTHER BOOT, GRUMBLING) A GREAT
MIS.	(164)	OURSELVES, YOULL PLEASE ALLOW ME TO LEAVE THE	HOUSE	. (HE TURNS TOWARDS THE INNER DOOR, HAVING LEFT HIS
BULL III	(138)	OF THEIR IRISH ODDITY. (HODSON COMES FROM THE	HOUSE	. LARRY SITS IN DORAN'S CHAIR AND READS). OH, BY THE
ARMS II	SD(25)	/LOUKA/ YES: SHE'S COMING. NICOLA GOES INTO THE	HOUSE	. LOUKA BRINGS THE COFFEE TO THE TABLE. /PETKOFF/
BULL III	(139)	EVENIN, MATT. GOODBYE. (HE GOES BACK INTO THE	HOUSE	. MATT MAKES FOR THE GATE. BROADBENT STOPS HIM.
HART I	(54)	NOT TO KNOW ME ON PURPOSE. I WILL LEAVE THE	HOUSE	. MAZZINI DUNN ENTERS FROM THE HALL. HE IS A LITTLE
CAPT	NOTES (302)	THE TYPE IN HIS MAN FROM SHROPSHIRE IN BLEAK	HOUSE	. MOST PUBLIC MEN AND ALL LAWYERS HAVE BEEN APPEALED
BUOY III	(45)	TWICE TO MY WEDDINGS LIKE A LAMB TO THE SLAUGHTER	HOUSE	. MY TWO WIVES WERE TRIUMPHANT. I BOUGHT NEW CLOTHES,
APPL II	(260)	THE PRODIGAL, SIR, HAS RETURNED TO HIS FATHER'S	HOUSE	. NOT POOR, NOT HUNGRY, NOT RAGGED, AS OF OLD. OH NO.
GETT	(279)	TO STAY, YOU WERE ALL SHOVING ME OUT OF THE	HOUSE	. NOW THAT I WANT TO GO, YOU WONT LET ME. /MRS
PHIL I	(84)	THERES NO NEXT FLOOR. WE'RE AT THE TOP OF THE	HOUSE	. NO, NO: YOU MUST INVENT SOME THUMPING LIE. I CANT
BASH II,1,	(99)	/LYDIA/ WELCOME, DEAR COUSIN, TO MY LONDON	HOUSE	. OF LATE YOU HAVE BEEN CHARY OF YOUR VISITS. /LUCIAN/
HART II	(89)	AT HIS BURSTING TEMPLES) OH, THIS IS A CRAZY	HOUSE	. OR ELSE I'M GOING CLEAN OFF MY CHUMP. IS SHE MAKING
O'FL	(226)	WITH YOU, O'FLAHERTY: SHOVE THEM INTO THE	HOUSE	. OUT WITH THE WHOLE DAMNED PACK OF YOU. /O'FLAHERTY/
HART II	(84)	I WASN'T USED TO THE WAYS OF THIS EXTRAORDINARY	HOUSE	. PLEASE FORGIVE ME. /MANGAN/ OH, THATS ALL RIGHT: I
MILL	PREFACE(111)	SELFISH AND CRUEL AS THE TYRANT OF A PRIVATE	HOUSE	. QUEEN ELIZABETH WAS A MAITRESSE FEMME; BUT SHE COULD
FANY	EPILOG (331)	WHY, OLD GILBEY IS STRAIGHT OUT OF THE MADRAS	HOUSE	. /BANNAL/ POOR OLD BARKER! /VAUGHAN/ UTTER
POSN	(458)	FIND A DOCTOR? THERES A DOCTOR IN THE VERY NEXT	HOUSE	. /BLANCO/ (MOPPING HIS DABBLED RED CREST AND TRYING
HART I	(82)	TAKE JOLLY GOOD CARE THAT THERE IS FOOD IN THE	HOUSE	. /CAPTAIN SHOTOVER/ (RAISING A STRANGE WAIL IN THE
HART I	(68)	THIS IS QUEER. I OUGHT TO WALK OUT OF THIS	HOUSE	. /CAPTAIN SHOTOVER/ WHY? /MANGAN/ WELL, MANY MEN
HART III	(130)	TWENTYFOUR YEARS AGO. WHAT IS WRONG WITH THE	HOUSE	. /CAPTAIN SHOTOVER/ WHAT! THE NUMSKULL SAID THERE
ARMS II	SD(26)	UNDER ALL THE CIRCUMSTANCES. LOUKA GOES INTO THE	HOUSE	. /CATHERINE/ MY DEAR PAUL: WHAT A SURPRISE FOR US! (
CATH 3,	SD(184)	AND LETS HER GO, EXPECTING HER TO RUN INTO THE	HOUSE	. /CLAIRE/ (PAUSING THOUGHTFULLY) IS SHE -- IS SHE
FANY I	SD(276)	BY ANY PROCESS SHORT OF FLINGING HER OUT OF THE	HOUSE	. /DORA/ (PLUNGING AT ONCE INTO PRIVILEGED INTIMACY
HART I	(64)	NONE THE LESS DELIGHTED TO FIND YOU IN OUR LITTLE	HOUSE	. /ELLIE/ (IN GREAT DISTRESS) I DONT KNOW WHAT TO DO.
HART II	(97)	YOU LITTLE MINX. REMEMBER THAT YOU ARE IN MY	HOUSE	. /ELLIE/ STUFF! WHY DONT YOU MIND YOUR OWN
BULL II	(108)	OR THE LIKE. /BROADBENT/ PERHAPS THERES A PUBLIC	HOUSE	. /FATHER DEMPSEY/ (GRIMLY) THERES SEVENTEEN. /AUNT
KING I	(181)	/NEWTON/ GEORGE FOX: YOU ARE AN INFIDEL. LEAVE MY	HOUSE	. /FOX/ (RISING) YOUR PHILOSOPHY HAS LED YOU TO THE
MIS.	(178)	BE SETTLED IN MRS TARLETON'S PRESENCE OR IN HER	HOUSE	. /GUNNER/ (PAINFULLY FRIGHTENED) WHY SHOULD I GO OUT
SUPR II	(66)	ABOUT SOMETHING ELSE. VIOLET'S COMING FROM THE	HOUSE	. /HECTOR/ I SHOULD ESTEEM IT A VERY GREAT FAVOR,
SUPR II	SD(64)	AND THEY DISAPPEAR ROUND THE CORNER TOWARDS THE	HOUSE	. /HECTOR/ I THINK I MAY GO SO FAR AS TO SAY THAT I

HART II (108)	THE VERY BURGLARS CANT BEHAVE NATURALLY IN THIS	HOUSE	. /HECTOR/ MY GOOD SIR: YOU MUST WORK OUT YOUR
BUOY II (18)	/SHE/ WELL, PASS DOUBLE QUICK. THIS ISNT A DOSS	HOUSE	. /HE/ NO; BUT IN THIS LONELY PLACE THE ARRIVAL OF ANY
GETT (336)	TONGUE. THATS ENOUGH TO KEEP YOU OUT OF MY	HOUSE	. /HOTCHKISS/ IT MUST BE RATHER A HOUSE OF CARDS. A
JITT II (48)	SAKE I AM PREPARED TO ENDURE YOUR PRESENCE IN MY	HOUSE	. /JITTA/ (WITH FAINT SURPRISE AND SOME IRONY) YOU
GENV II (59)	RECTOR HAS NO SOCIETY EXCEPT WHAT HE GETS IN MY	HOUSE	. /JUDGE/ THE RECTOR IS A FREEHOLDER. IF YOU ARE A
BULL III SD(120)	WORDS ON THE COMPANY, GOES CURTLY INTO THE	HOUSE	. /LARRY/ (STARING AFTER HIM) IS ANYTHING WRONG WITH
BASH II,1, (99)	/LUCIAN/ THERE IS A MAN I LIKE NOT HAUNTS THIS	HOUSE	. /LYDIA/ THOU SPEAKST OF CASHEL BYRON? /LUCIAN/ AYE,
CAND III (135)	ANGRY. I HAVE A GOOD MIND TO PACK YOU OUT OF THE	HOUSE	. /MORELL/ (TAKEN ABACK BY CANDIDA'S VIGOR, AND BY NO
GETT (336)	WORD, SAID IN THE RIGHT WAY-- AND DOWN COMES YOUR	HOUSE	. /MRS GEORGE/ THATS WHY I'LL DIE SOONER THAN LET YOU
GETT (328)	SCREAM. RING THE BELL. HAVE ME TURNED OUT OF THE	HOUSE	. /MRS GEORGE/ (WITH SUDDEN DEPTH OF FEELING) OH, IF
HART II (99)	SO, HESIONE. I MUST MAKE THE BEST OF MY RUINED	HOUSE	. /MRS HUSHABYE/ POOH! YOULL GET OVER IT. YOUR HOUSE
HART III (140)	WITHOUT FOUNDATIONS. I SHALL CALL IT HEARTBREAK	HOUSE	. /MRS HUSHABYE/ STOP, ELLIE; OR I SHALL HOWL LIKE AN
HART III (149)	AND THE POOR CLERGYMAN WILL HAVE TO GET A NEW	HOUSE	. /MRS HUSHABYE/ BUT WHAT A GLORIOUS EXPERIENCE! I
ARMS III (48)	OLD COAT HERE: THE BRAIDED ONE HE WEARS IN THE	HOUSE	. /NICOLA/ YES, MADAME. (HE GOES OUT). /PETKOFF/
BUOY IV (54)	OTHER FAMILY HE WOULD HAVE BEEN KICKED OUT OF THE	HOUSE	. /OLD BILL/ I LIKE THE FELLOW. /SIR FERDINAND/ LIKE
MILL I (154)	(TO PATRICIA) SMOOTH IT FOR HIM, ANGEL IN THE	HOUSE	. /PATRICIA/ (MOVING TO EPIFANIA'S CHAIR AND DOING
MIS. (198)	AEROPLANE OUT OF MY VINERY AND YOURSELF OUT OF MY	HOUSE	. /PERCIVAL/ (RISING, TO HYPATIA) I'M AFRAID I SHALL
ARMS II SD(38)	MAKES WAY PROUDLY FOR HER, AND THEN GOES INTO THE	HOUSE	. /RAINA/ I'M READY. WHATS THE MATTER? (GAILY) HAVE
SUPR I (27)	MR RAMSDEN. SHE HAD NO RIGHT TO COME TO YOUR	HOUSE	. /RAMSDEN/ (INDIGNANTLY) BUT I AM ONLY TOO ANXIOUS
DEVL I (20)	TONGUE. I WILL BEAR NO MORE OF THIS. LEAVE MY	HOUSE	. /RICHARD/ HOW DO YOU KNOW IT'S YOUR HOUSE UNTIL THE
ROCK I (202)	THE ARCHBISHOP WANTS YOU TO SAY IT, AT THE CHURCH	HOUSE	. /SIR ARTHUR/ DECIDEDLY I AM GOING MAD. /HILDA/ NO:
ROCK I (201)	FAMILY. YOUR SPEECH THIS AFTERNOON AT THE CHURCH	HOUSE	. /SIR ARTHUR/ AH, OF COURSE. I AM GOING DOTTY. THIRTY
GETT (317)	I SHALL WORK WHEN I'M MARRIED. I SHALL KEEP YOUR	HOUSE	. /SYKES/ OH, THAT! /REGINALD/ YOU CALL THAT WORK?
SUPR I (29)	OLD CATS, SIR. MY SISTER IS THE MISTRESS OF THIS	HOUSE	. /TANNER/ SHE WOULD PUT ME IN THE HOUSEKEEPER'S ROOM,
MIS. (174)	TARLETON/ WELL, I WONT HAVE ANY SOCIALISM IN MY	HOUSE	. /TARLETON/ (TO GUNNER) YOU HEAR WHAT MRS TARLETON
O'FL SD(219)	TERESA DRISCOLL, A PARLOR MAID, COMES FROM THE	HOUSE	. /TERESA/ YOURE TO COME UP TO THE DRAWING ROOM TO
MILL III (182)	HER BETTER THAN IF SHE HAD BEEN IN HER FATHER'S	HOUSE	. /THE MAN/ I CAN FIND YOU A FAMILY WHAT'LL DO IT
ARMS I (20)	YOU WOULD HAVE BEEN AS SAFE AS IN YOUR FATHER'S	HOUSE	. /THE MAN/ QUITE SURE? /RAINA/ (TURNING HER BACK ON
BUOY II (23)	ONE WHO CAN PUT TERRIBLE STRONG MAGICS ON THIS	HOUSE	. /THE NATIVE/ SIR: MAGICS ARE SUPERSTITIONS. PINK
DOCT IV (168)	ARTICLE ON HOW IT FEELS TO BE TURNED OUT OF THE	HOUSE	. /THE NEWSPAPER MAN/ (UNCONVINCED) YOU THINK SHE'D
SIM II SD(54)	IS SITTING AT THE END OF IT WITH HIS BACK TO THE	HOUSE	. SEATED NEAR HIM IS PRA. BOTH ARE BUSY WRITING.
SUPR II SD(61)	BY THE ARRIVAL OF MRS WHITEFIELD FROM THE	HOUSE	. SHE IS ACCOMPANIED BY THE AMERICAN GENTLEMAN, AND
O'FL SD(226)	STILL VIOLENTLY ABUSING ONE ANOTHER, INTO THE	HOUSE	. SIR PEARCE SLAMS THE DOOR UPON THEM SAVAGELY.
ROCK I (199)	NOTES FOR MY SPEECH THIS AFTERNOON AT THE CHURCH	HOUSE	. THE ARCHBISHOP TELLS ME THAT THE ANGLO-CATHOLICS ARE
GETT SD(259)	THE KITCHEN IS ONE OF THE FINEST ROOMS IN THE	HOUSE	. THE BISHOP HAS NEITHER THE INCOME NOR THE APPETITE
DEVL I (27)	THERE IS NO DANGER. (HE TAKES HER OUT OF THE	HOUSE	. THE REST CROWD TO THE DOOR TO FOLLOW HIM, EXCEPT
PRES (164)	SERJEANT-AT-ARMS RATHER THAN OF THE LEADER OF THE	HOUSE	. THERES NO USE IN MY TACKLING MRS BANGER: SHE WOULD
BULL III SD(117)	OF A SMALL GRASS PLOT BEFORE CORNELIUS DOYLE'S	HOUSE	. THEY HAVE FINISHED THEIR MEAL, AND ARE BURIED IN
ARMS II (34)	ME, SERGIUS. (LOUKA IS HEARD SINGING WITHIN THE	HOUSE	. THEY QUICKLY RELEASE EACH OTHER). I CANT PRETEND TO
CAPT I (224)	DOLLAR, BIKOUROS. I HAVE BROUGHT THEM TO YOUR	HOUSE	. THEY WILL PAY YOU, GIVE ME SOMETHING FOR BRINGING
WIDO II (37)	YOURSELF: YOU CAN BE HEARD ALL OVER THE	HOUSE	. WHAT IS THE MATTER? /BLANCHE/ (TOO ANGRY TO CARE
PYGM V (284)	OF IT THAT HAS COME MY WAY AND BEEN BUILT INTO MY	HOUSE	. WHAT MORE CAN YOU OR ANYONE ASK? /LIZA/ I WONT CARE
DOCT PREFACE(52)	BECAUSE INSUFFICIENTLY FINANCED, PRIVATE	HOUSE	. WHAT THE PUBLIC WANTS, THEREFORE, IS A CHEAP MAGIC
ROCK I (213)	END, BEGINNING WITH EVERY PANE OF GLASS IN THIS	HOUSE	. WHAT WILL HE GAIN BY IT? NEXT DAY A SCORE OR SO OF
BULL III SD(119)	I'LL HAVE SOME TOMORROW. HODSON GOES TO THE	HOUSE	. WHEN HE OPENS THE DOOR HE FINDS NORA AND AUNT JUDY
FABL PREFACE(91)	HONORIS CAUSA, COULD NOT TOLERATE A PIANO IN HIS	HOUSE	. WHEN ONE WAS PLAYED IN HIS HEARING BY HIS NEIGHBORS,
SIM I (37)	SHEW YOU THE SHORTEST WAY OUT? IT IS THROUGH THE	HOUSE	. WHERE DO YOU WISH TO GO, BY THE WAY? /THE
PYGM II (235)	OF LONG ACRE AND ENDELL STREET. /HIGGINS/ PUBLIC	HOUSE	. YES? /DOOLITTLE/ THE POOR MAN'S CLUB, GOVERNOR: WHY
BARB I (256)	OF RIGHT AND WRONG, IF HE HAD BEEN IN THE	HOUSE	. YOU KNOW, MY DEAR, YOUR FATHER WAS A VERY ATTRACTIVE
SUPR I (7)	YOU WERE TREATED AS A SON IN MY FRIEND'S	HOUSE	. YOU LIVED THERE; AND YOUR FRIENDS COULD NOT BE
MIS. (200)	US, MISS SZCZ? /LINA/ OLD PAL: THIS IS A STUFFY	HOUSE	. YOU SEEM TO THINK OF NOTHING BUT MAKING LOVE. ALL
SIM II (57)	" I SHALL BE OBLIGED TO OPEN FIRE ON GOVERNMENT	HOUSE	." NUMBER TWO, FROM THE COMMANDER OF THE BOMBAY
SHAK (142)	WITHOUT FOUNDATIONS. I SHALL CALL IT HEARTBREAK	HOUSE	." /SHOTOVER/ ENOUGH, ENOUGH. LET THE HEART BREAK IN
FANY PROL,SD(257)	THE END OF A SALOON IN AN OLD-FASHIONED COUNTRY	HOUSE	(FLORENCE TOWERS, THE PROPERTY OF COUNT O'DOWDA) HAS
SUPR I (26)	I WILL NOT HAVE THESE ABOMINATIONS UTTERED IN MY	HOUSE	(HE SMITES THE WRITING TABLE WITH HIS FIST). /TANNER/
DOCT PREFACE(32)	ON THE NEAREST CAT FROM THE HIGHEST WINDOW IN THE	HOUSE	(I PROTEST I DID IT MYSELF FROM THE FIRST FLOOR
JITT II (47)	QUITE RIGHT. I HAVE NO RIGHT TO BE IN ANY DECENT	HOUSE	(SHE TURNS TO THE DOOR). /LENKHEIM/ STOP: WHERE ARE
KING I (174)	/BARBARA/ A PRETTY HOUSE. A PRETTY PHILOSOPHER. A	HOUSE	KEPT FOR YOU TO MEET YOUR WOMEN IN. /MRS BASHAM/ (
MILL I (151)	DOORMATS ARE VERY USEFUL THINGS IF YOU WANT THE	HOUSE	KEPT TIDY, DEAR. THE TELEPHONE RINGS. SAGAMORE ATTENDS
JITT I (11)	TAKE THE LIFT, SIR? IT ISNT AS IF ANYONE IN THIS	HOUSE	KNEW YOU, AND FOR THAT MATTER YOU MEET PEOPLE ON THE
PRES (138)	OF THE LABOR PARTY APPEALED TO ME AND TO THE	HOUSE	LAST YEAR NOT TO THROW AWAY ALL THE LIBERTIES OF
HART II (112)	/MAZZINI/ WILL IT BE SAFE TO HAVE HIM IN THE	HOUSE	LIKE THAT? /GUINNESS/ WHY DIDNT YOU SHOOT HIM, SIR..
GETT (261)	IT PAYS HIM AND YOU, LET ALONE THE PLEASURE IN A	HOUSE	LIKE THIS (MRS BRIDGENORTH BOWS IN ACKNOWLEDGMENT OF
FANY II (287)	IF THEY KNEW, JO, THERED BE A CROWD ROUND THE	HOUSE	LOOKING UP AT US. YOU SHOULDNT KEEP THINKING ABOUT IT.
CAND II (113)	/MORELL/ YES; BUT SHE ISNT A SLAVE; AND THE	HOUSE	LOOKS AS IF I KEPT THREE. THAT MEANS THAT EVERYONE HAS
ROCK I (221)	CANT DO ANY WORK BEFORE YOU START FOR THE CHURCH	HOUSE	LUNCH. THE WHOLE MORNING IS GONE WITH THOSE PEOPLE
KING I (214)	BUT COME! MR NEWTON HAS ASKED US TO LEAVE HIS	HOUSE	MANY TIMES, AND WE MUST NOT FORGET THAT HE NEVER ASKED
BARB PREFACE(232)	WITH THE RESULT THAT THEY COME OUT OF THE TORTURE	HOUSE	MORE DANGEROUS THAN THEY WENT IN, AND RENEW THEIR EVIL
PHIL II (99)	YOU MIGHT THINK, WHEN YOURE AT HOME, YOU HAVE THE	HOUSE	MORE TO YOURSELF; AND WHEN YOU WANT TO HAVE YOUR
KING I (220)	ARE YOUR MANNERS, WOMAN? /MRS BASHAM/ IN THIS	HOUSE	MR NEWTON COMES FIRST. COME ALONG QUICK, ALL OF YOU;
KING I (194)	YOU OUT OF THE WINDOW IF YOU DONT GO. BUT MY	HOUSE	MUST HARBOR THE VILEST SCOUNDREL IN EUROPE WHILE HE
CAND I (82)	IT WAS GERMAN MEASLES. I BROUGHT IT INTO THE	HOUSE	MYSELF FROM THE PYCROFT STREET SCHOOL. A PARSON IS
SUPR II SD(48)	ON THE CARRIAGE DRIVE IN THE PARK OF A COUNTRY	HOUSE	NEAR RICHMOND AN OPEN TOURING CAR HAS BROKEN DOWN. IT
HART III (131)	UTTERWORD/ NOT A BIT. I ASSURE YOU, ALL THIS	HOUSE	NEEDS TO MAKE IT A SENSIBLE, HEALTHY, PLEASANT HOUSE,
WIDO II (28)	HANDS SARTORIUS ANOTHER LETTER). IT'S THE SORT OF	HOUSE	NOBODY CAN LIVE IN, YOU KNOW; BUT IT'S A NICE THING
HART PREFACE(24)	HAD NOT THAT SORT OF COURAGE: NEITHER HEARTBREAK	HOUSE	NOR HORSEBACK HALL HAD BRED IT, MUCH LESS THE SUBURBS.
GETT PREFACE(232)	MAN WHO HAS BEEN RECEIVED AS A FRIEND INTO THE	HOUSE	OF A CLERGYMAN FALLS IN LOVE WITH THE CLERGYMAN'S
METH PREFACE(R34)	OF YOUNG MEN OF THE PROFESSIONAL CLASS IN THE	HOUSE	OF A DOCTOR IN THE KENSINGTONIAN QUARTER OF LONDON.
WIDO I (3)	IS A VERY GRACEFUL FEMALE STATUE IN THE PRIVATE	HOUSE	OF A NOBLEMAN IN FRANKFURT. ALSO A ZOO. NEXT DAY,
MIS. (162)	(FOLLOWING HIM) DO, DO, DO, DO, DO. THIS IS THE	HOUSE	OF A RESPECTABLE SHOPKEEPER, ENORMOUSLY RICH. THIS IS
CAND I SD(79)	IN THE ROOM, MONEY BEING TOO SCARCE IN THE	HOUSE	OF AN EAST END PARSON TO BE WASTED ON SNOBBISH
GETT (336)	OUT OF MY HOUSE. /HOTCHKISS/ IT MUST BE RATHER A	HOUSE	OF CARDS. A WORD FROM ME TO GEORGE-- JUST THE RIGHT
DEVL I (25)	AND SAVED ME FROM HAVING MY SPIRIT BROKEN IN THIS	HOUSE	OF CHILDREN'S TEARS. I PROMISED HIM MY SOUL, AND SWORE
CLEO PRO2 (97)	HIM. /BELZANOR/ WHO ARE THOU THAT LAUGHEST IN THE	HOUSE	OF CLEOPATRA THE QUEEN, AND IN THE TEETH OF BELZANOR,
MTH3 (95)	MENAGERIE OF DEGENERATES THAT IS STILL CALLED THE	HOUSE	OF COMMONS? CONFUCIUS: YOU WILL NOT BELIEVE ME; AND I
CAPT NOTES (302)	BECAME PUBLIC THROUGH AN ATTEMPT TO MAKE THE	HOUSE	OF COMMONS ACT ON THEM. THIS BEING SO, I MUST ADD THAT
MTH2 (46)	HAVE A FOLLOWING, AND THINKS I COULD GET INTO THE	HOUSE	OF COMMONS AND HEAD A GROUP THERE. SO HE INSISTS ON
KING PREFACE(158)	HOUSE OF LORDS IS MORE REPRESENTATIVE THAN THE	HOUSE	OF COMMONS BECAUSE ITS MEMBERS ARE THERE AS THE SONS
DEVL EPILOG (81)	DEMAND FOR AN INQUIRY WAS DEFEATED IN THE	HOUSE	OF COMMONS BY THE COURT PARTY; AND WHEN HE AT LAST
SIM II (79)	STOCK EXCHANGE CLOSES: ONLY TWO MEMBERS LEFT.	HOUSE	OF COMMONS DECIMATED: ONLY FOURTEEN MEMBERS TO BE
METH PREFACE(R81)	REMAIN THE REPRESENTATIVE OF WESTMINSTER IN THE	HOUSE	OF COMMONS EVEN WHEN HE WAS WILLING. THE WESTMINSTER
BULL PREFACE(63)	THE DEMORALIZED OFFICIALS OF THE OCCUPATION. THE	HOUSE	OF COMMONS HAD TWENTY-FOUR HOURS CLEAR NOTICE, WITH
MTH2 (63)	AND LATER ON BY MY DUTIES AS LEADER OF THE	HOUSE	OF COMMONS IN THE DAYS WHEN PRIME MINISTERS WERE ALSO
GENV PREFACE(4)	WAS DESCRIBED BY THE PRIME MINISTER TO THE	HOUSE	OF COMMONS IN SECRET SESSION AS SO DESPERATE THAT IF
GENV II (64)	WHO FEEL AND THINK AS SHE DOES. WELL, THE	HOUSE	OF COMMONS IS EXACTLY LIKE CAMBERWELL IN THAT RESPECT.
ROCK I (213)	(CONCENTRATING HIMSELF ON HIS ADVERSARY IN THE	HOUSE	OF COMMONS MANNER) I WILL TELL THE NOBLE LORD WHAT I
POSN PREFACE(361)	SELECT COMMITTEE OF THE HOUSE OF LORDS AND THE	HOUSE	OF COMMONS ON THE STAGE PLAYS (CENSORSHIP) TOGETHER
UNPL PREFACE(R16)	HIS EVIDENCE BEFORE THE SELECT COMMITTEE OF THE	HOUSE	OF COMMONS ON THEATRES AND PLACES OF ENTERTAINMENT IN
APPL II (271)	AMANDA. (HE RISES AND BECOMES THE CONVENTIONAL	HOUSE	OF COMMONS ORATOR). MINISTERS COMPOSE THEMSELVES TO
AUGS (276)	/THE LADY/ STILL, IF A QUESTION WERE ASKED IN THE	HOUSE	OF COMMONS -- /AUGUSTUS/ THE GREAT ADVANTAGE OF BEING
GENV III (80)	TRUE, TRUE. I HAVE KNOWN MEN WHO COULD HOLD THE	HOUSE	OF COMMONS SPELLBOUND FOR HOURS; BUT MOST UNSAFE. MERE
APPL I (232)	WILL LEARN FROM HIS EXPLANATORY SPEECH IN THE	HOUSE	OF COMMONS THAT IT IS TO CHOOSE BETWEEN CABINET
APPL II (274)	PARTY LEADER WHO CAN DEPEND ON THE SUPPORT OF THE	HOUSE	OF COMMONS TO FORM A GOVERNMENT. HE MAY CALL ON YOU.
BULL III (137)	A COUNTRYMAN OF MY OWN, THE MORAL EFFECT ON THE	HOUSE	OF COMMONS WOULD BE IMMENSE! TREMENDOUS! PARDON MY
CAPT NOTES (300)	WAS AS NOTHING COMPARED TO HIS GETTING INTO THE	HOUSE	OF COMMONS, HOW HE DID IT I KNOW NOT; BUT THE THING
ROCK I (197)	MODERN FASHION OF SPEAKING DISRESPECTFULLY OF THE	HOUSE	OF COMMONS. IF IT GOES TOO FAR WE SHALL NOT HESITATE
ROCK I (197)	THE PARTY CLIQUES CARES A BRASS BUTTON FOR THE	HOUSE	OF COMMONS. (RISING) YOU WILL DO WHAT I ASK YOU AS TO

AUGS	(276)	IS THAT NOBODY TAKES THE SLIGHTEST NOTICE OF THE	HOUSE	OF COMMONS. NO DOUBT IT IS SOMETIMES NECESSARY FOR A
ROCK I	(200)	THAT I HAPPEN TO BE THE LEADER OF THE	HOUSE	OF COMMONS. /HILDA/ OH, WHAT IS THE USE OF LEADING THE
APPL I	(222)	FIRES OF SMITHFIELD TO BURN EVERY MEMBER OF THE	HOUSE	OF COMMONS. /MAGNUS/ I WAS NOT THINKING OF A
ROCK II	(239)	/SIR BEMROSE/ GOOD! THEN I'LL ANSWER FOR THE	HOUSE	OF COMMONS. /SIR DEXTER/ DONT BE SILLY. WHAT CAN YOU
ROCK II	(268)	OLD GUY IN WESTMINSTER ON THE SITE OF THE PRESENT	HOUSE	OF COMMONS. /THE DUKE/ DEMOCRACY, ARTHUR, DEMOCRACY.
BUOY 1	(10)	TO PARLIAMENT AND BRING YOUR CHANGES BEFORE THE	HOUSE	OF COMMONS. /SON/ TOO SLOW. CLASS WAR IS RUSHING ON US
MTH2	(46)	POWER OF LISTENING. HE DOESNT LISTEN EVEN IN THE	HOUSE	OF COMMONS. SAVVY RUSHES IN BREATHLESS, FOLLOWED BY
MIS. PREFACE	(88)	DESTRUCTIVE TO THE CHARACTER. IN CHURCH, IN THE	HOUSE	OF COMMONS, AT PUBLIC MEETINGS, WE SIT SOLEMNLY
JOAN PREFACE	(55)	LEAST AS ENJOYABLE AS AN ALL-NIGHT SITTING IN THE	HOUSE	OF COMMONS, AND MUCH MORE USEFUL. BUT IN ST JOAN I
BULL PREFACE	(27)	IN THE ELECTION OF A FORMIDABLE MINORITY IN THE	HOUSE	OF COMMONS, BESIDES ALLOWING HIM TO READ AND LEARN
ROCK II	(239)	DEXTER/ DONT BE SILLY. WHAT CAN YOU DO WITH THE	HOUSE	OF COMMONS, EXCEPT EMPTY IT WHENEVER YOU GET UP TO
ROCK I	(204)	PLACIDLY TO HIS CHAIR). IT'S JUST LIKE THE	HOUSE	OF COMMONS, EXCEPT THAT THE SPEECHES ARE SHORTER.
POSN PREFACE	(361)	EDWARDES, MR COMYNS CARR, THE SPEAKER OF THE	HOUSE	OF COMMONS, THE BISHOP OF SOUTHWARK, MR HALL CAINE, MR
HART PREFACE	(5)	IN THE SADDLE, BUT ON THE FRONT BENCH IN THE	HOUSE	OF COMMONS, WITH NOBODY TO CORRECT THEIR INCREDIBLE
DEVL EPILOG	(80)	BACKWARD IN CIVILIZATION. AS HE PUT IT TO THE	HOUSE	OF COMMONS, " WHILE WE REMEMBER THAT WE ARE CONTENDING
APPL II	(273)	SEEK A PARLIAMENTARY SEAT. /PROTEUS/ YOU IN THE	HOUSE	OF COMMONS! /MAGNUS/ (BLANDLY) IT IS MY INTENTION TO
LION PREFACE	(18)	DESCENT OF JESUS THROUGH JOSEPH FROM THE ROYAL	HOUSE	OF DAVID, AND YET DECLARE THAT NOT JOSEPH BUT THE HOLY
SUPR PREFACE	(R22)	THE RIGHT TO MAKE ONESELF AT HOME IN THE	HOUSE	OF GOD BY TAKING OFF THE HAT, OF EVERYTHING THAT HE
LION EPILOG	(150)	IT SEEMED TO THE BISHOPS AS NATURAL THAT THE	HOUSE	OF GOD SHOULD BE LOOTED WHEN HE ALLOWED GERMAN TO BE
HART I	(68)	YOU ARE BENEATH THE DOME OF HEAVEN, IN THE	HOUSE	OF GOD. WHAT IS TRUE WITHIN THESE WALLS IS TRUE
MIS. SD	(109)	IS TAKING HIS WEEKLY FRIDAY TO TUESDAY IN THE	HOUSE	OF HIS FATHER, JOHN TARLETON, WHO HAS MADE A GREAT
ARMS I	(19)	THESE THINGS TO SHEW YOU THAT YOU ARE NOT IN THE	HOUSE	OF IGNORANT COUNTRYFOLK WHO WOULD KILL YOU THE MOMENT
KING I SD	(161)	CHARLES'S GOLDEN DAYS". ACT I. THE LIBRARY IN THE	HOUSE	OF ISAAC NEWTON IN CAMBRIDGE IN THE YEAR 1680. IT IS A
O'FL	(215)	THEM. SHE SAYS WE'RE THE LOST TRIBES OF THE	HOUSE	OF ISRAEL AND THE CHOSEN PEOPLE OF GOD. SHE SAYS THAT
LION PREFACE	(27)	ADDRESSED EXCLUSIVELY TO " THE LOST SHEEP OF THE	HOUSE	OF ISRAEL." WHEN A WOMAN OF CANAAN BEGGED JESUS TO
CLEO NOTES	(207)	WITH GLAUCON AND POLEMARCHUS ON HIS WAY TO THE	HOUSE	OF KEPHALUS? " AND SO ON. CLEOPATRA. CLEOPATRA WAS
GENV III	(69)	YOU WILL REMEMBER THAT OUR SAVIOR WAS OF THE	HOUSE	OF KING DAVID. /THE WIDOW/ YOU WILL BE TELLING ME NEXT
MTH2	(65)	THE CHURCH? /CONRAD/ NO. /BURGE/ IS IT ABOUT THE	HOUSE	OF LORDS? /CONRAD/ NO. /BURGE/ IS IT ABOUT
FOUN	(215)	AND NOT LIKE A PROCESSION OF THE UNEMPLOYED. THE	HOUSE	OF LORDS ALWAYS GIVES CHARITY AND NEVER GIVES JUSTICE.
POSN PREFACE	(361)	IS REPORT FROM THE JOINT SELECT COMMITTEE OF THE	HOUSE	OF LORDS AND THE HOUSE OF COMMONS ON THE STAGE PLAYS (
POSN PREFACE	(375)	THE COMMITTEE ROOM SHUT, AND THE CORRIDORS OF THE	HOUSE	OF LORDS FILLED BY A WONDERING CROWD, TO WHOM IT HAD
MILL IV	(198)	DITCH, NO MATTER WHAT IT COSTS. TAKE HIM TO THE	HOUSE	OF LORDS IF NECESSARY. WE SHALL SEE WHOSE PURSE WILL
BARB II	(282)	DOGGEDLY, WITH A SENSE OF HEROICALLY DEFYING THE	HOUSE	OF LORDS IN THE PERSON OF LORD STEVENAGE) IF YOU WANT
KING PREFACE	(158)	INDISPENSABLE IN CABINETS. FOR INSTANCE, THE	HOUSE	OF LORDS IS MORE REPRESENTATIVE THAN THE HOUSE OF
POSN PREFACE	(377)	AS POSSIBLE. (I QUOTE THIS AS AN EXAMPLE TO THE	HOUSE	OF LORDS OF THE RIGHT THING TO SAY IN SUCH
UNPL PREFACE	(R15)	TO THE CENSORSHIP AS MANY RADICALS CLING TO THE	HOUSE	OF LORDS OR THE THRONE, OR AS DOMINEERING WOMEN SHUN
MILL PREFACE	(119)	BY NAME FROM THE MOST REACTIONARY MEMBERS OF THE	HOUSE	OF LORDS OR THE MILITARY CLUBS. A SOCIALIST PRIME
SIM II	(79)	MEMBERS TO BE FOUND: NONE OF CABINET RANK.	HOUSE	OF LORDS STILL MUSTERS FIFTY MEMBERS; BUT NOT ONE OF
POSN PREFACE	(369)	THE PEERS ON THE JOINT SELECT COMMITTEE. THE	HOUSE	OF LORDS THEN PROCEEDED TO ITS SELECTION. AS
FOUN	(216)	CHARITY AND NEVER GIVES JUSTICE. /MERCER/ THE	HOUSE	OF LORDS WILL FIND ITSELF UNEMPLOYED ONE OF THESE
ROCK II	(262)	WHAT IS LEFT OF YOUR BILL AND CARRIED IT, THE	HOUSE	OF LORDS WILL TURN IT DOWN; AND YOU WILL HAVE TO WAIT
FOUN	(218)	POLITICS. FOR YOU, A MAN, POLITICS MEANT THE	HOUSE	OF LORDS. FOR ME, A WOMAN, POLITICS MEANT HOLLOWAY
MTH2	(51)	DOMINIONS; TO DISESTABLISHMENT; TO REFORM OF THE	HOUSE	OF LORDS; TO A REVISED SCHEME OF TAXATION OF LAND
FOUN	(214)	/MERCER/ WHAT THE LORD CHANCELLOR SITS ON IN THE	HOUSE	OF LORDS, MISS. /ANASTASIA/ (CONTINUING HER READING)
BARB PREFACE	(233)	FOR A MASS OF MEN PRACTICALLY ALIKE: FELONY, THE	HOUSE	OF LORDS, THE FACTORY, THE STABLES, THE GIPSY
JITT III	(70)	ARE YOU ANGRY WITH HER FOR DARING TO SING IN THIS	HOUSE	OF MOURNING? OR ANGRY WITH ME FOR MAKING HER SING?
MTH3	(118)	TYRANT OR YOUR SLAVE. I WAS A PARLORMAID IN THE	HOUSE	OF ONE OF THE ACCOUNTANT GENERAL'S REMOTE ANCESTORS. (
METH PREFACE	(R82)	COULD NOT. ALSO, PLEASE NOTE, HE COULD DECORATE A	HOUSE	OF PLEASURE FOR A CARDINAL VERY BEAUTIFULLY WITH
LION PREFACE	(35)	AND MARK DESCRIBE IT AS TAKING PLACE IN THE	HOUSE	OF SIMON THE LEPER, WHERE IT IS OBJECTED TO AS A WASTE
KING I	(220)	/KNELLER/ I WILL GO HOME. I CANNOT EAT IN THIS	HOUSE	OF STRAIGHT LINES. /MRS BASHAM/ YOU WILL DO NOTHING OF
DEVL I	(26)	MEN WILL TAKE THIS CHILD AND RESCUE HER FROM THE	HOUSE	OF THE DEVIL? /JUDITH/ (COMING TO ESSIE AND THROWING
CLEO PRO2	(96)	PASS, O YOUNG CAPTAIN; AND BOW THE HEAD IN THE	HOUSE	OF THE QUEEN. /VOICE/ GO ANOINT THY JAVELIN WITH FAT
PYGM III SD	(244)	IS NOT SO LOFTY AS IT WOULD BE IN AN OLDER	HOUSE	OF THE SAME PRETENSION. THE WINDOWS ARE OPEN, GIVING
MTH3	(117)	OR A PARLORMAID OPENING THE DOOR OF THE	HOUSE	OF THE YOUNG WOMAN YOU WERE IN LOVE WITH? /THE
GETT	(338)	AT HIS TOUCH. /THE BISHOP/ COME! YOU ARE IN THE	HOUSE	OF YOUR FRIENDS. CAN WE HELP YOU? /MRS GEORGE/ (TO
MTH2	(76)	PLACE TO LIVE IN. /BURGE/ TRUE. IF YOU TAKE A	HOUSE	ON A NINETY-NINE YEARS LEASE. YOU SPEND A GOOD DEAL OF
HART III	(139)	RESISTED ME. WHATS THE MATTER, MR DUNN? IS THE	HOUSE	ON FIRE? /MAZZINI/ OH NO: NOTHING'S THE MATTER; BUT
PYGM III	(246)	HER SOME MONTHS AGO; AND SHE'S GETTING ON LIKE A	HOUSE	ON FIRE. I SHALL WIN MY BET. SHE HAS A QUICK EAR; AND
ROCK II	(256)	ARE, YOUR GRACE! I WILL CALL FOR YOU AT DOMESDAY	HOUSE	ON FRIDAY AT HALF PAST FOUR. AS I SHALL BRING A FEW
SUPR II SD	(48)	AN UNOBSTRUCTED VIEW OF THE WEST CORNER OF THE	HOUSE	ON HIS LEFT WERE HE NOT FAR TOO MUCH INTERESTED IN A
BUOY II SD	(18)	BY THE WATERSIDE, WHERE THERE IS A WOODEN	HOUSE	ON POSTS, WITH A LADDER FROM THE STOEP OR VERANDAH TO
HART I	(77)	I HAVE INVITED ALL SORTS OF PRETTY WOMEN TO THE	HOUSE	ON THE CHANCE OF GIVING YOU ANOTHER TURN. BUT IT HAS
SIM I SD	(36)	THE LAWN OF A STATELY	HOUSE	ON THE NORTH COAST OF A TROPICAL ISLAND IN THE PACIFIC
DEVL I SD	(3)	THE KITCHEN AND GENERAL DWELLING ROOM OF HER FARM	HOUSE	ON THE OUTSKIRTS OF THE TOWN OF WEBSTERBRIDGE. SHE IS
O'FL	(212)	HEIGHTH OF GRANDEUR; AND STOP SHE WILL AT EVERY	HOUSE	ON THE WAY TO SHEW HERSELF OFF AND TELL THEM WHERE
GETT	(274)	MR BRIDGENORTH: ARE YOU GOING TO LEAVE THIS	HOUSE	OR AM I? /REGINALD/ YOU ARE, I HOPE. (HE EMPHASIZES
GETT PREFACE	(202)	TO EFFECT SOME SORT OF SEGREGATION WITHIN THE	HOUSE	OR ELSE RUN A HEAVY RISK OF OVERSTRAINING THEIR
HART PREFACE	(28)	I AM AFRAID THEY DO NOT INCLUDE EITHER HEARTBREAK	HOUSE	OR HORSEBACK HALL. PLAGUE ON BOTH YOUR HOUSES!
GETT PREFACE	(233)	HIS LIFE FOR TWO WIVES: EITHER YOU GO OUT OF THE	HOUSE	OR I GO OUT OF IT." THE SITUATION IS NOT AT ALL
HART I	(68)	HERE ON YOUR DAUGHTER'S INVITATION. AM I IN HER	HOUSE	OR IN YOURS? /CAPTAIN SHOTOVER/ YOU ARE BENEATH THE
MTH2	(63)	I WILL UNDERTAKE TO PUT THE CASE TO THE	HOUSE	OR TO THE COUNTRY TO YOUR ENTIRE SATISFACTION. YOU
MILL PREFACE	(110)	PEER FIND THAT HE IS A NONENTITY IN A GRAND	HOUSE	ORGANIZED AND RULED BY HIS BUTLER? QUESTIONS LIKE
APPL INTRLUD	(243)	AND THE KING IS NOT A GENTLEMAN, I MUST TAKE A	HOUSE	OUTSIDE. I AM WRITING TO THE AGENTS ABOUT ONE NOW.
BARB I	(267)	OCCASIONALLY, IN THE STREETS AND IN PUBLIC	HOUSE	PARLORS BY MY NATURAL TALENT FOR STEPDANCING. LATER
CAND II	(114)	MORELL) JAMES: YOUVE NOT BEEN LOOKING AFTER THE	HOUSE	PROPERLY. /MORELL/ WHAT HAVE I DONE-- OR NOT DONE-- MY
BULL I	(90)	5 PER CENT WITH A LITTLE FARMING AND A SCRAP OF	HOUSE	PROPERTY IN THE NEAREST COUNTRY TOWN? WHAT AM I TO
DEST SD	(151)	IN TAVAZZANO ARE AT A LITTLE INN, THE FIRST	HOUSE	REACHED BY TRAVELLERS PASSING THROUGH THE PLACE FROM
DEVL I	(14)	THAT WOULD BE MORE IN YOUR WAY THAN GETTING THE	HOUSE	READY. (ESSIE COMES BACK). OH, HERE YOU ARE! (
ROCK I	(200)	THEIR INCLUSION IN THE NEXT CABINET. THE WHOLE	HOUSE	ROSE AT IT. LOOK AT THE PAPERS THIS MORNING! FULL OF
SUPR IV	(148)	THEYLL BE ABLE TO GET THAT DONE BEFORE I BUY THE	HOUSE	-- OR RATHER THE ABBEY? THEYRE BOTH ABBEYS. /VIOLET/
MILL I	(149)	YOU HADNT ANY WRONGS. YOU DROVE ME OUT OF THE	HOUSE	-- /EPIFANIA/ I DID NOT. I NEVER MEANT YOU TO GO. IT
JOAN 6	(136)	LIKE ANYONE ELSE. I WILL DO A LADY'S WORK IN THE	HOUSE	-- SPIN OR WEAVE -- AGAINST ANY WOMAN IN ROUEN. /THE
HART III	(147)	BRIGHTER. /NURSE GUINNESS/ (LOOKING UP AT THE	HOUSE	) IT'S MR HUSHABYE TURNING ON ALL THE LIGHTS IN THE
SUPR II	(57)	/STRAKER/ (CATCHING SIGHT OF ANN COMING FROM THE	HOUSE	) MISS WHITEFIELD, GENTLEMEN. (HE DISMOUNTS AND
O'FL	(221)	UP. /MRS O'FLAHERTY/ (CALLING FROM WITHIN THE	HOUSE	) TESSIE! TESSIE DARLINT! /TERESA/ (DISENGAGING
O'FL	(223)	OH! OH! OH! /SIR PEARCE/ (RUNNING OUT OF THE	HOUSE	) WHATS THIS INFERNAL NOISE? WHAT ON EARTH IS THE
3PLA PREFACE	(R31)	ANTONYS (THEY ARE TO BE FOUND IN EVERY PUBLIC	HOUSE	) WHO WOULD NO DOUBT BE GLAD ENOUGH TO BE TRANSFIGURED
ARMS II	(44)	(SNATCHING UP THE BAG, AND ESCAPING INTO THE	HOUSE	) YES, MAJOR. /CATHERINE/ OH, NEVER MIND, PAUL: DONT
BULL III	(140)	HODSON-- /HODSON/ (BEHIND THE CORNER OF THE	HOUSE	) YES, SIR. (HE HURRIES FORWARD). /BROADBENT/ HODSON:
ARMS II	(25)	POT AND CUPS ON THE TRAY, AND CARRIES IT INTO THE	HOUSE	) YOULL NEVER PUT THE SOUL OF A SERVANT INTO ME. MAJOR
ARMS II	(33)	THEM ON THE SOFIA ROUTE. (HE GOES TOWARDS THE	HOUSE	). COME ALONG. (SERGIUS IS ABOUT TO FOLLOW HIM WHEN
CAPT I	(234)	YOU AW, GAVNER. (HE GOES OFFICIOUSLY INTO THE	HOUSE	). LADY CICELY AND RANKIN SIT DOWN AS BEFORE TO
BULL III	(138)	THE PRICE, SIR. (HE FOLLOWS CORNELIUS INTO THE	HOUSE	). LARRY, NEWSPAPER STILL IN HAND, COMES BACK THROUGH
BULL III	(139)	PICKS IT UP AND CARRIES IT AWAY BEHIND THE	HOUSE	). /BROADBENT/ (BEAMING CANDIDATORIALLY) I MUST THANK
BULL III	(123)	WANT US. (SHE TAKES UP THE TRAY AND GOES INTO THE	HOUSE	). /BROADBENT/ (RISING AND GALLANTLY PROTESTING) OH,
ARMS II	(39)	FLIPPANTLY AWAY UP THE PATH TO THE CORNER OF THE	HOUSE	). /CATHERINE/ AND WHAT SHOULD I BE ABLE TO SAY TO
ARMS II	(41)	DETAIN YOU NO FURTHER. (HE TURNS TO GO INTO THE	HOUSE	). /CATHERINE/ (CATCHING HIM BY THE SLEEVE) OH, YOU
ARMS II	(29)	AGAINST THE RAIL OF THE STEPS LEADING TO THE	HOUSE	). /CATHERINE/ YOU LOOK SUPERB. THE CAMPAIGN HAS
BULL III	(134)	HE PASSES OUT OF SIGHT ROUND THE CORNER OF THE	HOUSE	). /DORAN/ (DAZED) HWAT SORT OF A FELLA IS HE AT ALL
MRS I	(194)	AS USUAL. COME IN AND TRY (MOVING TOWARDS THE	HOUSE	). /FRANK/ STOP A BIT. (SERIOUSLY) I WANT TO TAKE YOU
SIM I	(52)	FREE. FAREWELL (SHE POINTS HIS WAY THROUGH THE	HOUSE	). /IDDY/ (CLUTCHING AT HER ROBE) NO, NO. DO NOT
SIM II	(73)	WHERE WE OFTEN SIT. (HE LEADS THE WAY TO THE	HOUSE	). /KANCHIN/ IN THEORY. /JANGA/ IN FACT WE NEVER SIT
SIM II	(68)	AWAY, DISAPPEARING BETWEEN THE GARDEN AND THE	HOUSE	). /KANCHIN/ YOU SPEAK AS AN EMPRESS SHOULD SPEAK. (
CAPT I	(227)	TO SAY TO THAT SAME MOOR. (HE GOES INTO THE	HOUSE	). /LADY CICELY/ (WALKING ABOUT THE GARDEN, LOOKING
SIM II	(82)	USEFUL JOB. (HE FOLLOWS HYERING INTO THE	HOUSE	). /LADY FARWATERS/ (RISING) PROLA: SHALL I BRING YOU
ARMS II	(35)	GATEWAY, WHERE THEY ARE HIDDEN FROM THE	HOUSE	). /LOUKA (PLAINTIVELY) I MAY HAVE BEEN SEEN FROM THE
SIM II	(82)	WITH MY GARDENING BASKET. (SHE GOES INTO THE	HOUSE	). /MRS HYERING/ J'YOU THINK ITLL BE ALL RIGHT IF I GO

O'FL	(217)	A FRONT SEAT FOR HIMSELF. EH? (HE GOES INTO THE	HOUSE	). /MRS O'FLAHERTY/ SURE HE HAS THAT, YOUR HONOR. GOD
HART III	(146)	BE SEEN FOR A HUNDRED MILES (HE DASHES INTO THE	HOUSE	). /NURSE GUINNESS/ THE RECTORY IS NOTHING BUT A HEAP
O'FL	(221)	NOT VERY CONVINCINGLY, AND HURRIES INTO THE	HOUSE	). /O'FLAHERTY/ (ALONE) AND IF I DO GET A PENSION
MRS III	(222)	HIS WAY TO THE PORCH AND VANISHES INTO THE	HOUSE	). /PRAED/ CURIOUS THING IT MUST BE WRITING A SERMON
MRS III	(223)	TO THINK OF THAT NOW. HERE! (HE BOUNDS INTO THE	HOUSE	). /REV. S./ HE'S SO IMPETUOUS. I DONT KNOW WHAT TO DO
SIM II	(82)	ON, CHARLES. LETS GET TO WORK. (HE GOES INTO THE	HOUSE	). /SIR CHARLES/ (TO HIS WIFE, RISING) YOU MIGHT TAKE
CAPT I	(226)	AHRD ELLAM. (HE WITHDRAWS DISCREETLY INTO THE	HOUSE	). /SIR HOWARD/ (TO RANKIN) I AM SORRY TO INTRUDE ON
SIM II	(66)	I THINK IT'S AN ALBATROSS. (HE GOES INTO THE	HOUSE	). /VASHTI, MAYA, KANCHIN, JANGA/ (HISSING AFTER HIM)
SIM I	(51)	COME. (SHE GOES UP THE STEPS AND INTO THE	HOUSE	). THEY ALL RISE AND FOLLOW HER, EACH BESTOWING A WORD
CAPT I	SD(234)	YOUR LEDDYSHIP. THERE IS A SCUFFLING NOISE IN THE	HOUSE	; AND DRINKWATER SHOOTS OUT THROUGH THE DOORWAY ACROSS
KING I	(187)	KNOW NOR CARE WHERE THE KING IS. THIS IS MY	HOUSE	; AND I DEMAND TO BE LEFT IN PEACE IN IT. I AM ENGAGED
GENV II	(63)	UP ALL THE POLITICS I NEED WHEN I GET INTO THE	HOUSE	; AND I SHALL GET INTO THE HOUSE BECAUSE THERE ARE
LION I	(122)	HIM, POOR LAD. CARRY HIM GENTLY TO HIS	HOUSE	; AND LEAVE THE REST TO HEAVEN. /CENTURION/ TAKE HIM
DEVL I	(27)	WITH ME; RUN UP THE AMERICAN FLAG ON THE DEVIL'S	HOUSE	; AND MAKE A FIGHT FOR FREEDOM? (THEY SCRAMBLE OUT,
SUPR IV	(165)	DO WHEN YOU ARE GONE, WITH NO ONE BUT ANN IN THE	HOUSE	; AND SHE ALWAYS OCCUPIED WITH THE MEN! IT'S NOT TO
MILL IV	(197)	TO THAT. AS TO MISS SMITH, THIS IS A LICENSED	HOUSE	; AND SHE HAS AS MUCH RIGHT TO BE HERE AS YOU OR I.
SUPR I	(8)	WILL NOT HAVE IT. SHE MUST FORBID JOHN TANNER THE	HOUSE	; AND SO MUST YOU. THE PARLORMAID RETURNS. /OCTAVIUS/
BULL IV	(173)	ALREADY OWNS HALF ROSSCULLEN. DOOLAN'S IS A TIED	HOUSE	; AND THE BREWERS ARE IN THE SYNDICATE. AS TO
VWOO 2	(130)	IT MADE ME FEEL THAT I COULD DO WITH YOU IN THE	HOUSE	; AND THEN I COULD FALL IN LOVE WITH ANYONE I LIKED
BARB I	(252)	LIVE ON MY INCOME AS LONG AS WE ARE IN THE SAME	HOUSE	; BUT I CANT KEEP FOUR FAMILIES IN FOUR SEPARATE
SUPR II	(63)	FOR A RUN OCCASIONALLY: SHE IS TOO MUCH IN THE	HOUSE	; BUT IT WILL DO WHEN YOU COME BACK. /TANNER/ ABYSS
METH PREFACE	(R53)	THE PRIEST, WE COULD AT LEAST KEEP HIM OUT OF THE	HOUSE	; BUT WHAT OF THE MODERN DARWINIST SURGEON WHOM WE
MIS.	(199)	THE NEW SPORT OF AVIATION. YOU JUST SEE A NICE	HOUSE	; DROP IN; SCOOP UP THE MAN'S DAUGHTER; AND OFF WITH
BULL II	(108)	THE DISCUSSION, WHICH MAKES HIM ASHAMED OF HIS	HOUSE	; FOR HE GUESSES BROADBENT'S STANDARD OF COMFORT A
HART II	(111)	THEM SAME AS I WORKED IT HERE. I BREAK INTO THE	HOUSE	; PUT A FEW SPOONS OR DIAMONDS IN MY POCKET; MAKE A
PRES	(138)	QUITE RIGHT. /BALSQUITH/ THAT CARRIED THE	HOUSE	;-- /MITCHENER/ NATURALLY. /BALSQUITH/ -- AND THE
KING I	(174)	NOTHING WORSE THAN NELL. BUT I PROMISE YOU YOUR	HOUSE	SHALL BE A MONASTERY HENCEFORTH. AS CHARLES AND NELL
ANNA	(297)	IMPOSSIBLE, THAT A DAUGHTER OF THE IMPERIAL	HOUSE	SHOULD SPEAK TO ANYONE ALONE, WERE IT EVEN HER OWN
O'FL	(207)	SURE THE POOR WOMAN KISSED ME AND WENT ABOUT THE	HOUSE	SINGING IN HER OLD CRACKY VOICE THAT THE FRENCH WAS ON
HART PREFACE	(11)	DISPLAYING. THUS WERE THE FIRSTBORN OF HEARTBREAK	HOUSE	SMITTEN; AND THE YOUNG, THE INNOCENT, THE HOPEFUL
KING I	(172)	NEWTON. (LOOKING ROUND HER) AND WHO KEEPS YOUR	HOUSE	SO BEAUTIFULLY? I THOUGHT PHILOSOPHERS WERE LIKE
WIDO III	(50)	ON HIS KNEES TONIGHT, I WOULD WALK OUT OF THE	HOUSE	SOONER THAN ENDURE IT. (SHE GOES OUT EXCITEDLY).
ROCK I	(200)	SOCIALISM BREAKING UP THE FAMILY. FOR THE CHURCH	HOUSE	SPEECH THIS AFTERNOON. /SIR ARTHUR/ YES YES YES, OF
JITT III	(59)	SCIENCE NOR CARE ABOUT IT. IF I HAVE TO KEEP THE	HOUSE	SPICK AND SPAN I CANT ALWAYS KEEP MYSELF SPICK AND
DOCT PREFACE	(3)	WE DID, NO MAN'S NECK WOULD BE SAFE AND NO MAN'S	HOUSE	STABLE. BUT WE DO MAKE THE DOCTOR THE JUDGE, AND FINE
HART PREFACE	(3)	NO PESSIMIST: HE WAS NOT DISPOSED TO LEAVE THE	HOUSE	STANDING IF HE COULD BRING IT DOWN ABOUT THE EARS OF
HART PREFACE	(3)	HOUSE AND HORSEBACK HALL. WHERE HEARTBREAK	HOUSE	STANDS. HEARTBREAK HOUSE IS NOT MERELY THE NAME OF THE
MIS. PREFACE	(82)	TO MANY AN ORPHAN FONDER CARE IN A STRANGER'S	HOUSE	THAN IT WOULD HAVE RECEIVED FROM ITS ACTUAL PARENTS.
INCA PROLOG	(234)	LUXURY, IF YOU INSIST. CALL IT WHAT YOU PLEASE. A	HOUSE	THAT COSTS LESS THAN A HUNDRED THOUSAND DOLLARS A YEAR
GETT PREFACE	(247)	IT IS HIS HOUSE THAT HAS BEEN BROKEN INTO, OR HIS	HOUSE	THAT HAS BEEN BURNT; AND YOU WILL BE STARTLED BY THE
GETT PREFACE	(247)	BUT TELL THE MAGISTRATE OR FIREMAN THAT IT IS HIS	HOUSE	THAT HAS BEEN BROKEN INTO, OR HIS HOUSE THAT HAS BEEN
ARMS I	(19)	TO THE BALCONY BECAUSE OURS IS THE ONLY PRIVATE	HOUSE	THAT HAS TWO ROWS OF WINDOWS. THERE IS A FLIGHT OF
KING I	(188)	INFIDEL GALILEO! /NEWTON/ TAKE CARE, SIR. IN MY	HOUSE	THE GREAT GALILEO SHALL NOT BE CALLED AN INFIDEL BY
SUPR HANDBOK	(201)	BY-LAWS ARE MULTIPLIED; PUBLIC STEPS ARE TAKEN TO	HOUSE	THE MASSES DECENTLY; THE BARE-FOOTED GET BOOTS; RAGS
SIM II	(75)	VERSE OF THE NATIONAL ANTHEM AT THE MANSION	HOUSE	THE PROCEEDINGS WERE INTERRUPTED BY THE APPEARANCE OF
KING I	(210)	ALMIGHTY, FROM THE RAINBOW IN THE SKIES TO THE	HOUSE	THE SNAIL CARRIES ON HIS BACK, THAT IS NOT A CURVE,
MRS III	(221)	OVER HERE TODAY, AND TO INVITE THEM TO MAKE THIS	HOUSE	THEIR HOME. MY MOTHER THEN FOUND SHE MUST GO TO TOWN
CAPT I	SD(217)	THE NORTH EAST CORNER. AT THE GARDEN-DOOR OF THE	HOUSE	THERE APPEARS PRESENTLY A MAN WHO IS CLEARLY NO
KING I	(174)	OH! MR NEWTON: EITHER THIS FEMALE LEAVES THE	HOUSE	THIS INSTANT OR I DO. /BARBARA/ DO YOU KNOW, WOMAN,
FANY II	(296)	YOUR TONGUE, YOU YOUNG HUSSY; OR GO OUT OF MY	HOUSE	THIS INSTANT. /MARGARET/ I'M QUITE READY. (SHE TAKES
BUOY IV	(57)	EH? /SIR FERDINAND/ COMPLETELY. WHAT A	HOUSE	THIS IS! SHE WAS NOT A BIT SURPRISED, THOUGH SHE WAS
O'FL	(226)	IN THE WHOLE CREW OF YOU. IN WITH YOU INTO THE	HOUSE	THIS VERY MINUTE AND TEAR ONE ANOTHER'S EYES OUT IN
MILL IV	(192)	THANK YOU. /PATRICIA/ HAVE YOU MANY PEOPLE IN THE	HOUSE	THIS WEEK-END? /THE MANAGER/ LESS THAN USUAL, MADAM.
SUPR IV	(167)	BUT WHO EVER LOOKS AT IT WHEN IT HAS BEEN IN THE	HOUSE	THREE DAYS? I THOUGHT OUR PICTURES VERY LOVELY WHEN
BULL III	SD(117)	TO HIS LEFT, HE COULD PASS ROUND THE END OF THE	HOUSE	THROUGH AN UNKEMPT SHRUBBERY. THE MUTILATED REMNANT OF
ROCK I	(204)	THE JOKE. WHY THIS HILARITY? /DAVID/ TREAT THE	HOUSE	TO A BRIEF DESCRIPTION OF THIS FAMILY; AND YOU WILL
GLIM	(177)	/FERRUCCIO/ NOT WHILE THERES A BROOMSTICK IN THE	HOUSE	TO BREAK HER UGLY HEAD WITH. DO YOU SUPPOSE I'M GOING
SIM II	(66)	/IDDY/ (RISING) EXCUSE ME. I'M GOING INTO THE	HOUSE	TO GET THE FIELD GLASS. (HE GOES UP THE STEPS). /MRS
BASH II,1,	(99)	EVENTFUL NIGHT WHEN AS WE GATHERED WERE AT HOSKYN	HOUSE	TO HEAR A LECTURE BY HERR ABENDGASSE, HE PLACED A
MIS. PREFACE	(12)	ELDER ONES TOO, TWO ADULT PARENTS, IN SPITE OF A	HOUSE	TO KEEP AND AN INCOME TO EARN, CAN STILL INTERFERE TO
2TRU PREFACE	(10)	THEY ARE NEITHER IDLE NOR FREE. A LADY WITH A BIG	HOUSE	TO MANAGE, AND THE REARING OF A FAMILY TO SUPERVISE,
HART I	(67)	CAPTAIN IN THE PANTRY) PAPA: COME AND EXPLAIN THE	HOUSE	TO MR MANGAN. SHE GOES OUT WITH ELLIE. THE CAPTAIN
SUPR PREFACE	(R21)	IF HE BE POOR ENOUGH TO BE PUSHED OUT OF THE	HOUSE	TO OUTFACE HIS IGNOMINY BY DRUNKEN REJOICINGS. BUT
DOCT PREFACE	(35)	CRUEL OR HUMANE. THE CHINAMAN WHO BURNT DOWN HIS	HOUSE	TO ROAST HIS PIG WAS NO DOUBT HONESTLY UNABLE TO
BUOY II	(22)	THE DAY HAS DONE ITS WORST. /SHE/ IF YOU WANT A	HOUSE	TO SHADE YOU, BUILD ONE FOR YOURSELF. LEAVE MINE IN
HART III	(146)	OUT? /NURSE GUINNESS/ (RUNNING IN FROM THE	HOUSE	TO THE MIDDLE OF THE ESPLANADE) I DID, SIR. THE POLICE
HART III	(141)	IS QUITE CURED. THE PLACE MAY BE HEARTBREAK	HOUSE	TO YOU, MISS DUNN, AND TO THIS GENTLEMAN FROM THE CITY
ARMS II	SD(33)	OH, VERY WELL, VERY WELL. THEY GO INTO THE	HOUSE	TOGETHER AFFECTIONATELY. SERGIUS, LEFT ALONE WITH
DOCT III	(149)	TALKING HERE PRETTY FREELY ABOUT ME-- IN MY OWN	HOUSE	TOO. I DONT MIND THAT: I'M A MAN AND CAN TAKE CARE OF
POSN PREFACE	(410)	LEAST ATTEMPT ON HIS PART TO KEEP A DISORDERLY	HOUSE	UNDER COVER OF OPENING A THEATRE HE WOULD RISK HIS
JITT III	(63)	BELIEVED YOU COULD BE SO COARSE. NOBODY IN THIS	HOUSE	UNDERSTANDS ME, NEITHER MY MOTHER NOR YOU NOR ANYBODY.
FABL PREFACE	(71)	AND CLEANERS WILL NOT VENTURE INTO AN INFECTED	HOUSE	UNLESS WE MAKE A HORRIBLE STINK IN IT WITH BURNING
KING I	(176)	IN TWO FLIGHTS. /BARBARA/ I WILL NOT LEAVE THIS	HOUSE	UNTIL THAT PLAYER WOMAN HAS GONE FIRST. (SHE STRIDES
BUOY II	(22)	LIE DOWN AND SLEEP IN THE FRIENDLY SHADOW OF YOUR	HOUSE	UNTIL THE HEAT OF THE DAY HAS DONE ITS WORST. /SHE/ IF
GENV I	(35)	REFUSED TO LEAVE THE CHAMBER. SO HE ADJOURNED THE	HOUSE	UNTIL THE NEXT DAY; AND WHEN THE OPPOSITION TURNED UP
DEVL I	(20)	MY HOUSE. /RICHARD/ HOW DO YOU KNOW IT'S YOUR	HOUSE	UNTIL THE WILL IS READ? (THEY LOOK AT ONE ANOTHER
WIDO II	(43)	STONES. BUT, ON MY HONOR, I NEVER KNEW THAT MY	HOUSE	WAS A GLASS ONE UNTIL YOU POINTED IT OUT. I BEG YOUR
2TRU I	(29)	WHO KNOWS? IT MAY HAVE LURKED HERE SINCE THE	HOUSE	WAS BUILT. YOU NEVER CAN TELL. BUT YOU MUST NOT WORRY.
BULL PREFACE	(69)	SUPPLIES. IF THE OCCUPANTS REPORTED THE RAID, THE	HOUSE	WAS BURNT. THE BLACK AND TANS AND THE ORDINARY
BULL III	(119)	YUP WITH A THUMP AT THREE O'CLOCK? I THOUGHT THE	HOUSE	WAS FALLING. BUT THEN I'M A VERY LIGHT SLEEPER.
HART PREFACE	(10)	TO LIVE MUST MAKE A MERIT OF DYING. HEARTBREAK	HOUSE	WAS FAR TOO LAZY AND SHALLOW TO EXTRICATE ITSELF FROM
BARB III	(316)	WIFE HAS TREATED HIM TO IT EVER SINCE THE	HOUSE	WAS FOUNDED. IT IS MERE WASTE OF BREATH. IF THE
HART PREFACE	(4)	NEST IF NOT HERE? THE ALTERNATIVE TO HEARTBREAK	HOUSE	WAS HORSEBACK HALL, CONSISTING OF A PRISON FOR HORSES
BULL II	(103)	BEEN OPENED TO THEM. I DID NOT KNOW WHAT MY OWN	HOUSE	WAS LIKE, BECAUSE I HAD NEVER BEEN OUTSIDE IT. /NORA/
HART PREFACE	(5)	REVOLUTION ON THE SHELF. HEARTBREAK	HOUSE	WAS QUITE FAMILIAR WITH REVOLUTIONARY IDEAS ON PAPER.
HART II	(123)	/HECTOR/ IT IS A POSE LIKE ANY OTHER. IN THIS	HOUSE	WE KNOW ALL THE POSES: OUR GAME IS TO FIND OUT THE MAN
KING I	(175)	OF, IF YOU ARE THE DUCHESS OF CLEVELAND AND THIS	HOUSE	WERE WHAT YOU SAID IT WAS YOU WOULD BE ONLY TOO MUCH
ARMS III	(71)	FATHER'S BUSINESS. I CLIMBED THE BALCONY OF THIS	HOUSE	WHEN A MAN OF SENSE WOULD HAVE DIVED INTO THE NEAREST
MILL I	(149)	BUT REALLY A MAN CAPABLE OF FLOUNCING OUT OF THE	HOUSE	WHEN I WAS ON THE POINT OF PARDONING HIM AND GIVING
ARMS II	SD(38)	SHE TAKES HER TRAY, AND IS APPROACHING THE	HOUSE	WHEN RAINA RETURNS, WEARING A HAT AND JACKET IN THE
WIDO I	(19)	HAVE THE PLEASURE OF SEEING YOU SOMETIMES AT MY	HOUSE	WHEN WE RETURN TO ENGLAND. /COKANE/ (OVERWHELMED) MY
MIS.	(155)	TOO! WHAT SORT OF WOMAN IS THAT TO HAVE IN OUR	HOUSE	WHEN YOU KNOW THAT ALL HINDHEAD WILL BE CALLING ON US
GETT PREFACE	(222)	USE YOUR OWN MATURE CHARMS TO ATTRACT MEN TO THE	HOUSE	WHEN YOUR DAUGHTERS HAVE NO APTITUDE FOR THAT
INCA	(242)	THAT RATTLE AND BANG AND GUGGLE ALL OVER THE	HOUSE	WHENEVER ANYONE WASHES HIS HANDS. I KNOW. /THE
JITT III	(55)	AND A DOCTOR CANT HAVE THEM COMING TO HIS OWN	HOUSE	WHERE HIS WIFE AND DAUGHTER ARE. HE HAS TO KEEP A
MIS.	(181)	HINDHEAD AND EFFECTED AN UNLAWFUL ENTRY INTO HIS	HOUSE	WHERE I SECRETED MYSELF IN A PORTABLE TURKISH BATH
MIS.	(202)	LINA SZCZEPANOWSKA; AND I WILL NOT STAY IN THE	HOUSE	WHERE SUCH DISHONOR IS OFFERED ME. ADIEU. (SHE TURNS
MIS.	(198)	ONE'S PARENTS MEANS, JOEY. IT MEANS LIVING IN A	HOUSE	WHERE YOU CAN BE ORDERED TO LEAVE THE ROOM. IVE GOT TO
WIDO III	(65)	THE SAKE OF THAT, YOU COME BACK HERE-- INTO THE	HOUSE	WHERE YOU WERE REFUSED-- ORDERED OUT. (TRENCH'S FACE
METH PREFACE	(R46)	HARDLY A LABORER ATTACHED TO AN ENGLISH COUNTRY	HOUSE	WHO HAS NOT TAKEN A LITTER OF KITTENS OR PUPPIES TO
DEVL II	(30)	WHO ARE AFRAID OF IT. THERES A DANGER THAT THE	HOUSE	WILL CATCH FIRE IN THE NIGHT; BUT WE SHANT SLEEP ANY
SIM II	SD(74)	ON THE WELL PARAPET. SIR CHARLES RETURNS FROM THE	HOUSE	WITH A BATCH OF WIRELESS MESSAGES IN HIS HAND. /SIR
CAPT I	SD(227)	HEAVENLY PLACE. DRINKWATER RETURNS FROM THE	HOUSE	WITH A CHAIR. /DRINKWATER/ (PLACING THE CHAIR FOR SIR
DEVL I	(12)	CANT EXPECT ME TO DO ALL THE HEAVY WORK OF THE	HOUSE	WITH A GREAT LOUT LIKE YOU IDLING ABOUT. CHRISTY TAKES
GETT PREFACE	(242)	EXISTING CIRCUMSTANCES, ADVISE A WOMAN TO KEEP	HOUSE	WITH A MAN WITHOUT INSISTING ON HIS MARRYING HER,
ARMS II	(39)	ONLY TEN YEARS YOUNGER! (LOUKA COMES FROM THE	HOUSE	WITH A SALVER, WHICH SHE CARRIES HANGING DOWN BY HER
JOAN 6	(131)	IS STONED, TORN IN PIECES, DROWNED, BURNED IN HIS	HOUSE	WITH ALL HIS INNOCENT CHILDREN, WITHOUT A TRIAL,

CAPT I SD(234)	THEY WILL ADMIRE YOURS. DRINKWATER COMES FROM THE	HOUSE	WITH AN ITALIAN DRESSED IN A MUCH WORN SUIT OF BLUE
BASH PREFACE(89)	LOST ON THEM; BUT BEN WEBSTER BROUGHT DOWN THE	HOUSE	WITH CASHEL BYRON'S DECLAMATORY REPUDIATION OF THE
ROCK I (203)	OF SHEER DISLIKE OF ME. I REFUSE TO LIVE IN THIS	HOUSE	WITH HER A MOMENT LONGER. LADY CHAVENDER FOLLOWS HER
PYGM EPILOG (295)	SO SIMPLE. ELIZA'S DESIRE TO HAVE FREDDY IN THE	HOUSE	WITH HER SEEMED OF NO MORE IMPORTANCE THAN IF SHE HAD
ARMS II (34)	HER! MY HEART IS TOO FULL. (LOUKA COMES FROM THE	HOUSE	WITH HER TRAY. SHE GOES TO THE TABLE, AND BEGINS TO
MIS. (116)	BRUTALITY MAKES IT IMPOSSIBLE TO LIVE IN THE	HOUSE	WITH HIM. /JOHNNY/ (DEEPLY HURT) IT'S FOURTEEN YEARS,
FOUN (220)	THAT I REALLY COULD NOT LIVE IN THE SAME	HOUSE	WITH IT. I ADOPTED THE ORPHAN CHILD OF A CROSSING
LIED (203)	MORE TOO. I ASKED MRS BOMPAS TO WALK OUT OF THE	HOUSE	WITH ME-- TO LEAVE YOU-- TO GET DIVORCED FROM YOU AND
JITT II (46)	(WHINING PITIABLY) AND YOU COULD LIVE IN THE	HOUSE	WITH ME, AND TAKE MY CARE AND MY NURSING AND MY MONEY,
SUPR II SD(63)	DRESSED. AS HE COMES ALONG THE DRIVE FROM THE	HOUSE	WITH MRS WHITEFIELD HE IS SEDULOUSLY MAKING HIMSELF
SIM II SD(58)	FIVE LADIES ARE TAKING TEA. PRA COMES FROM THE	HOUSE	WITH SIR CHARLES AND HYERING. THEY HELP THEMSELVES TO
CAPT I (227)	HIN KICE AW SHOULD BE WORNTED. (HE GOES INTO THE	HOUSE	WITH SOFT STEPS). LADY CICELY SITS DOWN ON THE BENCH
POSN PREFACE(398)	DEFERENCE TO THE NEAR RELATIONS OF OUR REIGNING	HOUSE	WITH THAT REALM. HE WOULD CERTAINLY MAKE IT AN
CAPT I (225)	TO ASK, BIKOUROS. (HE GOES CHEERFULLY INTO THE	HOUSE	WITH THE KROOBOYS). /DRINKWATER/ JIST THORT EED TRAH
DOCT PREFACE(14)	OPERATING SURGEONS, WHO ARE USUALLY OUT OF THE	HOUSE	WITH THEIR FEE IN THEIR POCKETS BEFORE THE PATIENT HAS
BUOY III (37)	CHARACTERS. BUT NOBODY COULD LIVE IN THE SAME	HOUSE	WITH THEIR MOTHER. /SIR F./ (VERY GRAVELY) EXCUSE ME.
ARMS II SD(26)	TIED OVER HER THICK BLACK HAIR, COMES FROM THE	HOUSE	WITH TURKISH SLIPPERS ON HER BARE FEET, LOOKING
CAPT I SD(224)	TURNS TO GO, A MOORISH PORTER COMES FROM THE	HOUSE	WITH TWO KROOBOYS. /THE PORTER/ (AT THE DOOR,
MRS III (227)	VIVVUMS, RING THE GATE BELL. (HE GOES INTO THE	HOUSE	WITH UNRUFFLED SUAVITY). /CROFTS/ (WATCHING HIM WITH
APPL II (276)	BUT I AM HEARTBROKEN AT YOUR NOT COMING INTO THE	HOUSE	WITH US TO KEEP OLD ENGLAND IN FRONT AND LEAD A NEW
APPL INTRLUD(246)	NO MAN COULD CALL HIS SOUL HIS OWN IN THE SAME	HOUSE	WITH YOU, AND YET THAT MAN WAS UTTERLY INFATUATED WITH
POSN (441)	I KNOW THE ROAD HE TOOK; AND I'LL ASK AT EVERY	HOUSE	WITHIN SIGHT OF IT FOR A MILE OUT. COME, BOYS.
GETT (269)	COUNTRY TELLS ME THAT I CANT HAVE A CHILD IN MY	HOUSE	WITHOUT A MAN IN IT TOO; SO I TELL THE COUNTRY THAT IT
DOCT PREFACE(28)	IN A SURGICALLY DIRTY ROOM IN A SURGICALLY DIRTY	HOUSE	WITHOUT ANY ASSISTANCE, AND THAT THE MATERIALS FOR IT
LIED (191)	IN HAND; BID HIM FAREWELL; AND WALK OUT OF THE	HOUSE	WITHOUT CONCEALMENT OR SUBTERFUGE, FREELY AND
HART III (140)	STRANGELY HAPPY HOUSE, THIS AGONIZING HOUSE, THIS	HOUSE	WITHOUT FOUNDATIONS. I SHALL CALL IT HEARTBREAK HOUSE.
SHAK (142)	STRANGELY HAPPY HOUSE, THIS AGONIZING HOUSE, THIS	HOUSE	WITHOUT FOUNDATIONS. I SHALL CALL IT HEARTBREAK
2TRU PREFACE(5)	MAN WITH MONEY IN HIS POCKET COULD PASS A PUBLIC	HOUSE	WITHOUT GOING IN FOR A DRINK. THE OLD SOLDIER AND THE
2TRU PREFACE(5)	HEAR OF THE MULTIMILLIONAIRE PASSING THE PUBLIC	HOUSE	WITHOUT GOING IN AND DRINKING HIMSELF SILLY; AND WE
DEVL I (20)	ME THAT BEFORE? CHILDREN SUFFER ENOUGH IN THIS	HOUSE	WITHOUT-- (HE HURRIES REMORSEFULLY TO ESSIE). COME,
GLIM (183)	DEEPENS. /FERRUCCIO/ DOES YOUR FATHER DO THE	HOUSE	WORK WITH A GREAT GIRL LIKE YOU IDLING ABOUT?
ROCK I (199)	IT OUT. A LAUGH IN THE WRONG PLACE IN THE CHURCH	HOUSE	WOULD BE THE VERY DEVIL. WHERE DID YOU GET THAT
ARMS II (24)	WOULD GIVE YOU ANOTHER SITUATION? WHO IN THIS	HOUSE	WOULD DARE BE SEEN SPEAKING TO YOU EVER AGAIN? HOW
HART PREFACE(5)	MR ARNOLD BENNETT, AND MR JOHN GALSWORTHY, THE	HOUSE	WOULD HAVE BEEN OUT OF THE MOVEMENT. YOU WOULD FIND
ROCK I (200)	/SIR ARTHUR/ YES YES YES, OF COURSE. I WAS IN THE	HOUSE	YESTERDAY UNTIL THREE IN THE MORNING; AND MY BRAINS
BUOY IV (48)	FROM PANAMA. /OLD BILL/ GOOD. HAS SHE LEFT THE	HOUSE	YET? /NATIVE/ NOT WITHOUT ME. I DRIVE HER CAR. /OLD
KING I (174)	TO MR NEWTON, THE EMINENT PHILOSOPHER, IN WHOSE	HOUSE	YOU ARE AN UNINVITED GUEST. /BARBARA/ A PRETTY HOUSE.
ARMS I (18)	TO OUR HOSPITALITY. YOU DO NOT YET KNOW IN WHOSE	HOUSE	YOU ARE. I AM A PETKOFF. /THE MAN/ A PET WHAT?
JITT II (32)	WAS THAT AS YOU WERE SO MUCH IN AND OUT OF HIS	HOUSE	YOU MUST HAVE MET HER ONE TIME OR ANOTHER IF SHE WAS
ARMS III (50)	DO INDEED. BUT THEY DONT KNOW THAT IT WAS IN THIS	HOUSE	YOU TOOK REFUGE. IF SERGIUS KNEW, HE WOULD CHALLENGE
KING I (200)	KINDS OF FISH. /MRS BASHAM/ NO, SIR: IN THIS	HOUSE	YOU WILL HAVE TO BE CONTENT WITH A PROTESTANT DINNER.
FOUN (222)	A FAMILY MEANS RELATIONS. YOU CANT CALL YOUR	HOUSE	YOUR OWN. THE BROTHERS BORROW MONEY. THE SISTERS COME
BULL III SD(117)	EN BLOC. THE BACKGROUND TO THIS BREAKFAST IS THE	HOUSE	, A SMALL WHITE SLATED BUILDING, ACCESSIBLE BY A
PLES PREFACE(R10)	TOUR THROUGH THE PROVINCES WITH A DOLL'S	HOUSE	, ADDED CANDIDA TO ITS REPERTORY, TO THE GREAT
HART PREFACE(9)	BUT BEING AN IDLE HOUSE IT WAS A HYPOCHONDRIACAL	HOUSE	, ALWAYS RUNNING AFTER CURES. IT WOULD STOP EATING
GETT PREFACE(227)	CONSIDERATELY AT HOME AS ON A VISIT IN A STRANGE	HOUSE	, AND AS FRANKLY, KINDLY, AND EASILY IN A STRANGE
MILL IV (203)	HER, NO. WELL, BE IT SO. I SHALL SIT IN MY LONELY	HOUSE	, AND BE MYSELF, AND PILE UP MILLIONS UNTIL I FIND A
MTH1 II (24)	MERE CONVENIENCE OF ADAM: I WHO SPIN AND KEEP THE	HOUSE	, AND BEAR AND REAR CHILDREN, AND AM A WOMAN AND NOT A
MIS. PREFACE(56)	OF CHILDREN MAKING NOISE AND MISCHIEF IN THE	HOUSE	, AND BY THE DENIAL TO CHILDREN OF THE ELEMENTARY
SIM I SD(42)	HER ARM ROUND HIM). LADY FARWATERS COMES FROM THE	HOUSE	, AND PAUSES AT THE TOP OF THE STEPS TO TAKE IN WHAT
FOUN (221)	ONE OF MY FRIENDS. YOU CAN THEN INVITE ME TO YOUR	HOUSE	, AND PUT ON YOUR BEST COMPANY MANNERS FOR MY BENEFIT.
ARMS II SD(23)	WASHING SPREAD OUT TO DRY. A PATH RUNS BY THE	HOUSE	, AND RISES BY TWO STEPS AT THE CORNER, WHERE IT TURNS
FANY EPILOG (330)	FATHER WHEN HE'S GOING TO PUT HER OUT OF THE	HOUSE	, AND SAYS SHE'LL GO TOO. THEN THERES THE COMIC
GETT (269)	ABOUT MY BELONGINGS. I LIKE TO HAVE MY OWN	HOUSE	, AND TO HAVE IT TO MYSELF. I HAVE A VERY KEEN SENSE
MIS. (114)	GOVERNESS DID IT. I YELLED FIT TO BRING DOWN THE	HOUSE	, AND WENT INTO CONVULSIONS AND BRAIN FEVER AND THAT
DOCT PREFACE(69)	JELLY TO DRUNKARDS; BEEFSTEAKS AND STOUT IN ONE	HOUSE	, AND " URIC ACID FREE" VEGETARIAN DIET OVER THE WAY;
ARMS II (41)	TO SELECT! (LOUKA APPEARS AT THE DOOR OF THE	HOUSE	, ANNOUNCING CAPTAIN BLUNTSCHLI. SHE STANDS ASIDE AT
BULL IV (157)	/CORNELIUS/ I WISH HE'D NEVER SET FOOT IN MY	HOUSE	, BAD LUCK TO HIS FAT FACE! D'YE THINK HE'D LEND ME
O'FL (217)	HANDS WITH ME. COULD I TURN ON THE MAN IN HIS OWN	HOUSE	, BEFORE HIS OWN WIFE, WITH HIS MONEY IN MY POCKET AND
HART I (45)	DAUGHTER'S INVITATIONS? THIS IS A PRETTY SORT OF	HOUSE	, BY HEAVENS! A YOUNG AND ATTRACTIVE LADY IS INVITED
SUPR IV (147)	A FAIR OFFER. LET HIM PICK OUT THE MOST HISTORIC	HOUSE	, CASTLE, OR ABBEY THAT ENGLAND CONTAINS. THE VERY DAY
ARMS II SD(23)	THERE ARE FRUIT BUSHES ALONG THE PALING AND	HOUSE	, COVERED WITH WASHING SPREAD OUT TO DRY. A PATH RUNS
SIM II (75)	SPEAKING IN EMERGENCY MEETING AT THE MANSION	HOUSE	, DECLARES THAT REPORTS OF UTTERANCES BY ANGELS ARE
NEVR I (200)	YES. /THE YOUNG LADY/ YOU DONT OWN THE WHOLE	HOUSE	, DO YOU? /THE DENTIST/ NO. /THE YOUNG LADY/ I
SUPR II (50)	ON THE GRAVEL. OCTAVIUS IS COMING FROM THE	HOUSE	, DRESSED FOR MOTORING, BUT WITHOUT HIS OVERCOAT).
DEST (188)	TO JEST ABOUT SUCH THINGS. I CANNOT HAVE IT IN MY	HOUSE	, EXCELLENCY. /LIEUTENANT/ YES, DROP IT. YOURE MY
GETT (266)	SHE'S HARDLY A RESPONSIBLE HUMAN BEING OUT OF HER	HOUSE	, EXCEPT WHEN SHE'S MARKETING. /MRS BRIDGENORTH/ DOES
SIM I SD(41)	YOU. COME, PRA. SHE GOES UP THE STEPS INTO THE	HOUSE	, FOLLOWED BY PRA. THE CLERGYMAN, LEFT WITH THE FOUR
CAPT I (238)	CUTS HIM SHORT. HE FLIES FOR HIS LIFE INTO THE	HOUSE	, FOLLOWED BY THE ITALIAN). /BRASSBOUND/ YOUR LADYSHIP
BULL PREFACE(53)	COALS AND BLANKETS AND EMPLOYMENT IN COUNTRY	HOUSE	, GARDEN AND STABLE, OR AS BEATERS, HUNTSMEN AND THE
HART PREFACE(28)	OUR ARMADA IS IMPOTENT, IN THE BLOCKADER'S	HOUSE	, HE HAS ASSURED US, THERE ARE MANY MANSIONS; BUT I AM
HART I (65)	HER THOUGHTFULLY) THERES SOMETHING ODD ABOUT THIS	HOUSE	, HESIONE, AND EVEN ABOUT YOU. I DONT KNOW WHY I'M
GETT PREFACE(187)	WHERE THEY ARE PUBLICLY CLASSED WITH A MAN'S	HOUSE	, HIS OX, AND HIS ASS, AS HIS PURCHASED CHATTELS. IN
DOCT PREFACE(16)	BEFORE HE CAN AFFORD EVEN TO INSURE HIS LIFE. HIS	HOUSE	, HIS SERVANTS, AND HIS EQUIPAGE (OR AUTOPAGE) MUST
ARMS III (56)	TO OURSELVES; AND I SHALL BE MASTER IN MY OWN	HOUSE	, I PROMISE YOU. (HE THROWS THE LOGS DOWN AND KNEELS
GETT (317)	CONTRACT. I'LL NOT HAVE IT SO. IF I'M TO KEEP THE	HOUSE	, I SHALL EXPECT CECIL TO PAY ME AT LEAST AS WELL AS
GETT (274)	JUST TELLING ALICE, SIR, THAT IF YOU ENTERED THIS	HOUSE	, I SHOULD LEAVE IT. /REGINALD/ WELL, DONT LET ME
MRS IV (251)	WAS IT BUT STEALING? I'D BRING YOU UP IN MY OWN	HOUSE	, I WOULD. /VIVIE/ (QUIETLY) IN ONE OF YOUR OWN
MILL I (151)	PRAY? /PATRICIA/ WELL, I AM THE ANGEL IN THE	HOUSE	, IF YOU FOLLOW ME. /ALASTAIR/ (BLUBBERING) YOU ARE,
DOCT I SD(82)	WITH THE GASALIER AND THE VENETIAN BLINDS. THE	HOUSE	, IN FACT, WAS SO WELL FURNISHED IN THE MIDDLE OF THE
HART PREFACE(11)	LOVE IF THEY HAD NEVER READ ABOUT IT. HEARTBREAK	HOUSE	, IN SHORT, DID NOT KNOW HOW TO LIVE, AT WHICH POINT
GETT PREFACE(197)	IS IMPOSSIBLE. TWO CHILDREN MAKE A DOLL'S	HOUSE	, IN WHICH BOTH PARENTS AND CHILDREN BECOME MORBID IF
CAPT I SD(225)	HAND, COMES DOWN THE SIDE OF THE GARDEN NEXT THE	HOUSE	, INSTINCTIVELY MAINTAINING A DISTANCE BETWEEN HIMSELF
GETT (273)	HE MUSTNT. YOU TELL HIM THAT IF HE ENTERS THIS	HOUSE	, I'LL LEAVE IT; AND SO WILL EVERY DECENT MAN AND
UNPL PREFACE(R9)	WORLD CAN ATTRACT TO ITS EXHIBITIONS, ITS OPERA	HOUSE	, ITS CONCERTS AND ITS THEATRES. THE CLASSES EAGERLY
PHIL I (85)	ALREADY. CHARTERIS IS QUITE AT HOME IN OUR	HOUSE	, JO. /CUTHBERTSON/ I BEG BOTH YOUR PARDONS. HE'S
HART III (142)	I SHALL TAKE PARTICULAR CARE TO KEEP OUT OF YOUR	HOUSE	, LADY UTTERWORD. /LADY UTTERWORD/ YOU WILL BE QUITE
SIM II SD(82)	TIL IVE GONE. SHE SCUTTLES UP THE STEPS INTO THE	HOUSE	, LEAVING PROLA AND PRA ALONE TOGETHER. /PRA/ TELL ME
O'FL (220)	IF I LEAVE IT ON MY STOMACH. (SHE GOES INTO THE	HOUSE	, LEAVING THE TWO YOUNG PEOPLE ALONE TOGETHER).
APPL PREFACE(195)	THEN, WITH THE WAR ON OUR HANDS, THE CLEARING	HOUSE	, LIKE THE THAMES PIER, REMAINS ON PAPER; AND GATTIE
FOUN (215)	/THE LORD CHANCELLOR/ THAT REFERS TO MY PRIVATE	HOUSE	, MADAM. I DONT KEEP FOOD HERE. /MERCER/ I HAVE A
HART III (147)	/ELLIE/ (TENSE WITH EXCITEMENT) SET FIRE TO THE	HOUSE	, MARCUS. /MRS HUSHABYE/ MY HOUSE! NO. /HECTOR/ I
SUPR II (49)	GET OVER THAT ALL RIGHT. IF YOURE GOING UP TO THE	HOUSE	, MAY I ASK HOW LONG YOURE GOIN TO STAY? BECAUSE IF
GETT (303)	REGINALD. HE SHOULD HAVE KICKED YOU OUT OF THE	HOUSE	, MR HOTCHKISS. /REGINALD/ (RISING) HOW COULD I KICK
ROCK I (197)	TO BRING PROMINENT OFFENDERS TO THE BAR OF THE	HOUSE	, NO MATTER WHAT THEIR POSITION IS. /BASHAM/ ARTHUR:
BUOY III (35)	TO YOU, JULIA. FOR MY HOME IS HERE, IN DADDY'S	HOUSE	, NOT IN YOURS. DADDY IS GROWING OLD; AND OLD MEN
MIS. (198)	TO LEAVE THE ROOM. IVE GOT TO OBEY: IT'S HIS	HOUSE	, NOT MINE. /TARLETON/ WHO PAYS FOR IT? GO AND
HART PREFACE(3)	FOUR FASCINATING DRAMATIC STUDIES OF HEARTBREAK	HOUSE	, OF WHICH THREE, THE CHERRY ORCHARD, UNCLE VANYA, AND
HART III SD(139)	RICHLY COLORED SILK DRESSING-GOWN, COMES FROM THE	HOUSE	, ON LADY UTTERWORD'S SIDE. /MRS HUSHABYE/ OH! HERE
ROCK II (282)	WELL, WHETHER IT'S GETTING A BIG BILL THROUGH THE	HOUSE	, OR CARRYING A BIG MEETING OFF ITS FEET, OR WINNING A
POSN PREFACE(409)	BY ALLOWING HIS THEATRE TO BECOME A DISORDERLY	HOUSE	, OR FAILING TO PROVIDE A BUILDING WHICH COMPLIES WITH
GETT (316)	/LESBIA/ YES: I MUST HAVE MY OWN SEPARATE	HOUSE	, OR MY OWN SEPARATE PART OF A HOUSE. BOXER SMOKES: I
PPP (199)	A LIFETIME. FORMERLY IT WAS GEORGE'S. I KEPT HIS	HOUSE	, OR RATHER, HIS LODGINGS. I MENDED HIS CLOTHES. I
KING I (188)	FURY AND FACING HIM MENACINGLY) WILL YOU LEAVE MY	HOUSE	, OR SHALL I THROW YOU OUT THROUGH THE WINDOW?
MRS III SD(220)	READING THE STANDARD. HIS FATHER COMES FROM THE	HOUSE	, RED-EYED AND SHIVERY, AND MEETS FRANK'S EYE WITH
PHIL II (128)	TEA WITH HIM; AND IF MY DAUGHTER HAS GONE TO HIS	HOUSE	, SHE IS SIMPLY TAKING ADVANTAGE OF HIS INVITATION TO
NEVR IV (305)	FROM TIME TO TIME. I NEVER WAS MASTER IN MY OWN	HOUSE	, SIR: MY WIFE WAS LIKE YOUR YOUNG LADY: SHE WAS OF A

DOCT III (148)	TO IT, AS HE SAT FOR IT. MAY I SEND IT TO YOUR	HOUSE	, SIR PATRICK, FOR TWELVE GUINEAS? /SIR PATRICK/
DEVL III (66)	I DID, SIR. I FOUND HIM IN THE MINISTER'S	HOUSE	, SITTING AT TEA WITH THE LADY WITH HIS COAT OFF,
DEVL I SD(24)	HAWKINS. MRS DUDGEON, NOW AN INTRUDER IN HER OWN	HOUSE	, STANDS INERT, CRUSHED BY THE WEIGHT OF THE LAW ON
CAPT NOTES (300)	AND TALES HE HAS SINCE TOSSED TO US; BUT THE	HOUSE	, STRONG IN STUPIDITY, DID NOT UNDERSTAND HIM UNTIL IN
APPL PREFACE(187)	WHILST THE POSTMAN DELIVERS THE LETTERS AT THE	HOUSE	, TAKES THE CHRISTMAS BOXES, AND GETS THE WHOLE CREDIT
HART II (106)	ARE YOU FRIGHTENED, ALF? /MANGAN/ NO. IT AINT MY	HOUSE	, THANK GOD. /MRS HUSHABYE/ IF THEY CATCH A BURGLAR,
JITT III (57)	CHANCE OF OUR BEING ABLE TO MOVE INTO A BETTER	HOUSE	, THE FURNITURE AND PICTURES, IN EVERYTHING. THEN HE
BUOY III (37)	SPEND THE WHOLE DAY APART, THE WOMAN IN THE	HOUSE	, THE MAN IN THE OFFICE OR STUDY OR WORKSHOP. AND
MIS. SD(109)	THE HAT STAND, LEADING TO THE INTERIOR OF THE	HOUSE	, THE OTHER ON THE OPPOSITE SIDE AND AT THE OTHER END,
GETT PREFACE(201)	ALL: THEY ONLY GET ACCUSTOMED TO HAVING THE SAME	HOUSE	, THE SAME CHILDREN, AND THE SAME INCOME, WHICH IS
WIDO III (52)	IT OPEN) YOU CAN TAKE YOUR INDEPENDENCE OUT OF MY	HOUSE	, THEN. I WONT HAVE IT HERE. /LICKCHEESE/ (
HART III (140)	YES: THIS SILLY HOUSE, THIS STRANGELY HAPPY	HOUSE	, THIS AGONIZING HOUSE, THIS HOUSE WITHOUT
SHAK (142)	" YES: THIS SILLY HOUSE, THIS STRANGELY HAPPY	HOUSE	, THIS AGONIZING HOUSE, THIS HOUSE WITHOUT
LIED (191)	FEET TO TREAD. LET US GO OUT TOGETHER TO OUR OWN	HOUSE	, THIS EVENING, WITHOUT CONCEALMENT AND WITHOUT SHAME.
HART III (140)	HOUSE, THIS STRANGELY HAPPY HOUSE, THIS AGONIZING	HOUSE	, THIS HOUSE WITHOUT FOUNDATIONS. I SHALL CALL IT
SHAK (142)	HOUSE, THIS STRANGELY HAPPY HOUSE, THIS AGONIZING	HOUSE	, THIS HOUSE WITHOUT FOUNDATIONS. I SHALL CALL IT
HART I (48)	ON THE SOFA) I KNOW WHAT YOU MUST FEEL. OH, THIS	HOUSE	, THIS HOUSE! I COME BACK TO IT AFTER TWENTY-THREE
HART III (140)	IN THE CITY. /ELLIE/ (MUSICALLY) YES: THIS SILLY	HOUSE	, THIS STRANGELY HAPPY HOUSE, THIS AGONIZING HOUSE,
SHAK (142)	SHE MADE HER BED. /THE VIRGIN/ " YES: THIS SILLY	HOUSE	, THIS STRANGELY HAPPY HOUSE, THIS AGONIZING HOUSE,
KING I (218)	COURTS. HERE IS PASTOR FOX, A KING IN HIS MEETING	HOUSE	, THOUGH HIS MEETINGS ARE AGAINST THE LAW. HERE IS MR
MIS. SD(109)	SPRINGS FROM A BRIDGELIKE ARCH IN THE WALL OF THE	HOUSE	, THROUGH WHICH ONE COMES INTO A BIG HALL WITH TILED
BULL PREFACE(6)	AND OF THE CONFESSIONAL, AND OF THE PRIEST IN THE	HOUSE	, TO SEE HOW WEAK THESE FORCES ARE IN THE FACE OF
FANY II (289)	LIKE THIS. IF YOURE GOING TO TURN ME OUT OF THE	HOUSE	, TURN ME OUT: THE SOONER I GO THE BETTER. /DUVALLET/
ARMS II SD(23)	A CIGARET, IS STANDING BETWEEN THE TABLE AND THE	HOUSE	, TURNING HER BACK WITH ANGRY DISDAIN ON A MAN SERVANT
LION EPILOG (152)	IN BERLIN, THE CROWN PRINCE ROSE AND LEFT THE	HOUSE	, UNABLE TO ENDURE THE (I HOPE) VERY CLEAR AND FAIR
ROCK I (224)	AND MODERATE IN COUNSEL. BUT HERE, IN THIS CHURCH	HOUSE	, UNDER THE BANNER OF THE PRINCE OF PEACE, WE KNOW
BULL PREFACE(59)	HAD COME IN THE NIGHT AND BURIED IT IN HIS	HOUSE	, WHERE HIS MOTHER SAT ON IT, LIKE RACHEL ON LABAN'S
MIS. (179)	HINDHEAD, AND EFFECTED AN UNLAWFUL ENTRY INTO HIS	HOUSE	, WHERE I SECRETED MYSELF IN A PORTABLE TURKISH BATH--
FANY PROLOG (266)	VERY SHOCKINGLY. YOU INVITE ME TO THIS CHARMING	HOUSE	, WHERE I'M ABOUT TO ENJOY A CHARMING DINNER. AND JUST
HART III (130)	HECTOR. WHY DO YOU ASK HEAVEN TO DESTROY THIS	HOUSE	, WHICH COULD BE MADE QUITE COMFORTABLE IF HESIONE HAD
SUPR II SD(48)	OF TREES ROUND WHICH THE DRIVE SWEEPS TO THE	HOUSE	, WHICH IS PARTLY VISIBLE THROUGH THEM: INDEED TANNER,
ARMS II (32)	IN AN OLD COAT BELONGING TO THE MASTER OF THE	HOUSE	, WHO WAS AWAY AT THE WAR. /RAINA/ (RISING WITH
HART PREFACE(9)	FROM THE UNIVERSE." HYPOCHONDRIA. NOW HEARTBREAK	HOUSE	, WITH BUTLER AND BERGSON AND SCOTT HALDANE ALONGSIDE
HART III (131)	NEEDS TO MAKE IT A SENSIBLE, HEALTHY, PLEASANT	HOUSE	, WITH GOOD APPETITES AND SOUND SLEEP IN IT, IS
BULL PREFACE(54)	HIS FAMILY, HE WAS HANGED IN FULL VIEW OF HIS OWN	HOUSE	, WITH HIS WIVES AND CHILDREN AND GRANDCHILDREN
CLEO NOTES (204)	DID IN THE SAME TRADE, AND THAT HIS SUBURBAN	HOUSE	, WITH ITS BATH, ITS COTTAGE PIANO, ITS DRAWING ROOM
MRS PREFACE(154)	BE A FAR MORE TERRIBLE PLACE THAN MRS WARREN'S	HOUSE	, YET HELL IS STILL MORE DREADFUL. NOWADAYS THEY NO.
KING I (221)	YOU TO YOUR DINNER AT ONCE. /KNELLER/ IN THIS	HOUSE	, YOU SAID, MR NEWTON COMES FIRST. BUT YOU TAKE GOOD
FANY PROLOG (257)	COUNT/ MY STUDY IS AVAILABLE. AN OLD-FASHIONED	HOUSE	, YOU UNDERSTAND. WONT YOU SIT DOWN, MR SAVOYARD?
HART III (142)	DISTINGUISHED SOCIETY, MR DUNN. IF YOU WERE IN MY	HOUSE	, YOU WOULD FEEL EMBARRASSED. /MAZZINI/ I SHALL TAKE
LIED (200)	STAND HERE AND LET YOU INSULT MY WIFE IN HER OWN	HOUSE	, YOURE MISTAKEN. /HE/ (VERY UNCOMFORTABLE WITH HIS
HART I (48)	I KNOW WHAT YOU MUST FEEL, OH, THIS HOUSE, THIS	HOUSE	! I COME BACK TO IT AFTER TWENTY-THREE YEARS; AND IT
CAPT I (220)	SHOULD COME TO MOGADOR, OF ALL PLACES; AND TO MY	HOUSE	! I ONCE MET SIR HOWRRD HALLAM, YEARS AGO.
HART III (147)	SET FIRE TO THE HOUSE, MARCUS. /MRS HUSHABYE/ MY	HOUSE	! NO. /HECTOR/ I THOUGHT OF THAT; BUT IT WOULD NOT BE
HART III (130)	NUMSKULL SAID THERE WAS SOMETHING WRONG WITH MY	HOUSE	! /LADY UTTERWORD/ I SAID HASTINGS SAID IT; AND HE IS
ROCK I (233)	RUSHING AFTER HIM) NO, NO, SIR ARTHUR: THE CHURCH	HOUSE	! THE CHURCH HOUSE! YOUVE FORGOTTEN THAT YOU HAVE TO
HART I (49)	LOOKING FORWARD TO IT. AND NOW THE STATE OF THE	HOUSE	! THE WAY I'M RECEIVED! THE CASUAL IMPUDENCE OF THAT
HART I (82)	(RAISING A STRANGE WAIL IN THE DARKNESS) WHAT A	HOUSE	! WHAT A DAUGHTER! /MRS HUSHABYE/ (RAVING) WHAT A
ROCK I (233)	NO, NO, SIR ARTHUR: THE CHURCH HOUSE! THE CHURCH	HOUSE	! YOUVE FORGOTTEN THAT YOU HAVE TO LUNCH AT (HER

HOUSEBREAKER

DOCT PREFACE(3)	WE TAKE GOOD CARE NOT TO MAKE THE HANGMAN AND THE	HOUSEBREAKER	THE JUDGES OF THAT. IF WE DID, NO MAN'S NECK

HOUSEBREAKING

ROCK II (250)	READ THE HIDEOUS STORY OF THIS MONSTROUS ORGY OF	HOUSEBREAKING	AND MURDER, AND SWORN TO OURSELVES THAT NEVER,
POSN PREFACE(389)	FAR THAT A JUDGE CANNOT INFLICT THE PENALTY FOR	HOUSEBREAKING	ON A BURGLAR WHO CAN PROVE THAT HE FOUND THE

HOUSED

CYMB V (144)	AT YOUR EARNEST SUIT YOUR CHEST WAS SAFELY	HOUSED	IN MY CHAMBER; BUT WHERE WERE YOU? /IACHIMO/ I? I
BARB III (338)	MEAN? /UNDERSHAFT/ I FED YOU AND CLOTHED YOU AND	HOUSED	YOU. I TOOK CARE THAT YOU SHOULD HAVE MONEY ENOUGH TO
BARB III (339)	HYPOCRITE, BARBARA. HE WILL BE BETTER FED, BETTER	HOUSED	, BETTER CLOTHED, BETTER BEHAVED; AND HIS CHILDREN
ROCK PREFACE(167)	OWN TO DO WHAT I LIKE WITH," ARE BETTER FED AND	HOUSED	, NICER, AND MUCH MORE LEISURED, AND CONSEQUENTLY

HOUSEFUL

PYGM IV (266)	(VERY SULKY) YOU MAY TAKE THE WHOLE DAMNED	HOUSEFUL	IF YOU LIKE. EXCEPT THE JEWELS. THEYRE HIRED. WILL

HOUSEHOLD

GETT SD(295)	SHE IS THE TYPICAL SPOILT CHILD OF A CLERICAL	HOUSEHOLD	: ALMOST AS TERRIBLE A PRODUCT AS THE TYPICAL
GETT SD(295)	PRODUCT AS THE TYPICAL SPOILT CHILD OF A BOHEMIAN	HOUSEHOLD	: THAT IS, ALL HER CHILDISH AFFECTATIONS OF
BARB III (312)	A NIGHT OF IT WITH THE NOMINAL HEAD OF THIS	HOUSEHOLD	: THAT IS ALL. /LADY BRITOMART/ ANDREW MADE YOU
CLEO II (132)	AM I THEN THE MISTRESS OF THE QUEEN'S	HOUSEHOLD	? /CLEOPATRA/ (SHARPLY) NO: I AM THE MISTRESS OF
NEVR II (241)	MRS CLANDON) DOES NOBODY ASK A BLESSING IN THIS	HOUSEHOLD	? /PHILIP/ (INTERPOSING SMARTLY) LET US FIRST
PYGM EPILOG (299)	SCUTCHEON BY OPENING A SHOP, HE FOUND THE LITTLE	HOUSEHOLD	ALREADY CONVULSED BY A PRIOR ANNOUNCEMENT FROM
SUPR IV (172)	OF AN UNKNOWN FUTURE, FOR THE CARES OF A	HOUSEHOLD	AND A FAMILY, I BEG THAT NO MAN MAY SEIZE THE
POSN PREFACE(403)	WHO IS AT LEAST AN OFFICIAL OF THE KING'S	HOUSEHOLD	AND A NOMINEE OF THE GOVERNMENT, THE LORD
JOAN PREFACE(10)	CHALLENGED ANY WOMAN TO COMPETE WITH HER IN THE	HOUSEHOLD	ARTS OF THE MISTRESSES OF WELL FURNISHED HOUSES.
GETT PREFACE(253)	TO BE SAID FOR THE POLYGYNOUS OR POLYANDROUS	HOUSEHOLD	AS A SCHOOL FOR CHILDREN: CHILDREN REALLY DO
BULL III (117)	RENTS AND KEEPS HIS BOOKS AND CASH, KNOWN IN THE	HOUSEHOLD	AS " THE OFFICE." THIS CHAIR, LIKE THE TWO
APPL INTRLUD(253)	HUSBAND IN A MODEL HOUSEHOLD! AND WHEN THE MODEL	HOUSEHOLD	BECOMES A BORE, I AM THE DIVERSION. /MAGNUS/ WELL,
GETT PREFACE(231)	REALLY OF THREE EXCEPT IN THE SENSE THAT EVERY	HOUSEHOLD	BECOMES A HOUSEHOLD OF THREE WHEN A CHILD IS BORN,
MILL PREFACE(109)	YOU MAY FIND A MAITRESSE FEMME WHO RULES IN THE	HOUSEHOLD	BY A SORT OF DIVINE RIGHT. SHE MAY RULE AMIABLY BY
SUPR III (121)	WELL, WHAT PLACE HAVE SQUALLING BABIES AND	HOUSEHOLD	CARES IN THIS EXQUISITE PARADISE OF THE SENSES AND
GETT PREFACE(224)	OF THE TRUTH LIES BOTH WAYS. I ALSO KNOW OF A	HOUSEHOLD	CONSISTING OF THREE FAMILIES, A HAVING MARRIED
JITT III (53)	EVEN IF HALF OF IT WAS BEING HIS SLAVE AND HIS	HOUSEHOLD	DRUDGE. ALL THE SAME, I CANT SPEND MY WHOLE LIFE
HART I (75)	NO CHILD BROUGHT UP IN A STRICT PURITAN	HOUSEHOLD	EVER SUFFERED FROM PURITANISM AS I SUFFERED FROM
ROCK I (233)	JUST TURN KARL MARX INSIDE-OUT FOR THEM. (THE	HOUSEHOLD	GONG SOUNDS). LUNCH! COME ON: THAT WOMAN'S GIVEN
HART PREFACE(33)	IN THE ANECDOTE WHEN THE CART CONTAINING ALL HIS	HOUSEHOLD	GOODS LOST ITS TAILBOARD AT THE TOP OF THE HILL
3PLA PREFACE(R27)	BY CHARLES DICKENS: IN HIS PICTURE OF THE CLENNAM	HOUSEHOLD	IN LITTLE DORRIT: MRS DUDGEON BEING A REPLICA OF
PHIL II (120)	WITH THE PLEASURE OF RESTORING HAPPINESS TO THE	HOUSEHOLD	IN WHICH THE BEST HOPES OF YOUR LIFE ARE CENTRED
GETT PREFACE(253)	MOST POWERFUL ARGUMENTS FOR DIVORCE. AN UNHAPPY	HOUSEHOLD	IS A BAD NURSERY. THERE IS SOMETHING TO BE SAID
NEVR I (203)	AN AUTHORESS OF GREAT REPUTE-- IN MADEIRA. NO	HOUSEHOLD	IS COMPLETE WITHOUT HER WORKS. WE CAME TO ENGLAND
DOCT PREFACE(5)	CALL HIM IN WHEN THE SAME SYMPTOMS APPEAR IN HIS	HOUSEHOLD	IS HELD NOT TO HAVE DONE HIS UTMOST DUTY TO THE
GETT PREFACE(233)	WHAT AN HONORABLE AND SENSIBLE MAN DOES WHEN HIS	HOUSEHOLD	IS INVADED IS WHAT THE REVEREND JAMES MAVOR MORELL
MIS PREFACE(16)	INFLUENCE AND CARE ARE OFTEN DOMINANT IN THE	HOUSEHOLD	. AFFECTION, AS DISTINGUISHED FROM SIMPLE
MRS PREFACE(162)	HALLMARKED BY IT WITH THE APPROVAL OF THE ROYAL	HOUSEHOLD	. BUT AS SUCH STORIES CANNOT BE MADE PUBLIC
CLEO II (132)	(SHARPLY) NO: I AM THE MISTRESS OF THE QUEEN'S	HOUSEHOLD	. GO AND DO AS YOU ARE TOLD, OR I WILL HAVE YOU
DEVL I SD(16)	WIFE, BOTH FREE FROM THE CARES OF THE WILLIAM	HOUSEHOLD	. HAWKINS AT ONCE GOES BRISKLY TO THE TABLE AND
HART PREFACE(34)	CHARACTER GIVEN ME BY THE CHIEF OFFICER OF ITS	HOUSEHOLD	. HOWBEIT, THE FACT THAT MY PLAYS EFFECTED A
6CAL (104)	I WELL SEE WHO WEARS THE BREECHES IN THIS ROYAL	HOUSEHOLD	. I AM NOT SKILLED IN DEALING WITH FINE HANDSOME
CAND III (144)	EUGENE, TO SEE THE PICTURES OF THE HERO OF THAT	HOUSEHOLD	. JAMES AS A BABY! THE MOST WONDERFUL OF ALL
GENV I (45)	SUBVERSIVE KIND. THEY HAVE PENETRATED TO MY OWN	HOUSEHOLD	. MY WIFE IS A BUSY PROFESSIONAL WOMAN, AND MY
GETT (302)	TO PRAY THAT IT MIGHT NOT HAPPEN IN MY OWN	HOUSEHOLD	. PERHAPS IT WAS A PRESENTIMENT THAT IT MIGHT
CLEO III (145)	OF FTATATEETA, THE MISTRESS OF THE QUEEN'S	HOUSEHOLD	. /APOLLODORUS/ MY FRIEND: THIS IS A GREAT LADY,
CLEO III (146)	I AM FTATATEETA, THE MISTRESS OF THE QUEEN'S	HOUSEHOLD	. /CENTURION/ KEEP YOUR HANDS OFF OUR MEN,
CLEO III (147)	/APOLLODORUS/ OBEY THE MISTRESS OF THE QUEEN'S	HOUSEHOLD	. /FTATATEETA/ (IMPATIENTLY, AS THE PORTERS STOOP
MIS. PREFACE(6)	THEIR CHILDREN RUTHLESSLY TO MAKE MONEY FOR THE	HOUSEHOLD	. SUCH LEGISLATION HAS ALWAYS BEEN FURIOUSLY

DOCT PREFACE(45)	DEPENDENT ON IT WHEN DEATH THREATENS THE	HOUSEHOLD	. THAT DISTINCTION IS THE LINE THAT SEPARATES THE
FANY I (280)	NONE OF YOUR GAIETY HERE. THIS IS A RESPECTABLE	HOUSEHOLD	. YOUVE GONE AND GOT MY POOR INNOCENT BOY INTO
GETT PREFACE(236)	RECOIL AS FROM A PROFANATION, NO MORE WASHING OF	HOUSEHOLD	LINEN, DIRTY OR CLEAN, IN PUBLIC. WE MUST LEARN IN
JITT I SD(9)	AS THERE ARE NO BOOKS NOR PERSONAL BELONGINGS NOR	HOUSEHOLD	ODDS AND ENDS LYING ABOUT. THE TWO PHOTOGRAVURE
GETT PREFACE(197)	SOCIAL TRAINING A HOUSEHOLD OF TWENTY SURPASSES A	HOUSEHOLD	OF FIVE AS AN OXFORD COLLEGE SURPASSES AN
GETT PREFACE(231)	A CHILD IS BORN, AND MAY IN THE SAME WAY BECOME A	HOUSEHOLD	OF FOUR OR FOURTEEN IF THE UNION BE FERTILE
GETT PREFACE(231)	SO LITTLE TO SOME PEOPLE THAT THE ADDITION TO THE	HOUSEHOLD	OF HALF A DOZEN MORE WIVES OR HUSBANDS WOULD BE AS
GETT PREFACE(232)	EQUALLY HEARTBROKEN. WHEN THERE IS A SUCCESSFUL	HOUSEHOLD	OF ONE MAN AND TWO WOMEN THE SAME UNUSUAL
SIM II (57)	OF THEM WANT TO RAIN DESTRUCTION ON THIS LITTLE	HOUSEHOLD	OF OURS, AND THE OTHER HALF IS DETERMINED TO SINK
GETT PREFACE(231)	SIR WILLIAM AND LADY HAMILTON. THE SECRET OF THIS	HOUSEHOLD	OF THREE WAS NOT ONLY THAT BOTH THE HUSBAND AND
GETT PREFACE(231)	IN THE SENSE THAT EVERY HOUSEHOLD BECOMES A	HOUSEHOLD	OF THREE WHEN A CHILD IS BORN, AND MAY IN THE SAME
GETT PREFACE(231)	ONE SUCH RELATIONSHIP AT A TIME. WHAT IS CALLED A	HOUSEHOLD	OF THREE IS NEVER REALLY OF THREE EXCEPT IN THE
GETT PREFACE(197)	TRUE THAT FOR PURPOSES OF SOCIAL TRAINING A	HOUSEHOLD	OF TWENTY SURPASSES A HOUSEHOLD OF FIVE AS AN
HART II (101)	ME CRY. YOU KNOW, WHAT YOU SAID ABOUT MY MAKING A	HOUSEHOLD	PET OF HIM IS A LITTLE TRUE. PERHAPS HE OUGHT TO
HART II (100)	ALL. I SHOULD HAVE MADE A MAN OF MARCUS, NOT A	HOUSEHOLD	PET. /MRS HUSHABYE/ (FLAMING) YOU DARE! /ELLIE/
MTH3 (125)	IN ANOTHER HUNDRED YEARS WE SHALL BE SIMPLY THEIR	HOUSEHOLD	PETS. /BURGE-LUBIN/ (REACTING BUOYANTLY) NOT THE
POSN PREFACE(364)	THERE WAS THE KING. THE CENSOR IS A MEMBER OF HIS	HOUSEHOLD	RETINUE; AND AS A KING'S RETINUE HAS TO BE
CATH PREFACE(154)	BUT AS A HIGHLY DOMESTICATED GERMAN LADY WHOSE	HOUSEHOLD	ROUTINE WAS NOT AT ALL SO UNLIKE THAT OF QUEEN
BARB I (251)	YOU KNOW I HAVE NEVER INTERFERED IN THE	HOUSEHOLD	-- /LADY BRITOMART/ NO: I SHOULD THINK NOT. I DONT
HART III (131)	THAT THE STABLES ARE THE REAL CENTRE OF THE	HOUSEHOLD	; AND THAT IF ANY VISITOR WANTS TO PLAY THE PIANO
POSN PREFACE(392)	MAKES IT UNDESIRABLE THAT A MEMBER OF THE KING'S	HOUSEHOLD	SHOULD BE RESPONSIBLE FOR THE CHARACTER AND
VWOO 1 (120)	AS SHE WAS NEVER OUT AND HE WAS NEVER IN, THE	HOUSEHOLD	SHOULD HAVE BEEN A QUIET ONE; BUT THAT REMARK OF
POSN PREFACE(367)	CERTIFICATE FROM THE CHIEF OFFICER OF THE KING'S	HOUSEHOLD	THAT THE PLAY WAS A PROPER ONE. A TWO GUINEA
BULL I (93)	ON THE STRENGTH OF IT. IT HAS HELPED MY FATHER'S	HOUSEHOLD	THROUGH MANY A TIGHT PLACE. MY FATHER WAS HER
GENV PREFACE(3)	OF A DIRECT HIT NEXT TIME BLOWING ME AND MY	HOUSEHOLD	TO BITS. I CANNOT PRETEND THAT THIS TROUBLED ME
NEVR I (211)	RECOGNITION OF THE RIGHT OF EVERY MEMBER OF THE	HOUSEHOLD	TO INDEPENDENCE AND PRIVACY (HER EMPHASIS ON "
MILL PREFACE(111)	THE SAME MYSTERIOUS PERSONAL FORCE THAT MAKES THE	HOUSEHOLD	TYRANT, THE SCHOOL TYRANT, THE OFFICE TYRANT, THE
3PLA PREFACE(R27)	A PURITAN OF THE PURITANS. HE IS BROUGHT UP IN A	HOUSEHOLD	WHERE THE PURITAN RELIGION HAS DIED, AND BECOME,
MIS. (194)	CHEAP PERSON, MR TARLETON. I WAS BROUGHT UP IN A	HOUSEHOLD	WHICH COST AT LEAST SEVEN OR EIGHT TIMES THAT; AND
GETT PREFACE(253)	GOOD FOR CHILDREN. BUT IT IS JUST THE POLYGAMOUS	HOUSEHOLD	WHICH OUR MARRIAGE LAW ALLOWS TO BE BROKEN UP, AND
SIM II (56)	UNITED US ALL SIX, HAS ENDED IN A SINGLE LITTLE	HOUSEHOLD	WITH FOUR CHILDREN, WONDERFUL AND BEAUTIFUL, BUT
BARB PREFACE(209)	FAILURE OF LEVER'S BOOK TO PLEASE THE READERS OF	HOUSEHOLD	WORDS. THAT PAIN IN THE SELF-ESTEEM NOWADAYS
BARB PREFACE(207)	ROMANCE. IT WAS PUBLISHED BY CHARLES DICKENS IN	HOUSEHOLD	WORDS, AND PROVED SO STRANGE TO THE PUBLIC TASTE
CAND II SD(117)	CAREWORN. CANDIDA COMES IN. SHE HAS FINISHED HER	HOUSEHOLD	WORK AND TAKEN OFF THE APRON. SHE AT ONCE NOTICES
DEST (178)	A DUEL WITH BARRAS, A DOMESTIC SCENE, A BROKEN	HOUSEHOLD	, A PUBLIC SCANDAL, A CHECKED CAREER, ALL SORTS OF
JITT III (78)	DO YOU FORGET THAT I HAVE TO EARN BREAD FOR THE	HOUSEHOLD	, AND THAT YOUR OWN MONEY HARDLY PAYS FOR YOUR
DEVL I (20)	OF MY LATE FATHER, AND THE UNWORTHY HEAD OF THIS	HOUSEHOLD	, I BID YOU WELCOME. BY YOUR LEAVE, MINISTER
DEST (155)	THAT NOTHING SHORT OF HANGING YOU AND YOUR WHOLE	HOUSEHOLD	, INCLUDING THE LADY UPSTAIRS, WILL SATISFY ME.
MRS PREFACE(156)	EXAMINER, BEING AN OFFICER OF THE ROYAL	HOUSEHOLD	, PLACES THE KING IN THE POSITION OF SAYING TO THE
GETT PREFACE(225)	OTHER PURPOSE. AS TO THE CHILDREN OF THE TRIPLE	HOUSEHOLD	, THEY WERE NOT ONLY ON EXCELLENT TERMS WITH ONE
DEST (175)	TO MAKE A SCENE, TO FIGHT A DUEL, TO BREAK UP HIS	HOUSEHOLD	, TO INJURE HIS CAREER BY A SCANDAL, WHEN HE CAN
GENV I (42)	TO MAKE THEIR DREADFUL PROPAGANDA IN MY	HOUSEHOLD	! AND MY GRANDSON AT OXFORD HAS JOINED A
APPL INTRLUD(253)	WITH US. /ORINTHIA/ A MODEL HUSBAND IN A MODEL	HOUSEHOLD	! AND WHEN THE MODEL HOUSEHOLD BECOMES A BORE, I
		HOUSEHOLDER	
DOCT PREFACE(57)	WHEN THE LOCAL HEALTH AUTHORITY FORCES EVERY	HOUSEHOLDER	TO HAVE HIS SANITARY ARRANGEMENTS THOUGHT ABOUT
BARB PREFACE(241)	MODERN BURGLAR, WHEN CAUGHT AND OVERPOWERED BY A	HOUSEHOLDER	, USUALLY APPEALS, AND OFTEN, LET US HOPE, WITH
DOCT PREFACE(55)	DID NOT RAISE IT SUFFICIENTLY TO MAKE THE AVERAGE	HOUSEHOLDER	, WHO CANNOT EVADE REGULATIONS, DIE AS EARLY AS
		HOUSEHOLDS	
GETT PREFACE(210)	AND REARING OF CHILDREN AND THE ORDERING OF	HOUSEHOLDS	: THEY ARE QUARTERED ON THE WAGES OF THEIR
MIS. PREFACE(86)	BY OUR SENTIMENTAL MORALISTS ARE UNWORKABLE. WHEN	HOUSEHOLDS	AVERAGE TWELVE PERSONS WITH THE SEXES ABOUT
GETT PREFACE(239)	MUST EXTEND THE TERM CHILDLESS MARRIAGES TO COVER	HOUSEHOLDS	IN WHICH THE CHILDREN HAVE GROWN UP AND GONE
GETT PREFACE(242)	SONS OF THE PROPERTIED CLASSES, BROUGHT UP IN	HOUSEHOLDS	IN WHICH THE RATE OF EXPENDITURE, THOUGH TEN
BARB I (252)	POUNDS A YEAR. YOU SEE IT MEANS TWO ADDITIONAL	HOUSEHOLDS	. BESIDES, MY DEAR, YOU MUST MARRY SOON. I DONT
MIS. PREFACE(62)	THEY WERE BROUGHT UP IN WERE NO MORE AVERAGE	HOUSEHOLDS	THAN A MONTESSORI SCHOOL IS AN AVERAGE SCHOOL.
MIS. PREFACE(62)	THE MOST SACRED INSTITUTIONS OF HIS COUNTRY. THE	HOUSEHOLDS	THEY WERE BROUGHT UP IN WERE NO MORE AVERAGE
DOCT PREFACE(27)	ORDERS GIVEN FOR CHAMPAGNE JELLY AND OLD PORT IN	HOUSEHOLDS	WHERE SUCH LUXURIES MUST OBVIOUSLY BE ACQUIRED AT
GETT PREFACE(217)	LARGE HIS PRACTICE, KNOWS NOTHING OF THE MILLION	HOUSEHOLDS	WHICH HAVE NO SOLICITORS, AND WHICH NEVERTHELESS
BULL PREFACE(54)	THIS PRIVILEGE SHOULD EXCITE JEALOUSY IN OTHER	HOUSEHOLDS	, THREE OTHER DENSHAVIANS WERE HANGED WITH HIM.
		HOUSEKEEP	
BUOY IV (57)	ABOUT YOUR GRUB. SHE IS GLAD TO HAVE ONE MORE TO	HOUSEKEEP	FOR. YOU MAY CONSIDER YOURSELF ADOPTED. /SIR
		HOUSEKEEPER	
2TRU III (97)	THING AS A LADY. I HAVE THE INSTINCTS OF A GOOD	HOUSEKEEPER	: I WANT TO CLEAN UP THIS FILTHY WORLD AND KEEP
BUOY IV (51)	AT ALL. WHEN I HAD TO WORK, MY WIFE WAS ONLY MY	HOUSEKEEPER	: SHE SAW NEXT TO NOTHING OF ME EXCEPT WHEN I
LION PREFACE(78)	PREOCCUPATION WITH SEX JUST AS IN HER CAPACITY OF	HOUSEKEEPER	AND COOK SHE RELIEVES HIS PREOCCUPATION WITH
GETT PREFACE(238)	SOMETHING WORSE BY PUTTING THE WOMAN DOWN AS A	HOUSEKEEPER	AND INTRODUCING HER TO AN EMPLOYER WITHOUT
GETT (317)	THOUGHT IT WASNT WORK AT ALL. DOES YOUR PRESENT	HOUSEKEEPER	DO IT FOR NOTHING? /REGINALD/ BUT IT WILL BE
GENV I (45)	ABSOLUTELY DEPENDENT FOR OUR DOMESTIC WORK ON OUR	HOUSEKEEPER	FEODOROVNA BALLYBOUSHKA. WE WERE IDEALLY HAPPY
PYGM II (234)	A PLACE IN A FLOWER-SHOP. THIS GENTLEMAN AND MY	HOUSEKEEPER	HAVE BEEN HERE ALL THE TIME. (BULLYING HIM) HOW
GETT (317)	PAY ME AT LEAST AS WELL AS HE WOULD PAY A HIRED	HOUSEKEEPER	. I'LL NOT GO BEGGING TO HIM EVERY TIME I WANT A
KING I (172)	I HAVE NEVER NOTICED IT. THIS IS MRS BASHAM, MY	HOUSEKEEPER	. (HE SITS RESIGNEDLY). /NELLY/ YOU NEVER
BUOY IV (56)	REAL FATHER: I'M NOT ACCUSTOMED TO IT. I'M ONLY A	HOUSEKEEPER	. /OLD BILL/ WELL, MY CHILD, YOU CAN HAVE A REAL
KING I (172)	YOU NEVER NOTICED IT! YOU DONT DESERVE SUCH A	HOUSEKEEPER	. YOUR SERVANT, MRS BASHAM. MRS BASHAM BOWS
PYGM II (218)	A FROM B. (MRS PEARCE LOOKS IN: SHE IS HIGGINS'S	HOUSEKEEPER	). WHATS THE MATTER? /MRS PEARCE/ (HESITATING,
DEVL I (15)	WITH A PLEASANT SENSE OF BEING A MORE THOUGHTFUL	HOUSEKEEPER	THAN MRS DUDGEON). DO YOU KNOW ANY OF YOUR
HART II (107)	/MRS HUSHABYE/ WHAT HAS HAPPENED? /MAZZINI/ YOUR	HOUSEKEEPER	TOLD ME THERE WAS SOMEBODY UPSTAIRS, AND GAVE ME
SUPR I SD(3)	TWO HOUSEMAIDS AND A PARLORMAID DOWNSTAIRS, AND A	HOUSEKEEPER	UPSTAIRS WHO DOES NOT LET THEM SPARE
APPL INTRLUD(251)	HEALTHY JOLLY LUMPS OF CHILDREN AND YOUR COMMON	HOUSEKEEPER	WIFE AND THE RABBLE OF DOWDIES AND UPSTARTS AND
KING I SD(161)	VISITORS TO THE PHILOSOPHER. NEWTON'S	HOUSEKEEPER	, A MIDDLE AGED WOMAN OF VERY RESPECTABLE
KING I (167)	THIS LADY KNOWN TO YOU, GENTLEMEN. MRS BASHAM: MY	HOUSEKEEPER	, AND THE FAITHFUL GUARDIAN OF MY HOURS.
JITT I SD(9)	IT IS ALMOST DARK. MRS BILLITER, AN ELDERLY	HOUSEKEEPER	, HAS SOMETHING OF THE SAME UNDOMESTICATED AIR
PYGM II (236)	OR DID YOUR MISSUS HERE? /MRS PEARCE/ I AM THE	HOUSEKEEPER	, IF YOU PLEASE. I HAVE SENT FOR SOME CLOTHES
MRS III (220)	IT IS CLEARLY MY MOTHER'S DUTY, AS A PRUDENT	HOUSEKEEPER	, TO GO UP TO THE STORES AND ORDER A BARREL OF
CAND I SD(79)	ALTOGETHER THE ROOM IS THE ROOM OF A GOOD	HOUSEKEEPER	, VANQUISHED, AS FAR AS THE TABLE IS CONCERNED,
		HOUSEKEEPER'S	
SUPR I (29)	MOTHER, CONSIDERING WHAT TO DO. /TANNER/ OH! THE	HOUSEKEEPER'S	ROOM IS THE PENITENTIARY, I SUPPOSE; AND THE
SUPR I (46)	A MARRIED WOMAN YOU WOULD NOT LIKE SITTING IN THE	HOUSEKEEPER'S	ROOM AND BEING TREATED LIKE A NAUGHTY CHILD BY
SUPR I (44)	PRESENT TO ME, THE FILAGREE BRACELET, IN THE	HOUSEKEEPER'S	ROOM. /TANNER/ DO COME IN, VIOLET; AND TALK TO
SUPR I (29)	WHATS HAPPENING UPSTAIRS? /ANN/ VIOLET IS IN THE	HOUSEKEEPER'S	ROOM-- BY HERSELF, OF COURSE. /TANNER/ WHY NOT
SUPR I (29)	OF THIS HOUSE. /TANNER/ SHE WOULD PUT ME IN THE	HOUSEKEEPER'S	ROOM, TOO, IF SHE DARED, RAMSDEN. HOWEVER, I
BULL PREFACE(45)	NOT LIKE THE REHEARSALS. HIS OFFICER HAS NOT EVEN	HOUSEKEEPER'S	WORK TO KEEP HIM SANE. THE WORK OF ORGANIZING
		HOUSEKEEPERS	
ROCK II (263)	VALETS AND GAMEKEEPERS AND JOCKEYS, BUTLERS AND	HOUSEKEEPERS	AND LADIES' MAIDS AND SCULLERY MAIDS AND DEUCE
		HOUSEKEEPING	
PYGM EPILOG (302)	HOW MUCH ELIZA STILL MANAGES TO MEDDLE IN THE	HOUSEKEEPING	AT WIMPOLE STREET IN SPITE OF THE SHOP AND HER
BUOY III (29)	KNOWS EVERYTHING ABOUT IT, BUT I KNOW ALL ABOUT	HOUSEKEEPING	BECAUSE OUR MOTHER KNEW NOTHING ABOUT IT AND
JITT II (49)	YES, WITH ME. IT IS I WHO WILL HAVE TO PAY THE	HOUSEKEEPING	BILLS. BUT DONT BE AFRAID: I AM DONE WITH YOU.
PYGM II (226)	PAY HER WHATEVER IS NECESSARY: PUT IT DOWN IN THE	HOUSEKEEPING	BOOK. (IMPATIENTLY) WHAT ON EARTH WILL SHE
MIS. PREFACE(52)	A HIGH DEGREE OF CULTURE CANNOT ADD UP THEIR OWN	HOUSEKEEPING	BOOKS, THOUGH THEIR EDUCATION IN SIMPLE
MILL IV (189)	MORE COULD ANYONE ASK BUT A NICE HOTEL? ALL THE	HOUSEKEEPING	DONE FOR US: NO TROUBLE WITH THE SERVANTS: NO
CAND I SD(103)	TO THE DOOR. IT OPENS AND CANDIDA ENTERS IN HER	HOUSEKEEPING	DRESS. /CANDIDA/ ARE YOU GOING, EUGENE? (

JITT III (53)	OF COURSE NOT. /AGNES/ LIFE GOES ON, DOESNT IT?	HOUSEKEEPING	GOES ON: THE FUTURE HAS TO BE THOUGHT FOR AS
ARMS I (6)	INTO THE ROOM). /CATHERINE/ (BUSINESSLIKE, HER	HOUSEKEEPING	INSTINCTS AROUSED) I MUST SEE THAT EVERYTHING
GETT (261)	THE GREENGROCER, MAAM: THATS THE SECRET OF EASY	HOUSEKEEPING	. BLESS YOU, IT'S HIS BUSINESS. IT PAYS HIM AND
BUOY IV (60)	AND SOLVING CROSSWORD PUZZLES AS SHE TIRES OF	HOUSEKEEPING	. HER LOVE FOR ME IS VERY VARIABLE: IT TURNS TO
SUPR II (58)	SO EARLY IN THE MORNING. SHE WANTS TO FINISH HER	HOUSEKEEPING	. /OCTAVIUS/ I FLY, DEAREST ANN (HE KISSES HER
ARMS III (48)	YOU LIKE TO ORDER FROM SOFIA AGAINST A WEEK'S	HOUSEKEEPING	MONEY THAT THE COAT ISNT THERE. /CATHERINE/
KING I (199)	WITH ORDERS THAT WILL RUN AWAY WITH A FORTNIGHT'S	HOUSEKEEPING	MONEY; AND THAT WONT BE HALF WHAT THEYLL
POSN PREFACE(406)	TO FIGHT AGAINST THE FREE TICKETS AND DISORDERLY	HOUSEKEEPING	OF UNSCRUPULOUS COMPETITORS. THE DRAMATIC
BUOY IV (56)	BABZY. /DARKIE/ I DONT WANT TO BE SPOILT. I LIKE	HOUSEKEEPING	; AND I'M NOT SENTIMENTAL. IF I EVER WANT TO BE
WIDO II (34)	IS. /BLANCHE/ IT WOULD KEEP ME RATHER SHORT IN MY	HOUSEKEEPING	, DEAREST BOY, IF I HAD NOTHING OF MY OWN. BUT
GETT PREFACE(235)	THE WOMAN HAS A " SPHERE" OF HER OWN, THAT OF	HOUSEKEEPING	, IN WHICH THE MAN MUST NOT MEDDLE, WHILST HE
POSN PREFACE(414)	AGAINST THE ORDINARY LAWS AGAINST DISORDERLY	HOUSEKEEPING	, INDECENCY, BLASPHEMY, ETC., EXCEPT IN CASES
		HOUSEKNACKING	
WIDO III (60)	OLD HARRY WITH SLUM PROPERTIES, AND SPOIL THE	HOUSEKNACKING	GAME IF THEY PLEASE. THAT DIDNT MATTER IN THE
		HOUSEMAID	
2TRU PREFACE(4)	IN THOSE HARD EARNED HOURS SHE CEASES TO BE A	HOUSEMAID	AND CAN BE HERSELF; BUT THE LADY OF FASHION NEVER
OVER (177)	LIKE ME? I DONT MEAN LOVE ME: YOU MIGHT LOVE THE	HOUSEMAID	-- /GREGORY/ (VEHEMENTLY) NO! /MRS JUNO/ OH YES
DOCT III (151)	I MISSED A FIVE-POUND NOTE. IT WAS TRACED TO THE	HOUSEMAID	; AND SHE ACTUALLY SAID LOUIS HAD GIVEN IT TO HER
PYGM EPILOG (297)	ABLE TO AFFORD A MAID, COULD NOT AFFORD EVEN A	HOUSEMAID	, AND HAD TO SCRAPE ALONG AT HOME WITH AN
2TRU PREFACE(4)	IS VIRTUALLY AS COMPULSORY AS THE ROUTINE OF A	HOUSEMAID	, ITS DRESSING IS AS MUCH DICTATED AS HER UNIFORM,
MIS. PREFACE(22)	IN THAT CASE THE CULPRIT, A BOARDER, HAD KISSED A	HOUSEMAID	, OR POSSIBLY, BEING A HANDSOME YOUTH, BEEN KISSED
BASH II,1, (109)	EAGER DAME SINK THE GREAT LADY IN THE OBSEQUIOUS	HOUSEMAID	! OH, AT SUCH MOMENTS I COULD WISH THE COURT HAD
		HOUSEMAID'S	
2TRU PREFACE(4)	TO BE TIPPED THAN TO TIP. AND, AS I SURMISE, THE	HOUSEMAID'S	DAY OFF OR EVENING OFF IS REALLY OFF: IN THOSE
FABL PREFACE(82)	FOR CERTAIN THAT THE RECTOR IS THE FATHER OF HIS	HOUSEMAID'S	ILLEGITIMATE CHILD; AND AFTER THAT YOU MAY TELL
BULL PREFACE(45)	NO REAL WORK TO KEEP HIM FROM GOING MAD EXCEPT	HOUSEMAID'S	WORK: ALL THE REST IS FORCED EXERCISE, IN THE
		HOUSEMAIDS	
SUPR I SD(3)	VISIBLE: IT IS CLEAR THAT THERE ARE AT LEAST TWO	HOUSEMAIDS	AND A PARLORMAID DOWNSTAIRS, AND A HOUSEKEEPER
MIS. PREFACE(35)	DOWN TO SHEW THEM OFF; AND ACTING AS FOOTMEN AND	HOUSEMAIDS	TO ROYAL PERSONAGES. THE SOLE AND OBVIOUS CAUSE
2TRU PREFACE(4)	SUMS ON THEMSELVES, ARE NO HAPPIER THAN THEIR	HOUSEMAIDS	, IF SO HAPPY; FOR THE ROUTINE OF FASHION IS
		HOUSEOWNERS	
DOCT PREFACE(56)	OF CLASS DIFFERENCES. A COMMON COMPLAINT OF	HOUSEOWNERS	IS THAT THE PUBLIC HEALTH AUTHORITIES FREQUENTLY
		HOUSEPAINTER	
FABL III (109)	THEM MY DRAWINGS, THEY OFFERED TO MAKE ME A	HOUSEPAINTER	. I DONT WANT TO PAINT HOUSES: MY DESTINY IS TO
		HOUSE-DOOR	
DEVL I SD(4)	LEADING TO THE SCULLERY AND WASHHOUSE; AND THE	HOUSE-DOOR	, WITH ITS LATCH, HEAVY LOCK, AND CLUMSY WOODEN
		HOUSE-OWNING	
UNPL PREFACE(R17)	THE SUBJECT, THERE WOULD PROBABLY NOT BE A SINGLE	HOUSE-OWNING	NATIVE AMONG THEM WHO WOULD NOT CONCEIVE A
		HOUSES	
FABL III (109)	TO MAKE ME A HOUSEPAINTER. I DONT WANT TO PAINT	HOUSES	: MY DESTINY IS TO PAINT TEMPLES IN FRESCO. /THE
BARB PREFACE(218)	PERSONAL ONES. THEY ARE NOT CONTENT WITH HANDSOME	HOUSES	: THEY WANT HANDSOME CITIES. THEY ARE NOT CONTENT
BARB II (304)	WITH HIS WHISKY, HIS DISTILLERIES, AND HIS TIED	HOUSES	? ARE YOU GOING TO MAKE OUR SHELTER ANOTHER TIED
WIDO II (31)	WILL. /COKANE/ WHAT DESCRIPTION OF PROPERTIES?	HOUSES	? /LICKCHEESE/ TENEMENT HOUSES, LET FROM WEEK TO
BARB III (315)	AS WELL AS ALL THE OTHER SONS OF THE BIG BUSINESS	HOUSES	? /UNDERSHAFT/ YES: HE COULD LEARN THE OFFICE
CAND II (115)	DREADFUL PEOPLE WHO LIVE IN THESE HIDEOUS ROWS OF	HOUSES	? SERMONS AND SCRUBBING BRUSHES! WITH YOU TO PREACH
CYMB FORWORD(134)	IN, JUST AS AT ALL THE GREAT CONTINENTAL OPERA	HOUSES	A BALLET USED TO BE DE RIGUEUR. GOUNOD HAD TO
MRS PREFACE(174)	IN 1902 WITH THAT PRODUCED BY WIDOWERS'	HOUSES	ABOUT TEN YEARS EARLIER, THAT WHEREAS IN 1892 THE
UNPL PREFACE(R17)	THEM. HAD THE TWO PERFORMANCES OF WIDOWERS'	HOUSES	ACHIEVED BY MR GREIN BEEN MULTIPLIED BY FIFTY, IT
VWOO 1 (120)	HE SAID THERE IS NO FUTURE FOR THE GREAT	HOUSES	AND A GREAT FUTURE FOR TELEPHONES. /A/ AND YOU? HAD
CAPT I (226)	HAS ACQUIRED A HABIT OF WALKING INTO PEOPLE'S	HOUSES	AND BEHAVING AS IF SHE WERE IN HER OWN. /LADY CICELY/
GENV PREFACE(7)	REPLACED, BUT OF THE PLANT OF CIVILIZATION, THE	HOUSES	AND FACTORIES, THE RAILWAYS AND AIRWAYS, THE ORCHARDS
MTH4 II (184)	WERE THEMSELVES BLOWN INTO FRAGMENTS WITH THEIR	HOUSES	AND FAMILIES, WHILE THE TEN MILLION MEN LAY SNUGLY IN
BUOY III (32)	VERY POOR. YOU WILL HAVE TO LET YOUR COUNTRY	HOUSES	AND LIVE IN GATE LODGES AND GARDENERS' COTTAGES. YOUR
GENV PREFACE(3)	PRETEND THAT THIS TROUBLED ME MUCH: PEOPLE BUILD	HOUSES	AND LIVE ON THE SLOPES OF ETNA AND VESUVIUS AND AT
BARB III (330)	PLATE AND LINEN, ALL THAT FURNITURE AND THOSE	HOUSES	AND ORCHARDS AND GARDENS BELONG TO US. THEY BELONG TO
GETT PREFACE(227)	NOT LIMITED FOR MONEY REASONS; WHERE AT LEAST TWO	HOUSES	AND SOMETIMES THREE OR FOUR ARE THE RULE (NOT TO
APPL PREFACE(181)	CAN, IF RULERS OPPRESS US INTOLERABLY, BURN THEIR	HOUSES	AND TEAR THEM TO PIECES. THIS IS NOT SATISFACTORY.
BARB III (348)	COULD I LET IT GO; ONLY SHE THOUGHT IT WAS THE	HOUSES	AND THE KITCHEN RANGES AND THE LINEN AND CHINA, WHEN
WIDO III (56)	OUR FAULT? /SARTORIUS/ MY DEAR: IF WE MADE THE	HOUSES	ANY BETTER, THE RENTS WOULD HAVE TO BE RAISED SO MUCH
MTH4 I (174)	PITCH ON SUCH A SPOT TO LIVE? THE NEAREST	HOUSES	ARE AT A PLACE CALLED STRAND-ON-THE-GREEN: IT IS VERY
MRS PREFACE(164)	HAVE NO TWO-GUINEA CERTIFICATES TO PLEAD IF THEIR	HOUSES	ARE CONDUCTED VICIOUSLY. THEY KNOW THAT IF THEY LOSE
FABL PREFACE(71)	NOT USELESS: IT WAS NECESSARY. BUT, I URGED, THE	HOUSES	ARE NOT BEING DISINFECTED AT ALL. " OH YES THEY ARE"
WIDO II (26)	REPEATEDLY AGAINST DEALING WITH THESE TENEMENT	HOUSES	AS IF THEY WERE MANSIONS IN A WEST-END SQUARE. I HAVE
MIS. PREFACE(51)	GENTLEMEN WHO DISCUSS POLITICS IN COUNTRY	HOUSES	AT ELECTION TIME (AND AT NO OTHER TIME) AFTER THEIR
APPL INTRLUD(247)	I WAS PERFECTLY FAITHFUL TO THEM. I KEPT THEIR	HOUSES	BEAUTIFULLY; I FED THEM BETTER THAN THEY HAD EVER
GETT PREFACE(247)	" AFTER ALL, VERY FEW PEOPLE HAVE THEIR	HOUSES	BROKEN INTO; AND FEWER STILL HAVE THEM BURNT. DOES IT
GENV PREFACE(8)	AND DESTRUCTIVENESS THAT THEY WRECKED NOT MERELY	HOUSES	BUT WHOLE STREETS, AND SCATTERED BLAZING PHOSPHORUS
HART PREFACE(14)	OR LIE QUAKING IN BED, WHILST BOMBS CRASHED,	HOUSES	CRUMBLED, AND AIRCRAFT GUNS DISTRIBUTED SHRAPNEL ON
BARB III (346)	BY ALL MEN. /BARBARA/ POWER TO BURN WOMEN'S	HOUSES	DOWN AND KILL THEIR SONS AND TEAR THEIR HUSBANDS TO
DOCT PREFACE(71)	HALF-A-CROWN PER RE-VACCINATION PRODUCED RAIDS ON	HOUSES	DURING THE ABSENCE OF PARENTS, AND THE FORCIBLE
MTH4 II (184)	THEY HAD DUG FOR THEMSELVES. LATER ON EVEN THE	HOUSES	ESCAPED; BUT THEIR INHABITANTS WERE POISONED BY GAS
WIDO II (42)	TO SAVE MY MONEY IN ORDER TO PROVIDE ADDITIONAL	HOUSES	FOR THE HOMELESS, AND TO LAY BY A LITTLE FOR BLANCHE.
DOCT PREFACE(61)	ARE; FOR MANY VERY DESIRABLE PATIENTS IN COUNTRY	HOUSES	HAVE LATELY BEEN PERSUADED THAT THEIR FIRST DUTY IS
WIDO II (43)	TO SARTORIUS) WELL, PEOPLE WHO LIVE IN GLASS	HOUSES	HAVE NO RIGHT TO THROW STONES. BUT, ON MY HONOR, I
PYGM EPILOG (294)	ON THE RIGHT HAND OF THE DUCHESS; AND IN COUNTRY	HOUSES	HE SMOKED IN THE PANTRY AND WAS MADE MUCH OF BY THE
UNPL PREFACE(R25)	CHEATED, HALF COERCED INTO PAYING. IN WIDOWERS'	HOUSES	I HAVE SHEWN MIDDLE-CLASS RESPECTABILITY AND YOUNGER
POSN PREFACE(416)	OF THE EXTENT TO WHICH THEATRES ARE DISORDERLY	HOUSES	IN DISGUISE SIFTED TO THE BOTTOM. FOR IT IS ON THIS
HART PREFACE(4)	INTENSELY RUSSIAN PLAYS FITTED ALL THE COUNTRY	HOUSES	IN EUROPE IN WHICH THE PLEASURES OF MUSIC, ART,
FOUN (218)	WAS FOUND ON THE DOORSTEP OF ONE OF THE VERY BEST	HOUSES	IN PARK LANE. /THE LORD CHANCELLOR/ (OVERWHELMED) MY
FABL PREFACE(71)	I EXAMINED WAS FOR SULPHUR CANDLES TO DISINFECT	HOUSES	IN WHICH CASES OF FEVER HAD OCCURRED. I KNEW THAT
MRS PREFACE(151)	CHURCH ESTATES, THROUGH THE RENTS OF THE	HOUSES	IN WHICH IT IS PRACTISED. I COULD NOT HAVE DONE
WIDO III (54)	BY THE TOWER. BY MY ADVICE THAT MAN PUT HALF THE	HOUSES	INTO FIRST-CLASS REPAIR, AND LET THE OTHER HALF TO A
WIDO (1)	WIDOWERS'	HOUSES	.
MILL PREFACE(124)	IN LITTLE RED RIDING HOOD. WE ALL LIVE IN GLASS	HOUSES	. IS IT WISE TO THROW STONES AT THE JEWS? IS IT WISE
MRS PREFACE(177)	ITS REVENUE FROM ADVERTISEMENTS OF MRS WARREN'S	HOUSES	. MANY PEOPLE HAVE BEEN PUZZLED BY THE FACT THAT
WIDO II (42)	/TRENCH/ (DEFIANTLY) FROM INTEREST: NOT FROM	HOUSES	. MY HANDS ARE CLEAN AS FAR AS THAT GOES. INTEREST ON
MRS IV (251)	I WOULD. /VIVIE/ (QUIETLY) IN ONE OF YOUR OWN	HOUSES	. /MRS WARREN/ (SCREAMING) LISTEN TO HER! LISTEN TO
ROCK II (283)	OFFICE. THEY THINK THIS SIDE IS ONLY PRIVATE	HOUSES	. /SIR ARTHUR/ (GOING TO SEE) YES: THEY ALWAYS BREAK
JOAN PREFACE(10)	ARTS OF THE MISTRESSES OF WELL FURNISHED	HOUSES	. SHE UNDERSTOOD THE POLITICAL AND MILITARY SITUATION
APPL I (200)	MANSIONS, PARK GATES, AND PORTICOED COUNTRY	HOUSES	. THINK OF THE HORROR OF THAT ISLAND TO HIM! A
DOCT PREFACE(72)	AND MAKES IT SAFE FOR THEM TO RETURN TO THEIR	HOUSES	. TO ASSURE THEM THAT THE REAL SECRET IS SUNSHINE AND
BARB PREFACE(218)	MADE ILL BY THE ARCHITECTURE OF THEIR NEIGHBORS'	HOUSES	. TRADE PATTERNS MADE TO SUIT VULGAR PEOPLE DO NOT
GETT PREFACE(217)	OF ST JOHN: NAMELY, THAT WE ALL LIVE IN GLASS	HOUSES	. WE MAY TAKE IT, THEN, THAT THE IDEAL HUSBAND AND
GENV PREFACE(9)	UNDER THE PILES OF RUBBLE THAT HAD BEEN THEIR	HOUSES	. WE RAINED THESE MONSTER BOMBS ON GERMANY UNTIL THE
BARB I (252)	BUT I CANT KEEP FOUR FAMILIES IN FOUR SEPARATE	HOUSES	. YOU KNOW HOW POOR MY FATHER IS: HE HAS BARELY SEVEN
BULL PREFACE(51)	THEY WENT FROM 100 TO 300 YARDS AWAY FROM THE	HOUSES	(THESE DISTANCES WERE AFTERWARDS OFFICIALLY AVERAGED
DEVL III (61)	YOU WOULD HAVE FOUND THE STREETS BARRICADED, THE	HOUSES	LOOPHOLED, AND THE PEOPLE IN ARMS TO HOLD THE TOWN
FOUN (219)	WANT OF SOMETHING TO EAT. THERE WERE TWO PUBLIC	HOUSES	NEAR THE PRISON. ONE HAD A PLACARD UP " SAUSAGE AND

APPL II (263)	OUR COMMON FOREFATHERS BUILT AS THE COUNTRY	HOUSES	OF GOD. WHAT DID YOU DO WITH THEM? YOU SOLD THEM TO
POSN PREFACE(361)	TELLING THE STORY OF THE SELECT COMMITTEE OF BOTH	HOUSES	OF PARLIAMENT WHICH SAT LAST YEAR TO INQUIRE INTO THE
POSN PREFACE(407)	BE DEVIZED FOR SECURING THE ORDERLY CONDUCT OF	HOUSES	OF PUBLIC ENTERTAINMENT, DRAMATIC OR OTHER. LIBERTY
BULL PREFACE(69)	BY THE BLACK AND TANS HE WOULD BURN TWO COUNTRY	HOUSES	OF THE PROTESTANT GENTRY. THE COUNTRY HOUSES THAT
MIS. PREFACE(70)	NOT PRESS VERY HARDLY, AS, FOR INSTANCE, IN THE	HOUSES	OF THE VERY POOR, WHO CAN SEND THEIR CHILDREN TO PLAY
MIS. PREFACE(70)	THEIR CHILDREN TO PLAY IN THE STREETS, OR THE	HOUSES	OF THE VERY RICH, WHICH ARE SO LARGE THAT THE
HART I (75)	ARE LIKE THAT. THEY SPEND THEIR HOLIDAYS IN THE	HOUSES	OF THEIR RESPECTABLE SCHOOLFELLOWS. /LADY UTTERWORD/
BULL PREFACE(54)	HOWEVER, " IN A LOUD VOICE INVOKED RUIN UPON THE	HOUSES	OF THOSE WHO HAD GIVEN EVIDENCE AGAINST HIM"; AND
KING I (189)	(RISING) YOU SEE WHAT COMES OF FREQUENTING THE	HOUSES	OF YOUR INFERIORS. THEY FORGET THEMSELVES AND TAKE
BULL I (83)	NEVER REACH PADDINGTON: THERE ARE TOO MANY PUBLIC	HOUSES	ON THE WAY. SECOND, HE'S NOT AN IRISHMAN AT ALL.
ROCK II (269)	SWORD, WITH FLOGGINGS AND HANGINGS, BURNING THE	HOUSES	OVER THEIR HEADS AND BOMBING THEIR LITTLE STORES FOR
WIDO III (65)	ENTERPRISE-- TO BEFRIEND THE POOR BY HAVING THOSE	HOUSES	REBUILT, EH? (TRENCH MAINTAINS HIS ATTITUDE AND
UNPL PREFACE(R13)	IT THE FARFETCHED SCRIPTURAL TITLE OF WIDOWERS'	HOUSES	; AND HANDED IT OVER TO MR GREIN, WHO LAUNCHED IT AT
GETT PREFACE(193)	UP TO TWENTY YEARS FOR BREAKING INTO THEIR	HOUSES	; OF TREATING THEIR CHILDREN AS WILD BEASTS TO BE
JOAN PREFACE(46)	TO OUR OWN DAY (YOU CAN SEE PLENTY OF THE BURNT	HOUSES	STILL IN IRELAND), WITH THE RESULT THAT JOAN HAS
WIDO II (41)	ADVANTAGE IS TAKEN OF THAT TO MAKE THEM PAY FOR	HOUSES	THAT ARE NOT FIT FOR DOGS. WHY DONT YOU BUILD PROPER
BULL PREFACE(69)	HOUSES OF THE PROTESTANT GENTRY. THE COUNTRY	HOUSES	THAT WERE NOT BURNT WERE RAIDED AT NIGHT AND LAID
MIS. PREFACE(42)	BODIES AND TIMID SOULS IS SO COMMON IN COUNTRY	HOUSES	THAT YOU MAY SPEND HOURS IN THEM LISTENING TO STORIES
WIDO II (31)	COULD SCRAPE TOGETHER HE BOUGHT OLD HOUSES WITH:	HOUSES	THAT YOU WOULDNT HARDLY LOOK AT WITHOUT HOLDING YOUR
BUOY III (27)	HONG KONG. /THE PRIEST/ SIR: IN MANY OLD ENGLISH	HOUSES	THERE IS A ROOM SET APART AS A MEDITATION PARLOR.
POSN PREFACE(369)	HIM BY APPOINTING A SELECT COMMITTEE OF BOTH	HOUSES	TO INVESTIGATE THE SUBJECT. THE THEN CHANCELLOR OF
HART II (85)	MR HUSHABYE AT DINNER WHETHER THERE ARE ANY NICE	HOUSES	TO LET DOWN HERE. /MANGAN/ I LIKE THE PLACE. THE AIR
MRS PREFACE(180)	COULD DESIRE. I THEN MADE A TOUR OF THE PICTURE	HOUSES	TO SEE WHAT THE FILM CENSOR CONSIDERS ALLOWABLE. OF
CATH PREFACE(156)	WALLS OF NINETEEN OUT OF TWENTY ENGLISH COUNTRY	HOUSES	TO THIS DAY. AN ARTISTIC PRESENTMENT MUST NOT
FANY PROLOG (259)	WELL, I DONT LIVE IN IT. I FIND MODERN	HOUSES	UGLY. I DONT LIVE IN THEM: I HAVE A PALACE ON THE
BULL PREFACE(17)	HE FINDS ENGLISH SOCIETY AGREEABLE, AND ENGLISH	HOUSES	VERY COMFORTABLE, IRISH ESTABLISHMENTS BEING
HART PREFACE(33)	OF MANAGEMENT TO SUCH A DEGREE THAT UNLESS THE	HOUSES	WERE QUITE FULL EVERY NIGHT, PROFIT WAS IMPOSSIBLE.
HART II (111)	I DO IS INNOCENT AND PIOUS. I ENQUIRE ABOUT FOR	HOUSES	WHERE THE RIGHT SORT OF PEOPLE LIVE. I WORK IT ON
WIDO III (61)	IF THAT HAPPENS, THE MONEY SPENT IN IMPROVING THE	HOUSES	WILL BE THROWN AWAY: SIMPLY THROWN AWAY. WORSE THAN
WIDO II (31)	POUNDS HE COULD SCRAPE TOGETHER HE BOUGHT OLD	HOUSES	WITH: HOUSES THAT YOU WOULDNT HARDLY LOOK AT WITHOUT
MIS. PREFACE(17)	SCHOOLS, SEIZING ANY PRETEXT FOR FILLING THEIR	HOUSES	WITH CHILDREN EXACTLY AS SOME ECCENTRIC OLD LADIES
FABL II (105)	WILL HAVE TO FIND 88,454 CIVILIANS TO DUST THE	HOUSES	WITH VACUUM CLEANERS AND KEEP THE BANKS AND THE
HART PREFACE(15)	IN THEIR BEARING ON THE CHANCES WHETHER OUR	HOUSES	WOULD BE STANDING OR OURSELVES ALIVE NEXT MORNING,
GETT PREFACE(215)	WHO ARE RESOLVED TO BE MISTRESSES IN THEIR OWN	HOUSES	WOULD NOT BE THE ONLY ONES TO TAKE ADVANTAGE OF THE
SUPR IV (154)	IT). THANK YOU. BY THE WAY, MR MALONE, THOSE TWO	HOUSES	YOU MENTIONED-- THE ABBEYS. /MALONE/ YES? /VIOLET/
METH PREFACE(R60)	WHO ARE BORN AND BRED IN ENGLISH COUNTRY	HOUSES	, AND SENT FIRST TO ETON OR HARROW, AND THEN TO
METH PREFACE(R75)	IS CONTROVERSY. THEY BANISH THE BIBLE FROM THEIR	HOUSES	, AND SOMETIMES PUT INTO THE HANDS OF THEIR
ROCK PREFACE(166)	YOU, EXTERMINATE THEM; BUT DO NOT BURN THEIR	HOUSES	, AS YOU WILL NEED THEM TO LIVE IN. AND IT WAS THE
CAND I SD(77)	MONOTONY OF MILES AND MILES OF UNLOVELY BRICK	HOUSES	, BLACK IRON RAILINGS, STONY PAVEMENTS, SLATED ROOFS,
BARB PREFACE(224)	RECEIVE THE RENTS OF SPORTING PUBLIC	HOUSES	, BROTHELS, AND SWEATING DENS; OR THAT THE MOST
UNPL PREFACE(R17)	WAY BEING TO SIT IN SEPARATE FAMILIES IN SEPARATE	HOUSES	, EACH PERSON SILENTLY OCCUPIED WITH A BOOK, A PAPER,
MRS PREFACE(170)	THAT WHEN HE PRODUCED MY FIRST PLAY, WIDOWERS'	HOUSES	, EXACTLY THE SAME MISUNDERSTANDING AROSE. WHEN THE
WIDO III (56)	/BLANCHE/ IS IT NOT TRUE? ABOUT THE STATE OF THE	HOUSES	, I MEAN? /SARTORIUS/ (CALMLY) OH, QUITE TRUE.
WIDO II (31)	OF PROPERTIES? HOUSES? /LICKCHEESE/ TENEMENT	HOUSES	, LET FROM WEEK TO WEEK BY THE ROOM OR HALF ROOM:
GETT PREFACE(193)	CALLED EDUCATION; AND OF KEEPING PIANOS IN THEIR	HOUSES	, NOT FOR MUSICAL PURPOSES, BUT TO TORMENT THEIR
METH PREFACE(R69)	DIPLOMATISTS, OF THE MILITARISTS, OF THE COUNTRY	HOUSES	, OF THE TRADE UNIONS, OF EVERYTHING EPHEMERAL ON
DOCT PREFACE(72)	THE INCANTATION; AND BACK THEY GO TO THEIR	HOUSES	, SATISFIED. A RELIGIOUS CEREMONY-- A POETIC BLESSING
PLES PREFACE(R8)	VULGAR UNSOCIALISM: FOR INSTANCE, IN WIDOWERS'	HOUSES	, THE CLERGYMAN, WHO DOES NOT APPEAR ON THE STAGE AT
MRS PREFACE(177)	SIR GEORGE CROFTS, BUT BY THE LANDLORDS OF THEIR	HOUSES	, THE NEWSPAPERS WHICH ADVERTIZE THEM, THE
GETT PREFACE(227)	CONSTANTLY IN SOCIAL TRAINING IN OTHER PEOPLE'S	HOUSES	, THE RESULT IS TO PRODUCE A SET THAT, IN COMPARISON
BULL PREFACE(6)	(THAT SURVIVES ONLY IN IRELAND), BUT FOR THEIR	HOUSES	, THEIR PROPERTY, THEIR RIGHT TO LIVE IN THE COUNTRY
BARB PREFACE(239)	TACT AND GOOD TASTE OF THE LADIES OF OUR ROYAL	HOUSES	, WHO, THOUGH PRESUMABLY OF FULL NORMAL NATURAL
GETT PREFACE(193)	AND SOUNDS, UNHEALTHY SMELLS, AND INCONVENIENT	HOUSES	, WITH INHUMAN APATHY AND CALLOUSNESS. THEY HAD, AS
2TRU PREFACE(9)	NEW THING. ANYONE WHO HAS THE RUN OF OUR COUNTRY	HOUSES	, WITH THEIR GREAT PARKS AND GARDENS, THEIR STAFFS OF
UNPL PREFACE(R14)	RETURNING TO THE VEIN I HAD WORKED IN WIDOWERS'	HOUSES	, WROTE A THIRD PLAY, MRS WARREN'S PROFESSION, ON A
HART PREFACE(28)	HOUSE OR HORSEBACK HALL. PLAGUE ON BOTH YOUR	HOUSES	! MEANWHILE THE BOLSHEVIST PICKS AND PETARDS ARE AT
UNPL PREFACE(R10)	BECOME A VESTRYMAN: ME, THE AUTHOR OF WIDOWERS'	HOUSES	! THEN, LIKE ANY OTHER HARMLESS USEFUL CREATURE, I

HOUSEWIVES

SUPR HANDBOK(178)	POTATOES ARE PRODUCED TO SATISFY THE DEMAND OF	HOUSEWIVES	WHO DO NOT KNOW THE TECHNICAL DIFFERENCES BETWEEN

HOUSEWORK

BUOY III (33)	ALWAYS THOUGHT OF HER AS A WOMAN WHO DID HER OWN	HOUSEWORK	. I AM SURE I COULD LEARN. IS IT NOT EASIER FOR A
BUOY III (32)	THAT. /DARKIE/ NONE OF US WOMEN KNOWS HOW TO DO	HOUSEWORK	. /SIR F./ I AM AFRAID YOU WILL HAVE TO LEARN.
BUOY III (32)	COTTAGES. YOUR LADIES WILL HAVE TO DO THE	HOUSEWORK	. YOUR CLOTHES WILL HAVE TO LAST YOU FOR YEARS. I
SIM II (81)	SALLY: IF YOU HAVE GIVEN YOUR ORDERS FOR THE	HOUSEWORK	TODAY, GO AND COOK SOMETHING OR SEW SOMETHING OR
JITT I (15)	WHEN YOU ARE AWAY FROM ME, I PLOD THROUGH MY	HOUSEWORK	, AND JUST COUNT THE DAYS UNTIL-- UNTIL THIS (SHE

HOUSING

DOCT PREFACE(25)	HEAD OF CATTLE WOULD PROVIDE FOR THE BREEDING AND	HOUSING	OF ENOUGH MICROBES TO INOCULATE THE ENTIRE
MRS PREFACE(156)	READ THE FIRST REPORT OF THE COMMISSION ON THE	HOUSING	OF THE WORKING CLASSES (BLUEBOOK C4402, 1889); READ
GETT PREFACE(191)	THEY WERE CONTENT TO HAVE THE WHOLE NATIONAL	HOUSING	PROBLEM TREATED ON A BASIS OF ONE ROOM FOR TWO
PYGM EPILOG (295)	THEM, HIGGINS DECLINED TO BE BOTHERED ABOUT HER	HOUSING	PROBLEM WHEN THAT SOLUTION WAS SO SIMPLE. ELIZA'S
PYGM I (211)	PARK LANE, FOR INSTANCE. I'D LIKE TO GO INTO THE	HOUSING	QUESTION WITH YOU, I WOULD. /THE FLOWER GIRL/ (
DOCT PREFACE(25)	IS NOT EXPENSIVE. THE COST OF BREEDING AND	HOUSING	TWO HEAD OF CATTLE WOULD PROVIDE FOR THE BREEDING
SUPR HANDBOK(182)	AN INCREASE IN THE QUANTITY OF FOOD, CLOTHING,	HOUSING	, AND COMFORT AT THEIR PERSONAL DISPOSAL, AS WELL AS
ROCK I (202)	OUR INDUSTRIES IF WE MUST; NATIONALIZE EDUCATION,	HOUSING	, SCIENCE, ART, THE THEATRE, THE OPERA, EVEN THE

HOUSMAN

HART PREFACE(34)	MURRAY, JOHN MASEFIELD, ST JOHN HANKIN, LAURENCE	HOUSMAN	, ARNOLD BENNETT, JOHN GALSWORTHY, JOHN DRINKWATER,
POSN PREFACE(361)	MR CECIL RALEIGH, MR JOHN GALSWORTHY, MR LAURENCE	HOUSMAN	, SIR HERBERT BEERBOHM TREE, MR W.L. COURTNEY, SIR
POSN PREFACE(417)	BY PROFESSOR GILBERT MURRAY AND MR LAURENCE	HOUSMAN	, WHO, IN PURE KINDNESS TO THE MANAGERS, ASKED

HOUSTON

MIS. PREFACE(100)	MANIFESTO EVER WRITTEN, AS FAR AS I KNOW, IS	HOUSTON	CHAMBERLAIN'S FOUNDATIONS OF THE NINETEENTH CENTURY:
MILL PREFACE(125)	THAT HERR HITLER IN HIS YOUTH WAS FASCINATED BY	HOUSTON	CHAMBERLAIN'S FOUNDATIONS OF THE XIX CENTURY, AN

HOUT

CAND II (112)	THE MATTER? /BURGESS/ MR MORCHBANKS WILL BEAR ME	HOUT	: HE WAS A WITNESS. (VERY SOLEMNLY) YORE YOUNG WOMAN
CAND I (87)	YEARS AGO, YOU DONE ME A HIL TURN. YOU DONE ME	HOUT	OF A CONTRAC; AN WHEN I GEV YOU ARSH WORDS IN MY NATRAL
CAND I (91)	AT ALL. WHY, I KNOW A CLORGYMAN WHAT 'AS BIN KEP	HOUT	OF HIS JOB FOR YORRS BY THE BISHOP O LONDON, ALTHOUGH

HOUYHNHNMS

BASH II,1, (112)	THROUGH THE TOWN; BUT WE, THE RICH, ARE SLAVES TO	HOUYHNHNMS	: WE WAIT UPON THEIR COLDS, AND FROWST ALL DAY

HOVEL

MTH2 (40)	GOING TO MARRY A VILLAGE WOODMAN AND LIVE IN A	HOVEL	WITH HIM AND A LOT OF KIDS TUMBLING OVER ONE ANOTHER,

HOVERING

APPL PREFACE(192)	AT THE TABLE ON THE PLATFORM WITH HIS HAND	HOVERING	OVER THE BUTTONS, INTIMATING THAT THE MIRACLE WOULD

HOVERS

DOCT PREFACE(5)	NATION PALPITATING FOR DAYS WHILST THE PATIENT	HOVERS	IN PAIN AND FEVER BETWEEN LIFE AND DEATH, HIS FORTUNE

HOVIS

VWOO 2,SD(123)	ALMONDS, ALL ON THE COUNTER; CHEESE, BUTTER, AND	HOVIS	BREAD HANDY TO THE SCALES; AND, IN FRONT OF THE
VWOO 2 (123)	OF A POUND OF YOUR BEST BUTTER, A SMALL LOAF OF	HOVIS	, AND TWOPENNYWORTH OF SUGARED ALMONDS. /Z/ ANYTHING

VWOO	2	(126)	TWO AND TENPENCE, ISNT IT? /A/ I DONT KNOW. /Z/	HOVIS	, TUPPENCE HALFPENNY. THREE SHILLINGS AND A HALFPENNY.
				HOWARD	
CAPT II		(269)	IF SHE DOWNT. /LADY CICELY/ (BUSILY) GOODBYE,	HOWARD	: DONT BE ANXIOUS ABOUT ME; AND ABOVE ALL, DONT BRING
CAPT III		(276)	QUITE SAFE, THANK YE, SIR HOWRRD. /LADY CICELY/	HOWARD	: HE'S IN A HURRY. DONT MAKE HIM STOP TO TALK. /SIR
CAPT III		(277)	MISUNDERSTOOD. (DESPAIRINGLY) OH, IT'S DREADFUL,	HOWARD	: IT'S TERRIBLE! WHAT WOULD POOR MARY SAY IF SHE
CAPT II		(257)	/REDBROOK/ (WITH CHEERFUL TACT) TUT TUT, SIR	HOWARD	: WHATS THE USE OF TALKING BACK? COME ALONG: WE'LL
CAPT II		(263)	/LADY CICELY/ IS THERE REALLY ANY DANGER FOR	HOWARD	? /BRASSBOUND/ YES. DANGER FOR ALL OF US UNLESS I
CAPT II		(255)	(TO SIR HOWARD) COULDNT YOU HAVE HELPED HER,	HOWARD	? /SIR HOWARD/ NO. THIS MAN MAY BE IGNORANT ENOUGH
CAPT I		(229)	/LADY CICELY/ I NEVER KNEW YOU HAD A BROTHER,	HOWARD	? /SIR HOWARD/ (NOT PLEASED BY THIS REMARK) PERHAPS
CAPT I		(228)	OLD. /RANKIN/ AND WHERE MAY MILES BE NOW, SIR	HOWARD	? /SIR HOWARD/ (ABRUPTLY) DONT YOU KNOW THAT HE IS
CAPT I		(226)	PETS OF KROOBOYS! DID YOU NOTICE THEIR FACES,	HOWARD	? /SIR HOWARD/ I DID; AND I CAN CONFIDENTLY SAY,
CAPT III		(277)	DO YOU THINK HE'S SO GREATLY CHANGED AS THAT,	HOWARD	? /SIR HOWARD/ (FALLING BACK ON THE FATALISM OF THE
CAPT III		(283)	ON THE COUNSEL FOR THE PROSECUTION, WOULDNT YOU,	HOWARD	? /SIR HOWARD/ BUT THERE IS NO COUNSEL FOR THE
CAPT II		(260)	THAN GIVING HIM TEN YEARS PENAL SERVITUDE:	HOWARD	ADMITTED IT. SO YOU SEE HE'S NOT A BIT BAD REALLY.
BARB PREFACE		(228)	OF THE OLD SCHOOL. IT STILL, AS COMMISSIONER	HOWARD	AFFIRMS, " STICKS TO MOSES," WHICH IS FLAT NONSENSE
CAPT II		(251)	BY THE LITTLE DOOR, LEAVING BRASSBOUND AND SIR	HOWARD	ALONE TOGETHER). /SIR HOWARD/ (RISING) AND NOW,
CAPT I		(240)	HER HAND AT ONCE. HE HESITATES; THEN TURNS TO SIR	HOWARD	AND ADDRESSES HIM WITH WARNING EARNESTNESS).
CAPT I	SD	(234)	DOOR, WHILST DRINKWATER COMES FORWARD BETWEEN SIR	HOWARD	AND LADY CICELY. /DRINKWATER/ YR HONOR'S SERVANT. (
CAPT III		(279)	CAPTAIN KEARNEY. /KEARNEY/ (COMING BETWEEN SIR	HOWARD	AND LADY CICELY) WHEN WE PARTED YESTERDAY AHFTERNOON,
CAPT II		(248)	WITH CONSIDERABLE EMPHASIS, IF NECESSARY. (SIR	HOWARD	ASSENTS WITH A POLITE BUT INCREDULOUS NOD).
CAPT I	SD	(228)	FROM THE FLOWERBED AND SITS DOWN ON HER LEFT, SIR	HOWARD	BEING ON HER RIGHT. /LADY CICELY/ WHAT A PLEASANT
CAPT II		(266)	OUT SIR HOWARD) THIS IS THE INFIDEL, CADI. (SIR	HOWARD	BOWS TO SIDI, BUT, BEING AN INFIDEL, RECEIVES ONLY
CAPT III		(286)	WHAT PEOPLE TOLD YOU: IT'S NOT EVIDENCE. (SIR	HOWARD	CHOKES WITH INDIGNATION). /KEARNEY/ (CALMLY) ALLOW
CAPT III	SD	(275)	WONT EITHER. THERE! THEY SHAKE HANDS ON IT. SIR	HOWARD	COMES IN. /SIR HOWARD/ GOOD MORNING, MR RANKIN. I
CAPT III		(287)	LOVE WITH ME. SO HE NATURALLY OFFERED TO SWOP SIR	HOWARD	FOR ME. DONT YOU THINK THAT WAS NICE OF HIM, CAPTAIN
CAPT III		(273)	WE HAVE NO RIGHT TO JUDGE ONE ANOTHER; AND AS SIR	HOWARD	GETS 5,000 POUNDS A YEAR FOR DOING NOTHING ELSE BUT
CAPT II		(269)	CAPTAIN BRASSBOUND: I RELY ON YOU TO SEE THAT SIR	HOWARD	GETS SAFE TO MOGADOR. (WHISPERING) TAKE YOUR HAND
CAPT II	SD	(257)	COME ALONG! WE'LL MAKE YOU COMFORTABLE. SIR	HOWARD	GOES OUT THROUGH THE ARCH BETWEEN JOHNSON AND
CAPT II	SD	(244)	THIS EAH IS THE CORFEE AND COMMERCIAL ROOM. SIR	HOWARD	GOES TO THE TABLE AND SITS ON THE SADDLE, RATHER
CAPT III		(285)	ON THIS SUBJECT? /RANKIN/ (NAIVELY) YES. (SIR	HOWARD	GRUNTS EMPHATICALLY, AS WHO SHOULD SAY " I THOUGHT
CAPT I		(240)	HIM WITH WARNING EARNESTNESS). /BRASSBOUND/ SIR	HOWARD	HALLAM: I ADVISE YOU NOT TO ATTEMPT THIS EXPEDITION.
CAPT II		(265)	TAKES REFUGE BEHIND SIR HOWARD). /BRASSBOUND/ SIR	HOWARD	HALLAM: YOU HAVE ONE CHANCE LEFT. THE CADI OF KINTAFI
CAPT II		(270)	COMING TO LOOK FOR THE TWO BRITISH TRAVELLERS SIR	HOWARD	HALLAM AND LADY CICELY WAYNFLETE, IN THE CADI'S
CAPT II		(264)	CHARACTER ENOUGH. /BRASSBOUND/ WELL, THERES SIR	HOWARD	HALLAM FOR YOU! HE HAS CHARACTER ENOUGH. /A VOICE/
CAPT III		(281)	CHAHM ABOUT THE BRITISH ARISTOCRACY, SIR	HOWARD	HALLAM. ARE THEY ALL LIKE THAT? (HE TAKES THE
CAPT III		(283)	YOU ARE A MAN OF EXPERIENCE IN THESE MATTERS, SIR	HOWARD	HALLAM. IF YOU HAD TO CONDUCT THIS BUSINESS, HOW
CAPT III		(286)	(CALMLY) ALLOW THE LADY TO PRO-CEED, SIR	HOWARD	HALLAM. /SIR HOWARD/ (RECOVERING HIS SELF-CONTROL
CAPT III		(288)	(SIR HOWARD IS ABOUT TO PROTEST) NO, SIR	HOWARD	HALLAM; EXCUSE ME. IN MOMENTS OF PAHSSION I HAVE
CAPT I		(235)	/BRASSBOUND/ WHO ARE " WE"? /RANKIN/ THIS IS SIR	HOWARD	HALLAM, WHO WILL BE WELL KNOWN TO YE AS ONE OF HER
CAPT III		(286)	COULD CLAIM TO CARRY OFF SIR HOWARD, BECAUSE SIR	HOWARD	IS A CHRISTIAN. BUT AS I AM ONLY A WOMAN, HE HAD NO
CAPT III		(288)	IN THE LANGUAGE OF THE ENGLISH FORECASTLE-- (SIR	HOWARD	IS ABOUT TO PROTEST) NO, SIR HOWARD HALLAM; EXCUSE
CAPT II		(260)	HIS BADNESS? /LADY CICELY/ BLESS ME! YOUR UNCLE	HOWARD	IS ONE OF THE MOST HARMLESS OF MEN-- MUCH NICER THAN
CAPT III	SD	(282)	ON THE CAPTAIN'S RIGHT, BEHIND RANKIN AND SIR	HOWARD	. FINALLY BRASSBOUND APPEARS WITH LADY CICELY ON HIS
CAPT III		(287)	IN SPITE OF THE QUARREL BETWEEN HIMSELF AND SIR	HOWARD	. HE REFUSED TO GIVE UP EITHER OF US, AND WAS ON THE
CAPT II		(248)	GRIN). /BRASSBOUND/ MY MANNERS ARE ROUGH, SIR	HOWARD	. I HAVE NO WISH TO FRIGHTEN THE LADY. /SIR HOWARD/
CAPT II		(260)	AND SHE-- SHE-- /LADY CICELY/ YES: SO YOU TOLD	HOWARD	. (WITH GENUINE PITY FOR HIM) YOU MUST HAVE HAD A
CAPT I		(231)	LIVED! WE'LL MAKE AN EXCURSION TO THEM TOMORROW,	HOWARD	. /RANKIN/ THATS IMPOSSIBLE, MY LEDDY. THE NATIVES
CAPT III	SD	(282)	RANKIN HURRIES IN, AND TAKES HIS PLACE NEAR SIR	HOWARD	. /SIR HOWARD/ THIS IS MR RANKIN, CAPTAIN KEARNEY.
CAPT I		(239)	/LADY CICELY/ THAT DOESNT MATTER IN THE LEAST,	HOWARD	. THE IMPORTANT THING, CAPTAIN BRASSBOUND, IS: FIRST,
CAPT III		(283)	COUNSEL FOR THE PROSECUTION. YOU MUSTNT LET SIR	HOWARD	MAKE A SPEECH, CAPTAIN KEARNEY: HIS DOCTORS HAVE
CAPT III		(276)	IN A TENTATIVE STEALTHY WAY WHICH WOULD PUT SIR	HOWARD	ON HIS GUARD IF HE WERE IN A SUSPICIOUS FRAME OF
CAPT I		(238)	THATS WHAT ESCORTS ALWAYS DO. BUT SINCE SIR	HOWARD	PREFERS AN ESCORT, I THINK YOU HAD BETTER STAY AT
CAPT III		(276)	THE REST OF IT. THE FAMILY WILL BE FURIOUS. (SIR	HOWARD	QUAILS. SHE INSTANTLY FOLLOWS UP HER ADVANTAGE WITH)
CAPT II	SD	(253)	RIGHT, MUTTERING TO HIMSELF SO OMINOUSLY THAT SIR	HOWARD	QUIETLY GETS OUT OF HIS WAY BY CROSSING TO THE OTHER
CAPT II	SD	(246)	ADVANCES TO THE MIDDLE OF THE ROOM. SIR	HOWARD	RETIRES BEHIND THEM AND SEATS HIMSELF ON THE DIVAN,
CAPT III	SD	(283)	AS SHE STOPS AT THE TABLE ON HIS LEFT. SIR	HOWARD	RISES PUNCTILIOUSLY WHEN KEARNEY RISES AND SITS WHEN
CAPT II		(265)	TEARS) NAOW, NAOW. LISSEN, KEPN (POINTING TO SIR	HOWARD	): E'LL GIVE HUZ FAWV UNNERD RED UNS. (TO THE
CAPT I		(227)	A CHAIR. /DRINKWATER/ (PLACING THE CHAIR FOR SIR	HOWARD	) AWSKINK YR PAWDN FOR THE LIBBETY, SR AHRD. /SIR
CAPT II		(251)	YOU HAVE SEEN THIS UNBELIEVER (INDICATING SIR	HOWARD	) COME IN WITH US? /OSMAN/ YEA, AND THE SHAMELESS
CAPT II		(255)	CICELY/ (SYMPATHETICALLY) POOR WOMAN! (TO SIR	HOWARD	) COULDNT YOU EVER HAVE HELPED HER, HOWARD? /SIR HOWARD/
CAPT II		(244)	WHIMPERS). CORSE Y' AW. /LADY CICELY/ (TO SIR	HOWARD	) DID YOU EVER SEE SUCH A HELPLESS LOT OF POOR
CAPT II		(254)	BRASSBOUND CONTINUES, WITH AN EVIL GLANCE AT SIR	HOWARD	) I SHALL DO NO MORE THAN JUSTICE. /SIR HOWARD/ (
CAPT II		(248)	ER WEN SHE CAMS BAWCK AGIN. /BRASSBOUND/ (TO SIR	HOWARD	) I WISH YOU TO UNDERSTAND, SIR HOWARD, THAT IN THIS
CAPT II		(254)	CICELY, AND ADDS, POINTING CONTEMPTUOUSLY TO SIR	HOWARD	) LOOK AT HIM. YOU WOULD NOT TAKE THIS VIRTUOUSLY
CAPT II		(265)	THATS THE ACE OF TRUMPS. /BRASSBOUND/ (TO SIR	HOWARD	) NOW, HAVE YOU ANY OTHER CARD TO PLAY? ANY OTHER
CAPT II		(245)	YOUR MANNERS, YOU GUTTERSNIPE? (TURNING TO SIR	HOWARD	) THATS THE CURSE O THIS KIND O LIFE, SIR: YOU GOT TO
CAPT I		(235)	(TURNING THE SINGULAR LOOK AGAIN ON SIR	HOWARD	) THE FRIEND OF THE WIDOW! THE PROTECTOR OF THE
CAPT II		(266)	AT HIS RIGHT HAND. /OSMAN/ (POINTING OUT SIR	HOWARD	) THIS IS THE INFIDEL, CADI. (SIR HOWARD BOWS TO
CAPT II		(257)	JOHNSON! REDBROOK! SOME OF YOU THERE! (TO SIR	HOWARD	) YOU ASK FOR A LITTLE PRIVACY: YOU SHALL HAVE IT. I
CAPT III		(281)	IN A GROUP BEHIND KEARNEY. /KEARNEY/ (TO SIR	HOWARD	) YOU WILL BE GLAHD TO HEAR THAT I HAVE A VERRY GOOD
CAPT II		(245)	THE CAPN COMES, SIR. /DRINKWATER/ (FOLLOWING SIR	HOWARD	) YUSS; AN WHAWL YOURE WITIN, YLL TIKE YOUR HORDERS
CAPT II		(265)	HE SCRAMBLES AWAY AND TAKES REFUGE BEHIND SIR	HOWARD	). /BRASSBOUND/ SIR HOWARD HALLAM: YOU HAVE ONE
CAPT II		(254)	(HE MAKES A MOVEMENT AS IF TO RUSH AT SIR	HOWARD	). /LADY CICELY/ (RISING QUICKLY AND PUTTING HER
CAPT III		(287)	WHAT WAS HE TO DO? HE WASNT IN LOVE WITH SIR	HOWARD	; AND HE WAS IN LOVE WITH ME. SO HE NATURALLY OFFERED
CAPT I	SD	(235)	IN A SINGULAR AND RATHER DEADLY WAY AT SIR	HOWARD	; THEN WITH SOME SURPRISE AND UNEASINESS AT LADY
CAPT III		(273)	AT THE CASTLE. YOU MUSTNT MIND WHAT SIR	HOWARD	SAYS ABOUT HIM: YOU REALLY MUSTNT. /RANKIN/ BUT HIS
CAPT II		(252)	YES: WE KNOW IT. (HE IS GOING OUT WHEN SIR	HOWARD	SPEAKS). /SIR HOWARD/ YOU KNOW ALSO, MR JOHNSON, I
CAPT II	SD	(254)	FOR THE UNCLE OF A BRIGAND, WOULD YOU? SIR	HOWARD	STARTS. THE SHOCK IS TOO MUCH FOR HIM: HE SITS DOWN
CAPT III		(274)	WHAT D'YE MEAN? /LADY CICELY/ OH! DIDNT SIR	HOWARD	TELL YOU THAT? WHY, CAPTAIN BRASSBOUND TURNS OUT TO
CAPT III		(287)	/LADY CICELY/ (SPRINGING UP AGAIN) DID SIR	HOWARD	TELL YOU THE THINGS HE SAID ABOUT CAPTAIN
CAPT III		(289)	MY BARGE WILL BE READY TO TAKE OFF YOU AND SIR	HOWARD	TO THE SANTIAGO AT ONE O' CLAWK. (HE RISES). CAPTAIN
CAPT III		(287)	THAT CONVEY THAT IMPRESSION. /KEARNEY/ BUT SIR	HOWARD	TOLD ME YESTERDAY THAT CAPTAIN BRASSBOUND THREATENED
CAPT III		(286)	CAPTAIN KEARNEY, THEN CAPTAIN BRASSBOUND AND SIR	HOWARD	TURNED OUT TO BE RELATED TO ONE ANOTHER (SENSATION);
CAPT III		(284)	AND PUT PERSUASION ON THE AUTHORITIES. (SIR	HOWARD	TURNS AND LOOKS AT RANKIN WITH A SUDDEN DOUBT OF HIS
CAPT III		(285)	AS IN LEAGUE WITH THE SHEIKH TO DELIVER SIR	HOWARD	UP TO HIM. /RANKIN/ THAT WAS MY FIRST HASTY
CAPT III		(288)	NOW, CAPTAIN KEARNEY, DO YOU WANT ME-- DOES SIR	HOWARD	WANT ME-- DOES ANYBODY WANT ME TO GO INTO THE DETAILS
CAPT III		(276)	TO THE OTHER END OF THE TABLE, LOOKING AT SIR	HOWARD	WITH A TROUBLED, SORROWFULLY SYMPATHETIC AIR, BUT
CAPT III		(276)	AS IT HAPPENS, HE IS NOT). I'M SO SORRY FOR YOU,	HOWARD	, ABOUT THIS UNFORTUNATE INQUIRY. /SIR HOWARD/ (
CAPT I		(233)	YOU SO FRANKLY PROVES IT. YOU KNOW, REALLY,	HOWARD	, ALL THOSE POOR PEOPLE WHOM YOU TRY ARE MORE SINNED
CAPT III		(273)	OF YOURSELF IN YOUR BEST MOMENTS. HE FORGAVE SIR	HOWARD	, AND DID ALL HE COULD TO SAVE HIM. /RANKIN/ YE
CAPT II		(266)	MOUSE WITH ME, MAN. /DRINKWATER/ (ASIDE TO SIR	HOWARD	, AS BRASSBOUND TURNS CONTEMPTUOUSLY AWAY TO THE
CAPT II		(260)	CICELY/ DO YOU THINK SHE WOULD REALLY HAVE KILLED	HOWARD	, AS SHE THREATENED, IF HE HADNT SENT HER TO PRISON?
CAPT II		(257)	/LADY CICELY/ (PLACIDLY) BESIDES, REALLY,	HOWARD	, AS THE PROPERTY NOW COSTS 150 POUNDS A YEAR TO KEEP
CAPT III		(286)	DILEMMA. YOU SEE, HE COULD CLAIM TO CARRY OFF SIR	HOWARD	, BECAUSE SIR HOWARD IS A CHRISTIAN. BUT AS I AM ONLY
CAPT III		(290)	I GO. (HE NODS GLOOMILY. SHE GOES OUT WITH SIR	HOWARD	, FOLLOWING THE CAPTAIN AND HIS STAFF). /RANKIN/ (
CAPT I		(226)	SHE WERE IN HER OWN. /LADY CICELY/ BUT, MY DEAR	HOWARD	, I ASSURE YOU THE NATIVES LIKE IT. /RANKIN/ (
CAPT III		(278)	BELIEVE ANYTHING. THE PROPER THING FOR YOU TO DO,	HOWARD	, IS TO LET ME TELL THE EXACT TRUTH. THEN YOU CAN
CAPT III		(287)	BLAME ON CAPTAIN BRASSBOUND. SO HERE WE ARE. NOW,	HOWARD	, ISNT THAT THE EXACT TRUTH, EVERY WORD OF IT? /SIR
CAPT III		(278)	CICELY/ (WITH THE UTMOST GOODHUMOR) MY DEAR	HOWARD	, NOT A BIT. OF COURSE YOURE RIGHT: YOU KNOW HOW
CAPT II		(263)	AND THE REST COME IN THROUGH THE ARCH, WITH SIR	HOWARD	, STILL VERY CRUSTY AND DETERMINED. HE KEEPS CLOSE TO
CAPT II		(248)	(TO SIR HOWARD) I WISH YOU TO UNDERSTAND, SIR	HOWARD	, THAT IN THIS CASTLE, IT IS I WHO GIVE ORDERS, AND
CAPT I		(227)	THEY MUST WANT IT MORE THAN WE DO; AND YOU KNOW,	HOWARD	, THAT MAHOMETANS NEVER SPEND MONEY IN DRINK.
CAPT I		(231)	(INDIGNANTLY) OF COURSE NOT. YOU ALWAYS THINK,	HOWARD	, THAT NOTHING PREVENTS PEOPLE KILLING EACH OTHER BUT
CAPT II	SD	(266)	THE ROOM BEHIND THE TABLE AND ASSEMBLE NEAR SIR	HOWARD	, WHO STANDS HIS GROUND. DRINKWATER RUNS ACROSS TO
CAPT II		(243)	SHE IS, LIKE A BLOOMIN ORSPITTLE NASS. (SIR	HOWARD	, WITH A COPIOUS PAGRI ON HIS WHITE HAT, ENTERS

HOWARD'S

CAPT II	(260)	HE CANT HELP DOING IT. WHAT CAN YOU EXPECT? SIR	HOWARD'S	ALL RIGHT WHEN HE'S LEFT TO HIMSELF. WE CAUGHT A
BULL I	(78)	RIGHT: I WILL. (HE GIVES HIM A COPY OF EBENEZER	HOWARD'S	BOOK, AND SEVERAL PAMPHLETS). YOU UNDERSTAND THAT
CAPT III	(296)	THANK YOU. IVE HAD QUITE ENOUGH OF YOUR DUTY, AND	HOWARD'S	DUTY. WHERE WOULD YOU BOTH BE NOW IF I'D LET YOU DO
CAPT II	(270)	/BRASSBOUND/ IT IS NOT A BRITISH SHIP. (SIR	HOWARD'S	FACE FALLS). /LADY CICELY/ WHAT IS IT, THEN?
CAPT III	(275)	CADI DIDNT KNOW THAT CAPTAIN BRASSBOUND WAS SIR	HOWARD'S	NEPHEW, DID HE? /RANKIN/ NO. /LADY CICELY/ THEN HE
CAPT III	(274)	WHY, CAPTAIN BRASSBOUND TURNS OUT TO BE SIR	HOWARD'S	NEPHEW, THE SON OF THE BROTHER YOU KNEW. /RANKIN/ (
CAPT I	SD(235)	MARZO IMMEDIATELY HURRIES DOWN THE GARDEN ON SIR	HOWARD'S	RIGHT OUT OF THE NEIGHBORHOOD OF THE DOORWAY.
CAPT II	(258)	MOTHER'S COMPLEXION. BUT DIDNT YOU NOTICE SIR	HOWARD'S	TEMPER, HIS DOGGEDNESS, HIS HIGH SPIRIT: ABOVE ALL,

HOWBEIT

LION PREFACE	(79)	THEIR ENERGIES FOR LESS PRIMITIVE ACTIVITIES.	HOWBEIT	, PAUL SUCCEEDED IN STEALING THE IMAGE OF CHRIST
HART PREFACE	(34)	GIVEN ME BY THE CHIEF OFFICER OF ITS HOUSEHOLD.	HOWBEIT	, THE FACT THAT MY PLAYS EFFECTED A LODGMENT ON THE
HART PREFACE	(9)	WHICH ITS INVESTIGATORS CALLED NATURAL SELECTION.	HOWBEIT	, THERE WAS ONLY ONE RESULT POSSIBLE IN THE ETHICAL

HOWCEAN

CAPT I	(221)	HINDIES! JIST ACROST THERE, FATHER SAWD THET	HOWCEAN	(POINTING SEAWARD)! DEAR ME! WE CAMS HIN WITH
CAPT I	(223)	SUCKUS. IF AW WAS TO DO ORN THET THERE HETLENTIC	HOWCEAN	THE THINGS AW DID AS A BWOY IN THE WORTERLEOO ROWD,

HOWDYE

CAPT I	(234)	CHEF. /LADY CICELY/ (NODDING AFFABLY TO MARZO)	HOWDYE	DO? I LOVE ITALY. WHAT PART OF IT WERE YOU BORN IN?

HOWDYEDO

CAPT I	(232)	SAID THEYD KILL ME. BUT WHEN I MET THEM, I SAID	HOWDYEDO	? AND THEY WERE QUITE NICE. THE KINGS ALWAYS
CAPT II	(247)	YOU, LADY CICELY. /LADY CICELY/ (SHAKING HANDS)	HOWDYEDO	? OF COURSE I KNEW YOUR FATHER-- DUNHAM WASNT IT?
CAPT I	(236)	HIS LORDSHIP'S SISTER-IN-LAW. /LADY CICELY/	HOWDYEDO	, CAPTAIN BRASSBOUND? (HE BOWS GRAVELY). /SIR

HOWE

DEVL EPILOG	(81)	TO SIGN THE DISPATCHES; BUT AS THOSE ADDRESSED TO	HOWE	HAD NOT BEEN FAIR-COPIED, AND HE WAS NOT DISPOSED TO BE
DEVL III	(69)	MARCHED SOUTH FROM QUEBEC TO DO, AND WHAT GENERAL	HOWE	HAS MARCHED NORTH FROM NEW YORK TO DO: EFFECT A
DEVL III	(69)	AND VOICE) I HAVE JUST LEARNT, SIR, THAT GENERAL	HOWE	IS STILL IN NEW YORK. /SWINDON/ (THUNDERSTRUCK) GOOD
DEVL EPILOG	(81)	WHAT HAD HAPPENED ABOUT THE INSTRUCTIONS TO	HOWE	(THE SCENE IN WHICH I HAVE REPRESENTED HIM AS LEARNING
DEVL EPILOG	(81)	THESE WERE THE DISPATCHES INSTRUCTING SIR WILLIAM	HOWE	, WHO WAS IN NEW YORK, TO EFFECT A JUNCTION AT ALBANY

HOWKN

BULL II	(106)	DINTED A SLAB OF GRANITE) SURE ME FUT SLIPT.	HOWKN	I CARRY THREE MEN'S LUGGAGE AT WANST? /FATHER

HOWL

NEVR I	(202)	NO: IT'S ALL OVER. /THE YOUNG GENTLEMAN/ DID YOU	HOWL	? /THE YOUNG LADY/ OH, SOMETHING AWFUL. MR VALENTINE:
KING I	(211)	WAS STARING ME IN THE FACE. /JAMES/ WELL, WHY	HOWL	ABOUT IT? BRING OUT ANOTHER EDITION AND CONFESS THAT
MIS.	(113)	HAVE TRIED IT ON YOU UNTIL YOU FIRST LEARNT TO	HOWL	AND THEN TO BEHAVE YOURSELF. /BENTLEY/ (
ROCK I	(223)	COUNTRY: A RISE IN PRICES." THE MOB JUST GAVE ONE	HOWL	AND WENT FOR HIM. THEN THE POLICE DREW THEIR BATONS AND
NEVR III	(268)	FASHIONED MAN: HE THOUGHT IT UNFAIR, AND TRIED TO	HOWL	IT DOWN AS UNWOMANLY AND ALL THE REST OF IT. BUT THAT
HART III	(140)	HOUSE. /MRS HUSHABYE/ STOP, ELLIE; OR I SHALL	HOWL	LIKE AN ANIMAL. /MANGAN/ (BREAKS INTO A LOW
MILL I	(164)	EXTRAORDINARY LADY. /ALASTAIR/ (UTTERS A STIFLED	HOWL	)! /PATRICIA/ HE CANT FIND WORDS FOR HER, POOR DEAR.

HOWLED

NEVR II	(228)	LEARNT TO DO FROM MY MASTER HERBERT SPENCER. AM I	HOWLED	AT? NO: I'M INDULGED AS AN OLD FOGEY. I'M OUT OF
NEVR II	(228)	MY ST HELENA, FINCH. I SUPPOSE SHE WILL BE	HOWLED	AT AS I WAS; BUT SHE IS PREPARED FOR THAT. /M'COMAS/
NEVR II	(228)	AS I WAS; BUT SHE IS PREPARED FOR THAT. /M'COMAS/	HOWLED	AT! MY DEAR GOOD LADY: THERE IS NOTHING IN ANY OF
LADY PREFACE	(224)	BODIES? " " AN HE HAD BEEN A DOG THAT SHOULD HAVE	HOWLED	THUS, THEY WOULD HAVE HANGED HIM." THERE IS JUST AS

HOWLER

JOAN EPILOG	(162)	POLITICAL MISTAKES; AND THIS ONE WAS A VERITABLE	HOWLER	; FOR YOUR SPIRIT CONQUERED US, MADAM, IN SPITE OF

HOWLING

LIED	(194)	THANKFUL THAT YOU ARE ALIVE INSTEAD OF-- OF-- OF	HOWLING	ABOUT FIVESHILLINGSWORTH OF IVORY. DAMN YOUR FAN!
JOAN	6,SD(148)	THE SILENCE IS BROKEN BY SOMEONE FRANTICALLY	HOWLING	AND SOBBING. /WARWICK/ WHAT IN THE DEVIL'S NAME --?
BARB PREFACE	(240)	AND A CHRISTIAN IN THE MULTITUDE OF HUMAN WOLVES	HOWLING	FOR HIS BLOOD. THINK ALSO OF THIS: THAT AT THE VERY
MILL III	(186)	IS MY DEVOTED SLAVE. MAKE THAT POOR WOMAN STOP	HOWLING	IF YOU CAN. I AM GOING NOW. THERE IS NOT ENOUGH WORK
MTH5	(232)	TURNED TO POISON; AND HE PERISHED IN TORMENTS,	HOWLING	. I THEN PERCEIVED THAT I HAD PRODUCED A PREHISTORIC
HART III	(140)	ALFRED OFF. /ELLIE/ I LIKE HIM BEST WHEN HE IS	HOWLING	. /CAPTAIN SHOTOVER/ SILENCE! (MANGAN SUBSIDES
MTH5	(241)	IT, SIR: INDEED SHE DID. /THE FEMALE FIGURE/ (	HOWLING	LAMENTABLY) BOOHOO! OO! OOH! /THE HE-ANCIENT/
GLIM	(177)	WITH. DO YOU SUPPOSE I'M GOING TO LISTEN TO THE	HOWLING	OF A SHE-WOLF WHO WANTED ME TO ABSOLVE HER FOR
CLEO I	SD(117)	BODY, ITS BRAZEN BELL SHAPED LIKE THE HEAD OF A	HOWLING	WOLF. WHEN THEY REACH THE TRANSEPT, THEY STARE IN

HOWLS

PPP	SD(205)	WINDOW. /PHYLLIS/ I THINK IT'S RAINING. THE WIND	HOWLS	. /THE LANDLORD/ IT'S THANDERIN AND LAWTNIN. /FITZ/
MTH1 II	(22)	RUNNING WITH BLOOD! THE SHOUTS OF TRIUMPH! THE	HOWLS	OF RAGE! THE CURSES OF DESPAIR! THE SHRIEKS OF
HART III	(142)	HOWLS WHEN SHE TWISTS HIS HEART, JUST AS MANGAN	HOWLS	WHEN MY WIFE TWISTS HIS. /LADY UTTERWORD/ THAT IS
HART III	(142)	HOUSE IS. THAT POOR DEVIL UPSTAIRS WITH HIS FLUTE	HOWLS	WHEN SHE TWISTS HIS HEART, JUST AS MANGAN HOWLS WHEN

HOWLT

BULL I	(79)	IRELAND AS YOU DO MAY CALL ME ANYTHING. GIMMY A	HOWLT	O THAT WHISKY BOTTLE (HE REPLENISHES). /BROADBENT/ (
BULL III	(144)	/PATSY/ (MEDITATIVELY) BEDAD, IF DHAT PIG GETS A	HOWLT	O THE HANDLE O THE MACHINE-- (HE SHAKES HIS HEAD

HOWN

CAND I	(89)	NOT WISHIN TO BE HON BAD TERMS WITH MY	HOWN	DAUGHRTER'S USBAN. COME, JAMES: BE A KERISCHIN, AND
CAND I	(92)	GARN! D' YOU MEAN TO TELL ME-- YOUR	HOWN	FATHER! -- THAT CAB TOUTS OR SUCH LIKE, ORF THE
CAPT I	(238)	TO LADY CICELY) NAOW, LIDY: IT WOULDNT BE FOR YR	HOWN	GOOD. YER CAWNT HEXPECT A LOT O POOR HONEDDIKITED MEN
CAND I	(88)	I DIDNT HEAR YOU. /BURGESS/ OF COURSE I DID. I	HOWN	IT NOW. COME: I HARSK YOUR PARDON FOR THE LETTER I

HOWNED

CAND I	(87)	DONT GIT HINTO A FLUSTER ABOUT NOTHINK. IVE	HOWNED	I WAS WRONG. /MORELL/ HAVE YOU? I DIDNT HEAR YOU.

HOWNLY

CAPT I	(238)	THATS ENOUGH. GO. /DRINKWATER/ WEOLL, AW WAS	HOWNLY	A TEOLLN THE LIDY THET-- (A THREATENING MOVEMENT

HOWRRD

CAPT III	(284)	SIDI EL ASSIF. HE TOLD ME I SHOULD NEVER SEE SIR	HOWRRD	AGAIN, BECAUSE HIS MASTER KNEW HE WAS A CHRISTIAN AND
CAPT III	(284)	THE PARABLE? /RANKIN/ ON THE VERY DAY THAT SIR	HOWRRD	AND LADY CICELY STARTED ON THEIR EXCURSION I WAS
CAPT III	(272)	PRESIDE IN THIS; AND THAT LEAVES BUT ONE FOR SIR	HOWRRD	AND ONE FOR YOUR LEDDYSHIP. I COULD ALMOST BE TEMPTED
CAPT I	(219)	HEVER EAR O JADGE ELLAM? /RANKIN/ SIR	HOWRRD	HALLAM? /DRINKWATER/ THETS IM-- ENGINEST JADGE IN
CAPT I	(219)	LONDON NEWSPAPER), SHE DID. /RANKIN/ IS SHE SIR	HOWRRD	HALLAM'S SISTER-IN-LAW? /DRINKWATER/ DECEASED
CAPT I	(220)	OF ALL PLACES; AND TO MY HOUSE! I ONCE MET SIR	HOWRRD	HALLAM, YEARS AGO. /DRINKWATER/ (AMAZED) NAOW!
CAPT I	(220)	SOME INDIGNATION) I HOPE YOU DONT THINK I MET SIR	HOWRRD	IN THAT WAY. /DRINKWATER/ MAWT YEPPN TO THE
CAPT I	(228)	WELL, PERHAPS HARDLY AN ACQUAINTANCE, SIR	HOWRRD	. BUT I WAS A CLOSE FRIEND OF YOUR BROTHER MILES; AND
CAPT I	(239)	WE GO, MR RANKIN? /RANKIN/ TAKE MY ADVICE, SIR	HOWRRD	. DONT GO FAR. /BRASSBOUND/ I CAN TAKE YOU TO
CAPT I	(233)	HIS HANDS. /RANKIN/ I QUITE AGREE WITH YOU, SIR	HOWRRD	. I'LL SEND FELIX DRINKWOTTER FOR HIM (HE CLAPS HIS
CAPT I	(229)	IT FOR MILES' SAKE, THOUGH I AM NO LAWYER, SIR	HOWRRD	. /LADY CICELY/ I NEVER KNEW YOU HAD A BROTHER,
CAPT I	(231)	/RANKIN/ NAY, NAY: NOT EXACTLY THAT, SIR	HOWRRD	. /LADY CICELY/ (INDIGNANTLY) OF COURSE NOT. YOU
CAPT III	(276)	LAST NIGHT. /RANKIN/ QUITE SAFE, THANK YE, SIR	HOWRRD	. /LADY CICELY/ HOWARD: HE'S IN A HURRY. DONT MAKE
CAPT III	(274)	WITH A MOMENTARY SENSE OF ILL USAGE) I THINK SIR	HOWRRD	MIGHT HAVE TOLD ME THAT. /LADY CICELY/ OF COURSE HE
CAPT III	(274)	I HAD A CRACK WITH THE CADI AS WELL AS WITH SIR	HOWRRD	; AND THERE IS LITTLE QUESTION IN MY MIND BUT THAT
CAPT III	(285)	AS I UNDERSTAND IT, HE TRIED TO SMUGGLE SIR	HOWRRD	THROUGH UNDER THIS COMPACT, AND THE SHEIKH FOUND HIM

CAPT III (273) A PRECIOUS SCOUNDREL? DID YE NOT HEAR WHAT SIR HOWRRD TOLD ME ON THE YACHT LAST NIGHT? /LADY CICELY/ ALL A
CAPT I (228) CHANGING THE SUBJECT) AND HOW HAVE YE BEEN, SIR HOWRRD , SINCE OUR LAST MEETING THAT MORNING NIGH FORTY YEAR

HOWS
O'FL (220) AND HOW ARE YOU? /TERESA/ NICELY, THANK YOU. AND HOWS YOURSELF? /O'FLAHERTY/ FINELY, THANK GOD. (HE
BULL III (126) OR PATRONIZED, NODS INDEPENDENTLY. /DORAN/ HOWS YOURSELF, LARRY? /LARRY/ FINELY, THANK YOU. NO NEED TO

HOWTH
BUOY PREFACE(5) THE SKIES AND SEAS OF THE TWO GREAT BAYS BETWEEN HOWTH AND BRAY, WITH DALKEY ISLAND IN THE MIDDLE. I HAD

HOWVER
CAPT I (222) THER YNT NAOW AWM IN IT. SHE WERE A WUST HINJIN-- HOWVER THERE AGIN, YER SEE (POINTING SEAWARD)-- LEASTWAWS,
CAPT II (243) YUSS: SHOULD THINK THERE WORS DINEGER. IT'S HOWVER , THOW, AS IT MOWSTLY HIS BAW THE TAWM YOURE AWIKE. (

HOXTON
CAND I (81) IN SILENCE, WITH IMPLACABLE DISPARAGEMENT OF THE HOXTON ANARCHISTS IN EVERY LINE OF HER FACE. MORELL BURSTS
CAND I (79) /PROSERPINE/ ANOTHER LECTURE? /MORELL/ YES. THE HOXTON FREEDOM GROUP WANT ME TO ADDRESS THEM ON SUNDAY
CAND I (81) COMPANY. /MORELL/ THATLL DO: I'LL GO TO THE HOXTON GROUP OF FREEDOM INSTEAD. (SHE ENTERS THE ENGAGEMENT
CAND I SD(77) ALL THE PETTY FAUNA OF KINGSLAND, HACKNEY, AND HOXTON . A BANDSTAND, AN UNFURNISHED FORUM FOR RELIGIOUS,
PYGM I (211) WHERE I COME FROM? /THE NOTE TAKER/ (PROMPTLY) HOXTON . TITTERINGS. POPULAR INTEREST IN THE NOTE TAKER'S

HS
CAPT NOTES (306) SAY THAT IN ENGLAND HE WHO BOTHERS ABOUT HIS HS IS A FOOL, AND HE WHO RIDICULES A DROPPED H A SNOB. AS TO

HSH
MTH2 (87) FLAGS IN THE STREETS IN MY BEST CLOTHES; AND-- HSH ! (SHE JUMPS UP AND PRETENDS TO BE LOOKING FOR A BOOK

HUBBARD
FABL VI (122) GAME ON US, ARE YOU? /YOUTH 3/ IF YOU DO, MOTHER HUBBARD , YOULL NOT HAVE A HAPPY TIME WITH US. /TEACHER/ YOU

HUBBUB
2TRU PREFACE(12) WAILINGS ARISE. THE MOST ARTICULATE SOUNDS IN THE HUBBUB ARE TO THE EFFECT THAT THE WRETCHED SLAVES OF THE
O'FL SD(225) AND MENACES OF O'FLAHERTY, ONLY INCREASE THE HUBBUB . THEY ARE SOON ALL SPEAKING AT ONCE AT THE TOP OF
PYGM I (208) TO ASK HIM TO BUY A FLOWER OFF ME. (GENERAL HUBBUB , MOSTLY SYMPATHETIC TO THE FLOWER GIRL, BUT

HUBRIS
JOAN 5 (114) IS RISING AMONG US. IT IS THE CHASTISEMENT OF HUBRIS . /CHARLES/ YES: SHE THINKS SHE KNOWS BETTER THAN

HUCKSTERING
6CAL (95) THESE BASE RASCALS OF BURGESSES: THESE HUCKSTERING HOUNDS OF MERCHANTS WHO HAVE MADE THIS PORT OF

HUCKSTERS
LADY (244) THEM; AND TWAS THOSE BILLS, IN THE HANDS OF BASE HUCKSTERS , THAT WERE HIS UNDOING. /ELIZABETH/ (GRIMLY) THE

HUDDLE
BARB III (340) STRONG ENOUGH TO OVERTURN A SOCIAL SYSTEM, BUT HUDDLE THEM TOGETHER IN A CERTAIN HOUSE IN WESTMINSTER; AND
3PLA PREFACE(R32) ABSURD. BUT WHEN YOUR SHAKESPEARS AND THACKERAYS HUDDLE UP THE MATTER AT THE END BY KILLING SOMEBODY AND

HUDDLING
2TRU I (37) WHERE THE ELECTRIC SWITCH IS. /THE PATIENT/ (HUDDLING HERSELF UP IN THE BEDCLOTHES) WHAT ARE YOU DOING..

HUDIBRAS
BARB PREFACE(221) SHOULD PERPETUATE THE MEMORY OF THE AUTHOR OF HUDIBRAS WELL, IT CANNOT BE DENIED THAT THE ENGLISH ARE

HUE
APPL PREFACE(182) A TROUBLESOME CHAMPION OF LIBERTY IS TO RAISE A HUE AND CRY AGAINST HIM AS AN UNPATRIOTIC PERSON, AND LEAVE
MRS PREFACE(178) INDIFFERENT TO APHRODISIAC PLAYS, RAISE THE MORAL HUE AND CRY AGAINST PERFORMANCES OF MRS WARREN'S PROFESSION,

HUES
WIDO III SD(51) LINED THROUGHOUT WITH FURS PRESENTING ALL THE HUES OF THE TIGER. HIS SHIRT IS FASTENED AT THE BREAST WITH
SUPR I SD(3) BLUE, OF ONE OF THOSE INDEFINITELY MIXED HUES WHICH THE MODERN CLOTHIER HAS PRODUCED TO HARMONIZE

HUFF
FANY III (317) KNOW WHAT HAPPENS: COMPLAINTS AND QUARRELS AND HUFF AND OFFENCE AND BAD LANGUAGE AND BAD TEMPER AND REGULAR
SUPR III (135) AND IT ENDED IN NIETZSCHE'S GOING TO HEAVEN IN A HUFF . AND A GOOD RIDDANCE TOO. AND NOW, MY FRIEND, LET US
HART II (123) (A CHILDISHLY PLAINTIVE NOTE BREAKING INTO HIS HUFF) I HAVE NOT SAID A WORD AGAINST LADY UTTERWORD. THIS

HUFFED
FANY III (304) YOURE NO GOOD, NO GOOD TO ME, ANYHOW. /BOBBY/ (HUFFED) I'M SORRY, MISS KNOX. /MARGARET/ GOODBYE, MR
PHIL II (116) YOU MUST EXCUSE A DAUGHTER'S FEELINGS. /CRAVEN/ (HUFFED) IT EVIDENTLY DOESNT MAKE MUCH DIFFERENCE TO YOU,
GETT (276) TABLE NEAREST THE HEARTH.) /THE GENERAL/ (MUCH HUFFED) OH, WELL, IF LEO DOES NOT MIND, OF COURSE I HAVE NO
O'FL (211) THEM? WHAT BETTER IS ANYBODY? /SIR PEARCE/ (HUFFED , TURNING A COLD SHOULDER TO HIM) I AM SORRY THE

HUFFILY
GETT (284) THEM ALL OUT ALREADY, REGINALD. /LEO/ (A LITTLE HUFFILY) AFTER ALL, THERE ARE WORSE MEN THAN REGINALD. I
DOCT I (110) CAN; AND THEN I SHALL BE ALL RIGHT. /RIDGEON/ (HUFFILY) I AM NOT A CUREMONGER: IF YOU WANT CURES, YOU MUST
CAPT II (258) IS YOUR PET NAME, ISNT IT? /BRASSBOUND/ (HUFFILY) I AM NOT USUALLY CALLED SO TO MY FACE. /LADY
FANY III (301) YOU-- THAT WAY. /BOBBY/ (REMOVING HIS ARM RATHER HUFFILY) I BEG YOUR PARDON, I'M SURE. I THOUGHT YOU DID.
OVER (194) NEED WE GO ON FOOTLING ABOUT IT? /JUNO/ (HUFFILY) I DONT KNOW WHAT YOU CALL FOOTLING-- /MRS JUNO/ (
BULL III (139) THEY CALL A FREEHOLD FARMER A YEOMAN. /MATTHEW/ (HUFFILY) I DONT NEED TO BE INSTHRUCTED BE YOU, LARRY DOYLE.
CAND I (86) IS PRIVATE BETWEEN ME AND MR MORELL. /LEXY/ (HUFFILY) I HAVE NO INTENTION OF INTRUDING, I AM SURE, MR
HART III (143) TIRED OF YOU ALL, CLEVER AS YOU ARE. /MANGAN/ (HUFFILY) I NEVER SET UP TO BE CLEVER. /LADY UTTERWORD/ I
NEVR III (275) (INTERPOSING ADROITLY) I DO. /M'COMAS/ (HUFFILY) IN THAT CASE, SIR, YOU MUST NOT BE SURPRISED TO
MTH4 I (140) ELDERLY GENTLEMAN/ (PULLING HIMSELF TOGETHER HUFFILY) IT HAS NO EFFECT ON ME, MADAM. I FEAR MY
GETT (271) THE TABLE, NEAR THE STUDY DOOR). /THE GENERAL/ (HUFFILY) OH WELL, IF YOU REFUSE, YOU REFUSE. I SHALL NOT
HART II (113) /MRS HUSHABYE/ WHAT DO YOU SAY, ALF? /MANGAN/ (HUFFILY) OH, I DONT MATTER. I'M FORGOTTEN. THE BURGLAR HAS
OVER (191) GREGORY LOOKS AT JUNO. JUNO TURNS AWAY HIS HEAD HUFFILY). I MEAN, WHAT ARE WE GOING TO DO? /MRS LUNN/ WHAT
GETT (350) LESBIA. I SHALL NOT ASK YOU AGAIN. (HE SITS DOWN HUFFILY). /LESBIA/ YOU WILL, BOXER; BUT IT WILL BE NO USE.
WIDO III (64) WHY DONT YOU GO? (RED AND WINCING, HE STARTS HUFFILY TO GET HIS HAT FROM THE TABLE; BUT WHEN HE TURNS TO

HUFFISHLY
HART II (122) REALLY, ARIADNE IS THE LIMIT (HE MOVES AWAY HUFFISHLY TOWARDS THE WINDOWS). /HECTOR/ (COOLLY) SHE IS,

HUFFY
DOCT PREFACE(41) OFFER US ALL THE PIOUS PROTESTATIONS AND ALL THE HUFFY RECRIMINATIONS THAT ANY COMMON UNSCIENTIFIC MORTAL
SUPR II (65) FOR SAYING SO. /RAMSDEN/ (HALF APOLOGETIC, HALF HUFFY) THE YOUNG LADY WAS MARRIED SECRETLY; AND HER HUSBAND

HUG
2TRU II (66) ELSE IS LOOKING. AND ALL THE TIME I WANT TO HUG HIM (SHE BREAKS DOWN IN TEARS). /AUBREY/ OH FOR
MTH5 SD(205) A FIGURE LIKE A FARANDOLE. THEY NEITHER ROMP NOR HUG IN OUR MANNER. AT THE FIRST FULL CLOSE THEY CLAP THEIR
BULL IV (167) OF MY NATURE THAT I SHOULD HAVE SOMEBODY TO HUG OCCASIONALLY. BESIDES, IT'S GOOD FOR YOU: ITLL PLUMP OUT
MILL IV (201) (EXTRICATING HIMSELF GENTLY FROM EPIFANIA'S HUG) MR BLENDERBLAND: IT IS A MISTAKE TO GO INTO COURT IN

HUGE
DOCT PREFACE(31) OF ENGLAND, HE WOULD HAVE HAD TO WAIT FOR SOME HUGE ACCIDENTAL CALAMITY: A CHOLERA EPIDEMIC, A WAR, OR AN
MTH2 (72) CANNONS TRAINED ON EVERY CITY AND SEAPORT, AND HUGE AEROPLANES READY TO SPRING INTO THE AIR AND DROP BOMBS
GETT PREFACE(188) THOUGH WE ALL STILL ASSUME THE EXISTENCE OF A HUGE AND DANGEROUS MAJORITY WHICH REGARDS THE LEAST HINT OF

MTH2 (69) TASK WAS BEYOND HUMAN CAPACITY. WHAT WITH OUR HUGE ARMAMENTS, OUR TERRIBLE ENGINES OF DESTRUCTION, OUR
HART PREFACE(15) BEING UTTERED AMID THUNDERING APPLAUSE BEFORE HUGE AUDIENCES IN ENGLAND, AND THE MORE PRIVATE RECORDS OF
CATH 4,SD(187) BY A HEAVILY CURTAINED ARCH WITH THE HUGE BALLROOM OF THE PALACE. THE LIGHT IS SUBDUED BY RED
GETT SD(259) THE VICTORIAN CABINET-MAKERS ENCLOSED AND HID THE HUGE BLACK BEAMS OF HEWN OAK, AND OF ALL THE OTHER
LION PREFACE(61) CLASSES: SUCH STABILITY AS IT HAS IS DUE TO THE HUGE BLOCKS OF PEOPLE BETWEEN WHOM THERE IS EQUALITY OF
SUPR PREFACE(R15) TRIUMPHANT EVERYWHERE. CIVILIZED SOCIETY IS ONE HUGE BOURGEOISIE; NO NOBLEMAN DARES NOW SHOCK HIS
BARB III SD(326) SUGGESTS A FORTIFICATION, BECAUSE THERE IS A HUGE CANNON OF THE OBSOLETE WOOLWICH INFANT PATTERN PEERING
CLEO III SD(155) OF STEPS IN THE MIDDLE TO THE BROAD COPING. A HUGE CHAIN WITH A HOOK HANGS DOWN FROM THE LIGHTHOUSE CRANE
BARB PREFACE(242) MAN, HE BECOMES EQUALLY AN ANARCHIST. WHEN SOME HUGE CHANGE IN SOCIAL CONDITIONS, SUCH AS THE INDUSTRIAL
JOAN 2 (82) TO ANSWER THE ARCHBISHOP. /LA HIRE/ (WITH A HUGE CHUCKLE) WELL SAID, LASS! WELL SAID! /JOAN/ (
3PLA PREFACE(R31) MEN PERISH, SHAKESPEAR FINALLY STRAINS ALL HIS HUGE COMMAND OF RHETORIC AND STAGE PATHOS TO GIVE A
SUPR IV SD(142) SOMETHING PATHETIC ABOUT HIM AT TIMES, AS IF THE HUGE COMMERCIAL MACHINE WHICH HAS WORKED HIM INTO HIS FROCK
DOCT I (102) SCANDALOUS ADVERTISEMENTS OF PATENT MEDICINES! A HUGE COMMERCIAL SYSTEM OF QUACKERY AND POISON. WELL, WHOSE
APPL PREFACE(183) OUR INDUSTRIAL AND SOCIAL LIFE IS SET IN A HUGE COMMUNISTIC FRAMEWORK OF PUBLIC ROADWAYS, STREETS,
3PLA PREFACE(R21) OF HUMAN FOLLY AND VANITY), THEN, FOR THE HUGE COMPULSORILY SCHOOLED MASSES WHO READ ROMANCE OR
DOCT PREFACE(11) UNIONS TO THE GREAT EXCHANGES, WHICH MAKE UP THE HUGE CONFLICT WHICH WE CALL SOCIETY. BUT IT IS LESS
BARB III SD(326) BEHIND THE CANNON IS A TROLLEY CARRYING A HUGE CONICAL BOMBSHELL WITH A RED BAND PAINTED ON IT.
GETT PREFACE(222) TRADE UNIONISM AND UNORGANIZED CASUAL LABOR: A HUGE DIFFERENCE, NO DOUBT, AS TO ORDER AND COMFORT, BUT NOT
JOAN EPIL,SD(152) ARMS IN EMBROIDERY. EXCEPT FOR THE CANOPY AND THE HUGE DOWN PILLOWS THERE IS NOTHING TO DISTINGUISH IT FROM A
CATH 1 (164) I MUST MAKE MYSELF WHOLLY DRUNK (HE TAKES A HUGE DRAUGHT OF BRANDY). /VARINKA/ SOT! THE SERGEANT
MTH5 SD(214) ON THE ALTAR, AND THE PALL REMOVED. IT IS A HUGE EGG. /THE SHE-ANCIENT/ (FREEING HER ARMS FROM HER
DOCT PREFACE(13) TEMPT SURGEONS TO OPERATE ON THEM NOT ONLY WITH HUGE FEES, BUT WITH PERSONAL SOLICITATION. NOW IT CANNOT BE
CLEO PRO2,SD(102) BACK. YOU ARE THRUSTING ME ON THE SPEARHEADS. A HUGE GRIM WOMAN, HER FACE COVERED WITH A NETWORK OF TINY
CATH 1,SD(161) BE PUT BY A SLOVENLY MAN. IT DOES NOT CONCEAL HIS HUGE HAIRY CHEST, NOR HIS HALF-BUTTONED KNEE BREECHES, NOR
DEVL I SD(4) OF THE DOMESTIC ALTAR OF THE FIREPLACE, WITH ITS HUGE HOBS AND BOILER, AND ITS HINGED ARM ABOVE THE SMOKY
ARMS III (65) AH WELL, BLUNTSCHLI, YOU ARE RIGHT TO TAKE THIS HUGE IMPOSTURE OF A WORLD COOLLY. /RAINA/ (QUAINTLY TO
GETT PREFACE(207) OF THE VERY POOR IS COUNTERBALANCED BY A HUGE INFANTILE-MORTALITY IN THE SLUMS, WHILST THE VERY RICH
DOCT PREFACE(15) HAVE BEEN TRAINED AS DOMESTIC SERVANTS IN SOME HUGE INSTITUTION WITH LIFTS, VACUUM CLEANERS, ELECTRIC
CLEO PRO1 (90) TO ROME UNTIL THERE CAME A NEW ROME, RICH AND HUGE . AND I, RA, LAUGHED; FOR THE MINDS OF THE ROMANS
2TRU PREFACE(7) WITH ENVY OF THE POOR. BUT THE POOR ARE A HUGE MAJORITY AND THEY ARE SO DEMORALIZED BY THE NOTION THAT
MIS. PREFACE(94) EXTREMELY DANGEROUS IN AN EMPIRE IN WHICH A HUGE MAJORITY OF THE FELLOW SUBJECTS OF THE GOVERNING ISLAND
APPL PREFACE(181) PRIMITIVE ANSWER IS THAT AS WE ARE ALWAYS IN A HUGE MAJORITY WE CAN, IF RULERS OPPRESS US INTOLERABLY, BURN
3PLA PREFACE(R25) IT IS DONE. I LIKE EXPLAINING ITS MERITS TO THE HUGE MAJORITY WHO DONT KNOW GOOD WORK FROM BAD. IT DOES THEM
LION PREFACE(6) EXTREME SUSCEPTIBILITY TO IT. SETTING ASIDE THE HUGE MASS OF INCULCATED CHRIST-WORSHIP WHICH HAS NO REAL
LION PREFACE(59) HAVE GROTESQUELY DIFFERENT INCOMES, BUT IN THE HUGE MASS OF MANKIND VARIATION OF INCOME FROM INDIVIDUAL TO
LION PREFACE(10) AND A FEW ECCENTRIC ATHEISTS. IT CONSISTS OF A HUGE MASS OF WORLDLY PEOPLE, AND A SMALL PERCENTAGE OF
BARB PREFACE(237) WHO CHIPS A CORNER OF THE VENEERING FROM THE HUGE MEAT PACKING INDUSTRIES OF CHICAGO, AND SHEWS IT TO US
PYGM EPILOG (291) IMPULSES. THIS MAKES HIM A STANDING PUZZLE TO THE HUGE NUMBER OF UNCULTIVATED PEOPLE WHO HAVE BEEN BROUGHT UP
MIS. PREFACE(91) BUT IT IS CARRIED FAR ENOUGH TO INFLICT ON HUGE NUMBERS OF PEOPLE A MOST INJURIOUS ART STARVATION, AND
LION PREFACE(102) BEYOND WORDS: THE SACRISTAN WHO LENDS HIM A HUGE PAIR OF SLIPPERS); AND JESUS NEVER SUGGESTED THAT HIS
CATH 1,SD(161) HIS BUREAU IN THE WINTER PALACE, ST PETERSBURGH. HUGE PALATIAL APARTMENT: STYLE, RUSSIA IN THE XVIII CENTURY
DOCT I SD(82) HAUNCHED GILT LEGS ENDING IN SPHINX CLAWS. THE HUGE PIER-GLASS WHICH SURMOUNTS IT IS MOSTLY DISABLED FROM
BULL III SD(117) AN UNKEMPT SHRUBBERY, THE MUTILATED REMNANT OF A HUGE PLASTER STATUE, NEARLY DISSOLVED BY THE RAINS OF A
CLEO IV (175) WHERE A LIFE SIZE IMAGE OF RA, SEATED ON A HUGE PLINTH, TOWERS UP, WITH HAWK HEAD AND CROWN OF ASP AND
CAPT I SD(217) PAYS NO HEED TO IT, BEING ABSORBED IN TRIMMING A HUGE RED GERANIUM BUSH, TO ENGLISH EYES UNNATURALLY BIG,
3PLA PREFACE(R9) THE CRITICISM OF THE THEATRE CAME TO ME AS A HUGE RELIEF IN POINT OF BODILY EXERTION. THE DIFFERENCE
MIS. PREFACE(55) ON US AS A NECESSITY BY THE USE OF HORSES AND OF HUGE RETINUES; BUT FLOGGING HAS NEVER BEEN SO IMPOSED: IT
MIS. PREFACE(107) THE MILLIONAIRES WHO HAVE ACCIDENTALLY GAINED HUGE RICHES BY THE OCCASIONAL WINDFALLS OF OUR COMMERCE, THE
CAPT II SD(242) A TINY MOORISH TABLE IN THE MIDDLE; AND AT IT A HUGE SADDLE, WITH SADDLE CLOTHS OF VARIOUS COLORS, SHEWING
BARB PREFACE(234) INSTITUTION TURNING THE FACE OF EUROPE INTO ONE HUGE SARDONIC SMILE BY REFUSING TO STAY IN THE SAME HOTEL
METH PREFACE(R46) MERE CHAPTER OF ACCIDENTS IS ALWAYS DOING ON A HUGE SCALE WHAT THEY THEMSELVES ARE DOING ON A VERY SMALL
CLEO I SD(106) AND A VAST HORIZON COMES INTO RELIEF, BROKEN BY A HUGE SHAPE WHICH SOON REVEALS ITSELF IN THE SPREADING
BARB III SD(325) BETWEEN, THE TOPS OF ITS CHIMNEYS SPROUTING LIKE HUGE SKITTLES INTO THE MIDDLE DISTANCE. ACROSS THE CREST
PPP (200) FALLING OFF IN RELISH. /MAGNESIA/ (PICKING UP A HUGE SLICE) TAKE THIS, ADOLPHUS: IT IS THE LARGEST (SHE
MTH1 II SD(20) HE IS INSISTENTLY WARLIKE. HE IS EQUIPPED WITH HUGE SPEAR AND BROAD BRASS-BOUND LEATHER SHIELD; HIS CASQUE
GETT SD(260) TO OUR RIGHT IS THE IMMENSE FIREPLACE, WITH ITS HUGE SPIT LIKE A BABY CRANE, AND A COLLECTION OF OLD IRON
BULL II SD(97) UPWARD ACROSS THE PROSPECT FROM SOUTH TO NORTH. A HUGE STONE STANDS ON IT IN A NATURALLY IMPOSSIBLE PLACE, AS
BULL II (105) (REFERRING TO THE GUIDE BOOK) MURRAY SAYS THAT A HUGE STONE, PROBABLY OF DRUIDIC ORIGIN, IS STILL POINTED OUT
LION PROL,SD(105) LEGS, HOLDING UP HIS RIGHT FOREPAW, IN WHICH A HUGE THORN STICKS. HE SITS DOWN AND CONTEMPLATES IT. HE
BARB III (345) YOU ARE A SUFFICIENTLY PRACTICAL MAN? IT IS A HUGE UNDERTAKING, AN ENORMOUS RESPONSIBILITY. ALL THIS MASS
APPL PREFACE(191) BY OUR SYSTEM OF PRIVATE CAPITALISM IN SETTING UP HUGE VESTED INTERESTS IN DESTRUCTION, WASTE, AND DISEASE.
SUPR I SD(9) OLYMPIAN MAJESTY WITH WHICH A MANE, OR RATHER A HUGE WISP, OF HAZEL COLORED HAIR IS THROWN BACK FROM AN

HUGELY

LADY PREFACE(222) WHO DOTES WITHOUT DOUBTING; WHO KNOWS AND WHO IS HUGELY AMUSED AT THE ABSURDITY OF HIS INFATUATION FOR A
GENV IV (108) BARDO: YOU ARE A DAMNED FOOL. /BBDE/ (HUGELY AMUSED) HA HA! (TO THE JUDGE) THE INCIDENT IS
MIS. (148) BRITISH MORALITY IN A NUTSHELL! /TARLETON/ (HUGELY AMUSED) YES. HA HA! AWFUL HYPOCRITES, AINT WE? THEY
CAPT NOTES (300) QUALITATIVELY HIS INFERIOR, WAS QUANTITATIVELY SO HUGELY IN EXCESS OF HIM THAT IT PUT HIM IN PRISON, BUT HAD
BULL III (138) /LARRY/ WELL? WHAT HAS HAPPENED? /BROADBENT/ (HUGELY SELF-SATISFIED) I THINK IVE DONE THE TRICK THIS TIME.
BARB III (319) BETWEEN RIGHT AND WRONG. /UNDERSHAFT/ (HUGELY TICKLED) YOU DONT SAY SO! WHAT! NO CAPACITY FOR

HUGGING

MTH1 I (4) /EVE/ (TURNING AWAY FROM HIM WITH A SHRUG, AND HUGGING HER ANKLES) I SHOULD SOON GET TIRED OF THAT.
2TRU II SD(58) SEATS HERSELF ON THE RUG, AND LISTENS TO THEM, HUGGING HER KNEES AND HER UMBRELLA, AND TRYING TO LOOK AS
CAND III (132) IN MY PROFESSION? /MARCHBANKS/ (ON THE SOFA, HUGGING HIS ANKLES) OH, SHE FORGAVE YOU, JUST AS SHE
CAND III SD(129) HIMSELF WITHOUT RISING, AND SITS ON THE RUG HUGGING HIS ANKLES, ALSO QUITE UNEMBARRASSED. /CANDIDA/ OH,
BULL PREFACE(71) TOLERATE HOME RULE, IS NOW SUFFERING AND INDEED HUGGING HOME RULE ON A MUCH MORE HOMELY SCALE THAN THE HOME
PHIL II (127) AWAKE. /SYLVIA/ (TAKING CRAVEN'S LEFT ARM, AND HUGGING IT AFFECTIONATELY) DEAR OLD RIP VAN WINKLE!

HUGH

HART PREFACE(20) DROWNED, AMONG OTHERS. THE OTHERS INCLUDED SIR HUGH LANE; BUT AS HE HAD ONLY LAID THE COUNTRY UNDER GREAT
LION PREFACE(84) MEN HAVE DIED WORSE DEATHS: FOR EXAMPLE, HONEST HUGH LATIMER, WHO WAS BURNED BY US, WAS WORTH FIFTY STEPHENS
POSN PREFACE(369) NEWEST THING IN THE ADVANCED DRAMA. THERE WAS MR HUGH LAW, AN IRISH MEMBER, SON OF AN IRISH CHANCELLOR,
POSN PREFACE(376) ALL WANT TO PART WITH THE BOOKS. FOR INSTANCE, MR HUGH LAW, BEING AN IRISHMAN, WITH AN IRISHMAN'S SENSE OF HOW
GETT PREFACE(190) A FORGOTTEN CONFERENCE OF MARRIED MEN. THE LATE HUGH PRICE HUGHES, AN EMINENT METHODIST DIVINE, ONCE
LADY (206) ELIZABETH, GRANVILLE BARKER AS SHAKESPEAR, AND HUGH TABBERER AS THE WARDER.

HUGHES

GETT PREFACE(190) CONFERENCE OF MARRIED MEN. THE LATE HUGH PRICE HUGHES , AN EMINENT METHODIST DIVINE, ONCE ORGANIZED IN

HUGO

SIM I (43) TO THE ISLES. /THE CLERGYMAN/ HOW DO YOU DO, SIR HUGO ? /HYERING/ (SHAKING HANDS) NOT SIR HUGO. (
SIM I SD(43) STEPS, FOLLOWED BY SIR CHARLES FARWATERS AND BY HUGO HYERING C.B. AND MRS HYERING. HYERING IS THE FORMER
SIM I (43) MIDDLE OF THE OTHER STONE SEAT. /PRA/ THIS IS MR HUGO HYERING, POLITICAL SECRETARY TO THE ISLES. /THE
SIM I (43) DO, SIR HUGO? /HYERING/ (SHAKING HANDS) NOT SIR HUGO . (INTRODUCING) MRS HYERING. /MRS HYERING/ (SHAKING
BARB PREFACE(231) THAT THE SITUATION IS ONLY PARTLY NOVEL. VICTOR HUGO LONG AGO GAVE US THE EPIC OF THE CONVICT AND THE

HUGUENOT

BULL PREFACE(38) HAD BEEN GOVERNED BY AN ENGLISH VICEROY THROUGH A HUGUENOT BUREAUCRACY AND A JUDICIAL BENCH APPOINTED ON THE
BULL PREFACE(6) I AM AFRAID I MUST ADD, TO THEIR MERITS, THE HUGUENOT OF ULSTER IS A COWARD ONLY WHEN HE BREAKS HIS OWN
KING I (205) SERIOUSLY; AND NO ONE TAKES THEM SO. BUT YOUR HUGUENOT RANTERS PRETEND TO BE INSPIRED; AND FOOLISH PEOPLE

HUGUENOTS

BULL PREFACE(6) CATHOLIC CHURCH AT THE HEIGHT OF ITS POWER, THE HUGUENOTS HAVE ALWAYS WIELDED, AND STILL WIELD TO-DAY, A
POSN PREFACE(417) TRILOGY, AND THE BATHERS IN THE SECOND ACT OF LES HUGUENOTS , TO THE BALLETS OF WATER NYMPHS IN OUR CHRISTMAS

HULL

CAPT II	(252)	WORD ERE I GO OUT FROM HIS PRESENCE, O JOHNSON EL	HULL	. /JOHNSON/ HE WANTS THE DOLLAR. BRASSBOUND GIVES OSMAN
CAPT II	(245)	ALL SORTS. MY FATHER, SIR, WAS CAPN JOHNSON O	HULL	-- OWNED HIS OWN SCHOONER, SIR. WE'RE MOSTLY GENTLEMEN

HULLABALLOO

BULL IV	(148)	THEM STRAIGHT FOR HIM. OH, YOU NEVER HEARD SUCH A	HULLABALLOO	AS THERE WAS. THERE WAS MOLLY CRYIN ME CHANEY,

HULLO

MTH5	(220)	APPEAR ON THE STEPS, GRUMBLING). /ACIS/	HULLO	: WHATS THE MATTER? (HE GOES TO THE STEPS OF THE
ANNA	(293)	SITS DOWN). /SCHNEIDEKIND/ (INTO THE TELEPHONE)	HULLO	. NEVER MIND ALL THAT: IT'S ONLY A FELLOW HERE WHO HAS
CATH 1	(167)	I AM YOUR FRIEND. HAVE SOME DIAMONDS. (ROARING)	HULLO	THERE! DOGS, PIGS: HULLO! THE SERGEANT COMES IN.
GETT	(325)	SHE NOTICES COLLINS FOR THE FIRST TIME).	HULLO	, BILL: YOUVE GOT EM ALL ON TOO. GO AND HUNT UP A
BARB II	(299)	HE HALTS BETWEEN BARBARA AND THE DRUM. /BARBARA/	HULLO	, BILL! BACK ALREADY! /BILL/ (NAGGING AT HER) BIN
APPL I	(212)	MORE ARE YOU, WITH YOUR BLESSED ADVICE? /PLINY/	HULLO	, BILL! YOU HAVE BEEN HAVING YOUR MIND IMPROVED BY
2TRU III	(89)	PAULS SIDE, AND HAILS HIM NONCHALANTLY. /AUBREY/	HULLO	, FATHER, IS IT REALLY YOU? I THOUGHT I HEARD THE OLD
GENV III	(75)	THAT I CAN DECENTLY MENTION. /THE NEWCOMER/	HULLO	, MAAM! YOU KNOW, LADIES DONT SAY THINGS LIKE THAT IN
MTH4 II	(191)	HUMANITY HAS EVER GROANED UNDER. /THE ENVOY/	HULLO	, POPPA! STEADY! HOW DO YOU MAKE THAT OUT? /ZOZIM/
SUPR IV	(161)	LEFT THE TWO BRIGANDS TOGETHER TO TALK IT OUT.	HULLO	, TAVY! ANYTHING WRONG? /OCTAVIUS/ I MUST GO WASH MY
OVER	(180)	THATS RIGHT. (HE SITS BESIDE HER ON HER LEFT).	HULLO	! (HE RISES) THIS SOFA'S QUITE WARM. /MRS LUNN/ (
CLEO V	(195)	FROM BEHIND THE ROMAN LINE. /APOLLODORUS/	HULLO	! MAY I PASS? /CENTURION/ PASS APOLLODORUS THE
CATH 1	(167)	DIAMONDS. (ROARING) HULLO THERE! DOGS, PIGS:	HULLO	! THE SERGEANT COMES IN. /THE SERGEANT/ GOD BE
AUGS	(263)	HIS PAPER AND REPLACING HIS FEET ON THE FLOOR)	HULLO	! WHO ARE YOU? /THE CLERK/ THE STAFF (A SLIGHT
FABL VI	(129)	FEATHERS LIKE A BIRD, APPEARS SUDDENLY. /TEACHER/	HULLO	! WHO ARE YOU? WHAT ARE YOU DOING HERE? /THE
JOAN EPILOG	(160)	GO OFF SINGING THE OLD CHANTY: RUM TUM TRUMPLE --	HULLO	! WHO'S THAT KNOCKING AT THE DOOR? THEY LISTEN. A
DOCT II	(126)	/SIR PATRICK/ EH? EH? WHATS THAT? /WALPOLE/	HULLO	! YOU MUSTNT NEGLECT THIS, YOU KNOW. (ALL TOGETHER)
GETT	(281)	BISHOP/ (GOING TO LEO) GOOD MORNING, MY DEAR.	HULLO	! YOUVE BROUGHT REGINALD WITH YOU. THATS VERY NICE OF

HULLUCH

AUGS	(272)	WERE ORDERED TO OCCUPY THAT TERRIBLE QUARRY IN	HULLUCH	, AND YOU SWEPT INTO IT AT THE HEAD OF YOUR MEN LIKE

HULSE

INCA	(232)	ALFRED DRAYTON AS THE HOTEL-MANAGER, C. WORDLEY	HULSE	AS THE ARCHDEACON, AND RANDLE AYRTON AS THE INCA.

HUM

GENV PREFACE	(25)	OF AUSTRIANS WHO COULD NOT TO SAVE THEIR LIVES	HUM	A LINE OF DEUTSCHLAND UBER ALLES NOR COMPOSE A BAR OF
LIED	(197)	FARTHER). IF I BUTTON MY GLOVE, AND YOU WERE TO	HUM	A TUNE, DONT YOU THINK THAT-- /HE/ THE TABLEAU WOULD BE
LADY PREFACE	(222)	SOMETIMES A THOUSAND TWANGLING INSTRUMENTS WILL	HUM	ABOUT MINE EARS; AND SOMETIMES VOICES, THAT, IF I THEN
LION PREFACE	(64)	ON PAIN OF DEATH, HOWEVER CRUELLY INFLICTED, TO	HUM	ALL THE THEMES OF BEETHOVEN'S SYMPHONIES OR TO COMPLETE
SHAK	(141)	/SHAKES/ " THE SHARDBORNE BEETLE WITH HIS DROWSY	HUM	." /SHAV/ HAST NEVER HEARD OF ADAM LINDSAY GORDON?
LION II	(135)	A TRUMPET OR A DRUM OR THE CLASH OF STEEL OR THE	HUM	OF THE CATAPULT AS THE GREAT STONE FLIES, FIRE RUNS
FABL PREFACE	(91)	WITH A PIANO, AND ASKED TO SING OR WHISTLE OR	HUM	OR PLAY AS MANY OF THE LEADING THEMES OF THE SYMPHONIES,
FANY III	(308)	HIDE ME IN THE MEAT SAFE TIL THE COP GOES BY.	HUM	THE DEAR OLD MUSIC AS HIS STEP DRAWS NIGH. (SHE GOES
2TRU II	(62)	IS A LIE, AND A MURMUR OF PLEASED ASSENT WILL	HUM	UP FROM EVERY QUARTER OF THE GLOBE. IF SWEETIE HAD

HUMAN

BULL III	(121)	I TELL YOU, AN IRISH PEASANT'S INDUSTRY IS NOT	HUMAN	: IT'S WORSE THAN THE INDUSTRY OF A CORAL INSECT. AN
MIS.	(151)	OPPOSITE SEX. AND YET, WHY OPPOSITE? WE ARE ALL	HUMAN	: MALES AND FEMALES OF THE SAME SPECIES. WHEN THE
NEVR I SD	(208)	HER: PASSION IN HER IS HUMANITARIAN RATHER THAN	HUMAN	: SHE FEELS STRONGLY ABOUT SOCIAL QUESTIONS AND
SIM II	(61)	NEVER WILL LOVE ME. YOU HAVE NEVER LOVED ANYTHING	HUMAN	: WHY SHOULD YOU? NOTHING HUMAN IS GOOD ENOUGH TO BE
MTH2	(61)	WEALTH CAN BE CONTROLLED BY LEGISLATION OR BY ANY	HUMAN	ACTION WHATEVER. THEY OBEY FIXED SCIENTIFIC LAWS,
MRS PREFACE	(169)	WILL, PASSION, IMPULSE, WHIM, AS FACTORS IN	HUMAN	ACTION, I HAVE PLACED THEM SO NAKEDLY ON THE STAGE
POSN PREFACE	(384)	OF THE NEED FOR SETTING CERTAIN DEPARTMENTS OF	HUMAN	ACTIVITY ENTIRELY FREE FROM LEGAL INTERFERENCE. THIS
GETT PREFACE	(235)	MUST NOT MEDDLE, WHILST HE HAS ALL THE REST OF	HUMAN	ACTIVITY FOR HIS SPHERE: THE ONLY POINT AT WHICH THE
DOCT PREFACE	(13)	BUT IT HOLDS GOOD OVER THE ENTIRE FIELD OF	HUMAN	ACTIVITY. THE HARDEST-HEADED MATERIALIST WILL BECOME A
LION PREFACE	(53)	MUST PERFORCE BE LEFT OUT OF THE QUESTION IN	HUMAN	AFFAIRS UNTIL IT IS MADE PRACTICALLY APPLICABLE TO
HART PREFACE	(9)	AND THAT WAS THE BANISHMENT OF CONSCIENCE FROM	HUMAN	AFFAIRS, OR, AS SAMUEL BUTLER VEHEMENTLY PUT IT, " OF
PYGM EPILOG	(293)	IN THESE DIFFICULTIES, THIS BEING THE STATE OF	HUMAN	AFFAIRS, WHAT IS ELIZA FAIRLY SURE TO DO WHEN SHE IS
JOAN PREFACE	(36)	TWO DIFFERENT AND OPPOSITE IMPULSES, RIVALS FOR	HUMAN	ALLEGIANCE. I HAVE BEFORE ME THE LETTER OF A CATHOLIC
LION PREFACE	(18)	DIVINE KINGS INSIST A GOOD DEAL ON THEIR ROYAL	HUMAN	ANCESTORS. ALEXANDER, CLAIMING TO BE THE SON OF
BULL IV	(181)	IN THREE. IT IS A GODHEAD IN WHICH ALL LIFE IS	HUMAN	AND ALL HUMANITY DIVINE: THREE IN ONE AND ONE IN
OVER	(194)	MR LUNN IS FOOTLING. CANT WE ADMIT THAT WE'RE	HUMAN	AND HAVE DONE WITH IT? /JUNO/ I HAVE ADMITTED IT ALL
DOCT PREFACE	(58)	EXAGGERATION AND COWARDLY REFUSAL TO FACE A	HUMAN	AND NECESSARY SHARE OF THE RISK. THAT HAS ALWAYS BEEN
DOCT PREFACE	(46)	THE FOLLY OF TRUSTING TO VIVISECTORS TO HOLD THE	HUMAN	ANIMAL ANY MORE SACRED THAN THE OTHER ANIMALS BECOMES
HART I	(47)	GLAD. THE NATURAL TERM OF THE AFFECTION OF THE	HUMAN	ANIMAL FOR ITS OFFSPRING IS SIX YEARS. MY DAUGHTER
METH PREFACE	(R11)	THESE PAGES. POLITICAL INADEQUACY OF THE	HUMAN	ANIMAL. TEN MORE YEARS ELAPSED. NEO-DARWINISM IN
DOCT PREFACE	(38)	IS A RECOGNIZED METHOD OF TAMING THE YOUNG	HUMAN	ANIMAL. YET WE WERE ALL IN HYSTERICS OF INDIGNATION AT
ROCK PREFACE	(147)	IN LAW WE DRAW A LINE BETWEEN THE KILLING OF	HUMAN	ANIMALS AND NON-HUMAN ONES, SETTING THE LATTER APART
MTH1 II	(26)	UTTERLY LAZY AND WORTHLESS, AND THAT YOUR TAMED	HUMAN	ANIMALS MAY FIND WORK A BLASTING CURSE. A FINE DREAM,
MTH3	(115)	TO KNOW AND FEAR THE FEROCIOUS HATRED WITH WHICH	HUMAN	ANIMALS, LIKE ALL OTHER ANIMALS, TURN UPON ANY UNHAPPY
METH PREFACE	(R12)	PUBLIC WORK AS A SOCIALIST: NAMELY, WHETHER THE	HUMAN	ANIMAL, AS HE EXISTS AT PRESENT, IS CAPABLE OF SOLVING
GETT PREFACE	(242)	AND BUTLERS-- OF WHOM, IN THEIR ORDINARY	HUMAN	ASPECT, THERE ARE A GOOD MANY-- BECOME BARREN OLD
LION PREFACE	(58)	HUMAN EXPERIENCE AND ALL NATURAL UNCOMMERCIALIZED	HUMAN	ASPIRATION POINT TO THIS AS THE RIGHT PATH. THE GREEKS
MIS PREFACE	(46)	STATE OF THINGS IS PRACTICABLE IF WE PROCEED ON	HUMAN	ASSUMPTIONS AND NOT ON ACADEMIC ONES. IF ADULTS WILL
GENV PREFACE	(25)	FREAKS OF NATURE CALLED GREAT MEN MARK NOT	HUMAN	ATTAINMENT BUT HUMAN POSSIBILITY AND HOPE. THEY PROVE
DOCT PREFACE	(37)	THE ATTACK. NO KNOWLEDGE IS FINALLY IMPOSSIBLE OF	HUMAN	ATTAINMENT; FOR EVEN THOUGH IT MAY BE BEYOND OUR
LADY PREFACE	(219)	PLAYS WHERE THE SENSE OF SHAME IS USED AS A	HUMAN	ATTRIBUTE; AND THAT IS WHERE HAMLET IS ASHAMED, NOT OF
CLEO NOTES	(206)	TO ADMIT THAT THE AMERICAN IS HIS SUPERIOR AS A	HUMAN	BEING? I ASK THIS QUESTION BECAUSE THE SCARCITY OF
FANY EPILOG	(328)	IT AGREEABLE? CAN IT CONCEIVABLY DO GOOD TO ANY	HUMAN	BEING? IS IT DELICATE? DO SUCH PEOPLE REALLY EXIST?
GENV I	(47)	YOU KNOW. /COMMISSAR/ WELL? IS HE NOT A RATIONAL	HUMAN	BEING? /SHE/ OH NO: NOTHING AS COMMON AS THAT. I TELL
PYGM III	(256)	IDEA HOW FRIGHTFULLY INTERESTING IT IS TO TAKE A	HUMAN	BEING AND CHANGE HER INTO A QUITE DIFFERENT HUMAN
ROCK PREFACE	(148)	WHEN THE NECESSITY FOR KILLING A DANGEROUS	HUMAN	BEING ARISES, AS IT STILL DOES DAILY, THE ONLY
PYGM III	(256)	HUMAN BEING AND CHANGE HER INTO A QUITE DIFFERENT	HUMAN	BEING BY CREATING A NEW SPEECH FOR HER. IT'S FILLING
APPL PREFACE	(180)	CAN NO MORE EXIST WITHOUT A GOVERNMENT THAN A	HUMAN	BEING CAN EXIST WITHOUT A CO-ORDINATED CONTROL OF ITS
MIS. PREFACE	(20)	BY A MAN WHO CANNOT WRITE: A BOOK FROM WHICH NO	HUMAN	BEING CAN LEARN ANYTHING: A BOOK WHICH, THOUGH YOU MAY
PYGM III	(257)	/HIGGINS/ POSSIBLE SORT OF SOUND THAT A	HUMAN	BEING CAN MAKE-- /PICKERING/ WE HAVE TAKEN HER TO
FABL PREFACE	(66)	IT MAY EVEN, WHEN SOME FEAT IS REQUIRED WHICH A	HUMAN	BEING CAN PERFORM ONLY AFTER DRINKING A PINT OF
VWOO 3	(136)	RISING WRATHFULLY) THE MOST OFFENSIVE LIBERTY ONE	HUMAN	BEING CAN POSSIBLY TAKE WITH ANOTHER. WHAT BUSINESS IS
LADY PREFACE	(209)	AND GOATS WHERE, AS IT SEEMS TO ME, NO SANE	HUMAN	BEING CAN SEE ANYTHING BUT STARS HIGGLEDY-PIGGLEDY.
PHIL III	(133)	FACES. DO YOU KNOW THAT I HAVE NEVER HAD ONE	HUMAN	BEING CARE FOR ME SINCE I WAS BORN? /PARAMORE/ THATS
HART PREFACE	(10)	INOCULATIONS AND OPERATIONS. WHATEVER PART OF A	HUMAN	BEING COULD BE CUT OUT WITHOUT NECESSARILY KILLING HIM
JOAN PREFACE	(33)	ASK, SHOULD ANYONE TAKE THE TROUBLE TO ROAST A	HUMAN	BEING EXCEPT WITH THAT OBJECT? THEY CANNOT CONCEIVE
METH PREFACE	(R48)	WORD FOR WORD AS THEY STAND ON THE SHELVES IF NO	HUMAN	BEING HAD EVER BEEN CONSCIOUS, JUST AS THE TREES STAND
GETT PREFACE	(236)	ARE NOW COMPELLED TO ASSUME SILENTLY, THAT EVERY	HUMAN	BEING HAS A RIGHT TO SEXUAL EXPERIENCE, AND THAT THE
6CAL PREFACE	(89)	IN SHORT, BEHAVING HIMSELF LIKE AN UNRESTRAINED	HUMAN	BEING IN A VERY TRYING SITUATION INSTEAD OF LIKE A
SUPR III	(107)	LIFE TO THE EFFORT OF ORGANIZING ITSELF INTO THE	HUMAN	BEING IS NOT THE NEED FOR HIGHER LIFE BUT FOR A MORE
ROCK II	(256)	AND LET ME TRY TO CONVINCE YOU THAT A DUKE IS A	HUMAN	BEING LIKE YOURSELF? /ALOYSIA/ (REARING) ARE YOU
SIM II	(56)	SIMPLETON. IT WOULD BE IMPOSSIBLE TO CONCEIVE A	HUMAN	BEING OF LESS CONSEQUENCE IN THE WORLD. AND YET,
INCA	(247)	ON A DESERT ISLAND AND YOU WERE THE ONLY OTHER	HUMAN	BEING ON IT (HE STRIDES UP THE ROOM). /ERMYNTRUDE/ (
GETT PREFACE	(255)	THE CHILD EXCEPT PLACE IT IN THE CHARGE OF SOME	HUMAN	BEING OR ANOTHER, THE PARENT IS NO WORSE A CUSTODIAN
MIS. PREFACE	(12)	AND SILLY ENOUGH TO SUPPOSE THAT THEY KNOW WHAT A	HUMAN	BEING OUGHT TO BE, AND WHO STICK AT NOTHING IN THEIR
GETT PREFACE	(192)	CONSERVATIVE AT THE AGE AT WHICH EVERY HEALTHY	HUMAN	BEING OUGHT TO BE OBSTREPEROUSLY REVOLUTIONARY. AND
GETT	(266)	WIFE AND MOTHER THAT SHE'S HARDLY A RESPONSIBLE	HUMAN	BEING OUT OF HER HOUSE, EXCEPT WHEN SHE'S MARKETING.
2TRU II	(58)	KINDLY; BUT IF YOU TREAT A PRIVATE SOLDIER AS A	HUMAN	BEING THE RESULT IS DISASTROUS TO HIMSELF. HE
JOAN PREFACE	(7)	OF A MELODRAMATIC HEROINE AS IT IS POSSIBLE FOR A	HUMAN	BEING TO BE. LET US BE CLEAR ABOUT THE MEANING OF THE
PYGM I	(214)	NO RIGHT TO LIVE. REMEMBER THAT YOU ARE A	HUMAN	BEING WITH A SOUL AND THE DIVINE GIFT OF ARTICULATE
PYGM EPILOG	(297)	NORMAL-- OR SHALL WE SAY INEVITABLE? -- SORT OF	HUMAN	BEING. AT WORST THEY CALLED HER THE PUSHER; BUT TO

GENV IV (105)	NOT HITTITE: THAT IS ALL. /JEW/ A JEW IS A	HUMAN	BEING. HAS HE NOT A RIGHT OF WAY AND SETTLEMENT
ARMS III (56)	IF YOULL ONLY TALK TO ME SO AS TO REMIND ME I'M A	HUMAN	BEING. I GET TIRED OF BEING A SERVANT OCCASIONALLY.
PHIL I (78)	YOU USED? -- WITH YOUR FULL DEVELOPMENT AS A	HUMAN	BEING. I THINK THAT WAS HOW YOU PUT THE IBSENIST VIEW:
NEVR IV (298)	(RUNNING TO HIM) OH, NOW YOU LOOK QUITE LIKE A	HUMAN	BEING. MAYNT I HAVE JUST ONE DANCE WITH YOU? CAN YOU
SIM I (52)	EMBRACE) OH, MAYA, DARLING! SPEAK TO ME LIKE A	HUMAN	BEING. /MAYA/ THAT IS HOW I SPEAK TO YOU; BUT YOU DO
2TRU II (58)	/THE COUNTESS/ BUT SURELY I MAY TREAT HIM AS A	HUMAN	BEING. /TALLBOYS/ MOST CERTAINLY NOT. YOUR INTENTION
SIM I (46)	SOMETHING THAT IS ESSENTIAL TO A COMPLETE SOCIAL	HUMAN	BEING. /THE CLERGYMAN/ OH, I CANNOT BELIEVE THAT. THEY
FANY III (323)	ARE ONLY SONS-- GROWN-UP CHILDREN. HERE ONE IS A	HUMAN	BEING-- AN END IN HIMSELF. OH, MRS KNOX, IF ONLY YOUR
2TRU III (105)	IT. MY ACTION WAS INEXCUSABLE. BUT NO LADY-- NO	HUMAN	BEING-- HAS A RIGHT TO IMPOSE A FALSEHOOD ON ME. I DO
PYGM V (286)	THE GUTTER. WORK TIL YOU ARE MORE A BRUTE THAN A	HUMAN	BEING; AND THEN CUDDLE AND SQUABBLE AND DRINK TIL YOU
2TRU I SD(28)	SITS A MONSTER. IN SHAPE AND SIZE IT RESEMBLES A	HUMAN	BEING; BUT IN SUBSTANCE IT SEEMS TO BE MADE OF A
MTH5 (228)	DISTRACTION WITH YOUR VOLTAIRE. WHAT ABOUT YOUR	HUMAN	BEINGS? /ARJILLAX/ AYE: COME TO THEM. /PYGMALION/ I
KING I (217)	MAY WE ALL STOP BEING DUMB FLUNKEYS AND BE	HUMAN	BEINGS AGAIN? /CHARLES/ MR ROWLEY APOLOGIZES FOR HIS
LION PREFACE(62)	THE PRIMITIVE WANTS WHICH NATURE IMPOSES ON ALL	HUMAN	BEINGS ALIKE. WE KNOW THAT PEOPLE NEED BREAD AND BOOTS
DOCT PREFACE(50)	FROM THE ILLUMINATION OF NERO'S FEASTS BY BURNING	HUMAN	BEINGS ALIVE (ANOTHER INTERESTING EXPERIMENT) TO THE
MIS. PREFACE(71)	LEARNED THE LESSON THAT CHILDREN ARE INDEPENDENT	HUMAN	BEINGS AND HAVE RIGHTS. WANTED: A CHILD'S MAGNA
OVER (192)	/MRS LUNN/ NOT TO MENTION THAT AS WE ARE	HUMAN	BEINGS AND NOT REINDEER OR BARNDOOR FOWL, IF TWO MEN
GENV IV (101)	JUDGE/ WHY DO YOU SAY " ONLY"? THE SLAUGHTER OF	HUMAN	BEINGS AND THE DESTRUCTION OF CITIES ARE NOT ACTS TO
HART PREFACE(8)	IS THE CENTRAL TRUTH OF RELIGION, INASMUCH AS	HUMAN	BEINGS ARE PRODUCED BY THEIR ENVIRONMENT, THEIR SINS
KING II (232)	THE SAME. NO TWO CHILDREN ARE THE SAME. NO TWO	HUMAN	BEINGS ARE THE SAME. WHAT IS RIGHT FOR ONE IS WRONG
JOAN PREFACE(23)	WHICH MADE HER THE LEAST CAUTIOUS OF	HUMAN	BEINGS IN CIVIL AFFAIRS. THIS COMBINATION OF INEPT
SUPR HANDBOK(222)	SERVANTS. WHEN DOMESTIC SERVANTS ARE TREATED AS	HUMAN	BEINGS IT IS NOT WORTH WHILE TO KEEP THEM. THE
O'FL (226)	DO YOU HEAR ME SPEAKING TO YOU, WOMAN? ARE YOU	HUMAN	BEINGS OR ARE YOU WILD BEASTS? STOP THAT NOISE
FABL V (120)	YOU AGAIN AND AGAIN WE SHALL NEVER MAKE DECENT	HUMAN	BEINGS OUT OF CHEMICAL SALTS. WE MUST GET RID OF OUR
GETT PREFACE(217)	IDEAL HUSBAND AND THE IDEAL WIFE ARE NO MORE REAL	HUMAN	BEINGS THAN THE CHERUBIM. POSSIBLY THE GREAT MAJORITY
GETT PREFACE(218)	IN AN INSTANT THE NATURE OF THE RELATIONS OF TWO	HUMAN	BEINGS TO ONE ANOTHER. IF A MAN MARRIES A WOMAN AFTER
INCA (252)	PROVIDENCE ENTRUSTING THE CARE OF SIXTY MILLION	HUMAN	BEINGS TO THE ABILITIES OF CHIPS AND THE PIFFLER AND
MTH5 (218)	MONTHS THROUGH A DEVELOPMENT THAT ONCE COST	HUMAN	BEINGS TWENTY YEARS OF AWKWARD STUMBLING IMMATURITY
MIS. PREFACE(3)	ASCERTAINED THAT EVEN THE AMOEBA IS IMMORTAL.	HUMAN	BEINGS VISIBLY WEAR OUT, THOUGH THEY LAST LONGER THAN
LION PREFACE(66)	OBJECTION TO THAT INDIVIDUAL APPROPRIATION OF	HUMAN	BEINGS WHICH IS THE ESSENCE OF MATRIMONY AS TO THE
GENV PREFACE(17)	OF THEM IN WHICH THEY APPEAR AS ORDINARY	HUMAN	BEINGS WHO COULD BE PARALLELED FROM ANY CROWD OR ARMY.
POSN PREFACE(390)	WHO MAKE THEIR LIVING BY THE THEATRE ARE NORMAL	HUMAN	BEINGS WITH THE COMMON RIGHTS OF ENGLISH CITIZENS. IN
KING I (200)	HAVE FOUND THEM MUCH BETTER COMPANY THAN NINE	HUMAN	BEINGS. BUT NEVER MIND. SALLY WILL TELL ALL THE
JOAN PREFACE(18)	BE PART OF THE NORMAL PERMANENT EQUIPMENT OF ALL	HUMAN	BEINGS. JOAN'S MANLINESS AND MILITARISM. JOAN'S OTHER
MTH5 (227)	THE POINT, I HAVE SUCCEEDED IN MAKING ARTIFICIAL	HUMAN	BEINGS. REAL LIVE ONES, I MEAN. /INCREDULOUS VOICES/
MIS. PREFACE(56)	DENIAL TO CHILDREN OF THE ELEMENTARY RIGHTS OF	HUMAN	BEINGS. THE FIRST MAN WHO ENSLAVED AND " BROKE IN" AN
SUPR HANDBOK(212)	WASTE MATERIAL; WHEREAS IF THE GOODS CONSISTED OF	HUMAN	BEINGS, ALL THAT COULD BE DONE WOULD BE TO LET THEM
GENV IV (121)	YOU SEEM TO ME TO BE PERSONALLY HARMLESS	HUMAN	BEINGS, CAPABLE OF MEETING ONE ANOTHER AND CHATTING ON
MRS PREFACE(168)	WITH WHICH MY CHARACTERS BEHAVE LIKE	HUMAN	BEINGS, INSTEAD OF CONFORMING TO THE ROMANTIC LOGIC OF
GETT PREFACE(249)	WE MEET WITH THIS DIFFERENCE IN VALUE BETWEEN	HUMAN	BEINGS, WE MAY KNOW THAT WE ARE IN THE SLAVE-MARKET,
MTH5 (228)	(CRIES OF NO! THEY ARE NOT! COME TO THE	HUMAN	BEINGS! CONSPUEZ VOLTAIRE! CUT IT SHORT, PYG!
INCA (254)	COLLOQUIAL: A SINCERE FRIEND, A NATURAL	HUMAN	BEING, A GENIAL COMRADE, ONE EMINENTLY CALCULATED TO
MIS. PREFACE(33)	ITS RIGHTS, BEING CLEARLY THOSE OF ANY OTHER	HUMAN	BEING, ARE SUMMED UP IN THE RIGHT TO LIVE: THAT IS, TO
MIS. PREFACE(60)	PRODUCE, NOT A SELF-RELIANT, FREE, FULLY MATURED	HUMAN	BEING, BUT A GROWN-UP SCHOOLBOY OR SCHOOLGIRL, CAPABLE
GETT PREFACE(185)	DARE NOT AVOW: OWNERSHIP OF THE PERSON OF ANOTHER	HUMAN	BEING, FOR INSTANCE, AND HE NEVER TELLS THE TRUTH
BULL PREFACE(63)	ON ANY INTELLIGENT AND POLITICALLY EXPERIENCED	HUMAN	BEING, IS STRANGE ENOUGH-- THOUGH THE SECRET SHAME OF
LADY PREFACE(221)	SORE ON THE SUBJECT OF HER COMPLEXION; THAT NO	HUMAN	BEING, MALE OR FEMALE, CAN CONCEIVABLY ENJOY BEING
MTH4 II (178)	WAIT. THIS TALENT INVOLVES THE SHEDDING OF	HUMAN	BLOOD. /THE ORACLE/ ARE YOU A SURGEON, OR A DENTIST..
JOAN 6 (143)	HAVE TAKEN UP THE SWORD, EVEN TO THE SHEDDING OF	HUMAN	BLOOD, INCITING MEN TO SLAY EACH OTHER, INVOKING EVIL
LION PREFACE(73)	STROKE ITS DETESTABLE TRADITION OF PROPERTY IN	HUMAN	BODIES. BUT IT WILL LEAVE NATURE FREE TO EFFECT A
MTH5 (232)	THAT RIGHT; AND THEN I WENT AHEAD WITH A COMPLETE	HUMAN	BODY: ARMS AND LEGS AND ALL. HE WAS MY FIRST MAN.
KING PREFACE(158)	BEING IN THE WORLD; BUT IT WOULD BE A MUCH MORE	HUMAN	BODY IF IT WERE HALF-AND-HALF SONS AND DAUGHTERS. ALL
MIS. PREFACE(92)	TO STRUGGLE FOR TOLERATION. TO THEM AN UNDRAPED	HUMAN	BODY IS THE MOST MONSTROUS, THE MOST BLIGHTING, THE
DOCT PREFACE(72)	REVERENT TREATMENT OF EVERYTHING CAST OFF BY THE	HUMAN	BODY, EVEN TO NAIL CLIPPINGS AND HAIRS; AND OUR
SUPR III (121)	OF IT ALL THAT THE HUMAN WILL SHALL SAY TO THE	HUMAN	BRAIN: INVENT ME A MEANS BY WHICH I CAN HAVE LOVE,
BUOY III (33)	IT HARD TO BELIEVE THAT HE WILL EVER DIE. HE IS A	HUMAN	CALCULATING MACHINE. CALCULATING MACHINES DONT DIE.
MTH2 (69)	I AM NOT BLAMING YOU. YOUR TASK WAS BEYOND	HUMAN	CAPACITY. WHAT WITH OUR HUGE ARMAMENTS, OUR TERRIBLE
SUPR III (134)	BUT SUCH KINDNESS IS A DENIAL OF THE EXCLUSIVELY	HUMAN	CHARACTER OF THE SOUL. /THE STATUE/ AND WHO THE DEUCE
GENV IV (101)	IT IS NECESSARY FOR THE CULTIVATION OF THE	HUMAN	CHARACTER THAT A FIELD SHOULD BE RESERVED FOR WAR. MEN
BULL PREFACE(17)	OF HIS OWN SUPERIORITY IN THE DEEPER ASPECTS OF	HUMAN	CHARACTER. AS THE IRISH GENTLEMAN, TRACING HIS
DEVL EPILOG (82)	HIS DEATH, THACKERAY, WHO HAD AN INTENSE SENSE OF	HUMAN	CHARACTER, BUT WAS TYPICALLY STUPID IN VALUING AND
DOCT PREFACE(45)	AT THE THOUGHT OF LETTING THEM LOOSE ON A	HUMAN	CHILD. THE LADY WHO GETS HER CLOAK BY FLAYING A SABLE
AUGS (270)	HM! BEAUTIFUL, DID YOU SAY? /THE CLERK/ A	HUMAN	CHRYSANTHEMUM, SIR, BELIEVE ME. /AUGUSTUS/ IT WILL BE
BARB PREFACE(240)	UNNATURAL ABOMINATION UNDER RATIONAL AND KINDLY	HUMAN	CIRCUMSTANCES. THEN COMES THE CLIMAX OF IRONY AND
ROCK PREFACE(147)	AND POISONOUS SNAKES, THEIR INCOMPATIBILITY WITH	HUMAN	CIVILIZATION IS UNQUESTIONED. THIS DOES NOT EXCUSE THE
ROCK PREFACE(167)	EXPENSIVE AND TEDIOUS. YOU CAN EXTERMINATE ANY	HUMAN	CLASS NOT ONLY BY SUMMARY VIOLENCE BUT BY BRINGING UP
MTH4 I (143)	PEOPLE; AND-- /THE WOMAN/ THERE ARE ONLY TWO	HUMAN	CLASSES HERE: THE SHORTLIVED AND THE NORMAL. THE RULES
DEVL EPILOG (80)	THAT CERTAINTY OF THEIRS IS ONLY PART OF THE	HUMAN	COMEDY. THE AMERICAN UNIONIST IS OFTEN A SEPARATIST AS
SUPR III (103)	CONTRAST OF YOUR NEEDS WITH YOUR PRETENSIONS, NO	HUMAN	COMEDY, NOTHING BUT A PERPETUAL ROMANCE, A UNIVERSAL
APPL PREFACE(180)	OF THE PEOPLE: THAT, EVIDENTLY, IS NECESSARY: A	HUMAN	COMMUNITY CAN NO MORE EXIST WITHOUT A GOVERNMENT THAN
BULL PREFACE(11)	AND ARABS CANNOT OR WILL NOT SECURE THESE COMMON	HUMAN	CONDITIONS FOR ME IN NORTH AFRICA, I AM QUITE PREPARED
BARB III (346)	UNJUST WARS AND THINGS THAT I ABHOR. WHAT IS ALL	HUMAN	CONDUCT BUT THE DAILY AND HOURLY SALE OF OUR SOULS FOR
GETT PREFACE(258)	SAME TIME TO BE MADE SO GENERAL THAT ANY SORT OF	HUMAN	CONDUCT MAY BE BROUGHT WITHIN THEM BY A LITTLE SPECIAL
LION PREFACE(19)	BEFORE PILATE WAS MEANT AS AN EXAMPLE OF NORMAL	HUMAN	CONDUCT. LET US ADMIT THAT WITHOUT THE PROPER CLUES
3PLA PREFACE(R19)	IS, TO ME AT LEAST, AN INTOLERABLE PERVERSION OF	HUMAN	CONDUCT. THERE ARE TWO CLASSES OF STORIES THAT SEEM TO
SUPR PREFACE(R12)	AND CONVENTION CAN BE DRAMATIZED LIKE ALL OTHER	HUMAN	CONFLICTS: BUT THEY ARE PURELY JUDICIAL; AND THE FACT
DOCT PREFACE(17)	RETAINS HIS SELF-RESPECT MORE EASILY. THE	HUMAN	CONSCIENCE CAN SUBSIST ON VERY QUESTIONABLE FOOD. NO
GETT PREFACE(199)	AS CAREFULLY AS WHAT THEY CALL BADNESS; FOR THE	HUMAN	CONSTITUTION WILL NOT STAND VERY MUCH OF EITHER
PYGM EPILOG (298)	SHE COULD HAVE COME INTO ANY SORT OF SINCERE	HUMAN	CONTACT. IN THE RADIANCE OF THESE DISCOVERIES, AND THE
ROCK I (214)	AM IN THE GRIP OF ECONOMIC FORCES THAT ARE BEYOND	HUMAN	CONTROL. WHAT MORTAL MEN COULD DO THIS GOVERNMENT HAS
GENV IV (128)	STEM THE RUSH. AT LEAST ONE MAN SHALL STAND FOR	HUMAN	COURAGE AND DIGNITY WHEN THE RACE EXPIRES. /SIR O./
FANY EPILOG (328)	TO ITS PARENT: NO GIRL COULD SPEAK TO A YOUTH: NO	HUMAN	CREATURE COULD TEAR DOWN THE VEILS-- (APPEALING TO
SIM II (61)	IS GOOD ENOUGH TO BE LOVED. BUT EVERY DECENT	HUMAN	CREATURE HAS SOME CAPACITY FOR LOVING. LOOK AT ME!
SIM PREFACE(14)	BUT IF, DISCARDING THIS VIEW, YOU ASSUME THAT A	HUMAN	CREATURE IS CREATED FOR ITS OWN USE AND SHOULD HAVE
GETT (344)	GIVING IT UP) I DONT UNDERSTAND. I AM A WOMAN: A	HUMAN	CREATURE LIKE YOURSELVES. WILL YOU NOT TAKE ME AS I
SIM PREFACE(14)	PROPER ACCOUNT KEEPING. IN THE NATURE OF THINGS A	HUMAN	CREATURE MUST INCUR A CONSIDERABLE DEBT FOR ITS
MIS. (122)	BE AFRAID OF THE ARISTOCRACY, DEAR: THEYRE ONLY	HUMAN	CREATURES LIKE OURSELVES AFTER ALL; AND YOULL HOLD
MTH5 (234)	PYGMALION IS GOING TO SHEW YOU A PAIR OF	HUMAN	CREATURES WHO ARE ALL REFLEXES AND NOTHING ELSE. TAKE
SIM II (84)	THAN I HAVE EVER BEEN BORED BY ANY OTHER SET OF	HUMAN	CREATURES. COME, CONFESS: DID THEY NOT BORE YOU?
BARB II (291)	GREEK, THE MOST ARTIFICIAL AND SELF-SUPPRESSED OF	HUMAN	CREATURES, FROM HIS MEAL OF ROOTS, AND LETS LOOSE THE
JOAN 6 (145)	WANTING TO TAKE THEM AWAY FROM ME, OR FROM ANY	HUMAN	CREATURE, I KNOW THAT YOUR COUNSEL IS OF THE DEVIL,
SIM PREFACE(4)	CHANGES THAT TAKE PLACE IN THE OPERATION OF	HUMAN	CREDULITY AND INCREDULITY. I HAVE POINTED OUT ON A
DOCT PREFACE(77)	WITCHCRAFT OR PURE COMMERCIAL EXPLOITATION OF	HUMAN	CREDULITY AND FEAR OF DEATH. ADD TO THEM A GOOD DEAL
DOCT PREFACE(60)	NOR IN BIOMETRICS, NOR IN THE PSYCHOLOGY OF	HUMAN	CREDULITY, NOR IN THE INCIDENCE OF ECONOMIC PRESSURE.
CAPT III (285)	I SEE NO HARM SO FAR: ITS HUMAN FAWLLY, BUT NOT	HUMAN	CRIME. NOW THE COUNSEL FOR THE PROSECUTION CAN PROCEED
MILL PREFACE(112)	CREATES A SORT OF GRESHAM LAW BY WHICH THE BASER	HUMAN	CURRENCY DRIVES OUT THE NOBLER COINAGE. THIS IS QUITE
BARB PREFACE(240)	FOR SIXPENCE. THAT RIGHTEOUS AND HONORABLE HIGH	HUMAN	DEED IS NOT WASTED ON EUROPE, LET US HOPE, THOUGH IT
LADY PREFACE(228)	THAT SHE HAD REDUCED THE GREAT MAN TO THE COMMON	HUMAN	DENOMINATOR. IN SEIZING ON THESE TWO POINTS MR HARRIS
2TRU II (70)	STAGGER HIS IMAGINATION AND ALL THE PROBLEMS OF	HUMAN	DESTINY TO EMPLOY HIS MIND, AND HE GOES OUT AND SHOOTS
POSN PREFACE(384)	HIM THAT IT MUST BE SO, OR THE HIGHER AFFAIRS OF	HUMAN	DESTINY WILL SUFFER. SUCH SUBMISSION IS THE MORE
FABL III (113)	HERE: THE ARCHPRIEST, CHOOSER OF RULERS, LORD OF	HUMAN	DESTINY. AND YOUR CHOICE IS A GOVERNMENT OF TRAMPS!
FABL IV (114)	COPY. IT IS FOR THE NEW EDITION OF MY BOOK ON	HUMAN	DIET. ARE YOU READY? . . . RIGHT. THE HEADING IS
GETT PREFACE(221)	THERE IS NOTHING MORE WOUNDING TO OUR SENSE OF	HUMAN	DIGNITY THAN THE HUSBAND HUNTING THAT BEGINS IN EVERY
ROCK I (203)	NAG! ! I CONTROL MYSELF TO THE LIMIT OF	HUMAN	ENDURANCE WITH YOU ALL. BUT FLAVIA MAKES A STUDY OF
MIS. PREFACE(36)	ONCE REALIZE THAT A PERPETUAL HOLIDAY IS BEYOND	HUMAN	ENDURANCE, AND THAT " SATAN FINDS SOME MISCHIEF STILL
SUPR HANDBOK(198)	GUILLOTINE WAS USED IN FRANCE UP TO THE LIMIT OF	HUMAN	ENDURANCE, BOTH ON GIRONDINS AND JACOBINS. FOUQUIER
SUPR HANDBOK(188)	AND ACCEPT MORAL OBLIGATIONS BEYOND PRESENT	HUMAN	ENDURANCE, IS A THING THAT CONTEMPORARY MAN DOES NOT

METH PREFACE(R26)	OF DEVELOPMENT INTO NINE MONTHS BEFORE HE WAS	HUMAN	ENOUGH TO BREAK LOOSE AS AN INDEPENDENT BEING. AND
DOCT PREFACE(6)	EVEN WHEN, IF YOU ARE NOT FOND OF THEM, YOU ARE	HUMAN	ENOUGH TO FORGET EVERY PERSONAL GRUDGE BEFORE THE
BARB PREFACE(234)	WAYS A FIRM HOLD OF THE SCIENTIFIC FACT OF	HUMAN	EQUALITY, EXPRESSED BY BARBARA IN THE CHRISTIAN
FABL PREFACE(77)	OF NOODLES. THEY ARE EVIDENCE LIKE ANY OTHER	HUMAN	EVIDENCE; AND THEY FORCE ME TO THE CONCLUSION THAT
JOAN PREFACE(37)	REPRESENTING LIFE POSSIBLY AT ITS HIGHEST ACTUAL	HUMAN	EVOLUTION AND POSSIBLY AT ITS LOWEST, BUT NEVER AT ITS
SUPR HANDBOK(210)	THE SELECTIVE BREEDING OF MAN: IN OTHER TERMS, OF	HUMAN	EVOLUTION. WE MUST ELIMINATE THE YAHOO, OR HIS VOTE
BUOY II (21)	THAT SORT OF THING. I CAN STAND ALMOST ANYTHING	HUMAN	EXCEPT AN ENGLISH GENTLEMAN. /HE/ AND I CAN STAND
SIM PRO,3, (30)	I PRESUME TO TEACH OTHERS WITHOUT A COMPLETED	HUMAN	EXPERIENCE? HOW COULD I DEAL WITH CHILDREN IF I WERE
LION PREFACE(58)	AS WE SHOULD PUT IT NOWADAYS, " FOR NOTHING." ALL	HUMAN	EXPERIENCE AND ALL NATURAL UNCOMMERCIALIZED HUMAN
METH PREFACE(R17)	IS OFTEN A GOOD. NATURE HOLDS NO BRIEF FOR THE	HUMAN	EXPERIMENT: IT MUST STAND OR FALL BY ITS RESULTS. IF
METH PREFACE(R53)	MOB, BUT SIMPLY THAT IT IS IMPOSSIBLE BECAUSE THE	HUMAN	EXPERIMENTER CANNOT GET AT THE MOUSES'S MIND. AND THAT
MTH5 (231)	OF THE LIFE FORCE COULD MAKE MAGGOTS, BUT NOT	HUMAN	EYES OR EARS. I IMPROVED THE TISSUE UNTIL IT WAS
PYGM V (284)	IN MY LIFE. SNEERING DOESNT BECOME EITHER THE	HUMAN	FACE OR THE HUMAN SOUL. I AM EXPRESSING MY RIGHTEOUS
JOAN PREFACE(33)	HIS PARTY AND CLASS PREJUDICES ARE INVOLVED, THE	HUMAN	FACT REMAINS THAT THE BURNING OF JOAN OF ARC WAS A
3PLA PREFACE(R37)	EXPRESSED THEM ANY WORSE THAN GOETHE OR IBSEN?	HUMAN	FACULTY BEING WHAT IT IS, IS IT LIKELY THAT IN OUR
JOAN PREFACE(18)	FRANCIS GALTON AND OTHER MODERN INVESTIGATORS OF	HUMAN	FACULTY CALL A VISUALIZER. SHE SAW IMAGINARY SAINTS
LION PREFACE(5)	ITS COMPREHENSION DEPENDED ON A DEVELOPMENT OF	HUMAN	FACULTY SO RARE THAT ONLY ONE EXCEPTIONALLY GIFTED MAN
MILL PREFACE(124)	FANTASTIC FACTORS INTO MATHEMATICS, DESTROYING	HUMAN	FAITH IN ABSOLUTE MEASUREMENT, AND PLAYING AN
CLEO NOTES (209)	HAVE MADE ANY APPRECIABLE DIFFERENCE IN THE	HUMAN	FAUNA OF THESE ISLES? CERTAINLY I DO NOT. JULIUS
CAPT III (285)	MR RAHNKIN. WELL, I SEE NO HARM SO FAR: ITS	HUMAN	FAWLLY, BUT NOT HUMAN CRIME. NOW THE COUNSEL FOR THE
SUPR PREFACE(R32)	OF THE FICTIONIST AND THE COMMON SYMPATHIES OF	HUMAN	FEELING AND THOUGHT IN PRE-EMINENT DEGREE. THEY ARE
CAND III (133)	IS NOT A HEARTLESS LIE-- IF YOU HAVE A SPARK OF	HUMAN	FEELING LEFT IN YOU-- WILL YOU TELL ME WHAT HAS
MRS PREFACE(167)	BY THAT VERY RESISTANCE OF FACT AND LAW TO	HUMAN	FEELING WHICH CREATES DRAMA. IT IS THE DEUS EX MACHINA
MRS PREFACE(168)	OF IGNORING; NOT STAGE LOGIC, BUT, OF ALL THINGS,	HUMAN	FEELING. PEOPLE WITH COMPLETELY THEATRIFIED
MIS. PREFACE(84)	KEPT TOGETHER AT PRESENT BY FAMILY FEELING BUT BY	HUMAN	FEELING. THE FAMILY CULTIVATES SYMPATHY AND MUTUAL
MRS III (232)	INTELLECTUALLY; BUT IVE PLENTY OF HONEST	HUMAN	FEELING; AND THE OLD CROFTS BREED COMES OUT IN A SORT
MIS. PREFACE(78)	THEY DO NOT CONCEIVE THEIR ELDERS AS HAVING ANY	HUMAN	FEELINGS. SERVE THE ELDERS RIGHT, PERHAPS, FOR POSING
MRS PREFACE(167)	HAS TO FACE THE ACCUSATION THAT HIS PLAYS IGNORE	HUMAN	FEELING, AN ILLUSION PRODUCED BY THAT VERY RESISTANCE
HART III (141)	BUT WHAT A VERY NATURAL AND KINDLY AND CHARMING	HUMAN	FEELING, LADY UTTERWORD! /LADY UTTERWORD/ SO I
MRS PREFACE(173)	HERE AGAIN THE CLAMOR FOR NATURALNESS AND	HUMAN	FEELING, RAISED BY SO MANY CRITICS WHEN THEY ARE
BARB PREFACE(210)	IN COURTSHIP IS ENTIRELY PASSIVE; AND THAT THE	HUMAN	FEMALE FORM IS THE MOST BEAUTIFUL OBJECT IN NATURE.
SUPR PREFACE(R33)	A SERIOUS POSITIVE CHARACTER: THEY COULD PLACE A	HUMAN	FIGURE BEFORE YOU WITH PERFECT VERISIMILITUDE; BUT
MTH5 (226)	INCAPABLE OF MODELLING A THUMB NAIL, LET ALONE A	HUMAN	FIGURE. /MARTELLUS/ THAT DOES NOT MATTER: I HAVE DONE
METH PREFACE(R42)	A MOUNTAIN LANDSCAPE, OR A RAILWAY ACCIDENT IN A	HUMAN	FIGURE. TO CALL THIS NATURAL SELECTION IS A BLASPHEMY,
POSN PREFACE(417)	OF THE BATH, AND THE CHARM OF THE UNDRAPED	HUMAN	FIGURE, ARE EXPLOITED WITHOUT OFFENCE ON THE STAGE TO
MTH5 (247)	I AM AN ANIMATED BEING WITH A REASONABLE SOUL AND	HUMAN	FLESH SUBSISTING. IF YOUR AUTOMATA HAD BEEN PROPERLY
MTH5 (248)	THE BODY AND THE BRAIN, THE REASONABLE SOUL AND	HUMAN	FLESH SUBSISTING, AS ECRASIA SAYS, STAND BEFORE YOU
CLEO I (109)	WITH A HUNDRED ARROWS IN EACH; AND THEY LIVE ON	HUMAN	FLESH. /CAESAR/ WOULD YOU LIKE ME TO SHEW YOU A REAL
3PLA PREFACE(R21)	(A CONDITION GUARANTEED BY THE UNIFORMITY OF	HUMAN	FOLLY AND VANITY), THEN, FOR THE HUGE COMPULSORILY
DOCT PREFACE(17)	HEALTH, NOBODY IS EVER REALLY WELL); THEY EXPLOIT	HUMAN	FOLLY, VANITY, AND FEAR OF DEATH AS RUTHLESSLY AS
MILL PREFACE(115)	EUROPE NAPOLEON WAS FUNDAMENTALLY A COMMONPLACE	HUMAN	FOOL. IN SPITE OF HIS EARLY FAILURE IN THE EAST HE
2TRU PREFACE(25)	HIS FRANK METHOD OF TRIAL AND ERROR, HIS ENTIRELY	HUMAN	FOOTING, AND HIS LIABILITY TO REMOVAL AT A MOMENT'S
MILL PREFACE(124)	LIARS, AND FIENDS WHOSE ASSUMPTION OF THE	HUMAN	FORM IS THINNER THAN THAT OF THE WOLF IN LITTLE RED
GETT (327)	IF WOMAN YOU ARE INDEED AND NOT A FIEND IN	HUMAN	FORM-- /MRS GEORGE/ IS THIS OUT OF A BOOK? OR IS IT
GENV PREFACE(17)	LACKED THESE QUALITIES. THEY WERE NOT FIENDS IN	HUMAN	FORM; BUT THEY DID NOT KNOW WHAT TO DO WITH THE
MRS PREFACE(172)	POOR. NO: HAD I DRAWN MRS WARREN AS A FIEND IN	HUMAN	FORM, THE VERY PEOPLE WHO NOW REBUKE ME FOR FLATTERING
GETT PREFACE(188)	FIND THE AUSTERE SHELLEY DENOUNCED AS A FIEND IN	HUMAN	FORM, WHILST NELSON, WHO OPENLY LEFT HIS WIFE AND
BULL PREFACE(59)	NOT, OBSERVE, A TRIAL AS LITTLE UNFAIR AS	HUMAN	FRAILTY COULD MAKE IT, WHICH IS THE MOST THAT CAN BE
LADY PREFACE(215)	BELITTLE SUCH SAILORS. THEY ARE THE EMBLEMS OF	HUMAN	GENEROSITY; BUT SHAKESPEAR WAS NOT AN EMBLEM: HE WAS A
GENV PREFACE(10)	MINERALS, AND FINALLY INTO SUCH MIRACLES AS	HUMAN	GENIUSES, TAKING SOME GRAINS OF METAL AND A FEW SALTS
JOAN PREFACE(26)	THE WORK OF A MAN OF GENIUS, REMAINS A CREDIBLE	HUMAN	GOODYGOODY IN SPITE OF HER CREATOR'S INFATUATION. IT
MIS. PREFACE(20)	YOU ARE FORCED TO SIT, NOT IN A ROOM WITH SOME	HUMAN	GRACE AND COMFORT OF FURNITURE AND DECORATION, BUT IN
ROCK PREFACE(160)	POLICE INSPECTOR'S BELIEF THAT EVERY NORMAL	HUMAN	GROUP CONTAINS NOT ONLY A PERCENTAGE OF SAINTS BUT
METH PREFACE(R67)	THE DIVINE SENSE THAT LIBERTY IS A NEED VITAL TO	HUMAN	GROWTH. ACCORDINGLY, THOUGH IT WAS DIFFICULT ENOUGH TO
APPL PREFACE(194)	OR MOTOR LORRIES WITHOUT BEING TOUCHED BY A	HUMAN	HAND AND THEREFORE WITHOUT RISK OF BREAKAGE. IT WAS
SUPR PREFACE(R15)	THEY NOT MOLIERE AND MOZART, UPON WHOSE ART NO	HUMAN	HAND CAN IMPROVE? YOU WOULD LAUGH AT ME IF AT THIS
PYGM EPILOG (301)	AND NOBILITY, THE AUGUST MISSION AND DESTINY, OF	HUMAN	HANDWRITING. ELIZA ENDED BY ACQUIRING AN EXTREMELY
NEVR IV (288)	THE WINDOW, HAVING SOUNDED THE WHOLE GAMUT OF	HUMAN	HAPPINESS, FROM DESPAIR TO ECSTASY, IN FIFTY SECONDS).
PYGM II SD(217)	OF DIFFERENT SIZES, A LIFE-SIZE IMAGE OF HALF A	HUMAN	HEAD, SHEWING IN SECTION THE VOCAL ORGANS, AND A BOX
FABL IV (114)	LABOR OF BREEDING ANIMALS FOR FOOD, AND SUPPORTED	HUMAN	HEALTH AND LONGEVITY QUITE AS WELL, IF NOT BETTER,
CAND I (84)	THINK I'M JEALOUS? OH, WHAT A KNOWLEDGE OF THE	HUMAN	HEART YOU HAVE, MR LEXY MILL! HOW WELL YOU KNOW THE
GENV IV (122)	/BATTLER/ THIS IS THE MOST SHAMELESS BETRAYAL IN	HUMAN	HISTORY. GENERAL FLANCO: YOU OWE YOUR VICTORY TO MY
KING I (198)	AND A GOOD CATHOLIC, THANK GOD. BUT BEING	HUMAN	I AM ALSO A MAN OF SIN. I CONFESS IT; AND I DO MY
SUPR HANDBOK(188)	POPE IS A SAINT. HE IS NEVER WITHOUT AN ARRAY OF	HUMAN	IDOLS WHO ARE ALL NOTHING BUT SHAM SUPERMEN. THAT THE
POSN PREFACE(367)	SUCH CIRCUMSTANCES, MANAGERS WOULD BE MORE THAN	HUMAN	IF THEY DID NOT REGARD THE CENSORSHIP AS THEIR MOST
LION PREFACE(9)	UNLESS YOU KNOW SOMETHING OF THE HISTORY OF THE	HUMAN	IMAGINATION AS APPLIED TO RELIGION. NOT LONG AGO I
ROCK PREFACE(155)	MOST CRUEL AND OBSCENE METHOD OF KILLING THAT THE	HUMAN	IMAGINATION COULD CONCEIVE AT ITS VILEST WAS SPECIALLY
GETT PREFACE(226)	SITUATIONS THAT ONLY BY BEGLAMORING THE	HUMAN	IMAGINATION WITH A HYPNOTIC SUGGESTION OF WHOLLY
LION PREFACE(14)	IN WHICH THE REDEEMER, THOUGH CONCEIVED BY THE	HUMAN	IMAGINATION, IS NOT YET FOUND. HE IS AWAITED AND
LION PREFACE(19)	EQUIPMENT THAN A KNOWLEDGE OF THESE HABITS OF THE	HUMAN	IMAGINATION, ANYONE MAY NOW READ THE FOUR GOSPELS
LADY PREFACE(225)	TRADITION, OR INTERPRETATION, THAT POINTED TO ANY	HUMAN	IMPERFECTION IN THEIR HERO. THEY THUS LEAVE THEMSELVES
METH PREFACE(R18)	ANOTHER EXPERIMENT. WHAT HOPE IS THERE THEN OF	HUMAN	IMPROVEMENT? ACCORDING TO THE NEO-DARWINISTS, TO THE
LION PREFACE(75)	AND CONCEITED BORE; BUT IT WAS PARDONABLE AND	HUMAN	IN COMPARISON TO THE SLAUGHTER OF POOR ANANIAS AND
POSN PREFACE(382)	FOR MORALITY, WITH ALL THE DEAD WEIGHT OF	HUMAN	INERTIA AND SUPERSTITION TO HANG ON THE BACK OF THE
ROCK PREFACE(187)	THE ROMAN EMPIRE BEGAN WITH A WOLF SUCKLING TWO	HUMAN	INFANTS. IF THESE INFANTS HAD NOT BEEN WISER THAN
MIS. PREFACE(3)	BE CAPABLE OF OUTLIVING THE MEMORY OF THE OLDEST	HUMAN	INHABITANT, BUT THE FACT THAT NEW ONES ARE BORN
MIS. PREFACE(46)	GENERALLY, THERE ARE SCORES OF THOUSANDS OF	HUMAN	INSECTS GROPING THROUGH OUR DARKNESS BY THE FEEBLE
SUPR III (119)	(DETERMINEDLY) I SAY THE MOST LICENTIOUS OF	HUMAN	INSTITUTIONS: THAT IS THE SECRET OF ITS POPULARITY.
SUPR III (119)	NOT A RAP. MARRIAGE IS THE MOST LICENTIOUS OF	HUMAN	INSTITUTIONS-- /ANA/ JUAN! /THE STATUE/ (PROTESTING)
FABL PREFACE(77)	FORCE ME TO THE CONCLUSION THAT EVERY GRADE OF	HUMAN	INTELLIGENCE CAN BE CIVILIZED BY PROVIDING IT WITH A
GETT PREFACE(227)	SPECIAL FEELINGS WHICH ALTER THE NATURE OF	HUMAN	INTERCOURSE IS A MISCHIEVOUS ONE. THE WHOLE DIFFICULTY
MTH4 I (147)	INSENSIBILITY TO THE ELEMENTARY DECENCIES OF	HUMAN	INTERCOURSE. /THE MAN/ WHAT ARE DECENCIES? /THE
HART PREFACE(10)	NO ONE'S INSIDE WAS SAFE. THEY EXPLAINED THAT THE	HUMAN	INTESTINE WAS TOO LONG, AND THAT NOTHING COULD MAKE A
SIM II (61)	LOVED ANYTHING HUMAN: WHY SHOULD YOU? NOTHING	HUMAN	IS GOOD ENOUGH TO BE LOVED. BUT EVERY DECENT HUMAN
FANY PROLOG (263)	OFFERED TO COME JUST TO PLEASE HER! QUITE	HUMAN	. I WAS SURPRISED. /THE COUNT/ EXTREMELY KIND OF HIM.
PRES (152)	ORDERLY/ (CIVILLY) I DONT MIND THAT, SIR. IT'S	HUMAN	. IT'S ENGLISH. WHY COULDNT YOU HAVE SAID IT BEFORE..
OVER (184)	OR ASKED YOU TO HAVE A CUP OF TEA. IT'S NOT	HUMAN	. IT'S NOT RIGHT. LOVE HAS ITS RIGHTS AS WELL AS
CLEO II (130)	WOULD THAT IT HAD BEEN! VENGEANCE AT LEAST IS	HUMAN	. NO, I SAY: THOSE SEVERED RIGHT HANDS, AND THE BRAVE
MTH3 (132)	BUT IF YOU ARE NOT SURPRISED AT THIS YOU ARE NOT	HUMAN	. /CONFUCIUS/ I AM STAGGERED, JUST AS A MAN MAY BE
OVER (177)	VERY MUCH; AND I DO WANT TO BE AFFECTIONATE AND	HUMAN	. /GREGORY/ I OUGHT TO DRAW A LINE. /MRS JUNO/ SO YOU
KING I (195)	AN INSTANT WITHOUT SEEING THAT HE IS ONLY HALF	HUMAN	. /JAMES/ FLOG HIM THROUGH THE TOWN. FLOG HIM TO
BUOY III (35)	/MRS SECONDBORN/ WHATEVER IS NOT PERSONAL IS NOT	HUMAN	. THE WOMAN FROM PANAMA DASHES INTO THE TEMPLE, IN
JITT I (21)	IT'S NOT TRUE, BRUNO! I FEEL IT. IT IS NOT	HUMAN	. THERE IS SOMETHING ELSE AT THE BACK OF YOUR MIND.
MIS. (146)	ANY MAN'S LETTERS TO HIS CHILDREN. THEYRE NOT	HUMAN	. THEYRE NOT ABOUT HIMSELF OR THEMSELVES. THEYRE ABOUT
SUPR III (134)	IT LEADS TO AN INDISCRIMINATE CONTEMPT FOR THE	HUMAN	. TO A MAN, HORSES AND DOGS AND CATS ARE MERE SPECIES,
LADY (239)	BAD? O NO. HUMAN, MASTER WARDER.	HUMAN	. WE CALL ONE ANOTHER NAMES WHEN WE ARE OFFENDED, AS
LION PREFACE(12)	NATURAL THAT LITIGANTS SHOULD GIVE PRESENTS TO	HUMAN	JUDGES; AND THE BUYING OFF OF DIVINE WRATH BY ACTUAL
BULL PREFACE(28)	FULL OF AUTHENTIC EXAMPLES OF THE CONCURRENCE OF	HUMAN	KINDLINESS WITH POLITICAL RANCOR. SLAVES AND
POSN (465)	LIKE A CHILD WITH A NEW TOY: YOU AND YOUR BIT OF	HUMAN	KINDNESS! /THE WOMAN/ HOW MANY WOULD HAVE DONE IT
DOCT PREFACE(34)	THAT PARTICULAR ADDITION TO THE STORE OF	HUMAN	KNOWLEDGE MAY BE. A MAN WHO DID SO WOULD HAVE SHORT
MTH4 I (156)	PASSED AWAY THE IRISH RACE VANISHED FROM	HUMAN	KNOWLEDGE. AND THE DISPERSED JEWS DID THE SAME LEST
MTH2 (78)	ONE IS CLASSROOM JARGON: THE OTHER IS INSPIRED	HUMAN	LANGUAGE. /LUBIN/ (CALMLY REMINISCENT) ONE OF THE FEW
MTH5 (231)	LIFE FORCE USED TO SLIP SUDDENLY DOWN FROM ITS	HUMAN	LEVEL TO THAT OF A FUNGUS, SO THAT MEN FOUND THEIR
PRES (137)	! ! ! HAVE YOU NO REGARD FOR THE SANCTITY OF	HUMAN	LIFE? /BALSQUITH/ (MUCH RELIEVED) WELL, GETTING SHOT
BARB PREFACE(245)	AGAIN, HAVING MEANWHILE SPENT A GREAT DEAL OF	HUMAN	LIFE AND HAPPINESS IN THE TASK OF CHAINING AND FEEDING
MILL PREFACE(109)	NOW, YET IT RAISES A QUESTION THAT HAS TROUBLED	HUMAN	LIFE AND MOULDED HUMAN SOCIETY SINCE THE CREATION. THE
APPL PREFACE(183)	INSPECTION HAVE WE STOPPED THE MONSTROUS WASTE OF	HUMAN	LIFE AND WELFARE IT COST WHEN IT WAS LEFT UNCONTROLLED

GENV PREFACE(26)	AT LEAST A STRONG SUSPICION THAT THE TERM OF	HUMAN	LIFE CANNOT BE FIXED AT SEVENTY YEARS OR INDEED FIXED
DOCT PREFACE(25)	THE ENTIRE POPULATION OF THE GLOBE SINCE	HUMAN	LIFE FIRST APPEARED ON IT. BUT THE PRECAUTIONS
METH PREFACE(R29)	A HEREDITARY ONE, OR, TO PUT IT LESS DRILY, THAT	HUMAN	LIFE IS CONTINUOUS AND IMMORTAL. THE EVOLUTIONISTS
MTH3 (129)	BY DEMONSTRATING THAT THE TRUE EXPECTATION OF	HUMAN	LIFE IS SEVENTY-EIGHT POINT SIX. AND I WILL RESIST ANY
MTH4 II (180)	IT IS THE ONLY THING THAT MATTERS: THE VALUE OF	HUMAN	LIFE IS THE VALUE OF THE GREATEST LIVING MAN. CUT OFF
MTH2 (38)	TO IT). HERE IT IS: (READING) " THE TERM OF	HUMAN	LIFE MUST BE EXTENDED TO AT LEAST THREE CENTURIES."
MTH4 II (181)	(IT IS THE SAME THING), THE NOBLER PART OF	HUMAN	LIFE PERISHES. YOU MUST SAVE THE WORLD FROM THAT
MTH2 (68)	/FRANKLYN/ OUR PROGRAM IS ONLY THAT THE TERM OF	HUMAN	LIFE SHALL BE EXTENDED TO THREE HUNDRED YEARS. /LUBIN/
MIS. (171)	NEVER BEEN INVENTED. OF ALL THE DAMNABLE WASTE OF	HUMAN	LIFE THAT EVER WAS INVENTED, CLERKING IS THE VERY
MTH2 (80)	IN OUR PROGRAM THAT WE ADVOCATE THE EXTENSION OF	HUMAN	LIFE TO THREE HUNDRED YEARS! DUNREEN, AS LEADER OF
MTH3 (108)	IT SHEWED THAT THIS EXTENSION OF INDIVIDUAL	HUMAN	LIFE WAS POSSIBLE, AND HOW IT WAS LIKELY TO COME
MTH3 (93)	EFFECT, YOUR ESTIMATE OF THE AVERAGE DURATION OF	HUMAN	LIFE WILL BE UPSET. /BARNABAS/ (ALARMED) UPSET MY
ROCK PREFACE(147)	OF IT, NOT IN THE KILLING. THE SACREDNESS OF	HUMAN	LIFE. IN LAW WE DRAW A LINE BETWEEN THE KILLING OF
MTH3 (93)	THE GREATEST LIVING AUTHORITY ON THE DURATION OF	HUMAN	LIFE. WHO DARES DISPUTE IT? /BURGE-LUBIN/ NOBODY,
MTH3 (93)	THE GREATEST LIVING AUTHORITY ON THE DURATION OF	HUMAN	LIFE; AND-- /BARNABAS/ (INTERRUPTING) THE AMERICAN
DEST (154)	THEY SAY YOU ARE CAREFUL OF EVERYTHING EXCEPT	HUMAN	LIFE, EXCELLENCY. /NAPOLEON/ HUMAN LIFE, MY FRIEND, IS
LION PREFACE(78)	OF EVOLUTION, WHICH IS, THAT LIFE, INCLUDING	HUMAN	LIFE, IS CONTINUALLY EVOLVING, AND MUST THEREFORE BE
POSN PREFACE(392)	PLAYS. THE DRAMA, DEALING WITH ALL DEPARTMENTS OF	HUMAN	LIFE, IS NECESSARILY POLITICAL. RECENT EVENTS HAVE
DEST (154)	EXCEPT HUMAN LIFE, EXCELLENCY. /NAPOLEON/	HUMAN	LIFE, MY FRIEND, IS THE ONLY THING THAT TAKES CARE OF
ROCK PREFACE(149)	OF THE DOGMA OF THE UNCONDITIONAL SACREDNESS OF	HUMAN	LIFE, OR ANY OTHER INCARNATION OF LIFE; BUT IT COVERS
MTH3 (104)	IF YOU HAVE MISCALCULATED THE DURATION OF	HUMAN	LIFE, THAT IS NOT THE FAULT OF THE PERSONS WHOSE
ROCK PREFACE(155)	PRACTISED. THE OLD DOCTRINE OF THE SACREDNESS OF	HUMAN	LIFE, WHICH IN OUR IDIOT ASYLUMS AT DARENTH AND
MTH4 II (182)	WHEEL, BURNT ALIVE. NO SENSE OF THE SACREDNESS OF	HUMAN	LIFE! NO THOUGHT FOR MY WIFE AND CHILDREN! BITCH!
MTH2 (69)	INTERESTING. WHEN I WAS YOUNG I USED TO FEEL MY	HUMAN	LIMITATIONS VERY ACUTELY. /BURGE/ GOD KNOWS I HAVE
METH PREFACE(R46)	PERSEVERANCE, HIS CONSCIENTIOUSNESS REACHED THE	HUMAN	LIMIT. BUT HE NEVER GOT DEEPER BENEATH OR HIGHER ABOVE
MIS. PREFACE(9)	LIMIT TO PHYSICAL CRUELTY; AND THERE ARE ALSO	HUMAN	LIMITS TO IT. THERE IS AN ACTIVE SOCIETY WHICH BRINGS
SUPR HANDBOK(211)	OR A CHARTERED COMPANY FOR THE IMPROVEMENT OF	HUMAN	LIVE STOCK. BUT FOR THE PRESENT IT IS FAR MORE LIKELY
GENV PREFACE(23)	CONFUSED. POPULAR LOGIC ABOUT THEM IS, LIKE MOST	HUMAN	LOGIC, MERE ASSOCIATION OF IDEAS, OR, TO CALL IT BY
HART PREFACE(8)	THEY ARE USEFUL IN THE CONTINUAL STRUGGLE OF THE	HUMAN	MACHINE TO MAINTAIN ITS ENVIRONMENT IN A FAVORABLE
MIS. PREFACE(9)	QUITE JUSTIFIABLY BY RUSKIN AS HEAPS OF AGONIZING	HUMAN	MAGGOTS, STRUGGLING WITH ONE ANOTHER FOR SCRAPS OF
METH PREFACE(R30)	BLOOD AND BREEDING WERE EAGERLY SOUGHT AFTER IN	HUMAN	MARRIAGE. IN DEALING WITH PLANTS AND ANIMALS,
BULL PREFACE(19)	HIMSELF, WITHOUT ONE MOMENT OF ILLUSION AS TO THE	HUMAN	MATERIAL HE HAD TO COMMAND, WITHOUT ONE GUSH OF THE "
ROCK PREFACE(165)	A CIVILIZED STATE CAN BE MADE OUT OF ANY SORT OF	HUMAN	MATERIAL IS ONE OF OUR OLD RADICAL DELUSIONS. AS TO
SUPR HANDBOK(190)	DEMOCRACY CANNOT RISE ABOVE THE LEVEL OF THE	HUMAN	MATERIAL OF WHICH ITS VOTERS ARE MADE. SWITZERLAND
FABL V (119)	NOT AMONG ANGELS IN THE CLOUDS BUT ON EARTH AMONG	HUMAN	MEN AND WOMEN. /HERM./ THAT WAS NOT WHY THEY KILLED
FABL PREFACE(74)	AND THIS IS EXACTLY AS IT SHOULD BE, BECAUSE, AS	HUMAN	MENTAL CAPACITY VARIES FROM GRADE TO GRADE, THOSE WHO
FABL PREFACE(75)	RELIGION WAS CARRIED TO THE UTMOST REACH OF THE	HUMAN	MIND BY THE INDIAN JAINISTS, WHO RENOUNCED IDOLATRY
METH PREFACE(R29)	TOOK HEREDITY FOR GRANTED, SO DID EVERYBODY. THE	HUMAN	MIND HAS BEEN SOAKED IN HEREDITY AS LONG BACK AS WE
HART PREFACE(19)	HARDLY ONE OF THE EPOCH-MAKING WORKS OF THE	HUMAN	MIND MIGHT NOT HAVE BEEN ABORTED OR DESTROYED BY
METH PREFACE(R32)	FROM PLATO TO LEIBNITZ, HAD KEPT THE	HUMAN	MIND OPEN FOR THE THOUGHT OF THE UNIVERSE AS ONE IDEA
PRES (150)	/MITCHENER/ (GROANING) IT IS IMPOSSIBLE FOR THE	HUMAN	MIND TO CONCEIVE ANYTHING MORE DREADFUL THAN THIS.
METH PREFACE(R77)	AND THE REST, PERSIST IN TRYING TO CRAMP THE	HUMAN	MIND WITHIN THE LIMITS OF THESE GROTESQUE PERVERSIONS
LION PREFACE(18)	SUCH DOUBLE BELIEFS ARE ENTERTAINED BY THE	HUMAN	MIND WITHOUT UNEASINESS OR CONSCIOUSNESS OF THE
HART PREFACE(16)	NO NATIONAL FRONTIERS IN THE GREAT REALM OF THE	HUMAN	MIND, KEPT THE EUROPEAN COMITY OF THAT REALM LOFTILY
MTH2 (69)	BY OUR CIVILIZATION CANNOT BE SOLVED BY MERE	HUMAN	MUSHROOMS WHO DECAY AND DIE WHEN THEY ARE JUST
OVER PREFACE(159)	EFFORT, AIDED BY A SUPERHUMAN FACULTY FOR	HUMAN	NATURAL HISTORY; BUT THE RESULT WAS CURIOUSLY
MIS. (169)	ROBBERY OF THE POOR! IS THAT WHAT YOU CALL	HUMAN	NATURE? /TARLETON/ NO: THATS WHAT YOU CALL IT. COME,
MTH5 (242)	FOOLS. /THE MALE FIGURE/ DO YOU BLAME US FOR OUR	HUMAN	NATURE? /THE FEMALE FIGURE/ WE ARE FLESH AND BLOOD
NEVR IV (291)	GO ON. IT'S UNDERSTOOD THAT SELF IS PUT ASIDE.	HUMAN	NATURE ALWAYS BEGINS BY SAYING THAT. /CRAMPTON/ BUT I
BULL PREFACE(49)	OF THE MILITARY MIND CONTINUALLY TO IGNORE	HUMAN	NATURE AND CRY FOR THE MOON INSTEAD OF FACING MODERN
BULL PREFACE(33)	OF INDEPENDENCE. IT IS VAIN TO PLEAD THAT THIS IS	HUMAN	NATURE AND NOT CLASS WEAKNESS. THE JAPANESE HAVE
GETT (322)	YOU WOULD BE IN A MINORITY OF ONE. YOU MUST TAKE	HUMAN	NATURE AS IT IS. /SOAMES/ UPON WHAT COMPULSION MUST
LION PREFACE(78)	WAS STILL ON HIS BACK. THUS BUNYAN'S ALLEGORY OF	HUMAN	NATURE BREAKS THROUGH THE PAULINE THEOLOGY AT A
SIM I (40)	YOUR GODFATHERS AND GODMOTHERS COULD CHANGE YOUR	HUMAN	NATURE BY GIVING YOU AN UNUSUAL NAME IN BAPTISM. /THE
OVER PREFACE(168)	IS THAT NO NECESSARY AND INEVITABLE OPERATION OF	HUMAN	NATURE CAN REASONABLY BE REGARDED AS SINFUL AT ALL,
NEVR I (203)	/PHILIP/ (MATURELY) NO, DOLLY: MY KNOWLEDGE OF	HUMAN	NATURE CONFIRMS MR VALENTINE'S JUDGMENT. HE IS RIGHT.
JOAN PREFACE(40)	IN FREEDOM THAN POLITICAL AND ECCLESIASTICAL	HUMAN	NATURE COULD BEAR. IT IS EASY TO SAY THAT THE CHURCH
JITT PREFACE(3)	AND HIS HOPELESS INCAPACITY FOR REPRESENTING	HUMAN	NATURE DRAMATICALLY OR OTHERWISE, IN A FEW
LION PREFACE(3)	TO ADMIT THAT AFTER CONTEMPLATING THE WORLD AND	HUMAN	NATURE FOR NEARLY SIXTY YEARS, I SEE NO WAY OUT OF THE
PYGM EPILOG (289)	TRUE SEQUEL IS PATENT TO ANYONE WITH A SENSE OF	HUMAN	NATURE IN GENERAL, AND OF FEMININE INSTINCT IN
PHIL PREFACE(68)	BY CHANGING THE FAIR INTO A WOOLWORTH STORE. THE	HUMAN	NATURE IN IT IS STILL IN THE LATEST FASHION: INDEED I
DEST SD(149)	OF WORK, AND A CLEAR REALISTIC KNOWLEDGE OF	HUMAN	NATURE IN PUBLIC AFFAIRS, HAVING SEEN IT EXHAUSTIVELY
OVER PREFACE(160)	BE SETTLED BY BLOOD FEUD OR VENDETTA , AS LONG AS	HUMAN	NATURE INSISTS ON REVENGE, THE OFFICIAL ORGANIZATION
GETT PREFACE(202)	AS POSSIBLE OUT OF THE QUESTION, AND DEAL WITH	HUMAN	NATURE INSTEAD. FOR EVEN IF THERE COULD BE ANY REAL
GETT PREFACE(257)	THE LONG RUN OUR PRESENT PLAN OF TRYING TO FORCE	HUMAN	NATURE INTO A MOULD OF EXISTING ABUSES, SUPERSTITIONS,
NEVR II (230)	IS: IT'S NOT OUR FAULT. /PHILIP/ MY KNOWLEDGE OF	HUMAN	NATURE IS FAIRLY EXTENSIVE, MR M'COMAS; BUT I FIND IT
MTH4 I (165)	IT. IT IS RATHER PERSONAL AND IN BAD TASTE.	HUMAN	NATURE IS HUMAN NATURE, LONGLIVED OR SHORTLIVED, AND
GENV III (81)	HUMAN NATURE! BUT IT IS NOT NATURAL AT ALL: REAL	HUMAN	NATURE IS IN CONTINUAL CONFLICT WITH IT; FOR AMID ALL
GETT PREFACE(241)	IS ONLY 2, A FIGURE WHICH, IF WE ASSUME THAT	HUMAN	NATURE IS MUCH THE SAME IN WALWORTH AS IN WASHINGTON,
GETT PREFACE(193)	THEY HAD, AS TO ADULTS, A THEORY THAT	HUMAN	NATURE IS SO POOR THAT IT IS USELESS TO TRY TO MAKE
BARB PREFACE(239)	HAS FAITH IN THE KINDNESS AND INTELLIGENCE OF	HUMAN	NATURE IS THE FULMINATOR, NOW A HUNTED WRETCH, WITH
MIS. (169)	IT: YOULL GET NO JUSTICE HERE: WE DONT KEEP IT.	HUMAN	NATURE IS WHAT WE STOCK. /THE MAN/ HUMAN NATURE!
LION PREFACE(80)	SEX AND IS THEREFORE AN INERADICABLE PART OF	HUMAN	NATURE (WHY ELSE SHOULD CHRIST HAVE HAD TO ATONE FOR
MTH4 I (151)	COMMON A CONDITION WOULD BE UNDERSTOOD AS LONG AS	HUMAN	NATURE LASTED. TO EMBARRASS IS TO BRING A BLUSH TO THE
NEVR I (207)	THOUGH. /PHILIP/ I DOUBT IT. MY KNOWLEDGE OF	HUMAN	NATURE LEADS ME TO BELIEVE THAT IF HE HAD A LOT OF
NEVR I (213)	BUTTER FOR A FORTNIGHT PAST. NOW MY KNOWLEDGE OF	HUMAN	NATURE LEADS ME TO BELIEVE THAT WE HAD A FATHER, AND
NEVR I (211)	OF FAMILY LIFE, PHIL; AND YOUR EXPERIENCE OF	HUMAN	NATURE ONLY EXTENDS, SO FAR, TO ONE OF THEM. (
VWOO 3 (135)	CANT SAVE ANYTHING. /A/ I LOATHE SAVING. IT TURNS	HUMAN	NATURE SOUR. " CAST YOUR BREAD UPON THE WATERS; AND IT
NEVR II (231)	IT WILL DESERVE IT, MR M'COMAS. MY KNOWLEDGE OF	HUMAN	NATURE TEACHES ME NOT TO EXPECT TOO MUCH. /MRS
HART PREFACE(27)	IS THERE TO SAY EXCEPT THAT WAR PUTS A STRAIN ON	HUMAN	NATURE THAT BREAKS DOWN THE BETTER HALF OF IT, AND
JITT III (62)	HE WILL TELL YOU THAT THERE IS A CERTAIN SIDE TO	HUMAN	NATURE THAT MUST JUST BE RULED OUT IN JUDGING PEOPLE'S
CAPT NOTES (303)	AM AS NEARLY IMPARTIAL IN THE MATTER AS IT IS IN	HUMAN	NATURE TO BE. BESIDES, THERE IS NO STANDARD ENGLISH
HART III (136)	THE MEN DRINKING: IT'S HUMAN NATURE. BUT IT'S NOT	HUMAN	NATURE TO TELL EVERYBODY ABOUT IT. EVERY TIME ONE OF
GETT PREFACE(216)	DOUBT, IF IT WERE ALL THAT IT PRETENDS TO BE, AND	HUMAN	NATURE WERE WORKING SMOOTHLY WITHIN ITS LIMITS, THERE
GENV III (82)	FOREFRONT OF CIVILIZATION. THEN WHY DESPAIR OF	HUMAN	NATURE WHEN IT COSTS US SO MUCH TROUBLE TO CORRUPT
ROCK PREFACE(170)	NOTHING THAT CAN BE CHANGED MORE COMPLETELY THAN	HUMAN	NATURE WHEN THE JOB IS TAKEN IN HAND EARLY ENOUGH.
DOCT PREFACE(5)	TO GO WILDLY BEYOND THE ASCERTAINED STRAIN WHICH	HUMAN	NATURE WILL BEAR. IT IS SIMPLY UNSCIENTIFIC TO ALLEGE
LADY PREFACE(218)	IS THROWN INTO DESPAIR BY A COMPARISON OF ACTUAL	HUMAN	NATURE WITH THEORETICAL MORALITY, ACTUAL LAW AND
HART III (136)	DYEING THEIR HAIR AND THE MEN DRINKING: IT'S	HUMAN	NATURE. BUT IT'S NOT HUMAN NATURE TO TELL EVERYBODY
MIS. (122)	/MRS TARLETON/ OH NO: WE ALL DO THAT: THATS ONLY	HUMAN	NATURE. BUT YOU KNOW THEYVE NO NOTION OF DECENCY. I
LADY PREFACE(229)	WITH THE PLUTOCRACY TO ALL THE FAILINGS OF	HUMAN	NATURE. EVEN SHELLEY ADMITTED, 200 YEARS AFTER
LION PREFACE(77)	PROVIDED THEY HAVE SOME POINT OF CONTACT WITH	HUMAN	NATURE. HEDONISM WILL PASS THE PRAGMATIC TEST AS WELL
LADY PREFACE(232)	ANY REMEDY AT ALL, AND DID NOT MERELY DESPAIR OF	HUMAN	NATURE. HIS FIRST AND LAST WORD ON PARLIAMENT WAS "
GETT PREFACE(195)	THE INDIVIDUAL, THE DANGER OF IT DOES NOT LIE IN	HUMAN	NATURE. HOME LIFE AS WE UNDERSTAND IT IS NO MORE
GETT PREFACE(257)	WE MUST FINALLY ADAPT OUR INSTITUTIONS TO	HUMAN	NATURE. IN THE LONG RUN OUR PRESENT PLAN OF TRYING TO
NEVR I (217)	THE ENGLISH VARIETY, DOLL, TRUST MY KNOWLEDGE OF	HUMAN	NATURE. (HE RESUMES HIS POSITION ON THE HEARTH-RUG
POSN PREFACE(365)	TO CONTRADICT THEM, ALWAYS STRONG IN ENGLISH	HUMAN	NATURE. WHY THE MANAGERS LOVE THE CENSORSHIP. THE ONLY
KING I (198)	YOU HAVE NO HEAD FOR POLITICS AND NO KNOWLEDGE OF	HUMAN	NATURE. YOU NEED NOT BE ANXIOUS ABOUT ME. I WILL LEAVE
NEVR I (211)	AND I DONT THINK, JUDGING FROM MY KNOWLEDGE OF	HUMAN	NATURE-- WE DONT THINK THAT YOU (SPEAKING VERY
2TRU III (87)	IN YOUR LIFE BEFORE, THATS A HARD FACT OF	HUMAN	NATURE; AND IT'S ONE OF THE FACTS THAT RELIGION HAS TO
MTH4 I (165)	RATHER PERSONAL AND IN BAD TASTE. HUMAN NATURE IS	HUMAN	NATURE, LONGLIVED OR SHORTLIVED, AND ALWAYS WILL BE.
GENV III (82)	THE STREET, THE RESULT IS THAT HERE WE DESPAIR OF	HUMAN	NATURE, WHEREAS RUSSIA HAS HOPES THAT HAVE CARRIED HER
LION PREFACE(81)	MORALITY, BUT OF COURSE THE MAIN RESTRAINT IS	HUMAN	NATURE, WHICH HAS GOOD IMPULSES AS WELL AS BAD ONES,
SUPR HANDBOK(190)	THOSE WHOM THEY GOVERNED; SO, BY MERE FORCE OF "	HUMAN	NATURE," GOVERNMENT BY CONSENT OF THE GOVERNED HAS
MRS PREFACE(174)	ABOUT THEM THAT THEY FINALLY STOP BLAMING "	HUMAN	NATURE" FOR THEM, AND BEGIN TO SUPPORT MEASURES FOR
GENV III (81)	CRUEL OF ALL THE BEASTS. AND THIS, THEY SAY, IS	HUMAN	NATURE! BUT IT IS NOT NATURAL AT ALL: REAL HUMAN
MIS. (169)	KEEP IT. HUMAN NATURE IS WHAT WE STOCK. /THE MAN/	HUMAN	NATURE! DEBAUCHERY! GLUTTONY! SELFISHNESS! ROBBERY

PYGM EPILOG (298)	SHE CLUNG APPEARED IN ITS TRUE RELATION TO REAL	HUMAN	NEEDS AND WORTHY SOCIAL STRUCTURE, HE EFFECTED A
MIS. PREFACE(8)	THEM. THERE IS A POINT AT WHICH EVERY PERSON WITH	HUMAN	NERVES HAS TO SAY TO A CHILD " STOP THAT NOISE." BUT
GETT PREFACE(249)	PERSONS SOLD IS NEITHER RELIGIOUS NOR NATURAL NOR	HUMAN	NOR SUPER-HUMAN, BUT SIMPLY COMMERCIAL. THE CHURCH,
SIM PREFACE(18)	ALWAYS AVAILABLE TO CONSIDER WHETHER THESE	HUMAN	NUISANCES SHOULD NOT BE PUT OUT OF THEIR PAIN, OR OUT
GETT PREFACE(237)	OF HAPPINESS AS: PERHAPS THE MOST MISERABLE OF	HUMAN	OCCUPATIONS. NEVERTHELESS, THE AMERICAN CONSTITUTION
SUPR II (59)	TO ASSOCIATE WITH HER? HOW CAN I EVER HAVE ANY	HUMAN	OR DECENT RELATIONS WITH HER AGAIN, NOW THAT YOU HAVE
METH PREFACE(R42)	WITHOUT THE INTERVENTION OF ANY STOCK-BREEDER,	HUMAN	OR DIVINE, AND WITHOUT WILL, PURPOSE, DESIGN, OR EVEN
KING PREFACE(157)	A WOMAN. EVERY VOTE, TO BE VALID, MUST BE FOR A	HUMAN	PAIR, WITH THE RESULT THAT THE ELECTED BODY MUST
DOCT PREFACE(44)	HIS PRACTICE IS TRACKED DOWN TO ITS SOURCE IN	HUMAN	PASSION THERE IS A GREAT AND QUITE SINCERE POOHPOOHING
ROCK I (209)	TAKE THE PLACE OF EMOTION AND ECONOMICS OF HONEST	HUMAN	PASSION." WHEW! THAT TOOK A LONG BREATH. " THEY NEVER
SUPR III (109)	WILL NOT BE CATHOLIC ENOUGH: MEN WILL DIE FOR	HUMAN	PERFECTION, TO WHICH THEY WILL SACRIFICE ALL THEIR
SUPR III (90)	IS JUSTICE IN HELL: HEAVEN IS FAR ABOVE SUCH IDLE	HUMAN	PERSONALITIES. YOU WILL BE WELCOME IN HELL, SENORA.
JOAN PREFACE(23)	CAREER, AND MAKES HER A CREDIBLE HISTORICAL AND	HUMAN	PHENOMENON; BUT IT CLASHES MOST DISCORDANTLY BOTH WITH
LADY PREFACE(229)	CLASSES, WHICH IS WHAT ONE DEMANDS FROM A GREAT	HUMAN	POET, IS NOT THAT HE SHOULD FLATTER THE POOR AND
METH PREFACE(R27)	SPAN OF LIFE IS THREE-SCORE-AND-TEN. IT WIDENED	HUMAN	POSSIBILITIES TO THE EXTENT OF ENABLING US TO HOPE
GENV PREFACE(25)	CALLED GREAT MEN MARK NOT HUMAN ATTAINMENT BUT	HUMAN	POSSIBILITY AND HOPE. THEY PROVE THAT THOUGH WE IN THE
KING PREFACE(153)	FRESH. FOR INSTANCE, CHARLES MIGHT HAVE MET THAT	HUMAN	PRODIGY ISAAC NEWTON, AND NEWTON MIGHT HAVE MET THAT
SUPR HANDBOK(212)	HAPPY-GO-LUCKY INDUSTRIAL DISORDER, ALL THE	HUMAN	PRODUCTS, SUCCESSFUL OR NOT, WOULD HAVE TO BE THROWN
POSN PREFACE(383)	NO LESSON; AND HE HAS OPPOSED THE NEXT STEP IN	HUMAN	PROGRESS AS INDIGNANTLY AS IF NEITHER MANNERS,
GENV IV (112)	AS PIONEER I KNOW THAT THE REAL OBSTACLE TO	HUMAN	PROGRESS IS THE SORT OF MIND THAT HAS BEEN FORMED IN
JOAN PREFACE(50)	WILL HAVE BEFORE THEM NOT ONLY THE VISIBLE AND	HUMAN	PUPPETS, BUT THE CHURCH, THE INQUISITION, THE FEUDAL
METH PREFACE(R64)	AGAINST FISTICUFFS, ALL ATTEMPT TO INTRODUCE	HUMAN	PURPOSE AND DESIGN AND FORETHOUGHT INTO THE INDUSTRIAL
LION PREFACE(66)	THOUGH VINDICTIVENESS AND CRUELTY ARE AT LEAST	HUMAN	QUALITIES WHEN THEY ARE FRANKLY PROCLAIMED AND
SIM PREFACE(15)	AFFAIR IS THOUGHT OF AS A GRAND FINISH TO THE	HUMAN	RACE AND ALL ITS PROBLEMS, LEAVING THE SURVIVORS IN A
MIS. PREFACE(3)	SUCH A SHRIEK OF DESPAIR WOULD GO UP FROM THE	HUMAN	RACE AS NO OTHER CONCEIVABLE HORROR COULD PROVOKE.
FABL PREFACE(75)	PROPHETS, AND WHEN HE HAD RESOLVED TO DESTROY THE	HUMAN	RACE AS ONE OF HIS MISTAKES, WAS INDUCED TO MAKE AN
LADY PREFACE(219)	THE NATURAL AND PROPER SENTIMENTS OF THE	HUMAN	RACE AS SHAKESPEAR UNDERSTOOD THEM, AND NOT THE
MIS. (199)	FAMILY BE ROOTED OUT OF CIVILIZATION! LET THE	HUMAN	RACE BE BROUGHT UP IN INSTITUTIONS! /HYPATIA/ OH YES.
3PLA PREFACE(R20)	THE APPARENTLY INEVITABLE DESTRUCTION OF THE	HUMAN	RACE BY THE MARTIANS. ANOTHER EXAMPLE. AN AMERICAN
FABL PREFACE(69)	PROOF. NONE THE LESS, WITHOUT SUCH BELIEF THE	HUMAN	RACE CANNOT BE CIVILIZED AND GOVERNED, THOUGH THE TEN
VWOO 3 (140)	EASIER THAN YOU THINK. ABOUT FIVE PER CENT OF THE	HUMAN	RACE CONSISTS OF POSITIVE MASTERFUL ACQUISITIVE PEOPLE
GENV IV (113)	GOOD REASONS FOR DOING SO: IN SHORT, THAT THE	HUMAN	RACE DOES NOT AT PRESENT CONSIST EXCLUSIVELY OR EVEN
ROCK II (264)	THE HIGHEST ENLIGHTENMENT YET REACHED BY THE	HUMAN	RACE FROM THE TEMPLES OF BRAHMA THE THOUSANDFOLD WHO
GETT (266)	THINGS ABOUT HERSELF, BUT AS IF IT WAS THE WHOLE	HUMAN	RACE GIVING YOU A BIT OF ITS MIND. OH, WONDERFUL,
ROCK I (216)	BUT THERE IS STILL AN IMMENSE FRINGE OF THE	HUMAN	RACE GROWING UP TO A SENSE OF THE NECESSITY FOR
HART I (73)	IS THE DYNAMITE FOR? /HECTOR/ TO BLOW UP THE	HUMAN	RACE IF IT GOES TOO FAR. HE IS TRYING TO DISCOVER A
MIS. PREFACE(71)	INSTEAD OF, AS AT PRESENT, IMPRISONING THE	HUMAN	RACE IN DUSTY OR MUDDY THOROUGHFARES BETWEEN WALLS OF
MTH2 (81)	/CONRAD/ WELL, SOME AUTHORITIES HOLD THAT THE	HUMAN	RACE IS A FAILURE, AND THAT A NEW FORM OF LIFE, BETTER
MIS. PREFACE(3)	REMANUFACTURE OF THE LIFE STUFF BY WHICH THE	HUMAN	RACE IS PERPETUATED, THE LIFE FORCE EITHER WILL NOT OR
GENV IV (106)	AS TO OUR RACES, THEY ARE SO MIXED THAT THE WHOLE	HUMAN	RACE MUST BE DESCENDED FROM ABRAHAM; FOR EVERYBODY WHO
SIM II (60)	HE COMFORTS HIMSELF BY REMEMBERING THAT THE	HUMAN	RACE PRODUCED MOZART; BUT A WOMAN WHO PLAYS THE PIANO
DOCT I (95)	YOU, BLOOD-POISONING. NINETY-FIVE PER CENT OF THE	HUMAN	RACE SUFFER FROM CHRONIC BLOOD-POISONING, AND DIE OF
SUPR III (119)	HAS DONE MORE TO DESTROY THE CONSCIENCE OF THE	HUMAN	RACE THAN ANY OTHER SINGLE ERROR, COME, ANA! DO NOT
METH PREFACE(R63)	POLITICALLY ORGANIZED ATTEMPT TO PERSUADE THE	HUMAN	RACE THAT ALL PROGRESS, ALL PROSPERITY, ALL SALVATION,
SUPR HANDBOK(184)	GENERALLY KNOWN MODERN EXPERIMENT IN BREEDING THE	HUMAN	RACE TOOK PLACE IN A COMMUNITY WHICH DISCARDED BOTH
MTH4 I (161)	OF LIFE TO THREE HUNDRED YEARS HAS PROVIDED THE	HUMAN	RACE WITH CAPABLE LEADERS, AND MADE SHORT WORK OF SUCH
MTH4 III (197)	AND WE GO DOWN TO ANNIHILATION DRAGGING THE WHOLE	HUMAN	RACE WITH US. (HE PAUSES FOR BREATH). /THE ELDERLY
DOCT PREFACE(22)	THIS HAD BEEN EVEN APPROXIMATELY TRUE, THE WHOLE	HUMAN	RACE WOULD HAVE BEEN WIPED OUT BY THE PLAGUE LONG AGO,
JOAN 4 (100)	WHEN HE DAMNS, HE DAMNS THE SOULS OF THE ENTIRE	HUMAN	RACE. AGAINST THAT DREADFUL DESIGN THE CHURCH STANDS
GENV I (33)	JEW/ SOME OF THE GREATEST MEN HAVE DISLIKED THE	HUMAN	RACE. BUT FOR NOAH, ITS CREATOR WOULD HAVE DROWNED IT.
GENV III (83)	OF MAN: THAT IS, TO AN ENORMOUS MAJORITY OF THE	HUMAN	RACE. IT SIMPLY INDICATES MIXED ANCESTRY. /THE WIDOW/
MIS. (147)	LOSS. /TARLETON/ WELL, WHY NOT? AVERAGES OUT THE	HUMAN	RACE. MAKES THE NIGGER HALF AN ENGLISHMAN. MAKES THE
GENV IV (104)	OF AN ATTEMPT TO EXTERMINATE THE FLOWER OF THE	HUMAN	RACE. /BATTLER/ WHAT DO YOU MEAN? /THE JEW/ I AM A
PHIL II (96)	IS SET ABOVE THE HEALTH AND LIVES OF THE ENTIRE	HUMAN	RACE. /CUTHBERTSON/ (VEHEMENTLY) IT'S NOT IGNORANCE
GENV I (34)	OF ATTEMPTING TO EXTERMINATE A SECTION OF THE	HUMAN	RACE. /SHE/ WELL, IT SEEMS LIKE TAKING A LOT ON
O'FL (216)	WORLD TIL YOU KNOCK THE PATRIOTISM OUT OF THE	HUMAN	RACE. /SIR PEARCE/ STILL, WE -- /O'FLAHERTY/ WHISHT,
FABL I (103)	REPLACE THEM; BUT KILL THE WOMEN AND YOU KILL THE	HUMAN	RACE. /YOUNG WOMAN/ THAT WONT STOP WAR. SOMEBODY WILL
ROCK II (264)	FACES OF MY PEOPLE IN CEYLON, THE CRADLE OF THE	HUMAN	RACE. THERE YOU SEE MAN AS HE CAME FROM THE HAND OF
CATH PREFACE(154)	ARE ADMITTED WITH AWE BY THE REST OF THE	HUMAN	RACE. THEY SAY I THINK AN ENGLISHMAN A FOOL. WHEN I
SUPR HANDBOK(180)	IS INDISPENSABLE TO THE WEEDING OUT OF THE	HUMAN	RACE. WHEN THE CONCEPTION OF HEREDITY TOOK HOLD OF THE
GENV III (76)	/THE SECRETARY/ YOU ARE ALL ENEMIES OF THE	HUMAN	RACE. YOU ARE ALL ARMED TO THE TEETH AND FULL OF
METH PREFACE(R78)	OF THESE LEGENDS IS THE COMMON HERITAGE OF THE	HUMAN	RACE; AND THERE IS ONLY ONE INEXORABLE CONDITION
APPL PREFACE(193)	IN THE PROCESS, SAW IN GATTIE AN ENEMY OF THE	HUMAN	RACE, A WRECKER OF HOMES AND A STARVER OF INNOCENT
MILL PREFACE(124)	JEWS ARE THE NATURAL ENEMIES OF THE REST OF THE	HUMAN	RACE, AND THAT AS A STATE OF PERPETUAL WAR NECESSARILY
FABL IV (115)	THEIR ABLEST BIOLOGISTS HAD TO AGREE THAT THE	HUMAN	RACE, HAVING TRIED EATING EVERYTHING ON EARTH THAT WAS
GETT PREFACE(203)	WHICH EVERYTHING, EVEN THE VERY EXISTENCE OF THE	HUMAN	RACE, MUST BE SACRIFICED IF NECESSARY (AND THIS IS
FABL V (117)	OF ANY HUMAN SOCIETY: THE REPRODUCTION OF THE	HUMAN	RACE, THE MOST MENTIONABLE SUBJECT IN THE WORLD AND
SUPR HANDBOK(212)	IS NOTHING NEW IN PRIVATE ENTERPRISE THROWING ITS	HUMAN	REFUSE ON THE CHEAP LABOR MARKET AND THE WORKHOUSE;
SUPR III (124)	DO YOU KNOW THAT IT IS NOT THE GREATEST OF ALL	HUMAN	RELATIONS? FAR TOO GREAT TO BE A PERSONAL MATTER.
OVER PREFACE(157)	SIDES OF THE CASE, BETWEEN SPONTANEOUS	HUMAN	RELATIONS BETWEEN INDEPENDENT MEN AND WOMEN ON THE ONE
PYGM IV (265)	INTO THE GRATED TOSH, ELIZA. DONT YOU INSULT	HUMAN	RELATIONS BY DRAGGING ALL THIS CANT ABOUT BUYING AND
MIS. PREFACE(25)	INSTRUCTION IF I COULD HAVE GOT INTO ANY DECENT	HUMAN	RELATIONSHIP WITH THEM, AND IF THEY HAD NOT BEEN
MRS IV (242)	AN ARTIST, AND BELIEVING THAT THE MOST INTIMATE	HUMAN	RELATIONSHIPS ARE FAR BEYOND AND ABOVE THE SCOPE OF
GETT PREFACE(219)	HUMAN RELATIONS, AND EMBRACES ALL THE OTHER HIGH	HUMAN	RELATIONS. NOW THIS IS VIOLENTLY UNTRUE. EVERY ADULT
SUPR III (124)	ACCORDING TO YOU, LOVE IS THE SLIGHTEST OF ALL	HUMAN	RELATIONS. /DON JUAN/ HOW DO YOU KNOW THAT IT IS NOT
GETT PREFACE(219)	THE PARTIES IS THE MOST INTIMATE AND PERSONAL OF	HUMAN	RELATIONS, AND EMBRACES ALL THE OTHER HIGH HUMAN
SIM II (81)	THE END OF THE WORLD BUT THE BEGINNING OF REAL	HUMAN	RESPONSIBILITY. CHARLES AND I HAVE STILL OUR DUTIES:
MIS. PREFACE(30)	ALL THERE IS TO KNOW ABOUT ONESELF IS A NATURAL	HUMAN	RIGHT THAT SWEEPS AWAY ALL THE PRETENCES OF OTHERS TO
DOCT PREFACE(33)	TO KNOWLEDGE MUST BE REGARDED AS A FUNDAMENTAL	HUMAN	RIGHT. THE FACT THAT MEN OF SCIENCE HAVE HAD TO FIGHT
DOCT PREFACE(37)	AS THE ELEVATION OF CRUELTY TO THE RANK OF A	HUMAN	RIGHT. UNNECESSARY, BECAUSE NO VIVISECTOR CONFESSES TO
BARB PREFACE(243)	THE VERY GROUNDWORK OF INSTITUTIONS, RIDICULING	HUMAN	RIGHTS, EXTOLLING BRAINLESS METHODS AS " HISTORICAL,"
LION PREFACE(71)	SOLITUDE WHICH IS ONE OF THE MOST SACRED OF	HUMAN	RIGHTS, HE DOES SO BECAUSE HE HAS NO RIGHT TO IMPOSE
SUPR HANDBOK(196)	THE DYNAMITARD ASSERTS HIS CONCEPTION OF NATURAL	HUMAN	RIGHTS, THE FABIAN SOCIETY IS PATTED ON THE BACK JUST
2TRU PREFACE(13)	AUTOMATIC NOR ABSTRACT: IT MUST BE PERFORMED BY	HUMAN	RULERS AND AGENTS AS BEST THEY CAN. 3. THE BUSINESS OF
MTH5 (218)	THOUGH WE HAVE FOSSILS OF THEM. THEN YOU BECAME	HUMAN	; AND YOU PASSED IN FIFTEEN MONTHS THROUGH A
MIS. PREFACE(34)	OF ACTION WHEN CAPITALISM GOES THE WAY OF DRUIDIC	HUMAN	SACRIFICE (A MUCH LESS SLAUGHTEROUS INSTITUTION).
BULL PREFACE(57)	MISSIONARIES MIGHT DO WELL TO ADOPT THE RITE OF	HUMAN	SACRIFICE WHEN EVANGELIZING TRIBES IN WHOSE
BULL PREFACE(69)	PROBABLY SEE IN THESE CATASTROPHES A RITUAL OF	HUMAN	SACRIFICE WITHOUT WHICH THE SAVAGES OF THE TWENTIETH
DOCT PREFACE(32)	THAT A CALAMITY OF ANY SORT MUST BE EXPIATED BY A	HUMAN	SACRIFICE; SO THE WICKEDNESSES AND STUPIDITIES OF OUR
CLEO III (157)	THE HONOR OF ROME-- /CAESAR/ I DO NOT MAKE	HUMAN	SACRIFICES TO MY HONOR, AS YOUR DRUIDS DO. SINCE YOU
2TRU III (86)	ENEMIES WITHOUT GIVING QUARTER, AND OFFERING UP	HUMAN	SACRIFICES, AND THINKING YOU CAN DO WHAT YOU LIKE TO
GENV I (46)	OF THE MOST BARBAROUS KIND. THEY BELIEVE IN	HUMAN	SACRIFICES, IN WHAT THEY CALL THE REMISSION OF SINS BY
GETT PREFACE(187)	MARRIAGES AS ALL FANATICISMS ARE REINFORCED BY	HUMAN	SACRIFICES, IT HAS BEEN REDUCED TO A PRIVATE AND
DOCT PREFACE(39)	AND EVEN, WHEN THE CRUEL SACRIFICES ARE	HUMAN	SACRIFICES, OF POLITICAL ECONOMY, IT IS IDLE FOR THE
GENV III (81)	BEEN HEAPED A GROUNDWORK OF SAVAGE SUPERSTITIONS:	HUMAN	SACRIFICES, VENGEANCE, WARS OF CONQUEST AND RELIGION,
BARB PREFACE(228)	BEST OFFICERS THAT THEY WOULD WORK AS HARD FOR	HUMAN	SALVATION AS THEY DO AT PRESENT IF THEY BELIEVED THAT
BARB PREFACE(245)	THE OLD SCAPEGOAT AND SACRIFICIAL LAMB, WE DEIFY	HUMAN	SAVIORS, AND PRAY TO MIRACULOUS VIRGIN INTERCESSORS.
METH PREFACE(R30)	THE GARDEN OF EDEN, BUT ADAPTATIONS BY DELIBERATE	HUMAN	SELECTION OF THE MEDIEVAL WAR-HORSE TO MODERN RACING
DOCT PREFACE(6)	THAT; AND THE DOCTOR ASSURES YOU THAT ALL THAT	HUMAN	SKILL COULD DO HAS BEEN DONE. AND NOBODY HAS THE
SUPR HANDBOK(206)	IN 4 AND THEN REPLACE HIM BY A FRESH VICTIM. AND	HUMAN	SLAVERY, WHICH HAS REACHED ITS WORST RECORDED POINT
BULL PREFACE(26)	ANARCHIST AS FAR AS ANARCHISM IS PRACTICABLE IN	HUMAN	SOCIETY: THAT IS, HE IS AN INDIVIDUALIST, A
FABL V (117)	OUR BUSINESS IS THE VERY FIRST BUSINESS OF ANY	HUMAN	SOCIETY: THE REPRODUCTION OF THE HUMAN RACE, THE MOST
MTH2 (52)	ON EVERY PRINCIPLE THAT GOES TO THE ROOT OF	HUMAN	SOCIETY AND DESTINY; AND THE IMPOSSIBILITY OF KEEPING
GETT PREFACE(230)	HOUR. PHYSICALLY THERE IS NOTHING TO DISTINGUISH	HUMAN	SOCIETY FROM THE FARM-YARD EXCEPT THAT CHILDREN ARE
MIS. PREFACE(44)	CHILD MAY CORRUPT A WHOLE GENERATION AND MAKE	HUMAN	SOCIETY IMPOSSIBLE: THEREFORE THRASH THE VICE OUT OF
JOAN 4 (103)	NOT STOP UNTIL IT HAS BROUGHT THE WHOLE BODY OF	HUMAN	SOCIETY INTO SIN AND CORRUPTION, INTO WASTE AND RUIN.
APPL INTRLUD(253)	SECRET OF GOOD MANNERS; AND WITHOUT GOOD MANNERS	HUMAN	SOCIETY IS INTOLERABLE AND IMPOSSIBLE. /ORINTHIA/

GETT PREFACE(208)	IT WERE PHYSICALLY POSSIBLE TO INTRODUCE IT INTO	HUMAN	SOCIETY IT WOULD BE WRECKED BY AN OPPOSITE AND NOT
MILL PREFACE(109)	QUESTION THAT HAS TROUBLED HUMAN LIFE AND MOULDED	HUMAN	SOCIETY SINCE THE CREATION. THE LAW IS EQUAL BEFORE
FANY EPILOG (328)	TOO SUBTLE TO BE PUT INTO WORDS, WITHOUT WHICH	HUMAN	SOCIETY WOULD BE UNBEARABLE. PEOPLE COULD NOT TALK TO
2TRU PREFACE(13)	HERE IT IS. FUNDAMENTAL NATURAL CONDITIONS OF	HUMAN	SOCIETY. 1. GOVERNMENT IS NECESSARY WHEREVER TWO OR
ROCK PREFACE(188)	BE THE RUIN OF ALL KINGDOMS, ALL LAW, AND ALL	HUMAN	SOCIETY. IT MAY BE THE THOUGHT OF THE BEAST OF PREY
2TRU PREFACE(16)	AS TO THE FUNDAMENTAL CONDITIONS OF A STABLE	HUMAN	SOCIETY. OTHERWISE THE RESULT MIGHT BE AN ASSEMBLY OF
ROCK I (202)	FOUNDATION OF CHRISTIANITY, OF CIVILIZATION, OF	HUMAN	SOCIETY. /SIR ARTHUR/ THATS ENOUGH ABOUT THE
MTH4 I (158)	ON ASSUMPTIONS OF SOME SORT OR WE CANNOT FORM A	HUMAN	SOCIETY. /ZOO/ THE ASSUMPTIONS MUST BE SCIENTIFIC,
GETT PREFACE(194)	ARE SO THOROUGHLY HOME-BRED AS TO BE UNFIT FOR	HUMAN	SOCIETY. SO LITTLE IS EXPECTED OF THEM THAT IN
MTH3 (129)	CENTURIES OF LIFE, WILL DRIVE THEM MAD AND WRECK	HUMAN	SOCIETY. THIS DISCOVERY MUST BE KEPT A DEAD SECRET. (
LION PREFACE(50)	PAUL HAS SUCCEEDED IN EFFECTING THE SALVATION OF	HUMAN	SOCIETY. WHILST I WRITE, THE TURKS ARE SAID TO BE
JOAN 4 (105)	BECAUSE THERE MUST BE A KEYSTONE TO THE ARCH OF	HUMAN	SOCIETY; BUT WE HOLD OUR LANDS IN OUR OWN HANDS, AND
GENV IV (101)	THE QUESTION WHETHER THEY ARE FIT TO LIVE IN	HUMAN	SOCIETY, BUT NOT UNTIL THAT QUESTION HAS BEEN DECIDED
ROCK II (235)	AND ALL THE REST OF THE DEMOCRATIC DREGS OF	HUMAN	SOCIETY, WE COULDNT BE SURE OF A MAJORITY. HIS GOLDEN
BARB III (324)	OPEN THE GATES OF HEAVEN TO YOU, BUT TO TAKE A	HUMAN	SOUL FROM ME, AND TURN IT INTO THE SOUL OF A WOLF!
PYGM V (284)	DOESNT BECOME EITHER THE HUMAN FACE OR THE	HUMAN	SOUL. I AM EXPRESSING MY RIGHTEOUS CONTEMPT FOR
MILL PREFACE(132)	BULLETS WHICH THE DEVIL HAS READY TO SELL FOR A	HUMAN	SOUL. SIX OF THEM MAY HIT THE GLORYMONGER'S MARK VERY
MIS. (135)	OTHER MAN. AND BENEATH THAT COAT AND TROUSERS A	HUMAN	SOUL. TARLETON'S UNDERWEAR! (HE GOES OUT GRAVELY
PYGM V (281)	OF MANNERS, BUT HAVING THE SAME MANNER FOR ALL	HUMAN	SOULS: IN SHORT, BEHAVING AS IF YOU WERE IN HEAVEN,
BARB III (348)	THE LINEN AND CHINA, WHEN IT WAS REALLY ALL THE	HUMAN	SOULS TO BE SAVED: NOT WEAK SOULS IN STARVED BODIES,
LION PREFACE(60)	IN ADDITION TO THIS YOU DESIRE TO ALLOW THE TWO	HUMAN	SOULS WHICH ARE INSEPARABLE FROM THE CAPTAIN AND THE
JOAN PREFACE(36)	THEIR FUNCTION AS THE PASTORS OF THEIR FLOCKS OF	HUMAN	SOULS. BUT TO SAY THAT THE SOULS OF THE PEOPLE ARE NO
CLEO NOTES (204)	PROGRESS IN THE POPULAR SENSE OF EVOLUTION OF THE	HUMAN	SPECIES. THE NOTION THAT THERE HAS BEEN ANY SUCH
GENV PREFACE(14)	CHANGE IN THE NATURAL POLITICAL CAPACITY OF THE	HUMAN	SPECIES. THE COMEDIES OF ARISTOPHANES AND THE BIBLE
JOAN PREFACE(8)	ROMANCE, AND REGARDING WOMAN AS THE FEMALE OF THE	HUMAN	SPECIES, AND NOT AS A DIFFERENT KIND OF ANIMAL WITH
GETT PREFACE(226)	TOTAL DISUSE, HAVE LOST THE POWER OF KINDLY	HUMAN	SPEECH AND CAN ONLY SCOLD AND COMPLAIN: THERE ARE MEN
SIM I (52)	IS HOW I SPEAK TO YOU; BUT YOU DO NOT RECOGNIZE	HUMAN	SPEECH WHEN YOU HEAR IT: YOU CRAVE FOR SLANG AND SMALL
BULL PREFACE(41)	OF HOME RULE. THE GREAT MOVEMENTS OF THE	HUMAN	SPIRIT WHICH SWEEP IN WAVES OVER EUROPE ARE STOPPED ON
SUPR PREFACE(R39)	THEM TO YOU AS THE LATEST OUTPOURING OF THE	HUMAN	SPIRIT, AND, WORST OF ALL, KIDNAPS YOUNG PEOPLE AS
DOCT PREFACE(49)	AS TO THE DEGREE OF ACCURACY ATTAINABLE IN	HUMAN	STATEMENT), BUT NEVER DREAMS OF OFFERING ANY
MIS. PREFACE(97)	WOULD DROP DEAD. IF YOU TRY TO STRETCH IT TO FULL	HUMAN	STATURE WHEN IT IS TEN YEARS OLD, YOU WILL SIMPLY PULL
MRS PREFACE(158)	PARTICULAR SET OF TAPUS IN ADDITION TO THE COMMON	HUMAN	STOCK; AND THOUGH EACH OF THESE TAPUS LIMITS THE SCOPE
ROCK PREFACE(170)	CITY PLUTOCRATS, THOUGH THEY ARE FROM THE SAME	HUMAN	STOCK, ARE SO DIFFERENT THAT THEY CANNOT LIVE TOGETHER
3PLA PREFACE(R32)	WHO KNEW HUMAN WEAKNESS SO WELL, NEVER KNEW	HUMAN	STRENGTH OF THE CAESARIAN TYPE. HIS CAESAR IS AN
SUPR I (24)	SHE TO HIM, AND AS HORRIBLY FASCINATING. OF ALL	HUMAN	STRUGGLES THERE IS NONE SO TREACHEROUS AND REMORSELESS
SUPR HANDBOK(212)	ARE IN ORDINARY INDUSTRIES, EVEN A JOINT STOCK	HUMAN	STUD FARM (PIOUSLY DISGUISED AS A REFORMED FOUNDLING
DOCT PREFACE(46)	VERTEBRATE THAN THE DOG. VIVISECTING THE	HUMAN	SUBJECT. I HAVE IN MY HAND A PRINTED AND PUBLISHED
DOCT PREFACE(47)	AND YOU NOT ONLY SANCTION THE EXPERIMENT ON THE	HUMAN	SUBJECT, BUT MAKE IT THE FIRST DUTY OF THE VIVISECTOR.
DOCT PREFACE(68)	A CONSPIRACY TO EXPLOIT POPULAR CREDULITY AND	HUMAN	SUFFERING. ALREADY OUR M.O.H.S (MEDICAL OFFICERS OF
LION PREFACE(35)	AND BY REPRESENTING CHRIST AS SUPERIOR TO	HUMAN	SUFFERING. IT IS LUKE'S JESUS WHO HAS WON OUR HEARTS.
MIS. PREFACE(82)	AFFECTION AS DISTINGUISHED FROM THAT GENERAL	HUMAN	SYMPATHY WHICH HAS SECURED TO MANY AN ORPHAN FONDER
3PLA PREFACE(R34)	STAGE PLAYS DOES NOT PRESENT AN INFINITE SCOPE TO	HUMAN	TALENT; AND THE PLAYWRIGHTS WHO MAGNIFY ITS
JITT PREFACE(7)	THE ILL-ASSORTED PAIR SETTLE DOWN ON REASONABLE	HUMAN	TERMS, AND FIND LIFE BEARABLE AFTER ALL. TREBITSCH
WIDO II SD(25)	GOING BALD. A NERVOUS, WIRY, PERTINACIOUS	HUMAN	TERRIER, JUDGED BY HIS MOUTH AND EYES, BUT MISERABLY
JOAN PREFACE(18)	BUT ALSO A RATIONALISM CARRIED TO ITS ULTIMATE	HUMAN	TEST OF SUICIDE. YET EVEN IN THIS THE ILLUSION
LION PREFACE(98)	JEHOVAH MORE THAN KRISHNA, OR JESUS MORE OR LESS	HUMAN	THAN MAHOMET OR ZOROASTER OR CONFUCIUS. HE IS ACTUALLY
GENV PREFACE(7)	IS MUCH TO BE SAID FOR ENGLAND'S FULL SHARE OF	HUMAN	THOUGHTLESSNESS. IT IS SOMETIMES BETTER NOT TO THINK
PHIL II (121)	WELL, AT LEAST YOULL ADMIT THAT IT'S AMIABLE AND	HUMAN	TO HOPE THAT YOUR THEORY ABOUT JULIA IS RIGHT, BECAUSE
LION PREFACE(74)	SPIRIT). PETER'S FIRST HARANGUE SOFTENS US BY THE	HUMAN	TOUCH OF ITS EXORDIUM, WHICH WAS A QUAINT ASSURANCE TO
MIS. PREFACE(49)	WHO ALLEGED THAT HE HAD READ LOCKE ON THE	HUMAN	UNDERSTANDING, I ATTEMPTED TO READ THE BIBLE STRAIGHT
BUOY IV (52)	THERE ARE PLENTY OF RATTLERS AND GATERS OF THE	HUMAN	VARIETY IN PARK LANE? /SHE/ YES; AND YOU MAY BE ONE
FABL IV (115)	TO RESTRAIN IT. IT HAD ALSO BEEN NOTICED THAT	HUMAN	VEGETARIANS WERE RESTLESS, PUGNACIOUS, AND SAVAGELY
HART I (79)	TELL YOU I HAVE OFTEN THOUGHT OF THIS KILLING OF	HUMAN	VERMIN. MANY MEN HAVE THOUGHT OF IT. DECENT MEN ARE
SUPR HANDBOK(194)	HE CAN SHEW THAT MANY OF THE MOST DETESTABLE	HUMAN	VICES ARE NOT RADICAL, BUT ARE MERE REACTIONS OF OUR
SUPR III SD(135)	INFINITELY. THEN, VAGUELY, THERE IS A LIVE	HUMAN	VOICE CRYING SOMEWHERE. ONE SEES, WITH A SHOCK, A
OVER (182)	LITTLE CREATURES WITH SANDY HAIR. I DONT CONSIDER	HUMAN	VOLCANOES RESPECTABLE, AND I'M SO TIRED OF THE
MIS. PREFACE(75)	ONE IS TO PROVIDE FOR ALL THE CHILD'S REASONABLE	HUMAN	WANTS, ON WHICH POINT, IF YOU DIFFER FROM ME, I SHALL
3PLA PREFACE(R32)	HAS BEEN BEFOREHAND. BUT SHAKESPEAR, WHO KNEW	HUMAN	WEAKNESS SO WELL, NEVER KNEW HUMAN STRENGTH OF THE
LION PREFACE(96)	AND HISTORIANS, HAVING NO MORE BEARING ON	HUMAN	WELFARE THAN THE CONTROVERSY AS TO WHETHER UNCIAL OR
GETT PREFACE(205)	BE APPLIED TO IT EXCEPT THE TEST OF ITS EFFECT ON	HUMAN	WELFARE. THE SCIENCE AND ART OF POLITICS, POLITICAL
DOCT PREFACE(50)	SOME REGARD FOR AT LEAST THE APPEARANCES OF	HUMAN	WELFARE, WHEREAS A CURIOUS DEVIL MIGHT DESTROY THE
SUPR HANDBOK(211)	NEVERTHELESS, A GENERAL SECRET PUSHING OF THE	HUMAN	WILL IN THE REPUDIATED DIRECTION; SO THAT ALL SORTS OF
SUPR III (121)	IS IT NOT THE INEVITABLE END OF IT ALL THAT THE	HUMAN	WILL SHALL SAY TO THE HUMAN BRAIN: INVENT ME A MEANS
MIS. PREFACE(64)	SAKE. THE STRONGEST, FIERCEST FORCE IN NATURE IS	HUMAN	WILL. IT IS THE HIGHEST ORGANIZATION WE KNOW OF THE
BARB PREFACE(240)	A GENTLEMAN AND A CHRISTIAN IN THE MULTITUDE OF	HUMAN	WOLVES HOWLING FOR HIS BLOOD. THINK ALSO OF THIS: THAT
CLEO PRO1 (91)	DUTY AND OTHER MATTERS THAT CONCERNED NOT A MERE	HUMAN	WORM, AND THE GODS SMILED ON CAESAR; FOR HE LIVED THE
SIM PREFACE(12)	LEGAL NOVELTY AND IMPORTANCE OF ITS CRITERION OF	HUMAN	WORTH. I AM CAREFUL TO SAY LEGAL NOVELTY BECAUSE OF
LADY PREFACE(230)	IN AS YOU LIKE IT, AND MANY HONEST, BRAVE,	HUMAN	, AND LOYAL SERVANTS, BESIDE THE INEVITABLE COMIC
PYGM II (234)	(SWEETLY) WELL, WHAT WOULD A MAN COME FOR? BE	HUMAN	, GOVERNOR. /HIGGINS/ (DISARMED) ALFRED: DID YOU PUT
LION PREFACE(36)	DEMAND FOR SENTIMENT, AS FAR AS IT IS NOT SIMPLY	HUMAN	, IS MORE MANLY THAN WOMANLY); BUT THE CHRIST OF LUKE
GETT (302)	THAT UNLESS THE LAW OF MARRIAGE WERE FIRST MADE	HUMAN	, IT COULD NEVER BECOME DIVINE. /MRS BRIDGENORTH/ OH,
MIS. PREFACE(73)	AUTHORITY BY PERSUADING CHILDREN THAT HE IS NOT	HUMAN	, JUST AS LADIES USED TO PERSUADE THEM THAT THEY HAVE
LADY (239)	HIS CHARITY AND SELF-POSSESSION) BAD? O NO.	HUMAN	, MASTER WARDER, HUMAN. WE CALL ONE ANOTHER NAMES WHEN
DOCT PREFACE(46)	NEITHER SENSE NOR PURPOSE NOR LIFE NOR ANYTHING	HUMAN	, MUCH LESS GODLIKE, IN IT: BY THE METHOD, THAT IS, OF
DOCT PREFACE(40)	PSYCHOLOGICAL HYPOTHESIS, WHICH IS ALSO SIMPLE,	HUMAN	, OBVIOUS, AND PROBABLE. IT MAY BE AS WOUNDING TO THE
GETT PREFACE(231)	AND NEEDS (SOMETIMES SAID TO BE DISTINCTIVELY	HUMAN	, THOUGH BIRDS AND ANIMALS IN A STATE OF FREEDOM
MTH4 I (156)	DADDY, DADDY: I CAN HARDLY BELIEVE THAT YOU ARE	HUMAN	, YOU ARE SO STUPID. IT WAS WELL SAID OF YOUR PEOPLE

HUMANE

SUPR HANDBOK(197)	AND BLOODYMINDED FOR THE WAY OF THE CAUTIOUS AND	HUMANE	? IS ENGLAND ANY THE BETTER FOR THE WRECK OF
SUPR HANDBOK(222)	TRUST. THE PERFECT SERVANT, WHEN HIS MASTER MAKES	HUMANE	ADVANCES TO HIM, FEELS THAT HIS EXISTENCE IS
DOCT PREFACE(36)	NOT ENOUGH CIVIC VIRTUE TO MAKE HER HEALTHY IN A	HUMANE	AND ECONOMICAL WAY, WE SHOULD NOT HAVE ENOUGH TO
DEVL EPILOG (79)	REPORTS ARE VERY CLEVER AS CRITICISMS, AND ARE	HUMANE	AND ENLIGHTENED WITHIN CERTAIN ARISTOCRATIC LIMITS,
BARB PREFACE(214)	MUST THEREFORE BE RULED OUT IN FAVOR OF PURELY	HUMANE	AND HYGIENIC MEASURES. YET IN THE PRECISELY PARALLEL
METH PREFACE(R51)	AND CERTAINTY WITH WHICH BUTLER'S MIND MOVED TO	HUMANE	AND INSPIRING CONCLUSIONS WITH THE GROTESQUE
METH PREFACE(R53)	AND IT WAS DARWIN WHO PUT OUT WEISMANN'S	HUMANE	AND SENSIBLE EYE. HE BLINDED MANY ANOTHER EYE AND
MIS. PREFACE(34)	PUT ASIDE THE CONSIDERATIONS THAT NOW INDUCE ALL	HUMANE	AND THOUGHTFUL POLITICAL STUDENTS TO AGITATE FOR THE
LION I (114)	IT WAS A SILLY THING TO SAY. (IN A LOWER TONE,	HUMANE	AND URGENT) LAVINIA: DO CHRISTIANS KNOW HOW TO LOVE?
DOCT PREFACE(42)	WOMEN PRACTISING VIVISECTION AS SENSELESSLY AS A	HUMANE	BUTCHER, WHO ADORES HIS FOX TERRIER, WILL CUT A
MRS PREFACE(166)	INTELLECTUAL INTEREST, NOT ROMANTIC RHAPSODY BUT	HUMANE	CONCERN, ACCORDINGLY, I DO NOT FIND THOSE CRITICS WHO
DEVL III (76)	GENERAL BURGOYNE. /BURGOYNE/ I AM, SIR; AND I AM	HUMANE	ENOUGH TO BE GLAD OF IT. (RICHARD JUMPS DOWN FROM
DOCT PREFACE(37)	INVOLVES NO DESTRUCTION. AFTER SUCH TRIUMPHS OF	HUMANE	EXPERIMENT AND REASONING, IT IS USELESS TO ASSURE US
GENV I (44)	YOURSELF TO ME YESTERDAY AS A CULTIVATED AND	HUMANE	GENTLEMAN, INTERESTED IN THE CHURCH OF ENGLAND. AND
FABL PREFACE(77)	CHARLES II, HUMANE (INDEED, AS SOME THINK, TOO	HUMANE	IN HIS KINDNESS TO HIS DOZEN DOGS AND HALF DOZEN
UNPL PREFACE(R26)	PROFESSION WITH HONORABLE INDUSTRIES GUARDED BY A	HUMANE	INDUSTRIAL CODE AND A " MORAL MINIMUM" WAGE. HOW I
GENV PREFACE(15)	AWAITED ME IN SPITE OF POPE PIUS THE NINTH'S	HUMANE	INSTRUCTION TO THEM TO ABSOLVE ME ON THE PLEA OF
DOCT PREFACE(44)	TO IT ON THE PART EVEN OF THOSE WHO ARE NATURALLY	HUMANE	. IF THEY PASS ON FROM THE ROUTINE OF LECTURE
DOCT PREFACE(35)	TO LEARN ANYTHING FROM ANY EXPERIMENT, CRUEL OR	HUMANE	. THE CHINAMAN WHO BURNT DOWN HIS HOUSE TO ROAST HIS
FABL PREFACE(77)	HUMANELY TO HIS BEING BURNED. CHARLES II,	HUMANE	(INDEED, AS SOME THINK, TOO HUMANE IN HIS KINDNESS
BULL PREFACE(55)	IN CHARGE OF THE PROCEEDINGS IS " A SINGULARLY	HUMANE	MAN, AND IS VERY POPULAR AMONGST THE NATIVES OF EGYPT
DOCT PREFACE(43)	MADE BY CUTTING UP FROGS WITH SCISSORS. THE MOST	HUMANE	MAN, HOWEVER REPUGNANT THE OPERATION MAY BE TO HIM AT
PHIL II (121)	EQUALLY SCIENTIFIC, WHY NOT DEVOTE YOURSELF, AS A	HUMANE	MAN, TO PROVING THE AMIABLE THEORY RATHER THAN THE
METH PREFACE(R56)	MYSELF WHAT SPELL HAS FALLEN ON INTELLIGENT AND	HUMANE	MEN THAT THEY ALLOW THEMSELVES TO BE IMPOSED ON BY
SUPR HANDBOK(206)	WAS NEITHER THE MOST EFFECTIVE NOR THE LEAST	HUMANE	METHOD OF LABOR EXPLOITATION; AND THE WORLD IS NOW
DOCT PREFACE(37)	ALL REALLY WISH TO BE SPARED THAT KNOWLEDGE? ARE	HUMANE	METHODS REALLY TO BE PREFERRED TO CRUEL ONES? EVEN
DOCT PREFACE(36)	THE VIVISECTOR FROM DEVISING OR PUSHING THROUGH	HUMANE	METHODS, PREVENTS HIM FROM BRINGING ORDER OUT OF THE
BULL PREFACE(49)	THE PATENT FACT THAT THE MILITARY MIND AND THE	HUMANE	MIND CAN EXIST IN THE SAME PERSON; SO THAT AN OFFICER

DOCT PREFACE(40)	OF VIVISECTION DECLARE THEMSELVES THE MOST	HUMANE	OF MEN, INFLICTING SUFFERING ONLY TO RELIEVE IT,
DOCT PREFACE(37)	" YOU MEAN THAT YOU ARE NOT CLEVER OR	HUMANE	OR ENERGETIC ENOUGH TO FIND ONE." CRUELTY FOR ITS OWN
DOCT PREFACE(37)	CRUELTY ITSELF, WHICH IS PRECISELY THE KNOWLEDGE	HUMANE	PEOPLE WISH TO BE SPARED. BUT THE QUESTION REMAINS:
DOCT PREFACE(48)	LIKE MYSELF OF TELLING LIES. MOST SENSIBLE AND	HUMANE	PEOPLE WOULD, I HOPE, REPLY FLATLY THAT HONORABLE MEN
UNPL PREFACE(R7)	NOR THE COUNTRY THAT HAD RUINED IT. AS A	HUMANE	PERSON I DETESTED VIOLENCE AND SLAUGHTER, WHETHER IN
DOCT PREFACE(51)	AND GIVE VIVISECTIONISTS HEAVY DAMAGES AGAINST	HUMANE	PERSONS WHO ACCUSE THEM OF CRUELTY; THE EDITORS AND
MILL PREFACE(127)	AND AGENTS OF A POLITICAL CONSTITUTION APPLYING	HUMANE	PRINCIPLES WHICH NEITHER OF THEM MAY VIOLATE. IN THAT
NEVR I SD(208)	HER VOICE AND WAYS ARE ENTIRELY KINDLY AND	HUMANE	; AND SHE LENDS HERSELF CONSCIENTIOUSLY TO THE
ROCK PREFACE(164)	EXTERMINATION, MY PRESENT SUBJECT, WILL BECOME A	HUMANE	SCIENCE INSTEAD OF THE MISERABLE MIXTURE OF PIRACY,
SIM II (77)	OF A LIFE BUOY, THE PROPERTY OF THE ROYAL	HUMANE	SOCIETY. THERE CAN BE NO DOUBT THAT THE DISPARAGING
GETT PREFACE(222)	THEY MAY BE SUPERIOR INDIVIDUALS. THE CUBS OF A	HUMANE	TIGRESS WOULD STARVE; AND THE DAUGHTERS OF WOMEN WHO
DOCT IV (169)	ABSURDLY EXPRESSED AS IT IS, IS TOO SINCERE AND	HUMANE	TO BE RIDICULED) YES, B.B. DEATH MAKES PEOPLE GO ON
BARB PREFACE(244)	AND MADE TO UNDERSTAND THAT A STATE WHICH IS TOO	HUMANE	TO PUNISH WILL ALSO BE TOO THRIFTY TO WASTE THE LIFE
HART III (142)	PEOPLE, MOST ADVANCED, UNPREJUDICED, FRANK,	HUMANE	, UNCONVENTIONAL, DEMOCRATIC, FREE-THINKING, AND
		HUMANELY	
ROCK PREFACE(147)	SCIENTIFIC BASIS IF IT IS EVER TO BE CARRIED OUT	HUMANELY	AND APOLOGETICALLY AS WELL AS THOROUGHLY. KILLING
DOCT IV SD(156)	FROM THE INNER ROOM AND HASTENS BETWEEN THEM,	HUMANELY	CONCERNED, BUT PROFESSIONALLY ELATE AND
SUPR III (107)	BY WHICH EVEN THOSE WHO ARE CLEVER ENOUGH TO BE	HUMANELY	DISPOSED ARE PERSUADED TO BECOME THE MOST
ROCK PREFACE(159)	FORCED TO THE CONCLUSION THAT IF JESUS HAD BEEN	HUMANELY	EXTERMINATED HIS MEMORY WOULD HAVE LOST NINETYNINE
WIDO II (42)	TRENCH UNCONVINCED, BUT TALKED DOWN; COKANE	HUMANELY	PERPLEXED. SARTORIUS BENDS HIS BROWS; COMES FORWARD
PRES (135)	GO ON WORSE THAN EVER. SHOOT A FEW, PROMPTLY AND	HUMANELY	; AND THERE WILL BE AN END AT ONCE OF ALL
FABL PREFACE(77)	THAT SERVETUS MUST BE KILLED; BUT HE OBJECTED	HUMANELY	TO HIS BEING BURNED. CHARLES II, HUMANE (INDEED,
		HUMANITARIAN	
ROCK PREFACE(170)	FLESH EATER, THE MISSIONARY AND THE CANNIBAL, THE	HUMANITARIAN	AND THE SPORTSMAN-HUNTER, THE MILITARY
WIDO III (60)	A PUBLIC MAN. WE LIVE IN A PROGRESSIVE AGE; AND	HUMANITARIAN	IDEAS ARE ADVANCING AND MUST BE TAKEN INTO
METH PREFACE(R58)	OF DARWIN MAKES THE WHOLE WORLD KIN. ANOTHER	HUMANITARIAN	INTEREST IN DARWINISM WAS THAT DARWIN
ROCK PREFACE(156)	A STRENUOUS OUTCRY AGAINST IT, RAISED BY THE OLD	HUMANITARIAN	LEAGUE, AND VOICED IN PARLIAMENT BY THE IRISH
LION EPILOG (148)	AND CONSEQUENTLY IN A COMMON DOOM. ANDROCLES IS A	HUMANITARIAN	NATURALIST, WHOSE VIEWS SURPRISE EVERYBODY.
NEVR I SD(208)	SECRETLY EMBARRASS HER: PASSION IN HER IS	HUMANITARIAN	RATHER THAN HUMAN: SHE FEELS STRONGLY ABOUT
ROCK PREFACE(155)	AND SCIENTIFICALLY THAN AT PRESENT, BECAUSE THE	HUMANITARIAN	REVOLT AGAINST IT WOULD PROBABLY BECOME A
ROCK PREFACE(153)	AND AGAINST THE FACTS THERE IS A CHRONIC	HUMANITARIAN	REVOLT EXPRESSING ITSELF EITHER UNDERGROUND OR
SIM PREFACE(6)	SUNS AND THE LIKE. I AM NOT THINKING OF THE	HUMANITARIAN	REVOLT AGAINST EVERLASTING BRIMSTONE VOICED BY
PHIL II (114)	TO TALK, PARAMORE. BUT WHAT AM I TO SAY TO THE	HUMANITARIAN	SOCIETIES AND THE VEGETARIAN SOCIETIES THAT
ROCK PREFACE(155)	REVOLT AGAINST IT WOULD PROBABLY BECOME A	HUMANITARIAN	SUPPORT OF IT; AND THERE WOULD BE AN END OF THE
METH PREFACE(R58)	THE GENERAL CONCEPTION OF EVOLUTION PROVIDES THE	HUMANITARIAN	WITH A SCIENTIFIC BASIS, BECAUSE IT ESTABLISHES
		HUMANITARIANISM	
SUPR HANDBOK(177)	TO ATHEISM, FROM ATHEISM TO PANTHEISTIC	HUMANITARIANISM	, FROM GENERAL ILLITERACY TO GENERAL
		HUMANITARIANS	
METH PREFACE(R56)	ONLY FOOLS AND RASCALS COULD BEAR TO LIVE." THE	HUMANITARIANS	AND THE PROBLEM OF EVIL. YET THE HUMANITARIANS
METH PREFACE(R57)	IS STRUCK BY LIGHTNING. THAT DID NOT OCCUR TO THE	HUMANITARIANS	AT THE MOMENT: PEOPLE DO NOT REFLECT DEEPLY
METH PREFACE(R57)	AS WELL AS AN ENLARGED KNOWLEDGE OF FACTS TO THE	HUMANITARIANS	. HE DESTROYED THE OMNIPOTENCE OF GOD FOR
METH PREFACE(R56)	HUMANITARIANS AND THE PROBLEM OF EVIL. YET THE	HUMANITARIANS	WERE AS DELIGHTED AS ANYBODY WITH DARWINISM AT
METH PREFACE(R59)	ELEPHANT. WHY DARWIN PLEASED THE SOCIALISTS. THE	HUMANITARIANS	WERE NOT ALONE AMONG THE AGITATORS IN THEIR
SUPR HANDBOK(205)	IN OUR NEWSPAPERS AND IN OUR PULPITS. THE VERY	HUMANITARIANS	WHO ABHOR THEM ARE STIRRED TO MURDER BY THEM:
METH PREFACE(R59)	THE MILITARISTS WERE AS ENTHUSIASTIC AS THE	HUMANITARIANS	, THE SOCIALISTS AS THE CAPITALISTS. THE
DOCT PREFACE(38)	MUST HAVE SMILED SARDONICALLY AT SUCH INHUMAN	HUMANITARIANS	, WHOSE DAILY HABITS AND FASHIONABLE
NEVR II (247)	THAT? I'M A MAN, WITH THE FEELINGS OF OUR COMMON	HUMANITY	: HAVE I NO RIGHTS, NO CLAIMS? IN ALL THESE YEARS
METH PREFACE(R88)	OF ALL THE RELIGIONS THAT HAVE EVER TAKEN HOLD OF	HUMANITY	: NAMELY, THAT IT MUST BE, FIRST AND FUNDAMENTALLY,
2TRU II (80)	DEALING WITH MEN AND WOMEN MAKES ME FEEL MAD.	HUMANITY	ALWAYS FAILS ME: NATURE NEVER.
PHIL II (121)	THE SNARES OF IDEALISM; BUT I HAVE SOME COMMON	HUMANITY	AND COMMON SENSE. (HE REPLACES HIM IN THE EASY
LION PREFACE(4)	ECONOMICS. I SAY DISTINCTIVE, BECAUSE HIS COMMON	HUMANITY	AND HIS SUBJECTION TO TIME AND SPACE (THAT IS, TO
BARB PREFACE(226)	THAT IF THEY CONTENTED THEMSELVES WITH APPEALS TO	HUMANITY	AND PATRIOTISM, THE ARISTOCRACY, THOUGH IT WOULD
MRS PREFACE(175)	OF DECENT PEOPLE. THIS HIDEOUS REPUDIATION OF	HUMANITY	AND SOCIAL CONSCIENCE SO TOOK POSSESSION OF THE NEW
CLEO NOTES (207)	DIFFERENCE IN THE PLAY. I CAN ONLY IMITATE	HUMANITY	AS I KNOW IT. NOBODY KNOWS WHETHER SHAKESPEAR
JOAN EPIL,SD(160)	UP HER ARMS, AND TAKES REFUGE FROM DESPAIR OF	HUMANITY	BEFORE THE PICTURE OF THE VIRGIN. /THE SOLDIER/ (
3PLA PREFACE(R16)	A PASHA, INVITED ME TO FORGET THE COMMON BOND OF	HUMANITY	BETWEEN ME AND HIS COMPANY BY DEMANDING NOTHING
LION PREFACE(50)	BEATEN BY ANY FAILURE, AND WILL EVEN SUPERSEDE	HUMANITY	BY EVOLVING A HIGHER SPECIES IF WE CANNOT MASTER
BULL III (135)	REFORMS WHICH HAVE ALREADY BEEN CONFERRED ON	HUMANITY	BY THE LIBERAL PARTY, AND TRUSTING FOR FUTURE
MIS. PREFACE(91)	AS HOGS, SO LITTLE HAVE THEY CULTIVATED THEIR	HUMANITY	BY THE ONLY EFFECTIVE INSTRUMENT OF CULTURE: ART.
BULL IV (181)	IS A GODHEAD IN WHICH ALL LIFE IS HUMAN AND ALL	HUMANITY	DIVINE: THREE IN ONE AND ONE IN THREE. IT IS, IN
MIS. PREFACE(7)	THE JUST MAN MADE PERFECT: THAT IS, TO MAKE	HUMANITY	DIVINE. AND YOU WILL VITIATE THE EXPERIMENT IF YOU
GENV IV (124)	YOU. GOODBYE. CAN ANYONE EXPLAIN THIS? WHY IS	HUMANITY	DOOMED? /SECRETARY/ IT IS INTELLIGIBLE ENOUGH, AND
LION PREFACE(68)	DESCENDED FROM HIS THRONE IN HEAVEN TO TAKE ON	HUMANITY	FOR A TIME MIGHT REASONABLY DECLARE THAT THE
NEVR I SD(218)	OF GRAIN, AND TREATS HIM WITH A DISRESPECTFUL	HUMANITY	FOR WHICH HE IS SECRETLY GRATEFUL. /VALENTINE/ MAY
MTH4 II (181)	THE COMMON MAN, AND YOU CUT DOWN THE STATURE OF	HUMANITY	FROM THAT OF A GIANT TO THAT OF A NOBODY. I MATTER
BARB PREFACE(238)	BOMB WITHOUT STRIPPING THE MASK OF JUSTICE AND	HUMANITY	FROM THEMSELVES ALSO. BE IT NOTED THAT AT THIS VERY
BULL PREFACE(47)	AND ARE READY TO TAKE PART IN THEM AS IF THEIR	HUMANITY	HAD BEEN BLOWN OUT LIKE A CANDLE. YOU FIND THAT
NEVR III (265)	MR VALENTINE, THAT A LIFE DEVOTED TO THE CAUSE OF	HUMANITY	HAS ENTHUSIASMS AND PASSIONS TO OFFER WHICH FAR
MTH4 II (191)	IS THE MOST UNBEARABLE BURDEN OUR POOR TORTURED	HUMANITY	HAS EVER GROANED UNDER. /THE ENVOY/ HULLO, POPPA!
BARB PREFACE(245)	LIFE DEPENDS ON HIS USEFULNESS. HITHERTO, ALAS!	HUMANITY	HAS NEVER DARED FACE THESE HARD FACTS. WE
CLEO NOTES (207)	THE CONCLUSION, INVOLVED IN HIS FORMER ONE, THAT	HUMANITY	HAS PROGRESSED FROM WASHINGTON TO THE FIN DE SIECLE
SUPR PREFACE(R33)	BUT ALL SHAKESPEAR'S PROJECTIONS OF THE DEEPEST	HUMANITY	HE KNEW HAVE THE SAME DEFECT: THEIR CHARACTERS AND
BULL PREFACE(47)	UNDER FIRE IS A QUITE DIFFERENT THING FROM	HUMANITY	IN BARRACKS: WHEN THERE IS DANGER THE DIFFICULTY IS
MRS PREFACE(168)	TO BE ABLE TO ATTEND TO THE FAMILIAR FACTOR OF	HUMANITY	IN IT AS WELL AS TO THE UNFAMILIAR ONE OF A REAL
3PLA PREFACE(R21)	HIM IN BOOKS, A PERSISTENT MISREPRESENTATION OF	HUMANITY	IN LITERATURE GETS FINALLY ACCEPTED AND ACTED UPON.
LIED PREFACE(185)	BY FILLING IT IN WITH AN OBSERVED TOUCH OF ACTUAL	HUMANITY	INSTEAD OF WITH DOCTRINAIRE ROMANTICISM. NOTHING IN
DOCT PREFACE(48)	IN TORMENT I AM NOT LIKELY TO CONSIDER THAT HIS	HUMANITY	IS AMPLY VINDICATED BY ITS GENTLENESS. A COBRA'S
GENV IV (123)	AT GREENWICH FROM THREE AMERICAN OBSERVATORIES.	HUMANITY	IS DOOMED." THANK YOU. GOODBYE. CAN ANYONE EXPLAIN
BULL III (136)	AND IT CANNOT BE FAR DISTANT, GENTLEMEN, BECAUSE	HUMANITY	IS LOOKING FORWARD TO IT TOO, AND INSISTING ON IT
DOCT PREFACE(30)	TO OUR DOCTORS OF A REPUTATION FOR THE TENDEREST	HUMANITY	IS SO OBVIOUS, AND THE QUANTITY OF BENEVOLENT WORK
NEVR III (266)	/VALENTINE/ WELL, WHY NOT, IF THE CAUSE OF	HUMANITY	IS THE ONLY THING WORTH BEING SERIOUS ABOUT?
SUPR PREFACE(R32)	AND SHAKESPEAR'S PESSIMISM IS ONLY HIS WOUNDED	HUMANITY	. BOTH HAVE THE SPECIFIC GENIUS OF THE FICTIONIST
DOCT PREFACE(3)	LEG, IS ENOUGH TO MAKE ONE DESPAIR OF POLITICAL	HUMANITY	. BUT THAT IS PRECISELY WHAT WE HAVE DONE, AND THE
MTH4 II (179)	OTHER MEN, BECAUSE NINE-TENTHS OF ME IS COMMON	HUMANITY	. BUT THE OTHER TENTH IS A FACULTY FOR SEEING
DOCT PREFACE(30)	BEEN EXPRESSED BY THE MOST POPULAR SPOKESMEN OF	HUMANITY	. IF THE MEDICAL PROFESSION WERE TO OUTDO THE
CLEO NOTES (212)	TORMENTS AND PUBLIC EXECUTIONS FOR THE PASSION OF	HUMANITY	, ISLAM, SUBSTITUTING VOLUPTUOUSNESS FOR TORMENT (
NEVR I SD(209)	FROM THE ORDINARY RUN OF FASHIONABLE SEASIDE	HUMANITY	. MRS CLANDON COMES A LITTLE WAY INTO THE ROOM
DEST (183)	CAREER IS AT STAKE-- THE DESTINY OF EUROPE-- OF	HUMANITY	. /LIEUTENANT/ OH, BOTHER THE DESTINY OF HUMANITY!
NEVR III (277)	MAKE SOME ALLOWANCE FOR HIS FEELINGS? IN COMMON	HUMANITY	. /MRS CLANDON/ I NEVER DISCOVERED HIS FEELINGS. I
NEVR III (277)	AND HIS-- (SHE SHIVERS) THE REST OF HIS COMMON	HUMANITY	. /M'COMAS/ (WISTFULLY) WOMEN CAN BE VERY HARD,
BUOY II (24)	ON THE HIGHEST MENTAL PLANE ATTAINABLE BY	HUMANITY	. /THE NATIVE/ HOW DID YOU OBTAIN THAT DEGREE, SIR,
BARB II SD(273)	A COMMONPLACE OLD BUNDLE OF POVERTY AND HARD-WORN	HUMANITY	. SHE LOOKS SIXTY AND PROBABLY IS FORTY-FIVE. IF
ROCK PREFACE(170)	TO THE DEATH IN THE CREATION OF ARTIFICIAL	HUMANITY	. THERE IS NOTHING THAT CAN BE CHANGED MORE
LION PREFACE(68)	MIGHT REASONABLY DECLARE THAT THE ASSUMPTION OF	HUMANITY	MUST HAVE BEEN INCOMPLETE AT ITS MOST VITAL POINT
UNPL PREFACE(R25)	NO DOUBT ALL PLAYS WHICH DEAL SINCERELY WITH	HUMANITY	MUST WOUND THE MONSTROUS CONCEIT WHICH IT IS THE
LION PREFACE(4)	REVENGE OR PUNISHMENT, AND A FULL ASSUMPTION BY	HUMANITY	OF DIVINE RESPONSIBILITIES, HE WOULD HAVE CONFERRED
GETT PREFACE(195)	INTO LITTLE BRICK BOXES OF LITTLE PARCELS OF	HUMANITY	OF ILL-ASSORTED AGES, WITH THE OLD SCOLDING OR
DOCT PREFACE(30)	WHICH WOULD FOLLOW SUCH A REASSURANCE OF THE	HUMANITY	OF THE DOCTOR. NOT ONE DOCTOR IN A THOUSAND IS A
DOCT PREFACE(39)	AIRS WITH WHICH WE ARE SOMETIMES REFERRED TO THE	HUMANITY	OF THE MEDICAL PROFESSION AS A GUARANTEE THAT
BULL PREFACE(46)	IF IT WERE HUMANLY POSSIBLE TO MILITARIZE ALL THE	HUMANITY	OUT OF A MAN, THERE WOULD BE ABSOLUTELY NO DEFENCE

PYGM EPILOG (302)	AND THROW THEM BOTH BACK ON THEIR COMMON	HUMANITY	-- AND MAY THEY BE SPARED ANY SUCH TRIAL! -- WILL
GETT (284)	IN THE END YOU HAVE TO BE CONTENT WITH HIS COMMON	HUMANITY	; AND WHEN YOU COME DOWN TO THAT, YOU FIND OUT
PYGM V (284)	CARE A BIT FOR ME. /HIGGINS/ I CARE FOR LIFE, FOR	HUMANITY	; AND YOU ARE A PART OF IT THAT HAS COME MY WAY AND
GETT SD(295)	PLACID BALANCE HAVE DONE SOMETHING TO SAVE HER	HUMANITY	; BUT HER IMPETUOUS TEMPER AND ENERGETIC WILL,
SUPR I SD(16)	STILL MAKE MEN DREAM. VITALITY IS AS COMMON AS	HUMANITY	; BUT, LIKE HUMANITY, IT SOMETIMES RISES TO GENIUS;
ARMS II SD(28)	HIS IDEALS; BY HIS CONSEQUENT CYNICAL SCORN FOR	HUMANITY	; BY HIS JEJUNE CREDULITY AS TO THE ABSOLUTE
MIS. PREFACE(52)	IN THE WORLD FOR THAT INTUITION OF THE HIGHEST	HUMANITY	THAT WE, BEING MEMBERS ONE OF ANOTHER, MUST NOT
SUPR I (25)	THAT SORT. /TANNER/ ANN: WILL YOU HAVE THE COMMON	HUMANITY	TO TELL US WHAT THE MATTER IS? /ANN/ (HALF
BULL PREFACE(62)	MAKE THEMSELVES ABHORRED BY THE ASPIRING WILL OF	HUMANITY	TOWARDS DIVINITY. AS FOR THE EGYPTIANS, ANY MAN
BULL PREFACE(47)	EITHER KEEPS ITSELF OR GOES TO PIECES; FOR	HUMANITY	UNDER FIRE IS A QUITE DIFFERENT THING FROM HUMANITY
SUPR HANDBOK(180)	OF GIVING FANCY THE WIDEST POSSIBLE FIELD. TO CUT	HUMANITY	UP INTO SMALL CLIQUES, AND EFFECTIVELY LIMIT THE
BULL PREFACE(55)	CARRYING OUT THE EXECUTIONS," THAT " ALL POSSIBLE	HUMANITY	WAS SHEWN IN CARRYING THEM OUT," AND THAT " THE
BULL PREFACE(63)	ENOUGH-- THOUGH THE SECRET SHAME OF REVOLTED	HUMANITY	WILL MAKE CABINET MINISTERS SNATCH AT FANTASTIC
BULL PREFACE(8)	NO MATTER HOW BRAVELY HE FIGHTS, HISTORY AND	HUMANITY	WILL NEVER FORGIVE HIM: ENGLISH HISTORY AND
BULL PREFACE(63)	MINISTERS SNATCH AT FANTASTIC EXCUSES-- BUT WHAT	HUMANITY	WILL NOT FORGIVE OUR FOREIGN SECRETARY FOR IS HIS
MIS. PREFACE(79)	NOISE. BUT THE HEAD MASTER HAD NEVER ADMITTED ANY	HUMANITY	WITH US. WE HAD BEEN CAREFULLY BROKEN IN TO REGARD
BARB PREFACE(244)	THEY ARE NOT, ARE SYMPATHETIC ENOUGH TO CARE FOR	HUMANITY	, ABHORRING MURDER, AND NEVER COMMITTING IT UNTIL
ROCK II (264)	GALLERY OF MASTERPIECES THAT YOU CALL WESTERN	HUMANITY	, AND TELL ME, IF YOU DARE, THAT YOU ARE THE
SUPR HANDBOK(204)	LAW FORBADE MORE THAN FORTY LASHES IN THE NAME OF	HUMANITY	, AND THAT FLOGGINGS OF A THOUSAND LASHES WERE
BARB PREFACE(244)	WILL NOT RISK THEIR SKINS FOR THE GOOD OF	HUMANITY	, AND, WHEN THEY ARE NOT, ARE SYMPATHETIC ENOUGH TO
JITT III (79)	THAT EVER WAS WRITTEN-- BELONG NOT ONLY TO	HUMANITY	, BUT TO HER. AND I LOVE HER AS IF SHE WERE MY OWN
GETT PREFACE(256)	BY A SOLICITOR FOR ITS OWN SAKE AND THAT OF	HUMANITY	, COSTS AT LEAST 30 POUNDS OUT-OF-POCKET EXPENSES.
APPL I (235)	THE EXPEDIENT; FOR INTELLECTUAL INTEGRITY, FOR	HUMANITY	, FOR THE RESCUE OF INDUSTRY FROM COMMERCIALISM AND
BARB PREFACE(236)	RATHER THAN FROM PUBLIC SPIRIT, REASONABLENESS,	HUMANITY	, GENEROSITY, TENDERNESS, DELICACY, PITY AND
SUPR I SD(16)	VITALITY IS AS COMMON AS HUMANITY; BUT, LIKE	HUMANITY	, IT SOMETIMES RISES TO GENIUS; AND ANN IS ONE OF
BULL PREFACE(48)	THE LITERAL SENSE OF THE WORD; AND SO, WHAT WITH	HUMANITY	, LAZINESS, AND DOCILITY COMBINED, THEY MANAGE TO
BARB III (334)	THOUGHT, THE LOFTIEST POETRY YET ATTAINED BY	HUMANITY	, NO CAPITAL? MY CHARACTER! MY INTELLECT! MY
MIS. PREFACE(79)	TO OUR BETTER FEELINGS: THAT IS, TO OUR COMMON	HUMANITY	, NOT TO MAKE A NOISE. BUT THE HEAD MASTER HAD
DEST (180)	CAMPAIGN, THE DESTINY OF FRANCE, OF EUROPE, OF	HUMANITY	, PERHAPS, MAY DEPEND ON THE INFORMATION THOSE
UNPL PREFACE(R10)	CALLED ME MISTER, AND, WITH ITS FRANK, CHARMING	HUMANITY	, RESPECTED ME AS ONE WHO HAD DONE GOOD WORK IN MY
MIS. PREFACE(46)	DEATH, IT WOULD RID US AT ONCE OF THAT SCOURGE OF	HUMANITY	, THE AMATEUR POPE. AS AN IRISH PROTESTANT, I RAISE
MIS. PREFACE(81)	THIS SENSE THE CHILD CANNOT REALIZE ITS PARENT'S	HUMANITY	, THE PARENT CAN REALIZE THE CHILD'S; FOR THE
BULL PREFACE(8)	WILL NEVER FORGIVE HIM: ENGLISH HISTORY AND	HUMANITY	, TO THEIR CREDIT BE IT SAID, LEAST OF ALL. PLEASE
DEVL EPILOG (82)	DELICACY OF SENTIMENT, HIS FINE SPIRIT AND	HUMANITY	, WERE JUST THE QUALITIES TO MAKE HIM DISLIKED BY
CAPT I SD(225)	FLOWERED STRAW HAT. A WOMAN OF GREAT VITALITY AND	HUMANITY	, WHO BEGINS A CASUAL ACQUAINTANCE AT THE POINT
DEST (183)	HUMANITY. /LIEUTENANT/ OH, BOTHER THE DESTINY OF	HUMANITY	! (MAKING FOR HER) ONLY A KISS. /LADY/ (
		HUMANITY'S	
BARB PREFACE(215)	RAVISHER OR MURDERER, TO THE UTMOST LIMITS OF	HUMANITY'S	COMPARATIVELY NEGLIGIBLE IMPULSES IN THESE
		HUMANIZATION	
BULL PREFACE(62)	SUPPRESSION OF THE EMPIRE, AND, INCIDENTALLY, THE	HUMANIZATION	OF ITS SUPPORTERS BY THE STERNEST LESSONS OF
		HUMANIZE	
PLES PREFACE(R11)	WAS MORE THAN WILLING TO SHEW THAT THE DRAMA CAN	HUMANIZE	THESE THINGS AS EASILY AS THEY, IN THE WRONG HANDS,
		HUMANIZES	
UNPL PREFACE(R18)	HERSELF FOR AN INDEPENDENT WORKING LIFE,	HUMANIZES	HER WHOLE FAMILY IN AN ASTONISHINGLY SHORT TIME;
		HUMANLY	
NEVR II (255)	(INTERESTED) AH, NOW YOU ARE BEGINNING TO TALK	HUMANLY	AND SENSIBLY, MR VALENTINE. /VALENTINE/ (WITH A
MTH4 I (157)	YOUR IGNORANCE, YOUR BLINDNESS, YOUR IMBECILITY.	HUMANLY	I PITY YOU. INTELLECTUALLY I DESPISE YOU. /ZOO/
METH PREFACE(R89)	I AM NOT, I HOPE, UNDER MORE ILLUSION THAN IS	HUMANLY	INEVITABLE AS TO THE CRUDITY OF THIS MY BEGINNING OF
BULL PREFACE(46)	AND PROFESSIONALLY INCAPABLE, IF IT WERE	HUMANLY	POSSIBLE TO MILITARIZE ALL THE HUMANITY OUT OF A
INCA (257)	/THE INCA/ (RETURNING TO HER AND SPEAKING VERY	HUMANLY	) YOU ARE MAKING FUN OF ME. WHY DOES EVERYBODY MAKE
		HUMANS	
2TRU I (33)	/THE MONSTER/ NO: SHE GAVE THEM TO ME. THESE	HUMANS	ARE FULL OF HORRID DISEASES: THEY INFECT US POOR
ROCK PREFACE(148)	BRUTES. THIS WAS FOUNDED ON A GENERAL BELIEF THAT	HUMANS	HAVE IMMORTAL SOULS AND BRUTES NONE. NOWADAYS MORE
SIM PREFACE(4)	OF THE BIBLE WOULD HAVE REFUSED TO BELIEVE. THE	HUMANS	WHO HAVE LOST THEIR SIMPLE FAITH IN A FLAT EARTH AND
		HUMBLE	
BULL PREFACE(29)	AND KIND TO THEM, WITH SUBSTANTIAL RETURNS IN	HUMBLE	AFFECTION; SOLDIERS AND SAILORS OFTEN ADMIRE AND
GLIM (184)	SIGNOR. SANDRO IS VERY CLEVER; AND HE IS SO	HUMBLE	AND CHEERFUL AND GOOD-TEMPERED THAT PEOPLE DO NOT
HART PREFACE(39)	IS ALREADY PROVING IMPRACTICABLE; BUT BEFORE THE	HUMBLE	AND CONTRITE HEART CEASES TO BE DESPISED, THE
GLIM (174)	GIRL/ I KNOW THAT, FATHER; AND BELIEVE ME, I'M	HUMBLE	AND GOOD. I SWEAR TO YOU BY OUR LADY THAT IT IS NOT
METH PREFACE(R74)	AND ABOVE AND BELOW ALL HAVE BEEN MILLIONS OF	HUMBLE	AND OBSCURE PERSONS, SOMETIMES TOTALLY ILLITERATE,
JOAN EPILOG (158)	LIFE AGAINST DEATH, WITH THE HEART HIGH AND	HUMBLE	AND VOID OF MALICE, AND NOTHING COUNTING UNDER GOD
2TRU III (101)	/THE FATHER/ AND MEANWHILE MR MEEK-- THIS	HUMBLE	AND WORTHY SOLDIER-- IS TO REMAIN IN OBSCURITY AND
DOCT I (100)	BLENKINSOP? /BLENKINSOP/ IVE COME TO OFFER MY	HUMBLE	CONGRATULATIONS. OH DEAR! ALL THE GREAT GUNS ARE
KING I (166)	NOBLE FRIEND DO ME THE HONOR TO BE SEATED IN MY	HUMBLE	DWELLING? CHARLES BOWS AND TAKES THE ARMCHAIR WITH
GENV IV (93)	/BATTLER/ WHO ARE YOU? /SIR O./ ONLY A	HUMBLE	ENGLISHMAN, LISTENING MOST RESPECTFULLY TO YOUR
DOCT IV (157)	AS MANY PEOPLE AS I HAVE IN MY TIME YOULL FEEL	HUMBLE	ENOUGH ABOUT IT. COME AND LOOK AT HIM, COLLY. RIDGEON
ROCK I SD(210)	JOB (SAY A WATCHMAN) TO A CITY MISSIONARY OF	HUMBLE	EXTRACTION. HE IS AGGRESSIVELY MODEST, OR PRETENDS TO
MILL PREFACE(109)	HOW DOES AN OBSCURE VILLAGE PRIEST, THE SON OF	HUMBLE	FISHERFOLK, COME TO WEAR THE TRIPLE CROWN AND SIT IN
ROCK II (246)	ARE WITH YOU TO THE LAST MAN FOR IT. ACCEPT THE	HUMBLE	GRATITUDE OF A PAUPERIZED DUKE. /SIR DEXTER/ AND THE
MRS PREFACE(160)	HAS WOUNDED HIS NATIONAL VANITY. HE RESOLVES TO	HUMBLE	HER BY COMMITTING A RAPE UPON HER. HE ANNOUNCES HIS
PLES PREFACE(R13)	WANT NOR UNDERSTAND; FOR THE PUBLIC IS TOUCHINGLY	HUMBLE	IN SUCH MATTERS. FOR ALL THAT, THE COMMERCIAL LIMITS
PYGM V (271)	AND RESPECT MERIT IN EVERY CLASS OF LIFE, HOWEVER	HUMBLE	. THEM WORDS IS IN HIS BLOOMING WILL, IN WHICH, HENRY
CAND I (100)	YOU MAY BE A MASTER BUILDER WHERE I AM ONLY A	HUMBLE	JOURNEYMAN; FOR DONT THINK, MY BOY, THAT I CANNOT SEE
METH PREFACE(R78)	THEIR POWERS BUT FOR THEIR WEAKNESSES; THAT THE	HUMBLE	MIGHT BE EXALTED, AND THE PROUD REBUKED. PEOPLE WILL
POSN (443)	WE DO? WENT ON THE SPREE, NATURALLY. BUT I WAS	HUMBLE	MINDED. I DID AS THE REST DID. I GAVE MY MONEY IN AT
GETT SD(259)	ROOM. THIS IS NOT AT ALL BECAUSE HE IS A MAN OF	HUMBLE	MIND; BUT BECAUSE THE KITCHEN IS ONE OF THE FINEST
AUGS (273)	A GOVERNOR-GENERALSHIP IN THE TROPICS, OR MY	HUMBLE	MISSION HERE TO MAKE LITTLE PIFFLINGTON DO ITS BIT, I
LADY PREFACE(217)	HE WAS NOT A PARVENU TRYING TO COVER HIS	HUMBLE	ORIGIN WITH A PURCHASED COAT OF ARMS: HE WAS A
CLEO NOTES (207)	AS MORALISTS URGE US TO DO IN OUR CHILDHOOD), AND	HUMBLE	OURSELVES BEFORE THE ARROGANCE OF THE BIRDS OF
INCA (250)	HIMSELF. /ERMYNTRUDE/ OH, CAPTAIN, HOW COULD A	HUMBLE	PERSON LIKE MYSELF BE OF ANY INTEREST TO A PRINCE WHO
2TRU PREFACE(6)	NO VERY EXTRAORDINARY SUPPLY OF MONEY TO ENABLE A	HUMBLE	PERSON TO SAY " I WANT FOR NOTHING"; AND WHEN THAT
PYGM EPILOG (300)	CLASSES AT THE LONDON SCHOOL OF ECONOMICS, AND A	HUMBLE	PERSONAL APPEAL TO THE DIRECTOR OF THAT INSTITUTION
ROCK I (213)	SNUB HIM. HE IS DISGRACING HIS CLASS. AS A	HUMBLE	REPRESENTATIVE OF THAT CLASS I APOLOGIZE FOR HIM TO
POSN (461)	TO BE ONE, AND ONLY ONE; AND THAT ONE IS YOUR	HUMBLE	SERVANT. I CALL THAT TO THE NOTICE OF THE FOREMAN OF
DEVL I (18)	LADIES AND GENTLEMEN: YOUR SERVANT, YOUR VERY	HUMBLE	SERVANT. (WITH THIS COMPREHENSIVE INSULT, HE THROWS
SUPR III (134)	IT GETS TIRED OF THE WORLD, THE FLESH, AND YOUR	HUMBLE	SERVANT. /THE STATUE/ SUPERMAN IS A GOOD CRY; AND A
MIS. PREFACE(66)	IS THE VOICE OF GOD; AND I AM ONLY YOUR VERY	HUMBLE	SERVANT" HE SAYS AT ONCE " ALL RIGHT: TELL ME WHAT TO
KING I (176)	OR WOULD YOUR GRACE PREFER TO BE THROWN DOWN MY	HUMBLE	STAIRCASE BY MR ROWLEY? IT HAS TWENTYFOUR STEPS, IN
CLEO V (198)	HOW TO MAKE MEN SERVE HIM. /PERSIAN/ AY: MEN TOO	HUMBLE	TO BECOME DANGEROUS RIVALS TO HIM. /BELZANOR/ O
MIS. (188)	OUT WITH HIM. /BENTLEY/ (IN SCARED, SOBERED,	HUMBLE	TONES AS HE IS BORNE OFF) WHAT ARE YOU DOING? LET ME
BASH III (123)	LIKE A DEMON WITH ONE WHO, WHATSOE'ER HIS	HUMBLE	VIRTUES, WAS CLEARLY NOT A GENTLEMAN, MY SON! /ALL/
BARB PREFACE(216)	HIM, NOT A CHOICE BETWEEN OPULENT VILLAINY AND	HUMBLE	VIRTUE, BUT BETWEEN ENERGETIC ENTERPRISE AND COWARDLY
		HUMBLED	
MTH1 II (22)	IT, HEARD IT, FELT IT, RISKED IT, WILL FEEL A	HUMBLED	FOOL IN THE PRESENCE OF THE MAN WHO HAS. /EVE/ AND
BUOY IV (60)	HIMSELF BACK INTO HIS CHAIR. /MRS SECONDBORN/ (	HUMBLED	) WELL, DICK, I WILL SAY THAT YOU ARE WONDERFUL WHEN
PYGM EPILOG (300)	OVER AGAIN, AT LAST GENTLY INSISTED; AND ELIZA,	HUMBLED	TO THE DUST BY HAVING TO BEG FROM HIM SO OFTEN, AND
		HUMBLENESS	
BASH II,1, (112)	NOW LET ME LIFT THE COVER FROM MY SOUL. O WASTED	HUMBLENESS	! DELUDED DIFFIDENCE! HOW OFTEN HAVE I SAID,

			HUMBLER	
PRES	(161)	TO OUR BARE EXISTENCE THAN THE CATHEDRAL. EVEN	HUMBLER	APARTMENTS MIGHT MAKE THE SAME CLAIM. BUT WHICH IS
			HUMBLEST	
3PLA PREFACE	(R37)	TO SAY BETTER THAN HOMER OR SHAKESPEAR? BUT THE	HUMBLEST	AUTHOR, AND MUCH MORE A RATHER ARROGANT ONE LIKE
MILL PREFACE	(109)	PARENT AND NO LAW AT ALL FOR THE CHILD. IN THE	HUMBLEST	CABIN THAT CONTAINS A FAMILY YOU MAY FIND A
GETT	(292)	OF HIS DUTY OR HIS RISK ON THE SHOULDERS OF THE	HUMBLEST	DRUMMER BOY, I'D SHOOT HIM WITH MY OWN HAND.
MIS. PREFACE	(65)	ROOM OF A LOCAL COUNCIL OR CITY CORPORATION, THE	HUMBLEST	EMPLOYEES OF THE COMMITTEE FIND DEFENDERS IF THEY
GENV II	(57)	THE HIGHEST COURT CAN BE SET IN MOTION BY THE	HUMBLEST	INDIVIDUAL JUSTICE IS A MOCKERY. /SIR O./ OF COURSE
SUPR PREFACE	(R21)	INSIGNIFICANCE! HE SLINKS OUT OF THE WAY OF THE	HUMBLEST	PETTICOAT, HAPPY IF HE BE POOR ENOUGH TO BE PUSHED
DOCT PREFACE	(21)	WITCHES WHO PRESCRIBE SPELLS AND SELL CHARMS, THE	HUMBLEST	PROFESSIONAL HEALERS IN THIS COUNTRY ARE THE
CAND I	(101)	FOR THE GREAT HARVEST THAT ALL-- EVEN THE	HUMBLEST	-- SHALL ONE DAY REAP. AND LAST, BUT TRUST ME, NOT
			HUMBLY	
LADY	(250)	HER DESIRE TO BE EVER IN THE FASHION, AND TO DO	HUMBLY	AND DUTIFULLY WHATSO SHE SEETH EVERYBODY ELSE DOING.
LADY PREFACE	(215)	THE RANK THAT LOOKS AT THE MIDDLE CLASS, NOT	HUMBLY	AND ENVIOUSLY FROM BELOW, BUT INSOLENTLY FROM ABOVE.
WIDO I	(19)	WAVES HIM OFF, AND BEGINS TO WRITE). /TRENCH/ (	HUMBLY	AND GRATEFULLY) YES, OLD CHAP. THANKS AWFULLY. (BY
PYGM V	(283)	FROM YOUR IDIOTIC NOTIONS! I CONFESS THAT	HUMBLY	AND GRATEFULLY. AND I HAVE GROWN ACCUSTOMED TO YOUR
JOAN PREFACE	(5)	OF A SUPERIOR WOUNDS THEIR VANITY, BUT QUITE	HUMBLY	AND HONESTLY BECAUSE IT FRIGHTENS THEM. FEAR WILL
DEVL I	(23)	GIVE AND BEQUEATH MY SOUL INTO MY MAKER'S HANDS,	HUMBLY	ASKING FORGIVENESS FOR ALL MY SINS AND MISTAKES, AND
2TRU III	(86)	IS ALL RIGHT. DO JUSTICE; LOVE MERCY; AND WALK	HUMBLY	BEFORE YOUR GOD. THAT APPEALS TO A MAN IF ONLY IT
LADY	(248)	A WOMAN FOR THE TASTE OF THE TOWN. WHEREFORE I	HUMBLY	BEG YOUR MAJESTY TO GIVE ORDER THAT A THEATRE BE
DEST	(169)	THE SERVANT OF THE FRENCH REPUBLIC, FOLLOWING	HUMBLY	IN THE FOOTSTEPS OF THE HEROES OF CLASSICAL
NEVR IV	(289)	PRAY ALLOW ME. SIT DOWN, EVERYBODY. (THEY OBEY	HUMBLY	. GLORIA TAKES THE SADDLE-BAG CHAIR ON THE HEARTH.
DEST	(175)	THE TABLE) YOU ARE IMPERTINENT, MADAM. /LADY/ (	HUMBLY	) I BEG YOUR PARDON. CAESAR'S WIFE IS ABOVE
PHIL III	(133)	HIM TO HIDE HER FACE). /PARAMORE/ (FOLLOWING HER	HUMBLY	) I DONT DESERVE THIS FROM YOU: INDEED I DO NOT.
PHIL III	(138)	AGAIN) HE IS A BETTER MAN THAN YOU. /CHARTERIS/ (	HUMBLY	) I GRANT YOU THAT, MY DEAR. /JULIA/ (IMPETUOUSLY)
CAND II	(106)	TO THE BOOKCASE). /MARCHBANKS/ (APPROACHING HER	HUMBLY	) I HOPE I HAVNT OFFENDED YOU. PERHAPS I SHOULDNT
BULL IV	(166)	IVE NO RIGHT TO BE PARTICULAR. /BROADBENT/ (	HUMBLY	) I KNOW I'M NOT GOOD ENOUGH FOR YOU, NORA. BUT NO
HART II	(94)	WITH CONFIDENCE? WITH RESPECT? /MAZZINI/ (	HUMBLY	) I THINK THAT WHAT IS THE MATTER WITH ME IS THAT I
APPL I	(204)	I AM A BIT OF AN ENIGMA. PERHAPS I AM. /MAGNUS/ (	HUMBLY	) I WISH I COULD SEE THROUGH YOU, MR BOANERGES. BUT I
CLEO II	(130)	LIVES SHOULD BE AT THE MERCY OF SUCH FOOLS! (	HUMBLY	) LUCIUS SEPTIMIUS, PARDON ME: WHY SHOULD THE SLAYER
LIED	(190)	HERSELF ABRUPTLY AWAY) DONT BE SELFISH. /HE/ (	HUMBLY	) YES: I DESERVE THAT. I THINK IF I WERE GOING TO THE
JOAN 1	(57)	(RISING) NOW LISTEN TO ME, YOU. /STEWARD/ (	HUMBLY	) YES, SIR. /ROBERT/ WHAT AM I? /STEWARD/ WHAT ARE
HART II	(89)	MEN MADE FOOLS OF WITHOUT HYPNOTISM. /MANGAN/ (	HUMBLY	) YOU DONT DISLIKE TOUCHING ME, I HOPE. YOU NEVER
HART II	(112)	BOTH. /THE BURGLAR/ YES, CAPTAIN. (HE GOES OUT	HUMBLY	). /MAZZINI/ WILL IT BE SAFE TO HAVE HIM IN THE HOUSE
CAND II	(112)	PAPER FROM THE TABLE AND OFFERS IT. HE ACCEPTS IT	HUMBLY	). THANK YER, JAMES. (HE GOES BACK TO THE BIG CHAIR
6CAL	(99)	BUT WITH DUE RESPECT TO YOUR GREATNESS I WOULD	HUMBLY	SUBMIT TO YOUR MAJESTY THAT GOD MAY HAVE SOMETHING TO
JOAN 6	(144)	SINS I NOW RENOUNCE AND ABJURE AND DEPART FROM,	HUMBLY	THANKING YOU DOCTORS AND MASTERS WHO HAVE BROUGHT ME
MIS.	(180)	" FOUNDATION"? /PERCIVAL/ I APOLOGIZE MOST	HUMBLY	TO THE LADY AND HER FAMILY FOR MY CONDUCT-- (HE
MIS.	(181)	WAS NOT A SHRED OF FOUNDATION I APOLOGIZE MOST	HUMBLY	TO THE LADY AND HER FAMILY FOR MY CONDUCT AND I
LION II	(132)	WHICH IS THE GREEK SORCERER? /ANDROCLES/ (	HUMBLY	TOUCHING HIS FORELOCK) ME, YOUR WORSHIP. /CAESAR/ MY
BULL III SD	(126)	PRIEST; AND POOR MATTHEW, OUTFACED BY THE MILLER,	HUMBLY	TURNS THE BASKET UPSIDE DOWN AND SITS ON IT.
2TRU II SD	(60)	PLACE AND HOLD YOUR TONGUE. THE PATIENT OBEYS	HUMBLY	UNTIL THE COLONEL DELICATELY TURNS HIS HEAD AWAY,
FANY III	(302)	OUT SOONER OR LATER. (HE BEGINS HIS CONFESSION	HUMBLY	, AVOIDING HER GAZE). MEG: IT'S RATHER AWFUL: YOULL
WIDO II	(29)	HALLO! /LICKCHEESE/ (COMING BETWEEN THEM VERY	HUMBLY	, BUT IN MORTAL ANXIETY AND HASTE) LOOK HERE,
DEST	(189)	SATISFY YOU? BE OFF, BOTH OF YOU. /GIUSEPPE/ (	HUMBLY	, HIS LIPS TREMBLING) W-WILLINGLY, YOUR EXCELLENCY. (
FOUN	(218)	(CRUSHED) I'M SURE I BEG YOUR PARDON MOST	HUMBLY	, MISS. /THE LORD CHANCELLOR/ FORGET THE RUDENESS OF
			HUMBUG	
2TRU I	(34)	FAITH IN THE BOTTLE DOES. /THE MONSTER/ YOURE A	HUMBUG	: THATS WHAT YOU ARE. /THE DOCTOR/ FAITH IS HUMBUG.
DOCT I SD	(96)	THAT HE IS, SCIENTIFICALLY CONSIDERED, A COLOSSAL	HUMBUG	: THE FACT BEING THAT, THOUGH HE KNOWS JUST AS MUCH (
MTH4 II	(185)	FOR US IF YOU TELL US BEFOREHAND THAT IT IS ALL	HUMBUG	? /ZOO/ ONE WOULD NOT THINK SO; BUT IF YOU WONT
BULL IV	(153)	I CANNOT HELP THINKING THAT AN ENGLISHMAN WITH NO	HUMBUG	ABOUT HIM, WHO WILL TALK STRAIGHT COMMON SENSE AND
APPL I	(230)	DEMOCRACY IS A VERY REAL THING, WITH MUCH LESS	HUMBUG	ABOUT IT THAN MANY OLDER INSTITUTIONS. BUT IT MEANS,
MIS. PREFACE	(87)	FOR EVERYBODY CONCERNED. THE FAMILY IDEAL IS A	HUMBUG	AND A NUISANCE: ONE MIGHT AS REASONABLY TALK OF THE
BARB PREFACE	(229)	NEVER HAVE BEEN TAKEN IN BY SO TRANSPARENT A	HUMBUG	AS SNOBBY PRICE; AND CERTAINLY I DO NOT THINK SNOBBY
APPL I	(230)	I CANNOT SIT HERE AND LISTEN TO SUCH A WORD AS	HUMBUG	BEING APPLIED TO DEMOCRACY. I AM SORRY, SIR; BUT WITH
CATH PREFACE	(153)	POINT OF VIEW. IT WAS QUITE EASY FOR PATIOMKIN TO	HUMBUG	CATHERINE AS TO THE CONDITION OF RUSSIA BY CONDUCTING
SUPR III	(93)	ANA; AND DO NOT BE ALARMED: THERE IS PLENTY OF	HUMBUG	IN HELL (INDEED THERE IS HARDLY ANYTHING ELSE); BUT
APPL II	(257)	LESSONS. BUT WHEN IT COMES TO REAL BUSINESS	HUMBUG	IS NO USE: THEY PICK IT UP THEMSELVES TOO QUICKLY.
ROCK I	(221)	YOUR INNOCENCE, SRARTHUR, YOU DONT KNOW WHAT	HUMBUG	IS YET. WAIT TIL YOURE A LABOR LEADER. (HE WINKS AT
MTH3	(97)	VERY WELL. /BURGE-LUBIN/ SO HAVE YOU, YOU OLD	HUMBUG	. ALL THE SAME, I DONT KNOW HOW YOU STAND THE WORK
2TRU I	(34)	HUMBUG: THATS WHAT YOU ARE. /THE DOCTOR/ FAITH IS	HUMBUG	. BUT IT WORKS. /THE MONSTER/ THEN WHY DO YOU CALL IT
JITT II	(36)	EXPECT IT FROM YOU. OH, I AM SO TIRED OF ALL THIS	HUMBUG	. I TURNED TO YOU BECAUSE I HOPED YOU WOULD
MIS. PREFACE	(15)	IS IN THAT, AS IN SO MANY OTHER RESPECTS, A	HUMBUG	. OLD PEOPLE AND YOUNG PEOPLE CANNOT WALK AT THE SAME
JOAN 2	(79)	POETRY. /LA TREMOUILLE/ POETRY! I SHOULD CALL IT	HUMBUG	. /THE ARCHBISHOP/ YOU WOULD BE WRONG, MY FRIEND.
MTH5	(221)	OF YOU! HOLD YOUR SILLY TONGUE, YOU CONCEITED	HUMBUG	. WHAT DO YOU KNOW ABOUT IT? /ECRASIA/ I KNOW WHAT
MTH2	(53)	THEN. IT WAS THAT OLD DOTARD, THAT PLAYED-OUT OLD	HUMBUG	LUBIN. HE WAS PRIME MINISTER THEN, NOT I. /FRANKLYN/
2TRU PREFACE	(9)	AND PLUNDERED AND WORRIED AND TIRED, YOU CANNOT	HUMBUG	ME ON THIS POINT; I UNDERSTAND PERFECTLY WHY FLORENCE
BARB I	(271)	THE VERY CLEVER WAY IN WHICH YOU SYSTEMATICALLY	HUMBUG	ME. I HAVE FOUND YOU OUT. TAKE CARE BARBARA DOESNT.
BULL I	(83)	YOU DONT SERIOUSLY SUPPOSE THAT HAFFIGAN CAN	HUMBUG	ME, DO YOU? /DOYLE/ NO: HE'S TOO LAZY TO TAKE THE
APPL I	(207)	DONT FOLLOW THAT. /MAGNUS/ (SMILING) YOU CANNOT	HUMBUG	ME, MR BOANERGES. I SEE WHY YOU ARE A REPUBLICAN. IF
SUPR III	(93)	(INDEED THERE IS HARDLY ANYTHING ELSE); BUT THE	HUMBUG	OF DEATH AND AGE AND CHANGE IS DROPPED BECAUSE HERE
ROCK I	(211)	WHATEVER THE ACCIDENT OF BIRTH AND THE	HUMBUG	OF RANK MAY HAVE MADE ME I AM HERE AS A DELEGATE FROM
MTH2	(78)	(TO LUBIN) IF YOU WANT THE PROFESSIONAL	HUMBUG	OF REWRITING THE BIBLE IN WORDS OF FOUR SYLLABLES,
MTH2	(87)	(CARESSING HER) DARLING! WHAT A PRICELESS	HUMBUG	OLD LUBIN IS! /SAVVY/ OH, SWEET OLD THING! I LOVE
APPL PREFACE	(180)	REPORT THEM, WITHOUT OBSCURING IT IN A CLOUD OF	HUMBUG	). NOW FOR THE THREE ARTICLES OF THE DEFINITION.
MRS III	(222)	BROTHER AND SISTER-- THEY CANT KEEP UP THE POLITE	HUMBUG	THATS SO EASY FOR TEN MINUTES ON AN AFTERNOON CALL.
MIS. PREFACE	(73)	POSSIBILITIES ALWAYS CONCEALED BY THAT INFAMOUS	HUMBUG	THE CURRENT SCHOOLMASTER, WHO ACHIEVES A SPURIOUS
ANNA	(302)	AND HALF HUMBUGGED, SOMEBODY MUST FORCE THEM AND	HUMBUG	THEM. SOME ENERGETIC AND CAPABLE MINORITY MUST ALWAYS
GENV PREFACE	(13)	NOT WANT TO BE GOVERNED, AND THE PLUTOCRATS WHO	HUMBUG	THEM, THOUGH THEY ARE SO FAR DEMOCRATIC THAT THEY
MTH5	(221)	IT POINTED OUT. YOU DID NOT CALL ME A CONCEITED	HUMBUG	THEN. YOU STIFLED ME WITH CARESSES, YOU MODELLED ME
APPL PREFACE	(180)	A REALITY: IT IS ONLY A CRY BY WHICH DEMAGOGUES	HUMBUG	US INTO VOTING FOR THEM. IF YOU DOUBT THIS -- IF YOU
SUPR PREFACE	(R36)	AT THE WELTER OF ECCLESIASTICAL AND PROFESSIONAL	HUMBUG	WHICH SAVES THE FACE OF THE STUPID SYSTEM OF VIOLENCE
DOCT PREFACE	(17)	FROM UTTER CORRUPTION. FOR EVEN THE MOST HARDENED	HUMBUG	WHO EVER PRESCRIBED ETHER TONICS TO LADIES WHOSE NEED
APPL PREFACE	(188)	THE WORK IS NOT REALLY DOING IT: HE IS A POPULAR	HUMBUG	WHO IS MERELY DOING WHAT A PERMANENT OFFICIAL TELLS
GETT PREFACE	(195)	MR PECKSNIFF, WHO IS GENERALLY NO WORSE THAN A	HUMBUG	WITH A TURN FOR POMPOUS TALKING, IS REPRESENTED AS A
O'FL	(211)	YOU AT LAST, SIR. MAYBE YOUD RATHER HAVE ME	HUMBUG	YOU AND TELL YOU LIES AS I USED, JUST AS THE BOYS
ROCK I	(232)	PEOPLE! HOW YOU STICK TO YOUR POINT! AND WHAT A	HUMBUG	YOU ARE! DONT THINK YOU CAN IMPOSE ON ME WITH YOUR
MTH2	(78)	AND PRETENDING IT'S SOMETHING NEW, I CAN	HUMBUG	YOU TO YOUR HEART'S CONTENT. I CAN CALL GENESIS
BULL I	(83)	IS TO SIT THERE AND DRINK YOUR WHISKY WHILE YOU	HUMBUG	YOURSELF. HOWEVER, WE NEEDNT ARGUE ABOUT HAFFIGAN,
APPL I	(230)	PEOPLE HAVE FOUND OUT LONG AGO THAT DEMOCRACY IS	HUMBUG	, AND THAT INSTEAD OF ESTABLISHING RESPONSIBLE
ARMS II	(36)	OF THEM IS A HERO, ANOTHER A BUFFOON, ANOTHER A	HUMBUG	, ANOTHER PERHAPS A BIT OF A BLACKGUARD. (HE PAUSES,
SUPR HANDBOK	(191)	HAS NOW TO LEARN HOW TO FASCINATE, AMUSE, COAX,	HUMBUG	, FRIGHTEN, OR OTHERWISE STRIKE THE FANCY OF THE
OVER PREFACE	(155)	HIS OWN REMORSE, HE (OR SHE) MAY BE A LIAR AND A	HUMBUG	, PRETENDING TO BE BETTER THAN THE DETECTED
CAPT NOTES	(304)	WORK ON THE SUBJECT, IN SUCH WORDS AS PLUM, COME,	HUMBUG	, UP, GUN, ETC., MR SWEET'S EVIDENCE IS CONCLUSIVE.
3PLA PREFACE	(R23)	BISMARCKIAN MAN OF ACTION, IMPATIENT OF	HUMBUG	, WILL COMBINE WITH THE SUBTLETY AND SPIRITUAL ENERGY
MIS.	(121)	ALONE FOR GIVING A THING A PRETTY TURN! YOURE A	HUMBUG	, YOU KNOW, LORD SUMMERHAYS. JOHN DOESNT KNOW IT; AND
APPL II	(274)	WAYS ARE WORTH. /NICOBAR/ HYPOCRITE! /CRASSUS/	HUMBUG	! /LYSISTRATA/ I WISH YOUR MAJESTY EVERY SUCCESS.
MTH2	(66)	SUPPORT? /BURGE/ (HURLING THE EPITHET AT HIM)	HUMBUG	! /SAVVY/ STOP. (THEY ALL STOP SHORT IN THE
PYGM V	(288)	(RISING IN A FURY) WHAT! THAT IMPOSTOR! THAT	HUMBUG	! THAT TOADYING IGNORAMUS! TEACH HIM MY METHODS!
PHIL III	(140)	AT HER) ONLY SOMETIMES? /JULIA/ YOU FRAUD! YOU	HUMBUG	! YOU MISERABLE LITTLE PLASTER SAINT! (HE LOOKS
			HUMBUGGED	
METH PREFACE	(R68)	BENCHES IN PARLIAMENT, THE BRITISH PUBLIC CAN BE	HUMBUGGED	AND COERCED INTO BELIEVING AND SUFFERING

O'FL (212)	OF THE WAY. WHY SHOULD I READ THE PAPERS TO BE	HUMBUGGED	AND LIED TO BY THEM THAT HAD THE CUNNING TO STAY
BARB III (317)	HAVE THE POWER IN THIS MATTER; AND I AM NOT BE BE	HUMBUGGED	INTO USING IT FOR YOUR PURPOSES. /LADY BRITOMART/
JITT II (45)	(RISING ALSO) I HAVE HAD ENOUGH OF BEING	HUMBUGGED	. WHO WAS SHE? /JITTA/ (CLOSES HER LIPS
SIM II (58)	BY THE TIME THE FLEET REALIZES THAT IT HAS BEEN	HUMBUGGED	THE EMPIRE WILL BE TIRED OF IDDY. /VASHTI/ THE
ARMS II (31)	I CAME ACROSS. I'LL NEVER TRUST A SWISS AGAIN. HE	HUMBUGGED	US INTO GIVING HIM FIFTY ABLEBODIED MEN FOR TWO
ROCK II (235)	WELL WITHOUT CHAVENDER. BUT I HAD TO GIVE WAY. HE	HUMBUGGED	US. HE PRETENDED THAT WITHOUT HIS OLD GUARD OF
SUPR IV (152)	MY CONSENT! /RAMSDEN/ YOU HAVE DELIBERATELY	HUMBUGGED	US, SIR! /HECTOR/ HERE! I HAVE HAD JUST ABOUT
KING PREFACE(159)	PLAN BY WHICH OUR ELECTORATE CAN BE SIDE-TRACKED,	HUMBUGGED	, CHEATED, LIED TO, OR FRIGHTENED INTO TOLERATING
ANNA (302)	DO THEIR DUTY WITHOUT BEING HALF FORCED AND HALF	HUMBUGGED	, SOMEBODY MUST FORCE THEM AND HUMBUG THEM. SOME
		HUMBUGGING	
JOAN 1 (63)	YOU A VERY SIMPLE THING TO TAKE THIS GIRL AWAY,	HUMBUGGING	HER INTO THE BELIEF THAT YOU ARE TAKING HER TO
BUOY II (26)	MANY HUNDRED EARTHLY WIVES, YOU WERE	HUMBUGGING	ME. /THE NATIVE/ SIR: HOOCHLIPOOCHLI POSSESSES
GENV PREFACE(22)	WINDBAGS AMUSED AND HOPEFUL. WE ARE STILL	HUMBUGGING	OURSELVES INTO THE BELIEF THAT THE SWINGS TO THE
METH PREFACE(R68)	IN THE WORLD BETWEEN THE STATESMAN WHO IS	HUMBUGGING	THEM INTO FURTHERING HIS PERSONAL AMBITION AND
APPL II (257)	YOU GET NO THANKS FOR IT. THEY THINK YOU ARE ONLY	HUMBUGGING	THEM. /MAGNUS/ WELL, SO I AM, IN THE ELEMENTARY
PHIL III (141)	SOUNDS MUCH MORE LIKE THE TRUTH. COME! YOU WERE	HUMBUGGING	US, WERENT YOU? /CHARTERIS/ (ENIGMATICALLY) ASK
BULL I (92)	HOTLY) WHAT IS THERE BEHIND IT? DO YOU THINK I'M	HUMBUGGING	YOU? /BROADBENT/ DONT FLY OUT, OLD CHAP. I ONLY
O'FL (211)	I'M ABLE TO SIT HERE NOW AND TALK TO YOU WITHOUT	HUMBUGGING	YOU; AND THATS WHAT NOT ONE OF YOUR TENANTS OR
O'FL (212)	WHAT USE IS ALL THE LYING, AND PRETENDING, AND	HUMBUGGING	, AND LETTING ON, WHEN THE DAY COMES TO YOU THAT
		HUMBUG-PROOF	
BULL PREFACE(22)	EXPECTS ITS POLITICAL LEADERS TO BE CLEVER AND	HUMBUG-PROOF	. IT MAY BE THAT IF OUR RESOURCES INCLUDED THE
		HUMBUGS	
MIS. PREFACE(89)	TO EXPOSE AND DERIDE AND TWEAK THE NOSES OF OUR	HUMBUGS	AND PANJANDRUMS, LIKE VOLTAIRE OR DICKENS, WE ARE
SUPR III (78)	MEANS THAT HE HAS SOLD OUT TO THE PARLIAMENTARY	HUMBUGS	AND THE BOURGEOISIE. COMPROMISE! THAT IS HIS FAITH.
APPL INTRLUD(253)	THAT GREEDY SCHEMER PROTEUS? HE HUMBUGS YOU. HE	HUMBUGS	EVERYBODY. HE EVEN HUMBUGS HIMSELF; AND OF COURSE HE
APPL INTRLUD(253)	HE HUMBUGS YOU. HE HUMBUGS EVERYBODY. HE EVEN	HUMBUGS	HIMSELF; AND OF COURSE HE HUMBUGS THAT CABINET WHICH
3PLA PREFACE(R34)	THE PLAYWRIGHTS WHO MAGNIFY ITS DIFFICULTIES ARE	HUMBUGS	. THE SUMMIT OF THEIR ART HAS BEEN ATTAINED AGAIN
APPL INTRLUD(244)	A PRETTY EXCUSE. YOU ARE THE KING OF LIARS AND	HUMBUGS	, YOU CANNOT UNDERSTAND HOW A FALSEHOOD LIKE THAT
SUPR III (133)	FUNCTIONARIES AND THE HENCHMAN OF AMBITIOUS	HUMBUGS	; AND THE END WILL BE DESPAIR AND DECREPITUDE,
JOAN PREFACE(31)	FIELD, SHE WAS DOWN ON THEM AT ONCE FOR LIARS AND	HUMBUGS	; BUT SHE NEVER THOUGHT OF THEM AS HERETICS. SHE WAS
APPL INTRLUD(253)	HE EVEN HUMBUGS HIMSELF; AND OF COURSE HE	HUMBUGS	THAT CABINET WHICH IS A DISGRACE TO YOU: IT IS LIKE
ROCK I (221)	HIM BY THAT. (GENIALLY-- RISING). WHAT	HUMBUGS	WE PRIME MINISTERS HAVE TO BE, MR HIPNEY! YOU KNOW:
APPL INTRLUD(253)	DO YOU ENCOURAGE THAT GREEDY SCHEMER PROTEUS? HE	HUMBUGS	YOU. HE HUMBUGS EVERYBODY. HE EVEN HUMBUGS HIMSELF;
BULL I (86)	HYBRIDS THAT NOW MONOPOLIZE ENGLAND. HYPOCRITES,	HUMBUGS	, GERMANS, JEWS, YANKEES, FOREIGNERS, PARK LANERS,
		HUME	
LION PREFACE(94)	GROUNDS WHEN YOU HAVE TRIMMED OFF EVERYTHING THAT	HUME	OR GRIMM OR ROUSSEAU OR HUXLEY OR ANY MODERN BISHOP
LION PREFACE(94)	WAS EVER SUCH A PERSON AS JESUS OR NOT, WHEN	HUME	SAID THAT JOSHUA'S CAMPAIGNS WERE IMPOSSIBLE, WHATELY
METH PREFACE(R88)	STANDING UP TO ALL THE RATIONALISTIC BATTERIES OF	HUME	, VOLTAIRE, AND THE REST, COLLAPSE BEFORE THE ONSLAUGHT
		HUME'S	
LION PREFACE(94)	IMPOSSIBLE. ONLY FICTITIOUS CHARACTERS WILL STAND	HUME'S	SORT OF EXAMINATION: NOTHING WILL EVER MAKE EDWARD
		HUMILIATE	
DOCT PREFACE(27)	MUST FIND CHEAP TREATMENTS FOR CHEAP PEOPLE, OR	HUMILIATE	AND LOSE HIS PATIENTS EITHER BY PRESCRIBING BEYOND
MILL I (139)	LEAVING EVERYTHING TO ALASTAIR. /SAGAMORE/ TO	HUMILIATE	HIM? /EPIFANIA/ NO. TO RUIN HIM. TO DESTROY HIM.
GETT (335)	WERE TO ATTACK ME, I SHOULD SIMPLY DEFEAT HIM AND	HUMILIATE	HIM (HE GRADUALLY GETS HIS HANDS ON THE CHAIR AND
BULL I (81)	SHOULD HEAR AND RETURN). MISTHER BROADBENT: DONT	HUMILIATE	ME BEFORE A FELLA COUNTHRYMAN. LOOK HERE: ME CLOES
PHIL I (76)	THAT IS WORTHY OF YOU! TO USE BRUTE FORCE! TO	HUMILIATE	ME BEFORE HER! (SHE BURSTS INTO TEARS).
FOUN (209)	/BRABAZON/ THAT SPEECH WAS MEANT TO INSULT AND	HUMILIATE	ME. I MAKE IT A RULE TO FIGHT PEOPLE WHO ATTEMPT
FOUN (209)	A RULE TO FIGHT PEOPLE WHO ATTEMPT TO INSULT AND	HUMILIATE	ME. (THROWING AWAY HIS STICK) PUT UP YOUR HANDS.
		HUMILIATED	
MIS. (188)	HOPE SO. I HOPE SO. TARLETON: I'M BEYOND MEASURE	HUMILIATED	AND ANNOYED BY MY SON'S BEHAVIOR IN YOUR HOUSE. I
JOAN PREFACE(4)	THE EFFECT SHE WAS PRODUCING ON THE MEN WHOM SHE	HUMILIATED	BY BEING RIGHT WHEN THEY WERE WRONG, AND HAD
MILL PREFACE(123)	MUSSOLINI BECAUSE HE HAD A DEFEATED, PLUNDERED,	HUMILIATED	NATION TO RESCUE AND RESTORE, WHEREAS MUSSOLINI
SUPR IV (156)	ARE A NICE CREATURE-- A GOOD BOY. /OCTAVIUS/ (	HUMILIATED	) IS THAT ALL? /ANN/ (MISCHIEVOUSLY IN SPITE OF
MIS. (112)	AT THE WRITING TABLE, WHERE HE SITS, BITTERLY	HUMILIATED	, BUT AFRAID TO SPEAK LEST HE SHOULD BURST INTO
MILL PREFACE(121)	ISLES, PARLIAMENT, OPENLY FLOUTED, CHASTISED, AND	HUMILIATED	, COULD DO NOTHING. THE PEOPLE WERE DELIGHTED;
GENV IV (109)	I LIVE FOR NOTHING ELSE. I FOUND THEM DEFEATED,	HUMILIATED	, THE DOORMATS OF EUROPE. THEY NOW HOLD UP THEIR
		HUMILIATING	
METH PREFACE(R60)	INTO MONSTROUSLY RICH MEN. NOTHING COULD BE MORE	HUMILIATING	AND THREATENING TO THEM THAN THE VIEW THAT THE
PLES PREFACE(R7)	(THE INDEPENDENT), THREATENED TO END IN THE	HUMILIATING	DISCOVERY THAT THE NEW DRAMA, IN ENGLAND AT
DOCT II (121)	IT'S NOT THAT YOU WONT ASK ME AGAIN; BUT IT'S SO	HUMILIATING	. AND I DID SO LOOK FORWARD TO ONE EVENING IN MY
MIS. PREFACE(36)	BY THE DIGNITY OF ADULT WORK, THE EXCHANGE OF THE	HUMILIATING	LIABILITY TO PERSONAL ASSAULT FROM THE LAWLESS
MILL PREFACE(122)	KEPT IN A CONDITION OF PERMANENT, DECISIVE, AND	HUMILIATING	MILITARY INFERIORITY TO THE OTHER POWERS, AND
SUPR III (80)	HERE, MAY I ASK? /MENDOZA/ (REPUDIATING THIS	HUMILIATING	MISCONCEPTION) OH NO, NO, NO: NOTHING OF THE
UNPL PREFACE(R12)	OF ANY MAGNITUDE BY AN ENGLISH AUTHOR. IN THIS	HUMILIATING	NATIONAL EMERGENCY, I PROPOSED TO MR GREIN THAT
OVER PREFACE(156)	LIVES IN FLIRTATION, AND CONCEAL NOTHING BUT THE	HUMILIATING	SECRET THAT THEY HAVE NEVER GONE ANY FURTHER.
CAND I SD(79)	THEM, TO IMPOSE HIS AUTHORITY ON THEM WITHOUT	HUMILIATING	THEM, AND, ON OCCASION, TO INTERFERE IN THEIR
POSN PREFACE(389)	IS PRACTICALLY PLACED ABOVE THE LAW. IT IS ALMOST	HUMILIATING	TO HAVE TO DEMONSTRATE THE ESSENTIAL DIFFERENCE
SUPR PREFACE(R21)	WHEN MAN'S SEXUAL IMMUNITIES ARE MADE ACUTELY	HUMILIATING	TO HIM. WHEN THE TERRIBLE MOMENT OF BIRTH
POSN PREFACE(394)	OR A CABINET MINISTER, WOULD BE MUCH LESS	HUMILIATING	TO THE PERSONS IMMEDIATELY CONCERNED, THE
2TRU PREFACE(4)	DICTATED AS HER UNIFORM, ITS SNUBBINGS ARE AS	HUMILIATING	, AND ITS MONOTONY IS MORE TEDIOUS BECAUSE MORE
		HUMILIATION	
DEST SD(149)	REPEATED FAILURE AS A WOULD-BE AUTHOR,	HUMILIATION	AS A REBUFFED TIME SERVER, REPROOF AND
SUPR I (34)	HER HEAD, LEADING HER A LIFE OF ABJECT TERROR AND	HUMILIATION	BY THREATENING TO TELL ON HER. /ANN/ AND A VERY
PYGM EPILOG (297)	WITH ANYONE WITHIN HER REACH, AS AN UNBEARABLE	HUMILIATION	. COMMERCIAL PEOPLE AND PROFESSIONAL PEOPLE IN A
OVER (192)	WONT FIGHT. IF YOU BEAT ME MY WIFE WOULD SHARE MY	HUMILIATION	. IF I BEAT YOU, SHE WOULD SYMPATHIZE WITH YOU
CLEO IV SD(193)	WITH CLENCHED FISTS, IN SPEECHLESS RAGE AND	HUMILIATION	. /RUFIO/ THAT GAME IS PLAYED AND LOST,
PHIL I (78)	OF HAPPINESS. YOU REVENGED YOURSELF ON ME FOR THE	HUMILIATION	OF BEING THE SLAVE OF YOUR PASSION FOR ME. I WAS
MILL I (139)	BROUGHT UP ON AN INCOME OF SEVEN FIGURES? THE	HUMILIATION	OF IT! /SAGAMORE/ YOU TAKE AWAY MY BREATH.
HART PREFACE(38)	A GOOD SQUARE MEAL OF TEN YEARS REVENGE UPON AND	HUMILIATION	OF OUR PROSTRATE FOE, CAN ONLY BE GUESSED BY
NEVR III (270)	MY DESTINY, I SUPPOSE. AT LEAST SPARE ME THE	HUMILIATION	OF TRYING TO SAVE ME. (SHE SITS DOWN, WITH HER
ARMS I (5)	NOBLE: IT WAS TREASON TO THINK OF DISILLUSION OR	HUMILIATION	OR FAILURE. AND YET-- AND YET-- (SHE SITS DOWN
MTH4 II (182)	STRATEGY NEEDED TO WIN IT. (MAKING A POSE OF HIS	HUMILIATION	) BUT ENJOY YOUR TRIUMPH: YOU HAVE MADE ME--
LADY (246)	VERY SOUL: HE WILL WRING TEARS OF BLOOD FROM YOUR	HUMILIATION	; AND THEN HE WILL HEAL THE WOUND WITH
DEVL II (31)	ALMOST IN TEARS, AS IF THE VISIT WERE A PERSONAL	HUMILIATION	TO HER) BUT WHY DID YOU GO THERE? /ANDERSON/ (
PYGM EPILOG (301)	GRAVITY, BUT THE EFFORT THAT COST HER THE DEEPEST	HUMILIATION	WAS A REQUEST TO HIGGINS, WHOSE PET ARTISTIC
BULL PREFACE(45)	TO MAKE THEM KNEEL TO HIM AS AN ACT OF PERSONAL	HUMILIATION	, AND THEREBY PROVOKES A MUTINY AMONG MEN NOT
MIS. (140)	HAVE ANY FEELING FOR YOU EXCEPT ONE OF SHRINKING	HUMILIATION	, I CANT UNDERSTAND. /HYPATIA/ I DONT BLAME YOU
MIS. PREFACE(13)	REMORSE, OR IT MAY BE A SARCASM CAUSING SHAME AND	HUMILIATION	, OR IT MAY BE A SERMON CAUSING THE CHILD TO
MILL I (143)	BLACKGUARD. MY DISTRESS, MY DISGRACE, MY	HUMILIATION	, THE HORRIBLE MESS AND FAILURE I HAVE MADE OF
		HUMILIATIONS	
MIS. PREFACE(47)	AND THREATS OF HELL FIRE AND IMPOSITIONS AND	HUMILIATIONS	AND PETTY IMPRISONINGS AND SENDINGS TO BED AND
MILL PREFACE(119)	TO PREFER EVEN THE POORLIEST PAID JOB TO ITS	HUMILIATIONS	. THE ONLY WAY OF ESCAPE WAS FOR THE GOVERNMENT
SUPR I (33)	WERE TOUCHED UP FOR TELLING, A SENSITIVE BOY'S	HUMILIATIONS	MAY BE VERY GOOD FUN FOR ORDINARY THICKSKINNED
SUPR PREFACE(R16)	LEADING TO SORDID AND PROLONGED COMPLICATIONS AND	HUMILIATIONS	, HAVE BEEN DISCARDED ALTOGETHER AS UNWORTHY OF
MTH3 (123)	ON YOU, AND CONTRAST THEM WITH THE POVERTY! THE	HUMILIATIONS	! THE ANXIETIES! THE HEARTBREAK! THE

HUMILITY

BARB II (295) TO MAKE A RELIGIONI OF HIS COWARDICE BY PREACHING HUMILITY : WE KNOW BETTER THAN THAT. WE THREE MUST STAND
JOAN 6 (129) POVERTY, THE LIFEI OF AUSTERITY, AND THE RULE OF HUMILITY AND CHARITY, MAY BE THE FOUNDER OF A HERESY THAT
JOAN PREFACE(36) HAPPENS TO BEI POPE. THE CHURCHES MUST LEARN HUMILITY AS WELL AS TEACH IT. THE APOSTOLIC SUCCESSION
ROCK PREFACE(178) GALILEO'S ARGUMENT, OF PRIDE IN NOT HAVING HUMILITY ENOUGH TO ADMIT THAT IT HAD BEEN WRONG IN ITS
WIDO I (15) OBJECT. /SARTORIUS/ (CONDESCENDING TO TRENCH'S HUMILITY FROM THE MERE INSTINCT TO SEIZE AN ADVANTAGE, AND
ARMS II (32) PETKOFF: I WAS WRONG. (TO RAINA, WITH EARNEST HUMILITY) I BEG YOUR PARDON. I HAVE BEHAVED ABOMINABLY.
CAND III (143) WAITING TO HEAR YOUR BID. /MORELL/ (WITH PROUD HUMILITY) I HAVE NOTHING TO OFFER YOU BUT MY STRENGTH FOR
PYGM V (283) MY OWN SPARK OF DIVINE FIRE. BUT (WITH SUDDEN HUMILITY) I SHALL MISS YOU, ELIZA. (HE SITS DOWN NEAR HER
NEVR II (250) SIR? /CRAMPTON/ NO, THANK YOU. (WITH BITTER HUMILITY) I SUPPOSE THERES NO OBJECTION TO MY SITTING HERE
FANY III (314) NOT IN EITHER OF YOU. /GILBEY/ (WITH IRONIC HUMILITY) I'M SURE I'M OBLIGED TO YOU FOR YOUR GOOD
JOAN 5 (113) NOW SPEAKING. YOU CAME CLOTHED WITH THE VIRTUE OF HUMILITY ; AND BECAUSE GOD BLESSED YOUR ENTERPRISES
JOAN 6 (130) YOU WILL SEE A DIABOLICAL PRIDE AND A NATURAL HUMILITY SEATED SIDE BY SIDE IN THE SELFSAME SOUL. THEREFORE
BULL IV (180) YOU DO ME TOO MUCH HONOR, SIR. (WITH PRIESTLY HUMILITY TO LARRY) MR DOYLE: I AM TO BLAME FOR HAVING
BARB PREFACE(236) OF THE WICKED DOCTRINE OF DOCILITY IN POVERTY AND HUMILITY UNDER OPPRESSION; AND THEY ARE RENT BY THE MOST
MTH2 (85) FUTURE NOT ONLY BECAUSE, IF I MAY SAY SO IN ALL HUMILITY , I HAVE BEEN GIFTED WITH A CERTAIN POWER OF
ARMS II (37) A WOMAN UNDER ANY CIRCUMSTANCES. (WITH PROFOUND HUMILITY , UNCOVERING HIS HEAD) I BEG YOUR PARDON. /LOUKA/

HUMMING

BULL IV (158) AT EASE IN CONSEQUENCE, HE STROLLS ABOUT THE ROOM HUMMING DISTRACTEDLY). /NORA/ (STRUGGLING WITH HER TEARS)
VWOO 3 (141) SOUNDS, FROM THE COOING OF DOVES AND THE HUMMING OF BEES TO THE WIRELESS ECHOES OF BEETHOVEN AND
SIM II (55) GOT INTO THE HEADLINES AT HOME. THE CABLES ARE HUMMING WITH IDDY. IDDY HAS CONVULSED THE EMPIRE, CONFOUND

HUMMINGTOP

SIM I (40) MY NAME IS HAMMINGTAP. THE OLD FAMILY NAME IS HUMMINGTOP ; BUT MY GRANDFATHER CHANGED IT WHEN HE WAS AT

HUMOR

BULL I (88) MOMENTS FOR YOUR MOST IRRESISTIBLE STROKES OF HUMOR ? /BROADBENT/ HUMOR! I WAS PERFECTLY SERIOUS. WHAT
PHIL II (102) TO THEM) MAY I ASK, MR CHARTERIS, IS THIS THE NEW HUMOR ? /CHARTERIS/ (STILL TOO PREOCCUPIED WITH HIS OWN
CATH 4 (188) APPEALING, LIKE PRINCE PATIOMKIN, TO MY SENSE OF HUMOR ? /EDSTASTON/ SENSE OF HUMOR! HO! HA, HA! I LIKE
MILL I (142) OF A MILLION. /EPIFANIA/ HAVE YOU A SENSE OF HUMOR ? /SAGAMORE/ I TRY TO KEEP IT IN CHECK; BUT I AM
NEVR II (244) MISS. /DOLLY/ (TAKEN ABACK, RECOVERS HER GOOD HUMOR AFTER A LONG BREATH, AND SAYS SWEETLY) THANK YOU, DEAR
NEVR II (239) OF HIS OWN CALLOUSNESS TO INTENSELY ENJOY THE HUMOR AND ADROITNESS OF IT, PROCEEDS PLEASANTLY) FINCH: SOME
BUOY III (37) HER MATTER-OF-FACT HUSBAND. TO KEEP HER IN GOOD HUMOR AND HEALTH I HAD TO INVITE AND ENTERTAIN A SUCCESSION
GETT SD(295) SNOB OF THE FIRST WATER. HER FATHER'S SENSE OF HUMOR AND HER MOTHER'S PLACID BALANCE HAVE DONE SOMETHING TO
3PLA PREFACE(R38) PART, I CAN AVOUCH THAT SUCH POWERS OF INVENTION, HUMOR AND STAGE INGENUITY AS I HAVE BEEN ABLE TO EXERCISE IN
PHIL II (102) AM? YOUVE GOT YOUR HEAD SO STUFFED WITH THE NEW HUMOR AND THE NEW WOMAN AND THE NEW THIS, THAT, AND THE
MRS II (205) DOWN SHARPLY) OFF WITH YOU: VIVVUMS IS NOT IN A HUMOR FOR PETTING HER LITTLE BOY THIS EVENING. (SHE RISES
LIED (200) /HER HUSBAND/ (SHORTLY, SHEWING ILL HUMOR FOR THE FIRST TIME) OH! INDEED! (HE LEAVES HIS
SIM PREFACE(4) FUNDAMENTALLY THAN THAT WE ARE NO LONGER IN THE HUMOR FOR THEM WE REFILL OUR MINDS WITH THE MIRACLES OF
NEVR III (266) (SHE LOOKS SEARCHINGLY AT HIM. HIS SENSE OF HUMOR GETS THE BETTER OF HIM; AND HE ADDS QUAINTLY) ONLY, I
CATH 1 (172) /EDSTASTON/ HOW CAN ANYONE WITH A SENSE OF HUMOR HELP LAUGHING? POP OFF! (HE IS CONVULSED).
DOCT IV (160) HE IS. WE'LL ALLOW YOU TO WAIT A FEW MINUTES TO HUMOR HIM; BUT IF YOU TALK TO HIM, OUT YOU GO. HE MAY DIE AT
MILL I (143) NEVER TO EMPLOY A SOLICITOR WHO HAD NO SENSE OF HUMOR I WOULD WALK OUT OF THIS OFFICE AND DEPRIVE YOU OF A
LADY PREFACE(213) FROM STUPIDITY, BUT BECAUSE SCORN OVERCOMES HUMOR IN HIM. NOBODY EVER DREAMT OF REPROACHING MILTON'S
POSN PREFACE(432) THE PROSTITUTION, THE VIOLENCE, THE DRINKING-BAR HUMOR INTO WHICH THE LIGHT SHINES IN THE PLAY ARE LICENSED,
SUPR HANDBOK(193) MAKES ITS DESECRATION BY VILE LANGUAGE AND COARSE HUMOR INTOLERABLE; SO THAT AT LAST WE CANNOT BEAR TO HAVE IT
GETT (339) WE ARE BOTH FUNNY PEOPLE, LET US NOT FORGET THAT HUMOR IS A DIVINE ATTRIBUTE. /MRS GEORGE/ I KNOW NOTHING
BULL III (144) (SUDDENLY VERY SOLEMN) YES: THEIR SENSE OF HUMOR IS IN ABEYANCE: I NOTICED IT THE MOMENT WE LANDED.
BULL III (144) ! /LARRY/ YES, YOU. YOU SAY THE IRISH SENSE OF HUMOR IS IN ABEYANCE. WELL, IF YOU DRIVE THROUGH ROSSCULLEN
SUPR I SD(10) A SENSE OF HUMOR. JUST AT PRESENT THE SENSE OF HUMOR IS IN ABEYANCE. TO SAY THAT HE IS EXCITED IS NOTHING:
BARB I SD(259) COMPLEX FORM OF LOMAX'S COMPLAINT. HIS SENSE OF HUMOR IS INTELLECTUAL AND SUBTLE, AND IS COMPLICATED BY AN
APPL I (226) /AMANDA/ THIS IS A FREE COUNTRY, BILL. A SENSE OF HUMOR IS NOT A CRIME. AND WHEN THE KING IS NOT SETTING ME
NEVR IV SD(284) ANOTHER WITH A MELANCHOLY SENSE OF HUMOR, THOUGH HUMOR IS NOT THEIR STRONG POINT. /GLORIA/ SHAKE HANDS. (
LADY PREFACE(213) PITIES TOO MUCH; BUT THAT HE IS NOT INSENSIBLE TO HUMOR IS SHEWN NOT ONLY BY HIS APPRECIATION OF WILDE, BUT BY
LADY PREFACE(212) TO BE ALL THINGS TO ALL MEN, YET WHOSE PROUD HUMOR IT IS TO BE TO EVERY MAN, PROVIDED THE MAN IS EMINENT
GETT (293) THEM. /THE BISHOP/ NO. EDITH HAS NO SENSE OF HUMOR . AND IVE NEVER SEEN A MAN IN A JOCULAR MOOD ON HIS
SUPR PREFACE(R32) OF SOUND MORAL JUDGMENT WITH LIGHTHEARTED GOOD HUMOR ; BUT THEY ARE CONCERNED WITH THE DIVERSITIES OF THE
PHIL II (109) MAKE HIS WAY IN THIS COUNTRY. HE HAS NO SENSE OF HUMOR . GRACE COMES IN. HER DRESS, VERY CONVENIENT AND
BULL PREFACE(37) VOLTAIRE HAD AN IRREPRESSIBLE SENSE OF HUMOR . HE JOKED ABOUT HABAKKUK; AND JOKES ABOUT HABAKKUK
LADY PREFACE(213) WARD. YET HE KNOWS THE TASTE AND THE VALUE OF HUMOR . HE WAS ONE OF THE FEW MEN OF LETTERS WHO REALLY
CAPT I SD(217) DELICATE RESOLUTE FEATURES AND A TWINKLE OF MILD HUMOR . HE WEARS THE SUN HELMET AND PAGRI, THE
SUPR I (28) AS YOU MAY DISTORT IT TO GRATIFY YOUR MALICIOUS HUMOR . I HOPE, OCTAVIUS, NO SUSPICION OF ME IS POSSIBLE IN
MILL I (142) /EPIFANIA/ AND REMEMBER THIS. I HAVE NO SENSE OF HUMOR . I WILL NOT BE LAUGHED AT. /SAGAMORE/ I SHOULD NOT
CATH 2 (178) /CATHERINE/ DASHKOFF! YOU HAVE NO SENSE OF HUMOR . (SHE STEPS DOWN TO THE FLOOR LEVEL AND LOOKS
SUPR I SD(9) WHO WOULD BE LOST WITHOUT A SENSE OF HUMOR . JUST AT PRESENT THE SENSE OF HUMOR IS IN ABEYANCE.
BULL III (143) TO FIND THAT THE PEOPLE HERE SHEWED NO SENSE OF HUMOR . /BROADBENT/ (SUDDENLY VERY SOLEMN) YES: THEIR SENSE
BULL IV (153) YOU DONT UNDERSTAND MR KEEGAN'S PECULIAR VEIN OF HUMOR . /BROADBENT/ (INSTANTLY RECOVERING HIS CONFIDENCE)
GETT (332) INTO ALL SORTS OF WICKEDNESS TO KEEP THEM IN GOOD HUMOR . SINJON: BE OFF WITH YOU: THIS DOESNT CONCERN YOU.
SURP III SD(177) HEAR, HEAR! GENERAL LAUGHTER AND GOOD HUMOR . TANNER AND MENDOZA SHAKE HANDS. THE BRIGANDS DROP
BULL PREFACE(55) 4, EGYPT, 1906, ARE NOT LACKING IN UNCONSCIOUS HUMOR THE OFFICIAL WALRUS PLEDGES HIMSELF IN EVERY CASE
MILL IV (206) YOU WERE NOT ONE OF THE STROKES OF HIS INFINITE HUMOR . THEN I SAT DOWN AND TOOK UP A NEWSPAPER. AND
BARB II (293) YOU APPEAL VERY STRONGLY TO MY SENSE OF IRONIC HUMOR . UNDERSHAFT MUTELY OFFERS HIS HAND. THEY SHAKE.
NEVR I (222) (CRAMPTON RECEIVES THIS WITH A GROWL OF GRIM HUMOR . VALENTINE RINGS THE BELL, AND REMARKS IN A CHEERFUL
KING I (197) IN HER WAY PURPOSELY TO KEEP HER IN GOOD HUMOR . WHAT STRUCK ME MOST IN THE AFFAIR WAS THAT JACK
BARB I (268) AND MURDER. I FIND MYSELF IN A SPECIALLY AMIABLE HUMOR JUST NOW BECAUSE, THIS MORNING, DOWN AT THE FOUNDRY,
GETT (349) WONT SCOLD YOU TODAY. I FEEL IN PARTICULARLY GOOD HUMOR JUST NOW. /THE GENERAL/ MAY I ASK WHY, LESBIA?
CATH 4 (188) HA! I LIKE THAT. WOULD ANYBODY WITH A SENSE OF HUMOR MAKE A GUY OF A MAN LIKE THIS, AND THEN EXPECT HIM TO
FABL PREFACE(98) AND NATURAL SELECTION. THE SATIRICAL HUMOR OF ARISTOPHANES, THE WISECRACKS OF CONFUCIUS, THE
ARMS I (8) DESPERATE PREDICAMENT: EVEN WITH A SENSE OF THE HUMOR OF IT, WITHOUT, HOWEVER, THE LEAST INTENTION OF
LADY PREFACE(222) INVITING " MY LADY" TO LAUGH AT THE SEPULCHRAL HUMOR OF THE FACT THAT THOUGH SHE PAINT AN INCH THICK (
DEVL II (39) SHE IS PAINFULLY STRUGGLING TO GRASP IS NOT THE HUMOR OF THE SITUATION BUT ITS HORROR. HE TURNS TO THE
CLEO II (126) GENERAL HERE, CAESAR/ /CAESAR/ (TICKLED BY THE HUMOR OF THE SITUATION) AND ALSO THE EGYPTIAN GENERAL, EH..
SUPR HANDBOK(207) AS PRECARIOUSLY AS LION TAMERS DO, TAKING THE HUMOR OF THEIR SITUATION, AND THE DIGNITY OF THEIR
DOCT PREFACE(73) MUST LIQUEFY WHETHER THE SAINT IS IN THE HUMOR OR NOT, TO TRICK A HEATHEN INTO BEING A DUTIFUL
GETT SD(295) AND ENERGETIC WILL, UNRESTRAINED BY ANY TOUCH OF HUMOR OR SCEPTICISM, CARRY EVERYTHING BEFORE THEM. IMPERIOUS
SUPR II SD(61) AND THOUGH THEY FIND HIS VEIN OF EASY HUMOR RATHER AMUSING WHEN IT HAS CEASED TO PUZZLE THEM (AS
BARB II (299) YOU A LOT OF GOOD. /BILL/ (WITH SOUR MIRTHLESS HUMOR) AW WAS SIVIN ANATHER MENN'S KNEES AT THE TAWM. E WAS
CLEO PRO2 (103) WOMEN LAUGH TRIUMPHANTLY. /BELZANOR/ (WITH GRIM HUMOR) FTATATEETA: DAUGHTER OF A LONG-TONGUED, SWIVEL-EYED
MRS I (196) WANTS. /REV. S./ (SINKING INTO A FEEBLE VEIN OF HUMOR) I GREATLY DOUBT WHETHER SHE HAS AS MUCH MONEY AS YOU
DEST (164) NATURALLY MISLED ME. /LADY/ (RECOVERING HER GOOD HUMOR) IT WAS NOT YOUR FAULT, WAS IT? I'M SO GLAD YOURE
CAND III (129) BUT WITH A TOUCH OF HER WISE-HEARTED MATERNAL HUMOR) NO. BUT YOU MAY SAY ANYTHING YOU REALLY AND TRULY
GENV IV (92) NOT TO SMILE. /NEWCOMER/ (WHO HAS NO SENSE OF HUMOR) SMILE! HE WAS NOT SMILING: HE LAUGHED RIGHT OUT.
CAND II (122) SITTING BESIDE MARCHBANKS, STILL IN A BANTERING HUMOR) WELL, EUGENE: WHY ARE YOU SO SAD? DID THE ONIONS
CAPT III (280) TO HER? /KEARNEY/ (WITH GRAVELY DISSEMBLED HUMOR) WELL, I AHSKED THAT QUESTION TOO. I SAID, WHY DID
PHIL III (138) (SITTING DOWN AGAIN ON THE COUCH WITH RUEFUL HUMOR) WELL, YOU SHALL NOT EXPERIMENT ON ME ANY MORE. GO TO
ARMS III (63) WERE MAKING LOVE TO HER. /SERGIUS/ (WITH GRIM HUMOR) YOU SAW THAT? /RAINA/ ONLY TOO WELL. (SHE TURNS
INCA (247) OF LAUGHTER. HE STRUGGLES WITH HIS SENSE OF HUMOR). AT THE SAME TIME (HE SITS DOWN) THERE IS A CERTAIN
FANY PROLOG (264) I ASK? /SAVOYARD/ WELL, VAUGHAN HAS NO SENSE OF HUMOR ; AND IF YOU JOKE WITH HIM HE'LL THINK YOURE INSULTING
MILL I (153) THE SAME-- /EPIFANIA/ ADRIAN: I HAVE NO SENSE OF HUMOR ; AND YOU KNOW HOW IT ANNOYS ME WHEN YOU TALK THE SORT
MILL I (149) POLLY. SO THERE! /EPIFANIA/ I HAVE NO SENSE OF HUMOR ; BUT THIS STRIKES ME AS IRRESISTIBLY FUNNY. YOU
SUPR III (81) MOST MAGNIFICENT HEAD OF HAIR I EVER SAW. SHE HAD HUMOR ; SHE HAD INTELLECT; SHE COULD COOK TO PERFECTION; AND
DEST (185) LAUGHING AT IT. /NAPOLEON/ (A COLD RAY OF HUMOR STRIKING PALLIDLY ACROSS HIS GLOOM) WHAT SHALL WE DO
GETT (329) DIDNT YOU? /HOTCHKISS/ HE HAS MORE REAL SENSE OF HUMOR THAN SHE. HE'S BETTER BRED. THAT WAS NOT MY FAULT.
MIS. PREFACE(96) BY BIBLE SMASHERS WITHOUT ANY SENSE OF HUMOR THAT JONAH WOULD NOT HAVE FITTED INTO A WHALE'S GULLET
DOCT PREFACE(52) AND SELFISHNESS THEY FORCE THE DOCTORS TO HUMOR THEIR FOLLY AND IGNORANCE. HOW COMPLETE AND

FANY II (289)	TO IT, YOU WOULD UNDERSTAND THAT I'M NOT IN THE	HUMOR	TO BE GAPED AT WHILE YOURE TRYING TO PERSUADE YOURSELF
NEVR II (230)	YOU? /M'COMAS/ (TAKEN ABACK, BUT RALLYING HIS	HUMOR	TO MEET THE EMERGENCY) BECAUSE EIGHTEEN YEARS IS TOO
HART PREFACE(31)	WHICH HAD DRIVEN THEM TO THE THEATRE IN AN ILL	HUMOR	TO SEEK SOME SORT OF DISTRACTION, HAD ONLY TO EXPLOIT
PYGM II SD(218)	VARIES FROM GENIAL BULLYING WHEN HE IS IN A GOOD	HUMOR	TO STORMY PETULANCE WHEN ANYTHING GOES WRONG; BUT HE
GETT (329)	MY FAULT. /MRS GEORGE/ MY HUSBAND HAS A SENSE OF	HUMOR	TOO. /HOTCHKISS/ THE COAL MERCHANT? -- I MEAN THE
JOAN 2,SD(73)	IS NEITHER VULGAR NOR STUPID; AND HE HAS A CHEEKY	HUMOR	WHICH ENABLES HIM TO HOLD HIS OWN IN CONVERSATION.
BARB I SD(259)	TOWN. HE IS AFFLICTED WITH A FRIVOLOUS SENSE OF	HUMOR	WHICH PLUNGES HIM AT THE MOST INOPPORTUNE MOMENTS INTO
BULL IV (164)	/BROADBENT/ YES: I KNOW I HAVE A STRONG SENSE OF	HUMOR	WHICH SOMETIMES MAKES PEOPLE DOUBT WHETHER I AM QUITE
ARMS III SD(65)	AT BLUNTSCHLI, FALLS A VICTIM TO HER SENSE OF	HUMOR	, AND ACTUALLY LEANS BACK BABYISHLY AGAINST THE
MTH2 (60)	MR LUBIN. /LUBIN/ (ASSENTING WITH COMPLETE GOOD	HUMOR	, AND BECOMING ATTENTIVE, CLEAR, AND BUSINESSLIKE IN
O'FL PREFACE(202)	FOR A CENTURY, THOUGH HE SOON RECOVERS HIS GOOD	HUMOR	, AND CANNOT UNDERSTAND WHY THE SURVIVORS OF HIS WRATH
BASH PREFACE(91)	PRETENTIOUS, BARBAROUS AND CHILDISH IN ITS	HUMOR	, AND FULL OF MUSIC. IN SHORT, THE TASTE FOR IT, AS
BULL I (88)	TO IT, YOU DERIDE THEM FOR HAVING NO SENSE OF	HUMOR	, AND PLUME YOURSELF ON YOUR OWN WORTHLESSNESS AS IF
MRS III (227)	CONVERSATION) VERY. /CROFTS/ (WITH BRUTAL GOOD	HUMOR	, AS IF HE LIKED HER PLUCK) WELL, THATS NOT WHAT I
DOCT PREFACE(73)	HIS (OR HER) OTHER QUALIFICATIONS, A SENSE OF	HUMOR	, LEST HE (OR SHE) SHOULD COME AT LAST TO BELIEVE ALL
BULL IV (153)	AH! IT WAS ONLY YOUR DELIGHTFUL IRISH	HUMOR	, MR KEEGAN. OF COURSE, OF COURSE. HOW STUPID OF ME!
FOUN (214)	VOICE AND THE ENCOURAGING BEAM, TWINKLING WITH	HUMOR	, OF HIS TENDER GREY EYES." DO YOU MEAN TO TELL ME
SUPR II (53)	LOVE HAS NOT TOTALLY EXTINGUISHED YOUR SENSE OF	HUMOR	, TAVY. /OCTAVIUS/ THAT ANSWER WONT SATISFY HER.
CLEO NOTES (211)	OF ANY MERIT WHATEVER. AS TO CAESAR'S SENSE OF	HUMOR	, THERE IS NO MORE REASON TO ASSUME THAT HE LACKED IT
NEVR IV SD(284)	LOOK AT ONE ANOTHER WITH A MELANCHOLY SENSE OF	HUMOR	, THOUGH HUMOR IS NOT THEIR STRONG POINT. /GLORIA/
BULL PREFACE(21)	INTELLECTUALLY RIDICULOUS MEN, WITHOUT WIT OR	HUMOR	, TO GO ON CRUSADES AND MAKE SUCCESSFUL REVOLUTIONS,
CATH 1,SD(162)	AMONG THE BEST ON RECORD. HE HAS A WILD SENSE OF	HUMOR	, WHICH ENABLES HIM TO LAUGH AT HIMSELF AS WELL AS AT
CATH 4 (188)	TO MY SENSE OF HUMOR? /EDSTASTON/ SENSE OF	HUMOR	! HO! HA, HA! I LIKE THAT. WOULD ANYBODY WITH A
BULL I (88)	MOST IRRESISTIBLE STROKES OF HUMOR? /BROADBENT/	HUMOR	! I WAS PERFECTLY SERIOUS. WHAT DO YOU MEAN? DO YOU
JITT III (79)	OH LORD! IF YOU ONLY HAD THE SMALLEST SENSE OF	HUMOR	! /JITTA/ (PASSIONATELY) YOU CANT EVEN TRY TO

HUMORED

MTH1 II SD(20)	ADAM LOOKS WORRIED, LIKE A FARMER. EVE, BETTER	HUMORED	(HAVING GIVEN UP WORRYING), SITS AND SPINS AND

HUMOREDLY

DEST (176)	HOW COULD I TELL YOU THAT? /NAPOLEON/ (ILL	HUMOREDLY	, BEGINNING TO WALK ABOUT AGAIN IN ANGRY

HUMORIST

LION II (138)	AND BURN THE INCENSE. /LAVINIA/ HE IS NOT A	HUMORIST	: HE WAS RIGHT. YOU OUGHT TO KNOW THAT, CAPTAIN:
BULL II SD(111)	AS THE WHIMSICAL AFFECTATION OF A SHREWD IRISH	HUMORIST	AND INCORRIGIBLE SPENDTHRIFT. AUNT JUDY SEEMS TO
NEVR I SD(199)	STRAINED NOSTRILS STAMP IT AS THE GRAVITY OF THE	HUMORIST	. HIS EYES ARE CLEAR, ALERT, OF SCEPTICALLY
LION II (138)	OF MY PRIVATE PLEASURE. YOUR FRIEND HERE IS A	HUMORIST	. I LAUGHED AT HIS TELLING YOU TO THINK OF YOURSELF
CATH 1 (172)	THE JOKE TO THE EMPRESS: SHE IS BY WAY OF BEING A	HUMORIST	(HE TAKES HIM BY THE ARM, AND LEADS HIM TOWARDS
UNPL PREFACE(R21)	AS POET, STORYTELLER, CHARACTER DRAUGHTSMAN,	HUMORIST	, AND RHETORICIAN, HAS LEFT US NO INTELLECTUALLY
METH PREFACE(R9)	NOTHING ELSE. THE CELEBRATED BUFFOON WAS NOT A	HUMORIST	, BUT THE FAMOUS NATURALIST BUFFON. EVERY LITERATE
PYGM EPILOG (300)	BEARING ON THE FLOWER BUSINESS. HE, BEING A	HUMORIST	, EXPLAINED TO THEM THE METHOD OF THE CELEBRATED
LADY PREFACE(212)	WISSEND." FRANK HARRIS IS EVERYTHING EXCEPT A	HUMORIST	, NOT, APPARENTLY, FROM STUPIDITY, BUT BECAUSE
BULL III (144)	OF THAT IN A COUNTRY WHERE EVERY MAN IS A BORN	HUMORIST	! THINK OF WHAT IT MEANS! (IMPRESSIVELY) LARRY:

HUMORISTS

SUPR PREFACE(R40)	MY LITERARY BRAVURA (PUT IN TO PLEASE YOU): THE	HUMORISTS	ALONE, ODDLY ENOUGH, SERMONIZE ME, SCARED OUT OF
LADY PREFACE(213)	OF THEM MYSELF, WERE ALL, IN THEIR VARIOUS WAYS,	HUMORISTS	, " SIDNEY'S SISTER: PEMBROKE'S MOTHER." AND NOW

HUMOROUS

MILL PREFACE(109)	NOT PRETEND TO BE ANYTHING MORE THAN A COMEDY OF	HUMOROUS	AND CURIOUS CONTEMPORARY CHARACTERS SUCH AS BEN
BULL PREFACE(21)	GLADSTONE, SEEMS IRISH IN RESPECT OF A CERTAIN	HUMOROUS	BLACKGUARDISM, AND A POWER OF APPRECIATING ART AND
GETT SD(281)	HIS SHARP CHIN BY BRISTLING FORWARD, CLEVER	HUMOROUS	EYES, NOT WITHOUT A GLINT OF MISCHIEF IN THEM,
SUPR II SD(62)	AT BOTTOM, HE FIRST LEADS THE UNWARY, BY	HUMOROUS	IRREVERENCE, TO LEAVE POPULAR THEOLOGY OUT OF
CAND III (130)	AND ACTUALLY AT EASE WITH MORELL: EVEN IMPISHLY	HUMOROUS	) WELL? /MORELL/ HAVE YOU ANYTHING TO TELL ME?
BULL IV SD(151)	HEARTINESS, AS IT IS BY THIS TIME, FOR THE MORE	HUMOROUS	SPIRITS PRESENT, A QUESTION OF VOCIFERATION OR
DEVL II (32)	BUT-- /ANDERSON/ (GOING OVER TO HER WITH	HUMOROUS	TENDERNESS) COME, DEAR, YOURE NOT SO WICKED AS YOU
PHIL I SD(70)	IS HIMSELF LAUGHING, AND HIS CLEVER, IMAGINATIVE,	HUMOROUS	WAYS, CONTRAST STRONGLY WITH THE SINCERE TENDERNESS
BULL I (79)	ON YOUR OWN ACCOUNT PERHAPS, BUT ELOQUENT,	HUMOROUS	, A LOVER OF FREEDOM, AND A TRUE FOLLOWER OF THAT
CAPT I SD(225)	GOODLOOKING, SYMPATHETIC, INTELLIGENT, TENDER AND	HUMOROUS	, DRESSED WITH CUNNING SIMPLICITY NOT AS A
GETT SD(260)	OF FIFTY OR THEREABOUTS, PLACID, GENTLE, AND	HUMOROUS	, WITH DELICATE FEATURES AND FINE GREY HAIR WITH

HUMOROUSLY

CAND I SD(85)	WHO IN PRIVATE IS EASYGOING, AFFECTIONATE, AND	HUMOROUSLY	CONVIVIAL TO A FAULT. CORPOREALLY HE IS PODGY,
UNPL PREFACE(R9)	EXACTLY AS I SAW IT, TO BE APPLAUDED AS THE MOST	HUMOROUSLY	EXTRAVAGANT PARADOXER IN LONDON. THE ONLY
AUGS (278)	/AUGUSTUS/ (HAUGHTILY APPROACHING THE CLERK, WHO	HUMOROUSLY	MAKES A PARALYTIC ATTEMPT TO STAND AT ATTENTION)
DEVL II (34)	HIM AN IRONICAL BOW. ANDERSON RETURNS THE BOW	HUMOROUSLY	). COME: YOULL HAVE A CUP OF TEA, TO PREVENT YOU
NEVR II (227)	LONG SEPARATION). WHERES YOUR BEARD? /M'COMAS/ (	HUMOROUSLY	SOLEMN) WOULD YOU EMPLOY A SOLICITOR WITH A
ARMS II (42)	YOU REMEMBER HIM, DONT YOU? /SERGIUS/ (SALUTING	HUMOROUSLY	, AND THEN OFFERING HIS HAND WITH GREAT CHARM OF
CAND II (116)	PAPERS, AND ADDING, ACROSS TO PROSERPINE, HALF	HUMOROUSLY	, HALF ABSENTLY) WELL, MISS PROSSY, WHY HAVE YOU

HUMORS

MRS PREFACE(161)	OF THE CENSORSHIP, WHEREAS PLAYS IN WHICH THESE	HUMORS	AND FASCINATIONS ARE DISCARDED, AND THE SOCIAL
MRS PREFACE(161)	IN SHORT, BY DEPENDING WHOLLY ON THE COARSE	HUMORS	AND THE PHYSICAL FASCINATION OF SEX, THEY COMPLY WITH
SUPR PREFACE(R33)	MOTIVES ARE HIS OWN APPETITES AND INSTINCTS AND	HUMORS	. RICHARD III, TOO, IS DELIGHTFUL AS THE WHIMSICAL
3PLA PREFACE(R33)	OF MY DIABOLONIAN PURITAN OR MY REVIVAL OF THE	HUMORS	OF COOL AS A CUCUMBER, TOO MUCH SURPRISE AT THEM
3PLA PREFACE(R15)	CONTRARY, I AM, I PROTEST, AS ACCESSIBLE TO THE	HUMORS	OF THE ROGUE'S COMEDY OR THE RAKE'S PROGRESS AS TO
HART II (93)	SITS DOWN AT THE PORT END OF IT IN THE WORST OF	HUMORS	). /MAZZINI/ (FOLLOWING HER AND TAKING THE OTHER

HUMOUR

HART II (122)	TOO THANKFUL TO ANYONE WHO WILL KEEP HER IN GOOD	HUMOUR	FOR HIM. /HECTOR/ AND AS SHE HAS ALL THE SHOTOVER

HUMPH

HART I (59)	ELSE? /ELLIE/ OF COURSE NOT. /MRS HUSHABYE/	HUMPH	! (THE BOOK ON THE DRAWING-TABLE CATCHES HER EYE.

HUMPHRIES

ROCK I (210)	CHARMING AFFABILITY) WHAT! MY OLD FRIEND TOM	HUMPHRIES	! HOW HAVE YOU BEEN ALL THESE YEARS? SIT DOWN.

HUMPHRY

METH PREFACE(R10)	OF THE SUN, NEWTON'S THEORY OF GRAVITATION, SIR	HUMPHRY	DAVY'S INVENTION OF THE SAFETY-LAMP, THE DISCOVERY

HUMS

BULL II SD(112)	THEN SHE SETTLES HERSELF RESIGNEDLY TO WAIT, AND	HUMS	A SONG-- NOT AN IRISH MELODY, BUT A HACKNEYED ENGLISH

HUN

AUGS (266)	MAN: DO YOU WANT TO SEE PICTURE SHOWS WHEN THE	HUN	IS AT THE GATE? /THE CLERK/ (MOURNFULLY) I DONT NOW,
AUGS (282)	I SAID I WAS MY SISTER-IN-LAW AND THAT I WAS A	HUN	. HE LAPPED IT UP LIKE A KITTEN. . . . /AUGUSTUS/ YOU
AUGS (274)	ATTENTION) YES? /THE LADY/ SHE IS A GERMAN. A	HUN	. /AUGUSTUS/ YES, YES. SHE WOULD BE. CONTINUE. /THE
AUGS (267)	NO ROLLS. THE ONLY BAKER THAT BAKED ROLLS WAS A	HUN	; AND HE'S BEEN INTERNED. /AUGUSTUS/ QUITE RIGHT, TOO.
MTH2 (50)	THAT IS WHAT YOU FELLOWS NEVER WOULD REALIZE. THE	HUN	WAS AT THE GATE. OUR COUNTRY, OUR LIVES, THE HONOR OF
MTH2 (53)	WE DESERT THE COUNTRY AT SUCH A CRISIS? THE	HUN	WAS AT THE GATE. EVERYONE HAS TO MAKE SACRIFICES FOR THE
HART PREFACE(22)	TRENCHES WITH A GRIM DETERMINATION TO FIND THE	HUN	WHO HAD WOUNDED HIM AND PAY HIM OUT FOR IT. IT IS
MTH2 (50)	BY A DECLARATION OF PRINCIPLE. DO YOU THINK THE	HUN	WOULD EVER HAVE COME TO THE GATE IF HE HAD KNOWN THAT IT

HUNCHED

MTH2 SD(47)	IS JOINED BY SAVVY. THEY SIT THERE, SIDE BY SIDE,	HUNCHED	UP WITH THEIR ELBOWS ON THEIR KNEES AND THEIR CHINS

HUND

CATH 2 (178) ! ! /CATHERINE/ (LIKE A FISHFAG) SCHWEIG, DU HUND . (RESUMING HER IMPRESSIVE ROYAL MANNER) HAVE YOU NEVER

HUNDERD

BULL IV (157) IS HE AS READY AS THAT? WOULD HE LEN ME FIVE HUNDERD , D'YE THINK? /LARRY/ HE'LL LEND YOU MORE THAN THE

HUNDHERD

BULL I (80) THAN REASSURED) WHY SHOULDNT IT SATISFY ME? A HUNDHERD A YEAR IS TWELVE POUND A MONTH, ISNT IT?
BULL I (80) ME NACHER. BUT I WONT TAKE A PENNY MORE THAN A HUNDHERD A YEAR (HE LOOKS WITH RESTLESS CUNNING AT
BULL I (80) OUL MOTHER IN IRELAND. BUT NO MATTER: I SAID A HUNDHERD ; AND WHAT I SAID I'LL STICK TO, IF I HAVE TO

HUNDRED

SIM II (78) THERE WERE, PROLA? /PROLA/ FOUR. OR WAS IT FOUR HUNDRED ? /IDDY/ THERE WERE FOUR. THEIR NAMES WERE LOVE,
LIED (201) OF OUR FIRST ACTOR-MANAGERS HAVE OFFERED HER A HUNDRED A WEEK IF SHE'LL GO ON THE STAGE WHEN THEY START A
WIDO III (62) NOTHING; WHEREAS YOU WOULD HAVE LOST OVER FOUR HUNDRED A YEAR: A VERY SERIOUS MATTER FOR YOU. I HAD NO
MIS. (197) TO TAKE THAT GIRL OFF MY HANDS FOR FIFTEEN HUNDRED A YEAR: THATS ALL THAT CONCERNS ME. TELL HER WHO YOU
APPL PREFACE(180) INCOME. EQUAL CONSIDERATION FOR A PERSON WITH A HUNDRED A YEAR AND ONE WITH A HUNDRED THOUSAND IS -
2TRU PREFACE(4) OR PUBLIC WORK THAT THEY MIGHT AS WELL HAVE FIVE HUNDRED A YEAR AS FIFTY THOUSAND " FOR ALL THE GOOD IT DOES
GENV II (62) I HAVE BEEN A LOT IN THE PAPERS LATELY. IT'S SIX HUNDRED A YEAR FOR ME IF I GET IN. I SHALL BE THE PATRIOTIC
BARB III (333) CAN DO WITHOUT YOU. I MUST HAVE TWO THOUSAND FIVE HUNDRED A YEAR FOR TWO YEARS. AT THE END OF THAT TIME, IF I
GETT (294) HAVE TO CUT OFF AN INCH FROM MY RIGHT ARM THAN A HUNDRED A YEAR FROM MY MOTHER'S INCOME I OWE EVERYTHING TO
WIDO II (35) HUNDRED A YEAR. WELL, I WILL TAKE JUST SEVEN HUNDRED A YEAR FROM PAPA AT FIRST; AND THEN WE SHALL BE
ROCK II (260) FOR A DINNER UNTIL THEY VOTED THEMSELVES FOUR HUNDRED A YEAR OUT OF OUR POCKETS. /SIR BEMROSE/ (CARRIED
WIDO II (42) GIVE ME UNTIL I HAVE FIRST PAID YOU YOUR SEVEN HUNDRED A YEAR OUT OF IT. WHAT LICKCHEESE DID FOR ME, I DO
BARB II (284) AT THE NATIONAL SPORTIN CLUB WAS WORTH NIGH A HUNDRED A YEAR TO HIM. HE'S GEV EM UP NOW FOR RELIGION; SO
MILL IV (207) ISSUE OF FOUNDERS' SHARES FOR HER, WORTH THREE HUNDRED A YEAR TO HER. THEY CALLED IT LETTING HER IN ON THE
WIDO II (34) MATTER. DO YOU KNOW THAT I HAVE A BARE SEVEN HUNDRED A YEAR TO LIVE ON? /BLANCHE/ HOW DREADFUL!
MRS IV (244) THEM OFF WITH A SHILLING, I SHALL HAVE ONLY FOUR HUNDRED A YEAR. AND HE WONT DIE UNTIL HE'S THREE SCORE AND
WIDO II (36) OF COURSE, THAT WE SHALL LIVE ALWAYS ON SEVEN HUNDRED A YEAR. I INTEND TO GO AT MY PROFESSION IN EARNEST,
ROCK II (246) EVEN TO KEEP IT DUSTED. YOU CAN HAVE IT FOR A HUNDRED A YEAR. /SIR JAFNA/ TOO FAR FROM TOWN. /THE DUKE/
MIS. (197) PERCIVAL) I THINK YOU SAID YOUR PRICE WAS FIFTEEN HUNDRED A YEAR. TAKE IT, AND I WISH YOU JOY OF YOUR BARGAIN.
WIDO II (35) TOO PROUD TO OWE ANYTHING TO YOU. YOU HAVE SEVEN HUNDRED A YEAR. WELL, I WILL TAKE JUST SEVEN HUNDRED A YEAR
MIS. (121) ALL THE WAYS JOHN AND I HAD WHEN WE HAD BARELY A HUNDRED A YEAR. YOU SHOULD HAVE KNOWN ME WHEN I WAS FORTY!
WIDO II (35) RESTLESSLY ABOUT). WE REALLY CANNOT LIVE ON SEVEN HUNDRED A YEAR, HARRY; AND I DONT THINK IT QUITE FAIR OF YOU
GENV II (63) I WILL PAY YOU WHEN MY SHIP COMES HOME: THE SIX HUNDRED A YEAR, YOU KNOW. /SIR O./ WILL A FIVE POUND NOTE BE
GETT PREFACE(256) THERE IS NO DIFFERENCE IN THIS RESPECT BETWEEN A HUNDRED AND A QUADRILLION. DIVORCE IS THE ONE THING YOU MAY
MTH3 (116) IS YOUR AGE, MR ARCHBISHOP? /BURGE-LUBIN/ TWO HUNDRED AND EIGHTY-THREE, HE SAYS. THAT IS HIS LITTLE JOKE.
MTH3 (105) FOR YOUR AGE. /THE ARCHBISHOP/ MY AGE IS TWO HUNDRED AND EIGHTY-THREE. /BARNABAS/ (MOROSELY TRIUMPHANT)
MTH3 (106) IS A SWINDLER. /CONFUCIUS/ SEVENTY-EIGHT INTO TWO HUNDRED AND EIGHTY-THREE GOES MORE THAN THREE AND A HALF
KING PREFACE(154) THREE MIGHT HAVE MET. NOW ANYONE WHO CONSIDERS A HUNDRED AND FIFTIETH EDITION OF SWEET NELL OF OLD DRURY MORE
CURE (234) YOUNG FRIEND. BESIDES, I REALLY CANNOT EARN TWO HUNDRED AND FIFTY GUINEAS BY PLAYING SOOTHING SYRUP TO YOU.
CURE (232) I NEVER BREAK AN ENGAGEMENT, ESPECIALLY A TWO HUNDRED AND FIFTY GUINEA ONE. (SHE TURNS TOWARDS THE
MILL I (139) WELL, WHAT WAS THIRTY MILLIONS TO HIM? HE LOST A HUNDRED AND FIFTY MILLIONS. HE HAD PROMISED TO LEAVE ME TWO
MILL II (169) YOU INFINITE NOTHINGNESS! MY FATHER MADE A HUNDRED AND FIFTY MILLIONS. YOU NEVER MADE EVEN HALF A
LION PREFACE(57) HEAD), DR CRIPPEN'S TIME WAS WORTH, SAY, THREE HUNDRED AND FIFTY POUNDS A YEAR. CRITICIZE THIS ARRANGEMENT;
DOCT III (134) WE CAN TREAT YOU AS A FRIEND. WILL YOU LEND US A HUNDRED AND FIFTY POUNDS? /RIDGEON/ NO. /LOUIS/ (
MILL I (144) HIM THAT IF WITHIN SIX MONTHS HE HAD TURNED THAT HUNDRED AND FIFTY POUNDS INTO FIFTY THOUSAND, I WAS HIS. IF
MILL I (144) WHAT CONDITION? /EPIFANIA/ I WAS TO GIVE HIM ONE HUNDRED AND FIFTY POUNDS, AND TELL HIM THAT IF WITHIN SIX
MILL I (155) PROMISE TO MY FATHER. I HANDED HIM A CHEQUE FOR A HUNDRED AND FIFTY POUNDS. " MAKE THAT INTO FIFTY THOUSAND
MILL I (156) NEVER MISS THE PRICE. /ADRIAN/ IF I GIVE YOU MY HUNDRED AND FIFTY POUNDS, WILL YOU INVEST IT FOR ME?
MILL I (156) ALIVE MY HAND AND FORTUNE IF THEY COULD TURN MY HUNDRED AND FIFTY POUND CHEQUE INTO FIFTY THOUSAND WITHIN
MILL II (177) WELL, YOU KNOW BETTER NOW. I AM TO GIVE YOU A HUNDRED AND FIFTY POUNDS. IN SIX MONTHS YOU ARE TO INCREASE
MILL II (178) BORROW IT FROM THE CHAUFFEUR. HE WILL LEND YOU A HUNDRED AND FIFTY POUNDS ON MY ACCOUNT IF YOU DARE ASK HIM.
MILL IV (205) NOT EXPIRED. I WILL SHEW YOU HOW TO TURN YOUR HUNDRED AND FIFTY POUNDS INTO FIFTY THOUSAND. /THE DOCTOR/
MILL IV (207) AND THE PENSIONS THERE WAS A GAP EXACTLY ONE HUNDRED AND FIFTY POUNDS WIDE. HE WHO IS JUST AND EXACT
WIDO III (62) YOUR TEN THOUSAND POUNDS IN CONSOLS AND GET TWO HUNDRED AND FIFTY POUNDS A YEAR FOR IT INSTEAD OF SEVEN
DOCT I (88) REGULARLY EVERY FIFTEEN YEARS; AND IT'S FULLY A HUNDRED AND FIFTY SINCE YOURS WAS MADE LAST. THATS SOMETHING
MILL I (145) PUT HIM TO THE TEST? WHY DID YOU GIVE HIM THE HUNDRED AND FIFTY TO TRY HIS LUCK WITH? /EPIFANIA/ BOXING.
FABL II (107) WITH A PRESCRIPTION ON IT AND POCKET ANOTHER HUNDRED AND FIFTY THOUSAND. EVERY STATE IN EUROPE AND
FABL II (105) NEGRO HITLER, KETCHEWAYO THE SECOND, FOR A HUNDRED AND FIFTY THOUSAND. KETCH COULD AFFORD IT: HIS
MIS. PREFACE(74) HORROR; BUT YOU MAY AND DO KILL CHILDREN IN A HUNDRED AND FIFTY WAYS PROVIDED YOU DO NOT SHOOT THEM OR SET
JOAN PREFACE(49) NINETEENTH CENTURY AFTER AN ECLIPSE OF ABOUT FOUR HUNDRED AND FIFTY YEARS, THE RENASCENCE OF ANTIQUE
MIS. (153) /LINA/ I'LL TELL YOU WITH PLEASURE. FOR THE LAST HUNDRED AND FIFTY YEARS, NOT A SINGLE DAY HAS PASSED WITHOUT
MTH2 (39) AND SELF-CONCEIT, AND THAT I WAS NOT WITHIN A HUNDRED AND FIFTY YEARS OF THE EXPERIENCE AND WISDOM I WAS
MTH4 I (141) WOMAN/ (SMILING GRAVELY) IT MUST BE AT LEAST A HUNDRED AND FIFTY YEARS SINCE I LAST LAUGHED. BUT IF YOU DO
BARB III (334) MORE, OF COURSE. /CUSINS/ I WOULD HAVE TAKEN TWO HUNDRED AND FIFTY. HOW YOU CAN SUCCEED IN BUSINESS WHEN YOU
MILL I (144) POUNDS IN SIX MONTHS WITH A CAPITAL OF ONE HUNDRED AND FIFTY. /EPIFANIA/ HE DID. WISE AS MY FATHER WAS,
MILL I (156) MY BANK BALANCE AT PRESENT IS SOMEWHERE ABOUT A HUNDRED AND FIFTY. I SHOULD VERY MUCH LIKE TO KNOW HOW TO
GENV IV (96) FACTS UNTIL TWENTY YEARS AFTER. SOMETIMES A HUNDRED AND FIFTY. /JUDGE/ STILL, SIR MIDLANDER, YOU KNOW
KING I (164) FOURTEEN THOUSAND, FOUR HUNDRED MINUTES. SEVEN HUNDRED AND FIFTYSIX MILLION EIGHT HUNDRED AND SIXTYFOUR
MTH3 (121) LUTESTRING/ I DID MARRY. I MARRIED AGAIN ON MY HUNDRED AND FIRST BIRTHDAY. BUT OF COURSE I HAD TO MARRY AN
FABL II (108) ORDERED A SALUTE OF FIVE GUNS TO CELEBRATE THE HUNDRED AND FIRST BIRTHDAY OF THE PRESIDENT OF THE BOARD OF
KING I (164) AND SIXTY DAYS. TWO HUNDRED AND TEN THOUSAND TWO HUNDRED AND FORTY HOURS. TWELVE MILLION SIX HUNDRED AND
KING I (191) ME WHEN I WAS A BOY. LIVING AT THE HAGUE ON TWO HUNDRED AND FORTY POUNDS A YEAR FINISHED MY EDUCATION IN
LION PREFACE(97) WORD, AND YOU HAVE A TOTAL OF OVER THREE HUNDRED AND FORTY-TWO AND A QUARTER MILLION HERETICS TO
KING I (164) TWO HUNDRED AND FORTY HOURS. TWELVE MILLION SIX HUNDRED AND FOURTEEN THOUSAND, FOUR HUNDRED MINUTES. SEVEN
LION PREFACE(97) POPULATION OF THE FRENCH REPUBLIC IS ABOUT ONE HUNDRED AND FOURTEEN MILLIONS. THE FRENCH ARE NOT IN OUR
SIM PREFACE(3) PERFECT UNDERSTANDING COVERS MUCH MORE THAN NINE HUNDRED AND NINETY CASES OUT OF EVERY THOUSAND NEW PLAYS.
KING I (187) HE PROPS HIS HEAD ON HIS ELBOWS. /NEWTON/ TWELVE HUNDRED AND NINETY DAYS. AND IN THE VERY NEXT VERSE THIRTEEN
CATH 3 (186) HE HAS INSULTED THE EMPRESS. HE WILL RECEIVE A HUNDRED AND ONE BLOWS OF THE KNOUT. (HE LAUGHS AND GOES
MTH4 II (189) RECEPTION. ROYAL HONORS, MIND YOU! A SALUTE OF A HUNDRED AND ONE GUNS! THE STREETS LINED WITH TROOPS! THE
METH PREFACE(R49) YOU PUT IT DOWN A HUNDRED TIMES IT WILL JUMP UP A HUNDRED AND ONE TIMES; SO THAT IF YOU DESIRE ITS COMPANY AT
FANY III (307) YOU. (INTRODUCING) MONSIEUR DUVALLET: MISS FOUR HUNDRED AND SEVEN. MR BOBBY GILBEY. (DUVALLET BOWS). I
MTH3 (110) THAN FORTY-FIVE; AND MY REAL AGE WOULD BE ONE HUNDRED AND SEVENTEEN. WHAT WAS I TO DO? BLEACH MY HAIR?
SIM II (55) WANT OF CONSIDERATION FOR HIS POSITION. HE HAS A HUNDRED AND SEVENTEEN CHILDREN SURVIVING. /SIR CHARLES/ THEN
MTH3 (122) /MRS LUTESTRING/ I AM AT PRESENT IN MY TWO HUNDRED AND SEVENTY-FIFTH YEAR. YOU SUGGEST THAT I SHOULD
MTH3 (118) YOU ASKED ME MY AGE, MR CHIEF SECRETARY. I AM TWO HUNDRED AND SEVENTY-FOUR. /BURGE-LUBIN/ (GALLANTLY) YOU
MTH3 (134) AT LAST. /BURGE-LUBIN/ BUT FISHGUARD! TWO HUNDRED AND SEVENTY MILES! /THE NEGRESS/ THERE IS A
MTH3 (128) MAN SHOULD BE PRIVILEGED TO LIVE TO BE TWO HUNDRED AND SEVENTY-EIGHT, IT DOES SHORTEN MY LIFE,
MTH4 II (177) MY PRESENCE; AND I AM STILL A YOUNG WOMAN: ONE HUNDRED AND SEVENTY IF YOU WISH TO KNOW EXACTLY. /NAPOLEON/
MTH4 III (195) AS MUCH AS LOOKED AT YOU. THE ORACLE IS ONLY A HUNDRED AND SEVENTY; AND YOULL FIND IT HARD ENOUGH TO STAND
BARB III (340) LAST THEY GET THE COURAGE TO KILL; AND YOUR SIX HUNDRED AND SEVENTY FOOLS BECOME A GOVERNMENT. YOUR PIOUS
MTH4 III (202) HER. /THE ORACLE/ TAKE CARE. I HAVE BEEN HERE ONE HUNDRED AND SEVENTY YEARS. YOUR DEATH DOES NOT MEAN TO ME
DEVL I (21) DAY OF SEPTEMBER, ONE THOUSAND SEVEN HUNDRED AND SEVENTY SEVEN, I HEREBY REVOKE ALL FORMER WILLS
KING I (175) NOW ONE HUNDRED THOUSAND NIGHTS ARE ALMOST TWO HUNDRED AND SEVENTYFOUR YEARS. TO BE PRECISE, 273 YEARS 287
LION PREFACE(97) MILLION CHRISTIANS OUT OF A POPULATION OF THREE HUNDRED AND SIXTEEN AND A HALF MILLIONS. THE KING OF ENGLAND
METH PREFACE(R9) DAWN OF DARWINISM. ONE DAY EARLY IN THE EIGHTEEN HUNDRED AND SIXTIES, I, BEING THEN A SMALL BOY, WAS WITH MY
KING I (164) /NEWTON/ TWENTYFOUR YEARS, EIGHT THOUSAND SEVEN HUNDRED AND SIXTY DAYS. TWO HUNDRED AND TEN THOUSAND TWO
MTH2 (39) FOR LIFE. IF I THOUGHT I WAS GOING TO LIVE NINE HUNDRED AND SIXTY YEARS, I DONT THINK I SHOULD STAY IN THE
MTH2 (39) THING IT IS. /CONRAD/ IF I COULD COUNT ON NINE HUNDRED AND SIXTY YEARS I COULD MAKE MYSELF A REAL
FANY PROLOG (270) EXACTLY AND SCIENTIFICALLY FOR TWO THOUSAND TWO HUNDRED AND SIXTY YEARS. WHEN I SAY THAT THESE
KING I (164) MINUTES. SEVEN HUNDRED AND FIFTYSIX MILLION EIGHT HUNDRED AND SIXTYFOUR THOUSAND SECONDS. A LONG LONG LIFE.
MTH2 (83) THAT WOULD BE-- LET ME SEE-- FIVE TIMES THREE HUNDRED AND SIXTY-FIVE IS-- UM-- TWENTY-FIVE-- THIRTY-TWO--
KING I (164) EIGHT THOUSAND SEVEN HUNDRED AND SIXTY DAYS. TWO HUNDRED AND TEN THOUSAND TWO HUNDRED AND FORTY HOURS. TWELVE
GLIM (171) I'M VERY OLD; BUT IVE MY WITS ABOUT ME. I'M ONE HUNDRED AND THIRTEEN YEARS OLD, BY THE GRACE OF OUR LADY;
LADY PREFACE(221) IN SHAKESPEAR'S? IMAGINE HER READING THE HUNDRED AND THIRTIETH SONNET! " MY MISTRESS' EYES ARE

MTH2	(80)	THE POSITION OF WANTING TO ROB THE PEOPLE OF TWO	HUNDRED	AND THIRTY YEARS OF THEIR NATURAL LIFE. THE
PYGM II	(218)	TWENTY-FOUR DISTINCT VOWEL SOUNDS; BUT YOUR	HUNDRED	AND THIRTY BEAT ME. I CANT HEAR A BIT OF DIFFERENCE
MILL I	(162)	FORGIVE ALASTAIR FOR LETTING ME DOWN BY FOUR	HUNDRED	AND THIRTY POUNDS. /ALASTAIR/ SIXTEEN AND
MILL I	(161)	FIFTY THOUSAND POUNDS TO THE GOOD I WAS FOUR	HUNDRED	AND THIRTY POUNDS TO THE BAD. INSTEAD OF BRINGING ME
MILL I	(160)	AND RUN AWAY WHEN I INTERVENED. I WAS DOWN FOUR	HUNDRED	AND THIRTY POUNDS SIXTEEN AND SEVENPENCE BY THE
SIM II	(55)	POSTSCRIPT TO SAY THAT AS HE HAS BEEN MARRIED TWO	HUNDRED	AND THIRTYFOUR TIMES, AND COULD NOT HAVE LIVED ON
KING I	(187)	NINETY DAYS. AND IN THE VERY NEXT VERSE THIRTEEN	HUNDRED	AND THIRTYFIVE DAYS. FIVE MONTHS DIFFERENCE! AND
2TRU I	(28)	BACK INTO THE GLASS WITH A GASPING SCREAM). A	HUNDRED	AND THREE! IT'S ALL OVER. (IT COLLAPSES). THE DOOR
KING I	(176)	POSSIBLY BE UNFAITHFUL TO YOU IS TEN THOUSAND TWO	HUNDRED	AND TWENTY PLUS SEVEN FOR LEAP YEARS. YET YOU ALLEGE
JOAN EPILOG	(164)	VATICANA, THE SIXTEENTH DAY OF MAY, NINETEEN	HUNDRED	AND TWENTY. /DUNOIS/ (RAISING JOAN) HALF AN HOUR TO
MTH3	(126)	TO GROW UP. I BEGAN MY SERIOUS LIFE WHEN I WAS A	HUNDRED	AND TWENTY. ASIATICS CANNOT CONTROL ME: I AM NOT A
MTH2	(83)	TWENTY-FIVE-- THIRTY-TWO-- EIGHTEEN-- EIGHTEEN	HUNDRED	AND TWENTY-FIVE OUNCES A YEAR: JUST TWO OUNCES OVER
MILL IV	(206)	REMEMBER: MRS SOMEBODY OF CLAPHAM PARK, ONE	HUNDRED	AND TWENTYTWO THOUSAND POUNDS. SHE HAD NEVER DONE
VWOO 2	(126)	LONG: EIGHTY'S NO AGE HERE. GRANDFATHER WILL BE A	HUNDRED	AND TWO IN AUGUST. THATS BECAUSE HE'S NEVER HAD TO
GENV III	(65)	ONE OF THEM. THEY SETTLED WITH HER FOR THREE	HUNDRED	APIECE. BEGONIA MUST HAVE NETTED AT LEAST FOUR
METH PREFACE	(R89)	WHEN I WAS IN MY PRIME. IT IS MY HOPE THAT A	HUNDRED	APTER AND MORE ELEGANT PARABLES BY YOUNGER HANDS
CLEO I	(109)	TUSKS, AND LITTLE TAILS, AND SEVEN ARMS WITH A	HUNDRED	ARROWS IN EACH; AND THEY LIVE ON HUMAN FLESH.
ROCK I	(226)	THERE, PERHAPS. " WHO SAYS THAT WE NEED A	HUNDRED	BATTLESHIPS, GENTLEMEN? CHRISTIAN BROTHERHOOD IS A
GETT	(328)	ROSY LIKE YOUR OWN, NOW SCARRED AND RIVEN BY A	HUNDRED	BURNT-OUT FIRES? /HOTCHKISS/ (WILDLY) SLATE FIRES.
MTH5	(258)	TO SAY A THING THAT STILL LIVES AFTER THREE	HUNDRED	CENTURIES. I TOO WILL LEAVE WOMEN AND STUDY
MILL I	(158)	IN. WE LODGED THE MONEY AND GOT A BOOK OF A	HUNDRED	CHEQUES. WE TOOK A THEATRE. WE ENGAGED A FIRST RATE
GENV III	(85)	NO MIND AT ALL. THE JUDGE CAN HAVE HIS PICK OF A	HUNDRED	CLEVER WOMEN IN GENEVA; BUT WHAT HE NEEDS TO GIVE
METH PREFACE	(R30)	HAULAGE. HE KNEW THAT THERE ARE NEARLY TWO	HUNDRED	DIFFERENT SORTS OF DOGS, ALL CAPABLE OF BREEDING
PHIL II	(113)	MY THEORY. ANOTHER SACRIFICES 36 POUNDS-- THREE	HUNDRED	DOGS AT THREE FRANCS APIECE-- TO UPSET THE MONKEY
SUPR III	(104)	BEAST. ONE SPLENDID BODY IS WORTH THE BRAINS OF A	HUNDRED	DYSPEPTIC, FLATULENT PHILOSOPHERS. /DON JUAN/ YOU
BUOY II	(24)	(HE BENDS HIS NECK) IS HOOCHLIPOOCHLI. HE HAS A	HUNDRED	EARTHLY BRIDES; AND SHE WHO DWELLS WITHIN IS ONE OF
BUOY II	(26)	THE WOMAN HERE IS ONE OF HOOCHLIPOOCHLI'S MANY	HUNDRED	EARTHLY WIVES. YOU WERE HUMBUGGING ME. /THE NATIVE/
CLEO III	(153)	GOBLETS OF THE THINNEST IBERIAN CRYSTAL, AND A	HUNDRED	EGGS OF THE SACRED BLUE PIGEON. ON YOUR HONOR, LET
ARMS III	(73)	OF SHEETS AND BLANKETS, WITH TWO THOUSAND FOUR	HUNDRED	EIDER-DOWN QUILTS. I HAVE TEN THOUSAND KNIVES AND
JOAN 6	(141)	YOU REALIZE IT AT LAST. /LADVENU/ THERE ARE EIGHT	HUNDRED	ENGLISH SOLDIERS WAITING TO TAKE YOU TO THE
ROCK PREFACE	(183)	DOING SO; AND YOUR POLICE CAN SUPPLY YOU WITH A	HUNDRED	FACTS TO SUPPORT THE REASONS. IF IT IS YOUR WILL TO
MIS.	(161)	PUT YOU IN A WHEELBARROW AND RUN YOU ALONG, TWO	HUNDRED	FEET UP. /TARLETON/ (SHUDDERING) UGH! WELL, I'D DO
MTH5	(252)	A DOZEN LEGS: I WORKED WITH TWENTY HANDS AND A	HUNDRED	FINGERS: I LOOKED TO THE FOUR QUARTERS OF THE
SUPR I	(12)	FOR MY INFLUENCE. HE LEAVES YOU TWO THOUSAND FIVE	HUNDRED	FOR YOUR TROUBLE. HE LEAVES TAVY A DOWRY FOR HIS
MILL IV	(195)	/ADRIAN/ MY BROTHER GOT TWO THOUSAND FIVE	HUNDRED	FROM THE RAILWAY COMPANY WHEN AN ELECTRIC TRUCK
GETT	(318)	SAYING THAT SLATTOX IS ENTIRELY UNFIT TO HAVE TWO	HUNDRED	GIRLS IN HIS POWER AS ABSOLUTE SLAVES, THEN I SHALL
DOCT PREFACE	(3)	AND FINE HIM ANYTHING FROM SIXPENCE TO SEVERAL	HUNDRED	GUINEAS IF HE DECIDES IN OUR FAVOR. I CANNOT KNOCK
DOCT I	(93)	HE'S MADE QUITE THE FASHION. PEOPLE PAY HIM FIVE	HUNDRED	GUINEAS TO CUT IT OUT. THEY MIGHT AS WELL GET THEIR
DOCT I	(93)	HIS BROTHER-IN-LAW EXTIRPATED TONSILS FOR TWO	HUNDRED	GUINEAS UNTIL HE TOOK UP WOMEN'S CASES AT DOUBLE THE
KING I	(221)	MY TELESCOPE IT WILL GIVE YOU YOUR CHOICE OF A	HUNDRED	HEAVENS. /MRS BASHAM/ MR KNELLER: YOUR DINNER WILL
BULL PREFACE	(12)	WOULD NOT HAVE TOLERATED, THERE ARE, INDEED, A	HUNDRED	HORSES ON WHICH I COULD RIDE OFF IF I WISHED TO
ARMS III	(72)	TWENTY, NOBLE SWITZER. /BLUNTSCHLI/ I HAVE TWO	HUNDRED	HORSES. (THEY ARE AMAZED). HOW MANY CARRIAGES?
ARMS III	(73)	ALSO. /PETKOFF/ OH, I SHALL BE ONLY TOO GLAD. TWO	HUNDRED	HORSES! WHEW! /SERGIUS/ WHAT SAYS THE LADY?
MIS.	(195)	/PERCIVAL/ WE MIGHT DO WITH ANOTHER FIFTEEN	HUNDRED	IF MY FATHER WOULD CONTRIBUTE. BUT I SHOULD LIKE
MIS.	(123)	INSIDE AND HOW SHE EXPECTED TO LIVE TO BE OVER A	HUNDRED	IF SHE TOOK IT REGULARLY, AND ME LISTENING TO HER,
MILL IV	(194)	TOO MUCH. RIDICULOUS. A JURY MIGHT GIVE FIVE	HUNDRED	IF THERE WAS A CLEAR DISABLEMENT FROM EARNING, OR IF
MIS.	(135)	FOR HIS USUAL FIVE POUNDS; AND JOHN GAVE HIM A	HUNDRED	IN HIS BIG WAY, JUST LIKE A KING. /LORD SUMMERHAYS/
BUOY II	(25)	A HUNDRED YEARS BEHINDHAND IN SCIENCE AND SEVEN	HUNDRED	IN HISTORY YOU CANNOT HOPE FOR A DEGREE THERE. /THE
APPL PREFACE	(179)	ARE FORTY MILLIONS OF YOU AND HARDLY ROOM FOR SIX	HUNDRED	IN THE BASKET, THE BALLOON GOES UP AGAIN WITH MUCH
FABL VI	(131)	KNOW TOO MUCH. WE KNOW HOW TO MAKE CYCLOTRONS AND	HUNDRED	INCH TELESCOPES. WE HAVE HARNESSED ATOMIC ENERGY. HE
2TRU I	(28)	TO SEE INSTEAD OF SHAKING IT DOWN. IF IT'S OVER A	HUNDRED	I'M DONE FOR: I DARENT LOOK. OH, CAN IT BE THAT I'M
BARB III	(333)	UP TO FIVE THOUSAND A YEAR. THE TWO THOUSAND FIVE	HUNDRED	IS ONLY HALF PAY IN CASE I SHOULD TURN OUT A
MILL IV	(194)	IT'S NO USE, SAGAMORE. TWO THOUSAND FIVE	HUNDRED	. AND COSTS. NOT A PENNY LESS. /SAGAMORE/ TOO MUCH.
MILL IV	(195)	AND SHE SHALL PAY FOR THEM. TWO THOUSAND FIVE	HUNDRED	. AND MEDICAL EXPENSES. AND COSTS. /SAGAMORE/ AND
JOAN 5	(117)	WHEN SHE HAS ONLY TEN MEN TO DO THE WORK OF A	HUNDRED	. AND THEN SHE WILL FIND THAT GOD IS ON THE SIDE OF
GENV II	(50)	I HAD TEN FRANCS ON HIM; AND I HAVE WON A	HUNDRED	. HAD YOU ANYTHING ON? /THE SECRETARY/ (STILL MORE
WIDO II	(34)	/TRENCH/ WE MUST DO THE BEST WE CAN WITH SEVEN	HUNDRED	. I THINK WE OUGHT TO BE SELF-SUPPORTING. /BLANCHE/
BULL PREFACE	(18)	APPARENTLY, THAN THE ENGLISH CLIMATE WILL IN TWO	HUNDRED	. IT IS REINFORCED BY AN ARTIFICIAL ECONOMIC CLIMATE
KING I	(208)	HAVE BRIBED HIM TO INSULT ME. IT MAKES ME LOOK A	HUNDRED	. /CHARLES/ NONSENSE, DEAR. IT IS YOU TO THE LIFE.
MILL IV	(200)	NOSE. /SAGAMORE/ BUT HE WANTS TWO THOUSAND FIVE	HUNDRED	. /EPIFANIA/ (RISING STUPEFIED) TWO THOU-- (SHE
DOCT III	(135)	HAVE YOUR BIT TOO: I'LL GIVE YOU A CHEQUE FOR TWO	HUNDRED	. /RIDGEON/ WHY NOT CASH THE CHEQUE AT ONCE WITHOUT
MILL I	(162)	THE ELEPHANT GO FOR THIRTY POUNDS? HE COST TWO	HUNDRED	. /SAGAMORE/ DO NOT LET US WANDER FROM THE POINT.
MTH3	(108)	A MILLION YEARS: IF YOU HAVE ALREADY LIVED TWO	HUNDRED	. THERE IS NO QUESTION OF THREE HUNDRED YEARS. YOU
WIDO III	(62)	AND FIFTY POUNDS A YEAR FOR IT INSTEAD OF SEVEN	HUNDRED	. TRENCH, COMPLETELY OUT WITTED, STARES AT THEM IN
APPL PREFACE	(191)	THE PROSPERITY OF DIVES COSTS THE PRIVATION OF A	HUNDRED	LAZARUSES. THE TITLE BREAKAGES, LIMITED, WAS
GENV I	(38)	REVOLUTION. THERE MUST BE STILL AT LEAST FIFTEEN	HUNDRED	LEFT. /SHE/ BUT IS IT A MEMBER OF THE LEAGUE? /THE
METH PREFACE	(R18)	SORTS OF THINGS: PROVIDING THE CENTIPEDE WITH A	HUNDRED	LEGS, AND RIDDING THE FISH OF ANY LEGS AT ALL;
PYGM V	(278)	(SHE RESUMES HER STITCHING). AND THERE WERE A	HUNDRED	LITTLE THINGS YOU NEVER NOTICED, BECAUSE THEY CAME
JOAN 6	(142)	THAT YOU INTEND TO BETRAY HIM. THERE ARE EIGHT	HUNDRED	MEN AT THE GATE WHO WILL SEE THAT THIS ABOMINABLE
APPL PREFACE	(181)	PLAY THAN TO MAKE A GOOD LAW. AND THERE ARE NOT A	HUNDRED	MEN IN THE WORLD WHO CAN WRITE A PLAY GOOD ENOUGH TO
JOAN 6	(132)	ON THAT SCORE, MY LORD. THE NOBLE EARL HAS EIGHT	HUNDRED	MEN-AT-ARMS AT THE GATES. SHE WILL NOT SLIP THROUGH
MTH3	(100)	TO YOU, AND TO KNOW ALL THE TIME THAT YOU ARE TWO	HUNDRED	MILES AWAY, AND THAT I CANT TOUCH YOU? /THE
HART III	(146)	SEEN FOR MILES. /HECTOR/ IT SHALL BE SEEN FOR A	HUNDRED	MILES (HE DASHES INTO THE HOUSE). /NURSE GUINNESS/
FABL IV	(116)	IN BOOKS THAN I AM. HE WILL NEED PAPER FOR TWO	HUNDRED	MILLION COPIES. GOODBYE. HE TAKES OFF HIS
JOAN PREFACE	(47)	ASTRONOMERS WHO TELL US THAT THE SUN IS NEARLY A	HUNDRED	MILLION MILES AWAY AND THAT BETELGEUSE IS TEN TIMES
GENV IV	(120)	MONTH. /COMMISSAR/ THAT IS NOT MANY OUT OF TWO	HUNDRED	MILLION PEOPLE, GENERAL. THINK OF ALL THE RASCALS
MILL IV	(195)	FIVE HUNDRED POUNDS AND NOT TWO THOUSAND FIVE	HUNDRED	MILLIONS? /ADRIAN/ MY BROTHER GOT TWO THOUSAND FIVE
MILL I	(139)	FIFTY MILLIONS. HE HAD PROMISED TO LEAVE ME TWO	HUNDRED	MILLIONS. I WAS LEFT WITH A BEGGARLY THIRTY. IT
PRES	(142)	BY GERMANY AND FORCED TO PAY AN INDEMNITY OF FIVE	HUNDRED	MILLIONS. /BALSQUITH/ BUT YOU SAID THAT IF YOU GOT
MILL II	(167)	OF? ABOUT A FORTNIGHT. MY FATHER, WHEN HE HAD A	HUNDRED	MILLIONS, TRAVELLED THIRD CLASS AND NEVER SPENT MORE
DEST	(158)	WITH THE FASTEST HORSE IN THE CAMP. YOU ARRIVE A	HUNDRED	MINUTES LATE, ON FOOT. WHERE IS YOUR HORSE? /THE
KING I	(164)	MILLION SIX HUNDRED AND FOURTEEN THOUSAND, FOUR	HUNDRED	MINUTES. SEVEN HUNDRED AND FIFTYSIX MILLION EIGHT
KING I	(169)	CANNOT BELIEVE IT. THE PHILOSOPHER SEES A	HUNDRED	MIRACLES A DAY WHERE THE IGNORANT AND THOUGHTLESS
PHIL II	(113)	FRANCE! ONE FRENCHMAN EXPERIMENTS ON TWO	HUNDRED	MONKEYS TO DISPROVE MY THEORY. ANOTHER SACRIFICES 36
FANY PROLOG	(262)	ALL YOU WANT IS A FEW SAMPLE OPINIONS. OUT OF A	HUNDRED	NOTICES YOU WONT FIND MORE THAN FOUR AT THE OUTSIDE
UNPL PREFACE	(R24)	THERE ARE FIFTY WAYS OF SAYING YES, AND FIVE	HUNDRED	OF SAYING NO, BUT ONLY ONE WAY OF WRITING THEM DOWN.
2TRU II	(57)	CREDIT? /MEEK/ SORRY, COUNTESS: I HAVE ONLY TWO	HUNDRED	ON ME. YOU SHALL HAVE THE OTHER HUNDRED TOMORROW. (
MTH3	(121)	REGRET NOW IS THAT I SHALL DIE WHEN I AM THREE	HUNDRED	OR THEREABOUTS. THERE WAS ONLY ONE THING THAT MADE
MIS. PREFACE	(43)	SQUANDER AND RUIN GREAT ESTATES, NOR TOLERATE A	HUNDRED	OTHER ABSURD LIBERTIES THAT WE ALLOW TODAY BECAUSE
GETT PREFACE	(193)	THEY WERE VERY LIKE YOU AND ME. I COULD FILL A	HUNDRED	PAGES WITH THE TALE OF OUR IMBECILITIES AND STILL
ARMS III	(73)	NO. /BLUNTSCHLI/ I HAVE. I HAVE NINE THOUSAND SIX	HUNDRED	PAIRS OF SHEETS AND BLANKETS, WITH TWO THOUSAND FOUR
MTH4 I	(156)	AND KISSING THE GROUND MIGHT HAVE HAPPENED TO A	HUNDRED	PEOPLE. IT COULDNT HAVE HAPPENED TO A HUNDRED
VWOO 3	(133)	/A/ THAT MUST HAVE BEEN BETWEEN FOUR AND FIVE	HUNDRED	PER CENT PER ANNUM. SHYLOCK WOULD HAVE BLUSHED. /Z/
VWOO 1	(119)	WONT, ISNT IT? /A/ THERE ARE THREE OR FOUR	HUNDRED	PERSONS ON THIS SHIP. CANNOT YOU FIND ONE OF THEM
MILL II	(177)	THAT YOU NEVER DO. /EPIFANIA/ HOW MUCH IS TWO	HUNDRED	PIASTRES? /THE DOCTOR/ AT THE RATE OF EXCHANGE
MILL II	(176)	AND I FELT TEMPTED, I WOULD HAND THE WOMAN TWO	HUNDRED	PIASTRES AND TELL HER THAT UNLESS SHE WOULD GO OUT
LION PREFACE	(78)	NATURE BREAKS THROUGH THE PAULINE THEOLOGY AT A	HUNDRED	POINTS, HIS THEOLOGICAL ALLEGORY, THE HOLY WAR, WITH
MIS.	(173)	EVEN THAT MUCH GOOD. /TARLETON/ IF I GAVE YOU A	HUNDRED	POUND NOTE NOW TO GO AND HAVE A GOOD SPREE WITH, I
LION PREFACE	(59)	TO EVEN TO THE DEATH, WE MAY GIVE A CARPENTER A	HUNDRED	POUNDS A YEAR AND A JUDGE FIVE THOUSAND; BUT THE
DOCT PREFACE	(16)	INVALID MEANS ANYTHING FROM FIFTY TO FIVE	HUNDRED	POUNDS A YEAR FOR THE DOCTOR, OPERATIONS ENABLE A
MILL IV	(207)	HAVE A CIVIL LIST PENSION. SHE RECEIVED IT: A	HUNDRED	POUNDS A YEAR. I WENT TO THE GREAT METALLURGICAL
GENV PREFACE	(25)	KNOW AND RANKING THEM AS PASSING RICH ON FOUR	HUNDRED	POUNDS A YEAR WHEN THEY ARE LUCKY ENOUGH TO GET PAID
KING I	(194)	IN MY PALACE AT WHITEHALL WITH A PENSION OF FOUR	HUNDRED	POUNDS A YEAR. /JAMES/ WHAT! ! ! /CHARLES/ AND I,
MILL IV	(206)	SCIENCE AND EVERYTHING ABOUT MONEY. HE LEFT FOUR	HUNDRED	POUNDS AND A WIDOW: THE GOOD WOMAN WHO HAD BEEN A
MILL IV	(195)	HONOR AND SELF-RESPECT WORTH TWO THOUSAND FIVE	HUNDRED	POUNDS AND NOT TWO THOUSAND FIVE HUNDRED MILLIONS..
MILL I	(159)	HOLIDAY ALL THE BETTER. SAY THE CHEQUE IS FOR A	HUNDRED	POUNDS AND YOU HAVE NOT A PENNY AT THE BANK. YOU
BULL III	(130)	THAT WOULD NOT HAVE BEEN TEMPTED AS HARD BY A	HUNDRED	POUNDS AS YOUD BE BY FIVE SHILLINGS? NICK WAS TOO

MILL I (159)	OR A HOTEL MANAGER TO CASH ANOTHER CHEQUE FOR ONE	HUNDRED	POUNDS FOR YOU. THAT PROVIDES FOR THE PREVIOUS
WIDO II (31)	SIR; AND HE SHEWS HIS SENSE IN IT, TOO. EVERY FEW	HUNDRED	POUNDS HE COULD SCRAPE TOGETHER HE BOUGHT OLD HOUSES
2TRU PREFACE(5)	SOBER, WHEREAS THE PLUTOCRAT WHO HAS SPENT A	HUNDRED	POUNDS IN A DAY IN THE SEARCH FOR PLEASURE IS NOT
HART I (62)	WAS EMBROIDERED ON HIS BABYCLOTHES. AND FIVE	HUNDRED	POUNDS IN GOLD. /MRS HUSHABYE/ (LOOKING HARD AT
MILL I (158)	THOUSAND IN SIX MONTHS, AND THAT I HAD ONLY A	HUNDRED	POUNDS IN THE WORLD. HE JUMPED UP AND SAID " WHY,
MILL I (156)	ADVENTURER. YOU DONT KNOW HOW A MAN TO WHOM A	HUNDRED	POUNDS IS A CONSIDERABLE SUM FEELS IN THE ARMS OF A
MILL I (158)	THING, I TELL YOU. WHAT I DID WAS THIS. I HAD A	HUNDRED	POUNDS LEFT AFTER THE OPERA STUNT. I MET AN
BARB PREFACE(219)	DRURY LANE PANTOMIME; BUT HE ALWAYS PREFERS FIVE	HUNDRED	POUNDS TO FIVE HUNDRED SHILLINGS. NOW TO DEPLORE
2TRU II (57)	OF CREDIT CASHED FOR ME? I'D BETTER HAVE THREE	HUNDRED	POUNDS TO GO ON WITH. /MEEK/ (QUITE AT HIS EASE:
VWOO 1 (120)	RIGHT. I WAS RUDE. BUT A GOOD LAUGH IS WORTH A	HUNDRED	POUNDS TO ME. I FEEL A DIFFERENT MAN. FORGIVE ME.
DEVL I (21)	SIR, WRONG PHRASEOLOGY. " I GIVE AND BEQUEATH A	HUNDRED	POUNDS TO MY YOUNGER SON CHRISTOPHER DUDGEON, FIFTY
MILL I (159)	MANAGER TO CASH ANOTHER CHEQUE FOR YOU FOR TWO	HUNDRED	POUNDS, AND SO YOU GO SPENDING AND KITING FROM
BARB II (301)	YOU COULD DO A GREAT DEAL OF GOOD WITH A	HUNDRED	POUNDS. IF YOU WILL SET THIS GENTLEMAN'S MIND AT
PYGM IV (265)	OF THE JEWELLERY, WILL MAKE A BIG HOLE IN TWO	HUNDRED	POUNDS. WHY, SIX MONTHS AGO YOU WOULD HAVE THOUGHT
HART I (81)	PATENT LIFEBOAT I INVENTED? /MRS HUSHABYE/ FIVE	HUNDRED	POUNDS; AND I HAVE MADE IT LAST SINCE EASTER!
CAPT II (264)	(DIPLOMATICALLY) HE'S OFFERED A PRESENT OF FIVE	HUNDRED	QUID IF HE GETS SAFE BACK TO MOGADOR, GOVERNOR.
FABL PREFACE(76)	THAN PARADING IN OUR BEST CLOTHES EVERY SUNDAY. A	HUNDRED	RELIGIONS AND ONLY ONE SAUCE. AS IT IS, CHRISTIANITY
MTH4 I (163)	DO NOT KNOW HOW OLD YOU ARE: YOU LOOK ABOUT FIVE	HUNDRED	-- /THE ELDERLY GENTLEMAN/ FIVE HUNDRED! REALLY,
ARMS III (73)	THE SAME QUANTITY OF DESSERT SPOONS. I HAVE THREE	HUNDRED	SERVANTS. I HAVE SIX PALATIAL ESTABLISHMENTS,
BARB PREFACE(219)	BUT HE ALWAYS PREFERS FIVE HUNDRED POUNDS TO FIVE	HUNDRED	SHILLINGS. NOW TO DEPLORE THIS PREFERENCE AS SORDID,
MRS III (221)	THE STORES AND ORDER A BARREL OF WHISKY AND A FEW	HUNDRED	SIPHONS. /REV. S./ I DID NOT OBSERVE THAT SIR GEORGE
BARB III (327)	FIRST TRIAL IT HAS WIPED OUT A FORT WITH THREE	HUNDRED	SOLDIERS IN IT. /CUSINS/ (FROM THE PLATFORM) DUMMY
CLEO II (122)	TREASURY. /CAESAR/ (ENCOURAGINGLY) ONLY SIXTEEN	HUNDRED	TALENTS, POTHINUS. WHY COUNT IT IN SESTERCES? A
MIS. PREFACE(78)	INTENDING IT; AND IN NINETY-NINE CASES OUT OF A	HUNDRED	THE REASON IS THAT THEY DO NOT CONCEIVE THEIR ELDERS
MTH4 I (156)	A HUNDRED PEOPLE. IT COULDNT HAVE HAPPENED TO A	HUNDRED	THOUSAND: YOU KNOW THAT AS WELL AS I DO. AND WHAT A
MILL I (139)	YOU FORGET THE DEATH DUTIES. I HAVE BARELY SEVEN	HUNDRED	THOUSAND A YEAR. DO YOU KNOW WHAT THAT MEANS TO A
HART I (67)	A MAN, NOT LIKE A MOVY. YOU MEAN THAT YOU MAKE A	HUNDRED	THOUSAND A YEAR. /MANGAN/ I DONT BOAST. BUT WHEN I
HART I (68)	BROTHER. /CAPTAIN SHOTOVER/ THEN YOU ALSO MAKE A	HUNDRED	THOUSAND A YEAR, HEY? /MANGAN/ NO. I CANT SAY THAT.
HART I (67)	I DONT BOAST. BUT WHEN I MEET A MAN THAT MAKES A	HUNDRED	THOUSAND A YEAR, I TAKE OFF MY HAT TO THAT MAN, AND
UNPL PREFACE(R7)	BUT THAT OF AT LEAST SOME SEVENTY OR A	HUNDRED	THOUSAND CONTEMPORARY LONDON PLAYGOERS. TO FULFIL
CAPT II (252)	THE SULTAN OF MOROCCO MAY SEND SIDI'S HEAD WITH A	HUNDRED	THOUSAND DOLLARS BLOOD-MONEY TO THE COLONIAL OFFICE;
MILL I (160)	THE AMERICAN BOUGHT ALL THE RIGHTS BACK FOR FIVE	HUNDRED	THOUSAND DOLLARS, AND SOLD THEM TO AN AMERICAN
INCA PROLOG (234)	WHAT YOU PLEASE. A HOUSE THAT COSTS LESS THAN A	HUNDRED	THOUSAND DOLLARS A YEAR TO RUN IS INTOLERABLE TO ME.
APPL PREFACE(180)	FOR A PERSON WITH A HUNDRED A YEAR AND ONE WITH A	HUNDRED	THOUSAND IS IMPOSSIBLE. BUT NUMBER THREE: GOVERNMENT
KING I (175)	ALLOW A DAY-- OR SHALL I SAY A NIGHT? NOW ONE	HUNDRED	THOUSAND NIGHTS ARE ALMOST TWO HUNDRED AND
KING I (176)	PLUS SEVEN FOR LEAP YEARS. YET YOU ALLEGE ONE	HUNDRED	THOUSAND OCCASIONS, AND CLAIM TO HAVE LIVED FOR
FANY PROLOG (264)	LIKES A THING, YOU MAY TAKE YOUR OATH THERE ARE A	HUNDRED	THOUSAND PEOPLE IN LONDON THATLL LIKE IT IF THEY CAN
MIS. PREFACE(103)	OF THIRTEEN SHILLINGS A WEEK, " HERE IS ONE	HUNDRED	THOUSAND POUNDS: NOW YOU ARE WEALTHY." NOTHING CAN
ROCK II (241)	AT THAT. IT'S EASY ENOUGH TO GET A COUPLE OF	HUNDRED	THOUSAND POUNDS IF YOU ARE WILLING TO CALL IT A
FABL II (105)	/C.-IN-C./ THAT COCKNEY BLIGHTER? HE WANTED A	HUNDRED	THOUSAND POUNDS FOR IT, AND THE SCIENTIFIC
KING I (175)	UNFAITHFUL TO YOU A THOUSAND TIMES. /BARBARA/ A	HUNDRED	THOUSAND TIMES. /NEWTON/ FOR EACH UNFAITHFULNESS
KING I (185)	VERY VERY LARGE, MADAM. IT IS ONE MILLION THREE	HUNDRED	THOUSAND TIMES HEAVIER THAN THE EARTH. /LOUISE/ MY
MILL IV (209)	THREE: IT IS IRRESISTIBLE: IT IS A PULSE IN A	HUNDRED	THOUSAND. I LOVE IT: I CANNOT GIVE IT UP.
PYGM I (213)	80 POUNDS A YEAR, AND END IN PARK LANE WITH A	HUNDRED	THOUSAND. THEY WANT TO DROP KENTISH TOWN; BUT THEY
JOAN 2 (76)	DEAD. A DRUNKEN BLACKGUARD WHO HAS BEEN REBUKED A	HUNDRED	TIMES FOR SWEARING HAS FALLEN INTO A WELL, AND BEEN
3PLA PREFACE(R29)	OR OFTENER. NOT ONE OF MY CRITICS BUT HAS SEEN A	HUNDRED	TIMES IN HIS PAPER HOW SOME POLICEMAN OR FIREMAN OR
METH PREFACE(R49)	CLOTH BY CONVINCING YOU THAT IF YOU PUT IT DOWN A	HUNDRED	TIMES IT WILL JUMP UP A HUNDRED AND ONE TIMES; SO
ROCK II (244)	LETTERS UNTIL HE HAS AGREED TO PAY THEM FROM FIVE	HUNDRED	TO A THOUSAND A YEAR. HE CANT EVEN DIE WITHOUT
GENV III (82)	THE REST OF THE CIVILIZED WORLD IS FROM FIVE	HUNDRED	TO FIVE THOUSAND BEHIND IT. IN THE WEST THE VESTED
CLEO II (137)	WITH AN ARMY OUTNUMBERING YOUR LITTLE TROOP A	HUNDRED	TO ONE, IS IN POSSESSION OF ALEXANDRIA? /CAESAR/ (
2TRU II (57)	ONLY TWO HUNDRED ON ME. YOU SHALL HAVE THE OTHER	HUNDRED	TOMORROW. (HE HANDS HER
CYMB V (139)	BUT THIRTY SCORE AS FROM A CATAPULT FOUR	HUNDRED	TONS OF HORSE AND MAN IN ONE ENORMOUS SHOCK HURLED
JITT PREFACE(4)	I HAVE ONLY TO LIFT UP MY FINGER TO ATTRACT A	HUNDRED	TRANSLATORS. WHEN TREBITSCH VOLUNTEERED FOR THE JOB,
BARB III (347)	A COPY OF PLATO'S REPUBLIC, BUT A REVOLVER AND A	HUNDRED	UNDERSHAFT CARTRIDGES. THE BLOOD OF EVERY TURK HE
PLES PREFACE(R8)	THERE IS ONLY ONE RELIGION, THOUGH THERE ARE A	HUNDRED	VERSIONS OF IT. WE ALL HAD THE SAME THING TO SAY;
MILL I (159)	YOU WE HAD A CHEQUE BOOK? /ADRIAN/ BUT WHEN THE	HUNDRED	WAS GONE THE CHEQUES MUST HAVE BEEN DISHONORED.
ROCK PREFACE(162)	OF THIS SORT WOULD STILL HAVE LEFT UNSPECIFIED A	HUNDRED	WAYS IN WHICH WRECKERS OF COMMUNISM COULD HAVE
MTH2 (42)	YES: THEY ARE FRANKER, WHOLESOMER, BETTER IN A	HUNDRED	WAYS. AND YET I SQUIRM AT THEM. I CANNOT GET IT OUT
VWOO 1 (116)	CALL IT WHAT YOU LIKE, DEAR LADY; BUT I HAVE FIVE	HUNDRED	WORDS TO WRITE BEFORE LUNCH; AND I CANNOT DO THAT IF
ARMS II (31)	US INTO GIVING HIM FIFTY ABLEBODIED MEN FOR TWO	HUNDRED	WORN OUT CHARGERS. THEY WERENT EVEN EATABLE!
MTH4 I (171)	MEN LIVING SEVENTY YEARS AND THOSE LIVING THREE	HUNDRED	WOULD BE ALL THE GREATER; FOR TO A SHORTLIVER
JITT PREFACE(4)	WHEN TREBITSCH VOLUNTEERED FOR THE JOB, THE	HUNDRED	WOULD HAVE FLED FROM MY INVITATION AS ONE MAN. IT IS
FANY I (277)	/DORA/ A SPRINTER. HE SAID HE WAS THE FASTEST	HUNDRED	YARDS RUNNER IN ENGLAND. WE WERE ALL IN THE OLD
BASH II,1, (103)	BOB MELLISH TUCKED BENEATH HIS OXTER, SPRINTING A	HUNDRED	YARDS TO SHOW THE CROWD THE PERFECT PINK OF HIS
2TRU II (78)	FIELDING/ (INVISIBLE) FORTY HORSE. NINE	HUNDRED	YARDS, ABOUT, I MAKE IT. /MEEK/ RIFLES AT THE READY.
FANY I (278)	" DARLING, IF YOU CAN GET HOLY JOE TO SPRINT A	HUNDRED	YARDS, I'LL STAND YOU THAT SQUIFFER WITH THE GOLD
GENV PREFACE(26)	HEADMEN. IN MY METHUSELAH CYCLE I PUT IT AT THREE	HUNDRED	YEARS: A CENTURY OF CHILDHOOD AND ADOLESCENCE, A
MTH2 (45)	WELL, WHAT DO YOU THINK OF LIVING FOR SEVERAL	HUNDRED	YEARS? ARE YOU GOING TO HAVE A TRY FOR IT? /THE
MTH2 (87)	/HASLAM/ ABOUT OUR BEING ABLE TO LIVE THREE	HUNDRED	YEARS? FRANKLY NO, /CONRAD/ (TO SAVVY) NOR YOU, I
MTH2 (45)	THAT, SIR, IF HE THOUGHT IT MIGHT BE FOR SEVERAL	HUNDRED	YEARS? /CONRAD/ THATS TRUE. AND WHAT ABOUT
MTH4 III (195)	REALLY GOING TO SEE A WOMAN WHO HAS LIVED THREE	HUNDRED	YEARS? /ZOO/ STUFF! YOUD DROP DEAD IF A TERTIARY
MTH4 II (191)	HOW DO YOU MAKE THAT OUT? /ZOZIM/ WHAT IS THREE	HUNDRED	YEARS? SHORT ENOUGH, IF YOU ASK ME. WHY, IN THE OLD
MILL II (172)	MY ANCESTORS WERE MONEYLENDERS TO ALL EUROPE FIVE	HUNDRED	YEARS AGO: WE ARE NOW BANKERS TO ALL THE WORLD. /THE
FANY PROLOG (261)	THE SUCCESS MADE BY THE GENIUS OF GRIMALDI A	HUNDRED	YEARS AGO? MY DAUGHTER DOES NOT KNOW OF THE
POSN PREFACE(385)	MAY TURN OUT TO BE THE SALVATION OF THE RACE. A	HUNDRED	YEARS AGO NOBODY FORESAW THAT TOM PAINE'S CENTENARY
2TRU PREFACE(6)	PAY FOR THE NECESSITIES OF A CULTIVATED LIFE. A	HUNDRED	YEARS AGO SAMUEL WARREN WROTE A FAMOUS NOVEL ABOUT A
BUOY 1 (14)	CAN THEY DO EXCEPT STARVE OR COMMIT SUICIDE? A	HUNDRED	YEARS AGO THERE WERE KINGS TO SPUNGE ON. NOWADAYS
APPL PREFACE(188)	FROM THE EDITORIAL WASTE PAPER BASKETS OF A	HUNDRED	YEARS AGO. A THIRD ADDRESS, MORE UP-TO-DATE AND MUCH
LION PREFACE(57)	SILLY FOR DISCUSSION. HAMLET DISPOSED OF IT THREE	HUNDRED	YEARS AGO. " USE EVERY MAN AFTER HIS DESERTS, AND
JOAN PREFACE(34)	DEATH AT ITS WORST. JOAN WAS BURNT MORE THAN FIVE	HUNDRED	YEARS AGO. MORE THAN THREE HUNDRED YEARS LATER: THAT
MTH5 (219)	FANCY: THAT OLD GIRL HAS BEEN GOING FOR SEVEN	HUNDRED	YEARS AND HASNT HAD HER FATAL ACCIDENT YET; AND SHE
LADY (249)	PURSE. I TELL THEE, MASTER WILL, IT WILL BE THREE	HUNDRED	YEARS AND MORE BEFORE MY SUBJECTS LEARN THAT MAN
MTH2 (85)	ASK YOUR QUESTION. /LUBIN/ WHY DO YOU FIX THREE	HUNDRED	YEARS AS THE EXACT FIGURE? /FRANKLYN/ BECAUSE WE
MTH2 (82)	CITIZENS! OH! ARE THE CITIZENS TO LIVE THREE	HUNDRED	YEARS AS WELL AS THE STATESMEN? /CONRAD/ OF COURSE.
3PLA PREFACE(R33)	GIRONDIN, MIRRORED IN SHAKESPEAR'S ART TWO	HUNDRED	YEARS BEFORE THE REAL THING CAME TO MATURITY AND
METH PREFACE(R82)	IN; BUT HE COULD PAINT THE SUPERMAN THREE	HUNDRED	YEARS BEFORE NIETZSCHE WROTE ALSO SPRACH ZARATHUSTRA
JOAN PREFACE(34)	THREE HUNDRED YEARS LATER: THAT IS, ONLY ABOUT A	HUNDRED	YEARS BEFORE I WAS BORN, A WOMAN WAS BURNT ON
BUOY II (25)	KNOWLEDGE. /HE/ NOT AT OXFORD. UNLESS YOU ARE A	HUNDRED	YEARS BEHINDHAND IN SCIENCE AND SEVEN HUNDRED IN
GETT PREFACE(193)	CURED BY RADIUM, AND THAT MEN CAN LIVE FOR TWO	HUNDRED	YEARS BY DRINKING SOUR MILK. EVEN THESE CREDULITIES
MTH4 I (171)	FACE IT. THEREFORE I SAY THAT WE WHO LIVE THREE	HUNDRED	YEARS CAN BE OF NO USE TO YOU WHO LIVE LESS THAN A
MTH4 II (189)	IT. OUR BISHOPS AND PRIESTS PREVENTED US FOR TWO	HUNDRED	YEARS FROM FOLLOWING SUIT; AND WE HAVE NEVER
MTH4 I (155)	TO THE END, WHEN IT CAME AT LAST? HARDLY TWO	HUNDRED	YEARS HAD ELAPSED WHEN THE CLAIMS OF NATIONALITY
MTH4 I (161)	IS AN OLD STORY: THE EXTENSION OF LIFE TO THREE	HUNDRED	YEARS HAS PROVIDED THE HUMAN RACE WITH CAPABLE
MTH3 (112)	OF HIS BELIEF THAT HE WAS GOING TO LIVE THREE	HUNDRED	YEARS HE BECAME A CHANGED MAN. HE BEGAN TO TELL
MTH3 (108)	THAT GOSPEL WAS THAT MEN MUST LIVE THREE	HUNDRED	YEARS IF CIVILIZATION IS TO BE SAVED. IT SHEWED THAT
PLES PREFACE(R15)	CRITICS, HAS BEEN IN OPERATION IN LONDON FOR TWO	HUNDRED	YEARS IN SUPPORT OF ITALIAN OPERA. RETURNING NOW TO
JOAN PREFACE(34)	MORE THAN FIVE HUNDRED YEARS AGO. MORE THAN THREE	HUNDRED	YEARS LATER: THAT IS, ONLY ABOUT A HUNDRED YEARS
JOAN PREFACE(32)	AT THE FIRST TRIAL WHEN IT CANONIZED JOAN FIVE	HUNDRED	YEARS LATER? THE CHURCH UNCOMPROMISED BY ITS
LION PREFACE(67)	IS, THERE WILL YOUR HEART BE ALSO." EIGHTEEN	HUNDRED	YEARS LATER WE FIND A VERY DIFFERENT PERSON FROM
POSN PREFACE(392)	IT MUST BE REMEMBERED THAT IT WAS NOT UNTIL A	HUNDRED	YEARS LATER, IN THE REACTION AGAINST THE PURITANS,
DEST SD(151)	TO MAKE IT DIFFICULT FOR THE ROMANTICISTS OF A	HUNDRED	YEARS LATER TO CREDIT THE HITHERTO UNRECORDED LITTLE
DEST SD(152)	UNSPEAKABLY RIDICULOUS IN THE EYE OF HISTORY A	HUNDRED	YEARS LATER, BUT MONSTROUS AND HORRIBLE TO THE
MTH2 (88)	IT MEANS THAT THE FIRST MAN TO LIVE THREE	HUNDRED	YEARS MAYNT HAVE THE SLIGHTEST NOTION THAT HE IS
ANNA (298)	TO ME ALONE. DO YOU HEAR? I ORDER YOU. FOR SEVEN	HUNDRED	YEARS NO MEMBER OF YOUR FAMILY HAS EVER DISOBEYED AN
MTH1 II (31)	IS DREARY, DREARY! AND THERE IS YET NEARLY SEVEN	HUNDRED	YEARS OF IT TO ENDURE. /CAIN/ POOR MOTHER! YOU SEE,
MTH3 (122)	ANIMALISM IN WHICH WE LIVE FOR THE FIRST	HUNDRED	YEARS OF OUR LIFE IS WORSE IN THIS MATTER OF SEX
MTH3 (123)	AND CHINAMEN, I ASK MYSELF WHETHER EVEN THREE	HUNDRED	YEARS OF THOUGHT AND EXPERIENCE CAN SAVE YOU FROM

MTH3	(113)	DO NOT MAKE VOWS UNTIL DEATH WHEN DEATH IS THREE	HUNDRED	YEARS OFF. THEY RELAPSE INTO UNEASY SILENCE. THE
MTH4 II	(176)	INTO HER MOUTH, NOT BY A GOD, BUT BY A MAN THREE	HUNDRED	YEARS OLD, WHO HAS HAD THE CAPACITY TO PROFIT BY HIS
FANY PROLOG	(257)	MAN OF FIFTY, DRESSED WITH STUDIED ELEGANCE A	HUNDRED	YEARS OUT OF DATE, ADVANCING CORDIALLY TO SHAKE
GENV PREFACE	(14)	BY ANNOUNCING A DOMESTIC POLICY WHICH WAS A	HUNDRED	YEARS OUT OF FASHION, AND PROMISED NOTHING TO A WAR
MTH2	(54)	I THINK IT WAS TO CELEBRATE THE CONCLUSION OF THE	HUNDRED	YEARS PEACE WITH AMERICA. /FRANKLYN/ (SHAKING
MTH3	(129)	AND SISTERS WILL MEET AS STRANGERS AFTER A	HUNDRED	YEARS SEPARATION: THE TIES OF BLOOD WILL LOSE THEIR
JOAN 6	(130)	MERCY OF THE CHURCH IN DEALING WITH IT. FOR TWO	HUNDRED	YEARS THE HOLY OFFICE HAS STRIVEN WITH THESE
MTH1 II	(34)	STARS IN THEIR LITTLE TIME? IT TOOK ENOCH TWO	HUNDRED	YEARS TO LEARN TO INTERPRET THE WILL OF THE VOICE.
MTH2	(75)	NEW ARE RIPE FOR THEM. THEY DESERT THEM NOW TWO	HUNDRED	YEARS TOO SOON. /SAVVY/ I BELIEVE THE OLD PEOPLE ARE
MTH2	(72)	EUROPE. WHAT THEY NEEDED WAS A COUPLE OF	HUNDRED	YEARS TRAINING AND EXPERIENCE: WHAT THEY HAD
MTH4 I	(154)	GENTLEMAN/ YES: THE FIRST MAN TO LIVE THREE	HUNDRED	YEARS WAS AN ENGLISHMAN. THE FIRST, THAT IS, SINCE
MTH2	(73)	I GRANT YOU THAT IF WE COULD LIVE THREE	HUNDRED	YEARS WE SHOULD ALL BE, PERHAPS WISER, CERTAINLY
MTH3	(125)	INTO THE HANDS OF THE COLORED PEOPLE. IN ANOTHER	HUNDRED	YEARS WE SHALL BE SIMPLY THEIR HOUSEHOLD PETS.
MTH3	(123)	INGRATITUDE TOO! YOU DRAW A PENSION FOR THREE	HUNDRED	YEARS WHEN WE OWE YOU ONLY SEVENTY-EIGHT; AND YOU
MTH2	(88)	A SORT OF WAY, THAT PEOPLE MIGHT LIVE FOR THREE	HUNDRED	YEARS. BUT WHEN YOU CAME DOWN TO TIN TACKS, AND SAID
MILL IV	(205)	OF THE WEEK I HAD MADE ENOUGH TO SUPPORT ME FOR A	HUNDRED	YEARS. I DID IT HONESTLY AND LEGITIMATELY. I
MTH2	(39)	THAT CHOKES ME OFF. I COULDNT STICK IT FOR NINE	HUNDRED	YEARS. I SHOULD CHUCK IT. YOU KNOW, SOMETIMES, WHEN
MTH4 II	(191)	US THE POSSIBILITY THAT ANY OF US MAY LIVE THREE	HUNDRED	YEARS. I SOLEMNLY CURSE THAT POSSIBILITY. TO YOU IT
MTH3	(127)	COLD BLOOD BECAUSE THEIR CHILDREN WILL LIVE THREE	HUNDRED	YEARS. IT MUSTNT BE ALLOWED. /CONFUCIUS/ YOU CANNOT
MTH3	(111)	QUITE THAT. MY EXPECTATION OF LIFE IS ONLY THREE	HUNDRED	YEARS. /BARNABAS/ YOU WILL LAST OUT MY TIME ANYHOW:
MTH2	(69)	TO MORTAL MEN WHOSE WHOLE LIFE DOES NOT LAST A	HUNDRED	YEARS. /BURGE/ WE WON THE WAR: DONT FORGET THAT.
MTH3	(112)	COMMITTED MYSELF TO A LIFETIME OF THREE	HUNDRED	YEARS. /BURGE-LUBIN/ BUT HOW DO YOU DO IT? IS IT
JITT I	(24)	WEAK NOR AFRAID NOW; AND I PROMISE YOU TO LIVE A	HUNDRED	YEARS. /JITTA/ ALL THE UNHAPPINESSES ARE FORGOTTEN:
MTH2	(68)	THE TERM OF HUMAN LIFE SHALL BE EXTENDED TO THREE	HUNDRED	YEARS. /LUBIN/ (SOFTLY) EH? /BURGE/ (EXPLOSIVELY)
MTH2	(85)	WAIT FOR THEM. FEW INVESTMENTS FLOURISH FOR THREE	HUNDRED	YEARS. /SAVVY/ AND WHAT ABOUT BEFORE YOUR DEATH?
MTH3	(109)	SECRET BY WHICH YOU COULD ATTAIN THE AGE OF THREE	HUNDRED	YEARS. /THE ARCHBISHOP/ NO. NOTHING OF THE KIND.
MTH2	(37)	MY MIND AT LAST ABOUT THE TIME. I MAKE IT THREE	HUNDRED	YEARS. /THE CLERICAL GENTLEMAN/ (SITTING UP
MTH3	(109)	SAYING THAT I WAS CERTAINLY GOING TO LIVE THREE	HUNDRED	YEARS. SHE WAS SIXTY-EIGHT WHEN SHE DIED; AND THE
MTH4 II	(191)	IT MAY BE A BLESSING, BECAUSE YOU DO LIVE THREE	HUNDRED	YEARS. TO US, WHO LIVE LESS THAN A HUNDRED, WHOSE
LION PREFACE	(100)	AND RELIGIOUS WARS OF THE LAST FIFTEEN	HUNDRED	YEARS. WHEN THE LATE EXPLORER SIR HENRY STANLEY TOLD
MTH3	(108)	LIVED TWO HUNDRED. THERE IS NO QUESTION OF THREE	HUNDRED	YEARS. YOU HAVE MADE A SLIP AT THE VERY BEGINNING OF
MTH5	(261)	UPON ME WHEN ONE MAN REPENTED AND LIVED THREE	HUNDRED	YEARS; AND I WAITED TO SEE WHAT WOULD COME OF THAT.
SHAK	(140)	NEVER. (HE RISES). YOUNGER YOU ARE BY FULL THREE	HUNDRED	YEARS, AND THEREFORE CARRY A HEAVIER PUNCH THAN
2TRU III	(87)	CITADEL OF MODERN CIVILIZATION FOR THREE	HUNDRED	YEARS, HAS CRUMBLED LIKE THE WALLS OF JERICHO BEFORE
MTH3	(109)	WONDER TOO. THAT IS THE EXPLANATION OF THE THREE	HUNDRED	YEARS, MR SECRETARY. /CONFUCIUS/ IT IS VERY
MTH2	(84)	TO KNOW WHAT THEY ARE DOING. THEY WILL LIVE THREE	HUNDRED	YEARS, NOT BECAUSE THEY WOULD LIKE TO, BUT BECAUSE
CAND III	(146)	SEVENTY-FIVE. /MARCHBANKS/ (TURNING TO HER) IN A	HUNDRED	YEARS, WE SHALL BE THE SAME AGE. BUT I HAVE A BETTER
MTH2	(85)	IT OCCURRED TO YOU, LUBIN, THAT IF YOU LIVE THREE	HUNDRED	YEARS, YOUR DAUGHTERS WILL HAVE TO WAIT A DEVILISH
MTH2	(80)	WE ADVOCATE THE EXTENSION OF HUMAN LIFE TO THREE	HUNDRED	YEARS! DUNREEN, AS LEADER OF THE OPPOSITE PARTY,
MTH3	(108)	DISCOVERY THAT I WAS DESTINED TO LIVE THREE	HUNDRED	YEARS! I-- /CONFUCIUS/ (INTERRUPTING HIM) PARDON
MTH2	(81)	MY BEING LEADER OF THE PARTY FOR THE NEXT THREE	HUNDRED	YEARS! /BURGE/ WHAT! ! ! /LUBIN/ PERHAPS HARD ON
PHIL II	(120)	SCIENCE HAS RECEIVED FOR THE LAST THREE	HUNDRED	YEARS! /CHARTERIS/ NO, NO, NO. CONGRATULATE HIM ON
MTH2	(86)	HOME WITH HER MOTHER AND ON HER FATHER FOR THREE	HUNDRED	YEARS! THEYD MURDER HER IF SHE DIDNT MURDER THEM
MILL I	(158)	UP AND SAID " WHY, MAN ALIVE, IF YOU HAVE A	HUNDRED	YOU CAN OPEN A BANK ACCOUNT AND GET A CHEQUE BOOK."
MTH4 I	(171)	CAN BE OF NO USE TO YOU WHO LIVE LESS THAN A	HUNDRED	, AND THAT OUR TRUE DESTINY IS NOT TO ADVISE AND
SUPR HANDBOK	(209)	NOT REVISE ITS ARTICLES OF RELIGION ONCE IN THREE	HUNDRED	, EVEN WHEN THOSE ARTICLES AVOWEDLY BEGAN AS A
WIDO II	(35)	TO BE, HARRY. IF I WERE TO EAT UP HALF YOUR SEVEN	HUNDRED	, I SHOULD BE MAKING YOU TWICE AS POOR; BUT I'M
KING I	(201)	WHEN I AM PLAYING, ROWLEY DARLING. TWO OR THREE	HUNDRED	, MORE LIKELY. /FOX/ (RESUMING HIS SEAT IN THE
METH PREFACE	(R19)	AND TEN YEARS, HE CAN EQUALLY FIX IT AT THREE	HUNDRED	, OR THREE THOUSAND, OR EVEN AT THE GENUINE
2TRU II	(78)	THE READY. CUT-OFFS OPEN. SIGHTS UP TO EIGHTEEN	HUNDRED	, RIGHT OVER THEIR HEADS: NO HITTING. TEN ROUNDS
MTH4 II	(191)	THREE HUNDRED YEARS. TO US, WHO LIVE LESS THAN A	HUNDRED	, WHOSE FLESH IS AS GRASS, IT IS THE MOST UNBEARABLE
BARB III	(334)	/LOMAX/ DONE IN THE EYE! WHY, I GET ONLY EIGHT	HUNDRED	, YOU KNOW. /CUSINS/ BY THE WAY, MAC, I AM A
ARMS III	(55)	TWO HUNDRED! (IN A CRESCENDO OF DISMAY) FOUR	HUNDRED	! FOUR THOUSAND! ! NINE THOUSAND SIX HUNDRED! !
ARMS III	(55)	GLANCES OVER THEM). GREAT HEAVENS! SEVENTY! TWO	HUNDRED	! (IN A CRESCENDO OF DISMAY) FOUR HUNDRED! FOUR
MTH4 I	(163)	ABOUT FIVE HUNDRED-- /THE ELDERLY GENTLEMAN/ FIVE	HUNDRED	! REALLY, MADAM-- /ZOO/ (CONTINUING); BUT I KNOW,
MTH3	(122)	US THE FEW YEARS WE HAVE? YOU WHO HAVE THREE	HUNDRED	! /BURGE-LUBIN/ YOU ACCUSE ME OF LEVITY! MUST I
ARMS III	(55)	HUNDRED! FOUR THOUSAND! ! NINE THOUSAND SIX	HUNDRED	! ! ! WHAT ON EARTH AM I TO DO WITH THEM ALL?

HUNDREDS

INCA	(256)	DEATH IS LET LOOSE ON THEM. THEY GRUDGED A FEW	HUNDREDS	A YEAR FOR THEIR SALVATION: THEY NOW PAY MILLIONS A
BULL PREFACE	(49)	PRUSSIAN HEYDAY OF THE SYSTEM, WHEN FLOGGINGS OF	HUNDREDS	AND EVEN THOUSANDS OF LASHES WERE MATTERS OF
ROCK II	(267)	EXCHEQUER AND THE TREASURY AND EVEN THE CHILTERN	HUNDREDS	AND THE DUCHY OF LANCASTER-- WE HAVE NO DEPARTMENT
WIDO III	(53)	LOOKING MYSTERIOUSLY AT HIM) YOU AINT SPENT A FEW	HUNDREDS	IN REPAIRS SINCE WE PARTED, AVE YOU? (SARTORIUS,
MILL I	(157)	A FEW LESSONS FROM ALASTAIR IN THE ART OF TURNING	HUNDREDS	INTO TENS OF THOUSANDS. /EPIFANIA/ HIS EXAMPLE
DOCT PREFACE	(8)	OF A DOCTOR AS EFFECTUALLY AS ANY OF THE	HUNDREDS	OF CHILDREN WHO DIE EVERY DAY OF THE SAME DISEASES
METH PREFACE	(R21)	CREATED IN THE BEGINNING," THOUGH THERE WERE	HUNDREDS	OF COMMONPLACE SCOTCH GARDENERS, PIGEON FANCIERS,
MIS.	(195)	ONE OF MY THREE FATHERS (THE PRIEST) HAS MARRIED	HUNDREDS	OF COUPLES: COUPLES SELECTED BY ONE ANOTHER,
APPL PREFACE	(183)	TEACHERS, AND OFFICIALS OF ALL GRADES IN	HUNDREDS	OF DEPARTMENTS. WE HAVE FOUND BY BITTER EXPERIENCE
SIM II	(70)	DOES IT? WOULD IT BE REASONABLE TO TRY CASES IN	HUNDREDS	OF DIFFERENT LANDS AND LANGUAGES AND CREEDS AND
GETT	(356)	HYPOCRISIES, ITS JEALOUSIES AND SQUABBLES, ITS	HUNDREDS	OF DIVORCE CASES THAT NEVER COME INTO COURT, AS
O'FL	(209)	DUTY TO HAVE A MASS SAID FOR THE SOULS OF THE	HUNDREDS	OF GERMANS YOU SAY YOU KILLED" SAYS HE; " FOR MANY
DOCT PREFACE	(3)	SHILLINGS: HE WHO CUTS YOUR INSIDE OUT RECEIVES	HUNDREDS	OF GUINEAS, EXCEPT WHEN HE DOES IT TO A POOR PERSON
O'FL	(211)	IT CARRIES? DO YOU THINK I DONT KNOW THAT THERES	HUNDREDS	OF MEN AS BRAVE AS ME THAT NEVER HAD THE LUCK TO
GENV PREFACE	(11)	AND AIR RAIDS IN WHICH THE COMBATANTS ARE	HUNDREDS	OF MILES APART ON THE GROUND OR THOUSANDS OF FEET
APPL I	(237)	ONCE A YEAR. OUR NATIONAL REPAIR BILL RUNS UP TO	HUNDREDS	OF MILLIONS. I COULD NAME YOU A DOZEN INVENTIONS
SUPR III	(107)	DELIGHT, AND EGG THEIR GOVERNMENTS ON TO SPEND	HUNDREDS	OF MILLIONS OF MONEY IN THE SLAUGHTER, WHILST THE
SIM PREFACE	(9)	OF EVERYONE'S AMBITION IS AN UNEARNED INCOME; AND	HUNDREDS	OF MILLIONS OF THE COUNTRY'S INCOME ARE LAVISHED
KING I	(185)	WITH YOU. WHEN YOU THINK OF GRANDIOSE THINGS--	HUNDREDS	OF MILLIONS AND THINGS LIKE THAT-- YOU MUST
MTH2	(78)	OF MEN SPELLBOUND FOR CENTURIES, WHILST	HUNDREDS	OF MUCH MORE PLAUSIBLE AND AMUSING STORIES HAVE
OVER	(183)	LIST? NOT THE ONE I SHEW TO GREGORY: THERE ARE	HUNDREDS	OF NAMES ON THAT; BUT THE LITTLE PRIVATE LIST THAT
ANNA	(296)	IN YOUR IMAGINATION. I CAME ALONE. I AM ALONE.	HUNDREDS	OF OFFICERS TRAVEL EVERY DAY FROM HAKONSBURG TO
GENV III	(78)	TO HAVE ATTAINED CABINET RANK IN COMPETITION WITH	HUNDREDS	OF OTHER SUCCESSFUL AND AMBITIOUS COMPETITORS. /SIR
FANY EPILOG	(328)	THROAT, MAKING A NOISE LIKE A PHEASANT). YOU SEE	HUNDREDS	OF PLAYS EVERY YEAR. BUT TO ME, WHO HAVE NEVER SEEN
PYGM EPILOG	(289)	SUCH TRANSFIGURATIONS HAVE BEEN ACHIEVED BY	HUNDREDS	OF RESOLUTELY AMBITIOUS YOUNG WOMEN SINCE NELL
GENV I	(32)	THE PROTESTANTS ARE DISLIKED; AND ALL THEIR	HUNDREDS	OF SECTS DISLIKE ONEANOTHER, SO ARE THE CATHOLICS,
MTH2	(51)	BUSINESSES IN THE MIDLANDS? I CAN FIND YOU	HUNDREDS	OF THE MOST SORDID RASCALS, OR THE MOST DENSELY
MILL IV	(209)	A DANGEROUS OPERATION: HAVE YOU NOT PERFORMED	HUNDREDS	OF THEM? /THE DOCTOR/ OF A SURETY THERE IS NO WIT
BARB II	(298)	WE WANT THOUSANDS! TENS OF THOUSANDS!	HUNDREDS	OF THOUSANDS! I WANT TO CONVERT PEOPLE, NOT TO BE
HART PREFACE	(37)	BE DONE, ALSO FOR THE FIRST TIME IN THEIR LIVES.	HUNDREDS	OF THOUSANDS OF WOMEN HAVE BEEN TAKEN OUT OF THEIR
MIS. PREFACE	(89)	TO GO HOME; AND YOU WILL HAVE IN GREAT CAPITALS	HUNDREDS	OF THOUSANDS OF POUNDS SPENT EVERY NIGHT IN THE
APPL PREFACE	(185)	INCOME TAX AND SURTAX TO PROVIDE DOLES FOR SOME	HUNDREDS	OF UNEMPLOYED AND OLD AGE PENSIONERS. I HAVE NOT
MTH1 II	(27)	DIG ANY BETTER BECAUSE YOU HAVE BEEN DIGGING FOR	HUNDREDS	OF YEARS? I HAVE NOT LIVED AS LONG AS YOU; BUT I
MTH5	(210)	TRIVIALITIES OF OUR LIFE HERE. JUST THINK. I HAVE	HUNDREDS	OF YEARS TO LIVE: PERHAPS THOUSANDS. DO YOU SUPPOSE
GENV IV	(122)	BE DONE IN YOUR COUNTRIES. THEY REMAIN UNDONE FOR	HUNDREDS	OF YEARS; BUT THE FIRE AND THE POISON ARE ALWAYS UP
FABL PREFACE	(66)	AND KARL MARX ARRIVE ONLY ONCE AT INTERVALS OF	HUNDREDS	OF YEARS, WHILST CARPENTERS AND TAILORS,
BARB PREFACE	(246)	(I AM ONE) WHO KILL AND MAIM SHUNTERS BY	HUNDREDS	TO SAVE THE COST OF AUTOMATIC COUPLINGS, AND MAKE
MILL I	(159)	POUNDS. AND SO YOU GO SPENDING AND KITING FROM	HUNDREDS	TO THOUSANDS AND FROM RISKS OF EIGHTEEN MONTHS

HUNDREDTH

APPL I	(233)	OF IT IS UNKNOWN TO THE PEOPLE, AND THE REMAINING	HUNDREDTH	IS RESENTED BY THEM AS AN INVASION OF THEIR
CURE	(226)	ANY HARM IN BUYING THOSE SHARES. THIS IS THE FOUR	HUNDREDTH	TIME YOUVE SAID IT. /REGINALD/ (WILDLY) THEN WHY

HUNDREDTHS

APPL I	(233)	ONES. WE GET NO THANKS FOR IT BECAUSE NINETY NINE	HUNDREDTHS	OF IT IS UNKNOWN TO THE PEOPLE, AND THE REMAINING

HUNDREDWEIGHT

GETT PREFACE	(200)	WALK AT THE RATE OF FIVE MILES AN HOUR OR CARRY A	HUNDREDWEIGHT	CONTINUALLY ON THEIR BACKS. THEIR NORMAL

MTH2	(83)	OUNCES A YEAR: JUST TWO OUNCES OVER THE	HUNDREDWEIGHT	. /BURGE/ TWO MILLION TONS A YEAR, IN ROUND
BASH II,1,	(103)	SMARTLY TO HIS LEFT, CROSS-COUNTERED LIKE A	HUNDREDWEIGHT	OF BRICK--" /LUCIAN/ DEATH AND DAMNATION!
			HUNFORGIVIN	
CAND I	(89)	NO SIGN. HE LINGERS). I DIDNT HEXPECT TO FIND A	HUNFORGIVIN	SPIRIT IN YOU, JAMES. (MORELL STILL NOT
			HUNFRIENDLY	
CAND I	(89)	FEELING) OH, WELL, IF YOURE DETORMINED TO BE	HUNFRIENDLY	, I SPOSE I'D BETTER GO. (HE MOVES RELUCTANTLY
			HUNG	
PYGM II	(241)	BREAK IT. I DIDNT KNOW WHICH WAY TO LOOK. BUT I	HUNG	A TOWEL OVER IT, I DID. /HIGGINS/ OVER WHAT? /MRS
PYGM II	(235)	GIVE HIM A JAUNT. SON OF HER LANDLADY, HE IS. HE	HUNG	ABOUT ON THE CHANCE OF HER GIVING HIM ANOTHER RIDE
LADY PREFACE	(208)	POINT OF HIS CHIN WAS A MONSTROUS GOITRE, WHICH	HUNG	DOWN TO HIS COLLAR BONE, AND WAS VERY INADEQUATELY
GENV PREFACE	(10)	MANY SQUARE MILES AS IT WAS MEANT TO; BUT IF IT	HUNG	FIRE AND EXPLODED IN THE EARTH IT MIGHT START A
JOAN EPIL,SD	(152)	LIGHTED BY CANDLES OF PAINTED WAX. THE WALLS ARE	HUNG	FROM CEILING TO FLOOR WITH PAINTED CURTAINS WHICH STIR
MTH4 I	(160)	IS IN THE MIDDLE OF THE SEA. HE DECLARED HE HAD	HUNG	HIS HAT ON IT. /ZOO/ (LAUGHING) HE KNEW THAT
DEST SD	(162)	BUT BY NO MEANS WEAK: THE LITHE TENDER FIGURE IS	HUNG	ON A STRONG FRAME: THE HANDS AND FEET, NECK AND
DOCT I SD	(96)	MUSTER IN COMMON MEN REVEAL THEIR WEAKNESS WHEN	HUNG	ON HIS EGREGIOUS PERSONALITY. /B.B./ AHA! SIR COLENSO.
2TRU I	(29)	THERE IS A SHEET STEEPED IN CARBOLIC ACID ALWAYS	HUNG	OVER THE DOOR. /THE MONSTER/ (IN TEARS) NOT A BREATH
MTH3	(120)	HAVE NO CONCEPTION OF THE DREAD OF POVERTY THAT	HUNG	OVER US THEN, OR OF THE UTTER TIREDNESS OF FORTY YEARS'
POSN	(445)	NOW WITH THAT HORSE; AND HERE I AM WAITING TO BE	HUNG	UP AND FILLED WITH LEAD! WHAT CAME TO ME? WHAT MADE
GENV PREFACE	(18)	ENOUGH TO SUCCEED AS AN ARTIST, AND WAS THUS	HUNG	UP BETWEEN THE BOURGEOISIE FOR WHICH HE HAD NO INCOME
MTH2	(75)	POSSIBLE. /FRANKLYN/ PRECISELY. ADAM AND EVE WERE	HUNG	UP BETWEEN TWO FRIGHTFUL POSSIBILITIES. ONE WAS THE
2TRU PREFACE	(4)	FUN. THE VAMPIRE HAS A BETTER TIME THAN THE CALF	HUNG	UP BY THE HEELS WITH ITS THROAT CUT. THE MONEY-GETTER
ROCK PREFACE	(156)	WAS TORTURED SO FRIGHTFULLY BEFORE BEING	HUNG	UP IN A CAGE ON THE CHURCH TOWER TO STARVE TO DEATH IN
POSN	(450)	AS IT IS. AND A PRETTY COLOR YOULL BE WHEN YOURE	HUNG	WHITE AND SHOT RED. /BLANCO/ AINT SHE SPITEFUL.
PHIL I SD	(69)	OF LONDON. IT IS PAST TEN AT NIGHT. THE WALLS ARE	HUNG	WITH THEATRICAL ENGRAVINGS AND PHOTOGRAPHS: KEMBLE AS
			HUNGER	
CAND II	(107)	THINGS IF A CHILD WERE BY, CRYING BITTERLY WITH	HUNGER	? /PROSERPINE/ I SUPPOSE NOT. /MARCHBANKS/ WELL: I
SUPR III	(102)	DOWN FROM THEIR FOOL'S PARADISE BY THEIR BODIES:	HUNGER	AND COLD AND THIRST, AGE AND DECAY AND DISEASE, DEATH
FANY PREFACE	(255)	AND COWARDICE, OR INDEED ANYTHING BUT HOW TO KEEP	HUNGER	AND CONCUPISCENCE AND FASHIONABLE DRESSING WITHIN THE
2TRU II	(71)	ITS CYCLES OF EXULTANT VIGOR AND EXHAUSTION,	HUNGER	AND SATIETY, ITS LONGINGS FOR ACTION THAT CHANGE INTO
METH PREFACE	(R12)	GIVING HIM A RELIGION? A RELIGION MAY MAKE HIM	HUNGER	AND THIRST FOR RIGHTEOUSNESS; BUT WILL IT ENDOW HIM
BUOY II	(26)	US TO ADMINISTER IT. SOMETHING WITHIN ME MAKES ME	HUNGER	AND THIRST FOR RIGHTEOUSNESS. THAT SOMETHING MUST BE
LION PREFACE	(10)	SUNDAY CLOTHES, HAVE ROBUST CONSCIENCES, AND	HUNGER	AND THIRST, NOT FOR RIGHTEOUSNESS, BUT FOR RICH
FABL IV	(116)	BUTCHERS, BAR TENDERS, BREWERS, AND DISTILLERS.	HUNGER	AND THIRST, WHICH HAD FOR CENTURIES MEANT THE NEED
LION PREFACE	(79)	AND COOK SHE RELIEVES HIS PREOCCUPATION WITH	HUNGER	BY THE SIMPLE EXPEDIENT OF SATISFYING HIS APPETITE.
AUGS	(269)	IT? WELL, WHATS THE GOOD OF THAT IF I'M DEAD OF	HUNGER	BY THE TIME THEY COME BACK? /AUGUSTUS/ EVERYBODY
MTH4 I	(164)	THINGS I REBELLED AGAINST THEM; AND IN THEIR	HUNGER	FOR NEW LIGHTS AND NEW IDEAS THEY LISTENED TO ME AND
BARB II	(298)	THEM? I CANT TALK RELIGION TO A MAN WITH BODILY	HUNGER	IN HIS EYES. (ALMOST BREAKING DOWN) IT'S FRIGHTFUL.
MTH2	(69)	THAT THE MULTITUDES OF CHILDREN SLAIN BY	HUNGER	IN THE FIRST YEARS OF PEACE MADE US ALL WISH WE WERE
METH PREFACE	(R42)	CONSCIOUSNESS BEYOND THE BLIND WILL TO SATISFY	HUNGER	. IT IS TRUE THAT THIS BLIND WILL, BEING IN EFFECT A
BARB II	(276)	HARDENED, HALF WORN-OUT ELDERLY MAN, WEAK WITH	HUNGER	. /JENNY/ (SUPPORTING HIM) COME! PLUCK UP. I'LL GET
OVER	(184)	NOTHING BRINGS PEOPLE TO THEIR SENSES LIKE	HUNGER	. /JUNO/ (CONTEMPLATING THE FLOWER WITHOUT RAPTURE)
CAND II	(107)	THINGS WITH MY HEART CRYING OUT BITTERLY IN ITS	HUNGER	. /PROSERPINE/ THEN HOLD YOUR TONGUE. /MARCHBANKS/
SIM I	(38)	NOWHERE TO GO. /PROLA/ PERHAPS HE IS WEAK WITH	HUNGER	. /THE CLERGYMAN/ NO: IT'S NOT THAT. I HAVE BEEN
BARB III	(338)	SALVATION SHELTER I SAW POVERTY, MISERY, COLD AND	HUNGER	. YOU GAVE THEM BREAD AND TREACLE AND DREAMS OF
MTH1 II	(28)	THE SOUL ALONE: A LIFE WITHOUT CLODS OR SPADES,	HUNGER	OR FATIGUE-- /EVE/ SELFISH AND IDLE, CAIN. I KNOW.
ARMS I	(18)	VIGOR AND COURAGE). YOU SEE, SLEEP OR NO SLEEP,	HUNGER	OR NO HUNGER, TIRED OR NOT TIRED, YOU CAN ALWAYS DO A
FOUN	(218)	ME, A WOMAN, POLITICS MEANT HOLLOWAY GAOL AND THE	HUNGER	STRIKE. I REFUSED TO TAKE FOOD UNTIL I WAS SO
GETT PREFACE	(243)	WERE REALLY ONE ANSWER-- THAT POVERTY MEANS	HUNGER	, AN INTOLERABLE LACK OF VARIETY AND PLEASURE, AND,
GETT PREFACE	(243)	TO THIEVING, AND SOME REPLIED POVERTY, AND OTHERS	HUNGER	, AND OTHERS DESIRE FOR EXCITEMENT, NO ONE WOULD DENY
METH PREFACE	(R43)	REMAINED STILL POSSIBLE, THIS NEWLY SHEWN WAY OF	HUNGER	, DEATH, STUPIDITY, DELUSION, CHANCE, AND BARE
3PLA PREFACE	(R20)	STARVING TRAMP WHO CAN THINK OF NOTHING BUT HIS	HUNGER	, SEEMS TO BE UNABLE TO ESCAPE FROM THE OBSESSION OF
MIS. PREFACE	(105)	THAT EVERY VICTORY MEANS A DEFEAT; THAT FATIGUE,	HUNGER	, TERROR, AND DISEASE ARE THE RAW MATERIAL WHICH
ARMS I	(18)	YOU SEE, SLEEP OR NO SLEEP, HUNGER OR NO	HUNGER	, TIRED OR NOT TIRED, YOU CAN ALWAYS DO A THING WHEN
LION II	(131)	SAVED HIM FROM A LION THAT I'D JUST GOT MAD WITH	HUNGER	! A WILD ONE THAT CAME OUT OF THE FOREST NOT FOUR
			HUNGERFORD	
AUGS	(274)	FRIEND OF YOUR BROTHER AT THE WAR OFFICE,	HUNGERFORD	HIGHCASTLE: BLUELOO AS YOU CALL HIM: I DONT KNOW
AUGS	(282)	(INTO THE TELEPHONE) PUT ME THROUGH TO LORD	HUNGERFORD	HIGHCASTLE. . . . I'M HIS BROTHER, IDIOT. . . .
			HUNGRIER	
BUOY II	(20)	CONSUME MINE YOURSELF AFTER HE BRINGS IT? I AM	HUNGRIER	THAN YOU. /SHE/ YOU ARE NOT STARVING. A FAST WILL
			HUNGRILY	
GETT	(343)	SEE THERE, AT THE BACK OF GODSPEED? /SOAMES/ (	HUNGRILY	) GIVE US YOUR MESSAGE. /MRS GEORGE/ (WITH
ARMS I	(13)	MAN/ (GRINNING) YES: ISNT IT CONTEMPTIBLE? (	HUNGRILY	) I WISH I HAD SOME NOW. /RAINA/ ALLOW ME. (SHE
FABL III	(110)	YOU. (SHE HANDS HIM A TICKET). /THE TOURIST/ (	HUNGRILY	) THANK YOU. HE TAKES THE TICKET AND GOES INTO THE
			HUNGRY	
MRS II	(203)	I WANT ONE PERSON TO WAIT WITH ME. FRANK: ARE YOU	HUNGRY	? /FRANK/ NOT THE LEAST IN THE WORLD. COMPLETELY OFF
DEST	(186)	COME: DROP IT, GIUSEPPE: YOURE MAKING ME FEEL	HUNGRY	AGAIN. GIUSEPPE, WITH AN APOLOGETIC SHRUG, RETIRES
SUPR IV SD	(142)	LITTLE OF HIS OWN WAY AND LEFT HIS AFFECTIONS	HUNGRY	AND BAFFLED, AT THE FIRST WORD THAT FALLS FROM HIM IT
3PLA PREFACE	(R39)	CLEVER TO THOSE WHO HAVE NEVER HOPPED,	HUNGRY	AND CURIOUS, ACROSS THE FIELDS OF PHILOSOPHY,
METH PREFACE	(R65)	RUNAWAY CHILD'S SENSE OF FREEDOM BEFORE IT GETS	HUNGRY	AND LONELY AND FRIGHTENED. IN THIS PHASE WE DID NOT
BUOY II	(18)	OF ANY STRANGER MUST BE A GODSEND. BESIDES, I AM	HUNGRY	AND THIRSTY. /SHE/ MOST TRAMPS ARE. GET OUT. /HE/ NO:
BUOY IV	(51)	TO NOTHING OF ME EXCEPT WHEN I CAME HOME AT NIGHT	HUNGRY	AND TIRED AND DIRTY. WHEN I DID NOTHING BUT SEND
DEST	(160)	THE TABLE; AND SITS DOWN). IF YOU ONLY KNEW HOW	HUNGRY	AND TIRED I AM, YOUD HAVE MORE CONSIDERATION.
LION PROLOG	(107)	TO DENY IT. /ANDROCLES/ ONLY WHEN THEY WERE	HUNGRY	AND YOU WERE GETTING TOO STOUT, DEARIE. /MEGAERA/
SUPR HANDBOK	(229)	CONFLICTS. TWO STARVING MEN CANNOT BE TWICE AS	HUNGRY	AS ONE; BUT TWO RASCALS CAN BE TEN TIMES AS VICIOUS
BARB III	(339)	TERMS. TRY YOUR HAND ON MY MEN: THEIR SOULS ARE	HUNGRY	BECAUSE THEIR BODIES ARE FULL. /BARBARA/ AND LEAVE
HART I	(48)	TO RECEIVE ANYBODY, NO REGULAR MEALS, NOBODY EVER	HUNGRY	BECAUSE THEY ARE ALWAYS GNAWING BREAD AND BUTTER OR
DOCT PREFACE	(63)	ARE NOT EXPECTED TO FEED THE HUNGRY UNLESS THE	HUNGRY	CAN PAY; BUT A DOCTOR WHO ALLOWS A FELLOW-CREATURE TO
WIDO II	(30)	THE TABLE. HARDLY A PENNY OF THAT BUT THERE WAS A	HUNGRY	CHILD CRYING FOR THE BREAD IT WOULD HAVE BOUGHT. BUT
ROCK PREFACE	(166)	THE SOLDIERS WERE PEASANTS, AND ALL THE PEASANTS	HUNGRY	FOR PROPERTY, THE MILITARY ELEMENT ONLY ADDED TO THE
BARB PREFACE	(216)	BE PAINLESSLY BUT INEXORABLY KILLED, AND EVERY	HUNGRY	HALF NAKED CHILD FORCIBLY FATTENED AND CLOTHED, WOULD
MTH4 I	(154)	HINDOO KOOSH. CAN YOU WONDER THAT I TURN, WITH A	HUNGRY	HEART, TO THE MYSTERY AND BEAUTY OF THESE HAUNTED
MIS. PREFACE	(35)	AND DANGEROUS THINGS TO MAKE THEMSELVES TIRED AND	HUNGRY	IN THE EVENING. WHEN THEY ARE NOT INVOLVED IN WHAT
BASH II,1,	(102)	AS WE KNOW HE IS, SEEMED THIS TIME LIKELY TO GO	HUNGRY	. CASHEL WAS CLEARLY GROGGY AS HE SLIPPED THE SAILOR,
FABL III	(110)	WILL GIVE ME ANYTHING TO DO. I'M DEVILISHLY	HUNGRY	. HAVE YOU BY ANY CHANCE A CRUST OF BREAD TO SPARE..
LION PROL,SD	(105)	BUNDLE, IS VERY POORLY CLAD, AND SEEMS TIRED AND	HUNGRY	. HIS WIFE IS A RATHER HANDSOME PAMPERED SLATTERN,
FABL III	(111)	(HE STARTS TO GO). /THE GIRL/ STOP. YOU ARE	HUNGRY	. I'LL GET YOU SOME BREAD. (SHE GOES INTO THE
LION II	(128)	FOR US WITHOUT THAT? /ANDROCLES/ I'M GLAD HE'S	HUNGRY	. NOT THAT I WANT HIM TO SUFFER, POOR CHAP! BUT THEN
OVER	(184)	HIM ONE). GO AND DREAM OVER IT UNTIL YOU FEEL	HUNGRY	. NOTHING BRINGS PEOPLE TO THEIR SENSES LIKE HUNGER.
NEVR I	(210)	LANDLORD DOWNSTAIRS? /DOLLY/ DONT BE LONG. WE'RE	HUNGRY	. /MRS CLANDON/ (AGAIN REMONSTRATING) DOLLY, DEAR!
OVER	(191)	IS GETTING RIDICULOUS. /MRS LUNN/ I'M GETTING	HUNGRY	. /MRS JUNO/ DO YOU REALLY MIND, MRS LUNN? /MRS
LION II	(128)	THE NEW LION: LET THAT BE ENOUGH FOR YOU. HE'S	HUNGRY	. /SPINTHO/ (GROANING WITH HORROR) OH, LORD! CANT
GLIM	(179)	THATS RIGHT. SERVE ME LAST, GIULIETTA. SANDRO IS	HUNGRY	. /SQUARCIO/ (TO THE GIRL) COME COME! DO YOU NOT
GETT PREFACE	(235)	BULL-PUPS AND LEAVE THEIR WIVES AND CHILDREN	HUNGRY	. THAT BASIS IS THE PENALTY WE PAY FOR HAVING
ROCK II	(258)	PEOPLE WHO BURN GOOD FOOD WHEN PEOPLE ARE GOING	HUNGRY	. THEY CANT SET MATTERS RIGHT THEMSELVES; SO THEY
BULL IV	(179)	WORKERS HAVE LEFT IN MILLIONS BECAUSE IT IS A	HUNGRY	LAND, A NAKED LAND, AN IGNORANT AND OPPRESSED LAND.
CLEO V	(199)	FOR NUMIDIA TODAY. NOW TELL ME: IF YOU MEET A	HUNGRY	LION THERE, YOU WILL NOT PUNISH IT FOR WANTING TO EAT
JOAN PREFACE	(14)	APPETITE FOR FOOD IS NECESSARY TO THE LIFE OF THE	HUNGRY	MAN AND IS THEREFORE A PERSONAL APPETITE, WHEREAS THE
BUOY II	(20)	HOLY LADY; BUT WHAT ABOUT YOUR CONSCIENCE? A	HUNGRY	MAN ASKS YOU FOR FOOD. DARE YOU THROW HIM TO THE
CAND II	(112)	THE TABLE AND ASKS, WITH THE SICKLY CIVILITY OF A	HUNGRY	MAN) WHEN'S DINNER, JAMES? /MORELL/ NOT FOR A COUPLE

CLEO III (154) THE STAIR HEAD TO BE PAID. /APOLLODORUS/ HERE, YE HUNGRY ONES. (HE GIVES MONEY TO THE FIRST PORTER, WHO HOLDS
ROCK II (251) CHINK OF A SINGLE PENNY OF PUBLIC MONEY IN YOUR HUNGRY POCKET. (SHE TEARS OUT A CHAIR FROM UNDER THE TABLE
FOUN (219) I REFUSED TO TAKE FOOD UNTIL I WAS SO FRIGHTFULLY HUNGRY THAT WHEN THE GOVERNOR-- WHO WAS A PLUMP, CHUBBY,
DOCT PREFACE(63) BUTCHER AND BAKER ARE NOT EXPECTED TO FEED THE HUNGRY UNLESS THE HUNGRY CAN PAY; BUT A DOCTOR WHO ALLOWS A
LION PREFACE(25) HIM TO CURE THEM, WHEN MULTITUDES OF PEOPLE ARE HUNGRY , AND WHEN HIS DISCIPLES ARE TERRIFIED BY STORMS ON
MRS II (203) ME. I-- /VIVIE/ YOU HAVE HAD A LONG WALK AND ARE HUNGRY , MR PRAED: YOU SHALL HAVE YOUR SUPPER AT ONCE. I CAN
APPL II (260) HAS RETURNED TO HIS FATHER'S HOUSE. NOT POOR, NOT HUNGRY , NOT RAGGED, AS OF OLD. OH NO. THIS TIME HE RETURNS
DOCT PREFACE(64) DOCTOR EXCEPT AS A HEALER AND SAVIOR. HE MAY BE HUNGRY , WEARY, SLEEPY, RUN DOWN BY SEVERAL SUCCESSIVE

HUNK

BUOY II (18) MARRIED. HAVE YOU ANY MILK IN THE HOUSE? OR A HUNK OF BREAD AND AN ONION? /SHE/ NOT FOR YOU. /HE/ WHY
KING I (200) LIE. MY PENANCES ARE ALL REAL. /CHARLES/ WELL, A HUNK OF BREAD, A LUMP OF CHEESE, AND A BOTTLE OF ALE ARE

HUNNERDS

CAPT II (265) EAHS ANATHER LOT CAMMIN FROM THE SAHTH HEAST. HUNNERDS OF EM, THIS TAWM. THE OWL DEZZIT IS LAWK A BLOOMIN

HUNS

AUGS (265) NO IMAGINATION: THATS WHAT IT IS. BRING THE HUNS HERE; AND THEYLL QUARREL WITH THEM FAST ENOUGH.
AUGS (272) AND WERE CUT OFF AND MADE PRISONER BY THE HUNS . /AUGUSTUS/ YES, MADAM; AND WHAT WAS MY REWARD? THEY
AUGS (265) ONE ANOTHER: HOW CAN THEY HAVE GRUDGES AGAIN THE HUNS THAT THEY NEVER SAW? THEYVE NO IMAGINATION: THATS WHAT
ROCK PREFACE(188) WHO ARE LEARNED, FEAR OF THE GAULS AND GOTHS AND HUNS WHO ARE BARBARIANS, FEAR OF THE CARTHAGE YOU DESTROYED
HART PREFACE(20) SUDDENLY BURST INTO FURIOUS IMPRECATIONS ON " THE HUNS " AS MURDERERS, AND SHRIEKED FOR SAVAGE AND SATISFYING

HUNT

PRES (145) SHE'S MUSICAL AND ROMANTIC AND ALL THAT-- DONT HUNT : HATES POLITICS: STOPS IN TOWN ALL THE YEAR ROUND: ONE
MTH1 II (23) WOMAN SHALL MAKE ME LIVE MY FATHER'S LIFE. I WILL HUNT : I WILL FIGHT AND STRIVE TO THE VERY BURSTING OF MY
NEVR III (262) A CHAPTER MISSING. /MRS CLANDON/ (BEGINNING TO HUNT AMONG HER PROOFS) IS THERE? SURELY NOT. /GLORIA/ I
3PLA PREFACE(R10) TO HIM PLAYING MEANS PLAYING THE FOOL. HE CAN HUNT AND SHOOT AND TRAVEL AND FIGHT: HE CAN, WHEN SPECIAL
HART III (131) BECAUSE HE IS TOO LAZY AND PLEASURE-LOVING TO HUNT AND SHOOT. HE STRUMS THE PIANO, AND SKETCHES, AND RUNS
HART III (131) CONVENTION: EVERYBODY CAN SEE THAT THE PEOPLE WHO HUNT ARE THE RIGHT PEOPLE AND THE PEOPLE WHO DONT ARE THE
SUPR I (27) ROOF! GO AND DO YOUR MISERABLE DUTY, RAMSDEN. HUNT HER OUT INTO THE STREET. CLEANSE YOUR THRESHOLD FROM
BUOY II (23) AND I EXPECT A GOOD LUNCH AFTERWARDS. I CAN ALSO HUNT IF SOMEBODY WILL FETCH ME A SADDLED HORSE, AND STABLE
BUOY II (23) IT FOR ME AND TAKE IT OFF MY HANDS AGAIN WHEN THE HUNT IS OVER. I SHOULD BE AFRAID NOT TO FIGHT IF YOU PUT ME
CLEO III (153) HARBOR. STIR YOURSELVES, MY MILITARY FRIENDS: THE HUNT IS UP. (A CLANGOR OF TRUMPETS FROM SEVERAL POINTS
PRES (167) PREFER HER TO ME? /MRS FARRELL/ HE'S OUT O THE HUNT . HE'S ENGAGED TO ME. THE ORDERLY, OVERCOME BY THIS
DOCT PREFACE(45) ARE ALL CRUEL; YET THE TAME STAG HUNTER DOES NOT HUNT MEN; AND THE SPORTSMAN WHO LETS A LEASH OF GREYHOUNDS
MILL PREFACE(126) OR MARXISTS. A PERSECUTION IS ALWAYS A MAN HUNT ; AND MAN HUNTING IS NOT ONLY A VERY HORRIBLE SPORT BUT
AUGS (278) OFFICE STAFF? GOOD GOD! THEY WILL BE TAKING OUR HUNT SERVANTS NEXT. (CONFRONTING THE CLERK) WHAT DID THE
SUPR PREFACE(R20) LOVE INTEREST IS THE INTEREST OF SEEING THE WOMAN HUNT THE MAN DOWN. SHE MAY DO IT BY CHARMING HIM, LIKE
BASH II,1, (109) THE SLOT OF GILDED SNOBBERY, VENTRE A TERRE, WILL HUNT THROUGH LIFE WITH EAGER NOSE ON EARTH AND HANG THEE
GETT (325) HULLO, BILL: YOUVE GOT EM ALL ON TOO. GO AND HUNT UP A DRINK FOR JOSEPH: THERES A DEAR. (COLLINS GOES
BASH PREFACE(88) ADDRESSED THEMSELVES TO THE LITERATE ALONE. HUNT UP AN OLD MELODRAMA (SAY SWEENY TODD THE DEMON BARBER
FANY I (281) TO GET BOBBY OUT; AND IF YOU WONT FORK OUT, I'LL HUNT UP HOLY JOE. HE MIGHT GET IT OFF HIS BROTHER. THE
MILL PREFACE(130) AND HABITS OF SERFS. MILITARY GENIUSES COULD HUNT WITH SUCH PRODUCTS MORE EASILY THAN WITH A PACK OF
DOCT PREFACE(41) GETTING AWAY FROM THEIR DUTIES WITH RELIEF TO HUNT , TO GARDEN, TO KEEP BEES, TO GO INTO SOCIETY, AND THE

HUNTED

MTH4 I (144) OF AN ANIMAL WITH A NAME LIKE THAT. IT USED TO BE HUNTED AND SHOT IN THE BARBAROUS AGES. IT IS QUITE EXTINCT
JITT I SD(13) AFTERWARDS A VEILED LADY HURRIES IN LIKE A HUNTED CREATURE. HE FOLLOWS HER; SHUTS THE DOOR; AND COMES
GETT PREFACE(222) UP IN THE FAMILY CUPBOARD UNTIL THE PREY IS DULY HUNTED DOWN AND BAGGED: ALL THIS IS A MOTHER'S DUTY TODAY;
BASH III (121) OH, HIDE THEE, I IMPLORE: I CANNOT SEE THEE HUNTED DOWN LIKE THIS. THERE IS MY ROOM. CONCEAL THYSELF
METH PREFACE(R15) AND ELDON RULED THE ROOST AT HOME. ROUSSEAU WAS HUNTED FROM FRONTIER TO FRONTIER; KARL MARX STARVED IN EXILE
CAND I (97) ON SUCH OCCASIONS; BUT A CHANCE VISITOR IS. (THE HUNTED HORROR-STRICKEN EXPRESSION COMES OUT WITH SUDDEN
GETT PREFACE(252) WORLD TO THE OTHER, CHEATED, BEATEN, BULLIED, AND HUNTED INTO THE STREETS TO DISGUSTING OVERWORK, WITHOUT
BUOY II (22) /HE/ HE HUNTS, FISHES, AND FIGHTS. /SHE/ HAVE YOU HUNTED OR FISHED FOR ME? /HE/ NO. I HATE KILLING. /SHE/
FABL V (118) BE CUT TO PIECES THEY DOSED HIM WITH POISONS: I HUNTED OUT A CASE OF A WELL-KNOWN WOMAN WHO WAS GIVEN NINE
LADY PREFACE(209) OF ITS PREVIOUS OCCURRENCE IN THE LAST CYCLE. HE HUNTED OUT ALLUSIONS TO THIS FAVORITE THEORY IN HIS THREE
LION PROLOG (106) ALL RESPECTABLE PEOPLE DO, INSTEAD OF HAVING US HUNTED OUT OF HOUSE AND HOME FOR BEING DIRTY DISREPUTABLE
HART PREFACE(4) ANNEX FOR THE LADIES AND GENTLEMEN WHO RODE THEM, HUNTED THEM, TALKED ABOUT THEM, BOUGHT THEM AND SOLD THEM,
CAND I SD(93) EFFEMINATE, WITH A DELICATE CHILDISH VOICE, AND A HUNTED TORMENTED EXPRESSION AND SHRINKING MANNER THAT SHEW
BARB PREFACE(239) OF HUMAN NATURE IS THE FULMINATOR, NOW A HUNTED WRETCH, WITH NOTHING, APPARENTLY, TO SECURE HIS

HUNTER

BUOY III (43) SPITE OF HIS OUTRAGEOUS BOAST OF BEING A FORTUNE HUNTER ? /SHE/ YOU MAY LEAVE MONEY OUT OF THE QUESTION.
FABL VI (127) THE DISEMBODIED MUST INSPIRE THE SOLDIER AND THE HUNTER AS WELL AS THE PACIFIST AND PHILANTHROPIST. /YOUTH 1/
DOCT PREFACE(45) PLEAD, THAT WE ARE ALL CRUEL; YET THE TAME STAG HUNTER DOES NOT HUNT MEN; AND THE SPORTSMAN WHO LETS A LEASH
NEVR III (275) REGARDED BY THE YOUNG LADY'S FATHER AS A FORTUNE HUNTER . /VALENTINE/ SO I AM. DO YOU EXPECT MY WIFE TO LIVE
BUOY IV (54) LIKE THE FELLOW! LIKE AN IMPUDENT FORTUNE HUNTER : IN HEAVEN'S NAME, WHY? /OLD BILL/ HE ASKS

HUNTER'S

NEVR II (255) (WITH A GLEAM IN HIS EYE AT THE SUCCESS OF HIS HUNTER'S GUILE) OF COURSE! TWO INTELLIGENT PEOPLE LIKE US!

HUNTERS

DOCT PREFACE(23) THE DOCTORS THEMSELVES AS TO THE ANALYTIC MICROBE HUNTERS . THESE WITCH FINDERS WOULD GIVE YOU A CERTIFICATE
BULL IV (178) EFFICIENTLY SERVING THE CUPIDITY OF BASE MONEY HUNTERS . WE SPEND OUR LIVES EFFICIENTLY SNEERING AT HIM AND
BARB III (336) THE PLEASURE HUNTERS, THE MILITARY PROMOTION HUNTERS ; AND HE IS THEIR SLAVE. /UNDERSHAFT/ NOT
INCA (248) IT, YOU KNOW. /THE INCA/ MADAM, BE JUST. WHEN THE HUNTERS SURROUND THE LION, THE LION WILL SPRING. THE INCA
FABL VI (128) TO MAKE NUCLEAR BOMBS, OTHERS TO BE BIG GAME HUNTERS , JUDGES, EXECUTIONERS, AND KILLERS OF ALL SORTS,
DOCT PREFACE(38) MYSELF ON THE PLATFORM WITH FOXHUNTERS, TAME STAG HUNTERS , MEN AND WOMEN WHOSE CALENDAR WAS DIVIDED, NOT BY
BARB III (336) PART OF SOCIETY, THE MONEY HUNTERS, THE PLEASURE HUNTERS , THE MILITARY PROMOTION HUNTERS; AND HE IS THEIR
BARB III (336) BY THE MOST RASCALLY PART OF SOCIETY, THE MONEY HUNTERS , THE PLEASURE HUNTERS, THE MILITARY PROMOTION

HUNTING

MTH1 II (27) KNOW NOTHING. I KNOW THE CRAFT OF FIGHTING AND OF HUNTING : IN A WORD, THE CRAFT OF KILLING. WHAT CERTAINTY
MIS. PREFACE(53) SPORTSMAN (AND WAR IS FUNDAMENTALLY THE SPORT OF HUNTING AND FIGHTING THE MOST DANGEROUS OF THE BEASTS OF
BUOY II (21) " THATS QUITE ALL RIGHT, SONNY: DONT APOLOGIZE." HUNTING AND SHOOTING IS ALL RIGHT; BUT YOU NEED TO BE A
SUPR III (116) HIM THAT HIS BEAUTY WORSHIPPING AND HAPPINESS HUNTING AND WOMAN IDEALIZING WAS NOT WORTH A DUMP AS A
3PLA PREFACE(R22) THE SQUIRE WHO HAS NEVER SPARED AN HOUR FROM THE HUNTING FIELD TO DO A LITTLE PUBLIC WORK ON A PARISH COUNCIL
MIS. PREFACE(53) HIS NECK FOR FUN FIFTY TIMES EVERY WINTER IN THE HUNTING FIELD, AND AT BADAJOS SIEGES AND THE LIKE WILL RAM
BULL PREFACE(11) AS WELL IN AFRICA, OR WITH THE AMERICANS IN THE HUNTING GROUNDS OF THE RED MAN, TO CIVILIZE THESE PLACES;
APPL I (235) THE GULLIBILITY AND PRUDERY, THE HATING AND HUNTING INSTINCT OF THE VOTING MOB, AND CAST YOU DOWN FROM
MILL PREFACE(126) A PERSECUTION IS ALWAYS A MAN HUNT; AND MAN HUNTING IS NOT ONLY A VERY HORRIBLE SPORT BUT SOCIALLY A
MTH1 II (27) YOU, AM TIRED OF MYSELF WHEN I AM NOT FIGHTING OR HUNTING . SOONER THAN FACE A THOUSAND YEARS OF IT I SHOULD
KING I (195) ROARINGS. /CHARLES/ THAT WILL COME, JAMIE. I AM HUNTING OUT HIS RECORD; AND YOUR MAN JEFFRIES WILL SEE TO IT
HART I (62) TIGER FROM A HUNTING PARTY: ONE OF KING EDWARD'S HUNTING PARTIES IN INDIA. THE KING WAS FURIOUS: THAT WAS WHY
HART I (62) LIKE THAT. HE SAVED THE LIFE OF THE TIGER FROM A HUNTING PARTY: ONE OF KING EDWARD'S HUNTING PARTIES IN
CLEO PRO2 (104) MOTHER: YOUR GODS ARE ASLEEP OR AWAY HUNTING ; AND THE SWORD IS AT YOUR THROAT. BRING US TO WHERE
GETT PREFACE(221) TO OUR SENSE OF HUMAN DIGNITY THAN THE HUSBAND HUNTING THAT BEGINS IN EVERY FAMILY WHEN THE DAUGHTERS
SUPR HANDBOK(186) OF HOUNDS ONLY WORTH KEEPING FOR THE SPORT OF HUNTING WITH THEM. CAESAR'S CAPACITY FOR FIGHTING WITHOUT
PLES PREFACE(R10) RAISES DRAMATIC ART ABOVE IMPOSTURE AND PLEASURE HUNTING , AND ENABLES THE PLAYWRIGHT TO BE SOMETHING MORE
MRS IV (249) OF MONEY INSTEAD OF LIVING THE USUAL SHOOTING, HUNTING , DINING-OUT, TAILORING, LOAFING LIFE OF HIS SET
BULL IV (178) WE MAKE FOR THEM VERY EFFICIENTLY IN SHOOTING AND HUNTING , IN OPERATIONS FOR CANCER AND APPENDICITIS, IN
HART PREFACE(4) ART, LITERATURE, AND THE THEATRE HAD SUPPLANTED HUNTING , SHOOTING, FISHING, FLIRTING, EATING, AND DRINKING.
GENV PREFACE(24) AND DRINKING ALCOHOL AS PART OF THEIR DAILY DIET, HUNTING , SHOOTING, COURSING, READING TALES OF MURDER AND

HUNTLEY

PPP PREFACE(192) MISS IRENE VANBRUGH, MISS NANCY PRICE, MR G. P. HUNTLEY , MR CYRIL MAUDE, MR ERIC LEWIS, MR ARTHUR WILLIAMS,

HUNTRESS

PHIL II SD(103)	ALL THE MORE EXCITING TO THEM BECAUSE THE	HUNTRESS	AND HER PREY ALIKE MUST CONCEAL THE REAL OBJECT OF
FABL PREFACE(68)	ATHENE (MINERVA) THE THINKER, DIANA THE	HUNTRESS	, APHRODITE (VENUS) THE SEXMISTRESS. THEY REAPPEAR
LION II (128)	RATHER NOT. I COULDNT SACRIFICE TO DIANA: SHE'S A	HUNTRESS	, YOU KNOW, AND KILLS THINGS. /THE EDITOR/ THAT

HUNTS

MIS. PREFACE(92)	OF THE PAVEMENT. YOU HAVE THEM ORGANIZING	HUNTS	OF THE WOMEN WHO TEMPT THEM -- POOR CREATURES WHOM NO
SUPR HANDBOK(222)	NO FOXHUNTER IS SUCH A CAD AS TO PRETEND THAT HE	HUNTS	THE FOX TO TEACH IT NOT TO STEAL CHICKENS, OR THAT HE
FABL PREFACE(98)	THE BIBLE, HAVE BEEN FOLLOWED BY MASSACRES, WITCH	HUNTS	, CIVIL AND INTERNATIONAL WARS OF RELIGION, AND ALL
BUOY II (22)	OF DOORS. WHAT DOES HE WORK AT, PRAY? /HE/ HE	HUNTS	, FISHES, AND FIGHTS. /SHE/ HAVE YOU HUNTED OR FISHED

HUNTSMAN

SUPR PREFACE(R21)	AND MY DON JUAN IS THE QUARRY INSTEAD OF THE	HUNTSMAN	. YET HE IS A TRUE DON JUAN, WITH A SENSE OF

HUNTSMEN

ROCK II (263)	PAINTERS AND ALL SORTS, TO SAY NOTHING OF	HUNTSMEN	AND STABLEMEN AND GARDENERS, VALETS AND GAMEKEEPERS
BULL PREFACE(53)	COUNTRY HOUSE, GARDEN AND STABLE, OR AS BEATERS,	HUNTSMEN	AND THE LIKE, FROM THEM. BUT DENSHAWAI HAD NO SUCH

HUP

CAND I (90)	AGO, NO SENSIBLE MAN WOULD A THOUGHT O TAKIN	HUP	WITH YOUR HIDEARS. I HUSED TO WONDER YOU WAS LET PREACH

HUPPISHNESS

CAND I (88)	I DO IT? WHAT DOES IT LEAD TO BUT DRINK AND	HUPPISHNESS	IN WORKIN MEN? (HE SEATS HIMSELF MAGISTERIALLY

HUPSTAIRS

CAND II (109)	A DEPPITATION IN THE DININ ROOM; AND CANDY IS	HUPSTAIRS	HEDUCATING OF A YOUNG STITCHER GURL SHE'S

HURDLE

MTH1 II (33)	THE HURDLE BACK, LAZY HOUND! (HE REPLACES THE	HURDLE	ACROSS THE PASSAGE). /EVE/ THROUGH HIM AND HIS LIKE,
MTH1 II (33)	MOTHER. /ADAM/ (GRUMBLING) HE MIGHT HAVE PUT THE	HURDLE	BACK, LAZY HOUND! (HE REPLACES THE HURDLE ACROSS
MTH1 II SD(20)	THORN BRAKE WITH A PASSAGE THROUGH IT BARRED BY A	HURDLE	. THE TWO ARE SCANTILY AND CARELESSLY DRESSED IN
MTH1 II SD(20)	DIGGING WITHOUT RAISING HIS HEAD). CAIN KICKS THE	HURDLE	OUT OF HIS WAY, AND STRIDES INTO THE GARDEN. IN POSE,
MTH1 II (20)	/EVE/ (LOOKING ACROSS THE GARDEN TOWARDS THE	HURDLE	) HERE IS CAIN. /ADAM/ (UTTERING A GRUNT OF

HURL

6CAL PREFACE(89)	PLAY HAS NO MORAL WHATEVER. EVERY YEAR OR SO I	HURL	AT THEM A LONG PLAY FULL OF INSIDIOUS PROPAGANDA, WITH
BASH III (122)	/MELLISH/ INJURIOUS COPPER, IN THY TEETH I	HURL	THE LIE. I AM NO TRAINER, I. MY FATHER, A RESPECTED
GETT PREFACE(232)	CLERGYMAN, WHO HAS A TEMPER, IS FIRST TEMPTED TO	HURL	THE YOUTH INTO THE STREET BY BODILY VIOLENCE: AN
APPL PREFACE(193)	DUMP THE CRATES FROM TRUCK TO PLATFORM AND THEN	HURL	THEM INTO OTHER TRUCKS, SHATTERING BULBS, BATTERING

HURLED

GETT PREFACE(206)	MODERN ANTI-SOCIALIST NOODLE'S ORATION WILL BE	HURLED	AT HIM. AND HE WILL HAVE TO PROCEED WITHOUT THE
SUPR II SD(62)	BY HIM TO BE UNPACKED AT A MOMENT'S NOTICE AND	HURLED	AT THE HEAD OF ENGLISH LITERATURE, SCIENCE, AND ART,
METH PREFACE(R67)	OF SUCH AND SUCH A BRITISH LIBERTY WOULD BE	HURLED	FROM OFFICE IN A WEEK. THIS WAS NOT TRUE: THERE WAS
CYMB V (139)	TONS OF HORSE AND MAN IN ONE ENORMOUS SHOCK	HURLED	ON OUR SHAKEN LEGIONS. THEN THEIR CHARIOTS WITH EVERY
SUPR PREFACE(R15)	FOR INSTANCE, DON JUAN'S SUPERNATURAL ANTAGONIST	HURLED	THOSE WHO REFUSE TO REPENT INTO LAKES OF BURNING

HURLING

NEVR IV (296)	/PHILIP/ SH! /BOHUN/ (UNEXPECTEDLY BEGINNING BY	HURLING	A QUESTION STRAIGHT AT DOLLY) HAVE YOU ANY INTENTION
METH PREFACE(R55)	THAT IN THE YEAR 1906 I INDULGED MY TEMPER BY	HURLING	INVECTIVES AT THE NEO-DARWINIANS IN THE FOLLOWING
UNPL PREFACE(R9)	PROFOUNDLY AND WITTILY; WHEREAS DR JOHNSON, IN	HURLING	THAT EPITHET AT HIM, WAS BUT PICKING UP THE CHEAPEST
MTH2 (66)	LABORER. MAY I COUNT ON YOUR SUPPORT? /BURGE/ (	HURLING	THE EPITHET AT HIM) HUMBUG! /SAVVY/ STOP. (THEY
MIS. PREFACE(89)	MY EXCRUCIATION BY RISING WITH YELLS OF FURY AND	HURLING	THEIR PROGRAMS AND OPERA GLASSES AT THE MISCREANT,
PYGM IV (262)	DOOR). /LIZA/ (SNATCHING UP THE SLIPPERS, AND	HURLING	THEM AT HIM ONE AFTER THE OTHER WITH ALL HER FORCE)

HURLS

CATH 2 (175)	CHAIR. NARYSHKIN DEPRECATES WITH A GESTURE: SHE	HURLS	AN EMPHATIC REPETITION AT HIM) NOTHING! ! I WEAR A
GETT PREFACE(223)	CONVENIENT, NOT TO MENTION THE FOUL EPITHETS IT	HURLS	FREELY AT THOSE WHO ARE ASHAMED OF IT. UNPOPULARITY OF
2TRU II (64)	(RETURNING WITH A SILK CUSHION, WHICH SHE	HURLS	HARD AT AUBREY'S HEAD) THERE! AND NOW I GIVE YOU BOTH
SIM PRO,3, (35)	/THE Y.W./ (SCREAMING) NO. /THE E.O./ YES. (HE	HURLS	HER OVER). A SCREAM CUT SHORT BY A SPLASH. THE E. O.
PRES (156)	A PERSON OUT YOU SHOULD DO IT LIKE THIS. (SHE	HURLS	HIM FROM THE ROOM. HE IS HEARD FALLING HEADLONG
CURE (232)	HANDS YOUVE GOT! /STREGA/ THE IDEA! (SHE	HURLS	HIM TO THE CARPET). /REGINALD/ (ON THE FLOOR STARING
FANY III SD(306)	HIS PROTENDED COUNTENANCE A BOX ON THE CHEEK. HE	HURLS	HIMSELF ON HER. THEY WRESTLE. /BOBBY/ CAT! I'LL TEACH
MTH5 SD(238)	THE WOMAN! PYGMALION, SEEING WHAT IS HAPPENING,	HURLS	HIMSELF ON THE FEMALE FIGURE AND WRENCHES THE STONE
CLEO III (148)	AGAINST SICILIAN, CURSE YOU. TAKE THAT. (HE	HURLS	HIS PILUM AT APOLLODORUS, WHO DROPS EXPERTLY ON ONE
BARB II (309)	IT AHT O Y-- (BILL SNATCHES UP SHIRLEY'S MUG AND	HURLS	IT AT HER. SHE SLAMS THE LOFT DOOR AND VANISHES. THE
KING I (210)	AND GUNPOWDER MORE POWERFUL THAN THE STEAM WHICH	HURLS	THE STONES FROM ETNA IN ERUPTION, YET CANNOT YOU MAKE

HURRAH

CLEO III (165)	THE BOAT HAS REACHED HIM: HIP, HIP, HIP,	HURRAH	!
SIM II (64)	YOUR BURDENS ON ME, LAZY IDLE CHILDREN. /KANCHIN/	HURRAH	! ALL BURDENS ON PROLA. /JANGA/ THE BURDEN OF
PHIL III (135)	(TRANSPORTED) YOU HAVE CALLED ME PERCY!	HURRAH	! CHARTERIS AND CRAVEN COME IN. PARAMORE HASTENS TO
FABL I (102)	ALONG WAVING A NEWSPAPER AND CHEERING. /M. A. M./	HURRAH	! HAVE YOU HEARD THE NEWS? /YOUNG MAN/ NO. WHATS
BASH II,1, (103)	DUTCHMAN WENT TO GRASS, A BEATEN MAN." /LYDIA/	HURRAH	! HURRAH! HURRAH! OH, WELL DONE, CASHEL!
BASH II,1, (103)	WENT TO GRASS, A BEATEN MAN." /LYDIA/ HURRAH!	HURRAH	! HURRAH! OH, WELL DONE, CASHEL! /BASHVILLE/ " A
FABL I (102)	AND WHITE. YOU MAY KEEP IT. I'LL BUY ANOTHER.	HURRAH	! HURRAH! ! HURRAH! ! HE HANDS OVER THE PAPER
POSN (466)	BLANCO'S STANDING, RIGHT ALONG TO THE ELDER'S.	HURRAH	! (THEY RUSH OUT, DRAGGING THE ELDER WITH THEM).
BASH II,1, (103)	GRASS, A BEATEN MAN." /LYDIA/ HURRAH! HURRAH!	HURRAH	! OH, WELL DONE, CASHEL! /BASHVILLE/ " A SCENE OF
FABL I (102)	YOU MAY KEEP IT. I'LL BUY ANOTHER. HURRAH!	HURRAH	! ! HURRAH! ! ! HE HANDS OVER THE PAPER AND
FABL I (102)	KEEP IT. I'LL BUY ANOTHER. HURRAH! HURRAH! !	HURRAH	! ! ! HE HANDS OVER THE PAPER AND RUSHES AWAY,

HURRA-A-AY

FANY III (324)	(SHE SHAKES HANDS WITH HIM WARMLY). /BOBBY/	HURRA-A-AY	! AND SO SAY ALL OF US. DUVALLET, HAVING

HURRAY

BULL IV (150)	/AUNT JUDY/ (WAVING A HALF KNITTED SOCK) HIP HIP	HURRAY	! THE CHEERS ARE GIVEN WITH GREAT HEARTINESS, AS IT

HURRAY-AY-AY

JOAN 3 (93)	SHRILLY) THE MAID! THE MAID! GOD AND THE MAID!	HURRAY-AY-AY	! (HE SNATCHES UP THE SHIELD AND LANCE, AND

HURRICANE

PYGM II SD(224)	LIKE THIS. HIGGINS, THUS SCOLDED, SUBSIDES. THE	HURRICANE	IS SUCCEEDED BY A ZEPHYR OF AMIABLE SURPRISE.
SUPR I (36)	PASSIONS WOULD SWEEP IT AWAY LIKE A LEAF BEFORE A	HURRICANE	. IT IS THE BIRTH OF THAT PASSION THAT TURNS A
MILL I (164)	YOU MIGHT AS WELL TRY TO SEPARATE YOURSELF FROM A	HURRICANE	. (HE BECOMES SENTENTIOUS). LISTEN TO ME,
GENV IV (123)	SHALL SEE. I SHALL SWEEP THROUGH RURITANIA LIKE A	HURRICANE	. /COMMISSAR/ DO SO BY ALL MEANS, COMRADE BATTLER.
MTH2 (49)	WHEN THE SHIP OF STATE WEATHERED THE MIGHTIEST	HURRICANE	THAT HAS EVER BURST WITH EARTH-SHAKING VIOLENCE ON

HURRIED

PLES PREFACE(R8)	FORMER VISIT TO ITALY ON THE SAME BUSINESS I HAD	HURRIED	BACK TO BIRMINGHAM TO DISCHARGE MY DUTIES AS MUSICAL
CAPT III (284)	HIM OUT OF THE HANDS OF CAPTAIN BRASSBOUND, I	HURRIED	ON BOARD THE YACHT AND TOLD THE OWNER TO SCOUR THE
CLEO NOTES (203)	FOR BALDNESS. FOR THE SAKE OF CONCISENESS IN A	HURRIED	SITUATION I HAVE MADE CLEOPATRA RECOMMEND RUM. THIS,
CATH 4 (196)	ARCHWAY SHE STOPS AND TURNS TO EDSTASTON, WHO HAS	HURRIED	TO LIFT THE CURTAIN FOR HER). CAPTAIN: I WISH YOU
DEVL I (20)	MAN. /TITUS/ DO NOT LET YOURSELF BE ORDERED OR	HURRIED	, MR HAWKINS. /HAWKINS/ (VERY POLITELY AND

HURRIEDLY

SIM PRO,2, (27)	AND MADE FOR THE SEA AIR. /THE E.O./ (RISING	HURRIEDLY	) I CANT STAND ANY MORE OF THIS. (HE TAKES A

ROCK I	(198)	UP, THOROUGHLY ROUSED) I! ! ! ! /BASHAM/ (	HURRIEDLY	) NO: OF COURSE YOU COULDNT. ONLY, IT WOULD DO
DEST	(171)	YOU WILL BE EMPEROR OF FRANCE-- /NAPOLEON/ (	HURRIEDLY	) TAKE CARE. TREASON! /LADY/ (INSISTING) YES,
PRES	(162)	CORINTHIA/ FAREWELL, CREATURE. (BALSQUITH ENTERS	HURRIEDLY	). MR BALSQUITH: I AM GOING TO WAIT ON GENERAL
			HURRIES	
DEST	SD(173)	AVERTING HER HEAD. THE MOMENT HE TAKES THEM, SHE	HURRIES	ACROSS TO THE OTHER SIDE OF THE ROOM; SITS DOWN; AND
WIDO I	(19)	GRACIOUSLY WAVES HIM OFF TO JOIN BLANCHE. TRENCH	HURRIES	AFTER HER THROUGH THE GATE. THE LIGHT REDDENS AS THE
GETT	(286)	COME, ALICE (SHE VANISHES. MRS BRIDGENORTH	HURRIES	AFTER HER). /THE BISHOP/ THIS MEANS A DELAY. I SHALL
2TRU III	(109)	HIS WATERCOLORS, AND HIS K. C. B. (THE COLONEL	HURRIES	AWAY NOISELESSLY IN THE OPPOSITE DIRECTION),
SUPR IV	(155)	IS A FINANCIER OF BRIGANDS. (TANNER	HURRIES	AWAY TO OVERTAKE MALONE AND RAMSDEN. ANN STROLLS TO
SIM PRO,3,	(31)	OH, REALLY! SO SORRY TO HAVE TROUBLED YOU. (SHE	HURRIES	AWAY). /THE PRIEST/ (RESUMING HIS SEAT) YOU SHOULD
SUPR IV	(170)	BUT DOES NOT KNOW WHAT TO DO. MRS WHITEFIELD	HURRIES	BACK INTO THE VILLA. OCTAVIUS, MALONE, AND RAMSDEN
ARMS I	SD(7)	DRESSING TABLE, BLOWS OUT THE LIGHT THERE, AND	HURRIES	BACK TO BED IN THE DARK, NOTHING BEING VISIBLE BUT
CAND I	(96)	HAS THE BAG). NOW OPEN THE DOOR FOR ME. (HE	HURRIES	BEFORE HER AND OPENS THE DOOR). THANKS. (SHE GOES
CAPT I	SD(234)	HAVING BEEN VIOLENTLY KICKED. MARZO IMMEDIATELY	HURRIES	DOWN THE GARDEN ON SIR HOWARD'S RIGHT OUT OF THE
ARMS II	(42)	FOLLOWED BY SERGIUS). /PETKOFF/ (AS HE	HURRIES	DOWN THE STEPS) MY DEAR CAPTAIN BLUNTSCHLI--
CLEO III	SD(149)	SQUATTING AMONG THE BALES. THE BOATMAN, ALARMED,	HURRIES	DOWN THE STEPS OUT OF HARM'S WAY, BUT STOPS, WITH
CAND III	SD(134)	AT MORELL. SEEING THAT HE IS DISTRESSED, SHE	HURRIES	DOWN TO HIM, GREATLY VEXED. /CANDIDA/ YOU HAVE BEEN
PHIL II	SD(103)	PARAMORE, SEEING THE COLONEL APPARENTLY ILL,	HURRIES	DOWN TO HIM WITH HIS BEDSIDE MANNER IN FULL PLAY.
SUPR IV	(170)	THE CORNER OF THE LAWN; AND OCTAVIUS IMMEDIATELY	HURRIES	DOWN TO HIM). /TAVY/ (ASIDE TO TANNER, GRASPING HIS
MTH4 II	SD(182)	TO NAPOLEON'S RIGHT, WHILST THE ENVOY'S WIFE	HURRIES	EFFUSIVELY TO HIS LEFT. THE ENVOY MEANWHILE PASSES
BULL III	(140)	(BEHIND THE CORNER OF THE HOUSE) YES, SIR. (HE	HURRIES	FORWARD). /BROADBENT/ HODSON: THIS GENTLEMAN'S
CLEO II	(139)	AND BORROW HIS LEGIONS TO PUT OUT THE FIRE. (HE	HURRIES	HIM TO THE STEPS). /POTHINUS/ (SIGNIFICANTLY) YOU
ROCK I	SD(193)	HE READS THE TIMES UNTIL HIS SECRETARY	HURRIES	IN FROM HER OFFICE, WITH HER NOTEBOOK AND A SHEAF OF
DEVL II	(43)	THE DOOR. IT IS OPENED IN HER FACE BY ESSIE, WHO	HURRIES	IN FULL OF ANXIETY. THE SURPRISE IS SO DISAGREEABLE
JITT I	SD(13)	ROOM OPEN. IMMEDIATELY AFTERWARDS A VEILED LADY	HURRIES	IN LIKE A HUNTED CREATURE. HE FOLLOWS HER; SHUTS THE
6CAL	SD(100)	HOUND LIE. HANGING IS TOO GOOD FOR HIM. THE QUEEN	HURRIES	IN WITH HER LADIES IN GREAT CONCERN. THE MEN-AT-ARMS
MILL II	SD(170)	ENGLISH TOO WELL TO BE MISTAKEN FOR A NATIVE.	HURRIES	IN. /THE EGYPTIAN/ (PEREMPTORILY) WHATS THE
CATH	3,SD(183)	THE GARDEN GATE OPENED AND CLOSED. EDSTASTON	HURRIES	IN, WITH A CRY OF DELIGHT SHE THROWS HER ARMS ROUND
MRS I	(193)	/CROFTS/ (HASTILY) SHE'S CALLING US. (HE	HURRIES	IN). PRAED SHAKES HIS HEAD BODINGLY, AND IS
O'FL	(221)	TO SMILE AT DENNY, NOT VERY CONVINCINGLY, AND	HURRIES	INTO THE HOUSE). /O'FLAHERTY/ (ALONE) AND IF I DO
BARB II	(276)	UP WITH THE FOOD, MISS: E'S FAIR DONE. (JENNY	HURRIES	INTO THE SHELTER). ERE, BUCK UP, DADDY! SHE'S
JITT III	(56)	MRS HALDENSTEDT WANTS TO SPEAK TO YOU. (HE	HURRIES	INTO THE STUDY). /AGNES/ (SHAKING HER HEAD) YOU
CAPT III	SD(282)	WHAT ARE THEY DOING WITH THOSE PRISONERS? RANKIN	HURRIES	IN, AND TAKES HIS PLACE NEAR SIR HOWARD. /SIR
KING I	(220)	DOES NOT GET AT IT FIRST. LET US HURRY. (SHE	HURRIES	JAMES OUT). /MRS BASHAM/ WILL YOU TAKE THE PLAYER
2TRU III	(95)	/TALLBOYS/ I REALLY MUST-- (HE BREAKS AWAY AND	HURRIES	OFF ALONG THE BEACH PAST THE ABODE OF LOVE). /MRS
PYGM I	(213)	(SHE GATHERS HER SKIRTS ABOVE HER ANKLES AND	HURRIES	OFF TOWARDS THE STAND). /THE DAUGHTER/ BUT THE CAB--
DEST	(180)	WITH HIM. (GIUSEPPE, WITH UNRUFFLED READINESS,	HURRIES	OFF. NAPOLEON TURNS CURTLY TO THE LADY, SAYING) I
PHIL II	(109)	/THE PAGE/ (SERIOUSLY) INDEED, SIR? (HE	HURRIES	OFF). /CHARTERIS/ THAT BOY WILL MAKE HIS WAY IN THIS
MRS III	(223)	AIR. (THE CLERGYMAN, DAZED BUT OBEDIENT,	HURRIES	OFF). /FRANK/ WE MUST GET THE OLD GIRL BACK TO TOWN
CLEO IV	(192)	AWAY, LUCIUS; AND GIVE THE WORD. (LUCIUS	HURRIES	OUT AFTER BRITANNUS.) APOLLODORUS: LEND ME YOUR
ROCK I	SD(205)	AND GOES OUT. SIR ARTHUR LOOKS AT HILDA. SHE	HURRIES	OUT ALMOST ON TIPTOE. /SIR ARTHUR/ (TAKING HIS WIFE
BULL I	(81)	HE'S COMIN BACK. GOODBYE AND GOD BLESS YE. (HE	HURRIES	OUT ALMOST CRYING, THE 5 POUND NOTE AND ALL THE
DEST	(157)	UP HIS TRAY) CERTAINLY, EXCELLENCY. (HE	HURRIES	OUT BY THE INNER DOOR). /THE MAN'S VOICE/ (
MRS II	SD(207)	CROFTS, UNABLE TO RECOVER HIS PRESENCE OF MIND,	HURRIES	OUT OF THE COTTAGE. THE CLERGYMAN APPEARS AT THE
WIDO III	SD(55)	THE PARLORMAID LOOKS AT HER FACE, AND INSTANTLY	HURRIES	OUT OF THE ROOM ON TIPTOE WITH HER TRAY. /BLANCHE/
CLEO III	(156)	ISLAND. I MUST SEE WHAT THEIR BUSINESS IS. (HE	HURRIES	OUT PAST THE LIGHTHOUSE). /CAESAR/ (COMING AWAY
GETT	(263)	WEDDING. /THE GENERAL/ I CANT BEAR IT (HE	HURRIES	OUT THROUGH THE GARDEN DOOR). /COLLINS/ (PUTTING
BARB III	(323)	THANKS AWFULLY, OLD MAN. COME, MY OWNEST. (HE	HURRIES	OUT TO SECURE HIS SEAT IN THE CARRIAGE. SARAH
BULL IV	SD(149)	A YOUNG MAN, FEELING THAT HE MUST LAUGH OR BURST,	HURRIES	OUT. BARNEY PUTS AN IRON CONSTRAINT ON HIS FEATURES.
CLEO II	(136)	GET YOUR WOUND ATTENDED TO. GO. (THE SOLDIER	HURRIES	OUT. CAESAR COMES DOWN THE HALL BETWEEN RUFIO AND
CAND I	(92)	PAY FOR THE CAB; AND I DONT WANT THAT. (MORELL	HURRIES	OUT. CANDIDA PUTS DOWN HER HANDBAG; THEN TAKES OFF
CAPT II	SD(268)	LUGGAGE. OSMAN, AFTER A MOMENT OF STUPEFACTION,	HURRIES	OUT. LADY CICELY PUTS ON HER HAT AND PINS IT TO HER
FABL II	SD(105)	HAVE HEARD-- LORD O. BURSTS IN. THE SECRETARY	HURRIES	OUT. /OLDHAND/ ULSTERBRIDGE: HAVE YOU HEARD THE
CATH	2 (181)	GONE BEFORE YOU ARRIVED WITH THE MESSAGE. (HE	HURRIES	OUT. THE OTHER THREE, TOO TAKEN ABACK TO STOP HIM,
BASH II,1,	(111)	NEXT, ABLUTION; ELSE I SHALL BE TOTAL GULES. (HE	HURRIES	OUT.) /LYDIA/ HOW WELL HE SPEAKS! THERE IS A SILVER
CAND II	(110)	UP HER NOTE-BOOK AND PAPERS) THATS FOR ME. (SHE	HURRIES	OUT). /BURGESS/ (CALLING AFTER HER) OH, WE CAN
CLEO II	(139)	TO POTHINUS) I MUST GO TO SAVE THE LIBRARY. (HE	HURRIES	OUT). /CAESAR/ FOLLOW HIM TO THE GATE, POTHINUS. BID
JOAN	6 (147)	LORD, YOU MUST EXERCISE YOUR OWN AUTHORITY. (HE	HURRIES	OUT). /CAUCHON/ THESE ENGLISH ARE IMPOSSIBLE: THEY
PHIL I	(90)	I CANT. I'LL WAIT FOR YOU IN THE HALL. (SHE	HURRIES	OUT). /CRAVEN/ (FOLLOWING HER) BUT WHAT ON EARTH AM
HART II	(127)	ME, WILL YOU, LIKE A GOOD CHAP. GOODNIGHT. (HE	HURRIES	OUT). /HECTOR/ POOR WRETCH! OH WOMEN! WOMEN!
CAPT III	(281)	TO SOMEBODY BEFORE THE INQUIRY BEGINS. (SHE	HURRIES	OUT). /KEARNEY/ THERE IS SERTNLY A WONDERFUL CHAHM
HART I	(56)	OH DEAR! I BELIEVE HE IS WHISTLING FOR ME. (HE	HURRIES	OUT). /MRS HUSHABYE/ NOW MY FATHER IS A WONDERFUL
DEST	(194)	/GIUSEPPE/ GESU MARIA! (HE CROSSES HIMSELF AND	HURRIES	OUT). /NAPOLEON/ (THROWING DOWN THE LETTERS IN A
APPL I	(202)	TO HIS MAJESTY. I WILL SEE ABOUT IT. (HE	HURRIES	OUT). /PAMPHILIUS/ BE SEATED, MR BOANERGES.
DOCT I	(106)	TIME YOU TURN OUT YOUR WARDROBE. GOODBYE. (HE	HURRIES	OUT). /RIDGEON/ (LOOKING AFTER HIM) POOR CHAP! (
FANY PROLOG	(272)	I MUST HAVE JUST A LITTLE BRUSH UP: I-- (HE	HURRIES	OUT). /THE COUNT/ MY DEAR, YOU SHOULD BE IN THE
2TRU I	(49)	BEAT OUTSIDE. SPY OUT AND SEE. SAFETY FIRST (SHE	HURRIES	OUT). /THE BURGLAR/ WELL, FOR JUST THIS ONCE, SAFETY
MTH2	(44)	THE LINE, SIR. /FRANKLYN/ YES: ALL RIGHT (HE	HURRIES	OUT). THE PARLOR MAID GOES TO THE HEARTHRUG TO MAKE
JITT I	SD(26)	OVER HIM; KISSES HER HAND; CROSSES HERSELF; AND	HURRIES	OUT, CLOSING THE DOOR VERY SOFTLY BEHIND HER.
CATH	1,SD(163)	PEACE? THE SERGEANT SALUTES JOYFULLY AND	HURRIES	OUT, DIVINING THAT PATIOMKIN HAS INTENDED TO SEE THE
MILL IV	SD(197)	(TO ADRIAN) HAVE YOU HURT YOURSELF? THE MANAGER	HURRIES	OUT, GLAD TO ESCAPE FROM THE MELEE. /ADRIAN/ HURT
MIS.	(191)	I DONT GIVE DAMN FOR THE LOT OF YOU. (HE	HURRIES	OUT, RATHER AFRAID OF THE CONSEQUENCES OF THIS
JOAN	6,SD(151)	HIMSELF SOME MISCHIEF. AFTER HIM, QUICK. LADVENU	HURRIES	OUT, WARWICK URGING HIM. THE EXECUTIONER COMES IN BY
GETT	SD(272)	PLACIDITY QUITE UPSET, COMES IN WITH A LETTER;	HURRIES	PAST COLLINS; AND COMES BETWEEN LESBIA AND THE
CAND II	(109)	AT THE TRAGIC MASK PRESENTED TO HER, SHE	HURRIES	PAST HIM AT THE UTMOST POSSIBLE DISTANCE, KEEPING
DEVL I	(20)	SUFFER ENOUGH IN THIS HOUSE WITHOUT-- (HE	HURRIES	REMORSEFULLY TO ESSIE). COME, LITTLE COUSIN! NEVER
MRS I	(189)	SO. (VIVIE REAPPEARS WITH TWO MORE CHAIRS. HE	HURRIES	TO HER ASSISTANCE). ALLOW ME. /MRS WARREN/ (
CLEO V	(196)	HAS MADE SHORT WORK OF THEM. HERE HE COMES. (HE	HURRIES	TO HIS POST IN FRONT OF THE EGYPTIAN LINES).
FANY EPIL,SD(328)		THE CURTAIN. THE COUNT, DAZED AND AGITATED,	HURRIES	TO THE 4 CRITICS, AS THEY RISE, BORED AND WEARY,
PYGM II	(239)	THANK YOU, GOVERNOR. GOOD MORNING. (HE	HURRIES	TO THE DOOR, ANXIOUS TO GET AWAY WITH HIS BOOTY.
SUPR I	SD(16)	AND HER MOTHER; AND RAMSDEN SPRINGS UP AND	HURRIES	TO THE DOOR TO RECEIVE THEM. WHETHER ANN IS
MILL I	(165)	MR SAGAMORE (THEY SHAKE HANDS QUICKLY. SHE	HURRIES	TO THE DOOR). YOULL SEE. (SHE GOES OUT). /SAGAMORE/
ROCK I	(198)	SO MUCH OF YOUR TIME: I KNOW IT'S PRICELESS. (HE	HURRIES	TO THE DOOR; THEN HESITATES AND ADDS) BY THE WAY, I
APPL I	SD(258)	LIKE A MAN ASSURED OF AN ENTHUSIASTIC WELCOME,	HURRIES	TO THE QUEEN, AND SALUTES HER WITH A HANDSHAKE SO
CAND II	(114)	MARCHBANKS. BURGESS LOOKS ROUND, AMAZED. CANDIDA	HURRIES	TO THE SOFA). WHATS THE MATTER? ARE YOU ILL,
GETT	(342)	A GLASS OF WATER IN THE STUDY-- QUICK. (SOAMES	HURRIES	TO THE STUDY DOOR). /MRS GEORGE/ NO. (SOAMES
GETT	SD(323)	REGINALD AT THE GARDEN DOOR. MRS BRIDGENORTH	HURRIES	TO THE TOWER TO RECEIVE HER GUEST, AND GETS AS FAR
JOAN	6 (142)	THAT HE HAS SAVED YOU AT THE ELEVENTH HOUR! (HE	HURRIES	TO THE VACANT SEAT AT THE SCRIBES' TABLE, AND
CAND III	(138)	(AFFRIGHTEDLY) YES: I'D BETTER GO. (HE	HURRIES	TOWARDS THE DOOR; BUT CANDIDA PLACES HERSELF BEFORE
NEVR III	(263)	(GLORIA, IN UNGOVERNABLE APPREHENSION, RISES AND	HURRIES	TOWARDS THE DOOR). /MRS CLANDON/ (HALF RISING)
DEVL I	SD(5)	MUFFLED IN A PLAIN SHAWL AND GREY OVERCOAT. HE	HURRIES	, SHIVERING, TO THE FIRE, LEAVING MRS DUDGEON TO
			HURRY	
DOCT I	(106)	SEE HER. DO YOU HEAR? /EMMY/ OH, SHE AINT IN A	HURRY	: SHE DOESNT MIND HOW LONG SHE WAITS. (SHE GOES OUT).
AUGS	(281)	A RABBIT. I ASK MYSELF, WHY WAS SHE IN SUCH A	HURRY	? /THE LADY'S VOICE/ (FROM THE STREET) LORD
GETT	(266)	MAY I SEND UP WORD FROM YOU TO MISS EDITH TO	HURRY	A BIT WITH HER DRESSING? /MRS BRIDGENORTH/ DO.
GENV I	(31)	THE WORK. IF IT WERENT, AS I SAY, THAT THERES NO	HURRY	ABOUT IT, I SHOULD NEVER GET THROUGH IT. JUST LOOK
SUPR III	(77)	HILL. MENDOZA PRODUCES AN OPERA GLASS. THE OTHERS	HURRY	ACROSS TO THE ROAD AND DISAPPEAR TO THE NORTH).
MILL PREFACE(115)		OF FRANCE FOR HIS MARCH TO MOSCOW, ONLY TO	HURRY	BACK LEAVING HIS LEGIONS DEAD IN THE SNOW, AND
MTH1 I	(15)	A RING OF THE SNAKE). /ADAM/ THERE NEED BE NO	HURRY	EVEN THEN. /EVE/ I SEE YOU WILL PUT IT OFF UNTIL
GETT	(285)	ORANGE BLOSSOMS YET? /MRS BRIDGENORTH/ DO GO AND	HURRY	HER, LESBIA. /LESBIA/ (GOING OUT THROUGH THE TOWER)
BULL II	(107)	COULD HE BE LARRY, WOMAN ALIVE? LARRY'S IN NO	HURRY	HOME, IT SEEMS. I HAVNT SET EYES ON HIM. THIS IS HIS
BULL II	(110)	(CONTEMPTUOUSLY) ARRA HWAT UD HAPPEN TO HER?	HURRY	IN NOW, CORNY. COME, MR BROADBENT: I LEFT THE TEA ON
CLEO IV	(192)	MY ONLY SON? (HE CLAPS HIS HANDS. THE SLAVES	HURRY	IN TO THE TABLE). NO MORE OF THIS MAWKISH REVELLING:
JOAN	2 (86)	(HE SITS DOWN IN THE ROYAL CHAIR AS THEY ALL	HURRY	IN TO THEIR FORMER PLACES, CHATTERING AND WONDERING).
LION II	SD(140)	IN ETRUSCAN MASKS, WITH ROPES AND DRAG HOOKS,	HURRY	IN. /ONE OF THE SLAVES/ HOW MANY DEAD? /THE CALL BOY/

JOAN	6,SD(126)	NOBLES ARE JUST AS BAD. THE BISHOP'S ASSESSORS	HURRY	INTO THE HALL, HEADED BY CHAPLAIN DE STOGUMBER AND
DOCT	PREFACE(23)	IS ALWAYS IN A HURRY; BUT IT DOES NOT FOLLOW THAT	HURRY	IS THE CAUSE OF UNPUNCTUALITY: ON THE CONTRARY, WHAT
PHIL II	(128)	(HE GETS BETWEEN CRAVEN AND CUTHBERTSON). WHAT	HURRY	IS THERE? CANT YOU GIVE THE MAN TIME? /CRAVEN/
LIED	(198)	FORMALLY) I AM AT YOUR SERVICE. /HER HUSBAND/ NO	HURRY	. AFTER THE THEATRE WILL DO. /HE/ WE HAVE DECIDED NOT
MTH3	(104)	/BURGE-LUBIN/ STEADY, BARNABAS. DONT BE IN A	HURRY	. CONFUCIUS ENTERS. /THE ARCHBISHOP/ (RISING) GOOD
POSN	(461)	STOP A BIT, STOP A BIT. DONT YOU BE IN SUCH A	HURRY	. DONT LET HIM GO. NOT MUCH. BLANCO STANDS MOTIONLESS,
CAPT III	(276)	YE, SIR HOWRRD. /LADY CICELY/ HOWARD: HE'S IN A	HURRY	. DONT MAKE HIM STOP TO TALK. /SIR HOWARD/ VERY GOOD,
MIS.	(186)	(GOING TO HIM) SIP IT, DEAR. DONT BE IN A	HURRY	. GUNNER SIPS SLOWLY, EACH SIP MAKING HIS EYES WATER.
DEVL III	(77)	NOW, GENERAL, TIME PRESSES; AND AMERICA IS IN A	HURRY	. HAVE YOU REALIZED THAT THOUGH YOU MAY OCCUPY TOWNS
APPL I	(227)	HIS HEAD AT HER) TRAITOR! /PROTEUS/ I AM IN NO	HURRY	. HIS MAJESTY'S SPEECHES ARE VERY WISE AND
HART I	(80)	BEFORE HE CAN POINT HIS GUN AT ME. AND I MUST	HURRY	. I AM OLD: I HAVE NO TIME TO WASTE IN TALK (HE IS
ARMS II	(33)	YOU STAY HERE, MY DEAR SERGIUS: THERES NO	HURRY	. I HAVE A WORD OR TWO TO SAY TO PAUL. (SERGIUS
JITT II	(41)	SITS DOWN TO EXAMINE ITS CONTENTS. HE IS IN NO	HURRY	. IT CONTAINS NOTHING BUT THE MANUSCRIPT OF A BIGGISH
MRS III	(228)	OF THE INEVITABLE ROUTINE OF COURTSHIP) I'M IN NO	HURRY	. IT WAS ONLY JUST TO LET YOU KNOW IN CASE YOUNG
KING I	(220)	PROVIDED CHARLES DOES NOT GET AT IT FIRST. LET US	HURRY	. (SHE HURRIES JAMES OUT). /MRS BASHAM/ WILL YOU TAKE
MILL I	(141)	THIS EVENING. OR EVEN TOMORROW EVENING. THERES NO	HURRY	. /EPIFANIA/ YOU ARE A BRUTE, A BEAST, AND A PIG. MY
PYGM II	(242)	HIM AS A CLERGYMAN. YOU WONT SEE HIM AGAIN IN A	HURRY	. /HIGGINS/ I DONT WANT TO, ELIZA. DO YOU? /LIZA/ NOT
NEVR III	(274)	/DOLLY/ SERVE YOU RIGHT. YOU WERE IN TOO GREAT A	HURRY	. /PHILIP/ (PATTING HIM ON THE SHOULDER) NEVER MIND:
SUPR III	(137)	WE WERE ADVISED TO WAIT FOR IT; BUT I WAS IN A	HURRY	. /THE ROWDY ONE/ (IN AN AGONY OF APPREHENSION) AND
VWOO 2	(128)	NO MATTER HOW LONG YOU THINK. /A/ YOU ARE IN A	HURRY	. /Z/ WELL, I AM PAST THE AGE AT WHICH GIRLS MARRY
VWOO 2	(128)	WHY? HAVE YOU ANY INTENTIONS? /A/ DONT BE IN A	HURRY	. WEVE KNOWN EACH OTHER LESS THAN TEN MINUTES. /Z/ HOW
CLEO I	(112)	BETWEEN WHICH, AS THE PASSING TORCH MAKES THEM	HURRY	NOISELESSLY BACKWARDS, FIGURES OF MEN WITH WINGS AND
3PLA	PREFACE(R40)	YEARS OLD, IS STILL AHEAD OF OUR VOTERS. WE MUST	HURRY	ON; WE MUST GET RID OF REPUTATIONS: THEY ARE WEEDS IN
JOAN	6,SD(146)	WITH HER. THE EXECUTIONER AND HIS ASSISTANTS	HURRY	OUT THROUGH THE COURTYARD. /LADVENU/ YOU WICKED GIRL:
APPL I	SD(241)	COME ON, COME ON: IT'S EVER SO LATE. THEY ALL	HURRY	OUT, SEMPRONIUS AND PAMPHILIUS, ENTERING, HAVE TO
CAPT II	SD(265)	AY AY, SIR. /REDBROOK/ RIGHTO, GOVERNOR. THEY	HURRY	OUT, WITH A FEW OTHERS. DRINKWATER STARES AFTER THEM,
SUPR	HANDBOK(179)	ARE WE TO DO? II: PROPERTY AND MARRIAGE. LET US	HURRY	OVER THE OBSTACLES SET UP BY PROPERTY AND MARRIAGE.
DOCT	PREFACE(23)	OF A CAUSE. AN UNPUNCTUAL MAN IS ALWAYS IN A	HURRY	; BUT IT DOES NOT FOLLOW THAT HURRY IS THE CAUSE OF
CLEO II	(138)	/CAESAR/ FORGIVE ME, RUFIO; AND (ANXIOUSLY)	HURRY	THEM AS MUCH AS-- HE IS INTERRUPTED BY AN OUTCRY AS OF
DOCT V	(171)	I THINK I'D BETTER RUN OVER TO THE PRINTERS TO	HURRY	THEM UP. /JENNIFER/ OH, IF YOU WOULD BE SO GOOD, MR
MILL III	(183)	APOLOGY? AND NOW TO WORK, TO WORK. I AM IN A	HURRY	TO GET TO WORK. /THE MAN/ WELL, WHAT WORK CAN YOU DO?
MIS.	(176)	HAD THE POLICE IN. IF YOU HAD, YOUD NOT BE IN A	HURRY	TO HAVE THEM IN AGAIN. NOW, YOUNG MAN: CUT THE CACKLE;
PHIL III	SD(142)	NOT THINK ME UTTERLY VILE? CRAVEN AND PARAMORE	HURRY	TO HER IN THE GREATEST CONSTERNATION. /CRAVEN/ (
GETT	(326)	CECIL. REJJY. (STARTLED BY HIS URGENCY, THEY	HURRY	TO HIM). I'M FRIGHTFULLY SORRY TO DESERT ON THIS DAY;
MIS.	SD(152)	DOWN? THE GROUP BREAKS UP. JOHNNY AND BENTLEY	HURRY	TO THE PAVILION AND FETCH THE TWO WICKER CHAIRS.
HART II	(86)	TO OUTRUN HIS EXPENSES AND BE IN TOO GREAT A	HURRY	TO WAIT FOR HIS MARKET. I KNEW THAT THE SUREST WAY TO
BARB II	(276)	YOULL FIND REST AND PEACE AND APPINESS ERE.	HURRY	UP WITH THE FOOD, MISS: E'S FAIR DONE. (JENNY HURRIES
2TRU II	(75)	YESSIR. (HE GOES INTO THE PAVILION). /TALLBOYS/	HURRY	UP. (HE SETTLES HIMSELF COMFORTABLY AND TAKES OUT HIS
2TRU I	(49)	TO THE NURSE) DID YOU SPEAK? /THE NURSE/ NO.	HURRY	UP, WILL YOU. /THE BURGLAR/ IT MUST HAVE BEEN YOUR
GETT	(306)	AS UNCONCERNED AS POSSIBLE. /COLLINS/ SORRY TO	HURRY	YOU, MY LORD; BUT THE CHURCH HAS BEEN FULL THIS HOUR
POSN	(462)	IS NOT A HEALTHY PLACE FOR YOU. AS YOU ARE IN A	HURRY	, I'LL SELL YOU THE HORSE AT A REASONABLE FIGURE. NOW,
DEVL III	(73)	AND RETIRES BEHIND THE GALLOWS). YOU SEEM IN A	HURRY	, MR DUDGEON. /RICHARD/ (WITH THE HORROR OF DEATH
NEVR II	(249)	DISPARAGEMENT) AND MAKING HIS FORTUNE IN A	HURRY	, NO DOUBT. I KNOW WHAT HIS SIX WEEKS' EARNINGS COME
MTH3	(107)	COMPARATIVELY SHORT? /BURGE-LUBIN/ DONT BE IN A	HURRY	, OLD CHAP. (CONFUCIUS SITS DOWN AGAIN). THIS
LION	PREFACE(49)	OR COULD NOT BUTTON HIS ROBE WHEN HE WAS IN A	HURRY	, OR WHETHER HE LAUGHED OVER THE REPARTEES BY WHICH HE
MIS.	(178)	I'M WAITING FOR YOUR DECISION. I'M RATHER IN A	HURRY	, PLEASE. /GUNNER/ I NEVER SAID ANYTHING AGAINST THE
BULL III	(143)	ANY MESSAGE? /HODSON/ HE WAS IN TOO GREAT A	HURRY	, SIR. STARTED TO RUN HOME, SIR, AND LEFT HIS PIG
GENV I	(30)	/SHE/ OH, I CONDUCT IT ALL RIGHT. IT'S NEVER IN A	HURRY	, YOU KNOW. /HE/ BUT REALLY-- PARDON ME IF I AM TAKING

HURRYING

BULL IV	(156)	ME THINKING. THANK YOU. /BROADBENT/ (DELIGHTED,	HURRYING	ACROSS TO HIM TO SHAKE HANDS) NO, REALLY? YOU FIND
6CAL	(100)	SIR, WHAT IS THIS THEY TELL ME? /THE KING/ (	HURRYING	ACROSS TO INTERCEPT HER) MADAM: THIS IS NO PLACE
CAND I	(85)	DO YOU WALK WITH YOUR CHIN STUCK OUT BEFORE YOU,	HURRYING	ALONG WITH THAT EAGER LOOK IN YOUR EYES? YOU! WHO
MTH5	(208)	/THE MAIDEN/ (SHAKES HER HEAD)! /THE YOUTH/ (	HURRYING	BACK TO HER) WHAT IS THE MATTER? /THE MAIDEN/ (
ARMS III	(61)	DONT WANT TO KILL YOU IF I CAN HELP IT. /RAINA/ (	HURRYING	FORWARD ANXIOUSLY) I HAVE HEARD WHAT CAPTAIN
DEVL II	SD(29)	THE FIRST THING SHE SEES THERE IS HER HUSBAND,	HURRYING	HOME THROUGH THE RAIN. SHE GIVES A LITTLE GASP OF
HART III	(146)	MR HUSHABYE'S TURNED IT ON AGAIN. /THE BURGLAR/ (	HURRYING	IN AND APPEALING TO NURSE GUINNESS) HERE: WHERES
PYGM I	(206)	COMES INTO COLLISION WITH A FLOWER GIRL, WHO IS	HURRYING	IN FOR SHELTER, KNOCKING HER BASKET OUT OF HER
CYMB V	SD(141)	HE IS CONFRONTED WITH IACHIMO, BATTLE STAINED,	HURRYING	IN THE OPPOSITE DIRECTION. SEEING A BRITISH ENEMY
CYMB V	SD(141)	THE FASHION, LESS WITHOUT AND MORE WITHIN. HE IS	HURRYING	OFF WHEN HE IS CONFRONTED WITH IACHIMO, BATTLE
BARB II	(276)	YOULL BE ALL RIGHT THEN. /PRICE/ (RISING AND	HURRYING	OFFICIOUSLY TO TAKE THE OLD MAN OFF JENNY'S HANDS)
HART II	SD(110)	LADIES AND GENTLEMEN; AND THANK YOU KINDLY. HE IS	HURRYING	OUT WHEN HE IS CONFRONTED IN THE DOORWAY BY CAPTAIN
HART I	SD(48)	THE TABLE BACK TO ITS PLACE BY THE DOOR, AND IS	HURRYING	OUT WHEN SHE IS INTERCEPTED BY LADY UTTERWORD, WHO
MTH2	(47)	WHEN THE VISITOR HAS PASSED IN). /FRANKLYN/ (	HURRYING	PAST SAVVY TO HIS GUEST WITH THE FALSE CORDIALITY
CAND I	(92)	IS HORRIFIED TO FIND IT SO LATE). MY DARLING! (	HURRYING	TO HER AND SEIZING THE RUG STRAP, POURING FORTH HIS
CLEO IV	(179)	WHISPER) FTATATEETA, FTATATEETA. /FTATATEETA/ (	HURRYING	TO HER FROM THE TABLE AND PETTING HER) PEACE,
NEVR II	(260)	SINKING UPON THE BENCH) MOTHER! /MRS CLANDON/ (	HURRYING	TO HER IN ALARM) WHAT IS IT, DEAR? /GLORIA/ (WITH
DEVL II	(49)	(HE RUSHES OUT LIKE AN AVALANCHE). /ESSIE/ (	HURRYING	TO JUDITH) HE HAS GONE TO SAVE RICHARD, HASNT HE..
DEVL III	SD(71)	AT ONCE; AND THE SERGEANT AND PETTY OFFICERS,	HURRYING	TO THE BACK OF THE SQUARE, WITH A FEW WHISPERED
JITT I	SD(26)	AND SHAKES HER MANTLE STRAIGHT. SHE TURNS, AND IS	HURRYING	TO THE DOOR WHEN SHE FINDS THE BODY IN HER WAY. A
GENV IV	(124)	BE POSSIBLE ON THIS EARTH. /THE JEW/ (RISING AND	HURRYING	TO THE DOOR) EXCUSE ME. /SECRETARY/ NO USE RUNNING
CLEO V	(196)	GOES TO THE EGYPTIAN LINE. /CENTURION/ (	HURRYING	TO THE GANGWAY GUARD) ATTENTION THERE! CAESAR
MILL III	(179)	FISTS. I CAN SHOOT, IF NECESSARY. /THE WOMAN/ (	HURRYING	TO THE MAN AND HOLDING HIM) TAKE CARE, JOE. SHE'S
BARB II	SD(277)	LOITERING HERE. I MUST GET TO WORK AGAIN. SHE IS	HURRYING	TO THE SHELTER, WHEN THE NEWCOMER MOVES QUICKLY UP
METH	PREFACE(R27)	AS IT IS NOW CALLED: THIS POWER OF	HURRYING	UP INTO MONTHS A PROCESS WHICH WAS ONCE SO LONG AND

HURT

FANY II	(293)	WORST. THERES ONE GOOD THING ABOUT BEING HARD	HURT	: IT MAKES YOU SLEEP. I SLEPT IN THAT FILTHY CELL WITH
SUPR I	(25)	NOT EVEN WORSE THAN THAT. /OCTAVIUS/ IS SHE BADLY	HURT	? HAS THERE BEEN AN ACCIDENT? /RAMSDEN/ NO: NOTHING
MIS.	(149)	JOHN: ARE THEY KILLED? /LORD SUMMERHAYS/ ARE YOU	HURT	? IS ANYTHING BROKEN? CAN YOU STAND? /HYPATIA/ OH,
ARMS II	(37)	SLIGHTINGLY) OH! YOU WISH TO BE PAID FOR THE	HURT	? (HE PUTS ON HIS SHAKO, AND TAKES SOME MONEY FROM
HART III	(148)	GLASS FROM THE WINDOWS. /MAZZINI/ IS ANYONE	HURT	? /HECTOR/ WHERE DID IT FALL? /NURSE GUINNESS/ (IN
BARB II	(285)	TIRED? (LOOKING AT THE WOUNDED CHEEK) DOES IT	HURT	? /JENNY/ NO: IT'S ALL RIGHT NOW. IT WAS NOTHING.
ARMS III	(58)	FASCINATED, BUT ON HER GUARD). FFFF! DOES IT	HURT	? /LOUKA/ YES. /SERGIUS/ SHALL I CURE IT? /LOUKA/ (
BASH II,1,	(102)	NO MORE. OR STAY: HOW DID IT END? WAS CASHEL	HURT	? /LUCIAN/ (TO BASHVILLE) SKIP TO THE FINAL ROUND.
BASH II,2,	(117)	FROM THE STRUGGLING HEAP) MY LOVE, MY LOVE, ART	HURT	? /LYDIA/ NO, NO; BUT SAVE MY SORE OERMATCHED COUSIN.
MILL III	(182)	HAVE NOTHING BUT THE OLD GAS ENGINE THAT WOULDNT	HURT	A FLY, THOUGH IT BRINGS ME UNDER THE BLASTED WORKSHOP
LION II	(135)	HURT THE POOR GLADIATORS. /FERROVIUS/ IT DOES NOT	HURT	A MAN TO KILL HIM. /LAVINIA/ NOTHING BUT FAITH CAN SAVE
FABL	PREFACE(70)	UNCIVILIZED WAY. AS BURNING BRIMSTONE COULD NOT	HURT	A SPIRIT, THEY HAD TO BE ASSURED THAT THEIR BODIES
POSN	(460)	DRUNKEN LYING HOUND THAT WOULD GO FURTHER TO	HURT	A WOMAN ANY DAY THAN TO HELP HER. AND IF HE EVER DID A
ARMS II	(37)	DEFIANTLY AT HIM). A GENTLEMAN HAS NO RIGHT TO	HURT	A WOMAN UNDER ANY CIRCUMSTANCES. (WITH PROFOUND
HART I	(76)	WHAT AM I TO DO? I CANT FALL IN LOVE; AND I CANT	HURT	A WOMAN'S FEELINGS BY TELLING HER SO WHEN SHE FALLS IN
HART I	(49)	GOING ON IN THIS WAY; BUT I AM REALLY VERY MUCH	HURT	AND ANNOYED AND DISILLUSIONED: AND IF I HAD REALIZED IT
CAPT III	(287)	WHOLE TRUTH ABOUT ANYTHING! (SITTING DOWN, MUCH	HURT	AND DISCOURAGED) I'M SORRY YOU WISH CAPTAIN KEARNEY TO
BARB III	(318)	HAVE EXPLAINED TO ME YEARS AGO. I AM EXTREMELY	HURT	AND OFFENDED. ANY FURTHER DISCUSSION OF MY INTENTIONS
BULL IV	(165)	WITH YOU, IT'S NOT WANT OF FEELING. /BROADBENT/ (	HURT	AND PETULANT) IT'S YOU WHO HAVE NO FEELING. YOURE AS
NEVR II	(245)	WILL YOU EXCUSE ME? I AM AFRAID DOLLY IS	HURT	AND PUT OUT BY WHAT HAS PASSED. I MUST GO TO HER.
CLEO IV	(171)	MAN-- ONE WHO CAN LOVE AND HATE-- ONE WHOM I CAN	HURT	AND WHO WOULD HURT ME. /POTHINUS/ DOES CAESAR KNOW
LION	PROLOG (109)	KIND DOCTOR, UM'S AFFECTIONATE NURSEY. THAT DIDNT	HURT	AT ALL: NOT A BIT. JUST ONE MORE. JUST TO SHEW HOW THE
DOCT I	(86)	TIMES OUT OF TEN, EH? /SCHUTZMACHER/ (RATHER	HURT	AT SO MODERATE AN ESTIMATE) OH, MUCH OFTENER THAN THAT.
BULL IV	(146)	SHAME, BARNEY! THE POOR OLD WOMAN! AN SHE WAS	HURT	BEFORE, TOO, WHEN SHE SLIPPED ON THE STAIRS. /DORAN/
BULL IV	(146)	SLIPPED ON THE STAIRS. /DORAN/ BEDAD, MAAM, SHE'S	HURT	BEHIND NOW; FOR LARRY BOWLED HER OVER LIKE A SKITTLE. (
DEST	SD(149)	BY THE BASKING OF THE SWINE IN THE VILLAGES NOR	HURT	BY ITS COOL RECEPTION IN THE CHURCHES, BUT RUTHLESSLY
MRS IV	(249)	WOULD NOT SUCCEED. (MRS WARREN WINCES, DEEPLY	HURT	BY THE IMPLIED INDIFFERENCE TOWARDS HER AFFECTIONATE
MIS.	(117)	PROBABLY GETS AS MUCH AS HE GIVES IN THE WAY OF	HURT	FEELINGS. YOULL EXCUSE ME RAMBLING ON LIKE THIS ABOUT
JITT III	(58)	I DONT WANT TO MAKE A SCANDAL; AND I DONT WANT TO	HURT	HER: I WANT TO FIND OUT FROM HER WHAT SORT OF LIFE
PYGM II	(224)	MYSELF CLEARLY IT WAS BECAUSE I DID NOT WISH TO	HURT	HER DELICACY, OR YOURS. LIZA, REASSURED, STEALS BACK TO

FANY III	(298)	HER FEELINGS, SIR, YOU CAN MARRY HER. IF YOU	HURT	HER FEELINGS BY REFUSING, YOU HAD BETTER NOT TRY TO GET
GETT	(264)	BUT WHEN IT CAME TO THE POINT I COULDNT BEAR TO	HURT	HER FEELINGS. SHE'S A SENSITIVE, AFFECTIONATE, ANXIOUS
GETT	(264)	TEMPER TO PUT UP WITH HER, AND HOW DEEP IT WOULD	HURT	HER TO THINK IT WAS BECAUSE I DIDNT CARE FOR HER, I
JITT III	(58)	ME, IT'S BETTER NOT TO KNOW. YOU COULD NOT	HURT	HER WITHOUT HURTING YOURSELF AND EDITH WORSE. /AGNES/ I
PYGM V	(283)	IN A GIRL AS EASY AS SOME COULD TWIST HER ARMS TO	HURT	HER. MRS PEARCE WARNED ME. TIME AND AGAIN SHE HAS
BARB II	(300)	OR TWO TO POOR RUMMY MITCHENS! YOU REALLY DID	HURT	HER; AND SHE'S OLD. /BILL/ (CONTEMPTUOUSLY) NOT
FANY I	(280)	IN GAOL! /DORA/ OH, CHEER UP, OLD DEAR: IT WONT	HURT	HIM: LOOK AT ME AFTER FOURTEEN DAYS OF IT: I'M ALL THE
JOAN 2	(77)	WIND IS AGAINST HIM. /BLUEBEARD/ HOW CAN THE WIND	HURT	HIM AT ORLEANS? IT IS NOT ON THE CHANNEL. /LA HIRE/ IT
6CAL	(105)	TAKE HIM AWAY. /THE KING/ AWAY WITH HIM.	HURT	HIM NOT; BUT LET HIM NOT COME INTO THE QUEEN'S
BULL III	(122)	IT. /AUNT JUDY/ THAT WAS BECAUSE ANDY HAFFIGAN	HURT	HIM WITH A BRICK SO THAT HE WAS NEVER THE SAME AGAIN.
ARMS III	(61)	HE WONT BE ABLE TO TOUCH ME; AND I'LL NOT	HURT	HIM. IT WILL SAVE EXPLANATIONS. IN THE MORNING I SHALL
LION II SD	(143)	IN IT, AND PRETENDS TO PULL THE THORN OUT AND TO	HURT	HIMSELF. THE LION NODS REPEATEDLY. ANDROCLES HOLDS OUT
POSN PREFACE	(367)	LORD CHAMBERLAIN. A REFUSAL TO LICENCE DOES NOT	HURT	HIM, BECAUSE HE CAN PRODUCE ANOTHER PLAY: IT IS THE
WIDO II	(26)	/LICKCHEESE/ (DOUBTFULLY) THE VESTRY CANT	HURT	HIM, SIR. HE'S UNDER THE LOCAL GOVERNMENT BOARD.
GETT	(312)	AND HABITUALLY THREATENED TO DROP DEAD IF ANYBODY	HURT	HIS FEELINGS. YOU MAY HAVE NOTICED THAT PEOPLE WITH
MIS.	(187)	OH! BEASTS! BRUTES! /MRS TARLETON/ NOW DONT	HURT	HIS FEELINGS, POOR LITTLE LAMB! /LORD SUMMERHAYS/ (
MIS.	(135)	HE WAS A RATE COLLECTOR AND JOHN KEPT A SHOP. IT	HURT	HIS PRIDE TO HAVE TO BORROW MONEY SO OFTEN FROM JOHN;
GLIM	(186)	SINCERE SYMPATHY) POOR SIGNORINO! THAT MUST HAVE	HURT	HORRIBLY. /FERRUCCIO/ WHAT! YOU PITY ME FOR THE TOOTH
CLEO III	(159)	WHAT HAVE YOU BROUGHT ME? THE QUEEN WILL BE	HURT	IF I DO NOT LOOK AT IT. /RUFIO/ HAVE WE TIME TO WASTE
GETT	(279)	OH, DO STAY, REJJY. I SHALL REALLY BE	HURT	IF YOU DESERT US. /LESBIA/ BETTER STAY, REGINALD. YOU
MTH5	(215)	SPONGE IN IT. /THE MAIDEN/ SHUT YOUR EYES. ITLL	HURT	IF YOU DONT. /ANOTHER MAIDEN/ DONT BE SILLY. ONE WOULD
MIS. PREFACE	(61)	FROM IT, TO LIE WHEN THE TRUTH WOULD SHOCK OR	HURT	ITS ELDERS, TO BE ABOVE ALL THINGS OBEDIENT, AND TO BE
MIS. PREFACE	(81)	AND THE CONSEQUENCE IS THAT THE CHILD CAN	HURT	ITS PARENTS' FEELINGS MUCH MORE THAN ITS PARENTS CAN
MIS. PREFACE	(81)	OR CONTEMPT OR WANT OF INTEREST COULD POSSIBLY	HURT	ITS PARENT, AND THEREFORE EXPRESSES THEM ALL WITH AN
SIM PRO,2,	(29)	TO YOU I ALWAYS SAY; AND DONT CRY OUT UNTIL YOURE	HURT	. AFTER YOU, SIR. THEY DESCEND.
MIS.	(149)	CAN YOU STAND? /HYPATIA/ OH, YOU MUST BE	HURT	. ARE YOU SURE? SHALL I GET YOU SOME WATER? OR SOME
HART II	(103)	ONLY FIND SOME SORT OF CRUELTY THAT DIDNT REALLY	HURT	. BY THE WAY (SITTING DOWN BESIDE HIM ON THE ARM OF
KING I	(194)	UNTIL IT WAS EXHAUSTED; BUT IT STILL CAN	HURT	. HEAVEN KEEP HIM OUT OF YOUR HAND! THAT IS ALL I CAN
DEVL II	(42)	ELSE MATTERS. /JUDITH/ NO, NO, NO: I'M NOT	HURT	. /ANDERSON/ THANK HEAVEN FOR THAT! COME NOW: (
BASH II,2,	(118)	OH HEAVEN! THERE IS BLOOD UPON YOUR HIP. YOURE	HURT	. /CASHEL/ THE MORSEL IN YON WRETCH'S MOUTH WAS BITTEN
PYGM V	(283)	CAN TURN THE MACHINE ON. IT'S GOT NO FEELINGS TO	HURT	. /HIGGINS/ I CANT TURN YOUR SOUL ON. LEAVE ME THOSE
POSN	(439)	ON THE NEAREST BENCH). /ELDER DANIELS/ NOTHING TO	HURT	. THEYVE DRAWN A DROP OR TWO UNDER YOUR LEFT EYE.
ARMS II	(37)	WITH TEARS IN SPITE OF HERSELF) NO: I WANT MY	HURT	MADE WELL. /SERGIUS/ (SOBERED BY HER TONE) HOW? SHE
MTH5	(241)	LOOK AT ME LIKE THAT, MAM. I MEANT NO HARM. HE	HURT	ME: INDEED HE DID. /THE HE-ANCIENT/ THE CREATURE HAS
BARB II	(300)	EAH. AW BROWK YOUR JAWR. /JENNY/ NO, IT DIDNT	HURT	ME: INDEED IT DIDNT, EXCEPT FOR A MOMENT. IT WAS ONLY
MRS III	(231)	HA! HA! GO IT, LITTLE MISSIE, GO IT: IT DOESNT	HURT	ME AND IT AMUSES YOU. WHY THE DEVIL SHOULDNT I INVEST
PHIL II	(126)	THANK HEAVEN, I HAVE A HEART: THAT IS WHY YOU CAN	HURT	ME AS I CANNOT HURT YOU. AND YOU ARE A COWARD. YOU ARE
SUPR I	(21)	CALL ME RICKY-TICKY-TAVY. " MR ROBINSON" WOULD	HURT	ME CRUELLY. (SHE LAUGHS AND PATS HIS CHEEK WITH HER
JOAN 6	(135)	BESIDES, I CANNOT BEAR TO BE HURT; AND IF YOU	HURT	ME I WILL SAY ANYTHING YOU LIKE TO STOP THE PAIN. BUT I
JITT III	(75)	HAVE SAID IT. BUT PLEASE REMEMBER THAT YOU CAN	HURT	ME MORE THAN I CAN HURT YOU, BECAUSE YOU HAVE DONE
2TRU I	(36)	SAYING THAT. YOU KNOW IT'S NOT TRUE; AND IT DOES	HURT	ME SO. /THE NURSE/ YOU MUST NOT MIND WHAT A SICK PERSON
PHIL I	(82)	I SHALL PASS OUT AT THE FRONT; SO YOU WILL NOT	HURT	ME. GOODNIGHT. (HE APPROACHES THE DOOR). /JULIA/
MTH4 I	(168)	WORDS AT ME AS IF THEY WERE STONES, MEANING TO	HURT	ME. IT WAS THE INSTINCT TO KILL THAT YOU ROUSED IN ME.
HART II	(101)	/MRS HUSHABYE/ (MISCHIEVOUSLY) THAT WOULDNT	HURT	ME. PERHAPS IT COMES OFF AT NIGHT. /ELLIE/ (SO TAKEN
PHIL II	(110)	I'M SO GLAD. THAT WAS THE ONLY THING THAT REALLY	HURT	ME. /CHARTERIS/ JUST WHY SHE SAID IT. HOW ADORABLE OF
CLEO IV	(172)	LOVE AND HATE-- ONE WHOM I CAN HURT AND WHO WOULD	HURT	ME. /POTHINUS/ DOES CAESAR KNOW THIS? /CLEOPATRA/ YES.
SUPR II	(61)	AND YOU KNOW IT. YOU WOULD NEVER DO ANYTHING TO	HURT	ME. /TANNER/ WELL, IF YOU DONT WANT TO BE COMPROMISED,
MIS.	(115)	JOHNNY FRIGHTENED ME. YOU KNOW HOW EASY IT IS TO	HURT	ME; AND I'M TOO SMALL TO DEFEND MYSELF AGAINST JOHNNY.
DOCT I	(92)	SOMETIMES I SUSPECT MY SPINE. IT DOESNT EXACTLY	HURT	ME; BUT IT UNSETTLES ME COMPLETELY. I FEEL THAT
FABL III	(112)	YOULL ONLY BE WASTING YOUR TIME; BUT THAT WONT	HURT	ME, BECAUSE TIME IS OF NO VALUE TO ME: IT'S MY
CAPT II	(250)	A THING, CAPTAIN BRASSBOUND. I AM SURE IT WOULD	HURT	MR DRINKWATER. /DRINKWATER/ (LACHRYMOSELY) LIDY'S
JOAN EPILOG	(155)	JUST FANCY! DID IT HURT MUCH? /JOAN/ DID WHAT	HURT	MUCH? /CHARLES/ BEING BURNT. /JOAN/ OH, THAT! I
JOAN EPILOG	(155)	AM OUT OF THE BODY. /CHARLES/ JUST FANCY! DID IT	HURT	MUCH? /JOAN/ DID WHAT HURT MUCH? /CHARLES/ BEING
MILL IV	(197)	OUT, GLAD TO ESCAPE FROM THE MELEE. /ADRIAN/	HURT	MYSELF! HURT MYSELF! ! /EPIFANIA/ HAS HE BEEN RUN
MILL IV	(197)	WOMAN HAS HALF KILLED ME; AND SHE ASKS HAVE I	HURT	MYSELF! I FELL DOWN THE WHOLE FLIGHT OF STAIRS. MY
MILL IV	(197)	TO ESCAPE FROM THE MELEE. /ADRIAN/ HURT MYSELF!	HURT	MYSELF! ! /EPIFANIA/ HAS HE BEEN RUN OVER? /ADRIAN/
ROCK PREFACE	(159)	WERE NOT SATISFIED WITH SYMBOLIC CROSSES WHICH	HURT	NOBODY. THEY SOON GOT BUSY WITH " ACTS OF FAITH" WHICH
LADY PREFACE	(222)	SOUNDS AND SWEET AIRS THAT GIVE DELIGHT AND	HURT	NOT, SOMETIMES A THOUSAND TWANGLING INSTRUMENTS WILL
WIDO II	(30)	TO MEND A STAIRCASE THAT THREE WOMEN HAVE BEEN	HURT	ON, AND THAT WOULD HAVE GOT HIM PROSECUTED FOR
NEVR I	(200)	UP). WHY SHOULDNT YOU? IT'S YOUR BUSINESS TO	HURT	PEOPLE. (IT AMUSES HIM TO BE TREATED IN THIS FASHION:
BULL III	(121)	THROAT. /AUNT JUDY/ DEEDN WHY SHOULD THEY WANT TO	HURT	POOR CORNY? IT WAS HE THAT GOT MATT THE LEASE OF HIS
BULL III	(120)	(HASTILY) OH, IT DOESNT MATTER: I WAS NOT	HURT	-- AT LEAST-- ER-- /AUNT JUDY/ OH NOW WHAT A SHAME! AN
APPL INTRLUD	(244)	I HAVE SOMETHING IN ME THAT WINCES WHEN YOU ARE	HURT	-- OR PRETEND TO BE. /ORINTHIA/ (CONTEMPTUOUSLY) YES:
SUPR I	(9)	CALL ON ME! SAY I CANNOT SEE HIM. /OCTAVIUS/ (	HURT	) I AM SORRY YOU ARE TURNING MY FRIEND FROM YOUR DOOR
MTH5	(229)	WE WANT RESULTS, NOT EXPLANATIONS. /PYGMALION/ (	HURT	) I SEE I AM BORING YOU. NOT ONE OF YOU TAKES THE LEAST
PYGM IV	(266)	PICK UP TO EXPERIMENT ON. /HIGGINS/ (SHOCKED AND	HURT	) IS THAT THE WAY YOU FEEL TOWARDS US? /LIZA/ I DONT
MIS.	(116)	TO LIVE IN THE HOUSE WITH HIM. /JOHNNY/ (DEEPLY	HURT	) IT'S FOURTEEN YEARS, MOTHER, SINCE YOU HAD THAT ROW
PHIL III	(142)	WITH HIS HANDS IN HIS POCKETS). /CRAVEN/ (	HURT	) JULIA: YOU DONT TREAT ME RESPECTFULLY. I DONT WISH TO
CLEO III	(145)	SO YOU ARE THE CARPET MERCHANT? /APOLLODORUS/ (	HURT	) MY FRIEND: I AM A PATRICIAN. /SENTINEL/ A PATRICIAN!
HART I	(56)	I KNOW. PULLING THE DEVIL BY THE TAIL. /ELLIE/ (	HURT	) OH NO. NOT LIKE THAT. IT WAS AT LEAST DIGNIFIED. /MRS
2TRU I	(43)	YOU LOOK LIKE A CURATE. /THE BURGLAR/ (A LITTLE	HURT	) OH, NOT A CURATE. I HOPE I LOOK AT LEAST LIKE A
HART II	(87)	THAT SORT OF MAN. /MANGAN/ (SITTING UP, MUCH	HURT	) OH! DID SHE? AND YET SHE'D HAVE LET YOU MARRY ME.
LION I	(116)	ARE THE PROUDEST DEVILS ON EARTH. /LAVINIA/ (	HURT	) PRAY GOD THEN MY PRIDE MAY NEVER BECOME A FALSE
CLEO IV	(187)	DREADFUL TO THINK OF ANYONE BEING KILLED OR EVEN	HURT	; AND I HOPE NOTHING REALLY SERIOUS HAS-- (HER VOICE
JOAN 6	(135)	COULD UNDERSTAND? BESIDES, I CANNOT BEAR TO BE	HURT	; AND IF YOU HURT ME I WILL SAY ANYTHING YOU LIKE TO
MIS. PREFACE	(81)	PARENTS' FEELINGS MUCH MORE THAN ITS PARENTS CAN	HURT	THE CHILD'S, BECAUSE THE CHILD, EVEN WHEN THERE HAS
DOCT PREFACE	(37)	BUT NOT BY VIVISECTORS. THE RONTGEN RAYS NEED NOT	HURT	THE PATIENT; AND SPECTRUM ANALYSIS INVOLVES NO
LION II	(135)	JUST KEEP THINKING HOW CRUELLY YOU MIGHT	HURT	THE POOR GLADIATORS. /FERROVIUS/ IT DOES NOT HURT A MAN
LION PROLOG	(109)	OH, DID THE NASTY CRUEL LITTLE CHRISTIAN MAN	HURT	THE SORE PAW? (THE LION MOANS ASSENTINGLY BUT
JOAN EPILOG	(155)	THOU GO HANDLING FIRE AND THINKING IT WILL NOT	HURT	THEE. HOW HAST BEEN EVER SINCE? /CHARLES/ OH, NOT SO
LADY PREFACE	(228)	AND BE LIKED BY THEM, AND HIS RELUCTANCE TO	HURT	THEIR FEELINGS, LED HIM INTO AMIABLE FLATTERY EVEN WHEN
MIS. PREFACE	(25)	SUCH ADVANCES AS AGAINST FURTIVE ATTEMPTS TO	HURT	THEM ACCIDENTALLY IN THE FOOTBALL FIELD OR SMASH THEIR
LION EPILOG	(152)	PROCESSION OF DOCTORS GOES BY, BUT THE LIONS WILL	HURT	THEM JUST AS MUCH, AND THE SPECTATORS WILL ENJOY
MIS. PREFACE	(78)	NEVER KNOW WHAT IT MEANT TO BE HURT UNTIL SHE WAS	HURT	THROUGH HER CHILDREN. CHILDREN ARE EXTREMELY CRUEL
APPL INTRLUD	(244)	AGAIN. /MAGNUS/ (OBEYING) DONT PRETEND TO BE	HURT	UNLESS YOU REALLY ARE, DEAREST. IT WRINGS MY HEART.
MIS. PREFACE	(78)	THAT SHE WOULD NEVER KNOW WHAT IT MEANT TO BE	HURT	UNTIL SHE WAS HURT THROUGH HER CHILDREN. CHILDREN ARE
JOAN 4	(95)	FASHION? /THE CHAPLAIN/ WHY, MY LORD? CAN IT	HURT	US? /THE NOBLEMAN/ MEN CANNOT SERVE TWO MASTERS. IF
METH PREFACE	(R25)	WE HAVE TO PERSIST IN THEM EVEN WHEN THEY	HURT	US. WE CANNOT STOP BREATHING TO AVOID AN ATTACK OF
DOCT IV	(166)	DOCTOR. HE IS NOT TIRING ME; AND HE WILL BE SO	HURT	WHEN HE WAKES IF HE FINDS I HAVE PUT HIM AWAY. /SIR
DOCT PREFACE	(48)	STRONGLY OF THE VIVISECTORS WHO ARE SO DEEPLY	HURT	WHEN THEIR EVIDENCE IS SET ASIDE AS WORTHLESS. AN
CLEO IV	(187)	ONLY SAD; ONLY I AM SO SILLY, I CANNOT HELP BEING	HURT	WHEN YOU SPEAK COLDLY. OF COURSE YOU ARE QUITE RIGHT:
ARMS II	(37)	FEELING HER BRUISED ARMS) YOU KNOW HOW TO	HURT	WITH YOUR TONGUE AS WELL AS WITH YOUR HANDS. BUT I DONT
LION II	(137)	AND OUR LOVE SURROUND YOU. FAREWELL. NOTHING CAN	HURT	YOU: REMEMBER THAT, BROTHER. FAREWELL. ETERNAL GLORY,
GENV III	(67)	IN WHAT WAY COULD HIS SPEECH HAVE POSSIBLY	HURT	YOU? HE HAS MADE THAT SPEECH OVER AND OVER AGAIN. YOU
NEVR I	(222)	OH, IF YOU LIKE BEING HURT, ALL RIGHT. I'LL	HURT	YOU AS MUCH AS YOU LIKE, WITHOUT ANY EXTRA CHARGE FOR
NEVR I	(200)	OH, DONT SAY THAT. IT MAKES ME FEEL AS IF I HAD	HURT	YOU FOR THE SAKE OF FIVE SHILLINGS. /THE YOUNG LADY/ (
PHIL I	(86)	UNCOMMONLY WELL YOU LOOK, DAN! THE YEARS HAVNT	HURT	YOU MUCH. /CRAVEN/ (SUDDENLY BECOMING UNNATURALLY
HART II	(90)	ON THE LIGHT). OH, MR MANGAN, SIR, I HOPE I HAVNT	HURT	YOU PLUMPING INTO YOUR LAP LIKE THAT. (COMING TO HIM)
PHIL II	(126)	A HEART: THAT IS WHY YOU CAN HURT ME AS I CANNOT	HURT	YOU. AND YOU ARE A COWARD. YOU ARE GIVING HIM UP TO ME
VWOO 3	(138)	BY THE WAY, I MADE AN INCONSIDERATE REMARK WHICH	HURT	YOU. I DID NOT INTEND THAT. I SHOULD HAVE TOLD YOU
DEVL I	(20)	COUSIN! NEVER MIND ME! IT WAS NOT MEANT TO	HURT	YOU. (SHE LOOKS UP GRATEFULLY AT HIM. HER TEARSTAINED
SUPP III	(128)	IN THIS PALACE OF LIES A TRUTH OR TWO WILL NOT	HURT	YOU. YOUR FRIENDS ARE ALL THE DULLEST DOGS I KNOW. THEY
LION I	(120)	HAST TO THE POOR. COME, FRIEND: COURAGE! I MAY	HURT	YOUR BODY FOR A MOMENT; BUT YOUR SOUL WILL REJOICE IN
MTH4 I	(168)	WITH CRESTFALLEN COURTESY) I DID NOT MEAN TO	HURT	YOUR FEELINGS. I-- (SWALLOWING THE APOLOGY WITH AN
MILL IV	(197)	THE DOCTOR HERE AT ONCE. (TO ADRIAN) HAVE YOU	HURT	YOURSELF? THE MANAGER HURRIES OUT, GLAD TO ESCAPE FROM
CAND III	(144)	YOU KNOW HOW STRONG HE IS (I HOPE HE DIDNT	HURT	YOU): HOW CLEVER HE IS: HOW HAPPY. (WITH DEEPENING
JITT III	(75)	REMEMBER THAT YOU CAN HURT ME MORE THAN I CAN	HURT	YOU, BECAUSE YOU HAVE DONE NOTHING WRONG. YOU ARE

CURE	(237)	NATURE, SEE ANYTHING TO LOVE IN ME? I SHOULD	HURT	YOU, SHOCK YOU, PERHAPS-- YES: LET ME CONFESS IT-- I
NEVR I	(222)	PAIN IN MY DAY. /VALENTINE/ OH, IF YOU LIKE BEING	HURT	, ALL RIGHT. I'LL HURT YOU AS MUCH AS YOU LIKE, WITHOUT
ARMS III	(62)	HAPPILY EVER AFTER. /RAINA/ (TURNING AWAY DEEPLY	HURT	, ALMOST WITH A SOB IN HER VOICE) I NEVER SAID I WANTED
ROCK II	(270)	BUT LET IT BE A VOICE TO SQUEAL WITH WHEN THEYRE	HURT	, AND NOT TO PRETEND THEY KNOW MORE THAN GOD ALMIGHTY
DEVL II	(42)	WAS MY FAULT. COME: YOURE SAFE NOW; AND YOURE NOT	HURT	, ARE YOU? (HE TAKES HIS ARMS FROM HER TO SEE WHETHER
FANY PREFACE	(256)	CRITICS WHOM I DID NOT INTRODUCE WERE SOMEWHAT	HURT	, AS I SHOULD HAVE BEEN MYSELF UNDER THE SAME
PHIL I	(71)	THE STORY. SO MUCH THE BETTER. /GRACE/ (DEEPLY	HURT	, BUT CONTROLLING HERSELF) WHEN DID YOU BREAK IT OFF..
LIED	(203)	BE FOOLISH, TEDDY. I HOPE YOU WERE NOT REALLY	HURT	, HENRY. (SHE FEELS THE BACK OF HIS HEAD. HE
NEVR II	(235)	YOUR HANDS. /M'COMAS/ I AM THOROUGHLY VEXED AND	HURT	, MR CLANDON-- /PHILIP/ (INTERRUPTING HIM) YOU WILL
DEVL II	(42)	THATS RIGHT, THATS RIGHT. IF ONLY YOU ARE NOT	HURT	, NOTHING ELSE MATTERS. /JUDITH/ NO, NO, NO: I'M NOT
6CAL PREFACE	(89)	GRANDSON AND HIS QUEEN PHILIPPA. THEY WERE	HURT	, SHOCKED, SCANDALIZED AT THE SPECTACLE OF A MEDIEVAL
2TRU I SD	(40)	PATIENT'S VERY UNEXPECTED ATHLETICISM, BUT NOT	HURT	, SPRINGS UP. /THE NURSE/ QUICK, POPSY: TIE HER FEET.
SUPR IV	(153)	(TANNER AND OCTAVIUS RECOIL, OCTAVIUS RATHER	HURT	, TANNER CONSOLED BY THE SOLUTION OF THE MONEY
DOCT III	(145)	WELL, IF IT WOULD INTEREST YOU, AND IF IT WONT	HURT	, THATS ANOTHER MATTER. HOW MUCH WILL YOU GIVE ME TO
BASH II,1,	(101)	CHELSEA SNOB. MELLISH, WHOSE EPIGASTRIUM HAS BEEN	HURT	, TIS SAID, BY ACCIDENT AT WILTSTOKEN, LOOKED NONE THE
NEVR II	(233)	/M'COMAS/ I SHALL NOT PROCEED, SIR. I AM TOO	HURT	, TOO SHOCKED, TO PROCEED. /MRS CLANDON/ (STRUGGLING
MIS.	(116)	THIS YOUNG WHELP BEGINS TO CRY OUT BEFORE HE'S	HURT	, YOU TREAT ME AS IF I WERE A BRUTE AND A SAVAGE. /MRS
APPL I	(201)	IT. /PAMPHILIUS/ DONT CRY OUT BEFORE ORINTHIA IS	HURT	, YOUNG CHAP. I WAS GOING TO SAY THAT I SUPPOSE YOU

HURTED

O'FL	(208)	I WAS TIMID BY NATURE; AND WHEN THE OTHER BOYS	HURTED	ME, I'D WANT TO RUN AWAY AND CRY. BUT SHE WHALED ME

HURTING

LION II	(136)	GIVE UP OUR FAITH, BROTHER. WHY NOT DO IT WITHOUT	HURTING	ANYBODY? DONT FIGHT THEM. BURN THE INCENSE.
ROCK PREFACE	(179)	PUNCHESQUE SCHADENFREUDE COULD JUSTIFY HIM IN	HURTING	ANYONE'S FEELINGS. WHAT, THEN, WOULD HAVE BEEN HIS
GETT	(266)	THAT I NEVER TELL HER ANYTHING AT ALL FOR FEAR OF	HURTING	HER FEELINGS. YOU SEE, SHE'S SUCH AN OUT-AND-OUT
MIS.	(134)	AN AUTHOR. IVE NEVER SAID SO BEFORE FOR FEAR OF	HURTING	HIS FEELINGS, BECAUSE, AFTER ALL, THE LAD CANT HELP
CATH 4	(189)	WELL, OF COURSE, IF YOURE AN ILL-NATURED WOMAN,	HURTING	ME ON PURPOSE, I HAVE NOTHING MORE TO SAY.
CATH 4	(188)	/EDSTASTON/ WHY! WHY, BECAUSE THEYRE	HURTING	ME. /CATHERINE/ PEOPLE SOMETIMES LEARN THROUGH
ARMS II	(36)	YOU TO ME. /LOUKA/ (WINCING) NOT SO TIGHT: YOURE	HURTING	ME. /SERGIUS/ THAT DOESNT MATTER. YOU HAVE STAINED
NEVR I	(213)	DECISIVELY AND PUTTING AWAY THE STOOL) WE'RE	HURTING	YOU: LET'S DROP IT. WE DIDNT THINK YOUD MIND. I DONT
PYGM I	(209)	SENSIBILITY. CRIES OF DONT START HOLLERIN. WHO'S	HURTING	YOU? NOBODY'S GOING TO TOUCH YOU. WHATS THE GOOD OF
APPL INTRLUD	(244)	BUT I SHOULDNT DO IT WELL. I SHOULD BE AFRAID OF	HURTING	YOU ALL THE TIME. /ORINTHIA/ I BELIEVE YOU WOULD
BARB II	(289)	OR NOT? YOU NEVER SEEN IT. /BARBARA/ IVE SEEN IT	HURTING	YOU WHEN YOU WENT AGAINST IT. /BILL/ (WITH
APPL INTRLUD	(255)	STRONG THAT I CANNOT BREAK LOOSE WITHOUT	HURTING	YOU. MUST I CALL THE GUARD? /ORINTHIA/ DO, DO. IT
PYGM IV	(264)	LOW SPIRITS AND NOTHING ELSE. NOBODY'S	HURTING	YOU. NOTHING'S WRONG. YOU GO TO BED LIKE A GOOD GIRL
SUPR I	(21)	PIECE OF IMPERTINENCE. BUT I NEVER DREAMT OF ITS	HURTING	YOU. /RAMSDEN/ (BREEZILY, AS HE PATS HER
MRS IV	(241)	OF GETTING ON; BUT WE CANT DISCUSS THAT WITHOUT	HURTING	YOUR FEELINGS, FRANK, SINCE YOU ARE DETERMINED NOT
CAPT II	(261)	YOU COULD HAVE BEEN KIND AND FORBEARING WITH HER.	HURTING	YOUR UNCLE WONT DO HER ANY GOOD, YOU KNOW.
JITT III	(58)	NOT TO KNOW. YOU COULD NOT HURT HER WITHOUT	HURTING	YOURSELF AND EDITH WORSE. /AGNES/ I DONT WANT TO
BARB II	(288)	THAT NEVER LETS HIM GO) IT'S YOUR SOUL THATS	HURTING	YOU, BILL, AND NOT ME. WEVE BEEN THROUGH IT ALL
CAPT II	(247)	REDBROOK RAISE HIM). /LADY CICELY/ NOW THEYRE NOT	HURTING	YOU, MARZO. THEY COULDNT BE MORE GENTLE. /MARZO/
NEVR I	(215)	PURPOSELY, DELIBERATELY, WITH THE INTENTION OF	HURTING	YOU, WITH A WHIP BOUGHT FOR THE PURPOSE! WOULD YOU
PYGM I	(209)	AFTER HIM) THERE, THERE, THERE, THERE! WHO'S	HURTING	YOU, YOU SILLY GIRL? WHAT DO YOU TAKE ME FOR? /THE

HURTS

DOCT PREFACE	(42)	VULGARITY THAT INSTINCTIVELY STRIKES AT AND	HURTS	A THING THAT ANNOYS IT (AND ALL CHILDREN ARE
LION PROLOG	(109)	IS NOT TO BITE AND NOT TO SCRATCH, NOT EVEN IF IT	HURTS	A VERY VERY LITTLE. NOW MAKE VELVET PAWS. THATS RIGHT.
MTH4 I	(156)	TO ACT AS IF THEY WERE TRUE? CONTACT WITH TRUTH	HURTS	AND FRIGHTENS YOU: YOU ESCAPE FROM IT INTO AN
FANY PROLOG	(264)	NOT THAT HE DOESNT SEE A JOKE: HE DOES; AND IT	HURTS	HIM. A COMEDY SCENE MAKES HIM SORE ALL OVER: HE GOES
BULL IV	(175)	SMOULDERED INTO NOTHING BUT A DULL TEMPER THAT	HURTS	HIMSELF AND ALL AROUND HIM. I SAY LET HIM DIE, AND LET
LION PROL,SD	(105)	EXTRACT IT BY SCRAPING IT ALONG THE GROUND, AND	HURTS	HIMSELF WORSE. HE ROARS PITEOUSLY. HE LICKS IT AGAIN.
SUPR IV	(159)	LUCK. BUT I DONT THINK YOU QUITE KNOW HOW MUCH IT	HURTS	. /ANN/ YOU ARE SO SOFTHEARTED! IT'S QUEER THAT YOU
PHIL II	(110)	BUSINESS TO TELL IT TO ME. I DONT LIKE IT: IT	HURTS	. /GRACE/ (QUIETLY) IT'S ONLY THAT I LOVE YOU.
MIS.	(161)	/TARLETON/ DONT PROBE TOO DEEP, LINA. IT	HURTS	. /LINA/ YOU MUST GET OUT OF THE HABIT OF THINKING
MTH1 I	(8)	THAT IS TOO WONDERFUL. IT STIRS INSIDE ME. IT	HURTS	. /THE SERPENT/ IT NEARLY TORE ME ASUNDER. YET I AM
SUPR IV	(169)	/TANNER/ (GROANING) OH, THAT CLUTCH HOLDS AND	HURTS	. WHAT HAVE YOU GRASPED IN ME? IS THERE A FATHER'S
JOAN EPILOG	(157)	BUT THIS THING THAT THEY HAVE DONE AGAINST ME	HURTS	JUSTICE; DESTROYS FAITH; SAPS THE FOUNDATION OF THE
GETT	(335)	DUELS WITH SABRES. IVE MUSCLES OF IRON. NOTHING	HURTS	ME: NOT EVEN BROKEN BONES. FIGHTING IS ABSOLUTELY
MIS. PREFACE	(10)	THE CHILD'S GOOD. THE ASSAILANT MUST SAY " THIS	HURTS	ME MORE THAN IT HURTS YOU." THERE MUST BE HYPOCRISY AS
DOCT II	(118)	/MRS DUBEDAT/ THANK YOU. THANK YOU. NOTHING	HURTS	ME. GOODNIGHT. LOUIS GOES OUT THROUGH THE HOTEL
DEST	(168)	AFRAID. (SHE PRESSES HER HANDS ON HER HEART). IT	HURTS	ONLY TO IMAGINE IT. /NAPOLEON/ (INFLEXIBLY) WOULD YOU
BARB I SD	(263)	HAS LEARNT BY EXPERIENCE THAT HIS NATURAL GRIP	HURTS	ORDINARY PEOPLE UNLESS HE HANDLES THEM VERY CAREFULLY,
SUPR IV	(160)	ME AS A HUSBAND FOR ANN; BUT I LOVE ANN; AND IT	HURTS	RATHER. (HE RISES AND MOVES AWAY FROM HER TOWARDS THE
DOCT PREFACE	(48)	VINDICATED BY ITS GENTLENESS. A COBRA'S BITE	HURTS	SO LITTLE THAT THE CREATURE IS ALMOST, LEGALLY
POSN PREFACE	(426)	ITS TEETH: THE MORE DECAYED THEY ARE THE MORE IT	HURTS	TO TOUCH THEM. PREVENT DENTISTS AND DRAMATISTS FROM
MIS. PREFACE	(10)	ASSAILANT MUST SAY " THIS HURTS ME MORE THAN IT	HURTS	YOU." THERE MUST BE HYPOCRISY AS WELL AS CRUELTY. THE
BASH III	(127)	THE BLUE ANCHOR HOSTELRY ATTEND HIM; ASSUAGE HIS	HURTS	, AND BID BILL RICHARDSON LIMIT HIS ACCESS TO THE
NEVR III	(278)	KIND THINGS IN AN UNKIND WAY! PEOPLE WHOSE TOUCH	HURTS	, WHOSE VOICES JAR, WHOSE TEMPERS PLAY THEM FALSE, WHO
CATH 4	(194)	NEVER BE ABLE TO STAND UP AGAIN. OH LORD! HOW IT	HURTS	! (THEY SEIZE HIM BY THE SHOULDERS AND DRAG HIM UP).

HUS

ROCK PREFACE	(175)	GIORDANO BRUNO AND GALILEO, SERVETUS AND JOHN	HUS	AND THE HEROES OF FOXE'S BOOK OF MARTYRS STANDING OUT IN
JOAN PREFACE	(30)	THE WRATH FELL ON HIM IN HIS GRAVE? NEITHER	HUS	NOR WYCLIFFE WAS AS BLUNTLY DEFIANT AS JOAN: BOTH WERE
JOAN PREFACE	(30)	CHURCH TOLERATE THAT, WHEN IT HAD JUST DESTROYED	HUS	, AND HAD WATCHED THE CAREER OF WYCLIFFE WITH A GROWING
JOAN 4	(103)	HE IS SPREADING THIS HERESY EVERYWHERE. THE MAN	HUS	, BURNT ONLY THIRTEEN YEARS AGO AT CONSTANCE, INFECTED
BUOY PREFACE	(4)	WHAT LESS COULD MR SLUDGE SAY? OR JOHN	HUS	, WHO LET HIMSELF BE BURNT RATHER THAN RECANT HIS " I

HUSBAND

DEST	(174)	LETTER WRITTEN BY A WOMAN TO A MAN: A MAN NOT HER	HUSBAND	: A LETTER THAT MEANS DISGRACE, INFAMY-- /NAPOLEON/
GENV I	(39)	HE HAD CERTAIN WEAKNESSES. HE WAS AN AFFECTIONATE	HUSBAND	: I MAY EVEN SAY AN UXORIOUS ONE; BUT HE WAS VERY
GETT PREFACE	(231)	HE HAS NO WIVES AT ALL; NOR HAVE HIS WIVES ANY	HUSBAND	: IN SHORT, HE IS NOT WHAT WE CALL A MARRIED MAN.
MILL IV	(208)	YOU BEGIN BY THINKING YOU HAVE ONLY ONE	HUSBAND	: YOU FIND YOU HAVE A DOZEN. THERE IS A CREATURE YOU
OVER	(185)	PRESENT; BUT I'M ON THE LIST. I'M HER PROSPECTIVE	HUSBAND	: YOURE ONLY HER ACTUAL ONE. I'M THE ANTICIPATION:
FANY III	(315)	TO TREAT A MAN LIKE THAT? AN HONEST RESPECTABLE	HUSBAND	? AS IF HE WERE DIRT UNDER YOUR FEET? /KNOX/ LET
SUPR II	(54)	MAN, WHAT OTHER WORK HAS SHE IN LIFE BUT TO GET A	HUSBAND	? IT IS A WOMAN'S BUSINESS TO GET MARRIED AS SOON
DOCT I	(111)	/MRS DUBEDAT/ THEN CAN ANY DOCTOR CURE MY	HUSBAND	? OH, WHY DONT THEY DO IT? I HAVE TRIED SO MANY: I
CYMB V	(148)	IS IT TRUE THOU ART A WOMAN, AND THIS MAN THY	HUSBAND	? /IMOGEN/ I AM A WOMAN, AND THIS MAN MY HUSBAND.
GETT	(270)	EXPRESS IT? HANG IT ALL, LESBIA, DONT YOU WANT A	HUSBAND	? /LESBIA/ NO. I WANT CHILDREN; AND I WANT TO
MIS.	(153)	SPITE YOUR MOTHER? /PERCIVAL/ (QUICKLY) OR YOUR	HUSBAND	? /LINA/ I'M NOT MARRIED, AND WHY SHOULD I WANT TO
BUOY II	(18)	USELESS, EXCEPT TO COMMIT SUICIDE. HAVE YOU A	HUSBAND	? /SHE/ WHAT IS THAT TO YOU? /HE/ IF YOU HAVE, HE
DOCT II	(125)	/SIR PATRICK/ AND WHY ARNT YOU LIVING WITH YOUR	HUSBAND	? /THE MAID/ WE COULDNT AFFORD IT, SIR. I HAD
BUOY II	(19)	TO HER. VERY LUCKY BRING HER GIFTS. /HE/ HAS SHE	HUSBAND	? /THE NATIVE/ NO NO NO NO. SHE HOLY WOMAN. LIVE
GETT	(329)	YOU SURE YOULL ENJOY IT AS MUCH WHEN YOU ARE THE	HUSBAND	? SHE ISNT CLEVER, YOU KNOW. SHE'S ONLY
JITT II	(45)	NOT GIVE THE OTHER WOMAN AWAY, EVEN TO ME, YOUR	HUSBAND	? WERE THOSE HIS ORDERS? /JITTA/ (EXHAUSTED) I
DOCT V	(179)	(GABBLING AND STUTTERING) WHAT HUSBAND? WHOSE	HUSBAND	? WHICH HUSBAND? WHOM? HOW? WHAT? DO YOU MEAN
DOCT V	(179)	STUTTERING) WHAT HUSBAND? WHOSE HUSBAND? WHICH	HUSBAND	? WHOM? HOW? WHAT? DO YOU MEAN TO SAY THAT YOU
DOCT V	(179)	/RIDGEON/ (GABBLING AND STUTTERING) WHAT	HUSBAND	? WHOSE HUSBAND? WHICH HUSBAND? WHOM? HOW?
GETT	(328)	BETTER SUITED TO THAT YOUNG SAUCEBOX THAN HER	HUSBAND	? YOU ENJOYED HER COMPANY WHEN YOU WERE ONLY THE
HART II	(98)	DID YOU PICK UP MANGAN? HOW DID YOU PICK UP MY	HUSBAND	? YOU HAVE THE AUDACITY TO TELL ME THAT I AM A--
BUOY III	(46)	KEEP A HUSBAND ON THEM. /MRS SECONDBORN/ IS A	HUSBAND	A DOG OR A CAT TO BE KEPT AS A PET? I NEVER HEARD
PRES	(161)	HAS NO HIGH NOTES, EXCEPT WHEN SHE'S GIVING HER	HUSBAND	A PIECE OF HER MIND, OR CALLING DOWN THE STREET FOR
APPL INTRLUD	(246)	WITH YOUR BEAUTY WHEN HE MARRIED YOU. YOUR FIRST	HUSBAND	ACTUALLY FORCED A GOOD WIFE TO DIVORCE HIM SO THAT
OVER	(193)	ADVISABLE. /MRS LUNN/ (TO MRS JUNO) CAN YOUR	HUSBAND	AFFORD A SCANDAL, MRS JUNO? /MRS JUNO/ NO. /MRS
MILL I	(142)	YOU INSULT ME IN MY DISTRESS. YOU BACK UP MY	HUSBAND	AGAINST ME. YOU HAVE NO DECENCY, NO UNDERSTANDING.
GETT PREFACE	(212)	11-11 WIVES, OR THAT EACH WOMAN WHO CANNOT GET A	HUSBAND	ALL TO HERSELF SHALL DIVIDE HERSELF BETWEEN ELEVEN
HART I	(71)	ON HER RIGHT). /MRS HUSHABYE/ ONE'S SISTER'S	HUSBAND	ALWAYS IS, MR RANDALL. /LADY UTTERWORD/ DONT BE

JITT I (20)	I AM THE AUTHOR. THEY WILL FIND A BOOK BY YOUR	HUSBAND	AMONG MY THINGS: THAT IS ALL. (SHE IS ABOUT TO
JITT III (77)	HERSELF AS A SPECIAL CREATION, AND CONSIDER HER	HUSBAND	AN INFERIOR AND COMMON SORT OF ANIMAL. /JITTA/ YOU
OVER (185)	AND STRAIGHTFORWARDLY WITH ME. YOU CAN LEAVE	HUSBAND	AND CHILD, HOME, FRIENDS, AND COUNTRY, FOR MY SAKE,
CLEO II (134)	DESERT WITH MANY HORSEMEN, AND SLEW MY SISTER'S	HUSBAND	AND GAVE MY FATHER BACK HIS THRONE. (WISTFULLY) I
GETT (282)	ALFRED, TO SEND THAT SILLY GIRL BACK TO HER	HUSBAND	AND HER DUTY THAN TO TALK CLEVER AND MOCK AT YOUR
OVER (185)	ALL IN ALL TO ONE ANOTHER. OR YOU CAN TELL YOUR	HUSBAND	AND LET HIM JOLLY WELL PUNCH MY HEAD IF HE CAN. BUT
OVER (182)	IS ALWAYS FULL OF WOMEN WHO ARE IN LOVE WITH MY	HUSBAND	AND MEN WHO ARE IN LOVE WITH ME. WE ENCOURAGE IT
NEVR III (265)	RESULT WAS A BITTER DISAPPOINTMENT FOR BOTH MY	HUSBAND	AND MYSELF. SO YOU SEE, THOUGH I AM A MARRIED WOMAN,
GETT PREFACE(231)	HOUSEHOLD OF THREE WAS NOT ONLY THAT BOTH THE	HUSBAND	AND NELSON WERE DEVOTED TO LADY HAMILTON, BUT THAT
GENV IV (107)	THE FINGER OF THE WHOLE WORLD AT THE SLAYER OF MY	HUSBAND	AND SAY " YOU ARE GUILTY OF MURDER." YOU CAN PUT THE
HART III (138)	SOUND SOUL TO ITS NATURAL CAPTAIN, MY SPIRITUAL	HUSBAND	AND SECOND FATHER. SHE DRAWS THE CAPTAIN'S ARM
GETT PREFACE(217)	HOUSES. WE MAY TAKE IT, THEN, THAT THE IDEAL	HUSBAND	AND THE IDEAL WIFE ARE NO MORE REAL HUMAN BEINGS
KING II SD(223)	CATHERINE, AGED 42, ENTERS. SHE CONTEMPLATES HER	HUSBAND	AND THE UNTIDINESS HE HAS MADE, WITH A PORTUGUESE
VWOO 3 (138)	AND DEATH. /Z/ NOT ME, THANK YOU. ALL I WANT IS A	HUSBAND	AND THE USUAL CONSEQUENCES. /A/ THE SAME THING.
SUPR III (118)	CHASTITY, SENORA, SINCE IT TOOK THE FORM OF A	HUSBAND	AND TWELVE CHILDREN. WHAT MORE COULD YOU HAVE DONE
2TRU III (91)	THE SAME LODGING, AM I TO UNDERSTAND THAT YOU ARE	HUSBAND	AND WIFE? /SWEETIE/ WE MIGHT HAVE BEEN IF WE COULD
GETT PREFACE(226)	THE CONVENTION THAT THE NATURAL RELATION BETWEEN	HUSBAND	AND WIFE AND PARENT AND CHILD IS ONE OF INTENSE
BUOY III (39)	AND FORM A NEW RELATION WITH THEIR TEACHERS. ONLY	HUSBAND	AND WIFE COME TO FEEL THAT THEY BELONG TO ONEANOTHER
OVER PREFACE(157)	ON THE ONE HAND AND THE PROPERTY RELATION BETWEEN	HUSBAND	AND WIFE ON THE OTHER, NOT TO MENTION THE CONFUSION
MRS III (222)	IT DONT MATTER WHETHER THEYRE FATHER AND SON OR	HUSBAND	AND WIFE OR BROTHER AND SISTER-- THEY CANT KEEP UP
GETT PREFACE(257)	AS A PUNISHMENT AS IT IS AT PRESENT. SEND THE	HUSBAND	AND WIFE TO PENAL SERVITUDE IF YOU DISAPPROVE OF
GETT PREFACE(254)	BETWEEN PARENT AND CHILD MORE THAN BETWEEN	HUSBAND	AND WIFE. IF YOU PAY LESS THAN 40 POUNDS A YEAR
MTH1 I (18)	(INSTINCTIVELY MOVING HIS HAND TOWARDS HER)	HUSBAND	AND WIFE. /EVE/ (SLIPPING HER HAND INTO HIS) WIFE
HART II (89)	IS SHE MAKING A SWOP WITH YOU-- SHE TO HAVE YOUR	HUSBAND	AND YOU TO HAVE HERS? /ELLIE/ WELL, YOU DONT WANT
KING I (195)	BUT BETWEEN YOUR DAUGHTER MARY'S PROTESTANT	HUSBAND	AND YOU. /JAMES/ HE WILL HAVE TO CROSS THE SEAS TO
NEVR IV (288)	/BOHUN/ WE HAD BETTER WAIT UNTIL MRS CLANDON'S	HUSBAND	ARRIVES. /CRAMPTON/ WHAT D'Y' MEAN? I'M HER
OVER (182)	IT'S PLEASANT TO HAVE COMPANY. /JUNO/ AND IS YOUR	HUSBAND	AS INSENSIBLE AS YOURSELF! /MRS LUNN/ OH, GREGORY'S
MILL I (148)	IN HIS PRESENCE AND IN MINE TO SPEAK OF MY	HUSBAND	AS MR FITZFASSENDEN. HIS CHRISTIAN NAME IS NO
PYGM EPILOG (291)	MAN IN HIM, ACCORDING TO HER CONCEPTION OF A	HUSBAND	AS ONE TO WHOM SHE WOULD BE HIS NEAREST AND FONDEST
GENV I (40)	TIME; SO THEY THOUGHT THEY MIGHT AS WELL SHOOT MY	HUSBAND	AS THERE WAS NOBODY ELSE TO SHOOT. /SHE/ WHAT A
GETT (281)	POINTED OUT LONG AGO THAT A WOMAN WANTED A SUNDAY	HUSBAND	AS WELL AS A WEEKDAY ONE. BUT, AS USUAL, HE DIDNT
BUOY IV (51)	CHANGE IT. /OLD BILL/ A WORKING HUSBAND IS NO	HUSBAND	AT ALL. WHEN I HAD TO WORK, MY WIFE WAS ONLY MY
FANY II SD(285)	AND SOME SOLEMNITY. SHE IS SURPRISED TO SEE HER	HUSBAND	AT HOME DURING BUSINESS HOURS. /MRS KNOX/ WHAT
HART I (71)	MAN? /MRS HUSHABYE/ WELL, WHY SHOULDNT MY	HUSBAND	BE A HANDSOME MAN? /RANDALL/ (JOINING THEM AT THE
2TRU PREFACE(10)	SHOULD NOT BE AS HAPPY AS HER DAIRYMAID, OR HER	HUSBAND	BE AS HAPPY AS HIS GAMEKEEPER. THE RICHES OF THE
GETT PREFACE(213)	THEM FOR SUCH WORK. WHY SHOULD THE TAKING OF A	HUSBAND	BE IMPOSED ON THESE WOMEN AS THE PRICE OF THEIR
JITT PREFACE(6)	JITTA LIVES MISERABLY EVER AFTER, AND THAT HER	HUSBAND	BEARS MALICE, AND PRESENTS A CHARACTER-STUDY MUCH
LION PREFACE(78)	MAY LEAD TO PLACING THE DESIRE TO PLEASE WIFE OR	HUSBAND	BEFORE THE DESIRE TO PLEASE GOD, YET PREOCCUPATION
ARMS III (62)	MY BACK, JUST AS YOU TREAT ME AS YOUR AFFIANCED	HUSBAND	BEHIND HIS. BLUNTSCHLI: YOU KNEW OUR RELATIONS; AND
OVER (183)	GREGORY'S A SOLICITOR. I'M ACCUSTOMED TO MY	HUSBAND	BEING A SOLICITOR AND TELLING ME THINGS HE OUGHTNT
GENV I (38)	SIMPLY ONE CHARGE OF THE WILFUL MURDER OF MY LATE	HUSBAND	BY THE PRESIDENT OF THE EARTHLY PARADISE. /SHE/
GETT PREFACE(233)	SAME. IN A REAL MARRIAGE OF SENTIMENT THE WIFE OR	HUSBAND	CANNOT BE SUPPLANTED BY HALVES; AND SUCH A MARRIAGE
LIED SD(197)	THAT GLOVE ALONE: YOU LOOK LIKE A PICKPOCKET. HER	HUSBAND	COMES IN: A ROBUST, THICKNECKED, WELL GROOMED CITY
JITT III (70)	HAVE, I AM SURE WHAT WE OWE YOU, WITH YOUR DEAR	HUSBAND	COMING HERE EVERY DAY TO SET THE PAPERS IN ORDER,
GETT (300)	CHILDREN-- THE ELDEST ONLY FOUR YEARS OLD-- HER	HUSBAND	COMMITTED A MURDER, AND THEN ATTEMPTED TO COMMIT
JITT III (74)	TOLD HER? /JITTA/ (HER BORED MANNER WITH HER	HUSBAND	CONTRASTING STRONGLY WITH HER WARM INTEREST IN
GETT PREFACE(212)	NOW THE RIGHT TO BEAR CHILDREN WITHOUT TAKING A	HUSBAND	COULD NOT BE CONFINED TO WOMEN WHO ARE SUPERFLUOUS
GETT PREFACE(229)	SOMETIMES FIERCELY PUNISHED BY GIVING AN INJURED	HUSBAND	CRUSHING DAMAGES IN A DIVORCE SUIT (INJURED WIVES
NEVR III (274)	THE BACK, NEAR THE OTTOMAN). MRS CLANDON: YOUR	HUSBAND	DEMANDS THE CUSTODY OF HIS TWO YOUNGER CHILDREN, WHO
MTH3 (119)	THAN I REALLY WAS, UNTIL ONE DAY, LONG AFTER MY	HUSBAND	DIED AND MY CHILDREN WERE OUT IN THE WORLD WORKING
MILL II (174)	DOWNSTAIRS: WHO WAS HE? ONE DOES NOT THROW ONE'S	HUSBAND	DOWNSTAIRS. DID HE MAKE LOVE TO YOU? /EPIFANIA/ NO.
GETT PREFACE(220)	IS NEITHER VIRTUOUS, DIGNIFIED, NOR DECENT. NO	HUSBAND	EVER SECURED HIS DOMESTIC HAPPINESS AND HONOR, NOR
JITT II (38)	FAILED HIM. DONT FORGET THAT SHE IS A WOMAN WHOSE	HUSBAND	FAILED HER. /EDITH/ HOW DID HE FAIL HER? IF SHE HAD
GETT (299)	DOING PUBLIC WORK OUGHT TO GET MARRIED UNLESS HER	HUSBAND	FEELS ABOUT IT AS SHE DOES. I DONT BLAME YOU AT ALL
KING I (191)	BILL. AND YOU WILL HAVE TO FIND A PROTESTANT	HUSBAND	FOR ANNE: REMEMBER THAT. /JAMES/ YOU PRETEND YOU ARE
SUPR IV (160)	I DARESAY YOU ARE RIGHT TO PREFER JACK TO ME AS A	HUSBAND	FOR ANN; BUT I LOVE ANN; AND IT HURTS RATHER. (HE
LIED PREFACE(185)	THE NORTH OF SCOTLAND TO WRITE HOW HE LIED TO HER	HUSBAND	FOR DALY. IN HIS HANDS, IT SERVED ITS TURN VERY
POSN (465)	JACK. NOWS YOUR CHANCE, PETER. PASS ALONG A	HUSBAND	FOR FEEMY. OH MY! FEEMY! /FEEMY/ (SHORTLY) KEEP
DOCT I (108)	SHE THINKS IT'S LIFE AND DEATH TO HER	HUSBAND	FOR HER TO SEE YOU. /RIDGEON/ VALUES HER HUSBAND'S
DEVL III (50)	GALLANTRY). HOW LONG DO YOU ALLOW A BROKENHEARTED	HUSBAND	FOR LEAVE-TAKING, SERGEANT? /SERGEANT/ AS LONG AS
SIM II (56)	AND BEAUTIFUL, BUT STERILE. WHEN WE HAD TO FIND A	HUSBAND	FOR THE BLOSSOMING GIRLS, ONLY ONE MAN WAS FOUND
DOCT III (141)	IT WAS THE LAW THAT IF YOU HADNT HEARD OF YOUR	HUSBAND	FOR THREE YEARS YOU MIGHT MARRY AGAIN. SO AS SHE WAS
GETT PREFACE(234)	INJUSTICE OF FORBIDDING A WOMAN TO DIVORCE HER	HUSBAND	FOR UNFAITHFULNESS TO HIS MARRIAGE VOW, WHILST
FOUN (220)	BECAUSE IF A WOMAN CANT BULLY HER HUSBAND, HER	HUSBAND	GENERALLY BULLIES HER. YOU, MY LORD, YOU WILL, YOU
JITT II (50)	WIFE, DID YOU? I SEE. WHY COULD NOT YOUR STUPID	HUSBAND	GIVE YOU A TRIUMPHANT TOUR THROUGH EUROPE? WHY
HART III (148)	THE GRAVEL PIT, LAUGHING HARSHLY). /HECTOR/ ONE	HUSBAND	GONE. /CAPTAIN SHOTOVER/ THIRTY POUNDS OF GOOD
NEVR III (276)	/M'COMAS/ ON THE OTHER HAND, MRS CLANDON, YOUR	HUSBAND	HAD A GREAT HORROR OF ANYTHING GETTING INTO THE
DOCT II (116)	US. HAVE A GOOD CRY. /RIDGEON/ NO: DONT CRY. YOUR	HUSBAND	HAD BETTER NOT KNOW THAT WEVE BEEN TALKING ABOUT
OVER (193)	PREPARED TO PROMISE NEVER TO DO SO. I THINK YOUR	HUSBAND	HAS A RIGHT TO DEMAND THAT. THEN IF I SPEAK TO YOU
GETT (329)	BRED. THAT WAS NOT MY FAULT. /MRS GEORGE/ MY	HUSBAND	HAS A SENSE OF HUMOR TOO. /HOTCHKISS/ THE COAL
CAND I (103)	OF COURSE; UNLESS THE REVEREND GENTLEMAN YOUR	HUSBAND	HAS ANYTHING TO ADVANCE TO THE CONTRARY. /CANDIDA/
GENV IV (107)	YOU HAVE A SPECIFIC CASE. STATE IT. /WIDOW/ MY	HUSBAND	HAS BEEN MURDERED BY HIS SUCCESSOR. MY SON MUST
ARMS II (41)	HATE THE SERBS: THE EFFECT OF THE PEACE ON MY	HUSBAND	HAS BEEN TO MAKE HIM FEEL LIKE A LION BAULKED OF HIS
DEVL II (38)	YOUR HATE HELPS ME TO BE A BAD ONE. /JUDITH/ MY	HUSBAND	HAS BEEN VERY GOOD TO YOU. HE HAS FORGIVEN YOU FOR
DEVL III (63)	MEAN. I SAY THAT HE IS NOT MY HUSBAND-- THAT MY	HUSBAND	HAS ESCAPED. THIS MAN TOOK HIS PLACE TO SAVE HIM.
SUPR II (65)	THE YOUNG LADY WAS MARRIED SECRETLY; AND HER	HUSBAND	HAS FORBIDDEN HER, IT SEEMS, TO DECLARE HIS NAME. IT
ARMS II (41)	THIS HOUSE AT ONCE. (HE RAISES HIS EYEBROWS). MY	HUSBAND	HAS JUST RETURNED WITH MY FUTURE SON-IN-LAW; AND
SUPR II (65)	ON AN ALTAR TO BE WORSHIPPED. ANYHOW, VIOLET'S	HUSBAND	HAS NOT BEEN ENNOBLED. SO WHATS TO BE DONE?
GETT PREFACE(233)	ON A TOLERATED FOOTING, SHE WOULD SAY " MY	HUSBAND	HAS NOT ROOM IN HIS LIFE FOR TWO WIVES: EITHER YOU
HART II (102)	A MOUSTACHE LIKE A BRONZE CANDLESTICK AS YOUR	HUSBAND	HAS. THERE ARE THINGS NO DECENT WOMAN WOULD DO TO A
LIED (189)	AND TO LOVE ME, AND SO ON; BUT I CANT HELP MY	HUSBAND	HAVING DISAGREEABLE RELATIVES, CAN I? /HE/ (
KING PREFACE(156)	HOSPITAL OR MAKING DUKES OF HIS BASTARDS. AS A	HUSBAND	HE TOOK HIS MARRIAGE VERY SERIOUSLY, AND HIS SEX
GETT PREFACE(221)	WOUNDING TO OUR SENSE OF HUMAN DIGNITY THAN THE	HUSBAND	HUNTING THAT BEGINS IN EVERY FAMILY WHEN THE
BUOY III (43)	MY HANDS IN SPITE OF HIS PREACHING. WHEN I WANT A	HUSBAND	I CAN AFFORD TO PAY FOR HIM. /HE/ THAT IS VERY
MILL I (161)	HOW CAN I AFFORD TO LET YOU DIVORCE ME? AS YOUR	HUSBAND	I ENJOY A GOOD DEAL OF SOCIAL CONSIDERATION; AND THE
JITT I (17)	REMINDED OF HIM JUST NOW. /BRUNO/ BUT IT IS YOUR	HUSBAND	I MEAN. I HAVE CONVERTED HIM. /JITTA/ OH,
PYGM EPILOG (291)	IS TOO UGLY OR DISAGREEABLE TO FIND A WIFE OR A	HUSBAND	IF HE OR SHE WANTS ONE, WHILST MANY OLD MAIDS AND
GETT PREFACE(214)	THAT IS, IF EVERY WOMAN WERE WILLING TO TAKE A	HUSBAND	IF ONE COULD BE FOUND FOR HER, AND EVERY MAN WILLING
APPL INTRLUD(253)	FRIENDS FEEL AT HOME WITH US. /ORINTHIA/ A MODEL	HUSBAND	IN A MODEL HOUSEHOLD! AND WHEN THE MODEL HOUSEHOLD
PRES (165)	ABILITY AND FORCE OF CHARACTER CAN MAINTAIN HER	HUSBAND	IN COMPETITION WITH THE HUSBAND OF MRS BANGER. I
DEST (174)	/NAPOLEON/ WHY IS IT SENT TO ME? TO PUT THE	HUSBAND	IN MY POWER, EH? /LADY/ NO, NO: IT CAN BE OF NO USE
MILL IV (208)	YOU TAKE CARE, DOCTOR. SHE IS UNFAITHFUL TO HER	HUSBAND	IN WANTING TO MARRY YOU. SHE FLIRTED WITH ME: TOOK
DEST (174)	WROTE IT. /NAPOLEON/ THEN WHY NOT SEND IT TO HER	HUSBAND	INSTEAD OF TO ME? /LADY/ (COMPLETELY TAKEN ABACK)
HART I (81)	AS IT DID WHEN I WAS A BOY. WHY DOESNT YOUR	HUSBAND	INVENT SOMETHING? HE DOES NOTHING BUT TELL LIES TO
LIED (202)	HENRY: FOR HEAVEN'S SAKE-- /HE/ IT'S NO USE. YOUR	HUSBAND	IS A FOOL AND A BRUTE-- /HER HUSBAND/ WHATS THAT YOU
MILL I (138)	FOR ME TO KNOW WHO YOUR HUSBAND IS. /THE LADY/ MY	HUSBAND	IS A FOOL AND A BLACKGUARD. YOU WILL STATE THAT FACT
INCA (243)	WAR ON HIM. IT'S TOO BAD. /ERMYNTRUDE/ STILL, A MY	HUSBAND	IS A HUSBAND. I WISH I HAD ONE. /THE PRINCESS/ OH,
HART I (81)	NO, BY THUNDER! WHAT A DAMNED CREATURE A	HUSBAND	IS ANYHOW! /MRS HUSHABYE/ (TO THE CAPTAIN) WHAT
GETT PREFACE(202)	IN THE SCHOOLROOM IN CHARGE OF A GOVERNESS; THE	HUSBAND	IS AT HIS CLUB OR IN A SET WHICH IS NOT HIS WIFE'S;
MILL I (148)	TEETH ON EDGE) YOU HEAR THIS, MR SAGAMORE! MY	HUSBAND	IS CALLED " ALLY" BY THESE THIRD RATE PEOPLE! WHAT
MILL I (146)	ONE MOMENT. HOLD THE LINE. (TO EPIFANIA) YOUR	HUSBAND	IS DOWNSTAIRS, WITH A WOMAN. THEY WANT TO SEE ME.
GETT (335)	FRIGHTEN ME OR AMUSE ME; AND I ALWAYS WIN. YOUR	HUSBAND	IS IN ALL THESE RESPECTS AN AVERAGE MAN, PROBABLY.
HART II (94)	HIS FIRST YOUTH, IS HE? /MAZZINI/ AFTER ALL, NO	HUSBAND	IS IN HIS FIRST YOUTH FOR VERY LONG, MRS HUSHABYE.
GETT PREFACE(221)	A WOMAN WITHOUT PROPERTY OR MARKETABLE TALENT A	HUSBAND	IS MORE NECESSARY THAN A MASTER TO A DOG. THERE IS
BUOY IV (51)	WE CANNOT CHANGE IT. /OLD BILL/ A WORKING	HUSBAND	IS NO HUSBAND AT ALL. WHEN I HAD TO WORK, MY WIFE
GETT PREFACE(233)	ILLUSIONS OF LITERARY MASCULINITY. BESIDES, THE	HUSBAND	IS NOT NECESSARILY THE STRONGER MAN: AND APPEAL TO
LION PREFACE(70)	BUT A SLAVE, THE SELFISH WOMAN TO WHOM HER	HUSBAND	IS NOTHING BUT A SCAPEGOAT AND A BREADWINNER, ARE

APPL INTRLUD(250)	AND BORNE CHILDREN TO ONE OF THEM. BEING YOUR	HUSBAND	IS ONLY A JOB FOR WHICH ONE MAN WILL DO AS WELL AS
MILL II (174)	/EPIFANIA/ YES. BUT YOU NEED NOT BE AFRAID. MY	HUSBAND	IS OPENLY UNFAITHFUL TO ME AND CANNOT TAKE YOU INTO
DEVL III (61)	WITH STUDIED COURTESY) BELIEVE ME, MADAM, YOUR	HUSBAND	IS PLACING US UNDER THE GREATEST OBLIGATION BY
HART I (76)	DOOR LEADING TO THE HALL). /LADY UTTERWORD/ YOUR	HUSBAND	IS QUITE CHARMING, DARLING. HE HAS ACTUALLY
OVER PREFACE(158)	SUCH MATTERS. IN AN ELEGANT PLUTOCRACY, A JEALOUS	HUSBAND	IS REGARDED AS A BOOR. AMONG THE TRADESMEN WHO
HART I (49)	I MARRIED AT NINETEEN TO ESCAPE FROM IT. MY	HUSBAND	IS SIR HASTINGS UTTERWORD, WHO HAS BEEN GOVERNOR OF
6CAL (101)	SIR: THE KING IS INCAPABLE OF REVENGE: MY	HUSBAND	IS THE FLOWER OF CHIVALRY. /EUSTACHE/ YOU LITTLE
SUPR III (119)	SECRET OF ITS POPULARITY. AND A WOMAN SEEKING A	HUSBAND	IS THE MOST UNSCRUPULOUS OF ALL THE BEASTS OF PREY.
MILL II (177)	A HUSBAND WORTHY OF ME? /THE DOCTOR/ OH! THE	HUSBAND	IS TO BE TESTED TOO! THAT NEVER OCCURRED TO ME.
GETT PREFACE(221)	PROMISED, ONE OF THE SUREST METHODS TO OBTAIN A	HUSBAND	IS TO PRACTISE ON HIS SUSCEPTIBILITIES UNTIL HE IS
DOCT I (113)	BEWILDERED: THERES NOBODY DYING. /MRS DUBEDAT/ MY	HUSBAND	IS. /RIDGEON/ (PULLING HIMSELF TOGETHER) AH, YES: I
MILL I (138)	WILL IT WILL BE NECESSARY FOR ME TO KNOW WHO YOUR	HUSBAND	IS. /THE LADY/ MY HUSBAND IS A FOOL AND A
SUPR II (64)	WISHES. WOULD IT BE INDISCREET TO ASK WHO HER	HUSBAND	IS, IN CASE I SHOULD HAVE AN OPPORTUNITY OF
LIED (183)	HOW HE LIED TO HER	HUSBAND	. 1904.
LIED (204)	EH? /HE/ I SHOULD CALL IT HOW HE LIED TO HER	HUSBAND	.
JOAN 3 (91)	/JOAN/ (MATTER-OF-FACT) I WILL NEVER TAKE A	HUSBAND	. A MAN IN TOUL TOOK AN ACTION AGAINST ME FOR BREACH
BARB I (252)	OH, ADOLPHUS CUSINS WILL MAKE A VERY GOOD	HUSBAND	. AFTER ALL, NOBODY CAN SAY A WORD AGAINST GREEK: IT
DEVL III (71)	RUNNING TO SEE A MAN HANGED THATS NOT YOUR	HUSBAND	. AND HE'S NO BETTER THAN YOURSELF. I TOLD MY MAJOR
PYGM II (239)	WOMAN, GOVERNOR, JUST BECAUSE I'M NOT HER LAWFUL	HUSBAND	. AND SHE KNOWS IT TOO. CATCH HER MARRYING ME! TAKE
JOAN PREFACE(54)	HAS AN APHRODISIAC EFFECT ON ME OR ON MY WIFE OR	HUSBAND	. AND WHATEVER SUPERIOR PEOPLE MAY PRETEND, I CANNOT
HART I (46)	REMOTE PART OF THE EMPIRE WITH HER NUMSKULL OF A	HUSBAND	. AS A CHILD SHE THOUGHT THE FIGURE-HEAD OF MY SHIP,
GETT (326)	I ORDERED MY FIRST TON OF COALS FROM THAT WOMAN'S	HUSBAND	. AT THAT TIME I DID NOT KNOW THAT IT IS NOT TRUE
HART II (118)	THEY HAVE EVER BEEN. YOU ARE LOOKING FOR A RICH	HUSBAND	. AT YOUR AGE I LOOKED FOR HARDSHIP, DANGER, HORROR,
SUPR I (24)	BEGAN, THE GREAT ARTIST HAS BEEN KNOWN AS A BAD	HUSBAND	. BUT HE IS WORSE: HE IS A CHILD-ROBBER, A
BARB III (317)	JUST AS MUCH AS IT IS YOUR DUTY TO SUBMIT TO YOUR	HUSBAND	. COME, BIDDY! THESE TRICKS OF THE GOVERNING CLASS
LIED (203)	/SHE/ FOR MY SAKE, HENRY. AFTER ALL, HE'S MY	HUSBAND	. FORGIVE HIM. TAKE HIS HAND. (HENRY, DAZED, LETS
GETT PREFACE(214)	THE (TO THEM) UNBEARABLE CONDITION OF TAKING A	HUSBAND	. FROM BOTH CLASSES MAY, PERHAPS, BE SUBTRACTED FOR
CYMB V (148)	HUSBAND? /IMOGEN/ I AM A WOMAN, AND THIS MAN MY	HUSBAND	. HE WOULD HAVE SLAIN ME. /POSTHUMUS/ DO NOT HARP ON
PLES PREFACE(R18)	IT WITH PHOTOGRAPHS OF THE MUTILATED BODY OF HER	HUSBAND	. HERE WAS A SUFFICIENTLY SENSATIONAL CONFIRMATION
MILL IV (196)	MADAM: I DID NOT KNOW THAT THE GENTLEMAN WAS YOUR	HUSBAND	. HOWEVER, YOU ARE ALWAYS RIGHT. DO YOU WISH ME TO
PYGM II (238)	CHARITIES IN ONE WEEK FOR THE DEATH OF THE SAME	HUSBAND	. I DONT NEED LESS THAN A DESERVING MAN: I NEED
MRS IV (251)	A WIFE. I DONT WANT A MOTHER; AND I DONT WANT A	HUSBAND	. I HAVE SPARED NEITHER FRANK NOR MYSELF IN SENDING
GETT (284)	/THE BISHOP/ QUITE RIGHT, DEAR: STAND UP FOR YOUR	HUSBAND	. I HOPE YOU WILL ALWAYS STAND UP FOR ALL YOUR
INCA (243)	IT'S TOO BAD. /ERMYNTRUDE/ STILL, A HUSBAND IS A	HUSBAND	. I WISH I HAD ONE. /THE PRINCESS/ OH, HOW CAN YOU
OVER (175)	WONT EAT YOU. /GREGORY/ I'M NOT AFRAID OF YOUR	HUSBAND	. I'M AFRAID OF MY CONSCIENCE. /MRS JUNO/ (LOSING
MIS. (156)	HAVE YOU THINK ME AN UNPRINCIPLED MAN OR A BAD	HUSBAND	. I'M NOT. BUT IVE A SUPERABUNDANCE OF VITALITY.
KING PREFACE(156)	INTEREST, AND BEING A DISGRACEFULLY UNFAITHFUL	HUSBAND	. IT IS INFERRED THAT HE WAS POLITICALLY INFLUENCED
MILL I (163)	YOU FORGET THE DIGNITY OF YOUR POSITION AS MY	HUSBAND	. MR SAGAMORE: I HAVE CHANGED MY MIND ABOUT MY WILL.
DOCT I (113)	HIMSELF TOGETHER) AH, YES: I HAD FORGOTTEN YOUR	HUSBAND	. MRS DUBEDAT: YOU ARE ASKING ME TO DO A VERY
VWOO 1 (121)	IT: SHE SAID IT WOULD HELP ME TO GET A THRIFTY	HUSBAND	. MY FATHER TOLD ME TO BLUE IT ALL IN A LUMP WHILE I
MILL I (162)	AS A SINGLE WOMAN. I HAVE BECOME ACCUSTOMED TO A	HUSBAND	. NO: DECIDEDLY I WILL NOT DIVORCE ALASTAIR-- AT
NEVR II (232)	AND YOUR SISTERS' FATHER, AND MRS CLANDON'S	HUSBAND	. NOW! WHAT HAVE YOU TO SAY TO THAT? /DOLLY/ (
SUPR IV (166)	IT IS THE WORLD'S WILL THAT YOU SHOULD HAVE A	HUSBAND	. /ANN/ I DARESAY I SHALL, SOMEDAY. /TANNER/ BUT WHY
NEVR IV (289)	ARRIVES. /CRAMPTON/ WHAT D'Y' MEAN? I'M HER	HUSBAND	. /BOHUN/ (INSTANTLY POUNCING ON THE INCONSISTENCY
CLEO II (134)	AGAIN, NOW THAT I AM A QUEEN. I WOULD MAKE HIM MY	HUSBAND	. /CAESAR/ IT MIGHT BE MANAGED, PERHAPS; FOR IT WAS
SUPR III (95)	ARIGHT. HAVE YOU WARNED WHATSHISNAME? HER	HUSBAND	. /DON JUAN/ MY FRIEND OTTAVIO? NO: I HAVE NOT SEEN
JITT III (74)	MARRY HIM; FOR YOU MUSTNT TELL ANYONE EXCEPT YOUR	HUSBAND	. /EDITH/ YOU WANT ME TO MARRY HIM? /JITTA/ I DO.
HART I (64)	/MRS HUSHABYE/ (RISING) WHAT A LARK! HE IS MY	HUSBAND	. /ELLIE/ BUT HOW-- (SHE STOPS SUDDENLY; THEN TURNS
HART II (89)	HUSHABYE AND TELL HER THAT YOURE IN LOVE WITH HER	HUSBAND	. /ELLIE/ SHE KNOWS IT. /MANGAN/ YOU TOLD HER! !
MIS. (175)	I'LL TEACH YOU TO COME INTO MY HOUSE AND SHOOT MY	HUSBAND	. /GUNNER/ TEACH AWAY. I NEVER ASKED TO BE LET OFF.
HART I (81)	NEVER SEE YOU FROM BREAKFAST TO DINNER. I WANT MY	HUSBAND	. /HECTOR/ (BITTERLY) I MIGHT AS WELL BE YOUR
HART I (72)	DUNN. HOW DO YOU DO? /MRS HUSHABYE/ THIS IS MY	HUSBAND	. /HECTOR/ WE HAVE MET, DEAR. DONT INTRODUCE US ANY
HART II (121)	STRAIGHTENING UP) WHAT! BUT YOU ARE HER SISTER'S	HUSBAND	. /HECTOR/ WELL, IF YOU COME TO THAT, YOU ARE HER
LIED (194)	SWEAR IN MY PRESENCE. ONE WOULD THINK YOU WERE MY	HUSBAND	. /HE/ (AGAIN COLLAPSING ON THE STOOL) THIS IS SOME
BUOY II (21)	I AM HERE INSTEAD OF IN LONDON LOOKING FOR A RICH	HUSBAND	. /HE/ WE ARE GETTING ON LIKE OLD FRIENDS. EVIDENTLY
SIM I (50)	/LADY FARWATERS/ AND THE GIRLS WILL NEED A YOUNG	HUSBAND	. /IDDY/ (IMPLORINGLY) TWO YOUNG HUSBANDS, LADY
DEVL III (63)	TACT AND GENTLEMANLY FEELING SHEWN BY YOUR	HUSBAND	. /JUDITH/ (THROWING THE WORDS IN HIS FACE) OH, YOU
OVER (185)	ANOTHER MAN TO MY FACE! /MRS LUNN/ WHY, HE'S MY	HUSBAND	. /JUNO/ THAT TAKES AWAY THE LAST RAG OF EXCUSE FOR
HART II (124)	THE MAN HAS A ROOTED DELUSION THAT HE IS YOUR	HUSBAND	. /LADY UTTERWORD/ I KNOW. HE IS JEALOUS. AS IF HE
OVER (174)	ON THE BOAT-- YOU SPOKE TO ME OF YOUR POOR DEAR	HUSBAND	. /MRS JUNO/ (RELEASING HIM, QUITE REASSURED) IS
OVER (191)	JUNO? /JUNO/ I SHOULD ADVISE YOU TO DIVORCE YOUR	HUSBAND	. /MRS LUNN/ YOU WANT ME TO DRAG YOUR WIFE INTO
NEVR II (232)	FATHER, OR GLORIA'S FATHER, OR MY MOTHER'S	HUSBAND	. /M'COMAS/ OH, INDEED! WELL, SIR, LET ME TELL YOU
DEST (178)	ANY RISK NOW. SHE DOES NOT QUITE UNDERSTAND HER	HUSBAND	. /NAPOLEON/ I AM TO READ THE LETTER, THEN? (HE
SUPR I (11)	ME AS MUCH AS SHE LIKES. I MIGHT AS WELL BE HER	HUSBAND	. /RAMSDEN/ YOU CAN REFUSE TO ACCEPT THE
GETT (304)	THE HOPELESS ATTACHMENT: I SHALL ONLY BE THE	HUSBAND	. /REGINALD/ (SAVAGELY) WILL YOU TELL ME THIS, ANY
DEVL III (51)	IS HE ON THE WING? /JUDITH/ HE IS NO LONGER MY	HUSBAND	. /RICHARD/ (OPENING HIS EYES WIDE). EH? /JUDITH/
DOCT I (106)	/B.B./ DOWNSTAIRS. CHARMING WOMAN. TUBERCULOUS	HUSBAND	. /RIDGEON/ IS SHE THERE STILL? /EMMY/ (LOOKING
DOCT V (179)	/RIDGEON/ BY WHOM? ! ! ! /JENNIFER/ BY MY	HUSBAND	. /RIDGEON/ (GABBLING AND STUTTERING) WHAT
DOCT V (179)	THEY WERE ALL BOUGHT IN FOR ME THIS MORNING BY MY	HUSBAND	. /RIDGEON/ BY WHOM? ! ! ! /JENNIFER/ BY MY
DOCT V (172)	AN ADVANCE COPY OF MRS DUBEDAT'S LIFE OF HER LATE	HUSBAND	. /RIDGEON/ (READING THE TITLE) THE STORY OF A KING
GETT (316)	SOCIETY. WHAT SHE CLEARLY SHOULD NOT HAVE IS A	HUSBAND	. /SOAMES/ ANYTHING ELSE, MISS GRANTHAM? /LESBIA/
ANNA (297)	SPEAK TO ANYONE ALONE, WERE IT EVEN HER OWN	HUSBAND	. /THE GRAND DUCHESS/ YOU FORGET THAT THERE IS AN
6CAL (104)	ME TO SETTLE MY BUSINESS WITH YOUR HENPECKED	HUSBAND	. /THE QUEEN/ YOU SHALL SUFFER FOR THIS INSOLENCE. (
MTH1 I (18)	/EVE/ (SLIPPING HER HAND INTO HIS) WIFE AND	HUSBAND	. /THE SERPENT/ (LAUGHS)! ! ! /EVE/ (SNATCHING
ROCK II (281)	WOMEN FOLK. THAT WAS HER IDEAL OF A DELIGHTFUL	HUSBAND	. SHE FOUND TODAY THAT THE WORKING MAN DOESNT
JITT III SD(52)	VERY BUSY GOING THROUGH THE PAPERS OF HER LATE	HUSBAND	. SHE IS FEVERISHLY READING LETTERS, AND TEARING
GENV I (41)	FRIEND. SHE HAD TO. HORRIBLE. THEYVE SHOT HER	HUSBAND	. SHE SAYS SHE WILL SHOOT ME UNLESS THE LEAGUE STOPS
BUOY III (39)	GLAD TO BE RID OF YOUR CRAZY NOTIONS ABOUT YOUR	HUSBAND	. THE KIDS FILL HIS PLACE. /MRS THIRDBORN/ NOT AFTER
HART II (115)	MARRIED RIGHT UP TO THE HILT, LIKE MY DAUGHTER'S	HUSBAND	. THE MAN IS AT HOME ALL DAY, LIKE A DAMNED SOUL IN
DEVL III (63)	YOU SHALL NOT HANG HIM: THAT MAN IS NOT MY	HUSBAND	. THE OFFICERS LOOK AT ONE ANOTHER, AND WHISPER:
GETT PREFACE(251)	OF LENDING HER TOOTHBRUSH TO ANOTHER WOMAN AS HER	HUSBAND	. THE SENSE OF OUTRAGED MANHOOD WITH WHICH I FELT
JITT III (77)	THAT WAY. /LENKHEIM/ YES; BUT THEN HE WASNT YOUR	HUSBAND	. THELMA THOUGHT ME A MUCH FINER FELLOW THAN
BUOY III (37)	TO HER AND BECAME ONLY HER MATTER-OF-FACT	HUSBAND	. TO KEEP HER IN GOOD HUMOR AND HEALTH I HAD TO
LIED (191)	SHAME. REMEMBER! WE OWE SOMETHING TO YOUR	HUSBAND	. WE ARE HIS GUESTS HERE: HE IS AN HONORABLE MAN: HE
OVER (176)	CONSCIENCE WAS UNEASY WHEN YOU THOUGHT OF YOUR	HUSBAND	. WHAT MUST IT BE WHEN YOU THINK OF MY WIFE? /MRS
MTH5 (259)	ME. /EVE/ (APPEARING NEAR THE GROVE) HERE I AM,	HUSBAND	. YOU ARE VERY OLD. /A VOICE/ (IN THE HILLS) HA!
MILL I (138)	MAKE MY WILL, LEAVING EVERYTHING I POSSESS TO MY	HUSBAND	. YOU CAN HARDLY GO WRONG ABOUT THAT, I SUPPOSE.
CATH 1 (170)	BESIDES, IT IS NOT LUCKY TO BE CATHERINE'S	HUSBAND	. YOU KNOW WHAT HAPPENED TO PETER? /EDSTASTON/ (
DOCT I (109)	CASE. /MRS DUBEDAT/ DOCTOR: YOU MUST SAVE MY	HUSBAND	. YOU MUST. WHEN I EXPLAIN TO YOU, YOU WILL SEE THAT
MILL I (150)	MY WHAT, DID YOU SAY? /PATRICIA/ YOUR SUNDAY	HUSBAND	. YOU UNDERSTAND. WHAT MR ADRIAN BLENDERBLAND IS TO
ARMS III (57)	I BELIEVE YOU WOULD RATHER BE MY SERVANT THAN MY	HUSBAND	. YOU WOULD MAKE MORE OUT OF ME. OH, I KNOW THAT
VWOO 2 (129)	NOW THATS THE SORT OF MAN THAT WOULD SUIT ME AS A	HUSBAND	." I'D HAVE SAID IT EVEN IF YOU HADNT BEEN THE MARCO
MTH2 (79)	SKULL; AND YOU SAY, " THATS ADAM. THATS EVE'S	HUSBAND	." YOU TAKE THE SPECTACLED SCIENCE STUDENT FROM THE
DEVL EPILOG (85)	ACLAND. OTHERS HAVE NARRATED HOW LADY HARRIET'S	HUSBAND	KILLED HIMSELF IN A DUEL, BY FALLING WITH HIS HEAD
SUPR I (46)	YOU HAVE ALL BEEN TALKING ABOUT ME! IF MY	HUSBAND	KNEW IT HE WOULD NEVER LET ME SPEAK TO ANY OF YOU
JITT III (64)	EFFECT. /JITTA/ I HOPE NOT. TELL ME: DOES MY	HUSBAND	KNOW OF THIS NEW TURN? /FESSLER/ NOT YET. PERHAPS
DEVL II (36)	ME ABOUT THAT. I HATE AND DREAD YOU; AND MY	HUSBAND	KNOWS IT. IF YOU ARE NOT HERE WHEN HE COMES BACK, HE
LIED (192)	DEAREST, BELIEVE ME, NOTHING WILL HAPPEN. YOUR	HUSBAND	KNOWS THAT I AM CAPABLE OF DEFENDING MYSELF. UNDER
DOCT IV (162)	WILL SAY " LOOK AT THAT MISERABLE WOMAN: HER	HUSBAND	MADE HER MISERABLE." /MRS DUBEDAT/ NO, NEVER. YOU
OVER PREFACE(160)	TO MARRY AGAIN AFTER BEING DESERTED BY HER	HUSBAND	MAY BE MORE MERCIFUL THAN ALLOWING HER TO BE MOBBED
SUPR III (120)	OFF THE MASK WHEN THEIR BIRD IS IN THE NET. THE	HUSBAND	NEVER BECOMES NEGLIGENT, SELFISH, BRUTAL-- OH,
HART I (71)	/RANDALL/ (JOINING THEM AT THE WINDOW) ONE'S	HUSBAND	NEVER IS, ARIADNE (HE SITS BY LADY UTTERWORD, ON
JITT III (75)	YOU OWE IT TO YOUR POSITION AS AN INJURED	HUSBAND	NEVER TO SPEAK TO ME WHEN WE ARE ALONE AND THERE ARE
GETT (270)	THAT; SO I HAVE MADE UP MY MIND TO HAVE NEITHER	HUSBAND	NOR CHILDREN. /THE GENERAL/ BUT, GREAT HEAVENS, THE
DEVL III (76)	AFFECTIONATELY) WELL, WHAT DO YOU THINK OF YOUR	HUSBAND	NOW, EH? -- EH? ? -- EH? ? ? /JUDITH/ I AM
3PLA PREFACE(R15)	HAS PRESERVED FOR US OF THE CONVERSATION OF THE	HUSBAND	OF JULIET'S NURSE. NO: MY DISGUST WAS NOT MERE
PRES (165)	CAN MAINTAIN HER HUSBAND IN COMPETITION WITH THE	HUSBAND	OF MRS BANGER. I HAVE THE HONOR TO PROPOSE FOR YOUR

CYMB FORWORD(135)	BUT ONE. THE EXCEPTION IS THE HERO, OR RATHER THE	HUSBAND	OF THE HEROINE, LEONATUS POSTHUMUS. THE LATE CHARLES
GETT PREFACE(254)	THE WIFE IS THE PROPERTY OF THE HUSBAND OR THE	HUSBAND	OF THE WIFE IS NOT A WHIT LESS ABHORRENT AND
3PLA PREFACE(R29)	HAS HE EVER SEEN IT ADDED THAT THE SAVED WAS THE	HUSBAND	OF THE WOMAN THE SAVER LOVED, OR WAS THAT WOMAN
OVER (190)	SO VERY GOOD, MY DEAR, AS TO TAKE MY SENTIMENTAL	HUSBAND	OFF MY HANDS OCCASIONALLY, I SHALL BE MORE THAN
GETT PREFACE(233)	CAME INTO HER HOUSE AND PROPOSED TO ADORE HER	HUSBAND	ON A TOLERATED FOOTING, SHE WOULD SAY " MY HUSBAND
BUOY III (46)	ALL INDEPENDENT WOMEN DO WITH THEIR MEANS. KEEP A	HUSBAND	ON THEM. /MRS SECONDBORN/ IS A HUSBAND A DOG OR A
HART I (71)	I DONT KNOW. SHE QUARRELLED MORTALLY WITH MY	HUSBAND	ONLY TEN MINUTES AGO; AND I DIDNT KNOW ANYONE ELSE
SIM PRO;2, (27)	A WHITE WOMAN, THEYRE ALL SNOBS; AND THEY WANT A	HUSBAND	ONLY TO TAKE THEM HOME OUT OF THIS. /THE Y.W./ WHY,
MILL PREFACE(112)	VILLA. HAD CATHERINE II REIGNED OVER HER	HUSBAND	ONLY, SHE NEED NOT NOR COULD NOT HAVE HAD HIM
GETT PREFACE(250)	AND DESDEMONA. HOW STRONG WAS THE FEELING THAT A	HUSBAND	OR A WIFE IS AN ARTICLE OF PROPERTY, GREATLY
CAND I SD(91)	THEM, AND YET WOULD NOT SUSPECT EITHER HER	HUSBAND	OR HERSELF OF ANY SUCH IDEA, OR INDEED OF ANY
GETT PREFACE(209)	THE NUMBER OF WIVES PERMITTED TO A SINGLE	HUSBAND	OR OF HUSBANDS TO A SINGLE WIFE UNDER A MARRIAGE
GETT PREFACE(254)	THE THEORY THAT THE WIFE IS THE PROPERTY OF THE	HUSBAND	OR THE HUSBAND OF THE WIFE IS NOT A WHIT LESS
OVER PREFACE(168)	IS. IN JUST THE SAME WAY, I WANT THE UNFAITHFUL	HUSBAND	OR THE UNFAITHFUL WIFE IN A FARCICAL COMEDY NOT TO
GETT PREFACE(211)	CURED, MONOGAMY, IN THE SENSE OF HAVING ONLY ONE	HUSBAND	OR WIFE AT A TIME (FACILITIES FOR CHANGING ARE
GETT PREFACE(233)	TO JEALOUSY, SOMETIMES MAKE THE THREATENED	HUSBAND	OR WIFE HESITATE TO TAKE PROMPT STEPS AND DO THE
GETT PREFACE(211)	AND ECONOMICAL THAT NOBODY WOULD WANT TO SHARE A	HUSBAND	OR WIFE IF HE (OR SHE) COULD HAVE A SUFFICIENTLY
GETT PREFACE(186)	FOR TWENTY YEARS FOR IT, THE FREE AND INNOCENT	HUSBAND	OR WIFE OF THAT MURDERER SHOULD REMAIN BOUND BY THE
GETT PREFACE(218)	VOWS IN THE TECHNICAL DIVORCE COURT SENSE. NO	HUSBAND	OR WIFE YET BORN KEEPS THEM OR EVER CAN KEEP THEM IN
WIDO II (47)	A FOOL. /SARTORIUS/ THEN YOU WILL HAVE TO TAKE A	HUSBAND	OVER THIRTY, BLANCHE. YOU MUST NOT EXPECT TOO MUCH,
OVER (184)	I! I, A SOLICITOR! BRAVING THE RISK OF YOUR	HUSBAND	PUTTING ME INTO THE DIVORCE COURT AND MAKING ME A
GETT PREFACE(233)	HAS RESULTED IN THE IGNOMINIOUS DEFEAT OF THE	HUSBAND	QUITE AS OFTEN AS IN POETIC JUSTICE AS CONCEIVED IN
OVER (173)	BEAUTIFUL WOMAN, AND KNOWING THAT THERE IS A	HUSBAND	ROUND THE CORNER? I HAVE HAD THIS ACCURSED BOARD
OVER (174)	/GREGORY/ NO. IT WAS SOMETHING ABOUT YOUR LATE	HUSBAND	-- /MRS JUNO/ MY LATE HUSBAND! WHAT DO YOU MEAN?
DEVL III (63)	DONT KNOW WHAT YOU MEAN. I SAY THAT HE IS NOT MY	HUSBAND	-- THAT MY HUSBAND HAS ESCAPED. THIS MAN TOOK HIS
BUOY III (39)	I LIKED HIM BECAUSE HE WAS SO UNLIKE ME. (TO HER	HUSBAND	) AND IT WAS THE SAME WITH YOU, WASN'T IT, DICK?
DEVL I (11)	/MRS DUDGEON/ (TO HERSELF, THINKING OF HER	HUSBAND	) THIEF! THIEF! ! (SHE SHAKES HERSELF ANGRILY
KING II (223)	PUT UP WITH IT. /CHARLES/ (GETTING UP) I AM YOUR	HUSBAND	; AND I COUNT IT A GREAT PRIVILEGE. (HE KISSES
JITT I (17)	MAN! THE MOST HOPELESS MATERIALIST I KNOW IS MY	HUSBAND	; AND I DO NOT WANT TO BE REMINDED OF HIM JUST NOW.
SUPR II (66)	SAY NO MORE. WHOEVER HE IS, HE'S MISS RAWBNSN'S	HUSBAND	; AND I SHOULD BE GLAD FOR HER SAKE TO THINK BETTER
HART II (127)	I AM TIED TO HESIONE'S APRON-STRING; BUT I'M HER	HUSBAND	; AND IF I DID GO STARK STARING MAD ABOUT HER, AT
DOCT I (96)	ME, IVE BEEN TALKING TO THAT POOR GIRL. IT'S HER	HUSBAND	; AND SHE THINKS IT'S A CASE OF CONSUMPTION: THE
3PLA PREFACE(R30)	SAKE THAT HE OFFERED HIS LIFE TO SAVE HER BELOVED	HUSBAND	; AND THAT HIS EXPLICIT DENIAL OF HIS PASSION WAS
MTH1 I (18)	HE WILL BE TO YOU AND NOT TO ANY OTHER WOMAN IS	HUSBAND	; AND WHAT YOU WILL BE TO HIM AND NOT TO ANY OTHER
CATH 4 (197)	THINK OF HIM IN THAT WAY. AFTER ALL, HE WAS YOUR	HUSBAND	; AND WHATEVER HIS FAULTS MAY HAVE BEEN, IT IS NOT
ARMS I (17)	AFTER WHAT YOU HAVE JUST SAID ABOUT MY FUTURE	HUSBAND	; BUT I WILL GO OUT ON THE BALCONY AND SEE WHETHER
DEVL III (51)	DISPOSED OF UNCLE PETER. (SHE SHUDDERS). IS YOUR	HUSBAND	SAFE? IS HE ON THE WING? /JUDITH/ HE IS NO LONGER
GETT PREFACE(201)	SELDOM BROUGHT TO THAT TEST. THE TYPICAL BRITISH	HUSBAND	SEES MUCH LESS OF HIS WIFE THAN HE DOES OF HIS
PPP (199)	BRED CONTEMPT. NOW ALL THAT SHALL END. MY	HUSBAND	SHALL BE MY HERO, MY LOVER, MY PERFECT KNIGHT. HE
DOCT III (151)	SHALL BE IN MY PROPER PLACE, AT THE BEDSIDE. YOUR	HUSBAND	SHALL BE TREATED EXACTLY AS IF HE WERE A MEMBER OF
DOCT III (150)	A MOST GRATIFYING SURPRISE) MY DEAR LADY, YOUR	HUSBAND	SHALL HAVE ME. /MRS DUBEDAT/ BUT-- /B.B./ NOT A
SUPR IV SD(151)	TABLE, LOOKING ON IN HELPLESS ANNOYANCE AS HER	HUSBAND	SOARS TO HIGHER AND HIGHER MORAL EMINENCES WITHOUT
MIS. (136)	TO MANAGE IN JINGHISKAHN; AND I THINK YOU DO YOUR	HUSBAND	SOME INJUSTICE, MRS TARLETON. THEY PRETENDED TO LIKE
GETT (330)	BUT GEORGE GOES ON FOR EVER. /HOTCHKISS/ YES: A	HUSBAND	SOON BECOMES NOTHING BUT A HABIT. LISTEN: I SUPPOSE
DEVL I SD(16)	HER BREATH CONVULSIVELY THROUGH HER NOSE. HER	HUSBAND	SPEAKS. /UNCLE TITUS/ WELL, I HOPE HE WILL HAVE THE
JITT III (55)	AS I HAVE BEEN FOR MONTHS PAST, WHILE MY	HUSBAND	SPENT HOURS AND HOURS AND HOURS IN HIS STUDY,
GETT PREFACE(188)	SO THAT SHELLEY WAS SOMETHING MORE HATEFUL TO A	HUSBAND	THAN A HORSE THIEF: TO WIT, A WIFE THIEF, AND
OVER (189)	AND SO IS MY WIFE. DONT YOU SET UP TO BE A BETTER	HUSBAND	THAN I AM; FOR YOURE NOT. IVE OWNED I'M WRONG. YOU
MILL I (144)	ALL SOLICITORS YOU THINK YOU KNOW MORE ABOUT MY	HUSBAND	THAN I DO. WELL, I TELL YOU THAT ALASTAIR CAME BACK
ROCK I (206)	LIKE THAT. BUT IT'S BETTER TO SEE TOO LITTLE OF A	HUSBAND	THAN TOO MUCH OF HIM, ISNT IT? /LADY CHAVENDER/ I
SIM PRO;3, (30)	THAT BE? (TO THE PRIESTESS) YOU WOULDNT LIKE A	HUSBAND	THAT DIDNT EAT PLENTY OF MEAT, WOULD YOU? BUT THEN
KING II (226)	SAID IT I WOULD KILL HER. YOU ARE THE VERY BEST	HUSBAND	THAT EVER LIVED. /CHARLES/ (LAUGHING) OH! OH!
GETT (354)	/MRS GEORGE/ (SITTING DOWN) AND SO WILL MY	HUSBAND	THE COAL MERCHANT. /HOTCHKISS/ IF I WERE YOUR
GENV I (39)	THE LEAGUE OF NATIONS, WERE INTRODUCED BY MY LATE	HUSBAND	THE SIXTH PRESIDENT. HE OBSERVED THE CONSTITUTION
GENV I (39)	THE BUDGET WAS PASSED PROVIDING FOR TWO YEARS. MY	HUSBAND	THEN PROROGUED THE PARLIAMENT UNTIL THE END OF THAT
GETT (328)	THE FRIEND OF THE FAMILY-- WHEN THERE WAS THE	HUSBAND	THERE TO SHEW OFF AGAINST AND TO TAKE ALL THE
CLEO II (124)	AM NOT AFRAID. A QUEEN MUST NOT BE AFRAID. EAT MY	HUSBAND	THERE, IF YOU LIKE: HE IS AFRAID. /CAESAR/ (
CYMB V (144)	MAKES GOOD TO ME ALL YOU HAVE DONE, YOU AND MY	HUSBAND	THERE! /IACHIMO/ IT REMEDIES WHAT CAN BE REMEDIED.
CYMB V (145)	HAVE GRACE TO KNOW YOURSELF FOR WHAT YOU ARE. MY	HUSBAND	THINKS THAT ALL IS SETTLED NOW AND THIS A HAPPY
GETT (335)	DELIBERATELY) I SHALL PAY MY FIRST VISIT TO YOUR	HUSBAND	THIS AFTERNOON. /MRS GEORGE/ YOULL SEE WHAT HE'LL
MILL IV (196)	FIERCELY TO THE MANAGER) YOU HAVE ALLOWED MY	HUSBAND	TO BRING A WOMAN TO MY HOTEL AND REGISTER HER IN MY
APPL INTRLUD(246)	AND STUPIDER WOMEN. WHEN I BEGGED YOUR PRESENT	HUSBAND	TO COME BACK TO COURT FOR A WHILE FOR THE SAKE OF
GENV I (41)	IF THE LEAGUE DOES NOT BRING THE MURDERER OF MY	HUSBAND	TO JUSTICE MY SON WILL BE OBLIGED TO TAKE UP A BLOOD
MTH5 (235)	TODAY. /THE FEMALE FIGURE/ HOW CAN YOU EXPECT MY	HUSBAND	TO KNOW WHAT TO THINK OF YOU IF YOU GIVE HIM HIS
LIED (192)	FOR YOU: I HAVE THE TICKETS: WE WILL ASK YOUR	HUSBAND	TO LEND US THE CARRIAGE TO SHEW THAT THERE IS NO
LION PROLOG (106)	THEN WHY DONT YOU TREAT ME PROPERLY AND BE A GOOD	HUSBAND	TO ME? /ANDROCLES/ WHAT CAN I DO, MY DEAR?
POSN (465)	TWICE IN HER LIFE! I WANT SOMEBODY TO BE A GOOD	HUSBAND	TO ME NOW. /BLANCO/ ANY OFFER, GENTLEMEN, ON THAT
BARB I (261)	I YOUR PERMISSION, ADOLPHUS, TO INVITE MY OWN	HUSBAND	TO MY OWN HOUSE? /CUSINS/ (GALLANTLY) YOU HAVE MY
DEVL II (34)	WITH RESENTMENT, WHICH SHE HAS BEEN EXPECTING HER	HUSBAND	TO SHARE AND EXPRESS FOR HER AT EVERY INSULT OF
JITT II (33)	EDITH THAN IN THAT MOMENT WHEN I HAD TO ASK MY	HUSBAND	TO TELL YOU WHAT IT COST ME TO STAY AWAY. /AGNES/ (
MTH1 II (28)	I CAN MAKE BETTER USE OF MY TIME THAN TO PLAY THE	HUSBAND	TO THE CLAY BENEATH MY FEET. /ADAM/ DEVIL? WHAT NEW
GENV IV (107)	ME. I AM A MURDERESS (GENERAL CONSTERNATION). MY	HUSBAND	WANTED SATISFACTION OF ANOTHER KIND. HE GOT IT FROM
GENV I (40)	TO THE INSULT OF DEFEAT AT THE POLLS. BUT MY	HUSBAND	WAS A MILITARY GENIUS. HE HAD NO DIFFICULTY IN
DEVL I (8)	PENT UP BREATH AND SITS AT HER EASE AGAIN). YOUR	HUSBAND	WAS GREATLY TOUCHED AND IMPRESSED BY HIS BROTHER'S
DEST (157)	TO LISTEN) THATS NOT THE VOICE OF A WOMAN WHOSE	HUSBAND	WAS KILLED YESTERDAY. /GIUSEPPE/ HUSBANDS ARE NOT
CLEO II (142)	/CLEOPATRA/ BUT THEY DO GET KILLED. MY SISTER'S	HUSBAND	WAS KILLED IN BATTLE. YOU MUST NOT GO. LET HIM GO (
JITT III (77)	THELMA PETERSEN. THAT LASTED UNTIL SHE AND HER	HUSBAND	WENT BACK TO NORWAY. /JITTA/ OH, HOW DISGRACEFUL!
JITT I (13)	BY CHANCE? /THE LADY/ I ALWAYS FEEL AS IF MY	HUSBAND	WERE LYING IN WAIT FOR ME AT THE NEXT TURN. /THE
LION PREFACE(71)	TO WAIT IN GENTEEL IDLENESS AND USELESSNESS FOR A	HUSBAND	WHEN ALL HER HEALTHY SOCIAL INSTINCTS CALL HER TO
GETT PREFACE(238)	WIFE WHEN HE IS TIRED OF HER, AND THE WIFE THE	HUSBAND	WHEN ANOTHER MAN STRIKES HER FANCY? ONE MUST REPLY
JITT III (65)	THAT STOLE FROM ME MY RIGHT TO BE BESIDE MY	HUSBAND	WHEN HE DIED. /JITTA/ SHE DID NOT INTEND THAT. YOU
OVER (181)	/MRS LUNN/ WHAT ELOQUENCE! IT REMINDS ME OF MY	HUSBAND	WHEN HE WAS IN LOVE-- BEFORE WE WERE MARRIED. ARE
GENV IV (108)	YOURSELF. BUT I WILL SENTENCE THE SLAYER OF YOUR	HUSBAND	WHEN HIS OFFENCE IS PROVED; AND BY THAT ACT I WILL
MIS. (124)	FELLOW; BUT I NEVER COULD HAVE FANCIED HIM FOR A	HUSBAND	WHEN I WAS YOUR AGE. /HYPATIA/ YES; BUT HE HAS SOME
OVER (190)	MY PART, WILL DO MY BEST TO AMUSE YOUR EXCELLENT	HUSBAND	WHEN YOU FIND HIM TIRESOME. /JUNO/ I CALL THIS
LIED (191)	ALL LONDON AS SIMPLY AS I WILL DECLARE IT TO YOUR	HUSBAND	WHEN YOU SEE-- AS YOU SOON WILL SEE-- THAT THIS IS
DEVL II SD(28)	ON HARVESTS AND PRICES AT FAIRS; AN AFFECTIONATE	HUSBAND	WHO IS A TOWER OF STRENGTH TO HER: IN SHORT, THAT
OVER PREFACE(158)	WHO SUPPLY THAT PLUTOCRACY WITH ITS MEALS. A	HUSBAND	WHO IS NOT JEALOUS, AND REFRAINS FROM ASSAILING HIS
GETT (284)	SEW ON. BESIDES, NOTHING IS MORE DREADFUL THAN A	HUSBAND	WHO KEEPS TELLING YOU EVERYTHING HE THINKS, AND
DEST (176)	CREATURE, WITH A VERY ABLE AND AMBITIOUS	HUSBAND	WHO KNOWS HER THROUGH AND THROUGH: KNOWS THAT SHE
BUOY III (37)	ME FACE TO FACE WITH REALITY; PERHAPS TIED TO A	HUSBAND	WHO MAY BE ANYTHING FROM A CRIMINAL TO AN
GETT PREFACE(210)	WOULD TAKE A THOUSANDTH SHARE, IF NECESSARY, IN A	HUSBAND	WHO WAS A MAN IN A THOUSAND, RATHER THAN HAVE SOME
CURE (236)	STREGA, DONT YOU WANT A DEAR LITTLE DOMESTICATED	HUSBAND	WHO WOULD HAVE NO CONCERN BUT TO PLEASE YOU, NO
DEVL II (38)	JOY. /JUDITH/ (ANGRILY) I WOULD RATHER HAVE A	HUSBAND	WHOM EVERYBODY RESPECTS THAN-- THAN-- /RICHARD/ THAN
GETT PREFACE(237)	ACCEPT HIM. HIS CASE IS THE SAME AS THAT OF THE	HUSBAND	WHOSE WIFE TELLS HIM SHE NO LONGER CARES FOR HIM,
JITT III (55)	MARRY MY DAUGHTER. /FESSLER/ YOU SEE, THOUGH YOUR	HUSBAND	WILL BE REMEMBERED AS A GREAT PSYCHOLOGIST, HE HAD
SUPR IV (165)	WITH THE MEN! IT'S NOT TO BE EXPECTED THAT YOUR	HUSBAND	WILL CARE TO BE BOTHERED WITH AN OLD WOMAN LIKE ME.
MILL II (174)	SPECIES. FIVE MINUTES CONVERSATION WITH MY	HUSBAND	WILL CONVINCE YOU THAT HE AND I DO NOT BELONG TO THE
DOCT I (114)	AND OTHERS. I CAN PUT THE CASE TO THEM; AND YOUR	HUSBAND	WILL HAVE TO STAND OR FALL BY WHAT WE THINK OF HIM.
MIS. (170)	OF COURSE SHE HAD HER DUE; AND SHE FOUND A	HUSBAND	WITH IT, AND SET HIM UP IN BUSINESS WITH IT, AND
GETT (264)	AND AWAY SHE WOULD GO FROM HER HOME AND HER	HUSBAND	WITHOUT WITH-YOUR-LEAVE OR BY-YOUR-LEAVE. /MRS
OVER (175)	HOLD THEIR TONGUES. DONT BE SUCH A COWARD. MY	HUSBAND	WONT EAT YOU. /GREGORY/ I'M NOT AFRAID OF YOUR
MILL II (177)	/EPIFANIA/ INDEED! AND MY FATHER'S TEST FOR A	HUSBAND	WORTHY OF ME? /THE DOCTOR/ OH! THE HUSBAND IS TO
SUPR III (119)	TO DELUDE YOUR SUITORS INTO THE BELIEF THAT YOUR	HUSBAND	WOULD HAVE IN HIS HOME AN ANGEL WHO WOULD FILL IT
LIED (192)	ALL POETS I HAVE A PASSION FOR PUGILISM. YOUR	HUSBAND	WOULD MAKE A TOLERABLE SECOND-RATE HEAVY WEIGHT IF
SUPR IV (162)	NOT AN ANGEL. /TANNER/ IN SHORT-- TO PUT IT AS A	HUSBAND	WOULD PUT IT WHEN EXASPERATED TO THE POINT OF
GLIM (174)	A MOTHER-IN-LAW'S SIN IS VERY EXPENSIVE; FOR YOUR	HUSBAND	WOULD STINT YOU TO PAY FOR MASSES FOR HER SOUL. /THE

DOCT II (119)	VERY NICE PEOPLE. I CONFESS I WAS AFRAID THE	HUSBAND	WOULD TURN OUT AN APPALLING BOUNDER. BUT HE'S ALMOST
DEST (175)	BE SENT TO HER HUSBAND, ANSWER SIMPLY THAT THE	HUSBAND	WOULDNT READ IT. DO YOU SUPPOSE, YOU GOOSE, THAT A
BUOY III (39)	WAKE UP FROM YOUR DREAMS AND DELUSIONS ABOUT YOUR	HUSBAND	YOU HAVE YOUR CHILDREN TO LOVE. YOU MAY BE ONLY TOO
PYGM EPILOG (302)	AND IT IS NOTABLE THAT THOUGH SHE NEVER NAGS HER	HUSBAND	, AND FRANKLY LOVES THE COLONEL AS IF SHE WERE HIS
JITT III (73)	WOMAN. HAVE YOU QUITE FORGOTTEN THAT I HAVE A	HUSBAND	, AND THAT FOR YOUR FATHER'S SAKE I WAS UNFAITHFUL
GETT PREFACE(234)	THAT A WOMAN MAY HAVE AN INCORRIGIBLY UNFAITHFUL	HUSBAND	, AND YET BE MUCH BETTER OFF THAN IF SHE HAD AN
WIDO II (47)	TOO MUCH, MY CHILD. YOU WILL BE RICHER THAN YOUR	HUSBAND	, AND, I THINK, CLEVERER TOO. I AM BETTER PLEASED
DEST (175)	COMPROMISING A WIFE SHOULD NOT BE SENT TO HER	HUSBAND	, ANSWER SIMPLY THAT THE HUSBAND WOULDNT READ IT. DO
OVER (185)	PASSES BETWEEN MY WIFE AND MYSELF? YOURE NOT HER	HUSBAND	, ARE YOU? /JUNO/ NOT AT PRESENT; BUT I'M ON THE
MILL IV (202)	I, BECAUSE I AM A MILLIONAIRESS, CANNOT KEEP MY	HUSBAND	, CANNOT KEEP EVEN A LOVER, CANNOT KEEP ANYTHING BUT
GENV I (40)	OF RAISING AN ARMY TO AVENGE THIS OUTRAGE, MY	HUSBAND	, CRUSHED BY THE LOSS OF HIS MISTRESS, JUST MOPED AT
GETT (329)	FIEND THAT YOU ARE! /MRS GEORGE/ YOU AMUSED THE	HUSBAND	, DIDNT YOU? /HOTCHKISS/ HE HAS MORE REAL SENSE OF
CLEO II (134)	IS SOMEWHAT YOUNGER. /CLEOPATRA/ WOULD HE BE MY	HUSBAND	, DO YOU THINK, IF I ASKED HIM? /CAESAR/ VERY
CYMB V (149)	HOW? NONE! /IMOGEN/ ALL IS LOST. SHAME,	HUSBAND	, HAPPINESS, AND FAITH IN MAN. HE IS NOT EVEN SORRY.
DOCT I (113)	NOW IF YOU WILL ENTERTAIN FOR ME, AND BRING YOUR	HUSBAND	, HE WILL MEET ME; AND HE WILL MEET SOME OF THE MOST
FOUN (220)	I CAN BULLY, BECAUSE IF A WOMAN CANT BULLY HER	HUSBAND	, HER HUSBAND GENERALLY BULLIES HER. YOU, MY LORD,
DEVL II SD(29)	THE STREET. THE FIRST THING SHE SEES THERE IS HER	HUSBAND	, HURRYING HOME THROUGH THE RAIN. SHE GIVES A LITTLE
MIS. SD(150)	MRS TARLETON BETWEEN LORD SUMMERHAYS AND HER	HUSBAND	, HYPATIA BETWEEN PERCIVAL AND BENTLEY, AND JOHNNY
JITT III (75)	HAPPY. /LENKHEIM/ AS I UNFORTUNATELY AM ONLY YOUR	HUSBAND	, I SUPPOSE THERE IS NO USE MY TRYING. /JITTA/ (
LION PREFACE(67)	HIS WIFE, AND A MARRIED WOMAN TO PLEASE HER	HUSBAND	, INSTEAD OF DOING THE WORK OF GOD. THIS IS ANOTHER
PPP (206)	GOODNIGHT, SIR. SHE RETIRES. /MAGNESIA/ AND NOW,	HUSBAND	, LET US PERFORM OUR LAST SAD DUTY TO OUR FRIEND. HE
6CAL (101)	OF CHIVALRY. /EUSTACHE/ YOU LITTLE KNOW YOUR	HUSBAND	, MADAM. WE KNOW BETTER WHAT TO EXPECT FROM EDWARD
VWOO 1 (119)	NO BETTER THAN AN IDIOT, AND THAT YOU WERE A BAD	HUSBAND	, MOST LIKELY. /A/ YOU ARE QUITE RIGHT ON BOTH
NEVR I (223)	HM! A FATHER, TOO, PERHAPS, AS WELL AS A	HUSBAND	, MR CRAMPTON? /CRAMPTON/ THREE CHILDREN.
HART I (66)	/MRS HUSHABYE/ (TO MANGAN) DO YOU KNOW MY	HUSBAND	, MR MANGAN (SHE INDICATES HECTOR). /MANGAN/ (
FANY I SD(273)	OF THE ROOM. THE LADY IS A PLACID PERSON. HER	HUSBAND	, MR ROBIN GILBEY, NOT AT ALL PLACID, BURSTS
MILL I (150)	/PATRICIA/ ADRIAN IS MRS FITZFASSENDEN'S SUNDAY	HUSBAND	, MR SAGAMORE. /EPIFANIA/ MY WHAT, DID YOU SAY?
NEVR III (276)	TO SAY IS THIS. IN THE OLD ARRANGEMENT WITH YOUR	HUSBAND	, MRS CLANDON, YOU HAD HIM AT A TERRIBLE
VWOO 3 (143)	MY NOT APPRECIATING YOU. I WANT A FANCY SORT OF	HUSBAND	, NOT A COMMON VILLAGER THAT ANY WOMAN COULD PICK
DEST (176)	ANOTHER MAN, I SHOULD PRETEND TO GO ON LOVING MY	HUSBAND	, OR BE AFRAID TO TELL HIM OR ALL THE WORLD? BUT
DEVL III (54)	IN COLD BLOOD, CARING NOT HALF SO MUCH FOR YOUR	HUSBAND	, OR (RUTHLESSLY) FOR YOU (SHE DROOPS, STRICKEN)
DEVL III (63)	DO YOU MEAN THAT THIS GENTLEMAN IS NOT YOUR	HUSBAND	, OR MERELY-- I WISH TO PUT THIS WITH ALL DELICACY--
GETT (350)	WHATEVER IN THE RUMOR THAT I AM SEPARATED FROM MY	HUSBAND	, OR THAT THERE IS, OR EVER HAS BEEN, ANYTHING
JITT II SD(27)	REFUGE IN AN ILLNESS, AND IS KEEPING HER BED. HER	HUSBAND	, PROFESSOR ALFRED LENKHEIM, IS SITTING IN HIS STUDY
3PLA PREFACE(R30)	FOR A MARRIED WOMAN, AND DUTY TO HER ABSENT	HUSBAND	, SEALED HIS PASSION-PALPITATING LIPS. FROM THE
DEVL III (64)	(KEENLY, WITH A HALF SMILE) IF YOU ARE NOT HER	HUSBAND	, SIR, THE CASE IS NOT A SERIOUS ONE-- FOR HER. (
SIM PRO,3, (34)	VEAL, HAS FALLEN FOR A BROWN BISHOP; AND HER	HUSBAND	, THE WHITEST ENGLISH WEST-END WHITE, HAS BEEN
GETT PREFACE(238)	ECONOMIC SLAVERY AGAIN THE ROOT DIFFICULTY. THE	HUSBAND	, THEN, IS TO BE ALLOWED TO DISCARD HIS WIFE WHEN HE
DEVL I (13)	JUDITH IS MORE THAN TWENTY YEARS YOUNGER THAN HER	HUSBAND	, THOUGH SHE WILL NEVER BE AS YOUNG AS HE IN
BULL PREFACE(52)	KILLED AN ENGLISH FARMER'S WIFE. ABD-EL-NEBI, HER	HUSBAND	, TOOK THE MATTER TO HEART, NOT ALTOGETHER WITHOUT
JOAN PREFACE(8)	OF THE ATTRACTION, PURSUIT, AND CAPTURE OF A	HUSBAND	, WAS NOT HER BUSINESS: SHE HAD SOMETHING ELSE TO
LIED PREFACE(185)	IN THE THEATRE IS STALER THAN THE SITUATION OF	HUSBAND	, WIFE, AND LOVER, OR THE FUN OF KNOCKABOUT FARCE. I
DOCT PREFACE(6)	TO SAY TO THE NEWLY BEREFT FATHER, MOTHER,	HUSBAND	, WIFE, BROTHER, OR SISTER, " YOU HAVE KILLED YOUR
GETT PREFACE(208)	THOUGH UNABLE TO FIND OR UNWILLING TO ENTERTAIN A	HUSBAND	, WOULD LIKE TO OCCUPY THEMSELVES WITH THE REARING
GETT (330)	GEORGE/ OH, I DONT KNOW THAT I LOVE HIM. HE'S MY	HUSBAND	, YOU KNOW. BUT IF I GOT ANXIOUS ABOUT GEORGE'S
SUPR IV (152)	/MALONE/ YOUR WIFE! /TANNER/ YOU THE MISSING	HUSBAND	! ANOTHER MORAL IMPOSTOR! (HE SMITES HIS BROW,
MTH5 (240)	I. /THE FEMALE FIGURE/ (FONDLY) MY MAN! MY HERO	HUSBAND	! I AM PROUD OF YOU. I LOVE YOU. /MARTELLUS/ WE
PPP (195)	/LADY MAGNESIA/ (WAKING AND SITTING UP) MY	HUSBAND	! (ALL THE COLORS OF THE RAINBOW CHASE ONE ANOTHER
SIM PRO,3, (34)	BOOK. WEARS GLASSES. BI-FOCALS. /THE Y.W./ HER	HUSBAND	! OH, I SAY! /THE E.O./ (RISING DEFERENTIALLY)
HART I (82)	WHAT A FATHER! /HECTOR/ (FOLLOWING SUIT) WHAT A	HUSBAND	! /CAPTAIN SHOTOVER/ IS THERE NO THUNDER IN
HART I (71)	HECTOR. THEYVE MADE IT UP. /LADY UTTERWORD/ YOUR	HUSBAND	! THAT HANDSOME MAN? /MRS HUSHABYE/ WELL, WHY
OVER (174)	ABOUT YOUR LATE HUSBAND-- /MRS JUNO/ MY LATE	HUSBAND	! WHAT DO YOU MEAN? (CLUTCHING HIM,
CLEO II (124)	YOU LIKE: HE IS AFRAID. /CAESAR/ (STARTING) YOUR	HUSBAND	! WHAT DO YOU MEAN? /CLEOPATRA/ (POINTING TO
		HUSBANDMAN	
LION PREFACE(16)	AND AS INEXPLICABLE AS EVER, TAUGHT THE PRIMITIVE	HUSBANDMAN	, AND, AS WE MUST NOW AFFIRM, TAUGHT HIM QUITE
		HUSBANDMAN'S	
SUPR III (132)	BRAIN-- TO GRASP THIS KNOWLEDGE FOR ME AS THE	HUSBANDMAN'S	HAND GRASPS THE PLOUGH FOR ME. AND THIS" SAYS
		HUSBANDMEN	
BASH II,2, (113)	IN ATTENDANCE. /CETEWAYO/ IS THIS THE HALL OF	HUSBANDMEN	? /LUCIAN/ IT IS. /CETEWAYO/ ARE THESE ANAEMIC
		HUSBAND-HUNTING	
METH PREFACE(R87)	CHARACTER, PARADOXES OF CONVENTIONAL SOCIETY,	HUSBAND-HUNTING	, QUESTIONS OF CONSCIENCE, PROFESSIONAL
		HUSBAND'S	
OVER (185)	A DISAPPOINTMENT, DO YOU? WELL, I SUPPOSE EVERY	HUSBAND'S	A DISAPPOINTMENT. WHAT ABOUT YOURSELF? DONT TRY
JITT III (54)	DOCTOR FESSLER: IF YOU CAN TAKE NEITHER ME NOR MY	HUSBAND'S	AFFAIRS SERIOUSLY, I THINK YOU HAD BETTER LEAVE
MILL IV (203)	ACTION AGAINST PATRICIA SMITH FOR ALIENATING MY	HUSBAND'S	AFFECTIONS. DAMAGES TWENTY THOUSAND POUNDS.
CYMB FORWORD(136)	THAT IMOGEN IS SO DUTIFUL THAT SHE ACCEPTS HER	HUSBAND'S	ATTEMPT TO HAVE HER MURDERED WITH AFFECTIONATE
JITT III (80)	FOR YOU, MRS HALDENSTEDT. ALFRED HAS FOUND YOUR	HUSBAND'S	BOOK. IT IS A MASTERPIECE. HE WILL EDIT IT. HE
HART II (121)	/HECTOR/ WELL, IF YOU COME TO THAT, YOU ARE HER	HUSBAND'S	BROTHER. /RANDALL/ BUT YOU SEEM TO BE ON INTIMATE
LADY PREFACE(219)	REPULSIVE THAN HER RELATIONS WITH HER DECEASED	HUSBAND'S	BROTHER. HERE, TOO, SHAKESPEAR BETRAYS FOR ONCE
MILL IV (198)	MY WITNESS, MR SAGAMORE, HOW I GO IN FEAR OF MY	HUSBAND'S	BRUTAL VIOLENCE. HE IS STRONGER THAN I AM: HE CAN
DEST (156)	/GIUSEPPE/ FRENCH, EXCELLENCY. /NAPOLEON/ HER	HUSBAND'S	CHARGER, NO DOUBT. KILLED AT LODI, POOR FELLOW.
OVER (178)	/GREGORY/ SIBTHORPE! /MRS JUNO/ SIBTHORPE IS MY	HUSBAND'S	CHRISTIAN NAME. I OUGHTNT TO CALL HIM TOPS TO YOU
GETT (324)	COMING INTO MY SHOP AND TELLING ME THAT MY	HUSBAND'S	COALS WERE OUT OF PLACE IN YOUR CELLAR, AS NATURE
JITT I (19)	CONVENTIONAL AND SUPERFICIAL. BUT I AM YOUR	HUSBAND'S	COMRADE: WE WERE CHUMS AT SCHOOL: WE WERE AT
GETT (300)	THEM IN EVERY SORT OF WICKEDNESS. SURELY MY	HUSBAND'S	CONDUCT IS OF MORE IMPORTANCE TO ME THAN MR
JITT II SD(33)	BEEN DEEPLY WOUNDED BY THE CIRCUMSTANCES OF HER	HUSBAND'S	DEATH, AND IS STIFF AND SUSPICIOUS IN HER MANNER.
GETT (356)	TO ME WHEN ONCE I CROSS THE THRESHOLD OF YOUR	HUSBAND'S	HOUSE AND BREAK BREAD WITH HIM. THIS MARRIAGE BOND
GETT PREFACE(188)	THAN A BURGLAR: NAMELY, ONE WHO WOULD STEAL HER	HUSBAND'S	HOUSE FROM OVER HER HEAD, AND LEAVE HER DESTITUTE
JITT I (20)	/JITTA/ GOD OF HEAVEN! WHOSE NAME? /BRUNO/ YOUR	HUSBAND'S	. /JITTA/ (SPRINGING UP) ALFRED'S! /BRUNO/
DOCT I (108)	HUSBAND FOR HER TO SEE YOU. /RIDGEON/ VALUES HER	HUSBAND'S	LIFE AT HALF-A-CROWN! /EMMY/ WELL, IT'S ALL SHE
DOCT I (91)	(LOOKING IN) WILL YOU SEE A LADY THAT WANTS HER	HUSBAND'S	LUNGS CURED? /RIDGEON/ NO. HAVNT I TOLD YOU I
MILL I (150)	WITH WHOM I DISCUSS SUBJECTS THAT ARE BEYOND MY	HUSBAND'S	MENTAL GRASP, WHICH IS EXTREMELY LIMITED.
GENV III (66)	ABOLISHED THE INTELLECTUAL COMMITTEE, LEAVING MY	HUSBAND'S	MURDER STILL UNEXPIATED, THAT THROWS ME BACK ON
NEVR IV (289)	EYE, AND BEGINS) IN THIS FAMILY, IT APPEARS, THE	HUSBAND'S	NAME IS CRAMPTON: THE WIFE'S, CLANDON. THUS WE
NEVR IV (290)	CONVENIENCE AND DECENCY, WILL HAVE TO RESUME HER	HUSBAND'S	NAME (MRS CLANDON ASSUMES AN EXPRESSION OF THE
LIED SD(202)	THE FLOOR IN ORDER TO GET HER RIGHT ARM ROUND HER	HUSBAND'S	NECK. /SHE/ YOU SHANT, TEDDY: YOU SHANT. YOU WILL
GETT PREFACE(186)	(FOR INSTANCE, " MENTAL ANGUISH" CAUSED BY THE	HUSBAND'S	NEGLECT TO CUT HIS TOE-NAILS); BUT THERE IS ALWAYS
FANY I (281)	AND BOBBY ARE AS GOOD AS ENGAGED. MR KNOX IS MY	HUSBAND'S	PARTNER. MRS KNOX IS VERY RELIGIOUS; BUT SHE'S
GENV I (40)	ACQUITTED. UNFORTUNATELY THE SCANDAL DESTROYED MY	HUSBAND'S	POPULARITY. HE WAS DEFEATED AT THE NEXT ELECTION
LIED (189)	(BRIGHTENING UP) OH, OF COURSE THEY ARE YOUR	HUSBAND'S	RELATIVES: I FORGOT THAT. FORGIVE ME, AURORA. (HE
DEVL II (37)	A QUIET RESPECTABLE COUPLE, AND WAIT FOR YOUR	HUSBAND'S	RETURN? /JUDITH/ (RATHER ASHAMED OF HERSELF) IF
SUPR I (45)	APPROVES. I HAVE KEPT MY MARRIAGE A SECRET FOR MY	HUSBAND'S	SAKE. BUT NOW I CLAIM MY RIGHT AS A MARRIED WOMAN
DEVL II (34)	EVERY INSULT OF RICHARD'S) YOU ARE WELCOME FOR MY	HUSBAND'S	SAKE. (SHE BRINGS THE TEAPOT TO THE FIREPLACE AND
SUPR IV (168)	/ANN/ (SOFTLY) I MUST BE, FOR MY FUTURE	HUSBAND'S	SAKE. /TANNER/ FOR MINE! (CORRECTING HIMSELF
MIS. SD(121)	TAKES OUT HER DARNING MATERIALS AND ONE OF HER	HUSBAND'S	SOCKS. HYPATIA IS AT THE OTHER SIDE OF THE TABLE,
GETT (354)	THE COAL MERCHANT. /HOTCHKISS/ IF I WERE YOUR	HUSBAND'S	SUPERIOR HERE I SHOULD BE HIS SUPERIOR IN HEAVEN
JOAN PREFACE(11)	MAY HEAR VOICES TELLING HER THAT SHE MUST CUT HER	HUSBAND'S	THROAT AND STRANGLE HER CHILD AS THEY LIE ASLEEP;
OVER (186)	/JUNO/ (STERNLY) THIS IS NO WAY TO TAKE YOUR	HUSBAND'S	UNFAITHFULNESS. (TO LUNN) YOU OUGHT TO TEACH YOUR
JITT II (38)	INSULT MY MOTHER BY CONDOLING WITH HER ON HER	HUSBAND'S	UNFAITHFULNESS. THEY INSULT GOD BY DECLARING THAT
CYMB V (143)	HELP! HELP! /IMOGEN/ OH, LET ME DIE. I HEARD MY	HUSBAND'S	VOICE WHOM I THOUGHT DEAD; AND IN MY ECSTASY, THE
OVER (179)	(IN A THRILLING WHISPER) SH-SH-SH! THAT WAS MY	HUSBAND'S	VOICE. /GREGORY/ IMPOSSIBLE: IT'S ONLY OUR GUILTY
GETT (329)	STUDIED INSOLENCE) AND PRAY WHAT IS YOUR WRETCHED	HUSBAND'S	VULGAR CONVIVIALITY TO ME? /MRS GEORGE/ YOU LOVE

HUSBANDS

GETT (335) ONE OF THE OVERSIGHTS OF YOUR CODE OF HONOR FOR HUSBANDS : THE MAN WHO CAN BULLY THEM CAN INSULT THEIR WIVES
HART II (115) /ELLIE/ WHY DO WOMEN ALWAYS WANT OTHERS WOMEN'S HUSBANDS ? /CAPTAIN SHOTOVER/ WHY DO HORSE-THIEVES PREFER A
HART I (81) WANT TO BE MY BREADWINNER, LIKE THE OTHER POOR HUSBANDS ? /HECTOR/ NO, BY THUNDER! WHAT A DAMNED CREATURE
JOAN 3 (91) WIVES. DO YOU WANT TO BE LIKE A WOMAN WITH TWO HUSBANDS ? /JOAN/ (MATTER-OF-FACT) I WILL NEVER TAKE A
MILL IV (209) CHILD. ALL WIVES ARE ALL THESE WOMEN IN ONE, ALL HUSBANDS ALL THESE MEN IN ONE. WHAT DO THE UNMARRIED KNOW OF
ROCK I (208) AND FATHERS. YES, MY LORDS AND GENTLEMEN: HUSBANDS AND FATHERS. AND I VENTURE TO CLAIM YOUR UNANIMOUS
ROCK I (208) NOW SETTLED EXPERIENCED MEN, FAMILY MEN. WE ARE HUSBANDS AND FATHERS. YES, MY LORDS AND GENTLEMEN: HUSBANDS
SIM II (80) SUSPENSE HAS BEEN CREATED EVERYWHERE. HAPPY HUSBANDS AND FATHERS DISAPPEAR FROM THE FAMILY DINNER WITH
OVER PREFACE(163) THAT THERE ARE SUCH THINGS IN THE WORLD AS HUSBANDS AND LAWYERS AND DUELLING CODES AND THEORIES OF SIN
GETT PREFACE(187) SO ARE PEOPLE WHO HAVE DIVORCED THEIR WIVES OR HUSBANDS AND MARRIED AGAIN. AND YET MARRIAGE IS ENFORCED BY
SUPR III (118) OF WOMEN? /ANA/ I COULD HAVE HAD TWELVE HUSBANDS AND NO CHILDREN: THATS WHAT I COULD HAVE DONE,
OVER (173) WARM AFFECTION FROM THEM; BUT MY LOYALTY TO THEIR HUSBANDS AND THEIR HEARTHS AND THEIR HAPPINESS OBLIGES ME TO
DEVL II (32) BETTER FRIENDS TO THEIR ENEMIES THAN TO THEIR OWN HUSBANDS AND WIVES? COME: DEPEND ON IT, MY DEAR, YOU ARE
MIS. PREFACE(82) AN EXTREME AND OBVIOUS CASE; BUT THERE ARE MANY HUSBANDS AND WIVES WHO ARE TIRED OF THEIR CONSORTS, OR
GETT PREFACE(218) THE PEOPLE WHO ARE QUARRELSOME QUARREL WITH THEIR HUSBANDS AND WIVES JUST AS EASILY AS WITH THEIR SERVANTS AND
GETT PREFACE(246) ARE EQUALLY IF NOT MORE NECESSARY TO COMPEL OUR HUSBANDS AND WIVES TO RESPECT US; AND THAT SOCIETY WITHOUT
GETT PREFACE(225) AGAIN AND NEVER LOVED ANYONE EXCEPT THEIR OWN HUSBANDS AND WIVES. THE DOMESTIC DOCTRINAIRES ARE ALSO THE
GETT PREFACE(203) UNMARRIED COUPLE TO A DOZEN INFERIOR APATHETIC HUSBANDS AND WIVES, IF IT COULD BE PROVED THAT ILLICIT
BUOY III (38) IS IMPOSSIBLE. THEY SHOULD BE CONCUBINES, NOT HUSBANDS AND WIVES. ALL CONCUBINAGES ARE EXACTLY ALIKE. NO
SUPR HANDBOK(183) WITH, PEOPLE WOULD STILL CALL THEMSELVES HUSBANDS AND WIVES; DESCRIBE THEIR COMPANIONSHIPS AS
OVER PREFACE(167) AND WERE APT TO BLAME ONE ANOTHER, ESPECIALLY THE HUSBANDS AND WIVES, FOR THEIR CROSSNESS. BUT IT IS HAPPILY
MILL I (151) YOU CANT CALL YOUR SOUL YOUR OWN. AS SUNDAY HUSBANDS AND WIVES, JUST TO HAVE A GOOD TEARING BIT OF
JITT III (79) YOU WERE A CHUMP; AND SO YOU ARE. /LENKHEIM/ ALL HUSBANDS ARE CHUMPS, DEAR, AFTER THE FIRST MONTH OR SO.
DEST (157) WHOSE HUSBAND WAS KILLED YESTERDAY. /GIUSEPPE/ HUSBANDS ARE NOT ALWAYS REGRETTED, EXCELLENCY. (CALLING)
GETT PREFACE(209) RUIN OF THE COUNTRY, BECAUSE A WOMAN WITH SEVERAL HUSBANDS BEARS FEWER CHILDREN THAN A WOMAN WITH ONE, WHEREAS
BUOY III (34) THE WIVES OF CABINET MINISTERS WHOSE FATHERS AND HUSBANDS BEGAN ON FIVE SHILLINGS A WEEK: THEY BOAST OF IT.
LION PREFACE(70) DO NOT MAKE RECREANTS AND COWARDS OF THEM: THEIR HUSBANDS DO NOT CHAIN THEM TO THE CRADLE AND THE COOKING
PRES (137) NEITHER DO THE SUFFRAGETS. /BALSQUITH/ THEIR HUSBANDS DO. (TO THE ORDERLY) DID SHE KILL HIM? /THE
APPL INTRLUD(246) YOUNG THINGS LIKE YOU DONT REMEMBER THAT, THEIR HUSBANDS DO. THEY DONT NOTICE THE CHANGE. BESIDES, YOU
PYGM III (252) THERES LOTS OF WOMEN HAS TO MAKE THEIR HUSBANDS DRUNK TO MAKE THEM FIT TO LIVE WITH. (NOW QUITE AT
SUPR IV (168) GET INTO ALL SORTS OF HOT WATER. AND THEN THEIR HUSBANDS GET DRAGGED IN TOO, AND LIVE IN CONTINUAL DREAD OF
APPL INTRLUD(246) YOU HAVE BEEN MARRIED TWICE; AND BOTH YOUR HUSBANDS HAVE RUN AWAY FROM YOU TO MUCH PLAINER AND STUPIDER
SUPR HANDBOK(212) FACT THAT AS THE VAST MAJORITY OF WOMEN AND THEIR HUSBANDS HAVE, UNDER EXISTING CIRCUMSTANCES, NOT ENOUGH
GENV I (40) DO IT: I LOVED HER: I WOULD HAVE LET HER HAVE TEN HUSBANDS IF I HAD HAD THEM TO GIVE. BUT WHAT CAN YOU DO
GETT (332) AGAIN. /MRS GEORGE/ THATS TRUE. WOMEN DRIVE THEIR HUSBANDS INTO ALL SORTS OF WICKEDNESS TO KEEP THEM IN GOOD
GETT PREFACE(210) THEY ARE QUARTERED ON THE WAGES OF THEIR HUSBANDS . AT LEAST FOUR OUT OF FIVE OF OUR MEN COULD NOT
KING PREFACE(155) BUT ECLIPSED THE FACT THAT HE WAS THE BEST OF HUSBANDS . CATHERINE OF BRAGANZA, HIS WIFE, HAS BEEN MADE TO
GETT (284) I HOPE YOU WILL ALWAYS STAND UP FOR ALL YOUR HUSBANDS . (HE RISES AND GOES TO THE HEARTH, WHERE HE
KING II (226) HER) BELOVED: YOU WILL ONLY LOSE THE WORST OF HUSBANDS . /CATHERINE/ THAT IS A LIE: IF ANYONE ELSE SAID IT
BUOY III (37) MEN TO KEEP HER SUPPLIED WITH WHAT I CALL SUNDAY HUSBANDS . /MRS SECONDBORN/ THAT IS A PERFECTLY DIFFERENT
BUOY III (38) THERE SHOULD BE CONCUBINES AS WELL AS WIVES AND HUSBANDS . SOME MARRIAGES ARE BETWEEN COUPLES WHO HAVE NO
GETT PREFACE(212) DIVIDE HERSELF BETWEEN ELEVEN ALREADY MARRIED HUSBANDS . THUS THERE IS NO WAY OUT FOR US THROUGH POLYGYNY.
VWOO 3 (142) TO EDUCATE, TO MAKE REAL GENTLEMEN OF THEIR HUSBANDS . WHAT DO YOU INTEND TO MAKE OF ME, I WONDER? /Z/
GETT PREFACE(234) NOT NOW UNDER CONSIDERATION. ALSO, AFFECTIONATE HUSBANDS LIKE SAMUEL PEPYS, AND AFFECTIONATE WIVES OF THE
OVER (173) ARE EXTRAORDINARILY SCARCE IN MODERN SOCIETY. HUSBANDS LIVE LONGER THAN THEY USED TO; AND EVEN WHEN THEY
GETT PREFACE(196) OF BOOK); BUT IN ACTUAL LIFE SHE IS A NUISANCE. HUSBANDS MAY ESCAPE FROM HER WHEN THEIR BUSINESS COMPELS
GETT PREFACE(224) CHANGE. THE LADY WHO HAS MARRIED AND MANAGED FIVE HUSBANDS MUST BE MUCH MORE EXPERT AT IT THAN MOST MONOGAMIC
HART I (80) ACCORDINGLY. WHO ARE THE MEN THAT DO THINGS? THE HUSBANDS OF THE SHREW AND OF THE DRUNKARD, THE MEN WITH THE
BUOY III SD(29) INTRODUCED, AND SEAT THEMSELVES ON THE DIVAN, THE HUSBANDS ON OPPOSITE SIDES FROM THEIR WIVES. THE TWO JUNIORS
NEVR I (211) IS ANOTHER SORT OF FAMILY LIFE: A LIFE IN WHICH HUSBANDS OPEN THEIR WIVES' LETTERS, AND CALL ON THEM TO
GETT PREFACE(211) THUS IT APPEARS THAT IT IS THE SCARCITY OF HUSBANDS OR WIVES OF HIGH QUALITY THAT LEADS WOMEN TO
SUPR HANDBOK(220) AND TAKING THE QUOTIENT AS THE NUMBER OF WIVES OR HUSBANDS PERMITTED TO EACH PERSON) IS SECURED IN ENGLAND (
SUPR III (116) ALL. WOMEN HAVE TO PUT UP WITH FLESH-AND-BLOOD HUSBANDS -- AND LITTLE ENOUGH OF THAT TOO, SOMETIMES; AND
SIM II (83) AS A PASSION AND HAVE ENDED AS A HABIT, LIKE ALL HUSBANDS ; BUT OUTSIDE THAT ROUTINE THERE IS A LIFE OF THE
OVER PREFACE(157) FOR INSTANCE, ARE MUCH MORE JEALOUS OF THEIR HUSBANDS ' MOTHERS AND SISTERS THAN OF UNRELATED WOMEN WHOM
JITT III (74) VERY KIND OF JITTA TO INCLUDE ME IN THE NUMBER OF HUSBANDS SHE HAS APPARENTLY BEEN OFFERING YOU. BUT I HAVE NO
SUPR IV (166) I SHALL SEE IN THE GREASY EYES OF ALL THE OTHER HUSBANDS THEIR RELIEF AT THE ARRIVAL OF A NEW PRISONER TO
APPL INTRLUD(246) IF IT WERE NOT FOR THE NONENTITIES OF WIVES AND HUSBANDS THEY DRAG ABOUT WITH THEM, THERE WOULD BE NOBODY TO
GETT PREFACE(251) MANHOOD WITH WHICH I FELT MYSELF AND ALL OTHER HUSBANDS THUS REDUCED TO THE RANK OF A TOILET APPLIANCE GAVE
GETT PREFACE(209) OF WIVES PERMITTED TO A SINGLE HUSBAND OR OF HUSBANDS TO A SINGLE WIFE UNDER A MARRIAGE SYSTEM, IS NOT AN
BARB III (346) HOUSES DOWN AND KILL THEIR SONS AND TEAR THEIR HUSBANDS TO PIECES. /CUSINS/ YOU CANNOT HAVE POWER FOR GOOD
GETT PREFACE(234) TIED FOR LIFE TO ONE OF THE PERFECTLY " FAITHFUL" HUSBANDS WHO ARE SENTENCED TO A MONTH'S IMPRISONMENT
GETT PREFACE(235) ENCOURAGING AND ACCEPTING THE STANDARDS OF THE HUSBANDS WHO BUY MEAT FOR THEIR BULL-PUPS AND LEAVE THEIR
GETT (316) THE SOLUTION OF THE PROBLEM, YOU SEE, THEIR HUSBANDS WILL ALSO BE OUTCASTS; AND THE POOR LADIES WILL
GETT PREFACE(231) TO THE HOUSEHOLD OF HALF A DOZEN MORE WIVES OR HUSBANDS WOULD BE AS POSSIBLE AS THE ADDITION OF HALF A
SUPR III (119) FOR TWELVE CHILDREN BY TWELVE DIFFERENT HUSBANDS WOULD HAVE REPLENISHED THE EARTH PERHAPS MORE
ROCK I (205) /LADY CHAVENDER/ YOU ARE CERTAINLY THE BEST OF HUSBANDS , ARTHUR. YOU ARE THE BEST OF EVERYTHING. I DONT
MIS. (123) I THINK THEY MIGHT LEAVE THE DRAINS TO THEIR HUSBANDS , I SHOULDNT THINK MUCH OF A MAN THAT LEFT SUCH
SIM I (50) A YOUNG HUSBAND. /IDDY/ (IMPLORINGLY) TWO YOUNG HUSBANDS , LADY FARWATERS. OH PLEASE, TWO. /LADY FARWATERS/

HUSE

CAND II (110) (CUTTING HER SHORT) NO: YOUVE DONE IT NOW. NO HUSE A-TALKIN TO ME. I'LL LET YOU KNOW WHO I AM. (
CAND I (88) TAKIN IT FROM PEOPLE THAT MIGHT BE MAKIN A GOOD HUSE ON IT. /MORELL/ (WITH A HEAVY SIGH, SPEAKING WITH COLD

HUSED

CAND II (111) IT TO HOLD HIS ATTENTION) THATS THE SAME WHAT I HUSED TO THINK, MR MORCHBANKS. HI THOUGHT LONG ENOUGH THAT
CAND I (86) AT HER) YOURE NOT THE SAME YOUNG LADY AS HUSED TO TYPEWRITE FOR HIM? /PROSERPINE/ NO. /BURGESS/ (
CAND I (90) WOULD A THOUGHT O TAKIN HUP WITH YOUR HIDEARS. I HUSED TO WONDER YOU WAS LET PREACH AT ALL. WHY, I KNOW A

HUSETER

CAND I (89) STEPS DOORWARDS. THEN HE COMES BACK, WHINING). WE HUSETER GIT ON WELL ENOUGH, SPITE OF OUR DIFFERENT
CAND III (138) ARTER TWO SIPS. PEOPLE CARNT DRINK LIKE THEY HUSETER , (BUSTLING ACROSS TO THE HEARTH) WELL, JAMES: IT'S
CAND II (115) A BIT OF POETRY. CANDY TAKES ARTER ME THAT-A-WAY. HUSETER MAKE ME TELL ER FAIRY STORIES WHEN SHE WAS ONY A

HUSH

JOAN 6 (150) MY LORD: I KNOW THEY WERE FRENCH. /WARWICK/ HUSH ? SOMEONE IS COMING. CONTROL YOURSELF. LADVENU COMES
DEVL III SD(71) DRESS UP AND KEEP EM BACK, WILL YOU. CRIES OF HUSH AND SILENCE ARE HEARD AMONG THE TOWNSFOLK; AND THE
SUPR II (58) TAVY, DONT YOU? /OCTAVIUS/ SHE KNOWS I DO. /ANN/ HUSH . FOR SHAME, TAVY! /TANNER/ OH, I GIVE YOU LEAVE. I AM
HART II (89) THOUGH. /ELLIE/ (MAKING HER PASSES RHYTHMICALLY) HUSH . GO TO SLEEP. DO YOU HEAR? YOU ARE TO GO TO SLEEP, GO
GENV IV (123) THE TELEPHONE RINGS AGAIN. /ALL EXCEPT THE JUDGE/ HUSH . LET US HEAR THE NEWS. THE NEWS. THE NEWS. (THEY
SIM PRO,3, (33) INTO HER SEAT, FLABBERGASTED). /THE PRIESTESS/ HUSH . LOOK. THE LADY TOURIST RETURNS AND AGAIN GOES TO THE
GETT (343) IS SHE INSPIRED? /THE BISHOP/ MARVELLOUS. HUSH . /MRS GEORGE/ I HAVE EARNED THE RIGHT TO SPEAK. I HAVE
MTH4 III (199) /THE ELDERLY GENTLEMAN/ MAY I-- /ZOO/ (QUICKLY) HUSH . THE ORACLE IS GOING TO SPEAK. /THE ORACLE/ GO HOME,
JITT I (23) /BRUNO/ (COVERING HER MOUTH WITH HIS HAND) HUSH -- SH! (SHE LOOKS AFFRIGHTEDLY AT HIM: HE LOOKS
DEST (181) PERSONALLY I AM SORRY FOR YOU. I WOULD WILLINGLY HUSH UP THE AFFAIR IF IT WERE POSSIBLE. BUT I SHALL BE
JOAN 6 (128) IT SEEMS TO ME THAT THERE IS A CONSPIRACY HERE TO HUSH UP THE FACT THAT THE MAID STOLE THE BISHOP OF SENLIS'S
MTH5 (239) /THE NEWLY BORN/ OH! (SHE WEEPS). /STREPHON/ HUSH , DEAR: THATS CHILDISH. /THE NEWLY BORN/ (SUBSIDING
MILL III (180) SEARCH THE WHOLE BLOODY BASEMENT. /THE WOMAN/ HUSH , HUSH, JOE: DONT SPEAK TO THE LADY LIKE THAT. YOU SEE,
CLEO IV (185) WITH BONES IN IT, EH? /CAESAR/ (SHUDDERING) HUSH , HUSH, RUFIO. (HE LEAVES THE TABLE AND RETURNS TO THE
MILL III (180) THE WHOLE BLOODY BASEMENT. /THE WOMAN/ HUSH, HUSH , JOE: DONT SPEAK TO THE LADY LIKE THAT. YOU SEE, MAAM:
ARMS III (72) IS ACCUSTOMED TO A FIRST-RATE STABLE. /RAINA/ HUSH , MOTHER: YOURE MAKING ME RIDICULOUS. /BLUNTSCHLI/ OH
MRS III (224) THE SUN, I'LL SWEAR, AND VIVIE-- UGH! /PRAED/ HUSH , PRAY, THEYRE COMING. THE CLERGYMAN AND CROFTS ARE
WIDO II (37) HIM). /SARTORIUS/ (INTERRUPTING HER SEVERELY) HUSH , PRAY, BLANCHE: YOU ARE FORGETTING YOURSELF: YOU CAN
CLEO IV (185) BONES IN IT, EH? /CAESAR/ (SHUDDERING) HUSH, HUSH , RUFIO. (HE LEAVES THE TABLE AND RETURNS TO THE
MTH1 I (12) HOW? /THE SERPENT/ THAT IS THE GREAT SECRET. HUSH ! HE IS COMING. /ADAM/ (RETURNING) IS THERE ANOTHER

CAND II (106) WORK). /MARCHBANKS/ (STOPPING HER MYSTERIOUSLY) HUSH ! I GO ABOUT IN SEARCH OF LOVE; AND I FIND IT IN
DEVL III (54) HERSELF ON HER KNEES). I PRAY TO YOU-- /RICHARD/ HUSH ! (CALLING) COME IN. (THE SERGEANT UNLOCKS THE DOOR
SUPR III (94) SHOCKINGLY MUTILATED. MY POOR FATHER! /DON JUAN/ HUSH ! LISTEN! (TWO GREAT CHORDS ROLLING ON SYNCOPATED

HUSHABYE

HART III (132) MONEY? /MANGAN/ (MUCH ALARMED) WHATS THAT? MRS HUSHABYE : ARE MY AFFAIRS TO BE DISCUSSED LIKE THIS BEFORE
HART I (55) COME: I THOUGHT YOUD LIKE TO KNOW. EXCUSE ME, MRS HUSHABYE : THE STRANGE OLD GENTLEMAN-- /MRS HUSHABYE/ PAPA.
HART I (73) THAT I AM A THIEF, A PIRATE, OR A MURDERER. MRS HUSHABYE : WILL YOU EXCUSE ME A MOMENT? I MUST REALLY GO
HART II (125) AS A WOMAN CAN BE, YOU ARE A MADDENING DEVIL. HUSHABYE : YOU WILL NOT BELIEVE ME WHEN I TELL YOU THAT I
HART II (92) BODY) WHAT IS YOUR OBJECTION TO POOR MANGAN, MRS HUSHABYE ? HE LOOKS ALL RIGHT TO ME. BUT THEN I AM SO
HART I (55) OH! HOW CAN YOU TREAT A VISITOR LIKE THIS, MRS HUSHABYE ? /MRS HUSHABYE/ I THOUGHT YOU WERE GOING TO CALL
HART III (135) TO THAT YET, THANK GOD! WHAT DO YOU SAY, MRS HUSHABYE ? /MRS HUSHABYE/ OH, I SAY IT MATTERS VERY LITTLE
HART II SD(107) COMES IN AFTER RANDALL, AND GOES BETWEEN MRS HUSHABYE AND MANGAN. NURSE GUINNESS BRINGS UP THE REAR, AND
HART II (89) AS EASY AS THAT. SUPPOSE I GO STRAIGHT TO MRS HUSHABYE AND TELL HER THAT YOURE IN LOVE WITH HER HUSBAND.
HART II SD(106) IN EVENING DRESS) THEN HESIONE WINS HER BET. MRS HUSHABYE APPEARS IN THE PORT DOORWAY. SHE THROWS HER LEFT
HART II (85) THIS PART OF THE COUNTRY? I HEARD YOU ASK MR HUSHABYE AT DINNER WHETHER THERE ARE ANY NICE HOUSES TO LET
HART I SD(52) TO FEEL QUITE SURE THAT HE REALLY FORGETS. MRS HUSHABYE BURSTS INTO THE ROOM TEMPESTUOUSLY, AND EMBRACES
HART I SD(69) /THE GENTLEMAN/ I AM, AT LEAST A CONNEXION. MRS HUSHABYE COMES BACK. /MRS HUSHABYE/ HOW DO YOU DO? HOW GOOD
HART I SD(76) STRIKING HIMSELF ON THE CHEST) FOOL! GOAT! MRS HUSHABYE COMES BACK WITH THE CAPTAIN'S CAP. /HECTOR/ YOUR
HART II (90) HESSY! QUICK, DOTY DARLING, MISS HESSY! (MRS HUSHABYE COMES IN FROM THE HALL, FOLLOWED BY MAZZINI DUNN).
HART II (127) I'M REALLY VERY SLEEPY, SAY GOODNIGHT TO MRS HUSHABYE FOR ME, WILL YOU, LIKE A GOOD CHAP. GOODNIGHT. (HE
HART II (107) SOMEBODY UPSTAIRS, AND GAVE ME A PISTOL THAT MR HUSHABYE HAD BEEN PRACTISING WITH. I THOUGHT IT WOULD
HART I (45) OH, DONT THINK OF SUCH A THING, MISS. IF MRS HUSHABYE HAS FORGOTTEN ALL ABOUT IT, IT WILL BE A PLEASANT
HART I (66) DEAR! DEAR! WHAT AN ESCAPE! ELLIE, MY LOVE: MR HUSHABYE HAS JUST BEEN TELLING ME THE MOST EXTRAORDINARY--
HART II (97) HIM. /MAZZINI/ ARE YOU QUITE SURE, ELLIE? MRS HUSHABYE HAS MADE ME FEEL THAT I MAY HAVE BEEN THOUGHTLESS
HART III (148) WOULD ORDER HIS SOLDIERS TO TAKE COVER. MR HUSHABYE IS BEHAVING LIKE AN AMATEUR. MANGAN AND THE BURGLAR
HART I SD(62) STARES AT HER. HER CANDOR IS SO OBVIOUS THAT MRS HUSHABYE IS PUZZLED. /ELLIE/ GOODBYE, HESIONE. I'M VERY
HART II (94) HUSBAND IS IN HIS FIRST YOUTH FOR VERY LONG, MRS HUSHABYE . AND MEN CANT AFFORD TO MARRY IN THEIR FIRST YOUTH
HART I (55) AFRAID ELLIE IS NOT INTERESTED IN YOUNG MEN, MRS HUSHABYE . HER TASTE IS ON THE GRAVER, SOLIDER SIDE. /MRS
HART II (94) ! /MAZZINI/ THERE! YOU SEE, MRS HUSHABYE . I DONT WANT ELLIE TO LIVE ON RESIGNATION. /MRS
HART I (64) TEAK TABLE) MY REAL NAME, MISS DUNN, IS HECTOR HUSHABYE . I LEAVE YOU TO JUDGE WHETHER THAT IS A NAME ANY
HART II (95) HIMSELF TOGETHER) IT DOESNT MATTER ABOUT ME, MRS HUSHABYE . I THINK YOU LIKE ELLIE; AND THAT IS ENOUGH FOR
HART II (88) TO BELIEVE ME. I WANT TO BE NEAR YOUR FRIEND MRS HUSHABYE . I'M IN LOVE WITH HER. NOW THE MURDER'S OUT.
HART II (88) OUT. /ELLIE/ I WANT TO BE NEAR YOUR FRIEND MR HUSHABYE . I'M IN LOVE WITH HIM. (SHE RISES AND ADDS WITH A
HART III (139) I HOPE YOU DONT MIND MY BEING LIKE THIS, MR HUSHABYE . (HE SITS DOWN ON THE CAMPSTOOL). /MRS HUSHABYE/
HART I (74) COURSE, DEAR. /ELLIE/ THEN I'LL LEAVE YOU TO MR HUSHABYE . (SHE GOES OUT THROUGH THE HALL). /HECTOR/ THAT
HART II (105) TAKE HIS CHAINS WITH HIM? /MANGAN/ THATS RIGHT, HUSHABYE . KEEP THE PYJAMAS, MY LADY; AND MUCH GOOD MAY THEY
HART III (143) ALL THIS GOING TO END? /MAZZINI/ IT WONT END, MR HUSHABYE . LIFE DOESNT END: IT GOES ON. /ELLIE/ OH, IT CANT
HART I (66) (BENEVOLENTLY) ELLIE IS VERY NAUGHTY, MR HUSHABYE . OF COURSE SHE DOES NOT REALLY THINK THAT. (HE
HART II (94) OF INDUSTRY ARE WHAT YOU CALL FRAUDS, MRS HUSHABYE . OF COURSE THERE ARE SOME MANUFACTURERS WHO REALLY
HART II (97) NOW YOU MUST GO AWAY AND LEAVE ME TO TALK TO MRS HUSHABYE . /MAZZINI/ BUT I SHOULD LIKE TO HEAR. SHALL I BE
HART I SD(72) SMILING BENEVOLENTLY, BETWEEN MANGAN AND MRS HUSHABYE . /MRS HUSHABYE/ (INTRODUCING) MR MAZZINI DUNN,
HART II (92) TO HER PARTICULARLY. YOU WILL FIND HER WITH MR HUSHABYE PROBABLY. /GUINNESS/ I THINK NOT, DUCKY: MISS ADDY
HART III (132) SENSE. /MANGAN/ BUT IT ISNT RIGHT. IT-- (MRS HUSHABYE PUTS HER HAND ON HIS MOUTH). OH, VERY WELL. /LADY
HART I (51) HER EMPTY CUP) LADY UTTERWORD! DO YOU THINK MRS HUSHABYE REALLY EXPECTS ME? /LADY UTTERWORD/ OH, DONT ASK
HART III (141) SOLDIER OF FREEDOM. /MAZZINI/ OH, REALLY, MRS HUSHABYE -- /MANGAN/ A MEMBER OF HIS MAJESTY'S GOVERNMENT
HART II (102) SAID, YOU AND YOUR PRECIOUS FATHER, AND (TO MRS HUSHABYE) YOU TOO. SO I'M AN OBJECT, AM I? I'M A THING, AM
HART I (74) I'M DISAPPOINTED. (HE FOLLOWS RANDALL AND MRS HUSHABYE), ELLIE, HECTOR, AND LADY UTTERWORD ARE LEFT.
HART II (96) THE FACT IS, YOU DONT STRIKE ON MY BOX, MRS HUSHABYE ; AND I CERTAINLY DONT STRIKE ON YOURS. /MRS
HART II (95) LEARNT A GOOD DEAL ABOUT MYSELF FROM YOU, MRS HUSHABYE ; AND I'M AFRAID I SHALL NOT BE THE HAPPIER FOR
HART II (91) (MRS HUSHABYE SPLUTTERS). OH, YOU MAY LAUGH, MRS HUSHABYE ; BUT I MIGHT HAVE BEEN KILLED. /MRS HUSHABYE/ I
HART II (90) (COMING TO HIM) I WAS LOOKING FOR YOU, SIR. MRS HUSHABYE SAYS WILL YOU PLEASE-- (NOTICING THAT HE REMAINS
HART II (91) DOWN THE WHOLE FLIGHT AND NEVER WOKE UP. (MRS HUSHABYE SPLUTTERS). OH, YOU MAY LAUGH, MRS HUSHABYE; BUT I
HART II (97) (VERY CLEARLY AND STEADILY) PAPA. WHEN MRS HUSHABYE TAKES IT ON HERSELF TO EXPLAIN TO YOU WHAT I THINK
HART I (45) IT WAS FOR SOMETHING ELSE. I SUPPOSE IT WAS MRS HUSHABYE THAT INVITED YOU, DUCKY? /THE YOUNG LADY/ I
HART II (124) WITH A CERTAIN CONSIDERATION. I WILL NOT ALLOW HUSHABYE TO TAKE LIBERTIES WITH ME. I WILL NOT STAND YOUR
HART III (147) GUINNESS/ (LOOKING UP AT THE HOUSE) IT'S MR HUSHABYE TURNING ON ALL THE LIGHTS IN THE HOUSE AND TEARING
HART II SD(103) TO CRY LIKE A CHILD. ELLIE STARES AT THEM. MRS HUSHABYE , AT THE DISTRESSING SOUND HE MAKES, TAKES DOWN HER
HART II (92) (TROUBLED) YOU HAVE COMPLETELY UPSET ME, MRS HUSHABYE , BY ALL YOU HAVE SAID TO ME. THAT ANYONE COULD
HART I (54) THROUGH HIS). I MUST THANK YOU, MRS HUSHABYE , FOR YOUR KINDNESS TO MY DAUGHTER. I'M AFRAID SHE
HART II (106) TO THE DRAWING-TABLE. /MAZZINI/ OH, MY DEAR MRS HUSHABYE , I MIGHT HAVE KILLED HIM (HE THROWS THE PISTOL ON
HART II (91) AND HAS TO DRINK TOO LITTLE NOW. YOU KNOW, MRS HUSHABYE , I REALLY THINK HE HAS BEEN HYPNOTIZED. /GUINNESS/
HART II (123) SO WELL IN OTHER RESPECTS. /RANDALL/ REALLY, HUSHABYE , I THINK A MAN MAY BE ALLOWED TO BE A GENTLEMAN
HART I (66) TO DESCRIBE THEM. /CAPTAIN SHOTOVER/ (TO MRS HUSHABYE , INTRODUCING THE NEW COMER) SAYS HIS NAME IS
HART I SD(59) THAT SHE IS NOT ARGUING, BUT IN A DAYDREAM. MRS HUSHABYE , WATCHING HER INQUISITIVELY, GOES DELIBERATELY
HART II (92) HER IN WIDE-EYED AMAZEMENT) BLESS YOU, DEAR MRS HUSHABYE , WHAT ROMANTIC IDEAS OF BUSINESS YOU HAVE! POOR
HART I (46) MADAM, HAVE TWO DAUGHTERS. ONE OF THEM IS HESIONE HUSHABYE , WHO INVITED YOU HERE. I KEEP THIS HOUSE: SHE
HART I (70) HOW DARE YOU? (SHE MARCHES AT HIM PAST MRS HUSHABYE , WHO RETREATS AND JOINS MANGAN NEAR THE SOFA).
HART II (122) /RANDALL/ (RETURNING, MUCH TROUBLED) YOU SEE, HUSHABYE , YOU ARE WHAT WOMEN CONSIDER A GOOD-LOOKING MAN.
HART I (68) TO THE HALL). /MANGAN/ (FOLLOWING HIM) MRS HUSHABYE ! DO YOU MEAN TO SAY SHE BROUGHT ME DOWN HERE TO

HUSHABYEBABY

SIM I (49) IF YOU WILL ONLY TELL IT TO ME IN A GENTLE HUSHABYEBABY SORT OF WAY AND CALL ME IDDY. NOW GO ON, LADY

HUSHABYE'S

HART I (45) GUINNESS. THAT WAS OLD CAPTAIN SHOTOVER, MRS HUSHABYE'S FATHER. I HEARD HIM ROARING; BUT I THOUGHT IT WAS
HART I (47) GRACIOUS! IT'S MISS ADDIE, LADY UTTERWORD, MRS HUSHABYE'S SISTER: THE ONE I TOLD THE CAPTAIN ABOUT. (
HART III (146) FIRST. (THE LAMP LIGHTS UP AGAIN). THERE! MR HUSHABYE'S TURNED IT ON AGAIN. /THE BURGLAR/ (HURRYING IN

HUSHED

ANNA (291) SHE HAD. OH, FAR FAR BETTER. /SCHNEIDEKIND/ (IN HUSHED TONES) LEFT THE CHURCH? /STRAMMFEST/ (SHOCKED)

HUSHES

ARMS I (9) IN THE STREET. THE CHILL OF IMMINENT DEATH HUSHES THE MAN'S VOICE AS HE ADDS) DO YOU HEAR? IF YOU ARE

HUSITES

JOAN PREFACE(28) VILLAINY; THAT ALL HERETICS WERE ALBIGENSIANS OR HUSITES OR JEWS OR PROTESTANTS OF THE HIGHEST CHARACTER; AND
JOAN PREFACE(3) AND THE PROJECTOR OF A CRUSADE AGAINST THE HUSITES , SHE WAS IN FACT ONE OF THE FIRST PROTESTANT
ROCK PREFACE(177) TO LEAD A CRUSADE OF EXTERMINATION AGAINST THE HUSITES , THOUGH SHE WAS BURNT FOR SHARING THEIR HERESY.

HUSKILY

PHIL I (87) SOB FROM JULIA). DONT CRY, JULIA. /CUTHBERTSON/ (HUSKILY) I HOPE YOU MAY LONG BE SPARED, DAN. /CRAVEN/ TO

HUSKS

POSN (437) TO CLEAR OUT. ALLOW ME. (HE TAKES THE SACK OF HUSKS AND PUTS IT OUT OF THE WAY AGAINST THE PANELS OF THE
2TRU III (89) AND NEER-DO-WELL WHO WAS REDUCED TO EATING THE HUSKS THAT THE SWINE DID EAT. I AM NOT RUINED: I AM ROLLING

HUSKY

CLEO V (197) ON CAESAR'S ARM? WELL, NO MATTER-- (HE BECOMES HUSKY , AND TURNS AWAY TO RECOVER HIMSELF). /CAESAR/ WHERE

HUSSAR

CATH 2 (179) AHA! I KNEW IT. YOUR MAJESTY WORE THE HUSSAR UNIFORM. HE SAW HOW RADIANT! HOW SPLENDID! YOUR

HUSSARS

ANNA (292) FULL DRESS COURT UNIFORM OF THE PANDEROBAJENSKY HUSSARS . I GIVE YOU TWELVE HOURS TO CATCH HIM OR . . .
ANNA SD(304) AND APPEARS IN THE UNIFORM OF THE PANDEROBAJENSKY HUSSARS . /STRAMMFEST/ (PEERING THROUGH THE WINDOW) WHERE

HUSSIES
SIM II (55) VANCOUVER AND PRETORIA. " BURN HIM ALIVE AND HIS HUSSIES WITH HIM." DO YOU EXPECT ME TO THINK ABOUT SUCH

HUSSY
FANY I (275) SOMETHING ABOUT THE LAD, I'D HAVE JUGGINS PUT THE HUSSY INTO THE STREET. /JUGGINS/ (RETURNING AND ANNOUNCING)
FANY III (322) VIOLENTLY) HOLD YOUR TONGUE, YOU SHAMELESS YOUNG HUSSY . DONT YOU DARE SAY WHAT IT MEANS. /DUVALLET/ (
FOUN (217) BE OFF WITH YOU; AND BE ASHAMED OF YOURSELF, YOU HUSSY . /THE LORD CHANCELLOR/ GENTLY, MERCER, GENTLY. IT IS
POSN (454) WOMEN/ (CLAMORING ALL TOGETHER) SHUT UP, YOU HUSSY . YOURE A DISGRACE. HOW DARE YOU OPEN YOUR LIPS TO
FANY II (296) MUST BE TOLD. /KNOX/ HOLD YOUR TONGUE, YOU YOUNG HUSSY ; OR GO OUT OF MY HOUSE THIS INSTANT. /MARGARET/ I'M

HUSTLE
MTH2 (53) BUT AT ALL EVENTS I CAN GET THINGS DONE. I CAN HUSTLE : EVEN YOU WILL ADMIT THAT. BUT LUBIN! OH MY STARS,
POSN (451) NOW YOU KNOW. NOW THEN: WEVE WASTED ENOUGH TIME. HUSTLE WITH YOUR WITNESS THERE, WILL YOU? /BLANCO/ (
JOAN PREFACE(22) AFRAID OR CORRUPT. SHE COULD COAX AND SHE COULD HUSTLE , HER TONGUE HAVING A SOFT SIDE AND A SHARP EDGE. SHE

HUSTLED
GETT (273) TO STRUGGLE ALONG IN CONSTANT MONEY DIFFICULTIES, HUSTLED BY HIS SOLICITORS, MORALLY BULLIED BY THE BARMECIDE,
6CAL SD(97) HERE FOR TWELVE MONTHS. I'LL-- THE SIX BURGESSES, HUSTLED BY MEN-AT-ARMS, ENTER IN THEIR SHIRTS AND HALTERS,
SUPR III (78) ETC. (THE SOCIAL-DEMOCRATS AND THE ANARCHIST ARE HUSTLED INTO THE BACKGROUND. STRAKER, AFTER SUPERINTENDING
CAPT III (292) (THE REBUKE IS WELL RECEIVED; AND MARZO IS HUSTLED INTO THE BACKGROUND AND EXTINGUISHED). SHE WONT TAKE

HUSTLING
MIS. (119) ALWAYS TELEPHONING OR TELEGRAPHING: HE THINKS HES HUSTLING ALONG LIKE ANYTHING WHEN HES ONLY SENDING
BULL II SD(101) BUT ON THE INHABITANTS OF FATTER-FED, CROWDED, HUSTLING AND BUSTLING MODERN COUNTRIES SHE MAKES A VERY
DEVL III SD(71) WITH A FEW WHISPERED ORDERS AND SOME STEALTHY HUSTLING CAUSE IT TO OPEN AND ADMIT THE FUNERAL PROCESSION,
DEVL I (27) (THEY SCRAMBLE OUT, CHRISTY AMONG THEM, HUSTLING ONE ANOTHER IN THEIR HASTE) HA HA! LONG LIVE THE
DEVL III (71) OFFICERS, ENERGETICALLY LED BY THE SERGEANT, HUSTLING THE PERSONS WHO FIND THEMSELVES INSIDE THE SQUARE

HUT
2TRU II SD(51) ON THE LEFT. FROM THE NEIGHBORHOOD OF THE HUT A DATE PALM THROWS A LONG SHADOW; FOR IT IS EARLY
2TRU II SD(51) WE ARE IN A MILITARY CANTOONMENT. OPPOSITE THE HUT IS A PARTICOLORED CANVAS BATHING PAVILION WITH A FOLDING
2TRU II SD(51) THE ENTRANCE, AS SEEN FROM THE SAND DUNES THE HUT IS ON THE RIGHT AND THE PAVILION ON THE LEFT. FROM THE
2TRU II SD(74) AT HIM. HE DODGES HER AND RUNS OFF PAST THE HUT . AT THAT MOMENT TALLBOYS RETURNS WITH MEEK PAST THE
2TRU II SD(80) MEEK SALUTES AND TROTS SMARTLY OUT PAST THE HUT . /AUBREY/ BY JOVE! ! /THE COUNTESS/ WELL I NE-- (
2TRU II SD(75) A SIMILAR RECONNAISSANCE ROUND THE CORNER OF THE HUT . /THE COUNTESS/ HERE I AM AGAIN, YOU SEE. (SHE SMILES
2TRU II SD(51) CHAIR FOR USE BY HIS VISITORS IS AT HAND BY THE HUT . THOUGH WELL OVER FIFTY, HE IS STILL SLENDER, HANDSOME,
2TRU II SD(51) RANGE WHICH BOUNDS IT BEING VISIBLE. AN ARMY HUT ON THE HITHER SIDE, WITH A KLAXON ELECTRIC HORN
2TRU II SD(74) RETURNS WITH MEEK PAST THE OTHER SIDE OF THE HUT ; AND THE PATIENT, UNABLE TO CHECK HERSELF, CRASHES INTO
2TRU II SD(61) HIS CAP GALLANTLY AND BUSTLES OFF PAST THE HUT TO HIS INSPECTION. /THE PATIENT/ (RISING VENGEFULLY)

HUTCH
MIS. (201) ME TO COME AND LIVE WITH HIM IN THIS RRRRRRRABBIT HUTCH , AND TAKE MY BREAD FROM HIS HAND, AND ASK HIM FOR

HUTCHES
MIS. PREFACE(37) WORLD INSTEAD OF INMATES OF THE ENLARGED RABBIT HUTCHES WE CALL HOMES; TO LEARN MANNERS AND BECOME .

HUTS
BULL PREFACE(50) IN THE NILE DELTA. BESIDES THE DILAPIDATED HUTS AMONG THE REEDS BY THE ROADSIDE, AND THE PALM TREES,
2TRU II SD(51) MOTOR BICYCLE FROM THE SIDE OPPOSITE TO THE HUTS . /TALLBOYS/ DAMN THAT NOISE! THE UNSEEN RIDER
3PLA PREFACE(R33) HACKED OUT OF HIS PLAYS AS PEASANTS HAVE HACKED HUTS OUT OF THE COLISEUM, ARE BEGINNING TO VANISH FROM THE

HUXLEY
METH PREFACE(R55) THAN DARWIN HIMSELF, CEASED TO DAZZLE US WHEN HUXLEY AND TYNDALL AND SPENCER AND DARWIN PASSED AWAY, AND
LION PREFACE(89) THE MAIN DIFFERENCE THAT SET GLADSTONE AND HUXLEY BY THE EARS IS NOT ONE BETWEEN BELIEF IN SUPERNATURAL
SUPR PREFACE(R36) OF TRIBAL SOOTHSAYING AND IDOLATROUS RITES WHICH HUXLEY CALLED SCIENCE AND MISTOOK FOR AN ADVANCE ON THE
LION PREFACE(88) SALVATIONIST AND REJECT MORE MIRACLE STORIES THAN HUXLEY DID; AND YOU MAY UTTERLY REPUDIATE JESUS AS THE
LION PREFACE(94) OFF EVERYTHING THAT HUME OR GRIMM OR ROUSSEAU OR HUXLEY OR ANY MODERN BISHOP COULD REJECT AS FANCIFUL.
SUPR I SD(4) COBDEN; ENLARGED PHOTOGRAPHS OF MARTINEAU, HUXLEY , AND GEORGE ELIOT; AUTOTYPES OF ALLEGORIES BY MR
LION PREFACE(95) AND FORERUNNER RESPECTIVELY. IF HE IS BUILT LIKE HUXLEY , HE WILL TAKE THE SECULAR VIEW, IN SPITE OF ALL THAT
POSN PREFACE(382) EVOLUTIONISTS OF 1790-1830, OF DARWIN, WALLACE, HUXLEY , HELMHOLTZ, TYNDALL, SPENCER, CARLYLE, RUSKIN, AND
NEVR II (228) STUART MILL'S ESSAY ON LIBERTY (NOD); TO READ HUXLEY , TYNDALL, AND GEORGE ELIOT (THREE NODS); AND TO

HUXLEYS
LION PREFACE(95) IMPORTANT THING NOW IS THAT THE GLADSTONES AND HUXLEYS SHOULD NO LONGER WASTE THEIR TIME IRRELEVANTLY AND

HUZ
CAPT II (249) RIGHT, ISN'T IT? /DRINKWATER/ YUSS, AN HORDER HUZ ABAHT AS IF WE WAS KEB TAHTS! AN THE KEPN AFRIDE TO
CAPT I (223) ARFRICAR. DAOWNT HARFRICAR BELONG AS MUCH TO HUZ AS TO THEM? THETS WOT WE SY. ENNYWYS, THERE YNT NAOW
CAPT II (265) LISSEN, KEPN (POINTING TO SIR HOWARD): E'LL GIVE HUZ FAWV UNNERD RED UNS. (TO THE OTHERS) YNT YER SPOWK TO
CAPT I (223) DO IT? /DRINKWATER/ (SOMEWHAT ABASHED) SOME OF HUZ IS HANCONVERTED MEN, GAVNER; AN THEY SY: YOU SMAGGLES
CAPT I (227) HOOLIGAN! /DRINKWATER/ (DEPRECATINGLY) NIME GIV HUZ PORE THORTLESS LEDS BAW A GENT ON THE DILY CHRORNICLE.
CAPT I (238) CAWNT HEXPECT A LOT O POOR HONEDDIKITED MEN LAWK HUZ TO RAN AHRSEOLVS INTO DINEGER WITHAHT NAOW KEPN TO TEOLL
CAPT II (243) THE BENNY SEERAS: BLAOW ME IF SHE DIDNT! HARSKT HUZ WOT WE WAS FRAHTND OF. TYIN AP MAWTZOW'S WOUND, SHE IS.

HW
CAPT NOTES (306) OUT BY A GENERAL AGREEMENT TO PRONOUNCE WH AS HW , IS TEMPESTUOUSLY AUDIBLE, AND CANNOT BE DROPPED WITHOUT

HWAT
BULL III (123) NIGHT, AND PROPOSED TO MISS REILLY. /LARRY/ YOU HWAT ? ? ? (HE SCREAMS WITH LAUGHTER IN THE FALSETTO
BULL III (129) TO THE SEAT. BESIDES, I'M A SAXON. /DORAN/ A HWAT ? /BROADBENT/ A SAXON. AN ENGLISHMAN. /DORAN/ AN
BULL II (105) DIE-CAST. /CORNELIUS/ (IN BLANK BEWILDERMENT) HWAT ? /BROADBENT/ MURRAY DESCRIBES IT. ONE OF YOUR GREAT
SUPR IV (144) CAN WE DO? HE IS OUR CHAUFFEUR. /MALONE/ YOUR HWAT ? /VIOLET/ THE DRIVER OF OUR AUTOMOBILE. HE CAN DRIVE
BULL III (136) NOW: ALL WE WANT IS TO BE LET ALONE. /CORNELIUS/ HWAT ABOUT HOME RULE? /BROADBENT/ (RISING SO AS TO ADDRESS
BULL II (99) /KEEGAN/ FATHER! /PATSY/ (DESPERATELY) ARRA, HWAT AM I TO CALL YOU? FADHER DEMPSEY SEZ YOURE NOT A
BULL III (127) HAD ENOUGH OF HIS FOOLISH TALK AGEN LANLORDS. HWAT CALL HAS HE TO TALK ABOUT THE LAN, THAT NEVER WAS
BULL III (127) YOUR DISADVANTAGE. /MATTHEW/ (IMPLACABLE) THEN HWAT DID YOU MANE BE TALKIN ABOUT GIVIN HIM LAN? /DORAN/
BULL III (129) AN OLDER AND POSSIBLY FOOLISHER MAN. /CORNELIUS/ HWAT DOES IT MATTER TO US HWAT YOUR OPINIONS ARE? YOU KNOW
BULL III (135) (CONVENTIONALLY) /MATTHEW/ (STILL SUSPICIOUS) HWAT DOES REFORM MANE, SIR? DOES IT MANE ALTHERIN ANNYTHIN
BULL III (137) VACANTLY UNTIL HE IS OUT OF EARSHOT). /CORNELIUS/ HWAT D'YE THINK, FATHER DEMPSEY? /FATHER DEMPSEY/ (
SUPR IV (149) YOUVE NOT PLAYED THIS HAND STRAIGHT. /MALONE/ HWAT D'Y'MEAN? /HECTOR/ YOUVE OPENED A LETTER ADDRESSED TO
BULL III (131) HWERE HAVE YOU BEEN LIVING ALL THESE YEARS? AND HWAT HAVE YOU BEEN DREAMING OF? WHY, SOME O DHESE HONEST
BULL II (108) AT HIM). /CORNELIUS/ THE HOTEL! /FATHER DEMPSEY/ HWAT HOTEL? /AUNT JUDY/ INDEEDN YOURE NOT GOIN TO A HOTEL.
BULL III (127) WHAT MR HAFFIGAN SUFFERED. /MATTHEW/ NEVER MIND HWAT I SUFFERED, I KNOW WHAT I SUFFERED ADHOUT YOU TELLIN
BULL I (78) HOUR I'LL GO INTO IT WITH YOU. /TIM/ I TELL YOU HWAT . GIMME A PROSPECTUS. LEMMY TAKE IT HOME AND REFLECT ON
BULL III (127) LIKE DORAN AN MATT WERE KEP FROM OWNIN LAND. BUT HWAT MAN IN HIS SENSES EVER WANTED TO GIVE LAND TO PATSY
BULL III (134) ROUND THE CORNER OF THE HOUSE). /DORAN/ (DAZED) HWAT SORT OF A FELLA IS HE AT ALL AT ALL? /FATHER DEMPSEY/
SUPR IV (145) HE CONTINUES SLOWLY) NOW I DONT KNOW ON HWAT TERMS YOUNG PEOPLE ASSOCIATE IN ENGLISH SOCIETY; BUT IN
BULL IV (148) PICKED HIM UP HE HADNT A SCRATCH ON HIM, BARRN HWAT THE PIG DID TO HIS CLOES. PATSY HAD TWO FINGERS OUT O
BULL II (110) I GO FOR HER? /AUNT JUDY/ (CONTEMPTUOUSLY) ARRA HWAT UD HAPPEN TO HER? HURRY IN NOW, CORNY. COME, MR
BULL II (109) PATSY, BEFORE FATHER DEMPSEY? /PATSY/ WELL, HWAT WAS I TO DO? FATHER KEEGAN BID ME TELL YOU MISS NORA
BULL II (106) IF I LEFT YOUR HAMPER BEHIND IN THE WET GRASS; N HWAT WOULD THE MASTHER SAY IF I LEFT THE SAMMIN AND THE
BULL II (106) /PATSY/ AN WHOSE THINGS WAS I TO LAVE BEHIND? HWAT WOULD YOUR REVERENCE THINK IF I LEFT YOUR HAMPER BEHIND
BULL III (129) MAN. /CORNELIUS/ HWAT DOES IT MATTER TO US HWAT YOUR OPINIONS ARE? YOU KNOW THAT YOUR FATHER'S BOUGHT
BULL III (136) THE LOCAL CRICKET CLUB-- /CORNELIUS/ THE HWAT ! /DORAN/ NOBODY PLAYS BAT N BALL HERE, IF DHATS WHAT

BULL III (131) WORK A HORSE THAT COST YOU FIFTY GUINEAS. /DORAN/ HWAT ! ! ! /CORNELIUS/ (AGHAST) A POUND A-- GOD SAVE

HWATEVER

BULL II (108) THE LIKE OF HIM WOULD TELL YOU? SURE HE'D SAY HWATEVER WAS THE LEAST TROUBLE TO HIMSELF AND THE

HWATS

BULL III (131) (MATT SUBSIDES). NOW, NOW, NOW! COME, COME! HWATS ALL DHIS ABOUT PATSY FARRLL? HWY NEED YOU FALL OUT
BULL II (110) (HE TAKES HIS LOAD UP THE HILL). /CORNELIUS/ HWATS NORA DOIN AT THE ROUN TOWER? /AUNT JUDY/ OH, THE LORD
BULL IV (153) WE ALL HAVE TO STRETCH IT A BIT IN POLITICS: HWATS THE USE O PRETENDIN WE DONT? /BROADBENT/ (STIFFLY) I

HWEEL

BULL IV (145) LAUGH AT? /DORAN/ IT GOT ITS FUT INTO THE LITTLE HWEEL -- (HE IS OVERCOME AFRESH; AND THE REST COLLAPSE
BULL IV (157) LEND HIM 500 POUNDS ON THE MILL TO PUT IN A NEW HWEEL ; FOR THE OLD ONE'LL HARLY HOL TOGETHER. AN HAFFIGAN

HWEN

BULL III (134) HWEN IT WASNT YOURS IT WAS SOMEBODY ELSE'S; AND HWEN IT WAS NOBODY ELSE'S IT WAS OULD IRELAN'S. HOW THE
BULL III (134) ELSE EVER SINCE WE WAS CHILDHER BUT SUFFERINS. HWEN IT WASNT YOURS IT WAS SOMEBODY ELSE'S; AND HWEN IT WAS
BULL IV (148) DIVIL'S OWN LUCK, THAT ENGLISHMAN, ANNYWAY; FOR HWEN THEY PICKED HIM UP HE HADNT A SCRATCH ON HIM, BARRN

HWERE

BULL III (131) DECENT LIFE ON LESS? /FATHER DEMPSEY/ MAN ALIVE, HWERE HAVE YOU BEEN LIVING ALL THESE YEARS? AND HWAT HAVE
BULL IV (146) KEEGAN GLARES AT THEM). BEFORE BROADBINT KNEW HWERE HE WAS, THE PIG WAS UP HIS BACK AND OVER INTO HIS LAP;
BULL III (127) /CORNELIUS/ WE'RE TIRED OF HIM. HE DOESNT KNOW HWERE TO STOP. EVERY MAN CANT OWN LAND; AND SOME MEN MUST

HWERES

BULL II (109) DOES) THATS ALL RIGHT: ITLL BE NO TROUBLE AT ALL. HWERES NORA? /AUNT JUDY/ OH, HOW DO I KNOW? SHE SLIPPED

HWY

BULL II (109) THE FISH, THE BIRD, AND THE SACK. /AUNT JUDY/ AH, HWY CANT YOU HOLD YOUR TONGUE, PATSY, BEFORE FATHER
BULL III (142) IT PRETTY PINK, YOU BET. /MATTHEW/ (SCORNFULLY) HWY CANT YOU TELL A RAISONABLE LIE WHEN YOURE ABOUT IT?
BULL II (110) NORA WAS GONE TO THE ROUN TOWER. /AUNT JUDY/ AN HWY COULDNT YOU WAIT TO TELL US UNTIL FATHER DEMPSEY WAS
BULL III (131) COME, COME! HWATS ALL DHIS ABOUT PATSY FARRLL? HWY NEED YOU FALL OUT ABOUT HIM? /LARRY/ BECAUSE IT WAS BY
BULL III (126) ME! /FATHER DEMPSEY/ (ENCOURAGINGLY) YES, YOU. HWY NOT? /LARRY/ I'M AFRAID MY IDEAS WOULD NOT BE POPULAR

HYBRID

BULL PREFACE(16) HANGED AS A REBEL. WHEN I LOOK ROUND ME ON THE HYBRID COSMOPOLITANS, SLUM POISONED OR SQUARE PAMPERED, WHO

HYBRIDS

BULL I (86) NO, LARRY, NO. YOU ARE THINKING OF THE MODERN HYBRIDS THAT NOW MONOPOLIZE ENGLAND. HYPOCRITES, HUMBUGS,

HYDE

SUPR II (50) A SUCCESS? /OCTAVIUS/ I THINK SO. WE CAME FROM HYDE PARK CORNER HERE IN SEVENTEEN MINUTES. (THE CHAUFFEUR,
SUPR II (49) WATCH) I SUPPOSE YOU KNOW THAT WE HAVE COME FROM HYDE PARK CORNER TO RICHMOND IN TWENTY-ONE MINUTES. /THE
SIM II (77) NAVY WOULD NOT TAKE IT LYING DOWN. LATER, A HYDE PARK ORATOR WAS THROWN INTO THE SERPENTINE FOR SAYING
PYGM III (255) YOURS SINCE WE USED TO REVIEW THE VOLUNTEERS IN HYDE PARK TWENTY YEARS AGO. /HIGGINS/ (SULKILY) OH, WELL,
APPL II (257) HE LEARNT TO SPEAK SO BEAUTIFULLY, HE SAID " IN HYDE PARK." /MAGNUS/ YES; BUT WITH A CROWD TO STIMULATE HIM.
FABL PREFACE(79) AND FAILED, UNTIL ONE DAY, WALKING THROUGH HYDE PARK, HE HEARD A GOSPEL PREACHER CRY " LISTEN FOR THE
3PLA PREFACE(R24) CAUGHT THE EAR OF THE BRITISH PUBLIC ON A CART IN HYDE PARK, TO THE BLARING OF BRASS BANDS, AND THIS NOT AT

HYDROCHLORIC

FABL PREFACE(64) EXCRETION GOES WRONG THE BOTTLEMEN DOSE YOU WITH HYDROCHLORIC ACID OR CHALK-AND-OPIUM (" THE OLD MIXTURE")

HYDROCYANIC

MILL I (140) THE GLASS; AND THE SUPERNATANT FLUID WILL BE PURE HYDROCYANIC ACID, ONE SIP OF WHICH WILL KILL YOU LIKE A

HYDROPATHIC

MIS. PREFACE(24) IT THAN THE MANAGER OF A HOTEL WHICH BEGAN AS A HYDROPATHIC HAS OF THE WATER CURE. OR YOU CAN BUY A CHEAPER

HYDROPHOBIA

DOCT PREFACE(24) I HAVE HEARD THEM DENY THE EXISTENCE OF HYDROPHOBIA AS A SPECIFIC DISEASE DIFFERING FROM TETANUS. I
DOCT PREFACE(54) DOG NECESSARILY GOT HYDROPHOBIA. I MYSELF HEARD HYDROPHOBIA DISCUSSED IN MY YOUTH BY DOCTORS IN DUBLIN
DOCT PREFACE(54) SCEPTICISM OF AN EMINENT SURGEON AS TO WHETHER HYDROPHOBIA IS REALLY A SPECIFIC DISEASE OR ONLY ORDINARY
DOCT PREFACE(54) PERSON BITTEN BY A RABID DOG NECESSARILY GOT HYDROPHOBIA . I MYSELF HEARD HYDROPHOBIA DISCUSSED IN MY
DOCT PREFACE(54) THINKS THAT THE BITE OF A MAD DOG MEANS CERTAIN HYDROPHOBIA . IT SEEMED TO ME THAT THE PROPORTION OF DEATHS
DOCT PREFACE(54) AS TO THE PROPORTION OF DOG BITES THAT ENDED IN HYDROPHOBIA ; BUT NOBODY EVER GUESSED THAT THE CASES COULD
DOCT I (104) OF TREATING A SCARLET FEVER CASE WITH A SAMPLE OF HYDROPHOBIA SERUM FROM THE PASTEUR INSTITUTE, AND IT
DOCT PREFACE(54) ABOUT 100. THE VOGUE OF THE PASTEUR TREATMENT OF HYDROPHOBIA , FOR INSTANCE, WAS DUE TO THE ASSUMPTION BY THE

HYDRO-ELECTRIC

APPL I (208) YOURS IS A TRADE UNION SEAT, IS IT NOT? IF THE HYDRO-ELECTRIC WORKERS FEDERATION THROW YOU OVER, WHERE

HYERING

SIM II (57) OR WITH THEIR FISTS? WHAT DO THE ULTIMATUMS SAY, HYERING ? /HYERING/ (READING THEM) NUMBER ONE FROM THE
SIM II (63) OF OUR JOBS AS GOVERNOR AND POLITICAL SECRETARY, HYERING ? WILL THIS AFFECT OUR SALARIES? /HYERING/ THEY
SIM II (65) AND THAT SIR CHARLES IS A VOLUPTUOUS SULTAN AND HYERING A CO-RESPONDENT. THEY DONT LIVE IN A WORLD OF TRUTH:
SIM II SD(58) IS SITTING ON THE WESTERN STONE SEAT, WITH MRS HYERING BESIDE HER ON HER RIGHT. PROLA IS SITTING ON THE
SIM I SD(43) FOLLOWED BY SIR CHARLES FARWATERS AND BY HUGO HYERING C.B. AND MRS HYERING. HYERING IS THE FORMER
SIM II SD(54) SEATED NEAR HIM IS PRA. BOTH ARE BUSY WRITING. HYERING ENTERS. /SIR CHARLES/ MORNING, HYERING. /HYERING/
SIM II (82) THE ONLY UNQUESTIONABLY USEFUL JOB. (HE FOLLOWS HYERING INTO THE HOUSE). /LADY FARWATERS/ (RISING) PROLA:
SIM I SD(43) AND BY HUGO HYERING C.B. AND MRS HYERING. HYERING IS THE FORMER EMIGRATION OFFICER, NOW AN ELDERLY AND
SIM I SD(43) FARWATERS AND BY HUGO HYERING C.B. AND MRS HYERING , HYERING IS THE FORMER EMIGRATION OFFICER, NOW AN
SIM II (54) WRITING. HYERING ENTERS. /SIR CHARLES/ MORNING, HYERING . /HYERING/ MORNING. (HE SITS AT THE OTHER END OF
SIM I (43) (SHAKING HANDS) NOT SIR HUGO. (INTRODUCING) MRS HYERING . /MRS HYERING/ (SHAKING HANDS) C.B., IN CASE YOU
SIM II SD(58) PRA COMES FROM THE HOUSE WITH SIR CHARLES AND HYERING . THEY HELP THEMSELVES TO TEA. PRA ABSTAINS. /SIR
SIM II SD(70) THEMSELVES AS USUAL. THE TELEPHONE RINGS. HYERING RISES AND TAKES IT. /HYERING/ (TO THE ANGEL) EXCUSE
SIM II (70) THE ANGEL) EXCUSE ME. (TO THE TELEPHONE) YES? HYERING SPEAKING. . . . SOMEBODY WHAT? . . . OH! SOMEBODY
SIM II (56) HAS BEEN THE CENTRE OF THE BRITISH EMPIRE. YOU, HYERING , HAVE HAD THE SAME DIPLOMATIC SUCCESS IN THE EAST
SIM I (45) TWENTY YEARS AGO MY WIFE AND I, WITH MR AND MRS HYERING , JOINED THIS EASTERN GENTLEMAN AND HIS COLLEAGUE IN
SIM I (43) OF THE OTHER STONE SEAT. /PRA/ THIS IS MR HUGO HYERING , POLITICAL SECRETARY TO THE ISLES. /THE CLERGYMAN/

HYGIENE

DOCT PREFACE(80) COSTS MORE THAN HE IS WORTH IS DOOMED BY SOUND HYGIENE AS INEXORABLY AS BY SOUND ECONOMICS. 12. DO NOT TRY
DOCT PREFACE(71) TECHNIQUES, AND WILL HOLD GOOD WHETHER PUBLIC HYGIENE BE BASED ON THE POETIC FANCIES OF CHRISTIAN SCIENCE,
MIS. (123) THAT TIME. /HYPATIA/ THERE WAS A PHYSIOLOGY AND HYGIENE CLASS STARTED AT SCHOOL; BUT OF COURSE NONE OF OUR
DOCT PREFACE(61) TEMPERANCE, AND THE REST OF THE NEW FASHIONS IN HYGIENE . AT PRESENT THE TABLES HAVE BEEN TURNED ON MANY OLD
HART PREFACE(7) THIS IS WHAT HAS JUST HAPPENED IN OUR POLITICAL HYGIENE . POLITICAL SCIENCE HAS BEEN AS RECKLESSLY NEGLECTED
HART PREFACE(7) NOT ONE THAT COMPELS US TO CONDUCT A SOLVENT HYGIENE ON A CASH BASIS. SHE DEMORALIZES US WITH LONG
DOCT PREFACE(71) PROBLEMS. THE NOTION THAT THERAPEUTICS OR HYGIENE OR SURGERY IS ANY MORE OR LESS SCIENTIFIC THAN
DOCT PREFACE(29) HIS INCOME, AND AS THE ADVANCE OF SCIENTIFIC HYGIENE TENDS TO MAKE THE PRIVATE DOCTOR'S VISITS RARER, AND
DOCT PREFACE(69) HIM IS ONLY THE BEGINNING OF THAT ARMY OF PUBLIC HYGIENE WHICH WILL PRESENTLY TAKE THE PLACE IN GENERAL
METH PREFACE(R80) THING AS SMALLPOX, IT MAY COME TO THAT YET; FOR HYGIENE , AS IT FORCES ITS WAY INTO OUR SCHOOLS, IS BEING
GETT PREFACE(251) WE SHALL HAVE NO SYSTEMATIC INSTRUCTION IN SEXUAL HYGIENE , BECAUSE SUCH LECTURES AS ARE GIVEN IN GERMANY,
OVER PREFACE(169) REMEDY FOR THAT IS NOT SALVARSAN, BUT SOUND MORAL HYGIENE , THE FIRST FOUNDATION OF WHICH IS THE

HYGIENIC

NEVR I (206)	RECTOR'S WIFE ADVOCATES DRESS REFORM AND WEARS	HYGIENIC	BOOTS. (DOLLY FURTIVELY LOOKS AT HER OWN SHOE:
FANY III (313)	A MAN'S MIND. TALKING OF THAT, WHAT ABOUT THOSE	HYGIENIC	CORSET ADVERTISEMENTS THAT VINES AND JACKSON WANT
FABL PREFACE(90)	VACCINES, ANTITOXINS, VITAMINS, AND PROFESSEDLY	HYGIENIC	FOODS AND DRUGS AND DRINKS OF ALL SORTS. SUCH A
DOCT I (95)	MRS FOLJAMBE HAD THE RIGHT SPIRIT-- THE GENUINE	HYGIENIC	INSTINCT. SHE COULDNT STAND HER SISTER-IN-LAW BEING
DOCT PREFACE(28)	A YEAR BE HALF-A-CROWN. AND, ON THE OTHER HAND, A	HYGIENIC	MEASURE HAS ONLY TO BE ONE OF SUCH REFINEMENT,
BARB PREFACE(214)	BE RULED OUT IN FAVOR OF PURELY HUMANE AND	HYGIENIC	MEASURES. YET IN THE PRECISELY PARALLEL CASE OF A
DOCT PREFACE(73)	TERRIFIES SO MANY OF US: THE DANGER OF HAVING A	HYGIENIC	ORTHODOXY IMPOSED ON US. BUT WE MUST FACE THAT: IN
POSN PREFACE(417)	PANTOMIMES AND AT OUR VARIETY THEATRES, THE SOUND	HYGIENIC	PROPAGANDA OF THE BATH, AND THE CHARM OF THE
GETT PREFACE(204)	EVERYBODY. NOTHING COULD BE MORE INNOCENT, MORE	HYGIENIC	, MORE IMPORTANT TO THE SOCIAL WELFARE. BUT THE WAY

HYGIENIST

FABL PREFACE(90)	JESUS AND ST JAMES. MRS EDDY, A MUCH SOUNDER	HYGIENIST	THAN JENNER, PASTEUR, LISTER, AND THEIR DISCIPLES,

HYGIENISTS

DOCT PREFACE(20)	PRACTITIONERS NOW MAKE LARGE INCOMES AS	HYGIENISTS	, AND ARE RESORTED TO AS FREQUENTLY BY CULTIVATED
BARB PREFACE(229)	ULCERS TO DISTRICT VISITORS ARE CONVINCED	HYGIENISTS	, OR THAT THE CURIOSITY WHICH SOMETIMES WELCOMES

HYMN

DEVL I (17)	TO OFFER UP A PRAYER? /UNCLE TITUS/ OR SING A	HYMN	? /ANDERSON/ (RATHER HASTILY) I HAVE BEEN WITH OUR
LION PROL,SD(105)	FOREST SOUNDS, ROARING OF LIONS, CHRISTIAN	HYMN	FAINTLY. A JUNGLE PATH. A LION'S ROAR, A MELANCHOLY
FANY II (291)	SUPPOSE: YOU KNOW I LOVE SINGING A GOOD SWINGING	HYMN	; AND I FELT IT WAS RIDICULOUS TO GO HOME IN THE BUS
POSN (459)	AND SINGING DREADFUL DIRTY WICKED WORDS TO	HYMN	TUNES LIKE AS IF HE HAD SEVEN DEVILS IN HIM. /STRAPPER/
BARB II (297)	UP FROM THREE-AND-SIX TO FOUR-AND-TEN WITH THAT	HYMN	, PENNY BY PENNY AND VERSE BY VERSE, WAS A CAUTION. NOT

HYMNBOOKS

BARB III (324)	THE CHIEFS; AND THE CLERKS HAVE TALL HATS AND	HYMNBOOKS	AND KEEP UP THE SOCIAL TONE BY REFUSING TO

HYMNS

MIS. PREFACE(45)	PRINCE, AND LA ROCHEFOUCAULD'S MAXIMS, AND	HYMNS	ANCIENT AND MODERN, AND DE GLANVILLE'S APOLOGUE, AND
MIS. PREFACE(90)	BE LED TO THE DISCOVERY THAT JACKSON IN F AND	HYMNS	ANCIENT AND MODERN ARE NOT PERHAPS THE LAST WORD OF
FABL PREFACE(81)	THAT I HAD TO SUPPLY THE SERMON IN A RITUAL OF	HYMNS	AND LESSONS IN ALL RESPECTS LIKE A RELIGIOUS SUNDAY
MTH2 (57)	! ! /LUBIN/ YOU PROBABLY SANG SIXTY-SIX	HYMNS	. BUT AS I CANNOT BOAST EITHER YOUR ADMIRABLE VOICE OR
SIM II (54)	THEY PROPOSE TO DO NOTHING UNTIL THEN BUT SING	HYMNS	. THE IRISH FREE STATE ADMIRAL THREATENS TO SINK THEM
LION I (111)	THE PROFANITY AND BLASPHEMY OF SINGING CHRISTIAN	HYMNS	ON THE MARCH. I HAVE TO REPRIMAND YOU, CENTURION, FOR
FABL PREFACE(81)	THAT THE LESSONS WERE FROM BROWNING AND THE	HYMNS	WERE ASPIRATIONS TO " JOIN THE CHOIR INVISIBLE." LATER
METH PREFACE(R69)	A PRIME MINISTER WHO IS AN EMOTIONAL SINGER OF	HYMNS	, AND A GENERAL WHO IS A BIGOTED ROMAN CATHOLIC MAY BE
PLES PREFACE(R8)	IT BY SINGING REVOLUTIONARY LYRICS AND REPUBLICAN	HYMNS	, WE THOUGHT NOTHING OF SINGING THEM TO THE MUSIC OF

HYPATIA

MIS. (199)	FOR MAKING A FOOL OF MYSELF. I BEG YOUR PARDON.	HYPATIA	: I'M AWFULLY SORRY; BUT IVE MADE UP MY MIND THAT
MIS. (174)	OF THE COMPANY. /BENTLEY/ I SAY: HAS ANYBODY SEEN	HYPATIA	? SHE PROMISED TO COME OUT WITH ME; AND I CANT FIND
MIS. (116)	THAT ROW WITH ME FOR LICKING ROBERT AND GIVING	HYPATIA	A BLACK EYE BECAUSE SHE BIT ME. I PROMISED YOU THEN
MIS. SD(152)	THE TWO WICKER CHAIRS. JOHNNY GIVES HIS TO LINA.	HYPATIA	AND PERCIVAL TAKE THE CHAIRS AT THE WORKTABLE. LORD
MIS. (184)	BREAKING OUT LAMENTABLY) JOEY: HAVE YOU TAKEN	HYPATIA	AWAY FROM ME? /LORD SUMMERHAYS/ (SEVERELY)
MIS. SD(150)	TARLETON BETWEEN LORD SUMMERHAYS AND HER HUSBAND,	HYPATIA	BETWEEN PERCIVAL AND BENTLEY, AND JOHNNY TO
MIS. SD(120)	AND STICK FROM THE HAT STAND). MRS TARLETON AND	HYPATIA	COME BACK JUST AS THE TWO MEN ARE GOING OUT. HYPATIA
MIS. (191)	WONT YOU SIT DOWN? I'M VERY TIRED OF STANDING. (	HYPATIA	COMES FROM THE PAVILION AND TAKES A CHAIR AT THE
MIS. SD(115)	STILL VERY PLEASANT AND LIKEABLE AND UNAFFECTED.	HYPATIA	IS A TYPICAL ENGLISH GIRL OF A SORT NEVER CALLED
MIS. SD(121)	DARNING MATERIALS AND ONE OF HER HUSBAND'S SOCKS.	HYPATIA	IS AT THE OTHER SIDE OF THE TABLE, ON HER MOTHER'S
MIS. (131)	JOLLY GOOD CARE TO KEEP JOEY OUT OF THIS UNTIL	HYPATIA	IS PAST PRAYING FOR. JOHNNY AND LORD SUMMERHAYS
MIS. SD(177)	MRS TARLETON, WHO STARES STERNLY AT HYPATIA.	HYPATIA	IS THE FIRST TO RECOVER HER PRESENCE OF MIND.
MIS. (174)	SUBMISSIVENESS AND VIOLENCE) I CAN TELL YOU WHERE	HYPATIA	IS. I CAN TELL YOU WHERE JOEY IS. AND I SAY IT'S A
MIS. SD(177)	EXCEPT MRS TARLETON, WHO STARES STERNLY AT	HYPATIA	. HYPATIA IS THE FIRST TO RECOVER HER PRESENCE OF
MIS. (114)	TAKE ONE! " I TOOK ONE THE DAY AFTER I FIRST MET	HYPATIA	. I WENT AND BOUGHT HALF A DOZEN UNSHRINKABLE VESTS
MIS. (152)	BRITISH FLAG WAVES. HIS SON BENTLEY, ENGAGED TO	HYPATIA	. MR JOSEPH PERCIVAL, THE PROMISING SON OF THREE
MIS. SD(181)	BETWEEN PERCIVAL AND LINA. JOHNNY STOPS BESIDE	HYPATIA	. /PERCIVAL/ CERTAINLY. /TARLETON/ (UNEASILY) TAKE
MIS. (149)	HE'S LOST CONTROL. /MRS TARLETON/ LOOK, LOOK,	HYPATIA	. THERE ARE TWO PEOPLE IN IT. /BENTLEY/ THEYVE
MIS. (117)	ITLL HIT YOU AS WELL AS ME WHEN BUNNY MARRIES	HYPATIA	. WHEN ALL HYPATIA'S MONEY IS THROWN AWAY ON
MIS. (126)	ALL YOU KNOW ABOUT IT, MY LAD. HOW DO, PATSY! (	HYPATIA	KISSES HIM). HOW IS MY CHICKABIDDY? (HE KISSES MRS
MIS. (121)	FORTY! I TALKED LIKE A DUCHESS; AND IF JOHNNY OR	HYPATIA	LET SLIP A WORD THAT WAS LIKE OLD TIMES, I WAS DOWN
MIS. (181)	AND CUT IT SHORT. GET RID OF HIM. /MRS TARLETON/	HYPATIA	OUGHT TO HAVE HER CHARACTER CLEARED. /TARLETON/ YOU
MIS. (128)	SHE LIKES THEM! /MRS TARLETON/ BUNNY! TAKE	HYPATIA	OUT INTO THE GROUNDS FOR A WALK: THERES A GOOD BOY.
MIS. (183)	YOU TOO, MR PERCIVAL, FOE ENCOURAGING HER. (	HYPATIA	RETREATS TO THE PAVILION, AND EXCHANGES GRIMACES
MIS. SD(115)	WILL YOU. I'M NOT GOING TO TOUCH YOU. SH -- SH --	HYPATIA	RUSHES IN THROUGH THE INNER DOOR, FOLLOWED BY MRS
MIS. (180)	/BENTLEY/ " RICHLY DESERVE." /PERCIVAL/ (TO	HYPATIA	) DOES THAT SATISFY YOU, MISS TARLETON? /HYPATIA/
MIS. (198)	YOURSELF OUT OF MY HOUSE. /PERCIVAL/ (RISING, TO	HYPATIA	) I'M AFRAID I SHALL HAVE TO DINE AT THE BEACON,
MIS. (182)	SUMMERHAYS/ OH QUITE, QUITE. /PERCIVAL/ (TO	HYPATIA	) LORD SUMMERHAYS WOULD PROBABLY LIKE TO HEAR YOU
MIS. (194)	YOUR DAUGHTER TO BECOME MY WIDOW. /TARLETON/ (TO	HYPATIA	) WHY DIDNT YOU ACCEPT HIM, YOU YOUNG IDIOT? /LORD
MIS. SD(120)	COME BACK JUST AS THE TWO MEN ARE GOING OUT.	HYPATIA	SALUTES SUMMERHAYS FROM A DISTANCE WITH AN ENIGMATIC
MIS. SD(144)	I DONT KNOW. TARLETON RETURNS FROM THE VESTIBULE.	HYPATIA	SITS DOWN DEMURELY. /HYPATIA/ WELL, PAPA: HAVE YOU
MIS. (181)	OF UTTERING AN ABOMINABLE CALUMNY CONCERNING MISS	HYPATIA	TARLETON FOR WHICH THERE WAS NOT A SHRED OF
MIS. (180)	OF UTTERING AN ABOMINABLE CALUMNY CONCERNING MISS	HYPATIA	TARLETON, FOR WHICH THERE WAS NOT A SHRED OF
MIS. SD(137)	(HE GOES OUT WITH BENTLEY THROUGH THE PAVILION).	HYPATIA	THROWS ASIDE HER WORK WITH AN ENORMOUS SIGH OF
MIS. (154)	AFRAID SO. /MRS TARLETON/ OH WELL, NEVER MIND:	HYPATIA	WILL LEND THE LADY A GOWN. /LINA/ THANK YOU: I'M
MIS. (175)	ROTTER, YOU? /GUNNER/ (TO TARLETON) OH! IS	HYPATIA	YOUR DAUGHTER? AND JOEY IS MISTER PERCIVAL, IS HE?
MIS. SD(154)	YOU. /PERCIVAL/ THANK YOU. LINA GOES OUT WITH	HYPATIA	, AND PERCIVAL WITH JOHNNY. /MRS TARLETON/ WELL,
MIS. (182)	MR PERCIVAL. /PERCIVAL/ (FIRST BOWING TO	HYPATIA	, AND THEN TURNING WITH COLD CONTEMPT TO GUNNER, WHO
MIS. (122)	TO LEND THEM MONEY; AND YOU MUST NEVER DO THAT,	HYPATIA	, BECAUSE THEY NEVER PAY. HOW CAN THEY? THEY DONT
MIS. SD(162)	BETWEEN THE END OF THE SIDEBOARD AND THE WALL.	HYPATIA	, EXCITED, MISCHIEVOUS, HER EYES GLOWING, RUNS IN,
MIS. (165)	MISS TARLETON-- /HYPATIA/ (CARESSINGLY)	HYPATIA	, JOEY, PATSY, IF YOU LIKE. /PERCIVAL/ LOOK HERE:
MIS. (112)	LIKE, YOURE MISTAKEN. LET ME TELL YOU THAT EXCEPT	HYPATIA	, NOT ONE PERSON IN THIS HOUSE IS IN FAVOR OF HER
MIS. (151)	ALLUDED TO HER AS THE CHICKABIDDY. MY DAUGHTER	HYPATIA	, WHO HAS ALWAYS WANTED SOME ADVENTURE TO DROP OUT
MIS. SD(177)	(TURNING WHITE) YOU KNOW WHAT I SAW AND HEARD.	HYPATIA	, WITH A GLEAM OF TRIUMPH IN HER EYES, SLIPS
MIS. (124)	HES A SPLENDID ANIMAL -- /MRS TARLETON/ (SHOCKED)	HYPATIA	! HOW CAN YOU! THE THINGS THAT GIRLS SAY

HYPATIA'S

MIS. (181)	/MRS TARLETON/ STOP. MR PERCIVAL: I THINK, ON	HYPATIA'S	ACCOUNT, LORD SUMMERHAYS OUGHT TO BE TOLD ABOUT
MIS. (187)	LEAVE IT AT THAT. /BENTLEY/ I WANT TO KNOW TOO.	HYPATIA'S	ENGAGED TO ME. /HYPATIA/ BENTLEY: IF YOU INSULT ME
MIS. (126)	AND YOURE AN OLD JOSSER. (HE THROWS A CUSHION AT	HYPATIA'S	FEET AND SITS DOWN ON IT WITH HIS BACK AGAINST HER
MIS. (135)	I COULD ASK HER TO LET ME CHANCE JOHNNY'S AND	HYPATIA'S	FUTURE BY GOING INTO LITERATURE. BUT IT WAS NO
MIS. (117)	WELL AS ME WHEN BUNNY MARRIES HYPATIA. WHEN ALL	HYPATIA'S	MONEY IS THROWN AWAY ON LIBRARIES, WHERE WILL
MIS. SD(157)	RELIGION. LINA COMES IN. SHE HAS LEFT HER CAP IN	HYPATIA'S	ROOM, BUT HAS MADE NO OTHER CHANGE. SHE STOPS JUST

HYPERADRENAL

JOAN PREFACE(16)	ASTRAY AND LEFT HER INCURABLY HYPERPITUITARY OR	HYPERADRENAL	OR HYSTEROID OR EPILEPTOID OR ANYTHING BUT

HYPERAESTHESIA

HART PREFACE(31)	FROM THE BATTLEFIELD PRODUCED A CONDITION OF	HYPERAESTHESIA	IN WHICH ALL THE THEATRICAL VALUES WERE
HART PREFACE(11)	DID NOT SAVE ME FROM A CONSIDERABLE DEGREE OF	HYPERAESTHESIA	, THERE WERE OF COURSE SOME HAPPY PEOPLE TO
APPL PREFACE(191)	- OR, AS IT TURNED OUT, GIFTED -- WITH CHRONIC	HYPERAESTHESIA	, FEELING EVERYTHING VIOLENTLY AND EXPRESSING

HYPERBOLAS

KING I (213)	SUGAR LOAF AND CUT IT SLANTWISE, AND YOU WILL GET	HYPERBOLAS	AND PARABOLAS, ELLIPSES AND OVALS, WHICH LEONARDO

HYPERBOLE

BULL III (136)	ABOUT HOME RULE WITHOUT USING THE LANGUAGE OF	HYPERBOLE	, /DORAN/ SAVIN FADHER DEMPSEY'S PRESENCE, EH?
LADY PREFACE(229)	FOR THEM ALL," WE SHALL SEE MORE CIVILITY AND	HYPERBOLE	THAN SYCOPHANCY EVEN IN THE EARLIER AND MORE

HYPERBOLICAL

BASH PREFACE(89)	THE LISTENERS SHEWED UNMISTAKABLY THAT THEY LIKED	HYPERBOLICAL	RHETORIC AND DELIBERATELY ARTIFICIAL LANGUAGE.
JOAN PREFACE(42)	THE MEDIEVAL CRUSADES WHICH PROPOSED NOTHING MORE	HYPERBOLICAL	THAN THE RESCUE OF THE HOLY SEPULCHRE FROM THE
BULL PREFACE(70)	WAS THE USUAL COMBINATION OF MEAN SPITE WITH	HYPERBOLICAL	VIOLENCE. INDIANS WERE FORCED TO CRAWL PAST
LADY PREFACE(227)	NO DOUBT BY SHAKESPEAR'S VERBAL MAGIC, AND	HYPERBOLICAL	, AS SHAKESPEAR ALWAYS SEEMS TO PEOPLE WHO

HYPERPITUITARY

JOAN PREFACE(16)	HORMONES HAD GONE ASTRAY AND LEFT HER INCURABLY	HYPERPITUITARY	OR HYPERADRENAL OR HYSTEROID OR EPILEPTOID OR

HYPHENATED

INCA (255)	CRUMBLING? /ERMYNTRUDE/ EXCUSE ME! MINE WAS A	HYPHENATED	MILLIONAIRE. /THE INCA/ A HIGHFALUTIN

HYPNOTIC

METH PREFACE(R52)	PROCURED A COLONY OF MICE HIGHLY SUSCEPTIBLE TO	HYPNOTIC	SUGGESTION. HE SHOULD THEN HAVE HYPNOTIZED THEM
GETT PREFACE(226)	ONLY BY BEGLAMORING THE HUMAN IMAGINATION WITH A	HYPNOTIC	SUGGESTION OF WHOLLY UNNATURAL FEELINGS CAN IT BE
3PLA PREFACE(R26)	CRITICS WERE THE VICTIMS OF THE LONG COURSE OF	HYPNOTIC	SUGGESTION BY WHICH G.B.S. THE JOURNALIST

HYPNOTISM

HART II (89)	ME, THOUGH. IVE SEEN MEN MADE FOOLS OF BY	HYPNOTISM	, /ELLIE/ (STEADILY) BE QUIET. IVE SEEN MEN MADE
HART II (89)	BE QUIET. IVE SEEN MEN MADE FOOLS OF WITHOUT	HYPNOTISM	, /MANGAN/ (HUMBLY) YOU DONT DISLIKE TOUCHING ME.
GETT PREFACE(226)	OF HIS PRISONERS MAY CAUSE TO A GAOLER BY THE	HYPNOTISM	OF THE CONVENTION THAT THE NATURAL RELATION

HYPNOTIZE

HART II (89)	VERY REFRESHING. (WAKING A LITTLE) DONT YOU	HYPNOTIZE	ME, THOUGH. IVE SEEN MEN MADE FOOLS OF BY
HART II (118)	HIS ARM) YOU SHALL NOT RUN AWAY FROM ME. I CAN	HYPNOTIZE	YOU. YOU ARE THE ONLY PERSON IN THE HOUSE I CAN

HYPNOTIZED

MTH3 (131)	COMMON SENSE, YOU KNOW, THOSE TWO PEOPLE GOT US	HYPNOTIZED	: NOT A DOUBT OF IT. THEY MUST HAVE BEEN KIDDING
BULL PREFACE(14)	TOM BROADBENT AS INFATUATED IN POLITICS,	HYPNOTIZED	BY HIS NEWSPAPER LEADER-WRITERS AND PARLIAMENTARY
WIDO I SD(14)	WITHOUT A WORD, POINTS TO A SEAT. TRENCH, HALF	HYPNOTIZED	BY HIS OWN NERVOUSNESS AND THE IMPRESSIVENESS OF
GENV I (46)	WHEN WE DISCOVERED THAT SHE HAD BEEN	HYPNOTIZED	BY THIS ILLEGAL SOCIETY. I WARNED OUR SECRET
HART II (91)	EVEN IF YOU HAD BEEN, MR DUNN. SO ELLIE HAS	HYPNOTIZED	HIM. WHAT FUN! /MAZZINI/ OH NO, NO, NO. IT WAS
MIS. PREFACE(108)	THERE WERE NO COMPULSORY SCHOOLS AND NO CHILDREN	HYPNOTIZED	INTO THE BELIEF THAT THEY MUST TAMELY GO TO THEM
ROCK I (228)	CHAIR. THEY SIT CLOSE TOGETHER). YOU HAD ME HALF	HYPNOTIZED	. BUT FIRST, SHAKE HANDS. I WANT TO FEEL THAT YOU
HART II (91)	KNOW, MRS HUSHABYE, I REALLY THINK HE HAS BEEN	HYPNOTIZED	. /GUINNESS/ HIP NO WHAT, SIR? /MAZZINI/ ONE
MIS. (189)	(TO PERCIVAL) YOU CROWED PRETTY BIG OVER ME. YOU	HYPNOTIZED	ME. BUT WHEN YOU WERE PUT THROUGH THE FIRE
CAND III (127)	I'M SO SORRY, EUGENE. I THINK THE POKER MUST HAVE	HYPNOTIZED	ME. (SHE PUTS IT DOWN). /MARCHBANKS/ IT MADE ME
ARMS I (18)	PLEASE! (HE BECOMES MOTIONLESS, LIKE A	HYPNOTIZED	RABBIT, HIS FATIGUE GAINING FAST ON HIM. SHE
BARB III (336)	MY LOVE, WHAT POWER REALLY MEANS. /BARBARA/ (	HYPNOTIZED	) BEFORE I JOINED THE SALVATION ARMY, I WAS IN MY
METH PREFACE(R52)	TO HYPNOTIC SUGGESTION. HE SHOULD THEN HAVE	HYPNOTIZED	THEM INTO AN URGENT CONVICTION THAT THE FATE OF

HYPNOTIZING

HART II (91)	ONE EVENING AT HOME, AFTER WE HAD SEEN A	HYPNOTIZING	PERFORMANCE, THE CHILDREN BEGAN PLAYING AT IT;

HYPOCHONDRIA

HART PREFACE(9)	VEHEMENTLY PUT IT, " OF MIND FROM THE UNIVERSE."	HYPOCHONDRIA	. NOW HEARTBREAK HOUSE, WITH BUTLER AND BERGSON
JITT III (61)	WORRY TOO MUCH ABOUT YOUR FATHER. IT'S A SORT OF	HYPOCHONDRIA	; AND IT MAY MAKE YOU REALLY ILL. /EDITH/ (
JOAN PREFACE(16)	PURIFYING RELIGION AND BEING PURIFIED BY IT, BUT	HYPOCHONDRIA	, MELANCHOLIA, COWARDICE, STUPIDITY, CRUELTY,
DOCT PREFACE(12)	HALF-ALIVE PEOPLE WHO THROUGH VANITY, OR	HYPOCHONDRIA	, OR A CRAVING TO BE THE CONSTANT OBJECTS OF

HYPOCHONDRIAC

SUPR III (114)	DO TO SAVE MY SOUL; BUT I WAS NOT A SPIRITUAL	HYPOCHONDRIAC	ANY MORE THAN A BODILY ONE, AND WOULD NOT
SUPR III (114)	IMAGINARY DISEASES, I REPLIED THAT I WAS NOT A	HYPOCHONDRIAC	; SO THEY CALLED ME IGNORAMUS AND WENT THEIR

HYPOCHONDRIACAL

HART PREFACE(9)	WORLD OUTSIDE. BUT BEING AN IDLE HOUSE IT WAS A	HYPOCHONDRIACAL	HOUSE, ALWAYS RUNNING AFTER CURES. IT WOULD
DOCT PREFACE(16)	IS NEITHER AGREEABLE NOR PRACTICABLE. AND EVERY	HYPOCHONDRIACAL	RICH LADY OR GENTLEMAN WHO CAN BE PERSUADED

HYPOCHONDRIACS

DOCT PREFACE(17)	STRENGTH, AND PATIENCE ARE EXPLOITED BY SELFISH	HYPOCHONDRIACS	. THEY MUST DO ALL THESE THINGS OR ELSE RUN

HYPOCRISIES

SUPR HANDBOK(209)	CAN FALL TO PIECES WHEN THE VULGAR BELIEF IN ITS	HYPOCRISIES	AND IMPOSTURES CAN NO LONGER HOLD OUT AGAINST
MIS. PREFACE(14)	AND TORTURE WHICH WE DISGUISE UNDER SUCH	HYPOCRISIES	AS EDUCATION, TRAINING, FORMATION OF CHARACTER
BULL PREFACE(23)	WORK TO MANUFACTURE AND SUPPORT ENGLISH SHAMS AND	HYPOCRISIES	INSTEAD OF EXPOSING AND DENOUNCING THEM; IF HE
SUPR HANDBOK(211)	THE SUPERMAN MAY OPERATE IN SPITE OF ALL OUR	HYPOCRISIES	. ONE THING AT LEAST IS CLEAR TO BEGIN WITH. IF
METH PREFACE(R86)	COULD NOT FIND TEXTS MORE FUNDAMENTAL THAN THE	HYPOCRISIES	OF SHAM PURITANISM, OR THE MATRIMONIAL
FABL PREFACE(69)	MORAL DILEMMAS. IT DRIVES THEM TO FALSEHOODS,	HYPOCRISIES	, AND FORGERIES MOST DISTRESSING TO THEIR
GETT (356)	TRADESMEN'S SET. YOU KNOW ALL ITS SCANDALS AND	HYPOCRISIES	, ITS JEALOUSIES AND SQUABBLES, ITS HUNDREDS OF
GETT PREFACE(203)	JUMBLE OF SUPERSTITIONS AND INTERESTS, TABOOS AND	HYPOCRISIES	, WHICH COULD NOT BE RECONCILED IN ANY COHERENT

HYPOCRISY

MRS II (218)	KNOWS I MEAN ANOTHER. WHATS THE USE IN SUCH	HYPOCRISY	? IF PEOPLE ARRANGE THE WORLD THAT WAY FOR WOMEN,
SUPR I (39)	SCANDALOUS WOMAN, WILL YOU THROW AWAY EVEN YOUR	HYPOCRISY	? /ANN/ I AM NEVER HYPOCRITICAL WITH YOU, JACK.
JITT III (71)	HOME. /EDITH/ HAPPY! OH NO. BUT I AM DONE WITH	HYPOCRISY	AND CONVENTIONALITY; AND THAT IS SUCH A RELIEF
FANY PROLOG (260)	MUD AND EAST WIND; OUT OF VULGARITY AND UGLINESS,	HYPOCRISY	AND GREED, SUPERSTITION AND STUPIDITY. OUT OF ALL
MIS. PREFACE(10)	HURTS ME MORE THAN IT HURTS YOU." THERE MUST BE	HYPOCRISY	AS WELL AS CRUELTY. THE INJURY TO THE CHILD WOULD
MTH5 (261)	ON THE SHAME OF HIS SISTER PLANET: CRUELTY AND	HYPOCRISY	BECAME SO HIDEOUS THAT THE FACE OF THE EARTH WAS
SUPR HANDBOK(228)	DECLARED UNWHOLESOME. WHERE THERE IS NO RELIGION	HYPOCRISY	BECOMES GOOD TASTE. WHERE THERE IS NO KNOWLEDGE
BARB PREFACE(223)	DEFINITELY THAT IT REDUCED ITSELF TO ABSURDITY OR	HYPOCRISY	BY TAKING IT, ON THE FIRST POINT THE REPLY OF THE
MIS. PREFACE(81)	EVEN WHEN THERE HAS BEEN NONE OF THE DELIBERATE	HYPOCRISY	BY WHICH CHILDREN ARE TAKEN ADVANTAGE OF BY THEIR
CAPT II (256)	OF YOURSELF; FOR YOU ARE GOING TO SEE AT LAST THE	HYPOCRISY	IN THE SANCTIMONIOUS SPEECH OF THE JUDGE WHO IS
SUPR PREFACE(R21)	IN THAT DIRECTION. THERE ARE NO LIMITS TO MALE	HYPOCRISY	IN THIS MATTER. NO DOUBT THERE ARE MOMENTS WHEN
SUPR HANDBOK(204)	LABORATORY SUFFERS THE SLIGHTEST PAIN.	HYPOCRISY	IS AT ITS WORST; FOR WE NOT ONLY PERSECUTE
SUPR HANDBOK(219)	THOSE WHO HAVE SEEN THEIR PARENTS AS THEY ARE.	HYPOCRISY	IS NOT THE PARENT'S FIRST DUTY. THE VILEST
ROCK II (265)	I WILL NO LONGER BEAR IT. THE VEIL OF YOUR	HYPOCRISY	IS RENT BY YOUR OWN MOUTHS: I SHOULD DISHONOR MY
ROCK II (282)	IS REALLY THE BEGINNING OF HOPE, AND THE END OF	HYPOCRISY	. DO YOU THINK I DIDNT KNOW, IN THE DAYS OF MY
JOAN PREFACE(55)	ON THE FASHIONABLE PEOPLE WHOSE PLAYGOING IS A	HYPOCRISY	. I CANNOT HELP FEELING SOME COMPASSION FOR THEM
BULL IV (153)	LIFE HAS BEEN A PROTEST-- IT IS THE VICE OF	HYPOCRISY	. I WOULD ALMOST RATHER BE INCONSISTENT THAN
SUPR III SD(72)	ON WITH OUR PLAY; SO THAT WE MAY ENJOY IT WITHOUT	HYPOCRISY	. IF WE WERE REASONING, FAR-SIGHTED PEOPLE, FOUR
LION PREFACE(23)	HE IS APT TO ACCUSE PEOPLE WHO FEEL THAT WAY OF	HYPOCRISY	. LIKE THE LATE SAMUEL BUTLER, HE REGARDS DISEASE
CAPT NOTES (301)	VOICED A UNIVERSAL IMPULSE BY BLUNTLY DAMNING ITS	HYPOCRISY	. OF ALL THE ELOQUENCE OF THAT SILLY PARLIAMENT,
GENV IV (96)	AND YOU BOTH TAKE IT AS AN OUTBURST OF BRITISH	HYPOCRISY	. /BEGONIA/ A PIECE OF DAMNED CHEEK, I CALL IT. I
SUPR IV (163)	I CAN STAND EVERYTHING EXCEPT HER CONFOUNDED	HYPOCRISY	. THATS WHAT BEATS ME. /MRS WHITEFIELD/ (CARRIED
LION EPILOG (148)	TASTE, WHICH IN SUCH MATTERS PRACTICALLY MEANS	HYPOCRISY	. THE HOME SECRETARY AND THE JUDGES WHO TRY THE
BARB PREFACE(219)	LIMIT OF IMPUDENCE IN LYING AND CORRUPTION IN	HYPOCRISY	. THE UNIVERSAL REGARD FOR MONEY IS THE ONE
HART PREFACE(19)	REALLY A CHANGE AT ALL, BUT ONLY A RELIEF FROM	HYPOCRISY	. THINK, TOO, OF THOSE WHO, THOUGH THEY HAD
OVER PREFACE(168)	MORALITY, AND CAN BE KEPT IN COUNTENANCE ONLY BY	HYPOCRISY	. WHEN PEOPLE WERE ASHAMED OF SANITARY PROBLEMS,
UNPL PREFACE(R9)	BY MY ABNORMAL NORMALITY, THAT THE RESOURCE OF	HYPOCRISY	NEVER OCCURRED TO ME. BETTER SEE RIGHTLY ON A
LADY PREFACE(232)	ABOUT DRUNKENNESS AND ABOUT THE IDOLATRY AND	HYPOCRISY	OF OUR JUDICIAL SYSTEM; BUT HIS IMPLIED REMEDY WAS
FANY EPILOG (331)	ALL COME TO? AN ATTEMPT TO EXPOSE THE SUPPOSED	HYPOCRISY	OF THE PURITAN MIDDLE CLASS IN ENGLAND: PEOPLE
MRS II (216)	IN THE RIGHT OR WRONG OF THE THING! OH, THE	HYPOCRISY	OF THE WORLD MAKES ME SICK! LIZ AND I HAD TO WORK

SUPR III (127) FOR YOUR ATTACKING ME, BUT NOT FOR THE REVOLTING HYPOCRISY OF YOUR SUBSEQUENT PROCEEDINGS AS A STATUE. /THE
SUPR I (31) TO ME TO HAVE ABSOLUTELY NO CONSCIENCE-- ONLY HYPOCRISY ; AND YOU CANT SEE THE DIFFERENCE-- YET THERE IS A
BARB PREFACE(243) IS ORGANIZED ROBBERY; OUR MORALITY IS AN IMPUDENT HYPOCRISY ; OUR WISDOM IS ADMINISTERED BY INEXPERIENCED OR
SUPR PREFACE(R36) AND HIS YOUNG FRIEND CIVILITY; FORMALIST AND HYPOCRISY ; WILDHEAD, INCONSIDERATE, AND PRAGMATICK (WHO
JOAN PREFACE(54) FROM THE STALLS AND IN THE PRESS AN ATMOSPHERE OF HYPOCRISY SPREADS. NOBODY SAYS STRAIGHT OUT THAT GENUINE
GETT PREFACE(217) NOW, AND THAT THE ONLY CHANGE WOULD BE THAT HYPOCRISY WOULD NO LONGER BE COMPULSORY. INDEED, THIS CAN
FANY III (323) IF YOU WERE A FRENCHMAN, STIFLED IN PRUDERY, HYPOCRISY , AND THE TYRANNY OF THE FAMILY AND THE HOME, YOU
SUPR PREFACE(R16) IS IN DANGER OF PLUCKING. FAR FROM RELAPSING INTO HYPOCRISY , AS SGANARELLE FEARED, HE HAS UNEXPECTEDLY
BARB PREFACE(234) THE SANCTION OF SOUTH DAKOTA; TO GROTESQUE HYPOCRISY , CRUEL PERSECUTION, AND FINAL UTTER CONFUSION OF
METH PREFACE(R61) AND PIRACY OF THE FEUDAL BARONS, BUT THE HYPOCRISY , INHUMANITY, SNOBBERY, AND GREED OF THE
BARB PREFACE(215) MANHOOD INTO SCROFULA, COWARDICE, CRUELTY, HYPOCRISY , POLITICAL IMBECILITY, AND ALL THE OTHER FRUITS
ROCK PREFACE(155) SUPPORT OF IT; AND THERE WOULD BE AN END OF THE HYPOCRISY , THE VENAL SPECIAL PLEADING, AND THE CONCEALMENT

HYPOCRITE

2TRU PREFACE(5) THE MOST COMPLETE CONVICTION HE DENOUNCED ME AS A HYPOCRITE AND A LIAR, AFFIRMING IT TO BE A WELL-KNOWN AND
BULL IV (153) IGNORANT YOUTH, WHEN I SHOULD HAVE CALLED YOU A HYPOCRITE . /BROADBENT/ (REDDENING) A HYPOCRITE! /NORA/ (
SIM II (66) JANGA/ (HISSING AFTER HIM) LIAR. BABY. DASTARD. HYPOCRITE . /SIR CHARLES/ (LAUGHING) AN ALBATROSS! NOW
SUPR IV (163) OWN OPINION SO ELOQUENTLY EXPRESSED) OH, SHE IS A HYPOCRITE . SHE IS! SHE IS. ISNT SHE? /TANNER/ THEN WHY DO
SUPR IV (168) YOU WITH EVERY QUALITY. WELL, I TOO CAN BE A HYPOCRITE . YOUR FATHER'S WILL APPOINTED ME YOUR GUARDIAN,
MIS. PREFACE(65) PROVIDED ONLY THE EMPLOYEE, HOWEVER PATENT A HYPOCRITE OR INCORRIGIBLE A SLACKER, IS HAT IN HAND. BUT LET
SUPR III (97) THE SKY! /THE STATUE/ I CANT COMPLAIN. I WAS A HYPOCRITE ; AND IT SERVED ME RIGHT TO BE SENT TO HEAVEN.
BULL IV (154) ARE STILL SLOW, YOU SEE. BESIDES, CALLING ME A HYPOCRITE WAS TOO BIG A JOKE TO SWALLOW ALL AT ONCE, YOU
SUPR I (24) IS WORSE: HE IS A CHILD-ROBBER, A BLOOD-SUCKER, A HYPOCRITE , AND A CHEAT. PERISH THE RACE AND WITHER A
BARB III (339) THAT? /UNDERSHAFT/ YOU KNOW HE WILL. DONT BE A HYPOCRITE , BARBARA. HE WILL BE BETTER FED, BETTER HOUSED,
SUPR IV (168) FOR YOURS. YOU HAD BETTER MARRY WHAT YOU CALL A HYPOCRITE , JACK. WOMEN WHO ARE NOT HYPOCRITES GO ABOUT IN
2TRU II (66) SO WOULD YOU IF YOU WERE A WOMAN. DONT YOU BE A HYPOCRITE , POPSY: AT LEAST NOT WITH ME. /AUBREY/ AT LEAST
BULL PREFACE(59) BY HIS OWN JUDGMENT TO BE A PREVARICATOR, HYPOCRITE , TYRANT, AND COWARD OF THE FIRST WATER, PREENED
SUPR IV (168) /ANN/ BOA-CONSTRICTOR! ELEPHANT! /TANNER/ HYPOCRITE ! /ANN/ (SOFTLY) I MUST BE, FOR MY FUTURE
APPL II (274) MANNERS AND FRIENDLY WAYS ARE WORTH. /NICOBAR/ HYPOCRITE ! /CRASSUS/ HUMBUG! /LYSISTRATA/ I WISH YOUR
BULL IV (153) YOU A HYPOCRITE. /BROADBENT/ (REDDENING) A HYPOCRITE ! /NORA/ (HASTILY) OH I'M SURE YOU DONT THINK

HYPOCRITES

FABL PREFACE(64) INCORRIGIBLE LIARS? ARE PLAYERS IMPOSTORS AND HYPOCRITES ? WERE THE BIBLE CHRISTIANS RIGHT WHEN THEY
BARB PREFACE(236) IS UNSOUND AND THAT ALL RELIGIOUS MEN ARE HYPOCRITES AND ALLIES OF THEIR SWEATERS AND OPPRESSORS. THEY
METH PREFACE(R75) RELIGION IS A FRAUD, AND PARSONS AND TEACHERS HYPOCRITES AND LIARS. HE BECOMES INDIFFERENT TO RELIGION IF
SUPR IV (168) YOU CALL A HYPOCRITE, JACK. WOMEN WHO ARE NOT HYPOCRITES GO ABOUT IN RATIONAL DRESS AND ARE INSULTED AND
JOAN 6 (130) ERROR OF MISTAKING THESE SIMPLETONS FOR LIARS AND HYPOCRITES . THEY BELIEVE HONESTLY AND SINCERELY THAT THEIR
LION PREFACE(53) WE CAN HEAR THE REPLY, " WOE UNTO YOU, LIARS AND HYPOCRITES ; FOR YE HAVE THIS VERY DAY DIVIDED UP THE WEALTH
MIS. (148) /TARLETON/ (HUGELY AMUSED) YES. HA HA! AWFUL HYPOCRITES , AINT WE? THEY ARE INTERRUPTED BY EXCITED CRIES
BULL I (86) THE MODERN HYBRIDS THAT NOW MONOPOLIZE ENGLAND. HYPOCRITES , HUMBUGS, GERMANS, JEWS, YANKEES, FOREIGNERS,
DEST (194) HER OFF AND COMING BACK INTO THE ROOM) PAH! THE HYPOCRITES ! IF THE FRENCH SAID THAT, HOW THEY WOULD HOLD
JOAN 6 (126) AND CONTEMPT) AND YET THEY SAY ENGLISHMEN ARE HYPOCRITES ! YOU PLAY FOR YOUR SIDE, MY LORD, EVEN AT THE

HYPOCRITICAL

OVER PREFACE(155) WHAT IS MORE, THESE PROFESSIONS ARE NOT HYPOCRITICAL : THEY ARE FOR THE MOST PART QUITE SINCERE. THE
HART PREFACE(18) FOR EXAMPLE), WERE NOT DUPED FOR A MOMENT BY THE HYPOCRITICAL MELODRAMA THAT CONSOLED AND STIMULATED THE
BULL PREFACE(22) DISCOVERY THAT THE PLATITUDINIZING TWADDLER AND HYPOCRITICAL OPPORTUNIST WAS REALLY A MAN OF SOME PERCEPTION
MIS. PREFACE(15) GETTING RID OF IT ALTOGETHER ON MORE OR LESS HYPOCRITICAL PRETENCES) AND KEEPING IT CONTINUALLY AT HOME.
BARB PREFACE(222) AND PROFANEST FARCE CAN NO MORE DEPRIVE IT THAN A HYPOCRITICAL SERMON BY A SNOBBISH BISHOP CAN DESECRATE
OVER PREFACE(155) VIRTUE OF THE LIBERTINE IS THEREFORE NO MORE HYPOCRITICAL THAN THE PLEA OF NOT GUILTY WHICH IS ALLOWED TO
GETT PREFACE(214) WILL SERVE AS WELL AS ANOTHER; FOR IT WOULD BE HYPOCRITICAL TO PRETEND THAT THE DIFFICULTY IS A PRACTICAL
SUPR I (39) THROW AWAY EVEN YOUR HYPOCRISY? /ANN/ I AM NEVER HYPOCRITICAL WITH YOU, JACK. ARE YOU ANGRY? (SHE WITHDRAWS
OVER PREFACE(167) HAVE HAD YOU KILLED IN A MUCH LESS DISGUSTING, HYPOCRITICAL , AND UNFRIENDLY MANNER IF THE MATTER HAD BEEN
DOCT IV (168) LET US BE HONEST. TELL THE TRUTH, PADDY. DONT BE HYPOCRITICAL , RIDGEON. THROW OFF THE MASK, WALPOLE. ARE
BULL PREFACE(39) WITH FINLAND AND MACEDONIA RIDICULOUS AND HYPOCRITICAL , WHILST THE PRIEST TAKES ALL THE SPOILS, IN

HYPOCRITICALLY

SUPR HANDBOK(204) WITCHCRAFT WE DO BELIEVE IN, BUT CALLOUSLY AND HYPOCRITICALLY IN THE NAME OF THE EVANGELICAL CREED THAT OUR
POSN PREFACE(396) PROVIDED THE TREATMENT OF THE THEME IS GAILY OR HYPOCRITICALLY POPULAR, AND THE ENDING HAPPY, THE INDULGENCE
BARB PREFACE(223) AN ELABORATE MOCKERY OF THE ARMY. AND THEN EITHER HYPOCRITICALLY REBUKE ME FOR MOCKING, OR FOOLISHLY TAKE PART
WIDO II (24) MEET HIM UNTIL HE HAS SPOKEN TO ME. /BLANCHE/ (HYPOCRITICALLY) OF COURSE NOT, PAPA. I SHOULDNT HAVE

HYPOTENUSES

KING I (166) NUMBERS! NUMBERS! NUMBERS! SINES, COSINES, HYPOTENUSES , FLUXIONS, CURVES SMALL ENOUGH TO COUNT AS

HYPOTHECARY

MTH3 (107) OLD CHAP. (CONFUCIUS SITS DOWN AGAIN). THIS HYPOTHECARY , OR WHATEVER YOU CALL IT, IS PUT UP SERIOUSLY.

HYPOTHENUSE

FABL PREFACE(94) FIRST FIVE AND THE ONE ABOUT THE SQUARE OF THE HYPOTHENUSE . THE NEXT STEP WAS ALGEBRA, AGAIN WITHOUT A

HYPOTHESES

SUPR HANDBOK(184) OF THE CHURCH. ONE NEED NOT FURTHER PURSUE THESE HYPOTHESES : THEY ARE ONLY SUGGESTED HERE TO HELP THE READER
ROCK PREFACE(173) IT CAN ONLY SELECT THE MOST USEFUL WORKING HYPOTHESES AND INCULCATE THEM VERY MUCH AS IT INCULCATES
ROCK PREFACE(173) AS IN THE RULE OF THE ROAD. ALL THE PROVISIONAL HYPOTHESES MAY BE ILLUSIONS; BUT IF THEY CONDUCE TO
ROCK PREFACE(173) MOSTLY ILLUSORY, BUT, CRY THE PROFESSORS, ARE THE HYPOTHESES NEVER TO BE QUESTIONED? IS DISILLUSION TO BE
LADY PREFACE(211) WORK WAS NOT WASTED: IT IS BY EXHAUSTING ALL THE HYPOTHESES THAT WE REACH THE VERIFIABLE ONE; AND AFTER ALL,

HYPOTHESIS

MTH3 (105) THAT I HAVE LIVED NEARLY THREE CENTURIES? AS A HYPOTHESIS ? /BURGE-LUBIN/ WHAT IS A HYPOTHESIS?
MTH3 (105) AS A HYPOTHESIS? /BURGE-LUBIN/ WHAT IS A HYPOTHESIS ? /CONFUCIUS/ IT DOES NOT MATTER. I UNDERSTAND.
MIS. PREFACE(44) INTELLECTUAL SPECULATION, WITH ITS ROUTINE OF HYPOTHESIS AND VERIFICATION, INDUCTION AND DEDUCTION; OR
METH PREFACE(R66) A SUPREME BEING IN PRACTICAL POLITICS, SOME SUCH HYPOTHESIS HAD BEEN FOUND QUITE INDISPENSABLE, AND COULD NOT
MTH3 (106) ANSWER ME THAT. /CONFUCIUS/ CERTAINLY NOT. THE HYPOTHESIS IS THAT HE HAS WORKED CONTINUOUSLY SINCE 1910. WE
ROCK PREFACE(173) AS ANYTHING MORE THAN ANOTHER PROVISIONAL HYPOTHESIS . IT DIFFERS FROM THE OLD DUBLIN BRIMSTONE CREED
METH PREFACE(R36) AS IT GOES ALONG, WHEREAS A MAKER FOR IT IS A HYPOTHESIS . OF COURSE WE COULD GET NO FURTHER ON THESE
LADY PREFACE(223) HAVE IT SHE DID, IS AN EXTREMELY UNSHAKESPEARIAN HYPOTHESIS . " MEN HAVE DIED FROM TIME TO TIME, AND WORMS
METH PREFACE(R40) DESIGN COULD BE EXPLAINED WITHOUT RESORT TO THE HYPOTHESIS OF A PERSONAL DESIGNER. IF ONLY SOME GENIUS,
BARB PREFACE(209) OUT OF THE STENDHALIAN ATMOSPHERE. I EXCLUDE THE HYPOTHESIS OF COMPLETE ORIGINALITY ON LEVER'S PART, BECAUSE
BUOY PREFACE(6) HIS EXTRAORDINARY MENTAL GIFTS ANY LESS THAN HIS HYPOTHESIS OF GRAVITATION, WHICH MIGHT HAVE OCCURRED TO
FABL PREFACE(87) IN SOCIAL ORGANIZATION, ON A PROVISIONAL HYPOTHESIS OR FRAME OF REFERENCE (A NECESSARY TOOL OF
FABL PREFACE(87) THE WAY AND THE LIFE, HAVING ONLY A QUESTIONABLE HYPOTHESIS OR TWO TO OFFER; BUT THAT IS THE HEROIC LABEL
MIS. PREFACE(48) WHO BELIEVES THAT HE HAS MORE THAN A PROVISIONAL HYPOTHESIS TO GO UPON IS A BORN FOOL. HE MAY HAVE TO ACT
JOAN PREFACE(12) BEEN LOCKED UP. GRAVITATION, BEING A REASONED HYPOTHESIS WHICH FITTED REMARKABLY WELL INTO THE COPERNICAN
ROCK PREFACE(173) REGARD THIS AS ANYTHING MORE THAN A PROVISIONAL HYPOTHESIS WHICH, ON CONSIDERATION, I MUST DEFINITELY
DOCT PREFACE(40) BUT SCIENCE HAS TO CONSIDER ONLY THE TRUTH OF THE HYPOTHESIS , AND NOT WHETHER CONCEITED PEOPLE WILL LIKE IT
METH PREFACE(R88) UNTIL I COULD CONCEIVE IT AS A SCIENTIFIC HYPOTHESIS , EVEN THOUGH THE ABOMINATIONS, QUACKERIES,
3PLA PREFACE(R21) MADE BY WORKING OUT A METEOROLOGICAL OR ECONOMIC HYPOTHESIS , THE EXTENT TO WHICH IT IS CARRIED IN
DOCT PREFACE(40) FORWARD A STRICTLY SCIENTIFIC PSYCHOLOGICAL HYPOTHESIS , WHICH IS ALSO SIMPLE, HUMAN, OBVIOUS, AND

HYPOTHETICAL

ROCK PREFACE(179) IN DEBATE AND REPARTEE, FULL OF THE ILLUSTRATIVE HYPOTHETICAL CASES BELOVED OF LAWYERS (CALLED PARABLES IN

HYPROCISY

GETT PREFACE(195) AND EXACERBATED, PRODUCES DEBAUCHERY VEILED BY HYPROCISY , AN OVERWHELMING DEMAND FOR LICENTIOUS THEATRICAL

HYSTERIA

LION PREFACE(83)	HISTORY, AND NEVER " WORKED UP" AN AUDIENCE TO	HYSTERIA	. IT AIMS AT A PURELY NERVOUS EFFECT; IT BRINGS NO
BARB III (313)	DIED OF EMOTION. JENNY HILL SIMPLY GIBBERED WITH	HYSTERIA	. THE PRINCE OF DARKNESS PLAYED HIS TROMBONE LIKE A
MRS PREFACE(175)	OUTRAGING IT. THEY INFECTED EACH OTHER WITH THEIR	HYSTERIA	UNTIL THEY WERE FOR ALL PRACTICAL PURPOSES

HYSTERICAL

MRS IV (246)	GRAVELY ON SEEING MRS WARREN, WHO GREETS HER WITH	HYSTERICAL	CHEERFULNESS). WELL, DEARIE. SO HERE YOU ARE AT
BULL IV (164)	HAVE NO RIGHT TO RUIN MY WHOLE LIFE. YOU-- (A	HYSTERICAL	CONVULSION STOPS HIM). /NORA/ (ALMOST AWESTRUCK)
MTH4 I (144)	UNINTELLIGIBLY WITH MOMENTS OF SENSE DISTRESSED	HYSTERICAL	FOREIGN DRESS VERY FUNNY HAS CURIOUS FRINGE OF
3PLA PREFACE(R22)	NATION IN EUROPE TO THE MOST THEATRICAL AND	HYSTERICAL	. IS IT CLEAR NOW, WHY THE THEATRE WAS
2TRU II (73)	SEEM TO LIKE IT ANY BETTER. /AUBREY/ MOPS: YOURE	HYSTERICAL	. YOU FELT SPLENDID AN HOUR AGO; AND YOU WILL
BULL IV (162)	EYES OF NORA CRYNA-- /NORA/ (SPLUTTERING INTO A	HYSTERICAL	LAUGH AND CLUTCHING HIM CONVULSIVELY WITH HER
BULL PREFACE(47)	ANY THOROUGHNESS EXCEPT WHEN, IN AN OCCASIONAL	HYSTERICAL	OUTBURST OF TERROR AND VIOLENCE, THAT HACKNEYED
DOCT PREFACE(40)	ANSWERS THAT THE QUESTION CANNOT BE SETTLED BY	HYSTERICAL	PROTESTATIONS, AND THAT IF THE VIVISECTIONIST
HART PREFACE(23)	THAT THIS COULD NOT HAVE BEEN DONE BY A MOB OF	HYSTERICAL	RANTERS. THIS IS FORTUNATELY TRUE. TO PASS FROM
PYGM I (209)	A SORT OF INFORMER. /THE FLOWER GIRL/ (STILL	HYSTERICAL	) I TAKE MY BIBLE OATH I NEVER SAID A WORD-- /THE
CATH 4 (191)	WORD OF GERMAN; BUT THAT SOUNDED KIND. (BECOMING	HYSTERICAL	) LITTLE MOTHER, BEAUTIFUL LITTLE DARLING ANGEL
ROCK II (284)	TWO WORDS. " ENGLAND, ARISE." /HILDA/ (SUDDENLY	HYSTERICAL	) OH, MY GOD! I WILL GO OUT AND JOIN THEM (SHE
MRS PREFACE(152)	KNOWN THE EXULTATION OF SENDING THE PRESS INTO AN	HYSTERICAL	TUMULT OF PROTEST, OF MORAL PANIC, OF INVOLUNTARY
SUPR III (98)	/DON JUAN/ (WITH COLD DISGUST) YOU TALK LIKE A	HYSTERICAL	WOMAN FAWNING ON A FIDDLER. /THE DEVIL/ I AM NOT
PRES (155)	TO PUT MY FOOT DOWN-- /LADY CORINTHIA/ DONT BE	HYSTERICAL	, GENERAL. /MITCHENER/ HYSTERICAL! /MRS BANGER/
BULL PREFACE(46)	DESTRUCTIVE, CRUEL, DISHONEST, TYRANNICAL,	HYSTERICAL	, MENDACIOUS, ALARMISTS AT HOME AND TERRORISTS
BULL PREFACE(16)	A PENNY THE WORSE); BUT HE IS NEVER QUITE THE	HYSTERICAL	, NONSENSE-CRAMMED, FACT-PROOF, TRUTH-TERRIFIED,
PRES (155)	DONT BE HYSTERICAL, GENERAL. /MITCHENER/	HYSTERICAL	! /MRS BANGER/ DO YOU THINK WE ARE TO BE STOPPED

HYSTERICALLY

WIDO II (47)	TEMPTED HIM AFTER ALL. (SHE THROWS HER ARMS	HYSTERICALLY	ABOUT HIS NECK) PAPA: I DONT WANT TO MARRY: I
ROCK II (244)	DAMN THEM. (HE WIPES HIS BROW AND ADDS, RATHER	HYSTERICALLY	) EXCUSE ME, BOYS; BUT IF YOU SAW THE BLAYPORT
JITT III (69)	REALLY AND TRULY. /JITTA/ (BEGINNING TO LAUGH	HYSTERICALLY	) HOW FUNNY! /AGNES/ (HER CHUCKLES NOW
POSN (460)	OR WAS HE NOT? YES OR NO? /FEEMY/ A LITTLE	HYSTERICALLY	) I'LL TELL YOU FAST ENOUGH. DONT THINK I'M A
PYGM I (208)	A RIGHT TO SELL FLOWERS IF I KEEP OFF THE KERB. (	HYSTERICALLY	) I'M A RESPECTABLE GIRL: SO HELP ME, I NEVER
PPP (201)	RUSHES IN STRAIGHT TO MAGNESIA. /PHYLLIS/ (	HYSTERICALLY	) MY BELOVED MISTRESS, ONCE MORE WE MEET. (SHE
MRS IV (241)	PROPENSITY THAT WAY, DONT IT? /VIVIE/ (ALMOST	HYSTERICALLY	) OH YES: GO ON: DONT SPARE ME. I WAS
HART I (50)	(HE PLACES IT ON THE TRAY). /LADY UTTERWORD/ (	HYSTERICALLY	) PAPA: YOU CANT HAVE FORGOTTEN ME. I AM
CATH 4 (190)	EDSTASTON'S RIBS). /EDSTASTON/ (SHRIEKING	HYSTERICALLY	) YAGH! AH! (FURIOUSLY) IF YOUR MAJESTY DOES
JITT III SD(70)	JITTA, LEFT ALONE, BEGINS TO LAUGH AGAIN	HYSTERICALLY	, AND IS DISSOLVING INTO CONVULSIVE SOBS WHEN
PHIL II (126)	QUIETLY) NOTHING, DEAR. THERES NO ROW. /JULIA/ (	HYSTERICALLY	, TOTTERING AND STRETCHING OUT HER ARMS TO

HYSTERICS

APPL I (214)	WHY NOT, IF THE HORSE YOU HAVE GOT IS SUBJECT TO	HYSTERICS	? /BOANERGES/ NOT TO MENTION THAT YOU MAY HAVE
ROCK I (204)	/FLAVIA/ (IRRESISTIBLE AMUSEMENT STRUGGLING WITH	HYSTERICS	AND GETTING THE BETTER OF THEM) HA HA! HA HA HA!
APPL I (223)	ONLY POSSIBLE PRIME MINISTER, IN SPITE OF YOUR	HYSTERICS	AND TANTRUMS, YOUR SECRETIVENESS AND YOUR
2TRU I (38)	/THE NURSE/ YES. IT'S A CURE FOR SCREAMING AND	HYSTERICS	AND TANTRUMS. WHEN A WOMAN STARTS MAKING A ROW,
CAND III (136)	NO, NO: SHE'LL THINK IVE THROWN YOU INTO	HYSTERICS	. DONT LAUGH. BOISTEROUS VOICES AND LAUGHTER ARE
JITT III (69)	ME LAUGH ANY MORE: I AM AFRAID I SHALL GO INTO	HYSTERICS	. I AM STILL VERY FAR FROM WELL. /AGNES/ IT'S SUCH
MILL I (158)	UNTIL I FELL ON THE FLOOR OF MY BOX IN SCREAMING	HYSTERICS	. THE AUDIENCE HOOTED AND BOOED; BUT THEY COULD
DOCT PREFACE(38)	TAMING THE YOUNG HUMAN ANIMAL. YET WE WERE ALL IN	HYSTERICS	OF INDIGNATION AT THE CRUELTIES OF THE
MIS. (198)	I DONT GRUDGE YOU THAT. /TARLETON/ (ALMOST IN	HYSTERICS	) I USED TO THINK THAT THIS SORT OF THING WENT ON
CAND I (101)	ME, I'LL KILL MYSELF: I WONT BEAR IT. (ALMOST IN	HYSTERICS	) LET ME GO. TAKE YOUR HAND AWAY. /MORELL/ (WITH
SUPR III (82)	TO DO IT WITH. I HINTED AT MURDER: SHE WENT INTO	HYSTERICS	; AND AS I AM A LIVING MAN I WENT TO AMERICA SO

HYSTEROID

JOAN PREFACE(16)	HER INCURABLY HYPERPITUITARY OR HYPERADRENAL OR	HYSTEROID	OR EPILEPTOID OR ANYTHING BUT ASTEROID. SHE WOULD

IACHIMO

CYMB V (140)	HOPES OF ANY HELP FROM YOU. WHERE, THINK YOU, IS	IACHIMO	? /CAPTAIN/ I KNOW NOT. AND YET I THINK HE CANNOT
CYMB V SD(142)	THERE. MAKE FAST THE ROMAN. GUIDERIUS POUNCES ON	IACHIMO	AND DISARMS HIM. ARVIRAGUS PULLS POSTHUMUS BACK.
CYMB FORWORD(136)	BROTHERS AND CYMBELINE'S LONG LOST SONS; THAT	IACHIMO	IS NOW AN OCCUPANT OF THE PENITENT FORM AND VERY
CYMB V (139)	FIND OUT HOW FARES OUR RIGHT WING LED BY GENERAL	IACHIMO	. /CAPTAIN/ HE IS OUTGENERALLED. THERE'S NO RIGHT
CYMB V (143)	SINCE THOU LIV'ST. /IMOGEN/ MY PARAMOUR! (TO	IACHIMO	) OH, AS YOU ARE A GENTLEMAN, GIVE HIM THE LIE.
CYMB FORWORD(134)	PLAY AT THE OLD LYCEUM THEATRE, WHEN IRVING, AS	IACHIMO	, A STATUE OF ROMANTIC MELANCHOLY, STOOD DUMB ON THE
CYMB V SD(141)	HE IS HURRYING OFF WHEN HE IS CONFRONTED WITH	IACHIMO	, BATTLE STAINED, HURRYING IN THE OPPOSITE
CYMB FORWORD(136)	THESE INFANTILE JOYS, HAVING BECOME INTERESTED IN	IACHIMO	, IN IMOGEN, AND EVEN IN THE TWO LONG LOST PRINCES,
CYMB V (140)	/PHILARIO/ YOU WERE BEST COME WITH ME. FAILING	IACHIMO	, LUCIUS WILL REQUIRE YOUR TALE AT FIRST HAND.
CYMB V (141)	A BRITISH ENEMY HE DRAWS HIS SWORD. /POSTHUMUS/	IACHIMO	! PEACE, MAN: 'TIS I, POSTHUMUS. /IACHIMO/ PEACE IF
SUPR III (126)	THE DASTARDLY SEDUCER! WHAT SCENES OF IMOGEN AND	IACHIMO	! /ANA/ I MADE NO SCENES. I SIMPLY CALLED MY

IAGO

MRS PREFACE(153)	IN THE WAPPING GALLERY, WHO SHOUTS EXECRATIONS AT	IAGO	AND WARNINGS TO OTHELLO NOT TO BELIEVE HIM! BUT DEARER
MRS PREFACE(172)	ON RELIGION. ACCORDING TO THIS VIEW SUBALTERN	IAGO	IS AN ATTACK ON THE ARMY, SIR JOHN FALSTAFF AN ATTACK

IBERIAN

CLEO III (153)	UP IN IT TEN PRECIOUS GOBLETS OF THE THINNEST	IBERIAN	CRYSTAL, AND A HUNDRED EGGS OF THE SACRED BLUE

IBSEN

LION PREFACE(94)	A CROWN OF GLORY AS WELL! THAT WAS TOO MUCH FOR	IBSEN	: IT PROVOKED HIM TO EXCLAIM, P YOUR GOD IS AN OLD MAN
LION PREFACE(93)	ME NOTHING." THEN, TOO, THERE IS THE ATTITUDE OF	IBSEN	: THAT IRON MORALIST TO WHOM THE WHOLE SCHEME OF
3PLA PREFACE(R37)	HAVE EXPRESSED THEM ANY WORSE THAN GOETHE OR	IBSEN	? HUMAN FACULTY BEING WHAT IT IS, IS IT LIKELY THAT
3PLA PREFACE(R12)	IMPRACTICABLE FADDISTS FOR PRODUCING THE PLAYS OF	IBSEN	AND MAETERLINCK, THEN WHAT EPITHET IS CONTEMPTUOUS
UNPL PREFACE(R20)	BAYREUTH ON THE COSTLIEST SCALE; AND READERS OF	IBSEN	AND MAETERLINCK, AND PIANOFORTE STUDENTS OF WAGNER,
POSN PREFACE(419)	ZOLA, AND SWINBURNE, OR PRODUCE THE PLAYS OF	IBSEN	AND MR GRANVILLE BARKER, OR PRINT AN ORDINARY
BARB PREFACE(221)	I AM MET WITH NOTHING BUT VAGUE CACKLINGS ABOUT	IBSEN	AND NIETZSCHE, AND AM ONLY TOO THANKFUL THAT THEY ARE
METH PREFACE(R86)	HEAVENS. THE GIANTS OF THE THEATRE OF OUR TIME,	IBSEN	AND STRINDBERG, HAD NO GREATER COMFORT FOR THE WORLD
SIM PREFACE(3)	SOPHOCLES AND EURIPIDES, SHAKESPEAR AND GOETHE,	IBSEN	AND STRINDBERG, TOLSTOY AND TCHEKOV, TO SAY NOTHING OF
MRS PREFACE(165)	BE THAT THE EXAMINER WILL FIND HIS NATURAL LEVEL;	IBSEN	AND TOLSTOY THEIRS; SO NO HARM WILL BE DONE. THIS
MRS PREFACE(159)	THE CENSORSHIP, THOUGH IT CERTAINLY SUPPRESSES	IBSEN	AND TOLSTOY, AND WOULD SUPPRESS SHAKESPEAR BUT FOR THE
PHIL PREFACE(68)	CALLED THE UNINTELLIGENTSIA WAS AS UNCONSCIOUS OF	IBSEN	AS OF ANY OTHER POLITICAL INFLUENCE: QUARTER OF A
POSN PREFACE(399)	OF CHARACTER AND RANGE OF VISION WHICH MADE	IBSEN	CAPABLE OF IT ARE NOT TO BE EXPECTED FROM ANY
MRS PREFACE(153)	AND THE RUIN OF THE STATE AT HAND. EVEN THE	IBSEN	CHAMPIONS OF TEN YEARS AGO REMONSTRATE WITH ME JUST AS
PHIL I (89)	(OUTRAGED) DADDY! /CHARTERIS/ NOT AT THE	IBSEN	CLUB: QUITE THE CONTRARY. AFTER ALL, WHAT CAN WE DO..
PHIL PREFACE(68)	US IN 1889. THE STATE OF MIND REPRESENTED BY THE	IBSEN	CLUB IN THIS PLAY WAS FAMILIAR THEN TO OUR
PHIL I (88)	MANLY MEN AND DEUCE KNOWS WHAT ELSE. IS IT AT THE	IBSEN	CLUB THAT YOU SEE ALL THIS MANLINESS AND WOMANLINESS?
PHIL II SD(94)	ACT II. NEXT DAY AT NOON, IN THE LIBRARY OF THE	IBSEN	CLUB. A LONG ROOM, WITH GLASS DOORS HALF-WAY DOWN ON
PHIL I (87)	CLUB! I SHOULD BE LAUGHED OUT OF LONDON. THE	IBSEN	CLUB! COME, CUTHBERTSON! BACK ME UP. I'M SURE YOU
PHIL I (87)	BESIDES, NOW REALLY, SUCH A NAME FOR A CLUB! THE	IBSEN	CLUB! I SHOULD BE LAUGHED OUT OF LONDON. THE IBSEN
LADY PREFACE(233)	AS AUTOLYCUS DID: HE SAW IT, IF NOT EXACTLY AS	IBSEN	DID (FOR IT WAS NOT QUITE THE SAME WORLD), AT LEAST
PLES PREFACE(R9)	OF SHELLEY, SHALL HAVE REACHED THE VALLEYS. LET	IBSEN	EXPLAIN, IF HE CAN, WHY THE BUILDING OF CHURCHES AND
PHIL II (104)	COME, GENTLEMEN: LET US GO TO LUNCH IN THE	IBSEN	FASHION: THE UNSEXED FASHION. (HE TURNS AND GOES OUT,
PHIL I (73)	AND TO NOBODY ELSE. /CHARTERIS/ QUITE RIGHT.	IBSEN	FOR EVER! THATS EXACTLY MY OPINION. NOW TELL ME, DO I
LADY PREFACE(233)	THEY CANNOT PRODUCE POPULAR WORK. TAKE WAGNER AND	IBSEN	FOR INSTANCE! THEIR EARLIER WORKS ARE NO DOUBT MUCH
POSN PREFACE(399)	BE DIABOLICAL, IT IS NO EXAGGERATION TO SAY THAT	IBSEN	GAINED HIS OVERWHELMING REPUTATION BY UNDERTAKING A
POSN PREFACE(397)	WITHOUT RISK. THE PROHIBITED PLAYS OF BRIEUX AND	IBSEN	HAVE BEEN PERFORMED IN LONDON IN THIS WAY WITH
CYMB FORWORD(135)	WHO WITH HIS WIFE JANET ACHURCH BROKE THE ICE FOR	IBSEN	IN ENGLAND, USED TO CITE POSTHUMUS AS SHAKESPEAR'S
SUPR PREFACE(R35)	WAGNER IN TERMS OF POLYTHEISTIC MYTHOLOGY; AND	IBSEN	IN TERMS OF MID-XIX CENTURY PARISIAN DRAMATURGY.

3PLA PREFACE(R17) THEATRES TODAY. FOR INSTANCE, THE OBJECTION TO IBSEN IS NOT REALLY AN OBJECTION TO HIS PHILOSOPHY: IT IS A
SUPR PREFACE(R31) BEARABLE AFTER MEDIEVAL POESY THAN SCRIBE AFTER IBSEN . AS I SAT WATCHING EVERYMAN AT THE CHARTERHOUSE, I
PHIL PREFACE(68) HIDEOUSLY SLAUGHTERED WAS OFFERED TO THEM BY IBSEN . I MAKE NO ATTEMPT TO BRING THE PLAY UP TO DATE. I
SUPR PREFACE(R12) IN THE MIND TO (AS THEY THOUGHT) EMULATE IBSEN . I TAKE IT THAT WHEN YOU ASKED ME FOR A DON JUAN PLAY
3PLA PREFACE(R15) WANTED WAS TO CAPTURE SOME OF THE FASCINATION OF IBSEN . IT SEEMED TO THEM THAT MOST OF IBSEN'S HEROINES WERE
MIS. (130) /TARLETON/ BEEF! BE BLOWED! JOY OF LIFE. READ IBSEN . (HE GOES INTO THE PAVILION TO RELIEVE HIS
PHIL II (117) HENRIK? /CUTHBERTSON/ (IMPATIENTLY) IBSEN, MAN: IBSEN . (HE GOES OUT BY THE STAIRCASE DOOR, FOLLOWED BY
BARB PREFACE(208) HENRI BEYLE, ALIAS STENDHAL, CERTAINLY NEVER READ IBSEN . OF THE BOOKS THAT MADE LEVER POPULAR, SUCH AS
PHIL I SD(69) BUT NOT ELEONORA DUSE NOR ANY ONE CONNECTED WITH IBSEN . THE ROOM IS NOT RECTANGULAR, ONE CORNER BEING CUT
PLES PREFACE(R12) AUTHORS. AN ORIGINAL WORK BY A MAN OF GENIUS LIKE IBSEN MAY, OF COURSE, BAFFLE HIM AS IT BAFFLES MANY
3PLA PREFACE(R18) APPLAUD ITS PAINTER, AND THINK THE FUSS AGAINST IBSEN MEANS NOTHING MORE THAN THE CONVENTIONAL DISAPPROVAL
PYGM PREFACE(199) ABOUT AS CONCILIATORY TO CONVENTIONAL MORTALS AS IBSEN OR SAMUEL BUTLER. HIS GREAT ABILITY AS A PHONETICIAN (
3PLA PREFACE(R15) WERE NAUGHTY LADIES. AND THEY TRIED TO PRODUCE IBSEN PLAYS BY MAKING THEIR HEROINES NAUGHTY. BUT THEY TOOK
OVER PREFACE(161) PARISIAN SCHOOL WHICH DOMINATED THE STAGE UNTIL IBSEN PUT THEM OUT OF COUNTENANCE AND RELEGATED THEM TO
HART PREFACE(39) ARISTOPHANES, SHAKESPEAR AND MOLIERE, GOETHE AND IBSEN REMAIN FIXED IN THEIR EVERLASTING SEATS. HOW WAR
PHIL II (95) TURNS TO THE FIRE, AND AGAIN BURIES HERSELF IN IBSEN). /CUTHBERTSON/ (WITH EMPHATIC
PHIL I (73) OF HIM). EH, LITTLE PHILOSOPHER? NO, MY DEAR: IF IBSEN SAUCE IS GOOD FOR THE GOOSE, IT'S GOOD FOR THE GANDER
MRS PREFACE(152) EIGHT YEARS; AND I HAVE ONCE MORE SHARED WITH IBSEN THE TRIUMPHANT AMUSEMENT OF STARTLING ALL BUT THE
METH PREFACE(R87) STILL UNTOUCHED BY CREATIVE EVOLUTION IN 1920. IBSEN WAS DARWINIZED TO THE EXTENT OF EXPLOITING HEREDITY ON
FANY EPILOG (332) EVEN SUCH A PLAYED-OUT OLD BACK NUMBER AS IBSEN WOULD HAVE BEEN ASHAMED OF IT. HEART AND BRAIN,
POSN PREFACE(399) VIEWS, PERCEIVE THAT ANY NATION WHICH SUPPRESSED IBSEN WOULD PRESENTLY FIND ITSELF FALLING BEHIND THE NATIONS
PHIL II SD(94) BY A HANDSOME MANTELPIECE, WITH A BUST OF IBSEN , AND DECORATIVE INSCRIPTIONS OF THE TITLES OF HIS
UNPL PREFACE(R20) FROM THE EXPERIMENTS OF CHARLES CHARRINGTON WITH IBSEN , AND OF LUGNE POE WITH MAETERLINCK, UNDER
POSN PREFACE(390) OF SHAKESPEAR AND GOETHE, OF TOLSTOY AND IBSEN , AND THE MASTER THE HOLDER OF A PARTY APPOINTMENT
MRS PREFACE(159) ARISTOPHANES, EURIPIDES, SHAKESPEAR, GOETHE, IBSEN , AND TOLSTOY, NOT TO MENTION OUR OWN CONTEMPORARY
POSN PREFACE(368) IT WAS BECAUSE CERTAIN SEVERELY VIRTUOUS PLAYS BY IBSEN , BY M. BRIEUX, BY MR GRANVILLE BARKER, AND BY ME,
UNPL PREFACE(R22) IN THE MIDDLE? IT IS ASTONISHING TO ME THAT IBSEN , DEVOTING TWO YEARS TO THE PRODUCTION OF A THREE-ACT
3PLA PREFACE(R15) AS LYCEUM SHAKESPEAR, MUSICAL FARCE, OR SHAM IBSEN , FINALLY DISGUSTED ME, NOT BECAUSE I WAS PHARISAICAL,
UNPL PREFACE(R23) PRODUCED AT THE COST OF INTELLECTUAL OBSCURITY? IBSEN , INTERROGATED AS TO HIS MEANING, REPLIED " WHAT I
SUPR PREFACE(R36) EXACTLY WHAT IS COMPLAINED OF IN NIETZSCHE AND IBSEN , IS IT NOT? AND ALSO EXACTLY WHAT WOULD BE
UNPL PREFACE(R11) HAVE COME INTO EXISTENCE BUT FOR THE PLAYS OF IBSEN , JUST AS THE BAYREUTH FESTIVAL PLAYHOUSE WOULD NEVER
PHIL II SD(94) IT, IS A GREEN TABLE, LITTERED WITH JOURNALS. IBSEN , LOOKING DOWN THE ROOM, HAS THE DINING ROOM DOOR ON
PHIL II (117) (PUZZLED) HENRIK? /CUTHBERTSON/ (IMPATIENTLY) IBSEN , MAN: IBSEN. (HE GOES OUT BY THE STAIRCASE DOOR,
SUPR PREFACE(R31) CLASSICS), GOETHE, SHELLEY, SCHOPENHAUER, WAGNER, IBSEN , MORRIS, TOLSTOY, AND NIETZSCHE ARE AMONG THE WRITERS
FABL PREFACE(66) SHAKESPEAR, DANTE AND MICHAEL ANGELO, GOETHE AND IBSEN , NEWTON AND EINSTEIN, ADAM SMITH AND KARL MARX ARRIVE
GETT PREFACE(192) THE NATURAL SUPERIORS OF BEETHOVEN, OF RODIN, OF IBSEN , OF TOLSTOY AND ALL OTHER BENIGHTED FOREIGNERS. THOSE
UNPL PREFACE(R17) ALL THE CLASSIC DRAMATISTS, FROM ESCHYLUS TO IBSEN , ONLY GO TO THE THEATRE ON THE RARE OCCASIONS WHEN
PHIL II SD(94) THE SETTEE BEFORE THE FIRE, READING A VOLUME OF IBSEN , ONLY THE BACK OF HER HEAD BEING VISIBLE FROM THE
METH PREFACE(R86) OF GOETHE. HE, NO RICHER THAN SHAKESPEAR, IBSEN , OR STRINDBERG IN SPECIFIC TALENT AS A PLAYWRIGHT, IS
CATH PREFACE(157) ANY CONCERN WITH ONE ANOTHER: TOM ROBERTSON, IBSEN , PINERO, AND BARRIE MIGHT AS WELL HAVE BELONGED TO A
BARB PREFACE(207) THAT I AM ECHOING SCHOPENHAUER, NIETZSCHE, IBSEN , STRINDBERG, TOLSTOY, OR SOME OTHER HERESIARCH IN
UNPL PREFACE(R12) THAT NOBODY BELIEVES CANNOT BE PROVED TOO OFTEN. IBSEN , THEN, WAS THE HERO OF THE NEW DEPARTURE. IT WAS IN
BARB PREFACE(226) MONTAIGNE, MOLIERE, BEAUMARCHAIS, SWIFT, GOETHE, IBSEN , TOLSTOY, JESUS AND THE PROPHETS ALL THROWN IN (AS
POSN PREFACE(400) THE PLAYS OF EURIPIDES BECAUSE EURIPIDES, LIKE IBSEN , WAS A REVOLUTIONARY FREETHINKER. UNDER THE LORD
LION PREFACE(72) JUST AS WEAK, JUST AS COWARDLY AS SELF-DENIAL. IBSEN , WHO TAKES US INTO THE MATTER FAR MORE RESOLUTELY
MTH3 (124) UNSPARINGLY. AT THE CANONIZATION OF SAINT HENRIK IBSEN , YOU YOURSELF UNVEILED THE MONUMENT TO HIM WHICH
PHIL II (109) I KNOW FOR MAKING YOURSELF NASTY. /SYLVIA/ BOSH! IBSEN ! /CHARTERIS/ (TO THE PAGE) OFF WITH YOU, MY BOY: DR

IBSENISM

PHIL II (96) NOR SUPERSTITION, PARAMORE: IT'S SHEER DOWNRIGHT IBSENISM : THATS WHAT IT IS. IVE BEEN WANTING TO SIT
BARB PREFACE(208) TEN YEARS LATER, TO BE PERFUNCTORILY LABELLED IBSENISM ? I WAS NOT IBSENIST EVEN AT SECOND HAND; FOR
PHIL II (96) A SPLENDID FINE CREATURE: EVERY INCH A WOMAN. NO IBSENISM ABOUT HER! /PARAMORE/ I QUITE AGREE WITH YOU
BARB PREFACE(209) NOWADAYS CAUSES CRITICS TO RAISE A CRY OF IBSENISM . I THEREFORE ASSURE THEM THAT THE SENSATION FIRST
PHIL III (145) (OUTRAGED) SYMBOLIC! THAT IS AN ACCUSATION OF IBSENISM . WHAT DO YOU MEAN? /CHARTERIS/ SYMBOLIC OF THE
3PLA PREFACE(R24) THE LITTLE THEY KNOW IN MY QUINTESSENCE OF IBSENISM ; AND NOW THEY TURN THEIR GUNS-- THE GUNS I LOADED
BARB PREFACE(211) MISS BORCHARDT, WHO HAD READ MY QUINTESSENCE OF IBSENISM , AND TOLD ME THAT SHE SAW WHAT I HAD BEEN READING:
UNPL PREFACE(R13) FOLLOWING YEAR, 1893, WHEN THE DISCUSSION ABOUT IBSENISM , " THE NEW WOMAN," AND THE LIKE, WAS AT ITS

IBSENIST

BARB PREFACE(208) TO BE PERFUNCTORILY LABELLED IBSENISM? I WAS NOT IBSENIST EVEN AT SECOND HAND; FOR LEVER, THOUGH HE MAY HAVE
PHIL I (85) INTRODUCE YOU TO MR LEONARD CHARTERIS, THE FAMOUS IBSENIST PHILOSOPHER. /CRAVEN/ OH, WE KNOW ONE ANOTHER
PHIL I (78) A HUMAN BEING, I THINK THAT WAS HOW YOU PUT THE IBSENIST VIEW: OUR VIEW. SO I HAD TO BE CONTENT WITH A

IBSENITE

FANY EPILOG (328) TO ME THE MOST ORDINARY SORT OF OLD-FASHIONED IBSENITE DRIVEL. /THE COUNT/ (TURNING TO TROTTER, WHO IS ON
SUPR PREFACE(R20) DOCTOR IN ALL'S WELL THAT ENDS WELL (AN EARLY IBSENITE HEROINE) CAPTURES BERTRAM. BUT THE MATURE CASES ALL
PHIL II (108) FOR SHAME! HOWEVER, ANYTHING TO OBLIGE A FELLOW IBSENITE . I'LL BEAR YOUR AFFAIR IN MIND. BUT I THINK IT

IBSEN'S

SUPR PREFACE(R15) WITH PHILOSOPHIC FICTION BY SUCH PENS AS IBSEN'S AND TOLSTOY'S, DON JUAN HAD CHANGED HIS SEX AND
POSN PREFACE(418) BE CONSTRUED AS A SEDITIOUS LIBEL AS WELL. AS TO IBSEN'S BRAND (THE PLAY WHICH MADE HIM POPULAR WITH THE
FABL PREFACE(73) MERCHANTS, PILLORIED AS ALL OR NOTHINGS IN IBSEN'S BRAND. WHEN ONE LINK IN OUR MENTAL CHAIN SNAPPED WE
SIM PREFACE(16) HAD APPEARED ON THE STAGE BEFORE IN THE PERSON OF IBSEN'S BUTTON MOULDER. AND AS HISTORY ALWAYS FOLLOWS THE
GETT PREFACE(214) ARE, ON THE WHOLE, AN UGLY, MEAN, ILL-BRED RACE. IBSEN'S CHAIN STITCH. LET US NOT FORGET, HOWEVER, IN OUR
METH PREFACE(R87) IN HIS EMPEROR OR GALILEAN; BUT IT IS ONE OF IBSEN'S DISTINCTIONS THAT NOTHING WAS VALID FOR HIM BUT
LADY PREFACE(234) AS DEAD AS THE SECOND PART OF GOETHE'S FAUST OR IBSEN'S EMPEROR OR GALILEAN. HERE, THEN, SHAKESPEAR HAD A
CLEO NOTES (204) THE WHOLE, A RATHER LESS DIGNIFIED APPEARANCE IN IBSEN'S ENEMY OF THE PEOPLE THAN IN PLATO'S REPUBLIC. AND IN
3PLA PREFACE(R17) TELEGRAM) MAY AT ANY MOMENT PUT YOU IN HER PLACE, IBSEN'S EXPOSURE OF THE WORTHLESSNESS AND MEANNESS OF HER
UNPL PREFACE(R12) THEATRE. IT GOT ON ITS FEET BY PRODUCING IBSEN'S GHOSTS; BUT ITS SEARCH FOR UNACTED NATIVE DRAMATIC
SUPR HANDBOK(192) IN A DISEASED AND MORIBUND COMMUNITY IN WHICH IBSEN'S HEDDA GABLER WOULD BE THE TYPICAL WOMAN. BUT IT HAS
3PLA PREFACE(R15) OF IBSEN. IT SEEMED TO THEM THAT MOST OF IBSEN'S HEROINES WERE NAUGHTY LADIES. AND THEY TRIED TO
3PLA PREFACE(R37) THAT IF SHAKESPEAR HAD CONCEIVED GOETHE'S OR IBSEN'S IDEAS, HE WOULD HAVE EXPRESSED THEM ANY WORSE THAN
HART PREFACE(3) THEY DID NOT STRIKE ME IN THAT WAY. JUST AS IBSEN'S INTENSELY NORWEGIAN PLAYS EXACTLY FITTED EVERY
JOAN PREFACE(38) OF THE FACT THAT THE LAW OF EVOLUTION IS IBSEN'S LAW OF CHANGE. AND AS THE LAW OF GOD IN ANY SENSE OF
PHIL II SD(104) NOTHING ELSE FOR IT, HE BOLTS INTO THE RECESS ON IBSEN'S LEFT. /CUTHBERTSON/ GOOD MORNING, MISS CRAVEN. (
PHIL II (108) TO THE CLUB. (SHE GOES INTO THE RECESS ON IBSEN'S LEFT). THE PAGE ENTERS, CARRYING THE BRITISH MEDICAL
PHIL II (123) ONLY TOO DELIGHTED. (THEY GO INTO THE RECESS ON IBSEN'S LEFT, AND SIT THERE CHATTING IN WHISPERS, VERY
PHIL II (115) NERVES. PARAMORE THEN RETIRES TO THE RECESS ON IBSEN'S LEFT, AND THROWS HIMSELF ON THE DIVAN WITH A HALF
MIS. PREFACE(25) OF THEM TO GO ROUND. BUT EVEN THE FEW WHO, LIKE IBSEN'S MRS SOLNESS, HAVE " A GENIUS FOR NURSING THE SOULS
POSN PREFACE(400) PROHIBITS GHOSTS AND LICENSES ALL THE REST OF IBSEN'S PLAYS. AN ENLIGHTENED CENSORSHIP WOULD POSSIBLY
UNPL PREFACE(R23) I DOUBT IT, NOT BEING ONE OF THEM MYSELF) TO WHOM IBSEN'S PLAYS, AS THEY STAND, SPEAK SUFFICIENTLY FOR
PHIL PREFACE(66) BUT LIFE ITSELF WAS STAGGERING FROM THE IMPACT OF IBSEN'S PLAYS, WHICH REACHED US IN 1889. THE STATE OF MIND
LADY PREFACE(233) NOT QUITE THE SAME WORLD), AT LEAST WITH MUCH OF IBSEN'S POWER OF PENETRATING ITS ILLUSIONS AND IDOLATRIES,
PHIL II (122) INTEND TO MAKE ANY. (HE RETIRES TO THE RECESS ON IBSEN'S RIGHT, PICKING UP THE STEP-LADDER AS HE PASSES AND
PHIL II SD(94) DR PARAMORE IS ON THE DIVAN IN THE RECESS ON IBSEN'S RIGHT, READING THE BRITISH MEDICAL JOURNAL. HE IS
PLES PREFACE(R7) IN 1894, FLORENCE FARR, WHO HAD ALREADY PRODUCED IBSEN'S ROSMERSHOLM, WAS PLACED IN COMMAND OF THE AVENUE
GETT PREFACE(215) ALL DIRECTIONS IF A SINGLE THREAD OF IT BE CUT. IBSEN'S SIMILITUDE OF THE MACHINE-MADE CHAIN STITCH, WHICH
POSN PREFACE(399) MIGHT, WHILST SHRINKING EVEN WITH HORROR FROM IBSEN'S VIEWS, PERCEIVE THAT ANY NATION WHICH SUPPRESSED
POSN PREFACE(399) IT WOULD HAVE PERCEIVED THAT THOSE PLAYS OF IBSEN'S WHICH HAVE BEEN LICENSED WITHOUT QUESTION ARE
POSN PREFACE(398) IT WOULD UNDERSTAND IT BETTER. THE ONE PLAY OF IBSEN'S WHICH IS PROHIBITED ON THE ENGLISH STAGE, GHOSTS, IS

ICE

BULL I (79) TIM, WILL YOU COME WITH ME AND HELP TO BREAK THE ICE BETWEEN ME AND YOUR WARMHEARTED, IMPULSIVE COUNTRYMEN..
MTH2 (43) /CONRAD/ I SENT HER MY LAST BOOK. I CAN BREAK THE ICE BY ASKING HER WHAT SHE MADE OF IT. /FRANKLYN/ WHEN SHE
CYMB FORWORD(135) WHO WITH HIS WIFE JANET ACHURCH BROKE THE ICE FOR IBSEN IN ENGLAND, USED TO CITE POSTHUMUS AS
BULL I (83) VERY MAN TO TAKE WITH ME TO IRELAND TO BREAK THE ICE FOR ME. HE CAN GAIN THE CONFIDENCE OF THE PEOPLE THERE,
HART II (118) THE BRIDGE IN THE TYPHOON, OR FROZEN INTO ARCTIC ICE FOR MONTHS IN DARKNESS, THAN YOU OR THEY HAVE EVER BEEN.

FABL PREFACE(98)	EXHORTATIONS TO LOVE ONEANOTHER. HOMILIES CUT NO	ICE	IN ADMINISTRATIVE COUNCILS: THE LITERARY TALENT AND
METH PREFACE(R65)	NOT HAVE LIVED IN THE FIRE NOR UGOLINO IN THE	ICE	. BUT THE PHYSICISTS FOUND THEIR INTELLECTUAL VISION OF
SIM II (60)	I'M NOT: I FEEL AS IF YOUD GIVEN ME A STRAWBERRY	ICE	. THANK YOU, DEAR VASHTI, THANK YOU. YOU GIVE ME HOPE
FANY PROLOG (272)	ON, " THE ICE OF LIFE IS SLIPPERY." /TROTTER/	ICE	OF LIFE INDEED! YOU SHOULD BE EATING PENNY ICES AND
FANY PROLOG (272)	IT? /FANNY/ THATS NOT ALL. IT GOES ON, " THE	ICE	OF LIFE IS SLIPPERY." /TROTTER/ ICE OF LIFE INDEED! YOU
ARMS III (51)	LIKE HIM TO FIND OUT THAT THE STORY ABOUT THE	ICE	PUDDING WAS A-- A-- A-- YOU KNOW. /RAINA/ (WINCING) AH,
ARMS III (66)	INTERRUPTING HER SLIGHTINGLY) OH, I REMEMBER: THE	ICE	PUDDING. A PALTRY TAUNT, GIRL! MAJOR PETKOFF ENTERS, IN
ARMS II (44)	NOT ON YOUR FIRST DAY AT HOME. I'LL MAKE ANOTHER	ICE	PUDDING. TCH-CH-CH! (TOGETHER) /PETKOFF/ (YIELDING)
ARMS II (43)	I MADE A BEAUTIFUL ORNAMENT THIS MORNING FOR THE	ICE	PUDDING; AND THAT STUPID NICOLA HAS JUST PUT DOWN A PILE
ARMS II (44)	GO AND SLAM THAT BAG, TOO, DOWN ON MISS RAINA'S	ICE	PUDDING! (THIS IS TOO MUCH FOR NICOLA. THE BAG DROPS
BASH I (93)	NATURE IN OUR HEARTS THAW THE INTOLERABLE INCH OF	ICE	THAT BEARS THE WEIGHT OF ALL THE STAMPING WORLD, HEAR YE
FABL IV (115)	AS TEMPERATURE RISES, WATER CHANGES FROM SOLID	ICE	TO LIQUID FLUID, FROM LIQUID FLUID TO STEAM, FROM STEAM
METH PREFACE(R23)	ON THE ROAD WITH A BRUISED CHIN, OR SUPINE ON THE	ICE	WITH A BASHED OCCIPUT, BECOMES A BICYCLIST AND A SKATER.
APPL I (203)	DOWN. YOURE IN YOUR OWN HOUSE: CEREMONY CUTS NO	ICE	WITH ME. /MAGNUS/ (GRATEFULLY) THANK YOU. THE KING
BULL PREFACE(28)	RUSSIAN SOLDIERS UNDER WHOM THEY HAD BROKEN THE	ICE	WITH THEIR CANNON; EVEN THE RELATIONS BETWEEN

ICEBERG

CURE (226)	UP TO IT FOR SIX DAYS WITH THE COOLNESS OF AN	ICEBERG	AND THE CHEERFULNESS OF AN IDIOT. EVERY MEMBER OF IT

ICECAP

GENV IV (125)	OF YOU GENTLEMEN? /BBDE/ CAN YOU DEPEND ON THE	ICECAP	? I MUST GO HOME AT ONCE. THERE WILL BE A RUSH TO
GENV IV (125)	OF WASTE PAPER AND BE A MILLIONAIRE UNTIL THE	ICECAP	OVERTAKES HIM. IT MUST NOT BE. I WILL TAKE THE
GENV IV (124)	/SECRETARY/ NO USE RUNNING AWAY, MY FRIEND. THE	ICECAP	WILL OVERTAKE YOU WHEREVER YOU GO. /SECRETARY/ LET

ICECAPS

GENV IV (127)	OUT AND HAVING A TREMENDOUS SPREE BEFORE THE	ICECAPS	NIP US. HOW DOES THAT STRIKE YOU, GONNY? /BEGONIA/
GENV IV (124)	WILL TAKE US INTO THE AWFUL COLD OF SPACE. THE	ICECAPS	THAT WE HAVE ON THE NORTH AND SOUTH POLES WILL

ICED

GETT PREFACE(204)	OF BEER, OR, AMONG THE MORE LUXURIOUS CLASSES,	ICED	CLARET CUP, LEMON SQUASHES, AND THE LIKE. TO TAKE A
GENV I (43)	HE WILL RECOVER BEST AS HE IS. /SHE/ I HAVE SOME	ICED	LEMONADE IN MY THERMOS. SHALL I GIVE HIM SOME?
WIDO III (60)	ME ON FAIR TERMS FOR A DEPOT OF THE NORTH THAMES	ICED	MUTTON COMPANY. THEYLL BE KNOCKED DOWN INSIDE OF TWO
WIDO III (64)	TO ARRANGE ABOUT THE LEASE TO THE NORTH THAMES	ICED	MUTTON COMPANY? /TRENCH/ OH, I DONT MIND. I'M GOING
WIDO III (54)	THE OTHER HALF TO A NEW COMPANY: THE NORTH THAMES	ICED	MUTTON DEPOT COMPANY, OF WHICH I HOLD A FEW SHARES:

ICELAND

FANY III (307)	/DUVALLET/ PRACTISING JUJITSU OR THE NEW	ICELAND	WRESTLING. ADMIRABLE, MISS KNOX. THE ATHLETIC YOUNG

ICEPROOF

GENV IV (129)	THE LAST, AND SET AN EXAMPLE TO THE NEW RACE OF	ICEPROOF	MEN WHO WILL FOLLOW US. /SIR O./ STILL, YOU KNOW,

ICE-CAPS

METH PREFACE(R65)	THE COOLING OF THE SUN AND THE RETURN OF THE	ICE-CAPS	DOES NOT DEGRADE THE PESSIMIST: FOR EXAMPLE, THE

ICES

FANY PROLOG (272)	ICE OF LIFE INDEED! YOU SHOULD BE EATING PENNY	ICES	AND ENJOYING YOURSELF. I WONT HEAR ANOTHER WORD. THE
BASH II,2, (115)	HE OF WHOM CASHEL SPOKE? A DREADFUL THOUGHT	ICES	MY HEART. OH, WHY DID CASHEL LEAVE US AT THE DOOR?
BUOY III (43)	LOVE OF PET ANIMALS, LOVE OF WHISKY OR STRAWBERRY	ICES	, LOVE OF CRICKET OR LAWN TENNIS, ALSO LOVE OF MONEY

ICH

BASH II,1, (112)	NEGRO, DOTH THIS RUFFIAN PRECEDENCE TAKE OF ME. "	ICH	DIEN." DAMNATION! I SERVE. MY MOTTO SHOULD HAVE BEEN, "

ICILY

SUPR IV (148)	ISNT IT, LIKE YOURSELF? /VIOLET/ (	ICILY	PITYING HIS SENTIMENTALITY) REALLY, MR MALONE, I AM

ICONOCLASM

MILL PREFACE(133)	STILL PLEASE, IT WILL NO LONGER IMPOSE. FOR MERE	ICONOCLASM	IS A MISTAKE: THE ROUNDHEAD FOLLY (REALLY A
CAPT III (291)	ABACK. HIS FOLLOWERS, FAR FROM APPRECIATING HIS	ICONOCLASM	, ARE SHOCKED INTO SCANDALIZED SOBRIETY, EXCEPT

ICONOCLASMS

UNPL PREFACE(R9)	WANT OF SKILL COULD NOT EVEN IF THEY DURST. ITS	ICONOCLASMS	, SEDITIONS, AND BLASPHEMIES, IF WELL TURNED,

ICONOCLAST

LION PREFACE(48)	HERO. CHRISTIAN ICONOLATRY AND THE PERIL OF THE	ICONOCLAST	. I MUST NOW ABANDON THIS ATTITUDE, AND MAKE A
SUPR I (36)	BECOME A REFORMER, AND, LIKE ALL REFORMERS, AN	ICONOCLAST	. I NO LONGER BREAK CUCUMBER FRAMES AND BURN
MRS PREFACE(153)	DAYS REMONSTRATED WITH THEM. MR GREIN, THE HARDY	ICONOCLAST	WHO FIRST LAUNCHED MY PLAYS ON THE STAGE

ICONOGRAPHER

METH PREFACE(R84)	MATRIMONY, AND HE COULD NOT BECOME THE CONSCIOUS	ICONOGRAPHER	OF A RELIGION BECAUSE HE HAD NO CONSCIOUS
METH PREFACE(R87)	ME PROFESSIONALLY, DID NOT CONSTITUTE ME AN	ICONOGRAPHER	OF THE RELIGION OF MY TIME, AND THUS FULFIL MY

ICONOGRAPHIC

LION PREFACE(50)	NOT NEED THE PRESENT WAR TO SHEW THAT NEITHER THE	ICONOGRAPHIC	CHRIST NOR THE CHRIST OF ST PAUL HAS SUCCEEDED
LION PREFACE(48)	WE GET RID, TO BEGIN WITH, OF THE IDOLATROUS OR	ICONOGRAPHIC	WORSHIP OF CHRIST. BY THIS I MEAN LITERALLY

ICONOGRAPHY

METH PREFACE(R81)	BEEN QUITE CONTEMPTIBLE EXCEPT WHEN IMITATING THE	ICONOGRAPHY	AFTER THE RELIGION HAD BECOME A SUPERSTITION.
METH PREFACE(R80)	EXPLORERS AND DISCOVERERS, ON THE CONTRARY, THE	ICONOGRAPHY	AND HAGIOLOGY OF SCIENTISM ARE AS COPIOUS AS
JOAN PREFACE(15)	EATEN AND SLEPT LESS: THAT WAS ALL. THE MERE	ICONOGRAPHY	DOES NOT MATTER. ALL THE POPULAR RELIGIONS IN
METH PREFACE(R81)	HAS NEVER BEEN GREAT WHEN IT WAS NOT PROVIDING AN	ICONOGRAPHY	FOR A LIVE RELIGION. AND IT HAS NEVER BEEN QUITE
METH PREFACE(R90)	THE FIRST ATTEMPTS OF THE EARLY CHRISTIANS AT	ICONOGRAPHY	. IN THAT HOPE I WITHDRAW AND RING UP THE
JOAN PREFACE(16)	THE REST OF THE CATHOLIC HAGIOLOGY AS AN OBSOLETE	ICONOGRAPHY	OF EXPLODED MYTHS. IT WOULD BE RUBBED INTO HER
JOAN PREFACE(17)	NIGHTINGALE, WHO ALSO COMBINED A VERY SIMPLE	ICONOGRAPHY	OF RELIGIOUS BELIEF WITH A MIND SO EXCEPTIONALLY
METH PREFACE(R81)	MAN WILL ALWAYS BE AN EXPLOITER OF THE POPULAR	ICONOGRAPHY	, AND NOT ACCORDING TO HIS OWN PERSONAL

ICONOLATERS

LION PREFACE(49)	IT IS AT SUCH MOMENTS THAT YOU REALIZE THAT THE	ICONOLATERS	HAVE NEVER FOR A MOMENT CONCEIVED CHRIST AS A
LION PREFACE(49)	AN EXTRAORDINARY DISMAY AND HORROR AMONG THE	ICONOLATERS	. YOU WILL HAVE MADE THE PICTURE COME OUT OF ITS
LION PREFACE(49)	MAHOMETANISM, SHINTOISM, OR FIRE WORSHIP; AND THE	ICONOLATERS	, PLACIDLY CONTEMPTUOUS, WILL ONLY CLASSIFY YOU

ICONOLATRY

LION PREFACE(48)	NARRATIVES TELL US ABOUT THEIR HERO. CHRISTIAN	ICONOLATRY	AND THE PERIL OF THE ICONOCLAST. I MUST NOW

ICTHYOSAURUS

SUPR III (105)	HAVE EXISTED AND PERISHED. THE MEGATHERIUM, THE	ICTHYOSAURUS	HAVE PACED THE EARTH WITH SEVEN-LEAGUE STEPS

ICY

SUPR III (97)	EGOTIST SENT TO MY KINGDOM, AND YOU TAKEN TO THE	ICY	MANSIONS OF THE SKY! /THE STATUE/ I CANT COMPLAIN. I
HART II (119)	GO SLAUGHTERING SEALS AND WHALES IN GREENLAND'S	ICY	MOUNTAINS. THEY WONT LET WOMEN BE CAPTAINS. DO YOU WANT

IDDY

SIM II (60)	PEOPLE ARE LIKE ME OR NOT-- /LADY FARWATERS/ NO,	IDDY	: YOU ARE UNIQUE. /IDDY/ ANYHOW, I HAVE MADE A
SIM II (78)	FARWATERS/ WHAT ON EARTH IS THE MATTER WITH YOU,	IDDY	? HAVE YOU BEEN DRINKING? /IDDY/ (IN A GHASTLY
SIM II (65)	WHAT ABOUT THE PEOPLE WHO HAVE NO ORIGINAL IDEAS,	IDDY	? /PRA/ THE GREAT MAJORITY OF MANKIND? /IDDY/ THEYLL
SIM I (48)	ME MR HAMMINGTAP. I AM ACCUSTOMED TO BE CALLED	IDDY	AMONG FRIENDS. /MRS HYERING/ WHAT DOES IDDY STAND FOR?

SIM II (62)	EDITION. /KANCHIN/ THE LAND THAT BROUGHT FORTH	IDDY	BEGINS THE APOCALYPSE. /HYERING/ WHAT DO YOU MEAN? HAS
SIM II SD(69)	FLYING THIS WAY. /VASHTI/ IT'S SWOOPING DOWN.	IDDY	COMES FROM THE HOUSE AND TROTS DOWN THE STEPS WITH A
SIM II SD(59)	RAIN AND DEW. /MAYA/ SILENCE HIM, O YE STARS.	IDDY	COMES FROM THE HOUSE IN A CONDITION OF LAZY
SIM II SD(74)	SEATS. THE OTHERS SIT AS BEFORE, EXCEPT THAT	IDDY	DESERTS PROLA AND SITS ON THE WELL PARAPET. SIR CHARLES
SIM II (58)	HOW TO GET RID OF IDDY. /MAYA/ WE CANNOT ENDURE	IDDY	FOR EVER, PROLA. /PROLA/ YOU TWO CHOSE HIM, NOT I.
SIM II (55)	AT HOME. THE CABLES ARE HUMMING WITH IDDY.	IDDY	HAS CONVULSED THE EMPIRE, CONFOUND HIM! /HYERING/
SIM II (55)	AT THESE! /PRA/ ALL ABOUT IDDY. /SIR CHARLES/	IDDY	HAS GOT INTO THE HEADLINES AT HOME. THE CABLES ARE
SIM II (55)	ON ANY TERMS, AND INSISTS ON OUR PROSECUTING	IDDY	IF WE CANNOT WHITEWASH HIM. DELHI DECLARES THAT ANY
SIM II (58)	THE SEA TO ESCAPE FROM IDDY. /MAYA/ LET US THROW	IDDY	INTO THE SEA THAT HE MAY ESCAPE FROM HIMSELF. /VASHTI/
SIM II (58)	OF IDDY. /VASHTI/ IDDY IS A PESTILENCE. /MAYA/	IDDY	IS A BORE. /VASHTI/ LET US THROW OURSELVES INTO THE SEA
SIM II (58)	OF IDDY. /MAYA/ I AM TIRED OF IDDY. /VASHTI/	IDDY	IS A PESTILENCE. /MAYA/ IDDY IS A BORE. /VASHTI/ LET US
SIM I (48)	AT ALL. MY SISTER WAS THE KIDDY; SO I BECAME THE	IDDY	. DO PLEASE CALL ME THAT, AND BE KIND TO ME. I AM
SIM II (55)	HEADLINES AT HOME. THE CABLES ARE HUMMING WITH	IDDY	. IDDY HAS CONVULSED THE EMPIRE, CONFOUND HIM!
SIM II (74)	THERE ARE SUCH A LOT OF PRIESTS IN THE WORLD,	IDDY	. IT WOULD BE IMPOSSIBLE TO RESERVE SEATS FOR THEM ALL.
SIM I (49)	IN A GENTLE HUSHABYEBABY SORT OF WAY AND CALL ME	IDDY	. NOW GO ON, LADY FARWATERS. EXCUSE ME FOR INTERRUPTING
SIM II (58)	BE TIRED OF IDDY. /VASHTI/ THE WORLD IS TIRED OF	IDDY	. /MAYA/ I AM TIRED OF IDDY. /VASHTI/ IDDY IS A
SIM II (58)	US THROW OURSELVES INTO THE SEA TO ESCAPE FROM	IDDY	. /MAYA/ LET US THROW IDDY INTO THE SEA THAT HE MAY
SIM II (58)	YOU ARE WISE, PROLA. TELL US HOW TO GET RID OF	IDDY	. /MAYA/ WE CANNOT ENDURE IDDY FOR EVER, PROLA. /PROLA/
SIM II (55)	ON THE TABLE) LOOK AT THESE! /PRA/ ALL ABOUT	IDDY	. /SIR CHARLES/ IDDY HAS GOT INTO THE HEADLINES AT
SIM II (58)	THE WORLD IS TIRED OF IDDY. /MAYA/ I AM TIRED OF	IDDY	. /VASHTI/ IDDY IS A PESTILENCE. /MAYA/ IDDY IS A BORE.
SIM II (58)	IT HAS BEEN HUMBUGGED THE EMPIRE WILL BE TIRED OF	IDDY	. /VASHTI/ THE WORLD IS TIRED OF IDDY. /MAYA/ I AM
SIM I (49)	BE POLYGAMY. /PROLA/ YOU ARE IN THE EAST, MR	IDDY	. THE EAST IS POLYGAMOUS. TRY TO REMEMBER THAT
SIM I (51)	(HE GOES). /LADY FARWATERS/ CAST OUT FEAR,	IDDY	. WARM HEART. CLEAR MIND. THINK OF HAVING A THOUSAND
SIM II SD(78)	FOOLS OF THEM. /PRA/ WE MUST STOP MAKING FOOLS.	IDDY	RETURNS ALONE. SOMETHING STRANGE HAS HAPPENED TO HIM.
SIM I (49)	YOU SO LONG. /LADY FARWATERS/ YOU SEE,	IDDY	-- /IDDY/ OH, THANKS! /LADY FARWATERS/ (CONTINUING)--
SIM II (55)	THE CALIPH OF BRITISH ISLAM. HE DEMANDS THAT	IDDY	SHALL PUT AWAY ALL HIS WIVES EXCEPT FOUR. /HYERING/
SIM I (48)	IDDY AMONG FRIENDS. /MRS HYERING/ WHAT DOES	IDDY	STAND FOR? /THE CLERGYMAN/ WELL, IN OUR HOME I WAS
MTH4 I (152)	NICKNAMES, MY MOTHER THOUGHTLESSLY CALLED ME	IDDY	TOODLES. I WAS CALLED IDDY UNTIL I WENT TO SCHOOL, WHEN
SIM II (65)	/JANGA/ MUM! /VASHTI/ DUMB. /MAYA/ TIDDY	IDDY	UM. CARRY ON, DARLING. /IDDY/ PROLA CAN RULE THIS HOUSE
MTH4 I (152)	CALLED ME IDDY TOODLES. I WAS CALLED	IDDY	UNTIL I WENT TO SCHOOL, WHEN I MADE MY FIRST STAND FOR
MTH4 I (152)	REST OF THE WORLD. MY MOTHER SLIPPED BACK INTO	IDDY	WHEN HER FACULTIES BEGAN TO FAIL HER, POOR WOMAN; BUT I
SIM II (60)	/VASHTI/ IF IT IS ANY CONSOLATION TO YOU,	IDDY	, I CAN ASSURE YOU THAT I ALREADY HATE YOU SO INTENSELY
SIM II (66)	ANYBODY IN THE WORLD, OVER THE AGE OF SIX, EXCEPT	IDDY	, INVENT SUCH A RIDICULOUS EXCUSE FOR GOING TO HIS ROOM
SIM II (74)	OR GOATS? TELL ME THAT. /MAYA/ YOU ARE A SHEEP,	IDDY	, MY SWEET! THERE CAN BE NO DOUBT ABOUT THAT. /IDDY/ (
SIM II (79)	/PROLA/ HAS SHE LEFT A GREAT VOID IN YOUR HEART,	IDDY	, THAT GIRL WHO TURNED TO NOTHING IN YOUR ARMS? /IDDY/
SIM II (79)	/LADY FARWATERS/ (TROUBLED, HALF RISING) BUT,	IDDY	,-- /PROLA/ LET HIM GO. THE PIGEON KNOWS ITS WAY HOME.
SIM II (74)	THROUGH THE GARDEN, SOBBING). /MAYA/ OH, POOR	IDDY	! I'LL GO AND SOOTHE HIM WITH A THOUSAND KISSES. (SHE
		IDDY'S	
SIM II (68)	/PRA/ (RISING) THE ALBATROSS! ! /MAYA/ YES:	IDDY'S	ALBATROSS. LOOK! /JANGA/ FLYING ALL OVER THE TOWN.
		IDEA	
JOAN 4 (105)	HARDLY CARE, PROVIDED HE REIGN. IT IS AN ABSTRACT	IDEA	: A MERE FORM OF WORDS. /WARWICK/ BY NO MEANS. IT IS A
MIS. (129)	THATS AN IDEA. THATS A MOST INTERESTING	IDEA	: A MOST IMPORTANT IDEA. /MRS TARLETON/ YOU ALWAYS WERE
2TRU III (106)	ELDER/ MEDEA! MEDEA! /MRS MOPPLY/ IT ISNT AN	IDEA	: IT'S THE TRUTH. I WILL NEVER BELIEVE ANYTHING AGAIN
MTH1 II (21)	HE LAUGHED AT ME; AND THEN CAME MY GREAT	IDEA	: WHY NOT KILL HIM AS HE KILLED THE BEASTS? I STRUCK;
ROCK I (233)	MY BRAIN IS UNDERWORKED. DO YOU GRASP THAT	IDEA	? HAVE YOU EVER HEARD OF A RETREAT FOR THE MENTALLY
FABL I (103)	ON HIS KNEES) THAT IS AN IDEA. /YOUNG WOMAN/ WHAT	IDEA	? /YOUNG MAN/ YOURS. THERE IS A LOT OF MONEY IN IT.
SIM PRO,1, (25)	OFF THEM AND BE A MILLIONAIRE, I HAD RHODES'S	IDEA	ALL RIGHT. LET THE WHOLE EARTH BE ENGLAND, I SAID TO
ROCK PREFACE(149)	PRACTICABLE; BUT ITS DISCUSSION FAMILIARIZES THE	IDEA	AND CLEARS THE WAY FOR PRACTICABLE SUGGESTIONS. THE
JOAN 4 (106)	QUITE SO. THESE TWO IDEAS OF HERS ARE THE SAME	IDEA	AT BOTTOM. IT GOES DEEP, MY LORD. IT IS THE PROTEST OF
MTH3 (131)	ATTAIN TO MATURITY. /BURGE-LUBIN/ (GRASPING THE	IDEA	AT LAST) BY GEORGE, CONFUCIUS, YOURE RIGHT! I NEVER
BULL IV (167)	THINK THAT LARRY-- /BROADBENT/ (DISPOSING OF THE	IDEA	AT ONCE) LARRY! OH, THAT WOULDNT HAVE DONE AT ALL, NOT
METH PREFACE(R32)	MIND OPEN FOR THE THOUGHT OF THE UNIVERSE AS ONE	IDEA	BEHIND ALL ITS PHYSICALLY APPREHENSIBLE
NEVR II (237)	BUT I WAS UP TO HIS TRICKS, SIR. I SAW THE	IDEA	COMING INTO HIS HEAD AS HE STOOD THERE, THINKING WHAT
MIS. (135)	ACTOR. (BRIGHTENING) THERES AN IDEA IN THIS: AN	IDEA	FOR A PICTURE. WHAT A PITY YOUNG BENTLEY IS NOT A
SUPR III (109)	THIS. /DON JUAN/ USELESS: I CANNOT FENCE. EVERY	IDEA	FOR WHICH MAN WILL DIE WILL BE A CATHOLIC IDEA. WHEN
PYGM II (223)	FOOLISH. /HIGGINS/ (BECOMING EXCITED AS THE	IDEA	GROWS ON HIM) WHAT IS LIFE BUT A SERIES OF INSPIRED
SUPR IV (154)	VIOLET: I KNOW YOU WILL. /VIOLET/ I HAD NO	IDEA	HE COULD BE SO HEADSTRONG. IF HE GOES ON LIKE THAT,
PYGM III (256)	NO MISTAKE ABOUT THAT, MOTHER. BUT YOU HAVE NO	IDEA	HOW FRIGHTFULLY INTERESTING IT IS TO TAKE A HUMAN BEING
WIDO I (11)	YOU WOULDNT, SOMEHOW. WELL, LOOK HERE. I HAVE NO	IDEA	HOW YOU WILL RECEIVE THIS: IT MUST SEEM HORRIBLY
SIM I (37)	INDICATING THE FIGURES) BUT I ASSURE YOU I HAD NO	IDEA	I WAS INTRUDING ON CONSECRATED GROUND. /PRA/ YOU ARE
GENV II (63)	LOVE. /THE SECRETARY/ BUT SHE HASNT A POLITICAL	IDEA	IN HER HEAD. /SIR O./ SHE NEED NOT HAVE. THE WHIPS WILL
GENV III (85)	REST IS A SOFT-BOSOMED GOOSE WITHOUT A POLITICAL	IDEA	IN HER PRETTY HEAD. /BEGONIA/ GO ON: I AM USED TO IT. I
SUPR I (13)	HIS SEAT). /TANNER/ YOU HEAR HIM, TAVY! NOT AN	IDEA	IN HIS HEAD LATER THAN EIGHTEENSIXTY. WE CANT LEAVE ANN
HART PREFACE(5)	NEW HOME SECRETARY OR CHIEF OF POLICE, WITHOUT AN	IDEA	IN HIS HEAD THAT HIS GREAT-GRANDMOTHER MIGHT NOT HAVE
MIS. (135)	AMUSED EXCEPT THE ACTOR. (BRIGHTENING) THERES AN	IDEA	IN THIS: AN IDEA FOR A PICTURE. WHAT A PITY YOUNG
MILL I (143)	PRAY, SIT DOWN. /EPIFANIA/ YOU SEEM TO HAVE ONE	IDEA	IN YOUR HEAD, AND THAT IS TO GET YOUR CLIENTS TO SIT
SUPR III (108)	MATTERS JUST AS LITTLE. BUT THAT ABOUT PUTTING AN	IDEA	INTO A MAN'S HEAD IS STUFF AND NONSENSE. IN A BATTLE
SUPR III (108)	ANY OF THESE COWARDS BRAVE BY SIMPLY PUTTING AN	IDEA	INTO HIS HEAD. /THE STATUE/ STUFF! AS AN OLD SOLDIER I
BULL IV (155)	A QUEER WORLD: THATS CERTAIN. /BROADBENT/ YOUR	IDEA	IS A VERY CLEVER ONE, MR KEEGAN: REALLY MOST BRILLIANT:
2TRU PREFACE(23)	AS THAT OF THE BLUECOAT BOY; AND ST VINCENT'S	IDEA	IS CONSEQUENTLY LOST; BUT MODERN INDUSTRIAL EXPERIENCE
FABL PREFACE(85)	IS SUPPOSED TO BE A SUBSTITUTE FOR CIVIL WAR. THE	IDEA	IS THAT IF TWO BODIES OF CITIZENS DIFFER ON ANY PUBLIC
JOAN 4 (105)	AT ALL OF US, THROUGH THE CHURCH? /WARWICK/ HER	IDEA	IS THAT THE KINGS SHOULD GIVE THEIR REALMS TO GOD, AND
MTH2 (82)	THAT IS MY EXPERIENCE. /LUBIN/ QUITE SO. MY	IDEA	IS THAT WHILST WE SHOULD INTEREST THE ELECTORATE IN
JOAN PREFACE(11)	IMAGINATION IS SO VIVID THAT WHEN THEY HAVE AN	IDEA	IT COMES TO THEM AS AN AUDIBLE VOICE, SOMETIMES UTTERED
BULL I (76)	IDEA OF A WHISKY AND SODA. /TIM/ AN A VERY GOOD	IDEA	IT IS TOO. DHRINK IS THE CURSE O ME UNHAPPY COUNTHRY. I
GENV III (66)	YOU MUST ALLOW ME TO CARRY IT FOR YOU. I HAD NO	IDEA	IT WAS HEAVY. DO YOU KEEP ALL YOUR MONEY IN IT? /THE
2TRU I (47)	/THE BURGLAR/ STOP. SWEETIE! I HAVE ANOTHER	IDEA	. A REGULAR DAZZLER. LETS STAGE A KIDNAP. /THE NURSE/
MIS. (134)	(AGAIN IMPRESSED) THATS AN IDEA. THATS A NEW	IDEA	. I BELIEVE I OUGHT TO HAVE MADE JOHNNY AN AUTHOR. IVE
MIS. (132)	KNOW, THE SUPERMAN MAY COME. THE SUPERMAN'S AN	IDEA	. I BELIEVE IN IDEAS, READ WHATSHIS NAME. /LORD
JOAN 4 (107)	THERE YOU WILL FIND YET ANOTHER MOST DANGEROUS	IDEA	. I CAN EXPRESS IT ONLY BY SUCH PHRASES AS FRANCE FOR
INCA PROLOG (234)	MILLIONAIRE TO MARRY YOU. /ERMYNTRUDE/ THATS AN	IDEA	. I WILL (SHE VANISHES THROUGH THE CURTAINS). /THE
NEVR II (234)	HIS TRAY TO THE SERVICE TABLE. /PHILIP/ I HAVE AN	IDEA	. MR M'COMAS: THIS COMMUNICATION SHOULD BE MADE, SHOULD
ROCK I (227)	FROM THE FUTURE. /SIR ARTHUR/ THATS A CURIOUS	IDEA	. OF COURSE IF THERE ARE GHOSTS FROM THE PAST THERE
MIS. (129)	THATS A MOST INTERESTING IDEA: A MOST IMPORTANT	IDEA	. /MRS TARLETON/ YOU ALWAYS WERE ONE FOR IDEAS, JOHN.
GENV I (37)	HERE THEY ARE, MISS. BY GOSH, THATS A SPLENDID	IDEA	. /SHE/ THANK YOU. THAT IS ALL. GOOD MORNING.
GETT (281)	ONE. BUT, AS USUAL, HE DIDNT FOLLOW UP THE	IDEA	. /THE GENERAL/ (AGHAST) AM I TO UNDERSTAND-- /THE
FABL I (103)	THE NEWSPAPER DROP ON HIS KNEES) THAT IS AN	IDEA	. /YOUNG WOMAN/ WHAT IDEA? /YOUNG MAN/ YOURS. THERE IS
DEST (184)	ON THAT CONDITION. /LIEUTENANT/ THATS NOT A BAD	IDEA	. THANK YOU: I THINK I'LL TRY IT. /LADY/ DO. AND MIND,
MIS. (129)	NAPOLEON. /TARLETON/ (IMPRESSED) THATS AN	IDEA	. THATS A MOST INTERESTING IDEA: A MOST IMPORTANT IDEA.
MIS. (134)	LIKE HIM. /TARLETON/ (AGAIN IMPRESSED) THATS AN	IDEA	. THATS A NEW IDEA. I BELIEVE I OUGHT TO HAVE MADE
BULL PREFACE(10)	MUCH OBLIGED TO HIM, WHICH IS THE MODERN IMPERIAL	IDEA	. TO SINGE THE KING OF SPAIN'S BEARD; PICK HIS POCKET;
SUPR III (109)	IDEA FOR WHICH MAN WILL DIE WILL BE A CATHOLIC	IDEA	. WHEN THE SPANIARD LEARNS AT LAST THAT HE IS NO BETTER
SUPR III (109)	IS A COWARD TO THE BACKBONE, WILL FIGHT FOR AN	IDEA	LIKE A HERO. HE MAY BE ABJECT AS A CITIZEN; BUT HE IS
BULL PREFACE(9)	WAR NEXT DAY IF WE ARE FOOLS ENOUGH. A WAR FOR AN	IDEA	MAY BE A FOLLY; BUT IT IS NOT A DISHONOR. BOTH PARTIES
SUPR III (108)	CHURCH. /DON JUAN/ HAVE NO FEAR, COMMANDER: THIS	IDEA	OF A CATHOLIC CHURCH WILL SURVIVE ISLAM, WILL SURVIVE
PYGM IV (265)	/HIGGINS/ OH, LOTS OF THINGS. WHAT ABOUT YOUR OLD	IDEA	OF A FLORIST'S SHOP? PICKERING COULD SET YOU UP IN
PYGM III (245)	OH, I CANT BE BOTHERED WITH YOUNG WOMEN. MY	IDEA	OF A LOVABLE WOMAN IS SOMETHING AS LIKE YOU AS
MIS. (114)	GROW UP A BROKEN-SPIRITED SPANIEL, WHICH IS YOUR	IDEA	OF A MAN, I SUPPOSE. /JOHNNY/ JOLLY GOOD THING FOR YOU
LION PREFACE(102)	TO JESUS THAN A BRITISH PARSON, BECAUSE THE	IDEA	OF A PROFESSIONAL PRIEST IS UNFAMILIAR AND EVEN
BULL I (76)	WHISKY FOR HIMSELF) NOW THATS MY POOR ENGLISH	IDEA	OF A WHISKY AND SODA. /TIM/ AN A VERY GOOD IDEA IT IS
SUPR III (110)	CHILDREN AND REARING THEM. /ANA/ IS THAT YOUR	IDEA	OF A WOMAN'S MIND? I CALL IT CYNICAL AND DISGUSTING
SUPR III (109)	AND KILL ONE ANOTHER FOR THE GREAT CATHOLIC	IDEA	OF ABOLISHING SLAVERY. /THE DEVIL/ YES, WHEN THE
SUPR PREFACE(R34)	AS A RELIGIOUS OR POLITICAL IDEA, OR A GENERAL	IDEA	OF ANY SORT, WERE TO OCCUR TO HIM. HE IS TOLERABLE AS A
MTH4 I (158)	STORIES OF OUR RELIGION. AT FIRST WE HAD NO	IDEA	OF ASTRONOMICAL SPACE. WE BELIEVED THE SKY TO BE ONLY
MIS. (145)	IS A WONDERFUL ENTERTAINER. /TARLETON/ I THINK MY	IDEA	OF BRINGING UP A YOUNG GIRL HAS BEEN RATHER A SUCCESS.

LION PREFACE(12)	THE MORAL LAW WITHIN THEM REVOLTING AGAINST THE	IDEA	OF BUYING OFF THE DEITY WITH GOLD AND GIFTS, THOUGH
MIS. PREFACE(28)	SO AS TO MAKE THE PUBLIC FAMILIAR WITH THE	IDEA	OF COMPENSATION BEFORE HIS OWN TURN COMES. TABOO IN
SUPR III (106)	IMAGINATION GLOWS, THEIR ENERGIES RISE UP AT THE	IDEA	OF DEATH, THESE PEOPLE: THEY LOVE IT; AND THE MORE
DEVL III (78)	(PUGNACIOUS AND PATRIOTIC, REPUDIATING THE	IDEA	OF DEFEAT) 'TENTION. NOW THEN: COCK UP YOUR CHINS, AND
MIS. PREFACE(36)	SPACE BY PAPA. LOATHSOME AS WE HAVE MADE THE	IDEA	OF DUTY (LIKE THE IDEA OF WORK) WE MUST HABITUATE
CLEO V (198)	LONG ENOUGH. BESIDES: I HAVE ALWAYS DISLIKED THE	IDEA	OF DYING: I HAD RATHER BE KILLED. FAREWELL. /RUFIO/ (
METH PREFACE(R19)	ANXIOUSLY LOOKING. THE EARLY EVOLUTIONISTS. THE	IDEA	OF EVOLUTION, OR TRANSFORMATION AS IT IS NOW SOMETIMES
NEVR II SD(236)	EITHER BECAUSE HE IS OLD AND CHILLY, OR WITH SOME	IDEA	OF EXTENUATING THE UNFASHIONABLENESS OF HIS REEFER
BULL PREFACE(34)	SATURATED FROM HIS YOUTH UP WITH THE IMPERIAL	IDEA	OF FOREIGN RULE BY A SPIRITUALLY SUPERIOR INTERNATIONAL
NEVR I (223)	ME WHAT THE DEVIL THAT WAS TO ME. WELL, I HAVE AN	IDEA	OF GETTING MARRIED MYSELF. /CRAMPTON/ (WITH GRUMBLING
LION II (142)	CERTAINLY NOT. THERE HAS NEVER BEEN THE SLIGHTEST	IDEA	OF HARMING THEM. LADIES AND GENTLEMEN: YOU ARE ALL
JOAN 4 (107)	ME THAT THIS COUNTRY GIRL CAN RISE ABOVE THE	IDEA	OF HER VILLAGE FOR ITS VILLAGERS. BUT SHE CAN. SHE
DEVL II (39)	TO IT; TAKES IT DOWN; AND PUTS IT ON. THE	IDEA	OF HIMSELF AS A PARSON TICKLES HIM: HE LOOKS DOWN AT
JITT II (46)	WE WERE WAS PARADISE. DOES THAT GIVE YOU ANY	IDEA	OF HIS GREATNESS? /LENKHEIM/ OF YOUR MEANNESS, MORE
SUPR III (82)	FOR HOLDING UP TRAINS. IT WAS HE WHO HAD THE	IDEA	OF HOLDING UP MOTOR CARS IN THE SOUTH OF EUROPE: A
MIS. (117)	BUT UNFORTUNATELY, BEING VERY YOUNG, HE HAS NO	IDEA	OF HOW VERY LITTLE OF THAT SORT OF THING MOST OF US CAN
METH PREFACE(R53)	FOLLOWERS DID NOT THINK OF THIS. THEIR ONLY	IDEA	OF INVESTIGATION WAS TO IMITATE " NATURE" BY
WIDO II (36)	ABSOLUTELY DEPENDENT ON YOU; AND I DONT LIKE THE	IDEA	OF IT MYSELF. IF YOU EVEN MENTION SUCH A THING TO HIM
LION PREFACE(12)	BETWEEN ATONEMENT AND PUNISHMENT . THE PRIMITIVE	IDEA	OF JUSTICE IS PARTLY LEGALIZED REVENGE AND PARTLY
2TRU III (91)	SWEETIE, WAS IT? I NEVER DREAMT THAT THE	IDEA	OF MARRIAGE HAD OCCURRED TO EITHER OF US. IT CERTAINLY
MIS. (128)	AS A FATHER, HAVE YOU? /BENTLEY/ YES. THATS AN	IDEA	OF MINE. I KNEW A CHAP NAMED JOEY PERCIVAL AT OXFORD (
CURE (228)	THROW MYSELF OUT OF THE WINDOW. I CANT BEAR THE	IDEA	OF MUSIC. I DREAD IT, HATE IT, LOATHE IT. /THE DOCTOR/
SUPR IV (157)	YOU SEE, I SHALL HAVE TO LIVE UP ALWAYS TO YOUR	IDEA	OF MY DIVINITY; AND I DONT THINK I COULD DO THAT IF WE
ROCK I (198)	AT ALL SURE THAT THERE IS NOT SOMETHING IN HIS	IDEA	OF MY MAKING A SPEECH IN TRAFALGAR SQUARE. I HAVE NOT
DOCT II (120)	POOR INNOCENT YOUNG FELLOW-- HE HAS OF COURSE NO	IDEA	OF MY POSITION OR HOW BUSY I AM-- ACTUALLY WANTED ME TO
MTH4 I (165)	AND ALWAYS WILL BE. /ZOO/ THEN YOU GIVE UP THE	IDEA	OF PROGRESS? YOU CRY OFF THE TORCH, AND THE BRICK, AND
SIM PREFACE(16)	NOT BEEN INSTANTANEOUS AND UNANTICIPATED. AND THE	IDEA	OF PUNISHMENT NEVER ENTERED EITHER HIS MIND OR THE
GETT PREFACE(183)	NOT PHILOSOPHERS. WHEN THEY FINALLY GIVE UP THE	IDEA	OF REFORMING OUR MARRIAGE INSTITUTIONS BY PRIVATE
APPL INTRLUD(245)	TO YOUR AMANDAS AND LYSISTRATAS: CREATURES WHOSE	IDEA	OF ROMANCE IS A MINISTER IN LOVE WITH A DEPARTMENT, AND
HART I (59)	TELL HER ABOUT THEM? /MRS HUSHABYE/ THATS YOUR	IDEA	OF ROMANCE, IS IT? /ELLIE/ NOT ROMANCE, EXACTLY. IT
WIDO III (57)	THE BOOK FOR THE SAKE OF GRANDMAMMA? I HATE THE	IDEA	OF SUCH THINGS. I DONT WANT TO KNOW ABOUT THEM. I LOVE
DEVL III (62)	IF YOU WILL EXCUSE MY SAYING SO. HAVE YOU ANY	IDEA	OF THE AVERAGE MARKSMANSHIP OF THE ARMY OF HIS MAJESTY
GENV PREFACE(22)	LORD ACTON'S DICTUM THAT POWER CORRUPTS GIVES NO	IDEA	OF THE EXTENT TO WHICH FLATTERY, DEFERENCE, POWER, AND
METH PREFACE(R21)	INTO BEING AT AN ALMIGHTY WORD. WHAT A SUBLIME	IDEA	OF THE INFINITE MIGHT OF THE GREAT ARCHITECT, THE CAUSE
METH PREFACE(R73)	MECHANICAL CONCEPTION AS AGAINST THE DIVINE	IDEA	OF THE LIFE BREATHED INTO THE CLAY NOSTRILS OF ADAM,
DOCT PREFACE(59)	SWALLOW THE FALLACY WITHOUT A WRY FACE. IT HAS NO	IDEA	OF THE NEED FOR WHAT IS CALLED A CONTROL EXPERIMENT. IN
MRS PREFACE(152)	ITS DOORS FOR ONE NIGHT AND ONE AFTERNOON. SOME	IDEA	OF THE RESULTANT SENSATION MAY BE GATHERED FROM THE
GENV III (81)	IGNORANCE OF RUSSIA. NONE OF YOU SEEM TO HAVE ANY	IDEA	OF THE SORT OF WORLD YOU ARE LIVING IN. INTO THE VOID
PRES (163)	TO DO." BUT IT HAPPENS SOMETIMES THAT THEY GET AN	IDEA	OF THEIR OWN; AND THEN OF COURSE YOURE LANDED.
SUPR II (53)	I CAN TRUST HER TO YOU. WHAT WORRIES ME IS THE	IDEA	OF TRUSTING YOU TO HER. HAVE YOU READ MAETERLINCK'S
BARB III (328)	MY DEAR FATHER, I HAVE BEEN A FOOL: I HAD NO	IDEA	OF WHAT IT ALL MEANT: OF THE WONDERFUL FORETHOUGHT, THE
GETT (295)	/HOTCHKISS/ ARE YOU SURE YOU HAVE ANY ADEQUATE	IDEA	OF WHAT THE TRUTH ABOUT A MILITARY MAN REALLY IS?
GETT (307)	THANK YOU. /HOTCHKISS/ HAVE YOU THE LEAST	IDEA	OF WHAT THEY ARE TALKING ABOUT, MR ALDERMAN? /COLLINS/
MIS. PREFACE(24)	AND NAIL IT TO YOUR DOOR, THOUGH YOU HAVE NO MORE	IDEA	OF WHO PESTALOZZI WAS AND WHAT HE ADVOCATED OR HOW HE
MIS. PREFACE(33)	ITS HAUNTS, AND RELIGION ENOUGH TO HAVE SOME	IDEA	OF WHY IT IS ALLOWED ITS RIGHTS AND WHY IT MUST RESPECT
MIS. PREFACE(36)	AS WE HAVE MADE THE IDEA OF DUTY (LIKE THE	IDEA	OF WORK) WE MUST HABITUATE CHILDREN TO A SENSE OF
DOCT III (131)	BETTER TO ASK ME, DEAR. IT GIVES PEOPLE A WRONG	IDEA	OF YOU. /LOUIS/ BUT I WANT TO SPARE YOUR LITTLE
ROCK II (275)	/SIR ARTHUR/ MAY I ASK WHETHER THIS MATCH IS YOUR	IDEA	OR DAVID'S? SO FAR I DO NOT GATHER THAT HE HAS
FANY EPILOG (332)	/GUNN/ RUBBISH! /VAUGHN/ ROT! YOU MAY PUT THAT	IDEA	OUT OF YOUR HEAD, BANNAL. POOR AS THIS PLAY IS, THERES
MIS. (151)	YOU NEVER TOLD ME -- /PERCIVAL/ I HADNT THE LEAST	IDEA	-- ALL TOGETHER. AN EMBARRASSED PAUSE. /PERCIVAL/ I
INCA (237)	YOU. WHAT? OH YES, IT'S QUITE EASY. I HAD NO	IDEA	-- AM I TO HANG IT UP JUST AS IT WAS? THANK YOU. (SHE
APPL II (264)	FOR THE PRESENT, THAT IS ALL. THIS MAY BE A GREAT	IDEA	-- /VANHATTAN/ SURELY, SURELY. /MAGNUS/ IT MAY ALSO BE
WIDO III (51)	/THE PARLORMAID/ (INTENSELY REPUDIATING THE	IDEA	) O-O-O-O-H NO, SIR. QUITE THE GENTLEMAN, SIR!
LION PREFACE(76)	NUCLEUS FOR HIS NEW CHURCH. IT WAS A MONSTROUS	IDEA	; AND THE SHOCK OF IT, AS HE AFTERWARDS DECLARED,
CURE (228)	TO TRY THE MUSIC-CURE YET. IT WAS YOUR MOTHER'S	IDEA	; BUT I'LL CALL AND TELL HER TO WAIT A DAY OR TWO. I
OVER (181)	VERY ODD! /JUNO/ SHE SAID IT WAS AN EXCELLENT	IDEA	; THAT DOMESTIC FELICITY WAS MAKING US PERFECTLY
FANY PROLOG (261)	HERE, AND HAD SEEN A LOT OF PLAYS. HE HAD NO	IDEA	SHE'D BEEN AWAY IN VENICE ALL THE TIME. /THE COUNT/ OH,
JOAN 4 (105)	IDEA STRIKES AT US? /CAUCHON/ HOW DOES HER	IDEA	STRIKE AT YOU, EXCEPT AS IT STRIKES AT ALL OF US,
JOAN 4 (105)	POWER. WELL, DO YOU NOT SEE HOW THIS GIRL'S	IDEA	STRIKES AT US? /CAUCHON/ HOW DOES HER IDEA STRIKE AT
2TRU II (60)	THE REWARD? /TALLBOYS/ CERTAINLY SHE WOULD. GOOD	IDEA	THAT: WHAT? /THE COUNTESS/ YES, COLONEL, ISNT IT?
MIS. PREFACE(18)	BRUTAL, STUPID, UNSCRUPULOUS CLASS, WITH A FIXED	IDEA	THAT ALL ENJOYMENT CONSISTS IN UNDETECTED SINNING; AND
KING I (196)	FLATTERED WHEN I HEARD OF IT. I HAD NO	IDEA	THAT BARBARA PUT SO HIGH A PRICE ON MY BELIEF IN HER
LION PREFACE(23)	TODAY IS THAT HE EXPRESSLY REPUDIATES THE	IDEA	THAT FORMS OF RELIGION, ONCE ROOTED, CAN BE WEEDED OUT
LION PREFACE(76)	FLASHED UPON HIM ON THE ROAD TO DAMASCUS, THE	IDEA	THAT HE COULD NOT ONLY MAKE A RELIGION OF HIS TWO
LION PREFACE(69)	JESUS WAS A CELIBATE, AND SHRINK EVEN FROM THE	IDEA	THAT HIS BIRTH WAS A NATURAL ONE, YET CLING WITH
HART III (140)	DO FOR HER? /MANGAN/ DONT YOU RUN AWAY WITH THIS	IDEA	THAT I HAVE NOTHING. I-- /HECTOR/ OH, DONT EXPLAIN. WE
PYGM V (277)	YOU WILL JOLLY SOON SEE WHETHER SHE HAS AN	IDEA	THAT I HAVNT PUT INTO HER HEAD OR A WORD THAT I HAVNT
ROCK I (220)	SENTIMENTAL REVOLT AGAINST UNEMPLOYMENT. I HAD NO	IDEA	THAT IT HAD ACADEMIC PRETENSIONS. /HIPNEY/ LORD BLESS
MRS III (228)	NOW AS TO PRACTICAL MATTERS. YOU MAY HAVE AN	IDEA	THAT IVE FLUNG MY MONEY ABOUT; BUT I HAVNT: I'M RICHER
OVER (183)	HOPE FOR ME? /MRS LUNN/ OH, YES. GREGORY HAS AN	IDEA	THAT MARRIED WOMEN KEEP LISTS OF THE MEN THEYLL MARRY
MIS. PREFACE(73)	IT WILL BE NECESSARY TO SURPRISE THEM WITH THE	IDEA	THAT TEACHING IS WORK, AND THAT THE TEACHER IS TIRED
WIDO I (9)	WE MUST CERTAINLY SEE THAT, MR COKANE. I HAD NO	IDEA	THAT THE ARCHITECT OF COLOGNE CATHEDRAL LIVED SO
LION PREFACE(29)	OR THEIR WITNESSES, PILATE HAVING NATURALLY NO	IDEA	THAT THE PRISONER CONCEIVES HIMSELF AS GOING THROUGH AN
METH PREFACE(R48)	WE WERE INTELLECTUALLY INTOXICATED WITH THE	IDEA	THAT THE WORLD COULD MAKE ITSELF WITHOUT DESIGN,
SIM I (49)	ONEANOTHER. THEN THEY HIT OUT FOR THEMSELVES THE	IDEA	THAT THEY WERE NOT TO LOVE ONEANOTHER, BUT THAT THEY
FANY PROLOG (261)	BUT FROM WHAT BILLY BURJOYCE TOLD ME I GOT THE	IDEA	THAT YOUR DAUGHTER KNEW HER WAY ABOUT HERE, AND HAD
MIS. (195)	WAS NOTHING BUT THE BLINDFOLDED CHILD: PRETTY	IDEA	THAT, I THINK! I SHALL HAVE AS GOOD A CHANCE WITH
GENV II (55)	SECRETARY/ SHE TOLD ME ABOUT IT. BUT I HAD NO	IDEA	THE MAN WAS YOUR NEPHEW. I SEE HOW AWKWARD IT IS FOR
DOCT III (138)	A FUSS ABOUT IT. OF COURSE I'LL PAY IT. I HAD NO	IDEA	THE POOR FELLOW WAS HARD UP. I'M AS SHOCKED AS ANY OF
SUPR III (82)	UP MOTOR CARS IN THE SOUTH OF EUROPE: A WELCOME	IDEA	TO A DESPERATE AND DISAPPOINTED MAN. HE GAVE ME SOME
MILL I (152)	AND HAS NEVER, AS FAR AS I KNOW, CONTRIBUTED AN	IDEA	TO ANY OF THEM. /ALASTAIR/ BE FAIR TO HIM, EPPY. NO MAN
LION PREFACE(57)	THE MOMENT YOU TRY TO REDUCE THE SUNDAY SCHOOL	IDEA	TO FIGURES YOU FIND THAT IT BRINGS YOU BACK TO THE
CATH 1 (170)	MY WORD FOR IT. IT WILL STRIKE YOU AS A SPLENDID	IDEA	TO HAVE CONSCIENTIOUS SCRUPLES -- TO DESIRE THE
HART II (86)	HANDLE MONEY IS TO GIVE HIM SOME. I EXPLAINED MY	IDEA	TO SOME FRIENDS IN THE CITY, AND THEY FOUND THE MONEY;
VWOO 1 (121)	TAKE THAT AWAY FROM YOU ONCE YOUVE HAD IT." HIS	IDEA	WAS A WALKING TOUR, SPENDING THE NIGHTS IN THE BEST
JOAN PREFACE(30)	COMMON MORALITY OF CHRISTENDOM. AND ALTHOUGH THE	IDEA	WE CALL NATIONALISM WAS SO FOREIGN TO THE MEDIEVAL
MRS I (194)	/FRANK/ (RHAPSODICALLY) THEN YOU CAN HAVE NO	IDEA	WHAT A GIRL SHE IS. SUCH CHARACTER! SUCH SENSE! AND
INCA (247)	SITS DOWN) THERE IS A CERTAIN COARSE FUN IN THE	IDEA	WHICH COMPELS ME TO SMILE (HE TURNS UP HIS MOUSTACHE
LION PREFACE(76)	ATTACHING THE NAME OF JESUS CHRIST TO THE GREAT	IDEA	WHICH FLASHED UPON HIM ON THE ROAD TO DAMASCUS, THE
MTH3 (109)	CRANKS WHO HAD TALKED ONE ANOTHER INTO A FIXED	IDEA	WHICH HAD BECOME A MONOMANIA WITH THEM. IT WAS NOT
DOCT I (103)	ALL FEVERS. /B.B./ (SUDDENLY RISING TO THE NEW	IDEA	WITH IMMENSE INTEREST AND EXCITEMENT) WHAT! RIDGEON:
NEVR II (234)	ONLY THIS MORNING? /DOLLY/ (SEIZING THE	IDEA	WITH RAPTURE) OH YES, I DECLARE! /PHILIP/ THE VERY
HART I (64)	I HAVE BEEN AWAY FOR NEARLY A MONTH; AND I HAD NO	IDEA	YOU KNEW MY WIFE, OR THAT YOU WERE COMING HERE. I AM.
FANY PROLOG (257)	HIS HOST'S OBSOLETE COSTUME, CONTINUES) I HAD NO	IDEA	YOU WERE GOING TO APPEAR IN THE PIECE YOURSELF. /THE
MTH3 (99)	ME. THE PRESIDENT. BURGE-LUBIN. I HAD NO	IDEA	YOUR BEDROOM SWITCH WAS IN. I BEG YOUR PARDON. THE
SUPR III (108)	HOMES; BUT WHEN WE, TOO, FOUGHT FOR THAT MIGHTY	IDEA	, A CATHOLIC CHURCH, WE SWEPT THEM BACK TO AFRICA. /THE
2TRU I (41)	HONESTY IS THE BEST POLICY. I HAVE ANOTHER	IDEA	, AND A MUCH BETTER ONE. YOU LEAVE THIS TO ME. (HE
LIED (204)	(RUNNING BACK FROM THE BELL, DELIGHTED WITH THE	IDEA	, AND COMING BETWEEN THEM) OH HENRY, IF YOU WOULDNT
HART II (86)	YOUR FATHER'S MEASURE. I SAW THAT HE HAD A SOUND	IDEA	, AND THAT HE WOULD WORK HIMSELF SILLY FOR IT IF HE GOT
SUPR III (108)	TO FURTHER A UNIVERSAL PURPOSE-- FIGHTING FOR AN	IDEA	, AS THEY CALL IT. WHY WAS THE CRUSADER BRAVER THAN THE
MIS. (146)	ONE. /TARLETON/ (IMPRESSED, AS USUAL) THATS AN	IDEA	, CERTAINLY, I DONT THINK ANYBODY HAS EVER WRITTEN
MTH2 (69)	OWN GOVERNMENT. /LUBIN/ QUITE AN INTERESTING	IDEA	, DOCTOR. EXTRAVAGANT. FANTASTIC. BUT QUITE
2TRU II (70)	IT WAS A SORT OF FULFILMENT. BUT IT GIVES YOU AN	IDEA	, DOESNT IT, OF WHAT I MEAN? (SHE SITS DOWN AGAIN,
BARB PREFACE(213)	VOID, AND ASSUMING THAT EVERY PHILOSOPHICAL	IDEA	, EVERY HISTORIC THEORY, EVERY CRITICISM OF OUR MORAL,
CAPT II (261)	IRON-WILLED! STONEWALL JACKSON! THATS THE	IDEA	, ISNT IT? /BRASSBOUND/ (HOPELESSLY) YOU ARE LAUGHING
BULL I (76)	A LOCAL OPTIONIST TO THE BACKBONE. YOU HAVE NO	IDEA	, MR HAFFIGAN, OF THE RUIN THAT IS WROUGHT IN THIS
SUPR PREFACE(R34)	SO STUPENDOUS AS A RELIGIOUS OR POLITICAL	IDEA	, OR A GENERAL IDEA OF ANY SORT, WERE TO OCCUR TO HIM.

CAND I SD(91)	SUSPECT EITHER HER HUSBAND OR HERSELF OF ANY SUCH	IDEA	, OR INDEED OF ANY CONCERN WITH THE ART OF TITIAN. JUST
UNPL PREFACE(R19)	YOUNGER ACTOR-MANAGERS HAVE BEEN STRUCK WITH THE	IDEA	, QUITE NOVEL IN THEIR PROFESSION, OF PERFORMING
DEST SD(157)	INSUSCEPTIBLE TO THE NAPOLEONIC OR ANY OTHER	IDEA	, STUPENDOUSLY EGOTISTICAL, EMINENTLY QUALIFIED TO RUSH
MIS. (120)	PAVILION INTO THE GROUNDS). /JOHNNY/ NOT A BAD	IDEA	, THAT. /LORD SUMMERHAYS/ WHAT? /JOHNNY/ GOING TO MEET
HART PREFACE(38)	THAN ANY OTHER WAR OF OUR TIME A WAR FOR AN	IDEA	, THE CONQUERORS, CONFRONTED WITH A HEROIC TASK OF
LION PREFACE(57)	HIS MULTIPLE TO ONE THOUSAND." THE SUNDAY SCHOOL	IDEA	, WITH ITS PRINCIPLE " TO EACH THE INCOME HE DESERVES,"
MTH2 (85)	US. BUT WHAT A PITY! IT IS SUCH A FASCINATING	IDEA	! I THINK YOU ARE TOO HARD ON US PRACTICAL MEN; BUT
MIS. (114)	CANE! /BENTLEY/ PITY YOU HAVNT GOT MORE THAN ONE	IDEA	! IF YOU WANT TO KNOW, THEY DID TRY THAT ON ME ONCE,
ARMS I (9)	TO THE OTTOMAN AND SNATCHING THE CLOAK) A GOOD	IDEA	! I'LL KEEP THE CLOAK; AND YOULL TAKE CARE THAT NOBODY
BULL II (115)	BE MY WIFE? /NORA/ (PROMPTLY) DEED I WONT. THE	IDEA	! (LOOKING AT HIM MORE CAREFULLY) ARRA, COME HOME, MR
CURE (232)	I SAY, WHAT LOVELY HANDS YOUVE GOT! /STREGA/ THE	IDEA	! (SHE HURLS HIM TO THE CARPET). /REGINALD/ (ON THE
CAND II (106)	LOVE AFFAIRS. HOW DARE YOU SAY SUCH A THING? THE	IDEA	! (SHE TUCKS THE BOOK UNDER HER ARM, AND IS FLOUNCING
PYGM I (207)	DAUGHTER/ DO NOTHING OF THE SORT, MOTHER. THE	IDEA	! /THE MOTHER/ PLEASE ALLOW ME, CLARA. HAVE YOU ANY
MIS. (189)	WAS AFFIRMING MY MANHOOD. /MRS TARLETON/ WHAT AN	IDEA	! WHAT PUTS ALL THESE THINGS INTO YOUR HEAD? /GUNNER/
		IDEAL	
CAND II (114)	ALL HIS SOUL FOR THE WOMAN HE LOVES? THATS MY	IDEAL	: WHATS YOURS, AND THAT OF ALL THE DREADFUL PEOPLE WHO
CATH PREFACE(157)	BURBAGE AS AN ACTOR. PLAYWRIGHTS DO NOT WRITE FOR	IDEAL	ACTORS WHEN THEIR LIVELIHOOD IS AT STAKE: IF THEY DID,
LIED (192)	HOW COULD YOU? I HAVE FOLLOWED THE GREEK	IDEAL	AND NOT NEGLECTED THE CULTURE OF MY BODY. LIKE ALL
GETT PREFACE(216)	OF GUESSES; BUT AS ALL DEPARTURES FROM THE	IDEAL	ARE REGARDED AS DISGRACEFUL, EVIDENCE CANNOT BE
3PLA PREFACE(R38)	RAISE A SHRIEK OF CONCERN FOR THEIR KNIGHTLY	IDEAL	AS IF NOBODY HAD EVER QUESTIONED ITS SUFFICIENCY SINCE
PRES (164)	BE PERFECTLY IN EARNEST. HE SAYS HE HAS MET HIS	IDEAL	AT LAST, A REALLY SOLDIERLY WOMAN. SHE WILL SIT ON HIS
DOCT PREFACE(68)	HIS CLAIMS ARE IRRESISTIBLE; AND THIS IS THE	IDEAL	AT WHICH EVERY M.O.H. SHOULD AIM. BUT THE PROFESSION
OVER (190)	WE'RE NOT PERFECT; BUT AS LONG AS WE KEEP THE	IDEAL	BEFORE US-- /GREGORY/ HOW? /JUNO/ BY ADMITTING WE'RE
JOAN PREFACE(8)	HE WILL NEVER CATCH JOAN'S LIKENESS. HER	IDEAL	BIOGRAPHER MUST BE FREE FROM NINETEENTH CENTURY
3PLA PREFACE(R38)	TO BEAR THE WEIGHT OF A LIFE THAT WILL NOT GRANT	IDEAL	CONDITIONS TO THE LIVER. THIS ONE RAY OF PERCEPTION
METH PREFACE(R17)	WHY HE SHOULD BE SAVED. HE IS BY NO MEANS AN	IDEAL	CREATURE. AT HIS PRESENT BEST MANY OF HIS WAYS ARE SO
DEVL EPILOG (83)	AND DID HANDSOMELY AND LOFTILY. HE FELL, AND HIS	IDEAL	EMPIRE WAS DISMEMBERED, NOT THROUGH HIS OWN
BULL PREFACE(16)	THE ONLY SPOT ON EARTH WHICH STILL PRODUCES THE	IDEAL	ENGLISHMAN OF HISTORY. BLACKGUARD, BULLY, DRUNKARD,
PYGM EPILOG (296)	TO THE EFFECT THAT SHE WOULD HAVE IN FREDDY AN	IDEAL	ERRAND BOY. FREDDY HIMSELF WAS NEXT SOUNDED ON THE
JOAN PREFACE(9)	UNIQUE IN ART IN POINT OF BEING EVIDENTLY NOT AN	IDEAL	FACE BUT A PORTRAIT, AND YET SO UNCOMMON AS TO BE
ARMS II SD(29)	IT IS CLEAR THAT HERE OR NOWHERE IS RAINA'S	IDEAL	HERO. CATHERINE IS HARDLY LESS ENTHUSIASTIC ABOUT HIM
GETT PREFACE(217)	IN GLASS HOUSES. WE MAY TAKE IT, THEN, THAT THE	IDEAL	HUSBAND AND THE IDEAL WIFE ARE NO MORE REAL HUMAN
SUPR III (112)	RAW FORCE INTO HIGHER AND HIGHER INDIVIDUALS, THE	IDEAL	INDIVIDUAL BEING OMNIPOTENT, OMNISCIENT, INFALLIBLE,
O'FL PREFACE(203)	IS WHY I DID NOT ENDOW O'FLAHERTY V.C. WITH AN	IDEAL	IRISH COLLEEN FOR HIS SWEETHEART, AND GAVE HIM FOR HIS
MIS. PREFACE(87)	THE WORSE FOR EVERYBODY CONCERNED. THE FAMILY	IDEAL	IS A HUMBUG AND A NUISANCE: ONE MIGHT AS REASONABLY
MIS. (144)	NO. /HYPATIA/ SHALL I TELL YOU WHY? YOUR	IDEAL	IS AN OLD WOMAN. I DARESAY SHE'S GOT A YOUNG FACE; BUT
BULL IV (166)	TOO MUCH OF THE ANIMATED BEEFSTEAK ABOUT HER. THE	IDEAL	IS WHAT I LIKE. NOW LARRY'S TASTE IS JUST THE
LADY PREFACE(212)	IMPLIES; WHOSE VERY EXISTENCE IS AN INSULT TO THE	IDEAL	IT REALIZES; WHOSE EYE DISPARAGES, WHOSE RESONANT
GETT PREFACE(216)	OF MARRIAGE, REMOTENESS OF THE FACTS FROM THE	IDEAL	. BUT BEFORE WE ALLOW THIS TO DETER US FROM TOUCHING
DOCT IV (165)	LIFE, I HAVNT ALWAYS BEEN ABLE TO LIVE UP TO MY	IDEAL	. BUT IN MY OWN REAL WORLD I HAVE NEVER DONE ANYTHING
MILL PREFACE(117)	PARLIAMENTARY, DEMOCRACY WAS A DREAM, AN	IDEAL	. EVERYTHING WOULD BE WELL WHEN ALL MEN HAD VOTES,
GETT PREFACE(216)	AS A FACT IS NOT IN THE LEAST LIKE MARRIAGE AS AN	IDEAL	. IF IT WERE, THE SUDDEN CHANGES WHICH HAVE BEEN MADE
FANY PROLOG (258)	AT PRESENT, NOWHERE, EXCEPT AS A MEMORY AND AN	IDEAL	. (SAVOYARD INCLINES HIS HEAD RESPECTFULLY TO THE
SUPR IV (158)	IS EVER SO MUCH EASIER THAN LIVING UP TO AN	IDEAL	. OH, I SHALL ENRAPTURE JACK SOMETIMES! /OCTAVIUS/ (
DOCT III (144)	TOWARDS JUST AS ANY OTHER MAN STRIVES TOWARDS HIS	IDEAL	. /B.B./ (INTOLERANT) DONT TROUBLE TO EXPLAIN. I NOW
GENV IV (103)	FOR WOMEN, THE UTMOST PERIL FOR MEN: THAT IS THE	IDEAL	. /THE BETROTHED/ I SAY, SIGNOR: DO YOU TAKE ANY
MRS I (187)	FROM HER IDEAL. /VIVIE/ HER WHAT? ! /PRAED/ HER	IDEAL	. /VIVIE/ DO YOU MEAN HER IDEAL OF ME? /PRAED/ YES.
MRS I (186)	DONT MEAN THAT, BUT YOU ARE SO DIFFERENT FROM HER	IDEAL	. /VIVIE/ HER WHAT? ! /PRAED/ HER IDEAL. /VIVIE/ DO
GETT PREFACE(217)	I HAVE ANY KNOWLEDGE IS IN THE LEAST LIKE THE	IDEAL	MARRIAGE, I DO NOT MEAN THAT IT IS WORSE: I MEAN
GETT PREFACE(198)	WE ARE NOT THOUGHTLESSLY GLORIFYING IT AS THE	IDEAL	MARRIED STATE. THE GOSPEL OF LAODICEA. LET US TRY TO
GETT PREFACE(216)	WE REFER TO THE FACTS, WE DISCOVER THAT THE	IDEAL	MATRIMONY AND DOMESTICITY WHICH OUR BIGOTS IMPLORE US
2TRU I (43)	AT THE BEDSIDE). WE ARE GOING TO HAVE AN	IDEAL	NIGHT. NOW LISTEN. PICTURE TO YOURSELF A HEAVENLY
SIM II (65)	IF HE READ THE NEWSPAPERS. WE MUST HAVE AN	IDEAL	OF A BEAUTIFUL AND GOOD WORLD. WE MUST BELIEVE THAT TO
DOCT PREFACE(65)	HE HAS EVERY INDUCEMENT TO STRIVE TOWARDS THE	IDEAL	OF A CLEAN BILL OF HEALTH. HE HAS A SAFE, DIGNIFIED,
ROCK II (281)	TREATMENT OF THEIR WOMEN FOLK. THAT WAS HER	IDEAL	OF A DELIGHTFUL HUSBAND. SHE FOUND TODAY THAT THE
MIS. PREFACE(87)	THAN FAMILIES OF TEN WHICH ATTAIN THE BOER	IDEAL	OF BEING OUT OF SIGHT OF ONE ANOTHER'S CHIMNEY SMOKE.
APPL PREFACE(173)	TALENT BUT ON HIS CONFORMITY TO THE POPULAR	IDEAL	OF DIGNITY AND PERFECT BREEDING, HE HAS TO BE TRAINED,
2TRU PREFACE(20)	NAME ON A REGISTER OF VOTERS WE COULD REALIZE THE	IDEAL	OF EVERY MAN HIS OWN SOLON AND HIS OWN PLATO, AS TO
HART PREFACE(19)	A STANDARD OF INEVITABLE EVIL INSTEAD OF TO THE	IDEAL	OF LIFE MORE ABUNDANT. I CAN ANSWER FOR AT LEAST ONE
CYMB FORWORD(135)	MRS ALVING IN GHOSTS, THE SLAVERY TO AN INHUMAN	IDEAL	OF MARITAL FIDELITY WHICH LED HIM TO THIS VILLAINOUS
MRS I (187)	! /PRAED/ HER IDEAL. /VIVIE/ DO YOU MEAN HER	IDEAL	OF ME? /PRAED/ YES. /VIVIE/ WHAT ON EARTH IS IT
PRES (167)	AT MY FEET. /BALSQUITH/ (DOING SO) THAT IS MY	IDEAL	OF ROMANTIC HAPPINESS. IT COMMITS ME EXACTLY AS FAR AS
MIS. (150)	AND I CANT ANSWER FOR HIM SOCIALLY; BUT HE'S AN	IDEAL	PASSENGER FOR A FLYER. HE SAVED ME FROM A SMASH. /LORD
JITT III (62)	A PERSON YOU DONT KNOW. YOU SEE, EVERYBODY IS AN	IDEAL	PERSON TO US UNTIL WE MEET THEM; AND THEN,
SUPR PREFACE(R28)	GO UP TO THE BRIMS OF OUR HATS BY INSTINCT. OUR	IDEAL	PROSPERITY IS NOT THE PROSPERITY OF THE INDUSTRIAL
3PLA PREFACE(R18)	OFF THE SAME STAGE FOR HER CONTEMPT FOR THE	IDEAL	REPRESENTED BY A CARRIAGE, A FASHIONABLE DRESSMAKER,
FABL PREFACE(82)	AND HENRY IRVING, NOMINATED BY GALLUP POLL AS	IDEAL	RULERS, THE PEOPLE? AM I THE PEOPLE? WAS RUSKIN?
FANY PROLOG (258)	(SAVOYARD INCLINES HIS HEAD RESPECTFULLY TO THE	IDEAL	). BUT I AM BY NO MEANS AN IDEALOGUE. I AM NOT CONTENT
GENV II (58)	AN IDEALIST. /JUDGE/ NECESSARILY. JUSTICE IS AN	IDEAL	; AND I AM A JUDGE. WHAT, MAY I ASK, ARE YOU? /SIR
SUPR III (115)	OR REFINED ENOUGH TO SEEM TO REALIZE HIS	IDEAL	; AND SO HE WENT TO HIS GRAVE BELIEVING IN HIS DREAM.
GETT PREFACE(218)	YET BORN KEEPS THEM OR EVER CAN KEEP THEM IN THE	IDEAL	SENSE. MARRIAGE AS A MAGIC SPELL. THE TRUTH WHICH
LADY PREFACE(215)	FRANK WILL NOT HAVE HER AT ANY PRICE, BECAUSE HIS	IDEAL	SHAKESPEAR IS RATHER LIKE A SAILOR IN A MELODRAMA; AND
LADY PREFACE(225)	OR GAGS INTERPOLATED BY THE ACTORS. THIS	IDEAL	SHAKESPEAR WAS TOO WELL BEHAVED TO GET DRUNK;
GETT PREFACE(217)	FROM SOCIETY BEING ORGANIZED IN A DEFENCE OF ITS	IDEAL	SO JEALOUS AND IMPLACABLE THAT THE LEAST STEP FROM THE
BULL PREFACE(48)	IS JUST WHAT THE MILITARY SYSTEM AIMS AT. ITS	IDEAL	SOLDIER BEING, NOT A COMPLETE MAN, BUT A DOCILE UNIT
SUPR HANDBOK(188)	MISCONCEPTION OF ITS NATURE. MAN DOES DESIRE AN	IDEAL	SUPERMAN WITH SUCH ENERGY AS HE CAN SPARE FROM HIS
DOCT III (144)	UP TO BE EXACTLY A SUPERMAN; BUT STILL, IT'S AN	IDEAL	THAT I STRIVE TOWARDS JUST AS ANY OTHER MAN STRIVES
MRS II (208)	ME. PERFECT GENTLEMAN, PRADDY. ALWAYS WERE. MY	IDEAL	THROUGH LIFE. (HE RISES TO GO, BUT PAUSES A MOMENT
GENV II (58)	JUSTICE, AS YOU SAY, IS AN IDEAL, AND A VERY FINE	IDEAL	TOO; BUT WHAT I HAVE TO DEAL WITH IS POWER; AND POWER
BULL PREFACE(49)	WERE MATTERS OF ORDINARY ROUTINE, THIS DETESTABLE	IDEAL	WAS EVER REALIZED; BUT YOUR COURTS-MARTIAL ARE NOT
GENV PREFACE(13)	COULD BE TRUSTED TO DO NOTHING REVOLUTIONARY. OUR	IDEAL	WAS " A COMMONPLACE TYPE WITH A STICK AND A PIPE AND A
GETT PREFACE(217)	MAY TAKE IT, THEN, THAT THE IDEAL HUSBAND AND THE	IDEAL	WIFE ARE NO MORE REAL HUMAN BEINGS THAN THE CHERUBIM.
GENV III (65)	DOMESTIC PARAGON: A POLITICAL IDIOT. IN SHORT, AN	IDEAL	WIFE. THE WIDOW ENTERS ON THE ARM OF SIR ORPHEUS
SUPR I (24)	TO MAKE PRINTER'S INK TO SCOFF AT HER AND GLORIFY	IDEAL	WOMEN WITH. HE PRETENDS TO SPARE HER THE PANGS OF
GENV II (58)	ME TO CALL YOU SO-- JUSTICE, AS YOU SAY, IS AN	IDEAL	, AND A VERY FINE IDEAL TOO; BUT WHAT I HAVE TO DEAL
MIS. (144)	DOUBT OF IT. DONT INSIST. /HYPATIA/ IT'S NOT YOUR	IDEAL	, IS IT? /LORD SUMMERHAYS/ NO. /HYPATIA/ SHALL I TELL
MIS. PREFACE(87)	TALK OF THE BARRACK IDEAL, OR THE FORECASTLE	IDEAL	, OR ANY OTHER SUBSTITUTION OF THE MACHINERY OF SOCIAL
MIS. PREFACE(87)	ONE MIGHT AS REASONABLY TALK OF THE BARRACK	IDEAL	, OR THE FORECASTLE IDEAL, OR ANY OTHER SUBSTITUTION
DOCT IV (170)	AND THAT GIVES US A COMMON FAITH, A COMMON	IDEAL	, THAT NOBODY ELSE CAN QUITE HAVE. LIFE WILL ALWAYS BE
UNPL PREFACE(R25)	TO SOME A DIVINE ORDINANCE, TO SOME A ROMANTIC	IDEAL	, TO SOME A DOMESTIC PROFESSION FOR WOMEN, AND TO SOME
BULL PREFACE(13)	IS BENT ON CREATING A NEW IRELAND AFTER ITS OWN	IDEAL	, WHEREAS MY PLAY IS A VERY UNCOMPROMISING PRESENTMENT
		IDEALISM	
PYGM EPILOG (291)	OF HIS AFFECTIONS, HIS SENSE OF BEAUTY, AND HIS	IDEALISM	FROM HIS SPECIFICALLY SEXUAL IMPULSES. THIS MAKES
PLES PREFACE(R10)	SALUTARILY SHORTSIGHTED CHRISTIAN SOCIALIST	IDEALISM	. I AVAILED MYSELF OF IT IN CANDIDA, THE DRUNKEN
PHIL II (121)	AT ALL: I LOATHE IT AS I LOATHE ALL THE SNARES OF	IDEALISM	; BUT I HAVE SOME COMMON HUMANITY AND COMMON SENSE.
PLES PREFACE(R18)	WHICH WAS, WHETHER THE POLITICAL AND RELIGIOUS	IDEALISM	WHICH HAD INSPIRED GLADSTONE TO CALL FOR THE RESCUE
PLES PREFACE(R18)	STATES, WILL SURVIVE THE GENERAL ONSLAUGHT ON	IDEALISM	WHICH IS IMPLICIT, AND INDEED EXPLICIT, IN ARMS AND
PLES PREFACE(R18)	OF THE MODERN SCHOOL. FOR MY PART I HOPE NOT; FOR	IDEALISM	, WHICH IS ONLY A FLATTERING NAME FOR ROMANCE IN
		IDEALISMS	
2TRU III (110)	FROM ONE ANOTHER IN BEAUTIFUL IMPOSSIBLE	IDEALISMS	TO ENABLE THEM TO BEAR ONE ANOTHER'S COMPANY? THE
		IDEALIST	
GENV II SD(49)	TYPE, AND, ONE GUESSES, BEGAN AS A GENEVAN	IDEALIST	. AGE FIFTY OR THEREABOUTS. THERE IS A TELEPHONE ON
GENV II (58)	POWERS. /SIR O./ I AM AFRAID YOU ARE A BIT OF AN	IDEALIST	. /JUDGE/ NECESSARILY. JUSTICE IS AN IDEAL; AND I

O'FL PREFACE(202)	BY VOLUNTARY ENLISTMENT. THE HAPPY HOME OF THE	IDEALIST	MAY BECOME COMMON UNDER MILLENNIAL CONDITIONS. IT
DEST SD(150)	CIRCUMSTANCE, WHICH WOULD HAVE EMBARRASSED AN	IDEALIST	SOLDIER, HAS BEEN WORTH A THOUSAND CANNON TO
HART III (139)	AND HAS FAILED IGNOMINIOUSLY; WHILST YOU, AS AN	IDEALIST	, HAVE SUCCEEDED BRILLIANTLY. /MAZZINI/ I HOPE YOU
		IDEALISTIC	
PHIL I SD(84)	THE COLONEL'S BOYISHNESS. HE IS A MAN OF FERVENT	IDEALISTIC	SENTIMENT, SO FREQUENTLY OUTRAGED BY THE FACTS OF
		IDEALISTS	
APPL PREFACE(171)	UNREALITY OF BOTH DEMOCRACY AND ROYALTY AS OUR	IDEALISTS	CONCEIVE THEM. OUR LIBERAL DEMOCRATS BELIEVE IN A
CAPT III (297)	BY IT. /LADY CICELY/ OH, I SEE YOURE ONE OF THE	IDEALISTS	-- THE IMPOSSIBILISTS! WE HAVE THEM, TOO,
PLES PREFACE(R19)	IN THE WORLD WORKING ITSELF OUT AS FAST AS THE	IDEALISTS	WILL ALLOW IT; AND IF THEY WOULD ONLY LET IT ALONE
GENV IV (117)	THREE VOLUMES OF KARL MARX, THE THEORIES OF THE	IDEALISTS	, THE RANTING OF THE DEMAGOGUES: IN SHORT, THE
		IDEALIZATION	
CLEO NOTES (205)	CITIZEN'S IGNORANCE OF THE PAST COMBINES WITH HIS	IDEALIZATION	OF THE PRESENT TO MISLEAD AND FLATTER HIM. OUR
		IDEALIZATIONS	
DEVL I SD(3)	OF THE RIGHTS OF MAN. INTO THE MERITS OF THESE	IDEALIZATIONS	IT IS NOT HERE NECESSARY TO INQUIRE: SUFFICE
SUPR III (119)	WITH SIMULATED ACCOMPLISHMENTS AND DELUSIVE	IDEALIZATIONS	. WHEN YOUR SAINTED MOTHER, BY DINT OF
GETT PREFACE(194)	HIS ATTEMPTS TO MANUFACTURE ADMIRABLE HEROINES BY	IDEALIZATIONS	OF HOME-BRED WOMANHOOD ARE NOT ONLY ABSURD BUT
GETT (286)	TO ME. EVERYBODY OUGHT TO HAVE ONE OF THESE	IDEALIZATIONS	, LIKE DANTE'S BEATRICE. (HE CLASPS HIS HANDS
		IDEALIZE	
JITT III (62)	COMFORT HIM. STILL, YOU MUST BE CAREFUL NOT TO	IDEALIZE	A PERSON YOU DONT KNOW. YOU SEE, EVERYBODY IS AN
PYGM EPILOG (291)	HIGGINS COULD HAVE A PASSION FOR PHONETICS AND	IDEALIZE	HIS MOTHER INSTEAD OF ELIZA, WOULD SEEM TO THEM
APPL I (205)	OF COURSE NOT. IS IT NOT CURIOUS HOW PEOPLE	IDEALIZE	THEIR RULERS? IN THE OLD DAYS THE KING -- POOR
MTH5 (245)	STUDIES OF YOU, NOT PORTRAITS, OF COURSE: I SHALL	IDEALIZE	YOU A LITTLE. I HAVE COME TO THE CONCLUSION THAT
		IDEALIZED	
PYGM EPILOG (292)	WHEN THEY HAVE DEALT WITH MEN, AND BEEN SLAVISHLY	IDEALIZED	BY THE MEN OVER WHOM THEY HAVE FLOURISHED THE WHIP
DEVL I SD(3)	BOILED UP TO SHOOTING POINT, THE SHOOTING BEING	IDEALIZED	TO THE ENGLISH MIND AS SUPPRESSION OF REBELLION
		IDEALIZING	
SUPR III (116)	WORSHIPPING AND HAPPINESS HUNTING AND WOMAN	IDEALIZING	WAS NOT WORTH A DUMP AS A PHILOSOPHY OF LIFE; SO
		IDEALLY	
MTH5 (222)	/ECRASIA/ WRONG WITH THEM! INSTEAD OF BEING	IDEALLY	BEAUTIFUL NYMPHS AND YOUTHS, THEY ARE HORRIBLY
GENV I (45)	OUR HOUSEKEEPER FEODOROVNA BALLYBOUSHKA. WE WERE	IDEALLY	HAPPY WITH THIS EXCELLENT WOMAN FOR YEARS. IN HER
		IDEALOGUE	
FANY PROLOG (258)	TO THE IDEAL). BUT I AM BY NO MEANS AN	IDEALOGUE	. I AM NOT CONTENT WITH BEAUTIFUL DREAMS: I WANT
		IDEALS	
DEST SD(149)	COMMON IDEALS. NOT THAT HE IS INCAPABLE OF THESE	IDEALS	: ON THE CONTRARY, HE HAS SWALLOWED THEM ALL IN HIS
2TRU PREFACE(24)	CHURCH AND INTENTIONS OF THE EMPIRE (UNREALIZED	IDEALS	BOTH) I AM ON THE SIDE OF THE CHURCH. AS TO THE EVIL
MRS PREFACE(153)	THE WILD DUCK, EXCLAIMS THAT I HAVE SHATTERED HIS	IDEALS	. ACTUALLY HIS IDEALS! WHAT WOULD DR RELLING SAY?
GETT PREFACE(196)	GOOD THING. WE MUST BE REASONABLE IN OUR DOMESTIC	IDEALS	. I DO NOT THINK THAT LIFE AT A PUBLIC SCHOOL IS
ARMS I (5)	WHAT SERGIUS WOULD DO. OUR PATRIOTISM. OUR HEROIC	IDEALS	. I SOMETIMES USED TO DOUBT WHETHER THEY WERE
ROCK I (208)	IN THESE REALITIES THAT WAS MISSING IN THE	IDEALS	. I THANK YOU FOR THAT BURST OF APPLAUSE: WHICH I
DEST SD(149)	LOYALTY, PATRIOTISM OR ANY OF THE COMMON	IDEALS	. NOT THAT HE IS INCAPABLE OF THESE IDEALS: ON THE
SUPR PREFACE(R18)	WHICH HE STRAYS IN ALL DIRECTIONS AFTER SECONDARY	IDEALS	. THE ARTIST IS EITHER A POET OR A SCALLAWAG: AS
ROCK I (208)	WE HAVE CHERISHED HOPES AND STRIVEN TOWARDS	IDEALS	. WE HAVE ASPIRED TO THINGS THAT HAVE NOT BEEN
SUPR II SD(62)	BY DEMANDING WHETHER THE CARRYING OUT OF HIS	IDEALS	OF CONDUCT WAS NOT THE MANIFEST OBJECT OF GOD
ARMS I (13)	AGO. /RAINA/ (OUTRAGED IN HER MOST CHERISHED	IDEALS	OF MANHOOD) CHOCOLATE! DO YOU STUFF YOUR POCKETS
SIM PREFACE(18)	EMBODY ALL THE ARTISTIC, ROMANTIC, AND MILITARY	IDEALS	OF OUR CULTURED SUBURBS, ON THE DAY OF JUDGMENT NOT
FANY III (324)	RUN AWAY. YOU ARE NOT DAZZLED AND MISLED BY FALSE	IDEALS	OF PATRIOTIC ENTHUSIASM: YOUR HONEST AND SENSIBLE
SUPR HANDBOK(188)	HIS SUPERFINGERS AT ALL MAN'S PRESENT TRUMPERY	IDEALS	OF RIGHT, DUTY, HONOR, JUSTICE, RELIGION, EVEN
3PLA PREFACE(R18)	IN OTHER WORDS, A DISPARAGEMENT OF THE SOCIAL	IDEALS	OF THE POORER MIDDLE CLASS AND OF THE VAST
HART PREFACE(40)	EXPOSED THEY WILL HIDE UNDER THE MANTLE OF THE	IDEALS	ON THE STAGE JUST AS THEY DO IN REAL LIFE. AND THOUGH
ARMS I (16)	(DEEPLY WOUNDED, BUT STEADFASTLY LOYAL TO HER	IDEALS	) INDEED! WOULD YOU KNOW HIM AGAIN IF YOU SAW HIM..
ARMS II SD(28)	ONLY OF OTHERS, BUT OF HIMSELF, TO LIVE UP TO HIS	IDEALS	; BY HIS CONSEQUENT CYNICAL SCORN FOR HUMANITY; BY
MIS. PREFACE(15)	OR OF REALITIES OF ANY SORT, BUT ALWAYS OF	IDEALS	SUCH AS THE HOME, A MOTHER'S INFLUENCE, A FATHER'S
PLES PREFACE(R19)	ATTEMPTS TO FOUND OUR INSTITUTIONS ON THE	IDEALS	SUGGESTED TO OUR IMAGINATIONS BY OUR HALF-SATISFIED
SUPR HANDBOK(183)	AND CYNICAL VIEW OF MARRIAGE, DO HOMAGE TO ITS	IDEALS	WITH A SERIOUSNESS THAT SEEMS OLD FASHIONED IN
MRS PREFACE(170)	BESIDES THAT REPROACH TO ME FOR SHATTERING HIS	IDEALS	, COMPLAINS THAT MRS WARREN IS NOT WICKED ENOUGH, AND
SUPR III (110)	HE IS WELCOME TO HIS DREAMS, HIS FOLLIES, HIS	IDEALS	, HIS HEROISMS, PROVIDED THAT THE KEYSTONE OF THEM
ANNA (300)	THEY WERE DOGS: THEY HAD NO IMAGINATION, NO	IDEALS	, NO SENSE OF HONOR AND DIGNITY TO SUSTAIN THEM. /THE
3PLA PREFACE(R35)	ROBS THE THIEF, THAT GROVELS BEFORE ALL SORTS OF	IDEALS	, SOCIAL, MILITARY, ECCLESIASTICAL, ROYAL AND DIVINE,
MRS PREFACE(153)	THAT I HAVE SHATTERED HIS IDEALS. ACTUALLY HIS	IDEALS	! WHAT WOULD DR RELLING SAY? AND MR WILLIAM ARCHER
		IDEAS	
JITT I (18)	/BRUNO/ IT IS NOT HE WHO IS ROBBING ME OF MY	IDEAS	: IT IS I WHO AM ROBBING HIM OF HIS WIFE; AND THE LESS
MIS. (129)	UNDERWEAR. ANYBODY CAN SELL UNDERWEAR. TARLETON'S	IDEAS	: THATS WHATS DONE IT. IVE OFTEN THOUGHT OF PUTTING
SUPR PREFACE(R40)	STOCK. OTHERS ARE THE VICTIMS OF ASSOCIATION OF	IDEAS	: THEY CALL ME PESSIMIST BECAUSE MY REMARKS WOUND
SUPR PREFACE(R32)	OR A WORTHY LEADER: THEY HAVE NO CONSTRUCTIVE	IDEAS	: THEY REGARD THOSE WHO HAVE THEM AS DANGEROUS
GENV III (72)	IDEAS. /THE NEWCOMER/ WHERE DID RUSSIA GET HER	IDEAS	? FROM ENGLAND. IN RUSSIA KARL MARX WOULD HAVE BEEN
NEVR IV (301)	VERY SAFE, DIDNT YOU, BEHIND YOUR ADVANCED	IDEAS	? I AMUSED MYSELF BY UPSETTING THEM PRETTY EASILY.
CAND I (94)	FOOLISH IDEAS INTO YOUR ED? /MARCHBANKS/ FOOLISH	IDEAS	? OH, YOU MEAN SOCIALISM? NO. /BURGESS/ THATS RIGHT.
NEVR IV (300)	VALENTINE SEEMS RATHER TOO OLD FASHIONED IN HIS	IDEAS	ABOUT HIS OWN SEX TO LIKE BEING CALLED AN IDIOT. AND
PYGM II (232)	PICKERING, THAT WOMAN HAS THE MOST EXTRAORDINARY	IDEAS	ABOUT ME. HERE I AM, A SHY, DIFFIDENT SORT OF MAN. IVE
MRS IV (249)	DONT UNDERSTAND: YOUR HEAD IS FULL OF IGNORANT	IDEAS	ABOUT ME. WHAT DO THE PEOPLE THAT TAUGHT YOU KNOW
MILL III (183)	BOARDS THAT HAVE UPSET EVERYTHING AND GIVEN GIRLS	IDEAS	ABOVE THEIR STATION WITHOUT GIVING THEM THE MEANS TO
CAND I (102)	HER FROM HER SLAVERY TO THEM. I'LL PIT MY OWN	IDEAS	AGAINST THEM. YOU ARE DRIVING ME OUT OF THE HOUSE
GENV II (54)	THAT WENT IN FOR BEING CLEVER AND HAVING ORIGINAL	IDEAS	AND ALL THAT SORT OF CRANKINESS. BUT I BEAT THEM
DOCT I (88)	TO? WHY, RIGHT BACK TO MY POOR DEAR OLD FATHER'S	IDEAS	AND DISCOVERIES. HE'S BEEN DEAD NOW OVER FORTY YEARS.
LION PREFACE(5)	BUT TURNING OUR MODERN LIGHTS ON TO CERTAIN	IDEAS	AND DOCTRINES IN THEM WHICH DISENTANGLE THEMSELVES
GETT SD(259)	AS IF THE BUILDERS, ANTICIPATING OUR MODERN	IDEAS	AND INSTINCTIVELY DEFYING THEM, HAD RESOLVED TO SHEW
MIS. PREFACE(30)	BELONG TO A BYGONE ORDER OF EDUCATIONAL	IDEAS	AND INSTITUTIONS, AND THAT SCHOOLS ARE NOT NOW A BIT
CAND I (102)	BECAUSE YOU DARENT LET HER CHOOSE BETWEEN YOUR	IDEAS	AND MINE. YOU ARE AFRAID TO LET ME SEE HER AGAIN. (
BULL PREFACE(23)	CONSCIENCE AND HER QUICK TERRORS; WE MUST DEAL IN	IDEAS	AND POLITICAL PRINCIPLES SINCE WE CANNOT DEAL IN
CLEO NOTES (210)	COURIER KILLS HORSES-- ENABLES MEN WITH COMMON	IDEAS	AND SUPERSTITIONS TO DISTANCE ALL COMPETITORS IN THE
WIDO III (60)	WE LIVE IN A PROGRESSIVE AGE; AND HUMANITARIAN	IDEAS	ARE ADVANCING AND MUST BE TAKEN INTO ACCOUNT. BUT MY
SUPR PREFACE(R23)	CONFUSED AND ITS PURPOSE SO PERVERTED, THAT ITS	IDEAS	ARE MERE FANTASY TO COMMON MEN. WHETHER THE ARTIST
BARB III (340)	OF CONVEYING MY IDEAS. /LADY BRITOMART/ YOUR	IDEAS	ARE NONSENSE. YOU GOT ON BECAUSE YOU WERE SELFISH AND
SIM II (55)	DISCUSSIONS. EACH OF THEM MUST LEARN THAT ITS	IDEAS	ARE NOT EVERYBODY'S IDEAS. HERE IS A CABLEGRAM FROM
HART II (118)	WANTS AND HOBBIES. I SIT HERE WORKING OUT MY OLD	IDEAS	AS A MEANS OF DESTROYING MY FELLOW-CREATURES. I SEE MY
MIS. (133)	PEOPLE MAY FANCY. I DONT SET UP TO HAVE AS MANY	IDEAS	AS THE GOVERNOR; BUT WHAT IDEAS I HAVE ARE
BULL I (94)	ALL HARD HIT? /DOYLE/ NOT REALLY. I HAD ONLY TWO	IDEAS	AT THAT TIME: FIRST, TO LEARN TO DO SOMETHING; AND
ARMS I (5)	INTO MY EYES, THAT PERHAPS WE ONLY HAD OUR HEROIC	IDEAS	BECAUSE WE ARE SO FOND OF READING BYRON AND PUSHKIN,
JOAN PREFACE(8)	TO DENY THAT SAINTS EXIST, AND TO HOLD THAT NEW	IDEAS	CANNOT COME OTHERWISE THAN BY CONSCIOUS RATIOCINATION,
GENV III (82)	TAKE ITS ORDERS FROM MOSCOW. MOSCOW TOOK ALL ITS	IDEAS	FROM ENGLAND, AS THIS GENTLEMAN HAS TOLD YOU. MY
ROCK II (267)	OUR PROPER PLACE, THE DUSTBIN. YET THEY GOT THEIR	IDEAS	FROM US. KARL MARX THOUGHT IT ALL OUT IN BLOOMSBURY.
UNPL PREFACE(R16)	WAS OCCUPIED BY A GENTLEMAN, NOW DECEASED, WHOSE	IDEAS	HAD IN THE COURSE OF NATURE BECOME QUITE OBSOLETE. HE
3PLA PREFACE(R36)	BEGUN WORKING PROFESSIONALLY BEFORE HIS NEW	IDEAS	HAVE MASTERED HIM SUFFICIENTLY TO INSIST ON CONSTANT
LION PREFACE(97)	INSTEAD OF BEING, LIKE THE FOREFATHERS WHOSE	IDEAS	HE CLINGS TO, A SUBJECT OF A STATE PRACTICALLY WHOLLY
LION PREFACE(67)	RIGHT TO RISK HIS LIFE OR HIS LIVELIHOOD FOR HIS	IDEAS	HE NEEDS ONLY COURAGE AND CONVICTION TO MAKE HIS
MIS. (133)	TO HAVE AS MANY IDEAS AS THE GOVERNOR; BUT WHAT	IDEAS	I HAVE ARE CONSECUTIVE, AT ALL EVENTS. I CAN THINK AS

SUPR PREFACE(R39)	LEAST DOES NOT PRETEND THAT THERE ARE ANY MODERN	IDEAS	IN IT; WHEREAS YOUR ACADEMIC COPIER OF FOSSILS OFFERS
PHIL I (87)	EVERYTHING IS GOING TO THE DOGS THROUGH ADVANCED	IDEAS	IN THE YOUNGER GENERATION. /CHARTERIS/ OF COURSE. HE'S
JOAN PREFACE(13)	THE LESS AN ABLE LEADER OF MEN FOR IMAGINING HER	IDEAS	IN THIS WAY. THE EVOLUTIONARY APPETITE. WHAT THEN IS
BULL I (90)	AT THAT BLESSED OLD HEAD OF YOURS WITH ALL ITS	IDEAS	IN WATERTIGHT COMPARTMENTS, AND ALL THE COMPARTMENTS
GETT (182)	BUT SIMPLY THE SPONTANEOUS FALLING OF A PLAY OF	IDEAS	INTO THE FORM MOST SUITABLE TO IT, WHICH TURNED OUT TO
BARB I (257)	AND HE TOOK ADVANTAGE OF IT TO PUT THE WICKEDEST	IDEAS	INTO THEIR HEADS, AND MAKE THEM QUITE UNMANAGEABLE. I
CAND I (94)	OPE YOU AINT LETTIN JAMES PUT NO FOOLISH	IDEAS	INTO YOUR ED? /MARCHBANKS/ FOOLISH IDEAS? OH, YOU
MRS II (199)	YOU KNOW YOURSELF. DONT YOU GO TAKING ANY SILLY	IDEAS	INTO YOUR HEAD ABOUT ME. DO YOU HEAR? /FRANK/ (
3PLA PREFACE(R36)	MAKES ITS CHANNEL; AND THE TECHNICIAN WITHOUT	IDEAS	IS AS USELESS AS THE CANAL CONSTRUCTOR WITHOUT WATER,
BULL IV (156)	NO, REALLY? YOU FIND THAT CONTACT WITH ENGLISH	IDEAS	IS STIMULATING, EH? /KEEGAN/ I AM NEVER TIRED OF
APPL II (263)	IT IN A SMALL PARCEL AND SAY OUR GOODS AND OUR	IDEAS	. A POLITICAL UNION WITH US WILL BE JUST THE OFFICIAL
BARB PREFACE(207)	CERTAIN FACTS CONCERNING MY CONTACT WITH MODERN	IDEAS	. ABOUT HALF A CENTURY AGO, AN IRISH NOVELIST, CHARLES
FANY PROLOG (259)	I ASSURE YOU I AM A POOR MAN ACCORDING TO MODERN	IDEAS	. BUT I HAVE NEVER HAD ANYTHING LESS THAN THE VERY
SIM II (65)	OWN IDEAS, WHICH HAVE NOTHING TO DO WITH OUR	IDEAS	. CONSEQUENTLY-- THEREFORE-- ER-- ER-- WHAT WAS I
3PLA PREFACE(R11)	IT: HE DOES NOT PLAY WITH VOLUPTUOUS OR ROMANTIC	IDEAS	. FROM THE PLAY OF IDEAS-- AND THE DRAMA CAN NEVER BE
SIM II (55)	MUST LEARN THAT ITS IDEAS ARE NOT EVERYBODY'S	IDEAS	. HERE IS A CABLEGRAM FROM THE LEAGUE OF BRITISH
SUPR III (124)	I MUST THINK IT OVER. YOU ARE REALLY FULL OF	IDEAS	. HOW DID YOU COME TO THINK OF THIS ONE? /DON JUAN/ I
GENV III (74)	HAVE DIED OF HIS PERSONAL CONTACT WITH RUSSIAN	IDEAS	. I BLAME MYSELF FOR NOT HAVING BEEN MORE CONSIDERATE.
BUOY III (45)	LOGIC, ASSOCIATION OF IDEAS, MOSTLY NONSENSICAL	IDEAS	. INSTEAD OF ANALYSIS, EVERYTHING IN TOTALITARIAN
CAND I (102)	COWARDICE EITHER: I'M NOT AFRAID OF A CLERGYMAN'S	IDEAS	. I'LL FIGHT YOUR IDEAS. I'LL RESCUE HER FROM HER
CAND I (102)	AFRAID OF A CLERGYMAN'S IDEAS. I'LL FIGHT YOUR	IDEAS	. I'LL RESCUE HER FROM HER SLAVERY TO THEM. I'LL PIT
MIS. (132)	MAY COME. THE SUPERMAN'S AN IDEA. I BELIEVE IN	IDEAS	. READ WHATSHIS NAME. /LORD SUMMERHAYS/ READING IS A
JITT I (18)	CAN HELP HIM WITHOUT LETTING HIM ROB YOU OF YOUR	IDEAS	. /BRUNO/ IT IS NOT HE WHO IS ROBBING ME OF MY IDEAS:
PHIL II (110)	AND STARES AT HER). I QUITE AGREE WITH ALL YOUR	IDEAS	. /CHARTERIS/ (SCANDALIZED) THATS A NICE THING FOR A
BARB III (340)	MY DEAR: I HAVE NO OTHER MEANS OF CONVEYING MY	IDEAS	. /LADY BRITOMART/ YOUR IDEAS ARE NONSENSE. YOU GOT ON
SUPR I (11)	UNDER THE CONTROL OF AN OLD MAN WITH OBSOLETE	IDEAS	. /RAMSDEN/ (STUPENDED) MY IDEAS OBSOLETE! ! ! !
MIS. (130)	MONEY IN UNDERWEAR: THERES NONE IN WILD-CAT	IDEAS	. /TARLETON/ THERES MONEY IM ME, MADAM, NO MATTER WHAT
MIS. (130)	THE UNDERWEAR; BUT I SHALL COME IN STRONG ON THE	IDEAS	. /TARLETON/ YOU BE A GOOD BOY; AND PERHAPS I WILL.
GENV III (72)	AND THAT IS TO CONVERT THEM ALL TO ENGLISH	IDEAS	. /THE COMMISSAR/ BUT ALL THE WORLD IS IN REVOLT
GENV III (72)	THE ENGLISH THEMSELVES. THE FUTURE IS FOR RUSSIAN	IDEAS	. /THE NEWCOMER/ WHERE DID RUSSIA GET HER IDEAS? FROM
METH PREFACE(R19)	CAN READ BOTH, LIKE TO LEARN THE HISTORY OF THEIR	IDEAS	. SOME ARE SO ENTANGLED IN THE CURRENT CONFUSION OF
MILL IV (190)	AND HAD NEVER BEEN UP TO MUCH ACCORDING TO MODERN	IDEAS	. THEY HAD TO BE THROWN INTO THE STREET TO WANDER
MIS. (134)	TO HAVE BEEN A WRITER. I'M ESSENTIALLY A MAN OF	IDEAS	. WHEN I WAS YOUNG MAN I SOMETIMES USED TO PRAY THAT I
ARMS III (59)	SEEM TO ME TO GROW UP: THEY ALL HAVE SCHOOLBOY'S	IDEAS	. YOU DONT KNOW WHAT TRUE COURAGE IS. /SERGIUS/ (
3PLA PREFACE(R36)	WAGNER, MACLISE THAN MADOX BROWN. BESIDES, NEW	IDEAS	MAKE THEIR TECHNIQUE AS WATER MAKES ITS CHANNEL; AND
BUOY III (41)	A TEACHER AND A PREACHER. BUT AS HE HAD ORIGINAL	IDEAS	NO ONE WOULD EMPLOY HIM AS A PREACHER NOR LISTEN TO
SUPR I (11)	WITH OBSOLETE IDEAS. /RAMSDEN/ (STUPENDED) MY	IDEAS	OBSOLETE! ! ! ! ! ! /TANNER/ TOTALLY. I HAD
HART II (92)	BLESS YOU, DEAR MRS HUSHABYE, WHAT ROMANTIC	IDEAS	OF BUSINESS YOU HAVE! POOR DEAR MANGAN ISNT A BIT
CAPT III (298)	ODD A MATCH IT WOULD BE FOR ME ACCORDING TO THE	IDEAS	OF ENGLISH SOCIETY. /BRASSBOUND/ I CARE NOTHING ABOUT
METH PREFACE(R13)	THEMSELVES LIBERAL WHEN THEY ARE DEFENDING THE	IDEAS	OF HENRY VII, AND GENTLEMANLY WHEN THEY ARE OPPOSING
JOAN 4 (106)	KING AND HERSELF. /WARWICK/ QUITE SO. THESE TWO	IDEAS	OF HERS ARE THE SAME IDEA AT BOTTOM. IT GOES DEEP, MY
METH PREFACE(R13)	GENTLEMANLY WHEN THEY ARE OPPOSING TO THEM THE	IDEAS	OF RICHARD III. THUS THE EDUCATED MAN IS A GREATER
SUPR PREFACE(R13)	A SPANISH MONK, WAS PRESENTED, ACCORDING TO THE	IDEAS	OF THAT TIME, AS THE ENEMY OF GOD, THE APPROACH OF
ARMS I (5)	OUR IDEAS REAL! WHAT DO YOU MEAN? /RAINA/ OUR	IDEAS	OF WHAT SERGIUS WOULD DO. OUR PATRIOTISM. OUR HEROIC
BULL PREFACE(60)	" PREMATURE ENDEAVOURS TO THRUST WESTERN	IDEAS	ON AN EASTERN PEOPLE," BY WHICH HE MEANS THAT WHEN YOU
HART PREFACE(5)	HOUSE WAS QUITE FAMILIAR WITH REVOLUTIONARY	IDEAS	ON PAPER, IT AIMED AT BEING ADVANCED AND FREETHINKING,
CAPT III (280)	WILL NOT TALK NONSENSE TO CAPTAIN KEARNEY. YOUR	IDEAS	ON SOME SUBJECTS ARE REALLY HARDLY DECOROUS. /LADY
MIS. (147)	IN MY EMPLOYMENT: GIRLS AND YOUNG MEN. I HAD	IDEAS	ON THE SUBJECT. I USED TO GO TO THE PARENTS AND TELL
MIS. PREFACE(38)	AND ADVENTURE OF MAKING WORK BY INVENTING NEW	IDEAS	OR EXTENDING THE DOMAIN OF KNOWLEDGE, AND INSISTS ON A
BARB PREFACE(242)	UPON TO ADMINISTER ANY LAW THAT IS BASED ON	IDEAS	OR KNOWLEDGE LESS THAN HALF A CENTURY OLD, THEY
ARMS I (5)	REAL AFTER ALL. /CATHERINE/ (INDIGNANTLY) OUR	IDEAS	REAL! WHAT DO YOU MEAN? /RAINA/ OUR IDEAS OF WHAT
METH PREFACE(R34)	SUCH A BLASPHEMY. THIS EXQUISITE CONFUSION OF	IDEAS	ROUSED MY SENSE OF COMEDY. IT WAS CLEAR TO ME THAT THE
3PLA PREFACE(R11)	VOLUPTUOUS OR ROMANTIC IDEAS. FROM THE PLAY OF	IDEAS	-- AND THE DRAMA CAN NEVER BE ANYTHING MORE-- HE
MIS. (130)	HE WAS PROVIDENCE. THATS ONE OF TARLETON'S	IDEAS	; AND DONT YOU FORGET IT. /BENTLEY/ YOU ARE FULL OF
HART I (56)	PARENTS WERE POETS; AND THEY GAVE HIM THE NOBLEST	IDEAS	; BUT THEY COULD NOT AFFORD TO GIVE HIM A PROFESSION.
BARB III (317)	LIKE A RACEHORSE; CRAMMED WITH SECONDHAND	IDEAS	; DRILLED AND DISCIPLINED IN DOCILITY AND WHAT THEY
SUPR I SD(3)	IS IMPORTANT ON THE THRESHOLD OF A DRAMA OF	IDEAS	; FOR UNDER SUCH CIRCUMSTANCES EVERYTHING DEPENDS ON
SUPR III (109)	AM NOT NOW DEFENDING THE ILLUSORY FORMS THE GREAT	IDEAS	TAKE. I AM GIVING YOU EXAMPLES OF THE FACT THAT THIS
LADY PREFACE(227)	REALLY WAS) IS SO OVERCHARGED ACCORDING TO MODERN	IDEAS	THAT A REPLY ON THE GENERAL CASE IS NECESSARY.
BARB PREFACE(207)	ALL DRAMATIC MATERIAL THAT IS NOT COMMON AND ALL	IDEAS	THAT ARE NOT SUPERFICIAL. I THEREFORE VENTURE TO PUT
MIS. (132)	IT. YOU LIKE A BOOK WITH NOTHING IN IT BUT SOME	IDEAS	THAT THE CHAP THAT WRITES IT KEEPS WORRYING, LIKE A
CLEO NOTES (210)	WITHOUT ANY SPECIAL QUALITY OF MIND! NAY, WITH	IDEAS	THAT WERE WORN OUT BEFORE HE WAS BORN, AS NELSON'S AND
MIS. (118)	ONLY A BOY, AND HAD TO PRETEND TO TAKE IN ALL THE	IDEAS	THE GOVERNOR FED ME UP WITH. I DIDNT SEE IT; AND I
MTH4 I (164)	THEM; AND IN THEIR HUNGER FOR NEW LIGHTS AND NEW	IDEAS	THEY LISTENED TO ME AND ENCOURAGED ME TO REBEL. BUT MY
GETT SD(289)	OF HIS COLLAR, BUT TOO MUCH PREOCCUPIED WITH HIS	IDEAS	TO BE EMBARRASSED BY ANY CONCERN AS TO HIS APPEARANCE.
JOAN PREFACE(26)	A LIFE OF JOAN IN WHICH HE ATTRIBUTED JOAN'S	IDEAS	TO CLERICAL PROMPTING AND HER MILITARY SUCCESS TO AN
METH PREFACE(R28)	OF LANGUAGE DOES NOT IMPLY THE POSSESSION OF	IDEAS	TO EXPRESS: MEZZOFANTI, THE MASTER OF FIFTY-EIGHT
BULL PREFACE(35)	AN IRISH SECRETARY WHO HAS DARED TO APPLY ENGLISH	IDEAS	TO THE AFFAIRS OF THE GARRISON. WHEREUPON THE ENGLISH
PYGM EPILOG (298)	WITH WELLS, AND THAT THIS ACCESSIBILITY TO	IDEAS	WAS THE SECRET OF THEIR NICENESS. PEOPLE SHE HAD
ARMS I (5)	WALKS ABOUT EXCITEDLY). IT PROVES THAT ALL OUR	IDEAS	WERE REAL AFTER ALL. /CATHERINE/ (INDIGNANTLY) OUR
BARB PREFACE(221)	FUTURE OF THE NOVELTY AND FOREIGN ORIGIN OF THE	IDEAS	WHICH ARE NOW MAKING THEIR WAY INTO THE ENGLISH
GETT PREFACE(256)	OF DOMESTICITY, AND THE CURIOUS CONFUSION OF	IDEAS	WHICH MAKES SOME OF OUR BISHOPS IMAGINE THAT IN THE
UNPL PREFACE(R16)	FOR THE MOST PART THE GREATEST DREAD OF " NEW"	IDEAS	WHICH THE ABOLITION OF THE CENSORSHIP WOULD LET LOOSE
GENV I (39)	AND GOVERNED THE COUNTRY ACCORDING TO HIS OWN	IDEAS	WHILST THE PEOPLE ENJOYED THEMSELVES AND MADE MONEY IN
3PLA PREFACE(R36)	WHO FOR LACK OF NEW IDEAS, OR INDEED OF ANY	IDEAS	WORTH MENTIONING, ACHIEVE NO DISTINCTION OUTSIDE MUSIC
BULL III (126)	YES, YOU. WHY NOT? /LARRY/ I'M AFRAID MY	IDEAS	WOULD NOT BE POPULAR ENOUGH. /CORNELIUS/ I DONT KNOW
MIS. (133)	HE? YOU ARE RATHER ALL OVER THE SHOP WITH YOUR	IDEAS	, AINT YOU? /JOHNNY/ (HANDSOMELY) I'M NOT SAYING
LADY PREFACE(214)	I TAKE THIS TO BE ONE OF THE BRIGHTEST OF TYLER'S	IDEAS	, BECAUSE THE SONNETS ARE UNACCOUNTABLE AND OUT OF
SIM II (65)	WE MUST THEREFORE LIVE IN A WORLD OF ORIGINAL	IDEAS	, CREATED BY OURSELVES OUT OF OUR OWN NATURE. /IDDY/
BARB III (348)	I WISH I COULD CURE YOU OF MIDDLE-CLASS	IDEAS	, DOLLY. /CUSINS/ (GASPING) MIDDLE CL--! A SNUB! A
GENV III (72)	BUT ALL THE WORLD IS IN REVOLT AGAINST ENGLISH	IDEAS	, ESPECIALLY THE ENGLISH THEMSELVES. THE FUTURE IS FOR
HART II (86)	AND THEY FOUND THE MONEY; FOR I TAKE NO RISKS IN	IDEAS	, EVEN WHEN THEYRE MY OWN. YOUR FATHER, AND THE
3PLA PREFACE(R37)	IF SHAKESPEAR HAD CONCEIVED GOETHE'S OR IBSEN'S	IDEAS	, HE WOULD HAVE EXPRESSED THEM ANY WORSE THAN GOETHE
SIM II (65)	WHAT ABOUT THE PEOPLE WHO HAVE NO ORIGINAL	IDEAS	, IDDY? /PRA/ THE GREAT MAJORITY OF MANKIND? /IDDY/
MTH2 (67)	CAN GO IF HE LIKES; BUT I AM STILL OPEN TO NEW	IDEAS	, IF ONLY I CAN FIND THEM. /FRANKLYN/ (TO LUBIN) ARE
MIS. PREFACE(54)	MAKE ENGLAND A PARADISE, ACCORDING TO OUR PRESENT	IDEAS	, IN A FEW YEARS. THERE IS NO MYSTERY ABOUT IT: THE
HART I (48)	APPLES, AND, WHAT IS WORSE, THE SAME DISORDER IN	IDEAS	, IN TALK, IN FEELING. WHEN I WAS A CHILD I WAS USED
PHIL PREFACE(68)	FASHION: INDEED I AM FAR FROM SURE THAT ITS	IDEAS	, INSTEAD OF BEING 36 YEARS BEHIND THE TIMES, ARE NOT
MIS. (129)	IDEA. /MRS TARLETON/ YOU ALWAYS WERE ONE FOR	IDEAS	, JOHN. /TARLETON/ YOURE RIGHT, CHICKABIDDY. WHAT DO I
SUPR III (91)	GIRL OF 17, WITH HEAVY SPIRITS AND DECREPIT	IDEAS	, LIES ABOUT HER AGE? WELL, HERE WE HAVE NO BODIES:
BUOY III (45)	UNIVERSE, INSTEAD OF LOGIC, ASSOCIATION OF	IDEAS	, MOSTLY NONSENSICAL IDEAS. INSTEAD OF ANALYSIS,
MTH2 (62)	THING IN POLITICS. I AM NOT GIVING YOU MY OWN	IDEAS	, MR LUBIN, BUT JUST THE REGULAR ORTHODOX SCIENCE OF
FABL PREFACE(82)	AND SEXUAL PROMISCUITY WHICH IS ASSOCIATION OF	IDEAS	, NOT LOGIC. NO EMINENCE IN A SPECIFIC DEPARTMENT
MTH1 II (21)	I WAS A FOOL. BUT ABEL WAS A DISCOVERER, A MAN OF	IDEAS	, OF SPIRIT: A TRUE PROGRESSIVE. HE WAS THE DISCOVERER
3PLA PREFACE(R36)	MATHEMATICAL AND LINGUISTIC, WHO FOR LACK OF NEW	IDEAS	, OR INDEED OF ANY IDEAS WORTH MENTIONING, ACHIEVE NO
GENV PREFACE(23)	IS, LIKE MOST HUMAN LOGIC, MERE ASSOCIATION OF	IDEAS	, OR, TO CALL IT BY THE NEW NAME INVENTED BY ITS
FANY III (323)	FRANCE IS UNCONQUERABLE. WE IMPOSE OUR NARROW	IDEAS	, OUR PREJUDICES, OUR OBSOLETE INSTITUTIONS, OUR
CAND I (84)	WELL, WHEN YOU TALK TO ME, GIVE ME YOUR OWN	IDEAS	, SUCH AS THEY ARE, AND NOT HIS. YOU NEVER CUT A
SIM II (65)	WORLD OF TRUTH: THEY LIVE IN A WORLD OF THEIR OWN	IDEAS	, WHICH HAVE NOTHING TO DO WITH OUR IDEAS.
MTH1 II (20)	IN THE OLD FURROW. NO PROGRESS! NO ADVANCED	IDEAS	! NO ADVENTURES! WHAT SHOULD I BE IF I HAD STUCK TO
		IDEN	
LADY PREFACE(230)	BETWEEN THE STAGE COUNTRY GENTLEMAN ALEXANDER	IDEN	AND THE STAGE RADICAL JACK CADE, WE GET THE SHEPHERD IN
		IDENTICAL	
MIS. (127)	ABOUT THERE AS FRESH AS PAINT SOME OF THE	IDENTICAL	LITTLE LIVE CELLS THAT ADAM CHRISTENED IN THE
LADY PREFACE(219)	AS MR HARRIS POINTS OUT, THAT THEY ARE PRECISELY	IDENTICAL	WITH THE HEROES: MACBETH IS ONLY HAMLET

METH PREFACE(R73)	BODY AND A LIVE ONE: ARE PHYSICALLY AND CHEMICALLY	IDENTICAL	, AND THAT THE DIFFERENCE CAN BE ACCOUNTED FOR
		IDENTIFICATION	
3PLA PREFACE(R39)	AND THEIR INEVITABLE DILEMMAS AS TO MAKE THEIR	IDENTIFICATION	IMPOSSIBLE FOR THE MOMENT. IF SO, SO MUCH THE
CYMB FORWORD(135)	I REALLY COULD NOT KEEP MY COUNTENANCE OVER THE	IDENTIFICATION	OF GUIDERIUS BY THE MOLE ON HIS NECK. THAT
LADY PREFACE(209)	(WILLIAM HERBERT), AND PROMULGATED HIS OWN	IDENTIFICATION	OF MISTRESS MARY FITTON WITH THE DARK LADY.
LADY PREFACE(209)	SONNETS, IN WHICH HE ACCEPTED A PREVIOUS	IDENTIFICATION	OF MR W. H., THE " ONLIE BEGETTER" OF THE
DOCT PREFACE(9)	IT MEANS IN MANY INSTANCES (INCLUDING EVEN THE	IDENTIFICATION	OF PATHOGENIC BACILLI UNDER THE MICROSCOPE)
METH PREFACE(R61)	UTTERLY CORRUPTED BY AN ESSENTIALLY DIABOLICAL	IDENTIFICATION	OF SUCCESS IN LIFE WITH BIG PROFITS. THE
		IDENTIFIED	
LION PREFACE(17)	SECOND COMING; SO THAT THE TWO EVENTS BECOME	IDENTIFIED	AT LAST. THERE IS THE OTHER AND MORE ARTIFICIAL
LADY PREFACE(207)	THEATRE AS A MEMORIAL TO SHAKESPEAR, I HAVE	IDENTIFIED	THE DARK LADY WITH MISTRESS MARY FITTON. FIRST,
DOCT PREFACE(25)	PRECAUTIONARY PROCESSES. EVEN IF THE GERM WERE	IDENTIFIED	, COMPLETE PRECAUTIONS WOULD HARDLY PAY. IT IS
BULL PREFACE(59)	OFF, OR THRESHING, OR WHAT NOT. ONE OF THEM, WHEN	IDENTIFIED	, SAID " ALL MEN ARE ALIKE." HE HAD ONLY ONE EYE.
DOCT PREFACE(23)	IN WHICH THE CHARACTERISTIC BACILLUS HAD BEEN	IDENTIFIED	! WHEN THERE WAS NO BACILLUS IT WAS ASSUMED
		IDENTIFY	
LION I (114)	AMONG THESE PRISONERS YOU WILL PARTICULARLY	IDENTIFY	AN ARMORER NAMED FERROVIUS, OF DANGEROUS CHARACTER
SUPR HANDBOK(227)	THOSE WHO ADMIRE MODERN CIVILIZATION USUALLY	IDENTIFY	IT WITH THE STEAM ENGINE AND THE ELECTRIC
LION PREFACE(69)	SANCTIFY IT AND BRAND IT AS INFAMOUS; WHICH WILL	IDENTIFY	IT WITH VIRTUE AND WITH SIN SIMULTANEOUSLY.
KING I (215)	(PICKING UP A FRAGMENT AND TURNING IT OVER TO	IDENTIFY	IT) HAS THE KING TORN UP A WORK OF MINE? I LEAVE
MTH3 (111)	BATHING SEASON, WITH DOCUMENTS IN THE POCKETS TO	IDENTIFY	ME. I THEN TURNED UP IN A STRANGE PLACE, PRETENDING
BULL PREFACE(38)	" REBELS"; AND HE WOULD HAVE BEEN FORCED TO	IDENTIFY	THE CAUSE OF FREEDOM AND DEMOCRACY WITH THE CAUSE
SIM PRO;3,SD(30)	BAEDEKER IN HAND, HAS WANDERED IN, TRYING TO	IDENTIFY	THE IMAGES WITH THE AID OF HER BOOK. SHE NOW COMES
LION PREFACE(27)	JESUS. MATTHEW, LIKE MOST BIOGRAPHERS, STRIVES TO	IDENTIFY	THE OPINIONS AND PREJUDICES OF HIS HERO WITH HIS
HART PREFACE(26)	MENTION THEM WITHOUT ENABLING THE READER TO	IDENTIFY	THE PARTIES, WHICH WOULD NOT BE FAIR, AS THEY WERE
CYMB FORWORD(134)	AND INDIVIDUALITY, AND HAD NOTHING TO DO BUT	IDENTIFY	THEMSELVES BY MOLES ON THEIR NECKS, OR EXPLAIN WHY
MILL PREFACE(117)	IT WAS A DUMB PHANTOM WHICH EVERY STATESMAN COULD	IDENTIFY	WITH HIS OWN CONSCIENCE AND DREAD AS THE NEMESIS OF
POSN (447)	TO MAKE A MOVE TOWARDS HER WHEN SHE COMES IN TO	IDENTIFY	YOU. /BLANCO/ (RETREATING IN TERROR) A WOMAN? SHE
		IDENTIFYING	
SUPR PREFACE(R34)	FIELD PREACHER WHO ACHIEVED VIRTUE AND COURAGE BY	IDENTIFYING	HIMSELF WITH THE PURPOSE OF THE WORLD AS HE
LADY PREFACE(214)	TO SHAKESPEAR. THOUGH MR HARRIS FOLLOWED TYLER IN	IDENTIFYING	MARY FITTON AS THE DARK LADY, AND THE EARL OF
LION PREFACE(39)	TO BE HIS CONTEMPORARY (THERE IS NO GROUND FOR	IDENTIFYING	MATTHEW THE PUBLICAN WITH MATTHEW THE
		IDENTITY	
SUPR III SD(87)	VULGARITY, BUT STILL A RESEMBLANCE, EVEN AN	IDENTITY	. THE NAME TOO: DON JUAN TENORIO, JOHN TANNER.
BULL PREFACE(37)	A VAST BODY OF VOLTAIREANS. BUT THE ESSENTIAL	IDENTITY	OF THE FRENCH AND ENGLISH MOVEMENTS HAS BEEN
DEST SD(188)	AND FIERCELY AT HER TO SATISFY HIMSELF AS TO HER	IDENTITY	; FOR IT NOW BEGINS TO DARKEN RAPIDLY INTO NIGHT,
		IDEOLOGICALLY	
FABL PREFACE(83)	GOVERNMENT OF THE PEOPLE BY THE PEOPLE, PROFESSED	IDEOLOGICALLY	NOWADAYS BY ALL GOVERNMENTS AND OPPOSITIONS,
		IDEOLOGIES	
FABL PREFACE(86)	A CROSS CONFLICT BETWEEN FEUDAL AND PLUTOCRATIC	IDEOLOGIES	. THE FEUDAL PROPRIETARIAT IS ALL FOR WELL
		IDEOLOGY	
FABL PREFACE(69)	UP AGAINST GOD OF A RIVAL DEITY WITH A CONTRARY	IDEOLOGY	WAS RESENTED AS A MANICHEAN HERESY, BECAUSE PLAGUE
		IDIOCY	
METH PREFACE(R18)	SUGGESTIVE BIOLOGIST WHO WAS UNHAPPILY REDUCED TO	IDIOCY	BY NEO-DARWINISM, POINTED OUT THAT DEATH IS NOT AN
JITT III (78)	THE UNIVERSITY AT WHICH I AM A PROFESSOR; AND HIS	IDIOCY	IS NOT TAUGHT ANYWHERE. DO YOU FORGET THAT I HAVE TO
JITT III (78)	AN IDIOT? /LENKHEIM/ I MAY BE AN IDIOT; BUT MY	IDIOCY	IS THE ACCEPTED IDIOCY TAUGHT IN THE UNIVERSITY AT
AUGS (275)	-- /AUGUSTUS/ OH, NEVER MIND THAT. IT IS THE	IDIOCY	OF THE THING I LOOK AT. HE'LL LOSE HIS BET; AND SERVE
JITT III (78)	I MAY BE AN IDIOT; BUT MY IDIOCY IS THE ACCEPTED	IDIOCY	TAUGHT IN THE UNIVERSITY AT WHICH I AM A PROFESSOR;
SIM II (60)	ALWAYS MANAGED TO COME OUT WITH SOME STROKE OF	IDIOCY	THAT WAS EITHER SO FUNNY OR SO PITEOUS THAT I HAVE
METH PREFACE(R11)	I HABITUALLY DERIDED NEO-DARWINISM AS A GHASTLY	IDIOCY	, AND WOULD FALL ON ITS PROFESSORS SLAUGHTEROUSLY IN
		IDIOM	
FANY III (308)	AND ACCURATELY DESCRIBED IN YOUR NATIVE	IDIOM	AS A DAUGHTER OF JOY. /DUVALLET/ IT IS WHAT I THOUGHT.
		IDIOSYNCRASIES	
BULL PREFACE(21)	WITH THE CONTRAST BETWEEN THE ENGLISH AND IRISH	IDIOSYNCRASIES	. THE IRISHMAN MAKES A DISTINCTION WHICH THE
LION PREFACE(41)	IN SPITE OF THE SUSPICIONS ROUSED BY JOHN'S	IDIOSYNCRASIES	, HIS NARRATIVE IS OF ENORMOUS IMPORTANCE TO
		IDIOSYNCRASY	
FABL PREFACE(71)	ENOUGH TO HAVE WRITTEN TWENTY PLAYS, THE SHAVIAN	IDIOSYNCRASY	WHICH FASCINATES SOME OF THEM (OR USED TO) AND
MRS PREFACE(169)	WHICH HIS WHOLE WORK IS BUILT. FAR FROM IGNORING	IDIOSYNCRASY	, WILL, PASSION, IMPULSE, WHIM, AS FACTORS IN
		IDIOSYNCRATIC	
LION PREFACE(78)	PAUL'S THEORY OF ORIGINAL SIN WAS TO SOME EXTENT	IDIOSYNCRATIC	, HE TELLS US DEFINITELY THAT HE FINDS HIMSELF
JITT PREFACE(7)	THOSE WHO CAN SHOULD READ THE ORIGINAL, TO THE	IDIOSYNCRATIC	LITERARY QUALITY OF WHICH I HAVE BEEN
LADY PREFACE(213)	OF NEED, AND LEFT THE ROOM IN ANGER. HARRIS'S	IDIOSYNCRATIC	POWER OF PITY SAVED HIM FROM FEELING OR
SHAK PREFACE(135)	OF STAGECRAFT INTO FILMCRAFT MAY DESTROY THE	IDIOSYNCRATIC	PUPPET CHARM. TELEVISED PUPPETS COULD ENJOY
		IDIOSYNCRATICALLY	
CATH PREFACE(155)	NOR IS THE SKETCH OF CATHERINE COMPLETE EVEN	IDIOSYNCRATICALLY	, LEAVING HER POLITICS OUT OF THE
		IDIOT	
JOAN 3 (88)	DISAPPOINTED) IS THAT ALL? YOU INFERNAL YOUNG	IDIOT	: I HAVE A MIND TO PITCH YOU INTO THE RIVER. /THE
DEST (187)	OF THE AUSTRIANS. /NAPOLEON/ (PASSIONATELY) YOU	IDIOT	: I'LL HAVE YOU SHOT FOR LOSING THOSE DESPATCHES: I'LL
2TRU I (49)	FOR THE WINDOW). /THE PATIENT/ (STOPPING HIM)	IDIOT	: THE POLICE CANT TOUCH YOU IF I BACK YOU UP. IT'S I
FABL PREFACE(92)	BETWEEN THE UNCONSCIOUS GENIUS AND THE	IDIOT	? AGAIN, I DO NOT KNOW; BUT WE CAN AT LEAST CALL IN
JITT III (78)	TO BE TOMMY-ROT, OR DOES IT PROVE THAT YOU ARE AN	IDIOT	? /LENKHEIM/ I MAY BE AN IDIOT; BUT MY IDIOCY IS THE
MIS. (194)	(TO HYPATIA) WHY DIDNT YOU ACCEPT HIM, YOU YOUNG	IDIOT	? /LORD SUMMERHAYS/ I WAS TOO OLD. /TARLETON/ ALL
SUPR II (52)	SUCH A THING! /TANNER/ DONE WHAT, YOU MAUDLIN	IDIOT	? /OCTAVIUS/ YES, I AM AN IDIOT. JACK: IF YOU HAD
BULL I (92)	MY MOTIVES MUST BE A MAN OF GENIUS. BUT THAT THE	IDIOT	AND THE GENIUS SHOULD BE THE SAME MAN! HOW IS THAT
ROCK PREFACE(155)	OF THE SACREDNESS OF HUMAN LIFE, WHICH IN OUR	IDIOT	ASYLUMS AT DARENTH AND ELSEWHERE STILL TERRIFIES US
LION PREFACE(83)	AND PARTLY, SINCE EVEN THE MOST INFATUATED	IDIOT	CANNOT SPEND HIS LIFE ADMIRING HIMSELF, THE LESS
BARB PREFACE(208)	AT THE LUNATICS. I MYSELF HAVE HAD A VILLAGE	IDIOT	EXHIBITED TO ME AS SOMETHING IRRESISTIBLY FUNNY, ON
GENV III (85)	I KNOW YOUR OPINION OF ME: I AM THE ONLY PERFECT	IDIOT	IN GENEVA. BUT I GOT A MOVE ON THE LEAGUE; AND THATS
NEVR IV (300)	IDEAS ABOUT HIS OWN SEX TO LIKE BEING CALLED AN	IDIOT	. AND NOW HAD WE NOT BETTER GO AND SEE WHAT DOLLY IS
NEVR II (258)	PRAY? /VALENTINE/ OF COURSE NOT: I'M NOT SUCH AN	IDIOT	. AND YET MY HEART TELLS ME I SHOULD: MY FOOL OF A
SUPR HANDBOK(219)	SPECIALIST WITHOUT BEING IN THE STRICT SENSE AN	IDIOT	. DO NOT GIVE YOUR CHILDREN MORAL AND RELIGIOUS
CURE (226)	COOLNESS OF AN ICEBERG AND THE CHEERFULNESS OF AN	IDIOT	. EVERY MEMBER OF IT HAD A GO AT YOU; AND EVERYONE OF
DEVL III (64)	(IMPATIENTLY) CHRISTOPHER DUDGEON, YOU BLATANT	IDIOT	. GIVE YOUR FULL NAME. /SWINDON/ BE SILENT, PRISONER.
NEVR IV (300)	THAT RUDE. /VALENTINE/ I AM NOT A SENTIMENTAL	IDIOT	. I AM CURED OF SENTIMENT FOR EVER. (HE TURNS AWAY IN
JOAN 1 (60)	PRAYING! HA! YOU BELIEVE SHE PRAYS, YOU	IDIOT	. I KNOW THE SORT OF GIRL THAT IS ALWAYS TALKING TO
KING I (214)	FROM HIS BEING A PHILOSOPHER: THAT IS, HALF AN	IDIOT	. I TRUST YOUR MAJESTY WAS PLEASED WITH MY SKETCH OF
PYGM V (284)	AND WALKING ABOUT INTOLERANTLY) ELIZA: YOURE AN	IDIOT	. I WASTE THE TREASURES OF MY MILTONIC MIND BY
LION PREFACE(26)	OF JESUS'S INTELLIGENCE, THE PROPOSITION OF AN	IDIOT	. IF IT COULD BE PROVED TODAY THAT NOT ONE OF THE
PYGM V (286)	IT'S ALL YOULL GET UNTIL YOU STOP BEING A COMMON	IDIOT	. IF YOURE GOING TO BE A LADY, YOULL HAVE TO GIVE UP
GENV III (65)	NOTHING BEYOND. A DOMESTIC PARAGON: A POLITICAL	IDIOT	. IN SHORT, AN IDEAL WIFE. THE WIDOW ENTERS ON THE ARM
AUGS (282)	HUNGERFORD HIGHCASTLE. . . . I'M HIS BROTHER,	IDIOT	. . . . THAT YOU, BLUELOO? LADY HERE AT LITTLE
ARMS III (71)	WITH YOUR ACCOUNT OF YOURSELF. YOU ARE A ROMANTIC	IDIOT	. (BLUNTSCHLI IS UNSPEAKABLY TAKEN ABACK). NEXT TIME,
NEVR IV (300)	CONTEMPTUOUSLY) MOTHER: THIS MAN IS A SENTIMENTAL	IDIOT	. (SHE SWEEPS AWAY TO THE FIREPLACE). /MRS CLANDON/ (

SUPR II (52) WHAT, YOU MAUDLIN IDIOT? /OCTAVIUS/ YES, I AM AN IDIOT . JACK: IF YOU HAD HEARD HER VOICE! IF YOU HAD SEEN
INCA (248) BROOCH. /THE INCA/ NO , MADAM: YOU ARE ONLY AN IDIOT . /ERMYNTRUDE/ THANK YOU. /THE INCA/ MARK YOU: IT IS
SIM I (48) CLERGYMAN/ WELL, IN OUR HOME I WAS KNOWN AS THE IDIOT . /MRS HYERING/ OH! I AM SORRY: I DIDNT KNOW. /THE
SIM II (69) IT'S AN ANGEL. /JANGA/ OH GET OUT, YOU SILLY IDIOT . /PRA/ (LOOKING THROUGH THE GLASS) THAT IS NO BIRD.
2TRU I (37) BY. MY BEDSIDE LAMP IS NOT ENOUGH, YOU STUPID IDIOT . THE NURSE SWITCHES ON AGAIN, AND CALMLY RETURNS TO
ARMS III (67) SAY THAT I DID, SIR. /PETKOFF/ I KNOW THAT, YOU IDIOT . WAS IT TRUE? /NICOLA/ I AM SURE MISS RAINA IS
ROCK I (202) I KNOW THAT: I HAVE NOT YET BECOME A COMPLETE IDIOT . YOU KEEP SAYING THE FAMILY, THE FAMILY, THE FAMILY.
2TRU II (77) COMMUNICATION WITH THEM AND HAS GOT HOLD OF THAT IDIOT MEEK, WE MAY HAVE THEM DOWN ON US LIKE A SWARM OF
GETT (280) END OF THE SEASON, AND SOME PERFECTLY BLITHERING IDIOT OF A BOY TO BE QUITE WICKED WITH. I SO SELDOM FEEL
JOAN 1 (58) DRIVELLING SNIVELLING JIBBERING JABBERING IDIOT OF A STEWARD IN FRANCE. (HE STRIDES BACK TO THE
BULL I (92) RULE AND GLADSTONE MUST BE SIMPLY THE CHAMPION IDIOT OF ALL THE WORLD. YET THE MAN WHO COULD IN THE VERY
GETT (326) THREW ME, I CALLED AT THE SHOP AND MADE AN IDIOT OF MYSELF AS SHE DESCRIBED. /SYKES/ WELL, SUPPOSE YOU
SUPR IV (159) AND SENSIBLE? DO YOU WANT VIOLET TO BE AN IDIOT -- OR SOMETHING WORSE, LIKE ME? /OCTAVIUS/ SOMETHING
JITT III (78) THAT YOU ARE AN IDIOT? /LENKHEIM/ I MAY BE AN IDIOT ; BUT MY IDIOCY IS THE ACCEPTED IDIOCY TAUGHT IN THE
DEST (174) ARE ONLY TWO THINGS HE CAN DO-- LEATHER-BRAINED IDIOT THAT HE IS! -- SHUT HIMSELF UP IN MANTUA OR VIOLATE
SUPR III (86) DOGGREL TO ALL THE WORLD: HEAVENLY MUSIC TO ME! IDIOT THAT I AM TO WEAR MY HEART ON MY SLEEVE! (HE
MILL I (155) ALASTAIR PROPOSED TO ME-- HE WAS TOO GREAT AN IDIOT TO COMPREHEND HIS OWN AUDACITY-- I KEPT MY PROMISE TO
2TRU III (102) TURN HIS HAND TO EVERYTHING AND TO LOOK LIKE AN IDIOT WHEN HE FEELS LIKE ONE! I HAVE BEEN DRIVEN TO
FANY EPILOG (333) BEASTLY. YOU HATE IT. YOU THINK I'M A CONCEITED IDIOT , AND THAT I SHALL NEVER BE ABLE TO WRITE ANYTHING
VWOO 1 (119) /Z/ ONLY THAT YOU CONSIDER ME NO BETTER THAN AN IDIOT , AND THAT YOU WERE A BAD HUSBAND, MOST LIKELY. /A/
KING I (212) ME. I WILL NOT BEAR IT. /CHARLES/ DO NOT BE AN IDIOT , BARBARA: MR KNELLER IS PAYING YOU THE GREATEST
MTH5 (222) MODEL THEM. /ARJILLAX/ SKILFUL! YOU HIGH-NOSED IDIOT , I COULD TURN SUCH THINGS OUT BY THE SCORE WITH MY
SUPR IV (153) ALMOST IN TEARS, BUT OF VEXATION) OH, DONT BE AN IDIOT , TAVY. HECTOR'S ABOUT AS FIT TO BECOME A WORKMAN AS
MIS. PREFACE(74) OF SANE SOCIETY, OBVIOUS AS SUCH TO ANYONE BUT AN IDIOT , THAT IN ANY DECENT COMMUNITY, CHILDREN SHOULD FIND
SUPR III (137) FOR EM! LUTS TIKE TO THE MAHNTNS. /MENDOZA/ IDIOT , WHAT DO YOU KNOW ABOUT THE MOUNTAINS? ARE YOU A
NEVR III (281) VOICE; SUDDENLY FURIOUS WITH HIM FOR LEAVING HER) IDIOT !
BULL I (95) ELECTION. /DOYLE/ (JUMPING UP) OH, GET OUT, YOU IDIOT ! /BROADBENT/ (RISING ALSO, NOT A BIT SNUBBED) HA!
PHIL II (124) ASIDE TO JULIA AS HE GETS OUT OF THE EASY CHAIR) IDIOT ! SHE'LL HAVE YOU TURNED OUT OF THE CLUB FOR THIS.
DEST (164) LOOKING AFTER THEM WITH CONCENTRATED IRRITATION) IDIOT ! THE STRANGE LADY SMILES SYMPATHETICALLY. HE COMES
NEVR II (258) AND RETREATS A STEP). OH, WHAT A FOOL I AM! AN IDIOT ! YOU DONT UNDERSTAND: I MIGHT AS WELL TALK TO THE

IDIOTIC

LION PREFACE(56) DEEPER DISASTER, LAUGHING OUTRIGHT. WAS EVER SO IDIOTIC A PROJECT MOOTED AS THE ESTIMATION OF VIRTUE IN
DOCT V (177) AND KILLING YOU. /RIDGEON/ I AM SO HOPELESSLY IDIOTIC ABOUT YOU THAT I SHOULD NOT MIND IT A BIT. YOU WOULD
BARB PREFACE(245) AND FEEDING AND TORMENTING HIM, SEEMS TO ME IDIOTIC AND SUPERSTITIOUS, YET THAT IS WHAT WE DO TO MEN WHO
METH PREFACE(R71) WILL BE NOTICED, WAS FUNDAMENTALLY NOTHING BUT AN IDIOTIC ATTEMPT ON THE PART OF EACH BELLIGERENT STATE TO
2TRU PREFACE(25) FACE OF THIRTY MILLIONS OF UNEMPLOYED, AND WORLD IDIOTIC CONFERENCES AT WHICH EACH NATION IMPLORES ALL THE
2TRU II (54) SAXBY'S INSTRUCTIONS. DO YOU HEAR? STOP MAKING IDIOTIC FACES; AND GET A MOVE ON. SEND ME THE
FOUN (211) AS YOU SAY, NOTHING COULD HAVE BEEN MORE IDIOTIC . YOU OUGHT TO HAVE KNOWN BETTER. NO: THE CHURCH IS
PYGM V (283) THE OTTOMAN). I HAVE LEARNT SOMETHING FROM YOUR IDIOTIC NOTIONS: I CONFESS THAT HUMBLY AND GRATEFULLY. AND I
MIS. PREFACE(20) YOU MOVE, BEATEN IF YOU CANNOT PROVE BY ANSWERING IDIOTIC QUESTIONS THAT EVEN WHEN YOU ESCAPED FROM THE POUND
BULL PREFACE(63) SECOND EDITION OF THE INDIAN MUTINY. THAT THIS IDIOTIC ROMANCE, GROSS AND RIDICULOUS AS THE LIES OF
LION PREFACE(61) DO NOT HAPPEN TO HAVE A SHIP FOR HIM TO UNLOAD IS IDIOTIC ; FOR AS HE DOES FAR LESS MISCHIEF WITH HIS THROAT
OVER (181) THAT DOMESTIC FELICITY WAS MAKING US PERFECTLY IDIOTIC ; THAT SHE WANTED A HOLIDAY TOO. SO WE AGREED TO GO
JITT II (44) I WAS ONLY WAITING FOR THE PUBLICATION OF HIS IDIOTIC THEORY TO TEAR IT TO PIECES. YOU DONT SUPPOSE I
ROCK PREFACE(177) OF ITS DISCLOSURE, OR A THOUSAND SUCH. IT WAS IDIOTIC TO TRY TO ADAPT NATURE TO THE CHURCH INSTEAD OF
LION PREFACE(77) EVERY SOCIAL PRINCIPLE THAT IS NOT ABSOLUTELY IDIOTIC WORKS: AUTOCRACY WORKS IN RUSSIA AND DEMOCRACY IN
PRES (161) OF REMARKS WHICH ARE PERHAPS SOMETIMES RATHER IDIOTIC , I GET CERTAIN CONVICTIONS. THANKS TO YOU, I HAVE

IDIOTICALLY

BULL PREFACE(46) TO THIS INDICTMENT. BUT THE MILITARY SYSTEM IS SO IDIOTICALLY ACADEMIC AND IMPOSSIBLE, AND RENDERS ITS VICTIMS

IDIOTS

SUPR III (140) (BETWEEN HIS TEETH) GO ON. TALK POLITICS, YOU IDIOTS : NOTHING SOUNDS MORE RESPECTABLE. KEEP IT UP, I TELL
2TRU PREFACE(14) THINK THEY CAN BE HONESTLY FREE ALL THE TIME ARE IDIOTS : PEOPLE WHO SEEK WHOLE-TIME FREEDOM BY PUTTING THEIR
MTH5 (230) POOR DEVILS WERE VERY LITTLE BETTER THAN OUR IDIOTS : WE SHOULD NEVER DREAM OF LETTING ONE OF THEM
FABL VI (128) TO THE TWENTIETH CENTURY, AND MAY BE KILLED AS IDIOTS AND SAVAGES IF WE MEET A LATER AND HIGHER
2TRU PREFACE(14) TO PUBLIC GOVERNMENT HAS GROWN UP AMONG THE IDIOTS AND THIEVES, AND IS RESORTED TO HERE ONLY BECAUSE IT
BULL PREFACE(10) CORSAIRS WHO SHARED WITH THEM WHAT MODERN IDIOTS CALL " THE COMMAND OF THE SEA" (MUCH THE SEA CARES
JOAN PREFACE(4) AND HIS LIKE COULD NOT ENDURE BEING SHEWN UP AS IDIOTS EVERY TIME SOCRATES OPENED HIS MOUTH. SOCRATES,
ROCK PREFACE(190) THAT TIME PROFESSED SOCIALISM. BUT EVEN IF THESE IDIOTS HAD REALLY UNDERSTOOD WHAT THEY WERE TALKING ABOUT,
2TRU PREFACE(22) WHICH IT WOULD BE A COUNCIL OF TRAMPS AND VILLAGE IDIOTS . IT IS NOT DESIRABLE THAT AN ORDINARY PARISH PRIEST
SIM II (61) OF THE WISE ARE UNHEEDED. SILENCE FOR THE KING OF IDIOTS . /MAYA/ (ALSO ENSHRINING HERSELF) SPEAK, SOLOMON.
PYGM III (245) KEYS IN HIS TROUSER POCKETS) BESIDES, THEYRE ALL IDIOTS . /MRS HIGGINS/ DO YOU KNOW WHAT YOU WOULD DO IF YOU
FABL VI (128) GET BEYOND THE FIRST FORM, AND GROW UP TO BE IDIOTS OR SAVAGES. WE KILL THEM. BUT WE ARE OURSELVES A
JOAN 6 (138) THE ROOT OF THE MATTER THAN WE ARE THROWN BACK BY IDIOTS WHO UNDERSTAND NOTHING BUT HORSES. (TREMBLING WITH

IDLE

MTH1 II (28) DESTROYER. I KNOW YOU: I AM YOUR MOTHER. YOU ARE IDLE : YOU ARE SELFISH. IT IS LONG AND HARD AND PAINFUL TO
MTH1 II (29) BECAUSE HIS BROTHER CAN KEEP HIMSELF. BUT AM I IDLE ? IN REJECTING YOUR DRUDGERY, HAVE I NOT EMBRACED
SUPR I (36) OTHER PASSIONS WERE IN ME BEFORE; BUT THEY WERE IDLE AND AIMLESS-- MERE CHILDISH GREEDINESSES AND CRUELTIES,
MIS. (200) IT IS NOT HEALTHY. YOUR WOMEN ARE KEPT IDLE AND DRESSED UP FOR NO OTHER PURPOSE THAN TO BE MADE
2TRU PREFACE(8) SAVE UP FOR HOLIDAYS DURING WHICH THEY CAN BE IDLE AND RICH, IF NOT FOR LIFE, AT LEAST FOR AN HOUR. AN
METH PREFACE(R51) THE GROTESQUE STUPIDITIES AND CRUELTIES OF THE IDLE AND SILLY CONTROVERSY WHICH AROSE AMONG THE DARWINIANS
POSN (442) WORKING AND NOT WHEN HE'S DRUNK; BUT WHEN HE'S IDLE AND SOBER. OUR OWN NATURES TELL US TO DRINK WHEN WE
LION PREFACE(53) AS YOU HAVE TODAY; FOR THERE WILL ALWAYS BE THE IDLE AND THE INDUSTRIOUS, THE THRIFTY AND THE WASTEFUL, THE
DOCT PREFACE(33) FOR THE UNCONDITIONED PURSUIT OF KNOWLEDGE IS AS IDLE AS ALL DREAMS OF UNCONDITIONED ACTIVITY; BUT NONE THE
WIDO I (6) KNOW THE IMPORTANCE OF THESE THINGS; APPARENTLY IDLE CEREMONIAL TRIFLES, REALLY THE SPRINGS AND WHEELS OF A
FABL PREFACE(92) FOR ME, BECAUSE IT IS ALWAYS IN MY MOUTH." ASK AN IDLE CHILD WHAT IT IS DOING, AND IT WILL NOT CLAIM THAT IT
SIM II (64) RULE, PROLA. /PROLA/ ALL YOUR BURDENS ON ME. LAZY IDLE CHILDREN. /KANCHIN/ HURRAH! ALL BURDENS ON PROLA.
LION PREFACE(94) LIE BETWEEN THEM, THEY MUST NOT BE BURDENED WITH IDLE CONTROVERSIES AS TO WHETHER THERE WAS EVER SUCH A
KING I (167) HAS MUCH TO DO THIS MORNING. HE HAS NO TIME FOR IDLE CONVERSATION. /NEWTON/ I HAD FORGOTTEN TO MAKE THIS
BULL II (103) NOW WHAT IS IT? /NORA/ (EMBARRASSED) OH, ONLY IDLE CURIOSITY. I WANTED TO KNOW WHETHER YOU FOUND IRELAND--
MTH2 (73) PROFESSOR. IN ANY CASE I THINK A LITTLE PERFECTLY IDLE DISCUSSION WOULD DO BURGE GOOD. AFTER ALL, WE MIGHT AS
SUPR III (116) /DON JUAN/ THEN THE LADY, WHO HAD BEEN HAPPY AND IDLE ENOUGH BEFORE, BECAME ANXIOUS, PREOCCUPIED WITH ME,
MTH4 II (176) THAN THREE HOURS. /NAPOLEON/ YOU CAN KEEP THIS IDLE FABLE OF DISCOURAGEMENT FOR PEOPLE CREDULOUS ENOUGH TO
MTH2 (84) KNOW THEY MUST. /FRANKLYN/ DO NOT MISTAKE MERE IDLE FANCIES FOR THE TREMENDOUS MIRACLE-WORKING FORCE OF
JOAN 2 (82) MORE TITTERING. /JOAN/ (SCANDALIZED) YOU ARE AN IDLE FELLOW, BLUEBEARD; AND YOU HAVE GREAT IMPUDENCE TO
SUPR HANDBOK(214) KINGS; AND WITH MUST THERE IS NO ARGUING. IT IS IDLE FOR AN INDIVIDUAL WRITER TO CARRY SO GREAT A MATTER
DOCT PREFACE(39) ARE HUMAN SACRIFICES, OF POLITICAL ECONOMY, IT IS IDLE FOR THE VIVISECTOR TO PRETEND THAT HE IS INCAPABLE OF
KING I (165) MY MIND ON THESE I FIND MYSELF WANDERING OFF INTO IDLE GAMES OF SPECULATION ABOUT NUMBERS IN INFINITE SERIES,
BASH II,1, (107) HEARTED RATHER! /LYDIA/ BUT YOU NEED NOT BE AN IDLE GENTLEMAN. I CALL YOU ONE OF NATURE'S GENTLEMEN.
BUOY II (20) SLASHING TAILS, I AM FAR BETTER PROTECTED AGAINST IDLE GENTLEMEN HERE THAN I SHOULD BE IN PICCADILLY. /HE/
ROCK I (196) SO THAT SATAN MAY FIND MISCHIEF STILL FOR IDLE HANDS TO DO. NO, P.M.: THE RIGHT ALTERNATIVE IS MINE:
MIS. PREFACE(36) AND THAT " SATAN FINDS SOME MISCHIEF STILL FOR IDLE HANDS TO DO" AND IT WILL BE SEEN THAT WE HAVE NO RIGHT
PHIL I (81) ME AS SOMETHING MORE THAN THE AMUSEMENT OF AN IDLE HOUR. OH, LEONARD, LEONARD, YOUVE NEVER GIVEN ME A
HART PREFACE(9) AS THE UNCULTURED WORLD OUTSIDE. BUT BEING AN IDLE HOUSE IT WAS A HYPOCHONDRIACAL HOUSE, ALWAYS RUNNING
SUPR III (90) IS JUSTICE IN HELL: HEAVEN IS FAR ABOVE SUCH IDLE HUMAN PERSONALITIES. YOU WILL BE WELCOME IN HELL,
SUPR IV (155) AND RAMSDEN, ANN STROLLS TO THE STEPS WITH AN IDLE IMPULSE TO TORMENT OCTAVIUS). /ANN/ WONT YOU GO WITH
GETT PREFACE(244) DEATH. UNTIL THEN, ALL TALK OF " PURIFICATION" IS IDLE . IT IS FOR THAT REASON THAT I LAY LITTLE STRESS ON
MILL IV (205) AND HAPPINESS, BUT ALL THIS TALK IS IDLE . THIS LADY HAS EASILY FULFILLED THE CONDITION IMPOSED
ROCK I (229) PERFECTLY SANITARY. NO NEWSPAPERS, NO LETTERS, NO IDLE LADIES. NO BOOKS EXCEPT IN THE AFTERNOON AS A REST FROM
GENV PREFACE(12) A THIRD OF THEIR WEEKLY EARNINGS OR MORE TO AN IDLE LANDLORD AS IF THAT WERE A LAW OF NATURE; BUT A
LIED (192) YOU ARE DIVORCED, WE SHALL GO THROUGH WHATEVER IDLE LEGAL CEREMONY YOU MAY DESIRE. I ATTACH NO IMPORTANCE
MIS. PREFACE(3) IF WE COULD GET IT FOR NOTHING; BUT THAT SORT OF IDLE LIKING IS NOT WILL. IT IS AMAZING -- CONSIDERING THE

ROCK II (240)	HONESTLY FREE OF INCOME TAX AND MAKE THESE LAZY	IDLE	LUBBERS OF LANDLORDS SWEAT FOR IT. I CALL THAT THE
OVER PREFACE(156)	MAY, AS NAPOLEON SAID, BE THE OCCUPATION OF THE	IDLE	MAN JUST AS MEN ARE THE PREOCCUPATION OF THE IDLE
HART II (125)	OF THE IDLE MAN. WELL, IF EVER THERE WAS AN	IDLE	MAN ON EARTH, HIS NAME IS RANDALL UTTERWORD. /RANDALL/
MIS. (112)	GOVERNOR ISNT GIVING HIS DAUGHTER MONEY FOR AN	IDLE	MAN TO LIVE ON HER. YOURE ON TRIAL HERE BECAUSE MY
HART II (126)	NAPOLEON SAID THAT WOMAN IS THE OCCUPATION OF THE	IDLE	MAN. BUT HE ADDED THAT SHE IS THE RELAXATION OF THE
HART II (125)	WHEN HE SAID THAT WOMEN ARE THE OCCUPATION OF THE	IDLE	MAN. WELL, IF EVER THERE WAS AN IDLE MAN ON EARTH, HIS
PLES PREFACE(R11)	TO THE GREAT ASTONISHMENT OF ITS AUDIENCES. IN AN	IDLE	MOMENT IN 1895 I BEGAN THE LITTLE SCENE CALLED THE MAN
2TRU PREFACE(10)	THE POOR IN A LUMP. BUT THEN THEY ARE NEITHER	IDLE	NOR FREE. A LADY WITH A BIG HOUSE TO MANAGE, AND THE
PYGM II (238)	BE AFRAID THAT I'LL SAVE IT AND SPARE IT AND LIVE	IDLE	ON IT. THERE WONT BE A PENNY OF IT LEFT BY MONDAY: I'LL
MILL PREFACE(129)	THE SERVICE OF THE COMMUNITY, OR, IF THEY ARE	IDLE	OR INCORRIGIBLY RECALCITRANT, HANDED OVER TO THE
ROCK I (232)	YOU KNOW. BRACING. /THE LADY/ CURIOUS, HOW	IDLE	PEOPLE ARE ALWAYS CLAMORING TO BE BRACED! LIKE
BARB PREFACE(213)	THE POOR MAN TO SEE HIS CHILDREN STARVE WHILST	IDLE	PEOPLE OVERFEED PET DOGS WITH THE MONEY THAT MIGHT FEED
ROCK I (232)	TO BE BRACED! LIKE TROUSERS. /SIR ARTHUR/	IDLE	PEOPLE! HOW YOU STICK TO YOUR POINT! AND WHAT A
BULL PREFACE(37)	MAY HAPPEN SO. " THE ISLAND OF THE SAINTS" IS NO	IDLE	PHRASE. RELIGIOUS GENIUS IS ONE OF OUR NATIONAL
PRES (157)	ARE. TO YOU A WOMAN'S HONOR IS NOTHING, AND THE	IDLE	PLEASURE OF THE MOMENT IS EVERYTHING. /MITCHENER/ THIS
MTH1 II (30)	HE STEALS AND KILLS FOR HIS FOOD; AND MAKES UP	IDLE	POEMS OF LIFE AFTER DEATH; AND DRESSES UP HIS
SUPR HANDBOK(177)	HAND ALL THE WORK THAT HE USED TO SHIRK WITH AN	IDLE	PRAYER. HE MUST, IN EFFECT, CHANGE HIMSELF INTO THE
GETT (344)	(TROUBLED) YOU ARE PAINING AND TIRING ME WITH	IDLE	QUESTIONS. YOU ARE DRAGGING ME BACK TO MYSELF. YOU ARE
MTH2 (85)	SUBJECT. MAY I PUT JUST ONE QUESTION TO YOU? AN	IDLE	QUESTION, SINCE NOTHING CAN COME OF IT; BUT STILL--
BULL IV (170)	BE NO MORE NEGLECT, NO MORE LONELINESS, NO MORE	IDLE	REGRETTINGS AND VAIN-HOPINGS IN THE EVENINGS BY THE
MIS. PREFACE(36)	PREVENTS US FROM DOING IT -- WE SHOULD HAVE NO	IDLE	RICH AND INDEED PROBABLY NO RICH, SINCE THERE IS NO
ROCK PREFACE(152)	MACHINERY OF AMUSEMENT AND PROTECTION FOR THE	IDLE	RICH CLASSES CREATED BY THE PRIVATE PROPERTY SYSTEM. BY
SUPR I (7)	BY JOHN TANNER, M.I.R.C., MEMBER OF THE	IDLE	RICH CLASS. /OCTAVIUS/ (SMILING) BUT JACK-- /RAMSDEN/
SUPR HANDBOK(173)	BY JOHN TANNER, M.I.R.C. (MEMBER OF THE	IDLE	RICH CLASS). PREFACE TO THE REVOLUTIONIST'S HANDBOOK. "
2TRU PREFACE(8)	THE GRAVE. I WOULD AND COULD LIVE THE LIFE OF THE	IDLE	RICH IF I LIKED IT; AND MY SOLE REASON FOR NOT LIVING
2TRU PREFACE(9)	WAKES ARE ON, SO I HAVE HAD MY AFTERNOONS AS AN	IDLE	RICH MAN, AND KNOW ONLY TOO WELL WHAT IT IS LIKE. IT
2TRU PREFACE(3)	THEM UNBEARABLY MISERABLE. BUT WHO HAS PITIED THE	IDLE	RICH OR REALLY BELIEVED THAT THEY HAVE A WORSE TIME OF
BARB II SD(273)	THE WHITEWASHED WALLS OF THE YARD WOULD DRIVE ANY	IDLE	RICH PERSON STRAIGHT TO THE MEDITERRANEAN. BUT THESE
2TRU PREFACE(5)	SYSTEM, WITH ITS GOLDEN EXCEPTIONS OF	IDLE	RICHERY AND ITS LEADEN RULE OF ANXIOUS POVERTY, IS AS
DOCT PREFACE(16)	PRACTICE BECOMES MORE AND MORE CONFINED TO THE	IDLE	RICH. THE PROPER ADVICE FOR MOST OF THEIR AILMENTS IS
2TRU PREFACE(8)	OFFER, THE PRIZE OF ADMISSION TO THE RANKS OF THE	IDLE	RICH, CAN POSSIBLY CONFER EITHER HAPPINESS OR HEALTH OR
MIS. PREFACE(77)	THE RESTLESS GLOBE-TROTTING VAGABONDAGE OF THE	IDLE	RICH, WANDERING FROM HOTEL TO HOTEL AND NEVER REALLY
ROCK I (232)	I GIVE YOU UP. YOU ARE FACTPROOF. I AM LAZY, I AM	IDLE	; AND I AM BREAKING DOWN FROM OVERWORK. HOW LOGICAL!
GETT (306)	THE CHURCH HAS FAILED. I SHALL PUT ASIDE ALL	IDLE	SOCIAL DISTINCTIONS AND APPEAL TO THE MUNICIPALITY.
BULL II (105)	AND THE LIKE. TAKE NO NOTICE OF THEM. IT'S ALL	IDLE	STORIES AND SUPERSTITION. /BROADBENT/ (SOMEWHAT
MIS. PREFACE(4)	IN. THEREFORE LET US GIVE UP TELLING ONE ANOTHER	IDLE	STORIES, AND REJOICE IN DEATH AS WE REJOICE IN BIRTH;
METH PREFACE(R43)	TO PASS. HAD I NOT PRELUDED WITH THE APPARENTLY	IDLE	STORY OF MY REVIVAL OF THE CONTROVERSIAL METHODS OF
NEVR I (223)	BRINGS IT TO THE CABINET, CONTINUING IN THE SAME	IDLE	STRAIN) I REALLY SHOULD LIKE TO KNOW YOUR FAMILY, MR
JOAN EPILOG (153)	COWARDLY EVASION OF THE ISSUE, TESTIMONY MADE OF	IDLE	TALES THAT COULD NOT IMPOSE ON A PLOUGHBOY. YET OUT OF
LION PREFACE(47)	OF THE MATTER FOR ITSELF AT ALL. IT IS THEREFORE	IDLE	TO BEGIN DISPUTING WITH THE READER AS TO WHAT HE SHOULD
KING PREFACE(157)	IN EQUAL NUMBERS. UNTIL THIS IS ACHIEVED IT IS	IDLE	TO PRATE ABOUT POLITICAL DEMOCRACY AS EXISTING, OR EVER
2TRU PREFACE(12)	REPAID, THE SYSTEM BECAME SO EXTENSIVE THAT THE	IDLE	UPSTART RICH BECAME A DEFINITELY MISCHIEVOUS AND
2TRU PREFACE(11)	IT IS HIS DUTY TO TELL YOU THAT YOU ARE AN	IDLE	USELESS GLUTTON AND DRUNKARD AND THAT YOU ARE GOING TO
MILL PREFACE(128)	SELFISHNESS IN INDUSTRY, AND GLORIFICATION OF	IDLE	USELESSNESS IN THE FACE OF THE DEGRADING MISERY OF THE
GETT PREFACE(234)	FOR LIFE TO A CRIMINAL, A DRUNKARD, A LUNATIC, AN	IDLE	VAGRANT, OR A PERSON WHOSE RELIGIOUS FAITH WAS CONTRARY
BULL PREFACE(11)	BECAUSE THEY IMAGINE THAT A KING OR A CHIEF IS AN	IDLE	VOLUPTUARY WITH LOTS OF MONEY, LEISURE, AND POWER OVER
LADY (248)	TO GOOD WORKS. I HAVE ALSO STOLE FROM A BOOK OF	IDLE	WANTON TALES TWO OF THE MOST DAMNABLE FOOLISHNESSES IN
SUPR III (131)	APPETITE IN THE ACT OF GRATIFYING IT? IS A FIELD	IDLE	WHEN IT IS FALLOW? CAN THE COMMANDER EXPEND HIS
MTH1 II (34)	GO ON WITH YOUR SPINNING; AND DO NOT SIT THERE	IDLE	WHILE I AM STRAINING MY MUSCLES FOR YOU. /EVE/ (SLOWLY
OVER PREFACE(156)	IDLE MAN JUST AS MEN ARE THE PREOCCUPATION OF THE	IDLE	WOMAN; BUT THE MASS OF MANKIND IS TOO BUSY AND TOO POOR
PYGM II (228)	AND TAKE RIDES IN TAXIS. IF YOURE NAUGHTY AND	IDLE	YOU WILL SLEEP IN THE BACK KITCHEN AMONG THE BLACK
ROCK II (247)	NOT ONLY YOUR IDLERS BUT OUR IDLERS: ALL THE	IDLE	YOUNG GENTLEMEN WHO DO NOTHING BUT WASTE THEIR OWN TIME
FANY III (326)	MARRY MARGARET! /JUGGINS/ (CONTINUING) AS AN	IDLE	YOUNGER SON, UNABLE TO SUPPORT MYSELF, OR EVEN TO
ROCK II (244)	OF THE FINANCIERS AND ENTREPRENEURS BY A USELESS,	IDLE	, AND PREDATORY LANDED CLASS. /SIR ARTHUR/ (CHUCKLING)
LION PREFACE(43)	WOULD HAVE BEEN THAT ALL THESE INQUIRIES ARE	IDLE	, BECAUSE IF JESUS HAD WISHED TO ESCAPE, HE COULD HAVE
2TRU PREFACE(10)	IT IS NOT BECAUSE COUNTRYHOUSE LIFE IS	IDLE	, BUT BECAUSE ITS ACTIVITIES ARE UNCONGENIAL AND
MTH1 II (29)	OR SPADES, HUNGER OR FATIGUE-- /EVE/ SELFISH AND	IDLE	, CAIN. I KNOW. /CAIN/ SELFISH, YES: A LIFE IN WHICH NO
JOAN PREFACE(35)	ANY PRIEST OR BODY OF PRIESTS, AS LAZY, DRUNKEN,	IDLE	, DISSOLUTE, AND UNWORTHY OF THEIR GREAT CHURCH AND
CAND II SD(105)	BEEN REPLACED AT THE TABLE. MARCHBANKS, ALONE AND	IDLE	, IS TRYING TO FIND OUT HOW THE TYPEWRITER WORKS.
LION PREFACE(57)	DO WITH HIM IS TO DO NOTHING: THAT IS, TO BE AS	IDLE	, LAZY, AND HEARTLESS IN DEALING WITH HIM AS HE IS IN
CLEO IV (182)	MIND. TODAY YOU ARE TO BE LIKE OTHER PEOPLE:	IDLE	, LUXURIOUS, AND KIND. (SHE STRETCHES HER HAND TO HIM
JOAN 6 (124)	AT IT ELEVEN WEEKS! /CAUCHON/ WE HAVE NOT BEEN	IDLE	, MY LORD. WE HAVE HELD FIFTEEN EXAMINATIONS OF THE
MIS. PREFACE(77)	BEING DERELICT OF GOD AND MAN, THE MISERY OF THE	IDLE	, POOR OR RICH. AND THIS IS ONE OF THE MISERIES OF
3PLA PREFACE(R10)	BOTH OF THEM FASHIONABLY DRESSED AND EXQUISITELY	IDLE	, POSING AGAINST BACKGROUNDS OF DRAWING ROOM AND DAINTY
CAND II (114)	IT ALL? /MARCHBANKS/ (FIRING UP) YES, TO BE	IDLE	, SELFISH, AND USELESS: THAT IS, TO BE BEAUTIFUL AND
CAND II (114)	AND WHERE THERE IS NOTHING TO DO BUT TO BE	IDLE	, SELFISH, AND USELESS. /CANDIDA/ (JARRED) OH, JAMES!

IDLENESS

MRS I (195)	(SEVERELY) YES. I ADVISED YOU TO CONQUER YOUR	IDLENESS	AND FLIPPANCY, AND TO WORK YOUR WAY INTO AN
SUPR III (121)	CHILDLESS LABORER IS MORE TORMENTED BY HIS WIFE'S	IDLENESS	AND HER CONSTANT DEMANDS FOR AMUSEMENT AND
METH PREFACE(R15)	ON PROFITEERING, AND IS TAUGHT TO HONOR PARASITIC	IDLENESS	AND LUXURY, LEARNS TO SHOOT AND RIDE AND KEEP FIT
LION PREFACE(71)	IS CONDEMNED BY HER PARENTS TO WAIT IN GENTEEL	IDLENESS	AND USELESSNESS FOR A HUSBAND WHEN ALL HER HEALTHY
MIS. PREFACE(21)	BEEN TAUGHT TO DIE RATHER THAN ENDURE. AND SO	IDLENESS	AND WORTHLESSNESS ON THE ONE HAND AND A PRETENCE OF
MIS. PREFACE(35)	THE SOLE AND OBVIOUS CAUSE OF THE NOTION THAT	IDLENESS	IS DELIGHTFUL AND THAT HEAVEN IS A PLACE WHERE
OVER PREFACE(156)	LAYS TO VIRTUE. STILL, WHEREVER THERE IS	IDLENESS	OR EVEN A REASONABLE SUPPLY OF ELEGANT LEISURE
CAPT I (224)	CHOSEN THEIR CALLING THROUGH A LOVE OF LUXURIOUS	IDLENESS	): I HAVE BROUGHT TO YOUR HOUSE A CHRISTIAN DOG AND
GETT PREFACE(208)	BECOME WORKERS SUPPORTING THE MALES IN LUXURY AND	IDLENESS	UNTIL THE QUEEN HAS FOUND HER MATE, WHEN THE QUEEN
MIS. PREFACE(73)	LIKE -- OFTEN TURNS OUT WELL AFTERWARDS, AS IF	IDLENESS	WERE A SIGN OF ABILITY AND CHARACTER. A MUCH MORE

IDLER

HART I SD(44)	NOT EXPENSIVELY DRESSED, EVIDENTLY NOT A SMART	IDLER	. WITH A SIGH OF WEARY RESIGNATION SHE COMES TO THE
HART PREFACE(25)	TIME WITH URGENT PRACTICAL WORK, HAD TO LEAVE TO	IDLER	PEOPLE, OR TO PROFESSIONAL RHETORICIANS, THE
SUPR PREFACE(R28)	MY SOCIALISM FOR MILLIONAIRES) LEFT WORD THAT NO	IDLER	WAS TO INHERIT HIS ESTATE. THE BENT BACKS STRAIGHTENED
SUPR HANDBOK(219)	DOES. HE WHO CANNOT, TEACHES. A LEARNED MAN IS AN	IDLER	WHO KILLS TIME WITH STUDY. BEWARE OF HIS FALSE
ROCK PREFACE(160)	THE MAN WHO STOLE THE COMMON FROM THE GOOSE. THE	IDLER	, THAT COMMON ENEMY OF MANKIND WHO ROBS EVERYBODY ALL

IDLER'S

DOCT PREFACE(12)	THE OCCURRENCE HIMSELF FOR THE SAKE OF GETTING AN	IDLER'S	PENSION AT THE EXPENSE OF THE RAILWAY COMPANY, BEING

IDLERS

ROCK II (247)	COMPEL THE IDLERS, NOT ONLY YOUR IDLERS BUT OUR	IDLERS	: ALL THE IDLE YOUNG GENTLEMEN WHO DO NOTHING BUT
MILL IV (210)	HERE: THE WEALTH THEY CREATE IS THROWN AWAY ON	IDLERS	AND THEIR PARASITES, WHILST POVERTY, DIRT, DISEASE,
ROCK II (247)	WE SHALL COMPEL THE IDLERS, NOT ONLY YOUR	IDLERS	BUT OUR IDLERS: ALL THE IDLE YOUNG GENTLEMEN WHO DO
BULL IV (179)	FROM ENGLAND TO IRELAND! /KEEGAN/ JUST AS OUR	IDLERS	HAVE FOR SO MANY GENERATIONS TAKEN MONEY FROM IRELAND
ROCK II (247)	THEY ARE WORKING ALREADY. WE SHALL COMPEL THE	IDLERS	. NOT ONLY YOUR IDLERS BUT OUR IDLERS: ALL THE IDLE
METH PREFACE(R72)	SELECTION OF WORKERS AS FITTER TO SURVIVE THAN	IDLERS	; WHILST THE WESTERN POWERS ARE DRIFTING AND
MIS. PREFACE(22)	HAD BEEN TAKEN, AND ALL THE DISLOYAL WASTERS AND	IDLERS	SHEWN STERNLY TO THE DOOR, THE SCHOOL WOULD NOT HAVE
BULL IV (179)	IS THE MAKING OF GOLF LINKS AND HOTELS TO BRING	IDLERS	TO A COUNTRY WHICH WORKERS HAVE LEFT IN MILLIONS
BULL IV (179)	OPPRESSED LAND. /BROADBENT/ BUT, HANG IT ALL, THE	IDLERS	WILL BRING MONEY FROM ENGLAND TO IRELAND! /KEEGAN/
LION PREFACE(58)	HOW TO PREVENT THE THEFT OF THAT SUBSISTENCE BY	IDLERS	, SHOULD BE CAREFULLY DISSOCIATED; FOR THE TRIUMPHANT

IDLEST

ROCK I (232)	FROM OVERWORK. HOW LOGICAL! /THE LADY/ ALL THE	IDLEST	AND LAZIEST OF MY PATIENTS SLAVE FROM MORNING TO
GENV IV (109)	I AM, ALL THAT YOU ARE DOING HERE WOULD SEEM THE	IDLEST	TRIFLING. /BATTLER/ (SHOUTING) WHO IS THE MASTER?

IDLING

GLIM (183)	DO THE HOUSE WORK WITH A GREAT GIRL LIKE YOU	IDLING	ABOUT? SQUARCIO IS A FOOL, AFTER ALL. /GIULIA/ NO,

DEVL I (12)	WORK OF THE HOUSE WITH A GREAT LOUT LIKE YOU	IDLING	ABOUT. CHRISTY TAKES THE WINDOW BAR OUT OF ITS
ROCK II (258)	WHEN THEY HAVE NO LIBERTY. THEY ARE SICK OF	IDLING	AND LOAFING ABOUT ON DOLES WHEN THEY ARE NOT DRUDGING
LION PREFACE(57)	MAY QUITE RATIONALLY COMPEL HIM TO ABSTAIN FROM	IDLING	BY WHATEVER MEANS WE EMPLOY TO COMPEL HIM TO ABSTAIN
ROCK PREFACE(161)	SEVERE LAWS AGAINST ANY INTERFERENCE WITH HIS	IDLING	. IT WAS THE BUSINESS OF THE SOVIET TO MAKE ALL
		IDLY	
DOCT IV SD(159)	AND REPORTS, BUT ONLY TO SELL THEM TO	IDLY	CURIOUS PEOPLE, HAS NOTHING BUT HONOR TO LOSE BY
JOAN 3,SD(89)	RAGE. THE WIND DROPS; AND THE PENNON FLAPS	IDLY	DOWN THE LANCE; BUT DUNOIS IS TOO MUCH OCCUPIED WITH
GETT PREFACE(234)	TO A MONTH'S IMPRISONMENT OCCASIONALLY FOR	IDLY	LEAVING THEIR WIVES IN CHILDBIRTH WITHOUT FOOD, FIRE,
GENV IV (117)	DUTIES OF MY CLASS AND MY FAITH. I COULD NOT SIT	IDLY	READING AND TALKING WHILST THE CIVILIZATION ESTABLISHED
NEVR II (238)	PLEASED TO MEET YOU AGAIN. (SHE WANDERS	IDLY	ROUND THE TABLE, EXCHANGING A GRIMACE WITH VALENTINE ON
		IDOL	
METH PREFACE(R39)	PASSIONS COULD BE NOTHING BUT AN ANTHROPOMORPHIC	IDOL	: NO MATTER: PEOPLE AT LARGE COULD NOT CONCEIVE A GOD
METH PREFACE(R39)	WHOSE DENIAL OF GOD WAS SIMPLY A DENIAL OF THE	IDOL	AND A DEMONSTRATION AGAINST AN UNBEARABLE AND MOST
SUPR HANDBOK(217)	OF A FLESH AND BLOOD ONE. WHEN THE WOODEN	IDOL	DOES NOT ANSWER THE PEASANT'S PRAYER, HE BEATS IT: WHEN
SUPR HANDBOK(217)	PRAYER, HE BEATS IT: WHEN THE FLESH AND BLOOD	IDOL	DOES NOT SATISFY THE CIVILIZED MAN, HE CUTS ITS HEAD
METH PREFACE(R39)	AND OF VERY EVIL PASSIONS TOO. THEY IMPOSED THIS	IDOL	IN PRACTICE ON THE CHURCH ITSELF, IN SPITE OF THE FIRST
LION I (116)	MY SOUL BEFORE THE PEOPLE THAT THIS HIDEOUS	IDOL	IS GOD, AND THAT ALL THIS WICKEDNESS AND FALSEHOOD IS
MTH5 (225)	MARBLE REMAINS MARBLE, AND THE GRAVEN IMAGE AN	IDOL	. AS I HAVE BROKEN MY IDOLS, AND CAST AWAY MY CHISEL
JOAN 2 (71)	AM AN ARCHBISHOP; AND AN ARCHBISHOP IS A SORT OF	IDOL	. AT ANY RATE HE HAS TO LEARN TO KEEP STILL AND SUFFER
APPL INTRLUD(254)	ALL I CAN DO IS TO DRAW THE LINE AT BEING A CRUEL	IDOL	. (HE LOOKS AT HIS WATCH) NOW I MUST REALLY BE OFF. AU
JOAN 2 (71)	YOU HAVE THE PATIENCE TO STAND THERE LIKE A STONE	IDOL	. /THE ARCHBISHOP/ YOU SEE, I AM AN ARCHBISHOP; AND AN
LION PREFACE(64)	LIFE OF AN HONEST MAN INSTEAD OF THAT OF A CRUEL	IDOL	. THERE HAS ALSO BEEN A PROPAGANDA OF A SOULLESS
KING I (181)	GOD! SHAME ON YOU, ISAAC NEWTON, FOR MAKING AN	IDOL	OF AN ARCHBISHOP! THERE IS NO CREDULITY LIKE THE
SIM II (64)	/PROLA/ BE QUIET, YOU TWO. YOU SHALL NOT MAKE AN	IDOL	OF ME. /KANCHIN/ WE SHALL MAKE YOU THE EMPRESS OF THE
DEST (192)	WITHOUT KNOWLEDGE, SO THAT THEY MAKE AN	IDOL	OF ME; WHILST THE HIGH ARE UNSCRUPULOUS WITHOUT
LADY PREFACE(225)	WITH AN UNCONQUERABLE STYLE WHICH IS THE MAN. THE	IDOL	OF THE BARDOLATERS. THERE IS EVEN AN ADVANTAGE IN
ARMS I (4)	ME THE NEWS. SERGIUS IS THE HERO OF THE HOUR, THE	IDOL	OF THE REGIMENT. /RAINA/ TELL ME, TELL ME. HOW WAS IT?
METH PREFACE(R65)	OF OUR GREAT POETS, CALLED THE ANTHROPOMORPHIC	IDOL	OLD NOBODADDY, AND GIBED AT HIM IN TERMS WHICH THE
CLEO IV (184)	FOUR/ (HOLDING THEIR GLASSES TOGETHER BEFORE THE	IDOL	) SEND US THY VOICE, FATHER NILE. THE DEATH CRY OF A
APPL I (207)	YOURE KING. /MAGNUS/ AND WHAT IS THE KING? AN	IDOL	SET UP BY A GROUP OF PLUTOCRATS SO THAT THEY CAN RULE
BARB PREFACE(228)	HIS DAUGHTER IS ANY LESS OBVIOUSLY A TRIBAL	IDOL	THAN DAGON OR CHEMOSH. FURTHER, THERE IS STILL TOO MUCH
METH PREFACE(R39)	AN UNBEARABLE AND MOST UNCHRISTIAN IDOLATRY. THE	IDOL	WAS, AS SHELLEY HAD BEEN EXPELLED FROM OXFORD FOR
DOCT PREFACE(51)	TO DIE THAT THEY WILL CLING FRANTICALLY TO ANY	IDOL	WHICH PROMISES TO CURE ALL THEIR DISEASES, AND CRUCIFY
SUPR HANDBOK(217)	IS A DEVICE FOR COMBINING THE INERTIA OF A WOODEN	IDOL	WITH THE CREDIBILITY OF A FLESH AND BLOOD ONE. WHEN THE
ROCK PREFACE(188)	WORSE THAN EVER, FEAR OF IMPERIAL CAESAR, THE	IDOL	YOU HAVE YOURSELF CREATED, AND FEAR OF ME, THE
MILL PREFACE(123)	WHINING ABOUT IT. HE AT ONCE BECAME A POPULAR	IDOL	, AND HAD THE REGULAR EXECUTIVE FORCES SO COMPLETELY
LION PREFACE(88)	THE BLESSED VIRGIN HERSELF TO THE STATUS OF AN	IDOL	, CONCENTRATED SALVATIONISM TO A POINT AT WHICH THE
FABL PREFACE(73)	BIBLE WAS TRUE. IF JEHOVAH WAS A BARBAROUS TRIBAL	IDOL	, IRRECONCILABLE WITH THE GOD OF MICAH, THEN THERE WAS
APPL INTRLUD(254)	A REAL MAN WOULD NEVER DO AS A KING. I AM ONLY AN	IDOL	, MY LOVE; AND ALL I CAN DO IS TO DRAW THE LINE AT
3PLA PREFACE(R27)	THE HEROES OF THE LOFTIEST POETRY, OUR NEWEST	IDOL	, THE SUPERMAN, CELEBRATING THE DEATH OF GODHEAD, MAY
GENV PREFACE(14)	THE NEXT BIG BOSS CAME ALONG AND BECAME A POPULAR	IDOL	, WORSHIPPED AT THE POLLS BY 99 PER CENT MAJORITIES.
		IDOLATER	
JOAN PREFACE(30)	BUT AS A HERETIC, BLASPHEMER, SORCERESS AND	IDOLATER	, HER ALLEGED OFFENCES WERE NOT POLITICAL OFFENCES
BULL PREFACE(16)	ENGLISHMAN THE DUPE OF EVERY CHARLATAN AND THE	IDOLATER	OF EVERY NUMSKULL, I PERCEIVE THAT IRELAND IS THE
JOAN PREFACE(6)	HARLOT, NOT A WITCH, NOT A BLASPHEMER, NO MORE AN	IDOLATER	THAN THE POPE HIMSELF, AND NOT ILL CONDUCTED IN ANY
SIM PRO,3, (31)	NATURE BY WHICH WE ALL LIVE. BUT OF COURSE TO AN	IDOLATER	THEY ARE IDOLS. /THE Y.W./ YOU TALK A LOT ABOUT
ANNA (299)	HER HAND). /THE GRAND DUCHESS/ (INDULGENTLY)	IDOLATER	! WHEN WILL YOU LEARN THAT OUR STRENGTH HAS NEVER
		IDOLATERS	
SIM II (67)	YOU PROVOKE ME TO BOX YOUR EARS, YOU ABOMINABLE	IDOLATERS	? GET UP THIS INSTANT. GO AND SCRUB THE FLOORS.
BARB II (295)	WE THREE TO DO WITH THE COMMON MOB OF SLAVES AND	IDOLATERS	? (HE SITS DOWN AGAIN WITH A SHRUG OF CONTEMPT
SIM PRO,3, (31)	STEADY ON, YOU. WHO ARE YOU CALLING HEATHEN	IDOLATERS	? LOOK AT ALL THOSE IMAGES. I SHOULD SAY, IF YOU
KING I (188)	ONLY A FOOL WOULD SET UP THESE SUPERSTITIOUS	IDOLATERS	AGAINST THE ROYAL SOCIETY, FOUNDED BY YOUR ROYAL
LION PREFACE(97)	WAY OF RELIGIOUS INSTRUCTION, TO REGARD AS GROSS	IDOLATERS	CONSIGNED TO ETERNAL PERDITION, BUT WHOSE FAITH I
FABL PREFACE(78)	AND PLAYWRIGHT DOES NOT SHAKE THE FAITH OF MY	IDOLATERS	IN THE LEAST. FACTS COUNT FOR NOTHING. I AM TOLD
METH PREFACE(R79)	OR ST PETER'S, ARE FIRE-DOOMED HEATHENS AND	IDOLATERS	. ALL THE SWEETNESS OF RELIGION IS CONVEYED TO THE
SUPR HANDBOK(217)	SLAYS A KING AND HE WHO DIES FOR HIM ARE ALIKE	IDOLATERS	. ROYALTY. KINGS ARE NOT BORN: THEY ARE MADE BY
SUPR HANDBOK(217)	THE ARISTOCRACY, OF IDOLS; THE DEMOCRACY, OF	IDOLATERS	. THE POPULACE CANNOT UNDERSTAND THE BUREAUCRACY:
GETT PREFACE(228)	AND THIS LATTER VIEW WILL PERHAPS PREVAIL IF THE	IDOLATERS	OF MARRIAGE PERSIST IN REFUSING ALL PROPOSALS FOR
3PLA PREFACE(R34)	COULD NOT FOLLOW THE STORY OF GLOSTER. BOTH THESE	IDOLATERS	OF THE BARD MUST HAVE THOUGHT FORBES ROBERTSON MAD
SIM PRO,3, (31)	UNDERSTAND. /THE PRIESTESS/ I FIND THESE HEATHEN	IDOLATERS	VERY TRYING. IS IT REALLY KIND TO TREAT THEM
MILL PREFACE(124)	WOULD LEARN THAT THE GERMANS ARE A RACE OF SAVAGE	IDOLATERS	, MURDERERS, LIARS, AND FIENDS WHOSE ASSUMPTION OF
		IDOLATRIES	
LION PREFACE(80)	OF PRINCES, BY CASTING ALL THE QUACKERIES AND	IDOLATRIES	WHICH NOW USURP AND MALVERSATE THE POWER OF GOD
LADY PREFACE(233)	OF IBSEN'S POWER OF PENETRATING ITS ILLUSIONS AND	IDOLATRIES	, AND WITH ALL SWIFT'S HORROR OF ITS CRUELTY AND
LADY PREFACE(232)	NO MEANS A POPULAR MOVEMENT; AND, LIKE ALL SUCH	IDOLATRIES	, IT WAS EXCITED BY THE MAGIC OF SHAKESPEAR'S ART
		IDOLATROUS	
BULL PREFACE(18)	WITH FACTS, THE ACTUAL DISTINCTION BETWEEN THE	IDOLATROUS	ENGLISHMAN AND THE FACT-FACING IRISHMAN, OF THE
BUOY PREFACE(6)	REFRAINING FROM SOME PARAPHRASE OF " AN EVIL AND	IDOLATROUS	GENERATION CLAMORS FOR A MIRACLE." BUT AS MAHOMET
LADY PREFACE(232)	REMEDY WAS PERSONAL SOBRIETY AND FREEDOM FROM	IDOLATROUS	ILLUSION IN SO FAR AS HE HAD ANY REMEDY AT ALL,
LADY PREFACE(222)	NOT, WAS WHAT MR HARRIS IN ONE PASSAGE CALLS IT:	IDOLATROUS	. IF IT HAD BEEN, SHE MIGHT HAVE BEEN ABLE TO
SIM PREFACE(9)	THE WHOLE BUSINESS OF RITUAL RELIGION AS	IDOLATROUS	. THE BELL, HE SAID, " STRUCK ON HIS HEART."
LION PREFACE(48)	MORE HE HAD." WE GET RID, TO BEGIN WITH, OF THE	IDOLATROUS	OR ICONOGRAPHIC WORSHIP OF CHRIST. BY THIS I MEAN
SUPR PREFACE(R36)	OF SHELLEY, THE REVIVAL OF TRIBAL SOOTHSAYING AND	IDOLATROUS	RITES WHICH HUXLEY CALLED SCIENCE AND MISTOOK FOR
JOAN PREFACE(23)	BUT IT CLASHES MOST DISCORDANTLY BOTH WITH THE	IDOLATROUS	ROMANCE THAT HAS GROWN UP ROUND HER, AND THE
		IDOLATRY	
FABL PREFACE(75)	HUMAN MIND BY THE INDIAN JAINISTS, WHO RENOUNCED	IDOLATRY	AND BLOOD SACRIFICE LONG BEFORE MICAH, AND
LADY PREFACE(232)	HE WAS CONCERNED ABOUT DRUNKENNESS AND ABOUT THE	IDOLATRY	AND HYPOCRISY OF OUR JUDICIAL SYSTEM; BUT HIS
GENV PREFACE(22)	MOBS AND MONARCHS BEING PRODUCTS OF POLITICAL	IDOLATRY	AND IGNORANCE. THE WIDER THE SUFFRAGE, THE GREATER
3PLA PREFACE(R33)	HARRIS, HAVE ALWAYS KEPT AS FAR ON THIS SIDE	IDOLATRY	AS I. AS TO OUR ORDINARY UNCRITICAL CITIZENS, THEY
KING I (182)	OF HELL? /FOX/ HOW SHALL I ROOT OUT THE SIN OF	IDOLATRY	FROM THIS LAND? WORSHIP YOUR GOD, WOMAN, NOT A
LADY PREFACE(217)	UNLESS THERE HAD BEEN, NOT ONLY IDOLATRY, BUT	IDOLATRY	FULSOME ENOUGH TO IRRITATE JONSON INTO AN EXPRESS
DOCT PREFACE(42)	AWAY FROM THE GOD OF HIS FATHERS TO THE SENSUOUS	IDOLATRY	IN WHICH HE ENDED HIS DAYS. IN THE SAME WAY WE FIND
MIS. PREFACE(100)	THEIR PROPER PLACE AS AMUSING VULGARITIES. ARTIST	IDOLATRY	. BUT THERE ARE MORE DANGEROUS INFLUENCES THAN
SUPR PREFACE(R27)	OF A SCOTCH MISSIONARY INTO CRUDE AFRICAN	IDOLATRY	. I DO NOT KNOW WHETHER YOU HAVE ANY ILLUSIONS LEFT
FABL PREFACE(80)	MY CRITICISMS OF SHAKESPEAR STOPPED THIS SIDE OF	IDOLATRY	. IT MAY SEEM THAT BETWEEN A ROMAN CATHOLIC WHO
FABL PREFACE(79)	KNOW BETTER. TO RETURN TO THE INVETERACY OF	IDOLATRY	. TEN YEARS AGO DISCIPLES OF A RIVAL CELEBRITY WERE
SUPR HANDBOK(217)	GOLDEN RULE IS THAT THERE ARE NO GOLDEN RULES.	IDOLATRY	. THE ART OF GOVERNMENT IS THE ORGANIZATION OF
SUPR HANDBOK(217)	THE ART OF GOVERNMENT IS THE ORGANIZATION OF	IDOLATRY	. THE BUREAUCRACY CONSISTS OF FUNCTIONARIES; THE
LION PREFACE(50)	THAN A DECLARATION OF SENTIMENT OR A LABEL OF	IDOLATRY	. THE DOCTRINES IN WHICH JESUS IS THUS CONFIRMED
METH PREFACE(R39)	AGAINST AN UNBEARABLE AND MOST UNCHRISTIAN	IDOLATRY	. THE IDOL WAS, AS SHELLEY HAD BEEN EXPELLED FROM
LADY PREFACE(217)	AS HE GAINED THE MEANS TO KEEP IT UP. THIS SIDE	IDOLATRY	. THERE IS ANOTHER MATTER WHICH I THINK MR HARRIS
LADY PREFACE(218)	HIS DISCLAIMER, HE DID NOT STOP " THIS SIDE	IDOLATRY	." IF, THEREFORE, EVEN JONSON FELT HIMSELF FORCED
GENV PREFACE(20)	THE MOMENT IT MADE HITLER A FIGURE HEAD, POPULAR	IDOLATRY	MADE A PROPHET AND A HERO OF HIM, AND GAVE HIM A
3PLA PREFACE(R23)	I SEE THAT THE NINETEENTH CENTURY HAS CROWNED THE	IDOLATRY	OF ART WITH THE DEIFICATION OF LOVE, SO THAT EVERY
BUOY PREFACE(6)	AND SELF-STYLED SCIENTIFIC SOCIALISTS IN THEIR	IDOLATRY	OF DARWIN AND MARX, THE SCIENTIST WHO SOLVES THE
APPL PREFACE(171)	TO POLITICAL PRINCIPLES IS ONLY A MASK FOR OUR	IDOLATRY	OF EMINENT PERSONS, THE APPLE CART EXPOSES THE
3PLA PREFACE(R22)	WERE BECOMING THE INSTRUMENTS OF A SYSTEMATIC	IDOLATRY	OF SENSUOUSNESS, I WOULD HOLD IT GOOD STATESMANSHIP
MIS. PREFACE(101)	HIS DUE. IN THUS DELIVERING OUR CHILDREN FROM THE	IDOLATRY	OF THE ARTIST, WE SHALL NOT DESTROY FOR THEM THE
JOAN PREFACE(22)	LORDS AND KINGS AND PRELATES AS SUCH WITHOUT	IDOLATRY	OR SNOBBERY, SEEING AT A GLANCE HOW MUCH THEY WERE
LION PREFACE(102)	CARRYING SUBSERVIENCE TO THE STATE TO A PITCH OF	IDOLATRY	THAT ENDED IN THE THEORY OF THE DIVINE RIGHT OF

MILL PREFACE(132)	CALLED MILITARY GLORY. IT WAS THIS IGNORANCE AND	IDOLATRY	THAT FIRST EXALTED NAPOLEON AND THEN SMASHED HIM.
HART PREFACE(35)	SOMETIMES PRODUCED SUCH DEVELOPMENTS OF EROTIC	IDOLATRY	THAT MEN WHO WERE NOT ONLY ENTHUSIASTIC AMATEURS OF
FABL PREFACE(78)	I AM ASSUMED TO BE THE PROPRIETOR. IF THIS IS NOT	IDOLATRY	THE WORD HAS NO MEANING. THE FACT THAT I AM
SIM I (41)	THE PAINT ON A HARD WOODEN IMAGE. I WONDER IS IT	IDOLATRY	TO ADORE YOU? ST PETER IN ROME IS ONLY A BRONZE
SUPR II (54)	AT LEAST SO I'M TOLD. THEY NEVER EXPOSED THEIR	IDOLATRY	TO THE TEST OF DOMESTIC FAMILIARITY; AND IT LASTED
SUPR HANDBOK(202)	AFFAIRS WE HAD ASSUMED THAT THE SYCOPHANCY AND	IDOLATRY	WHICH ENCOURAGED CHARLES I TO UNDERVALUE THE
LADY PREFACE(232)	BY THE BRITISH PUBLIC WAS ANOTHER MATTER. THE	IDOLATRY	WHICH EXASPERATED BEN JONSON WAS BY NO MEANS A
LADY PREFACE(218)	I SUBMIT TO MR HARRIS THAT BY RULING OUT THIS	IDOLATRY	, AND ITS POSSIBLE EFFECT IN MAKING SHAKESPEAR
POSN PREFACE(384)	WHO REGARDED THE ONE MEASURE AS A FACILITATION OF	IDOLATRY	, AND THE OTHER AS A CONDONATION OF THE
LADY PREFACE(217)	EVER. " I LOVED THE MAN," SAYS BEN, " THIS SIDE	IDOLATRY	, AS WELL AS ANY," NOW WHY IN THE NAME OF COMMON
LADY PREFACE(217)	QUALIFICATION UNLESS THERE HAD BEEN, NOT ONLY	IDOLATRY	, BUT IDOLATRY FULSOME ENOUGH TO IRRITATE JONSON
3PLA PREFACE(R35)	GUILT AND INNOCENCE, AND CONSEQUENTLY REVENGE AND	IDOLATRY	, HAVE NO MEANING. SUCH MEN MUST REWRITE ALL THE
DOCT PREFACE(71)	LOVE AND DREAD OF THE MARVELLOUS, AND POPULAR	IDOLATRY	, TO INDUCE THE POOR TO COMPLY WITH THE SANITARY
JOAN 6 (143)	I CONFESS TO THE SIN OF SEDITION, TO THE SIN OF	IDOLATRY	, TO THE SIN OF DISOBEDIENCE, TO THE SIN OF PRIDE,
2TRU PREFACE(22)	BE TOO SACERDOTAL; FOR THAT IS THE METHOD OF	IDOLATRY	, WHICH SUBSTITUTES FOR RATIONAL AUTHORITY THE
METH PREFACE(R61)	IN 1867. THE REVOLT AGAINST ANTHROPOMORPHIC	IDOLATRY	, WHICH WAS, AS WE HAVE SEEN, THE SECRET OF

IDOLIZATION

GENV PREFACE(21)	TWENTY. SO DID LOUIS NAPOLEON, BACKED BY POPULAR	IDOLIZATION	OF HIS UNCLE, WHO HAD BECOME A NATIONAL HERO, AS

IDOLIZATIONS

JOAN PREFACE(23)	READERS WOULD PROBABLY LIKE TO KNOW HOW THESE	IDOLIZATIONS	AND REACTIONS HAVE AFFECTED THE BOOKS THEY ARE

IDOLIZE

BARB PREFACE(232)	OVERMEASURE. AND WITH WHAT RESULT? HE BEGINS TO	IDOLIZE	HIMSELF, TO RESPECT HIMSELF, TO LIVE UP TO THE
BULL PREFACE(19)	" KISS ME, HARDY" EMOTION WHICH ENABLED NELSON TO	IDOLIZE	HIS CREWS AND HIS STAFF, WITHOUT FORGETTING EVEN IN
LADY PREFACE(218)	ABOUT WHO IDOLIZED SHAKESPEAR AS AMERICAN LADIES	IDOLIZE	PADEREWSKI, AND WHO CARRIED BARDOLATRY, EVEN IN THE

IDOLIZED

BARB PREFACE(210)	VIOLENTLY ON THE HEAD. A SENTENCE DENOUNCING THE	IDOLIZED	FORM AS UGLY HAS BEEN LARGELY QUOTED. THE ENGLISH
BULL PREFACE(66)	HIM SPRING UP. UNTIL THEN, MEN OF BOTH PARTIES	IDOLIZED	HIM WITHOUT KNOWING WHY, JUST AS THEY HAD FORMERLY
FABL PREFACE(78)	AND ITS POLICY OF FREE TRADE. I AM MYSELF MUCH	IDOLIZED	. I RECEIVE ALMOST DAILY LETTERS FROM DEVOUT
SIM II (62)	BEING LOVED IN RETURN, OR THE FALSEHOOD OF BEING	IDOLIZED	. /MAYA/ SOLOMON HAS SPOKEN. /VASHTI/ STUPENDOUS.
GETT PREFACE(188)	A TROIS WITH SIR WILLIAM AND LADY HAMILTON, WAS	IDOLIZED	, SHELLEY MIGHT HAVE HAD AN ILLEGITIMATE CHILD IN
JOAN PREFACE(31)	TO THE PATRIOTIC NATIONALIST POPULACE, WHO	IDOLIZED	JOAN'S MEMORY. THE ENGLISH WERE GONE; AND A VERDICT
BULL PREFACE(66)	WITHOUT KNOWING WHY, JUST AS THEY HAD FORMERLY	IDOLIZED	LORD CROMER AND LORD MILNER WITHOUT KNOWING WHY.
LADY PREFACE(218)	THERE MUST HAVE BEEN MANY PEOPLE ABOUT WHO	IDOLIZED	SHAKESPEAR AS AMERICAN LADIES IDOLIZE PADEREWSKI,
MTH4 I (155)	INTOLERABLE BORES. THE COMMUNITIES WHICH HAD ONCE	IDOLIZED	THEM AS THE INCARNATION OF ALL THAT IS ADORABLE IN
BARB PREFACE(232)	VERY CHRISTIANLY. HE IS NOT ONLY FORGIVEN: HE IS	IDOLIZED	, RESPECTED, MADE MUCH OF, ALL BUT WORSHIPPED.

IDOLIZES

BULL PREFACE(19)	THE FAINTEST INKLING OF THE REALITY WHICH HE	IDOLIZES	AS TOMMY ATKINS. PERHAPS YOU HAVE NEVER THOUGHT OF
SUPR IV (167)	OF MAN NEVER MARRIES? /TANNER/ WHAT! A MAN WHO	IDOLIZES	WOMEN! WHO SEES NOTHING IN NATURE BUT ROMANTIC

IDOLIZING

LION EPILOG (148)	YOU CAN MAKE OF ANY SILLY-CLEVER GENTLEMAN BY	IDOLIZING	HIM. WE ARE STILL SO EASILY IMPOSED ON BY SUCH

IDOLS

SIM PRO,3, (31)	THE OTHER LEG. /THE PRIEST/ THOSE IMAGES ARE NOT	IDOLS	: THEY ARE PERSONIFICATIONS OF THE FORCES OF NATURE BY
SUPR HANDBOK(198)	MAKE UP OUR MINDS THAT MAN WILL RETURN TO HIS	IDOLS	AND HIS CUPIDITIES, IN SPITE OF ALL " MOVEMENTS" AND
FABL V (118)	NINETEENTH CENTURY THAT THEY GAVE UP BELIEVING IN	IDOLS	AND PRIESTS, AND TOOK TO BELIEVING IN MEDICINE MEN AND
FABL PREFACE(75)	IDOLS BUT HORSE IDOLS, CAT IDOLS, ELEPHANT	IDOLS	AND WHAT NOT? THE STATUES OF THE JAINIST SAGES AND
MILL IV (210)	EMPERORS, CONQUERORS, PONTIFFS AND ALL THE OTHER	IDOLS	ARE SWEPT AWAY SOONER OR LATER; AND ALL THE KING'S
FABL PREFACE(75)	FIND? IDOLS EVERYWHERE. NOT EVEN ANTHROPOMORPHIC	IDOLS	BUT HORSE IDOLS, CAT IDOLS, ELEPHANT IDOLS AND WHAT
FABL PREFACE(75)	INTO A JAINIST TEMPLE TODAY: WHAT DO YOU FIND?	IDOLS	EVERYWHERE. NOT EVEN ANTHROPOMORPHIC IDOLS BUT HORSE
SIM I (37)	/PRA/ IDOLS! /THE CLERGYMAN/ NO, OF COURSE NOT	IDOLS	. I MEANT THOSE GODS AND GODDESSES-- /PRA/ THEY ARE
SUPR I (36)	BURN GORSE BUSHES; I SHATTER CREEDS AND DEMOLISH	IDOLS	. /ANN/ (BORED) I AM AFRAID I AM TOO FEMININE TO SEE
SIM PRO,3, (31)	ALL LIVE. BUT OF COURSE TO AN IDOLATER THEY ARE	IDOLS	. /THE Y,W,/ YOU TALK A LOT ABOUT RELIGION HERE. CANT
GENV PREFACE(25)	SPORTSMEN, AND DEVOUT BELIEVERS IN ANCIENT TRIBAL	IDOLS	. THE GENIUSES THEMSELVES ARE STEEPED IN VULGAR
SUPR HANDBOK(217)	THE BUREAUCRACY: IT CAN ONLY WORSHIP THE NATIONAL	IDOLS	. THE SAVAGE BOWS DOWN TO IDOLS OF WOOD AND STONE: THE
SUPR HANDBOK(217)	TO IDOLS OF WOOD AND STONE: THE CIVILIZED MAN TO	IDOLS	OF FLESH AND BLOOD. A LIMITED MONARCHY IS A DEVICE FOR
MILL PREFACE(134)	ARTICLES, AND WORSHIP THE BLOODTHIRSTY TRIBAL	IDOLS	OF NOAH AND SAMUEL WITH A GRAVITY AND SINCERITY THAT
SUPR HANDBOK(217)	THE NATIONAL IDOLS. THE SAVAGE BOWS DOWN TO	IDOLS	OF WOOD AND STONE: THE CIVILIZED MAN TO IDOLS OF FLESH
SIM I (37)	/THE CLERGYMAN/ OH, EXCUSE ME. I THOUGHT-- THOSE	IDOLS	-- /PRA/ IDOLS! /THE CLERGYMAN/ NO, OF COURSE NOT
SUPR HANDBOK(217)	CONSISTS OF FUNCTIONARIES; THE ARISTOCRACY, OF	IDOLS	; THE DEMOCRACY, OF IDOLATERS. THE POPULACE CANNOT
SUPR HANDBOK(218)	REPUBLICS CAN NO MORE DISPENSE WITH NATIONAL	IDOLS	THAN MONARCHIES WITH PUBLIC FUNCTIONARIES. GOVERNMENT
LION EPILOG (148)	HIM. WE ARE STILL SO EASILY IMPOSED ON BY SUCH	IDOLS	THAT ONE OF THE LEADING PASTORS OF THE FREE CHURCHES
SUPR HANDBOK(188)	IS A SAINT. HE IS NEVER WITHOUT AN ARRAY OF HUMAN	IDOLS	WHO ARE ALL NOTHING BUT SHAM SUPERMEN. THAT THE REAL
POSN PREFACE(382)	BLASPHEMIES AND SACRILEGES OF MAHOMET AGAINST THE	IDOLS	WHOM HE DETHRONED TO MAKE WAY FOR HIS CONCEPTION OF
METH PREFACE(R62)	BETWEEN THEM TOPPLED OVER TWO CLOSELY RELATED	IDOLS	, AND BECAME THE PROPHETS OF TWO NEW CREEDS. WHY
MTH5 (225)	AND THE GRAVEN IMAGE AN IDOL. AS I HAVE BROKEN MY	IDOLS	, AND CAST AWAY MY CHISEL AND MODELLING TOOLS, SO WILL
FABL PREFACE(75)	NOT EVEN ANTHROPOMORPHIC IDOLS BUT HORSE	IDOLS	, CAT IDOLS, ELEPHANT IDOLS AND WHAT NOT? THE STATUES
FABL PREFACE(75)	EVEN ANTHROPOMORPHIC IDOLS BUT HORSE IDOLS, CAT	IDOLS	, ELEPHANT IDOLS AND WHAT NOT? THE STATUES OF THE
SIM I (37)	OH, EXCUSE ME. I THOUGHT-- THOSE IDOLS-- /PRA/	IDOLS	! /THE CLERGYMAN/ NO, OF COURSE NOT IDOLS. I MEANT

IDYLL

LION PREFACE(33)	AT THE VERY OUTSET HE ACHIEVES THE MOST CHARMING	IDYLL	IN THE BIBLE: THE STORY OF MARY CROWDED OUT OF THE INN
WIDO II (33)	SIR, CHARMED. LIFE HERE IS AN IDYLL-- A PERFECT	IDYLL	. WE WERE JUST DWELLING ON IT. /SARTORIUS/ (SLYLY)
WIDO II (33)	CHARMED, MY DEAR SIR, CHARMED. LIFE HERE IS AN	IDYLL	-- A PERFECT IDYLL. WE WERE JUST DWELLING ON IT.

IDYLLICALLY

O'FL (226)	HIS PIPE, AND BEGINS TO FILL IT. /O'FLAHERTY/ (	IDYLLICALLY	) WHAT A DISCONTENTED SORT OF AN ANIMAL A MAN

IF-POSSIBLE-COMIC

PLES PREFACE(R11)	BY PEOPLE WITH AN EXPENSIVE AIR, ATTENDED BY AN	IF-POSSIBLE-COMIC	WAITER, I WAS MORE THAN WILLING TO SHEW

IFS

JOAN 5 (116)	IS ON HIS SIDE. /JOAN/ AH! IF, IF, IF, IF! IF	IFS	AND ANS WERE POTS AND PANS THERE'D BE NO NEED OF
SUPR HANDBOK(199)	MELIORIST THEN RECONSIDER HIMSELF AND HIS ETERNAL	IFS	AND ANS WHICH NEVER BECOME POTS AND PANS. WHILST MAN
GETT PREFACE(214)	TO GIVE THE UNMARRIED WOMAN A CHANCE. THESE	IFS	WILL NOT WORK. WE MUST RECOGNIZE TWO CLASSES OF OLD

IGH

CAND II (115)	STORIES WHEN SHE WAS ONY A LITTLE KIDDY NOT THAT	IGH	(INDICATING A STATURE OF TWO FEET OR THEREABOUTS).

IGHBRED

CAND I (95)	GOODBYE, MR MORCHBANKS: I KNOW YOURE TOO	IGHBRED	TO TAKE MY PLEASANTRY IN BAD PART. (HE AGAIN OFFERS

IGHTEEN

BULL III (141)	YOU THAT CAWNT BE MOVED UNTIL YOUVE RAN AP	IGHTEEN	MONTHS RENT. OI ONCE RAN AP FOUR WEEKS IN LEMBETH

IGNATIUS

APPL INTRLUD(247)	BACK TO THEIR CABBAGES. LOOK AT THE OLD CREATURE	IGNATIUS	IS LIVING WITH NOW! SHE GIVES YOU HIS REAL
APPL INTRLUD(247)	HIS REAL MEASURE. /MAGNUS/ AN EXCELLENT WOMAN.	IGNATIUS	IS QUITE HAPPY WITH HER. I NEVER SAW A MAN SO
LION PREFACE(86)	THAT FREDERICK WAS ANTICHRIST AND TORQUEMADA AND	IGNATIUS	LOYOLA MEN AFTER THE VERY HEART OF JESUS. NEITHER

IGNOBLE

LION PREFACE(94)	TO WHOM THE WHOLE SCHEME OF SALVATION WAS ONLY AN	IGNOBLE	ATTEMPT TO CHEAT GOD; TO GET INTO HEAVEN WITHOUT

MIS. PREFACE(99)	PICTURE OF A BEWILDERED SOUL CANNOT DISGUISE THE	IGNOBLE	IRRELEVANCE OF THE RETORT OF GOD WITH WHICH IT
3PLA PREFACE(R24)	BY WAY OF HOMAGE TO THE SANCTITY OF THE	IGNOBLE	PRIVATE LIFE TO WHICH HE IS CONDEMNED BY HIS
CLEO IV (190)	AND CLEOPATRA) HEARKEN TO ME, CAESAR. IT MAY BE	IGNOBLE	; BUT I ALSO MEAN TO LIVE AS LONG AS I CAN. /CAESAR/
DOCT III (152)	FACE TO TELL ME ANY WRONG THING HE HAS DONE, ANY	IGNOBLE	THOUGHT HE HAS UTTERED. THEY HAVE ALWAYS CONFESSED
ARMS II (33)	THAT I COULD NEVER DO A BASE DEED, OR THINK AN	IGNOBLE	THOUGHT. /SERGIUS/ MY LADY AND MY SAINT! (HE
6CAL PREFACE(90)	ALL INTERPRETERS OF LIFE IN ACTION, NOBLE OR	IGNOBLE	, FIND THEIR INSTRUMENT IN THE THEATRE; AND ALL THE
CLEO IV (190)	BUT I DONT WANT TO DIE. /CAESAR/ (SADLY) OH,	IGNOBLE	, IGNOBLE! /LUCIUS/ (COMING FORWARD BETWEEN CAESAR
CLEO IV (190)	DONT WANT TO DIE. /CAESAR/ (SADLY) OH, IGNOBLE,	IGNOBLE	! /LUCIUS/ (COMING FORWARD BETWEEN CAESAR AND

IGNOMINIOUS

SUPR IV (166)	SALE OF MY BIRTHRIGHT, SHAMEFUL SURRENDER,	IGNOMINIOUS	CAPITULATION, ACCEPTANCE OF DEFEAT. I SHALL
HART PREFACE(27)	MORE BRAVELY THAN THE TRAITOR BOLO FACED THE	IGNOMINIOUS	CERTAINTY OF IT? BOLO TAUGHT US ALL HOW TO DIE:
BULL PREFACE(70)	WATER SUPPLY. OF COURSE NOTHING HAPPENED BUT AN	IGNOMINIOUS	CLIMB DOWN; BUT THE INCIDENT ILLUSTRATES MY
GETT PREFACE(233)	MAN; AND APPEAL TO FORCE HAS RESULTED IN THE	IGNOMINIOUS	DEFEAT OF THE HUSBAND QUITE AS OFTEN AS IN
LION PREFACE(16)	AND TO HOLD THAT BELIEF IN THE FACE OF THE MOST	IGNOMINIOUS	DEFEATS BY VEGETARIAN WRESTLERS AND RACERS AND
MTH4 I (153)	WOULD HAVE BEEN A NOBLER AND HAPPIER LOT THAN THE	IGNOMINIOUS	EASE OF MY PRESENT LONGEVITY. /ZOO/ LONGEVITY!
LADY (243)	/THE MAN/ (SITTING UP AS MAJESTICALLY AS HIS	IGNOMINIOUS	POSTURE ALLOWS) WOMAN! YOU HAVE STRUCK WILLIAM
SUPR I (33)	BUT TO THE BOY HIMSELF THEY ARE SO ACUTE, SO	IGNOMINIOUS	, THAT HE CANNOT CONFESS THEM-- CANNOT BUT DENY

IGNOMINIOUSLY

MTH4 I (166)	BUT I LITTLE THOUGHT I SHOULD LIVE TO HAVE IT	IGNOMINIOUSLY	APPLIED TO MYSELF. YOU HAVE ACTUALLY
MRS PREFACE(160)	OCCURS TO HIM. HE WILL ASSAULT THE DUENNA, AND BE	IGNOMINIOUSLY	EXPELLED FROM THE PALACE BY HIS INDIGNANT
JITT PREFACE(3)	VIEW TO IMMEDIATE PRODUCTION. THE EVASION FAILED	IGNOMINIOUSLY	. MY WIFE CAME TO ME AND SAID THAT THE YOUNG
NEVR III (269)	CRUSHINGLY). I BEG YOUR PARDON. (HE SITS DOWN	IGNOMINIOUSLY	ON THE OTTOMAN). /GLORIA/ I CANNOT BELIEVE
MIS. PREFACE(69)	PLACID SMILE, THAT HE WOULD ALMOST CERTAINLY BE	IGNOMINIOUSLY	PLUCKED. AND HE IS SO LITTLE ASHAMED OF OR
PHIL II (124)	CERTAINLY, CERTAINLY. (HE FOLLOWS PARAMORE	IGNOMINIOUSLY	). /GRACE/ (TO JULIA, WITH QUIET
HART III (139)	MAN, HAS TRIED TO UNDRESS HIMSELF AND HAS FAILED	IGNOMINIOUSLY	; WHILST YOU, AS AN IDEALIST, HAVE SUCCEEDED

IGNOMINY

SUPR PREFACE(R21)	TO BE PUSHED OUT OF THE HOUSE TO OUTFACE HIS	IGNOMINY	BY DRUNKEN REJOICINGS. BUT WHEN THE CRISIS IS OVER
SUPR I (47)	RING LIKE THE REST OF US, RAMSDEN. THE CUP OF OUR	IGNOMINY	IS FULL.
SUPR IV (166)	AT THE ARRIVAL OF A NEW PRISONER TO SHARE THEIR	IGNOMINY	. THE YOUNG MEN WILL SCORN ME AS ONE WHO HAS SOLD

IGNORAMUS

KING I (221)	NO HEAVEN. YOU HAVE ABOLISHED THE SKY. /NEWTON/	IGNORAMUS	! THERE MAY BE STARS BEYOND OUR VISION BIGGER THAN
2TRU PREFACE(13)	HAPPENS THAT MR GILBERT CHESTERTON, WHO IS NOT AN	IGNORAMUS	AND NOT IN THE LEAST TERRIFIED, AND WHOSE VERY
SUPR III (114)	THAT I WAS NOT A HYPOCHONDRIAC; SO THEY CALLED ME	IGNORAMUS	AND WENT THEIR WAY. THE DOCTORS OF DIVINITY BADE
GENV II (63)	ELSE. /THE SECRETARY/ BUT SHE IS A COMPLETE	IGNORAMUS	. SHE WILL GIVE HERSELF AWAY EVERY TIME SHE OPENS
DOCT PREFACE(6)	TREATMENT JUST AS MUCH AS THE MOST CREDULOUS	IGNORAMUS	THAT EVER PAID SIXPENCE FOR A BOTTLE OF STRONG
POSN PREFACE(411)	FUNCTIONARY. TO BE RESPONSIBLE TO EVERY FANATICAL	IGNORAMUS	WHO CHOOSES TO PROSECUTE HIM FOR EXHIBITING A CAST
KING II (229)	LATIN IS NO USE: JACK CHURCHILL, WHO IS AN	IGNORAMUS	, IS WORTH FIFTY SCHOLARS. IF ORANGE BILLY DIES
LADY PREFACE(215)	AWAY THE FAMILIAR PLEA OF THE BARDOLATROUS	IGNORAMUS	, THAT SHAKESPEAR'S COARSENESS WAS PART OF THE
PYGM V (288)	THAT IMPOSTOR! THAT HUMBUG! THAT TOADYING	IGNORAMUS	! TEACH HIM MY METHODS! MY DISCOVERIES! YOU

IGNORAMUSES

MIS. PREFACE(70)	PLACES, THOUGH THEY TURN OUT BLACKGUARDS AND	IGNORAMUSES	AND BOOBIES GALORE, TURN THEM OUT WITH THE
FABL PREFACE(85)	OUR DIPLOMATISTS THE WORST. THIS WILL SHOCK OUR	IGNORAMUSES	AS A STUPENDOUS HERESY AND A MAD PARADOX. LET US
METH PREFACE(R40)	ARRANGEMENT; AND SCIENCE WAS STRANGLED BY BIGOTED	IGNORAMUSES	CLAIMING INFALLIBILITY FOR THEIR INTERPRETATION
MIS. PREFACE(54)	TO SAY THAT HE WOULD RATHER SEE AN ENGLAND OF	IGNORAMUSES	THAN AN ENGLAND OF COWARDS AND SLAVES. AND IF
MIS. PREFACE(54)	ONE, AS WE HAVE AT PRESENT AN ENGLAND OF	IGNORAMUSES	WHO ARE ALSO COWARDS AND SLAVES, AND
BULL IV (152)	THE CHARLATANS, THE-- THE-- THE FOOLS AND	IGNORAMUSES	WHO CORRUPT THE MULTITUDE BY THEIR WEALTH, OR
2TRU PREFACE(13)	POLITICS RELIGION AND ECONOMICS WITH TERRIFIED	IGNORAMUSES	WHO UNDERSTAND NEITHER WHAT THEY ARE DEFENDING
JOAN PREFACE(16)	WAS A MARTYR, AND HIS PERSECUTORS INCORRIGIBLE	IGNORAMUSES	, AND THAT ST TERESA'S HORMONES HAD GONE ASTRAY
METH PREFACE(R16)	WHO, HOWEVER GENEROUS BY NATURE, ARE BY EDUCATION	IGNORAMUSES	, DUPES, SNOBS, AND SPORTSMEN TO WHOM FIGHTING
BULL PREFACE(38)	THE BOGEY-ATHEIST OF THREE GENERATIONS OF ENGLISH	IGNORAMUSES	, INSTEAD OF THE LEGITIMATE SUCCESSOR OF MARTIN

IGNORANCE

SUPR III (104)	OF FOLLY, AND IMAGINATION ACCUSING STUPIDITY OF	IGNORANCE	: WHEREAS, ALAS! STUPIDITY HAS ALL THE KNOWLEDGE,
HART PREFACE(15)	OF EDUCATION, ART, SCIENCE, AND RELIGION FROM OUR	IGNORANCE	AND BARBARISM, AND LEFT US GLORYING GROTESQUELY IN
SUPR III (104)	UP OBSTACLES TO ITSELF AND DESTROYS ITSELF IN ITS	IGNORANCE	AND BLINDNESS. IT NEEDS A BRAIN, THIS IRRESISTIBLE
GENV PREFACE(16)	SUBJECTS ACCORDINGLY. NOW THIS POLITICAL	IGNORANCE	AND DELUSION IS CURABLE BY SIMPLE INSTRUCTION AS
METH PREFACE(R11)	IT ON THE PEOPLE AS A CRUSADE, AND ESPECIALLY THE	IGNORANCE	AND ERRORS OF THE VICTORS OF WESTERN EUROPE WHEN
MIS. PREFACE(27)	UP AGAINST THE ABUSE OF SCHOOLS TO KEEP PEOPLE IN	IGNORANCE	AND ERROR, SO THAT THEY MAY BE INCAPABLE OF
DOCT PREFACE(9)	AGAINST A CHARGE OF MALPRACTICE BY A PLEA OF	IGNORANCE	AND FALLIBILITY, HIS PLEA IS RECEIVED WITH FLAT
MIS. PREFACE(47)	THE DISEASES THEY THEMSELVES DIE OF DAILY, SO OUR	IGNORANCE	AND HELPLESSNESS SET US CLAMORING FOR SPIRITUAL
MILL PREFACE(132)	SLAUGHTER CALLED MILITARY GLORY. IT WAS THIS	IGNORANCE	AND IDOLATRY THAT FIRST EXALTED NAPOLEON AND THEN
JOAN PREFACE(35)	THAT OF THE JESUITS WITH PRIESTLY APATHY AND	IGNORANCE	AND INDISCIPLINE. THE MOST BIGOTED ULSTER
O'FL PREFACE(202)	NO BETTER MAY BE, FOR ENGLAND, KNOWING THAT THE	IGNORANCE	AND INSULARITY OF THE IRISHMAN IS A DANGER TO
FANY PROL,SD(266)	TURN FOR WRITING, AND NEGATIVELY BY A COMFORTABLE	IGNORANCE	AND LACK OF INTUITION WHICH HIDES FROM HIM ALL THE
APPL I (235)	AT LEAST IT STOOD ABOVE THE TYRANNY OF POPULAR	IGNORANCE	AND POPULAR POVERTY. TODAY ONLY THE KING STANDS
POSN PREFACE(426)	PORNOGRAPHERS MAY MAKE ON ME BY APPEALING TO THE	IGNORANCE	AND PREJUDICES OF COMMON JURORS, THEN I WELCOME
GENV PREFACE(14)	FORCES ITS WAY PIECEMEAL IN SPITE OF STAGNANT	IGNORANCE	AND SELFISHNESS. BESIDES, THERE ARE ALWAYS ANCIENT
MIS. PREFACE(43)	LIBERTY WE MUST LET EVERYONE TAKE; BUT RISKS OF	IGNORANCE	AND SELF-HELPLESSNESS ARE ANOTHER MATTER. NOT ONLY
MTH2 (39)	OF IT I REALIZED THAT I WAS WALKING WITH MY OWN	IGNORANCE	AND SELF-CONCEIT, AND THAT I WAS NOT WITHIN A
DOCT PREFACE(76)	ALMROTH. WHAT ELSE CAN HE DO, EXCEPT CONFESS HIS	IGNORANCE	AND STARVE? BUT NOW PLEASE OBSERVE HOW " THE
3PLA PREFACE(R22)	THAN THEY EVER WERE BY PLAYING ON THEIR FORMER	IGNORANCE	AND SUPERSTITION. NAY, WHY SHOULD I SAY WILL BE..
GENV III (82)	BEHIND IT. IN THE WEST THE VESTED INTERESTS IN	IGNORANCE	AND SUPERSTITION ARE SO OVERWHELMING THAT NO
APPL I (235)	BY THE PRESS, WHICH CAN ORGANIZE AGAINST YOU THE	IGNORANCE	AND SUPERSTITION, THE TIMIDITY AND CREDULITY, THE
BULL III (133)	CAN BEAR TO SEE HER BEGGING HER BREAD FROM THE	IGNORANCE	AND SUPERSTITION OF MEN LIKE YOU? I WOULD HAVE
DOCT I (107)	MY LAD. WHEN YOU KNOW AS MUCH AS I KNOW OF THE	IGNORANCE	AND SUPERSTITION OF THE PATIENTS, YOULL WONDER
JOAN PREFACE(45)	FOUNDED ON A FAIR OBSERVATION OF HER OBVIOUS	IGNORANCE	AND TEMERITY, WERE AT WORK AGAINST HER. AND AS SHE
MIS. PREFACE(43)	AGE OF 21 YEARS BUT OF 21 SECONDS. THE RISKS OF	IGNORANCE	AND WEAKNESS. THE DIFFICULTY WITH CHILDREN IS THAT
GETT (319)	THE UNFORTUNATE ELDEST CHILDREN OF THEIR YOUTHFUL	IGNORANCE	AND WILFULNESS? WHICH PARENT IS TO OWN THE
NEVR II (229)	BACK TO ENGLAND IT IS IMPOSSIBLE TO LEAVE THEM IN	IGNORANCE	ANY LONGER. (AGITATED) FINCH: I CANNOT BRING
MIS. PREFACE(29)	A FICTITIOUS DELICACY) ARE, IN EFFECT, ADVOCATING	IGNORANCE	AS A SAFEGUARD AGAINST PRECOCITY. IF IGNORANCE
GENV PREFACE(7)	DAILY EMERGENCIES WITHIN THE LIMITS OF THEIR	IGNORANCE	AS BEST THEY CAN. IF THEIR VISION IS VULGAR AND
POSN PREFACE(422)	DISPLAY OF THOUGHTLESSNESS AND HISTORICAL	IGNORANCE	AS THIS PARAGRAPH OF ITS REPORT IMPLIES DESERVES
JOAN PREFACE(31)	AS HERETICS. SHE WAS IN A STATE OF INVINCIBLE	IGNORANCE	AS TO THE CHURCH'S VIEW; AND THE CHURCH COULD NOT
GENV II SD(49)	NATIONS, ALL IN A CONDITION OF INVINCIBLE	IGNORANCE	AS TO THE SPIRIT OF GENEVA AND THE CONSTITUTION OF
BULL IV (180)	SO FOOLISH IN HIS CLEVERNESS, I CANNOT IN MY	IGNORANCE	BE SURE WHICH OF YOU IS THE MORE DEEPLY DAMNED;
GETT PREFACE(255)	DUTY PERFORMED BY OFFICIALS, WILL, AS POVERTY AND	IGNORANCE	BECOME THE EXCEPTION INSTEAD OF THE RULE, GIVE WAY
JOAN PREFACE(33)	POPE IS ON HIS KNEES IN THE DUST CONFESSING HIS	IGNORANCE	BEFORE THE THRONE OF GOD, ASKING ONLY THAT AS TO
FABL PREFACE(95)	MOST ATTRACTIVE MAN) AND LEFT ME ENCOURAGED IN MY	IGNORANCE	BY MY OBSERVATION THAT THOUGH HE WAS SCRUPULOUS
SUPR HANDBOK(228)	BECOMES GOOD TASTE. WHERE THERE IS NO KNOWLEDGE	IGNORANCE	CALLS ITSELF SCIENCE. IF THE WICKED FLOURISH AND
GETT PREFACE(192)	SNOBBERIES AND PARTISANERIES, AS	IGNORANCE	CAN UNDERSTAND AND IRRESPONSIBILITY RELISH. WHAT
METH PREFACE(R10)	OF THE NEO-DARWINIANS. THIS PARTICULAR SORT OF	IGNORANCE	DOES NOT ALWAYS OR OFTEN MATTER. BUT IN DARWIN'S
GENV III (81)	YOU ARE LIVING IN. INTO THE VOID CREATED BY THIS	IGNORANCE	HAS BEEN HEAPED A GROUNDWORK OF SAVAGE
GETT PREFACE(245)	OF THE FACTS. NO DOUBT THIS IS A VERY FORMIDABLE	IGNORANCE	IN A COUNTRY WHERE THE FIRST CRY OF THE SOUL IS "
KING PREFACE(155)	HIT ON THAT SIMPLE DEVICE UNTIL LONG AFTER. MY	IGNORANCE	IN THESE MATTERS IS STUPENDOUS; BUT I REFUSE TO
ARMS I (19)	ME! THINK OF THAT! /RAINA/ YOU SHEWED GREAT	IGNORANCE	IN THINKING THAT IT WAS NECESSARY TO CLIMB UP TO
METH PREFACE(R40)	SOCIALLY AND POLITICALLY POWERFUL	IGNORANCE	INCONCEIVABLE BY THOMAS AQUINAS OR EVEN ROGER
BULL PREFACE(43)	THAT HIS COUNTRY MAY BE GOVERNED ACCORDING TO HIS	IGNORANCE	INSTEAD OF THE WISDOM OF THE PRIVY COUNCIL, HE IS
MIS. PREFACE(29)	TO BE SAID FOR IT UP TO THE AGE AT WHICH	IGNORANCE	IS A DANGER INSTEAD OF A SAFEGUARD, EVEN AS IT IS,
DOCT PREFACE(33)	A DESIRABLE THING, THOUGH ANY FOOL CAN PROVE THAT	IGNORANCE	IS BLISS, AND THAT " A LITTLE KNOWLEDGE IS A
DOCT PREFACE(33)	OWNER'S BACK WAS TURNED. WHEN GRAY SAID " WHERE	IGNORANCE	IS BLISS, ' TIS FOLLY TO BE WISE," HE FORGOT THAT
DOCT PREFACE(52)	IGNORANCE. HOW COMPLETE AND INCONSIDERATE THEIR	IGNORANCE	IS CAN ONLY BE REALIZED BY THOSE WHO HAVE SOME
SUPR III (104)	A BRAIN, THIS IRRESISTIBLE FORCE, LEST IN ITS	IGNORANCE	IT SHOULD RESIST ITSELF. WHAT A PIECE OF WORK IS

SUPR HANDBOK(219)	OF HIS FALSE KNOWLEDGE: IT IS MORE DANGEROUS THAN	IGNORANCE	. ACTIVITY IS THE ONLY ROAD TO KNOWLEDGE. EVERY
JOAN PREFACE(22)	VERY CAPABLE: A BORN BOSS. JOAN'S IMMATURITY AND	IGNORANCE	. ALL THIS, HOWEVER, MUST BE TAKEN WITH ONE HEAVY
LADY (245)	MERCIFUL PRINCE. I MAKE ALLOWANCE FOR YOUR RUSTIC	IGNORANCE	. BUT REMEMBER THAT THERE ARE THINGS WHICH BE
3PLA PREFACE(R40)	RID OF REPUTATIONS: THEY ARE WEEDS IN THE SOIL OF	IGNORANCE	. CULTIVATE THAT SOIL, AND THEY WILL FLOWER MORE
FABL V (120)	SAND PICKED UP ON THE MARGIN OF THE OCEAN OF OUR	IGNORANCE	. HE WAS A SILLY FELLOW WHO THOUGHT THAT THE WORLD
BARB II (280)	MARK OF IT, YOU SILLY YOUNG LUMP OF CONCEIT AND	IGNORANCE	. HIT A GIRL IN THE JAW AND ONY MAKE HER CRY! IF
DOCT PREFACE(52)	THEY FORCE THE DOCTORS TO HUMOR THEIR FOLLY AND	IGNORANCE	. HOW COMPLETE AND INCONSIDERATE THEIR IGNORANCE
KING I (170)	I SPEND MY LIFE CONTEMPLATING THE OCEAN OF MY	IGNORANCE	. I ONCE BOASTED OF HAVING PICKED UP A PEBBLE ON
ROCK II (270)	BOUND HAND AND FOOT BY OUR OWN FOLLY AND	IGNORANCE	. IT TOOK THE HEART OUT OF OLD HIPNEY; AND NOW I'M
MIS. PREFACE(59)	INCOMPETENT AND ILL-MANNERED PERSON THAN LEFT IN	IGNORANCE	. READING, WRITING, AND ENOUGH ARITHMETIC TO USE
BASH I (95)	IT AS MEN ANNOUNCE A CELEBRATED NAME. FORGIVE MY	IGNORANCE	. /CASHEL/ I BLESS IT, LYDIA. I HAVE FORGOT YOUR
MTH2 (88)	WE EARNED ON FALSE PRETENCES IN THE DAYS OF OUR	IGNORANCE	. /CONRAD/ I DARESAY. BUT CREATIVE EVOLUTION
KING I (170)	AS MYSELF. I SUFFER GREATLY FROM SHAME AT MY	IGNORANCE	. /NEWTON/ SHAME WILL NOT HELP YOU, PASTOR. I
GETT (340)	MIND MY CALLING HIM THAT, DID HE? IT WAS ONLY MY	IGNORANCE	. /THE BISHOP/ NOT AT ALL. (HE OPENS THE STUDY
WIDO II (44)	HARRY. PERHAPS IT WILL BE AS WELL TO LEAVE HER IN	IGNORANCE	. /TRENCH/ (ANXIOUSLY) BUT I MUST EXPLAIN NOW.
SUPR HANDBOK(190)	OF DODGING POPULAR ENTHUSIASMS AND DUPING POPULAR	IGNORANCE	. THE POLITICIAN WHO ONCE HAD TO LEARN HOW TO
JOAN 4 (104)	MESSIRE DE STOGUMBER, ON THE GROUND OF INVINCIBLE	IGNORANCE	. THE THICK AIR OF YOUR COUNTRY DOES NOT BREED
GENV PREFACE(22)	MONARCHS BEING PRODUCTS OF POLITICAL IDOLATRY AND	IGNORANCE	. THE WIDER THE SUFFRAGE, THE GREATER THE
METH PREFACE(R14)	INSTEAD OF DRIFTING DOWN THE MIDSTREAM OF MERE	IGNORANCE	. THERE IS NO WAY OUT THROUGH THE SCHOOLMASTER.
GENV PREFACE(15)	TO THEM TO ABSOLVE ME ON THE PLEA OF INVINCIBLE	IGNORANCE	. WE WERE BOTH TAUGHT TO WORSHIP " A TENTH RATE
PHIL II (96)	HUMAN RACE. /CUTHBERTSON/ (VEHEMENTLY) IT'S NOT	IGNORANCE	NOR SUPERSTITION, PARAMORE: IT'S SHEER DOWNRIGHT
POSN PREFACE(410)	SINCERE SECTARIAN BIGOTRY WITH A COMPLETE	IGNORANCE	OF ART AND HISTORY. EVEN WHEN THEY HAVE SOME
MILL PREFACE(120)	AND WERE WRECKING THEM IN THEIR HELPLESS	IGNORANCE	OF BUSINESS. AS ONE INDIGNANT MASTER-FASCIST SAID
2TRU PREFACE(18)	THEIR PEOPLE, BUT BECAUSE THE OLD PRIESTS'	IGNORANCE	OF ECONOMICS AND POLITICAL SCIENCE BLINDED THEM TO
MIS. PREFACE(97)	SELECTION IS NEITHER POSSIBLE NOR DESIRABLE.	IGNORANCE	OF EVIL IS NOT VIRTUE BUT IMBECILITY: ADMIRING IT
GENV PREFACE(15)	DEFICIENT POLITICAL CAPACITY. IT IS LARGELY	IGNORANCE	OF FACTS, CREATING A VACUUM INTO WHICH ALL SORTS
MIS. PREFACE(100)	THAN RAGTIMES WAITING FOR PEOPLE BROUGHT UP IN	IGNORANCE	OF FINE ART. NOTHING IS MORE PITIABLY RIDICULOUS
FABL PREFACE(79)	RUSSIA. WHAT DAMNS OUR FOREIGN POLICY HERE IS OUR	IGNORANCE	OF HISTORY OF HOME AFFAIRS. IN THE IMAGINATION OF
GENV III (81)	DEAD IN A FORTNIGHT. IT IS EVIDENT ALSO THAT HER	IGNORANCE	OF HOW HER OWN COUNTRY IS CONDUCTED IS AS COMPLETE
JITT PREFACE(4)	CLAIM KNOWLEDGE OF THE GERMAN LANGUAGE NOR PLEAD	IGNORANCE	OF IT. I AM LIKE MOST LITERARY PERSONS: I HAVE
APPL II (258)	HARD FOR US TO SHARE YOUR ENTHUSIASM IN COMPLETE	IGNORANCE	OF ITS CAUSE. /VANHATTAN/ THAT IS TRUE, MAAM. I AM
GETT PREFACE(204)	MEANS GOVERNING A COUNTRY ACCORDING TO THE	IGNORANCE	OF ITS MAJORITIES IS NEVER MORE DISASTROUS THAN
BULL II (116)	AND HE HAS NO SUSPICION OF THE FACT, OR OF HER	IGNORANCE	OF IT, THAT WHEN AN ENGLISHMAN IS SENTIMENTAL HE
MIS. PREFACE(57)	IT NEED NOT TROUBLE US. BUT IT IS A FACT THAT	IGNORANCE	OF LATIN AND GREEK AND MATHEMATICS CLOSES CERTAIN
HART PREFACE(5)	COMMONS, WITH NOBODY TO CORRECT THEIR INCREDIBLE	IGNORANCE	OF MODERN THOUGHT AND POLITICAL SCIENCE BUT
POSN PREFACE(421)	ELECTIONEERING. NOTHING IS MORE ALARMING THAN THE	IGNORANCE	OF OUR PUBLIC MEN OF THE COMMONPLACES OF OUR
MIS. PREFACE(95)	SO POTENT A FACTOR IN EVOLUTION AS TO KEEP IT IN	IGNORANCE	OF RADIATION OR CAPILLARY ATTRACTION. EVEN IF YOU
MRS PREFACE(176)	IT AND WELCOMED IT WITH THAT EXPRESS OBJECT.	IGNORANCE	OF REAL LIFE COULD HARDLY GO FURTHER. I WAS DEEPLY
GENV III (81)	OWN COUNTRY IS CONDUCTED IS AS COMPLETE AS HER	IGNORANCE	OF RUSSIA. NONE OF YOU SEEM TO HAVE ANY IDEA OF
3PLA PREFACE(R34)	INTERESTING CHARACTER. IT WAS THE AGE OF GROSS	IGNORANCE	OF SHAKESPEAR AND INCAPACITY FOR HIS WORKS THAT
MIS. PREFACE(95)	IT WOULD BE AS ABSURD TO KEEP A CHILD IN DELUSIVE	IGNORANCE	OF SO POTENT A FACTOR IN EVOLUTION AS TO KEEP IT
ARMS I (14)	WHY, HOW IS IT THAT YOUVE JUST BEATEN US? SHEER	IGNORANCE	OF THE ART OF WAR, NOTHING ELSE. (INDIGNANTLY) I
SUPR PREFACE(R9)	OF OUR OWN VIEWS OF LIFE. SO YOU CANNOT PLEAD	IGNORANCE	OF THE CHARACTER OF THE FORCE YOU SET IN MOTION.
HART I (46)	MY WRETCHED CHILDREN, WHOM YOU HAVE BROUGHT UP IN	IGNORANCE	OF THE COMMONEST DECENCIES OF SOCIAL INTERCOURSE?
GETT PREFACE(245)	ARE SOUND ENOUGH: WHAT IS WRONG WITH US IS	IGNORANCE	OF THE FACTS. NO DOUBT THIS IS A VERY FORMIDABLE
DOCT III (141)	PATRICK/ YOU LET HER RISK IMPRISONMENT IN HER	IGNORANCE	OF THE LAW? /LOUIS/ WELL, I RISKED IMPRISONMENT
DOCT PREFACE(53)	AGAINST THE PUBLIC. STATISTICAL ILLUSIONS. PUBLIC	IGNORANCE	OF THE LAWS OF EVIDENCE AND OF STATISTICS CAN
BULL PREFACE(26)	NOT A WHIT MORE FOOLISH THAN WE WHO LAUGH AT HIS	IGNORANCE	OF THE NATURE OF POETRY WHILST WE TAKE IT AS A
BULL PREFACE(37)	AND ENGLISH MOVEMENTS HAS BEEN OBSCURED BY THE	IGNORANCE	OF THE ORDINARY ENGLISHMAN, WHO, INSTEAD OF
CLEO NOTES (205)	IF IT WERE NOT THAT THE ORDINARY CITIZEN'S	IGNORANCE	OF THE PAST COMBINES WITH HIS IDEALIZATION OF THE
MIS. PREFACE(30)	TO A PROPOSAL OF MARRIAGE, SHE SHOULD DO SO IN	IGNORANCE	OF THE RELATION SHE IS UNDERTAKING. WHEN THIS
JITT PREFACE(3)	PAMPHLETEER, WHO HAD BEEN ALLOWED TO DISPLAY HIS	IGNORANCE	OF THE RUDIMENTS OF STAGE TECHNIQUE, AND HIS
MTH2 (83)	TO DIE BEFORE THEIR WORK IS DONE, AND THEIR OWN	IGNORANCE	OF THE SPLENDID WORK THERE IS FOR THEM TO DO.
GETT (293)	SAY THIS. WHEN I PROPOSED TO EDITH I WAS IN UTTER	IGNORANCE	OF WHAT I WAS LETTING MYSELF IN FOR LEGALLY.
GENV PREFACE(24)	A HATRED OF LEARNING AND DISCIPLINE, AND A DENSE	IGNORANCE	OF WHAT LIFE IS TO NINE TENTHS OF THEIR
GETT (290)	YOU DONT WISH ANY MAN TO GIVE YOU HIS HAND IN	IGNORANCE	OF YOUR DISGRACE; BUT YOU HAD BETTER ALLOW US TO
NEVR III (277)	YOUR CHILDREN AWAY FROM YOU AND BRING THEM UP IN	IGNORANCE	OF YOUR VERY NAME, HOW WOULD YOU FEEL? WHAT WOULD
GETT PREFACE(244)	SEEMS TO BE NO BOTTOM TO THE ABYSS OF PUBLIC	IGNORANCE	ON THE SUBJECT, I AM COMPELLED TO WARN MY READERS
GENV IV (104)	PEOPLE GOOD GOVERNMENT, AS FAR AS THEIR FOLLY AND	IGNORANCE	PERMIT. WHAT MORE DO THEY NEED? /THE NEWCOMER/
HART II (86)	AND AN ATTEMPT AT PATRONAGE OF HER	IGNORANCE	). /MANGAN/ OF COURSE YOU DONT UNDERSTAND: WHAT DO
PYGM EPILOG (301)	AND NOT IN THE LEAST FUNNY (WHICH WAS ONLY HER	IGNORANCE	), TOOK HIS ADVICE WITH ENTIRE GRAVITY. BUT THE
ARMS III (57)	THE WAY I TREAT A STABLEBOY. THATS ONLY YOUR	IGNORANCE	; AND DONT YOU FORGET IT. AND DONT BE SO READY TO
GENV IV (97)	IT'S BETTER THAN PECKHAM ANYHOW. /BBDE/ EXCUSE MY	IGNORANCE	; BUT WHAT IS PECKHAM? /BEGONIA/ OH! HE DOESNT
METH PREFACE(R30)	CONCEIVED HIMSELF A PILLAR. BUT THIS WAS ONLY HIS	IGNORANCE	; FOR A MAN MAY DENY HIS DESCENT FROM AN APE AND
GETT (355)	ITS PLACE. YOU WOULD RATHER LET A CHILD PERISH IN	IGNORANCE	THAN HAVE IT TAUGHT BY A RIVAL SECTARY. YOU TALK
MRS I (188)	YOU MAY BACK ME TO WIN. BUT IF I HIT HARDER IN MY	IGNORANCE	THAN I NEED, REMEMBER THAT IT IS YOU WHO REFUSE TO
FABL PREFACE(84)	NOT BY INCURABLE MENTAL INCAPACITY, BUT BY AN	IGNORANCE	THAT IS ESSENTIALLY MATHEMATICAL. NONE OF OUR
METH PREFACE(R19)	WITH CIRCUMSTANTIAL SELECTION BY THEIR HISTORICAL	IGNORANCE	THAT THEY ARE PUZZLED BY ANY DISTINCTION BETWEEN
FABL PREFACE(90)	THEMSELVES FROM WHAT IN THEIR ABYSMAL	IGNORANCE	THEY CALL MEDIEVAL BARBARISM WHEN THEY ARE IN FACT
HART PREFACE(22)	HAVE LAUGHED AT. THUS THE NATURAL CONFUSION OF	IGNORANCE	WAS INCREASED BY A DELIBERATELY PROPAGATED
SUPR I (28)	AND WE ARE NOT TO LEARN WHO HE IS! IN OUR	IGNORANCE	WE ARE TO SHAKE HIM BY THE HAND; TO INTRODUCE HIM
MIS. PREFACE(29)	IGNORANCE AS A SAFEGUARD AGAINST PRECOCITY. IF	IGNORANCE	WERE PRACTICABLE THERE WOULD BE SOMETHING TO BE
FANY PROLOG (270)	DONT KNOW; AND I SHANT SPOIL YOU BY DISPELLING AN	IGNORANCE	WHICH, IN MY OPINION, IS HIGHLY BECOMING TO YOUR
MIS. PREFACE(89)	OF IMPOSTURE THAT THRIVES ON THIS COMBINATION OF	IGNORANCE	WITH DESPAIRING ENDURANCE IS INCALCULABLE. GIVEN A
JOAN PREFACE(23)	THIS COMBINATION OF INEPT YOUTH AND ACADEMIC	IGNORANCE	WITH GREAT NATURAL CAPACITY, PUSH, COURAGE,
METH PREFACE(R88)	WISDOM IS MORE DANGEROUS THAN MERE OPPORTUNIST	IGNORANCE	, AND THAT SOMEBODY MUST TAKE THE GARDEN OF EDEN
O'FL (224)	IN IRELAND WHERE IVE BEEN IMPOSED ON AND KEPT IN	IGNORANCE	, AND TO DIE WHERE THE DIVIL HIMSELF WOULDNT TAKE
DOCT PREFACE(73)	OF HIS CORRUPTION AND AN EXPLOITER OF HIS	IGNORANCE	, AND WILL FIND ITSELF LAUNCHED UPON THAT
JOAN 2 (75)	GRANDFATHER SAY? /CHARLES/ THAT JUST SHEWS YOUR	IGNORANCE	, BLUEBEARD. MY GRANDFATHER HAD A SAINT WHO USED
DOCT PREFACE(62)	WILL BLAME, NOT ITS OWN APATHY, SUPERSTITION, AND	IGNORANCE	, BUT THE DEPRAVITY OF THE DOCTORS. NOTHING COULD
BARB PREFACE(220)	PRIESTCRAFT, KINGCRAFT, DEMAGOGY, MONOPOLY,	IGNORANCE	, DRINK, WAR, PESTILENCE, NOR ANY OTHER OF THE
MIS. PREFACE(4)	PUT ON IMMORTALITY. PRACTISE AS YOU WILL ON HIS	IGNORANCE	, HIS FEARS, AND HIS IMAGINATION WITH BRIBES OF
BULL III (132)	THATS TRUE. YOU HOLD YOUR TONGUE AS BEFITS YOUR	IGNORANCE	, MATTHEW HAFFIGAN; AND TRUST YOUR PRIEST TO DEAL
MIS. PREFACE(60)	THIS PRECOCITY IS DISABLED BY POVERTY,	IGNORANCE	, NARROWNESS, AND A HIDEOUS POWER OF LIVING
DOCT PREFACE(16)	SCIENTIFIC PROFESSIONAL WORK TO SAVE HIM FROM THE	IGNORANCE	, OBSOLESCENCE, AND ATROPHY OF SCIENTIFIC
APPL PREFACE(186)	APT TO ABUSE ANY POWER OF CONTROL WE HAVE, OUR	IGNORANCE	, OUR PASSIONS, OUR PRIVATE AND IMMEDIATE
POSN PREFACE(390)	OF THE MAGISTRATE'S PERSONAL CAPRICE, PREJUDICE,	IGNORANCE	, SUPERSTITION, TEMPER, STUPIDITY, RESENTMENT,
PHIL II (96)	MEN HAVE TO PUT UP WITH NOWADAYS, MR CUTHBERTSON.	IGNORANCE	, SUPERSTITION, SENTIMENTALITY: THEY ARE ALL ONE.
SUPR PREFACE(R36)	OF GOOD FAMILY AND HIGH FEEDING); THAT BRISK LAD	IGNORANCE	, TALKATIVE, BY-ENDS OF FAIRSPEECH AND HIS
MILL PREFACE(130)	VALUE. BUT WE MUST ALSO ELIMINATE THE MASS OF	IGNORANCE	, WEAKNESS, AND TIMIDITY WHICH FORCE THEM TO TREAT
MTH4 I (157)	IN MY ENLIGHTENMENT; AND I RECOIL FROM YOUR	IGNORANCE	, YOUR BLINDNESS, YOUR IMBECILITY. HUMANLY I PITY
MILL I (155)	/EPIFANIA/ BRAINS! BY YOUR OWN FOLLY, YOUR	IGNORANCE	, YOUR CRIMINAL INSTINCTS, AND THE LUCK THAT
JOAN 5 (119)	ALONE, TRUSTING TO YOUR OWN CONCEIT, YOUR OWN	IGNORANCE	, YOUR OWN HEADSTRONG PRESUMPTION, YOUR OWN
ROCK II (265)	FROM ENGLAND, AND LEAVE YOU TO PERISH IN YOUR	IGNORANCE	, YOUR VAIN CONCEIT, AND YOUR ABOMINABLE MANNERS.
BARB III (345)	EMPTY BOX). INFERNAL NONSENSE! PURE SCIENTIFIC	IGNORANCE	! (HE GOES IN). /SARAH/ AM I ALL RIGHT, BILTON?
GENV I (46)	BUT YOU DONT UNDERSTAND. OH, WHAT DREADFUL	IGNORANCE	! /COMMISSAR/ LET US PASS ON TO ANOTHER POINT.
BULL I (86)	THE DULLNESS! THE HOPELESSNESS! THE	IGNORANCE	! THE BIGOTRY! /BROADBENT/ (MATTER-OF-FACTLY)
CAND II (120)	HE HAS THROWN IT AWAY AND DEGRADED HIMSELF IN HIS	IGNORANCE	! WILL HE FORGIVE ME THEN, DO YOU THINK?

IGNORANCES

DOCT PREFACE(60)	THERAPEUTICS. TO ALL THESE BLUNDERS AND	IGNORANCES	DOCTORS ARE NO LESS SUBJECT THAN THE REST OF US.
HART PREFACE(24)	THE EMPIRE SICK WITH ITS INCONTINENCES, ITS	IGNORANCES	, ITS FEROCITIES, ITS PANICS, AND ITS ENDLESS AND
MIS. PREFACE(72)	AND STUPIDITIES AND RANCORS AND INEPTITUDES AND	IGNORANCES	, WOULD OPERATE AS POWERFULLY AMONG CHILDREN AS

IGNORANT

ROCK II (244)	QUARTER AS RENT TO THE LANDLORD. THE LABORER IS	IGNORANT	: HE THINKS HE IS ROBBED BY THE LANDLORD; BUT THE
2TRU III (111)	HIS FEET, RISING AND THICKENING ROUND HIM). I AM	IGNORANT	: I HAVE LOST MY NERVE AND AM INTIMIDATED: ALL I

MTH3 (119)	WHICH COOK AND I USED TO READ. I WAS VERY	IGNORANT	: IT DID NOT SEEM SO IMPOSSIBLE TO ME AS TO AN
MILL PREFACE(109)	AND ANOTHER FOR THE FEEBLE, ONE LAW FOR THE	IGNORANT	AND ANOTHER FOR THE LEARNED, ONE LAW FOR THE BRAVE
HART PREFACE(22)	WAS PRODIGIOUSLY OUTNUMBERED BY THE COMPARATIVELY	IGNORANT	AND CHILDISH. REMEMBER THAT THESE PEOPLE HAD TO BE
CAND I (80)	TELL THEM YOU CANT COME. THEYRE ONLY HALF A DOZEN	IGNORANT	AND CONCEITED COSTERMONGERS WITHOUT FIVE SHILLINGS
ROCK I (213)	WILL BE IN PRISON WITH THEIR HEADS BROKEN. A FEW	IGNORANT	AND COWARDLY PEOPLE WHO HAVE STILL ANY MONEY TO
FABL III (112)	WHAT TO DO, THEY WONT DO IT, AND TELL ME I'M	IGNORANT	AND CRAZY. AND SO I AM: I KNOW IT ONLY TOO WELL.
BULL III (130)	LANDLORD. DO YOU THINK, BECAUSE YOURE POOR AND	IGNORANT	AND HALF-CRAZY WITH TOILING AND MOILING MORNING
CAPT III (292)	MAN NOWHERE. /JOHNSON/ (SEVERELY) DONT YOU BE A	IGNORANT	AND IMMORAL FOREIGNER. (THE REBUKE IS WELL
METH PREFACE(R68)	THE PEOPLE, UNTAUGHT OR MISTAUGHT, ARE SO	IGNORANT	AND INCAPABLE POLITICALLY THAT THIS IN ITSELF WOULD
DOCT PREFACE(15)	AS HE CAN GIVE WITHOUT COST MERELY BY BEING LESS	IGNORANT	AND MORE ACCUSTOMED TO SICK-BEDS THAN HIS PATIENTS.
BULL IV (179)	BECAUSE IT IS A HUNGRY LAND, A NAKED LAND, AN	IGNORANT	AND OPPRESSED LAND. /BROADBENT/ BUT, HANG IT ALL,
MIS. PREFACE(12)	HOPELESSLY WARPED AND WASTED BY PARENTS WHO ARE	IGNORANT	AND SILLY ENOUGH TO SUPPOSE THAT THEY KNOW WHAT A
HART PREFACE(3)	WAS DELIVERING THE WORLD OVER TO THE CONTROL OF	IGNORANT	AND SOULLESS CUNNING AND ENERGY, WITH THE FRIGHTFUL
METH PREFACE(R59)	ENGLAND THAT HER CRIMINALS, HER DRUNKARDS, HER	IGNORANT	AND STUPID MASSES, WERE THE VICTIMS OF
SIM PRO,2, (27)	THEY WONT LOOK AT A WHITE MAN. THEY TELL ME I'M	IGNORANT	AND THAT I SMELL BAD. /THE Y.W./ WELL, SO YOU DO.
KING I (169)	SEES A HUNDRED MIRACLES A DAY WHERE THE	IGNORANT	AND THOUGHTLESS SEE NOTHING BUT THE DAILY ROUND,
GETT PREFACE(225)	SOCIETY OF PROFLIGACY, POOR PEOPLE BEING OFTEN SO	IGNORANT	AND UNCULTIVATED THAT THEY HAVE NOTHING TO OFFER
SIM PREFACE(3)	THE SIMPLEST ARE THOSE IN WHICH THE JOURNALIST IS	IGNORANT	AND UNCULTIVATED, AND THE AUTHOR IS ASSUMING A HIGH
MTH2 (61)	SHOULD THE OCCASION ARISE, TO DEAL WITH ALL THESE	IGNORANT	AND UNPRACTICAL PEOPLE IN A CONCLUSIVE AND
BUOY III (35)	YOU THINK I DONT KNOW; BUT I DO. AM I WICKED AND	IGNORANT	AND UNREASONABLE? /SECONDBORN/ OCCASIONALLY, MY
BUOY III (34)	/SECONDBORN/ MY DEAR: THE WORLD IS SO WICKED AND	IGNORANT	AND UNREASONABLE THAT I MUST GET AWAY FROM IT
KING I (170)	I AM SINFUL ENOUGH TO BE GLAD THAT YOU ARE AS	IGNORANT	AS MYSELF. I SUFFER GREATLY FROM SHAME AT MY
MTH5 (230)	ANYTHING. /PYGMALION/ HE MIGHT IF HE WERE SO	IGNORANT	AS NOT TO BE ABLE TO DISTINGUISH BETWEEN WOOD AND
BULL III (142)	WOT OI SY. /MATTHEW/ (FULL OF SCORN FOR A MAN SO	IGNORANT	AS TO BE UNABLE TO PRONOUNCE THE WORD CONNAUGHT,
MRS I (185)	SLEEPING, CYCLING, AND WALKING, I'M A MORE	IGNORANT	BARBARIAN THAN ANY WOMAN COULD POSSIBLY BE WHO
O'FL (210)	HAS IT EVER DONE HERE IN IRELAND? IT'S KEPT ME	IGNORANT	BECAUSE IT FILLED UP MY MOTHER'S MIND, AND SHE
METH PREFACE(R80)	DISCOVERS THAT THEY MIGHT HAVE BEEN WRITTEN BY AN	IGNORANT	BUT CURIOUS AND OBSERVANT NURSERYMAID, AND COULD
CLEO III (150)	EXULTANTLY, TO THE CENTURION) NOW YOU SEE WHAT AN	IGNORANT	COMMON CREATURE YOU ARE! /CENTURION/ (CURTLY)
O'FL (212)	HOW WOULD A GENTLEMAN LIKE YOU KNOW WHAT A POOR	IGNORANT	CONCEITED CREATURE I WAS WHEN I WENT FROM HERE INTO
OVER PREFACE(166)	BE THAT OF A PHILOSOPHIC ADVENTURER TEMPTING AN	IGNORANT	COUNTRY GIRL, OR OF A TRAGICALLY SERIOUS POET
ARMS I (19)	TO SHEW YOU THAT YOU ARE NOT IN THE HOUSE OF	IGNORANT	COUNTRYFOLK WHO WOULD KILL YOU THE MOMENT THEY SAW
BULL III (142)	WHERES ME PIG? GOD FORGIMMY FOR TALKIN TO A POOR	IGNORANT	CRAYCHER LIKE YOU! /HODSON/ (GRINNING WITH
BARB PREFACE(213)	BY DINT OF SHEER " BRILLIANCY" IS PART OF THAT	IGNORANT	CREDULITY WHICH IS THE DESPAIR OF THE HONEST
KING I (212)	MOVEMENTS BY IT. AND NOW COMES THIS PAINTER, THIS	IGNORANT	DAUBER WHO, WERE IT TO SAVE HIS SOUL-- IF HE HAS A
MTH2 (61)	AND SOCIALISM AND SO FORTH IS FOUNDED ON THE	IGNORANT	DELUSION THAT WAGES AND THE PRODUCTION AND
MIS. PREFACE(103)	THE MACHINE. IT IS ONLY IN UNSKILLED HANDS UNDER	IGNORANT	DIRECTION THAT MACHINERY IS DANGEROUS. WE CAN NO
MTH3 (126)	EXPRESSED IT FOR ME. I FELT, EVEN WHEN I WAS AN	IGNORANT	DOMESTIC SLAVE, THAT WE HAD THE POSSIBILITY OF
MTH2 (48)	COME TO BELIEVE THAT EVERYONE THEY SPEAK TO IS AN	IGNORANT	DUPE AND A BORN FOOL INTO THE BARGAIN. /BURGE/ (
HART PREFACE(6)	OF THE FRONT BENCH CAN EDIFY OR DEBAUCH AN	IGNORANT	ELECTORATE AT WILL. THUS OUR DEMOCRACY MOVES IN A
BARB PREFACE(238)	THE RESPONSIBLE PARTIES. HIS POVERTY HAS LEFT HIM	IGNORANT	ENOUGH TO BE DUPED BY THE PRETENCE THAT THE
MIS. (178)	FEELING WOULD HAVE UTTERED EVEN IF HE HAD BEEN	IGNORANT	ENOUGH TO BELIEVE IT. MISS TARLETON'S CONDUCT,
GETT PREFACE(228)	MUCH BY THOSE BELOW IT AS THOSE ABOVE IT, AND YET	IGNORANT	ENOUGH TO BE PROUD OF IT, AND TO HOLD ITSELF UP AS
POSN PREFACE(411)	HANDS AND NOT LEFT AT THE DISPOSAL OF EVERY BIGOT	IGNORANT	ENOUGH TO BE UNAWARE OF THE SOCIAL DANGERS OF
CAPT II (255)	HER, HOWARD? /SIR HOWARD/ NO. THIS MAN MAY BE	IGNORANT	ENOUGH TO SUPPOSE THAT WHEN I WAS A STRUGGLING
MTH5 (249)	IT IS AS EASY TO UNDERSTAND AS ANY OTHER	IGNORANT	ERROR. WHAT ARTIST IS AS GREAT AS HIS OWN WORKS?
DOCT PREFACE(58)	THEM AS LEPERS. NO DOUBT THERE IS A GOOD DEAL OF	IGNORANT	EXAGGERATION AND COWARDLY REFUSAL TO FACE A HUMAN
DOCT I (99)	IT IS ONLY THE HALF-TRUTHS THAT ARE DANGEROUS.	IGNORANT	FADDISTS PICK UP SOME SUPERFICIAL INFORMATION ABOUT
BULL PREFACE(3)	AND GUESSED WRONGLY, WHILST STUPIDER AND MORE	IGNORANT	FELLOW-PILGRIMS GUESSED RIGHTLY). JOHN BULL'S OTHER
DOCT PREFACE(23)	OF SMALLPOX AMONG THEM, SHE WAS SNUBBED AS AN	IGNORANT	FEMALE WHO DID NOT KNOW THAT SMALLPOX CAN BE
CAPT II (245)	HERE, SIR, AS YOULL FIND, EXCEPT THE POOR	IGNORANT	FOREIGNER AND THAT THERE SCUM OF THE SUBMERGED
GENV IV (93)	SAID IT. /NEWCOMER/ OH, DONT TALK NONSENSE, YOU	IGNORANT	FOREIGNER. PLEBISCITES ARE UNENGLISH, THOROUGHLY
PYGM II (220)	DIRT. /MRS PEARCE/ HOW CAN YOU BE SUCH A FOOLISH	IGNORANT	GIRL AS TO THINK YOU COULD AFFORD TO PAY MR
PYGM IV (266)	OF FEELING. /LIZA/ I'M SORRY. I'M ONLY A COMMON	IGNORANT	GIRL; AND IN MY STATION I HAVE TO BE CAREFUL. THERE
PYGM V (286)	I WANT A LITTLE KINDNESS. I KNOW I'M A COMMON	IGNORANT	GIRL, AND YOU A BOOK-LEARNED GENTLEMAN; BUT I'M NOT
CAND I SD(85)	BY OVERFEEDING AND COMMERCIAL SUCCESS. A VULGAR	IGNORANT	GUZZLING MAN, OFFENSIVE AND CONTEMPTUOUS TO PEOPLE
MRS PREFACE(156)	ENOUGH INTO THINGS TO BE ABLE TO SAY NO, HOW MANY	IGNORANT	HALF-STARVED GIRLS WILL BELIEVE YOU ARE SPEAKING
MRS IV (249)	WHAT YOU DONT UNDERSTAND; YOUR HEAD IS FULL OF	IGNORANT	IDEAS ABOUT ME. WHAT DO THE PEOPLE THAT TAUGHT YOU
KING I (179)	AND RITUAL THEY WILL PASS AS HOLY MEN WITH THE	IGNORANT	. AND THERE ARE GREAT MYSTERIES THAT MUST BE
FANY III (314)	AS ALL THAT. /MRS KNOX/ I DONT SAY SHE WAS	IGNORANT	. BUT I DO SAY THAT SHE DIDNT KNOW WHAT WE KNOW: I
BUOY III (41)	ARE POLITICALLY AND SCIENTIFICALLY OBSOLETE AND	IGNORANT	. EVEN IN THE ELEMENTARY SCHOOLS CHILDREN SPEND
SIM PRO,2, (28)	WELL; BUT OF THE GREAT GAME OF LIFE THEY ARE	IGNORANT	. HERE, WHERE THEY ARE IN THE MIDST OF LIFE AND
BARB PREFACE(215)	POOR MEAN? IT MEANS LET HIM BE WEAK. LET HIM BE	IGNORANT	. LET HIM BECOME A NUCLEUS OF DISEASE. LET HIM BE A
PYGM IV (264)	SUBJECTIVE. /LIZA/ I DONT UNDERSTAND. I'M TOO	IGNORANT	. /HIGGINS/ IT'S ONLY IMAGINATION. LOW SPIRITS AND
SIM PREFACE(4)	TRIBESMAN WAS AS CAPABLE MENTALLY AS HIMSELF, BUT	IGNORANT	. THAT IS MY ATTITUDE WHEN I WRITE PREFACES. MY
FANY III (317)	PRIDE? BUT IVE NOTICED IT ALL MY LIFE: WE'RE	IGNORANT	. WE DONT REALLY KNOW WHATS RIGHT AND WHATS WRONG.
CAPT NOTES (304)	THE EXPERT PHONETICIAN. THIS IS NO MERE RASH AND	IGNORANT	JIBE OF MY OWN AT THE EXPENSE OF MY ENGLISH
JOAN 4 (103)	PIOUS MEN, ARE THRUST INTO THE KENNEL BY EVERY	IGNORANT	LABORER OR DAIRYMAID WHOM THE DEVIL CAN PUFF UP
POSN PREFACE(415)	WOULD HAVE DENOUNCED THAT CHIEF CONSTABLE AS AN	IGNORANT	LIBELLER OF A NOBLE PROFESSION. BUT THE CONSTABLE
DOCT V (173)	ASKED HIM WHY, HE SAID THAT PRIVATE DOCTORS WERE	IGNORANT	LICENSED MURDERERS. /RIDGEON/ THAT IS WHAT THE
2TRU III (87)	THIS FOOLING, BOTH OF YOU. YOU, SIR, ARE NOT AN	IGNORANT	MAN: YOU KNOW THAT THE UNIVERSE IS WRECKED.
DOCT PREFACE(20)	MAGICAL CURES FOR DISEASE. TO A SUFFICIENTLY	IGNORANT	MAN EVERY CAPTAIN OF A TRADING SCHOONER IS A
LION PREFACE(83)	EFFECT; IT BRINGS NO ENLIGHTENMENT; THE MOST	IGNORANT	MAN HAS ONLY TO BECOME INTOXICATED WITH HIS OWN
MIS. PREFACE(51)	A PAGE OF PLATO, AND IS ADMITTEDLY A DANGEROUSLY	IGNORANT	MAN POLITICALLY, IS NEVERTHELESS A SOCRATES
CLEO PRO1 (93)	YE SHALL SEE; AND YE SHALL MARVEL, AFTER YOUR	IGNORANT	MANNER, THAT MEN TWENTY CENTURIES AGO WERE ALREADY
CLEO NOTES (204)	MATERIAL CONDITIONS OF THEIR EXISTENCE. THE MORE	IGNORANT	MEN ARE, THE MORE CONVINCED ARE THEY THAT THEIR
APPL II (276)	/LYSISTRATA/ NEVER FEAR, SIR, IT IS NOT THE MOST	IGNORANT	NATIONAL CROWD THAT WILL COME OUT ON TOP, BUT THE
KING I (173)	EVER MET WHO DID NOT THINK AN ACTRESS MUST BE AN	IGNORANT	NINNY-- EXCEPT SCHOOLBOYS, WHO THINK SHE IS A
ROCK I (220)	COMMUNISM, AND THAT WHOEVER DOESNT KNOW IT IS AN	IGNORANT	NOBODY OR A HALF-EDUCATED COLLEGE FOOL; AND YOULL
WIDO III (56)	WHO WRITE SUCH BOOKS AS THESE SHOULD BE SO	IGNORANT	OF PRACTICAL BUSINESS. ONE WOULD SUPPOSE, TO READ
CATH PREFACE(154)	MOTIVE OF A PLAY THAT WILL LEAVE THE READER AS	IGNORANT	OF RUSSIAN HISTORY AS HE MAY BE NOW BEFORE HE HAS
METH PREFACE(R69)	WOULD BE AFRAID OF THESE IF THEY WERE NOT TOO	IGNORANT	OF SOCIETY AND HISTORY TO APPRECIATE THE RISK, AND
FABL PREFACE(90)	THOUGH ITS GHOST STILL WALKS BECAUSE DOCTORS ARE	IGNORANT	OF STATISTICS, AND, I MUST ADD, BECAUSE IT IS
CURE (234)	THATS THE NAME OF THE TUNE TOO. YOU SEEM QUITE	IGNORANT	OF THE BEST MUSIC. DONT YOU KNOW RUM TUM TIDDLE,
MIS. PREFACE(88)	TO THE ENGLISHMAN OR AMERICAN, SO SURPRISINGLY	IGNORANT	OF THE BIBLE, IS THAT THE AUTHORIZED ENGLISH
MTH5 (230)	WOOD AND SOFT IRON. IN THOSE DAYS THEY WERE VERY	IGNORANT	OF THE DIFFERENCES BETWEEN THINGS, BECAUSE THEIR
MTH3 (97)	/CONFUCIUS/ ONLY AN ENGLISHMAN COULD BE SO	IGNORANT	OF THE NATURE OF GOVERNMENT AS TO SUPPOSE THAT A
FABL PREFACE(89)	AND LEAKING PIPES. HE MAY, LIKE JENNER, BE SO	IGNORANT	OF THE RUDIMENTS OF STATISTICS AS TO BELIEVE THAT
BULL PREFACE(4)	AT THE END OF WHICH THE UNIONISTS, QUITE AS	IGNORANT	OF WHAT THE PEOPLE OF ENGLAND WERE THINKING ABOUT
JOAN PREFACE(10)	DISREGARDED; JOAN'S PEOPLE COULD NOT AFFORD TO BE	IGNORANT	OF WHAT WAS GOING ON IN THE FEUDAL WORLD. THEY WERE
O'FL (223)	NATURAL FEELINGS FOR YOU; FOR IT'S ONLY A SILLY	IGNORANT	OLD COUNTRYWOMAN YOU ARE WITH ALL YOUR FINE TALK
ROCK I (220)	DOWN ON THE STUFF YOU WERE TAUGHT AT COLLEGE AS	IGNORANT	OLDFASHIONED TRASH. LOOK AT THAT GIRL ALOYSIA
SUPR HANDBOK(185)	THE UNINTENTIONAL CHILD SLAUGHTER THAT GOES ON BY	IGNORANT	PARENTS IN PRIVATE HOMES, NUMBERED ONLY 300, COULD
DOCT PREFACE(65)	SHABBY COAT, THE WOLF AT THE DOOR, THE TYRANNY OF	IGNORANT	PATIENTS, THE WORK-DAY OF 24 HOURS, AND THE
DOCT PREFACE(20)	UNDERSTAND QUITE WELL WHAT THEY ARE DOING AS BY	IGNORANT	PEOPLE WHO ARE SIMPLY DUPES. BONE-SETTERS MAKE
JOAN 6 (130)	AND IT KNOWS THAT THEY BEGIN ALWAYS BY VAIN AND	IGNORANT	PERSONS SETTING UP THEIR OWN JUDGMENT AGAINST THE
JOAN PREFACE(10)	BUT THIS DOES NOT MEAN THAT JOAN WAS AN	IGNORANT	PERSON, OR THAT SHE SUFFERED FROM THE DIFFIDENCE
GENV I (31)	ARE THEY DOING TO CORRECT THE MISTAKES OF OUR	IGNORANT	POLITICIANS? /SHE/ WELL, WE HAVE THEIR NAMES ON
APPL I (235)	WHILST YOU PUT THE ODIUM OF ALL OUR RESISTANCE TO	IGNORANT	POPULAR CLAMOR ON ME. I ASK YOU, BEFORE YOU PLAY
MRS PREFACE(162)	I HAVE DESCRIBED WERE FIRST PRODUCED, AND A FEW	IGNORANT	PROTESTS BY CHURCHMEN AGAINST MUCH BETTER PLAYS
GENV II (58)	EXISTENCE OF WHICH I MUST CONFESS I WAS ENTIRELY	IGNORANT	-- HAS FOUND THE PROCEDURE; AND THE COURT WILL BACK
MTH4 II (185)	WILL THEN BEGIN ALL OVER AGAIN AS HALF-STARVED	IGNORANT	SAVAGES, AND FIGHT WITH BOOMERANGS AND POISONED
METH PREFACE(R54)	I FOUND MYSELF REGARDED AS A BLASPHEMER AND AN	IGNORANT	SENTIMENTALIST BECAUSE WHENEVER THE NEO-DARWINIAN
DOCT PREFACE(31)	AND DR JOHNSON AND RUSKIN AND MARK TWAIN ARE	IGNORANT	SENTIMENTALISTS, JUST AS HE COMPLIES WITH ANY OTHER
DOCT PREFACE(49)	BURGLAR IS A PUBLIC BENEFACTOR AND THE POLICE ARE	IGNORANT	SENTIMENTALISTS. NO HIGHWAY ROBBER HAS YET HARROWED
DOCT PREFACE(47)	AFTERWARDS TO PROTECT IT FROM WHAT HE DEEMS THE	IGNORANT	SENTIMENTALITY OF THE LAITY. WHEN THE PUBLIC
BULL PREFACE(11)	A FOOL'S NOTION. IT IS AT BOTTOM THE FOLLY OF THE	IGNORANT	SIMPLETONS WHO LONG TO BE KINGS AND CHIEFS BECAUSE
KING I (169)	THE DAILY ROUND, THE COMMON TASK. JOSHUA WAS AN	IGNORANT	SOLDIER. HAD HE BEEN A PHILOSOPHER HE WOULD HAVE

MTH2 (78)	SCIENCE KNOWS NOTHING OF IT. THEN SCIENCE IS MORE	IGNORANT	THAN THE CHILDREN AT ANY VILLAGE SCHOOL. /CONRAD/
DOCT PREFACE(15)	PATIENTS ARE FOR THE MOST PART SO POOR AND SO	IGNORANT	THAT GOOD ADVICE WOULD BE RESENTED AS IMPRACTICABLE
JOAN 5 (118)	PROUD AND DISOBEDIENT. I AM A POOR GIRL, AND SO	IGNORANT	THAT I DO NOT KNOW A FROM B. HOW COULD I BE PROUD?
DOCT PREFACE(73)	FREE OF SUPERSTITION. IF ITALIAN PEASANTS ARE SO	IGNORANT	THAT THE CHURCH CAN GET NO HOLD OF THEM EXCEPT BY
BARB PREFACE(242)	MAGISTRATES, BECAUSE MANY OF THEM ARE SO OLD AND	IGNORANT	THAT WHEN THEY ARE CALLED UPON TO ADMINISTER ANY
VWOO 3 (135)	EDUCATED CUSTOMER. OF COURSE, WHEN PEOPLE ARE TOO	IGNORANT	TO KNOW THE NAMES OF WHAT THEY EAT, THAT IS ANOTHER
CLEO II (138)	GO DOWN TO POSTERITY AS A BARBAROUS SOLDIER TOO	IGNORANT	TO KNOW THE VALUE OF BOOKS? /CAESAR/ THEODOTUS: I
DOCT PREFACE(71)	COMPLY WITH THE SANITARY REGULATIONS THEY ARE TOO	IGNORANT	TO UNDERSTAND. AS I HAVE ELSEWHERE CONFESSED, I
MILL PREFACE(132)	NATION IS MADE UP FOR THE MOST PART OF PEOPLE TOO	IGNORANT	TO UNDERSTAND EFFICIENT GOVERNMENT, AND TAUGHT, AS
MIS. PREFACE(47)	MUCH BETTER THAN SOCRATES OR SOLON? IT IS THIS	IGNORANT	UPPISHNESS THAT DOES THE MISCHIEF. A STRANGER ON
APPL I (234)	WITH FOOLISH FACTIONS IN PARLIAMENT AND WITH	IGNORANT	VOTERS IN THE CONSTITUENCIES? THE SCIENTISTS WILL
JOAN 6 (147)	NOT UNDERSTAND A WORD WE WERE SAYING. IT IS THE	IGNORANT	WHO SUFFER. COME, OR WE SHALL BE LATE FOR THE END.
DOCT III (147)	WELL, WHAT IS OUR FRIEND DUBEDAT? A VICIOUS AND	IGNORANT	YOUNG MAN WITH A TALENT FOR DRAWING. /LOUIS/ THANK
DOCT III (147)	THEN, WHAT ARE MANY OF MY PATIENTS? VICIOUS AND	IGNORANT	YOUNG MEN WITHOUT A TALENT FOR ANYTHING. IF I WERE
BULL IV (153)	/KEEGAN/ (QUIETLY) SIR: THERE WAS A TIME, IN MY	IGNORANT	YOUTH, WHEN I SHOULD HAVE CALLED YOU A HYPOCRITE.
DOCT PREFACE(43)	THE HEART VISIBLE TO STUDENTS. ONE, A BARBAROUS,	IGNORANT	, AND THOUGHTLESS WAY, IS TO STICK LITTLE FLAGS
LADY PREFACE(229)	KNOW THAT THEY ARE DIRTY, DRUNKEN, FOUL-MOUTHED,	IGNORANT	, GLUTTONOUS, PREJUDICED: IN SHORT, HEIRS TO THE
PYGM EPILOG (297)	THEM. SHE WAS, IN SHORT, AN UTTER FAILURE, AN	IGNORANT	, INCOMPETENT, PRETENTIOUS, UNWELCOME, PENNILESS,
GENV II (50)	MORE GRAVELY) I AM AFRAID YOU WILL THINK ME VERY	IGNORANT	, MISS BROWN; BUT I HAVE NEVER HEARD OF MR
BULL PREFACE(22)	HIS POPULARITY BY PRETENDING TO BE RUDER, MORE	IGNORANT	, MORE SENTIMENTAL, MORE SUPERSTITIOUS, MORE STUPID
UNPL PREFACE(R18)	UNFIT FOR CIVILIZED INTERCOURSE: GRACELESS,	IGNORANT	, NARROW-MINDED TO A QUITE APPALLING DEGREE. IN
ROCK I (194)	DOORSTEP. /SIR ARTHUR/ IT'S ALL SO FOOLISH-- SO	IGNORANT	, POOR CHAPS! (HE THROWS THE TIMES ON THE TABLE
DOCT PREFACE(51)	LAY CAPACITY. HE IS MADE OF THE SAME CLAY AS THE	IGNORANT	, SHALLOW, CREDULOUS, HALF-MISEDUCATED, PECUNIARILY
JOAN PREFACE(38)	OF MILLIONS OF MEN AND WOMEN, MOSTLY POOR AND	IGNORANT	, SHOULD COMPETE SUCCESSFULLY IN THE SELECTION OF
GETT SD(262)	SIMPLICITY AND DIGNITY OF CHARACTER. HE IS	IGNORANT	, STUPID, AND PREJUDICED, HAVING BEEN CAREFULLY
ROCK PREFACE(167)	AND FOR CULTURAL PURPOSES HAS TO BE CLASSED AS	IGNORANT	, THOUGH HE KNOWS THINGS THAT UNIVERSITY PROFESSORS
BULL IV (173)	TO SUCH MEN? THEY ARE TOO SMALL, TOO POOR, TOO	IGNORANT	, TOO SIMPLEMINDED TO HOLD IT AGAINST US: YOU MIGHT
SUPR IV (151)	THIS IS THE HIGHBORN SOCIAL TONE IVE SPOILT BE ME	IGNORANT	, UNCULTIVATED BEHAVIOR! MAKIN LOVE TO A MARRIED

IGNORANTLY

DOCT PREFACE(7)	THE AUTHORITY OF SCRIPTURE, AND ANOTHER FOR	IGNORANTLY	AND SUPERSTITIOUSLY ACCEPTING IT AS A GUIDE TO
JOAN 6 (131)	WRETCH SUSPECTED OF HERESY, PERHAPS QUITE	IGNORANTLY	AND UNJUSTLY, IS STONED, TORN IN PIECES, DROWNED,
DOCT I (99)	BUT WHEN I THINK OF THE AVERAGE MEN OF YOUR DAY,	IGNORANTLY	BLEEDING AND CUPPING AND PURGING, AND SCATTERING
SUPR II (59)	OF A CYNICAL, CUNNING, AVARICIOUS, DISILLUSIONED,	IGNORANTLY	EXPERIENCED, FOUL-MINDED OLD WOMAN WHOM SHE CALLS
SUPR HANDBOK(201)	CONTEMPORARIES; AND WE CONCLUDE (USUALLY QUITE	IGNORANTLY	) THAT THE ABUSES EXPOSED BY THEM ARE THINGS OF
CYMB FORWORD(134)	VERSES WERE CUT OUT AS A MATTER OF COURSE; AND I	IGNORANTLY	THANKED HEAVEN FOR IT. WHEN I READ THE ACT AS
METH PREFACE(R48)	ENLIGHTENMENT AND EMANCIPATION FOR WHICH HE WAS	IGNORANTLY	UNGRATEFUL. EVEN NOW, WHEN BUTLER'S EMINENCE IS

IGNORE

MIS. PREFACE(90)	BLESSED SELECTIVE FACULTY WHICH ENABLES US TO	IGNORE	A GOOD DEAL OF DISAGREEABLE NOISE IF THERE IS A
SUPR PREFACE(R28)	NO GENTLEMAN AFTER ALL? HOWEVER, IT WAS EASY TO	IGNORE	A RICH MAN'S SOLECISM. THE UNGENTLEMANLY CLAUSE WAS
BULL PREFACE(68)	UPON THIS INTERESTING BUT HOPELESS ATTEMPT TO	IGNORE	BRITISH RULE THE GOVERNMENT LET LOOSE A SPECIALLY
DOCT PREFACE(39)	A CRAZE FOR DRINK CAN; AND NOBODY WHO ATTEMPTS TO	IGNORE	CRUELTY AS A POSSIBLE FACTOR IN THE ATTRACTION OF
BULL IV SD(145)	AUNT JUDY IS QUIETLY BUSY. NORA IS TRYING TO	IGNORE	DORAN AND ATTEND TO HER GAME. ON THE OTHER HAND DORAN
BULL PREFACE(70)	OFFENCE AND DEFENCE IN TERMS OF AIRPLANES WHICH	IGNORE	HIS WATERLOO RIDGES, AND THE INEVITABLE NATIONALIST
MRS PREFACE(167)	HE HAS TO FACE THE ACCUSATION THAT HIS PLAYS	IGNORE	HUMAN FEELING, AN ILLUSION PRODUCED BY THAT VERY
BULL PREFACE(49)	OF THE MILITARY MIND CONTINUALLY TO	IGNORE	HUMAN NATURE AND CRY FOR THE MOON INSTEAD OF FACING
FABL PREFACE(84)	THREE. THE FOURTH DIMENSION IS THAT OF TIME. TO	IGNORE	IT IS TO BE PRE-EINSTEIN, WHICH IS AS OUT-OF-DATE AS
GETT PREFACE(183)	BY THE SIMPLE PROCESS OF PROMISING ONE ANOTHER TO	IGNORE	IT, MARRIAGE NEVERTHELESS INEVITABLE. NOW MOST LAWS
MIS. PREFACE(18)	IT DOES AT PRESENT IS PRODUCED BY OUR EFFORTS TO	IGNORE	IT, OR TO SMOTHER IT UNDER A HEAP OF SENTIMENTAL LIES
2TRU II (69)	MAKERS OF OUR DOMESTIC INSTITUTIONS HAVE TRIED TO	IGNORE	. AND NOW THAT SWEETIE GOES SHOUTING THEM ALL OVER
POSN PREFACE(389)	OR A SANITARY INSPECTOR; BUT IT IS IMPOSSIBLE TO	IGNORE	THE CARELESSNESS WITH WHICH EVEN DISTINGUISHED
SUPR III (124)	JUAN: WE KNOW THE LIBERTINE'S PHILOSOPHY. ALWAYS	IGNORE	THE CONSEQUENCES TO THE WOMAN. /DON JUAN/ THE
MRS PREFACE(161)	BY SEX SERIOUSLY FACED AND DEALT WITH, INEVITABLY	IGNORE	THE OFFICIAL FORMULA AND ARE SUPPRESSED. IF THE OLD
MRS PREFACE(165)	TRAPPED THEM IN EXCEPTIONAL NUMBERS, PROCEEDS TO	IGNORE	THEIR SENSES AND RUTHLESSLY IMPROVE THEIR MINDS? BUT
MIS. PREFACE(59)	THEM, YET THERE IS NO GREATER CRUELTY THAN TO	IGNORE	THEM. I HAVE COMPLAINED SUFFICIENTLY OF WHAT I

IGNORED

HART I (54)	BEHIND HIM). /LADY UTTERWORD/ I WILL NOT BE	IGNORED	AND PRETENDED TO BE SOMEBODY ELSE. I WILL HAVE IT
MRS PREFACE(158)	OF A DRAMA IN WHICH LOVE SHOULD BE AS EFFECTIVELY	IGNORED	AS CHOLERA IS AT PRESENT, THERE IS NOT THE SLIGHTEST
SUPR PREFACE(R15)	WILLIAM BLAKE AS SUPERFICIALLY AS THE XVIII HAD	IGNORED	HOGARTH OR THE XVII BUNYAN, HAD GOT PAST THE
HART PREFACE(15)	LOSS OF THEIR EFFICIENCY BECAME TOO GLARING TO BE	IGNORED	. REMONSTRANCES AND WARNINGS WERE MET EITHER WITH AN
JOAN PREFACE(53)	MUST STAND. TO THE CRITICS, LEST THEY SHOULD FEEL	IGNORED	. TO A PROFESSIONAL CRITIC (I HAVE BEEN ONE MYSELF)
DOCT PREFACE(28)	BEYOND THE RESOURCES OF PRIVATE PRACTICE, TO BE	IGNORED	OR ANGRILY DENOUNCED AS A FAD. TRADE UNIONISM AND
OVER PREFACE(166)	THIS HIGHLY DEVELOPED CLASS, SEX CAN NO LONGER BE	IGNORED	OR CONVENTIONALIZED OR DISTORTED BY THE PLAYWRIGHT
3PLA PREFACE(R24)	CITIZEN HAS EVER SINCE QUOTED THE APOLOGY AND	IGNORED	THE FANFARE. WHEN AN ACTRESS WRITES HER MEMOIRS, SHE
2TRU PREFACE(3)	OUR CONVENTIONAL AND ROMANTIC WRITERS HAVE	IGNORED	THOSE HORRORS, DWELLING PLEASANTLY ON THE ELEGANCES
ROCK II (250)	THEY CLUNG TO THEIR ANCIENT HOMESTEADS AND	IGNORED	YOUR INFAMOUS NOTICES TO QUIT? WOULD IT SURPRISE
ROCK PREFACE(153)	ARE TOO OBVIOUS OR BECOME TOO SCANDALOUS TO BE	IGNORED	, WHEN THEY OFTEN ADVOCATE EMIGRATION OR BIRTH

IGNORES

KING I (203)	DOES WEAK AID AFFORD; SHE TRUSTS HER BALANCE, AND	IGNORES	HER SWORD. VIRTUE IS SLOW TO TAKE WHATS NOT HER OWN,

IGNORING

DEST (175)	REAL PERSONS IN YOUR ROMANCES. /LADY/ (POLITELY	IGNORING	A SPEECH WHICH IS TO HER ONLY A BREACH OF GOOD
SUPR I (18)	/ANN/ (RESUMING IN THE SAME GENTLE VOICE,	IGNORING	HER MOTHER'S BAD TASTE) MAMMA KNOWS THAT SHE IS NOT
MRS II (203)	GOING TO THE DOOR OF THE KITCHEN AND OPENING IT,	IGNORING	HER MOTHER) NOW, ABOUT SUPPER? (ALL RISE EXCEPT
ARMS III (73)	/RAINA/ (MUTINOUSLY) HE'S NOT. /CATHERINE/ (	IGNORING	HER)-- I SHALL NOT STAND IN THE WAY OF HER
NEVR II (245)	HER PART AGAINST ME, YOU MEAN. /MRS CLANDON/ (	IGNORING	HIM) GLORIA: WILL YOU TAKE MY PLACE WHILST I AM
NEVR II (246)	WISH TO JOIN THEM IN INSULTING ME? /VALENTINE/ (	IGNORING	HIM) I'M OVERWHELMED, MISS CLANDON. IT'S ALL MY
JITT II (50)	AGAIN;-- /LENKHEIM/ I NEVER WILL. /JITTA/ (STILL	IGNORING	HIS PROTESTS)-- BUT YOU WILL COME TO BELIEVE EVERY
MRS PREFACE(169)	ON WHICH HIS WHOLE WORK IS BUILT, FAR FROM	IGNORING	IDIOSYNCRASY, WILL, PASSION, IMPULSE, WHIM, AS
ROCK PREFACE(155)	VENAL SPECIAL PLEADING, AND THE CONCEALMENT OR	IGNORING	OF FACTS WHICH ARE IMPOSED ON US AT PRESENT BECAUSE
SUPR I SD(17)	TO HIS MAGISTERIAL SEAT AT THE WRITING TABLE,	IGNORING	TANNER, AND OPENS THE PROCEEDINGS. /RAMSDEN/ I AM
SUPR IV (168)	HIMSELF SAVAGELY) I MEAN FOR HIS. /ANN/ (	IGNORING	THE CORRECTION) YES, FOR YOURS. YOU HAD BETTER
GENV III (75)	BUT THEIR CATSPAW. THEY FLOUT US OPENLY BY	IGNORING	THE COVENANT AND MAKING UNILATERAL TREATIES THAT
WIDO I (14)	THINK HE HAS SUCH WONDERFUL TACT. /SARTORIUS/ (	IGNORING	THE DIGRESSION) I HAVE JUST HAD A WORD WITH MY
PHIL II (119)	WISH TO PURSUE THE CONVERSATION). /CHARTERIS/ (	IGNORING	THE HINT, AND COOLLY SITTING DOWN BESIDE HIM) WHY
POSN (448)	DRUNK-- AT LEAST NOT AS DRUNK AS THAT. /BLANCO/ (	IGNORING	THE INTERRUPTION)-- AND YOU FOUND A MAN WITHOUT A
MTH4 I (149)	ELDERLY GENTLEMAN/ (VEHEMENTLY) NO. /THE MAN/ (	IGNORING	THE INTERRUPTION) BLESS YOU FOR TAKING HIM OFF MY
NEVR IV (285)	YOU CAN HEAR HIS MIND WORKING. /GLORIA/ (	IGNORING	THE JIBE) WHERE IS HE? /VALENTINE/ BOUGHT A FALSE
PLES PREFACE(R15)	IN THE WAY OF THE PERFORMANCE OF MY PLAYS BY	IGNORING	THE MAJORITY OF THE MANAGER'S CUSTOMERS: NAY, BY
CLEO NOTES (207)	OF THE BIRDS OF ARISTOPHANES. MY REASON THEN FOR	IGNORING	THE POPULAR CONCEPTION OF PROGRESS IN CAESAR AND
LADY PREFACE(233)	THE BRITISH PUBLIC, AND NEVER FORGAVE IT FOR	IGNORING	THEIR BEST WORK AND ADMIRING THEIR SPLENDID
DOCT III (141)	RASCAL. (ALL CRYING OUT TOGETHER) /LOUIS/ (	IGNORING	THEIR OUTCRY) SHE WAS MARRIED TO THE STEWARD OF A
CAPT I (236)	FOR A TRIP INTO THE MOUNTAINS. /BRASSBOUND/ (	IGNORING	THIS ANNOUNCEMENT) WHO IS THE LADY? /RANKIN/ LADY
FABL PREFACE(88)	THE LATEST VIEWS ARE THOSE OF BASTIAT AND COBDEN,	IGNORING	THOSE OF CAIRNES AND MILL, IS SUCCESSFUL,
SUPR PREFACE(R15)	THE TIME THE POLITE CRITICS OF THE XIX CENTURY,	IGNORING	WILLIAM BLAKE AS SUPERFICIALLY AS THE XVIII HAD
MRS PREFACE(168)	THIS LOGIC RUTHLESSLY OVERBOARD, I AM ACCUSED OF	IGNORING	, NOT STAGE LOGIC, BUT, OF ALL THINGS, HUMAN
FABL PREFACE(97)	THE RUSSIAN BOLSHEVIKS WENT RUINOUSLY WRONG BY	IGNORING	" THE INEVITABILITY OF GRADUALNESS" AND ATTEMPTING

IH

CAPT II (245)	YNT IT? (FEROCIOUSLY) OO A YOU ORDERIN ABAHT,	IH	? /SIR HOWARD/ (RISING QUIETLY, AND TAKING REFUGE

II

MIS. PREFACE(104)	OF NAPOLEON, THE FICKLENESS OF CATHERINE	II	: IN SHORT, ALL THE CHILDISHNESSES OF ALL THE DESPOTS
SUPR HANDBOK(179)	A SUPERMAN THAN CALVIN. WHAT THEN ARE WE TO DO?	II	: PROPERTY AND MARRIAGE. LET US HURRY OVER THE OBSTACLES

BUOY II (18)	ACT	II	: THE ADVENTURE. THE SHORE OF A BROAD WATER STUDDED WITH
MTH2 (35)	PART	II	: THE GOSPEL OF THE BROTHERS BARNABAS. IN THE FIRST YEARS
POSN PREFACE(405)	REJECTED STATEMENT. THE REJECTED STATEMENT, PART	II	: THE LICENSING OF THEATRES. THE DISTINCTION BETWEEN
DOCT PREFACE(53)	INOCULATION, BY WHICH VOLTAIRE, CATHERINE	II	AND LADY MARY WORTLEY MONTAGU SO CONFIDENTLY EXPECTED TO
JOAN 2 (71)	SCENE	II	CHINON, IN TOURAINE. AN END OF THE THRONE-ROOM IN THE
DOCT PREFACE(32)	DESCRIPTION OF THE TREATMENT OF CHARLES	II	IN HIS LAST ILLNESS TO SEE HOW STRONGLY HIS PHYSICIANS
MTH4 II (175)	ACT	II	. A COURTYARD BEFORE THE COLUMNED PORTICO OF A TEMPLE.
MILL II (166)	ACT	II	. A DISMAL OLD COFFEE ROOM IN AN ANCIENT RIVERSIDE INN.
MTH1 II (20)	ACT	II	. A FEW CENTURIES LATER. MORNING. AN OASIS IN
SIM II (54)	ACT	II	. A FINE FORENOON SOME YEARS LATER. THE GARDEN IS
SIM PRO,2, (26)	SCENE	II	. A GRASSY CLIFF TOP OVERHANGING THE SEA. A SEAT FOR
2TRU II (51)	ACT	II	. A SEA BEACH IN A MOUNTAINOUS COUNTRY. SAND DUNES RISE
DOCT II (115)	ACT	II	. AFTER DINNER ON THE TERRACE AT THE STAR AND GARTER,
CLEO II (118)	ACT	II	. ALEXANDRIA. A HALL ON THE FIRST FLOOR OF THE PALACE,
KING PREFACE(153)	NELL GWYNN, AND NELL'S PRINCIPAL LOVER AS CHARLES	II	. AS NELL WAS A LIVELY AND LOVABLE ACTRESS, IT WAS EASY
WIDO II (24)	ACT	II	. IN THE LIBRARY OF A HANDSOMELY APPOINTED VILLA AT
MRS II (198)	ACT	II	. INSIDE THE COTTAGE AFTER NIGHTFALL. LOOKING EASTWARD
APPL II (257)	ACT	II	. LATER IN THE AFTERNOON. THE TERRACE OF THE PALACE. A
CAPT II (242)	ACT	II	. MIDDAY. A ROOM IN A MOORISH CASTLE. A DIVAN SEAT RUNS
DEVL II (28)	ACT	II	. MINISTER ANDERSON'S HOUSE IS IN THE MAIN STREET OF
PHIL II (94)	ACT	II	. NEXT DAY AT NOON, IN THE LIBRARY OF THE IBSEN CLUB. A
GENV II (49)	ACT	II	. OFFICE OF THE SECRETARY OF THE LEAGUE OF NATIONS.
FANY II (285)	ACT	II	. ON THE AFTERNOON OF THE SAME DAY, MRS KNOX IS WRITING
SUPR II (48)	ACT	II	. ON THE CARRIAGE DRIVE IN THE PARK OF A COUNTRY HOUSE
NEVR II (225)	ACT	II	. ON THE TERRACE AT THE MARINE HOTEL. IT IS A SQUARE
SUPR HANDBOK(175)	SIR ROBERT GIFFEN. ESSAYS IN FINANCE, VOL.	II	. P. 393. FOREWORD. A REVOLUTIONIST IS ONE WHO DESIRES TO
BULL II (97)	ACT	II	. ROSSCULLEN. WESTWARD A HILLSIDE OF GRANITE ROCK AND
BASH II,1, (99)	ACT	II	. SCENE 1. LONDON. A ROOM IN LYDIA'S HOUSE. ENTER LYDIA
METH PREFACE(R69)	III AND ELICITED LIBERAL PAMPHLETS FROM CATHERINE	II	. STATESMEN ARE AFRAID OF THE SUBURBS, OF THE NEWSPAPERS,
KING II (223)	ACT	II	. THE BOUDOIR OF CATHERINE OF BRAGANZA, CHARLES'S QUEEN,
CAND II (105)	ACT	II	. THE SAME DAY LATER IN THE AFTERNOON. THE SAME ROOM. THE
HART II (84)	ACT	II	. THE SAME ROOM, WITH THE LIGHTS TURNED UP AND THE
ROCK II (234)	ACT	II	. THE SAME SCENE ON THE 10TH NOVEMBER AT 9.30 IN THE
ARMS II (23)	ACT	II	. THE SIXTH OF MARCH, 1886. IN THE GARDEN OF MAJOR
BARB II (273)	ACT	II	. THE YARD OF THE WEST HAM SHELTER OF THE SALVATION ARMY
SIM PREFACE(9)	GEORGE FOX, THOUGH BOTH CROMWELL AND CHARLES	II	LIKED THE MAN AND ADMIRED HIM. NOW THE HERETIC IN RUSSIA
GENV PREFACE(5)	FRIGHTENED ENGLAND IS CAPABLE OF ANYTHING. PHILIP	II	OF SPAIN FRIGHTENED HER. LOUIS XIV OF FRANCE FRIGHTENED
GENV PREFACE(5)	FRIGHTENED HER. NAPOLEON FRIGHTENED HER. WILHELM	II	OF THE GERMAN REICH FRIGHTENED HER. BUT INSTEAD OF
METH PREFACE(R82)	ANGELO COULD NOT VERY WELL BELIEVE IN JULIUS	II	OR LEO X, OR IN MUCH THAT THEY BELIEVED IN; BUT HE COULD
MILL PREFACE(112)	REALM HAD BEEN A TEN-ROOMED VILLA. HAD CATHERINE	II	REIGNED OVER HER HUSBAND ONLY, SHE NEED NOT NOR COULD NOT
LADY PREFACE(212)	PERISHED ON THE SCAFFOLD FOR BLOWING ALEXANDER	II	TO FRAGMENTS, MAY PERHAPS HAVE ECHOED HAMLET'S OH GOD,
KING I SD(187)	THE DUKE OF YORK, THE DUKE, AFTERWARDS JAMES	II	, COMES IN PRECIPITATELY. /JAMES/ (IMPERIOUSLY) WHERE IS
GENV PREFACE(23)	TO INDIVIDUAL, FROM WILLIAM RUFUS TO CHARLES	II	, FROM NERO TO MARCUS AURELIUS, FROM MONMOUTH AND PRINCE
FABL PREFACE(77)	HE OBJECTED HUMANELY TO HIS BEING BURNED. CHARLES	II	, HUMANE (INDEED, AS SOME THINK, TOO HUMANE IN HIS
SUPR HANDBOK(217)	AT A CRITICAL AGE, AS IN THE CASE OF CHARLES	II	, THE SUBJECT BECOMES SANE AND NEVER COMPLETELY RECOVERS
CATH 1,SD(161)	DO MOST WITH THE STILL ABLER EMPRESS CATHERINE	II	, WHO IS NOT A RUSSIAN BUT A GERMAN, BY NO MEANS

III

BUOY III (27)	ACT	III	: THE DISCUSSION. A DRAWINGROOM IN BELGRAVE SQUARE.
SUPR HANDBOK(185)	IN A COMMUNITY WHICH DISCARDED BOTH INSTITUTIONS.	III	: THE PERFECTIONIST EXPERIMENT AT ONEIDA CREEK. IN 1848
MTH3 (89)	PART	III	: THE THING HAPPENS. A SUMMER AFTERNOON IN THE YEAR 2170
METH PREFACE(R69)	OFFICIALS, WHICH WOULD HAVE SCANDALIZED GEORGE	III	AND ELICITED LIBERAL PAMPHLETS FROM CATHERINE II.
HART PREFACE(19)	OF JESUS AND ST FRANCIS TO THE MORALS OF RICHARD	III	AND THE MADNESS OF DON QUIXOTE EXTREMELY IRKSOME. BUT
SUPR HANDBOK(203)	TO PLUME OURSELVES ON OUR SUPERIORITY TO EDWARD	III	AT THE SURRENDER OF CALAIS. AND THE DEMOCRATIC AMERICAN
MILL PREFACE(132)	A WAR. IT WAS NOT ONLY THE LAST CARD OF NAPOLEON	III	BEFORE HE LOST THE GAME: IT PLAYED A CONSIDERABLE PART
OVER PREFACE(165)	OUR ARTIFICIAL LIGHT. WHEN GARRICK PLAYED RICHARD	III	IN SLASHED TRUNK HOSE AND PLUMES, IT WAS NOT BECAUSE HE
MILL III (179)	ACT	III	. A BASEMENT IN THE COMMERCIAL ROAD. AN ELDERLY MAN,
2TRU III (81)	ACT	III	. A NARROW GAP LEADING DOWN TO THE BEACH THROUGH MASSES
SIM PRO,3, (29)	SCENE	III	. A SHELF OF ROCK HALF WAY DOWN THE CLIFF FORMS AN
GENV III (65)	ACT	III	. AFTERNOON IN THE LOUNGE OF A FASHIONABLE RESTAURANT
FANY III (297)	ACT	III	. AGAIN IN THE GILBEY'S DINING ROOM. AFTERNOON. THE
DEVL III (50)	ACT	III	. EARLY NEXT MORNING THE SERGEANT, AT THE BRITISH
SUPR III (71)	ACT	III	. EVENING IN THE SIERRA NEVADA. ROLLING SLOPES OF BROWN
DOCT III (131)	ACT	III	. IN DUBEDAT'S STUDIO. VIEWED FROM THE LARGE WINDOW THE
HART III (129)	ACT	III	. IN THE GARDEN, HECTOR, AS HE COMES OUT THROUGH THE
ARMS III (46)	ACT	III	. IN THE LIBRARY AFTER LUNCH. IT IS NOT MUCH OF A
MRS III (220)	ACT	III	. IN THE RECTORY GARDEN NEXT MORNING, WITH THE SUN
MTH4 III (194)	ACT	III	. INSIDE THE TEMPLE. A GALLERY OVERHANGING AN ABYSS.
JITT III (52)	ACT	III	. MRS HALDENSTEDT IS IN HER SITTING-ROOM WITH ALFRED AND
BARB III (311)	ACT	III	. NEXT DAY AFTER LUNCH LADY BRITOMART IS WRITING IN THE
BULL III (117)	ACT	III	. NEXT MORNING BROADBENT AND LARRY ARE SITTING AT THE
PHIL III (132)	ACT	III	. PARAMORE'S RECEPTION ROOM IN SAVILE ROW. VIEWING THE
CAND III (127)	ACT	III	. PAST TEN IN THE EVENING. THE CURTAINS ARE DRAWN, AND
NEVR III (261)	ACT	III	. THE CLANDONS' SITTING ROOM IN THE HOTEL. AN EXPENSIVE
WIDO III (49)	ACT	III	. THE DRAWING-ROOM IN SARTORIUS'S HOUSE IN BEDFORD
CLEO III (144)	ACT	III	. THE EDGE OF THE QUAY IN FRONT OF THE PALACE, LOOKING
LION PREFACE(94)	TELLS YOU DISPROVES THE EXISTENCE OF WILLIAM	III	. THE GOSPEL NARRATIVES IN THE MAIN GIVE YOU A BIOGRAPHY
METH PREFACE(R13)	THEY ARE OPPOSING TO THEM THE IDEAS OF RICHARD	III	. THUS THE EDUCATED MAN IS A GREATER NUISANCE THAN THE
CAPT III (272)	ACT	III	. TORRID FORENOON FILTERED THROUGH SMALL MOORISH WINDOWS
BASH III (119)	ACT	III	. WILTSTOKEN. A ROOM IN THE WARREN LODGE. LYDIA AT HER
PHIL I SD(69)	(AFTER MACLISE), SIR HENRY IRVING AS RICHARD	III	(AFTER LONG), ELLEN TERRY, MRS KENDAL, ADA REHAN, SARAH
SUPR PREFACE(R14)	JUST AS IT MADE PETER A BOLDER KING THAN GEORGE	III	; BUT AS IT WAS, AFTER ALL, ONLY A NEGATIVE
OVER PREFACE(165)	COMBINATION OF THE STATE ROBES OF GEORGE	III	WITH SUCH SCRAPS OF OLDER FASHIONS AS SEEMED TO
CYMB FORWORD(133)	A HAPPY ENDING TO KING LEAR, CIBBER'S RICHARD	III	, A LOVE SCENE IN THE TOMB OF THE CAPULETS BETWEEN ROMEO
6CAL (93)	TOLD? GOGSWOONS, WHY WAS I NOT TOLD? (EDWARD	III	, AGED 35, DASHES FROM HIS PAVILION, FOAMING). OUT! (
LADY PREFACE(220)	AND TO CONDEMN THEM AS OUT OF CHARACTER, RICHARD	III	, IMMEDIATELY AFTER PITYING HIMSELF BECAUSE " THERE IS
6CAL SD(93)	THE LAST DAY OF THE SIEGE. THE PAVILION OF EDWARD	III	, KING OF ENGLAND, IS ON YOUR LEFT AS YOU FACE THE
SUPR PREFACE(R33)	OWN APPETITES AND INSTINCTS AND HUMORS. RICHARD	III	, TOO, IS DELIGHTFUL AS THE WHIMSICAL COMEDIAN WHO STOPS
DEVL EPILOG (82)	A CENTURY AGO BECAUSE THEY PREFERRED GEORGE	III	, WERE QUITE PREPARED TO LOSE SOUTH AFRICA TODAY BECAUSE

IKY

APPL I (209)	CANNOT PRETEND TO YOUR GIFTS, AM VERY GLAD THAT	IKY	CANNOT UPSET ME AS LONG AS I AM THE NEPHEW OF MY UNCLE.
APPL I (209)	THE MULTITUDE! /BOANERGES/ YOURE THINKING OF	IKY	JACOBUS? HE IS ONLY A TALKER. (SNAPPING HIS FINGERS) I

IKY'S

APPL I (209)	AND MINE. /BOANERGES/ THAT'S TRUE. BUT I CAN TALK	IKY'S	HEAD OFF. /MAGNUS/ LUCKY MAN: YOU HAVE ALL THE TRUMPS

IL

SUPR III (98)	IN THE FRENCH MANNER) VIVAN LE FEMMINE! VIVA	IL	BUON VINO! /THE STATUE/ (TAKING UP THE TUNE AN OCTAVE
MILL PREFACE(122)	DIFFERENT; BUT HE HAD ONE QUALITY IN COMMON WITH	IL	DUCE: HE KNEW WHAT THE VICTORIOUS ALLIES WOULD FIGHT FOR
MILL PREFACE(121)	BLIND TO THE FACT STARING THEM IN THE FACE THAT	IL	DUCE, KNOWING WHAT THE PEOPLE WANTED AND GIVING IT TO
MILL PREFACE(121)	STUART MILL'S ESSAY ON LIBERTY. MUSSOLINI, NOW	IL	DUCE, NEVER EVEN LOOKED ROUND: HE WAS BUSY SWEEPING UP
FANY III (308)	SIR, THAT MISS KNOX IS A LADY ABSOLUTELY COMME	IL	FAUT? /DUVALLET/ PERFECTLY. BUT THE OTHER? /JUGGINS/
SUPR PREFACE(R13)	TO REPENT; BUT IN WHAT TERMS! " OUI, MA FOI!	IL	FAUT S'AMENDER, ENCORE VINGT OU TRENTE ANS DE CETTE
SUPR PREFACE(R16)	GROUP THEMSELVES PATHETICALLY TO SING " PROTEGGA	IL	GIUSTO CIELO"; THEY GRASP FORMIDABLE LEGAL AND SOCIAL
BUOY III (44)	EXPERIENCE IS MOTHERHOOD. CELIBACY FOR A WOMAN IS	IL	GRAN RIFIUTO, THE GREAT REFUSAL OF HER DESTINY, OF THE
JITT PREFACE(5)	HEART: THE VILLAIN MAY, LIKE THE WICKED COUNT IN	IL	TROVATORE, LIVE ONLY TO CENTUPLICAR LA MORTE OF THE HERO

		ILE	
CAPT I (227)	SAY, TOUCHING HIS FORELOCK) AWLL ENG ABAHT WITHIN	ILE	, GAVNER, HIN KICE AW SHOULD BE WORNTED. (HE GOES INTO
		ILIAD	
JOAN PREFACE(25)	PECKSNIFFIAN. SAMUEL BUTLER BELIEVED THE	ILIAD	TO BE A BURLESQUE OF GREEK JINGOISM AND GREEK
		ILIADS	
3PLA PREFACE(R37)	ACHILLES AND AJAX AS HEROES TO THE WORLD IN THE	ILIADS	. IN DUE TIME CAME SHAKESPEAR, WHO SAID, VIRTUALLY: I
		ILL	
CURE (233)	YOUVE NO RIGHT TO BULLY ME LIKE THIS. I'M	ILL	: I CANT BEAR IT. I'LL THROW MYSELF OUT OF THE WINDOW.
DOCT I (101)	ARE ALL CLERKS AND SHOPMEN. THEY DARENT BE	ILL	: THEY CANT AFFORD IT, AND WHEN THEY BREAK DOWN, WHAT
BARB II (282)	HIS NAME IN HER NOTE BOOK). /BILL/ OO'S JENNY	ILL	? AND WOT CALL AS SHE TO PRY FOR ME? /BARBARA/ I DONT
JITT II (44)	AWAY FOR? /JITTA/ HAVE YOU FORGOTTEN THAT I AM	ILL	? I CAN HARDLY STAND. I MUST LIE DOWN. /ALFRED/ WELL,
SUPR IV (170)	(RUNNING BETWEEN ANN AND TANNER) ARE YOU	ILL	? /ANN/ (REELING, WITH A SUPREME EFFORT) I HAVE
MTH3 (101)	TABLE. /BURGE-LUBIN/ WHATS THE MATTER? ARE YOU	ILL	? /BARNABAS/ (CHOKING) NO. I-- (HE COLLAPSES INTO THE
DOCT I (102)	/WALPOLE/ (INTERESTED) WHAT? YOURE NEVER	ILL	? /B.B./ NEVER. /WALPOLE/ THATS INTERESTING. I BELIEVE
PHIL II (112)	WHATS THE MATTER, PARAMORE? /JULIA/ ARE YOU	ILL	? /CUTHBERTSON/ NO BAD NEWS, I HOPE? /PARAMORE/ (
JITT II (29)	FIRST? /FESSLER/ BUT DIDNT YOU KNOW THAT HE WAS	ILL	? /LENKHEIM/ OH, I KNEW ABOUT HIS HEART AND SO FORTH.
SUPR IV (160)	HIS HEAD) WHATS THE MATTER, TAVY? ARE YOU	ILL	? /OCTAVIUS/ NO, NOTHING, NOTHING. /MRS WHITEFIELD/ (
DOCT I (98)	MUST BE A GERM: ELSE HOW COULD THE PATIENT BE	ILL	? /SIR PATRICK/ CAN YOU SHEW ME THE GERM OF OVERWORK..
SUPR IV (160)	THAT AWFUL OLD IRISHMAN. ARE YOU SURE YOURE NOT	ILL	? WHATS THE MATTER? /OCTAVIUS/ (AFFECTIONATELY) IT'S
FABL V (118)	FROM THE SHOCK OR DIE, WHEN THE PATIENT WAS	ILL	ALL OVER AND COULD NOT BE CUT TO PIECES THEY DOSED HIM
2TRU III (106)	TO HER. SHE WAS A HORRID SELFISH GIRL, ALWAYS	ILL	AND COMPLAINING, AND NEVER SATISFIED, NO MATTER HOW MUCH
BARB II (288)	IT, AW TELL YOU. CHACK IT. AW'M SICK O YOUR JENNY	ILL	AND ER SILLY LITTLE FICE. /BARBARA/ THEN WHY DO YOU KEEP
WIDO III (50)	PREYING ON YOUR SPIRITS, I MUST INSIST ON BEING	ILL	AND HAVE SOMETHING PREYING ON MINE. AND INDEED, MY GIRL,
2TRU I (28)	ME FROM MY SUFFERINGS? WHAT RIGHT HAS SHE TO GET	ILL	AND MAKE ME ILL LIKE THIS? MEASLES: THATS WHAT SHE'S
MIS. PREFACE(99)	THUS SPAKE ZOROASTER IS LESS COMFORTING TO THE	ILL	AND UNHAPPY THAN THE PSALMS; BUT IT IS MUCH TRUER,
PHIL II (116)	SHOULDER). /JULIA/ SILLY: ONLY THINK! DAD'S NOT	ILL	AT ALL. IT WAS ONLY A MISTAKE OF DR PARAMORE'S. OH,
MRS IV SD(245)	BLACK SILK MANTLE. SHE IS PITIABLY ANXIOUS AND	ILL	AT EASE: EVIDENTLY PANIC-STRICKEN. /MRS WARREN/ (TO
BULL IV (158)	THAT HE HAS NOTHING ELSE TO SAY, AND BEING	ILL	AT EASE IN CONSEQUENCE, HE STROLLS ABOUT THE ROOM
CAND I (95)	NOTICED THAT HE SAID SOMETHING FUNNY; BUT I AM SO	ILL	AT EASE WITH STRANGERS; AND I NEVER CAN SEE A JOKE. I'M
CLEO III SD(155)	AT THE PARAPET LOOKING OUT ANXIOUSLY, EVIDENTLY	ILL	AT EASE. BRITANNUS COMES OUT OF THE LIGHTHOUSE DOOR.
MRS I (187)	I KNOW FAR LESS THAN YOU DO. /PRAED/ (VERY	ILL	AT EASE) IN THAT CASE-- (HE STOPS, QUITE AT A LOSS.
BULL III SD(125)	THE SAKE OF THEIR APPEARANCE. MATTHEW HAFFIGAN,	ILL	AT EASE, COASTS THE GARDEN SHYLY ON THE SHRUBBERY SIDE
MTH2 SD(54)	BRINGS OUT THE FACT THAT THEY ARE UNHAPPY MEN,	ILL	AT EASE, SQUARE PEGS IN ROUND HOLES, WHILST HE
FANY III (318)	YOU THAT IS THE CORRECT THING. (THEY SIT DOWN,	ILL	AT EASE, WHILST HE PLACES THE TRAY ON THE TABLE. HE THEN
LION PREFACE(46)	THE MODERN PHYSICIAN TELLS HIS PATIENT THAT HE IS	ILL	BECAUSE EVERY DROP OF HIS BLOOD IS SWARMING WITH A
DOCT PREFACE(17)	OF THE MALADE IMAGINAIRE (WHO IS ALWAYS REALLY	ILL	BECAUSE, AS THERE IS NO SUCH THING AS PERFECT HEALTH,
AUGS (268)	THEY GOT THE CHANCE. /AUGUSTUS/ BEAMISH: IT'S AN	ILL	BIRD THAT FOULS ITS OWN NEST. /THE CLERK/ IT WASNT ME
SUPR PREFACE(R25)	MISGOVERNMENT, WILL RUIN US IF OUR CITIZENS ARE	ILL	BRED. WHEN WE TWO WERE BORN, THIS COUNTRY WAS STILL
BARB PREFACE(218)	NOSES AT THEIR NEIGHBORS' DRAINS, AND ARE MADE	ILL	BY THE ARCHITECTURE OF THEIR NEIGHBORS' HOUSES. TRADE
BARB III (339)	PEOPLE, ABJECT PEOPLE, DIRTY PEOPLE, ILL FED,	ILL	CLOTHED PEOPLE. THEY POISON US MORALLY AND PHYSICALLY:
SIM PREFACE(9)	AND GENTLEMEN WHILST LABORERS ARE UNDERFED,	ILL	CLOTHED, AND SLEEPING TWO OR THREE IN A BED AND TEN IN A
JOAN PREFACE(6)	MORE AN IDOLATER THAN THE POPE HIMSELF, AND NOT	ILL	CONDUCTED IN ANY SENSE APART FROM HER SOLDIERING, HER
CATH PREFACE(159)	ME EXCLAIM, " HOW OFT THE SIGHT OF MEANS TO DO	ILL	DEEDS MAKES DEEDS ILL DONE! " BUT BURBAGE MAY HAVE
BARB II (309)	SAMMUN ELSE EZ. WERES IT GORN? BLY ME IF JENNY	ILL	DIDNT TIKE IT ARTER ALL! /RUMMY/ (SCREAMING AT HIM
CATH PREFACE(159)	THE SIGHT OF MEANS TO DO ILL DEEDS MAKES DEEDS	ILL	DONE! " BUT BURBAGE MAY HAVE FLOURISHED THE PROMPT COPY
CAND I SD(77)	STONY PAVEMENTS, SLATED ROOFS, AND RESPECTABLY	ILL	DRESSED OR DISREPUTABLY WORSE DRESSED PEOPLE, QUITE
BARB III (339)	OF POOR PEOPLE, ABJECT PEOPLE, DIRTY PEOPLE,	ILL	FED, ILL CLOTHED PEOPLE. THEY POISON US MORALLY AND
MTH2 (62)	A LITTLE SO AS TO LET THEM DOWN WITHOUT CREATING	ILL	FEELING IN THE WORKING-CLASS ELECTORATE. IN SHORT, I CAN
PYGM V (280)	HER VEXATION) OH WELL, JUST TO SHEW THERES NO	ILL	FEELING. I'LL BE BACK IN A MOMENT. (SHE GOES OUT).
PPP SD(195)	DAGGER NERVOUSLY GRIPPED IN HIS RIGHT HAND BODE	ILL	FOR THE SLEEPING LADY. PROVIDENTIALLY SHE SNEEZES ON THE
JITT II (36)	HE WAS TOO CONSIDERATE TO LET YOU KNOW HOW	ILL	HE WAS. /EDITH/ HE TOLD EVERYONE ELSE. WE WERE LEFT IN
MIS. PREFACE(47)	QUITE THE CONTRARY HAPPENS. JUST AS OUR	ILL	HEALTH DELIVERS US INTO THE HANDS OF MEDICAL QUACKS AND
LIED (200)	ACQUAINTANCE. /HER HUSBAND/ (SHORTLY, SHEWING	ILL	HUMOR FOR THE FIRST TIME) OH! INDEED! (HE LEAVES HIS
HART PREFACE(31)	WHICH HAD DRIVEN THEM TO THE THEATRE IN AN	ILL	HUMOR TO SEEK SOME SORT OF DISTRACTION, HAD ONLY TO
DEST (176)	HOW COULD I TELL YOU THAT? /NAPOLEON/ (	ILL	HUMOREDLY, BEGINNING TO WALK ABOUT AGAIN IN ANGRY
MILL I (153)	BE CONTENT WITH A SINGLE OPINION. WHEN I FEEL	ILL	I ALWAYS CONSULT AT LEAST HALF A DOZEN DOCTORS. THE
DEVL I (6)	MY FAULT. WHEN WE GOT TO NEVINSTOWN WE FOUND HIM	ILL	IN BED. HE DIDNT KNOW US AT FIRST. THE MINISTER SAT UP
INCA (244)	FOR A WEEK. TELL HIM TO CALL TOMORROW: SAY I'M	ILL	IN BED. I CANT: I WONT: I DARENT: YOU MUST GET RID OF
ROCK PREFACE(183)	AND WELL INFORMED OPINION AND SENTIMENTAL AND	ILL	INFORMED IMPULSE. /JESUS/ NEVERTHELESS, OPINION IS A
BASH II,1, (104)	AGAIN? /LYDIA/ NO, LUCIAN. HE HATH USED ME VERY	ILL	. HE SHOULD HAVE TOLD ME. I WILL NE'ER FORGIVE HIM. SAY,
SUPR I (13)	OF ABUSING-- /TANNER/ DONT, TAVY: YOULL MAKE ME	ILL	. I AM NOT A MAN OF HONOR: I AM A MAN STRUCK DOWN BY A
2TRU I (37)	CAN BE SO THOUGHTLESS AND CLUMSY WHEN I AM SO	ILL	. I AM SUFFERING HORRIBLY. SHUT THAT WINDOW AND SWITCH
MTH4 I (141)	GENTLEMAN/ (NERVED BY INDIGNATION) I AM NOT	ILL	. I HAVE NEVER HAD A DAY'S ILLNESS IN MY LIFE. /THE
2TRU II (52)	SAXBY HAS JUST RETURNED TO THE BASE, SERIOUSLY	ILL	. I HAVE TAKEN OVER FROM HIM. I AM COLONEL TALLBOYS.
JITT II (31)	BE ABLE TO CALL ON THEM. I HAVE BEEN REALLY TOO	ILL	. I HOPE THEY KNOW THAT. /FESSLER/ (WITH AFFECTIONATE
MILL II (173)	NOR ATTRACTIVE TO ME EXCEPT WHEN THEY ARE	ILL	. I KNOW TOO MUCH ABOUT THEM, INSIDE AND OUT. YOU ARE
MILL IV (206)	A PRIME MINISTER WHEN HE IMAGINED HIMSELF TO BE	ILL	. I WENT TO HIM AND TOLD HIM THAT IT WAS THE WILL OF
FABL PREFACE(90)	AS IT CALLS IN THE DOCTOR WHEN THE PATIENT IS NOT	ILL	. IN THE ARMY SOME THIRTY INOCULATIONS ARE PRACTICALLY
MIS. (174)	AGO; AND THAT YOUR VOICE SOUNDED AS IF YOU WERE	ILL	. (SHE COMES BETWEEN TARLETON AND THE MAN). IS ANYTHING
DOCT PREFACE(53)	WENT TO BED OR CONSIDERED THEMSELVES AS SERIOUSLY	ILL	. NEITHER JENNER, NOR ANY OTHER DOCTOR EVER, AS FAR AS I
MTH4 I (152)	MY KNEES ARE TREMBLING. I FEAR I AM REALLY	ILL	. NOT SO YOUNG AS I WAS. /ZOO/ I NOTICED THAT YOU ARE
CAND II (114)	ARE YOU ILL, EUGENE? /MARCHBANKS/ NO: NOT	ILL	. ONLY HORROR! HORROR! HORROR! (HE BOWS HIS HEAD ON
BARB I (260)	CHOLLY: THE VULGARITY OF IT POSITIVELY MAKES ME	ILL	. /BARBARA/ IT'S ALL RIGHT, MOTHER: CHOLLY IS QUITE
JOAN 6 (133)	BUT THE BISHOP SENT ME SOME CARP; AND IT MADE ME	ILL	. /CAUCHON/ I AM SORRY. I TOLD THEM TO SEE THAT IT WAS
JITT III (61)	SORT OF HYPOCHONDRIA; AND IT MAY MAKE YOU REALLY	ILL	. /EDITH/ (SCORNFULLY) YES, I KNOW. WHAT CANT BE CURED
OVER (174)	NOTHING! (RISING ANXIOUSLY) NONSENSE: YOURE	ILL	. /GREGORY/ NO. IT WAS SOMETHING ABOUT YOUR LATE
BASH II,1, (101)	YOUR HAND-- A CHAIR-- /BASHVILLE/ MADAM: YOURE	ILL	. /LYDIA/ PROCEED. WHAT YOU HAVE READ I DO NOT
DEVL II (35)	/CHRISTY/ (COMING FURTHER IN) MOTHER'S VERY	ILL	. /RICHARD/ WELL, DOES SHE WANT TO SEE ME? /CHRISTY/
CURE (232)	TO HER PLAINTIVELY) DONT YOU SEE THAT I AM	ILL	. /STREGA/ I SEE THAT YOU ARE MENTALLY AFFLICTED. BUT
CURE (231)	LEAVE THE ROOM. /REGINALD/ BUT, YOU KNOW, I AM	ILL	. /STREGA/ THEN GO TO BED, AND SEND FOR A DOCTOR. (SHE
SUPR III (97)	WITH LOVE AND JOY-- /DON JUAN/ YOU ARE MAKING ME	ILL	. /THE DEVIL/ THERE! (APPEALING TO THE STATUE) YOU
MTH4 I (141)	HIS SOBS CHOKE HIM). /THE WOMAN/ YOU SEE, YOU ARE	ILL	. /THE ELDERLY GENTLEMAN/ (NERVED BY INDIGNATION) I AM
GENV IV (124)	/SECRETARY/ LET HIM ALONE. THE SHOCK HAS MADE HIM	ILL	. /THE JEW/ NO: NOT THAT. I MUST TELEPHONE (HE GOES
BUOY III (30)	HE ALWAYS CALLS IN A DIFFERENT DOCTOR WHEN HE IS	ILL	. /THE YOUTH/ HE PICKS UP HIS SOLICITOR FOR THE JOB,
PYGM V (276)	/LIZA/ BUT OF COURSE YOU ARE: YOU ARE NEVER	ILL	. SO GLAD TO SEE YOU AGAIN, COLONEL PICKERING. (HE
JITT III (69)	ME TO MAKE YOU TALK AND LAUGH SO MUCH, AND YOU SO	ILL	. YOURE VERY PALE, DEAR. CAN I GET YOU ANYTHING?
SIM I (39)	AND PREACH; BUT IT WAS ONLY TO MAKE THEMSELVES	ILL	LAUGHING AT ME. THOUGH PERHAPS I SHOULDNT SAY THAT. SOME
2TRU I (28)	WHAT RIGHT HAS SHE TO GET ILL AND MAKE ME	ILL	LIKE THIS? MEASLES: THATS WHAT SHE'S GOT. MEASLES!
LADY PREFACE(217)	AS A GENTLEMAN UNDER A CLOUD THROUGH HIS FATHER'S	ILL	LUCK IN BUSINESS, AND NEVER FOR A MOMENT AS A MAN OF THE
SUPR IV (159)	TAVY. /OCTAVIUS/ I HAVE NO HOPE, ANN: I ACCEPT MY	ILL	LUCK. BUT I DONT THINK YOU QUITE KNOW HOW MUCH IT HURTS.
GETT PREFACE(237)	EVEN DOES IT. YET WE EXPECT HIM TO FACE HIS	ILL	LUCK, AND NEVER DREAM OF FORCING THE WOMAN TO ACCEPT
BULL IV (154)	OF THOSE TALES OF UNMERITED MISFORTUNE, OF CRUEL	ILL	LUCK, OF RELENTLESS PERSECUTION BY DESTINY, WHICH
MIS. PREFACE(10)	AND AT LEAST IT WAS NOT A TRIVIAL VIEW, NOR AN	ILL	MEANT ONE. IT WAS MUCH MORE RESPECTABLE THAN THE GENERAL
WIDO II (30)	ARE NOT GOING THE RIGHT WAY ABOUT IT IN SPEAKING	ILL	OF MR SARTORIUS. /LICKCHEESE/ HAVE I SAID ONE WORD
LION PREFACE(25)	DANGER SO STRONGLY, THAT WHEN PEOPLE WHO WERE NOT	ILL	OR IN TROUBLE CAME TO HIM AND ASKED HIM TO EXERCISE HIS
DOCT PREFACE(6)	MUST BELIEVE IN WHAT YOU HAVE. WHEN YOUR CHILD IS	ILL	OR YOUR WIFE DYING, AND YOU HAPPEN TO BE VERY FOND OF
LION PREFACE(37)	THE PRISONER WILL NOT SPEAK TO HIM. WHEN JESUS IS	ILL	RECEIVED IN A SAMARITAN VILLAGE JAMES AND JOHN PROPOSE
PPP (201)	HAIR AT THE BACK OF THE BUST'S HEAD: IT MAKES HIM	ILL	). YAH, I CANNOT. I CANNOT. NOT EVEN YOUR BUST,
JITT I (24)	YOUR MIND. I HAVE KNOWN ALL ALONG THAT YOU WERE	ILL	; AND MY ONLY FEAR WAS THAT THAT (SHE REPEATS HIS
CAPT I (220)	GOOD. THEY COME TO ME FOR MEDICINE WHEN THEY ARE	ILL	; AND THEY CALL ME THE CHRISTIAN WHO IS NOT A THIEF.
DOCT IV (158)	PAPER THIS MORNING SAYING THAT LOUIS IS SERIOUSLY	ILL	; AND THIS MAN WANTS TO INTERVIEW HIM ABOUT IT. HOW CAN
DOCT I (107)	CANT ALL BE GENIUSES LIKE YOU. EVERY FOOL CAN GET	ILL	; BUT EVERY FOOL CANT BE A GOOD DOCTOR: THERE ARE NOT
NEVR II (254)	SHE CONTINUES INDIFFERENTLY) I THOUGHT HE WAS	ILL	; BUT HE RECOVERED HIMSELF. HE WOULDNT WAIT FOR YOU. I

SIM PREFACE(13)	LIVE ON THIS EARTH; AND I CONSIDER IT MONEY VERY	ILL	SPENT. FOR IF THE PEOPLE WHO LIVE ON MY EARNINGS WERE
SUPR III (97)	OF THAT PRIEST-RIDDEN PLACE. YOU HAVE HEARD ME	ILL	SPOKEN OF; AND YET, BELIEVE ME, I HAVE HOSTS OF FRIENDS
NEVR I SD(218)	MAN OF ABOUT SIXTY, WITH AN ATROCIOUSLY OBSTINATE	ILL	TEMPERED GRASPING MOUTH, AND A DOGMATIC VOICE. THERE IS
6CAL SD(103)	PAROXYSM OF TEARS: HAS COMPLETELY DISCHARGED HIS	ILL	TEMPER. IT DAWNS ON HIM THAT THROUGH PETER HE MAY GET
PHIL I (78)	YOU OF HABITUAL AND INTOLERABLE JEALOUSY AND	ILL	TEMPER; OF INSULTING ME ON IMAGINARY PROVOCATION; OF
MIS. PREFACE(29)	EVEN WHEN THIS EXCUSE OF BAD MANNERS,	ILL	TEMPER, AND BRUTISHNESS (FOR THAT IS WHAT IT COMES TO)
MIS. PREFACE(56)	WERE INNOCENT OF ANYTHING WORSE THAN STUPIDITY,	ILL	TEMPER, AND INABILITY TO DISCOVER OTHER METHODS OF
3PLA PREFACE(R13)	AT A MOMENT WHEN MISS ELLEN TERRY WAS TOO	ILL	TO APPEAR, THE THEATRE HAD TO BE CLOSED AFTER A BRIEF
DOCT PREFACE(6)	CASES WHERE THE PATIENT IS AN ADULT AND NOT TOO	ILL	TO DECIDE THE STEPS TO BE TAKEN. WE ARE SUBJECT TO
HART PREFACE(13)	WHERE THE EVIDENCE AS TO THEIR BEING KILLED BY	ILL	TREATMENT WAS SO UNEQUIVOCAL THAT THE VERDICT WOULD
CAPT III (274)	SO. /RANKIN/ (WITH A MOMENTARY SENSE OF	ILL	USAGE) I THINK SIR HOWRRD MIGHT HAVE TOLD ME THAT. /LADY
CLEO II (138)	/RUFIO/ (WITH A SUDDEN SPLUTTER OF RAGING	ILL	USAGE, COMING DOWN TO CAESAR AND SCOLDING HIM) CAN I
BULL III (130)	/MATTHEW/ WAS PATSY FARRLL EVER ILL USED AS I WAS	ILL	USED? TELL ME DHAT. /LARRY/ HE WILL BE, IF EVER HE GETS
BULL III (130)	OWN A FEW FIELDS. /MATTHEW/ WAS PATSY FARRLL EVER	ILL	USED AS I WAS ILL USED? TELL ME DHAT. /LARRY/ HE WILL
PHIL I (79)	LETTERS; AND THEN REPRESENTING YOURSELF AS AN	ILL	USED SAINT AND MARTYR WANTONLY BETRAYED AND DESERTED BY
PLES PREFACE(R16)	THEM WITH ALL THE SUBTLETY NEEDED TO CONCEAL MY	ILL	WILL FROM MYSELF AS WELL AS FROM THE MANAGER. THE MAIN
PLES PREFACE(R16)	I HAVE NONE TO COMPLAIN OF. I HAVE COME UPON NO	ILL	WILL, NO INACCESSIBILITY, ON THE PART OF THE VERY FEW
DOCT PREFACE(65)	DEPENDS, NOT ON THE NUMBER OF PEOPLE WHO ARE	ILL	, AND WHOM HE CAN KEEP ILL, BUT ON THE NUMBER OF PEOPLE
DOCT PREFACE(65)	OF PEOPLE WHO ARE ILL, AND WHOM HE CAN KEEP	ILL	, BUT ON THE NUMBER OF PEOPLE WHO ARE WELL. HE IS
MIS. (115)	THE USE? WHATS HAPPENED? /MRS TARLETON/ ARE YOU	ILL	, CHILD? (THEY GET HIM UP). THERE, THERE, PET! IT'S
CAND II (114)	HURRIES TO THE SOFA). WHATS THE MATTER? ARE YOU	ILL	, EUGENE? /MARCHBANKS/ NO: NOT ILL. ONLY HORROR!
PHIL II SD(103)	HEAVING. PARAMORE, SEEING THE COLONEL APPARENTLY	ILL	, HURRIES DOWN TO HIM WITH HIS BEDSIDE MANNER IN FULL
GETT (342)	HER FROM FALLING) WHATS THE MATTER? ARE YOU	ILL	, MRS COLLINS? (HE GETS HER BACK INTO HER CHAIR).
2TRU I (28)	/THE MONSTER/ OH! OH! ! OH! ! ! I AM SO	ILL	! SO MISERABLE! OH, I WISH I WERE DEAD. WHY DOESNT SHE
BULL III (141)	CAUSE YOU MIDE IT BY CHACKIN A FEW STOWNS DAHN A	ILL	! WELL, WOT PRAWCE MAW GRENFAWTHER, OI SHOULD LAWK TO
		ILLBRED	
JOAN 4 (104)	SAW SOMETHING OF THE MAHOMETANS. THEY WERE NOT SO	ILLBRED	AS I HAD BEEN LED TO BELIEVE. IN SOME RESPECTS THEIR
KING I (218)	GUTTER DIRT. /CHARLES/ FOR SHAME, NELLY! IT WAS	ILLBRED	OF YOU TO REPROACH HER GRACE FOR THE MOST AMIABLE
		ILLEGAL	
ROCK II (259)	WILL NOT ENFORCE YOUR DECISIONS IF THEY ARE	ILLEGAL	. THE CIVIL SERVANTS WILL SABOTAGE YOU EVEN IF THEY
POSN PREFACE(396)	AND PROSTITUTION-- FOR INSTANCE, AN UNSUCCESSFUL	ILLEGAL	OPERATION (SUCCESSFUL ONES ARE TOLERATED) OR
APPL PREFACE(178)	ABOLISH THE SEA; THAT I AM GOING TO MAKE BATHING	ILLEGAL	; THAT I AM OUT TO RUIN OUR CARRYING TRADE AND LAY
GENV I (46)	DISCOVERED THAT SHE HAD BEEN HYPNOTIZED BY THIS	ILLEGAL	SOCIETY. I WARNED OUR SECRET POLICE, FORMERLY KNOWN
ROCK PREFACE(163)	UNDER A CRIMINAL CODE OF HAVING TAKEN A SINGLE	ILLEGAL	STEP, BUT QUITE EASY TO CONVINCE ANY REASONABLE BODY
HART II (116)	DOES ANY MODERN GIRL BELIEVE THAT THE LEGAL AND	ILLEGAL	WAYS OF GETTING MONEY ARE THE HONEST AND DISHONEST
		ILLEGALITY	
HART PREFACE(14)	REASON. IN EUROPEAN COURTS THERE WAS VINDICTIVE	ILLEGALITY	: IN AMERICAN COURTS THERE WAS RAVING LUNACY. IT
		ILLEGIBLE	
AUGS (277)	LADY/ (PUZZLING OVER IT) IT IS REALLY ALMOST	ILLEGIBLE	. I THINK THE BEGINNING IS MEANT FOR " DEAREST
		ILLEGITIMATE	
GETT PREFACE(188)	HAMILTON, WAS IDOLIZED. SHELLEY MIGHT HAVE HAD AN	ILLEGITIMATE	CHILD IN EVERY COUNTY IN ENGLAND IF HE HAD DONE
GETT PREFACE(203)	ON THESE VIEWS, HE IS BOUND TO PREFER ONE HEALTHY	ILLEGITIMATE	CHILD TO TEN RICKETY LEGITIMATE ONES, AND ONE
FABL PREFACE(82)	THAT THE RECTOR IS THE FATHER OF HIS HOUSEMAID'S	ILLEGITIMATE	CHILD; AND AFTER THAT YOU MAY TELL ME THAT THE
		ILLHUMOREDLY	
GENV III (67)	ON THE LEAGUE LAST NIGHT? /THE SECRETARY/ (	ILLHUMOREDLY	) YES. HALF ABOUT HARROW AS A NURSERY FOR
MIS. (162)	AHA! ARNT YOU GLAD IVE CAUGHT YOU? /PERCIVAL/ (	ILLHUMOREDLY	TURNING AWAY FROM HER AND COMING TOWARDS THE
		ILLIBERAL	
POSN PREFACE(408)	IN WHICH THE LORD CHAMBERLAIN IS EQUALLY	ILLIBERAL	, THAT PARTICULAR IS THE ASSUMPTION THAT A DRAPED
POSN PREFACE(408)	CALLED MUSIC HALLS) HAS BEEN VERY FAR FROM	ILLIBERAL	, EXCEPT IN THE ONE PARTICULAR IN WHICH THE LORD
		ILLIBERALLY	
PYGM EPILOG (297)	AND HAD TO SCRAPE ALONG AT HOME WITH AN	ILLIBERALLY	TREATED GENERAL SERVANT. UNDER SUCH
POSN PREFACE(408)	TO STAMP OUT THE THEATRE, OR EVEN TO TREAT IT	ILLIBERALLY	, WOULD HAVE A CHANCE OF ADOPTION. MUNICIPAL
		ILLICIT	
GETT PREFACE(239)	REFUSING TO SUBMIT TO THE CONDEMNATION, FORMING	ILLICIT	CONNECTIONS TO AN EXTENT WHICH THREATENS TO
SUPR PREFACE(R11)	SORT OF PLAYS WHICH TRADE ON THE TRADITION THAT	ILLICIT	LOVE AFFAIRS ARE AT ONCE VICIOUS AND DELIGHTFUL, WE
LION PREFACE(95)	FOR SAYING THAT IF A MODERN GIRL ACCOUNTED FOR AN	ILLICIT	PREGNANCY BY SAYING SHE HAD CONCEIVED OF THE HOLY
GETT PREFACE(229)	DIRECTLY PROSECUTED; AND THIS IMPUNITY EXTENDS TO	ILLICIT	RELATIONS BETWEEN UNMARRIED PERSONS WHO HAVE REACHED
MRS PREFACE(161)	IF THE OLD RULE AGAINST THE EXHIBITION OF	ILLICIT	SEX RELATIONS ON THE STAGE WERE REVIVED, AND THE
GETT PREFACE(184)	SO CONVINCINGLY IN LES HANNETONS, AN AVOWEDLY	ILLICIT	UNION IS OFTEN FOUND IN PRACTICE TO BE AS TYRANNICAL
GETT PREFACE(183)	CITE THE EXAMPLE OF GEORGE ELIOT, WHO FORMED AN	ILLICIT	UNION WITH LEWES. THEY QUOTE A SAYING ATTRIBUTED TO
GETT PREFACE(203)	ONE AND A HALF, HE WOULD BE BOUND TO ENCOURAGE	ILLICIT	UNIONS AND DISCOURAGE AND EVEN PENALIZE MARRIAGE.
GETT PREFACE(203)	HUSBANDS AND WIVES. IF IT COULD BE PROVED THAT	ILLICIT	UNIONS PRODUCE THREE CHILDREN EACH AND MARRIAGES
GETT PREFACE(183)	THE BOLDER AND MORE REBELLIOUS SPIRITS FORM	ILLICIT	UNIONS, DEFIANTLY SENDING CARDS ROUND TO THEIR
		ILLICITLY	
BULL II SD(111)	IS REVIVED BY THE PRODUCTION OF A BOTTLE OF	ILLICITLY	DISTILLED WHISKY, CALLED POTCHEEN, WHICH HE HAS
UNPL PREFACE(R26)	TO ATTACH THEMSELVES TO BREADWINNERS, LICITLY OR	ILLICITLY	, ON PAIN OF HEAVY PRIVATION AND DISADVANTAGE; BUT
		ILLITERACIES	
BASH PREFACE(89)	HAVE OCCASION TO DO, I FIND IN THEM SUCH	ILLITERACIES	AS HE EXITS, SHE EXITS, THEY EXIT ETC. ETC.
		ILLITERACY	
DOCT IV SD(159)	SPIRITS THROUGH A DAILY STRUGGLE WITH HIS OWN	ILLITERACY	AND THE PRECARIOUSNESS OF HIS EMPLOYMENT. HE HAS
ROCK PREFACE(171)	OF FUTURE CITIZENS. ALL WILL AGREE TO EXTERMINATE	ILLITERACY	BY COMPULSORY READING, WRITING, AND ARITHMETIC:
6CAL PREFACE(89)	PLAY WAS THE EXPOSURE IT ELICITED OF THE QUAINT	ILLITERACY	OF OUR MODERN LONDON JOURNALISTS. THEIR ONLY
SUPR HANDBOK(177)	TO PANTHEISTIC HUMANITARIANISM, FROM GENERAL	ILLITERACY	TO GENERAL LITERACY, FROM ROMANCE TO REALISM,
		ILLITERATE	
SHAK PREFACE(137)	FICTITIOUS FIGURE SHAXPER OR SHAGSPER THE	ILLITERATE	BUMPKIN. ENOUGH TOO FOR MY FEELING THAT THE REAL
MILL PREFACE(135)	I COMMIT A MURDER PRECISELY AS IF I WERE THE MOST	ILLITERATE	CALL BOY? POLITICALLY WE ALL HAVE AT LEAST THE
SHAK PREFACE(136)	LOST, COULD NOT POSSIBLY HAVE BEEN WRITTEN BY AN	ILLITERATE	CLOWN AND POACHER WHO COULD HARDLY WRITE HIS OWN
SHAK PREFACE(136)	WHAT DOES FOLLOW IS THAT SHAKESPEAR WAS NOT AN	ILLITERATE	CLOWN BUT A WELL READ GRAMMAR-SCHOOLED SON IN A
CATH PREFACE(158)	BEFORE I WROTE FOR HER, BUT NOT FOR PLAYING	ILLITERATE	COCKNEY FLOWER-MAIDENS. AND IN THE CASE WHICH IS
MIS. PREFACE(69)	AND THE COSTER KNOWS THAT HIS SON WILL BECOME AN	ILLITERATE	HOOLIGAN IF HE IS LEFT TO THE STREETS, THERE IS
DOCT PREFACE(62)	I MADE THE ARTIST A RASCAL, THE JOURNALIST AN	ILLITERATE	INCAPABLE, AND ALL THE DOCTORS " ANGELS." BUT I
JOAN PREFACE(10)	CASE AND SHAKESPEAR'S IS THAT SHAKESPEAR WAS NOT	ILLITERATE	. HE HAD BEEN TO SCHOOL, AND KNEW AS MUCH LATIN
HART PREFACE(16)	THEMSELVES INTO THE ORGY AS SHAMELESSLY AS THE	ILLITERATE	. THE CHRISTIAN PRIEST JOINING IN THE WAR DANCE
2TRU II (54)	NOW OR YOU WERE LYING WHEN YOU SAID YOU WERE	ILLITERATE	. WHICH IS IT? /MEEK/ I DONT SEEM TO BE ABLE TO
JOAN PREFACE(10)	PURPOSES, NONE AT ALL. JOAN WAS ABSOLUTELY	ILLITERATE	. " I DO NOT KNOW A FROM B" SHE SAID. BUT MANY
JOAN PREFACE(9)	HAS BEEN BASED ON THE ASSUMPTION THAT HE WAS AN	ILLITERATE	LABORER, IN THE FACE OF THE PLAINEST EVIDENCE
BASH PREFACE(89)	AND PLAYS ALIKE SOON CAME TO BE WRITTEN BY	ILLITERATE	MASTERS OF THE VERNACULAR; AND I MYSELF WELCOMED
FABL PREFACE(95)	UNHONORED AND UNSUNG WHILST MEN AND WOMEN TOTALLY	ILLITERATE	OR AT MOST SELFTAUGHT TO READ AND WRITE IN THEIR
FABL PREFACE(75)	PHILOSOPHIC CREEDS TO THE NARROW INTELLIGENCES OF	ILLITERATE	PEASANTS AND OF CHILDREN. EIGHT THOUSAND YEARS
FOUN (215)	YOU NOTHING BUT THE VITUPERATIVE RAVINGS OF AN	ILLITERATE	PENNY-A-LINER BLINDED BY PARTY PASSION. /MERCER/
DOCT IV (159)	TO GET THEM WRONG. THAT COMES OF BELONGING TO AN	ILLITERATE	PROFESSION, WITH NO QUALIFICATIONS AND NO PUBLIC
APPL PREFACE(187)	OF HIS DUTIES; AND WE ELECT ANOTHER EQUALLY	ILLITERATE	SUCCESSOR ON SIMILAR GROUNDS. BUT BY THIS TIME
VWOO 3 (137)	REFUSE TO MARRY SOME RIDICULOUS VILLAGE MAIDEN OR	ILLITERATE	WIDOW WITH WHOM I COULD NOT HOLD A MOMENT'S

APPL PREFACE(187) IT MAY WORK VERY WELL; FOR OUR POSTMAN, THOUGH ILLITERATE , MAY BE A VERY CAPABLE FELLOW; AND THE BOY WHO
METH PREFACE(R74) OF HUMBLE AND OBSCURE PERSONS, SOMETIMES TOTALLY ILLITERATE , SOMETIMES UNCONSCIOUS OF HAVING ANY RELIGION AT
GENV PREFACE(24) HAVE NOT ONLY NEWTONS AND EINSTEINS, BUT OBSCURE ILLITERATE " LIGHTNING CALCULATORS," TO WHOM THE ANSWERS TO
2TRU II (53) NOT EDUCATIONALLY QUALIFIED, SIR. /TALLBOYS/ ILLITERATE ! ARE YOU NOT ASHAMED? /MEEK/ NO, SIR.

ILLITERATES

GENV PREFACE(16) DUMB. THEY ARE MORE DANGEROUS THAN SIMPLETONS AND ILLITERATES BECAUSE ON THE STRENGTH OF THEIR IRRELEVANT

ILLNATURED

APPL INTRLUD(249) I SHOULD LIKE THAT. AND THE PUBLIC WOULD THINK IT ILLNATURED . /ORINTHIA/ OH, YOU KNOW WHAT I MEAN. DIVORCE
PYGM PREFACE(200) HENCE. HE WAS, I BELIEVE, NOT IN THE LEAST AN ILLNATURED MAN: VERY MUCH THE OPPOSITE, I SHOULD SAY; BUT HE

ILLNESS

DOCT PREFACE(70) ON THE VITAL STATISTICS OF HIS DISTRICT OF THE ILLNESS AND DEATHS IT CAUSES, WHILST IT WOULD TAKE FROM HIM
DOCT PREFACE(24) " TAKES": THAT IS, UNLESS IT PRODUCES PERCEPTIBLE ILLNESS AND DISABLEMENT. SOMETIMES BOTH DOCTOR AND PATIENT
DOCT I (93) WITHOUT LEAVING HIM ANY THE WORSE, EXCEPT FOR THE ILLNESS AND THE GUINEAS IT COSTS HIM. I KNEW THE WALPOLES
DOCT PREFACE(4) PERSON WHO DOES NOT FEEL THAT THE TRAGEDY OF ILLNESS AT PRESENT IS THAT IT DELIVERS YOU HELPLESSLY INTO
DOCT PREFACE(17) IN THE MOMENT HE STOPS GOING OUT; AND THEREFORE ILLNESS HAS SPECIAL TERRORS FOR HIM, AND SUCCESS NO CERTAIN
2TRU II SD(57) OF A NATIVE SERVANT. ALL TRACES OF THE PATIENT'S ILLNESS HAVE DISAPPEARED: SHE IS SUNBURNT TO THE COLOR OF
MTH4 I (141) I AM NOT ILL. I HAVE NEVER HAD A DAY'S ILLNESS IN MY LIFE. /THE WOMAN/ MAY I ADVISE YOU? /THE
DOCT I (102) (SUNNILY) I AM NEVER SICK. NEVER HAD A DAY'S ILLNESS IN MY LIFE. THATS WHAT ENABLES ME TO SYMPATHIZE WITH
O'FL (207) WOMAN, ALWAYS MOST LOYAL. WHENEVER THERE IS AN ILLNESS IN THE ROYAL FAMILY, SHE ASKS ME EVERY TIME WE MEET
DOCT PREFACE(79) INTEREST IN ILL-HEALTH. 3. REMEMBER THAT AN ILLNESS IS A MISDEMEANOR; AND TREAT THE DOCTOR AS AN
KING I (184) DEAR, AND SO HELPFUL WHEN THERE IS ANY TROUBLE OR ILLNESS . HE PICKED HER UP OUT OF THE GUTTER; BUT THE GOOD
DOCT PREFACE(65) POSITION, BASED WHOLLY ON THE PREVALENCE OF ILLNESS . IT IS TRUE THERE ARE GRAVE SCANDALS IN THE PUBLIC
2TRU I (29) I HAVE NEVER NEGLECTED THE SMALLEST SYMPTOM OF ILLNESS . SHE HAS HAD DOCTORS IN ATTENDANCE ON HER ALMOST
DOCT PREFACE(7) THE BIBLE IS VERY CLEAR AS TO THE TREATMENT OF ILLNESS . THE EPISTLE OF JAMES, CHAPTER V., CONTAINS THE
2TRU I (45) SO SHAMEFULLY? YOU THINK YOU ARE IN A STATE OF ILLNESS . YOURE NOT: YOURE IN A STATE OF SIN. SELL THE
2TRU II (71) FAST, WITH THE RESULT THAT I HAVE FORGOTTEN WHAT ILLNESS MEANS; AND IF I RAN AWAY FROM YOU TWO NEITHER OF YOU
MIS. PREFACE(79) MASTER WAS BROUGHT DOWN TO EARTH BY THE SUDDEN ILLNESS OF HIS WIFE. IN THE CONFUSION THAT ENSUED IT BECAME
DOCT PREFACE(5) PSYCHOLOGICAL FACT TO BE REMEMBERED: A SERIOUS ILLNESS OR A DEATH ADVERTIZES THE DOCTOR EXACTLY AS A
MIS. PREFACE(79) ONE NOT SUBJECT TO ERROR OR SUFFERING OR DEATH OR ILLNESS OR MORTALITY. CONSEQUENTLY SYMPATHY WAS IMPOSSIBLE;
DOCT PREFACE(69) HAVE BEEN MERE ADVENTURERS IN THE PRIVATE ILLNESS SERVICE. TO PUT IT ANOTHER WAY, A HOST OF MEN AND
DOCT PREFACE(32) OF THE TREATMENT OF CHARLES II IN HIS LAST ILLNESS TO SEE HOW STRONGLY HIS PHYSICIANS FELT THAT THEIR
MTH2 (59) CONVALESCENCE. IT IS THE PART THAT MAKES THE ILLNESS WORTH WHILE. /SAVVY/ (HALF-RISING) PERHAPS I'D
JITT II SD(27) DULY CERTIFIED. JITTA HAS TAKEN REFUGE IN AN ILLNESS , AND IS KEEPING HER BED. HER HUSBAND, PROFESSOR
DOCT IV (161) ABOUT-- ABOUT-- ER-- WELL, A FEW WORDS ON YOUR ILLNESS , AND YOUR PLANS FOR THE SEASON. /LOUIS/ MY PLANS
MTH5 (211) COMFORT MAKES WINTER A TORTURE, SPRING AN ILLNESS , SUMMER AN OPPRESSION, AND AUTUMN ONLY A RESPITE.
MILL IV (207) AND NO MAJESTY! BUT ALL THIS TOOK TIME. THE ILLNESS , THE NURSE, THE FUNERAL, THE DISPOSAL OF THE
DOCT PREFACE(13) TO AWAIT THE NATURAL CURE WOULD MEAN A MONTH'S ILLNESS , THEN HE IS CLEARLY JUSTIFIED IN RECOMMENDING THE
BARB PREFACE(219) AND UNDENIABLY AS THE WANT OF IT REPRESENTS ILLNESS , WEAKNESS, DISGRACE, MEANNESS AND UGLINESS. NOT THE
DOCT PREFACE(70) WILL CARRY HIM TO SOLVENCY THROUGH A MORASS OF ILLNESS , WHILST THE LEAST ATTEMPT AT PLAIN DEALING WITH
JITT III (70) BEING MORE THAN AN ANGEL TO ME IN SPITE OF YOUR ILLNESS , WORDS CAN NEVER SAY. JUST LIE QUIET WHERE YOU ARE;

ILLNESSES

2TRU I (31) WELL IN SPITE OF THE FORTUNE I HAVE SPENT ON HER ILLNESSES ? THERE MUST BE SOME DEEP-ROOTED CAUSE. TELL ME
SUPR III (121) EXPENSES, THEIR WORRIES, THEIR TRIALS, THEIR ILLNESSES AND AGONIES AND RISKS OF DEATH, THEIR RETINUE OF
DOCT PREFACE(20) OR THE NEAREST QUACK): IT IS THE ART OF CURING ILLNESSES . IT DOES HAPPEN EXCEPTIONALLY THAT A PRACTISING
DOCT PREFACE(5) OPERATIONS AND MANUFACTURE AND PROLONG LUCRATIVE ILLNESSES . THE ONLY ONES WHO CAN CLAIM TO BE ABOVE
DOCT PREFACE(79) AND ANNOUNCEMENTS OF INDIVIDUAL CASES, OF ALL ILLNESSES OF DOCTORS OR IN THEIR FAMILIES. 10. MAKE IT
BARB III (338) DO THEY MATTER? THEY ARE ONLY THE ACCIDENTS AND ILLNESSES OF LIFE: THERE ARE NOT FIFTY GENUINE PROFESSIONAL
BARB PREFACE(245) PUT UP WITH THEIR VICES, AS WE PUT UP WITH THEIR ILLNESSES , UNTIL THEY GIVE MORE TROUBLE THAN THEY ARE

ILLOGICAL

MRS PREFACE(173) ENOUGH TO LAUGH AT IT); BUT IN BOTH CASES IT IS ILLOGICAL , AND IN BOTH CASES NATURAL. I REPEAT, THE CRITICS

ILLOGICALITIES

MIS. PREFACE(58) REASONS, AND AFFECTIONATE REASONS FOR ALL THESE ILLOGICALITIES . CHILDREN DO NOT WANT TO BE TREATED

ILLOGICALLY

LION PREFACE(18) EXAMPLE OF AUGUSTUS, CLAIMED THE TITLE OF GOD. ILLOGICALLY , SUCH DIVINE KINGS INSIST A GOOD DEAL ON THEIR

ILL-ADVISED

HART PREFACE(13) OF THEIR CONVICTIONS. THOSE WHO DID SO WERE VERY ILL-ADVISED FROM THE POINT OF VIEW OF THEIR OWN PERSONAL

ILL-ASSORTED

GETT PREFACE(195) BRICK BOXES OF LITTLE PARCELS OF HUMANITY OF ILL-ASSORTED AGES, WITH THE OLD SCOLDING OR BEATING THE
GETT PREFACE(240) THE COUPLES: A VERY DESIRABLE THING WHEN THEY ARE ILL-ASSORTED . ALSO, IT MAKES PEOPLE MUCH MORE WILLING TO
JITT PREFACE(6) TRANSLATOR'S TREACHERIES HERE AND THERE, THAT THE ILL-ASSORTED PAIR SETTLE DOWN ON REASONABLE HUMAN TERMS, AND

ILL-BRED

GETT PREFACE(214) GOVERNED AND ARE, ON THE WHOLE, AN UGLY, MEAN, ILL-BRED RACE. IBSEN'S CHAIN STITCH. LET US NOT FORGET,

ILL-CONDITIONED

METH PREFACE(R47) AND SNOBBISHLY, PERSUADED HIM THAT BUTLER WAS TOO ILL-CONDITIONED AND NEGLIGIBLE TO BE ANSWERED. THAT THEY

ILL-CONDUCTED

POSN PREFACE(389) ONE KNOWS BETTER THAN A MAGISTRATE THAT A SINGLE ILL-CONDUCTED FAMILY MAY DEMORALIZE A WHOLE STREET, NO
MRS PREFACE(163) ALL, AND THAT WHEN HE WAS ONCE SATISFIED THAT THE ILL-CONDUCTED HERO WAS A GERMAN AND NOT AN ENGLISH OFFICER,
HART I (75) CORRECT THING, YOU CAN DO JUST WHAT YOU LIKE. AN ILL-CONDUCTED , CARELESS WOMAN GETS SIMPLY NO CHANCE. AN
HART I (75) CARELESS WOMAN GETS SIMPLY NO CHANCE. AN ILL-CONDUCTED , CARELESS MAN IS NEVER ALLOWED WITHIN ARMS

ILL-DRESSED

PYGM PREFACE(201) FULL, ACCURATE, LEGIBLE SCRIPT FOR OUR NOBLE BUT ILL-DRESSED LANGUAGE; BUT HE WAS LED PAST THAT BY HIS

ILL-FEELING

DEVL III (60) NECESSITY AND MILITARY DUTY, WITHOUT ANY PERSONAL ILL-FEELING . /RICHARD/ OH, QUITE SO. THAT MAKES ALL THE
MTH4 II (187) WHY NOT LIVE AND LET LIVE? THERES NOT A SCRAP OF ILL-FEELING ON OUR SIDE. WE SHOULD WELCOME A COLONY OF

ILL-HEALTH

DOCT PREFACE(79) INTERESTS THE WORST IS THE VESTED INTEREST IN ILL-HEALTH . 3. REMEMBER THAT AN ILLNESS IS A MISDEMEANOR;
DOCT PREFACE(68) THE LOCAL PRIVATE DOCTORS ARE MAKING OUT OF THE ILL-HEALTH OF THEIR PATIENTS. IF A COMPETITOR CAN PROVE THAT
DOCT PREFACE(63) BUT THE TRUE DOCTOR IS INSPIRED BY A HATRED OF ILL-HEALTH , AND A DIVINE IMPATIENCE OF ANY WASTE OF VITAL

ILL-HUMORED

CLEO II (140) FINE TALKING. (HE GETS AWAY FROM CAESAR WITH AN ILL-HUMORED SHRUG, AND GOES TO THE BALCONY FOR ANOTHER LOOK

ILL-HUMOREDLY

HART I (71) WINDOW-SEAT AND SITS DOWN, TURNING AWAY FROM THEM ILL-HUMOREDLY AND LOOKING INTO THE GARDEN, WHERE HECTOR AND
GLIM (177) HAVE A HEADACHE: THATS ALL. (HE THROWS HIMSELF ILL-HUMOREDLY ON A BENCH AT THE TABLE OUTSIDE THE INN.
BULL III (140) THE SHRUBBERY). /LARRY/ (THROWING THE PAPER ILL-HUMOREDLY ON THE CHAIR) LOOK HERE, TOM! HERE, I SAY!
CLEO III (160) BRITANNUS GOES INTO THE LIGHTHOUSE. /RUFIO/ (ILL-HUMOREDLY) ARE YOU REALLY GOING TO WAIT HERE FOR THIS
NEVR I (207) /PHILIP/ (THROWING AWAY DOLLY'S ARM AND COMING ILL-HUMOREDLY TOWARDS THE OPERATING CHAIR) THAT WRETCHED

ILL-LUCK

O'FL PREFACE(202) WHOM ARE ANY THE LESS IRKSOME WHEN THEY HAPPEN BY ILL-LUCK TO BE ALSO OUR FATHERS, OUR MOTHERS, OUR WIVES AND

DEST SD(149) MANAGER. WITHAL, HE IS NO SPOILED CHILD. POVERTY, ILL-LUCK , THE SHIFTS OF IMPECUNIOUS SHABBY-GENTILITY,

ILL-MANNERED
MIS. PREFACE(59) I HAVE THE UTTERMOST CONTEMPT FOR A TEACHER SO ILL-MANNERED AND INCOMPETENT AS TO BE UNABLE TO MAKE A CHILD
MIS. PREFACE(59) READ AND WRITE WITH TEARS BY AN INCOMPETENT AND ILL-MANNERED PERSON THAN LEFT IN IGNORANCE. READING,
LADY PREFACE(215) LACK OF MIDDLE-CLASS TRAINING. THEY ARE ROWDY, ILL-MANNERED , ABUSIVE, MISCHIEVOUS, FOND OF QUOTING OBSCENE
UNPL PREFACE(R18) NATURE, THEY ARE, BY HOME TRAINING, SO INCREDIBLY ILL-MANNERED , THAT NOT EVEN THEIR INTEREST AS MEN OF

ILL-NATURE
HART II (85) PURPOSE. /ELLIE/ ON PURPOSE! /MANGAN/ NOT OUT OF ILL-NATURE , YOU KNOW. AND YOULL ADMIT THAT I KEPT A JOB FOR

ILL-NATURED
CATH 4 (188) /EDSTASTON/ OH, WELL, OF COURSE, IF YOURE AN ILL-NATURED WOMAN, HURTING ME ON PURPOSE, I HAVE NOTHING

ILL-NOURISHED
CAPT I SD(217) CIVILIZATION. HIS FRAME AND FLESH ARE THOSE OF AN ILL-NOURISHED LAD OF SEVENTEEN; BUT HIS AGE IS INSCRUTABLE:
WIDO I SD(3) COKANE, IS PROBABLY OVER 40, POSSIBLY 50: AN ILL-NOURISHED , SCANTY-HAIRED GENTLEMAN, WITH AFFECTED

ILL-REGULATED
HART III (141) LITTLE SELF-CONTROL; BUT TO ME IT IS ONLY A VERY ILL-REGULATED AND RATHER UNTIDY VILLA WITHOUT ANY STABLES.

ILL-TEMPER
MIS. (202) ABOUT IT, JOHNNY. /JOHNNY/ (SHORTLY, BUT WITHOUT ILL-TEMPER) OH! IS THAT SO? /HYPATIA/ THE CAT'S OUT OF THE

ILL-TEMPERED
DOCT PREFACE(42) AND THINK CHILDREN OUGHT TO BE BEATEN. THE ILL-TEMPERED VULGARITY THAT INSTINCTIVELY STRIKES AT AND
GETT PREFACE(234) AND YET BE MUCH BETTER OFF THAN IF SHE HAD AN ILL-TEMPERED , PEEVISH, MALICIOUSLY SARCASTIC ONE, OR WAS

ILL-TREATED
JOAN PREFACE(13) AS SHE WAS A PRETTY GIRL, AND HAD BEEN ABOMINABLY ILL-TREATED AND FINALLY DONE TO DEATH BY A SUPERSTITIOUS

ILL-TREATING
DEVL I (20) WRATH) WHO HAS BEEN MAKING HER CRY? WHO HAS BEEN ILL-TREATING HER? BY GOD-- /MRS DUDGEON/ (RISING AND

ILL-TREATMENT
LION PREFACE(65) OF MALICIOUS, DELIBERATE, COSTLY AND DEGRADING ILL-TREATMENT OF CRIMINALS FOR THE SAKE OF THESE MARGINAL
GETT PREFACE(243) PHENOMENON, PRODUCED BY OUR UNDERPAYMENT AND ILL-TREATMENT OF WOMEN WHO TRY TO EARN AN HONEST LIVING. I

ILL-USAGE
BARB PREFACE(227) PREACHING, BUT NOT PREACHING SUBMISSION; DARING ILL-USAGE AND ABUSE, BUT NOT PUTTING UP WITH MORE OF IT THAN

ILL-WILL
MTH4 II (192) BECAUSE I HAVE RISEN FOR THE MOMENT FAR ABOVE ANY ILL-WILL TO YOU OR TO ANY FELLOW-CREATURE; BUT I AM YOUR

ILL'S
BARB II (289) TO SPIT IN TODGER FAIRMAWL'S EYE. AW BESHED JENNY ILL'S FICE; AN NAR AW'LL GIT ME AOWN FICE BESHED AND CAM

ILLS
LADY PREFACE(229) PREJUDICED: IN SHORT, HEIRS TO THE PECULIAR ILLS OF POVERTY AND SLAVERY, AS WELL AS CO-HEIRS WITH THE
CYMB V (141) HAVE THEM FALL NO MORE. YOU SOME PERMIT TO SECOND ILLS WITH ILLS, EACH ELDER WORSE, AND MAKE THEM DREAD IT, TO
CYMB V (141) FALL NO MORE. YOU SOME PERMIT TO SECOND ILLS WITH ILLS , EACH ELDER WORSE, AND MAKE THEM DREAD IT, TO THE
GETT PREFACE(195) FOR BEHAVING LIKE OLD PEOPLE, AND ALL THE OTHER ILLS , MENTIONABLE AND UNMENTIONABLE, THAT ARISE FROM

ILLTREAT
2TRU I (38) I AM A POOR WOMAN IN A HOSPITAL WHOM YOU CAN ILLTREAT AS YOU PLEASE? DO YOU KNOW WHAT WILL HAPPEN TO YOU

ILLUDE
3PLA PREFACE(R23) ENERGY OF THE MAN OF THOUGHT WHOM SHAMS CANNOT ILLUDE OR INTEREST. THAT COMBINATION WILL BE ON ONE SIDE;

ILLUDED
SHAK PREFACE(136) PERFECTLY THAT THE SPECTATORS WILL BE COMPLETELY ILLUDED , THE RESULT WOULD BE THE DEATH OF PUPPETRY; FOR IT

ILLUMINATED
JOAN 4,SD(94) IN A HANDSOME CHAIR TURNING OVER THE LEAVES OF AN ILLUMINATED BOOK OF HOURS. THE NOBLEMAN IS ENJOYING HIMSELF:
MILL I SD(137) OF THE ROOM. THE FACES OF THE CLIENTS ARE THUS ILLUMINATED BY THE WINDOW WHILST HIS OWN COUNTENANCE IS IN
JOAN 4 (94) OF RICH BLACK WRITING IN BEAUTIFUL BORDERS, AND ILLUMINATED PICTURES CUNNINGLY INSET. BUT NOWADAYS, INSTEAD
2TRU III SD(81) TO ACCOMMODATE TWO PERSONS; ITS RECESSES ARE ILLUMINATED ROSILY BY BULBS WRAPPED IN PINK PAPER; AND SOME
MTH4 I (159) HIM, CAN YOU NOT? /THE ELDERLY GENTLEMAN/ (ILLUMINATED) OH HOW TRUE! OF COURSE, OF COURSE. THERE IS A

ILLUMINATING
JOAN EPILOG (158) RELIGHTING THEMSELVES AT THE SAME MOMENT, AND ILLUMINATING HIS ARMOUR AND SURCOAT CHEERFULLY) I HAVE KEPT

ILLUMINATION
LIED (198) THEM UNDER HENRY'S NOSE). /HE/ AS WITH A SUDDEN ILLUMINATION OF GLAD SURPRISE) WHY, THESE ARE MY POEMS!
DOCT PREFACE(50) IT JUSTIFIES ANY SORT OF CONDUCT, FROM THE ILLUMINATION OF NERO'S FEASTS BY BURNING HUMAN BEINGS ALIVE
OVER PREFACE(166) BE A MIRROR OF SUCH ACCURACY AND INTENSITY OF ILLUMINATION THAT THEY SHALL BE ABLE TO GET GLIMPSES OF
SUPR III (117) WERE DOWN FOR THE FIRST TIME, WHAT AN ASTOUNDING ILLUMINATION ! I HAD BEEN PREPARED FOR INFATUATION, FOR

ILLUMINATIONS
LION PREFACE(82) WITH ALL SORTS OF FINE QUALITIES AND OCCASIONAL ILLUMINATIONS , BUT ALWAYS HOPELESSLY IN THE TOILS OF SIN,

ILLUSAGE
GENV PREFACE(17) THEY HAD TO MAKE THEIR VICTIMS DIE OF ILLUSAGE INSTEAD OF BY MILITARY LAW. UNDER SUCH

ILLUSION
HART I SD(43) POST AND THE SIDES. ANOTHER DOOR STRAINS THE ILLUSION A LITTLE BY BEING APPARENTLY IN THE SHIP'S PORT
NEVR II (258) FACE THAT: I MUST HAVE ONE ILLUSION LEFT: THE ILLUSION ABOUT YOU. I LOVE YOU. (HE TURNS TOWARDS HER AS IF
2TRU PREFACE(5) WINES CULMINATING IN CIGARS AND LIQUEURS; BUT THE ILLUSION AND THE RESULTS ARE COGNATE. I THEREFORE PLEAD FOR
LION PREFACE(51) WAY THROUGH SUCH A MASS OF POPULAR PASSION AND ILLUSION AS STANDS BETWEEN US AND A SENSE OF THE VALUE OF
GETT PREFACE(255) THAN ADOPTED PARENTS IS PROBABLY AS COMPLETE AN ILLUSION AS THE NOTION THAT THEY ARE ANY BETTER, SEE NO
LADY PREFACE(213) A FORECAST PROVED TRUE. WILDE, THOUGH UNDER NO ILLUSION AS TO THE FOLLY OF THE QUITE UNSELFISH SUIT-AT-LAW
BULL PREFACE(19) FINALLY NAPOLEON HIMSELF, WITHOUT ONE MOMENT OF ILLUSION AS TO THE HUMAN MATERIAL HE HAD TO COMMAND, WITHOUT
LADY PREFACE(232) WAS PERSONAL SOBRIETY AND FREEDOM FROM IDOLATROUS ILLUSION IN SO FAR AS HE HAD ANY REMEDY AT ALL, AND DID NOT
DOCT PREFACE(55) THE CASE OF A PROPHYLACTIC ENFORCED BY LAW, THIS ILLUSION IS INTENSIFIED GROTESQUELY, BECAUSE ONLY VAGRANTS
BUOY III (39) YOU. LET US LOOK AT THIS MATHEMATICALLY. THE SEX ILLUSION IS NOT A FIXED QUANTITY: NOT WHAT MATHEMATICIANS
SUPR HANDBOK(201) CONCEIT OF CIVILIZATION. AFTER ALL, THE PROGRESS ILLUSION IS NOT SO VERY SUBTLE. WE BEGIN BY READING THE
MIS. PREFACE(107) IS A GHASTLY DEFECT. FREEDOM FROM IMAGINATIVE ILLUSION IS THEREFORE NO GUARANTEE WHATEVER OF NOBILITY OF
MTH5 (254) AND A DEEP THING: IT IS AN ACT OF LIFE AND NOT AN ILLUSION . ART IS AN ILLUSION. /ARJILLAX/ THAT IS FALSE. THE
GENV III (73) HE WILLS--" /THE JUDGE/ PARDON ME! THAT IS AN ILLUSION . I HAVE GONE INTO THAT QUESTION; AND I CAN ASSURE
MTH5 (254) IS AN ACT OF LIFE AND NOT AN ILLUSION. ART IS AN ILLUSION . /ARJILLAX/ THAT IS FALSE. THE STATUE COMES TO
APPL PREFACE(187) IS NOT A DEMOCRATIC REALITY: IT IS A DEMOCRATIC ILLUSION . THE BOY, WHEN HE HAS ABILITY ENOUGH TO TAKE
OVER PREFACE(165) OF MOOD RATHER THAN AT DIRECT SIMULATIVE ILLUSION . THE THEATRE, AS I FIRST KNEW IT, WAS A PLACE OF
OVER PREFACE(165) AND FLATS WHICH DESTROYED BOTH ATMOSPHERE AND ILLUSION . THIS WAS TOLERATED, AND EVEN INTENSELY ENJOYED,
SUPR HANDBOK(194) OF SUBJECTS IN SPITE OF IT. VII: PROGRESS AN ILLUSION . UNFORTUNATELY THE EARNEST PEOPLE GET DRAWN OFF
MTH5 (237) WE ARE PART OF A COSMIC SYSTEM. FREE WILL IS AN ILLUSION . WE ARE THE CHILDREN OF CAUSE AND EFFECT. WE ARE
ROCK II (281) A POOR MAN? /BARKING/ OH, THAT WAS A GIRLISH ILLUSION . YOU SEE, SHE HAD A GLIMPSE TODAY, AT THE

SUPR III (131)	YOU WILL SEE NOTHING BUT AN INFINITE COMEDY OF	ILLUSION	. YOU WILL DISCOVER THE PROFOUND TRUTH OF THE
SUPR III (91)	/DON JUAN/ YOU SEE, SENORA, THE LOOK WAS ONLY AN	ILLUSION	. YOUR WRINKLES LIED, JUST AS THE PLUMP SMOOTH SKIN
NEVR II (258)	NO, NO: I CANT FACE THAT: I MUST HAVE ONE	ILLUSION	LEFT: THE ILLUSION ABOUT YOU. I LOVE YOU. (HE
JOAN PREFACE(26)	AN UNNATURAL FICTION TO BE EXPLAINED AWAY AS AN	ILLUSION	MANUFACTURED BY PRIESTS AND SOLDIERS, BUT A
ROCK PREFACE(173)	WHY DO YE WRONG ONE TO ANOTHER? " I HAVE NO	ILLUSION	OF BEING FREE TO SAY AND WRITE WHAT I PLEASE. I
SUPR HANDBOK(201)	CHANGES THAT MONEY MAKES. STILL, THEY PRODUCE AN	ILLUSION	OF BUSTLING PROGRESS; AND THE READING CLASS INFERS
GETT PREFACE(209)	REASON, THOUGH MEN MAY CONSENT TO IT UNDER THE	ILLUSION	OF CHIVALRY. IT IS A SIMPLE MATTER OF NECESSITY;
BULL PREFACE(44)	WHICH AT LEAST CREATES AND MAINTAINS AN	ILLUSION	OF DEMOCRACY. AMERICA, AS FAR AS ONE CAN ASCERTAIN,
BULL PREFACE(20)	DEBRUEYS OR VILLENEUVE (WHO HAD NOT EVEN THE	ILLUSION	OF HEROISM WHEN HE WENT LIKE A LAMB TO THE
SUPR HANDBOK(199)	ALONG WHICH WE ARE EVOLVING. THIS IS INDEED THE	ILLUSION	OF ILLUSIONS; FOR IT GIVES US INFALLIBLE AND
SUPR PREFACE(R37)	OF LITERARY VIRTUOSITY, IS NOT FOUNDED ON ANY	ILLUSION	OF MINE AS TO THE PERMANENCE OF THOSE FORMS OF
SUPR HANDBOK(186)	OF THE TINKERING, THERE MAY BE AN OCCASIONAL	ILLUSION	OF MORAL EVOLUTION, AS WHEN THE VICTORY OF THE
MIS. PREFACE(93)	AND THEATRICAL REPRESENTATIONS IN WHICH AN	ILLUSION	OF NATURAL CLOTHESLESSNESS IS PRODUCED AND MADE
SUPR HANDBOK(194)	GET DRAWN OFF THE TRACK OF EVOLUTION BY THE	ILLUSION	OF PROGRESS. ANY SOCIALIST CAN CONVINCE US EASILY
SUPR HANDBOK(199)	CAPABLE OF NET PROGRESS. THERE WILL ALWAYS BE AN	ILLUSION	OF PROGRESS, BECAUSE WHEREVER WE ARE CONSCIOUS OF
JITT PREFACE(6)	IN PROPORTION AS A PLAY SUCCEEDS IN PRODUCING AN	ILLUSION	OF REAL LIFE, IT MUST DISPENSE WITH THE FRANTIC
BULL PREFACE(44)	CONCESSION OF NATURAL RIGHTS, AND KEEPS UP AN	ILLUSION	OF SAFEGUARDING THEM BY AN ELABORATE MACHINERY OF
BULL PREFACE(22)	ENTERPRISES TO A MUDDLED SUCCESS, AND CREATE AN	ILLUSION	OF SOME MIRACULOUS AND DIVINE INNATE ENGLISH
2TRU PREFACE(6)	MONSTROUS THAT IT MAY NOW BE DISMISSED AS AN	ILLUSION	OF THE POOR WHO KNOW NOTHING OF THE LIVES OF THE
OVER PREFACE(163)	ON OUR STAGE IS RIDICULOUSLY DESTRUCTIVE TO THE	ILLUSION	OF THE SCENE. YET PUGILISTS AND GLADIATORS WILL
CLEO NOTES (206)	FROM OUT THE AZURE MAIN. AGAIN, THERE IS THE	ILLUSION	OF " INCREASED COMMAND OVER NATURE," MEANING THAT
BASH PREFACE(88)	THEY ARE SAYING; BUT IT CANNOT IMPOSE ANY SUCH	ILLUSION	ON A PROFESSIONALLY SKILLED LISTENER. THEN THERE
JOAN PREFACE(18)	HUMAN TEST OF SUICIDE. YET EVEN IN THIS THE	ILLUSION	PERSISTED; AND SHE ANNOUNCED HER RELAPSE AS
METH PREFACE(R22)	TURNED ZOOLOGIST, DECLARED THAT SPECIES WERE AN	ILLUSION	PRODUCED BY THE SHORTNESS OF OUR INDIVIDUAL LIVES,
MRS PREFACE(167)	THAT HIS PLAYS IGNORE HUMAN FEELING, AN	ILLUSION	PRODUCED BY THAT VERY RESISTANCE OF FACT AND LAW TO
CLEO NOTES (210)	IS THEREFORE MORE LIKELY THAN NOT TO BE AN	ILLUSION	PRODUCED BY THE INCAPACITY OF HIS ADVERSARY. AT ALL
SUPR III (118)	THEM AND DESPERATELY STROVE TO RECOVER THEIR	ILLUSION	; BUT THEY NOW SEEMED THE EMPTIEST OF INVENTIONS:
METH PREFACE(R89)	TO LIVE FOR EVER. I AM NOT, I HOPE, UNDER MORE	ILLUSION	THAN IS HUMANLY INEVITABLE AS TO THE CRUDITY OF
METH PREFACE(R15)	EDUCATION. ALLOPATHY HAS PRODUCED THE POISONOUS	ILLUSION	THAT IT ENLIGHTENS INSTEAD OF DARKENING. THE
3PLA PREFACE(R26)	YOU, MY FRIEND, NOW READING THIS SENTENCE. THE	ILLUSION	THAT MAKES YOU THINK ME SO ORIGINAL IS FAR SUBTLER
MRS PREFACE(169)	COMPLETELY THE DRAMATIST IS EMANCIPATED FROM THE	ILLUSION	THAT MEN AND WOMEN ARE PRIMARILY REASONABLE BEINGS,
BULL PREFACE(56)	PENAL SERVITUDE. THIS WAS THE REALITY BEHIND THE	ILLUSION	THAT SOOTHED US AFTER BOMBARDING ALEXANDRIA. THE
ROCK PREFACE(174)	COMPLAIN, BECAUSE I DO NOT SHARE THE PROFESSORIAL	ILLUSION	THAT THERE IS ANY MORE FREEDOM FOR DISILLUSIONISTS
HART PREFACE(12)	THE GENERAL CRAZINESS. MEN WERE SEIZED WITH THE	ILLUSION	THAT THEY COULD WIN THE WAR BY GIVING AWAY MONEY.
ROCK PREFACE(175)	INTOLERANCES OF FASCISM AND COMMUNISM CREATES AN	ILLUSION	THAT THEY DO NOT EXIST ELSEWHERE; BUT THEY EXIST
CLEO NOTES (209)	HAVE NOT BEEN TOO MUCH IMPOSED ON BY THE DRAMATIC	ILLUSION	TO WHICH ALL GREAT MEN OWE PART OF THEIR REPUTATION
DOCT PREFACE(56)	AND NEGLECT. THERE IS ANOTHER STATISTICAL	ILLUSION	WHICH IS INDEPENDENT OF CLASS DIFFERENCES. A COMMON
JOAN PREFACE(11)	AND EXPLAIN WHY THE APPLES WERE FALLING. SUCH AN	ILLUSION	WOULD HAVE INVALIDATED NEITHER THE THEORY OF
OVER PREFACE(165)	IN FACT, THE MORE SCENERY YOU HAVE THE LESS	ILLUSION	YOU PRODUCE. THE WISE PLAYWRIGHT, WHEN HE CANNOT
SUPR III (102)	ANIMAL AT ALL: YOU ARE A GHOST, AN APPEARANCE, AN	ILLUSION	, A CONVENTION, DEATHLESS, AGELESS: IN A WORD,
BARB PREFACE(245)	IF A MAN CANNOT LOOK EVIL IN THE FACE WITHOUT	ILLUSION	, HE WILL NEVER KNOW WHAT IT REALLY IS, OR COMBAT
NEVR III (274)	I AM SORRY TO HAVE TO DISABUSE YOU OF ANY SUCH	ILLUSION	, MISS DOROTHEA. /DOLLY/ (COOING ECSTATICALLY)
BULL PREFACE(15)	DOYLE'S SPECIAL CONTRIBUTION WAS THE FREEDOM FROM	ILLUSION	, THE POWER OF FACING FACTS, THE NERVOUS INDUSTRY,
		ILLUSIONPROOF	
JOAN PREFACE(13)	MIGHT HAVE BEEN PLANNED BY NAPOLEON OR ANY OTHER	ILLUSIONPROOF	GENIUS. THEY CAME TO JOAN AS AN INSTRUCTION
		ILLUSIONS	
BUOY IV (50)	I RATHER LIKE HIM. /SHE/ YES: SO DO I. HE HAS NO	ILLUSIONS	ABOUT HIMSELF NOR ABOUT ME. AFTER ALL, IF HE TURNS
LADY PREFACE(215)	HE WAS A MAN AND THE AUTHOR OF HAMLET, WHO HAD NO	ILLUSIONS	ABOUT HIS MOTHER. IN WEAK MOMENTS ONE ALMOST
ROCK II (281)	SOCIETY; AND WE ARE THROUGH WITH IT! WE HAVE NO	ILLUSIONS	ABOUT IT, EVEN IF WE ARE FIT FOR NOTHING BETTER. I
SUPR IV (158)	ECSTASY-- WHISPERING) I CANT: HE HAS NO	ILLUSIONS	ABOUT ME. I SHALL SURPRISE JACK THE OTHER WAY.
MIS. PREFACE(81)	WITH THEIR EXPERIENCE OF LIFE HAVE NONE OF THE	ILLUSIONS	ABOUT THE CHILD THAT THE CHILD HAS ABOUT THE
HART PREFACE(18)	OF THE YOUNG MEN THEMSELVES! MANY OF THEM HAD NO	ILLUSIONS	ABOUT THE POLICY THAT LED TO THE WAR: THEY WENT
BULL PREFACE(18)	BUT YOU WILL NOT SUSPECT HIM OF HAVING HAD ANY	ILLUSIONS	ABOUT THE CONTEMPORARY BRITISH PRIVATE; WHILST AS
DOCT PREFACE(6)	TO CALL THEM IN JUST THE SAME. NAPOLEON HAD NO	ILLUSIONS	ABOUT THEM; BUT HE HAD TO DIE UNDER THEIR
ANNA (299)	STRENGTH HAS NEVER BEEN IN OURSELVES, BUT IN YOUR	ILLUSIONS	ABOUT US? (SHE SHAKES OFF HER KINDLINESS, AND
GETT PREFACE(220)	ANY DISCUSSION TENDING TO STRIP IT OF ITS	ILLUSIONS	AND GET AT ITS REAL NATURAL HISTORY IS NERVOUSLY
LADY PREFACE(233)	WITH MUCH OF IBSEN'S POWER OF PENETRATING ITS	ILLUSIONS	AND IDOLATRIES, AND WITH ALL SWIFT'S HORROR OF ITS
JOAN PREFACE(11)	WHOSE TEMPTATIONS PRESENT THEMSELVES UNDER THESE	ILLUSIONS	ARE NOT RESPONSIBLE FOR THEIR ACTIONS, AND MUST BE
MIS. PREFACE(67)	ACTION, IN COMMITTEE OR OTHERWISE, CAN RETAIN ANY	ILLUSIONS	AS TO THE APPALLING EFFECTS ON OUR NATIONAL
JOAN PREFACE(5)	BUT NEITHER FRANK NOR DISINTERESTED, HAD NO	ILLUSIONS	AS TO THE NATURE OF HIS POPULARITY. WHEN HE WAS
BULL PREFACE(23)	ENOUGH, BUT CLEVER ENOUGH TO DO THIS, WE HAVE NO	ILLUSIONS	AS TO THE EXISTENCE OF ANY MYSTERIOUS IRISH PLUCK,
BUOY III (39)	OF MARRIAGE. /MRS SECONDBORN/ BESIDES, THE	ILLUSIONS	DONT AFFECT PEOPLE WHO HAVE COMMON SENSE. I NEVER
GETT PREFACE(219)	IT IS A RELATION BESET WITH WILDLY EXTRAVAGANT	ILLUSIONS	FOR INEXPERIENCED PEOPLE, AND THAT EVEN THE MOST
SUPR PREFACE(R30)	TO THE PHILISTINE. EVERY MAN WHO RECORDS HIS	ILLUSIONS	IS PROVIDING DATA FOR THE GENUINELY SCIENTIFIC
SUPR HANDBOK(209)	THE MINDS OF MEN WHOSE PRESENT FAITH IN THESE	ILLUSIONS	IS THE CEMENT OF OUR SOCIAL SYSTEM, CAN BE
BUOY III (39)	/SECONDBORN/ NOT QUITE. I HAD MY SHARE OF THE	ILLUSIONS	, BUT WHEN THEY VANISHED THEY DID NOT MATTER MUCH.
CLEO NOTES (206)	WITH A MAUSER RIFLE. ALL SUCH NOTIONS ARE	ILLUSIONS	. GO BACK TO THE FIRST SYLLABLE OF RECORDED TIME,
ARMS II SD(23)	OF THE ACCURATE CALCULATOR WHO HAS NO	ILLUSIONS	, HE WEARS A WHITE BULGARIAN COSTUME: JACKET WITH
SUPR IV (157)	TAVY: I WOULDNT FOR WORLDS DESTROY YOUR	ILLUSIONS	. I CAN NEITHER TAKE YOU NOR LET YOU GO. I CAN SEE
DOCT PREFACE(53)	HAVE TO DECIDE AGAINST THE PUBLIC. STATISTICAL	ILLUSIONS	. PUBLIC IGNORANCE OF THE LAWS OF EVIDENCE AND OF
SUPR III (114)	AMONG ALL THE CONFLICTS OF INTERESTS AND	ILLUSIONS	. /THE STATUE/ YOU MEAN THE MILITARY MAN. /DON
JOAN PREFACE(11)	CONCLUSIONS OF GENIUS SOMETIMES ASSUME SIMILAR	ILLUSIONS	. SOCRATES, LUTHER, SWEDENBORG, BLAKE SAW VISIONS
ROCK PREFACE(172)	BEING MOSTLY MORE OR LESS DUPED THEMSELVES BY THE	ILLUSIONS	. UNFORTUNATELY THEY ALLOW THE ILLUSIONS TO FALL
BULL PREFACE(15)	THE NERVOUS ENERGY, AND THE FREEDOM FROM ROMANTIC	ILLUSIONS	(OFTEN CALLED CYNICISM) OF SUCH FOREIGNERS FOR
SUPR PREFACE(R27)	IDOLATRY. I DO NOT KNOW WHETHER YOU HAVE ANY	ILLUSIONS	LEFT ON THE SUBJECT OF EDUCATION, PROGRESS, AND SO
GETT PREFACE(232)	NOTION TO THE CONTRARY BEING ONE OF THE	ILLUSIONS	OF LITERARY MASCULINITY. BESIDES, THE HUSBAND IS
SUPR III (117)	FOR INFATUATION, FOR INTOXICATION, FOR ALL THE	ILLUSIONS	OF LOVE'S YOUNG DREAM; AND LO! NEVER WAS MY
BARB I SD(260)	IS NOT MERCIFUL ENOUGH TO BLIND HIM WITH THE	ILLUSIONS	OF LOVE, HE IS OBSTINATELY BENT ON MARRYING
GETT PREFACE(219)	MUST GET MARRIED TO SECURE A LIVELIHOOD; AND THE	ILLUSIONS	OF SEXUAL ATTRACTION WILL CAUSE THE IMAGINATION OF
HART PREFACE(11)	IN THE MADHOUSE, WHEN THE LUNATICS, EXALTED BY	ILLUSIONS	OF SPLENDID TALENT AND VISIONS OF A DAWNING
ROCK PREFACE(172)	THEY POSSESS (THIS IS ONE OF THEIR INCULCATED	ILLUSIONS	) IS THREATENED BY THE DICTATORSHIPS WHICH ARE
ROCK PREFACE(173)	THE ROAD. ALL THE PROVISIONAL HYPOTHESES MAY BE	ILLUSIONS	; BUT IF THEY CONDUCE TO BENEFICIAL CONDUCT THEY
SUPR HANDBOK(199)	WE ARE EVOLVING. THIS IS INDEED THE ILLUSION OF	ILLUSIONS	; FOR IT GIVES US INFALLIBLE AND APPALLING
DOCT PREFACE(14)	CONQUERED. DOCTORS ARE NO MORE PROOF AGAINST SUCH	ILLUSIONS	THAN OTHER MEN. CAN ANYONE THEN DOUBT THAT UNDER
ROCK PREFACE(172)	BY THE ILLUSIONS. UNFORTUNATELY THEY ALLOW THE	ILLUSIONS	TO FALL BEHIND THE TIMES AND BECOME INCREDIBLE, AT
SUPR III (104)	SOONER THAN FACE THESE REALITIES, PILING UP	ILLUSIONS	TO HIDE THEM, AND CALLING ITSELF CLEVERNESS,
ROCK PREFACE(172)	IT IS THE IMPORTANCE OF KEEPING OUR INCULCATED	ILLUSIONS	UP TO DATE THAT THROWS OUR HIGHER PROFESSIONAL
DOCT PREFACE(52)	SOME KNOWLEDGE OF VITAL STATISTICS, AND OF THE	ILLUSIONS	WHICH BESET PUBLIC HEALTH LEGISLATION. WHAT THE
MRS IV (240)	THE GAIETY OF BRUSSELS. YOU ARE WELCOME TO ANY	ILLUSIONS	YOU MAY HAVE LEFT ON THESE SUBJECTS: I HAVE NONE.
LION PREFACE(32)	THIS SHEWS A GREAT POWER OF SEEING THROUGH VULGAR	ILLUSIONS	, AND A CAPACITY FOR A HIGHER MORALITY THAN HAS
DEST SD(149)	THE FRENCH REVOLUTION. HE IS IMAGINATIVE WITHOUT	ILLUSIONS	, AND CREATIVE WITHOUT RELIGION, LOYALTY,
MTH5 (243)	I WAS REALLY A KING OF KINGS. (TO THE OTHERS)	ILLUSIONS	, FAREWELL: WE ARE GOING TO OUR THRONES. (HE
BUOY III (36)	MYSELF WHAT IS CALLED FALLING IN LOVE. I HAD	ILLUSIONS	, INFATUATIONS, IMPULSES THAT WERE UTTERLY
BUOY III (42)	HE IS THE MAN I AM IN LOVE WITH: THE OBJECT OF MY	ILLUSIONS	, MY MADNESS. IF HE FOLLOWED ME ACROSS THE
CAND III (132)	OUR SOULS, AND NOT OUR FOLLIES AND VANITIES AND	ILLUSIONS	, NOR OUR COLLARS AND COATS, NOR ANY OTHER OF THE
HART PREFACE(8)	WILL, AND SO FORTH, ARE, THEY TAUGHT, MERE	ILLUSIONS	, PRODUCED BECAUSE THEY ARE USEFUL IN THE
ROCK PREFACE(172)	LIKELIEST OUTCOME IS AN ELABORATE CREED OF USEFUL	ILLUSIONS	, TO BE DISCARDED BIT BY BIT AS THE CHILD IS
3PLA PREFACE(R22)	ENABLES EVERY PENMAN TO PLAY ON THEIR ROMANTIC	ILLUSIONS	, WILL BE LED BY THE NOSE FAR MORE COMPLETELY THAN
		ILLUSIVE	
OVER PREFACE(164)	SCENERY (IN MOST MODERN PLAYS SCENERY IS NOT	ILLUSIVE	: EVERYTHING VISIBLE IS AS REAL AS IN YOUR DRAWING
OVER PREFACE(164)	FOR EXAMPLE, THE MAIN OBJECTION TO THE USE OF	ILLUSIVE	SCENERY (IN MOST MODERN PLAYS SCENERY IS NOT
		ILLUSORY	
SUPR PREFACE(R22)	MORE FEAR OF WOMEN'S PURSUIT THAN LOVE OF THEIR	ILLUSORY	BEAUTY. BUT ORDINARY MEN CANNOT PRODUCE REALLY

SUPR III (109)	HAVE HIS TURN TOO. BUT I AM NOT NOW DEFENDING THE	ILLUSORY	FORMS THE GREAT IDEAS TAKE. I AM GIVING YOU
ROCK PREFACE(173)	UNTIL BETTER ONES ARRIVE. TOLERATION MOSTLY	ILLUSORY	. BUT, CRY THE PROFESSORS, ARE THE HYPOTHESES NEVER
CLEO NOTES (210)	IT MAY, HOWEVER, BE SAID THAT PEACE HATH HER	ILLUSORY	REPUTATIONS NO LESS THAN WAR. AND IT IS CERTAINLY
FABL PREFACE(85)	CHECKS AND SAFEGUARDS AGAINST DESPOTISM NOW SO	ILLUSORY	, AND GIVES THEM AS MUCH EFFECTIVENESS AS THEIR
JOAN PREFACE(17)	OF THE VOICES. THAT THE VOICES AND VISIONS WERE	ILLUSORY	, AND THEIR WISDOM ALL JOAN'S OWN, IS SHEWN BY THE

ILLUSTRATE

GETT PREFACE(232)	EVEN FOR UNCONVENTIONAL PEOPLE. LET ME	ILLUSTRATE	BY REFERENCE TO A FICTITIOUS CASE: THE ONE
BASH II,1, (99)	OF ILLUSTRATION. /LUCIAN/ WHAT RIGHT HAD HE TO	ILLUSTRATE	HIS POINT UPON MY PERSON? WAS I HIS ASSISTANT
ROCK PREFACE(157)	HORROR FROM A PROPOSAL TO PUNISH THEM. LET ME	ILLUSTRATE	MY ATTITUDE BY A VERY FAMOUS, INDEED FAR TOO
JOAN PREFACE(22)	PLENTY OF MANAGING WOMEN AMONG US OF THAT AGE WHO	ILLUSTRATE	PERFECTLY THE SORT OF PERSON SHE WOULD HAVE
LION PREFACE(63)	ON THE VIEWS OF JESUS. WHEN SWIFT HAD OCCASION TO	ILLUSTRATE	THE CORRUPTION OF OUR CIVILIZATION BY MAKING A
2TRU PREFACE(5)	HIS CASE IS HARDLY A FAIR ONE. BUT IT SERVES TO	ILLUSTRATE	THE MORAL OF MY PLAY, WHICH IS, THAT OUR
SUPR PREFACE(R20)	CAPTURES BERTRAM. BUT THE MATURE CASES ALL	ILLUSTRATE	THE SHAKESPEARIAN LAW. THE ONE APPARENT
JOAN PREFACE(46)	RIGHT IN THEIR VIEW OF THE FACTS. AS IT IS, THEY	ILLUSTRATE	THE TOO LITTLE CONSIDERED TRUTH THAT THE FASHION
LION PREFACE(24)	ENTERTAINS HIS HEARERS WITH FABLES (PARABLES) TO	ILLUSTRATE	THEM. HE HAS NO SYNAGOGUE OR REGULAR
MIS. PREFACE(106)	OF NAPOLEON, WITH THEIR ATMOSPHERE OF GLORY,	ILLUSTRATE	THIS. IN THE RUSSIAN CAMPAIGN NAPOLEON'S MARSHALS
MILL PREFACE(130)	TO RICHARD CROMWELL OR THE DUKE OF REICHSTADT TO	ILLUSTRATE	THIS. IT IS OCCURRING EVERY DAY IN COMMERCIAL
MIS. PREFACE(59)	THE DIFFICULTY IS TO KNOW WHERE TO STOP. TO	ILLUSTRATE	THIS, LET US CONSIDER THE MAIN DANGER OF CHILDISH
GETT PREFACE(205)	IS DONE, AND THAT OF THE OFFICIAL BEGINS. TO	ILLUSTRATE	, THERE IS NO NEED FOR THE POLICE OFFICER WHO

ILLUSTRATED

GETT PREFACE(197)	CASE WAS AN EXTREME ONE, IT WAS AN EXTREME THAT	ILLUSTRATED	A TENDENCY. SIR WALTER SCOTT'S FATHER, WHEN HIS
2TRU I (44)	A COPY OF THE LADY'S PICTORIAL. IT CONTAINED AN	ILLUSTRATED	ACCOUNT OF YOUR JEWELS. CAN YOU GUESS WHAT
BASH PREFACE(91)	TAUGHT TO READ, HAVE PLENTY OF DRAMATICALLY	ILLUSTRATED	BIBLES AND SHAKESPEARS LEFT IN THEIR WAY, WITH
METH PREFACE(R51)	THE STULTIFICATION AND DAMNATION WHICH ENSUED ARE	ILLUSTRATED	BY A COMPARISON OF THE EASE AND CERTAINTY WITH
LION PREFACE(35)	FROM UNPLEASANTNESS, AND HIS SENTIMENTALITY, ARE	ILLUSTRATED	BY HIS VERSION OF THE WOMAN WITH THE OINTMENT.
JITT PREFACE(6)	TRUE, AS THE LATE ST JOHN HANKIN POINTED OUT AND	ILLUSTRATED	BY HIS PLAYS WITH HAPPY ENDINGS, THAT THE
2TRU I SD(37)	THE NURSE SITS DOWN; TAKES OUT A LEAF CUT FROM AN	ILLUSTRATED	JOURNAL; AND PROCEEDS TO STUDY IT ATTENTIVELY.
BARB PREFACE(219)	DIFFERENCE BETWEEN THE CHRISTMAS NUMBER OF THE	ILLUSTRATED	LONDON NEWS AND THE KELMSCOTT CHAUCER IS SILLY:
MILL IV SD(188)	IS SPRAWLING HAPPILY ON THE LONG SEAT, READING AN	ILLUSTRATED	MAGAZINE. PATRICIA, IN HER GLADDEST SUMMER RAGS,
GENV I SD(29)	SHE IS NOT AT WORK. SHE IS SMOKING AND READING AN	ILLUSTRATED	MAGAZINE WITH HER HEELS ON THE TABLE. A THERMOS
GENV IV SD(87)	BEGONIA AND HER YOUNG MAN HAVE ONE EXCESSIVELY	ILLUSTRATED	NEWSPAPER BETWEEN THEM. HE HAS HIS ARM ROUND HER
CAND II (112)	JUST TO PASS THE TIME. (MORELL TAKES AN	ILLUSTRATED	PAPER FROM THE TABLE AND OFFERS IT. HE ACCEPTS
FANY III SD(297)	THE ARMCHAIR, CROUCHING OVER THE FIRE, READING AN	ILLUSTRATED	PAPER. HE IS A PRETTY YOUTH, OF VERY SUBURBAN
MILL IV SD(188)	DAINTY SHADES. NEAR IT IS A TABLE WITH ALL THE	ILLUSTRATED	PAPERS AND MAGAZINES TO HAND. FARTHER DOWN THE
CAND I SD(92)	STUCK THROUGH IT, A HANDBAG, AND A SUPPLY OF	ILLUSTRATED	PAPERS. /MORELL/ (SHOCKED AT HIS REMISSNESS)
SUPR III (137)	LOUISA'S PORTRAIT. IT WILL BE PUBLISHED IN THE	ILLUSTRATED	PAPERS. YOU BLENCH. IT WILL BE YOUR DOING,
MILL IV (199)	SAFE NOW, LADIES AND GENTLEMEN. (HE PICKS UP HIS	ILLUSTRATED	PAPER, AND RETIRES WITH IT TO ONE OF THE REMOTER
BASH PREFACE(91)	AND SHAKESPEARS LEFT IN THEIR WAY, WITH THE	ILLUSTRATED	PASSAGES PRINTED UNDER THE PICTURES, IT WILL
DEVL EPILOG (79)	WITHIN CERTAIN ARISTOCRATIC LIMITS, BEST	ILLUSTRATED	PERHAPS BY HIS DECLARATION, WHICH NOW SOUNDS SO
CYMB FORWORD(136)	CHILD THAT ONE OF THE BOOKS I DELIGHTED IN WAS AN	ILLUSTRATED	SHAKESPEAR, WITH A PICTURE AND TWO OR THREE
2TRU III (110)	US: OUR SUNBATHERS, GRINNING AT US FROM EVERY	ILLUSTRATED	SUMMER NUMBER OF OUR MAGAZINES, ARE NUDER THAN
POSN PREFACE(361)	IMBECILITY AND MISCHIEVOUSNESS COULD NOT BE FULLY	ILLUSTRATED	WITHIN THE LIMITS OF DECORUM IMPOSED ON THE

ILLUSTRATES

BULL PREFACE(70)	BUT AN IGNOMINIOUS CLIMB DOWN; BUT THE INCIDENT	ILLUSTRATES	MY CONTENTION THAT OUR AUTHORITY, WHEN IT IS TOO
DEVL EPILOG (82)	OF BANISHING HIM FROM PARLIAMENT. THE EPISODE	ILLUSTRATES	THE CURIOUS PERVERSION OF THE ENGLISH SENSE OF

ILLUSTRATING

METH PREFACE(R81)	MASTERS BY IMITATION WHEN THEY SHOULD HAVE BEEN	ILLUSTRATING	A FAITH OF THEIR OWN. CONTEMPLATE, IF YOU CAN
MTH4 I (163)	NOT ABOUT IMAGES. /THE ELDERLY GENTLEMAN/ I WAS	ILLUSTRATING	-- NOT, I HOPE, QUITE INFELICITOUSLY-- THE
BULL PREFACE(19)	TOMMY ATKINS, PERHAPS YOU HAVE NEVER THOUGHT OF	ILLUSTRATING	THE CONTRAST BETWEEN ENGLISH AND IRISH BY MOORE
GENV PREFACE(6)	OLD COMMENT ON THE ANGLO-IRISH SITUATION AS	ILLUSTRATING	THE DIFFICULTY OF DRIVING IN DOUBLE HARNESS
2TRU PREFACE(17)	TURNING ITS CATHEDRALS INTO HISTORICAL MUSEUMS	ILLUSTRATING	THE INFAMIES OF ECCLESIASTICAL HISTORY AND

ILLUSTRATION

POSN PREFACE(417)	AND INCONSIDERATE PEOPLE SEIZED EAGERLY ON THIS	ILLUSTRATION	AS IF IT WERE A SUCCESSFUL ATTEMPT TO PROVE
NEVR III (267)	WITH GLORIA? /VALENTINE/ A GREAT DEAL. BY WAY OF	ILLUSTRATION	. DURING THIS WHOLE CENTURY, MY DEAR MRS
CLEO NOTES (206)	HAS ACCUMULATED A LITTLE: THAT IS ALL. ONE MORE	ILLUSTRATION	. IS THE ENGLISHMAN PREPARED TO ADMIT THAT THE
BASH II,1, (99)	FORM. /LYDIA/ POOH! THAT WAS BUT BY WAY OF	ILLUSTRATION	. /LUCIAN/ WHAT RIGHT HAD HE TO ILLUSTRATE HIS
APPL PREFACE(195)	YOU ALL THIS MECHANICAL STUFF MERELY BY WAY OF	ILLUSTRATION	. WHAT I HAVE COME TO CONSULT YOU ABOUT IS A
BULL PREFACE(20)	THEATRICAL FOREIGNER. THE VALUE OF THE	ILLUSTRATION	LIES IN THE FACT THAT NELSON AND WELLINGTON
BULL PREFACE(66)	SHEWED NO OTHER INTEREST IN THE MATTER: ANOTHER	ILLUSTRATION	OF HOW HOPELESS IT IS TO INDUCE ONE MODERN
LION PREFACE(64)	AND COULD NOT SEE THEM. THIS IS A TYPICAL	ILLUSTRATION	OF THE ABSURDITIES AND CRUELTIES INTO WHICH WE
POSN PREFACE(362)	REPORT OF THE JOINT SELECT COMMITTEE IS A CAPITAL	ILLUSTRATION	OF THIS TENDENCY. THE CASE AGAINST THE
METH PREFACE(R52)	NATURALLY NEITHER BLIND NOR STUPID IS A TELLING	ILLUSTRATION	OF WHAT DARWIN UNINTENTIONALLY DID TO THE MINDS
LADY PREFACE(227)	OUT (THOUGH HE DOES NOT USE THIS PARTICULAR	ILLUSTRATION	) PAUL VERONESE IS AN ANCHORITE COMPARED TO
MTH2 (83)	IN THE COUNTRY. LET ME ASSUME FOR THE SAKE OF	ILLUSTRATION	THAT EACH PERSON WOULD HAVE TO CONSUME, SAY,
MIS. PREFACE(96)	IT IS TO BE READ IT MUST BE READABLE. TAKE FOR AN	ILLUSTRATION	THE STORY OF ELISHA AND THE BEARS. TO THE
GETT PREFACE(204)	LEMON SQUASHES, AND THE LIKE. TO TAKE A MORAL	ILLUSTRATION	, THE WILL TO SUPPRESS MISCONDUCT AND SECURE

ILLUSTRATIONS

SUPR HANDBOK(205)	OF CONDUCT THAN THE PASSIONS OF A MOB. THE	ILLUSTRATIONS	GIVEN ABOVE ARE COMMONPLACES TAKEN FROM THE
BARB PREFACE(208)	I KNOW NOTHING BUT THE NAMES AND SOME OF THE	ILLUSTRATIONS	, BUT THE STORY OF THE DAY'S RIDE AND LIFE'S
SUPR I (11)	THE GREYHAIRED; AND I WAS FULL OF ARGUMENTS AND	ILLUSTRATIONS	. I SAID THE PROPER THING WAS TO COMBINE THE
METH PREFACE(R46)	COME TO THE END OF THE INNUMERABLE INSTANCES AND	ILLUSTRATIONS	OF WHICH THE BOOK MAINLY CONSISTS. DARWIN
FABL IV (116)	TYPESCRIPT. LEAVE THE TYPE AND THE FORMAT AND THE	ILLUSTRATIONS	TO THE PRINTER: HE IS A BETTER ARTIST IN BOOKS

ILLUSTRATIVE

MRS PREFACE(162)	OF RETURNING THE ARTICLE, PRINTED IT WITH THE	ILLUSTRATIVE	EXAMPLES OMITTED, AND NOTHING LEFT BUT THE
ROCK PREFACE(179)	AND READY IN DEBATE AND REPARTEE, FULL OF THE	ILLUSTRATIVE	HYPOTHETICAL CASES BELOVED OF LAWYERS (CALLED

ILLUSTRATIVELY

METH PREFACE(R41)	I DO NOT REMEMBER HOW THIS ANIMAL IMPOSED HIMSELF	ILLUSTRATIVELY	ON THE EVOLUTION CONTROVERSY; BUT THERE WAS

ILLUSTRIOUS

PYGM PREFACE(199)	TOWARDS THE END OF THE EIGHTEEN-SEVENTIES, THE	ILLUSTRIOUS	ALEXANDER MELVILLE BELL, THE INVENTOR OF VISIBLE
MTH3 (108)	ARCHBISHOP) YOU WISH US TO UNDERSTAND THAT THE	ILLUSTRIOUS	ANCESTORS OF THE ACCOUNTANT GENERAL COMMUNICATED
HART PREFACE(17)	FROM THE ROLL OF OUR PEERAGE, CHANGING THE KING'S	ILLUSTRIOUS	AND HISTORICALLY APPROPRIATE SURNAME FOR THAT OF
HART PREFACE(33)	A COMMITTEE WAS FORMED; AND ALL SORTS OF	ILLUSTRIOUS	AND INFLUENTIAL PERSONS LENT THEIR NAMES TO A
METH PREFACE(R13)	ROBBER BARON, AND THE PROFITEER, AS MODELS OF THE	ILLUSTRIOUS	AND THE SUCCESSFUL. IN VAIN DO THE PROPHETS WHO
GLIM (176)	MIGHT KILL YOUR EXCELLENCY; AND, AS YOU SAY, MY	ILLUSTRIOUS	BARON MIGHT BREAK ME ON THE WHEEL FOR YOUR
MTH4 I (154)	GEM SET IN A SILVER SEA! CAN I, A SCION OF THE	ILLUSTRIOUS	BRITISH RACE, EVER FORGET THAT WHEN THE EMPIRE
SUPR III (97)	THE PLEASURE OF AGAIN RECEIVING A VISIT FROM THE	ILLUSTRIOUS	COMMANDER OF CALATRAVA? (COLDLY) DON JUAN,
JOAN PREFACE(4)	IN WHOM THE MOST VENERABLE HIERARCHY AND THE MOST	ILLUSTRIOUS	DYNASTY CONVERGED, HER PRETENSIONS AND
GLIM (179)	BE THE SAME TO HIM AS IF HE GOT IT FROM YOUR	ILLUSTRIOUS	FATHER. /SQUARCIO/ STUPID: THE COUNT IS CLEVERER
CLEO NOTES (208)	THAT CLEOPATRA WAS WELL EDUCATED. HER FATHER, THE	ILLUSTRIOUS	FLUTE BLOWER, WAS NOT AT ALL A PARENT OF THE
ROCK I SD(193)	RESIDENCE OF THE BRITISH PRIME MINISTER. THE	ILLUSTRIOUS	HOLDER OF THAT OFFICE, SIR ARTHUR CHAVENDER, IS
BUOY IV (53)	FATHER. /THE NATIVE/ (TO HER) SIR FLOPPER, THE	ILLUSTRIOUS	LAW SERVANT OF GOD, HAS WAITED UNTIL YOUR
FANY III (324)	FALL BACK ON IT DOES NOT MATTER." THINK OF YOUR	ILLUSTRIOUS	NELSON, ALWAYS BEATEN ON LAND, ALWAYS VICTORIOUS
MTH4 III (200)	/ZOO/ THE SAME REPLY, WORD FOR WORD, THAT YOUR	ILLUSTRIOUS	PREDECESSOR, AS YOU CALL HIM, GOT FIFTEEN YEARS
MTH4 III (199)	TO REPEAT THE SIGNAL FAVOR CONFERRED ON MY	ILLUSTRIOUS	PREDECESSOR, SIR FULLER EASTWIND, AND TO ANSWER
MTH3 (94)	SAGE. ENTERS. /BURGE-LUBIN/ (JOCULARLY) WELL,	ILLUSTRIOUS	SAGE-AND-ONIONS, HOW ARE YOUR POOR SORE FEET?

IM

CAPT I (219)	WITH VOYLENCE. BLESS IS AWT, AW SY NATHINK AGIN	IM	: AWM ALL FER LOR MAWSEOLF, AW EM. /RANKIN/ WELL?

SUPR III	(83)	DOES HE MEAN BY MAKIN OUT THAT SHE EVER LOOKED AT	IM	? (RELUCTANTLY RESUMING HIS COUCH ON THE TURF) HEAR HIM
BARB II	(289)	WITH HIS DRUMSTICK). /BILL/ GOWIN TO MERRY	IM	? /BARBARA/ YES. /BILL/ (FERVENTLY) GAWD ELP IM!
CAND II	(111)	YORR HE IS. JUST YOU KEEP YOUR HEYE ON	IM	AND SEE. (RISING MOMENTOUSLY) I'M SORRY, JAMES, TO AVE
BARB II	(309)	US. AOL MENN, WOT O'CLOCK THIS MAWNIN WAS IT WEN	IM	AS THEY CALL SNOBBY PRAWCE WAS SIVED? /BARBARA/ (
BARB II	(299)	ME A SETTERDA NAWT. AW EDNT JAST NAO SHAOW WIV	IM	AT ALL. ARF THE STREET PRYED; AN THE TATHER ARF LARFED
CAPT I	(222)	WAW, ITS THE NIME IS BLESSED MATHER GIVE	IM	AT ER KNEE. BLESS IS LITTLE AWT! THER YNT NAOW AWM IN
BARB II	(309)	UP HIS CAP. I WAS UP HERE ALL THE TIME AN SEE	IM	DO IT. /BILL/ WOT! STOWL MAW MANNEY! WAW DIDNT YOU CALL
PPP	(204)	UP IN TRAFALGAR SQUARE. /THE LANDLORD/ AUSHD PAT	IM	IN THE CESTERN AN WORSH IT AHT OF IM. PHYLLIS COMES BACK
BARB II	(284)	POTATO. /BILL/ (SULLENLY) AW AINT AFRIDE OF	IM	. AW AINT AFRIDE OF ENNYBODY. BAT E CAN LICK ME. SHE'S
BARB II	(300)	MIKES A MENN THET SORE THAT IZ LAWF'S A BURDN TO	IM	. AW WOWNT EV IT. AW TELL YOU; SAO TIKE YOUR MANNEY AND
CAPT III	(292)	SITCH PUSSON: ITS THET YOU DUNNO WHERE TO LOOK FR	IM	. (THE IMPLICATION THAT HE IS SUCH A PERSON IS SO
PPP	(204)	AUSHD PAT IM IN THE CESTERN AN WORSH IT AHT OF	IM	. PHYLLIS COMES BACK WITH A DOCTOR. /PHYLLIS/ THE MEDICAL
PPP	(205)	HIM ABOUT. /THE LANDLORD/ NAOW, NAOW, THET YNT	IM	. /THE DOCTOR/ WHAT, YOU! HE POUNCES ON THE LANDLORD AND
MIS.	(130)	NONE IN WILD-CAT IDEAS. /TARLETON/ THERES MONEY	IM	ME, MADAM, NO MATTER WHAT I GO INTO. /MRS TARLETON/ DONT
APPL I	(230)	THAT I GET BLAMED FOR EVERYTHING THAT GOES WRONG	IM	MY DEPARTMENT. /MAGNUS/ AH! BUT WHAT A DESPOT YOU ARE,
CAPT III	(292)	/MARZO/ (TRYING TO REPEAT HIS SUCCESS)	IM	ONLY DAM PIRATE. SHE SAINT, I TELL YOU-- NO TAKE ANY MAN
PRES	(148)	IS. (CHUCKLING) COULDNT HELP LARFIN WHEN I SOR	IM	OP IT. /MITCHENER/ (HIGHLY INCENSED) HOW DARE YOU
CAPT I	(219)	/RANKIN/ SIR HOWRRD HALLAM? /DRINKWATER/ THETS	IM	-- ENGINEST JADGE IN HINGLAND! -- AWLUS GIVES THE KET WEN
BARB II	(284)	YOU WAS SPEAKIN ON? /SHIRLEY/ THATS HIM. /BILL/	IM	THAT WRASTLED IN THE MUSIC AWL? /SHIRLEY/ THE
SIM II	(79)	. . . GOOD! PUT ME ON TO IT. (TO THE OTHERS)	IM	THROUGH TO LONDON REGIONAL. LISTEN: I'LL REPEAT IT AS IT
CAPT I	(223)	IF WE GOWS DAHN ON AHR BLOOMIN BENDED KNEES TO	IM	TO DO IT. /RANKIN/ (DRILY) AND DO YE GO DOWN ON YOUR
CAND II	(116)	MR MARCHBANKS. HE'S MAD. /BURGESS/ MAD! WHAT!	IM	TOO! ! /PROSERPINE/ MAD AS A MARCH HARE. HE DID
BARB II	(284)	TO SHIRLEY, WITH UNDISSEMBLED MISGIVING) IS THET	IM	YOU WAS SPEAKIN ON? /SHIRLEY/ THATS HIM. /BILL/ IM THAT
CAND I	(93)	I CAN SEE THAT. BE SURE YOU HINTRODOOCE ME TO	IM	, CANDY. (HE LOOKS AT HIS WATCH ANXIOUSLY). I CAN ONY
CAPT II	(265)	UNNERD RED UNS. (TO THE OTHERS) YNT YER SPOWK TO	IM	, MISTE JORNSON-- MISTE REDBROOK-- /BRASSBOUND/ (CUTTING
SUPR IV	(144)	WHEN WEVE AD YOU AS LONG TO POLISH UP AS WEVE AD	IM	, PERHAPS YOULL BEGIN TO LOOK A LITTLE BIT UP TO IS MARK.
BARB II	(289)	IM? /BARBARA/ YES. /BILL/ (FERVENTLY) GAWD ELP	IM	! GAW-AW-AW-AWD ELP IM! /BARBARA/ WHY? DO YOU THINK HE
CAPT III	(292)	ENGLAND! /MARZO/ (TRYING TO REPEAT HIS SUCCESS)	IM	! IM ONLY DAM PIRATE. SHE SAINT, I TELL YOU-- NO TAKE
BARB II	(289)	(FERVENTLY) GAWD ELP IM! GAW-AW-AW-AWD ELP	IM	! /BARBARA/ WHY? DO YOU THINK HE WONT BE HAPPY WITH

IMAGE

MTH5	(225)	YOU WILL, MARBLE REMAINS MARBLE, AND THE GRAVEN	IMAGE	AN IDOL. AS I HAVE BROKEN MY IDOLS, AND CAST AWAY MY
CLEO I	SD(106)	STILL CLEARS, UNTIL THE UPRAISED EYES OF THE	IMAGE	ARE DISTINGUISHED LOOKING STRAIGHT FORWARD AND UPWARD
KING II	(227)	TO ME. /CHARLES/ YES, ONCE, WITH THE WOMAN WHOSE	IMAGE	AS BRITANNIA IS ON EVERY BRITISH PENNY, AND WILL
OVER PREFACE	(166)	NOTHING. ONLY BY GIVING THEM BACK SOME MONSTROUS	IMAGE	CAN THE MIRROR AMUSE THEM OR TERRIFY THEM. IT IS NOT
LION PREFACE	(49)	ANY DAY) THAT CHRIST IS NOT THE LIFELESS HARMLESS	IMAGE	HE HAS HITHERTO BEEN TO YOU, BUT A RALLYING CENTRE FOR
DOCT PREFACE	(72)	DEADLY INSULT TO THE BLESSED VIRGIN TO PLACE HER	IMAGE	IN A COTTAGE THAT IS NOT KEPT UP TO THAT HIGH STANDARD
CLEO IV	SD(183)	THE PRIEST COMES TO THE TABLE AND PLACES THE	IMAGE	IN THE MIDDLE OF IT. THE LIGHT BEGINS TO CHANGE TO THE
FABL PREFACE	(69)	CHURCH AGAINST THE WORSHIPPERS OF HER WHITE	IMAGE	IN THE NEXT VILLAGE, SATANIC SOLUTION OF THE PROBLEM
CLEO II	SD(121)	A SEATED MAN WITH THE HEAD OF A HAWK. BEFORE THE	IMAGE	IS A BRONZE TRIPOD, ABOUT AS LARGE AS A THREE-LEGGED
KING I	(182)	/MRS BASHAM/ THE ARCHBISHOP IS NOT A GRAVEN	IMAGE	. AND WHEN HE IS OFFICIATING HE IS NOT IN THE LIKENESS
SIM I	(41)	LIVING LIPS INSTEAD OF THE PAINT ON A HARD WOODEN	IMAGE	. I WONDER IS IT IDOLATRY TO ADORE YOU? ST PETER IN
APPL PREFACE	(187)	BY THE VILLAGE AS SUCH. HERE YOU HAVE THE PERFECT	IMAGE	OF A POPULARLY ELECTED CABINET MINISTER AND THE CIVIL
METH PREFACE	(R67)	BUT THEY RESTRAINED THEMSELVES BY SETTING UP AN	IMAGE	OF A PUBLIC OPINION WHICH WOULD NOT TOLERATE ANY
LION PREFACE	(79)	HOWBEIT, PAUL SUCCEEDED IN STEALING THE	IMAGE	OF CHRIST CRUCIFIED FOR THE FIGURE-HEAD OF HIS
ARMS I	SD(3)	WOODEN SHRINE, BLUE AND GOLD, WITH AN IVORY	IMAGE	OF CHRIST, AND A LIGHT HANGING BEFORE IT IN A PIERCED
APPL PREFACE	(179)	I THINK YOU WILL ADMIT THAT THE BALLOON AS AN	IMAGE	OF DEMOCRACY CORRESPONDS TO THE PARLIAMENTARY FACTS.
BASH III	(121)	MADE TO BLACKEN OTHER'S EYES, STILL BATTER AT THE	IMAGE	OF DIVINITY? I LOATHE THEE. HENCE FROM MY HOUSE AND
ROCK PREFACE	(184)	WHAT HOLDS ME TOGETHER STANDING BEFORE YOU IN THE	IMAGE	OF GOD. /PILATE/ THAT IS WELL ARGUED; BUT WHAT IS
PYGM II	SD(217)	TUNING-FORKS OF DIFFERENT SIZES, A LIFE-SIZE	IMAGE	OF HALF A HUMAN HEAD, SHEWING IN SECTION THE VOCAL
NEVR I	(220)	SAYS HE'S ONLY FIFTY SEVEN AND HE THINKS ME THE	IMAGE	OF HIS MOTHER AND HE HATES HIS DAUGHTER AND-- (SHE IS
CLEO IV	SD(177)	THE GAP IN THE COLONNADE, AND COMES DOWN PAST THE	IMAGE	OF RA AND PAST THE TABLE TO CAESAR. HER RETINUE,
CLEO IV	(175)	THE ROOF, EXCEPT IN THE MIDDLE, WHERE A LIFE SIZE	IMAGE	OF RA, SEATED ON A HUGE PLINTH, TOWERS UP, WITH HAWK
FABL PREFACE	(68)	AND WAGING CIVIL WAR IN THE NAME OF THE BLACK	IMAGE	OF THE BLESSED VIRGIN IN THEIR PARISH CHURCH AGAINST
CLEO I	(107)	FIND. AND HERE AT LAST IS THEIR SENTINEL-- AN	IMAGE	OF THE CONSTANT AND IMMORTAL PART OF MY LIFE, SILENT,
CLEO II	SD(121)	LOOKING ABOUT HIM, SEES IN THE NEAREST CORNER AN	IMAGE	OF THE GOD RA, REPRESENTED AS A SEATED MAN WITH THE
MTH5	(225)	INSPIRATION BE SATISFIED WITH ANY IMAGE, EVEN AN	IMAGE	OF THE TRUTH? IN THE END THE INTELLECTUAL CONSCIENCE
JOAN EPILOG	(164)	A SPECIAL CHAPEL TO HER, AND TO PLACE HER	IMAGE	ON ITS ALTAR IN EVERY SUCH CHURCH. AND IT SHALL BE
SIM I	(41)	TO ADORE YOU? ST PETER IN ROME IS ONLY A BRONZE	IMAGE	; BUT HIS FEET HAVE BEEN WORN AWAY BY THE KISSES OF
CLEO IV	SD(189)	ORANGE, AGAINST WHICH THE COLONNADE AND THE GREAT	IMAGE	SHEW DARKLIER AND DARKLIER. /RUFIO/ CAESAR: ENOUGH OF
LION PREFACE	(49)	MUST LOOK TO YOURSELVES; FOR YOU HAVE BROUGHT THE	IMAGE	TO LIFE; AND THE MOB MAY NOT BE ABLE TO BEAR THAT
GETT	(268)	THE HEART HAS ITS PREFERENCES, LESBIA. ONE	IMAGE	, AND ONE ONLY, GETS INDELIBLY-- /LESBIA/ YES. EXCUSE
ARMS I	SD(7)	OF THE LIGHT IN THE PIERCED BALL BEFORE THE	IMAGE	, AND THE STARLIGHT SEEN THROUGH THE SLITS AT THE TOP
JITT I	(24)	LYING ON THE FLOOR). /JITTA/ (FLINCHING AT THE	IMAGE	, BUT STEADFAST IN HER THOUGHT) HAVE NO FEAR, BRUNO.
MTH5	(225)	CAN SO NOBLE AN INSPIRATION BE SATISFIED WITH ANY	IMAGE	, EVEN AN IMAGE OF THE TRUTH? IN THE END THE
BASH I	(94)	SOLITUDES. /CASHEL/ A SYLVAN GOD! A GOAT-EARED	IMAGE	! DO YOUR STATUES SPEAK? WALK? HEAVE THE CHEST WITH

IMAGE-MAKERS

METH PREFACE	(R79)	TO THE WORLD BY THE HANDS OF STORY-TELLERS AND	IMAGE-MAKERS	. WITHOUT THEIR FICTIONS THE TRUTHS OF RELIGION

IMAGE-MAKING

MTH5	(245)	PYGMALION'S DUSTBIN, NOT CURED YOU OF THIS SILLY	IMAGE-MAKING	? /ARJILLAX/ WHY DID YOU MODEL THEM AS YOUNG

IMAGES

MTH4 I	(166)	YOU REMEMBER? THE SLAVERY OF THE SHORTLIVED TO	IMAGES	AND METAPHORS. /THE ELDERLY GENTLEMAN/ (AGHAST) DO
MTH5	(247)	A REAL LIVING CREATURE. AS YOU GROW UP YOU MAKE	IMAGES	AND PAINT PICTURES. THOSE OF YOU WHO CANNOT DO THAT
MTH5	(220)	TO CRITICIZE YOUR BUSTS, THOUGH I CANNOT MAKE	IMAGES	ANY MORE THAN YOU CAN PLAY? /ARJILLAX/ ANY FOOL CAN
SIM PRO,3,	(31)	THE BOOT IS ON THE OTHER LEG. /THE PRIEST/ THOSE	IMAGES	ARE NOT IDOLS: THEY ARE PERSONIFICATIONS OF THE
SIM PRO,3,SD	(34)	AN ENGLISH MALE TOURIST ENTERS FROM AMONG THE	IMAGES	. HE IS ON THE YOUNG SIDE OF MIDDLE AGE, WITH
SIM PRO,3,	(31)	YOU CALLING HEATHEN IDOLATERS? LOOK AT ALL THOSE	IMAGES	. I SHOULD SAY, IF YOU ASK ME, THAT THE BOOT IS ON
MTH4 I	(163)	MADAM. METAPHORS MERELY. /ZOO/ IMAGES, IMAGES,	IMAGES	. I WAS TALKING ABOUT MEN, NOT ABOUT IMAGES. /THE
MTH4 I	(163)	IMAGES. I WAS TALKING ABOUT MEN, NOT ABOUT	IMAGES	. /THE ELDERLY GENTLEMAN/ I WAS ILLUSTRATING-- NOT, I
SIM PRO,3,SD	(32)	FOR STAYING, MOVES AWAY RELUCTANTLY TOWARDS THE	IMAGES	. /THE PRIESTESS/ (CALLING AFTER HER IMPERIOUSLY)
SIM PRO,3,SD	(29)	OF DUSKY YELLOW SILK ON HER LEFT NEAREST THE	IMAGES	. /THE Y.W./ YOU KNOW, TO ME THIS IS A FUNNY SORT OF
MTH5	(246)	/THE SHE-ANCIENT/ WHAT YOU CALL WORKS OF ART.	IMAGES	. WE CALL THEM DOLLS. /ARJILLAX/ JUST SO. YOU HAVE NO
MTH5	(225)	IS ONLY THE BEGINNING OF YOUR DISILLUSION WITH	IMAGES	OF ALL SORTS. AS YOUR HAND BECAME MORE SKILFUL AND
FABL PREFACE	(92)	TO LOOK AT ANYTHING WE DO NOT NOTICE THAT THE	IMAGES	OF EVERYTHING ELSE WITHIN OUR RANGE OF VISION ARE
KING I	(216)	HANDS MEAN TO YOU. BUT THE HAND THAT CAN DRAW THE	IMAGES	OF GOD AND REVEAL THE SOUL IN THEM, AND IS INSPIRED
MTH5	(224)	I TOO HAD THIS DREAM. I TOO FOUND ONE DAY THAT MY	IMAGES	OF LOVELINESS HAD BECOME VAPID, UNINTERESTING,
SIM PRO,3,SD	(29)	BETWEEN THE SEA AND A SERIES OF GIGANTIC	IMAGES	OF ORIENTAL DEITIES IN SHALLOW ALCOVES CUT IN THE
MTH5	(225)	DISCARDING THE FLEETING FLESHLY LURE, AND MAKING	IMAGES	OF THE MIND THAT FASCINATES TO THE END. BUT HOW CAN
MTH5	(224)	AM THE MAN. I WILL PLACE IN YOUR THEATRE SUCH	IMAGES	OF THE NEWLY BORN AS MUST SATISFY EVEN ECRASIA'S
MILL PREFACE	(133)	TO ENFORCE THE SECOND COMMANDMENT BY SMASHING THE	IMAGES	SOON SMASHED THE SECOND COMMANDMENT. GIVE AWAY THE
SIM PRO,3,SD	(30)	IN HAND, HAS WANDERED IN, TRYING TO IDENTIFY THE	IMAGES	WITH THE AID OF HER BOOK. SHE NOW COMES BEHIND THE
MILL PREFACE	(133)	DRESSED-UP PERFORMERS ARE ONLY AMATEURS, AND THE	IMAGES	WORKS OF ART, AND THE DUPES AND WORSHIPPERS WILL
MTH4 I	(165)	MADAM, IS THE SEED OF THE CHURCH. /ZOO/ MORE	IMAGES	, DADDY! THE BLOOD OF THE SHORTLIVED FALLS ON STONY
MTH5	(218)	PRETTY TOYS, AS YOU SEE: A PLAYHOUSE, PICTURES,	IMAGES	, FLOWERS, BRIGHT FABRICS, MUSIC: ABOVE ALL,
MTH4 I	(163)	METAPHORS, MADAM, METAPHORS MERELY. /ZOO/ IMAGES,	IMAGES	, IMAGES. I WAS TALKING ABOUT MEN, NOT ABOUT IMAGES.
MTH4 I	(163)	METAPHORS, MADAM. METAPHORS MERELY. /ZOO/	IMAGES	, IMAGES, IMAGES. I WAS TALKING ABOUT MEN, NOT ABOUT

IMAGINABLE

GETT PREFACE	(245)	THE POSSIBILITY OF THE MOST HORRIBLE CRIME	IMAGINABLE	: THAT OF THE PERSON WHO, WHEN SUFFERING FROM
INCA	(252)	OF MEN OF GENIUS ARE ALWAYS THE GREATEST DUFFERS	IMAGINABLE	. /THE INCA/ PRECISELY. THAT IS WHAT PROVES THAT

IMAGINAIRE

DOCT PREFACE	(17)	THEY NURSE THE DELUSIONS OF THE MALADE	IMAGINAIRE	(WHO IS ALWAYS REALLY ILL BECAUSE, AS THERE IS

IMAGINARY

GENV IV (114)	A PERFECT FIEND, JEALOUS, QUARRELSOME, FULL OF	IMAGINARY	AILMENTS, AS TOUCHY AS MR BATTLER, AS BUMPTIOUS AS
DOCT PREFACE(26)	OTHER DOCTORS WHO ARE DENOUNCING THE DANGER AS	IMAGINARY	AND OPSONIN AS A CRAZE OR A FAD, OBVIOUSLY DO SO
HART I SD(78)	A SWORD-STICK. HE FIGHTS A DESPERATE DUEL WITH AN	IMAGINARY	ANTAGONIST, AND AFTER MANY VICISSITUDES RUNS HIM
ROCK I SD(208)	LOOKS INSPIRED AND TRIUMPHANT. HE ADDRESSES AN	IMAGINARY	ASSEMBLY. /SIR ARTHUR/ " MY LORDS AND GENTLEMEN:
ROCK I SD(224)	STARTS VIOLENTLY AS HIS EYE, SWEEPING ROUND THE	IMAGINARY	ASSEMBLY, LIGHTS ON A WOMAN IN GREY ROBES
LION PREFACE(77)	MEN AND WOMANLY WOMEN AND WHAT NOT, ALL OF THEM	IMAGINARY	ATLASES CARRYING IMAGINARY WORLDS ON THEIR
DOCT PREFACE(56)	WOULD TAKE A GOOD DEAL OF BRANDY TO CANCEL. THIS	IMAGINARY	CASE EXPLAINS THE ACTUAL CASE OF THE SANITARY
BULL PREFACE(51)	AND THE FEELING IN THE VILLAGE WAS MUCH AS IF OUR	IMAGINARY	CHINESE OFFICERS, ON BEING INTERFERED WITH IN
MRS PREFACE(160)	IN LOVE WITH HIM UNDER THE INFLUENCE OF HIS	IMAGINARY	CRIME AGAINST HER. FINALLY SHE CONSENTS TO MARRY
MIS. PREFACE(105)	GLORIES: HE ALSO TERRIFIES HIMSELF WITH	IMAGINARY	DANGERS, HE DOES NOT EVEN PICTURE WHAT THESE
JOAN PREFACE(18)	IMAGINARY SAINTS: JUST AS SOME OTHER PEOPLE SEE	IMAGINARY	DIAGRAMS AND LANDSCAPES WITH NUMBERS DOTTED ABOUT
MIS. PREFACE(77)	IF THEY KNEW HOW, TRAVELLING IS SURROUNDED WITH	IMAGINARY	DIFFICULTIES AND TERRORS. IN SHORT, THE DIFFICULTY
HART I SD(66)	EXPRESSION, STANDING A LITTLE ON AN ENTIRELY	IMAGINARY	DIGNITY, WITH A DULL COMPLEXION, STRAIGHT,
SUPR III (114)	TO SAVE MY BODY, AND OFFERED ME QUACK CURES FOR	IMAGINARY	DISEASES. I REPLIED THAT I WAS NOT A
HART II (113)	(IN A STRANGELY CALM VOICE, STARING INTO AN	IMAGINARY	DISTANCE) HIS HEART IS BREAKING: THAT IS ALL. (
MTH5 (247)	OF YOU WHO CANNOT DO THAT MAKE STORIES ABOUT	IMAGINARY	DOLLS. OR YOU DRESS YOURSELVES UP AS DOLLS AND ACT
BARB III (347)	YOU-- YOU-- OH! FOR MY DRUM! (HE FLOURISHES	IMAGINARY	DRUMSTICKS). /BARBARA/ (ANGERED BY HIS LEVITY)
APPL PREFACE(187)	OF DEMOCRATIC CHOICE. IT IS ALWAYS BEST TO TAKE	IMAGINARY	EXAMPLES: THEY OFFEND NOBODY. IMAGINE THEN THAT WE
ROCK I (209)	SMITES THE TABLE AND PAUSES, GLARING ROUND AT HIS	IMAGINARY	HEARERS). I SEE THAT WE ARE OF ONE MIND, MY LORDS
HART II (123)	NEVER WASTE JEALOUSY ON A REAL MAN: IT IS THE	IMAGINARY	HERO THAT SUPPLANTS US ALL IN THE LONG RUN.
MTH4 II (191)	FRAGMENT OF LIFE THAT WAS GRANTED TO THEM TO AN	IMAGINARY	IMMORTALITY. THEY CRUCIFIED THE PROPHET WHO TOLD
MILL II (172)	TO BE DONE IN THE WORLD BESIDES ATTENDING RICH	IMAGINARY	INVALIDS. /EPIFANIA/ BUT IF YOU ARE WELL PAID?
PRES (143)	YOU SPEND YOUR LIVES IN AN ECSTASY OF TERROR OF	IMAGINARY	INVASIONS. I DONT BELIEVE YOU EVER GO TO BED
MILL PREFACE(125)	EVERYBODY TO READ. ITS ETHNOLOGY WAS NOT WHOLLY	IMAGINARY	. A SMATTERING OF MENDELISM IS ALL THAT ONE NEEDS
DOCT PREFACE(29)	THAT DOCTORS HAVE THEIR USES, REAL AS WELL AS	IMAGINARY	. BUT JUST AS THE BEST CARPENTER OR MASON WILL
GENV IV (89)	AS POSSIBLE; BUT OUR APPARENT PRIVACY IS QUITE	IMAGINARY	. GENERAL CONSTERNATION. THEY ALL SIT UP AS IN
GENV IV (113)	YOU OF THEM. HE WILL SHEW YOU THAT THEY ARE ALL	IMAGINARY	. HE WILL FILL YOUR HEARTS WITH LOVE OF HIMSELF;
2TRU PREFACE(7)	TO PRODUCE UNLIMITED DAYDREAMS OF BEQUESTS FROM	IMAGINARY	LONG LOST UNCLES IN AUSTRALIA OR A LUCKY TICKET IN
FABL PREFACE(87)	WELL BE THE TOWN CRIER OFFERING A REWARD FOR AN	IMAGINARY	LOST DOG. HOW ARE WE TO BEGIN? SIXTY YEARS AGO
MTH2 (61)	ALL THIS FUSS ABOUT THE LABOR PARTY, WITH ITS	IMAGINARY	NEW PRINCIPLES AND NEW POLITICS. THE LABOR MEMBERS
2TRU PREFACE(13)	HAS LATELY TAKEN ME TO TASK FOR THE ENTIRELY	IMAGINARY	OFFENCE OF ADVOCATING GOVERNMENT BY A COMMITTEE OF
BULL I (89)	HAVE LEARNT TO LIVE IN A REAL WORLD AND NOT IN AN	IMAGINARY	ONE. I OWE MORE TO YOU THAN TO ANY IRISHMAN.
UNPL PREFACE(R18)	NOT LIVE REAL LIVES, THEY MAY AT LEAST READ ABOUT	IMAGINARY	ONES, AND PERHAPS LEARN FROM THEM TO DOUBT WHETHER
FABL V (118)	CALCULATE, THEY ACCEPTED THEM AS GIFTS FROM SOME	IMAGINARY	PARADISE THEY CALLED HEAVEN. WHEN ONE OF THEIR
UNPL PREFACE(R7)	BUT MY OWN LAZINESS TO MY POWER OF CONJURING UP	IMAGINARY	PEOPLE IN IMAGINARY PLACES, AND FINDING PRETEXTS
DOCT PREFACE(53)	OF VACCINATION. JENNER HIMSELF ALLUDED TO THIS	IMAGINARY	PHENOMENON BEFORE THE INTRODUCTION OF VACCINATION,
METH PREFACE(R73)	LIFE AND DEATH WITH AN EMPTY PHRASE DENOTING AN	IMAGINARY	PHYSICAL FORCE. THESE PROFESSIONAL FACTION FIGHTS
MTH4 I (170)	NEVER OF ANY REAL HELP TO YOU. YOU DRAW WONDERFUL	IMAGINARY	PICTURES OF US, AND WRITE FICTITIOUS TALES AND
UNPL PREFACE(R7)	TO MY POWER OF CONJURING UP IMAGINARY PEOPLE IN	IMAGINARY	PLACES, AND FINDING PRETEXTS FOR THEATRICAL SCENES
JOAN PREFACE(48)	SLIGHTLY MORE LIKE THE ORIGINALS THAN THOSE	IMAGINARY	PORTRAITS OF ALL THE POPES FROM SAINT PETER ONWARD
PHIL I (78)	JEALOUSY AND ILL TEMPER; OF INSULTING ME ON	IMAGINARY	PROVOCATION; OF POSITIVELY BEATING ME; OF STEALING
POSN PREFACE(374)	PRIVATELY CIRCULATED PAMPHLETS, AND OTHER REAL OR	IMAGINARY	RARITIES, SUCH MANIACS WILL CHEERFULLY PAY FIVE
DOCT PREFACE(8)	ALL THIS SUPPOSED EXACTNESS AND INFALLIBILITY IS	IMAGINARY	; AND TO TREAT A DOCTOR AS IF HIS MISTAKES WERE
JOAN PREFACE(18)	OF HUMAN FACULTY CALL A VISUALIZER. SHE SAW	IMAGINARY	SAINTS JUST AS SOME OTHER PEOPLE SEE IMAGINARY
OVER PREFACE(165)	AT HOME) IS THAT IT IS UNCONVINCING; WHILST THE	IMAGINARY	SCENERY WITH WHICH THE AUDIENCE TRANSFIGURES A
GENV PREFACE(26)	BUT NOBODY CAN FORESEE WHAT PERIODS MY	IMAGINARY	SENATORS WILL REPRESENT. THE PACE OF EVOLUTIONARY
LION II (138)	SO REAL A THING THAT WHEN IT COMES CLOSE, ALL THE	IMAGINARY	THINGS -- ALL THE STORIES, AS YOU CALL THEM --
MTH4 I (156)	AND FRIGHTENS YOU: YOU ESCAPE FROM IT INTO AN	IMAGINARY	VACUUM IN WHICH YOU CAN INDULGE YOUR DESIRES AND
CAPT III SD(291)	CHARACTER OF A CIRCUS RINGMASTER, FLOURISHING AN	IMAGINARY	WHIP AND EGGING ON THE REST TO WILDER EXERTIONS. A
HART I SD(78)	HE DOES SO. HE LOOKS STRAIGHT INTO THE EYES OF AN	IMAGINARY	WOMAN; SEIZES HER BY THE ARMS; AND SAYS IN A DEEP
FABL PREFACE(65)	BLACKSMITH JOE GARGERY. I WAS LIVING IN AN	IMAGINARY	WORLD. DEEPLY AS I WAS INTERESTED IN POLITICS,
LION PREFACE(77)	WHAT NOT, ALL OF THEM IMAGINARY ATLASES CARRYING	IMAGINARY	WORLDS ON THEIR UNSUBSTANTIAL SHOULDERS. THE EDEN
BULL PREFACE(56)	INTRODUCED INTO EGYPT BY THE ENGLISH IN 1882 WAS	IMAGINARY	, AND THAT THE REAL WORK OF COPING WITH EGYPTIAN
MIS. PREFACE(56)	AND FROM THE PEOPLE WHO REALLY PROFIT BY IT TO	IMAGINARY	" FOREIGN SCOUNDRELS," AND TO SECURE A MONOPOLY OF

IMAGINATION

AUGS (265)	AGAIN THE HUNS THAT THEY NEVER SAW? THEYVE NO	IMAGINATION	: THATS WHAT IT IS. BRING THE HUNS HERE; AND
GETT (269)	BUT LOVE-- /LESBIA/ OH, LOVE! HAVE YOU NO	IMAGINATION	? DO YOU THINK I HAVE NEVER BEEN IN LOVE WITH
NEVR II (257)	OH, DONT YOU SEE WHAT YOU HAVE SET TO WORK IN MY	IMAGINATION	? /GLORIA/ I HOPE YOU ARE NOT GOING TO BE SO
JOAN EPILOG (161)	TORMENT IN EVERY AGE TO SAVE THOSE THAT HAVE NO	IMAGINATION	? /JOAN/ WELL, IF I SAVED ALL THOSE HE WOULD
MTH4 II (179)	POSSESSES. /THE ORACLE/ YOU MEAN THAT YOU HAVE NO	IMAGINATION	? /NAPOLEON/ (FORCIBLY) I MEAN THAT I HAVE THE
SUPR III (104)	STUPIDITY ACCUSING IMAGINATION OF FOLLY, AND	IMAGINATION	ACCUSING STUPIDITY OF IGNORANCE: WHEREAS, ALAS!
SUPR III (104)	ALAS! STUPIDITY HAS ALL THE KNOWLEDGE, AND	IMAGINATION	ALL THE INTELLIGENCE. /THE DEVIL/ AND A PRETTY
LION PREFACE(15)	FROM ALL THAT, HIS REFORMATION WAS A TRIUMPH OF	IMAGINATION	AND A TRIUMPH OF CHEAPNESS. IT BROUGHT YOU
2TRU II (70)	ALL THE MIRACLES OF THE UNIVERSE TO STAGGER HIS	IMAGINATION	AND ALL THE PROBLEMS OF HUMAN DESTINY TO EMPLOY
MRS IV (238)	THOUGHT OUR WHOLE RELATIONS WERE ALTERED IN YOUR	IMAGINATION	AND CONSCIENCE, AS YOU PUT IT, THE MOMENT THOSE
SUPR PREFACE(R19)	AND FECUNDITY, BUT SUPERIOR TO HIM IN	IMAGINATION	AND CUNNING. THE DON JUAN PLAY, HOWEVER, IS TO
GETT SD(275)	IMPORTANT. SHE HAS MORE THAN COMMON	IMAGINATION	AND NO MORE THAN COMMON CONCEPTION AND
METH PREFACE(R52)	CLEVER AND STUDIOUS MAN, NOT WITHOUT ROOTS OF	IMAGINATION	AND PHILOSOPHY IN HIM WHICH DARWINISM KILLED AS
HART PREFACE(35)	OF PRETTY PICTURES OF PRETTY SAINTS ASSAILED THE	IMAGINATION	AND SENSES THROUGH STAINED-GLASS WINDOWS; AND
HART PREFACE(10)	THEY WERE NOT CLEVER ENOUGH TO APPEAL TO THE	IMAGINATION	AND SOCIABILITY OF THE HEARTBREAKERS BY THE ARTS
MTH1 I (10)	THAT IS THE WORD THAT MEANS BOTH THE BEGINNING IN	IMAGINATION	AND THE END IN CREATION. /EVE/ FIND ME A WORD
PYGM EPILOG (294)	FOR HIM. THE SOMETHING APPEARED VAGUELY TO HIS	IMAGINATION	AS A PRIVATE SECRETARYSHIP OR A SINECURE OF SOME
LION PREFACE(9)	YOU KNOW SOMETHING OF THE HISTORY OF THE HUMAN	IMAGINATION	AS APPLIED TO RELIGION. NOT LONG AGO I ASKED A
SUPR II (60)	TO YOUR MOTHER, AND HELP HER TO POISON RHODA'S	IMAGINATION	AS SHE HAS POISONED YOURS. IT IS THE TAME
GETT SD(275)	OR ANYTHING ELSE THAT HAPPENS TO STRIKE HER	IMAGINATION	AS SOUNDING INTELLECTUALLY IMPORTANT. SHE HAS
NEVR II SD(225)	AMBITION STANDS REBUKED AS VULGARITY, AND	IMAGINATION	AS TREASON TO THE ABOUNDING SUFFICIENCY AND
2TRU II (62)	YOU, MY SWEETIE, LIE AND LIE AND LIE UNTIL YOUR	IMAGINATION	BURSTS. /THE PATIENT/ (THROWING HERSELF MOODILY
SUPR HANDBOK(227)	TRYING TO REPLACE THEM WITH SOMETHING BETTER. THE	IMAGINATION	CANNOT CONCEIVE A VILER CRIMINAL THAN HE WHO
CLEO IV (182)	EXCEPT THE SOURCE OF THE NILE." /CAESAR/ (HIS	IMAGINATION	CATCHING FIRE) AND WHY NOT SEE THAT? CLEOPATRA:
ROCK PREFACE(155)	AND OBSCENE METHOD OF KILLING THAT THE HUMAN	IMAGINATION	COULD CONCEIVE AT ITS VILEST WAS SPECIALLY
METH PREFACE(R50)	UNNOTICED OR UNDISCOVERED, WHICH ONLY REQUIRE	IMAGINATION	ENOUGH TO FIT THEM TO THE EVOLUTION OF AN
CLEO IV (175)	MEN. GIVE ME A GOOD TALKER-- ONE WITH WIT AND	IMAGINATION	ENOUGH TO LIVE WITHOUT CONTINUALLY DOING
JOAN PREFACE(12)	THIS ENTIRELY REASONABLE NECESSITY CAME TO HER	IMAGINATION	FIRST AS AN ORDER FROM GOD DELIVERED THROUGH THE
2TRU PREFACE(7)	WHICH THEY WERE BORN, AND HAVE TO DEPEND ON THEIR	IMAGINATION	FOR THEIR NOTIONS OF WHAT IT IS LIKE TO BE IN
ROCK PREFACE(175)	OF FOXE'S BOOK OF MARTYRS STANDING OUT IN OUR	IMAGINATION	FROM THOUSANDS OF FORGOTTEN MARTYRDOMS. GALILEO
ARMS III (70)	LOOK AT ME. SHE, RICH, YOUNG, BEAUTIFUL, WITH HER	IMAGINATION	FULL OF FAIRY PRINCES AND NOBLE NATURES AND
DOCT II SD(117)	AND HIS ARTIST'S POWER OF APPEALING TO THE	IMAGINATION	GAINS HIM CREDIT FOR ALL SORTS OF QUALITIES AND
MIS. PREFACE(105)	IN THE MILITARY CODE. A VERY LITTLE REALISTIC	IMAGINATION	GIVES AN AMBITIOUS PERSON ENORMOUS POWER OVER
SUPR III (106)	BUT ON DEATH SHE SPENT ALL SHE HAD. THEIR	IMAGINATION	GLOWS, THEIR ENERGIES RISE UP AT THE IDEA OF
JOAN PREFACE(11)	AS SAINT FRANCIS AND SAINT JOAN DID. IF NEWTON'S	IMAGINATION	HAD BEEN OF THE SAME VIVIDLY DRAMATIC KIND HE
MILL I (148)	I ADMITTED HIM TO MY WORLD, THE WORLD WHICH MY	IMAGINATION	HAD PEOPLED WITH HEROES AND SAINTS. NEVER BEFORE
VWOO 2 (127)	WAY TO BE HAPPY AND LONGLIVED. /A/ BUT IF YOUR	IMAGINATION	HAS ONLY ONE VILLAGE IN IT IT MUST BE PRETTY
SUPR HANDBOK(181)	OF HEREDITY TOOK HOLD OF THE SCIENTIFIC	IMAGINATION	IN THE MIDDLE OF LAST CENTURY, ITS DEVOTEES
MIS. PREFACE(105)	BETTER A HOPELESS WORLD. THE WISE MAN KNOWS THAT	IMAGINATION	IS NOT ONLY A MEANS OF PLEASING HIMSELF AND
JOAN PREFACE(11)	THEIR OWN. THERE ARE PEOPLE IN THE WORLD WHOSE	IMAGINATION	IS SO VIVID THAT WHEN THEY HAVE AN IDEA IT COMES
MTH1 I (10)	LILITH THAT NEVER WAS. SHE DID NOT KNOW THEN THAT	IMAGINATION	IS THE BEGINNING OF CREATION. YOU IMAGINE WHAT
KING I (181)	" IN THE BEGINNING"! THINK OF IT IF YOU HAVE ANY	IMAGINATION	. AND BECAUSE SOME FOOL IN A STEEPLEHOUSE,
APPL INTRLUD(251)	JOB. /ORINTHIA/ YOU THINK SO BECAUSE YOU HAVE NO	IMAGINATION	. AND YOU DONT KNOW ME BECAUSE I HAVE NEVER LET
MIS. PREFACE(104)	TO DO WITH IT EXCEPT FOR PURELY SECULAR REASONS.	IMAGINATION	. BEFORE WE CAN CLEARLY UNDERSTAND HOW BALEFUL
SUPR III (82)	THE JEW ALWAYS BECOMES LEADER, BY HIS BRAINS AND	IMAGINATION	. BUT WITH ALL MY PRIDE OF RACE I WOULD GIVE
MIS. PREFACE(105)	OVER THE MULTITUDINOUS VICTIMS OF THE ROMANTIC	IMAGINATION	. FOR THE ROMANCER NOT ONLY PLEASES HIMSELF WITH
BULL I (87)	ACROSS THE TABLE) IT'S ALL DREAMING, ALL	IMAGINATION	. HE CANT BE RELIGIOUS. THE INSPIRED CHURCHMAN
APPL PREFACE(192)	THAT GATTIE HAD ANY WORKS, EXCEPT IN HIS FERVID	IMAGINATION	. HE MENTIONED " THE COMPANY." THAT WAS MORE
BULL I (85)	MY HEART: AN IRISHMAN'S HEART IS NOTHING BUT HIS	IMAGINATION	. HOW MANY OF ALL THOSE MILLIONS THAT HAVE LEFT

ANNA (296)	THAT? /THE GRAND DUCHESS/ (IMPETUOUSLY) IN YOUR	IMAGINATION	. I CAME ALONE. I AM ALONE. HUNDREDS OF OFFICERS
MTH4 I (163)	IF THEIR STRENGTH EVER EXISTED OUTSIDE YOUR	IMAGINATION	. I DO NOT KNOW HOW OLD YOU ARE: YOU LOOK ABOUT
LION PREFACE(46)	BECAUSE IN SOME MYSTERIOUS WAY IT APPEALS TO HIS	IMAGINATION	. IF YOU ASK HIM WHY HE BELIEVES THAT THE SUN IS
NEVR IV (302)	PROUDLY) KEEP YOUR OWN GLORIA! THE GLORIA OF YOUR	IMAGINATION	. (HER EMOTION BEGINS TO BREAK THROUGH HER
PYGM IV (264)	UNDERSTAND. I'M TOO IGNORANT. /HIGGINS/ IT'S ONLY	IMAGINATION	. LOW SPIRITS AND NOTHING ELSE. NOBODY'S HURTING
NEVR IV (301)	WHAT DO YOU MEAN? /VALENTINE/ THE GLORIA OF MY	IMAGINATION	. /GLORIA/ (PROUDLY) KEEP YOUR OWN GLORIA: THE
JOAN 1 (67)	THEY COME FROM GOD. /ROBERT/ THEY COME FROM YOUR	IMAGINATION	. /JOAN/ OF COURSE. THAT IS HOW THE MESSAGES OF
BUOY III (37)	BUT REALLY DOES NOT EXIST AT ALL EXCEPT IN MY	IMAGINATION	. SO NOW YOU KNOW, ALL OF YOU. LET US CHANGE THE
MIS. PREFACE(105)	SENSING THEM; AND THIS I WILL CALL THE REALISTIC	IMAGINATION	. TAKE FOR EXAMPLE MARRIAGE AND WAR. ONE MAN HAS
MIS. PREFACE(104)	THINGS AS THEY ARE NOT: THIS I CALL THE ROMANTIC	IMAGINATION	. THE OTHER IS THE POWER TO IMAGINE THINGS AS
PLES PREFACE(R7)	AT LEAST, WAS A FIGMENT OF THE REVOLUTIONARY	IMAGINATION	. THIS WAS NOT TO BE ENDURED. I HAD RASHLY TAKEN
APPL I (198)	I MEAN; AND HE HAD AN ODDLY LIMITED SORT OF	IMAGINATION	. WHAT I MEAN IS THAT HE COULDNT IMAGINE
MIS. (152)	YOUR COUNTRYWOMEN HAVE ALWAYS APPEALED TO OUR	IMAGINATION	. WOMEN OF DESTINY! BEAUTIFUL! MUSICAL!
HART III (143)	BE REGARDED MERELY AS A SUCCESSFUL MAN. I HAVE AN	IMAGINATION	LIKE ANYONE ELSE. I HAVE A PRESENTIMENT-- /MRS
AUGS (277)	YES: IT IS, ISNT IT? LUCY APPEALS TO THE	IMAGINATION	LIKE NO OTHER WOMAN. BY THE WAY (HANDING OVER
BULL PREFACE(55)	TORTURE FOR WHICH THE MILITARY AND BUREAUCRATIC	IMAGINATION	LUSTS. SO, AS THEY HAD ROOM FOR ONLY ONE MAN ON
SUPR HANDBOK(223)	VIRTUE OR VICE IN HIM, HOWEVER CLOSELY THE	IMAGINATION	MAY ASSOCIATE THEM. VIRTUE CONSISTS, NOT IN
LION PREFACE(14)	WILLING TO BE HANGED FOR IT IN YOUR STEAD" ? OUR	IMAGINATION	MUST COME TO OUR RESCUE. WHY NOT, INSTEAD OF
BULL I (87)	OUT OF HIM LIKE THAT DREAMING. AN IRISHMAN'S	IMAGINATION	NEVER LETS HIM ALONE, NEVER CONVINCES HIM, NEVER
METH PREFACE(R56)	AFTER ALL, YOU CANNOT UNDERSTAND MOSES WITHOUT	IMAGINATION	NOR SPURGEON WITHOUT METAPHYSICS; BUT YOU CAN BE
BULL I (91)	OF NEW YORK. I WANT IRELAND TO BE THE BRAINS AND	IMAGINATION	OF A BIG COMMONWEALTH, NOT A ROBINSON CRUSOE
ARMS II SD(28)	HARDIHOOD, THE HIGH SPIRIT, AND THE SUSCEPTIBLE	IMAGINATION	OF AN UNTAMED MOUNTAINEER CHIEFTAIN. BUT HIS
SUPR III (104)	THE OTHER OF ITS OWN DEFECT: STUPIDITY ACCUSING	IMAGINATION	OF FOLLY, AND IMAGINATION ACCUSING STUPIDITY OF
DOCT PREFACE(31)	A MAHOMET LEARNS THAT IF HE WISHES TO STRIKE THE	IMAGINATION	OF HIS TRIBE-- AND WITHOUT DOING THAT HE CANNOT
MTH2 (78)	OF THE GARDEN OF EDEN HAS SURVIVED AND HELD THE	IMAGINATION	OF MEN SPELLBOUND FOR CENTURIES, WHILST HUNDREDS
FABL PREFACE(79)	OUR IGNORANCE OF HISTORY OF HOME AFFAIRS. IN THE	IMAGINATION	OF OUR AMATEUR POLITICIANS ENGLAND IS A UTOPIA
JOAN PREFACE(14)	ST CATHERINE, BUT THE DRAMATIZATION BY JOAN'S	IMAGINATION	OF THAT PRESSURE UPON HER OF THE DRIVING FORCE
LION PREFACE(16)	YET ANOTHER PERSISTENT BELIEF HAS BESET THE	IMAGINATION	OF THE RELIGIOUS EVER SINCE RELIGION SPREAD
HART PREFACE(25)	THE PRESENTATION OF THE WAR TO THE REASON AND	IMAGINATION	OF THE COUNTRY AND THE WORLD IN SPEECHES, POEMS,
DOCT PREFACE(21)	KNOWS WHY! VIRGINIA SNAKE ROOT FASCINATES THE	IMAGINATION	OF THE HERBALIST AS MERCURY USED TO FASCINATE
CATH PREFACE(156)	TO LET SLIP A WORD THAT COULD BLUDGEON THE	IMAGINATION	OF THE READER BY REMINDING HIM OF THE BOARDS AND
SHAK PREFACE(135)	IMPOSSIBLE FOR LIVING ACTORS, KEEPS THE	IMAGINATION	OF THE SPECTATORS CONTINUOUSLY STIMULATED. WHEN
LION PREFACE(5)	BEEN MILITANT ATHEISTS, BUT FOR SOME REASON THE	IMAGINATION	OF WHITE MANKIND HAS PICKED OUT JESUS OF
GETT PREFACE(219)	THE ILLUSIONS OF SEXUAL ATTRACTION WILL CAUSE THE	IMAGINATION	OF YOUNG MEN TO ENDOW HER WITH EVERY
MRS IV (238)	DOES IT MAKE ANY DIFFERENCE? I MEAN IN YOUR	IMAGINATION	OR CONSCIENCE; FOR OF COURSE IT MAKES NO REAL
GENV IV (101)	POWER OVER THE IMAGINATION, AND THROUGH THE	IMAGINATION	OVER THE CHARACTERS AND POWERS OF MANKIND. /THE
JOAN PREFACE(12)	SANE; BUT ITS FORM PROVES THAT HER DRAMATIC	IMAGINATION	PLAYED TRICKS WITH HER SENSES. HER POLICY WAS
SUPR III (104)	BY THE REALITIES LEARNT FROM TOIL AND POVERTY:	IMAGINATION	RESOLVED TO STARVE SOONER THAN FACE THESE
KING I (185)	PASCAL, TEACHED ME THIS. YOU MUST NEVER LET YOUR	IMAGINATION	RUN AWAY WITH YOU. WHEN YOU THINK OF GRANDIOSE
LION PREFACE(14)	THE REDEEMER IS ONCE FOUND (OR INVENTED BY THE	IMAGINATION	) IS TO BELIEVE IN THE EFFICACY OF THE
BULL I (87)	SAVES EVERYTHING EXCEPT IMAGINATION, IMAGINATION,	IMAGINATION	; AND IMAGINATION'S SUCH A TORTURE THAT YOU CANT
MIS. PREFACE(105)	AND ROUTED ENEMIES IN THE FIELD. THAT IS ROMANTIC	IMAGINATION	; AND THE MISCHIEF IT DOES IS INCALCULABLE. IT
2TRU II (69)	PLANNING ROBBERIES. OF COURSE I KNOW IT'S MOSTLY	IMAGINATION	; BUT THE FUN IS IN THE PLANNING AND THE
MTH1 I (12)	DO CARE. IT IS THAT CARE THAT WILL PROMPT YOUR	IMAGINATION	; INFLAME YOUR DESIRES; MAKE YOUR WILL
SUPR PREFACE(R29)	AND THEN LEAVE HIS WORKS ENTIRELY TO THE READER'S	IMAGINATION	; SO THAT AT THE END OF THE BOOK YOU WHISPER TO
DOCT PREFACE(52)	ITS FLESH, IS KEPT AT A GREATER DISTANCE IN OUR	IMAGINATION	THAN OUR FOSTER MOTHER THE COW. AT ALL EVENTS,
LION PREFACE(34)	HAS THIS STORY CONQUERED AND FASCINATED OUR	IMAGINATION	THAT MOST OF US SUPPOSE ALL THE GOSPELS TO
BULL PREFACE(57)	HUMAN SACRIFICE WHEN EVANGELIZING TRIBES IN WHOSE	IMAGINATION	THAT PRACTICE IS INSEPARABLY BOUND UP WITH
MIS. PREFACE(104)	UP THE CONFUSION MADE BY OUR USE OF THE WORD	IMAGINATION	TO DENOTE TWO VERY DIFFERENT POWERS OF MIND. ONE
MIS. PREFACE(3)	ON THE PART OF THE LIFE FORCE. PEOPLE WITH NO	IMAGINATION	TRY TO MAKE THINGS WHICH WILL LAST FOR EVER, AND
JOAN PREFACE(12)	HE WAS MORE FANTASTIC THAN JOAN, BECAUSE HIS	IMAGINATION	WAS NOT DRAMATIC BUT MATHEMATICAL AND THEREFORE
ARMS I (5)	AND HIS SOLDIERSHIP MIGHT NOT PROVE MERE	IMAGINATION	WHEN HE WENT INTO A REAL BATTLE. I HAD AN UNEASY
MIS. PREFACE(79)	BUT WHAT YOU REALLY ARE MAY SEEM PLEASANT TO THE	IMAGINATION	WHEN THE TREATMENT IS ABOVE YOUR MERITS; BUT IN
GETT PREFACE(226)	SITUATIONS THAT ONLY BY BEGLAMORING THE HUMAN	IMAGINATION	WITH A HYPNOTIC SUGGESTION OF WHOLLY UNNATURAL
OVER PREFACE(159)	HAS BEEN INVESTED BY THE POPULAR HISTORICAL	IMAGINATION	WITH ALL THE EXTRAVAGANCES OF A MESSALINA OR A
MIS. PREFACE(4)	AS YOU WILL ON HIS IGNORANCE, HIS FEARS, AND HIS	IMAGINATION	WITH BRIBES OF PARADISES AND THREATS OF HELLS,
MTH4 I (161)	THINGS OF WHICH IT HAD SOME REAL KNOWLEDGE. BUT	IMAGINATION	WITH MICROSCOPES, WORKING ON A TERRIFYING
MTH4 I (161)	PRODUCE! WHATEVER THE SCIENTIFIC PEOPLE MAY SAY,	IMAGINATION	WITHOUT MICROSCOPES WAS KINDLY AND OFTEN
MTH4 II (179)	(FORCIBLY) I MEAN THAT I HAVE THE ONLY	IMAGINATION	WORTH HAVING: THE POWER OF IMAGINING THINGS AS
JOAN PREFACE(15)	ANY OTHER AUGUSTINIAN MONK: HE HAD A MORE VIVID	IMAGINATION	, AND HAD PERHAPS EATEN AND SLEPT LESS: THAT WAS
GENV IV (101)	QUALITY THAT GIVES WAR ITS UNIQUE POWER OVER THE	IMAGINATION	, AND THROUGH THE IMAGINATION OVER THE
SUPR I (36)	SAVE OUR SCALPS FROM THE RED INDIANS. YOU HAVE NO	IMAGINATION	, ANN. I AM TEN TIMES MORE DESTRUCTIVE NOW THAN
LION PREFACE(19)	THAN A KNOWLEDGE OF THESE HABITS OF THE HUMAN	IMAGINATION	, ANYONE MAY NOW READ THE FOUR GOSPELS WITHOUT
UNPL PREFACE(R7)	HAVE CONJURED SO AS TO INTEREST NOT ONLY MY OWN	IMAGINATION	, BUT THAT OF AT LEAST SOME SEVENTY OR A HUNDRED
BARB PREFACE(207)	THE CONFLICT BETWEEN REAL LIFE AND THE ROMANTIC	IMAGINATION	, CRITICS NEVER AFFILIATE ME TO MY COUNTRYMAN
BULL PREFACE(18)	IRISHMAN, WITH A FAR SUBTLER AND MORE FASTIDIOUS	IMAGINATION	, HAS ONE EYE ALWAYS ON THINGS AS THEY ARE. IF
BULL PREFACE(18)	THAT THE ENGLISHMAN IS WHOLLY AT THE MERCY OF HIS	IMAGINATION	, HAVING NO SENSE OF REALITY TO CHECK IT. THE
BULL I (87)	WORKING. IT SAVES EVERYTHING EXCEPT IMAGINATION,	IMAGINATION	, IMAGINATION; AND IMAGINATION'S SUCH A TORTURE
BULL I (87)	IT SAVES WORKING. IT SAVES EVERYTHING EXCEPT	IMAGINATION	, IMAGINATION, IMAGINATION; AND IMAGINATION'S
LION PREFACE(14)	WHICH THE REDEEMER, THOUGH CONCEIVED BY THE HUMAN	IMAGINATION	, IS NOT YET FOUND. HE IS AWAITED AND EXPECTED
METH PREFACE(R56)	YOU CAN BE A THOROUGHGOING NEO-DARWINIAN WITHOUT	IMAGINATION	, METAPHYSICS, POETRY, CONSCIENCE, OR DECENCY.
ANNA (300)	BUT THAT WAS BECAUSE THEY WERE DOGS: THEY HAD NO	IMAGINATION	, NO IDEALS, NO SENSE OF HONOR AND DIGNITY TO
MTH5 (254)	IMPULSES ON TO THE PLANE OF BEAUTY, OF	IMAGINATION	, OF ROMANCE, OF POETRY, OF ART, OF-- /ACIS/
SUPR III (115)	WELL, I FOUND THAT WHEN I HAD TOUCHED A WOMAN'S	IMAGINATION	, SHE WOULD ALLOW ME TO PERSUADE MYSELF THAT SHE
MIS. PREFACE(79)	REVERSE. WHEN I WAS A VERY SMALL BOY, MY ROMANTIC	IMAGINATION	, STIMULATED BY EARLY DOSES OF FICTION, LED ME
DOCT PREFACE(36)	THE BUSINESS COMES TO BE DONE, THE SAME WANT OF	IMAGINATION	, THE SAME STUPIDITY AND CRUELTY, THE SAME
NEVR II (258)	ME TO BELIEVE MY EYES, MY HEART, MY INSTINCTS, MY	IMAGINATION	, WHICH ARE ALL TELLING ME THE MOST MONSTROUS
MIS. PREFACE(107)	OFTEN CONSISTS NOT ONLY IN A LACK OF ROMANTIC	IMAGINATION	, WHICH LACK IS A MERIT, BUT OF THE REALISTIC,
MIS. PREFACE(107)	BUT OF THE REALISTIC, CONSTRUCTIVE, UTOPIAN	IMAGINATION	, WHICH LACK IS A GHASTLY DEFECT. FREEDOM FROM
JITT III (65)	GOING OVER AND OVER THAT DREADFUL TIME IN MY	IMAGINATION	, WITH NO RELIEF BUT JUST THINKING HOW I CAN
DEST SD(157)	MAN WITHOUT FEAR, WITHOUT REVERENCE, WITHOUT	IMAGINATION	, WITHOUT SENSE, HOPELESSLY INSUSCEPTIBLE TO THE
BARB PREFACE(207)	AND POWERFULLY BY DINT OF MERE ROMANCE-FED	IMAGINATION	, WITHOUT COURAGE, WITHOUT MEANS, WITHOUT
MTH3 (117)	THAT THE REALITY? HOW THESE THINGS GROW IN OUR	IMAGINATION	! BUT MAY I SAY, MRS LUTESTRING, THAT THE

IMAGINATION'S

BULL I (87)	EXCEPT IMAGINATION, IMAGINATION, IMAGINATION; AND	IMAGINATION'S	SUCH A TORTURE THAT YOU CANT BEAR IT WITHOUT

IMAGINATIONS

OVER PREFACE(167)	THE MORE INTERESTING BECOME THE IMPULSES AND	IMAGINATIONS	AND REASONINGS, IF ANY, OF THE PEOPLE WHO
PLES PREFACE(R19)	OUR INSTITUTIONS ON THE IDEALS SUGGESTED TO OUR	IMAGINATIONS	BY OUR HALF-SATISFIED PASSIONS, INSTEAD OF ON A
JOAN PREFACE(14)	NEED. THE DIVERSE MANNERS IN WHICH OUR	IMAGINATIONS	DRAMATIZE THE APPROACH OF THE SUPERPERSONAL
SIM II (67)	MINDS. /MAYA/ WE HAVE NO MINDS. /VASHTI/ WE HAVE	IMAGINATIONS	. /KANCHIN/ WE HAVE MADE THIS HOUSE A TEMPLE.
DOCT PREFACE(43)	AS LITTLE AS POSSIBLE BY USING THEIR BRAINS AND	IMAGINATIONS	. THUS WE HAVE, AS PART OF THE ROUTINE OF
GENV PREFACE(15)	INCLUDED A PERCENTAGE OF THINKERS WHO HAD THEIR	IMAGINATIONS	OBSESSED BY UTOPIAS IN WHICH PERFECTLY WISE
MTH3 (129)	THE TIES OF BLOOD WILL LOSE THEIR INNOCENCE. THE	IMAGINATIONS	OF MEN, LET LOOSE OVER THE POSSIBILITIES OF
PYGM EPILOG (303)	LOVE LIKE ANY COMMON MAN. WE ALL HAVE PRIVATE	IMAGINATIONS	OF THAT SORT, BUT WHEN IT COMES TO BUSINESS, TO
METH PREFACE(R73)	THAT WENT FAR BEYOND THE COMPARATIVELY UNINFORMED	IMAGINATIONS	OF THE AUTHORS OF THE BOOK OF GENESIS, REGARDED
OVER PREFACE(163)	OF EARNESTNESS TO BE ACCEPTED BY THE WILLING	IMAGINATIONS	OF THE YOUNGER SPECTATORS AS A DESPERATE
GETT (311)	OF THE CHURCH, AND ITS INFLUENCE ON THE SOULS AND	IMAGINATIONS	OF THE PEOPLE, VERY SOON BEGIN TO GO RAPIDLY TO
2TRU PREFACE(19)	THAT IT BECAME NECESSARY TO PRACTISE ON THE	IMAGINATIONS	OF THE POOR TO THE EXTENT OF MAKING THEM
MRS PREFACE(168)	HUMAN FEELING. PEOPLE WITH COMPLETELY THEATRIFIED	IMAGINATIONS	TELL ME THAT NO GIRL WOULD TREAT HER MOTHER AS
PYGM EPILOG (289)	AND INDEED, WOULD HARDLY NEED TELLING IF OUR	IMAGINATIONS	WERE NOT SO ENFEEBLED BY THEIR LAZY DEPENDENCE
BULL IV (178)	IT EFFICIENTLY, AND OUR LIBRARY TO FUDDLE THE FEW	IMAGINATIONS	YOUR DISTILLERIES WILL SPARE, AND OUR REPAIRED
MTH1 I (10)	SNAKE INTERLACED WITH ME; AND NOW THERE ARE TWO	IMAGINATIONS	, TWO DESIRES, TWO WILLS TO CREATE WITH. /EVE/

IMAGINATIVE

GETT (281)	DID YOU KNOW? /THE BISHOP/ OH, I SHOULD SAY MOST	IMAGINATIVE	AND CULTIVATED YOUNG WOMEN FEEL LIKE THAT. I

SUPR III (111)	STRONG TO BE CONTROLLED BY HER BODILY, AND TOO	IMAGINATIVE	AND MENTALLY VIGOROUS TO BE CONTENT WITH MERE
SUPR III (121)	PRUDENT, THE THRIFTILY SELFISH AND AMBITIOUS, THE	IMAGINATIVE	AND POETIC, THE LOVERS OF MONEY AND SOLID
ARMS II SD(28)	IN A PARISIAN SALON, SHEWING THAT THE CLEVER	IMAGINATIVE	BARBARIAN HAS AN ACUTE CRITICAL FACULTY WHICH
PYGM EPILOG (291)	THAT REMARKABLE MOTHERS ARE UNCOMMON. IF AN	IMAGINATIVE	BOY HAS A SUFFICIENTLY RICH MOTHER WHO HAS
MIS. PREFACE(9)	THE COCK WOULD COME DOWN THE CHIMNEY. LESS	IMAGINATIVE	BUT EQUALLY DISHONEST PEOPLE TOLD ME I SHOULD GO
BASH PREFACE(91)	THE ELIZABETHAN STYLE HAS MANY CHARMS FOR	IMAGINATIVE	CHILDREN. IT IS BLOODY, BOMBASTIC, VIOLENT,
SUPR III (94)	OF LOVE BECAUSE THEY HAVE NO BODIES. SHEER	IMAGINATIVE	DEBAUCHERY! FAUGH! /ANA/ HAS EVEN DEATH FAILED
SUPR III SD(72)	STORIES, AND A POSITION WHICH LENDS ITSELF TO	IMAGINATIVE	DECORATION. THE RANKS OF UNSKILLED LABOR OFFER
MIS. PREFACE(107)	WHICH LACK IS A GHASTLY DEFECT. FREEDOM FROM	IMAGINATIVE	ILLUSION IS THEREFORE NO GUARANTEE WHATEVER OF
LION PREFACE(82)	LUKE) MUCH WEAKER IN POWER OF THOUGHT THAN IN	IMAGINATIVE	LITERARY ART. HENCE WE FIND LUKE CREDITED WITH
MIS. PREFACE(3)	LIVE FOR EVER THEMSELVES, BUT THE INTELLIGENTLY	IMAGINATIVE	MAN KNOWS VERY WELL THAT IT IS WASTE OF LABOR TO
BULL PREFACE(15)	THE SHARPENED WITS, THE SENSITIVE PRIDE OF THE	IMAGINATIVE	MAN WHO HAS FOUGHT HIS WAY UP THROUGH SOCIAL
SUPR III SD(72)	THE TRAMP, ARE EQUALLY ENTITLED. FURTHER, THE	IMAGINATIVE	MAN, IF HIS LIFE IS TO BE TOLERABLE TO HIM, MUST
JITT I (14)	UNSMILING MOUTHS AND TRAGIC EYES NOT ONLY MAKE	IMAGINATIVE	MEN FANCY UNFATHOMABLE DEPTHS IN THEIR NATURES,
JOAN 1,SD(60)	WIDE APART AND BULGING AS THEY OFTEN DO IN VERY	IMAGINATIVE	PEOPLE, A LONG WELL-SHAPED NOSE WITH WIDE
JOAN PREFACE(15)	VISION. AND WHEN IN THE CASE OF EXCEPTIONALLY	IMAGINATIVE	PERSONS, ESPECIALLY THOSE PRACTISING CERTAIN
BARB III (346)	SO HORRIBLY ABUSED AS THE INTELLECTUAL POWER, THE	IMAGINATIVE	POWER, THE POETIC, RELIGIOUS POWER THAT CAN
JOAN PREFACE(47)	MY OWN AGE AGAINST THE CHARGE OF BEING LESS	IMAGINATIVE	THAN THE MIDDLE AGES. I AFFIRM THAT THE
DEST SD(149)	DEPARTMENT DURING THE FRENCH REVOLUTION. HE IS	IMAGINATIVE	WITHOUT ILLUSIONS, AND CREATIVE WITHOUT
PHIL I SD(70)	AT WHICH HE IS HIMSELF LAUGHING, AND HIS CLEVER,	IMAGINATIVE	, HUMOROUS WAYS, CONTRAST STRONGLY WITH THE
SUPR HANDBOK(181)	TASTES AND RANGE OF HIS CLASS, AND OF A CLEVER,	IMAGINATIVE	, INTELLECTUAL, HIGHLY CIVILIZED JEWESS, MIGHT
SUPR III (129)	OPINIONATED; NOT PROGRESSIVE, ONLY FACTIOUS; NOT	IMAGINATIVE	, ONLY SUPERSTITIOUS; NOT JUST, ONLY VINDICTIVE;

IMAGINATIVENESS

3PLA PREFACE(R13)	TO A FAR MORE CULTIVATED SENSUOUSNESS AND	IMAGINATIVENESS	THAN THE MUSICAL FARCES IN WHICH OUR STAGE

IMAGINE

MTH1 I (11)	SERPENT/ LILITH DID NOT IMAGINE HIM SO. HE CAN	IMAGINE	: HE CAN WILL: HE CAN DESIRE: HE CAN GATHER HIS LIFE
MTH4 I (169)	TOLERATED YOUR OPINIONS SO FAR IS MORE THAN I CAN	IMAGINE	: I CAN ONLY CONJECTURE THAT YOU HAVE CONTRIBUTED
BULL PREFACE(29)	A PRIESTHOOD REPUTED THE RICHEST IN THE WORLD!	IMAGINE	A CATHOLIC MIDDLE CLASS CONTINUALLY DEFEATED IN THE
MTH2 (86)	YOUR DEATH? SUPPOSE THEY DIDNT GET MARRIED!	IMAGINE	A GIRL LIVING AT HOME WITH HER MOTHER AND ON HER
POSN PREFACE(400)	CONSIDER, FOR EXAMPLE, THE CHRISTMAS PANTOMIMES.	IMAGINE	A JUDGE OF THE HIGH COURT, OR AN ARCHBISHOP, OR A
MTH5 (259)	BUT THEY HAVE ALL GONE). AFTER ALL, I CAN	IMAGINE	A LOVER NOBLER THAN ANY OF YOU. (SHE GOES INTO THE
PHIL II (109)	I'M AFRAID TO FACE YOU AFTER LAST NIGHT. CAN YOU	IMAGINE	A MORE HORRIBLE SCENE? DONT YOU HATE THE VERY SIGHT
MIS. (125)	SAY, IF JOHN HADNT SUITED ME. /HYPATIA/ I CAN	IMAGINE	ALL SORTS OF MEN I COULD FALL IN LOVE WITH; BUT I
CAND II (120)	AS SO MANY MEN DO, ESPECIALLY POETIC MEN, WHO	IMAGINE	ALL WOMEN ARE ANGELS! SUPPOSE HE ONLY DISCOVERS THE
MILL I (152)	WHO HAS CUT ME OUT WITH EPPY. /PATRICIA/ I CANT	IMAGINE	ANY MAN CUTTING YOU OUT WITH ANY WOMAN, DEAR.
POSN PREFACE(429)	PLAY WERE PROSECUTED. TO MAKE IT CLEARER, LET US	IMAGINE	ANY OTHER OFFENDER-- SAY A COMPANY PROMOTER WITH A
SIM I (46)	THEY SEEMED TO ME TO BE QUITE PERFECT. I CANNOT	IMAGINE	ANYONE MORE PERFECT THAN MAYA. /PRA/ WELL, WHAT DID
MTH5 (209)	MARKEDLY DISENCHANTED) NUMBERS! ! ! I CANNOT	IMAGINE	ANYTHING DRIER OR MORE REPULSIVE. /THE MAIDEN/ THEY
APPL I (198)	OF IMAGINATION. WHAT I MEAN IS THAT HE COULDNT	IMAGINE	ANYTHING HE DIDNT SEE; BUT HE COULD IMAGINE THAT
FANY III (303)	NICE MAN AND WENT TO HAVE A DANCE MYSELF. I CANT	IMAGINE	ANYTHING MORE INNOCENT AND MORE HAPPY. ALL THE BAD
BULL PREFACE(30)	BECAUSE IT PROCLAIMS YOUR OWN GRIEVANCE! AND	IMAGINE	BEING BOUND TO SUBMIT TO ALL THIS BECAUSE THE
BULL PREFACE(29)	FAR FROM SO SPHERICAL AS PROTESTANTS ALLEGE!	IMAGINE	BEING FORBIDDEN TO READ THIS PREFACE BECAUSE IT
GETT PREFACE(234)	WHOSE RELIGIOUS FAITH WAS CONTRARY TO HER OWN.	IMAGINE	BEING MARRIED TO A LIAR, A BORROWER, A MISCHIEF
BULL PREFACE(29)	OF YOUR AFFAIRS VERIFIED IN THE CONFESSIONAL!	IMAGINE	BEING ONE OF A PEASANTRY REPUTED THE POOREST IN THE
SIM II (59)	GOING TO TAKE IS THIS. WE HAVE NEVER BEEN ABLE TO	IMAGINE	ETERNITY PROPERLY. ST JOHN OF PATMOS STARTED THE
HART PREFACE(19)	" GERMAN LOSSES." THEY WERE OUR LOSSES AS WELL.	IMAGINE	EXULTING IN THE DEATH OF BEETHOVEN BECAUSE BILL
JITT II (27)	WEEK. /LENKHEIM/ HOW? /FESSLER/ JUST CONSIDER.	IMAGINE	HAVING TO CONSOLE BRUNO'S WIDOW WHEN I'M ENGAGED TO
LADY PREFACE(221)	HAS PUT HIMSELF SO SUCCESSFULLY IN SHAKESPEAR'S?	IMAGINE	HER READING THE HUNDRED AND THIRTIETH SONNET! " MY
PHIL II (110)	YOU CANT FORGET THAT HORRIBLE SCENE LAST NIGHT.	IMAGINE	HER SAYING I HAD KISSED HER WITHIN THE LAST TWO
MTH1 I (11)	/EVE/ WHY? /THE SERPENT/ LILITH DID NOT	IMAGINE	HIM SO. HE CAN IMAGINE: HE CAN WILL: HE CAN DESIRE:
MRS III (222)	(RISING AND FLINGING DOWN HIS PAPER) BUT JUST	IMAGINE	HIS TELLING CROFTS TO BRING THE WARRENS OVER HERE!
2TRU I (37)	RETURNS TO THE BEDSIDE. /THE PATIENT/ I CANT	IMAGINE	HOW ANYONE CAN BE SO THOUGHTLESS AND CLUMSY WHEN I
MIS. (143)	HAVE FALLEN IN LOVE WITH ME. YOU CAN NEVER	IMAGINE	HOW DELIGHTED I WAS TO FIND THAT INSTEAD OF BEING
MRS II (208)	END TO ANOTHER EXCEPT THE GOV'NOR; SO YOU CAN	IMAGINE	HOW JOLLY DULL IT PANS OUT FOR HER. (TO HIS FATHER)
CAPT I (232)	TO RANKIN, SITTING DOWN AGAIN RESIGNEDLY) YOU CAN	IMAGINE	HOW MUCH USE THERE IS IN TALKING TO A WOMAN WHO
METH PREFACE(R33)	AND CREATIVE EVOLUTION, IT IS DIFFICULT TO	IMAGINE	HOW THIS NEW DEPARTURE OF DARWIN'S COULD POSSIBLY
FANY PROLOG (260)	THE SORT OF PEOPLE WE ARE, MR SAVOYARD. YOU CAN	IMAGINE	HOW WE FEEL HERE. /SAVOYARD/ RATHER OUT OF IT, EH..
JITT III (67)	SHE LEFT HIM. /AGNES/ (SHAKING HER HEAD) I CANT	IMAGINE	HOW WOMEN CAN BRING THEMSELVES TO BEHAVE SO. WHAT
GETT (341)	I THINK I SHOULD MARRY AGAIN LEST ANYONE SHOULD	IMAGINE	I HAD FOUND MARRIAGE UNHAPPY WITH ALICE. /SOAMES/ (
MRS I (187)	PLENTY OF MONEY TO MAKE THINGS SMOOTH. BUT DONT	IMAGINE	I KNOW ANYTHING ABOUT MY MOTHER. I KNOW FAR LESS
PYGM III (249)	SCIENCE OR ANYTHING ELSE? WHAT THE DEVIL DO YOU	IMAGINE	I KNOW OF PHILOSOPHY? /MRS HIGGINS/ (WARNINGLY) OR
FANY III (298)	HAVE BEEN RATHER EXCEPTIONAL; AND SHE'LL	IMAGINE	I MEAN I'M FONDER OF HER THAN I CAN EVER BE OF
DOCT IV (165)	YOU HAVE. I KNOW WHAT YOU ALL THINK OF ME. DONT	IMAGINE	I'M SORE ABOUT IT. I FORGIVE YOU. /WALPOLE/ (
DEST (168)	PRESSES HER HANDS ON HER HEART). IT HURTS ONLY TO	IMAGINE	IT. /NAPOLEON/ (INFLEXIBLY) WOULD YOU HAVE COME FOR
MTH5 (251)	ALAS! I COULD NOT CREATE IT: I COULD ONLY	IMAGINE	IT. /THE SHE-ANCIENT/ I, LIKE ARJILLAX, FOUND OUT
PRES (161)	BOOK. MINE-- SUCH AS THEY ARE-- ARE MY OWN. I	IMAGINE	IT'S SOMETHING LIKE THIS. THERE IS AN OLD SAYING
FABL PREFACE(69)	THE FACT THAT EVIL IS EVIL. THUS THE WORLD, AS WE	IMAGINE	IT, IS CROWDED WITH ANTHROPOMORPHIC SUPERNATURAL
AUGS (274)	ON EARTH DID HE DO THAT FOR? /THE LADY/ I CANT	IMAGINE	. BUT THIS I KNOW, SHE MADE A BET WITH HIM THAT SHE
2TRU PREFACE(8)	THAN ANYTHING ELSE OF AN ACCEPTED KIND THAT I CAN	IMAGINE	. FOR, JUST AS THE BEAN-FEASTER CAN LIVE LIKE A LORD
MIS. (150)	A BIRD. /PERCIVAL/ HOW HE KEPT HIS HEAD I CANT	IMAGINE	. FRANKLY, I DIDNT. THE PASSENGER, ALSO BEGOGGLED,
DOCT PREFACE(31)	FAR FROM BEING AS SUPERIOR TO SUCH TRIBES AS WE	IMAGINE	. IT IS VERY DOUBTFUL INDEED WHETHER PETER THE GREAT
PHIL I (74)	DEUCE IS CALLING AT THIS HOUR? /GRACE/ I CANT	IMAGINE	. (THEY LISTEN GUILTILY. THE DOOR OF THE FLAT IS
BULL IV (172)	COMPLACENTLY) SHE'S RATHER FULL OF IT, AS YOU MAY	IMAGINE	. POOR NORA! WELL, MR KEEGAN, AS I SAID, I BEGIN TO
JITT III (68)	THE WEIGHT YOU HAVE TAKEN OFF MY MIND! YOU CANT	IMAGINE	. /JITTA/ HAVE I? THEN I HAVE DONE WHAT I CAME TO
DOCT IV (164)	BEEN THINKING-- THINKING. I'M CLEVERER THAN YOU	IMAGINE	. /SIR PATRICK/ (WHISPERING TO RIDGEON) YOUVE GOT
GENV III (85)	ATTRACTION YOU CAN FIND IN MY CONVERSATION I CANT	IMAGINE	. /THE SECRETARY/ GENEVA IS SO FULL OF MENTAL PEOPLE
NEVR III (274)	CHAPTER SEVENTEEN OR THEREABOUTS, I SHOULD	IMAGINE	. /VALENTINE/ (MUCH PUT OUT BY THIS PLEASANTRY) NO:
MIS. (157)	THE BIBLE FOR? /MRS TARLETON/ I'M SURE I CANT	IMAGINE	. SHE CANT BE RIGHT IN HER HEAD. /LORD SUMMERHAYS/
DOCT III (134)	LOOKING FORWARD TO YOUR VISIT MORE THAN YOU CAN	IMAGINE	. SHES TAKEN QUITE A FANCY TO YOU, RIDGEON. THE POOR
SIM II (73)	ANGEL IS FAR FROM BEING THE PERFECT ORGANISM YOU	IMAGINE	. THERE IS ALWAYS SOMETHING BETTER. /VASHTI/
MIS. (153)	NEAREST LINA) BAD THING TO AEROPLANE ON, I SHOULD	IMAGINE	. TOO JUMPY. BEEN UP MUCH? /LINA/ NOT IN AN
CAND I (101)	IT'S AN OLD STORY: YOULL FIND IT IN THE BIBLE. I	IMAGINE	KING DAVID, IN HIS FITS OF ENTHUSIASM, WAS VERY LIKE
JITT I (17)	MATERIALIST YOU KNOW: THE VERY LAST MAN YOU COULD	IMAGINE	LENDING HIMSELF TO SUCH A MYSTICAL SPECULATION!
MRS IV (250)	GOOD SOCIETY, AND HAS THE AIR OF BEING A LADY.	IMAGINE	ME IN A CATHEDRAL TOWN! WHY, THE VERY ROOKS IN THE
MIS. (167)	WHAT A PRETTY GIRL! VERY PRETTY. I CAN	IMAGINE	MYSELF FALLING IN LOVE WITH HER WHEN I WAS YOUR AGE
CURE (235)	/REGINALD/ RATHE-E-E-ERRR. THATS HOW I ALWAYS DO	IMAGINE	MYSELF. /STREGA/ RIGHT. NOW LISTEN. (SHE PLAYS THE
GETT (301)	ACTUALLY DONE-- THINGS THAT EVERYBODY DOES, I	IMAGINE	-- WOULD EXPOSE ME, IF I WERE FOUND OUT AND
MTH1 I (10)	YOU IMAGINE WHAT YOU DESIRE; YOU WILL WHAT YOU	IMAGINE	; AND AT LAST YOU CREATE WHAT YOU WILL. /EVE/ HOW
UNPL PREFACE(R20)	WITH THE ORIGINALITY AND GENIUS OF THE AUTHOR.	IMAGINE	SHAKESPEAR CONFRONTED WITH SIR HENRY IRVING AT A
MTH5 (225)	OF YOUR INSPIRATION BY ECRASIA AND THE FOOLS WHO	IMAGINE	SHE SPEAKS WITH AUTHORITY? LET US HAVE THEM ALL SET
GETT PREFACE(228)	INDEED. THE MORAL IS, DO NOT THROW ANY. IF WE CAN	IMAGINE	SHELLEY AND QUEEN VICTORIA ARGUING OUT THEIR
MTH1 II (30)	PERHAPS THIS STRONG BRAVE SON OF MINE, WHO COULD	IMAGINE	SOMETHING BETTER, AND COULD DESIRE WHAT HE IMAGINED,
MTH1 I (11)	BE UNABLE TO CREATE WITHOUT NEW EYES. YOU CAN	IMAGINE	SUCH AN END; BUT YOU CANNOT DESIRE IT, THEREFORE
MRS I (190)	MY DEAR KITTY: YOU THINK I'M OFFENDED. DONT	IMAGINE	THAT: PRAY DONT. BUT YOU KNOW I OFTEN NOTICE THINGS
CURE (235)	BEAUTIFUL WOMEN WHO ARE PROUD OF YOU. CAN YOU	IMAGINE	THAT? /REGINALD/ RATHE-E-E-ERRR. THATS HOW I ALWAYS
BULL PREFACE(11)	WHO LONG TO BE KINGS AND CHIEFS BECAUSE THEY	IMAGINE	THAT A KING OR A CHIEF IS AN IDLE VOLUPTUARY WITH
JITT III (77)	OF IT. /JITTA/ (MORE DIGNIFIED THAN EVER) IF YOU	IMAGINE	THAT ANY RELATIONS THAT COULD EXIST BETWEEN MRS
MIS. PREFACE(34)	SOMETIMES BETTER PARENTS IN EFFECT THAN THOSE WHO	IMAGINE	THAT CHILDREN ARE AS CAPABLE OF HAPPINESS AS ADULTS.
SUPR III (130)	HELL, AS YOU ARE WEARIED NOW, YOU WILL NO LONGER	IMAGINE	THAT EVERY SWING FROM HEAVEN TO HELL IS AN
ROCK II (238)	CORRUPTED LIKE THIS! ARE YOU SUCH A DUPE AS TO	IMAGINE	THAT FREE ENGLISHMEN WILL TOLERATE SUCH A MONSTROUS
MIS. PREFACE(68)	IN HIS CLASS: ONLY FOOLS AND ROMANTIC NOVICES	IMAGINE	THAT FREEDOM IS A MERE MATTER OF THE READINESS OF
JOAN PREFACE(19)	HAVE BEEN ADDRESSED TO A CHILD YOUNG ENOUGH TO	IMAGINE	THAT HE WAS IN EARNEST. JOAN MUST THEREFORE AS A
MIS. (140)	FEELING OF EARLY YOUTH FOR LATE AGE, OR	IMAGINE	THAT I HAVE ANY FEELING FOR YOU EXCEPT ONE OF
NEVR II (253)	DESCRIBE THINGS TO ME; NO DOUBT I SHALL PRESENTLY	IMAGINE	THAT I REMEMBER THEM. BUT I REALLY REMEMBER NOTHING.
GETT PREFACE(186)	CELIBATES AND BY COMFORTABLY MARRIED PEOPLE WHO	IMAGINE	THAT IF OTHER COUPLES ARE UNCOMFORTABLE IT MUST BE

GETT PREFACE(186)	THEIR OWN FAULT, JUST AS RICH PEOPLE ARE APT TO	IMAGINE	THAT IF OTHER PEOPLE ARE POOR IT SERVES THEM RIGHT.
GETT PREFACE(256)	OF IDEAS WHICH MAKES SOME OF OUR BISHOPS	IMAGINE	THAT IN THE PHRASE " WHOM GOD HATH JOINED," THE WORD
BULL PREFACE(38)	IS THE CONCLUSIVE REPLY TO THE SHALLOW PEOPLE WHO	IMAGINE	THAT IRELAND DELIVERED UP TO THE IRISH DEMOCRACY--
HART II (92)	BY ALL YOU HAVE SAID TO ME, THAT ANYONE COULD	IMAGINE	THAT I-- I, A CONSECRATED SOLDIER OF FREEDOM, IF I
GETT (317)	POOR MAN'S DAUGHTER. /SYKES/ BUT SURELY YOU DONT	IMAGINE	THAT I'M GOING TO LET EDITH WORK WHEN WE'RE MARRIED.
DOCT III (143)	ALL THIS IS NO GOOD. YOU DONT UNDERSTAND. YOU	IMAGINE	THAT I'M SIMPLY AN ORDINARY CRIMINAL. /WALPOLE/ NOT
POSN PREFACE(368)	THIS INFLUENCED PUBLIC OPINION; BUT THOSE WHO	IMAGINE	THAT IT COULD INFLUENCE BRITISH GOVERNMENTS LITTLE
ROCK PREFACE(173)	IT IS AS BADLY EDUCATED AS OUR PRESENT ONES, WILL	IMAGINE	THAT IT HAS ANY FINAL AND ETERNAL TRUTHS TO
MTH2 (55)	INEFFABLE COMFORTABLENESS) MY DEAR BURGE: IF YOU	IMAGINE	THAT IT IS POSSIBLE TO BE WITHIN TEN MILES OF YOUR
DOCT PREFACE(14)	TO GO ON, AND THAT PATIENTS ARE ENCOURAGED TO	IMAGINE	THAT MODERN SURGERY AND ANESTHESIA HAVE MADE
GETT PREFACE(255)	HIGHLY QUESTIONABLE AT FIRST SIGHT TO THOSE WHO	IMAGINE	THAT ONLY PARENTS SPOIL CHILDREN, YET THOSE WHO
UNPL PREFACE(R12)	PLEASANT PEOPLE WITH " INDEPENDENT" INCOMES WHO	IMAGINE	THAT SUCH SORDID MATTERS DO NOT TOUCH THEIR OWN
DOCT PREFACE(28)	OF THE SAVAGE RANCOR THAT SO AMAZES PEOPLE WHO	IMAGINE	THAT THE CONTROVERSY CONCERNING VACCINATION IS A
GETT PREFACE(256)	USEFUL. THE COST OF DIVORCE. BUT PLEASE DO NOT	IMAGINE	THAT THE EVILS OF INDISSOLUBLE MARRIAGE CAN BE CURED
DOCT PREFACE(71)	KNOWLEDGE. BUT I MAY REMIND THOSE WHO CONFUSEDLY	IMAGINE	THAT THE MEDICAL PROBLEM IS ALSO THE SCIENTIFIC
APPL I (198)	IMAGINE ANYTHING HE DIDNT SEE; BUT HE COULD	IMAGINE	THAT WHAT HE DID SEE WAS DIVINE AND HOLY AND
CURE (235)	HERE. DONT IMAGINE YOURSELF GOING INTO BATTLE.	IMAGINE	THAT YOU HAVE JUST BEEN IN A BATTLE; AND THAT YOU
BULL PREFACE(29)	HAD VIRTUALLY NO OTHER WAY OF GETTING MARRIED!	IMAGINE	THE CHURCH RATES REVIVED IN THE FORM OF AN
LION PREFACE(100)	AND BOSSUET, AND THE NORTH IN ST PAUL AND CALVIN.	IMAGINE	THE EFFECT OF TRYING TO GOVERN INDIA OR EGYPT FROM
BULL PREFACE(29)	WITH REBELLION AGAINST THE TYRANNY OF THE CHURCH.	IMAGINE	THE FEELINGS OF AN ENGLISH FARMER IF THE PARSON
BULL PREFACE(50)	JUST AS AN ENGLISH FARMER KEEPS POULTRY. TRY TO	IMAGINE	THE FEELINGS OF AN ENGLISH VILLAGE IF A PARTY OF
MIS. (143)	MEN. GOOD FOR NOTHING ELSE AT LAST. OH, YOU CANT	IMAGINE	THE FIENDISH SELFISHNESS OF THE OLD PEOPLE AND THE
POSN PREFACE(430)	SENSE OF MEN OF THE WORLD. YOU HAVE ONLY TO	IMAGINE	THE PRIVY COUNCIL AS CONSISTING OF MEN OF THE WORLD
SHAK PREFACE(136)	BY PUNCH-AND-JUDY SQUEAKS AND THE LIKE. I CAN	IMAGINE	THE PUPPETS SIMULATING LIVING PERFORMERS SO
BULL II (113)	DYING TO SEE YOU, OF COURSE. I DARESAY YOU CAN	IMAGINE	THE SENSATION AN ENGLISHMAN LIKE YOU WOULD MAKE
UNPL PREFACE(R20)	AT ONE OF THE SCHOOL FOR SCANDAL. IT IS EASY TO	IMAGINE	THE SPEECHES THAT MIGHT PASS ON SUCH OCCASIONS. FOR
ARMS II (38)	AND DOWN THE GARDEN IN A BROWN STUDY. /CATHERINE/	IMAGINE	THEIR MEETING THAT SWISS AND HEARING THE WHOLE
OVER PREFACE(159)	REMARK THAT VERY FEW PEOPLE WOULD EVER	IMAGINE	THEMSELVES IN LOVE IF THEY HAD NEVER READ ANYTHING
MIS. PREFACE(14)	CONDITION OF NERVOUS FEEBLENESS, AND AT LAST	IMAGINE	THEMSELVES UNABLE TO WORK UNDER CONDITIONS OF BUSTLE
MIS. PREFACE(92)	CHILDREN BROUGHT UP IN FREEDOM. YOU HAVE MEN WHO	IMAGINE	THEMSELVES TO BE MINISTERS OF RELIGION OPENLY
3PLA PREFACE(R11)	THAT THEIR INFLUENCE IS ANY NOBLER WHEN THEY	IMAGINE	THEMSELVES CHRISTIANS THAN WHEN THEY KNOW THEMSELVES
SUPR HANDBOK(188)	HE CALLS GREAT MEN OR HEROES, BECAUSE HE WILL	IMAGINE	THEM, NOT AS TRUE SUPERMEN, BUT AS HIMSELF ENDOWED
APPL PREFACE(187)	TO TAKE IMAGINARY EXAMPLES: THEY OFFEND NOBODY.	IMAGINE	THEN THAT WE ARE THE INHABITANTS OF A VILLAGE. WE
MRS I (184)	FOR SHY AND SINCERE SOULS. /VIVIE/ YES, I	IMAGINE	THERE MUST HAVE BEEN A FRIGHTFUL WASTE OF TIME.
SUPR III (108)	BUT MEN NEVER REALLY OVERCOME FEAR UNTIL THEY	IMAGINE	THEY ARE FIGHTING TO FURTHER A UNIVERSAL PURPOSE--
ROCK PREFACE(174)	OF REVOLUTIONISTS, AND BY CHURCHES WHO	IMAGINE	THEY POSSESS THE ETERNAL TRUTH ABOUT EVERYTHING, TO
MIS. PREFACE(104)	ROMANTIC IMAGINATION. THE OTHER IS THE POWER TO	IMAGINE	THINGS AS THEY ARE WITHOUT ACTUALLY SENSING THEM;
MIS. PREFACE(104)	DIFFERENT POWERS OF MIND. ONE IS THE POWER TO	IMAGINE	THINGS AS THEY ARE NOT: THIS I CALL THE ROMANTIC
BULL PREFACE(29)	THE ONLY EFFICIENT UNIVERSITIES IN THE COUNTRY!	IMAGINE	TRYING TO GET A MODERN EDUCATION IN A SEMINARY OF
3PLA PREFACE(R37)	INFERIOR TO THE BEST WORKS OF THEIR FORERUNNERS.	IMAGINE	WAGNER DYING AFTER COMPOSING RIENZI, OR SHELLEY
MTH5 (210)	POISONS WITH IT TO MAKE US DELIRIOUS ENOUGH TO	IMAGINE	WE ARE ENJOYING OURSELVES; AND THEN HAVING TO PASS
MTH3 (120)	YOUR OWN WELL-FED NATURAL EXUBERANCE. YOU CANNOT	IMAGINE	WHAT ALCOHOL WAS TO AN UNDERFED POOR WOMAN. I HAD
MIS. PREFACE(78)	HAD BETTER WAIT AND SEE; FOR NOBODY NOW ALIVE CAN	IMAGINE	WHAT CUSTOMS AND INSTITUTIONS WOULD GROW UP IN
APPL INTRLUD(249)	IT WHEN THEY NEED A CHANGE. /MAGNUS/ BUT I CANT	IMAGINE	WHAT I SHOULD DO WITHOUT JEMIMA. /ORINTHIA/ NOBODY
GENV IV (91)	IN THE WORLD: THAT IS MY VISION. I LEAVE YOU TO	IMAGINE	WHAT I THINK OF THE MOB OF BAGMEN FROM FIFTY POTTY
APPL PREFACE(192)	OF WATER WAS THEN SET AT MY FEET. I COULD NOT	IMAGINE	WHAT I WAS EXPECTED TO DO WITH THE WATER OR WHAT WAS
BUOY 1 (14)	THOUGHT A GOOD DEAL OVER THIS. I HAVE TRIED TO	IMAGINE	WHAT OLD JOHN SHAKESPEAR OF STRATFORD-UPON-AVON,
NEVR II (237)	SIR. YES, SIR, I ASSURE YOU, SIR. YOU WOULD NEVER	IMAGINE	WHAT RESPECTABLE PROFESSIONAL GENTLEMEN FROM LONDON
POSN PREFACE(391)	IMPLIES CAN ONLY BE APPRECIATED BY THOSE WHO CAN	IMAGINE	WHAT THE EFFECT ON THE MIND MUST BE OF THE DUTY OF
MIS. PREFACE(10)	AND THE OTHER IS THE ATTRIBUTE OF A GOD, ONE CAN	IMAGINE	WHAT THE LIVES OF THIS GENTLEMAN'S CHILDREN WOULD
BULL PREFACE(59)	GOT ANYWHERE FOR THE LIKE MISCONDUCT. ONE CAN	IMAGINE	WHAT WOULD HAVE HAPPENED TO THE MAN, PRISONER OR
MTH1 I (10)	IMAGINATION IS THE BEGINNING OF CREATION. YOU	IMAGINE	WHAT YOU DESIRE; YOU WILL WHAT YOU IMAGINE; AND AT
APPL INTRLUD(249)	DO WITHOUT JEMIMA. /ORINTHIA/ NOBODY ELSE CAN	IMAGINE	WHAT YOU DO WITH HER. BUT YOU NEED NOT DO WITHOUT
INCA (244)	HIM A PERCEPTIBLE SHOCK). I AM QUITE AT A LOSS TO	IMAGINE	WHY I SHOULD TREAT A PERFECT STRANGER NAMED DUVAL: A
JITT III (72)	SHE WOULD NOT DISAPPOINT YOU? IT IS EASY TO	IMAGINE	WONDERFUL WOMEN WORTHY OF YOUR FATHER'S LOVE. BUT
PHIL I (86)	LEANING AGAINST IT AND ADMIRING CRAVEN). JUST	IMAGINE	YOU BEING DAN CRAVEN! /CRAVEN/ JUST IMAGINE YOU
PHIL I (86)	JUST IMAGINE YOU BEING DAN CRAVEN! /CRAVEN/ JUST	IMAGINE	YOU BEING JO CUTHBERTSON, THOUGH! THATS A FAR MORE
SUPR I (19)	THAT I SHOULD BE RHODA'S GUARDIAN? /ANN/ I CANT	IMAGINE	YOU DOING ANYTHING DISGRACEFUL, GRANNY. /TANNER/ (
PYGM IV (264)	SHOULDNT BOTHER ABOUT IT IF I WERE YOU. I SHOULD	IMAGINE	YOU WONT HAVE MUCH DIFFICULTY IN SETTLING YOURSELF
DOCT III (143)	SCOUNDREL. IT'S JUST ARGUING IN A CIRCLE. AND YOU	IMAGINE	YOURE A MAN OF SCIENCE! /B.B./ I-- I-- I-- I HAVE A
CURE (235)	/STREGA/ WITH CHOPIN'S POLONAISE IN A FLAT. NOW,	IMAGINE	YOURSELF GOING INTO BATTLE. (HE RUNS AWAY AS
CURE (235)	EVER. HAVE YOU NO PITY? /STREGA/ COME HERE. DONT	IMAGINE	YOURSELF GOING INTO BATTLE. IMAGINE THAT YOU HAVE
MIS. (140)	REPROACH YOU! I WAS AN OLD FOOL. BUT HOW YOU CAN	IMAGINE	, AFTER THAT, THAT I CAN SUSPECT YOU OF THE SMALLEST
FANY I (274)	AFRAID HE IS INCORRIGIBLE. MY BROTHER, AS YOU MAY	IMAGINE	, FEELS THAT THIS LAST ESCAPADE HAS GONE BEYOND THE
JOAN PREFACE(37)	IN THE HANDS OF GOD, AND NOT, AS SIMPLE PRIESTS	IMAGINE	, GOD IN THE HANDS OF THE CHURCH; SO IF HE ANSWERS
GENV I (35)	HE BECAME PRIME MINISTER? /SHE/ (BORED) CANT	IMAGINE	, I'M SURE. /NEWCOMER/ HE SAID HE HAD BEEN RETURNED
MIS. PREFACE(24)	BUY A CHEAPER PLATE INSCRIBED KINDERGARTEN, AND	IMAGINE	, OR LEAVE OTHERS TO IMAGINE, THAT FROEBEL IS THE
SUPR II (65)	CONSIDERATE. /OCTAVIUS/ WE FEEL THAT, AS YOU MAY	IMAGINE	, PRETTY DEEPLY. /RAMSDEN/ (TESTILY) IT IS SOME
MIS. PREFACE(24)	KINDERGARTEN, AND IMAGINE, OR LEAVE OTHERS TO	IMAGINE	, THAT FROEBEL IS THE GOVERNING GENIUS OF YOUR
3PLA PREFACE(R17)	AND THEIR SELFISHNESS UTTERLY ANNIHILATED.	IMAGINE	, THEN, THE RESULT OF CONDUCTING THEATRES ON THE
MTH1 I (10)	TWO WILLS TO CREATE WITH. /EVE/ TO DESIRE, TO	IMAGINE	, TO WILL, TO CREATE. THAT IS TOO LONG A STORY. FIND
BARB III (328)	AND JAM AND CREAM FOR THREEPENCE I REALLY CANNOT	IMAGINE	! -- STILL YOU MUST REMEMBER THAT RESTAURANTS BREAK
FANY I (274)	A CERTAIN DEGREE OF REPROBATION." " AS YOU MAY	IMAGINE	! " AND WE KNOW NO MORE ABOUT IT THAN THE BABE

IMAGINED

MTH1 I (10)	/THE SERPENT/ SHE IMAGINED IT. /EVE/ WHAT IS	IMAGINED	? /THE SERPENT/ SHE TOLD IT TO ME AS A MARVELLOUS
MTH1 II (22)	THAT THEY MAY IN TURN CREATE MORE MEN. I HAVE	IMAGINED	A GLORIOUS POEM OF MANY MEN, OF MORE MEN THAN THERE
MTH1 I (11)	/EVE/ FIND ME A WORD FOR THE STORY LILITH	IMAGINED	AND TOLD YOU IN YOUR SILENT LANGUAGE: THE STORY
CAPT NOTES (301)	THERE-- SO REFRESHINGLY DIFFERENT FROM THE SCENES	IMAGINED	BY BLOODY-MINDED CLERKS WHO ESCAPE FROM THEIR
MILL PREFACE(135)	NUMBERS UNLESS AND UNTIL THEY DEVELOP THE VRIL	IMAGINED	BY BULWER-LYTTON WHICH WILL ENABLE ONE PERSON TO
HART PREFACE(4)	AND SETTLED DOWN LATER INTO THE TYPES OF BEAUTY	IMAGINED	BY THE PREVIOUS GENERATION OF PAINTERS. THEY TOOK
GENV PREFACE(19)	AND LOUIS NAPOLEON UNDER THE SECOND REPUBLIC,	IMAGINED	HE HAD ONLY TO APPEAR IN THE STREETS WITH A FLAG TO
MILL IV (206)	LISTEN. I ONCE CURED A PRIME MINISTER WHEN HE	IMAGINED	HIMSELF TO BE ILL. I WENT TO HIM AND TOLD HIM THAT
DEST (168)	FOR THE DESPATCHES? /LADY/ (OVERCOME BY THE	IMAGINED	HORROR) DONT ASK ME. I MUST HAVE COME. /NAPOLEON/
JOAN PREFACE(5)	INNOCENT AS THIS AT THE AGE OF SEVENTY, IT MAY BE	IMAGINED	HOW INNOCENT JOAN WAS AT THE AGE OF SEVENTEEN. NOW
GETT PREFACE(232)	BY REFERENCE TO A FICTITIOUS CASE: THE ONE	IMAGINED	IN MY OWN PLAY CANDIDA WILL DO AS WELL AS ANOTHER.
MTH1 I (10)	WILLED IT SO. WHEN LILITH TOLD ME WHAT SHE HAD	IMAGINED	IN OUR SILENT LANGUAGE (FOR THERE WERE NO WORDS
VWOO 2 (128)	TRAVELLING JUST DESTROYED THE WORLD FOR ME AS I	IMAGINED	IT. GIVE ME THIS VILLAGE ALL THE TIME. /A/ HAD YOU
MTH1 I (10)	DID LILITH WORK THIS MIRACLE? /THE SERPENT/ SHE	IMAGINED	IT. /EVE/ WHAT IS IMAGINED? /THE SERPENT/ SHE TOLD
DOCT III (133)	HER SHRINE A CHAPEL MORE BEAUTIFUL THAN WAS EVER	IMAGINED	. I CANT PASS THE SHOPS WITHOUT WRESTLING WITH THE
MTH5 (226)	FRIEND. I DO NOT COME EMPTY-HANDED TODAY, AS YOU	IMAGINED	. ON THE CONTRARY, I BRING WITH ME SUCH A WORK OF
HART PREFACE(33)	OF THE WAR ON THE LONDON THEATRES MAY NOW BE	IMAGINED	. THE BEDS AND THE BEVIES DROVE EVERY HIGHER FORM
BARB PREFACE(232)	OUTDOES IN VILLAINY THE WORST THAT HAS EVER BEEN	IMAGINED	OF THE BUCCANEERS OF THE SPANISH MAIN, CAPTAIN KIDD
BULL IV (159)	WHEN ONE GOT MAUDLIN AND CALLED IRELAND ERIN, AND	IMAGINED	ONE WAS REMEMBERING THE DAYS OF OLD, AND SO FORTH.
SUPR HANDBOK(209)	IS THE CEMENT OF OUR SOCIAL SYSTEM, CAN BE	IMAGINED	ONLY BY THOSE WHO KNOW HOW SUDDENLY A CIVILIZATION
JITT III (72)	LOVE. BUT THE REAL PERSON ALWAYS KILLS THE	IMAGINED	PERSON. /EDITH/ HE SAID THAT ONCE. /JITTA/ WELL, IS
METH PREFACE(R71)	FAR WORSE THAN THE BLACKEST PESSIMIST HAD EVER	IMAGINED	POSSIBLE. CIRCUMSTANTIAL SELECTION IN FINANCE. HOW
MIS. PREFACE(75)	HER EXPENSE. NO MORE MONSTROUS INJUSTICE COULD BE	IMAGINED	THAN THAT THE BURDEN OF REARING THE CHILDREN SHOULD
FANY III SD(297)	UNTRAINED AND UNSATISFACTORY, HIS PARENTS HAVING	IMAGINED	THAT DOMESTIC RESTRICTION IS WHAT THEY CALL "
O'FL PREFACE(203)	THE WAR EVERYONE EXCEPT THE SOLDIERS AT THE FRONT	IMAGINED	THAT NOTHING BUT AN EXTREME ASSERTION OF OUR MOST
APPL PREFACE(196)	SOMETHING GREAT IN A MAN WHO, HAVING NOT ONLY	IMAGINED	THEM BUT INVENTED THEIR MACHINERY, COULD, FAR FROM
MTH1 II (30)	SOMETHING BETTER, AND COULD DESIRE WHAT HE	IMAGINED	, MIGHT ALSO BE ABLE TO WILL WHAT HE DESIRED UNTIL
ROCK PREFACE(190)	BEGGAR MYSELF IN THIS FASHION, PEOPLE WHO	IMAGINED	, MORE SPECIFICALLY, THAT A SOCIALIST COULD NOT

IMAGINES

VWOO 2 (126)	ABOUT WHAT HE'LL DO OR WHERE HE'LL GO. HE JUST	IMAGINES	AND IMAGINES. IT'S THE ONLY WAY TO BE HAPPY AND
BARB III (340)	YOUR PIOUS MOB FILLS UP BALLOT PAPERS AND	IMAGINES	IT IS GOVERNING ITS MASTERS; BUT THE BALLOT PAPER

MRS I (185)	TO READ LAW: NOT FOR A HOLIDAY, AS MY MOTHER	IMAGINES	. I HATE HOLIDAYS. /PRAED/ YOU MAKE MY BLOOD RUN
VWOO 2 (126)	HE'LL DO OR WHERE HE'LL GO. HE JUST IMAGINES AND	IMAGINES	. IT'S THE ONLY WAY TO BE HAPPY AND LONGLIVED. /A/
LION PREFACE(56)	WHY NOT DISTRIBUTE ACCORDING TO MERIT? " HERE ONE	IMAGINES	JESUS, WHOSE SMILE HAS BEEN BROADENING DOWN THE
BULL PREFACE(39)	ENGLAND IS NOTHING BUT THE POPE'S POLICEMAN. SHE	IMAGINES	SHE IS HOLDING THE VATICAN CARDINALS AT BAY WHEN
CAPT III (276)	SUCH A CREATURE IS: WHEN SHE HAS A GRIEVANCE, AND	IMAGINES	SOME INNOCENT PERSON TO BE THE AUTHOR OF IT. /LADY
CAPT NOTES (304)	IN PHONETIC SPELLING OF THE SOUNDS HE UTTERS. HE	IMAGINES	THAT A DEPARTURE FROM CONVENTIONAL SPELLING
METH PREFACE(R24)	OF WHICH IS RANK HERESY TO THE NEO-DARWINIAN, WHO	IMAGINES	THAT IF YOU STOP CIRCUMSTANTIAL SELECTION, YOU NOT
DOCT PREFACE(78)	THE SAME. SCIENCE BECOMES DANGEROUS ONLY WHEN IT	IMAGINES	THAT IT HAS REACHED ITS GOAL. WHAT IS WRONG WITH
DOCT PREFACE(50)	WHO MAKES IT IS ETHICALLY IMBECILE; AND WHOEVER	IMAGINES	THAT IT IS A SCIENTIFIC CLAIM HAS NOT THE FAINTEST
DOCT PREFACE(49)	AND YOUR NATURAL CONTEMPT FOR HIS STUPIDITY, HE	IMAGINES	THAT YOU ARE ATTACKING SCIENCE. YET HE HAS NO

IMAGINING

ARMS I (16)	WHEN I THINK OF HIM CHARGING THE WINDMILLS AND	IMAGINING	HE WAS DOING THE FINEST THING-- (HE CHOKES WITH
JOAN PREFACE(13)	SHE WAS NONE THE LESS AN ABLE LEADER OF MEN FOR	IMAGINING	HER IDEAS IN THIS WAY. THE EVOLUTIONARY APPETITE.
JITT III (77)	YOU HAVE DECEIVED ME? /LENKHEIM/ NOW DONT BEGIN	IMAGINING	THAT I AM A DON JUAN. TO BE PRECISE, I HAVE KISSED
FABL PREFACE(98)	AMATEURS WHO INFEST OUR PARLIAMENTS AND PARTIES,	IMAGINING	THAT IT CAN BE SOLVED BY GIVING ALL OF US
OVER (180)	OF THE ROMANCE OF A JOURNEY IS THAT A MAN KEEPS	IMAGINING	THAT SOMETHING MIGHT HAPPEN; AND HE CANT DO THAT
ROCK PREFACE(177)	WAS NOT IN INTERFERING WITH HIS LIBERTY, BUT IN	IMAGINING	THAT THE SECRET OF THE EARTH'S MOTION COULD BE
ROCK I (214)	SEND IT TO THE FUNDS FOR THE RELIEF OF DISTRESS,	IMAGINING	THAT THEY ARE RANSOMING THEIR RICHES. YOU, LADIES
BARB III (321)	AND APPLAUSE OF MY NEWSPAPERS, AND THE DELIGHT OF	IMAGINING	THAT YOU ARE A GREAT STATESMAN. GOVERNMENT OF YOUR
MTH4 II (179)	THE ONLY IMAGINATION WORTH HAVING: THE POWER OF	IMAGINING	THINGS AS THEY ARE, EVEN WHEN I CANNOT SEE THEM.
GLIM (186)	AND THEY GAVE IT TO ME. I DREAMED AND ROMANCED:	IMAGINING	THINGS AS I WANTED THEM, NOT AS THEY REALLY ARE.
POSN PREFACE(382)	ENLIGHTENMENT. THIS CAN BE BROUGHT HOME TO US BY	IMAGINING	WHAT WOULD HAVE BEEN THE EFFECT OF APPLYING TO ALL

IMBECILE

PHIL I (79)	HAVE I BECOME A DRUNKARD, OR A CRIMINAL, OR AN	IMBECILE	? /CHARTERIS/ YOU HAVE BECOME WHAT IS INFINITELY
HART PREFACE(9)	REPARABLE IN OUR TIME. IT MAY BE ASKED HOW SO	IMBECILE	AND DANGEROUS A CREED EVER CAME TO BE ACCEPTED BY
BULL PREFACE(48)	WHY, THEIRS BUT TO DO AND DIE," TO THE MORAL	IMBECILE	AND POLITICAL SLUGGARD THESE CONDITIONS ARE AS
DOCT PREFACE(30)	AND THE CONTEMPT OF ABLE THINKERS FOR HIS	IMBECILE	CASUISTRY, HAVE BEEN EXPRESSED BY THE MOST POPULAR
METH PREFACE(R52)	BE TRANSMITTED, AND YET WEISMANN WAS NOT A BORN	IMBECILE	. HE WAS AN EXCEPTIONALLY CLEVER AND STUDIOUS MAN,
OVER (192)	/JUNO/ IT'S QUITE PLAIN TO ANYONE BUT AN	IMBECILE	. IF YOU TELL ME IVE DONE SOMETHING WRONG YOU
MILL I (146)	FOR MAKING A MESS OF MY LIFE AND MARRYING AN	IMBECILE	. I, EPIFANIA OGNISANTI DI PARERGA, SAW MYSELF AS
DOCT PREFACE(64)	SAVAGE AND UNMANAGEABLE, AND THE PATIENT ONES	IMBECILE	. PERHAPS THEY DO, TO SOME EXTENT, AND THE PAY IS
JOAN 1 (62)	(TO THE STEWARD) GO WITH HER, YOU, YOU DITHERING	IMBECILE	. STAY WITHIN CALL; AND KEEP YOUR EYE ON HER. I
AUGS (267)	I DID NOT KNOW THAT I WAS TALKING TO AN	IMBECILE	. YOU OUGHT TO BE ASHAMED OF YOURSELF. THERE MUST
MILL I (155)	LOOK INCREDULOUS, ADRIAN, BUT HE DID. YES: THIS	IMBECILE	MADE FIFTY THOUSAND POUNDS AND WON EPIFANIA
PHIL I (79)	BECOME A DRUNKARD, A-- /JULIA/-- A CRIMINAL, AN	IMBECILE	OR A HORROR. YOU SAID THAT BEFORE. (SHE SITS DOWN
DOCT PREFACE(50)	OR DYNAMITARDS. THE MAN WHO MAKES IT IS ETHICALLY	IMBECILE	; AND WHOEVER IMAGINES THAT IT IS A SCIENTIFIC
SUPR IV (172)	SEIZE THE OCCASION TO GET HALF DRUNK AND UTTER	IMBECILE	SPEECHES AND COARSE PLEASANTRIES AT MY EXPENSE, WE
SUPR HANDBOK(226)	GENERAL IN A NATION IS ITS CAESAR, THE LEAST	IMBECILE	STATESMAN ITS SOLON, THE LEAST CONFUSED THINKER ITS
PHIL I (77)	MIGHT HAVE TURNED OUT A DRUNKARD, A CRIMINAL, AN	IMBECILE	, A HORROR TO YOU; AND YOU COULDNT HAVE RELEASED
AUGS PREFACE(261)	BUT OBSTRUCTIVELY FUSSY, SELF-IMPORTANT,	IMBECILE	, AND DISASTROUS, SAVE FOR THE SATISFACTION OF
PRES (152)	DO NOT KNOW WHAT I HAVE TO PUT UP WITH. THIS	IMBECILE	, INCOMPETENT, UNSOLDIERLY DISGRACE TO THE UNIFORM

IMBECILES

ROCK II (265)	AND MY BRAINS, GOVERN THIS ROOMFUL OF NEEDY	IMBECILES	, BUT I NOW CAST YOU OFF. I RETURN TO INDIA TO
HART III (141)	BE MARRIED TO MY SISTER. /HECTOR/ ALL HEARTBROKEN	IMBECILES	. /MAZZINI/ OH NO. SURELY, IF I MAY SAY SO, RATHER
BULL PREFACE(23)	ALTHOUGH THERE WAS NO LACK AMONG US OF FLUENT	IMBECILES	, WITH MAJESTIC PRESENCES AND OCEANS OF DIGNITY

IMBECILITIES

GETT PREFACE(193)	I COULD FILL A HUNDRED PAGES WITH THE TALE OF OUR	IMBECILITIES	AND STILL LEAVE MUCH UNTOLD; BUT WHAT I HAVE
JOAN PREFACE(8)	KIND OF ANIMAL WITH SPECIFIC CHARMS AND SPECIFIC	IMBECILITIES	. JOAN'S GOOD LOOKS. TO PUT THE LAST POINT

IMBECILITY

MIS. PREFACE(97)	DESIRABLE. IGNORANCE OF EVIL IS NOT VIRTUE BUT	IMBECILITY	: ADMIRING IT IS LIKE GIVING A PRIZE FOR HONESTY
LADY PREFACE(229)	WHOSE BREATH WAS RANK, AND WHOSE POLITICAL	IMBECILITY	AND CAPRICE MOVED CORIOLANUS TO SAY TO THE ROMAN
POSN PREFACE(361)	IT WAS ALLEGED BY MYSELF AND OTHERS THAT AS ITS	IMBECILITY	AND MISCHIEVOUSNESS COULD NOT BE FULLY
BARB PREFACE(217)	LETHAL CHAMBER. BUT AS, THANKS TO OUR POLITICAL	IMBECILITY	AND PERSONAL COWARDICE (FRUITS OF POVERTY,
MTH4 I (157)	RECOIL FROM YOUR IGNORANCE, YOUR BLINDNESS, YOUR	IMBECILITY	. HUMANLY I PITY YOU. INTELLECTUALLY I DESPISE
MILL I (149)	NIGHT OF LEGITIMATE BLISS WOULD BE CAPABLE OF ANY	IMBECILITY	. /ALASTAIR/ PARDONING ME! PARDONING ME FOR
MRS III (226)	/FRANK/ EVER SO PEACEFUL, AND RELIEVED FROM THE	IMBECILITY	OF THE LITTLE BOY'S FATHER AND THE
HART PREFACE(23)	OF ENGLAND WAS SILENT AND INVISIBLE, ALL ITS	IMBECILITY	WAS DEAFENING THE HEAVENS WITH ITS CLAMOR AND
BARB PREFACE(215)	COWARDICE, CRUELTY, HYPOCRISY, POLITICAL	IMBECILITY	, AND ALL THE OTHER FRUITS OF OPPRESSION AND
BULL PREFACE(45)	OF THE FACT THAT MILITARY SERVICE PRODUCES MORAL	IMBECILITY	, FEROCITY, AND COWARDICE, AND THAT THE DEFENCE
MTH4 I (142)	IF YOU CANNOT DISCRIMINATE BETWEEN HAY FEVER AND	IMBECILITY	, I CAN ONLY SAY THAT YOUR ADVANCED YEARS CARRY
BARB III (322)	AND ALL THAT. /SARAH/ YOU DONT MIND CHOLLY'S	IMBECILITY	, PAPA, DO YOU? /LOMAX/ (MUCH TAKEN ABACK) OH I

IMITATE

MIS. (194)	THAT SINGLE NOTE THAT NO NIGHTINGALE CAN	IMITATE	? THAT IS WHAT HAPPENED IN THE WOODS WHEN I WAS
CLEO IV (168)	IF SHE WERE QUEEN? /CHARMIAN/ BECAUSE YOU TRY TO	IMITATE	CAESAR IN EVERYTHING; AND HE LETS EVERYBODY SAY WHAT
DOCT I (99)	IMITATOR, JUST AS MEN IMITATE EACH OTHER, GERMS	IMITATE	EACH OTHER. THERE IS THE GENUINE DIPHTHERIA BACILLUS
DOCT I (99)	LITTLE CREATURES HAS AN IMITATOR, JUST AS MEN	IMITATE	EACH OTHER, GERMS IMITATE EACH OTHER. THERE IS THE
MILL I (157)	ATTAINED BY MORTAL MAN. HE FOUND THAT HE COULD	IMITATE	GRAMOPHONE RECORDS WITH THE GREATEST FACILITY; AND
CAND I (84)	CUT A POORER FIGURE THAN WHEN YOU ARE TRYING TO	IMITATE	HIM. /LEXY/ (STUNG) I TRY TO FOLLOW HIS EXAMPLE,
CAND I (84)	(STUNG) I TRY TO FOLLOW HIS EXAMPLE, NOT TO	IMITATE	HIM. /PROSERPINE/ (COMING AT HIM AGAIN ON HER WAY
CAND I (85)	ON HER WAY BACK TO HER WORK) YES, YOU DO: YOU	IMITATE	HIM. WHY DO YOU TUCK YOUR UMBRELLA UNDER YOUR LEFT
CLEO NOTES (207)	ANY ESSENTIAL DIFFERENCE IN THE PLAY, I CAN ONLY	IMITATE	HUMANITY AS I KNOW IT. NOBODY KNOWS WHETHER
METH PREFACE(R39)	PARENTS, FELL FAR SHORT IN THEIR ATTEMPTS TO	IMITATE	IT, BUT IT WAS NOT ITS SOCIAL VICES THAT BROUGHT IT
BULL PREFACE(18)	AND EAST ANGLIA CANNOT PRODUCE AND DO NOT WANT TO	IMITATE	. HOW CAN I SKETCH THE BROAD LINES OF THE CONTRAST
MIS. PREFACE(11)	ONE OF THE SUCCESSES OF THE ALMIGHTY: THEREFORE	IMITATE	ME IN EVERY PARTICULAR OR I WILL HAVE THE SKIN OFF
FANY PROLOG (261)	WHAT WAS IT AFTER ALL BUT A STUPID ATTEMPT TO	IMITATE	THE SUCCESS MADE BY THE GENIUS OF GRIMALDI A HUNDRED
PYGM PREFACE(203)	THE ATTEMPT OF A PHONETICALLY UNTAUGHT PERSON TO	IMITATE	THE VULGAR DIALECT OF THE GOLF CLUB; AND I AM SORRY
METH PREFACE(R53)	OF THIS. THEIR ONLY IDEA OF INVESTIGATION WAS TO	IMITATE	" NATURE" BY PERPETRATING VIOLENT AND SENSELESS

IMITATED

HART PREFACE(30)	UNDERSTOOD BUT INTENSELY ENJOYED AN ARTIST WHO	IMITATED	COCKS CROWING AND PIGS SQUEAKING. BUT THE PEOPLE

IMITATES

MIS. (157)	GET EM, CHICKABIDDY. I UNDERSTAND. (HE	IMITATES	A JUGGLER TOSSING UP BALLS). EH? /LINA/ (GOING TO
BARB PREFACE(231)	SEEN SPEAKING IN THE PUBLIC STREET: IN SHORT, SHE	IMITATES	CHRIST. BILL'S CONSCIENCE REACTS TO THIS JUST AS
INCA (249)	CREATURES. I HAVE NOTHING AGAINST THEM. PONGO	IMITATES	FARMYARD SOUNDS -- COCK-CROWING AND THAT SORT OF
SUPR I SD(42)	UNCONCERNED AS POSSIBLE. OCTAVIUS INSTINCTIVELY	IMITATES	HER. /THE MAID/ THE CAB IS AT THE DOOR, MAAM. /MISS

IMITATING

BARB III (350)	LADY BRITOMART'S RIBS WITH HER FINGER TIPS AND	IMITATING	A BICYCLE HORN) PIP! PIP! /LADY BRITOMART/ (
CATH 1 (166)	RIDICULOUS STIFF GESTURES OF HIS HEAD AND ARMS,	IMITATING	A PUPPET) YOU ARE CAPTAIN WHATHISNAME; AND YOUR
ROCK II (264)	ONE. THIS PRIMITIVE SAVAGE DARES TO ACCUSE ME OF	IMITATING	HIM: ME, WITH THE BLOOD IN MY VEINS OF CONQUERORS
DEVL II (45)	TAKE HIM HIS OWN COAT. I KNOW WHAT HE'LL SAY-- (	IMITATING	RICHARD'S SARDONIC MANNER) " ANXIOUS ABOUT MY
METH PREFACE(R81)	IT HAS NEVER BEEN QUITE CONTEMPTIBLE EXCEPT WHEN	IMITATING	THE ICONOGRAPHY AFTER THE RELIGION HAD BECOME A
MTH5 (248)	SPEAK, ARJILLAX: YOU WHO HAVE ADVANCED FROM	IMITATING	THE LIGHTLY LIVING CHILD TO THE INTENSELY LIVING
CATH 1,SD(161)	APARTMENT: STYLE, RUSSIA IN THE XVIII CENTURY	IMITATING	THE VERSAILLES DU ROI SOLEIL. EXTRAVAGANT LUXURY.

IMITATION

INCA (245)	HELP IT. I AM AMUSED. THE OTHER WAS MERELY AN	IMITATION	: A FAILURE, I ADMIT. /ERMYNTRUDE/ YOU INTIMATED
ROCK II (265)	IF YOU DARE, THAT YOU ARE THE ORIGINAL AND I THE	IMITATION	. DO YOU NOT FEAR THE LIGHTNING? THE EARTHQUAKE?
MIS. PREFACE(31)	GO AND DO LIKEWISE BY PUTTING HIS VICTIMS INTO AN	IMITATION	NEST AND BOTTLING AND EXHIBITING THEM AS AIDS TO "

6CAL SD(104) OF THE QUEEN, UNTIL IT DEVELOPS INTO A STARTLING IMITATION OF A DOG FIGHT. /THE QUEEN/ (TEARING THE TWO DOGS
6CAL (105) GEE-UP, NEDDY. (HE FINISHES WITH A SPIRITED IMITATION OF A DONKEY'S BRAY). /THE KING/ THAT IS HOW THEY
BARB PREFACE(217) COWARDICE (FRUITS OF POVERTY, BOTH), THE BEST IMITATION OF A GOOD LIFE NOW PROCURABLE IS LIFE ON AN
MIS. PREFACE(99) ONLY A VERY FOOLISH PERSON WOULD SUBSTITUTE THE IMITATION OF CHRIST FOR TREASURE ISLAND AS A PRESENT FOR A
MTH5 (217) COMPANIONS HERE WILL TEACH YOU HOW TO KEEP UP AN IMITATION OF HAPPINESS DURING YOUR FOUR YEARS BY WHAT THEY
PYGM IV SD(267) HER FEELINGS BY A WILD PANTOMIME IN WHICH AN IMITATION OF HIGGINS'S EXIT IS CONFUSED WITH HER OWN
GETT (319) THE REAL THING AS WELL AS WE LIKE AN ARTISTIC IMITATION OF IT? IS NOT THE REAL THING ACCURSED? ARE NOT
GETT (319) GOES A LONG WAY WITH THEM; AND THEY LIKE A GOOD IMITATION OF IT BETTER THAN THE REAL THING, AS EVERY NURSE
MILL PREFACE(134) MEANS BEING PUT THROUGH THIS PROCESS, OR THE BEST IMITATION OF IT THAT OUR CHILDREN'S PARENTS CAN AFFORD. THE
ROCK II (265) HAS BETRAYED ITSELF. I AM NIGGER, I AM BAD IMITATION OF THAT EATER OF UNCLEAN FOODS, NEVER SUFFICIENTLY
MTH3 (105) SECRETARY. /BURGE-LUBIN/ (RISING IN INSTINCTIVE IMITATION OF THE ARCHBISHOP) HONOR US BY TAKING A SEAT, O
WIDO II (36) ANGRILY; AND HER VOICE IS NO LONGER EVEN AN IMITATION OF THE VOICE OF A LADY AS SHE EXCLAIMS) I HATE
METH PREFACE(R81) AGO TO ACHIEVE THE EFFECTS OF THE OLD MASTERS BY IMITATION WHEN THEY SHOULD HAVE BEEN ILLUSTRATING A FAITH OF

IMITATIONS
DOCT PREFACE(27) NASTY, DANGEROUS AND SCIENTIFICALLY SPURIOUS IMITATIONS AS ORDINARY VACCINATION, WHICH WILL PROBABLY BE

IMITATIVE
METH PREFACE(R83) BEAUTIFUL." IN OUR DAY IT HAS FALLEN TO BE THE IMITATIVE AND VOLUPTUOUS. IN BOTH PERIODS THE WORD
3PLA PREFACE(R37) HAVE BEEN WELL ENOUGH ESTABLISHED. THE EARLY IMITATIVE WORKS OF GREAT MEN ARE USUALLY CONSPICUOUSLY

IMITATOR
DOCT I (99) ONE OF THESE INTERESTING LITTLE CREATURES HAS AN IMITATOR , JUST AS MEN IMITATE EACH OTHER, GERMS IMITATE

IMITATORS
LADY PREFACE(215) THE MODELS OF THIS TYPE (I SAY NOTHING OF MERE IMITATORS OF IT) BELOW THE RANK THAT LOOKS AT THE MIDDLE
LION PREFACE(83) MISCHIEVOUS OF THEM. THE NET RESULT IS THAT THE IMITATORS OF THE APOSTLES, WHETHER THEY ARE CALLED HOLY
BASH II,1, (103) THIS SAMPLE OF COLONIAL SMARTNESS WILL NOT FIND IMITATORS ON THIS SIDE. THE LOSERS SETTLED UP LIKE

IMMACULATE
GETT PREFACE(248) ITSELF ABSOLUTELY AN OBSCENE THING, AND THAT AN IMMACULATE CONCEPTION IS A MIRACLE. SO UNWHOLESOME AN
METH PREFACE(R76) MEANS AN ETERNITY OF BLAZING BRIMSTONE; THAT THE IMMACULATE CONCEPTION MEANS THAT SEX IS SINFUL AND THAT
SIM PRO,3, (31) WITH YOU. THE FATHER, THE SON, THE SPIRIT, THE IMMACULATE MOTHER-- /THE L.T./ EXCUSE ME. WE ARE NOT

IMMATURE
METH PREFACE(R14) ALL IF THEY DID NOT ACT AS PRISONS IN WHICH THE IMMATURE ARE KEPT FROM WORRYING THE MATURE) THAT SAVE US
SUPR PREFACE(R16) OF GALLANTRY, AFTER BECOMING, AT MOST, TWO IMMATURE INTRIGUES LEADING TO SORDID AND PROLONGED
CAND I (81) IS A CONCEITEDLY WELL INTENTIONED, ENTHUSIASTIC, IMMATURE NOVICE, WITH NOTHING POSITIVELY UNBEARABLE ABOUT
JOAN PREFACE(44) THE POPULACE AND THE VANITY AND SILLINESS OF AN IMMATURE PRINCE BY EXPLOITING A FEW OF THOSE LUCKY
MTH2 (68) DOWN TO POSTERITY AS ONE OF A EUROPEAN GROUP OF IMMATURE STATESMEN AND MONARCHS WHO, DOING THE VERY BEST FOR

IMMATURITY
MTH5 (218) HUMAN BEINGS TWENTY YEARS OF AWKWARD STUMBLING IMMATURITY AFTER THEY WERE BORN. THEY HAD TO SPEND FIFTY
JOAN PREFACE(22) EDGE. SHE WAS VERY CAPABLE: A BORN BOSS. JOAN'S IMMATURITY AND IGNORANCE. ALL THIS, HOWEVER, MUST BE TAKEN
MTH3 (122) PEOPLE NOT UNDERSTAND THAT AS THE CONFUSION AND IMMATURITY AND PRIMITIVE ANIMALISM IN WHICH WE LIVE FOR THE
BULL PREFACE(43) AT 21 BY HIS OWN INEXPERIENCE AND FOLLY AND IMMATURITY INSTEAD OF BY THE EXPERIENCE AND SAGACITY OF HIS
MTH3 (126) TO MATURE, AND ARE THE MOST HELPLESS DURING THEIR IMMATURITY . I KNOW NOW THAT IT TOOK ME A WHOLE CENTURY TO

IMMEASURABLE
FABL IV (116) SUBSTANTIAL EVEN AT TEMPERATURES THAT ARE QUITE IMMEASURABLE AND HARDLY CONCEIVABLE. IT FOLLOWED LOGICALLY
JOAN PREFACE(5) IS A MYSTERY WHICH CANNOT BE REASONED AWAY. BEING IMMEASURABLE IT IS UNBEARABLE WHEN THERE IS NO PRESUMPTION
KING I (216) BUT I CANNOT MEASURE IT IN A PINT POT. BEAUTY IS IMMEASURABLE . /NEWTON/ I CAN MEASURE GRAVITATION. NOTHING

IMMEASURABLY
SUPR III (105) MAGNIFICENCE OF BODY HAS BEEN TRIED. THINGS IMMEASURABLY GREATER THAN MAN IN EVERY RESPECT BUT BRAIN

IMMEDIATE
GENV IV (98) OF TRUTH AND IMPORTANCE, AND THUS PRODUCE IMMEDIATE ACTION AND ENTHUSIASTIC FAITH AND OBEDIENCE. MY
POSN PREFACE(414) OR SANITARY DEFECT IN THE BUILDING NECESSITATES IMMEDIATE ACTION FOR THE PROTECTION OF THE PUBLIC AGAINST
SIM PREFACE(18) EXPERIMENT IN GROUP MARRIAGE I AM ADVOCATING THE IMMEDIATE ADOPTION OF THAT METHOD OF PEOPLING THE WORLD FOR
BULL PREFACE(13) THEATRE BY MESSRS VEDRENNE AND BARKER, AND ITS IMMEDIATE AND ENORMOUS POPULARITY WITH DELIGHTED AND
SIM II (57) THE IMPERIAL PROVINCE OF HOLY ISLAND DEMANDS THE IMMEDIATE AND EXEMPLARY COMBUSTION OF THE ABOMINABLE
DOCT PREFACE(56) SOUND, PROBABLY THE RESULT WOULD BE AN IMMEDIATE AND STARTLING REDUCTION IN CHILD MORTALITY,
METH PREFACE(R67) UP WITH IN THE ABSTRACT, AND NO HARDSHIP SHORT OF IMMEDIATE AND SUDDEN STARVATION THAT IT WOULD NOT AND DID
SHAK PREFACE(135) THIS FEAT, AND WAS GRATIFIED BY MR LANCHESTER'S IMMEDIATE APPROVAL. I HAVE LEARNT PART OF MY CRAFT AS
FABL PREFACE(75) THIS IS AS TRUE AS EVER. NOT ONLY ARE THE IMMEDIATE BLACK CONVERTS OF OUR MISSIONARIES INFERIOR IN
MIS. PREFACE(7) AT ALL UNLIKE WHAT THEY WOULD BE IF THERE WERE NO IMMEDIATE CONSANGUINITY BETWEEN THEM, AND ONE WERE WHITE AND
ROCK PREFACE(148) COMPUNCTION ABOUT SACRIFICING OTHERS TO THEIR OWN IMMEDIATE CONVENIENCE. TO PUNISH SUCH PERSONS IS RIDICULOUS:
GENV IV (126) YOU USE ALL YOUR INFLUENCE AT ROME TO OBTAIN AN IMMEDIATE DECISION FROM THE CHURCH AGAINST THIS STORY?
BULL PREFACE(4) CONCEIVABLY BENEFIT ANYONE IN ENGLAND, HAD THE IMMEDIATE EFFECT OF EXTINGUISHING ITS NOBLE AUTHOR
APPL PREFACE(186) THAT IT GOES WHERE IT IS MOST WANTED AND GIVES IMMEDIATE EMPLOYMENT. THIS IS THE BEST I CAN DO WITHOUT
GENV IV (121) WHICH CALLS FOR NOTHING SHORT OF YOUR IMMEDIATE EXECUTION. THE LEADERS AND THE BRITISH CONTINGENT,
BARB PREFACE(207) CRITICS NEVER AFFILIATE ME TO MY COUNTRYMAN AND IMMEDIATE FORERUNNER, CHARLES LEVER, WHILST THEY CONFIDENTLY
MRS II SD(203) PRAED PUTS HIS HAT ON THE DRESSER. THERE IS AN IMMEDIATE IMPROVEMENT IN THE COMPANY'S BEHAVIOR. CROFTS
APPL PREFACE(186) OUR IGNORANCE, OUR PASSIONS, OUR PRIVATE AND IMMEDIATE INTERESTS ARE CONSTANTLY IN CONFLICT WITH THE
MILL PREFACE(113) AND, IF THEY DID, WOULD NOT SACRIFICE THEIR OWN IMMEDIATE INTERESTS TO THE PERMANENT INTERESTS OF THE NATION
ROCK PREFACE(176) NOT ABHORRED, IT IS QUITE CREDIBLE THAT BOTH HIS IMMEDIATE JUDGES AND THE POPE BELIEVED WITH AT LEAST HALF
APPL PREFACE(195) IF YOUR MIND WAS NOT LARGE ENOUGH TO GRASP THE IMMEDIATE NECESSITY FOR A NEW CENTRAL CLEARING HOUSE IN
MRS PREFACE(167) THAT RESISTANCE, MAKES THE FALL OF THE CURTAIN AN IMMEDIATE NECESSITY, SINCE DRAMA ENDS EXACTLY WHERE
MRS III (228) STROLLS ACROSS TO THE SUNDIAL TO GET OUT OF HIS IMMEDIATE NEIGHBORHOOD). /CROFTS/ (NOT AT ALL DISCOURAGED,
GENV PREFACE(3) THE NEWS OF THE DAMAGE REACHING BEYOND ITS IMMEDIATE NEIGHBORHOOD. ONE NIGHT EARLY IN THE RESUMED WAR I
METH PREFACE(R49) THUS WITHOUT ANY CONSCIOUSNESS OR ANY PURPOSE, IMMEDIATE OR ULTERIOR, HE MUST HAVE KNOWN VERY LITTLE ABOUT
CLEO II (122) IT IS CAESAR'S DUTY TO HIS COUNTRY TO REQUIRE IMMEDIATE PAYMENT. /CAESAR/ (BLANDLY) AH, I FORGOT. I HAVE
MILL PREFACE(128) IN THE GENERAL INTEREST AND NOT SOLELY IN THE IMMEDIATE PERSONAL INTEREST OF THE DECIDER. IT WAS ARGUED BY
MIS. PREFACE(6) IS TO TREAT THE CHILD AS THE PROPERTY OF ITS IMMEDIATE PHYSICAL PARENTS, AND TO ALLOW THEM TO DO WHAT
FABL PREFACE(86) IS TO BE DONE? I AM ASKED EVERY WEEK WHAT IS MY IMMEDIATE PRACTICAL REMEDY FOR ALL THIS. ALSO WHAT IS MY
SIM PREFACE(18) ADOPTION OF THAT METHOD OF PEOPLING THE WORLD FOR IMMEDIATE PRACTICE BY MY READERS. GROUP MARRIAGE IS A FORM
GENV PREFACE(19) WENT BY TRAIN) WAS WITHIN HIS GRASP. HE HAD THE IMMEDIATE PRECEDENT OF KURT EISNER'S SUCCESSFUL PUTSCH TO
SUPR PREFACE(R30) THIRD ACT OF THE ENSUING COMEDY IS SUITABLE FOR IMMEDIATE PRODUCTION AT A POPULAR THEATRE WE NEED NOT
JITT PREFACE(3) RESPONSIBLE MANAGER OF A THEATRE WITH A VIEW TO IMMEDIATE PRODUCTION. THE EVASION FAILED IGNOMINIOUSLY. MY
DOCT PREFACE(25) WHICH THE DOCTORS, FORGETTING EVERYTHING BUT THE IMMEDIATE QUARREL, NAIVELY EXCUSE THEMSELVES BY ADMITTING,
MTH2 (68) IS VERY EVIDENT. YOU ARE NOW, MR LUBIN, WITHIN IMMEDIATE REACH OF YOUR SEVENTIETH YEAR. MR JOYCE BURGE IS
2TRU PREFACE(23) GIVE THEM EITHER TITLE, RANK, OR UNIFORM, AS THE IMMEDIATE RESULT WILL BE THEIR PARTIAL DISABLEMENT BY THE
BARB PREFACE(217) AND BELIEVED AS UNDERSHAFT ACTS AND BELIEVES, THE IMMEDIATE RESULT WOULD BE A REVOLUTION OF INCALCULABLE
GETT PREFACE(207) PRESENT FIGURE, OR TO INCREASE IT, WE MUST TAKE IMMEDIATE STEPS TO INDUCE PEOPLE OF MODERATE MEANS TO MARRY
SUPR PREFACE(R13) IMPRESSES US IN EL BURLADOR DE SEVILLA IS NOT THE IMMEDIATE URGENCY OF REPENTANCE, BUT THE HEROISM OF DARING
MIS. PREFACE(18) REGARD FOR THE INTERESTS, EITHER REMOTE OR IMMEDIATE , OF THE CHILDREN. THIS SYSTEM TENDS TO PRODUCE A

IMMEDIATELY
O'FL (226) BEINGS OR ARE YOU WILD BEASTS? STOP THAT NOISE IMMEDIATELY : DO YOU HEAR? (YELLING) ARE YOU GOING TO DO
O'FL SD(226) SIR PEARCE SLAMS THE DOOR UPON THEM SAVAGELY. IMMEDIATELY A HEAVENLY SILENCE FALLS ON THE SUMMER
BULL II (98) AWAY PAST THE STONE TOWARDS THE BROW OF THE HILL. IMMEDIATELY A YOUNG LABORER, HIS FACE DISTORTED WITH TERROR,
DOCT PREFACE(58) FINGER; AND THAT IF THIS JOINT BE AMPUTATED IMMEDIATELY AFTER BIRTH, TYPHUS FEVER WILL DISAPPEAR. HAD
PYGM EPILOG (292) INDICATIONS SHE HAS HERSELF GIVEN THEM. ALMOST IMMEDIATELY AFTER ELIZA IS STUNG INTO PROCLAIMING HER
PHIL II (129) NOT GOOD FOR YOUR LIVER, CRAVEN, TO RUSH ABOUT IMMEDIATELY AFTER LUNCH. /CUTHBERTSON/ HIS LIVER'S CURED.
LADY PREFACE(220) TO CONDEMN THEM AS OUT OF CHARACTER, RICHARD III, IMMEDIATELY AFTER PITYING HIMSELF BECAUSE " THERE IS NO

POSN PREFACE(393)	OF THOSE PREVAILING IN ST. JAMES'S PALACE.	IMMEDIATELY	AFTER THIS, THE LORD CHAMBERLAIN LICENSED THE
GENV I (39)	FELT FREE FOR THE FIRST TIME IN THEIR LIVES.	IMMEDIATELY	AFTER THE ELECTIONS THE BUDGET WAS PASSED
CLEO III SD(153)	CENTURION AND HIS GUARD RUN OFF NORTHWARD; AND	IMMEDIATELY	AFTERWARDS THE BUCINA SOUNDS. THE FOUR PORTERS
JITT I SD(13)	THE VISITOR, LEAVING THE DOOR OF THE ROOM OPEN.	IMMEDIATELY	AFTERWARDS A VEILED LADY HURRIES IN LIKE A
MIS. (177)	ACROSS THE GARDEN WITH PERCIVAL IN HOT PURSUIT.	IMMEDIATELY	AFTERWARDS SHE APPEARS AGAIN, AND RUNS INTO THE
LADY PREFACE(213)	TO WILDE WITH MIRACULOUS PRECISION EXACTLY WHAT	IMMEDIATELY	AFTERWARDS HAPPENED TO HIM, AND WARNED HIM TO
LADY PREFACE(224)	AND WHEN HE DISCUSSES THE SCENE WITH HORATIO	IMMEDIATELY	AFTER, HE UTTERLY FORGETS HER, THOUGH HE IS
HART PREFACE(20)	FINE ARTS, NO GREAT STRESS WAS LAID ON THAT LOSS.	IMMEDIATELY	AN AMAZING FRENZY SWEPT THROUGH THE COUNTRY. MEN
LION EPILOG (147)	THE SECOND IS BY LEADING THE HERD TO WAR, WHICH	IMMEDIATELY	AND INFALLIBLY MAKES THEM FORGET EVERYTHING,
MRS PREFACE(180)	FILM TO BE MADE FOR THIS PURPOSE. THE FILM CENSOR	IMMEDIATELY	BANNED THE PART OF THE FILM WHICH GAVE THE
MIS. PREFACE(32)	TO IT BY, SAY, THE COLLEGE OF HERALDS, SHOULD	IMMEDIATELY	BE SKINNED ALIVE WITH A BIRCH ROD. IT MIGHT EVEN
LION PREFACE(39)	AND THEREUPON HANDED ONE TO JUDAS, WHO ATE IT AND	IMMEDIATELY	BECAME POSSESSED BY THE DEVIL. THIS IS MORE
BULL PREFACE(4)	WHICH HAD UP TO THAT MOMENT BEEN A TOPICAL PLAY,	IMMEDIATELY	BECAME A HISTORICAL ONE. BROADBENT IS NO LONGER
APPL PREFACE(186)	FALL TO NOTHING, AS THE STOCK EXCHANGE WOULD	IMMEDIATELY	BECOME A MARKET IN WHICH THERE WERE ALL SELLERS
NEVR IV SD(285)	MY DEAR. THANK YOU. VALENTINE ARRIVES. GLORIA	IMMEDIATELY	BECOMES DELIBERATELY HAUGHTY. /VALENTINE/ EXCUSE
MILL IV (195)	OBLITERATED ALL CONSCIOUSNESS OF WHAT HAPPENED	IMMEDIATELY	BEFORE THE ASSAULT: THE LAST THING I CAN
ROCK PREFACE(190)	REPROACH ME BECAUSE I, BEING A SOCIALIST, DO NOT	IMMEDIATELY	BEGGAR MYSELF IN THIS FASHION. PEOPLE WHO
DOCT I (82)	IS STILL QUITE PRESENTABLE. /EMMY/ (ENTERING AND	IMMEDIATELY	BEGINNING TO DUST THE COUCH) THERES A LADY
ARMS III SD(69)	CLOCK OF WHICH THE SPRING HAS BEEN TOUCHED,	IMMEDIATELY	BEGINS TO FOLD HIS ARMS. /BLUNTSCHLI/ (BEFORE
KING I (207)	LIE TO ITSELF: IT OVERTHROWS THE ROMAN CHURCH AND	IMMEDIATELY	BUILDS ITSELF ANOTHER NEARER HOME AND MAKES YOU
JOAN 4 (98)	ON THEM AND DROVE THEM ON TO THE BRIDGE, WHICH	IMMEDIATELY	BURST INTO FLAMES AND CRUMBLED UNDER THEM,
APPL II SD(265)	WITH SEMPRONIUS, HEADS THE PROCESSION, FOLLOWED	IMMEDIATELY	BY THE TWO LADY MINISTERS. THE QUEEN RISES AS
SIM PREFACE(16)	OF THEM. UNFORTUNATELY THE WORD TRIBUNAL	IMMEDIATELY	CALLS UP VISIONS NOT ONLY OF JUDGMENT BUT OF
PYGM V SD(281)	WITH HIGGINS. HE RISES AND JOINS HER THERE. SHE	IMMEDIATELY	COMES BACK INTO THE ROOM AND MAKES FOR THE DOOR;
CLEO II SD(123)	TO BEHAVE LIKE A QUEEN? /CAESAR/ YES. CLEOPATRA	IMMEDIATELY	COMES DOWN TO THE CHAIR OF STATE; SEIZES
MTH4 II SD(182)	DE SIECLE. THEY FILE IN UNDER THE PORTICO. ZOO	IMMEDIATELY	COMES OUT IMPERIOUSLY TO NAPOLEON'S RIGHT,
POSN PREFACE(394)	WOULD BE MUCH LESS HUMILIATING TO THE PERSONS	IMMEDIATELY	CONCERNED, THE INHERENT VICES OF THE INSTITUTION
ROCK PREFACE(167)	FORMS OF CAPITALIZATION AND ARE RUNNING SHORT OF	IMMEDIATELY	CONSUMABLE GOODS, PRESENTING THE SPECTACLE OF
HART PREFACE(23)	DELUSION AND FOLLY, THE CRITICAL READER WILL	IMMEDIATELY	COUNTERPLEAD THAT ENGLAND ALL THIS TIME WAS
JOAN PREFACE(48)	TALES OF ALL KINDS. THE PROPORTION OF MARVEL TO	IMMEDIATELY	CREDIBLE STATEMENT IN THE LATEST EDITION OF THE
PHIL III SD(136)	SHE CROSSES TO THAT SIDE BEHIND THE TABLE; AND HE	IMMEDIATELY	CROSSES TO THE OPPOSITE SIDE IN FRONT OF IT,
MILL PREFACE(122)	MYSELF, ALSO UNDERSTOOD THE SITUATION, AND WAS	IMMEDIATELY	DENOUNCED BY THE REFUGEES AND THEIR CHAMPIONS AS
ARMS I (14)	RAISES HIS HEAD AND LOOKS GRATEFULLY AT HER: SHE	IMMEDIATELY	DRAWS BACK AND SAYS STIFFLY) YOU MUST EXCUSE ME:
DEVL III (51)	OF THEM. (HE GOES OUT, LOCKING THE DOOR. RICHARD	IMMEDIATELY	DROPS HIS RAFFISH MANNER AND TURNS TO JUDITH
DOCT PREFACE(54)	ONE HAS VACCINATION MARKS: THE OTHER HAS NONE.	IMMEDIATELY	EITHER THE VACCINISTS OR THE ANTI-VACCINISTS
BARB I SD(265)	A FACE AT LOMAX, WHOSE TOO LONG SUPPRESSED MIRTH	IMMEDIATELY	EXPLODES IN AGONIZED NEIGHINGS. /LADY BRITOMART/
GETT PREFACE(211)	AS A MOTHER, POLYGYNY AND POLYANDRY WOULD	IMMEDIATELY	FALL INTO SINCERE DISREPUTE, BECAUSE MONOGAMY IS
HART PREFACE(4)	VACUUM; AND AS NATURE, ABHORRING THE VACUUM,	IMMEDIATELY	FILLED IT UP WITH SEX AND WITH ALL SORTS OF
CLEO II SD(127)	TRY, ACHILLAS. (CALLING) GUARD THERE. THE LOGGIA	IMMEDIATELY	FILLS WITH CAESAR'S SOLDIERS, WHO STAND, SWORD
HART PREFACE(26)	OF ACTION TO ELECT THEM TOO. THE ELECTION THAT	IMMEDIATELY	FOLLOWED THE ARMISTICE WAS PERHAPS THE MADDEST
MRS III (233)	HARSHLY; AND HE STARTS BACK INVOLUNTARILY. ALMOST	IMMEDIATELY	FRANK APPEARS AT THE PORCH WITH HIS RIFLE).
LION PREFACE(36)	THE CHRIST. THIS IS NOTEWORTHY BECAUSE JESUS	IMMEDIATELY	GIVES THEM A DELIBERATE EXHIBITION OF MIRACLES,
HART PREFACE(22)	HIS BROTHER WOULD BE KILLED AT THE FRONT,	IMMEDIATELY	HE WOULD THROW UP HIS WORK AND TAKE UP THE WAR
PPP SD(194)	MAGNESIA SWITCHES OFF THE ELECTRIC LIGHT, AND	IMMEDIATELY	HEARS THE ANGELS QUITE DISTINCTLY. THEY SING
CAPT I SD(234)	APPEARANCE OF HAVING BEEN VIOLENTLY KICKED. MARZO	IMMEDIATELY	HURRIES DOWN THE GARDEN ON SIR HOWARD'S RIGHT
SUPR IV (170)	WITHDRAWS TO THE CORNER OF THE LAWN; AND OCTAVIUS	IMMEDIATELY	HURRIES DOWN TO HIM). /TAVY/ (ASIDE TO TANNER,
MILL PREFACE(118)	HIM TO LOOK UP INTO THE SKY. THE DIPLOMATISTS	IMMEDIATELY	INDULGED THEMSELVES WITH A PRODIGIOUSLY
MIS. (178)	SIR, YOULL HAVE THE GOODNESS TO COME OUT WITH ME	IMMEDIATELY	. I HAVE SOME BUSINESS WITH YOU WHICH CANT BE
APPL INTRLUD(250)	SHE DIES! WILL YOU DIE TOO? /MAGNUS/ NOT	IMMEDIATELY	. I SHALL HAVE TO CARRY ON AS BEST I CAN WITHOUT
NEVR II (234)	MORE TO COME STILL, THANK YOU. THEY WILL BE HERE	IMMEDIATELY	. (SHE GOES INTO THE HOTEL). THE WAITER TAKES
PHIL I (82)	YOU DEMAND, ON CONDITION THAT YOU COME AWAY	IMMEDIATELY	. ON MY SACRED WORD OF HONOR AS A GENTLEMAN-- AS
BASH III (125)	LOVE ME? /BASHVILLE/ TIS SAID: NOW LET ME LEAVE	IMMEDIATELY	. /LYDIA/ IN TAKING, BASHVILLE, THIS MOST
DOCT I SD(83)	SHE DETECTS DUST ON THE CONSOLE AND IS DOWN ON IT	IMMEDIATELY	. /REDPENNY/ (JUMPING UP AND FOLLOWING HER)
INCA (239)	HIGHNESS? I SHOULD LIKE TO SET ABOUT MY DUTIES	IMMEDIATELY	. /THE PRINCESS/ OH YES, I THINK SO. OH
WIDO I SD(6)	SISTER OR YOUR FATHER'S? THIS SHOT TELLS	IMMEDIATELY	. THE GENTLEMAN IS PERCEPTIBLY INTERESTED.
APPL PREFACE(181)	THE STREETS. EVERYONE WHO SAW THEM DOING IT	IMMEDIATELY	JOINED IN THE RUSH. THEY RAN SIMPLY BECAUSE
JOAN PREFACE(49)	IS MENTIONED FATALISTICALLY ONLY TO BE FORGOTTEN	IMMEDIATELY	LIKE A PASSING VAGUE APPREHENSION. TO SHAKESPEAR
MILL IV (193)	KNOWS SHE CAN DEPEND ON ME. (HE GOES OUT, BUT	IMMEDIATELY	LOOKS IN AGAIN TO SAY) YOUR FRIEND MR SAGAMORE,
MTH4 II (179)	LIKE TO DO, AND PARTLY BECAUSE, IF I STOP, I	IMMEDIATELY	LOSE MY POWER AND BECOME A BEGGAR IN THE LAND
CAPT NOTES (306)	AUDIBLE, AND CANNOT BE DROPPED WITHOUT BEING	IMMEDIATELY	MISSED. THE LONDON H IS SO COMPARATIVELY QUIET
GENV I (46)	OVER HER. SHE REFUSED TO DO ANY WORK THAT WAS NOT	IMMEDIATELY	NECESSARY, ON THE GROUND THAT THE END OF THE
MRS I (183)	OF CHARACTER ON HIS PART. BUT HE DOES NOT	IMMEDIATELY	OBEY). /PRAED/ BY THE WAY, THOUGH, HADNT WE
UNPL PREFACE(R8)	THE REMAINING NINETY PER CENT BEING ABNORMAL. I	IMMEDIATELY	PERCEIVED THE EXPLANATION OF MY WANT OF SUCCESS
LADY PREFACE(221)	THAT SHAKESPEAR'S REVULSIONS, AS THE SONNET	IMMEDIATELY	PRECEDING SHEWS, WERE AS VIOLENT AS HIS ARDORS,
METH PREFACE(R54)	OF THE ACCIDENTS OF OUR COMPETITIVE COMMERCE, AND	IMMEDIATELY	PROCEEDS TO DIG HIS GRAVE WITH HIS TEETH. BUT
MIS. PREFACE(31)	NOT NOW WHAT THEY WERE WHEN YOU WERE A BOY." I	IMMEDIATELY	PROCURED THE TIME SHEETS OF HALF A DOZEN MODERN
MIS. PREFACE(108)	THEIR LIVES IN EXTIRPATING FOR THE SAKE OF AN	IMMEDIATELY	QUIET AND FINALLY DISASTROUS LIFE.
DEVL I (5)	DOOR? (SHE SEES THAT THE GIRL IS ASLEEP, AND	IMMEDIATELY	RAISES A CLAMOR OF HEARTFELT VEXATION). WELL,
DOCT PREFACE(5)	MUCH SOUGHT AFTER THAT THEIR CURED PATIENTS ARE	IMMEDIATELY	REPLACED BY FRESH ONES. AND THERE IS THIS
DEVL EPILOG (81)	HIM TO RETURN TO AMERICA INTO CAPTIVITY. BURGOYNE	IMMEDIATELY	RESIGNED ALL HIS APPOINTMENTS; AND THIS
FABL PREFACE(84)	OUTSTRIPS IT BECAUSE, BEING FASTER, IT IS MORE	IMMEDIATELY	RESPONSIVE TO THE CONTINUAL NEED FOR REFORMS AND
PHIL II SD(103)	FIRST MAKES FOR THE STAIRCASE DOOR. JULIA	IMMEDIATELY	RETREATS TO IT, BARRING HIS PATH. HE DOUBLES
GETT (262)	IS OR ISNT. (HE GOES OUT THROUGH THE TOWER, AND	IMMEDIATELY	RETURNS FOR A MOMENT TO ANNOUNCE) THE GENERAL.
GENV IV SD(115)	FOREIGN SECRETARY, SIR ORPHEUS MIDLANDER. FLANCO	IMMEDIATELY	RISES; CLICKS HIS HEELS; AND SALUTES SIR ORPHEUS
HART II SD(107)	THE ROOM AND RELEASES HIM. - ELLIE FOLLOWS, AND	IMMEDIATELY	RUNS ACROSS TO THE BACK OF HER FATHER'S CHAIR,
DOCT I (86)	GOODBYE. (HE GOES OUT WITH RIDGEON, WHO RETURNS	IMMEDIATELY	). /REDPENNY/ OLD PADDY CULLEN WAS HERE BEFORE
ARMS I SD(7)	SILHOUETTED IN BLACK UPON IT. THE SHUTTERS CLOSE	IMMEDIATELY	; AND THE ROOM IS DARK AGAIN. BUT THE SILENCE IS
FABL PREFACE(65)	ANY NORMAL PERSON, BUT WHEN IT WAS PUT TO ME, I	IMMEDIATELY	SAID DOGBERRY, I WAS ONCE SHEWN THE DAGGER WITH
POSN PREFACE(362)	THAT SOMETHING MUST BE DONE, THEY	IMMEDIATELY	SET TO WORK TO FACE THE SITUATION AND DISCOVER
METH PREFACE(R49)	MOVEMENT. HIS PROOF IS THAT THE BUTTERFLY	IMMEDIATELY	SETTLES AGAIN ON THE FLOWER, AND REPEATS THE
ANNA (291)	TREASON TO THE REVOLUTION, MY LAD; AND THEY WOULD	IMMEDIATELY	SHOOT YOU, UNLESS YOU CRIED AND ASKED TO SEE
APPL PREFACE(178)	FAMILIAR WITH IT TRUST IT LEAST. YOU WILL NOT	IMMEDIATELY	SHRIEK OUT THAT I DO NOT BELIEVE IN THE SEA;
JITT II (49)	/LENKHEIM/ YOU CAN STAND AS WELL AS I CAN. (SHE	IMMEDIATELY	SITS DOWN OBSTINATELY AT THE WRITING-TABLE).
MTH4 III SD(198)	THE ELDERLY GENTLEMAN IS KNOCKED FLAT; BUT AS HE	IMMEDIATELY	SITS UP AGAIN DAZEDLY IT IS CLEAR THAT HE IS
ARMS I SD(12)	HER WITH A SLAM, LOCKING IT VIOLENTLY. THE MAN	IMMEDIATELY	STEPS OUT FROM BEHIND THE CURTAIN, SHEATHING HIS
MRS PREFACE(151)	PROSPECTS AT THE OUTSET OF MY CAREER. MY PLAY WAS	IMMEDIATELY	STIGMATIZED BY THE LORD CHAMBERLAIN, WHO BY ACT
METH PREFACE(R14)	YOU THROW A BUCKET OF MUD OVER IT, WHEN IT WILL	IMMEDIATELY	TAKE EXTRAORDINARY PAINS TO LICK THE MUD OFF,
CAPT II (253)	YOU SHOULD HAVE TAKEN MY WARNING. /SIR HOWARD/ (	IMMEDIATELY	TAKING THE TONE OF COLD DISGUST FOR MORAL
MTH5 (240)	FEEL CALLED. (SEEING THE BODY OF PYGMALION, AND	IMMEDIATELY	TAKING A STERNER TONE) WHAT! A CHILD LOST! A
BULL PREFACE(68)	ROYAL ASSENT AND BECAME A STATUTE OF THE REALM.	IMMEDIATELY	THE BRITISH OFFICERS ON SERVICE IN IRELAND
MTH3 SD(91)	DIAL; PUTS ANOTHER PEG IN; AND PRESSES A BUTTON.	IMMEDIATELY	THE SILVERY SCREEN VANISHES; AND IN ITS PLACE
UNPL PREFACE(R14)	THE BUILDING OF ROBINSON CRUSOE'S FIRST BOAT. I	IMMEDIATELY	THREW IT ASIDE, AND, RETURNING TO THE VEIN I HAD
FABL PREFACE(97)	AN ADVANCE, THEY ARE SO ASHAMED OF IT THAT THEY	IMMEDIATELY	THROW AWAY ALL CREDIT FOR IT BY PROTESTING THAT
MRS I SD(197)	MRS WARREN APPEARS ON THE THRESHOLD, AND IS	IMMEDIATELY	TRANSFIXED, RECOGNIZING THE CLERGYMAN. /VIVIE/ (
DOCT PREFACE(32)	OUT OF THE WINDOW WILL ALWAYS FALL ON ITS LEGS,	IMMEDIATELY	TRIES THE EXPERIMENT ON THE NEAREST CAT FROM THE
NEVR IV (301)	PART KINDLY. /GLORIA/ (ENORMOUSLY RELIEVED, AND	IMMEDIATELY	TURNING HER BACK ON HIM DELIBERATELY) GOODBYE. I
MRS II SD(199)	A MOMENT, TEMPTED. AT LAST SHE KISSES HIM, AND	IMMEDIATELY	TURNS AWAY, OUT OF PATIENCE WITH HERSELF. /MRS
KING PREFACE(157)	VOTES FOR WOMEN TO ABSURDITY; FOR THE WOMEN	IMMEDIATELY	USED THEIR VOTE TO KEEP WOMEN OUT OF PARLIAMENT.
JITT I SD(25)	SHE DASHES INTO THE BEDROOM, AND REAPPEARS ALMOST	IMMEDIATELY	WITH HER BLOUSE ON, ARRANGING IT WITH NERVOUS
CAPT I (227)	CHRORNICLE, LIDY. (RANKIN RETURNS. DRINKWATER	IMMEDIATELY	WITHDRAWS, STOPPING THE MISSIONARY FOR A MOMENT

IMMEMORIAL

LION PREFACE(28)	AND RETURN TO LIFE. HE ATTACHES TO HIMSELF THE	IMMEMORIAL	TRIBAL CEREMONY OF EATING THE GOD, BY BLESSING

IMMENSE

MIS. SD(126)	THE TIP FOR YOU. BENTLEY AND MR TARLETON (AN	IMMENSE	AND GENIAL VETERAN OF TRADE) COME INTO VIEW AND
MILL II SD(166)	OLD COFFEE ROOM IN AN ANCIENT RIVERSIDE INN. AN	IMMENSE	AND HIDEOUS SIDEBOARD OF THE MURKIEST MAHOGANY

BARB PREFACE(237)	SOOTHING AND CHEERING THE VICTIMS WITH HOPES OF	IMMENSE	AND INEXPENSIVE HAPPINESS IN ANOTHER WORLD WHEN THE
DEVL I SD(16)	IS A WIRY LITTLE TERRIER OF A MAN, WITH AN	IMMENSE	AND VISIBLY PURSEPROUD WIFE, BOTH FREE FROM THE
DOCT PREFACE(59)	AND I CANNOT RESIST PROFESSOR KARL PEARSON'S	IMMENSE	CONTEMPT FOR, AND INDIGNANT SENSE OF GRAVE SOCIAL
POSN PREFACE(380)	IN AMERICA BY THE POLICE IN CONSEQUENCE OF AN	IMMENSE	CROWD OF DISORDERLY PERSONS HAVING BEEN ATTRACTED TO
3PLA PREFACE(R37)	ALSO TAKES CAESAR FOR HIS HERO, AND EXPLAINS THE	IMMENSE	DIFFERENCE IN SCOPE BETWEEN THE PERFECT KNIGHT
CATH 1,SD(161)	IS HALF DRESSED IN AN UNFASTENED SHIRT AND AN	IMMENSE	DRESSING-GOWN, ONCE GORGEOUS, NOW FOOD-SPLASHED AND
FANY III (323)	AGAINST INJUSTICE AND VIOLENCE? (RISING, WITH	IMMENSE	ELAN) YOUR DAUGHTER, MADAM, IS SUPERB. YOUR COUNTRY
LADY PREFACE(224)	MEN, NOT ONLY BECAUSE IT IS DIAGNOSTIC OF THAT	IMMENSE	ENERGY OF LIFE WHICH WE CALL GENIUS, BUT BECAUSE ITS
SUPR III (110)	FOR HER PURPOSES MORE THAN A FRACTION OF THE	IMMENSE	ENERGY SHE HAS LEFT AT HIS DISPOSAL BY SAVING HIM
METH PREFACE(R17)	THE RULERS ARE EQUALLY INTIMIDATED BY THE	IMMENSE	EXTENSION AND CHEAPENING OF THE MEANS OF SLAUGHTER
GETT SD(259)	OF THE PALACE. IN THE WALL TO OUR RIGHT IS THE	IMMENSE	FIREPLACE, WITH ITS HUGE SPIT LIKE A BABY CRANE, AND
ROCK I (216)	OCCURRED TO SOME EXTENT; BUT THERE IS STILL AN	IMMENSE	FRINGE OF THE HUMAN RACE GROWING UP TO A SENSE OF
ROCK PREFACE(176)	AS A CHILD I THOUGHT OF THE EARTH AS BEING AN	IMMENSE	GROUND FLOOR WITH A STAR STUDDED CEILING WHICH WAS
POSN PREFACE(390)	ACT FOR HAVING FAILED NOT ONLY TO APPRECIATE THE	IMMENSE	IMPORTANCE OF THE THEATRE AS A MOST POWERFUL
DOCT I (103)	/B.B./ (SUDDENLY RISING TO THE NEW IDEA WITH	IMMENSE	INTEREST AND EXCITEMENT) WHAT! RIDGEON: DID YOU
UNPL PREFACE(R9)	SOON MY PRIVILEGES WERE ENORMOUS AND MY WEALTH	IMMENSE	. I HAD A PROMINENT PLACE RESERVED FOR ME ON A
ROCK PREFACE(152)	POLICE OFFICERS, SCAVENGERS, AND OPERATORS OF THE	IMMENSE	MACHINERY OF AMUSEMENT AND PROTECTION FOR THE IDLE
SIM PREFACE(15)	WE DARE BRING IT INTO PLAY, WOULD TELL US THAT AN	IMMENSE	MAJORITY OF THE PRISONERS AT THE BAR WILL BE NEITHER
METH PREFACE(R11)	EVOLUTIONIST, BUT AS THE EVOLUTIONIST, WITH THE	IMMENSE	MAJORITY WHO NEVER READ HIS BOOKS, THE FEW WHO NEVER
BULL IV (146)	COTCH HIM IN HER APERN WIDHOUT INTINDIN TO. (	IMMENSE	MERRIMENT). /AUNT JUDY/ AH, FOR SHAME, BARNEY! THE
MIS. PREFACE(41)	CONTINENTS AND FOUNDING RELIGIONS, OPENS UP	IMMENSE	NEW POSSIBILITIES OF MISCHIEF. TEACH A CHILD TO
LION PREFACE(79)	AND RUSKIN, HAVE DEFIED THE TYRANNY OF SEX, BUT	IMMENSE	NUMBERS OF ORDINARY CITIZENS OF BOTH SEXES HAVE,
BUOY 1 (15)	SPORT TOO RUINOUS AND VICIOUS FOR MEN ENNOBLED BY	IMMENSE	POWER AND ITS SPLENDID POSSIBILITIES. /FATHER/ POWER
APPL PREFACE(186)	WE CANNOT GOVERN OURSELVES; YET IF WE ENTRUST THE	IMMENSE	POWERS AND REVENUES WHICH ARE NECESSARY IN AN
BULL III (135)	RETHRENCHMENT MANE NOW? /BROADBENT/ IT MEANS AN	IMMENSE	REDUCTION IN THE BURDEN OF THE RATES AND TAXES.
BARB II (307)	BODGER. YOU REMEMBER THE CHORUS. " FOR THEE	IMMENSE	REJOICING-- IMMENSO GIUBILO-- IMMENSO GIUBILO." (
BULL IV (165)	HER VIOLENTLY TO HIS BREAST, WITH A CROW OF	IMMENSE	RELIEF AND TRIUMPH) AH, THATS RIGHT, THATS RIGHT:
DOCT PREFACE(30)	IN THE KINGDOM WOULD GAIN SUBSTANTIALLY BY THE	IMMENSE	RELIEF AND RECONCILIATION WHICH WOULD FOLLOW SUCH A
BARB III (318)	/UNDERSHAFT/ (RISING) MY DEAR BOY: THIS IS AN	IMMENSE	RELIEF TO ME. AND I TRUST IT MAY PROVE AN EQUALLY
MTH2 (60)	WITH YOUR VOLCANIC ENERGY. /BURGE/ (WITH AN	IMMENSE	SENSE OF POWER) NO, BY GEORGE! /FRANKLYN/ I THINK I
MTH1 I SD(3)	ACT I. THE GARDEN OF EDEN. AFTERNOON. AN	IMMENSE	SERPENT IS SLEEPING WITH HER HEAD BURIED IN A THICK
MTH5 SD(214)	SILVER DISHES PIERCED WITH HOLES, CLOTHS, AND	IMMENSE	SPONGES. THE REST CARRY WANDS WITH RIBBONS, AND
PYGM IV (262)	YOUNG AGAIN. ANYHOW, IT WAS A GREAT SUCCESS: AN	IMMENSE	SUCCESS. I WAS QUITE FRIGHTENED ONCE OR TWICE
DOCT I (98)	THE PUDDING IS IN THE EATING, YOU KNOW. IT WAS AN	IMMENSE	SUCCESS. IT ACTED LIKE MAGIC ON THE LITTLE PRINCE.
PYGM EPILOG (299)	YOU NOT LIKE TO BE ASSURED THAT THE SHOP WAS AN	IMMENSE	SUCCESS, THANKS TO ELIZA'S CHARMS AND HER EARLY
HART III (134)	EVENING! /LADY UTTERWORD/ YOU MUST HAVE GIVEN AN	IMMENSE	SUM TO THE PARTY FUNDS, MR MANGAN. /MANGAN/ NOT A
MIS. PREFACE(48)	TO SAY IT, BECAUSE OPTIMISTIC LIES HAVE SUCH	IMMENSE	THERAPEUTIC VALUE THAT A DOCTOR WHO CANNOT TELL THEM
HART III (137)	CAN LIVE VERY COMFORTABLY ON HIS REPUTATION FOR	IMMENSE	WEALTH. /ELLIE/ I CANNOT COMMIT BIGAMY, LADY
HART I (45)	SUDDENLY: AN ANCIENT BUT STILL HARDY MAN WITH AN	IMMENSE	WHITE BEARD, IN A REEFER JACKET WITH A WHISTLE
BULL III (137)	THE MORAL EFFECT ON THE HOUSE OF COMMONS WOULD BE	IMMENSE	! TREMENDOUS! PARDON MY SAYING THESE FEW WORDS:
		IMMENSELY	
FANY III (322)	ENGLISH AND AMERICAN GIRLS DO. THAT IS WHY I SO	IMMENSELY	ADMIRE THE ENGLISH PEOPLE. YOU ARE SO FREE-- SO
MRS I (194)	THE INVITATION? /FRANK/ (INCREDULOUS, BUT	IMMENSELY	AMUSED) IS THAT VIVIE'S MOTHER? /PRAED/ YES.
BULL IV SD(148)	SOILED AND DISORDERED AS TO HIS MOTORING COAT:	IMMENSELY	IMPORTANT AND SERIOUS AS TO HIMSELF. HE MAKES HIS
PYGM EPILOG (302)	THAN THE INFATUATION OF COMMONER SOULS. SHE IS	IMMENSELY	INTERESTED IN HIM. SHE HAS EVEN SECRET MISCHIEVOUS
HART II (112)	THEIR BATTLES OVER AGAIN AND ENJOY THEMSELVES	IMMENSELY	. /LADY UTTERWORD/ (IRRITABLY) YOU ARE NOT
PYGM II (231)	ON TO PICKERING, WHO IS ENJOYING THE CONVERSATION	IMMENSELY	). IT IS THESE LITTLE THINGS THAT MATTER,
		IMMENSITY	
APPL II (258)	SAY WHETHER I EXAGGERATE THE IMPORTANCE -- THE	IMMENSITY	-- OF AN OCCASION THAT CANNOT BE EXAGGERATED.
		IMMENSO	
BARB II (308)	THE STREET OUTSIDE) OFF WE GO. PLAY UP, THERE!	IMMENSO	GIUBILO. (HE GIVES THE TIME WITH HIS DRUM; AND THE
BARB II (307)	" FOR THEE IMMENSE REJOICING-- IMMENSO GIUBILO--	IMMENSO	GIUBILO." (WITH DRUM OBBLIGATO) RUM TUM TI TUM TUM,
BARB II (307)	THE CHORUS. " FOR THEE IMMENSE REJOICING--	IMMENSO	GIUBILO-- IMMENSO GIUBILO." (WITH DRUM OBBLIGATO)
		IMMERSED	
MTH3 (92)	YOU NEVER LOOK WHERE YOU ARE GOING WHEN YOU ARE	IMMERSED	IN YOUR CALCULATIONS. SOME DAY YOU WILL WALK INTO
		IMMERSES	
ROCK I SD(209)	TAKES UP A BIG BLUE ONE, IN THE STUDY OF WHICH HE	IMMERSES	HIMSELF PROFOUNDLY. /HILDA/ (FLINGING-THE-DOOR
		IMMERSION	
FABL PREFACE(73)	IN HIS BOOK CALLED FATHER AND SON, THE	IMMERSION	HAD WASHED ALL THE FATHER'S PIOUS CREDULITY OUT OF
FABL PREFACE(73)	OF A PLYMOUTH BROTHER, AND WAS BAPTIZED BY TOTAL	IMMERSION	, OF WHICH HE WROTE A HIGHLY ENTERTAINING
		IMMIGRANT	
BULL PREFACE(18)	THERE IS AN IRISH CLIMATE, WHICH WILL STAMP AN	IMMIGRANT	MORE DEEPLY AND DURABLY IN TWO YEARS, APPARENTLY,
		IMMIGRATION	
BULL PREFACE(12)	THEY FEEL STRONG ENOUGH. IF NATIONS ARE TO LIMIT	IMMIGRATION	, INTER-MARRIAGE WITH FOREIGNERS, AND EVEN
		IMMINENT	
ROCK PREFACE(163)	SORT OF MURDER, A CORNERER WHO FINDS HIMSELF IN	IMMINENT	DANGER OF DETECTION AND LIQUIDATION BY THE OGPU
ARMS I (9)	BY A SHARP FUSILLADE IN THE STREET. THE CHILL OF	IMMINENT	DEATH HUSHES THE MAN'S VOICE AS HE ADDS) DO YOU
HART PREFACE(38)	OR A DEMAGOGIC CLAPTRAP, IS NOW A POSSIBILITY SO	IMMINENT	THAT HARDLY BY TRYING TO SUPPRESS IT IN OTHER
		IMMOBILITY	
FABL PREFACE(94)	ONLY BY STEALTH COULD I RELIEVE THE TORTURE OF	IMMOBILITY	BY STEALTHILY EXCHANGING PUNCHES (CALLED " THE
		IMMOBILIZATION	
FABL PREFACE(89)	WHO HAS BEEN TAUGHT TO PRESCRIBE DIGITALIS AND	IMMOBILIZATION	, PLUS A DIET OF ALCOHOLIC STIMULANTS, FOR
		IMMODERATELY	
GETT PREFACE(199)	GOOD MAN IS VERY MUCH MORE DANGEROUS THAN AN	IMMODERATELY	BAD MAN: THAT IS WHY SAVONAROLA WAS BURNT AND
GETT PREFACE(199)	HAVE TOO MUCH OF A GOOD THING. THE TRUTH IS, AN	IMMODERATELY	GOOD MAN IS VERY MUCH MORE DANGEROUS THAN AN
SUPR PREFACE(R40)	WHICH SHALL BE THE CLOSING CADENCE OF THIS	IMMODERATELY	LONG LETTER FROM YOURS FAITHFULLY, G. BERNARD
		IMMODEST	
JOAN 6 (143)	I HAVE BLASPHEMED ABOMINABLY BY WEARING AN	IMMODEST	DRESS, CONTRARY TO THE HOLY SCRIPTURE AND THE
		IMMORAL	
POSN PREFACE(383)	DOING SO HE NEVER REALIZED THAT IT HAD EVER BEEN	IMMORAL	: CONSEQUENTLY ITS EARLY STRUGGLES TAUGHT HIM NO
KING I (205)	JUST UTTERED BY ELEANOR GWYN ARE NOT PROFANE AND	IMMORAL	: THEY ARE MAD AND FOOLISH. /LOUISE/ ALL THE LESS
POSN PREFACE(381)	TO ESTABLISHED MANNERS AND CUSTOMS IS IMMORAL. AN	IMMORAL	ACT OR DOCTRINE IS NOT NECESSARILY A SINFUL ONE: ON
MRS PREFACE(171)	WHAT IS, ACCORDING TO HER LIGHTS, THE LEAST	IMMORAL	ALTERNATIVE, IT IS NONE THE LESS INFAMOUS OF SOCIETY
METH PREFACE(R61)	OF THE BOURGEOISIE TO SOCIETY WAS GROSSLY	IMMORAL	AND DISASTROUS, AND THAT THE WHITED WALL OF STARCHED
POSN PREFACE(382)	WOULD NOT HAVE BEEN PUBLISHED, AS THEY WERE ALL	IMMORAL	AND HERETICAL IN THE VERY HIGHEST DEGREE, AND GAVE
POSN PREFACE(381)	MY LIVELIHOOD. IF I WERE PREVENTED FROM PRODUCING	IMMORAL	AND HERETICAL PLAYS, I SHOULD CEASE TO WRITE FOR THE
POSN PREFACE(380)	IN GENERAL PRACTICE, I AM A SPECIALIST IN	IMMORAL	AND HERETICAL PLAYS. MY REPUTATION HAS BEEN GAINED
MRS PREFACE(151)	SUPERMONARCHICAL POWER OVER OUR THEATRES, AS "	IMMORAL	AND OTHERWISE IMPROPER FOR THE STAGE." ITS
DOCT III (139)	BY THAT, MAY I ASK? /LOUIS/ NOW, I'M ONLY AN	IMMORAL	ARTIST; BUT IF YOUD TOLD ME THAT JENNIFER WASNT
BARB PREFACE(213)	POOR," AND SUCH PHRASES ARE AS INTOLERABLE AND AS	IMMORAL	AS " DRUNKEN BUT AMIABLE," " FRAUDULENT BUT A GOOD
POSN PREFACE(384)	CIVILIZATION UNTIL THE CHINESE LATELY TOOK TO	IMMORAL	COURSES BY PERMITTING RAILWAY CONTRACTORS TO

SIM II (65)	AND THAT PROLA AND VASHTI AND MAYA ARE A TROOP OF	IMMORAL	DANCING GIRLS, AND THAT SIR CHARLES IS A VOLUPTUOUS
POSN PREFACE(385)	WITHOUT HERETICS AND ADVOCATES OF SHOCKINGLY	IMMORAL	DOCTRINES. THE INQUISITION AND THE STAR CHAMBER,
POSN PREFACE(400)	LORD CHAMBERLAIN, WE CAN SMUGGLE A GOOD DEAL OF	IMMORAL	DRAMA AND ALMOST AS MUCH COARSELY VULGAR AND
CAPT III (292)	/JOHNSON/ (SEVERELY) DONT YOU BE A IGNORANT AND	IMMORAL	FOREIGNER. (THE REBUKE IS WELL RECEIVED; AND MARZO
SUPR III (125)	HER WOMANHOOD. /ANA/ YOU MEAN THAT IT WAS AN	IMMORAL	IMPULSE. /DON JUAN/ NATURE, MY DEAR LADY, IS WHAT
POSN PREFACE(381)	IS CONTRARY TO ESTABLISHED MANNERS AND CUSTOMS IS	IMMORAL	. AN IMMORAL ACT OR DOCTRINE IS NOT NECESSARILY A
POSN PREFACE(413)	GIVEN OR CONTEMPLATED IS HERETICAL OR	IMMORAL	. D. THE LICENSING AREA SHALL BE NO LESS THAN THAT
SUPR III (125)	/DON JUAN/ NATURE, MY DEAR LADY, IS WHAT YOU CALL	IMMORAL	. I BLUSH FOR IT; BUT I CANNOT HELP IT. NATURE IS A
CYMB FORWORD(137)	TO SHAKESPEAR'S REHANDLING, WHICH HE ABHORRED AS	IMMORAL	. NOBODY HAS EVER AGREED WITH HIM. WILL IT BE
MRS PREFACE(171)	OF THE BOLDEST AND MOST SPECIOUS DEFENCES OF AN	IMMORAL	LIFE FOR POOR WOMEN THAT HAS EVER BEEN PENNED."
MRS PREFACE(171)	VICE WHICH SHE ORGANIZES. IT IS NO DEFENCE OF AN	IMMORAL	LIFE TO SAY THAT THE ALTERNATIVE OFFERED BY SOCIETY
BARB I (256)	WERE OTHER DIFFERENCES. I REALLY CANNOT BEAR AN	IMMORAL	MAN. I AM NOT A PHARISEE, I HOPE; AND I SHOULD NOT
MRS PREFACE(161)	AS VOID IN ITS GENERAL TENDENCY OF " ANYTHING	IMMORAL	OR OTHERWISE IMPROPER FOR THE STAGE." BUT LET NOBODY
UNPL PREFACE(R14)	DOES NOT IN ITS GENERAL TENDENCY CONTAIN ANYTHING	IMMORAL	OR OTHERWISE IMPROPER FOR THE STAGE," AND THAT THE
MRS III (225)	VIV: THERES A FREEMASONRY AMONG THOROUGHLY	IMMORAL	PEOPLE THAT YOU KNOW NOTHING OF. YOUVE TOO MUCH
POSN PREFACE(413)	WOULD STOP THE EVASIONS BY WHICH HERETICAL AND	IMMORAL	PLAYS ARE NOW PERFORMED IN SPITE OF THE LORD
POSN PREFACE(412)	THEM, AND BECAUSE THE MANY HERETICAL AND	IMMORAL	PLAYS WHICH NOW PASS THE LORD CHAMBERLAIN BECAUSE HE
FANY EPILOG (328)	SIR: IF IT HAD BEEN WHAT PEOPLE CALL AN	IMMORAL	PLAY, I SHOULDNT HAVE MINDED A BIT. (VAUGHAN IS
POSN (453)	YOU LIAR! /BLANCO/ I ACCUSE THE FAIR EUPHEMIA OF	IMMORAL	RELATIONS WITH EVERY MAN IN THIS TOWN, INCLUDING
POSN (453)	AND DRAMATICALLY) SHERIFF: I ACCUSE FEEMY OF	IMMORAL	RELATIONS WITH STRAPPER. /FEEMY/ OH YOU LIAR!
MRS PREFACE(176)	COURT, WHICH DECLARED THAT THE PLAY WAS NOT	IMMORAL	; ACQUITTED DALY; AND MADE AN END OF THE ATTEMPT TO
FABL PREFACE(81)	ALL OWENITES, MARXISTS, AND DARWINISTS AS	IMMORAL	; BUT IT MUST BE BORNE IN MIND THAT ALL
GETT PREFACE(202)	EVEN AGAINST ITS ENERVATING HAPPINESS. WANTED: AN	IMMORAL	STATESMAN. WE NOW SEE THAT THE STATESMAN WHO
POSN PREFACE(399)	BEEN LICENSED WITHOUT QUESTION ARE FUNDAMENTALLY	IMMORAL	TO AN ALTOGETHER EXTRAORDINARY DEGREE. EVERY ONE OF
GETT (313)	EVER, I'LL HAVE NOTHING TO DO WITH IT. I CALL IT	IMMORAL	TO HAVE A MARRIAGE FOR A TERM OF YEARS. IF THE
BARB III (315)	ELSE, ANDREW. DO YOU SUPPOSE THIS WICKED AND	IMMORAL	TRADITION CAN BE KEPT UP FOR EVER? DO YOU PRETEND
POSN PREFACE(381)	ADVANCE IN THOUGHT AND CONDUCT IS BY DEFINITION	IMMORAL	UNTIL IT HAS CONVERTED THE MAJORITY. FOR THIS REASON
POSN PREFACE(385)	THESE LIBERATORS MAY THEMSELVES HAVE WITH	IMMORAL	VIEWS. A MAN WITH THE STRONGEST CONVICTION OF THE
LION PREFACE(73)	WAY, A SOCIALISTIC WAY, AN ATHEISTIC WAY, AN	IMMORAL	WAY, AND THAT THE VANGUARD OUGHT TO BE ASHAMED OF
MIS. PREFACE(44)	WHICH AT FIRST APPEAR SEDITIOUS, BLASPHEMOUS, AND	IMMORAL	, AND WHICH DEEPLY SHOCK PEOPLE WHO NEVER THINK
BARB I (268)	CAN YOU? AT LEAST UNLESS YOURE DOWNRIGHT	IMMORAL	, DONT YOU KNOW. /UNDERSHAFT/ YOU HARDLY APPRECIATE
SUPR HANDBOK(211)	REPUDIATION OF SUCH PROPOSALS AS INDECENT AND	IMMORAL	, WITH, NEVERTHELESS, A GENERAL SECRET PUSHING OF
POSN PREFACE(396)	MALE CHARACTERS IN THE PIECE WAS DESCRIBED AS "	IMMORAL	," THE EXAMINER OF PLAYS OBJECTED TO THAT PASSAGE,

IMMORALISM

FANY PROLOG (271)	AND INSULT. AND NOW I'M TOLD THAT I'M A CENTRE OF	IMMORALISM	! OF MODERN MINXISM! A TRIFLER WITH THE MOST

IMMORALIST

FANY PROLOG (271)	A BEL ESPRIT, A WIT, AN IRRESPONSIBLE, A PARISIAN	IMMORALIST	, TRES CHIC. /TROTTER/ I! /FANNY/ THERES QUITE A

IMMORALITIES

POSN PREFACE(383)	HAVE BECOME ESTABLISHED RELIGIONS; AND FRESH	IMMORALITIES	ARE PERSECUTED IN THEIR NAME. THE TRUTH IS THAT
POSN PREFACE(383)	AS THEY ARE, ARE DISGUISED BY THE PROMOTION OF	IMMORALITIES	INTO MORALITIES WHICH IS CONSTANTLY GOING ON.
POSN PREFACE(382)	BE THE SON OF GOD, ARE ALL EXAMPLES OF SHOCKING	IMMORALITIES	(EVERY IMMORALITY SHOCKS SOMEBODY), THE
OVER PREFACE(168)	BUT THAT WE SHALL NOT ATTEMPT TO DEFEND OUR	IMMORALITIES	, IS A STANDARD VIEW IN ENGLAND, AND WAS

IMMORALITY

POSN PREFACE(410)	BETWEEN MORALITY AND VIRTUE, BETWEEN	IMMORALITY	AND VICE, BETWEEN CONSCIENTIOUS HERESY AND MERE
POSN PREFACE(384)	BECAUSE THE ARGUMENTS AGAINST TOLERATING	IMMORALITY	ARE THE SAME AS THE ARGUMENTS AGAINST TOLERATING
POSN PREFACE(412)	THEM TO ACCEPT THE RESPONSIBILITY FOR HERESY OR	IMMORALITY	BY LICENSING THEM, AND BECAUSE THE MANY HERETICAL
POSN PREFACE(381)	A CENSOR IS NEVER INTENTIONALLY A PROTECTOR OF	IMMORALITY	. HE ALWAYS AIMS AT THE PROTECTION OF MORALITY.
POSN PREFACE(383)	CONSTANTINOPLE. HE HAS NEVER WILLINGLY TOLERATED	IMMORALITY	. HE DID NOT ADOPT ANY INNOVATION UNTIL IT HAD
POSN PREFACE(381)	BUT ON PUBLIC GROUNDS. THE DEFINITION OF	IMMORALITY	. IN DEALING WITH THE QUESTION OF THE CENSORSHIP,
MRS PREFACE(154)	SALVATION ARMY OF COMPLICITY IN MY OWN SCANDALOUS	IMMORALITY	. IT WILL SEEM TO THEM THAT PEOPLE WHO WOULD
GETT (314)	LET DO WHAT THEY WANT TO, THEN I CALL IT SIMPLE	IMMORALITY	. (SHE GOES INDIGNANTLY TO THE OAK CHEST, AND
PYGM II (239)	RATHER DRAW THE LINE AT ENCOURAGING THAT SORT OF	IMMORALITY	. /DOOLITTLE/ TELL HER SO, GOVERNOR: TELL HER SO.
OVER (194)	BUT, MY PRECIOUS, THIS IS THE MOST HORRIBLE	IMMORALITY	. /MRS LUNN/ I DONT INTEND TO GIVE UP MEETING
SUPR PREFACE(R16)	HE HAS UNEXPECTEDLY DISCOVERED A MORAL IN HIS	IMMORALITY	. THE GROWING RECOGNITION OF HIS NEW POINT OF
MRS PREFACE(171)	ARE NOT MORALITY AND IMMORALITY, BUT TWO SORTS OF	IMMORALITY	. THE MAN WHO CANNOT SEE THAT STARVATION,
POSN PREFACE(385)	BUT CENSORSHIPS, MADE RUTHLESS WAR ON IMPIETY AND	IMMORALITY	. THE RESULT WAS ONCE FAMILIAR TO ENGLISHMEN,
FANY PREFACE(255)	OF SALVATION AND DAMNATION, NOT OF MORALITY AND	IMMORALITY	. THE WORD MORALITY, IF WE MET IT IN THE BIBLE,
POSN PREFACE(389)	RESTRAIN ITS MEMBERS ON THE GROUND THAT THEIR	IMMORALITY	MAY CORRUPT THEIR NEIGHBORS. HE CAN PREVENT ANY
POSN PREFACE(382)	OF HAMPDEN AND OF WASHINGTON; THE REVOLTING	IMMORALITY	OF LUTHER IN NOT ONLY MARRYING WHEN HE WAS A
POSN PREFACE(384)	MOMENT A FEW BOLD ENGLISHWOMEN VENTURED ON THE	IMMORALITY	OF RIDING ASTRIDE THEIR HORSES, A PRACTICE THAT
GETT PREFACE(203)	WORTHLESS AND UNAMIABLE PEOPLE GENERALLY, NOR THE	IMMORALITY	OF THE COUPLES CONDEMNED TO CELIBACY BY
SUPR III (124)	HAVE YOU NOT OFTEN EXPRESSED YOUR DISGUST AT THE	IMMORALITY	OF THE ENGLISH NATION, IN WHICH WOMEN AND MEN OF
KING I (205)	HE WILL WRITE SUCH A BOOK ON THE PROFANENESS AND	IMMORALITY	OF THE STAGE AS WILL EITHER KILL THE THEATRE OR
POSN PREFACE(382)	ARE ALL EXAMPLES OF SHOCKING IMMORALITIES (EVERY	IMMORALITY	SHOCKS SOMEBODY), THE SUPPRESSION AND EXTINCTION
POSN PREFACE(381)	REASON IT IS OF THE MOST ENORMOUS IMPORTANCE THAT	IMMORALITY	SHOULD BE PROTECTED JEALOUSLY AGAINST THE ATTACKS
GETT PREFACE(230)	THEY WILL NO LONGER ALLOW THE LAW TO TAKE	IMMORALITY	SO EASILY. BOTH MEN AND WOMEN WILL BE FORCED TO
BARB I (256)	WRONGNESS. JUST AS ONE DOESNT MIND MEN PRACTISING	IMMORALITY	SO LONG AS THEY OWN THAT THEY ARE IN THE WRONG BY
BARB I (256)	SO I COULDNT FORGIVE ANDREW FOR PREACHING	IMMORALITY	WHILE HE PRACTISED MORALITY. YOU WOULD ALL HAVE
POSN PREFACE(381)	EVERYTHING DEPENDS ON THE CORRECT USE OF THE WORD	IMMORALITY	, AND A CAREFUL DISCRIMINATION BETWEEN THE POWERS
POSN PREFACE(386)	CANNOT CLAIM THE PRIVILEGES OF HERESY OR	IMMORALITY	, BECAUSE NO CASE CAN BE MADE OUT IN SUPPORT OF
MRS PREFACE(171)	FOR THE ALTERNATIVES OFFERED ARE NOT MORALITY AND	IMMORALITY	, BUT TWO SORTS OF IMMORALITY. THE MAN WHO CANNOT
POSN PREFACE(384)	TO SUCH SUPPRESSION, THE TOTAL SUPPRESSION OF	IMMORALITY	, ESPECIALLY IN MATTERS OF RELIGION AND SEX,
POSN PREFACE(382)	THE TRAIN TRAVEL AT SIXTY MILES AN HOUR. IT IS	IMMORALITY	, NOT MORALITY, THAT NEEDS PROTECTION: IT IS
POSN PREFACE(382)	THAT NEEDS PROTECTION: IT IS MORALITY, NOT	IMMORALITY	, THAT NEEDS RESTRAINT; FOR MORALITY, WITH ALL
UNPL PREFACE(R15)	IF HE REALLY PROTECTS THE PUBLIC AGAINST MY	IMMORALITY	, WHY DOES NOT THE PUBLIC PAY HIM FOR THE
3PLA PREFACE(R22)	PURSUIT OF PLEASURE SUNK IT IN " PROFANENESS AND	IMMORALITY	"? I HAVE, I THINK, ALWAYS BEEN A PURITAN IN MY

IMMORALLY

BARB III (327)	OLD RASCAL; BUT IT'S ALL HORRIBLY, FRIGHTFULLY,	IMMORALLY	, UNANSWERABLY PERFECT. SARAH ARRIVES. /SARAH/

IMMORTAL

LION PREFACE(8)	STONED, SCOURGED, AND KILLED; AND HE WAS A GOD,	IMMORTAL	AND ALL-POWERFUL, ABLE TO RAISE THE DEAD AND CALL
CLEO II (139)	IN TEN GENERATIONS OF MEN, THE WORLD GAINS AN	IMMORTAL	BOOK. /CAESAR/ (INFLEXIBLE) IF IT DID NOT FLATTER
LION PREFACE(39)	THIS MAN LETTERS, HAVING NEVER LEARNT? " JOHN THE	IMMORTAL	EYE-WITNESS. JOHN, MOREOVER, CLAIMS TO BE NOT ONLY
KING I (189)	REQUESTS. HE STAYED HERE TO HEAP INSULTS ON THE	IMMORTAL	GALILEO, WHOSE SHOE LATCHET HE IS UNWORTHY TO
CLEO I (107)	(STARTING VIOLENTLY, AND CLUTCHING HIS SWORD)	IMMORTAL	GODS! /THE GIRL/ OLD GENTLEMAN: DONT RUN AWAY.
LION PREFACE(42)	INTO THE AUDACIOUS HINT THAT HE, JOHN, IS HIMSELF	IMMORTAL	IN THE FLESH. STILL, HE DOES NOT MISS THE
DOCT IV (165)	TO LIVE. IVE ESCAPED FROM MYSELF. I'M IN HEAVEN,	IMMORTAL	IN THE HEART OF MY BEAUTIFUL JENNIFER. I'M NOT
MTH2 (76)	THIS WAY. IT IS CLEAR THAT WHEN ADAM AND EVE WERE	IMMORTAL	IT WAS NECESSARY THAT THEY SHOULD MAKE THE EARTH AN
LION PREFACE(16)	RIGHTLY, THAT GOD IS IN THE SEED, AND THAT GOD IS	IMMORTAL	. AND THUS IT BECAME THE TEST OF GODHEAD THAT
MTH4 II (181)	MADE ME POPULAR, POWERFUL, FAMOUS, HISTORICALLY	IMMORTAL	. BUT I FORESEE THAT IF I GO ON TO THE END IT WILL
MIS. PREFACE(3)	ARE BORN CONCLUSIVELY PROVES THAT THEY ARE NOT	IMMORTAL	. DO AWAY WITH DEATH AND YOU DO AWAY WITH THE NEED
MIS. PREFACE(3)	BY NO MEANS ASCERTAINED THAT EVEN THE AMOEBA IS	IMMORTAL	. HUMAN BEINGS VISIBLY WEAR OUT, THOUGH THEY LAST
METH PREFACE(R19)	TIMES AS LONG AS A DOG, AND A TURTLE BE ALMOST	IMMORTAL	. IN THE CASE OF MAN, THE OPERATION HAS OVERSHOT
3PLA PREFACE(R34)	WHOM NOBODY DREAMS OF MOCKING WITH THE WORD	IMMORTAL	. IT IS THE PHILOSOPHY, THE OUTLOOK ON LIFE, THAT
MTH5 (253)	WHAT IS YOUR DESTINY? /THE HE-ANCIENT/ TO BE	IMMORTAL	. /THE SHE-ANCIENT/ THE DAY WILL COME WHEN THERE
MTH4 I (162)	THE INDIVIDUAL PERISHES; BUT THE RACE IS	IMMORTAL	. THE ACORN OF TODAY IS THE OAK OF THE NEXT
METH PREFACE(R29)	IT LESS DRILY, THAT HUMAN LIFE IS CONTINUOUS AND	IMMORTAL	. THE EVOLUTIONISTS TOOK HEREDITY FOR GRANTED. SO
3PLA PREFACE(R31)	BE GLAD ENOUGH TO BE TRANSFIGURED BY SOME POET AS	IMMORTAL	LOVERS. WOE TO THE POET WHO STOOPS TO SUCH FOLLY!
BULL PREFACE(37)	WITH KING WILLIAM! " (OF GLORIOUS, PIOUS, AND	IMMORTAL	MEMORY); BUT IT MAY HAPPEN SO. " THE ISLAND OF THE
MTH4 I (154)	SO FLIPPANTLY. ARE YOU AWARE, MADAM, THAT AT THAT	IMMORTAL	MOMENT THE ENGLISH RACE HAD LOST INTELLECTUAL
BULL III (136)	IN MEMORY OF OUR GREAT PARTY AND OF THE	IMMORTAL	NAME OF OUR GRAND OLD LEADER. /DORAN/ (
CLEO I (107)	IS THEIR SENTINEL-- AN IMAGE OF THE CONSTANT AND	IMMORTAL	PART OF MY LIFE, SILENT, FULL OF THOUGHTS, ALONE IN

LADY (238) MAN/ (EAGERLY) SNAPPER-UP OF -- (HE GASPS) OH! IMMORTAL PHRASE! (HE WRITES IT DOWN). THIS MAN IS A
LADY (242) TRUTH. THE POWER I SPEAK OF IS THE POWER OF IMMORTAL POESY. FOR KNOW THAT VILE AS THIS WORLD IS, AND
LION PREFACE(16) THAT WHEN THE REDEEMER COMES HE WILL BE IMMORTAL ; HE WILL GIVE US HIS BODY TO EAT AND HIS BLOOD TO
BASH II,2, (114) IN THE WORKS OF NEWTON AND IN THE PLAYS OF THE IMMORTAL SHAKESPEAR. THERE IS NOT ONE OF ALL THE THOUSANDS
ROCK PREFACE(148) HE HIMSELF SHOULD BE SPARED BECAUSE HE HAS AN IMMORTAL SOUL AND A RABBIT HAS NONE IS AS HOPELESSLY OUT OF
FABL VI (128) /TEACHER/ THAT MAKES NO DIFFERENCE. WHAT IS AN IMMORTAL SOUL BUT A DISEMBODIED THOUGHT? I HAVE RECEIVED
DOCT PREFACE(45) AS THE STEP FROM A PHYSICAL ORGANISM TO AN IMMORTAL SOUL. THAT CONCEIT HAS BEEN TAKEN OUT OF ALL OUR
SIM PRO,3, (32) OUT IN A NET AND EMPTIED ME OUT. I BROUGHT UP MY IMMORTAL SOUL. THEY GAVE ME WHAT I THOUGHT WAS A NICE CUP OF
ROCK PREFACE(148) WAS FOUNDED ON A GENERAL BELIEF THAT HUMANS HAVE IMMORTAL SOULS AND BRUTES NONE. NOWADAYS MORE AND MORE
SUPR IV (157) SEEMS TO ME SUCH A STRIKING PROOF THAT WE HAVE IMMORTAL SOULS. /OCTAVIUS/ OH! (HE HASTILY SITS DOWN AT
POSN (450) HIS HAIR). /ELDER DANIELS/ OH, THINK OF YOUR IMMORTAL SOUL, MAN, NOT OF YOUR FOOLISH FACE. /BLANCO/ I
FANY PROLOG (270) BUT IN THE SENSE GIVEN TO IT FOR ALL TIME BY THE IMMORTAL STAGIRITE. /FANNY/ WHO IS THE STAGIRITE? /TROTTER/
HART III (148) /MAZZINI/ OH, POOR MANGAN! /HECTOR/ ARE YOU IMMORTAL THAT YOU NEED PITY HIM? OUR TURN NEXT. THEY WAIT
DOCT PREFACE(22) PATHOGENIC GERMS. THEY CONCEIVE MICROBES AS IMMORTAL UNTIL SLAIN BY A GERMICIDE ADMINISTERED BY A DULY
SHAK (142) WE PUPPETS SHALL REPLAY OUR SCENE. MEANWHILE, IMMORTAL WILLIAM DEAD AND TURNED TO CLAY MAY STOP A HOLE TO
SUPR HANDBOK(214) THAT THEY CAN LIVE FOR EVER, ARE SEEKING FOR SOME IMMORTAL WORK INTO WHICH THEY CAN BUILD THE BEST OF
PPP PREFACE(192) COMPANY. AS THE BILL BAILEY SONG HAS NOT PROVED IMMORTAL , ANY EQUALLY APPROPRIATE DITTY OF THE MOMENT MAY
LION PREFACE(39) MOCK MODESTY, ADDS THAT HE MUST NOT CLAIM TO BE IMMORTAL , AS THE DISCIPLES CONCLUDED, FOR CHRIST DID NOT
MTH4 II (191) GOING TO LAST OUT FOR EVER AND EVER AND EVER. IMMORTAL , YOU THOUGHT YOURSELVES. WERE YOU ANY HAPPIER

IMMORTALITY
MTH1 I (14) BURDEN OF IMMORTALITY IS LIFTED FROM YOU. /EVE/ IMMORTALITY ? WHAT IS THAT? /THE SERPENT/ MY NEW WORD FOR
LION PREFACE(89) BY ATONEMENT MUST REJECT ALSO BELIEF IN PERSONAL IMMORTALITY AND IN MIRACLES IS AS BASELESS AS THE NOTION
LION PREFACE(89) SINS BRINGS ITS KARMA, ALSO INSIST ON INDIVIDUAL IMMORTALITY AND METEMPSYCHOSIS IN ORDER TO PROVIDE AN
LION PREFACE(88) NO CRITERION. NOR IS BELIEF IN INDIVIDUAL IMMORTALITY ANY CRITERION. THEOSOPHISTS, REJECTING VICARIOUS
BUOY PREFACE(3) ARE THE SPIRITUALISTS. THEY BELIEVE IN PERSONAL IMMORTALITY AS FAR AS ANY MORTAL CAN BELIEVE IN AN
MIS. PREFACE(3) THE LIFE FORCE EITHER WILL NOT OR CANNOT ACHIEVE IMMORTALITY EXCEPT IN VERY LOW ORGANISMS: INDEED IT IS BY NO
JITT II (42) POINTING TO THE MANUSCRIPT) HE HAS SACRIFICED HIS IMMORTALITY FOR YOUR BENEFIT. /LENKHEIM/ (ANGRILY) ROT. WHY
DOCT IV (162) OF WHEN THEY THINK OF ME. THAT IS THE SORT OF IMMORTALITY I WANT. YOU CAN MAKE THAT FOR ME, JENNIFER.
MTH1 I (14) INVENT THINGS EVERY DAY NOW THAT THE BURDEN OF IMMORTALITY IS LIFTED FROM YOU. /EVE/ IMMORTALITY? WHAT IS
MIS. PREFACE(3) WERE TO CONVINCE US THAT OUR DREAM OF PERSONAL IMMORTALITY IS NO DREAM BUT A HARD FACT, SUCH A SHRIEK OF
3PLA PREFACE(R39) FOR ME: I SHALL PERHAPS ENJOY A FEW YEARS OF IMMORTALITY . BUT THE WHIRLIGIG OF TIME WILL SOON BRING MY
MTH4 I (157) AND THE MORTAL BOLGE BLUEBIN BARLOW PUTS ON IMMORTALITY . ON THIS GROUND I AM YOUR EQUAL, EVEN IF YOU
MIS. PREFACE(4) BECOME INCORRUPTIBLE, AND THIS MORTAL PUT ON IMMORTALITY . PRACTISE AS YOU WILL ON HIS IGNORANCE, HIS
DOCT IV (162) AND DO IT AS NOBODY ELSE CAN. PROMISE ME THAT IMMORTALITY . PROMISE ME YOU WILL NOT MAKE A LITTLE HELL OF
DOCT IV (163) FLAMES. YOU ARE MY HOLD ON THE WORLD: YOU ARE MY IMMORTALITY . PROMISE. /MRS DUBEDAT/ I'M LISTENING. I SHALL
MTH2 (75) ON ANY SINGLE CREATURE THE TERRIBLE BURDEN OF IMMORTALITY . /LUBIN/ I SEE. THE OLD MUST MAKE ROOM FOR THE
MTH4 II (191) OF LIFE THAT WAS GRANTED TO THEM TO AN IMAGINARY IMMORTALITY . THEY CRUCIFIED THE PROPHET WHO TOLD THEM TO
MTH1 II (33) TO SIT AND BROOD UNDER THE TERROR OF ETERNITY, OF IMMORTALITY . THINK OF IT, MAN: TO HAVE NO ESCAPE! TO BE
LION PREFACE(88) THE WEIGHT SUSPENDED FROM IT. BELIEF IN PERSONAL IMMORTALITY NO CRITERION. NOR IS BELIEF IN INDIVIDUAL
KING I (180) STONE SOON FINDS HIMSELF BEGINNING TO DOUBT THE IMMORTALITY OF THE SOUL. HE ENDS BY DOUBTING THE EXISTENCE
FABL VI (128) OR FOURTH FORM BELIEVE IN WHAT THEY CALL THE IMMORTALITY OF THE SOUL. /YOUTH 1/ (CONTEMPTUOUSLY) YES,
SUPR PREFACE(R22) USE OF THEIR LIMBS, OF THAT ANCIENT SYMBOL OF IMMORTALITY , THE RIGHT TO MAKE ONESELF AT HOME IN THE HOUSE

IMMORTALIZE
LADY PREFACE(208) IMPORTANCE. I THOUGHT IT WOULD BE FRIENDLY TO IMMORTALIZE HIM, AS THE SILLY LITERARY SAYING IS, MUCH AS

IMMORTALIZED
BUOY IV (59) BORES IN LITERATURE, MERE NAMES INCIDENTALLY IMMORTALIZED BY A FEW LINES IN A GREAT POEM? /MRS
LADY PREFACE(208) THE SILLY LITERARY SAYING IS, MUCH AS SHAKESPEAR IMMORTALIZED MR W. H., AS HE SAID HE WOULD, SIMPLY BY

IMMORTALS
MTH5 SD(241) THE FEMALE AUTOMATON HARDLY DARES TO SOB. THE IMMORTALS CONTEMPLATE THEM WITH SHAME AND LOATHING. THE
MTH4 II (187) ON OUR SIDE. WE SHOULD WELCOME A COLONY OF IMMORTALS -- WE MAY ALMOST CALL YOU THAT-- IN THE BRITISH

IMMOVABLE
JOAN PREFACE(31) UNTHINKABLE. THUS AN IRRESISTIBLE FORCE MET AN IMMOVABLE OBSTACLE, AND DEVELOPED THE HEAT THAT CONSUMED
MIS. PREFACE(77) COULD AFFORD A TRIP ROUND THE WORLD, WHO ARE MORE IMMOVABLE THAN ALDGATE PUMP. TO OTHERS, WHO WOULD MOVE IF
FABL PREFACE(69) WHEN THE PEOPLE BELIEVE THAT THE EARTH IS FLAT, IMMOVABLE , AND THE CENTRE OF THE UNIVERSE, AND COPERNICUS

IMMOVABLES
GENV IV SD(87) AND SHEW UP ALL THE GILDING AND GRANDEUR OF THE IMMOVABLES . THE DOOR IS AT THE SIDE, ON THE RIGHT OF THE

IMMOVABLY
DEST (177) OF MY SENSES. (TO HER) BEGONE. /LADY/ (SEATED IMMOVABLY) NOT WITHOUT THAT LETTER. /NAPOLEON/ BEGONE, I
MTH2 (77) LEGS AND THROW HIM DOWNSTAIRS. /LUBIN/ (STILL IMMOVABLY SCEPTICAL) AND WHAT DOES SCIENCE SAY TO THIS FAIRY

IMM-PAWSIBL
APPL II (262) A BARBAROUS PAST. FORTUNATELY, IT'S IMPOSSIBLE -- IMM-PAWSIBL . THE OLD WARCRY WOULD NOT APPEAL TO THE

IMMUNE
DOCT PREFACE(26) CHILD IN THE WORLD COULD BE RENDERED ABSOLUTELY IMMUNE FROM ALL DISEASE DURING ITS ENTIRE LIFE BY TAKING
DOCT PREFACE(52) OR BY VACCINATION, WERE NOT, AS HE HAD SUPPOSED, IMMUNE FROM SMALLPOX, HE ASCRIBED THE CASES OF IMMUNITY
DOCT I (98) IN A WEEK HE WAS ALL RIGHT AGAIN, AND ABSOLUTELY IMMUNE FROM TYPHOID FOR THE REST OF HIS LIFE. THE FAMILY
SIM II (80) WHILST THE LAWYERS AND CLERGY ARE COMPARATIVELY IMMUNE . A SITUATION OF TERRIBLE SUSPENSE HAS BEEN CREATED
DOCT III (140) FROM WHICH HE WAS, SCIENTIFICALLY SPEAKING, IMMUNE . BUT THAT DOES NOT AFFECT THE FUNDAMENTAL TRUTH OF

IMMUNITIES
SUPR PREFACE(R21) NO DOUBT THERE ARE MOMENTS WHEN MAN'S SEXUAL IMMUNITIES ARE MADE ACUTELY HUMILIATING TO HIM. WHEN THE
UNPL PREFACE(R9) PATIENTLY LISTENED TO MY HARANGUES. I ENJOYED THE IMMUNITIES OF IMPECUNIOSITY WITH THE OPPORTUNITIES OF A

IMMUNITY
DOCT PREFACE(71) FOR THIS OR THAT CEREMONY OF WITCHCRAFT, BUT FOR IMMUNITY FROM DISEASE, AND PAYING, TOO, IN A RATIONAL WAY.
DOCT PREFACE(55) THE CHEST, PROLONGS LIFE, AND CONFERS COMPARATIVE IMMUNITY FROM DISEASE; FOR THE STATISTICS SHEW THAT THE
POSN PREFACE(363) ARE SO VICIOUS THAT THEIR PRESENT PRACTICAL IMMUNITY FROM PROSECUTION MUST BE PUT AN END TO; BUT NO
SUPR HANDBOK(185) A HANDFUL OF PEOPLE, WHO, AFTER THIRTY YEARS OF IMMUNITY FROM THE UNINTENTIONAL CHILD SLAUGHTER THAT GOES ON
BASH II,1, (105) LIKE ALL WOMEN, LYDIA, YOU HAVE THE COURAGE OF IMMUNITY . TO STRIKE YOU WERE AGAINST HIS CODE OF HONOR; BUT
DOCT PREFACE(52) IMMUNE FROM SMALLPOX, HE ASCRIBED THE CASES OF IMMUNITY WHICH HAD FORMERLY MISLED HIM TO A DISEASE OF THE

IMMUNIZATION
DOCT PREFACE(74) WRIGHT IN THE THEORY AND PRACTICE OF SECURING IMMUNIZATION FROM BACTERIAL DISEASES BY THE INOCULATION OF "
DOCT PREFACE(24) A TWO-HOURS CAB FARE. ECONOMIC DIFFICULTIES OF IMMUNIZATION . I HAVE HEARD DOCTORS AFFIRM AND DENY ALMOST
DOCT PREFACE(75) MIGHT NOT HAVE TAKEN PLACE AGAINST THE WHOLE IMMUNIZATION MOVEMENT IN THERAPEUTICS. THE SITUATION WAS
DOCT PREFACE(78) OF PARACELSUS. WE CALL THEM BY DIFFERENT NAMES: IMMUNIZATION OR RADIOTHERAPY OR WHAT NOT; BUT THE DREAMS

IMMUNIZER
FABL PREFACE(90) EXALTING EVERY LABORATORY VIVISECTOR AND QUACK IMMUNIZER ABOVE JESUS AND ST JAMES. MRS EDDY, A MUCH SOUNDER

IMMUNIZERS
FABL PREFACE(90) OF PANACEAS, PROPHYLACTICS, ELIXIRS, IMMUNIZERS , VACCINES, ANTITOXINS, VITAMINS, AND PROFESSEDLY

IMMURED
NEVR III SD(261) AGAINST THE BLACK MARBLE CENOTAPH IN WHICH IT IS IMMURED . /MRS CLANDON/ FIVE! I DONT THINK WE NEED WAIT ANY

IMMUTABLE
MTH2 (61) POLITICS. THE LABOR MEMBERS WILL FIND THAT THE IMMUTABLE LAWS OF POLITICAL ECONOMY TAKE NO MORE NOTICE OF
MTH2 (62) THIS ABOUT WAGES AND DISTRIBUTION BEING FIXED BY IMMUTABLE LAWS OF POLITICAL ECONOMY IS OBSOLETE ROT.

		IMMUTABLY	
2TRU III (87)	DETERMINISM: THE STARS IN THEIR ORBITS OBEYED	IMMUTABLY	FIXED LAWS; AND WHEN WE TURNED FROM SURVEYING
		IMOGEN	
SUPR III (126)	TO THE DASTARDLY SEDUCER! WHAT SCENES OF	IMOGEN	AND IACHIMO! /ANA/ I MADE NO SCENES. I SIMPLY CALLED
CYMB V SD(142)	GUIDERIUS, ARVIRAGUS, PISANIO, WITH LUCIUS AND	IMOGEN	AS FIDELE: BOTH OF THEM PRISONERS GUARDED BY BRITISH
CYMB FORWORD(136)	FORM AND VERY UNLIKE HIS OLD SELF; AND THAT	IMOGEN	IS SO DUTIFUL THAT SHE ACCEPTS HER HUSBAND'S ATTEMPT
CYMB V (141)	AND MAKE THEM DREAD IT, TO THE DOERS' THRIFT; BUT	IMOGEN	IS YOUR OWN: DO YOUR BEST WILLS, AND MAKE ME BLEST TO
CYMB V (143)	MET ME WITH A BLOW. /POSTHUMUS/ HER VOICE. 'TIS	IMOGEN	. OH, DEAREST HEART, THOU LIVEST. OH, YOU GODS, WHAT
CYMB V (148)	EACH ONE HERE, IT SEEMS, IS SOMEONE ELSE. (TO	IMOGEN	) GO CHANGE YOUR DRESS FOR ONE BECOMING TO YOUR SEX
CYMB V (143)	YOUR HELP. MY LORD POSTHUMUS: YOU NE'ER KILLED	IMOGEN	TILL NOW. HELP! HELP! /IMOGEN/ OH, LET ME DIE. I
CYMB V (141)	LIV'D TO PUT ON THIS: SO HAD YOU SAV'D THE NOBLE	IMOGEN	TO REPENT, AND STRUCK ME (WRETCH) MORE WORTH YOUR
CYMB FORWORD(136)	JOYS, HAVING BECOME INTERESTED IN IACHIMO, IN	IMOGEN	, AND EVEN IN THE TWO LONG LOST PRINCES, I WANTED TO
CYMB V (141)	THE PART I CAME WITH; SO I'LL DIE FOR THEE, O	IMOGEN	, EVEN FOR WHOM MY LIFE IS EVERY BREATH A DEATH; AND
		IMOGENE	
LADY PREFACE(220)	OF A BROKEN MAN; NOR IS CLOTEN'S COMMENT THAT IF	IMOGENE	DOES NOT APPRECIATE IT, " IT IS A VICE IN HER EARS
		IMOGEN'S	
CYMB FORWORD(136)	IN THE REVELATION THAT POLYDORE AND CADWAL ARE	IMOGEN'S	LONG LOST BROTHERS AND CYMBELINE'S LONG LOST SONS;
		IMP	
JOAN 4 (99)	HALF A DOZEN BATTLES? NO, MY LORD: ANY TRUMPERY	IMP	COULD DO THAT MUCH IF THE GIRL COULD BE DAMNED AT ALL.
CAND III (133)	SHALL FEEL HER HANDS TOUCH ME. /MORELL/ YOU YOUNG	IMP	, DO YOU KNOW HOW DANGEROUS IT IS TO SAY THAT TO ME? OR
MRS II (210)	YOU? /MRS WARREN/ (RISING BREATHLESS) YOU YOUNG	IMP	! /VIVIE/ EVERYBODY KNOWS MY REPUTATION, MY SOCIAL
		IMPACT	
BULL IV (150)	WRECKED: AN AGED AND INFIRM LADY HAS SUFFERED AN	IMPACT	FOR WHICH I FEEL PERSONALLY RESPONSIBLE, THOUGH MY
METH PREFACE(R74)	AND TORTURE CHAMBERS THAT MAKES IT REEL AT THE	IMPACT	OF EVERY ADVANCE IN SCIENCE, INSTEAD OF BEING
PHIL PREFACE(68)	BUT LIFE ITSELF WAS STAGGERING FROM THE	IMPACT	OF IBSEN'S PLAYS, WHICH REACHED US IN 1889. THE STATE
HART PREFACE(15)	IMPOSSIBLE WAY. WHAT REALLY HAPPENED WAS THAT THE	IMPACT	OF PHYSICAL DEATH AND DESTRUCTION, THE ONE REALITY
MTH2 (52)	SOLD THE PASS! /FRANKLYN/ WHEN THE TERRIBLE	IMPACT	OF REAL WARFARE SWEPT YOUR PARLIAMENTARY SHAM WARFARE
		IMPAIR	
POSN PREFACE(422)	TO VICE OR CRIME. (F) TO BE CALCULATED TO	IMPAIR	FRIENDLY RELATIONS WITH ANY FOREIGN POWER. (G) TO BE
		IMPAIRING	
DOCT I SD(81)	THAT AGE INCREASES HER QUALIFICATION INSTEAD OF	IMPAIRING	IT. BEING AN INDUSTRIOUS, AGREEABLE, AND POPULAR
		IMPALED	
GETT PREFACE(238)	OF WOMEN IS ACHIEVED, WE SHALL HAVE TO REMAIN	IMPALED	ON THE OTHER HORN OF THE DILEMMA AND MAINTAIN
		IMPART	
CURE (235)	I HAVE A CONFESSION TO MAKE, A CONFIDENCE TO	IMPART	. YOUR PLAYING DRAWS IT FROM ME. LISTEN, STREGA (SHE
CYMB FORWORD(138)	MUCH ABOUT WHAT NAT LEE DID IN HIS ATTEMPTS TO	IMPART	RESTORATION GENTILITY TO SHAKESPEAR, OR ABOUT THOMAS
		IMPARTED	
MIS. PREFACE(79)	WAS BEYOND DESCRIPTION: FORTUNATELY FOR ME, IT	IMPARTED	SUCH A GHASTLINESS TO MY VOICE AND ASPECT AS I,
		IMPARTIAL	
BARB PREFACE(209)	RELENTED OVER PICKWICK, THEY DID NOT BECOME	IMPARTIAL	: THEY SIMPLY CHANGED SIDES, AND BECAME FRIENDS
FANY PROLOG (267)	TO ABOUT THE PLAY. HOW CAN YOU EXPECT ME TO BE	IMPARTIAL	? GOD FORBID THAT I SHOULD SET UP TO BE A JUDGE,
ROCK I (227)	I SHOULD LIKE TO HAVE THE OPINION OF AN	IMPARTIAL	AND DISINTERESTED GHOST. /THE LADY/ AS I LISTEN TO
BULL PREFACE(34)	AND ABYSMALLY INFERIOR TO, MY OWN. FINALLY, I AM	IMPARTIAL	AS TO YOUR INTERESTS BECAUSE THEY ARE BOTH EQUALLY
MRS PREFACE(158)	PERSONS WILL VOTE FOR A COMPLETE TAPU, AND AN	IMPARTIAL	CLEAN SWEEP FROM THE BOARDS OF MRS WARREN AND
GENV PREFACE(22)	TO SECURE SUBSTANTIAL DEMOCRACY, WHICH MEANS	IMPARTIAL	GOVERNMENT FOR THE GOOD OF THE GOVERNED BY
CAPT NOTES (303)	ENGLISH, BUT IRISH ENGLISH; SO I AM AS NEARLY	IMPARTIAL	IN THE MATTER AS IT IS IN HUMAN NATURE TO BE.
BULL PREFACE(34)	I BELIEVE IN NEITHER OF YOUR RELIGIONS. I AM	IMPARTIAL	IN YOUR CONFLICTS OF CUSTOM AND SENTIMENT BECAUSE
BULL PREFACE(33)	BETWEEN TWO NATIVES. HE SAYS, IN EFFECT, " I AM	IMPARTIAL	IN YOUR RELIGIOUS DISPUTES BECAUSE I BELIEVE IN
MTH3 (95)	JUSTICE IS IMPARTIALITY. ONLY STRANGERS ARE	IMPARTIAL	. /BURGE-LUBIN/ IT ENDS IN THE PUBLIC SERVICES
SUPR HANDBOK(219)	TREATISE IS POSTPONED UNTIL ITS AUTHOR ATTAINS	IMPARTIAL	JUDGMENT AND PERFECT KNOWLEDGE. IF A HORSE COULD
MIS. PREFACE(13)	BECAUSE IT IS INEVITABLE. YOU CANNOT HOLD AN	IMPARTIAL	JUDICIAL INQUIRY EVERY TIME A CHILD MISBEHAVES
ARMS III (65)	EXCLAIMING) JUDGE HER, BLUNTSCHLI. YOU, THE COOL	IMPARTIAL	MAN: JUDGE THE EAVESDROPPER. LOUKA STANDS HER
FABL PREFACE(89)	THAT HE (OR SHE) HAS COMPLETELY MASTERED THESE	IMPARTIAL	PHYSICAL AND MATHEMATICAL THEORIES, THE TOP PANEL
GENV IV (89)	THE YOUNG GENTLEMAN IS THE PUBLIC. /THE JUDGE/ AN	IMPARTIAL	SPECTATOR, EH? /THE BETROTHED/ NO, MY LORD. VERY
GENV IV (98)	AM IN SPIRIT, I RESPECTFULLY SUGGEST THAT IF AN	IMPARTIAL	STRANGER WERE PRESENT HIS IMPRESSION WOULD BE THAT
DOCT PREFACE(4)	NO LESS, AND WHAT OTHER MEN DARE PRETEND TO BE	IMPARTIAL	WHERE THEY HAVE A STRONG PECUNIARY INTEREST ON ONE
FABL PREFACE(64)	DILEMMA. IN SPITE OF ITS AUTHOR'S EFFORTS TO BE	IMPARTIAL	, IT IS CONVINCING AND CONVERTING AS TO HIS
		IMPARTIALITY	
POSN PREFACE(371)	IT SHOOK THE CONFIDENCE OF THE AUTHORS IN ITS	IMPARTIALITY	AND ITS SERIOUSNESS. OF COURSE IT WAS NOT ABLE
LADY PREFACE(229)	LIVE POLITICAL ISSUE IN SHAKESPEAR'S TIME, BUT OF	IMPARTIALITY	IN JUDGING CLASSES, WHICH IS WHAT ONE DEMANDS
CAPT III (278)	YOU MUST GIVE YOUR EVIDENCE WITH ABSOLUTE	IMPARTIALITY	. (SHE NODS, AS IF THOROUGHLY IMPRESSED AND
MTH3 (95)	IT. WHY SHOULD IT BE SO? /CONFUCIUS/ JUSTICE IS	IMPARTIALITY	. ONLY STRANGERS ARE IMPARTIAL. /BURGE-LUBIN/
		IMPARTIALLY	
MIS. PREFACE(93)	NEED FOR A RELIGION AND ITS RIGHT TO AN	IMPARTIALLY	COMMUNICATED HISTORICAL OBJECTIVE KNOWLEDGE OF
APPL I (225)	RELIGIOUS SECTS THAN I CAN COUNT, TO RULE THEM	IMPARTIALLY	I MUST NOT BELONG TO ANY OF THEM; AND THEY ALL
2TRU PREFACE(14)	TO SELECT RULERS WHO WILL GOVERN RIGHTEOUSLY AND	IMPARTIALLY	IN ACCORDANCE WITH THE FUNDAMENTAL NATURAL
		IMPARTING	
ROCK PREFACE(172)	TIMES THAT RELIGIOUS EDUCATION CONSISTED IN	IMPARTING	TO CHILDREN CERTAIN ETERNAL, FINAL, AND ABSOLUTE
		IMPARTS	
SUPR IV (152)	MARRIED A WORKER (HIS AMERICAN PRONUNCIATION	IMPARTS	AN OVERWHELMING INTENSITY TO THIS SIMPLE AND
GETT (353)	(SARDONICALLY) IN LANGUAGE WHOSE EXCESS	IMPARTS	THE POWER THEY FEEL SO WELL. /MRS GEORGE/ THOUGH
		IMPASSABLE	
SUPR III (100)	OF DEVIL'S BRIDGES); BUT THE GULF OF DISLIKE IS	IMPASSABLE	AND ETERNAL. AND THAT IS THE ONLY GULF THAT
SUPR III (100)	ANGELIC AND THE DIABOLIC TEMPERAMENT. WHAT MORE	IMPASSABLE	GULF COULD YOU HAVE? THINK OF WHAT YOU HAVE SEEN
ROCK I (194)	LATE; BUT REALLY THE STREETS ARE BECOMING QUITE	IMPASSABLE	WITH THE CROWDS OF UNEMPLOYED. I TOOK A TAXI; BUT
MIS. (195)	OH, THE GULF THAT LIES BETWEEN THEM! THE	IMPASSABLE	, ETERNAL GULF! AND SO I'M TO BUY THE BRUTE FOR
		IMPASSIONED	
BULL PREFACE(4)	THINKING ABOUT AS LORD ROSEBERY, ENTERED UPON AN	IMPASSIONED	DEFENCE OF THE EMPLOYMENT OF CHINESE LABOR IN
3PLA PREFACE(R28)	DICK WAS A PURITAN IN THIS RESPECT ALSO: A MAN	IMPASSIONED	ONLY FOR SAVING GRACE, AND NOT TO BE LED OR
3PLA PREFACE(R19)	THE DRAMATIC DANCER; THE EXQUISITE DECLAIMER OF	IMPASSIONED	POESY, THE RARE ARTIST WHO, BRINGING SOMETHING
BARB PREFACE(223)	PRIMITIVE SEXUAL EXCITEMENT: SUCH PHRASES AS "	IMPASSIONED	POETRY" OR " PASSIONATE LOVE OF TRUTH" HAVE
		IMPATIENCE	
MIS. PREFACE(89)	BORED OR THADDLED AT, OR TO EXPRESS OUR NATURAL	IMPATIENCE	AND DERISION OF BORES AND THADDLERS, AND WHEN A
BULL PREFACE(14)	WORLD AND WAS MOVED ONLY TO DISLIKE, MISTRUST,	IMPATIENCE	AND EVEN EXASPERATION BY HIS OWN COUNTRYMEN; THAT
PYGM V (268)	HIGGINS/ YES, DEAR. GOOD MORNING. (HE CHECKS HIS	IMPATIENCE	AND KISSES HER, WHILST THE PARLOR-MAID GOES OUT).
JITT III SD(52)	HER SIGHS AND EXCLAMATIONS OF DISAPPOINTMENT AND	IMPATIENCE	ARE GETTING ON THE NERVES OF ALFRED, WHO IS
HART I (66)	PLEASURE OF TELLING IT TO YOU. BUT IN A MOMENT OF	IMPATIENCE	AT BEING TURNED OUT OF THE ROOM, I THREW IT AWAY
DEST SD(157)	ATTRIBUTABLE BY A SUPERFICIAL OBSERVER TO HIS	IMPATIENCE	AT NOT BEING PROMPTLY ATTENDED TO BY THE STAFF OF

SUPR I SD(17)	LATE MR WHITEFIELD WOULD BE GRATIFIED ALMOST TO	IMPATIENCE	BY THE LONG FACES OF THE MEN (EXCEPT TANNER, WHO
BARB I SD(259)	AGAINST IMPULSES OF INHUMAN RIDICULE AND FIERCE	IMPATIENCE	HAS SET UP A CHRONIC STRAIN WHICH HAS VISIBLY
ARMS II (42)	HIS ADDRESS, KEEPING CATHERINE IN AN AGONY OF	IMPATIENCE	. AS HE HANDS HER THE CARD, PETKOFF, HATLESS,
FANY I SD(278)	TO HIS FACE? GILBEY CLUTCHES AT HIS HAIR IN HIS	IMPATIENCE	. /DORA/ WELL, WHAT WOULD HE CALL HIM? AFTER
NEVR I SD(208)	OF HAUGHTY HIGH-MINDEDNESS, RAGING WITH THE	IMPATIENCE	OF A METTLESOME DOMINATIVE CHARACTER PARALYZED BY
DOCT PREFACE(63)	INSPIRED BY A HATRED OF ILL-HEALTH, AND A DIVINE	IMPATIENCE	OF ANY WASTE OF VITAL FORCES. UNLESS A MAN IS LED
JOAN 6 (138)	WHICH EXPOSE HER TO MINOR PENANCES? I SHARE THE	IMPATIENCE	OF HIS LORDSHIP AS TO THESE MINOR CHARGES. ONLY,
CAND II (106)	WELL, UPON MY WORD! /MARCHBANKS/ (WITH PETULANT	IMPATIENCE	) AH, DONT SAY THOSE STUPID THINGS TO ME: THEY
BULL III (127)	I'M GOIN OURA DHIS. I-- /DORAN/ (WITH VIOLENT	IMPATIENCE	) ARRA WHO'S GOIN TO GIVE YOUR LAN TO PATSY, YOWL
CAPT III (276)	THE AUTHOR OF IT. /LADY CICELY/ (WITH A TOUCH OF	IMPATIENCE	) OH, QUITE. THATLL BE MADE CLEAR ENOUGH. I CAN
SUPR IV (159)	IS THOROUGHLY WOMANLY AT HEART. /ANN/ (WITH SOME	IMPATIENCE	) WHY DO YOU SAY THAT? IS IT UNWOMANLY TO BE
CAND II (123)	HAVE YOU RECEIVED IT? /MORELL/ (WITH RESTRAINED	IMPATIENCE	) YES, YES! I GOT IT. /LEXY/ IT WAS REPLY PAID.
ARMS I (18)	WANT TO BE TROUBLESOME. (SHE SHAKES HIM IN HER	IMPATIENCE	). I AM NOT INDIFFERENT, DEAR YOUNG LADY, I
JOAN 5 (113)	OF BURGUNDY. /JOAN/ TREATY! (SHE STAMPS WITH	IMPATIENCE	). /CHARLES/ WELL, WHY NOT, NOW THAT I AM CROWNED
CAND III (133)	WHY, THE FLAMING SWORD (MORELL STAMPS WITH	IMPATIENCE	)-- WELL, IN PLAIN PROSE, I LOVED HER SO
CATH 1,SD(163)	AND HAS PLAYED THIS COMEDY OF FURY AND EXHAUSTED	IMPATIENCE	TO CONCEAL HIS INTEREST IN THE VISITOR. /VARINKA/
3PLA PREFACE(R10)	THE THEATRE: THEY HAVE NEITHER THE PHILOSOPHER'S	IMPATIENCE	TO GET TO REALITIES (REALITY BEING THE ONE THING
HART PREFACE(21)	IT WAS TO THE ACTUAL COMBATANTS. I EXPRESSED MY	IMPATIENCE	VERY FREELY, AND FOUND THAT MY VERY
LION PREFACE(68)	FAMILY ENTANGLEMENTS. IT IS EVIDENT FROM HIS	IMPATIENCE	WHEN PEOPLE EXCUSED THEMSELVES FROM FOLLOWING HIM
CLEO II (119)	SPEAK FOR THE KING. /POTHINUS/ (SUPPRESSING HIS	IMPATIENCE	WITH DIFFICULTY) THE KING WISHED TO SAY THAT THE
BULL PREFACE(33)	OF SO MONSTROUSLY INHUMAN A PRETENSION, AND OUR	IMPATIENCE	WITH SO GROSS A CONFUSION OF THE MUTUALLY
JOAN PREFACE(4)	SHE MADE NO SECRET OF HER OPINION OF THEM OR HER	IMPATIENCE	WITH THEIR FOLLY; AND SHE WAS NAIVE ENOUGH TO
BULL II SD(112)	FOR LARRY. AT LAST SHE GIVES IT UP WITH A SOB OF	IMPATIENCE	, AND RETREATS TO THE HOARY FOOT OF THE TOWER,
DOCT III (153)	HIM. I AM HIS WIFE. I KNOW HE HAS LITTLE FAULTS:	IMPATIENCE	, SENSITIVENESS, EVEN LITTLE SELFISHNESSES THAT
DEVL III (72)	STEPS AS HE DESCENDS. /RICHARD/ (WITH SUPPRESSED	IMPATIENCE	, TO BRUDENELL) LOOK HERE, SIR: THIS IS NO PLACE

IMPATIENT

POSN PREFACE(375)	OCCURRED. FOR IT MUST BE REMEMBERED THAT, HOWEVER	IMPATIENT	AND CONTEMPTUOUS I MIGHT FEEL OF THE INTELLECTUAL
MTH4 I (146)	BEAR THESE UNNATURAL ARRANGEMENTS. /THE MAN/ (	IMPATIENT	AND HELPLESS) YOU SHOULDNT HAVE COME AMONG US.
BULL PREFACE(54)	HAD GIVEN EVIDENCE AGAINST HIM"; AND DARWEESH WAS	IMPATIENT	AND PRESUMED TO TELL THE HANGMAN TO BE QUICK. BUT
CLEO II SD(118)	QUICK WITTED, BUT OF COMMON MIND AND CHARACTER;	IMPATIENT	AND UNABLE TO CONTROL HIS TEMPER. HE HAS FINE
6CAL (101)	A THOUSAND FAVORS AND GRACES AND PRESENTS. I AM	IMPATIENT	AND UNGRATEFUL, EVER ASKING, ASKING, ASKING. HAVE
JITT I (19)	SPENDING OUR PRICELESS MOMENTS LIKE THIS. I AM AS	IMPATIENT	AS YOU ARE: I LONG FOR YOU BEYOND ALL EXPRESSION.
MTH2 (44)	GRAVES. (THE PARLOR MAID RETURNS. FRANKLYN IS	IMPATIENT	AT THE INTERRUPTION). WELL? WHAT IS IT NOW? /THE
WIDO III SD(54)	ON WHICH SHE COLLECTS THE COFFEE CUPS, SARTORIUS,	IMPATIENT	AT THE INTERRUPTION, RISES AND MOTIONS LICKCHEESE
PYGM III (259)	GO DOWNSTAIRS). /MRS HIGGINS/ (RISES WITH AN	IMPATIENT	BOUNCE, AND RETURNS TO HER WORK AT THE
DOCT PREFACE(64)	CONSTANT RISK OF INFECTION. ONE WONDERS WHY THE	IMPATIENT	DOCTORS DO NOT BECOME SAVAGE AND UNMANAGEABLE, AND
MIS. PREFACE(61)	HANDS ALL YOUR LIFE, AND ARE GENERALLY RATHER	IMPATIENT	FOR THE DAY WHEN HE WILL EARN HIS OWN LIVING AND
PHIL PREFACE(68)	INFLUENCE: QUARTER OF A CENTURY ELAPSED BEFORE AN	IMPATIENT	HEAVEN RAINED GERMAN BOMBS DOWN ON THEM TO WAKE
CLEO II (138)	RUFIO, PATIENCE. /RUFIO/ PATIENCE! WHO IS	IMPATIENT	HERE, YOU OR I? WOULD I BE HERE, IF I COULD NOT
PYGM II (230)	YOUVE MISLAID ANYTHING OR WHEN YOU GET A LITTLE	IMPATIENT	. NOW IT DOESNT MATTER BEFORE ME: I'M USED TO IT.
CAND III (146)	MY HEART. LET ME GO NOW. THE NIGHT OUTSIDE GROWS	IMPATIENT	. /CANDIDA/ GOODBYE. (SHE TAKES HIS FACE IN HER
BASH II,1, (112)	/LYDIA/ LET US HASTE, MY LOVE: THE COACHMAN IS	IMPATIENT	. /CASHEL/ DID HE GUESS HE STAYS FOR CASHEL BYRON,
MTH5 (214)	OF COURSE SHE ONLY HALF UNDERSTANDS, AND IS VERY	IMPATIENT	. /THE SHE-ANCIENT/ VERY WELL. BRING HER OUT INTO
MIS. (191)	OF THIS DEFIANCE, WHICH HAS PROVOKED JOHNNY TO AN	IMPATIENT	MOVEMENT TOWARDS HIM). /HYPATIA/ THANK GOODNESS
BARB III (319)	LEFT BUT THE STAGE, IS THERE? (STEPHEN MAKES AN	IMPATIENT	MOVEMENT). WELL, COME! IS THERE ANYTHING YOU KNOW
CLEO III (157)	OF OCCUPATION HERE. /CAESAR/ WELL? /BRITANNUS/ (	IMPATIENT	OF CAESAR'S SLOWNESS TO GRASP THE SITUATION) WELL,
LION PREFACE(23)	MISERY IN THE WORLD. HE BREAKS THE SABBATH; IS	IMPATIENT	OF CONVENTIONALITY WHEN IT IS UNCOMFORTABLE OR
3PLA PREFACE(R23)	OF THE STRONG-MINDED BISMARCKIAN MAN OF ACTION,	IMPATIENT	OF HUMBUG, WILL COMBINE WITH THE SUBTLETY AND
ARMS I (15)	WHY SHOULD HE PULL AT HIS HORSE? /THE MAN/ (	IMPATIENT	OF SO STUPID A QUESTION) IT'S RUNNING AWAY WITH
LION PREFACE(99)	IN ANY DIRECTION, WHICH MAKES THEM EQUALLY	IMPATIENT	OF SYSTEMATIC DESPOTISM AND SYSTEMATIC GOOD
MIS. PREFACE(22)	FROM IT INTO THE PULPIT. THE ABLEST AND MOST	IMPATIENT	OF THEM WERE OFTEN SO IRRITATED BY THE AWKWARD,
CAPT I (236)	(HE BOWS GRAVELY). /SIR HOWARD/ (A LITTLE	IMPATIENT	OF THESE QUESTIONS, WHICH STRIKE HIM AS SOMEWHAT
BULL IV (174)	PLUNDER YOU AFTERWARDS. /BROADBENT/ (A LITTLE	IMPATIENT	OF THIS UNBUSINESSLIKE VIEW) YES, YES; BUT YOU
GETT PREFACE(243)	FOR SOME REASON SCIENTIFIC WRITERS ARE PERVERSELY	IMPATIENT	OF THIS VIEW, AND, TO DISCREDIT IT, QUOTE POLICE
MIS. PREFACE(88)	AND UNNATURAL CONVENTIONS AS THIS THAT MAKE US SO	IMPATIENT	OF WHAT WE CALL FAMILY FEELING. EVEN APART FROM
MTH4 III (197)	YOUNG TAKING AN INTEREST IN POLITICS. IT IS AN	IMPATIENT	QUESTION; BUT IT IS A PRACTICAL QUESTION, AN
HART II (105)	WITHOUT YOUR LUGGAGE, MR MANGAN. /ELLIE/ (	IMPATIENT	) GO, GO: WHY DONT YOU GO? IT IS A HEAVENLY
JITT I (15)	MORTAL BE HAPPY? /JITTA/ (SUDDENLY PROSAIC AND	IMPATIENT	) YES: ALFRED CAN. A GLASS OF WINE AND A CIGAR CAN
JITT II (35)	AT THE BEGINNING OF EVERYTHING INSTEAD. /EDITH/ (	IMPATIENT	) YOU NEED NOT SPEAK TO ME LIKE THAT. YOU KNOW
ARMS III (56)	TELLING ME NOT TO MIND THE MAJOR BEING A LITTLE	IMPATIENT	; FOR THEY KNEW WHAT A GOOD SERVANT I WAS-- AFTER
MRS IV SD(243)	BRACES VIVIE. SHE THROWS IT AWAY FROM HER WITH AN	IMPATIENT	SHAKE, AND FORCES HERSELF TO STAND UP, THOUGH NOT
CLEO II (141)	ME. /RUFIO/ (COMING BACK INTO THE LOGGIA, MORE	IMPATIENT	THAN EVER) NOW CAESAR: HAVE YOU DONE TALKING? THE
CAND III (145)	THE WORDS) I KNOW THE HOUR WHEN IT STRIKES. I AM	IMPATIENT	TO DO WHAT MUST BE DONE. /MORELL/ (WHO HAS ALSO
SUPR III (130)	THEM. THEY MIGHT BE MEN OF FIFTY. /DON JUAN/ I AM	IMPATIENT	TO GET THERE. IS THE WORD BEAUTY EVER MENTIONED;
CLEO IV (178)	WITH HER BEAUTY THAT YOU DO NOT SEE THAT SHE IS	IMPATIENT	TO REIGN IN EGYPT ALONE, AND THAT HER HEART IS SET
LION PREFACE(9)	NOT MAKE SENSE OF THEM, NOR EVEN BE ABLE WITHOUT	IMPATIENT	WEARINESS TO PERSEVERE IN THE TASK OF GOING
MRS PREFACE(175)	ITSELF. THE MAGISTRATE, NATURALLY SOMEWHAT	IMPATIENT	WHEN HE FOUND THAT WHAT HE HAD TO READ WAS A
CLEO PRO1 (93)	IS A WOLF THAT MAY COME TO YOUR OWN DOOR. ARE YE	IMPATIENT	WITH ME? DO YE CRAVE FOR A STORY OF AN UNCHASTE
DEST (176)	HAUGHTY MANNER, OF WHICH HE IS HIMSELF SOMEWHAT	IMPATIENT	, AND SAYS SUSPICIOUSLY, LOWERING HIS VOICE) WHO
JOAN 1 (61)	NOT ANGER HER: GIVE HER WHAT SHE WANTS. /JOAN/ (	IMPATIENT	, BUT FRIENDLY) THEY ALL SAY I AM MAD UNTIL I TALK
JOAN 3 (90)	WHICH IS THE WAY TO THE BRIDGE? /DUNOIS/ YOU ARE	IMPATIENT	, MAID. /JOAN/ IS THIS A TIME FOR PATIENCE? OUR
BULL IV (180)	EH? (LARRY, WITH A SHRUG, HALF COMIC, HALF	IMPATIENT	, TURNS AWAY UP THE HILL, BUT PRESENTLY STROLLS
MTH5 (220)	THAT TO DO WITH IT? (HE IS HALF DERISIVE, HALF	IMPATIENT	, WHOLLY RESOLVED NOT TO TAKE HER SERIOUSLY IN
FANY I (278)	CACKLING ABOUT YOUR SQUIFFER? /DORA/ OH, AINT HE	IMPATIENT	! WELL, IT DOES YOU CREDIT, OLD DEAR. AND YOU

IMPATIENTLY

NEVR II (258)	AND STANDS ON HER GUARD WRATHFULLY. HE SPRINGS UP	IMPATIENTLY	AND RETREATS A STEP). OH, WHAT A FOOL I AM! AN
AUGS (282)	TELEPHONE, WAVING HER DISENGAGED HAND BEHIND HER	IMPATIENTLY	AT THEM TO STOP MAKING A NOISE) SH-SH-SH-SH-SH!
LION PREFACE(6)	DID. I HAVE HEARD THIS FEELING EXPRESSED FAR MORE	IMPATIENTLY	BY PERSONS BROUGHT UP IN ENGLAND AS CHRISTIANS
HART I (59)	MUCH; AND I SHALL ALWAYS BE-- /MRS HUSHABYE/ (	IMPATIENTLY	COMPLETING THE SENTENCE AND PRANCING AWAY
JITT I (10)	PROMISED TO LEAVE ME SOMETHING. /MRS BILLITER/ (	IMPATIENTLY	GROPING IN HER PURSE AND EXTRACTING A TIP) THATS
MTH1 II SD(34)	NOR KILLING. SHE SPINS RESIGNEDLY; HE DIGS	IMPATIENTLY	.
MRS III SD(229)	GRASS; AND LOOKS CUNNINGLY AT HER. SHE TURNS AWAY	IMPATIENTLY	. /CROFTS/ I'M A GOOD DEAL OLDER THAN YOU.
NEVR IV (292)	AND SYPHON FOR YOU, SIR. (BOHUN WAVES HIS HAND	IMPATIENTLY	. THE WAITER PLACES A LARGE GLASS JUG AND THREE
CAPT II (248)	YOU STEBLISH YR HAWTHORITY. (BRASSBOUND TURNS	IMPATIENTLY	ON HIM: HE RETREATS REMONSTRATING) NAH, NAH,
PYGM III SD(250)	HIS DISASTROUS JOURNEY BY THROWING HIMSELF SO	IMPATIENTLY	ON THE DIVAN THAT HE ALMOST BREAKS IT. MRS
CLEO III (164)	AT THE PARAPET). /RUFIO/ (TO APOLLODORUS,	IMPATIENTLY	) AND BY WHAT ROAD ARE WE TO WALK TO THE
FANY II (289)	TO ANYBODY, I SUPPOSE. BUT THEY DO. (RISING	IMPATIENTLY	) AND REALLY I'D RATHER GO OUT AND ASSAULT
DEST (157)	OUT BY THE INNER DOOR). /THE MAN'S VOICE/ (	IMPATIENTLY	) ARE YOU ALL ASLEEP HERE? THE OTHER DOOR IS
GENV IV (108)	NO DUEL THEN? /BATTLER/ DO NOT TORMENT ME. (	IMPATIENTLY	) BARDO: YOU ARE A DAMNED FOOL. /BBDE/ (HUGELY
PYGM V (275)	OR TELL HER HOW SPLENDID SHE'D BEEN. /HIGGINS/ (	IMPATIENTLY	) BUT SHE KNEW ALL ABOUT THAT. WE DIDNT MAKE
HART II (119)	EAT, BUT YOU WILL NOT LIVE. /ELLIE/ (SITTING UP	IMPATIENTLY	) BUT WHAT CAN I DO? I AM NOT A SEA CAPTAIN: I
DEVL III (64)	WHATS YOUR NAME? /CHRISTY/ CHRISTY. /RICHARD/ (	IMPATIENTLY	) CHRISTOPHER DUDGEON, YOU BLATANT IDIOT. GIVE
WIDO I (11)	EAGERNESS). NOW, IF IT WERE COKANE-- /BLANCHE/ (	IMPATIENTLY	) COKANE! /TRENCH/ (TERRIFIED) NO, NOT COKANE.
AUGS (277)	INTERRUPTED BY A KNOCK AT THE DOOR). /AUGUSTUS/ (	IMPATIENTLY	) COME IN. (THE CLERK ENTERS, CLEAN SHAVEN AND
CLEO II (125)	MAKE THEM BOTH A PRESENT OF CYPRUS. /POTHINUS/ (	IMPATIENTLY	) CYPRUS IS OF NO USE TO ANYBODY. /CAESAR/ NO
CAPT III (289)	YES. IT IS TRUE-- AS FAR AS IT GOES. /KEARNEY/ (	IMPATIENTLY	) DO YOU WAWNT IT TO GO ANY FURTHER? /MARZO/
NEVR IV (292)	IN THEIR STYLE OF DRESSING. /MRS CLANDON/ (	IMPATIENTLY	) DO YOU SUPPOSE I CHOOSE THEIR CLOTHES FOR
JITT II (32)	MATTER? NEED WE GOSSIP ABOUT IT? /LENKHEIM/ (	IMPATIENTLY	) DONT BE SO SUPERIOR. I LIKE GOSSIP. EVERYBODY
WIDO I (10)	GOT TO KNOW HIM FIRST, HAVNT YOU? /BLANCHE/ (	IMPATIENTLY	) EVERYBODY IS AFRAID OF PAPA: I'M SURE I DONT
MTH2 (60)	THINGS: PRINCIPLES ARE SETTLED THINGS. /CONRAD/ (	IMPATIENTLY	) GREAT HEAVENS! -- /LUBIN/ (INTERRUPTING HIM
HART III (143)	MAKE FUN OF ME; BUT IF YOU ONLY KNEW-- /HECTOR/ (	IMPATIENTLY	) HOW IS ALL THIS GOING TO END? /MAZZINI/ IT
WIDO III (49)	DOCTOR TODAY ABOUT OUR GOING ABROAD. /BLANCHE/ (	IMPATIENTLY	) I AM QUITE WELL; AND I WILL NOT GO ABROAD. I
MTH5 (212)	THAT FINISHES IT. YOU DISLIKE ME. /THE MAIDEN/ (	IMPATIENTLY	) I TELL YOU AGAIN, I DO NOT DISLIKE YOU; BUT
MTH4 II (185)	AMBROSE. I WARNED YOU. /THE ENVOY/ BUT-- /ZOO/ (	IMPATIENTLY	) I WONDER WHAT ZOZIM IS DOING. HE OUGHT TO BE
PHIL II (117)	/CRAVEN/ (PUZZLED) HENRIK? /CUTHBERTSON/ (	IMPATIENTLY	) IBSEN, MAN: IBSEN. (HE GOES OUT BY THE

WIDO I (19) I SHALL BE AWFULLY OBLIGED TO YOU. /COKANE/ (IMPATIENTLY) LEAVE ME, LEAVE ME: YOU DISTURB ME. (HE WAVES
INCA (251) THE GREAT --/THE INCA/ (INTERRUPTING HER IMPATIENTLY) MADAM: IF YOU ASK ME, I CONSIDER BEDROCK A
GETT (354) ARE AS INGRAINED A SNOB AS EVER. /HOTCHKISS/ (IMPATIENTLY) MY DEAR ANTHONY: I FIND YOU MERELY RIDICULOUS
SUPR III (112) GO AHEAD BY ALL MEANS. /DON JUAN/ (SOMEWHAT IMPATIENTLY) MY POINT, YOU MARBLE-HEADED OLD MASTERPIECE,
DEVL III (74) MAKES A GESTURE AS IF TO TOUCH HIM. HE RECOILS IMPATIENTLY) NO: GO AWAY, GO AWAY: YOULL UNNERVE ME. TAKE
BARB I (262) SEEM NEVER TO DESERT YOU. ACCORDINGLY-- ER-- (IMPATIENTLY) NOW I HAVE FORGOTTEN WHAT I WAS GOING TO SAY.
JITT I (21) NAME TACKED ON TO IT AS BRUNO'S. /JITTA/ (IMPATIENTLY) OH YES, YES! I KNOW ALL THAT. IT SOUNDS LIKE A
LIED (188) MADNESS, YOUR RASHNESS, YOUR IMPRUDENCE! /SHE/ (IMPATIENTLY) OH, BE SENSIBLE, HENRY. CANT YOU SEE WHAT A
MIS. (140) I KNOW THAT. WHEN MEN OF MY AGE-- /HYPATIA/ (IMPATIENTLY) OH, DO TALK ABOUT YOURSELF WHEN YOU MEAN
PRES (138) OF IT, THAT AFFAIR OF THE CURATE-- /MITCHENER/ (IMPATIENTLY) OH, DAMN THAT CURATE. IVE HEARD OF NOTHING BUT
SUPR II (52) NOT TIRED OF PLAYING WITH YOU YET. /OCTAVIUS/ (IMPATIENTLY) OH, DONT BE A FOOL, JACK. DO YOU SUPPOSE THIS
DOCT III (141) WHAT ARE TO DO WITH THIS DAISY! /LOUIS/ (IMPATIENTLY) OH, GO AND DO WHATEVER THE DEVIL YOU PLEASE.
PHIL II (122) MY-- WHAT DID YOU CALL YOUR SOUL? /PARAMORE/ (IMPATIENTLY) OH, GO ON, GO ON: FINISH WHAT YOU WERE GOING
MIS. (154) I'M DOING A BIT OF DREAMING MYSELF. /HYPATIA/ (IMPATIENTLY) OH, IT'S ALL RIGHT, MAMMA. JOHNNY: LOOK AFTER
ARMS III (57) SHOULD ALWAYS STAND BY ANOTHER. /LOUKA/ (RISING IMPATIENTLY) OH, I MUST BEHAVE IN MY OWN WAY. YOU TAKE ALL
CAND I (80) END BRANCH. THURSDAY, FIRST CONFIRMATION CLASS. (IMPATIENTLY) OH, I'D BETTER TELL THEM YOU CANT COME. THEYRE
SUPR III (93) YOU BEHAVED SO DISGRACEFULLY TO ME? /DON JUAN/ (IMPATIENTLY) OH, I BEG YOU NOT TO BEGIN TALKING ABOUT LOVE.
GETT (270) SURE OF IT. I NEVER MEANT-- /LESBIA/ (RISING IMPATIENTLY) OH, MY DEAR BOXER, DO PLEASE TRY TO THINK OF
GETT (303) REALLY, BOXER! YOU MUST NOT-- /THE GENERAL/ (IMPATIENTLY) OH, OF COURSE I DONT MEAN THAT YOU USED THOSE
BULL III (122) HIM, MISS DOYLE? WHO CAN BLAME HIM? /LARRY/ (IMPATIENTLY) OH, RUBBISH! WHATS THE GOOD OF THE MAN THATS
O'FL (221) /MRS O'FLAHERTY/ COME, CHILD, COME. /TERESA/ (IMPATIENTLY) OH, SURE I'M COMING. (SHE TRIES TO SMILE AT
SUPR II (64) I ASK WHAT OTHER OBJECTION APPLIES? /TANNER/ (IMPATIENTLY) OH, TELL HIM, TELL HIM. WE SHALL NEVER BE ABLE
SUPR IV (148) BOTH ABBEYS. /VIOLET/ (PUTTING THAT ASIDE RATHER IMPATIENTLY) OH, WELL, LET US TALK SENSE, MR MALONE. YOU
DEVL III (52) ATLANTIC AND MAKE AMERICA A NATION. /JUDITH/ (IMPATIENTLY) OH, WHAT DOES ALL THAT MATTER? /RICHARD/ (
MILL IV (200) ON HIS BEHALF AD MISERICORDIAM. /EPIFANIA/ (IMPATIENTLY) OH, WE ARE WASTING TIME; AND I HAVE MORE
BARB II (300) YOU-- /JENNY/ (DISTRESSED) OH NO-- /BILL/ (IMPATIENTLY) TELL Y' AW DID: CAWNT YOU LISTEN TO WOTS BEIN
PHIL I (86) DISPLAYING SOME EMOTION). /CHARTERIS/ (A LITTLE IMPATIENTLY) THE FACT IS, CUTHBERTSON, CRAVEN'S A DEVOUT
MTH4 II (177) YOU ON YOUR IMPRESSIVENESS, MADAM. /THE ORACLE/ (IMPATIENTLY) TIME! TIME! TIME! TIME! /NAPOLEON/ YOU
MIS. (115) /MRS TARLETON/ WAS IT A WASP? /BENTLEY/ (IMPATIENTLY) WASP BE DASHED! /MRS TARLETON/ OH BUNNY!
WIDO III (55) ARE MRS LICKCHEESE AND THE CHIL-- /SARTORIUS/ (IMPATIENTLY) WE HAVE BUSINESS TO TRANSACT, BLANCHE. YOU CAN
APPL I (212) /NICOBAR/ I DONT SEE THAT. WE -- /PROTEUS/ (IMPATIENTLY) WELL, IF YOU DONT, THEN FOR HEAVEN'S SAKE
PYGM IV (264) PRAYERS. " THANK GOD IT'S ALL OVER! " /HIGGINS/ (IMPATIENTLY) WELL, DONT YOU THANK GOD IT'S ALL OVER? NOW
PYGM III (246) HOW COULD YOU BE SO SILLY, HENRY? /HIGGINS/ (IMPATIENTLY) WELL, SHE MUST TALK ABOUT SOMETHING. (HE
PHIL II (111) AND THROWS HERSELF INTO A CHAIR. /CRAVEN/ (IMPATIENTLY) WHAT IS THE MATTER? HAS EVERY ONE GONE MAD
PYGM II (226) PUT IT DOWN IN THE HOUSEKEEPING BOOK. (IMPATIENTLY) WHAT ON EARTH WILL SHE WANT WITH MONEY?
PYGM II (226) YOU MUST LOOK AHEAD A LITTLE. /HIGGINS/ (IMPATIENTLY) WHATS TO BECOME OF HER IF I LEAVE HER IN THE
APPL INTRLUD(245) THEIR FADS AND THEIR ELECTION CHANCES. (RISING IMPATIENTLY) WHO COULD TALK TO SUCH PEOPLE? IF IT WERE NOT
DEVL III (66) SIR. /SERGEANT/ (SHOUTING) SILENCE. /RICHARD/ (IMPATIENTLY) YAH! (TO CHRISTY) HE WANTS TO KNOW AM I
ARMS II (30) ALWAYS APPEARS AT THE RIGHT MOMENT. /CATHERINE/ (IMPATIENTLY) YES: SHE LISTENS FOR IT. IT IS AN ABOMINABLE
BULL I (84) HOME AGAIN? TO-- /DOYLE/ (INTERRUPTING HIM VERY IMPATIENTLY) YES, YES: I KNOW ALL THAT AS WELL AS YOU DO.
ROCK II (258) THAT THEYD SUBMIT TO ANYTHING. /SIR DEXTER/ (IMPATIENTLY) YES, YES: WE KNOW THE CANT OF ALL THE
CLEO IV (169) OUT OF YOU. (THE LADIES LAUGH. CLEOPATRA RISES IMPATIENTLY). BEGONE, ALL OF YOU. I WILL SPEAK WITH
PHIL II (111) ANSWERING WHEN HE'S SPOKEN TO? (JULIA WRITHES IMPATIENTLY). COME, COME (TENDERLY): WONT MY PET TELL HER
SUPR IV (146) MONEY IF YOU HAVE TO WORK FOR IT? (SHE RISES IMPATIENTLY). IT'S ALL NONSENSE, MR MALONE: YOU MUST ENABLE
DEST (157) STOP. LET HER COME. /VOICE/ GIUSEPPE! ! (IMPATIENTLY). /GIUSEPPE/ LET ME GO, EXCELLENCY. IT IS MY
FABL V (117) WHICH IT WAS NOT MENTIONED. (HE SHUTS THE BOOK IMPATIENTLY). /ROSE/ THAT SEEMS HARDLY POSSIBLE. OUR
ARMS II (40) AND BE VERY POLITE TO HIM. DONT DELAY. HERE (IMPATIENTLY SNATCHING THE SALVER FROM HER): LEAVE THAT HERE;
BULL I (91) COMPROMISE OR LAXITY. FOR INSTANCE-- /DOYLE/ (IMPATIENTLY SPRINGING UP AND WALKING ABOUT) FOR INSTANCE,
ARMS II (24) YOUR FATHER BE LEFT ON HIS LITTLE FARM? (SHE IMPATIENTLY THROWS AWAY THE END OF HER CIGARET, AND STAMPS
MTH1 I (16) /THE SERPENT/ (LAUGHS)! ! ! /EVE/ (TURNING IMPATIENTLY TO THE SNAKE) THAT HEART-BITING SOUND AGAIN! DO
JOAN 2 (82) CHUCKLE) WELL SAID, LASS! WELL SAID! /JOAN/ (IMPATIENTLY TO THE ARCHBISHOP) OH, MY LORD, WILL YOU SEND
JOAN EPILOG (154) DID HE GET IN? WHERE ARE MY PEOPLE? (HE GOES IMPATIENTLY TO THE BED, AND SWINGS THE RATTLE. A RUSH OF
JITT II (41) MOMENT. ALWAYS SPOILING EVERYTHING. (SHE TURNS IMPATIENTLY TO THE WINDOW, AND STANDS WITH HER BACK TO THEM,
PHIL II (116) ELSE'S? (HE PATS HER CHEEK, MOLLIFIED. JULIA IMPATIENTLY TURNS AWAY FROM THEM). COME TO THE SMOKING ROOM;
JITT I (13) ALWAYS MY WIFE. /JITTA/ (RECOILING FROM HIM IMPATIENTLY , AND THROWING HER CLOAK ON THE COUCH) OH YES:
CLEO III (147) MISTRESS OF THE QUEEN'S HOUSEHOLD. /FTATATEETA/ (IMPATIENTLY , AS THE PORTERS STOOP TO LIFT THE BALES) QUICK,
ARMS I (12) NO: I HAVE NOT BEEN TO BED. /THE OFFICER/ (IMPATIENTLY , COMING BACK INTO THE ROOM) YOUR NEIGHBORS HAVE
GETT (318) AS TO THE TERM OF THE AGREEMENT. /REGINALD/ (IMPATIENTLY , LEAVING THE HEARTH AND GOING BEHIND SOAMES)
CAND I (83) AS HE TAKES OUT A CIGARET). /PROSERPINE/ (IMPATIENTLY , PULLING THE LETTER SHE HAS BEEN WORKING AT OFF

IMPEACHMENT
GETT PREFACE(205) HE DID NOT WANT THE BOY CURED WOULD HAVE DESERVED IMPEACHMENT FOR GROSS TYRANNY. BUT A STATESMAN TOLERATING

IMPECUNIOSITY
MTH2 (64) TO THE PEOPLE: YOU BELONGED TO THE IMPECUNIOUS. IMPECUNIOSITY AND BROKEN BOOTS ARE THE LOT OF THE
UNPL PREFACE(R9) TO MY HARANGUES, I ENJOYED THE IMMUNITIES OF IMPECUNIOSITY WITH THE OPPORTUNITIES OF A MILLIONAIRE. IF

IMPECUNIOUS
MTH2 (64) NEVER BELONGED TO THE PEOPLE: YOU BELONGED TO THE IMPECUNIOUS . IMPECUNIOSITY AND BROKEN BOOTS ARE THE LOT OF
DEST SD(149) SPOILED CHILD, POVERTY, ILL-LUCK, THE SHIFTS OF IMPECUNIOUS SHABBY-GENTILITY, REPEATED FAILURE AS A WOULD-BE

IMPEDIMENT
AUGS (263) WHO ARE YOU? /THE CLERK/ THE STAFF (A SLIGHT IMPEDIMENT IN HIS SPEECH ADDS TO THE IMPRESSION OF
SHAK (140) THE BOWELS OF THE LAND HAVE WE MARCHED ON WITHOUT IMPEDIMENT . SHALL I STILL CALL YOU CAMPBELL? /ROB/ (IN A

IMPELLED
GENV IV (112) A MIGHTY MOVEMENT IN THE HISTORY OF THE WORLD. IMPELLED BY IT I HAVE STRETCHED OUT MY HAND AND LIFTED MY
ROCK PREFACE(149) WHICH I RECOMMEND TO THOSE READERS WHO MAY FEEL IMPELLED TO RAMBLE AWAY AT THIS POINT INTO THE PROSINGS

IMPENETRABLE
DOCT I SD(108) AND SHUTS THE DOOR. RIDGEON, WHO HAS PUT ON AN IMPENETRABLE AND RATHER DISTANT PROFESSIONAL MANNER, TURNS
CLEO IV (189) OF POTHINUS. (LOFTILY, WRAPPING HIMSELF UP IN AN IMPENETRABLE DIGNITY) LET THE QUEEN OF EGYPT NOW GIVE HER
2TRU III SD(112) OF SHIFTING WHITE CLOUD; THERE IS LEFT ONLY FOG: IMPENETRABLE FOG; BUT THE INCORRIGIBLE PREACHER WILL NOT BE
CURE (226) BEFORE YOUR FATUOUS SELF-SATISFACTION, YOUR IMPENETRABLE INABILITY TO SEE ANY REASON WHY YOU SHOULDNT
JITT I (16) EYES, BUT HE SAW NOTHING: HIS SELF-CONCEIT IS IMPENETRABLE . HIS CHEERFUL GRIN KILLED MY CONSCIENCE. I
SUPR I SD(4) ABOVE THE MANTELSHELF, IS A FAMILY PORTRAIT OF IMPENETRABLE OBSCURITY. A CHAIR STANDS NEAR THE WRITING
BASH III (120) THOUSANDS THIRTY-NINE. I TELL THEE, LYDIA, ON THE IMPENETRABLE SARCOLOBE THAT HOLDS HIS SEEDLING BRAIN THESE

IMPENETRABLY
MTH4 I (146) HERE. ALL I CAN TELL YOU IS THAT SHE WAS THE MOST IMPENETRABLY STUPID WOMAN I HAVE EVER MET IN THE WHOLE

IMPENITENCE
SUPR PREFACE(R13) DON JUAN CASTS BACK TO THE ORIGINAL IN POINT OF IMPENITENCE ; BUT IN PIETY HE FALLS OFF GREATLY. TRUE, HE

IMPENITENT
SUPR I SD(43) FAVORABLY. VIOLET APPEARS AT THE DOOR. SHE IS AS IMPENITENT AND SELF-POSSESSED A YOUNG LADY AS ONE WOULD
CAPT NOTES (301) IN SPAIN OR SCOTLAND. HE IS, I REGRET TO ADD, AN IMPENITENT AND UNASHAMED DANDY: SUCH BOOTS, SUCH A HAT,
METH PREFACE(R9) SAID AS ANY NEO-DARWINIAN NOWADAYS. HE DIED IMPENITENT , AND DID NOT MENTION ME IN HIS WILL. TWENTY

IMPERATIVE
SUPR HANDBOK(190) THE NEED FOR THE SUPERMAN IS, IN ITS MOST IMPERATIVE ASPECT, A POLITICAL ONE. WE HAVE BEEN DRIVEN TO
GETT PREFACE(203) BUT WHAT IS NOW MAKING SOME ACTION IN THE MATTER IMPERATIVE IS NEITHER THE SUFFERINGS OF THOSE WHO ARE TIED
MIS. PREFACE(29) IT HAS NO APPLICATION TO CHILDREN EXCEPT AS AN IMPERATIVE REASON FOR TRAINING THEM TO RESPECT OTHER
JOAN EPILOG (166) THOUGH OCCASIONALLY ERRONEOUS, ARE STILL IMPERATIVE ; SO IF YOU WILL BE GOOD ENOUGH TO EXCUSE ME -- (

IMPERATIVELY
KING I (170) DRURY LANE ACTRESS? /MRS BASHAM/ (TURNING IMPERATIVELY TO CHARLES) OH, I COULDNT ALLOW THAT, MR

IMPERCEPTIBLE

POSN PREFACE(395) WITH THESE SAME JESTS SLURRED OVER SO AS TO BE IMPERCEPTIBLE BY EVEN THE MOST PRURIENT SPECTATOR. THE

IMPERFECT

SUPR III (105) ARE THEY NOW? FOSSILS IN MUSEUMS, AND SO FEW AND IMPERFECT AT THAT, THAT A KNUCKLE BONE OR A TOOTH OF ONE OF
SIM PREFACE(18) BUT IN EFFECT MUCH EASIER THAN THE PRESENT VERY IMPERFECT BARGAIN. THIS INVOLVES A NEW SOCIAL CREED. A NEW
BARB I (255) (DESPERATELY) I DARESAY WE HAVE BEEN THE VERY IMPERFECT CHILDREN OF A VERY PERFECT MOTHER; BUT I DO BEG
CAPT I SD(218) THEY CANNOT BE INDICATED, SAVE IN THE ABOVE IMPERFECT MANNER, WITHOUT THE AID OF A PHONETIC ALPHABET. HE

IMPERFECTION

LADY PREFACE(225) OR INTERPRETATION, THAT POINTED TO ANY HUMAN IMPERFECTION IN THEIR HERO. THEY THUS LEAVE THEMSELVES WITH
FABL PREFACE(65) I CALL THE LIFE FORCE, WHEN NOT DEFEATED BY THE IMPERFECTION OF ITS MORTAL INSTRUMENTS, ALWAYS TAKES CARE

IMPERFECTIONS

MIS. PREFACE(4) WILL IT BE POSSIBLE FOR ME TO CONCEIVE MY PRESENT IMPERFECTIONS (AND WHAT I CANNOT CONCEIVE I CANNOT
LADY PREFACE(222) OF HIS INFATUATION FOR A WOMAN OF WHOSE MORTAL IMPERFECTIONS NOT ONE ESCAPES HIM: A MAN ALWAYS EXCHANGING

IMPERFECTLY

UNPL PREFACE(R22) BECAUSE IN HIS TIME THE ACTING OF PLAYS WAS VERY IMPERFECTLY DIFFERENTIATED FROM THE DECLAMATION OF VERSES;
DOCT PREFACE(9) TO THE FACTS THAT MEDICAL SCIENCE IS AS YET VERY IMPERFECTLY DIFFERENTIATED FROM COMMON CUREMONGERING
DOCT PREFACE(34) TO KNOWLEDGE. IT IS A RIGHT THAT IS AS YET VERY IMPERFECTLY RECOGNIZED IN PRACTICE. BUT IN THEORY IT IS
MTH4 II SD(182) THE ENVOY, A TYPICAL POLITICIAN, LOOKS LIKE AN IMPERFECTLY REFORMED CRIMINAL DISGUISED BY A GOOD TAILOR.
2TRU II SD(51) ANNOUNCING THE APPROACH OF A POWERFUL AND VERY IMPERFECTLY SILENCED MOTOR BICYCLE FROM THE SIDE OPPOSITE TO
BARB I SD(259) AT THE MOST INOPPORTUNE MOMENTS INTO PAROXYSMS OF IMPERFECTLY SUPPRESSED LAUGHTER. CUSINS IS A SPECTACLED
PPP (199) HIS HAIR NEEDED CUTTING OR HIS COUNTENANCE WAS IMPERFECTLY WASHED, I POINTED IT OUT TO HIM. THE TROUBLE
BARB I (260) (LOMAX ENTERS, CONTROLLING HIS FEATURES VERY IMPERFECTLY , AND PLACES HIMSELF VAGUELY BETWEEN SARAH AND

IMPERIAL

DEVL EPILOG (80) ARE APT TO BE DISRUPTIONISTS AS REGARDS THAT IMPERIAL ANCIENT OF DAYS, THE EMPIRE OF CHINA. BOTH ARE
SIM II (56) IN THE WORLD. AND YET, LOOK! THERE IS THE IMPERIAL ARMADA, IN WHICH EVERY PETTY PROVINCE INSISTS ON
CATH 2,SD(174) MIDDLE OF THE ROOM, STANDS A GILT CHAIR, WITH THE IMPERIAL ARMS CARVED AND THE IMPERIAL MONOGRAM EMBROIDERED.
BULL PREFACE(31) CLING CLOSER THAN BROTHERS TO THAT AND ANY OTHER IMPERIAL ASSET THAT CAN BE EXPLOITED FOR THE PROTECTION OF
CATH 2 (179) WITHOUT PERFORMING ACROBATIC FEATS IN THE IMPERIAL BED. /EDSTASTON/ I KNOW NOTHING ABOUT HER MAJESTY'S
CATH 1 (172) GO AND LOOK THROUGH THE KEYHOLE OF THE IMPERIAL BED-CHAMBER; AND BRING ME WORD WHETHER THE EMPRESS
LION II SD(127) THE ARENA DESCENDS FROM THE FLOOR LEVEL UNDER THE IMPERIAL BOX. ON BOTH SIDES OF THIS PASSAGE STEPS ASCEND TO
CYMB V (149) FOR BY THIS GENTLEMAN'S REPORT AND MINE I HOPE IMPERIAL CAESAR WILL REKNIT HIS FAVOUR WITH THE RADIANT
ROCK PREFACE(188) FEAR OF IT AND NOW FEAR WORSE THAN EVER, FEAR OF IMPERIAL CAESAR, THE IDOL YOU HAVE YOURSELF CREATED, AND
CATH 2,SD(174) LITTLE IN FRONT OF THE LINE OF COURTIERS, BY THE IMPERIAL CHAIR. SILENCE, BROKEN ONLY BY THE YAWNS AND
LION I (112) FACT THAT YOU MAY BE CALLED ON TO APPEAR IN THE IMPERIAL CIRCUS AT ANY TIME FROM TOMORROW ONWARDS ACCORDING
SUPR PREFACE(R28) AND MELODRAMAS ARE BLUSTERING ABOUT OUR IMPERIAL DESTINY; BUT OUR EYES AND HEARTS TURN EAGERLY TO
MILL PREFACE(114) SOCIAL OUTLOOK. HIS ASSUMPTION OF THE IMPERIAL DIADEM, HIS RIDICULOUS ATTEMPT TO ESTABLISH THE
MILL PREFACE(114) MAKE A COURT FOR HIMSELF, HIS SILLY INSISTENCE ON IMPERIAL ETIQUETTE WHEN HE WAS A DETHRONED AND MORIBUND
SIM II (57) OF THE PORT EARNESTLY BEGS THE COMMANDERS OF THE IMPERIAL FLEET TO SUSPEND ACTION FOR ANOTHER DAY, AS HIS
SUPR HANDBOK(198) HER HEAD WAS OFF. AND WHAT CAME OF IT ALL? THE IMPERIAL FRANCE OF THE ROUGON MACQUART FAMILY, AND THE
LION I (112) TO DEFEND THEMSELVES, IF THEY CHOOSE, AGAINST THE IMPERIAL GLADIATORS. /LAVINIA/ CAPTAIN: IS THERE NO HOPE
ANNA (296) HE TURNS IMPRESSIVELY TO THE GRAND DUCHESS) YOUR IMPERIAL HIGHNESS DESIRES ME TO ADDRESS YOU AS COMRADE?
ANNA (299) DAMN THEIR TRIFLING! /STRAMMFEST/ I THANK YOUR IMPERIAL HIGHNESS FROM THE BOTTOM OF MY HEART FOR THAT
INCA (249) AS FAR AS I CAN RECOLLECT THE NAME, IT IS HIS IMPERIAL HIGHNESS PRINCE EITEL WILLIAM FREDERICK GEORGE
ANNA (302) /STRAMMFEST/ I AM AT A LOSS TO UNDERSTAND YOUR IMPERIAL HIGHNESS. YOU SEEM TO ME TO CONTRADICT YOURSELF.
ANNA (296) WHY DONT YOU LAUGH? DONT YOU APPRECIATE HER IMPERIAL HIGHNESS'S JOKE? /SCHNEIDEKIND/ (SUDDENLY
ANNA (297) ETERNALLY IMPOSSIBLE, THAT A DAUGHTER OF THE IMPERIAL HOUSE SHOULD SPEAK TO ANYONE ALONE, WERE IT EVEN
BULL PREFACE(34) HE HAS BEEN SATURATED FROM HIS YOUTH UP WITH THE IMPERIAL IDEA OF FOREIGN RULE BY A SPIRITUALLY SUPERIOR
BULL PREFACE(10) BE VERY MUCH OBLIGED TO HIM, WHICH IS THE MODERN IMPERIAL IDEA. TO SINGE THE KING OF SPAIN'S BEARD; PICK HIS
PYGM PREFACE(199) REVIEW TO COMMISSION AN ARTICLE FROM SWEET ON THE IMPERIAL IMPORTANCE OF HIS SUBJECT. WHEN IT ARRIVED, IT
CLEO PRO1 (92) ACCUSTOMED TO THIS KIND OF KILLING; FOR THOU HAST IMPERIAL INSTINCTS. WILT THOU THEREFORE KILL THE LESSER DOG
PYGM PREFACE(199) THAN OF PHONETICS. ONCE, IN THE DAYS WHEN THE IMPERIAL INSTITUTE ROSE IN SOUTH KENSINGTON, AND JOSEPH
GENV PREFACE(22) TO THE LEFT ARE DEMOCRATIC AND THOSE TO THE RIGHT IMPERIAL . THEY ARE ONLY SWINGS FROM FAILURE TO FAILURE TO
BULL PREFACE(56) NATIVE COURTS SET UP TO FLATTER OUR SENSE OF IMPERIAL JUSTICE HAD, APPARENTLY, ABOUT AS MUCH TO DO WITH
CATH 2 (179) HER. (TO CATHERINE) TRUST ME: HE HAS SEEN YOUR IMPERIAL MAJESTY BEFORE. /CATHERINE/ (TO EDSTASTON) YOU
CATH 2 (174) HER ACCENT IS GERMAN). /NARYSHKIN/ (FORMALLY) HER IMPERIAL MAJESTY IS AWAKE. (THE COURT FALLS ON ITS KNEES).
INCA (254) BUT YOU KNOW NOW THAT BENEATH THE TRAPPINGS OF IMPERIAL MAJESTY THERE IS A MAN: SIMPLE, FRANK, MODEST,
CATH 4 (193) STEADY, DEAREST: IT IS THE EMPRESS. CALL HER YOUR IMPERIAL MAJESTY, CALL HER STAR OF THE NORTH, LITTLE MOTHER,
CATH 2 (179) SAME, YOU WERE VERY VERY VERY ANXIOUS TO SEE HER IMPERIAL MAJESTY. YOU BLUSHED WHEN THE PRINCE SPOKE OF HER.
INCA (254) HAS COME FOR ME TO MAKE A REVELATION. IT IS YOUR IMPERIAL MAJESTY'S TURN NOW TO BRACE YOURSELF. TO STEEL
INCA (245) TO PRESENT YOU WITH THIS TRIFLING TOKEN OF HIS IMPERIAL MAJESTY'S REGARD. I DO CONSIDER THEM SATISFACTORY.
CATH 2 (178) PRINCESS DASHKOFF/ SCANDALOUS! AN INSULT TO YOUR IMPERIAL MAJESTY! /CATHERINE/ DASHKOFF: YOU HAVE NO SENSE
LION I (112) INTO THE ARENA WITH THE WILD BEASTS OF THE IMPERIAL MENAGERIE, AND WILL SUFFER THE CONSEQUENCES. THE
MILL IV (207) OUT THE PRIME MINISTER. HE HAS BOWLED OUT THE IMPERIAL METALLURGICAL TRUST. HE HAS SETTLED THE WIDOW'S
BULL PREFACE(64) CITIZENS? IS IT NOT CLEARLY BECAUSE THE WHOLE IMPERIAL MILITARY SYSTEM OF COERCION AND TERRORISM IS
ANNA (298) (MAKING AN IMPULSIVE MOVEMENT TOWARDS HER) MY IMPERIAL MISTRESS -- /THE GRAND DUCHESS/ STOP. I HAVE ONE
CATH 2,SD(174) GILT CHAIR, WITH THE IMPERIAL ARMS CARVED AND THE IMPERIAL MONOGRAM EMBROIDERED. THE COURT IS IN ATTENDANCE,
LION PREFACE(99) WOULD PRACTICALLY DISQUALIFY HIM FOR HIGH IMPERIAL OFFICE. A CALVINIST VICEROY OF INDIA AND A
BULL PREFACE(9) TIGHT LITTLE ISLAND," DESPISED SPAIN FOR HER IMPERIAL POLICY, AND SAW HER LOSE HER PLACE, NOT ONLY AMONG
DEST (193) YOU ON BUSINESS PRINCIPLES; HE ENSLAVES YOU ON IMPERIAL PRINCIPLES; HE BULLIES YOU ON MANLY PRINCIPLES; HE
SIM II (57) THREE: " I HAVE REPEATEDLY INFORMED YOU THAT THE IMPERIAL PROVINCE OF HOLY ISLAND DEMANDS THE IMMEDIATE AND
ROCK II (260) GREATEST LAND, AND THE BIRTHPLACE OF THE NOBLEST IMPERIAL RACE, THAT EVER GOD CREATED. /SIR ARTHUR/ LOUD AND
CATH 4,SD(188) TO ALLOW CATHERINE TO ENTER. SHE IS IN FULL IMPERIAL REGALIA, AND STOPS STERNLY JUST WHERE SHE HAS
HART PREFACE(39) OF FIGHTING FOR HIS COUNTRY AGAINST ENGLAND; IMPERIAL ROMANOFF, SAID TO HAVE PERISHED MISERABLY BY A MORE
DOCT PREFACE(72) REACTION AGAINST THE VOLUPTUOUS BATHING OF THE IMPERIAL ROMANS WHICH MADE DIRTY HABITS A PART OF CHRISTIAN
SUPR HANDBOK(202) ON THE HEAD ARE SO COMMON A PART OF OUR IMPERIAL ROUTINE THAT THE LAST DOZEN OF THEM HAS NOT CALLED
BULL PREFACE(70) HANDS AND KNEES. THE EFFECT WAS TO MAKE BRITISH IMPERIAL RULE RIDICULOUS IN EUROPE, AND IMPLACABLY RESENTED
LION II (135) CONQUER: CAESAR HIMSELF WILL NOT BE SAFE IN HIS IMPERIAL SEAT IF ONCE THAT SPIRIT GETS LOOSE IN ME. OH,
CLEO PRO1 (92) POWER CRUMBLED IN HIS HAND, EVEN AS THE POWER OF IMPERIAL SPAIN CRUMBLED WHEN IT WAS SET AGAINST YOUR FATHERS
PLES PREFACE(R19) PROGRESS, SCIENCE, MORALS, RELIGION, PATRIOTISM, IMPERIAL SUPREMACY, NATIONAL GREATNESS AND ALL THE OTHER
MILL PREFACE(133) APPLE CART. IT SEEMED AN ASTUTE STROKE OF GERMAN IMPERIAL TACTICS TO SEND LENIN SAFELY THROUGH GERMANY TO
POSN PREFACE(397) BE DEMOLISHED, AS WAS THE CASE RECENTLY WITH THE IMPERIAL THEATRE AFTER IT HAD PASSED INTO THE HANDS OF THE
LION EPILOG (148) PULPIT MAY BE AS PERILOUS TO A MAN'S SOUL AS AN IMPERIAL THRONE. ALL MY ARTICULATE CHRISTIANS, THE READER
LION PREFACE(18) SOONER OR LATER TO VERY EMINENT PERSONS IN ROMAN IMPERIAL TIMES, AND THAT MODERN THEOLOGIANS, FAR FROM
CATH 4 (189) ASK YOUR MAJESTY NOT TO PUT THE POINT OF YOUR IMPERIAL TOE BETWEEN MY RIBS. I AM TICKLESOME. /CATHERINE/
LION PREFACE(18) INTERPOLATION BORROWED FROM THE GREEK AND ROMAN IMPERIAL TRADITION. BUT EXPERIENCE SHEWS THAT SIMULTANEOUS
SIM II (55) HERE IS A CABLEGRAM FROM THE LEAGUE OF BRITISH IMPERIAL WOMANHOOD, VANCOUVER AND PRETORIA. " BURN HIM ALIVE

IMPERIALISM

MIS. (148) SHEW IT TO YOU TOMORROW. THATS THE GOOD SIDE OF IMPERIALISM : IT'S UNSELFISH. I DESPISE THE LITTLE
SUPR PREFACE(R28) A WAVE FROM A FLAG OR A BLAST FROM A BRASS BAND? IMPERIALISM ? NOT A BIT OF IT. OBSEQUIOUSNESS, SERVILITY,
MTH2 (63) SOCIETY OF HIS OWN DAY BY AGREEING TO CALL HIS IMPERIALISM CHRISTIANITY. MIND: I MUST NOT GO AHEAD OF THE
LION EPILOG (152) VERY CLEAR AND FAIR EXPOSITION OF AUTOCRATIC IMPERIALISM GIVEN BY THE ROMAN CAPTAIN TO HIS CHRISTIAN
SUPR HANDBOK(218) DISCOVERY OF A TRUSTWORTHY ANTHROPOMETRIC METHOD. IMPERIALISM . EXCESS OF INSULARITY MAKES A BRITON AN
BULL III (136) UNION JACK-- THAT DETESTABLE SYMBOL OF A DECADENT IMPERIALISM -- BE REPLACED BY A FLAG AS GREEN AS THE ISLAND

IMPERIALIST

LADY PREFACE(212) THE ATHEIST A CATHOLIC MYSTIC, TO THE BISMARCKIAN IMPERIALIST AN ANACHARSIS KLOOTZ, TO ANACHARSIS KLOOTZ A
GENV PREFACE(12) TO BE TOLERATED AS AN INSTITUTION, WAR AND IMPERIALIST DIPLOMACY PERSIST NONE THE LESS. CIVILIZATION'S
BULL PREFACE(10) INVINCIBLE ARMADA FOR LITTLE ENGLAND, THE MODERN IMPERIALIST DOES NOT BELIEVE IN THE LORD OF HOSTS; BUT THE
GENV I (36) IT. /NEWCOMER/ NO: I DONT HOLD WITH KIPLING. TOO IMPERIALIST FOR ME. I'M A DEMOCRAT. /SHE/ BUT NOT A BUSINESS
BULL PREFACE(63) PRESENCE OF THE VICTIMS' FAMILIES UNDER THE LATE IMPERIALIST GOVERNMENT), NOT ONLY PERMITTED AND DEFENDED THE

FOUN (216)	WELL, MADAM, TO MAKE HIM A CONSERVATIVE AND AN	IMPERIALIST	I SHOULD HAVE TO RAISE HIS SALARY VERY
SUPR HANDBOK(218)	MAKES A COLONIST AN IMPERIALIST. A COLONIAL	IMPERIALIST	IS ONE WHO RAISES COLONIAL TROOPS, EQUIPS A
SUPR HANDBOK(218)	OF LOCAL SELF-ASSERTION MAKES A COLONIST AN	IMPERIALIST	. A COLONIAL IMPERIALIST IS ONE WHO RAISES
SUPR HANDBOK(218)	EXCESS OF INSULARITY MAKES A BRITON AN	IMPERIALIST	. EXCESS OF LOCAL SELF-ASSERTION MAKES A
DEVL EPILOG (79)	IT IS SUFFICIENT TO SAY THAT BURGOYNE WAS AN	IMPERIALIST	. HE SYMPATHIZED WITH THE COLONISTS; BUT WHEN
ROCK PREFACE(174)	ARE SILENT ABOUT THE SUPPRESSION OF LIBERTY IN	IMPERIALIST	JAPAN, THOUGH IN JAPAN IT IS A CRIME TO HAVE "
ROCK PREFACE(157)	HE WAS A RIOTER AND A COMMUNIST. FROM THE ROMAN	IMPERIALIST	POINT OF VIEW HE WAS A TRAITOR. FROM THE
APPL II (258)	OWE AMERICA THAT OLD WAR DEBT. AND WITH A MAD	IMPERIALIST	PRESIDENT LIKE BOSSFIELD! NO YOU WOULDNT, MY
LION EPILOG (152)	CAPTAIN TO HIS CHRISTIAN PRISONERS. NO ENGLISH	IMPERIALIST	WAS INTELLIGENT AND EARNEST ENOUGH TO DO THE
DOCT PREFACE(14)	BELIEVES THAT THERE IS NOTHING LIKE LEATHER. THE	IMPERIALIST	WHO REGARDS THE CONQUEST OF ENGLAND BY A FOREIGN
SUPR HANDBOK(218)	INTO INSOLUBLE CONFLICT WITH THE INSULAR BRITISH	IMPERIALIST	, " CUTS THE PAINTER" AND BREAKS UP THE EMPIRE.
		IMPERIALISTS	
MTH2 (52)	OF SOCIALISTS AND ANTI-SOCIALISTS, OF JINGO	IMPERIALISTS	AND LITTLE ENGLANDERS, OF CAST-IRON
METH PREFACE(R16)	UNDER SUCH CIRCUMSTANCES EXCEPT TO MILITARIST	IMPERIALISTS	IN CHRONIC TERROR OF INVASION AND SUBJUGATION,
SIM PREFACE(18)	AS WELL TO REMIND OUR WESTERN AND VERY INSULAR	IMPERIALISTS	THAT MARRIAGE IN THE BRITISH EMPIRE IS
		IMPERIALLY	
PHIL III SD(136)	SCORN; SWEEPS ACROSS TO THE COUCH; AND SITS DOWN	IMPERIALLY	. WITH A GREAT SIGH OF RELIEF HE DROPS INTO
BULL PREFACE(64)	GREY AS VALID THAT MAIN ASSET OF " THINKING	IMPERIALLY	," THE CONVICTION THAT WE ARE ALL GOING TO BE
		IMPERIL	
JOAN 4 (108)	(RISING ALSO, BUT IN PROTEST) I WILL NOT	IMPERIL	MY SOUL. I WILL UPHOLD THE JUSTICE OF THE CHURCH. I
2TRU II (55)	DOES WHEN ON ACTIVE SERVICE ANY ACT CALCULATED TO	IMPERIL	THE SUCCESS OF HIS MAJESTY'S FORCES OR ANY PART
		IMPERILLING	
MIS. (202)	YET LOWER AND BE AN ACTRESS OR AN OPERA SINGER,	IMPERILLING	MY SOUL BY THE WICKED LIE OF PRETENDING TO BE
		IMPERIOUS	
3PLA PREFACE(R18)	HAVE VITALITY ENOUGH TO MAKE ANY OF OUR INSTINCTS	IMPERIOUS	: WE CAN BE MADE TO LIVE ON PRETENCES, AS THE
GETT SD(295)	OR SCEPTICISM, CARRY EVERYTHING BEFORE THEM.	IMPERIOUS	AND DOGMATIC, SHE TAKES COMMAND OF THE PARTY AT
INCA (255)	AUDIENCE (SHE FALLS BACK INTO HER SEAT AT THE	IMPERIOUS	WAVE OF HIS HAND) SO (HE CLICKS HIS HEELS).
		IMPERIOUSLY	
ARMS I SD(4)	MOTHER, CATHERINE PETKOFF, A WOMAN OVER FORTY,	IMPERIOUSLY	ENERGETIC, WITH MAGNIFICENT BLACK HAIR AND EYES,
CATH 2 (177)	/PATIOMKIN/ DONT SCOLD, LL MOTHER. /CATHERINE/ (	IMPERIOUSLY	) GO. /PATIOMKIN/ (RISING UNSTEADILY) YES: GO.
NEVR IV (297)	SIT DOWN. /M'COMAS/ I-- /BOHUN/ (WAVING HIM DOWN	IMPERIOUSLY	) NO: SIT DOWN, SIT DOWN. M'COMAS SITS DOWN
CATH 4 (194)	BAND STRIKES UP A REDOWA. /CATHERINE/ (CALLING	IMPERIOUSLY	) PATIOMKIN! (THE MUSIC STOPS SUDDENLY). HERE!
SIM PRO,3, (32)	THE IMAGES. /THE PRIESTESS/ (CALLING AFTER HER	IMPERIOUSLY	) WHERE HAVE YOU SPENT ETERNITY SO FAR, MAY I
KING I (187)	JAMES II, COMES IN PRECIPITATELY. /JAMES/ (	IMPERIOUSLY	) WHERE IS HIS MAJESTY THE KING? /NEWTON/ (
CLEO IV (176)	HE NOT ESCAPED? /RUFIO/ NO. /CAESAR/ (RISING	IMPERIOUSLY	) WHY NOT? YOU HAVE BEEN GUARDING THIS MAN
MILL IV (204)	COME HERE (SHE STRETCHES OUT HER HAND TO HIM	IMPERIOUSLY	). /THE DOCTOR/ (COMING TO HER AND FEELING HER
MTH4 II SD(182)	IN UNDER THE PORTICO. ZOO IMMEDIATELY COMES OUT	IMPERIOUSLY	TO NAPOLEON'S RIGHT, WHILST THE ENVOY'S WIFE
INCA (240)	PRINCESS SITS DOWN FORLORNLY. ERMYNTRUDE TURNS	IMPERIOUSLY	TO THE MANAGER). HER HIGHNESS WILL REQUIRE THIS
		IMPERISHABLE	
DOCT V (177)	YOU DID NOT PAINT THOSE PICTURES WHICH ARE MY	IMPERISHABLE	JOY AND PRIDE: YOU DID NOT SPEAK THE WORDS THAT
DOCT V (177)	YOU ARE HAPPY. YOU ARE WELL. HIS WORKS ARE AN	IMPERISHABLE	JOY AND PRIDE FOR YOU. /JENNIFER/ AND YOU THINK
FANY PROLOG (258)	FROM THE PAST A VAST TREASURE OF BEAUTY-- OF	IMPERISHABLE	MASTERPIECES OF POETRY, OF PAINTING, OF
APPL I (237)	SHOULD HAVE UNBREAKABLE GLASS, UNBREAKABLE STEEL,	IMPERISHABLE	MATERIALS OF ALL SORTS. BUT FOR THEM OUR GOODS
		IMPERSONAL	
MIS. PREFACE(85)	THE CHILD IS NOT. WOE TO THE OLD IF THEY HAVE NO	IMPERSONAL	INTERESTS, NO CONVICTIONS, NO PUBLIC CAUSES TO
MIS. PREFACE(36)	THAT ITS DISCIPLINE IS THE DISCIPLINE OF	IMPERSONAL	NECESSITY, NOT THAT OF WANTON PERSONAL COERCION.
MILL PREFACE(112)	DIFFICULTIES AS WELL AS OUT OF ETERNAL AND	IMPERSONAL	ONES. AS LONG AS AN INDIVIDUAL OF THEIR CALIBRE
GETT PREFACE(223)	IT, AND LEGISLATE ON IT, WHOLLY AS IF IT WERE AN	IMPERSONAL	ONE, IS TO MAKE A HIGHER DEMAND THAN MOST PEOPLE
GETT PREFACE(225)	DOCTRINAIRES ARE ALSO THE DULL PEOPLE. THE	IMPERSONAL	RELATION OF SEX MAY BE JUDICIALLY RESERVED FOR
CLEO NOTES (209)	OF TRAVEL AND CAMPAIGN HISTORIES IN A STYLE SO	IMPERSONAL	THAT THE AUTHENTICITY OF THE LATER VOLUMES IS
GETT PREFACE(223)	IT IS VERY HARD TO MAKE AN AVERAGE CITIZEN TAKE	IMPERSONAL	VIEWS OF ANY SORT IN MATTERS AFFECTING PERSONAL
GETT PREFACE(223)	AT THOSE WHO ARE ASHAMED OF IT. UNPOPULARITY OF	IMPERSONAL	VIEWS. UNFORTUNATELY IT IS VERY HARD TO MAKE AN
GETT PREFACE(207)	ENDS IN VIEW: HIS BEING PUBLIC, FARSIGHTED, AND	IMPERSONAL	, AND THOSE OF MULTITUDES OF THE ELECTORATE
SUPR PREFACE(R23)	OF OTHERS. HERE WOMAN MEETS A PURPOSE AS	IMPERSONAL	, AS IRRESISTIBLE AS HER OWN; AND THE CLASH IS
GETT PREFACE(223)	THAT WE SHOULD DEAL WITH THE SEXUAL RELATION AS	IMPERSONAL	, IT SEEMS TO THEM TO MEAN THAT WE SHOULD
		IMPERSONALITY	
GETT PREFACE(223)	HENCE THEIR RECOIL FROM IT. BUT PROMISCUITY AND	IMPERSONALITY	ARE NOT THE SAME THING. NO MAN EVER YET FELL
GETT PREFACE(223)	AS " A STEADY IMPROVEMENT IN GENERAL MORALITY."	IMPERSONALITY	IS NOT PROMISCUITY. THERE IS, TOO, A REALLY
GETT PREFACE(219)	EVEN UNDER THE MOST UNNATURAL CONDITIONS. THE	IMPERSONALITY	OF SEX. IT IS NECESSARY TO LAY SOME STRESS ON
		IMPERSONALLY	
MTH3 (124)	MR PRESIDENT. BUT LET US LOOK AT THE POSITION	IMPERSONALLY	. CAN YOU DENY THAT WHAT IS HAPPENING IS THAT
		IMPERSONATE	
METH PREFACE(R66)	ANYBODY IF THERE HAD NOT BEEN SOMEBODADDY TO	IMPERSONATE	. WE DID NOT SEE THE SIGNIFICANCE OF THE FACT
MRS PREFACE(163)	TO RESTRAIN SIR HENRY IRVING FROM PRESUMING TO	IMPERSONATE	SAMSON OR DAVID ON THE STAGE, THOUGH ANY OTHER
		IMPERSONATED	
METH PREFACE(R66)	THAT, IN SHORT, NOBODADDY COULD NOT HAVE	IMPERSONATED	ANYBODY IF THERE HAD NOT BEEN SOMEBODADDY TO
SUPR IV (149)	YOUVE OPENED A LETTER ADDRESSED TO ME. YOUVE	IMPERSONATED	ME AND STOLEN A MARCH ON THIS LADY. THATS
MRS PREFACE(178)	AGAINST INDECENCY. IT SUMMONED THE ACTRESS WHO	IMPERSONATED	MRS WARREN TO THE POLICE COURT, AND OFFERED HER
		IMPERSONATES	
SUPR PREFACE(R31)	FROM MOZART; AND I HEREBY AUTHORIZE ANY ACTOR WHO	IMPERSONATES	HIM, TO SING " DALLA SUA PACE" (IF HE CAN) AT
SUPR PREFACE(R11)	NOT SO THE ENGLISH ACTRESS. THE HEROINE SHE	IMPERSONATES	IS NOT ALLOWED TO DISCUSS THE ELEMENTAL
UNPL PREFACE(R23)	RELIGIOUS CONDITIONS UNDER WHICH THE CHARACTER HE	IMPERSONATES	IS SUPPOSED TO BE ACTING. DEFINITE CONCEPTIONS
		IMPERSONATING	
HART I (50)	SO DO NOT TRY TO INGRATIATE YOURSELF HERE BY	IMPERSONATING	HER (HE WALKS FIRMLY AWAY TO THE OTHER SIDE
		IMPERSONATOR	
CATH PREFACE(158)	KINGSTON, WHO FIRST MADE HER REPUTATION AS AN	IMPERSONATOR	OF THE MOST DELIGHTFULLY FEATHER-HEADED AND
		IMPERTINENCE	
SUPR HANDBOK(217)	IF YOU ARE ON GOOD TERMS WITH YOURSELF IT IS AN	IMPERTINENCE	: IF ON BAD, AN INJURY. THE GOLDEN RULE IS THAT
DEST (171)	STRUGGLING WITH HAPPY TEARS) YES, I KNOW IT IS AN	IMPERTINENCE	IN ME TO TELL YOU WHAT YOU MUST KNOW FAR BETTER
MTH4 I (144)	UNDER HIS CHIN. /THE GENTLEMAN/ THIS IS A GROSS	IMPERTINENCE	. AN INSULT. /THE WOMAN/ (REPLACING HER
SUPR I (21)	TO THINK THAT GRANNY IS RATHER A PIECE OF	IMPERTINENCE	. BUT I NEVER DREAMT OF ITS HURTING YOU.
CAND I SD(79)	OCCASION, TO INTERFERE IN THEIR BUSINESS WITHOUT	IMPERTINENCE	. HIS WELL-SPRING OF ENTHUSIASM AND SYMPATHETIC
PHIL II SD(95)	THE BOOKSTAND TO SEE WHO IS THE AUTHOR OF THIS	IMPERTINENCE	. /PARAMORE/ (TO SYLVIA, STIFFLY) I BEG YOUR
FANY EPILOG (328)	THING HAS AMUSING PASSAGES. DISMISS THE REST AS	IMPERTINENCE	. /THE COUNT/ MR TROTTER: IT IS EASY FOR YOU TO
BULL III (137)	MY SAYING THESE FEW WORDS: NOBODY FEELS THEIR	IMPERTINENCE	MORE THAN I DO. GOOD MORNING, GENTLEMEN. HE
UNPL PREFACE(R14)	ON THE CONTRARY, I STRENUOUSLY RESENT THAT	IMPERTINENCE	ON HIS PART. BUT I MUST SUBMIT IN ORDER TO
SUPR I (9)	I MUST SAY THAT OF ALL THE CONFOUNDED PIECES OF	IMPERTINENCE	-- WELL, IF THESE ARE ANARCHIST MANNERS, I HOPE
ARMS II (39)	WILL BE ALL OVER BETWEEN YOU. /RAINA/ (WITH COOL	IMPERTINENCE	) OH, I KNOW SERGIUS IS YOUR PET. I SOMETIMES
GETT (324)	THE ROOF? /HOTCHKISS/ I REMEMBER THAT DEPLORABLE	IMPERTINENCE	WITH SHAME AND CONFUSION. YOU WERE KIND ENOUGH
BULL IV (180)	THE OTHER. /LARRY/ IN EITHER CASE IT WOULD BE AN	IMPERTINENCE	, MR KEEGAN, AS YOUR APPROVAL IS NOT OF THE
HART PREFACE(20)	ABOUT THE LUSITANIA SEEMED ALMOST A HEARTLESS	IMPERTINENCE	, THOUGH I WAS WELL ACQUAINTED PERSONALLY WITH

CLEO II SD(133)	TO GOVERN. CAESAR, QUITE DUMBFOUNDED BY THIS	IMPERTINENCE	, TURNS IN HIS CHAIR AND STARES AT HER.
GETT (294)	BY THIS? WHAT THE-- /REGINALD/ CONFOUND YOUR	IMPERTINENCE	, WHAT DO YOU-- (BOTH HIGHLY INCENSED)
SUPR III (139)	ALL ENJOYED YOUR VISITS VERY MUCH. /VIOLET/ WHAT	IMPERTINENCE	! (SHE TURNS HER BACK ON HIM, AND GOES UP THE
BARB III (343)	OR I WILL KILL YOU. BUT YOUR LOVE! DAMN YOUR	IMPERTINENCE	! /CUSINS/ (GRINNING) I MAY NOT BE ABLE TO
		IMPERTINENCES	
CATH PREFACE(158)	IN THE CASE WHICH IS PROVOKING ME TO ALL THESE	IMPERTINENCES	, I AM QUITE SURE THAT MISS GERTRUDE KINGSTON,
		IMPERTINENT	
3PLA PREFACE(R20)	ON ITS SCIENTIFIC PLANE: NOTHING COULD BE MORE	IMPERTINENT	AND IRRITATING. YET MR WELLS HAS HAD TO PRETEND
LION II (132)	SAYING WHAT THEY LIKE TO ME. THEY ARE ALMOST AS	IMPERTINENT	AS THE GLADIATORS. WHICH IS THE GREEK SORCERER?
KING I (167)	TO SAY TO ISAAC NEWTON. IT IS NOT ALTOGETHER AN	IMPERTINENT	CURIOSITY. MY TRADE, WHICH IS A VERY UNUSUAL
CATH 3 (186)	HOLY NICHOLAS, LITTLE BEAUTY. /CLAIRE/ DONT BE	IMPERTINENT	. HOW CAN I GET ADMISSION TO THE PALACE? /THE
HART II (110)	GO, ESPECIALLY IF HE IS GOING TO BE GREEDY AND	IMPERTINENT	. /THE BURGLAR/ (QUICKLY) ALL RIGHT, LADY, ALL
FANY PROLOG (268)	OF THE WHOLE CAMBRIDGE FABIAN SOCIETY, KITTENS.	IMPERTINENT	LITTLE KITTENS. BLAME THEM. SMACK THEM. I GUESS
GLIM (182)	BE ASKED FOR FAVORS, GIULIACCIA, NOT TO BE ASKED	IMPERTINENT	QUESTIONS. /GIULIA/ WHAT WOULD YOU DO IF A
PYGM I (212)	DAUGHTER/ (VIOLENTLY) WILL YOU PLEASE KEEP YOUR	IMPERTINENT	REMARKS TO YOURSELF. /THE NOTE TAKER/ DID I SAY
CAPT I (236)	OF THESE QUESTIONS, WHICH STRIKE HIM AS SOMEWHAT	IMPERTINENT	) LET US COME TO BUSINESS, IF YOU PLEASE. WE ARE
GETT (269)	MY DEAR LESBIA: YOU KNOW I DONT WISH TO BE	IMPERTINENT	; BUT THESE ARE NOT CORRECT VIEWS FOR AN ENGLISH
AUGS (278)	MADE A COPY OF THAT PAPER. /AUGUSTUS/ KEEP YOUR	IMPERTINENT	SURMISES TO YOURSELF, SIR. REMEMBER THAT YOU ARE
CAPT II (250)	IS SUBJECT TO FITS OF INSOLENCE. IF HE IS	IMPERTINENT	TO YOUR LADYSHIP, OR DISOBEDIENT, YOU HAVE MY
BULL I (92)	HIM WITH SOMETHING LIKE AWE). I DONT WISH TO BE	IMPERTINENT	, AS YOU KNOW, LARRY; BUT ARE YOU SURE SHE HAS
DEST (175)	(OFFENDED, COMING OFF THE TABLE) YOU ARE	IMPERTINENT	, MADAM. /LADY/ (HUMBLY) I BEG YOUR PARDON.
		IMPERTINENTLY	
CLEO IV (167)	FOOL. DO YOU KNOW WHY I ALLOW YOU ALL TO CHATTER	IMPERTINENTLY	JUST AS YOU PLEASE, INSTEAD OF TREATING YOU AS
		IMPERTURBABILITY	
HART II (124)	COOL AND IMPERTURBABLE IN THE FACE OF A BURGLAR.	IMPERTURBABILITY	IS ALMOST TOO STRONG A POINT OF MINE. BUT (
ARMS II SD(23)	VALUES HIMSELF ON HIS RANK IN SERVITUDE, AND THE	IMPERTURBABILITY	OF THE ACCURATE CALCULATOR WHO HAS NO
		IMPERTURBABLE	
POSN PREFACE(372)	IN ACTING ENABLED ME TO MAINTAIN AN APPEARANCE OF	IMPERTURBABLE	GOOD-HUMOR, WAS EQUALLY FURIOUS. THE FRICTION
HART II (124)	HERE. I HAVE REMAINED ABSOLUTELY COOL AND	IMPERTURBABLE	IN THE FACE OF A BURGLAR. IMPERTURBABILITY IS
DEVL III (69)	REASON FOR OUR GIVING WAY. /BURGOYNE/ (	IMPERTURBABLE	) SUPPOSE I RESIGN MY COMMAND TO YOU. WHAT
NEVR I (210)	THE CLANDONS LOOK SURPRISED, EXCEPT PHIL, WHO IS	IMPERTURBABLE	). IF HE WOULDNT MIND WAITING JUST TWO
		IMPERTURBABLY	
3PLA PREFACE(R26)	OF THE BYRON-ROBERTSON SCHOOL, IN WHICH THE	IMPERTURBABLY	IMPUDENT COMEDIAN, AFTERWARDS SHELVED BY THE
ARMS III (48)	I'LL GIVE YOU SIX TO ONE. /BLUNTSCHLI/ (	IMPERTURBABLY	) IT WOULD BE ROBBING YOU, MAJOR. MADAME IS
NEVR I (205)	/DOLLY/ (EMPHATICALLY) TWENTY-SEVEN. /PHILIP/ (	IMPERTURBABLY	) THIRTY-THREE. /DOLLY/ STUFF. /PHILIP/ (TO
		IMPERVIOUS	
BULL I (90)	COMPARTMENTS, AND ALL THE COMPARTMENTS WARRANTED	IMPERVIOUS	TO ANYTHING IT DOESNT SUIT YOU TO UNDERSTAND.
MRS PREFACE(155)	THEATRICAL, WHILST THE THEATRE ITSELF REMAINS	IMPERVIOUS	TO COMMON SENSE, RELIGION, SCIENCE, POLITICS, AND
FABL PREFACE(63)	PROGRESS, AND GULLIVER'S TRAVELS, STICK IN MINDS	IMPERVIOUS	TO THE EPISTLES OF PAUL, THE SERMONS OF BUNYAN,
METH PREFACE(R9)	SOME MONKEYS HAVE NO TAILS, BUT MY UNCLE WAS AS	IMPERVIOUS	TO WHAT DARWIN REALLY SAID AS ANY NEO-DARWINIAN
		IMPETUOSITY	
JOAN 5 (114)	WE SHOULD CONQUER THE EARTH, NO DOUBT. PLUCK AND	IMPETUOSITY	ARE GOOD SERVANTS IN WAR, BUT BAD MASTERS: THEY
NEVR II (248)	YOU. /CRAMPTON/ YOU! /VALENTINE/ (WITH GROWING	IMPETUOSITY	) YES: I. I SAT NEXT HER; AND I NEVER SAID A
		IMPETUOUS	
PYGM II SD(218)	BUT FOR HIS YEARS AND SIZE, RATHER LIKE A VERY	IMPETUOUS	BABY " TAKING NOTICE" EAGERLY AND LOUDLY, AND
PYGM EPILOG (292)	HER WRATH WHEN HE HAD GONE TOO FAR WITH HIS	IMPETUOUS	BULLYING, AND YOU WILL SEE THAT ELIZA'S INSTINCT
SUPR III SD(87)	HANDSOME FACE, PALER AND COLDER, WITHOUT TANNER'S	IMPETUOUS	CREDULITY AND ENTHUSIASM, AND WITHOUT A TOUCH OF
BARB PREFACE(227)	DUST AND MUD OF THE SLUMS; ROUSING MARCHES AND	IMPETUOUS	DITHYRAMBS RISE TO THE HEAVENS FROM PEOPLE AMONG
DOCT I SD(109)	IS EXCITED AND FLASHES THEM WIDE OPEN; IS SOFTLY	IMPETUOUS	IN HER SPEECH AND SWIFT IN HER MOVEMENTS; AND IS
BULL III SD(125)	MERELY CRUEL AND SENSELESS FUN, AND A VIOLENT AND	IMPETUOUS	INTOLERANCE OF OTHER TEMPERAMENTS AND OTHER
NEVR II (243)	(SERVING GLORIA WITH FOWL) OH NO, MISS: HE'S TOO	IMPETUOUS	. HE'S AT THE BAR. /M'COMAS/ (PATRONIZINGLY) A
MRS III (223)	(HE BOUNDS INTO THE HOUSE). /REV. S./ HE'S SO	IMPETUOUS	. I DONT KNOW WHAT TO DO WITH HIM, MR PRAED.
NEVR II (259)	COURAGE! (HE DRAWS HER TO HIM; KISSES HER WITH	IMPETUOUS	STRENGTH; AND LAUGHS BOYISHLY). NOW YOUVE DONE IT,
GETT SD(295)	HAVE DONE SOMETHING TO SAVE HER HUMANITY; BUT HER	IMPETUOUS	TEMPER AND ENERGETIC WILL, UNRESTRAINED BY ANY
JOAN PREFACE(5)	JOAN WAS A WOMAN OF ACTION, OPERATING WITH	IMPETUOUS	VIOLENCE ON THEIR BODIES. THAT, NO DOUBT, IS WHY
BULL I SD(74)	PORTENTOUSLY SOLEMN, SOMETIMES JOLLY AND	IMPETUOUS	, ALWAYS BUOYANT AND IRRESISTIBLE, MOSTLY
ARMS II (41)	BACK IS TURNED, CATHERINE SWOOPS ON HIM WITH	IMPETUOUS	, URGENT, COAXING APPEAL). CAPTAIN BLUNTSCHLI: I
		IMPETUOUSLY	
CAPT II SD(269)	A LITTLE TOWARDS HIS MEN; AND THE CADI COMES	IMPETUOUSLY	FORWARD BETWEEN HIM AND LADY CICELY. /THE CADI/
BARB II (306)	AND SAVED THROUGH YOU. /CUSINS/ (RETURNING	IMPETUOUSLY	FROM THE SHELTER WITH A FLAG AND A TROMBONE, AND
APPL I SD(209)	A YOUNG LADY, DRESSED FOR WALKING, RUSHES IN	IMPETUOUSLY	. /THE YOUNG LADY/ PAPA: I CANNOT FIND THE
MTH2 SD(41)	AN ITALIAN YOUTH IN A GOZZOLI PICTURE, COMES IN	IMPETUOUSLY	. SHE SEEMS TO HAVE NOTHING ON BUT HER SHORT
6CAL SD(93)	STILL FLYING. THE BLACK PRINCE, AGED 17, ARRIVES	IMPETUOUSLY	PAST THE QUEEN'S TENT, A GROOM RUNNING AFTER
BARB III (330)	FROM THE TOWN WITH A BOUQUET. /LADY BRITOMART/ (	IMPETUOUSLY	) ANDREW: YOU SHOULDNT HAVE LET ME SEE THIS
PHIL III (138)	(HUMBLY) I GRANT YOU THAT, MY DEAR. /JULIA/ (	IMPETUOUSLY	) DONT CALL ME YOUR DEAR. AND WHAT DO YOU MEAN
JOAN 5 (116)	AND PANS THERE'D BE NO NEED OF TINKERS. (RISING	IMPETUOUSLY	) I TELL YOU, BASTARD, YOUR ART OF WAR IS NO
CATH 3 (186)	WILL MAKE YOUR SALVATION HIS CHARGE. /CLAIRE/ (	IMPETUOUSLY	) I WILL GIVE YOU (SHE IS ABOUT TO SAY FIFTY
ANNA (296)	(EAGERLY) WHERE IS THAT? /THE GRAND DUCHESS/ (	IMPETUOUSLY	) IN YOUR IMAGINATION. I CAME ALONE. I AM ALONE.
CAND I (101)	OF FINDING WORDS FOR DIVINE TRUTH. /MARCHBANKS/ (	IMPETUOUSLY	) IT'S THE GIFT OF THE GAB, NOTHING MORE AND
MTH5 (223)	ENDURE ITS VAPID EMPTINESS. (HE MOUNTS THE ALTAR	IMPETUOUSLY	) LISTEN TO ME, ALL OF YOU; AND DO YOU, ECRASIA,
DEVL II (47)	ESSIE! /ESSIE/ (RUNNING IN) YES. /ANDERSON/ (	IMPETUOUSLY	) OFF WITH YOU AS HARD AS YOU CAN RUN, TO THE
CAND I (92)	UNNERSTANNIN. AIN WE, JAMES? /MORELL/ (	IMPETUOUSLY	) OH BOTHER YOUR UNDERSTANDING! YOUVE KEPT ME
JITT III (60)	FATHER. /AGNES/ YOU DARE-- /EDITH/ (CONTINUING	IMPETUOUSLY	) OH, I KNOW VERY WELL HOW TIDY YOU KEPT HIS
APPL I (236)	BEFORE HE BEGINS, IF YOU ASK ME. /LYSISTRATA/ (	IMPETUOUSLY	) WHAT SORT OF ANIMALS ARE YOU -- YOU MEN? THE
GLIM (173)	BRIDE HAS A DOWRY-- /THE GIRL/ (INTERRUPTING HIM	IMPETUOUSLY	) YES, YES: OH BLESSED BE SAINT BARBARA FOR
PHIL III (134)	AWAY FROM HIM). WHAT DO YOU MEAN? /PARAMORE/ (	IMPETUOUSLY	) YOU MUST SEE WHAT I MEAN. CONTRADICT THE RUMOR
ROCK I (233)	THAT WOMAN'S GIVEN ME AN APPETITE. (HE GOES OUT	IMPETUOUSLY	THROUGH THE MASKED DOOR). /HILDA/ (RUSHING
MIS. SD(200)	HER CAP ON, AND HER GOGGLES IN HER HAND, COMES	IMPETUOUSLY	THROUGH THE INNER DOOR. /LINA/ (ON THE STEPS)
ARMS III (72)	OF AN ESTABLISHMENT, HERE GOES! (HE DARTS	IMPETUOUSLY	TO THE TABLE; SEIZES THE PAPERS IN THE BLUE
JOAN 1 (69)	CAN STOP THEM WITH GOD ON OUR SIDE. (SHE RISES	IMPETUOUSLY	, AND GOES AT HIM, UNABLE TO SIT QUIET ANY
		IMPETUS	
O'FL PREFACE(201)	SET A PERILOUS PACE FOR HIM. IRISH SOLDIERS GIVE	IMPETUS	TO THOSE MILITARY OPERATIONS WHICH REQUIRE FOR THEIR
LADY PREFACE(224)	IS NO LONGER SHAKESPEAR: ALL THE BITE, THE	IMPETUS	, THE STRENGTH, THE GRIM DELIGHT IN HIS OWN POWER OF
		IMPIETY	
6CAL (99)	HEAD OR TAIL OF THIS, BOY? IS HE ACCUSING ME OF	IMPIETY	? IF HE IS, BY GOD-- /EUSTACHE/ SIR, IS IT FOR ME
POSN PREFACE(385)	NOTHING BUT CENSORSHIPS, MADE RUTHLESS WAR ON	IMPIETY	AND IMMORALITY. THE RESULT WAS ONCE FAMILIAR TO
JOAN 5 (119)	YOUR OWN HEADSTRONG PRESUMPTION, YOUR OWN	IMPIETY	IN HIDING ALL THESE SINS UNDER THE CLOAK OF A TRUST
CLEO II (119)	WISHED TO SAY THAT THE GODS WOULD NOT SUFFER THE	IMPIETY	OF HIS SISTER TO GO UNPUNISHED. /PTOLEMY/ (HASTILY)
		IMPIOUS	
MILL PREFACE(113)	THE COMMON MAN WILL BELIEVE HIM TO BE INSANE OR	IMPIOUS	: WHEN MEASURES OF THAT COMPLEXION ARE NECESSARY, AS
METH PREFACE(R35)	THAT HIS GUESTS WOULD VANISH PRECIPITATELY IF THE	IMPIOUS	CHALLENGE WERE UTTERED, LEAVING HIM ALONE WITH A
KING I (203)	IT IS TRUE. BUT BEWARE HOW YOU LET THESE BOLD	IMPIOUS	FELLOWS EXTINGUISH HOPE IN YOU. THEIR DAY IS SHORT;

KING I (203) UNCERTAIN PRAISE! THE WORLD IS MADE FOR THE BOLD IMPIOUS MAN WHO STOPS AT NOTHING, SEIZES ALL HE CAN. JUSTICE

IMPISH

LADY PREFACE(224) I LAY STRESS ON THIS IRONY OF SHAKESPEAR'S, THIS IMPISH REJOICING IN PESSIMISM, THIS EXULTATION IN WHAT
LADY PREFACE(223) OF GLOSTER, INTO WHOM SHAKESPEAR PUT ALL HIS OWN IMPISH SUPERIORITY TO VULGAR SENTIMENT, EXCLAIMS " AND THIS

IMPISHLY

CAND III (130) AND ACTUALLY AT EASE WITH MORELL! EVEN IMPISHLY HUMOROUS) WELL? /MORELL/ HAVE YOU ANYTHING TO TELL
BARB II (305) TO TAKE HIS OWN BUSINESS FROM HIM. /CUSINS/ (IMPISHLY) PURE SELF-SACRIFICE ON BODGER'S PART, CLEARLY!

IMPISHNESS

ROCK PREFACE(178) EVEN WITH THE FULLEST ALLOWANCE FOR THE STRAIN OF IMPISHNESS WITH WHICH THE LIFE FORCE ENDOWS THOSE OF US WHO

IMPLACABILITY

METH PREFACE(R62) BY THE EAR. MARX HAD, TOO, WHAT DARWIN HAD NOT: IMPLACABILITY AND A FINE JEWISH LITERARY GIFT, WITH TERRIBLE

IMPLACABLE

NEVR I (211) EXCITEMENT, DIGNIFIED BUT DOGGED, LADYLIKE BUT IMPLACABLE : THE MANNER OF THE OLD GUARD) PHIL: TAKE CARE.
2TRU II (66) ME THAT WHAT WAS TO BE DREADED IN WOMEN WAS THEIR IMPLACABLE CONSTANCY. BUT YOU! FICKLE! I SHOULD THINK SO.
APPL I (222) /LYSISTRATA/ (WHO HAS BEEN LISTENING WITH IMPLACABLE CONTEMPT TO THE DISCUSSION, SUDDENLY BREAKS IN IN
SUPR IV SD(143) BEING A VERY OBVIOUS COCKNEY, INSPIRES HIM WITH IMPLACABLE CONTEMPT, AS A STUPID ENGLISHMAN WHO CANNOT EVEN
ARMS III (56) RATHER FORLORNLY ON HIS CALVES, DAUNTED BY HER IMPLACABLE DISDAIN) YOU HAVE A GREAT AMBITION IN YOU, LOUKA.
CAND I (81) (SHE ENTERS THE ENGAGEMENT IN SILENCE, WITH IMPLACABLE DISPARAGEMENT OF THE HOXTON ANARCHISTS IN EVERY
INCA (255) I SHALL BE BEATEN IN CONSEQUENCE, BECAUSE MY MOST IMPLACABLE ENEMY, THOUGH ONLY FEW MONTHS FURTHER AWAY FROM
NEVR I (220) TO FORGET THEM. (HIS FEATURES SETTLE INTO AN IMPLACABLE FROWN). /DOLLY/ (LOOKING CRITICALLY AT HIM). I
BULL PREFACE(64) BECAUSE I AM HAMPERED, AS AN IRISHMAN, BY MY IMPLACABLE HOSTILITY TO ENGLISH DOMINATION. MISTRUSTING MY
DOCT IV SD(160) IN SPITE OF THEMSELVES, EXCEPT RIDGEON, WHO IS IMPLACABLE . B.B. IS ENTIRELY SYMPATHETIC AND FORGIVING.
MIS. PREFACE(46) ANARCHISTS ARE TEMPTED TO PREACH A VIOLENT AND IMPLACABLE RESISTANCE TO ALL LAW AS THE ONLY REMEDY; AND THE
LION I (125) /SPINTHO/ I NEVER SAID THEY DIDNT. /FERROVIUS/ (IMPLACABLE) DO THEY OR DO THEY NOT? /SPINTHO/ THEY DO!
BULL III (127) COMPARIN YOU TO YOUR DISADVANTAGE. /MATTHEW/ (IMPLACABLE) THEN HWAT DID YOU MANE BE TALKIN ABOUT GIVIN
GETT PREFACE(217) IN A DEFENCE OF ITS IDEAL SO JEALOUS AND IMPLACABLE THAT THE LEAST STEP FROM THE STRAIGHT PATH MEANS
BARB I SD(259) VISIBLY WRECKED HIS CONSTITUTION. HE IS A MOST IMPLACABLE , DETERMINED, TENACIOUS, INTOLERANT PERSON WHO BY

IMPLACABLY

CAPT II (271) A STRONG POSITION, CAPTAIN BRASSBOUND (LOOKING IMPLACABLY AT HIM) YOU ARE LAID BY THE HEELS, MY FRIEND, AS
POSN (447) MORNING, STRAPPER. NOT A DOUBT OF IT. /BLANCO/ (IMPLACABLY CONTEMPTUOUS) GO HOME AND WASH YOURSELF, YOU
BULL PREFACE(29) AS A CONFESSOR AND SPIRITUAL PASTOR WHILST BEING IMPLACABLY DETERMINED TO SEIZE THE FIRST OPPORTUNITY OF
6CAL SD(101) PLACE ON HIS CHAIR OF STATE WITH HIS ARMS FOLDED IMPLACABLY . THE QUEEN FOLLOWS HIM SLOWLY AND DESOLATELY.
BULL PREFACE(70) BRITISH IMPERIAL RULE RIDICULOUS IN EUROPE, AND IMPLACABLY RESENTED IN INDIA. IN EGYPT THE BRITISH
APPL I (227) TO SOFTEN IT) A CONSTITUTIONAL KING. /PROTEUS/ (IMPLACABLY) A DUMB KING. /MAGNUS/ HM! WHAT NEXT?
DEVL I (9) IN THIS WORLD AND THE NEXT. /MRS DUDGEON/ (IMPLACABLY) HE WILL BE PUNISHED FOR IT. HE WILL BE PUNISHED
JOAN 4 (108) I WILL SPARE HER IF I CAN. /THE CHAPLAIN/ (IMPLACABLY) I WOULD BURN HER WITH MY OWN HANDS. /CAUCHON/ (
GETT (321) MAKE YOU UNDERSTAND, NOTHING WILL. /SOAMES/ (IMPLACABLY) I'M STILL AWAITING MY INSTRUCTIONS. THEY LOOK
NEVR III (271) DONT BE ANGRY-- /GLORIA/ (INTERRUPTING HIM IMPLACABLY) IS IT TRUE? DID YOU EVER SAY THAT BEFORE? DID
PHIL I (81) THE TABLE). AND NOW DO PRAY COME ALONG. /JULIA/ (IMPLACABLY) YOU CAN GO! THERE IS NOTHING TO PREVENT YOU. I
2TRU PREFACE(17) IN SHORT, ADDRESSING ITSELF SOLEMNLY AND IMPLACABLY TO A ROOT-AND-BRANCH EXTERMINATION OF EVERYTHING

IMPLANT

BASH II,1, (108) MY SPRINGING MUSCLE AND UNTIRING HEART? DID I IMPLANT THE INSTINCT IN THE RACE THAT FOUND A USE FOR THESE,

IMPLANTED

POSN (443) OUT, FLYING IN THE FACE OF THE NATURAL TASTES IMPLANTED IN US ALL FOR A GOOD PURPOSE? NOT IF I WAS TO

IMPLEMENTS

KING I (199) KNELLER, THE NEW DUTCH PAINTER, WITH A LOAD OF IMPLEMENTS CONNECTED WITH HIS TRADE, HAD GOT IN IN SPITE OF
HART PREFACE(5) HARDY, AND, GENERALLY SPEAKING, ALL THE LITERARY IMPLEMENTS FOR FORMING THE MIND OF THE PERFECT MODERN
MTH5 SD(214) WITH A CEREMONIAL ROBE, AND CARRIES TWO IMPLEMENTS LIKE LONG SLENDER SAWS. SHE COMES TO THE ALTAR

IMPLICATED

POSN PREFACE(432) LICENCE THE CONDITION THAT ALL THE PASSAGES WHICH IMPLICATED GOD IN THE HISTORY OF BLANCO POSNET MUST BE

IMPLICATION

JOAN PREFACE(18) MAY THEREFORE ACCEPT AS A FLAT FACT, CARRYING NO IMPLICATION OF UNSOUNDNESS OF MIND, THAT JOAN WAS WHAT
CAPT I (221) AS I COULD JUDGE. /DRINKWATER/ (EMBRACING THE IMPLICATION) COURSE E WORS, GAVNER. EV AW SAID A WORD AGIN
FANY EPILOG (329) BY EVERY WORD OF THIS PLAY, EVERY TONE, EVERY IMPLICATION ; THAT YOU DID NOT SIT THERE SHRINKING IN EVERY
LION PREFACE(33) NOT ONLY SAVES TIME, BUT AVOIDS THE ABSURD IMPLICATION THAT CHRIST WAS MERELY GOING THROUGH A
CAPT III (292) ITS THET YOU DUNNO WHERE TO LOOK FR IM. (THE IMPLICATION THAT HE IS SUCH A PERSON IS SO INTOLERABLE THAT
METH PREFACE(R67) AS OUR ABLEST CHURCHMAN HAS SAID, THE REAL IMPLICATION WAS THAT HE WAS EITHER A FOOL, A BIGOT, OR A
BARB PREFACE(210) MUST HERE AFFIRM, WITH AS MUCH GENTLENESS AS THE IMPLICATION WILL BEAR, THAT IT HAS YET TO BE PROVED THAT
CLEO NOTES (205) BE ASSUMED AS INDEED IT GENERALLY IS ASSUMED BY IMPLICATION , THAT A MURDER COMMITTED WITH A POISONED ARROW
MRS PREFACE(151) WAS PROHIBITED, I MYSELF BEING BRANDED BY IMPLICATION , TO MY GREAT DAMAGE, AS AN UNSCRUPULOUS AND

IMPLICATIONS

ROCK PREFACE(173) IN THE EXISTENCE OF HELL BUT A WHOLE SERIES OF IMPLICATIONS AS TO THE NATURE AND CHARACTER OF GOD. NOW THAT
MTH3 (117) IN ORDER. BUT WE DO NOT COMMIT OURSELVES TO THE IMPLICATIONS OF THE WORD HORROR. /THE ARCHBISHOP/ BY THE

IMPLICIT

BULL PREFACE(70) ALMOST EVERY ONE OF THESE FRONTIERS HAS A NEW WAR IMPLICIT IN IT, BECAUSE THE SOLDIER RECOGNIZES NO
UNPL PREFACE(R23) ACTING. DEFINITE CONCEPTIONS OF THESE ARE ALWAYS IMPLICIT IN THE BEST PLAYS, AND ARE OFTEN THE KEY TO THEIR
PLES PREFACE(R18) THE GENERAL ONSLAUGHT ON IDEALISM WHICH IS IMPLICIT , AND INDEED EXPLICIT, IN ARMS AND THE MAN AND THE

IMPLICITLY

MIS. PREFACE(91) THE CREATOR IS EXPLICITLY PRAYED TO, AND IMPLICITLY CONVICTED OF INDECENCY EVERY DAY. AN ASSOCIATION

IMPLIED

LION PREFACE(48) A PRECIS OF THE GOSPEL NARRATIVES I HAVE NOT IMPLIED ANY ESTIMATE EITHER OF THEIR CREDIBILITY OR OF THEIR
POSN PREFACE(400) DRUDGERY UPON AN OFFICIAL OF THE CLASS IMPLIED BY THE DEMAND FOR AN ENLIGHTENED CENSORSHIP FALLS
3PLA PREFACE(R12) STALLS TO THE WHOLE AUDITORIUM, CONSIDER WHAT IS IMPLIED BY THE FACT THAT THE PRICES (ALL MUCH TOO HIGH, BY
SUPR PREFACE(R26) BURKE'S LANGUAGE GAVE GREAT OFFENCE BECAUSE THE IMPLIED EXCEPTIONS TO ITS UNIVERSAL APPLICATION MADE IT A
JOAN PREFACE(33) THE FINAL CRITICISM OF ITS PHYSICAL SIDE IS IMPLIED IN THE REFUSAL OF THE MARQUESAS ISLANDERS TO BE
MRS IV (249) SUCCEED. (MRS WARREN WINCES, DEEPLY HURT BY THE IMPLIED INDIFFERENCE TOWARDS HER AFFECTIONATE INTENTION.
APPL INTRLUD(245) I KNOW IT. BUT I DID NOT SAY IT. /ORINTHIA/ YOU IMPLIED IT. YOU MEANT IT. WHEN THOSE RIDICULOUS POLITICAL
CAPT III SD(279) ADDRESSING A LADY, BUT ALSO WITH AN EMPHATICALLY IMPLIED REBUKE, AS AN AMERICAN ADDRESSING AN ENGLISH PERSON
LADY PREFACE(232) AND HYPOCRISY OF OUR JUDICIAL SYSTEM; BUT HIS IMPLIED REMEDY WAS PERSONAL SOBRIETY AND FREEDOM FROM
METH PREFACE(R30) REPUDIATED WAS COUSINSHIP WITH THE APE, AND THE IMPLIED SUSPICION OF A RUDIMENTARY TAIL, BECAUSE HE THOUGHT
NEVR IV (299) I SAID ANYTHING INSULTING? /GLORIA/ YOU HAVE IMPLIED THAT MY PAST HAS BEEN LIKE YOURS. THAT IS THE WORST
METH PREFACE(R60) ON IT MORE POTENT THAN OWEN HAD EVER CLAIMED. IT IMPLIED THAT STREET ARABS ARE PRODUCED BY SLUMS AND NOT BY
MRS PREFACE(176) HIM; AND EVEN THEN, SINCE HIS VINDICATION IMPLIED THE CONDEMNATION OF THE PRESS, WHICH WAS BY THAT
PLES PREFACE(R18) UNROMANTIC (BUT ALL THE MORE DRAMATIC) FACTS IMPLIED TO THEM A DENIAL OF THE EXISTENCE OF COURAGE,
MIS. (134) FOR ME. (WITH A SNORT AND A NOD TO EMPHASIZE THE IMPLIED WARNING, HE RETREATS TO THE TURKISH BATH, AND LOLLS

IMPLIES

POSN PREFACE(391) OF THE MAN WHO EXERCISES IT. AND WHAT THIS IMPLIES CAN ONLY BE APPRECIATED BY THOSE WHO CAN IMAGINE
POSN PREFACE(422) IGNORANCE AS THIS PARAGRAPH OF ITS REPORT IMPLIES DESERVES TO BE HALED BEFORE THE TRIBUNAL IT HAS
FABL PREFACE(82) NOT LOGIC. NO EMINENCE IN A SPECIFIC DEPARTMENT IMPLIES EVEN ORDINARY ABILITY IN ANY OTHER, NOR DOES ANY
POSN PREFACE(400) FALLS THROUGH THE MOMENT WE REALIZE WHAT IT IMPLIES IN PRACTICE. ANOTHER MATERIAL DIFFICULTY IS THAT NO

BULL PREFACE(40)	FOR AN ENGLISHMAN TO UNDERSTAND ALL THAT THIS	IMPLIES	. A CONQUERED NATION IS LIKE A MAN WITH CANCER: HE
DOCT PREFACE(55)	MUSIC, A PEW IN CHURCH, ANYTHING, IN SHORT, THAT	IMPLIES	MORE MEANS AND BETTER NURTURE THAN THE MASS OF
FANY EPILOG (328)	PRIVATE REASONS FOR MY DISCOMPOSURE. THIS PLAY	IMPLIES	OBSCURE, UNJUST, UNKIND REPROACHES AND MENACES TO
LADY PREFACE(211)	CONTRARY OF EVERYTHING THAT THIS DESCRIPTION	IMPLIES	; WHOSE VERY EXISTENCE IS AN INSULT TO THE IDEAL IT
GETT SD(260)	TO YOU WITHOUT OFFENCE, BECAUSE HIS TONE ALWAYS	IMPLIES	THAT HE DOES IT WITH YOUR KIND PERMISSION. WITHAL BY
LION PREFACE(39)	ANY PROTEST OR EXCITING ANY COMMENT. IT ALSO	IMPLIES	THAT JESUS DELIBERATELY BEWITCHED JUDAS IN ORDER TO
CLEO NOTES (211)	IN ITS POPULAR BRITISH SENSE OF SELF-DENIAL,	IMPLIES	THAT MAN IS VICIOUS BY NATURE, AND THAT SUPREME
SUPR HANDBOK(223)	AND VICES. NO SPECIFIC VIRTUE OR VICE IN A MAN	IMPLIES	THE EXISTENCE OF ANY OTHER SPECIFIC VIRTUE OR VICE
JOAN PREFACE(29)	NOT ENOUGH," FOR WHICH OMISSION, AND THE LIE IT	IMPLIES	, THEY WILL NEED EDITH'S INTERCESSION WHEN THEY ARE
		IMPLORE	
BASH III (121)	COME ONE, COME ALL! /LYDIA/ OH, HIDE THEE, I	IMPLORE	: I CANNOT SEE THEE HUNTED DOWN LIKE THIS. THERE IS
MTH4 III (201)	GO BACK AND CONNIVE AT A BLASPHEMOUS LIE. I	IMPLORE	GUIDANCE. THE PYTHONESS WALKS IN ON THE GALLERY
JOAN 6 (125)	HER? NO. HAVE WE CEASED TO EXHORT HER; TO	IMPLORE	HER TO HAVE PITY ON HERSELF; TO COME TO THE BOSOM OF
JOAN 6 (135)	PREACHERS AND DOCTORS TO THIS WOMAN TO EXHORT AND	IMPLORE	HER TO SAVE HER SOUL AND BODY FROM THE FIRE: WE
GETT (332)	AND IRRITABLE THAT YOU WOULD BE THE FIRST TO	IMPLORE	ME TO TAKE TO IT AGAIN. /MRS GEORGE/ THATS TRUE.
BARB PREFACE(210)	OWN CASE IS A SPECIALLY HARD ONE, BECAUSE, WHEN I	IMPLORE	THE CRITICS WHO ARE OBSESSED WITH THE
MTH4 III (202)	BECOME INCAPABLE OF IT THROUGH MY STAY HERE. I	IMPLORE	TO BE ALLOWED TO STAY. /THE ORACLE/ MY FRIEND: IF
GETT PREFACE(216)	IDEAL MATRIMONY AND DOMESTICITY WHICH OUR BIGOTS	IMPLORE	US TO PRESERVE AS THE CORNER-STONE OF OUR SOCIETY IS
LADY (247)	HE MAKES A NOTE OF IT). /THE DARK LADY/ MADAM: I	IMPLORE	YOU GIVE ME LEAVE TO GO. I AM DISTRACTED WITH GRIEF
FOUN (220)	BUT THE TUMULT OF MY EMOTIONS CARRIES ME AWAY. I	IMPLORE	YOU NOT TO KEEP ME WAITING. MY SOUL, MY SOUL IS
DOCT III (155)	THAT YOU CAN DO IT AND THAT NOBODY ELSE CAN. I	IMPLORE	YOU NOT TO REFUSE WHAT I AM GOING TO ASK YOU TO DO.
BULL III (133)	I APPRECIATE YOUR REALLY BRILLIANT ELOQUENCE, I	IMPLORE	YOU NOT TO DESERT THE GREAT LIBERAL PRINCIPLE OF
CATH 2 (175)	DASHKOFF/ GOD KNOWS, LITTLE MOTHER, WE ALL	IMPLORE	YOU TO GIVE YOUR WONDERFUL BRAIN A REST. THAT IS WHY
MTH1 I (9)	NEED NOT. THERE WILL BE NO PAIN FOR HIM. HE WILL	IMPLORE	YOU TO LET HIM DO HIS SHARE. HE WILL BE IN YOUR
OVER (177)	IMPLORE YOU TO SIT STILL AND BE NICE. /GREGORY/ I	IMPLORE	YOU TO RUN AWAY. I BELIEVE I CAN TRUST MYSELF TO LET
OVER (177)	GRAB YOU ROUND THE NECK AND DISGRACE MYSELF. I	IMPLORE	YOU TO SIT STILL AND BE NICE. /GREGORY/ I IMPLORE
MIS. (204)	MISS SZCZEPANOWSKA: MY SON IS VERY DEAR TO ME. I	IMPLORE	YOU TO WAIT UNTIL TOMORROW MORNING. /LINA/ THERE MAY
FANY EPILOG (328)	/THE COUNT/ GENTLEMEN: DO NOT SPEAK TO ME. I	IMPLORE	YOU TO WITHHOLD YOUR OPINION. I AM NOT STRONG ENOUGH
CATH 4 (192)	MOTHER: DONT BE CRUEL: UNTIE ME. OH, I BEG AND	IMPLORE	YOU. DONT BE UNKIND. I SHALL GO MAD. /CATHERINE/ YOU
MTH4 I (172)	OH, STEADY! STEADY! PRAY! PRAY! REFLECT, I	IMPLORE	YOU. IT IS POSSIBLE TO COLONIZE WITHOUT
DEVL III (55)	TO HIM) ONLY ONE THING MORE-- I ENTREAT, I	IMPLORE	YOU. LET ME BE PRESENT IN THE COURT. I HAVE SEEN
ANNA (298)	EVERYTHING: I SWEAR ANYTHING: PUT IT DOWN, I	IMPLORE	YOU. /THE GRAND DUCHESS/ (THROWING IT ON THE TABLE)
6CAL (99)	OUR NAKED CONDITION THAT SHAKES US. WE KNEEL TO	IMPLORE	YOUR KING'S MERCY FOR OUR WRETCHED AND STARVING
DEVL III (53)	/JUDITH/ THEN WHY NOT TRY TO SAVE YOURSELF? I	IMPLORE	YOU-- LISTEN. YOU SAID JUST NOW THAT YOU SAVED HIM
		IMPLORED	
LIED (203)	GET DIVORCED FROM YOU AND MARRY ME. I BEGGED AND	IMPLORED	HER TO DO IT THIS VERY NIGHT. IT WAS HER REFUSAL
BARB II (304)	IS BODGER THE WHISKY MAN? DO YOU REMEMBER HOW WE	IMPLORED	THE COUNTY COUNCIL TO STOP HIM FROM WRITING
		IMPLORES	
2TRU PREFACE(25)	WORLD IDIOTIC CONFERENCES AT WHICH EACH NATION	IMPLORES	ALL THE OTHERS TO ABSORB ITS UNEMPLOYED BY A
BULL PREFACE(35)	THE ENGLISH GOVERNMENT ABJECTLY REMOVES HIM, AND	IMPLORES	HIM, AS A GENTLEMAN AND A LOYAL ENGLISHMAN, NOT TO
2TRU II (59)	WOMAN! -- HAS ACTUALLY SENT ME THE RANSOM. SHE	IMPLORES	ME TO PAY IT AND RELEASE HER CHILD. SHE IS AFRAID
DOCT I (110)	THE SIDE. ANOTHER MAN BEGS TO BE TAKEN ABOARD. HE	IMPLORES	THE CAPTAIN OF THE RAFT TO SAVE HIM. BUT THE
MRS PREFACE(160)	HER. HE ANNOUNCES HIS PURPOSE. SHE REMONSTRATES,	IMPLORES	, FLIES TO THE DOORS AND FINDS THEM LOCKED, CALLS
		IMPLORING	
DEST (175)	WE WERE AT SCHOOL TOGETHER. SHE HAS WRITTEN TO ME	IMPLORING	ME TO PREVENT THE LETTER FALLING INTO YOUR HANDS.
SUPR IV (169)	YES, YES, YES. /TANNER/ NO. /ANN/ (COAXING--	IMPLORING	-- ALMOST EXHAUSTED) YES. BEFORE IT IS TOO LATE
ROCK II (280)	SOME MANNERS INTO YOU. /DAVID/ (APPALLED AND	IMPLORING	) ALOYSIA! (HE TRIES TO TAKE HER IN HIS ARMS).
WIDO II (46)	ME TO KILL YOU. /THE PARLORMAID/ (PROTESTING AND	IMPLORING	, BUT IN A CAREFULLY SUBDUED VOICE) LET ME GO,
		IMPLORINGLY	
DEVL II (35)	THAT ENMITY-- (SHE GRASPS HIS HAND AND LOOKS	IMPLORINGLY	AT HIM, DOING BOTH WITH AN INTENSITY THAT CHECKS
DEVL III SD(68)	RESOLUTELY) NOT ONE WORD MORE. COME. SHE LOOKS	IMPLORINGLY	AT HIM, BUT IS OVERBORNE BY HIS DETERMINATION.
MTH3 (134)	THE PEG OUT OF HER SWITCHBOARD). /BURGE-LUBIN/ (	IMPLORINGLY	) NO: STOP: LET ME EXPLAIN: HOLD THE LINE JUST
DEST (182)	DELAY ME, YOU KNOW. DUTY, MADAM, DUTY. /LADY/ (	IMPLORINGLY	) OH, SIR, WHAT ARE YOU GOING TO DO TO MY POOR
DOCT IV (161)	/MRS DUBEDAT/ YES, YES: YOU KNOW I WILL. (	IMPLORINGLY	) ONLY, MY LOVE, MY LOVE, DONT TALK: IT WILL
SIM I (50)	AND THE GIRLS WILL NEED A YOUNG HUSBAND. /IDDY/ (	IMPLORINGLY	) TWO YOUNG HUSBANDS, LADY FARWATERS. OH PLEASE,
CURE (225)	IN BUYING THOSE SHARES. (CLUTCHING THE DOCTOR	IMPLORINGLY	) WONT YOU BELIEVE ME, DOCTOR? I NEVER MEANT
SIM PRO,1, (24)	/WILKS/ CHUCK HER YOURSELF. WHAT CAN I DO? (	IMPLORINGLY	TO HER) IF YOUD ONLY HAVE THE GOODNESS TO GO,
DEVL III (74)	(SEVERELY) FALL BACK. (HE OBEYS). /RICHARD/ (	IMPLORINGLY	TO THOSE AROUND HIM, AND FINALLY TO BURGOYNE, AS
DEST (189)	THE WAY. /GIUSEPPE/ YOU CANT MISS IT. BESIDES (	IMPLORINGLY	, LAYING HIS HAND ON HIS SLEEVE) I AM ONLY A
WIDO II (36)	IT'S ONLY A QUESTION OF MONEY. /BLANCHE/ (	IMPLORINGLY	, THE VOICE SOFTENING AND REFINING FOR THE LAST
		IMPLY	
SUPR IV (145)	BUT IN AMERICA THAT NOTE WOULD BE CONSIDERED TO	IMPLY	A VERY CONSIDERABLE DEGREE OF AFFECTIONATE INTIMACY
GENV IV (119)	YOU ARE CONSCIOUS HAS ANY LIMITS? DOES IT NOT	IMPLY	A WORLD STATE WITH MR BATTLER OR SIGNOR BOMBARDONE OR
FABL PREFACE(82)	OTHER, NOR DOES ANY SPECIFIC PERSONAL DEPRAVITY	IMPLY	GENERAL DEPRAVITY. I MAY FAIRLY CLAIM TO BE AN ADEPT
NEVR IV (299)	THAT IS THE WORST OF INSULTS. /VALENTINE/ I	IMPLY	NOTHING OF THE SORT. I DECLARE THAT MY PAST HAS BEEN
3PLA PREFACE(R24)	CALLED IN FROM THE OUTSIDE, WHAT CAN HE DO BUT	IMPLY	THAT HIS FRIEND'S TRANSCENDENT ABILITY AS A DRAMATIST
GENV IV (113)	UNCLE O? /SIR O./ I UNDERSTOOD THE SECRETARY TO	IMPLY	THAT HOWEVER LARGE-MINDED YOUR VIEW OF THE BROTHERHOOD
GETT (301)	MAN AS ANY HERE. /THE GENERAL/ (OUTRAGED) DO YOU	IMPLY	THAT I HAVE BEEN GUILTY OF CONDUCT THAT WOULD EXPOSE
3PLA PREFACE(R32)	ITS RUINOUS GLAMOR, TO WORSHIP IT, DEIFY IT, AND	IMPLY	THAT IT ALONE MAKES OUR LIFE WORTH LIVING, IS NOTHING
3PLA PREFACE(R20)	A YOUNG LADY MANUFACTURED FOR THE PURPOSE, AND TO	IMPLY	THAT IT IS ON HER ACCOUNT ALONE THAT HE FEELS
SUPR PREFACE(R21)	WHOLE DRUDGERY OF CREATION ON ONE SEX, AND THEN	IMPLY	THAT NO FEMALE OF ANY WOMANLINESS OR DELICACY WOULD
MIS. PREFACE(5)	BUT SUCH POSERS ARE UNPOPULAR, BECAUSE THEY	IMPLY	THAT OUR LITTLE CUSTOMS, OR, AS WE OFTEN CALL THEM,
MTH3 (97)	HE WOULD BE SHOT. /BURGE-LUBIN/ STUFF! DO YOU	IMPLY	THAT THE ADMINISTRATION OF WHICH I AM PRESIDENT IS NO
BARB II (295)	(IN A WHITE FURY) DO I UNDERSTAND YOU TO	IMPLY	THAT YOU CAN BUY BARBARA? /UNDERSHAFT/ NO; BUT I CAN
LIED (199)	(WITH AN AIR OF GREAT SURPRISE) DO YOU MEAN TO	IMPLY	THAT YOU DONT BELIEVE ME? /HER HUSBAND/ DO YOU EXPECT
METH PREFACE(R28)	EVEN EXCEPTIONAL COMMAND OF LANGUAGE DOES NOT	IMPLY	THE POSSESSION OF IDEAS TO EXPRESS: MEZZOFANTI, THE
MRS PREFACE(174)	THEM IN PUBLIC, ONLY ONE WRITER HAS VENTURED TO	IMPLY	THIS TIME THAT THE POVERTY MENTIONED BY MRS WARREN HAS
DOCT PREFACE(14)	OR SPEAK TO THE PUBLIC ABOUT OPERATIONS, THEY	IMPLY	, AND OFTEN SAY IN SO MANY WORDS, THAT CHLOROFORM HAS
LION PREFACE(5)	OURSELVES. WHY JESUS MORE THAN ANOTHER? I DO NOT	IMPLY	, HOWEVER, THAT THESE DOCTRINES WERE PECULIAR TO
		IMPLYING	
GETT SD(289)	TALKS TO OTHER PEOPLE WITH A SWEET FORBEARANCE (	IMPLYING	A KINDLY CONSIDERATION FOR THEIR STUPIDITY) WHICH
CAPT NOTES (303)	TO FELIX DRINKWATER ALSO I OWE SOME APOLOGY FOR	IMPLYING	THAT ALL HIS VOWEL PRONUNCIATIONS ARE
APPL I (218)	OWN OPINIONS AND NOT OURS. WE CANNOT HAVE YOU	IMPLYING	THAT EVERYTHING THAT IS OF ANY VALUE IN OUR
LION PREFACE(35)	" THIS DAY SHALT THOU BE WITH ME IN PARADISE,"	IMPLYING	THAT HE WILL SPEND THE THREE DAYS OF HIS DEATH
CATH PREFACE(157)	TOO MUCH; FOR I CAN REMEMBER A TIME (I AM NOT	IMPLYING	THAT IT IS YET WHOLLY PAST) WHEN THE ART OF WRITING
JOAN PREFACE(53)	I COULD HARDLY BE EXPECTED TO STULTIFY MYSELF BY	IMPLYING	THAT JOAN'S HISTORY IN THE WORLD ENDED UNHAPPILY
FABL PREFACE(87)	NO PANACEA, I AM TOLD THAT I AM NOT CONSTRUCTIVE,	IMPLYING	THAT PRACTICAL PEOPLE ARE CONSTRUCTIVE AND DO KNOW.
DEVL III (65)	MINISTER? /CHRISTY/ OF COURSE I DO (	IMPLYING	THAT SWINDON MUST BE AN ASS NOT TO KNOW IT).
METH PREFACE(R34)	REPEATEDLY AND INDIGNANTLY CONTRADICTED IT, AND	IMPLYING	THAT THE ATHEIST CHAMPION WAS FAR TOO PIOUS A MAN
JOAN PREFACE(47)	SCIENTIFIC. I MUST NOT, BY THE WAY, BE TAKEN AS	IMPLYING	THAT THE EARTH IS FLAT, OR THAT ALL OR ANY OF OUR
LION PREFACE(23)	BUT THAT HE IS NOT THERE TO BE ANOINTED ALWAYS,	IMPLYING	THAT YOU SHOULD NEVER LOSE A CHANCE OF BEING HAPPY
DEVL I (13)	WOULDNT MIND SHUTTING THE DOOR! (JUDITH SMILES,	IMPLYING	" HOW STUPID OF ME! " AND SHUTS IT WITH AN
		IMPOASSIBLE	
CAPT I (219)	BE DONE EAH WITHAHT A HESCORT. /RANKIN/ IT'S	IMPOASSIBLE	: TH' WOULD OALL B' MURRDERED. MOROCCO IS NOT
		IMPOLITELY	
GETT (355)	SOLEMNLY DECLARE THAT BETWEEN THIS WOMAN, AS YOU	IMPOLITELY	CALL HER, AND ME, I SEE NO BARRIER THAT MY
UNPL PREFACE(R13)	I, BEING AT THAT TIME IN SOME PRACTICE AS WHAT IS	IMPOLITELY	CALLED A MOB ORATOR, MADE A SPEECH BEFORE THE

IMPOLITENESS

MTH3	(135)	(SHAKING HIS HEAD, SHOCKED AT THE PRESIDENT'S	IMPOLITENESS	) NO. NO, NO, NO, NO, NO. OH, THESE ENGLISH!

IMPORT

UNPL PREFACE	(R20)	PHILOSOPHY THAT A DRAMATIC WORK OF SERIOUS POETIC	IMPORT	CAN BECOME POPULAR. IN THE CASE OF THE FIRST PART OF
BULL PREFACE	(44)	OF A STANDARD WAGE, AND TO IMPOSE CRUSHING	IMPORT	DUTIES ON EVERY ENGLISH TRADE THAT FLOURISHES IN THE
BARB PREFACE	(213)	MUST NECESSARILY BE EITHER A FOREIGN	IMPORT	, OR ELSE A FANTASTIC SALLY (IN RATHER QUESTIONABLE

IMPORTANCE

GENV I	(30)	THANK YOU; BUT MY BUSINESS IS OF GREAT	IMPORTANCE	: I MUST SEE YOUR CHIEF. THIS IS NOT THE HEAD
GENV IV	(110)	NO POLICE. THE LADY IS RAISING A POINT OF GENERAL	IMPORTANCE	: ONE WE MUST SETTLE BEFORE WE CAN COME TO ANY
2TRU I	(43)	HAVE SOMETHING TO PROPOSE TO YOU OF THE GREATEST	IMPORTANCE	: SOMETHING THAT MAY MAKE ANOTHER WOMAN OF YOU
MIS. PREFACE	(58)	IN LIFE: INDEED THE WANT WILL SURVIVE THEIR	IMPORTANCE	: SUPERSTITION IS NOWHERE STRONGER THAN IN THE
MTH5	(250)	A BEAUTIFUL NOSE AND AN UGLY ONE IS OF SUPREME	IMPORTANCE	: THAT IT IS INDEED THE ONLY THING THAT MATTERS.
LION PREFACE	(87)	ECONOMIC, AND MORAL VIEWS OF THE CHRIST HAVE NO	IMPORTANCE	: THE ATONEMENT IS EVERYTHING; AND WE ARE SAVED
MTH4 I	(174)	DO NOT TOLERATE RUINS. WAS LONDON A PLACE OF ANY	IMPORTANCE	? /THE ELDERLY GENTLEMAN/ (AMAZED) WHAT!
SUPR PREFACE	(R21)	THE TERRIBLE MOMENT OF BIRTH ARRIVES, ITS SUPREME	IMPORTANCE	AND ITS SUPERHUMAN EFFORT AND PERIL, IN WHICH THE
2TRU PREFACE	(10)	EXERCISE AND OCCUPATION AND SENSE OF SOCIAL	IMPORTANCE	AND UTILITY TO KEEP THEM ON VERY GOOD TERMS WITH
PLES PREFACE	(R13)	FOR OUR SOCIAL WELFARE. THE THEATRE IS GROWING IN	IMPORTANCE	AS A SOCIAL ORGAN. BAD THEATRES ARE AS
ROCK PREFACE	(179)	PASSION PLAY IMPOSSIBLE. THE QUESTION IS OF SUCH	IMPORTANCE	AT THE PRESENT CRISIS, WHEN THE KINGDOMS ARE
SUPR III	(90)	FROM SHEER LOVE OF SERVITUDE, AND MAGNIFY YOUR	IMPORTANCE	FOR THE SAKE OF DIGNIFYING THEIR SERVICE-- THE
MIS. PREFACE	(57)	WANT TO LEARN THEM AS LONG AS THEY ARE OF ANY	IMPORTANCE	IN LIFE: INDEED THE WANT WILL SURVIVE THEIR
GETT	(332)	WAYS. FIRST, HE TALKS AS IF THE ONLY THING OF ANY	IMPORTANCE	IN LIFE WAS WHICH PARTICULAR WOMAN HE SHALL
ARMS II SD	(25)	UNAMBITIOUS EXCEPT AS TO HIS INCOME AND HIS	IMPORTANCE	IN LOCAL SOCIETY, BUT JUST NOW GREATLY PLEASED
DOCT PREFACE	(50)	SETTLED DOUBTFUL POINTS OF THE GREATEST	IMPORTANCE	IN NAVAL WARFARE. ACCORDING TO VIVISECTIONIST
POSN PREFACE	(408)	THERE IS NOT A MUNICIPAL AUTHORITY OF ANY	IMPORTANCE	IN THE COUNTRY IN WHICH A PROPOSAL TO STAMP OUT
2TRU PREFACE	(17)	REDISCOVERS THE CHURCH SYSTEM, A TREMENDOUS	IMPORTANCE	IS GIVEN TO A CLEAR UNDERSTANDING OF THE CATHOLIC
WIDO I SD	(5)	RESOLUTE CLEAN-SHAVEN MOUTH, GIVE HIM AN AIR OF	IMPORTANCE	. HE WEARS A LIGHT GREY FROCK-COAT WITH SILK
LADY PREFACE	(208)	ON THAT OR ANY OTHER SUBJECT, OF THE SLIGHTEST	IMPORTANCE	. I THOUGHT IT WOULD BE FRIENDLY TO IMMORTALIZE
GENV IV	(99)	PRONUNCIATION OF THE CLASSICS IS A MATTER OF NO	IMPORTANCE	. IT IS A MATTER OF SUPREME IMPORTANCE. /JUDGE/
PRES	(144)	OF THE MOON IS BECOMING ONE OF THE GREATEST	IMPORTANCE	. IT WILL BE REACHED AT NO VERY DISTANT DATE. CAN
LADY PREFACE	(227)	TOUCHY PEOPLE WHO HAVE NO GENIUS ATTACH SO MUCH	IMPORTANCE	. NO READER WHO HAD NOT BEEN TAMPERED WITH BY THE
MTH1 II	(31)	WHO HAS GROWN UP AND WANTS TO IMPRESS ME WITH HIS	IMPORTANCE	. OH, IT IS DREARY, DREARY! AND THERE IS YET
ROCK I	(200)	IS A LIAR, IS A VITAL QUESTION OF THE FIRST	IMPORTANCE	. /HILDA/ BUT THEYRE BOTH LIARS. /SIR ARTHUR/ OF
GENV IV	(99)	OF NO IMPORTANCE. IT IS A MATTER OF SUPREME	IMPORTANCE	. /JUDGE/ WE DO NOT QUESTION ITS IMPORTANCE, SIR
MRS I	(190)	WELL, SHE HAS BEEN STUFFING YOU NICELY WITH HER	IMPORTANCE	. /PRAED/ BUT YOUNG PEOPLE ARE PARTICULARLY
GENV I	(37)	/THE WIDOW/ BUT I MUST SEE SOMEBODY-- SOMEBODY OF	IMPORTANCE	. /SHE/ WELL, I'M SORRY. THERES NOBODY BUT ME. I
DEVL III	(69)	MAY KNOW THAT WE ARE DEALING WITH AN OFFICER OF	IMPORTANCE	. /SWINDON/ POOH! /BURGOYNE/ HE WILL BE FULLY
WIDO II	(40)	HAVE KNOWN YOUR OWN MIND ON A POINT OF SUCH VITAL	IMPORTANCE	. /TRENCH/ (MUCH INJURED) I OUGHT TO HAVE
FABL PREFACE	(95)	UNDERSTAND MATHEMATICS AND REALIZE THEIR ENORMOUS	IMPORTANCE	. SOME RESULTS. IS IT TO BE WONDERED AT THAT WITH
MIS. PREFACE	(50)	LEARNING AND LOVE SPORT. IF WE ARE TO DISCUSS THE	IMPORTANCE	OF ART, LEARNING, AND INTELLECTUAL CULTURE, THE
GETT PREFACE	(213)	IN THAT WAY. PLATO LONG AGO POINTED OUT THE	IMPORTANCE	OF BEING GOVERNED BY MEN WITH SUFFICIENT SENSE OF
BULL I	(87)	THAT TEACHES HIM THE SANCTITY OF LIFE AND THE	IMPORTANCE	OF CONDUCT IS SENT AWAY EMPTY; WHILE THE POOR
SUPR I SD	(9)	CANNOT RESIST FINERY, BUT FROM A SENSE OF THE	IMPORTANCE	OF EVERYTHING HE DOES WHICH LEADS HIM TO MAKE AS
ROCK PREFACE	(172)	MORE AND MORE DISASTROUSLY TO ABSURDITY.	IMPORTANCE	OF FREE THOUGHT. LET ME TRY TO STRAIGHTEN THIS
SUPR HANDBOK	(180)	OF THE SUPERMAN. AT THIS POINT WE PERCEIVE THE	IMPORTANCE	OF GIVING FANCY THE WIDEST POSSIBLE FIELD. TO CUT
LION PREFACE	(92)	IT IS TACITLY RESERVED FOR THE OTHER FELLOW. THE	IMPORTANCE	OF HELL IN THE SALVATION SCHEME. THE SERIOUSNESS
DEVL EPILOG	(83)	BUT BECAUSE LORD GEORGE GERMAIN OVERESTIMATED THE	IMPORTANCE	OF HIS KENTISH HOLIDAY, AND UNDERESTIMATED THE
PYGM PREFACE	(199)	COMMISSION AN ARTICLE FROM SWEET ON THE IMPERIAL	IMPORTANCE	OF HIS SUBJECT. WHEN IT ARRIVED, IT CONTAINED
GETT PREFACE	(237)	GOOD FOR HIM TO BE ENCOURAGED TO EXAGGERATE THE	IMPORTANCE	OF HIS SHORT SPAN IN THIS VALE OF TEARS RATHER
SIM PREFACE	(11)	IT IS TO DRAW ATTENTION TO THE LEGAL NOVELTY AND	IMPORTANCE	OF ITS CRITERION OF HUMAN WORTH. I AM CAREFUL TO
MIS. PREFACE	(59)	OF A CHILD'S LIBERTY BEFORE IT CAN APPRECIATE THE	IMPORTANCE	OF ITS LIBERTY, OR FORESEE THAT THESE
ROCK PREFACE	(172)	THEY FIND THEMSELVES SHORT OF MONEY. IT IS THE	IMPORTANCE	OF KEEPING OUR INCULCATED ILLUSIONS UP TO DATE
ROCK PREFACE	(169)	AGITATE FOR THE EXTERMINATION OF THE UNMUSICAL.	IMPORTANCE	OF LAZINESS FOR FALLOWING. SOME OF THESE
BARB PREFACE	(221)	AND OF AN EARNEST AND CONSTANT SENSE OF THE	IMPORTANCE	OF MONEY. IT DRIVES ONE ALMOST TO DESPAIR OF
DOCT PREFACE	(12)	PERSONS SO INCAPABLE OF APPRECIATING THE RELATIVE	IMPORTANCE	OF PRESERVING THEIR BODILY INTEGRITY (INCLUDING
GETT PREFACE	(235)	AS TO WHICH SEX SHALL CORRUPT THE OTHER MOST.	IMPORTANCE	OF SENTIMENTAL GRIEVANCES. ANY TOLERABLE WESTERN
CLEO II SD	(120)	AT HIS GIRDLE. HIS SERIOUS AIR AND SENSE OF THE	IMPORTANCE	OF THE BUSINESS IN HAND IS IN MARKED CONTRAST TO
POSN PREFACE	(375)	WAY, NOT ONLY FOR THE SAKE OF THE DIGNITY AND	IMPORTANCE	OF THE MATTER WITH WHICH IT HAD TO DEAL, AND IN
CATH 2	(176)	(SHE PACES THE CHAMBER WITH A DEEP SENSE OF THE	IMPORTANCE	OF THE MUSEUM), IT SHALL BE ONE OF THE WONDERS OF
LION PREFACE	(101)	SACRED DIET OF LONG PIG. HERE THEN COMES IN THE	IMPORTANCE	OF THE REPUDIATION BY JESUS OF PROSELYTISM. HIS
MRS PREFACE	(158)	CAN HARDLY HAVE CONSIDERED THE NUMBER AND	IMPORTANCE	OF THE SUBJECTS WHICH ARE ACTUALLY BANISHED FROM
HART PREFACE	(35)	BROUGHT UP TO CARE; AND A SENSE OF THE NATIONAL	IMPORTANCE	OF THE THEATRE IS NOT BORN IN MANKIND: THE
JOAN PREFACE	(15)	OF THE HALLUCINATIONS WITHOUT REGARD TO THE VITAL	IMPORTANCE	OF THE THINGS THEY SYMBOLIZE. IF JOAN WERE REBORN
POSN PREFACE	(390)	HAVING FAILED NOT ONLY TO APPRECIATE THE IMMENSE	IMPORTANCE	OF THE THEATRE AS A MOST POWERFUL INSTRUMENT FOR
PLES PREFACE	(R13)	OF SCIENCE IS CONVINCINGLY WRITTEN, THE NATIONAL	IMPORTANCE	OF THE THEATRE WILL BE AS UNQUESTIONED AS THAT OF
SUPR HANDBOK	(214)	ON THE OTHER HAND A SENSE OF THE SOCIAL	IMPORTANCE	OF THE TINKER'S MARRIAGE HAS BEEN STEADILY
WIDO I	(6)	AH, YOU ARE YOUNG, DEAR BOY: YOU DONT KNOW THE	IMPORTANCE	OF THESE THINGS: APPARENTLY IDLE CEREMONIAL
METH PREFACE	(R63)	IT IS HARDLY POSSIBLE TO EXAGGERATE THE	IMPORTANCE	OF THIS PREPARATION FOR DARWINISM BY A VAST
POSN PREFACE	(378)	INSIGNIFICANT LITTLE BOOKS BEING OF ANY	IMPORTANCE	OR HAVING CAUSED ME OR ANYBODY ELSE ANY TROUBLE,
O'FL	(210)	OF THE WAR? OF THE INTERESTS AT STAKE? OF THE	IMPORTANCE	-- I MAY ALMOST SAY -- IN FACT I WILL SAY -- THE
APPL II	(258)	AND THEN YOU SHALL SAY WHETHER I EXAGGERATE THE	IMPORTANCE	-- THE IMMENSITY -- OF AN OCCASION THAT CANNOT BE
LADY	(244)	EIGHTH. /SHAKESPEAR/ (SWELLING WITH INTOLERANT	IMPORTANCE	) NAME NOT THAT INORDINATE MAN IN THE SAME BREATH
KING I	(187)	IT. I AM ENGAGED IN RESEARCHES OF THE MOST SACRED	IMPORTANCE	; AND FOR THEM I REQUIRE SOLITUDE. DO YOU HEAR,
INCA	(240)	INQUIRY FOR ROOMS FROM AN ENGLISH FAMILY OF	IMPORTANCE	; AND I VENTURE TO ASK YOU TO LET ME KNOW HOW
MILL PREFACE	(128)	POPULATION ARE CAPABLE OF MAKING DECISIONS OF ANY	IMPORTANCE	; AND WITHOUT MANY DAILY DECISIONS CIVILIZATION
PYGM EPILOG	(295)	FREDDY IN THE HOUSE WITH HER SEEMED OF NO MORE	IMPORTANCE	THAN IF SHE HAD WANTED AN EXTRA PIECE OF BEDROOM
BARB PREFACE	(243)	TO ACCEPT BUT TO UPHOLD AS A MATTER OF SUCH VITAL	IMPORTANCE	THAT A LAWBREAKER AT LARGE IS HARDLY TO BE
POSN PREFACE	(381)	FOR THIS REASON IT IS OF THE MOST ENORMOUS	IMPORTANCE	THAT IMMORALITY SHOULD BE PROTECTED JEALOUSLY
ROCK PREFACE	(161)	PLEASED, WHEREAS IN FACT IT WAS OF LIFE-OR-DEATH	IMPORTANCE	THAT THEY SHOULD REDOUBLE THEIR ACTIVITY AND
DEVL II	(31)	BE GLAD TO SEE HIM FOR A MOMENT ON A MATTER OF	IMPORTANCE	TO HIMSELF, AND THAT IF HE WOULD LOOK IN HERE
PRES	(144)	MILITARY IN ITS WAY OF THINKING TO ATTACH ANY	IMPORTANCE	TO IT. /MITCHENER/ (LOSING HIS TEMPER) YOU ARE
GETT	(300)	SURELY MY HUSBAND'S CONDUCT IS OF MORE	IMPORTANCE	TO ME THAN MR BALFOUR'S OR MR ASQUITH'S. IF I HAD
DOCT PREFACE	(30)	OF MEDICAL KINDNESS. DOCTORS AND VIVISECTION. THE	IMPORTANCE	TO OUR DOCTORS OF A REPUTATION FOR THE TENDEREST
METH PREFACE	(R31)	AND THEREBY MADE A CONTRIBUTION OF EXTRAORDINARY	IMPORTANCE	TO OUR UNDERSTANDING OF UNINJURED CREATURES. THE
METH PREFACE	(R32)	CUVIER AND ST HILAIRE. IT IS OF THE UTMOST	IMPORTANCE	TO SCIENCE." THE RUPTURE GOETHE MEANT WAS ABOUT
MIS. PREFACE	(31)	WOULD PROBABLY BE CANED. I DO NOT ATTACH ANY	IMPORTANCE	TO SUCH MODERNITIES IN SCHOOL FURNITURE. THE
FOUN	(211)	OLD ENOUGH TO BE MY MOTHER. I ATTACH SOME	IMPORTANCE	TO THAT DISTINCTION; SO BE GOOD ENOUGH TO BEAR IT
INCA	(238)	THINK YOU COULD BE HAPPY WITH ME? I ATTACH SUCH	IMPORTANCE	TO THAT. /ERMYNTRUDE/ (GUSHING) OH, I KNOW I
LIED	(192)	IDLE LEGAL CEREMONY YOU MAY DESIRE. I ATTACH NO	IMPORTANCE	TO THE LAW: MY LOVE WAS NOT CREATED IN ME BY THE
KING I	(179)	THE BIBLE). IT MAY PROVE OF THE GREATEST	IMPORTANCE	TO THE WORLD. I BEG YOU TO ALLOW ME TO PROCEED
JOAN PREFACE	(10)	DICTATE THEM AND ATTACH FULL AND INDEED EXCESSIVE	IMPORTANCE	TO THEM. WHEN SHE WAS CALLED A SHEPHERD LASS TO
GETT	(272)	I'M SURE SHE WILL AGREE WITH ME. I ATTACH	IMPORTANCE	TO THIS AS AN AFFIRMATION OF SOLIDARITY IN THE
LION PREFACE	(41)	IDIOSYNCRASIES. HIS NARRATIVE IS OF ENORMOUS	IMPORTANCE	TO THOSE WHO GO TO THE GOSPELS FOR A CREDIBLE
DOCT PREFACE	(19)	THING SHOULD BEFALL US. IT IS OF THE MOST EXTREME	IMPORTANCE	TO US THAT THE EXPERTS ON WHOSE ASSURANCE WE FACE
DOCT PREFACE	(80)	AND TEETH AND EYESIGHT AND OTHER MATTERS OF	IMPORTANCE	TO YOU WILL BE ATTENDED TO. BE PARTICULARLY
LION PREFACE	(23)	A PROSELYTIST, A POINT OF CONSIDERABLE PRACTICAL	IMPORTANCE	TODAY IS THAT HE EXPRESSLY REPUDIATES THE IDEA
GENV IV	(99)	DANGEROUS. HE SWITCHES YOU OFF TO SOMETHING OF NO	IMPORTANCE	WHATEVER. /SIR O./ I DID NOT INTEND THAT. I
DOCT III	(152)	LUNG IS ATTACKED. /MRS DUBEDAT/ (ATTACHING NO	IMPORTANCE	WHATEVER TO BLENKINSOP) DO YOU MEAN THAT ELDERLY
AUGS	(270)	LADY I HAVE JUST RECEIVED NEWS OF THE GREATEST	IMPORTANCE	WHICH WILL OCCUPY MY ENTIRE ATTENTION FOR THE
AUGS	(278)	IT) OH, HOW IMPRUDENT! EVERYBODY WOULD GUESS ITS	IMPORTANCE	WITH YOUR NAME ON IT. FORTUNATELY I HAVE SOME
GENV III	(71)	DIFFICULT TO ACCUSTOM MYSELF TO THE EXAGGERATED	IMPORTANCE	YOU ALL ATTACH TO SEX IN THESE WESTERN COUNTRIES.
LION PREFACE	(87)	PERSONAL AND POLITICAL, WHICH ARE NOW OF PRESSING	IMPORTANCE	, AND INSTRUCTING HIS DISCIPLES TO CARRY THEM OUT
GETT SD	(276)	NOTHING. SHE RUNS IN FUSSILY, FULL OF HER OWN	IMPORTANCE	, AND SWOOPS ON LESBIA, WHO IS MUCH LESS DISPOSED
GENV IV	(98)	IS TO PROPAGATE A BURNING CONVICTION OF TRUTH AND	IMPORTANCE	, AND THUS PRODUCE IMMEDIATE ACTION AND
APPL PREFACE	(194)	ON ME TO UNFOLD A NEW SCHEME OF MUCH GREATER	IMPORTANCE	, AS HE DECLARED, THAN HIS TRUCKS. HE WAS VERY

SUPR I SD(3)	ACTIVE CIVIL LIFE THAN MEN GET HIS BROAD AIR OF	IMPORTANCE	, HIS DIGNIFIED EXPECTATION OF DEFERENCE, HIS
APPL PREFACE(191)	TOLD THAT HE HAD MADE AN INVENTION OF FIRST-RATE	IMPORTANCE	, I WAS INCREDULOUS, AND CONCLUDED THAT THE
MIS. PREFACE(87)	WISHES TO DECEIVE HIM AS TO HIS INCOME AND SOCIAL	IMPORTANCE	, IS IN EFFECT BROKEN UP BY SCHOOL LIFE, BY
SUPR II (64)	WE DO, IN CONFIDENCE. /RAMSDEN/ (WITH AN AIR OF	IMPORTANCE	, LEST MALONE SHOULD SUSPECT A MISALLIANCE) HER
GENV IV (99)	IMPORTANCE. /JUDGE/ WE DO NOT QUESTION ITS	IMPORTANCE	, SIR MIDLANDER; BUT IT IS OUTSIDE THE
DOCT I SD(81)	REDPENNY, CHRISTIAN NAME UNKNOWN AND OF NO	IMPORTANCE	, SITS AT WORK IN A DOCTOR'S CONSULTING ROOM. HE
		IMPORTANT	
LION PREFACE(87)	JESUS, AS GUIDES TO CONDUCT, ARE INTERESTING AND	IMPORTANT	: THE REST IS MERE PSYCHOPATHY AND SUPERSTITION.
DOCT I (93)	THE DIFFERENCE IT MAKES; BUT I SUPPOSE THEY FEEL	IMPORTANT	AFTER IT. YOU CANT GO OUT TO DINNER NOW WITHOUT
GETT (315)	DONT BE SOULLESS, ANTHONY. /LESBIA/ I HAVE A VERY	IMPORTANT	AMENDMENT. IF THERE ARE ANY CHILDREN, THE MAN MUST
GETT (271)	SERVICES TO THE COMMUNITY AS A GREENGROCER ARE AS	IMPORTANT	AND AS DIGNIFIED AS MINE AS A SOLDIER? /COLLINS/
BULL IV SD(148)	AND DISORDERED AS TO HIS MOTORING COAT: IMMENSELY	IMPORTANT	AND SERIOUS AS TO HIMSELF. HE MAKES HIS WAY TO THE
BULL III (128)	WHAT DO YOU SAY? /BROADBENT/ (DEPRECATORY, BUT	IMPORTANT	AND SMILING) OH, I HAVE NO CLAIM WHATEVER TO THE
KING PREFACE(154)	UNIVERSE. THERE IS ANOTHER CLASH WHICH IS	IMPORTANT	AND TOPICAL IN VIEW OF THE HOLD THAT PROFESSIONAL
NEVR I (211)	THE DIGNITY OF THE OCCASION, RISES, LOOKING	IMPORTANT	AND UNCOMPROMISING. SHE CROSSES TO THE WINDOW, AND
GETT (293)	HE HAPPENED TO RECOLLECT THAT HE HAD A RATHER	IMPORTANT	APPOINTMENT TO MARRY EDITH. HE SAID THE SOONER I
DOCT PREFACE(41)	EXPERIMENTS WOULD BE QUITE AS INTERESTING AND	IMPORTANT	AS ANY YET UNDERTAKEN BY THE VIVISECTORS. THEY
KING II (225)	AND LET HER ROT THERE. /CHARLES/ SHE IS NOT SO	IMPORTANT	AS THAT, BELOVED. NOR AM I. AND WE MUST FORGIVE
DOCT PREFACE(49)	SINCE THE WORLD BEGAN HAVE PRODUCED NOTHING SO	IMPORTANT	AS THE INNOCENT AND HONORABLE DISCOVERY OF
MIS. PREFACE(61)	YOUR KNOWING BETTER THAN YOUR ELDERS, ARE JUST AS	IMPORTANT	AS THOSE OF THE SERMON ON THE MOUNT; BUT NO ONE
PLES PREFACE(R17)	FORMULA OF TREATING BAD AS GOOD AND GOOD AS BAD,	IMPORTANT	AS TRIVIAL AND TRIVIAL AS IMPORTANT, SERIOUS AS
GETT (316)	BEST. /LEO/ (TO THE BISHOP) BAPTISM IS NEARLY AS	IMPORTANT	AS VACCINATION: ISNT IT? /THE BISHOP/ IT USED TO
GETT PREFACE(234)	IT PROTECTS ITSELF. DIVORCE. ALL THIS HAS AN	IMPORTANT	BEARING ON THE QUESTION OF DIVORCE. DIVORCE
METH PREFACE(R25)	BETWEEN THE EFFORTS TO ACQUIRE A HABIT ARE	IMPORTANT	BECAUSE, AS WE HAVE SEEN, THEY RECUR NOT ONLY FROM
LION PREFACE(25)	MEN WHO POSSESS SUCH POWERS, BUT HAVE FAR MORE	IMPORTANT	BUSINESS IN THE WORLD THAN TO EXHIBIT THEM, TO BE
MILL IV (200)	OH, WE ARE WASTING TIME; AND I HAVE MORE	IMPORTANT	BUSINESS TO SETTLE. GIVE HIM A TEN POUND NOTE AND
MTH3 (135)	IF-- (CONFUCIUS RETURNS) CONFUCIUS: I HAVE SOME	IMPORTANT	BUSINESS AT FISHGUARD. THE IRISH AIR SERVICE CAN
WIDO III (51)	MR LICKCHEESE WANTS TO SEE YOU VERY PARTICLAR. ON	IMPORTANT	BUSINESS, YOUR BUSINESS, HE TOLD ME TO SAY.
INCA (243)	REALLY. OH, WHAT SHALL I DO? /THE MANAGER/ ON	IMPORTANT	BUSINESS, HE SAYS, YOUR HIGHNESS. CAPTAIN DUVAL.
MTH2 (78)	HIM FORCIBLY) LUBIN: HAS THIS STUPENDOUSLY	IMPORTANT	COMMUNICATION WHICH PROFESSOR BARNABAS HAS JUST
DEST (159)	PISTOLS AND HIS HORSE AND HIS DESPATCHES-- MOST	IMPORTANT	DESPATCHES-- AND LET ME GO AWAY WITH THEM. (
FABL II (106)	I SHALL HAVE TO DO IT. /OLDHAND/ YOU HAVE A VERY	IMPORTANT	DIPLOMATIC POINT THERE, I ADMIT; BUT IT MUST STAND
POSN PREFACE(371)	MAY NOT BE GREAT POEMS, OR EDIFYING SERMONS, OR	IMPORTANT	DOCUMENTS, OR CHARMING ROMANCES: OUR TRIBAL
2TRU II (79)	YOU ABOUT. SHALL I DRAW UP THE REPORT, SIR?	IMPORTANT	ENGAGEMENT: ENEMY ROUTED: NO BRITISH CASUALTIES.
CLEO NOTES (210)	YEARS OPENLY SCANDALOUS, THE DIFFERENCE WAS NOT	IMPORTANT	ENOUGH TO BE NOTICED. IT MAY, HOWEVER, BE SAID
MIS. PREFACE(58)	TOO EARLY. AND THIS BRINGS ME TO AN	IMPORTANT	FACTOR IN THE CASE: THE FACTOR OF EVOLUTION.
LION PREFACE(33)	THE CHRONICLER WRITING FOR THE SAKE OF RECORDING	IMPORTANT	FACTS, TO THE ARTIST, TELLING THE STORY FOR THE
ARMS III (72)	THE SARANOFFS ARE KNOWN AS THE RICHEST AND MOST	IMPORTANT	FAMILIES IN THE COUNTRY. OUR POSITION IS ALMOST
BULL PREFACE(9)	THE WAY TO LOOK AT IT. THE QUESTION IS STILL MORE	IMPORTANT	FOR ENGLAND THAN FOR IRELAND. IN SPITE OF
GETT PREFACE(234)	PRESSING NEED FOR ADMITTING OTHER AND FAR MORE	IMPORTANT	GROUNDS FOR DIVORCE. IF WE TAKE A DOCUMENT LIKE
PPP (196)	A MOMENT. /FITZ/ (CALLING TO ADOLPHUS) SOMETHING	IMPORTANT	HAPPENED? WHAT IS IT? /ADOLPHUS/ (WITHOUT) MY
APPL II (260)	VERY VERY LONG TIME AGO. I TAKE IT THAT SOMETHING	IMPORTANT	HAS HAPPENED SINCE YESTERDAY. /VANHATTAN/ IT HAS.
PPP (195)	LIGHT). /ADOLPHUS/ (WITHOUT) SOMETHING MOST	IMPORTANT	HAS HAPPENED. I MUST COME IN FOR A MOMENT. /FITZ/
MIS. (129)	AN IDEA. THATS A MOST INTERESTING IDEA: A MOST	IMPORTANT	IDEA. /MRS TARLETON/ YOU ALWAYS WERE ONE FOR
CAPT II (250)	MR DRINKWATER WONT MIND MY MENTIONING IT. IT'S SO	IMPORTANT	IF HE'S TO ATTEND ON MARZO. /BRASSBOUND/ WHAT IS
SUPR HANDBOK(180)	FOR SPEED, OR SHEEP FOR MUTTON. WHAT IS REALLY	IMPORTANT	IN MAN IS THE PART OF HIM THAT WE DO NOT YET
POSN PREFACE(362)	LESS WELL KNOWN TO THE GENERAL PUBLIC, BUT	IMPORTANT	IN THE WORLD OF THE THEATRE. THE PUBLICATION OF A
BULL PREFACE(47)	EXCUSE IS MADE, IS THAT DISCIPLINE IS SUPREMELY	IMPORTANT	IN WAR. NOW MOST SOLDIERS HAVE NO EXPERIENCE OF
MTH2 (79)	TO ARGUE IT IN AN ECCLESIASTICAL COURT. BUT	IMPORTANT	IS HARDLY A WORD I SHOULD ATTACH TO IT. /BURGE/
POSN PREFACE(393)	WAS JUSTIFIED, IS OF NO CONSEQUENCE. WHAT IS	IMPORTANT	IS THAT IT WAS SURE TO BE MADE, JUSTLY OR
GETT (316)	WELL. /LESBIA/ THAT REMINDS ME OF SOMETHING VERY	IMPORTANT	. BOXER BELIEVES IN VACCINATION: I DO NOT. THERE
APPL PREFACE(180)	NUMBER TWO: GOVERNMENT FOR THE PEOPLE, IS MOST	IMPORTANT	. DEAN INGE PUT IT PERFECTLY FOR US WHEN HE CALLED
GENV I (37)	AM I TO TAKE THAT SERIOUSLY? MY BUSINESS IS	IMPORTANT	. I CAME HERE TO PLACE IT BEFORE A BODY OF PERSONS
BUOY PREFACE(6)	AND THE INTERPRETATION OF THE BIBLE AS FAR MORE	IMPORTANT	. IN THIS VALUATION, WHICH SEEMS SO QUEER TO US
FOUN (211)	GIVE ME A START. AND THERES ANOTHER THING: VERY	IMPORTANT	. I-- OH, BY THE WAY, WONT YOU SIT DOWN? EXCUSE
GETT PREFACE(207)	AGAINST ANY CHILDBEARING. THIS LAST CAUSE IS	IMPORTANT	. IT CANNOT BE REMOVED BY ANY ECONOMIC
MRS I SD(195)	50. EXTERNALLY HE IS PRETENTIOUS, BOOMING, NOISY,	IMPORTANT	. REALLY HE IS THAT OBSOLESCENT SOCIAL PHENOMENON
MILL II (172)	I NEED BY WORK WHICH I VENTURE TO THINK MORE	IMPORTANT	. /EPIFANIA/ (THROWING HIM AWAY AND MOVING ABOUT
MTH2 (76)	I WISH YOU WOULD, YOU KNOW. IT'S IMPORTANT, VERY	IMPORTANT	. /FRANKLYN/ WELL, CONSIDER IT THIS WAY. IT IS
CAND II SD(122)	'ANG IT ALL! LEXY MILL COMES IN, ANXIOUS AND	IMPORTANT	. /LEXY/ (HASTENING TO SHAKE HANDS WITH CANDIDA)
KING I (167)	GENTLEMEN MORE INTERESTING AND INFINITELY MORE	IMPORTANT	. /MRS BASHAM/ (POSTED BEHIND NEWTON'S CHAIR)
PYGM II (231)	/HIGGINS/ CERTAINLY. QUITE RIGHT. MOST	IMPORTANT	. /MRS PEARCE/ I MEAN NOT TO BE SLOVENLY ABOUT HER
NEVR III (279)	RISING) I QUITE AGREE WITH YOU. I THINK IT'S MOST	IMPORTANT	. /M'COMAS/ THERE CAN BE NO OBJECTION TO THAT, I
FABL V (117)	MENTIONABLE SUBJECT IN THE WORLD AND THE MOST	IMPORTANT	. /SHAMROCK/ WELL, IVE BEEN THROUGH EVERY SCRAP OF
GETT SD(275)	STRIKE HER IMAGINATION AS SOUNDING INTELLECTUALLY	IMPORTANT	. SHE HAS MORE THAN COMMON IMAGINATION AND NO MORE
GETT (340)	AT THIRTEEN SHILLINGS A TON. /THE BISHOP/ THATS	IMPORTANT	. THANK YOU FOR TELLING ME. /MRS GEORGE/ I HAVE
GENV IV (99)	TECHNIQUE. YOU WERE TALKING OF SOMETHING REALLY	IMPORTANT	. THAT IS DANGEROUS. HE SWITCHES YOU OFF TO
MTH2 (76)	(TO FRANKLYN) I WISH YOU WOULD, YOU KNOW, IT'S	IMPORTANT	, VERY IMPORTANT. /FRANKLYN/ WELL, CONSIDER IT
PHIL II (95)	MY MENTIONING IT WHEN I SAY THAT IT MAY THROW AN	IMPORTANT	LIGHT ON HER FATHER'S CASE. THE FIRST THING, OF
GETT (317)	REJJY. /EDITH/ YOU ARE FORGETTING THE VERY	IMPORTANT	MATTER OF MONEY. /COLLINS/ AH! MONEY! NOW WE'RE
MIS. PREFACE(29)	ON RESPECT FOR THEIR OWN IN THESE AS IN OTHER	IMPORTANT	MATTERS WHICH ARE EQUALLY DANGEROUS: FOR EXAMPLE,
GETT PREFACE(214)	A PREMIUM ON WANT OF SELF-RESPECT IN CERTAIN VERY	IMPORTANT	MATTERS; AND THE CONSEQUENCE IS THAT WE ARE VERY
2TRU PREFACE(22)	SHOULD KNOW WHAT THEY ARE TALKING ABOUT. ANOTHER	IMPORTANT	MODERN DISCOVERY IS THAT GOVERNMENT IS NOT A
BARB PREFACE(221)	IN LONDON, THE SECOND ACT WAS REPORTED IN AN	IMPORTANT	NORTHERN NEWSPAPER AS A WITHERING ATTACK ON THE
KING I (167)	MANY QUESTIONS AS SHE PLEASES; FOR I AM FAR LESS	IMPORTANT	NOW IN ENGLAND THAN JACK THE FISH HAWKER. /MRS
SUPR PREFACE(R25)	FACT THAT THIS INITIATIVE IS POLITICALLY THE MOST	IMPORTANT	OF ALL THE INITIATIVES, BECAUSE OUR POLITICAL
SUPR I SD(3)	INCLUDED. HOW OLD IS ROEBUCK? THE QUESTION IS	IMPORTANT	ON THE THRESHOLD OF A DRAMA OF IDEAS; FOR UNDER
PHIL II (95)	WELL, SINCE YOU ASK ME, YES: PERHAPS A MOST	IMPORTANT	ONE. I HAVE DISCOVERED SOMETHING THAT HAS HITHERTO
JOAN PREFACE(53)	CANONIZED IS A DIFFERENT MATTER, AND A MORE	IMPORTANT	ONE. SO I AM AFRAID THE EPILOGUE MUST STAND. TO
MIS. PREFACE(21)	DID NOT LEARN MY SCHOOL LESSONS, HAVING MUCH MORE	IMPORTANT	ONES IN HAND, WITH THE RESULT THAT I HAVE NOT
ROCK I (222)	THEM: YOU NEEDNT BOTHER. THERE ARE TWO OR THREE	IMPORTANT	ONES THAT YOU OUGHT TO ANSWER: I HAVE PUT THEM
DOCT PREFACE(34)	OF 500 DEGREES FAHRENHEIT, NO MATTER HOW	IMPORTANT	OR INTERESTING THAT PARTICULAR ADDITION TO THE
BUOY PREFACE(6)	IN THE FACTS OF HISTORY, NOTHING COULD BE MORE	IMPORTANT	OR MORE SCIENTIFIC; AND THE FACT THAT THE RESULT
BULL PREFACE(13)	OF COURSE), WHO, TWELVE YEARS AGO, PLAYED AN	IMPORTANT	PART IN THE HISTORY OF THE MODERN ENGLISH STAGE AS
MIS. PREFACE(77)	15. MERE WONDERING AND STARING AT THINGS IS AN	IMPORTANT	PART OF A CHILD'S EDUCATION: THAT IS WHY CHILDREN
2TRU PREFACE(10)	TO PEOPLE BROUGHT UP TO IT IS A NECESSARY AND	IMPORTANT	PART OF A WELL ORDERED LIFE. THE LANDED GENTRY
BARB PREFACE(221)	THEM TO INSIST ON THEIR OWN MERITS AS AN	IMPORTANT	PART OF THEIR OWN BUSINESS. THE SALVATION ARMY,
LION PREFACE(21)	EGYPT. WE MAY FORGET THEM, AND PROCEED TO THE	IMPORTANT	PART OF THE NARRATIVE, WHICH SKIPS AT ONCE TO THE
ROCK I (228)	HOW TO CURE YOURSELF? THE TWENTY GUINEAS IS AN	IMPORTANT	PART OF THE CURE. IT WILL MAKE YOU TAKE IT
SUPR HANDBOK(181)	OR THAT A CONFLICT OF TEMPERAMENT IS NOT A HIGHLY	IMPORTANT	PART OF WHAT BREEDERS CALL CROSSING. ON THE
PYGM PREFACE(202)	AS PHONETICIANS, AND THAT THEY ARE AMONG THE MOST	IMPORTANT	PEOPLE IN ENGLAND AT PRESENT, IT WILL SERVE ITS
SIM II (80)	LIES IN THE FACT THAT NOT ONLY IS IT OUR MOST	IMPORTANT	PEOPLE WHO ARE VANISHING, BUT THAT IT IS THE MOST
UNPL PREFACE(R9)	EVERY WEEK TO SAY MY SAY AS IF I WERE THE MOST	IMPORTANT	PERSON IN THE KINGDOM. MY PLEASING TOIL WAS TO
BARB PREFACE(236)	AND ABHORRED, THE POLICEMAN BEING A MUCH MORE	IMPORTANT	PERSON THAN ANY OF THE PERSONS OF THE TRINITY, AND
GENV IV (124)	OF JUDGES AND GENERALS. A MOMENT AGO WE WERE	IMPORTANT	PERSONS: THE FATE OF EUROPE SEEMED TO DEPEND ON
GENV IV (95)	GENTLEMEN. ALLOW ME TO RECALL YOU TO THE	IMPORTANT	POINT REACHED BY SIR MIDLANDER. /SIR O./ WHAT WAS
JOAN 6 (127)	YOUR PURPOSE. /THE CHAPLAIN/ BUT SOME OF THE MOST	IMPORTANT	POINTS HAVE BEEN REDUCED ALMOST TO NOTHING. FOR
BULL III (136)	NOR SHOULD THE LIGHTER, BUT STILL MOST	IMPORTANT	QUESTION OF THE SPORTS OF THE PEOPLE BE FORGOTTEN.
LION PREFACE(41)	IS EITHER ALIVE OR DEAD, AND NEVER CONSIDER THE	IMPORTANT	QUESTION HOW MUCH ALIVE HE IS); AND THAT MEN
MTH4 III (200)	FOR IT; AND YOU GOT IT. AND JUST THINK OF ALL THE	IMPORTANT	QUESTIONS YOU MIGHT HAVE ASKED. SHE WOULD HAVE
NEVR IV (290)	BOHUN, WE HAD PERHAPS BETTER DISPOSE OF THE	IMPORTANT	QUESTIONS FIRST. /BOHUN/ M'COMAS: THERE WILL BE NO
NEVR IV (290)	M'COMAS: THERE WILL BE NO DIFFICULTY ABOUT THE	IMPORTANT	QUESTIONS. THERE NEVER IS. IT IS THE TRIFLES THAT
GETT PREFACE(208)	IT WOULD BE WRECKED BY AN OPPOSITE AND NOT LESS	IMPORTANT	REVOLT OF WOMEN: THAT IS, THE REVOLT AGAINST
BULL I (92)	TO WHAT I AM GOING TO SAY; FOR IT'S A NEW AND	IMPORTANT	SCIENTIFIC THEORY OF THE ENGLISH NATIONAL
ANNA (296)	/THE GRAND DUCHESS/ (PRETENDING TO WHISPER AN	IMPORTANT	SECRET) WHERE HE HAS ALWAYS BEEN. /STRAMMFEST/ (
FABL PREFACE(81)	PRAYER. WHEN I WAS INVITED TO ADDRESS THE MOST	IMPORTANT	SECULAR SOCIETY IN ENGLAND I FOUND THAT I HAD TO

APPL PREFACE(181)	IT WAS STARTED BY A RUNAWAY COW. THAT COW HAD AN	IMPORTANT	SHARE IN MY EDUCATION AS A POLITICAL PHILOSOPHER;
MIS. PREFACE(28)	REVOLT AGAINST THEIR INDUSTRIAL SLAVERY. THE MOST	IMPORTANT	SIMPLE FUNDAMENTAL ECONOMIC TRUTH TO IMPRESS ON A
GENV PREFACE(23)	IS, IF WORTH EMPLOYING AT ALL, AS NECESSARY AND	IMPORTANT	SOCIALLY AS THE ABLEST DIRECTOR. EQUALITY BETWEEN
ROCK I (210)	ARTHUR/ (STARTING FROM HIS PREOCCUPATION WITH	IMPORTANT	STATE DOCUMENTS, AND ADVANCING PAST THE FIREPLACE
SUPR IV (145)	ON ME, AND THAT I HAVE TO BE CONSULTED IN ANY	IMPORTANT	STEP HE MAY PROPOSE TO TAKE. /VIOLET/ I AM SURE
MIS. PREFACE(28)	THE MIND, THE LESS COURAGE THERE IS TO FACE	IMPORTANT	SUBJECTS OBJECTIVELY. THE ABLEST AND MOST HIGHLY
PYGM PREFACE(202)	IT, AND WHO KEEP ALL THE BEST PLACES FOR LESS	IMPORTANT	SUBJECTS WHICH THEY PROFESS WITHOUT ORIGINALITY
POSN PREFACE(394)	RELIGIOUS LEADERS ARE MORE INTERESTING AND MORE	IMPORTANT	SUBJECTS FOR THE DRAMATIST THAN GREAT CONQUERORS.
APPL PREFACE(195)	INTO A FULLFED ELECTRICIAN, WAS STUPENDOUSLY MORE	IMPORTANT	THAN ANY RIDICULOUS MELODRAMA. HE ADMITTED THAT
APPL INTRLUD(253)	WORK. /ORINTHIA/ WHAT WORK HAVE YOU THAT IS MORE	IMPORTANT	THAN BEING WITH ME? /MAGNUS/ NONE. /ORINTHIA/
KING I (184)	THEM! WHAT ELSE HAVE YOU TO DO THAT IS MORE	IMPORTANT	THAN MY BUSINESS WITH YOU? /NEWTON/ MANY OTHER
SUPR PREFACE(R22)	AS IF THE KITCHEN AND THE NURSERY WERE LESS	IMPORTANT	THAN THE OFFICE IN THE CITY. WHEN HIS SWAGGER IS
DOCT I (113)	IF YOU CAN CONVINCE ME THAT HIS LIFE IS MORE	IMPORTANT	THAN THE WORST LIFE I AM NOW SAVING. BUT YOU MUST
MIS. PREFACE(12)	LARGE FAMILIES. THESE RIGHTS HAVE NOW BECOME MORE	IMPORTANT	THAN THEY USED TO BE, BECAUSE THE MODERN PRACTICE
MTH3 (116)	DAY BEFORE ME. /BARNABAS/ HAVE YOU ANYTHING MORE	IMPORTANT	THAN THIS THING, IF IT'S TRUE? /BURGE-LUBIN/ OH,
DOCT I (95)	OUGHT TO BE COMPULSORY! IT'S TEN TIMES MORE	IMPORTANT	THAN VACCINATION. /SIR PATRICK/ HAVE YOU HAD YOUR
DOCT PREFACE(73)	OF BY-LAWS AND THE LIKE; THEREFORE IT WILL BE	IMPORTANT	THAT EVERY M.O.H. SHALL HAVE, WITH HIS (OR HER)
DOCT I (91)	INOCULATE AND KILL. THATS MY DISCOVERY; THE MOST	IMPORTANT	THAT HAS BEEN MADE SINCE HARVEY DISCOVERED THE
POSN PREFACE(398)	ADJUSTED THAT HE IS TYRANNICAL JUST WHERE IT IS	IMPORTANT	THAT HE SHOULD BE TOLERANT, AND TOLERANT JUST
HART PREFACE(10)	(BY WHICH THEY MEANT THEIR PRACTICES) WAS SO	IMPORTANT	THAT NO CONSIDERATION FOR THE INTERESTS OF ANY
MIS. PREFACE(107)	MUCH WORSE THAN OURSELVES, AND WHY IT IS SO	IMPORTANT	THAT SUBMISSIVENESS SHOULD NO LONGER BE
MIS. PREFACE(69)	PRACTICE; AND THIS IS WHAT MAKES IT SO	IMPORTANT	THAT THE ESTABLISHED PRACTICE SHOULD BE A SOUND
BARB I (262)	RECOLLECTION IS PERFECTLY CORRECT. IT IS MOST	IMPORTANT	THAT YOU SHOULD BE GOOD; AND I DO BEG YOU FOR ONCE
FOUN (216)	MAN TO ADVISE ME AND BE A FATHER TO ME, IT'S VERY	IMPORTANT	THAT YOU SHOULD BE QUITE ALL RIGHT, ISNT IT? /THE
LION PREFACE(7)	DEFEAT AND DISGRACE. WAS JESUS A MARTYR? IT IS	IMPORTANT	THEREFORE THAT WE SHOULD CLEAR OUR MINDS OF THE
BARB PREFACE(219)	SPOT IN OUR SOCIAL CONSCIENCE. MONEY IS THE MOST	IMPORTANT	THING IN THE WORLD. IT REPRESENTS HEALTH,
HART II (104)	THE SOFA) I SHOULD LET HIM HAVE IT, MY DEAR. THE	IMPORTANT	THING IS NOT TO HAVE THE LAST WORD, BUT TO HAVE
MTH4 I (156)	OF THE AIR, OR EVEN THE SLIME OF THE DITCH? THE	IMPORTANT	THING IS THAT WHEN MY CREATOR TOOK IT, WHATEVER IT
LION PREFACE(95)	THAT A PIOUS FAMILY CAN DO TO PREVENT HIM. THE	IMPORTANT	THING NOW IS THAT THE GLADSTONES AND HUXLEYS
BULL I (88)	REASSURED) OF COURSE I AM. OUR GUIDANCE IS THE	IMPORTANT	THING. WE ENGLISH MUST PLACE OUR CAPACITY FOR
JOAN PREFACE(33)	BY SIMPLE SOULS WHOSE RATIONAL FAITH IN MORE	IMPORTANT	THINGS HAS BECOME BOUND UP WITH A QUITE IRRATIONAL
GETT (341)	OF YOUR FELLOW CREATURES, AND ALL THE REALLY	IMPORTANT	THINGS THAT MAKE MEN WORK AND STRIVE INSTEAD OF
AUGS (276)	ATTENTION. YOU SEE, THERE ARE ALWAYS SO MANY MORE	IMPORTANT	THINGS TO BE ATTENDED TO. FAMILY MATTERS, AND SO
KING I (164)	AM MOST HEARTILY ASHAMED. THERE ARE SO MANY MORE	IMPORTANT	THINGS TO BE WORKED AT: THE TRANSMUTATIONS OF
CAPT I (239)	THAT DOESNT MATTER IN THE LEAST, HOWARD. THE	IMPORTANT	THING, CAPTAIN BRASSBOUND, IS: FIRST, THAT WE
LION EPILOG (151)	LOOMS AS A HIGHLY SPOKEN OF AND DOUBTLESS MOST	IMPORTANT	THING, LIKE GREEK TRAGEDY, OR CLASSICAL MUSIC, OR
PYGM EPILOG (289)	AND DOMINATES, AND TEACHES, AND BECOMES	IMPORTANT	TO A SPINSTER, AS HIGGINS WITH ELIZA, SHE ALWAYS,
JOAN PREFACE(15)	THE MODERN EDUCATION WHICH JOAN ESCAPED. IT IS	IMPORTANT	TO EVERYONE NOWADAYS TO UNDERSTAND THIS, BECAUSE
PLES PREFACE(R17)	HE HAS FOUND BY EXPERIENCE THAT IT IS MORE	IMPORTANT	TO HAVE A FEW BITS OF CHOCOLATE TO EAT IN THE
DOCT PREFACE(49)	NO BURGLAR CONTENDS THAT AS IT IS ADMITTEDLY	IMPORTANT	TO HAVE MONEY TO SPEND, AND AS THE OBJECT OF
DOCT IV (158)	SEEING ME, AND SENT IN WORD THAT HIS BUSINESS WAS	IMPORTANT	TO LOUIS, IS A NEWSPAPER MAN. A PARAGRAPH APPEARED
MIS. PREFACE(34)	BETTER FOR IT. CHILDREN'S HAPPINESS. ALSO IT IS	IMPORTANT	TO PUT THE HAPPINESS OF THE CHILDREN RATHER
FANY PROLOG (272)	/FANNY/ I KNOW. DONT SCOLD ME: I HAD SOMETHING	IMPORTANT	TO SAY TO HIM. /THE COUNT/ I SHALL ASK HIM TO TAKE
JITT I (20)	SPEAK TO YOU ABOUT MY BOOK. I HAVE SOMETHING VERY	IMPORTANT	TO SAY TO YOU ABOUT IT. /JITTA/ (A LITTLE
DEVL II (33)	OWN INVITATION. YOU LEFT WORD YOU HAD SOMETHING	IMPORTANT	TO TELL ME. /ANDERSON/ I HAVE A WARNING WHICH IT
GETT (346)	BISHOP/ WAIT A MOMENT, BOXER. CECIL HAS SOMETHING	IMPORTANT	TO TELL US. /SYKES/ WEVE DONE IT. THATS ALL.
GETT PREFACE(204)	COULD BE MORE INNOCENT, MORE HYGIENIC, MORE	IMPORTANT	TO THE SOCIAL WELFARE. BUT THE WAY OF THE PEOPLE
APPL I (238)	BECAUSE THE EFFICIENCY OF THE POST OFFICE IS AS	IMPORTANT	TO THEM AS TO THE GENERAL PUBLIC. /AMANDA/ STUFF!
MTH4 I (167)	BUT HAVE YOU NOTICED SOMETHING MUCH MORE	IMPORTANT	TO YOURSELF: THAT IS, THAT YOU HAVE NEVER ASKED US
MTH2 (79)	YEARS OF OFFICE FOR THE LIBERAL PARTY SEEM SO	IMPORTANT	TO YOU, MR BURGE, IF YOU HAD ANOTHER TWO AND A
PRES (146)	COMES IN. /MITCHENER/ MRS FARRELL: IVE A VERY	IMPORTANT	VISIT TO PAY: I SHALL WANT MY FULL DRESS UNIFORM
BULL III SD(126)	SESSION ASSUMES A PORTENTOUS AIR, AS IF SOMETHING	IMPORTANT	WERE COMING. /CORNELIUS/ PRAPS YOULL EXPLAIN,
LION PREFACE(20)	THE DIALECT OF PALESTINE. THESE DISTINCTIONS ARE	IMPORTANT	, AS YOU WILL FIND IF YOU READ HOLINSHED OR
LION PREFACE(43)	THE CONSENSUS ON THIS POINT IS	IMPORTANT	, BECAUSE IT PROVES THE ABSOLUTE SINCERITY OF
PLES PREFACE(R17)	GOOD AS BAD, IMPORTANT AS TRIVIAL AND TRIVIAL AS	IMPORTANT	, SERIOUS AS LAUGHABLE AND LAUGHABLE AS SERIOUS,

IMPORTANTLY

MTH4 I (144)	TO VISIT US? /THE ELDERLY GENTLEMAN/ (	IMPORTANTLY	) OUR PRIME MINISTER, MR BADGER BLUEBIN, HAS
DEST (182)	INTERCEPTS HIM. /LADY/ LIEUTENANT. /LIEUTENANT/ (	IMPORTANTLY	) YOU MUSNT DELAY ME, YOU KNOW. DUTY, MADAM,
ARMS III (49)	RIGHT. I'LL SEE TO IT. (HE GOES TO THE DOOR	IMPORTANTLY	, BUT HESITATES ON THE THRESHOLD). BY THE BYE,
DEST (158)	THE LETTERS AND DESPATCHES? /THE LIEUTENANT/ (	IMPORTANTLY	, RATHER PLEASED THAN OTHERWISE AT HAVING SOME

IMPORTATION

DOCT PREFACE(23)	KNOW THAT SMALLPOX CAN BE PRODUCED ONLY BY THE	IMPORTATION	OF ITS SPECIFIC MICROBE. IF THIS WAS THE LINE

IMPORTED

MTH3 (97)	YOU ARE CONGENITALLY INCAPABLE. ACCORDINGLY, YOU	IMPORTED	EDUCATED NEGRESSES AND CHINESE TO GOVERN YOU. SINCE
CAND I SD(77)	OF CARPET GARDENING, AND A SANDPIT, ORIGINALLY	IMPORTED	FROM THE SEASIDE FOR THE DELIGHT OF CHILDREN, BUT
MTH3 (95)	CHINAMAN TO TAKE PART IN OUR PUBLIC SERVICES, AND	IMPORTED	NATIVES OF SCOTLAND FOR THAT PURPOSE. WE HAVE DONE
BULL PREFACE(15)	IS, I HAVE NO TRACE IN ME OF THE COMMERCIALLY	IMPORTED	NORTH SPANISH STRAIN WHICH PASSES FOR ABORIGINAL
MTH3 (96)	HE WAS NOT AN ENGLISHMAN: HE WAS A FRENCHMAN. HE	IMPORTED	PARLIAMENTS FROM FRANCE. /BURGE-LUBIN/ (SURPRISED)
APPL I (220)	WHERE LABOR IS CHEAP. WE LIVE IN COMFORT ON THE	IMPORTED	PROFITS OF THAT CAPITAL. WE ARE ALL LADIES AND

IMPORTS

ROCK II (237)	FOREIGN TRADE IN PROTECTED INDUSTRIES. STATE	IMPORTS	ONLY, TO BE SOLD AT STATE REGULATED PRICES. /SIR

IMPORTUNATE

BASH II,2, (114)	HORRIBLE CLIMAX! ALL-UNDOING SPITE! -- TH'	IMPORTUNATE	CLUTCHING OF THE COWARD'S HAND FROM WEARIED
BARB PREFACE(227)	COLLECTORS OF RATES, TAXES, AND RENT; NO	IMPORTUNATE	HOPES NOR EXACTING DUTIES; NOTHING BUT THE REST
BASH III (124)	LIFE WERE WORTH LIVING! HAD I ANY CHOICE IN THIS	IMPORTUNATE	RELATIONSHIP? NONE, AND UNTIL THAT HIGH
GETT (315)	EACH OCCASION. AT SUCH TIMES HE IS SUPERFLUOUS,	IMPORTUNATE	, AND RIDICULOUS. /COLLINS/ BUT WHERE IS HE TO

IMPORTUNITY

SUPR PREFACE(R25)	THE SUPPRESSION OF RAPINE AND DISCOURAGEMENT OF	IMPORTUNITY	, WITHOUT BEING DRIVEN TO VERY SERIOUS

IMPOSE

MILL I (144)	WHENEVER A MAN ASKED ME TO MARRY HIM I SHOULD	IMPOSE	A CONDITION ON MY CONSENT. /SAGAMORE/ (ATTENTIVE)
GETT PREFACE(237)	AN ACT OF ENSLAVEMENT. BUT IT IS NO WORSE THAN TO	IMPOSE	A CONTINUATION OF MARRIAGE ON PEOPLE WHO HAVE CEASED
2TRU III (105)	BUT NO LADY-- NO HUMAN BEING-- HAS A RIGHT TO	IMPOSE	A FALSEHOOD ON ME. I DO NOT REGRET MY ACTION. I HAVE
UNPL PREFACE(R15)	OF THEIR SUPPORTERS, THEN HE CAN SUPPRESS IT, AND	IMPOSE	A MULCT OF 50 POUNDS ON EVERYBODY WHO TAKES PART IN A
MIS. PREFACE(36)	DO" AND IT WILL BE SEEN THAT WE HAVE NO RIGHT TO	IMPOSE	A PERPETUAL HOLIDAY ON CHILDREN. IF WE DID, THEY
BULL PREFACE(7)	WHY WAS IT THAT THE PRIESTS HAD NO POWER TO	IMPOSE	A ROMAN CATHOLIC LEADER ON THE HOME RULE MOVEMENT
POSN PREFACE(364)	IN CAMERA IF AND WHEN IT PLEASES. 5. THE POWER TO	IMPOSE	A VETO ON THE PRODUCTION OF PLAYS IS TO BE ABOLISHED
BASH PREFACE(88)	UNDERSTAND WHAT THEY ARE SAYING; BUT IT CANNOT	IMPOSE	ANY SUCH ILLUSION ON A PROFESSIONALLY SKILLED
SUPR III (118)	WORLD. I SAW THEN HOW USELESS IT IS TO ATTEMPT TO	IMPOSE	CONDITIONS ON THE IRRESISTIBLE FORCE OF LIFE; TO
BULL PREFACE(44)	BEHIND THE BULWARK OF A STANDARD WAGE, AND TO	IMPOSE	CRUSHING IMPORT DUTIES ON EVERY ENGLISH TRADE THAT
LION PREFACE(71)	RIGHTS, HE DOES SO BECAUSE HE HAS NO RIGHT TO	IMPOSE	ECCENTRIC STANDARDS OF EXPENDITURE AND UNSOCIAL
SIM II (75)	DENOUNCES THE REPORTS AS NONSENSE THAT WOULD NOT	IMPOSE	EVEN ON THE SOCIETY FOR PSYCHICAL RESEARCH. HIS
CAND I SD(79)	WITHOUT SETTING HIMSELF UP AGAINST THEM, TO	IMPOSE	HIS AUTHORITY ON THEM WITHOUT HUMILIATING THEM, AND,
GETT PREFACE(249)	BUT MAMMON OVERREACHED HIMSELF WHEN HE TRIED TO	IMPOSE	HIS DOCTRINE OF INALIENABLE PROPERTY ON THE CHURCH
BARB PREFACE(231)	PRECEPT THE LAW AND PUBLIC OPINION TEACH HIM TO	IMPOSE	HIS WILL ON OTHERS BY ANGER, VIOLENCE, AND CRUELTY,
MIS. PREFACE(66)	EMPLOYEE HAS IN HIM THE SAME FIERCE IMPULSE TO	IMPOSE	HIS WILL WITHOUT RESPECT FOR THE WILL OF OTHERS.
3PLA PREFACE(R20)	UP IMPOSING CELIBACY ON OUR PRIESTS; BUT WE STILL	IMPOSE	IT ON OUR ART, WITH THE VERY UNDESIRABLE AND
POSN PREFACE(394)	THING FOR COURT CEREMONIES; BUT TO ATTEMPT TO	IMPOSE	IT ON THE DRAMA IS ABOUT AS SENSIBLE AS AN ATTEMPT TO
METH PREFACE(R11)	CINEMA-FED ROMANTICISM WHICH MADE IT POSSIBLE TO	IMPOSE	IT ON THE PEOPLE AS A CRUSADE, AND ESPECIALLY THE
MILL PREFACE(133)	THOUGH IT WILL STILL PLEASE, IT WILL NO LONGER	IMPOSE	. FOR MERE ICONOCLASM IS A MISTAKE: THE ROUNDHEAD
GETT PREFACE(237)	TO WHICH MODERN DEMOCRACY COMMITS US, TO	IMPOSE	MARRIAGE ON TWO UNMARRIED PEOPLE WHO DO NOT DESIRE TO

MIS. PREFACE(84)	CHANGE THEIR BEHAVIOR AS CIRCUMSTANCES CHANGE. TO	IMPOSE	ON A CITIZEN OF LONDON THE FAMILY DUTIES OF A
JOAN EPILOG (153)	TESTIMONY MADE OF IDLE TALES THAT COULD NOT	IMPOSE	ON A PLOUGHBOY. YET OUT OF THIS INSULT TO JUSTICE,
JOAN 4 (100)	EXPLANATION. THE WOMAN'S MIRACLES WOULD NOT	IMPOSE	ON A RABBIT: SHE DOES NOT CLAIM THEM AS MIRACLES
KING I (195)	AND HIS SILLY POPISH PLOT THAT SHOULD NOT	IMPOSE	ON A RABBIT. NO MAN WITH EYES IN HIS HEAD COULD LOOK
JOAN 6 (140)	IS A GRAIN OF WORLDLY SENSE IN IT SUCH AS MIGHT	IMPOSE	ON A SIMPLE VILLAGE MAIDEN. /JOAN/ IF WE WERE AS
MILL PREFACE(131)	PLEASE NOTE THAT NAPOLEON DID NOT AND COULD NOT	IMPOSE	ON BOURRIENNE AND TALLEYRAND, NOR EVEN ON THE MORE
INCA (241)	ADVANTAGE OF HER HIGHNESS'S GRACIOUSNESS. YOU	IMPOSE	ON HER WITH YOUR STORIES. YOU GIVE HER A ROOM NOT FIT
APPL PREFACE(171)	ANTI-DEMOCRATIC ROYALIST VOTE AGAINST HIM, AND	IMPOSE	ON HIM A RIVAL IN THE PERSON OF THE ONLY PUBLIC MAN
MRS II (206)	MRS WARREN, FLUSHING A LITTLE AT HER FAILURE TO	IMPOSE	ON HIM IN THE CHARACTER OF A THEATRICALLY DEVOTED
MTH4 II (175)	THE GOD, AND SO ON. THAT SORT OF THING DOES NOT	IMPOSE	ON ME: I USE IT MYSELF TO IMPOSE ON SIMPLETONS. I
ROCK I (232)	AND WHAT A HUMBUG YOU ARE! DONT THINK YOU CAN	IMPOSE	ON ME WITH YOUR MEDITATION PARLOR AND YOUR DIGNIFIED
ROCK PREFACE(183)	A DEAD THING AND IMPULSE A LIVE THING. YOU CANNOT	IMPOSE	ON ME WITH YOUR REASONABLE AND WELL INFORMED OPINION.
JITT II (38)	NO MORE OF THE POOR CHILD BUSINESS: IT DOES NOT	IMPOSE	ON ME HOW AM I TO FIND HER? /JITTA/ (
DOCT PREFACE(39)	DOES NOT, UNFORTUNATELY FOR MY OWN COMFORT,	IMPOSE	ON ME VIVISECTORS CAN HARDLY PRETEND TO BE BETTER
METH PREFACE(R37)	TO DO WITH RELIGION, OR BEING SERIOUS ENOUGH TO	IMPOSE	ON OR CONFUSE ANY PROPERLY EDUCATED CHILD OVER THE
MTH4 II (191)	ABSOLUTELY INSANE: AND SUICIDAL. NEVERTHELESS WE	IMPOSE	ON OURSELVES ABSTINENCES AND DISCIPLINES AND STUDIES
MTH4 II (175)	THING DOES NOT IMPOSE ON ME: I USE IT MYSELF TO	IMPOSE	ON SIMPLETONS. I BELIEVE THAT WHAT IS, IS. I KNOW
3PLA PREFACE(R32)	RESPECT FOR THEM AT ALL: SUCH MAUDLIN TRICKS MAY	IMPOSE	ON TEA-DRUNKARDS, NOT ON ME. BESIDES, I HAVE A
BARB PREFACE(209)	TO CARRY THINGS OFF BETTER THAN HE DID; TO	IMPOSE	ON THE PEOPLE WHO SAW THROUGH HIM; TO FASCINATE
ROCK PREFACE(182)	YOUR PEOPLE THAT I SHOULD SIT IN THIS CHAIR AND	IMPOSE	ON THEM THE PEACE OF ROME THAN THAT THEY SHOULD BE
GETT PREFACE(192)	CONSTITUTIONAL GOVERNMENT, ANY COUNTERFEIT COULD	IMPOSE	ON THEM. ANY ATHEIST COULD PASS HIMSELF OFF ON THEM
METH PREFACE(R68)	AND SUFFERING EVERYTHING THAT IT PAYS TO	IMPOSE	ON THEM, AND THAT ANY FALSE EXCUSE FOR AN UNPOPULAR
VWOO 2 (130)	THE LOCAL AUTHORITY-- TO A POINT AT WHICH YOU CAN	IMPOSE	ON UNOBSERVANT AND UNWARY TRAVELLERS. YOU HAVE HAD
GENV IV (96)	UNDERTAKE ANY LARGER CARES THAT PROVIDENCE MAY	IMPOSE	ON US. MEANWHILE WE SHOULD FEEL VERY UNEASY IF ANY
GENV IV (96)	/BBDE/ A MOST ASTUTE SPEECH. BUT IT CANNOT	IMPOSE	ON US. /JUDGE/ IT HAS IMPOSED ON BOTH OF YOU. IT IS A
KING I (166)	THE ARMCHAIR WITH EASY GRACE. /FOX/ I MUST NOT	IMPOSE	ON YOU BY CLAIMING THE GENTLEMAN AS MY FRIEND. WE MET
BARB PREFACE(218)	GRATUITOUSLY OUT OF SHEER FOLLY AND ABJECTNESS,	IMPOSE	ONLY ON THOSE WHO WANT TO BE IMPOSED ON. THE REASON
SUPR I (35)	DO YOU THINK THAT ANYTHING IS STRONG ENOUGH TO	IMPOSE	OUGHTS ON A PASSION EXCEPT A STRONGER PASSION STILL?
GETT PREFACE(236)	IN THESE MATTERS TO MIND OUR OWN BUSINESS AND NOT	IMPOSE	OUR INDIVIDUAL NOTIONS OF PROPRIETY ON ONE ANOTHER,
FANY III (323)	ALAS, CAN ONLY FIGHT. FRANCE IS UNCONQUERABLE. WE	IMPOSE	OUR NARROW IDEAS, OUR PREJUDICES, OUR OBSOLETE
SUPR HANDBOK(205)	ENOUGH TO SEE THAT NOTHING BUT BRUTE COERCION CAN	IMPOSE	OUR SELFISH WILL ON OTHERS. COWARDICE IS UNIVERSAL:
MILL IV (200)	YOU. YOUR CHEEK, YOUR GLUTTONY, YOUR OBSTINACY	IMPOSE	RESPECT ON ME. I THREW A HALF BAKED GENTLEMAN
SUPR HANDBOK(213)	STATE OR BY SOME ORGANIZATION STRONG ENOUGH TO	IMPOSE	RESPECT UPON THE STATE. THE NOVELTY OF ANY SUCH
SUPR HANDBOK(190)	TIME AND BY MORALLY SUICIDAL COERCIVE METHODS,	IMPOSE	SUPER-HUMANITY ON THOSE WHOM THEY GOVERNED; SO, BY
MIS. PREFACE(22)	MORE RESPONSIBLE AND ANXIOUS ONES. THEY COULD NOT	IMPOSE	THE HEROIC ATTITUDE ON THEIR EMPLOYERS; NOR WOULD
BARB PREFACE(212)	INFERIOR WHITE RACES FOUND THEMSELVES TO	IMPOSE	THEIR DOMINATION ON THE COLORED RACES BY PRIESTCRAFT,
LADY PREFACE(233)	MEN WITH THESE POWERS THAT THEY ARE FORCED TO	IMPOSE	THEIR FULLEST EXERCISE ON THE WORLD BECAUSE THEY

IMPOSED

MIS. PREFACE(55)	OF HUGE RETINUES; BUT FLOGGING HAS NEVER BEEN SO	IMPOSED	: IT HAS ALWAYS BEEN A VICE, CRAVED FOR ON ANY
LION PREFACE(53)	AND THE STERN COMPULSION OF NATURE, HAD NOT	IMPOSED	A COMMON RULE ON THE HALF DOZEN ROBINSON CRUSOES WHO
2TRU I (48)	AND OF THE FAMILY DOCTOR FOR HER HEALTH, THE	IMPOSED	AFFECTION OF UNINTERESTING BROTHERS AND SISTERS, THE
JOAN PREFACE(55)	CONTINUOUS PLAYING, BARRING THE ONE INTERVAL	IMPOSED	BY CONSIDERATIONS WHICH HAVE NOTHING TO DO WITH ART.
MILL IV (205)	THIS LADY HAS EASILY FULFILLED THE CONDITION	IMPOSED	BY MY MOTHER. BUT I HAVE NOT FULFILLED THE CONDITION
GETT PREFACE(215)	TO MAKE MARRIAGE MORE AND MORE ONE OF THE CUSTOMS	IMPOSED	BY NECESSITY ON THE POOR, WHILST THE FREER FORM OF
GETT PREFACE(240)	WITHOUT RESORTING TO THE SHAMEFUL SHIFTS	IMPOSED	BY OUR LAW, YET THE FIGURES JUST GIVEN TO THE ROYAL
MILL IV (205)	MY MOTHER. BUT I HAVE NOT FULFILLED THE CONDITION	IMPOSED	BY THE LADY'S FATHER. /EPIFANIA/ YOU NEED NOT
MIS. PREFACE(33)	ALTOGETHER UNACCOUNTABLE MANNER WITHIN THE LIMITS	IMPOSED	BY THE SIMILAR RIGHTS OF ITS NEIGHBORS, AND THE
METH PREFACE(R41)	CAMMYLEOPARD), I DO NOT REMEMBER HOW THIS ANIMAL	IMPOSED	HIMSELF ILLUSTRATIVELY ON THE EVOLUTION CONTROVERSY;
MTH4 II (188)	OF COURSE YOU KNOW AS WELL AS I DO THAT HE HAS	IMPOSED	HIMSELF ON MY PARTY JUST TO SPY ON ME. I DONT DENY
SUPR HANDBOK(182)	ON STRINGENT PUBLIC OR COLLECTIVE CONDITIONS,	IMPOSED	IN THE INTEREST OF THE GENERAL WELFARE WITHOUT ANY
INCA (256)	I WAS SWEPT AWAY BY A PASSION NOT MY OWN, WHICH	IMPOSED	ITSELF ON ME. BY MYSELF I AM NOTHING. I DARE NOT
MIS. PREFACE(57)	TRUE; FOR THERE IS NO LABOR THAT MIGHT NOT BE	IMPOSED	ON A CHILD OR AN ADULT ON THE SAME PRETEXT; BUT AS A
ROCK II (270)	OR LORD KNOWS WHAT SILLINESS THAT SHOULDNT HAVE	IMPOSED	ON A CHILD OF FOUR. THAT WAS THE END OF DEMOCRACY
APPL PREFACE(172)	IN PARLIAMENT, WITH A DOCILITY WHICH CANNOT BE	IMPOSED	ON A KING WHO WORKS AT HIS JOB; FOR THE KING WORKS
O'FL (224)	YOU ASK ME TO LIVE IN IRELAND WHERE IVE BEEN	IMPOSED	ON AND KEPT IN IGNORANCE, AND TO DIE WHERE THE DIVIL
FABL PREFACE(74)	OF VACCINATION ON EVIDENCE THAT COULD NOT HAVE	IMPOSED	ON ANY COMPETENT STATISTICIAN, AND WAS PICKED UP BY
BULL PREFACE(63)	RIDICULOUS AS THE LIES OF FALSTAFF, SHOULD HAVE	IMPOSED	ON ANY INTELLIGENT AND POLITICALLY EXPERIENCED HUMAN
GENV IV (96)	BUT IT CANNOT IMPOSE ON US. /JUDGE/ IT HAS	IMPOSED	ON BOTH OF YOU. IT IS A PERFECTLY HONEST SPEECH MADE
FABL PREFACE(69)	AND GOVERNING ARE MOSTLY TOO CLEVER TO BE	IMPOSED	ON BY FAIRY TALES, AND IN ANY CASE HAVE TO DEAL WITH
LION EPILOG (148)	BY IDOLIZING HIM. WE ARE STILL SO EASILY	IMPOSED	ON BY SUCH IDOLS THAT ONE OF THE LEADING PASTORS OF
CLEO NOTES (209)	THE GALLIC WARS, I HOPE I HAVE NOT BEEN TOO MUCH	IMPOSED	ON BY THE DRAMATIC ILLUSION TO WHICH ALL GREAT MEN
BULL IV (180)	CAN KEEP BOTH FOR MY FRIEND HERE, WHO IS STILL	IMPOSED	ON BY THEM. I KNOW THEIR VALUE. /KEEGAN/ YOU MEAN
METH PREFACE(R56)	AND HUMANE MEN THAT THEY ALLOW THEMSELVES TO BE	IMPOSED	ON BY THIS RABBLE OF DOLTS, BLACKGUARDS, IMPOSTORS,
PHIL II (125)	TO ME? /GRACE/ DO YOU SUPPOSE I AM A MAN, TO BE	IMPOSED	ON BY THIS SORT OF RUBBISH? /JULIA/ (GETTING UP
POSN PREFACE(383)	THE BEGINNING OF THE WORLD. TOLERATION MUST BE	IMPOSED	ON HIM AS A MYSTIC AND PAINFUL DUTY BY HIS SPIRITUAL
ROCK PREFACE(157)	CRUELTY WHICH HAS BEEN MORTIFIED BY THE RESTRAINT	IMPOSED	ON IT BY CIVILIZATION. TAKE THE CASE OF THE
HART II (110)	NOT BILLY DUNN. THIS IS BILLY DUNN. WHY HAVE YOU	IMPOSED	ON ME? /THE BURGLAR/ (INDIGNANTLY TO MAZZINI) HAVE
BUOY III (28)	BE IMPOSED ON YOU. /SIR FERDINAND/ NOTHING CAN BE	IMPOSED	ON ME. THE ATMOSPHERE HERE IS MOST UNSUITABLE. DOES
CATH PREFACE(156)	I AM DEPARTING FROM A RULE WHICH I HAVE HITHERTO	IMPOSED	ON MYSELF SO RIGIDLY THAT I NEVER PERMIT MYSELF,
POSN PREFACE(361)	BE FULLY ILLUSTRATED WITHIN THE LIMITS OF DECORUM	IMPOSED	ON THE PRESS, IT COULD ONLY BE DEALT WITH BY A
CYMB FORWORD(133)	IN THE CRUDE LITERARY BUTCHERIES SUCCESSFULLY	IMPOSED	ON THE PUBLIC AND THE CRITICS AS SHAKESPEAR'S PLAYS
BARB PREFACE(212)	THE SLAVE-MORALITY AS HAVING BEEN INVENTED AND	IMPOSED	ON THE WORLD BY SLAVES MAKING A VIRTUE OF NECESSITY
MRS PREFACE(173)	CONSPICUOUS REACTIONISTS AGAINST THE RESTRAINTS	IMPOSED	ON THEM IN CHILDHOOD BY THEIR FATHER'S PROFESSION.
GETT PREFACE(221)	A MASS OF EXORBITANT AND IRRELEVANT CONDITIONS	IMPOSED	ON THEM ON FALSE PRETENCES TO ENABLE NEEDY PARENTS
SUPR I (32)	WHICH YOU BULLIED THE OTHER GIRLS: YOUR VIRTUE	IMPOSED	ON THEM. BUT TELL ME THIS: DID YOU EVER KNOW A GOOD
GETT PREFACE(213)	SUCH WORK. WHY SHOULD THE TAKING OF A HUSBAND BE	IMPOSED	ON THESE WOMEN AS THE PRICE OF THEIR RIGHT TO
MIS. PREFACE(55)	CENTURY. THIS FOULNESS, WE CAN PLEAD, WAS	IMPOSED	ON US AS A NECESSITY BY THE USE OF HORSES AND OF
MIS. PREFACE(83)	ADMIT THEM TO OUR INTIMACY, BUT TO HAVE A PERSON	IMPOSED	ON US AS A BROTHER MERELY BECAUSE HE HAPPENS TO HAVE
ROCK PREFACE(155)	THE CONCEALMENT OR IGNORING OF FACTS WHICH ARE	IMPOSED	ON US AT PRESENT BECAUSE EXTERMINATION FOR THE
GENV PREFACE(8)	ALL OF IT THAT ACHIEVED ITS PURPOSE OF RUIN HAS	IMPOSED	ON US THE ADDED BURDEN OF REPAIRING WHAT WE HAVE
SIM PREFACE(5)	THEIR SOCIAL USES. THEY HAVE BEEN INVENTED AND	IMPOSED	ON US TO SECURE CERTAIN LINES OF BEHAVIOR AS EITHER
DOCT PREFACE(73)	OF US: THE DANGER OF HAVING A HYGIENIC ORTHODOXY	IMPOSED	ON US. BUT WE MUST FACE THAT: IN SUCH CROWDED AND
BUOY III (28)	BE GIVEN HERE. BUT NO RELIGIOUS SERVICE IS TO BE	IMPOSED	ON YOU. /SIR FERDINAND/ NOTHING CAN BE IMPOSED ON
GENV I (44)	HANDS ARE NOT BLOODSTAINED, COMRADE. I HAVE NOT	IMPOSED	ON YOU. YOU HAVE NOT QUITE RECOVERED YET, I THINK. I
CAPT III (274)	I CANNOT SAY THAT, LEDDY CEECILY. I DOUBT HE HAS	IMPOSED	ON YOUR GOOD NATURE AND SWEET DISPOSEETION. I HAD A
BARB PREFACE(218)	ABJECTNESS, IMPOSE ONLY ON THOSE WHO WANT TO BE	IMPOSED	ON. THE REASON WHY THE INDEPENDENT INCOME-TAX PAYERS
METH PREFACE(R70)	AND THE UNITED STATES OF AMERICA COULD HAVE	IMPOSED	PEACE ON THE WORLD, AND NURSED MODERN CIVILIZATION
FABL PREFACE(84)	CONTROLLED PRICES, RATIONED FOOD AND CLOTHING,	IMPOSED	PURCHASE TAXES ON LUXURIES, AND INCREASED THE
METH PREFACE(R39)	NOTHING ELSE, AND OF VERY EVIL PASSIONS TOO. THEY	IMPOSED	THIS IDOL IN PRACTICE ON THE CHURCH ITSELF, IN SPITE
O'FL (222)	AND FEAR AND TROUBLE. IVE BEEN MADE A FOOL OF AND	IMPOSED	UPON ALL MY LIFE. I THOUGHT THAT COVETIOUS STHREAL
MILL PREFACE(113)	PLEASE. WHEN A MENTALITY IS CREATED AND A CODE	IMPOSED	, THE BORN RULER, THE MOSES OR LENIN, IS NO LONGER

IMPOSES

MIS. PREFACE(8)	IS RIGHT AND WHAT HE DISAPPROVES OF IS WRONG; WHO	IMPOSES	A CORRESPONDING CONDUCT ON THE CHILD BY A SYSTEM OF
SUPR HANDBOK(189)	VICARIOUSLY; BUT MARRIAGE ITSELF SUCCESSFULLY	IMPOSES	CELIBACY ON MILLIONS OF UNMARRIED NORMAL MEN AND
POSN PREFACE(381)	NOW MORALITY IS EXTREMELY VALUABLE TO SOCIETY. IT	IMPOSES	CONVENTIONAL CONDUCT ON THE GREAT MASS OF PERSONS
MIS. PREFACE(8)	THE CONVENTIONAL GOOD FATHER WHO DELIBERATELY	IMPOSES	HIMSELF ON HIS SON AS A GOD; WHO TAKES ADVANTAGE OF
LION PREFACE(90)	EXCEPT TO PEOPLE UPON WHOM THE DELUSION	IMPOSES	, " THE HIGHER CRITICISM." HISTORICAL RESEARCH AND
LION PREFACE(62)	TO THE SUPPLY OF THE PRIMITIVE WANTS WHICH NATURE	IMPOSES	ON ALL HUMAN BEINGS ALIKE, WE KNOW THAT PEOPLE NEED
MIS. PREFACE(91)	BY ART. ALL THE WHOLESOME CONDITIONS WHICH ART	IMPOSES	ON APPETITE ARE WAIVED: INSTEAD OF CULTIVATED MEN
MIS. PREFACE(83)	US TO SPEND OUR CHILDHOOD WITH THEM, AND THUS	IMPOSES	ON US A CURIOUS RELATION IN WHICH FAMILIARITY
SUPR PREFACE(R20)	THE THEATRE, THAT LAST SANCTUARY OF UNREALITY, IT	IMPOSES	ONLY ON THE INEXPERIENCED, IN SHAKESPEAR'S PLAYS THE
POSN PREFACE(412)	OF DOMESTIC AND FOREIGN POLICY, AND THAT IT	IMPOSES	THE LIMITS OF ETIQUET ON THE HISTORICAL DRAMA. 5. A
JOAN PREFACE(48)	OVER FOUR TIMES AS MANY MONTHS; FOR THE THEATRE	IMPOSES	UNITIES OF TIME AND PLACE FROM WHICH NATURE IN HER
DOCT I SD(96)	MAKES INTERRUPTION OR INATTENTION IMPOSSIBLE, AND	IMPOSES	VENERATION AND CREDULITY ON ALL BUT THE STRONGEST

IMPOSING

ROCK PREFACE(153)	OUR POLITICAL CONSTITUTIONS VERY UNSTABLE; AND	IMPOSING	AN HABITUAL DISINGENUOUSNESS ON CONSERVATIVE
NEVR IV SD(286)	ONE. HIS BEARING AS HE ENTERS IS SUFFICIENTLY	IMPOSING	AND DISQUIETING; BUT WHEN HE SPEAKS, HIS POWERFUL
ROCK PREFACE(153)	CATASTROPHE ARRIVES, IT IS DISGUISED UNDER AN	IMPOSING	ARRAY OF DOCTORS' NAMES FOR MORIBUNDITY. THE
JOAN 2,SD(71)	NOTHING OF THE ECCLESIASTIC ABOUT HIM EXCEPT HIS	IMPOSING	BEARING, AND THE LORD CHAMBERLAIN, MONSEIGNEUR DE
SUPR I SD(9)	OF HAZEL COLORED HAIR IS THROWN BACK FROM AN	IMPOSING	BROW, SUGGEST JUPITER RATHER THAN APOLLO. HE IS
3PLA PREFACE(R20)	THE INSTANCE OF MARTIN LUTHER WE LONG AGO GAVE UP	IMPOSING	CELIBACY ON OUR PRIESTS; BUT WE STILL IMPOSE IT ON
JITT III (58)	HER OUT? /LENKHEIM/ (MEETING HER EYE WITH	IMPOSING	FIRMNESS) SOLELY FOR YOUR OWN SAKE, MRS
METH PREFACE(R88)	TIME. ALSO I SUPPLIED THE PUBLISHED WORK WITH AN	IMPOSING	FRAMEWORK CONSISTING OF A PREFACE, AN APPENDIX
MILL I SD(152)	WHEN HE COMES IN? ADRIAN BLENDERBLAND, AN	IMPOSING	MAN IN THE PRIME OF LIFE, BEARDED IN THE VICTORIAN
APPL PREFACE(177)	ELECTED BY VOTE SHOULD NOT ESCAPE BY WEARING ITS	IMPOSING	MASK. I DELIVERED MYSELF AS FOLLOWS: YOUR
2TRU PREFACE(15)	THE STATE, THE REALM, THE REPUBLIC, OR ANY OTHER	IMPOSING	NAME THAT DID NOT GIVE AWAY ITS CENTRAL PURPOSE.
GETT PREFACE(255)	CAN TAKE IS THAT AS THE STATE, IN SPITE OF ITS	IMPOSING	NAME, CAN, WHEN ALL IS SAID, DO NOTHING WITH THE
JOAN 4,SD(94)	WORK WRITING. AT THE OTHER SIDE OF THE TABLE AN	IMPOSING	NOBLEMAN, AGED 46, IS SEATED IN A HANDSOME CHAIR
BARB II (290)	OUT! /CUSINS/ YOU KNOW, I DO NOT ADMIT THAT I AM	IMPOSING	ON BARBARA. I AM QUITE GENUINELY INTERESTED IN THE
METH PREFACE(R45)	IT IS THEIR BUSINESS TO PRODUCE TRANSFORMATION BY	IMPOSING	ON FLOWERS AND ANIMALS A SELECTION FROM WITHOUT.
GENV III (85)	AND I DINE TOGETHER? /BEGONIA/ OH, I FEEL I AM	IMPOSING	ON YOU: I HAVE DINED WITH YOU THREE TIMES ALREADY.
APPL II (273)	I SAY, WHATS THE GAME? /MAGNUS/ THERE IS NO	IMPOSING	ON YOU, PRIME MINISTER. THE GAME IS, OF COURSE,
METH PREFACE(R11)	HAVE AWKWARD CONSEQUENCES. DARWIN WAS GIVEN AN	IMPOSING	REPUTATION AS NOT ONLY AN EVOLUTIONIST, BUT AS THE
NEVR I SD(208)	RULING OUT ALL ATTEMPT AT SEX ATTRACTION AND	IMPOSING	RESPECT ON FRIVOLOUS MANKIND AND FASHIONABLE
MIS. PREFACE(8)	ANY MORE THAN WITH GROWN-UP PEOPLE WITHOUT	IMPOSING	RULES OF CONDUCT ON THEM. THERE IS A POINT AT WHICH
ROCK I SD(193)	ARE THE SPACIOUS WINDOWS. EVERYTHING IS ON AN	IMPOSING	SCALE, INCLUDING AN OBLONG TABLE ACROSS THE MIDDLE
INCA SD(244)	IN MILITARY UNIFORM, ADVANCES WITH A MARKED AND	IMPOSING	STAGE WALK; STOPS; ORDERS THE TREMBLING MANAGER BY
GENV I SD(37)	OF A GORGEOUS AND OPULENT SOUTHERN BEAUTY. HER	IMPOSING	STYLE AND DRESS AT ONCE REDUCE THE YOUNG LADY OF
WIDO I SD(5)	CARRIAGE, HIS INCISIVE, DOMINEERING UTTERANCE AND	IMPOSING	STYLE, WITH HIS STRONG AQUILINE NOSE AND RESOLUTE
BULL PREFACE(39)	OPPRESSED UNDER JUDICIAL FORMS WHICH CONFER THE	IMPOSING	TITLE OF JUSTICE ON A CRUDE SYSTEM OF BLUDGEONING
MTH5 (220)	TO TAKE HER SERIOUSLY IN SPITE OF HER BEAUTY AND	IMPOSING	TONE). /ECRASIA/ WELL, HAVE YOU EVER HESITATED TO
OVER (179)	AND DRESSING VERY CAREFULLY. SHE IS A TALL,	IMPOSING	, HANDSOME, LANGUID WOMAN, WITH FLASHING DARK EYES
SUPR III SD(73)	AND A MEPHISTOPHELEAN AFFECTATION WHICH IS FAIRLY	IMPOSING	, PERHAPS BECAUSE THE SCENERY ADMITS OF A LARGER

IMPOSINGLY

JOAN 1,SD(66)	BUT REMAINS STANDING TO INFLATE HIMSELF MORE	IMPOSINGLY	. JOAN COMES IN, FULL OF GOOD NEWS. /JOAN/ JACK
GENV I (30)	FOR INTELLECTUAL CO-OPERATION LODGED IN SOME	IMPOSINGLY	MONUMENTAL STRUCTURE. /SHE/ OH, ISNT IT
BULL III (136)	/BROADBENT/ (RISING SO AS TO ADDRESS THEM MORE	IMPOSINGLY	) I REALLY CANNOT TELL YOU WHAT I FEEL ABOUT HOME
JOAN 1 (61)	SQUARELY ON THE TABLE, AND INFLATES HIS CHEST	IMPOSINGLY	TO CURE THE UNWELCOME AND ONLY TOO FAMILIAR

IMPOSITION

LION PREFACE(81)	HOWEVER, DID NOT GET HIS GREAT REPUTATION BY MERE	IMPOSITION	AND REACTION. IT IS ONLY IN COMPARISON WITH JESUS
JOAN PREFACE(54)	TWO LONG INTERVALS OF RELIEF) IS AN INTOLERABLE	IMPOSITION	. NOBODY SAYS " I HATE CLASSICAL TRAGEDY AND
MIS. PREFACE(32)	WITH ITS ACCOMPANYING CLASS DISTINCTIONS AND	IMPOSITION	OF SNOBBERY ON CHILDREN AS A NECESSARY PART OF
METH PREFACE(R78)	AS IT IS UNINTELLIGIBLE. AND THIS IS BECAUSE THE	IMPOSITION	OF THE LEGENDS AS LITERAL TRUTHS AT ONCE CHANGES
LION PREFACE(80)	A MORE MONSTROUS IMPOSITION PERPETRATED THAN THE	IMPOSITION	OF THE LIMITATIONS OF PAUL'S SOUL UPON THE SOUL
MIS. PREFACE(98)	OF A VERY REMARKABLE ORIENTAL RACE; AND THE	IMPOSITION	OF THIS LITERATURE, ON WHATEVER FALSE PRETENCES,
LION PREFACE(80)	THERE HAS REALLY NEVER BEEN A MORE MONSTROUS	IMPOSITION	PERPETRATED THAN THE IMPOSITION OF THE

IMPOSITIONS

MIS. PREFACE(47)	AND TERRIFYINGS AND THREATS OF HELL FIRE AND	IMPOSITIONS	AND HUMILIATIONS AND PETTY IMPRISONINGS AND
FABL PREFACE(93)	ON. THE SCHOOLMASTER DOES NOT TEACH. HE CANES OR	IMPOSITIONS	OR " KEEPS IN" THE PUPILS WHO CANNOT ANSWER
MIS. PREFACE(21)	WITS; AND WHEN THIS DOES NOT SUFFICE WE SCRIBBLE	IMPOSITIONS	, OR SUFFER EXTRA IMPRISONMENTS -- " KEEPING IN"

IMPOSSIBILISTS

CAPT III (297)	OH, I SEE YOURE ONE OF THE IDEALISTS-- THE	IMPOSSIBILISTS	! WE HAVE THEM, TOO, OCCASIONALLY, IN OUR

IMPOSSIBILITIES

LADY PREFACE(211)	OF MINE IS A BRIEF TRIFLE, AND FULL OF MANIFEST	IMPOSSIBILITIES	AT THAT; WHILST MR HARRIS'S PLAY IS SERIOUS
DOCT PREFACE(36)	OF WITHOUT VISITING IT IN A BALLOON. BOTH THESE	IMPOSSIBILITIES	HAVE BEEN ACHIEVED, BUT NOT BY VIVISECTORS.
POSN PREFACE(400)	LITTLE EXCEPT STAGNANT MEDIOCRITY. THE PRACTICAL	IMPOSSIBILITIES	OF CENSORSHIP. THERE IS, BESIDES, A CRUSHING
CATH PREFACE(156)	SANE AND SKILLED AUTHOR WRITES PLAYS THAT PRESENT	IMPOSSIBILITIES	TO THE ACTOR OR TO THE STAGE ENGINEER. IF,

IMPOSSIBILITY

APPL PREFACE(180)	THE PEOPLE CANNOT GOVERN. THE THING IS A PHYSICAL	IMPOSSIBILITY	, EVERY CITIZEN CANNOT BE A RULER ANY MORE
FABL PREFACE(89)	THEORY HE TAUGHT THAT A STATE PARCEL POST IS AN	IMPOSSIBILITY	, FOR WHEN HE RETURNED TO ENGLAND AFTER
JITT I (22)	SHUDDERING) NO, NO: IT IS INHUMAN: A MOCKERY, AN	IMPOSSIBILITY	, /BRUNO/ I KNOW I AM PUTTING YOUR LOVE TO THE
MIS. PREFACE(93)	SOME SORT OF RELIGION. SECULAR EDUCATION IS AN	IMPOSSIBILITY	, SECULAR EDUCATION COMES TO THIS: THAT THE
UNPL PREFACE(R19)	THE MORE COMPLETELY DOES HE GET CONVINCED OF THE	IMPOSSIBILITY	OF ACHIEVING AN AUTHENTIC REPRESENTATION OF
ROCK PREFACE(154)	AS IN THE FRENCH REVOLUTION, BUT WHEN THE	IMPOSSIBILITY	OF DOING THIS (EXCEPT IN THE SPECIAL CASE OF
MILL PREFACE(136)	WHO WEARY US WITH THEIR BLITHERINGS ABOUT THE	IMPOSSIBILITY	OF EQUALITY WHEN THEY ARE AT A LOSS FOR ANY
MTH2 (52)	TO THE ROOT OF HUMAN SOCIETY AND DESTINY; AND THE	IMPOSSIBILITY	OF KEEPING SUCH A TEAM TOGETHER WILL FORCE YOU
APPL INTRLUD(250)	/MAGNUS/ I FORGET. I THINK I WAS EXPLAINING THE	IMPOSSIBILITY	OF MY WIFE CHANGING PLACES WITH YOU.
POSN PREFACE(409)	FROM WHICH CENTRAL CONTROL IS FREE: NAMELY, THE	IMPOSSIBILITY	OF PLANNING THEATRICAL TOURS WITHOUT THE
MIS. PREFACE(93)	BY THE DISCONTINUANCE OF RELIGIOUS EDUCATION. THE	IMPOSSIBILITY	OF SECULAR EDUCATION. NOW CHILDREN MUST BE
DOCT PREFACE(9)	CONTENTION IS, OF COURSE, THAT A BAD DOCTOR IS AN	IMPOSSIBILITY	), BUT BETWEEN PRACTITIONERS OF EQUAL EMINENCE
6CAL PREFACE(90)	OF ACTING. A GOOD PLAY WITH BAD PARTS IS NOT AN	IMPOSSIBILITY	; BUT IT IS A MONSTROSITY. A BAD PLAY WITH
METH PREFACE(R17)	MASTERY OF THE ENTIRE GLOBE: THAT IS, IN AN	IMPOSSIBILITY	THAT WILL YET SEEM POSSIBLE IN DETAIL TO
POSN PREFACE(401)	TO PROTECT THE PUBLIC. IT WAS THIS PRACTICAL	IMPOSSIBILITY	THAT PREVENTED THE LONDON COUNTY COUNCIL FROM
OVER PREFACE(168)	DEMANDS, NOT THAT WE SHOULD BEHAVE MORALLY (AN	IMPOSSIBILITY	TO OUR SINFUL NATURE) BUT THAT WE SHALL NOT
DOCT PREFACE(24)	INOCULATORY METHODS MOST IN VOGUE IS AN ECONOMIC	IMPOSSIBILITY	UNDER OUR PRIVATE PRACTICE SYSTEM. THEY BUY
POSN PREFACE(364)	TO THE CONTRARY, WHICH IS A CONSTITUTIONAL	IMPOSSIBILITY	, COULD HAVE RELIEVED THE COMMITTEE FROM THE

IMPOSSIBLE

JOAN 6 (137)	I HAVE HAD, WERE NOT FROM GOD, THEN THAT IS	IMPOSSIBLE	: I WILL NOT DECLARE IT FOR ANYTHING IN THE
PYGM EPILOG (293)	BEYOND ALL BEARING, THE UNION BECOMES	IMPOSSIBLE	: IT ENDS IN THE WEAKER PARTY BEING EITHER
OVER (179)	SH-SH-SH! THAT WAS MY HUSBAND'S VOICE. /GREGORY/	IMPOSSIBLE	: IT'S ONLY OUR GUILTY FANCY. /A WOMAN'S VOICE/
CLEO I (110)	PERPLEXEDLY) YES, I-- (QUITE PANICSTRICKEN) NO:	IMPOSSIBLE	: MADNESS, MADNESS! (DESPERATELY) BACK TO
WIDO II (39)	LIKE A SAVAGE. /SARTORIUS/ LIVE ON YOUR INCOME!	IMPOSSIBLE	: MY DAUGHTER IS ACCUSTOMED TO A PROPER
ROCK I (198)	ABOUT IT FOR A FORTNIGHT. HOWEVER, OF COURSE IT'S	IMPOSSIBLE	: SAY NO MORE: SO LONG. (HE GOES OUT). /SIR
SIM PREFACE(10)	FOR HIM TO BECOME A GENTLEMAN. TOLERATION IS	IMPOSSIBLE	: THE HERETIC-SABOTEUR WILL NOT TOLERATE THE
MIS. PREFACE(44)	CORRUPT A WHOLE GENERATION AND MAKE HUMAN SOCIETY	IMPOSSIBLE	: THEREFORE THRASH THE VICE OUT OF HIM, AND SO ON
JOAN 6 (147)	(HE HURRIES OUT). /CAUCHON/ THESE ENGLISH ARE	IMPOSSIBLE	: THEY WILL THRUST HER STRAIGHT INTO THE FIRE.
MTH4 I (172)	/ZOO/ ABNORMAL, YOU MEAN. WHAT YOU ASK IS	IMPOSSIBLE	: WE WEED THEM ALL OUT. /THE ELDERLY GENTLEMAN/
ARMS II (33)	REGIMENTS. /SERGIUS/ (PROTESTING) MY DEAR MADAM,	IMPOSSIBLE	: YOU-- /CATHERINE/ (STOPPING HIM PLAYFULLY) YOU
APPL I (222)	HIS MAJESTY'S HAND, AND MAKING MY SITUATION HERE	IMPOSSIBLE	? GUILTY SILENCE. /PROTEUS/ (PROCEEDING
DEVL III (70)	IN AN IMPREGNABLE POSITION. /SWINDON/ (APPALLED)	IMPOSSIBLE	? /BURGOYNE/ (COLDLY) I BEG YOUR PARDON?
OVER PREFACE(165)	WHO ARE HAPPIEST WHEN THEY ARE MOST UNNATURAL AND	IMPOSSIBLE	AND ABSURD, BUT FOR AUDIENCES AS WELL. I HAVE
GETT PREFACE(201)	OF COURSE NOBODY EXPECTS THEM TO DO ANYTHING SO	IMPOSSIBLE	AND SO UNWHOLESOME, YET THE LAW THAT REGULATES
GENV PREFACE(13)	FOR PERFECT DEMOCRACY OF COURSE MAKES DEMOCRACY	IMPOSSIBLE	AND THE ADVENTURES OF CROMWELL, NAPOLEON, HITLER,
LION PREFACE(99)	OR IN THE WESTMINSTER CONFESSION ARE WILDLY	IMPOSSIBLE	AS POLITICAL CONSTITUTIONS FOR MODERN EMPIRES. A
6CAL PREFACE(90)	FUTILITY OF THE MELANCHOLY JAQUES; AND MILLAMANT,	IMPOSSIBLE	AS SHE IS, STILL PRODUCES THE USUAL COMPLIMENTS
CYMB V (140)	AGAIN. BUT THATS IMPOSSIBLE. /PHILARIO/ NOT SO	IMPOSSIBLE	AS THAT THIS WITLESS SAVAGE CYMBELINE, WHOSE
GETT PREFACE(191)	ME BACK TO WHAT THEY WOULD HAVE CONSIDERED AN	IMPOSSIBLE	ASCETICISM. BUT THEY PAID NO PENALTY OF WHICH
UNPL PREFACE(R14)	CHARLES WYNDHAM COULD ACT, IN A PLAY WHICH WAS	IMPOSSIBLE	AT HIS THEATRE: A FEAT COMPARABLE TO THE BUILDING
METH PREFACE(R53)	ENOUGH TO OVERAWE THE MOB, BUT SIMPLY THAT IT IS	IMPOSSIBLE	BECAUSE THE HUMAN EXPERIMENTER CANNOT GET AT THE
KING PREFACE(159)	TO BE DONE? GIVING ALL WOMEN THE VOTE MAKES IT	IMPOSSIBLE	BECAUSE IT ONLY DOUBLES THE RESISTANCE TO ANY
METH PREFACE(R25)	OR THE NEW ONE CREATED, WHEN SUDDENLY THE	IMPOSSIBLE	BECOMES POSSIBLE AND THE HABIT IS FORMED. THE
MIS. PREFACE(29)	THEIR OWN RELATION TO THE CHILD MAKES THE SUBJECT	IMPOSSIBLE	BETWEEN THEM) WE ARE VIRTUALLY ARRANGING TO HAVE
GETT PREFACE(217)	PATH MEANS EXPOSURE AND RUIN, IT IS ALMOST	IMPOSSIBLE	BY ANY EXTRAVAGANCE OF MISCONDUCT TO PROVOKE

UNPL PREFACE(R18)	THEIR OWN ORBIT, OR ITS STAGNANT ISOLATION MADE	IMPOSSIBLE	BY THE CONDITIONS OF WORKING CLASS LIFE, MANNERS
BULL PREFACE(57)	AVAILABLE FORM OF OFFICIAL LYNCH LAW, WERE MADE	IMPOSSIBLE	BY THE JEALOUSY OF THE " LOYAL" (TO ENGLAND)
CLEO PRO1 (91)	AND APPROVED; AND ON THE FIELD OF PHARSALIA THE	IMPOSSIBLE	CAME TO PASS; THE BLOOD AND IRON YE PIN YOUR
MRS PREFACE(158)	FROM THE STAGE ALTOGETHER. THOSE WHO THINK THIS	IMPOSSIBLE	CAN HARDLY HAVE CONSIDERED THE NUMBER AND
MILL PREFACE(122)	POWERS HAD EITHER TO RENEW THE WAR OR TEAR UP THE	IMPOSSIBLE	CLAUSES WITH A GOOD GRACE. BUT THEY COULD NOT
NEVR IV (283)	FROM THEM AT THEIR AGE. IF YOURE GOING TO MAKE	IMPOSSIBLE	CONDITIONS OF THIS KIND, WE MAY AS WELL GO BACK
DEST SD(151)	THEY FIGHT ALL DAY AND MARCH ALL NIGHT, COVERING	IMPOSSIBLE	DISTANCES AND APPEARING IN INCREDIBLE PLACES, NOT
MILL PREFACE(113)	THE SEEDS OF HALF A DOZEN NEW WARS AND IS	IMPOSSIBLE	ENOUGH IN ITS CONDITIONS TO MAKE ITS VIOLATION
APPL INTRLUD(252)	SO JOLLY, NO CABINET SO TACTFUL THAT IT IS	IMPOSSIBLE	EVER TO GET TIRED OF THEM. JEMIMA HAS HER
JOAN PREFACE(32)	HAD HE LIVED LONGER. IT IS THEREFORE BY NO MEANS	IMPOSSIBLE	FOR A PERSON TO BE EXCOMMUNICATED AS A HERETIC,
ROCK PREFACE(157)	AGAINST THE CITY (HE DECLARED THAT IT WAS	IMPOSSIBLE	FOR A RICH MAN TO ENTER THE KINGDOM OF HEAVEN),
PYGM PREFACE(199)	MAN CAN TEACH HIMSELF WHAT IT SOUNDS LIKE. IT IS	IMPOSSIBLE	FOR AN ENGLISHMAN TO OPEN HIS MOUTH WITHOUT
3PLA PREFACE(R39)	NOWADAYS. EVEN WERE THEY DEAR, IT WOULD STILL BE	IMPOSSIBLE	FOR ANY PUBLIC-SPIRITED CITIZEN OF THE WORLD TO
OVER PREFACE(164)	THE ACTORS RATHER INSISTING THAT IT SHALL BE	IMPOSSIBLE	FOR ANY SPECTATOR TO MISTAKE A STAGE KISS FOR A
DOCT PREFACE(7)	IT WOULD HAVE LIVED. IT WAS, OF COURSE,	IMPOSSIBLE	FOR ANY MAN OF SENSE AND HONOR TO ASSUME DIVINE
MIS. PREFACE(12)	WORLD HOLDS GOOD BECAUSE IN LARGE FAMILIES IT IS	IMPOSSIBLE	FOR EACH CHILD TO RECEIVE WHAT SCHOOLMASTERS CALL
SUPR II (64)	BEHIND. THERE ARE CIRCUMSTANCES WHICH MAKE IT	IMPOSSIBLE	FOR HER TO COME ON SUCH AN EXPEDITION. /HECTOR/ (
LADY PREFACE(215)	ARE SUFFICIENTLY HETERODOX TO MAKE IT ALMOST	IMPOSSIBLE	FOR HIM TO RISK PERHAPS FIVE YEARS OF A SLENDER
LION PREFACE(80)	FOR THE SIN OF ALL FUTURE GENERATIONS?) IT WAS	IMPOSSIBLE	FOR HIM TO DECLARE THAT SIN, EVEN IN ITS
LION PREFACE(14)	MAN STILL IN HIS OLD DIFFICULTY; FOR IF IT WAS	IMPOSSIBLE	FOR HIM TO PROCURE RAMS AND GOATS AND SHEKELS,
JITT III (57)	ALL HIS PROFESSIONAL ENGAGEMENTS IT WAS UTTERLY	IMPOSSIBLE	FOR HIM TO HAVE GIVEN MUCH OF HIS TIME TO ANY
SIM PREFACE(10)	HIS FANATICAL HATRED OF A SYSTEM WHICH MAKES IT	IMPOSSIBLE	FOR HIM TO BECOME A GENTLEMAN. TOLERATION IS
MRS PREFACE(168)	ARE SO WELL KNOWN THAT IT IS ALMOST	IMPOSSIBLE	FOR ITS SLAVES TO WRITE TOLERABLE LAST ACTS TO
SHAK PREFACE(135)	THEIR UNVARYING INTENSITY OF FACIAL EXPRESSION,	IMPOSSIBLE	FOR LIVING ACTORS, KEEPS THE IMAGINATION OF THE
GETT PREFACE(257)	AND THE CASE IS ONE WHICH NEEDS IT. 4. MAKE IT	IMPOSSIBLE	FOR MARRIAGE TO BE USED AS A PUNISHMENT AS IT IS
METH PREFACE(R88)	MY OWN IRISH EIGHTEENTH-CENTURYISM MADE IT	IMPOSSIBLE	FOR ME TO BELIEVE ANYTHING UNTIL I COULD CONCEIVE
JOAN 6 (137)	THAT I HAVE DONE THEM BY THE ORDER OF GOD: IT IS	IMPOSSIBLE	FOR ME TO SAY ANYTHING ELSE. IF ANY CHURCHMAN
DOCT PREFACE(62)	AFFORD FEES ON THE HIGHEST SCALE, HAS MADE IT	IMPOSSIBLE	FOR ME TO SHARE THAT HOSTILITY TO THE DOCTOR AS A
NEVR I (206)	TO STAY HERE FOR ANY LENGTH OF TIME, IT WILL BE	IMPOSSIBLE	FOR ME TO ACCEPT YOUR KIND INVITATION TO LUNCH. (
NEVR I (203)	THE PLEASURE OF ENTERTAINING? IT'S REALLY QUITE	IMPOSSIBLE	FOR ME TO LUNCH AT THE MARINE HOTEL WITH TWO
UNPL PREFACE(R13)	I SAW THAT THE VERY QUALITIES WHICH HAD MADE IT	IMPOSSIBLE	FOR ORDINARY COMMERCIAL PURPOSES IN 1885 MIGHT BE
APPL PREFACE(180)	I MENTIONED IT ONLY TO REMIND YOU THAT IT SEEMS	IMPOSSIBLE	FOR STATESMEN TO MAKE SPEECHES ABOUT DEMOCRACY,
POSN PREFACE(394)	IF APPLIED IN ALL DIRECTIONS, WOULD MAKE IT	IMPOSSIBLE	FOR THE QUEEN TO RECEIVE A TURKISH AMBASSADOR
POSN PREFACE(394)	BE LICENSED BY THE LORD CHAMBERLAIN IT WOULD BE	IMPOSSIBLE	FOR THE KING TO ALLOW THE LICENCE TO BE ISSUED,
PRES (150)	THATS WHAT E'S FOR. /MITCHENER/ (GROANING) IT IS	IMPOSSIBLE	FOR THE HUMAN MIND TO CONCEIVE ANYTHING MORE
3PLA PREFACE(R39)	DILEMMAS AS TO MAKE THEIR IDENTIFICATION	IMPOSSIBLE	FOR THE MOMENT. IF SO, SO MUCH THE BETTER FOR ME:
MILL PREFACE(122)	THAT THE TIME HAD ARRIVED WHEN IT WOULD BE QUITE	IMPOSSIBLE	FOR THE ALLIES TO BEGIN THE WAR OVER AGAIN TO
LION PREFACE(58)	SHALL BE ANYTHING TO EAT OR DRINK IT WILL BE	IMPOSSIBLE	FOR US TO THINK OF NOBLER THINGS, OR LIVE A
SUPR I (18)	AND THAT OF MR TANNER; FOR I FEAR IT IS	IMPOSSIBLE	FOR US TO UNDERTAKE A JOINT ARRANGEMENT. /ANN/ (
KING I (174)	THIS IS THE SCIENTIFIC BUSINESS WHICH MADE IT	IMPOSSIBLE	FOR YOU TO SEE ME THIS MORNING. /CHARLES/ BE
2TRU II (58)	RELATION-- ANY HINT OF FAMILIARITY WITH HIM-- IS	IMPOSSIBLE	FOR YOU. /THE COUNTESS/ BUT SURELY I MAY TREAT
2TRU III (110)	THEMSELVES FROM ONE ANOTHER IN BEAUTIFUL	IMPOSSIBLE	IDEALISMS TO ENABLE THEM TO BEAR ONE ANOTHER'S
MIS. PREFACE(6)	EXTENSION OF SUCH LEGISLATION AT PRESENT WOULD BE	IMPOSSIBLE	IF IT WERE NOT THAT THE PARENTS AFFECTED BY IT
APPL I (198)	AND OMNIPOTENT AND ETERNAL AND EVERYTHING THAT IS	IMPOSSIBLE	IF ONLY IT LOOKED SPLENDID ENOUGH, AND THE ORGAN
LION EPILOG (150)	THE GERMANS! " THE INCIDENT WOULD HAVE BEEN	IMPOSSIBLE	IN A COUNTRY WHERE THE CHURCH WAS AS POWERFUL AS
GETT PREFACE(255)	AS THEY BEST MAY. SUCH FREEDOM IS, OF COURSE,	IMPOSSIBLE	IN OUR PRESENT POVERTY-STRICKEN CIRCUMSTANCES. AS
LION PREFACE(14)	PROCURE RAMS AND GOATS AND SHEKELS, HOW MUCH MORE	IMPOSSIBLE	IS IT FOR HIM TO FIND A NEIGHBOR WHO WILL
LION PREFACE(89)	WAS MEANT FOR THE SERVICE OF HIS FATHER, THE MORE	IMPOSSIBLE	IT BECOMES FOR US TO BELIEVE THAT HE WAS TALKING
UNPL PREFACE(R6)	NOT SPLENETIC OVER OUR VARIANCE. JUDGE THEN, HOW	IMPOSSIBLE	IT WAS FOR ME TO WRITE FICTION THAT SHOULD
POSN PREFACE(402)	FORCES ON THE CONTINENT WILL UNDERSTAND HOW	IMPOSSIBLE	IT WOULD BE TO PROCURE INSPECTORS WHOSE
GETT (182)	WITH THE TIME SPREAD OVER A LONG PERIOD, WOULD BE	IMPOSSIBLE	.
MRS PREFACE(159)	TO DEFEND HIM. A COMPLETE TAPU IS POLITICALLY	IMPOSSIBLE	. A COMPLETE TOLERATION IS EQUALLY IMPOSSIBLE TO
SUPR I (37)	BUT THE MORAL PASSION MADE OUR CHILDISH RELATIONS	IMPOSSIBLE	. A JEALOUS SENSE OF MY NEW INDIVIDUALITY AROSE
HART PREFACE(38)	THE TASK THEY WERE DOING WHAT THEY COULD TO MAKE	IMPOSSIBLE	. ALAS! HEGEL WAS RIGHT WHEN HE SAID THAT WE
JOAN 6 (137)	IN SPITE OF ANY MAN ALIVE. THAT IS WHAT I MEAN BY	IMPOSSIBLE	. AND IN CASE THE CHURCH SHOULD BID ME DO
BASH I (95)	OWNS THIS PARK! A LADY MARRY A PRIZEFIGHTER!	IMPOSSIBLE	. AND YET THE PRIZEFIGHTER MUST MARRY HER. ENTER
FANY III (327)	LIEUTENANT? /DUVALLET/ IN FRANCE IT WOULD BE	IMPOSSIBLE	. BUT HERE-- AH! (KISSING HIS HAND) LA BELLE
GETT PREFACE(217)	THE PAPERS, THE PRETENCE OF NOT KNOWING BECOMES	IMPOSSIBLE	. BUT IT IS HARDLY TOO MUCH TO SAY THAT IF YOU
APPL PREFACE(180)	HUNDRED A YEAR AND ONE WITH A HUNDRED THOUSAND IS	IMPOSSIBLE	. BUT NUMBER THREE: GOVERNMENT BY THE PEOPLE, IS
KING I (185)	AND GOING TO THE TABLE TO COAX HIM) AH! YOU ARE	IMPOSSIBLE	. BUT YOU WILL MAKE ME A LOVE POTION, WILL YOU
JOAN 6 (136)	/JOAN/ -- PROVIDED IT DOES NOT COMMAND ANYTHING	IMPOSSIBLE	. CAUCHON SINKS BACK IN HIS CHAIR WITH A HEAVY
MRS II (201)	THINK: IT'S IMPOSSIBLE. /CROFTS/ OF COURSE IT'S	IMPOSSIBLE	. DONT BE A FOOL, KITTY. /MRS WARREN/ (NETTLED)
HART PREFACE(33)	HOUSES WERE QUITE FULL EVERY NIGHT, PROFIT WAS	IMPOSSIBLE	. EVEN BARE SOLVENCY COULD NOT BE ATTAINED
JOAN PREFACE(45)	AND HERSELF INTO THE BARGAIN; AND THAT WAS	IMPOSSIBLE	. FROM THE MOMENT WHEN SHE FAILED TO STIMULATE
2TRU I (30)	THERE WAS THAT MAN AT FOLKESTONE: HE WAS	IMPOSSIBLE	. HE TORE ASIDE THE CURTAIN AND LET THE BLAZING
JITT I (18)	HUSBAND I MEAN. I HAVE CONVERTED HIM. /JITTA/ OH,	IMPOSSIBLE	. HE WOULD NEVER BELIEVE A THING LIKE THAT. DONT
JOAN 5 (118)	TO HIM) OH, MY LORD, DO NOT SAY THAT. IT IS	IMPOSSIBLE	. I A WITCH! /THE ARCHBISHOP/ PETER CAUCHON
JOAN 5 (120)	BEARD. /BLUEBEARD/ YOU KNOW, THE WOMAN IS QUITE	IMPOSSIBLE	. I DONT DISLIKE HER, REALLY; BUT WHAT ARE YOU TO
FOUN (214)	/ANASTASIA/ (PRODUCING A NEWSPAPER) QUITE	IMPOSSIBLE	. I HAVE HERE AN ARTICLE ON SIR CARDONIUS, HEADED
WIDO II (36)	IMPOSSIBLE. /BLANCHE/ IMPOSSIBLE! /TRENCH/ YES,	IMPOSSIBLE	. I HAVE RESOLVED NOT TO TAKE ANY MONEY FROM YOUR
MIS. (204)	I'LL COME. /LORD SUMMERHAYS/ NO, NO, BENTLEY.	IMPOSSIBLE	. I SHALL NOT ALLOW IT. /MRS TARLETON/ DO YOU
MTH5 (256)	LANGUAGE. ANOTHER CENTURY OR TWO AND IT WILL BE	IMPOSSIBLE	. I SHALL HAVE TO BE RELIEVED BY A YOUNGER
JITT II (43)	ONLY HE DIES ROMANTICALLY! ANYHOW THIS THING IS	IMPOSSIBLE	. I WONT DO IT. /JITTA/ WHY? /LENKHEIM/ BECAUSE
LION PREFACE(52)	POOR, HE WILL INFORM US THAT SUCH AN OPERATION IS	IMPOSSIBLE	. IF HE SELLS HIS SHARES AND HIS LANDS, THEIR
MRS PREFACE(158)	SCOPE OF THE DRAMATIST, IT DOES NOT MAKE DRAMA	IMPOSSIBLE	. IF THE EXAMINER WERE TO REFUSE TO LICENSE PLAYS
SIM PREFACE(17)	IS TRUSTWORTHY AND COMPULSORY UNEMPLOYMENT MADE	IMPOSSIBLE	. IN FACT IT IS SO DEFINITE THAT IT FINALLY TAKES
METH PREFACE(R40)	SUFFERING AND INJUSTICE. BUT A DISORDERLY GOD WAS	IMPOSSIBLE	. IN THE MIDDLE AGES A COMPROMISE HAD BEEN MADE
MIS. PREFACE(74)	GROUND THAT IT IS FANTASTIC OR MAD OR APPARENTLY	IMPOSSIBLE	. IT IS THE SENSIBLE SCHEMES, UNFORTUNATELY, THAT
BARB PREFACE(226)	IN SUCH A WAY AS TO MAKE THAT EVERYDAY INFAMY	IMPOSSIBLE	. I, WHO HAVE PREACHED AND PAMPHLETEERED LIKE ANY
PHIL III (134)	HIM OFF, CRYING) NO, NO, NO, NO. I CANNOT. IT'S	IMPOSSIBLE	. (SHE GOES TOWARDS THE DOOR). /PARAMORE/ (
BUOY II (25)	A SOLID TWENTY POUNDS FOR IT. /THE NATIVE/ IT IS	IMPOSSIBLE	. KNOWLEDGE AND WISDOM CANNOT BE PURCHASED LIKE
LION I (116)	CRUEL DEATHS ON ME. I TELL YOU, IT IS PHYSICALLY	IMPOSSIBLE	. LISTEN, CAPTAIN: DID YOU EVER TRY TO CATCH A
LION PREFACE(94)	SAME LINES, THAT THE CAMPAIGNS OF NAPOLEON WERE	IMPOSSIBLE	. ONLY FICTITIOUS CHARACTERS WILL STAND HUME'S
BUOY III (40)	YOU TAKE YOUR UNIVERSITY DEGREE. /THE WIDOWER/	IMPOSSIBLE	. OUR FATHER GAVE US ALL THE MONEY WE NEEDED ON
GENV PREFACE(9)	AND MUNITION FACTORIES MADE RETALIATION IN KIND	IMPOSSIBLE	. OUR FLAME THROWING FROM TANKS FINISHED THE
MILL IV (194)	IN THE SOLAR PLEXUS? /ADRIAN/ STRIKE A WOMAN!	IMPOSSIBLE	. /ALASTAIR/ ROT! IF A WOMAN STARTS FIGHTING SHE
MIS. (184)	GAME VERY STRICTLY, AS A SINGLE-HANDED GAME, IT'S	IMPOSSIBLE	. /BENTLEY/ (SUDDENLY BREAKING OUT LAMENTABLY)
WIDO II (35)	NOT A WORD TO SAY AGAINST THAT. /TRENCH/ IT'S	IMPOSSIBLE	. /BLANCHE/ IMPOSSIBLE! /TRENCH/ YES,
CAPT II (268)	CERTAINLY. SIDI SMILES GRAVELY. /SIR HOWARD/	IMPOSSIBLE	. /BRASSBOUND/ YOU DONT KNOW WHAT YOURE DOING.
JOAN 6 (141)	VOICES HAVE DECEIVED YOU? /JOAN/ OH NO: THAT IS	IMPOSSIBLE	. /CAUCHON/ IMPOSSIBLE! THEY HAVE LED YOU
MRS II (201)	HIM! YOUR DAUGHTER TO MY SON! ONLY THINK: IT'S	IMPOSSIBLE	. /CROFTS/ OF COURSE IT'S IMPOSSIBLE. DONT BE A
MILL I (151)	ALL RIGHT. BUT AS EVERYDAY PARTNERS THEYRE JUST	IMPOSSIBLE	. /EPIFANIA/ SO I AM THE SUNDAY WIFE. (TO
ROCK I (221)	CRUSH ME IF I DONT CLEAR IT OFF BEFORE IT BECOMES	IMPOSSIBLE	. /HILDA/ BUT I KEEP TELLING YOU, SIR ARTHUR,
JOAN 6 (137)	THE CHURCH THE ERROR AND FOLLY OF COMMANDING THE	IMPOSSIBLE	. /JOAN/ IF YOU COMMAND ME TO DECLARE THAT ALL
APPL INTRLUD(253)	GOOD MANNERS HUMAN SOCIETY IS INTOLERABLE AND	IMPOSSIBLE	. /ORINTHIA/ WOULD ANY OTHER WOMAN STAND YOUR
CYMB V (140)	SAY CASSIVELAUNUS IS ALIVE AGAIN. BUT THATS	IMPOSSIBLE	. /PHILARIO/ NOT SO IMPOSSIBLE AS THAT THIS
GETT (313)	GOING IS IN HIGHER HANDS. /LESBIA/ ANTHONY! YOURE	IMPOSSIBLE	. /SOAMES/ (TAKING UP HIS PEN) YOU WONT TAKE MY
2TRU II (76)	/AUBREY/ YOU DONT SAY SO! /THE COUNTESS/ OH,	IMPOSSIBLE	. /TALLBOYS/ NOT A DOUBT OF IT. SHE'S A FRAUD:
SUPR I (10)	WILL DOWN ON THE WRITING TABLE). /RAMSDEN/ YOU!	IMPOSSIBLE	. /TANNER/ IT'S ONLY TOO HIDEOUSLY TRUE. (HE
LION I (115)	ARE LAUGHING AT ME. /LAVINIA/ AT YOU, CAPTAIN!	IMPOSSIBLE	. /THE CAPTAIN/ THEN YOU ARE FLIRTING WITH ME.
GENV III (86)	YOU TO ACT AS CLERK TO THE COURT. /THE SECRETARY/	IMPOSSIBLE	. /THE JUDGE/ IT SEEMS SO NOW; BUT I THINK YOU
BARB II (295)	BUT I CAN BUY THE SALVATION ARMY. /CUSINS/ QUITE	IMPOSSIBLE	. /UNDERSHAFT/ YOU SHALL SEE. ALL RELIGIOUS
DOCT I (94)	BLOOD-POISONING. /RIDGEON/ BLOOD-POISONING!	IMPOSSIBLE	. /WALPOLE/ I TELL YOU, BLOOD-POISONING.
MRS III (226)	MAKE MISTAKES. IT'S NO USE, VIV: YOUR MOTHER'S	IMPOSSIBLE	. SHE MAY BE A GOOD SORT; BUT SHE'S A BAD LOT, A
METH PREFACE(R70)	A FIST AT THEM, MAKES A EUROPEAN CIVILIZATION	IMPOSSIBLE	. SUCH PEACE AND PROSPERITY AS WE ENJOYED BEFORE
GENV PREFACE(11)	WITH THE HOPE THAT THE ATOMIC BOMB HAS MADE WAR	IMPOSSIBLE	. THAT HOPE HAS OFTEN BEEN ENTERTAINED BEFORE.
MTH4 III SD(195)	BY SHUDDERING NEGATIVELY, INTIMATE THAT IT IS	IMPOSSIBLE	. THE ELDERLY GENTLEMAN MANAGES TO GET ON HIS

MIS. (200)	INTO THE AIR: RIGHT UP INTO THE BLUE. /PERCIVAL/	IMPOSSIBLE	. THE FRAME'S TWISTED. THE PETROL HAS GIVEN OUT;
MTH5 (226)	WE HAVE SURPASSED ALL OUR COMPETITORS. /ECRASIA/	IMPOSSIBLE	. THE GREATEST THINGS IN ART CAN NEVER BE
MIS. PREFACE(22)	BUT FILLED. BUT SO HONEST AN ATTITUDE WAS	IMPOSSIBLE	. THE MASTERS MUST HAVE HATED THE SCHOOL MUCH
FABL PREFACE(67)	IS IMPOSSIBLE, BECAUSE EQUALITY OF OPPORTUNITY IS	IMPOSSIBLE	. THE PRESENT COMBINATION OF CULTURE AND
ROCK PREFACE(179)	OF HIS KINGDOM ON EARTH? A MODERN PASSION PLAY	IMPOSSIBLE	. THE QUESTION IS OF SUCH IMPORTANCE AT THE
LION PREFACE(63)	BUT HIGHLY ECONOMICAL TO AN EXTENT THAT NOW SEEMS	IMPOSSIBLE	. THE SPORTSMEN, THE MUSICIANS, THE PHYSICISTS,
CLEO II (122)	/POTHINUS/ (AGHAST) FORTY MILLION SESTERCES!	IMPOSSIBLE	. THERE IS NOT SO MUCH MONEY IN THE KING'S
GENV I (47)	TEACH THAT BLASPHEMY OR DOES IT NOT? /COMMISSAR/	IMPOSSIBLE	. THERE ARE NO POOR IN RUSSIA. /BISHOP/ OH! (HE
MTH5 (225)	YOU; AND YOU SEE I AM NONE THE WORSE. /MARTELLUS/	IMPOSSIBLE	. THEY ARE ALL SMASHED. (HE RISES, LAUGHING).
PHIL I (83)	THE TWO FATHERS! /JULIA/ (SITTING ON THE FLOOR)	IMPOSSIBLE	. THEY DONT KNOW ONE ANOTHER, /CHARTERIS/
BUOY III (38)	BASTARDS, THOUGH DOMESTIC LIFE WITH THEM IS	IMPOSSIBLE	. THEY SHOULD BE CONCUBINES, NOT HUSBANDS AND
PYGM EPILOG (296)	OF THE SOCIAL LADDER ON WHICH RETAIL TRADE IS	IMPOSSIBLE	. THIS DIFFICULTY WAS REMOVED BY AN EVENT HIGHLY
GETT PREFACE(197)	COMMUNITY IN WHICH AN EXCESS OF SENTIMENTALITY IS	IMPOSSIBLE	. TWO CHILDREN MAKE A DOLL'S HOUSE, IN WHICH BOTH
CLEO II (122)	AND A TALENT IS WORTH A RACEHORSE. I SAY IT IS	IMPOSSIBLE	. WE HAVE BEEN AT STRIFE HERE, BECAUSE THE KING'S
CAPT NOTES (303)	MAKES THE ART OF RECORDING SPEECH ALMOST	IMPOSSIBLE	. WHAT IS MORE, IT PLACES THE MODERN DRAMATIST
FABL PREFACE(67)	NOW WITHOUT CULTURED HOMES CIVILIZATION IS	IMPOSSIBLE	. WITHOUT CULTURE POSSIBLE IN EVERY HOME
GENV PREFACE(14)	BUT THIS DOES NOT MEAN THAT ENLIGHTENMENT IS	IMPOSSIBLE	. WITHOUT IT OUR ATTEMPTS AT DEMOCRACY WILL WRECK
ROCK I (198)	A WONDERFULLY SOOTHING EFFECT. /HILDA/ BUT IT'S	IMPOSSIBLE	. YOU HAVE A CONFERENCE EVERY MONTH UNTIL
MTH3 (108)	INTERRUPTING HIM) PARDON ME. SUCH A DISCOVERY WAS	IMPOSSIBLE	. YOU HAVE NOT MADE IT YET. YOU MAY LIVE A
GETT (357)	HOST, TO BREAK THE COVENANT OF BREAD AND SALT, IS	IMPOSSIBLE	. YOU MAY TAKE ME HOME WITH YOU, POLLY: YOU HAVE
GENV IV (114)	NO: I HAVE SAID ENOUGH. YOU KNOW NOW WHAT AN	IMPOSSIBLE	JOB I HAVE HERE AS SECRETARY TO THE LEAGUE OF
CLEO I (109)	DO YOU SUPPOSE THAT I BELIEVE YOU ARE REAL, YOU	IMPOSSIBLE	LITTLE DREAM WITCH? /CLEOPATRA/ (GIGGLING AND
MTH3 (110)	BEGAN TO CALL ME THE WANDERING JEW. YOU SEE HOW	IMPOSSIBLE	MY POSITION WAS. I FORESAW THAT IN TWENTY YEARS
SUPR III (119)	LADY TO THREE DIFFERENT FATHERS IS NOT	IMPOSSIBLE	NOR CONDEMNED BY PUBLIC OPINION. THAT SUCH A LADY
PYGM PREFACE(202)	PROFESSOR HIGGINS IN THE FLOWER-GIRL IS NEITHER	IMPOSSIBLE	NOR UNCOMMON. THE MODERN CONCIERGE'S DAUGHTER WHO
LADY PREFACE(227)	BESIDE THOSE OF TITIAN OR PAUL VERONESE, IT IS	IMPOSSIBLE	NOT TO BE STRUCK BY THE ABSENCE IN THE FLORENTINE
MTH3 (110)	MAN, HE ISNT DEAD. /CONFUCIUS/ IT IS SOCIALLY	IMPOSSIBLE	NOT TO DO WHAT EVERYBODY ELSE DOES. ONE MUST DIE
GETT PREFACE(196)	DEVOTION HE INSPIRES SO EXTRAVAGANT, THAT IT IS	IMPOSSIBLE	NOT TO SEE THAT THE REVOLT AGAINST CONVENTIONAL
UNPL PREFACE(R12)	HAS HIMSELF DESCRIBED HOW I PROVED THE MOST	IMPOSSIBLE	OF COLLABORATORS. LAYING VIOLENT HANDS ON HIS
DOCT PREFACE(37)	LEADERS OF THE ATTACK. NO KNOWLEDGE IS FINALLY	IMPOSSIBLE	OF HUMAN ATTAINMENT; FOR EVEN THOUGH IT MAY BE
3PLA PREFACE(R20)	TO BE LAID DOWN UNTIL FINISHED. LOVE INTEREST IS	IMPOSSIBLE	ON ITS SCIENTIFIC PLANE: NOTHING COULD BE MORE
CYMB FORWORD(133)	THAT SHAKESPEAR'S PLAYS AS WRITTEN BY HIM ARE	IMPOSSIBLE	ON THE STAGE, WHICH HAD PRODUCED A HAPPY ENDING
HART PREFACE(34)	A COMMERCIALLY SOUND SPECULATION, NOW BECAME AN	IMPOSSIBLE	ONE. ACCORDINGLY, ATTEMPTS ARE BEING MADE TO
MILL PREFACE(116)	THEY HAVE DONE THAN EITHER DECLARE MODERN WAR	IMPOSSIBLE	OR ELSE KEEP THROWING MASSES OF INFANTRY IN THE
HART I (59)	GIRLS OF YOUR AGE FALL IN LOVE WITH ALL SORTS OF	IMPOSSIBLE	PEOPLE, ESPECIALLY OLD PEOPLE. /ELLIE/ I LIKE MR
BUOY III (34)	THEY HAD ONE DAUGHTER. /MRS SECONDBORN/ A QUITE	IMPOSSIBLE	PERSON. /SIR F./ IN WHAT WAY? /DARKIE/ SHE CAN
CAPT III (276)	NEED YOUR COMMISERATION, CICELY. THE WOMAN WAS AN	IMPOSSIBLE	PERSON, HALF MAD, HALF DRUNK. DO YOU UNDERSTAND
BULL II SD(97)	NORTH. A HUGE STONE STANDS ON IT IN A NATURALLY	IMPOSSIBLE	PLACE, AS IF IT HAD BEEN TOSSED UP THERE BY A
FABL PREFACE(93)	CERTAINLY, THOSE WHO FORGET EVERYTHING ARE	IMPOSSIBLE	POLITICALLY; AND I HAVE OFTEN WISHED I HAD THE
SUPR III (123)	WITH THE GRATIFICATION OF PERSONAL FANCIES, THE	IMPOSSIBLE	REALIZATION OF BOYS' AND GIRLS' DREAMS OF BLISS,
APPL II (262)	REVERSION TO A BARBAROUS PAST. FORTUNATELY, IT'S	IMPOSSIBLE	-- IMM-PAWSIBL. THE OLD WARCRY WOULD NOT APPEAL
CATH 1 (173)	COME ALONG, DARLING. /EDSTASTON/ (STRUGGLING)	IMPOSSIBLE	-- /VARINKA/ COME, COME, COME. /EDSTASTON/ NO.
PYGM PREFACE(200)	ARTICLE, BEING LIBELLOUS, HAD TO BE RETURNED AS	IMPOSSIBLE	; AND I HAD TO RENOUNCE MY DREAM OF DRAGGING ITS
MIS. PREFACE(80)	ILLNESS OR MORTALITY. CONSEQUENTLY SYMPATHY WAS	IMPOSSIBLE	; AND IF THE UNFORTUNATE LADY DID NOT PERISH, IT
BULL II (104)	BUT THE DEEP UNDERSTANDING IN HIS EYES MAKES THAT	IMPOSSIBLE	; AND SHE ONLY LOOKS AT HIM EARNESTLY AND GOES.
SIM PREFACE(15)	IS EASY TO SAY THAT TO DIVINE JUSTICE NOTHING IS	IMPOSSIBLE	; BUT THE MORE DIVINE THE JUSTICE THE MORE
METH PREFACE(R69)	NEVER DOES BREAK OUT UNTIL IT SEEMS HOPELESS AND	IMPOSSIBLE	; FOR RULERS WHO THINK IT POSSIBLE TAKE CARE TO
BARB PREFACE(243)	A REVOLUTIONARY WRITER, BECAUSE OUR LAWS MAKE LAW	IMPOSSIBLE	; OUR LIBERTIES DESTROY ALL FREEDOM; OUR PROPERTY
2TRU PREFACE(14)	THE GOVERNMENT. IN BIG CIVILIZATIONS THIS IS	IMPOSSIBLE	; SO THE FIRST BUSINESS OF THE GOVERNMENT IS TO
PYGM PREFACE(201)	THE ADVENTURE OF ELIZA DOOLITTLE WOULD HAVE BEEN	IMPOSSIBLE	; STILL, AS WILL BE SEEN, THERE ARE TOUCHES OF
WIDO III (55)	(SHE TRIES TO TEAR THE BOOK ACROSS. FINDING THIS	IMPOSSIBLE	SHE THROWS IT VIOLENTLY INTO THE FIREPLACE. IT
FABL PREFACE(74)	TOTALLY CATHOLIC CHURCH OR COMMUNIST STATE IS AN	IMPOSSIBLE	SIMPLIFICATION OF SOCIAL ORGANIZATION. IT IS
3PLA PREFACE(R38)	IMPROVEMENTS: THE ACTION IS NOT CARRIED ON BY	IMPOSSIBLE	SOLILOQUYS AND ASIDES; AND MY PEOPLE GET ON AND
2TRU II (62)	HAVE BELIEVED HER. BUT SHE HAS NO SOONER MADE THE	IMPOSSIBLE	STATEMENT THAT SHE IS A COUNTESS, AND THAT THE
BULL PREFACE(20)	OUTRAGE TO THE GOVERNED AND A FINALLY	IMPOSSIBLE	TASK FOR THE GOVERNOR. I DARESAY SOME ENGLISHMAN
GENV IV (103)	BY AN ARISTOCRACY OF ACROBATS? /BBDE/ IS IT MORE	IMPOSSIBLE	THAN YOUR BRITISH ARISTOCRACY OF FOXHUNTERS?
BULL PREFACE(20)	HE MAY PLEAD WITH SOME TRUTH THAT THOUGH IT SEEMS	IMPOSSIBLE	THAT ANY OTHER COUNTRY THAN ENGLAND COULD PRODUCE
GENV III (75)	THEM. WE SHAME THEM. WE MAKE THINGS DIFFICULT OR	IMPOSSIBLE	THAT USED TO BE EASY. YOU DONT KNOW WHAT THE
HART III (144)	REVOLUTION, OR SOME FRIGHTFUL SMASH-UP: IT SEEMED	IMPOSSIBLE	THAT WE COULD BLUNDER AND MUDDLE ON ANY LONGER.
METH PREFACE(R69)	KNOW THAT A REVOLUTION ALWAYS SEEMS HOPELESS AND	IMPOSSIBLE	THE DAY BEFORE IT BREAKS OUT, AND INDEED NEVER
GENV PREFACE(17)	WHEN FURTHER OVERCROWDING BECAME PHYSICALLY	IMPOSSIBLE	THEY COULD DO NOTHING WITH THEIR UNWALLED
MTH1 I (8)	ANOTHER NEW WORD. /THE SERPENT/ A MIRACLE IS AN	IMPOSSIBLE	THING THAT IS NEVERTHELESS POSSIBLE. SOMETHING
MIS. (192)	SUMMERHAYS: A FAMILY IS AN AWFUL THING, AN	IMPOSSIBLE	THING. CAT AND DOG. PATSY: I'M ASHAMED OF YOU.
GENV PREFACE(6)	THE DRAWBACK TO ENGLAND'S CAPACITY FOR DOING	IMPOSSIBLE	THINGS WHEN IN DANGER IS HER INCAPACITY FOR DOING
FANY III (323)	TOO PIGHEADED TO ADMIT THAT THERE IS ANYTHING	IMPOSSIBLE	TO A FRENCHMAN: WE WERE QUITE SATISFIED WHEN OUR
METH PREFACE(R56)	OF GOD IS TO MAKE GOD A DEMON. BELIEF IN GOD WAS	IMPOSSIBLE	TO ANY THOUGHTFUL PERSON WITHOUT BELIEF IN THE
MIS. PREFACE(7)	SO EXTENSIVELY AND PROFOUNDLY THAT IT IS	IMPOSSIBLE	TO ASCERTAIN WHAT THE REAL NATURAL RELATIONS OF
BARB III (321)	PATRONAGE) REALLY, MY DEAR FATHER, IT IS	IMPOSSIBLE	TO BE ANGRY WITH YOU. YOU DONT KNOW HOW ABSURD
MTH2 SD(38)	WITH A FRANK SCHOOLBOYISHNESS THAT MAKES IT	IMPOSSIBLE	TO BE UNKIND TO HIM, AND EXPLODES INTO OBVIOUSLY
LION PREFACE(20)	YOU THAT HE SAW THIS OR DID THAT, AND YOU FIND IT	IMPOSSIBLE	TO BELIEVE HIM, YOU LOSE PATIENCE WITH HIM, AND
MTH3 (110)	TO BE SEVENTY-FIVE; MY APPEARANCE WOULD MAKE IT	IMPOSSIBLE	TO BELIEVE THAT I WAS MORE THAN FORTY-FIVE; AND
ARMS III (52)	THAT THRILLING VOICE, I ADMIRE YOU; BUT I FIND IT	IMPOSSIBLE	TO BELIEVE A SINGLE WORD YOU SAY. /RAINA/ (
SIM II (56)	TURNED OUT? AN IMPOTENT SIMPLETON. IT WOULD BE	IMPOSSIBLE	TO CONCEIVE A HUMAN BEING OF LESS CONSEQUENCE IN
ROCK PREFACE(163)	IN ANY HIGHLY CIVILIZED STATE. IT MAY BE QUITE	IMPOSSIBLE	TO CONVICT A FORESTALLER OR REGRATOR UNDER A
MIS. SD(172)	OF A CLOCK WITH A LIGHT DANCING STEP. HE FINDS IT	IMPOSSIBLE	TO COVER HER WITH THE PISTOL: SHE IS ALWAYS TOO
SUPR PREFACE(R25)	BE PASSED OVER WITHOUT CULPABLE FRIVOLITY. IT IS	IMPOSSIBLE	TO DEMONSTRATE THAT THE INITIATIVE IN SEX
HART I SD(66)	AND FEATURES SO ENTIRELY COMMONPLACE THAT IT IS	IMPOSSIBLE	TO DESCRIBE THEM. /CAPTAIN SHOTOVER/ (TO MRS
LION PREFACE(33)	BE SAVED AND THOSE WHO DO NOT, DAMNED; BUT IT IS	IMPOSSIBLE	TO DISCOVER WHETHER HE MEANS ANYTHING BY A STATE
PYGM PREFACE(199)	ANOTHER PHONETIC VETERAN, WERE MEN WHOM IT WAS	IMPOSSIBLE	TO DISLIKE. HENRY SWEET, THEN A YOUNG MAN, LACKED
DOCT PREFACE(25)	AS A POINT IN THEIR FAVOR, THAT IT IS OFTEN	IMPOSSIBLE	TO DISTINGUISH THE DISEASE PRODUCED BY THEIR
HART I (50)	TO THINK OF ALL THEIR GOOD POINTS OR IT WOULD BE	IMPOSSIBLE	TO ENDURE THEM. BUT WHEN THEY ARE AWAY, WE
HART PREFACE(22)	WHO HAD WOUNDED HIM AND PAY HIM OUT FOR IT. IT IS	IMPOSSIBLE	TO ESTIMATE WHAT PROPORTION OF US, IN KHAKI OR
OVER PREFACE(156)	INACCESSIBILITY OF THE FACTS. ALSO, IT IS	IMPOSSIBLE	TO ESTIMATE ITS PREVALENCE. A PRACTICE TO WHICH
POSN PREFACE(371)	COULD DISCUSS, AND WHICH I MYSELF HAVE FOUND IT	IMPOSSIBLE	TO EXPOSE IN THE PRESS BECAUSE NO EDITOR OF A
DOCT PREFACE(36)	SEEMED REASONABLE ENOUGH TO DECLARE THAT IT WAS	IMPOSSIBLE	TO FIND WHETHER OR NOT THERE WAS A STONE INSIDE A
NEVR IV (285)	HAUGHTY. /VALENTINE/ EXCUSE ME; BUT IT'S	IMPOSSIBLE	TO FIND A SERVANT TO ANNOUNCE ONE: EVEN THE NEVER
MIS. PREFACE(56)	IRON DUKE OF WELLINGTON COMPLAINED THAT IT WAS	IMPOSSIBLE	TO GET AN ORDER OBEYED IN THE BRITISH ARMY EXCEPT
PRES (163)	PARTY DEMANDS VOTES FOR WOMEN. THAT MAKES IT	IMPOSSIBLE	TO GIVE THEM, BECAUSE IT WOULD BE YIELDING TO
HART III (139)	OH NO: NOTHING'S THE MATTER; BUT REALLY IT'S	IMPOSSIBLE	TO GO TO SLEEP WITH SUCH AN INTERESTING
LION PREFACE(17)	EXPERIENCE CONFIRMS HIS EVIDENT BELIEF THAT IT IS	IMPOSSIBLE	TO GOVERN WITHOUT IT IN CERTAIN PHASES OF
3PLA PREFACE(R12)	THAT THIS DIVERSITY IN THE AUDIENCE MAKES IT	IMPOSSIBLE	TO GRATIFY EVERY ONE OF ITS UNITS BY THE SAME
LION II (132)	SPOILSPORT. THERE ARE MEN IN WHOSE PRESENCE IT IS	IMPOSSIBLE	TO HAVE ANY FUN: MEN WHO ARE A SORT OF WALKING
POSN PREFACE(389)	A MAGISTRATE OR A SANITARY INSPECTOR; BUT IT IS	IMPOSSIBLE	TO IGNORE THE CARELESSNESS WITH WHICH EVEN
MIS. PREFACE(6)	SMALL CLASS WHICH KEEPS PLENTY OF SERVANTS IT IS	IMPOSSIBLE	TO INDUCE PARENTS TO KEEP THEIR CHILDREN AT HOME
ROCK PREFACE(156)	STATE FLOGGING WOULD CEASE BECAUSE IT WOULD BE	IMPOSSIBLE	TO INDUCE ANY DECENT CITIZEN TO FLOG ANOTHER.
NEVR II (229)	AND NOW THAT WE HAVE COME BACK TO ENGLAND IT IS	IMPOSSIBLE	TO LEAVE THEM IN IGNORANCE ANY LONGER. (
MIS. (116)	DECLARE, MAMMA, THAT JOHNNY'S BRUTALITY MAKES IT	IMPOSSIBLE	TO LIVE IN THE HOUSE WITH HIM. /JOHNNY/ (DEEPLY
DEST SD(150)	IS MAKING HIMSELF USEFUL: INDEED, IT IS EVEN NOW	IMPOSSIBLE	TO LIVE IN ENGLAND WITHOUT SOMETIMES FEELING HOW
UNPL PREFACE(R22)	TO BE UTTERING. NOW IT IS NOT A WHIT LESS	IMPOSSIBLE	TO MAKE A MODERN PRACTICAL STAGE PLAY
MTH3 (119)	TO READ. I WAS VERY IGNORANT: IT DID NOT SEEM SO	IMPOSSIBLE	TO ME AS TO AN EDUCATED WOMAN. YET I FORGOT ALL
UNPL PREFACE(R19)	HE STILL HOLDS HIS OWN SO WELL THAT IT IS NOT	IMPOSSIBLE	TO MEET OLD PLAYGOERS WHO HAVE WITNESSED PUBLIC
BARB I (251)	THEM; AND WHAT I DO KNOW IS SO PAINFUL! IT IS SO	IMPOSSIBLE	TO MENTION SOME THINGS TO YOU-- (HE STOPS,
MIS. PREFACE(67)	QUARRELSOMENESS WHICH MAKES POLITICAL REFORM AS	IMPOSSIBLE	TO MOST ENGLISHMEN AS TO HOGS. CERTAIN SECTIONS
JOAN PREFACE(18)	ABLE TO PERFORM FEATS OF MEMORY AND ARITHMETIC	IMPOSSIBLE	TO NON-VISUALIZERS. VISUALIZERS WILL UNDERSTAND
MIS. PREFACE(71)	LIKE ALL SIMPLE AND OBVIOUS ARRANGEMENTS, SEEMS	IMPOSSIBLE	TO PEOPLE BROUGHT UP AS CHILDREN ARE NOW. STILL,
POSN PREFACE(413)	AS TO BE PHYSICALLY POSSIBLE, BE MENTALLY	IMPOSSIBLE	TO PERSONS OF TASTE AND ENLIGHTENMENT. 8.
MIS. PREFACE(106)	WAS A COMPLETER REALIST THAN NAPOLEON. IT WAS	IMPOSSIBLE	TO PERSUADE WELLINGTON THAT HE WAS BEATEN UNTIL

DOCT PREFACE(9)	OF EQUAL EMINENCE AND AUTHORITY. USUALLY IT IS	IMPOSSIBLE	TO PERSUADE THE JURY THAT THESE FACTS ARE FACTS.
ROCK PREFACE(170)	THE VARIETY OF OUR TEMPERAMENTS MAKES IT	IMPOSSIBLE	TO PLEASE EVERYBODY. THE QUAKER AND THE
POSN PREFACE(392)	WHAT INDEED NEEDED NO DEMONSTRATION-- THAT IT IS	IMPOSSIBLE	TO PREVENT INFERENCES BEING MADE, BOTH AT HOME
POSN PREFACE(424)	IS A FIXTURE, SHE MAY HISS AND HOOT AND MAKE IT	IMPOSSIBLE	TO PROCEED WITH THE PERFORMANCE, EVEN ALTHOUGH
GETT PREFACE(255)	MERELY TECHNICAL. UNTIL WE ABOLISH POVERTY IT IS	IMPOSSIBLE	TO PUSH RATIONAL MEASURES OF ANY KIND VERY FAR:
BULL PREFACE(61)	EVEN AFTER THE TRIAL, AT WHICH IT HAD BEEN	IMPOSSIBLE	TO PUSH THE MEDICAL EVIDENCE FURTHER THAN TO SAY
LION PREFACE(8)	WITHOUT PREJUDICE. WHEN I WAS YOUNG IT WAS	IMPOSSIBLE	TO READ THEM WITHOUT FANTASTIC CONFUSION OF
SUPR HANDBOK(193)	OR A FURTIVE FACETIOUSNESS THAT MAKES IT	IMPOSSIBLE	TO READ THE COMMENT ALOUD IN COMPANY. ALL THIS
BUOY III (44)	CHILD BEARING IS AN EXPERIENCE WHICH IT IS	IMPOSSIBLE	TO REGRET. IT IS DEFINITELY ORDAINED.
SIM II (74)	A LOT OF PRIESTS IN THE WORLD, IDDY. IT WOULD BE	IMPOSSIBLE	TO RESERVE SEATS FOR THEM ALL. /IDDY/ OH, I MEANT
GENV PREFACE(26)	IN THE MIDDLE OF THE NINETEENTH CENTURY, IT IS	IMPOSSIBLE	TO RESIST AT LEAST A STRONG SUSPICION THAT THE
MRS PREFACE(157)	AMOUNTS, I FEAR, TO A BLUNT YES; FOR IT SEEMS	IMPOSSIBLE	TO ROOT OUT OF AN ENGLISHMAN'S MIND THE NOTION
GETT PREFACE(212)	MONOGAMICALLY SUPERFLUOUS WOMEN, YET IT IS QUITE	IMPOSSIBLE	TO SAY OF ANY GIVEN UNMARRIED WOMAN THAT SHE IS
HART PREFACE(22)	WHICH AT LAST OVERREACHED ITSELF AND MADE IT	IMPOSSIBLE	TO STOP THE WAR BEFORE WE HAD NOT ONLY ACHIEVED
DOCT PREFACE(40)	IS PASSED OVER AS SUCH A HOPELESS FOOL THAT IT IS	IMPOSSIBLE	TO TAKE ANY INTEREST IN HIM. WHY NOT TEST THE
NEVR II (230)	IS FAIRLY EXTENSIVE, MR M'COMAS; BUT I FIND IT	IMPOSSIBLE	TO TAKE THE INHABITANTS OF THIS ISLAND SERIOUSLY.
OVER PREFACE(162)	AND FRANKNESS THAT WOULD HAVE SEEMED UTTERLY	IMPOSSIBLE	TO THACKERAY OR DICKENS IF THEY HAD BEEN TOLD
MRS PREFACE(159)	IMPOSSIBLE. A COMPLETE TOLERATION IS EQUALLY	IMPOSSIBLE	TO THE EXAMINER, BECAUSE HIS OCCUPATION WOULD BE
METH PREFACE(R42)	OF INERT AND DEAD MATTER, BUT ETERNALLY	IMPOSSIBLE	TO THE SPIRITS AND SOULS OF THE RIGHTEOUS. IF IT
APPL PREFACE(183)	WE HAVE FOUND BY BITTER EXPERIENCE THAT IT IS	IMPOSSIBLE	TO TRUST FACTORIES, WORKSHOPS, AND MINES TO
FABL V (117)	OH, THEY WERE THE DAMNEDEST FOOLS! IT IS	IMPOSSIBLE	TO UNDERSTAND HOW THEY KEPT GOING FOR A WEEK,
JOAN PREFACE(24)	OWN STYLE WAS FULLY FORMED AND HARDENED, IT IS	IMPOSSIBLE	TO VERIFY THIS GUESS. HIS FINGER IS NOT
PYGM II (230)	YOU SEE, SHE'LL BE A PUPIL; AND TEACHING WOULD BE	IMPOSSIBLE	UNLESS PUPILS WERE SACRED. IVE TAUGHT SCORES OF
METH PREFACE(R75)	POPULAR CONSENT IS INDISPENSABLE, AND WILL BE	IMPOSSIBLE	UNTIL THE STATESMAN CAN APPEAL TO THE VITAL
HART PREFACE(15)	THE WAR DID NOT CHANGE MEN'S MINDS IN ANY SUCH	IMPOSSIBLE	WAY. WHAT REALLY HAPPENED WAS THAT THE IMPACT OF
FABL PREFACE(64)	HAS JUST BEEN PUBLISHED. IT WOULD HAVE BEEN	IMPOSSIBLE	WHEN I WROTE THE DOCTOR'S DILEMMA. IN SPITE OF
BARB PREFACE(243)	TOLERATED ON ANY PLEA. SUCH AN ATTITUDE BECOMES	IMPOSSIBLE	WHEN THE ONLY MEN WHO CAN MAKE THEMSELVES HEARD
SUPR HANDBOK(209)	OF STEPHENSONS. ALTHOUGH NATIONAL CHRISTIANITY IS	IMPOSSIBLE	WITHOUT A NATION OF CHRISTS. BUT DOES ANY MAN
SUPR PREFACE(R12)	LENGTH OF A DEFECT (UNIVERSALITY OF CHARACTER IS	IMPOSSIBLE	WITHOUT A SHARE OF VULGARITY); AND EVEN IF YOU
FABL PREFACE(96)	SUPPORT A GOOSE ON THE COMMON, THUS MAKING IT	IMPOSSIBLE	WITHOUT NATIONALIZATION TO SUBSTITUTE
FABL PREFACE(87)	SINGING AT THE TOP OF MY VOICE THAT DEMOCRACY IS	IMPOSSIBLE	WITHOUT SCIENTIFIC ANTHROPOMETRY. I MIGHT AS WELL
SIM PREFACE(3)	A MONKEY. YET THERE IS AN ANALOGY. A COCO-NUT IS	IMPOSSIBLE	WITHOUT A SUITABLE CLIMATE; AND A PLAY IS
SIM PREFACE(3)	WITHOUT A SUITABLE CLIMATE; AND A PLAY IS	IMPOSSIBLE	WITHOUT A SUITABLE CIVILIZATION. IF AUTHOR AND
APPL PREFACE(184)	CORPORATE ACTION. NOW CORPORATE ACTION IS	IMPOSSIBLE	WITHOUT A GOVERNING BODY. IT MAY BE THE CENTRAL
LION PREFACE(101)	MOST HIGHLY VALUED. YET, I REPEAT, GOVERNMENT IS	IMPOSSIBLE	WITHOUT A RELIGION: THAT IS, WITHOUT A BODY OF
HART III (143)	HAVE A PRESENTIMENT-- /MRS HUSHABYE/ OH, YOU ARE	IMPOSSIBLE	, ALFRED. HERE I AM DEVOTING MYSELF TO YOU; AND
BULL PREFACE(7)	THAT MAKES THE POSITION OF THE ORANGEMEN SO	IMPOSSIBLE	, AND BREAKS IN THEM THE SPIRIT THAT ANIMATES
MIS. PREFACE(105)	BEGINS IN SILLY AND SELFISH EXPECTATIONS OF THE	IMPOSSIBLE	, AND ENDS IN SPITEFUL DISAPPOINTMENT, SOUR
FABL PREFACE(68)	AND BUSINESS ABILITY. SUCH EQUATIONS ARE WILDLY	IMPOSSIBLE	, AND HAVE NOTHING TO DO WITH THE INSANE
DOCT I SD(96)	AUDIENCE, AND MAKES INTERRUPTION OR INATTENTION	IMPOSSIBLE	, AND IMPOSES VENERATION AND CREDULITY ON ALL BUT
BULL PREFACE(46)	MILITARY SYSTEM IS SO IDIOTICALLY ACADEMIC AND	IMPOSSIBLE	, AND RENDERS ITS VICTIMS SO INCAPABLE OF
LION PREFACE(78)	THAT RODE REFORMADOES," IS, AS A WHOLE, ABSURD,	IMPOSSIBLE	, AND, EXCEPT IN PASSAGES WHERE THE ARTISTIC OLD
FABL PREFACE(67)	POSSIBLE IN EVERY HOME DEMOCRATIC CIVILIZATION IS	IMPOSSIBLE	, BECAUSE EQUALITY OF OPPORTUNITY IS IMPOSSIBLE.
APPL INTRLUD(254)	MIND YOUR TEA. I WILL GIVE YOU YOUR TEA. /MAGNUS/	IMPOSSIBLE	, BELOVED. JEMIMA DOES NOT LIKE TO BE KEPT
ARMS II (42)	HE MUST GO AT ONCE. /SERGIUS/ (SARDONICALLY)	IMPOSSIBLE	, BLUNTSCHLI. WE WANT YOU HERE BADLY. WE HAVE TO
JITT II (39)	FOR HER! I CALL IT ABOMINABLE. /JITTA/ DONT BE	IMPOSSIBLE	, DEAR. ABOMINABLE OR NOT, IT EXPLAINS HER
JOAN PREFACE(46)	OF OUR CLOTHES, AND THAT IT IS DIFFICULT, IF NOT	IMPOSSIBLE	, FOR MOST PEOPLE TO THINK OTHERWISE THAN IN THE
HART PREFACE(12)	TRAVELLING MUST BE STOPPED, OR, THAT BEING	IMPOSSIBLE	, GREATLY HINDERED. ALL PRETENCES ABOUT FINE ART
KING I (176)	HAVE LIVED FOR NEARLY THREE CENTURIES, AS THAT IS	IMPOSSIBLE	, IT IS CLEAR THAT YOU HAVE BEEN MISINFORMED
GETT (273)	BESIDES, LEO'S COMING. THEYD MEET. IT'S	IMPOSSIBLE	, LESBIA. /LESBIA/ OH, I FORGOT THAT. THAT
INCA (246)	AND BUY SOMETHING NICE WITH THE MONEY. /THE INCA/	IMPOSSIBLE	, MADAM. A DESIGN BY THE INCA MUST NOT BE
FANY II (289)	THE BETTER. /DUVALLET/ (RISING QUICKLY) THAT IS	IMPOSSIBLE	, MADEMOISELLE. YOUR FATHER HAS HIS POSITION TO
CAPT I (231)	TO THEM TOMORROW, HOWARD. /RANKIN/ THATS	IMPOSSIBLE	, MY LEDDY. THE NATIVES ARE VERRA DANGEROUS.
HART I (48)	LYING ON THE STEPS, THE SERVANTS SPOILT AND	IMPOSSIBLE	, NOBODY AT HOME TO RECEIVE ANYBODY, NO REGULAR
APPL INTRLUD(250)	MY WIFE CHANGING PLACES WITH YOU. /ORINTHIA/ WHY	IMPOSSIBLE	, PRAY? /MAGNUS/ I CANNOT MAKE YOU UNDERSTAND:
DOCT I (98)	IT. /SIR PATRICK/ SUPPOSE THERES NO GERM? /B.B./	IMPOSSIBLE	, SIR PATRICK: THERE MUST BE A GERM: ELSE HOW
BULL PREFACE(26)	NOW NOTHING CAN BE MORE ANOMALOUS, AND AT BOTTOM	IMPOSSIBLE	, THAN A CONSERVATIVE PROTESTANT PARTY STANDING
ANNA (297)	CONSENT. IT IS IMPOSSIBLE, UTTERLY, ETERNALLY	IMPOSSIBLE	, THAT A DAUGHTER OF THE IMPERIAL HOUSE SHOULD
2TRU II (72)	ASTRONOMICAL AND ENDLESS AND INCONCEIVABLE AND	IMPOSSIBLE	, THAT I SHALL JUST GO STARK RAVING MAD AND BE
MIS. PREFACE(74)	THINGS. IT IS SO FANTASTIC, SO MAD, SO APPARENTLY	IMPOSSIBLE	, THAT NO SCHEME OF REFORM NEED EVER HENCEFORTH
METH PREFACE(R74)	TEMPORALITIES AND LEGENDS THAT ARE MAKING BELIEF	IMPOSSIBLE	, THOUGH THEY ARE THE STOCK-IN-TRADE OF ALL THE
ANNA (297)	THIS IS THE LAST STRAW: I CANNOT CONSENT. IT IS	IMPOSSIBLE	, UTTERLY, ETERNALLY IMPOSSIBLE, THAT A DAUGHTER
LION PREFACE(94)	NOT. WHEN HUME SAID THAT JOSHUA'S CAMPAIGNS WERE	IMPOSSIBLE	, WHATELY DID NOT WRANGLE ABOUT IT: HE PROVED, ON
2TRU PREFACE(12)	MAINTAINING A PARLIAMENT TO MAKE ANY CHANGE	IMPOSSIBLE	, WITH CHURCHES SCHOOLS AND UNIVERSITIES TO
AUGS (275)	DOES HE TAKE ME FOR A FOOL? /THE LADY/ OH,	IMPOSSIBLE	! HE IS JEALOUS OF YOUR INTELLECT. THE BET IS AN
HART II (112)	ANOTHER BURGLAR MAY TURN UP. /MAZZINI/ OH,	IMPOSSIBLE	! I HOPE NOT. /RANDALL/ WHY NOT? THERE IS MORE
CATH 1 (171)	THIS VERY INSTANT. /EDSTASTON/ IN THESE BOOTS?	IMPOSSIBLE	! I MUST CHANGE. /PATIOMKIN/ NONSENSE! YOU
MTH2 (63)	BE WRONG. /BURGE/ (IN A BURST OF IRONY) OH NO.	IMPOSSIBLE	! IMPOSSIBLE! /LUBIN/ YES, MR BARNABAS, THOUGH
CLEO IV (174)	HAVE HAD YOUR HAIR CUT! BUT NOT YOUR BEARD--?	IMPOSSIBLE	! (HE SNIFFS AT RUFIO'S BEARD). YES, PERFUMED,
MRS I (192)	ALL I KNOW, I MIGHT BE HER FATHER. /PRAED/ YOU!	IMPOSSIBLE	! /CROFTS/ (CATCHING HIM UP CUNNINGLY) YOU KNOW
MTH2 (63)	(IN A BURST OF IRONY) OH NO. IMPOSSIBLE!	IMPOSSIBLE	! /LUBIN/ YES, MR BARNABAS, THOUGH I DO NOT
CLEO II (137)	TO LOOK OUT), /CAESAR/ WHAT, ABLAZE ALREADY!	IMPOSSIBLE	! /RUFIO/ YES, FIVE GOOD SHIPS, AND A BARGE
WIDO II (36)	AGAINST THAT. /TRENCH/ IT'S IMPOSSIBLE. /BLANCHE/	IMPOSSIBLE	! /TRENCH/ YES, IMPOSSIBLE. I HAVE RESOLVED NOT
PRES (133)	RESIGNED. /MITCHENER/ BUT HOW? WHY? OH,	IMPOSSIBLE	! THE PROCLAMATION OF MARTIAL LAW LAST TUESDAY
JOAN 6 (141)	YOU? /JOAN/ OH NO: THAT IS IMPOSSIBLE. /CAUCHON/	IMPOSSIBLE	! THEY HAVE LED YOU STRAIGHT TO YOUR
3PLA PREFACE(R18)	MUST THEREFORE PROCEED UPON GENTEEL ASSUMPTIONS.	IMPOSSIBLE	! YOU WILL EXCLAIM. BUT YOU ARE WRONG: NOTHING

IMPOSSIBLY

BARB PREFACE(220)	IS CHEAPENED TO WORTHLESSNESS FOR SOME, AND MADE	IMPOSSIBLY	DEAR TO OTHERS, THAT IS BECOMES A CURSE. IN
MRS PREFACE(175)	TEN GUINEAS A YEAR WITH BOARD AND LODGING IS AN	IMPOSSIBLY	LOW WAGE FOR A BARMAID. IT GOES ON TO CITE MR
CAPT NOTES (305)	ACCURATELY ENOUGH; BUT HE WOULD RHYME IT QUITE	IMPOSSIBLY	TO NICE, WHICH TOMPKINS WOULD HAVE PRONOUNCED AS

IMPOSTOR

LION PREFACE(26)	WOULD EXPOSE THEIR HERO TO CONDEMNATION AS AN	IMPOSTOR	AMONG PEOPLE WHOSE GOOD OPINION WAS OF GREAT
LION PREFACE(8)	WAY. THAT WAS WHY HE TREATED JESUS AS AN	IMPOSTOR	AND A BLASPHEMER WHERE WE SHOULD HAVE TREATED HIM
SUPR HANDBOK(203)	HIM; THE PHYSICIAN IS STILL THE CREDULOUS	IMPOSTOR	AND PETULANT SCIENTIFIC COXCOMB WHOM MOLIERE
MTH3 (94)	TOMFOOLERY, OF COURSE. I SHALL PUT THIS AMERICAN	IMPOSTOR	IN HIS PLACE. (HE GOES OUT). /BURGE-LUBIN/ (
MIS. PREFACE(78)	FOR POSING AS SUPERHUMAN! THE PENALTY OF THE	IMPOSTOR	IS NOT THAT HE IS FOUND OUT (HE VERY SELDOM IS)
ROCK PREFACE(157)	POINT OF VIEW OF THE HIGH PRIEST A HERETIC AND AN	IMPOSTOR	. FROM THE POINT OF VIEW OF THE MERCHANTS HE WAS A
JOAN PREFACE(44)	IN THE VOICES, AND REGARDED HER AS A LIAR AND	IMPOSTOR	. IT IS HARD TO CONCEIVE ANYTHING MORE INFURIATING
DEVL III (67)	NAME IS DUDGEON, SIR, RICHARD DUDGEON. HE IS AN	IMPOSTOR	. /BURGOYNE/ (BRUSQUELY) NONSENSE, SIR: YOU HANGED
BARB PREFACE(213)	PHILOSOPHER, AND THE OPPORTUNITY OF THE RELIGIOUS	IMPOSTOR	. THE GOSPEL OF ST ANDREW UNDERSHAFT. IT IS THIS
LION PREFACE(40)	OF THE CHRISTIANS, THAT JESUS WAS EITHER AN	IMPOSTOR	OR THE VICTIM OF A DELUSION. NOW ALL THE
SHAK (139)	FOR ALL TIME. HITHER I RAGING COME AN INFAMOUS	IMPOSTOR	TO CHASTIZE, WHO IN AN ECSTASY OF SELF-CONCEIT
LION PREFACE(43)	OF JESUS'S DECLARATION THAT HE WAS A GOD. NO	IMPOSTOR	WOULD HAVE ACCEPTED SUCH DREADFUL CONSEQUENCES
LION PREFACE(43)	WITHOUT AN EFFORT TO SAVE HIMSELF. NO	IMPOSTOR	WOULD HAVE BEEN NERVED TO ENDURE THEM BY THE
METH PREFACE(R66)	OF BEING A RIDICULOUS FICTION, MIGHT BE ONLY AN	IMPOSTOR	, AND THAT THE EXPOSURE OF THIS KOEPENIK CAPTAIN OF
POSN PREFACE(394)	THE PREFACES TO WHICH MAHOMET IS CRITICIZED AS AN	IMPOSTOR	, OR OF THE OLDER BOOKS IN WHICH HE IS REVILED AS
DOCT PREFACE(23)	WAS SAVED BY SIMPLY CALLING THE BACILLUS AN	IMPOSTOR	, OR PSEUDO-BACILLUS. THE SAME BOUNDLESS CREDULITY
JOAN PREFACE(11)	PROVE THAT SHE WAS MAD, THAT SHE WAS A LIAR AND	IMPOSTOR	, THAT SHE WAS A SORCERESS (SHE WAS BURNED FOR
FOUN (215)	ARE STERN WITH THE WORTHLESS AND MERCILESS TO THE	IMPOSTOR	, YET YOUR MATURE WISDOM AND UNPARALLELED LEGAL
SUPR IV (152)	/TANNER/ YOU THE MISSING HUSBAND! ANOTHER MORAL	IMPOSTOR	! (HE SMITES HIS BROW, AND COLLAPSES INTO
PYGM V (288)	NEPEAN. /HIGGINS/ (RISING IN A FURY) WHAT! THAT	IMPOSTOR	! THAT HUMBUG! THAT TOADYING IGNORAMUS! TEACH

IMPOSTORS

KING I (178)	FOX, GEORGE FOX: RISE UP: TESTIFY: UNMASK THESE	IMPOSTORS	: DRAG THEM DOWN FROM THEIR PULPITS AND THEIR
FABL PREFACE(64)	ARE WE SIMPLY INCORRIGIBLE LIARS? ARE PLAYERS	IMPOSTORS	AND HYPOCRITES? WERE THE BIBLE CHRISTIANS RIGHT

LION PREFACE(28)	HE FEARS THAT THIS MAY LEAD TO THE APPEARANCE OF	IMPOSTORS	CLAIMING TO BE HIMSELF, AND DECLARES EXPLICITLY
2TRU PREFACE(23)	MAKE SUPERNATURAL PRETENSIONS. THEY MUST NOT BE	IMPOSTORS	. A VOCATION FOR POLITICS, THOUGH ESSENTIALLY A
BARB III (347)	AND TYRANNICAL THAN ALL THE FOOLS, RASCALS, AND	IMPOSTORS	. I WANT A POWER SIMPLE ENOUGH FOR COMMON MEN TO
JOAN PREFACE(44)	ARE MESSENGERS OF GOD, OR THEY ARE BLASPHEMOUS	IMPOSTORS	. IN THE MIDDLE AGES THE GENERAL BELIEF IN
KING I (212)	AND A SNARE, AND YOUR PROTESTANT ARCHBISHOPS	IMPOSTORS	. /NEWTON/ YOU DO NOT KNOW THE WORST, SIR. I HAVE
LION PREFACE(28)	AND REPEATEDLY THAT NO MATTER WHAT WONDERS THESE	IMPOSTORS	MAY PERFORM, HIS OWN COMING WILL BE UNMISTAKEABLE,
JOAN PREFACE(14)	MUST UNDERSTAND THAT VISIONARIES ARE NEITHER	IMPOSTORS	NOR LUNATICS. IT IS ONE THING TO SAY THAT THE
METH PREFACE(R56)	IMPOSED ON BY THIS RABBLE OF DOLTS, BLACKGUARDS,	IMPOSTORS	, QUACKS, LIARS, AND, WORST OF ALL, CREDULOUS
BUOY III (41)	OR WRITE IT EASILY. /THE WIDOWER/ WE ARE NOT	IMPOSTORS	, SIR FERDINAND, BECAUSE WE RAN AWAY FROM OUR

IMPOSTURE

LION PREFACE(60)	FRANCE AND THE UNITED STATES FOR EXAMPLE, IS AN	IMPOSTURE	AND A DELUSION. IT REDUCES JUSTICE AND LAW TO A
PLES PREFACE(R10)	IS THE FUNCTION THAT RAISES DRAMATIC ART ABOVE	IMPOSTURE	AND PLEASURE HUNTING, AND ENABLES THE PLAYWRIGHT
SUPR PREFACE(R33)	OFFS WITH PEOPLE'S HEADS, WE ARE REVOLTED AT THE	IMPOSTURE	AND REPUDIATE THE CHANGELING. FAULCONBRIDGE,
DOCT PREFACE(17)	BECOMES, THE MORE THEY ARE COMPELLED TO LIVE BY	IMPOSTURE	AND THE LESS BY THAT REALLY HELPFUL ACTIVITY OF
SUPR PREFACE(R24)	MIND THAT IS NOT STRONG ENOUGH TO SEE THROUGH THE	IMPOSTURE	AND TO USE THE GREAT MASTERS OF ARTS AS WHAT THEY
SUPR III (120)	PROVE, ANA? ONLY THAT THE HERO IS AS GROSS AN	IMPOSTURE	AS THE HEROINE. /ANA/ IT IS ALL NONSENSE: MOST
MIS. PREFACE(20)	FEED YOUR SOULS, YOU ARE FORCED TO READ A HIDEOUS	IMPOSTURE	CALLED A SCHOOL BOOK, WRITTEN BY A MAN WHO CANNOT
LION PREFACE(48)	WHILST OTHERS WILL SCOFF AT IT AS A PLANNED	IMPOSTURE	IN WHICH LAZARUS ACTED AS A CONFEDERATE. BETWEEN
GETT PREFACE(195)	NAME UNTIL THE REAL THING IS LOATHED BECAUSE THE	IMPOSTURE	IS LOATHSOME. LITERARY TRADITIONS SPRING UP IN
MTH4 II (176)	TO THAT MAN FACE TO FACE, WITHOUT MUMMERY OR	IMPOSTURE	. /THE VEILED WOMAN/ YOU SEEM TO BE AN UNUSUALLY
ARMS III (65)	WELL, BLUNTSCHLI, YOU ARE RIGHT TO TAKE THIS HUGE	IMPOSTURE	OF A WORLD COOLLY. /RAINA/ (QUAINTLY TO
GETT PREFACE(235)	DOES NOT NEED TO PROTECT HER AGAINST A SIMILAR	IMPOSTURE	ON HIS PART, BECAUSE HE CANNOT BEAR CHILDREN. NO
GENV I (44)	WHAT RIGHT HAD YOU TO PRACTISE SUCH A CRUEL	IMPOSTURE	ON ME? (HE RISES: THE COMMISSAR HELPS HIM) NO: I
METH PREFACE(R13)	IN VAIN DO THE PROPHETS WHO SEE THROUGH THIS	IMPOSTURE	PREACH AND TEACH A BETTER GOSPEL: THE INDIVIDUALS
HART PREFACE(7)	THAT FRESH AIR IS A FAD, AND SANITATION AN	IMPOSTURE	SET UP TO MAKE PROFITS FOR PLUMBERS, THEN SUDDENLY
MIS. PREFACE(89)	AS THEY DO WHEN RICHTER CONDUCTS IT, THE MASS OF	IMPOSTURE	THAT THRIVES ON THIS COMBINATION OF IGNORANCE WITH
DOCT PREFACE(73)	AND IS CONTINUALLY URGED BY ITS DISLIKE OF THE	IMPOSTURE	TO STRIVE TO MAKE THE PEASANT SUSCEPTIBLE TO THE
METH PREFACE(R84)	WERE AT LEAST IN REVOLT AGAINST FALSEHOOD AND	IMPOSTURE	, AND WERE NOT ONLY, AS THEY CLAIMED, " CHASTENING

IMPOSTURES

SUPR HANDBOK(209)	WHEN THE VULGAR BELIEF IN ITS HYPOCRISIES AND	IMPOSTURES	CAN NO LONGER HOLD OUT AGAINST ITS FAILURES AND
JOAN PREFACE(47)	ANY OF OUR AMAZING CREDULITIES ARE DELUSIONS OR	IMPOSTURES	. I AM ONLY DEFENDING MY OWN AGE AGAINST THE
2TRU PREFACE(13)	FUNDAMENTALLY, DISCARDING THE PROTESTANT	IMPOSTURES	ON ENGLISH HISTORY WHICH INSPIRED THE VIGOROUS
METH PREFACE(R87)	OF CONSCIENCE, PROFESSIONAL DELUSIONS AND	IMPOSTURES	, ALL WORKED INTO A SERIES OF COMEDIES OF MANNERS
METH PREFACE(R88)	EVEN THOUGH THE ABOMINATIONS, QUACKERIES,	IMPOSTURES	, VENALITIES, CREDULITIES, AND DELUSIONS OF THE

IMPOTENCE

SUPR III (121)	FREE FOR THE FEAR OF OLD AGE AND UGLINESS AND	IMPOTENCE	AND DEATH. THE CHILDLESS LABORER IS MORE TORMENTED
CLEO II SD(118)	HABIT OF BEING IN LEADING STRINGS, THE MIXTURE OF	IMPOTENCE	AND PETULANCE, THE APPEARANCE OF BEING EXCESSIVELY
POSN PREFACE(395)	THE LICENSER WITH THE EXCEPTION OF A REFERENCE TO	IMPOTENCE	AS A GROUND FOR DIVORCE WHICH NO ENGLISH ACTRESS
POSN PREFACE(430)	HIS PROFESSIONAL EXPERIENCE WITH A SENSE OF THE	IMPOTENCE	OF JUDGES AND LAWS AND COURTS TO DEAL
CLEO V (200)	THAT. /CLEOPATRA/ (PETTISH AND CHILDISH IN HER	IMPOTENCE	) NO; NOT WHEN A ROMAN SLAYS AN EGYPTIAN. ALL THE
BULL PREFACE(21)	THE NEED FOR CARRYING OFF THE WORTHLESSNESS AND	IMPOTENCE	THAT ACCOMPANY IT, PRODUCE IN ALL NATIONS A GAY,
DEST (165)	/LADY/ (BREAKING DOWN IN THE CHILDISH RAGE OF	IMPOTENCE	, AND THROWING HERSELF IN TEARS ON THE CHAIR LEFT

IMPOTENT

METH PREFACE(R86)	EMPYREAN WHILST THEY ARE GNASHING THEIR TEETH IN	IMPOTENT	FURY IN THE MUD, OR AT BEST FINDING AN ACID
HART PREFACE(28)	AND AGAINST THAT BLOCKADE OUR ARMADA IS	IMPOTENT	. IN THE BLOCKADER'S HOUSE, HE HAS ASSURED US,
2TRU PREFACE(20)	ENOUGH TO ASSUME DICTATORSHIP AND KICK ASIDE THE	IMPOTENT	OFFICIAL GOVERNMENT UNTIL HE HAD COMPLETELY MUZZLED
SIM II (56)	AND HOW HAS THIS PARAGON TURNED OUT? AN	IMPOTENT	SIMPLETON. IT WOULD BE IMPOSSIBLE TO CONCEIVE A

IMPOTENTLY

MTH4 II (184)	STATUE THE WAR GOD OF TURANIA IS NOW GIBBERING	IMPOTENTLY	. /ZOO/ SERVE HIM RIGHT! WAR GOD INDEED! /THE

IMPRACTICABLE

DOCT PREFACE(15)	SO IGNORANT THAT GOOD ADVICE WOULD BE RESENTED AS	IMPRACTICABLE	AND WOUNDING. WHEN YOU ARE SO POOR THAT YOU
3PLA PREFACE(R12)	NEW CENTURY THEATRE, AND THE STAGE SOCIETY ARE	IMPRACTICABLE	FADDISTS FOR PRODUCING THE PLAYS OF IBSEN AND
ROCK PREFACE(159)	ALL GOVERNMENTS IT HAS REMAINED PARADOXICAL AND	IMPRACTICABLE	, A TYPICAL ACKNOWLEDGMENT OF IT WAS THE
LION PREFACE(59)	INDIVIDUAL IS UNKNOWN, BECAUSE IT IS RIDICULOUSLY	IMPRACTICABLE	, AS A DEVICE FOR PERSUADING A CARPENTER THAT
DOCT PREFACE(79)	ALIVE IS OF INFINITE VALUE IS LEGISLATIVELY	IMPRACTICABLE	. NO DOUBT THE HIGHER THE LIFE WE SECURE TO
FABL PREFACE(74)	A DAIRY FARMER AND HIS MILKMAIDS. CATHOLICISM	IMPRACTICABLE	. THE LESSON OF THIS IS THAT A TOTALLY
SUPR II (60)	TO YOU. /ANN/ YOU ARE SO UTTERLY UNREASONABLE AND	IMPRACTICABLE	. WHAT CAN I DO? /TANNER/ DO! BREAK YOUR
LION PREFACE(19)	FORCE US TO SHOVE THEM ASIDE IN EMERGENCIES AS	IMPRACTICABLE	LUNATICS WHEN THEY ASK US TO MEET VIOLENCE AND
GETT (322)	MY REASON TELLS ME AT PRESENT IS THAT YOU ARE AN	IMPRACTICABLE	LUNATIC. /SOAMES/ DOES THAT HELP? /HOTCHKISS/
BARB PREFACE(233)	ARE NO ABSOLUTE SCOUNDRELS, THOUGH THERE ARE	IMPRACTICABLE	PEOPLE OF WHOM I SHALL TREAT PRESENTLY. EVERY
HART PREFACE(39)	AND THE WORST IT THREATENS IS ALREADY PROVING	IMPRACTICABLE	; BUT BEFORE THE HUMBLE AND CONTRITE HEART
FABL PREFACE(64)	BE, WHEN THESE TREATMENTS FAIL, OR WHEN THEY ARE	IMPRACTICABLE	, THEY TELL YOU SYMPATHETICALLY THAT YOU MUST

IMPRECATIONS

HART PREFACE(20)	IN THEIR NEWSPAPERS, SUDDENLY BURST INTO FURIOUS	IMPRECATIONS	ON " THE HUNS" AS MURDERERS, AND SHRIEKED FOR
PYGM III SD(250)	ON HIS WAY; EXTRICATING HIMSELF WITH MUTTERED	IMPRECATIONS	; AND FINISHING HIS DISASTROUS JOURNEY BY

IMPREGNABLE

2TRU III (87)	THE UNIVERSE OF ISAAC NEWTON, WHICH HAS BEEN AN	IMPREGNABLE	CITADEL OF MODERN CIVILIZATION FOR THREE HUNDRED
SUPR HANDBOK(190)	HER SOCIAL PROBLEMS SIMPLIFIED IN THE SAME WAY BY	IMPREGNABLE	NATURAL FORTIFICATIONS AND A POPULATION EDUCATED
LADY (245)	MEN TO YOUR FEET, AND FOUNDED YOUR THRONE ON THE	IMPREGNABLE	ROCK OF YOUR PROUD HEART, A STONY ISLAND IN A
VWOO 3 (137)	A POST OFFICE. WHILE I COMMAND BOTH I AM IN AN	IMPREGNABLE	STRATEGIC POSITION. /Z/ WELL, I DONT LIKE TO SAY
ROCK PREFACE(166)	LANDED PROPRIETORS THAT MADE LENIN'S POSITION	IMPREGNABLE	, AND PROVIDED TROTSKY AND STALIN WITH THE RED

IMPREGNATION

SUPR III (110)	SEPARATE CREATURE WHOSE SOLE FUNCTION WAS HER OWN	IMPREGNATION	! FOR MARK WHAT HAS HAPPENED. FIRST, MAN HAS

IMPRESARIO

FANY PROLOG (265)	PARDON. /THE COUNT/ THIS IS MR SAVOYARD, YOUR	IMPRESARIO	, MY DEAR. /FANNY/ (SHAKING HANDS) HOW DO YOU

IMPRESCRIPTIBLE

2TRU II SD(52)	HIS REPLIES, HE SOMEHOW SUGGESTS THAT THERE IS AN	IMPRESCRIPTIBLE	JOKE SOMEWHERE BY AN INVISIBLE SMILE WHICH

IMPRESS

CATH 1 (164)	THE ENGLISH. /VARINKA/ AND YOU THINK YOU WILL	IMPRESS	AN ENGLISHMAN BY RECEIVING HIM AS YOU ARE NOW, HALF
BULL PREFACE(27)	AND MANNING, THE GENERAL RUN OF MANKIND TAKES ITS	IMPRESS	FROM THE ATMOSPHERE IN WHICH IT IS BROUGHT UP. IN
SUPR PREFACE(R31)	DRAMATISTS WHO INVENTED SOCRATES AND DR JOHNSON,	IMPRESS	ME MORE DEEPLY THAN THE ROMANTIC PLAYWRIGHTS. EVER
MTH1 II (31)	WHO HAS GROWN UP AND WANTS TO	IMPRESS	ME WITH HIS IMPORTANCE. OH, IT IS DREARY, DREARY!
MTH4 III (194)	SORT OF THING IS GOT UP TO IMPRESS YOU, NOT TO	IMPRESS	ME. /THE ELDERLY GENTLEMAN/ I WISH YOU WOULD LET IT
VWOO 2 (125)	NOT A DETECTIVE. IT IS PEOPLE'S CHARACTERS THAT	IMPRESS	ME; I CANT TELL YOU THE COLOR OF HER HAIR OR THE
MIS. PREFACE(28)	IMPORTANT SIMPLE FUNDAMENTAL ECONOMIC TRUTH TO	IMPRESS	ON A CHILD IN COMPLICATED CIVILIZATIONS LIKE OURS IS
LION I (111)	THEM TO SHAVE EVERY DAY, NOT EVERY WEEK. YOU WILL	IMPRESS	ON THEM PARTICULARLY THAT THERE MUST BE AN END TO
BULL PREFACE(32)	TO INTIMIDATION, FOR LET ME HALT A MOMENT HERE TO	IMPRESS	ON YOU, O ENGLISH READER, THAT NO FACT HAS BEEN MORE
MIS. PREFACE(55)	BOYS WERE FLOGGED WHEN CRIMINALS WERE HANGED, TO	IMPRESS	THE AWFUL WARNING ON THEM. BOYS WERE FLOGGED AT
MIS. PREFACE(55)	ON THEM. BOYS WERE FLOGGED AT BOUNDARIES, TO	IMPRESS	THE BOUNDARIES ON THEIR MEMORY. OTHER METHODS AND
CLEO NOTES (208)	WE SHOULD EXPECT THE ANCESTORS OF MR PODSNAP TO	IMPRESS	THE CULTIVATED ITALIANS OF THEIR TIME. I AM TOLD
2TRU II (53)	IT'S OF NO CONSEQUENCE, SIR. IT WAS ONLY TO	IMPRESS	THE HEADMAN. /TALLBOYS/ INNDEED. WHO PICKED YOU FOR
2TRU II (53)	RESPONSIBLE PERSON, WITH SUFFICIENT STYLE TO	IMPRESS	THE NATIVE HEADMAN TO WHOM COLONEL SAXBY'S LETTER
DEVL III (72)	THE SOLEMNITY OF THE OCCASION, AS YOU CALL IT, TO	IMPRESS	THE PEOPLE WITH YOUR OWN DIGNITY-- HANDEL'S MUSIC

BUOY III (32)	WILL HAVE TO LAST YOU FOR YEARS. I AM HERE TO	IMPRESS	THESE HARD FACTS ON YOU. /THE WIDOWER/ BUT SURELY
MTH4 III (194)	/THE ELDERLY GENTLEMAN/ I WISH YOU WOULD LET IT	IMPRESS	US, THEN, MADAM. I AM DEEPLY IMPRESSED; BUT YOU ARE
BUOY II (19)	YOU BY OFFERING TO PAY FOR MY ENTERTAINMENT? OR	IMPRESS	YOU BY INTRODUCING MYSELF AS A GRADUATE OF OXFORD
MTH4 II (185)	ROBE, AND PUT ON A WIG AND A LONG FALSE BEARD, TO	IMPRESS	YOU SILLY PEOPLE. I HAVE TO PUT ON A PURPLE MANTLE.
MTH4 II (176)	THE USUAL MUMMERY, AS YOU RIGHTLY CALL IT, TO	IMPRESS	YOUR FRIEND THE ENVOY. AS YOU ARE SUPERIOR TO THAT
MTH4 III (194)	SO? /ZOO/ NO. THIS SORT OF THING IS GOT UP TO	IMPRESS	YOU, NOT TO IMPRESS ME. /THE ELDERLY GENTLEMAN/ I
		IMPRESSED	
BULL III (138)	TALK; AND IT WENT HOME. THEY WERE GREATLY	IMPRESSED	: EVERYONE OF THOSE MEN BELIEVES IN ME AND WILL
CAPT III (278)	IMPARTIALITY. (SHE NODS, AS IF THOROUGHLY	IMPRESSED	AND REPROVED, AND GAZES AT HIM WITH THE STEADFAST
JOAN PREFACE(27)	BOTH OF THEM WERE BAPTIZED AS PROTESTANTS, AND	IMPRESSED	BY ALL THEIR SCHOOLING AND MOST OF THEIR READING
BULL III (137)	HE'LL DO FOR US RIGHT ENOUGH. /MATTHEW/ (DEEPLY	IMPRESSED	BY BROADBENT, AND UNABLE TO UNDERSTAND THEIR
NEVR IV (286)	(MAKING IT A POINT OF HONOR NOT TO BE	IMPRESSED	BY HIM) DO I LOOK LIKE IT? MY NAME IS VALENTINE.
DEVL I (8)	EASE AGAIN). YOUR HUSBAND WAS GREATLY TOUCHED AND	IMPRESSED	BY HIS BROTHER'S AWFUL DEATH. (MRS DUDGEON
POSN PREFACE(430)	IT IS INEVITABLE THAT A JUDGE SHOULD BE DEEPLY	IMPRESSED	BY HIS PROFESSIONAL EXPERIENCE WITH A SENSE OF THE
KING I SD(166)	I THANK YOU (HE PASSES IN). SALLY, INTENSELY	IMPRESSED	BY MR ROWLEY, GOES OUT. /FOX/ AM I ADDRESSING THE
MIS. PREFACE(58)	OF EVOLUTION. DOCILITY AND DEPENDENCE. IF ANYONE,	IMPRESSED	BY MY VIEW THAT THE RIGHTS OF A CHILD ARE
GETT (306)	TO HOTCHKISS'S LEFT. /HOTCHKISS/ (RISING,	IMPRESSED	BY THE ALDERMANIC GOWN) IVE NOT HAD THE PLEASURE.
APPL I (211)	ALICE HAPPENED TO DROP IN. SHE WAS GREATLY	IMPRESSED	BY THE PRESIDENT. THEY ALL LAUGH UPROARIOUSLY AT
SUPR IV (145)	NEAREST CHAIR OF THE TWO BOOKS ON IT). /MALONE/ (	IMPRESSED	BY THIS ATTENTION) THANK YOU. (HE SITS DOWN,
MILL PREFACE(134)	AS DEPENDENT ON THEM AS THEY ON HIM. BUT I FEAR I	IMPRESSED	HIM MOST BY ADDING, QUITE UNTRULY, THAT NO
PYGM PREFACE(201)	MIGHT HAVE SET THE THAMES ON FIRE. AS IT WAS, HE	IMPRESSED	HIMSELF PROFESSIONALLY ON EUROPE TO AN EXTENT THAT
MRS II (213)	WITH BRAZEN ENERGY, AND SITS DOWN. VIVIE IS	IMPRESSED	IN SPITE OF HERSELF). D'YOU KNOW WHAT YOUR
2TRU III SD(112)	DISPERSES (OR THE READER PUTS DOWN THE BOOK)	IMPRESSED	IN THE ENGLISH MANNER WITH THE PENTECOSTAL FLAME
MRS III SD(229)	IS FINAL. I WONT GO BACK FROM IT. CROFTS IS NOT	IMPRESSED	. HE GRINS; LEANS FORWARD WITH HIS ELBOWS ON HIS
GENV IV (95)	BUT AS YOU KNEW YOU WERE QUITE SAFE, WE WERE NOT	IMPRESSED	. /BBDE/ YOU ARE QUITE RIGHT, EXCELLENCY. IT WAS
JOAN 2 (77)	IS TRUE THAT DE BAUDRICOURT SEEMS EXTRAORDINARILY	IMPRESSED	. /LA HIRE/ DE BAUDRICOURT IS A BLAZING ASS; BUT
MTH4 II (185)	KNOW, AS A MATTER OF EXPERIENCE, THAT YOU WILL BE	IMPRESSED	. THE ORACLE WILL FRIGHTEN YOU OUT OF YOUR WITS. (
JOAN PREFACE(15)	STRONGLY THROUGHOUT LIFE WHEN IT HAS BEEN WELL	IMPRESSED	, THUS ALL THE THINKING OF THE HALLUCINATED ADULT
AUGS (271)	DESCRIBING MYSELF SO, MADAM; BUT NO DOUBT I HAVE	IMPRESSED	MY COUNTRYMEN -- AND (BOWING GALLANTLY) MAY I SAY
FABL PREFACE(70)	NOT FOR ANY ECONOMIC MISDEMEANOR. THIS VIEW WAS	IMPRESSED	ON ME IN MY CHILDHOOD. I NOW REGARD IT AS A MUCH
CLEO NOTES (208)	THE UNADULTERATED BRITON WHO FOUGHT CAESAR AND	IMPRESSED	ROMAN OBSERVERS MUCH AS WE SHOULD EXPECT THE
ARMS I (19)	A MAJOR. /THE MAN/ (PRETENDING TO BE DEEPLY	IMPRESSED	) A MAJOR! BLESS ME! THINK OF THAT! /RAINA/ YOU
SUPR III (124)	GROUNDS, NOT ON PERSONAL ONES. /THE STATUE/ (	IMPRESSED	) A VERY CLEVER POINT THAT, JUAN: I MUST THINK IT
MTH2 (81)	BIG ENOUGH TO TAKE US INTO A NEW AGE. /LUBIN/ (	IMPRESSED	) FANCY MY BEING LEADER OF THE PARTY FOR THE NEXT
CAPT III (274)	A BREEGAND. /LADY CICELY/ (APPARENTLY DEEPLY	IMPRESSED	) I WONDER WHETHER HE CAN BE, MR RANKIN. IF YOU
CAPT I (222)	YER WOT E IS, YR HONOR? /RANKIN/ (NOT AT ALL	IMPRESSED	) IF YE WILL BE SO GOOD, MR DRINKWOTTER.
CATH 1 (167)	IS ON THE OTHER SIDE. /PATIOMKIN/ (SURPRISED AND	IMPRESSED	) IS IT? YOU ARE LEARNED! YOU ARE A DOCTOR! YOU
GLIM (175)	HAND). DO YOU KNOW WHO I AM, DOG? /SQUARCIO/ (	IMPRESSED	) NO, YOUR EXCELLENCY. /THE FRIAR/ I AM FERRUCCIO,
NEVR II (235)	YACHT BUILDER, AN EMINENT MAN HERE. /WAITER/ (	IMPRESSED	) OH, BEG PARDON, SIR, I'M SURE. A SON OF MR
PYGM IV (264)	OF ME? /HIGGINS/ (ENLIGHTENED, BUT NOT AT ALL	IMPRESSED	) OH, THATS WHATS WORRYING YOU, IS IT? (HE
MILL I (137)	RINGS. /SAGAMORE/ (LISTENING) YES? . . . (	IMPRESSED	) OH! SEND HER UP AT ONCE. A TRAGIC LOOKING
MTH1 II (25)	HERE ONLY TO MAKE LIFE GLORIOUS FOR US? /ADAM/ (	IMPRESSED	) THAT IS A GREAT THOUGHT, CERTAINLY. /EVE/ (
MIS. (129)	BACKED HIMSELF AGAINST NAPOLEON. /TARLETON/ (	IMPRESSED	) THATS AN IDEA, THATS A MOST INTERESTING IDEA: A
MIS. (134)	HAVE BEEN VERY LIKE HIM. /TARLETON/ (AGAIN	IMPRESSED	) THATS AN IDEA, THATS A NEW IDEA. I BELIEVE I
CAND III (143)	MY DESOLATION, MY HEART'S NEED. /CANDIDA/ (	IMPRESSED	) THATS A GOOD BID, EUGENE. NOW I KNOW HOW TO MAKE
WIDO I (9)	COUNT FURSTENBERG-STAMMHEIM." /SARTORIUS/ (MUCH	IMPRESSED	) WE MUST CERTAINLY SEE THAT, MR COKANE. I HAD NO
ANNA (292)	ELOPED! /SCHNEIDEKIND/ (NOT PARTICULARLY	IMPRESSED	) YES, SIR. /STRAMMFEST/ ANNAJANSKA, THE
MTH4 II (192)	FROM WHICH WE HAVE BOTH PROCEEDED. /ZOZIM/ (	IMPRESSED	) YOU SPOKE THAT PIECE VERY WELL, DADDY. I COULDNT
GLIM (188)	AND ITSELF PART OF THE INFINITE. /SANDRO/ (	IMPRESSED	) YOUR EXCELLENCY SPEAKS LIKE A CRAZY BUT VERY
LION PREFACE(25)	ON HIM BEFORE MY EYES, AND I WILL BE REALLY	IMPRESSED	; BUT MERE CURES OF AILMENTS THAT HAVE OFTEN BEEN
CLEO IV SD(183)	WITH HIM. THE THREE MEN ARE DETERMINED NOT TO BE	IMPRESSED	; BUT THEY FEEL CURIOUS IN SPITE OF THEMSELVES.
MTH4 III (195)	WOULD LET IT IMPRESS US, THEN, MADAM. I AM DEEPLY	IMPRESSED	; BUT YOU ARE SPOILING THE EFFECT. /ZOO/ YOU JUST
SUPR PREFACE(R40)	BOOK HAS DONE VERY WELL. THE STRONG CRITICS ARE	IMPRESSED	; THE WEAK INTIMIDATED; THE CONNOISSEURS TICKLED
APPL PREFACE(172)	HAVE COME INTO CONTACT WITH MONARCHS HAVE BEEN SO	IMPRESSED	THAT THEY HAVE ATTRIBUTED TO THEM EXTRAORDINARY
DOCT PREFACE(61)	OF ALL KINDS, THAT THE PUBLIC WAS SUFFICIENTLY	IMPRESSED	TO MAKE IT POSSIBLE FOR THE DOCTORS TO OPEN THEIR
DEST SD(150)	THE FOLLOWING STORY HAS BEEN ENACTED, THAT THEY,	IMPRESSED	WITH THE LATER GLORY OF " L'EMPEREUR," HAVE
BULL PREFACE(21)	IS ALMOST BEYOND BELIEF) TO MAKE. THE ENGLISHMAN,	IMPRESSED	WITH THE DISSOLUTENESS OF THE FAITHLESS WITS OF
MTH4 II (185)	ELDERLY GENTLEMAN/ BUT DO YOU EXPECT US TO BE	IMPRESSED	, AFTER THIS? /ZOO/ I DONT EXPECT ANYTHING. I
MIS. (146)	MIND NOT ALTOGETHER A NATURAL ONE. /TARLETON/ (	IMPRESSED	, AS USUAL) THATS AN IDEA, CERTAINLY. I DONT THINK
NEVR III SD(274)	TO THE OTTOMAN, AND SITS DOWN). DOLLY, DULY	IMPRESSED	, FOLLOWS AND SITS BESIDE HIM ON HIM RIGHT.
MTH2 (82)	WITH HIS CONSIDERING CAP ON) I ADMIT THAT I AM	IMPRESSED	, GENTLEMEN. I WILL GO SO FAR AS TO SAY THAT YOUR
DOCT IV SD(160)	IN LANGUOR AND DRAMA IN DEATH. THEY ARE ALL	IMPRESSED	, IN SPITE OF THEMSELVES, EXCEPT RIDGEON, WHO IS
CLEO III (145)	STANDS HIGH WITH CAESAR. /SENTINEL/ (NOT AT ALL	IMPRESSED	, POINTING TO THE CARPETS) AND WHAT IS ALL THIS
		IMPRESSES	
BULL I (95)	WELL, EVERYTHING YOU TELL ME ABOUT HER	IMPRESSES	ME FAVORABLY. SHE SEEMS TO HAVE THE FEELINGS OF A
3PLA PREFACE(R24)	FANFARE. WHEN AN ACTRESS WRITES HER MEMOIRS, SHE	IMPRESSES	ON YOU IN EVERY CHAPTER HOW CRUELLY IT TRIED HER
SUPR PREFACE(R13)	CHOOSES TO LEARN FROM HIS BOOK. WHAT ATTRACTS AND	IMPRESSES	US IN EL BURLADOR DE SEVILLA IS NOT THE IMMEDIATE
		IMPRESSING	
GENV IV (98)	THE EIGHTEENTH CENTURY; BUT OF WHAT USE IS IT FOR	IMPRESSING	A MODERN CROWD? AND YOUR SLOGANS ARE HOPELESSLY
		IMPRESSION	
CYMB FORWORD(134)	NOT DONE SO FOR MANY YEARS, AND HAD THE COMMON	IMPRESSION	ABOUT IT THAT IT WAS A COBBLED-UP AFFAIR BY
WIDO I (21)	BUT I DESIRE THAT THERE MAY BE NO WRONG	IMPRESSION	AS TO MY DAUGHTER'S-- ER-- BREEDING. AS TO
GENV II (62)	DO YOU THINK YOU WILL BE ABLE TO MAKE A BETTER	IMPRESSION	AT THE MEETINGS? YOU ARE NOT A POLITICIAN, ARE
CATH PREFACE(154)	WHAT WAS BEST WORTH SAYING, I BEG TO CORRECT YOUR	IMPRESSION	BY ASSURING YOU THAT WHAT BYRON SAID WAS ALL
SUPR IV (158)	JACK THE OTHER WAY. GETTING OVER AN UNFAVORABLE	IMPRESSION	IS EVER SO MUCH EASIER THAN LIVING UP TO AN
LION PREFACE(39)	PURPOSE THAN TO FULFIL THE OLD PROPHECIES. THE	IMPRESSION	IS MORE UNPLEASANT, BECAUSE, AS JOHN, UNLIKE
PPP SD(193)	AGAINST THE WALL NEAR THE BED. THE GENERAL	IMPRESSION	IS ONE OF BRIGHTNESS, BEAUTY, AND SOCIAL
SUPR III (82)	COULD NOT DENY IT; NEITHER COULD I ERADICATE THE	IMPRESSION	IT MADE ON HER MIND. I COULD HAVE GOT ROUND ANY
CAPT III (287)	THEN: PLEASE DONT SAY THINGS THAT CONVEY THAT	IMPRESSION	. /KEARNEY/ BUT SIR HOWARD TOLD ME YESTERDAY THAT
HART I (51)	HE DIDNT FORGET YOU AFTER ALL! YOU HAVE MADE AN	IMPRESSION	. /THE CAPTAIN/ (GLOOMILY) YOUTH! BEAUTY!
BULL II SD(101)	MODERN COUNTRIES SHE MAKES A VERY DIFFERENT	IMPRESSION	. THE ABSENCE OF ANY SYMPTOMS OF COARSENESS OR
HART I SD(48)	PRECIPITATE IN SPEECH AND ACTION THAT THE FIRST	IMPRESSION	(ERRONEOUS) IS ONE OF COMIC SILLINESS. /LADY
GENV PREFACE(4)	ALLIES' LOSSES WERE NOT GIVEN AT ALL, THE	IMPRESSION	LEFT BEING THAT THE ALLIES HAD KILLED OR TAKEN
JOAN PREFACE(24)	OF LENIN IN 1917. IT ENDS IN MERE SCURRILITY. THE	IMPRESSION	LEFT BY IT IS THAT THE PLAYWRIGHT, HAVING BEGUN
LIED (200)	RESENTMENT). /HE/ (HASTENING TO IMPROVE THE	IMPRESSION	MADE BY HIS MENDACITY) I SHOULD NEVER HAVE DREAMT
MRS PREFACE(168)	THAT A DISTINGUISHED CRITIC HAS SUMMED UP THE	IMPRESSION	MADE ON HIM BY MRS WARREN'S PROFESSION, BY
FABL PREFACE(76)	TO BE A LIE, AND HE TOLD IT WITHOUT A BLUSH, THE	IMPRESSION	MADE ON ME WAS SO SHOCKING THAT I HAVE FELT EVER
LION PREFACE(38)	READER CAN NOW FIND ANY CLUE; AND GIVES THE	IMPRESSION	OF AN EDUCATED, NOT TO SAY SOPHISTICATED MYSTIC,
CLEO NOTES (204)	PLAY WHICH SHALL CONVEY TO THE GENERAL PUBLIC AN	IMPRESSION	OF ANTIQUITY IS TO MAKE THE CHARACTERS SPEAK
NEVR I SD(199)	OF THIRTY OR THEREABOUTS. HE DOES NOT GIVE THE	IMPRESSION	OF BEING MUCH OF A WORKMAN: THE PROFESSIONAL
MRS PREFACE(166)	INEVITABLY PRODUCES AT FIRST AN OVERWHELMING	IMPRESSION	OF COLDNESS AND INHUMAN RATIONALISM. BUT THIS
CLEO NOTES (211)	TO THE CROWD. HENCE, IN ORDER TO PRODUCE AN	IMPRESSION	OF COMPLETE DISINTERESTEDNESS AND MAGNANIMITY, HE
SUPR I SD(4)	OF A MAN WHO DOES NOT UNDERSTAND THEM), AND AN	IMPRESSION	OF DUPONT'S ENGRAVING OF DELAROCHE'S BEAUX ARTS
METH PREFACE(R33)	TO IT. THIS SLUMP NOT ONLY HEIGHTENED THE	IMPRESSION	OF ENTIRE NOVELTY WHEN DARWIN BROUGHT THE SUBJECT
MRS PREFACE(163)	MEANT TO PRODUCE, A VERY STRONG AND VERY PAINFUL	IMPRESSION	OF EVIL. I DO NOT DOUBT FOR A MOMENT THAT THE
CLEO NOTES (212)	I AM RIGHT IN ASSUMING THAT THE WAY TO PRODUCE AN	IMPRESSION	OF GREATNESS IS BY EXHIBITING A MAN, NOT AS
MRS PREFACE(168)	OF THIS RESISTANCE PRODUCES SO STRONG AN	IMPRESSION	OF HEARTLESSNESS NOWADAYS THAT A DISTINGUISHED
AUGS (263)	(A SLIGHT IMPEDIMENT IN HIS SPEECH ADDS TO THE	IMPRESSION	OF INCOMPETENCE PRODUCED BY HIS AGE AND
2TRU II SD(52)	SMILE WHICH UNHAPPILY PRODUCES AT TIMES AN	IMPRESSION	OF IRONY. HE SALUTES; HANDS THE LETTER TO THE
LADY PREFACE(217)	HIS DEATH, AND IS CLEARLY MEANT TO HEIGHTEN THE	IMPRESSION	OF SHAKESPEAR'S PRODIGIOUS NATURAL ENDOWMENTS BY
MTH2 SD(47)	MR HASLAM, OUR RECTOR. BURGE CONVEYS AN	IMPRESSION	OF SHINING LIKE A CHURCH WINDOW; AND HASLAM
PYGM III SD(249)	ELIZA, WHO IS EXQUISITELY DRESSED, PRODUCES AN	IMPRESSION	OF SUCH REMARKABLE DISTINCTION AND BEAUTY AS SHE
LION PREFACE(6)	WAS JESUS A COWARD? I KNOW QUITE WELL THAT THIS	IMPRESSION	OF SUPERIORITY IS NOT PRODUCED ON EVERYONE, EVEN

PYGM EPILOG (296)	HE HAD NOT QUITE RECOVERED FROM THE DAZZLING	IMPRESSION	OF THE DAY BEFORE. THEY BROKE THE MATTER TO
MTH5 (222)	AGAIN AND YET AGAIN UNTIL YOU RECEIVE THE FULL	IMPRESSION	OF THE INTENSITY OF MIND THAT IS STAMPED ON THEM;
MRS PREFACE(167)	TO REVIVE GENUINE DRAMA PRODUCES THE DISAGREEABLE	IMPRESSION	OF THE PEDANT WHO ATTEMPTS TO START A SERIOUS
LION PREFACE(9)	FROM PAINTERS AND POETS, YOU CAME OUT WITH AN	IMPRESSION	OF THEIR CONTENTS THAT WOULD HAVE ASTONISHED A
UNPL PREFACE(R19)	ACTED. BUT IF I HAD NOT READ THEM AS WELL, MY	IMPRESSION	OF THEM WOULD BE NOT MERELY INCOMPLETE, BUT
CAPT III (272)	OR THEYLL GIVE CAPTAIN KEARNEY QUITE A FALSE	IMPRESSION	OF WHAT HAPPENED. /RANKIN/ BUT YE CANNOT SEE
MTH3 (121)	FROM A SLEDGE-HAMMER COULD PRODUCE THE SMALLEST	IMPRESSION	ON ANY OF US? /MRS LUTESTRING/ WELL, YOU SEE, IT
BARB PREFACE(207)	NOVEL WHEN I WAS A CHILD; AND IT MADE AN ENDURING	IMPRESSION	ON ME. THE HERO WAS A VERY ROMANTIC HERO, TRYING
SUPR HANDBOK(179)	THOUGH IRREFUTABLE, WILL NEVER MAKE ANY SERIOUS	IMPRESSION	ON PROPERTY. THE KNELL OF THAT OVERRATED
CAPT III (275)	ARE. BUT DONT YOU THINK HE WOULD MAKE A BETTER	IMPRESSION	ON THE AMERICAN CAPTAIN IF HE WERE A LITTLE MORE
DEST (187)	MOUTH OF A CANNON: NOTHING LESS COULD MAKE ANY	IMPRESSION	ON YOU. (BAYING AT HIM) DO YOU HEAR? DO YOU
BULL IV (163)	BEASTLY. IT MUST HAVE MADE A MOST UNFAVORABLE	IMPRESSION	ON YOU. /NORA/ OH, SURE IT'S ALL RIGHT. SAY NO
BUOY III (36)	MY BEST TO ACT FOR HIM WITHOUT MAKING THE LEAST	IMPRESSION	ON YOUR VERY INTERESTING RELATIVES, I REALLY DO
NEVR IV SD(286)	POWER OF INTENSELY CRITICAL LISTENING, RAISE THE	IMPRESSION	PRODUCED BY HIM TO ABSOLUTE TREMENDOUSNESS. /THE
METH PREFACE(R50)	PRODUCED BY A MOTOR BUS, AND THE AUDILE	IMPRESSION	PRODUCED BY ITS HOOTER. BUT IF YOU ALLOW YOURSELF
METH PREFACE(R50)	AUTOMATICALLY AND PROMPTLY ENOUGH TO THE VISUAL	IMPRESSION	PRODUCED BY A MOTOR BUS, AND THE AUDILE
METH PREFACE(R49)	SELECTION REACTS PROMPTLY TO A VISUAL	IMPRESSION	PRODUCED BY THE LIZARD'S MOVEMENT. HIS PROOF IS
FANY PROLOG (267)	SET UP TO BE A JUDGE, OR DO MORE THAN RECORD AN	IMPRESSION	; BUT MY IMPRESSIONS CAN BE INFLUENCED; AND IN
FANY PROLOG (270)	BELIEVE THAT MY CRITICISM IS MERELY A PERSONAL	IMPRESSION	; THAT-- /FANNY/ YOU ALWAYS SAID IT WAS.
MIS. PREFACE(97)	IS ABOUT BEARS; AND IT LEAVES THE CHILD WITH AN	IMPRESSION	THAT CHILDREN WHO POKE FUN AT OLD GENTLEMEN AND
LION PREFACE(5)	AND RECALCITRANCE, PRODUCED AN IRRESISTIBLE	IMPRESSION	THAT CHRIST, THOUGH REJECTED BY HIS POSTERITY AS
CATH PREFACE(154)	RELATIONS. IN SHORT, IF BYRON LEAVES YOU WITH AN	IMPRESSION	THAT HE SAID VERY LITTLE ABOUT CATHERINE, AND
MIS. PREFACE(68)	WHICH SENSIBLE PEOPLE THROW THEM OFF, CREATES AN	IMPRESSION	THAT IF WE ONLY TAKE JOHNSON'S ADVICE TO FREE OUR
POSN PREFACE(374)	MY STATEMENT HAD NOT UNNATURALLY CREATED THE	IMPRESSION	THAT IT MUST BE A SCANDALOUS DOCUMENT; AND A
HART III (136)	FOR THIS (TOUCHING HER FOREHEAD) UNDER THE	IMPRESSION	THAT IT WAS A TRANSFORMATION; BUT IT IS ALL
SUPR I (13)	WITH SUCH VEHEMENCE THAT TANNER RECOILS UNDER THE	IMPRESSION	THAT IT IS BEING THROWN AT HIS HEAD). /TANNER/
MTH3 (134)	VERY RECKLESSLY FOR SOME TIME PAST UNDER THE	IMPRESSION	THAT MY LIFE WOULD BE SO SHORT THAT IT WAS NOT
DOCT I SD(109)	AND HARDENS HIS MANNER STILL MORE. HE HAS AN	IMPRESSION	THAT SHE IS VERY WELL DRESSED; BUT SHE HAS A
WIDO I (14)	MY DAUGHTER, DR TRENCH; AND I FIND HER UNDER THE	IMPRESSION	THAT SOMETHING HAS PASSED BETWEEN YOU WHICH IT IS
LION PREFACE(98)	OF DEATH OR CHRISTIANITY BUT FOR A VAGUE	IMPRESSION	THAT THESE LOST ONES ARE ALL BEING CONVERTED
NEVR IV SD(286)	GOES INTO THE GARDEN, LEADING THE WAY UNDER THE	IMPRESSION	THAT THE STRANGER IS FOLLOWING HIM. THE MAJESTIC
MRS PREFACE(179)	TO LONDON FROM THE COUNTRY UNDER THE MISTAKEN	IMPRESSION	THAT THERE IS ALWAYS EMPLOYMENT THERE FOR
MRS PREFACE(175)	WRITERS ABANDONED ALL SELF-RESTRAINT UNDER THE	IMPRESSION	THAT THEY WERE UPHOLDING VIRTUE INSTEAD OF
SIM PREFACE(13)	BY OUR RULERS TO STOP THE PROPAGANDA UNDER THE	IMPRESSION	THAT THIS WOULD STOP THE THOUGHTS; BUT THERE WAS
BARB PREFACE(221)	POSTHUMOUS WAY OF ALL FLESH MAKING SO LITTLE	IMPRESSION	THAT WHEN, SOME YEARS LATER, I PRODUCE PLAYS IN
GENV IV (98)	THAT IF AN IMPARTIAL STRANGER WERE PRESENT HIS	IMPRESSION	WOULD BE THAT YOU TWO GENTLEMEN ARE THREATENING
MIS. PREFACE(97)	NOT NICE CHILDREN, WHICH IS A HIGHLY DESIRABLE	IMPRESSION	, AND JUST AS MUCH AS A CHILD IS CAPABLE OF
FABL PREFACE(72)	I TELL THESE ANECDOTES BECAUSE THEY GIVE AN	IMPRESSION	, BETTER THAN ANY ABSTRACT ARGUMENT COULD, OF THE

IMPRESSIONIST

METH PREFACE(R10)	DRAMATIC OR DESCRIPTIVE MUSIC BEFORE WAGNER; NO	IMPRESSIONIST	PAINTING BEFORE WHISTLER; WHILST AS TO MYSELF,

IMPRESSIONS

FANY PROLOG (267)	OR DO MORE THAN RECORD AN IMPRESSION; BUT MY	IMPRESSIONS	CAN BE INFLUENCED; AND IN THIS CASE YOURE
FANY PROLOG (262)	HAVE SECURED MR TROTTER. I HAVE READ HIS PLAYFUL	IMPRESSIONS	. /SAVOYARD/ WELL, I WAS RATHER IN A FUNK ABOUT
ROCK PREFACE(180)	WHILST THE CLEVERER ONES SELDOM RECONSIDER THE	IMPRESSIONS	THEY HAVE RECEIVED AS LITTLE CHILDREN. MOST

IMPRESSIVE

JOAN PREFACE(12)	AT IT. YET HIS THEORY OF GRAVITATION IS NOT SO	IMPRESSIVE	A MENTAL FEAT AS HIS ASTOUNDING CHRONOLOGY, WHICH
SUPR PREFACE(R22)	BEAUTY. BUT ORDINARY MEN CANNOT PRODUCE REALLY	IMPRESSIVE	ART-WORKS. THOSE WHO CAN ARE MEN OF GENIUS: THAT
SUPR PREFACE(R22)	HIM UNTIL HE IS SECURED FOR EVER! IF THE REALLY	IMPRESSIVE	BOOKS AND OTHER ART-WORKS OF THE WORLD WERE
CLEO II (119)	SPEAK. /THEODOTUS/ (IN A SQUEAK WHICH HE MAKES	IMPRESSIVE	BY SHEER SELF-OPINIONATIVENESS) PEACE FOR THE
PRES (152)	SHE PASSES HIM CONTEMPTUOUSLY AND SITS DOWN WITH	IMPRESSIVE	CONFIDENCE IN THE CHAIR NEXT THE FIREPLACE. LADY
DEVL II (49)	AND SPEAKING WITH SOMETHING OF HIS OLD QUIET AND	IMPRESSIVE	CONVICTION) YOU DONT KNOW THE MAN YOURE MARRIED
PYGM IV (267)	ON A HEARTLESS GUTTERSNIPE. (HE GOES OUT WITH	IMPRESSIVE	DECORUM, AND SPOILS IT BY SLAMMING THE DOOR
NEVR IV SD(286)	THE ROOM TO THE END OF THE TABLE, WHERE, WITH	IMPRESSIVE	DELIBERATION, HE TAKES OFF THE FALSE NOSE AND
CATH 2 (175)	WHAT A LIAR YOU ARE! (DASHKOFF CURTSIES WITH	IMPRESSIVE	DIGNITY). AND YOU THINK YOU ARE FLATTERING ME!
ARMS III (69)	SHE MARRY INTO THE NOBILITY. (HE GOES OUT WITH	IMPRESSIVE	DISCRETION, LEAVING THEM ALL STARING AFTER HIM).
BULL PREFACE(37)	ACHIEVEMENTS ON HIS MONUMENT AT FERNEY THE MOST	IMPRESSIVE	EPITAPH IN EUROPE, THEN MADE THE MOST EARNEST OF
FANY I (274)	SO, BETWEEN OURSELVES, I SHALL, WITH DUE AND	IMPRESSIVE	FORMALITY, FORGIVE BOBBY LATER ON; BUT FOR THE
SUPR I (7)	AND ADDRESSES HIM AT CLOSE QUARTERS WITH	IMPRESSIVE	GRAVITY). NOW, OCTAVIUS, I KNOW THAT MY DEAD
PYGM PREFACE(199)	J. ELLIS WAS STILL A LONDON PATRIARCH, WITH AN	IMPRESSIVE	HEAD ALWAYS COVERED BY A VELVET SKULL CAP, FOR
SIM I SD(38)	BUT THE YEARS HAVE ONLY MADE HER BEAUTY MORE	IMPRESSIVE	. /THE CLERGYMAN/ (GAPING AT HER IN UNDISGUISED
2TRU III (101)	LADY. (TO TALLBOYS) BY THE WAY, COLONEL, THE	IMPRESSIVE	OLD PARTY IN THE SHRINE IS MY FATHER. /TALLBOYS/
2TRU II (53)	DID YOU INDEED? YOU CONSIDER YOURSELF AN	IMPRESSIVE	PERSON, EH? YOU THINK YOU CARRY ABOUT WITH YOU
BULL I SD(73)	ADVERTISEMENT OF A STEAMSHIP COMPANY, AN	IMPRESSIVE	PORTRAIT OF GLADSTONE, AND SEVERAL CARICATURES OF
JOAN PREFACE(6)	OF THE CORONATION OF CHARLES VII. IT IS THE MORE	IMPRESSIVE	REVERSAL BY A UNANIMOUS POSTERITY, CULMINATING IN
CATH 2 (178)	(LIKE A FISHFAG) SCHWEIG, DU HUND. (RESUMING HER	IMPRESSIVE	ROYAL MANNER) HAVE YOU NEVER BEEN TAUGHT, SIR,
WIDO II (42)	HIMSELF FOR A SPRING; AND ADDRESSES HIMSELF, WITH	IMPRESSIVE	SIGNIFICANCE, TO TRENCH). AND NOW, DR TRENCH, MAY
MIS. SD(180)	FOR WHICH THERE WAS NOT A SHRED OF FOUNDATION.	IMPRESSIVE	SILENCE WHILST BENTLEY WRITES. /BENTLEY/ "
POSN PREFACE(377)	AND GAVE AWAY THE WHOLE CASE BY HANDING ME, WITH	IMPRESSIVE	SIMPLICITY AND COURTESY, HIS TWO COPIES OF THE
MTH5 (223)	HE WAS NOT SATISFIED; FOR THE TEMPLE WAS NO MORE	IMPRESSIVE	THAN IT HAD BEEN BEFORE, EXCEPT THAT THERE WAS A
AUGS (271)	HIGH COMPLIMENT OF DECLARING THAT I AM NEVER MORE	IMPRESSIVE	THAN WHEN I HAVE NOTHING TO SAY. /THE LADY/ I
APPL PREFACE(181)	BECAUSE EVERYONE ELSE WAS DOING IT. IT WAS MOST	IMPRESSIVE	TO SEE THOUSANDS OF PEOPLE SWEEPING ALONG AT FULL
POSN PREFACE(376)	WHILST THE MAJORITY REGARDED IT AS AN AUGUST AND	IMPRESSIVE	VINDICATION OF THE MAJESTY OF PARLIAMENT, THE
MIS. PREFACE(29)	WHETHER BY WAY OF DELICACY AND POETRY OR TOO	IMPRESSIVE	WARNING, BUT THE PLAIN FACT IS THAT IN REFUSING

IMPRESSIVELY

LION I (120)	I'M NOT A CHRISTIAN: I'M A MAN. (FERROVIUS RISES	IMPRESSIVELY	AND TOWERS OVER HIM. LENTULUS BECOMES WHITE
NEVR IV SD(286)	BUT WHEN HE SPEAKS, HIS POWERFUL MENACING VOICE,	IMPRESSIVELY	ARTICULATED SPEECH, STRONG INEXORABLE MANNER,
APPL I SD(238)	THEN THE VOICE OF THE PRIME MINISTER BREAKS IT	IMPRESSIVELY	AS HE ADDRESSES THE KING. /PROTEUS/ YOU HEAR
ROCK PREFACE(161)	OF ATTENDING TO THEM, SO THAT HE MIGHT THE MORE	IMPRESSIVELY	ASK THE REST OF THE STAFF WHETHER THEY YET
APPL I (218)	I HAVE TO KEEP. (HE STRAIGHTENS UP AND BECOMES	IMPRESSIVELY	ELOQUENT). AT THIS MOMENT MY CUE IS TO SHEW
PHIL I SD(92)	RETURNS. INSTEAD OF ENTERING, HE STANDS	IMPRESSIVELY	IN THE DOORWAY WITH ONE HAND IN THE BREAST OF
SUPR I (30)	PERPLEXED, GOES OUT. /RAMSDEN/ (FACING TANNER	IMPRESSIVELY	) AND MORALITY, SIR? WHAT IS TO BECOME OF
GETT (310)	DECLINE THE MISSION. /THE GENERAL/ (RISING	IMPRESSIVELY	) BE GOOD ENOUGH TO GIVE ME THAT RING, MR
APPL II (271)	NOT THE MOMENT FOR YOUR TOMFOOLERIES. /PROTEUS/ (	IMPRESSIVELY	) BILL IS RIGHT, AMANDA. (HE RISES AND BECOMES
MTH4 I (153)	BOOBY OR SOMETHING. /THE ELDERLY GENTLEMAN/ (	IMPRESSIVELY	) BOLGE BLUEBIN, MADAM: A HISTORICAL NAME. LET
CAPT II (268)	HIM TO MOROCCO AND DELIVER HIM UP THERE. /SIDI/ (	IMPRESSIVELY	) BRASSBOUND: I AM IN MINE OWN HOUSE AND AMID
CLEO I (111)	(SPRINGING UP FULL OF HOPE) WHAT! /CAESAR/ (	IMPRESSIVELY	) BUT HE EATS GIRLS (SHE RELAPSES) AND CATS.
MTH4 II (187)	A CURIOUSLY CARVED TOP. /ZOZIM/ (IN THE DOORWAY,	IMPRESSIVELY	) HAIL, STRANGERS! /ALL/ (REVERENTLY) HAIL!
MTH4 II (175)	HE IS ON HER RIGHT: SHE ON HIS LEFT. /NAPOLEON/ (	IMPRESSIVELY	) I AM THE MAN OF DESTINY. /THE VEILED WOMAN/ (
SUPR II (69)	WELL. ALL RIGHT. IT AINT MY BUSINESS. /TANNER/ (	IMPRESSIVELY	) I TRUST, ENRY, THAT, AS BETWEEN EMPLOYER AND
BULL III (135)	ANNYTHIN DHATS AS IT IS NOW? /BROADBENT/ (	IMPRESSIVELY	) IT MEANS, MR HAFFIGAN, MAINTAINING THOSE
BULL III (144)	IS A BORN HUMORIST! THINK OF WHAT IT MEANS! (	IMPRESSIVELY	) LARRY: WE ARE IN THE PRESENCE OF A GREAT
MTH4 I (143)	ME AT ONCE WHO YOU ARE. /THE ELDERLY GENTLEMAN/ (	IMPRESSIVELY	) MADAM, I AN A RETIRED GENTLEMAN, FORMERLY
DOCT IV (167)	MAKING HER PROMISE NEVER TO MARRY AGAIN. /B.B./ (	IMPRESSIVELY	) MRS DUBEDAT IS NOT IN A POSITION TO CARRY THE
CAND II (111)	HIM? /MARCHBANKS/ I DONT THINK SO. /BURGESS/ (	IMPRESSIVELY	) NO MORE YOU WOULDNT. THATS THE DANGER ON IT.
PHIL III (142)	AND I BELIEVE HIM, AND FEEL THE BETTER FOR IT. (	IMPRESSIVELY	) NOW, CHARTERIS: PARAMORE AND YOU STAND TODAY
NEVR II (233)	MEAN? AM I TO UNDERSTAND? IS IT-- /PHILIP/ (	IMPRESSIVELY	) STEADY, FINCH. THINK IT OUT SLOWLY AND
PYGM II (241)	LONG, GENTLEMEN. (HE TURNS TO GO). /HIGGINS/ (	IMPRESSIVELY	) STOP. YOULL COME REGULARLY TO SEE YOUR
CAPT III (288)	LANGUAGE OF TWO ANGRY MEN? /KEARNEY/ (RISING	IMPRESSIVELY	) THE UNITED STATES NAVY WILL HAVE NO HAHND IN
NEVR II (235)	LUNCH WITH HIS FAMILY, PERHAPS, SIR? /PHILIP/ (	IMPRESSIVELY	) WILLIAM: HE DOES NOT KNOW THAT WE ARE HIS
CAND I (91)	A BISHOP YOURSELF, I DUSSENT TAKE THE BET. (VERY	IMPRESSIVELY	) YOU AND YOUR CREW ARE GITTIN HINFLUENTIAL: I
MTH3 (129)	SIGN OF WEAKNESS ABOUT IT. /CONFUCIUS/ (VERY	IMPRESSIVELY	) YOU WILL REGRET IT IF YOU DO. /BARNABAS/ WHAT
ROCK II (271)	/HIPNEY/ (RISING WITH A CHUCKLE) AHA! (	IMPRESSIVELY	) YOU TAKE IT FROM ME, YOU THREE GENTLEMEN: ALL
SUPR III (137)	AND TO NOBODY, SEE? /MENDOZA/ (TURNING ON HIM	IMPRESSIVELY	) YOUNG MAN: IF I AM TRIED, I SHALL PLEAD

ANNA (296) /STRAMMFEST/ (GROWLING AT HIM) YAH! (HE TURNS IMPRESSIVELY TO THE GRAND DUCHESS) YOUR IMPERIAL HIGHNESS
BULL III SD(137) MORE THAN I DO. GOOD MORNING, GENTLEMEN. HE TURNS IMPRESSIVELY TO THE GATE, AND TROTS AWAY, CONGRATULATING
NEVR III (274) CLANDON. VERY SERIOUS NEWS INDEED. (HE PASSES IMPRESSIVELY TO THE OTTOMAN, AND SITS DOWN). DOLLY, DULY

IMPRESSIVENESS

JOAN 6,SD(133) SEEMS TO REQUIRE FOR THE COMPLETE SUCCESS OF ITS IMPRESSIVENESS . /THE INQUISITOR/ (KINDLY/ SIT DOWN, JOAN.
WIDO I SD(14) HALF HYPNOTIZED BY HIS OWN NERVOUSNESS AND THE IMPRESSIVENESS OF SARTORIUS, SITS DOWN HELPLESSLY.
CAND I (83) UP; LOOKS AT IT; AND ADDS, WITH EVEN GREATER IMPRESSIVENESS) EXTREMELY BEAUTIFUL. HOW FINE HER EYES
DEVL I (17) AT THE BEDROOM DOOR. /JUDITH/ (WITH GENTLE IMPRESSIVENESS) FRIENDS, MRS DUDGEON. (SHE TAKES THE CHAIR
JOAN 1 (63) HANDS OFF HER. /POULENGEY/ (WITH DELIBERATE IMPRESSIVENESS) I SHOULD AS SOON THINK OF THE BLESSED
APPL II (259) /VANHATTAN/ (RISING TO GIVE HIS WORDS MORE IMPRESSIVENESS) SIR: THE DEBT IS CANCELLED. THE FRONTIER NO
MTH4 II (177) IN SPITE OF MYSELF. I COMPLIMENT YOU ON YOUR IMPRESSIVENESS , MADAM. /THE ORACLE/ (IMPATIENTLY) TIME!

IMPRESSIVE-LOOKING

MTH2 SD(37) BARNABAS. IN THE FIRST YEARS AFTER THE WAR AN IMPRESSIVE-LOOKING GENTLEMAN OF 50 IS SEATED WRITING IN A

IMPRINTING

3PLA PREFACE(R30) MUTELY ATTESTING HIS PASSION BY SURREPTITIOUSLY IMPRINTING A HEARTBROKEN KISS ON A STRAY LOCK OF HER HAIR

IMPRISON

MIS. PREFACE(22) MUCH MORE THAN THE BOYS DID. JUST AS YOU CANNOT IMPRISON A MAN WITHOUT IMPRISONING A WARDER TO SEE THAT HE
2TRU II (71) THE SHACKLES AND THROW DOWN ALL THE WALLS THAT IMPRISON A RESPECTABLE WOMAN. /THE PATIENT/ WELL, WHAT ABOUT
BARB PREFACE(244) RESTRAINING DISHONEST ONES. THAT IS WHY WE DO NOT IMPRISON DOGS. WE EVEN TAKE OUR CHANCE OF THEIR FIRST BITE.
BARB PREFACE(239) BEAST" TO SHREDS. DRAG HIM TO THE SCAFFOLD. IMPRISON HIM FOR LIFE. LET ALL CIVILIZED STATES BAND
BARB PREFACE(214) AND DELIBERATELY DO HIM A MALICIOUS INJURY: SAY, IMPRISON HIM FOR YEARS. ONE WOULD NOT SUPPOSE THAT IT NEEDED
CLEO II (140) IN HIS EAR) BESIDES, MY FRIEND: EVERY EGYPTIAN WE IMPRISON MEANS IMPRISONING TWO ROMAN SOLDIERS TO GUARD HIM.
BULL PREFACE(5) FOR SELF-GOVERNMENT, THERE WOULD BE NO NEED TO IMPRISON NATIONALISTS EITHER IN INDIA OR EGYPT; SO THAT, IN
POSN PREFACE(389) MAY DEMORALIZE A WHOLE STREET, NO MAGISTRATE CAN IMPRISON OR OTHERWISE RESTRAIN ITS MEMBERS ON THE GROUND
GETT PREFACE(252) BE DISPOSED OF. BUT IF YOU HANG THE PARENTS, OR IMPRISON THE PARENTS, OR TAKE THE CHILDREN OUT OF THE

IMPRISONED

APPL I (199) BUT WHAT ABOUT HIS DYING OF SOLITUDE? WAS HE IMPRISONED ? /SEMPRONIUS/ NO. HIS YACHT STRUCK A REEF AND
MIS. PREFACE(108) BELIEF THAT THEY MUST TAMELY GO TO THEM AND BE IMPRISONED AND BEATEN AND OVER-TASKED IN THEM, WE SHALL HAVE
APPL PREFACE(182) AUTOCRATS. ON THE CONTRARY, ONE OF THEM HAD BEEN IMPRISONED AND TORTURED FOR HIS RESISTANCE TO THE DESPOTISM
MIS. PREFACE(41) THUS A BABY HAS TO BE PRETTY CLOSELY GUARDED AND IMPRISONED BECAUSE IT CANNOT TAKE CARE OF ITSELF. IT HAS
BULL PREFACE(54) THEN DARWEESH WAS A BIT OF A BRIGAND: HE HAD BEEN IMPRISONED FOR BEARING FALSE WITNESS; AND HIS RESISTANCE TO
MTH4 I (160) TO CONFESS TO IT BEFORE, LEST I SHOULD BE IMPRISONED FOR BLASPHEMY, OR EVEN BURNT ALIVE. /ZOO/
MIS. PREFACE(45) THAT HE MUST NOT RELEASE A MAN WHO HAS BEEN IMPRISONED FOR BLASPHEMY, AS HIS REMARKS WERE PAINFUL TO THE
GENV PREFACE(19) FLAT ON THE PAVEMENT TO AVOID THE BULLETS. HE WAS IMPRISONED FOR EIGHT MONTHS FOR HIS ESCAPADE, NOT HAVING
GETT (300) HORRIBLE MURDERER. THEY WOULD NOT EVEN KEEP HIM IMPRISONED FOR LIFE. FOR TWENTY YEARS SHE HAD TO LIVE
GENV III (73) ANY PERSON OBNOXIOUS TO THE GOVERNMENT CAN BE IMPRISONED FOR OPENING HIS MOUTH OR DIPPING HIS PEN IN THE
BARB III (346) IT FOR AN INCOME. I HAVE SOLD IT TO ESCAPE BEING IMPRISONED FOR REFUSING TO PAY TAXES FOR HANGMEN'S ROPES AND
BULL PREFACE(54) TO HIS CREDIT. HE AND ABD-EL-NEBI (WHO HAD BEEN IMPRISONED FOR THEFT) WERE THE ONLY DISREPUTABLE CHARACTERS
BARB PREFACE(241) CALLS HIS PAPER: THE FREETHINKER; AND HAS BEEN IMPRISONED FOR " BAD TASTE" UNDER THE LAW AGAINST BLASPHEMY.
MIS. PREFACE(76) FREEDOM. I AM SURE THAT A CHILD SHOULD NOT BE IMPRISONED IN A SCHOOL. I AM NOT SO SURE THAT IT SHOULD NOT
GENV III (68) COMMERCIALLY AND SOCIALLY RUINED? HAVE YOU BEEN IMPRISONED IN CONCENTRATION CAMPS COMMANDED BY HOOLIGANS?
MIS. PREFACE(76) NOT SOMETIMES BE DRIVEN OUT INTO THE OPEN -- IMPRISONED IN THE WOODS AND ON THE MOUNTAINS, AS IT WERE.
JITT III (61) HE WAS ALIVE, AND MUCH GREATER, I THINK OF HIM IMPRISONED IN THESE WALLS, LONGING FOR HIS PROPER HAPPINESS,
GENV III (73) GONE A LITTLE TOO FAR IN DEALING WITH SEX; THEY IMPRISONED STREET CORNER SPEAKERS ON CHARGES OF OBSTRUCTING
BULL PREFACE(28) OR AS THE ITALIANS LOVED THEM BEFORE THEY IMPRISONED THE POPE IN THE VATICAN. THEY LOVE THEIR
MIS. (190) IN THE WRONG. YOU WOULD THEN BE CHARGED AND IMPRISONED UNTIL THINGS QUIETED DOWN. /GUNNER/ AND YOU CALL
MIS. PREFACE(88) HAVE BEEN SNUBBED, SCOLDED, BULLIED, BEATEN AND IMPRISONED WHENEVER WE DARED TO RESENT BEING BORED OR
SUPR HANDBOK(196) IS DENOUNCED AS A MISLEADER OF THE PEOPLE, AND IMPRISONED WITH HARD LABOR TO SHEW HIM HOW MUCH SINCERITY
CAPT II (255) HANDS THE REDRESS THE LAW DENIED HER, YOU HAD HER IMPRISONED , AND FORCED HER TO WRITE YOU AN APOLOGY AND
FABL PREFACE(77) BEEN REPEALED IN SCOTLAND. SO FAR I HAVE NOT BEEN IMPRISONED , AS POORER MEN HAVE BEEN IN MY TIME, FOR
GENV II (58) OVERCOME BY AN ABLER RIVAL AND DULY PROSCRIBED, IMPRISONED , EXILED OR ASSASSINATED IN HIS TURN. SUCH A
MTH4 II (181) TO THE END IT WILL LEAVE ME EXECRATED, DETHRONED, IMPRISONED , PERHAPS EXECUTED. YET IF I STOP FIGHTING I
LION PREFACE(55) YOU RESIST THE SELLING UP YOU ARE BLUDGEONED AND IMPRISONED , THE PROCESS BEING EUPHEMISTICALLY CALLED THE

IMPRISONING

MIS. PREFACE(22) DID. JUST AS YOU CANNOT IMPRISON A MAN WITHOUT IMPRISONING A WARDER TO SEE THAT HE DOES NOT ESCAPE, THE
ANNA (302) THE UPPER HAND? ARE THEY NOT HANGING, SHOOTING, IMPRISONING AS MUCH AS EVER WE DID? DO THEY EVER TELL THE
HART PREFACE(39) AND THE ARMY THEY RESCUED IS BUSY IN COLOGNE IMPRISONING EVERY GERMAN WHO DOES NOT SALUTE A BRITISH
GETT PREFACE(193) FROM MERE THOUGHTLESSNESS, THINKING NOTHING OF IMPRISONING MEN AND WOMEN FOR PERIODS UP TO TWENTY YEARS FOR
SIM PREFACE(10) FOR READING THE WORKS OF THOMAS PAINE, OR IMPRISONING POOR MEN FOR MAKING SCEPTICAL JOKES ABOUT THE
MIS. PREFACE(71) TO BE ENCOUNTERED, INSTEAD OF, AS AT PRESENT, IMPRISONING THE HUMAN RACE IN DUSTY OR MUDDY THOROUGHFARES
CLEO II (140) MY FRIEND: EVERY EGYPTIAN WE IMPRISON MEANS IMPRISONING TWO ROMAN SOLDIERS TO GUARD HIM. EH? /RUFIO/
MTH4 I (164) RIGHT: THEY CAN GOVERN YOU ONLY BY BEATING YOU, IMPRISONING YOU, TORTURING YOU, KILLING YOU IF YOU DISOBEY

IMPRISONINGS

MIS. PREFACE(47) FIRE AND IMPOSITIONS AND HUMILIATIONS AND PETTY IMPRISONINGS AND SENDINGS TO BED AND STANDING IN CORNERS AND

IMPRISONMENT

MIS. PREFACE(51) WHO IS CONVERSANT WITH THE CLASS IN WHICH CHILD IMPRISONMENT AND COMPULSORY SCHOOLING IS CARRIED OUT TO THE
MIS. PREFACE(50) LATIN HAD NOT BEEN MADE THE EXCUSE FOR MY SCHOOL IMPRISONMENT AND DEGRADATION. WHY WE LOATHE LEARNING AND
POSN PREFACE(427) FOR THE SUPPRESSION OF MOTOR CARS, THE VIRTUAL IMPRISONMENT AND ENSLAVEMENT OF THE YOUNG, THE PASSING OF
BULL PREFACE(58) COURT OF DISCIPLINE, WHICH AWARDED HIM TWO YEARS IMPRISONMENT AND FIFTY LASHES. WITHOUT RUDELY CALLING THIS A
MIS. PREFACE(51) AND PARAPHRASES FORCED ON ALL YOUNG PEOPLE BY IMPRISONMENT AND FLOGGING AND SCOLDING, THERE WILL NOT BE A
JOAN PREFACE(34) JUDGED THIS MATTER WHEN SHE HAD TO CHOOSE BETWEEN IMPRISONMENT AND THE STAKE, AND CHOSE THE STAKE, AND THEREBY
JOAN 6,SD(133) CHAIN. SHE WEARS A PAGE'S BLACK SUIT. HER LONG IMPRISONMENT AND THE STRAIN OF THE EXAMINATIONS WHICH HAVE
MIS. PREFACE(14) TRUE EXPLANATION OF THE MONSTROUS SYSTEM OF CHILD IMPRISONMENT AND TORTURE WHICH WE DISGUISE UNDER SUCH
BULL PREFACE(56) SIX TO SEVEN YEARS PENAL SERVITUDE, THREE TO IMPRISONMENT FOR A YEAR WITH HARD LABOR AND FIFTY LASHES,
DOCT III (141) HER IGNORANCE OF THE LAW? /LOUIS/ WELL, I RISKED IMPRISONMENT FOR HER SAKE. I COULD HAVE BEEN HAD UP FOR IT
JOAN PREFACE(18) HAD GAINED NOTHING BY HER RECANTATION BUT CLOSE IMPRISONMENT FOR LIFE THAT SHE WITHDREW IT, AND DELIBERATELY
DOCT III (141) SOMEHOW. /SIR PATRICK/ YOU LET HER RISK IMPRISONMENT IN HER IGNORANCE OF THE LAW? /LOUIS/ WELL, I
SUPR HANDBOK(221) AND ROB THE RICH CITIZEN WHOSE MONEY HE DESIRES. IMPRISONMENT IS AS IRREVOCABLE AS DEATH. CRIMINALS DO NOT
ROCK PREFACE(163) WELL, BE REMITTED AFTER A WHILE. AS FOUR YEARS IMPRISONMENT IS CONSIDERED ENOUGH FOR ANY REASONABLE SORT OF
DOCT PREFACE(44) THE USELESS AND DETESTABLE TORTURE OF SOLITARY IMPRISONMENT IS SHEWN AT ITS WORST WITHOUT THE INTRODUCTION
JOAN 6 (145) TO THE END OF THY EARTHLY DAYS IN PERPETUAL IMPRISONMENT . /JOAN/ (RISING IN CONSTERNATION AND TERRIBLE
SIM PREFACE(17) THEIR LIVES SHALL BE TAKEN BY THE SLOW TORTURE OF IMPRISONMENT . THEN WE HAVE A MASS OF PEOPLE WHO THINK THAT
GETT PREFACE(234) FAITHFUL" HUSBANDS WHO ARE SENTENCED TO A MONTH'S IMPRISONMENT OCCASIONALLY FOR IDLY LEAVING THEIR WIVES IN
SUPR HANDBOK(201) THE HOPE IS NOT FULFILLED; BUT THE LIFELONG IMPRISONMENT OF PENNILESS MEN FOR DEBT CEASES; FACTORY ACTS
BARB PREFACE(238) BY APPROVING EVERY DAY OF SENTENCES OF YEARS OF IMPRISONMENT SO INFERNAL IN THEIR UNNATURAL STUPIDITY AND
MILL I (159) TO THOUSANDS AND FROM RISKS OF EIGHTEEN MONTHS IMPRISONMENT TO FIVE YEARS, TEN YEARS, FOURTEEN YEARS EVEN.
BARB PREFACE(214) BEDS IF SUCH STUPID VILLAINIES AS SENTENCES OF IMPRISONMENT WERE NOT COMMITTED DAILY. IT IS USELESS TO
BARB PREFACE(245) IT, AT LEAST, IS IRREVOCABLE-- AS IF ONE HOUR OF IMPRISONMENT WERE NOT AS IRREVOCABLE AS ANY EXECUTION! IF A
GETT PREFACE(193) WILD BEASTS TO BE TAMED BY A SYSTEM OF BLOWS AND IMPRISONMENT WHICH THEY CALLED EDUCATION; AND OF KEEPING
SUPR HANDBOK(202) SLOW MISERY AND DEGRADATION OF MODERN REFORMED IMPRISONMENT WITH AS LITTLE REMORSE AS LAUD AND HIS STAR
MIS. PREFACE(59) WHAT I SUFFERED THROUGH THE PROCESS OF ASSAULT, IMPRISONMENT , AND COMPULSORY LESSONS THAT TAUGHT ME
GENV IV (118) YOU BY A JEWISH GENTLEMAN OF UNLAWFUL ARREST AND IMPRISONMENT , ASSAULT, ROBBERY, AND DENIAL OF HIS RIGHT TO
JOAN PREFACE(14) PENCE THE WORSE, FACE POVERTY, INFAMY, EXILE, IMPRISONMENT , DREADFUL HARDSHIP, AND DEATH. EVEN THE
BARB PREFACE(240) PROCEED TO TORTURE HIM, AFTER THEIR MANNER, BY IMPRISONMENT , FOR REFUSING TO FASTEN HIS TEETH IN THE
POSN PREFACE(397) PENALTIES OF DEFYING IT, NO POWERS OF ARREST OR IMPRISONMENT , IN SHORT, NONE OF THE GUARANTEES OF
MIS. PREFACE(39) BUT FINITE. WHEN LEARNING IS ONLY AN EXCUSE FOR IMPRISONMENT , IT IS AN INSTRUMENT OF TORTURE WHICH BECOMES
BULL IV (155) IN CHARACTER ARE PUT TO THE HORRIBLE TORTURE OF IMPRISONMENT , NOT FOR HOURS BUT FOR YEARS, IN THE NAME OF
MIS. PREFACE(52) EVERYWHERE WE FIND THE SAME RESULT. THE IMPRISONMENT , THE BEATING, THE TAMING AND LAMING, THE
MIS. PREFACE(72) TO SUE PEDAGOGUES AND OTHERS FOR ASSAULT AND IMPRISONMENT , THERE WOULD BE AN AMAZING CHANGE IN THE

ROCK PREFACE(163) ONLY " WEEDING THE GARDEN"); AND THE SENTENCE OF IMPRISONMENT , THOUGH IT MAY SEEM SEVERE TO US IN VIEW OF
BARB PREFACE(215) WICKEDNESS WITH WHICH WE SCATTER SENTENCES OF IMPRISONMENT , TORTURE IN THE SOLITARY CELL AND ON THE PLANK
JOAN 6 (145) IN CONSTERNATION AND TERRIBLE ANGER) PERPETUAL IMPRISONMENT ! AM I NOT THEN TO BE SET FREE? /LADVENU/ (

IMPRISONMENTS
MIS. PREFACE(21) SUFFICE WE SCRIBBLE IMPOSITIONS, OR SUFFER EXTRA IMPRISONMENTS -- " KEEPING IN" WAS THE PHRASE IN MY TIME --

IMPRISONS
MTH5 (255) BLOOD IS NECESSARY. IT DIES. /THE HE-ANCIENT/ IT IMPRISONS US ON THIS PETTY PLANET AND FORBIDS US TO RANGE
GENV II (58) WHOM HAS HIS PROSCRIPTION LIST OF ENEMIES WHOM HE IMPRISONS , EXILES, OR MURDERS AT HIS PLEASURE UNTIL HE IS

IMPROBABILITY
2TRU III (91) BECAUSE I FELT I COULD NOT LIVE WITHOUT YOU. THE IMPROBABILITY OF THAT STATEMENT IS THE MEASURE OF MY
GENV PREFACE(3) IS GREATER. HOODWINKED HEROISM. IT WAS THIS IMPROBABILITY WHICH MADE PRE-ATOMIC AIR RAIDING FUTILE AS A

IMPROBABLE
LADY PREFACE(217) GREAT MEN, BEN JONSON'S EVIDENCE DISPOSES OF SO IMPROBABLE A NOTION AT ONCE AND FOR EVER. " I LOVED THE
PLES PREFACE(R17) REJECTED THESE CIRCUMSTANCES AS FANTASTICALLY IMPROBABLE AND CYNICALLY UNNATURAL, IT WAS NOT NECESSARY TO
SIM II (81) ENGLISH PEOPLE; AND WE SHALL NOT DO ANYTHING SO IMPROBABLE AS DISAPPEAR. /SIR CHARLES/ (TO HIS WIFE) DO NOT
HART I (63) I'M VERY SORRY. I SEE NOW THAT IT SOUNDS VERY IMPROBABLE AS I TELL IT. BUT I CANT STAY IF YOU THINK THAT
2TRU III (109) RECKLESS A LIAR, WOULD DARE TO INVENT FIGURES SO IMPROBABLE AS MEN AND WOMEN WITH THEIR MINDS STRIPPED
JOAN PREFACE(13) GOD FOR HER. NOT THAT SUCH A BELIEF WOULD BE MORE IMPROBABLE OR FANTASTIC THAN SOME MODERN BELIEFS WHICH WE
2TRU III (91) OR DID I NOT? /AUBREY/ HEAVENLY. THAT ALSO SEEMS IMPROBABLE ; BUT IT IS GOSPEL TRUTH. /THE ELDER/ WRETCHED
JOAN PREFACE(47) IS TRUE, AND THAT EVERYTHING THAT IS MAGICAL, IMPROBABLE , EXTRAORDINARY, GIGANTIC, MICROSCOPIC,
PYGM EPILOG (289) THE TRANSFIGURATION IT RECORDS SEEMS EXCEEDINGLY IMPROBABLE , IS COMMON ENOUGH. SUCH TRANSFIGURATIONS HAVE

IMPROBABLY
POSN PREFACE(403) BY MR ASQUITH AND MR BALFOUR MIGHT NOT IMPROBABLY COST MORE AND LAST LONGER THAN A CIVIL WAR. AND

IMPROPER
PYGM III (255) (AGGRIEVED) DO YOU MEAN THAT MY LANGUAGE IS IMPROPER ? /MRS HIGGINS/ NO, DEAREST: IT WOULD BE QUITE
INCA (238) WORE MY JEWELS AND ONE OF MY DRESSES AT A RATHER IMPROPER BALL WITH HER YOUNG MAN; AND MY UNCLE SAW HER.
POSN PREFACE(371) THEY ARE DISCUSSED ARE IMPROPER CONVERSATIONS, IMPROPER BOOKS, IMPROPER PLAYS, AND SHOULD NOT BE ALLOWED.
MIS. (185) SIMPLY AND UNAFFECTEDLY. DID YOU WITNESS ANY IMPROPER CONDUCT ON MY PART WHEN YOU WERE IN THE BATH?
POSN PREFACE(371) BOOKS, OR PLAYS IN WHICH THEY ARE DISCUSSED ARE IMPROPER CONVERSATIONS, IMPROPER BOOKS, IMPROPER PLAYS, AND
FANY EPILOG (331) AUTHOR, ANYHOW, WITH, OF COURSE, THE INEVITABLE IMPROPER FEMALE: THE MRS TANQUERAY, IRIS, AND SO FORTH.
MTH4 I (146) WHAT IS A SHILLING? WHAT IS AN INTRODUCTION? IMPROPER FEMALE DOESNT MAKE SENSE. /THE ELDERLY GENTLEMAN/
MTH4 I (145) SPOKE TO ME WITHOUT ANY INTRODUCTION, LIKE ANY IMPROPER FEMALE. AND SHE HAS MADE OFF WITH MY SHILLING. /THE
HART PREFACE(35) PARADED IN THEIR BEST CLOTHES; WHERE STORIES OF IMPROPER FEMALES LIKE POTIPHAR'S WIFE, AND EROTIC POETRY
UNPL PREFACE(R14) TENDENCY CONTAIN ANYTHING IMMORAL OR OTHERWISE IMPROPER FOR THE STAGE," AND THAT THE LORD CHAMBERLAIN
MRS PREFACE(151) OVER OUR THEATRES, AS " IMMORAL AND OTHERWISE IMPROPER FOR THE STAGE." ITS PERFORMANCE WAS PROHIBITED, I
MRS PREFACE(161) TENDENCY OF " ANYTHING IMMORAL OR OTHERWISE IMPROPER FOR THE STAGE." BUT LET NOBODY CONCLUDE THEREFORE
POSN PREFACE(399) SHOULD BE STRUCK OUT AS UNBEARABLY HORRIFYING AND IMPROPER . BUT COMPLIANCE WITH THESE CONDITIONS WOULD
BARB I (270) YOU CANNOT GO NOW, ANDREW: IT WOULD BE MOST IMPROPER . SIT DOWN. WHAT WILL THE SERVANTS THINK?
GETT PREFACE(204) TRANSLATED INTO ENGLISH, AS ITS SUBJECT WAS TOO IMPROPER . THE LIMITS OF DEMOCRACY. NOW IF ENGLAND HAD BEEN
WIDO II (32) TRY TO SHOVE THE BLAME ON TO ME? /COKANE/ A MOST IMPROPER OBSERVATION TO ADDRESS TO A GENTLEMAN, MR
BARB III (315) /LADY BRITOMART/ IT WOULD BE MOST UNNATURAL AND IMPROPER OF YOU TO LEAVE IT TO ANYONE ELSE, ANDREW. DO YOU
POSN PREFACE(401) INNOCENT PHRASE HAS OFTEN BEEN MADE OFFENSIVELY IMPROPER ON THE STAGE BY POPULAR LOW COMEDIANS, WITH THE
POSN (449) BE HANGED IN A PROPER STATE OF MIND THAN IN AN IMPROPER ONE. BUT IT WONT MAKE ANY DIFFERENCE TO US: MAKE NO
MRS PREFACE(163) THINKS ME A BLACKGUARD, AND MY PLAY A GROSSLY IMPROPER ONE, BECAUSE, LIKE TOLSTOY'S DOMINION OF DARKNESS,
POSN PREFACE(371) ARE IMPROPER CONVERSATIONS, IMPROPER BOOKS, IMPROPER PLAYS, AND SHOULD NOT BE ALLOWED. THE CENSOR MAY
PYGM V (269) I REALLY THINK HE SUSPECTED US OF SOME IMPROPER PURPOSE. /MRS HIGGINS/ WELL, OF COURSE HE DID. WHAT
BARB III (313) HE NEVER DOES A PROPER THING WITHOUT GIVING AN IMPROPER REASON FOR IT. /CUSINS/ HE CONVINCED ME THAT I HAVE
GETT (349) DEAR LESBIA, THAT I WAS NOT USING THE WORD IN ITS IMPROPER SENSE. I AM SOMETIMES UNFORTUNATE IN MY CHOICE OF
2TRU II (68) TALKING TO HIM. HE ONLY TOLD ME HALF A DOZEN IMPROPER STORIES TO SHEW HOW OPENMINDED HE WAS. I NEVER
BARB III (313) CONVINCED ME THAT I HAVE ALL MY LIFE BEEN DOING IMPROPER THINGS FOR PROPER REASONS. /LADY BRITOMART/
GETT PREFACE(258) BY PROVIDING MEANS FOR DISSOLVING ALL UNHAPPY, IMPROPER , AND INCONVENIENT MARRIAGES. AND, AS IT IS OUR
GETT PREFACE(232) AN IMPULSE NATURAL, PERHAPS, BUT VULGAR AND IMPROPER , AND NOT OPEN, ON CONSIDERATION, TO DECENT MEN.
POSN PREFACE(371) ABORTION, CONTAGIOUS DISEASES, AND NUDITY ARE IMPROPER , AND THAT ALL CONVERSATIONS, OR BOOKS, OR PLAYS IN
LIED (191) OR LATER. /SHE/ NO, HENRY. I WILL DO NOTHING IMPROPER , NOTHING DISHONORABLE. (SHE SITS DOWN PLUMP ON

IMPROPERLY
MIS. (177) AND BLACKGUARDLY LIE THAT THIS LADY BEHAVED IMPROPERLY IN MY PRESENCE? /GUNNER/ (TURNING WHITE) YOU
NEVR IV (284) HER HAND) MY DEAR: I'M AFRAID I SPOKE VERY IMPROPERLY OF YOUR MOTHER THIS AFTERNOON. /GLORIA/ OH, DONT

IMPROPRIETY
POSN PREFACE(417) LOCKWOOD WHETHER A LAW SUFFICIENT TO RESTRAIN IMPROPRIETY IN BOOKS WOULD ALSO RESTRAIN IMPROPRIETY IN
POSN PREFACE(417) RESTRAIN IMPROPRIETY IN BOOKS WOULD ALSO RESTRAIN IMPROPRIETY IN PLAYS. SIR WILLIAM REPLIED: " I SHOULD SAY
POSN PREFACE(401) SHE SUCCEEDED IN TURNING WHAT WAS MEANT AS AN IMPROPRIETY INTO AN INOFFENSIVE STROKE OF REALISM; YET IT IS
POSN PREFACE(412) OF ITS OFFICIAL LICENCE TO THE MOST EXTREME IMPROPRIETY THAT THE LOWEST SECTION OF LONDON PLAYGOERS WILL

IMPROVE
SUPR PREFACE(R15) AND MOZART, UPON WHOSE ART NO HUMAN HAND CAN IMPROVE ? YOU WOULD LAUGH AT ME IF AT THIS TIME OF DAY I
METH PREFACE(R23) HAD ANYTHING TO DO WITH IT; FOR THOUGH YOU MAY IMPROVE AT EACH BICYCLING LESSON DURING THE LESSON, WHEN YOU
MILL PREFACE(126) FRONTIER ARE ALL EXACTLY ALIKE, AND THAT THEY IMPROVE BY CONTINUOUS INBREEDING. NOW HERR HITLER IS NOT A
6CAL PREFACE(91) WITH SHOCK, DAMN THEIR EYES! I HAVE HAD TO IMPROVE CONSIDERABLY ON THE STORY AS TOLD BY THAT ABSURD OLD
UNPL PREFACE(R18) BY THE CONDITIONS OF WORKING CLASS LIFE, MANNERS IMPROVE ENORMOUSLY. IN THE MIDDLE CLASSES THEMSELVES THE
MILL IV (189) MEN, AND RUINED THE OLD PLACE BY TRYING TO IMPROVE IT BY GETTING RID OF THE OLD THINGS IN IT. IT WAS ON
MTH5 (219) THE WORLD TO PLAY WITH BECAUSE THEY PROMISED TO IMPROVE IT. THEY DID NOT IMPROVE IT; AND THEY WOULD HAVE
MTH5 (219) BECAUSE THEY PROMISED TO IMPROVE IT. THEY DID NOT IMPROVE IT; AND THEY WOULD HAVE WRECKED IT HAD THEIR POWER
VWOO 1 (119) /Z/ WHAT BOOKS WOULD YOU RECOMMEND ME TO READ TO IMPROVE MY MIND? /A/ (SHOUTING FURIOUSLY) STEWARD. /Z/ OH,
KING I (167) EXCEPT TO WASTE OUR HOST'S INVALUABLE TIME AND TO IMPROVE MY OWN, IF HE WILL BE GOOD ENOUGH TO ALLOW ME SUCH A
CYMB FORWORD(136) ARE VERY VARIOUS. WHEN A MEDIOCRE ARTIST TRIES TO IMPROVE ON A GREAT ARTIST'S WORK THE EFFECT IS RIDICULOUS OR
GENV PREFACE(10) IF NOT OF THE WORLD. THEY MAY YET CHEAPEN AND IMPROVE ON IT. OR THEY MAY DISCOVER A GAS LIGHTER THAN AIR,
CAND II (110) THE LAST WORD, AND YET HALF INCLINED TO TRY TO IMPROVE ON IT, HE LOOKS AFTER HER FOR A MOMENT; THEN
DOCT II (123) SERIOUSLY, NOW? /SCHUTZMACHER/ NO. YOU CANT IMPROVE ON NATURE IN TELLING STORIES ABOUT GENTLEMEN LIKE MR
OVER (187) MR LUNN AND MYSELF. WE CAN HARDLY BE EXPECTED TO IMPROVE ONE ANOTHER'S MORALS. (HE PASSES BEHIND THE
NEVR I (205) YOU, MR VALENTINE. /DOLLY/ YOU WERE GOING TO IMPROVE OUR MINDS, I THINK. /VALENTINE/ THE FACT IS, YOUR--
LIED (200) WITH GROWING RESENTMENT). /HE/ (HASTENING TO IMPROVE THE IMPRESSION MADE BY HIS MENDACITY) I SHOULD NEVER
APPL PREFACE(195) SIMILARLY, GATTIE WAS NOT CONTENT TO IMPROVE THE LUGGAGE ARRANGEMENTS OF OUR RAILWAYS: HE WOULD
2TRU III (109) THIEF. /AUBREY/ (RISING) IF I MAY BE ALLOWED TO IMPROVE THE OCCASION FOR A MOMENT-- GENERAL CONSTERNATION.
WIDO III (57) TO SUFFER ANY MORE. I HAVE MADE UP MY MIND TO IMPROVE THE PROPERTY, AND GET IN QUITE A NEW CLASS OF
HART II (94) WE SHOULD SPEND TOO MUCH ON EVERYTHING. WE SHOULD IMPROVE THE QUALITY OF THE GOODS AND MAKE THEM TOO DEAR. WE
MTH5 (249) WORKS? HE CAN CREATE MASTERPIECES; BUT HE CANNOT IMPROVE THE SHAPE OF HIS OWN NOSE. /ACIS/ THERE! WHAT HAVE
GETT (274) /LESBIA/ DONT YOU TWO BEGIN TO QUARREL. THAT WONT IMPROVE THE SITUATION. /MRS BRIDGENORTH/ I THINK YOU MIGHT
DOCT PREFACE(29) UNDER EXISTING CONDITIONS MUST FINALLY BE, NOT TO IMPROVE THE TECHNICAL QUALITY OF THE WORK DONE BY ITS
GETT PREFACE(241) WE WERE TO SPARE THEIR FEELINGS WE SHOULD NEVER IMPROVE THE WORLD AT ALL. TO LET THEM FRIGHTEN US, AND THEN
SUPR HANDBOK(194) TO THE END OF THE REFORMERS' PATHS WE SHOULD IMPROVE THE WORLD PRODIGIOUSLY. BUT THERE IS NO MORE HOPE IN
MTH2 (80) DECEIVE YOURSELF. IT'S ONLY THE POLITICIANS WHO IMPROVE THE WORLD SO GRADUALLY THAT NOBODY CAN SEE THE
MRS PREFACE(165) PROCEEDS TO IGNORE THEIR SENSES AND RUTHLESSLY IMPROVE THEIR MINDS? BUT I PROTEST AGAIN THAT THE LURE WAS
NEVR I (204) SUCCESSFULLY RESISTED ALL OUR MOTHER'S EFFORTS TO IMPROVE THEM. /VALENTINE/ (DUBIOUSLY) HM! /DOLLY/ (
NEVR I (204) BE WITHOUT THEM. READ THEM, MR VALENTINE: THEYLL IMPROVE YOUR MIND. /DOLLY/ BUT NOT TILL WEVE GONE, PLEASE.
SUPR I (37) I AM YOUR GUARDIAN; AND IT IS MY DUTY TO IMPROVE YOUR MIND. /ANN/ THE LOVE COMPACT IS OVER, THEN, IS
MTH3 (120) FACES) /MRS LUTESTRING/ A LITTLE ALCOHOL WOULD IMPROVE YOUR TEMPER AND MANNERS, AND MAKE YOU MUCH EASIER TO

IMPROVED
KING PREFACE(159) IS NO CABINET IN EUROPE THAT WOULD NOT BE VITALLY IMPROVED BY HAVING ITS MALE TAIL CUT OFF AND FEMALE HEADS

SUPR HANDBOK(187)	A LUTHER PLUS A GOETHE, THE WORLD WILL BE NO MORE	IMPROVED	BY ITS HEROES THAN A BRIXTON VILLA IS IMPROVED BY
APPL I (212)	HULLO, BILL! YOU HAVE BEEN HAVING YOUR MIND	IMPROVED	BY SOMEBODY. /BOANERGES/ WHAT DO YOU MEAN? ISNT IT
BARB PREFACE(219)	A VERY INSPIRING CALL TO ARMS; NOR IS IT REALLY	IMPROVED	BY SUBSTITUTING SAINTS FOR CRANKS. BOTH TERMS
GETT PREFACE(194)	CORRUPT, PRODUCE SOCIABLER MEN. WOMEN, TOO, ARE	IMPROVED	BY THE ESCAPE FROM HOME PROVIDED BY WOMEN'S
3PLA PREFACE(R14)	IN THE THEATRE. I DID NOT FIND THAT MATTERS WERE	IMPROVED	BY THE LADY PRETENDING TO BE " A WOMAN WITH A
SUPR HANDBOK(187)	IMPROVED BY ITS HEROES THAN A BRIXTON VILLA IS	IMPROVED	BY THE PYRAMID OF CHEOPS. THE PRODUCTION OF SUCH
CLEO NOTES (204)	FACT THAT THE WORLD, INSTEAD OF HAVING BEEN	IMPROVED	IN 67 GENERATIONS OUT OF ALL RECOGNITION, PRESENTS,
VWOO 3 (134)	ITEM: I HAVE SHARPENED MY FACULTIES, AND GREATLY	IMPROVED	IN OBSERVATION AND MATHEMATICS. /Z/ COULDNT YOU PUT
DEST SD(180)	WITHOUT CAP, SWORD OR GLOVES, AND MUCH	IMPROVED	IN TEMPER AND SPIRITS BY HIS MEAL, CHOOSES THE
MILL PREFACE(124)	WERE JEWS, SURELY THE AVERAGE GERMAN CAN BE	IMPROVED	. I AM TOLD THAT CHILDREN BRED FROM IRISH COLLEENS
SUPR III (128)	MY EYES AT THE WORLD AND SAW THAT IT COULD BE	IMPROVED	. I TELL YOU THAT IN THE PURSUIT OF MY OWN
NEVR I (204)	HM? PHIL: HE PREFERS PEOPLE WHOSE MINDS ARE	IMPROVED	. /PHILIP/ IN THAT CASE WE SHALL HAVE TO INTRODUCE
MIS. PREFACE(37)	A COUPLE OF YEARS, THEIR EFFECT WOULD BE VASTLY	IMPROVED	. THE NEW LAZINESS, THE CHILD OF THE FUTURE, THEN,
JOAN PREFACE(52)	THEIR HEARTFELT INSTRUCTIONS AS TO HOW IT CAN BE	IMPROVED	, THEY POINT OUT THAT BY THE EXCISION OF THE
MIS. PREFACE(3)	PROBABLY BE SUPERSEDED IN HALF THAT TIME BY AN	IMPROVED	MACHINE ANSWERING THE SAME PURPOSE. HE ALSO KNOWS
BARB I (268)	MONEY, I DEVOTE TO EXPERIMENTS AND RESEARCHES IN	IMPROVED	METHODS OF DESTROYING LIFE AND PROPERTY. I HAVE
METH PREFACE(R73)	AND THAT THERE IS NO REASON TO DOUBT THAT WITH	IMPROVED	METHODS THEY WILL PRESENTLY BE ABLE TO DEMONSTRATE
BULL IV (181)	TALK! /BROADBENT/ OH TUT, TUT, LARRY! THEY	IMPROVED	MY MIND: THEY RAISED MY TONE ENORMOUSLY. I FEEL
DOCT PREFACE(45)	EVER OCCUR TO HER THAT HER VEAL CUTLET MIGHT BE	IMPROVED	ON BY A SLICE OF TENDER BABY. NOW THERE WAS A TIME
DOCT PREFACE(35)	THE LONDON COUNTY COUNCIL, IT WOULD BE ENORMOUSLY	IMPROVED	; AND THE AVERAGE LIFETIME OF LONDONERS WOULD BE
MIS. (148)	NONSENSE! DONT BE SELFISH. THINK HOW YOUVE	IMPROVED	THE OTHER CHAPS. LOOK AT THE SPANISH EMPIRE! BAD
MTH5 (231)	COULD MAKE MAGGOTS, BUT NOT HUMAN EYES OR EARS. I	IMPROVED	THE TISSUE UNTIL IT WAS SUSCEPTIBLE TO A HIGHER
OVER PREFACE(167)	AND SECOND IN REAL LIFE, THEY WOULD BE GREATLY	IMPROVED	THEREBY EVEN AS ENTERTAINMENTS; FOR I HAVE NEVER
MIS. PREFACE(4)	WHICH CAN ONLY BE A BEING THAT CANNOT BE	IMPROVED	UPON. AFTER ALL, WHAT MAN IS CAPABLE OF THE INSANE
ARMS II (29)	/CATHERINE/ YOU LOOK SUPERB. THE CAMPAIGN HAS	IMPROVED	YOU, SERGIUS. EVERYBODY HERE IS MAD ABOUT YOU. WE
PYGM II (241)	THEM IN WITHOUT THAT. IF YOU WANT ELIZA'S MIND	IMPROVED	, GOVERNOR, YOU DO IT YOURSELF WITH A STRAP. SO
VWOO 3 (135)	MATTER. /Z/ WELL, ANYHOW, YOUR MANNERS HAVE	IMPROVED	, HAVNT THEY? /A/ I DONT KNOW. I KNOW THAT THEY
VWOO 3 (134)	ABOUT THE LEARNING. BUT SEE HOW YOUR MANNERS HAVE	IMPROVED	! /A/ MY MANNERS! ! /Z/ YES. WHY, ON THAT SHIP

IMPROVEMENT

METH PREFACE(R18)	EXPERIMENT. WHAT HOPE IS THERE THEN OF HUMAN	IMPROVEMENT	? ACCORDING TO THE NEO-DARWINISTS, TO THE
METH PREFACE(R30)	A VIEW TO THE PRODUCTION OF NEW VARIETIES AND THE	IMPROVEMENT	AND MODIFICATION OF SPECIES HAD BEEN PRACTISED
METH PREFACE(R18)	TO THE MECHANISTS, NO HOPE WHATEVER, BECAUSE	IMPROVEMENT	CAN COME ONLY THROUGH SOME SENSELESS ACCIDENT
GETT PREFACE(223)	IT WAS: A RESULT WHICH IS REGARDED AS " A STEADY	IMPROVEMENT	IN GENERAL MORALITY." IMPERSONALITY IS NOT
GENV IV (90)	CONSPIRACIES DISCUSSED, MAY PRODUCE A GREAT	IMPROVEMENT	IN MORALS. /THE WIDOW/ I PROTEST. ALL THINGS
MRS PREFACE(164)	HISTORY OF POPULAR ART IS MORE AMAZING THAN THE	IMPROVEMENT	IN MUSIC-HALLS THAT THIS SIMPLE ARRANGEMENT HAS
MRS II SD(203)	HIS HAT ON THE DRESSER. THERE IS AN IMMEDIATE	IMPROVEMENT	IN THE COMPANY'S BEHAVIOR. CROFTS TAKES DOWN HIS
JOAN PREFACE(38)	THOUGH ALL SOCIETY IS FOUNDED ON INTOLERANCE, ALL	IMPROVEMENT	IS FOUNDED ON TOLERANCE, OR THE RECOGNITION OF
SUPR HANDBOK(188)	POSSIBLE TO US. IV: MAN'S OBJECTION TO HIS OWN	IMPROVEMENT	. BUT WOULD SUCH A CHANGE BE TOLERATED IF MAN
DOCT PREFACE(57)	TAKEN: THE NET RESULT AT FIRST IS SURE TO BE AN	IMPROVEMENT	. NOT UNTIL ATTENTION HAS BEEN EFFECTUALLY
MTH2 (81)	THE WORLD SO GRADUALLY THAT NOBODY CAN SEE THE	IMPROVEMENT	. THE NOTION THAT NATURE DOES NOT PROCEED BY
CAPT III SD(283)	IT; AND THE REST REGARD IT AS AN UNQUESTIONABLE	IMPROVEMENT	. THE OFFICERS FALL BACK GALLANTLY TO ALLOW HER
SUPR HANDBOK(211)	A PRIVATE SOCIETY OR A CHARTERED COMPANY FOR THE	IMPROVEMENT	OF HUMAN LIVE STOCK. BUT FOR THE PRESENT IT IS
JOAN PREFACE(52)	GO IN MY HANDS. SOME WELL-MEANT PROPOSALS FOR THE	IMPROVEMENT	OF THE PLAY. I HAVE TO THANK SEVERAL CRITICS ON
LION PREFACE(101)	HIS OWN, OR OUR JEWISH CANONICAL LITERATURE AS AN	IMPROVEMENT	ON HINDOO SCRIPTURE, IS TO OFFER OLD LAMPS FOR
DOCT PREFACE(22)	WERE DIPPED IN CARBOLIC OIL, WHICH WAS A GREAT	IMPROVEMENT	ON NOT DIPPING THEM IN ANYTHING AT ALL AND
BARB PREFACE(216)	AND CLOTHED, WOULD NOT THAT BE AN ENORMOUS	IMPROVEMENT	ON OUR EXISTING SYSTEM, WHICH HAS ALREADY
3PLA PREFACE(R33)	THAN AN OFFER OF MY CAESAR TO THE PUBLIC AS AN	IMPROVEMENT	ON SHAKESPEAR'S, AND IN FACT, THAT IS THEIR
MIS. PREFACE(90)	IMPROVING IN ITS MANNERS; AND WHAT WITH THIS	IMPROVEMENT	ON THE ONE HAND, AND ON THE OTHER THAT BLESSED
CLEO NOTES (204)	OF PROGRESSIVE TEMPERAMENT WILL TESTIFY THAT THE	IMPROVEMENT	SINCE HE WAS A BOY IS ENORMOUS. NOW IF WE COUNT
DOCT PREFACE(56)	TO THE CHILDREN'S TEETH, THERE WOULD BE AN	IMPROVEMENT	WHICH IT WOULD TAKE A GOOD DEAL OF BRANDY TO
BULL PREFACE(10)	WOULD RECOGNIZE THE ARRANGEMENT AS AN ENORMOUS	IMPROVEMENT	, AND BE VERY MUCH OBLIGED TO HIM, WHICH IS THE

IMPROVEMENTS

3PLA PREFACE(R38)	DONE. TRUE, MY PLAYS HAVE THE LATEST MECHANICAL	IMPROVEMENTS	: THE ACTION IS NOT CARRIED ON BY IMPOSSIBLE
MILL PREFACE(129)	MOUTHS, WOULD AT FIRST PRODUCE SOME STRIKING	IMPROVEMENTS	IN THE WORKING OF THE PUBLIC SERVICES,
WIDO III (60)	THE PRESENT VALUATION, WITH THE COST OF THE	IMPROVEMENTS	THROWN IN. LEAVE THINGS AS THEY ARE; AND YOU
CLEO NOTES (204)	PLATO, AND ADD TOGETHER THE SUCCESSIVE ENORMOUS	IMPROVEMENTS	TO WHICH EACH OF THEM HAS TESTIFIED, IT WILL

IMPROVES

SUPR HANDBOK(203)	ENOUGH TO SET THE MANTRAP OF RHAMPSINITIS	IMPROVES	ON IT BY BARBED WIRE; THE MODERN GENTLEMAN WHO IS
LION PREFACE(70)	AS THE GENERAL CONDUCT OF MARRIED COUPLES	IMPROVES	, BECOMES MUCH WORSE. THE SELFISH MAN TO WHOM HIS

IMPROVIDENT

BULL I (79)	AND ALL THE QUALITIES OF YOUR RACE: RASH AND	IMPROVIDENT	BUT BRAVE AND GOODNATURED; NOT LIKELY TO SUCCEED
BULL III (123)	MERCY, SHE REFUSED ME. /LARRY/ THAT WAS EXTREMELY	IMPROVIDENT	OF HER. (BEGINNING TO REFLECT) BUT LOOK HERE:
HART PREFACE(29)	WAS DANGEROUSLY EXHAUSTED. HER OPPONENTS, EQUALLY	IMPROVIDENT	, WENT AS MUCH TOO CLOSE TO BANKRUPTCY AS

IMPROVIN

SUPR II (52)	UNPERTURBED) YES. WELL, THIS CONVERSATION IS VERY	IMPROVIN	; BUT IVE GOT TO LOOK AFTER THE CAR; AND YOU TWO

IMPROVING

MRS IV (241)	/FRANK/ OH, DONT MIND MY FEELINGS. GIVE ME SOME	IMPROVING	ADVICE BY ALL MEANS: IT DOES ME EVER SO MUCH GOOD.
LION PREFACE(70)	PREPOSTEROUSNESS IN MARRIAGE, INSTEAD OF	IMPROVING	AS THE GENERAL CONDUCT OF MARRIED COUPLES
MIS. (132)	OF TENNIS? /BENTLEY/ OH, LETS HAVE SOME MORE	IMPROVING	CONVERSATION. WOULDNT YOU RATHER, JOHNNY?
MIS. PREFACE(90)	WHEEZING AND SNARLING AND BRAYING, IS STEADILY	IMPROVING	IN ITS MANNERS; AND WHAT WITH THIS IMPROVEMENT ON
GETT PREFACE(186)	BUT THERE IS A VERY PRESSING QUESTION OF	IMPROVING	ITS CONDITIONS. I HAVE NEVER MET ANYBODY REALLY IN
MRS I (184)	OF LIFE, WASTE OF EVERYTHING. BUT THINGS ARE	IMPROVING	, DO YOU KNOW, I HAVE BEEN IN A POSITIVE STATE OF
BARB II (309)	IT TO YOU. /BILL/ (HIS VOICE AND ACCENT SUDDENLY	IMPROVING	) NOT IF AW WIZ TO STAWVE FOR IT. AW AINT TO BE
CYMB FORWORD(133)	FOREWORD. THE PRACTICE OF	IMPROVING	SHAKESPEAR'S PLAYS, MORE ESPECIALLY IN THE MATTER
MIS. (127)	JOHN? /TARLETON/ YES. DONT INTERRUPT ME WHEN I'M	IMPROVING	THE BOY'S MIND. WHERE WAS I? THIS REPULSIVE MASK
GENV PREFACE(21)	HIS INITIAL CONQUESTS WELCOME AND PERMANENT BY	IMPROVING	THE CONDITION OF THE INHABITANTS. ON THE CONTRARY
WIDO III (61)	NEW STREET. IF THAT HAPPENS, THE MONEY SPENT IN	IMPROVING	THE HOUSES WILL BE THROWN AWAY: SIMPLY THROWN

IMPROVISE

METH PREFACE(R28)	THEM MEN WHO MASTER SYSTEMS OF SHORTHAND AND	IMPROVISE	NEW SYSTEMS OF THEIR OWN AS EASILY AS THEY LEARNT

IMPROVISED

MILL PREFACE(121)	SHIRTS AND APPLIED THE NECESSARY COERCION. SUCH	IMPROVISED	BODIES ATTRACTED YOUNG MEN OF MILITARY TASTES AND
JOAN EPIL,SD(158)	QUARTER. A ROUGH MALE VOICE IS HEARD TROLLING AN	IMPROVISED	TUNE. RUM TUM TRUMPLEDUM, BACON FAT AND

IMPROVIZE

MTH2 (43)	SHE IS A BOLSHEVIST AND NOTHING ELSE. SHE HAS TO	IMPROVIZE	HER MANNERS AND HER CONDUCT AS SHE GOES ALONG.

IMPRUDENCE

INCA PROLOG (233)	TO A FATHER? YOUR MARRIAGE WAS A MOST DISASTROUS	IMPRUDENCE	. IT GAVE YOU HABITS THAT ARE ABSOLUTELY BEYOND
LIED (188)	HEAVEN FOR YOUR MADNESS, YOUR RASHNESS, YOUR	IMPRUDENCE	! /SHE/ (IMPATIENTLY) OH, BE SENSIBLE, HENRY.

IMPRUDENT

AUGS (278)	COMES BACK TO THE TABLE TO LOOK AT IT) OH, HOW	IMPRUDENT	! EVERYBODY WOULD GUESS ITS IMPORTANCE WITH YOUR
LIED (188)	OH, HOW COULD I HAVE BEEN SO MAD! SO RASH! SO	IMPRUDENT	! /HE/ THANK HEAVEN FOR YOUR MADNESS, YOUR

IMPUDENCE

CAND I (87)	USED THE WRONG WORD. I SHOULD HAVE SAID DAMN YOUR	IMPUDENCE	: THATS WHAT ST PAUL OR ANY HONEST PRIEST WOULD
GENV III (84)	PAY FOR IT? /THE WIDOW/ IS THERE ANY END TO YOUR	IMPUDENCE	? I HAVE NEVER DINED WITH A JEW IN MY LIFE. /THE
O'FL (218)	AND WAS IT THE BELGIANS LEARNED YOU SUCH BRAZEN	IMPUDENCE	? /O'FLAHERTY/ THE BELGIANS IS GOOD MEN; AND THE

BARB PREFACE(219) TO STRAIN TOWARDS THE EXTREME POSSIBLE LIMIT OF IMPUDENCE IN LYING AND CORRUPTION IN HYPOCRISY. THE
ARMS III (57) WE'RE ALONE. IT'S TOO SHARP AND IMPUDENT; AND IMPUDENCE IS A SORT OF FAMILIARITY: IT SHEWS AFFECTION FOR
CATH 4 (188) EITHER TIME. IVE BEEN CARRIED. I CALL IT INFERNAL IMPUDENCE . /CATHERINE/ TAKE CARE WHAT YOU SAY. /EDSTASTON/
JOAN PREFACE(43) WILL FORGET HIS CLOTH AND DAMN THE CURATE'S IMPUDENCE , THE MORE OBEDIENT A MAN IS TO ACCREDITED
HART I (49) OF THE HOUSE! THE WAY I'M RECEIVED! THE CASUAL IMPUDENCE OF THAT WOMAN GUINNESS, OUR OLD NURSE! REALLY
MIS. PREFACE(48) SO CANNOT BE SAVED. AND THIS IS SIMPLY A PIECE OF IMPUDENCE ON YOUR PART, AS YOU KNOW NOTHING ABOUT IT EXCEPT
JOAN 2 (82) ARE AN IDLE FELLOW, BLUEBEARD; AND YOU HAVE GREAT IMPUDENCE TO ANSWER THE ARCHBISHOP. /LA HIRE/ (WITH A HUGE
DOCT PREFACE(49) VERY WORST. INDEED, NO CRIMINAL HAS YET HAD THE IMPUDENCE TO ARGUE AS EVERY VIVISECTOR ARGUES. NO BURGLAR
JOAN 1 (59) DO YOU MEAN TO SAY THAT THAT GIRL, WHO HAD THE IMPUDENCE TO ASK TO SEE ME TWO DAYS AGO, AND WHOM I TOLD YOU
KING I (165) FOX THE QUAKER, IN HIS LEATHER BREECHES, HAD THE IMPUDENCE TO CALL. /NEWTON/ (INTERESTED) GEORGE FOX? IF HE
JOAN 6 (122) I AM AWARE OF THAT FACT. WILL IT PLEASE YOUR IMPUDENCE TO FIND THE BISHOP OF BEAUVAIS FOR ME, AND GIVE
MIS. (112) YOUR BAD MANNERS AND YOUR CONCEIT, AND THE DAMNED IMPUDENCE YOU THINK CLEVER. /BENTLEY/ (DEEPLY WOUNDED AND
JOAN 1 (60) VOICE/ BE YOU CAPTAIN? /ROBERT/ YES, DAMN YOUR IMPUDENCE , I BE CAPTAIN. COME UP HERE. (TO THE SOLDIERS IN
SUPR I (15) AS ANY OF THE REST OF YOU. CULTIVATE A LITTLE IMPUDENCE , RAMSDEN; AND YOU WILL BECOME QUITE A REMARKABLE
2TRU I (44) THINKING ABOUT YOU. /THE PATIENT/ JUST LIKE HER IMPUDENCE ! HOW DID SHE KNOW ABOUT ME? /THE BURGLAR/
MTH3 (125) OUTSIDE THEIR OFFICES. /BARNABAS/ CONFOUND THEIR IMPUDENCE ! I HAD GIFTS ENOUGH TO FIND YOU OUT, ANYHOW.
2TRU III (108) FOR YOU, SIR. /TALLBOYS/ FOR ME! DAMN THEIR IMPUDENCE ! I NEVER ASKED FOR ONE. /MEEK/ NO, SIR; BUT
PHIL II (95) HIS VISITOR UP HERE, I SHOULD NOT OBJECT. THE IMPUDENCE ! (HE DASHES HIS PAPER DOWN ON THE CHAIR).
PYGM V (285) /HIGGINS/ (DISAGREEABLY SURPRISED) DAMN HIS IMPUDENCE ! (HE RECOILS AND FINDS HIMSELF SITTING ON HIS
KING I (210) TO IT. /BARBARA/ CHARLES! YOU ARE OBSCENE. THE IMPUDENCE ! (SHE SITS). /KNELLER/ THE BEAUTY, MADAM. CLEAR
PRES (166) PUT ME SLIPPER ACRDSS YOU. (SHE RINGS OFF). THE IMPUDENCE ! (TO MITCHENER) BLESS YOU, ME CHILDHER, MAY YOU
LADY (243) PUTS HIS ARMS ABOUT HER). /THE LADY/ UNMEASURED IMPUDENCE ! ON YOUR LIFE, TAKE YOUR HANDS FROM ME. THE DARK
PRES (162) COMPULSORY MILITARY SERVICE. /MITCHENER/ INFERNAL IMPUDENCE ! /BALSQUITH/ THE LABOR PARTY IS TAKING THE SAME
DOCT III (149) AND GOES FOR HIS HAT). /RIDGEON/ DAMN HIS IMPUDENCE ! /B.B./ I SHOULDNT BE AT ALL SURPRISED TO LEARN
CAND I (87) YOU, JAMES. /MORELL/ (STARTING UP) CONFOUND YOUR IMPUDENCE ! /BURGESS/ (RETREATING, WITH ALMOST LACHRYMOSE
DEVL III (69) SIX HOURS TO CLEAR OUT. /SWINDON/ WHAT MONSTROUS IMPUDENCE ! /BURGOYNE/ WHAT SHALL WE DO, EH? /SWINDON/
HART II (114) UTTERWORD/ I KNOW VERY WELL WHAT YOU MEANT. THE IMPUDENCE ! /ELLIE/ WHAT ON EARTH DO YOU MEAN? /CAPTAIN
DOCT III (132) INTENDED TO FINISH THEM. /LOUIS/ CONFOUND HIS IMPUDENCE ! WHAT THE DEVIL DOES HE TAKE ME FOR? NOW THAT
UNPL PREFACE(R15) " ALLOWS" ITS PERFORMANCE (CONFOUND HIS IMPUDENCE !). IN SPITE OF THIS CERTIFICATE HE STILL RETAINS

IMPUDENT
JOAN 6 (139) DRESS. FOR THE LAST TIME, WILL YOU PUT OFF THAT IMPUDENT ATTIRE, AND DRESS AS BECOMES YOUR SEX? /JOAN/ I
JOAN 1 (61) ME. POLLY AND JACK AND -- /ROBERT/ POLLY! ! YOU IMPUDENT BAGGAGE, DO YOU DARE CALL SQUIRE BERTRAND DE
LION PREFACE(8) UTTERING WHAT SEEMED TO HIM AN APPALLING AND IMPUDENT BLASPHEMY. THE FACT THAT THE BLASPHEMY WAS TO JESUS
3PLA PREFACE(R26) SCHOOL, IN WHICH THE IMPERTURBABLY IMPUDENT COMEDIAN, AFTERWARDS SHELVED BY THE REACTION TO
DEST (177) IN HER FACE) PSHA! FLATTERY! FLATTERY! COARSE, IMPUDENT FLATTERY! /LADY/ (SPRINGING UP WITH A BRIGHT
BUOY IV (54) FELLOW. /SIR FERDINAND/ LIKE THE FELLOW! LIKE AN IMPUDENT FORTUNE HUNTER! IN HEAVEN'S NAME, WHY? /OLD BILL/
BARB PREFACE(243) PROPERTY IS ORGANIZED ROBBERY; OUR MORALITY IS AN IMPUDENT HYPOCRISY; OUR WISDOM IS ADMINISTERED BY
MIS. PREFACE(104) AS MUCH FLOGGING AND HANGING, AS MUCH IMPUDENT INJUSTICE ON THE BENCH AND LUSTFUL RANCOR IN THE
HART II (100) ME IF YOU DARE. /MRS HUSHABYE/ WELL, OF ALL THE IMPUDENT LITTLE FIENDS I EVER MET! HECTOR SAYS THERE IS A
GENV II (61) BROWN? /SIR O./ DO WITH HER! SQUASH HER, IMPUDENT LITTLE SLUT. SHE IS NOBODY: SHE DOESNT MATTER. THE
LADY (248) OF WHICH A WOMAN GOETH IN MAN'S ATTIRE AND MAKETH IMPUDENT LOVE TO HER SWAIN, WHO PLEASETH THE GROUNDLINGS BY
POSN SD(447) COMES IN. SHE IS A YOUNG WOMAN OF 23 OR 24, WITH IMPUDENT MANNERS, BATTERED GOOD LOOKS, AND DIRTY-FINE DRESS.
SUPR I (14) (VERY DELIBERATELY) MR TANNER: YOU ARE THE MOST IMPUDENT PERSON I HAVE EVER MET. /TANNER/ (SERIOUSLY) I
SUPR I (15) I SUPPOSE. /TANNER/ NO: I AM ONLY THE MOST IMPUDENT PERSON YOUVE EVER MET. THATS YOUR NOTION OF A
MIS. PREFACE(47) QUACKS AND CREATES A PASSIONATE DEMAND FOR IMPUDENT PRETENCES THAT DOCTORS CAN CURE THE DISEASES THEY
HART PREFACE(16) AND GOETHE, WERE KEPT IN COUNTENANCE BY THE MOST IMPUDENT REPUDIATIONS OF EVERY DECENCY OF CIVILIZATION AND
ARMS III (57) ALL, UNLESS WHEN WE'RE ALONE. IT'S TOO SHARP AND IMPUDENT ; AND IMPUDENCE IS A SORT OF FAMILIARITY: IT SHEWS
KING I (219) I AM NO BETTER MYSELF. /BARBARA/ NO BETTER! YOU IMPUDENT SLUT. /NELL/ WELL, NO WORSE, IF YOU LIKE. ONE
PYGM V (288) MYSELF. /HIGGINS/ (WONDERING AT HER) YOU DAMNED IMPUDENT SLUT, YOU! BUT IT'S BETTER THAN SNIVELLING; BETTER
O'FL (225) TOP OF THEIR VOICES. /MRS O'FLAHERTY/ (SOLO) YOU IMPUDENT YOUNG HEIFER, HOW DAR YOU SAY SUCH A THING TO ME..
JOAN PREFACE(44) OF THE EAR OF THE REIGNING SOVEREIGN, BY AN IMPUDENT YOUNG UPSTART PRACTISING ON THE CREDULITY OF THE

IMPUDENTLY
SUPR HANDBOK(201) OFFICE, LIKE THOSE POOR BOURBONS WHO HAVE BEEN SO IMPUDENTLY BLAMED FOR A UNIVERSAL CHARACTERISTIC, HAD LEARNT
MIS. PREFACE(10) THE SIN OF STEALING FIRE FROM THE ALTAR: A SIN SO IMPUDENTLY PRACTISED BY POPES, PARENTS, AND PEDAGOGUES, THAT
MIS. PREFACE(18) TO TREAT CHILDHOOD FRANKLY AS A STATE OF SIN, AND IMPUDENTLY PROCLAIM THE MONSTROUS PRINCIPLE THAT LITTLE
MIS. PREFACE(104) AND THE FLATTERERS OF DEMOCRACY ARE AS IMPUDENTLY SERVILE TO THE SUCCESSFUL, AND INSOLENT TO COMMON

IMPULSE
ROCK PREFACE(183) /JESUS/ NEVERTHELESS, OPINION IS A DEAD THING AND IMPULSE A LIVE THING. YOU CANNOT IMPOSE ON ME WITH YOUR
MIS. PREFACE(95) DIVINE SPARK; AND NO RESOLUTION NOT TO CALL THIS IMPULSE AN IMPULSE OF LOYALTY TO THE FELLOWSHIP OF THE HOLY
PRES (133) RIGHT. (BALSQUITH HAS A STRONG CONTROVERSIAL IMPULSE AND IS EVIDENTLY GOING TO DISPUTE THIS PROFESSION OF
BARB II (306) A THOUSAND PEOPLE FALL ON THEIR KNEES WITH ONE IMPULSE AND PRAY? COME WITH US TO THE MEETING. BARBARA
CAPT NOTES (301) UNTIL IN AN INSPIRED MOMENT HE VOICED A UNIVERSAL IMPULSE BY BLUNTLY DAMNING ITS HYPOCRISY. OF ALL THE
MIS. PREFACE(83) LITTLE CHILDREN" HAS BECOME AN AFFECTIONATE IMPULSE DEEP IN OUR NATURE. NOW THERE IS NO SUCH IMPULSE TO
SUPR III (115) ALARMED ME; FOR THE FIRST MEANT THAT THE LADY'S IMPULSE HAD BEEN SOLELY TO THROW DOWN MY FORTIFICATIONS AND
GETT SD(295) OF CONSCIENTIOUS SCRUPLE AND RELIGIOUS IMPULSE HAVE BEEN APPLAUDED AND DEFERRED TO UNTIL SHE HAS
MTH5 (261) BEST OF ALL, THEY ARE STILL NOT SATISFIED: THE IMPULSE I GAVE THEM IN THAT DAY WHEN I SUNDERED MYSELF IN
MIS. PREFACE(18) INTERVALS BETWEEN THE MOMENTS OF AFFECTIONATE IMPULSE IS JUST THAT FEELING THAT LEADS THEM TO AVOID THEIR
LADY PREFACE(212) WORK OF ONE WHOSE FIXED PRACTICE AND UNGOVERNABLE IMPULSE IT IS TO KICK CONVENTIONAL DIGNITY WHENEVER HE SEES
JOAN PREFACE(21) SHE WAS A WOMAN OF POLICY AND NOT OF BLIND IMPULSE . IN WAR SHE WAS AS MUCH A REALIST AS NAPOLEON: SHE
SUPR III (125) WOMANHOOD. /ANA/ YOU MEAN THAT IT WAS AN IMMORAL IMPULSE . /DON JUAN/ NATURE, MY DEAR LADY, IS WHAT YOU CALL
ROCK PREFACE(183) INFORMED OPINION AND SENTIMENTAL AND ILL INFORMED IMPULSE . /JESUS/ NEVERTHELESS, OPINION IS A DEAD THING AND
GETT PREFACE(232) THE YOUTH INTO THE STREET BY BODILY VIOLENCE: AN IMPULSE NATURAL, PERHAPS, BUT VULGAR AND IMPROPER, AND NOT
DEVL II (40) /RICHARD/ (FOLDING HER IN HIS ARMS WITH AN IMPULSE OF COMPASSION FOR HER DISTRESS) MY POOR GIRL!
CATH 2 (178) AT PATIOMKIN, HE GURGLES BRUTISHLY; SHE HAS AN IMPULSE OF DISGUST). HOG. (SHE KICKS HIM AS HARD AS SHE
SUPR IV (160) HAS AN IMPULSE TO KISS HIM AND THEN ANOTHER IMPULSE OF DISTASTE WHICH PREVENTS HER; FINALLY RUNS AWAY
MTH5 (254) YOUR TASTES AND SENSES HAD OVERLAID THE DIRECT IMPULSE OF LIFE IN YOU, AND BECAUSE I CARED ONLY FOR OUR
MIS. PREFACE(95) AND NO RESOLUTION NOT TO CALL THIS IMPULSE AN IMPULSE OF LOYALTY TO THE FELLOWSHIP OF THE HOLY GHOST, OR
ROCK PREFACE(149) FOR THE EXTERMINATION OF FASCISTS, IN INDIA THE IMPULSE OF MOSLEMS AND HINDUS TO EXTERMINATE ONE ANOTHER IS
SUPR III (125) AND WERE THE OUTCOME OF A PERFECTLY SIMPLE IMPULSE OF MY MANHOOD TOWARDS HER WOMANHOOD. /ANA/ YOU MEAN
SUPR IV (156) TO LOVE ME? /ANN/ (LOOKING AT HIM WITH A FAINT IMPULSE OF PITY) TAVY, MY DEAR, YOU ARE A NICE CREATURE-- A
DOCT V (174) (RAISING HER HEAD A LITTLE WITH A QUITE GENTLE IMPULSE OF PRIDE) YOU THINK IT ONLY MATTERED BECAUSE I HEARD
NEVR III (263) THE TEA TABLE). /GLORIA/ (LOOKING ROUND WITH AN IMPULSE OF TERROR) AND THE OTHER GENTLEMAN? /WAITER/ (
ROCK PREFACE(149) TO EXTERMINATE ONE ANOTHER IS COMPLICATED BY THE IMPULSE OF THE BRITISH EMPIRE TO EXTERMINATE BOTH WHEN THEY
2TRU PREFACE(16) TO THE PUBLIC WELFARE IN OBEDIENCE TO THE IMPULSE OF THE HOLY GHOST WITHIN THEM. THIS IMPULSE WAS
METH PREFACE(R83) THE EIGHTEENTH CENTURY PASSION MEANT IRRESISTIBLE IMPULSE OF THE LOFTIEST KIND: FOR EXAMPLE A PASSION FOR
GETT (343) YOUR ARMS, AND THE VOLUME OF ALL THE SEAS IN ONE IMPULSE OF YOUR SOULS. A MOMENT ONLY; BUT WAS IT NOT
CAPT II (268) /SIR HOWARD AND BRASSBOUND/ (WITH THE SAME IMPULSE) NO, NO. /LADY CICELY/ (EAGERLY) YES, YES.
LADY PREFACE(227) BY THE EXCESSIVE SUSCEPTIBILITY TO THE NORMAL IMPULSE SHEWN IN THE WHOLE MASS OF HIS WRITINGS. THIS LATTER
GETT PREFACE(229) THEIR PREJUDICES ARE CHALLENGED, HAVE NO OTHER IMPULSE THAN TO CALL THE CHALLENGER NAMES, AND, WHEN THE
METH PREFACE(R18) DOES NOT DISCOURAGE THOSE WHO BELIEVE THAT THE IMPULSE THAT PRODUCES EVOLUTION IS CREATIVE. THEY HAVE
SIM PREFACE(15) CONCEIT IN THEIR EMANCIPATION AND AN EXULTANT IMPULSE TO ABUSE IT. THE SUBSTITUTION OF IRRESPONSIBILITY
OVER (172) SATISFACTION IS DEATH. /MRS JUNO/ YES; BUT THE IMPULSE TO COMMIT SUICIDE IS SOMETIMES IRRESISTIBLE.
POSN PREFACE(365) HOSTILE BODIES BY THE OPERATION OF THE MERE IMPULSE TO CONTRADICT THEM, ALWAYS STRONG IN ENGLISH HUMAN
DEST SD(173) FROM HER BOSOM. FOR A MOMENT SHE HAS AN INTENSE IMPULSE TO DASH THEM IN HIS FACE. BUT HER GOOD BREEDING CUTS
SUPR III SD(140) THE BRIGANDS, STRUGGLING WITH AN OVERWHELMING IMPULSE TO HIDE BEHIND ONE ANOTHER, LOOK AS UNCONCERNED AS
MIS. PREFACE(66) AND THE EMPLOYEE HAS IN HIM THE SAME FIERCE IMPULSE TO IMPOSE HIS WILL WITHOUT RESPECT FOR THE WILL OF
MTH4 I (168) TO ME. I FEEL HOT ALL OVER. I HAVE A HORRIBLE IMPULSE TO INJURE YOU. WHAT HAVE YOU DONE TO ME? /THE
NEVR IV (289) WANT YOU TO THINK OVER IT WHEN YOU FEEL YOUR NEXT IMPULSE TO INTERRUPT ME. /VALENTINE/ (DAZED) THIS IS SIMPLY
SUPR IV (160) TAVY. GOODBYE, DEAR. (SHE PATS HIS CHEEK; HAS AN IMPULSE TO KISS HIM AND THEN ANOTHER IMPULSE OF DISTASTE
BARB PREFACE(229) WE SHOULD BEWARE OF ASSUMING THAT THE IMPULSE TO MAKE THEM WAS PIOUS OR THAT THE INTEREST OF THE
MIS. (140) FOR A CHILD COMPANION, BUT BY THE INNOCENT IMPULSE TO PLACE THE DELICACY AND WISDOM AND SPIRITUALITY OF
CLEO II SD(127) NEWLY-ACQUIRED DIGNITY AS A QUEEN, AND A STRONG IMPULSE TO PUT OUT HER TONGUE AT HIM. SHE TAKES NO PART IN
NEVR IV SD(302) DUMB WITH PANIC, LOOKS AT THEM WITH AN OBVIOUS IMPULSE TO RUN AWAY. /DOLLY/ (BREAKING THE SILENCE) NUMBER

SUPR HANDBOK(204)	AS IT HAS ALWAYS BEEN, MURDEROUS EXCITEMENT: THE	IMPULSE	TO SLAUGHTER IS UNIVERSAL; AND MUSEUMS ARE SET UP
MRS IV (252)	AT HER FIERCELY FOR A MOMENT WITH A SAVAGE	IMPULSE	TO STRIKE HER) NO, THANK YOU. GOODBYE. /VIVIE/ (
MIS. PREFACE(83)	IMPULSE DEEP IN OUR NATURE. NOW THERE IS NO SUCH	IMPULSE	TO SUFFER OUR SISTERS AND BROTHERS, OUR AUNTS AND
OVER SD(171)	AND IS, IN FACT, YIELDING TO AN IRRESISTIBLE	IMPULSE	TO THROW HIS ARMS ROUND HER. /THE LADY/ DONT-- OH
SUPR IV (156)	RAMSDEN. ANN STROLLS TO THE STEPS WITH AN IDLE	IMPULSE	TO TORMENT OCTAVIUS). /ANN/ WONT YOU GO WITH THEM,
NEVR II (258)	YOU. I LOVE YOU. (HE TURNS TOWARDS HER AS IF THE	IMPULSE	TO TOUCH HER WERE UNGOVERNABLE: SHE RISES AND STANDS
SUPR HANDBOK(182)	AS PROPERTY, AND WILL BE MODIFIED BY THE	IMPULSE	TOWARDS HIM JUST AS EFFECTUALLY. THE PRACTICAL
MIS. PREFACE(95)	A FOOL IS FORCED TO APPEAL TO THE CHILD'S VITAL	IMPULSE	TOWARDS PERFECTION, TO THE DIVINE SPARK; AND NO
2TRU PREFACE(16)	THE IMPULSE OF THE HOLY GHOST WITHIN THEM. THIS	IMPULSE	WAS THEIR VOCATION. THEY WERE CALLED FROM ABOVE, NOT
MIS. PREFACE(56)	THE CHOICE OF THIS ONE BETRAYED THE SENSUAL	IMPULSE	WHICH MAKES THE PRACTICE AN ABOMINATION. BUT WHEN
POSN PREFACE(376)	AND TO KICK ME OUT OF THE ROOM WAS THE PASSIONATE	IMPULSE	WHICH PREVAILED IN SPITE OF ALL THE REMONSTRANCES OF
CAND III (128)	AND HIS ARMS ON HER LAP, AND SPEAKS WITH GROWING	IMPULSE	, HIS BLOOD BEGINNING TO STIR). MAY I SAY SOME
MRS PREFACE(169)	FAR FROM IGNORING IDIOSYNCRASY, WILL, PASSION,	IMPULSE	, WHIM, AS FACTORS IN HUMAN ACTION, I HAVE PLACED
		IMPULSES	
OVER PREFACE(167)	THE CONSEQUENCES, THE MORE INTERESTING BECOME THE	IMPULSES	AND IMAGINATIONS AND REASONINGS, IF ANY, OF THE
MTH5 (248)	BEFORE YOU UNMASKED AS MERE MACHINERY, AND YOUR	IMPULSES	ARE SHEWN TO BE NOTHING BUT REFLEXES, YOU ARE
LION PREFACE(81)	MAIN RESTRAINT IS HUMAN NATURE, WHICH HAS GOOD	IMPULSES	AS WELL AS BAD ONES, AND REFRAINS FROM THEFT AND
MRS PREFACE(169)	LOGIC ABOUT DUTY, AND TO DISGUISE EVEN HIS OWN	IMPULSES	FROM HIMSELF IN THIS WAY, FINDS THE PICTURE AS
BARB PREFACE(215)	LIMITS OF HUMANITY'S COMPARATIVELY NEGLIGIBLE	IMPULSES	IN THESE DIRECTIONS? SUPPOSE WE WERE TO ABOLISH
MIS. (164)	THE SON OF THREE FATHERS. I MISTRUST THESE WILD	IMPULSES	. /HYPATIA/ TAKE CARE. YOURE LETTING THE MOMENT
PYGM EPILOG (291)	AND HIS IDEALISM FROM HIS SPECIFICALLY SEXUAL	IMPULSES	. THIS MAKES HIM A STANDING PUZZLE TO THE HUGE
BARB I SD(259)	TEMPERAMENT AND A HIGH CONSCIENCE AGAINST	IMPULSES	OF INHUMAN RIDICULE AND FIERCE IMPATIENCE HAS SET
GETT PREFACE(205)	STATE ORGANIZED SO AS TO CARRY OUT EXACTLY THE	IMPULSES	OF THE AVERAGE SOLDIER WOULD NOT LAST A YEAR. THE
MTH5 (254)	REFINED. I DID MY BEST TO LIFT YOUR PREHISTORIC	IMPULSES	ON TO THE PLANE OF BEAUTY, OF IMAGINATION, OF
PYGM EPILOG (298)	HAD BEEN UNLOCKED ALL THE TIME, AND THAT THE	IMPULSES	SHE HAD SO CAREFULLY STRUGGLED WITH AND STIFLED FOR
BUOY III (36)	FALLING IN LOVE. I HAD ILLUSIONS, INFATUATIONS,	IMPULSES	THAT WERE UTTERLY UNREASONABLE AND IRRESISTIBLE.
METH PREFACE(R57)	OF AN EVIL WILL, OR COULD RECONCILE IT WITH OUR	IMPULSES	TOWARDS JUSTICE, MERCY, AND A HIGHER LIFE. A
ROCK PREFACE(148)	UNABLE TO RESTRAIN THEIR VIOLENT OR ACQUISITIVE	IMPULSES	, AND HAVE NO COMPUNCTION ABOUT SACRIFICING OTHERS
JOAN PREFACE(36)	AND SCIENCE ARE TWO DIFFERENT AND OPPOSITE	IMPULSES	, RIVALS FOR HUMAN ALLEGIANCE. I HAVE BEFORE ME THE
		IMPULSIVE	
MILL I (155)	IT HIMSELF, GAVE HIM A SORT OF GREATNESS. I AM	IMPULSIVE	: I KEPT MY WORD AND MARRIED HIM INSTANTLY. THEN,
DOCT III (134)	YOU WANT TO SOUND MY WRETCHED LUNG. (WITH	IMPULSIVE	CANDOR) MY DEAR RIDGEON: I'LL BE FRANK WITH YOU.
BULL I (79)	TO BREAK THE ICE BETWEEN ME AND YOUR WARMHEARTED,	IMPULSIVE	COUNTRYMEN? /TIM/ WILL I COME TO MADAGASCAR OR
PHIL I SD(84)	FIGURE, AND BEING, IN FACT, A GOOD-NATUREDLY	IMPULSIVE	CREDULOUS PERSON WHO, AFTER AN ENTIRELY
SUPR I SD(16)	IT; THOUGH HER POSE IS FASHIONABLY FRANK AND	IMPULSIVE	. SHE INSPIRES CONFIDENCE AS A PERSON WHO WILL DO
ANNA (298)	SHOTS. HE VANISHES). /STRAMMFEST/ (MAKING AN	IMPULSIVE	MOVEMENT TOWARDS HER) MY IMPERIAL MISTRESS -- /THE
BARB (206)	CAME INTO OUR DRAMATIC LITERATURE WITH ALL THE	IMPULSIVE	POWER OF AN ORIGINAL WORK SHORTLY BEFORE MAJOR
BULL IV (162)	TO SPEAK, SO PAINFUL THAT HE CONTINUES WITH	IMPULSIVE	SYMPATHY) NO: DONT TRY TO SPEAK: IT'S ALL RIGHT
FOUN (221)	THAT YOU ARE TOO YOUNG, TOO IRRESPONSIBLE, TOO	IMPULSIVE	TO BE ANYTHING MORE TO ME THAN AN EXTREMELY
		IMPULSIVELY	
GETT (268)	WHY I'M GOING TO BE AN OLD MAID. /THE GENERAL/ (	IMPULSIVELY	APPROACHING HER) DONT SAY THAT, LESBIA. IT'S NOT
PHIL I (70)	DIGNIFIED QUIETNESS OF THE WOMAN. /CHARTERIS/ (	IMPULSIVELY	CLASPING GRACE) MY DEAREST LOVE. /GRACE/ (
BARB II (307)	THINK I AM WRONG TO TAKE THE MONEY? /BARBARA/ (	IMPULSIVELY	GOING TO HER AND KISSING HER) NO, NO: GOD HELP
CAND III (142)	A WOUNDED ANIMAL). I CANT SPEAK-- /CANDIDA/ (	IMPULSIVELY	GOING TO HIM) AH, DEAREST-- /MARCHBANKS/ (IN
PHIL II (125)	METHOD IN A MILDER FORM: REASONABLE AND	IMPULSIVELY	GOODNATURED INSTEAD OF TRAGIC) I KNOW I WAS
SUPR III (78)	WAY AGAIN. WELL, I'LL THINK ABOUT IT. /DUVAL/ (	IMPULSIVELY	RUSHING ACROSS TO STRAKER) MON FRERE! (HE
CATH 4 (198)	YOU WISH. THE STOVE, BY ALL MEANS. /EDSTASTON/ (	IMPULSIVELY	) AH, MADAM, ABOLISH THE STOVE: BELIEVE ME,
BULL I (79)	I FEEL SURE YOU WOULD, MR HAFFIGAN. /TIM/ (	IMPULSIVELY	) DAMN IT! CALL ME TIM. A MAN THAT TALKS ABOUT
2TRU III (92)	OF YOUR DETERMINISM, SIR. /THE FATHER/ (RISING	IMPULSIVELY	) DETERMINISM IS GONE, SHATTERED, BURIED WITH A
PYGM III (250)	DAUGHTER CLARA. /LIZA/ HOW DO YOU DO? /CLARA/ (	IMPULSIVELY	) HOW DO YOU DO? (SHE SITS DOWN ON THE OTTOMAN
ARMS I (10)	HIS SABRE AND FACES THE DOOR, WAITING). /RAINA/ (	IMPULSIVELY	) I'LL HELP YOU. I'LL SAVE YOU. /THE MAN/ YOU
PYGM V (277)	I'M ONLY A SQUASHED CABBAGE LEAF-- /PICKERING/ (	IMPULSIVELY	) NO. /LIZA/ (CONTINUING QUIETLY) -- BUT I OWE
MIS. (160)	YOU? /LINA/ ONLY A POINT OF HONOR? /TARLETON/ (	IMPULSIVELY	) NO, BY GOD! A POINT OF AFFECTION AS WELL.
SUPR IV (153)	TREAT ME AS A FRIEND: DRAW ON ME. /OCTAVIUS/ (	IMPULSIVELY	) OR ON ME. /MALONE/ (WITH FIERCE JEALOUSY) WHO
JITT I (13)	THE WORLD WITH OUR LOVE. /JITTA/ (EMBRACING HIM	IMPULSIVELY	) SHALL WE? /BRUNO/ THERE IS MY WIFE. ALWAYS MY
SUPR II (67)	SENTIMENT) THATS VERY ENGLISH. (APPEALING TO HER	IMPULSIVELY	) VIOLET: DAD'S BOUND TO FIND US OUT SOMEDAY.
MTH5 (234)	GREAT OF YOU, DARLING STREPHON! (SHE KISSES HIM	IMPULSIVELY	). /STREPHON/ (PASSIONATELY) LET ME ALONE.
APPL II SD(277)	POCKETS HER HANDKERCHIEF; SHAKES THE KING'S HANDS	IMPULSIVELY	; AND GOES WITH AMANDA. THE KING PLUNGES INTO
PHIL I (83)	OH, GO TO THE DEUCE. (HE DISENGAGES HIMSELF	IMPULSIVELY	; AND SHE, AS IF HE HAD FLUNG HER DOWN, FALLS
PPP (194)	MISSING) NOT UNDER THE CIRCUMSTANCES. /PHYLLIS/ (	IMPULSIVELY	THROWING HERSELF ON HER KNEES BY HER MISTRESS'S
OVER (187)	NOT BRAG ABOUT SINNING WITH MY WIFE. (HE TURNS	IMPULSIVELY	TO HIS WIFE; MAKES HER RISE; AND TAKES HER
ARMS II SD(30)	A DAINTY EASTERN CAP OF GOLD TINSEL. SERGIUS GOES	IMPULSIVELY	TO MEET HER. POSING REGALLY, SHE PRESENTS HER
JITT I SD(26)	WAY. A FLUSH OF REMORSE COMES OVER HER. SHE TURNS	IMPULSIVELY	TO THE VASE; TAKES OUT A HANDFUL OF ROSES; AND
PHIL II (115)	(PARAMORE TURNS STIFFLY AWAY. CRAVEN FOLLOWS HIM	IMPULSIVELY	, EXCLAIMING REMORSEFULLY) WELL, PERHAPS IT WAS
DEVL III (52)	THAT ALL NIGHT? YOUR DEATH WILL BE AT MY DOOR. (	IMPULSIVELY	, SHE GIVES HIM HER HAND, AND ADDS, WITH INTENSE
		IMPULSIVENESS	
WIDO I (12)	AND THEN PUTS HER HANDS INTO HIS WITH CALCULATED	IMPULSIVENESS	, HE SNATCHES HER INTO HIS ARMS WITH A CRY OF
		IMPUNITY	
MIS. (170)	OF? /THE MAN/ ARE WOMEN TO BE RUINED WITH	IMPUNITY	? /TARLETON/ I HAVNT RUINED ANY WOMAN THAT I'M
GENV IV (101)	WE NOT CREATE ONE BEFORE WE ARE DESTROYED BY THE	IMPUNITY	AND GLORIFICATION OF MURDER? /BBDE/ PEACE MAY
GENV PREFACE(20)	MASSACRED ALL HIS POLITICAL RIVALS NOT ONLY WITH	IMPUNITY	BUT WITH FULL PARLIAMENTARY APPROVAL. LIKE ST PETER
MRS PREFACE(167)	A PRETENCE OF COMPLIANCE OR DEFIED WITH COMPLETE	IMPUNITY	BY ANY REASONABLY STRONG-MINDED PERSON. NOBODY CAN
GETT PREFACE(246)	MAKES THIS OUTRAGE ABSOLUTELY LEGAL. YOU MAY WITH	IMPUNITY	DO TO THE PERSON TO WHOM YOU ARE MARRIED WHAT YOU
CAPT I (229)	A THING WHICH PROBABLY COULD HARDLY BE DONE WITH	IMPUNITY	EVEN HERE IN MOROCCO, UNDER THE MOST BARBAROUS OF
GETT PREFACE(229)	WAY), IS NOT NOW DIRECTLY PROSECUTED; AND THIS	IMPUNITY	EXTENDS TO ILLICIT RELATIONS BETWEEN UNMARRIED
ROCK PREFACE(189)	ITSELF FROM STAGNATION AND PUTREFACTION, DECLARE	IMPUNITY	FOR CRITICISM. THIS MEANS IMPUNITY NOT ONLY FOR
HART PREFACE(12)	SIMPLY THAT A SOLDIER COULD DO WHAT HE LIKED WITH	IMPUNITY	IN CIVIL LIFE, WAS NOT THE LAW OF THE LAND, AND
LION PREFACE(92)	THEN WE CAN BE AS WICKED AS WE LIKE WITH	IMPUNITY	INSIDE THE SECULAR LAW, EVEN FROM SELF-REPROACH,
POSN PREFACE(397)	IN THIS WAY WITH COMPLETE IMPUNITY. BUT THE	IMPUNITY	IS NOT CONFINED TO CONDEMNED THEATRES. NOT LONG AGO
ROCK PREFACE(184)	GOVERNMENT IS CRUEL; FOR NOTHING IS SO CRUEL AS	IMPUNITY	. A SALUTARY SEVERITY-- /JESUS/ OH PLEASE! YOU
GETT PREFACE(229)	AND CRIME, IN ORDER THAT MEN MAY BE VICIOUS WITH	IMPUNITY	. ADULTERY, FOR INSTANCE, THOUGH IT IS SOMETIMES
POSN PREFACE(397)	PERFORMED IN LONDON IN THIS WAY WITH COMPLETE	IMPUNITY	. BUT THE IMPUNITY IS NOT CONFINED TO CONDEMNED
JOAN 4 (95)	YOUR GREATNESS PRIVILEGES YOU TO BE SO WITH	IMPUNITY	. BUT YOUR LORDSHIP KNOWS VERY WELL THAT I AM NOT
MRS PREFACE(162)	IT IS SLIGHTED AS A BLACKGUARD AGITATING FOR	IMPUNITY	. CONSEQUENTLY NOTHING CAN REALLY SHAKE THE
GETT (335)	WHO CAN BULLY THEM CAN INSULT THEIR WIVES WITH	IMPUNITY	. TELL HIM IF YOU DARE. IF I CHOOSE TO TAKE TEN
ROCK PREFACE(189)	DECLARE IMPUNITY FOR CRITICISM. THIS MEANS	IMPUNITY	NOT ONLY FOR PROPOSITIONS WHICH, HOWEVER NOVEL,
MILL IV (199)	THREATEN ME. BLACKMAIL ME. YOU CAN ALL DO IT WITH	IMPUNITY	NOW. /SAGAMORE/ (BEHIND HER CHAIR) DONT TAKE IT
MILL PREFACE(118)	FROM EXPERIENCE THAT THEY MIGHT WITH PERFECT	IMPUNITY	TELL THE NATION ONE THING ON TUESDAY AND THE
BARB PREFACE(241)	WHOSE CONSENT, COUNSEL, OR SILENCE MAY SECURE	IMPUNITY	TO THE PRINCIPAL. IF YOU INSTITUTE PUNISHMENT AS
GENV III (66)	IF OUR RELATIVES COULD BE MURDERED WITH	IMPUNITY	WE SHOULD HAVE PEOPLE SHOOTING THEM ALL OVER THE
METH PREFACE(R64)	IN SHORT, ON " DOING THE OTHER FELLOW DOWN" WITH	IMPUNITY	, ALL INTERFERENCE BY A GUIDING GOVERNMENT, ALL
DOCT PREFACE(8)	WOULD NOT HAVE DIED. AND HE DOES SO NOT ONLY WITH	IMPUNITY	, BUT WITH PUBLIC APPLAUSE, THOUGH THE LOGICAL
HART PREFACE(7)	IT UTTERLY AND SCANDALOUSLY, IF NOT WITH ABSOLUTE	IMPUNITY	, YET WITHOUT ANY EVIL CONSEQUENCES THAT ANYONE
		IMPURITY	
GETT PREFACE(216)	THEY DO MEAN CELIBATE, THEN MARRIAGE IS LEGALIZED	IMPURITY	, A CONCLUSION WHICH IS OFFENSIVE AND INHUMAN.
		IMPUTATION	
LION I (112)	THAT AS THE EMPEROR IS A DIVINE PERSONAGE, HER	IMPUTATION	OF CRUELTY IS NOT ONLY TREASON, BUT SACRILEGE. I
POSN PREFACE(376)	THAT IT MUST BE CLEARED AT ALL COSTS OF THE	IMPUTATION	OF HAVING PROCURED MORE THAN ONE COPY EACH OF MY

IMPUTE
PRES (158) SUCH SUSPICIONS INVITE THE CONDUCT THEY IMPUTE . (SHE RAISES THE PISTOL). YOU NEED NOT BE ALARMED:
SUPR I (27) HELP HER. (TURNING ON TANNER) HOW DARE YOU, SIR, IMPUTE SUCH MONSTROUS INTENTIONS TO ME? I PROTEST AGAINST

IMPUTED
LION PREFACE(79) IN IT AND COME OUT WHITER THAN SNOW, CANNOT BE IMPUTED TO HIM ON HIS OWN AUTHORITY. " I COME AS AN
JOAN 6 (136) MORE ESPECIALLY AS TO THE ACTS AND WORDS THAT ARE IMPUTED TO YOU IN THIS TRIAL BY THE PROMOTER HERE, WILL YOU

IMPUTES
LION PREFACE(27) WOULD BE AS SHEEP AMONG WOLVES. MATTHEW IMPUTES BIGOTRY TO JESUS. MATTHEW, LIKE MOST BIOGRAPHERS,
JOAN 6 (137) SHAKES HIS HEAD PITIFULLY. /D'ESTIVET/ SHE IMPUTES TO THE CHURCH THE ERROR AND FOLLY OF COMMANDING THE

IMPUTING
JOAN 6 (143) THEM, AND STUBBORNLY AND MOST BLASPHEMOUSLY IMPUTING THESE SINS TO ALMIGHTY GOD. I CONFESS TO THE SIN OF

INABILITY
LION PREFACE(99) RULE; FOR IRELAND, THE STANDING INSTANCE OF THE INABILITY OF THE ENGLISH TO COLONIZE WITHOUT EXTERMINATION
3PLA PREFACE(R38) ARE FOUNDED ON A PASSION FOR DEATH BORN OF INABILITY TO BEAR THE WEIGHT OF A LIFE THAT WILL NOT GRANT
MIS. PREFACE(56) OF ANYTHING WORSE THAN STUPIDITY, ILL TEMPER, AND INABILITY TO DISCOVER OTHER METHODS OF MAINTAINING ORDER
HART PREFACE(19) IN DEATH FOR ITS OWN SAKE, WHICH WAS AT BOTTOM AN INABILITY TO REALIZE THAT THE DEATHS WERE REAL DEATHS AND
MIS. PREFACE(91) VIRTUE, AND SANCTITY, WITH SUCH AN APPALLING INABILITY TO RECOGNIZE IT OR LOVE IT WHEN IT ARRIVES THAT IT
CURE (226) YOUR FATUOUS SELF-SATISFACTION, YOUR IMPENETRABLE INABILITY TO SEE ANY REASON WHY YOU SHOULDNT HAVE BOUGHT
MIS. PREFACE(46) OF HIS NOTIONS OF GOVERNMENT, AND HIS SIMPLE INABILITY TO UNDERSTAND WHY HE SHOULD NOT USE AND MAKE LAWS

INACCESSIBILITY
OVER PREFACE(156) THEMSELVES, WHICH IS HARDLY FAIR TO THE PRACTICE. INACCESSIBILITY OF THE FACTS. ALSO, IT IS IMPOSSIBLE TO
PLES PREFACE(R16) TO COMPLAIN OF. I HAVE COME UPON NO ILL WILL, NO INACCESSIBILITY , ON THE PART OF THE VERY FEW MANAGERS WITH

INACCESSIBLE
NEVR I (212) ABOUT IT. (SHE SITS DOWN, PANTING). /DOLLY/ (INACCESSIBLE TO RHETORIC) SEE TWENTIETH CENTURY PARENTS,

INACCURACY
DOCT IV SD(159) CURIOUS PEOPLE, HAS NOTHING BUT HONOR TO LOSE BY INACCURACY AND UNVERACITY), HE HAS PERFORCE BECOME A

INACCURATELY
GETT PREFACE(221) MAY BE FOOLISH; BUT THEY ARE ONLY EXPRESSING INACCURATELY A VERY REAL NEED FOR THE DISENTANGLEMENT OF

INACTIVE
ARMS II (33) IN THE WORLD; WHILST I HAVE HAD TO SIT AT HOME INACTIVE -- DREAMING-- USELESS-- DOING NOTHING THAT COULD

INADEQUACY
METH PREFACE(R37) NOTHING BUT BELIEF IN A NURSERY BOGEY, AND ITS INADEQUACY IS DEMONSTRATED BY A TOY LOGICAL DILEMMA, NEITHER
ROCK PREFACE(161) THE FACT THAT ORDERS ARE MEANT TO BE EXECUTED. INADEQUACY OF PENAL CODES. NOW BEING MINISTER OF TRANSPORT,
METH PREFACE(R11) NEVER PUBLISHED, VARIEGATE THESE PAGES. POLITICAL INADEQUACY OF THE HUMAN ANIMAL. TEN MORE YEARS ELAPSED.
POSN PREFACE(421) CHAMBER WAS CREATED BY HENRY VII: THAT IS, THE INADEQUACY OF THE ORDINARY LAW. " WE CONSIDER," SAYS THE

INADEQUATE
2TRU III (104) MEAN? /TALLBOYS/ IF YOU CONSIDER MY EXPRESSION INADEQUATE I AM WILLING TO AMEND IT. LET US PUT IT THAT I
PPP SD(193) BEAUTY, AND SOCIAL AMBITION, DAMPED BY SOMEWHAT INADEQUATE MEANS. A CERTAIN AIR OF THEATRICALITY IS PRODUCED
LION PREFACE(3) HAVE BEEN ONE OR TWO GROTESQUE ATTEMPTS AT IT BY INADEQUATE PEOPLE, SUCH AS THE KINGDOM OF GOD IN MUNSTER,

INADEQUATELY
LADY PREFACE(208) WHICH HUNG DOWN TO HIS COLLAR BONE, AND WAS VERY INADEQUATELY BALANCED BY A SMALLER ONE ON HIS RIGHT EYELID.
BULL PREFACE(64) I FEAR I HAVE STATED THEIR CASE VERY UNFAIRLY AND INADEQUATELY , BECAUSE I AM HAMPERED, AS AN IRISHMAN, BY MY

INADMISSIBLE
DEVL EPILOG (84) THEIR WAY TO BENNINGTON. ANSWER: THIS ARTICLE IS INADMISSIBLE IN ANY EXTREMITY. SOONER THAN THIS ARMY WILL
LION I (111) AFFAIRS. IN A ROMAN SOLDIER SUCH DEPENDENCE IS INADMISSIBLE . LET ME SEE NO MORE OF IT WHILST WE ARE IN THE
O'FL PREFACE(203) ADAPTED TO ITS PURPOSE WAS VOTED UTTERLY INADMISSIBLE ; AND IN DUE COURSE THE BRITISH GOVERNMENT,
GETT PREFACE(243) DAUGHTERS OF THEIR FRIENDS. THIS BEING MORALLY INADMISSIBLE , A DEMAND ARISES FOR A CHEAP TEMPORARY
METH PREFACE(R73) GROUNDS. FIRST, THAT VITALITY IS SCIENTIFICALLY INADMISSIBLE , BECAUSE IT CANNOT BE ISOLATED AND

INADVERTENTLY
BASH PREFACE(87) QUOTE ME DERISIVELY, HE SHOULD DO SO IN PERIL OF INADVERTENTLY LIGHTING ON A PURPLE PATCH FROM HAMLET OR

INALIENABLE
LION PREFACE(93) DO. EVERY MAN TO WHOM SALVATION IS OFFERED HAS AN INALIENABLE NATURAL RIGHT TO SAY " NO, THANK YOU: I PREFER
GETT PREFACE(249) HIMSELF WHEN HE TRIED TO IMPOSE HIS DOCTRINE OF INALIENABLE PROPERTY ON THE CHURCH UNDER THE GUISE OF
BARB PREFACE(222) TOGETHER, TAKES FROM THAT DIVINE PRESENCE AN INALIENABLE SANCTITY OF WHICH THE GROSSEST AND PROFANEST

INANE
3PLA PREFACE(R9) FOR THREE YEARS; AND THE SOUL OF HIM HAS BECOME INANE AND IS FEEDING UNNATURALLY ON HIS BODY. AND I WAS
DOCT III SD(131) HAND AND A SCYTHE SLUNG ON ITS BACK, SMILES WITH INANE MALICE AT LOUIS, WHO, IN A MILKMAN'S SMOCK MUCH
MIS. PREFACE(35) AS CONVENTIONALLY CONCEIVED, IS A PLACE SO INANE , SO DULL, SO USELESS, SO MISERABLE, THAT NOBODY HAS

INANIMATE
APPL I (206) THAT YOU ARE ANIMATE MATTER AS DISTINGUISHED FROM INANIMATE . /BOANERGES/ (NOT QUITE LIKING THIS) I THINK I'D
PPP SD(205) THROUGH A GHASTLY QUADRILLE, AT LAST SINK INANIMATE ON THE CARPET. /MAGNESIA/ (LISTENING AT THE

INAPPREHENSIBLE
JOAN PREFACE(5) VICTIMS ABSOLUTELY UNREASONABLE, AND THEREFORE INAPPREHENSIBLE BY THEMSELVES. NAPOLEON, ALSO POSSESSED OF

INAPPROPRIATE
SUPR PREFACE(R33) WITHOUT, AND THE EXTERNAL FORCE IS GROTESQUELY INAPPROPRIATE EXCEPT WHEN IT IS QUITE CONVENTIONAL, AS IN

INAPT
PYGM I (209) WHATS A COPPER'S NARK? /THE BYSTANDER/ (INAPT AT DEFINITION) IT'S A-- WELL, IT'S A COPPER'S NARK, AS

INAPTITUDE
LION PREFACE(99) OF THEIR HISTORY, IS REALLY ONLY AN INCURABLE INAPTITUDE FOR THEOLOGY, AND INDEED FOR CO-ORDINATED THOUGHT
JOAN PREFACE(20) MILITARY SERVICE IS FOUNDED, NOT ON ANY NATURAL INAPTITUDE THAT MEN DO NOT SHARE, BUT ON THE FACT THAT

INARTICULATE
SUPR PREFACE(R17) TO PECKSNIFF, YET IF YOU SEPARATE THE REAL HERO, INARTICULATE AND UNINTELLIGIBLE TO HIMSELF EXCEPT IN FLASHES
PHIL I (83) ANY SORT OF SENSE OR CHARACTER? (SHE GIVES AN INARTICULATE CRY, AND THROWS HERSELF SOBBING ON HIS BREAST).
WIDO II (38) I SHALL FIND YOU ALONE WHEN I COME BACK. (AN INARTICULATE EXCLAMATION BURSTS FROM TRENCH. SHE GOES OUT,
ROCK II SD(264) IS CHOKING WITH INDIGNATION, AND FOR THE MOMENT INARTICULATE . /SIR BEMROSE/ THIS IS AWFUL. WE CANNOT DO
MIS. (112) LAUGH) TRY IT, MY SON. (BENTLEY GIVES AN INARTICULATE SOB OF RAGE), FIGHTING ISNT IN YOUR LINE. YOURE
NEVR I SD(224) WELL DOWN ON THE CHAIR. CRAMPTON MAKES AN INARTICULATE SOUND IN THE MOUTHPIECE AND TRIES TO LAY HANDS
MIS. (187) IN YOUR PIPE AND SMOKE IT, MY BOY. /BENTLEY/ (INARTICULATE WITH FURY AND SUPPRESSED TEARS) OH! BEASTS!
NEVR II (244) IT. I CALL ALL OF YOU TO WITNESS-- (HE BECOMES INARTICULATE , AND IS ABOUT TO STRIKE HIS FIST RECKLESSLY ON

INARTICULATELY
ARMS I (21) YOU ARE NOT GOING ASLEEP, ARE YOU? (HE MURMURS INARTICULATELY : SHE RUNS TO HIM AND SHAKES HIM). DO YOU

INARTISTIC

MTH5 (255) THE ANCIENTS BEING INARTISTIC. THEY ARE DAMNABLY INARTISTIC . /ECRASIA/ (TRIUMPHANT) AH! OUR GREATEST
MTH5 (255) AND ECRASIA IS RIGHT ABOUT THE ANCIENTS BEING INARTISTIC . THEY ARE DAMNABLY INARTISTIC. /ECRASIA/ (
DOCT III (142) IT: YOU CHAPS DID. IT'S ALWAYS THE WAY WITH THE INARTISTIC PROFESSIONS: WHEN THEYRE BEATEN IN ARGUMENT THEY

INASMUCH

POSN PREFACE(413) IS AN ENTIRELY DIFFERENT MATTER FROM CENSORSHIP, INASMUCH AS A THEATRE, BEING NOT ONLY A STAGE, BUT A PLACE
HART PREFACE(8) PREDESTINATION IS THE CENTRAL TRUTH OF RELIGION, INASMUCH AS HUMAN BEINGS ARE PRODUCED BY THEIR ENVIRONMENT,

INATTENTION

DOCT I SD(96) AND ITS AUDIENCE, AND MAKES INTERRUPTION OR INATTENTION IMPOSSIBLE, AND IMPOSES VENERATION AND CREDULITY

INATTENTIVE

BASH II,1, (107) NO WORK FOR YOU. /CASHEL/ THOU DOST ARRAIGN THE INATTENTIVE FATES THAT WEAVE MY THREAD OF LIFE IN RUDER

INAUDIBLE

CAPT NOTES (306) QUIET AT ALL TIMES, AND SO COMPLETELY INAUDIBLE IN WH, THAT IT PROBABLY FELL OUT OF USE SIMPLY BY

INAUDIBLY

BARB I (251) SUPPOSE YOU MEAN YOUR FATHER. /STEPHEN/ (ALMOST INAUDIBLY) YES. /LADY BRITOMART/ MY DEAR: WE CANT GO ON ALL

INAUGURATE

METH PREFACE(R24) SELECTION, YOU NOT ONLY STOP DEVELOPMENT BUT INAUGURATE A RAPID AND DISASTROUS DEGENERATION. LET US FIX
BARB III (340) WHEN YOU SHOOT, YOU PULL DOWN GOVERNMENTS, INAUGURATE NEW EPOCHS, ABOLISH OLD ORDERS AND SET UP NEW. IS

INAUGURATED

GETT PREFACE(190) THEM FROM THE LAWS OF HEALTH AND TEMPERANCE; INAUGURATED A LIFE-LONG HONEYMOON; AND PLACED THEIR
BARB II (306) IN AN ECSTASY OF MISCHIEF) THE MILLENNIUM WILL BE INAUGURATED BY THE UNSELFISHNESS OF UNDERSHAFT AND BODGER.
GENV PREFACE(14) SHOULD BE NO MILITARY CONTROLS AND A NEW WORLD INAUGURATED IN WHICH EVERYBODY WAS TO BE BOTH EMPLOYED AND
3PLA PREFACE(R32) NOR IN THE EPOCH, NOW FAST WANING, WHICH HE INAUGURATED . IT COST SHAKESPEAR NO PANG TO WRITE CAESAR
FANY III (323) IF THAT CONQUEST OF EUROPE BY FRANCE WHICH INAUGURATED THE NEW AGE AFTER THE REVOLUTION HAD ONLY BEEN
SUPR PREFACE(R28) DECADENT PHASE OF PANEM ET CIRCENSES IS BEING INAUGURATED UNDER OUR EYES. OUR NEWSPAPERS AND MELODRAMAS
GETT PREFACE(249) SO HOLY INDEED THAT IT COULD NOT BE VALIDLY INAUGURATED WITHOUT THE BLESSING OF THE CHURCH. AND BY THIS
ROCK PREFACE(175) IT. THE CASE OF GALILEO IN THE EPOCH WHICH JESUS INAUGURATED , OR AT LEAST IN WHICH HIS NAME WAS HABITUALLY

INAUGURATING

GENV PREFACE(7) BATTLE OF HASTINGS DID NOT KNOW THAT THEY WERE INAUGURATING FEUDALISM FOR FOUR CENTURIES, NOR THE RED ROSES

INAUGURATION

GETT PREFACE(221) STATE OF MATRIMONY": IT IS AS OFTEN AS NOT THE INAUGURATION OF A LIFELONG SQUABBLE, A CORRODING GRUDGE,

INBORN

FABL PREFACE(88) DOING SET SUMS IN ALGEBRA BY RULE OF THUMB ABOVE INBORN MATHEMATICAL COMPREHENSION BY STATESMEN WHO CANNOT
METH PREFACE(R28) CONDENSED INTO AN INSTINCTIVE AND UNCONSCIOUS INBORN ONE, FACTORS WHICH FORMERLY HAD TO BE CONSIDERED ONE
FABL PREFACE(68) SO FAR ARE UNGOVERNABLE BY ABSTRACT THOUGHT. OUR INBORN SENSE OF RIGHT AND WRONG, OF GRACE AND SIN, MUST BE

INBRED

MILL PREFACE(125) AND CHINESE LAUNDRYMEN ARE FAR SUPERIOR TO INBRED IRISH OR CHINESE. HERR HITLER IS NOT A TYPICAL

INBREEDING

SUPR PREFACE(R27) VOTERS TO BE FOUND TODAY? NOWHERE. PLUTOCRATIC INBREEDING HAS PRODUCED A WEAKNESS OF CHARACTER THAT IS TOO
MILL PREFACE(126) ALIKE, AND THAT THEY IMPROVE BY CONTINUOUS INBREEDING . NOW HERR HITLER IS NOT A STUPID GERMAN. I

INCA

INCA (251) MILLIONS OF HEROES. HAS IT PRODUCED MORE THAN ONE INCA ? (HE RESUMES HIS SEAT). /ERMYNTRUDE/ FORTUNATELY
INCA (247) IS THE TRUTH, DOES ITS RECOGNITION CONSTITUTE THE INCA A COXCOMB? OTHER POTENTATES HAVE MOUSTACHES: EVEN
INCA (249) CANNONS. THE WORLD WILL ONE DAY DO JUSTICE TO THE INCA AS THE MAN WHO KEPT THE PEACE WITH NOTHING BUT HIS
INCA (253) A MERE PRESIDENT! /THE INCA/ WELL, WHY NOT! AN INCA CAN DO NOTHING. HE IS TIED HAND AND FOOT. A
INCA (248) SURROUND THE LION, THE LION WILL SPRING. THE INCA HAD KEPT THE PEACE FOR YEARS. THOSE WHO ATTACKED HIM
INCA (248) BLOOD, BROWN BLOOD, YELLOW BLOOD, BLUE BLOOD. THE INCA HAD NEVER SHED A DROP. /ERMYNTRUDE/ HE HAD ONLY TALKED.
INCA (252) PERUSALEM, WHERE EVERY FOOL IS A SOLDIER. BUT THE INCA HAS A THOUSAND OTHER RESOURCES. HE IS AN ARCHITECT.
INCA (251) TURN HIM LOOSE IN PASTURE AND HE IS LOST. THE INCA HAS DEFEATED ALL THESE GENERALS AGAIN AND AGAIN AT
INCA (243) ENEMY EVERYWHERE EXCEPT IN PERUSALEM, BECAUSE THE INCA HAS MADE WAR ON EVERYBODY. AND I SHALL HAVE TO PRETEND
INCA (249) MANNER) BUT YOU WILL PLEASE UNDERSTAND THAT THE INCA HAS NO DESIRE TO PIN YOU TO ANY PARTICULAR SON. THERE
INCA (246) CARE, MADAM! THIS BROOCH WAS DESIGNED BY THE INCA HIMSELF. ALLOW ME TO EXPLAIN THE DESIGN. IN THE CENTRE,
INCA (250) AFTER A TIME. I SUGGEST THAT YOU MIGHT PREFER THE INCA HIMSELF. /ERMYNTRUDE/ OH, CAPTAIN, HOW COULD A HUMBLE
INCA (243) DUVAL! NONSENSE! THE USUAL THING. IT IS THE INCA HIMSELF, INCOGNITO. /THE PRINCESS/ OH, SEND HIM AWAY.
INCA (254) I AM NO CAPTAIN. I -- /ERMYNTRUDE/ YOU ARE THE INCA IN DISGUISE. /THE INCA/ GOOD HEAVENS! HOW DO YOU KNOW
INCA (252) INCA/ PRECISELY. THAT IS WHAT PROVES THAT THE INCA IS A MAN OF GENIUS. HIS RELATIVES ARE DUFFERS.
INCA (253) INDIA-RUBBER STAMP. AN EMPEROR IS A PUPPET. THE INCA IS NOT ALLOWED TO MAKE A SPEECH: HE IS COMPELLED TO
INCA (246) SULKILY). THE POSITION OF DAUGHTER-IN-LAW TO THE INCA IS NOT COMPATIBLE WITH THE TASTES OF A PIG. (HE
INCA (252) /THE INCA/ (TRIUMPHANTLY) THAT IS JUST WHAT THE INCA IS PLAYING FOR, MADAM. IT IS WHY HE CONSENTED TO THE
INCA (243) THEY JUST MARRY YOU TO ANYONE THEY LIKE. THE INCA IS TO COME AND LOOK AT ME, AND PICK OUT WHICHEVER OF
INCA (248) MY HEAD. I SHOULD GO MAD. ARE YOU QUITE SURE THE INCA ISNT MAD? /THE INCA/ HOW CAN HE BE MAD, MADAM? WHAT
INCA (232) HULSE AS THE ARCHDEACON, AND RANDLE AYRTON AS THE INCA .
INCA (252) UNCLE WOULD HAVE BEEN AS GREAT A MAN AS THE INCA . AND -- WELL, EVERYBODY KNOWS WHAT THE INCA'S UNCLE
INCA (243) OH, SEND HIM AWAY. OH, I'M SO AFRAID OF THE INCA . I'M NOT PROPERLY DRESSED TO RECEIVE HIM; AND HE IS SO
INCA (246) ALONE. YOU PRESENTED IT TO ME ON BEHALF OF THE INCA . IT IS MINE. YOU SAID MY APPEARANCE WAS SATISFACTORY.
INCA (248) THE CONDITION OF THE PEOPLE WHO DISAGREE WITH THE INCA . /ERMYNTRUDE/ THEN I AM A LUNATIC BECAUSE I DONT LIKE
INCA (253) BE A REPUBLIC. /ERMYNTRUDE/ THEN GOODBYE TO THE INCA . /THE INCA/ ON THE CONTRARY, MADAM, THE INCA WILL THEN
INCA SD(244) JEWEL CASE IN HIS HAND, RETURNS, USHERING IN THE INCA . /THE MANAGER/ CAPTAIN DUVAL. THE INCA, IN MILITARY
INCA (248) EXPECTED THAT YOU SHOULD SEE EYE TO EYE WITH THE INCA . THAT WOULD BE PRESUMPTION. IT IS FOR YOU TO ACCEPT
INCA (245) HA! /ERMYNTRUDE/ (FRIGIDLY) I ASKED COULD THE INCA LAUGH. I DID NOT ASK COULD YOU LAUGH. /THE INCA/ THAT
INCA (246) /THE INCA/ IMPOSSIBLE, MADAM. A DESIGN BY THE INCA MUST NOT BE EXHIBITED FOR SALE IN THE SHOP WINDOW OF A
INCA (229) THE INCA OF PERUSALEM: AN ALMOST HISTORICAL COMEDIETTA.
INCA (232) THE INCA OF PERUSALEM WAS PERFORMED FOR THE FIRST TIME IN
INCA (243) AN OFFICER ASKS TO SEE YOU ON BEHALF OF THE INCA OF PERUSALEM. /THE PRINCESS/ (RISING DISTRACTEDLY) OH,
INCA (242) A BOY WHO NEVER SAW ME! ONE OF THE SONS OF THE INCA OF PERUSALEM. /ERMYNTRUDE/ INDEED? WHICH SON? /THE
INCA (245) BUSINESS? /THE INCA/ I COME ON BEHALF OF THE INCA OF PERUSALEM. /ERMYNTRUDE/ THE ALLERHOCHST? /THE INCA/
INCA (247) I MARRY THE INCA'S SON, CAPTAIN, I SHALL MAKE THE INCA ORDER YOU TO CUT OFF THAT MOUSTACHE. IT IS TOO
INCA (252) /THE INCA/ AHA! THE FOOLS TALK OF CRUSHING THE INCA ; BUT THEY LITTLE KNOW THEIR MAN. TELL ME THIS. WHY DID
INCA (248) WITHOUT QUESTION OR DEMUR THE ASSURANCE OF YOUR INCA THAT THE BROOCH IS A MASTERPIECE. /ERMYNTRUDE/ MY
INCA (246) OMINOUSLY) I AM SORRY TO HAVE TO REPORT TO THE INCA THAT YOU HAVE NO SOUL FOR FINE ART. (HE RISES
INCA (252) LEFT NO SYMPHONIES IN ST HELENA. SEND THE INCA TO ST HELENA, MADAM, AND THE WORLD WILL CROWD THITHER
INCA (250) CAN YOU NAME A SINGLE MAN IN THE ENTOURAGE OF THE INCA WHO IS NOT A BORN FOOL? /ERMYNTRUDE/ OH, HOW CAN YOU
INCA (252) A REPUBLIC, LIKE FRANCE AFTER 1871, AND THE INCA WILL BE SENT TO ST HELENA. /THE INCA/ (TRIUMPHANTLY)
INCA (246) FUMING). /ERMYNTRUDE/ SO MUCH THE BETTER. THE INCA WILL HAVE TO REDEEM IT TO SAVE HIMSELF FROM THAT
INCA (253) THE INCA. /THE INCA/ ON THE CONTRARY, MADAM, THE INCA WILL THEN HAVE HIS FIRST REAL CHANCE. HE WILL BE
INCA (247) INCA/ YOUR APPEARANCE IS NOT SATISFACTORY. THE INCA WOULD NOT ALLOW HIS SON TO MARRY YOU IF THE BOY WERE ON
INCA (248) MY INCA! OH, COME! I LIKE THAT. HE IS NOT MY INCA YET. /THE INCA/ HE IS EVERYBODY'S INCA, MADAM. HIS
INCA PREFACE(231) QUITE WELL HAVE AFFORDED TO LAUGH AT THE DOOMED INCA , I AM IN ANOTHER DIFFICULTY. I MAY BE SUPPOSED TO BE
INCA SD(244) IN THE INCA. /THE MANAGER/ CAPTAIN DUVAL. THE INCA , IN MILITARY UNIFORM, ADVANCES WITH A MARKED AND
INCA (248) IS NOT MY INCA YET. /THE INCA/ HE IS EVERYBODY'S INCA , MADAM. HIS REALM WILL YET EXTEND TO THE CONFINES OF
INCA (253) A COME DOWN FOR HIM? THINK OF IT! AFTER BEING INCA , TO BE A MERE PRESIDENT! /THE INCA/ WELL, WHY NOT!
INCA (248) THAT THE BROOCH IS A MASTERPIECE. /ERMYNTRUDE/ MY INCA ! OH, COME! I LIKE THAT. HE IS NOT MY INCA YET. /THE

		INCADISPARAGEMENT	
INCA (245)	SEVERELY PUNISHABLE! -- IN PERUSALEM. IT IS CALLED	INCADISPARAGEMENT	. /ERMYNTRUDE/ HOW CHEERFUL! CAN HE
INCA (251)	/ERMYNTRUDE/ (SHOCKED) OH, CAPTAIN! TAKE CARE!	INCADISPARAGEMENT	. /THE INCA/ I REPEAT, GROSSLY OVERRATED.
		INCALCULABLE	
2TRU III (88)	ALL IS CAPRICE: THE CALCULABLE WORLD HAS BECOME	INCALCULABLE	: PURPOSE AND DESIGN, THE PRETEXTS FOR ALL THE
BARB PREFACE(217)	THE IMMEDIATE RESULT WOULD BE A REVOLUTION OF	INCALCULABLE	BENEFICENCE. TO BE WEALTHY, SAYS UNDERSHAFT, IS
LION PREFACE(4)	RESPONSIBILITIES, HE WOULD HAVE CONFERRED AN	INCALCULABLE	BENEFIT ON MANKIND, BECAUSE THESE DISTINCTIVE
LION PREFACE(49)	ITS PEDESTAL, THE STORY BECOME REAL, WITH ALL THE	INCALCULABLE	CONSEQUENCES THAT MAY FLOW FROM THIS TERRIFYING
MIS. PREFACE(89)	OF IGNORANCE WITH DESPAIRING ENDURANCE IS	INCALCULABLE	. GIVEN A PUBLIC TRAINED FROM CHILDHOOD TO
MIS. PREFACE(105)	ROMANTIC IMAGINATION; AND THE MISCHIEF IT DOES IS	INCALCULABLE	. IT BEGINS IN SILLY AND SELFISH EXPECTATIONS
APPL PREFACE(195)	WHAT WE HAVE LOST BY NOT LETTING HIM DO IT IS	INCALCULABLE	. SIMILARLY, GATTIE WAS NOT CONTENT TO IMPROVE
JITT PREFACE(4)	IS FOR ME TO SAY THAT MY PERSONAL DEBT TO HIM IS	INCALCULABLE	. WHEN THE HORRIBLE CATASTROPHE OF THE WAR HAD
SUPR HANDBOK(223)	COUNT FURTHER THAN HIS TEN FINGERS IT IS AN	INCALCULABLE	MYRIAD. THE DIFFERENCE BETWEEN THE SHALLOWEST
SUPR III (81)	HER HIGHLY STRUNG TEMPERAMENT MADE HER UNCERTAIN,	INCALCULABLE	, VARIABLE, CAPRICIOUS, CRUEL, IN A WORD,
		INCANDESCENT	
PHIL I SD(69)	PIECE OF MUSIC ON THE DESK IS WHEN OTHER LIPS.	INCANDESCENT	LIGHTS, WELL SHADED, ARE ON THE PIANO AND
		INCANTATION	
DOCT PREFACE(72)	SAVE MONEY AT THEIR EXPENSE. SO YOU PERFORM THE	INCANTATION	; AND BACK THEY GO TO THEIR HOUSES, SATISFIED. A
		INCANTATIONS	
DOCT PREFACE(71)	I HAVE MYSELF BEEN RESPONSIBLE FOR RIDICULOUS	INCANTATIONS	WITH BURNING SULPHUR, EXPERIMENTALLY PROVED TO
SUPR HANDBOK(204)	PUBLIC HEALTH AUTHORITIES DELIBERATELY GO THROUGH	INCANTATIONS	WITH BURNING SULPHUR (WHICH THEY KNOW TO BE
		INCAPABLE	
BULL PREFACE(19)	THE NORMAL BRITISH OFFICER OF THAT TIME WAS AN	INCAPABLE	AMATEUR (AS HE STILL IS) AND THE NORMAL BRITISH
DOCT PREFACE(35)	RIGHT: IT ONLY PROVED THAT THE CHINAMAN WAS AN	INCAPABLE	COOK AND, FUNDAMENTALLY, A FOOL. TAKE ANOTHER
SUPR HANDBOK(226)	AGE OR CONDITION IS WITHOUT ITS HEROES. THE LEAST	INCAPABLE	GENERAL IN A NATION IS ITS CAESAR, THE LEAST
MRS PREFACE(163)	HAVE DESCRIBED, AND WHICH HE LICENSED, WAS QUITE	INCAPABLE	IN MANUSCRIPT OF PRODUCING ANY PARTICULAR EFFECT
MTH3 (97)	IS AN ART OF WHICH YOU ARE CONGENITALLY	INCAPABLE	, ACCORDINGLY, YOU IMPORTED EDUCATED NEGRESSES AND
BULL PREFACE(46)	POLITICALLY REACTIONARY, AND PROFESSIONALLY	INCAPABLE	, IF IT WERE HUMANLY POSSIBLE TO MILITARIZE ALL
SUPR HANDBOK(177)	NOT HELP THEMSELVES, THE GOD OF THE LAZY AND	INCAPABLE	. THE NINETEENTH CENTURY DECIDED THAT THERE IS
HART PREFACE(22)	POSSESS, AND A COMPREHENSION OF WHICH THEY WERE	INCAPABLE	. WHEN THE ARMISTICE AT LAST SET ME FREE TO TELL
SUPR HANDBOK(228)	ITSELF, AND THE UNEXPECTED ALWAYS HAPPENS, HOW	INCAPABLE	MUST MAN BE OF LEARNING FROM EXPERIENCE!
SUPR I (13)	AGAINST JACK. HE IS A MAN OF HONOR, AND	INCAPABLE	OF ABUSING-- /TANNER/ DONT, TAVY: YOULL MAKE ME
BUOY IV (54)	/SIR FERDINAND/ MY REASON IS THAT I AM TOTALLY	INCAPABLE	OF ADVISING YOU ON THE SUBJECT OF YOUR
OVER PREFACE(162)	OR AMUSING STORIES SUITED TO PEOPLE WHO ARE	INCAPABLE	OF ANY INTEREST IN PSYCHOLOGY, BUT THE FINE ARTIST
MIS. (174)	SUDDENLY BREAKING OUT AGGRESSIVELY, BEING	INCAPABLE	OF ANY MIDDLE WAY BETWEEN SUBMISSIVENESS AND
ARMS III (51)	ON HIM) IF YOU ARE INCAPABLE OF GRATITUDE YOU ARE	INCAPABLE	OF ANY NOBLE SENTIMENT. EVEN ANIMALS ARE GRATEFUL.
SIM PREFACE(4)	I WRITE PREFACES, MY NEWSPAPER CRITICS MAY SEEM	INCAPABLE	OF ANYTHING BETTER THAN THE TRASH THEY WRITE; BUT
2TRU III (83)	THERE IS THAT SIDE TO IT, AND THAT FOR PEOPLE	INCAPABLE	OF ANYTHING BETTER-- MERE ANIMALS AS YOU MIGHT
DOCT PREFACE(12)	FASHIONABLE OPERATIONS A SPRINKLING OF PERSONS SO	INCAPABLE	OF APPRECIATING THE RELATIVE IMPORTANCE OF
DOCT V (179)	SHAKE ME. YOU ARE SO UTTERLY, SO WILDLY WRONG; SO	INCAPABLE	OF APPRECIATING LOUIS-- /RIDGEON/ OH! (TAKING UP
SUPR II (59)	IN THAT ABOMINABLE WAY? /ANN/ I KNOW YOU ARE	INCAPABLE	OF BEHAVING BADLY-- /TANNER/ THEN WHY DID YOU LIE
MTH4 I (170)	TO CONCEAL FROM YOURSELVES THE TRUTH THAT YOU ARE	INCAPABLE	OF BEING HELPED BY US. YOUR PRIME MINISTER
DOCT III (153)	HERE IN THIS ROOM JUST BEFORE YOU CAME; AND HE IS	INCAPABLE	OF BREAKING HIS WORD. THAT WAS HIS ONLY REAL
BULL PREFACE(47)	AND IMPOSSIBLE, AND RENDERS ITS VICTIMS SO	INCAPABLE	OF CARRYING IT OUT WITH ANY THOROUGHNESS EXCEPT
APPL PREFACE(192)	WHICH IT SHOULD BE REPEATED. I WAS BY THAT TIME	INCAPABLE	OF CHOOSING; SO I SAID THE SOONER THE BETTER; AND
GETT PREFACE(191)	WERE A BLACK-COATED ARMY OF CALAMITY. THEY WERE	INCAPABLE	OF COMPREHENDING THE INDUSTRIES THEY WERE ENGAGED
BULL PREFACE(39)	THAT IS WHY IT IS ONLY THE SMALL-MINDED IRISH,	INCAPABLE	OF CONCEIVING WHAT RELIGIOUS FREEDOM MEANS TO A
MILL PREFACE(114)	ALWAYS DOES WHAT WAS DONE LAST TIME BECAUSE HE IS	INCAPABLE	OF CONCEIVING ANYTHING BETTER, MAKES THE BEST
DEST SD(151)	HOWEVER, LIKES MIRACLES AND HEROES, AND IS QUITE	INCAPABLE	OF CONCEIVING THE ACTION OF SUCH FORCES AS
LADY PREFACE(234)	CONTEMPORARIES WITHOUT PERCEIVING THAT THEY WERE	INCAPABLE	OF DEALING WITH THE PROBLEMS RAISED BY THEIR OWN
DOCT IV SD(159)	BY A CONGENITAL ERRONEOUSNESS WHICH RENDERS HIM	INCAPABLE	OF DESCRIBING ACCURATELY ANYTHING HE HEARS. AS THE
APPL II (268)	ABOUT THAT. WHEN AN HONEST MAN FINDS HIMSELF	INCAPABLE	OF DISCHARGING THE DUTIES OF A PUBLIC POST, HE
GETT PREFACE(218)	ONE ANOTHER; BUT THESE LAST ARE PEOPLE WHO ARE	INCAPABLE	OF DISLIKING ANYBODY. IF THEY DO NOT QUARREL, IT
APPL PREFACE(187)	BOY WHO READS THE ADDRESSES FOR HIM MAY BE QUITE	INCAPABLE	OF DOING ANYTHING MORE. BUT THIS DOES NOT ALWAYS
MIS. (181)	NOW? /PERCIVAL/ OF COURSE. (GUNNER, WHO IS NOW	INCAPABLE	OF DOING ANYTHING ON HIS OWN INITIATIVE, SIGNS).
NEVR I (202)	A LOT OF QUESTIONS? /THE YOUNG LADY/ (AS IF	INCAPABLE	OF DOING SUCH A THING) OH NO. /PHILIP/ GLAD TO
DOCT PREFACE(43)	CRUEL, NOR PARTICULARLY GENEROUS, BUT SIMPLY	INCAPABLE	OF ETHICAL JUDGMENT OR INDEPENDENT ACTION. JUST SO
MTH5 (227)	IS UNFORTUNATE THAT PYGMALION IS CONSTITUTIONALLY	INCAPABLE	OF EXHIBITING ANYTHING WITHOUT FIRST GIVING A
ARMS III (51)	INDIGNANT PROTEST) AND SO HE BECOMES A CREATURE	INCAPABLE	OF FAITH AND OF GRATITUDE. /BLUNTSCHLI/ (MAKING A
SIM II (66)	FEEL THAT IT'S RIGHT. /PROLA/ AND IF THEY ARE	INCAPABLE	OF FEELING IT? /JANGA/ KILL. /KANCHIN/ KILL.
DEST (176)	THAT SILLY WOMEN LIE ABOUT: KNOWS THAT SHE IS	INCAPABLE	OF FIDELITY TO ANY PRINCIPLE OR ANY PERSON; AND
PYGM EPILOG (301)	TO WRITE. HE DECLARED THAT SHE WAS CONGENITALLY	INCAPABLE	OF FORMING A SINGLE LETTER WORTHY OF THE LEAST OF
MTH2 (72)	THE INK DRIED ON IT. THE STATESMEN OF EUROPE WERE	INCAPABLE	OF GOVERNING EUROPE. WHAT THEY NEEDED WAS A COUPLE
ARMS III (51)	/RAINA/ GRATITUDE! (TURNING ON HIM) IF YOU ARE	INCAPABLE	OF GRATITUDE YOU ARE INCAPABLE OF ANY NOBLE
GETT (331)	HAPPY WHEN SHE FINDS YOU OUT? /HOTCHKISS/ SHE'S	INCAPABLE	OF HAPPINESS. BUT SHE'S NOT INCAPABLE OF THE
BULL PREFACE(18)	ALWAYS REMAIN CONSTITUTIONALLY AND CONGENITALLY	INCAPABLE	OF HAVING, THE FAINTEST INKLING OF THE REALITY
MTH4 III (202)	PEOPLE TO WHOM NOTHING IS REAL. I HAVE BECOME	INCAPABLE	OF IT THROUGH MY STAY HERE. I IMPLORE TO BE
GENV II (55)	IN FIRST-RATE STYLE. THE WOMAN HERSELF IS QUITE	INCAPABLE	OF IT. THERE MUST BE SOMEBODY BEHIND HER. CAN IT
METH PREFACE(R49)	ANY VISIBLE EFFECT ON PUBLIC OPINION, I MUST BE	INCAPABLE	OF LEARNING FROM EXPERIENCE, AND AM THEREFORE A
PRES (168)	TO THE ARMY HE AND CHUBBS-JENKINSON WILL BE FOUND	INCAPABLE	OF MAINTAINING DISCIPLINE. THEY WILL BE SACKED AND
MIS. PREFACE(19)	UNDERSTAND AND DONT CARE ABOUT, AND ARE THEREFORE	INCAPABLE	OF MAKING YOU UNDERSTAND OR CARE ABOUT. IN A
JOAN PREFACE(55)	NOTICE OF IT THAN EINSTEIN OF THE PEOPLE WHO ARE	INCAPABLE	OF MATHEMATICS. I WRITE IN THE CLASSICAL MANNER
LION PREFACE(83)	OF THE PEOPLE WHO, BEING INTELLIGENT ENOUGH TO BE	INCAPABLE	OF MERE DULL SELF-RIGHTEOUSNESS, AND HIGHLY
METH PREFACE(R75)	MECHANICAL OR CHEMICAL FACTS THAT WE HAVE BECOME	INCAPABLE	OF METAPHYSICAL TRUTH, AND TRY TO CAST OUT
MTH5 (226)	LOST YOUR ARTISTIC SENSES. THE MAN IS UTTERLY	INCAPABLE	OF MODELLING A THUMB NAIL, LET ALONE A HUMAN
DEST SD(162)	OVER HER BODY. EVEN THE LIEUTENANT, ORDINARILY	INCAPABLE	OF OBSERVATION, CAN SEE A THING WHEN IT IS PAINTED
METH PREFACE(R12)	ARE THE ARDENT INSTRUMENTS. BUT IF MAN IS REALLY	INCAPABLE	OF ORGANIZING A BIG CIVILIZATION, AND CANNOT
POSN PREFACE(381)	CONDUCT ON THE GREAT MASS OF PERSONS WHO ARE	INCAPABLE	OF ORIGINAL ETHICAL JUDGMENT, AND WHO WOULD BE
LION PREFACE(8)	FOUND TO BE OBSESSED BY A DELUSION; DECLARED	INCAPABLE	OF PLEADING; AND SENT TO AN ASYLUM: THAT IS THE
DEVL EPILOG (80)	OF THE FACT THAT MANKIND, BEING FOR THE MOST PART	INCAPABLE	OF POLITICS, ACCEPTS VITUPERATION AS AN EASY AND
DOCT PREFACE(39)	IS IDLE FOR THE VIVISECTOR TO PRETEND THAT HE IS	INCAPABLE	OF PRACTISING CRUELTY FOR PLEASURE OR PROFIT OR
FABL PREFACE(96)	THE DAY FOR THEMSELVES AND THEIR FAMILIES, ARE SO	INCAPABLE	OF PUTTING TWO AND TWO TOGETHER POLITICALLY THAT
6CAL (101)	/THE QUEEN/ OH, YOU MISTAKE, SIR: THE KING IS	INCAPABLE	OF REVENGE: MY HUSBAND IS THE FLOWER OF CHIVALRY.
LION PREFACE(76)	FASCINATION WITHOUT UNDERSTANDING IT, AND BEING	INCAPABLE	OF RISING TO IT, DRAGS IT DOWN TO ITS LEVEL BY
ARMS III (67)	WAS IT TRUE? /NICOLA/ I AM SURE MISS RAINA IS	INCAPABLE	OF SAYING ANYTHING THAT IS NOT TRUE, SIR.
JOAN 5 (114)	EVERYONE ELSE. /JOAN/ (DISTRESSED, BUT NAIVELY	INCAPABLE	OF SEEING THE EFFECT SHE IS PRODUCING) BUT I DO
METH PREFACE(R40)	BY THOMAS AQUINAS OR EVEN ROGER BACON, WAS	INCAPABLE	OF SO CONVENIENT AN ARRANGEMENT; AND SCIENCE WAS
MIS. PREFACE(28)	IN IGNORANCE AND ERROR, SO THAT THEY MAY BE	INCAPABLE	OF SUCCESSFUL REVOLT AGAINST THEIR INDUSTRIAL
APPL II (268)	TO BE A CONSTITUTIONAL MONARCH. I AM BY NATURE	INCAPABLE	OF THE NECESSARY SELF-EFFACEMENT. /AMANDA/ WELL,
FANY EPILOG (332)	REPEATEDLY PROVED THAT SHAW IS PHYSIOLOGICALLY	INCAPABLE	OF THE NOTE OF PASSION. /BANNAL/ YES, I KNOW.
GETT (331)	SHE'S INCAPABLE OF HAPPINESS. BUT SHE'S NOT	INCAPABLE	OF THE PLEASURE OF HOLDING A MAN AGAINST HIS WILL.
MTH4 I (157)	TO THE BLOCKHEADS AND THE MUCKRAKERS WHO ARE	INCAPABLE	OF THEIR OWN GLORIOUS DESTINY, AND UNCONSCIOUS OF
DEST SD(149)	OR ANY OF THE COMMON IDEALS. NOT THAT HE IS	INCAPABLE	OF THESE IDEALS: ON THE CONTRARY, HE HAS SWALLOWED
PYGM EPILOG (291)	BY PARENTAL FASCINATION. NOW, THOUGH ELIZA WAS	INCAPABLE	OF THUS EXPLAINING TO HERSELF HIGGINS'S FORMIDABLE
3PLA PREFACE(R12)	BY THE VERY WISEACRES AFOREMENTIONED, WHO, QUITE	INCAPABLE	OF UNDERSTANDING THE LESSON, WOULD THEREUPON SET
MIS. PREFACE(30)	CAN JUSTIFY SUCH A RISK. THERE MAY BE PEOPLE	INCAPABLE	OF UNDERSTANDING THAT THE RIGHT TO KNOW ALL THERE
PYGM II (228)	WHAT SHE'S DOING. /HIGGINS/ HOW CAN SHE? SHE'S	INCAPABLE	OF UNDERSTANDING ANYTHING. BESIDES, DO ANY OF US
GETT (271)	THAT IS WHAT AN ENGLISH GENTLEMAN SEEMS	INCAPABLE	OF UNDERSTANDING. (SHE SITS DOWN AT THE END OF
SIM II (71)	ENGLAND. /THE ANGEL/ I AM AFRAID MOST OF THEM ARE	INCAPABLE	OF UNDERSTANDING THE WAYS OF HEAVEN. THEY GO
PHIL II (98)	WILL KNOW HOW I LOVED THAT WOMAN. BUT SHE WAS	INCAPABLE	OF VALUING A TRUE MAN'S AFFECTION. DO YOU KNOW,
LION PREFACE(71)	PRACTISE VIRTUES THAT UNATTACHED INDIVIDUALS ARE	INCAPABLE	OF. IT IS TRUE THAT TOO MUCH OF THIS DOMESTIC

METH PREFACE(R68)	UNTAUGHT OR MISTAUGHT, ARE SO IGNORANT AND	INCAPABLE	POLITICALLY THAT THIS IN ITSELF WOULD NOT GREATLY
JITT III (77)	BRUNO, YOU ONLY SHEW FOR THE THOUSANDTH TIME HOW	INCAPABLE	YOU ARE OF UNDERSTANDING EITHER HIM OR ME.
DOCT PREFACE(62)	THE ARTIST A RASCAL, THE JOURNALIST AN ILLITERATE	INCAPABLE	, AND ALL THE DOCTORS " ANGELS." BUT I DID NOT GO
		INCAPABLES	
HART PREFACE(23)	AFFORD TO DO. THE DUMB CAPABLES AND THE NOISY	INCAPABLES	. CONFRONTED WITH THIS PICTURE OF INSENSATE
DOCT PREFACE(65)	PRACTITIONER WILL ACCEPT, AND WHERE, THEREFORE,	INCAPABLES	OR DRUNKARDS GET AUTOMATICALLY SELECTED FOR THE
HART PREFACE(23)	THE CAPABLE PEOPLE WENT AND DID IT; BUT THE	INCAPABLES	WOULD BY NO MEANS GET OUT OF THE WAY: THEY FUSSED
INCA (252)	MY SOUL, CAPTAIN, IF ALL THE INCA'S GENERALS ARE	INCAPABLES	, AND ALL HIS RELATIVES DUFFERS, PERUSALEM WILL
		INCAPACITIES	
SUPR II SD(62)	THEIR STUPIDITIES, AND TO REPRESENT THEIR VARIOUS	INCAPACITIES	AS POINTS OF GOOD BREEDING. ENGLISH LIFE SEEMS
		INCAPACITY	
ARMS III SD(46)	WITH A MIXTURE OF ENVIOUS IRRITATION AT HIS OWN	INCAPACITY	AND AWESTRUCK WONDER AT AN ABILITY WHICH SEEMS TO
LION PREFACE(89)	AS AN INFALLIBLE CURE FOR GUILT, AND A CONGENITAL	INCAPACITY	FOR BELIEVING THIS, OR (THE SAME THING) DESIRING
GENV PREFACE(6)	FOR DOING IMPOSSIBLE THINGS WHEN IN DANGER IS HER	INCAPACITY	FOR DOING POSSIBLE THINGS (EXCEPT REPEATING WHAT
3PLA PREFACE(R34)	WAS THE AGE OF GROSS IGNORANCE OF SHAKESPEAR AND	INCAPACITY	FOR HIS WORKS THAT PRODUCED THE INDISCRIMINATE
3PLA PREFACE(R24)	PRIVATE LIFE TO WHICH HE IS CONDEMNED BY HIS	INCAPACITY	FOR PUBLIC LIFE. THUS SHAKESPEAR, AFTER
JITT PREFACE(3)	RUDIMENTS OF STAGE TECHNIQUE, AND HIS HOPELESS	INCAPACITY	FOR REPRESENTING HUMAN NATURE DRAMATICALLY OR
ROCK II (267)	PLENTY OF HARD DRIVING COURAGE, AND A COMPLETE	INCAPACITY	FOR SEEING ANY SIDE OF A QUESTION BUT HIS OWN. A
PLES PREFACE(R16)	MANAGER. THE MAIN DIFFICULTY, OF COURSE, IS THE	INCAPACITY	FOR SERIOUS DRAMA OF THOUSANDS OF PLAYGOERS OF
CLEO NOTES (210)	LIKELY THAN NOT TO BE AN ILLUSION PRODUCED BY THE	INCAPACITY	OF HIS ADVERSARY, AT ALL EVENTS, CAESAR MIGHT
FABL PREFACE(84)	MISGOVERNMENT ARE CAUSED, NOT BY INCURABLE MENTAL	INCAPACITY	, BUT BY AN IGNORANCE THAT IS ESSENTIALLY
3PLA PREFACE(R24)	THEIR CRAFT. NATURALLY, MAKING A VIRTUE OF THEIR	INCAPACITY	, THEY EITHER REPUDIATE PREFACES AS SHAMEFUL, OR
		INCARCERATION	
FANY II (289)	REGRETTABLE INCIDENT WHICH LED TO YOUR DAUGHTER'S	INCARCERATION	. I GOT A FORTNIGHT WITHOUT THE OPTION OF A
		INCARNATE	
FABL VI (130)	THAT YOU ARE ONE OF THE DISEMBODIED, AGAIN	INCARNATE	? /RAPHAEL/ WHY NOT? EVOLUTION CAN GO BACKWARDS
JOAN PREFACE(44)	HAD TO DEPEND ON THOSE WHO ACCEPTED HER AS AN	INCARNATE	ANGEL AGAINST THOSE WHO ADDED TO AN INTENSE
CYMB V (139)	OR DEAD. THE CRACKBRAINED WELSHMEN RAGED LIKE	INCARNATE	DEVILS. /PHILARIO/ YES: THEY THOUGHT WE WERE THE
ANNA (292)	THE SWINE SAYS THAT THE GRAND DUCHESS IS A DEVIL	INCARNATE	. (INTO THE TELEPHONE) FILTHY TRAITOR: IS THAT
HART II (125)	IS-- /LADY UTTERWORD/ LAZINESS! YOU ARE LAZINESS	INCARNATE	. YOU ARE SELFISHNESS ITSELF. YOU ARE THE MOST
BULL II SD(111)	SPENDTHRIFT. AUNT JUDY SEEMS TO HIM AN	INCARNATE	JOKE. THE LIKELIHOOD THAT THE JOKE WILL PALL AFTER
UNPL PREFACE(R21)	TO THE ACTOR THE SORT OF PERSON HE MEANT HIM TO	INCARNATE	, WHAT A LIGHT THEY WOULD SHED, NOT ONLY ON THE
		INCARNATED	
SUPR III (116)	BUT IT WAS NOT MUSIC, PAINTING, POETRY, AND JOY	INCARNATED	IN A BEAUTIFUL WOMAN. I RAN AWAY FROM IT. I RAN
		INCARNATES	
SUPR PREFACE(R23)	CONSCIOUSNESS OF LIFE AND THE WOMAN WHO	INCARNATES	ITS FECUNDITY, IS TRUE IN SOME DEGREE OF ALL
SUPR PREFACE(R23)	OF COURSE; BUT WHAT IS TRUE OF THE GREAT MAN WHO	INCARNATES	THE PHILOSOPHIC CONSCIOUSNESS OF LIFE AND THE
		INCARNATION	
MTH4 I (155)	COMMUNITIES WHICH HAD ONCE IDOLIZED THEM AS THE	INCARNATION	OF ALL THAT IS ADORABLE IN THE WARM HEART AND
BULL II SD(101)	AN INVALID WITHOUT THE EXCUSE OF DISEASE, AN	INCARNATION	OF EVERYTHING IN IRELAND THAT DROVE HIM OUT OF
LADY PREFACE(214)	PARTICULARLY FOND OF HER. THAT SHE WAS A SIMPLE	INCARNATION	OF EXTRAVAGANT MATERNAL PRIDE LIKE THE MOTHER OF
NEVR I SD(208)	FORMIDABLE PERSON THAN HER MOTHER. SHE IS THE	INCARNATION	OF HAUGHTY HIGH-MINDEDNESS, RAGING WITH THE
NEVR IV (285)	YOULL LIKE HIM, MISS CLANDON: HE'S THE VERY	INCARNATION	OF INTELLECT. YOU CAN HEAR HIS MIND WORKING.
ROCK PREFACE(149)	SACREDNESS OF HUMAN LIFE, OR ANY OTHER	INCARNATION	OF LIFE; BUT IT COVERS ONLY A CORNER OF THE
BARB III (342)	SOFTENS). /UNDERSHAFT/ MY DEAR: YOU ARE THE	INCARNATION	OF MORALITY. (SHE SNORTS). YOUR CONSCIENCE IS
PRES (151)	MOMENT-- WHATEVER HIS PERSONAL FRAILTIES-- THE	INCARNATION	OF OUR NATIONAL DESTINY. /THE ORDERLY/ WHAT I'M
LION PREFACE(16)	LED THE FIRST MEN WHO CONCEIVED GOD AS CAPABLE OF	INCARNATION	TO BELIEVE THAT THEY COULD ACQUIRE A SPARK OF
		INCARNATIONS	
SUPR III (116)	TO BE. I DARESAY YOU ALL WANT TO MARRY LOVELY	INCARNATIONS	OF MUSIC AND PAINTING AND POETRY. WELL, YOU
		INCA-ESS	
INCA (254)	BUT I HAD RATHER YOU DID NOT MENTION IT TO THE	INCA-ESS	, IF YOU DONT MIND. /ERMYNTRUDE/ THIS IS REALLY
		INCA'S	
INCA (246)	HALF A MILLION PERUSALEM DOLLARS, MADAM. THE	INCA'S	DESIGN CONSTITUTES IT A WORK OF ART. AS SUCH, IT IS
INCA (252)	BUT BLESS MY SOUL, CAPTAIN, IF ALL THE	INCA'S	GENERALS ARE INCAPABLES, AND ALL HIS RELATIVES
INCA (248)	MADAM? WHAT IS SANITY? THE CONDITION OF THE	INCA'S	MIND. WHAT IS MADNESS? THE CONDITION OF THE PEOPLE
INCA (247)	UP AND DOWN SEVERAL TIMES)? NO! I SAY NO. THE	INCA'S	MOUSTACHE IS SO WATCHED AND STUDIED THAT IT HAS MADE
INCA (247)	THE FACE. THIS MOUSTACHE IS AN EXACT COPY OF THE	INCA'S	MOUSTACHE. WELL, DOES THE WORLD OCCUPY ITSELF WITH
INCA (252)	I BELIEVE IN INDIVIDUAL GENIUS. THAT IS THE	INCA'S	SECRET. IT MUST BE. WHY, HANG IT ALL, MADAM, IF IT
INCA (249)	MY BUSINESS. YOU WANT ME TO MARRY ONE OF THE	INCA'S	SONS: I FORGET WHICH. /THE INCA/ AS FAR AS I CAN
INCA (247)	AND SMILES). /ERMYNTRUDE/ WHEN I MARRY THE	INCA'S	SON, CAPTAIN, I SHALL MAKE THE INCA ORDER YOU TO CUT
INCA (249)	THE SWORD OF THE SPIRIT: IN OTHER WORDS, ON THEIR	INCA'S	TALK, THAN ON THEIR MURDEROUS CANNONS. THE WORLD WILL
INCA (252)	THE INCA. AND -- WELL, EVERYBODY KNOWS WHAT THE	INCA'S	UNCLE WAS. /ERMYNTRUDE/ MY EXPERIENCE IS THAT THE
INCA (252)	ALL, MADAM, IF IT WERE A MERE FAMILY MATTER, THE	INCA'S	UNCLE WOULD HAVE BEEN AS GREAT A MAN AS THE INCA, AND
		INCAS	
INCA (244)	HIGHNESS, AND PERFECTLY CAPABLE OF TACKLING TEN	INCAS	IF NECESSARY. I WILL ARRANGE THE MATTER. (TO THE
		INCAUTIOUS	
DEST SD(171)	YOU SEE: I SHEW MY CONFIDENCE IN YOU. THIS	INCAUTIOUS	ECHO OF THE LIEUTENANT UNDOES HER. NAPOLEON
BULL II (110)	WHICH IS SUPPOSED TO WALK DOWN THE THROATS OF	INCAUTIOUS	SLEEPERS AND CAUSE THEM TO PERISH IN A SLOW
		INCAUTIOUSLY	
GETT PREFACE(197)	TENDENCY. SIR WALTER SCOTT'S FATHER, WHEN HIS SON	INCAUTIOUSLY	EXPRESSED SOME RELISH FOR HIS PORRIDGE, DASHED
METH PREFACE(R34)	AND AN ANECDOTE WAS RELATED OF A MAN WHO, HAVING	INCAUTIOUSLY	SCOFFED AT THE MISSION OF MESSRS MOODY AND
		INCENDIARIES	
DOCT PREFACE(36)	ASKED, DO NOT I, AS A PUBLIC-SPIRITED MAN, EMPLOY	INCENDIARIES	TO SET IT ON FIRE, WITH A HEROIC DISREGARD OF
DOCT PREFACE(35)	ARGUED IN THE SAME WAY ABOUT ROME. HE EMPLOYED	INCENDIARIES	TO SET IT ON FIRE; AND HE PLAYED THE HARP IN
		INCENDIARY	
SUPR HANDBOK(196)	WAS UNDERSTOOD AS EQUIVALENT TO CUT-THROAT AND	INCENDIARY	? NOT BECAUSE THE ENGLISH HAVE THE SMALLEST
SUPR PREFACE(R39)	AND TO GO WRONG AT INCONVENIENT MOMENTS, AND WITH	INCENDIARY	POSSIBILITIES. THESE ARE THE FAULTS OF MY
BARB PREFACE(215)	DO TEN TIMES LESS HARM AS A PROSPEROUS BURGLAR,	INCENDIARY	, RAVISHER OR MURDERER, TO THE UTMOST LIMITS OF
		INCENSE	
LION II (137)	HIM WITH A PANG OF REMORSE) ANDROCLES: BURN THE	INCENSE	: YOULL BE FORGIVEN. LET MY DEATH ATONE FOR BOTH. I
LION II (139)	DOWN THE FLAG IN THE DAY OF BATTLE AND BURNT THE	INCENSE	? SONS TAKE AFTER THEIR MOTHERS, YOU KNOW. DO YOU
LION II (139)	CAPTAIN/ LAVINIA: COME DOWN TO EARTH. BURN THE	INCENSE	AND MARRY ME. /LAVINIA/ HANDSOME CAPTAIN: WOULD YOU
LION I (113)	TO YOU THAT IF YOU CANNOT BURN A MORSEL OF	INCENSE	AS A MATTER OF CONVICTION, YOU MIGHT AT LEAST DO SO
CLEO II SD(121)	AS LARGE AS A THREE-LEGGED STOOL, WITH A STICK OF	INCENSE	BURNING ON IT. RUFIO, WITH ROMAN RESOURCEFULNESS AND
LION I (116)	A MOUSE. WELL, CAPTAIN, IF I TOOK A PINCH OF	INCENSE	IN MY HAND AND STRETCHED IT OUT OVER THE ALTAR FIRE,
CLEO IV SD(183)	SPHINX WITH A TINY TRIPOD BEFORE IT. A MORSEL OF	INCENSE	IS SMOKING IN THE TRIPOD. THE PRIEST COMES TO THE
BULL PREFACE(25)	TO THEM WHEN THEY ARE CONDUCTED WITH CANDLES OR	INCENSE	. FOR EXAMPLE, I WAS NEVER CONFIRMED, ALTHOUGH THE
LION II (136)	HURTING ANYBODY? DONT FIGHT THEM. BURN THE	INCENSE	. /FERROVIUS/ BURN THE INCENSE! NEVER. /LAVINIA/
LION II (136)	YOUR HEART. I SAY, THINK OF YOURSELF AND BURN THE	INCENSE	. /LAVINIA/ HE IS NOT A HUMORIST: HE WAS RIGHT. YOU
LION II (128)	BE OBSTINATE. COME WITH ME AND DROP THE PINCH OF	INCENSE	ON THE ALTAR. THATS ALL YOU NEED DO TO BE LET OFF.

LION I (115)	HIM ZEUS. CALL HIM WHAT YOU WILL AS YOU DROP THE	INCENSE	ON THE ALTAR FLAME! HE WILL UNDERSTAND. /LAVINIA/
LION I (113)	CEREMONY EFFECTED BY DROPPING A PINCH OF	INCENSE	ON THE ALTAR, AFTER WHICH THE PRISONER IS AT ONCE
CLEO II SD(121)	PROMPTLY SEIZES THE TRIPOD; SHAKES OFF THE	INCENSE	; BLOWS AWAY THE ASH; AND DUMPS IT DOWN BEHIND
LION I (115)	STRANGE THING, CAPTAIN, THAT A LITTLE PINCH OF	INCENSE	SHOULD MAKE ALL THAT DIFFERENCE. RELIGION IS SUCH A
BUOY III (47)	IN MY RESTLESS TEENS. I DETESTED IT. THE SCENT OF	INCENSE	SICKENS ME. (TO HIM) COME, YOU. WE MUST THINK IT
LION II (136)	THEM. BURN THE INCENSE. /FERROVIUS/ BURN THE	INCENSE	! NEVER. /LAVINIA/ THAT IS ONLY PRIDE, FERROVIUS.
		INCENSED	
PYGM II (241)	(SHE PUTS OUT HER TONGUE AT HIM. HE IS SO	INCENSED	BY THIS THAT PICKERING PRESENTLY FINDS IT NECESSARY
METH PREFACE(R34)	SANKEY WAS TO BE STRUCK DEAD ON THE SPOT BY AN	INCENSED	DEITY, NOTHING COULD EFFECT A MORE CONVINCING
ROCK I (197)	WHERE THEY WOULD BE REALLY USEFUL. /SIR ARTHUR/ (	INCENSED	) BASHAM! I MUST TELL YOU THAT WE ARE QUITE
CATH 1 (168)	STAKE A MILLION ROUBLES ON YOU. /EDSTASTON/ (	INCENSED	) DAMN YOU! DO YOU TAKE ME FOR A PRIZE-FIGHTER?
CAND II (109)	EASY CHAIR, AND SITS DOWN). /PROSERPINE/ (HIGHLY	INCENSED	) HE'LL BE ALL RIGHT NOW THAT HE HAS THE ADVANTAGE
PRES (148)	LARFIN WHEN I SOR IM OP IT. /MITCHENER/ (HIGHLY	INCENSED	) HOW DARE YOU INDULGE IN THIS UNSEEMLY MIRTH IN
POSN (436)	AND HIS VIGILANCE COMMITTEE, INDEED! /BABSY/ (	INCENSED	) OH, WELL! IF PEOPLE ARE GOING TO TAKE THE PART
GETT (294)	YOUR IMPERTINENCE, WHAT DO YOU-- (BOTH HIGHLY	INCENSED	) /HOTCHKISS/ EASY, REJJY. EASY, OLD MAN. STEADY,
JITT I (10)	JUST RIGHT FOR TWO, AINT IT? /MRS BILLITER/ (	INCENSED	) WHAT DO YOU MEAN, WITH YOUR " JUST RIGHT FOR
		INCENTIVE	
MILL PREFACE(110)	OF THE STATE. A SOCIETY WHICH DEPENDS ON THE	INCENTIVE	OF PRIVATE PROFIT IS DOOMED. AND WHAT ABOUT
2TRU PREFACE(25)	INCENTIVE TO SEEK ELECTION EXCEPT THE VOCATIONAL	INCENTIVE	; FOR SUCCESS, IN THE FIRST INSTANCE, MEANS, NOT
DOCT PREFACE(69)	A HOST OF MEN AND WOMEN WHO HAVE NOW A STRONG	INCENTIVE	TO BE MISCHIEVOUS AND EVEN MURDEROUS ROGUES WILL
DOCT PREFACE(69)	HAVE A MUCH STRONGER, BECAUSE A MUCH HONESTER,	INCENTIVE	TO BE NOT ONLY GOOD CITIZENS BUT ACTIVE
UNPL PREFACE(R16)	SYSTEM HAS BROUGHT SUCCESS NOT ONLY HAVE NO	INCENTIVE	TO CHANGE IT FOR ANOTHER WHICH WOULD EXPOSE THEM
MRS PREFACE(177)	WARREN'S PROFESSION, AND A CORRESPONDINGLY STRONG	INCENTIVE	TO CONCEAL, FROM THEIR OWN CONSCIENCES NO LESS
MRS PREFACE(177)	LARGE AND POWERFUL CLASS WITH A STRONG PECUNIARY	INCENTIVE	TO PROTECT MRS WARREN'S PROFESSION, AND A
2TRU PREFACE(25)	AND EQUAL NEIGHBORS AND WORKMATES. THEY HAVE NO	INCENTIVE	TO SEEK ELECTION EXCEPT THE VOCATIONAL INCENTIVE;
POSN PREFACE(380)	IN THESE MATTERS, I HAVE NO OTHER EFFECTUAL	INCENTIVE	TO WRITE PLAYS, AS I AM NOT DEPENDENT ON THE
		INCE-INCE-ISTASTANEOUSLY	
CATH 1 (166)	DARLING. CROSS EYE. SEES EVERYTHING. READ LERRER	INCE-INCE-ISTASTANEOUSLY	. KINDLY GIVE ME VINEGAR BORLE.
		INCESSANT	
INCA PREFACE(231)	BY THE SACRIFICE OF EVERY RECREATIVE ACTIVITY TO	INCESSANT	AND VEHEMENT WAR WORK, INCLUDING A HEARTBREAKING
SUPR III (127)	MY LIFE. THAT IS THE WORKING WITHIN ME OF LIFE'S	INCESSANT	ASPIRATION TO HIGHER ORGANIZATION, WIDER, DEEPER,
FABL PREFACE(77)	SCEPTICS, WHILST I SUFFER NOTHING WORSE THAN	INCESSANT	ATTEMPTS TO CONVERT ME. ALL THE RELIGIONS AND
METH PREFACE(R31)	GOVERNORS OF OUR VITAL FORCES DO NOT HOLD THEIR	INCESSANT	CONVERSATIONS THROUGH THE NERVES, AND, POSITIVELY,
LION PREFACE(74)	AND BE BAPTIZED. TO THIS THE OTHER APOSTLES ADDED	INCESSANT	DENUNCIATIONS OF THE JEWS FOR HAVING CRUCIFIED
MIS. PREFACE(15)	THE GOODNATURED AND SOUND PEOPLE WOULD PREFER THE	INCESSANT	NOISE TO THE INCESSANT SILENCE. BUT THAT CHOICE IS
MIS. PREFACE(15)	PEOPLE WOULD PREFER THE INCESSANT NOISE TO THE	INCESSANT	SILENCE. BUT THAT CHOICE IS NOT THRUST UPON US BY
		INCESSANTLY	
LION PREFACE(24)	STRESS ON BAPTISM OR VOWS, AND PREACHES CONDUCT	INCESSANTLY	. HE ADVOCATES COMMUNISM, THE WIDENING OF THE
MTH5 SD(205)	AS IF TIME HAD WORKED OVER EVERY INCH OF IT	INCESSANTLY	THROUGH WHOLE GEOLOGIC PERIODS. HIS HEAD IS
		INCEST	
JOAN 6 (132)	ANY INCITEMENT BE RECONCILED TO NAKEDNESS AND	INCEST	AND POLYGAMY AND THE LIKE. BUT WE ARE CONFRONTED
POSN PREFACE(371)	BEEN SUPPORTED BY A LARGE BODY OF PEOPLE TO WHOM	INCEST	IS A TABOOED SUBJECT WHICH MUST NOT BE MENTIONED ON
JOAN 6 (130)	THE SPRING, THEY BEGIN WITH POLYGAMY, AND END BY	INCEST	. HERESY AT FIRST SEEMS INNOCENT AND EVEN LAUDABLE;
POSN PREFACE(400)	BECAUSE, LIKE HAMLET, IT MENTIONS THE SUBJECT OF	INCEST	; BUT AN ENLIGHTENED CENSORSHIP MIGHT SUPPRESS ALL
POSN PREFACE(371)	TO KNOW ANYTHING: ALL THAT THEY DO KNOW IS THAT	INCEST	, PROSTITUTION, ABORTION, CONTAGIOUS DISEASES, AND
		INCESTUOUS	
POSN PREFACE(384)	APPROVE OF IT, BUT BY THE PEOPLE WHO REGARD IT AS	INCESTUOUS	. CATHOLIC EMANCIPATION AND THE ADMISSION OF JEWS
POSN PREFACE(398)	WERE MADE IN IT. HE WOULD DISALLOW THE	INCESTUOUS	RELATIONSHIP BETWEEN THE KING AND QUEEN. HE WOULD
		INCH	
2TRU II SD(51)	STILL SLENDER, HANDSOME, WELL SET UP, AND EVERY	INCH	A COMMANDING OFFICER. HIS FULL STYLE AND TITLE IS
GENV II SD(56)	UNDER FORTY, IN FACT, BUT VERY GRAVE AND EVERY	INCH	A JUDGE. /THE SECRETARY/ I AM DESOLATE AT HAVING
KING II (234)	PULLS COMPLETE HIS TOILET). NOW YOU LOOK EVERY	INCH	A KING. (MAKING HIM A FORMAL CURTSEY) YOUR MAJESTY'S
GENV IV SD(90)	! THE DICTATOR ENTERS, DOMINANT, BRUSQUE, EVERY	INCH	A MAN OF DESTINY. /BOMBARDONE/ IS THIS THE SO-CALLED
GETT SD(323)	WALL) MRS GEORGE, MY LORD. MRS GEORGE IS EVERY	INCH	A MAYORESS IN POINT OF STYLISH DRESSING; AND SHE DOES
VWOO 3,SD(133)	APRON. HE IS IN HIS SHIRTSLEEVES, AND LOOKS EVERY	INCH	A SHOPKEEPER. Z COMES IN THROUGH THE POST OFFICE, VERY
ARMS II (31)	WITH MOCK ENTHUSIASM) AH, HE WAS A SOLDIER: EVERY	INCH	A SOLDIER! IF ONLY I HAD BOUGHT THE HORSES FOR MY
PHIL II (96)	I BELIEVE YOU. A SPLENDID FINE CREATURE: EVERY	INCH	A WOMAN. NO IBSENISM ABOUT HER! /PARAMORE/ I QUITE
PRES (159)	MRS BANGER IS A MAN IN PETTICOATS. I AM EVERY	INCH	A WOMAN; BUT I FIND IT CONVENIENT TO WORK WITH HER.
LION PREFACE(61)	SELLING OUR SOULS AND BODIES BY THE POUND AND THE	INCH	AFTER WASTING HALF THE DAY HAGGLING OVER THE PRICE.
CAND I (81)	WITH HIS LIPS CAREFULLY CLOSED A FULL HALF	INCH	FROM EACH CORNER FOR THE SAKE OF A FINICKING
GETT (294)	ON MY PROPERTY. I'D RATHER HAVE TO CUT OFF AN	INCH	FROM MY RIGHT ARM THAN A HUNDRED A YEAR FROM MY
MTH4 I (163)	CALL GIANTS, MUST HAVE BEEN ABOUT QUARTER OF AN	INCH	HIGH. /THE ELDERLY GENTLEMAN/ I AM NOT HERE TO BANDY
PHIL II (125)	MAD. /GRACE/ NOT A BIT MAD. YOU CALCULATED TO AN	INCH	HOW FAR YOU COULD GO, WHEN HE IS PRESENT TO STAND
METH PREFACE(R42)	THIS PROCESS, BY WHICH THE SPECIES GAINS, SAY, AN	INCH	IN REACH, WILL REPEAT ITSELF UNTIL THE GIRAFFE'S NECK
MIS. PREFACE(31)	OF THE WEIGHT OF A POUND AND THE LENGTH OF AN	INCH	. AND SOMETIMES A SCOUNDREL WHO HAS RIFLED A BIRD'S
BASH II,1, (103)	WORTHINGTON, WHO SHEWED HIMSELF A SPORTSMAN EVERY	INCH	. BARELY THE BET WAS BOOKED, WHEN, AT THE REELING
KING I (172)	IS, MR NEWTON; BUT YOU LOOK ONE, EVERY	INCH	. YOUR SERVANT, SIR. (SHE CURTSIES TO HIM). /NEWTON/
JOAN 4 (104)	BEFORE THE WORLD, AND SUBMIT HERSELF TO THE LAST	INCH	OF HER SOUL TO HER CHURCH, TO THE FIRE SHE SHALL GO IF
BASH I (93)	WELL OF NATURE IN OUR HEARTS THAN THE INTOLERABLE	INCH	OF ICE THAT BEARS THE WEIGHT OF ALL THE STAMPING WORLD,
MTH5 SD(205)	RETICULATIONS, AS IF TIME HAD WORKED OVER EVERY	INCH	OF IT INCESSANTLY THROUGH WHOLE GEOLOGIC PERIODS. HIS
PHIL II (107)	THERE ARE FORTY MILLIONS OF THEM TO EVERY SQUARE	INCH	OF LIVER. PARAMORE DISCOVERED THEM FIRST; AND NOW HE
BULL PREFACE(31)	WILL NOT RELAX THEIR DETERMINATION TO HOLD EVERY	INCH	OF THE GOVERNMENT OF IRELAND THAT THEY CAN GRASP; BUT
GETT (313)	A DAY! /SOAMES/ OFF THE PATH IS OFF THE PATH. AN	INCH	OR A MILE: WHAT DOES IT MATTER? /LEO/ IF THE MARRIAGE
METH PREFACE(R42)	STARVATION. ALL THE ANIMALS WHO HAPPEN TO BE AN	INCH	OR SO ABOVE THE AVERAGE WILL BE BETTER FED AND STRONGER
METH PREFACE(R42)	THE GROUND. THEN THE ANIMALS WHO HAPPEN TO BE AN	INCH	OR TWO SHORT OF THE AVERAGE WILL DIE OF STARVATION. ALL
SUPR II (56)	IN IT AS THAT CAR AND ME IF YOU DONT GIT THE LAST	INCH	OUT OF US BOTH. /TANNER/ (SOOTHINGLY) ALL RIGHT,
WIDO II (27)	YOUR HANDS? IF I FIND THAT YOU HAVE STEPPED AN	INCH	OUTSIDE THE LETTER OF THE LAW, MR LICKCHEESE, I WILL
BARB II (280)	(THREATENING HIM)? /SHIRLEY/ (NOT BUDGING AN	INCH	) WILL YOU BOX TODGER FAIRMILE IF I PUT HIM ON TO YOU?
BULL IV (146)	SIX YARDS SIDEWAYS AT WAN JUMP IF HE CLEARED AN	INCH	; AND HE'D A CLEARED SEVEN IF DOOLAN'S GRANMOTHER HADNT
NEVR II (228)	(RESOLUTELY) YES: I HAVE NOT GONE BACK ONE	INCH	; AND I HAVE EDUCATED GLORIA TO TAKE UP MY WORK WHEN I
NEVR IV SD(293)	THE HARLEQUIN'S DRESS IS MADE OF LOZENGES, AN	INCH	SQUARE, OF TURQUOISE BLUE SILK AND GOLD ALTERNATELY.
FABL VI (131)	MUCH. WE KNOW HOW TO MAKE CYCLOTRONS AND HUNDRED	INCH	TELESCOPES. WE HAVE HARNESSED ATOMIC ENERGY. HE COULDNT
LADY PREFACE(222)	HUMOR OF THE FACT THAT THOUGH SHE PAINT AN	INCH	THICK (WHICH THE DARK LADY MAY HAVE DONE), TO YORICK'S
MRS PREFACE(168)	WITH A FLINTY SOCIAL PROBLEM THAT NEVER YIELDS AN	INCH	TO MERE SENTIMENT. I GO FURTHER THAN THIS. I DECLARE
SUPR I SD(9)	RESTLESS BLUE EYE, JUST THE THIRTY-SECONDTH OF AN	INCH	TOO WIDE OPEN), POSSIBLY A LITTLE MAD. HE IS CAREFULLY
POSN PREFACE(432)	GREGORY AND MR YEATS NOT ONLY WOULD NOT YIELD AN	INCH	, BUT INSISTED, WITHIN THE DUE LIMITS OF GALLANT
ROCK PREFACE(178)	WAS ITS VISIBLE TANGIBLE SYMBOL ON EARTH A SINGLE	INCH	, IT LOST A GREAT OPPORTUNITY, AS IT HAS SINCE LOST
BARB I (253)	THE UNDERSHAFT QUICK FIRERS! THE UNDERSHAFT TEN	INCH	! THE UNDERSHAFT DISAPPEARING RAMPART GUN! THE
		INCHES	
KING I (217)	IT WAS YOU WHO CAPTIVATED ME WITH YOUR SEVENTY	INCHES	AND YOUR GOOD LOOKS. /BARBARA/ AY, FLATTER HIM.
2TRU I (48)	HOW DARINGLY MODERN! SHOES: HEELS ONLY TWO	INCHES	BUT NO USE FOR THE MOUNTAINS. WHAT A THEME FOR A
MIS. (166)	EYES. THE MAN'S HEAD RISES FROM THE LUNETTE A FEW	INCHES	FROM HIS NOSE. HE RECOILS FROM THE BATH WITH A
CYMB V (139)	TO HIS HELMET) -- WELL! SEE THEIR WORK! TWO	INCHES	FURTHER DOWN I HAD BEEN BLIND OR DEAD. THE
POSN PREFACE(391)	SENSE, A BUSY-BODY, A MAN TO WHOM A MATTER OF TWO	INCHES	IN THE LENGTH OF A GENTLEMAN'S SWORD OR THE ABSENCE
HART II (117)	MY SOUL FROM THE POVERTY THAT IS DAMNING ME BY	INCHES	. CAPTAIN SHOTOVER/ RICHES WILL DAMN YOU TEN TIMES
HART II (117)	THE KICKING AND SWEARING THAT WAS DAMNING ME BY	INCHES	. /ELLIE/ (RELEASING HIM) I SHALL PRETEND TO SELL

MIS. (137)	(RISING RELUCTANTLY) I PROMISED YOU TWO	INCHES	MORE ROUND MY CHEST THIS SUMMER. I TRIED EXERCISES
SUPR II (56)	ALONG IN A LEATHER COAT AND GOGGLES, WITH TWO	INCHES	OF DUST ALL OVER HIM, AT SIXTY MILES AN HOUR AND THE
GENV III (65)	GOOD-NATURED, ABLE TO SEE EVERYTHING WITHIN SIX	INCHES	OF HER NOSE AND NOTHING BEYOND. A DOMESTIC PARAGON: A
CLEO IV (187)	GALLERY ARCH SIXTY FEET ABOVE GROUND, WITH THREE	INCHES	OF STEEL IN HIS RIBS. HE IS AS DEAD AS POMPEY. WE ARE
GETT PREFACE(191)	THE FINE EDGE OF THEIR FACULTIES AND THE LAST FEW	INCHES	OF THEIR CHESTS WITHOUT BEING ANY THE LESS FIT FOR
BULL IV (162)	A GOOD BROAD CHEST, EH? NOT LESS THAN FORTY-TWO	INCHES	-- NO: DONT FUSS: NEVER MIND THE CONVENTIONS: WE'RE
DEST (186)	WOULD HAVE MADE A MAN OF ME IF I HAD BEEN A FEW	INCHES	TALLER. BUT IT ALWAYS MEANT MAKING ME WORK; AND I AM
MRS II (199)	ASSURANCE) WELL, YOU HAVE GOT A NICE HEALTHY TWO	INCHES	THICK OF CHEEK ALL OVER YOU. I DONT KNOW WHERE YOU
PHIL III (136)	YOU. /CHARTERIS/ YES? (HE ROLLS THE CHAIR A FEW	INCHES	TOWARDS HER). /JULIA/ COME HERE, I SAY. I AM NOT
BASH II,1, (111)	YOUNG MAN, HOW COMES IT THAT A FELLOW OF YOUR	INCHES	, SO DEFT A WRESTLER AND SO BOLD A SPIRIT, CAN STOOP

INCIDENCE

DOCT PREFACE(60)	IN THE PSYCHOLOGY OF HUMAN CREDULITY, NOR IN THE	INCIDENCE	OF ECONOMIC PRESSURE. FURTHER, THEY MUST BELIEVE,

INCIDENT

JOAN 4 (102)	VIEW OF WHAT WOULD OTHERWISE BE A VERY HORRIBLE	INCIDENT	? /CAUCHON/ YES: IT IS A PAINFUL DUTY: EVEN, AS
CAPT III (286)	OVERWHELMED BY THE UNEXPECTED PROFUSION OF	INCIDENT	AND CHARACTER IN HER STORY) WELL, WHAT HAPPENED
BULL PREFACE(53)	WERE SENT OFF TO CAMP IN THEIR CARRIAGES; AND THE	INCIDENT	ENDED FOR THAT DAY. NO ENGLISH MOB, UNDER SIMILAR
BULL PREFACE(70)	HAPPENED BUT AN IGNOMINIOUS CLIMB DOWN; BUT THE	INCIDENT	ILLUSTRATES MY CONTENTION THAT OUR AUTHORITY, WHEN
MIS. (140)	YOUNG MAN WHO COMES A-COURTING IS AS FAMILIAR AN	INCIDENT	IN MY LIFE AS COFFEE FOR BREAKFAST. OF COURSE, HE'S
ROCK PREFACE(155)	IN TREATING IT AS A HARMLESS AND NECESSARY	INCIDENT	IN PRISON ROUTINE. UNFORTUNATELY THE WHOLE QUESTION
GENV PREFACE(4)	AIR FORCE IN " THE BATTLE OF BRITAIN" AND IN AN	INCIDENT	IN SOUTH AMERICA IN WHICH THREE BRITISH WARSHIPS
SUPR HANDBOK(203)	AS BACON WAS, AS TO VINDICTIVE CRUELTY, AN	INCIDENT	IN THE SOUTH AFRICAN WAR, WHEN THE RELATIVES AND
GENV IV (108)	(HUGELY AMUSED) HA HA! (TO THE JUDGE) THE	INCIDENT	IS CLOSED. AN ATTRACTIVE AND VERY VOLUBLE
POSN PREFACE(430)	GOT ONLY ONE VOTE: THAT OF MR HARCOURT. BUT THE	INCIDENT	IS NOT THE LESS SIGNIFICANT. LORD GORELL CARRIED
MRS PREFACE(179)	NOTHING THAT NOW MATTERS WERE IT NOT FOR A RECENT	INCIDENT	. BEFORE DESCRIBING THIS I MUST EXPLAIN THAT WITH
3PLA PREFACE(R25)	IT DOES NOT CONTAIN A SINGLE EVEN PASSABLY NOVEL	INCIDENT	. EVERY OLD PATRON OF THE ADELPHI PIT WOULD, WERE
BARB PREFACE(229)	TO DRAMATIC ORATORY, WITH PLENTY OF THRILLING	INCIDENT	. FOR MY PART, WHEN I HEAR A CONVERT RELATING THE
SUPR III (139)	THE UNFORTUNATE MANNERS OF YOUR CLASS CLOSES THE	INCIDENT	. FOR THE FUTURE, YOU WILL PLEASE ADDRESS ME WITH
LION PREFACE(34)	GIVES THE CHARM OF SENTIMENTAL ROMANCE TO EVERY	INCIDENT	. THE ANNUNCIATION, AS DESCRIBED BY MATTHEW, IS
DEVL III (64)	ANDERSON, THAT YOU MUST NOT BUILD ON THIS LITTLE	INCIDENT	. WE ARE BOUND TO MAKE AN EXAMPLE OF SOMEBODY.
BULL PREFACE(54)	BRITISH INVASION IS THE ONLY OFFICIALLY RECORDED	INCIDENT	OF HIS LIFE WHICH IS ENTIRELY TO HIS CREDIT. HE AND
SUPR HANDBOK(193)	IN SHORT, POPULAR PRUDERY IS ONLY A MERE	INCIDENT	OF POPULAR SQUALOR: THE SUBJECTS WHICH IT TABOOS
POSN PREFACE(372)	PART OF ITS BUSINESS THAT LED TO THE COMIC	INCIDENT	OF THE COMMITTEE'S SUDDEN DISCOVERY THAT I HAD
ROCK PREFACE(180)	READER AND SPECTATOR. IT MAY BE ASKED WHY THE	INCIDENT	OF THE TRIAL AND EXECUTION MUST FAIL ON THE STAGE,
METH PREFACE(R34)	QUITE VENTURING TO QUESTION THE TRUTH OF THE	INCIDENT	-- FOR THEY NATURALLY DID NOT CARE TO RUN THE RISK
PYGM I (206)	BY A RATTLING PEAL OF THUNDER, ORCHESTRATES THE	INCIDENT	). /THE FLOWER GIRL/ NAH THEN, FREDDY: LOOK WH' Y'
NEVR II SD(245)	WATCH HER IN EMBARRASSED SILENCE, FEELING THE	INCIDENT	TO BE A VERY PAINFUL ONE. THE WAITER DISCREETLY
SIM II (76)	PERSONS, DECLARED THAT THE MANSION HOUSE	INCIDENT	WAS QUITE INCOMPREHENSIBLE TO HIM, AS HE COULD NOT
FANY II (289)	ON MY ACCOUNT. I WAS CONCERNED IN THE REGRETTABLE	INCIDENT	WHICH LED TO YOUR DAUGHTER'S INCARCERATION. I GOT A
LION EPILOG (150)	SERVE GOD RIGHT, FOR CREATING THE GERMANS! " THE	INCIDENT	WOULD HAVE BEEN IMPOSSIBLE IN A COUNTRY WHERE THE
3PLA PREFACE(R21)	OF THE NEW AGE. WHEN I CAME TO THAT TOUCHING	INCIDENT	, I BECAME AS PAOLO AND FRANCESCA: " IN THAT BOOK I
OVER PREFACE(164)	NO DOUBT THAT ONCE IT IS DECIDED TO REPRESENT AN	INCIDENT	, IT WILL BE OFFENSIVE, NO MATTER WHETHER IT BE A
BULL PREFACE(60)	THIRTY YEARS HAVE BEEN CROWNED BY THE DENSHAWAI	INCIDENT	, WHAT WILL EGYPT BE LIKE AT THE END OF ANOTHER
BULL PREFACE(62)	MAN CRADLED BY THE NILE WHO, AFTER THE DENSHAWAI	INCIDENT	, WILL EVER VOLUNTARILY SUBMIT TO BRITISH RULE, OR

INCIDENTAL

SUPR HANDBOK(183)	THAT CONJUGATION IS THE ONE PURELY ACCIDENTAL AND	INCIDENTAL	CONDITION OF MARRIAGE. CONJUGATION IS ESSENTIAL
SUPR PREFACE(R12)	SUCH PLAYS SOMETIMES OBTAIN ARE DUE TO THE	INCIDENTAL	CONVENTIONAL MELODRAMA WITH WHICH THE EXPERIENCED
PLES PREFACE(R10)	MIGHT HAVE BEEN ACCEDED TO, IN SPITE OF MANY	INCIDENTAL	DIFFICULTIES. NAY, IF ONLY I HAD MADE THE POET A
DOCT PREFACE(56)	WOULD AN ANTI-BRANDY PARTY BE LISTENED TO. THAT	INCIDENTAL	GOOD WOULD BE THE SUBSTITUTION OF ATTENTION TO
DOCT PREFACE(56)	THE DIRECT HARM DONE BY IT WOULD OUTWEIGH THE	INCIDENTAL	GOOD, WOULD AN ANTI-BRANDY PARTY BE LISTENED TO.
DOCT PREFACE(57)	BY FIVE PER THOUSAND WHILST THE ATTENTION	INCIDENTAL	TO IT IS REDUCING THE DEATH-RATE FIFTEEN PER
OVER PREFACE(157)	SO COMPLICATED BY ORDINARY LIKES AND DISLIKES, BY	INCIDENTAL	WOUNDS TO VANITY OR GRATIFICATIONS OF IT, AND BY
DOCT PREFACE(57)	WHICH HAVE NO MERITS AT ALL, EITHER DIRECT OR	INCIDENTAL	, MAY BE BROUGHT INTO HIGH REPUTE BY STATISTICS.

INCIDENTALLY

ROCK PREFACE(166)	EGGS, COULD NOT BE EXTERMINATED SUMMARILY WITHOUT	INCIDENTALLY	EXTERMINATING THE WHOLE RUSSIAN NATION. THE WAY
BUOY IV (59)	THE GREATEST BORES IN LITERATURE, MERE NAMES	INCIDENTALLY	IMMORTALIZED BY A FEW LINES IN A GREAT POEM?
HART PREFACE(8)	ENVIRONMENT IN A FAVORABLE CONDITION, A PROCESS	INCIDENTALLY	INVOLVING THE RUTHLESS DESTRUCTION OR
FABL PREFACE(85)	EFFECTIVENESS AS THEIR AIRY NATURE IS CAPABLE OF.	INCIDENTALLY	IT GIVES STALIN THE BEST RIGHT OF ANY LIVING
LION PREFACE(79)	BUT IT HAS MADE PAUL THE ETERNAL ENEMY OF WOMAN.	INCIDENTALLY	IT HAS LED TO MANY FOOLISH SURMISES ABOUT
LION PREFACE(86)	AS THE MISCHIEF WHICH FOLLOWED PROVES; BUT THEY	INCIDENTALLY	LET LOOSE THE SAYINGS OF JESUS IN OPEN
DEST SD(151)	REPUBLICAN INSTITUTIONS ON THEM; SO THAT IN	INCIDENTALLY	LOOTING THEM IT MERELY MAKES FREE WITH THE
LION PREFACE(66)	AND MADE HIM WORSE BY TORTURE AND DEGRADATION,	INCIDENTALLY	MAKING OURSELVES WORSE IN THE PROCESS. IT DOES
POSN PREFACE(366)	AND SIR HERBERT TREE, BECAUSE THEY ARE ONLY	INCIDENTALLY	MANAGERS AND MEN OF BUSINESS: PRIMARILY THEY
BUOY PREFACE(6)	OF THE PROPHET DANIEL AND JOHN OF PATMOS, AND	INCIDENTALLY	OF SHAKESPEAR AND MYSELF, WILL MAKE A LONGER
PLES PREFACE(R19)	BENEFICIAL EXERCISE OF RESPECTING THEMSELVES, AND	INCIDENTALLY	RESPECTING ME, WE SHOULD ALL GET ALONG MUCH
BARB II (302)	HER IN PRAYER. (HE SKULKS OFF THROUGH THE GATE,	INCIDENTALLY	STEALING THE SOVEREIGN ON HIS WAY OUT BY
BULL PREFACE(62)	DEFEAT, AND SUPPRESSION OF THE EMPIRE, AND,	INCIDENTALLY	, THE HUMANIZATION OF ITS SUPPORTERS BY THE

INCIDENTS

SUPR PREFACE(R17)	THAT IS, DISSECT OUT THE ABSURD SENSATIONAL	INCIDENTS	AND PHYSICAL VIOLENCES OF A BORROWED STORY FROM
MIS. PREFACE(106)	GOVERNMENT BY BULLIES. THESE PICTURESQUE MARTIAL	INCIDENTS	ARE BEING REPRODUCED EVERY DAY IN OUR ORDINARY
OVER PREFACE(164)	FOR WHATEVER QUESTION THERE ARISES AS TO WHAT	INCIDENTS	ARE PROPER FOR REPRESENTATION ON THE STAGE OR NOT,
FABL PREFACE(64)	RIGHT WHEN THEY DISOWNED BUNYAN BECAUSE THE	INCIDENTS	HE DESCRIBED HAD NEVER OCCURRED NOR THE CHARACTERS
MILL PREFACE(121)	HIS WORK LIKE A PARLIAMENTARY MAN TO DISCUSS "	INCIDENTS	." ALL HE SAID WAS " I TAKE THE RESPONSIBILITY FOR
BULL PREFACE(35)	IT IN THE FACE OF THE NATIONALIST ENEMY. SUCH	INCIDENTS	NATURALLY DO NOT SHAKE THE STURDY CONVICTION OF
MIS. PREFACE(44)	OF THE OTHER DISAGREEABLE, DANGEROUS, OR BRACING	INCIDENTS	OF FREEDOM. THE EXPEDIENCY OF TOLERATION HAS BEEN
3PLA PREFACE(R19)	THEATRES, REALISTICALLY SIMULATING THE	INCIDENTS	OF LIFE, CANNOT TOUCH IT WITHOUT INDECORUM. CAN
MIS. PREFACE(85)	OF THE PATERNAL HOME MUST REMAIN ONE OF NORMAL	INCIDENTS	OF MARRIAGE. THE PARENT IS LEFT LONELY AND THE
3PLA PREFACE(R19)	YOU WILL. BUT ANY SUCH REALISTIC TREATMENT OF THE	INCIDENTS	OF SEX IS QUITE OUT OF THE QUESTION. THE SINGER,
MRS PREFACE(161)	IN ORDER FROM THE OFFICIAL POINT OF VIEW. THE	INCIDENTS	OF SEX WHICH THEY CONTAIN, THOUGH CARRIED IN BOTH
OVER PREFACE(164)	AND TREATMENT ON THE STAGE OF THE PHYSICAL	INCIDENTS	OF SEX. ON THE FRENCH STAGE A KISS IS AS OBVIOUS A
HART PREFACE(33)	THE DARK LADY OF THE SONNETS, WAS ONE OF THE	INCIDENTS	OF THAT APPEAL. AFTER SOME YEARS OF EFFORT THE
SUPR PREFACE(R10)	ATTRACTION, AND YET FORBIDDEN TO EXHIBIT THE	INCIDENTS	OF THAT ATTRACTION OR EVEN TO DISCUSS ITS NATURE.
BULL PREFACE(46)	AFRICAN WARS, THE DREYFUS AFFAIR IN FRANCE, THE	INCIDENTS	OF THE ANTI-MILITARIST CAMPAIGN BY THE
JOAN EPILOG (162)	WILL REMEMBER ME FOR YOUR SAKE, THOUGH THE	INCIDENTS	OF THE CONNECTION WERE PERHAPS A LITTLE
SUPR HANDBOK(203)	ENGLISH OFFICER DID IN SOUTH AFRICA. THE	INCIDENTS	OF THE WHITE INVASION OF AFRICA IN SEARCH OF
MRS III (220)	UP EVERY NIGHT WITH HIM UNTIL FOUR, RECALLING THE	INCIDENTS	OF YOUR FIERY YOUTH, IT IS CLEARLY MY MOTHER'S
HART PREFACE(26)	SYSTEM, " GIVING THEM THE COUPON." OTHER	INCIDENTS	WERE SO GROTESQUE THAT I CANNOT MENTION THEM
3PLA PREFACE(R22)	PRODUCED (OFTEN HAVE BEEN PRODUCED, IN FACT) BY	INCIDENTS	WHICH, IF LEFT TO THE OPERATION OF NATURAL AND
3PLA PREFACE(R25)	ECCENTRICITY. NOW THIS, IF IT APPLIES TO THE	INCIDENTS	, PLOT, CONSTRUCTION, AND GENERAL PROFESSIONAL AND

INCINERATED

JOAN PREFACE(53)	CROOK TO SHEW THE CANONIZED JOAN AS WELL AS THE	INCINERATED	ONE; FOR MANY A WOMAN HAS GOT HERSELF BURNT BY

INCIPIENT

BULL I SD(75)	AS HE IS SECRETLY PURSUED BY THE HORRORS OF	INCIPIENT	DELIRIUM TREMENS. /HAFFIGAN/ TIM HAFFIGAN, SIR, AT
POSN SD(438)	HAS A FAIRLY RESOLUTE MOUTH, THOUGH THE FIRE OF	INCIPIENT	DELIRIUM TREMENS IS IN HIS EYE. HIS ARMS ARE BOUND
PYGM EPILOG (300)	LEARNING BOOKKEEPING AND TYPEWRITING WITH	INCIPIENT	JUNIOR CLERKS, MALE AND FEMALE, FROM THE

INCISIVE

WIDO I SD(5)	WELL PRESERVED, AND OF UPRIGHT CARRIAGE. HIS	INCISIVE	, DOMINEERING UTTERANCE AND IMPOSING STYLE, WITH

INCISIVELY

ROCK II (253)	MAYOR, TO THE LAST DROP OF OUR BLOOD. /BASHAM/ (	INCISIVELY	RE-ENTERING THE CONVERSATION; THEY HAD FORGOTTEN

		INCITEMENT	
JOAN 6 (132)	BECAUSE SOUND AND SENSIBLE MEN WILL NOT UNDER ANY	INCITEMENT	BE RECONCILED TO NAKEDNESS AND INCEST AND
POSN PREFACE(386)	THIS VINDICATION AND ENNOBLEMENT MIGHT ACT AS AN	INCITEMENT	TO AN ACTUAL ASSASSINATION AS WELL AS TO
POSN PREFACE(386)	OF CENSORSHIP; AND IT SEEMS HARD TO JUSTIFY AN	INCITEMENT	TO IT ON ANTI-CENSORIAL PRINCIPLES. THE VERY
		INCITING	
JOAN 6 (143)	THE SWORD, EVEN TO THE SHEDDING OF HUMAN BLOOD,	INCITING	MEN TO SLAY EACH OTHER, INVOKING EVIL SPIRITS TO
POSN PREFACE(426)	I CLAIM FULL LIBERTY TO WRITE AND PERFORM A PLAY	INCITING	THE COUNTRY TO THAT WAR WITHOUT INTERFERENCE FROM
METH PREFACE(R15)	MATTER IF IT WERE, A BODY OF SCHOOLMASTERS	INCITING	THEIR PUPILS TO INFINITESIMAL PECCADILLOES WITH THE
POSN PREFACE(386)	BY DEED" OR SOCIOLOGICAL EXPERIMENT. A PLAY	INCITING	TO SUCH AN ASSASSINATION CANNOT CLAIM THE
		INCIVIL	
CYMB V (146)	/CYMBELINE/ HE WAS A PRINCE. /GUIDERIUS/ A MOST	INCIVIL	ONE: THE WRONGS HE DID ME WERE NOTHING PRINCE-LIKE;
		INCIVILITY	
LION PREFACE(33)	OF SYROPHENICIAN RACE, WHICH PROBABLY EXCUSED ANY	INCIVILITY	TO HER IN MARK'S EYES. HE REPRESENTS THE FATHER
		INCLINATION	
JOAN 4,SD(97)	CAUCHON ACCEPTS THE PLACE OF HONOR WITH A GRAVE	INCLINATION	. WARWICK FETCHES THE LEATHER STOOL CARELESSLY,
KING I (187)	DOOR, CALLING) SALLY! /LOUISE/ (WITH A GRACIOUS	INCLINATION	OF HER HEAD) MONSIEUR-- /NEWTON/ I WISH YOUR
BULL IV (172)	BEGIN TO SEE MY WAY. /KEEGAN/ (WITH A COURTEOUS	INCLINATION	) THE CONQUERING ENGLISHMAN, SIR. WITHIN 24
DOCT III (153)	JUST FOR A FEW MINUTES. (HE ASSENTS WITH A GRAVE	INCLINATION	, AND SITS ON THE SOFA. SHE SITS ON THE EASEL
		INCLINATIONS	
HART II (92)	OR THAT I SHOULD EVER HAVE DREAMED OF FORCING HER	INCLINATIONS	IN ANY WAY, IS A MOST PAINFUL BLOW TO MY--
SUPR III (90)	HERE? WHY AM I HERE? I, WHO SACRIFICED ALL MY	INCLINATIONS	TO WOMANLY VIRTUE AND PROPRIETY! /DON JUAN/
		INCLINE	
MTH3 SD(114)	FROM THAT OF THE MEN, WHO RISE AS SHE ENTERS, AND	INCLINE	THEIR HEADS WITH INSTINCTIVE AWE. SHE COMES TO THE
		INCLINED	
MIS. (135)	AS A SPECTATOR SEES A PLAY, LAUGH IF YOU FEEL	INCLINED	: NO MAN SEES THE COMIC SIDE OF IT MORE THAN I. IN
FOUN (218)	UNGOVERNABLE APPETITE, AND WAS NATURALLY RATHER	INCLINED	TO BE STOUT, I TRIED POLITICS. FOR YOU, A MAN,
FABL PREFACE(64)	(MENS SANA IN CORPORE SANO) AND MORE AND MORE	INCLINED	TO BELIEVE THAT AN UNHEALTHY BODY IS THE RESULT OF
CYMB FORWORD(138)	MASQUE. BUT IF THEY ARE HALFHEARTED ABOUT IT, AND	INCLINED	TO COMPROMISE BY LEAVING OUT THE MASQUE AND THE
GETT (264)	FROM HOME. /MRS BRIDGENORTH/ DID YOU EVER FEEL	INCLINED	TO RUN AWAY, COLLINS? /COLLINS/ OH YES MAAM, YES:
CAND II (110)	THE TRIUMPH OF HAVING THE LAST WORD, AND YET HALF	INCLINED	TO TRY TO IMPROVE ON IT, HE LOOKS AFTER HER FOR A
		INCLINES	
FANY PROLOG (258)	EXCEPT AS A MEMORY AND AN IDEAL. (SAVOYARD	INCLINES	HIS HEAD RESPECTFULLY TO THE IDEAL). BUT I AM BY NO
SUPR III (80)	DREGS. /TANNER/ COME! YOU ARE A WIT. (MENDOZA	INCLINES	HIS HEAD, FLATTERED). MAY ONE ASK YOU A BLUNT
		INCLOODIN	
CAPT I (220)	OF THE SCHOONER THENKSGIVIN, AN IS CREW,	INCLOODIN	MAWSEOLF, WILL SEE THE LIDY AN JADGE ELLAM THROUGH
		INCLUDE	
MTH3 (107)	WHAT ABOUT MY FACTS? /CONFUCIUS/ IF YOUR FACTS	INCLUDE	A CASE OF A MAN LIVING 283 YEARS, I ADVISE YOU TO
PYGM EPILOG (296)	CONVERSATIONAL QUALIFICATIONS WERE EXPECTED TO	INCLUDE	A GROUNDING IN THE NOVELS OF MR H. G. WELLS. SHE
HART PREFACE(28)	ARE MANY MANSIONS; BUT I AM AFRAID THEY DO NOT	INCLUDE	EITHER HEARTBREAK HOUSE OR HORSEBACK HALL. PLAGUE ON
3PLA PREFACE(R33)	WITH SHAKESPEAR CRITICISM SO LIMITED AS NOT TO	INCLUDE	EVEN THE PREFACES OF DR JOHNSON AND THE UTTERANCES
BULL PREFACE(8)	IF EVER A BOOK OF SPIES BE WRITTEN, IT WILL	INCLUDE	EXAMPLES OF COURAGE, CONVICTION, PERSEVERANCE, AND
VWOO 2,SD(123)	ARE AVAILABLE FOR CUSTOMERS. THE GOODS FOR SALE	INCLUDE	GINGER BEER IN STONE BOTTLES, TABLETS OF MILK
JOAN PREFACE(36)	WE MUST BROADEN CATHOLICISM SUFFICIENTLY TO	INCLUDE	HER IN ITS CHARTER. OUR CHURCHES MUST ADMIT THAT NO
LION PREFACE(84)	BEEN TORMENTED IN THEIR CHILDHOOD IN HIS NAME	INCLUDE	HIM IN THEIR GENERAL LOATHING OF EVERYTHING
LION PREFACE(84)	AS A SENTIMENTAL PACIFIST AND AN ASCETIC,	INCLUDE	HIM IN THEIR GENERAL DISLIKE OF THAT TYPE OF
OVER PREFACE(159)	AUTHORS OF SAINTLY TEMPERAMENT ARE FORCED TO	INCLUDE	IN THEIR RETINUE COUNTESSES OF ARDENT COMPLEXION
LION PREFACE(96)	A BLASPHEMOUS BOOK, THE SALVATION ARMY MIGHT NOW	INCLUDE	IT AMONG ITS PUBLICATIONS WITHOUT SHOCKING ANYONE. I
LION PREFACE(40)	NARRATIVES WRITTEN IN THE FIRST CENTURY A. D. I	INCLUDE	JOHN, BECAUSE THOUGH IT MAY BE CLAIMED THAT HE
APPL INTRLUD(250)	ME. /ORINTHIA/ MIGHT NOT CARRYING ON WITHOUT HER	INCLUDE	MARRYING ME? /MAGNUS/ MY DEAR ORINTHIA, I HAD
JITT III (74)	KIND OF YOU, EDITH, AND VERY KIND OF JITTA TO	INCLUDE	ME IN THE NUMBER OF HUSBANDS SHE HAS APPARENTLY BEEN
LION PREFACE(84)	SHAKESPEAR; AND PEOPLE WHO DISLIKE THEATRE MAY	INCLUDE	MOLIERE IN THAT DISLIKE WITHOUT EVER HAVING READ A
GENV IV (128)	GOING TO HAPPEN? MY CLASSICAL EDUCATION DID NOT	INCLUDE	SCIENCE. /COMMISSAR/ I AWAIT INSTRUCTIONS. THE
PYGM PREFACE(200)	WAY. I DARESAY HIS PAPERS, IF HE HAS LEFT ANY,	INCLUDE	SOME SATIRES THAT MAY BE PUBLISHED WITHOUT TOO
PLES PREFACE(R19)	ALONE AND LEARN TO RESPECT REALITY, WHICH WOULD	INCLUDE	THE BENEFICIAL EXERCISE OF RESPECTING THEMSELVES,
DOCT PREFACE(48)	ALL THE CUSTOMARY ETHICAL OBLIGATIONS (WHICH	INCLUDE	THE OBLIGATION TO TELL THE TRUTH) ARE SUSPENDED,
GENV IV (128)	INSTRUCTIONS. THE MARXIAN DIALECTIC DOES NOT	INCLUDE	THE QUANTUM THEORY. I MUST CONSULT MOSCOW. (HE GOES
LION PREFACE(96)	HAVE PRODUCED THIS SUDDEN CLEARING OF THE AIR	INCLUDE	THE TRANSFORMATION OF MANY MODERN STATES, NOTABLY
DOCT PREFACE(62)	WE FIND THAT THE FASHIONS OF THE YEAR	INCLUDE	TREATMENTS, OPERATIONS, AND PARTICULAR DRUGS AS WELL
		INCLUDED	
SUPR HANDBOK(201)	THE OFFICERS' MESS OF OUR MOST SELECT REGIMENT	INCLUDED	A FLOGGING CLUB PRESIDED OVER BY THE SENIOR
GENV PREFACE(15)	YET THESE BARBARIANS, LIKE OUR OWN AT PRESENT,	INCLUDED	A PERCENTAGE OF THINKERS WHO HAD THEIR IMAGINATIONS
CLEO NOTES (206)	BUT EVEN IF MAN'S INCREASED COMMAND OVER NATURE	INCLUDED	ANY INCREASED COMMAND OVER HIMSELF (THE ONLY SORT
MIS. PREFACE(67)	CEASING TO EXPECT MORE OF ONE'S OWN WAY THAN IS	INCLUDED	IN THE GREATEST COMMON MEASURE OF THE COMMITTEE,
SIM I (50)	VASHTI AND MAYA, BUT ALL THE LADIES HERE, ARE	INCLUDED	IN THE SUPERFAMILY COMPACT. /IDDY/ OH, HOW NICE AND
METH PREFACE(R47)	ACCOUNTING FOR THE WHOLE OF NATURAL HISTORY. HE	INCLUDED	IT UNDER THE HEADING OF EVOLUTION, THOUGH IT WAS
SUPR I SD(3)	FOR TWO GUINEAS, FIRST CLASS FARES BOTH WAYS	INCLUDED	. HOW OLD IS ROEBUCK? THE QUESTION IS IMPORTANT ON
GENV III (75)	I AM THE RUTHLESS ENEMY OF EVERY NATION, MY OWN	INCLUDED	. LET ME BE FRANK. I HATE THE LOT OF YOU. /ALL THE
2TRU I (46)	MOUNTAIN AND THE FLOOD FOR SEVEN GUINEAS, TIPS	INCLUDED	. NOW YOU SHALL HAVE AN ETERNITY WITH YOUR MOPS IN
POSN PREFACE(370)	DRAMA, LICENSED BY THE LORD CHAMBERLAIN,	INCLUDED	PLAYS WHICH COULD BE DESCRIBED ONLY BEHIND CLOSED
SIM PREFACE(7)	BEEN CONTEMPORARY WITH EUROPEANS WHOSE AMUSEMENTS	INCLUDED	SEEING CRIMINALS BROKEN ON THE WHEEL). THEREFORE
HART PREFACE(20)	FARCE, HAD BEEN DROWNED, AMONG OTHERS, THE OTHERS	INCLUDED	SIR HUGH LANE; BUT AS HE HAD ONLY LAID THE COUNTRY
BASH PREFACE(90)	PUZZLE, IN SPITE OF THE ACTING OF CASTS WHICH	INCLUDED	SUCH ACCOMPLISHED COMEDIANS AS CHARLES QUATERMAINE,
2TRU II (72)	YOU WITH THE ANIMALS AND THEIR WAYS, JUST AS I	INCLUDED	SWEETIE AND THE SERGEANT. /THE COUNTESS/ YOU LET
BULL PREFACE(22)	AND HUMBUG-PROOF. IT MAY BE THAT IF OUR RESOURCES	INCLUDED	THE ARMED FORCE AND VIRTUALLY UNLIMITED MONEY WHICH
2TRU II (72)	SUGARY TONGUED BLACKGUARD. (RELEASING HIM) NO: I	INCLUDED	YOU WITH THE ANIMALS AND THEIR WAYS, JUST AS I
		INCLUDES	
VWOO 2 (131)	ASK HOW MUCH THAT EXPRESSION " LOOKING AFTER ME"	INCLUDES	? LET ME BE CLEAR ON THE POINT. AS A MATTER OF
MIS. PREFACE(87)	US THAT THOUGH THE POPULAR CONCEPTION OF HEAVEN	INCLUDES	A HOLY FAMILY, IT DOES NOT ATTACH TO THAT FAMILY
BASH PREFACE(88)	A NEGLIGIBLE ONE EVEN IN THE THEATRE; FOR IT	INCLUDES	A LARGE BODY OF INTELLIGENT MANUAL AND OPEN AIR
2TRU I SD(27)	BED AND THE YOUNG LADY AN INVALID. THE FURNITURE	INCLUDES	A VERY HANDSOME DRESSING TABLE WITH SILVER-BACKED
SUPR I SD(43)	THE RUTHLESS ELEGANCE OF HER EQUIPMENT, WHICH	INCLUDES	A VERY SMART HAT WITH A DEAD BIRD IN IT, MARK A
FABL PREFACE(84)	AND ADAPTATIONS TO CHANGING CIRCUMSTANCES. IT	INCLUDES	ALL THE CONVENTIONAL DEMOCRATIC CHECKS AND
SIM I (48)	PROPOSAL DISHONORABLE, MR HAMMINGTAP, UNLESS IT	INCLUDES	ALL THE LADIES OF THE FAMILY. YOU WILL NOT BE
JITT PREFACE(3)	DECEMBER 1869. THE LIST OF HIS ORIGINAL WORKS	INCLUDES	EIGHT NOVELS AND VOLUMES OF STORIES, AND SIX OR
CAPT I SD(217)	TO THE MOORISH MIND. THE VIEW FROM THE GARDEN	INCLUDES	MUCH ATLANTIC OCEAN AND A LONG STRETCH OF SANDY
APPL I (225)	WHO DO NOT BELONG TO THEM AS ATHEISTS, MY COURT	INCLUDES	SEVERAL PERFECTLY RESPECTABLE WIVES AND MOTHERS
LION PREFACE(80)	IN THE PLAIN FACT THAT AS WHAT HE CALLED SIN	INCLUDES	SEX AND IS THEREFORE AN INERADICABLE PART OF HUMAN
LION PREFACE(100)	ARE NEITHER FRENCH NOR CHRISTIAN NOR MODERNIST	INCLUDES	SOME THIRTY MILLIONS OF NEGROES WHO ARE
MTH2 (78)	HAS TO ACCOUNT FOR EVERYTHING; AND EVERYTHING	INCLUDES	THE BIBLE. /FRANKLYN/ THE BOOK OF GENESIS IS A PART
GENV IV (115)	COMMUNISM HE HAS MY SYMPATHY. /COMMISSAR/ WHICH	INCLUDES	THE HELP OF YOUR GUNS AND SOLDIERS. /BBDE/ I CANNOT
GETT PREFACE(209)	WILL EVER SUCCEED OR DESERVE TO SUCCEED UNLESS IT	INCLUDES	THE RECOGNITION OF AN ABSOLUTE RIGHT TO SEXUAL
MIS. PREFACE(33)	A TASTE FOR INFANTICIDE. AND THIS RIGHT TO LIVE	INCLUDES	, AND IN FACT IS, THE RIGHT TO BE WHAT THE CHILD

		INCLUDING	
FANY I SD(273)	DINING-ROOM CHAIRS, RANGED AGAINST THE WALLS, AND	INCLUDING	A BABY ROCKING-CHAIR ON THE LADY'S SIDE OF THE
HART PREFACE(20)	THAT SEVERAL WELL-KNOWN FIRST-CLASS PASSENGERS,	INCLUDING	A FAMOUS THEATRICAL MANAGER AND THE AUTHOR OF A
PYGM II SD(233)	DUSTMAN, CLAD IN THE COSTUME OF HIS PROFESSION,	INCLUDING	A HAT WITH A BACK BRIM COVERING HIS NECK AND
INCA PREFACE(231)	ACTIVITY TO INCESSANT AND VEHEMENT WAR WORK,	INCLUDING	A HEARTBREAKING MASS OF FUSSING AND CADGING AND
MILL PREFACE(121)	OF MILITARY TASTES AND OLD SOLDIERS, INEVITABLY	INCLUDING	A PERCENTAGE OF RUFFIANS AND SADISTS. THIS FRINGE
MIS. (177)	INTO THE PAVILION, FINDING IT FULL OF PEOPLE,	INCLUDING	A STRANGER, SHE STOPS; BUT PERCIVAL, FLUSHED AND
CYMB FORWORD(134)	THAT IT WAS A COBBLED-UP AFFAIR BY SEVERAL HANDS,	INCLUDING	A VISION IN PRISON ACCOMPANIED BY SCRAPS OF QUITE
ROCK I SD(193)	WINDOWS. EVERYTHING IS ON AN IMPOSING SCALE,	INCLUDING	AN OBLONG TABLE ACROSS THE MIDDLE OF THE ROOM,
POSN PREFACE(414)	EDIFICATION, INSTRUCTION, OR ENTERTAINMENT (	INCLUDING	ANOTHER THEATRE) WOULD DRAW THE PUBLIC AWAY FROM
BARB II (307)	CONVERTED IT. WE CONVERT EVERYTHING TO GOOD HERE,	INCLUDING	BODGER. YOU REMEMBER THE CHORUS. " FOR THEE
LION PREF,FN(43)	UNJUSTLY AND ACCEPTED THE PERSONS OF THE WICKED (	INCLUDING	BY
MIS. PREFACE(72)	MAGNA CHARTA OR DECLARATION OF RIGHTS BY WAY OF	INCLUDING	CHILDREN IN THE CONSTITUTION IS A QUESTION ON
LION PREFACE(98)	BLASPHEMY AT ALL, TO TREAT ALL THE RELIGIONS,	INCLUDING	CHRISTIANITY, AS BLASPHEMOUS WHEN PARADED BEFORE
MRS PREFACE(151)	AND VERY LUCRATIVE TO GREAT CITY ESTATES,	INCLUDING	CHURCH ESTATES, THROUGH THE RENTS OF THE HOUSES IN
SUPR III (90)	WILL FIND EVERYTHING HERE THAT A LADY CAN DESIRE,	INCLUDING	DEVILS WHO WILL SERVE YOU FROM SHEER LOVE OF
BULL PREFACE(41)	ALSO THE NATIVE LANGUAGE OF HALF THE WORLD,	INCLUDING	ENGLAND. EVERY ELECTION IS FOUGHT ON NATIONALIST
DOCT PREFACE(9)	DIAGNOSIS, THOUGH IT MEANS IN MANY INSTANCES (	INCLUDING	EVEN THE IDENTIFICATION OF PATHOGENIC BACILLI
MRS PREFACE(176)	HARDLY BEEN ABLE TO APPROACH AN AMERICAN CITY,	INCLUDING	EVEN THOSE CITIES WHICH HAD HEAPED APPLAUSE ON HIM
JITT PREFACE(3)	AND VOLUMES OF STORIES, AND SIX OR SEVEN PLAYS,	INCLUDING	FRAU GITTA'S SUHNE, OF WHICH THE PRESENT WORK IS A
LION PREFACE(78)	CONDITION OF EVOLUTION, WHICH IS, THAT LIFE,	INCLUDING	HUMAN LIFE, IS CONTINUALLY EVOLVING, AND MUST
LION PREFACE(32)	THAT MANY WOMEN HAD COME WITH JESUS TO JERUSALEM,	INCLUDING	MARY MAGDALENE, OUT OF WHOM HE HAD CAST SEVEN
SUPR IV (145)	STAYIN HERE IN GRANNIDA WITH A PARTY OF ENGLISH,	INCLUDING	MY SON HECTOR. /VIOLET/ (CONVERSATIONALLY) YES.
METH PREFACE(R27)	ANY APPARENT EFFORT OF MEMORY. MOST PEOPLE,	INCLUDING	MYSELF, PLAY CHESS (WHEN THEY PLAY IT AT ALL)
PLES PREFACE(R7)	POUNDS 2 SHILLINGS 5 PENCE PER REPRESENTATION (	INCLUDING	NINE MATINEES). A PUBLISHER RECEIVING 1700 POUNDS
LION PREFACE(4)	FROM THE JEWS AND THE BARABBASQUES GENERALLY,	INCLUDING	OURSELVES. WHY JESUS MORE THAN ANOTHER? I DO NOT
GENV PREFACE(21)	AS WE HAD IN RENDERING BY THE SAME METHODS (	INCLUDING	POISON GAS) IN THE NORTH WEST PROVINCES OF INDIA,
DOCT PREFACE(61)	HAD BEEN CONDUCTED FOR MANY YEARS BY LAYMEN,	INCLUDING	QUACKS AND FADDISTS OF ALL KINDS, THAT THE PUBLIC
LION PREFACE(98)	HE WAS DOGMATIZING; AND MANY PESSIMIST SAGES,	INCLUDING	SHAKESPEAR, WHOSE HERO BEGGED HIS FRIEND TO
6CAL SD(96)	AND A GROUP OF NOBLEMEN ATTENDANT ON THE KING,	INCLUDING	SIR WALTER MANNY AND THE LORDS DERBY, NORTHAMPTON,
BARB PREFACE(227)	PRACTISING WHAT THE WORLD WILL LET THEM PRACTISE,	INCLUDING	SOAP AND WATER, COLOR AND MUSIC. THERE IS DANGER
CURE (226)	OF IT HAD A GO AT YOU; AND EVERYONE OF THEM,	INCLUDING	SOME OF THE CLEVEREST CROSS-EXAMINERS IN LONDON,
BUOY III (34)	THINGS A LADY OUGHT NOT TO KNOW. /MRS THIRDBORN/	INCLUDING	SOME THINGS NOBODY OUGHT TO KNOW. BUT IT IS NOT
JOAN PREFACE(52)	SEVERAL CRITICS ON BOTH SIDES OF THE ATLANTIC,	INCLUDING	SOME WHOSE ADMIRATION FOR MY PLAY IS MOST
HART I SD(43)	MAHOGANY ARTICLE, ODDLY UPHOLSTERED IN SAILCLOTH,	INCLUDING	THE BOLSTER, WITH A COUPLE OF BLANKETS HANGING
DOCT PREFACE(12)	IMPORTANCE OF PRESERVING THEIR BODILY INTEGRITY (	INCLUDING	THE CAPACITY FOR PARENTAGE) AND THE PLEASURE OF
DOCT I (114)	OF HIS FAVORITE MODEL FOR THE WHOLE TREATMENT,	INCLUDING	THE CURE? /MRS DUBEDAT/ YOU ARE VERY GENEROUS.
MILL PREFACE(129)	IN THE WORKING OF THE PUBLIC SERVICES,	INCLUDING	THE ELIMINATION OF DUD DIGNITARIES AND THE GENERAL
DEST (155)	SHORT OF HANGING YOU AND YOUR WHOLE HOUSEHOLD,	INCLUDING	THE LADY UPSTAIRS, WILL SATISFY ME. /GIUSEPPE/ WE
FABL PREFACE(99)	BE THE MAINSTAY OF PEACE BECAUSE ALL THE STATES (	INCLUDING	THE ONE) WILL BE AFRAID OF IT. WHEN THE SECRET IS
LADY PREFACE(229)	MORE CIRCUMSTANTIAL AND MORE ABUSIVE. EVERYBODY,	INCLUDING	THE WORKERS THEMSELVES, KNOW THAT THEY ARE DIRTY,
PYGM II SD(218)	AND CARELESS ABOUT HIMSELF AND OTHER PEOPLE,	INCLUDING	THEIR FEELINGS. HE IS, IN FACT, BUT FOR HIS YEARS
JOAN PREFACE(20)	WHO MANAGE THEIR OWN AFFAIRS AND OTHER PEOPLE'S,	INCLUDING	THOSE OF THEIR MENFOLK, AND ARE ENTIRELY MASCULINE
GENV II (53)	YOU HAVE PRODUCED A FIRST CLASS POLITICAL CRISIS,	INCLUDING	WHAT PROMISES TO BE A WORLD WAR, AND MADE AN
POSN (453)	OF IMMORAL RELATIONS WITH EVERY MAN IN THIS TOWN,	INCLUDING	YOURSELF, SHERIFF. I SAY THIS IS A CONSPIRACY TO
APPL I (210)	ON ME TODAY WITH SOME OF HIS COLLEAGUES --	INCLUDING	, I HOPE, YOURSELF -- TO DISCUSS THE CRISIS. (
		INCLUSION	
ROCK I (200)	ARE; BUT THE DIVISION MIGHT HAVE AFFECTED THEIR	INCLUSION	IN THE NEXT CABINET. THE WHOLE HOUSE ROSE AT IT.
		INCLUSIVE	
BULL IV (168)	FRIDAY TO TUESDAY, RAILWAY TICKET AND HOTEL ALL	INCLUSIVE	, I TELL YOU, NORA, I'M GOING TO DEVELOP THIS
		INCOGNITA	
GETT (339)	AND FACING HER, BREATHLESS) MRS COLLINS! YOU ARE	INCOGNITA	APPASSIONATA! /MRS GEORGE/ YOU READ MY LETTERS,
GETT (285)	THAT FASCINATES ME. /MRS BRIDGENORTH/ DO YOU MEAN	INCOGNITA	APPASSIONATA? /THE BISHOP/ YES. /THE GENERAL (
GETT (285)	THERE REALLY IS SOMETHING FASCINATING ABOUT	INCOGNITA	, SHE NEVER GIVES HER ADDRESS. THATS A GOOD SIGN.
		INCOGNITO	
MTH4 I (144)	IS REALLY THE EMPEROR OF TURANIA TRAVELLING	INCOGNITO	. I UNDERSTAND HE HAS A QUESTION TO PUT TO THE
INCA (243)	THE USUAL THING. IT IS THE INCA HIMSELF,	INCOGNITO	. /THE PRINCESS/ OH, SEND HIM AWAY. OH, I'M SO
		INCOHERENT	
PLES PREFACE(R10)	WAS THE HIGHER BUT VAGUER AND TIMIDER VISION, THE	INCOHERENT	, MISCHIEVOUS, AND EVEN RIDICULOUS
		INCOME	
FABL PREFACE(67)	INCOME IS AN OBVIOUS COROLLARY. YES; BUT HOW MUCH	INCOME	? A NATIONAL DIVIDEND OF, SAY, THIRTEEN SHILLINGS A
BARB PREFACE(234)	AND DUCHESSES, IN WHICH ALL THE GRADES OF	INCOME	AND CASTE REPRESENT DISTINCT ANIMALS WHO MUST NOT BE
ARMS II SD(25)	ABOUT 50, NATURALLY UNAMBITIOUS EXCEPT AS TO HIS	INCOME	AND HIS IMPORTANCE IN LOCAL SOCIETY, BUT JUST NOW
GENV PREFACE(23)	EQUALITY BETWEEN THEM IS EITHER EQUALITY OF	INCOME	AND OF INCOME ONLY OR AN OBVIOUS LIE. EQUALITY OF
SUPR HANDBOK(208)	A THOUSAND CHANGES ON THE DIFFERENT SCALES OF	INCOME	AND PRESSURE OF POPULATION, FIRMLY BELIEVING ALL THE
MTH3 (104)	YOU DO NOT COMPREHEND THE RELATION BETWEEN	INCOME	AND PRODUCTION. /BARNABAS/ I UNDERSTAND MY OWN
MIS. PREFACE(87)	AND EVERYONE WISHES TO DECEIVE HIM AS TO HIS	INCOME	AND SOCIAL IMPORTANCE, IS IN EFFECT BROKEN UP BY
MILL IV (196)	HOW CAN I AFFORD TO LOSE A CLIENT WITH SUCH AN	INCOME	AND SUCH A TEMPER? HER TANTRUMS ARE WORTH TWO OR
GENV PREFACE(18)	UP BETWEEN THE BOURGEOISIE FOR WHICH HE HAD NO	INCOME	AND THE WORKING CLASS FOR WHICH HE HAD NO CRAFT. BUT
SIM PREFACE(9)	INCOME; AND HUNDREDS OF MILLIONS OF THE COUNTRY'S	INCOME	ARE LAVISHED ANNUALLY ON LADIES AND GENTLEMEN WHILST
JITT PREFACE(4)	NINETEENTH CENTURY I WAS DERIVING A SUBSTANTIAL	INCOME	AS A PLAYWRIGHT FROM AMERICA AND CENTRAL EUROPE. NOT
BARB I (252)	FOR YOU AND THE OTHER CHILDREN TO LIVE ON MY	INCOME	AS LONG AS WE ARE IN THE SAME HOUSE; BUT I CANT KEEP
LION PREFACE(61)	THAT WE MUST BEGIN BY HOLDING THE RIGHT TO AN	INCOME	AS SACRED AND EQUAL, JUST AS WE NOW BEGIN BY HOLDING
GETT PREFACE(202)	TWO CASES OF THE SINGLE ROOM AND THE UNEARNED	INCOME	AS THE EXTREMES, WE MIGHT PERHAPS LOCATE AT A GUESS
LION PREFACE(61)	DESTROYED IN ALL DIRECTIONS BY INEQUALITY OF	INCOME	BETWEEN CLASSES: SUCH STABILITY AS IT HAS IS DUE TO
LADY PREFACE(215)	FOR HIM TO RISK PERHAPS FIVE YEARS OF A SLENDER	INCOME	BY AN APPEAL TO A PREJUDICED ORTHODOX JURY; AND THEY
BARB I (251)	BUT THE WILL SAYS ALSO THAT IF HE INCREASES HIS	INCOME	BY HIS OWN EXERTIONS, THEY MAY DOUBLE THE INCREASE.
BARB I (257)	BRITOMART/ BUT AFTER ALL, STEPHEN, OUR PRESENT	INCOME	COMES FROM ANDREW. /STEPHEN/ (SHOCKED) I NEVER KNEW
MTH3 (110)	BEFORE THE 1969 ACT FOR THE REDISTRIBUTION OF	INCOME	ENTITLED ME TO A HANDSOME RETIRING PENSION. OWING TO
LION PREFACE(57)	ASKED AT THE BEGINNING. WHAT DO YOU GIVE A MAN AN	INCOME	FOR? OBVIOUSLY TO KEEP HIM ALIVE. SINCE IT IS
PYGM II (222)	FOR A LESSON. TWO-FIFTHS OF A MILLIONAIRE'S	INCOME	FOR A DAY WOULD BE SOMEWHERE ABOUT 60 POUNDS. IT'S
PYGM II (222)	CONTINUING) SHE OFFERS ME TWO-FIFTHS OF HER DAY'S	INCOME	FOR A LESSON. TWO-FIFTHS OF A MILLIONAIRE'S INCOME
DOCT PREFACE(29)	OF THE MEDICAL PROFESSION TODAY IS TO SECURE AN	INCOME	FOR THE PRIVATE DOCTOR; AND TO THIS CONSIDERATION ALL
GETT PREFACE(210)	SHARE IN A FIRST-RATE MAN. SUBSTITUTE THE WORD	INCOME	FOR THE WORD MAN, AND YOU WILL HAVE THE QUESTION AS
LION PREFACE(59)	BUT IN THE HUGE MASS OF MANKIND VARIATION OF	INCOME	FROM INDIVIDUAL TO INDIVIDUAL IS UNKNOWN, BECAUSE IT
WIDO III (62)	OF BEING AVARICIOUS, HARRY. TWO THIRDS OF YOUR	INCOME	GONE AT ONE BLOW. AND I MUST SAY IT SERVES YOU RIGHT.
LION PREFACE(57)	SCHOOL IDEA, WITH ITS PRINCIPLE " TO EACH THE	INCOME	HE DESERVES," IS REALLY TOO SILLY FOR DISCUSSION.
CURE (236)	GATHERED TO AND CHERISHED, A BREADWINNER ON WHOSE	INCOME	I CAN LIVE WITHOUT THE SORDID HORRORS OF HAVING TO
LION PREFACE(55)	BETTER. THE NEED FOR A DRASTIC REDISTRIBUTION OF	INCOME	IN ALL CIVILIZED COUNTRIES IS NOW AS OBVIOUS AND AS
HART PREFACE(37)	OF HIS DEATH DUTIES, HE IS LUCKY IF HIS NET	INCOME	IS 10,000 POUNDS, THOUGH HIS NOMINAL PROPERTY REMAINS
FABL PREFACE(67)	THIS CLOSED THE CORRESPONDENCE. EQUALITY OF	INCOME	IS AN OBVIOUS COROLLARY. YES; BUT HOW MUCH INCOME? A
WIDO II (42)	TRENCH). AND NOW, DR TRENCH, MAY I ASK WHAT YOUR	INCOME	IS DERIVED FROM? /TRENCH/ (DEFIANTLY) FROM
WIDO I (22)	MORTGAGE FROM WHICH, IF I MISTAKE NOT, HIS ENTIRE	INCOME	IS DERIVED. THE TRUTH IS, MR COKANE, I AM QUITE WELL
NEVR II (250)	THERES A PRETENCE THAT I DONT GET THEM. WHY, HIS	INCOME	IS MOSTLY FEES, SIR; AND I UNDERSTAND THERES A
NEVR II (250)	PUT ON A WIG AND GOWN TO SHEW WHAT HE IS. IF MY	INCOME	IS MOSTLY TIPS, AND THERES A PRETENCE THAT I DONT GET
GENV PREFACE(23)	AND OF INCOME ONLY OR AN OBVIOUS LIE. EQUALITY OF	INCOME	IS PRACTICABLE ENOUGH: ANY SPORTING PEER WITH HIS
MIS. PREFACE(35)	AND THAT WHOEVER IS NOT BORN TO AN INDEPENDENT	INCOME	IS STRIVING FOR ONE OR LONGING FOR ONE BECAUSE IT
FABL PREFACE(78)	LETTERS FROM DEVOUT SHAVIANS WHO BELIEVE THAT MY	INCOME	IS UNLIMITED, MY KNOWLEDGE AND WISDOM INFINITE, MY
DOCT PREFACE(29)	EVERY ADVANCE OF SCIENCE THAT THREATENS HIS	INCOME	. AND AS THE ADVANCE OF SCIENTIFIC HYGIENE TENDS TO
BULL PREFACE(15)	FOREIGNERS FOR THE MANAGEMENT OF HIS SOURCES OF	INCOME	. AT ALL EVENTS I AM PERSUADED THAT A MODERN NATION

MILL IV (194) YOUR FATHER FOUNDED: YOU DONT REALLY EARN YOUR INCOME . BESIDES, HANG IT ALL! A MAN ACCUSING A WOMAN OF
BUOY III (31) NOT TAXED, AS THEY ARE CLASSED AS CAPITAL, NOT AS INCOME . CONSEQUENTLY IT HAS BEEN POSSIBLE FOR YOUR FATHER
APPL PREFACE(180) IT, SO DO I. THAT IS WHY I INSIST ON EQUALITY OF INCOME . EQUAL CONSIDERATION FOR A PERSON WITH A HUNDRED A
BARB I (252) /STEPHEN/ OF COURSE I WAS THINKING ONLY OF HIS INCOME . HOWEVER, HE IS NOT LIKELY TO BE EXTRAVAGANT. /LADY
BASH II,1, (110) SUM. /LYDIA/ THOU SILLY CASHEL, TIS BUT A WEEK'S INCOME . I DID PROPOSE TO GIVE THEE THREE TIMES THAT FOR
BARB III (346) IT FOR A PROFESSORSHIP. I HAVE SOLD IT FOR AN INCOME . I HAVE SOLD IT TO ESCAPE BEING IMPRISONED FOR
GETT (294) RIGHT ARM THAN A HUNDRED A YEAR FROM MY MOTHER'S INCOME . I OWE EVERYTHING TO HER CARE OF ME. EDITH, IN
PYGM EPILOG (289) AND THAT, AGAIN, WILL DEPEND ON HER AGE AND INCOME . IF SHE IS AT THE END OF HER YOUTH, AND HAS NO
HART PREFACE(37) CHANGE MADE BY THE WAR IN THE DISTRIBUTION OF INCOME . IT SEEMS ONLY THE OTHER DAY THAT A MILLIONAIRE WAS
WIDO III (61) MY LESSON; AND I'M GOING TO STICK TO MY PRESENT INCOME . IT'S LITTLE ENOUGH FOR ME AS IT IS. /SARTORIUS/ IT
NEVR IV (297) THE STRENGTH OF YOUR POSITION LIES IN YOUR INCOME . (HE CLAPS ON THE FALSE NOSE, AND IS AGAIN
LION PREFACE(61) OF PEOPLE BETWEEN WHOM THERE IS EQUALITY OF INCOME . JESUS AS ECONOMIST. IT SEEMS THEREFORE THAT WE MUST
SUPR IV (157) FOR A MAN IN LONDON IF HE HAS A COMFORTABLE INCOME . /OCTAVIUS/ (CONSIDERABLY COOLED, BUT BELIEVING
BARB II (286) I WOULDNT HAVE YOUR CONSCIENCE, NOT FOR ALL YOUR INCOME . /UNDERSHAFT/ I WOULDNT HAVE YOUR INCOME, NOT FOR
PHIL I (77) BE SUPPORTED AND PENSIONED IN OLD AGE OUT OF HIS INCOME . THATS THE ADVANCED VIEW: OUR VIEW. BESIDES, IF YOU
LION PREFACE(58) VIRTUE." WE ALL STRIVE TOWARDS AN INDEPENDENT INCOME . WE ALL KNOW AS WELL AS JESUS DID THAT IF WE HAVE TO
GETT SD(259) ROOMS IN THE HOUSE. THE BISHOP HAS NEITHER THE INCOME NOR THE APPETITE TO HAVE HIS COOKING DONE THERE. THE
DEVL II SD(28) POULTRY, PIGS NOR CATTLE; A STEADY AND SUFFICIENT INCOME NOT DIRECTLY DEPENDENT ON HARVESTS AND PRICES AT
MIS. PREFACE(77) BY THE WAY, I VERY NEARLY DID, MY PROFESSIONAL INCOME NOT HAVING AS YET BEGUN TO SPROUT). THERE ARE MASSES
MILL I (139) THIRTY. IT BROKE HIS HEART. /SAGAMORE/ STILL, AN INCOME OF A MILLION AND A HALF-- /EPIFANIA/ MAN: YOU FORGET
DOCT PREFACE(27) OFF THAN THE PATIENT) TO ASSUME THAT THE AVERAGE INCOME OF AN ENGLISH FAMILY IS ABOUT 2000 POUNDS A YEAR, AND
MILL I (139) KNOW WHAT THAT MEANS TO A WOMAN BROUGHT UP ON AN INCOME OF SEVEN FIGURES? THE HUMILIATION OF IT! /SAGAMORE/
2TRU PREFACE(12) THE RIGHT TO LIVE FOR NOTHING ON THE FUTURE INCOME OF THE COUNTRY UNTIL THEIR MONEY WAS RETURNED: A
CAPT I (230) OF THE WEST INDIAN SUGAR INDUSTRY CONVERTED THE INCOME OF THE ESTATE INTO AN ANNUAL LOSS OF ABOUT 150 POUNDS
BARB PREFACE(224) LOVELY WAYS OF LIFE. HE HAS ONLY TO FOLLOW UP THE INCOME OF THE SWEET LADIES TO ITS INDUSTRIAL SOURCE, AND
MIS. PREFACE(103) LIKE SAYING TO A LABORER BROUGHT UP ON A FAMILY INCOME OF THIRTEEN SHILLINGS A WEEK, " HERE IS ONE HUNDRED
MILL I (142) SHOULD NOT DREAM OF LAUGHING AT A CLIENT WITH AN INCOME OF THREE QUARTERS OF A MILLION. /EPIFANIA/ HAVE YOU A
BUOY III (43) AND WITH WHAT I COULD SPARE I HAVE DOUBLED MY INCOME ON THE MONEY MARKET. I HAVE INHERITED MY FATHER'S
SUPR HANDBOK(182) DEVELOPED PUBLIC CONDITIONS AS TO PLACE ITS INCOME ON THE SAME FOOTING AS THAT OF A PROPERTYLESS
GENV PREFACE(23) BETWEEN THEM IS EITHER EQUALITY OF INCOME AND OF INCOME ONLY OR AN OBVIOUS LIE. EQUALITY OF INCOME IS
FABL PREFACE(68) NEW READERS SATURATED WITH THE COMMON NOTION THAT INCOME OUGHT TO VARY WITH MENTAL CAPACITY, PERSONAL TALENT,
FABL PREFACE(68) TO DO WITH THE INSANE MISDISTRIBUTION OF NATIONAL INCOME PRODUCED BY NINETEENTH CENTURY PLUTOCRACY. AND SO I
MIS. PREFACE(38) OWN PERSON (IT IS RETINUE THAT EATS UP THE BIG INCOME) WITHOUT WORKING TOO HARD OR TOO LONG FOR QUITE AS
LION PREFACE(60) IS NARROWED TO A HANDFUL OF PERSONS OF SIMILAR INCOME ; AND BEAUTY AND HEALTH BECOME THE DREAMS OF ARTISTS
SIM PREFACE(9) THE OBJECT OF EVERYONE'S AMBITION IS AN UNEARNED INCOME ; AND HUNDREDS OF MILLIONS OF THE COUNTRY'S INCOME
LION PREFACE(58) THE GREEKS SAID, " FIRST SECURE AN INDEPENDENT INCOME ; AND THEN PRACTISE VIRTUE." WE ALL STRIVE TOWARDS AN
WIDO II (39) ASKING HER TO BE CONTENT TO LIVE ON MY OWN LITTLE INCOME ; AND YET SHE TURNED ON ME AS IF I'D BEHAVED LIKE A
LION PREFACE(59) QUESTION OF THE PROPORTION IN WHICH THE NATIONAL INCOME SHALL BE DISTRIBUTED CAN HAVE ONLY ONE ANSWER. ALL
LION PREFACE(55) UNPRACTICAL NOTION THAT IN SOME WAY A MAN'S INCOME SHOULD BE GIVEN HIM, NOT TO ENABLE HIM TO LIVE, BUT
PYGM EPILOG (294) AS MRS EYNSFORD HILL TO LIVE IN EARLSCOURT ON AN INCOME SO PITIABLY SMALLER THAT I HAVE NOT THE HEART TO
APPL PREFACE(185) NOT GET ANY OF IT. THE OTHER PAYERS OF SURTAX AND INCOME TAX AND DEATH DUTIES WOULD SAVE THE INTEREST THEY NOW
ROCK II (240) PLEDGED NOW TO GIVE US OUR PAY HONESTLY FREE OF INCOME TAX AND MAKE THESE LAZY IDLE LUBBERS OF LANDLORDS
HART PREFACE(37) 50,000 POUNDS A YEAR. TODAY, WHEN HE HAS PAID HIS INCOME TAX AND SUPER TAX, AND INSURED HIS LIFE FOR THE
APPL PREFACE(185) POSSESSIONS; BUT I AM AN OLD MAN PAYING ENOUGH IN INCOME TAX AND SURTAX TO PROVIDE DOLES FOR SOME HUNDREDS OF
2TRU PREFACE(22) FACED: OUR CLANDESTINE METHODS OF VIOLATING IT BY INCOME TAX AND SURTAX, WHICH MEAN ONLY " WHAT A THIEF STOLE
MILL IV (200) OF THE MONTH. I SUBSCRIBE A GUINEA A YEAR TO THE INCOME TAX PAYERS' DEFENCE LEAGUE; BUT THAT IS ALL:
VWOO 3 (133) SALISBURY DOES ALL THAT WHEN HE MAKES OUT THE INCOME TAX RETURN. YOURE NOT EXPECTED TO DO FIGURES IN THIS
BULL PREFACE(29) CHURCH RATES REVIVED IN THE FORM OF AN UNOFFICIAL INCOME TAX SCIENTIFICALLY ADJUSTED TO YOUR TAXABLE CAPACITY
ROCK II (257) IN THE POUND! ! /SIR DEXTER/ NEVER MIND MY INCOME TAX, IF WHAT YOU SAID JUST NOW MEANS ANYTHING IT
ROCK II (257) TO KNOW BETTER, ARE ALWAYS COMPLAINING OF THE INCOME TAX, /THE DUKE/ BUT FIVE SHILLINGS IN THE POUND,
DOCT PREFACE(63) CLASSES, HIS FEES HAVE TO BE GRADUATED LIKE THE INCOME TAX, THE SUCCESSFUL FASHIONABLE DOCTOR MAY WEED HIS
ROCK II (240) A BATTLESHIP, AND THEN DOCK A QUARTER OFF IT FOR INCOME TAX, WE CANT SET FOOT ON SHORE WITHOUT BEING RENTED
GENV IV (99) AND SECOND THAT HE WANTED YOUR MONEY TO PAY HIS INCOME TAX-- A HIGHLY PATRIOTIC MOTIVE-- WOULD YOU ACCEPT
ROCK II (249) OF MY UNFORTUNATE FELLOW LANDLORDS IN THE FORM OF INCOME TAX, SURTAX, AND ESTATE DUTIES-- WHAT YOU CALL DEATH
FABL PREFACE(84) MORE GRUDGINGLY WITH A VIEW TO EQUALITY OF INCOME THAN THE KREMLIN. STALIN'S RUSSO-FABIAN SLOGAN,
BARB I (251) EXERTIONS ARE MUCH MORE LIKELY TO DECREASE HIS INCOME THAN TO INCREASE IT. SARAH WILL HAVE TO FIND AT LEAST
LION PREFACE(55) TO EACH PERSON THE EXACT PORTION OF THE NATIONAL INCOME THAT HE OR SHE HAS PRODUCED. TO A CHILD IT SEEMS THAT
LION PREFACE(63) EQUAL DISTRIBUTION OF THE SURPLUS OF THE NATIONAL INCOME THAT IS NOT ABSORBED BY SIMPLE COMMUNISM. JUDGE NOT.
JITT II SD(33) HOME TO KEEP AND A FAMILY TO MANAGE ON A SLENDER INCOME THAT SHE IS SET DOWN AS MUCH OLDER AND LESS
LION PREFACE(56) THE LATE MR BARNEY BARNATO RECEIVED AS HIS LAWFUL INCOME THREE THOUSAND TIMES AS MUCH MONEY AS AN ENGLISH
FABL PREFACE(67) IS THREATENED. CONSEQUENTLY THE BASIC INCOME TO BE AIMED AT MUST BE SUFFICIENT TO ESTABLISH
BUOY PREFACE(4) A DOWNSTART GENTLEMAN DRIVEN BY LACK OF UNEARNED INCOME TO BECOME AN INCOMPETENT MERCHANT AND HARP ON HIS
MIS. PREFACE(12) ADULT PARENTS, IN SPITE OF A HOUSE TO KEEP AND AN INCOME TO EARN, CAN STILL INTERFERE TO A DISASTROUS EXTENT
LION PREFACE(60) REASONS FOR OBJECTING TO CLASS STRATIFICATION OF INCOME WHICH HAVE HEAPED THEMSELVES UP SINCE THE TIME OF
DOCT PREFACE(16) SATISFY HIS OWN REQUIREMENTS, ABOVE ALL, THE INCOME WHICH PROVIDES FOR THESE OUTGOINGS STOPS THE MOMENT
BULL PREFACE(17) BY AN ATTEMPT TO KEEP A PARK AND A STABLE ON AN INCOME WHICH WOULD NOT JUSTIFY AN ENGLISHMAN IN VENTURING
FABL PREFACE(68) CALLED CAPITAL, TO EXPERIMENT WITH; FOR THE BASIC INCOME WILL KEEP THEM IN THE NORMAL GROOVES. SO MUCH FOR THE
APPL PREFACE(185) ADVOCATED IT STRONGLY FOR YEARS BEFORE I HAD ANY INCOME WORTH TAXING. BUT I COULD NOT DO IT IF THE GOVERNMENT
BULL I (95) THOUGH WE MUST FACE THE FACT THAT IN ENGLAND HER INCOME WOULD HARDLY MAINTAIN HER IN THE LOWER MIDDLE CLASS--
BARB PREFACE(217) LIFE NOW PROCURABLE IS LIFE ON AN INDEPENDENT INCOME , ALL SENSIBLE PEOPLE AIM AT SECURING SUCH AN INCOME,
BARB PREFACE(217) ALL SENSIBLE PEOPLE AIM AT SECURING SUCH AN INCOME , AND ARE, OF COURSE, CAREFUL TO LEGALIZE AND
ROCK PREFACE(170) BY GIVING THEM ALL THE SAME EDUCATION AND INCOME , AND RANKING THEM ALL IN THE SAME CLASS. FOR
ROCK II (237) PUBLIC SERVICE FOR ALL, IRRESPECTIVE OF INCOME , AS IN WAR TIME. /SIR DEXTER/ SLAVERY. CALL IT BY
HART III (132) NONSENSE, MR MANGAN! IT ALL TURNS ON YOUR INCOME , DOESNT IT? /MANGAN/ WELL, IF YOU COME TO THAT, HOW
DEST (176) KNOWS THAT SHE HAS LIED TO HIM ABOUT HER AGE, HER INCOME , HER SOCIAL POSITION, ABOUT EVERYTHING THAT SILLY
2TRU PREFACE(6) OF THE FUNERAL OF A SHIPPING MAGNATE WHOSE INCOME , IF THE CAPITAL VALUE OF THE PROPERTY LEFT BY HIM BE
PYGM II (221) SHILLING, BUT AS A PERCENTAGE OF THIS GIRL'S INCOME , IT WORKS OUT AS FULLY EQUIVALENT TO SIXTY OR
BARB II (286) ALL YOUR INCOME. /UNDERSHAFT/ I WOULDNT HAVE YOUR INCOME , NOT FOR ALL YOUR CONSCIENCE, MR SHIRLEY. (HE GOES
FABL PREFACE(67) ABILITY AND MENTAL SCOPE, THE SAME BASIC INCOME , OR RATION, OR MINIMUM WAGE, OR NATIONAL DIVIDEND,
WIDO I (22) ONE ANOTHER). /SARTORIUS/ (VERY DELIBERATELY) MY INCOME , SIR, IS DERIVED FROM THE RENTAL OF A VERY EXTENSIVE
GETT PREFACE(202) THE SAME HOUSE, THE SAME CHILDREN, AND THE SAME INCOME , WHICH IS QUITE A DIFFERENT MATTER. THE
MIS. PREFACE(32) OUR RIDICULOUS MISDISTRIBUTION OF THE NATIONAL INCOME , WITH ITS ACCOMPANYING CLASS DISTINCTIONS AND
BARB PREFACE(217) LIVE BY MEANS OF WHAT IS CALLED " AN INDEPENDENT INCOME " WOULD BE THE SHORTEST WAY TO THE LETHAL CHAMBER.
WIDO II (39) BEHAVED LIKE A SAVAGE. /SARTORIUS/ LIVE ON YOUR INCOME ! IMPOSSIBLE: MY DAUGHTER IS ACCUSTOMED TO A PROPER
PYGM III (258) HER OWN LIVING WITHOUT GIVING HER A FINE LADY'S INCOME ! IS THAT WHAT YOU MEAN? /PICKERING/ (INDULGENTLY,

INCOME-TAX

BARB PREFACE(218) TO BE IMPOSED ON. THE REASON WHY THE INDEPENDENT INCOME-TAX PAYERS ARE NOT SOLID IN DEFENCE OF THEIR POSITION

INCOME-TAXED

ROCK II (245) OFFERS; AND ON THAT THREE AND A HALF I SHALL BE INCOME-TAXED AND SURTAXED, JAFNA'S GRANDSONS WILL GO TO

INCOMES

DOCT PREFACE(28) THE EXTINCTION OF A CONSIDERABLE PART OF THEIR INCOMES ; A PART, TOO, THAT IS EASILY AND REGULARLY EARNED,
LION PREFACE(52) WOMAN ONE VOTE, AND UNIVERSAL SUFFRAGE AND EQUAL INCOMES AND ALL SORTS OF MODERN POLITICAL MEASURES. EVEN IN
BARB PREFACE(224) ANYBODY EXCEPT SWEET OLD LADIES WITH INDEPENDENT INCOMES AND GENTLE AND LOVELY WAYS OF LIFE. HE HAS ONLY TO
MIS. PREFACE(35) OUT THAT THE WRETCHED PEOPLE WHO HAVE INDEPENDENT INCOMES AND NO USEFUL OCCUPATION, DO THE MOST AMAZINGLY
DOCT PREFACE(20) UNQUALIFIED PRACTITIONERS NOW MAKE LARGE INCOMES AS HYGIENISTS, AND ARE RESORTED TO AS FREQUENTLY BY
APPL PREFACE(185) AND REDISTRIBUTING IT AMONG PEOPLE WHO HAVE NO INCOMES AT ALL, I COULD DO NOTHING BY MYSELF. WHAT COULD I
DOCT PREFACE(29) BY GENERATIONS OF APOTHECARY-DOCTORS WHOSE INCOMES DEPENDED ON THE QUANTITY OF DRUGS THEY COULD INDUCE
MRS PREFACE(177) THE STREETS, AS IF VICIOUS WOMEN WITH INDEPENDENT INCOMES EVER WENT THERE. THESE ARE THE PEOPLE WHO, INDULGENT
HART PREFACE(37) OF THE SCALE MILLIONS OF PERSONS HAVE HAD REGULAR INCOMES FOR THE FIRST TIME IN THEIR LIVES; AND THEIR MEN
LION PREFACE(59) EVER HAS BEEN, BUT THE DIFFERENCES BETWEEN CLASS INCOMES , ALREADY THERE IS ECONOMIC EQUALITY BETWEEN
LION PREFACE(59) OF ROBBERS, AND HAVE GROTESQUELY DIFFERENT INCOMES , BUT IN THE HUGE MASS OF MANKIND VARIATION OF
LION PREFACE(63) FOR WHICH, THEREFORE, THEY MUST HAVE INDIVIDUAL INCOMES , FOREIGN TRAVEL IS AN OBVIOUS INSTANCE. WE ARE SO
BUOY III (31) BE TAXED LIKE EVERYONE ELSE, IF YOU HAVE ANY INCOMES . HAVE YOU? /THE WIDOWER/ ALL I KNOW IS THAT WHAT
BUOY IV (55) BILL/ NO THEY WONT. THEY CAN LIVE ON THEIR WIVES' INCOMES , I TOOK CARE OF THAT. /SIR FERDINAND/ WELL, THAT IS

ROCK II (237)	/BASHAM/ DOUBLING OF THE SURTAX ON UNEARNED	INCOMES	. /SIR DEXTER/ YES: TAKE OUR LAST PENNY! AND WHEN
DOCT PREFACE(69)	THEY WILL HAVE NO ANXIETY WHATEVER ABOUT THEIR	INCOMES	. THE FUTURE OF PRIVATE PRACTICE. IT MUST NOT BE
GENV III (73)	ANY DOCTRINE THAT THREATENS ITS EXISTENCE OR THE	INCOMES	OF ITS RULERS. THE ONLY DIFFERENCE IS THAT IN RUSSIA
ROCK II (244)	BUT AS A SANE MAN OF BUSINESS. IF YOU DESTROY THE	INCOMES	OF OUR LANDED GENTRY WHERE WILL YOU FIND THE CAPITAL
LION PREFACE(59)	SO: IT ALWAYS WILL BE SO. IT IS TRUE THAT THE	INCOMES	OF ROBBERS VARY CONSIDERABLY FROM INDIVIDUAL TO
BUOY III (32)	ALL THE KING'S MEN CANNOT BRING BACK THE UNEARNED	INCOMES	OF THE NINETEENTH CENTURY. THE SOCIALISTS AND TRADE
LION PREFACE(59)	INDIVIDUAL; AND THE VARIATION IS REFLECTED IN THE	INCOMES	OF THEIR PARASITES. THE COMMERCIALIZATION OF CERTAIN
DOCT PREFACE(68)	HAVE BEEN IN CHARGE; AND NOT TO THE SIZE OF THE	INCOMES	THE LOCAL PRIVATE DOCTORS ARE MAKING OUT OF THE
BUOY III (29)	WE ARE ENTIRELY DEPENDENT ON OUR FATHER FOR OUR	INCOMES	WE CAN DEFEND OURSELVES AGAINST HIS TYRANNY ONLY BY
HART PREFACE(6)	CHERRY ORCHARD. EVEN THOSE WHO LIVED WITHIN THEIR	INCOMES	WERE REALLY KEPT GOING BY THEIR SOLICITORS AND
MTH3 (106)	NOT ROBBED THE EXCHEQUER BY DRAWING FIVE OR SIX	INCOMES	WHEN HE WAS ONLY ENTITLED TO ONE? ANSWER ME THAT.
APPL PREFACE(183)	COMMUNISM AND THE DRASTIC TAXATION OF UNEARNED	INCOMES	WHICH FINANCES IT WERE TO STOP, OUR PRIVATE
HART PREFACE(4)	WHEN THEY COULD, THEY LIVED WITHOUT SCRUPLE ON	INCOMES	WHICH THEY DID NOTHING TO EARN. THE WOMEN IN THEIR
UNPL PREFACE(R12)	THEM AND THE PLEASANT PEOPLE WITH " INDEPENDENT"	INCOMES	WHO IMAGINE THAT SUCH SORDID MATTERS DO NOT TOUCH
BUOY III (31)	WITH HIS DEATH, WHICH CANNOT NOW BE FAR OFF. YOUR	INCOMES	WILL BE TAXED LIKE EVERYONE ELSES, IF YOU HAVE ANY
BUOY III (40)	IS FINISHED. SIR FERDINAND HAS TOLD US THAT OUR	INCOMES	WILL STOP WHEN OUR FATHER DIES. HE HAS ADVISED US
BUOY IV (55)	AS YOU INSTRUCTED ME, THAT THE SOURCE OF THEIR	INCOMES	WOULD DRY UP AT YOUR DEATH, AND THEY MUST THEN FEND
LION PREFACE(59)	EXCEPTIONAL TALENTS HAS ALSO PRODUCED EXCEPTIONAL	INCOMES	, DIRECT AND DERIVATIVE. PERSONS WHO LIVE ON RENT OF
BUOY III (31)	CHANCELLOR OF THE EXCHEQUER MAY TAX MONEY MARKET	INCOMES	, EITHER AS SUCH OR AS GAMBLING. IN THAT CASE THE
BUOY III (38)	WE ARE DEALING WITH THE HARD CASH OF YOUR	INCOMES	, NOT WITH SOLOMON AND MAHOMET. WE ARE NOT MORMONS.
SUPR I (14)	ASHAMED OF OURSELVES, OF OUR RELATIVES, OF OUR	INCOMES	, OF OUR ACCENTS, OF OUR OPINIONS, OF OUR

INCOMMODE

APPL I (203)	DO THEY INCOMMODE YOU? /BOANERGES/ OH, THEY DONT	INCOMMODE	ME. I AM READY TO HAVE OUR TALK OUT IN TRAFALGAR
APPL I (203)	PASSES? /MAGNUS/ MY PRIVATE SECRETARIES. DO THEY	INCOMMODE	YOU? /BOANERGES/ OH, THEY DONT INCOMMODE ME. I AM

INCOMMODED

BULL IV (165)	THING THIS WILL BE FOR BOTH OF US. /NORA/ (	INCOMMODED	AND NOT AT ALL ENRAPTURED BY HIS ARDOR) YOURE

INCOMMUNICABLE

METH PREFACE(R65)	FOUND THEIR INTELLECTUAL VISION OF THE WORLD	INCOMMUNICABLE	TO THOSE WHO WERE NOT BORN WITH IT. IT CAME

INCOMPATIBILITY

ROCK PREFACE(160)	WHICH IS ALWAYS INCORRIGIBLE SOCIAL	INCOMPATIBILITY	AND NOTHING ELSE. THE RUSSIAN EXPERIMENT.
ROCK PREFACE(170)	IT IS POSSIBLE TO GET RID OF THEIR SOCIAL	INCOMPATIBILITY	BY GIVING THEM ALL THE SAME EDUCATION AND
MIS. PREFACE(81)	TAKE A VERY COMMON INSTANCE OF THIS AGONIZING	INCOMPATIBILITY	. A WIDOW BRINGS UP HER SON TO MANHOOD. HE
NEVR III (276)	(NOBODY'S FAULT, YOU KNOW, BUT PURELY ACCIDENTAL	INCOMPATIBILITY	OF TASTES); WHEN HE IS DEPRIVED BY THAT
ROCK PREFACE(165)	ANY RUSSIAN OF BEING A LADY OR A GENTLEMAN.	INCOMPATIBILITY	OF PEASANTRY WITH MODERN CIVILIZATION.
ROCK PREFACE(151)	CHARLES'S PRIVATE CHARACTER. IT WAS SOLELY FOR	INCOMPATIBILITY	OF POLITICS THAT HE WAS ELIMINATED, OR "
DOCT I SD(96)	CHEERING, REASSURING, HEALING BY THE MERE	INCOMPATIBILITY	OF DISEASE OR ANXIETY WITH HIS WELCOME
ROCK PREFACE(147)	KILLED. AS TO TIGERS AND POISONOUS SNAKES, THEIR	INCOMPATIBILITY	WITH HUMAN CIVILIZATION IS UNQUESTIONED.

INCOMPATIBLE

JITT III (62)	REALLY WAS LONELY HERE OWING TO YOUR MOTHER BEING	INCOMPATIBLE	AND ALL THAT, THEN I QUITE AGREE IT WAS A MERCY
PHIL I (80)	I WONT, MY DEAR. THATS FLAT. WE'RE INTELLECTUALLY	INCOMPATIBLE	. /JULIA/ BUT WHY? WE COULD BE SO HAPPY. YOU
CLEO NOTES (205)	OF MAN WITH WHOM THE COMMON LABORER IS SOCIALLY	INCOMPATIBLE	. THE SAME THING IS TRUE OF HORSES AND DOGS.
MIS. PREFACE(67)	WINDS AND THE WEATHER. SUCH A STATE OF MIND IS	INCOMPATIBLE	NOT ONLY WITH THE DEMOCRATIC INTRODUCTION OF
SUPR III (75)	AND THEY HAVE PUT BEFORE US THREE DISTINCT AND	INCOMPATIBLE	VIEWS OF SOCIAL-DEMOCRACY. /THE THREE MEN IN
LION PREFACE(72)	SUICIDE. NOW TO SAY OF ANY INSTITUTION THAT IT IS	INCOMPATIBLE	WITH BOTH THE CONTEMPLATIVE AND ADVENTUROUS
MILL PREFACE(126)	DANGEROUS ONE, AS IT REVIVES A PRIMITIVE INSTINCT	INCOMPATIBLE	WITH CIVILIZATION: INDEED CIVILIZATION RESTS
ROCK PREFACE(170)	LORD LONSDALE IS NOT IN THE LEAST SOCIALLY	INCOMPATIBLE	WITH DEAN INGE, THOUGH A REALLY CRITICAL
BULL PREFACE(43)	THAT THE SATISFACTION OF NATURAL RIGHTS WAS	INCOMPATIBLE	WITH GOOD GOVERNMENT THAT HIS COURTIERS CALLED
GETT PREFACE(219)	EVEN HATRED, CRUELTY, AND CONTEMPT ARE NOT	INCOMPATIBLE	WITH IT; AND JEALOUSY AND MURDER ARE AS NEAR TO
BULL PREFACE(20)	DEGREE EFFICIENT, AND BOTH IN THE HIGHEST DEGREE	INCOMPATIBLE	WITH ONE ANOTHER ON ANY OTHER FOOTING THAN ONE
SUPR HANDBOK(180)	AND EQUALITY, AS ALL ECONOMISTS KNOW, IS	INCOMPATIBLE	WITH PROPERTY. BESIDES, EQUALITY IS AN
PHIL I (77)	ME AT ANY TIME IF YOU FOUND OUR COMPANIONSHIP	INCOMPATIBLE	WITH-- WHAT WAS THE EXPRESSION YOU USED? --

INCOMPATIBLES

ROCK PREFACE(151)	WOULD HAVE BEEN MURDER. BUT AS THEY WERE ALSO	INCOMPATIBLES	WITH BRITISH CIVILIZATION, IT WAS ONLY

INCOMPETENCE

DEVL III (69)	/BURGOYNE/ (FORCIBLY) JOBBERY AND SNOBBERY,	INCOMPETENCE	AND RED TAPE. (HE HOLDS UP THE DISPATCH AND
APPL I (226)	A BUNGLER, AND EVERYBODY BELIEVES IT. JOBBERY AND	INCOMPETENCE	ARE THE TWO SORTS OF MUD THAT STICK TO US. NO
GENV PREFACE(26)	NEXT DISCOVERY. MEANWHILE HERE WE ARE, WITH OUR	INCOMPETENCE	ARMED WITH ATOMIC BOMBS. NOW POWER CIVILIZES
NEVR II (235)	A SOLICITOR! /PHILIP/ FINCH: YOUR PROFESSIONAL	INCOMPETENCE	IS APPALLING, WILLIAM: YOUR SAGACITY PUTS US
CAND I (96)	(RELAPSING INTO DEJECTION) NO: COWARDICE,	INCOMPETENCE	. MRS MORELL'S QUITE RIGHT. /CANDIDA/ OF COURSE
AUGS (263)	IN HIS SPEECH ADDS TO THE IMPRESSION OF	INCOMPETENCE	PRODUCED BY HIS AGE AND APPEARANCE). /AUGUSTUS/
BULL III (122)	AWAY ALL THE LAND, AND THEN, WHEN YOUR ECONOMIC	INCOMPETENCE	PRODUCES ITS NATURAL AND INEVITABLE RESULTS,
SUPR HANDBOK(201)	EXAMPLE, WE REMEMBERED THE MALADMINISTRATION AND	INCOMPETENCE	REVEALED BY THE CRIMEAN WAR AS PART OF A BYGONE
MTH2 (87)	TOO. TO ME THE AWFUL THING ABOUT THEIR POLITICAL	INCOMPETENCE	WAS THAT THEY HAD TO KILL THEIR OWN SONS. IT

INCOMPETENT

DEST SD(149)	TIME SERVER, REPROOF AND PUNISHMENT AS AN	INCOMPETENT	AND DISHONEST OFFICER, AN ESCAPE FROM DISMISSAL
MIS. PREFACE(59)	TO LEARN TO READ AND WRITE WITH TEARS BY AN	INCOMPETENT	AND ILL-MANNERED PERSON THAN LEFT IN IGNORANCE.
MIS. PREFACE(59)	CONTEMPT FOR A TEACHER SO ILL-MANNERED AND	INCOMPETENT	AS TO BE UNABLE TO MAKE A CHILD LEARN TO READ
MILL IV (206)	AN HOUR. /EPIFANIA/ THAT COMES OF MARRYING AN	INCOMPETENT	DREAMER. ARE YOU GOING TO BEG FOR HER? I WARN
SUPR HANDBOK(188)	LIVING SUBSTITUTE FOR IT HE CAN FIND. HIS LEAST	INCOMPETENT	GENERAL IS SET UP AS AN ALEXANDER; HIS KING IS
CLEO PRO2,SD(95)	WHEN IT WILL NOT: AN EFFECTIVE SERGEANT, AN	INCOMPETENT	GENERAL, A DEPLORABLE DICTATOR. WOULD, IF
GENV PREFACE(16)	BETWEEN A FIRST FLOOR HEAVEN AND A BASEMENT HELL.	INCOMPETENT	GOVERNMENTS ARE THE CRUELLEST. THE NEED FOR
SUPR HANDBOK(218)	UNSOLVED. DEMOCRACY SUBSTITUTES ELECTION BY THE	INCOMPETENT	MANY FOR APPOINTMENT BY THE CORRUPT FEW.
KING PREFACE(159)	ARE AVAILABLE, HAVE THEIR PROPER PLACES FILLED BY	INCOMPETENT	MEN: THERE IS NO CABINET IN EUROPE THAT WOULD
BUOY PREFACE(4)	DRIVEN BY LACK OF UNEARNED INCOME TO BECOME AN	INCOMPETENT	MERCHANT AND HARP ON HIS GENTILITY. WHEN I TAKE
GENV PREFACE(22)	THEMSELVES REACTIONS FROM THE BANKRUPTCIES OF	INCOMPETENT	MONARCHS, BOTH MOBS AND MONARCHS BEING PRODUCTS
2TRU PREFACE(21)	GOVERNMENT IS A MIXTURE OF A HAPORTH OF VERY	INCOMPETENT	OFFICIAL GOVERNMENT WITH AN INTOLERABLE DEAL OF
SUPR III (109)	CROSS, WILL SURVIVE EVEN THAT VULGAR PAGEANT OF	INCOMPETENT	SCHOOLBOYISH GLADIATORS WHICH YOU CALL THE ARMY.
MILL IV (205)	I CAME TO THIS HOTEL AS A SCULLERY MAID: THE MOST	INCOMPETENT	SCULLERY MAID THAT EVER BROKE A DINNER SERVICE.
MTH2 (69)	LEFT YOU TO FINISH IT. AND YOU WERE SO UTTERLY	INCOMPETENT	THAT THE MULTITUDES OF CHILDREN SLAIN BY HUNGER
PRES (167)	TO BE A SERGEANT? /MITCHENER/ YOURE TOO UTTERLY	INCOMPETENT	TO DISCHARGE THE DUTIES OF A SERGEANT. YOU ARE
JOAN 1 (58)	BUT THE PRIVILEGE OF BEING THE WORST, MOST	INCOMPETENT	, DRIVELLING SNIVELLING JIBBERING JABBERING
PYGM EPILOG (297)	SHE WAS, IN SHORT, AN UTTER FAILURE, AN IGNORANT,	INCOMPETENT	, PRETENTIOUS, UNWELCOME, PENNILESS, USELESS
PRES (152)	KNOW WHAT I HAVE TO PUT UP WITH. THIS IMBECILE,	INCOMPETENT	, UNSOLDIERLY DISGRACE TO THE UNIFORM HE SHOULD
HART PREFACE(25)	HIM THE WHOLE COUNTRY SEEMED MAD, FUTILE, SILLY,	INCOMPETENT	, WITH NO HOPE OF VICTORY EXCEPT THE HOPE THAT

INCOMPLETE

LION PREFACE(68)	THAT THE ASSUMPTION OF HUMANITY MUST HAVE BEEN	INCOMPLETE	AT ITS MOST VITAL POINT IF HE WERE A CELIBATE.
SUPR I (6)	SORT OF THING THAT SHE THINKS A MAN'S CHARACTER	INCOMPLETE	IF HE IS NOT AMBITIOUS. SHE KNOWS THAT IF SHE
METH PREFACE(R26)	INDEPENDENT BEING. AND EVEN THEN HE WAS STILL SO	INCOMPLETE	THAT HIS PARENTS MIGHT WELL HAVE EXCLAIMED " GOOD
MTH5 (230)	THOUGH THEIR ANALYSIS WAS TOO SUPERFICIAL AND	INCOMPLETE	TO DETECT IT. YOU MUST REMEMBER THAT THESE POOR
UNPL PREFACE(R19)	WELL, MY IMPRESSION OF THEM WOULD BE NOT MERELY	INCOMPLETE	, BUT VIOLENTLY DISTORTED AND FALSIFIED. IT IS

INCOMPLETENESS

ROCK PREFACE(178)	MOSTLY OPEN TO PRECISELY THE SAME REPROACHES.	INCOMPLETENESS	OF THE GREAT TRIALS. NO DOUBT GALILEO MISSED

INCOMPREHENSIBLE

FABL V (118)	TO MAKE THEM GO EVEN THAT FAR. THEIR CALENDAR IS	INCOMPREHENSIBLE	: THEY COULD NOT FIX THEIR FESTIVALS NOR
ROCK II (237)	AT STATE REGULATED PRICES. /SIR DEXTER/ ROT!	INCOMPREHENSIBLE	AND UNHEARD-OF ROT. /BASHAM/ COMPULSORY
O'FL PREFACE(202)	AND HE WILL STAY IN IRELAND AND DIE FOR HER; FOR,	INCOMPREHENSIBLE	AS IT SEEMS TO AN ENGLISHMAN, IRISH

BASH PREFACE(88) OTHERWISE IT DOES NOT EXIST FOR THEM EXCEPT AS AN INCOMPREHENSIBLE BORE. THERE WAS A TIME WHEN NOT ONLY THE
HART PREFACE(30) FOUND THE DRAMATIC PART OF IT UTTERLY INCOMPREHENSIBLE . HE DID NOT KNOW HOW TO PLAY HIS PART OF
BUOY III (39) YOU EVERY DAY, AND CAN GET NOTHING OUT OF YOU BUT INCOMPREHENSIBLE RAVINGS ABOUT VARIABLES AND FUNCTIONS. YOUR
GENV I (47) OUR POLICE HAVE FOUND MOST OF THE ARTICLES INCOMPREHENSIBLE ; BUT THERE IS ONE, THE EIGHTEENTH, WHICH
BULL PREFACE(26) FLOCK WITH TWO FINGERS, HE BECOMES HORRIFICALLY INCOMPREHENSIBLE TO THE IRISH PROTESTANT CHURCHMAN, WHO, ON
METH PREFACE(R79) COMPREHENSIBLE. THE LAW OF INVERSE SQUARES IS AS INCOMPREHENSIBLE TO THE COMMON MAN AS THE ATHANASIAN CREED.
SIM II (76) THAT THE MANSION HOUSE INCIDENT WAS QUITE INCOMPREHENSIBLE TO HIM, AS HE COULD NOT CONCEIVE HOW THE
MILL PREFACE(124) FAITH IN ABSOLUTE MEASUREMENT, AND PLAYING AN INCOMPREHENSIBLE TRICK WITH THE SACRED VELOCITY OF LIGHT,

INCONCEIVABLE
2TRU II (72) THAT IS OPPRESSIVELY ASTRONOMICAL AND ENDLESS AND INCONCEIVABLE AND IMPOSSIBLE, THAT I SHALL JUST GO STARK
BULL PREFACE(27) HE WOULD BE DENOUNCED FROM THE ALTAR AS AN ALMOST INCONCEIVABLE BLASPHEMER; AND HIS EDUCATIONAL OPPORTUNITIES
METH PREFACE(R40) SOCIALLY AND POLITICALLY POWERFUL IGNORANCE INCONCEIVABLE BY THOMAS AQUINAS OR EVEN ROGER BACON, WAS
6CAL PREFACE(90) MORE THAN A PLAYWRIGHT'S DIRECT BUSINESS IS AS INCONCEIVABLE BY THEM AS A MEDIEVAL KING. NOW A PLAYWRIGHT'S
METH PREFACE(R83) NOR OF ELECTRONS DANCING IN VORTICES OF INCONCEIVABLE ENERGY; BUT PRAY CAN ANYONE EXPLAIN THE LAST
MTH5 (251) IN THE HARDPRESSED HEART OF THE EARTH, WHERE THE INCONCEIVABLE HEAT OF THE SUN STILL GLOWS, THE STONE LIVES
METH PREFACE(R50) REFUTABLE. DO NOT TOO HASTILY SAY THAT THIS IS INCONCEIVABLE , TO CIRCUMSTANTIAL SELECTION ALL MECHANICAL
LION II (131) CAESAR. I MEAN THAT WE FORGIVE YOU. /METELLUS/ AN INCONCEIVABLE LIBERTY! DO YOU NOT KNOW, WOMAN, THAT THE
PHIL I (88) BUT A MAN WAS FOUND READY TO TAKE THAT INCONCEIVABLE LIE ON HIS CONSCIENCE. /JULIA/ (FIRING UP) IF
GENV IV (116) ALWAYS IS OUT OF PLACE AMONG TALKERS. /BBDE/ INCONCEIVABLE NOTHINGNESS THAT YOU ARE, DO YOU DARE TO CLASS
SUPR PREFACE(R36) AND YET, INSTEAD OF EXCLAIMING " SEND THIS INCONCEIVABLE SATANIST TO THE STAKE," THE RESPECTABLE
SUPR III (113) POETRY OF THEIR LOVES AND NESTINGS, THAT IT IS INCONCEIVABLE THAT LIFE, HAVING ONCE PRODUCED THEM, SHOULD,
BULL PREFACE(3) OF GLADSTONIAN LIBERALISM, WHEN IT WAS UTTERLY INCONCEIVABLE THAT AN ACT OF CONSTITUTIONAL REFORM WHICH HAD

INCONCEIVABLY
MTH5 (228) HOLDING HIS BRAIN IN FORM AND OPERATION WITH AN INCONCEIVABLY POWERFUL GRIP, THE URGE OF EVOLUTION: ALL

INCONGRUITIES
2TRU II SD(52) AWARE. THE DISPATCH RIDER SEEMS CONSCIOUS OF HIS INCONGRUITIES ; FOR, THOUGH VERY PROMPT, CONCISE, AND

INCONGRUITY
SUPR PREFACE(R34) OF THEIR DISAPPOINTMENT OR THE COMEDY OF THEIR INCONGRUITY , AND THE FIELD PREACHER WHO ACHIEVED VIRTUE AND

INCONGRUOUS
JOAN PREFACE(27) A NINETEENTH-TWENTIETH CENTURY ENVIRONMENT IS AS INCONGRUOUS A FIGURE AS SHE WOULD APPEAR WERE SHE TO WALK
BUOY III SD(27) AS ONLY CHINESE ART COULD MAKE IT. A MOST INCONGRUOUS FIGURE ENTERS: A MIDDLE-AGED TWENTIETH CENTURY
UNPL PREFACE(R12) TOUCH THEIR OWN LIVES. THE RESULT WAS REVOLTINGLY INCONGRUOUS ; FOR THOUGH I TOOK MY THEME SERIOUSLY ENOUGH, I
METH PREFACE(R85) GENTLE CREATIONS WITHOUT SCRUPLE, NO MATTER HOW INCONGRUOUS THEY MAY BE. AND ALL THE TIME HIS VITAL NEED FOR
DEVL III (73) OBSERVATIONS SEEM TO STRIKE MR DUDGEON AS INCONGRUOUS UNDER THE CIRCUMSTANCES, YOU HAD BETTER OMIT

INCONGRUOUSLY
LADY PREFACE(219) IDENTICAL WITH THE HEROES: MACBETH IS ONLY HAMLET INCONGRUOUSLY COMMITTING MURDERS AND ENGAGING IN
BARB III (315) HIM INTO THE WORLD; BUT HE CHOSE HIS PARENTS VERY INCONGRUOUSLY , I THINK. I SEE NOTHING OF MYSELF IN HIM, AND

INCONSEQUENT
CATH PREFACE(158) OF THE MOST DELIGHTFULLY FEATHER-HEADED AND INCONSEQUENT INGENUES, THOUGHT ME MORE THAN USUALLY MAD WHEN

INCONSIDERATE
SUPR I (21) OH, I WONDER CAN YOU BE RIGHT! HAVE I BEEN INCONSIDERATE ? (SHE TURNS TO OCTAVIUS, WHO IS SITTING
LIED (194) STICKS ARE DISCONNECTED). OH, HOW COULD YOU BE SO INCONSIDERATE ? /HE/ I BEG YOUR PARDON. I WILL BUY YOU A
OVER PREFACE(162) ART AND MORALITY. IT IS RIDICULOUS TO SAY, AS INCONSIDERATE AMATEURS OF THE ARTS DO, THAT ART HAS NOTHING
POSN PREFACE(384) THEFT; AND THIS IS WHY THE CENSOR SEEMS TO THE INCONSIDERATE AS OBVIOUSLY DESIRABLE A FUNCTIONARY AS THE
METH PREFACE(R89) I DID NOT CUT THESE CEREBRAL CAPERS IN MERE INCONSIDERATE EXUBERANCE. I DID IT BECAUSE THE WORST
BULL PREFACE(55) ARRANGEMENT THROUGH SAID SULEIMAN KHEIRALLAH'S INCONSIDERATE INDISPOSITION MADE THE EXECUTION OF DARWEESH
MIS. PREFACE(9) A STRAIGHTFORWARD WAY THAT IT DOES NOT PAY TO BE INCONSIDERATE . ALSO, PERHAPS, THAT MAMMA, WHO MADE THE
PYGM V (275) (CONSCIENCE STRICKEN) PERHAPS WE WERE A LITTLE INCONSIDERATE . IS SHE VERY ANGRY? /MRS HIGGINS/ (
GETT PREFACE(232) ON CONSIDERATION, TO DECENT MEN, EVEN COARSE AND INCONSIDERATE MEN ARE RESTRAINED FROM IT BY THE FACT THAT
2TRU I (37) NURSE SWITCHES THE LIGHT OFF. /THE PATIENT/ SO INCONSIDERATE OF YOU! THE NURSE SWITCHES THE LIGHTS ON
CAPT II (269) (FUMBLING IN HIS BREAST) PEACE, PEACE, THOU INCONSIDERATE ONE. (HE TAKES OUT A LETTER). /BRASSBOUND/
METH PREFACE(R23) LONG NECK, LIKE THE GIRAFFE. THIS SEEMS ABSURD TO INCONSIDERATE PEOPLE AT THE FIRST BLUSH; BUT IT IS WITHIN
POSN PREFACE(417) STAGE IT WOULD BE SHOCKING." ALL THE STUPID AND INCONSIDERATE PEOPLE SEIZED EAGERLY ON THIS ILLUSTRATION AS
MTH3 (130) PEOPLE CALLED A DAMNED BLACKGUARD WHEN SOME INCONSIDERATE PERSON WANTED TO TELL THE PUBLIC MORE THAN WAS
BULL PREFACE(33) UNTIL PUBLIC DISASTERS COMPEL A TERRIFIED AND INCONSIDERATE REARRANGEMENT, INNUMERABLE EXPERIMENTS IN
VWOO 3 (138) I KNOW YOU DIDNT MEAN IT. BY THE WAY, I MADE AN INCONSIDERATE REMARK WHICH HURT YOU. I DID NOT INTEND THAT.
SUPR HANDBOK(206) AS YOU CAN A LABORER. BUT THIS NATURAL CHECK ON INCONSIDERATE SELFISHNESS IS ITSELF CHECKED, PARTLY BY OUR
DOCT PREFACE(52) HUMOR THEIR FOLLY AND IGNORANCE. HOW COMPLETE AND INCONSIDERATE THEIR IGNORANCE IS CAN ONLY BE REALIZED BY
DOCT PREFACE(28) THE ANTI-VACCINATOR IS DOING A CRUEL, RUINOUS, INCONSIDERATE THING IN A MOOD OF MALIGNANT FOLLY: ALL THIS,
DOCT PREFACE(63) WELL WHILST THEMSELVES SUBMITTING TO SPECIALLY INCONSIDERATE TREATMENT. THE BUTCHER AND BAKER ARE NOT
SUPR PREFACE(R36) CIVILITY; FORMALIST AND HYPOCRISY; WILDHEAD, INCONSIDERATE , AND PRAGMATICK (WHO WERE CLEARLY YOUNG

INCONSIDERATENESS
DOCT PREFACE(27) AND RETAIN A SPARK OF COMMON SENSE. THIS SORT OF INCONSIDERATENESS GETS CURED ONLY IN THE CLASSES WHERE
POSN PREFACE(390) RIGHTS OF ENGLISH CITIZENS. IN THIS EXTREMITY OF INCONSIDERATENESS IT IS NOT SURPRISING THAT THEY ALSO DID

INCONSISTENCY
NEVR IV (289) HER HUSBAND. /BOHUN/ (INSTANTLY POUNCING ON THE INCONSISTENCY BETWEEN THIS AND HIS PREVIOUS STATEMENT) YOU
LION PREFACE(69) OF US IS AT HEART A GOOD CHRISTIAN SEXUALLY. INCONSISTENCY OF THE SEX INSTINCT. BUT THE QUESTION IS NOT
PHIL I (87) /CRAVEN/ (TACTLESSLY HARPING ON CUTHBERTSON'S INCONSISTENCY) WELL, YOU KNOW, THIS IS UNEXPECTED: NOW IT'S
MIS. PREFACE(62) THE RESULT THAT YOUR VICTIM, BEWILDERED BY YOUR INCONSISTENCY , CONCLUDES THAT THERE IS NO USE TRYING TO

INCONSISTENT
BULL IV (153) THE VICE OF HYPOCRISY. I WOULD ALMOST RATHER BE INCONSISTENT THAN INSINCERE. /KEEGAN/ DO NOT BE OFFENDED,
LION PREFACE(42) MISS THE SIGNIFICANT SAYINGS ALTOGETHER, HOWEVER INCONSISTENT THEY MAY BE WITH THE DOCTRINE HE IS CONSCIOUSLY

INCONSISTENTLY
BARB PREFACE(215) HIM BE POOR. SERVE HIM RIGHT! ALSO-- SOMEWHAT INCONSISTENTLY -- BLESSED ARE THE POOR! NOW WHAT DOES THIS

INCONTINENCES
HART PREFACE(24) ENGLAND WAS MAKING THE EMPIRE SICK WITH ITS INCONTINENCES , ITS IGNORANCES, ITS FEROCITIES, ITS PANICS,

INCONTINENT
BASH II,1, (107) TO BEGIN MY LIFE A SPEECHLESS BABE, HAIRLESS, INCONTINENT , HOBBLING UPON ALL FOURS, A NURSE'S NUISANCE..

INCONTROVERTIBLE
MILL PREFACE(124) HISTORIAN OR PSYCHO-ANALYST CAN BRING A MASS OF INCONTROVERTIBLE EVIDENCE TO PROVE THAT IT WOULD HAVE BEEN

INCONVENIENCE
GETT PREFACE(184) MARRIAGE LAWS MEANS EITHER DOWNRIGHT RUIN OR SUCH INCONVENIENCE AND DISABLEMENT AS A PRUDENT MAN OR WOMAN
MIS. PREFACE(52) AND ONLY POSSIBLE WAY OF DEALING WITH EVIL OR INCONVENIENCE , " AINT NOBODY TO BE WHOPPED FOR THIS HERE.."
HART PREFACE(36) PLACE OF PENANCE IN WHICH WE SUFFER SO MUCH INCONVENIENCE ON THE SLENDEREST CHANCE OF GAINING A SCRAP OF
SUPR PREFACE(R12) UNFORTUNATE HABIT-- YOU NOW, I HOPE, FEEL ITS INCONVENIENCE -- OF NOT EXPLAINING YOURSELF, I HAVE HAD TO
HART II (108) JUST NOR RIGHT THAT WE SHOULD BE PUT TO A LOT OF INCONVENIENCE TO GRATIFY YOUR MORAL ENTHUSIASM, MY FRIEND.
FANY III (309) (ADVANCING TO THE MIDDLE OF THE TABLE) WOULD IT INCONVENIENCE YOU, SIR, IF I WERE TO GIVE YOU A MONTH'S
MIS. PREFACE(48) TEACHER'S WORD AS TO WHICH CHILD HAS CAUSED LEAST INCONVENIENCE " HE WOULD PROBABLY BE UNFROCKED, IF NOT

INCONVENIENCED
METH PREFACE(R67) RESULT, THE PEOPLE WHO DID NOT FEEL IN THE LEAST INCONVENIENCED BY BEING NO LONGER GOVERNED BY NOBODADDY SOON

METH PREFACE(R67) BY NOBODADDY SOON FOUND THEMSELVES VERY ACUTELY INCONVENIENCED BY BEING GOVERNED BY FOOLS AND COMMERCIAL
DEVL III (73) UNTIL-- ER-- UNTIL MR DUDGEON CAN NO LONGER BE INCONVENIENCED BY THEM. (BRUDENELL, WITH A SHRUG, SHUTS HIS

INCONVENIENCES

GETT PREFACE(184) OVER RATHER THAN FACE. AND THESE DISABLEMENTS AND INCONVENIENCES ARE NOT EVEN THE PRICE OF FREEDOM; FOR, AS
3PLA PREFACE(R16) OURSELVES CAN IT PREVENT US FROM REALIZING ITS INCONVENIENCES . A PLAY THAT DOES NOT DO THIS FOR THE
PRES (163) CONVENIENCES OF DEMOCRACY WITHOUT ITS OCCASIONAL INCONVENIENCES . /MITCHENER/ WHAT ARE ITS CONVENIENCES, I
MTH3 (131) NOT TO BELIEVE IT NOW THAT YOU REALIZE ITS INCONVENIENCES . THAT IS THE ENGLISH METHOD. IT MAY NOT WORK

INCONVENIENT

POSN PREFACE(387) BECAUSE IT REFERS TO POLITICAL FACTS, BECOME SO INCONVENIENT AND INOPPORTUNE THAT FOREIGN OFFICES TAKE THE
PHIL II (99) OF THE MATTER. WELL, THE FACT IS, IT'S NOT SO INCONVENIENT AS YOU MIGHT THINK. WHEN YOURE AT HOME, YOU
AUGS (270) SIR, BELIEVE ME. /AUGUSTUS/ IT WILL BE EXTREMELY INCONVENIENT FOR ME TO SEE HER; BUT THE COUNTRY IS IN
CAPT II (261) THEY CAN ALWAYS DEPEND ON YOU; BUT ISNT IT RATHER INCONVENIENT FOR YOURSELF WHEN YOU CHANGE YOUR MIND?
GETT PREFACE(193) UGLY SIGHTS AND SOUNDS, UNHEALTHY SMELLS, AND INCONVENIENT HOUSES, WITH INHUMAN APATHY AND CALLOUSNESS.
MILL PREFACE(126) FOR PLUNDERING RAIDS AND COUPS D'ETAT AGAINST INCONVENIENT LIBERALS OR MARXISTS. A PERSECUTION IS ALWAYS A
GETT PREFACE(258) MEANS FOR DISSOLVING ALL UNHAPPY, IMPROPER, AND INCONVENIENT MARRIAGES. AND, AS IT IS OUR CAUTIOUS CUSTOM TO
SUPR PREFACE(R39) PERSON, LIABLE TO GO OUT AND TO GO WRONG AT INCONVENIENT MOMENTS, AND WITH INCENDIARY POSSIBILITIES.
DOCT PREFACE(43) FLOG HIM FOR NOT TELLING A LIE IF THE BOY TELLS INCONVENIENT OR DISRESPECTFUL TRUTHS, BECAUSE IT IS
MRS III (232) IN THE FACE OF SOCIETY, SOCIETY DOESNT ASK ANY INCONVENIENT QUESTIONS; AND IT MAKES PRECIOUS SHORT WORK OF
BULL PREFACE(55) SAID BETTER NOT; AND HE ESCAPED. THIS WAS VERY INCONVENIENT ; FOR THE NUMBER OF FLOGGEES HAD BEEN MADE UP
HART I (75) /LADY UTTERWORD/ CHILDREN ARE CERTAINLY VERY INCONVENIENT SOMETIMES. BUT INTELLIGENT PEOPLE CAN ALWAYS
POSN PREFACE(427) AND RELIGIOUS, AT MOMENTS WHICH MAY BE EXTREMELY INCONVENIENT TO THE GOVERNMENT. IS IT CERTAIN THAT A
APPL I (241) MAY I ASK? /PAMPHILIUS/ WELL, IT WOULD BE RATHER INCONVENIENT , WOULDNT IT, IF WE HAD TO BE TOLD EVERYTHING

INCORPORATED

MRS PREFACE(163) OF PHYSICIANS, THE ROYAL ACADEMY OF ARTS, THE INCORPORATED LAW SOCIETY, AND CONVOCATION WERE ABOLISHED,

INCORPORATION

LADY PREFACE(232) AND WHAT THE ENGLISH CONSTITUTION NEEDED WAS THE INCORPORATION OF WHIG PRINCIPLES OF INDIVIDUAL LIBERTY.

INCORPOREAL

SUPR III SD(86) THE PALLOR REVEALS A MAN IN THE VOID, AN INCORPOREAL BUT VISIBLE MAN, SEATED, ABSURDLY ENOUGH, ON

INCORRECT

MIS. (163) TO DISCUSS. /PERCIVAL/ I WILL DO NOTHING INCORRECT . /HYPATIA/ OH, DONT BE AFRAID, LITTLE BOY: YOULL
INCA (257) DONT BE AFRAID. I PROMISE TO REFUSE ANY INCORRECT PROPOSALS. /THE INCA/ (ENCHANTED) OH! CHARMING

INCORRECTLY

DOCT PREFACE(74) VACCINES" MADE OF THEIR OWN BACTERIA: A PRACTICE INCORRECTLY CALLED VACCINETHERAPY (THERE IS NOTHING VACCINE

INCORRIGIBLE

MIS. PREFACE(65) ONLY THE EMPLOYEE, HOWEVER PATENT A HYPOCRITE OR INCORRIGIBLE A SLACKER, IS HAT IN HAND. BUT LET THE MOST
LADY PREFACE(215) CONTEMPT FOR THE TRADESMAN AND MECHANIC, AND HIS INCORRIGIBLE ADDICTION TO SMUTTY JOKES. HE DOES US THE
JOAN 2,SD(73) OF A YOUNG DOG ACCUSTOMED TO BE KICKED, YET INCORRIGIBLE AND IRREPRESSIBLE. BUT HE IS NEITHER VULGAR NOR
CLEO III (157) WORTH MORE THAN POMPEY'S WAS-- THAN CATO'S IS. O INCORRIGIBLE BRITISH ISLANDER: AM I A BULL DOG, TO SEEK
CLEO NOTES (212) FIGHT. IF THIS BE TRUE, HE MUST HAVE BEEN AN INCORRIGIBLE COMEDIAN. BUT EVEN IF WE WAIVE THIS STORY, OR
FABL PREFACE(82) CIVILIZED PERSONS EXCEPT CERTIFIED LUNATICS AND INCORRIGIBLE CRIMINALS MUST FOR ELEMENTARY PURPOSES BE HELD
BULL PREFACE(48) TO THE WILLIAM TELL TEMPERAMENT. JUST AS THE MOST INCORRIGIBLE CRIMINAL IS ALWAYS, WE ARE TOLD, THE BEST
LADY PREFACE(221) CLEAR THAT TO THE LAST THERE WAS IN SHAKESPEAR AN INCORRIGIBLE DIVINE LEVITY, AN INEXHAUSTIBLE JOY THAT
JOAN 6 (147) (ALSO ON HIS FEET AGAIN) THAT MAN IS AN INCORRIGIBLE FOOL. /CAUCHON/ BROTHER MARTIN: SEE THAT
JOAN PREFACE(16) THAT GALILEO WAS A MARTYR, AND HIS PERSECUTORS INCORRIGIBLE IGNORAMUSES, AND THAT ST TERESA'S HORMONES HAD
BUOY 1 (16) IF I WERE YOU I WOULDNT. /FATHER/ OH, YOU ARE INCORRIGIBLE . I TELL YOU AGAIN YOU ARE TOO CLEVER: YOU KNOW
ROCK I (232) (CALLING AFTER HER GAILY) HA HA! INCORRIGIBLE, INCORRIGIBLE . (HE TAKES HER CARD FROM THE TABLE, AND
MRS I (197) ALMOST TO TEARS) I LEAVE YOU, SIR. YOU ARE INCORRIGIBLE . (HE TURNS TOWARDS THE GATE). /FRANK/ (
MRS II (205) BETTER. VIVVUMS MUSTNT LECTURE: HER LITTLE BOY'S INCORRIGIBLE . (HE ATTEMPTS TO TAKE HER FACE CARESSINGLY IN
FANY I (274) DID NOT REACH ME UNTIL TO-DAY. I AM AFRAID HE IS INCORRIGIBLE . MY BROTHER, AS YOU MAY IMAGINE, FEELS THAT
FABL VI (127) EXECUTE CRIMINALS WHO HAVE NO CONSCIENCE AND ARE INCORRIGIBLE . THEY ARE OLD EXPERIMENTS OF THE LIFE FORCE.
ANNA (301) BREAST BY THEM. /THE GRAND DUCHESS/ OH, YOU ARE INCORRIGIBLE . YOU ARE MAD, INFATUATED. YOU WILL NOT BELIEVE
MTH2 (64) LIBERAL ONES. /BURGE/ IN SHORT, LUBIN, YOURE INCORRIGIBLE . YOU DONT BELIEVE ANYTHING IS GOING TO CHANGE.
GENV PREFACE(26) HAS GIVEN WAY TO A DOUBT WHETHER NATURE IS NOT AN INCORRIGIBLE KANGAROO. WHAT IS CERTAIN IS THAT NEW
SUPR II (58) PAST ALL SALVATION HE'D HAVE FOUND OUT WHAT AN INCORRIGIBLE LIAR YOU ARE. /ANN/ YOU MISUNDERSTAND, JACK. I
FABL PREFACE(64) MYSELF: ARE WE ALL MENTAL CASES? ARE WE SIMPLY INCORRIGIBLE LIARS? ARE PLAYERS IMPOSTORS AND HYPOCRITES..
2TRU III SD(112) THERE IS LEFT ONLY FOG: IMPENETRABLE FOG; BUT THE INCORRIGIBLE PREACHER WILL NOT BE DENIED HIS PERORATION,
CLEO V (198) A SIGH, RAISING HIS HANDS AND GIVING CAESAR UP AS INCORRIGIBLE) FAREWELL. (THEY SHAKE HANDS). /CAESAR/ (
APPL I (231) TO DO NOW? THATS WHAT I WANT TO KNOW. /AMANDA/ (INCORRIGIBLE) I SUGGEST A LITTLE COMMUNITY SINGING (SHE
PYGM V (289) CARELESS, VIGOROUS VOICE SHEWS THAT HE IS INCORRIGIBLE). /LIZA/ (DISDAINFULLY) BUY THEM YOURSELF. (
GETT PREFACE(246) PERSONS, MEANS TYRANNY AND SLAVERY. IF THE INCORRIGIBLE SENTIMENTALISTS HERE RAISE THEIR LITTLE PIPE OF
ROCK PREFACE(160) JUSTIFICATION FOR EXTERMINATION, WHICH IS ALWAYS INCORRIGIBLE SOCIAL INCOMPATIBILITY AND NOTHING ELSE. THE
BULL II SD(111) AFFECTATION OF A SHREWD IRISH HUMORIST AND INCORRIGIBLE SPENDTHRIFT. AUNT JUDY SEEMS TO HIM AN
JOAN 6 (146) THE DIN) SHE IS A RELAPSED HERETIC, OBSTINATE, INCORRIGIBLE , AND ALTOGETHER UNWORTHY OF THE MERCY WE HAVE
PYGM V (279) IS UNCONSCIOUS OF HIS APPROACH. /PICKERING/ HE'S INCORRIGIBLE , ELIZA. YOU WONT RELAPSE, WILL YOU? /LIZA/
FABL III (112) BRIGADE. OR YOU MAY BE CLASSED AS DANGEROUS AND INCORRIGIBLE , IN WHICH CASE YOULL BE LIQUIDATED. /THE
ROCK I (232) /SIR ARTHUR/ (CALLING AFTER HER GAILY) HA HA! INCORRIGIBLE , INCORRIGIBLE. (HE TAKES HER CARD FROM THE
SUPR I (40) HER ARMS AWAY WITH PERFECT DIGNITY) YOU ARE INCORRIGIBLE , JACK. BUT YOU SHOULD NOT JEST ABOUT OUR
CLEO I (112) IS HE THAT HAS TURNED YOU INTO A ROMAN. /CAESAR/ INCORRIGIBLE , OH, INCORRIGIBLE! AWAY! (HE FOLLOWS HER,
CLEO I (112) YOU INTO A ROMAN. /CAESAR/ INCORRIGIBLE, OH, INCORRIGIBLE ! AWAY! (HE FOLLOWS HER, THE BUCINA SOUNDING
LION I (115) BUT SUCH A VERY HANDSOME CAPTAIN. /THE CAPTAIN/ INCORRIGIBLE ! (URGENTLY) LISTEN TO ME. THE MEN IN THAT

INCORRIGIBLY

JOAN PREFACE(22) AND THIS MUCH SWEARING SHE ALLOWED TO THE INCORRIGIBLY BLASPHEMOUS LA HIRE EQUALLY WITH HERSELF. THE
MILL PREFACE(129) SERVICE OF THE COMMUNITY, OR, IF THEY ARE IDLE OR INCORRIGIBLY RECALCITRANT, HANDED OVER TO THE POLICE. UNDER
DOCT PREFACE(77) BEGINNING TO BE SO SUSPICIOUS OF DRUGS, AND THE INCORRIGIBLY SUPERSTITIOUS PEOPLE SO PROFUSELY SUPPLIED WITH
2TRU III (93) ELDER/ A SAINT! SAY RATHER THE RUINED SON OF AN INCORRIGIBLY SUPERSTITIOUS MOTHER. RETIRE NOW-- FROM THE
GETT PREFACE(234) PEPYS' DIARY, WE LEARN THAT A WOMAN MAY HAVE AN INCORRIGIBLY UNFAITHFUL HUSBAND, AND YET BE MUCH BETTER OFF

INCORRUPTIBLE

2TRU III (88) FORTY YEARS. MY SON, WHOM I BROUGHT UP TO BE AN INCORRUPTIBLE GODFEARING ATHEIST, HAS BECOME A THIEF AND A
CLEO III (151) CENTURION IS AT HAND; AND THE ROMAN SOLDIER IS INCORRUPTIBLE WHEN HIS OFFICER IS LOOKING. I MUST CARRY YOUR
MIS. PREFACE(4) AND REBIRTH THAT THIS CORRUPTIBLE SHALL BECOME INCORRUPTIBLE , AND THIS MORTAL PUT ON IMMORTALITY. PRACTISE
MTH4 I (157) IN ME KINDLES AND GLOWS, THE CORRUPTIBLE BECOMES INCORRUPTIBLE , AND THE MORTAL BOLGE BLUEBIN BARLOW PUTS ON
NEVR II SD(226) IN HIS YOUTH TO BE TRUTHFUL, MAGNANIMOUS, AND INCORRUPTIBLE , BUT HAD NEVER SUCCEEDED IN MAKING THAT HABIT

INCREASE

SUPR HANDBOK(192) ON. OUR NOTION OF TREATING A MOTHER IS, NOT TO INCREASE HER SUPPLY OF FOOD, BUT TO CUT IT OFF BY FORBIDDING
2TRU PREFACE(14) TO EVADE HIS SHARE IN THE LABOR OF PRODUCTION, TO INCREASE HIS SHARE IN THE DISTRIBUTION OF THE PRODUCT, AND
DOCT PREFACE(65) DEATH-RATE GOES UP HIS CREDIT GOES DOWN. AS EVERY INCREASE IN HIS SALARY DEPENDS ON THE ISSUE OF A PUBLIC
METH PREFACE(R42) ANIMALS IS FOUR FEET, AND THAT THEY INCREASE IN NUMBERS UNTIL A TIME COMES WHEN ALL THE TREES
LION PREFACE(92) VIEW OF JESUS IS POWERFULLY REINFORCED BY THE INCREASE IN OUR DAY OF THE NUMBER OF PEOPLE WHO HAVE HAD THE
BULL PREFACE(62) OF THE NATIVE NEWSPAPERS AND A CONSIDERABLE INCREASE IN THE ARMY OF OCCUPATION! AND LORD CROMER WRITES
DOCT PREFACE(69) OUT OF COUNTENANCE AND PERISH, EVERY YEAR SEES AN INCREASE IN THE NUMBER OF PERSONS EMPLOYED IN THE PUBLIC
MRS PREFACE(155) OF PERFORMING MRS WARREN'S PROFESSION WERE AN INCREASE IN THE NUMBER OF PERSONS ENTERING THAT PROFESSION
SUPR HANDBOK(182) OF PROPERTY WOULD MEAN NOTHING EXCEPT AN INCREASE IN THE QUANTITY OF FOOD, CLOTHING, HOUSING, AND
ROCK PREFACE(154) A CHANCELLOR OF THE EXCHEQUER APOLOGIZING FOR AN INCREASE IN THE SURTAX, A FASCIST DICTATOR ORGANIZING A
APPL I (233) BY THEM AS AN INVASION OF THEIR LIBERTY OR AN INCREASE IN THEIR TAXATION. IT WEARS OUT THE STRONGEST MAN,
MILL II (177) AND FIFTY POUNDS. IN SIX MONTHS YOU ARE TO INCREASE IT TO FIFTY THOUSAND. HOW IS THAT FOR A TEST? /THE
BARB I (251) MUCH MORE LIKELY TO DECREASE HIS INCOME THAN TO INCREASE IT. SARAH WILL HAVE TO FIND AT LEAST ANOTHER 800

GETT PREFACE(207)	THE POPULATION AT ITS PRESENT FIGURE, OR TO	INCREASE	IT, WE MUST TAKE IMMEDIATE STEPS TO INDUCE PEOPLE
BARB I (251)	INCOME BY HIS OWN EXERTIONS, THEY MAY DOUBLE THE	INCREASE	. /LADY BRITOMART/ CHARLES LOMAX'S EXERTIONS ARE
2TRU PREFACE(8)	WILL PROPITIATE A SPITEFUL DEITY OR	INCREASE	MY BALANCE IN A SALVATION BANK IN A WORLD BEYOND
CLEO NOTES (207)	OF MACHINERY THERE, AND A CONSEQUENT "	INCREASE	OF COMMAND OVER NATURE" WHICH MAKES MANY OF OUR
BULL PREFACE(64)	WHICH HAVE OF LATE STUMBLED INTO AN ENORMOUS	INCREASE	OF MATERIAL WEALTH WITHOUT HAVING MADE ANY
GENV PREFACE(16)	BY SIMPLE INSTRUCTION AS TO THE FACTS WITHOUT ANY	INCREASE	OF POLITICAL CAPACITY, I AM ENDING AS A SAGE WITH A
FABL PREFACE(88)	IS NOW QUITE INSUFFICIENT IN VIEW OF THE ENORMOUS	INCREASE	OF PUBLIC FUNCTIONS INVOLVED BY MODERN SOCIALISM.
MTH4 I (171)	FOR TO A SHORTLIVER INCREASE OF YEARS IS ONLY	INCREASE	OF SORROW; BUT TO A LONGLIVER EVERY EXTRA YEAR IS A
WIDO II (43)	DOUBT OF IT, MY DEAR SIR: NOT A DOUBT OF IT. THE	INCREASE	OF THE POPULATION IS AT THE BOTTOM OF IT ALL.
MTH4 I (171)	WOULD BE ALL THE GREATER; FOR TO A SHORTLIVER	INCREASE	OF YEARS IS ONLY INCREASE OF SORROW; BUT TO A
BARB PREFACE(214)	OUR CHANCES OF EVER GETTING THEM BACK, AND	INCREASE	OUR CHANCES OF BEING SHOT BY THE ROBBER IF WE ARE
MTH4 I (169)	THE COLONIZERS ARE OF OPINION THAT WE SHOULD	INCREASE	OUR NUMBERS AND COLONIZE. THE CONSERVATIVES HOLD
METH PREFACE(R18)	BODILY CONTRIVANCE TO MAINTAIN OUR ACTIVITY AND	INCREASE	OUR RESOURCES. VOLUNTARY LONGEVITY. AMONG OTHER
MTH4 I (159)	CERTAINLY NOT. ANY SUCH INVESTIGATION COULD ONLY	INCREASE	THE DISGUST WITH WHICH HE INSPIRES ME, AND MAKE ME
LION PREFACE(35)	PARISIAN STAGE. THERE IS A DISTINCT ATTEMPT TO	INCREASE	THE FEMININE INTEREST ALL THROUGH. THE SLIGHT LEAD
O'FL SD(225)	AND THE PROTESTS AND MENACES OF O'FLAHERTY, ONLY	INCREASE	THE HUBBUB. THEY ARE SOON ALL SPEAKING AT ONCE AT
PYGM I (209)	NOT KNOWING WHAT THE MATTER IS, CROWD IN AND	INCREASE	THE NOISE WITH QUESTION AND ANSWER: WHATS THE ROW?
GENV PREFACE(13)	TO RE-ORGANIZE PRODUCTION COLLECTIVELY SO AS TO	INCREASE	THE PRODUCT AND BRING THE HIGHEST CULTURE WITHIN
DOCT PREFACE(53)	IF THE EFFECT OF A PROPHYLACTIC IS ACTUALLY TO	INCREASE	THE PROPORTION TO TWENTY PER CENT, THE PUBLICATION
GENV PREFACE(16)	THEY LIVE. I CANNOT CHANGE THEIR MINDS; BUT I CAN	INCREASE	THEIR KNOWLEDGE. A LITTLE KNOWLEDGE IS A DANGEROUS
GENV PREFACE(13)	SLAVES ALIVE AND EFFICIENT, USE THEIR POWERS TO	INCREASE	THEIR REVENUES AND SUPPRESS RESISTANCE TO THEIR
SUPR PREFACE(R9)	LOVES AND COMFORTS PRAYED FOR BY DESDEMONA: THEY	INCREASE	, EVEN AS YOUR DAYS DO GROW, NO MERE PIONEERING
SUPR I (26)	OF HER HIGHEST PURPOSE AND GREATEST FUNCTION-- TO	INCREASE	, MULTIPLY, AND REPLENISH THE EARTH. AND INSTEAD OF

INCREASED

HART PREFACE(22)	AT. THUS THE NATURAL CONFUSION OF IGNORANCE WAS	INCREASED	BY A DELIBERATELY PROPAGATED CONFUSION OF NURSERY
DOCT PREFACE(58)	THE TROUBLES OF CONSUMPTIVE PATIENTS ARE GREATLY	INCREASED	BY THE GROWING DISPOSITION TO TREAT THEM AS
HART PREFACE(15)	WAS URGENTLY NECESSARY THAT PRODUCTION SHOULD BE	INCREASED	BY THE MOST SCIENTIFIC ORGANIZATION AND ECONOMY OF
CLEO NOTES (206)	REMAINS THAT IT IS ONLY BY RUNNING AWAY FROM THE	INCREASED	COMMAND OVER NATURE TO COUNTRY PLACES WHERE NATURE
CLEO NOTES (206)	HAVE REPLACED FOUR ON FOOT. BUT EVEN IF MAN'S	INCREASED	COMMAND OVER NATURE INCLUDED ANY INCREASED COMMAND
CLEO NOTES (206)	THE AZURE MAIN. AGAIN, THERE IS THE ILLUSION OF "	INCREASED	COMMAND OVER NATURE," MEANING THAT COTTON IS CHEAP
CLEO NOTES (206)	MAN'S INCREASED COMMAND OVER NATURE INCLUDED ANY	INCREASED	COMMAND OVER HIMSELF (THE ONLY SORT OF COMMAND
FABL IV (115)	AND REACH. WITH THE ENDING OF WARS THEIR NUMBERS	INCREASED	ENORMOUSLY; BUT TO THE FEW BORN THINKERS WHO STILL
GENV PREFACE(7)	OF LATE. BUT THE PERILS OF THE SITUATION HAVE	INCREASED	ENORMOUSLY. MEN ARE WHAT THEY WERE; BUT WAR HAS
BULL PREFACE(66)	EULOGIES WHICH WERE HEAPED ON HIM BY BOTH PARTIES	INCREASED	IN VOLUME; AND AN ATTEMPT WHICH I MADE TO CALL
SIM PREFACE(17)	TO OVERCOME THESE PREJUDICES WE NEED A GREATLY	INCREASED	INTOLERANCE OF SOCIALLY INJURIOUS CONDUCT AND AN
JOAN 2 (79)	HOW IT HAS BEEN DONE, AND MY FAITH WILL NOT BE	INCREASED	, BUT AS FOR THE OTHERS, IF THEY FEEL THE THRILL
DOCT PREFACE(58)	ON THE OTHER HAND CANCER AND MADNESS HAVE	INCREASED	(STATISTICALLY) TO AN APPALLING EXTENT. THE
MTH4 I (159)	WISDOM WE HAD. ALL I CAN GRANT YOU IS THAT THEY	INCREASED	OUR KNOWLEDGE. /ZOO/ NONSENSE! CONSCIOUSNESS OF A
FABL PREFACE(86)	BOTH PARTIES INSIST ON THE SUPREME NECESSITY FOR	INCREASED	PRODUCTION; BUT AS THE PLUTOCRATS DO ALL THEY CAN
FABL PREFACE(67)	MUST BE LEVELLED UP, NOT DOWN, TO THIS QUOTA BY	INCREASED	PRODUCTION. WHEN THE QUOTA IS ACHIEVED,
MIS. (202)	I HAVE MADE TEN POUNDS A MINUTE. /JOHNNY/ (WITH	INCREASED	RESPECT) HAVE YOU INDEED? I DIDNT KNOW: YOULL
FABL PREFACE(84)	CLOTHING, IMPOSED PURCHASE TAXES ON LUXURIES, AND	INCREASED	THE BUREAUCRACY BOTH IN NUMBERS AND POWER WHILST
METH PREFACE(R21)	LITTLE BY LITTLE FROM A SMALL BEGINNING, AND HAS	INCREASED	THROUGH THE ACTIVITY OF THE ELEMENTAL FORCES
GETT PREFACE(198)	THE LATE SAMUEL BUTLER WITH A CONVICTION THAT	INCREASED	WITH HIS EXPERIENCE OF LIFE, PREACHED THE GOSPEL

INCREASES

JOAN EPILOG (155)	AM BUT A DREAM THAT THOURT DREAMING. (THE LIGHT	INCREASES	: THEY BECOME PLAINLY VISIBLE AS HE SITS UP) THOU
PRES (142)	IT INCREASES THE DANGER TENFOLD, BECAUSE IT	INCREASES	GERMAN JEALOUSY OF OUR MILITARY SUPREMACY.
DOCT I SD(81)	THE FURTHER GREAT ADVANTAGE OVER THEM THAT AGE	INCREASES	HER QUALIFICATION INSTEAD OF IMPAIRING IT. BEING
BARB I (251)	YEAR. /STEPHEN/ BUT THE WILL SAYS ALSO THAT IF HE	INCREASES	HIS INCOME BY HIS OWN EXERTIONS, THEY MAY DOUBLE
HART III SD(147)	ONE ANOTHER'S ARMS IN WILD EXCITEMENT. THE LIGHT	INCREASES	. /MAZZINI/ (ANXIOUSLY) THE LIGHT IS GETTING
PYGM I SD(211)	POPULAR INTEREST IN THE NOTE TAKER'S PERFORMANCE	INCREASES	. /THE SARCASTIC ONE/ (AMAZED) WELL, WHO SAID I
CLEO I SD(116)	TUMULT OF ARMED MEN IS HEARD. CLEOPATRA'S TERROR	INCREASES	. THE BUCINA SOUNDS CLOSE AT HAND, FOLLOWED BY A
PRES (142)	/MITCHENER/ ON THE CONTRARY, MY DEAR FELLOW, IT	INCREASES	THE DANGER TENFOLD, BECAUSE IT INCREASES GERMAN
2TRU III SD(100)	GUN IN ACTION REACHES THEIR EARS FROM AFAR. IT	INCREASES	TO SHATTERING INTENSITY AS IT APPROACHES. THEY ALL
MTH1 I SD(19)	EVE'S FACE LIGHTS UP WITH INTENSE INTEREST, WHICH	INCREASES	UNTIL AN EXPRESSION OF OVERWHELMING REPUGNANCE

INCREASING

SIM PREFACE(3)	PREFACE ON DAYS OF JUDGMENT. THE	INCREASING	BEWILDERMENT OF MY JOURNALIST CRITICS AS TO WHY I
APPL II SD(271)	SINCERE FRIENDSHIP. RENEWED MURMURS OF SYMPATHY.	INCREASING	EMOTION. /PROTEUS/ WE HAVE HAD OUR DISAGREEMENTS
DOCT PREFACE(53)	THE PERCENTAGE BY EIGHTY PER CENT INSTEAD OF	INCREASING	IT BY FIVE, BECAUSE THE PUBLIC, LEFT TO ITSELF
HART PREFACE(15)	OF TOIL REDUCES PRODUCTION HEAVILY INSTEAD OF	INCREASING	IT, THE FACTORY LAWS WERE SUSPENDED, AND MEN AND
MTH4 I (159)	AND OMNISCIENT. THUS OUR DISCOVERIES, INSTEAD OF	INCREASING	OUR WISDOM, ONLY DESTROYED THE LITTLE CHILDISH
KING PREFACE(156)	WAS IN THE LINE OF EVOLUTION, WHICH LEADS TO AN	INCREASING	SEPARATION OF THE UNIQUE AND INTENSELY PERSONAL
BULL PREFACE(62)	FOR BRINGING IN A PRESS LAW AND FOR CONSIDERABLY	INCREASING	THE ARMY OF OCCUPATION." JUST THINK OF IT! IN A
CLEO NOTES (205)	IS CLEARLY ROOM FOR GREAT CHANGES IN THE WORLD BY	INCREASING	THE PERCENTAGE OF INDIVIDUALS WHO ARE CAREFULLY
ROCK PREFACE(169)	FOR US: OTHERS VALUE IT BECAUSE IT ENRICHES US BY	INCREASING	THE PRODUCT PER HOUR. SOME OF US WOULD LIKE TO
DOCT PREFACE(56)	CHILD MORTALITY, LEADING TO FURTHER LEGISLATION	INCREASING	THE QUANTITY OF BRANDY TO A GALLON. NOT UNTIL THE

INCREDIBILITIES

CAPT NOTES (304)	A POINT OF HONOR OF BELIEF IN ABSTRACTIONS AND	INCREDIBILITIES	? AND SO I AM COMPELLED TO HIDE LADY

INCREDIBILITY

LION PREFACE(25)	TO THE ACCEPTANCE OF CHRISTIANITY, BECAUSE THEIR	INCREDIBILITY	(IF THEY WERE NOT INCREDIBLE THEY WOULD NOT

INCREDIBLE

CAPT NOTES (300)	HAVE NOT MADE HIM THE HERO OF MY PLAY, BECAUSE SO	INCREDIBLE	A PERSONAGE MUST HAVE DESTROYED ITS LIKELIHOOD--
METH PREFACE(R75)	OF METAPHYSICAL TRUTH, AND TRY TO CAST OUT	INCREDIBLE	AND SILLY LIES BY CREDIBLE AND CLEVER ONES,
MTH4 I (154)	THESE ISLANDS. I REPEAT, THESE ISLANDS WERE THEN,	INCREDIBLE	AS IT NOW SEEMS, THE CENTRE OF THE BRITISH
MIS. PREFACE(92)	STATUES, THEATRES, AND PRETTY COLORS. AND	INCREDIBLE	AS IT SEEMS, THESE UNHAPPY LUNATICS ARE LEFT AT
MIS. PREFACE(55)	NINETEENTH CENTURY WILL BECOME AS FORGOTTEN AND	INCREDIBLE	AS THE CONDITION OF THE CORRIDORS OF PALACES AND
METH PREFACE(R56)	TAIL, AND HIS ABODE OF BURNING BRIMSTONE, WAS AN	INCREDIBLE	BOGEY; BUT THE EVIL ATTRIBUTED TO HIM WAS REAL
GENV PREFACE(6)	INVADING ARMIES, WAS A FEAT WHICH STILL SEEMS	INCREDIBLE	EVEN NOW THAT IT HAS ACTUALLY BEEN ACHIEVED; YET
BULL PREFACE(67)	MADE RIDICULOUS. WHAT ACTUALLY HAPPENED WOULD BE	INCREDIBLE	IF THERE WERE NOT SO MANY LIVING WITNESSES OF IT.
HART PREFACE(5)	HOUSE OF COMMONS, WITH NOBODY TO CORRECT THEIR	INCREDIBLE	IGNORANCE OF MODERN THOUGHT AND POLITICAL SCIENCE
BULL PREFACE(63)	CRITICIZE OR REPUDIATE THEM, ON THE GROUND-- HOW	INCREDIBLE	IT NOW APPEARS! -- THAT ABD-EL-NEBI AND HASSAN
METH PREFACE(R38)	DESIGN, NO GUIDING INTELLIGENCE? THE THING WAS	INCREDIBLE	. IN VAIN DID HELMHOLTZ DECLARE THAT " THE EYE
GENV I (48)	IS DEAD. /POSKY/ WAS HE EVER ALIVE? TO ME HE WAS	INCREDIBLE	. /SHE/ I SUPPOSE MY THERMOS IS OF NO USE NOW.
LION PREFACE(87)	THE PARTHENOGENETIC BIRTH, AND THE MORE	INCREDIBLE	MIRACLES ARE REJECTED AS INVENTIONS; AND SUCH
DEST SD(151)	COVERING IMPOSSIBLE DISTANCES AND APPEARING IN	INCREDIBLE	PLACES, NOT BECAUSE EVERY SOLDIER CARRIES A FIELD
LION PREFACE(45)	IN THE GOSPELS WHICH THEY CONSIDER CREDIBLE AND	INCREDIBLE	RESPECTIVELY, THEIR LISTS WOULD BE DIFFERENT IN
PHIL I (88)	A WOMANLY WOMAN? /CHARTERIS/ (DARKLY) IT SOUNDS	INCREDIBLE	; BUT A MAN WAS FOUND READY TO TAKE THAT
JOAN PREFACE(47)	WHO BALANCE BETELGEUSE BY DESCRIBING THE	INCREDIBLE	SMALLNESS OF THE ATOM, AND A HOST OF OTHER MARVEL
BULL PREFACE(36)	THE HEADSHIP OF HER OWN CHURCH. IT MAY SEEM	INCREDIBLE	THAT LONG AFTER THE LAST ORANGEMAN SHALL LAY DOWN
LION PREFACE(25)	BECAUSE THEIR INCREDIBILITY (IF THEY WERE NOT	INCREDIBLE	THEY WOULD NOT BE MIRACLES) MAKES PEOPLE
MRS PREFACE(164)	WERE SUPPOSED TO ENLIVEN THE SQUALID DULNESS,	INCREDIBLE	TO THE YOUNGER GENERATION, OF THE MUSIC-HALLS
MIS. PREFACE(101)	ART HAS ALWAYS BEEN BAFFLED AND SNUBBED, IS	INCREDIBLE	TO THOSE WHO HAVE NOT WITNESSED AND UNDERSTOOD
LION PREFACE(44)	THIS QUESTION, AND HAVE ACCEPTED THE CREDIBLE AND	INCREDIBLE	WITH EQUAL COMPLACENCY. I HAVE DONE THIS BECAUSE
ROCK PREFACE(172)	THE ILLUSIONS TO FALL BEHIND THE TIMES AND BECOME	INCREDIBLE	, AT WHICH POINT THEY BECOME EXCEEDINGLY
LION PREFACE(19)	ARE, TO A MODERN EDUCATED PERSON, NONSENSICAL AND	INCREDIBLE	, WHILST THE APOSTLES ARE UNREADABLE. BUT WITH
LION II (143)	FRANTIC EXCITEMENT. /THE EMPEROR/ MY FRIENDS, AN	INCREDIBLE	! AN AMAZING THING! HAS HAPPENED. I CAN NO

INCREDIBLY

UNPL PREFACE(R18)	ENOUGH BY NATURE, THEY ARE, BY HOME TRAINING, SO	INCREDIBLY	ILL-MANNERED, THAT NOT EVEN THEIR INTEREST AS MEN
JOAN PREFACE(41)	UNDERSTAND CAPITALISM. IN THE UNITED STATES AN	INCREDIBLY	SAVAGE PERSECUTION OF RUSSIANS TOOK PLACE DURING

		INCREDULITY	
LION PREFACE(5)	BELIEF, AND YET HAVE, IN THE TEETH OF DOGGED	INCREDULITY	AND RECALCITRANCE, PRODUCED AN IRRESISTIBLE
SIM II (75)	CHARLES/ (READING) " JUDGMENT DAY. WIDESPREAD	INCREDULITY	AS TO ANYTHING HAVING REALLY HAPPENED. REPORTED
LION PREFACE(47)	HAD A QUITE DIFFERENT FASHION OF CREDULITY AND	INCREDULITY	FROM THE VENERABLE BEDE AND PIERS PLOWMAN AND
MTH3 SD(111)	SECRETARY AND THE PRESIDENT LOOK VERY GLUM. THEIR	INCREDULITY	IS VANQUISHED AT LAST. /BURGE-LUBIN/ LOOK HERE.
SIM PREFACE(4)	PLACE IN THE OPERATION OF HUMAN CREDULITY AND	INCREDULITY	. I HAVE POINTED OUT ON A FORMER OCCASION THAT
MTH3 (117)	VENERABLE PRELATE, SHEWS NO SIGN OF SURPRISE OR	INCREDULITY	. /BURGE-LUBIN/ SHE DOESNT TAKE IT SERIOUSLY.
LION PREFACE(30)	OF THE PROMISED SECOND COMING, AND BORE OUT THE	INCREDULITY	OF PILATE AND THE JEWS. AND AS MATTHEW WRITES AS
DOCT PREFACE(9)	FROM LAYMEN WHO KNOW, BECAUSE HE HAS BROUGHT THE	INCREDULITY	ON HIMSELF. IF HE ESCAPES, HE CAN ONLY DO SO BY
DOCT PREFACE(9)	AND FALLIBILITY. HIS PLEA IS RECEIVED WITH FLAT	INCREDULITY	; AND HE GETS LITTLE SYMPATHY, EVEN FROM LAYMEN
BULL III (142)	/MATTHEW/ (STARTING UP, MORE IN SCANDALIZED	INCREDULITY	THAN IN ANGER) D'YE HAVE THE FACE TO SET UP
LION PREFACE(19)	BEWILDERMENT, AND WITHOUT THE CONTEMPTUOUS	INCREDULITY	WHICH SPOILS THE TEMPER OF MANY MODERN ATHEISTS,
POSN (448)	(SHE RECEIVES THE ASSURANCE WITH CONTEMPTUOUS	INCREDULITY	, AND SITS DOWN ON THE STEP OF THE SHERIFF'S
SUPR II (50)	CAR. (THE CHAUFFEUR LOOKS AT TANNER WITH COOL	INCREDULITY	, AND TURNS TO THE CAR, WHISTLING A POPULAR AIR
		INCREDULOUS	
ARMS III (70)	HAD PRICKED HIM AND INTERRUPTING BLUNTSCHLI IN	INCREDULOUS	AMAZEMENT) EXCUSE ME, BLUNTSCHLI: WHAT DID YOU
DOCT I (103)	POOR OLD FATHER TALKING AGAIN. /B.B./ (RISING IN	INCREDULOUS	AMAZEMENT) YOUR FATHER! BUT, LORD BLESS MY
BULL PREFACE(31)	PROTESTANT PUGNACITY. IF ANY ENGLISHMAN FEELS	INCREDULOUS	AS TO THIS VIEW OF PROTESTANTISM AS AN
JOAN PREFACE(18)	WHO HAVE NEVER READ GALTON WILL BE PUZZLED AND	INCREDULOUS	. BUT A VERY LITTLE INQUIRY AMONG THEIR
CAPT II (248)	NECESSARY. (SIR HOWARD ASSENTS WITH A POLITE BUT	INCREDULOUS	NOD). /DRINKWATER/ EAH, EAH! LADY CICELY
CAND I (83)	LET YOU KNOW THAT HE WAS COMING. /MORELL/ (HALF	INCREDULOUS	) BUT HE HASNT CALLED HERE FOR THREE YEARS. ARE
BULL I (84)	ANDY HAFFIGAN OF ROSSCULLEN. /BROADBENT/ (STILL	INCREDULOUS	) BUT HIS BROGUE? /DOYLE/ HIS BROGUE! A FAT
BULL II (103)	IT'S THE FUNNIEST JOKE IN THE WORLD. /NORA/ (	INCREDULOUS	) GALONG WITH YOU! /KEEGAN/ (SPRINGING UP
ARMS III (50)	ROOM). /BLUNTSCHLI/ (DEEPLY CONCERNED, AND HALF	INCREDULOUS	) NO! YOU DONT MEAN THAT, DO YOU? /RAINA/ (
MILL I (155)	/ALASTAIR/ WHY NOT? /EPIFANIA/ YOU MAY WELL LOOK	INCREDULOUS	, ADRIAN. BUT HE DID. YES: THIS IMBECILE MADE
APPL PREFACE(191)	MADE AN INVENTION OF FIRST-RATE IMPORTANCE, I WAS	INCREDULOUS	, AND CONCLUDED THAT THE INVENTION WAS ONLY A
PHIL II (125)	I HAVE REFUSED HIS OFFER TO MARRY ME. /JULIA/ (	INCREDULOUS	, BUT HOPEFUL) YOU HAVE REFUSED! /GRACE/ YES;
MRS I (194)	FRANK) WILL YOU ACCEPT THE INVITATION? /FRANK/ (	INCREDULOUS	, BUT IMMENSELY AMUSED) IS THAT VIVIE'S MOTHER?
2TRU PREFACE(5)	OF THE RICH AS OF THE POOR. WE ARE ALL AMAZED AND	INCREDULOUS	, LIKE THE SOLDIER, WHEN WE HEAR OF THE
		INCREDULOUSLY	
BULL II SD(107)	LOOKS ROUND FOR LARRY; IS PUZZLED; THEN STARES	INCREDULOUSLY	AT BROADBENT. /AUNT JUDY/ SURELY TO GOODNESS
NEVR II (248)	DAUGHTER THATS MADE A MAN OF ME. /CRAMPTON/ (	INCREDULOUSLY	) ARE YOU IN LOVE WITH MY DAUGHTER?
BULL IV (149)	SOLEMNLY) NO: I AM A TEETOTALLER. /AUNT JUDY/ (	INCREDULOUSLY	) ARRA SINCE WHEN? /BROADBENT/ SINCE THIS
CAND I (92)	TO THE VIRGIN)? HE GAVE US THAT. /BURGESS/ (	INCREDULOUSLY	) GARN! D' YOU MEAN TO TELL ME-- YOUR HOWN
DEVL III (50)	AND HAS MADE A RARE GOOD BREAKFAST. /JUDITH/ (	INCREDULOUSLY	) HE IS IN GOOD SPIRITS! /SERGEANT/ TIP TOP,
MIS. (122)	SET, THEYLL SHOCK YOU AT FIRST. /HYPATIA/ (	INCREDULOUSLY	) HOW? /MRS TARLETON/ WELL, THE THINGS THEY
CAND II (122)	WHEN YOU TORTURE HIM AND LAUGH. /CANDIDA/ (	INCREDULOUSLY	) I TORTURE JAMES! NONSENSE, EUGENE: HOW YOU
CLEO V (197)	WELL, WHAT SAY YOU TO YOURSELF? /RUFIO/ (	INCREDULOUSLY	) I! I A GOVERNOR! WHAT ARE YOU DREAMING
CAND II (119)	I FEEL A LITTLE JEALOUS SOMETIMES. /MORELL/ (	INCREDULOUSLY	) OF PROSSY? /CANDIDA/ (LAUGHING) NO, NO,
NEVR III (264)	ON THE LIPS, BEFORE EVERYBODY. /MRS CLANDON/ (	INCREDULOUSLY	) PHIL! DOLLY! ARE YOU JOKING? (THEY SHAKE
SUPR I (35)	YOUD NEVER HAVE LET ME CALL MY OWN. /ANN/ (	INCREDULOUSLY	) WHAT? /TANNER/ MY SOUL. /ANN/ OH, DO BE
NEVR I (220)	YOU HAVE A CURIOUS LOOK OF MY MOTHER. /DOLLY/ (	INCREDULOUSLY	) YOUR MOTHER! ! ! QUITE SURE YOU DONT MEAN
DEVL II (47)	HAVE (JUDITH RISES BREATHLESS, AND STARES AT HIM	INCREDULOUSLY	)-- THE CHESTNUT MARE, IF SHE'S FRESH--
NEVR II (227)	THE UMBRELLA) DONT YOU KNOW ME? /MRS CLANDON/ (	INCREDULOUSLY	, LOOKING HARD AT HIM) ARE YOU FINCH M'COMAS?
ARMS III (52)	(GASPING) I! I! ! ! (SHE POINTS TO HERSELF	INCREDULOUSLY	, MEANING " I, RAINA PETKOFF, TELL LIES! " HE
CAND III (143)	I'M LOST. HE CANNOT BEAR THE BURDEN. /MORELL/ (	INCREDULOUSLY	, RAISING HIS HEAD AND VOICE WITH COMIC
		INCUBATE	
METH PREFACE(R18)	ITS YOUNG INSIDE ITS BODY, AND THE FOWL TO	INCUBATE	HERS OUTSIDE IT; OFFERING US, WE MAY SAY, OUR
		INCUBATING	
JOAN PREFACE(17)	CRY OF BACK TO THE MIDDLE AGES, WHICH HAS BEEN	INCUBATING	EVER SINCE THE PRE-RAPHAELITE MOVEMENT BEGAN,
		INCUBATION	
MTH5 (254)	OF TODAY ARE THE MEN AND WOMEN OF THE NEXT	INCUBATION	. I HOLD UP THE MARBLE FIGURE BEFORE THE MOTHER
MTH5 (233)	SYSTEM CAPABLE OF INTERNAL NOURISHMENT AND	INCUBATION	. /ECRASIA/ WHY DID YOU NOT FIND OUT HOW TO MAKE
		INCUBUS	
SIM II (59)	KEEN. /MAYA/ PRA: WE BESEECH THEE. ABOLISH THE	INCUBUS	. /VASHTI/ GIVE HIM PEACE THAT WE MAY HAVE REST.
		INCULCATE	
ROCK PREFACE(173)	THAT IT HAS ANY FINAL AND ETERNAL TRUTHS TO	INCULCATE	: IT CAN ONLY SELECT THE MOST USEFUL WORKING
JOAN PREFACE(36)	NO PLACE FOR FREETHINKERS: NAY, WHICH DOES NOT	INCULCATE	AND ENCOURAGE FREETHINKING WITH A COMPLETE BELIEF
ROCK PREFACE(172)	UTOPIA WILL SEEK FOR ABSOLUTE TRUTH IN ORDER TO	INCULCATE	IT THOUGH THE HEAVENS FALL. NOR DO I ADVISE A
MIS. PREFACE(82)	IS APT TO BE MORBID; AND WE ARE PROBABLY WRONG TO	INCULCATE	ITS DELIBERATE CULTIVATION. THE NATURAL COURSE IS
MIS. PREFACE(54)	BREAK THE SPIRIT THAT REVOLTS AGAINST HIM, AND TO	INCULCATE	SUBMISSION, EVEN TO OBSCENE ASSAULT, AS A DUTY. A
MIS. PREFACE(36)	COMMUNITY FOR WHAT THEY CONSUME AND ENJOY, AND	INCULCATE	THE REPAYMENT AS A POINT OF HONOR. IF WE DID THAT
2TRU PREFACE(12)	WITH CHURCHES SCHOOLS AND UNIVERSITIES TO	INCULCATE	THE SACREDNESS OF PRIVATE PROPERTY AND PARTY
ROCK PREFACE(173)	SELECT THE MOST USEFUL WORKING HYPOTHESES AND	INCULCATE	THEM VERY MUCH AS IT INCULCATES STANDARD BEHAVIOR
MIS. PREFACE(60)	IS USELESS TO EXPECT PARENTS AND SCHOOLMASTERS TO	INCULCATE	THIS UPPISHNESS. SUCH UNAMIABLE PRECEPTS AS ALWAYS
CLEO NOTES (212)	INFLUENTIAL FAMILIES TO GO ROUND) FORCES US TO	INCULCATE	, BUT AS SIMPLY DOING WHAT HE NATURALLY WANTS TO
		INCULCATED	
MIS. PREFACE(63)	SCHOOL. THE COMINGS OF AGE OF CHILDREN. ALL THIS	INCULCATED	ADULT DOCILITY, WHICH WRECKS EVERY CIVILIZATION
ROCK PREFACE(173)	THEY CONDUCE TO BENEFICIAL CONDUCT THEY MUST BE	INCULCATED	AND ACTED ON BY GOVERNMENTS UNTIL BETTER ONES
MIS. PREFACE(102)	WILL GIVE IT THE SLIP IF IT IS NOT RELIGIOUSLY	INCULCATED	AND STRONGLY SAFE-GUARDED. BESIDES, MEN ARE BORN
MIS. PREFACE(35)	POSSIBLE IS DONE TO INTENSIFY THE PRISONER'S	INCULCATED	AND UNNATURAL NOTION THAT WORK IS AN EVIL. IN
METH PREFACE(R88)	PSEUDO-SCIENTIFIC CURE-MONGERS, ALL SEDULOUSLY	INCULCATED	BY MODERN " SECONDARY EDUCATION," WERE SO
LION PREFACE(6)	TO IT. SETTING ASIDE THE HUGE MASS OF	INCULCATED	CHRIST-WORSHIP WHICH HAS NO REAL SIGNIFICANCE
LION PREFACE(17)	ARTIFICIAL SIDE OF THIS BELIEF, ON WHICH IT IS AN	INCULCATED	DREAD. THE RULER WHO APPEALS TO THE PROSPECT OF
GETT PREFACE(220)	THAT WHAT HAS LED THEM ASTRAY IS A SEDULOUSLY	INCULCATED	FALSE NOTION THAT THE RELATION THEY ARE TEMPTED
FABL PREFACE(72)	WAS MADE MISERABLE BY A DREAD OF HELL SEDULOUSLY	INCULCATED	FROM HIS INFANCY. HIS REACTION AGAINST IT CARRIED
ROCK PREFACE(172)	THEY THINK THEY POSSESS (THIS IS ONE OF THEIR	INCULCATED	ILLUSIONS) IS THREATENED BY THE DICTATORSHIPS
ROCK PREFACE(172)	OF MONEY. IT IS THE IMPORTANCE OF KEEPING OUR	INCULCATED	ILLUSIONS UP TO DATE THAT THROWS OUR HIGHER
GETT PREFACE(221)	WHAT IS MORE, AS THE SAME FANTASTIC ERRORS ARE	INCULCATED	IN MEN, AND THE CONSCIENTIOUS ONES THEREFORE FEEL
MIS. PREFACE(107)	IMPORTANT THAT SUBMISSIVENESS SHOULD NO LONGER BE	INCULCATED	. AND YET AS LONG AS YOU HAVE THE COMPULSORY
DOCT PREFACE(61)	FASHIONS AND EPIDEMICS. A DEMAND, HOWEVER, CAN BE	INCULCATED	. THIS IS THOROUGHLY UNDERSTOOD BY FASHIONABLE
MIS. PREFACE(107)	AS WE KNOW IT, WE SHALL HAVE SUBMISSIVENESS	INCULCATED	. WHAT IS MORE, UNTIL THE ACTIVE HOURS OF CHILD
MIS. PREFACE(107)	US ARE A FEW SPIRITS RELATIVELY FREE FROM THIS	INCULCATED	PARALYSIS. SOMETIMES BECAUSE THEY ARE
OVER PREFACE(157)	TWO PASSIONS IN PRACTICE. BESIDES, JEALOUSY IS AN	INCULCATED	PASSION, FORCED BY SOCIETY ON PEOPLE IN WHOM IT
ROCK PREFACE(174)	I SAY ANYTHING THAT COULD BREAK THE CAREFULLY	INCULCATED	POPULAR FAITH IN CAPITALISM THE SILENCE IS SO
MIS. PREFACE(89)	NATIVE STRENGTH TO BREAK THE BONDS OF THIS	INCULCATED	REVERENCE AND TO EXPOSE AND DERIDE AND TWEAK THE
MIS. PREFACE(107)	WHATEVER OF NOBILITY OF CHARACTER: THAT IS WHY	INCULCATED	SUBMISSIVENESS MAKES US SLAVES TO PEOPLE MUCH
BARB PREFACE(220)	OF THE LATTER HALF OF THE XIX CENTURY, STEADILY	INCULCATED	THE NECESSITY AND MORALITY OF A CONSCIENTIOUS
DOCT PREFACE(53)	NOR ANY OTHER DOCTOR EVER, AS FAR AS I KNOW,	INCULCATED	THE POPULAR NOTION THAT EVERYBODY GOT SMALLPOX AS
ROCK PREFACE(170)	WILL NOT AGREE AS TO THE FAITHS AND HABITS TO BE	INCULCATED	UPON THE CHILDREN OF THE COMMUNITY IN ORDER THAT
MIS. PREFACE(85)	SUPERIMPOSES ON IT A PAINFUL BURDEN OF FORCED,	INCULCATED	, SUGGESTED, AND ALTOGETHER UNNECESSARY AFFECTION
		INCULCATES	
MIS. PREFACE(98)	SO SILLY AS IT LOOKS. IT IS TRUE THAT THE BIBLE	INCULCATES	HALF A DOZEN RELIGIONS: SOME OF THEM BARBAROUS;
ROCK PREFACE(173)	HYPOTHESES AND INCULCATE THEM VERY MUCH AS IT	INCULCATES	STANDARD BEHAVIOR THROUGHOUT THAT VAST FIELD OF

INCULCATING

ROCK PREFACE(191)	MODEL EDUCATIONAL ESTABLISHMENTS EVER DREAMS OF	INCULCATING	. AYOT ST LAWRENCE, 22ND OCTOBER 1933.

INCULCATION

METH PREFACE(R15)	WHY, WHILST MOST PEOPLE'S MINDS SUCCUMB TO	INCULCATION	AND ENVIRONMENT, A FEW REACT VIGOROUSLY: HONEST
MIS. PREFACE(103)	IS NOT A NATURAL ONE. IT IS A MATTER OF	INCULCATION	. IF PEOPLE ARE BROUGHT UP TO BE SLAVES, IT IS
MIS. PREFACE(52)	CHILDREN IS CONCERNED, NOTHING BUT THE DELIBERATE	INCULCATION	OF A ROUTINE OF COMPLAINT, SCOLDING, PUNISHMENT,
SIM PREFACE(17)	ITS CRUELTIES, TOGETHER WITH A SUFFICIENT SCHOOL	INCULCATION	OF SOCIAL RESPONSIBILITY TO MAKE EVERY CITIZEN
SIM PREFACE(7)	CHILDREN, FAR FROM BEING PROTECTED AGAINST THE	INCULCATION	OF THE BELIEF IN BRIMSTONE, ARE EXPOSED TO IT IN
APPL I (235)	TAKE COMMAND OF OUR SCHOOLS AND PUT A STOP TO THE	INCULCATION	UPON YOUR UNFORTUNATE CHILDREN OF SUPERSTITIONS

INCULPATED

BULL PREFACE(56)	WHEN AN OFFENCE WAS REPORTED, DESCENDED ON THE	INCULPATED	VILLAGE; SEIZED EVERYBODY CONCERNED; AND PLIED

INCUR

SIM PREFACE(14)	IN THE NATURE OF THINGS A HUMAN CREATURE MUST	INCUR	A CONSIDERABLE DEBT FOR ITS NURTURE AND EDUCATION (IF
GETT PREFACE(213)	TO ALL THE MEAN SHIFTS OF ELECTIONEERING AND	INCUR	ALL ITS HEAVY EXPENSES FOR THE SAKE OF A SEAT IN
BULL PREFACE(24)	DO NOT HESITATE TO TEACH THAT ALL METHODISTS	INCUR	DAMNATION. IN IRELAND ALL THAT THE MEMBER OF THE IRISH
HART I (57)	OUT INTO BUSINESS ON A LARGE SCALE, HE HAD TO	INCUR	LIABILITIES. WHEN THE BUSINESS WENT INTO LIQUIDATION
BASH PREFACE(90)	A SINGLE WORD OF IT WAS, IT WAS BELIEVED, TO	INCUR	THE CURSE IN THE LAST CHAPTER OF REVELATIONS. EVEN IN

INCURABLE

DOCT I SD(81)	SHE HAS THE COMPLEXION OF A NEVER-WASHED GYPSY,	INCURABLE	BY ANY DETERGENT; AND SHE HAS, NOT A REGULAR BEARD
MIS. PREFACE(39)	OF ADAM BECOMES FIRST A BLESSING AND THEN AN	INCURABLE	HABIT. AND IN VIEW OF THAT DAY WE MUST NOT GRUDGE
LION PREFACE(99)	EVERY CHAPTER OF THEIR HISTORY, IS REALLY ONLY AN	INCURABLE	INAPTITUDE FOR THEOLOGY, AND INDEED FOR
ROCK I (229)	IT IN ONE WORD, A BAD CASE OF FRIVOLITY, POSSIBLY	INCURABLE	. /SIR ARTHUR/ FRIVOLITY! DID I UNDERSTAND YOU TO
FABL PREFACE(84)	SHAM-DEMOCRATIC MISGOVERNMENT ARE CAUSED, NOT BY	INCURABLE	MENTAL INCAPACITY, BUT BY AN IGNORANCE THAT IS
BARB II (276)	ONY A JUMPED-UP, JERKED-OFF, ORSPITTLE-TURNED-OUT	INCURABLE	OF AN OLE WORKIN MAN: WHO CARES ABOUT YOU? EH?

INCURABLES

BUOY IV (54)	CYRIL IS A DOCTOR, HEAD OF A MENTAL HOSPITAL FOR	INCURABLES	. HE IS THE MAN YOU SHOULD CONSULT. LAWYERS ARE
LION PREFACE(58)	THAN IF THEY WERE HANDSOMELY PENSIONED OFF AS	INCURABLES	. JESUS HAD MORE SENSE THAN TO PROPOSE ANYTHING

INCURABLY

JOAN PREFACE(16)	ST TERESA'S HORMONES HAD GONE ASTRAY AND LEFT HER	INCURABLY	HYPERPITUITARY OR HYPERADRENAL OR HYSTEROID OR
MIS. PREFACE(51)	OF LITERATURE AND MATHEMATICS WILL HAVE BEEN	INCURABLY	PREJUDICED AGAINST THEM. EVERYONE WHO IS
ARMS III (71)	CHANCES IN LIFE? /BLUNTSCHLI/ (PROMPTLY) AN	INCURABLY	ROMANTIC DISPOSITION. I RAN AWAY FROM HOME TWICE
ARMS III (70)	HAS SPOILED ALL HIS CHANCES IN LIFE THROUGH AN	INCURABLY	ROMANTIC DISPOSITION, A MAN-- /SERGIUS/ (STARTING

INCURRED

ROCK PREFACE(160)	PROTECTED FROM HAVING HIS OWN POCKET PICKED,	INCURRED	NO PENALTY, AND HAD ACTUALLY PASSED THE MOST SEVERE
BULL IV (150)	MY OLD FRIEND MR LAURENCE DOYLE UNFORTUNATELY	INCURRED	THE FIRST EFFECTS OF HER VERY NATURAL RESENTMENT. I
PLES PREFACE(R13)	THAT THEY CAN ALL POINT TO HONORABLE LOSSES	INCURRED	THROUGH AIMING " OVER THE HEADS OF THE PUBLIC," AND

INCURRING

MIS. PREFACE(78)	FORMAL ACKNOWLEDGMENT OF THE OBLIGATIONS IT IS	INCURRING	AND A KNOWLEDGE OF THE FACT THAT THESE OBLIGATIONS
MIS. PREFACE(10)	TIMES (HE VERY NEARLY DID, BY THE WAY) WITHOUT	INCURRING	ANY DANGER OF BEING REMOVED TO AN ASYLUM, OR EVEN

INCURSIONS

PYGM EPILOG (296)	BY FREDDY'S MOTHER. CLARA, IN THE COURSE OF HER	INCURSIONS	INTO THOSE ARTISTIC CIRCLES WHICH WERE THE

INDEBTED

PRES (152)	OF SATISFACTION) AND NOW, LADIES, TO WHAT AM I	INDEBTED	-- /MRS BANGER/ LET ME INTRODUCE US. I AM ROSA
JITT PREFACE(4)	IT IS NOT FOR ME TO SAY HOW FAR ENGLISH DRAMA IS	INDEBTED	TO HERR TREBITSCH FOR ITS PRESENT PRESTIGE ABROAD.
MTH2 (78)	MADE TO US: A COMMUNICATION FOR WHICH I SHALL BE	INDEBTED	TO HIM ALL MY LIFE LONG: HAS THIS, I SAY, NO DEEPER
BARB (206)	MAJOR BARBARA WAS BEGUN. THE PLAY, INDEED, STANDS	INDEBTED	TO HIM IN MORE WAYS THAN ONE. G.B.S.
DEVL III (63)	BLACK CAP AND SO FORTH? I AM SURE WE ARE GREATLY	INDEBTED	TO THE ADMIRABLE TACT AND GENTLEMANLY FEELING SHEWN
HART PREFACE(34)	DRAMA OF THE KIND I DEALT IN ALIVE; SO THAT I WAS	INDEBTED	TO THE EMPEROR OF AUSTRIA FOR MAGNIFICENT
BARB I (265)	NOT AT ALL. /UNDERSHAFT/ MR CUSINS: I AM MUCH	INDEBTED	TO YOU FOR EXPLAINING SO PRECISELY. (TURNING TO
FANY PROLOG (266)	MY DAUGHTER. (THEY ALL BOW). WE ARE VERY GREATLY	INDEBTED	TO YOU, GENTLEMEN, FOR SO KINDLY INDULGING HER
KING I (173)	/NEWTON/ (VERY SERIOUSLY) I SHALL BE MUCH	INDEBTED	TO YOU, MADAM, IF YOU WILL COMMUNICATE TO ME THE

INDEBTEDNESS

APPL PREFACE(185)	THEY MIGHT WRITE OFF THAT MUCH OF THEIR CAPITAL	INDEBTEDNESS	. THE RESULT WOULD BE A BIGGER DIVIDEND FOR THE

INDECENCIES

MRS PREFACE(171)	TO OUR LAWGIVERS TO PUNISH SILLY AND NEGLIGIBLE	INDECENCIES	WITH A FEROCITY UNKNOWN IN DEALING WITH, FOR

INDECENCY

GETT PREFACE(248)	TO PUT IT IN CHRISTIAN TERMS, AN ACCUSATION OF	INDECENCY	AGAINST GOD, IS THE NOTION THAT SEX, WITH ALL ITS
BULL PREFACE(40)	FOX DO THESE THINGS WITHOUT THE SMALLEST SENSE OF	INDECENCY	AND DISHONOR, BUT THEY CANNOT MUZZLE HIS
MRS PREFACE(178)	THAT THEY WERE SIMPLY STUPID MEN WHO THOUGHT THAT	INDECENCY	CONSISTS, NOT IN EVIL, BUT IN MENTIONING IT. I
MIS. PREFACE(91)	EXPLICITLY PRAYED TO, AND IMPLICITLY CONVICTED OF	INDECENCY	EVERY DAY. AN ASSOCIATION OF VICE AND SIN WITH
MRS PREFACE(178)	PERFORMANCE, FELL BACK ON A LOCAL BYE-LAW AGAINST	INDECENCY	. IT SUMMONED THE ACTRESS WHO IMPERSONATED MRS
MTH4 I (142)	TO EXPLAIN. DECENCY CANNOT BE DISCUSSED WITHOUT	INDECENCY	. /THE WOMAN/ I CANNOT UNDERSTAND YOU AT ALL. I
POSN PREFACE(421)	ENTERTAINMENTS EXCEPT COMMON POLICE CASES OF	INDECENCY	. THE REASON GIVEN IS THAT FOR WHICH THE STAR
OVER PREFACE(163)	ARE OFTEN SCANDALIZED BY WHAT THEY CONSIDER THE	INDECENCY	OF THE ENGLISH STAGE, AND THAT FRENCH ACTRESSES
POSN PREFACE(421)	REPORT, " THAT THE LAW WHICH PREVENTS OR PUNISHES	INDECENCY	, BLASPHEMY AND LIBEL IN PRINTED PUBLICATIONS (IT
POSN PREFACE(414)	ORDINARY LAWS AGAINST DISORDERLY HOUSEKEEPING,	INDECENCY	, BLASPHEMY, ETC., EXCEPT IN CASES WHERE SOME
POSN PREFACE(381)	MAGISTRACY AND THE WHOLE BODY OF LAW. BLASPHEMY,	INDECENCY	, LIBEL, TREASON, SEDITION, OBSCENITY, PROFANITY,

INDECENCY'S

SUPR HANDBOK(225)	STRONG ENOUGH TO MASTER HER. DECENCY. DECENCY IS	INDECENCY'S	CONSPIRACY OF SILENCE. EXPERIENCE. MEN ARE WISE

INDECENT

3PLA PREFACE(R19)	COMPARE WITH IT THE TREATMENT OF LOVE, FRANKLY	INDECENT	ACCORDING TO OUR NOTIONS, IN ORIENTAL FICTION. IN
SUPR HANDBOK(211)	MEAN A BLATANT REPUDIATION OF SUCH PROPOSALS AS	INDECENT	AND IMMORAL, WITH, NEVERTHELESS, A GENERAL SECRET
POSN PREFACE(417)	THE POLICE WOULD SIMPLY ARREST HER ON A CHARGE OF	INDECENT	EXPOSURE. THE EXTENT TO WHICH THIS OBVIOUS
DOCT PREFACE(38)	METHODS. WE SENT OUR SONS TO PUBLIC SCHOOLS WHERE	INDECENT	FLOGGING IS A RECOGNIZED METHOD OF TAMING THE YOUNG
POSN PREFACE(408)	A DRAPED FIGURE IS DECENT AND AN UNDRAPED ONE IS	INDECENT	. IT IS USELESS TO POINT TO ACTUAL EXPERIENCE,
POSN PREFACE(421)	THE REPORT) IN THE CASE OF A PLAY:-- (A) TO BE	INDECENT	. (B) TO CONTAIN OFFENSIVE PERSONALITIES, (C) TO
GENV II (60)	OF THOSE THINGS THAT ARE NOT DONE. CASTOR OIL IS	INDECENT	. MOTOR OIL IS ALL RIGHT. /JUDGE/ WELL, YOU NEED
GENV IV (90)	PRIVATE ARE NOT EVIL; BUT THEY MAY BE EXTREMELY	INDECENT	. /BEGONIA/ WE'D BETTER CHANGE THE SUBJECT, I
SUPR HANDBOK(192)	CONSEQUENTLY WE HAVE NO LANGUAGE FOR THEM EXCEPT	INDECENT	LANGUAGE. WE THEREFORE HAVE TO DECLARE THEM UNFIT
POSN PREFACE(410)	IT MORE EXACTLY, BETWEEN A NAKED FIGURE AND AN	INDECENT	ONE. THEY OFTEN COMBINE A NARROW BUT TERRIBLY
MIS. (123)	NICE GOOD WOMEN A THING IS EITHER DECENT OR	INDECENT	; AND IF IT'S INDECENT, WE JUST DONT MENTION IT OR
6CAL PREFACE(89)	OF KING EDWARD THE SEVENTH SEEMED UNNATURAL AND	INDECENT	TO THEM, AND THEY RENT THEIR GARMENTS ACCORDINGLY.
CLEO PRO1 (91)	BOLDLY, AND WAS NOT FOREVER REBUKING US FOR OUR	INDECENT	WAYS OF CREATION, AND HIDING OUR HANDIWORK AS A
DOCT PREFACE(37)	CLAIMS ANY GENERAL FUNDAMENTAL RIGHT TO BE CRUEL,	INDECENT	, BECAUSE THERE IS AN ACCEPTED CONVENTION TO
MIS. PREFACE(30)	TABOO WHICH RULES THE SUBJECT OUT ALTOGETHER AS	INDECENT	, HAS NO AGE LIMIT. IT MEANS THAT AT NO MATTER WHAT
DOCT PREFACE(37)	BLUSH IT MAY SEEM NOT ONLY UNNECESSARY, BUT EVEN	INDECENT	, TO DISCUSS SUCH A PROPOSITION AS THE ELEVATION OF
JOAN 6 (139)	SECOND, SHE WEARS MEN'S CLOTHES, WHICH IS	INDECENT	, UNNATURAL, AND ABOMINABLE; AND IN SPITE OF OUR
MIS. (123)	A THING IS EITHER DECENT OR INDECENT; AND IF IT'S	INDECENT	, WE JUST DONT MENTION IT OR PRETEND TO KNOW ABOUT

INDECENTLY

MRS PREFACE(175) UNTIL THEY WERE FOR ALL PRACTICAL PURPOSES INDECENTLY MAD. THEY FINALLY FORCED THE POLICE TO ARREST
POSN PREFACE(384) AND THEIR SOLDIERS TO WEAR CLOTHES WHICH INDECENTLY REVEALED THE FACT THAT THEY HAD LEGS AND WAISTS
GETT PREFACE(229) BUT DEALT WITH IT WILL BE, DECENTLY OR INDECENTLY ; FOR THE PRESENT STATE OF THINGS IN ENGLAND IS

INDECISION

WIDO II (36) SHE TAKES IT OVER HIS SHOULDER WITH EQUAL INDECISION . THEY ARE BOTH TRYING HARD TO CONCILIATE ONE

INDECISIVE

DOCT IV (159) /THE NEWSPAPER MAN/ (LOOKING ROUND AND MAKING INDECISIVE ATTEMPTS AT NOTES) THIS IS THE STUDIO. I SUPPOSE.

INDECOROUS

CATH PREFACE(154) LOVE INTEREST ON AN ENORMOUS AND UTTERLY INDECOROUS SCALE. CATHERINE KEPT THIS VAST GUIGNOL THEATRE

INDECORUM

JOAN PREFACE(24) DEFEND IT AGAINST THE CHARGE OF EXTRAVAGANT INDECORUM . BUT ITS PURPOSE WAS NOT TO DEPICT JOAN, BUT TO
3PLA PREFACE(R19) THE INCIDENTS OF LIFE, CANNOT TOUCH IT WITHOUT INDECORUM . CAN ANY DILEMMA BE MORE COMPLETE? LOVE IS
SUPR I SD(17) ON THE CORNER OF THE WRITING TABLE WITH STUDIED INDECORUM . OCTAVIUS GIVES MRS WHITEFIELD A CHAIR NEXT ANN.

INDEED

GLIM (184) THROW THE CARDINAL OUT OF THE WINDOW. /FERRUCCIO/ INDEED : AND PRAY WHY? /GIULIA/ HE WILL PAY THIRTY CROWNS
NEVR II (226) WITH THEM THAT IS VERY TAKING, SIR, VERY TAKING INDEED : ESPECIALLY THE YOUNG LADY AND GENTLEMAN. /THE
WIDO II (34) DREADFUL! /TRENCH/ BLANCHE: IT'S VERY SERIOUS INDEED : I ASSURE YOU IT IS. /BLANCHE/ IT WOULD KEEP ME
AUGS (274) OR TWO. FINALLY HE BECAME BLUELOO. /THE LADY/ OH, INDEED : I DIDNT KNOW. WELL, BLUELOO IS SIMPLY INFATUATED
FANY II (295) DEVIL. THEN I DONT KNOW WHAT I SHALL DO: I DONT INDEED : ITLL KILL ME. /MARGARET/ YOU SHOULDNT HAVE PRAYED
MTH1 II (22) THE SHRIEKS OF TORMENT! THAT WILL BE LIFE INDEED : LIFE LIVED TO THE VERY MARROW: BURNING,
LADY PREFACE(220) AWAY OUR PITY. DE PROFUNDIS WAS DE PROFUNDIS INDEED : WILDE WAS TOO GOOD A DRAMATIST TO THROW AWAY SO
CATH 4 (189) TOE BETWEEN MY RIBS. I AM TICKLESOME. /CATHERINE/ INDEED ? ALL THE MORE REASON FOR YOU TO TREAT ME WITH
MILL I (143) NOT AT YOUR MISFORTUNES, BUT AT YOU. /EPIFANIA/ INDEED ? AM I SO COMIC A FIGURE IN MY MISERY? /SAGAMORE/
MIS. (166) /TARLETON/ (THE NAME CONVEYING NOTHING TO HIM) INDEED ? AND HOW IS SHE? QUITE WELL, I HOPE, EH? /THE
BARB I (269) BOSH! THERE ARE NO SCOUNDRELS. /UNDERSHAFT/ INDEED ? ARE THERE ANY GOOD MEN? /BARBARA/ NO. NOT ONE.
BUOY IV (49) KNOW. HE WANTS TO MARRY ME. /OLD BILL/ DOES HE INDEED ? DO YOU WANT TO MARRY HIM? /SHE/ I AM CONSIDERING
DEST (154) OF EUROPE, EH? WHY ONLY EUROPE? /GIUSEPPE/ WHY, INDEED ? EMPEROR OF THE WORLD, EXCELLENCY! WHY NOT? (HE
DOCT III (138) SEEN MINNIE'S MARRIAGE LINES. /LOUIS/ (COOLLY) INDEED ? HAVE YOU SEEN JENNIFER'S? /RIDGEON/ (RISING IN
HART I (59) I LIKE OTHELLO. /MRS HUSHABYE/ DO YOU INDEED ? HE WAS JEALOUS, WASNT HE? /ELLIE/ OH, NOT THAT. I
NEVR III (274) REMARK THAT MAKES A LOT OF MISCHIEF. /DOLLY/ OH, INDEED ? HMHM! /PHILIP/ AHAH! (HE GOES TO THE HEARTH AND
PHIL II (96) FEELING THAT HE IS IN THE PRESENCE OF SCIENCE) INDEED ? HOW WILL YOU DO THAT? /PARAMORE/ OH, EASILY
KING II (232) I NOT DO WHAT MY MOTHER DID? /CHARLES/ WHY NOT, INDEED ? I DARESAY YOU WILL DO IT VERY WELL, BELOVED. THE
MIS. (202) /JOHNNY/ (WITH INCREASED RESPECT) HAVE YOU INDEED ? I DIDNT KNOW: YOULL EXCUSE MY MISTAKE, I HOPE. BUT
JOAN 4 (99) VIEWS THAN YOU GIVE HIM CREDIT FOR. /WARWICK/ INDEED ? IN WHAT WAY? LISTEN TO THIS, MESSIRE JOHN.
NEVR I (211) WITH A SPRING) THAT WEVE GROWN UP. /MRS CLANDON/ INDEED ? IN WHAT WAY HAVE I GIVEN YOU ANY REASON TO
MTH2 (40) /HASLAM/ SHE IS GOING TO LEAVE YOU? /FRANKLYN/ INDEED ? I'M SORRY. IS IT OUR FAULT, MR HASLAM? /HASLAM/
GENV II (62) HEARD THE NEWS? LORD MIDDLESEX IS DEAD. /SIR O./ INDEED ? LET ME SEE. MIDDLESEX? I DONT ATTACH ANY
MTH4 I (169) YOUR LIKE. /THE ELDERLY GENTLEMAN/ (INTERESTED) INDEED ? PRAY, MAY I ASK WHAT IT IS? I AM A KEEN
OVER (180) HERE IS A ROMANCE. /MRS LUNN/ (FAINTLY IRONICAL) INDEED ? /JUNO/ YES. YOUVE GUESSED, OF COURSE, THAT I'M A
WIDO II (25) (LOOKING UP FROM HIS WRITING, DISPLEASED) INDEED ? /LICKCHEESE/ YES, SIR. DR TRENCH ASKED HIS WAY OF
MTH2 (61) /FRANKLYN/ (WITH INTEREST AND SOME SURPRISE) INDEED ? /LUBIN/ YES. IT OCCURRED QUITE AT THE BEGINNING OF
SUPR I (12) WHY DIDNT HE APPOINT TAVY? /RAMSDEN/ AH! WHY INDEED ? /OCTAVIUS/ I WILL TELL YOU. HE SOUNDED ME ABOUT
WIDO II (24) TRENCH. /BLANCHE/ (WITH AFFECTED INDIFFERENCE) INDEED ? /SARTORIUS/ " INDEED? "! IS THAT ALL YOU HAVE TO
SIM I (48) TO TELL YOU THIS-- SHE KISSED ME. /SIR CHARLES/ INDEED ? THAT SHEWS THAT SHE CONTEMPLATES A UNION WITH YOU.
ROCK I (213) MAKE YOU SIT UP AND DO SOMETHING. /SIR ARTHUR/ INDEED ? THATS INTERESTING. MAY I ASK WHAT? /OXFORD YOUTH/
DEST (158) WITH HIS CAP AND WHIP ON THE TABLE) AH! WHERE INDEED ? THATS JUST WHAT I SHOULD LIKE TO KNOW, GENERAL. (
NEVR II (251) A MOMENT. /CRAMPTON/ (LOOKING STEADILY AT HER) INDEED ? THATS SURPRISING. YOU MEET YOUR FATHER AFTER
ROCK I (215) SOMETHING ALL RIGHT. /SIR ARTHUR/ (BRIGHTENING) INDEED ? WHAT IS IT? /BLEE/ (WITH INTENSE CONTEMPT) YOUR
INCA (242) THE SONS OF THE INCA OF PERUSALEM. /ERMYNTRUDE/ INDEED ? WHICH SON? /THE PRINCESS/ I DONT KNOW. THEY HAVNT
2TRU II (53) /MEEK/ I VOLUNTEERED, SIR. /TALLBOYS/ DID YOU INDEED ? YOU CONSIDER YOURSELF AN IMPRESSIVE PERSON, EH?
WIDO II (24) AFFECTED INDIFFERENCE) INDEED? /SARTORIUS/ " INDEED ? "! IS THAT ALL YOU HAVE TO SAY TO ME? OH, VERY
MIS. PREFACE(74) ADMITTED THAT THE FOXES HAVE THE BEST OF IT; AND INDEED A GLANCE AT OUR PHEASANTS, OUR DEER, AND OUR CHILDREN
PPP (204) HAS SET INSIDE HIM. THE OFFICER WAS RIGHT: HE IS INDEED A LIVING STATUE. MAGNESIA FLINGS HERSELF ON THE STONY
CLEO IV (171) HIS EYES KEENLY TO HERS) IS CLEOPATRA THEN INDEED A QUEEN, AND NO LONGER CAESAR'S PRISONER AND SLAVE..
BARB I SD(260) MERE FORCE OF CHARACTER PRESENTS HIMSELF AS-- AND INDEED ACTUALLY IS-- CONSIDERATE, GENTLE, EXPLANATORY, EVEN
MRS PREFACE(151) TO PROSTITUTION TO KEEP BODY AND SOUL TOGETHER. INDEED ALL ATTRACTIVE UNPROPERTIED WOMEN LOSE MONEY BY BEING
LION PREFACE(82) SPURIOUS BY PAULINE THEOLOGIANS BECAUSE PAUL, AND INDEED ALL THE APOSTLES, ARE REPRESENTED IN IT AS VERY
PHIL III (134) WITH THEATRICAL PATHOS) YOU ARE RIGHT THERE, I AM INDEED ALONE IN THE WORLD. /PARAMORE/ (TIMIDLY APPROACHING
O'FL (216) I HOPE YOURE PROUD OF HIM. /MRS O'FLAHERTY/ AND INDEED AND I AM, YOUR HONOR. IT'S THE BRAVE BOY HE IS; AND
JITT III (69) TO THINK I HAVE SET YOURS. /AGNES/ YOU HAVE: INDEED AND INDEED YOU HAVE. I AM SURE WHAT WE OWE YOU, WITH
GETT (327) AGONY. (RISING) FATAL WOMAN-- IF WOMAN YOU ARE INDEED AND NOT A FIEND IN HUMAN FORM-- /MRS GEORGE/ IS THIS
CAPT III (273) ATLAS. /LADY CICELY/ (DELIGHTED) NO! /RANKIN/ INDEED AND THEY DID. THE POOR CADI IS SO TARRIFIED BY ALL HE
APPL PREFACE(186) BEST I CAN DO WITHOUT GOVERNMENT INTERFERENCE: INDEED ANY OTHER WAY OF DEALING WITH MY SPARE MONEY WOULD BE
FANY PREFACE(255) OF GOOD AND EVIL, OF COURAGE AND COWARDICE, OR INDEED ANYTHING BUT HOW TO KEEP HUNGER AND CONCUPISCENCE AND
SUPR PREFACE(R29) AGREES WITH THEM CAN POSSIBLY BE A DRAMATIST, OR INDEED ANYTHING ELSE THAT TURNS UPON A KNOWLEDGE OF MANKIND.
MIS. PREFACE(102) ARE AMONG THE THINGS THEY DO NOT UNDERSTAND, AND INDEED ARE NOT AT PRESENT ALLOWED TO UNDERSTAND. THEY CAN BE
BARB PREFACE(217) A GOOD LIFE BEFORE ALL THE OTHER DUTIES-- WHICH INDEED ARE NOT DUTIES AT ALL WHEN THEY CONFLICT WITH IT, BUT
TRFL (83) THE CIRCUS CLOWN WITH THE RINGMASTER: WHAT ELSE INDEED ARE THE PASSAGES BETWEEN MONSIEUR JOURDAIN AND HIS
METH PREFACE(R81) THE DEATH OF ART, BUT A GLORIOUS REBIRTH OF IT. INDEED ART HAS NEVER BEEN GREAT WHEN IT WAS NOT PROVIDING AN
BULL II SD(111) NEITHER HOSPITABLE REMONSTRANCE NOR SURPRISE. INDEED AUNT JUDY WANTS TO GET RID OF HIM WHILST SHE MAKES A
PRES (133) HIMSELF INTO MITCHENER'S CHAIR) YES: IT IS INDEED BALSQUITH. IT HAS COME TO THIS: THAT THE ONLY WAY THE
PYGM V (281) SORRY TO MISS YOUR WEDDING. /DOOLITTLE/ I SHOULD INDEED BE HONORED BY YOUR CONDESCENSION, MAAM; AND MY POOR
PPP (198) FACE LIGHTS UP WITH HEAVENLY RADIANCE)! HAVE I INDEED BEEN FOUND WORTHY TO BE THE FIRST CLOTHES-MARTYR?
BARB PREFACE(244) ALLOWANCES. ALL MEN MAKE VERY LARGE ALLOWANCES INDEED BEFORE THEY STAKE THEIR OWN LIVES IN A WAR TO THE
DOCT PREFACE(33) FORCE, DESIRES TO BE GODLIKE, IT IS STUPID, AND INDEED BLASPHEMOUS AND DESPAIRING, TO HOPE THAT THE THIRST
MIS. PREFACE(34) THIS SOCIETY CANNOT GO WITH ANY CERTAINTY, AND INDEED CAN ONLY GO THIS FAR RATHER APOLOGETICALLY AND
HART PREFACE(40) MAY BE BETTER THINGS TO REVEAL, IT MAY NOT, AND INDEED CANNOT, BE MILITARILY EXPEDIENT TO REVEAL THEM WHILST
MILL PREFACE(126) INSTINCT INCOMPATIBLE WITH CIVILIZATION: INDEED CIVILIZATION RESTS FUNDAMENTALLY ON THE COMPACT THAT
LION PREFACE(97) PRACTICALLY WHOLLY CHRISTIAN, IS NOW CROWDED, AND INDEED CONSIDERABLY OVERCROWDED, INTO A CORNER OF AN EMPIRE
FABL PREFACE(78) NO MEANING. THE FACT THAT I AM ASCERTAINABLY, AND INDEED CONSPICUOUSLY, ONLY A SUPERANNUATED (NOT
GETT PREFACE(190) TO CONSIDER THE SUBJECT. NOTHING CAME OF IT (NOR INDEED COULD HAVE COME OF IT IN THE ABSENCE OF WOMEN); BUT
DOCT PREFACE(32) ALL ON THE SIDE OF VIVISECTION IS THE MIGHTY AND INDEED DIVINE FORCE OF CURIOSITY. HERE WE HAVE NO DECAYING
PLES PREFACE(R9) CAN ONLY COME WHEN THE WORK IS DONE, AND INDEED DONE WITH: THAT IS TO SAY, WHEN THE DEVELOPMENT,
POSN PREFACE(407) OF CARRYING ON A LEGITIMATE DRAMATIC BUSINESS. INDEED EVERYBODY CONNECTED WITH THE THEATRICAL PROFESSION
JOAN PREFACE(10) COULD AND DID DICTATE THEM AND ATTACH FULL AND INDEED EXCESSIVE IMPORTANCE TO THEM. WHEN SHE WAS CALLED A
PLES PREFACE(R18) ONSLAUGHT ON IDEALISM WHICH IS IMPLICIT, AND INDEED EXPLICIT, IN ARMS AND THE MAN AND THE NATURALIST
ROCK PREFACE(157) LET ME ILLUSTRATE MY ATTITUDE BY A VERY FAMOUS, INDEED FAR TOO FAMOUS, EXAMPLE OF THE POPULAR CONCEPTION OF
GENV PREFACE(26) OF HUMAN LIFE CANNOT BE FIXED AT SEVENTY YEARS OR INDEED FIXED AT ALL. IF WE MASTER THE ART OF LIVING INSTEAD
LION PREFACE(99) ONLY AN INCURABLE INAPTITUDE FOR THEOLOGY, AND INDEED FOR CO-ORDINATED THOUGHT IN ANY DIRECTION, WHICH
UNPL PREFACE(R9) WHICH MANY WOULD LIKE TO SAY, BUT DARE NOT, AND INDEED FOR WANT OF SKILL COULD NOT EVEN IF THEY DURST. ITS
PLES PREFACE(R11) PERSUADE THOSE WHO HAD ASKED FOR IT THAT THEY HAD INDEED GOT IT. A CHAPTER IN CYRIL MAUDE'S HISTORY OF THE
MTH5 (232) CONCEIVE. /ARJILLAX/ IF YOU MODELLED HIM, HE MUST INDEED HAVE BEEN A SPECTACLE. /PYGMALION/ OH, IT WAS NOT HIS
MTH5 (241) ME LIKE THAT, MAM. I MEANT NO HARM. HE HURT ME: INDEED HE DID. /THE HE-ANCIENT/ THE CREATURE HAS KILLED THAT
MIS. PREFACE(101) AS AN ARTIST, TARTUFFE IS NOT ALWAYS A PRIEST. INDEED HE IS NOT ALWAYS A RASCAL: HE IS OFTEN A WEAK MAN
GENV PREFACE(13) BY HIS POLITICAL PROGRAM, WHICH FEW UNDERSTOOD: INDEED HE ONLY HALF UNDERSTOOD IT HIMSELF. WHEN MR WINSTON
INCA (253) OUGHT TO HAVE BEEN SHOT BEFORE HE WAS FORTY, AS INDEED HE VERY NEARLY WAS. TAKE THIS FROM ME: HEREDITARY
LADY PREFACE(230) REGICIDE AND TRANSFIGURING THE REPUBLICANS. INDEED HERO-WORSHIPPERS HAVE NEVER FORGIVEN HIM FOR
FANY I (277) ME NOT TO BEGIN BY TELLING YOU HE'S QUITE SAFE. INDEED HE'S IN THE SAFEST PLACE IN THE WORLD, AS ONE MAY
LION PREFACE(100) MILLIONS OF NEGROES WHO ARE SUSCEPTIBLE, AND INDEED HIGHLY SUSCEPTIBLE, OF CONVERSION TO THOSE
BARB PREFACE(220) VIEWS WILL NOT PERPLEX YOU IN THE LEAST. UNLESS INDEED HIS CONSTANT SENSE THAT HE IS ONLY THE INSTRUMENT OF

MIS. PREFACE(106)	BUT YOU CAN ALWAYS BLUFF THE ROMANTIC PERSON:	INDEED	HIS GRASP OF REAL CONSIDERATIONS IS SO FEEBLE THAT
MILL I (138)	DI PARERGA. /SAGAMORE/ (BOWING) OH! I AM	INDEED	HONORED. PRAY BE SEATED. /EPIFANIA/ SIT DOWN
BULL PREFACE(71)	OR TOLERATE HOME RULE, IS NOW SUFFERING AND	INDEED	HUGGING HOME RULE ON A MUCH MORE HOMELY SCALE THAN
PHIL PREFACE(68)	NATURE IN IT IS STILL IN THE LATEST FASHION:	INDEED	I AM FAR FROM SURE THAT ITS IDEAS, INSTEAD OF BEING
CLEO I (113)	OF THEIR SLAVES. /CLEOPATRA/ I AM NOT AFRAID.	INDEED	I AM NOT AFRAID. /FTATATEETA/ WE SHALL SEE WHO IS
JOAN 4 (96)	THE WITCH AND BEAT THE BASTARD ALL IN GOOD TIME.	INDEED	I AM WAITING AT PRESENT FOR THE BISHOP OF BEAUVAIS,
WIDO I (20)	TO RISE, BUT CHECKS HIMSELF TO ADD) UNLESS	INDEED	I CAN ASSIST YOU IN ANY WAY? BY CLEARING UP ANY
LADY (248)	DRIVE THEIR NOBLER FELLOWS FROM THE STAGE, WHERE	INDEED	I CANNOT HAVE MY LADY PHYSICIAN PRESENTED AT ALL, SHE
PHIL III (133)	HER HUMBLY) I DONT DESERVE THIS FROM YOU:	INDEED	I DO NOT. /JULIA/ (RATING HIM) THEN WHY DO YOU
BARB II (285)	ANGRY WITH HIM, DO YOU? /JENNY/ OH NO, NO, NO:	INDEED	I DONT, MAJOR, BLESS HIS POOR HEART! (BARBARA
LIED (195)	IT'S VERY NICE OF YOU; AND I APPRECIATE IT:	INDEED	I DO; BUT IT'S NOT SEASONABLE JUST AT PRESENT. NOW
JITT II (33)	BUT IN MY SICK ROOM I WAS WITH YOU IN SPIRIT.	INDEED	I HAVE NEVER BEEN CLOSER TO YOU AND POOR EDITH THAN
ROCK II (283)	THEY MAKE A STAND, THE COWARDS? /LADY CHAVENDER/	INDEED	I HOPE THEY WONT. WHAT ARE YOU THINKING OF, HILDA?
HART I (54)	SLEEP IN ARIADNE'S OLD ROOM. /LADY UTTERWORD/	INDEED	I SHALL DO NOTHING OF THE SORT. THAT LITTLE HOLE! I
PLES PREFACE(R10)	PERFORMANCES, THEY ADMIRED THE PLAY GENEROUSLY:	INDEED	I THINK THAT IF ANY OF THEM HAD BEEN YOUNG ENOUGH TO
NEVR IV (292)	ONES! YOU HAVE NOT SEEN THEM, MR BOHUN; AND	INDEED	I THINK YOU WOULD AGREE WITH ME THAT THERE IS
JITT III (59)	HAVE BEEN SO GOOD. I WILL THINK OVER YOUR ADVICE:	INDEED	I WILL. /LENKHEIM/ (ENCOURAGINGLY) DO. (HE WAVES
CAND III (135)	I MEAN-- I-- I'M VERY SORRY. I WONT DO IT AGAIN:	INDEED	I WONT. I'LL LET HIM ALONE. /MORELL/ (INDIGNANTLY,
JOAN PREFACE(12)	THEREFORE EXTRAORDINARILY SUSCEPTIBLE TO NUMBERS:	INDEED	IF ALL HIS WORKS WERE LOST EXCEPT HIS CHRONOLOGY WE
BASH PREFACE(91)	HAMLET INTO MODERN VERNACULAR ENGLISH." BUT	INDEED	IF THE ALIENATION OF OUR YOUNG FROM ELIZABETHAN
NEVR I (219)	HIM AWAY OURSELVES. MY MOTHER WOULD BE VERY GLAD	INDEED	IF YOU WOULD COME TOO. /CRAMPTON/ (GRATEFULLY, AFTER
AUGS (271)	SO WONDERFULLY! /AUGUSTUS/ IT WOULD BE STRANGE	INDEED	IF, AFTER SITTING ON THIRTY-SEVEN ROYAL COMMISSIONS,
LADY PREFACE(232)	FOR BELIEVING THAT SHAKESPEAR DIED GAME, AND	INDEED	IN A STATE OF LEVITY WHICH WOULD HAVE BEEN CONSIDERED
SUPR HANDBOK(195)	ENERGY. WE DO NOT DESIRE THE END ENOUGH:	INDEED	IN MOST CASES WE DO NOT EFFECTIVELY DESIRE IT AT ALL.
BARB PREFACE(217)	SOCIETY, ON THE OTHER HAND, BEHAVED VERY BADLY	INDEED	IN ORGANIZING ITSELF SO STUPIDLY THAT A GOOD LIFE
BARB PREFACE(226)	JESUS AND THE PROPHETS ALL THROWN IN (AS	INDEED	IN SOME SORT I ACTUALLY AM, STANDING AS I DO ON ALL
BULL IV (177)	IT IS CALLED THE ISLAND OF THE SAINTS; BUT	INDEED	IN THESE LATER YEARS IT MIGHT BE MORE FITLY CALLED
DOCT IV (166)	THATS REAL. /MRS DUBEDAT/ DONT SPARE ME, DEAR.	INDEED	INDEED YOU WILL NOT TIRE ME. LEAN ON ME WITH ALL YOUR
LION PREFACE(70)	WE HAVE SEEN TO BE ENTIRELY PRACTICABLE, AND	INDEED	INEVITABLE IF OUR CIVILIZATION IS TO BE SAVED FROM
2TRU PREFACE(12)	THIS SORT OF LIFE HAS BEEN MADE POSSIBLE, AND	INDEED	INEVITABLE, BY WHAT WILLIAM COBBETT, WHO HAD A STURDY
GETT PREFACE(255)	MARTIAL LAW THAT WOULD BE QUITE UNNECESSARY AND	INDEED	INTOLERABLE IN A PROSPEROUS COMMUNITY. BUT, HOWEVER
PRES (166)	LOVE YOU. (INTO THE TELEPHONE) IT'S LIKELY	INDEED	I'D FRIGHTEN THE MAN OFF WITH ANY SUCH NONSENSE AT MY
NEVR II (252)	INTOLERABLE. HE ADDS HASTILY) NO! I'M NOT ANGRY:	INDEED	I'M NOT. WAIT, WAIT! GIVE ME A LITTLE TIME TO THINK.
BASH PREFACE(90)	NOT AS A MOCKERY, BUT AS GENUINE TRAGEDY, WHICH	INDEED	IT ALSO IS. IT WAS THE LITERARY FUN THAT PROVED A
METH PREFACE(R88)	COMEDY COULD BE DETACHED AND PLAYED BY ITSELF:	INDEED	IT COULD HARDLY BE PLAYED AT FULL LENGTH OWING TO THE
BARB II (300)	AW BROWK YOUR JAWR. /JENNY/ NO, IT DIDNT HURT ME:	INDEED	IT DIDNT, EXCEPT FOR A MOMENT. IT WAS ONLY THAT I WAS
CLEO NOTES (205)	THE PAGAN ANOTHER. IT MIGHT AS WELL BE ASSUMED AS	INDEED	IT GENERALLY IS ASSUMED BY IMPLICATION, THAT A MURDER
MIS. PREFACE(83)	OUT AT THE DOOR THE LOVER COMES IN AT THE WINDOW.	INDEED	IT HAPPENS NOW OFTENER THAN IT USED TO, BECAUSE
BUOY 1 (13)	/FATHER/ THE RUSSIAN MADNESS WILL NOT LAST.	INDEED	IT HAS COLLAPSED ALREADY. I NOW INVEST ALL MY SAVINGS
MIS. PREFACE(3)	ACHIEVE IMMORTALITY EXCEPT IN VERY LOW ORGANISMS:	INDEED	IT IS BY NO MEANS ASCERTAINED THAT EVEN THE AMOEBA IS
CLEO NOTES (212)	OF HIS LIGHTHEARTEDNESS AND ADVENTUROUSNESS.	INDEED	IT IS CLEAR FROM HIS WHOLE HISTORY THAT WHAT HAS BEEN
JITT I (19)	STROKE OF LUCK FOR US THAT HE KNOWS NOTHING-- IF	INDEED	IT IS ONLY LUCK, AND NOT HIS SUBCONSCIOUS KNOWLEDGE
METH PREFACE(R13)	IS A GREATER NUISANCE THAN THE UNEDUCATED ONE:	INDEED	IT IS THE INEFFICIENCY AND SHAM OF THE EDUCATIONAL
OVER PREFACE(156)	MAY HAVE NO EXISTENCE. IT IS OFTEN ASSUMED --	INDEED	IT IS THE OFFICIAL ASSUMPTION OF THE CHURCHES AND THE
MIS. PREFACE(52)	STREETS AFTER TWENTY-ONE YEARS PENAL SERVITUDE.	INDEED	IT IS WORSE; FOR THE CONVICT, HAVING LEARNT BEFORE
DEVL I (13)	/MRS ANDERSON/ (WITH COMPLACENT AMIABILITY) YES,	INDEED	IT IS. PERHAPS YOU HAD RATHER I DID NOT INTRUDE ON
GETT PREFACE(245)	AS ANY OTHER CONTAGIOUS DISEASE DOES; THAT	INDEED	IT OFTEN HITS THE INNOCENT AND MISSES THE GUILTY
JOAN PREFACE(53)	WELL INTENTIONED BUT DISASTROUS COUNSELLORS:	INDEED	IT PROBABLY WILL HAPPEN WHEN I AM NO LONGER IN
LION PREFACE(56)	PUZZLED HEAD WITH A POTSHERD AND BE DUMB, UNLESS	INDEED	IT STRIKES HIM THAT GOD IS THE ULTIMATE MAKER, AND
GETT (284)	BE REGINALD OVER AGAIN. IT WASNT WORTH CHANGING:	INDEED	IT WASNT. /LEO/ THEN IT'S A MISTAKE TO GET MARRIED.
LION PREFACE(96)	THAN IN THE SIXTEEN HALF CENTURIES PRECEDING:	INDEED	IT WOULD BE EASIER TO SUSTAIN THE THESIS THAT THE
BULL IV (162)	LITTLE CAMBRIC HANDKERCHIEFS-- /NORA/ (SOBBING)	INDEED	IT'S A COMMON COTTON ONE. /BROADBENT/ OF COURSE IT'S
MRS PREFACE(165)	HIS INDULGENCE MUST BE A VERY EXCITING PLAY	INDEED	. ACCORDINGLY, I FIND ONE CRITIC SO EXPLICIT AS TO
BUOY IV (54)	HER. DIDNT YOU NOTICE IT? /SIR FERDINAND/ I DID	INDEED	. AND I HAVE COME TO TELL YOU I CAN NO LONGER ACT AS
ARMS III (50)	/RAINA/ (TURNING, WITH SUDDEN EARNESTNESS) I DO	INDEED	. BUT THEY DONT KNOW THAT IT WAS IN THIS HOUSE YOU
SUPR IV (165)	/VIOLET/ (VERY DECIDEDLY) I SHOULD THINK NOT,	INDEED	. DONT CRY, DEAR: I'M ONLY GOING TO THE HOTEL. /MRS
BULL III (125)	WITH THEM ALL) MOST HAPPY, MR DORAN. VERY PLEASED	INDEED	. DORAN, NOT QUITE SURE WHETHER HE IS BEING COURTED
BARB PREFACE(230)	I LOATHE AS I LOATHE ALL GIBBETS) BECOMES DEEP	INDEED	. FORGIVENESS, ABSOLUTION, ATONEMENT, ARE FIGMENTS:
MRS III (222)	HERE. REALLY MOST CHARMING. /REV. S./ YES: IT IS	INDEED	. FRANK WILL TAKE YOU FOR A WALK, MR PRAED, IF YOU
JITT I SD(11)	RATHER IRRESOLUTELY, AND LOOKING VERY CAREWORN	INDEED	. HE IS WELL DRESSED, ON THE VERGE OF FIFTY, GOING
NEVR III (273)	HER BACK TO THEM). /PHILIP/ (SIGNIFICANTLY) OH,	INDEED	. HMHM! /DOLLY/ AHAH! /PHILIP/ YOU SEEM IN
2TRU I (37)	/THE ELDERLY LADY/ (WHISPERING) I WILL	INDEED	. HOW KIND OF YOU! YOU WILL LET ME KNOW IF
DEVL III (68)	ARE UNALTERED, GENERAL. /BURGOYNE/ AH,	INDEED	. I AM SORRY. GOOD MORNING, MR DUDGEON. GOOD MORNING,
OVER (173)	I VALUE SUCH AFFECTIONATE REGARD VERY HIGHLY	INDEED	. I AM SURROUNDED WITH WOMEN WHO ARE MOST DEAR TO ME.
FANY PROLOG (262)	FIRST MAN I WENT FOR WAS TROTTER. /THE COUNT/ OH	INDEED	. I AM VERY GLAD YOU HAVE SECURED MR TROTTER. I HAVE
OVER (176)	HINT THAT YOU HAD A WIFE. /GREGORY/ I DID	INDEED	. I DISCUSSED THINGS WITH YOU THAT ONLY MARRIED
CAND II (105)	(EARNESTLY) I ASSURE YOU I DIDNT. I DIDNT	INDEED	. I ONLY TURNED A LITTLE WHEEL. IT GAVE A SORT OF
PYGM II (218)	SHE'S QUITE A COMMON GIRL, SIR. VERY COMMON	INDEED	. I SHOULD HAVE SENT HER AWAY, ONLY I THOUGHT PERHAPS
VWOO 3 (138)	/Z/ (REMORSEFULLY) OH, I DIDNT KNOW: I DIDNT	INDEED	. I WAS ONLY JOKING. (SHE SITS AGAIN) I WOULDNT HAVE
AUGS (276)	BY NO MEANS, MADAM. IT MATTERS VERY MUCH	INDEED	. IF THIS SPY WERE TO OBTAIN POSSESSION OF THE LIST,
DOCT I (102)	VERY SENSIBLE, BLENKINSOP: VERY SENSIBLE	INDEED	. I'M DELIGHTED TO SEE THAT YOU DISAPPROVE OF DRUGS.
PHIL I (92)	WENT STRAIGHT OFF. /CUTHBERTSON/ VERY KIND OF HER	INDEED	. I'M REALLY ASHAMED-- /CRAVEN/ DONT MENTION IT, JO:
LION PROLOG (106)	YOU. /MEGAERA/ BLAME ME! I SHOULD THINK NOT	INDEED	. IS IT MY FAULT THAT I'M MARRIED TO YOU?
WIDO II (36)	DO YOU OBJECT? /TRENCH/ (EARNESTLY) I DO NOT	INDEED	. IT'S ONLY A QUESTION OF MONEY. /BLANCHE/ (
CAND II (116)	FEET OR THEREABOUTS). /MORELL/ (PREOCCUPIED) AH,	INDEED	. (HE BLOTS THE TELEGRAM AND GOES OUT). /PROSERPINE/
NEVR III (274)	FROM YOUR FATHER, MISS CLANDON. VERY SERIOUS NEWS	INDEED	. (HE PASSES IMPRESSIVELY TO THE OTTOMAN, AND SITS
NEVR III (263)	LIKE THIS: VERY PLEASANT AND INVIGORATING	INDEED	. (HE TAKES THE TRAY FROM THE CENTRE TABLE AND PUTS
NEVR IV (286)	HE DARES) MY NAME IS CRAMPTON, SIR. /BOHUN/ OH,	INDEED	. (PASSING HIM OVER WITHOUT FURTHER NOTICE AND
WIDO I (9)	AND ARCHLY) AH, EXCELLENT, EXCELLENT: VERY GOOD	INDEED	. (SERIOUSLY) BUT DO YOU KNOW, MISS SARTORIUS, THERE
NEVR IV (288)	TIMELY, MISS, VERY THOUGHTFUL AND CONSIDERATE	INDEED	. (TO MRS CLANDON, TIMIDLY BUT EXPECTANTLY) ANYTHING
NEVR III (280)	VERY BRIGHT AND PLEASANT, VERY GAY AND INNOCENT	INDEED	. (TO PHIL) TICKETS DOWNSTAIRS AT THE OFFICE, SIR,
NEVR IV (293)	CHOICE AND CLASSY, VERY GENTEEL AND HIGH TONED	INDEED	. MIGHT BE THE SON AND DAUGHTER OF A DEAN, SIR, I
BULL IV (170)	WILL BE A PERSON OF VERY CONSIDERABLE CONSEQUENCE	INDEED	. PLAY YOUR NEW PART WELL, AND THERE WILL BE NO MORE
WIDO I (21)	AN ATTITUDE OF PATRONAGE AND ENCOURAGEMENT) AH,	INDEED	. QUITE SO, QUITE SO. (HE WRITES) " -- ENTIRELY FOR
SUPR II (63)	RAMSDEN? /RAMSDEN/ I SHOULD THINK IT VERY LIKELY	INDEED	. /ANN/ YOU DONT OBJECT, DO YOU, MOTHER? /MRS
BULL IV (168)	HAVE YOU? /NORA/ (INDIGNANTLY) NOT LIKELY,	INDEED	. /BROADBENT/ WELL, WE MUSNT BE STIFF AND STAND-OFF,
SUPR III (116)	ABOUT THE OTHER, UNLESS ONE WAS VERY HARD HIT	INDEED	. /DON JUAN/ THEN THE LADY, WHO HAD BEEN HAPPY AND
CATH 4 (194)	PATS HIS CHEEK). /CLAIRE/ (SNORTING) SO I SEE,	INDEED	. /EDSTASTON/ DONT BE ANGRY, DEAREST: IN THIS COUNTRY
MRS IV (243)	I'M EXTREMELY DISAPPOINTED IN CROFTS: I AM	INDEED	. /FRANK/ I'M NOT IN THE LEAST. I FEEL HE'S PERFECTLY
JITT III (65)	FOR ME. (CRYING) I DIDNT DESERVE IT: I DIDNT	INDEED	. /JITTA/ THERE, DEAR, THERE! DONT TORTURE YOURSELF.
GENV IV (124)	IT IS INTELLIGIBLE ENOUGH, AND VERY SERIOUS	INDEED	. /JUDGE/ IT IS NOT INTELLIGIBLE TO ME. WILL YOU
GETT (313)	THE DOCUMENT WE ARE DRAFTING? /SOAMES/ SHE HAS	INDEED	. /LESBIA/ THAT SOUNDS AS IF YOU DISAPPROVED.
BULL II (116)	OVER THAT STONE. IT WAS AN ACCIDENT: IT WAS	INDEED	. /NORA/ YES, OF COURSE IT WAS. JUST TAKE MY ARM, MR
CLEO IV (177)	/RUFIO/ (SARCASTICALLY) VERY HANDSOME OF YOU,	INDEED	. /POTHINUS/ SO BE IT: YOU ARE THE MASTER. OUR GODS
ROCK I (200)	WORK AND ATTEND SO MANY DEBATES AS WELL: YOU WILL	INDEED	. /SIR ATTHUR/ MISS HANWAYS: I WISH I COULD PERSUADE
JOAN 4 (94)	YOU TAKE OUR SITUATION VERY COOLLY. VERY COOLLY	INDEED	. /THE NOBLEMAN/ (SUPERCILIOUS) WHAT IS THE MATTER?
WIDO II (36)	TO HIM YOU WILL BREAK OFF THE MATCH: YOU WILL	INDEED	. /TRENCH/ (OBSTINATELY) I CANT HELP THAT. /BLANCHE/
MRS IV (250)	VIVIE: I MEANT TO HAVE BEEN MORE WITH YOU: I DID	INDEED	. /VIVIE/ IT'S NO USE, MOTHER: I AM NOT TO BE CHANGED
JOAN 4 (98)	THAT THE SEIGNEUR DUNOIS IS A VERY ABLE COMMANDER	INDEED	. /WARWICK/ YOUR LORDSHIP IS THE FLOWER OF COURTESY.
PHIL I (91)	I'M EXCESSIVELY VEXED ABOUT JULIA'S CONDUCT: I AM	INDEED	. SHE CANT BEAR TO BE CROSSED IN THE SLIGHTEST THING,
GETT (264)	MAAM. SHE NEVER GAVE THEM A CHANCE: SHE DIDNT	INDEED	. SHE NEVER UNDERSTOOD THAT MARRIED PEOPLE SHOULD
CAND I (96)	/MARCHBANKS/ (EARNESTLY) NO: I SHOULD LIKE TO,	INDEED	. THANK YOU VERY MUCH. BUT-- BUT-- /MORELL/ BUT--
GETT PREFACE(228)	OTHER CAMP; AND MOST OF IT WILL STICK VERY HARD	INDEED	. THE MORAL IS, DO NOT THROW ANY. IF WE CAN IMAGINE
NEVR II (250)	AND AN HONOR TO US, MR CRAMPTON, VERY KIND	INDEED	. THE MORE YOU ARE AT HOME HERE, SIR, THE BETTER FOR
PYGM V (281)	I HAVNT SAID I WANTED YOU BACK AT ALL. /LIZA/ OH,	INDEED	. THEN WHAT ARE WE TALKING ABOUT? /HIGGINS/ ABOUT
DEVL III (75)	WHOSE DEAREST PRAYER HAS BEEN GRANTED. /SWINDON/	INDEED	. THEN YOU ARE JUST IN TIME TO TAKE YOUR PLACE ON THE
GETT (356)	VULGARITY. /MRS GEORGE/ (RISING PROMPTLY) OH,	INDEED	. THEN YOURE NOT COMING HOME WITH ME, YOUNG MAN. I'M

GETT SD(323)	OF STYLISH DRESSING; AND SHE DOES IT VERY WELL	INDEED	. THERE IS NOTHING QUIET ABOUT MRS GEORGE: SHE IS NOT
CAPT III (289)	UNLESS YOU LIKE TO BEHAVE YOURSELF VERY NICELY	INDEED	. WHAT HOUR DID YOU SAY WE WERE TO LUNCH AT, CAPTAIN
DOCT I (86)	TO BE THE FIRST TO CONGRATULATE YOU. /RIDGEON/	INDEED	. WHO TAUGHT YOU TO SPEAK OF SIR PATRICK CULLEN AS
WIDO I (16)	MORE? /TRENCH/ (MUCH PUZZLED, BUT GRATEFUL) NO	INDEED	. YOU ARE REALLY VERY GOOD. MANY THANKS. SINCE YOU
CAND II (110)	HO! I'M A SILLY OLE FAT'EAD, AM I? HO,	INDEED	(GASPING)! HALL RIGHT, MY GURL! HALL RIGHT. YOU
GETT (306)	IN MY GOWN. /HOTCHKISS/ (STAGGERED) VERY PLEASED	INDEED	(HE SITS DOWN AGAIN). /THE BISHOP/ PERSONALLY I
LION PREFACE(98)	AWHILE," WOULD SAY DOGMATIZING VERY PERNICIOUSLY.	INDEED	MANY PREACHERS AND SAINTS DECLARE, SOME OF THEM IN
SIM PREFACE(12)	A FULL EQUIVALENT OF WHAT WE CONSUME, AND	INDEED	MORE. ON THE CONTRARY, EVERY INDUCEMENT TO SHIRK THAT
METH PREFACE(R43)	CHANCE, AND BARE SURVIVAL WAS ALSO POSSIBLE: WAS	INDEED	MOST CERTAINLY THE WAY IN WHICH MANY APPARENTLY
JOAN PREFACE(31)	OF THE PROBLEMS PRESENTED TO HER SEEMED, AND	INDEED	MOSTLY WERE, THE PLAINEST COMMONSENSE, AND THEIR
OVER PREFACE(155)	WHO BELIEVE THEM TO BE RETROGRADE, ARE OFTEN, AND	INDEED	MOSTLY, THE LAST PEOPLE IN THE WORLD TO ENGAGE IN
METH PREFACE(R86)	HAD NO GREATER COMFORT FOR THE WORLD THAN WE:	INDEED	MUCH LESS; FOR THEY REFUSED US EVEN THE
LION PREFACE(44)	WAS ONE WHICH HE BELIEVED THAT HE COULD, AND	INDEED	MUST FULFIL. TWO EVANGELISTS DECLARE THAT IN HIS LAST
MILL PREFACE(116)	WHO UNDER SIMILAR CIRCUMSTANCES COULD AND	INDEED	MUST HAVE BECOME KINGS IF THEY HAD BEEN UNGOVERNABLE
LION PREFACE(16)	TO RISE AGAIN FOR EVER AND EVER. YOU MAY, AND	INDEED	MUST, USE JOHN BARLEYCORN " RIGHT BARBAROUSLEE,"
POSN PREFACE(392)	POLITICAL. RECENT EVENTS HAVE SHEWN-- WHAT	INDEED	NEEDED NO DEMONSTRATION-- THAT IT IS IMPOSSIBLE TO
METH PREFACE(R69)	AND IMPOSSIBLE THE DAY BEFORE IT BREAKS OUT, AND	INDEED	NEVER DOES BREAK OUT UNTIL IT SEEMS HOPELESS AND
ARMS I (5)	AT BUCHAREST. REAL LIFE IS SO SELDOM LIKE THAT!	INDEED	NEVER, AS FAR AS I KNEW IT THEN. (REMORSEFULLY) ONLY
BULL PREFACE(42)	GARRISON HACK TOGETHER INTO THE DUSTBIN. THERE IS	INDEED	NO GREATER CURSE TO A NATION THAN A NATIONALIST
SUPR HANDBOK(177)	THE NINETEENTH CENTURY DECIDED THAT THERE IS	INDEED	NO SUCH GOD; AND NOW MAN MUST TAKE IN HAND ALL THE
CATH 1 (168)	THE SERGEANT OUT, NOT MALICIOUSLY BUT FROM HABIT,	INDEED	NOT NOTICING THAT HE DOES IT). DARLING: HAVE SOME
BARB PREFACE(222)	BUT ACTUALLY OUTSIDE THEIR KNOWLEDGE OF SOCIETY.	INDEED	NOTHING COULD BE MORE IRONICALLY CURIOUS THAN THE
METH PREFACE(R80)	CREATIVE EVOLUTION IS ALREADY A RELIGION, AND IS	INDEED	NOW UNMISTAKEABLY THE RELIGION OF THE TWENTIETH
KING I (180)	ME THAT THE TRANSMUTATION OF METALS, AND	INDEED	OF ALL SUBSTANCES, MUST BE POSSIBLE. IT IS OCCURRING
CAND I SD(91)	HER HUSBAND OR HERSELF OF ANY SUCH IDEA, OR	INDEED	OF ANY CONCERN WITH THE ART OF TITIAN. JUST NOW SHE
3PLA PREFACE(R36)	AND LINGUISTIC, WHO FOR LACK OF NEW IDEAS, OR	INDEED	OF ANY IDEAS WORTH MENTIONING, ACHIEVE NO DISTINCTION
BULL PREFACE(11)	AND TRIBAL COMMUNITIES, AND A VERY LARGE ALLOY	INDEED	OF BRIGANDAGE IN OUR EXPLORATIONS AND COLONIZATIONS.
CYMB FORWORD(135)	HAS ALWAYS BEEN THE CURSE OF SERIOUS DRAMA, AND	INDEED	OF SERIOUS LITERATURE OF ANY KIND. IT IS SO
GETT PREFACE(196)	IN ANY SENSE FOR MORE THAN A VERY SMALL FRACTION	INDEED	OF THE TIME HE DEVOTES TO BUSINESS AND TO RECREATIONS
KING PREFACE(156)	MERRY MONARCH AND HIS WOMEN. ON THE STAGE, AND	INDEED	OFF IT, HE IS REPRESENTED AS HAVING PRACTICALLY NO
JOAN PREFACE(14)	THEY WILL NOT BE A PENNY THE BETTER, AND ARE	INDEED	OFTEN MANY PENCE THE WORSE, FACE POVERTY, INFAMY,
BULL PREFACE(41)	IN ENGLAND IS SICKENING ENOUGH TO SERIOUS PEOPLE:	INDEED	ONE EVENING'S MAFFICKING IN LONDON PRODUCED A
GETT PREFACE(186)	BREAKS DOWN IN PRACTICE. SOUTH CAROLINA HAS	INDEED	PASSED WHAT IS CALLED A FREAK LAW DECLARING THAT A
DOCT PREFACE(7)	BY ANSWERING THIS IN THE AFFIRMATIVE, OR	INDEED	PRETENDING TO BE ABLE TO ANSWER IT AT ALL. AND ON
MIS. PREFACE(36)	FROM DOING IT -- WE SHOULD HAVE NO IDLE RICH AND	INDEED	PROBABLY NO RICH, SINCE THERE IS NO DISTINCTION IN
DOCT V (176)	BUT SURELY-- I DID NOT MEAN TO OFFEND YOU,	INDEED	-- BUT YOU MUST BE AT LEAST TWENTY YEARS OLDER THAN I
CLEO I (110)	TWO. I MEANT TO SACRIFICE THE WHITE CAT-- I DID	INDEED	-- I (CAESAR, WHO HAS SLIPPED DOWN FROM THE
ARMS II (39)	/CATHERINE/ (OPENING HER EYES VERY WIDELY	INDEED	) WELL, UPON MY WORD! /RAINA/ (CAPRICIOUSLY: HALF
SUPR I (7)	ALTHOUGH (HERE HE SUDDENLY BECOMES VERY SERIOUS	INDEED	) YOU HAVE ONE GREAT DRAWBACK. /OCTAVIUS/ (
MIS. PREFACE(86)	THEY AVERAGE THREE THE RESULTS MAY BE VERY BAD	INDEED	; AND TO LUMP THE TWO TOGETHER UNDER THE GENERAL TERM
LION II (128)	BE LET OFF. /ANDROCLES/ NO: THANK YOU VERY MUCH	INDEED	; BUT I REALLY MUSTNT. /THE EDITOR/ WHAT! NOT TO
MTH5 (241)	HIS KNEES) OH DONT, SIR. DONT. SHE DID IT, SIR:	INDEED	SHE DID. /THE FEMALE FIGURE/ (HOWLING LAMENTABLY)
JOAN PREFACE(3)	WESTERN EUROPE BEFORE SHE WAS OUT OF HER TEENS (	INDEED	SHE NEVER GOT OUT OF THEM), IT IS HARDLY SURPRISING
3PLA PREFACE(R13)	COMPANY. THIS MAY HAVE BEEN SHAKESPEAR'S FAULT:	INDEED	SIR HENRY LATER ON COMPLAINED THAT HE HAD LOST A
CYMB FORWORD(133)	EXACTLY AS SHAKESPEAR WROTE THEM, THERE WAS	INDEED	SOME DEMUR; BUT IT WAS EXPRESSED OUTSIDE THE THEATRE
GETT PREFACE(225)	CLASSED WITH SHREWS AND WIFE-BEATERS: THEY ARE	INDEED	SOMETIMES HELD UP AS MODELS OF DOMESTICITY BECAUSE
SUPR II SD(48)	THE HOUSE, WHICH IS PARTLY VISIBLE THROUGH THEM:	INDEED	TANNER, STANDING IN THE DRIVE WITH HIS BACK TO US,
OVER PREFACE(161)	IS THE DRAMATIC SUBJECT PAR EXCELLENCE, AND	INDEED	THAT A PLAY THAT IS NOT ABOUT ADULTERY IS NOT A PLAY
GETT PREFACE(249)	UNDERSTAND THAT IT WAS A HOLY STATE: SO HOLY	INDEED	THAT IT COULD NOT BE VALIDLY INAUGURATED WITHOUT THE
CATH PREFACE(157)	FOR HEROES WITH TWENTY ARMS LIKE AN INDIAN GOD.	INDEED	THE ACTOR OFTEN INFLUENCES THE AUTHOR TOO MUCH; FOR I
LION PREFACE(102)	DISCIPLE, HAD HIS PLACE IN THE SCHEME OF THINGS.	INDEED	THE APOSTLES MADE THIS AN EXCUSE FOR CARRYING
GETT (312)	I AM SPEAKING TECHNICALLY, NOT IN BOXER'S MANNER.	INDEED	THE BISHOPS THEMSELVES WENT SO FAR IN THAT DIRECTION
HART PREFACE(36)	WITH RHEIMS THE GLOOMIEST OF LITTLE CONVENTICLES:	INDEED	THE CATHEDRAL MUST, FROM THE PURITAN POINT OF VIEW,
METH PREFACE(R38)	ENOUGH TO SAY THAT EVERY MAN MAKES HIS OWN EYES:	INDEED	THE EMBRYOLOGISTS HAD ACTUALLY CAUGHT HIM DOING IT.
POSN PREFACE(419)	HOW WOULD THE PROCTOR LIVE WITHOUT FEES, UNLESS	INDEED	THE GOVERNMENT GAVE HIM A SALARY FOR DOING NOTHING..
SUPR HANDBOK(199)	ON THE LINES ALONG WHICH WE ARE EVOLVING. THIS IS	INDEED	THE ILLUSION OF ILLUSIONS; FOR IT GIVES US INFALLIBLE
LION PREFACE(18)	MAY HAVE BEEN UNCONSCIOUS OF THE CONTRADICTION:	INDEED	THE INTERPOLATORS THEMSELVES MUST HAVE BEEN
LADY PREFACE(214)	THE MOST CHARMING OF ALL SHAKESPEAR'S OLD WOMEN,	INDEED	THE MOST CHARMING OF ALL HIS WOMEN, YOUNG OR OLD, IS
LION PREFACE(61)	BY HOLDING THE RIGHT TO LIFE AS SACRED AND EQUAL.	INDEED	THE ONE RIGHT IS ONLY A RESTATEMENT OF THE OTHER. TO
MTH5 (250)	AN UGLY ONE IS OF SUPREME IMPORTANCE: THAT IT IS	INDEED	THE ONLY THING THAT MATTERS. /THE SHE-ANCIENT/ THAT
GETT PREFACE(254)	BONDAGE WILL GO THE WAY OF CONJUGAL BONDAGE:	INDEED	THE ORDER OF REFORM SHOULD RATHER BE PUT THE OTHER
JOAN PREFACE(25)	MAY BE SAID TO HAVE LET JOAN OFF VERY EASILY. BUT	INDEED	THE PERSONAL ADVENTURES OF THE CHARACTERS ARE SO
SUPR PREFACE(R33)	DESCRIPTIONS OF INSTINCTIVE TEMPERAMENTS:	INDEED	THE PLAY OF CORIOLANUS IS THE GREATEST OF
MIS. PREFACE(68)	BEFORE SCHOOLS LIKE BEDALES WERE FOUNDED:	INDEED	THE PRACTICE WAS COMMON ENOUGH IN ELEMENTARY SCHOOLS
HART PREFACE(23)	LEAVE THE RABBLE RAVING TO ITS HEARTS' CONTENT.	INDEED	THE RAVING WAS USEFUL TO THE EFFICIENT, BECAUSE, AS
BARB PREFACE(237)	OF THE POOR AND OF THE POLICE AT THE SAME TIME.	INDEED	THE RELIGIOUS BODIES, AS THE ALMONERS OF THE RICH,
MIS. PREFACE(58)	AS LONG AS THEY ARE OF ANY IMPORTANCE IN LIFE:	INDEED	THE WANT WILL SURVIVE THEIR IMPORTANCE: SUPERSTITION
LION PREFACE(58)	WE SHALL NEVER HAVE A DECENT SOCIAL LIFE.	INDEED	THE WHOLE ATTRACTION OF OUR PRESENT ARRANGEMENT LIES
LION PREFACE(77)	THE STREET," THE THING HAPPENS OFTEN ENOUGH; FOR	INDEED	THE WORLD IS FULL OF THESE ADAMS AND SMITHS AND MEN
GETT PREFACE(192)	ON THE STRENGTH OF A STAGGERING LACK OF VIRTUE.	INDEED	THEIR ONLY CONCEPTION OF THE MEANING OF THE WORD
LADY (249)	I WILL BE DUST BENEATH THE FEET OF THE HORSES, IF	INDEED	THERE BE ANY HORSES THEN, AND MEN BE STILL RIDING
MIS. PREFACE(50)	QUITE A CONSIDERABLE DEGREE OF BODILY CULTURE:	INDEED	THERE IS A CONTINUAL OUTCRY AGAINST THE SACRIFICE OF
SUPR III (93)	BE ALARMED: THERE IS PLENTY OF HUMBUG IN HELL (	INDEED	THERE IS HARDLY ANYTHING ELSE); BUT THE HUMBUG OF
JOAN PREFACE(24)	AS LIKELY AS NOT, THIS IS WHAT ACTUALLY HAPPENED:	INDEED	THERE IS ONLY ONE OTHER APPARENT WAY OF ACCOUNTING
HART PREFACE(16)	OF GREEK HISTORY WERE NOT SURPRISED BY IT.	INDEED	THESE STUDENTS THREW THEMSELVES INTO THE ORGY AS
KING I (171)	REAL WOMEN IN THEM, ARE THEY NOT? /MRS BASHAM/	INDEED	THEY ARE NOT, MR ROWLEY. THEY ARE NOT LIKE WOMEN AT
ROCK PREFACE(171)	BY COMPULSORY READING, WRITING, AND ARITHMETIC:	INDEED	THEY HAVE ALREADY DONE SO. BUT ALL WILL NOT AGREE ON
METH PREFACE(R78)	AND ROMAN CATHOLICS. FREETHINKERS READ THE BIBLE:	INDEED	THEY SEEM TO BE ITS ONLY READERS NOW EXCEPT THE
MTH2 (49)	BURGE, PRETTY WELL KNOWN THROUGHOUT EUROPE, AND	INDEED	THROUGHOUT THE WORLD, AS THE MAN WHO-- UNWORTHILY
2TRU PREFACE(16)	COULD SELDOM COME TO A UNANIMOUS DECISION, IF	INDEED	TO ANY DECISION EXCEPT IN THE NEGATIVE AGAINST A
UNPL PREFACE(R17)	WHO WOULD NOT CONCEIVE A VISIT TO THE THEATRE, OR	INDEED	TO ANY PUBLIC ASSEMBLY, ARTISTIC OR POLITICAL, AS AN
APPL I (203)	SAID TO A KING BEFORE? /MAGNUS/ I AM VERY GLAD	INDEED	TO HEAR IT, MR BOANERGES. I THOUGHT I HAD ALREADY
APPL I (209)	IS IN USE, AS YOU MIGHT SAY. I AM VERY PLEASED	INDEED	TO MAKE THE ACQUAINTANCE OF THE PRINCESS ROYAL. THEY
GETT PREFACE(212)	CASTE YOU PAY ANOTHER PERSON OF VERY AUGUST CASTE	INDEED	TO MAKE YOUR DAUGHTER MOMENTARILY ONE OF HIS SIXTY OR
HART I (69)	OF YOU TO COME! /THE GENTLEMAN/ I AM VERY GLAD	INDEED	TO MAKE YOUR ACQUAINTANCE, HESIONE. (INSTEAD OF
PYGM III (250)	HIGGINS/ (CORDIALLY) QUITE RIGHT: I'M VERY GLAD	INDEED	TO SEE YOU. /PICKERING/ HOW DO YOU DO, MISS
JOAN PREFACE(11)	JOAN HAD TO WORK AS A HIRED SERVANT WORKS, OR	INDEED	TO WORK AT ALL WHEN SHE PREFERRED TO GO TO
GLIM (187)	HAS TURNED YOUR JEST INTO EARNEST. /SANDRO/ IT IS	INDEED	TRUE, SIR, THAT THOSE WHO COME UNDER THE SPECIAL
SUPR III (95)	AND YOU, FATHER, HAVE FORGOTTEN MY NAME. YOU ARE	INDEED	TURNED TO STONE. /THE STATUE/ MY DEAR: I AM SO MUCH
BUOY II (25)	WITH HIM. /THE NATIVE/ THEN, SIR, YOU MUST	INDEED	VENERATE ME; FOR THE DOCTRINES OF MY TEACHERS HAVE
DOCT PREFACE(31)	TO SUCH TRIBES AS HE IMAGINE, IT IS VERY DOUBTFUL	INDEED	WHETHER PETER THE GREAT COULD HAVE EFFECTED THE
PYGM EPILOG (289)	TO BE CAPABLE OF IT, CONSIDERS VERY SERIOUSLY	INDEED	WHETHER SHE WILL PLAY FOR BECOMING THAT BACHELOR'S
POSN PREFACE(421)	OR SEDITIOUS PLAYS AND THEIR AUTHORS, AND	INDEED	WITH ALL CHARGES AGAINST THEATRICAL ENTERTAINMENTS
JOAN PREFACE(24)	A SINGLE POINT OF CONTACT WITH THE REAL JOAN, NOR	INDEED	WITH ANY MORTAL WOMAN THAT EVER WALKED THIS EARTH.
BULL II SD(107)	TRANQUILLITY, KINDLY WITHOUT CONCERN FOR OTHERS:	INDEED	WITHOUT MUCH CONCERN FOR HERSELF: A CONTENTED PRODUCT
GETT PREFACE(230)	NEITHER POLITICALLY NOR PERSONALLY FREE, IN WHICH	INDEED	WOMEN ARE CALLED WOMANLY ONLY WHEN THEY REGARD
MILL I (139)	WELL, IF ALASTAIR PREFERS HER TO YOU SHE MUST BE	INDEED	WORTH KNOWING. I SHALL CERTAINLY MAKE HIM INTRODUCE
JITT III (80)	HAPPINESS OF OUR LIVES. YOU ARE OUR GOOD ANGEL:	INDEED	YOU ARE. OH, YOU ARE A LUCKY MAN, MR LENKHEIM, TO
BASH II,1, (106)	NOW, FAREWELL. YOU MUST NOT COME AGAIN, UNLESS	INDEED	YOU CAN SOME DAY LOOK IN MY EYES AND SAY: LYDIA: MY
LADY (242)	THOUGH YOU SPAKE WITH THE TONGUES OF ANGELS, AS	INDEED	YOU DO, YET KNOW THAT I AM THE KING OF WORDS-- /THE
APPL PREFACE(179)	YOU HAVE NO ADDRESS, AND ARE JUST A TRAMP -- IF	INDEED	YOU EXIST AT ALL." YOU WILL NOTICE THAT I AM TOO
LIED (189)	AN UNMARRIED WOMAN! HOW I WISH THEY HAD! /SHE/	INDEED	YOU HAVE NO RIGHT TO WISH ANYTHING OF THE SORT. THEY
JITT III (69)	I HAVE SET YOURS. /AGNES/ YOU HAVE: INDEED AND	INDEED	YOU HAVE. I AM SURE WHAT WE OWE YOU, WITH YOUR DEAR
PHIL I (81)	LEONARD, LEONARD, YOUVE NEVER GIVEN ME A CHANCE:	INDEED	YOU HAVNT. I'LL TAKE PAINS; I'LL READ; I'LL TRY TO
MIS. PREFACE(40)	IS ALWAYS THE CALCULUS TO FALL BACK ON, UNLESS	INDEED	YOU INSIST ON HIS LEARNING MUSIC, AND PROCEED TO HIT
HART I (47)	WITH THE TEA-THINGS ON IT, TO ELLIE'S SIDE)	INDEED	YOU NEVER WERE MORE MISTAKEN. SHE IS IN ENGLAND THIS
HART I (81)	RIGHT: I OUGHT TO SUPPORT MY WIFE. /MRS HUSHABYE/	INDEED	YOU SHALL DO NOTHING OF THE SORT: I SHOULD NEVER SEE

CAPT III (289) TO HEAVEN. WE DO WHAT WE LIKE NOW. /LADY CICELY/ INDEED YOU WILL DO NOTHING OF THE SORT, MARZO, UNLESS YOU
DOCT IV (166) REAL. /MRS DUBEDAT/ DONT SPARE ME, DEAR. INDEED INDEED YOU WILL NOT TIRE ME. LEAN ON ME WITH ALL YOUR
MIS. (155) CHICKABIDDY: I'LL TACKLE EM. /MRS TARLETON/ INDEED YOULL DO NOTHING OF THE KIND: YOULL STAY HERE QUIETLY
SUPR PREFACE(R14) WHETHER WE MIGHT NOT HAVE DONE AS HE DID, UNLESS INDEED YOUR FASTIDIOUSNESS HAD SAVED YOU FROM THE EMPRESS
LADY (244) THEM SHORT) HOW KNOW YOU THAT KING HARRY WAS INDEED YOUR FATHER? /ELIZABETH/ ZOUNDS! NOW BY-- (SHE
GETT PREFACE(254) CONSENT TO THE SALVATION OF THE CHILD, UNLESS, INDEED , A HINT FROM A POLICE INSPECTOR CONVINCED THEM THAT
BULL PREFACE(12) GRAND JURIES WOULD NOT HAVE TOLERATED. THERE ARE, INDEED , A HUNDRED HORSES ON WHICH I COULD RIDE OFF IF I
JITT II (51) DID HE INDEED, CONFOUND HIM! /JITTA/ HE DID INDEED , ALFRED; AND I FORBID YOU TO CONFOUND HIM.
DOCT PREFACE(70) AND SUPERSTITIONS OF PRIVATE PRACTICE, BEING, INDEED , ALL DERIVED FROM IT. SUCH MONSTROSITIES AS
DOCT PREFACE(50) THERE ARE MANY MORE WAITING TO BE DISCOVERED. INDEED , ALL PATHS LEAD TO KNOWLEDGE; BECAUSE EVEN THE
3PLA PREFACE(R20) TO SING THE OLD MAIDS OF ENGLAND?): RATHER, INDEED , AN INSISTENCE ON THE BLINDING AND NARROWING POWER
BULL II (105) HEARD OF IT! /FATHER DEMPSEY/ (VERY SERIOUSLY INDEED , AND EVEN A LITTLE SEVERELY) DONT BELIEVE ANY SUCH
HART I (58) ALL HIS MONEY BEING THROWN AWAY? /ELLIE/ HE DID INDEED , AND NEVER UTTERED A REPROACH TO MY FATHER. HE
FABL PREFACE(77) TO HIS BEING BURNED. CHARLES II, HUMANE (INDEED , AS SOME THINK, TOO HUMANE IN HIS KINDNESS TO HIS
LION PREFACE(82) MORE THAN BY ANY QUALITIES OF MIND OR CHARACTER. INDEED , BUT FOR THE EPISTLES, WE SHOULD HAVE A VERY POOR
2TRU II (59) TO ME, AND NOT TO MEEK? /THE COUNTESS/ I WILL INDEED , COLONEL. I AM SO SORRY, AND I THOROUGHLY
JITT II (51) OF US WHAT IS BEST FOR US. /LENKHEIM/ DID HE INDEED , CONFOUND HIM! /JITTA/ HE DID INDEED, ALFRED; AND I
ARMS I (19) STAIRS! HOW GRAND! YOU LIVE IN GREAT LUXURY INDEED , DEAR YOUNG LADY. /RAINA/ DO YOU KNOW WHAT A LIBRARY
MIS. PREFACE(46) RIGHT, SHOULD BE DEALT WITH AS A BLASPHEMER: AS, INDEED , GUILTY OF THE UNPARDONABLE SIN AGAINST THE HOLY
CLEO NOTES (207) THAT HE COULD NOT HAVE MADE THEM SO, UNLESS, INDEED , HE HAD PLAYED THE LITERARY MAN AND MADE QUINCE SAY,
JOAN PREFACE(25) AND THE OTHER HEROINES OF THE POEM VERY UNCHASTE INDEED , HE MAY BE SAID TO HAVE LET JOAN OFF VERY EASILY.
CAPT I (229) SUBDUING HIS VOICE) YES: HE DID NOT LIVE LONG: INDEED , HE NEVER CAME BACK TO ENGLAND. IT MUST BE NEARLY
PYGM V (277) OF HIS OUTBURST. /MRS HIGGINS/ VERY NICELY PUT, INDEED , HENRY. NO WOMAN COULD RESIST SUCH AN INVITATION.
CLEO IV (187) RETURNING) WHY DO YOU SAY THAT, CAESAR? INDEED, INDEED , I AM NOT HIDING ANYTHING. YOU ARE WRONG TO TREAT ME
3PLA PREFACE(R36) SKILL OF THE MASTERS WAS BY NO MEANS SUPERLATIVE. INDEED , I DEFY ANYONE TO PROVE THAT THE GREAT EPOCH MAKERS
SUPR III (81) JUST AS I SHALL HAVE MY TURN AT THE SAVOY. INDEED , I HAVE HAD A TURN THERE ALREADY-- AS WAITER.
CLEO IV (187) FEARS RETURNING) WHY DO YOU SAY THAT, CAESAR? INDEED , INDEED, I AM NOT HIDING ANYTHING. YOU ARE WRONG TO
POSN PREFACE(433) AND BE INDICTABLE ACCORDINGLY; UNLESS, INDEED , IT CAN PERSUADE THE COURTS TO RECOGNIZE IT AS A NEW
DEST SD(150) OF POLITICAL RUBBISH, IS MAKING HIMSELF USEFUL: INDEED , IT IS EVEN NOW IMPOSSIBLE TO LIVE IN ENGLAND
UNPL PREFACE(R20) OF A COMPLETE MISUNDERSTANDING OF ITS PHILOSOPHY: INDEED , IT IS NOT TOO MUCH TO SAY THAT IT IS ONLY BY A
MRS PREFACE(166) STONE AND FORTY, AS SHE OFTEN IS IN GERMANY. INDEED , IT NEEDED NO WAGNER TO CONVINCE THE PUBLIC OF THIS.
DOCT I (105) TELL PEOPLE, THE OPERATION WILL DO THEM NO HARM: INDEED , IVE KNOWN THE NERVOUS SHAKE-UP AND THE FORTNIGHT IN
APPL II (260) SINCE YESTERDAY. /VANHATTAN/ IT HAS. IT HAS INDEED , KING MAGNUS. /MAGNUS/ THEN WHAT IS IT? I HAVE NOT
KING I (161) IS NO HOUR TO CALL ON MR NEWTON. /THE MAID/ NO INDEED , MAAM. AND LOOK AT ME! NOT DRESSED TO OPEN THE DOOR
NEVR IV (292) STIMULATING, VERY ENTERTAINING AND INSTRUCTIVE INDEED , MAAM. /BOHUN/ (RESUMING COMMAND OF THE
NEVR IV (287) IT'S VERY KIND OF YOU: VERY LADYLIKE AND AFFABLE INDEED , MAAM; BUT I SHOULD FEEL AT A GREAT DISADVANTAGE OFF
MRS I (182) AMONG ITS PENDANTS). /PRAED/ VERY KIND OF YOU INDEED , MISS WARREN. (SHE SHUTS THE GATE WITH A VIGOROUS
MRS IV (243) PRESENT, YOURS EVER SO DEVOTEDLY. /PRAED/ WE DO INDEED , MISS WARREN. I DECLARE YOU ARE THE MOST SPLENDIDLY
NEVR II (238) AT FIRST, MISS; BUT RESIGNED: VERY RESIGNED INDEED , MISS. (HE TAKES THE STICK AND COAT INTO THE
WIDO I (19) THEM ON A SUBJECT THAT CONCERNS YOU. /SARTORIUS/ INDEED , MR COKANE! WELL, THE COMMUNICATION COULD NOT BE IN
MTH3 (117) LUTESTRING? /MRS LUTESTRING/ I TAKE IT SERIOUSLY INDEED , MR PRESIDENT. I SEE NOW THAT I WAS NOT MISTAKEN AT
GLIM (182) TO YOUR FATHER FOR VENGEANCE-- /SQUARCIO/ IF INDEED , MY DAUGHTER, THERE BE ANY SOUL LEFT WHEN THE BODY
WIDO III (50) BEING ILL AND HAVE SOMETHING PREYING ON MINE. AND INDEED , MY GIRL, THERE IS NO USE IN OUR GOING ON AS WE HAVE
DOCT PREFACE(49) IS SIMPLY CRIMINAL ANARCHISM AT ITS VERY WORST. INDEED , NO CRIMINAL HAS YET HAD THE IMPUDENCE TO ARGUE AS
PPP (201) MR BASTABLE IS DYING. /PHYLLIS/ (WITH CONCERN) INDEED , SIR? I HOPE HE WILL NOT THINK IT UNFEELING OF ME
PHIL II (109) WITH EXPECTATION. /THE PAGE/ (SERIOUSLY) INDEED , SIR? (HE HURRIES OFF). /CHARTERIS/ THAT BOY WILL
FANY III (297) IVE BEEN TALKING TO DORA ABOUT YOU. /JUGGINS/ INDEED , SIR? /BOBBY/ YES. DORA SAYS YOUR NAME CANT BE
MRS III (227) AWARE THAT I'M NOT A YOUNG LADY'S MAN. /VIVIE/ INDEED , SIR GEORGE? /CROFTS/ NO; AND TO TELL YOU THE
WIDO II (32) (HIS SUPPRESSED SPLEEN BREAKING OUT) OH INDEED , SIR. BUT I SUPPOSE YOULL TAKE YOUR SHARE WHEN YOU
PRES (149) YOUD APPRECIATE MY QUALITIES THEN: YOU WOULD INDEED , SIR. I SHANT NEVER DO MYSELF JASTICE AT SOLJERIN,
NEVR II (237) HE IS: VERY PLEASANT, VE-RY OFFHAND AND AFFABLE INDEED , SIR. (AGAIN CHANGING HIS TEMPO TO SAY TO
PYGM II (236) BETTER GO, MRS PEARCE. /MRS PEARCE/ I THINK SO, INDEED , SIR. (SHE GOES, WITH DIGNITY). /PICKERING/ THE
NEVR II (243) SIR. BUT DOING WELL NOW, SIR: VERY SATISFACTORY INDEED , SIR. NOTHING LESS THAN FIFTY GUINEAS, SIR.
NEVR IV (288) FOR ME, SIR, WITH THAT BALL: VERY BUSY EVENING INDEED , SIR. /BOHUN/ (INEXORABLY) WE SHALL WANT YOU. /MRS
NEVR IV (304) TO MEET YOU IN ANY WAY, VERY HAPPY AND PLEASED INDEED , SIR. /PHILIP/ (REAPPEARING) HE COMES. (HE WAVES
NEVR IV (305) OUT VERY COMFORTABLE, VERY ENJOYABLE AND HAPPY INDEED , SIR-- FROM TIME TO TIME. I NEVER WAS MASTER IN MY
NEVR II (249) /WAITER/ WE GET ON TOGETHER VERY WELL, VERY WELL INDEED , SIR, CONSIDERING THE DIFFERENCE IN OUR STATIONS. (
WIDO III (51) ON MY BUSINESS? /THE PARLORMAID/ YES, SIR. BUT INDEED , SIR, YOUD SCARCELY KNOW HIM. /SARTORIUS/ (
MILL IV (192) SHUTTING IT. THE SIGNATURE SURPRISES HIM). OH, INDEED , SIR! WE ARE HONORED. /ALASTAIR/ ANYTHING WRONG?
BARB (206) SHORTLY BEFORE MAJOR BARBARA WAS BEGUN. THE PLAY, INDEED , STANDS INDEBTED TO HIM IN MORE WAYS THAN ONE.
DEST SD(162) LAPPELS, NO GRECO-TALLIEN SHAM CHITON, NOTHING, INDEED , THAT THE PRINCESSE DE LAMBALLE MIGHT NOT HAVE WORN.
SUPR HANDBOK(204) AS IT WAS TO SOLOMON SPOILING REHOBOAM: INDEED , THE COMPARISON IS UNFAIR TO THE JEWS IN VIEW OF THE
LION PREFACE(38) MARK, AND THE URBANE EASY-MINDED CHARMER OF LUKE. INDEED , THE JEWS SAY OF HIM " HOW KNOWETH THIS MAN LETTERS,
HART III (148) ARE RUNNING! /NURSE GUINNESS/ THINK OF THEM, INDEED , THE MURDERING BLACKGUARDS! WHAT NEXT? A TERRIFIC
GETT PREFACE(238) THEY MUST BECOME MATRIMONIAL AGENCIES, UNLESS, INDEED , THEY ARE PREPARED TO BECOME SOMETHING WORSE BY
GETT PREFACE(217) BE THAT HYPOCRISY WOULD NO LONGER BE COMPULSORY. INDEED , THIS CAN HARDLY BE CALLED GUESSING: THE EVIDENCE IS
DOCT PREFACE(37) IS NOT AN ATTACK ON THE RIGHT TO KNOWLEDGE: WHY, INDEED , THOSE WHO HAVE THE DEEPEST CONVICTION OF THE
PLES PREFACE(R12) NOT " BACKERS") IS BY NO MEANS AN UNKNOWN EVENT. INDEED , TO ANYONE WHO CAN ESTIMATE, EVEN VAGUELY, THE
ARMS III (47) IT'S VERY GOOD OF YOU, BLUNTSCHLI: IT IS INDEED , TO LET YOURSELF BE PUT UPON IN THIS WAY. NOW ARE
PHIL I (75) JULIA, JULIA! THIS IS TOO BAD. /JULIA/ IS IT, INDEED , TOO BAD? WHAT ARE YOU DOING UP HERE WITH THAT
MIS. PREFACE(85) A MARRIAGE, VARIES FROM ONE TO TWENTY: INDEED , WHEN A WIDOWER WITH A FAMILY MARRIES A WIDOW WITH A
UNPL PREFACE(R22) INDUCE THE ENGLISH PUBLIC TO BUY AND READ PLAYS. INDEED , WHY SHOULD THEY, WHEN THEY FIND NOTHING IN THEM
BASH PREFACE(87) NINETEENTH CENTURY BLANK VERSE, OF COURSE, NOR INDEED , WITH A VERY FEW EXCEPTIONS, ANY POST-SHAKESPEAREAN
PYGM EPILOG (289) OF THE STORY NEED NOT BE SHEWN IN ACTION, AND INDEED , WOULD HARDLY NEED TELLING IF OUR IMAGINATIONS WERE
LADY (238) YOU JUDGE TOO MUCH BY THE COURT, SIR. THERE, INDEED , YOU MAY SAY OF FRAILTY THAT ITS NAME IS WOMAN. /THE
O'FL (217) FOR FINDING THE RIGHT WORD! A BIG BOSTHOON HE IS INDEED , YOUR HONOR. OH, TO THINK OF THE TIMES AND TIMES I
PRES (137) ARMY AS LAWLESS AS THEMSELVES. CLOUTED HER HEAD INDEED ! A PURELY CIVIL PROCEDURE. /THE ORDERLY/ ANY
MILL II (177) SO. YOU COULD NEVER PASS THE TEST. /EPIFANIA/ INDEED ! AND MY FATHER'S TEST FOR A HUSBAND WORTHY OF ME..
MIS. (203) WRONG END OF THE STICK IN MORAL QUESTIONS. /LINA/ INDEED ! AND WHAT DO YOU CONCLUDE FROM THAT, MISTER
FANY III (316) AM AS GREAT A SINNER AS YOURSELF. /GILBEY/ OH, INDEED ! AND WHO TOLD YOU I WAS A SINNER? /MRS GILBEY/
DEVL III (53) YOU HAVE ACTED. /RICHARD/ (WITH SOME SCORN) INDEED ! BUT IF I DONT GO THROUGH WITH IT, WHERE WILL THE
BULL II (109) HIS PROPER NAME, THE SAME AS I DO? FATHER KEEGAN INDEED ! CANT YOU TELL THE DIFFERENCE BETWEEN YOUR PRIEST
LION II (127) EDITOR/ YOU KNOW NOTHING ABOUT IT. THE PEOPLE INDEED ! DO YOU SUPPOSE WE WOULD KILL A MAN WORTH PERHAPS
PYGM II (224) AS THE GIRL VERY PROPERLY SAYS, GARN! MARRIED INDEED ! DONT YOU KNOW THAT A WOMAN OF THAT CLASS LOOKS A
2TRU III (101) OLD PARTY IN THE SHRINE IS MY FATHER. /TALLBOYS/ INDEED ! HAPPY TO MEET YOU, SIR, THOUGH I CANNOT
FABL III (109) I'M NOT A MEDIOCRITY: I'M A GENIUS. /THE MATRON/ INDEED ! HAVE YOU A JOB OF ANY SORT? /THE TOURIST/ NO.
WIDO II (33) FACE HER JUST NOW. /SARTORIUS/ (RALLYING HIM) INDEED ! HA, HA! THE LAUGH, THE FIRST THEY HAVE HEARD FROM
CATH 3 (184) HER CLOSE? /EDSTASTON/ FAIRLY CLOSE. /CLAIRE/ INDEED ! HOW CLOSE? NO: THATS SILLY OF ME: I WILL TELL
ARMS III (59) WHAT TRUE COURAGE IS. /SERGIUS/ (IRONICALLY) INDEED ! I AM WILLING TO BE INSTRUCTED. (HE SITS ON THE
PHIL III (137) ONCE GAVE ME THE BENEFIT OF THE DOUBT. /JULIA/ INDEED ! I NEVER TOLD YOU SO. IF YOU CANNOT BEHAVE LIKE A
FOUN (218) TO SAY SUCH A THING? A WORKHOUSE DOORSTEP INDEED ! I WAS FOUND ON THE DOORSTEP OF ONE OF THE VERY
KING I (165) YOU MUST KEEP SALLY OUT OF HIS WAY. /MRS BASHAM/ INDEED ! IF HE TRIES ANY OF HIS TRICKS ON SALLY I SHALL SEE
ARMS III (55) /LOUKA/ (PROUDLY) MY OWN FASHION. /NICOLA/ INDEED ! IF THE MISTRESS CATCHES YOU, SHE'LL TALK TO YOU. (
NEVR II (237) MY INFERNAL WIFE. /VALENTINE/ (COOLLY) OH INDEED ! INTERESTING MEETING! (HE RESUMES HIS STUDY OF
CAND II (108) MILL! ! ! A FINE MAN TO BREAK MY HEART ABOUT, INDEED ! I'D RATHER HAVE YOU THAN MR MILL. /MARCHBANKS/ (
PYGM II (225) POINT BY HER INSENSIBILITY TO HIS ELOCUTION) OH, INDEED ! I'M MAD, AM I? VERY WELL, MRS PEARCE: YOU NEEDNT
MRS II (210) (MUTTERING) ALL I HAVE TO SAY ON THE SUBJECT, INDEED ! (AGAIN RAISING HER VOICE ANGRILY) DO YOU KNOW WHO
LIED (200) SHEWING ILL HUMOR FOR THE FIRST TIME) OH! INDEED ! (HE LEAVES HIS HEARTH AND BEGINS TO APPROACH
JOAN 6 (136) TERRIBLY AVENGED. /COURCELLES/ (MUTTERS) NOODLE INDEED ! (HE SITS DOWN, MUCH DISCONTENTED). /THE
HART I (50) THE ROOM). /LADY UTTERWORD/ INGRATIATING MYSELF INDEED ! (WITH DIGNITY) VERY WELL, PAPA. (SHE SITS DOWN
DEST (158) OF THAT HORSE. /NAPOLEON/ (ANGRILY SARCASTIC) INDEED ! (WITH SUDDEN MISGIVING) WHERE ARE THE LETTERS AND
SUPR II (64) THAT, MALONE-- AT LEAST NOT ALTOGETHER. /HECTOR/ INDEED ! MAY I ASK WHAT OTHER OBJECTION APPLIES? /TANNER/
MILL II (174) A MALE OF YOUR SPECIES. /EPIFANIA/ MY SPECIES INDEED ! MEN ARE A DIFFERENT AND VERY INFERIOR SPECIES.
WIDO II (28) IT FOR ME. /SARTORIUS/ (GLANCING AT COKANE) INDEED ! MR COKANE EVIDENTLY DID IT WITH GREAT TACT.
MILL II (166) MAN. /EPIFANIA/ (OPENING HER EYES WIDE) INDEED ! NOT THAT I AM DENYING IT; BUT WHAT HAS IT TO DO
OVER (187) ARMS, RESOLVED NOT TO BUDGE). /GREGORY/ OH! INDEED ! OH, ALL RIGHT. IF YOU COME TO THAT -- (HE CROSSES
MRS I (181) (SHE RESUMES HER WORK). /THE GENTLEMAN/ INDEED ! PERHAPS-- MAY I ASK ARE YOU MISS VIVIE WARREN?

DEVL III	(59)	MINISTER IN THIS TOWN. /BURGOYNE/ (INTERESTED)	INDEED !	PRAY, MR ANDERSON, WHAT DO YOU GENTLEMEN BELIEVE?
2TRU II	(79)	NOW, SIR. NO MORE TROUBLE FROM THEM. /TALLBOYS/	INDEED !	QUARTERMASTER'S CLERK, INTERPRETER, INTELLIGENCE
PHIL III	(142)	(INDIGNANTLY) HOW IS HE GOING TO TAKE IT,	INDEED !	REALLY, PAPA, THIS IS TOO MUCH. IF MRS CUTHBERTSON
POSN	(436)	MEN HE LYNCHES, HE AND HIS VIGILANCE COMMITTEE,	INDEED !	/BABSY/ (INCENSED) OH, WELL! IF PEOPLE ARE GOING
HART I	(55)	AFTER MAZZINI). " GRAVER, SOLIDER TASTES,"	INDEED !	/ELLIE/ (AGHAST) YOU DONT MEAN THAT YOU WERE
DEVL II	(36)	CHILD) IT IS NOT BECAUSE I LIKE YOU. /RICHARD/	INDEED !	/JUDITH/ YES: I HAD RATHER YOU DID GO THAN MISTAKE
HART II	(93)	/MRS HUSHABYE/ (SCORNFULLY) POOR DEAR MANGAN	INDEED !	/MAZZINI/ BUT HE DOESNT KNOW ANYTHING ABOUT
MTH4 II	(178)	NOT AT ALL. THEY ADORE ME. /THE ORACLE/	INDEED !	/NAPOLEON/ I HAVE NEVER SHED BLOOD WITH MY OWN
CURE	(234)	HIM SPRAWLING OVER THE KEYBOARD)! BEAUTIFUL DOLL	INDEED !	/REGINALD/ OH, I SAY! LOOK HERE: THATS THE NAME
LION I	(112)	SILENCE! HOLD YOUR TONGUE, THERE. PERSECUTION,	INDEED !	/THE CAPTAIN/ (UNMOVED AND SOMEWHAT SARDONIC)
MTH4 II	(184)	IMPOTENTLY. /ZOO/ SERVE HIM RIGHT! WAR GOD	INDEED !	/THE ENVOY/ (COMING BETWEEN HIS WIFE AND ZOO) I
NEVR II	(227)	OH, VERY PLEASANT, SIR, VERY AFFABLE AND PLEASANT	INDEED !	/THE GENTLEMAN/ YOU LIKE HIS FATHER! (HE LAUGHS
MTH4 I	(143)	/THE ELDERLY GENTLEMAN/ (AGAIN SNORTING) HM!	INDEED !	/THE WOMAN/ HAVE YOU BEEN SENT HERE TO MAKE YOUR
NEVR IV	(301)	THAT NOW SHE CAN DO AS SHE LIKES WITH HIM)	INDEED !	/VALENTINE/ BUT WHY DID I DO IT? BECAUSE I WAS
FANY EPILOG	(332)	WOULD HAVE BEEN ASHAMED OF IT. HEART AND BRAIN,	INDEED !	/VAUGHAN/ YOU HAVE NEITHER ONE NOR THE OTHER.
NEVR II	(236)	JUST TALKING ABOUT YOUR FRIEND, SIR. /VALENTINE/	INDEED !	/WAITER/ (SMOOTHLY MELODIOUS) YES, SIR. GREAT
CAND III	(138)	WITHOUT DISASTER). /BURGESS/ (INDIGNANTLY) STUFF	INDEED !	THAT GURL DUNNO WHAT CHAMPAGNE IS! POMMERY AND
CAPT I	(227)	GRIN) WRORNGFULLY HACQUITTID! /SIR HOWARD/	INDEED !	THATS THE FIRST CASE OF THE KIND I HAVE EVER MET.
KING I	(165)	TWO MEN OUGHT TO MEET. /MRS BASHAM/ THOSE TWO MEN	INDEED !	THE HONOR OF MEETING YOU OUGHT TO BE ENOUGH FOR
MIS.	(114)	ME PITY YOU. /BENTLEY/ " ROMANCE OF BUSINESS"	INDEED !	THE REAL ROMANCE OF TARLETON'S BUSINESS IS THE
MTH3	(102)	ROBBER OF HIS COUNTRY'S EXCHEQUER! POOR FELLOW	INDEED !	WAIT TIL I CATCH HIM. /BURGE-LUBIN/ HOW CAN YOU
MTH3	(103)	THEM I CANNOT BE A PROPER ARCHBISHOP. /BARNABAS/	INDEED !	WELL, IN MY DEPARTMENT THE WORD THIEF SURVIVES,
NEVR II	(232)	FATHER, OR MY MOTHER'S HUSBAND. /M'COMAS/ OH,	INDEED !	WELL, SIR, LET ME TELL YOU THAT WHETHER YOU LIKE
BULL IV	(171)	MADE A VERY GOOD MATCH, LET ME TELL YOU. /NORA/	INDEED !	WELL, SOME PEOPLE MIGHT SAY HE'S NOT DONE SO BADLY
LIED	(198)	DO. /HE/ WE HAVE DECIDED NOT TO GO. /HER HUSBAND/	INDEED !	WELL, THEN, SHALL WE ADJOURN TO MY SNUGGERY?
CLEO V	(197)	ARMIES TO CONQUER ON YOUR WAY HOME? /CAESAR/	INDEED !	WELL, WHAT SAY YOU TO YOURSELF? /RUFIO/ (
MILL I	(139)	I HAD FORGOTTEN THAT. /EPIFANIA/ HAD YOU	INDEED !	WELL, WILL YOU PLEASE GIVE YOUR MIND TO IT FOR A
DOCT III	(135)	SUGGEST IT IF I DIDNT WANT THE MONEY. /RIDGEON/	INDEED !	WELL, YOU WILL HAVE TO FIND SOME OTHER MEANS OF
HART II	(124)	FORCES MEN TO DISCUSS YOU. /LADY UTTERWORD/ OH	INDEED !	WHAT ABOUT YOUR FATAL GIFT OF BEAUTY? /HECTOR/
PYGM III	(245)	/MRS HIGGINS/ OH! DONT THEY? SMALL TALK	INDEED !	WHAT ABOUT YOUR LARGE TALK? REALLY, DEAR, YOU
CLEO V	(201)	/CLEOPATRA/ (PROUDLY) BEAUTY FROM ROME TO EGYPT	INDEED !	WHAT CAN ROME GIVE ME THAT EGYPT CANNOT GIVE ME..
MRS II	(210)	AND SAYING NOTHING). YOU AND YOUR WAY OF LIFE,	INDEED !	WHAT NEXT? (SHE LOOKS AT VIVIE AGAIN. NO REPLY).
MTH4 I	(160)	FOR BLASPHEMY, OR EVEN BURNT ALIVE. /ZOO/	INDEED !	WHAT OPINION IS THAT? /THE ELDERLY GENTLEMAN/ (
PPP	(203)	AHSE DAHN. /THE POLICEMAN/ (OFFENDED) POLICEMAN,	INDEED !	WHERES YOUR MANNERS? /FITZ/ OFFICER-- /THE
VWOO 3	(136)	YOU. IT'S MY BUSINESS AS MUCH AS YOURS. /A/ OH,	INDEED !	WHO DOES THIS SHOP BELONG TO? I MEAN TO WHOM DOES
CAPT I	(240)	YOU NOT TO ATTEMPT THIS EXPEDITION. /SIR HOWARD/	INDEED !	WHY? /BRASSBOUND/ YOU ARE SAFE HERE. I WARN YOU,
PYGM III	(246)	HER YOU WOULDNT HAVE ASKED HER. /MRS HIGGINS/	INDEED !	WHY? /HIGGINS/ WELL, IT'S LIKE THIS. SHE'S A
BULL II	(115)	GLAD OF THAT? /NORA/ (UP IN ARMS AT ONCE) GLAD	INDEED !	WHY SHOULD I BE GLAD? AS WEVE WAITED EIGHTEEN
ARMS I	(16)	WOUNDED, BUT STEADFASTLY LOYAL TO HER IDEALS)	INDEED !	WOULD YOU KNOW HIM AGAIN IF YOU SAW HIM? /THE
FANY PROLOG	(272)	ICE OF LIFE IS SLIPPERY." /TROTTER/ ICE OF LIFE	INDEED !	YOU SHOULD BE EATING PENNY ICES AND ENJOYING
PRES	(148)	N YOUR RISKS N YOUR BRAVERY N YOUR SELF-CONTHROL	INDEED !	" WHY DONT YOU CONTHROL YOURSELF? " I SEZ TO
O'FL	(219)	BECAUSE YOU SAVE THAT BY THE KING FEEDING HIM." "	INDEED !	" SAYS I: " I SUPPOSE IF I'D SIX SONS, YOUD STOP
			INDEEDN	
BULL II	(108)	HOTEL! /FATHER DEMPSEY/ HWAT HOTEL? /AUNT JUDY/	INDEEDN	YOURE NOT GOIN TO A HOTEL. YOULL STAY WITH US. I'D
			INDEFATIGABLE	
MIS.	(118)	I'M AFRAID NOT. HES A PERFECT WHIRLWIND.	INDEFATIGABLE	AT PUBLIC WORK. WONDERFUL MAN, I THINK.
GENV III	(84)	FASHION. AND YOU HAVE BOUNDLESS AMBITION AND	INDEFATIGABLE	PERTINACITY: YOU NEVER STOP ASKING FOR WHAT
ROCK PREFACE	(169)	HOW MANY LAZY ANCESTORS IT TAKES TO PRODUCE AN	INDEFATIGABLE	PRODIGY; BUT IT IS CERTAIN THAT DYNASTIES OF
DOCT PREFACE	(19)	ARE NEVER OUT OF A JOB BECAUSE THEY ARE STRONG,	INDEFATIGABLE	, AND SKILFUL, AND WHO THEREFORE ARE BOLD IN A
METH PREFACE	(R12)	IS A VERY COMPLICATED ONE, THE MOST DEVOTED AND	INDEFATIGABLE	, THE MOST ABLE AND DISINTERESTED STUDENTS OF
			INDEFENSIBLE	
DEVL EPILOG	(79)	IN 1876, EVIDENTLY REGARDED HIS POSITION AS	INDEFENSIBLE	. NOWADAYS, IT IS SUFFICIENT TO SAY THAT
MRS PREFACE	(152)	NONE THE LESS THE INJURY DONE ME, NOW ADMITTEDLY	INDEFENSIBLE	, WAS REAL AND CONSIDERABLE, AND THE INJURY TO
			INDEFINABLY	
SUPR PREFACE	(R37)	OR ITS COLOR, YET, LIKE THE PASTEL, THEY GROW	INDEFINABLY	SHABBY, AND WILL GROW SHABBIER UNTIL THEY CEASE
			INDEFINITELY	
SUPR I SD	(3)	BLACK NOR PERCEPTIBLY BLUE, OF ONE OF THOSE	INDEFINITELY	MIXED HUES WHICH THE MODERN CLOTHIER HAS
			INDELIBLY	
GETT	(268)	LESBIA. ONE IMAGE, AND ONE ONLY, GETS	INDELIBLY	-- /LESBIA/ YES. EXCUSE MY INTERRUPTING YOU SO
			INDELICACY	
DEST	(190)	/NAPOLEON/ (WALKING ABOUT) YOU ARE GUILTY OF	INDELICACY	: OF UNWOMANLINESS. IS THAT COSTUME PROPER?
SUPR III	(82)	OBJECTION; BUT NO WOMAN CAN STAND A SUSPICION OF	INDELICACY	AS TO HER PERSON. MY ENTREATIES WERE IN VAIN: SHE
GETT PREFACE	(236)	CASES, NO MORE LETTERS READ IN COURT WITH AN	INDELICACY	THAT MAKES EVERY SENSITIVE PERSON SHUDDER AND
			INDELICATE	
FABL PREFACE	(64)	AND SAWBONESES, WAKENED UP BY AN EXTRAORDINARILY	INDELICATE	ADVENTURER NAMED SIGMUND FREUD, AND BY THE ABLE
APPL I	(217)	MATTERS TO A HEAD. /MAGNUS/ IT WAS PERHAPS	INDELICATE	. BUT YOU ALL ALLUDE SO FREELY TO YOUR OWN POWERS
SUPR III	(123)	NO LONGER BE ABBREVIATED AND HALF SUPPRESSED AS	INDELICATE	. THE SOBER DECENCY, EARNESTNESS, AND AUTHORITY
SUPR PREFACE	(R21)	PEOPLE AND THEN DISPARAGE IT AS UNWORTHY AND	INDELICATE	. WE LAUGH AT THE HAUGHTY AMERICAN NATION BECAUSE
PHIL I	(90)	AWKWARD: UPON MY LIFE IT IS. THAT WAS A MOST	INDELICATE	THING OF YOU TO SAY PLUMP OUT BEFORE US ALL: THAT
GETT	(317)	AS WELL AS YOURS, YOU KNOW. /LEO/ DONT BE	INDELICATE	, REJJY. /EDITH/ YOU ARE FORGETTING THE VERY
			INDEMNITIES	
ANNA	(299)	THAT BEOTIA WILL ALLOW NO ANNEXATIONS AND NO	INDEMNITIES	, AND MERELY WISHES TO ESTABLISH THE KINGDOM OF
			INDEMNITY	
ROCK II	(259)	CALL A MEETING OF PARLIAMENT TO PASS AN ACT OF	INDEMNITY	FOR ALL MY PROCEEDINGS. /SIR DEXTER/ YOU CANNOT
PRES	(142)	TO BE INVADED BY GERMANY AND FORCED TO PAY AN	INDEMNITY	OF FIVE HUNDRED MILLIONS. /BALSQUITH/ BUT YOU SAID
			INDEPENDENCE	
SUPR II	(60)	DUTY OF MANHOOD AND WOMANHOOD IS A DECLARATION OF	INDEPENDENCE	: THE MAN WHO PLEADS HIS FATHER'S AUTHORITY IS
PYGM V	(287)	HAVE KINDNESS, I'LL HAVE INDEPENDENCE. /HIGGINS/	INDEPENDENCE	? THATS MIDDLE CLASS BLASPHEMY. WE ARE ALL
GETT	(269)	AND CLEANLINESS AND ORDER. I AM PROUD OF MY	INDEPENDENCE	AND JEALOUS FOR IT. I HAVE A SUFFICIENTLY
MIS. PREFACE	(59)	TRUTH, VERY FEW ADULTS CARE TO BE CALLED ON FOR	INDEPENDENCE	AND ORIGINALITY: THEY ALSO ARE BEWILDERED AND
NEVR I	(211)	OF THE RIGHT OF EVERY MEMBER OF THE HOUSEHOLD TO	INDEPENDENCE	AND PRIVACY (HER EMPHASIS ON " PRIVACY" IS
BULL PREFACE	(33)	WAS SEEN IN ENGLAND. IT COST THE AMERICAN WAR OF	INDEPENDENCE	AND THE IRISH VOLUNTEER MOVEMENT TO OBTAIN THE
BARB III	(328)	FOR EVERY WANT OF YOUR WORKMEN MAY SAP THEIR	INDEPENDENCE	AND WEAKEN THEIR SENSE OF RESPONSIBILITY. AND
2TRU I	(48)	THEIR DISTANCE, THE INVASION OF HER PRIVACY AND	INDEPENDENCE	AT EVERY TURN BY QUESTIONS AS TO WHERE SHE HAS
GETT PREFACE	(215)	POINT NOTHING BUT THE ACHIEVEMENT OF ECONOMIC	INDEPENDENCE	BY WOMEN, WHICH IS ALREADY SEEN CLEARLY AHEAD
MIS.	(203)	MISTER JOHNNY? /JOHNNY/ WELL, OBVIOUSLY, THAT	INDEPENDENCE	FOR WOMEN IS WRONG AND SHOULDNT BE ALLOWED. FOR
FABL II	(106)	OF DIAMONDS. THE FELLOW MADE A DECLARATION OF	INDEPENDENCE	FOR ZULULAND WITH HIMSELF AS EMPEROR. CAPETOWN,
PYGM V	(285)	FATHER AND ALL THE WORLD! WHY DID YOU TAKE MY	INDEPENDENCE	FROM ME? WHY DID I GIVE IT UP? I'M A SLAVE
SUPR HANDBOK	(198)	HAVE LIFTED A FINGER IN THE CAUSE OF AMERICAN	INDEPENDENCE	IF THEY HAD FORESEEN ITS REALITY? NO: WHAT
DEVL EPILOG	(80)	THE ANTI-BURGOYNE TRADITION OF AMERICAN	INDEPENDENCE	IN ENGLISH POLITICS, ABANDONED GLADSTONE AND
BARB III	(318)	SHE WONT INTERFERE WITH YOU ANY MORE: YOUR	INDEPENDENCE	IS ACHIEVED: YOU HAVE WON YOUR LATCHKEY. DONT
APPL II	(260)	BLANDLY TRIUMPHANT) I DO, SIR. THE DECLARATION OF	INDEPENDENCE	IS CANCELLED. THE TREATIES WHICH ENDORSED IT
BULL PREFACE	(43)	GRANDMOTHER, HE IS ASSERTING A NATURAL RIGHT TO	INDEPENDENCE	. EVEN IF HOME RULE WERE AS UNHEALTHY AS AN
GETT	(317)	/EDITH/ THEN DONT GRUDGE ME MY SELF-RESPECT AND	INDEPENDENCE	. I INSIST ON IT IN FAIRNESS TO YOU, CECIL.
GETT	(349)	SORT OF WAY. BUT I PREFER MY DIGNITY AND MY	INDEPENDENCE	. I'M AFRAID I THINK THIS RAGE FOR HAPPINESS

BULL PREFACE(33)	THE NATIONALIST MARK OF TODAY IN THE MATTER OF	INDEPENDENCE	. IT IS VAIN TO PLEAD THAT THIS IS HUMAN NATURE
PYGM V (287)	OR A PUPPY. IF I CANT HAVE KINDNESS, I'LL HAVE	INDEPENDENCE	. /HIGGINS/ INDEPENDENCE? THATS MIDDLE CLASS
SIM II (62)	FROM THE EMPIRE. /KANCHIN/ ENGLAND STRIKES FOR	INDEPENDENCE	. /JANGA/ DOWNING STREET DECLARES FOR A RIGHT
HART PREFACE(38)	DOMESTIC CAGES AND TASTED BOTH DISCIPLINE AND	INDEPENDENCE	. THE THOUGHTLESS AND SNOBBISH MIDDLE CLASSES
BULL PREFACE(20)	WITH ONE ANOTHER ON ANY OTHER FOOTING THAN ONE OF	INDEPENDENCE	. THE GOVERNMENT OF NELSON BY WELLINGTON OR OF
BULL IV (150)	" GOD BLESS YOU, SIR! "), THAT LOVE OF	INDEPENDENCE	(A DEFIANT VOICE, " THATS IT!
GETT PREFACE(239)	AND IN SO DOING IT MUST ACHIEVE FOR THEM ECONOMIC	INDEPENDENCE	OF MEN. AND WHEN THIS IS DONE, CAN WE FEEL SURE
GETT PREFACE(238)	THE QUESTION REMINDS US THAT UNTIL THE ECONOMIC	INDEPENDENCE	OF WOMEN IS ACHIEVED, WE SHALL HAVE TO REMAIN
WIDO III (52)	THE DOOR, AND HOLDING IT OPEN) YOU CAN TAKE YOUR	INDEPENDENCE	OUT OF MY HOUSE, THEN. I WONT HAVE IT HERE.
MTH4 I (155)	WERE EVER FOREMOST IN THE STRUGGLE FOR NATIONAL	INDEPENDENCE	; AND THE WORLD RANG CONTINUALLY WITH THE STORY
APPL II (261)	THE OLD WARCRY OF SINN FEIN, AND FIGHT FOR OUR	INDEPENDENCE	TO THE LAST DROP OF OUR BLOOD? /VANHATTAN/ I
SUPR II (60)	CAPE IF YOU LIKE. THAT WILL BE A DECLARATION OF	INDEPENDENCE	WITH A VENGEANCE. YOU CAN WRITE A BOOK ABOUT IT
BULL PREFACE(28)	PAPAL REACTION, AND OF HARDY INDIVIDUALISM AND	INDEPENDENCE	WITH DESPOTISM AND SUBJUGATION. THAT VIOLENT
DEST (192)	AS THE GREAT CHAMPION OF FREEDOM AND NATIONAL	INDEPENDENCE	, HE CONQUERS AND ANNEXES HALF THE WORLD, AND
BULL I (86)	AND SPIRIT IS THE IRISH PARTY. LOOK AT ITS	INDEPENDENCE	, ITS DETERMINATION, ITS DEFIANCE OF BAD
MRS II (210)	YOURE TRYING TO TALK? DO YOU WANT TO SHEW YOUR	INDEPENDENCE	, NOW THAT YOURE A GREAT LITTLE PERSON AT
DEVL EPILOG (82)	RECESS CAME AT A CRITICAL PERIOD OF THE WAR OF	INDEPENDENCE	, SAID THAT THE LORDS COULD NOT BE EXPECTED TO
BULL IV (150)	OF INDEPENDENCE (A DEFIANT VOICE, " THATS IT!	INDEPENDENCE	! "), THAT INDIGNANT SYMPATHY WITH THE CAUSE OF
		INDEPENDENT	
MIS. (201)	ME. I AM STRONG: I AM SKILFUL: I AM BRAVE: I AM	INDEPENDENT	: I AM UNBOUGHT: I AM ALL THAT A WOMAN OUGHT TO
MIS. (159)	HIM. COME NOW! YOURE A WOMAN OF THE WORLD: YOURE	INDEPENDENT	: YOU MUST HAVE DRIVEN LOTS OF MEN CRAZY. YOU
MIS. PREFACE(60)	CAPABLE OF NOTHING IN THE WAY OF ORIGINAL OR	INDEPENDENT	ACTION EXCEPT OUTBURSTS OF NAUGHTINESS IN THE
DOCT PREFACE(43)	BUT SIMPLY INCAPABLE OF ETHICAL JUDGMENT OR	INDEPENDENT	ACTION. JUST SO DO WE FIND A CROWD OF PETTY
DEVL EPILOG (80)	AS A FEDERATION OF BRITISH COLONIES OR AS AN	INDEPENDENT	AFRIKANDER UNITED STATES. IN ALL THESE CASES THE
MRS II (217)	LIFE WORTH? WITHOUT SELF-RESPECT! WHY AM I	INDEPENDENT	AND ABLE TO GIVE MY DAUGHTER A FIRST-RATE
GENV III (73)	IN IRELAND; THEY DISMISSED EDITORS WHO WERE TOO	INDEPENDENT	AND OUTSPOKEN; THEY BURNT THE BOOKS OF NOVELISTS
BARB III (349)	SKIRT) BARBARA: WHEN WILL YOU LEARN TO BE	INDEPENDENT	AND TO ACT AND THINK FOR YOURSELF? I KNOW AS
DOCT PREFACE(70)	WHO ARE IN GREAT DEMAND CAN BE AS HIGH-HANDED AND	INDEPENDENT	AS EMPLOYEES ARE IN ALL CLASSES WHEN A DEARTH IN
METH PREFACE(R26)	BEFORE HE WAS HUMAN ENOUGH TO BREAK LOOSE AS AN	INDEPENDENT	BEING, AND EVEN THEN HE WAS STILL SO INCOMPLETE
SUPR HANDBOK(190)	FRANCE AND THE UNITED STATES, WHICH ARE AVOWEDLY	INDEPENDENT	DEMOCRATIC REPUBLICS, ARE NEITHER HEALTHY,
GETT PREFACE(239)	THE SOLUTION OF THE PROBLEM OF FINDING	INDEPENDENT	EMPLOYMENT FOR WOMEN MAY CAUSE A GREAT NUMBER OF
APPL I (235)	YOU CONTINUE TO SUPPORT ME AS A SEPARATE AND	INDEPENDENT	ESTATE OF THE REALM, I AM YOUR SCAPEGOAT: YOU
LION PREFACE(52)	NOT POSSIBLY HAVE BEEN REALIZED BY A SERIES OF	INDEPENDENT	EXPLOSIONS OF PERSONAL RIGHTEOUSNESS ON THE PART
MIS. PREFACE(71)	MEANWHILE LEARNED THE LESSON THAT CHILDREN ARE	INDEPENDENT	HUMAN BEINGS AND HAVE RIGHTS. WANTED: A CHILD'S
WIDO III (51)	MASTER, AND NOT YOU: DONT THINK IT. NOW THAT I'M	INDEPENDENT	IN RESPECT OF MONEY-- /SARTORIUS/ (CROSSING
MIS. PREFACE(35)	HOLIDAY, AND THAT WHOEVER IS NOT BORN TO AN	INDEPENDENT	INCOME IS STRIVING FOR ONE OR LONGING FOR ONE
LION PREFACE(58)	THEN PRACTISE VIRTUE." WE ALL STRIVE TOWARDS AN	INDEPENDENT	INCOME. WE ALL KNOW AS WELL AS JESUS DID THAT IF
BARB PREFACE(218)	WHO WANT TO BE IMPOSED ON. THE REASON WHY THE	INDEPENDENT	INCOME-TAX PAYERS ARE NOT SOLID IN DEFENCE OF
LION PREFACE(58)	RIGHT PATH. THE GREEKS SAID, " FIRST SECURE AN	INDEPENDENT	INCOME; AND THEN PRACTISE VIRTUE." WE ALL STRIVE
BARB PREFACE(224)	MONEY FROM ANYBODY EXCEPT SWEET OLD LADIES WITH	INDEPENDENT	INCOMES AND GENTLE AND LOVELY WAYS OF LIFE. HE
MIS. PREFACE(35)	I POINT OUT THAT THE WRETCHED PEOPLE WHO HAVE	INDEPENDENT	INCOMES AND NO USEFUL OCCUPATION, DO THE MOST
MRS PREFACE(177)	WOMEN TO THE STREETS, AS IF VICIOUS WOMEN WITH	INDEPENDENT	INCOMES EVER WENT THERE. THESE ARE THE PEOPLE
BARB PREFACE(217)	OF A GOOD LIFE NOW PROCURABLE IS LIFE ON AN	INDEPENDENT	INCOME, ALL SENSIBLE PEOPLE AIM AT SECURING SUCH
BARB PREFACE(217)	ATTEMPT TO LIVE BY MEANS OF WHAT IS CALLED " AN	INDEPENDENT	INCOME" WOULD BE THE SHORTEST WAY TO THE LETHAL
LION PREFACE(24)	CONCEPTION OF SOCIETY IN WHICH YOU ARE NOT AN	INDEPENDENT	INDIVIDUAL BUT A MEMBER OF SOCIETY, YOUR
MIS. (198)	AND SUPPORT YOURSELF AS I DID IF YOU WANT TO BE	INDEPENDENT	. /HYPATIA/ I WANTED TO AND YOU WOULDNT LET ME.
POSN PREFACE(412)	DRAMA. 5. A CENSORSHIP OF A MORE ENLIGHTENED AND	INDEPENDENT	KIND, EXERCISED BY THE MOST EMINENT AVAILABLE
CAND I (80)	/PROSERPINE/ GUILD OF ST MATTHEW ON MONDAY.	INDEPENDENT	LABOR PARTY, GREENWICH BRANCH, ON THURSDAY.
ROCK I (197)	THE SYNDICALISTS, THE OFFICIAL LABOR PARTY, THE	INDEPENDENT	LABOR PARTY, THE SALVATION ARMY, THE CHURCH ARMY
ROCK PREFACE(149)	OF THE CLASS OF LADIES AND GENTLEMEN OF SO-CALLED	INDEPENDENT	MEANS HAS ALREADY BEEN ACCOMPLISHED; AND AN
GETT PREFACE(215)	COUPLES LIVE, WOULD, IF THEY WERE POSSESSED OF	INDEPENDENT	MEANS, HAVE EVERY INDUCEMENT TO ADOPT THE NEW
OVER PREFACE(157)	CASE, BETWEEN SPONTANEOUS HUMAN RELATIONS BETWEEN	INDEPENDENT	MEN AND WOMEN ON THE ONE HAND AND THE PROPERTY
BULL III (121)	HE'S BOUGHT HIS FARM IN THE LAND PURCHASE. HE'S	INDEPENDENT	NOW. /NORA/ IT'S MADE A GREAT CHANGE, LARRY.
LION PREFACE(5)	IS A STEP IN MORAL EVOLUTION WHICH IS	INDEPENDENT	OF ANY INDIVIDUAL PREACHER. IF JESUS HAD NEVER
PYGM V (285)	COULD GO BACK TO MY FLOWER BASKET! I SHOULD BE	INDEPENDENT	OF BOTH YOU AND FATHER AND ALL THE WORLD! WHY
BARB PREFACE(233)	HIS SITUATION. IN SHORT, THOUGH CHARACTER IS	INDEPENDENT	OF CIRCUMSTANCES, CONDUCT IS NOT; AND OUR MORAL
DOCT PREFACE(56)	THERE IS ANOTHER STATISTICAL ILLUSION WHICH IS	INDEPENDENT	OF CLASS DIFFERENCES. A COMMON COMPLAINT OF
GETT PREFACE(242)	INSISTING ON HIS MARRYING HER, UNLESS SHE IS	INDEPENDENT	OF CONVENTIONAL SOCIETY (A STATE OF THINGS
DOCT PREFACE(28)	THAT IS EASILY AND REGULARLY EARNED, SINCE IT IS	INDEPENDENT	OF DISEASE, AND BRINGS EVERY PERSON BORN INTO
SUPR HANDBOK(214)	WE SHALL PRESENTLY MAKE THEIR BODILY NOURISHMENT	INDEPENDENT	OF HIM. BUT THEY ARE STILL RIFF-RAFF; AND TO
SIM II (83)	THERE IS A LIFE OF THE INTELLECT THAT IS QUITE	INDEPENDENT	OF IT. WHAT HAVE I BEEN TO YOU IN THAT LIFE? A
MRS IV (250)	WHY YOU CONTINUE YOUR BUSINESS NOW THAT YOU ARE	INDEPENDENT	OF IT. YOUR SISTER, YOU TOLD ME, HAS LEFT ALL
LION PREFACE(73)	SOLUTION IS TO MAKE THE INDIVIDUAL ECONOMICALLY	INDEPENDENT	OF MARRIAGE AND THE FAMILY, AND TO MAKE MARRIAGE
GETT PREFACE(258)	DECENT AND HONORABLE BY MAKING WOMEN ECONOMICALLY	INDEPENDENT	OF MEN, AND (IN THE YOUNGER SON SECTION OF THE
DOCT I SD(96)	THE SOUND OF HIS VOICE; HE IS A BORN HEALER, AS	INDEPENDENT	OF MERE TREATMENT AND SKILL AS ANY CHRISTIAN
VWOO 3 (140)	YOU ALREADY HAVE ME-- AS AN EMPLOYER. AND YOU ARE	INDEPENDENT	OF ME, AND CAN LEAVE ME IF YOU ARE NOT
MILL PREFACE(112)	IN THE CONTESTS OF CHARACTER AND TALENT WHICH ARE	INDEPENDENT	OF MONEY. IF MOSES IS THE ONLY TRIBESMAN CAPABLE
DEVL II (32)	LOFTY, SELF-RESPECTING, DETERMINED TO BE	INDEPENDENT	OF ONE ANOTHER, CAREFUL OF HOW THEY SPEAK OF ONE
MIS. PREFACE(85)	DO WELL TO GET RID OF BY MAKING RELATIVES AS	INDEPENDENT	OF ONE ANOTHER AS POSSIBLE. THE FATE OF THE
APPL PREFACE(177)	TUNNEL. BUT CERTAIN FACTS ABOUT THE SEA ARE QUITE	INDEPENDENT	OF OUR FEELINGS TOWARDS IT. IF I TAKE IT FOR
BULL PREFACE(31)	IN NEED OF PARLIAMENTARY AND OFFICIAL FORCES	INDEPENDENT	OF ROME. THEY WILL GET NOT ONLY THE PROTESTANT
OVER PREFACE(157)	E. THE CONVENTION OF JEALOUSY. THAT JEALOUSY IS	INDEPENDENT	OF SEX IS SHEWN BY ITS INTENSITY IN CHILDREN,
GETT PREFACE(222)	OF DESTITUTION THAT THE MEANS FOR MAKING WOMEN	INDEPENDENT	OF THE COMPULSORY SALE OF THEIR PERSONS, IN
DOCT PREFACE(70)	BY A PUBLIC OFFICER WHOSE SALARY WAS COMPLETELY	INDEPENDENT	OF THE NUMBER OF VACCINATIONS PERFORMED BY HIM,
PLES PREFACE(R16)	DEPENDENT ON THEM, AND THAT NO MANAGER IS WHOLLY	INDEPENDENT	OF THEM; BUT I CAN NO MORE WRITE WHAT THEY WANT
GETT PREFACE(258)	SECTION OF THE UPPER CLASSES) MEN ECONOMICALLY	INDEPENDENT	OF WOMEN. WE ALSO HAVE TO BRING OURSELVES INTO
BUOY III (39)	ARE SIX, WHEN THEY GO TO SCHOOL AND BEGIN TO BE	INDEPENDENT	OF YOU AND FORM A NEW RELATION WITH THEIR
GENV I (32)	SERVICE I MAY BE ABLE TO RENDER WILL BE ENTIRELY	INDEPENDENT	OF YOUR OFFICIAL WORK HERE. /SHE/ LOOK HERE: I
MIS. PREFACE(75)	THEY PASS AWAY FROM HER INTO THE COMMUNITY AS	INDEPENDENT	PERSONS, MARRYING STRANGERS, WORKING FOR
DOCT PREFACE(65)	OF HEALTH. HE HAS A SAFE, DIGNIFIED, RESPONSIBLE,	INDEPENDENT	POSITION BASED WHOLLY ON THE PUBLIC HEALTH;
POSN PREFACE(373)	BEING ABLE TO SECURE GREATER PUBLICITY FOR IT BY	INDEPENDENT	PUBLICATION ON MY OWN ACCOUNT; AND AS, FURTHER,
SIM II (63)	WE HAD BETTER PROCLAIM THE UNEXPECTED ISLES AN	INDEPENDENT	REPUBLIC AND SECURE THE NEW JOBS FOR OURSELVES.
GENV II (51)	DOMINION OF JACKSONSLAND HAS DECLARED ITSELF AN	INDEPENDENT	REPUBLIC. /BEGONIA/ IT OUGHT TO BE ASHAMED OF
PLES PREFACE(R7)	ACTUAL ESTABLISHMENT OF A " NEW THEATRE" (THE	INDEPENDENT	), THREATENED TO END IN THE HUMILIATING
BULL IV (171)	FACE IF IT IS TRUE-- AT ALL EVENTS ITLL MAKE US	INDEPENDENT	; FOR IF THE WORST COMES TO THE WORST, WE CAN
LION PREFACE(33)	KINGDOM OF GOD," WHICH SUGGESTS THAT HE WAS AN	INDEPENDENT	SEEKER. MARK EARNS OUR GRATITUDE BY MAKING NO
DEVL III (64)	EXPLAINING. /BURGOYNE/ I THINK WE SHOULD PREFER	INDEPENDENT	TESTIMONY, IF YOU DONT MIND. THE SERGEANT, WITH
3PLA PREFACE(R12)	COLOMBE'S BIRTHDAY, AND THE CENCI; IF THE	INDEPENDENT	THEATRE, THE NEW CENTURY THEATRE, AND THE STAGE
UNPL PREFACE(R17)	DEADLOCK WAS COMPLETE. THE PLAY WAS READY; THE	INDEPENDENT	THEATRE WAS READY; AND THE CAST WAS READY; BUT
UNPL PREFACE(R16)	MONEY AT THE DOORS, A SUPPORT WITH WHICH THE	INDEPENDENT	THEATRE COULD NOT AFFORD TO DISPENSE, WAS OUT OF
UNPL PREFACE(R17)	CLOSED MY CAREER AS PLAYWRIGHT IN ORDINARY TO THE	INDEPENDENT	THEATRE. FORTUNATELY, THOUGH THE STAGE IS BOND,
UNPL PREFACE(R14)	THE PLAYWRIGHT, THE PLAY WAS EVERYTHING THAT THE	INDEPENDENT	THEATRE COULD DESIRE: RATHER MORE, IF ANYTHING,
UNPL PREFACE(R12)	GREIN FOLLOWED UP THE CAMPAIGN IN LONDON WITH HIS	INDEPENDENT	THEATRE. IT GOT ON ITS FEET BY PRODUCING IBSEN'S
UNPL PREFACE(R13)	AND THE LIKE, WAS AT ITS HEIGHT, I WROTE FOR THE	INDEPENDENT	THEATRE THE TOPICAL COMEDY CALLED THE
UNPL PREFACE(R13)	STYLE. THE VOLUME, FORMING NUMBER ONE OF THE	INDEPENDENT	THEATRE SERIES OF PLAYS, NOW EXTINCT, IS A
UNPL PREFACE(R13)	IN 1885 MIGHT BE EXACTLY THOSE NEEDED BY THE	INDEPENDENT	THEATRE IN 1892. SO I COMPLETED IT BY A THIRD
PLES PREFACE(R10)	DID NOT SEE THE FOOTLIGHTS UNTIL MY OLD ALLY THE	INDEPENDENT	THEATRE, MAKING A PROPAGANDIST TOUR THROUGH THE
PLES PREFACE(R7)	NEW DRAMATISTS, MYSELF, DISCOVERED BY THE	INDEPENDENT	THEATRE (AT MY OWN SUGGESTION); DR JOHN
PLES PREFACE(R15)	MINE WOULD STILL LEAVE FORLORN HOPES LIKE THE	INDEPENDENT	THEATRE ITS REASON FOR EXISTING. THE COMMITTEE
MRS PREFACE(170)	AN EXCEPTIONALLY ABOMINABLE POLICE CASE. MY OLD	INDEPENDENT	THEATRE MANAGER, MR GREIN, BESIDES THAT REPROACH
JOAN PREFACE(43)	THINKING FOR THEMSELVES, AND THE ABLEST AND MOST	INDEPENDENT	THINKERS ARE CONTENT TO UNDERSTAND THEIR OWN
POSN PREFACE(413)	WOULD RUIN THE THEATRE SPIRITUALLY BY DRIVING ALL	INDEPENDENT	THINKERS FROM THE DRAMA INTO THE UNCENSORED
BUOY III (46)	MEANS? THAT ALSO IS THE QUESTION. /HE/ WHAT ALL	INDEPENDENT	WOMEN DO WITH THEIR MEANS. KEEP A HUSBAND ON
GETT PREFACE(239)	WOMEN FOR WHOM THE LABOR EXCHANGES ARE FINDING	INDEPENDENT	WORK? WILL NOT MANY WOMEN NOW ENGAGED IN
UNPL PREFACE(R18)	AND HER INSISTENCE ON QUALIFYING HERSELF FOR AN	INDEPENDENT	WORKING LIFE, HUMANIZES HER WHOLE FAMILY IN AN
CURE (236)	FROM THE PIANO) MY CHILD! I AM A HARD, STRONG,	INDEPENDENT	, MUSCULAR WOMAN. HOW CAN YOU, WITH YOUR

MIS. (202) ME THAT THE MOMENT A WOMAN BECOMES PECUNIARILY INDEPENDENT , SHE GETS HOLD OF THE WRONG END OF THE STICK IN
WIDO III (65) TOLD YOU. YOU, WHO WERE SO DISINTERESTED, SO INDEPENDENT , THAT YOU COULD NOT ACCEPT ANYTHING FROM MY
BULL PREFACE(6) CHRISTIAN COUNTRIES WHICH ARE POLITICALLY INDEPENDENT , THE CLERICALS ARE STRUGGLING, NOT TO REGAIN
GETT PREFACE(213) WOMEN OF ADMIRABLE CHARACTER, STRONG, CAPABLE, INDEPENDENT , WHO DISLIKE THE DOMESTIC HABITS OF MEN; HAVE
UNPL PREFACE(R12) TIES BETWEEN THEM AND THE PLEASANT PEOPLE WITH " INDEPENDENT " INCOMES WHO IMAGINE THAT SUCH SORDID MATTERS
GETT (349) OF THE MORNING I AM STILL UNMARRIED! STILL INDEPENDENT ! STILL MY OWN MISTRESS! STILL A GLORIOUS

INDEPENDENTLY
BULL III SD(126) WHETHER HE IS BEING COURTED OR PATRONIZED, NODS INDEPENDENTLY . /DORAN/ HOWS YOURSELF, LARRY? /LARRY/
CLEO NOTES (211) OR SUCCESS IN ANY PARTICULAR INSTANCE QUITE INDEPENDENTLY OF CONVENTION AND MORAL GENERALIZATION. HE
DOCT PREFACE(25) PARENTS OF HAVING CONTRACTED THIS DISEASE INDEPENDENTLY OF THE INOCULATION, AN EXCUSE WHICH NATURALLY
ROCK PREFACE(174) INTO A PREDATORY CAPITALIST STATE, EITHER INDEPENDENTLY OR AS PART OF A JAPANESE ASIATIC HEGEMONY, ALL

INDEPENDENT'S
PLES PREFACE(R7) (HIS PLAY THE BLACK CAT HAD BEEN ONE OF THE INDEPENDENT'S SUCCESSES); AND MR W.B. YEATS, A GENUINE

INDEPENDENTS
UNPL PREFACE(R13) WAS SUFFICIENTLY EXCITING: THE SOCIALISTS AND INDEPENDENTS APPLAUDED ME FURIOUSLY ON PRINCIPLE; THE
FABL PREFACE(76) BY OUR MISSIONARIES, WHO ARE PRACTICALLY ALL INDEPENDENTS . COMMON TO THESE IRRECONCILABLE FAITHS IS THE

INDEPINDENT
BULL III (129) SAY BUT AN ENGLISH PRODESTN MIGHTNT HAVE A MORE INDEPINDENT MIND ABOUT THE LAN, AN BE LESS AFEERD TO SPAKE

INDESCRIBABLE
BASH II,2, (117) DOWN WITH A CRASH. SCREAMS FROM ITS OCCUPANTS. INDESCRIBABLE CONFUSION.) /CASHEL/ (DRAGGING LYDIA FROM THE
BASH II,1, (103) OH, WELL DONE, CASHEL! /BASHVILLE/ " A SCENE OF INDESCRIBABLE EXCITEMENT ENSUED; FOR IT WAS NOW QUITE
SIM II (79) ECHOES THE NEWS). EXTRAORDINARY DISAPPEARANCES. INDESCRIBABLE PANIC. STOCK EXCHANGE CLOSES: ONLY TWO MEMBERS
DOCT IV (165) THE GOOD FIGHT, AND NOW IT'S ALL OVER, THERES AN INDESCRIBABLE PEACE. (HE FEEBLY FOLDS HIS HANDS AND UTTERS
DOCT III (149) WELL! ! ! (HE GIVES THE SITUATION UP AS INDESCRIBABLE , AND GOES FOR HIS HAT). /RIDGEON/ DAMN HIS
GETT (281) A FAIRY PRINCE, SOMETIMES SOMEBODY QUITE INDESCRIBABLE , AND SOMETIMES NOBODY AT ALL. /LEO/ YES:

INDEX
WIDO I (8) THE OTHER POCKET). THANK YOU. (HE CONSULTS THE INDEX FOR ROLANDSECK). /BLANCHE/ SUGAR, DR TRENCH? /TRENCH/
DOCT I (90) AND IN FIFTEEN MINUTES I'LL GIVE YOU HIS OPSONIN INDEX IN FIGURES. IF THE FIGURE IS ONE, INOCULATE AND CURE:
GENV I (31) AT THIS NICE LITTLE JOB THEYVE GIVEN ME! A CARD INDEX OF ALL THE UNIVERSITIES WITH THE NAMES AND ADDRESSES
MRS PREFACE(164) WORK. THE CONCLAVE WHICH COMPILES THE EXPURGATORY INDEX OF THE ROMAN CATHOLIC CHURCH IS THE MOST AUGUST,
ROCK PREFACE(174) NOMINALLY A FREE STATE, ONE OF MY BOOKS IS ON THE INDEX ; AND I HAVE NO DOUBT ALL THE REST WILL FOLLOW AS SOON
BULL PREFACE(29) WHERE EVERY MODERN BOOK WORTH READING IS ON THE INDEX , AND THE EARTH IS STILL REGARDED, NOT PERHAPS AS
GENV I SD(29) TO HAVE BEEN WORKING AT THE COMPILATION OF A CARD INDEX , AS THERE ARE CARDS SCATTERED ABOUT, AND AN OPEN CASE
DOCT PREFACE(26) WITHOUT ANY REFERENCE TO THE PATIENT'S " OPSONIC INDEX " AT THE MOMENT OF INOCULATION, AND THOUGH THOSE OTHER

INDIA
LION PREFACE(99) FOR HIGH IMPERIAL OFFICE. A CALVINIST VICEROY OF INDIA AND A PARTICULAR BAPTIST SECRETARY OF STATE FOR
DEVL EPILOG (79) LED BURGOYNE, A PROFESSED ENEMY OF OPPRESSION IN INDIA AND ELSEWHERE, TO ACCEPT HIS AMERICAN COMMAND WHEN SO
ROCK II (265) UNTIL NOW I HAVE SUPPORTED THE CONNECTION BETWEEN INDIA AND ENGLAND BECAUSE I KNEW THAT IN THE COURSE OF
BULL PREFACE(34) THE MAINTENANCE OF ABSOLUTE INJUSTICE AS BETWEEN INDIA AND ENGLAND." IT WILL BE OBSERVED THAT NO ENGLISHMAN,
BARB I (250) YOUVE BEEN AT HARROW AND CAMBRIDGE. YOUVE BEEN TO INDIA AND JAPAN. YOU MUST KNOW A LOT OF THINGS, NOW; UNLESS
GENV PREFACE(11) THE NEW BOMB WITH RUSSIA, THE THIRD. VILLAGES IN INDIA ARE STILL WIPED OUT TO " LARN" THEIR MOSTLY HARMLESS
ROCK PREFACE(174) AND EDITORS SWEPT AWAY, NOT ONLY IN IRELAND AND INDIA BUT IN LONDON IN MY TIME, TO BE TAKEN IN BY TENNYSON'S
PYGM III (253) /PICKERING/ DONT ASK ME. IVE BEEN AWAY IN INDIA FOR SEVERAL YEARS; AND MANNERS HAVE CHANGED SO MUCH
BULL PREFACE(70) FURTHER PANICS AND ATROCITIES WILL ENSUE BEFORE INDIA IS LEFT TO GOVERN ITSELF AS MUCH AS IRELAND AND EGYPT
HART PREFACE(14) NOTABLY ON THE WEST COAST OF NORTH AMERICA AND IN INDIA . BUT THE MORAL PESTILENCE, WHICH WAS UNQUESTIONABLY A
ROCK II (265) /SIR ARTHUR/ THAT ONE WORD NIGGER WILL COST US INDIA . HOW COULD DEXY BE SUCH A FOOL AS TO LET IT SLIP!
PRES (135) ONLY TO A COUNCIL OF WAR. IT ANSWERS PERFECTLY IN INDIA : IF ANYONE OBJECTS, SHOOT HIM DOWN. /BALSQUITH/ BUT
BULL PREFACE(70) RIDICULOUS IN EUROPE, AND IMPLACABLY RESENTED IN INDIA : THE BRITISH DOMINATION DIED OF DENSHAWAI;
BUOY 1 (12) /SON/ WE DO. WE DID IT IN IRELAND. WE DID IT IN INDIA . IT HAS ALWAYS BEEN SO. WE RESIST CHANGES UNTIL THE
SIM II (55) POLYGAMY WOULD BE AN INSULT TO THE RELIGIONS OF INDIA . /PRA/ THE CULTURAL MINISTER AT DELHI ADDS A
PYGM I (211) NOTE TAKER/ CHELTENHAM, HARROW, CAMBRIDGE, AND INDIA . /THE GENTLEMAN/ QUITE RIGHT. (GREAT LAUGHTER.
HART I (62) PARTY: ONE OF KING EDWARD'S HUNTING PARTIES IN INDIA . THE KING WAS FURIOUS: THAT WAS WHY HE NEVER HAD HIS
LION PREFACE(15) VICARIOUS, AND IS NOT YET UNIVERSALLY SO. IN INDIA MEN PAY WITH THEIR OWN SKINS, TORTURING THEMSELVES
BULL PREFACE(5) PRESSURE OF THE HOME RULE AGITATIONS IN EGYPT AND INDIA MORE THAN IN IRELAND; FOR THE IRISH, NOW CONFIDENT
LION PREFACE(100) CALVIN. IMAGINE THE EFFECT OF TRYING TO GOVERN INDIA OR EGYPT FROM BELFAST OR FROM THE VATICAN! THE
BULL PREFACE(5) BE NO NEED TO IMPRISON NATIONALISTS EITHER IN INDIA OR EGYPT; SO THAT, IN EFFECT, THE NATIVES HAVE
BULL PREFACE(34) ENGLISHMAN IS SUFFICIENT TO ENSURE THE WELFARE OF INDIA OR IRELAND, IT OUGHT TO SUFFICE EQUALLY FOR ENGLAND.
PYGM V (287) YOU SHALL MARRY THE GOVERNOR-GENERAL OF INDIA OR THE LORD-LIEUTENANT OF IRELAND, OR SOMEBODY WHO
ROCK II (265) AND BY THE JUSTICE OF BRAHMA IT MUST END IN INDIA RULING ENGLAND JUST AS I, BY MY WEALTH AND MY BRAINS,
ROCK PREFACE(149) STATES FOR THE EXTERMINATION OF FASCISTS. IN INDIA THE IMPULSE OF MOSLEMS AND HINDUS TO EXTERMINATE ONE
ROCK II (265) IMBECILES. BUT I NOW CAST YOU OFF. I RETURN TO INDIA TO DETACH IT WHOLLY FROM ENGLAND, AND LEAVE YOU TO
PYGM I (214) FROM INDIA TO MEET YOU. /HIGGINS/ I WAS GOING TO INDIA TO MEET YOU. /PICKERING/ WHERE DO YOU LIVE? /HIGGINS/
PYGM I (214) /PICKERING/ (WITH ENTHUSIASM) I CAME FROM INDIA TO MEET YOU. /HIGGINS/ I WAS GOING TO INDIA TO MEET
ROCK II (269) PUT DOWN THE PEOPLE IN EGYPT, IN IRELAND, AND IN INDIA WITH FIRE AND SWORD, WITH FLOGGINGS AND HANGINGS,
SIM II (56) HATED YOU; BUT DELHI SUPPORTED YOU; AND SINCE INDIA WON DOMINION STATUS DELHI HAS BEEN THE CENTRE OF THE
POSN PREFACE(386) THE TSAR OF RUSSIA OR THE GOVERNOR-GENERAL OF INDIA WOULD HARDLY CARE TO SEE PERFORMED IN THEIR CAPITALS
GENV PREFACE(21) POISON GAS) IN THE NORTH WEST PROVINCES OF INDIA , AND HAD ALREADY COMPLETED IN AUSTRALIA, NEW ZEALAND,
POSN PREFACE(427) THE PASSING OF PRESS LAWS (ESPECIALLY IN EGYPT, INDIA , AND IRELAND), EXACTLY AS THEY SHRIEK FOR A
LION PREFACE(96) OVERFLOW THE FRONTIERS OF ALL THE CHURCHES. IN INDIA , FOR EXAMPLE, THERE ARE LESS THAN FOUR MILLION
BULL PREFACE(33) ONE PERSON WE WILL NOT ENDURE. THE ENGLISHMAN IN INDIA , FOR EXAMPLE, STANDS, A VERY STATUE OF JUSTICE,
LION PREFACE(77) AMERICA; ATHEISM WORKS IN FRANCE, POLYTHEISM IN INDIA , MONOTHEISM THROUGHOUT ISLAM, AND PRAGMATISM, OR
MTH4 I (155) WHERE THERE WAS STILL A NATIONALIST QUESTION, TO INDIA , PERSIA, AND COREA, TO MOROCCO, TUNIS, AND TRIPOLI.
GETT PREFACE(209) BRITISH EMPIRE, AND IS AS PRACTICABLE HERE AS IN INDIA , THERE IS A GOOD DEAL TO BE SAID AGAINST IT, AND
BULL PREFACE(70) FROM DENSHAWAI OR THE BLACK AND TAN TERROR. IN INDIA , WHICH IS STILL STRUGGLING FOR SELF-GOVERNMENT, AND
LION PREFACE(48) AND MANY THEOSOPHISTS AND LOVERS OF THE WISDOM OF INDIA , WHO NEVER ENTER A CHRISTIAN CHURCH EXCEPT AS

INDIAN
BULL PREFACE(34) GOVERNMENT THAT DOES ABSOLUTE JUSTICE AS BETWEEN INDIAN AND INDIAN, BEING WHOLLY PREOCCUPIED WITH THE
GENV III (76) SHE IS HEAVEN KNOWS WHAT MIXTURE OF SPANIARD AND INDIAN AND SAVAGE. /THE WIDOW/ MEN WITH RED BLOOD IN THEM DO
MIS. (131) OF MY CLUB, WHICH CONSISTS MOSTLY OF RETIRED INDIAN CIVIL SERVANTS? WE LOOK ON AT THE MUDDLE AND THE
SUPR PREFACE(R31) OF MENDOZA LIMITED I TRACE BACK TO A CERTAIN WEST INDIAN COLONIAL SECRETARY, WHO, AT A PERIOD WHEN HE AND I
PYGM I (214) LINES. /THE GENTLEMAN/ I AM MYSELF A STUDENT OF INDIAN DIALECTS; AND-- /THE NOTE TAKER/ (EAGERLY) ARE YOU?
PYGM III (255) TO LIVE THERE WITH HENRY. WE WORK TOGETHER AT MY INDIAN DIALECTS; AND WE THINK IT MORE CONVENIENT-- /MRS
SIM I SD(36) 17 AND 20. THEY ARE MAGICALLY BEAUTIFUL IN THEIR INDIAN DRESSES, SOFTLY BRILLIANT, MAKING THE TROPICAL
KING I (201) THEY WANT ME TO RECITE MY BIG SPEECH FROM THE INDIAN EMPEROR. BUT I CANT DO THAT WITHOUT PROPER DRAPERY:
KING I (204) COME! GIVE US ONE OF CYDARA'S SPEECHES FROM THE INDIAN EMPEROR. IT WAS IN THAT THAT YOU BURST ON THE WORLD
BULL IV (154) OF CONSCIENCE ENJOYED BY THE SUBJECTS OF OUR INDIAN EMPIRE. /LARRY/ NO DOUBT; BUT MAY WE VENTURE TO ASK
CAPT NOTES (302) OF INVENTION CONCERNING THE STORY OF THE WEST INDIAN ESTATE WHICH SO VERY NEARLY SERVES AS A PEG TO HANG
CAPT III (276) PEOPLE WILL NEVER UNDERSTAND ABOUT THE WEST INDIAN ESTATE. THEYLL THINK YOURE THE WICKED UNCLE OUT OF
BASH II,1, (112) IN IT; FOR BY SO MUCH AS THE NE'ER SUBDUED INDIAN EXCELS THE SERVILE NEGRO, DOTH THIS RUFFIAN
CATH PREFACE(157) WRITE PARTS FOR HEROES WITH TWENTY ARMS LIKE AN INDIAN GOD, INDEED THE ACTOR OFTEN INFLUENCES THE AUTHOR TOO
HART I SD(43) OF WATER COLOR, A TUMBLER OF DISCOLORED WATER, INDIAN INK, PENCILS, AND BRUSHES ON IT. THE DRAWING-BOARD IS
ROCK II SD(264) AN ATMOSPHERE OF AWE BEHIND HIM, IN WHICH THE INDIAN IS CHOKING WITH INDIGNATION, AND FOR THE MOMENT
CAPT I (229) MILES DIED, HE LEFT AN ESTATE IN ONE OF THE WEST INDIAN ISLANDS. IT WAS IN CHARGE OF AN AGENT WHO WAS A
FABL PREFACE(75) TO THE UTMOST REACH OF THE HUMAN MIND BY THE INDIAN JAINISTS, WHO RENOUNCED IDOLATRY AND BLOOD SACRIFICE
BULL PREFACE(46) BUT NEVER TO RULE; AND WHEN AN EMERGENCY LIKE THE INDIAN MUTINY COMES, HE BREAKS DOWN; AND THE SITUATION HAS
BULL PREFACE(63) AND ASIA BY A COLOSSAL SECOND EDITION OF THE INDIAN MUTINY. THAT THIS IDIOTIC ROMANCE, GROSS AND
HART I (68) WILL BREAK IT OFF. TAKE MY ADVICE: MARRY A WEST INDIAN NEGRESS: THEY MAKE EXCELLENT WIVES. I WAS MARRIED TO
SIM PREFACE(19) THE LEAVES, LET US HOPE THEY NEVER WILL. ON THE INDIAN OCEAN, APRIL 1935. THE FIRST PERFORMANCE OF THE
BULL PREFACE(34) OR WOULD TOLERATE A PROPOSAL TO ESTABLISH THE INDIAN OR IRISH SYSTEM IN GREAT BRITAIN. YET IF THE JUSTICE

BULL IV (155)	MUST BE HELL, AND THAT WE ARE ALL HERE, AS THE	INDIAN	REVEALED TO ME-- PERHAPS HE WAS SENT TO REVEAL IT TO
BARB III (343)	YOU LOVE THE OPPRESSED RACES, THE NEGRO, THE	INDIAN	RYOT, THE UNDERDOG EVERYWHERE. DO YOU LOVE THE
PHIL II (107)	BUT WE ALWAYS THOUGHT THAT IT WAS PARTLY HIS	INDIAN	SERVICE, AND PARTLY HIS EATING AND DRINKING TOO MUCH.
KING II SD(223)	AND BREECHES, SHIRT AND CRAVAT, WRAPPED IN AN	INDIAN	SILK DRESSING GOWN, IS ASLEEP ON A COUCH. HIS COAT
PHIL I SD(69)	SHIRT, AND TURNS OVER A GARNET COLORED SCARF OF	INDIAN	SILK, SECURED BY A TURQUOISE RING. HE WEARS BLUE
CAPT I (230)	YES. A FEW YEARS AGO THE COLLAPSE OF THE WEST	INDIAN	SUGAR INDUSTRY CONVERTED THE INCOME OF THE ESTATE
HART I (47)	HIGH HEAVEN THEY HAVE GIVEN THIS INNOCENT CHILD	INDIAN	TEA: THE STUFF THEY TAN THEIR OWN LEATHER INSIDES
MTH3 (125)	ME AS I STAND HERE, YOU WOULD HAVE TO APPOINT AN	INDIAN	TO SUCCEED ME. I TAKE PRECEDENCE TODAY NOT AS AN
MIS. PREFACE(65)	WE WILL ALLOW A VILLAGE OF EGYPTIAN FELLAHEEN OR	INDIAN	TRIBESMEN TO LIVE THE LOWEST LIFE THEY PLEASE AMONG
SUPR HANDBOK(204)	AND TO STEAL BIRDS' EGGS AND KEEP THEM AS THE RED	INDIAN	USED TO KEEP SCALPS. COERCION WITH THE LASH IS AS
SUPR HANDBOK(225)	A BONE ARE LOVERS OF ANIMALS. THE NORTH AMERICAN	INDIAN	WAS A TYPE OF THE SPORTSMAN WARRIOR GENTLEMAN. THE
BULL PREFACE(34)	THAT DOES ABSOLUTE JUSTICE AS BETWEEN INDIAN AND	INDIAN	, BEING WHOLLY PREOCCUPIED WITH THE MAINTENANCE OF

INDIANS

BULL PREFACE(8)	RISKING THEIR LIVES TO INTRODUCE IT IN PERSIA,	INDIANS	AND EGYPTIANS WHO ARE READY TO SACRIFICE ALL THEY
METH PREFACE(R78)	SAINTS WITH PLEASURE. BUT SUCH FARE IS SHIRKED BY	INDIANS	AND ROMAN CATHOLICS. FREETHINKERS READ THE BIBLE:
POSN PREFACE(387)	ENTERTAIN VERY SERIOUSLY A PROPOSAL TO EXCLUDE	INDIANS	FROM THEM, AND TO SUPPRESS THE PLAY COMPLETELY IN
FANY III (320)	AND BE ASHAMED OF YOURSELVES, BEHAVING LIKE WILD	INDIANS	. /DORA'S VOICE/ (SCREAMING) OH! OH! OH! DONT,
SUPR I (36)	STRATAGEMS TO SAVE OUR SCALPS FROM THE RED	INDIANS	. YOU HAVE NO IMAGINATION, ANN. I AM TEN TIMES MORE
BULL PREFACE(70)	OF MEAN SPITE WITH HYPERBOLICAL VIOLENCE.	INDIANS	WERE FORCED TO CRAWL PAST OFFICIAL BUILDINGS ON
DEVL EPILOG (85)	HIS SWORD. IN CONNECTION WITH THE REFERENCE TO	INDIANS	WITH SCALPING KNIVES, WHO, WITH THE TROOPS HIRED
DEVL III (57)	ARE HESSIANS, BRUNSWICKERS, GERMAN DRAGOONS, AND	INDIANS	WITH SCALPING KNIVES. THESE ARE THE COUNTRYMEN ON
POSN PREFACE(407)	IN UNIFORM, GENTLEMEN NOT IN EVENING DRESS,	INDIANS	, OR WHAT NOT; BUT WHEN DISORDER IS STOPPED,
DEVL EPILOG (85)	CAMP AS A PRISONER OF WAR, WHEN ANOTHER PARTY OF	INDIANS	, SENT BY HER BETROTHED, CLAIMED HER. THE WYANDOTTE

INDIARUBBER

MIS. (137)	MY CHEST THIS SUMMER. I TRIED EXERCISES WITH AN	INDIARUBBER	EXPANDER; BUT I WASNT STRONG ENOUGH: INSTEAD OF
APPL I (205)	IT HALF SO SILLY AS OUR PRETENCE THAT HE IS AN	INDIARUBBER	STAMP? THE ANCIENT ROMAN EMPEROR-GOD HAD NOT
APPL I (205)	AM HOME SECRETARY, BY JINGO! NOBODY WILL MAKE AN	INDIARUBBER	STAMP OF BILL BOANERGES: TAKE THAT FROM ME.
APPL I (206)	BILL BOANERGES, EH? /MAGNUS/ PRECISELY. THE	INDIARUBBER	STAMP THEORY WILL NOT WORK, MR BOANERGES. THE
APPL I (206)	THE BIT AND UNSUCCESSFUL THE ATTEMPT. BUT THE	INDIARUBBER	STAMP THEORY BREAKS DOWN IN EVERY REAL
APPL I (212)	NONE? /BOANERGES/ DONT TALK SILLY, NICK. THIS	INDIARUBBER	STAMP THEORY DOESNT WORK. WHAT MAN HAS EVER
APPL I (205)	WILL BE SETTLED BY A LIVING PERSON AND NOT BY AN	INDIARUBBER	STAMP. /BOANERGES/ IT WILL BE SETTLED BY THE
APPL I (204)	AM I RIGHT? /BOANERGES/ YOU ARE, KING MAGNUS. AN	INDIARUBBER	STAMP. THATS WHAT YOU HAVE GOT TO BE; AND DONT
APPL I (206)	SHEWS THAT WE ARE SOMETHING MORE THAN A PAIR OF	INDIARUBBER	STAMPS. YOU ARE UP AGAINST MY BRAINS, SUCH AS
APPL I (204)	KNOW WHAT THEY CALL THAT IN BELGIUM? /MAGNUS/ AN	INDIARUBBER	STAMP, I THINK. AM I RIGHT? /BOANERGES/ YOU
APPL I (205)	CONSTITUTED DEMOCRATIC MINISTER. /MAGNUS/ ANOTHER	INDIARUBBER	STAMP, EH? /BOANERGES/ AT PRESENT, PERHAPS. BUT
PYGM II SD(217)	BURNERS ATTACHED TO A GAS PLUG IN THE WALL BY AN	INDIARUBBER	TUBE, SEVERAL TUNING-FORKS OF DIFFERENT SIZES, A

INDIA-RUBBER

BULL I (74)	A VERY WET CLIMATE, SIR. I'D BETTER PACK YOUR	INDIA-RUBBER	OVERALLS. /BROADBENT/ DO. WHERES MR DOYLE?
INCA (253)	A CONSTITUTIONAL MONARCH IS OPENLY CALLED AN	INDIA-RUBBER	STAMP. AN EMPEROR IS A PUPPET. THE INCA IS NOT

INDICATE

SUPR HANDBOK(192)	WERE REALLY FOUNDED ON PUBLIC OPINION, IT WOULD	INDICATE	AN ATTITUDE OF DISGUST AND RESENTMENT TOWARDS THE
MTH4 I (152)	I DISCOVERED THAT THE NAME JOSEPH WAS SUPPOSED TO	INDICATE	AN UNMANLY PRUDERY BECAUSE OF SOME OLD STORY ABOUT
GETT PREFACE(245)	WHERE FRANTIC DENIALS AND FURIOUS SUPPRESSIONS	INDICATE	EVERYWHERE THE COWARDICE AND WANT OF FAITH WHICH
DEVL II (39)	HER MOUTH HASTILY WITH THE HAND SHE HAS RAISED TO	INDICATE	HIM, AND STANDS STARING AFFRIGHTEDLY). /THE
GENV PREFACE(15)	LABELS WHICH NONE OF THEM CAN DEFINE, AND WHICH	INDICATE	TENETS WHICH NONE OF THEM ACCEPT AS PRACTICAL RULES
POSN PREFACE(412)	ITS APPLICATION TO POLITICAL PLAYS IS TAKEN TO	INDICATE	THE ATTITUDE OF THE CROWN ON QUESTIONS OF DOMESTIC
FABL PREFACE(91)	IF THE ANSWER BE YES, THEY CAN BE INVITED TO	INDICATE	THE BOOKS THEY KNOW. I AM QUITE AWARE OF THE
DOCT PREFACE(21)	DOCTOR ABOUT SOME OF THE ORDINARY SYMPTOMS WHICH	INDICATE	THE NEED FOR A HOLIDAY AND A CHANGE. THE DOCTOR
PYGM III (249)	MAKES SIGNS OVER HIS MOTHER'S HEAD TO ELIZA TO	INDICATE	TO HER WHICH LADY IS HER HOSTESS). ELIZA, WHO IS
SUPR PREFACE(R17)	THOUGH THE LINES PUT INTO THE ACTOR'S MOUTH TO	INDICATE	TO THE PIT THAT HAMLET IS A PHILOSOPHER ARE FOR THE

INDICATED

MTH2 SD(37)	INSTEAD OF BEHIND, COMBINE WITH THE PROSPERITY	INDICATED	BY HIS SURROUNDINGS, AND HIS AIR OF PERSONAL
LION PROLOG (108)	LION. HE STEALS CAUTIOUSLY TOWARDS THE SPOT	INDICATED	BY MEGAERA. SHE RISES WITH AN EFFORT AND TOTTERS
GETT PREFACE(208)	THE ADVANCE IN SOCIAL ORGANIZATION AND CONSCIENCE	INDICATED	BY SUCH PAYMENTS INVOLVED ALSO THE OPENING UP OF
DOCT PREFACE(46)	WITH THE GERMICIDE MODIFIED IN THE DIRECTION	INDICATED	BY THE EXPERIMENTS MADE ON THE TWO PATIENTS AND
NEVR IV (297)	MAY NOT HAVE COMMITTED YOURSELF IN THE DIRECTION	INDICATED	BY THIS YOUNG LADY. (M'COMAS IS ABOUT TO
SIM I (47)	A UNION BETWEEN HIM AND OUR GIRLS IS CLEARLY	INDICATED	. /THE CLERGYMAN/ YOU MEAN THAT I OUGHT TO MARRY
ROCK II (282)	A COTTAGE NEAR A GOOD GOLF LINKS SEEMS TO BE	INDICATED	. WHAT WOULD YOU LIKE? /LADY CHAVENDER/ BUT YOUR
LION PREFACE(91)	THAN ARCHBISHOP USSHER DID. I HAVE THEREFORE	INDICATED	LITTLE MORE OF THE DISCOVERIES THAN ARCHBISHOP
WIDO III (53)	SEE IT. (HE DOUBLES THE BOOK BACK AT THE PLACE	INDICATED	, AND HANDS IT TO SARTORIUS). /SARTORIUS/ SO
CAPT I SD(218)	AMAZING TO ALL BUT COCKNEYS, THEY CANNOT BE	INDICATED	, SAVE IN THE ABOVE IMPERFECT MANNER, WITHOUT THE

INDICATES

2TRU III (108)	THERE. /TALLBOYS/ THIS CANNOT BE TRUE, MEEK. IT	INDICATES	A DEGREE OF INTELLIGENCE OF WHICH NO GOVERNMENT IS
CAPT NOTES (304)	THAT A DEPARTURE FROM CONVENTIONAL SPELLING	INDICATES	A DEPARTURE FROM THE CORRECT STANDARD ENGLISH OF
MIS. PREFACE(93)	ON THE MOUNTAINS TO HIDE THEM, I SUBMIT THAT THIS	INDICATES	A THOROUGHLY HEALTHY STATE ON THE PART OF THE
HART I (66)	MANGAN) DO YOU KNOW MY HUSBAND, MR MANGAN (SHE	INDICATES	HECTOR). /MANGAN/ (GOING TO HECTOR, WHO MEETS HIM
BULL IV (163)	DETAIN YOU LONG. MAY I ASK YOU TO SIT DOWN. (HE	INDICATES	HER CHAIR WITH OPPRESSIVE SOLEMNITY. SHE SITS DOWN
MILL IV (193)	TO MYSELF. I SUPPOSE YOU MEAN THIS AND THIS (HE	INDICATES	HIS INJURIES). WELL, THEY ARE WHAT YOUR WIFE HAS
LION PREFACE(39)	THAN THE OTHER ACCOUNTS, IN WHICH JESUS OPENLY	INDICATES	JUDAS WITHOUT ELICITING ANY PROTEST OR EXCITING
GENV III (83)	AN ENORMOUS MAJORITY OF THE HUMAN RACE. IT SIMPLY	INDICATES	MIXED ANCESTRY. /THE WIDOW/ AH, THAT IS THE SECRET
DOCT IV (168)	THAT A DISREGARD OF THE USUAL ARRANGEMENTS	INDICATES	REAL DEPRAVITY? /WALPOLE/ I DONT MIND HIS
FOUN (214)	(TAKING THE PAPER AND READING AT THE PLACE HE	INDICATES	) " HOW MUCH LONGER WILL THE NATION ALLOW THIS
ROCK I SD(193)	SILVER TRAY, WITH COFFEE AND MILK FOR ONE PERSON,	INDICATES	SIR ARTHUR'S UNOFFICIAL SEAT. IN THE CORNER
CAND III SD(127)	TABLE HAS BEEN CLEARED AND TIDIED: EVERYTHING	INDICATES	THAT THE DAY'S WORK IS OVER. CANDIDA AND
KING I (179)	OF THE PROPHECIES IN THE BOOK OF DANIEL. (HE	INDICATES	THE BIBLE). IT MAY PROVE OF THE GREATEST
CAND III (144)	CHAIR). BRING ME THAT CHAIR, EUGENE. (SHE	INDICATES	THE EASY CHAIR. HE FETCHES IT SILENTLY, EVEN WITH
JOAN 6 (141)	DO YOU SEE THAT MAN WHO STANDS BEHIND YOU (HE	INDICATES	THE EXECUTIONER)? /JOAN/ (TURNING AND LOOKING AT
DOCT V (171)	THE ADVANCE COPIES OF YOUR BOOK HAVE COME. (HE	INDICATES	THE NEW BOOKS). /JENNIFER/ (POUNCING ON A COPY,
ROCK I (211)	HEARD OF YOU, MR BLEE. WILL YOU SIT HERE? (HE	INDICATES	THE PRESIDENTIAL CHAIR ON THE OXFORD YOUTH'S
APPL I SD(203)	NOT NOTICED IT. FORGIVE ME: FORCE OF HABIT. HE	INDICATES	TO SEMPRONIUS THAT HE WISHES TO SIT NEAR
JITT I (24)	HERE WITH A-- WITH A (HE CANNOT SAY IT, AND	INDICATES	, BY A GESTURE, THE FIGURE OF A DEAD MAN LYING ON

INDICATING

DEST SD(157)	EYE CAN PERCEIVE A CERTAIN MORAL DEPTH,	INDICATING	A MORE PERMANENT AND MOMENTOUS GRIEVANCE. ON
SUPR HANDBOK(203)	FACT THAT THEY ARE ACCEPTED WITHOUT PROTEST AS	INDICATING	A NATURAL AND PROPER COURSE OF PUBLIC CONDUCT
CAND II (115)	WHEN SHE WAS ONY A LITTLE KIDDY NOT THAT IGH (	INDICATING	A STATURE OF TWO FEET OR THEREABOUTS). /MORELL/ (
LION I (118)	THE WAY TO MANAGE THEM, EH! THIS FINE FELLOW (	INDICATING	ANDROCLES, WHO COMES TO HIS LEFT, AND MAKES
BARB II (300)	WOT AW DAN TO ER IS NOT ON ME MAWND-- WOT SHE (	INDICATING	BARBARA) MAWT CALL ON ME CONSCIENCE-- NO MORE
FANY III (307)	YOUNG ENGLISHWOMAN IS AN EXAMPLE TO ALL EUROPE. (	INDICATING	BOBBY) YOUR INSTRUCTOR, NO DOUBT. MONSIEUR-- (HE
DEVL III (72)	WILL, SIR, AND THOSE OF YOUR ACCOMPLICES HERE (	INDICATING	BURGOYNE AND SWINDON): I SEE LITTLE DIVINITY
GENV III (71)	THERE IS ROOM FOR YOU HERE, DAME BEGONIA (	INDICATING	CHAIR ON HIS RIGHT). /BEGONIA/ (TAKING IT) THERE
CATH 4 (189)	THE DOOR. THE SOLDIERS RISE). STOP. ROLL THAT (	INDICATING	EDSTASTON) NEARER. (THE SOLDIERS OBEY). NOT SO
HART I (72)	DUNN, LADY UT-- OH, I FORGOT: YOUVE MET. (	INDICATING	ELLIE) MISS DUNN. /MAZZINI/ (WALKING ACROSS THE
PYGM III (249)	(TO MRS HILL) WHAT DO YOU KNOW OF SCIENCE? (	INDICATING	FREDDY) WHAT DOES HE KNOW OF ART OR SCIENCE OR
CLEO III (152)	(TO THE PORTERS) FOLLOW THIS LADY (	INDICATING	FTATATEETA); AND OBEY HER. THE PORTERS RISE AND
NEVR I (218)	THANK YOU; BUT WONT THIS YOUNG LADY-- (	INDICATING	GLORIA, WHO IS CLOSE TO THE CHAIR)? /GLORIA/
MTH5 (256)	OURSELVES FROM THAT TYRANNY. IT IS THIS STUFF (	INDICATING	HER BODY), THIS FLESH AND BLOOD AND BONE AND ALL
HART II (122)	UP. SHE MAKES ME WEAR THESE RIDICULOUS THINGS (	INDICATING	HIS ARAB COSTUME) BECAUSE SHE THINKS ME ABSURD IN
PYGM V (270)	ACCOSTS HIM WITH VEHEMENT REPROACH. /DOOLITTLE/ (	INDICATING	HIS OWN PERSON) SEE HERE! DO YOU SEE THIS? YOU
DOCT PREFACE(79)	HAVE INSCRIBED ON IT, IN ADDITION TO THE LETTERS	INDICATING	HIS QUALIFICATIONS, THE WORDS " REMEMBER THAT I
MIS. PREFACE(32)	WOULD BE TO SEE THAT EVERY CHILD WORE A BADGE	INDICATING	ITS CLASS IN SOCIETY, AND THAT EVERY CHILD SEEN

DEVL I	(19)	ALLOWANCE OF GOOD LOOKS. /ANDERSON/ (QUIETLY	INDICATING	JUDITH) SIR: YOU ARE IN THE PRESENCE OF MY WIFE.
LION I	(117)	CHAFF THEM. LEAVE THEM TO THE LIONS. /LENTULUS/ (	INDICATING	LAVINIA, WHO IS STILL LOOKING TOWARDS THE ARCHES
HART II	(99)	DONT UNDERSTAND HOW YOUR MARRYING THAT OBJECT (	INDICATING	MANGAN) WILL CONSOLE YOU FOR NOT BEING ABLE TO
CAPT I	(236)	YOU SEE WHAT MY MEN ARE LIKE. THAT RASCAL (	INDICATING	MARZO) WOULD CUT A THROAT FOR A DOLLAR IF HE HAD
BARB II	(296)	REALLY ARE AN INFERNAL OLD RASCAL. /UNDERSHAFT/ (	INDICATING	PETER SHIRLEY, WHO HAS JUST COME FROM THE SHELTER
CAPT II	(251)	AND JOHNSON); YOU HAVE SEEN THIS UNBELIEVER (	INDICATING	SIR HOWARD) COME IN WITH US? /OSMAN/ YEA, AND
ARMS III	(58)	SHOULD NOT TRIFLE WITH A SERVANT. /SERGIUS/ (	INDICATING	THE BRUISE WITH A MERCILESS STROKE OF HIS
ARMS II	(27)	CAN SEE IT; SO YOUD BETTER HAVE ALL THAT (	INDICATING	THE CLOTHES ON THE BUSHES) PUT SOMEWHERE ELSE.
PYGM II	(225)	PEARCE/ YOU SEE NOW WHAT COMES OF BEING SAUCY. (	INDICATING	THE DOOR) THIS WAY, PLEASE. /LIZA/ (ALMOST IN
SIM I	(37)	I MIGHT CUT ACROSS THROUGH YOUR GROUNDS. (	INDICATING	THE FIGURES) BUT I ASSURE YOU I HAD NO IDEA I WAS
ARMS II	(40)	(LOUKA STOPS). HE WILL HAVE TO GO THAT WAY (	INDICATING	THE GATE OF THE STABLEYARD). TELL NICOLA TO BRING
LION I	(119)	BE SEEN WITH YOU. /LENTULUS/ HAW! GOOD! (	INDICATING	THE KNEELING FERROVIUS). IS THIS ONE OF THE
DOCT III	(136)	ANYWHERE YOU CAN. TAKE THIS CHAIR, SIR PATRICK (	INDICATING	THE ONE ON THE THRONE). UP-Z-Z-Z! (HELPING HIM
MTH5	(221)	PRESIDING OVER THE INFANCY OF YOUR MASTER HERE (	INDICATING	THE OTHER SCULPTOR), MARTELLUS. /MARTELLUS/ (A
SIM I	(44)	ALL. (HE SITS ON LADY FARWATERS' RIGHT). /PRA/ (	INDICATING	THE PARAPET OF THE WELL) YOU HAD BETTER SIT HERE.
CLEO PRO2	(97)	THEE BLACK. (TO BELZANOR) WHAT HAS THIS MORTAL (	INDICATING	THE PERSIAN) TOLD YOU? /BELZANOR/ HE SAYS THAT
MILL III	(183)	DOWN TO HIS ACCOUNTS). /EPIFANIA/ (TO THE WOMAN,	INDICATING	THE PILE OF COATS) WHAT DO YOU DO WITH THESE WHEN
SIM PRO,3,	(32)	I HAVE NO DESIRE TO SPEAK TO YOU. /THE Y.W./ (	INDICATING	THE PRIEST) FALLEN IN LOVE WITH HIM, HAVE YOU?
APPL I	(203)	THE THRONE OFTENER THAN THAT. /BOANERGES/ (	INDICATING	THE SECRETARIES WITH A JERK OF HIS HEAD) WHAT
NEVR II	(240)	CLANDON/ MR VALENTINE: WILL YOU TAKE THAT SIDE (	INDICATING	THE SIDE NEXT THE PARAPET) WITH GLORIA? (
CLEO IV	(166)	PHILOSOPHY OF PYTHAGORAS. /CLEOPATRA/ HAS SHE (	INDICATING	THE SLAVE) BECOME PROFICIENT IN THE PHILOSOPHY OF
MILL II	(168)	CONFESS I LOOKED FORWARD TO A BETTER LUNCH THAN (	INDICATING	THE TABLE) THAT. /EPIFANIA/ OHO! SO THAT IS WHAT
BARB III	(327)	SEEN EVERYTHING? I'M SORRY I WAS CALLED AWAY. (	INDICATING	THE TELEGRAMS) GOOD NEWS FROM MANCHURIA.
BARB III	(330)	SHOULDNT HAVE! THATS ALL. TO THINK OF ALL THAT (	INDICATING	THE TOWN) BEING YOURS! AND THAT YOU HAVE KEPT IT
KING I	(185)	GOOD MONSIEUR NIEUTON: DO NOT BE SO FANCIFUL. (	INDICATING	THE WINDOW) LOOK AT IT. LOOK AT IT. IT IS MUCH
NEVR II	(241)	WILLIAM; AND ONE LARGE FOR THIS GENTLEMAN (	INDICATING	VALENTINE). LARGE APOLLINARIS FOR MR M'COMAS.
BULL II	(99)	ACQUIRED AIR OF HELPLESSNESS AND SILLINESS,	INDICATING	, NOT HIS REAL CHARACTER, BUT A CUNNING DEVELOPED

INDICATION

SIM II	(54)	THE TABLE AFTER HAVING AN ACKNOWLEDGMENT OF PRA'S	INDICATION	OF A SALAAM). ANYTHING FRESH? /SIR CHARLES/ (
LION PREFACE	(20)	RECORD OF ITS HAVING BEEN TOLD TO JESUS, NOR ANY	INDICATION	OF HIS HAVING ANY KNOWLEDGE OF IT. THE NARRATIVE,

INDICATIONS

PYGM III	(251)	SLOWLY IN AN EASTERLY DIRECTION. THERE ARE NO	INDICATIONS	OF ANY GREAT CHANGE IN THE BAROMETRICAL
PYGM EPILOG	(292)	SHORTLY TO THOSE WHO HAVE NOT GUESSED IT FROM THE	INDICATIONS	SHE HAS HERSELF GIVEN THEM. ALMOST IMMEDIATELY
PYGM PREFACE	(200)	THAT LESS EXPERT MORTALS SHOULD REQUIRE FULLER	INDICATIONS	WAS BEYOND SWEET'S PATIENCE. THEREFORE, THOUGH

INDICTABLE

POSN PREFACE	(433)	IT WILL, I PRESUME, BECOME A CONSPIRACY, AND BE	INDICTABLE	ACCORDINGLY; UNLESS, INDEED, IT CAN PERSUADE THE
CYMB FORWORD	(137)	SOLD OR EXHIBITED AS THE ORIGINAL. THE FRAUD IS	INDICTABLE	. BUT WHEN IT COMES TO COMPLETE FORGERY, AS IN
DOCT V	(177)	AM A DOCTOR: I HAVE NOTHING TO FEAR. IT IS NOT AN	INDICTABLE	OFFENCE TO CALL IN B.B. PERHAPS IT OUGHT TO BE;
MRS PREFACE	(155)	IT, ITS PERFORMANCE MIGHT WELL BE MADE AN	INDICTABLE	OFFENCE. NOW LET US CONSIDER HOW SUCH RECRUITING

INDICTED

DOCT PREFACE	(9)	THEMSELVES IN AN AWKWARD POSITION IF THEY WERE	INDICTED	FOR ALLOWING A CUSTOMER TO DIE, OR FOR BURNING A
POSN PREFACE	(423)	AND TO PERFORM THE PLAY UNTIL HIS ACCUSERS HAD	INDICTED	HIM AT LAW, AND OBTAINED THE VERDICT OF A JURY
LION PREFACE	(8)	AND THE HEAD MASTER OF ETON. IF JESUS HAD BEEN	INDICTED	IN A MODERN COURT, HE WOULD HAVE BEEN EXAMINED BY
GETT PREFACE	(216)	BE OBTAINED; FOR WHEN THE WHOLE COMMUNITY IS	INDICTED	, NOBODY WILL GO INTO THE WITNESS-BOX FOR THE

INDICTMENT

METH PREFACE	(R13)	IF NOT IN THE DOCK PLEADING TO A POMPOUSLY WORDED	INDICTMENT	FOR SEDITION AGAINST THE EXPLOITERS. OUR SCHOOLS
DOCT PREFACE	(63)	DOCTOR'S HARDSHIPS. A REVIEW OF THE COUNTS IN THE	INDICTMENT	I HAVE BROUGHT AGAINST PRIVATE MEDICAL PRACTICE
SUPR HANDBOK	(207)	AFFECTION. LET IT BE REPEATED THEREFORE THAT NO	INDICTMENT	IS HERE LAID AGAINST THE WORLD ON THE SCORE OF
BULL PREFACE	(46)	MAN, THERE WOULD BE ABSOLUTELY NO DEFENCE TO THIS	INDICTMENT	. BUT THE MILITARY SYSTEM IS SO IDIOTICALLY
JOAN PREFACE	(29)	COWARDS CAPABLE OF PLEADING TO AN INTELLIGIBLE	INDICTMENT	. THE POINT NEED BE NO FURTHER LABORED. JOAN WAS
MRS PREFACE	(154)	LEARNT THAT MRS WARREN'S DEFENCE OF HERSELF AND	INDICTMENT	OF SOCIETY IS THE THING THAT MOST NEEDS SAYING,
JOAN 6	(127)	LORD: WE HAVE BEEN AT GREAT PAINS TO DRAW UP AN	INDICTMENT	OF THE MAID ON SIXTYFOUR COUNTS. WE ARE NOW TOLD
PYGM III	(251)	(STARTLED) DEAR ME! /LIZA/ (PILING UP THE	INDICTMENT	) WHAT CALL WOULD A WOMAN WITH THAT STRENGTH IN
SUPR III	(129)	REALITIES. YOU WOULD HAVE TO PLEAD GUILTY TO MY	INDICTMENT	; BUT FORTUNATELY FOR YOUR SELF-RESPECT, MY
BARB PREFACE	(235)	AS EVERY MAN'S LIBERTY IS AT THE MERCY OF A MORAL	INDICTMENT	WHICH ANY FOOL CAN TRUMP UP AGAINST EVERYONE WHO
SUPR IV	(163)	AND A COQUETTE AND SO FORTH IS A TRUMPED-UP MORAL	INDICTMENT	WHICH MIGHT BE BROUGHT AGAINST ANYBODY. WE ALL
ROCK PREFACE	(158)	TO THE BAR. HE WAS GUILTY ON EVERY COUNT OF THE	INDICTMENT	, AND ON MANY MORE THAT HIS ACCUSERS HAD NOT THE

INDICTMENTS

HART PREFACE	(12)	SOLDIERS WERE ACQUITTED, EVEN ON FULLY PROVED	INDICTMENTS	FOR WILFUL MURDER, UNTIL AT LAST THE JUDGES AND

INDIES

CAPT I	(221)	OF MINE. YEARS AGO. HE WENT OUT TO THE WEST	INDIES	. /DRINKWATER/ THE WUST HINDIES! JIST ACROST THERE,
CAPT I	(229)	THIRTY YEARS AGO NOW THAT HE DIED IN THE WEST	INDIES	ON HIS PROPERTY THERE. /RANKIN/ (SURPRISED) HIS
CAPT I	(230)	IT. IN THE COURSE OF A HOLIDAY TRIP TO THE WEST	INDIES	, I FOUND THAT THIS DISHONEST AGENT HAD LEFT THE

INDIFFERENCE

GETT PREFACE	(245)	INTO PEOPLE'S MINDS, AND THEIR SELF-RIGHTEOUS	INDIFFERENCE	AND INTOLERANCE SOON CHANGE INTO LIVELY CONCERN
HART PREFACE	(8)	HALF CENTURY. IT IS DIFFICULT TO SAY WHETHER	INDIFFERENCE	AND NEGLECT ARE WORSE THAN FALSE DOCTRINE; BUT
DEST	(176)	(MEETING HIS ANGRY SEARCHING GAZE WITH TRANQUIL	INDIFFERENCE	AS SHE SITS LOOKING UP AT HIM) A VAIN, SILLY,
SUPR II SD	(63)	WOULD LET HER ALONE, ACCEPTING BOREDOM AND	INDIFFERENCE	AS THEIR COMMON LOT; AND THE POOR LADY WANTS TO
LION I	(118)	I SUPPOSE SHE THINKS I CARE. (WITH AN AIR OF	INDIFFERENCE	HE STROLLS WITH METELLUS TO THE EAST SIDE OF
WIDO III	(64)	CORNERS OF HIS MOUTH: WITH A HEAVY ASSUMPTION OF	INDIFFERENCE	HE WALKS STRAIGHT BACK TO HIS CHAIR, AND PLANTS
PYGM EPILOG	(302)	SLIPPERS"; YET SHE HAS A SENSE, TOO, THAT HIS	INDIFFERENCE	IS DEEPER THAN THE INFATUATION OF COMMONER
MIS. PREFACE	(92)	IN NATURE, AND, AT ITS AVERAGE, AN OBJECT OF	INDIFFERENCE	. IF EVERY RAG OF CLOTHING MIRACULOUSLY DROPPED
NEVR II SD	(246)	SHE DESCENDS THE STEPS WITH COLD DISGUSTED	INDIFFERENCE	. THEY ALL LOOK AFTER HER, AND SO DO NOT NOTICE
LION PREFACE	(17)	WHO ARE CONVINCED, AND WHO ARE HORRIFIED AT THE	INDIFFERENCE	OF THE IRRELIGIOUS TO THE APPROACHING DOOM, AND
MRS PREFACE	(169)	THE MORE POWERFULLY HE INSISTS ON THE RUTHLESS	INDIFFERENCE	OF THEIR GREAT DRAMATIC ANTAGONIST, THE
MRS PREFACE	(170)	PRODUCT, NOT OF INDIVIDUAL HARPAGONS, BUT OF THE	INDIFFERENCE	OF VIRTUOUS YOUNG GENTLEMEN TO THE CONDITION OF
LIED	(200)	MRS BOMPAS ARE RELATIONS OF PERFECT COLDNESS-- OF	INDIFFERENCE	-- /HER HUSBAND/ (SCORNFULLY) SAY IT AGAIN:
GENV I	(42)	WHAT TO DO OR WHERE TO GO HERE. I AM MET WITH	INDIFFERENCE	-- WITH APATHY-- WHEN I REVEAL A STATE OF
CAPT I	(237)	WEST COAST. /DRINKWATER/ (AFFECTING AN IRONIC	INDIFFERENCE	) GOW ORN, GOW ORN. SR AHRD EZ ERD WITNESSES TO
BULL II	(113)	DEAL ABOUT YOU FROM LARRY. /NORA/ (WITH BITTER	INDIFFERENCE	) HAVE YOU NOW? WELL, THATS A GREAT HONOR, I'M
WIDO II	(24)	FOR YOU-- FROM TRENCH. /BLANCHE/ (WITH AFFECTED	INDIFFERENCE	) INDEED? /SARTORIUS/ " INDEED? "! IS THAT
NEVR I	(214)	SHE ADDS, OVER HER SHOULDER, WITH STUDIED	INDIFFERENCE	) ON BOARD THE STEAMER, THE FIRST OFFICER DID
MRS II	(209)	RATHER ROUGHLY). /MRS WARREN/ (GALLED BY VIVIE'S	INDIFFERENCE	) WHAT DO YOU KNOW OF MEN, CHILD, TO TALK THAT
NEVR I	(224)	READY TO HIS HAND, CHATTING ON WITH PROVOKING	INDIFFERENCE	), AND SO YOU ADVISE ME NOT TO GET MARRIED, MR
WIDO I	(18)	DOWN THE PENCIL AND LEANS BACK WITH OSTENTATIOUS	INDIFFERENCE	), OF COURSE IT IS NO BUSINESS OF MINE: I ONLY
MIS.	(134)	AND LOLLS AGAINST IT WITH AN AIR OF GOOD-HUMORED	INDIFFERENCE	). /TARLETON/ WELL, WHO DENIES IT? YOURE QUITE
LIED	(201)	YOU, IT SEEMS. YOU REGARD HER WITH COLDNESS, WITH	INDIFFERENCE	; AND YOU HAVE THE COOL CHEEK TO TELL ME SO TO
GETT PREFACE	(246)	SUFFERING FROM THOSE THEY DISLIKE OR REGARD WITH	INDIFFERENCE	; THAT HEALTHY MARRIAGES ARE PARTNERSHIPS OF
MIS. PREFACE	(15)	ARE LEFT OUT OF ACCOUNT, CHILDREN CAN STAND WITH	INDIFFERENCE	SIGHTS, SOUNDS, SMELLS, AND DISORDERS THAT
DEST	(168)	IS FEAR. IT IS FEAR THAT MAKES MEN FIGHT: IT IS	INDIFFERENCE	THAT MAKES THEM RUN AWAY: FEAR IS THE
PHIL I SD	(84)	AND RECREATIVE EMOTION, AND ITS DISILLUSIONED	INDIFFERENCE	TO ADVENTURE AND ENJOYMENT, EXCEPT AS A MEANS
CLEO II SD	(121)	ON IT. RUFIO, WITH ROMAN RESOURCEFULNESS AND	INDIFFERENCE	TO FOREIGN SUPERSTITIONS, PROMPTLY SEIZES THE
DOCT PREFACE	(44)	OF VIVISECTION WHICH SOON PRODUCES COMPLETE	INDIFFERENCE	TO IT ON THE PART EVEN OF THOSE WHO ARE
BULL PREFACE	(9)	ENGLAND THAN FOR IRELAND, IN SPITE OF ENGLAND'S	INDIFFERENCE	TO IT. IN IRELAND WE ARE STILL SANE: WE DO NOT
MTH4 II	(178)	I HAVE THE VIRTUES OF A LABORER: INDUSTRY AND	INDIFFERENCE	TO PERSONAL COMFORT. BUT I MUST RULE, BECAUSE I
POSN PREFACE	(399)	OBJECTIONS TO THE TENDENCY OF THE PLAY. THIS	INDIFFERENCE	TO THE LARGER ISSUES OF A THEATRICAL
LION PREFACE	(99)	BY EXTERMINATING THE NATIVES, HAS BEEN DUE TO OUR	INDIFFERENCE	TO THE SALVATION OF OUR SUBJECTS. IRELAND IS
MRS PREFACE	(170)	THE REPUTABLE DAUGHTER WHO CANNOT ENDURE HER. HER	INDIFFERENCE	TO THE ULTIMATE SOCIAL CONSEQUENCES OF HER
GENV IV SD	(115)	VERY SIGNIFICANTLY WITH HIS CONTEMPTUOUS	INDIFFERENCE	TO THE TWO LEADERS. SIR ORPHEUS, AS BEFORE,

PYGM EPILOG (289)	SOME REASON IN IT. WHEN HIGGINS EXCUSED HIS	INDIFFERENCE	TO YOUNG WOMEN ON THE GROUND THAT THEY HAD AN
MRS IV (249)	(MRS WARREN WINCES, DEEPLY HURT BY THE IMPLIED	INDIFFERENCE	TOWARDS HER AFFECTIONATE INTENTION. VIVIE,
MIS. PREFACE(81)	PARENT, AND THEREFORE EXPRESSES THEM ALL WITH AN	INDIFFERENCE	WHICH HAS GIVEN RISE TO THE TERM ENFANT
METH PREFACE(R75)	SENSE FOUNDED ON HIS OBSERVATION OF THIS. BUT	INDIFFERENCE	WILL NOT GUIDE NATIONS THROUGH CIVILIZATION TO
DOCT PREFACE(44)	BUT INTO RESEARCH WORK, THEY CARRY THIS ACQUIRED	INDIFFERENCE	WITH THEM INTO THE LABORATORY, WHERE ANY
NEVR II (255)	MERITS. (SHE TURNS AWAY FROM HIM WITH INFINITE	INDIFFERENCE	, AND SITS DOWN WITH HER BOOK ON THE GARDEN
PHIL II (122)	TO SAY. /CHARTERIS/ (SUDDENLY AFFECTING COMPLETE	INDIFFERENCE	, AND RISING CARELESSLY) I DONT KNOW THAT I WAS
NEVR III (272)	DOLLY AND PHIL. (SHE SITS DOWN WITH SLIGHTING	INDIFFERENCE	, AT THE END OF THE TABLE NEAREST THE WINDOW).
CAPT III SD(290)	HIMSELF SAVAGELY. REDBROOK, TRAINED TO AFFECT	INDIFFERENCE	, GRINS CYNICALLY; WINKS AT BRASSBOUND; AND
NEVR II (238)	HIS POLITE ATTENTION, AND DOLLY'S UNCONCERNED	INDIFFERENCE	, LEAVE CRAMPTON ON THE FOOTING OF A CASUAL
GETT PREFACE(232)	RELATION IS NO LONGER REALLY VALUED; AND THIS	INDIFFERENCE	, LIKE THE TRIPLE BOND OF AFFECTION WHICH
BULL I SD(73)	BUT THIS IS THE EFFECT OF BACHELOR UNTIDINESS AND	INDIFFERENCE	, NOT WANT OF MEANS; FOR NOTHING THAT DOYLE AND

INDIFFERENT

ROCK II (277)	OUT FROM AMONG THE THOUSAND LADIES TO WHOM HE IS	INDIFFERENT	? TO USE YOUR OWN EXPRESSION, DOES HE COME ALL
SIM PREFACE(15)	THAT I, AT ALL EVENTS, WILL GO TO HELL. AS TO THE	INDIFFERENT	AND THE SCEPTICAL, I MAY DO THEM THE MISCHIEF
PYGM IV SD(262)	OUT). ELIZA TRIES TO CONTROL HERSELF AND FEEL	INDIFFERENT	AS SHE RISES AND WALKS ACROSS TO THE HEARTH TO
BULL I SD(73)	UP PATIENTLY WITH A GREAT DEAL OF TROUBLE AND	INDIFFERENT	HEALTH, THE LUGGAGE BELONGS TO BROADBENT, WHO
CLEO IV SD(193)	GOOD AND PATIENT. HE GOES, PREOCCUPIED AND QUITE	INDIFFERENT	. SHE STANDS WITH CLENCHED FISTS, IN SPEECHLESS
METH PREFACE(R75)	A CONTRADICTION IN TERMS; AND A STATESMAN WHO IS	INDIFFERENT	ON PRINCIPLE, A LAISSER-FAIRE OR MUDDLE-THROUGH
PYGM EPILOG (298)	ACQUAINTANCES TO WHOM SHE HAD BEEN A TEDIOUS OR	INDIFFERENT	OR RIDICULOUS AFFLICTION, DROPPED HER: OTHERS
POSN PREFACE(418)	EXCEPT IN A BROADLY CULTIVATED AND TOLERANT (OR	INDIFFERENT	) MODERN CITY. THE LIGHTER PLAYS WOULD BE NO
HART II (96)	YOU KNOW WHAT HAPPENED TO ME. /ELLIE/ (UTTERLY	INDIFFERENT	) OH, I DARESAY I CAN WAKE HIM. IF NOT, SOMEBODY
BARB II (287)	AND STRETCHES HIS LEGS IN AN ATTEMPT TO SEEM	INDIFFERENT	). /BARBARA/ WELL, IF YOURE HAPPY, WHY DONT YOU
METH PREFACE(R75)	THE ESTABLISHMENT OF THE PERFECT CITY OF GOD. AN	INDIFFERENT	STATESMAN IS A CONTRADICTION IN TERMS; AND A
CAND II (107)	THE WEATHER. /MARCHBANKS/ WOULD YOU TALK ABOUT	INDIFFERENT	THINGS IF A CHILD WERE BY, CRYING BITTERLY WITH
CAND II (107)	SUPPOSE NOT. /MARCHBANKS/ WELL: I CANT TALK ABOUT	INDIFFERENT	THINGS WITH MY HEART CRYING OUT BITTERLY IN ITS
CAND II (107)	ABOUT? /PROSERPINE/ (SNUBBING HIM) TALK ABOUT	INDIFFERENT	THINGS. TALK ABOUT THE WEATHER. /MARCHBANKS/
DOCT PREFACE(41)	OVERCOME THEIR NATURAL REPUGNANCE AND BECOME	INDIFFERENT	TO ANYTHING THEY DO OFTEN ENOUGH. IT IS THIS
MRS PREFACE(178)	THERE. THESE ARE THE PEOPLE WHO, INDULGENT OR	INDIFFERENT	TO APHRODISIAC PLAYS, RAISE THE MORAL HUE AND
MIS. PREFACE(91)	SUPPOSE THAT UNCULTIVATED PEOPLE ARE MERELY	INDIFFERENT	TO HIGH AND NOBLE QUALITIES. THEY HATE THEM
GETT (341)	FOR MONEY INSTEAD OF BEING SELFISHLY AND LAZILY	INDIFFERENT	TO IT. FOR HER SAKE YOU WOULD COME TO CARE IN
PHIL II (102)	THEM. YOU CANNOT HAVE CHANGED SO MUCH AS TO BE	INDIFFERENT	TO ME! WHOEVER MAY HAVE STRUCK YOUR FANCY FOR
MRS IV (239)	USE, PRADDY. VIV IS A LITTLE PHILISTINE. SHE IS	INDIFFERENT	TO MY ROMANCE, AND INSENSIBLE TO MY BEAUTY.
MRS PREFACE(177)	ATTACKED BY PERSONS AND PAPERS NOTORIOUSLY	INDIFFERENT	TO PUBLIC MORALS ON ALL OTHER OCCASIONS. THE
METH PREFACE(R75)	AND TEACHERS HYPOCRITES AND LIARS. HE BECOMES	INDIFFERENT	TO RELIGION IF HE HAS LITTLE CONSCIENCE, AND
METH PREFACE(R61)	THAT THE TYPE OF CHARACTER WHICH REMAINS	INDIFFERENT	TO THE WELFARE OF ITS NEIGHBORS AS LONG AS ITS
BARB I SD(249)	WELL MANNERED AND YET APPALLINGLY OUTSPOKEN AND	INDIFFERENT	TO THE OPINION OF HER INTERLOCUTORS, AMIABLE AND
BULL PREFACE(25)	CONVENIENT AND SOCIALLY ELIGIBLE) BECAUSE HE IS	INDIFFERENT	TO THE FORM OF PROTESTANTISM, PROVIDED IT IS
DOCT PREFACE(21)	BEFORE 1860, WHO WERE USUALLY CONTEMPTUOUS OF OR	INDIFFERENT	TO THE GERM THEORY AND BACTERIOLOGICAL
DEVL I (6)	WORK ITS RIGHT NAME. (CHRISTY, SOULLESSLY	INDIFFERENT	TO THE STRIFE OF GOOD AND EVIL, STARES AT THE
BARB II (296)	REVOLUTION. /CUSINS/ -- UNSELFISH-- /UNDERSHAFT/	INDIFFERENT	TO THEIR OWN INTERESTS, WHICH SUITS ME EXACTLY.
NEVR II (250)	TOO CURIOUS ABOUT HIM TO BE COLD, BUT SUPREMELY	INDIFFERENT	TO THEIR KINSHIP. HE GREETS HER WITH A GROWL).
DEVL II (32)	FELLOW CREATURES IS NOT TO HATE THEM, BUT TO BE	INDIFFERENT	TO THEM; THATS THE ESSENCE OF INHUMANITY. AFTER
GETT PREFACE(224)	WE DO WE FALL IN LOVE WITH ONE PERSON, AND REMAIN	INDIFFERENT	TO THOUSANDS OF OTHERS WHO PASS BEFORE OUR EYES
MIS. (153)	AND ASK QUESTIONS; BUT THEN IT'S INHUMAN TO BE	INDIFFERENT	, AS IF YOU DIDNT CARE. /LINA/ I'LL TELL YOU
SUPR II SD(62)	CULTURE HE FINDS ENGLISH PEOPLE EITHER TOTALLY	INDIFFERENT	, AS THEY VERY COMMONLY ARE TO ALL CULTURE, OR
2TRU I SD(28)	DEEPEST CONCERN FOR THE INVALID, THE DOCTOR IS	INDIFFERENT	, BUT KEEPS UP HIS BEDSIDE MANNER CAREFULLY,
ARMS I (18)	(SHE SHAKES HIM IN HER IMPATIENCE). I AM NOT	INDIFFERENT	, DEAR YOUNG LADY, I ASSURE YOU. BUT HOW IS IT
LION I SD(110)	TIRED AND DUSTY; BUT THE SOLDIERS ARE DOGGED AND	INDIFFERENT	, THE CHRISTIANS LIGHTHEARTED AND DETERMINED TO
METH PREFACE(R75)	LESS BY THE SAINTS THAN BY THE VAST MASS OF THE	INDIFFERENT	, WHO NEITHER ACT NOR REACT IN THE MATTER.
ARMS I (18)	MOONLIGHT. I'LL SAVE YOU. OH, HOW CAN YOU BE SO	INDIFFERENT	! YOU WANT ME TO SAVE YOU, DONT YOU? /THE MAN/

INDIFFERENTLY

MIS. PREFACE(43)	ADULTS AND ADULTS. WE SHALL NOT ALWAYS LOOK ON	INDIFFERENTLY	AT FOOLISH MARRIAGES AND FINANCIAL
ARMS II (34)	RELEASE EACH OTHER). I CANT PRETEND TO TALK	INDIFFERENTLY	BEFORE HER: MY HEART IS TOO FULL. (LOUKA
LION II SD(137)	GLADIATORS GO BACK TO THEIR FORMER PLACES	INDIFFERENTLY	. THE CALL BOY SHRUGS HIS SHOULDERS AND SQUATS
NEVR II (254)	THAT HE IS ALONE WITH GLORIA. SHE CONTINUES	INDIFFERENTLY	) I THOUGHT HE WAS ILL; BUT HE RECOVERED
LION PREFACE(22)	HE PREACHES IN THE SYNAGOGUES AND IN THE OPEN AIR	INDIFFERENTLY	, JUST AS THEY COME. HE REPEATEDLY SAYS, " I

INDIGENCE

GETT PREFACE(222)	MOTHER'S SQUEAMISHNESS BY LIFELONG CELIBACY AND	INDIGENCE	. TO ASK A YOUNG MAN HIS INTENTIONS WHEN YOU KNOW

INDIGENOUS

2TRU II SD(58)	HER KNEES AND HER UMBRELLA, AND TRYING TO LOOK AS	INDIGENOUS	AS POSSIBLE. /TALLBOYS/ THANK YOU. (HE SITS
CAPT III SD(279)	AND CLIMATICALLY IN THE DIRECTION OF THE	INDIGENOUS	NORTH AMERICAN, WHO IS ALREADY IN POSSESSION OF

INDIGENT

HART II (99)	OLD MAID LIVING ON A PITTANCE FROM THE SICK AND	INDIGENT	ROOMKEEPERS' ASSOCIATION. BUT MY HEART IS BROKEN,

INDIGESTION

SIM PRO,2, (27)	Y.W./ WELL, SO YOU DO. YOU SMELL OF DRINK AND	INDIGESTION	AND SWEATY CLOTHES. YOU WERE QUITE DISGUSTING
METH PREFACE(R82)	AND MENDELSSOHN, STAINER AND PARRY, WHICH SPREAD	INDIGESTION	AT OUR MUSICAL FESTIVALS UNTIL I PUBLICLY TOLD
PPP (203)	INFORM YOU THAT MY FRIEND HAD AN ACUTE ATTACK OF	INDIGESTION	. NO CARBONATE OF SODA BEING AVAILABLE, HE

INDIGNANT

SUPR IV SD(143)	AND UNLUCKY SPECIES, BUT OCCASIONALLY WITH	INDIGNANT	ALARM WHEN THE OLD GENTLEMAN SHEWS SIGNS OF
PYGM V (269)	YOU OFFERED A REWARD? /MRS HIGGINS/ (RISING IN	INDIGNANT	AMAZEMENT) YOU DONT MEAN TO SAY YOU HAVE SET THE
CAND I SD(98)	ABACK, BUT NOT DISCONCERTED; AND HE SOON BECOMES	INDIGNANT	AND CONTEMPTUOUS. /MORELL/ (SITTING DOWN TO HAVE
BULL III (122)	NATURAL AND INEVITABLE RESULTS, GET VIRTUOUSLY	INDIGNANT	AND KILL THE PEOPLE THAT CARRY OUT YOUR LAWS.
FANY II (293)	AS THEY HAD TREATED THE STUDENTS. DUVALLET GOT	INDIGNANT	AND REMONSTRATED WITH A POLICEMAN, WHO WAS SHOVING
NEVR III (267)	HAS NO LONGER ANYTHING TO FEAR). /MRS CLANDON/ (	INDIGNANT	AT HIS ASSURANCE) WHAT DO YOU MEAN? /VALENTINE/ (
JOAN 2 (80)	LISTENS), THE DUKE OF -- (THE CHATTER CONTINUES.	INDIGNANT	AT HIS FAILURE TO COMMAND A HEARING, HE SNATCHES
DEST (162)	OH, LIEUTENANT! /LADY/ (AFFRIGHTED, BUT HIGHLY	INDIGNANT	AT HIS HAVING DARED TO TOUCH HER) GENTLEMEN: I
BULL PREFACE(28)	OF PRIESTS. DO NOT BE DISTRACTED BY THE SHRIEK OF	INDIGNANT	DENIAL FROM THE CATHOLIC PAPERS AND FROM THOSE WHO
CAPT II (247)	FROZEN OUT OF HIS FACE EXCEPT ONE OF EXTREME AND	INDIGNANT	DUMBFOUNDEDNESS). WILL YOU ASK YOUR STRONG FRIEND
JOAN 6 (145)	CHARITY. YOU PROMISED ME MY LIFE; BUT YOU LIED (	INDIGNANT	EXCLAMATIONS). YOU THINK THAT LIFE IS NOTHING BUT
SUPR PREFACE(R13)	THE POLICE, TEMPORAL AND SPIRITUAL; AND WHEN AN	INDIGNANT	FATHER SEEKS PRIVATE REDRESS WITH THE SWORD, DON
MRS PREFACE(160)	BE IGNOMINIOUSLY EXPELLED FROM THE PALACE BY HIS	INDIGNANT	FATHER-IN-LAW. TO HIS HORROR, WHEN HE PROCEEDS TO
CAPT II (254)	LOOK AT HIM. YOU WOULD NOT TAKE THIS VIRTUOUSLY	INDIGNANT	GENTLEMAN FOR THE UNCLE OF A BRIGAND, WOULD YOU..
MTH4 III (197)	ELDERLY GENTLEMAN/ THERE! EVEN THE ORACLE IS	INDIGNANT	. (TO THE ENVOY) DO NOT ALLOW YOURSELF TO BE PUT
LION EPILOG (152)	THE LION LOOSE ON THE MAN, YOU WOULD BE JUSTLY	INDIGNANT	. NOW THAT WE MAY NO LONGER SEE A MAN HANGED, WE
CLEO II SD(125)	FIERCER AND DOGGEDER, AND BRITANNUS HAUGHTILY	INDIGNANT	. /RUFIO/ (CONTEMPTUOUSLY) EGYPT FOR THE
MTH4 I SD(166)	STRICTLY TO HEEL. THE ELDERLY GENTLEMAN RETURNS,	INDIGNANT	. /ZOO/ HERE HE IS YOU CAN RELEASE THE PIER
PHIL I SD(84)	FACTS OF LIFE THAT HE HAS ACQUIRED AN HABITUALLY	INDIGNANT	MANNER, WHICH UNEXPECTEDLY BECOMES ENTHUSIASTIC OR
MILL PREFACE(120)	IN THEIR HELPLESS IGNORANCE OF BUSINESS. AS ONE	INDIGNANT	MASTER-FASCIST SAID TO ME " THEY WERE LISTENING TO
SUPR I SD(10)	A FOOLSCAP DOCUMENT WHICH HE THRUSTS UNDER THE	INDIGNANT	NOSE OF RAMSDEN AS HE EXCLAIMS /TANNER/ RAMSDEN:
ARMS III (51)	WAYS BY ALL SORTS OF PEOPLE. /RAINA/ (RISING IN	INDIGNANT	PROTEST) AND SO HE BECOMES A CREATURE INCAPABLE OF
NEVR I (215)	DO YOU THINK? (GLORIA UTTERS AN EXCLAMATION OF	INDIGNANT	REPULSION). THAT WOULD HAVE BEEN YOUR LAST
SUPR II (67)	PAY UP AT THE SAME TIME. /VIOLET/ (ALARMED AND	INDIGNANT	) DO YOU MEAN TO WORK? DO YOU WANT TO SPOIL OUR
OVER (186)	HIS MISCONDUCT WITH MY WIFE. /GREGORY/ (DEEPLY	INDIGNANT	) HOW DARE YOU, SIR, ASPERSE THE CHARACTER OF THAT
BARB III (350)	HORN) PIP! PIP! /LADY BRITOMART/ (HIGHLY	INDIGNANT	) HOW DARE YOU SAY PIP! PIP! TO ME, SARAH? YOU
AUGS (276)	YOUR POST. OF COURSE. /AUGUSTUS/ (AMAZED AND	INDIGNANT	) I LOSE MY POST! WHAT ARE YOU DREAMING ABOUT,
MTH5 (217)	THEIR HANDS AND SHOUT FOR JOY. /THE NEWLY BORN/ (	INDIGNANT	) I MAY LIVE! SUPPOSE THERE HAD BEEN ANYTHING
CATH 1 (165)	AT FIRST SIGHT, EH? /EDSTASTON/ (SHOCKED AND	INDIGNANT	) I THINK NOTHING OF THE SORT; AND I'LL TROUBLE
AUGS (273)	MADAM. /THE LADY/ (SURPRISED AND RATHER	INDIGNANT	) IS IT? WHO TOLD YOU? WAS IT ONE OF YOUR GERMAN

HART I (46)	HE BECAME RICH. ARE YOU HIS DAUGHTER? /ELLIE/ (	INDIGNANT	) NO: CERTAINLY NOT. I AM PROUD TO BE ABLE TO SAY
JITT III (54)	I KNOW HE THOUGHT SO HIMSELF. /FESSLER/ (	INDIGNANT	) OH NO: HE WAS THE MOST MODEST OF MEN. I AM SURE
CAND III (136)	/MORELL/ (CONTEMPTUOUSLY) NO. /MARCHBANKS/ (	INDIGNANT	) OH! /MORELL/ (TO EUGENE) YOU BEGAN IT: THIS
JOAN 6 (137)	WHAT IT MAY BE. /THE ASSESSORS/ (SHOCKED AND	INDIGNANT	) OH! THE CHURCH CONTRARY TO GOD! WHAT DO YOU
INCA (247)	SUDDENLY) WOMAN: DO NOT BE A FOOL. /ERMYNTRUDE/ (	INDIGNANT	) WELL! /THE INCA/ YOU MUST LOOK FACTS IN THE
JITT II (36)	ABACK) EDITH, DEAR-- /EDITH/ (DOWNRIGHT AND	INDIGNANT	) WHY DO YOU TREAT ME AS IF I WERE A LITTLE GIRL,
CATH 2 (179)	LADY TO CONFIRM ME. /VARINKA/ (PRETENDING TO BE	INDIGNANT	) YES: YOU PROTESTED. BUT, ALL THE SAME, YOU WERE
FANY III (322)	I HAVE TWO DAUGHTERS. /KNOX/ (RISING, VIRTUOUSLY	INDIGNANT	) YOU SIT THERE AFTER CARRYING ON WITH MY
GETT (291)	THAT MAN HIS CHANCE. /THE GENERAL/ (GENEROUSLY	INDIGNANT	) YOUR COMMANDING OFFICER, SIR, WAS MY FRIEND
FANY PROLOG (263)	TOO MUCH FUSS ABOUT ART (THE COUNT IS EXTREMELY	INDIGNANT	). BUT THATS ONLY HIS MODESTY, BECAUSE ART IS HIS
MRS IV (244)	AT ONE ANOTHER, FRANK UNRUFFLED, PRAED DEEPLY	INDIGNANT	). LET ME TELL YOU, GARDNER, THAT IF YOU DESERT
DOCT PREFACE(59)	KARL PEARSON'S IMMENSE CONTEMPT FOR, AND	INDIGNANT	SENSE OF GRAVE SOCIAL DANGER IN, THE UNSKILLED
GENV IV (123)	A FINGER ON HER WE SHOULD-- PARDON ME IF IN MY	INDIGNANT	SURPRISE AT YOUR BREACH OF THE PEACE I AM UNABLE
BULL IV (150)	VOICE, " THATS IT! INDEPENDENCE! "), THAT	INDIGNANT	SYMPATHY WITH THE CAUSE OF OPPRESSED NATIONALITIES
DEVL I (19)	SHE LOOKS SHOCKED, AND SITS DOWN AMID A MURMUR OF	INDIGNANT	SYMPATHY FROM HIS RELATIVES. ANDERSON, SENSIBLE
POSN PREFACE(416)	SUCH ABUSES, AND DENY, WITH PERFECT SINCERITY AND	INDIGNANT	VEHEMENCE, THAT THEY EXIST EXCEPT, PERHAPS, IN
MRS PREFACE(165)	LESS THAN ARDENT YOUNG ENTHUSIASTS, ARE EQUALLY	INDIGNANT	WITH ME. THEY REVILE ME AS LACKING IN PASSION, IN
CAPT II (258)	TORN. /LADY CICELY/ YOU SHOULD NOT GET VIRTUOUSLY	INDIGNANT	WITH PEOPLE. IT BURSTS CLOTHES MORE THAN ANYTHING
ARMS III SD(70)	/CATHERINE/ (HAUGHTILY) RAINA! RAINA, EQUALLY	INDIGNANT	, ALMOST SNORTS AT THE LIBERTY. /LOUKA/ I HAVE A
MRS IV (242)	TO THE TRUTH. /PRAED/ (RISING, STARTLED AND	INDIGNANT	, AND PRESERVING HIS POLITENESS WITH AN EFFORT) I
DOCT PREFACE(47)	PATIENTS ARE EXPERIMENTED ON WERE AS LOUD, AS	INDIGNANT	, AS HIGH-MINDED AS EVER, IN SPITE OF THE FEW
DOCT I (107)	UGLY OLD DEVIL, AND NO MISTAKE. /EMMY/ (HIGHLY	INDIGNANT	, CALLING AFTER HIM) YOURE NO BEAUTY YOURSELF. (
CAND III (142)	RAISES HIS HAND TO SILENCE HER). DONT TRY TO LOOK	INDIGNANT	, CANDIDA-- /CANDIDA/ TRY! /MORELL/ (CONTINUING)
SUPR IV SD(143)	BUSINESS IS THAT OF YOURS? STRAKER, NOW HIGHLY	INDIGNANT	, COMES BACK FROM THE STEPS AND CONFRONTS THE
SUPR HANDBOK(207)	BY CROWDS OF RESPECTABLE, CHARITABLE, VIRTUOUSLY	INDIGNANT	, HIGH-MINDED CITIZENS, WHO, THOUGH THEY ACT
BARB II (290)	LOOKING AFTER HIM) I WONDER! /BARBARA/ DOLLY! (	INDIGNANT	, IN HER MOTHER'S MANNER). /CUSINS/ YES, MY DEAR,
2TRU PREFACE(19)	THE CHURCH LOST IT UNTIL THE EMPIRE, VIRTUOUSLY	INDIGNANT	, TOOK IT ON ITSELF TO REFORM THE CHURCH, ALL THE
		INDIGNANTLY	
CAND II (105)	ALL THE SAME, ARNT THEY? /PROSERPINE/ (SOMEWHAT	INDIGNANTLY	: ANY SUCH DISCUSSION, EXCEPT BY WAY OF
ARMS I SD(10)	DOMINATED AT LAST BY THE VOICE OF CATHERINE,	INDIGNANTLY	ADDRESSING AN OFFICER WITH WHAT DOES THIS MEAN,
POSN PREFACE(415)	MR GEORGE ALEXANDER PROTESTED VIGOROUSLY AND	INDIGNANTLY	AGAINST MY ADMISSION THAT THEATRES, LIKE
NEVR II (245)	THATS WHAT YOU MEAN, EH? /VALENTINE/ (RISING	INDIGNANTLY	AND ADDRESSING GLORIA) MISS CLANDON: I--
DOCT III (142)	MORE THIS WAY, SIR PATRICK. (SIR PATRICK TURNS	INDIGNANTLY	AND GLARES AT HIM). OH, THATS TOO MUCH. /SIR
JITT II (45)	SHE WAS. YOU KNOW ALL ABOUT IT. /JITTA/ (RISING	INDIGNANTLY	AND LETTING HERSELF GO) YOU ARE MAD, AND GROSSLY
POSN PREFACE(383)	HE HAS OPPOSED THE NEXT STEP IN HUMAN PROGRESS AS	INDIGNANTLY	AS IF NEITHER MANNERS, CUSTOMS, NOR THOUGHT HAD
ARMS III (70)	INSTEAD OF RAINA. (SHE IS ABOUT TO BREAK OUT	INDIGNANTLY	AT HIM: HE STOPS HER BY EXCLAIMING TESTILY) DONT
NEVR III (271)	THERE IS BETWEEN THE TWO. (GLORIA TURNS	INDIGNANTLY	AWAY FROM HIM. HE CONTINUES, TO MRS CLANDON) I
POSN (451)	WITH YOUR WITNESS THERE, WILL YOU? /BLANCO/ (	INDIGNANTLY	BRINGING DOWN HIS FIST ON THE BAR) SWEAR THE
METH PREFACE(R34)	DECLARING THAT BRADLAUGH HAD REPEATEDLY AND	INDIGNANTLY	CONTRADICTED IT, AND IMPLYING THAT THE ATHEIST
APPL I (226)	REPUTATIONS THAT THEY LOSE NO OPPORTUNITY OF	INDIGNANTLY	DENYING THAT THEY HAVE EVER YIELDED TO
MTH3 (92)	REPLACED BY THE BLANK SCREEN)-- /BURGE-LUBIN/ (	INDIGNANTLY	HOLDING DOWN HIS BUTTON) DONT CUT US OFF,
METH PREFACE(R75)	TO RELIGION IF HE HAS LITTLE CONSCIENCE, AND	INDIGNANTLY	HOSTILE TO IT IF HE HAS A GOOD DEAL. THE SAME
APPL PREFACE(178)	NOT TAKE THAT AS A PERSONAL INSULT AND ASK ME	INDIGNANTLY	IF I CONSIDER YOU INFERIOR TO A FISH. WELL, YOU
PRES (157)	/MITCHENER/ CERTAINLY I AM IN EARNEST, MOST	INDIGNANTLY	IN EARNEST. /LADY CORINTHIA/ (THROWING DOWN THE
HART III (131)	FROM AN OPEN WINDOW ABOVE. SHE RAISES HERSELF	INDIGNANTLY	IN THE HAMMOCK). RANDALL: YOU HAVE NOT GONE TO
CURE (232)	AT HER HANDS) NO, YOU SHANT. (SHE RISES	INDIGNANTLY	. HE HOLDS ON TO HER HANDS, BUT EXCLAIMS
DEVL II SD(33)	MY FATHER'S ESTATE? JUDITH THROWS DOWN THE SPOON	INDIGNANTLY	. /ANDERSON/ (QUITE UNRUFFLED, AND HELPING
APPL II SD(272)	UPROAR. PROTEUS FLINGS HIMSELF INTO HIS CHAIR	INDIGNANTLY	. /BALBUS/ SHAME! /NICOBAR/ SHUT UP, YOU B --
NEVR IV SD(296)	BUT WHAT ABOUT DOROTHEE-EE-A? M'COMAS RISES	INDIGNANTLY	. /CRAMPTON/ (ANXIOUSLY, RISING TO RESTRAIN
NEVR IV SD(292)	(FURIOUS, RISING) CHILDISH! MRS CLANDON RISES	INDIGNANTLY	. /M'COMAS/ CRAMPTON, YOU PROMISED-- /VALENTINE/
GENV IV SD(121)	THE BRITISH CONTINGENT, EXCEPT THE NEWCOMER, RISE	INDIGNANTLY	. /NEWCOMER/ HEAR HEAR! HEAR HEAR! HEAR HEAR!
FOUN SD(210)	CRIES HOLD! ENOUGH! THE LORD CHANCELLOR ENTERS	INDIGNANTLY	. /THE LORD CHANCELLOR/ WHATS THIS? WHO IS THIS
MTH5 SD(205)	HE WAKES UP AND STARES ABOUT HIM. THE COUPLE STOP	INDIGNANTLY	. THE REST STOP. THE MUSIC STOPS. THE YOUTH WHOM
DOCT PREFACE(4)	THE MEDICAL PROFESSION. AGAIN I HEAR THE VOICES	INDIGNANTLY	MUTTERING OLD PHRASES ABOUT THE HIGH CHARACTER
DOCT III (152)	SHALL TAKE MR DUBEDAT'S. /MRS DUBEDAT/ TURNING	INDIGNANTLY	ON HIM) I SEE WHAT IT IS. OH! IT IS ENVIOUS,
3PLA PREFACE(R16)	OF MAKING THE THEATRE A TEMPLE OF PLEASURE,	INDIGNANTLY	REFUSE TO CHANGE THE THEATRICAL PROFESSION FOR
NEVR I (213)	WE HAVE A RIGHT TO KNOW, MOTHER. /MRS CLANDON/ (	INDIGNANTLY	) AH! YOU INSIST. /GLORIA/ DO YOU INTEND THAT
PRES (137)	(RELIEVED) OH: IS THAT ALL? /MITCHENER/ (MOST	INDIGNANTLY	) ALL! A CIVILIAN SHOOTS DOWN ONE OF HIS
BULL IV (158)	HIS APPLICATION TO BROADBENT). /AUNT JUDY/ (	INDIGNANTLY	) AS IF HE HADNT SEEN ENOUGH O BORRYIN WHEN HE
DEVL I (18)	USUAL, LOOKING AFTER THE LADIES! /UNCLE TITUS/ (	INDIGNANTLY	) BE ASHAMED OF YOURSELF, SIR-- /RICHARD/ (
SUPR I (27)	HAD NO RIGHT TO COME TO YOUR HOUSE. /RAMSDEN/ (	INDIGNANTLY	) BUT I AM ONLY TOO ANXIOUS TO HELP HER. (
LION II (133)	IS NOTHING IN THE RULES AGAINST IT. /SECUTOR/ (	INDIGNANTLY	) CAESAR: IS IT A DIRTY TRICK OR IS IT NOT?
WIDO II (48)	HIS GROUND RIGIDLY). /TRENCH/ (TURNING AWAY	INDIGNANTLY	) COME ON, COKANE. /COKANE/ CERTAINLY, HARRY,
ANNA (298)	YOUR OWN SAKE, COMRADE -- /THE GRAND DUCHESS/ (	INDIGNANTLY	) COMRADE! YOU! ! ! GO. (SHE FIRES TWO MORE
CAPT I (237)	TO BE CALLED BRANDYFACED JACK. /DRINKWATER/ (	INDIGNANTLY	) EAH, AW SY! NAH LOOK EAH, KEPN: MAW NIME IS
SUPR III (76)	(STUBBORNLY) NO MORE AINT WE. /MENDOZA/ (	INDIGNANTLY	) HAVE I TAKEN MORE THAN MY SHARE? /THE SULKY
JITT II (43)	PRETENDED TO THINK MUCH OF THE BOOK. /JITTA/ (	INDIGNANTLY	) HE THOUGHT THE WORLD OF IT. IT WAS HIS
CATH 4 (189)	OF TORTURE. WILL THEY BE NEEDED? /CATHERINE/ (	INDIGNANTLY	) HOW DARE YOU NAME SUCH ABOMINATIONS TO A
FOUN (218)	A WORKHOUSE DOORSTEP! /ANASTASIA/ (RISING MOST	INDIGNANTLY	) HOW DARE YOU PRESUME TO SAY SUCH A THING? A
PHIL III (142)	AGO. HOW ARE YOU GOING TO TAKE IT? /JULIA/ (	INDIGNANTLY	) HOW IS HE GOING TO TAKE IT, INDEED! REALLY,
DOCT III (145)	YOU GIVE ME TO LET YOU DO IT? /WALPOLE/ (RISING	INDIGNANTLY	) HOW MUCH! WHAT DO YOU MEAN? /LOUIS/ WELL,
CATH 4 (192)	CAPTAIN EDSTASTON: YOU ARE A BOOBY. /EDSTASTON/ (	INDIGNANTLY	) I AM NOTHING OF THE KIND. I HAVE BEEN
DEST (191)	NOT AFRAID TO BE MEAN AND SELFISH. /NAPOLEON/ (	INDIGNANTLY	) I AM NEITHER MEAN NOR SELFISH. /LADY/ OH, YOU
ARMS III (53)	WHEN DID YOU SEND IT TO ME? /RAINA/ (	INDIGNANTLY	) I DID NOT SEND IT TO YOU. (SHE TURNS HER HEAD
AUGS (263)	TO THE DOGS, IF YOU ASK ME. /AUGUSTUS/ (RISING	INDIGNANTLY	) I DO NOT ASK YOU, SIR; AND I WILL NOT ALLOW
CAND I (84)	ANY FEELING AGAINST MRS MORELL. /PROSERPINE/ (	INDIGNANTLY	) I HAVE NO FEELING AGAINST HER. SHE'S VERY
ARMS I (18)	PETKOFF. /THE MAN/ A PET WHAT? /RAINA/ (RATHER	INDIGNANTLY	) I MEAN THAT I BELONG TO THE FAMILY OF THE
ARMS I (14)	IGNORANCE OF THE ART OF WAR, NOTHING ELSE. (	INDIGNANTLY	) I NEVER SAW ANYTHING SO UNPROFESSIONAL.
PYGM II (231)	MUST NOT SWEAR BEFORE THE GIRL. /HIGGINS/ (	INDIGNANTLY	) I SWEAR! (MOST EMPHATICALLY) I NEVER SWEAR.
APPL I (204)	NOT AT ALL, I ASSURE YOU -- /BOANERGES/ (	INDIGNANTLY	) I WAS NOT ALLUDING TO MY PERSONAL APPEARANCE.
CAPT I (233)	ON THEM, YOU WOULD FIND THEM QUITE NICE TO YOU. (	INDIGNANTLY	) I WONT HAVE THIS POOR MAN TRAMPLED ON MERELY
ARMS III (49)	TAKEN OFF THEIR BACKS. /SERGIUS/ (STIFFENING	INDIGNANTLY	) I'LL SAY SO. (HE STRIDES TO THE DOOR). AND IF
HART II (126)	(WHICH IS QUITE TRUE). /RANDALL/ (WAKING UP	INDIGNANTLY	) I'M NOT. YOU ARE MOST CRUEL, ARIADNE. (
FANY III (303)	YOU WERE THAT SORT OF GIRL. /MARGARET/ (RISING	INDIGNANTLY	) I'M NOT. YOU MUSTNT PRETEND TO THINK THAT I'M
JOAN 5 (119)	COUNSELS ALWAYS WRONG? /THE ARCHBISHOP/ (	INDIGNANTLY	) IT IS WASTE OF TIME ADMONISHING YOU. /CHARLES/
JOAN 2 (73)	AM NOT INTERESTED IN THE NEWEST TOYS. /CHARLES/ (	INDIGNANTLY	) IT ISNT A TOY. (SULKILY) HOWEVER, I CAN GET
SUPR III (83)	/STRAKER/ (SCRAMBLING UP ON HIS KNEES MOST	INDIGNANTLY	) LOOK HERE: LOUISA STRAKER IS MY SISTER, SEE..
NEVR IV (299)	IN COMPARISON WITH YOURS. /MRS CLANDON/ (MOST	INDIGNANTLY	) MR VALENTINE! /VALENTINE/ WELL, WHAT AM I TO
DOCT III (146)	CLEAR YOUR MIND OF CANT, WALPOLE. /WALPOLE/ (	INDIGNANTLY	) MY MIND IS PERFECTLY CLEAR OF CANT. /B.B./
CAPT III (291)	STUDS. I KNOW WHATS IN YOUR MIND. /DRINKWATER/ (	INDIGNANTLY	) NAOW YER DOWNT: NORT A BIT ON IT. WOTS IN MAW
LIED (196)	NAME OF BOMPAS OCCUR IN ANY OF THE POEMS? /HE/ (	INDIGNANTLY	) NO. /SHE/ YOURE QUITE SURE? /HE/ OF COURSE I
BULL IV (168)	BY SPEAKING TO THEM BEFORE-- HAVE YOU? /NORA/ (	INDIGNANTLY	) NOT LIKELY, INDEED. /BROADBENT/ WELL, WE MUSNT
SUPR I (19)	DONE ANYTHING OF THE SORT, HAVE YOU? /RAMSDEN/ (	INDIGNANTLY	) NO, SIR. /MRS WHITEFIELD/ (PLACIDLY) WELL,
CAPT I (231)	NOT EXACTLY THAT, SIR HOWRRD. /LADY CICELY/ (	INDIGNANTLY	) OF COURSE NOT. YOU ALWAYS THINK, HOWARD, THAT
MRS II (217)	OR EVEN GO INTO THE FACTORY? /MRS WARREN/ (	INDIGNANTLY	) OF COURSE NOT. WHAT SORT OF MOTHER DO YOU TAKE
SUPR II (56)	POSITIVELY PREFERS HER MOTHER TO ANN. SHE-- (	INDIGNANTLY	) OH, I SAY! /OCTAVIUS/ WHATS THE MATTER?
MTH5 (224)	AND, IT SEEMS, EMPTY-HEADED? /ECRASIA/ (	INDIGNANTLY	) OH, SHAME! YOU DARE DISPARAGE MARTELLUS,
MTH5 (209)	AND THINK ABOUT NUMBERS. /THE YOUTH/ (RISING	INDIGNANTLY	) OH, THIS IS TOO MUCH. I HAVE SUSPECTED YOU FOR
SUPR III (88)	NOW BUT TO MAKE THE BEST OF IT. /THE OLD WOMAN/ (	INDIGNANTLY	) OH! AND I MIGHT HAVE BEEN SO MUCH WICKEDER!
ARMS I (5)	ALL OUR IDEAS WERE REAL AFTER ALL. /CATHERINE/ (	INDIGNANTLY	) OUR IDEAS REAL! WHAT DO YOU MEAN? /RAINA/
BULL III (141)	BE TIKEN IN BY MY AOWL MEN, PEDDY. /MATTHEW/ (	INDIGNANTLY	) PADDY YOURSELF! HOW DAR YOU CALL ME PADDY?
MTH5 (226)	YOU KNOW HIM QUITE WELL. PYGMALION. /ECRASIA/ (	INDIGNANTLY	) PYGMALION! THAT SOULLESS CREATURE! A
MRS I (192)	NOT YOUR DAUGHTER, IS SHE? /PRAED/ (RISING	INDIGNANTLY	) REALLY, CROFTS--! /CROFTS/ NO OFFENCE, PRAED.
DEVL III (64)	WE WAIT. GIVE THE LADY A NEWSPAPER. /RICHARD/ (	INDIGNANTLY	) SHAME! /BURGOYNE/ (KEENLY, WITH A HALF
PHIL II (100)	YOU THAT SHE WANTS TO MARRY ME? /CUTHBERTSON/ (	INDIGNANTLY	) SHE HAS MENTIONED THAT YOU WANT TO MARRY HER.
PHIL II (95)	QUITE WELL, I HOPE? /SYLVIA/ (TURNING HER HEAD	INDIGNANTLY	) SH-- SH-- SH! PARAMORE TURNS, SURPRISED.

BULL IV (148)	TO BLAZES. (NORA OFFENDED, RISES). /KEEGAN/ (	INDIGNANTLY	) SIR! /DORAN/ (QUICKLY) SAVIN YOUR PRESENCE,
ARMS III (62)	FAVORS I NEVER ENJOYED. /BLUNTSCHLI/ (JUMPING UP	INDIGNANTLY	) STUFF! RUBBISH! I HAVE RECEIVED NO FAVORS.
CAND III (138)	AND BARELY ESCAPES WITHOUT DISASTER). /BURGESS/ (	INDIGNANTLY	) STUFF INDEED! THAT GURL DUNNO WHAT CHAMPAGNE
SUPR I (20)	MY VIEWS ARE TOO ADVANCED FOR HIM. /RAMSDEN/ (	INDIGNANTLY	) THEY ARE NOT. I DENY IT. /ANN/ OF COURSE NOT.
DEVL II (36)	TRUTH, YOU WILL USE IT TO TORMENT ME. /RICHARD/ (	INDIGNANTLY	) TORMENT! WHAT RIGHT HAVE YOU TO SAY THAT? DO
DEST (176)	YOU ARE ALL THE SAME, YOU WOMEN. /LADY/ (	INDIGNANTLY	) WE ARE NOT ALL THE SAME, ANY MORE THAN YOU
DOCT III (148)	THAT. (HE ALSO RETRIEVES HIS HAT). /LOUIS/ (	INDIGNANTLY	) WELL, OF ALL THE MEAN-- (WORDS FAIL HIM)!
FANY III (315)	NEVER SAID A HARSH WORD TO YOU. /GILBEY/ (RISING	INDIGNANTLY	) WHAT RIGHT HAVE YOU TO TREAT A MAN LIKE THAT?
MTH5 (235)	WAY SHE HAS BEEN GOING ON! /THE NEWLY BORN/ (	INDIGNANTLY	) WHAT DO YOU MEAN? HOW HAVE I BEEN GOING ON..
MTH2 (43)	SHE HASNT READ A WORD OF IT. /CONRAD/ (RISING	INDIGNANTLY	) WHAT! /FRANKLYN/ (INEXORABLY) NOT A WORD OF
HART III (137)	NOT ESCAPE IF I CHOSE TO TAKE YOU. /MANGAN/ (	INDIGNANTLY	) WHAT! DO YOU MEAN TO SAY YOU ARE GOING TO
PHIL III (145)	DONT BE ALARMED. IT'S ALL OFF. /SYLVIA/ (RISING	INDIGNANTLY	) WHAT! YOUVE CHUCKED GRACE TOO! WHAT A
DOCT V (171)	BRUSH AND CRAYON AND IN THE EASEL? /JENNIFER/ (	INDIGNANTLY	) YES: MOST DISGRACEFUL. THEY WRITE QUITE
CLEO IV (170)	I AM QUEEN OF EGYPT, AND NOT YOU? /FTATATEETA/ (	INDIGNANTLY	). YOU ARE LIKE THE REST OF THEM. YOU WANT TO BE
PHIL I (78)	ME IF I HAD NEVER MET YOU! /CHARTERIS/ (RISING	INDIGNANTLY	) YOU UNGENEROUS WRETCH! IS THIS YOUR GRATITUDE
CAPT I (224)	HAS SIXTEEN SHOTS IN THE MAGAZINE. /DRINKWATER/ (	INDIGNANTLY	) YUSS; AND THE PEOPLE THAT SELLS SICH THINGS
JOAN 6 (134)	OF MY DUTY BY THIS WOMAN. (HE SITS DOWN	INDIGNANTLY	). /CAUCHON/ I HAVE WARNED YOU BEFORE, JOAN,
WIDO III (63)	SHORTLY) I DONT KNOW THAT I AM. (SARTORIUS RISES	INDIGNANTLY	). /LICKCHEESE/ EASY ONE MOMENT, MR SARTORIUS. (
DEST (165)	HE SNATCHES THE HANDKERCHIEF RUDELY). GENERAL! (	INDIGNANTLY	). /NAPOLEON/ (TAKING THE OTHER HANDKERCHIEF
SIM PRO,3, (32)	DARE YOU? REALLY! REALLY! ! (SHE GOES OUT	INDIGNANTLY	). /THE PRIESTESS/ ANOTHER CONQUEST, PRA? /THE
MTH4 I (142)	INTELLIGIBLY-- /THE ELDERLY GENTLEMAN/ (SNORTS	INDIGNANTLY	)! /THE WOMAN/ (CONTINUING)-- AND WHY YOU ARE
BULL II (105)	STORIES AND SUPERSTITION. /BROADBENT/ (SOMEWHAT	INDIGNANTLY	; FOR TO BE REBUKED BY AN IRISH PRIEST FOR
LADY (244)	WANTONING WITH A BASEBORN SERVANT. /SHAKESPEAR/ (	INDIGNANTLY	SCRAMBLING TO HIS FEET) BASEBORN! I, A
BARB II (278)	ER, AW YER? PUT AP YOUR ENDS. /RUMMY/ (RUNNING	INDIGNANTLY	TO HIM TO SCOLD HIM) OH, YOU GREAT BRUTE-- (HE
SUPR III SD(95)	I HAVE NOT SEEN HIM SINCE ANA ARRIVED. ANA COMES	INDIGNANTLY	TO LIGHT. /ANA/ WHAT DOES THIS MEAN? OTTAVIO
HART II (110)	WHY HAVE YOU IMPOSED ON ME? /THE BURGLAR/ (	INDIGNANTLY	TO MAZZINI) HAVE YOU BEEN GIVING YOURSELF OUT TO
KING I (174)	YOU TO MEET YOUR WOMEN IN. /MRS BASHAM/ (COMING	INDIGNANTLY	TO THE MIDDLE OF THE ROOM) OH! MR NEWTON:
GETT (314)	TO. THEN I CALL IT SIMPLE IMMORALITY. (SHE GOES	INDIGNANTLY	TO THE OAK CHEST, AND PERCHES HERSELF ON IT
DEST (177)	MUCH GOOD MAY THEY DO YOU. GOODBYE. (SHE GOES	INDIGNANTLY	TOWARDS THE INNER DOOR). /NAPOLEON/ MY OWN--!
WIDO I (12)	IF YOU HADNT HELPED ME OUT WITH IT. /BLANCHE/ (	INDIGNANTLY	TRYING TO BREAK LOOSE FROM HIM) I DIDNT HELP YOU
PLES PREFACE(R9)	DRAMATIST AS ENEMIES TO BE PIOUSLY GLORIFIED OR	INDIGNANTLY	VILIFIED. IN SUCH CHEAP WARES I DO NOT DEAL.
DEST (170)	YOU HAVE NEVER TRIED IT, GENERAL. /NAPOLEON/ (	INDIGNANTLY	, FORGETTING ALL ABOUT BRUTUS AND SCIPIO) WHAT
CAND III (135)	INDEED I WONT. I'LL LET HIM ALONE. /MORELL/ (	INDIGNANTLY	, WITH AN AGGRESSIVE MOVEMENT TOWARDS EUGENE)
DOCT PREFACE(48)	HE HAD ANY OTHER CRIMES TO CONFESS, REPLIED	INDIGNANTLY	" WHAT DO YOU TAKE ME FOR? " REMINDS US VERY

INDIGNATION

METH PREFACE(R24)	WORLD AS A SEPARATE INDIVIDUAL IS TO YELL WITH	INDIGNATION	: THAT YELL WHICH SHAKESPEAR THOUGHT THE MOST
BARB PREFACE(246)	AND GUILT, REWARD AND PUNISHMENT, VIRTUOUS	INDIGNATION	AND PARDON, INSTEAD OF STANDING UP TO THE FACTS
JOAN PREFACE(24)	IT IS THE FASHION TO DISMISS THIS WITH VIRTUOUS	INDIGNATION	AS AN OBSCENE LIBEL; AND I CERTAINLY CANNOT
3PLA PREFACE(R35)	AND PATRIOTIZED, THAT CONCEIVES VIRTUOUS	INDIGNATION	AS SPIRITUALLY NUTRITIOUS, THAT MURDERS THE
POSN PREFACE(368)	PRESENT OPERATION OF THE CENSORSHIP, AND THEIR	INDIGNATION	AT BEING HANDED OVER TO A DOMESTIC OFFICIAL AS
JOAN EPILOG (163)	/THE GENTLEMAN/ (EMPHATICALLY, TO MARK HIS	INDIGNATION	AT THE INTERRUPTION) -- BY THE BISHOP OF ORLEANS
DOCT PREFACE(38)	HUMAN ANIMAL, YET WE WERE ALL IN HYSTERICS OF	INDIGNATION	AT THE CRUELTIES OF THE VIVISECTORS. THESE, IF
DOCT PREFACE(51)	IN SYMPATHETIC READERS A TRANSPORT OF VIRTUOUS	INDIGNATION	AT THE EXPENSE OF THE MEDICAL PROFESSION. I
BULL PREFACE(63)	GOVERNMENT (STILL SIMMERING WITH VIRTUOUS	INDIGNATION	AT THE FLOGGING OF CHINAMEN AND THE MILITARY
GENV III (68)	TO SHUT ME OUT OF THE WORLD; BUT YOU BURN WITH	INDIGNATION	BECAUSE YOU YOURSELF HAVE BEEN SHUT OUT OF YOUR
ROCK II SD(246)	QUITE TRANSFIGURED, IS JUBILANT. ALOYSIA GLOWS	INDIGNATION	. BLEE AND THE MAYOR, DOGGEDLY WEARING THEIR
CAPT II SD(257)	WALKS UP AND DOWN THE ROOM, NURSING HIS	INDIGNATION	. IN DOING SO HE UNCONSCIOUSLY ENTERS UPON AN
MRS III SD(231)	IS TO BE SYMPATHETIC. HE TAKES REFUGE IN GENEROUS	INDIGNATION	. /CROFTS/ SHE OUGHT TO HAVE HAD MORE
DEVL III SD(71)	HIS POCKET. THEN HE RAISES HIS VOICE IN VIRTUOUS	INDIGNATION	. /THE SERGEANT/ ME TAKE MONEY IN THE EXECUTION
ROCK II (252)	LIBERALS CANT UNDERSTAND ANYTHING BUT VIRTUOUS	INDIGNATION	. /THE MAYOR/ WHO ARE YOU CALLING A LIBERAL? I
6CAL SD(105)	WELL SAID, LASS. HE NUDGES HER, TO HER EXTREME	INDIGNATION	. /THE KING/ HEAR THAT, DEAREST: HE CALLS THEE
METH PREFACE(R44)	AS IT SEEMED, WAS RECEIVED WITH HORROR AND	INDIGNATION	. THE TIDE HAS NOW TURNED; AND EVERY PUNY
APPL PREFACE(195)	TO SHEW UNMISTAKEABLE SIGNS OF DISAPPOINTMENT AND	INDIGNATION	. " YOU DO NOT SEEM TO UNDERSTAND ME," HE SAID.
BULL PREFACE(47)	THEM-- " NATIVES," AND THEIR HONEST AND GENEROUS	INDIGNATION	KNOWS NO BOUNDS; THEY FEEL ABOUT THEM LIKE MEN,
SIM PREFACE(11)	CORPUS ACT, AND THE LIKE, TO HAVE ANY VIRTUOUS	INDIGNATION	LEFT TO SPARE FOR THE BLUNDERS AND EXCESSES INTO
DOCT III (135)	REFUSE? /RIDGEON/ DO I MEAN--! (LETTING HIS	INDIGNATION	LOOSE) OF COURSE I REFUSE, MAN. WHAT DO YOU TAKE
BULL PREFACE(58)	CLIENTS, WHOSE CONDUCT HAD " CAUSED THE UNANIMOUS	INDIGNATION	OF ALL EGYPTIANS." " CLEMENCY," THEY SAID, " WAS
MIS. PREFACE(17)	AND WHITEWASHED. THE VERY PEOPLE WHO READ WITH	INDIGNATION	OF SQUEERS AND CREAKLE IN THE NOVELS OF DICKENS
BULL PREFACE(50)	EVERYBODY IN CHINA KNEW, AND THAT THE PRETENDED	INDIGNATION	OF THE FARMERS WAS A CLOAK FOR HATRED OF THE
MIS. (177)	GUNNER, AND SPEAKING WITH DEEP BUT CONTAINED	INDIGNATION	) AM I TO UNDERSTAND YOU AS DARING TO PUT
DEVL II (46)	NOT SPARE YOU. /ANDERSON/ (RISING IN GENEROUS	INDIGNATION	) AND YOU THINK THAT I WILL LET A MAN WITH THAT
NEVR II (234)	M'COMAS) IS IT YOU, SIR? /M'COMAS/ (RENERVED BY	INDIGNATION	) CERTAINLY NOT. MY CHILDREN KNOW HOW TO BEHAVE
GENV II (50)	THEM AT ANY MOMENT. /BEGONIA/ (FLUSHING WITH	INDIGNATION	) DO YOU MEAN THAT THEYVE BROKEN UP OUR DEAR
CAND II (110)	OLD FATHEAD! /BURGESS/ (RISING, BREATHLESS WITH	INDIGNATION	) HO! I'M A SILLY OLE FAT'EAD, AM I? HO,
MTH4 I (141)	YOU ARE ILL. /THE ELDERLY GENTLEMAN/ (NERVED BY	INDIGNATION	) I AM NOT ILL. I HAVE NEVER HAD A DAY'S ILLNESS
CAPT I (220)	ON MAW KERRICKTER, AW DID. /RANKIN/ (WITH SOME	INDIGNATION	) I HOPE YOU DONT THINK I MET SIR HOWRRD IN THAT
ARMS III (65)	HAD STRUCK HIM, AND SPEAKING WITH QUIET BUT DEEP	INDIGNATION	) I WILL PROVE THAT THAT, AT LEAST, IS A
MTH4 I (146)	FOR YOU. /THE ELDERLY GENTLEMAN/ (NERVED BY	INDIGNATION	) MAY I ASK WHY? I AM A VICE-PRESIDENT OF THE
JOAN 6 (142)	(WHO HAS BEEN LISTENING WITH GROWING ALARM AND	INDIGNATION	) MY LORD: DO YOU MEAN THAT YOU ARE GOING TO
MTH4 I (152)	DADDY. /THE ELDERLY GENTLEMAN/ (STIMULATED BY	INDIGNATION	) MY NAME, I REPEAT, IS JOSEPH POPHAM BOLGE
SUPR I (45)	OUR REAL REGARD FOR YOU. /VIOLET/ (FLUSHING WITH	INDIGNATION	) OH! YOU THINK ME A WICKED WOMAN, LIKE THE
DEVL I (8)	SNEERS. ANDERSON BREAKS OFF TO DEMAND WITH SOME	INDIGNATION	) WELL, WASNT IT ONLY NATURAL, MRS DUDGEON? HE
MTH3 (123)	ARCHBISHOP/ (WHO HAS CAUGHT THE INFECTION OF HER	INDIGNATION	) WHAT HIGHER EMPLOYMENTS ARE YOU CAPABLE OF?
BULL III (122)	TO AMERICA FOR IT. /BROADBENT/ (GLOWING WITH	INDIGNATION	) WHO CAN BLAME HIM, MISS DOYLE? WHO CAN BLAME
CAPT II (245)	IS SCANDALIZED; AND THERE IS A GENERAL THRILL OF	INDIGNATION	). BETTER EV NAOW FEMBLY, AN RAWSE AHT OF IT,
NEVR III (266)	MOUTH TO PROTEST: SHE CUTS HIM SHORT WITH SOME	INDIGNATION	). OH, DO YOU THINK, LITTLE AS I UNDERSTAND
CAPT III (286)	YOU: IT'S NOT EVIDENCE. (SIR HOWARD CHOKES WITH	INDIGNATION	). /KEARNEY/ (CALMLY) ALLOW THE LADY TO
SUPR IV (151)	AWAY TOWARDS THE GATE, HIS ELBOWS QUIVERING WITH	INDIGNATION	). /TANNER/ ANOTHER MADMAN! THESE MEN IN LOVE
BULL II (114)	LOSES HIS HEAD AND SEIZES HER ARMS, TO HER GREAT	INDIGNATION	). STOP LAUGHING: DO YOU HEAR? I AM IN EARNEST:
LION PREFACE(26)	WAS IRRITATED BEYOND MEASURE, AND REFUSED WITH AN	INDIGNATION	WHICH THEY, NOT SEEING ROUSSEAU'S POINT, MUST
BULL PREFACE(59)	BUSINESS, YET NOT SO PITIABLE AS THE VIRTUOUS	INDIGNATION	WITH WHICH JUDGE LYNCH, HIMSELF PROVABLE BY HIS
ROCK II SD(264)	BEHIND HIM, IN WHICH THE INDIAN IS CHOKING WITH	INDIGNATION	, AND FOR THE MOMENT INARTICULATE. /SIR BEMROSE/
OVER PREFACE(156)	WITHOUT RAISING AN ALARM WITH THE NOISIEST	INDIGNATION	, ARE CLEARLY EXAMPLES OF THE FACT THAT MOST
PHIL I (88)	MONSTROUS; BUT IT'S TRUE. /CRAVEN/ (WITH RISING	INDIGNATION	, AS HE BEGINS TO DRAW THE INEVITABLE
BARB PREFACE(226)	THE WORK OF MEN WHO HAD OBSERVED THAT VIRTUOUS	INDIGNATION	, CAUSTIC CRITICISM, CONCLUSIVE ARGUMENT AND
SUPR IV SD(149)	GATE, AND ADMITS HECTOR, WHO, SNORTING WITH	INDIGNATION	, COMES UPON THE LAWN, AND IS MAKING FOR HIS
GETT PREFACE(218)	SURPRISE AND HIS WIFE'S EQUALLY IRRATIONAL	INDIGNATION	, THAT HIS WIFE IS A STRANGER TO HIM, AND THE
CAND III (131)	YOU THINK THAT WOULD HAVE SAVED US! VIRTUOUS	INDIGNATION	: OH, YOU ARE NOT WORTHY TO LIVE IN THE SAME
SUPR III (126)	AND THEN, HEAVENS! WHAT TRANSPORTS OF VIRTUOUS	INDIGNATION	: WHAT OVERWHELMING DEFIANCE TO THE DASTARDLY

INDIGNITIES

GETT PREFACE(258)	HETERODOXY, CONTAGIOUS DISEASE, OUTRAGES,	INDIGNITIES	, PERSONAL ABUSE, " MENTAL ANGUISH," CONDUCT
GETT PREFACE(241)	NOT BE FORGOTTEN THAT THE REFUSAL TO ACCEPT THE	INDIGNITIES	, RISKS, HARDSHIPS, SOFTSHIPS, AND DIVIDED

INDIGNITY

GETT PREFACE(190)	WHOSE OBJECTION TO MARRIAGE IS THE INTOLERABLE	INDIGNITY	OF BEING SUPPOSED TO DESIRE OR LIVE THE MARRIED
GETT (333)	MRS COLLINS, IF I CANT GET A THING WITHOUT THE	INDIGNITY	OF FIGHTING FOR IT, I DO WITHOUT IT. /MRS GEORGE/

INDIRECT

GETT PREFACE(252)	NURSE, AND OF ALL THE OTHER VICTIMS, DIRECT AND	INDIRECT	, ARISES WITH ITS INVARIABLE REFRAIN: " WHY DID

INDIRECTLY

POSN PREFACE(364)	MEMBERS HAVE DISCOVERED A METHOD OF DOING THIS	INDIRECTLY	. AND SO ON, AND SO FORTH. THE THING IS TO BE

INDISCIPLINE

JOAN PREFACE(35)	JESUITS WITH PRIESTLY APATHY AND IGNORANCE AND	INDISCIPLINE	. THE MOST BIGOTED ULSTER ORANGEMAN OR

2TRU PREFACE(20) OCCASIONALLY-- RIOTERS. THE RESULTANT DISORDER, INDISCIPLINE , AND BREAKDOWN OF DISTRIBUTION, PRODUCED A

INDISCREET

POSN PREFACE(431) PREVENT EVEN ITS PERFORMANCE IN IRELAND BY SOME INDISCREET CASTLE OFFICIALS IN THE ABSENCE OF THE LORD
NEVR I (220) MY SISTER MEANS: WELL, MR CRAMPTON; BUT SHE IS INDISCREET . NOW DOLLY: OUTSIDE! (HE TAKES HER TOWARDS THE
MTH3 (118) LUTESTRING! YOU SPEAK AS IF I WERE A NOTORIOUSLY INDISCREET PERSON. BARNABAS! HAVE I SUCH A REPUTATION?
JITT III (57) CLOSER TO HER) DEAR LADY! MAY I ASK YOU A VERY INDISCREET QUESTION? I SHALL NOT BE IN THE LEAST OFFENDED
SUPR II (64) I SHALL RESPECT THE LADY'S WISHES. WOULD IT BE INDISCREET TO ASK WHO HER HUSBAND IS, IN CASE I SHOULD HAVE

INDISCRETION

SUPR PREFACE(R16) ARE WRECKED AND PUBLIC CAREERS UNDONE BY A SINGLE INDISCRETION . A MAN HAD BETTER HAVE ALL THE STATUES IN
DEST (175) ASSUMPTION OF SUPERIORITY) YOU HAVE COMMITTED AN INDISCRETION . I PARDON YOU. IN FUTURE, DO NOT PERMIT
GETT PREFACE(221) TO WHICH HE CAN BE LEGALLY HELD, OR ELSE INTO AN INDISCRETION WHICH HE MUST REPAIR BY MARRIAGE ON PAIN OF

INDISCRETIONS

NEVR I (203) THE RESULT OF LONG PRACTICE IN CHECKING DOLLY'S INDISCRETIONS). THE FACT IS, MR VALENTINE, WE ARE THE

INDISCRIMINATE

SUPR III (134) OF THE PURSUIT OF THE SUPERHUMAN: IT LEADS TO AN INDISCRIMINATE CONTEMPT FOR THE HUMAN. TO A MAN, HORSES AND
FABL PREFACE(93) BUT SECURE VICTORY IN EXAMINATIONS FOR THE INDISCRIMINATE ENCYCLOPEDIC MEMORY, WHICH IS THE MOST
3PLA PREFACE(R34) AND INCAPACITY FOR HIS WORKS THAT PRODUCED THE INDISCRIMINATE EULOGIES WITH WHICH WE ARE FAMILIAR. IT WAS
POSN PREFACE(407) MANNERS. IT IS, HOWEVER, QUITE ARGUABLE THAT THE INDISCRIMINATE ISSUE OF FREE ADMISSIONS, THOUGH AN
POSN PREFACE(406) OF ITS DISGUISE IS STRIPPED BY THE VIRTUALLY INDISCRIMINATE ISSUE OF FREE TICKETS TO THE MEN. ACCESS TO
GENV IV (116) DEVASTATION OF YOUR OWN COUNTRY AND AN INDISCRIMINATE MASSACRE OF ITS INHABITANTS. /FLANCO/ THAT IS
MIS. PREFACE(91) HAS REVEALED TO THEM AND NURSED IN THEM, WE GET INDISCRIMINATE RAPACITY IN PURSUIT OF PLEASURE AND A PARADE
GETT PREFACE(224) CAN SAVE THEIR WIVES AND DAUGHTERS FROM QUITE INDISCRIMINATE RAPINE. DOMESTIC CHANGE OF AIR. OUR RELIEF AT
MIS. PREFACE(104) EXCESS OF MUTILATION, RAPINE, AND DELIRIOUS INDISCRIMINATE SLAUGHTER OF HELPLESS NON-COMBATANTS, OLD AND

INDISCRIMINATELY

GENV IV (110) EXCEPT SIR O./ (VOCIFEROUSLY) NO. /SIR O./ NOT INDISCRIMINATELY . /THE BRITISH CONTINGENT/ HEAR HEAR! /SIR
DOCT I (104) THAT IVE USED ALL SORTS OF ANTI-TOXINS ABSOLUTELY INDISCRIMINATELY , WITH PERFECTLY SATISFACTORY RESULTS. I

INDISPENSABLE

PLES PREFACE(R8) ITSELF, THERE MAY BE NO END; BUT THE CONFLICT IS INDISPENSABLE : NO CONFLICT, NO DRAMA. CERTAINLY IT IS EASY
MILL PREFACE(113) THE BORN RULER, THE MOSES OR LENIN, IS NO LONGER INDISPENSABLE : ROUTINE GOVERNMENT BY DUNDERHEADS BECOMES
3PLA PREFACE(R17) DRESSES, NICE DRAWING ROOMS AND NICE PEOPLE, ARE INDISPENSABLE : TO BE UNGENTEEL IS WORSE THAN TO FAIL. I USE
MRS III (230) WE HOLD MOST OF THE CAPITAL; AND YOUR MOTHER'S INDISPENSABLE AS MANAGING DIRECTOR. YOUVE NOTICED, I
METH PREFACE(R39) ATHEIST HOME DEAD ON A SHUTTER (THE SHUTTER WAS INDISPENSABLE BECAUSE IT MARKED THE UTTER UNPREPAREDNESS OF
APPL PREFACE(173) TO TRAIN HIMSELF, TO ACCEPT GOOD MANNERS AS AN INDISPENSABLE CONDITION OF HIS INTERCOURSE WITH HIS
SUPR HANDBOK(181) TO HER. THEREFORE MARRIAGE, WHILST IT IS MADE AN INDISPENSABLE CONDITION OF MATING, WILL DELAY THE ADVENT OF
KING I (179) A RELIGION FOR HIMSELF. A READYMADE CHURCH IS AN INDISPENSABLE CONVENIENCE FOR MOST OF US. THE INNER LIGHT
APPL PREFACE(187) HIMSELF TO THE NEW POSTMAN AS AN ESTABLISHED AND INDISPENSABLE FEATURE OF THE POSTAL SYSTEM, AND FINALLY
DOCT I SD(81) DOMESTIC LABORATORY ASSISTANT, AND MAKING HIMSELF INDISPENSABLE GENERALLY, IN RETURN FOR UNSPECIFIED
MIS. PREFACE(57) OR MATHEMATICS ON THE GROUND THAT THEY ARE AN INDISPENSABLE GYMNASTIC FOR THE MENTAL POWERS. IT WOULD BE
METH PREFACE(R25) LONG SURVIVE ITS UTILITY, AND IF OTHER AND STILL INDISPENSABLE HABITS AND MODIFICATIONS HAVE BEEN BUILT ON
KING PREFACE(158) EXTENDED, DETAILED CRITICISM BY WOMEN HAS BECOME INDISPENSABLE IN CABINETS, FOR INSTANCE, THE HOUSE OF LORDS
MILL PREFACE(114) ANY PLAUSIBILITY THAT WILLIAM THE CONQUEROR WAS INDISPENSABLE IN ENGLAND: HE WANTED ENGLAND AND GRABBED IT.
SIM PREFACE(11) LIQUIDATED, CONVERTED, OR INTIMIDATED. BUT IT WAS INDISPENSABLE IN ITS PRIME. THE BOLSHEVIKS, INFECTED AS THEY
POSN PREFACE(386) CAN BE MADE OUT IN SUPPORT OF ASSASSINATION AS AN INDISPENSABLE INSTRUMENT OF PROGRESS. NOW IT HAPPENS THAT WE
FABL PREFACE(67) AND WHO NOT. WHAT IS MORE, THEY ARE ALL EQUALLY INDISPENSABLE . AN INDUSTRIAL MAGNATE ONCE WROTE ASKING ME
ROCK II (266) SUCH A HOLD ON THE COUNTRY. WE MUST FACE IT: HE'S INDISPENSABLE . I'LL JUST GO AND ASSURE HIM THAT WE HAVE NO
SIM PRO,1, (24) WHOLE WORLD. I WONDER AM I A DISPENSABLE OR AN INDISPENSABLE . (SHE GOES OUT THROUGH THE RAILWAY DOOR).
ROCK PREFACE(170) VARYING FROM WEEKS TO YEARS. STANDARD RELIGION INDISPENSABLE . NEVERTHELESS THERE WILL BE CONFLICTS TO THE
MTH3 (98) ARE NEVER LIKED. I AM NOT LIKEABLE; BUT I AM INDISPENSABLE . /BURGE-LUBIN/ OH, CHEER UP, OLD MAN: THERES
SIM PRO,1, (24) OFFICE; AND IT HAD BETTER BE ME THAN HIM. I AM INDISPENSABLE . /THE Y.W./ WHAT A WORD! DISPENSABLES AND
MTH4 III (201) /THE ELDERLY GENTLEMAN/ NO, AMBROSE: YOU ARE INDISPENSABLE . THERE IS NO ONE ELSE. /THE ENVOY/ VERY WELL.
CATH PREFACE(154) COMMITTING REAL ATROCITIES, NOT FORGETTING THE INDISPENSABLE LOVE INTEREST ON AN ENORMOUS AND UTTERLY
MILL PREFACE(112) AS AN INDIVIDUAL OF THEIR CALIBRE REMAINS THE INDISPENSABLE MAN (OR WOMAN) DOING THINGS THAT THE COMMON
OVER PREFACE(161) THEY WERE WRONG IN ASSUMING THAT SEX IS AN INDISPENSABLE MOTIVE IN POPULAR PLAYS. THE PLAYS OF MOLIERE
NEVR I (206) OR DEAD. AM I TO INFER THAT YOU HAVE OMITTED THAT INDISPENSABLE PART OF YOUR SOCIAL EQUIPMENT? (THEY CONFIRM
BARB PREFACE(222) ABBEY. BUT IN OUR PROFESSIONAL PLAYGOERS THIS INDISPENSABLE PRELIMINARY CONCEPTION OF SANCTITY SEEMS
DOCT PREFACE(11) THE RADICALS WHO USED TO ADVOCATE, AS AN INDISPENSABLE PRELIMINARY TO SOCIAL REFORM, THE STRANGLING
BULL PREFACE(33) OF THEM THAT HE CAN GOVERN THEM TOLERABLY. THE INDISPENSABLE PRELIMINARY TO DEMOCRACY IS THE REPRESENTATION
BULL PREFACE(33) IS THE REPRESENTATION OF EVERY INTEREST: THE INDISPENSABLE PRELIMINARY TO JUSTICE IS THE ELIMINATION OF
BARB PREFACE(228) OFF SUPPLIES AT ONCE IF IT BEGAN TO PREACH THAT INDISPENSABLE REVOLT AGAINST POVERTY WHICH MUST ALSO BE A
ROCK PREFACE(165) OF THE PRETENSION OF THEIR OWN CLASS TO BE INDISPENSABLE), ALLOWED THEIR PARENTS TO BE DESCRIBED AS
AUGS PREFACE(261) SO TO THIS DAY. HE GAVE US HIS WORD THAT HE WAS INDISPENSABLE ; AND WE TOOK IT.
MIS. PREFACE(84) AND SISTERS. THE PARENT SEEMS LIKELY TO REMAIN INDISPENSABLE ; BUT THERE IS NO REASON WHY THAT NATURAL TIE
DOCT PREFACE(70) WHEN A DEARTH IN THEIR LABOR MARKET MAKES THEM INDISPENSABLE ; BUT THE AVERAGE DOCTOR IS NOT IN THIS
MRS PREFACE(154) WHO HOLD THE WIDELY WHISPERED VIEW THAT IT IS AN INDISPENSABLE SAFETY-VALVE FOR THE PROTECTION OF DOMESTIC
LADY PREFACE(211) AND HIGH ACADEMIC DISTINCTION IN ADDITION TO THE INDISPENSABLE SCHOLARSHIP AND LITERARY REPUTATION, ARE
PYGM EPILOG (301) CERTAIN QUALITIES AND SHAPES OF PAPER BECAME INDISPENSABLE TO HER. SHE COULD NOT EVEN ADDRESS AN ENVELOPE
ROCK II (243) THAT THE OWNERS OF ALL THE MILES OF LAND THAT ARE INDISPENSABLE TO MY SCHEME, AND THAT WITHOUT IT WOULD NOT BE
BUOY III (37) BESIDES, TAKE MY CASE. MY LATE WIFE AND I WERE SO INDISPENSABLE TO ONEANOTHER THAT A SEPARATION WOULD HAVE
MIS. PREFACE(18) SEND THEM TO ARE WELL CONDUCTED, BENEFICIAL, AND INDISPENSABLE TO THE SUCCESS OF THE CHILDREN IN AFTER LIFE.
DOCT PREFACE(51) A PASSION OF CRUELTY IN MAN JUST BECAUSE IT IS INDISPENSABLE TO THE FULNESS OF HIS KNOWLEDGE. THOU ART THE
POSN PREFACE(396) UNINSTRUCTED MASS OF POPULAR SENTIMENT-- IS INDISPENSABLE TO THE CENSORSHIP AS IT EXISTS TODAY IN
SUPR HANDBOK(180) OF BAD BREEDING ALSO; AND BAD BREEDING IS INDISPENSABLE TO THE WEEDING OUT OF THE HUMAN RACE. WHEN THE
METH PREFACE(R66) SOME SUCH HYPOTHESIS HAD BEEN FOUND QUITE INDISPENSABLE , AND COULD NOT BE REPLACED BY A MERE GODDESS
METH PREFACE(R75) DRIVING FORCE OF AN UNDELUDED POPULAR CONSENT IS INDISPENSABLE , AND WILL BE IMPOSSIBLE UNTIL THE STATESMAN
ROCK PREFACE(171) A STANDARD RELIGION. YET A STANDARD RELIGION IS INDISPENSABLE , HOWEVER COMPLETELY IT MAY SHED THE OLD
SIM PRO,1, (25) MUST BE LEFT IN THE OFFICE" I SAYS. " I AM INDISPENSABLE " I SAYS. AND ALL THE TIME I KNEW THAT NOBODY

INDISPENSABLES

SIM PRO,1, (24) /THE Y.W./ WHAT A WORD! DISPENSABLES AND INDISPENSABLES : THERE YOU HAVE THE WHOLE WORLD. I WONDER AM

INDISPOSED

DEST SD(150) OF MEN WITHOUT MONEY, IN RAGS, AND CONSEQUENTLY INDISPOSED TO STAND MUCH DISCIPLINE, ESPECIALLY FROM UPSTART
DOCT I SD(87) GRUNTS FOR ARTICULATE SPEECH, AND GENERALLY INDISPOSED , AT HIS AGE, TO MAKE MUCH SOCIAL EFFORT. HE

INDISPOSITION

BULL PREFACE(55) THROUGH SAID SULEIMAN KHEIRALLAH'S INCONSIDERATE INDISPOSITION MADE THE EXECUTION OF DARWEESH TEDIOUS, AS HE

INDISSOLUBILITY

GETT PREFACE(226) SHOULD HAVE BEEN ESTABLISHED SHEWS THAT THE INDISSOLUBILITY OF MARRIAGE CREATES SUCH INTOLERABLE

INDISSOLUBLE

GETT PREFACE(187) SACERDOTAL VIEW OF MARRIAGE AS A SACRED AND INDISSOLUBLE COVENANT, BECAUSE, THOUGH REINFORCED BY UNHAPPY
GETT PREFACE(256) IS AS CHEAP AS MARRIAGE, MARRIAGE WILL REMAIN INDISSOLUBLE FOR ALL EXCEPT THE HANDFUL OF PEOPLE TO WHOM
GETT PREFACE(256) BUT PLEASE DO NOT IMAGINE THAT THE EVILS OF INDISSOLUBLE MARRIAGE CAN BE CURED BY DIVORCE LAWS
GETT PREFACE(250) PROPERTY ON THE CHURCH UNDER THE GUISE OF INDISSOLUBLE MARRIAGE. FOR THE CHURCH TRIED TO SHELTER THIS
GETT PREFACE(240) FIRST CONDITION OF ITS MAINTENANCE. A THOUSAND INDISSOLUBLE MARRIAGES MEAN A THOUSAND MARRIAGES AND NO
GETT PREFACE(186) CHURCH BY ASSENTING VERBALLY TO THE DOCTRINE OF INDISSOLUBLE MARRIAGE, BUT NOBODY WORTH COUNTING BELIEVES
GETT PREFACE(186) IF NOT BY THE TEMPORAL COURTS, BY THE POPE. INDISSOLUBLE MARRIAGE IS AN ACADEMIC FIGMENT, ADVOCATED ONLY
GETT PREFACE(226) IT, " BEFORE COMPANY," AND HERE THE EFFECTS OF INDISSOLUBLE MARRIAGE-FOR-BETTER-FOR-WORSE ARE VERY PLAINLY
GETT PREFACE(216) WHICH HAVE BEEN MADE ON THE CONTINENT FROM INDISSOLUBLE ROMAN CATHOLIC MARRIAGE TO MARRIAGE THAT CAN BE
GETT PREFACE(185) ENGLISH CIVIL MARRIAGE, SACRAMENTAL MARRIAGE, INDISSOLUBLE ROMAN CATHOLIC MARRIAGE, MARRIAGE OF DIVORCED

GETT PREFACE(258) IT IS CLEAR THAT NO MARRIAGE IS ANY LONGER INDISSOLUBLE ; AND THE SENSIBLE THING TO DO THEN IS TO GRANT

INDISTINGUISHABLE

GENV IV (97) NOT ON THE NORTH. /BEGONIA/ WHAT DO YOU MEAN-- INDISTINGUISHABLE ? IT MAYNT BE AS DISTANGAY AS MAYFAIR;
MILL PREFACE(119) OF POLITICAL HELPLESSNESS IN WHICH THEY WERE INDISTINGUISHABLE EXCEPT BY NAME FROM THE MOST REACTIONARY
GENV IV (97) MR BATTLER, IS A PART OF LONDON WHICH IS TOTALLY INDISTINGUISHABLE FROM ANY OTHER PART OF LONDON, EXCEPT THAT
GENV IV (97) ADJACENT TO CAMBERWELL AND EQUALLY AND ENTIRELY INDISTINGUISHABLE FROM IT. /BEGONIA/ DONT YOU BELIEVE HIM,
METH PREFACE(R26) EMBRYONIC LIFETIME, DURING PART OF WHICH HE WAS INDISTINGUISHABLE FROM AN EMBRYONIC DOG, AND HAD NEITHER A
DOCT PREFACE(24) AT THEIR WORST ARE BAD ENOUGH TO BE INDISTINGUISHABLE FROM THOSE OF THE MOST DISCREDITABLE AND

INDIVIDUAL

JOAN PREFACE(32) ON SUFFICIENT EVIDENCE IT WILL DECLARE THAT INDIVIDUAL A SAINT. THUS, AS REVELATION MAY COME BY WAY OF
APPL PREFACE(183) CORPORATE ACTION INVOLVES MORE GOVERNMENT THAN INDIVIDUAL ACTION. THUS GOVERNMENT, WHICH USED TO BE A
APPL PREFACE(183) GETTING ALONG IS THE WAY OF CORPORATE ACTION, NOT INDIVIDUAL ACTION; AND CORPORATE ACTION INVOLVES MORE
DOCT PREFACE(79) NOT EFFECT RESUSCITATION. THE THEORY THAT EVERY INDIVIDUAL ALIVE IS OF INFINITE VALUE IS LEGISLATIVELY
CATH 1,SD(161) CLAIM TO BE THE CLEVEREST AND MOST ATTRACTIVE INDIVIDUAL ALIVE. NOW SHE NOT ONLY TOLERATES PATIOMKIN LONG
OVER PREFACE(158) AND GOES ON NOT ONLY BETWEEN CLASS AND CLASS AND INDIVIDUAL AND INDIVIDUAL, BUT IN THE SELFSAME BREAST IN A
METH PREFACE(R63) THAT ALL PROGRESS, ALL PROSPERITY, ALL SALVATION, INDIVIDUAL AND SOCIAL, DEPEND ON AN UNRESTRAINED CONFLICT
OVER PREFACE(155) THEM, BUT BECAUSE THE FRICTION SET UP BETWEEN THE INDIVIDUAL AND THE COMMUNITY BY THE EXPRESSION OF UNUSUAL
LADY PREFACE(232) FACT THAT IN HIS DAY WHAT ENGLISH LAND NEEDED WAS INDIVIDUAL APPROPRIATION AND CULTIVATION, AND WHAT THE
LION PREFACE(67) WHICH IS THE ESSENCE OF MATRIMONY AS TO THE INDIVIDUAL APPROPRIATION OF WEALTH. A MARRIED MAN, HE SAID,
LION PREFACE(66) WE FIND JESUS MAKING THE SAME OBJECTION TO THAT INDIVIDUAL APPROPRIATION OF HUMAN BEINGS WHICH IS THE
METH PREFACE(R60) ACCEPTANCE OF THE CONGENITAL CHARACTER OF THE INDIVIDUAL AS THE DETERMINING FACTOR IN HIS DESTINY HAD BEEN
MIS. PREFACE(12) EACH CHILD TO RECEIVE WHAT SCHOOLMASTERS CALL " INDIVIDUAL ATTENTION." THE CHILDREN MAY RECEIVE A GOOD DEAL
MIS. PREFACE(12) THE CHILDREN MAY RECEIVE A GOOD DEAL OF INDIVIDUAL ATTENTION FROM ONE ANOTHER IN THE SHAPE OF
SUPR III (112) INTO HIGHER AND HIGHER INDIVIDUALS, THE IDEAL INDIVIDUAL BEING OMNIPOTENT, OMNISCIENT, INFALLIBLE, AND
JOAN PREFACE(32) SUCH, THE SUPREMACY OF PRIVATE JUDGMENT FOR THE INDIVIDUAL BEING THE QUINTESSENCE OF PROTESTANTISM;
UNPL PREFACE(R15) INFLUENCE, MOVING ONLY AT THE PROMPTINGS OF INDIVIDUAL BENEVOLENCE TO INDIVIDUALS, MAKES NICE LITTLE
LION PREFACE(24) OF SOCIETY IN WHICH YOU ARE NOT AN INDEPENDENT INDIVIDUAL BUT A MEMBER OF SOCIETY, YOUR NEIGHBOR BEING
DOCT PREFACE(80) NO DOUBT THE HIGHER THE LIFE WE SECURE TO THE INDIVIDUAL BY WISE SOCIAL ORGANIZATION, THE GREATER HIS
LION PREFACE(64) THAT THERE ARE LIMITS TO THE NUMBER OF CUBITS AN INDIVIDUAL CAN ADD TO HIS STATURE MORALLY OR PHYSICALLY, AND
MILL PREFACE(110) WORLD'S WELFARE DEPENDS ON OPERATIONS BY WHICH NO INDIVIDUAL CAN MAKE MONEY, WHILST ITS RUIN BY WAR AND DRINK
BARB PREFACE(213) PLANE AS A MATTER OF COURSE, IT IS THAT NO INDIVIDUAL CAN MAKE MORE THAN A MINUTE CONTRIBUTION TO IT.
DOCT PREFACE(79) BY SPECIAL STATISTICS AND ANNOUNCEMENTS OF INDIVIDUAL CASES, OF ALL ILLNESSES OF DOCTORS OR IN THEIR
UNPL PREFACE(R25) NOT ONLY WITH THE COMEDY AND TRAGEDY OF INDIVIDUAL CHARACTER AND DESTINY, BUT WITH THOSE SOCIAL
METH PREFACE(R87) POLITICS, NATURAL CHRISTIANITY, NATIONAL AND INDIVIDUAL CHARACTER, PARADOXES OF CONVENTIONAL SOCIETY,
MIS. PREFACE(75) WE NEED IS TO ORGANIZE IT SO THAT INSTEAD OF THE INDIVIDUAL CHILD FASTENING LIKE A PARASITE ON ITS OWN
2TRU PREFACE(14) OF THE LABOR AND LEISURE INVOLVED. THUS THE INDIVIDUAL CITIZEN HAS TO BE COMPELLED NOT ONLY TO BEHAVE
SUPR I SD(16) BECOMES TRANSFIGURED, AND THE PUNY LIMITS OF INDIVIDUAL CONSCIOUSNESS ARE SUDDENLY MADE INFINITE BY A
HART PREFACE(10) THAT NO CONSIDERATION FOR THE INTERESTS OF ANY INDIVIDUAL CREATURE, WHETHER FROG OR PHILOSOPHER, MUCH LESS
LION PREFACE(63) DEMAND IN WHICH MEN WILL NEED AND USE MONEY OR INDIVIDUAL CREDIT, AND FOR WHICH, THEREFORE, THEY MUST HAVE
ROCK II (255) I AM JUST AS MUCH AGAINST CABINET DICTATORSHIP AS INDIVIDUAL DICTATORSHIP. WHAT I WANT DONE IS THE WILL OF THE
SIM PREFACE(13) CAPITALIST PLANTERS, MADE THE QUESTION OF WHETHER INDIVIDUAL DOGS AND MEN ARE WORTH THEIR SALT FAMILIAR TO ME
LION PREFACE(73) THE PRACTICAL SOLUTION IS TO MAKE THE INDIVIDUAL ECONOMICALLY INDEPENDENT OF MARRIAGE AND THE
MRS PREFACE(151) IS NOT ONLY CARRIED ON WITHOUT ORGANIZATION BY INDIVIDUAL ENTERPRISE IN THE LODGINGS OF SOLITARY WOMEN,
LION PREFACE(70) THAT MARRIAGE BECOMES AN INTOLERABLE OBSTACLE TO INDIVIDUAL EVOLUTION. AND THAT IS WHY THE REVOLT AGAINST
METH PREFACE(R38) EVERYWHERE, AND MUST BE SOMETHING BIGGER THAN THE INDIVIDUAL EYE-MAKING MAN, ONLY THE STUPIDEST MUCKRAKERS
LION PREFACE(70) AND AT THE SAME TIME PRODUCES A GREATER NEED FOR INDIVIDUAL FREEDOM IN PURSUIT OF A HIGHER EVOLUTION. THE
BARB PREFACE(243) ARE PROPORTIONATE, NOT TO THE FREEDOM OF THE INDIVIDUAL FROM A CODE, BUT TO THE COMPLEXITY AND SUBTLETY
INCA (252) AND THE PIFFLER AND JACK JOHNSON. I BELIEVE IN INDIVIDUAL GENIUS. THAT IS THE INCA'S SECRET. IT MUST BE.
MILL PREFACE(114) GENIUS AND POLITICAL CAPACITY IN A SINGLE INDIVIDUAL GIVES THAT INDIVIDUAL HIS OPPORTUNITY. NAPOLEON,
SUPR HANDBOK(177) GENTLEMAN CAN APPEAR AS MERE BY-PRODUCTS OF MAN'S INDIVIDUAL GREED AND FOLLY, WHAT MIGHT WE NOT HOPE FOR AS A
SUPR HANDBOK(179) THREATEN THE EXISTENCE OF THE RACE, BUT ONLY THE INDIVIDUAL HAPPINESS OF ITS UNITS, AND FINALLY THE
SUPR HANDBOK(182) OF THE GENERAL WELFARE WITHOUT ANY REGARD FOR INDIVIDUAL HARD CASES, PEOPLE IN LANCASHIRE STILL SPEAK OF
MRS PREFACE(170) SHEWED HIM THAT SLUMS ARE THE PRODUCT, NOT OF INDIVIDUAL HARPAGONS, BUT OF THE INDIFFERENCE OF VIRTUOUS
MILL PREFACE(114) CAPACITY IN A SINGLE INDIVIDUAL GIVES THAT INDIVIDUAL HIS OPPORTUNITY, NAPOLEON, IF HE HAD BEEN BORN A
MTH3 (108) IS TO BE SAVED. IT SHEWED THAT THIS EXTENSION OF INDIVIDUAL HUMAN LIFE WAS POSSIBLE, AND HOW IT WAS LIKELY TO
LION PREFACE(89) OF OUR SINS BRINGS ITS KARMA, ALSO INSIST ON INDIVIDUAL IMMORTALITY AND METEMPSYCHOSIS IN ORDER TO
LION PREFACE(88) IMMORTALITY NO CRITERION. NOR IS BELIEF IN INDIVIDUAL IMMORTALITY ANY CRITERION. THEOSOPHISTS,
LION PREFACE(63) CREDIT, AND FOR WHICH, THEREFORE, THEY MUST HAVE INDIVIDUAL INCOMES. FOREIGN TRAVEL IS AN OBVIOUS INSTANCE.
AUGS (272) ANY BRITISH BATTLE EVER BEEN WON EXCEPT BY A BOLD INDIVIDUAL INITIATIVE? I SAY NOTHING OF PROFESSIONAL
SUPR PREFACE(R15) OF THE DOLL'S HOUSE AND ASSERTING HERSELF AS AN INDIVIDUAL INSTEAD OF A MERE ITEM IN A MORAL PAGEANT. NOW IT
SUPR HANDBOK(189) OF THE RACE WOULD STILL SHATTER THE OPPOSITION OF INDIVIDUAL INSTINCTS, NOT ONLY DO THE BEES AND THE ANTS
SUPR HANDBOK(189) OF UNMARRIED NORMAL MEN AND WOMEN. IN SHORT, THE INDIVIDUAL INSTINCT IN THIS MATTER, OVERWHELMING AS IT IS
MILL PREFACE(114) BUT WILLIAM HAD ALL THE QUALITIES THAT MAKE AN INDIVIDUAL IRRESISTIBLE: THE PHYSICAL STRENGTH AND FEROCITY
METH PREFACE(R24) YOUR SON WHEN HE ENTERS THE WORLD AS A SEPARATE INDIVIDUAL IS TO YELL WITH INDIGNATION: THAT YELL WHICH
LION PREFACE(59) OF MANKIND VARIATION OF INCOME FROM INDIVIDUAL TO INDIVIDUAL IS UNKNOWN, BECAUSE IT IS RIDICULOUSLY
METH PREFACE(R19) FATAL ACCIDENT MAKES AN END OF THE INDIVIDUAL . ALL THAT IS NECESSARY TO MAKE HIM EXTEND HIS
SIM PREFACE(4) OF VISION VARIES ENORMOUSLY FROM INDIVIDUAL TO INDIVIDUAL . BETWEEN THE SUPERSTATESMAN WHOSE VISION
GETT PREFACE(183) ALL LAWS OUGHT TO BE, STRONGER THAN THE STRONGEST INDIVIDUAL . CERTAINLY THE MARRIAGE LAW IS. THE ONLY PEOPLE
JOAN PREFACE(38) GHOST AS IT FLASHES WITH UNERRING AIM UPON THE INDIVIDUAL . NOR CAN ANY COLLEGE OF CARDINALS PRAY
JOAN PREFACE(32) WISDOM MAY COME AS A DIVINE REVELATION TO AN INDIVIDUAL . ON SUFFICIENT EVIDENCE IT WILL DECLARE THAT
MIS. PREFACE(63) SHOULD BE A SERIES OF COMING OF AGES FOR EVERY INDIVIDUAL . THE MAMMALS HAVE THEIR FIRST COMING OF AGE WHEN
GENV II (57) COURT CAN BE SET IN MOTION BY THE HUMBLEST INDIVIDUAL JUSTICE IS A MOCKERY. /SIR O./ OF COURSE I AGREE
METH PREFACE(R23) OCCURS AGAIN. THE RACE LEARNS EXACTLY AS THE INDIVIDUAL LEARNS. YOUR SON RELAPSES, NOT TO THE VERY
2TRU PREFACE(14) BEING HIS LEISURE. 8. LEISURE IS THE SPHERE OF INDIVIDUAL LIBERTY: LABOR IS THE SPHERE OF SLAVERY. 9.
2TRU PREFACE(13) THE GOOD OF THE COMMUNITY INVOLVES A MAXIMUM OF INDIVIDUAL LIBERTY FOR ALL ITS MEMBERS THE RULERS HAVE AT
2TRU PREFACE(13) OF AGREEMENT AS TO THE NECESSARY SACRIFICE OF INDIVIDUAL LIBERTY TO THE GOOD OF THE COMMUNITY. 5. THE
MILL PREFACE(117) CENTURY, IT WAS STILL BELIEVED THAT BRITISH INDIVIDUAL LIBERTY FORBAD PARLIAMENT TO DO ANYTHING THAT IT
ROCK PREFACE(172) PROFESSIONAL CLASSES INTO WILD ALARM WHEN THE INDIVIDUAL LIBERTY OF THOUGHT, SPEECH, AND CONSCIENCE WHICH
LADY PREFACE(232) WAS THE INCORPORATION OF WHIG PRINCIPLES OF INDIVIDUAL LIBERTY, SHAKESPEAR AND THE BRITISH PUBLIC. I
LION PREFACE(89) SINNER. THE BELIEF IN THE PROLONGATION OF INDIVIDUAL LIFE BEYOND THE GRAVE IS FAR MORE REAL AND VIVID
DOCT PREFACE(34) SERVICE HE MAY EVEN HAVE TO THROW AWAY HIS INDIVIDUAL LIFE TO SAVE THE LIFE OF THE COMMUNITY. IT IS
METH PREFACE(R18) APPARENTLY CHANGEABLE AT WILL IS THE DURATION OF INDIVIDUAL LIFE. WEISMANN, A VERY CLEVER AND SUGGESTIVE
APPL I (208) EH? YOU ADMITTED JUST NOW THAT EVEN A MODEST INDIVIDUAL LIKE MYSELF HAD GIVEN YOUR THRONE A SHAKE OR TWO.
METH PREFACE(R22) WERE AN ILLUSION PRODUCED BY THE SHORTNESS OF OUR INDIVIDUAL LIVES, AND THAT THEY WERE CONSTANTLY CHANGING AND
GETT PREFACE(200) AND ITS EFFECT ON THE CHARACTER OF THE INDIVIDUAL MAY EASILY BE DISASTROUS. FOR BETTER FOR WORSE.
MIS. PREFACE(5) OUR FATHER WHICH ART IN HEAVEN," TWO VERY LIMITED INDIVIDUAL MORTALS SHOULD BE ALLOWED TO APPEAR AT ITS
HART PREFACE(8) ALTER OUR DESTINY. STILL, AS CALVINISM GAVE THE INDIVIDUAL NO CLUE AS TO WHETHER HE HAD DRAWN A LUCKY NUMBER
GETT PREFACE(236) TO MIND OUR OWN BUSINESS AND NOT IMPOSE OUR INDIVIDUAL NOTIONS OF PROPRIETY ON ONE ANOTHER, EVEN IF IT
FABL VI SD(122) WEARING UNIFORMS WITH SIX SLEEVE STRIPES. THEIR INDIVIDUAL NUMBERS ARE ON THEIR CAPS. NUMBERS 1, 2, 3, ARE
CAPT III (288) AM I TO STAND HERE IN THE ABSENCE OF ANY INDIVIDUAL OF MY OWN SEX AND REPEAT THE LANGUAGE OF TWO
MILL PREFACE(112) OUT OF ETERNAL AND IMPERSONAL ONES. AS LONG AS AN INDIVIDUAL OF THEIR CALIBRE REMAINS THE INDISPENSABLE MAN (
JITT III (56) PEOPLE SLEEP IN THE SAME WAY. EVERY CASE IS AN INDIVIDUAL ONE. YOU MUST READ IT, FESSLER. /FESSLER/ (
POSN PREFACE(403) IS ESSENTIALLY A MATTER, NOT BETWEEN ONE PRIVATE INDIVIDUAL OR BODY AND ANOTHER, BUT BETWEEN A PUBLIC
GETT PREFACE(255) TO LEAVE IT AT THE IRRESPONSIBLE DISPOSAL OF ANY INDIVIDUAL OR COUPLE OF INDIVIDUALS AS A MERE SMALL PARCEL
GETT PREFACE(220) TRANSCENDS THE PERSONAL INTERESTS OF ANY INDIVIDUAL OR EVEN OF ANY TEN GENERATIONS OF INDIVIDUALS
MIS. PREFACE(70) THEY ARE BETTER THAN NO MANNERS AT ALL. AND NO INDIVIDUAL OR FAMILY CAN POSSIBLY TEACH THEM. THEY CAN BE
LION PREFACE(67) DIVIDING WITH WOMEN AND MEN THE ALLEGIANCE THE INDIVIDUAL OWES TO GOD WITHIN HIM. THIS RAISES THE PRACTICAL
MTH4 I (162) WE STORE SUSTENANCE FOR FUTURE COMMUNITIES. THE INDIVIDUAL PERISHES; BUT THE RACE IS IMMORTAL. THE ACORN OF
LION PREFACE(5) IN MORAL EVOLUTION WHICH IS INDEPENDENT OF ANY INDIVIDUAL PREACHER. IF JESUS HAD NEVER EXISTED (AND THAT
LION PREFACE(55) SIMPLE AND DIRECT VILLAGE EXAMPLES OF APPARENT INDIVIDUAL PRODUCTION TURN OUT ON A MOMENT'S EXAMINATION TO
LION PREFACE(54) IS THE ORDER OF THE DAY. AN ATTEMPT TO RETURN TO INDIVIDUAL PROPERTIES AS THE BASIS OF OUR PRODUCTION WOULD
MIS. PREFACE(60) UNSCRUPULOUS, THE PREDATORY, IF HERE AND THERE AN INDIVIDUAL REFUSES TO BE DOCILE, TEN DOCILE PERSONS WILL
METH PREFACE(R59) OF CAPITALISM IS THE BELIEF IN THE EFFICACY OF INDIVIDUAL RIGHTEOUSNESS. ROBERT OWEN MADE DESPERATE EFFORTS
LION PREFACE(59) OF ROBBERS VARY CONSIDERABLY FROM INDIVIDUAL TO INDIVIDUAL ; AND THE VARIATION IS REFLECTED IN THE INCOMES
MIS. PREFACE(13) MORE POWER OF WORKING ON THE AFFECTIONS OF THE INDIVIDUAL SCHOLAR IN THE INTIMATE WAY THAT, FOR EXAMPLE,

MIS. PREFACE(69)	THAT DO NOT EXIST; AND THE PRIVATE ENTERPRISE OF	INDIVIDUAL	SCHOOLMASTERS APPEALING TO A GROUP OF WELL-TO-DO
FABL PREFACE(82)	NEVERTHELESS WE CANNOT LEGISLATE FOR EVERY	INDIVIDUAL	SEPARATELY, NOR PROVIDE A SPECIAL POLICEMAN TO
JOAN 4 (107)	IT GOES DEEP, MY LORD. IT IS THE PROTEST OF THE	INDIVIDUAL	SOUL AGAINST THE INTERFERENCE OF PRIEST OR PEER
JOAN PREFACE(37)	ARE SIFTED UNTIL AT THE END OF THE PROCESS AN	INDIVIDUAL	STANDS SUPREME AS THE VICAR OF CHRIST. BUT WHEN
METH PREFACE(R69)	LITTLE WHAT THE OPINIONS OR SUPERSTITIONS OF THE	INDIVIDUAL	STATESMEN CONCERNED MAY BE. A KAISER WHO IS A
LION PREFACE(72)	FAMILY TIES AS THE CLAIM OF A PARTICULAR KIND OF	INDIVIDUAL	TO BE FREE FROM THEM BECAUSE THEY HAMPER HIS OWN
MILL PREFACE(126)	COMES THE RISK WE RUN WHEN WE ALLOW A DOMINANT	INDIVIDUAL	TO BECOME A DESPOT. THERE IS A STORY TOLD OF A
LION PREFACE(21)	IS INSUFFICIENT AS A DEDICATION OF THE	INDIVIDUAL	TO GOD, AND HAS SUBSTITUTED THE RITE OF BAPTISM.
SUPR HANDBOK(180)	AND EFFECTIVELY LIMIT THE SELECTION OF THE	INDIVIDUAL	TO HIS OWN CLIQUE, IS TO POSTPONE THE SUPERMAN
LION PREFACE(59)	THE INCOMES OF ROBBERS VARY CONSIDERABLY FROM	INDIVIDUAL	TO INDIVIDUAL; AND THE VARIATION IS REFLECTED IN
LION PREFACE(59)	THE HUGE MASS OF MANKIND VARIATION OF INCOME FROM	INDIVIDUAL	TO INDIVIDUAL IS UNKNOWN, BECAUSE IT IS
SIM PREFACE(4)	WORLD. THIS SORT OF VISION VARIES ENORMOUSLY FROM	INDIVIDUAL	TO INDIVIDUAL. BETWEEN THE SUPERSTATESMAN WHOSE
GENV PREFACE(23)	MUSICAL OR MATHEMATICAL OR MILITARY CAPACITY FROM	INDIVIDUAL	TO INDIVIDUAL, FROM WILLIAM RUFUS TO CHARLES II,
LION PREFACE(62)	INSTRUMENT CALLED MONEY A MEANS OF ENABLING EVERY	INDIVIDUAL	TO ORDER AND PAY FOR THE PARTICULAR THINGS HE
PLES PREFACE(R16)	AND EXAGGERATING THE POWER OF THE TALENTED	INDIVIDUAL	TO PREVAIL AGAINST THEM; WHILST I HAVE ACQUIRED
MIS. PREFACE(68)	FREEDOM IS A MERE MATTER OF THE READINESS OF THE	INDIVIDUAL	TO SNAP HIS FINGERS AT CONVENTION. IT IS TRUE
SUPR III (114)	BUT THE PURPOSE OF LIFE, AND THEREBY ENABLE THE	INDIVIDUAL	TO WORK FOR THAT PURPOSE INSTEAD OF THWARTING AND
MIS. PREFACE(13)	MINISTER HAS OF WORKING ON THE AFFECTIONS OF ANY	INDIVIDUAL	VOTER, CHILDREN AS NUISANCES, EXPERIENCED
SIM PREFACE(9)	DOES NOT NOW MATTER A PENNY TO THE STATE OR THE	INDIVIDUAL	WHETHER A CITIZEN BELONGS TO ONE PERSUASION OR
MTH3 (115)	LIKE ALL OTHER ANIMALS, TURN UPON ANY UNHAPPY	INDIVIDUAL	WHO HAS THE MISFORTUNE TO BE UNLIKE THEMSELVES IN
ROCK PREFACE(152)	TRACT OF LAND BECOMES THE PRIVATE PROPERTY OF AN	INDIVIDUAL	WHO HAS TO DEPEND ON IT FOR HIS SUBSISTENCE, THE
LION PREFACE(63)	PAY BECAUSE THE PRICE IS BEYOND THE MEANS OF ANY	INDIVIDUAL	WORKER. BUT EVEN WHEN THE UTMOST ALLOWANCE IS
SUPR HANDBOK(214)	WITH MUST THERE IS NO ARGUING. IT IS IDLE FOR AN	INDIVIDUAL	WRITER TO CARRY SO GREAT A MATTER FURTHER IN A
NEVR II (228)	STANDING FOR LIBERTY AND THE RIGHTS OF THE	INDIVIDUAL	, AS I LEARNT TO DO FROM MY MASTER HERBERT
METH PREFACE(R26)	NOT ONLY FROM EFFORT TO EFFORT IN THE CASE OF THE	INDIVIDUAL	, BUT FROM GENERATION TO GENERATION IN THE CASE
OVER PREFACE(158)	ONLY BETWEEN CLASS AND CLASS AND INDIVIDUAL AND	INDIVIDUAL	, BUT IN THE SELFSAME BREAST IN A SERIES OF
GENV I (33)	SOIL BY ITS RESPONSIBLE RULER. I, AS A RUINED	INDIVIDUAL	, CAN DO NOTHING. BUT THE LEAGUE OF NATIONS CAN
FABL PREFACE(66)	GIVES SOME NEEDED EXTRAORDINARY QUALITY TO SOME	INDIVIDUAL	, DOES NOT BOTHER ABOUT HIS OR HER MORALS. IT MAY
GENV PREFACE(23)	OR MILITARY CAPACITY FROM INDIVIDUAL TO	INDIVIDUAL	, FROM WILLIAM RUFUS TO CHARLES II, FROM NERO TO
PLES PREFACE(R16)	ACQUIRED THE POLITICIAN'S HABIT OF REGARDING THE	INDIVIDUAL	, HOWEVER TALENTED, AS HAVING NO CHOICE BUT TO
MRS PREFACE(179)	IN MRS WARREN'S PROFESSION, SOCIETY, AND NOT ANY	INDIVIDUAL	, IS THE VILLAIN OF THE PIECE; BUT IT DOES NOT
KING PREFACE(158)	SHARED BY WOMEN AND MEN, AND, WHEN IT QUITS THE	INDIVIDUAL	, PRODUCES IN BOTH ALIKE THE DISSOLUTION WE CALL
JOAN PREFACE(37)	BUT THE WORD MADE FLESH: THAT IS, THE UNAVERAGED	INDIVIDUAL	, REPRESENTING LIFE POSSIBLY AT ITS HIGHEST
GETT PREFACE(194)	LIKE REASONABLE PROPORTIONS IN THE LIFE OF THE	INDIVIDUAL	, THE DANGER OF IT DOES NOT LIE IN HUMAN NATURE.
SIM PREFACE(8)	THERE IS NO PERSONAL LIFE AFTER DEATH FOR THE	INDIVIDUAL	, THE TEACHING BEING THAT OF ECCLESIASTES IN OUR
POSN PREFACE(427)	SOME SORT. AND THOUGH THESE ARE ONLY RISKS TO THE	INDIVIDUAL	, TO THE COMMUNITY THEY ARE CERTAINTIES. IT IS
DOCT PREFACE(45)	PUBLIC DISLIKE SURGING UP IN A MOMENT AGAINST AN	INDIVIDUAL	, YOU MUST WATCH ONE WHO DOES SOMETHING UNUSUAL,

INDIVIDUALISM

BULL PREFACE(28)	REVOLUTION WITH PAPAL REACTION, AND OF HARDY	INDIVIDUALISM	AND INDEPENDENCE WITH DESPOTISM AND
SIM PREFACE(10)	MAHOMET, AND FROM WORLD CATHOLICISM TO NATIONAL	INDIVIDUALISM	AT THE REFORMATION, ALL LED TO THE PERSECUTION
BULL PREFACE(25)	TO THE EXTREMEST PRACTICABLE DEGREE OF	INDIVIDUALISM	, IT IS TRUE THAT THEY TALK OF CHURCH AND
DOCT PREFACE(66)	OF HIGHLY QUALIFIED EXPERTS ON TRIVIAL JOBS. THE	INDIVIDUALISM	OF PRIVATE PRACTICE LEADS TO AN APPALLING
2TRU PREFACE(19)	TO A CURIOUS ADULTERATION OF THEIR DOCTRINE OF	INDIVIDUALISM	, OR THE RIGHT OF PRIVATE JUDGMENT, WITH MOST

INDIVIDUALIST

UNPL PREFACE(R25)	ON WHICH I AM, LIKE MOST SOCIALISTS, AN EXTREME	INDIVIDUALIST	. I BELIEVE THAT ANY SOCIETY WHICH DESIRES TO
ROCK PREFACE(166)	FANATICALLY COMMUNIST GOVERNMENT AND THE FIERCELY	INDIVIDUALIST	PEASANT PROPRIETOR, WHO WANTED THE PRODUCE OF
BULL PREFACE(36)	MOVEMENT IN ENGLAND IN OPPOSITION TO THE	INDIVIDUALIST	SECULARISTS OF THE URBAN PROLETARIAT; BUT THEY
BARB PREFACE(224)	CERTAIN COINS AS TAINTED IS AN UNPRACTICAL	INDIVIDUALIST	SUPERSTITION. NONE THE LESS THE FACT THAT ALL
BULL PREFACE(26)	PRACTICABLE IN HUMAN SOCIETY: THAT IS, HE IS AN	INDIVIDUALIST	, A FREETHINKER, A SELF-HELPER, A WHIG, A
JOAN PREFACE(49)	HIS FIGURES ARE ALL INTENSELY PROTESTANT,	INDIVIDUALIST	, SCEPTICAL, SELF-CENTERED IN EVERYTHING BUT
GENV III (76)	POLITICIAN. YOUR POSE IS THAT OF THE RUGGED	INDIVIDUALIST	, THE ISOLATIONIST, AT BOTTOM AN ANARCHIST.

INDIVIDUALISTIC

BULL PREFACE(37)	WAS THE PHILOSOPHIC CHAMPION OF THEIR PROTESTANT,	INDIVIDUALISTIC	, DEMOCRATIC DEISM AGAINST THE STATE CHURCH

INDIVIDUALISTS

GETT PREFACE(185)	EITHER TO HIMSELF OR ANYONE ELSE, WITH THOSE	INDIVIDUALISTS	WHO IN THE NINETEENTH CENTURY DREAMT OF DOING

INDIVIDUALITIES

MIS. PREFACE(4)	DOWN THE BURDEN OF OUR WRETCHED LITTLE MAKESHIFT	INDIVIDUALITIES	FOR EVER AT EACH LIFT TOWARDS THE GOAL OF

INDIVIDUALITY

LADY PREFACE(214)	IN ALL'S WELL THAT ENDS WELL. IT HAS A CERTAIN	INDIVIDUALITY	AMONG THEM WHICH SUGGESTS A PORTRAIT. MR
SUPR I (37)	RELATIONS IMPOSSIBLE. A JEALOUS SENSE OF MY NEW	INDIVIDUALITY	AROSE IN ME-- /ANN/ YOU HATED TO BE TREATED AS
METH PREFACE(R60)	AND HABITS FORMED. SUCH A ROUTINE WOULD DESTROY	INDIVIDUALITY	IF ANYTHING COULD. YET INDIVIDUALS COME OUT
MIS. PREFACE(4)	RETAIN THEIR SINFUL NATURE: THAT IS TO SAY, THEIR	INDIVIDUALITY	. AND THIS SORT OF HELL, HOWEVER CONVENIENT AS
CYMB FORWORD(135)	TO BRING THE OTHERS BACK TO DRAMATIC ACTIVITY AND	INDIVIDUALITY	, I SHOULD LIKE TO HAVE RETAINED CORNELIUS AS
ROCK I (203)	ALL THE THINGS I WANTED FOR YOU UNTIL I HAVE NO	INDIVIDUALITY	LEFT. IF I TAKE UP A BOOK YOU WANT ME TO READ
JOAN PREFACE(38)	SUB-CONSCIOUS INTENTION OF HIS SELF-PRESERVING	INDIVIDUALITY	MUST BE TO FIND A TRUSTWORTHY SERVANT FOR HIS
APPL II (264)	YOUR FLAG. STILL, WE CLING TO THE LITTLE SCRAP OF	INDIVIDUALITY	YOU HAVE LEFT US. IF WE MUST MERGE, AS YOU
CYMB FORWORD(134)	WHICH THE CHARACTERS LOST ALL THEIR VITALITY AND	INDIVIDUALITY	, AND HAD NOTHING TO DO BUT IDENTIFY
JOAN PREFACE(41)	WELL INFORMED SENSE OF THE VALUE OF ORIGINALITY,	INDIVIDUALITY	, AND ECCENTRICITY, THE RESULT WILL BE
MTH5 (251)	ARE STILL THE MOUNTAINS, EACH WITH ITS NAME, ITS	INDIVIDUALITY	, ITS UPSTANDING STRENGTH AND MAJESTY, ITS

INDIVIDUALLY

UNPL PREFACE(R17)	WERE CORDONED BY THE POLICE AND EXAMINED	INDIVIDUALLY	AS TO THEIR VIEWS ON THE SUBJECT, THERE WOULD
APPL I (221)	BOATS AND CARS, SIR: THE FINEST ON EARTH, AND ALL	INDIVIDUALLY	DESIGNED. NO CHEAP MASS PRODUCTION STUFF THERE.
JOAN PREFACE(22)	SNOBBERY, SEEING AT A GLANCE HOW MUCH THEY WERE	INDIVIDUALLY	GOOD FOR, SHE HAD THE RESPECTABLE
POSN PREFACE(381)	FORM OF IT GRIEVOUSLY INJURES AND HINDERS ME	INDIVIDUALLY	, BUT ON PUBLIC GROUNDS, THE DEFINITION OF
BARB PREFACE(228)	THEY BELIEVED THAT DEATH WOULD BE THE END OF THEM	INDIVIDUALLY	, THEY AND THEIR FOLLOWERS HAVE A BAD HABIT OF

INDIVIDUAL'S

MIS. PREFACE(43)	MUST BE REGULATED BY SOME THEORY OF THE	INDIVIDUAL'S	RIGHTS. THOUGH THE RIGHT TO LIVE IS ABSOLUTE,

INDIVIDUALS

UNPL PREFACE(R26)	ITS ROMANTIC FOLLIES AND WITH THE STRUGGLES OF	INDIVIDUALS	AGAINST THOSE FOLLIES, MAY BE CALLED, BY
JOAN PREFACE(13)	FAR TRANSCENDING THE PURPOSE OF KEEPING THESE	INDIVIDUALS	ALIVE AND PROSPEROUS AND RESPECTABLE AND SAFE
MIS. PREFACE(37)	READING IN SECLUSION, BUT AS MEMBERS OF A BODY OF	INDIVIDUALS	ALL PURSUING CULTURE, TALKING CULTURE, THINKING
GETT PREFACE(220)	CONSTANTLY AND RUTHLESSLY USED AS A BAIT, BOTH BY	INDIVIDUALS	AND BY SOCIETY, ANY DISCUSSION TENDING TO STRIP
MIS. PREFACE(64)	IS THE CONSTANT ATTEMPTS MADE BY THE WILLS OF	INDIVIDUALS	AND CLASSES TO THWART THE WILLS AND ENSLAVE THE
MIS. PREFACE(64)	THWART THE WILLS AND ENSLAVE THE POWERS OF OTHER	INDIVIDUALS	AND CLASSES. THE POWERS OF THE PARENT AND THE
MILL PREFACE(110)	UNLESS THEY ARE RESTRAINED BY LAW; FOR ORDINARY	INDIVIDUALS	ARE HELPLESS IN THEIR HANDS. ARE THEY TO BE THE
LION PREFACE(71)	AND CHILDREN, PRACTISE VIRTUES THAT UNATTACHED	INDIVIDUALS	ARE INCAPABLE OF. IT IS TRUE THAT TOO MUCH OF
UNPL PREFACE(R25)	OUTGROWN BUT NOT MODIFIED, AND WHICH " ADVANCED"	INDIVIDUALS	ARE THEREFORE FORCED TO EVADE. THE SCENE WITH
GETT PREFACE(255)	DISPOSAL OF ANY INDIVIDUAL OR COUPLE OF	INDIVIDUALS	AS A MERE SMALL PARCEL OF PRIVATE PROPERTY. THE
PLES PREFACE(R14)	OF 1834, TO THE PAUPERIZATION OF PRIVATE	INDIVIDUALS	BY PUBLIC DOLES, IF WE WANT A THEATRE WHICH
METH PREFACE(R60)	DESTROY INDIVIDUALITY IF ANYTHING COULD. YET	INDIVIDUALS	COME OUT FROM IT AS DIFFERENT AS PITT FROM FOX,
METH PREFACE(R18)	SENSE ENOUGH TO DECAY AND DIE ON PURPOSE, BUT THE	INDIVIDUALS	DO NOT SEEM TO HAVE CALCULATED VERY REASONABLY:
JOAN PREFACE(13)	BUT THAT THERE ARE FORCES AT WORK WHICH USE	INDIVIDUALS	FOR PURPOSES FAR TRANSCENDING THE PURPOSE OF
METH PREFACE(R18)	ONLY FOR THE SURVIVAL OF SPECIES IN WHICH THE	INDIVIDUALS	HAVE SENSE ENOUGH TO DECAY AND DIE ON PURPOSE.
MILL PREFACE(135)	PREVENTIVE OF ANY ATTEMPT AT OPPRESSION, FOR THAT	INDIVIDUALS	HERE AND THERE POSSESS A POWER OF DOMINATION
BARB PREFACE(233)	AND TEMPERAMENT, THE CONDUCT AND MORALS OF THE	INDIVIDUALS	IN EACH GROUP ARE AS PREDICABLE AND AS ALIKE IN
2TRU PREFACE(13)	SELFISH OR UNEXPECTED BEHAVIOR ON THE PART OF	INDIVIDUALS	IN SOCIAL AFFAIRS. 4. THIS BUSINESS CAN BE DONE
LION PREFACE(59)	DISTRIBUTE THE PRODUCT OF THE LAND AMONG ALL THE	INDIVIDUALS	IN THE COMMUNITY. EQUAL DISTRIBUTION. WHEN THAT
MTH4 I (172)	COULD BE PLACED IN CHARGE OF ONE OF THOSE NORMAL	INDIVIDUALS	. /ZOO/ ABNORMAL, YOU MEAN. WHAT YOU ASK IS

GETT PREFACE(222)	IT ARE BAD PARENTS, THOUGH THEY MAY BE SUPERIOR	INDIVIDUALS	. THE CUBS OF A HUMANE TIGRESS WOULD STARVE; AND
SUPR HANDBOK(199)	BY THE BEST NOURISHED AND CULTIVATED NORMAL	INDIVIDUALS	. WE MUST THEREFORE FRANKLY GIVE UP THE NOTION
APPL PREFACE(184)	OF INDUSTRY AND CONTROL BY SEPARATE PRIVATE	INDIVIDUALS	KEPT IN ORDER BY THEIR COMPETITION FOR OUR
ROCK PREFACE(155)	WE STILL SNATCH AT EVERY EXCUSE FOR DECLARING	INDIVIDUALS	OUTSIDE THE PROTECTION OF LAW AND TORTURING THEM
UNPL PREFACE(R23)	DEAL OF THE FAMILY AND PERSONAL HISTORY OF THE	INDIVIDUALS	REPRESENTED, SHOULD NEVERTHELESS GIVE THE
LION PREFACE(62)	SOME MEN FANCY OR CAN USE, IT IS NECESSARY THAT	INDIVIDUALS	SHOULD BE ABLE TO HAVE THINGS MADE TO THEIR
GETT PREFACE(220)	ANY INDIVIDUAL OR EVEN OF ANY TEN GENERATIONS OF	INDIVIDUALS	THAT IT SHOULD BE HELD TO BE AN ACT OF
SUPR HANDBOK(208)	HAPPENED TO NATIONS AS TO PRIVATE FAMILIES AND	INDIVIDUALS	THAT THEY HAVE FLOURISHED AND DECAYED, REPENTED
DEVL EPILOG (84)	THE GENERALS OF THE UNITED STATES NEVER PERMIT	INDIVIDUALS	TO BE PILLAGED. ANSWER: NOTED. PROPOSITION 3.
MIS. PREFACE(69)	SHOULD BE A SOUND ONE, AND SO USELESS FOR CLEVER	INDIVIDUALS	TO DISPARAGE IT UNLESS THEY CAN ORGANIZE AN
CLEO NOTES (205)	IN THE WORLD BY INCREASING THE PERCENTAGE OF	INDIVIDUALS	WHO ARE CAREFULLY BRED AND GENTLY NURTURED, EVEN
METH PREFACE(R60)	DESOLATING DEAD LEVEL THAN IN THE CASE OF THE	INDIVIDUALS	WHO ARE BORN AND BRED IN ENGLISH COUNTRY HOUSES,
JOAN PREFACE(49)	MAKE EPOCHS RATHER THAN BY VULGARLY AMBITIOUS	INDIVIDUALS	WHO MAKE ROWS, THE DIVINITY WHICH SHAPES OUR
METH PREFACE(R13)	IMPOSTURE PREACH AND TEACH A BETTER GOSPEL: THE	INDIVIDUALS	WHOM THEY CONVERT ARE DOOMED TO PASS AWAY IN A
MILL PREFACE(128)	BY SIMPLE LIBERALISM, THE TYRANNY OF THE TALENTED	INDIVIDUALS	WILL REMAIN. AGAIN I ASK WHAT ARE WE TO DO WITH
SUPR PREFACE(R12)	DISCOUNTENANCES THE WOMAN. NOW THE CONFLICTS OF	INDIVIDUALS	WITH LAW AND CONVENTION CAN BE DRAMATIZED LIKE
METH PREFACE(R61)	CONCEIVABLY BE THE WORK OF ENVIRONMENT ACTING ON	INDIVIDUALS	WITHOUT ANY CHARACTER OR INTELLECTUAL
LION PREFACE(93)	AND HAPPIER THAN A NATION OF WESLEYS; AND ITS	INDIVIDUALS	WOULD BE HIGHER IN THE EVOLUTIONARY SCALE. AT
MILL PREFACE(125)	RECESSIVES, HAVE EXISTED AND KEEP CROPPING UP AS	INDIVIDUALS	, AND EXCITING ANTIPATHIES OR AFFINITIES QUITE
DOCT PREFACE(70)	PRACTICE, THUS PROTECTED, WOULD ITSELF PROTECT	INDIVIDUALS	, AS FAR AS SUCH PROTECTION IS POSSIBLE, AGAINST
APPL INTRLUD(252)	OF US LIKES THEM AND THE OTHER DOESNT, NOT ONLY	INDIVIDUALS	, BUT WHOLE SORTS OF PEOPLE. FOR INSTANCE, YOUR
UNPL PREFACE(R15)	AT THE PROMPTINGS OF INDIVIDUAL BENEVOLENCE TO	INDIVIDUALS	, MAKES NICE LITTLE PLACES TO JOB NICE LITTLE
SUPR III (112)	TO BUILD UP THAT RAW FORCE INTO HIGHER AND HIGHER	INDIVIDUALS	, THE IDEAL INDIVIDUAL BEING OMNIPOTENT,

INDIVISIBLE

SUPR IV (169)	MY FREEDOM, FOR MY HONOR, FOR MY SELF, ONE AND	INDIVISIBLE	. /ANN/ YOUR HAPPINESS WILL BE WORTH THEM ALL.
BULL PREFACE(3)	WAS THAT IRELAND WAS POLITICALLY ONE AND	INDIVISIBLE	, AND, CONSEQUENTLY, THAT WHEN HOME RULE CAME,

INDIVISIBLY

KING I (165)	IN INFINITE SERIES, AND DIVIDING CURVES INTO	INDIVISIBLY	SHORT TRIANGLE BASES. HOW SILLY! WHAT A WASTE

INDOLENT

BARB PREFACE(215)	EMBRACED AS ST FRANCIS EMBRACED IT. IF A MAN IS	INDOLENT	, LET HIM BE POOR. IF HE CHOOSES TO SPEND HIS URBAN

INDOMITABLE

GETT SD(323)	STILL A TURN OF DELICATE BEAUTY AND PRIDE IN HER	INDOMITABLE	CHIN; BUT HER CHEEKS ARE WASTED AND LINED, HER
3PLA PREFACE(R27)	NEED OF HIS NATURE. WITH ALL HIS MOTHER'S	INDOMITABLE	SELFFULNESS, BUT WITH PITY INSTEAD OF HATRED AS

INDOMITABLY

NEVR IV (290)	HAVE TO CALL HIMSELF MR CLANDON. (CRAMPTON LOOKS	INDOMITABLY	RESOLVED TO DO NOTHING OF THE SORT). NO DOUBT

INDOOR

2TRU PREFACE(9)	PARKS AND GARDENS, THEIR STAFFS OF RETAINERS,	INDOOR	AND OUTDOOR, AND THE LOCAL PUBLIC WORK THAT IS ALWAYS
BASH PREFACE(88)	ON AN ELIZABETHAN STAGE, WITH TRAVERSES FOR THE	INDOOR	SCENES, AND WITH ONLY ONE INTERVAL AFTER THE SECOND

INDOORS

BUOY II (23)	AWAKE. /HE/ THEN HADNT YOU BETTER LET ME SLEEP	INDOORS	? /SHE/ THE SAXOPHONE WOULD KEEP YOU AWAKE. /HE/ ON
GLIM SD(183)	THE WOODEN PLATTERS AND FRAGMENTS OF THE MEAL	INDOORS	, FERRUCCIO IS LEFT ALONE WITH GIULIA. THE GLOAMING
MRS I (182)	GOOD OF YOU, MISS WARREN! /VIVIE/ WILL YOU COME	INDOORS	; OR WOULD YOU RATHER SIT OUT HERE AND TALK?
MIS. PREFACE(15)	TO ONE OF THE PARTIES. WHEN THEY ARE SITTING	INDOORS	THEY CANNOT ENDURE THE SAME DEGREES OF TEMPERATURE
CAPT I (234)	AN E AWITES YR COMMAWNDS. /RANKIN/ SHALL WE GO	INDOORS	TO SEE HIM? /SIR HOWARD/ I THINK WE HAD BETTER HAVE
BASH II,1, (112)	WE WAIT UPON THEIR COLDS, AND FROWST ALL DAY	INDOORS	, IF THEY BUT COUGH OR SPURN THEIR HAY. /BASHVILLE/

INDOORY

VWOO 1 (120)	AND WOULD YOU BELIEVE IT, MY MOTHER WAS THAT	INDOORY	THAT SHE GRUDGED HAVING TO GO OUT AND DO HER

INDUCE

MILL I (159)	YOU HAVE NOT A PENNY AT THE BANK, YOU MUST THEN	INDUCE	A FRIEND OR A HOTEL MANAGER TO CASH ANOTHER CHEQUE
DOCT PREFACE(76)	A NEGATIVE PHASE OF COOKING ACTIVITY, AND MIGHT	INDUCE	A POSITIVE ONE. AND THUS IT HAPPENS THAT THE REFUSAL
GETT PREFACE(239)	THE ONLY DISCOMFORT SUFFICIENTLY IRKSOME TO	INDUCE	A WOMAN TO BREAK UP HER HOME, AND ECONOMIC DEPENDENCE
MIS. PREFACE(34)	IT WE MUST PUT ASIDE THE CONSIDERATIONS THAT NOW	INDUCE	ALL HUMANE AND THOUGHTFUL POLITICAL STUDENTS TO
SUPR HANDBOK(228)	TO RECRUIT FOR MONASTERIES AND CONVENTS THAN TO	INDUCE	AN ARAB WOMAN TO UNCOVER HER MOUTH IN PUBLIC, OR A
MILL I (159)	YOU, ON PAIN OF EIGHTEEN MONTHS HARD LABOR, TO	INDUCE	ANOTHER FRIEND OR HOTEL MANAGER TO CASH ANOTHER
ROCK PREFACE(156)	WOULD CEASE BECAUSE IT WOULD BE IMPOSSIBLE TO	INDUCE	ANY DECENT CITIZEN TO FLOG ANOTHER. AMONG US A
MILL III (184)	FOR FOURTEEN POUNDS. TELL HIM THAT IF HE CAN	INDUCE	BOLTON'S TO PART FROM IT AT THAT FIGURE YOU WILL GIVE
HART II (91)	WAS SUCH A TERRIBLE LESSON TO HER: NOTHING WOULD	INDUCE	HER TO TRY SUCH A THING AGAIN. /MRS HUSHABYE/ THEN
SUPR IV (154)	IT FOR HIS HOTEL BILL. I'LL SEE WHETHER I CAN	INDUCE	HIM TO ACCEPT IT. NOT NOW, OF COURSE, BUT PRESENTLY.
AUGS (272)	MILITARY STRATEGY, DECLARED THAT NOTHING WOULD	INDUCE	HIM TO DEPRIVE MY COUNTRY OF MY SERVICES, AND SET ME
POSN PREFACE(377)	TO BE ABLE TO ASSURE ME THAT NOTHING SHOULD	INDUCE	HIM TO GIVE UP MY STATEMENT OR PREVENT HIM FROM
POSN PREFACE(366)	BY AN UNKNOWN MAN MAY ATTRACT HIM SUFFICIENTLY TO	INDUCE	HIM TO GIVE THAT UNKNOWN MAN A TRIAL; BUT THIS DOES
NEVR II SD(226)	WHICH ARE NOT SUFFICIENTLY SUCCULENT TO	INDUCE	HIM TO PERSEVERE WITH THEM. /THE GENTLEMAN/ (YAWNING
APPL II (269)	CLEVERER THAN I AM. BUT I HAVE NEVER BEEN ABLE TO	INDUCE	HIM TO TAKE ANY INTEREST IN PARLIAMENTARY POLITICS.
PHIL III (145)	VERY GOOD FRIENDS, I HOPE; BUT NOTHING WOULD	INDUCE	ME TO MARRY YOU. (SHE TAKES THE EASY CHAIR AT THE
MTH2 (53)	ON THAT SUBJECT MY LIPS ARE CLOSED. NOTHING WILL	INDUCE	ME TO SAY ONE WORD AGAINST THE OLD MAN. I NEVER HAVE;
BULL PREFACE(50)	OTHER COUNTRIES), IT WOULD BE VERY DIFFICULT TO	INDUCE	MEN OF CAPACITY AND CHARACTER TO ENTER IT. AND IN
BULL PREFACE(66)	ANOTHER ILLUSTRATION OF HOW HOPELESS IT IS TO	INDUCE	ONE MODERN NATION, PREOCCUPIED AS IT NECESSARILY IS
GETT PREFACE(203)	EXISTENCE OF THE MOST UNBEARABLE HARDSHIPS WILL	INDUCE	OUR STATESMEN TO MOVE SO LONG AS THE VICTIMS SUBMIT
MIS. PREFACE(6)	KEEPS PLENTY OF SERVANTS IT IS IMPOSSIBLE TO	INDUCE	PARENTS TO KEEP THEIR CHILDREN AT HOME INSTEAD OF
GETT PREFACE(207)	TO INCREASE IT, WE MUST TAKE IMMEDIATE STEPS TO	INDUCE	PEOPLE OF MODERATE MEANS TO MARRY EARLIER AND TO HAVE
GETT PREFACE(224)	CARRIED EVEN TO SUCH FASTIDIOUSNESS AS TO	INDUCE	PEOPLE TO SAY QUITE COMMONLY THAT THERE IS ONLY ONE
ROCK II (262)	OF EXTERMINATION? I DONT THINK YOU WILL EVER	INDUCE	RESPECTABLE BRITONS TO WEAR RED-WHITE-AND-BLUE
UNPL PREFACE(R22)	AND THE RESULT IS THAT IT IS VERY DIFFICULT TO	INDUCE	THE ENGLISH PUBLIC TO BUY AND READ PLAYS. INDEED, WHY
MILL PREFACE(127)	EVASIVE AS HIS COLLEAGUE; BUT HE ALSO FAILED TO	INDUCE	THE NEWCOMER TO FORGO HIS PROMISED PRIVILEGE. AT LAST
BULL IV (152)	TO BE PREPARED TO TAKE THE NECESSARY STEPS TO	INDUCE	THE PEOPLE TO VOTE FOR YOU. THAT IS HOW PEOPLE
DOCT PREFACE(71)	DREAD OF THE MARVELLOUS, AND POPULAR IDOLATRY, TO	INDUCE	THE POOR TO COMPLY WITH THE SANITARY REGULATIONS THEY
DOCT PREFACE(29)	DEPENDED ON THE QUANTITY OF DRUGS THEY COULD	INDUCE	THEIR PATIENTS TO SWALLOW. THESE TWO CASES OF
PLES PREFACE(R13)	WANT AND UNDERSTAND, OR EVEN ENOUGH OF IT TO	INDUCE	THEM TO SWALLOW AT THE SAME TIME A GREAT DEAL THAT
2TRU PREFACE(15)	WORK AND A FAITH IN ITS BENEFICENCE WHICH WILL	INDUCE	THEM TO TAKE VOWS TO ABSTAIN FROM ANY PROFIT THAT IS
LION PREFACE(73)	PROTESTING AT EVERY STEP THAT NOTHING WILL	INDUCE	US TO GO; THAT IT IS A RIDICULOUS WAY, A DISGRACEFUL
PHIL I (74)	ANY EXCEPTION. I HAD A GOOD DEAL OF TROUBLE TO	INDUCE	YOU TO COME AND SEE US. YOU WERE VERY COY.
MRS PREFACE(165)	NO PAINS TO MAKE KNOWN THAT MY PLAYS ARE BUILT TO	INDUCE	, NOT VOLUPTUOUS REVERIE BUT INTELLECTUAL INTEREST,

INDUCED

DOCT PREFACE(62)	INDUCED EPIDEMICS, PROVING THAT EPIDEMICS CAN BE	INDUCED	BY TRADESMEN, AND THEREFORE BY DOCTORS. THE DOCTOR'S
DOCT PREFACE(62)	OF BEING GENUINE: FASHIONS, AFTER ALL, ARE ONLY	INDUCED	EPIDEMICS, PROVING THAT EPIDEMICS CAN BE INDUCED BY
DOCT PREFACE(51)	AT ALL SURPRISED IF WHAT I HAVE WRITTEN ABOVE HAS	INDUCED	IN SYMPATHETIC READERS A TRANSPORT OF VIRTUOUS
DOCT PREFACE(54)	A SPECIFIC DISEASE OR ONLY ORDINARY TETANUS	INDUCED	(AS TETANUS WAS THEN SUPPOSED TO BE INDUCED) BY A
SIM PREFACE(5)	RULERS. I LEARNED THIS EARLY IN LIFE. MY NURSE	INDUCED	ME TO ABSTAIN FROM CERTAIN TROUBLESOME ACTIVITIES BY
MIS. PREFACE(49)	BOOKS: FOR EXAMPLE, THOUGH NOTHING WOULD HAVE	INDUCED	ME TO READ THE BUDGET OF STUPID PARTY LIES THAT
SUPR III (99)	OF IT; BUT AS A MATTER OF FACT NOTHING COULD HAVE	INDUCED	ME TO STAY THERE. I SIMPLY LEFT IT AND ORGANIZED
DOCT PREFACE(54)	INDUCED (AS TETANUS WAS THEN SUPPOSED TO BE	INDUCED	) BY A LACERATED WOUND, THERE WERE NO STATISTICS
APPL PREFACE(195)	BREAKAGES, LIMITED, WOULD DO NOTHING FOR HIM, I	INDUCED	SOME LESS EMBARRASSED PUBLIC PERSONS TO TAKE A RIDE
GETT SD(259)	ADROIT COMPLAINTS OF THE DISCOMFORT OF THE PLACE,	INDUCED	THE ECCLESIASTICAL COMMISSIONERS TO GIVE HIM SOME
PYGM PREFACE(199)	AND JOSEPH CHAMBERLAIN WAS BOOMING THE EMPIRE, I	INDUCED	THE EDITOR OF A LEADING MONTHLY REVIEW TO COMMISSION
POSN PREFACE(429)	PROSPECTUS-- PLEADING IN COURT THAT HE HAD	INDUCED	THE LORD CHAMBERLAIN TO ISSUE A CERTIFICATE THAT THE
FANY PROLOG (265)	IS A MEMBER OF THE NEW ACADEMIC COMMITTEE. HE	INDUCED	THEM TO GO IN FOR A UNIFORM LIKE THE FRENCH ACADEMY;

GETT PREFACE(243)	USED. IF A PRISONFUL OF THIEVES WERE ASKED WHAT	INDUCED	THEM TO TAKE TO THIEVING, AND SOME REPLIED POVERTY,
METH PREFACE(R39)	NEITHER PARENTS, PARSONS, NOR PEDAGOGUES COULD BE	INDUCED	TO ADOPT THAT ARTICLE. ST JOHN MIGHT SAY THAT " GOD
FABL PREFACE(75)	THE HUMAN RACE AS ONE OF HIS MISTAKES, WAS	INDUCED	TO MAKE AN EXCEPTION IN THE CASE OF NOAH AND HIS
2TRU PREFACE(12)	PEOPLE WITH ANY MONEY TO SPARE THAT THEY CAN BE	INDUCED	TO PART WITH IT ONLY ON CONDITION THAT THE
DOCT PREFACE(32)	AS SHE WAS BY THE SERPENT, BEFORE HE COULD BE	INDUCED	TO PLUCK THE APPLE FROM THE TREE OF KNOWLEDGE. I
POSN PREFACE(401)	STILL FALL INTO ARREAR. NO COMMITTEE COULD BE	INDUCED	TO UNDERTAKE SUCH A TASK. THE ATTACHMENT OF AN
BARB III (315)	SON. /UNDERSHAFT/ DO YOU REALLY THINK SO? HE HAS	INDUCED	US TO BRING HIM INTO THE WORLD; BUT HE CHOSE HIS
GENV II (54)	ON EARTH YOU THINK YOU HAVE BEEN DOING? WHAT	INDUCED	YOU TO DO IT? /THE SECRETARY/ I DIDNT DO IT. IT WAS
		INDUCEMENT	
GETT PREFACE(215)	WERE POSSESSED OF INDEPENDENT MEANS, HAVE EVERY	INDUCEMENT	TO ADOPT THE NEW CONDITIONS INSTEAD OF THE OLD
MIS. PREFACE(62)	OF SULKY RESENTMENT, WHICH IS AN ADDITIONAL	INDUCEMENT	TO PACK HIM OFF TO SCHOOL. IN SCHOOL, HE FINDS
SIM PREFACE(12)	CONSUME, AND INDEED MORE. ON THE CONTRARY, EVERY	INDUCEMENT	TO SHIRK THAT PRIMARY DUTY IS CONTINUALLY BEFORE
VWOO 3 (138)	SERVICES IN THE SHOP, AND WISH TO OFFER YOU EVERY	INDUCEMENT	TO STAY HERE PERMANENTLY. /Z/ TEN POUNDS EXTRA,
DOCT PREFACE(65)	THE CONSTITUENCY UNDER HIS CHARGE, HE HAS EVERY	INDUCEMENT	TO STRIVE TOWARDS THE IDEAL OF A CLEAN BILL OF
MRS PREFACE(169)	AND THAT NOT ONE OF THESE WOMEN HAD ANY	INDUCEMENT	TO SUPPORT IT EXCEPT THEIR BELIEF IN THE
MRS III (229)	I'M GONE. /VIVIE/ I AM PROOF AGAINST EVEN THAT	INDUCEMENT	, SIR GEORGE. DONT YOU THINK YOUD BETTER TAKE
		INDUCEMENTS	
SUPR HANDBOK(211)	THE COST OF DIRECT STATE EXPERIMENTS, AND PROVIDE	INDUCEMENTS	TO PRIVATE PERSONS TO ACHIEVE SUCCESSFUL
BULL PREFACE(53)	THE LIKE, FROM THEM. BUT DENSHAWAI HAD NO SUCH	INDUCEMENTS	TO SUBMIT TO THEIR THOUGHTLESS AND SELFISH
		INDUCES	
LION PREFACE(11)	HAT, AND PRAISE HIM AS A SAINT; BUT IF HE	INDUCES	THEM TO ACTUALLY DO IT, THEY BURN HIM AS A PUBLIC
GETT PREFACE(190)	ITS WORST ASPECT AS A SLAVERY TO PLEASURE WHICH	INDUCES	TWO PEOPLE TO ACCEPT SLAVERY TO ONE ANOTHER HAS
		INDUCING	
MIS. PREFACE(3)	THAN A LABORIOUS SIXPENCE; BUT THE DIFFICULTY OF	INDUCING	A MAN TO MAKE ANY SERIOUS EFFORT TO OBTAIN 50
MIS. PREFACE(39)	IS ANOTHER MATTER. BUT MOST OF THE DIFFICULTY OF	INDUCING	CHILDREN TO LEARN WOULD DISAPPEAR IF OUR DEMANDS
MIS. PREFACE(4)	OBTAIN 50 POUNDS IS NOTHING TO THE DIFFICULTY OF	INDUCING	HIM TO MAKE A SERIOUS EFFORT TO KEEP ALIVE. THE
MIS. PREFACE(85)	THE FATE OF THE FAMILY. THE DIFFICULTY OF	INDUCING	PEOPLE TO TALK SENSIBLY ABOUT THE FAMILY IS THE
GETT PREFACE(195)	OVER THE HEAD OF HIMSELF AND HIS DAUGHTERS BY	INDUCING	PEOPLE TO PAY HIM MORE FOR HIS SERVICES THAN THEY
NEVR IV (296)	CAN YOU, IN RETURN, POINT OUT TO ME ANY WAY OF	INDUCING	THEM TO HOLD THEIR TONGUES? /MRS CLANDON/ DOLLY,
		INDUCTION	
MIS. PREFACE(44)	WITH ITS ROUTINE OF HYPOTHESIS AND VERIFICATION,	INDUCTION	AND DEDUCTION; OR EVEN INTO SO RAPID AND INTUITIVE
FANY PROLOG (257)	FANNY'S FIRST PLAY.	INDUCTION	, THE END OF A SALOON IN AN OLD-FASHIONED COUNTRY
FABL PREFACE(76)	UNDER DURESS. BUT ONE DAY I WAS PRESENT AT THE	INDUCTION	OF A RECTOR. WHEN THE BISHOP ASKED THE POSTULANT
FANY PREFACE(255)	HER GOD. THE CRITICS WHOM I HAVE LAMPOONED IN THE	INDUCTION	TO THIS PLAY UNDER THE NAMES OF TROTTER, VAUGHAN,
		INDULGE	
MTH2 (61)	OF COURSE, AS FAR AS IT MAY BE ADVISABLE TO	INDULGE	AND FLATTER THEM A LITTLE SO AS TO LET THEM DOWN
NEVR II (253)	IN SPITE OF HERSELF, AND RESIGNS HERSELF TO	INDULGE	HIM A LITTLE). LISTEN NOW. WHAT I WANT TO ASK YOU IS
SUPR II (52)	ABOUT THE CAR, BUT PRESENTLY SAUNTERS OFF TO	INDULGE	IN A CIGARET). /TANNER/ THATS A VERY MOMENTOUS
DEST (167)	THAT HIS VICTORY IS COMPLETE, AND THAT HE MAY NOW	INDULGE	IN A LITTLE PLAY WITH HIS VICTIM. HE COMES BACK AND
JOAN 3 (91)	JOAN: ONLY COMPANY OFFICERS ARE ALLOWED TO	INDULGE	IN DISPLAYS OF PERSONAL COURAGE. BESIDES, YOU MUST
SIM II (66)	SUCH A RIDICULOUS EXCUSE FOR GOING TO HIS ROOM TO	INDULGE	IN HIS POOR LITTLE SECRET VICE OF CIGARET SMOKING..
2TRU PREFACE(11)	AND THE DRUGS, HIS CHILDREN WILL STARVE. IF YOU	INDULGE	IN SUCH A LUXURY AS A CLERICAL SPIRITUAL ADVISER IT
MRS PREFACE(167)	FATE, OR IN THE REALITY OF THE FIGURES WHO	INDULGE	IN SUCH PATHOS. SITTING AT SUCH PLAYS WE DO NOT
APPL I (201)	SOMETHING ABOUT ORINTHIA. DONT. IF YOU	INDULGE	IN SUPPOSITION ON THAT SUBJECT, YOU WILL LOSE YOUR
KING I (179)	INHOSPITABLE AS TO DRIVE AWAY MY GUESTS MERELY TO	INDULGE	IN THE TRIFLING PURSUIT OF MATHEMATICAL CALCULATION,
PRES (148)	IT. /MITCHENER/ (HIGHLY INCENSED) HOW DARE YOU	INDULGE	IN THIS UNSEEMLY MIRTH IN THE PRESENCE OF YOUR
MILL I (163)	ASK? /EPIFANIA/ ALL-IN WRESTLING. WHEN YOU NEXT	INDULGE	IN YOUR FAVORITE SPORT OF WIFE BEATING, LOOK OUT FOR
JOAN EPILOG (161)	GOOD. I AM WELL CONNECTED, YOU SEE; AND THEY	INDULGE	ME. /JOAN/ POOR OLD JOHN! WHAT BROUGHT THEE TO THIS
GETT PREFACE(246)	A LITTLE PRIVATE ALSATIA IN WHICH WE CAN	INDULGE	OURSELVES AS WE PLEASE WITHOUT REPROACH OR
CLEO IV (176)	/CAESAR/ (WITH AN AIR OF DOING IT EXPRESSLY TO	INDULGE	RUFIO) WELL, WELL: LET US HAVE HIM. /RUFIO/ (
GETT (321)	/COLLINS/ WELL, THE SINGLE ONES CANT AFFORD TO	INDULGE	THEIR AFFECTIONS THE SAME AS MARRIED PEOPLE.
NEVR IV (298)	(FOLLOWING HIM) WELL, NEVER MIND. WE MUST	INDULGE	THEM A LITTLE. CAN YOU GET US SOMETHING TO WEAR,
MTH4 I (156)	FROM IT INTO AN IMAGINARY VACUUM IN WHICH YOU CAN	INDULGE	YOUR DESIRES AND HOPES AND LOVES AND HATES WITHOUT
		INDULGED	
POSN PREFACE(370)	CENSORSHIP, THE THEATRE IS NOT RESPECTED. IT IS	INDULGED	AND DESPISED AS A DEPARTMENT OF WHAT IS POLITELY
NEVR II (228)	MASTER HERBERT SPENCER. AM I HOWLED AT? NO: I'M	INDULGED	AS AN OLD FOGEY. I'M OUT OF EVERYTHING, BECAUSE IVE
ROCK PREFACE(190)	MOST, BE A LITTLE ECCENTRIC AT THE COST OF BEING	INDULGED	AS SLIGHTLY CRACKED. ON THE OTHER HAND THE
GENV PREFACE(22)	TO THE UTMOST, BUT A DELIGHTFUL SPORT TO BE	INDULGED	FOR ITS OWN SAKE, AND ASSERTED AND REASSERTED BY
POSN PREFACE(369)	INSTITUTION AND AN ABOMINABLE NUISANCE TO BOOT,	INDULGED	HIM BY APPOINTING A SELECT COMMITTEE OF BOTH HOUSES
JOAN PREFACE(38)	ABERNETHY, THE FAMOUS DOCTOR, WAS ASKED WHY HE	INDULGED	HIMSELF WITH ALL THE HABITS HE WARNED HIS PATIENTS
DOCT PREFACE(42)	WOULD LOSE THEIR EMPLOYMENT AND STARVE IF THEY	INDULGED	IN ANY PECULIARITY, A RESPECTABLE MAN WILL LIE
ROCK PREFACE(174)	IS NO EXCUSE FOR THE EXTRAVAGANCES OF CENSORSHIP	INDULGED	IN BY JEJUNE GOVERNMENTS OF REVOLUTIONISTS, AND BY
SIM PREFACE(5)	TROUBLESOME ACTIVITIES BY THREATENING THAT IF I	INDULGED	IN THEM THE COCK WOULD COME DOWN THE CHIMNEY. THIS
FOUN (211)	/BRABAZON/ EXACTLY. BUT I SHOULD NOT HAVE BEEN	INDULGED	. I WAS TOO YOUNG. HOW DID I KNOW WHAT WAS GOOD FOR
METH PREFACE(R55)	ELSE. ACCORDINGLY, I FIND THAT IN THE YEAR 1906 I	INDULGED	MY TEMPER BY HURLING INVECTIVES AT THE
O'FL (212)	/SIR PEARCE/ OH, THATS ALL RIGHT: SHE MUST BE	INDULGED	ON AN OCCASION LIKE THIS. I'M SORRY MY WIFE IS IN
LION EPILOG (150)	INDULGED THEIR PASSIONS, JUST AS THEY HAD ALWAYS	INDULGED	THEIR CLASS PREJUDICES AND COMMERCIAL INTERESTS,
LION EPILOG (150)	NO APOLOGIES OR EXCUSES, GOOD OR BAD. THEY SIMPLY	INDULGED	THEIR PASSIONS, JUST AS THEY HAD ALWAYS INDULGED
JITT III (66)	ONLY FANCIES: OF COURSE; AND I WOULDNT HAVE	INDULGED	THEM FOR THE WORLD; BUT A MAN MIGHT. WHAT I CANT
MILL PREFACE(118)	UP INTO THE SKY. THE DIPLOMATISTS IMMEDIATELY	INDULGED	THEMSELVES WITH A PRODIGIOUSLY EXPENSIVE WAR, AFTER
LION PREFACE(66)	QUALITIES WHEN THEY ARE FRANKLY PROCLAIMED AND	INDULGED	, THEY ARE LOATHSOME WHEN THEY ASSUME THE ROBES OF
		INDULGENCE	
CAND III (145)	I REFUSE IT. I BUILD A CASTLE OF COMFORT AND	INDULGENCE	AND LOVE FOR HIM, AND STAND SENTINEL ALWAYS TO
ANNA PREFACE(287)	OWN ART AS ELEPHANTINE. WE SHOULD RATHER CRAVE	INDULGENCE	AS THREE NOVICES FRESH FROM THE AWFUL LEGITIMACY
SUPR IV SD(143)	BRITISH RACE, AND TREATS HIM NORMALLY WITH THE	INDULGENCE	DUE TO AN INFERIOR AND UNLUCKY SPECIES, BUT
POSN PREFACE(398)	THEM IS DISPROVED BY THE PLAIN FACT THAT HIS	INDULGENCE	GOES AS FAR AS THE POLICE, AND SOMETIMES FURTHER
CAND I (99)	I WONT ALLOW. DONT FORCE ME TO SHEW YOU THE	INDULGENCE	I SHOULD SHEW TO A CHILD. BE A MAN. /MARCHBANKS/
HART PREFACE(12)	AND MAGISTRATES DID NOT ALWAYS MANIFEST ITSELF IN	INDULGENCE	. NO PERSON UNLUCKY ENOUGH TO BE CHARGED WITH ANY
HART PREFACE(12)	CROSS DID NOT CARRY WITH IT A PERPETUAL PLENARY	INDULGENCE	. UNFORTUNATELY THE INSANITY OF THE JURIES AND
MRS PREFACE(165)	PEOPLE TO INFER THAT A PLAY WHICH OVERSTEPPED HIS	INDULGENCE	MUST BE A VERY EXCITING PLAY INDEED. ACCORDINGLY,
MIS. PREFACE(65)	UNTRUSTWORTHY IN EVERY WAY WITHOUT EXHAUSTING THE	INDULGENCE	OF THE COUNTRY HOUSE. BUT LET HIM DARE TO BE "
POSN PREFACE(396)	HYPOCRITICALLY POPULAR, AND THE ENDING HAPPY, THE	INDULGENCE	OF THE LORD CHAMBERLAIN CAN BE COUNTED ON. ON THE
LION PREFACE(35)	THE PARABLE OF THE PRODIGAL SON, APPEALING TO THE	INDULGENCE	ROMANCE HAS ALWAYS SHEWN TO CHARLES SURFACE AND
MTH4 III (196)	THE ENVOY IS UNHINGED. I THROW MYSELF UPON YOUR	INDULGENCE	-- /ZOO/ (INTERRUPTING HIM INTOLERANTLY) DONT
NEVR II (234)	ME AS YOUR SON? /WAITER/ (WITH RESPECTFUL	INDULGENCE	) YES, SIR. ANYTHING YOU PLEASE, SIR. /PHILIP/
GETT PREFACE(188)	LAXITY OF CONDUCT IS WINKED AT WITH GRINNING	INDULGENCE	; SO THAT WE FIND THE AUSTERE SHELLEY DENOUNCED
BULL II (116)	HIM THERE IS SOMETHING DIVINE IN THE SYMPATHETIC	INDULGENCE	SHE SUBSTITUTES FOR THE ANGRY DISGUST WITH WHICH
POSN PREFACE(368)	WHILST THOSE WHOSE PRACTICE IT IS TO STRAIN HIS	INDULGENCE	TO THE UTMOST WERE ALMOST RAPTUROUS IN HIS
MIS. PREFACE(34)	PEOPLE WHO REGARD HAPPINESS AS A VERY EXCEPTIONAL	INDULGENCE	TO WHICH CHILDREN ARE BY NO MEANS ENTITLED,
CAND I SD(91)	AND IS LOOKING AT THEM WITH AN AMUSED MATERNAL	INDULGENCE	WHICH IS HER CHARACTERISTIC EXPRESSION. SHE IS A
PHIL II (125)	OH, IF YOU HAD A SCRAP OF SELF-RESPECT, THEIR	INDULGENCE	WOULD MAKE YOU CREEP ALL OVER. I UNDERSTAND NOW
GETT PREFACE(255)	AS OFTEN SPOILT BY SEVERITY AND COLDNESS AS BY	INDULGENCE	, AND THAT THE NOTION THAT NATURAL PARENTS ARE
DEST SD(149)	THE ALPS WITH RESPECT AND THE ANTHILLS WITH	INDULGENCE	, NEITHER DISGUSTED BY THE BASKING OF THE SWINE
		INDULGENCES	
MIS. PREFACE(65)	OF HARSH TREATMENT. GRATUITIES ARE VOTED,	INDULGENCES	AND HOLIDAYS ARE PLEADED FOR, DELINQUENCIES ARE
GETT PREFACE(250)	NOT BE THROWN ON THE SCRAP-HEAP WITH THE SALE OF	INDULGENCES	AND THE LIKE; AND SO THE REFORMATION LEFT
APPL PREFACE(173)	AND TO LEAVE TO THE LESS HIGHLY PLACED SUCH	INDULGENCES	AS TEMPERS, TANTRUMS, BULLYINGS, SNEERINGS,
DOCT I SD(81)	TO WALK. SHE HAS USED HER UGLINESS TO SECURE	INDULGENCES	UNATTAINABLE BY CLEOPATRA OR FAIR ROSAMUND, AND

2TRU PREFACE(15)	THAT IS NOT SHARED BY ALL THE REST, AND FROM ALL	INDULGENCES	WHICH MIGHT BLUNT THEIR CONSCIENCES OR SUBJECT
SIM PREFACE(7)	LED TO A TRADE IN ABSOLUTIONS, PARDONS, AND	INDULGENCES	WHICH PROVED BY THE HARDNESS OF THE CASH THE
		INDULGENT	
MRS PREFACE(178)	EVER WENT THERE. THESE ARE THE PEOPLE WHO,	INDULGENT	OR INDIFFERENT TO APHRODISIAC PLAYS, RAISE THE
INCA (249)	PITYINGLY; SHRUGS HIS SHOULDERS; THEN, WITH	INDULGENT	PATERNAL CONTEMPT) EXCELLENT LADS, MADAM. VERY
BARB III (321)	PUTTING HIS HAND ON HIS FATHER'S SHOULDER WITH	INDULGENT	PATRONAGE) REALLY, MY DEAR FATHER, IT IS
MTH5 (206)	YOU ARE GOING? /THE ANCIENT/ (MILD, BLAND, AND	INDULGENT	) I DID NOT KNOW THERE WAS A NURSERY HERE, OR I
UNPL PREFACE(R7)	FOR HIGH FUNCTIONS. FASHIONABLE LIFE, OPEN ON	INDULGENT	TERMS TO UNENCUMBERED " BRILLIANT" PERSONS, I
GENV I (39)	WOULD HAVE STOOD FOR IT. AND HE WAS MUCH TOO	INDULGENT	TO HIS ENEMIES. NATURALLY, WHENEVER HE WON AN
JOAN PREFACE(41)	THEY ARE ENOUGH TO SHEW THAT BETWEEN A MAXIMUM OF	INDULGENT	TOLERATION AND A RUTHLESSLY INTOLERANT TERRORISM
LION II (133)	HIM I SHOULD NOT HAVE HAD THE MONEY. /CAESAR/ (	INDULGENT	, LAUGHING) YOU ROGUES: THERE IS NO END TO YOUR
		INDULGENTLY	
CAND I (98)	AND KINDNESS. (MORELL, FIRM AS A ROCK, LOOKS	INDULGENTLY	AT HIM). DONT LOOK AT ME IN THAT SELF-COMPLACENT
CATH 2 (178)	(SHE STEPS DOWN TO THE FLOOR LEVEL AND LOOKS	INDULGENTLY	AT PATIOMKIN. HE GURGLES BRUTISHLY; SHE HAS AN
MRS I (191)	TEA? /MRS WARREN/ YES, DEARIE. (SHE LAUGHS	INDULGENTLY	AT PRAED'S GRAVITY, AND PATS HIM ON THE CHEEK AS
CAND I (81)	HE HAS WON OVER BY A DOGLIKE DEVOTION, LOOKS UP	INDULGENTLY	FROM THE CHURCH REFORMER, AND REMARKS) WELL,
DOCT II (127)	A FORMIDABLE GRUNT. B.B. LAUGHS AND PATS HIM	INDULGENTLY	ON THE SHOULDER) GOODNIGHT. GOODNIGHT.
WIDO III (52)	HOUSE, THEN. I WONT HAVE IT HERE. /LICKCHEESE/ (	INDULGENTLY	) COME, SARTORIUS: DONT BE STIFFNECKED. I COME
APPL II (262)	GERMANY CALL IT? /VANHATTAN/ (SHAKING HIS HEAD	INDULGENTLY	) FRANCE AND GERMANY? THESE QUEER OLD
MTH3 (130)	DASHES OUT IN A FURY). /BURGE-LUBIN/ (LAUGHING	INDULGENTLY	) HE WILL KEEP THE SECRET ALL RIGHT. I KNOW
CLEO IV (193)	/CLEOPATRA/ HAVE YOU FORGOTTEN ME? /CAESAR/ (	INDULGENTLY	) I AM BUSY NOW, MY CHILD, BUSY. WHEN I RETURN
ANNA (299)	(HE KISSES HER HAND). /THE GRAND DUCHESS/ (	INDULGENTLY	) IDOLATER! WHEN WILL YOU LEARN THAT OUR
MRS II (210)	AT SCHOOL? DONT BE A FOOL, CHILD. /VIVIE/ (	INDULGENTLY	) THATS ALL YOU HAVE TO SAY ON THE SUBJECT, IS
CATH 2 (178)	TAVERN AND LOW COMPANY FOR THE REST OF THE DAY. (	INDULGENTLY	) THERE! (SHE TAKES A PILLOW FROM THE BED AND
BULL I (79)	BOTTLE (HE REPLENISHES). /BROADBENT/ (SMILING	INDULGENTLY	) WELL, TIM, WILL YOU COME WITH ME AND HELP TO
BULL III (137)	D'YE THINK, FATHER DEMPSEY? /FATHER DEMPSEY/ (	INDULGENTLY	) WELL, HE HASNT MUCH SENSE, GOD HELP HIM; BUT
DOCT II (120)	WHAT! /SIR PATRICK/ (GRUNTS)! /B.B./ (	INDULGENTLY	) WELL, WELL, IT WAS REALLY HARDLY BORROWING;
CLEO II (131)	OF HIS BRITISH SECRETARY IS INEXHAUSTIBLE, SMILES	INDULGENTLY	). /RUFIO/ IT IS NO USE TALKING TO HIM,
PYGM III (258)	INCOME! IS THAT WHAT YOU MEAN? /PICKERING/ (	INDULGENTLY	, BEING RATHER BORED) OH, THAT WILL BE ALL
		INDULGES	
SUPR HANDBOK(203)	OF CALAIS, AND THE DEMOCRATIC AMERICAN OFFICER	INDULGES	IN TORTURE IN THE PHILIPPINES JUST AS THE
		INDULGING	
FANY PROLOG (266)	GREATLY INDEBTED TO YOU, GENTLEMEN, FOR SO KINDLY	INDULGING	HER WHIM. (THE DRESSING BELL SOUNDS. THE COUNT
CYMB FORWORD(137)	OF CONSCIENCE AND HAVE NO APOLOGY TO MAKE FOR	INDULGING	IN A VARIATION ON THE LAST ACT OF CYMBELINE. I
DOCT PREFACE(39)	OF IT. THOSE WHO ACCUSE VIVISECTORS OF	INDULGING	THE WELL-KNOWN PASSION OF CRUELTY UNDER THE CLOAK
		INDUSTRIAL	
METH PREFACE(R62)	CAPITALISTS SHEWED THAT MARX HAD NEVER BREATHED	INDUSTRIAL	AIR, AND HAD DUG HIS CASE OUT OF BLUEBOOKS IN THE
MILL PREFACE(129)	OUR PRESENT PROLETARIAT TO DEAL WITH, REESTABLISH	INDUSTRIAL	ANARCHY AND HERITABLE PRIVATE PROPERTY IN LAND
APPL PREFACE(183)	DEVELOPMENT OF SOCIALISM AND COMMUNISM. OUR	INDUSTRIAL	AND SOCIAL LIFE IS SET IN A HUGE COMMUNISTIC
BULL PREFACE(71)	AND THE CATHOLIC HAVE BEEN THE BULWARK OF THE	INDUSTRIAL	CAPITALISTS AGAINST THE GROWING POLITICAL POWER
UNPL PREFACE(R26)	WITH HONORABLE INDUSTRIES GUARDED BY A HUMANE	INDUSTRIAL	CODE AND A " MORAL MINIMUM" WAGE. HOW I CAME,
2TRU PREFACE(12)	WHEN JOINT STOCK COMPANIES WERE FORMED TO RUN BIG	INDUSTRIAL	CONCERNS WITH MONEY RAISED ON THE STILL MORE
APPL I (237)	HE REPRESENTS BREAKAGES, LIMITED, THE BIGGEST	INDUSTRIAL	CORPORATION IN THE COUNTRY. /LYSISTRATA/ (
MRS PREFACE(156)	(SACRED WORD, HOME!) ISSUED BY THE WOMEN'S	INDUSTRIAL	COUNCIL (HOME INDUSTRIES OF WOMEN IN LONDON,
SUPR HANDBOK(212)	ORDINARY POVERTY. IN OUR PRESENT HAPPY-GO-LUCKY	INDUSTRIAL	DISORDER, ALL THE HUMAN PRODUCTS, SUCCESSFUL OR
MIS. PREFACE(36)	COERCION. THE EAGERNESS OF CHILDREN IN OUR	INDUSTRIAL	DISTRICTS TO ESCAPE FROM SCHOOL TO THE FACTORY IS
SUPR HANDBOK(179)	VITAL MATTER THAN MERE PERSONAL INEQUITIES IN	INDUSTRIAL	ECONOMY. NO SUCH CONFLICT WAS PERCEIVED WHILST
SIM PREFACE(13)	PENAL POOR LAW FOR WORKERS THROWN OUT OF OUR	INDUSTRIAL	ESTABLISHMENTS AS " TOO OLD AT FORTY." AS I
2TRU PREFACE(23)	VINCENT'S IDEA IS CONSEQUENTLY LOST; BUT MODERN	INDUSTRIAL	EXPERIENCE CONFIRMS IT; FOR THE LATEST
BULL IV (174)	YES, MR KEEGAN: THIS PLACE MAY HAVE AN	INDUSTRIAL	FUTURE, OR IT MAY HAVE A RESIDENTIAL FUTURE: I
METH PREFACE(R30)	OF THE MEDIEVAL WAR-HORSE TO MODERN RACING AND	INDUSTRIAL	HAULAGE. HE KNEW THAT THERE ARE NEARLY TWO
BARB PREFACE(242)	AND NINETEENTH CENTURIES, THROWS OUR LEGAL AND	INDUSTRIAL	INSTITUTIONS OUT OF DATE, ANARCHISM BECOMES
BULL PREFACE(71)	SMALLER. NOW IT HAPPENS THAT PROTESTANT ULSTER IS	INDUSTRIAL	IRELAND AND CATHOLIC IRELAND AGRICULTURAL
BULL PREFACE(50)	DEPENDENT FOR ITS RECRUITS ON THE REFUSE OF	INDUSTRIAL	LIFE, AND FOR ITS OFFICERS ON THE ARISTOCRATIC
MIS. PREFACE(103)	THAN WE CAN FEED AND CLOTHE THEM WITHOUT	INDUSTRIAL	MACHINERY. SHATTER THE MACHINE, AND YOU GET
SUPR III (105)	SUBMARINE TORPEDO BOAT. THERE IS NOTHING IN MAN'S	INDUSTRIAL	MACHINERY BUT HIS GREED AND SLOTH: HIS HEART IS
FABL PREFACE(67)	IS MORE, THEY ARE ALL EQUALLY INDISPENSABLE. AN	INDUSTRIAL	MAGNATE ONCE WROTE ASKING ME DID I REALIZE THAT
FABL IV (115)	WOULD NOT MAKE POLITICAL ALLIANCES, NOR ENGAGE IN	INDUSTRIAL	MASS PRODUCTION OR WAGE WORLD WARS. ATOMIC BOMBS
FANY PROLOG (259)	ON 1500 POUNDS A YEAR; WHILST OUR WRETCHED VULGAR	INDUSTRIAL	MILLIONAIRES ARE SPENDING TWENTY THOUSAND ON THE
HART III (133)	/MANGAN/ PEOPLE THINK I HAVE. PEOPLE THINK I'M AN	INDUSTRIAL	NAPOLEON. THATS WHY MISS ELLIE WANTS TO MARRY ME.
SUPR PREFACE(R28)	OUR IDEAL PROSPERITY IS NOT THE PROSPERITY OF THE	INDUSTRIAL	NORTH, BUT THE PROSPERITY OF THE ISLE OF WIGHT,
CLEO NOTES (207)	IF LIFE IS CROWNED BY ITS SUCCESS AND DEVOTION IN	INDUSTRIAL	ORGANIZATION AND INGENUITY, WE HAD BETTER WORSHIP
APPL I (237)	AS THE GREAT THUNDERING DYNAMOS OF OUR BIG	INDUSTRIAL	PLANTS. I DO IT; BUT IT COSTS TWICE AS MUCH AS IT
MTH3 (110)	FOR SOME YEARS I WAS IN CONTINUAL TROUBLE. THE	INDUSTRIAL	POLICE ROUNDED ME UP AGAIN AND AGAIN, REFUSING TO
BARB PREFACE(216)	COBDEN-SANDERSON, IN SAYING THIS, HE SOLVED THE	INDUSTRIAL	PROBLEM AT A STROKE. AT PRESENT WE SAY CALLOUSLY
APPL II (262)	WE FIND HERE EVERYTHING WE ARE ACCUSTOMED TO: OUR	INDUSTRIAL	PRODUCTS, OUR BOOKS, OUR PLAYS, OUR SPORTS, OUR
SUPR HANDBOK(189)	THE PERPETUAL SHIFTING OF CONDITIONS PRODUCED BY	INDUSTRIAL	PROGRESS.) EVEN IF THIS SELECTIVE AGENCY HAD NOT
BULL PREFACE(71)	AGAINST THE GROWING POLITICAL POWER OF THE	INDUSTRIAL	PROLETARIAT ORGANIZED IN TRADE UNIONS, LABOR
METH PREFACE(R10)	OF ELECTRICITY, THE APPLICATION OF STEAM TO	INDUSTRIAL	PURPOSES, AND THE PENNY POST. IT WAS JUST THE
BULL III (132)	DESCRIPTION) ARE WE, MATT? /LARRY/ FOR MODERN	INDUSTRIAL	PURPOSES YOU MIGHT JUST AS WELL BE, BARNEY. YOURE
MRS PREFACE(176)	THAT YOU CANNOT CHEAPEN WOMEN IN THE MARKET FOR	INDUSTRIAL	PURPOSES WITHOUT CHEAPENING THEM FOR OTHER
SUPR PREFACE(R25)	PROSECUTION OF DYNASTIC WARS, HAS BECOME THE	INDUSTRIAL	REORGANIZATION OF BRITAIN, THE CONSTRUCTION OF A
BARB PREFACE(242)	HUGE CHANGE IN SOCIAL CONDITIONS, SUCH AS THE	INDUSTRIAL	REVOLUTION OF THE EIGHTEENTH AND NINETEENTH
METH PREFACE(R60)	TO THE SUPERIORITY OF YOUR OWN CHARACTER! THE	INDUSTRIAL	REVOLUTION HAD TURNED NUMBERS OF GREEDY DULLARDS
JOAN PREFACE(41)	UNDER THE STRAIN OF AN UNSKILLED ATTEMPT AT	INDUSTRIAL	REVOLUTION BY SOCIALISTS WHO UNDERSTOOD SOCIALISM
METH PREFACE(R16)	TO WHOM THE ORGANIZATION BY THE NATION OF ITS OWN	INDUSTRIAL	SERVICES WOULD MEAN CHECKMATE. FINANCIAL
APPL I (238)	YOUR ONE SUPPORTER IN THE CABINET ADMITS THAT THE	INDUSTRIAL	SITUATION IS TOO STRONG FOR HER. I DO NOT PRETEND
LADY PREFACE(230)	THING IS TRUE OF MR HARRIS'S OWN PLAYS AND MINE.	INDUSTRIAL	SLAVERY IS NOT COMPATIBLE WITH THAT FREEDOM OF
MIS. PREFACE(28)	BE INCAPABLE OF SUCCESSFUL REVOLT AGAINST THEIR	INDUSTRIAL	SLAVERY. THE MOST IMPORTANT SIMPLE FUNDAMENTAL
MIS. PREFACE(6)	OR ARE LESS POWERFUL, IN THE CASE OF MANUAL AND	INDUSTRIAL	SLAVERY. SENSATIONALLY BAD CASES FALL INTO TWO
BARB PREFACE(224)	FOLLOW UP THE INCOME OF THE SWEET LADIES TO ITS	INDUSTRIAL	SOURCE, AND THERE HE WILL FIND MRS WARREN'S
LION PREFACE(57)	FOR HIM INSTEAD OF BASING, AS WE DO, OUR WHOLE	INDUSTRIAL	SYSTEM ON SUCCESSIVE COMPETITIVE WAVES OF
MIS. PREFACE(35)	NOTHING TO BE DONE, IS OUR SCHOOL SYSTEM AND OUR	INDUSTRIAL	SYSTEM. THE SCHOOL IS A PRISON IN WHICH WORK IS A
METH PREFACE(R64)	HUMAN PURPOSE AND DESIGN AND FORETHOUGHT INTO THE	INDUSTRIAL	WELTER BEING " CONTRARY TO THE LAWS OF POLITICAL
2TRU PREFACE(17)	IN THE FIRST INSTANCE BY THE GROUP OF PEASANTS OR	INDUSTRIAL	WORKERS WITH WHOM THE POSTULANT'S DAILY LIFE HAS
JOAN PREFACE(43)	GIVEN? THE GOVERNMENT OF THE WORLD, POLITICAL,	INDUSTRIAL	, AND DOMESTIC, HAS TO BE CARRIED ON MOSTLY BY
DOCT PREFACE(11)	AND ARTISTIC CONSPIRACY, AND THE INNUMERABLE	INDUSTRIAL	, COMMERCIAL, AND FINANCIAL CONSPIRACIES, FROM
		INDUSTRIALISM	
FANY PROLOG (258)	KINGS MAY SUCCEED. I FOUND ENGLAND BEFOULED WITH	INDUSTRIALISM	: WELL, I DID WHAT BYRON DID: I SIMPLY REFUSED
		INDUSTRIALISTS	
FABL PREFACE(66)	CARPENTERS AND TAILORS, STOCKBROKERS AND PARSONS,	INDUSTRIALISTS	AND TRADERS ARE ALL FORTHCOMING IN THOUSANDS
ROCK PREFACE(152)	BUT I MAY DO MUCH BETTER BY LETTING MY LAND TO	INDUSTRIALISTS	FOR THE ERECTION OF FACTORIES. THEY
		INDUSTRIALLY	
LION PREFACE(54)	OUT AND ROPE YOU IN AND FINALLY STRIKE YOU DEAD	INDUSTRIALLY	AS THOROUGHLY AS ST PETER HIMSELF. THERE IS NO
FABL PREFACE(66)	MILLIONS OF " HANDS" (CORRECTLY SO CALLED	INDUSTRIALLY	) ARE BORN, BUT AS THEY ARE HELPLESS WITHOUT
SUPR III SD(72)	DO, THE WORLD WOULD BE COMPELLED TO REFORM ITSELF	INDUSTRIALLY	, AND ABOLISH SLAVERY AND SQUALOR, WHICH EXIST
BULL PREFACE(44)	AND AGAIN BY ENGLAND. UNABLE TO COMPETE WITH US	INDUSTRIALLY	, SHE HAS DESTROYED OUR INDUSTRIES BY THE BRUTE

INDUSTRIES

ROCK I (223)	WILL SOON SEE THE ONE THING THAT CAN REVIVE OUR	INDUSTRIES	AND SAVE OUR BELOVED COUNTRY: A RISE IN PRICES."
SIM PREFACE(11)	COMMISSARS WHO HAD TO MAKE THE RUSSIAN	INDUSTRIES	AND TRANSPORT SERVICES WORK, FOUND THEMSELVES
FABL PREFACE(84)	THE LABOR PARTY IN ENGLAND NATIONALIZED AS MANY	INDUSTRIES	AS IT COULD MANAGE, AND REGULATED PRIVATE
BULL PREFACE(44)	WITH US INDUSTRIALLY, SHE HAS DESTROYED OUR	INDUSTRIES	BY THE BRUTE FORCE OF PROHIBITIVE TAXATION. SHE
UNPL PREFACE(R26)	AND MRS WARREN'S PROFESSION WITH HONORABLE	INDUSTRIES	GUARDED BY A HUMANE INDUSTRIAL CODE AND A " MORAL
ROCK I (202)	NATIONALIZE THE LAND IF YOU WILL; NATIONALIZE OUR	INDUSTRIES	IF WE MUST; NATIONALIZE EDUCATION, HOUSING,
SUPR HANDBOK(212)	FOR DIVIDENDS, JUST AS THEY ARE IN ORDINARY	INDUSTRIES	. EVEN A JOINT STOCK HUMAN STUD FARM (PIOUSLY
ROCK II (237)	COLLECTIVE FARMING. NATIONALIZATION OF FERTILIZER	INDUSTRIES	. NITROGEN FROM THE AIR. POWER FROM THE TIDES.
ROCK II (237)	PROHIBITION OF PRIVATE FOREIGN TRADE IN PROTECTED	INDUSTRIES	. STATE IMPORTS ONLY, TO BE SOLD AT STATE
MRS PREFACE(156)	(BLUEBOOK C4402, 1889); READ THE REPORT ON HOME	INDUSTRIES	(SACRED WORD, HOME!) ISSUED BY THE WOMEN'S
METH PREFACE(R69)	POPULAR DEMAND FOR DIRECT ACTION BY THE ORGANIZED	INDUSTRIES	(" SYNDICALISM"); AND WRECKED THE CENTRE OF
BARB PREFACE(237)	OF THE VENEERING FROM THE HUGE MEAT PACKING	INDUSTRIES	OF CHICAGO, AND SHEWS IT TO US AS A SAMPLE OF
MRS PREFACE(156)	ISSUED BY THE WOMEN'S INDUSTRIAL COUNCIL (HOME	INDUSTRIES	OF WOMEN IN LONDON, 1897, 1S.); AND ASK YOURSELF
ROCK PREFACE(164)	BUSINESS ORGANIZERS NOTHING COULD BE DONE IN THE	INDUSTRIES	; AND THE HOPE THAT PICKED MEMBERS OF THE
FABL PREFACE(96)	NOW (1949) RAGING ON THE NATIONALIZATION OF OUR	INDUSTRIES	; YET NOT ONE WORD IS SAID NOR A FIGURE GIVEN AS
BULL PREFACE(44)	WITH UNINTELLIGENT RANCOR, IN WRECKING ALL THE	INDUSTRIES	THAT WERE BASED ON THE POVERTY OF OUR PEOPLE
GETT PREFACE(192)	THEY WERE INCAPABLE OF COMPREHENDING THE	INDUSTRIES	THEY WERE ENGAGED IN, THE LAWS UNDER WHICH THEY
APPL I (222)	PROSPERITY THAT COMES OF YOUR LEAVING OUR VITAL	INDUSTRIES	TO BIG BUSINESS MEN AS LONG AS THEY KEEP YOUR

INDUSTRIOUS

BULL III (121)	AS AN INDUSTRIOUS DECENT MAN. /BROADBENT/ WAS HE	INDUSTRIOUS	? THATS REMARKABLE, YOU KNOW, IN AN IRISHMAN.
BARB II (274)	ANDS ON. IN A PROPER STATE OF SOCIETY I AM SOBER,	INDUSTRIOUS	AND HONEST: IN ROME, SO TO SPEAK, I DO AS THE
BULL III (121)	THE LEASE OF HIS FARM, AND STOOD UP FOR HIM AS AN	INDUSTRIOUS	DECENT MAN. /BROADBENT/ WAS HE INDUSTRIOUS?
FANY III (326)	TO MISS KNOX'S HAND. BUT AS A SOBER, HONEST, AND	INDUSTRIOUS	DOMESTIC SERVANT, WHO HAS, I TRUST, GIVEN
MILL PREFACE(114)	ASSUMPTION THAT THEY ARE ALWAYS WRONG. THE	INDUSTRIOUS	DUNDERHEAD WHO ALWAYS DOES WHAT WAS DONE LAST
BARB III (321)	TO ME. YOU ARE VERY PROPERLY PROUD OF HAVING BEEN	INDUSTRIOUS	ENOUGH TO MAKE MONEY; AND IT IS GREATLY TO YOUR
HART PREFACE(9)	CAREERS TO SHAMELESS RASCALS, PROVIDED THEY WERE	INDUSTRIOUS	ENOUGH. IT IS TRUE THAT THIS MOTIVE OPERATED
METH PREFACE(R44)	WHEN I DESCRIBED DARWIN AS " AN INTELLIGENT AND	INDUSTRIOUS	PIGEON FANCIER," THAT BLASPHEMOUS LEVITY, AS IT
GENV III (79)	COUNTRY SOLELY BECAUSE HE IS SO THOUGHTFUL AND	INDUSTRIOUS	THAT HIS FELLOW-COUNTRYMEN ARE HOPELESSLY BEATEN
DOCT I SD(81)	QUALIFICATION INSTEAD OF IMPAIRING IT. BEING AN	INDUSTRIOUS	, AGREEABLE, AND POPULAR OLD SOUL, SHE IS A
GENV IV (104)	EXCLUDE THE CHINESE? BECAUSE THE CHINAMAN IS SO	INDUSTRIOUS	, SO FRUGAL, SO TRUSTWORTHY, THAT NOBODY WILL
LADY PREFACE(216)	GIVE CONTINUAL SCANDAL TO THE PIOUS, SERIOUS,	INDUSTRIOUS	, SOLVENT BOURGEOIS. NO OTHER CLASS IS
LION PREFACE(53)	TODAY; FOR THERE WILL ALWAYS BE THE IDLE AND THE	INDUSTRIOUS	, THE THRIFTY AND THE WASTEFUL, THE DRUNKEN AND
2TRU PREFACE(6)	FOURTEEN THOUSAND TIMES AS SOBER, HONEST, AND	INDUSTRIOUS	, WHICH WOULD LEAD TO THE QUAINT CONCLUSION THAT
BULL III (121)	REMARKABLE, YOU KNOW, IN AN IRISHMAN. /LARRY/	INDUSTRIOUS	! THAT MAN'S INDUSTRY USED TO MAKE ME SICK,

INDUSTRIOUSLY

GENV IV (111)	IN THESE EXPRESSIONS THAT YOU MAINTAIN SO	INDUSTRIOUSLY	. DO YOU NOT FIND IT VERY TIRESOME TO HAVE TO
BULL I (79)	THE IRISH SECRETARY. EH? /BROADBENT/ (LAUGHING	INDUSTRIOUSLY	) CAPITAL. YOUR IRISH WIT HAS SETTLED THE
LION PROLOG (109)	THE LION NODS INTELLIGENTLY AND LICKS HIS PAW	INDUSTRIOUSLY	). CLEVER LITTLE LIONY-PIONY! UNDERSTANDS

INDUSTRY

MIS. PREFACE(86)	POLITICAL AS THE ORGANIZATION OF AN ARMY OR AN	INDUSTRY	: FATHERS BEING NO MORE EXPECTED TO BE SENTIMENTAL
DOCT PREFACE(49)	TO PUT A STOP TO BURGLARY IS TO PUT A STOP TO	INDUSTRY	? ALL THE VIVISECTIONS THAT HAVE BEEN PERFORMED
BULL PREFACE(44)	HIMSELF, HAVING THE ALTERNATIVE OF STOPPING OUR	INDUSTRY	ALTOGETHER, HE VERY NATURALLY AND PROPERLY AVAILED
FABL PREFACE(97)	AND ATTEMPTING A CATASTROPHIC TRANSFER OF	INDUSTRY	AND AGRICULTURE FROM PRIVATE TO PUBLIC OWNERSHIP,
APPL PREFACE(184)	TO CHOOSE, NOT BETWEEN GOVERNMENTAL CONTROL OF	INDUSTRY	AND CONTROL BY SEPARATE PRIVATE INDIVIDUALS KEPT IN
HART I (56)	HIM BOSS MANGAN, DONT THEY? HE IS A NAPOLEON OF	INDUSTRY	AND DISGUSTINGLY RICH, ISNT HE? WHY ISNT YOUR
WIDO II (42)	CONTEMPTUOUSLY OF ME BECAUSE I HAVE APPLIED MY	INDUSTRY	AND FORETHOUGHT TO THE MANAGEMENT OF OUR PROPERTY,
MTH4 II (178)	AND HABITS. I HAVE THE VIRTUES OF A LABORER:	INDUSTRY	AND INDIFFERENCE TO PERSONAL COMFORT. BUT I MUST
DEST (192)	THE SHOPKEEPER, HE PURSUES HIS PURPOSE WITH THE	INDUSTRY	AND STEADFASTNESS THAT COME FROM STRONG RELIGIOUS
HART II (94)	/MAZZINI/ I AM AFRAID ALL THE CAPTAINS OF	INDUSTRY	ARE WHAT YOU CALL FRAUDS, MRS HUSHABYE. OF COURSE
CAPT I (230)	YEARS AGO THE COLLAPSE OF THE WEST INDIAN SUGAR	INDUSTRY	CONVERTED THE INCOME OF THE ESTATE INTO AN ANNUAL
APPL PREFACE(192)	THAT THE ADOPTION OF HIS PLAN WOULD RELEASE FROM	INDUSTRY	ENOUGH MEN TO UTTERLY OVERWHELM THE CENTRAL EMPIRES
LADY (248)	ADVANCEMENT OF WOMEN OF HIGH NATURE AND FRUITFUL	INDUSTRY	EVEN AS YOUR MAJESTY IS: THE ONE A SKILFUL
CAND III (145)	AT EACH PHRASE) HIS STRENGTH FOR MY DEFENCE! HIS	INDUSTRY	FOR MY LIVELIHOOD! HIS DIGNITY FOR MY POSITION!
CAND III (143)	MY HONESTY FOR YOUR SURETY, MY ABILITY AND	INDUSTRY	FOR YOUR LIVELIHOOD, AND MY AUTHORITY AND POSITION
APPL I (235)	INTEGRITY, FOR HUMANITY, FOR THE RESCUE OF	INDUSTRY	FROM COMMERCIALISM AND OF SCIENCE FROM
MIS. PREFACE(11)	TO ANYONE. THE MANUFACTURE OF MONSTERS, THIS	INDUSTRY	IS BY NO MEANS PECULIAR TO CHINA. THE CHINESE (
METH PREFACE(R22)	TO US. WE HAVE SINCE COME TO THINK THAT ITS	INDUSTRY	IS LESS CONTINUOUS: THAT THE CLOCK STOPS FOR A LONG
BULL III (121)	EVEN AS A BOY. I TELL YOU, AN IRISH PEASANT'S	INDUSTRY	IS NOT HUMAN: IT'S WORSE THAN THE INDUSTRY OF A
OVER PREFACE(156)	SOCIETY DO NOT KNOW HOW THE OTHER SECTIONS LIVE.	INDUSTRY	IS THE MOST EFFECTIVE CHECK ON GALLANTRY. WOMEN
SUPR PREFACE(R36)	OF VIOLENCE AND ROBBERY WHICH WE CALL LAW AND	INDUSTRY	. EVEN ATHEISTS REPROACH ME WITH INFIDELITY AND
BARB III (328)	OH, MAGNIFICENT. A PERFECT TRIUMPH OF MODERN	INDUSTRY	. FRANKLY, MY DEAR FATHER, I HAVE BEEN A FOOL: I
MRS PREFACE(175)	THE FACT THAT AGRICULTURE IN ENGLAND IS A RUINED	INDUSTRY	. IF POVERTY DOES NOT MATTER AS LONG AS IT IS
POSN (440)	BY LICKING THEIR YOUNG INTO HABITS OF HONEST	INDUSTRY	. /STRAPPER/ IF I HADNT PROMISED ELDER DANIELS HERE
GENV IV (100)	AND AEROPLANE CRASHES ARE NOT THE OBJECTS OF THE	INDUSTRY	. THEY ARE ITS ACCIDENTS. THEY OCCUR IN SPITE OF
BULL III (121)	INDUSTRY IS NOT HUMAN: IT'S WORSE THAN THE	INDUSTRY	OF A CORAL INSECT. AN ENGLISHMAN HAS SOME SENSE
APPL PREFACE(193)	WAS THREATENED, THE EXPLOITERS OF THE GREAT	INDUSTRY	OF REPAIRING OUR RAILWAY TRUCKS (EVERY TIME A
ROCK PREFACE(168)	MORE LABORIOUS), STRAINS ALL THE WIT AND	INDUSTRY	OF THE RUSSIAN RULERS; AND OCCASIONAL SIDESLIPS
METH PREFACE(R51)	TOLD HIM BEFOREHAND. SO WITH THE PATIENCE AND	INDUSTRY	ON WHICH MEN OF SCIENCE PRIDE THEMSELVES, HE CUT
DOCT PREFACE(18)	FOUND HIS SELF-RESPECT ON SOBRIETY, HONESTY AND	INDUSTRY	; BUT A NAPOLEON NEEDS NO SUCH PROPS FOR HIS SENSE
DOCT PREFACE(18)	IN FRESCO PAINTING MORE CONSCIENTIOUSNESS AND	INDUSTRY	THAN GO TO THE MAKING OF THE REPUTATIONS OF A DOZEN
BARB PREFACE(216)	OF EARNING IT: ON THE CONTRARY, WE ALLOW OUR	INDUSTRY	TO BE ORGANIZED IN OPEN DEPENDENCE ON THE
GENV PREFACE(22)	JOB WHICH STRAINS THEIR MENTAL CAPACITY AND	INDUSTRY	TO THE UTMOST, BUT A DELIGHTFUL SPORT TO BE
BULL III (121)	IN AN IRISHMAN. /LARRY/ INDUSTRIOUS! THAT MAN'S	INDUSTRY	USED TO MAKE ME SICK, EVEN AS A BOY. I TELL YOU, AN
METH PREFACE(R46)	THE EVIDENCE THAT EXISTS IN THE WORLD. DARWIN'S	INDUSTRY	WAS ENORMOUS. HIS PATIENCE, HIS PERSEVERANCE, HIS
MIS. PREFACE(36)	AND UNNATURAL NOTION THAT WORK IS AN EVIL. IN	INDUSTRY	WE ARE OVERWORKED AND UNDERFED PRISONERS. UNDER
FABL PREFACE(86)	AND LAISSER-FAIRE, THE PROLETARIAT ALL FOR STATE	INDUSTRY	WITH ABOLITION OF FEUDAL PRIVILEGE AND REPLACEMENT
UNPL PREFACE(R26)	THEMSELVES IN REASONABLE COMFORT BY THEIR	INDUSTRY	WITHOUT SELLING THEIR AFFECTIONS AND THEIR
SUPR HANDBOK(212)	AND THE WORKHOUSE; AND THE REFUSE OF THE NEW	INDUSTRY	WOULD PRESUMABLY BE BETTER BRED THAN THE STAPLE
MILL PREFACE(128)	LAZINESS IN POLITICS, SHAMELESS SELFISHNESS IN	INDUSTRY	, AND GLORIFICATION OF IDLE USELESSNESS IN THE FACE
FABL PREFACE(86)	THE PLUTOCRATS DO ALL THEY CAN TO SABOTAGE STATE	INDUSTRY	, AND THE PROLETARIANS TO SABOTAGE PRIVATE
BULL PREFACE(32)	ARE IN ENGLAND, YOU GET A GOVERNING CLASS WITHOUT	INDUSTRY	, CHARACTER, COURAGE, OR REAL EXPERIENCE; AND UNDER
BULL IV (173)	POUNDS OUT OF LAND THAT HAFFIGAN, WITH ALL HIS	INDUSTRY	, COULD NOT MAKE OR LOSE TEN SHILLINGS OUT OF.
APPL PREFACE(174)	NO LONGER DARE EVEN TO TALK OF NATIONALIZING ANY	INDUSTRY	, HOWEVER SOCIALLY VITAL, THAT HAS A FARTHING OF
HART II (92)	A HALFPENNY AN HOUR RUTHLESSLY! A CAPTAIN OF	INDUSTRY	, I THINK YOU CALL HIM, DONT YOU? ARE YOU GOING TO
MIS. PREFACE(86)	IT IS BIG ENOUGH TO LEND A HAND TO THE FAMILY	INDUSTRY	, IS AN INVESTMENT IN WHICH THE ONLY DANGER IS THAT
MIS. PREFACE(38)	TO DRIVING ALL PERSONS OF A CERTAIN AGE OUT OF	INDUSTRY	, LEAVING THEM TO FIND SOMETHING EXPERIMENTAL TO
BULL PREFACE(22)	AS WELL AS OF STRONG CONSTITUTION, PEG-AWAY	INDUSTRY	, PERSONAL AMBITION, AND PARTY KEENNESS. ENGLISH
CAND I SD(85)	AND SOCIALLY WHOLESOME TRIUMPH OF THE ABILITY,	INDUSTRY	, SHREWDNESS, AND EXPERIENCE IN BUSINESS OF A MAN
GENV PREFACE(20)	COME TO TERMS WITH THE CAPTAINS OF FINANCE AND	INDUSTRY	, THE BANKERS, AND THE CONSERVATIVES WHO REALLY
BULL PREFACE(15)	ILLUSION, THE POWER OF FACING FACTS, THE NERVOUS	INDUSTRY	, THE SHARPENED WITS, THE SENSITIVE PRIDE OF THE
METH PREFACE(R57)	SUCH SKILLED DIRECTION, SUCH VIGILANT	INDUSTRY	, WAS QUITE UNINTENTIONAL? WOULD HE NOT CONCLUDE
MIS. PREFACE(102)	STATESMEN ARE MANIFESTLY NO MORE " CAPTAINS OF	INDUSTRY	" OR SCIENTIFIC POLITICIANS THAN OUR BOOKMAKERS ARE
HART II (94)	THEN THE CREATURE IS A FRAUD EVEN AS A CAPTAIN OF	INDUSTRY	! /MAZZINI/ I AM AFRAID ALL THE CAPTAINS OF

INEBRIATE

SUPR III SD(74)	MAN COULD DESIRE). EXCEPT THE BULLFIGHTING	INEBRIATE	THERE IS ONLY ONE PERSON IN THE COMPANY WHO LOOKS

INEBRIATED

CLEO IV (185)	SO RUFIO: HE KNOWS WELL THE RED VINTAGE THAT HAS	INEBRIATED	HER). /RUFIO/ (IN A LOW TONE) THERE IS SOME

INEBRIATES

ROCK I (233)	THAT MY AUNT WAS SENT TO. BUT THAT IS FOR	INEBRIATES	. /SIR ARTHUR/ THE ONE I'M GOING TO IS FOR THE

INEFFABLE

NEVR IV (305) (CONTEMPLATING THE DEFEATED DUELLIST OF SEX WITH INEFFABLE BENIGNITY) CHEER UP, SIR, CHEER UP. EVERY MAN IS
MTH2 (55) /LUBIN/ (SEATING HIMSELF IN BURGE'S CHAIR WITH INEFFABLE COMFORTABLENESS) MY DEAR BURGE: IF YOU IMAGINE
CAPT I (227) DELIGHT) NAOW, GAVNER. (HALF WHISPERING, WITH AN INEFFABLE GRIN) WRORNGFULLY HACQUITTID! /SIR HOWARD/
MTH4 I (170) THE HOLY ISLANDS AND SPOKEN FACE TO FACE WITH THE INEFFABLE ONES. HE WILL PRETEND THAT ALL THE MEASURES HE
BARB PREFACE(227) DEBTOR'S PRISON, WHO TELLS THE NEWCOMER OF ITS INEFFABLE PEACE AND SECURITY: NO DUNS; NO TYRANNICAL
CATH 4 (198) JEALOUSY) FOR YOUR LOVER? /CATHERINE/ (WITH AN INEFFABLE SMILE) NO: FOR MY MUSEUM.

INEFFECTIVE

HART PREFACE(6) IN A VACUUM WOULD HAVE LEFT THEM HELPLESS AND INEFFECTIVE IN PUBLIC AFFAIRS. EVEN IN PRIVATE LIFE THEY
BULL PREFACE(34) UNION OR THE EMPIRE. YOU MAY BUY A COMMON AND NOT INEFFECTIVE VARIETY OF IRISH PROTESTANT BY DELEGATING YOUR

INEFFECTUAL

JITT I (11) TO THE DOOR SO FORMIDABLY THAT THE GIRL, AFTER AN INEFFECTUAL GRIMACE, HAS TO GO). THE MOMENT THE GENTLEMAN IS
BARB II (293) MR UNDERSHAFT: I AM IN MANY WAYS A WEAK, TIMID, INEFFECTUAL PERSON; AND MY HEALTH IS FAR FROM SATISFACTORY.

INEFFICIENCY

APPL I (238) IN THE NEXT TWO YEARS WITHOUT AN ARTICLE ON THE INEFFICIENCY AND CORRUPTION OF ALL GOVERNMENT DEPARTMENTS,
METH PREFACE(R13) THAN THE UNEDUCATED ONE: INDEED IT IS THE INEFFICIENCY AND SHAM OF THE EDUCATIONAL SIDE OF OUR SCHOOLS
MILL PREFACE(132) SUCH AN EXPOSURE OF THE OBSOLESCENCE AND INEFFICIENCY OF PROFITMONGERING METHODS THAT IT TOOK YEARS
BULL IV (174) ONLY TWO QUALITIES IN THE WORLD: EFFICIENCY AND INEFFICIENCY , AND ONLY TWO SORTS OF PEOPLE: THE EFFICIENT

INEFFICIENT

2TRU II (73) ON EARTH DO YOU MEAN BY THAT? /THE PATIENT/ YES: INEFFICIENT FERTILIZERS. WE DO NOTHING BUT CONVERT GOOD FOOD
2TRU II (73) WE, WE THREE GLORIOUS ADVENTURERS? JUST THREE INEFFICIENT FERTILIZERS. /AUBREY/ WHAT ON EARTH DO YOU MEAN
BULL IV (174) ONLY TWO SORTS OF PEOPLE: THE EFFICIENT AND THE INEFFICIENT . IT DONT MATTER WHETHER THEYRE ENGLISH OR
BULL IV (175) IT'S HARD ON HAFFIGAN. IT'S ALWAYS HARD ON THE INEFFICIENT . /LARRY/ PAH! WHAT DOES IT MATTER WHERE AN OLD
PYGM EPILOG (299) EDUCATED AT CHEAP, PRETENTIOUS, AND THOROUGHLY INEFFICIENT SCHOOLS, KNEW A LITTLE LATIN. IT WAS VERY

INEFFICIENTLY

BULL IV (178) AFTER ALL? MR BROADBENT SPENDS HIS LIFE INEFFICIENTLY ADMIRING THE THOUGHTS OF GREAT MEN, AND

INELASTIC

JOAN PREFACE(50) INSPIRATION ALWAYS BEATING AGAINST THEIR TOO INELASTIC LIMITS: ALL MORE TERRIBLE IN THEIR DRAMATIC FORCE

INELIGIBLE

PYGM EPILOG (294) TRUE THAT ELIZA'S SITUATION DID NOT SEEM WHOLLY INELIGIBLE . HER FATHER, THOUGH FORMERLY A DUSTMAN, AND NOW

INEPT

POSN PREFACE(378) MORE SERVICEABLE TO HIS COLLEAGUES THAN THEIR OWN INEPT COUP DE THEATRE WOULD HAVE BEEN IF HE HAD NOT SPOILED
BULL PREFACE(48) ARE ALWAYS TO BE OBEYED THOUGHTLESSLY, HOWEVER INEPT OR DISHONORABLE THEY MAY BE. AS THE LATE LAUREATE SAID
NEVR II (253) MY DEAR CHILD. (THE ENDEARMENT IS SO PLAINTIVELY INEPT THAT SHE SMILES IN SPITE OF HERSELF, AND RESIGNS
JOAN PREFACE(23) BEINGS IN CIVIL AFFAIRS. THIS COMBINATION OF INEPT YOUTH AND ACADEMIC IGNORANCE WITH GREAT NATURAL

INEPTITUDE

UNPL PREFACE(R8) PROVIDED IT IS A NOVEL AT ALL, AND NOT MERELY AN INEPTITUDE . I WAS NOT CONVINCED THAT THE PUBLISHERS' VIEW

INEPTITUDES

AUGS (278) MY BUSINESS WITH THIS LADY TO REPEAT THIS MAN'S INEPTITUDES ? /THE CLERK/ NO. I COME BECAUSE THE WAITER
MIS. PREFACE(72) ITS VULGARITIES AND STUPIDITIES AND RANCORS AND INEPTITUDES AND IGNORANCES, WOULD OPERATE AS POWERFULLY
PYGM EPILOG (298) AS A BABY; BUT NOBODY HATES A BABY FOR ITS INEPTITUDES , OR THINKS THE WORSE OF IT FOR TRYING TO EAT

INEPTLY

BULL PREFACE(35) THE CONFUSED AIMS OF ENGLISH CABINETS STRUGGLING INEPTLY WITH THE BURDENS OF EMPIRE, AND BIASSED BY THE

INEQUALITY

SUPR HANDBOK(194) AND TRAINING, IS ENORMOUS. HE CAN SHEW THAT INEQUALITY AND INIQUITOUS DISTRIBUTION OF WEALTH AND
BARB PREFACE(234) TO FOUND MORAL INSTITUTIONS ON A BASIS OF MORAL INEQUALITY CAN LEAD TO NOTHING BUT UNNATURAL REIGNS OF THE
BARB PREFACE(234) FOUND POLITICAL INSTITUTIONS ON A BASIS OF SOCIAL INEQUALITY HAVE ALWAYS PRODUCED LONG PERIODS OF DESTRUCTIVE
LION PREFACE(60) THE POLITICAL AND BIOLOGICAL OBJECTIONS TO INEQUALITY . BUT THERE ARE OTHER REASONS FOR OBJECTING TO
MILL PREFACE(135) VRIL AS ANYTHING ELSE. IT IS THE FINAL REALITY OF INEQUALITY . IT IS EASY TO EQUALIZE THE DOMINATORS WITH THE
LION PREFACE(54) HAS MADE SHORT WORK OF THE PRIMITIVE PLEAS FOR INEQUALITY . THE PHARISEES THEMSELVES HAVE ORGANIZED
LION PREFACE(61) BUT ACTUALLY DESTROYED IN ALL DIRECTIONS BY INEQUALITY OF INCOME BETWEEN CLASSES: SUCH STABILITY AS IT
SIM II (80) TITLED LADIES' LEAGUE OF SOCIAL SERVICE, ON THE INEQUALITY OF SACRIFICE AS BETWEEN THE WEST END AND THE
MIS. PREFACE(103) BEEN EDUCATED TO WANT IT. THEY CHOOSE SLAVERY AND INEQUALITY ; AND ALL THE OTHER EVILS ARE AUTOMATICALLY ADDED
FABL PREFACE(68) WHEN THE QUOTA IS ACHIEVED, ARITHMETICAL INEQUALITY WILL NO LONGER MATTER; FOR THE EUGENIC TEST IS

INEQUITABLE

SUPR HANDBOK(179) AND THE SOCIAL LABOR BURDEN IN A GROTESQUELY INEQUITABLE MANNER) DID NOT THREATEN THE EXISTENCE OF THE

INEQUITIES

SUPR HANDBOK(179) WITH SOME MORE VITAL MATTER THAN MERE PERSONAL INEQUITIES IN INDUSTRIAL ECONOMY. NO SUCH CONFLICT WAS

INERADICABLE

LION PREFACE(80) HE CALLED SIN INCLUDES SEX AND IS THEREFORE AN INERADICABLE PART OF HUMAN NATURE (WHY ELSE SHOULD CHRIST
ROCK PREFACE(156) OF USE; BUT THE SADIST MANIA FOR FLOGGING SEEMS INERADICABLE ; FOR AFTER A PARTIALLY SUCCESSFUL ATTEMPT TO

INERT

METH PREFACE(R42) NATURE IS NOTHING BUT A CASUAL AGGREGATION OF INERT AND DEAD MATTER, BUT ETERNALLY IMPOSSIBLE TO THE
DEVL I SD(24) DUDGEON, NOW AN INTRUDER IN HER OWN HOUSE, STANDS INERT , CRUSHED BY THE WEIGHT OF THE LAW ON WOMEN, ACCEPTING

INERTIA

POSN PREFACE(382) FOR MORALITY, WITH ALL THE DEAD WEIGHT OF HUMAN INERTIA AND SUPERSTITION TO HANG ON THE BACK OF THE PIONEER,
DOCT PREFACE(78) OF " I AM LEARNING," AND PRAY FOR CREDULITY AND INERTIA AS WISE MEN PRAY FOR SCEPTICISM AND ACTIVITY. SUCH
MIS. PREFACE(76) POLYTECHNIC EXCURSION AND THE TOURIST AGENCY, OUR INERTIA IS STILL APPALLING. I CONFESS TO HAVING ONCE SPENT
METH PREFACE(R73) METAPHYSICAL AS WELL AS PHYSICAL OVERCOMERS OF INERTIA , SINCE THE DISCOVERY OF EVOLUTION AS THE METHOD OF
APPL PREFACE(193) A CONCILIATORY MANNER WITH DUE ALLOWANCE FOR THE INERTIA OF A SOMEWHAT UNIMAGINATIVE OFFICIALDOM WHICH HAD
SUPR HANDBOK(217) A LIMITED MONARCHY IS A DEVICE FOR COMBINING THE INERTIA OF A WOODEN IDOL WITH THE CREDIBILITY OF A FLESH AND
METH PREFACE(R73) OF MATTER IN MOTION (BRIEFLY, THAT CAN OVERCOME INERTIA), IS ESSENTIALLY A MECHANISTIC CONCEPTION. HERE WE

INERTLY

HART II (90) SIR! (SHE SHAKES HIM; AND HE IS ROLLING INERTLY OFF THE CHAIR ON THE FLOOR WHEN SHE HOLDS HIM UP AND

INESTIMABLE

BULL PREFACE(34) RULERS OVER YOU. IN RETURN FOR WHICH YOU GET THE INESTIMABLE BENEFIT OF A GOVERNMENT THAT DOES ABSOLUTE
BARB II (305) IN THE MORNING. IS IT BODGER'S FAULT THAT THIS INESTIMABLE GIFT IS DEPLORABLY ABUSED BY LESS THAN ONE PER
HART PREFACE(19) NO CHILDREN OF THEIR OWN TO LOSE, YET KNEW THE INESTIMABLE LOSS TO THE WORLD OF FOUR YEARS OF THE LIFE OF A

INEVITABILITY

FABL PREFACE(97) BOLSHEVIKS WENT RUINOUSLY WRONG BY IGNORING " THE INEVITABILITY OF GRADUALNESS" AND ATTEMPTING A CATASTROPHIC

INEVITABLE

MIS. PREFACE(93) THE INSTRUMENT OF SOMETHING ETERNAL, DIVINE, AND INEVITABLE : YOU CANNOT EVADE IT THE MOMENT THE
BARB II (293) SHOULD I WASTE YOUR TIME IN DISCUSSING WHAT IS INEVITABLE ? /UNDERSHAFT/ YOU MEAN THAT YOU WILL STICK AT
PYGM EPILOG (297) AS A RATIONAL AND NORMAL-- OR SHALL WE SAY INEVITABLE ? -- SORT OF HUMAN BEING. AT WORST THEY CALLED

POSN PREFACE(427)	ANYTHING FOR A QUIET LIFE", AND WHO WILL MAKE THE	INEVITABLE	ABUSES OF FREEDOM BY OUR BLACKGUARDS AN EXCUSE
SUPR III (120)	TO BE NEXT BEFORE MINE; AND I MUST ACCEPT THE	INEVITABLE	AND MAKE THE BEST OF THE COMPANIONSHIP. MANY SUCH
CAND I SD(85)	HONESTLY REGARDS HIS COMMERCIAL PROSPERITY AS THE	INEVITABLE	AND SOCIALLY WHOLESOME TRIUMPH OF THE ABILITY,
SUPR HANDBOK(195)	MEASURE WHICH WAS AS OBVIOUSLY NECESSARY AND	INEVITABLE	AS ANY POLITICAL MEASURE HAS EVER BEEN OR IS EVER
METH PREFACE(R89)	NOT, I HOPE, UNDER MORE ILLUSION THAN IS HUMANLY	INEVITABLE	AS TO THE CRUDITY OF THIS MY BEGINNING OF A BIBLE
LION PREFACE(58)	SMITTEN WITH THE DEGENERACY WHICH SEEMS TO BE THE	INEVITABLE	BIOLOGICAL PENALTY OF COMPLETE PARASITISM. THEY
FABL PREFACE(96)	THIS ARRANGEMENT WAS ACCEPTED AS FINAL AND	INEVITABLE	BY ABLE AND BENEVOLENT PUBLIC MEN LIKE THOMAS DE
DOCT PREFACE(80)	HAS BECOME CONSTANTLY MORE PRESSING AS THE	INEVITABLE	COLLISIONS BETWEEN THE MARCH OF DISCOVERY IN
LADY PREFACE(230)	BRAVE, HUMAN, AND LOYAL SERVANTS, BESIDE THE	INEVITABLE	COMIC ONES. EVEN IN THE JINGO PLAY, HENRY V, WE
OVER PREFACE(167)	FINALLY TEDIOUS BECAUSE THE HEART OF THEM, THE	INEVITABLE	CONJUGAL INFIDELITY, IS ALWAYS EVADED. EVEN ITS
DOCT PREFACE(8)	MALICIOUS OR CORRUPT MALPRACTICES (AN	INEVITABLE	DEDUCTION FROM THE POSTULATE THAT THE DOCTOR,
MIS. PREFACE(82)	THINK TOO HARDLY OF HIM BECAUSE HE HAD OBEYED THE	INEVITABLE	DESTINY OF A MAN TO LEAVE HIS FATHER AND MOTHER
MIS. PREFACE(54)	THE MEN THEY HATE AND FEAR, AS IF THIS WERE THE	INEVITABLE	DESTINY OF MANKIND. AND NATURALLY, WHEN THEY GROW
3PLA PREFACE(R20)	THAT HE FEELS CONCERNED ABOUT THE APPARENTLY	INEVITABLE	DESTRUCTION OF THE HUMAN RACE BY THE MARTIANS.
3PLA PREFACE(R39)	TRANSFIGURE THE ETERNAL STAGE PUPPETS AND THEIR	INEVITABLE	DILEMMAS AS TO MAKE THEIR IDENTIFICATION
ROCK PREFACE(168)	RUSSIAN RULERS; AND OCCASIONAL SIDESLIPS MUST BE	INEVITABLE	DURING THESE YEARS WHEN THE ABLEST AND OLDEST
LION PREFACE(84)	ON BAPTISM AND TRANSUBSTANTIATION. MEANWHILE THE	INEVITABLE	EFFECT OF DROPPING THE PECULIAR DOCTRINES OF
SUPR III (121)	OF THE SENSES AND EMOTIONS? IS IT NOT THE	INEVITABLE	END OF IT ALL THAT THE HUMAN WILL SHALL SAY TO
3PLA PREFACE(R39)	UNIVERSAL READING, CHEAP NEWSPAPERS, AND THE	INEVITABLE	ENSUING DEMAND FOR NOTABILITIES OF ALL SORTS,
HART PREFACE(19)	AND DELIBERATELY WORK TO A STANDARD OF	INEVITABLE	EVIL INSTEAD OF TO THE IDEAL OF LIFE MORE
APPL I (240)	SCAFFOLD, SPINNING OUT HIS PRAYERS TO PUT OFF THE	INEVITABLE	EXECUTION AS LONG AS POSSIBLE. NOTHING THAT YOU
MIS. (140)	YOU OF THE SMALLEST FEELING FOR ME EXCEPT THE	INEVITABLE	FEELING OF EARLY YOUTH FOR LATE AGE, OR IMAGINE
JOAN PREFACE(51)	MURDER, BUT THE GODS LAUGH AT THE MURDERERS. THE	INEVITABLE	FLATTERIES OF TRAGEDY. HERE THEN WE HAVE A REASON
DOCT PREFACE(47)	IN THE VIVISECTOR'S POSITION: THAT IS, HIS	INEVITABLE	FORFEITURE OF ALL CLAIM TO HAVE HIS WORD
GETT (330)	ONE DAY SHE CAME TO ME AND TOLD ME THAT THE	INEVITABLE	HAD HAPPENED. I HAD TACT ENOUGH NOT TO ASK HER
LION PREFACE(70)	HAVE SEEN TO BE ENTIRELY PRACTICABLE, AND INDEED	INEVITABLE	IF OUR CIVILIZATION IS TO BE SAVED FROM COLLAPSE,
GENV PREFACE(26)	WILL BE THE FATAL ACCIDENT WHICH IS STATISTICALLY	INEVITABLE	IF WE LIVE LONG ENOUGH. IN SHORT, IT IS NOT
FANY EPILOG (331)	GOOD AS THE AUTHOR, ANYHOW. WITH, OF COURSE, THE	INEVITABLE	IMPROPER FEMALE: THE MRS TANQUERAY, IRIS, AND SO
POSN PREFACE(393)	INVASION WAS RIDICULED. THE GERMAN PRESS DREW THE	INEVITABLE	INFERENCE THAT THE LORD CHAMBERLAIN WAS AN
PHIL I (88)	WITH RISING INDIGNATION, AS HE BEGINS TO DRAW THE	INEVITABLE	INFERENCES) DO YOU MEAN TO SAY THAT SOMEBODY HAD
POSN PREFACE(402)	THE PROPER AUTHORITY. THIS PLAN WOULD COMBINE THE	INEVITABLE	INTOLERANCE OF AN ENLIGHTENED CENSORSHIP WITH THE
METH PREFACE(R37)	THE FLIPPANCY OF THE SCEPTICISM. THE RESULT WAS	INEVITABLE	. ALL WHO WERE STRONGMINDED ENOUGH NOT TO BE
LION PREFACE(72)	RIDICULOUS ABOUT A MARRIED PHILOSOPHER BECOMES	INEVITABLE	. AND YET THE CELIBATE IS STILL MORE RIDICULOUS
MTH5 (238)	AND THE QUEEN LOGICAL AND PREDETERMINED AND	INEVITABLE	. AND YET THEY ARE NOT TWO LOGICAL AND
MTH3 (132)	COME TO REGARD SOME SUCH DEVELOPMENT AS THIS AS	INEVITABLE	. IF I HAD NOT THUS PREPARED MYSELF TO BE
LION PREFACE(89)	THE SECULAR VIEW NATURAL, NOT RATIONAL, THEREFORE	INEVITABLE	. IT MUST THEREFORE BE TAKEN AS A FLAT
GENV PREFACE(4)	WE KNEW NOTHING OF. ALL THIS WAS NECESSARY AND	INEVITABLE	. IT WAS DANGEROUS TO TELL THE TRUTH ABOUT
WIDO II (40)	MUST BE PAID, DEAR BOY. IT IS INEVITABLE, HARRY,	INEVITABLE	. (TRENCH TURNS AWAY PETULANTLY. SARTORIUS LOOKS
MTH5 (237)	THE IRRESISTIBLE, THE IRRESPONSIBLE, THE	INEVITABLE	. MY NAME IS OZYMANDIAS, KING OF KINGS: LOOK ON
GETT PREFACE(183)	ONE ANOTHER TO IGNORE IT. MARRIAGE NEVERTHELESS	INEVITABLE	. NOW MOST LAWS ARE, AND ALL LAWS OUGHT TO BE,
WIDO II (43)	YOU MEDDLE IN BUSINESS MATTERS. I TOLD YOU IT WAS	INEVITABLE	. /TRENCH/ (DAZED) DO YOU MEAN TO SAY THAT I AM
BARB PREFACE(220)	HER LOVER THE EURIPIDEAN REPUBLICAN NATURAL AND	INEVITABLE	. THAT, HOWEVER, IS NOT NEW, EVEN ON THE STAGE.
GENV PREFACE(13)	AND UPSTART PRESIDENTS OF SOUTH AMERICAN HISTORY	INEVITABLE	. THERE NEVER HAS BEEN AND NEVER WILL BE A
MTH5 (238)	INEVITABLE, BUT ONE LOGICAL AND PREDETERMINED AND	INEVITABLE	. THEREFORE CONFOUND NOT THE PERSONS, NOR DIVIDE
BULL PREFACE(19)	VULGAR AFFECTATION, WAS QUITE NATURAL AND	INEVITABLE	. WELLINGTON'S FORMULA FOR THAT KIND OF THING WAS
MIS. PREFACE(13)	OR NURSE IT IS NOT ARGUED ABOUT BECAUSE IT IS	INEVITABLE	. YOU CANNOT HOLD AN IMPARTIAL JUDICIAL INQUIRY
GETT PREFACE(206)	CLUB. DEMOCRACY AS TO THE THING TO BE DONE MAY BE	INEVITABLE	(HENCE THE VITAL NEED FOR A DEMOCRACY OF
SUPR HANDBOK(198)	GOOD HEAVENS!) ARE BUT PRELIMINARIES TO THE	INEVITABLE	LATER STAGE, NOW THREATENING US, IN WHICH THE
3PLA PREFACE(R21)	EVEN IN THIS ECONOMIC UTOPIA WE FIND THE	INEVITABLE	LOVE AFFAIR. THE HERO, WAKING UP IN A DISTANT
PLES PREFACE(R16)	AS A MATTER OF INSTINCT I FIGHT AGAINST THE	INEVITABLE	MISREPRESENTATION OF THEM WITH ALL THE SUBTLETY
BULL PREFACE(70)	WHICH IGNORE HIS WATERLOO RIDGES. AND THE	INEVITABLE	NATIONALIST REBELLIONS AGAINST THESE MILITARY
OVER PREFACE(168)	DOCTRINE OF ORIGINAL SIN IS THAT NO NECESSARY AND	INEVITABLE	OPERATION OF HUMAN NATURE CAN REASONABLY BE
ROCK PREFACE(179)	PENALTY, INSTEAD OF A GOD GOING THROUGH AN	INEVITABLE	ORDEAL AS A PRELUDE TO THE ESTABLISHMENT OF HIS
MTH4 I (142)	SAY THAT YOUR ADVANCED YEARS CARRY WITH THEM THE	INEVITABLE	PENALTY OF DOTAGE. /THE WOMAN/ I AM ONE OF THE
DOCT PREFACE(26)	WERE NOT ACCIDENTS, BUT PERFECTLY ORDERLY AND	INEVITABLE	PHENOMENA FOLLOWING THE INJECTION OF DANGEROUSLY
LION PREFACE(29)	PRISONER CONCEIVES HIMSELF AS GOING THROUGH AN	INEVITABLE	PROCESS OF TORMENT, DEATH, AND BURIAL AS A
LADY PREFACE(224)	THERE IS JUST AS MUCH SHAKESPEAR HERE AS IN THE	INEVITABLE	QUOTATION ABOUT THE SWEET SOUTH AND THE BANK OF
MTH5 (238)	REPUGNANTLY ON MY SENSORIUM, WHO KNOWS THAT THE	INEVITABLE	RESPONSE TO THAT STIMULUS MAY NOT BE A MESSAGE TO
METH PREFACE(R65)	INSISTENCE ON MODERN DEMOCRATIC DEGRADATION AS AN	INEVITABLE	RESULT OF SOLAR SHRINKAGE, ARE NOT DEHUMANIZED AS
DOCT PREFACE(8)	FOR MALPRACTICE, HE HAS TO STRUGGLE AGAINST THE	INEVITABLE	RESULT OF HIS FORMER PRETENCES TO INFINITE
DOCT PREFACE(62)	DOCTOR AS A MAN WHICH EXISTS AND IS GROWING AS AN	INEVITABLE	RESULT OF THE PRESENT CONDITION OF MEDICAL
3PLA PREFACE(R16)	MANAGERS ASTONISHED AT THIS UNEXPECTED BUT QUITE	INEVITABLE	RESULT OF THE ATTEMPT TO PLEASE HIM. WHEREAS, HAD
BULL III (122)	ECONOMIC INCOMPETENCE PRODUCES ITS NATURAL AND	INEVITABLE	RESULTS, GET VIRTUOUSLY INDIGNANT AND KILL THE
MRS III (228)	AS IF A FEW PRELIMINARY REFUSALS WERE PART OF THE	INEVITABLE	ROUTINE OF COURTSHIP) I'M IN NO HURRY. IT WAS
BARB PREFACE(227)	ABUSE, BUT NOT PUTTING UP WITH MORE OF IT THAN IS	INEVITABLE	; AND PRACTISING WHAT THE WORLD WILL LET THEM
GETT PREFACE(184)	DECENT PEOPLE. MARRIAGE REMAINS PRACTICALLY	INEVITABLE	; AND THE SOONER WE ACKNOWLEDGE THIS, THE SOONER
MILL PREFACE(129)	PERSONS WHO CAN ONLY WORK A ROUTINE, A RELAPSE IS	INEVITABLE	; AND THE DESTRUCTION BY THE DOMINATORS OF THE
JOAN PREFACE(52)	TWENTIETH CENTURY. ALL I CLAIM IS THAT BY THIS	INEVITABLE	SACRIFICE OF VERISIMILITUDE I HAVE SECURED IN THE
BULL PREFACE(65)	AS ENGLISH RULE IN EGYPT, AND THAT THIS IS THE	INEVITABLE	SPIRIT OF ALL COERCIVE MILITARY RULE, THEY WILL
ROCK PREFACE(168)	WATCHES NEXT." THE CONSTANT CORRECTION OF THE	INEVITABLE	SWERVES TOWARDS ONE EXTREME OR THE OTHER,
POSN PREFACE(430)	TO LORD GORELL'S JUDGMENT ON ALL POINTS. IT IS	INEVITABLE	THAT A JUDGE SHOULD BE DEEPLY IMPRESSED BY HIS
PLES PREFACE(R15)	SEEM TO THEM VALIDLY HEROIC OR VENERABLE. IT IS	INEVITABLE	THAT ACTORS SHOULD SUFFER MORE THAN MOST OF US
MTH3 SD(103)	AFRAID OF HIM; AND IT SEEMS QUITE NATURAL AND	INEVITABLE	THAT HE SHOULD SPEAK FIRST. /THE ARCHBISHOP/ GOOD
GETT PREFACE(230)	IN SEX MATTERS; AND WHEN THEY FIND THAT THIS IS	INEVITABLE	THEY WILL RAISE THE QUESTION OF WHAT BEHAVIOR
GETT PREFACE(221)	WHEN THE DAUGHTERS BECOME MARRIAGEABLE; BUT IT IS	INEVITABLE	UNDER EXISTING CIRCUMSTANCES; AND THE PARENTS WHO
3PLA PREFACE(R31)	OUR SYSTEM OF MORALS AND RELIGION, DELIVERED THE	INEVITABLE	VERDICT OF THAT SYSTEM ON US THROUGH THE MOUTH OF
GETT (330)	I HAD TACT ENOUGH NOT TO ASK HER WHAT THE	INEVITABLE	WAS; AND I GATHERED PRESENTLY THAT SHE HAD TOLD
CAND I SD(78)	A TRAVELLING CLOCK IN A LEATHER CASE (THE	INEVITABLE	WEDDING PRESENT), AND ON THE WALL ABOVE A LARGE
GETT (182)	BUT I FIND IN PRACTICE THAT THE GREEK FORM IS	INEVITABLE	WHEN DRAMA REACHES A CERTAIN POINT IN POETIC AND
ARMS I (13)	WHEN THAT NOURISHMENT IS EXHAUSTED HE ACCEPTS THE	INEVITABLE	WITH PATHETIC GOODHUMOR, AND SAYS, WITH GRATEFUL
SUPR HANDBOK(189)	BUT THE REPLACEMENT OF THE OLD UNINTELLIGENT,	INEVITABLE	, ALMOST UNCONSCIOUS FERTILITY BY AN
METH PREFACE(R73)	CEASE TO BOGGLE AT THE NAME VITALIST, OR AT THE	INEVITABLE	, ANCIENT, POPULAR, AND QUITE CORRECT USE OF THE
CAND I (83)	OUT OF HIS KNOWLEDGE. (HE RESIGNS HIMSELF TO THE	INEVITABLE	, AND GOES OUT). LEXY LOOKS AFTER HIM WITH
MTH5 (238)	LIKEWISE. THE KING LOGICAL AND PREDETERMINED AND	INEVITABLE	, AND THE QUEEN LOGICAL AND PREDETERMINED AND
UNPL PREFACE(R26)	THE COMMERCIAL MAKESHIFTS WHICH THE DEFECTS MAKE	INEVITABLE	, AND WHO OFTEN, LIKE SARTORIUS AND MRS WARREN,
MTH5 (238)	THEY ARE NOT TWO LOGICAL AND PREDETERMINED AND	INEVITABLE	, BUT ONE LOGICAL AND PREDETERMINED AND
2TRU PREFACE(12)	SORT OF LIFE HAS BEEN MADE POSSIBLE, AND INDEED	INEVITABLE	, BY WHAT WILLIAM COBBETT, WHO HAD A STURDY SENSE
WIDO II (40)	(SOFTLY) RENT MUST BE PAID, DEAR BOY. IT IS	INEVITABLE	, HARRY, INEVITABLE. (TRENCH TURNS AWAY
POSN PREFACE(402)	MINISTER IT WAS SUGGESTED THAT IF A CENSORSHIP BE	INEVITABLE	, PROVISION SHOULD BE MADE FOR AN APPEAL FROM THE

INEVITABLES

2TRU II (64)	MARRY HIM, JUST TO PUT HIM ON THE LIST OF THE	INEVITABLES	THAT I MUST PUT UP WITH WILLYNILLY, LIKE GETTING

INEVITABLY

LADY PREFACE(212)	POWER OF CONVICTION. THE STORY, AS HE TELLS IT,	INEVITABLY	AND IRRESISTIBLY DISPLACES ALL THE VULGAR, MEAN,
MILL PREFACE(131)	NAPOLEON BONAPARTE, FIRST CONSUL AND EMPEROR, AS	INEVITABLY	AS BOURRIENNE REMAINED A SPECULATOR, LITTERATEUR
MRS PREFACE(161)	OF ANY POLYANDROUS GROUP WILL, WHEN THEY GROW UP,	INEVITABLY	BE CONFRONTED, AS THOSE OF MRS WARREN'S GROUP ARE
MTH4 II (180)	HAVE TO CONVINCE HIM THAT IF HE HESITATES HE WILL	INEVITABLY	BE SHOT AT DAWN BY HIS OWN COMRADES FOR
BULL PREFACE(3)	OUTSIDE THE CAMP TO WHAT MUST THEN	INEVITABLY	BECOME A ROMAN CATHOLIC HOME RULE GOVERNMENT OF
BULL PREFACE(45)	PEOPLES WILL CLING TO IT VOLUNTARILY, IT WILL	INEVITABLY	BECOME A MILITARY TYRANNY TO PREVENT THEM FROM
MILL PREFACE(112)	TRIBESMAN CAPABLE OF MAKING A CODE OF LAWS, HE	INEVITABLY	BECOMES LAWGIVER TO ALL THE TRIBES, AND, EQUALLY
SIM PREFACE(6)	THAT ALL MY ROMAN CATHOLIC FELLOW CHILDREN WOULD	INEVITABLY	BURN IN BLAZING BRIMSTONE TO ALL ETERNITY, AND
LION PREFACE(23)	CONVERT A MAN BROUGHT UP IN ANOTHER CREED, YOU	INEVITABLY	DEMORALIZE HIM. HE ACTS ON THIS VIEW HIMSELF, AND
METH PREFACE(R54)	CIRCUMSTANTIAL SELECTION MUST INVARIABLY AND	INEVITABLY	DEVELOP IN THE LONG RUN. UNCONTROLLED QUALITIES
GETT PREFACE(232)	FOR THE REALLY INTIMATE AFFECTION OF THE THIRD	INEVITABLY	DRIVES OUT THE OTHER. THE DRIVEN-OUT PARTY MAY
CATH PREFACE(155)	IS, THIS PLAY GREW OUT OF THE RELATIONS WHICH	INEVITABLY	EXIST IN THE THEATRE BETWEEN AUTHORS AND ACTORS.
3PLA PREFACE(R14)	OR EYE FOR COLOR, THE SEARCH FOR UNIVERSALITY	INEVITABLY	FLUNG THE MANAGERS BACK ON THE INSTINCT OF SEX AS

GETT PREFACE(200) TOLERANCE SO LONG ACCORDED TO MONKS AND NUNS IS INEVITABLY GIVING WAY TO A VERY GENERAL AND VERY NATURAL
MRS PREFACE(161) CREATED BY SEX SERIOUSLY FACED AND DEALT WITH, INEVITABLY IGNORE THE OFFICIAL FORMULA AND ARE SUPPRESSED.
MILL PREFACE(121) YOUNG MEN OF MILITARY TASTES AND OLD SOLDIERS, INEVITABLY INCLUDING A PERCENTAGE OF RUFFIANS AND SADISTS.
LION PREFACE(78) WITH DOMESTIC AFFECTION. THIS VIEW OF THE CASE INEVITABLY LED HIM TO INSIST THAT A WIFE SHOULD BE RATHER A
MRS PREFACE(180) ALL THE EVIL EFFECTS OF SUCH CORRUPT CONTROL ARE INEVITABLY PRODUCED GRATUITOUSLY BY CENSORS WITH THE BEST
MRS PREFACE(166) ITS REMORSELESS LOGIC AND IRON FRAMEWORK OF FACT, INEVITABLY PRODUCES AT FIRST AN OVERWHELMING IMPRESSION OF
2TRU PREFACE(21) WITHOUT WHICH THE VOCATION OF THE PRIEST IS INEVITABLY PUSHED OUT BY THE VOCATION OF THE ROBBERS AND THE
APPL I (240) THAT IF I SIGN THIS ULTIMATUM, I SHALL NOT INEVITABLY RELAPSE INTO THE CONDUCT THAT MY NATURE
POSN PREFACE(398) DO NOTHING OF THE SORT. ON THE CONTRARY, IT WOULD INEVITABLY SUPPRESS IT MORE COMPLETELY THAN THE LORD
POSN PREFACE(428) HIS PATH. CONSIDER HOW THE VOLUNTARY SYSTEM MUST INEVITABLY WORK. THE JOINT SELECT COMMITTEE EXPRESSLY URGES
MILL PREFACE(112) BECOMES LAWGIVER TO ALL THE TRIBES, AND, EQUALLY INEVITABLY , IS FORCED TO ADD TO WHAT HE CAN UNDERSTAND OF

INEXACT
JOAN PREFACE(51) IT MAY GIVE THE ESSENTIAL TRUTH OF IT, GIVES AN INEXACT PICTURE OF SOME ACCIDENTAL FACTS. IT GOES ALMOST

INEXCUSABLE
2TRU III (105) THE LADY HAS A RIGHT TO IT. MY ACTION WAS INEXCUSABLE . BUT NO LADY-- NO HUMAN BEING-- HAS A RIGHT TO

INEXHAUSTIBLE
LADY PREFACE(221) IN SHAKESPEAR AN INCORRIGIBLE DIVINE LEVITY, AN INEXHAUSTIBLE JOY THAT DERIDED SORROW? THINK OF THE POOR
POSN PREFACE(365) EXAMINER OF PLAYS A CHERISHED PRIVILEGE AND AN INEXHAUSTIBLE JOY. THIS ERROR WAS NOT REMOVED BY THE
3PLA PREFACE(R20) MOST EASILY BAFFLED OF ALL INSTINCTS, IS INEXHAUSTIBLE , AND THAT THE FIELD OF THE ENGLISH ROMANCER
CLEO II (131) MORAL EYE-TO-BUSINESS OF HIS BRITISH SECRETARY IS INEXHAUSTIBLE , SMILES INDULGENTLY). /RUFIO/ IT IS NO USE
SUPR PREFACE(R31) FOLLOWED, RECOMMENDED WEBB, THE ENCYCLOPEDIC AND INEXHAUSTIBLE , TO FORM HIMSELF INTO A COMPANY FOR THE

INEXORABILITY
BARB PREFACE(230) AN UNMERCIFUL PERSON, I DO NOT THINK THAT THE INEXORABILITY OF THE DEED ONCE DONE SHOULD BE DISGUISED BY

INEXORABLE
BARB PREFACE(230) FOILED BOTH WAYS. HE FINDS THE SALVATION ARMY AS INEXORABLE AS FACT ITSELF. IT WILL NOT PUNISH HIM: IT WILL
METH PREFACE(R78) HERITAGE OF THE HUMAN RACE; AND THERE IS ONLY ONE INEXORABLE CONDITION ATTACHED TO THEIR HEALTHY ENJOYMENT,
MTH3 (97) YOUR ANARCHY FORCED YOU AT LAST TO RECOGNIZE TWO INEXORABLE FACTS. FIRST, THAT GOVERNMENT IS ABSOLUTELY
MRS PREFACE(167) IN THE STAGE PATHOS THAT ACCEPTS THEM AS AN INEXORABLE FATE, OR IN THE REALITY OF THE FIGURES WHO
MRS IV (236) AFTER TEA. (HE MURMURS). NO USE GROANING: I'M INEXORABLE . (HE TAKES THE OPPOSITE SEAT DISCONSOLATELY).
2TRU PREFACE(5) AND A LIAR, AFFIRMING IT TO BE A WELL-KNOWN AND INEXORABLE LAW OF NATURE THAT NO MAN WITH MONEY IN HIS
METH PREFACE(R63) THAT TRADE UNIONISM IS A VAIN DEFIANCE OF THE INEXORABLE LAWS OF POLITICAL ECONOMY, JUST AS THE
ROCK I (219) HIPNEY, I WISH I HAD TIME TO EXPLAIN TO YOU THE INEXORABLE LAWS OF POLITICAL ECONOMY. I-- /HIPNEY/ (
NEVR IV SD(286) VOICE, IMPRESSIVELY ARTICULATED SPEECH, STRONG INEXORABLE MANNER, AND A TERRIFYING POWER OF INTENSELY
2TRU PREFACE(21) EXCLUSIVELY WITH MANAGING DIRECTORS; AND TO THAT INEXORABLE NATURAL FACT WE SHALL ALWAYS HAVE TO COME BACK.
JOAN PREFACE(17) AND BLINDNESS TO THE CALLS AND VISIONS OF THE INEXORABLE POWER THAT MADE US, AND WILL DESTROY US IF WE
LION II (138) CALL THEM -- FADE INTO MERE DREAMS BESIDE THAT INEXORABLE REALITY. I KNOW NOW THAT I AM NOT DYING FOR
WIDO I (13) GIRL. /TRENCH/ (HOTLY) COKANE! /COKANE/ (INEXORABLE) HER FATHER SEEMS TO BE A PERFECT GENTLEMAN. I
HART II (97) LIKE TO HEAR. SHALL I BE IN THE WAY? /ELLIE/ (INEXORABLE) I HAD RATHER TALK TO HER ALONE. /MAZZINI/ (
MIS. (152) REMONSTRATING) BUT IT'S NOT GOOD SENSE. /LINA/ (INEXORABLE) SAY FISH CHURCH. /TARLETON/ FISH CHURCH. /LINA/
BARB PREFACE(245) VIRGIN INTERCESSORS. WE ATTRIBUTE MERCY TO THE INEXORABLE ; SOOTHE OUR CONSCIENCES AFTER COMMITTING MURDER
GLIM (186) YOU. IF YOU HAD PITIED ME! IF YOU HAD BEEN LESS INEXORABLE THAN DEATH ITSELF, I SHOULD HAVE BROKEN DOWN AND
GETT (331) ANY WOMAN CAN PICK UP. NOT FOR ME, THANK YOU. (INEXORABLE , SHE TURNS TOWARDS THE TOWER TO GO). /HOTCHKISS/
SUPR HANDBOK(177) CONCLUSION. THE DESPAIR OF INSTITUTIONS, AND THE INEXORABLE " YE MUST BE BORN AGAIN," WITH MRS POYSER'S

INEXORABLY
DOCT PREFACE(80) THAN HE IS WORTH IS DOOMED BY SOUND HYGIENE AS INEXORABLY AS BY SOUND ECONOMICS. 12. DO NOT TRY TO LIVE FOR
SUPR IV (153) THATS NOT GOING TO CHANGE. (HE PASSES HIS FATHER INEXORABLY BY, AND GOES TO VIOLET). COME, MRS MALONE: YOUVE
MIS. PREFACE(83) MARRY LATER, THE FACTS OF AGE AND TIME STILL INEXORABLY CONDEMN MOST PARENTS TO COMPARATIVE SOLITUDE WHEN
FANY III (325) /JUGGINS/ YOUR BOY AND MISS DELANEY WILL BE INEXORABLY CONDEMNED BY RESPECTABLE SOCIETY TO SPEND THE
APPL II (267) O'CLOCK. IT NOW A QUARTER PAST. /MAGNUS/ ARE YOU INEXORABLY DETERMINED TO FORCE THIS ISSUE TO ITS LOGICAL
BARB PREFACE(215) SAY, 365 POUNDS A YEAR, SHALL BE PAINLESSLY BUT INEXORABLY KILLED, AND EVERY HUNGRY HALF NAKED CHILD
GETT (318) ARE PEOPLE TO DO BUT SHOOT SOMEBODY? /SOAMES/ (INEXORABLY) I'M WAITING FOR MY INSTRUCTIONS AS TO THE TERM
HART II (108) OUT, WHILE YOU HAVE THE CHANCE. /THE BURGLAR/ (INEXORABLY) NO. I MUST WORK MY SIN OFF MY CONSCIENCE. THIS
MTH2 (43) (RISING INDIGNANTLY) WHAT! /FRANKLYN/ (INEXORABLY) NOT A WORD OF IT. /CONRAD/ (BEATEN) WELL, I
SUPR IV (149) HAVE FINISHED SPEAKING TO YOUR FATHER. /HECTOR/ (INEXORABLY) NO, VIOLET: I MEAN TO HAVE THIS THING OUT.
NEVR I (213) DOLLY GENTLY AND SITS DOWN AGAIN). /GLORIA/ (INEXORABLY) WE HAVE A RIGHT TO KNOW, MOTHER. /MRS CLANDON/
NEVR IV (288) BALL: VERY BUSY EVENING INDEED, SIR. /BOHUN/ (INEXORABLY) WE SHALL WANT YOU. /MRS CLANDON/ (POLITELY)
GETT (356) SO YOURE NOT COMING HOME WITH ME. /HOTCHKISS/ (INEXORABLY) YES, I AM. /MRS GEORGE/ NO. /HOTCHKISS/ YES.
ARMS II (35) SHALL BE DISGRACED. (SHE STRUGGLES: HE HOLDS HER INEXORABLY). OH, WILL YOU LET GO? /SERGIUS/ (LOOKING
POSN (462) AGAIN. I'M DONE WITH YOU. /BLANCO/ (POINTING INEXORABLY TO NESTOR) DRUNK IN CHURCH. DISTURBING THE

INEXPENSIVE
UNPL PREFACE(R20) LUGNE POE WITH MAETERLINCK, UNDER COMPARATIVELY INEXPENSIVE CONDITIONS, TO THOSE OF THE WAGNER FESTIVAL
BARB PREFACE(237) CHEERING THE VICTIMS WITH HOPES OF IMMENSE AND INEXPENSIVE HAPPINESS IN ANOTHER WORLD WHEN THE PROCESS OF

INEXPERIENCE
BULL PREFACE(43) HE INSISTS ON GUIDING HIMSELF AT 21 BY HIS OWN INEXPERIENCE AND FOLLY AND IMMATURITY INSTEAD OF BY THE
NEVR I SD(208) METTLESOME DOMINATIVE CHARACTER PARALYZED BY THE INEXPERIENCE OF HER YOUTH, AND UNWILLINGLY DISCIPLINED BY
UNPL PREFACE(R14) THAT FORCE JUSTIFIED ITSELF IN SPITE OF THE INEXPERIENCE OF THE PLAYWRIGHT. THE PLAY WAS EVERYTHING THAT
POSN PREFACE(403) SOUND, IT BEARS ALL THE MARKS OF THAT PRACTICAL INEXPERIENCE WHICH LEADS MEN TO BELIEVE THAT ARBITRATION

INEXPERIENCED
NEVR I (215) CHILDREN, ALL OF YOU; BUT YOU ARE STILL VERY INEXPERIENCED AND CONSEQUENTLY SOMETIMES VERY UNSYMPATHETIC.
MRS PREFACE(178) FOUND MUNICIPAL COUNCILLORS QUITE SO SIMPLE AND INEXPERIENCED AS THIS. AT ALL EVENTS I DO NOT PROPOSE TO
SUPR PREFACE(R20) SANCTUARY OF UNREALITY, IT IMPOSES ONLY ON THE INEXPERIENCED . IN SHAKESPEAR'S PLAYS THE WOMAN ALWAYS TAKES
VWOO 3 (141) IT ALL GOT TO DO WITH YOU AND ME? /A/ YOU ARE INEXPERIENCED , YOU DONT KNOW. YOU ARE THE DUPE OF
VWOO 2 (128) A WIDOWER KNOW WHAT TO EXPECT FROM A WOMAN. AN INEXPERIENCED MAN EXPECTS THE EARTH. /A/ HOW DO YOU KNOW
VWOO 1 (118) COULD GET FROM A WOMAN. DONT YOU THINK SO? /A/ INEXPERIENCED MEN THINK THERE IS SOMETHING WONDERFUL YOU CAN
BARB PREFACE(243) IMPUDENT HYPOCRISY; OUR WISDOM IS ADMINISTERED BY INEXPERIENCED OR MALEXPERIENCED DUPES, OUR POWER WIELDED BY
GETT PREFACE(244) EASY TO DISSOLVE UNIONS CONTRACTED BY YOUNG AND INEXPERIENCED PEOPLE IN THE EVENT OF THEIR TURNING OUT
GETT PREFACE(219) BESET WITH WILDLY EXTRAVAGANT ILLUSIONS FOR INEXPERIENCED PEOPLE, AND THAT EVEN THE MOST EXPERIENCED
JOAN PREFACE(4) ELIZABETH. BUT SHE WAS TOO YOUNG AND RUSTICAL AND INEXPERIENCED TO HAVE ANY SUCH ARTS. WHEN SHE WAS THWARTED
SUPR I (14) WAY. BUT SHE IS ONLY A WOMAN, AND A YOUNG AND INEXPERIENCED WOMAN AT THAT. /TANNER/ RAMSDEN: I BEGIN TO
GETT PREFACE(232) WITH THE CLERGYMAN'S WIFE, AND, BEING YOUNG AND INEXPERIENCED , DECLARES HIS FEELINGS, AND CLAIMS THAT HE,
SUPR I (20) AS YOU. /ANN/ I FEEL THAT I AM TOO YOUNG, TOO INEXPERIENCED , TO DECIDE. MY FATHER'S WISHES ARE SACRED TO

INEXPLICABLE
LION PREFACE(16) THE MOST WONDERFUL OF ALL THE MIRACLES AND AS INEXPLICABLE AS EVER, TAUGHT THE PRIMITIVE HUSBANDMAN, AND,
BUOY III (43) MY CASE IS A SPECIFIC ONE OF ANIMAL MAGNETISM, AS INEXPLICABLE AS THE TERRESTRIAL MAGNETISM THAT DRAGS A STEEL
METH PREFACE(R65) A FAITH THAT THE UNIVERSE WAS ORDERED HOWEVER INEXPLICABLE BY US ITS ORDER MIGHT BE, AND THEREFORE A SENSE
BUOY PREFACE(5) THEM FAR BEHIND. YET THERE ARE THE MOMENTS OF INEXPLICABLE HAPPINESS OF WHICH MR J. B. PRIESTLEY SPOKE IN
BUOY PREFACE(4) TALENT THAT WAY. SO I HAD; BUT THAT FACT REMAINS INEXPLICABLE . WHAT LESS COULD MR SLUDGE SAY? OR JOHN HUS,
PYGM EPILOG (296) PERSON, AND TO HER OWN MOTHER AS IN SOME INEXPLICABLE WAY A SOCIAL FAILURE, HAD NEVER SEEN HERSELF IN
SUPR PREFACE(R10) BUT YOU MUST NOT EXPECT ME TO ADOPT YOUR INEXPLICABLE , FANTASTIC, PETULANT, FASTIDIOUS WAYS: YOU

INEXPLICABLY
SUPR PREFACE(R14) INTERESTING YOU, ATTRACTING YOU, TEMPTING YOU, INEXPLICABLY FORCING YOU TO RANGE THE HERO WITH HIS ENEMY
2TRU II SD(51) FOR THERE IS SOMETHING EXASPERATINGLY AND INEXPLICABLY WRONG ABOUT HIM. HE WEARS A PITH HELMET WITH A

INEXPRESSIBLE
CATH 4,SD(198) IN CHILDLIKE AWE BY VARINKA, AND WITH QUITE INEXPRESSIBLE FEELINGS BY CATHERINE. WHEN HE IS OUT OF SIGHT
SIM I (42) PEOPLE. I ONLY KNOW THAT YOU FILL MY HEART WITH INEXPRESSIBLE LONGINGS. /MAYA/ WE ARE THE AWAKENING.

SUPR I (45)	BE INSULTED. /OCTAVIUS/ (RAISING HIS HEAD WITH	INEXPRESSIBLE	RELIEF) YOU ARE MARRIED! /VIOLET/ YES; AND I
GENV III (85)	GENEVA IS SO FULL OF MENTAL PEOPLE THAT IT IS AN	INEXPRESSIBLE	RELIEF TO MEET SOME CHEERFUL PERSON WITH
SIM I (47)	STILL, SOMEHOW, I SEEM TO LOVE THEM ALL IN AN	INEXPRESSIBLE	SORT OF WAY. ONLY, IF THERE WERE ANY QUESTION
		INEXPRESSIBLY	
SUPR I (21)	FRIEND RICKY-TICKY-TAVY (HE BLUSHES AND LOOKS	INEXPRESSIBLY	FOOLISH). /MRS WHITEFIELD/ (RISING AND
JITT I (15)	/BRUNO/ DEAREST LOVE: YOU CAN, YOU DO MAKE ME	INEXPRESSIBLY	HAPPY. SO HAPPY, THAT EVERY TIME YOU GO AWAY
PPP (202)	SHAKING THE FROTH OUT OF A FLAGON. /ADOLPHUS/ HOW	INEXPRESSIBLY	SOOTHING TO THE CHEST! A DELICIOUS NUMBNESS
CAND I SD(94)	FOLGATE? DOWN IN SURREY, ISNT IT? BURGESS,	INEXPRESSIBLY	TICKLED, BEGINS TO SPLUTTER WITH LAUGHTER.
		INEXPRESSIVE	
CATH 4 (195)	RECOIL FROM ONE ANOTHER, AND REMAIN UTTERLY	INEXPRESSIVE	). /CATHERINE/ (PUSHING EDSTASTON TOWARDS
CAPT III SD(282)	CONFIDENCE IN HIS INNOCENCE. JOHNSON SOLID AND	INEXPRESSIVE	, REDBROOK UNCONCERNED AND DEBONAIR, MARZO
		INEXTRICABLY	
BARB PREFACE(224)	DISEASE, AND ALL THE EVIL FRUITS OF POVERTY, AS	INEXTRICABLY	AS WITH ENTERPRISE, WEALTH, COMMERCIAL PROBITY,
AUGS PREFACE(261)	WHO REGARDED THE PROWESS OF THE BRITISH ARMY AS	INEXTRICABLY	BOUND UP WITH HIGHCASTLE PRESTIGE. BUT OUR
METH PREFACE(R38)	SEEMED TO INVOLVE LETTING THE BOGEY COME BACK, SO	INEXTRICABLY	HAD WE MANAGED TO MIX UP BELIEF IN THE BOGEY'S
FABL PREFACE(89)	ASS'S BRIDGE: THE THEORY OF RENT, AND WITH IT	INEXTRICABLY	THE THEORY OF EXCHANGE VALUE. UNLESS A
		INFALLIBILITY	
2TRU III (88)	HERE WAS MY FAITH: HERE I FOUND MY DOGMA OF	INFALLIBILITY	: I, WHO SCORNED ALIKE THE CATHOLIC WITH HIS
JOAN PREFACE(33)	WILL, CANONIZE GALILEO WITHOUT COMPROMISING SUCH	INFALLIBILITY	AS IT CLAIMS FOR THE POPE, IF NOT WITHOUT
JOAN PREFACE(33)	FOR THE POPE, IF NOT WITHOUT COMPROMISING THE	INFALLIBILITY	CLAIMED FOR THE BOOK OF JOSHUA BY SIMPLE SOULS
METH PREFACE(R40)	WAS STRANGLED BY BIGOTED IGNORAMUSES CLAIMING	INFALLIBILITY	FOR THEIR INTERPRETATION OF THE BIBLE, WHICH
ROCK PREFACE(173)	WORKERS, WHO HAVE SOMEHOW WON THAT FAITH IN THEIR	INFALLIBILITY	FORMERLY ENJOYED BY OUR PRIESTS. NO FUTURE
FABL PREFACE(77)	NO LESS THAN IN THE VICARAGE OF THE POPE AND HIS	INFALLIBILITY	IN COUNCIL WITH THE COLLEGE OF CARDINALS,
JOAN PREFACE(32)	PROTESTANT READERS THAT THE FAMOUS DOGMA OF PAPAL	INFALLIBILITY	IS BY FAR THE MOST MODEST PRETENSION OF THE
DOCT PREFACE(8)	POISON USED. NOW ALL THIS SUPPOSED EXACTNESS AND	INFALLIBILITY	IS IMAGINARY; AND TO TREAT A DOCTOR AS IF HIS
DOCT PREFACE(10)	MARK, THUS EVEN THE LAYMAN HAS TO BE TAUGHT THAT	INFALLIBILITY	IS NOT QUITE INFALLIBLE, BECAUSE THERE ARE TWO
BUOY PREFACE(5)	WOULD LOSE THEIR REPUTATION FOR OMNISCIENCE AND	INFALLIBILITY	. BUT MAGIC AND MIRACLE, AS FAR AS THEY ARE
JOAN PREFACE(32)	NOT ONE OF THE ACTS FOR WHICH THE CHURCH CLAIMS	INFALLIBILITY	. PERHAPS I HAD BETTER INFORM MY PROTESTANT
3PLA PREFACE(R33)	AGAINST A HITHERTO UNQUESTIONED PERFECTION AND	INFALLIBILITY	. SUCH CRITICISMS ARE NO MORE NEW THAN THE
MILL PREFACE(124)	OF ESTABLISHED PHYSICAL SCIENCE BY DENYING THE	INFALLIBILITY	OF NEWTON, INTRODUCING FANTASTIC FACTORS INTO
LION PREFACE(90)	OR ATTACKING THE PAPER FORTIFICATIONS OF THE	INFALLIBILITY	OF THE BIBLE, HAVE HARDLY ANYTHING TO DO WITH
LION PREFACE(9)	STATES, WHERE THE OLD TRADITION OF THE VERBAL	INFALLIBILITY	OF " THE BOOK OF BOOKS" LINGERS MORE STRONGLY
DOCT PREFACE(8)	THE DOCTOR'S CARE. RECOIL OF THE DOGMA OF MEDICAL	INFALLIBILITY	ON THE DOCTOR. ON THE OTHER HAND, WHEN THE
BUOY PREFACE(6)	OFF THE SCIENTIFIC TARGET IN HIS ATTRIBUTION OF	INFALLIBILITY	TO ARCHBISHOP USSHER THAN MOST MODERN
		INFALLIBLE	
METH PREFACE(R62)	NOTHING AGAINST HIM. NOW MARX WAS BY NO MEANS	INFALLIBLE	: HIS ECONOMICS, HALF BORROWED, AND HALF
SUPR HANDBOK(199)	INDEED THE ILLUSION OF ILLUSIONS; FOR IT GIVES US	INFALLIBLE	AND APPALLING ASSURANCE THAT IF OUR POLITICAL
APPL I (205)	AND WAS ACTUALLY CALLED GOD AND WORSHIPPED AS	INFALLIBLE	AND OMNISCIENT, THAT WAS MONSTROUS -- /BOANERGES/
MTH4 I (158)	MILES OF SPACE AND WORSHIPPED THE ASTRONOMER AS	INFALLIBLE	AND OMNISCIENT, THEY BUILT TEMPLES FOR HIS
MTH4 I (159)	MAN, WHO WAS WORSHIPPED, LIKE THE ASTRONOMER, AS	INFALLIBLE	AND OMNISCIENT, THUS OUR DISCOVERIES, INSTEAD OF
FABL PREFACE(89)	PROPHYLACTIC PROVES THAT THE PROPHYLACTIC IS	INFALLIBLE	AND THAT COMPULSION TO USE IT WILL ABOLISH THE
JOAN PREFACE(32)	DEMOCRACIES, OUR INFALLIBLE MEDICAL COUNCILS, OUR	INFALLIBLE	ASTRONOMERS, OUR INFALLIBLE JUDGES, AND OUR
LION PREFACE(47)	PROTESTANT AS TO WHY HE REGARDS NEWTON AS AN	INFALLIBLE	AUTHORITY, AND ST THOMAS AQUINAS OR THE POPE AS
OVER (194)	DIE SOME TIME OR OTHER; YET THAT DOESNT MAKE THEM	INFALLIBLE	AUTHORITIES ON MORALS, DOES IT? /GREGORY/ I WAS
LION PREFACE(89)	BELIEF IN THE EFFICACY OF THE CRUCIFIXION AS AN	INFALLIBLE	CURE FOR GUILT, AND A CONGENITAL INCAPACITY FOR
JOAN PREFACE(32)	OF THE KIND IN EXISTENCE. COMPARED WITH OUR	INFALLIBLE	DEMOCRACIES, OUR INFALLIBLE MEDICAL COUNCILS, OUR
MILL I (141)	PIECES IN HIS FACE). /SAGAMORE/ (BEAMING) IT'S	INFALLIBLE	. AND NOW THAT YOU HAVE BLOWN OFF STEAM, SUPPOSE
NEVR II (258)	AND YOUR KNOWLEDGE AND YOUR EXPERIENCE ARE NOT	INFALLIBLE	. AT LEAST I HOPE NOT. /VALENTINE/ I MUST BELIEVE
MILL I (140)	A PRESCRIPTION FOR THEM? /SAGAMORE/ I DO. IT'S	INFALLIBLE	. /EPIFANIA/ YOU ARE SURE THAT THEY HAVE ALL DIED
METH PREFACE(R27)	CONSCIOUS CALCULATION AT ALL; AND THE RESULT IS	INFALLIBLE	. YET SOME OF THESE NATURAL ARITHMETICIANS HAVE
JOAN PREFACE(32)	MEDICAL COUNCILS, OUR INFALLIBLE ASTRONOMERS, OUR	INFALLIBLE	JUDGES, AND OUR INFALLIBLE PARLIAMENTS, THE POPE
JOAN PREFACE(32)	COMPARED WITH OUR INFALLIBLE DEMOCRACIES, OUR	INFALLIBLE	MEDICAL COUNCILS, OUR INFALLIBLE ASTRONOMERS, OUR
MILL IV (198)	WHAT IS TOKO? /ALASTAIR/ SHE KNOWS. TOKO IS AN	INFALLIBLE	MEDICINE FOR CALMING THE NERVES. A PUNCH IN THE
JOAN PREFACE(32)	ASTRONOMERS, OUR INFALLIBLE JUDGES, AND OUR	INFALLIBLE	PARLIAMENTS, THE POPE IS ON HIS KNEES IN THE DUST
LION PREFACE(79)	TO HIM ON HIS OWN AUTHORITY. " I COME AS AN	INFALLIBLE	PATENT MEDICINE FOR BAD CONSCIENCES" IS NOT ONE
MILL PREFACE(135)	BEING AVAILABLE FOR EVERYBODY, AND THEREFORE AN	INFALLIBLE	PREVENTIVE OF ANY ATTEMPT AT OPPRESSION. FOR THAT
LION PREFACE(45)	TO BELIEVE THE BIBLE IN THE OLD LITERAL WAY AS AN	INFALLIBLE	RECORD AND REVELATION, AND REJECTING THAT VIEW
LION PREFACE(88)	NOTION THAT MATTHEW'S MANUSCRIPT IS A LITERAL AND	INFALLIBLE	RECORD OF FACTS, NOT SUBJECT TO THE ERRORS THAT
BULL PREFACE(71)	I HAD OCCASION TO POINT OUT THAT MARX WAS NOT	INFALLIBLE	; BUT HE LEFT ME WITH A VERY STRONG DISPOSITION
METH PREFACE(R76)	THEY DO AND THEY DO NOT; THAT THE BIBLE IS AN	INFALLIBLE	SCIENTIFIC MANUAL, AN ACCURATE HISTORICAL
GETT (291)	BILLITER IS NOT A GENTLEMAN? /HOTCHKISS/ BY AN	INFALLIBLE	SIGN: ONE OF THOSE TRIFLES THAT STAMP A MAN. HE
HART III (142)	IT SEEMS QUITE NATURAL. /LADY UTTERWORD/ AN	INFALLIBLE	SIGN THAT YOU ARE NOT NOW IN REALLY DISTINGUISHED
DOCT PREFACE(7)	GAINED THEIR NAME BY BELIEVING THAT THE BIBLE IS	INFALLIBLE	, AND TAKING THEIR BELIEF QUITE SERIOUSLY. THE
LION EPILOG (151)	POOR FREETHINKER FOR SAYING THAT ST JAMES WAS NOT	INFALLIBLE	, AND TO SEND ONE OF THE PECULIAR PEOPLE TO
SUPR III (112)	IDEAL INDIVIDUAL BEING OMNIPOTENT, OMNISCIENT,	INFALLIBLE	, AND WITHAL COMPLETELY, UNILLUDEDLY
MIS. PREFACE(67)	WITH HIM AND DO NOT INTEND TO TREAT HIM AS	INFALLIBLE	, ARE PITIABLE AS FAR AS THEY ARE ANYTHING BUT
DOCT PREFACE(10)	HAS TO BE TAUGHT THAT INFALLIBILITY IS NOT QUITE	INFALLIBLE	, BECAUSE THERE ARE TWO QUALITIES OF IT TO BE HAD
BUOY PREFACE(6)	AM OBVIOUSLY NEITHER OMNIPOTENT, OMNISCIENT, NOR	INFALLIBLE	, BEING NOT ONLY NOT A GOD NOR EVEN THE
MTH2 (74)	WRONG, AND EVEN THE LIBERAL PARTY HAS NOT BEEN	INFALLIBLE	, THE MEN OF SCIENCE HAVE ALWAYS BEEN WRONG.
MILL I (144)	BUT MY FATHER COULD HAVE THOUGHT OF SUCH A REAL,	INFALLIBLE	, UNSENTIMENTAL TEST. I GAVE HIM MY SACRED
		INFALLIBLY	
SUPR PREFACE(R27)	INTO MERE FASHIONABLE FOLLY OR CANTING CHARITY AS	INFALLIBLY	AS A SAVAGE CONVERTS THE PHILOSOPHICAL THEOLOGY
MIS. PREFACE(47)	RULES OF RIGHT AND WRONG CONDUCT; TO DISCRIMINATE	INFALLIBLY	BETWEEN VIRTUOUS AND VICIOUS CHARACTER; AND THIS
LION EPILOG (147)	BY LEADING THE HERD TO WAR, WHICH IMMEDIATELY AND	INFALLIBLY	MAKES THEM FORGET EVERYTHING, EVEN THEIR MOST
DOCT PREFACE(8)	ALSO THAT ON DISSECTING A DEAD BODY HE CAN	INFALLIBLY	PUT HIS FINGER ON THE CAUSE OF DEATH, AND, IN
MRS PREFACE(151)	ATTRACTIVE UNPROPERTIED WOMEN LOSE MONEY BY BEING	INFALLIBLY	VIRTUOUS OR CONTRACTING MARRIAGES THAT ARE NOT
3PLA PREFACE(R19)	BE THE ONLY THEME THAT TOUCHES ALL YOUR AUDIENCE	INFALLIBLY	, YOUNG AND OLD, RICH AND POOR, AND YET LOVE IS
		INFAME	
BULL PREFACE(37)	OF THE TECHNICAL DIFFERENCE BETWEEN VOLTAIRE'S "	INFAME	" AND DR CLIFFORD'S. ONE WAS THE UNREFORMED ROMAN
		INFAMIES	
2TRU PREFACE(17)	INTO HISTORICAL MUSEUMS ILLUSTRATING THE	INFAMIES	OF ECCLESIASTICAL HISTORY AND EXPRESSLY ENTITLING
MILL PREFACE(118)	WITH A MEANNESS AND CRUELTY WHICH REVIVED ALL THE	INFAMIES	OF THE POOR LAW OF A CENTURY AGO (THE DAYS OF
METH PREFACE(R55)	TWOPENNY-HALFPENNY TORQUEMADAS WALLOWING IN THE	INFAMIES	OF THE VIVISECTOR'S LABORATORY, AND SOLEMNLY
		INFAMOUS	
GETT PREFACE(188)	AS TO THE BEAUTY AND HOLINESS OF MARRIAGE AS	INFAMOUS	AND ABHORRENT, I SOMETIMES WONDER WHY IT IS SO
UNPL PREFACE(R13)	MERITS OR EVEN ITS DEMERITS; AND I AT ONCE BECAME	INFAMOUS	AS A PLAYWRIGHT. THE FIRST PERFORMANCE WAS
MRS PREFACE(176)	SUCH PLAYS AS YOU NEVER CAN TELL, WRITTEN BY THE	INFAMOUS	AUTHOR OF MRS WARREN'S PROFESSION, AND ACTED BY THE
WIDO III (57)	US WHEN SUCH THINGS ARE WRITTEN ABOUT US IN THAT	INFAMOUS	BOOK? /SARTORIUS/ (COLDLY AND A LITTLE WISTFULLY)
DOCT PREFACE(10)	BUT SUCH BEHAVIOR IS CONSIDERED LITTLE SHORT OF	INFAMOUS	BY HIS COLLEAGUES. WHY DOCTORS DO NOT DIFFER. THE
ROCK PREFACE(165)	AS GENUINE PROLETARIANS, AND TRANSFERRED FROM THE	INFAMOUS	CATEGORY OF INTELLIGENTSIA TO THE HONORABLE ONE OF
DOCT PREFACE(4)	PROFESSION HAS NOT A HIGH CHARACTER: IT HAS AN	INFAMOUS	CHARACTER, I DO NOT KNOW A SINGLE THOUGHTFUL AND
ROCK PREFACE(175)	AT THEM A DAMNING CONTRAST BETWEEN THEIR	INFAMOUS	CORRUPTION AND MENDACITY AND HIS OWN UPRIGHT
PYGM IV (267)	DONT YOU HIT ME. /HIGGINS/ HIT YOU! YOU	INFAMOUS	CREATURE, HOW DARE YOU ACCUSE ME OF SUCH A THING..
GETT PREFACE(228)	FOR REFORM AND TREATING THOSE WHO ADVOCATE IT AS	INFAMOUS	DELINQUENTS. NEITHER VIEW IS OF ANY USE EXCEPT AS A
MIS. PREFACE(75)	THEY ARE PROVIDED GRUDGINGLY AND ON CONDITIONS	INFAMOUS	ENOUGH TO DRAW DOWN ABUNDANT FIRE FROM HEAVEN UPON
MIS. PREFACE(73)	OR EAT: POSSIBILITIES ALWAYS CONCEALED BY THAT	INFAMOUS	HUMBUG THE CURRENT SCHOOLMASTER, WHO ACHIEVES A
SHAK (139)	AN AGE BUT FOR ALL TIME. HITHER I RAGING COME AN	INFAMOUS	IMPOSTOR TO CHASTIZE, WHO IN AN ECSTASY OF
APPL PREFACE(194)	IN THE DESIRABILITY OF ITS ABOLISHING ITSELF AS	INFAMOUS	. THE LAST TIME I SAW HIM HE CALLED ON ME TO UNFOLD

GETT PREFACE(254)	A THOROUGHLY RASCALLY COUPLE MAKING A LIVING BY	INFAMOUS	MEANS AND BRINGING UP THEIR CHILDREN TO THEIR
ROCK II (250)	TO THEIR ANCIENT HOMESTEADS AND IGNORED YOUR	INFAMOUS	NOTICES TO QUIT? WOULD IT SURPRISE YOU TO LEARN
METH PREFACE(R62)	SHIRT FRONTS CONCEALED AND DEFENDED THE MOST	INFAMOUS	OF ALL TYRANNIES AND THE BASEST OF ALL ROBBERIES,
MRS PREFACE(171)	LEAST IMMORAL ALTERNATIVE, IT IS NONE THE LESS	INFAMOUS	OF SOCIETY TO OFFER SUCH ALTERNATIVES. FOR THE
POSN PREFACE(411)	INTO POWER, IT IS NOT TOO MUCH TO ASK THAT SUCH	INFAMOUS	POWERS OF OPPRESSION SHOULD BE KEPT IN RESPONSIBLE
ANNA (300)	HOPELESS SQUALID MISERY? YOU WOULD FILL THOSE	INFAMOUS	PRISONS AGAIN WITH THE NOBLEST SPIRITS IN THE
MRS PREFACE(173)	A MORDANT CONTRAST BETWEEN HIM AND THE WOMAN OF	INFAMOUS	PROFESSION, WITH HER WELL BROUGHT-UP,
BULL PREFACE(60)	WAS ABOLISHING THE BASTINADO AS " A HORRIBLE AND	INFAMOUS	PUNISHMENT." IN 1906 LORD CROMER GUARANTEES
DOCT III (143)	MIND TO TAKE YOU BY THE SCRUFF OF YOUR NECK, YOU	INFAMOUS	RASCAL, AND GIVE YOU A SOUND THRASHING. /LOUIS/ I
APPL I (238)	OF PUTTING IN NEW GLASS. AND IT IS TRUE. IT IS	INFAMOUS	; IT IS OUTRAGEOUS; BUT IF I ATTEMPT TO FIGHT THEM
LION PREFACE(69)	TO IT; WHICH WILL SANCTIFY IT AND BRAND IT AS	INFAMOUS	; WHICH WILL IDENTIFY IT WITH VIRTUE AND WITH SIN
PRES (156)	A TRANSPORT OF RAGE) HOW DARE YOU REPEAT THAT	INFAMOUS	SLANDER! (HE RINGS THE BELL VIOLENTLY). IF THIS
DOCT V (171)	DAY, AND ALL THEY DRANK, I REALLY THINK IT IS	INFAMOUS	THAT THEY SHOULD WRITE LIKE THAT. I HOPE YOU HAVE
MRS IV (242)	TO MENTION THEM. AND YET I CANT TELL YOU. THE TWO	INFAMOUS	WORDS THAT DESCRIBE WHAT MY MOTHER IS ARE RINGING
SUPR IV (168)	AT HIM) NOW, JACK! BEHAVE YOURSELF. /TANNER/	INFAMOUS	, ABANDONED WOMAN! DEVIL! /ANN/ BOA-CONSTRICTOR!
SUPR I (7)	RED CLOTH). I HAVE IN MY HAND A COPY OF THE MOST	INFAMOUS	, THE MOST SCANDALOUS, THE MOST MISCHIEVOUS, THE
SUPR III (116)	I BECAME FAMOUS FOR RUNNING AWAY FROM IT. /ANA/	INFAMOUS	, YOU MEAN. /DON JUAN/ I DID NOT RUN AWAY FROM YOU.
SUPR I (46)	ANGER EXTINGUISHES IT. /VIOLET/ YOU! OH, HOW	INFAMOUS	! HOW ABOMINABLE! HOW DISGRACEFULLY YOU HAVE ALL

INFAMOUSLY

JITT II (38)	AGAIN, PACING UP AND DOWN). OH, IF YOU KNEW HOW	INFAMOUSLY	ALL THOSE PEOPLE WHO CALL ON US MISUNDERSTAND

INFAMY

MIS. (168)	MAN/ WHAT IF I DO? WHAT HAS THAT TO DO WITH YOUR	INFAMY	AND MY MOTHER'S DOOM? /TARLETON/ THERE, YOU SEE!
MRS PREFACE(172)	HERSELF ABOVE ITS VILEST BRANCHES. THE DEGREES IN	INFAMY	ARE AS NUMEROUS AND AS SCRUPULOUSLY OBSERVED AS THE
JOAN PREFACE(24)	BUT HE MAY HAVE TRIED TO REDEEM IT FROM DOWNRIGHT	INFAMY	BY SHEDDING A MOMENTARY GLAMOR ON THE FIGURE OF THE
BARB PREFACE(226)	SOCIETY IN SUCH A WAY AS TO MAKE THAT EVERYDAY	INFAMY	IMPOSSIBLE. I, WHO HAVE PREACHED AND PAMPHLETEERED
BULL IV (177)	THESE IS THE FINE FLOWER OF THE WORLD'S CROP OF	INFAMY	. BUT THE DAY MAY COME WHEN THESE ISLANDS SHALL LIVE
BARB PREFACE(216)	BUT BETWEEN ENERGETIC ENTERPRISE AND COWARDLY	INFAMY	. HIS CONDUCT STANDS THE KANTIAN TEST, WHICH PETER
JITT PREFACE(3)	THEATRE WAS ONE NOT OF GOOD REPUTE, BUT OF	INFAMY	. I WAS RATED IN THE THEATRICAL WORLD OF LONDON AS AN
MIS. (174)	WHERE JOEY IS. AND I SAY IT'S A SCANDAL AND AN	INFAMY	. IF PEOPLE ONLY KNEW WHAT GOES ON IN THIS SO-CALLED
PHIL I (88)	COMPLIMENT. WHY, THE PLACE MUST BE A DEN OF	INFAMY	. /CUTHBERTSON/ (EMPHATICALLY) SO IT IS, CRAVEN: SO
GENV III (71)	BOLSHEVIKS AND PROTESTANTS WOULD ALLOW SUCH AN	INFAMY	. THEY WILL ALL GO TO HELL FOR IT. AS TO MY LOVING
BULL PREFACE(12)	RIFFRAFF WHO SET UP LITTLE HELLS OF ANARCHY AND	INFAMY	JUST BEYOND THE BORDER, AND THUS COMPEL US TO ADVANCE
DEST (174)	NOT HER HUSBAND: A LETTER THAT MEANS DISGRACE,	INFAMY	-- /NAPOLEON/ A LOVE LETTER? /LADY/ (
LADY PREFACE(212)	HE HAS LIFTED THE CHICAGO ANARCHISTS OUT OF THEIR	INFAMY	, AND SHEWN THAT, COMPARED WITH THE CAPITALISM THAT
JOAN PREFACE(14)	INDEED OFTEN MANY PENCE THE WORSE, FACE POVERTY,	INFAMY	, EXILE, IMPRISONMENT, DREADFUL HARDSHIP, AND DEATH.
GETT PREFACE(252)	HELP THAT BRINGS, NOT RESCUE, BUT EXPOSURE AND	INFAMY	, YET REVENGING HERSELF TERRIBLY IN THE END BY

INFANCY

UNPL PREFACE(R24)	HIGHLY DEVELOPED GRAMMATICALLY, IS STILL IN ITS	INFANCY	AS A TECHNICAL SPEECH NOTATION: FOR EXAMPLE, THERE
BARB III (317)	BLESSED FOUNDLING NOWADAYS IS SNAPPED UP IN HIS	INFANCY	BY BARNARDO HOMES, OR SCHOOL BOARD OFFICERS, OR
GENV IV (112)	IS THE SORT OF MIND THAT HAS BEEN FORMED IN ITS	INFANCY	BY THE JEWISH SCRIPTURES. THAT OBSTACLE I MUST SMASH
FABL PREFACE(72)	BY A DREAD OF HELL SEDULOUSLY INCULCATED FROM HIS	INFANCY	. HIS REACTION AGAINST IT CARRIED HIM INTO
MTH3 (132)	THEME) OH, YOURE QUITE RIGHT. WE ARE ONLY IN OUR	INFANCY	. I OUGHT TO BE IN A PERAMBULATOR, WITH A NURSE
2TRU III (90)	SURE. /THE ELDER/ MY SON WAS CALLED POPSY IN HIS	INFANCY	. I PUT A STOP TO IT, ON PRINCIPLE, WHEN HE ENTERED
SIM II (84)	CHILDREN DID NOT VANISH LIKE EUPHORION IN THEIR	INFANCY	. THEY GREW UP TO BORE ME MORE INTENSELY THAN I HAVE
MTH5 (221)	ME AS THE GENIUS OF ART PRESIDING OVER THE	INFANCY	OF YOUR MASTER HERE (INDICATING THE OTHER
2TRU PREFACE(9)	OR OTHER (POSSIBLY WHEN I WAS ASSURED IN MY	INFANCY	THAT SOME NASTY MEDICINE WAS DELICIOUS) MADE UP MY
GETT PREFACE(210)	WE KILL SO MANY OF OUR MALE CHILDREN IN	INFANCY	THAT WE ARE LEFT WITH A SURPLUS OF ADULT WOMEN WHICH
MILL PREFACE(127)	THE SON OF HIS FATHER, HE HAS BEEN TRAINED FROM	INFANCY	TO BEHAVE WELL IN HARNESS AND BLINKERS, HE MAY GO AS
GENV PREFACE(24)	THAN COMMON LITERARY ABILITY. MOZART, ABLE IN HIS	INFANCY	TO DO ANYTHING HE PLEASED IN MUSIC, FROM THE
CAPT NOTES (304)	BUT WHAT DOES THAT MATTER TO PEOPLE TRAINED FROM	INFANCY	TO MAKE A POINT OF HONOR OF BELIEF IN ABSTRACTIONS
MIS. PREFACE(83)	A HABIT OF DEPENDENCE AND EXPECTATION FORMED IN	INFANCY	WHICH NATURALLY ATTACHES A CHILD TO ITS PARENTS OR

INFANT

MTH5 (208)	WHAT! AND BE AS MISERABLE AS YOU? /THE ANCIENT/	INFANT	: ONE MOMENT OF THE ECSTASY OF LIFE AS WE LIVE IT
MTH5 (214)	TWO YOUNG MEN. /THE SHE-ANCIENT/ (TO STREPHON)	INFANT	: YOU ARE ONLY AT THE BEGINNING OF IT ALL. (TO ACIS)
LION PREFACE(36)	OF JESUS PIOUS MEN AND WOMEN HAIL THE	INFANT	AS THE CHRIST. THE BAPTIST HIMSELF IS NOT CONVINCED;
ROCK I (218)	BITS, AND TURNED MILLIONS AND MILLIONS OF THEIR	INFANT	CHILDREN OUT TO STARVE IN THE SNOW OR STEAL AND BEG
GETT (300)	LIFE, FOR THE SAKE, THEY SAID, OF HIS WIFE AND	INFANT	CHILDREN. AND SHE COULD NOT GET A DIVORCE FROM THAT
FABL PREFACE(72)	CANNOT BE SAID FOR MORE COMPLICATED SCHEMES OF	INFANT	CIVILIZATION. IF THEY BEGIN WITH LAW'S SERIOUS CALL,
ROCK PREFACE(172)	GENTLEMAN, FOUND MYSELF, AT THE DAWN OF MY	INFANT	CONSCIENCE, ABSOLUTELY CONVINCED THAT ALL ROMAN
AUGS (268)	WE HAVE TO. WE DROPPED IT FOR A WHILE; BUT THE	INFANT	DEATH RATE WENT UP SOMETHING FRIGHTFUL. /AUGUSTUS/
SUPR III (119)	TO SPURN INTO THE GUTTER FOR BEARING ONE UNLAWFUL	INFANT	IS NO DOUBT TRUE; BUT DARE YOU SAY SHE IS LESS
BARB I (253)	AT HARROW THEY CALLED ME THE WOOLWICH	INFANT	. AT CAMBRIDGE IT WAS THE SAME. A LITTLE BRUTE AT
FOUN (210)	YOU REMEMBER THE MATTER OF BRABAZON, AN	INFANT	. COME, NOW! FRANKLY AS MAN TO MAN YOU DO REMEMBER
FOUN (210)	/BRABAZON/ OF COURSE THERE IS. WELL, I'M THE	INFANT	. I'M BRABAZON. I'LL CALL THEE HAMLET! KING!
FABL PREFACE(96)	THAN THE INFINITESIMAL CALCULUS TO A NEWLY BORN	INFANT	. POLITICAL CONTROVERSY IS NOW (1949) RAGING ON THE
FOUN (210)	TO MAN YOU DO REMEMBER THE MATTER OF BRABAZON, AN	INFANT	. /THE LORD CHANCELLOR/ THERE IS SUCH A CASE, I
FOUN (210)	BUSINESS. IN THE MATTER OF BRABAZON, AN	INFANT	. /THE LORD CHANCELLOR/ IF YOU ARE A SOLICITOR, SIR,
METH PREFACE(R20)	AS THE PHRASE WENT THEN, DID NOT PERPLEX MY	INFANT	MIND IN THE LEAST: I KNEW PERFECTLY WELL, WITHOUT
SUPR PREFACE(R19)	DEVELOPMENT OF POVERTY, CELIBACY, PROSTITUTION,	INFANT	MORTALITY, ADULT DEGENERACY, AND EVERYTHING THAT WISE
BARB III SD(326)	THERE IS A HUGE CANNON OF THE OBSOLETE WOOLWICH	INFANT	PATTERN PEERING ACROSS IT AT THE TOWN. THE CANNON IS
VWOO 1 (120)	WHEN HE WAS A CHILD, HE WON A PRIZE AS THE	INFANT	PEDESTRIAN. AND WOULD YOU BELIEVE IT, MY MOTHER WAS
ANNA (290)	PAPER. YOU MIGHT AS WELL SEND REPORTS TO AN	INFANT	SCHOOL. (HE THROWS HIS HEAD ON THE TABLE WITH A
GETT (292)	BURKE SEEM LIKE THE MEDALS THEY GIVE CHILDREN IN	INFANT	SCHOOLS IN COMPARISON. I'M NOT ALLOWED TO MAKE ANY
FABL IV (116)	IS FOR THE TENTH EDITION OF MY PRIMER FOR	INFANT	SCHOOLS IN THE RUDIMENTARY BIOLOGY SERIES. I HAVE
BUOY 1 (13)	OWN VILLAINOUS HISTORY. HE RUINED HIMSELF; HIS	INFANT	SON DIED OF POVERTY; AND TWO OF HIS CHILDREN
BULL III (123)	TIME AT THE TOWER. /LARRY/ WELL, YOU ARE A NICE	INFANT	TO BE LET LOOSE IN THIS COUNTRY! FANCY THE POTCHEEN
MTH5 (208)	ON THE STEPS AS HE GOES OUT) AND DONT YOU FORGET,	INFANT	, THAT ONE MOMENT OF THE ECSTASY OF LIFE AS I LIVE IT
DEST SD(152)	AND HORRIBLE TO THE CONTEMPORARY NORTH ITALIAN	INFANT	, TO WHOM NOTHING WOULD SEEM MORE NATURAL THAN THAT

INFANTICIDE

MIS. PREFACE(33)	OR PASTEUR OR THE NEAREST PERSON WITH A TASTE FOR	INFANTICIDE	. AND THIS RIGHT TO LIVE INCLUDES, AND IN FACT
3PLA PREFACE(R22)	UP OF HOMES, DUELLING, MURDER, SUICIDE AND	INFANTICIDE	WILL BE PRODUCED (OFTEN HAVE BEEN PRODUCED, IN

INFANTILE

MIS. PREFACE(59)	AS AN ADULT WOULD BE TO MOCK AND DESTROY IT.	INFANTILE	DOCILITY AND JUVENILE DEPENDENCE ARE, LIKE DEATH,
CYMB FORWORD(136)	WITH AFFECTIONATE DOCILITY, I CANNOT SHARE THESE	INFANTILE	JOYS, HAVING BECOME INTERESTED IN IACHIMO, IN
MIS. PREFACE(9)	ANNOYING YOU BY A PERFECTLY HEALTHY AND NATURAL	INFANTILE	PROCEDURE, IS OFFENDING GOD. THIS IS A BLASPHEMOUS

INFANTILE-MORTALITY

GETT PREFACE(207)	OF THE VERY POOR IS COUNTERBALANCED BY A HUGE	INFANTILE-MORTALITY	IN THE SLUMS, WHILST THE VERY RICH ARE

INFANTRY

MILL PREFACE(117)	WAR IMPOSSIBLE OR ELSE KEEP THROWING MASSES OF	INFANTRY	IN THE OLD FASHION AGAINST SLAUGHTERING MACHINERY
BULL PREFACE(56)	THE MILITARY MOUNTED POLICE, AND THE MOUNTED	INFANTRY	. A FEW SPARE SENTENCES OF FLOGGING SHOULD HAVE
DEVL III (58)	20TH, 21ST, 24TH, 47TH, 53RD, AND 62ND BRITISH	INFANTRY	. ONE OFFICER IS A MAJOR GENERAL OF THE ROYAL
CYMB V (140)	CONSORT'S HEAD, COULD THUS DEFEAT ROMAN-TRAINED	INFANTRY	. /CAPTAIN/ 'TIS MY BELIEF THAT OLD BELARIUS,
ARMS III (74)	YOURE SURE TO BE ASKED TO GET RID OF SOME OF THE	INFANTRY	OF THE TIMOK DIVISION. SEND THEM HOME BY WAY OF LOM
DEVL III SD(70)	OF SOLDIERS WITH FIXED BAYONETS, HALF BRITISH	INFANTRY	, HALF HESSIANS, TRAMP QUICKLY INTO THE MIDDLE OF

INFANTS

BARB PREFACE(238)	AND PROSTITUTION, TO SUCH WHOLESALE MASSACRE OF	INFANTS	AS HEROD NEVER DREAMT OF, TO PLAGUE, PESTILENCE AND
MIS. PREFACE(24)	THEMSELVES AS STUDENTS AND DISTRACT CLASSES OF	INFANTS	BY THEIR DESPERATE ENDEAVORS TO BEAT TWO IN A BAR
ROCK PREFACE(187)	WITH A WOLF SUCKLING TWO HUMAN INFANTS. IF THESE	INFANTS	HAD NOT BEEN WISER THAN THEIR FOSTERMOTHER YOUR

MIS. PREFACE(97) NONSENSE ABOUT THE BAD EFFECT OF BIBLE STORIES ON INFANTS . BUT LET NO ONE THINK THAT A CHILD OR ANYONE ELSE
ROCK PREFACE(187) ROMAN EMPIRE BEGAN WITH A WOLF SUCKLING TWO HUMAN INFANTS . IF THESE INFANTS HAD NOT BEEN WISER THAN THEIR
AUGS (268) OF OUR GALLANT SOLDIERS, NOT OF YOUR SQUALLING INFANTS . /THE CLERK/ IF YOU WANT SOLDIERS YOU MUST HAVE
HART PREFACE(17) MOTHERS SHALL BUT SMILE WHEN THEY BEHOLD THEIR INFANTS QUARTERED BY THE HANDS OF WAR," WAS A SHAKESPEAREAN
MTH5 (262) BECOME ALL LIFE AND NO MATTER, AND BECAUSE THESE INFANTS THAT CALL THEMSELVES ANCIENTS ARE REACHING OUT
METH PREFACE(R75) THE DEADLIEST DULLNESS, COMPELLING THESE WRETCHED INFANTS TO SIT OUT THE DISCOURSES OF SECULARIST LECTURERS (
MIS. PREFACE(38) OF CHILDREN WORKING FOR THEIR LIVING WITH INFANTS TOILING IN A FACTORY FOR TEN HOURS A DAY OR BOYS

INFATUATE

BARB PREFACE(209) DON QUIXOTE AND PICKWICK: HE HAS NOT EVEN THE INFATUATE COURAGE OF TAPPERTIT, BUT WE DARE NOT LAUGH AT

INFATUATED

NEVR III (280) HOW IS A MAN TO LOOK DIGNIFIED WHEN HE'S INFATUATED ? /GLORIA/ (ANGRILY) DONT SAY THOSE THINGS TO
CLEO IV (170) ARE INFATUATED WITH THIS OLD MAN? /CLEOPATRA/ INFATUATED ? WHAT DOES THAT MEAN? MADE FOOLISH, IS IT
PYGM V (286) NATURAL. /HIGGINS/ IN SHORT, YOU WANT ME TO BE AS INFATUATED ABOUT YOU AS FREDDY? IS THAT IT? /LIZA/ NO I
ARMS III (53) THEM: THE NURSE, YOUR PARENTS, SERGIUS: I'M YOUR INFATUATED ADMIRER. /RAINA/ (PLEASED) REALLY? /BLUNTSCHLI/
GETT PREFACE(251) MAY BE LEARNT FROM SHAKESPEAR. HIS MOST INFATUATED AND PASSIONATE LOVERS ARE ANTONY AND OTHELLO; YET
JOAN PREFACE(45) SHE MUST HAVE SEEMED, TO ALL WHO WERE NOT INFATUATED BY HER, SO INSUFFERABLE THAT NOTHING BUT AN
LADY PREFACE(216) INDUSTRIOUS, SOLVENT BOURGEOIS. NO OTHER CLASS IS INFATUATED ENOUGH TO BELIEVE THAT GENTLEMEN ARE BORN AND NOT
LION PREFACE(83) SEAT IN HEAVEN, AND PARTLY, SINCE EVEN THE MOST INFATUATED IDIOT CANNOT SPEND HIS LIFE ADMIRING HIMSELF, THE
BULL PREFACE(14) WILLING TO ALLOW ME TO REPRESENT TOM BROADBENT AS INFATUATED IN POLITICS, HYPNOTIZED BY HIS NEWSPAPER
PYGM III SD(250) BOWS AND SITS DOWN IN THE ELIZABETHAN CHAIR, INFATUATED . /HIGGINS/ (SUDDENLY) BY GEORGE, YES: IT ALL
ANNA (301) DUCHESS/ OH, YOU ARE INCORRIGIBLE. YOU ARE MAD, INFATUATED . YOU WILL NOT BELIEVE THAT WE ROYAL DIVINITIES
MRS III (226) LADY AT EVER SUCH A DISADVANTAGE. NO, VIV: YOUR INFATUATED LITTLE BOY WILL HAVE TO STICK TO YOU IN ANY CASE.
DOCT PREFACE(8) BARRISTER IS AS SUPERSTITIOUS AS THE DOCTOR IS INFATUATED ; AND THE PECULIAR GOES UNPITIED TO HIS CELL,
SUPR PREFACE(R20) OR VANITY, OR CLING TO THEM IN A ROMANTICALLY INFATUATED WAY, SUCH EFFEMINATES DO NOT COUNT IN THE WORLD
AUGS (274) OH, INDEED: I DIDNT KNOW. WELL, BLUELOO IS SIMPLY INFATUATED WITH MY SISTER-IN-LAW; AND HE HAS RASHLY LET OUT
CLEO IV (170) /POTHINUS/ IT IS THE COMMON TALK THAT YOU ARE INFATUATED WITH THIS OLD MAN? /CLEOPATRA/ INFATUATED? WHAT
PHIL III (140) /JULIA/ (DELIBERATELY) I HAVE SEEN YOU VERY MUCH INFATUATED WITH THIS DEPRAVED CREATURE WHO HAS NO MORAL
APPL INTRLUD(246) SAME HOUSE WITH YOU, AND YET THAT MAN HAS UTTERLY INFATUATED WITH YOUR BEAUTY WHEN HE MARRIED YOU, YOUR FIRST
BUOY IV (53) YOURS OF A CHARWOMAN. OH, WHY, WHY AM I INFATUATED WITH YOU? I KNOW SO MANY APPARENTLY SUPERIOR

INFATUATEDLY

3PLA PREFACE(R20) CANNOT BE COURAGEOUS AND KIND AND FRIENDLY UNLESS INFATUATEDLY IN LOVE WITH SOMEBODY (IS NO POET MANLY ENOUGH

INFATUATION

3PLA PREFACE(R32) I HAVE A TECHNICAL OBJECTION TO MAKING SEXUAL INFATUATION A TRAGIC THEME. EXPERIENCE PROVES THAT IT IS
LADY PREFACE(222) AND WHO IS HUGELY AMUSED AT THE ABSURDITY OF HIS INFATUATION FOR A WOMAN OF WHOSE MORTAL IMPERFECTIONS NOT
2TRU II (67) I DONT PRETEND TO BE. BUT I MAY TELL YOU THAT MY INFATUATION FOR POPSY, WHICH I NOW SEE WAS WHAT REALLY
SUPR III (126) MADE ME THINK SO TOO? I ALSO HAD MY MOMENTS OF INFATUATION IN WHICH I GUSHED NONSENSE AND BELIEVED IT.
BARB PREFACE(211) DEMONSTRATION OF THE FOLLY OF THAT OUTWORN INFATUATION . BUT EVEN THE LESS RECKLESSLY SUPERFICIAL
SUPR III (84) I FORGET THE REST. CALL IT MADNESS IF YOU WILL-- INFATUATION . I AM AN ABLE MAN, A STRONG MAN: IN TEN YEARS I
SUPR III (116) MAN WITH THE ARTIST NATURE, AS HE CALLED HIS INFATUATION . I THANKED HIM FOR TEACHING ME TO USE MY EYES
JOAN PREFACE(26) HUMAN GOODYGOODY IN SPITE OF HER CREATOR'S INFATUATION . IT IS THE DESCRIPTION RATHER THAN THE
2TRU III (91) OF THAT STATEMENT IS THE MEASURE OF MY INFATUATION . /SWEETIE/ DONT YOU BE SO SPITEFUL. DID I GIVE
SUPR IV (151) HECTOR KNOWS IT; AND YET HE PERSISTS IN HIS INFATUATION . TAKE HIM HOME AND LOCK HIM UP. /MALONE/ (
PYGM EPILOG (302) TOO, THAT HIS INDIFFERENCE IS DEEPER THAN THE INFATUATION OF COMMONER SOULS. SHE IS IMMENSELY INTERESTED
GETT PREFACE(220) VOWS MADE UNDER THE INFLUENCE OF ITS TRANSIENT INFATUATION SO SACRED AND ENDURING, THAT ONLY AN ATROCIOUSLY
MILL I (162) PAPERS WITH THAT THING? TO HAVE THE STORY OF MY INFATUATION TOLD IN HEADLINES IN EVERY RAG IN LONDON!
GETT (327) OF THE WAR SAVED ME. ON THE FIELD OF BATTLE THE INFATUATION WORE OFF. THE BILLITER AFFAIR MADE A NEW MAN OF
SUPR III (117) ASTOUNDING ILLUMINATION! I HAD BEEN PREPARED FOR INFATUATION , FOR INTOXICATION, FOR ALL THE ILLUSIONS OF
3PLA PREFACE(R32) BAWDRY ITS HORSELAUGH AT THE EXPENSE OF SEXUAL INFATUATION , IF IT MUST; BUT TO ASK US TO SUBJECT OUR SOULS

INFATUATIONS

NEVR III (265) TO OFFER WHICH FAR TRANSCEND THE SELFISH PERSONAL INFATUATIONS AND SENTIMENTALITIES OF ROMANCE. THOSE ARE NOT
BARB II (294) A GROWN-UP DAUGHTER IS THE MOST DANGEROUS OF ALL INFATUATIONS . I APOLOGIZE FOR MENTIONING MY OWN PALE, COY,
DOCT PREFACE(13) RECOGNIZES THIS IN THE CASE OF THE AMATORY INFATUATIONS OF THE ADOLESCENTS WHO SEE ANGELS AND HEROES IN
BULL PREFACE(21) CONTRAST BETWEEN THIS FASHION AND THE ENERGETIC INFATUATIONS THAT HAVE ENABLED INTELLECTUALLY RIDICULOUS
BUOY III (36) WHAT IS CALLED FALLING IN LOVE. I HAD ILLUSIONS, INFATUATIONS , IMPULSES THAT WERE UTTERLY UNREASONABLE AND

INFECT

MIS. PREFACE(32) TO THE FOLLIES WITH WHICH OUR COMMERCIALISM WOULD INFECT ANY SYSTEM THAT IT WOULD TOLERATE AT ALL. BUT
BARB PREFACE(215) POISONOUS CONGERIES OF SLUMS. LET HIS DAUGHTERS INFECT OUR YOUNG MEN WITH THE DISEASES OF THE STREETS, AND
JOAN 4 (108) LET HER PERISH. LET HER BURN. LET HER NOT INFECT THE WHOLE FLOCK. IT IS EXPEDIENT THAT ONE WOMAN DIE
2TRU I (33) THEM; AND YOU DOCTORS PRETEND THAT IT IS WE THAT INFECT THEM. YOU OUGHT ALL TO BE STRUCK OFF THE REGISTER.
2TRU I (33) THESE HUMANS ARE FULL OF HORRID DISEASES: THEY INFECT US POOR MICROBES WITH THEM; AND YOU DOCTORS PRETEND

INFECTED

JOAN 4 (103) HUS, BURNT ONLY THIRTEEN YEARS AGO AT CONSTANCE, INFECTED ALL BOHEMIA WITH IT. A MAN NAMED WCLEEF, HIMSELF AN
BULL IV SD(145) IN AN ECSTASY OF MISCHIEVOUS MIRTH WHICH HAS INFECTED ALL HIS FRIENDS. THEY ARE SCREAMING WITH LAUGHTER,
JOAN PREFACE(16) INOCULATIONS OF INFECTED BACTERIA AND SERUM FROM INFECTED ANIMALS, AND AGAINST OLD AGE BY SURGICAL
SIM PREFACE(11) WAS INDISPENSABLE IN ITS PRIME. THE BOLSHEVIKS, INFECTED AS THEY WERE WITH ENGLISH LIBERAL AND AGNOSTIC
JOAN PREFACE(16) ALL POSSIBLE INFECTIONS BY INOCULATIONS OF INFECTED BACTERIA AND SERUM FROM INFECTED ANIMALS, AND
MRS PREFACE(175) UPHOLDING VIRTUE INSTEAD OF OUTRAGING IT. THEY INFECTED EACH OTHER WITH THEIR HYSTERIA UNTIL THEY WERE FOR
FABL PREFACE(71) STRIPPERS AND CLEANERS WILL NOT VENTURE INTO AN INFECTED HOUSE UNLESS WE MAKE A HORRIBLE STINK IN IT WITH
BULL PREFACE(50) ALL THE ATROCITIES OF MILITARY RULE, AND BECOME INFECTED IN THE END WITH THE CHRONIC PANIC CHARACTERISTIC OF
2TRU I (32) USE INOCULATING WHEN THE PATIENT IS ALREADY FULLY INFECTED . /THE ELDERLY LADY/ BUT I HAVE FOUND IT SO
GETT PREFACE(252) YOUTH, OF THE YOUNG WIFE, OF THE MOTHER, OF THE INFECTED NURSE, AND OF ALL THE OTHER VICTIMS, DIRECT AND
POSN PREFACE(427) CHILD IS MAIMED OR DROWNED AND SOME YOUNG MAN INFECTED WITH DISEASE; AND POLITICAL ASSASSINATIONS HAVE
CAPT III SD(290) EYES AND THE WORKING OF HIS MOUTH SHEW THAT HE IS INFECTED WITH THE GENERAL EXCITEMENT; BUT HE BRIDLES HIMSELF
JOAN 6 (146) SUNDERED FROM HER BODY. /THE INQUISITOR/ INFECTED WITH THE LEPROSY OF HERESY. /CAUCHON/ A MEMBER OF
DOCT PREFACE(53) BEFORE VACCINATION WAS INVENTED. THAT DOCTORS GET INFECTED WITH THESE DELUSIONS, AND ARE IN THEIR

INFECTING

SUPR HANDBOK(181) ARE WE TO TRY TO CORRECT OUR DISEASED STOCKS BY INFECTING OUR HEALTHY STOCKS WITH THEM? CLEARLY THE

INFECTION

2TRU I (29) AFTER IT. /THE DOCTOR/ THAT WAS A SPECIFIC INFECTION : A GERM, A MICROBE. /THE MONSTER/ ME! PUT IT ALL
HART PREFACE(10) THEY HAD TO FALL BACK COARSELY ON THE TERROR OF INFECTION AND DEATH. THEY PRESCRIBED INOCULATIONS AND
DOCT PREFACE(58) ARE TO A LARGE EXTENT PREVENTED. THE DANGERS OF INFECTION AND THE WAY TO AVOID IT ARE BETTER UNDERSTOOD THAN
CAND I (82) A PARSON IS LIKE A DOCTOR, MY BOY: HE MUST FACE INFECTION AS A SOLDIER MUST FACE BULLETS. (HE CLAPS LEXY
DOCT PREFACE(24) HEARD DOCTORS DENY THAT THERE IS SUCH A THING AS INFECTION . I HAVE HEARD THEM DENY THE EXISTENCE OF
DOCT PREFACE(64) CONDITIONS MUST BE ADDED THE CONSTANT RISK OF INFECTION . ONE WONDERS WHY THE IMPATIENT DOCTORS DO NOT
DOCT PREFACE(70) ADMINISTRATION AND VIGILANT PREVENTION OF INFECTION . SUCH ABSURD PANIC SCANDALS AS THAT OF THE LAST
DOCT I (95) WITH NUCIFORM SACS, MAKING THEMSELVES CENTRES OF INFECTION . THE OPERATION OUGHT TO BE COMPULSORY: IT'S TEN
DOCT PREFACE(58) SINCE PEOPLE EXPOSED THEMSELVES RECKLESSLY TO THE INFECTION OF CONSUMPTION AND PNEUMONIA IN THE BELIEF THAT
MTH3 (123) /THE ARCHBISHOP/ (WHO HAS CAUGHT THE INFECTION OF HER INDIGNATION) WHAT HIGHER EMPLOYMENTS ARE
3PLA PREFACE(R23) TO ANDROGYNOUS HEROES ON THE STAGE; AND IF THE INFECTION SPREADS UNTIL THE DEMOCRATIC ATTITUDE BECOMES
DOCT PREFACE(17) BY DEPUTY, THOUGH HE IS EXCEPTIONALLY EXPOSED TO INFECTION , AND HAS TO FACE ALL WEATHERS AT ALL HOURS OF THE
DOCT PREFACE(58) WAS OUT OF ALL PROPORTION TO THE DANGER OF INFECTION , AND WAS ACCOMPANIED BY APPARENT BLINDNESS TO THE
LION PREFACE(23) LEPER. A WOMAN, APPARENTLY TO PROTECT HIM AGAINST INFECTION , POURS A COSTLY UNGUENT ON HIS HEAD, AND IS
DOCT PREFACE(58) FORMERLY HELD BY LEPROSY, BUT THE SCARE OF INFECTION , THOUGH IT SETS EVEN DOCTORS TALKING AS IF THE

INFECTIONS

JOAN PREFACE(16) FORTIFIED WITH ANTIBODIES AGAINST ALL POSSIBLE INFECTIONS BY INOCULATIONS OF INFECTED BACTERIA AND SERUM

INFECTIOUS

CAND III (130)	IVE GOT THAT FAR. BUT DONT BE AFRAID. HEROICS ARE	INFECTIOUS	: I CAUGHT THE DISEASE FROM YOU. I SWORE NOT TO
FABL III (111)	NOT TAKE ME: HE SAID I WAS TOO DIRTY AND PROBABLY	INFECTIOUS	AND VERMINOUS. THE MEDICAL OFFICER QUARANTINED
DOCT PREFACE(24)	OBSERVER AS SYDENHAM DREAMT OF SMALLPOX BEING	INFECTIOUS	. I HAVE HEARD DOCTORS DENY THAT THERE IS SUCH A
NEVR II (255)	AM I INSPIRING? /VALENTINE/ YES. STRENGTH'S	INFECTIOUS	. /GLORIA/ WEAKNESS IS, I KNOW. /VALENTINE/ (
DOCT PREFACE(24)	NO MORE DREAMT OF CONSUMPTION AND PNEUMONIA BEING	INFECTIOUS	THAN THEY NOW DREAM OF SEA-SICKNESS BEING
ROCK PREFACE(159)	OF DOCTRINE, WERE BURNT ALIVE. CRUELTY IS SO	INFECTIOUS	THAT THE VERY COMPASSION IT ROUSES IS INFURIATED
DOCT PREFACE(24)	THAN THEY NOW DREAM OF SEA-SICKNESS BEING	INFECTIOUS	, OR THAN SO GREAT A CLINICAL OBSERVER AS
BULL PREFACE(64)	OF TEN PITCHED BATTLES. AS COWARDICE IS HIGHLY	INFECTIOUS	, WOULD IT NOT BE DESIRABLE TO SUPERSEDE

INFECTIOUSNESS

DOCT PREFACE(58)	AND WAS ACCOMPANIED BY APPARENT BLINDNESS TO THE	INFECTIOUSNESS	OF SMALLPOX, WHICH HAS SINCE BEEN WORKED UP

INFECTS

DOCT PREFACE(39)	THERE IS IN MAN A SPECIFIC LUST FOR CRUELTY WHICH	INFECTS	EVEN HIS PASSION OF PITY AND MAKES IT SAVAGE. SIMPLE

INFELICITOUSLY

MTH4 I (163)	I WAS ILLUSTRATING-- NOT, I HOPE, QUITE	INFELICITOUSLY	-- THE GREAT MARCH OF PROGRESS. I WAS SHEWING

INFER

JOAN 4 (99)	TO LOOK VERY DUBIOUS) WELL, WHAT ARE WE TO	INFER	FROM ALL THIS, MY LORD? HAS THE MAID CONVERTED YOU..
LION PREFACE(80)	BACK WHEN HE CAUGHT SIGHT OF THE CROSS, WE MUST	INFER	FROM HIS TEACHING THAT HE WOULD HAVE TOLD BUNYAN IN
MRS PREFACE(165)	IT WAS NATURAL ENOUGH FOR THOUGHTLESS PEOPLE TO	INFER	THAT A PLAY WHICH OVERSTEPPED HIS INDULGENCE MUST BE A
FABL PREFACE(94)	OF CHEESE. I HAD ENOUGH MATHEMATICAL FACULTY TO	INFER	THAT IF A EQUALS B AND B EQUALS C, A MUST EQUAL C. BUT
FABL PREFACE(94)	EQUALS C, A MUST EQUAL C. BUT I HAD WIT ENOUGH TO	INFER	THAT IF A QUART OF BRANDY EQUALS THREE BIBLES, AND
METH PREFACE(R31)	A HORRIBLY INJURED DOG CAN DIE, LEAVING US TO	INFER	THAT WE SHALL PROBABLY PERISH LIKEWISE IF WE GRUDGE
DOCT PREFACE(51)	PATHS AND GOES DOWN THAT ONE, IT IS SCIENTIFIC TO	INFER	THAT WHAT ATTRACTS HIM IS NOT KNOWLEDGE, SINCE THERE
MTH4 I (170)	ON THE SACKS). /THE ELDERLY GENTLEMAN/ AM I TO	INFER	THAT YOU DENY MY RIGHT TO LIVE BECAUSE I ALLOWED
NEVR I (206)	YOU: AND THATS A FATHER, ALIVE OR DEAD. AM I TO	INFER	THAT YOU HAVE OMITTED THAT INDISPENSABLE PART OF YOUR
JITT PREFACE(5)	OF ABSORPTION, THAT I MANAGED AT LAST TO DIVINE,	INFER	, GUESS, AND CO-INVENT THE STORY OF GITTA, OR JITTA,
LION PREFACE(32)	SCRIBES BUT AS ONE HAVING AUTHORITY: THAT IS, WE	INFER	, HE PREACHES HIS OWN DOCTRINE AS AN ORIGINAL MORALIST
POSN PREFACE(373)	OF FAITH ON THE PART OF THE CHAIRMAN, WHO, I	INFER	, WAS NOT IN AGREEMENT WITH THE SUPPRESSIVE MAJORITY.

INFERENCE

GETT PREFACE(225)	FROM THOSE WHO LIVE IN SMALL FAMILIES. THE	INFERENCE	IS THAT CHANGES OF PARTNERS ARE NOT IN THEMSELVES
INCA (238)	YOUR HIGHNESS? /THE PRINCESS/ (STRUCK BY THE	INFERENCE	) I SUPPOSE HE MUST HAVE BEEN. I WONDER! YOU
BARB I (254)	/LADY BRITOMART/ (RATHER TAKEN ABACK BY THIS	INFERENCE	) OH NO. TO DO ANDREW JUSTICE, THAT WAS NOT THE
METH PREFACE(R51)	HIM BEFOREHAND. WEISMANN THEN GRAVELY DREW THE	INFERENCE	THAT ACQUIRED HABITS CANNOT BE TRANSMITTED. AND
METH PREFACE(R55)	OF THIS SUPREME SENSE; TO MISS THE OBVIOUS	INFERENCE	THAT IT IS THE QUALITY THAT DISTINGUISHES THE
SHAK PREFACE(136)	OWN NAME. THIS IS UNQUESTIONABLY TRUE. BUT THE	INFERENCE	THAT SHAKESPEAR DID NOT WRITE THEM DOES NOT
POSN PREFACE(393)	RIDICULED. THE GERMAN PRESS DREW THE INEVITABLE	INFERENCE	THAT THE LORD CHAMBERLAIN WAS AN ANTI-GERMAN
POSN PREFACE(393)	LORD CHAMBERLAIN LICENSED THE PLAY. WHETHER THE	INFERENCE	, AS FAR AS THE LORD CHAMBERLAIN WAS CONCERNED,

INFERENCES

POSN PREFACE(392)	DEMONSTRATION-- THAT IT IS IMPOSSIBLE TO PREVENT	INFERENCES	BEING MADE, BOTH AT HOME AND ABROAD, FROM THE
FABL PREFACE(70)	PEOPLE WERE NOT LOGICAL ENOUGH TO DRAW SUBVERSIVE	INFERENCES	. THEY SWALLOWED THE CONTRADICTION CHEERFULLY.
PHIL I (88)	INDIGNATION, AS HE BEGINS TO DRAW THE INEVITABLE	INFERENCES	) DO YOU MEAN TO SAY THAT SOMEBODY HAD THE

INFERIOR

JITT III (77)	A SPECIAL CREATION, AND CONSIDER HER HUSBAND AN	INFERIOR	AND COMMON SORT OF ANIMAL. /JITTA/ YOU FORGET THAT
SUPR IV SD(143)	TREATS HIM NORMALLY WITH THE INDULGENCE DUE TO AN	INFERIOR	AND UNLUCKY SPECIES, BUT OCCASIONALLY WITH
GETT PREFACE(203)	ENERGETIC AND CAPABLE UNMARRIED COUPLE TO A DOZEN	INFERIOR	APATHETIC HUSBANDS AND WIVES. IF IT COULD BE PROVED
DEVL EPILOG (83)	THE DIFFICULTY OF CONQUERING THOSE REMOTE AND	INFERIOR	CREATURES, THE COLONISTS, AND KING GEORGE AND THE
SUPR HANDBOK(218)	SOCIAL ORGANIZATION. THE RELATION OF SUPERIOR TO	INFERIOR	EXCLUDES GOOD MANNERS, EDUCATION. WHEN A MAN
FABL PREFACE(75)	THE IMMEDIATE BLACK CONVERTS OF OUR MISSIONARIES	INFERIOR	IN CHARACTER BOTH TO THE UNCONVERTED AND THE BORN
LIED SD(188)	SOUTH KENSINGTON FEMALE OF ABOUT 37, HOPELESSLY	INFERIOR	IN PHYSICAL AND SPIRITUAL DISTINCTION TO THE
SUPR HANDBOK(175)	SOCIAL ORDER, IS NOT A REVOLUTIONIST, IS AN	INFERIOR	. AND YET REVOLUTIONS HAVE NEVER LIGHTENED THE
SUPR HANDBOK(221)	EMBARRASS THE SUPERIOR, AND ARE DISGRACED BY THE	INFERIOR	. GREAT MEN REFUSE TITLES BECAUSE THEY ARE JEALOUS
2TRU II (58)	IS ONE OF A SUPERIOR ADDRESSING A VERY DISTANT	INFERIOR	. NEVER LET HIM ADDRESS YOU ON HIS OWN INITIATIVE.
ARMS III (59)	BENEATH YOU, I WOULD DARE TO BE THE EQUAL OF MY	INFERIOR	. WOULD YOU DARE AS MUCH IF YOU LOVED ME? NO: IF
JOAN PREFACE(37)	SELECTION AND ELECTION ARE OF THE SUPERIOR BY THE	INFERIOR	(THE CARDINAL VICE OF DEMOCRACY), WITH THE RESULT
JOAN PREFACE(38)	MAY BE INSPIRED. THE CONSCIOUS PRAYER OF THE	INFERIOR	MAY BE THAT HIS CHOICE MAY LIGHT ON A GREATER THAN
SUPR HANDBOK(220)	MORMONS, IS WRECKED BY THE REVOLT OF THE MASS OF	INFERIOR	MEN WHO ARE CONDEMNED TO CELIBACY BY IT; FOR THE
BARB PREFACE(209)	NOT THROWING A STONE AT A CREATURE OF ANOTHER AND	INFERIOR	ORDER, BUT MAKING A CONFESSION, WITH THE EFFECT
ROCK PREFACE(149)	THE EXTERMINATION OF WHAT THE EXTERMINATORS CALL	INFERIOR	RACES IS AS OLD AS HISTORY. " STONE DEAD HATH NO
BARB PREFACE(212)	SUPERIOR WHITE RACE TO SUBJUGATE THE MINDS OF THE	INFERIOR	RACES WHOM THEY WISHED TO EXPLOIT, AND WHO WOULD
JITT III (78)	TO BE HER INSURANCE POLICY. NO DOUBT I AM BRUNO'S	INFERIOR	; BUT I DRAW THE LINE AT HELPING HIM TO ROB HIS
GENV PREFACE(15)	BECAUSE I BELIEVED THAT CATHOLICS WERE AN	INFERIOR	SPECIES WHO WOULD ALL GO TO HELL WHEN THEY DIED;
MILL II (174)	MY SPECIES INDEED! MEN ARE A DIFFERENT AND VERY	INFERIOR	SPECIES. FIVE MINUTES CONVERSATION WITH MY HUSBAND
ROCK PREFACE(150)	GLASSES, REGARD ALL DIFFERENTLY COLORED FOLK AS	INFERIOR	SPECIES. LADIES AND GENTLEMEN CLASS REBELLIOUS
BULL I (89)	SOMETHING IN AMERICA AND A FEW OTHER REMOTE AND	INFERIOR	SPOTS; BUT IN THE MAIN IT IS BY LIVING WITH YOU AND
APPL PREFACE(178)	INSULT AND ASK ME INDIGNANTLY IF I CONSIDER YOU	INFERIOR	TO A FISH. WELL, YOU MUST PLEASE BE EQUALLY
JOAN 1,SD(70)	MADE A FOOL OF BY A CRAZY FEMALE, AND A SOCIAL	INFERIOR	TO BOOT, SCRATCHES HIS HEAD AND SLOWLY COMES BACK
SUPR PREFACE(R19)	SMOKED OUT AND UNLOADED OF HIS HONEY BY BEINGS	INFERIOR	TO HIMSELF IN SIMPLE ACQUISITIVENESS,
BULL PREFACE(10)	FOR ALL THAT, THOUGH ENGLAND'S FLEET WAS FAR MORE	INFERIOR	TO IT THAN THE GERMAN FLEET WILL EVER AGAIN BE TO
UNPL PREFACE(R19)	WHENEVER, AS OCCASIONALLY HAPPENS, THE ADAPTER IS	INFERIOR	TO THE AUTHOR. THE LIVING AUTHOR CAN PROTECT
3PLA PREFACE(R37)	WORKS OF GREAT MEN ARE USUALLY CONSPICUOUSLY	INFERIOR	TO THE BEST WORKS OF THEIR FORERUNNERS. IMAGINE
GETT (326)	BECAUSE IT SEEMED CHEAP. IT PROVED UNEXPECTEDLY	INFERIOR	TO THE FAMILY SILKSTONE; AND IN THE IRRITATION INTO
CLEO NOTES (206)	CAESAR'S ROME. YET THE COCKNEY PROLETARIAN IS SO	INFERIOR	TO THE VILLAGE LABORER THAT IT IS ONLY BY STEADY
MIS. (133)	PUT US IN THE BACK ROW. IT ISNT A FACT THAT WE'RE	INFERIOR	TO THEM: IT'S A PUT-UP JOB; AND IT'S THEY THAT HAVE
MRS PREFACE(179)	RENTS, ADVERTISEMENTS, OR DIVIDENDS, ARE GROSSLY	INFERIOR	TO THEM IN MORAL SENSE AND PUBLIC RESPONSIBILITY.
BULL PREFACE(34)	AND SENTIMENTS ARE DIFFERENT FROM, AND ABYSMALLY	INFERIOR	TO, MY OWN. FINALLY, I AM IMPARTIAL AS TO YOUR
METH PREFACE(R54)	LESSEN THE SEVERITY OF THE STRUGGLE AND PRESERVE	INFERIOR	VARIETIES FROM THE EFFORTS OF NATURE TO WEED THEM
BARB PREFACE(212)	BY THE NECESSITY IN WHICH THE NUMERICALLY	INFERIOR	WHITE RACES FOUND THEMSELVES TO IMPOSE THEIR
APPL II (273)	YOU MEAN. THE COMMON MAN IS THE SUPERIOR, NOT THE	INFERIOR	, OF THE TITLED MAN. /MAGNUS/ THAT IS WHY I AM
CAPT NOTES (300)	ON THAT OCCASION CIVILIZATION, QUALITATIVELY HIS	INFERIOR	, WAS QUANTITATIVELY SO HUGELY IN EXCESS OF HIM
GETT (328)	DISAGREED WITH YOU? /HOTCHKISS/ (WITHERINGLY)	INFERIOR	! /MRS GEORGE/ THANK YOU. ANYTHING ELSE?

INFERIORITY

JOAN PREFACE(6)	RESULT COULD HAVE BEEN PRODUCED BY A CRAPULOUS	INFERIORITY	AS WELL AS BY A SUBLIME SUPERIORITY, THE
GENV IV (96)	MILITARY OR NAVAL INFERIORITY, ESPECIALLY NAVAL	INFERIORITY	. I WARN YOU-- I BEG YOU-- DO NOT FRIGHTEN US.
PYGM EPILOG (302)	LONGER DARES TO TEASE HER BY ASSUMING AN ABYSMAL	INFERIORITY	OF FREDDY'S MIND TO HIS OWN. HE STORMS AND
SUPR PREFACE(R21)	ITS BOOTS AND THEN PROVES THE MORAL AND PHYSICAL	INFERIORITY	OF THE NEGRO BY THE FACT THAT HE IS A SHOEBLACK;
MILL PREFACE(122)	OF PERMANENT, DECISIVE, AND HUMILIATING MILITARY	INFERIORITY	TO THE OTHER POWERS, AND ESPECIALLY TO FRANCE.
BARB PREFACE(231)	HE IS PLACED IN A POSITION OF UNBEARABLE MORAL	INFERIORITY	, AND STRIVES BY EVERY MEANS IN HIS POWER TO
GENV IV (96)	TO PLACE US IN A POSITION OF MILITARY OR NAVAL	INFERIORITY	, ESPECIALLY NAVAL INFERIORITY. I WARN YOU-- I

INFERIORS

GETT PREFACE(211)	AND THE INFERIORS. IF WE COULD GET RID OF OUR	INFERIORS	AND SCREW UP OUR AVERAGE QUALITY UNTIL MEDIOCRITY
MIS. PREFACE(66)	CORIOLANUS IS PLAYED ON HIM IN HIS TURN BY HIS	INFERIORS	, EVERYWHERE WE SEE THE CUNNING SUCCEEDING IN THE
LADY PREFACE(218)	SHAKESPEAR SPOKE AND WROTE OF BRICKLAYERS AS HIS	INFERIORS	, HE MUST HAVE FELT IT A LITTLE HARD THAT BEING A
GETT PREFACE(211)	BEST PEOPLE, BUT FROM THE MEDIOCRITIES AND THE	INFERIORS	, IF WE COULD GET RID OF OUR INFERIORS AND SCREW
KING I (189)	SEE WHAT COMES OF FREQUENTING THE HOUSES OF YOUR	INFERIORS	, THEY FORGET THEMSELVES AND TAKE LIBERTIES. AND
LADY PREFACE(216)	SOCIAL SUPERIORS AND INSOLENCE TOWARDS SOCIAL	INFERIORS	, THE EASY WAYS WITH SERVANTS WHICH IS SEEN NOT

			INFERNAL	
WIDO III	(52)	PUT YOU DOWNSTAIRS BY THE BACK OF YOUR NECK, YOU	INFERNAL	BLACKGUARD. /LICKCHEESE/ (NOT A BIT RUFFLED, HANGS
ARMS II	(44)	GOT OUT OF HAND WHILE I WAS AWAY. I'LL TEACH HIM.	INFERNAL	BLACKGUARD! THE SACK NEXT SATURDAY! I'LL CLEAR
PRES	(164)	PRIVATE BUSINESS WITH MRS FARRELL. OUTSIDE, YOU	INFERNAL	BLACKGUARD. /THE ORDERLY/ (ARGUING, AS USUAL)
MTH2	(72)	SINGLE THING YOU DID TO HELP US DURING THE WHOLE	INFERNAL	BUSINESS? /CONRAD/ WE'RE NOT BLAMING YOU: YOU
PHIL II	(110)	OF THE WOMEN I LOVE IS ONLY EQUALLED BY THE	INFERNAL	CONSTANCY OF THE WOMEN WHO LOVE ME. WELL, WELL! I
NEVR II	(236)	HAND OVER HIS FOREHEAD). I HAVE NOT GOT OVER THAT	INFERNAL	GAS YET. HE GOES TO THE IRON CHAIR, SO THAT HE CAN
BASH II,2,	(113)	THOSE CHIMNEYS THE FULIGINOUS ALTARS OF SOME	INFERNAL	GOD. I NOW PERCEIVE THE ENGLISH DARE NOT LOOK UPON
CATH 4	(188)	COME EITHER TIME. IVE BEEN CARRIED. I CALL IT	INFERNAL	IMPUDENCE. /CATHERINE/ TAKE CARE WHAT YOU SAY.
PRES	(162)	BY COMPULSORY MILITARY SERVICE. /MITCHENER/	INFERNAL	IMPUDENCE! /BALSQUITH/ THE LABOR PARTY IS TAKING
METH PREFACE	(R86)	GOETHE IS OLYMPIAN: THE OTHER GIANTS ARE	INFERNAL	IN EVERYTHING BUT THEIR VERACITY AND THEIR
BARB PREFACE	(238)	DAY OF SENTENCES OF YEARS OF IMPRISONMENT SO	INFERNAL	IN THEIR UNNATURAL STUPIDITY AND PANIC-STRICKEN
APPL II	(265)	HAVE IT YOUR OWN WAY, DEAREST. WHERE ARE THESE	INFERNAL	MINISTERS? THEYRE LATE. /THE QUEEN/ (LOOKING OUT
PHIL II	(113)	OF DEATH! ON THE STRENGTH OF THREE DOGS AND AN	INFERNAL	MONKEY? /PARAMORE/ (UTTERLY CONTEMPTUOUS OF
O'FL	(223)	PEARCE/ (RUNNING OUT OF THE HOUSE) WHATS THIS	INFERNAL	NOISE? WHAT ON EARTH IS THE MATTER? /O'FLAHERTY/
MIS.	(187)	MEAN IT: DONT CRY. /LORD SUMMERHAYS/ STOP THAT	INFERNAL	NOISE, SIR: DO YOU HEAR? STOP IT INSTANTLY.
PRES	(160)	AM ABLE TO SEE WITH AN UNPREJUDICED EYE WHAT	INFERNAL	NONSENSE IT IS. BUT I TELL YOU PLAINLY, LADY
BARB III	(345)	SAY! (BILTON STOLIDLY HANDS HIM THE EMPTY BOX).	INFERNAL	NONSENSE! PURE SCIENTIFIC IGNORANCE! (HE GOES
BUOY II	(23)	ARE AN INHOSPITABLE WRETCH, /SHE/ AND YOU ARE AN	INFERNAL	NUISANCE (SHE GOES INTO THE HOUSE AND SLAMS THE
LION PREFACE	(81)	SCOTS AND LITERAL SWISS, IT BECOMES THE MOST	INFERNAL	OF FATALISMS; AND THE LIVES OF CIVILIZED CHILDREN
BARB II	(293)	YOU ARE, AS FAR AS I AM ABLE TO GATHER, A MOST	INFERNAL	OLD RASCAL; BUT YOU APPEAL VERY STRONGLY TO MY
BARB II	(296)	EXCELLENT. /CUSINS/ (REVOLTED) YOU REALLY ARE AN	INFERNAL	OLD RASCAL. /UNDERSHAFT/ (INDICATING PETER
HART II	(125)	BEAR IT, I TELL YOU. WILL YOU LISTEN TO ME, YOU	INFERNAL	-- (HE CHOKES). /LADY UTTERWORD/ WELL: GO ON. WHAT
LION II	(145)	TO UNDO THE CLASP OF HIS BROOCH) FRIENDS! YOU	INFERNAL	SCOUNDREL (THE LION GROWLS) -- DONT LET HIM GO.
DEVL III	(67)	BOUND, AND SEIZING SWINDON BY THE THROAT) YOU	INFERNAL	SCOUNDREL-- THE SERGEANT RUSHES TO THE RESCUE FROM
MILL PREFACE	(111)	THE WORST CASES, THE POLITICAL USURPER MAY BE AN	INFERNAL	SCOUNDREL, RUTHLESS IN MURDER, TREACHERY, AND
SIM PREFACE	(7)	CRIMES, BUT THOUGH WE KNOW OF THESE FAILURES OF	INFERNAL	TERRORISM WE HAVE NO RECORD OF ITS SUCCESSES. WE
HART II	(125)	WELL: GO ON. WHAT WERE YOU GOING TO CALL ME? AN	INFERNAL	WHAT? WHICH UNPLEASANT ANIMAL IS IT TO BE THIS
NEVR II	(237)	CONSPIRACY. THIS IS MY FAMILY! MY CHILDREN! MY	INFERNAL	WIFE. /VALENTINE/ (COOLLY) OH INDEED! INTERESTING
PRES	(139)	(BALSQUITH, REASSURED, SITS DOWN). BUT WHAT AN	INFERNAL	YOUNG FOOL CHUBBS-JENKINSON IS, NOT TO KNOW THE
JOAN 3	(88)	(FURIOUSLY DISAPPOINTED) IS THAT ALL? YOU	INFERNAL	YOUNG IDIOT: I HAVE A MIND TO PITCH YOU INTO THE
			INFERNALLY	
DOCT II	(128)	PICTURES ARE SO AGREEABLE, AND THE GOOD PEOPLE SO	INFERNALLY	DISAGREEABLE AND MISCHIEVOUS, THAT I REALLY CANT
PHIL III	(141)	SPOIL EVERYTHING LIKE THIS. /CRAVEN/ THIS IS MOST	INFERNALLY	PERPLEXING. I CANT BELIEVE THAT YOU INSULTED
			INFERNO	
SUPR III	(128)	THROUGH ALL THE CIRCLES OF THE FOOLISH ITALIAN'S	INFERNO	THAN THROUGH THE PLEASURES OF EUROPE. THAT IS WHAT
			INFERRED	
LION PREFACE	(36)	I HAVE CALLED THE ROUSSEAU VIEW OF MIRACLES AS	INFERRED	FROM MATTHEW. LUKE SHEWS ALL A ROMANCER'S
O'FL PREFACE	(202)	EXPERIENCE AND OBSERVATION WHAT ANYONE MIGHT HAVE	INFERRED	FROM THE RECORDS OF IRISH EMIGRATION, THAT ALL AN
SUPR IV	(146)	MR MALONE. HECTOR WANTS TO MARRY ME. /MALONE/ I	INFERRED	FROM YOUR NOTE THAT HE MIGHT. WELL, MISS ROBINSON,
JOAN PREFACE	(35)	ANTI-CLERICALISM. I MUST NOT LEAVE IT TO BE	INFERRED	HERE THAT ONE CANNOT BE AN ANTI-CLERICAL AND A GOOD
KING PREFACE	(156)	BEING A DISGRACEFULLY UNFAITHFUL HUSBAND. IT IS	INFERRED	THAT HE WAS POLITICALLY INFLUENCED BY WOMEN,
SUPR II SD	(48)	ALL AFFECT THE GENTLEMAN IN HIS SPEECH, IT MAY BE	INFERRED	THAT HIS SMART APPEARANCE IS A MARK OF RESPECT TO
HART PREFACE	(16)	DANGERS (AS IN FACT THEY ARE), LEAVING IT TO BE	INFERRED	THAT OUR OWN MILITARISM AND OUR OWN POLITICAL
JOAN PREFACE	(49)	WHENEVER HE DESCRIBES ANYONE ELSE, I HAVE	INFERRED	THAT THESE GOOD-NATURED YOUNG MEN WERE VERY LIKE
			INFERS	
SUPR HANDBOK	(201)	OF BUSTLING PROGRESS; AND THE READING CLASS	INFERS	FROM THEM THAT THE ABUSES OF THE EARLY VICTORIAN
LADY PREFACE	(215)	WHO HAVE THE VERY CHARACTERISTICS FROM WHICH HE	INFERS	THAT SHAKESPEAR WAS AT A SOCIAL DISADVANTAGE THROUGH
			INFEST	
FABL PREFACE	(98)	TO THE WELL-INTENTIONED UTOPIAN AMATEURS WHO	INFEST	OUR PARLIAMENTS AND PARTIES, IMAGINING THAT IT CAN BE
APPL PREFACE	(194)	ME A VIVID ACCOUNT OF THE PIRATES WHO USED TO	INFEST	THE THAMES BELOW LONDON BRIDGE BEFORE THE DOCKS WERE
CAPT I	(233)	A WOMAN WHO ADMIRES THE FACES OF THE RUFFIANS WHO	INFEST	THESE PORTS, MR RANKIN. CAN ANYTHING BE DONE IN THE
LADY	(243)	JADES AND LIGHT-O'-LOVES AND FLY-BY-NIGHTS THAT	INFEST	THIS PALACE OF MINE, MAY WILLIAM SHAKESPEAR BE? /THE
			INFESTED	
GENV IV	(116)	/FLANCO/ YOU MEAN THAT YOU HAVE POLICED A PLACE	INFESTED	BY SAVAGES. A CHILD COULD HAVE DONE IT WITH A
JOAN PREFACE	(19)	THE SAFEST WAY OF TRAVELLING THROUGH A COUNTRY	INFESTED	WITH HOSTILE TROOPS AND BANDS OF MARAUDING
FABL PREFACE	(93)	MOST DISABLING OF ALL MEMORIES. UNIVERSITIES ARE	INFESTED	WITH PEDANTS WHO HAVE ALL RECORDED HISTORY AT THEIR
			INFIDEL	
CATH 4	(190)	YOU DISCUSS THE BLASPHEMIES OF THAT ABOMINABLE	INFIDEL	? AGH! ! (SHE HAS AGAIN APPLIED HER TOE). OH!
MTH2	(78)	PULLING MY LEG BY TRYING TO MAKE OUT THAT I AM AN	INFIDEL	? /LUBIN/ IT'S VERY INTERESTING AND AMUSING, BURGE;
KING I	(188)	MY HOUSE THE GREAT GALILEO SHALL NOT BE CALLED AN	INFIDEL	BY ANY POPISH BLOCKHEAD, PRINCE OR NO PRINCE.
CAPT II	(268)	A JUST MAN FULFILS ITSELF WITHOUT MANY WORDS. THE	INFIDEL	CADI, THY CAPTIVE, FALLS TO MY SHARE. /BRASSBOUND/ (
KING I	(188)	I KNOW YOU. YOU ARE A FOLLOWER OF THE ARCH	INFIDEL	GALILEO! /NEWTON/ TAKE CARE, SIR. IN MY HOUSE THE
METH PREFACE	(R9)	PREFACE. THE	INFIDEL	HALF CENTURY. THE DAWN OF DARWINISM. ONE DAY EARLY
METH PREFACE	(R72)	FOR, THROUGHOUT ALL THE GODLESS WELTER OF THE	INFIDEL	HALF-CENTURY, DARWINISM HAS BEEN ACTING NOT ONLY
KING I	(181)	A HAND ON HIS SHOULDER). MR NEWTON: THE WORD	INFIDEL	IS NOT ONE TO BE USED HASTILY BETWEEN US THREE. OLD
KING I	(181)	SINFULLY WASTED. /NEWTON/ GEORGE FOX: YOU ARE AN	INFIDEL	. LEAVE MY HOUSE. /FOX/ (RISING) YOUR PHILOSOPHY
BUOY II	(24)	BUT HERE YOU ARE A HEATHEN, A BARBARIAN, AN	INFIDEL	. MENTALLY WE ARE NOT ON THE SAME PLANE.
KING I	(181)	LED YOU TO THE CONCLUSION THAT GEORGE FOX IS AN	INFIDEL	. SO MUCH THE WORSE FOR YOUR PHILOSOPHY! THE LORD
KING I	(181)	WAS TO ALEXANDER THE GREAT, WAS CALLED AN	INFIDEL	. YOU YOURSELF, IN SPITE OF YOUR INTEREST IN THE
PLES PREFACE	(R8)	NONCONFORMIST DIVINE," THAN I WAS TO THEM " AN	INFIDEL	." THERE IS ONLY ONE RELIGION, THOUGH THERE ARE A
KING I	(188)	HAVE BEEN THROWN BY YOUR FRIEND AND PROTEGE, THE	INFIDEL	PHILOSOPHER NEWTON. /CHARLES/ GET UP, MAN: DONT PLAY
KING I	(211)	DONE? /NEWTON/ SIR: YOU BEGAN IT, YOU AND THIS	INFIDEL	QUAKER. I HAVE DEVOTED MONTHS OF MY LIFE TO THE
METH PREFACE	(R35)	WERE UTTERED, LEAVING HIM ALONE WITH A SOLITARY	INFIDEL	UNDER SENTENCE OF EXTERMINATION IN FIVE MINUTES,
BUOY 1	(13)	INSTANTLY OR DIE; WITH MAHOMET THE SLAYING OF THE	INFIDEL	WAS A PASSPORT TO HEAVEN; WITH DOMINIC AND HIS DOGS
CAPT II	(266)	/OSMAN/ (POINTING OUT SIR HOWARD) THIS IS THE	INFIDEL	, CADI. (SIR HOWARD BOWS TO SIDI, BUT, BEING AN
CAPT II	(266)	CADI. (SIR HOWARD BOWS TO SIDI, BUT, BEING AN	INFIDEL	, RECEIVES ONLY THE HAUGHTIEST STARE IN
LION PREFACE	(100)	PARIS FROM THE GRIP OF THE MODERN SCIENTIFIC "	INFIDEL	," AND TO RAISE THE CRY OF " BACK TO THE APOSTLES:
BULL PREFACE	(37)	HE THINKS OF VOLTAIRE AS A FRENCH "	INFIDEL	," INSTEAD OF AS THE CHAMPION OF THE LAITY AGAINST
			INFIDELITIES	
OVER PREFACE	(167)	BUT IT IS HAPPILY BY NO MEANS TRUE THAT CONJUGAL	INFIDELITIES	ALWAYS PRODUCE TRAGIC CONSEQUENCES, OR THAT
OVER PREFACE	(157)	BE JEALOUS OF B AND NOT OF C, AND WILL TOLERATE	INFIDELITIES	ON THE PART OF D WHILST BEING FURIOUSLY ANGRY
MIS. PREFACE	(82)	DISAPPOINTED IN THEM, OR ESTRANGED FROM THEM BY	INFIDELITIES	; AND THESE PARENTS, IN LOSING A SON OR A
			INFIDELITY	
SUPR PREFACE	(R36)	LAW AND INDUSTRY. EVEN ATHEISTS REPROACH ME WITH	INFIDELITY	AND ANARCHISTS WITH NIHILISM BECAUSE I CANNOT
JITT PREFACE	(6)	THAT IN REAL LIFE THE CONSEQUENCES OF CONJUGAL	INFIDELITY	ARE SELDOM EITHER SO SERIOUS AS THEY ARE ASSUMED
LION PREFACE	(20)	HOLY GHOST, AND THAT HE MUST NOT ACCUSE HER OF	INFIDELITY	BECAUSE OF HER BEARING A SON OF WHICH HE IS NOT
JITT I	(20)	THAT A MAN CAN BE GUILTY OF TO A WOMAN EXCEPT THE	INFIDELITY	THAT I WOULD WELCOME WITH DELIGHT TO EXCUSE MY
OVER PREFACE	(167)	THE HEART OF THEM, THE INEVITABLE CONJUGAL	INFIDELITY	, IS ALWAYS EVADED. EVEN ITS CONSEQUENCES ARE
			INFIDELIUM	
SIM I	(45)	A BISHOP IS NEEDED HERE: A BISHOP IN PARTIBUS	INFIDELIUM	. PROVIDENCE SEEMS TO HAVE THROWN YOU ON THIS
			INFIDELS	
KING I	(212)	I AM A CHRISTIAN LADY. CHARLES ALWAYS ENCOURAGES	INFIDELS	AND LIBERTINES TO BLASPHEME. AND NOW HE ENCOURAGES
LION I	(122)	OF THE MOB: THEY LISTEN TO ME IN SILENCE; AND	INFIDELS	ARE OFTEN CONVERTED BY A STRAIGHT HEART-TO-HEART
JOAN 4	(104)	THIS BEFORE. MEN GO TO THE EAST TO CONVERT THE	INFIDELS	. AND THE INFIDELS PERVERT THEM. THE CRUSADER COMES

JOAN 4 (104) GO TO THE EAST TO CONVERT THE INFIDELS. AND THE INFIDELS PERVERT THEM. THE CRUSADER COMES BACK MORE THAN
LION PREFACE(88) PEOPLE WHOM PETER WOULD HAVE STRUCK DEAD AS WORSE INFIDELS THAN SIMON MAGUS; AND THE ATONEMENT IS PREACHED BY
LION EPILOG (152) FLAT-EARTH MEN, SCOFFERS AT THE LABORATORIES, OR INFIDELS WHO REFUSE TO KNEEL DOWN WHEN A PROCESSION OF
BARB I (269) OF THEM THROUGH MY HANDS: SCOUNDRELS, CRIMINALS, INFIDELS , PHILANTHROPISTS, MISSIONARIES, COUNTY

INFIGHTING

MILL IV (203) HEAVIER THAN I; AND I CANNOT KEEP MY HEAD AT INFIGHTING AS YOU CAN. YOU DO NOT SUIT. I THROW YOU TO

INFINITE

MTH4 II (192) THEY ARE ENOUGH FOR ME, BECAUSE THESE THINGS ARE INFINITE AND ETERNAL, AND CAN MAKE TEN OF MY YEARS AS LONG
METH PREFACE(R16) UNEASINESS BE ENTRUSTED TO INFINITE WISDOM AND INFINITE BENEVOLENCE ARE PLACED IN THE HANDS OF ROMANTIC
SUPR HANDBOK(188) NOT AS TRUE SUPERMEN, BUT AS HIMSELF ENDOWED WITH INFINITE BRAINS, INFINITE COURAGE, AND INFINITE MONEY. THE
SUPR I SD(16) OF INDIVIDUAL CONSCIOUSNESS ARE SUDDENLY MADE INFINITE BY A MYSTIC MEMORY OF THE WHOLE LIFE OF THE RACE TO
MTH5 (218) IF YOU SHOULD TURN OUT TO BE A PERSON OF INFINITE CAPACITY, YOU WILL NO DOUBT FIND LIFE INFINITELY
3PLA PREFACE(R12) UNITS BY THE SAME LUXURY, SINCE IN THAT DOMAIN OF INFINITE CAPRICE, ONE MAN'S MEAT IS ANOTHER MAN'S POISON,
SUPR III (131) TO HIGHER THINGS, YOU WILL SEE NOTHING BUT AN INFINITE COMEDY OF ILLUSION. YOU WILL DISCOVER THE PROFOUND
BULL PREFACE(39) GETS NOTHING OUT OF IRELAND BUT INFINITE TROUBLE, INFINITE CONFUSION AND HINDRANCE IN HER OWN LEGISLATION, A
CAND III (135) THAN GIVE YOU A MOMENT'S PAIN. /CANDIDA/ (WITH INFINITE CONTEMPT FOR THIS PUERILITY) MUCH GOOD YOUR DYING
SUPR HANDBOK(188) BUT AS HIMSELF ENDOWED WITH INFINITE BRAINS, INFINITE COURAGE, AND INFINITE MONEY. THE MOST TROUBLESOME
GETT (334) MARRIAGE NOR THE INTELLIGENCE TO UNDERSTAND ITS INFINITE DISHONOR WILL MAKE THE ENGLAND OF THE FUTURE. (SHE
APPL INTRLUD(253) WE TWO ALSO HAVE OUR ORBITS, AND MUST KEEP AN INFINITE DISTANCE BETWEEN US TO AVOID A DISASTROUS
APPL INTRLUD(253) THERE IS NOT ONLY A POWERFUL ATTRACTION BUT AN INFINITE DISTANCE. WHEN THE ATTRACTION BECOMES STRONGER THAN
CLEO I SD(106) LOOKING STRAIGHT FORWARD AND UPWARD IN INFINITE FEARLESS VIGIL, AND A MASS OF COLOR BETWEEN ITS
BARB II (306) I LIVE THE MORE PROOF I SEE THAT THERE IS AN INFINITE GOODNESS THAT TURNS EVERYTHING TO THE WORK OF
SUPR III SD(94) MAJESTIC OLD MAN. BUT HE WAIVES HIS MAJESTY WITH INFINITE GRACE; WALKS WITH A FEATHER-LIKE STEP; AND MAKES
MILL IV (206) ME WHETHER YOU WERE NOT ONE OF THE STROKES OF HIS INFINITE HUMOR. THEN I SAT DOWN AND TOOK UP A NEWSPAPER, AND
NEVR II (255) PERSONAL MERITS. (SHE TURNS AWAY FROM HIM WITH INFINITE INDIFFERENCE, AND SITS DOWN WITH HER BOOK ON THE
GENV PREFACE(26) AS NATURAL DEATH: IT IS LIFE THAT IS NATURAL AND INFINITE . HOW LONG, THEN, WOULD IT TAKE US TO MATURE INTO
SUPR HANDBOK(224) APPEARS, TO THE LATTER, TRIFLING; TO THE FORMER, INFINITE . IN A STUPID NATION THE MAN OF GENIUS BECOMES A
GLIM (188) FROM FINITE TO INFINITE, AND ITSELF PART OF THE INFINITE . /SANDRO/ (IMPRESSED) YOUR EXCELLENCY SPEAKS LIKE
DOCT PREFACE(8) THE INEVITABLE RESULT OF HIS FORMER PRETENCES TO INFINITE KNOWLEDGE AND UNERRING SKILL. HE HAS TAUGHT THE
APPL I (205) ROMAN EMPEROR-GOD HAD NOT INFINITE WISDOM, INFINITE KNOWLEDGE, INFINITE POWER; BUT HE HAD SOME: PERHAPS
2TRU III (87) TURNED FROM SURVEYING THEIR VASTNESS TO STUDY THE INFINITE LITTLENESS OF THE ATOMS, THERE TOO WE FOUND THE
CATH 1 (162) (WHOM (CROSSING HIMSELF) MAY GOD IN HIS INFINITE MERCY DAMN ETERNALLY!), IS IN THE ANTECHAMBER AND
METH PREFACE(R21) AT AN ALMIGHTY WORD. WHAT A SUBLIME IDEA OF THE INFINITE MIGHT OF THE GREAT ARCHITECT, THE CAUSE OF ALL
SUPR HANDBOK(188) WITH INFINITE BRAINS, INFINITE COURAGE, AND INFINITE MONEY. THE MOST TROUBLESOME OPPOSITION WILL ARISE
MILL II (169) YOU DARE THINK SUCH THINGS OF MY FATHER! YOU INFINITE NOTHINGNESS! MY FATHER MADE A HUNDRED AND FIFTY
METH PREFACE(R36) BUT HE DID NOT REALLY BELIEVE THAT INFINITY WAS INFINITE OR THAT THE ETERNAL WAS ALSO SEMPITERNAL: HE
APPL I (205) HAD NOT INFINITE WISDOM, INFINITE KNOWLEDGE, INFINITE POWER; BUT HE HAD SOME: PERHAPS EVEN AS MUCH AS HIS
CLEO IV (191) DOES CAESAR DESPAIR? /CAESAR/ (WITH INFINITE PRIDE) HE WHO HAS NEVER HOPED CAN NEVER DESPAIR.
VWOO 3 (142) LIGHTNING FLASH WHICH TURNS THE BLACK NIGHT INTO INFINITE RADIANCE. IT WILL BE DARK AGAIN BEFORE YOU CAN
CAND III (140) MASTER. I ASSERT NO SUCH RIGHT. /CANDIDA/ (WITH INFINITE REPROACH) YOU DONT KNOW! OH, JAMES! JAMES! (TO
SUPR III SD(87) OF A GHOSTLY CLARIONET TURNING THIS TUNE INTO INFINITE SADNESS: THE YELLOWISH PALLOR MOVES: THERE IS AN
MIS. PREFACE(39) MUST NOT GRUDGE CHILDREN THEIR SHARE OF IT. THE INFINITE SCHOOL TASK. THE QUESTION OF CHILDREN'S WORK,
3PLA PREFACE(R34) OF PRACTICABLE STAGE PLAYS DOES NOT PRESENT AN INFINITE SCOPE TO HUMAN TALENT; AND THE PLAYWRIGHTS WHO
POSN (440) HANDS OF THE VIGILANCE COMMITTEE. /BLANCO/ (WITH INFINITE SCORN) YOU AND YOUR ROTTEN ELDER, AND YOUR ROTTEN
KING I (212) THE SIMPLEST EQUATION, OR AS MUCH AS CONCEIVE AN INFINITE SERIES OF NUMBERS! THIS FELLOW SUBSTITUTES FOR MY
KING I (165) INTO IDLE GAMES OF SPECULATION ABOUT NUMBERS IN INFINITE SERIES, AND DIVIDING CURVES INTO INDIVISIBLY SHORT
SUPR IV SD(141) BALUSTRADE OF A FLAGGED PLATFORM ON THE EDGE OF INFINITE SPACE AT THE TOP OF THE HILL. BETWEEN US AND THIS
GENV III (76) INTO FRONTIERS. /THE COMMISSAR/ ONLY BECAUSE INFINITE SPACE IS TOO MUCH FOR US TO MANAGE. BE REASONABLE.
SIM I (51) FLOWERS; BREATHE THE AIR; OPEN YOUR SOUL TO THE INFINITE SPACE OF THE SKY. NATURE ALWAYS HELPS. /IDDY/ (
KING I (211) CALCULATED THAT GOD DEALS IN MILLIONS OF MILES OF INFINITE SPACE, BE SUCH AN UTTER FOOL AS TO LIMIT ETERNITY,
NEVR II (234) SHOULD BE MADE, SHOULD IT NOT, BY A MAN OF INFINITE TACT? /M'COMAS/ IT WILL REQUIRE TACT, CERTAINLY.
METH PREFACE(R21) THE INFINITE, IT WOULD SURELY REQUIRE A GREATER INFINITE TO CAUSE THE CAUSES OF EFFECTS THAN TO PRODUCE THE
BULL PREFACE(39) IN ENGLAND. SHE GETS NOTHING OUT OF IRELAND BUT INFINITE TROUBLE, INFINITE CONFUSION AND HINDRANCE IN HER
DOCT PREFACE(79) THE THEORY THAT EVERY INDIVIDUAL ALIVE IS OF INFINITE VALUE IS LEGISLATIVELY IMPRACTICABLE. NO DOUBT THE
PYGM EPILOG (299) HAD NOT WITHERED HIM, NOR COULD CUSTOM STALE HIS INFINITE VARIETY IN HALF AN HOUR. HIS PLEASANT NEATNESS AND
LION PREFACE(60) OF ALL, MARRIAGE BECOMES A CLASS AFFAIR: THE INFINITE VARIETY OF CHOICE WHICH NATURE OFFERS TO THE YOUNG
METH PREFACE(R16) COULD HARDLY WITHOUT UNEASINESS BE ENTRUSTED TO INFINITE WISDOM AND INFINITE BENEVOLENCE ARE PLACED IN THE
BARB III (337) REELED AND CRUMBLED UNDER ME, I WAS SAFE WITH AN INFINITE WISDOM WATCHING ME, AN ARMY MARCHING TO SALVATION
APPL I (205) STAMP? THE ANCIENT ROMAN EMPEROR-GOD HAD NOT INFINITE WISDOM, INFINITE KNOWLEDGE, INFINITE POWER; BUT HE
MTH5 (261) THEY HAVE DONE SEEMS BUT THE FIRST HOUR OF THE INFINITE WORK OF CREATION, YET I WILL NOT SUPERSEDE THEM
GLIM (188) CLOUDS TO THE EVERLASTING SEA, FROM FINITE TO INFINITE , AND ITSELF PART OF THE INFINITE. /SANDRO/ (
METH PREFACE(R21) THE ENS ENTIUM! FOR IF WE WOULD COMPARE THE INFINITE , IT WOULD SURELY REQUIRE A GREATER INFINITE TO
FABL PREFACE(78) MY INCOME IS UNLIMITED, MY KNOWLEDGE AND WISDOM INFINITE , MY NAME A GUARANTEE OF SUCCESS FOR ANY

INFINITELY

APPL PREFACE(177) AS USUAL, IN A COMPLETELY ABSTRACT GUISE AS AN INFINITELY BENEFICENT PRINCIPLE IN WHICH WE MUST TRUST
MILL PREFACE(134) INFINITELY PITIABLE; IF THEY DID NOT ALSO MAKE HIM INFINITELY DANGEROUS. HE WILL FEED HIS MIND ON EMPTY PHRASES
MILL IV (209) MEN IN ONE. WHAT DO THE UNMARRIED KNOW OF THIS INFINITELY DANGEROUS HEART TEARING EVERCHANGING LIFE OF
MTH2 (69) THE THOUGHT OF THEIR BEING ENTRUSTED EVEN TO AN INFINITELY EXPERIENCED AND BENEVOLENT GOD, MUCH LESS TO
MTH5 (218) OF INFINITE CAPACITY, YOU WILL NO DOUBT FIND LIFE INFINITELY INTERESTING. HOWEVER, ALL YOU HAVE TO DO NOW IS
SUPR III SD(135) THERE IS NOTHING: ALL EXISTENCE SEEMS SUSPENDED INFINITELY . THEN, VAGUELY, THERE IS A LIVE HUMAN VOICE
UNPL PREFACE(R21) SHORT, THE FACT THAT A SKILFULLY WRITTEN PLAY IS INFINITELY MORE ADAPTABLE TO ALL SORTS OF ACTING THAN
HART PREFACE(27) AT BOTTOM, PEACE IS NOT ONLY BETTER THAN WAR, BUT INFINITELY MORE ARDUOUS. DID ANY HERO OF THE WAR FACE THE
KING I (167) I FIND YOU TWO GENTLEMEN MORE INTERESTING AND INFINITELY MORE IMPORTANT. /MRS BASHAM/ (POSTED BEHIND
3PLA PREFACE(R19) DECORUM IS OBSERVED. THE RESULT IS THAT THEY ARE INFINITELY MORE INSTRUCTIVE AND ENJOYABLE THAN OUR ROMANCES,
MTH4 II (177) MEASURE MINE? /THE ORACLE/ YES: BY A FIGURE INFINITELY NEAR TO ZERO. EVEN IN US THE FORCE IS NEGLIGIBLE
MILL PREFACE(134) WITH A GRAVITY AND SINCERITY THAT WOULD MAKE HIM INFINITELY PITIABLE IF THEY DID NOT ALSO MAKE HIM INFINITELY
MTH1 II (28) THAT IT IS THE GATE OF ANOTHER LIFE: A LIFE INFINITELY SPLENDID AND INTENSE: A LIFE OF THE SOUL ALONE: A
PYGM III (258) HALF SOLVED IT ALREADY. /MRS HIGGINS/ NO, YOU TWO INFINITELY STUPID MALE CREATURES: THE PROBLEM OF WHAT IS TO
DEST SD(162) LESS AT EASE THAN BEFORE. SHE IS ADVANCING IN AN INFINITELY WELL BRED MANNER TO PAY HER RESPECTS TO HIM WHEN
PHIL I (79) AN IMBECILE? /CHARTERIS/ YOU HAVE BECOME WHAT IS INFINITELY WORSE THAN ALL THREE TOGETHER: A JEALOUS

INFINITESIMAL

BUOY PREFACE(5) BIBLE, AND WAS ASHAMED OF HIS INVENTION OF THE INFINITESIMAL CALCULUS UNTIL LEIBNIZ MADE IT FASHIONABLE.
FABL PREFACE(96) TO WINNERS OF THE MATHEMATICAL TRIPOS THAN THE INFINITESIMAL CALCULUS TO A NEWLY BORN INFANT. POLITICAL
DOCT PREFACE(76) VERY MUCH TOO POWERFUL, AND THAT A COMPARATIVELY INFINITESIMAL DOSE WOULD NOT PRECIPITATE A NEGATIVE PHASE OF
MTH4 II (181) VALUE OF THE GREATEST LIVING MAN. CUT OFF THAT INFINITESIMAL LAYER OF GREY MATTER WHICH DISTINGUISHES MY
KING I (169) THREE TIMES; FOR IT MUST HAVE STOPPED FOR AN INFINITESIMAL MOMENT WHEN IT TURNED BACK, AND AGAIN WHEN IT
METH PREFACE(R15) A BODY OF SCHOOLMASTERS INCITING THEIR PUPILS TO INFINITESIMAL PECCADILLOES WITH THE OBJECT OF PROVOKING THEM

INFINITESIMALLY

METH PREFACE(R14) AND THE HOMEOPATHISTS DOSE YOU, THEY GIVE YOU AN INFINITESIMALLY ATTENUATED DOSE. IF THEY GAVE YOU THE VIRUS
DOCT PREFACE(76) PERCEPTIBLE QUANTITIES, WILL, WHEN TAKEN IN INFINITESIMALLY SMALL QUANTITIES, PROVOKE JUST THE OPPOSITE

INFINITIVES

SUPR PREFACE(R38) ESPECIALLY IF HE TAKES CARE NOT TO SPLIT HIS INFINITIVES . AND SO WITH YOUR DOCTORS OF MUSIC, WHO, WITH
BASH II,1, (99) A THOROUGHBRED COMMERCIAL STATESMAN, SPLITS HIS INFINITIVES , WHICH I, POOR SLAVE, MUST REUNITE, THOUGH ALL

INFINITUDE

SUPR III (131) REPEATED; NAY MORE, THAT IN THE UNTHINKABLE INFINITUDE OF TIME THE SUN THROWS OFF THE EARTH AND CATCHES

INFINITY

METH PREFACE(R36) COULD SEE BUT A LITTLE WAY IN ANY DIRECTION INTO INFINITY . BUT HE DID NOT REALLY BELIEVE THAT INFINITY WAS
METH PREFACE(R36) AS LONG A LINE OF MAKERS AS YOU PLEASE; BUT AN INFINITY OF MAKERS IS UNTHINKABLE AND EXTRAVAGANT: IT IS NO
FABL V (121) SO WILL ALL THE OTHER GRAINS. /SHAMROCK/ IN THE INFINITY OF TIME, WHEN THE OCEANS DRY UP AND MAKE NO MORE

METH PREFACE(R36) INTO INFINITY. BUT HE DID NOT REALLY BELIEVE THAT INFINITY WAS INFINITE OR THAT THE ETERNAL WAS ALSO

INFIRM
GENV I SD(42) BISHOP ENTERS. HE IS OLD, SOFT, GENTLE AND RATHER INFIRM . /THE BISHOP/ EXCUSE ME; BUT DOES ANYONE HERE SPEAK
BULL IV (150) A PUBLIC BUILDING HAS BEEN WRECKED: AN AGED AND INFIRM LADY HAS SUFFERED AN IMPACT FOR WHICH I FEEL

INFIRMARY
MRS II (217) AND NOTHING TO LOOK FORWARD TO BUT THE WORKHOUSE INFIRMARY . DONT YOU BE LED ASTRAY BY PEOPLE WHO DONT KNOW
BARB II (284) I WANT TO SEE THEM TWO MEET. I'LL TAKE HIM TO THE INFIRMARY WHEN IT'S OVER. /BILL/ (TO SHIRLEY, WITH

INFIRMITIES
APPL I (240) THE PLEDGE, WE WERE NOT EQUALLY CERTAIN THAT THE INFIRMITIES OF HIS NATURE WOULD ALLOW HIM TO KEEP IT. MY
MTH4 I (172) WITH ONE BE UNHAPPY BECAUSE HE HAS NOT TWO? BUT INFIRMITIES OF MIND AND TEMPER ARE QUITE ANOTHER MATTER. IF
MIS. (142) MY HOLIER FEELINGS, AT LEAST YOU KNOW THE BODILY INFIRMITIES OF THE OLD. YOU KNOW THAT I DARENT EAT ALL THE

INFIRMITY
APPL I (240) HIM TO KEEP IT. MY NATURE IS ALSO SUBJECT TO INFIRMITY . ARE YOU SATISFIED, MR PROTEUS, THAT IF I SIGN
NEVR II SD(226) BE LAUGHED AT. THERE IS NO SIGN OF STUPIDITY OR INFIRMITY OF WILL ABOUT HIM: ON THE CONTRARY, HE WOULD PASS

INFLAME
MTH1 I (12) IS THAT CARE THAT WILL PROMPT YOUR IMAGINATION; INFLAME YOUR DESIRES; MAKE YOUR WILL IRRESISTIBLE; AND

INFLAMED
MIS. PREFACE(91) GLORIOUS) APPETITES AND PROPENSITIES ARE AT ONCE INFLAMED BY STARVATION AND UNEDUCATED BY ART. ALL THE
SUPR HANDBOK(197) MORE SHEEPISHLY, LET A FEW STRONGMINDED PURITANS, INFLAMED BY THE MASTERPIECES OF JEWISH REVOLUTIONARY

INFLAMMATION
LION PROLOG (109) OUT. NOW LICK JM'S PAW TO TAKE AWAY THE NASTY INFLAMMATION . SEE? (HE LICKS HIS OWN HAND. THE LION NODS

INFLATE
JOAN 1,SD(66) TO HIS MAGISTERIAL CHAIR, BUT REMAINS STANDING TO INFLATE HIMSELF MORE IMPOSINGLY. JOAN COMES IN, FULL OF GOOD

INFLATES
JOAN 1 (61) DOWN HIS TWO FISTS SQUARELY ON THE TABLE, AND INFLATES HIS CHEST IMPOSINGLY TO CURE THE UNWELCOME AND ONLY
CAPT III SD(290) RECENT PROCEEDINGS AND MADE A DRAMATIC SPEECH, INFLATES HIS CHEST, CURLS HIS SCANTY MOUSTACHE, AND THROWS

INFLATING
ARMS III (49) NOT NECESSARY. HIS SIGNATURE WILL DO. /PETKOFF/ (INFLATING HIS CHEST AND THUMPING IT) AH WELL, I THINK WEVE

INFLEXIBILITY
WIDO III (50) BLANCHE? /BLANCHE/ I THOUGHT YOU ADMIRED INFLEXIBILITY : YOU HAVE ALWAYS PRIDED YOURSELF ON IT.
WIDO III (50) MORE, PERHAPS, IF IT IS ONLY FOR THE SAKE OF INFLEXIBILITY THAT YOU ARE STANDING OUT-- /BLANCHE/ I AM NOT

INFLEXIBLE
FANY II SD(296) KNOX TRIES TO PRAY AND CANNOT. MARGARET STANDS INFLEXIBLE .
2TRU II (62) THAT HE IS AN ATHEIST, AND LIKE ALL ATHEISTS, AN INFLEXIBLE MORALIST? HE SAID I MIGHT BECOME A PREACHER IF I
POSN PREFACE(383) WORLD TO STAGNATION, WHICH IS THE PENALTY OF AN INFLEXIBLE MORALITY. WHAT TOLERATION MEANS, THIS MUST BE
DOCT PREFACE(18) ETHICAL ENERGY ENOUGH FOR MORE THAN ONE REALLY INFLEXIBLE POINT OF HONOR. ANDREA DEL SARTO, LIKE LOUIS
CLEO II (139) MEN, THE WORLD GAINS AN IMMORTAL BOOK. /CAESAR/ (INFLEXIBLE) IF IT DID NOT FLATTER MANKIND, THE COMMON
LIED (191) (SHE SITS DOWN PLUMP ON THE STOOL AND LOOKS INFLEXIBLE). /HE/ IF YOU DID, YOU WOULD NO LONGER BE
WIDO III (50) REPLY; THEN ADDS IN A LOWER TONE) NEED YOU BE SO INFLEXIBLE , BLANCHE? /BLANCHE/ I THOUGHT YOU ADMIRED

INFLEXIBLY
DEST SD(166) SOME DEVICE TO OUTWIT HIM. HE MEETS HER REGARD INFLEXIBLY . /LADY/ (RISING AT LAST WITH A QUIET LITTLE
DEST (168) HEART). IT HURTS ONLY TO IMAGINE IT. /NAPOLEON/ (INFLEXIBLY) WOULD YOU HAVE COME FOR THE DESPATCHES? /LADY/

INFLEXION
BULL IV SD(151) CAN BE HEARD OUTSIDE SAYING GOODNIGHT IN EVERY INFLEXION KNOWN TO PARLIAMENTARY CANDIDATES. NORA, AUNT

INFLEXIONS
CLEO II (119) THE KING'S WORD! /PTOLEMY/ (WITHOUT ANY VOCAL INFLEXIONS : HE IS EVIDENTLY REPEATING A LESSON) TAKE NOTICE

INFLICT
BARB PREFACE(214) SUGGESTED BY THE POLICE STATISTICS IS THAT WE INFLICT ATROCIOUS INJURIES ON THE BURGLARS WE CATCH IN ORDER
POSN PREFACE(389) GROUND THAT HE MIGHT USE THEM TO COMMIT MURDER OR INFLICT MALICIOUS INJURY, HE HAS NO GENERAL POWER TO PREVENT
MIS. (199) YOU OUT. /PERCIVAL/ I REALLY HAVE NO RIGHT TO INFLICT MYSELF ON YOU, DROPPING IN AS I DID-- /TARLETON/ OUT
MIS. PREFACE(91) SUPPRESS OXYGEN. BUT IT IS CARRIED FAR ENOUGH TO INFLICT ON HUGE NUMBERS OF PEOPLE A MOST INJURIOUS ART
KING I (199) ARE WORSE PENANCES THAN ANY PRIEST DARE INFLICT ON YOU. TRY BARBARA: A WEEK WITH HER IS WORSE THAN A
POSN PREFACE(389) IS SOMETIMES CARRIED SO FAR THAT A JUDGE CANNOT INFLICT THE PENALTY FOR HOUSEBREAKING ON A BURGLAR WHO CAN

INFLICTED
GETT PREFACE(230) COMMITTED ON WOMEN OUTSIDE MARRIAGE, CAN STILL BE INFLICTED BY MEN ON THEIR WIVES WITHOUT LEGAL REMEDY. AT ALL
MILL IV (197) IN QUICKLY) HE DECLARES THAT HIS INJURIES WERE INFLICTED BY YOU WHEN YOU LAST MET, MRS FITZFASSENDEN.
OVER PREFACE(159) OF THE SAVAGE PUNISHMENTS THAT ARE LEGALLY INFLICTED FOR ABERRATIONS AND ABSURDITIES TO WHICH NO SANELY
SUPR HANDBOK(204) AND THAT FLOGGINGS OF A THOUSAND LASHES WERE INFLICTED ON ENGLISH SOLDIERS IN THE XVIII AND XIX
JOAN PREFACE(34) MOST SENSATIONALLY FRIGHTFUL OF THESE ATROCITIES INFLICTED ON ITS VICTIM THE MISERY, DEGRADATION, AND
LION PREFACE(12) COURSE THAT THIS COMPENSATING SUFFERING SHOULD BE INFLICTED ON THE WRONGDOER FOR THE SAKE OF ITS DETERRENT
LION PREFACE(75) AN ORATION TO THE COUNCIL, IN WHICH HE FIRST INFLICTED ON THEM A TEDIOUS SKETCH OF THE HISTORY OF ISRAEL,
SUPR HANDBOK(204) IN THE XVIII AND XIX CENTURIES, AND WOULD BE INFLICTED STILL BUT FOR THE CHANGE IN THE BALANCE OF
LION PREFACE(64) BE COMPELLED ON PAIN OF DEATH, HOWEVER CRUELLY INFLICTED , TO HUM ALL THE THEMES OF BEETHOVEN'S SYMPHONIES

INFLICTING
MIS. PREFACE(41) TO SECURE THEM, NOT BY THE RIDICULOUS METHOD OF INFLICTING ARTIFICIAL INJURIES ON THE PERSONS WHO HAVE NOT
GLIM (178) IS TO RULE AND TO FIGHT. RULING IS NOTHING BUT INFLICTING CRUELTIES ON WRONGDOERS: FIGHTING IS NOTHING BUT
OVER PREFACE(159) IN FACT AS THEY DO IN CONVENTION BY DELIBERATELY INFLICTING INJURIES -- SOMETIMES ATROCIOUS INJURIES -- ON
DOCT PREFACE(40) DECLARE THEMSELVES THE MOST HUMANE OF MEN, INFLICTING SUFFERING ONLY TO RELIEVE IT, SCRUPULOUS IN THE

INFLICTION
BARB PREFACE(244) THEIR NURTURE. THE SECOND IS THAT THE DELIBERATE INFLICTION OF MALICIOUS INJURIES WHICH NOW GOES ON UNDER THE

INFLICTS
JOAN PREFACE(25) CLOTHES ON, SHE DEFENDS AGNES WITH HER SWORD, AND INFLICTS APPROPRIATE MUTILATIONS ON HER ASSAILANTS, CAN BE
DOCT PREFACE(48) IS ALMOST, LEGALLY SPEAKING, A VIVISECTOR WHO INFLICTS NO PAIN. BY GIVING HIS VICTIMS CHLOROFORM BEFORE
MIS. PREFACE(28) EFFORT THE EQUIVALENT OF WHAT HE OR SHE CONSUMES, INFLICTS ON THE COMMUNITY PRECISELY THE SAME INJURY THAT A
DEVL I SD(24) AS PROOFS OF THE GREATNESS OF THE POWER THAT INFLICTS THEM, AND OF HER OWN WORMLIKE INSIGNIFICANCE. FOR

INFLUENCE
PHIL PREFACE(68) AS UNCONSCIOUS OF IBSEN AS OF ANY OTHER POLITICAL INFLUENCE : QUARTER OF A CENTURY ELAPSED BEFORE AN IMPATIENT
3PLA PREFACE(R11) NOT ONLY A CUSTOMER'S INFLUENCE BUT A FINANCIER'S INFLUENCE : SO MUCH SO, THAT THE WAY IS SMOOTHEST FOR THOSE
BULL PREFACE(25) PARSON HAS NO PRIESTLY CHARACTER AND NO PRIESTLY INFLUENCE : THE HIGH CHURCH CURATE OF COURSE EXISTS AND HAS
SUPR III (80) HONEST MEN CAN NEVER EXERCISE ANY REAL POLITICAL INFLUENCE : THERE ARE TOO FEW OF THEM. UNTIL A MOVEMENT
JOAN 6 (128) DO YOU SUGGEST THAT I AM UNDER DIABOLICAL INFLUENCE ? /COURCELLES/ I SUGGEST NOTHING, MY LORD. BUT IT
SUPR I (39) A PRICKED BLADDER). BUT I AM SORRY YOU THOUGHT MY INFLUENCE A BAD ONE. /TANNER/ I DONT SAY IT WAS A BAD ONE.
BUOY IV (51) YOU, MR BUOYANT. I EXPECTED YOU TO USE ALL YOUR INFLUENCE AGAINST ME. YOU ARE A MODEL FATHER-IN-LAW. /SHE/ I
CLEO PRO1 (92) MY HOME IN EGYPT; AND I DESIRE CONSIDERATION AND INFLUENCE AMONG YOU." AND THEY SAID, " WE KNEW WELL THOU

MIS. PREFACE(16)	BEG THE QUESTION OF WHAT A HOME AND A MOTHER'S	INFLUENCE	AND A FATHER'S CARE AND SO FORTH REALLY COME TO IN
FABL PREFACE(76)	WITH THE INTELLECTUAL HONESTY NECESSARY TO ITS	INFLUENCE	AND AUTHORITY. SHAKE THAT AUTHORITY, AND
MIS. PREFACE(16)	CONTACT WITH THEIR VALETS AND LADY'S-MAIDS, WHOSE	INFLUENCE	AND CARE ARE OFTEN DOMINANT IN THE HOUSEHOLD.
MRS IV (249)	HOW CAN YOU KEEP IT UP WITHOUT MY MONEY AND MY	INFLUENCE	AND LIZZIE'S FRIENDS? CANT YOU SEE THAT YOURE
MTH2 (71)	REPRESENT SOMETHING WHICH HAS HAD FAR TOO MUCH	INFLUENCE	AND POPULARITY IN THIS COUNTRY SINCE JOSEPH
GENV IV (126)	/SIR O./ MAY I SUGGEST THAT YOU USE ALL YOUR	INFLUENCE	AT ROME TO OBTAIN AN IMMEDIATE DECISION FROM THE
CAPT I (230)	AND SOLICITOR GENERAL, WHO APPRECIATED MY	INFLUENCE	AT THE COLONIAL OFFICE. AND SO I GOT THE ESTATE
POSN PREFACE(368)	OPINION; BUT THOSE WHO IMAGINE THAT IT COULD	INFLUENCE	BRITISH GOVERNMENTS LITTLE KNOW HOW REMOTE FROM
3PLA PREFACE(R11)	THAT IT IS EXOTIC, AND IS NOT ONLY A CUSTOMER'S	INFLUENCE	BUT A FINANCIER'S INFLUENCE: SO MUCH SO, THAT THE
LION I (122)	THE BRETHREN; BUT WHEN I COME, ALL THIS STOPS: MY	INFLUENCE	CALMS THE PASSIONS OF THE MOB: THEY LISTEN TO ME
UNPL PREFACE(R15)	TEN VOTES BY ABOLISHING HIM. PRIVATE POLITICAL	INFLUENCE	CANNOT TOUCH HIM; FOR SUCH PRIVATE INFLUENCE,
PRES (159)	CAUCUS AND THE POLLING BOOTH. WE SHOULD LOSE OUR	INFLUENCE	COMPLETELY UNDER SUCH A STATE OF AFFAIRS. THE NEW
CAND II (125)	COMMITTEE OF THE COUNTY COUNCIL, AND HAS SOME	INFLUENCE	IN THE MATTER OF CONTRACTS. (BURGESS WAKES UP AT
3PLA PREFACE(R11)	BUT THERE IS NO REASON TO SUPPOSE THAT THEIR	INFLUENCE	IS ANY NOBLER WHEN THEY IMAGINE THEMSELVES
DEVL EPILOG (79)	PROMOTION ON ANY OTHER GROUND THAN THAT OF FAMILY	INFLUENCE	. AS A PARLIAMENTARY CANDIDATE, BURGOYNE TOOK OUR
MIS. (118)	ANYTHING: I'M A CHILD TO HIM STILL: I HAVE NO	INFLUENCE	. BESIDES, YOU KNOW HOW TO HANDLE MEN. SEE HOW YOU
SUPR I (12)	YOU OUGHT TO BE PRETTY WELL OBLIGED TO ME FOR MY	INFLUENCE	. HE LEAVES YOU TWO THOUSAND FIVE HUNDRED FOR YOUR
SUPR I (12)	YOU HAVE ADMITTED THAT HE MADE IT UNDER YOUR	INFLUENCE	. /TANNER/ YOU OUGHT TO BE PRETTY WELL OBLIGED TO
PRES (159)	BY BEAUTY, BY CHARM. THE MEN WHO ARE NOT HAVE NO	INFLUENCE	. THE SALIC LAW, WHICH FORBADE WOMEN TO OCCUPY A
MTH2 (48)	IS THE MOVE TO BE? YOU ARE A MAN OF ENORMOUS	INFLUENCE	. WE KNOW THAT. WEVE ALWAYS KNOWN IT. WE HAVE TO
HART PREFACE(8)	GOING TO THE DEVIL VERY PRECIPITATELY UNDER THE	INFLUENCE	OF A PSEUDO-SCIENCE AS DISASTROUS AS THE BLACKEST
FABL IV (114)	CENTURY THE TRIBES OF NEW ZEALAND HAD, UNDER THE	INFLUENCE	OF BRITISH COLONISTS, LEFT OFF EATING THEIR
METH PREFACE(R59)	ENCOURAGED BY DARWIN'S INSISTENCE ON THE	INFLUENCE	OF ENVIRONMENT. PERHAPS THE STRONGEST MORAL
MTH3 (112)	/THE ARCHBISHOP/ NO. HE WAS SHOT. UNDER THE	INFLUENCE	OF HIS BELIEF THAT HE WAS GOING TO LIVE THREE
MRS PREFACE(160)	SHE IS REALLY FALLING IN LOVE WITH HIM UNDER THE	INFLUENCE	OF HIS IMAGINARY CRIME AGAINST HER. FINALLY SHE
MIS. PREFACE(86)	AT ALL. UNDER SUCH CIRCUMSTANCES PHRASES LIKE THE	INFLUENCE	OF HOME LIFE, THE FAMILY, THE DOMESTIC HEARTH, AND
GETT PREFACE(220)	INTENSELY PERSONAL, AND THE VOWS MADE UNDER THE	INFLUENCE	OF ITS TRANSIENT INFATUATION SO SACRED AND
APPL II (264)	WAS ON THE CARDS. WHEN I WAS YOUNG, AND UNDER THE	INFLUENCE	OF OUR FAMILY TRADITION, WHICH OF COURSE NEVER
GETT PREFACE(226)	OF ONE'S FAMILY IS TO BE A MONSTER. UNDER THE	INFLUENCE	OF THE EMOTION THUS MANUFACTURED THE MOST
MIS. PREFACE(13)	SCHOOL THE SYSTEM MAY BE BAD; BUT THE PERSONAL	INFLUENCE	OF THE HEAD MASTER HAS TO BE EXERTED, WHEN IT IS
GETT PREFACE(201)	RESULT IS THAT WHEN TWO PEOPLE ARE UNDER THE	INFLUENCE	OF THE MOST VIOLENT, MOST INSANE, MOST DELUSIVE,
3PLA PREFACE(R11)	CAN SEE NO VALIDITY WHATEVER IN THE VIEW THAT THE	INFLUENCE	OF THE RICH JEWS ON THE THEATRE IS ANY WORSE THAN
3PLA PREFACE(R11)	RICH JEWS ON THE THEATRE IS ANY WORSE THAN THE	INFLUENCE	OF THE RICH OF ANY OTHER RACE. OTHER QUALITIES
MRS PREFACE(155)	I HAVE POINTED OUT AGAIN AND AGAIN THAT THE	INFLUENCE	OF THE THEATRE IN ENGLAND IS GROWING SO GREAT THAT
DOCT PREFACE(40)	SERIES OF EXPERIMENTS ON PERSONS UNDER THE	INFLUENCE	OF VOLUPTUOUS ECSTASY, SO AS TO ASCERTAIN ITS
METH PREFACE(R60)	DISCOVERING IN THE ENVIRONMENT OF AN ORGANISM AN	INFLUENCE	ON IT MORE POTENT THAN OWEN HAD EVER CLAIMED. IT
2TRU PREFACE(18)	SO CORRUPTED BY ITS OWN PROPERTY, AND BY THE	INFLUENCE	ON IT OF THE LAY PROPRIETORS, THAT IT LOST ALL ITS
FABL PREFACE(93)	EXCEEDING 32 WORDS ON THEIR RESPECTIVE STYLES AND	INFLUENCE	ON RENAISSANCE ART. GIVE THE DATES OF SIX OF
GETT (311)	THE SPIRITUAL INTERESTS OF THE CHURCH, AND ITS	INFLUENCE	ON THE SOULS AND IMAGINATIONS OF THE PEOPLE, VERY
3PLA PREFACE(R11)	APPEAL SPECIALLY TO THE JEWISH TASTE. ENGLISH	INFLUENCE	ON THE THEATRE, AS FAR AS THE STALLS ARE
3PLA PREFACE(R11)	JEWS. ALL THAT CAN FAIRLY BE SAID OF THE JEWISH	INFLUENCE	ON THE THEATRE IS THAT IT IS EXOTIC, AND IS NOT
SUPR PREFACE(R9)	ME: ITS MORALS, ITS MANNERS, ITS PHILOSOPHY, ITS	INFLUENCE	ON THE YOUNG, ARE FOR YOU TO JUSTIFY. YOU WERE OF
PRES (160)	TALENT-- WHO WIELD A LEGITIMATE, A REFINING	INFLUENCE	OVER THE MEN. (SHE SITS DOWN GRACEFULLY, SMILING,
DEST SD(150)	CAPORAL, AS HE IS STILL IN THE STAGE OF GAINING	INFLUENCE	OVER THEM BY DISPLAYS OF PLUCK. HE IS NOT IN A
KING PREFACE(158)	MUCH; FOR IN OLIGARCHIES WOMEN EXERCISE SO MUCH	INFLUENCE	PRIVATELY AND IRRESPONSIBLY THAT THE CLEVEREST OF
APPL PREFACE(171)	PRIME MINISTER TO DEPRIVE HIM OF THE RIGHT TO	INFLUENCE	PUBLIC OPINION THROUGH THE PRESS AND PLATFORM: IN
GETT PREFACE(220)	PROFESSION, PROMISE, OR PROPOSAL MADE UNDER ITS	INFLUENCE	SHOULD BIND ANYBODY; AND THAT ITS GREAT NATURAL
BARB PREFACE(238)	LESS PERSONAL POWER THAN ANY POLICEMAN, AND LESS	INFLUENCE	THAN ANY CHAIRMAN OF A TRUST, ARE RESPONSIBLE. AT
JOAN PREFACE(39)	TO THE FULL EXTENT TO WHICH IT COULD CONTROL OR	INFLUENCE	THE TEMPORAL POWER, IT ENFORCED CONFORMITY BY
3PLA PREFACE(R11)	OF THE WHOLE COMMUNITY, SHOULD ENABLE THEM TO	INFLUENCE	THE THEATRE (AND EVERYTHING ELSE IN THE MARKET);
MIS. PREFACE(101)	PERSONS WHO ARE ALSO CONNOISSEURS IN ART. THE	INFLUENCE	THEY CAN EXERCISE ON YOUNG PEOPLE WHO HAVE BEEN
FOUN (211)	MENTION IT. WELL, YOU KNOW: I WANT SOME GOOD HOME	INFLUENCE	TO STEADY ME. YOU SEE YOU CANT STEADY ME: YOURE
3PLA PREFACE(R11)	THE BOX OFFICE WILL NEVER BECOME AN ENGLISH	INFLUENCE	UNTIL THE THEATRE TURNS FROM THE DRAMA OF ROMANCE
JOAN 6 (128)	IT IS ONLY ANOTHER EXAMPLE OF THE DIABOLICAL	INFLUENCE	WHICH THIS WOMAN EXERCISES OVER THE COURT. (HE
DOCT III (136)	AS HE GOES. /LOUIS/ BUT YOU MUST HAVE GREAT	INFLUENCE	WITH THEM. YOU MUST KNOW SUCH LOTS OF THINGS ABOUT
DEVL I (11)	OR TWO) MRS DUDGEON: I USED TO HAVE SOME LITTLE	INFLUENCE	WITH YOU. WHEN DID I LOSE IT? /MRS DUDGEON/ (
DOCT PREFACE(32)	DOCTOR'S OCCUPATION AND SEVEN-EIGHTHS OF HIS	INFLUENCE	WOULD BE GONE. THE HIGHER MOTIVE. THE TREE OF
FANY PROLOG (266)	/FANNY/ OH, I WOULD NOT FOR THE WORLD TRY TO	INFLUENCE	YOUR OPINION. /TROTTER/ BUT YOU DO: YOU ARE
MIS. PREFACE(15)	BUT ALWAYS OF IDEALS SUCH AS THE HOME, A MOTHER'S	INFLUENCE	, A FATHER'S CARE, FILIAL PIETY, DUTY, AFFECTION,
MTH2 (48)	NOW. /SAVVY/ IT'S NO USE SAYING YOU HAVE NO	INFLUENCE	, DADDY. HEAPS OF PEOPLE SWEAR BY YOU. /BURGE/ (
UNPL PREFACE(R15)	INFLUENCE CANNOT TOUCH HIM; FOR SUCH PRIVATE	INFLUENCE	, MOVING ONLY AT THE PROMPTINGS OF INDIVIDUAL
GETT PREFACE(203)	MOMENT; AND YET IT INFLUENCES, OR IS BELIEVED TO	INFLUENCE	, SO MANY VOTES, THAT NO GOVERNMENT WILL TOUCH THE

INFLUENCED

FABL IV (114)	THEIR PRISONERS OF WAR. THE BRITISH THEMSELVES,	INFLUENCED	BY A PROPHET WHOSE NAME HAS COME DOWN TO US IN
FANY EPILOG (329)	DELIVER HIS JUDGMENT FIRST; SO THAT HE MAY NOT BE	INFLUENCED	BY THE AUTHORITY OF HIS ELDERS. YOU ARE THE
KING PREFACE(156)	HUSBAND. IT IS INFERRED THAT HE WAS POLITICALLY	INFLUENCED	BY WOMEN, ESPECIALLY BY LOUISE DE KEROUALLE, WHO,
MRS II (201)	HE WILL. BUT HAS YOUR BOY'S CONDUCT EVER BEEN	INFLUENCED	BY YOUR REASONS? /CROFTS/ YOU CANT MARRY HER;
GENV IV (127)	/FLANCO/ YOU SHOCK ME. THE CHURCH CANNOT BE	INFLUENCED	. IT KNOWS THE TRUTH AS GOD KNOWS IT, AND WILL
POSN PREFACE(368)	WERE LICENSED WITHOUT DEMUR. NO DOUBT THIS	INFLUENCED	PUBLIC OPINION; BUT THOSE WHO IMAGINE THAT IT
FANY PROLOG (267)	RECORD AN IMPRESSION; BUT MY IMPRESSIONS CAN BE	INFLUENCED	; AND IN THIS CASE YOURE INFLUENCING THEM

INFLUENCES

POSN PREFACE(365)	EVERY INTEREST HAS ITS OPPOSITION, ALL THESE	INFLUENCES	HAD CREATED HOSTILE BODIES BY THE OPERATION OF
2TRU PREFACE(15)	THEIR CONSCIENCES: OR SUBJECT THEM TO THE FAMILY	INFLUENCES	SO BITTERLY DEPRECATED BY JESUS. THIS NATURAL "
MIS. PREFACE(100)	ARTIST IDOLATRY. BUT THERE ARE MORE DANGEROUS	INFLUENCES	THAN RAGTIMES WAITING FOR PEOPLE BROUGHT UP IN
CATH PREFACE(157)	ARMS LIKE AN INDIAN GOD. INDEED THE ACTOR OFTEN	INFLUENCES	THE AUTHOR TOO MUCH; FOR I CAN REMEMBER A TIME (
LION PREFACE(49)	TO YOU, BUT A RALLYING CENTRE FOR REVOLUTIONARY	INFLUENCES	WHICH ALL ESTABLISHED STATES AND CHURCHES FIGHT,
POSN PREFACE(365)	LOVE THE CENSORSHIP. THE ONLY ONE OF THESE	INFLUENCES	WHICH SEEMS TO BE GENERALLY MISUNDERSTOOD IS THAT
GETT PREFACE(203)	GOVERNMENT COULD ACT FOR A MOMENT; AND YET IT	INFLUENCES	, OR IS BELIEVED TO INFLUENCE, SO MANY VOTES,

INFLUENCING

FANY PROLOG (266)	YOUR OPINION. /TROTTER/ BUT YOU DO: YOU ARE	INFLUENCING	ME VERY SHOCKINGLY. YOU INVITE ME TO THIS
HART PREFACE(4)	PROPRIETORS, OR ANY CHANCE OF SHARING OR	INFLUENCING	THEIR ACTIVITIES. BUT THEY SHRANK FROM THAT
FANY PROLOG (267)	CAN BE INFLUENCED; AND IN THIS CASE YOURE	INFLUENCING	THEM SHAMELESSLY ALL THE TIME. /FANNY/ DONT MAKE

INFLUENTIAL

PLES PREFACE(R14)	IN BIG CITIES: IT SHOULD BE FEASIBLE TO FORM	INFLUENTIAL	COMMITTEES, PREFERABLY WITHOUT ANY ACTORS,
CAPT III (296)	YOU ARE THE NEPHEW OF A GREAT BIGWIG, AND HAVE	INFLUENTIAL	CONNEXIONS, AND GOOD FRIENDS AMONG THEM, LOTS OF
PLES PREFACE(R14)	TO THEIR ORDINARY BUSINESS. IF THE COMMITTEE IS	INFLUENTIAL	ENOUGH, THE OFFER WILL BE ACCEPTED. IN THAT
CLEO NOTES (212)	POSITIONS (NOT HAVING ENOUGH GREAT MEN IN OUR	INFLUENTIAL	FAMILIES TO GO ROUND) FORCES US TO INCULCATE,
BULL IV (168)	BUT, MY DEAR, DOOLAN'S A PUBLICAN: A MOST	INFLUENTIAL	MAN. BY THE WAY, I ASKED HIM IF HIS WIFE WOULD
ROCK PREFACE(157)	FROM THE SNOBBISH POINT OF VIEW, ALWAYS A VERY	INFLUENTIAL	ONE, HE WAS A PENNILESS VAGRANT. FROM THE POLICE
MTH2 (47)	THAT IT INHERIT SHALL DISSOLVE, AND, LIKE THIS	INFLUENTIAL	PAGEANT FADED, LEAVE NOT A RACK BEHIND." THATS
HART PREFACE(33)	WAS FORMED; AND ALL SORTS OF ILLUSTRIOUS AND	INFLUENTIAL	PERSONS LENT THEIR NAMES TO A GRAND APPEAL TO
MTH4 II (178)	A VERY EXTRAORDINARY PERSON: MY FAMILY IS NOT	INFLUENTIAL	; AND WITHOUT THIS TALENT I SHOULD CUT NO

INFLUENTIALLY

POSN PREFACE(394)	OF THEIR CATHEDRAL IN A CITY OCCUPIED LARGELY AND	INFLUENTIALLY	BY JEWS. COURT ETIQUET IS NO DOUBT AN
CLEO PRO2,SD(95)	GENERAL, A DEPLORABLE DICTATOR, WOULD, IF	INFLUENTIALLY	CONNECTED, BE EMPLOYED IN THE TWO LAST

INFLUENZA

PYGM III (251)	EVERY SPRING. /LIZA/ (DARKLY) MY AUNT DIED OF	INFLUENZA	: SO THEY SAID. /MRS EYNSFORD HILL/ (CLICKS HER
PYGM III (251)	Y-E-E-E-ES, LORD LOVE YOU! WHY SHOULD SHE DIE OF	INFLUENZA	? SHE COME THROUGH DIPHTHERIA RIGHT ENOUGH THE
PYGM III (251)	A WOMAN WITH THAT STRENGTH IN HER HAVE TO DIE OF	INFLUENZA	? WHAT BECOME OF HER NEW STRAW HAT THAT SHOULD
PYGM III (251)	I'M SURE I HOPE IT WONT TURN COLD. THERES SO MUCH	INFLUENZA	ABOUT. IT RUNS RIGHT THROUGH OUR WHOLE FAMILY
HART III (141)	/LADY UTTERWORD/ THANK YOU, HESIONE; BUT THE	INFLUENZA	IS QUITE CURED. THE PLACE MAY BE HEARTBREAK HOUSE

HART III (141)	BUT I KNOW NOW THAT IT WAS ONLY THE LAST OF MY	INFLUENZA	. I FOUND THAT I WAS NOT REMEMBERED AND NOT
MTH3 (119)	ALWAYS KILL YOURSELF, AS COOK DID; BUT THAT WAS	INFLUENZA	, LONG LIFE IS COMPLICATED, AND EVEN TERRIBLE; BUT
2TRU I (29)	/THE MONSTER/ MEASLES! HE MISTOOK IT FOR	INFLUENZA	. /THE ELDERLY LADY/ IT WAS SO UNEXPECTED! SUCH A
MILL I (160)	/ALASTAIR/ WAS IT MY FAULT? THE ELEPHANT GOT	INFLUENZA	. THE MINISTRY OF HEALTH CLOSED ME DOWN AND
HART PREFACE(14)	IS THE USUAL ACCOMPANIMENT OF WAR WAS CALLED	INFLUENZA	, WHETHER IT WAS REALLY A WAR PESTILENCE OR NOT
2TRU I (32)	IT SO NECESSARY MYSELF. I WAS INOCULATED AGAINST	INFLUENZA	THREE YEARS AGO; AND I HAVE HAD IT ONLY FOUR TIMES
DOCT PREFACE(10)	SAME PRICE. DURING THE FIRST GREAT EPIDEMIC OF	INFLUENZA	TOWARDS THE END OF THE NINETEENTH CENTURY A LONDON

INFORM

2TRU II (56)	INSTANTLY. TAKE THEM BACK ON YOUR DAMNED BICYCLE.	INFORM	HIM THAT BRITISH OFFICERS ARE NOT ORIENTALS, AND DO
POSN PREFACE(405)	OUT THESE ACTS NEVER GO TO A MANUFACTURER AND	INFORM	HIM THAT UNLESS HE MANUFACTURES WOOLLENS INSTEAD OF
POSN PREFACE(376)	FOR FURTHER EXAMINATION. THE CHAIRMAN WAS THEN TO	INFORM	ME COLDLY THAT THE COMMITTEE DID NOT DESIRE TO HAVE
ARMS III (68)	/PETKOFF/ (EXASPERATED) RAINA: WILL YOU KINDLY	INFORM	ME, IF I AM NOT ASKING TOO MUCH, WHICH OF THESE
JOAN PREFACE(32)	CHURCH CLAIMS INFALLIBILITY. PERHAPS I HAD BETTER	INFORM	MY PROTESTANT READERS THAT THE FAMOUS DOGMA OF PAPAL
APPL PREFACE(185)	I COULD BURN ALL MY SHARE CERTIFICATES AND	INFORM	THE SECRETARIES OF THE COMPANIES THAT THEY MIGHT
LION PREFACE(52)	ALL THAT HE HAS AND GIVE IT TO THE POOR, HE WILL	INFORM	US THAT SUCH AN OPERATION IS IMPOSSIBLE. IF HE SELLS
KING I (167)	MEN'S SOULS. /CHARLES/ GOOD. WELL, PASTOR, I MUST	INFORM	YOU I HAVE NO BUSINESS HERE EXCEPT TO WASTE OUR
LION I (112)	TO THE REQUIREMENTS OF THE MANAGERS. I MAY	INFORM	YOU THAT AS THERE IS A SHORTAGE OF CHRISTIANS JUST
NEVR IV (287)	YOU WILL EXCUSE HIM, MRS CLANDON, WHEN I	INFORM	YOU THAT HE IS MY FATHER. /WAITER/ (HEARTBROKEN) OH
MTH4 I (153)	BOLGE BLUEBIN, MADAM: A HISTORICAL NAME. LET ME	INFORM	YOU THAT I CAN TRACE MY FAMILY BACK FOR MORE THAN A
MTH4 I (156)	ELDERLY GENTLEMAN/ IT IS MY TURN NOW, MADAM, TO	INFORM	YOU THAT I DO NOT UNDERSTAND A SINGLE WORD YOU ARE
GETT (292)	GENERAL/ AS A BRITISH GENERAL, SIR, I HAVE TO	INFORM	YOU THAT IF ANY OFFICER UNDER MY COMMAND VIOLATED THE
PPP (203)	(BOWING) SIR: TO YOU. /FITZ/ (BOWING) I MAY	INFORM	YOU THAT MY FRIEND HAD AN ACUTE ATTACK OF
MTH4 II (191)	BAGHDAD HISTORICAL SOCIETY I AM IN A POSITION TO	INFORM	YOU THAT THE COMMUNITIES WHICH TOOK THIS MONSTROUS
2TRU I (46)	I THINK YOU WILL FEEL MORE AT EASE WITH US IF I	INFORM	YOU THAT WE ARE LADIES AND GENTLEMEN. MY OWN RANK--
BASH III (119)	POLICE. /POLICEMAN/ MADAM, IT DOES; AND I MAY NOW	INFORM	YOU THAT WHAT YOU TERM A LOCAL FESTIVAL IS A MOST
PRES (153)	THEMSELVES. /MITCHENER/ I AM SORRY TO HAVE TO	INFORM	YOU, MADAM, THAT THE GOVERNMENT HAS GIVEN UP THAT

INFORMAL

DOCT I SD(81)	A LEADER OF HIS PROFESSION, AND AMOUNTING TO AN	INFORMAL	APPRENTICESHIP AND A TEMPORARY AFFILIATION.
CLEO II (122)	OF MONEY. /BRITANNUS/ (DISAPPROVING OF THESE	INFORMAL	EXPRESSIONS) MY MASTER WOULD SAY THAT THERE IS A

INFORMALLY

MTH4 I (144)	UNDERSTAND HE HAS A QUESTION TO PUT TO THE ORACLE	INFORMALLY	. I HAVE COME SOLELY TO VISIT THE COUNTRY. /THE

INFORMANT

ARMS III (63)	ABOUT YOUR FRIEND WHO WAS BURNT. HE WAS NOT MY	INFORMANT	. /RAINA/ WHO THEN? (SUDDENLY GUESSING THE

INFORMATION

DOCT I (99)	IGNORANT FADDISTS PICK UP SOME SUPERFICIAL	INFORMATION	ABOUT GERMS; AND THEY WRITE TO THE PAPERS AND
MIS. PREFACE(25)	ME, AND WHOM I SHOULD CERTAINLY HAVE PESTERED FOR	INFORMATION	AND INSTRUCTION IF I COULD HAVE GOT INTO ANY
DEST (174)	THESE PAPERS CONTAIN? I'LL TELL YOU. FIRST, MY	INFORMATION	AS TO BEAULIEU'S RETREAT. THERE ARE ONLY TWO
DEST (174)	BEEN BETRAYED, AND HAS SENT YOU TO INTERCEPT THE	INFORMATION	AT ALL HAZARDS, AS IF THAT COULD SAVE HIM FROM
VWOO 2 (125)	THATS A POLICE CALL. /A/ YOU NEED NOT POINT THE	INFORMATION	AT ME. I AM NOT THE CRIMINAL. /Z/ OH, IT ISNT A
NEVR II (232)	IS MY FATHER, I SHALL DECLINE TO ENTERTAIN THE	INFORMATION	FOR A MOMENT. /M'COMAS/ AND PRAY WHY? /PHILIP/
SUPR HANDBOK(203)	SEAT OF WAR IN SOMALILAND MENTIONING THAT CERTAIN	INFORMATION	HAS BEEN GIVEN BY A PRISONER OF WAR " UNDER
MTH3 (95)	FOR THAT PURPOSE, WE HAVE DONE WELL. YOUR	INFORMATION	HERE IS ALWAYS TWENTY YEARS OUT OF DATE.
BASH PREFACE(90)	HIM; BUT WHEN MARIE CORELLI EXPANDED THIS CONCISE	INFORMATION	INTO A NOVEL IN HER OWN PASSIONATE AND RICHLY
PYGM EPILOG (300)	AND AN ARTICLE ON METAPHYSICS AND COMBINED THE	INFORMATION	. HE SUGGESTED THAT THEY SHOULD COMBINE THE
CAPT III (284)	OF MINE GAVE THE CADI OF THE DISTRICT SERTN	INFORMATION	. IN CAWNSEQUENCE OF THAT INFORMATION THE CADI
CAPT III (284)	THROUGH HAVING SPRAINED HIS AHNKLE, GAVE ME SERTN	INFORMATION	. IN CAWNSEQUENCE OF THAT INFORMATION THE
WIDO I (20)	TO WAIT UNTIL YOU VOLUNTEERED THE NECESSARY	INFORMATION	. /SARTORIUS/ HM! MAY I ASK WHAT YOU HAVE SAID,
2TRU II (60)	GOVERNMENT IS OFFERING A SUBSTANTIAL REWARD FOR	INFORMATION	. /THE COUNTESS/ (JUMPING UP EXCITEDLY)
BULL PREFACE(69)	IN PETTY BATTLES. THOSE WHO GAVE WARNINGS OR	INFORMATION	OF ANY HELPFUL KIND TO THEM WERE MERCILESSLY
JOAN PREFACE(33)	MATTERS ON WHICH HE HAS CLEARLY MORE SOURCES OF	INFORMATION	OPEN TO HIM THAN ANYONE ELSE HIS DECISION SHALL
DEST (180)	I CANNOT PERSUADE THIS LADY TO GIVE ME MUCH	INFORMATION	; BUT THERE CAN BE NO DOUBT THAT THE MAN WHO
CAPT III (284)	SERTN INFORMATION. IN CAWNSEQUENCE OF THAT	INFORMATION	THE CADI STIMULATED HIMSELF TO SOME TEN KNOTS AN
CAPT III (284)	ME SERTN INFORMATION. IN CAWNSEQUENCE OF THAT	INFORMATION	THE SANTIAGO MADE THE TWENTY KNOTS TO MOGADOR
DEST (180)	EUROPE, OF HUMANITY, PERHAPS, MAY DEPEND ON THE	INFORMATION	THOSE DESPATCHES CONTAIN. /LIEUTENANT/ YES, I
MILL III (183)	YOU OR I? /EPIFANIA/ I DID. I THANK YOU FOR THE	INFORMATION	YOU HAVE GIVEN ME: IT HAS BEEN INSTRUCTIVE AND
DEST (174)	GENERAL: LET US MAKE A FAIR DIVISION. TAKE THE	INFORMATION	YOUR SPIES HAVE SENT YOU ABOUT THE AUSTRIAN
MTH4 I (157)	AND CARBON IN MY FLESH. I THANK THEM FOR THE	INFORMATION	, AND TELL THEM THAT THERE ARE BLACKBEETLES IN
MTH2 (71)	MIND: IT HAS NOT BEEN STORED WITH THE BEST	INFORMATION	, NOR CULTIVATED BY INTERCOURSE WITH EDUCATED
OVER PREFACE(163)	WE MAY DO ANY DAY IF WE COME WITHIN REACH OF SUCH	INFORMATION	, THAT FRENCH ACTORS ARE OFTEN SCANDALIZED BY
APPL I (227)	ARTICLES, SPICED WITH EXCLUSIVE BACKSTAIRS	INFORMATION	, THAT DONT SEEM TO THEM TO HAVE ANYTHING TO DO

INFORMED

2TRU II (79)	ANY FURTHER RANK OF WHICH I HAVE NOT BEEN	INFORMED	? /MEEK/ NO SIR. /TALLBOYS/ QUITE SURE YOURE NOT A
GETT PREFACE(192)	AND SUBSTITUTING FOR POLITICAL ARTICLES	INFORMED	BY AT LEAST SOME PRETENCE OF KNOWLEDGE OF
BULL PREFACE(53)	TO THE THRESHING-FLOOR; SHEWN THE WOUNDED WOMAN;	INFORMED	BY GESTURES THAT THEY DESERVED TO HAVE THEIR
JOAN PREFACE(12)	OF THE DISCOVERY. IF NEWTON HAD BEEN	INFORMED	BY PYTHAGORAS THAT THE MOON WAS MADE OF GREEN
PYGM PREFACE(201)	THREE COPIES OF IT DURING MY LIFETIME; AND I AM	INFORMED	BY THE PUBLISHERS THAT ITS CLOISTERED EXISTENCE IS
ROCK I (215)	OF TRADE ARE NOT WHOLLY WANTING. SOME OF THE BEST	INFORMED	CITY AUTHORITIES ARE OF OPINION THAT THIS YEAR WILL
LION PREFACE(48)	CREDIBILITY OR OF THEIR TRUTH. I HAVE SIMPLY	INFORMED	HIM OR REMINDED HIM, AS THE CASE MAY BE, OF WHAT
POSN PREFACE(369)	OF PLAYS OF REMARKABLE PROMISE. MR HARCOURT	INFORMED	HIS LEADERS THAT HE WAS GOING TO TAKE UP THE
ROCK PREFACE(183)	AND WELL INFORMED OPINION AND SENTIMENTAL AND ILL	INFORMED	IMPULSE. /JESUS/ NEVERTHELESS, OPINION IS A DEAD
CAPT I (236)	CAPTAIN BRASSBOUND. /BRASSBOUND/ YOU WERE RIGHTLY	INFORMED	. THAT IS MY BUSINESS. /LADY CICELY/ THEN WHY WONT
UNPL PREFACE(R8)	SURGERY. HE TESTED MY EYESIGHT ONE EVENING, AND	INFORMED	ME THAT IT WAS QUITE UNINTERESTING TO HIM BECAUSE
POSN PREFACE(377)	SUBJECT TO STAGE FRIGHT. WHEN MR SAMUEL HAD	INFORMED	ME THAT THE COMMITTEE HAD NO FURTHER QUESTIONS TO
ROCK PREFACE(183)	EVER ASCERTAIN, BUT BETWEEN REASONABLE AND WELL	INFORMED	OPINION AND SENTIMENTAL AND ILL INFORMED IMPULSE.
ROCK PREFACE(183)	CANNOT IMPOSE ON ME WITH YOUR REASONABLE AND WELL	INFORMED	OPINION. IF IT IS YOUR WILL TO CRUCIFY ME, I CAN
JOAN PREFACE(41)	LIBERTY TO SHOCK CONVENTIONAL PEOPLE, AND A WELL	INFORMED	SENSE OF THE VALUE OF ORIGINALITY, INDIVIDUALITY,
POSN PREFACE(373)	IN CAMERA. WHEN THE DOORS WERE OPENED AGAIN I WAS	INFORMED	SIMPLY THAT THE COMMITTEE WOULD NOT HEAR MY
GENV IV (116)	MR BATTLER MAY BE A USEFUL CIVILIAN. I AM	INFORMED	THAT HE IS POPULAR WITH THE LOWER MIDDLE CLASS. BUT
HART I (47)	I AM NOT AT HOME. IF SHE ASKS FOR ME, LET HER BE	INFORMED	THAT I AM EXTREMELY OLD, AND HAVE TOTALLY FORGOTTEN
FANY II (289)	A MAGNIFICENT MOULINET, I MUST SAY-- AND WAS	INFORMED	THAT I HAD BEEN GUILTY OF AN ACT OF COWARDICE, BUT
JOAN 6 (150)	HE IS VERY GRAVE AND COMPOSED. /WARWICK/ I AM	INFORMED	THAT IT IS ALL OVER, BROTHER MARTIN. /LADVENU/ (
BULL PREFACE(53)	THEY SHOULD HAVE BEEN SEVERELY REPRIMANDED AND	INFORMED	THAT THEY HAD THEMSELVES TO THANK FOR WHAT HAPPENED
2TRU III (84)	ON THE VERY FIRST PAGE OF IT. " I AM FOR CERTAIN	INFORMED	THAT THIS OUR CITY WILL BE BURNED WITH FIRE FROM
BULL IV (154)	STORY HAVE YOU HEARD ABOUT THAT? /LARRY/ I AM	INFORMED	THAT WHEN THE DEVIL CAME FOR THE BLACK HEATHEN, HE
MRS III (221)	/REV. S./ (APPALLED) WHAT! ! ! /FRANK/ CROFTS	INFORMED	US AT BREAKFAST THAT YOU TOLD HIM TO BRING MRS
SIM II (57)	OF HIS PERSON." NUMBER THREE: " I HAVE REPEATEDLY	INFORMED	YOU THAT THE IMPERIAL PROVINCE OF HOLY ISLAND
DOCT PREFACE(79)	FORTUNE TELLERS. 9. KEEP THE PUBLIC CAREFULLY	INFORMED	, BY SPECIAL STATISTICS AND ANNOUNCEMENTS OF
WIDO I (20)	BY CLEARING UP ANY POINT ON WHICH YOU ARE NOT	INFORMED	, FOR INSTANCE? OR EVEN, IF I MAY SO FAR PRESUME
POSN PREFACE(431)	OBVIOUSLY MORE DEEPLY CONSIDERED AND BETTER	INFORMED	, THOUGH I SAY IT THAT SHOULD NOT. AT ALL EVENTS, I

INFORMER

POSN PREFACE(411)	WHO HAS STUDIED HIS POWERS AS A COMMON	INFORMER	IN ORDER THAT HE MAY EXTORT MONEY FOR REFRAINING
POSN PREFACE(411)	DANGERS OF PERSECUTION. BESIDES, THE COMMON	INFORMER	IS NOT ALWAYS A SINCERE BIGOT WHO BELIEVES HE IS
POSN PREFACE(410)	MANAGERS NOT TO ABUSE THE POWERS OF THE COMMON	INFORMER	. AS IT IS, IT HAS BEEN FOUND NECESSARY, IN ORDER
PYGM I (209)	SAY. WHAT ELSE WOULD YOU CALL IT? A SORT OF	INFORMER	. /THE FLOWER GIRL/ (STILL HYSTERICAL) I TAKE MY
POSN PREFACE(411)	BUT WHEN THAT IS NO LONGER AVAILABLE, THE COMMON	INFORMER	MUST BE DISARMED IF THE MANAGER IS TO ENJOY
POSN PREFACE(410)	THIS DISQUALIFICATION OF THE COMMON	INFORMER	SHOULD BE EXTENDED TO THE INITIATION OF ALL

INFORMER'S

POSN PREFACE(420)	COMBINE THIS WITH THE ABOLITION OF THE COMMON	INFORMER'S	POWER TO INITIATE PROCEEDINGS; AND YOU WILL HAVE

INFORMERS

POSN PREFACE(368) VIGILANCE SOCIETIES AND MUNICIPALITIES AND COMMON INFORMERS IN A COUNTRY WHERE A LARGE SECTION OF THE

INFORMING

POSN PREFACE(430) CENSORSHIP PARAGRAPH BY PARAGRAPH, SUDDENLY INFORMING HIS COLLEAGUES THAT THEY HAD BEEN WRONG ALL
GENV IV (123) WAS YOUR ATTITUDE ALSO. BUT I HAD THE HONOR OF INFORMING YOU EXPLICITLY-- VERY EXPLICITLY, MR BATTLER--

INFRA

DOCT I (85) ANY NOTICE. AND I'M AFRAID YOULL THINK IT RATHER INFRA DIG. /RIDGEON/ OH, I HAVE AN OPEN MIND. WHAT WAS THE

INFREQUENT

CAND I SD(77) PUSH." EVEN THE POLICEMEN AND THE CHAPELS ARE NOT INFREQUENT ENOUGH TO BREAK THE MONOTONY. THE SUN IS SHINING

INFREQUENTLY

SUPR III (124) ME SO INTERESTING A HERO OF LEGEND, I WAS NOT INFREQUENTLY MET IN SOME SUCH WAY AS THIS. THE LADY WOULD
MIS. PREFACE(9) CAUGHT, THEY ARE TREATED AS CRIMINALS; AND NOT INFREQUENTLY THE POLICE HAVE SOME TROUBLE TO SAVE THEM FROM

INFRINGEMENT

MIS. PREFACE(41) BE CARRIED ABOUT (THE MOST COMPLETE CONCEIVABLE INFRINGEMENT OF ITS LIBERTY) UNTIL IT CAN WALK. BUT NOBODY
METH PREFACE(R67) ANY GOVERNMENT WHICH PROPOSED SUCH AND SUCH AN INFRINGEMENT OF SUCH AND SUCH A BRITISH LIBERTY WOULD BE

INFURIATE

BARB PREFACE(240) HIS TRIUMPH OVER ALL THE PRISONS AND SCAFFOLDS OF INFURIATE EUROPE EXCEPT THE REVOLVER IN HIS POCKET AND HIS
BUOY PREFACE(6) OF THE TIMES (AS THEY ALL ASSUME), THEY INFURIATE ME. INSTEAD OF REMINDING THEM CALMLY THAT, LIKE

INFURIATED

GETT PREFACE(185) WHETHER HE WISHES TO ABOLISH MARRIAGE, IS INFURIATED BY A SENSE OF UNANSWERABLE QUIBBLING WHEN THE
ROCK PREFACE(175) INSTEAD OF DEFENDING HIS RIGHT TO CRITICIZE HE INFURIATED HIS ACCUSERS BY LAUNCHING AT THEM A DAMNING
MILL I (145) IT WAS DURING OUR HONEYMOON-- WHEN HIS COLDNESS INFURIATED ME TO SUCH A DEGREE THAT I WENT FOR HIM WITH MY
MIS. (117) TOO FAMILIAR TO ME. IT GENERALLY MEANS THAT SOME INFURIATED PERSON IS TRYING TO THRASH BENTLEY. NOBODY HAS
ROCK I (201) AND WEVE DONE NOTHING. /SIR ARTHUR/ (AGAIN INFURIATED) HOW CAN THE BUSIEST MAN IN ENGLAND FIND TIME TO
ROCK PREFACE(159) INFECTIOUS THAT THE VERY COMPASSION IT ROUSES IS INFURIATED TO TAKE REVENGE BY STILL VILER CRUELTIES. THE

INFURIATES

GETT SD(289) A KINDLY CONSIDERATION FOR THEIR STUPIDITY) WHICH INFURIATES THOSE WHOM HE DOES NOT SUCCEED IN AMUSING. THEY

INFURIATING

JOAN PREFACE(44) IMPOSTOR. IT IS HARD TO CONCEIVE ANYTHING MORE INFURIATING TO A STATESMAN OR A MILITARY COMMANDER, OR TO A

INFUSION

METH PREFACE(R21) INFUSORIANS, AS COMMON WATER WAS FOUND TO BE AN INFUSION OF THEM. IN THE EIGHTEENTH CENTURY NATURALISTS WERE

INFUSORIAN

METH PREFACE(R21) CENTURY NATURALISTS WERE VERY KEEN ON THE INFUSORIAN AMOEBAS, AND WERE MUCH STRUCK BY THE WAY IN WHICH

INFUSORIANS

METH PREFACE(R21) NEW WORLD OF HITHERTO INVISIBLE CREATURES CALLED INFUSORIANS , AS COMMON WATER WAS FOUND TO BE AN INFUSION OF

INGE

FABL PREFACE(91) UP HIS WINDOW AND ROAR CURSES AT THEM. BUT IF DR INGE HAD BEEN BROUGHT UP ON BEETHOVEN INSTEAD OF ON
APPL PREFACE(180) FOR THE PEOPLE, IS MOST IMPORTANT. DEAN INGE PUT IT PERFECTLY FOR US WHEN HE CALLED DEMOCRACY A FORM
GENV PREFACE(16) FROM MOSES TO MARX, AND FROM PLATO TO RUSKIN AND INGE ; BUT A QUESTION AS TO A POINT OF EXISTING LAW OR THE
APPL PREFACE(185) FOR THE SATISFACTION OF OUR RELIGIOUS NEEDS. DEAN INGE TELLS US THAT OUR GENERAL ELECTIONS HAVE BECOME PUBLIC
FABL PREFACE(91) OF THE POSSIBILITY OF MISLEADING RESULTS. DR INGE , AN UNQUESTIONABLY TOP NOTCHER, WHEN HE WAS DEAN OF ST
FABL PREFACE(94) FORGET SOME THINGS THEY HAD BETTER REMEMBER. DR INGE , COMMENTING ON THE IRISH QUESTION, POINTED OUT HOW
SIM II (70) TO ONE OF YOUR BIG GUNS-- A DEAN-- NAME OF INGE , I THINK. I ANNOUNCED IT TO HIM LAST NIGHT IN A DREAM.
ROCK PREFACE(170) NOT IN THE LEAST SOCIALLY INCOMPATIBLE WITH DEAN INGE , THOUGH A REALLY CRITICAL NATURALIST WOULD AS SOON

INGENIOUS

HART PREFACE(32) RESULTING COMPLICATIONS AND SCANDALS EXQUISITELY INGENIOUS AND AMUSING, NOR THEIR EQUALLY VERDANT FLAPPERS
KING PREFACE(155) WITH A MONSTROUS MEMORY; HE WAS ALSO A MOST INGENIOUS AND DEXTEROUS MAKER OF APPARATUS. HE MADE HIS OWN
INCA (247) OF EVERY CAPITAL ON THE CIVILIZED GLOBE SELL INGENIOUS CARDBOARD REPRESENTATIONS OF THEIR FACES ON WHICH,
METH PREFACE(R50) EXPLANATION THAT WILL FIT THE CASE IF ONLY HE IS INGENIOUS ENOUGH AND GOES FAR ENOUGH TO FIND IT. DARWIN
PHIL I (79) IN CASE YOU SHOULD TURN OUT BADLY. /JULIA/ VERY INGENIOUS , AND PRAY, HAVE I BECOME A DRUNKARD, OR A
METH PREFACE(R57) BROUGHT ABOUT BY SUCH ELABORATE MACHINERY, SUCH INGENIOUS PREPARATION, SUCH SKILLED DIRECTION, SUCH VIGILANT
METH PREFACE(R22) METHOD OF EVOLUTION. LAMARCK, WHILST MAKING MANY INGENIOUS SUGGESTIONS AS TO THE REACTION OF EXTERNAL CAUSES
PRES (161) /MITCHENER/ YOUR ARGUMENTS ARE SO DEVILISHLY INGENIOUS THAT I FEEL CONVINCED YOU GOT THEM OUT OF SOME
MTH3 (109) YEARS, MR SECRETARY. /CONFUCIUS/ IT IS VERY INGENIOUS , MR ARCHBISHOP, AND VERY WELL TOLD. /BURGE-LUBIN/
DOCT PREFACE(43) SEE THE FLAGS JUMP. THE OTHER, AN ELEGANT, INGENIOUS , WELL-INFORMED, AND INSTRUCTIVE WAY, IS TO PUT A

INGENIOUSLY

METH PREFACE(R38) THING THAN A WATCH, A MAN WITH ALL HIS ORGANS INGENIOUSLY CONTRIVED, CORDS AND LEVERS, GIRDERS AND
DOCT III (137) HAT ON THE HEAD OF THE LAY FIGURE, THEREBY INGENIOUSLY DESTROYING THE DIGNITY OF THE CONCLAVE. HE THEN
SUPR III (107) SOMETHING MORE CONSTANTLY, MORE RUTHLESSLY, MORE INGENIOUSLY DESTRUCTIVE WAS NEEDED; AND THAT SOMETHING WAS
BULL PREFACE(4) FRIEND AND FABIAN COLLEAGUE, MR SIDNEY WEBB, AND INGENIOUSLY FOISTED ON THE LIBERALS BY MYSELF AND OTHER

INGENUES

CATH PREFACE(158) MOST DELIGHTFULLY FEATHER-HEADED AND INCONSEQUENT INGENUES , THOUGHT ME MORE THAN USUALLY MAD WHEN I PERSUADED

INGENUITY

FANY EPILOG (331) OLD STAGE CONVENTIONS AND PUPPETS WITHOUT THE OLD INGENUITY AND THE OLD ENJOYMENT. AND A FEEBLE AIR OF
3PLA PREFACE(R38) THAT SUCH POWERS OF INVENTION, HUMOR AND STAGE INGENUITY AS I HAVE BEEN ABLE TO EXERCISE IN PLAYS PLEASANT
GETT (182) ON THE ATTENTION OF THE AUDIENCE AND ON THE INGENUITY OF THE PLAYWRIGHT IS MUCH LESS; BUT I FIND IN
BARB PREFACE(211) NOT MERELY DEFEND IT WITH THE MOST DISCONCERTING INGENUITY , BUT ACTUALLY PROVE IT TO BE A POSITIVE DUTY THAT
CLEO NOTES (207) AND DEVOTION IN INDUSTRIAL ORGANIZATION AND INGENUITY , WE HAD BETTER WORSHIP THE ANT AND THE BEE (AS

INGENUOUS

JITT II SD(33) IN HER MANNER. HER DAUGHTER IS YOUNG AND INGENUOUS , WITH A STRONG CHARACTER. A PASSION OF GRIEF FOR

INGENUOUSLY

DOCT III (137) MY DEAR WALPOLE, I AM SORRY. (HE PLACES HIS HAND INGENUOUSLY ON WALPOLE'S SHOULDER AND LOOKS FRANKLY AT HIM).
WIDO I (15) CHARACTER. IF YOU WERE NOT SERIOUS-- /TRENCH/ (INGENUOUSLY) BUT I WAS PERFECTLY SERIOUS. I WANT TO MARRY

INGENUOUSNESS

CAND III (145) BESIDE HER CHAIR AND EMBRACING HER WITH BOYISH INGENUOUSNESS) IT'S ALL TRUE, EVERY WORD. WHAT I AM YOU

INGERSOLL

LION PREFACE(88) WHOSE VIEWS OF THE MIRACLES ARE THOSE OF INGERSOLL AND BRADLAUGH. LUTHER, WHO MADE A CLEAN SWEEP OF

INGERSOLL'S

MIS. PREFACE(45) WATTS'S RHYMES, AND NIETZSCHE'S GAY SCIENCE, AND INGERSOLL'S MISTAKES OF MOSES, AND THE SPEECHES AND

INGE'S

GENV PREFACE(6) THE LESSONS OF THE WAR AND PROVES THE TRUTH OF DR INGE'S OLD COMMENT ON THE ANGLO-IRISH SITUATION AS

		INGES	
BULL III (141)	OF A JOB IN WINTER. THEY TOOK THE DOOR OFF ITS	INGES	AND THE WINDER AHT OF ITS SESHES ON ME, AN GEV MAW
		INGESTION	
LION PREFACE(85)	BUT AS TO WHETHER IT WAS A SYMBOLIC OR A REAL	INGESTION	OF DIVINE SUBSTANCE, PRODUCED PERSECUTION,
		INGINE	
BULL III (143)	CONSTERNATION) HOLY MOSES! DONT TELL ME IT'S THE	INGINE	HE WANTS TO TAKE ME ON. /HODSON/ WOT ELSE? /MATTHEW/
BULL III (143)	WHY DIDNT YOU TELL ME THAT BEFORE? THE DIVIL AN	INGINE	HE'LL GET ME ON THIS DAY. (HIS EAR CATCHES AN
		INGLES	
SUPR III (140)	AT TANNER. /THE OFFICER/ WHO ARE THESE MEN, SENOR	INGLES	? /TANNER/ MY ESCORT. MENDOZA, WITH A
		INGRAINED	
GETT (354)	FRIED FISH EVERY FRIDAY AND LIKE IT. YOU ARE AS	INGRAINED	A SNOB AS EVER. /HOTCHKISS/ (IMPATIENTLY) MY DEAR
BULL III (135)	IS A MOST BRILLIANT SPEAKER; BUT HE'S A TORY: AN	INGRAINED	OLD-FASHIONED TORY. /CORNELIUS/ N HOW D'YE MAKE
		INGRATE	
MIS. (170)	FREE LIBRARY. THERES NO HARM IN THAT. /TARLETON/	INGRATE	! I SUPPLY YOU WITH FREE BOOKS; AND THE USE YOU
BASH I (96)	BY THY BELT INVITES MY FIST. /MELLISH/ (WEEPING)	INGRATE	! O WRETCHED LOT! WHO WOULD A TRAINER BE? O
		INGRATES	
3PLA PREFACE(R24)	WITHOUT WILL, OR HEART, AS THEY CALL IT.	INGRATES	: WHO WAS IT THAT DIRECTED YOUR ATTENTION TO THE
		INGRATIATE	
CAPT I SD(218)	HIS MANNER SHEWS AN EARNEST DISPOSITION TO	INGRATIATE	HIMSELF WITH THE MISSIONARY, PROBABLY FOR SOME
HART I (50)	ARIADNE A PERFECT FIEND; SO DO NOT TRY TO	INGRATIATE	YOURSELF HERE BY IMPERSONATING HER (HE WALKS
		INGRATIATING	
HART I (50)	TO THE OTHER SIDE OF THE ROOM). /LADY UTTERWORD/	INGRATIATING	MYSELF INDEED! (WITH DIGNITY) VERY WELL,
SUPR II SD(63)	BLACK BEARD, CLEAR, WELL SHAPED EYES, AND AN	INGRATIATING	VIVACITY OF EXPRESSION. HE IS, FROM THE
		INGRATITUDE	
GENV IV (122)	VICTORY TO MY AID. WILL YOU BE SUCH A MONSTER OF	INGRATITUDE	AS TO DESERT ME NOW? /FLANCO/ I OWE MY VICTORY
AUGS (272)	(WITH EMOTION) I HAD MY FIRST TASTE OF THE	INGRATITUDE	OF MY OWN COUNTRY AS I MADE MY WAY BACK TO OUR
LION PREFACE(92)	LAW, EVEN FROM SELF-REPROACH, WHICH BECOMES MERE	INGRATITUDE	TO THE SAVIOR. ON THE OTHER HAND, IF CHRIST DID
MTH3 (123)	ARE ONLY THE HEAD OF A DEPARTMENT? /BARNABAS/	INGRATITUDE	TOO! YOU DRAW A PENSION FOR THREE HUNDRED YEARS
DEST SD(151)	TO BE GRATEFUL TO IT, AND PERHAPS WOULD BE IF	INGRATITUDE	WERE NOT THE PROVERBIAL FAILING OF THEIR
MTH3 (122)	OF ME. THERE ARE MOMENTS WHEN YOUR LEVITY, YOUR	INGRATITUDE	, YOUR SHALLOW JOLLITY, MAKE MY GORGE RISE SO
AUGS (272)	KNOW. HOW SHAMEFULLY YOU HAVE BEEN TREATED! WHAT	INGRATITUDE	! BUT THE COUNTRY IS WITH YOU. THE WOMEN ARE
		INGREDIENT	
FABL V (120)	WE NEVER AGREED ON THE LAST MILLIGRAM OF EACH	INGREDIENT	; AND IT IS THAT MILLIGRAM THAT DETERMINES
MTH5 (227)	AGES; BUT NOTHING CAME OF THEM UNTIL THE	INGREDIENT	WHICH THE OLD CHRONICLER CALLED THE BREATH OF
DOCT PREFACE(21)	IN WHICH VIRGINIA SNAKE ROOT WILL BE AN	INGREDIENT	, HEAVEN KNOWS WHY! VIRGINIA SNAKE ROOT
		INGREDIENTS	
SUPR HANDBOK(178)	FOR A COMPLETELY CONVINCING PRESCRIPTION OF HIS	INGREDIENTS	. CERTAIN COMMON AND OBVIOUS MISTAKES MAY BE
CLEO NOTES (203)	PART RUBBED TILL IT SPROUTS." CONCERNING THESE	INGREDIENTS	, MY FELLOW-DRAMATIST GILBERT MURRAY, WHO, AS A
		INGRESS	
BULL PREFACE(11)	IN ENGLAND. I DEMAND OF EVERY NATION RIGHT OF	INGRESS	AND EGRESS, ROADS, POLICE, AN EFFICIENT POST OFFICE,
GENV I (36)	UP A DICTATORSHIP AND OBSTRUCTING THE LAWFUL	INGRESS	OF DULY ELECTED MEMBERS TO THE LEGISLATIVE CHAMBER.
		INGROWING	
DOCT PREFACE(3)	MORE THE MUTILATOR IS PAID. HE WHO CORRECTS THE	INGROWING	TOE-NAIL RECEIVES A FEW SHILLINGS: HE WHO CUTS
		INHABITANT	
MIS. PREFACE(3)	OF OUTLIVING THE MEMORY OF THE OLDEST HUMAN	INHABITANT	. BUT THE FACT THAT NEW ONES ARE BORN
		INHABITANTS	
GENV PREFACE(8)	AND HAVING TO HOUSE AND FEED THEIR SURVIVING	INHABITANTS	AFTER WRECKING THEIR WATER MAINS, ELECTRIC POWER
MILL IV (211)	BUT WE SHALL HAVE TO LIQUIDATE ALL THE ADULT	INHABITANTS	AND BEGIN WITH THE NEWLY BORN, AND THE FIRST
DOCT PREFACE(72)	TRANSFIGURE IT. IN ENGLAND, WHERE SO MANY OF THE	INHABITANTS	ARE TOO GROSS TO BELIEVE IN POETIC FAITHS, TOO
GENV I (38)	CAPITAL CONTAINED MORE THAN TWO THOUSAND WHITE	INHABITANTS	BEFORE THE LAST REVOLUTION. THERE MUST BE STILL
APPL I (231)	MINISTER OF A COUNTRY WHERE THE ONLY THINGS THE	INHABITANTS	CAN BE SERIOUS ABOUT ARE FOOTBALL AND
BULL PREFACE(51)	PIGEON-SHOOTING THERE THE YEAR BEFORE LAST. THE	INHABITANTS	COMPLAINED AND MEMORIALIZED; BUT THEY OBTAINED
BULL PREFACE(59)	OF THE VILLAGE AND THE CRUCIFIXION OF ALL ITS	INHABITANTS	COULD PRESERVE THE BRITISH EMPIRE. THAT DEFENCE
2TRU III (107)	IS TO BECOME OF OUR UNHAPPY COUNTRY IF ALL ITS	INHABITANTS	DESERT IT FOR AN OUTLANDISH PLACE IN WHICH EVEN
BUOY 1 (14)	ATOMIC BOMBS, AND WIPE OUT A CITY AND ALL ITS	INHABITANTS	IN A THOUSANDTH OF A SECOND. /SON/ WHAT DOES
GENV PREFACE(10)	ABOVE A CITY COULD CONVERT THAT CITY AND ITS	INHABITANTS	INTO A HEAP OF FLAMING GAS IN A FRACTION OF A
GENV PREFACE(21)	AND PERMANENT BY IMPROVING THE CONDITION OF THE	INHABITANTS	. ON THE CONTRARY HE MADE HIS NAME EXECRATED
MTH2 (68)	WIPE OUT OF EXISTENCE MANY MILLIONS OF ITS	INHABITANTS	. /BURGE/ LESS THAN A MILLION. /FRANKLYN/ THAT
GENV IV (116)	OWN COUNTRY AND AN INDISCRIMINATE MASSACRE OF ITS	INHABITANTS	. /FLANCO/ THAT IS MY PROFESSION. I AM A
GENV IV (116)	OF THE ENEMIES OF MY COUNTRY, AND SLAUGHTER THEIR	INHABITANTS	. /NEWCOMER/ DO YOU CALL THE LAWFULLY
HART PREFACE(3)	EXPLOITING AND EVEN FLATTERING THEIR CHARM. THE	INHABITANTS	. TCHEKOV'S PLAYS, BEING LESS LUCRATIVE THAN
GENV IV (100)	BUSINESS IS TO BURN THE HOMES AND KILL THEIR	INHABITANTS	. THAT IS NOT A PART OF CIVILIZATION: IT IS A
GENV PREFACE(11)	STILL WIPED OUT TO " LARN" THEIR MOSTLY HARMLESS	INHABITANTS	NOT TO SNIPE AT BRITISH SOLDIERS. THE ALARM IS
FABL I (103)	A POISON GAS LIGHTER THAN AIR! IT MAY KILL THE	INHABITANTS	OF A CITY; BUT IT WILL LEAVE THE CITY STANDING
GENV PREFACE(27)	THROUGH THE STRATOSPHERE OF KILLING ALL THE	INHABITANTS	OF A CITY WITHOUT DAMAGING ITS BUILDINGS OR
GENV III (81)	THE LADY IS WRONG AS TO THE FACTS, BECAUSE THE	INHABITANTS	OF A COUNTRY CONDUCTED AS SHE SUPPOSES RUSSIA TO
APPL PREFACE(187)	THEY OFFEND NOBODY. IMAGINE THEN THAT WE ARE THE	INHABITANTS	OF A VILLAGE. WE HAVE TO ELECT SOMEBODY FOR THE
BULL II SD(101)	COMMONPLACE ENOUGH TO IRISH EYES; BUT ON THE	INHABITANTS	OF FATTER-FED, CROWDED, HUSTLING AND BUSTLING
MIS. PREFACE(92)	RAG OF CLOTHING MIRACULOUSLY DROPPED FROM THE	INHABITANTS	OF LONDON AT NOON TOMORROW (SAY AS A
GENV I (33)	THE JESUITS, THE FREEMASONS. YOU TELL ME THAT THE	INHABITANTS	OF PECKHAM ARE DISLIKED: NO DOUBT THEY DESERVE
BULL PREFACE(10)	BY FORCE WHEN IT WAS REBUILT, ALL THE REASONABLE	INHABITANTS	OF THAT TOWN WOULD RECOGNIZE THE ARRANGEMENT AS
ROCK PREFACE(152)	HIS SUBSISTENCE, THE RELATION BETWEEN HIM AND THE	INHABITANTS	OF THAT TRACT BECOMES AN ECONOMIC ONE; AND IF
LION PREF,FN(43)	ANTICIPATION PRACTICALLY ALL THE WHITE	INHABITANTS	OF THE BRITISH ISLES
3PLA PREFACE(R20)	A TALE OF THE INVASION OF THE EARTH BY THE	INHABITANTS	OF THE PLANET MARS: A CAPITAL STORY, NOT TO BE
GENV PREFACE(3)	OF THE BOMBARDMENTS ONLY FROM TEN TO FIFTEEN	INHABITANTS	OF THESE ISLANDS WERE KILLED BY AIR RAIDS EVERY
LION PREFACE(97)	THE FAITH; BUT WHAT FAITH IS NOW THE FAITH? THE	INHABITANTS	OF THIS ISLAND WOULD, WITHIN THE MEMORY OF
MTH4 I (147)	WILD CREATURES, DESCENDANTS OF THE ABORIGINAL	INHABITANTS	OF THIS COAST. THEY USED TO BE CALLED THE
NEVR II (230)	MR M'COMAS; BUT I FIND IT IMPOSSIBLE TO TAKE THE	INHABITANTS	OF THIS ISLAND SERIOUSLY. /M'COMAS/ I PRESUME,
LION PREFACE(100)	SECURE AT LEAST THE LIVES OF THE UNFORTUNATE	INHABITANTS	OUT OF WHOSE LABOR IT COULD BE MADE. AT THIS
BARB PREFACE(244)	OF DIVIDING THE WEALTH OF THE COUNTRY AMONG ITS	INHABITANTS	SHALL BE SO CONDUCTED THAT NO CRUMB SHALL, SAVE
PRES (143)	NO SECURITY. WHAT A FRIGHTFUL THING! HOW DO THE	INHABITANTS	SLEEP WITH THE POSSIBILITY OF INVASION, OF
BUOY 1 (15)	CHEMICAL SALTS TO BLOW THIS HOUSE AND ALL ITS	INHABITANTS	TO SMITHEREENS, A GLASS RETORT, A PESTLE AND
MTH4 II (184)	LATER ON EVEN THE HOUSES ESCAPED; BUT THEIR	INHABITANTS	WERE POISONED BY GAS THAT SPARED NO LIVING SOUL.
BULL III SD(117)	THEIR GERMINATION IS A MYSTERY TO THE OLDEST	INHABITANTS	, TO WHOSE MEANS AND TASTES THEY ARE TOTALLY
		INHABITED	
GENV I SD(29)	FOR CENTRAL HEATING IN A CELLAR THAN FOR AN	INHABITED	APARTMENT, IS TO THE TYPIST'S RIGHT, THE PRESS
HART PREFACE(32)	BEDROOM IN THE FLATS BENEATH AND ABOVE, ALL THREE	INHABITED	BY COUPLES CONSUMED WITH JEALOUSY. WHEN THESE
AUGS (265)	ROUND. /AUGUSTUS/ (RISING ANGRILY) THIS TOWN IS	INHABITED	BY DASTARDS, I SAY IT WITH A FULL SENSE OF
MTH5 (246)	SAKE DONT TELL US THAT THE EARTH WAS ONCE	INHABITED	BY OZYMANDIASES AND CLEOPATRAS. LIFE IS HARD
HART III (141)	RATHER UNTIDY VILLA WITHOUT ANY STABLES. /HECTOR/	INHABITED	BY--? /ELLIE/ A CRAZY OLD SEA CAPTAIN AND A YOUNG

		INHERENT	
FABL PREFACE(98)	WEALTH DISTRIBUTION, WHICH PLUTOCRACY, WITH ITS	INHERENT	CLASS WARFARE, HAS HOPELESSLY FAILED TO SOLVE, WILL
MRS PREFACE(163)	I HASTEN TO ADD THAT I BELIEVE THESE EVILS TO BE	INHERENT	IN THE NATURE OF ALL CENSORSHIP, AND NOT MERELY A
MIS. PREFACE(28)	BY THE DENIAL OF CHILDREN'S RIGHTS, NOR IS IT	INHERENT	IN THE NATURE OF SCHOOLS. I MENTION IT ONLY BECAUSE
POSN PREFACE(394)	TO THE PERSONS IMMEDIATELY CONCERNED, THE	INHERENT	VICES OF THE INSTITUTION WOULD NOT BE APPRECIABLY
GETT PREFACE(209)	OF THE INSTITUTION OF MONOGAMY IS NOT ANY	INHERENT	VICIOUSNESS IN POLYGYNY OR POLYANDRY, BUT THE HARD
		INHERENTLY	
POSN PREFACE(368)	COMMUNITY STILL BELIEVES THAT ART OF ALL KINDS IS	INHERENTLY	SINFUL. WHY THE GOVERNMENT INTERFERED. IT MAY NOW
		INHERIT	
SUPR PREFACE(R28)	FOR MILLIONAIRES) LEFT WORD THAT NO IDLER WAS TO	INHERIT	HIS ESTATE, THE BENT BACKS STRAIGHTENED
KING I (164)	A WILD, EXTRAVAGANT, WEAK MAN: SO THEY TELL ME. I	INHERIT	HIS WILDNESS, HIS EXTRAVAGANCE, HIS WEAKNESS, IN THE
MTH2 (47)	TEMPLES, THE GREAT GLOBE ITSELF: YEA, ALL THAT IT	INHERIT	SHALL DISSOLVE, AND, LIKE THIS INFLUENTIAL PAGEANT
WIDO I (21)	EXPRESSED. /SARTORIUS/ " THE YOUNG LADY WILL	INHERIT	THE BULK OF HER FATHER'S FORTUNE, AND WILL BE
KING II (230)	PROTESTANT WIFE WHO WOULD BRING YOU A SON TO	INHERIT	THE CROWN AND SAVE ALL THIS KILLING OF MONMOUTH AND
ROCK PREFACE(188)	THEIR SIN: THE MEN WHOM I FILL WITH FAITH SHALL	INHERIT	THE EARTH. I SAY TO YOU CAST OUT FEAR. SPEAK NO MORE
BUOY IV (50)	THERE MAY BE NONE FOR YOUR DAUGHTER. SHE MAY	INHERIT	YOUR GENIUS. /OLD BILL/ SHE DOES. BUT MY GENIUS
SHAK (142)	THE GREAT GLOBE ITSELF, YEA, ALL WHICH IT	INHERIT	, SHALL DISSOLVE-- /SHAV/ -- AND LIKE THIS FOOLISH
		INHERITANCE	
BARB III (330)	STEPHEN. WHY SHOULD NOT ADOLPHUS SUCCEED TO THE	INHERITANCE	? I COULD MANAGE THE TOWN FOR HIM; AND HE CAN
BARB III (330)	YOU ARE TRYING TO PUT ME OFF THE SUBJECT OF THE	INHERITANCE	BY PROFANE JOKES. WELL, YOU SHANT. I DONT ASK IT
BARB II (294)	(IN TOWERING EXCITEMENT) IT IS THE UNDERSHAFT	INHERITANCE	. I SHALL HAND ON MY TORCH TO MY DAUGHTER. SHE
BARB III (346)	TO SELL YOUR SOUL FOR ME ANY MORE THAN FOR THIS	INHERITANCE	. /CUSINS/ IT IS NOT THE SALE OF MY SOUL THAT
BARB III (330)	TO ME. I BELONG TO IT. IT IS THE UNDERSHAFT	INHERITANCE	. /LADY BRITOMART/ IT IS NOT. YOUR RIDICULOUS
CAPT II (255)	WITH THE DEATH OF MY MOTHER AND THE THEFT OF MY	INHERITANCE	. /SIR HOWARD/ AS TO YOUR INHERITANCE, SIR, IT
BARB III (330)	THAT NOISY BANGING FOUNDRY MAY BE THE UNDERSHAFT	INHERITANCE	; BUT ALL THAT PLATE AND LINEN, ALL THAT
MILL I (139)	YOU ARE RIGHT. MAKE IT A CONDITION OF THE	INHERITANCE	THAT WITHIN A MONTH FROM MY FUNERAL HE MARRIES A
HART PREFACE(6)	LIFE THEY WERE OFTEN HELPLESS MASTERS OF THEIR	INHERITANCE	, LIKE THE PEOPLE IN TCHEKOV'S CHERRY ORCHARD.
CAPT II (255)	THEFT OF MY INHERITANCE. /SIR HOWARD/ AS TO YOUR	INHERITANCE	, SIR, IT WAS YOURS WHENEVER YOU CAME FORWARD TO
		INHERITANCES	
GENV PREFACE(14)	AND THESE ARE NOT THE WORK OF ADULT SUFFRAGE, BUT	INHERITANCES	FROM FEUDAL AND ECCLESIASTICAL SYSTEMS WHICH
		INHERITED	
BARB III (330)	I DONT ASK IT ANY LONGER FOR STEPHEN: HE HAS	INHERITED	FAR TOO MUCH OF YOUR PERVERSITY TO BE FIT FOR IT.
NEVR I SD(218)	AS A PROSPEROUS MASTER-MANUFACTURER IN A BUSINESS	INHERITED	FROM AN OLD FAMILY IN THE ARISTOCRACY OF TRADE.
FANY PROLOG (258)	SO FEW OF US KNOW THEM WHEN WE SEE THEM. WE HAVE	INHERITED	FROM THE PAST A VAST TREASURE OF BEAUTY-- OF
GETT (273)	THE FAMILY PROPERTY WAS ALL MORTGAGED WHEN HE	INHERITED	IT. HE HAD TO STRUGGLE ALONG IN CONSTANT MONEY
NEVR IV (305)	AND MASTERFUL DISPOSITION, WHICH MY SON HAS	INHERITED	, BUT IF I HAD MY LIFE TO LIVE TWICE OVER, I'D DO
METH PREFACE(R23)	UNTIL IT WAS ADDED UNTO HIM. HOW ACQUIREMENTS ARE	INHERITED	. BUT WHEN YOUR SON TRIES TO SKATE OR BICYCLE IN
BUOY III (43)	DOUBLED MY INCOME ON THE MONEY MARKET. I HAVE	INHERITED	MY FATHER'S FLAIR FOR FINANCE. MONEY MAKES ITSELF
MTH4 I (153)	THEIR NAMES, BOLGE AND BLUEBIN; AND I HOPE I HAVE	INHERITED	SOMETHING OF THEIR MAJESTIC SPIRIT. WELL, THEY
MTH5 (260)	THEMSELVES IN WITH THE WORMS. MY CLEVER ONES HAVE	INHERITED	THE EARTH. ALL'S WELL. (SHE FADES AWAY). /ADAM/ I
INCA (251)	IF I WERE YOU. /ERMYNTRUDE/ BUT HASNT ANY OF THEM	INHERITED	THE FAMILY GENIUS? SURELY, IF PROVIDENCE HAS
		INHERITORS	
BULL PREFACE(11)	ARE NOT ONLY NATIVES WITHIN OUR OWN FRONTIERS BUT	INHERITORS	OF THE EARTH. ENGLAND HAS RIGHTS IN IRELAND AS
		INHIBITED	
LION PREFACE(96)	COLENSO, FOR SAYING THE SAME THING OPENLY, WAS	INHIBITED	FROM PREACHING AND ACTUALLY EXCOMMUNICATED, EIGHT
		INHIBITING	
MIS. PREFACE(42)	AND THE PAID DEPUTIES OF PARENTS ARE ALWAYS	INHIBITING	AND PROHIBITING AND PUNISHING AND SCOLDING AND
		INHIBITION	
MIS. PREFACE(57)	BECOME A PLEASURE PURCHASABLE IN OUR STREETS, AND	INHIBITION	A GROWN-UP HABIT THAT CHILDREN PLAY AT. " GO AND
MIS. PREFACE(68)	OF US LIVE IN A CONDITION OF QUITE UNNECESSARY	INHIBITION	, WEARING UGLY AND UNCOMFORTABLE CLOTHES, MAKING
		INHIBITIVE	
APPL PREFACE(176)	NECESSARY TO THE WHOLE COMMUNITY, THIS PURELY	INHIBITIVE	CHECK ON TYRANNY HAS BECOME A STRANGLEHOLD ON
BULL II SD(111)	ANY SPECIAL INSISTENCE IS NEEDED; FOR THE ENGLISH	INHIBITIVE	INSTINCT DOES NOT SEEM TO EXIST IN ROSSCULLEN.
MIS. PREFACE(52)	THE ARREST OF DEVELOPMENT, THE ATROPHY OF ALL	INHIBITIVE	POWER EXCEPT THE POWER OF FEAR, ARE REAL: THE
		INHOSPITABLE	
KING I (179)	I WOULD NOT HAVE YOU BELIEVE THAT I COULD BE SO	INHOSPITABLE	AS TO DRIVE AWAY MY GUESTS MERELY TO INDULGE IN
HART II (108)	ME, WONT YOU? /HECTOR/ NO, I'M SORRY TO BE	INHOSPITABLE	; BUT WILL YOU KINDLY LEAVE THE HOUSE? /THE
BUOY II (23)	WEARILY) YOU HAVE THE LAST WORD. YOU ARE AN	INHOSPITABLE	WRETCH. /SHE/ AND YOU ARE AN INFERNAL NUISANCE
		INHOSPITABLY	
DEVL I (13)	KNOCKS AT THE HOUSE DOOR: SHE TURNS AND CRIES	INHOSPITABLY	) COME IN. (JUDITH ANDERSON, THE MINISTER'S
		INHUMAN	
JITT I (22)	BY A SOLEMN VOW, I-- (SHUDDERING) NO, NO: IT IS	INHUMAN	: A MOCKERY, AN IMPOSSIBILITY. /BRUNO/ I KNOW I AM
SUPR III (125)	THESE CONDITIONS BECAUSE THEY WERE EXORBITANT AND	INHUMAN	: IT WAS THEIR EXTRAORDINARY IRRELEVANCE THAT
BULL PREFACE(33)	US DIVIDED BETWEEN OUR DERISION OF SO MONSTROUSLY	INHUMAN	A PRETENSION, AND OUR IMPATIENCE WITH SO GROSS A
PLES PREFACE(R17)	ACCUSE ME, IN VARIOUS TERMS AND DEGREES, OF AN	INHUMAN	AND FREAKISH WANTONNESS; OF PREOCCUPATION WITH " THE
MIS. PREFACE(63)	EVERY CIVILIZATION AS IT IS WRECKING OURS, IS	INHUMAN	AND UNNATURAL. WE MUST RECONSIDER OUR INSTITUTION OF
GETT PREFACE(183)	ANARCHICAL ACTION. BECAUSE OUR MARRIAGE LAW IS	INHUMAN	AND UNREASONABLE TO THE POINT OF DOWNRIGHT .
GETT PREFACE(193)	UNHEALTHY SMELLS, AND INCONVENIENT HOUSES, WITH	INHUMAN	APATHY AND CALLOUSNESS. THEY HAD, AS TO ADULTS, A
METH PREFACE(R50)	SELECTION CO-OPERATING WITH A FORCE AS	INHUMAN	AS WE CONCEIVE MAGNETISM TO BE CAN FIND A LOGICAL
OVER PREFACE(161)	AS NEARLY SEXLESS AS ANYTHING NOT ABSOLUTELY	INHUMAN	CAN BE; AND SOME OF SHAKESPEAR'S PLAYS ARE SEXUALLY
DOCT PREFACE(64)	SNATCHED AN HOUR'S SLEEP. TO THE STRAIN OF SUCH	INHUMAN	CONDITIONS MUST BE ADDED THE CONSTANT RISK OF
GETT PREFACE(250)	MARRIAGE. FOR THE CHURCH TRIED TO SHELTER THIS	INHUMAN	DOCTRINE AND FLAT CONTRADICTION OF THE GOSPEL BY
DOCT PREFACE(38)	PRESENT, MUST HAVE SMILED SARDONICALLY AT SUCH	INHUMAN	HUMANITARIANS, WHOSE DAILY HABITS AND FASHIONABLE
CYMB FORWORD(135)	LINES OF MRS ALVING IN GHOSTS, THE SLAVERY TO AN	INHUMAN	IDEAL OF MARITAL FIDELITY WHICH LED HIM TO THIS
GETT PREFACE(216)	IMPURITY, A CONCLUSION WHICH IS OFFENSIVE AND	INHUMAN	. MARRIAGE AS A FACT IS NOT IN THE LEAST LIKE
MTH5 (254)	HAVE, ECRASIA! /ECRASIA/ INHUMAN! /ACIS/ YES:	INHUMAN	, WHY DONT YOU FALL IN LOVE WITH SOMEONE? /ECRASIA/
BUOY IV (59)	THIS CANT ABOUT THEIR BEING SOULLESS, DEAD,	INHUMAN	MECHANISMS IS CONTRARY TO THE PLAINEST FACTS OF LIFE
MTH5 (253)	/ACIS/ (INTERRUPTING HER DISGUSTEDLY) WHAT AN	INHUMAN	MIND YOU HAVE, ECRASIA! /ECRASIA/ INHUMAN! /ACIS/
GETT PREFACE(201)	THE MERE FORCE OF FACTS WOULD MAKE AN END TO THIS	INHUMAN	NONSENSE IN A MONTH, IF NOT SOONER; BUT IT IS VERY
MRS PREFACE(166)	FIRST AN OVERWHELMING IMPRESSION OF COLDNESS AND	INHUMAN	RATIONALISM. BUT THIS WILL SOON PASS AWAY. WHEN THE
BARB I SD(259)	AND A HIGH CONSCIENCE AGAINST IMPULSES OF	INHUMAN	RIDICULE AND FIERCE IMPATIENCE HAS SET UP A CHRONIC
SUPR HANDBOK(184)	BY OFFERING TO REVIVE ALL THE OLD	INHUMAN	STRINGENCY AND IRREVOCABILITY OF MARRIAGE, TO
GETT PREFACE(256)	OF MARRIAGE, IF OUR DOMESTIC LAWS ARE KEPT SO	INHUMAN	THAT THEY AT LAST PROVOKE A FURIOUS GENERAL
MIS. (153)	TO BE CURIOUS AND ASK QUESTIONS; BUT THEN IT'S	INHUMAN	TO BE INDIFFERENT, AS IF YOU DIDNT CARE. /LINA/ I'LL
MIS. PREFACE(75)	THAT YOU ARE SOCIALLY A FOOL AND PERSONALLY AN	INHUMAN	WRETCH. THE OTHER IS THAT THESE WANTS SHOULD BE
MTH4 II (182)	MURDERESS! MONSTER! SHE-DEVIL! UNNATURAL,	INHUMAN	WRETCH! YOU DESERVE TO BE HANGED, GUILLOTINED,
MTH5 (254)	AN INHUMAN MIND YOU HAVE, ECRASIA! /ECRASIA/	INHUMAN	! /ACIS/ YES: INHUMAN. WHY DONT YOU FALL IN LOVE
		INHUMANITY	
BARB PREFACE(244)	RUFFIAN, THE GAMBLER, AND THE BEGGAR, MAY WITHOUT	INHUMANITY	BE HANDED OVER TO THE LAW, AND MADE TO UNDERSTAND
DEVL II (32)	TO BE INDIFFERENT TO THEM; THATS THE ESSENCE OF	INHUMANITY	. AFTER ALL, MY DEAR, IF YOU WATCH PEOPLE
METH PREFACE(R54)	LOGIC, OR MY NATURAL ABHORRENCE OF ITS SICKENING	INHUMANITY	. THE GREATEST OF THESE IS SELF-CONTROL. AS THERE
MIS. PREFACE(78)	ACQUAINTANCE, TEMPORARILY OR PERMANENTLY, WITHOUT	INHUMANITY	. THUS BOTH PARTIES WOULD BE ON THEIR GOOD

MRS PREFACE(168)	DECLARE THAT THE REAL SECRET OF THE CYNICISM AND	INHUMANITY	OF WHICH SHALLOWER CRITICS ACCUSE ME IS THE
METH PREFACE(R61)	PIRACY OF THE FEUDAL BARONS, BUT THE HYPOCRISY,	INHUMANITY	, SNOBBERY, AND GREED OF THE BOURGEOISIE, WHO
		INHUMANLY	
PRES (134)	WOMEN TO HOLLOWAY AND KILLING THEM SLOWLY AND	INHUMANLY	BY RUINING THEIR HEALTH; AND IT DOES NO GOOD: THEY
LADY PREFACE(219)	ASSUMPTION THAT FEMALE RELIGION MEANS AN	INHUMANLY	FEROCIOUS CHASTITY. BUT FOR THE MOST PART
DOCT PREFACE(64)	AS THOSE OF PAGET SHEW, ARE SOMETIMES MISERABLY,	INHUMANLY	POOR UNTIL THEY ARE PAST THEIR PRIME. IN SHORT,
		INIGO	
PYGM III SD(244)	ELIZABETHAN CHAIR ROUGHLY CARVED IN THE TASTE OF	INIGO	JONES. ON THE SAME SIDE A PIANO IN A DECORATED CASE.
		INIMITABLE	
FANY PROLOG (258)	WE CAN REPRODUCE MANY OF THEM. WE CAN BUY A FEW	INIMITABLE	ORIGINALS. WE CAN SHUT OUT THE NINETEENTH
		INIQUITIES	
BULL PREFACE(7)	WILDERNESS AGAINST ONE OR OTHER OF THE MANIFOLD	INIQUITIES	AND FALSEHOODS OF OUR CIVILIZATION? I THINK IF I
BULL III (140)	RATHER THAN WANT OF HEART THAT ALLOWS SUCH	INIQUITIES	TO DISGRACE SOCIETY. /HODSON/ (PROSAICALLY) YES,
		INIQUITOUS	
PHIL III (144)	ARE GOING SMOOTHLY. NOW YOU SAID TODAY, AT THAT	INIQUITOUS	CLUB, THAT YOU WERE NOT A WOMANLY WOMAN. VERY
SUPR HANDBOK(194)	IS ENORMOUS. HE CAN SHEW THAT INEQUALITY AND	INIQUITOUS	DISTRIBUTION OF WEALTH AND ALLOTMENT OF LABOR
		INIQUITY	
KING I (178)	AM I TO HOLD MY PEACE IN THE FACE OF THIS	INIQUITY	? WHEN THE BELL RINGS TO ANNOUNCE SOME PITIFUL
2TRU PREFACE(21)	GOVERNMENT EXISTS TO SECURE, AND THAT ALL THIS	INIQUITY	ARISES AUTOMATICALLY WHEN WE THOUGHTLESSLY ALLOW A
LION PREFACE(55)	CALLED THE MAINTENANCE OF LAW AND ORDER.	INIQUITY	CAN GO NO FURTHER. BY THIS TIME NOBODY WHO KNOWS
CLEO II (119)	/PTOLEMY/ OH YES-- WILL NOT MAINTAIN SUCH	INIQUITY	THEY WILL GIVE HER HEAD TO THE AXE EVEN AS HER
		INITIAL	
GETT PREFACE(198)	TO GET DRUNK AT LEAST ONCE A DAY? APART FROM THE	INITIAL	ABSURDITY OF ACCEPTING AS PERMANENT A STATE OF
BASH I (96)	AND MY NAME'S BOB MELLISH. /CASHEL/ CHANGE THY	INITIAL	AND BE TRULY HIGHT HELLISH. AS FOR THY DOG, WHY DOST
GENV PREFACE(21)	CAESAR NOR A MAHOMET, HE FAILED TO MAKE HIS	INITIAL	CONQUESTS WELCOME AND PERMANENT BY IMPROVING THE
PLES PREFACE(R12)	TROUBLE, THE RISK OF HEAVY LOSS, AND THE	INITIAL	EXPENSE AND THOUGHT, INVOLVED BY THE PRODUCTION OF A
SUPR HANDBOK(195)	NO COMMUNITY HAS EVER YET PASSED BEYOND THE	INITIAL	PHASES IN WHICH ITS PUGNACITY AND FANATICISM ENABLED
		INITIALS	
ROCK II (274)	THE TIMES; AND YOU WOULDNT HAVE TO CHANGE YOUR	INITIALS	. NO BOTHER ABOUT YOUR CLOTHES AT THE LAUNDRY, FOR
SUPR III (82)	LIKE A BOY: I CUT HER NAME ON THE TREES AND HER	INITIALS	ON THE SOD. WHEN I AM ALONE I LIE DOWN AND TEAR MY
		INITIATE	
SUPR PREFACE(R21)	NO FEMALE OF ANY WOMANLINESS OR DELICACY WOULD	INITIATE	ANY EFFORT IN THAT DIRECTION. THERE ARE NO LIMITS
FABL V (119)	FROM THE LIVING BODY TO PERPETUATE THE RACE. TO	INITIATE	BIRTHS THEY HAD TO PRACTISE PERSONAL CONTACTS WHICH
MIS. (193)	I DONT DENY THAT I ENJOYED IT, BUT I DID NOT	INITIATE	IT. AND I BEGAN BY RUNNING AWAY. /TARLETON/ SO
POSN PREFACE(420)	THE ABOLITION OF THE COMMON INFORMER'S POWER TO	INITIATE	PROCEEDINGS; AND YOU WILL HAVE GONE AS FAR AS SEEMS
		INITIATED	
LION PREFACE(23)	THIS DAY A CHRISTIAN WOULD BE IN RELIGION A JEW	INITIATED	BY BAPTISM INSTEAD OF CIRCUMCISION, AND ACCEPTING
MRS PREFACE(164)	AND EXISTING INSTITUTIONS. ALL PROGRESS IS	INITIATED	BY CHALLENGING CURRENT CONCEPTIONS, AND EXECUTED
MRS I (186)	IN MY LIFE. I CLEARED ALL MY EXPENSES, AND GOT	INITIATED	INTO THE BUSINESS WITHOUT A FEE INTO THE BARGAIN.
		INITIATION	
LION PREFACE(84)	TO THE GENTILES. THE JEWS HAD THEIR OWN RITE OF	INITIATION	: THE RITE OF CIRCUMCISION; AND THEY WERE
SUPR I (44)	A WOMAN CAN HAVE, AND MOTHERHOOD HER SOLEMN	INITIATION	INTO WOMANHOOD; AND THAT THE FACT OF YOUR NOT
POSN PREFACE(410)	OF THE COMMON INFORMER SHOULD BE EXTENDED TO THE	INITIATION	OF ALL PROCEEDINGS OF A CENSORIAL CHARACTER
		INITIATIONS	
BULL PREFACE(25)	WHICH HOLDS ITS OWN AS A RESPECTABLE HABIT, THE	INITIATIONS	ARE PERFUNCTORY, THE OMISSIONS REGARDED AS
		INITIATIVE	
AUGS (272)	BATTLE EVER BEEN WON EXCEPT BY A BOLD INDIVIDUAL	INITIATIVE	? I SAY NOTHING OF PROFESSIONAL JEALOUSY: IT
GENV III (75)	THE LEAGUE OF NATIONS DOES ANYTHING ON ITS OWN	INITIATIVE	AND ON PRINCIPLE, IT PRODUCES, NOT PEACE, BUT
PHIL I (74)	HAD ENOUGH OF IT; AND AT NO TIME HAVE I TAKEN THE	INITIATIVE	AND PERSECUTED WOMEN WITH MY ADVANCES AS WOMEN
BARB PREFACE(212)	WE CAN JUDGE FOR OURSELVES WHETHER THE	INITIATIVE	CAME FROM ABOVE OR BELOW. MY OBJECT HERE IS NOT
SUPR PREFACE(R20)	HAVE SET UP A FEEBLE ROMANTIC CONVENTION THAT THE	INITIATIVE	IN SEX BUSINESS MUST ALWAYS COME FROM THE MAN, IS
SUPR PREFACE(R25)	IT IS IMPOSSIBLE TO DEMONSTRATE THAT THE	INITIATIVE	IN SEX TRANSACTIONS REMAINS WITH WOMAN, AND HAS
SUPR PREFACE(R22)	OF LIFE." THE PRETENCE THAT WOMEN DO NOT TAKE THE	INITIATIVE	IS PART OF THE FARCE. WHY, THE WHOLE WORLD IS
SUPR PREFACE(R25)	TO VERY SERIOUS REFLECTIONS ON THE FACT THAT THIS	INITIATIVE	IS POLITICALLY THE MOST IMPORTANT OF ALL THE
SUPR PREFACE(R20)	IN SHAKESPEAR'S PLAYS THE WOMAN ALWAYS TAKES THE	INITIATIVE	. IN HIS PROBLEM PLAYS AND HIS POPULAR PLAYS
ROCK II (255)	THE PEOPLE. I AM FOR THE REFERENDUM. I AM FOR THE	INITIATIVE	. WHEN A MAJORITY OF THE PEOPLE ARE IN FAVOR OF A
BULL PREFACE(48)	CONVICT, SO THE MAN WITH LEAST CONSCIENCE AND	INITIATIVE	MAKES THE BEST BEHAVED SOLDIER, AND THAT NOT
MIS. PREFACE(52)	HOW TO SET ABOUT IT, HOWEVER LAMED HIS POWER OF	INITIATIVE	MAY HAVE BECOME THROUGH DISUSE; BUT THE CHILD
GENV I (33)	ALONE CAN CALL UNRIGHTEOUS RULERS TO ACCOUNT. THE	INITIATIVE	MUST BE TAKEN BY ITS COMMITTEE FOR INTELLECTUAL
GETT PREFACE(212)	DO ANYTHING OF THE SORT. THE MAN ALONE HAS ANY	INITIATIVE	; BUT HE HAS NO ACCESS TO THE WOMAN; BESIDES, AS
2TRU II (58)	INFERIOR. NEVER LET HIM ADDRESS YOU ON HIS OWN	INITIATIVE	, OR CALL YOU ANYTHING BUT " MY LADY." IF THERE
MIS. (181)	WHO IS NOW INCAPABLE OF DOING ANYTHING ON HIS OWN	INITIATIVE	, SIGNS). NOW STAND UP AND READ YOUR DECLARATION
		INITIATIVES	
SUPR PREFACE(R25)	IS POLITICALLY THE MOST IMPORTANT OF ALL THE	INITIATIVES	, BECAUSE OUR POLITICAL EXPERIMENT OF DEMOCRACY,
		INJA	
BULL III (137)	AN ENGLISH EXPEDITION HAD BEEN BET IN A BATTLE IN	INJA	SOMEWHERE; AN HE WAS AS PLEASED AS PUNCH! LARRY TOLD
		INJECT	
DOCT PREFACE(24)	BUY SOME STUFF FROM SOMEBODY FOR A SHILLING, AND	INJECT	A PENNYWORTH OF IT UNDER THEIR PATIENT'S SKIN FOR
DOCT PREFACE(46)	REMEDY FOR PULMONARY TUBERCULOSIS, WHICH WAS, TO	INJECT	A POWERFUL GERMICIDE DIRECTLY INTO THE CIRCULATION BY
DOCT I (91)	AS YOU CALL IT. EH? /RIDGEON/ PRECISELY. TO	INJECT	A VACCINE INTO A PATIENT WITHOUT FIRST TESTING HIS
DOCT I (103)	DISEASE; PREPARE FROM IT A SUITABLE ANTI-TOXIN;	INJECT	IT THREE TIMES A DAY QUARTER OF AN HOUR BEFORE MEALS;
DOCT I (98)	FIRST, DONT BE AFRAID OF THEM: SECOND,	INJECT	THEM A QUARTER OF AN HOUR BEFORE MEALS, THREE TIMES A
		INJECTED	
DEVL II (47)	REDDENS; THE FLESHY PURSES UNDER HIS EYES BECOME	INJECTED	WITH HOT BLOOD; THE MAN OF PEACE VANISHES,
		INJECTION	
DOCT PREFACE(26)	ORDERLY AND INEVITABLE PHENOMENA FOLLOWING THE	INJECTION	OF DANGEROUSLY STRONG " VACCINES" AT THE WRONG
		INJINE	
BULL IV (146)	MACHINERY, N LARRY DOYLE IN THE ROAD STARTIN THE	INJINE	WID A BED WINCH. AT THE FIRST PUFF OF IT THE PIG LEP
		INJOORED	
BULL II (107)	ANYBODY ELSE. WELL, WHAT CANT BE CURED MUST BE	INJOORED	. COME ON IN, ALL OF YOU. YOU MUST BE DYIN FOR YOUR
		INJUDICIOUSLY	
MTH4 I (170)	RIGHT TO LIVE BECAUSE I ALLOWED MYSELF-- PERHAPS	INJUDICIOUSLY	-- TO GIVE YOU A SLIGHT SCOLDING? /ZOO/ IS IT
		INJUN	
NEVR I (216)	PERFECTLY. NOT LIKE ME. /DOLLY/ HONEST	INJUN	? MRS CLANDON GASPS FAINTLY; BUT HER POWERS OF
NEVR I (216)	OF REMONSTRANCE ARE EXHAUSTED. /VALENTINE/ HONEST	INJUN	! /DOLLY/ THEN OFF WITH YOU AND BRING HIM UP.

INJUNCTION

FABL PREFACE(75)	US TO LOVE OUR FELLOW-CREATURES, YET TO OBEY AN	INJUNCTION	TO HOLD ACCURSED ALL WHO DO GOOD WORKS OTHERWISE

INJURE

GETT PREFACE(241)	IS NOT USED TO IT AND THEREFORE FEARS THAT IT MAY	INJURE	HIM. EVERY ADVANCE IN CIVILIZATION FRIGHTENS THESE
DEST (175)	TO FIGHT A DUEL, TO BREAK UP HIS HOUSEHOLD, TO	INJURE	HIS CAREER BY A SCANDAL, WHEN HE CAN AVOID IT ALL BY
MIS. PREFACE(21)	SEDITIOUS LITTLE NUISANCE; AND THAT NOTHING COULD	INJURE	ME IN CHARACTER AND DEGRADE THEIR OCCUPATION MORE
LION PREFACE(51)	MEMBERS ONE OF ANOTHER; SO THAT YOU CANNOT	INJURE	OR HELP YOUR NEIGHBOR WITHOUT INJURING OR HELPING
DEST (174)	BEEN SENT TO YOU OUT OF SHEER MALICE: SOLELY TO	INJURE	THE WOMAN WHO WROTE IT. /NAPOLEON/ THEN WHY NOT SEND
JOAN PREFACE(5)	FOR MENTAL GIANTS WHO NEITHER HATE NOR INTEND TO	INJURE	THEIR FELLOWS TO REALIZE THAT NEVERTHELESS THEIR
GETT (337)	A GENTLEMAN, I'LL NEVER DO ANYTHING TO ANNOY OR	INJURE	YOU EXCEPT THAT I RESERVE THE RIGHT TO GIVE YOU A
MTH4 I (168)	I FEEL HOT ALL OVER. I HAVE A HORRIBLE IMPULSE TO	INJURE	YOU. WHAT HAVE YOU DONE TO ME? /THE ELDERLY
SUPR HANDBOK(229)	YOU NOR ALLOWS YOU TO FORGIVE YOURSELF. IF YOU	INJURE	YOUR NEIGHBOR, BETTER NOT DO IT BY HALVES.

INJURED

MIS. PREFACE(13)	WHEN HE IS SO PUNISHED, IS THE PERSON WHOM HE HAS	INJURED	ALLOWED TO ACT AS JUDGE, JURY, AND EXECUTIONER. IT
BULL PREFACE(61)	DENSHAWAI AFFRAY SOME NATIVES STONED AND SEVERELY	INJURED	AN IRRIGATION INSPECTOR. TWO DAYS AGO THREE NATIVES
CLEO NOTES (210)	OUT OF THE QUESTION THAT WHEN HIS HEAD WAS	INJURED	AT THE BATTLE OF THE NILE, AND HIS CONDUCT BECAME
METH PREFACE(R31)	NERVES, AND, POSITIVELY, HOW MISERABLY A HORRIBLY	INJURED	DOG CAN DIE, LEAVING US TO INFER THAT WE SHALL
GETT PREFACE(229)	IT IS SOMETIMES FIERCELY PUNISHED BY GIVING AN	INJURED	HUSBAND CRUSHING DAMAGES IN A DIVORCE SUIT (INJURED
JITT III (75)	INSUFFERABLE. YOU OWE IT TO YOUR POSITION AS AN	INJURED	HUSBAND NEVER TO SPEAK TO ME WHEN WE ARE ALONE AND
POSN PREFACE(407)	COMPETITORS. THE DRAMATIC AUTHOR IS EQUALLY	INJURED	, HE FINDS THAT UNLESS HE WRITES PLAYS WHICH MAKE
WIDO II (40)	A POINT OF SUCH VITAL IMPORTANCE. /TRENCH/ (MUCH	INJURED	) I OUGHT TO HAVE KNOWN! COKANE: IS THIS
MTH3 (118)	PLACE BEFORE THE END OF THE WEEK. /BURGE-LUBIN/ (	INJURED	) REALLY, MRS LUTESTRING! YOU SPEAK AS IF I WERE A
PYGM III (255)	FOR HER AT A GARDEN PARTY. /HIGGINS/ (DEEPLY	INJURED	) WELL I MUST SAY-- /PICKERING/ (INTERRUPTING HIM)
PPP (198)	THINK OF YOUR MISSPENT LIFE-- /ADOLPHUS/ (MUCH	INJURED	) WHOSE MISSPENT LIFE? /MAGNESIA/ (CONTINUING
GETT PREFACE(229)	HUSBAND CRUSHING DAMAGES IN A DIVORCE SUIT (	INJURED	WIVES ARE NOT CONSIDERED IN THIS WAY), IS NOT NOW
PHIL I (76)	TEARS OFF HER MANTLE): I AM A MOST UNHAPPY AND	INJURED	WOMAN; BUT I AM NOT THE FOOL YOU TAKE ME TO BE. I AM
AUGS (273)	ONE OF YOUR GERMAN BROTHERS-IN-LAW? /AUGUSTUS/ (	INJURED	, REMONSTRATING) I HAVE ONLY THREE GERMAN

INJURES

POSN PREFACE(381)	MERELY BECAUSE THE EXISTING FORM OF IT GRIEVOUSLY	INJURES	AND HINDERS ME INDIVIDUALLY, BUT ON PUBLIC GROUNDS.
BUOY III (41)	WORK ON UNCONGENIAL SUBJECTS IS OVERWORK WHICH	INJURES	THE BRAIN PERMANENTLY. SO WE ARE NOT UNIVERSITY

INJURIES

MILL IV (199)	DUE TO MR BLENDERBLAND WITHOUT MENTIONING HIS	INJURIES	? /EPIFANIA/ THERE IS NO COMPENSATION DUE TO MR
MIS. PREFACE(88)	THIS. THE VIOLENCE DONE TO OUR SOULS BY IT LEAVES	INJURIES	AND PRODUCES SUBTLE MALADIES WHICH HAVE NEVER BEEN
BULL PREFACE(61)	OFF HIS DONKEY AND KICKED HIM IN THE STOMACH: HIS	INJURIES	ARE SERIOUS. IN THE LATTER CASE THEFT APPEARS TO
MILL IV (199)	WANT TO SETTLE THIS BUSINESS OF MR BLENDERBLAND'S	INJURIES	BEFORE WE GO INTO THE MATRIMONIAL QUESTION.
NEVR I (220)	WE SHALL LIKE YOU WHEN YOU ARE BROODING OVER YOUR	INJURIES	. /PHILIP/ (WHO HAS ENTERED THE ROOM UNOBSERVED,
MILL IV (199)	NO MORE OF MR BLENDERBLAND AND HIS RIDICULOUS	INJURIES	. /SAGAMORE/ DO BE A LITTLE REASONABLE, MRS
BARB PREFACE(214)	POLICE STATISTICS IS THAT WE INFLICT ATROCIOUS	INJURIES	ON THE BURGLARS WE CATCH IN ORDER TO MAKE THE REST
MIS. PREFACE(41)	BY THE RIDICULOUS METHOD OF INFLICTING ARTIFICIAL	INJURIES	ON THE PERSONS WHO HAVE NOT YET MASTERED THEM, BUT
METH PREFACE(R51)	AND IT WOULD NEVER HAVE OCCURRED TO HIM THAT	INJURIES	OR ACCIDENTS COMING FROM EXTERNAL SOURCES AGAINST
OVER PREFACE(159)	INFLICTING INJURIES -- SOMETIMES ATROCIOUS	INJURIES	-- ON THE PARTIES CONCERNED. FEW PEOPLE HAVE ANY
OVER PREFACE(159)	THEY DO IN CONVENTION BY DELIBERATELY INFLICTING	INJURIES	-- SOMETIMES ATROCIOUS INJURIES -- ON THE PARTIES
MILL IV (193)	SUPPOSE YOU MEAN THIS AND THIS (HE INDICATES HIS	INJURIES	). WELL, THEY ARE WHAT YOUR WIFE HAS DONE TO ME.
NEVR I (220)	THAT WAS DONE ME ONCE: THATS ALL. I DONT FORGET	INJURIES	; AND I DONT WANT TO FORGET THEM. (HIS FEATURES
MILL IV (197)	(CUTTING IN QUICKLY) HE DECLARES THAT HIS	INJURIES	WERE INFLICTED BY YOU WHEN YOU LAST MET, MRS
BARB PREFACE(244)	IS THAT THE DELIBERATE INFLICTION OF MALICIOUS	INJURIES	WHICH NOW GOES ON UNDER THE NAME OF PUNISHMENT BE

INJURING

OVER (172)	BUT SURELY YOU CAN DO AS YOU PLEASE WITHOUT	INJURING	ANYONE, MRS JUNO, THAT IS THE WHOLE SECRET OF YOUR
LION PREFACE(51)	YOU CANNOT INJURE OR HELP YOUR NEIGHBOR WITHOUT	INJURING	OR HELPING YOURSELF. GOD IS YOUR FATHER: YOU ARE
KING I (170)	YOU OUGHT TO BE ASHAMED OF YOURSELF, MR NEWTON,	INJURING	THE POOR GENTLEMEN'S BRAINS WITH SUCH OUTLANDISH

INJURIOUS

MIS. PREFACE(91)	TO INFLICT ON HUGE NUMBERS OF PEOPLE A MOST	INJURIOUS	ART STARVATION, AND TO CORRUPT A GREAT DEAL OF THE
SIM PREFACE(17)	NEED A GREATLY INCREASED INTOLERANCE OF SOCIALLY	INJURIOUS	CONDUCT AND AN UNCOMPROMISING ABANDONMENT OF
BASH III (122)	THIS ONE'S BYRON'S TRAINER, MELLISH. /MELLISH/	INJURIOUS	COPPER, IN THY TEETH I HURL THE LIE. I AM NO
GETT PREFACE(225)	IS THAT CHANGES OF PARTNERS ARE NOT IN THEMSELVES	INJURIOUS	OR UNDESIRABLE. PEOPLE ARE NOT DEMORALIZED BY THEM
CLEO III (153)	(EXCITEDLY RUSHING UP THE STEPS) OH THOU	INJURIOUS	PORTER! OH THOU UNNATURAL SON OF A SHE-CAMEL! (
ROCK I (230)	WILL LOSE IT. A BRAIN UNDEREXERCISED IS FAR MORE	INJURIOUS	TO HEALTH THAN AN UNDEREXERCISED BODY. YOU KNOW
MIS. PREFACE(14)	FORCED, TO SIT STILL AND NOT SPEAK, WHICH IS	INJURIOUS	TO ITS HEALTH, UNNATURAL, UNJUST, AND THEREFORE
MRS PREFACE(151)	IS PRACTISED. I COULD NOT HAVE DONE ANYTHING MORE	INJURIOUS	TO MY PROSPECTS AT THE OUTSET OF MY CAREER. MY
DOCT PREFACE(31)	IT BECAME THE FASHION IN SPITE OF ITS BEING SO	INJURIOUS	TO THOSE WHO FOLLOW IT. MAKING ALL POSSIBLE
BASH II,1, (106)	WHAT'S HECUBA TO HIM OR HE TO HECUBA? /LUCIAN/	INJURIOUS	UPSTART! IF BY HECUBA THOU POINTEST DARKLY AT MY

INJURY

BARB PREFACE(214)	SEIZE A MAN AND DELIBERATELY DO HIM A MALICIOUS	INJURY	: SAY, IMPRISON HIM FOR YEARS. ONE WOULD NOT SUPPOSE
MRS PREFACE(152)	OR NO LORD CHAMBERLAIN. NONE THE LESS THE	INJURY	DONE ME, NOW ADMITTEDLY INDEFENSIBLE, WAS REAL AND
PHIL II (113)	BREATHES HARD AT THEM). /CRAVEN/ (HIS SENSE OF	INJURY	GROWING ON HIM) AM I TO UNDERSTAND, PARAMORE, THAT
POSN PREFACE(414)	FOR THE PROTECTION OF THE PUBLIC AGAINST PHYSICAL	INJURY	. F. NO LICENCE SHALL BE REFUSED ON THE GROUND THAT
POSN PREFACE(389)	USE THEM TO COMMIT MURDER OR INFLICT MALICIOUS	INJURY	. HE HAS NO GENERAL POWER TO PREVENT CITIZENS FROM
SUPR HANDBOK(217)	YOURSELF IT IS AN IMPERTINENCE: IF ON BAD, AN	INJURY	. THE GOLDEN RULE IS THAT THERE ARE NO GOLDEN RULES.
GETT PREFACE(188)	AS AGAINST ONE WHO THREATENS US WITH A MORTAL	INJURY	. WHAT IS THE ELEMENT IN HIS PROPOSALS THAT PRODUCES
2TRU III (99)	HAVE YOU CONSIDERED THE POSSIBILITY OF A SERIOUS	INJURY	-- /TALLBOYS/ (CUTTING HIM SHORT) MY UMBRELLA IS
PYGM I (211)	/THE FLOWER GIRL/ (STILL NURSING HER SENSE OF	INJURY	) AINT NO CALL TO MEDDLE WITH ME, HE AINT. /THE
GETT (278)	REJJY? /REGINALD/ (WITH AN UNBEARABLE SENSE OF	INJURY	) I SHOULDNT MIND A BIT IF IT WERE FOR LEO'S SAKE.
OVER (183)	/JUNO/ (RISING, WITH A GROWING SENSE OF	INJURY	) LOOK HERE, MRS LUNN: DO YOU THINK A MAN'S HEART IS
ROCK PREFACE(160)	SETS A HORRIBLE EXAMPLE OF CRUELTY AND MALICIOUS	INJURY	; COSTS A GOOD DEAL OF MONEY THAT MIGHT BE BETTER
MIS. PREFACE(28)	INFLICTS ON THE COMMUNITY PRECISELY THE SAME	INJURY	THAT A THIEF PRODUCES, AND WOULD, IN ANY HONEST
NEVR I (220)	/CRAMPTON/ (VINDICTIVELY) NO, NOT A SORROW. AN	INJURY	THAT WAS DONE ME ONCE: THATS ALL. I DONT FORGET
BULL PREFACE(54)	DID ENSUE. ABD-EL-NEBI, IN CONSIDERATION OF THE	INJURY	TO HIS WIFE, WAS ONLY SENTENCED TO PENAL SERVITUDE
MRS PREFACE(152)	INDEFENSIBLE, WAS REAL AND CONSIDERABLE, AND THE	INJURY	TO SOCIETY MUCH GREATER; FOR WHEN THE WHITE SLAVE
MIS. PREFACE(10)	THERE MUST BE HYPOCRISY AS WELL AS CRUELTY. THE	INJURY	TO THE CHILD WOULD BE FAR LESS IF THE VOLUPTUARY SAID
CAPT II (266)	SULTAN IF ENGLAND DEMANDS SATISFACTION FOR ANY	INJURY	TO YOU. IF WE CAN HOLD THE SHEIKH IN PARLEY UNTIL THE
BULL PREFACE(53)	THE ELDERS AND WATCHMEN, AND SAVED FROM FURTHER	INJURY	, BUT NOT BEFORE THEY HAD BEEN SEVERELY KNOCKED

INJUSTICE

3PLA PREFACE(R24)	TO TELL LESS THAN THE TRUTH I SHOULD DO MYSELF AN	INJUSTICE	AND DECEIVE MY READERS. AS TO THE CRITIC THUS
HART II (102)	AND LISTENED TO SUCH UNFAIRNESS, SUCH LIES, SUCH	INJUSTICE	AND PLOTTING AND BACKBITING AND SLANDERING OF ME,
BULL III (141)	O DISEASE IS ZHOURAGASSID? DIDJEVER SUFFER FROM	INJUSTICE	AND STARVATION? DHATS THE IRISH DISEASE. IT'S
FANY III (323)	OUT THE TEETH OF POLICEMEN AS A PROTEST AGAINST	INJUSTICE	AND VIOLENCE? (RISING, WITH IMMENSE ELAN) YOUR
BULL PREFACE(34)	PREOCCUPIED WITH THE MAINTENANCE OF ABSOLUTE	INJUSTICE	AS BETWEEN INDIA AND ENGLAND." IT WILL BE OBSERVED
MIS. PREFACE(75)	BEEN BUILT UP AT HER EXPENSE. NO MORE MONSTROUS	INJUSTICE	COULD BE IMAGINED THAN THAT THE BURDEN OF REARING
POSN PREFACE(375)	VERY MUCH BETTER THAN ITS MAJORITY DESERVED, AN	INJUSTICE	FOR WHICH I NOW APOLOGIZE. I DID NOT, HOWEVER,
BARB I (271)	YOURSELF SUCH AN INJUSTICE, AND BARBARA SUCH AN	INJUSTICE	. AS FOR MYSELF, I FLATLY DENY IT: I HAVE DONE MY
METH PREFACE(R40)	UNJUST GOD; FOR NATURE WAS FULL OF SUFFERING AND	INJUSTICE	. BUT A DISORDERLY GOD WAS IMPOSSIBLE. IN THE
CAPT II (255)	DID. I REPEAT, IT WAS A HARD CASE-- A FRIGHTFUL	INJUSTICE	, BUT IT COULD NOT BE REMEDIED. /BRASSBOUND/ YOU
MTH2 (55)	ACUTELY AWARE OF IT, YOU DO YOURSELF THE GREATEST	INJUSTICE	. HOW ARE YOU? AND HOW ARE YOUR GOOD NEWSPAPER
MILL IV (202)	FOR ANYBODY. MY MILLIONS ARE IN THEMSELVES AN	INJUSTICE	. I SPEAK OF THE JUSTICE OF HEAVEN. /ALASTAIR/ OH
CAPT II (256)	NOTHING OF ENGLISH SOCIETY, AND DRIVEN MAD BY	INJUSTICE	. /BRASSBOUND/ YOUR DEFENCE-- /SIR HOWARD/ (
BARB I (272)	HIM. /LADY BRITOMART/ THE OTHERS DO. THAT IS THE	INJUSTICE	OF A WOMAN'S LOT. A WOMAN HAS TO BRING UP HER

GETT PREFACE(234) REFORMERS ARE SO MUCH PREOCCUPIED WITH THE INJUSTICE OF FORBIDDING A WOMAN TO DIVORCE HER HUSBAND FOR
SUPR HANDBOK(208) IN MONEY OR IN THOUGHT, THEY FEEL DEEPLY THE INJUSTICE OF FOREIGNERS, WHO ALLOW THEM NO CREDIT FOR THIS
MRS II (212) HER) OH, I WONT BEAR IT: I WONT PUT UP WITH THE INJUSTICE OF IT. WHAT RIGHT HAVE YOU TO SET YOURSELF UP
FABL PREFACE(97) LASSALLE IN GERMANY HAD ALREADY DEMONSTRATED THE INJUSTICE OF ITS " IRON LAW OF WAGES," ENGLAND'S SHAMEFACED
MRS IV (252) ARE THE ONLY ONE THAT EVER TURNED ON ME. OH, THE INJUSTICE OF IT! THE INJUSTICE! THE INJUSTICE! I ALWAYS
SUPR III (80) YOU. WE NATURALLY HAVE MODERN VIEWS AS TO THE INJUSTICE OF THE EXISTING DISTRIBUTION OF WEALTH: OTHERWISE
MIS. PREFACE(104) AS MUCH FLOGGING AND HANGING, AS MUCH IMPUDENT INJUSTICE ON THE BENCH AND LUSTFUL RANCOR IN THE PULPIT, AS
MIS. PREFACE(13) BUT HIS CONSCIENCE TO SHIELD THE CHILD FROM INJUSTICE OR UNKINDNESS. THE ACTION MAY BE A TORRENT OF
CAPT NOTES (303) HAVE BEEN APPEALED TO BY VICTIMS OF THIS SENSE OF INJUSTICE -- THE MOST UNHELPABLE OF AFFLICTIONS IN A SOCIETY
PHIL II (113) FEEL NOW. (WRITHING UNDER A SENSE OF INTOLERABLE INJUSTICE) IT'S THE FAULT OF THE WICKEDLY SENTIMENTAL LAWS
PHIL II (120) WOULD PLEASE YOU. /CHARTERIS/ (DEPRECATING THIS INJUSTICE TO HIS GOOD FEELING) MY DEAR FELLOW! /PARAMORE/ I
LION PREFACE(19) LUNATICS WHEN THEY ASK US TO MEET VIOLENCE AND INJUSTICE WITH DUMB SUBMISSION IN THE BELIEF THAT THE
BARB I (271) I CANNOT BEAR TO HEAR YOU DOING YOURSELF SUCH AN INJUSTICE , AND BARBARA SUCH AN INJUSTICE. AS FOR MYSELF, I
LADY PREFACE(212) HARRIS, IN HIS SONIA, HAS RESCUED HER FROM THAT INJUSTICE , AND ENSHRINED HER AMONG THE SAINTS. HE HAS
LION PREFACE(50) AND ENCOURAGED TO FIND THAT WE WERE DOING HIM AN INJUSTICE , AND THAT THE NIMBUS THAT SURROUNDS HIS HEAD IN
APPL I (234) ME HASTEN TO ADD, THEIR HATRED OF OPPRESSION AND INJUSTICE , AND THEIR CONTEMPT FOR THE CHICANERIES AND FALSE
MIS. (136) JINGHISKAHN; AND I THINK YOU DO YOUR HUSBAND SOME INJUSTICE , MRS TARLETON. THEY PRETENDED TO LIKE ME BECAUSE
NEVR II (237) ON). I SEEM TO HAVE DONE THE YOUNG GENTLEMAN AN INJUSTICE , SIR, HAVNT I, SIR? /CRAMPTON/ RRRH! (HE STOPS
CAPT NOTES (302) SERIOUSLY, AND, WHEN THE LAW IS ON THE SIDE OF INJUSTICE , WILL NOT ACCEPT THE SITUATION, AND ARE DRIVEN
MRS IV (252) ME. OH, THE INJUSTICE OF IT! THE INJUSTICE! THE INJUSTICE ! I ALWAYS WANTED TO BE A GOOD WOMAN. I TRIED
MRS IV (252) EVER TURNED ON ME. OH, THE INJUSTICE OF IT! THE INJUSTICE ! THE INJUSTICE! I ALWAYS WANTED TO BE A GOOD

INJUSTICES

BULL III (142) HAVE THE FACE TO SET UP ENGLAND AGEN IRELAND FOR INJUSTICES AN WRONGS AN DISTHRESS AN SUFFERIN? /HODSON/ (
CLEO PRO1 (92) OF GOD THE SCOURGE OF YOUR BOASTINGS AND YOUR INJUSTICES AND YOUR LUSTS AND STUPIDITIES. AND NOW, WOULD YE

INK

MTH2 (72) YOUR PEACE TREATY WAS A SCRAP OF PAPER BEFORE THE INK DRIED ON IT. THE STATESMEN OF EUROPE WERE INCAPABLE OF
SIM II (76) ABOUT TWEAKING THE LORD MAYOR'S NOSE, POURING INK INTO THE PRIME MINISTER'S HAT, AND SINGING DERISIVELY
BARB II (304) WONT YOU? JENNY: GO IN AND FETCH A PEN AND INK . (JENNY RUNS TO THE SHELTER DOOR). /UNDERSHAFT/ DO NOT
DEST (153) EXCELLENCY: I OBEY. /NAPOLEON/ SOME RED INK . /GIUSEPPE/ ALAS! EXCELLENCY, THERE IS NONE.
GENV III (73) FOR OPENING HIS MOUTH OR DIPPING HIS PEN IN THE INK . /SIR O./ YES; BUT WHOSE FAULT IS THAT? YOUR RUSSIAN
ANNA (295) COME OUT OF IT, YOU FOOL! YOURE UPSETTING THE INK . SCHNEIDEKIND EMERGES, RED IN THE FACE WITH SUPPRESSED
MIS. (180) SITS DOWN HELPLESSLY AND DIPS THE PEN IN THE INK .) I HOPE WHAT YOU ARE SIGNING IS NO MERE FORM OF WORDS
SUPR I (24) MOTHER'S MILK AND BLACKENS IT TO MAKE PRINTER'S INK TO SCOFF AT HER AND GLORIFY IDEAL WOMEN WITH. HE
MRS IV (253) AND IS IN THE ACT OF DIPPING HER PEN IN THE INK WHEN SHE FINDS FRANK'S NOTE. SHE OPENS IT UNCONCERNEDLY
FANY III SD(297) IT IS DRAPED IN ITS ORDINARY CLOTH, WITH PEN AND INK , AN EXERCISE-BOOK, AND SCHOOL-BOOKS ON IT. BOBBY GILBEY
ARMS III SD(46) OLD CANISTER FULL OF PENS, AN EGGCUP FILLED WITH INK , AND A DEPLORABLE SCRAP OF HEAVILY USED PINK BLOTTING
GENV PREFACE(6) CAPABLE OF SAVING BILLIONSWORTH OF BRITISH TIME, INK , AND PAPER, BY SPELLING ENGLISH SPEECH SOUNDS
HART I SD(43) COLOR, A TUMBLER OF DISCOLORED WATER, INDIAN INK , PENCILS, AND BRUSHES ON IT. THE DRAWING-BOARD IS SET

INKHORN

JOAN PREFACE(15) THINK THEY SEE THEM. LUTHER, WHEN HE THREW HIS INKHORN AT THE DEVIL, WAS NO MORE MAD THAN ANY OTHER
CLEO II SD(120) HE IS CAREFULLY DRESSED IN BLUE, WITH PORTFOLIO, INKHORN , AND REED PEN AT HIS GIRDLE. HIS SERIOUS AIR AND

INKLING

MIS. PREFACE(25) DUTY AND DISCIPLINE, AND A CLERGYMAN WITH AN INKLING OF RELIGION, THOUGH THERE ARE NOTHING LIKE ENOUGH OF
DOCT PREFACE(49) THAT YOU ARE ATTACKING SCIENCE, YET HE HAS NO INKLING OF THE METHOD AND TEMPER OF SCIENCE. THE POINT AT
BULL PREFACE(18) CONGENITALLY INCAPABLE OF HAVING, THE FAINTEST INKLING OF THE REALITY WHICH HE IDOLIZES AS TOMMY ATKINS.
MIS. PREFACE(104) THE SMALLEST PRETENCE TO CULTURE, OR THE LEAST INKLING OF WHAT THE GREAT PROPHETS VAINLY TRIED TO MAKE THE

INK-BOTTLE

MRS IV SD(245) AT HER; PUTS HIS NOTE CAREFULLY ON THE INK-BOTTLE , SO THAT VIVIE CANNOT FAIL TO FIND IT WHEN NEXT

INKSTAND

CAPT III SD(272) A PRESIDENTIALLY ELBOWED CHAIR BEHIND IT, AND AN INKSTAND AND PAPER READY FOR THE SITTER, A COUPLE OF CHEAP
DEVL I (12) (LINGERING AT THE FIRE) YOUD BETTER PUT THE INKSTAND INSTEAD, FOR THE LAWYER. /MRS DUDGEON/ THATS NO
DEVL I SD(16) CHAIR NEAREST THE SOFA, CHRISTY HAVING LEFT THE INKSTAND THERE. HE PUTS HIS HAT ON THE FLOOR BESIDE HIM, AND
CAPT III SD(272) LITTLE TRAY WITH A JUG AND SOME GLASSES NEAR THE INKSTAND WHEN LADY CICELY'S VOICE IS HEARD AT THE DOOR.
DEVL III SD(55) ALSO DRAPED IN MAROON, WITH A BELL, A HEAVY INKSTAND , AND WRITING MATERIALS ON IT. SEVERAL CHAIRS ARE
2TRU I SD(27) OUT, A LOUIS QUINZE WRITING TABLE AND CHAIR WITH INKSTAND , BLOTTER, AND CABINET OF STATIONERY, A MAGNIFICENT
DEVL I (15) STAND OF STUFFED BIRDS UNDER A GLASS CASE, AND AN INKSTAND , WHICH HE PLACES ON THE TABLE). GOOD MORNING, MR

INKY

GETT PREFACE(205) OPENED AN ABSCESS ON HER PUPIL'S HEAD WITH AN INKY PENKNIFE. HER OBJECT WAS ENTIRELY LAUDABLE: HER HEART
GETT PREFACE(205) TOLERATING AMATEUR SURGICAL PRACTICE WITH INKY PENKNIVES IN SCHOOL WOULD BE A VERY BAD MINISTER OF

INLAID

NEVR III SD(261) FIREPLACE, ITS CENTRE COMPARTMENT CLOSED BY AN INLAID DOOR, AND ITS CORNERS ROUNDED OFF WITH CURVED PANES
CLEO IV SD(173) IN HAND, AND FOLLOWED BY A SLAVE CARRYING AN INLAID STOOL. AFTER MANY STAIRS THEY EMERGE AT LAST INTO A
CAND II (114) ME WITH A NICE NEW ONE, WITH AN IVORY BACK INLAID WITH MOTHER-OF-PEARL? /MARCHBANKS/ (SOFTLY AND
FANY I (278) THERES ONE IN A SHOP IN GREEN STREET, IVORY INLAID , WITH GOLD KEYS AND RUSSIA LEATHER BELLOWS; AND

INLETS

METH PREFACE(R38) CHEMICAL RETORTS, CARBURETTORS, VENTILATORS, INLETS AND OUTLETS, TELEPHONE TRANSMITTERS IN HIS EARS,

INMATES

HART PREFACE(3) PICKAXE WITH A WILL. HE TREATED THE CASE OF THE INMATES AS ONE OF OPIUM POISONING, TO BE DEALT WITH BY
MIS. PREFACE(37) TO BECOME CITIZENS OF THE WORLD INSTEAD OF INMATES OF THE ENLARGED RABBIT HUTCHES WE CALL HOMES; TO

INMOST

SUPR I (32) AT GETTING THROUGH HIS GUARD AND SURPRISING HIS INMOST SECRETS. /ANN/ WHAT NONSENSE! ALL BECAUSE YOU USED
SUPR I (24) MASK OF CONVENTION FROM THEM, TO SURPRISE THEIR INMOST SECRETS, KNOWING THAT THEY HAVE THE POWER TO ROUSE
SUPR I (32) SILLY BOY'S TRICKS! AND YOU CALL SUCH THINGS INMOST SECRETS! BOYS' SECRETS ARE JUST LIKE MEN'S; AND YOU

INN

MILL II (167) SCENERY. AND YET YOU CHOOSE THIS FILTHY OLD INN AND SAY " HOW JOLLY! " WHAT IS THE USE OF BEING A
MRS IV SD(235) SATURDAY AFTERNOON. THE CHIMNEYS OF LINCOLN'S INN AND THE WESTERN SKY BEYOND ARE SEEN THROUGH THE WINDOW.
DEST (157) AS A SOLDIER. /A MAN'S VOICE/ (OUTSIDE, AT THE INN DOOR, SHOUTING) HERE, SOMEONE. HOLLO! LANDLORD! WHERE
MILL I SD(137) YOUNG SOLICITOR, IS IN HIS OFFICE IN LINCOLN'S INN FIELDS. IT IS A FINE MORNING IN MAY. THE ROOM, AN OLD
DEST (154) HOW YOU ENJOY LOOKING ON AT ME WHILST I KEEP THE INN FOR YOU AND WAIT ON YOU! WELL, I SHALL ENJOY LOOKING ON
DEST (154) ALL THAT TO YOU. BESIDES, WHAT WOULD BECOME ON MY INN IF I WERE EMPEROR? SEE HOW YOU ENJOY LOOKING ON AT ME
LION PREFACE(33) THE BIBLE: THE STORY OF MARY CROWDED OUT OF THE INN INTO THE STABLE AND LAYING HER NEWLY-BORN SON IN THE
GLIM (176) OF MY SIGHT WHEN YOU HAVE TOLD ME WHERE THE NEXT INN IS. /SQUARCIO/ I'M SORRY TO THWART YOUR EXCELLENCY; BUT
MILL II SD(166) A DISMAL OLD COFFEE ROOM IN AN ANCIENT RIVERSIDE INN . AN IMMENSE AND HIDEOUS SIDEBOARD OF THE MURKIEST
GLIM (177) ILL-HUMOREDLY ON A BENCH AT THE TABLE OUTSIDE THE INN . GIULIA RETURNS WITH A TABLECLOTH AND BEGINS PREPARING
MRS II (200) /CROFTS/ DONT KNOW. I SUPPOSE HE CAN SLEEP AT THE INN . /MRS WARREN/ HAVNT YOU ROOM FOR HIM, SAM? /REV. S./
GLIM (171) NEAR THIS, DAUGHTER? THE BOY MENTIONED AN INN . /THE GIRL/ THERE IS AN INN, FATHER, NOT TWENTY YARDS
DEVL II (47) OFF WITH YOU AS HARD AS YOU CAN RUN, TO THE INN . TELL THEM TO SADDLE THE FASTEST AND STRONGEST HORSE
GLIM SD(171) IN THE FIFTEENTH CENTURY A. D. GLOAMING. AN INN ON THE EDGE OF AN ITALIAN LAKE. A STONE CROSS WITH A
DEST (156) VOICE/ (CALLING FROM SOME DISTANT PART OF THE INN) GIUSEP-PE! (THE VOICE IS VERY MUSICAL, AND THE TWO
GLIM (179) I DROPPED THEM. (HE GOES BACK INTO THE INN). GIULIA RETURNS WITH SANDRO. /GIULIA/ THIS IS THE LAD,
GLIM (177) SIR. GIULIA IS A GOOD GIRL. (HE GOES INTO THE INN). /FERRUCCIO/ (SHOUTING AFTER HIM) MUST THE RICH DIE
GLIM (177) SOMEBODY, YOU MUST BEAT ME. (SHE GOES INTO THE INN). /SQUARCIO/ I ADVISE YOU NOT TO TRY THAT, EXCELLENCY.
MILL II (166) " HOW JOLLY! " I LOOK ROUND AT THIS ROTTEN OLD INN TRYING TO PRETEND THAT IT'S A RIVERSIDE HOTEL. WE HAVE
GLIM SD(187) WHO HAS COME STEALING ROUND THE CORNER OF THE INN WITH A FISHING NET, CASTS IT OVER FERRUCCIO, AND DRAWS
MRS PREFACE(160) NUMBER TWO. A GERMAN OFFICER FINDS HIMSELF IN AN INN WITH A FRENCH LADY WHO HAS WOUNDED HIS NATIONAL VANITY.

DEST	SD(157)	BEING PROMPTLY ATTENDED TO BY THE STAFF OF THE	INN	, BUT IN WHICH A MORE DISCERNING EYE CAN PERCEIVE A
GLIM	(171)	THE BOY MENTIONED AN INN. /THE GIRL/ THERE IS AN	INN	, FATHER, NOT TWENTY YARDS AWAY. IT'S KEPT BY MY FATHER,
DEST	(185)	GIUSEPPE'S EAR) YOU ARE THROWN AWAY IN THIS	INN	, GIUSEPPE. (HE SITS DOWN AND PLACES GIUSEPPE BEFORE
GLIM	(175)	HE IS A DEVIL FOR WOMEN; AND ONCE HE IS IN THE	INN	, MY FATHER WILL DO THE REST. /THE FRIAR/ (IN A RICH
DEST	SD(151)	THE BEST QUARTERS IN TAVAZZANO ARE AT A LITTLE	INN	, THE FIRST HOUSE REACHED BY TRAVELLERS PASSING THROUGH
GLIM	(175)	AS HE SPRINGS UP AND RUSHES TO THE DOOR OF THE	INN	, WHICH HE BATTERS WITH A STONE). HO THERE, SQUARCIO,

INNATE

BULL	PREFACE(22)	CREATE AN ILLUSION OF SOME MIRACULOUS AND DIVINE	INNATE	ENGLISH QUALITY THAT ENABLES A GENERAL TO BECOME A
METH	PREFACE(R20)	FIRE, AIR, EARTH, AND WATER, EFFECTED BY THE TWO	INNATE	FORCES OF ATTRACTION AND REPULSION, OR LOVE AND HATE.

INNDEED

2TRU	II (53)	IT WAS ONLY TO IMPRESS THE HEADMAN. /TALLBOYS/	INNDEED	. WHO PICKED YOU FOR THIS DUTY? /MEEK/ SERGEANT,

INNER

PYGM	EPILOG (302)	COLONEL TO SAY ANYTHING OF THE SORT) DEEPENS HER	INNER	CERTAINTY THAT SHE IS " NO MORE TO HIM THAN THEM
MTH2	(84)	ITS NECESSITY, WILL DO IT RELUCTANTLY, UNDER	INNER	COMPULSION, AS ALL GREAT EFFORTS ARE MADE. THEY WILL
METH	PREFACE(R50)	YOU CAN ONLY TELL HIM OUT OF THE DEPTHS OF YOUR	INNER	CONVICTION THAT HE IS A FOOL AND A LIAR. BUT AS THIS,
DEST	(194)	UP THEIR HANDS IN PIOUS HORROR! (HE GOES TO THE	INNER	DOOR AND HOLDS IT OPEN, SHOUTING) HALLO! GIUSEPPE!
JITT	II SD(27)	LEADING TO AN INNER ROOM. THE WINDOW FACES THE	INNER	DOOR FROM THE OPPOSITE SIDE; AND THERE IS A
DOCT	III SD(131)	NEAR SIDE OF THIS DOOR. IN THE CORNER NEAR THE	INNER	DOOR IS A LITTLE TEA-TABLE. A LAY FIGURE, IN A
MIS.	SD(116)	COME. THE TWO LADIES GO OUT THROUGH THE	INNER	DOOR WITH BENTLEY, WHO TURNS DERISIVELY AT THE DOOR TO
DEST	(184)	INTO WAFTING HIM A KISS, AND RUNS OUT THROUGH THE	INNER	DOOR, ELECTRIFIED, HE BURSTS INTO A VOLLEY OF
JITT	II SD(31)	YOU. LENKHEIM GOES OUT FOR A MOMENT THROUGH THE	INNER	DOOR, JITTA COMES IN, LANGUID, AND DRESSED AS LENKHEIM
MIS.	SD(200)	IN HER HAND, COMES IMPETUOUSLY THROUGH THE	INNER	DOOR, /LINA/ (ON THE STEPS) MR PERCIVAL: CAN WE GET
MIS.	SD(203)	MYSELF. MRS TARLETON COMES IN SOFTLY THROUGH THE	INNER	DOOR, /MRS TARLETON/ DONT MAKE TOO MUCH NOISE. THE
MIS.	SD(174)	SEND? MRS TARLETON COMES IN HASTILY THROUGH THE	INNER	DOOR, /MRS TARLETON/ (ON THE STEPS) IS ANYTHING THE
MIS.	SD(156)	OF COURSE. MRS TARLETON COMES BACK THROUGH THE	INNER	DOOR, /MRS TARLETON/ WELL I NEVER! JOHN: I DONT THINK
JITT	II SD(27)	AND THE OTHER A ROUND TABLE ON THE SIDE NEAR THE	INNER	DOOR, THERE IS A CHAIR AT IT WITH ITS BACK TO THE WALL
MIS.	SD(154)	RISING) COME WITH ME. LINA FOLLOWS HER TO THE	INNER	DOOR, THEY ALL RISE. /JOHNNY/ (TO PERCIVAL) I'LL SHEW
DEST	(181)	(LOOKING ABOUT HIM ON HIS WAY TO THE	INNER	DOOR) BY THE WAY, GENERAL, DID I GIVE YOU MY SWORD OR
DEST	(157)	GIUSEPPE OFF) MY MAN AT LAST. (POINTING TO THE	INNER	DOOR) GO. ATTEND TO YOUR BUSINESS: THE LADY IS CALLING
DOCT	III (149)	TO SEE YOU, IF YOU DONT MIND. (HE GOES TO THE	INNER	DOOR). AND NOW, BEFORE SHE COMES IN, ONE WORD. YOUVE
MRS	II (205)	HIM SHORT) YOU ARE VERY TIRESOME. (SHE OPENS THE	INNER	DOOR). HAVE YOU ROOM FOR FRANK THERE? HE'S
DEST	(189)	EXCELLENCY. (HE GOES RELUCTANTLY TOWARDS THE	INNER	DOOR). HEAVEN PROTECT ME! (TO THE LIEUTENANT) AFTER
MIS.	(136)	ONE ON SPECIAL OCCASIONS. (SHE GOES TO THE	INNER	DOOR). JOHNNY: WHEN HE COMES BACK ASK HIM WHERE WE'RE
BULL	IV (157)	HIS COAT AND CAP, AND LEAVES THE ROOM THROUGH THE	INNER	DOOR). NORA RETURNS TO HER CHAIR AND SHUTS UP THE
MRS	IV (246)	NOT WAIT. THE FACT IS-- (VIVIE IS HEARD AT THE	INNER	DOOR). /FRANK/ SH! TOO LATE. SHE'S COMING. /MRS
MIS.	(176)	THE YOUNG GENTLEMAN. (SHE GOES OUT THROUGH THE	INNER	DOOR). /GUNNER/ THERE YOU ARE! IT'S ALL OF A PIECE
MIS.	(191)	COME ALONG WITH ME. (SHE LEADS THE WAY TO THE	INNER	DOOR). /GUNNER/ (FOLLOWING HER OBEDIENTLY) THANK YOU
MIS.	(158)	YOU WANT, OF COURSE. (SHE GOES OUT THROUGH THE	INNER	DOOR). /LORD SUMMERHAYS/ WILL YOU FORGIVE MY
DEST	(179)	GENERAL. (SHE TURNS COOLLY TOWARDS THE	INNER	DOOR). /NAPOLEON/ (ANGRILY FLINGING THE PACKET ON THE
DEST	(157)	CALLING) COMING, LADY, COMING. (HE MAKES FOR THE	INNER	DOOR). /NAPOLEON/ (ARRESTING HIM WITH A STRONG HAND
DEST	(177)	YOU. GOODBYE. (SHE GOES INDIGNANTLY TOWARDS THE	INNER	DOOR). /NAPOLEON/ MY OWN--! STOP. COME BACK. COME
DOCT	III (137)	I'LL FETCH YOU A CHAIR. (HE MAKES FOR THE	INNER	DOOR). /RIDGEON/ (STOPPING HIM) YOU SHALL NOT LEAVE
MIS.	(155)	SPRUNG UP OUT OF THE EARTH (SHE MAKES FOR THE	INNER	DOOR). /TARLETON/ NO: DONT YOU TROUBLE, CHICKABIDDY:
MIS.	(145)	ADVENTURES SOMETIMES. (SHE GOES OUT THROUGH THE	INNER	DOOR). /TARLETON/ SHE HAD ME THERE, THOUGH SHE DOESNT
DEST	(157)	CERTAINLY, EXCELLENCY. (HE HURRIES OUT BY THE	INNER	DOOR). /THE MAN'S VOICE/ (IMPATIENTLY) ARE YOU ALL
BULL	IV SD(145)	SIDEBOARD. KEEGAN'S HAT IS ON THE ONE NEAREST THE	INNER	DOOR; AND HIS STICK IS LEANING AGAINST IT. A THIRD
DOCT	III SD(131)	ON A DAIS) A LITTLE TO THE LEFT, OPPOSITE THE	INNER	DOOR, AND AN EASEL TO THE RIGHT, OPPOSITE THE OUTER
MIS.	SD(115)	YOU. SH -- SH -- HYPATIA RUSHES IN THROUGH THE	INNER	DOOR, FOLLOWED BY MRS TARLETON, AND THROWS HERSELF ON
BULL	IV SD(161)	RETURNING NEWLY WASHED AND COMBED THROUGH THE	INNER	DOOR, HAS SEEN HER CONDITION, FIRST WITH SURPRISE AND
MIS.	(164)	ME TO LEAVE THE HOUSE. (HE TURNS TOWARDS THE	INNER	DOOR, HAVING LEFT HIS CAP IN THE BEDROOM). /HYPATIA/ (
BULL	IV (157)	THE OFFICE FOR A BIT. (HE WITHDRAWS THROUGH THE	INNER	DOOR, OBVIOUSLY TO PREPARE HIS APPLICATION TO
JOAN	6,SD(122)	STOOL FOR THE PRISONER. ALL THESE ARE AT THE	INNER	END OF THE HALL. THE FURTHER END IS OPEN TO THE
JOAN	6,SD(122)	DOWN THE GREAT HALL FROM THE MIDDLE OF THE	INNER	END, THE JUDICIAL CHAIRS AND SCRIBES' TABLE ARE TO THE
SUPR	I SD(16)	FELL. SHE IS TO HIM THE REALITY OF ROMANCE, THE	INNER	GOOD SENSE OF NONSENSE, THE UNVEILING OF HIS EYES, THE
KING	I (219)	VILLAINS. VALUE HIM RATHER FOR HIS FLASHES OF THE	INNER	LIGHT? DID HE NOT STOP THE BUTCHERING OF THE
LION	PREFACE(72)	A VIRTUE AT ALL; BUT THEN THE FOLLOWING OF THE	INNER	LIGHT AT ALL COSTS IS LARGELY SELF-INDULGENCE, WHICH
METH	PREFACE(R74)	MOVEMENT TOWARDS THE PURSUIT OF A LIGHT CALLED AN	INNER	LIGHT BECAUSE EVERY MAN MUST SEE IT WITH HIS OWN EYES
KING	I (203)	HOPE IN YOU. THEIR DAY IS SHORT; BUT THE	INNER	LIGHT IS ETERNAL. /JAMES/ I AM SAFE IN THE BOSOM OF MY
KING	I (178)	MONSTER CALLED A CHURCH TO ENTER YOUR MIND YOUR	INNER	LIGHT IS LIKE AN EXTINGUISHED CANDLE; AND YOUR SOUL IS
KING	I (179)	AN INDISPENSABLE CONVENIENCE FOR MOST OF US. THE	INNER	LIGHT MUST EXPRESS ITSELF IN MUSIC, IN NOBLE
KING	I (207)	ARE SNARES OF THE DIVVLE. BUT WHY NOT FOLLOW THE	INNER	LIGHT THAT HAS SAVED YOU FROM THE CHURCHES? BE
LION	EPILOG (147)	HAVE-AND-HOLDERS. PEOPLE WHO ARE SHEWN BY THEIR	INNER	LIGHT THE POSSIBILITY OF A BETTER WORLD BASED ON THE
LION	PREFACE(68)	PERSUADED AT LAST THAT NO MAN COULD FOLLOW HIS	INNER	LIGHT UNTIL HE WAS FREE FROM THEIR COMPULSION. THE
KING	I (203)	/LOUISE/ TAKE THE GENTLEMAN'S MIND OFF HIS	INNER	LIGHT, NELL. GIVE US A SPEECH. /NELL/ THEY DONT WANT A
UNPL	PREFACE(R11)	WRITTEN FOR THE THEATRES INSTEAD OF FROM ITS OWN	INNER	NECESSITY. STILL, A THING THAT NOBODY BELIEVES CANNOT
SUPR	III (107)	IS NOT THE POWER OF LIFE BUT OF DEATH; AND THE	INNER	NEED THAT HAS NERVED LIFE TO THE EFFORT OF ORGANIZING
DOCT	IV SD(156)	IN ANY DANGER OF THAT. SIR RALPH COMES FROM THE	INNER	ROOM AND HASTENS BETWEEN THEM, HUMANELY CONCERNED, BUT
BULL	I SD(73)	HAND WALL IS THE FIREPLACE, AND THE DOOR OF AN	INNER	ROOM BETWEEN THE FIREPLACE AND OUR OBSERVANT SPARROW.
DOCT	IV (170)	GO TO THE DOOR. /MRS DUBEDAT/ (COMING FROM THE	INNER	ROOM WONDERFULLY AND BEAUTIFULLY DRESSED, AND RADIANT,
BULL	I SD(73)	BAG AND A STRAP OF RUGS. HE CARRIES THEM INTO THE	INNER	ROOM. HE IS A RESPECTABLE VALET, OLD ENOUGH TO HAVE
DOCT	III SD(133)	PUZZLED BY HIS FORMAL MANNER; THEN GOES INTO THE	INNER	ROOM. /LOUIS/ (FLIPPANTLY) I SAY: DONT LOOK SO GRAVE.
DOCT	IV SD(157)	HIM, COLLY. RIDGEON AND SIR PATRICK GO INTO THE	INNER	ROOM. /WALPOLE/ I APOLOGIZE, B.B. BUT IT'S
DOCT	IV SD(157)	BUT ALWAYS GENTLE, COMES BETWEEN THEM FROM THE	INNER	ROOM. SHE WEARS A NURSE'S APRON. /MRS DUBEDAT/ SIR
JITT	II SD(27)	CORRIDOR; THE OTHER, ON THEIR LEFT, LEADING TO AN	INNER	ROOM. THE WINDOW FACES THE INNER DOOR FROM THE
DOCT	IV (156)	WITH BAD NEWS IN HIS FACE, ENTERS FROM THE	INNER	ROOM). WELL: WHATS UP? /SIR PATRICK/ GO IN AND SEE.
DOCT	III SD(131)	THE LEFT AT THE NEAR END. THE DOOR LEADING TO THE	INNER	ROOMS IS IN THE OPPOSITE WALL, AT THE FAR END. THE
MRS	IV SD(235)	THE WALL, NEAR A DOOR COMMUNICATING WITH THE	INNER	ROOMS. IN THE OPPOSITE WALL IS THE DOOR LEADING TO THE
DEST	SD(152)	A COUCH NEAR IT; ANOTHER DOOR, LEADING TO THE	INNER	ROOMS, BETWEEN IT AND THE VINEYARD; AND THE TABLE IN
MRS	IV (243)	(SHE MOVES A FEW STEPS TOWARDS THE DOOR OF THE	INNER	ROOM, AND STOPS CLOSE TO PRAED TO SAY) I SHALL NEED
MRS	IV SD(245)	FRANK POINTS EXPRESSIVELY TO THE DOOR OF THE	INNER	ROOM, BUT SAYS NOTHING. /MRS WARREN/ (SITTING DOWN
GENV	IV (109)	I AM NOT DEAF; BUT WHEN ONE IS LISTENING TO THE	INNER	VOICE IT IS NOT EASY TO CATCH EXTERNAL NOISES.
SUPR	I SD(4)	AS THE BLINDS WILL PERMIT. ON HIS LEFT IS THE	INNER	WALL, WITH A STATELY BOOKCASE, AND THE DOOR NOT QUITE
SUPR	III (114)	HE WHO SEEKS IN CONTEMPLATION TO DISCOVER THE	INNER	WILL OF THE WORLD, IN INVENTION TO DISCOVER THE MEANS

INNERMOST

JOAN	PREFACE(51)	WRITER OF HIGH TRAGEDY AND COMEDY, AIMING AT THE	INNERMOST	ATTAINABLE TRUTH, MUST NEEDS FLATTER CAUCHON
JITT	I (17)	FRUIT IF ITS ROOTS LIE DEEP ENOUGH IN THEIR	INNERMOST	CONVICTION. /JITTA/ BRUNO: THAT MUST BE RIGHT. IT
2TRU	I (48)	ALL THESE DEVICES FOR WORRYING HER TO DEATH THE	INNERMOST	UPPERMOST LIFE IN HER RISES LIKE MILK IN A BOILING

INNIMY

BULL	I (78)	NEVER FEAR, SIR. WE KNOW HOW TO RESPICT A BRAVE	INNIMY	. /BROADBENT/ WHAT I REALLY DREAD IS

INNISKILLING

BULL	PREFACE(56)	FELLOW VILLAGERS AND THE OFFICERS AND MEN OF THE	INNISKILLING	DRAGOONS, THE MILITARY MOUNTED POLICE, AND THE

INNKEEPER

DEST	(190)	LAYING HIS HAND ON HIS SLEEVE) I AM ONLY A POOR	INNKEEPER	: YOU ARE A MAN OF FAMILY. /LIEUTENANT/ THERES
DEST	SD(152)	BLACK-CURLED BULLET HEADED GRINNING LITTLE	INNKEEPER	OF 40. NATURALLY AN EXCELLENT HOST, HE IS IN THE
DEST	(160)	IF EVER-- /NAPOLEON/ (SHOUTING FURIOUSLY FOR THE	INNKEEPER	) GIUSEPPE! (TO THE LIEUTENANT, OUT OF ALL
DEST	(186)	HEAVEN! SO I TAUGHT MYSELF TO COOK AND BECAME AN	INNKEEPER	; AND NOW I KEEP SERVANTS TO DO THE WORK, AND HAVE
DEST	(157)	ME GO, EXCELLENCY. IT IS MY POINT OF HONOR AS AN	INNKEEPER	TO COME WHEN I AM CALLED. I APPEAL TO YOU AS A
DEST	SD(162)	PERCEPTIBLY EXCEEDS THAT OF NAPOLEON AND THE	INNKEEPER	, AND LEAVES HER AT NO DISADVANTAGE WITH THE
DEST	SD(162)	TO THE PRIVILEGES OF RANK AND BEAUTY. THE	INNKEEPER	, WHO HAS EXCELLENT NATURAL MANNERS, IS HIGHLY

		INNKEEPERS	
LADY PREFACE(231)	HAD FINALLY TO DROP DON QUIXOTE'S TROUBLES WITH	INNKEEPERS	DEMANDING TO BE PAID FOR HIS FOOD AND LODGING,
DEST (154)	SIDEBOARD) EVERY MAN TO HIS TRADE, EXCELLENCY. WE	INNKEEPERS	HAVE PLENTY OF CHEAP WINE: WE THINK NOTHING OF
DEST (185)	TRUE, LIEUTENANT; QUITE TRUE. YOU ARE ALL LIKE	INNKEEPERS	NOW IN FRANCE: YOU HAVE TO BE POLITE TO
		INNOCENCE	
KING I (175)	SHALL WE STRIKE OFF YOUR AGE FOR THE DAYS OF	INNOCENCE	? /NELL/ FIVE AT MOST. /BARBARA/ BE SILENT, YOU.
LIED (199)	TO ME. /HE/ DOES NOT THAT PROVE THEIR PERFECT	INNOCENCE	? SHE WOULD HAVE SHEWN THEM TO YOU AT ONCE IF SHE
METH PREFACE(R46)	OF A MAN WHO INSISTS ON CONTINUING TO PROVE HIS	INNOCENCE	AFTER HE HAS BEEN ACQUITTED. YOU ASSURE HIM THAT
BARB PREFACE(246)	THEIR COUNTRIES BY TRUSTING TO THE HOCUS-POCUS OF	INNOCENCE	AND GUILT, REWARD AND PUNISHMENT, VIRTUOUS
JOAN PREFACE(31)	POOR JOAN. MARK AND ANDREW WOULD HAVE SHARED HER	INNOCENCE	AND HER FATE HAD THEY BEEN DEALT WITH BY THE
APPL I (222)	OH, THATS CHILDISH. /MAGNUS/ CHILDREN IN THEIR	INNOCENCE	ARE SOMETIMES VERY PRACTICAL, MR COLONIAL
JOAN 5 (120)	BECAUSE HE IS THE FRIEND OF EVERYONE; AND IN MY	INNOCENCE	I BELIEVED THAT YOU WHO NOW CAST ME OUT WOULD BE
JOAN EPILOG (153)	THE NOONDAY SUN ON THE HILLTOP; THE WHITE ROBE OF	INNOCENCE	IS CLEANSED FROM THE SMIRCH OF THE BURNING
MILL IV (198)	OF THE LOWER NATURE AGAINST THE HIGHER. MY	INNOCENCE	IS HELPLESS. DO YOUR WORST. (SHE SITS DOWN IN
MRS IV (242)	NEITHER OF YOU KNOW ANYTHING. YOUR GUESSES ARE	INNOCENCE	ITSELF COMPARED TO THE TRUTH. /PRAED/ (RISING,
MTH2 (60)	THE PRIVILEGE OF MY AGE AND OF MY TRANSPARENT	INNOCENCE	. I HAVE NOT TO STRUGGLE WITH YOUR VOLCANIC
CAPT III SD(282)	AND STEADFAST SMIRK A CHEERFUL CONFIDENCE IN HIS	INNOCENCE	. JOHNSON SOLID AND INEXPRESSIVE, REDBROOK
BARB II (310)	HIS HEAD) YOU MAKE TOO MUCH OF HIM, MISS, IN YOUR	INNOCENCE	. /BARBARA/ (GOING TO HIM) PETER: I'M LIKE YOU
POSN (443)	THAT WHEN I WAS DRUNK I WAS IN A STATE OF	INNOCENCE	. TEMPTATIONS AND BAD COMPANY AND EVIL THOUGHTS
MTH3 (129)	SEPARATION: THE TIES OF BLOOD WILL LOSE THEIR	INNOCENCE	. THE IMAGINATIONS OF MEN, LET LOOSE OVER THE
POSN PREFACE(416)	DEFENDED AND PRIVATELY AMUSED BY MR ALEXANDER'S	INNOCENCE	. TO ACCEPT A WEST END MANAGER AS AN EXPERT IN
VWOO 3 (142)	ABOUT GRATIFYING MY SENSES IS ONLY YOUR VIRGIN	INNOCENCE	. WE SHALL GET QUITE AWAY FROM THE WORLD OF SENSE.
MTH3 (122)	YOU SUGGEST THAT I SHOULD TAKE ADVANTAGE OF THE	INNOCENCE	OF A CHILD OF THIRTY, AND MARRY IT. /THE
MTH3 (122)	HAVE YOU EVER TRIED TO TAKE ADVANTAGE OF THE	INNOCENCE	OF A LITTLE CHILD FOR THE GRATIFICATION OF YOUR
DOCT PREFACE(41)	FOR INSTANCE, THE ASCERTAINMENT OF THE GUILT OR	INNOCENCE	OF AN ACCUSED PERSON A MUCH EXACTER PROCESS THAN
JOAN PREFACE(23)	EASIER THAN THEY ARE, AND, LIKE MAHOMET IN HIS	INNOCENCE	OF ANY WORLD BUT THE TRIBAL WORLD, WROTE LETTERS
METH PREFACE(R57)	A THEORY OF COLLISIONS: THAT IS, A THEORY OF THE	INNOCENCE	OF MUCH APPARENTLY DESIGNED DEVILRY. IN THIS WAY
CLEO II (134)	THAT I WANTED HIM TO? /CAESAR/ (TOUCHED BY HER	INNOCENCE	OF THE BEAUTIFUL YOUNG MAN'S CHARACTER) MY POOR
POSN PREFACE(427)	ABUSED JUST AS CERTAINLY AS THE COMPLAISANCE AND	INNOCENCE	OF THE CENSORSHIP IS ABUSED AT PRESENT. IT WILL
3PLA PREFACE(R10)	WITH NAGGING RELATIVES. THESE PEOPLE PRESERVE THE	INNOCENCE	OF THE THEATRE: THEY HAVE NEITHER THE
3PLA PREFACE(R16)	THE CLERKS, WHO, AS I HAVE SAID, PRESERVE THE	INNOCENCE	OF THE THEATRE, WOULD NOT DARE TO LET THEMSELVES
GETT PREFACE(257)	THEREBY MAKING THE TREATMENT OF WHAT YOU CONSIDER	INNOCENCE	ON BOTH SIDES THE SAME AS THE TREATMENT OF WHAT
FANY I (281)	LIKE YOU THAT TAKE ADVANTAGE OF A CHILD'S	INNOCENCE	OUGHT TO BE WHIPPED THROUGH THE STREETS. /DORA/
WIDO II (41)	THE MONEY YOU TAKE? /SARTORIUS/ (PITYING HIS	INNOCENCE	) MY YOUNG FRIEND: THESE POOR PEOPLE DO NOT KNOW
2TRU II SD(77)	TO HIM PAST THE COUNTESS WITH AN AIR OF DISARMING	INNOCENCE	; FALLS ON HER KNEES; LIFTS HER PALMS; AND SMITES
ROCK PREFACE(180)	OF THEM REMAIN IN THIS CONDITION OF INTELLECTUAL	INNOCENCE	TO THE END OF THEIR LIVES, WHILST THE CLEVERER
GETT PREFACE(251)	WILL BE CONSIDERED A CORRUPTION OF THAT YOUTHFUL	INNOCENCE	WHICH NOW SUBSISTS ON NASTY STORIES AND WHISPERED
3PLA PREFACE(R35)	NOR RELISHED BY MEN IN WHOSE PHILOSOPHY GUILT AND	INNOCENCE	, AND CONSEQUENTLY REVENGE AND IDOLATRY, HAVE NO
JOAN PREFACE(31)	HER OWN UNCONSCIOUSNESS OF IT, WHICH WE CALL HER	INNOCENCE	, AND HER FRIENDS CALLED HER SIMPLICITY. HER
GETT (282)	IS GUILTY: AND WE WONT ALLOW HIM TO PROVE HIS	INNOCENCE	, BECAUSE IT WOULD BE AGAINST PUBLIC MORALS IF HE
GETT PREFACE(249)	GAVE ITS BLESSING TO MARRIAGE, DID NOT, IN ITS	INNOCENCE	, FATHOM THESE COMMERCIAL TRADITIONS. CONSEQUENTLY
CLEO NOTES (212)	THEORIES OF MORAL RESPONSIBILITY, GUILT,	INNOCENCE	, REWARD, PUNISHMENT, AND THE REST OF IT, THAT
LADY (238)	MEN? /THE BEEFEATER/ NOW THE LORD BLESS YOUR	INNOCENCE	, SIR, DO YOU THINK YOU ARE THE ONLY PRETTY MAN IN
ROCK I (221)	RISING AND TAKING IT RATHER PITYINGLY) BLESS YOUR	INNOCENCE	, SRARTHUR, YOU DONT KNOW WHAT HUMBUG IS YET. WAIT
		INNOCENCY	
CLEO PRO1 (89)	AND NOTHING WRITTEN THEREON (TO SIGNIFY THE	INNOCENCY	OF YOUR MINDS). HEAR ME, YE WOMEN WHO ADORN
		INNOCENT	
FANY PROLOG (267)	MY DEAR YOUNG LADY-- /FANNY/ I DONT MEAN MORALLY	INNOCENT	: EVERYBODY WHO READS YOUR ARTICLES KNOWS YOURE AS
GENV II (55)	THEM AT ONCE. /THE SECRETARY/ THEY ARE QUITE	INNOCENT	: THEY KNOW NO MORE ABOUT IT THAN I DID. THE WHOLE
JOAN PREFACE(27)	IS NATURAL ENOUGH. MARK TWAIN, THE	INNOCENT	ABROAD, WHO SAW THE LOVELY CHURCHES OF THE MIDDLE
MIS. PREFACE(77)	OF THEM, THE DISTRACTION OF SEEING THE WORLD, IS	INNOCENT	AND BENEFICIAL. ALSO IT IS CHILDISH, BEING A
OVER PREFACE(156)	ON THE STRENGTH OF IT. ON THE OTHER HAND, THE	INNOCENT	AND CONVENTIONAL PEOPLE WHO REGARD GALLANT
JOAN 6 (130)	AND END BY INCEST. HERESY AT FIRST SEEMS	INNOCENT	AND EVEN LAUDABLE; BUT IT ENDS IN SUCH A MONSTROUS
FANY I (279)	ROAD MYSELF: ROTTEN LUCK, WASNT IT? I TRIED THE	INNOCENT	AND GENTEEL AND ALL THE REST; BUT BOBBY'S HAT DONE
POSN PREFACE(407)	ISSUE OF FREE ADMISSIONS, THOUGH AN APPARENTLY	INNOCENT	AND GOOD-NATURED, AND CERTAINLY A HIGHLY POPULAR
DOCT III (142)	NOT ONLY HIM BUT EVERYBODY CONNECTED WITH HIM,	INNOCENT	AND GUILTY ALIKE. ITLL THROW HIS BOARD AND LODGING
GETT PREFACE(198)	FOR THE CHILDREN THEMSELVES, IS NOT ALWAYS THE	INNOCENT	AND HIGHMINDED PRACTICE IT PROFESSES TO BE; AT ALL
DOCT PREFACE(49)	BEGAN HAVE PRODUCED NOTHING SO IMPORTANT AS THE	INNOCENT	AND HONORABLE DISCOVERY OF RADIOGRAPHY; AND ONE OF
GETT PREFACE(245)	DISEASE DOES; THAT INDEED IT OFTEN HITS THE	INNOCENT	AND MISSES THE GUILTY BECAUSE THE GUILTY KNOW THE
FANY III (303)	HAVE A DANCE MYSELF. I CANT IMAGINE ANYTHING MORE	INNOCENT	AND MORE HAPPY. ALL THE BAD PART WAS DONE BY OTHER
AUGS PREFACE(261)	THE SHEWING-UP OF AUGUSTUS SCANDALIZED ONE OR TWO	INNOCENT	AND PATRIOTIC CRITICS WHO REGARDED THE PROWESS OF
HART II (111)	DID, AS YOU WELL KNOW, CAPTAIN. BUT WHAT I DO IS	INNOCENT	AND PIOUS. I ENQUIRE ABOUT FOR HOUSES WHERE THE
SIM I (39)	AFTER TAKING THE AFTERNOON SERVICE. " YOU LOOK SO	INNOCENT	AND RESPECTABLE" THEY SAID. " JUST WHAT WE WANT! "
METH PREFACE(R35)	AND THE JUSTICE OF HIS DISCRIMINATION BETWEEN THE	INNOCENT	AND THE GUILTY. IN VAIN DID I APPEAL TO THE
GETT PREFACE(245)	MAY OR MAY NOT HAVE ORIGINATED, CONTAMINATES THE	INNOCENT	AND THE GUILTY ALIKE ONCE IT IS LAUNCHED EXACTLY AS
GETT PREFACE(257)	ON THE OTHER HAND, YOU THINK A COUPLE PERFECTLY	INNOCENT	AND WELL CONDUCTED, DO NOT CONDEMN THEM ALSO TO
BULL IV (150)	HAVE HAD A SOMEWHAT AGITATING DAY: A VALUABLE AND	INNOCENT	ANIMAL HAS LOST ITS LIFE: A PUBLIC BUILDING HAS
JOAN EPILOG (157)	THE FEET OF MEN AND SPIRITS ALIKE WHEN THE	INNOCENT	ARE SLAIN IN THE NAME OF LAW, AND THEIR WRONGS ARE
FANY PROLOG (267)	EVERYBODY WHO READS YOUR ARTICLES KNOWS YOURE AS	INNOCENT	AS A LAMB. /TROTTER/ WHAT! /FANNY/ YES, MR
FANY III (314)	/GILBEY/ OH, COME, MRS KNOX! GIRLS ARE NOT SO	INNOCENT	AS ALL THAT. /MRS KNOX/ I DONT SAY SHE WAS
FANY PROLOG (267)	UNDERSTAND WHAT IT MEANS TO PAPA. YOURE NOT SO	INNOCENT	AS HE IS. /TROTTER/ (REMONSTRATING) MY DEAR YOUNG
MIS. PREFACE(82)	EVERYTHING THEY CARE FOR. NO PARENT'S LOVE IS AS	INNOCENT	AS THE LOVE OF A CHILD: THE EXCLUSION OF ALL
HART PREFACE(31)	BY DAMSELS (CALLED FLAPPERS) OFTEN AS	INNOCENT	AS THEMSELVES, CROWDED THE THEATRES TO THE DOORS.
JOAN PREFACE(5)	CONTRAST WITH NAPOLEON. IF SOCRATES WAS AS	INNOCENT	AS THIS AT THE AGE OF SEVENTY, IT MAY BE IMAGINED
APPL PREFACE(193)	HUMAN RACE, A WRECKER OF HOMES AND A STARVER OF	INNOCENT	BABES. HE FOUGHT THEM UNDAUNTEDLY; BUT THEY WERE
MTH2 (50)	MOTHERS AND DAUGHTERS. THE TENDER FLESH OF OUR	INNOCENT	BABES, WERE AT STAKE. WAS THAT A TIME TO ARGUE
LION PREFACE(13)	WHOLE TRANSACTION. FOR EXAMPLE, THE SHEDDING OF	INNOCENT	BLOOD CANNOT BE BALANCED BY THE SHEDDING OF GUILTY
FANY I (280)	RESPECTABLE HOUSEHOLD. YOUVE GONE AND GOT MY POOR	INNOCENT	BOY INTO TROUBLE. IT'S THE LIKE OF YOU THATS THE
HART PREFACE(31)	FEMALE OF HIS SPECIES. IT GAVE HIM AN ENTIRELY	INNOCENT	BUT DELIGHTFUL PLEASURE MERELY TO SEE A FLAPPER.
METH PREFACE(R79)	DAY BEFORE THE SUN WAS CREATED, OR TO BETRAY AN	INNOCENT	CALF-LOVE FOR THE VIRGIN MARY, WOULD BUY HIM A
SUPR I (30)	THAT? /TANNER/ MEANING A WEEPING MAGDALEN AND AN	INNOCENT	CHILD BRANDED WITH HER SHAME. NOT IN OUR CIRCLE,
HART I (47)	NOW BEFORE HIGH HEAVEN THEY HAVE GIVEN THIS	INNOCENT	CHILD INDIAN TEA: THE STUFF THEY TAN THEIR OWN
JOAN 5 (109)	LIKES HIS COMRADE. /DUNOIS/ YOU NEED IT, POOR	INNOCENT	CHILD OF GOD. YOU HAVE NOT MANY FRIENDS AT COURT.
GETT PREFACE(228)	OF HOLIES IN THE TEMPLE OF HONORABLE MOTHERHOOD,	INNOCENT	CHILDHOOD, MANLY VIRTUE, AND SWEET AND WHOLESOME
GETT PREFACE(258)	IN PUBLIC, TO THE GREAT DISTRESS AND DISGRACE OF	INNOCENT	CHILDREN AND RELATIVES, WHILST THE GROUNDS HAVE AT
GETT PREFACE(245)	WE SO GLIBLY SAY " SERVE THEM RIGHT," BUT QUITE	INNOCENT	CHILDREN AND INNOCENT PARENTS, SMITTEN BY A
JOAN 6 (131)	PIECES, DROWNED, BURNED IN HIS HOUSE WITH ALL HIS	INNOCENT	CHILDREN, WITHOUT A TRIAL, UNSHRIVEN, UNBURIED SAVE
POSN PREFACE(422)	UNDERSTANDING, HAD A COMPARATIVELY DEFINITE AND	INNOCENT	CLAUSE BEEN ADDED FORBIDDING THE AFFIRMATION OR
PRES (157)	CONFOUND IT, MADAM, CAN YOU NOT RECEIVE AN	INNOCENT	COMPLIMENT WITHOUT SUSPECTING ME OF DISHONORABLE
JOAN 2 (79)	OFTEN -- I DO NOT SAY ALWAYS -- VERY SIMPLE AND	INNOCENT	CONTRIVANCES BY WHICH THE PRIEST FORTIFIES THE
MRS PREFACE(154)	CENSORSHIP OF THE MINOR THEATRE CRITIC, NOR OF AN	INNOCENT	COURT OFFICIAL LIKE THE LORD CHAMBERLAIN'S
JOAN 6 (147)	BUT IT IS A TERRIBLE THING TO SEE A YOUNG AND	INNOCENT	CREATURE CRUSHED BETWEEN THESE MIGHTY FORCES, THE
JOAN PREFACE(13)	BISHOP, IT MUST BE ASSUMED THAT SHE WAS THE	INNOCENT	DUPE OF THESE DELUSIONS. THE TWENTIETH CENTURY
HART II (92)	NO SENSE? LOOK AT THE BRUTE! THINK OF POOR WEAK	INNOCENT	ELLIE IN THE CLUTCHES OF THIS SLAVEDRIVER, WHO
SUPR III (133)	THAT WARMTH OF HEART, SINCERE UNFORCED AFFECTION,	INNOCENT	ENJOYMENT, AND WARM, BREATHING, PALPITATING
MRS PREFACE(174)	BY A LITTLE PLEA IN A THEATRICAL PAPER WHICH IS	INNOCENT	ENOUGH TO THINK THAT TEN GUINEAS A YEAR WITH BOARD
LION PREFACE(83)	CANNOT SPEND HIS LIFE ADMIRING HIMSELF, THE LESS	INNOCENT	EXCITEMENT OF PUNISHING OTHER PEOPLE FOR NOT
MRS I (191)	/CROFTS/ OH, DONT BE ALARMED: IT'S QUITE AN	INNOCENT	FEELING, THATS WHAT PUZZLES ME ABOUT IT. WHY, FOR
APPL INTRLUD(254)	I HATE BEATING PEOPLE. BUT THERE WOULD BE SOME	INNOCENT	FUN IN OUTWITTING HIM. /ORINTHIA/ MAGNUS: YOU ARE A
HART I (79)	/HECTOR/ PRECISELY. WELL, DARE YOU KILL HIS	INNOCENT	GRANDCHILDREN? /CAPTAIN SHOTOVER/ THEY ARE MINE
GETT PREFACE(186)	INTO PRISON FOR TWENTY YEARS FOR IT, THE FREE AND	INNOCENT	HUSBAND OR WIFE OF THAT MURDERER SHOULD REMAIN
MRS PREFACE(180)	PRIVATE EXHIBITION OF THE FILM THAT IT WAS QUITE	INNOCENT	I WROTE TO THE CENSOR, BEGGING HIM TO EXAMINE THE
MIS. (140)	CHILDHOOD FOR A CHILD COMPANION, BUT BY THE	INNOCENT	IMPULSE TO PLACE THE DELICACY AND WISDOM AND

METH PREFACE(R76)	LIE AND CHEAT AND MURDER AND THEN WASH OURSELVES	INNOCENT	IN THE BLOOD OF THE LAMB ON SUNDAY AT THE COST OF A
NEVR III (280)	MAAM: VERY BRIGHT AND PLEASANT, VERY GAY AND	INNOCENT	INDEED. (TO PHIL) TICKETS DOWNSTAIRS AT THE
JOAN EPILOG (166)	AM OF THE DEAD, TESTIFIED THAT DAY THAT YOU WERE	INNOCENT	. BUT I DO NOT SEE HOW THE INQUISITION COULD
2TRU II (67)	ASTONISHING BREAKAWAY, HAS BEEN, SO FAR, QUITE	INNOCENT	. CAN YOU BELIEVE THAT, YOU CLOD? /THE COUNTESS/
CLEO IV (185)	HER VOICE ALMOST FAILING) NOTHING. I AM	INNOCENT	. (SHE APPROACHES HIM AFFECTIONATELY). DEAR
MRS IV (245)	WARREN/ OH, YOU NEVER CAN SEE WHY NOT: YOURE TOO	INNOCENT	. MR FRANK: DID SHE SAY ANYTHING TO YOU? /FRANK/ (
MILL I (149)	/ALASTAIR/ NO, I TELL YOU. IT WAS QUITE	INNOCENT	. /EPIFANIA/ (TO PATRICIA) WAS HE IN YOUR ARMS OR
JOAN 3 (92)	ARE NOT ANSWERED. YOURS MAY BE: YOU ARE YOUNG AND	INNOCENT	. /JOAN/ OH YES: YOU ARE RIGHT. I WILL PRAY: I WILL
PYGM III (253)	I FIND THE NEW SMALL TALK DELIGHTFUL AND QUITE	INNOCENT	. /MRS EYNSFORD HILL/ (RISING) WELL, AFTER THAT, I
SIM II (59)	/MAYA/ WHEN WE WERE HAPPY. /VASHTI/ WHEN HE WAS	INNOCENT	. /PRA/ YOU RAISED THIS STRANGE SPIRIT. I CANNOT
OVER (178)	THIS. I HAVE BEEN PUSHED OVER A PRECIPICE. I'M	INNOCENT	. THIS WILD JOY, THIS EXQUISITE TENDERNESS, THIS
JOAN 6 (147)	CALL HER INNOCENT! /THE INQUISITOR/ OH, QUITE	INNOCENT	. WHAT DOES SHE KNOW OF THE CHURCH AND THE LAW?
JOAN PREFACE(5)	AT THE AGE OF SEVENTY, IT MAY BE IMAGINED HOW	INNOCENT	JOAN WAS AT THE AGE OF SEVENTEEN. NOW SOCRATES WAS
POSN (464)	HARD ON IT HIMSELF? WHY SHOULD HE GO HARD ON THE	INNOCENT	KID AND GO SOFT ON A ROTTEN THING LIKE ME? WHY DID
O'FL (207)	AND ALWAYS HAS BEEN, THAT EVER TAUGHT A POOR	INNOCENT	LAD LIKE MYSELF TO PRAY NIGHT AND MORNING TO ST
POSN PREFACE(378)	B" AMONG MY MOST VALUED LITERARY TROPHIES. AN	INNOCENT	LADY TOLD ME AFTERWARDS THAT SHE NEVER KNEW THAT I
MIS. (145)	SHE HAD ME THERE, THOUGH SHE DOESNT KNOW IT, POOR	INNOCENT	LAMB! PUBLIC SCANDAL EXAGGERATES ENORMOUSLY, OF
ARMS II (31)	OF THAT CONSUMMATE SOLDIER, MAJOR: SIMPLY TWO	INNOCENT	LITTLE CHILDREN. /RAINA/ WHAT WAS HE LIKE?
DEST (158)	I TELL YOU, GENERAL, IF EVER I CATCH THAT	INNOCENT	LOOKING YOUTH, I'LL SPOIL HIS BEAUTY, THE SLIMY
DEST (158)	(ADVANCING FROM THE HEARTH TO THE TABLE) WHAT	INNOCENT	LOOKING YOUTH? PULL YOURSELF TOGETHER, SIR, WILL
GETT PREFACE(222)	" PLUCKS THE ROSE FROM THE FAIR FOREHEAD OF AN	INNOCENT	LOVE, AND SETS A BLISTER THERE", AND THEN CALMLY
CAPT II (254)	HOWARD/ I SHALL MEET IT, I TRUST, AS BECOMES AN	INNOCENT	MAN AND AN UPRIGHT JUDGE. WHAT DO YOU CHARGE
DEVL II (47)	DEATH, TONY-- YOUR SURE DEATH, IF GOD WILL LET	INNOCENT	MEN BE MURDERED. THEY WILL NOT LET YOU SEE HIM:
2TRU III (98)	WE WERENT EVEN KILLING THE WRONG PEOPLE. IT WAS	INNOCENT	MEN KILLING ONE ANOTHER. /THE PATIENT/ JUST FOR THE
ROCK PREFACE(182)	MISCHIEF SUCH AS STONINGS AND CRUCIFIXIONS OF	INNOCENT	MEN, HOW AM I TO JUDGE WHETHER IT IS HE WHO IS
2TRU I (28)	MEASLES! AND SHE'S GIVEN THEM TO ME, A POOR	INNOCENT	MICROBE THAT NEVER DID HER ANY HARM. AND SHE SAYS
OVER PREFACE(155)	ACTUALLY OCCURS AMONG QUITE ORDINARY PEOPLE,	INNOCENT	OF ALL UNCONVENTIONAL VIEWS CONCERNING IT. THE
APPL PREFACE(178)	OF MEDIEVAL MONARCHY AND FEUDALISM. I AM QUITE	INNOCENT	OF ANY SUCH EXTRAVAGANCES. ALL I MEAN IS THAT
MIS. PREFACE(56)	AND TOLERATED ON ALL HANDS BY PEOPLE WHO WERE	INNOCENT	OF ANYTHING WORSE THAN STUPIDITY, ILL TEMPER, AND
DOCT PREFACE(25)	INTRODUCE INTO THE PATIENT'S SYSTEM MAY BE QUITE	INNOCENT	OF THE CATASTROPHE, AND THAT THE CASUAL DIRT
BARB PREFACE(238)	AND OF ALL THESE, THE HORSES ALONE ARE	INNOCENT	OF THE GUILT HE IS AVENGING: HAD HE BLOWN ALL
LADY PREFACE(227)	EVER PUT ANY CONSTRUCTION BUT THE OBVIOUS AND	INNOCENT	ONE ON THESE PASSAGES. BUT THE GENERAL VOCABULARY
JOAN PREFACE(6)	WERE EQUALLY GLAD TO BE RID OF HER. WAS JOAN	INNOCENT	OR GUILTY? AS THIS RESULT COULD HAVE BEEN PRODUCED
GETT PREFACE(245)	THEM RIGHT," BUT QUITE INNOCENT CHILDREN AND	INNOCENT	PARENTS, SMITTEN BY A CONTAGION WHICH, NO MATTER IN
JOAN PREFACE(51)	ONLY AS MECHANISM. IT IS, I REPEAT, WHAT NORMALLY	INNOCENT	PEOPLE DO THAT CONCERNS US: AND IF JOAN HAD NOT
JOAN PREFACE(51)	US: AND IF JOAN HAD NOT BEEN BURNT BY NORMALLY	INNOCENT	PEOPLE IN THE ENERGY OF THEIR RIGHTEOUSNESS HER
LION PREFACE(98)	IT DOES NOT SAY SO. NO DOUBT THERE ARE MANY	INNOCENT	PEOPLE IN ENGLAND WHO TAKE CHARLEMAGNE'S VIEW, AND
MIS. PREFACE(19)	IS, ON THE WHOLE, NOTHING ON EARTH INTENDED FOR	INNOCENT	PEOPLE SO HORRIBLE AS A SCHOOL. TO BEGIN WITH, IT
LION PREFACE(13)	MIGHT QUITE POSSIBLY LEAD TO OUR PUTTING SOME	INNOCENT	PERSON -- THE MORE INNOCENT THE BETTER -- TO A
CAPT III (276)	IS WHEN SHE HAS A GRIEVANCE, AND IMAGINES SOME	INNOCENT	PERSON TO BE THE AUTHOR OF IT. /LADY CICELY/ (WITH
GENV IV (101)	THIS DOES NOT JUSTIFY YOUNG MEN IN SLAUGHTERING	INNOCENT	PERSONS AT RANDOM. IT WOULD JUSTIFY ME IN
ROCK PREFACE(147)	MURDERER TO THE SLAUGHTER OF MILLIONS OF QUITE	INNOCENT	PERSONS. WHILST ASSENTING TO THESE PROCEEDINGS, AND
POSN PREFACE(401)	TO YOU FOR A MOMENT, MISS? " YET THAT APPARENTLY	INNOCENT	PHRASE HAS OFTEN BEEN MADE OFFENSIVELY IMPROPER ON
ARMS III (68)	(ENIGMATICALLY) THE WORLD IS NOT SUCH AN	INNOCENT	PLACE AS WE USED TO THINK, PETKOFF. /BLUNTSCHLI/ (
FANY PROLOG (271)	GREAT HEAVENS! HOW IS IT POSSIBLE THAT A FEW	INNOCENT	PLEASANTRIES SHOULD BE SO FRIGHTFULLY
2TRU II (70)	TO EMPLOY HIS MIND, AND HE GOES OUT AND SHOOTS AN	INNOCENT	POLICEMAN BECAUSE HE CAN THINK OF NOTHING MORE
MIS. (147)	BE A NECESSARY RELATION, BUT IT CAN NEVER BE AN	INNOCENT	RELATION. YOUD DIE RATHER THAN ALLUDE TO IT. DEPEND
MIS. (147)	BETWEEN THE YOUNG AND THE OLD SHOULD BE AN	INNOCENT	RELATION. IT SHOULD BE SOMETHING THEY COULD TALK
APPL INTRLUD(251)	DEFY YOU TO MAKE ME MORE HAPPY THAN OUR STRANGELY	INNOCENT	RELATIONS HAVE ALREADY MADE ME. /ORINTHIA/ (RISING
POSN PREFACE(416)	AND A SPECIAL POLICE, WAS BROUGHT OUT BY AN	INNOCENT	REMARK MADE BY SIR WILLIAM GILBERT, WHO, WHEN
MILL I (149)	MIND HOW I KNOW IT. I DO. /ALASTAIR/ IT WAS QUITE	INNOCENT	; BUT WHERE COULD I GO TO WHEN YOU DROVE ME OUT OF
O'FL (206)	PITCH OF TIREDNESS OF IT THAT WHEN A POOR LITTLE	INNOCENT	SLIP OF A BOY IN THE STREET THE OTHER NIGHT DREW
LION PREFACE(13)	TO OUR PUTTING SOME INNOCENT PERSON -- THE MORE	INNOCENT	THE BETTER -- TO A CRUEL DEATH TO BALANCE THE
ROCK PREFACE(158)	HIS ACCUSERS HAD NOT THE WIT TO FRAME. IF HE WAS	INNOCENT	THEN THE WHOLE WORLD WAS GUILTY. TO ACQUIT HIM WAS
OVER (190)	POLYANDRY. /MRS LUNN/ I WISH YOU WOULDNT CALL	INNOCENT	THINGS BY OFFENSIVE NAMES, MR JUNO. WHAT DO YOU
LION PREFACE(77)	RELATION, WHICH UNTIL THEN HAD SEEMED QUITE	INNOCENT	TO THEM; AND THERE IS NO GETTING OVER THE HARD FACT
GENV IV (100)	WITH LAYING A MINE IN THE HIGH SEAS TO SLAUGHTER	INNOCENT	TRAVELLERS WHOSE INTENTIONS TOWARDS YOURSELF, YOUR
6CAL (94)	HER TO DIE! THEY ARE TRYING TO MURDER HER AND OUR	INNOCENT	UNBORN CHILD. THINK OF THAT, BOY: OH, THINK OF THAT
PYGM II SD(219)	THE PATHOS OF THIS DEPLORABLE FIGURE, WITH ITS	INNOCENT	VANITY AND CONSEQUENTIAL AIR, TOUCHES PICKERING,
DOCT II (128)	WHAT WILL HE BE A SOURCE OF FOR THAT POOR	INNOCENT	WIFE OF HIS, WHEN SHE FINDS HIM OUT? /RIDGEON/
JOAN 6 (129)	THEY ARE BEYOND THE BELIEF OF HONEST MEN AND	INNOCENT	WOMEN; YET THEY ALL BEGAN WITH SAINTLY SIMPLETONS.
JOAN 1 (58)	DEPRECATINGLY) OH, SIR: YOU ALWAYS GIVE MY MOST	INNOCENT	WORDS SUCH A TURN! /ROBERT/ I WILL GIVE YOUR NECK
BARB PREFACE(238)	ENOUGH TO BE DUPED BY THE PRETENCE THAT THE	INNOCENT	YOUNG BRIDE AND BRIDEGROOM, PUT FORTH AND CROWNED
DOCT II (120)	HAS TO LEAVE HER A GOOD DEAL ALONE; AND THE POOR	INNOCENT	YOUNG FELLOW-- HE HAS OF COURSE NO IDEA OF MY
WIDO II (31)	ANXIETY) JUST LISTEN TO THIS! WELL, YOU ARE AN	INNOCENT	YOUNG GENTLEMAN. DO YOU SUPPOSE HE SACKED ME
HART PREFACE(7)	GANGRENE, SLAUGHTERING RIGHT AND LEFT UNTIL THE	INNOCENT	YOUNG HAVE PAID FOR THE GUILTY OLD, AND THE ACCOUNT
GENV II (53)	IT WAS OPENED BY THE CONSERVATIVE CANDIDATE: AN	INNOCENT	YOUNG LAD ROLLING IN MONEY. HE SAW THAT I WAS A CUT
POSN PREFACE(408)	OR IN A DANCE, ARE AT THEIR BEST NOT ONLY	INNOCENT	, BUT REFINING IN THEIR EFFECT, WHEREAS THOSE
MILL I (160)	USED TO MONEY; AND IT TRANSFIGURED HIM. I, POOR	INNOCENT	, HAD NO SUSPICION THAT MONEY COULD WORK SUCH
POSN PREFACE(401)	THE THEATRE, MIGHT CONVERT ANY DIALOGUE, HOWEVER	INNOCENT	, INTO JUST THE SORT OF ENTERTAINMENT AGAINST WHICH
GETT PREFACE(204)	THE REACH OF EVERYBODY. NOTHING COULD BE MORE	INNOCENT	, MORE HYGIENIC, MORE IMPORTANT TO THE SOCIAL
ANNA (292)	SIR. /STRAMMFEST/ ANNAJANSKA, THE BEAUTIFUL, THE	INNOCENT	, MY MASTER'S DAUGHTER! (HE BURIES HIS FACE IN
JOAN 6 (128)	ISSUES ON WHICH WE MAY HAVE TO DECLARE HER	INNOCENT	, SHE MAY ESCAPE US ON THE GREAT MAIN ISSUE OF
POSN PREFACE(380)	THE REPRESENTATION WAS LAWFUL AND THE INTENTION	INNOCENT	, SINCE WHEN IT HAS BEEN REPEATEDLY PERFORMED. I AM
MILL I (152)	THEY MAY BE. /EPIFANIA/ THEY ARE PERFECTLY	INNOCENT	, SO FAR. I AM NOT QUITE CONVINCED THAT I LOVE
SUPR I (28)	CONFUSEDLY. AND YET YOU KNOW PERFECTLY WELL HE'S	INNOCENT	, TAVY. /RAMSDEN/ (EXHAUSTED) I AM GLAD YOU ADMIT
HART PREFACE(11)	OF HEARTBREAK HOUSE SMITTEN; AND THE YOUNG, THE	INNOCENT	, THE HOPEFUL EXPIATED THE FOLLY AND WORTHLESSNESS
GETT PREFACE(245)	TAKE ELABORATE PRECAUTIONS AGAINST IT, WHILST THE	INNOCENT	, WHO HAVE BEEN EITHER CAREFULLY KEPT FROM ANY
JOAN 6 (147)	THE CHURCH AND THE LAW. /CAUCHON/ YOU CALL HER	INNOCENT	! /THE INQUISITOR/ OH, QUITE INNOCENT. WHAT DOES

INNOCENTLY

OVER PREFACE(156)	A GENTLEMAN AND A LADY CANNOT BE ALONE TOGETHER	INNOCENTLY	. AND THAT IS MANIFEST BLAZING NONSENSE, THOUGH
ARMS III (71)	TURNING AND STARING AT ONE ANOTHER. HE PROCEEDS	INNOCENTLY	) ALL THAT ADVENTURE WHICH WAS LIFE OR DEATH TO
DEST (169)	(FURIOUSLY) I AM NO FRENCHMAN. /LADY/ (	INNOCENTLY	) I THOUGHT YOU SAID YOU WON THE BATTLE OF LODI
HART I (62)	/MRS HUSHABYE/ -- DE ROUGEMONT? /ELLIE/ (	INNOCENTLY	) NO: DE LAROCHEJAQUELIN. A FRENCH FAMILY. A
SUPR I (21)	ANCESTOR DON JUAN. /RAMSDEN/ DON JUAN! /ANN/ (	INNOCENTLY	) OH, IS THERE HARM IN IT? I DIDNT KNOW. THEN I
ARMS II (34)	FEELS THE NEED OF SOME RELIEF AFTER IT. /LOUKA/ (	INNOCENTLY	) PERHAPS YOU WOULD LIKE SOME COFFEE, SIR? (SHE
DOCT V (176)	IT BECAUSE I WAS IN LOVE WITH YOU. /JENNIFER/ (	INNOCENTLY	SURPRISED) IN LO-- YOU! AN ELDERLY MAN!
DEST (176)	CARE: DO YOU HEAR? YOU MAY GO TOO FAR. /LADY/ (	INNOCENTLY	TURNING HER FACE TO HIM) WHATS THE MATTER?

INNOCENTS

LION PREFACE(88)	REJECT MATTHEW'S STORY OF THE MASSACRE OF THE	INNOCENTS	AND THE FLIGHT INTO EGYPT WITHOUT CEREMONY. THE
LION PREFACE(21)	TURNS ON THE CREDIBILITY OF THE MASSACRE OF THE	INNOCENTS	AND THE FLIGHT INTO EGYPT. WE MAY FORGET THEM, AND

INNOCUOUS

POSN PREFACE(390)	AND WHAT WHOLESOME, WHAT POISONOUS AND WHAT	INNOCUOUS	: WHAT HE CAN DO IS TO PREVENT ANYBODY WHO HAS NOT

INNOVATING

JOAN PREFACE(32)	VIRTUE WHOSE PRIVATE JUDGMENT IS PRIVILEGED. MANY	INNOVATING	SAINTS, NOTABLY FRANCIS AND CLARE, HAVE BEEN IN

INNOVATION

METH PREFACE(R10)	THE SUREST WAY TO PRODUCE AN EFFECT OF DARING	INNOVATION	AND ORIGINALITY WAS TO REVIVE THE ANCIENT
2TRU PREFACE(18)	AND IN NO WAY PLEDGED AGAINST CHANGE AND	INNOVATION	AS SUCH, BUT ESSENTIALLY THE SYSTEM IS THAT OF
MTH2 (77)	MEAT-EATING, THE OTHER WAS HORRIFIED AT THE	INNOVATION	, WITH THE FEROCITY WHICH IS STILL CHARACTERISTIC
CYMB FORWORD(133)	THE LATE WILLIAM POEL, INTRODUCED THE STARTLING	INNOVATION	OF PERFORMING THE PLAYS IN THE WEST END OF LONDON
POSN PREFACE(383)	TOLERATED IMMORALITY. HE DID NOT ADOPT ANY	INNOVATION	UNTIL IT HAD BECOME MORAL; AND THEN HE ADOPTED
SIM PREFACE(17)	ENJOYED THE HIGHEST RESPECTABILITY, IS AN	INNOVATION	WHICH SHOULD BE CARRIED OUT WITH THE UTMOST

INNOVATOR

DOCT PREFACE(77)	AND THE OPSONIST THAT OTHER REMARKABLE	INNOVATOR	, THE SWEDISH MASSEUR, WHO DOES NOT THEORIZE ABOUT

INNQUERY

CAPT III (290)	O' CLAWK. (HE RISES). CAPTAIN BRASSBOUND: THIS	INNQUERY	HAS ELICITED NO REASON WHY I SHOULD DETAIN YOU OR

INNUMERABLE

MIS. PREFACE(45)	TWO CENTURIES DESTROYED THE NATURAL HAPPINESS OF	INNUMERABLE	CHILDREN BY PERSUADING PIOUS PARENTS THAT IT IS
GENV PREFACE(13)	ADVENTURES OF CROMWELL, NAPOLEON, HITLER, AND THE	INNUMERABLE	CONQUISTADORES AND UPSTART PRESIDENTS OF SOUTH
BULL PREFACE(33)	A TERRIFIED AND INCONSIDERATE REARRANGEMENT.	INNUMERABLE	EXPERIMENTS IN LOCAL GOVERNMENT HAVE SHEWN THAT
SUPR III (112)	ARE WE AGREED THAT LIFE IS A FORCE WHICH HAS MADE	INNUMERABLE	EXPERIMENTS IN ORGANIZING ITSELF; THAT THE
DOCT PREFACE(11)	THE LITERARY AND ARTISTIC CONSPIRACY, AND THE	INNUMERABLE	INDUSTRIAL, COMMERCIAL, AND FINANCIAL
METH PREFACE(R46)	IT LONG BEFORE WE HAVE COME TO THE END OF THE	INNUMERABLE	INSTANCES AND ILLUSTRATIONS OF WHICH THE BOOK
JOAN 6 (131)	EVEN WHEN GUILTY, IF REPENTANCE FOLLOWS SIN.	INNUMERABLE	LIVES OF HERETICS HAVE BEEN SAVED BECAUSE THE
JOAN PREFACE(3)	LATER, TO SAY NOTHING OF CATALINA DE ERAUSO AND	INNUMERABLE	OBSCURE HEROINES WHO HAVE DISGUISED THEMSELVES
LION PREFACE(69)	FOR THE GRATIFICATION OF SEX AND RAISE UP	INNUMERABLE	OBSTACLES TO IT; WHICH WILL SANCTIFY IT AND

INOCULATE

DOCT I (90)	OPSONIN INDEX IN FIGURES. IF THE FIGURE IS ONE,	INOCULATE	AND CURE: IT IT'S UNDER POINT EIGHT, INOCULATE AND
DOCT I (91)	INOCULATE AND CURE: IT IT'S UNDER POINT EIGHT,	INOCULATE	AND KILL. THATS MY DISCOVERY: THE MOST IMPORTANT
JOAN PREFACE(40)	VIRTUALLY COMPULSORY BAPTISM. BUT COMPULSION TO	INOCULATE	IS OBJECTED TO AS A CRUDELY UNSCIENTIFIC AND
DOCT PREFACE(25)	THE GERM HAS NOT YET BEEN DETECTED, WHAT YOU	INOCULATE	IS SIMPLY UNDEFINED MATTER THAT HAS BEEN SCRAPED
PHIL II (107)	AS WELL AS VACCINATED. BUT IT WAS TOO LATE TO	INOCULATE	POOR PAPA. ALL THEY COULD DO WAS TO PROLONG HIS
DOCT PREFACE(25)	THE BREEDING AND HOUSING OF ENOUGH MICROBES TO	INOCULATE	THE ENTIRE POPULATION OF THE GLOBE SINCE HUMAN
SUPR III (133)	SNATCH THE BABIES FROM THE WATER SPRINKLING AND	INOCULATE	THEM WITH DISEASE TO SAVE THEM FROM CATCHING IT
DOCT I (90)	DEPENDS ON YOUR INOCULATING AT THE RIGHT MOMENT.	INOCULATE	WHEN THE PATIENT IS IN THE NEGATIVE PHASE AND YOU
DOCT I (90)	PATIENT IS IN THE NEGATIVE PHASE AND YOU KILL:	INOCULATE	WHEN THE PATIENT IS IN THE POSITIVE PHASE AND YOU
METH PREFACE(R14)	THAT PARALYSE ORDINARY MINDS. WHEN THE DOCTORS	INOCULATE	YOU AND THE HOMEOPATHISTS DOSE YOU, THEY GIVE YOU
METH PREFACE(R14)	THEY WANT TO RID YOU OF A DISEASE OR A SYMPTOM,	INOCULATE	YOU WITH THAT DISEASE OR GIVE YOU A DRUG THAT

INOCULATED

DOCT PREFACE(75)	WHEN SIR ALMROTH WRIGHT POINTED OUT THAT IF YOU	INOCULATED	A PATIENT WITH PATHOGENIC GERMS AT A MOMENT WHEN
PHIL II (107)	AND NOW HE DECLARES THAT EVERYBODY SHOULD BE	INOCULATED	AGAINST THEM AS WELL AS VACCINATED. BUT IT WAS
2TRU I (32)	BUT I HAVE FOUND IT SO NECESSARY MYSELF. I WAS	INOCULATED	AGAINST INFLUENZA THREE YEARS AGO; AND I HAVE HAD
HART PREFACE(10)	KNOWLEDGE, THEY OPERATED AND VIVISECTED AND	INOCULATED	AND LIED ON A STUPENDOUS SCALE, CLAMORING FOR AND
DOCT PREFACE(26)	THE TROUBLE DOES NOT END WITH THE MATTER TO BE	INOCULATED	. THERE IS THE QUESTION OF THE CONDITION OF THE
DOCT I (90)	THE UPS AND DOWNS, AS THE CASE MAY BE. IF WE HAD	INOCULATED	JANE MARSH WHEN HER BUTTER FACTORY WAS ON THE
DOCT I (104)	WITH PERFECTLY SATISFACTORY RESULTS. I	INOCULATED	THE LITTLE PRINCE WITH YOUR STUFF, RIDGEON,
DOCT I (104)	OUGHT TO HAVE BEEN. THE CONSEQUENCE WAS THAT I	INOCULATED	THE TYPHOID CASE FOR TETANUS AND THE TETANUS CASE

INOCULATING

DOCT I (90)	THE NEGATIVE PHASE. EVERYTHING DEPENDS ON YOUR	INOCULATING	AT THE RIGHT MOMENT. INOCULATE WHEN THE PATIENT
2TRU I (32)	I DONT BELIEVE IN INOCULATIONS. BUT IT IS NO USE	INOCULATING	WHEN THE PATIENT IS ALREADY FULLY INFECTED. /THE
DOCT PREFACE(26)	A FEW DOCTORS HAVE NOW LEARNT THE DANGER OF	INOCULATING	WITHOUT ANY REFERENCE TO THE PATIENT'S " OPSONIC

INOCULATION

DOCT I (103)	INOCULATION! DO YOU MEAN SMALLPOX	INOCULATION	? /SIR PATRICK/ YES. IN THE PRIVACY OF OUR
2TRU I (32)	WILL SEE WHAT CAN BE DONE. SHE SHALL HAVE BOTH AN	INOCULATION	AND A NEW PRESCRIPTION. WILL THAT SET YOUR MIND
DOCT PREFACE(25)	TO DISTINGUISH THE DISEASE PRODUCED BY THEIR	INOCULATION	AND THE DISEASE THEY HAVE ACCUSED THE PATIENT OF
DOCT PREFACE(52)	VACCINATION IS CARRIED OUT WITH AN ANTI-JENNERIAN	INOCULATION	BECAUSE THE PUBLIC WOULD HAVE IT SO IN SPITE OF
DOCT I (91)	DONT DIE NOW. /SIR PATRICK/ AND MINE DO WHEN MY	INOCULATION	CATCHES THEM IN THE NEGATIVE PHASE, AS YOU CALL
DOCT I (105)	REST. THAT IS WHY SIR PATRICK'S FATHER FOUND THAT	INOCULATION	CURED ALL FEVERS. IT STIMULATED THE PHAGOCYTES.
DOCT I (90)	ALWAYS RHYTHMICAL, YOU KNOW-- AND THAT WHAT THE	INOCULATION	DOES IS TO STIMULATE THE UPS AND DOWNS, AS THE
DOCT PREFACE(75)	LYING THAT WAS NECESSARY TO SAVE THE CREDIT OF	INOCULATION	IN THOSE DAYS WAS PRODIGIOUS; AND HAD IT NOT
2TRU I (32)	IT EVERY FEBRUARY. DO, TO PLEASE ME, GIVE HER AN	INOCULATION	. I FEEL SUCH A RESPONSIBILITY IF ANYTHING IS
DOCT I (88)	PROUD OF. BUT YOUR DISCOVERY'S NOT NEW. IT'S ONLY	INOCULATION	. MY FATHER PRACTISED INOCULATION UNTIL IT WAS
DOCT I (103)	HE SAID WHAT YOU SAY. NO MORE DRUGS. NOTHING BUT	INOCULATION	. /B.B./ (ALMOST CONTEMPTUOUSLY) INOCULATION!
DOCT I (88)	WAS RIGHT AFTER ALL. YOUVE BROUGHT US BACK TO	INOCULATION	. /RIDGEON/ I KNOW NOTHING ABOUT SMALLPOX. MY
DOCT PREFACE(26)	OF TOBACCO AND PAPERS OF PINS. THE PERILS OF	INOCULATION	. THE TROUBLE DOES NOT END WITH THE MATTER TO BE
DOCT PREFACE(25)	WELL. ANYTHING MAY HAPPEN AS THE RESULT OF SUCH	INOCULATION	. YET THIS IS THE ONLY STUFF OF THE KIND WHICH
DOCT PREFACE(74)	IMMUNIZATION FROM BACTERIAL DISEASES BY THE	INOCULATION	OF " VACCINES" MADE OF THEIR OWN BACTERIA: A
JOAN PREFACE(40)	TYPICAL MODERN EXAMPLE AND CONTRAST IS COMPULSORY	INOCULATION	REPLACING WHAT WAS VIRTUALLY COMPULSORY BAPTISM.
DOCT PREFACE(25)	BUT THE PRECAUTIONS NECESSARY TO INSURE THAT THE	INOCULATION	SHALL CONSIST OF NOTHING ELSE BUT THE REQUIRED
DOCT I (89)	FROM JANE'S CASE? /RIDGEON/ I FOUND OUT THAT THE	INOCULATION	THAT OUGHT TO CURE SOMETIMES KILLS. /SIR
DOCT I (88)	NEW. IT'S ONLY INOCULATION. MY FATHER PRACTISED	INOCULATION	UNTIL IT WAS MADE CRIMINAL IN EIGHTEEN-FORTY.
DOCT I (103)	FATHER USED TO DECLARE HIS BELIEF THAT SMALLPOX	INOCULATION	WAS GOOD, NOT ONLY FOR SMALLPOX, BUT FOR ALL
DOCT PREFACE(75)	KILL HIM, WHEREAS IF YOU MADE PRECISELY THE SAME	INOCULATION	WHEN THE COOKING POWER WAS RISING TO ONE OF ITS
BARB PREFACE(214)	WHO SUFFERS FROM IT AND PUNISHING THEM BY	INOCULATION	WITH SMALLPOX, I SHOULD BE LAUGHED AT; FOR
DOCT PREFACE(29)	PRACTICE IT IS FOUND THAT A SUFFICIENTLY SMALL	INOCULATION	WITH TYPHOID RALLIES OUR POWERS TO RESIST THE
DOCT PREFACE(25)	CONTRACTED THIS DISEASE INDEPENDENTLY OF THE	INOCULATION	, AN EXCUSE WHICH NATURALLY DOES NOT MAKE THE
DOCT PREFACE(26)	THE PATIENT'S " OPSONIC INDEX" AT THE MOMENT OF	INOCULATION	, AND THOUGH THOSE OTHER DOCTORS WHO ARE
DOCT PREFACE(26)	WAS UNLUCKY, THAT THE RESULTS WERE NOT DUE TO THE	INOCULATION	, BUT TO SOME OTHER CAUSE: A FAVORITE AND NOT
DOCT PREFACE(27)	EQUALLY VAUNTED FORERUNNER, EIGHTEENTH CENTURY	INOCULATION	, BY A PURELY REACTIONARY LAW MAKING ALL SORTS
DOCT PREFACE(53)	ATTRIBUTED IT TO THE OLDER PRACTICE OF SMALLPOX	INOCULATION	, BY WHICH VOLTAIRE, CATHERINE II AND LADY MARY
DOCT PREFACE(24)	KNOWN; AND DOCTORS, TO SAVE THE CREDIT OF THE	INOCULATION	, HAVE BEEN DRIVEN TO ACCUSE THEIR PATIENT OR
DOCT PREFACE(27)	PUBLIC HOSPITALS. WHEN IT COMES TO PROPHYLACTIC	INOCULATION	, THE ALTERNATIVE LIES BETWEEN THE COMPLETE
DOCT PREFACE(24)	NOR THE PATIENT IS QUITE SATISFIED UNLESS THE	INOCULATION	" TAKES": THAT IS, UNLESS IT PRODUCES
DOCT I (103)	BUT INOCULATION. /B.B./ (ALMOST CONTEMPTUOUSLY)	INOCULATION	! DO YOU MEAN SMALLPOX INOCULATION? /SIR

INOCULATIONISTS

MTH2 (52)	QUAKERS, OF CHRISTIAN SCIENTISTS AND COMPULSORY	INOCULATIONISTS	, OF SYNDICALISTS AND BUREAUCRATS: IN SHORT,

INOCULATIONS

DOCT I (89)	COULD HAVE TOLD YOU THAT. IVE TRIED THESE MODERN	INOCULATIONS	A BIT MYSELF. IVE KILLED PEOPLE WITH THEM; AND
HART PREFACE(10)	TERROR OF INFECTION AND DEATH. THEY PRESCRIBED	INOCULATIONS	AND OPERATIONS. WHATEVER PART OF A HUMAN BEING
FABL PREFACE(90)	THE PATIENT IS NOT ILL. IN THE ARMY SOME THIRTY	INOCULATIONS	ARE PRACTICALLY COMPULSORY; AND VACCINATION IS
DOCT PREFACE(76)	RALPH BLOOMFIELD BONINGTON'S WAY OF ADMINISTERING	INOCULATIONS	AS IF THEY WERE SPOONFULS OF SQUILLS MAY
2TRU I (32)	MRS MOPPLY: I NEVER SAID THAT I DONT BELIEVE IN	INOCULATIONS	. BUT IT IS NO USE INOCULATING WHEN THE PATIENT
JOAN PREFACE(16)	ANTIBODIES AGAINST ALL POSSIBLE INFECTIONS BY	INOCULATIONS	OF INFECTED BACTERIA AND SERUM FROM INFECTED
2TRU I (32)	COMES BACK). DOCTOR: I KNOW YOU DONT BELIEVE IN	INOCULATIONS	; BUT I CANT HELP THINKING SHE OUGHT TO HAVE
2TRU I (34)	YOU SEE, IT'S EASIER TO BELIEVE IN BOTTLES AND	INOCULATIONS	THAN IN ONESELF AND IN THAT MYSTERIOUS POWER
DOCT PREFACE(76)	NOT LED HIM TO THE CONCLUSION THAT THE CUSTOMARY	INOCULATIONS	WERE VERY MUCH TOO POWERFUL, AND THAT A
SUPR HANDBOK(203)	MODERN FORM OF PATENT MEDICINES AND PROPHYLACTIC	INOCULATIONS	, IS RAMPANT; THE LANDOWNER WHO IS NO LONGER
2TRU I (34)	AS A RHINOCEROS. CURSE YOUR SILLY BOTTLES AND	INOCULATIONS	! WHY DONT YOU CHUCK THEM AND TURN FAITH

INOCULATORY

DOCT PREFACE(24)	A DOCTOR IS THE OBJECTION THAT PROPHYLAXIS BY THE	INOCULATORY	METHODS MOST IN VOGUE IS AN ECONOMIC

INOFFENSIVE

MTH5 (248)	MODELLED, AND SAW THEM VANISH IN AN INSTANT INTO	INOFFENSIVE	DUST. /THE SHE-ANCIENT/ SPEAK, ARJILLAX: YOU WHO
NEVR II (240)	TABLE! /WAITER/ (HOLDING THE CHAIR FOR HIM WITH	INOFFENSIVE	ENCOURAGEMENT) THIS END, SIR. (CRAMPTON
POSN PREFACE(401)	TURNING WHAT WAS MEANT AS AN IMPROPRIETY INTO AN	INOFFENSIVE	STROKE OF REALISM; YET IT IS NONE THE LESS CLEAR

INOPERATIVE

GETT PREFACE(187)	IT HAS BEEN REDUCED TO A PRIVATE AND SOCIALLY	INOPERATIVE	ECCENTRICITY BY THE INTRODUCTION OF CIVIL

		INOPPORTUNE	
BARB I SD(259)	SENSE OF HUMOR; WHICH PLUNGES HIM AT THE MOST	INOPPORTUNE	MOMENTS INTO PAROXYSMS OF IMPERFECTLY SUPPRESSED
POSN PREFACE(387)	TO POLITICAL FACTS, BECOME SO INCONVENIENT AND	INOPPORTUNE	THAT FOREIGN OFFICES TAKE THE TROUBLE TO HAVE
		INOPPORTUNELY	
HART II (109)	WE SHALL HAVE TO TAKE UP A COLLECTION FOR THIS	INOPPORTUNELY	CONTRITE SINNER. /LADY UTTERWORD/ BUT TWENTY
SUPR PREFACE(R32)	BETWEEN THE DORRIT AND CLENNAM FAMILIES SO	INOPPORTUNELY	DISCOVERED BY MONSIEUR RIGAUD BLANDOIS. THE
		INORDINATE	
GETT PREFACE(189)	TO ATTACK MARRIAGE BECAUSE IT THWARTED HIS	INORDINATE	AFFECTIONS AND PREVENTED HIM FROM MAKING LIFE A
LADY (244)	WITH INTOLERANT IMPORTANCE) NAME NOT THAT	INORDINATE	MAN IN THE SAME BREATH WITH STRATFORD'S WORTHIEST
		INORDINATELY	
JOAN PREFACE(53)	THEIR LAST TRAINS: AND CURSE ME FOR WRITING SUCH	INORDINATELY	LONG AND INTOLERABLY DREARY AND MEANINGLESS
MTH4 I (161)	TO CREDIT EVERY ADVANCE IN CIVILIZATION TO YOUR	INORDINATELY	LONG LIVES. DO YOU NOT KNOW THAT THIS QUESTION
2TRU PREFACE(21)	MAJORITY ARE FORCED TO MAINTAIN A MINORITY	INORDINATELY	RICH AND PASSIONATELY CONVINCED THAT LABOR IS
		INQUEST	
CURE (229)	I'M NOT TREATING YOU WITH A VIEW TO A CORONER'S	INQUEST	. YOU KNOW, DONT YOU, THAT OPIUM IS A POISON?
BARB II (281)	/SHIRLEY/ I DID. ME AGE COME OUT AT A CORONER'S	INQUEST	ON ME DAUGHTER. /BARBARA/ STEADY? /SHIRLEY/
DOCT PREFACE(79)	MAKING IT THE SUBJECT OF A REASONABLY CONDUCTED	INQUEST	; AND EXECUTE THE DOCTOR, IF NECESSARY, AS A DOCTOR,
		INQUIRE	
DEVL I SD(3)	THESE IDEALIZATIONS IT IS NOT HERE NECESSARY TO	INQUIRE	: SUFFICE IT TO SAY, WITHOUT PREJUDICE, THAT THEY
WIDO I (14)	A FATHER-- THE FATHER OF A MOTHERLESS GIRL-- TO	INQUIRE	INTO AT ONCE. MY DAUGHTER, PERHAPS FOOLISHLY, HAS
POSN PREFACE(361)	BOTH HOUSES OF PARLIAMENT WHICH SAT LAST YEAR TO	INQUIRE	INTO THE WORKING OF THE CENSORSHIP, AGAINST WHICH IT
CLEO PRO2 (99)	BUT ONLY THE HIGH GODS. WE WENT A JOURNEY TO	INQUIRE	OF PTOLEMY WHY HE HAD DRIVEN CLEOPATRA INTO SYRIA,
BASH III (119)	SHORT, A PRIZEFIGHT. MY SOLE PURPOSE HERE IS TO	INQUIRE	WHETHER YOUR LADYSHIP ANY BAD CHARACTERS THIS
		INQUIRED	
NEVR II (244)	I SUPPOSE THE PORTUGUESE RELIGION. I NEVER	INQUIRED	. /DOLLY/ THE SERVANTS COME IN LENT AND KNEEL DOWN
		INQUIRER	
UNPL PREFACE(R18)	IN WELCOMING A POSSIBLE CUSTOMER IN EVERY	INQUIRER	CAN CORRECT THEIR HABIT OF TREATING EVERYBODY WHO
		INQUIRES	
SUPR HANDBOK(218)	THAT IS WHY MOST MEN DREAD IT. THE DUKE	INQUIRES	CONTEMPTUOUSLY WHETHER HIS GAMEKEEPER IS THE EQUAL
		INQUIRIES	
JOAN 6 (129)	THAT WE HAVE SENT TO THE GIRL'S VILLAGE TO MAKE	INQUIRIES	ABOUT HER; AND THERE IS PRACTICALLY NOTHING
JOAN 6 (135)	THAT IS NOT SO, MASTER, EXCEPT WHEN THE	INQUIRIES	ARE CARRIED ON BY PEOPLE WHO DO NOT KNOW THEIR
LION PREFACE(43)	OF THE EVANGELISTS WOULD HAVE BEEN THAT ALL THESE	INQUIRIES	ARE IDLE, BECAUSE IF JESUS HAD WISHED TO ESCAPE,
2TRU II (76)	ANXIOUS TO GET RID OF ME; SO I DID NOT PRESS MY	INQUIRIES	, BUT THAT ACCOUNTS FOR THE MAROONS. /TALLBOYS/
		INQUIRING	
JOAN 6 (128)	A DOZEN OTHER THINGS WHICH YOU WERE DILIGENTLY	INQUIRING	INTO UNTIL MY ARRIVAL. THERE IS NOT A VILLAGE GIRL
JOAN 6,SD(146)	SILENCE. CAUCHON TURNS TO THE INQUISITOR WITH AN	INQUIRING	LOOK. THE INQUISITOR NODS AFFIRMATIVELY. THEY RISE
SUPR III (124)	MY ADVANCES, PROVIDED THEY WERE HONORABLE. ON	INQUIRING	WHAT THAT PROVISO MEANT, I FOUND THAT IT MEANT
MIS. PREFACE(49)	MY DISAPPEARANCE; THERETHROUGH. IT MAY BE WORTH	INQUIRING	WHERE I SHOULD HAVE GONE TO. I SHOULD SAY THAT
		INQUIRINGLY	
PHIL I (76)	A MOVEMENT TOWARDS THE DOOR, BUT STOPS AND LOOKS	INQUIRINGLY	AT CHARTERIS AS JULIA SPRINGS UP TO INTERCEPT
MRS IV (240)	CONCERNED) MY DEAR MISS WARREN: I-- (LOOKING	INQUIRINGLY	AT FRANK) IS ANYTHING THE MATTER? /FRANK/ SHE
MTH2 SD(40)	GOES OUT WITH THE LETTERS). THE TWO BROTHERS LOOK	INQUIRINGLY	AT HASLAM. /HASLAM/ SILLY GIRL! GOING TO MARRY
SUPR II SD(57)	NOTE IN ITS CHEERFULNESS, THEY TURN AND LOOK	INQUIRINGLY	AT HIM. BUT HE IS BUSY WITH HIS PAPER; AND
BULL I (76)	NOT TOO STHRONG. (BROADBENT STOPS AND LOOKS	INQUIRINGLY	AT HIM). SAY HALF-AN-HALF. (BROADBENT, SOMEWHAT
MTH4 I (141)	WOMAN/ (LOOKING AT HER HANDS, AND THEN LOOKING	INQUIRINGLY	AT HIM) WHERE? /THE ELDERLY GENTLEMAN/ (
LION II (140)	IN WILD APPLAUSE. THE GLADIATORS LISTEN AND LOOK	INQUIRINGLY	AT ONE ANOTHER), /THE EDITOR/ WHATS UP NOW?
SUPR III SD(140)	LOOKS HARD AT THE BRIGANDS; AND THEN	INQUIRINGLY	AT TANNER. /THE OFFICER/ WHO ARE THESE MEN,
WIDO I (7)	ALLOW ME TO INTRODUCE YOU TO-- ER--? (HE LOOKS	INQUIRINGLY	AT THE GENTLEMAN, WAITING FOR THE NAME). /THE
NEVR IV (288)	(CRAMPTON ASSENTS WITH A GRUNT. THE WAITER LOOKS	INQUIRINGLY	AT VALENTINE). /VALENTINE/ I LIKE CUCUMBER.
PHIL I (86)	ANGUISH IN HER VOICE) DADDY! (CUTHBERTSON LOOKS	INQUIRINGLY	ROUND AT HER), /CRAVEN/ THERE, THERE, MY DEAR: I
JOAN EPILOG (161)	DE STOGUMBER, AT YOUR SERVICE. (HE LOOKS AT THEM	INQUIRINGLY	) DID YOU SAY ANYTHING? I AM A LITTLE DEAF,
NEVR I (204)	(DUBIOUSLY) HM! /DOLLY/ (ECHOING HIM	INQUIRINGLY	) HM? PHIL: HE PREFERS PEOPLE WHOSE MINDS ARE
MIS. (160)	T-A-R-L-E-T-O-N. ER--? (SHE LOOKS AT HIM	INQUIRINGLY	). /TARLETON/ (PROMPTLY) FIFTY-EIGHT. /LINA/
NEVR II (241)	MOTHER AND MISS GLORIA AS BEFORE; AND-- (TURNING	INQUIRINGLY	TO CRAMPTON) EH? /CRAMPTON/ (SCOWLING AND
MTH2 SD(67)	BROTHERS BARNABAS, DADDY, LUBIN AND BURGE TURN	INQUIRINGLY	TO FRANKLYN, SUSPECTING A MOVE TO FORM A NEW
		INQUIRY	
JOAN EPILOG (153)	YOUR BONNET ABOUT THE MAID. HAVE YOU BEEN AT THE	INQUIRY	? /LADVENU/ I HAVE GIVEN MY TESTIMONY. /CHARLES/ IS
DOCT PREFACE(40)	WITHOUT LABORATORY EXPERIMENTS BY A SIMPLE	INQUIRY	ADDRESSED TO THE NEAREST POLICEMAN, OR, FAILING HIM,
JOAN PREFACE(18)	BE PUZZLED AND INCREDULOUS, BUT A VERY LITTLE	INQUIRY	AMONG THEIR ACQUAINTANCES WILL REVEAL TO THEM THAT
CAPT III (281)	A MOMENT. I WANT TO SPEAK TO SOMEBODY BEFORE THE	INQUIRY	BEGINS. (SHE HURRIES OUT). /KEARNEY/ THERE IS
MIS. PREFACE(13)	INEVITABLE. YOU CANNOT HOLD AN IMPARTIAL JUDICIAL	INQUIRY	EVERY TIME A CHILD MISBEHAVES ITSELF. TO ALLOW THE
INCA (240)	YOUR HIGHNESS; BUT I HAVE RECEIVED AN URGENT	INQUIRY	FOR ROOMS FROM AN ENGLISH FAMILY OF IMPORTANCE; AND
JOAN EPILOG (153)	THE LYING SENTENCE AND THE PITILESS FIRE. AT THIS	INQUIRY	FROM WHICH I HAVE JUST COME, THERE WAS SHAMELESS
MIS. PREFACE(69)	HOUR IN REMEDYING IT. THE COSTER MAY RESENT THE	INQUIRY	INSTEAD OF BEING AMUSED BY IT; BUT HIS ANSWER, IF
JOAN EPILOG (163)	KNOWN AS THE MAID, HAVING BEEN THE SUBJECT OF AN	INQUIRY	INSTITUTED BY THE BISHOP OF ORLEANS -- /JOAN/ (
SIM PREFACE(16)	BEING, COMING LITERALLY OUT OF THE BLUE; BUT HIS	INQUIRY	IS NOT WHETHER YOU BELIEVE IN TWEEDLEDUM OR
GETT PREFACE(203)	WHEN THEY TAKE THE REMEDY INTO THEIR OWN HANDS AN	INQUIRY	IS SOON BEGUN. BUT WHAT IS NOW MAKING SOME ACTION IN
MIS. (165)	EMPTY. HIS EXHAUSTION DISABLES HIM FROM FURTHER	INQUIRY	. HE DABS HIS BROW WITH HIS HANDKERCHIEF, AND WALKS
CAPT III (276)	SO SORRY FOR YOU, HOWARD, ABOUT THIS UNFORTUNATE	INQUIRY	. /SIR HOWARD/ (SWINGING ROUND ON HIS CHAIR,
JOAN 6 (129)	THAT MEN OF SUFFICIENTLY LARGE MIND TO CONDUCT AN	INQUIRY	LIKE THIS WOULD CONSIDER SERIOUS. I AGREE WITH MY
CAPT III (275)	THAT WE ARE BOUND NOT TO REPEAT ANYTHING AT THE	INQUIRY	THAT THE CADI SAID. HE DIDNT KNOW, YOU SEE. /RANKIN/
MRS PREFACE(156)	WAY. BUT ALAS! THAT CERTAIN KIND TURNS OUT ON	INQUIRY	TO BE SIMPLY THE PRETTY, DAINTY KIND: THAT IS, THE
DEVL EPILOG (81)	OF GERMAIN'S NEGLECT, BURGOYNE'S DEMAND FOR AN	INQUIRY	WAS DEFEATED IN THE HOUSE OF COMMONS BY THE COURT
JOAN PREFACE(31)	WERE TRAPS, IS THAT IT HAS THE SUPPORT OF THE	INQUIRY	WHICH REHABILITATED HER TWENTYFIVE YEARS LATER. BUT
CAPT III (272)	HANDSOME SHEIKH SIDI? I MUST SEE THEM BEFORE THE	INQUIRY	, OR THEYLL GIVE CAPTAIN KEARNEY QUITE A FALSE
AUGS (279)	HIS HAND) STOP. REMEMBER: IF THERE SHOULD BE AN	INQUIRY	, YOU MUST BE ABLE TO SWEAR THAT YOU NEVER SHEWED
CAPT III (272)	DOWN) HOW NICE YOUVE MADE THE ROOM FOR THE	INQUIRY	! /RANKIN/ (DOUBTFULLY) I COULD WISH THERE WERE
		INQUISITION	
JOAN PREFACE(31)	AND HER FATE HAD THEY BEEN DEALT WITH BY THE	INQUISITION	: THAT IS WHY THEIR ACCOUNTS OF THE TRIAL ARE AS
SIM PREFACE(18)	THEM IS A CRUEL WASTE OF TIME. THERE SHOULD BE AN	INQUISITION	ALWAYS AVAILABLE TO CONSIDER WHETHER THESE HUMAN
JOAN PREFACE(42)	STRICT LEGALITY OF PROCEDURE AS JOAN HAD FROM THE	INQUISITION	AND FROM THE SPIRIT OF THE MIDDLE AGES EVEN WHEN
SIM PREFACE(10)	THE STAR CHAMBER IF IT HAD CALLED ITSELF AN	INQUISITION	AND GIVEN LAUD THE OFFICIAL TITLE BORNE BY
SIM PREFACE(17)	FINALLY TAKES THE MATTER OUT OF THE HANDS OF THE	INQUISITION	AND MAKES AN OVERDRAFT AN ORDINARY OFFENCE TO BE
SIM PREFACE(11)	ORGANIZED THE TCHEKA. NOW THE TCHEKA, BEING AN	INQUISITION	AND NOT AN ORDINARY POLICE COURT DEALING UNDER
JOAN PREFACE(39)	TO AN EXTENT THAT WOULD HAVE HORRIFIED THE	INQUISITION	AND STAGGERED ARCHBISHOP LAUD. OUR CREDULITY IS
POSN PREFACE(385)	ADVOCATES OF SHOCKINGLY IMMORAL DOCTRINES, THE	INQUISITION	AND THE STAR CHAMBER, WHICH WERE NOTHING BUT
DOCT PREFACE(78)	SCEPTICISM AND ACTIVITY. SUCH ABOMINATIONS AS THE	INQUISITION	AND THE VACCINATION ACTS ARE POSSIBLE ONLY IN
JOAN 6 (129)	STAMPED OUT IN TIME. THE RECORDS OF THE HOLY	INQUISITION	ARE FULL OF HISTORIES WE DARE NOT GIVE TO THE
SIM PREFACE(12)	BEFORE US. WE ARE TAUGHT TO THINK OF AN	INQUISITION	AS A TRIBUNAL WHICH HAS TO DECIDE WHETHER WE
SIM PREFACE(10)	COUNTRIES IN WHICH THE REFORMATION TRIUMPHED THE	INQUISITION	BECAME SO UNPOPULAR THAT ITS NAME WAS CAREFULLY
FABL PREFACE(77)	CROPPED HAD I LIVED IN THE DAYS OF THE BRITISH	INQUISITION	CALLED THE STAR CHAMBER. NOWADAYS NONCONFORMITY
SIM PREFACE(10)	ABOUT THE PARTHENOGENESIS OF JESUS. THUS THE	INQUISITION	CAME TO BE REMEMBERED IN ENGLAND ONLY AS AN

SIM PREFACE(14)	ABOLISHED THE LADY AND GENTLEMAN EXACTLY AS THE	INQUISITION	CARRIED OUT THE EXECUTIVE WORK OF A CATHOLIC
JOAN EPILOG (166)	THAT YOU WERE INNOCENT. BUT I DO NOT SEE HOW THE	INQUISITION	COULD POSSIBLY BE DISPENSED WITH UNDER EXISTING
JOAN 6 (131)	HOLY OFFICE WOULD DEAL WITH THEM. BEFORE THE HOLY	INQUISITION	EXISTED, AND EVEN NOW WHEN ITS OFFICERS ARE NOT
SIM PREFACE(18)	AN INQUISITION. THE PRECEDENTS ESTABLISHED BY THE	INQUISITION	FURNISH THE MATERIAL FOR A NEW LEGAL CODE.
HART PREFACE(10)	POPE, NOR PARLIAMENT DARE EVER HAVE CLAIMED. THE	INQUISITION	ITSELF WAS A LIBERAL INSTITUTION COMPARED TO THE
2TRU III (93)	MORE HORRIBLE THAN ALL THE ATROCITIES OF THE	INQUISITION	. ITS SPREAD OF ENLIGHTENMENT HAS BEEN A SPREAD
JOAN PREFACE(7)	STAKE TO BEAT THE ROMAN CATHOLIC CHURCH AND THE	INQUISITION	. THE EASIEST WAY TO MAKE THESE INSTITUTIONS THE
SIM PREFACE(18)	INVOLVES A NEW HERESY. A NEW HERESY INVOLVES AN	INQUISITION	. THE PRECEDENTS ESTABLISHED BY THE INQUISITION
JOAN PREFACE(29)	ECCLESIASTICAL COURTS AND THE COURTS OF THE	INQUISITION	(JOAN WAS TRIED BY A COMBINATION OF THE TWO)
SIM PREFACE(10)	TO DEVELOP A NEW JUDICIAL ORGAN, CALLED THE	INQUISITION	OR HOLY OFFICE, TO DEAL WITH HERESY; AND THOUGH
ROCK PREFACE(162)	THAT IS WHY THE RUSSIANS WERE FORCED TO SET UP AN	INQUISITION	OR STAR CHAMBER, CALLED AT FIRST THE CHEKA AND
JOAN 6,SD(122)	THE COURT BEING THE BISHOP'S COURT WITH THE	INQUISITION	PARTICIPATING; HENCE THERE ARE TWO RAISED CHAIRS
JOAN 6 (124)	MYSELF -- THAT IS, TO ASSOCIATE THE HOLY	INQUISITION	-- WITH THE BISHOP'S COURT. I DID NOT AT FIRST
SIM PREFACE(10)	BURNED BOTH. CONCEIVE, THEN, OUR HORROR WHEN THE	INQUISITION	SUDDENLY ROSE UP AGAIN IN RUSSIA. IT BEGAN AS
JOAN PREFACE(7)	GOT A FAR FAIRER TRIAL FROM THE CHURCH AND THE	INQUISITION	THAN ANY PRISONER OF HER TYPE AND IN HER
SIM PREFACE(18)	LEGAL CODE. CODIFICATION ENABLES THE WORK OF THE	INQUISITION	TO BE DONE BY AN ORDINARY COURT OF LAW.
JOAN PREFACE(28)	OF THE HIGHEST CHARACTER; AND THAT THE	INQUISITION	WAS A CHAMBER OF HORRORS INVENTED EXPRESSLY AND
JOAN PREFACE(29)	AFTER SITTING FOR MANY WEEKS. THE MODERN MILITARY	INQUISITION	WAS NOT SO SQUEAMISH. IT SHOT HER OUT OF HAND;
2TRU PREFACE(18)	QUARREL BETWEEN THE CHURCH AND THE SPANISH	INQUISITION	WAS THE RESULT. BUT THE RICHES OF THE CHURCH
SUPR HANDBOK(207)	MONSTERS DO. THE FIRES OF SMITHFIELD AND OF THE	INQUISITION	WERE LIGHTED BY EARNESTLY PIOUS PEOPLE, WHO WERE
JOAN 4 (97)	OF YOUR REVEREND LORDSHIP TO DENOUNCE HER TO THE	INQUISITION	, AND HAVE HER BURNT FOR THAT OFFENCE. /CAUCHON/
POSN PREFACE(385)	OF THE STAR CHAMBER. SPAIN DID NOT GET RID OF THE	INQUISITION	, AND PAID FOR THAT OMISSION BY BECOMING A
SIM PREFACE(18)	DONE BY AN ORDINARY COURT OF LAW. THEREUPON THE	INQUISITION	, AS SUCH, DISAPPEARS, PRECISELY AS THE TCHEKA
JOAN PREFACE(52)	NOT ONLY THEMSELVES BUT THE CHURCH AND THE	INQUISITION	, JUST AS WARWICK HAS TO MAKE THE FEUDAL SYSTEM
JOAN PREFACE(50)	VISIBLE AND HUMAN PUPPETS, BUT THE CHURCH, THE	INQUISITION	, THE FEUDAL SYSTEM, WITH DIVINE INSPIRATION
JOAN PREFACE(42)	BUT CAN ANY OF THE MODERN SUBSTITUTES FOR THE	INQUISITION	, THE SPECIAL TRIBUNALS AND COMMISSIONS, THE
JOAN PREFACE(52)	MATTERS AS THE CHURCH, THE FEUDAL SYSTEM, THE	INQUISITION	, THE THEORY OF HERESY AND SO FORTH, ALL OF
LION PREFACE(86)	THE PERSECUTIONS IN ALBI AND ELSEWHERE, THE	INQUISITION	, THE " WARS OF RELIGION" WHICH FOLLOWED THE
JOAN PREFACE(42)	OF THE HOLY SEPULCHRE FROM THE SARACENS. THE	INQUISITION	, WITH ITS ENGLISH EQUIVALENT THE STAR CHAMBER,

INQUISITIONARY

SIM PREFACE(14)	THIS OBVIOUS CONCLUSION; BUT IT MAKES THE SPECIAL	INQUISITIONARY	WORK OF THE TCHEKA INTELLIGIBLE. FOR THE

INQUISITIONS

SIM PREFACE(12)	THE TESTS OF FITNESS TO LIVE ACCEPTED BY THE OLD	INQUISITIONS	. THE PUBLIC NEVER DREAMS OF AN ECONOMIC TEST
SIM PREFACE(10)	BORNE BY TORQUEMADA. IN THE END ALL THE SPECIFIC	INQUISITIONS	PETERED OUT, NOT IN THE LEAST THROUGH A GROWTH
SIM PREFACE(18)	THE SIMPLETON IS NOW CLEAR ENOUGH. WITH AMATEUR	INQUISITIONS	UNDER ONE NAME OR ANOTHER OR NO NAME AT WORK IN

INQUISITIVE

JITT I (16)	FIRST: I HARDLY DARED GO HOME AND FACE ALFRED'S	INQUISITIVE	EYES. BUT HE SAW NOTHING: HIS SELF-CONCEIT IS
WIDO I (10)	TACT! THATS NOT TACT: THATS INQUISITIVENESS.	INQUISITIVE	PEOPLE ALWAYS HAVE A LOT OF PRACTICE IN GETTING
WIDO II (29)	JUDGE OF THE CIRCUMSTANCES THAN I AM. /COKANE/ (	INQUISITIVE	) I THINK YOU OUGHT TO HEAR THE CIRCUMSTANCES,
WIDO I (22)	/COKANE/ (AGAIN OBSEQUIOUS, BUT STILL	INQUISITIVE	) WHAT A REMARKABLE COINCIDENCE! IN WHAT

INQUISITIVELY

NEVR I (200)	SHE SHAKES HER DRESS INTO ORDER: LOOKS	INQUISITIVELY	ABOUT HER; AND GOES TO THE BROAD WINDOW). YOU
WIDO I (17)	THE HOTEL; AND COKANE, WHO HAS BEEN HANGING ABOUT	INQUISITIVELY	, EMERGES FROM THE SHRUBBERY). /TRENCH/ (
HART I SD(59)	BUT IN A DAYDREAM. MRS HUSHABYE, WATCHING HER	INQUISITIVELY	, GOES DELIBERATELY BACK TO THE SOFA AND

INQUISITIVENESS

MIS. PREFACE(15)	IF THE MAIN FACTORS OF NOISE, RESTLESSNESS, AND	INQUISITIVENESS	ARE LEFT OUT OF ACCOUNT, CHILDREN CAN STAND
WIDO I (10)	(CONTEMPTUOUSLY) TACT! THATS NOT TACT: THATS	INQUISITIVENESS	. INQUISITIVE PEOPLE ALWAYS HAVE A LOT OF

INQUISITOR

JOAN 6 (143)	I WILL NOT SIT DOWN. /CAUCHON/ MASTER	INQUISITOR	: THIS MAN HAS CALLED ME A TRAITOR TO MY FACE
JOAN 6,SD(147)	THE MAY DAYLIGHT. ONLY THE BISHOP AND THE	INQUISITOR	ARE LEFT IN THE COURT. /CAUCHON/ (TURNING TO GO)
JOAN EPIL,SD(165)	FRANCE. THE VISION FADES. THE ARCHBISHOP AND THE	INQUISITOR	ARE NOW SEEN ON THE RIGHT AND LEFT OF CAUCHON.
JOAN 6,SD(122)	RAISED CHAIRS SIDE BY SIDE FOR THE BISHOP AND THE	INQUISITOR	AS JUDGES. ROWS OF CHAIRS RADIATING FROM THEM AT
JOAN 6 (140)	SAVE YOU. HIS LORDSHIP IS TRYING TO SAVE YOU. THE	INQUISITOR	COULD NOT BE MORE JUST TO YOU IF YOU WERE HIS OWN
JOAN 6 (123)	YOUR REVERENCE IS MOST WELCOME. WE HAVE NO	INQUISITOR	IN ENGLAND, UNFORTUNATELY; THOUGH WE MISS HIM
JOAN 6 (123)	ST DOMINIC. HE IS ACTING AS DEPUTY FOR THE CHIEF	INQUISITOR	INTO THE EVIL OF HERESY IN FRANCE. BROTHER JOHN:
DOCT PREFACE(30)	A SOUTH SEA BUCCANEER, OR A PHILOSOPHER FROM AN	INQUISITOR	. FOR HERE WE LOOK IN VAIN FOR EITHER AN ECONOMIC
GETT PREFACE(193)	A SENSELESS STUPIDITY THAT WOULD HAVE REVOLTED AN	INQUISITOR	. IN SHORT, DEAR READER, THEY WERE VERY LIKE YOU
JOAN PREFACE(51)	BY THE TEMPORAL SITUATION. NEITHER DOES THE	INQUISITOR	LEMAITRE, IN SUCH SCANTY ACCOUNTS OF HIM AS ARE
JOAN PREFACE(49)	TYRANT AND A BULLY INSTEAD OF A CATHOLIC, AND THE	INQUISITOR	LEMAITRE WOULD HAVE BEEN A SADIST INSTEAD OF A
JOAN 6,SD(146)	TO THE INQUISITOR WITH AN INQUIRING LOOK. THE	INQUISITOR	NODS AFFIRMATIVELY. THEY RISE SOLEMNLY, AND
JOAN PREFACE(50)	CONCERN US. THE RASCALLY BISHOP AND THE CRUEL	INQUISITOR	OF MARK TWAIN AND ANDREW LANG ARE AS DULL AS
JOAN 6,SD(148)	UNCONCEALED HOSTILITY. THEN CAUCHON FOLLOWS THE	INQUISITOR	OUT. WARWICK LOOKS ROUND. FINDING HIMSELF ALONE,
JOAN 6,SD(136)	SINKS BACK IN HIS CHAIR WITH A HEAVY SIGH. THE	INQUISITOR	PURSES HIS LIPS AND FROWNS. LADVENU SHAKES HIS
JOAN 6 (126)	GOOD MORNING, MASTER DE STOGUMBER. (TO THE	INQUISITOR	) CHAPLAIN TO THE CARDINAL OF ENGLAND. /THE
JOAN 6,SD(123)	ESPECIALLY ON OCCASIONS LIKE THE PRESENT. THE	INQUISITOR	SMILES PATIENTLY, AND BOWS. HE IS A MILD ELDERLY
JOAN 6 (129)	CONSIDER SERIOUS. I AGREE WITH MY COLLEAGUE THE	INQUISITOR	THAT IT IS ON THE COUNT OF HERESY THAT WE MUST
JOAN 6,SD(146)	THERE IS A DEAD SILENCE. CAUCHON TURNS TO THE	INQUISITOR	WITH AN INQUIRING LOOK. THE INQUISITOR NODS
JOAN 6 (128)	HERESY IS MY PECULIAR BUSINESS: I AM HERE AS AN	INQUISITOR	, NOT AS AN ORDINARY MAGISTRATE. STICK TO THE
JOAN 6 (125)	ELOQUENCE, TO THE DISGUST OF CAUCHON AND THE	INQUISITOR	, WHO HAVE LISTENED TO HIM SO FAR WITH

INQUISITORS

MIS. PREFACE(66)	AS THEY CALL IT -- WITH THE RUTHLESSNESS OF GRAND	INQUISITORS	. CUNNING, UNSCRUPULOUS CHILDREN LEARN ALL THE
LION PREFACE(45)	IN VACCINATION WITH THE CRUEL FANATICISM OF	INQUISITORS	. I AN CONVINCED THAT IF A DOZEN SCEPTICS WERE

IN'T

BASH I (95)	END ALL BETWEEN US. AND YET THERE'S NO DISHONOR	IN'T	: YOUR LAWYER, WHO LET YOUR LODGE TO ME, WILL VOUCH ME

INS

APPL I (220)	PER CENT WERE ONLY A PARCEL OF SILLIES PLAYING AT	INS	AND OUTS. TO MAKE DEMOCRACY WORK IN CRASSUS'S WAY WE

INSANE

MTH4 II (191)	GENTLEMAN/ NATURALLY WE ARE NOT ABSOLUTELY	INSANE	AND SUICIDAL. NEVERTHELESS WE IMPOSE ON OURSELVES
GETT PREFACE(199)	LIFE SPENT IN PRAYER AND ALMSGIVING IS REALLY AS	INSANE	AS A LIFE SPENT IN CURSING AND PICKING POCKETS: THE
LION PREFACE(83)	COMPENSATION FOR ALL THIS PRIVATION IS PARTLY AN	INSANE	CONCEIT OF BEING THE ELECT OF GOD, WITH A RESERVED
MILL II (174)	SEE. ENORMOUS SELF-CONFIDENCE. RECKLESS AUDACITY.	INSANE	EGOTISM. APPARENTLY SEXLESS. /EPIFANIA/ SEXLESS! WHO
UNPL PREFACE(R7)	BETWEEN THEM. BUT TO OBTAIN A LIVELIHOOD BY THIS	INSANE	GIFT, I MUST HAVE CONJURED SO AS TO INTEREST NOT ONLY
JOAN PREFACE(11)	FOR THEIR ACTIONS, AND MUST BE TREATED AS	INSANE	. BUT THE SEERS OF VISIONS AND THE HEARERS OF
GENV I (45)	/BISHOP/ I CANNOT BEAR THIS! THE MAN IS	INSANE	. I SUBSCRIBE TO THE SOCIETY ALMOST BEYOND MY MEANS.
BUOY IV (54)	I WERE A MEDICAL ADVISER I SHOULD CERTIFY THEM AS	INSANE	. /OLD BILL/ AND ME? /SIR FERDINAND/ WELL, HARDLY
OVER (187)	GREGORY ARE SUCH FRIENDS, MRS JUNO. /JUNO/ THIS	INSANE	MAGNANIMITY-- /MRS LUNN/ DONT YOU THINK YOUVE SAID
FABL PREFACE(68)	IMPOSSIBLE, AND HAVE NOTHING TO DO WITH THE	INSANE	MISDISTRIBUTION OF NATIONAL INCOME PRODUCED BY
MILL I SD(137)	CLIENTS OR POSSIBLE ASSAULT BY VIOLENT OR	INSANE	ONES. THE DOOR IS ON HIS RIGHT TOWARDS THE FARTHER
MILL PREFACE(113)	AT WHICH THE COMMON MAN WILL BELIEVE HIM TO BE	INSANE	OR IMPIOUS: WHEN MEASURES OF THAT COMPLEXION ARE
GENV PREFACE(13)	WELL DRESSED FEMALE TO RULE OVER THEM. THIS	INSANE	PRESCRIPTION FOR PERFECT DEMOCRACY OF COURSE MAKES
GENV I (46)	WE WERE ABOUT TO HAVE HER CERTIFIED AS	INSANE	-- MOST RELUCTANTLY; FOR WE LOVED OUR DEAR
MIS. PREFACE(4)	UPON. AFTER ALL, WHAT MAN IS CAPABLE OF THE	INSANE	SELF-CONCEIT OF BELIEVING THAT AN ETERNITY OF HIMSELF
BARB PREFACE(241)	AFTER TORTURE, FOR ITS CENTRAL MYSTERY AN	INSANE	VENGEANCE BOUGHT OFF BY A TRUMPERY EXPIATION. BUT
LION PREFACE(31)	HIS DELUSION IS A VERY COMMON DELUSION AMONG THE	INSANE	, AND THAT SUCH INSANITY IS QUITE CONSISTENT WITH THE
GETT PREFACE(201)	ARE UNDER THE INFLUENCE OF THE MOST VIOLENT, MOST	INSANE	, MOST DELUSIVE, AND MOST TRANSIENT OF PASSIONS, THEY
GETT PREFACE(218)	THAT IT SHALL NOT HAPPEN, ARE EITHER INSINCERE,	INSANE	, OR HOPELESSLY STUPID. THERE IS SOME SENSE IN A

INCA PROLOG (234) AND MAKES FOR THE DOOR, GRUMBLING ALL THE TIME). INSANE , SENSELESS EXTRAVAGANCE! (BARKING) WORTHLESSNESS!

INSANELY
METH PREFACE(R30) UNCONSCIOUS OF HEREDITY, OR SCEPTICAL, MEN WERE INSANELY CREDULOUS ABOUT IT: THEY NOT ONLY BELIEVED IN THE
SIM PREFACE(12) PROPERTY, WHICH, WHEN IT IS INSANELY EXTENDED TO THE COMMON EARTH OF THE COUNTRY, MEANS
LADY PREFACE(213) AND EVENTS PRESENTLY PROVED TO WILDE HOW INSANELY HE HAD BEEN ADVISED IN TAKING THE ACTION, AND HOW
MTH4 I (141) NAME OF A BUTTERFLY. /THE ELDERLY GENTLEMAN/ (INSANELY) I GIVE UP. I CAN BEAR THIS NO LONGER. IT IS

INSANITARY
DOCT PREFACE(52) THE RATES AND MORE PUBLIC INTERFERENCE WITH THE INSANITARY , BECAUSE INSUFFICIENTLY FINANCED, PRIVATE HOUSE.

INSANITY
GETT PREFACE(252) BLINDNESS AND STERILITY, PAIN AND DISFIGUREMENT, INSANITY AND DEATH AMONG US WITH THE CERTAINTY THAT WE ARE
LION PREFACE(31) COMMON DELUSION AMONG THE INSANE, AND THAT SUCH INSANITY IS QUITE CONSISTENT WITH THE RETENTION OF THE
CLEO NOTES (210) WORSHIP ACCORDED BY ALL RACES TO CERTAIN FORMS OF INSANITY , BUT CAESAR'S VICTORIES WERE ONLY ADVERTISEMENTS
GENV III (81) FIND IT SOPHISTICATED TO THE VERGE OF SUICIDAL INSANITY . THIS MAKES TROUBLE FOR YOU AS FOREIGN SECRETARY.
GETT PREFACE(199) ENDING IN INSANITY OR CRIME. THE FACT THAT THE INSANITY MAY BE PRIVILEGED, AS SAVONAROLA'S WAS UP TO THE
HART PREFACE(12) A PERPETUAL PLENARY INDULGENCE. UNFORTUNATELY THE INSANITY OF THE JURIES AND MAGISTRATES DID NOT ALWAYS
GETT PREFACE(199) WITHOUT SERIOUS PSYCHOLOGICAL MISCHIEF, ENDING IN INSANITY OR CRIME. THE FACT THAT THE INSANITY MAY BE
JOAN PREFACE(41) A LINE SOMEWHERE BETWEEN ALLOWABLE CONDUCT AND INSANITY OR CRIME, IN SPITE OF THE RISK OF MISTAKING SAGES
2TRU PREFACE(17) PRODUCE GENERAL HORROR OR BE TAKEN AS PROOFS OF INSANITY THEIR AUTHORITY WOULD COLLAPSE. HENCE THE NEED FOR
GETT PREFACE(258) SUCH AS ADULTERY, CRUELTY, DRUNKENNESS, FELONY, INSANITY , VAGRANCY, NEGLECT TO PROVIDE FOR WIFE AND

INSATIABLE
MIS. PREFACE(50) WHOM A LITERARY EDUCATION CAN BE OF ANY USE ARE INSATIABLE : THEY WILL READ AND STUDY FAR MORE THAN IS GOOD
MIS. PREFACE(14) CHILD IS A RESTLESS, NOISY LITTLE ANIMAL, WITH AN INSATIABLE APPETITE FOR KNOWLEDGE, AND CONSEQUENTLY A
KING II (224) WHICH MEANT MEN AND MONEY. FOR BOTH, BARBARA IS INSATIABLE . GRAB, GRAB, GRAB. WHEN ONE IS DONE WITH
2TRU II (66) SUITED, WERE WE? /AUBREY/ YOU HAD ACQUIRED AN INSATIABLE TASTE FOR COMMERCIAL TRAVELLERS. YOU COULD SAMPLE
VWOO 1 (119) SHIP. CANNOT YOU FIND ONE OF THEM WITH THE SAME INSATIABLE THIRST FOR CONVERSATION AS YOURSELF? /Z/ WELL!

INSATIABLY
SUPR I (32) MY DEAR LADY MEPHISTOPHELES, TEMPTED. YOU WERE INSATIABLY CURIOUS AS TO WHAT A BOY MIGHT BE CAPABLE OF, AND

INSAWD
CAPT II (263) ON THE ORAWZN WIV ABAHT FIFTY MEN. THYLL BE EAH INSAWD O TEN MINNITS, THEY WILL. /LADY CICELY/ THE SHEIKH!

INSCRIBE
JOAN PREFACE(29) A STATUE TO HER, BUT TOOK PARTICULAR CARE NOT TO INSCRIBE ON THE PEDESTAL " PATRIOTISM IS NOT ENOUGH," FOR

INSCRIBED
FABL III SD(109) ISLE OF WIGHT, A BUILDING OF STEEL AND GLASS IS INSCRIBED ANTHROPOMETRIC LABORATORY. ON THE TERRACE BEFORE
FABL IV SD(114) IN THE ISLE OF WIGHT: BUT THE BUILDING IS NOW INSCRIBED DIET COMMISSIONERS. A COMMISSIONER IN CAP AND GOWN
MILL II SD(166) AND PLAYING A FLAGEOLET. UNDERNEATH THE SOW IS INSCRIBED IN TALL LETTERS THE PIG AND WHISTLE. BETWEEN THESE
MIS. PREFACE(24) OF THE WATER CURE. OR YOU CAN BUY A CHEAPER PLATE INSCRIBED KINDERGARTEN, AND IMAGINE, OR LEAVE OTHERS TO
MIS. PREFACE(24) CRECHE. NO DOUBT THE NEW BRASS PLATES ARE BEING INSCRIBED MONTESSORI INSTITUTE, AND WILL BE USED WHEN THE
DOCT PREFACE(79) FOR A DOCTOR USING A BRASS PLATE TO HAVE INSCRIBED ON IT, IN ADDITION TO THE LETTERS INDICATING HIS
MILL II SD(166) DOOR, WHICH STANDS WIDE OPEN AND HAS COFFEE ROOM INSCRIBED ON IT, IS TO THE RIGHT OF ANYONE CONTEMPLATING THE
MIS. PREFACE(24) AND YOU CAN EASILY BUY A SECONDHAND BRASS PLATE INSCRIBED PESTALOZZIAN INSTITUTE AND NAIL IT TO YOUR DOOR,
PHIL II SD(94) BETWEEN IT AND THE MIDDLE OF THE ROOM. PLACARDS INSCRIBED SILENCE ARE CONSPICUOUSLY EXHIBITED HERE AND
MILL I SD(137) AND BESIDE IT A STAND OF BLACK TIN BOXES INSCRIBED WITH CLIENTS' NAMES. SO FAR, THE PLACE PROCLAIMS
HART PREFACE(27) HOMES TODAY, TO FIND THE OLD FAMILIAR SIGNPOST INSCRIBED " TO STRATFORD, 1 MILE," AND AT THE END OF THE

INSCRIBING
2TRU PREFACE(20) WAS NONSENSE. NEVERTHELESS IT WAS ASSUMED THAT BY INSCRIBING EVERY MAN'S NAME ON A REGISTER OF VOTERS WE COULD

INSCRIPTION
OVER (173) STICKING UP, IF I MAY PUT IT THAT WAY, WITH THE INSCRIPTION : TRESPASSERS WILL BE PROSECUTED. HOW WE ALL
ARMS III (67) TAKEN WHAT? /PET<OFF/ YOUR PHOTOGRAPH, WITH THE INSCRIPTION : " RAINA, TO HER CHOCOLATE CREAM SOLDIER: A
MIS. PREFACE(23) STICKS TO ME, I HAVE NEVER YET SEEN A LATIN INSCRIPTION ON A TOMB THAT I COULD TRANSLATE THROUGHOUT. OF
2TRU III SD(81) LIKE A POINTED ARCH, AND SURMOUNTING IT WITH THE INSCRIPTION SN PAULS. THE GROTTO TO THE LEFT IS MUCH WIDER.
MTH3 (124) TO HIM WHICH BEARS ON ITS PEDESTAL THE NOBLE INSCRIPTION , " I CAME NOT TO CALL SINNERS, BUT THE

INSCRIPTIONS
LION PREFACE(91) LATIN AUTHORS, AND WRITERS OF ANCIENT ANONYMOUS INSCRIPTIONS ARE THROWN AT OUR HEADS AS THE SOURCES OF THIS
GENV I SD(29) FOOLSCAP FROM WHICH SHE HAS BEEN COPYING THE CARD INSCRIPTIONS . BUT AT PRESENT SHE IS NOT AT WORK. SHE IS
PHIL II SD(94) MANTELPIECE, WITH A BUST OF IBSEN, AND DECORATIVE INSCRIPTIONS OF THE TITLES OF HIS PLAYS. THERE ARE CIRCULAR
LADY PREFACE(209) HIS HAND OCCASIONALLY AT DECIPHERING ANCIENT INSCRIPTIONS , READING THEM AS PEOPLE SEEM TO READ THE

INSCRUTABLE
CAPT I SD(217) AN ILL-NOURISHED LAD OF SEVENTEEN; BUT HIS AGE IS INSCRUTABLE : ONLY THE ABSENCE OF ANY SIGN OF GREY IN HIS
SIM I SD(36) THEM. THEIR EXPRESSIONS ARE INTENT, GRAVE, AND INSCRUTABLE . THEY FACE SOUTH WITH THEIR BACKS TO THE SEA.
CAND III (144) HE TAKES THE VISITOR'S CHAIR HIMSELF, AND SITS, INSCRUTABLE . WHEN THEY ARE ALL SETTLED SHE BEGINS, THROWING
PYGM PREFACE(201) REDUCED IT IN HIS OWN PRACTICE TO THE MOST INSCRUTABLE OF CRYPTOGRAMS. HIS TRUE OBJECTIVE WAS THE
METH PREFACE(R33) ACCORDINGLY, AGNOSTICS. THEY HAD TURNED FROM THE INSCRUTABLE QUESTION OF WHY THINGS EXISTED, TO THE SPADE

INSCRUTABLY
CLEO IV SD(169) THESE MATTERS. THE LADIES LAUGH. CLEOPATRA LOOKS INSCRUTABLY AT HIM. /CHARMIAN/ I SEE YOU DO NOT KNOW THE
DEST (188) COAT, AND PAUSES FOR PERMISSION). /NAPOLEON/ (INSCRUTABLY) IF YOU DARE. /LADY/ THANK YOU. (SHE OPENS HIS

INSECT
BULL II (99) YOU FOOLISH MAN, GET UP. ARE YOU AFRAID OF A POOR INSECT BECAUSE I PRETENDED IT WAS TALKING TO ME? /PATSY/
BULL II SD(97) HE IS ROUSED FROM HIS TRANCE BY THE CHIRP OF AN INSECT FROM A TUFT OF GRASS IN A CREVICE OF THE STONE. HIS
BULL II SD(97) TAKES OFF HIS HAT TO THE TUFT, ADDRESSING THE INSECT IN A BROGUE WHICH IS THE JOCULAR ASSUMPTION OF A
MRS III SD(229) KNEES TO PROD WITH HIS STICK AT SOME UNFORTUNATE INSECT IN THE GRASS; AND LOOKS CUNNINGLY AT HER. SHE TURNS
BULL III (121) HUMAN: IT'S WORSE THAN THE INDUSTRY OF A CORAL INSECT . AN ENGLISHMAN HAS SOME SENSE ABOUT WORKING: HE
MILL I (156) SUCCEEDED; AND I FOUND MYSELF TIED FOR LIFE TO AN INSECT . /ALASTAIR/ YOU MAY SAY WHAT YOU LIKE; BUT YOU WERE
METH PREFACE(R59) CAN CATCH HIM, AND SO HARDY OF CONSTITUTION THAT INSECT POWDER WILL HAVE NO MORE EFFECT ON HIM THAN
MTH4 I (162) LITERATURE. WE MAY BE INSECTS; BUT LIKE THE CORAL INSECT WE BUILD ISLANDS WHICH BECOME CONTINENTS: LIKE THE
PYGM IV (263) /HIGGINS/ YOU WON MY BET! YOU! PRESUMPTUOUS INSECT ! I WON IT. WHAT DID YOU THROW THOSE SLIPPERS AT ME

INSECTS
MTH4 I (162) AND PAGES AND VOLUMES AND CHAPTERS AND CORAL INSECTS AND BEES AND ACORNS AND STONES AND MOUNTAINS. /THE
2TRU II (71) THE ANIMALS AND THEIR WAYS, THE BIRDS AND INSECTS AND REPTILES. EVERY DAY IS A DAY OF ADVENTURE WITH
MIS. PREFACE(46) GENERALLY, THERE ARE SCORES OF THOUSANDS OF HUMAN INSECTS GROPING THROUGH OUR DARKNESS BY THE FEEBLE
MTH4 I (162) TO A BIBLE, A BIBLE TO A LITERATURE. WE MAY BE INSECTS ; BUT LIKE THE CORAL INSECT WE BUILD ISLANDS WHICH
DEST SD(149) DISDAINFUL OF TWO HORDES OF MISCHIEVOUS INSECTS WHICH ARE THE FRENCH AND AUSTRIAN ARMIES. TWO DAYS
APPL INTRLUD(248) SIXTEEN HOURS A DAY FOR THIRTY YEARS, LIKE CORAL INSECTS , MAKE THEM GREAT. WHAT ARE THEY FOR? THESE DULL

INSECURITY
GETT PREFACE(188) THAN MARY WOLLSTONECRAFT ARE UNABLE TO FACE THE INSECURITY AND DISCREDIT OF THE VAGABONDAGE WHICH IS THE

INSENSATE
HART PREFACE(23) NOISY INCAPABLES, CONFRONTED WITH THIS PICTURE OF INSENSATE DELUSION AND FOLLY, THE CRITICAL READER WILL

INSENSIBILITY

BULL PREFACE(32)	BULLIED ENGLAND INTO CONCEDING HOME RULE; FOR THE	INSENSIBILITY	OF THE ENGLISH GOVERNING CLASSES TO
BULL PREFACE(14)	HIS POWER OF TAKING HIMSELF SERIOUSLY, AND HIS	INSENSIBILITY	TO ANYTHING FUNNY IN DANGER AND DESTRUCTION,
PYGM II (225)	/HIGGINS/ (WOUNDED IN HIS TENDEREST POINT BY HER	INSENSIBILITY	TO HIS ELOCUTION) OH, INDEED! I'M MAD, AM I?
MTH4 I (147)	HAVE BELIEVED IN THE EXISTENCE OF SUCH SCANDALOUS	INSENSIBILITY	TO THE ELEMENTARY DECENCIES OF HUMAN

INSENSIBLE

OVER (182)	AS YOURSELF! /MRS LUNN/ OH, GREGORY'S NOT	INSENSIBLE	: VERY FAR FROM IT; BUT I AM THE ONLY WOMAN IN
OVER (182)	WORLD FOR HIM. /JUNO/ BUT YOU? ARE YOU REALLY AS	INSENSIBLE	AS YOU SAY YOU ARE? /MRS LUNN/ I NEVER SAID
OVER (182)	TO HAVE COMPANY. /JUNO/ AND IS YOUR HUSBAND AS	INSENSIBLE	AS YOURSELF! /MRS LUNN/ OH, GREGORY'S NOT
OVER (182)	I NEVER SAID ANYTHING OF THE KIND. I'M NOT AT ALL	INSENSIBLE	BY NATURE; BUT (I DONT KNOW WHETHER YOUVE
NEVR I SD(224)	AIMLESSLY, THEN SUBSIDE AND DROP. HE IS QUITE	INSENSIBLE	. VALENTINE THROWS ASIDE THE MOUTHPIECE QUICKLY;
MTH5 (210)	HAVE STOLEN OUT AT NIGHT WHEN YOU WERE ALL LYING	INSENSIBLE	-- QUITE DISGUSTING, I CALL IT-- AND WANDERED
HART II (90)	YOU PLEASE-- (NOTICING THAT HE REMAINS QUITE	INSENSIBLE	) OH, MY GOOD LORD, I HOPE I HAVNT KILLED HIM.
LADY PREFACE(213)	HAVE SAID, HE PITIES TOO MUCH; BUT THAT HE IS NOT	INSENSIBLE	TO HUMOR IS SHEWN NOT ONLY BY HIS APPRECIATION OF
MRS IV (239)	PHILISTINE. SHE IS INDIFFERENT TO MY ROMANCE, AND	INSENSIBLE	TO MY BEAUTY. /VIVIE/ MR PRAED: ONCE FOR ALL,

INSENSIBLY

MRS PREFACE(167)	AT LAST SO ROOTED, THAT CRITICISM OF THE THEATRE	INSENSIBLY	CEASES TO BE CRITICISM AT ALL, AND BECOMES MORE

INSEPARABLE

BARB PREFACE(220)	LIFE ITSELF IS A CURSE. FOR THE TWO THINGS ARE	INSEPARABLE	: MONEY IS THE COUNTER THAT ENABLES LIFE TO BE
SUPR I (21)	SHE GOES PAST HER MOTHER TO OCTAVIUS) AND JACK'S	INSEPARABLE	FRIEND RICKY-TICKY-TAVY (HE BLUSHES AND LOOKS
PRES (135)	OF GOVERNMENT, PUBLIC OPINION IS MIND. MIND IS	INSEPARABLE	FROM MATTER. SHOOT DOWN THE MATTER AND YOU KILL
LION PREFACE(60)	YOU DESIRE TO ALLOW THE TWO HUMAN SOULS WHICH ARE	INSEPARABLE	FROM THE CAPTAIN AND THE CABIN BOY, AND WHICH
APPL PREFACE(175)	TO SOCIALISM AND CAPITALISM. WE HAVE TO SOLVE TWO	INSEPARABLE	MAIN PROBLEMS: THE ECONOMIC PROBLEM OF HOW TO

INSEPARABLES

PHIL I (86)	HERE ARE ALL OUR YOUNG PEOPLE BOSOM FRIENDS,	INSEPARABLES	; AND YET THEY NEVER SAID A WORD OF IT TO US.

INSEPARABLY

BULL PREFACE(57)	TRIBES IN WHOSE IMAGINATION THAT PRACTICE IS	INSEPARABLY	BOUND UP WITH RELIGION. IT SUGGESTS THAT THE

INSERT

APPL I (227)	HANDS OF MEN MUCH RICHER THAN I, WHO WOULD NOT	INSERT	A SINGLE PARAGRAPH AGAINST THEIR OWN INTERESTS EVEN
MRS PREFACE(162)	TO FACE THIS, AND HAD PLEDGED HIMSELF TO	INSERT	THE ARTICLE UNALTERED (THE PARTICULARITY OF THE

INSERTED

2TRU III (111)	THE FATAL WORD NOT HAS BEEN MIRACULOUSLY	INSERTED	INTO ALL OUR CREEDS: IN THE DESECRATED TEMPLES
FABL PREFACE(78)	WERE NEVER REPORTED, AND MY LETTERS AND ARTICLES	INSERTED	ONLY WHEN I COULD COMBINE WHAT I BELIEVED AND
POSN PREFACE(379)	TO THOSE RECOMMENDATIONS WHICH WERE OBVIOUSLY	INSERTED	SOLELY TO CONCILIATE THE MAJORITY AND GET THE

INSET

JOAN 4 (94)	BORDERS, AND ILLUMINATED PICTURES CUNNINGLY	INSET	. BUT NOWADAYS, INSTEAD OF LOOKING AT BOOKS, PEOPLE

INSIDE

DOCT PREFACE(36)	TO FIND WHETHER OR NOT THERE WAS A STONE	INSIDE	A MAN'S BODY EXCEPT BY EXPLORING IT WITH A KNIFE, OR
SIM PRO?1, (23)	OH LORD! /THE Y.W./ WELL, YOU CAN MAKE YOUR	INSIDE	ALL RIGHT IF YOU EAT PROPERLY AND STOP DRINKING AND
MIS. (123)	-- BEGAN TALKING ABOUT WHAT SOUR MILK DID IN HER	INSIDE	AND HOW SHE EXPECTED TO LIVE TO BE OVER A HUNDRED IF
MILL II (173)	WHEN THEY ARE ILL. I KNOW TOO MUCH ABOUT THEM,	INSIDE	AND OUT, YOU ARE PERFECTLY WELL. /EPIFANIA/ LIAR.
APPL I (215)	A POWERFUL HAND, AND SWINGS IT FORWARD TO THE	INSIDE	CORNER OF SEMPRONIUS'S TABLE, WHERE SHE STANDS
MILL PREFACE(134)	WITHOUT HIM; BUT THAT WILL NOT GIVE HIM THE	INSIDE	GRIP. A LATE RICH SHIPOWNER, ENGAGED IN A QUARREL
DOCT I (95)	TAKE THE SPONGES OUT, AND WAS STITCHING THEM UP	INSIDE	HER WHEN THE NURSE MISSED THEM. SOMEHOW, I'D MADE
APPL I (199)	FRIENDLY AND KINDLY. IT SHEWS HE HAD SOMETHING	INSIDE	HIM AFTER ALL. /SEMPRONIUS/ NOT A BIT. HE NEVER
PPP (204)	WOTJEMEAN? /MAGNESIA/ THE PLASTER HAS SET	INSIDE	HIM. THE OFFICER WAS RIGHT: HE IS INDEED A LIVING
FANY III (315)	DOWN TO THE BOTTOM OF THE HILL. HE HAS NO POWERS	INSIDE	HIMSELF TO KEEP HIM STEADY; SO LET HIM CLING TO THE
CAND III (131)	THE REVEREND JAMES MUST HAVE HIDDEN SOMEWHERE	INSIDE	HIS BLACK COAT: THE MAN THAT CANDIDA LOVED. YOU CANT
LION II (144)	A LAUGH). /THE EMPEROR/ (STANDING ON A CHAIR	INSIDE	HIS BOX AND LOOKING OVER THE WALL) SORCERER: I
GETT PREFACE(217)	SPEAKING FOR MYSELF, I CAN SAY THAT I KNOW THE	INSIDE	HISTORY OF PERHAPS HALF A DOZEN MARRIAGES. ANY FAMILY
BARB II (274)	KNOW WOTS INSIDE THE LAW AND WOTS OUTSIDE IT; AND	INSIDE	IT I DO AS THE CAPITALISTS DO: PINCH WOT I CAN LAY ME
GENV III (69)	SPEECHES OUTSIDE YOUR PARLIAMENT HOUSE INSTEAD OF	INSIDE	IT. BUT TO ME THE PERSECUTION IS A MATTER OF LIFE AND
APPL PREFACE(180)	PERORATION TO PIECES AND SEE WHAT THERE REALLY IS	INSIDE	IT. (BY THE WAY, LINCOLN DID NOT REALLY DECLAIM IT
METH PREFACE(R18)	THE SEA; ENABLING THE MAMMAL TO GESTATE ITS YOUNG	INSIDE	ITS BODY, AND THE FOWL TO INCUBATE HERS OUTSIDE IT;
MTH5 (242)	DEVILS; BUT THEY ARE MAKING ME FEEL UNEASY IN MY	INSIDE	. I NEVER HAD SUCH A SENSATION BEFORE. /MARTELLUS/ I
MILL II (175)	THE DIGESTION OF AN OSTRICH. I HAVE A CLOCKWORK	INSIDE	. I SLEEP EIGHT HOURS LIKE A LOG. WHEN I WANT
DOCT PREFACE(5)	WRONG WITH HIS THROAT, OR HAS A PAIN IN HIS	INSIDE	. IF A DOCTOR EFFECTS SOME TRUMPERY CURE WITH A WET
POSN PREFACE(375)	LEAKED OUT THAT SOMETHING TERRIBLE WAS HAPPENING	INSIDE	. IT COULD NOT BE ANOTHER LICENSED PLAY TOO
BARB III (345)	ON LIST SLIPPERS, MISS: THATS ALL. WEVE GOT EM	INSIDE	. (SHE GOES IN). /STEPHEN/ (VERY SERIOUSLY TO
BARB I (266)	LAUGH IF YOU WANT TO, CHOLLY? IT'S GOOD FOR YOUR	INSIDE	. /LADY BRITOMART/ BARBARA: YOU HAVE HAD THE
ROCK II (268)	HIM A WALKING TALKING SHELL OF A MAN WITH NOTHING	INSIDE	. THE ONLY MAN THAT EVER HAD A PROPER UNDERSTANDING
SIM PRO,1, (23)	TO BE MADE HAPPY. YOU OUGHT TO BE HAPPY FROM THE	INSIDE	. THEN YOU WOULDNT NEED THINGS TO MAKE YOU HAPPY.
BARB II (281)	AND THE DEVIL OUT OF YOU THERE WHEN THEY GET YOU	INSIDE	. YOU MIND WHAT YOURE ABOUT: THE MAJOR HERE IS THE
BARB II (282)	YOURE THE MAN THAT JENNY HILL WAS PRAYING FOR	INSIDE	JUST NOW. (SHE ENTERS HIS NAME IN HER NOTE BOOK).
FANY PROLOG (264)	BESIDES, BANNAL'S KNOWLEDGE OF THE THEATRE IS AN	INSIDE	KNOWLEDGE. WE KNOW HIM; AND HE KNOWS US. HE KNOWS THE
MTH1 I (8)	BIRTH. /EVE/ OH! THAT IS TOO WONDERFUL. IT STIRS	INSIDE	ME. IT HURTS. /THE SERPENT/ IT NEARLY TORE ME
BARB II (280)	TODGER FAIRMILE'D DONE IT, SHE WOULDNT A GOT UP	INSIDE	O TEN MINUTES, NO MORE THAN YOU WOULD IF HE GOT ON TO
CAPT III (284)	SANTIAGO MADE THE TWENTY KNOTS TO MOGADOR HARBOR	INSIDE	OF FIFTY-SEVEN MINUTES. BEFORE NOON NEXT DAY A
KING I (190)	FATE OF OUR FATHER. THEY WILL HAVE YOUR HEAD OFF	INSIDE	OF FIVE YEARS UNLESS YOU JUMP INTO THE NEAREST
MIS. PREFACE(8)	TO THANK HIS STARS THAT HIS FATHER RESPECTED THE	INSIDE	OF HIS HEAD WHILST CUFFING THE OUTSIDE OF IT; AND
ARMS I (14)	LADY! YOU CAN ALWAYS TELL AN OLD SOLDIER BY THE	INSIDE	OF HIS HOLSTERS AND CARTRIDGE BOXES. THE YOUNG ONES
MTH5 (217)	I WAS RATHER YOUNG WHEN I SAID THAT; BUT THE	INSIDE	OF MY HEAD IS CHANGING VERY RAPIDLY. I SHOULD LIKE TO
APPL I (239)	ME, BILL, I'LL DRIVE YOU OUT OF YOUR CONSTITUENCY	INSIDE	OF TWO MONTHS. /BOANERGES/ HO! YOU WILL, WILL YOU..
WIDO III (60)	ICED MUTTON COMPANY. THEYLL BE KNOCKED DOWN	INSIDE	OF TWO YEAR TO MAKE ROOM FOR THE NEW NORTH AND SOUTH
MIS. PREFACE(4)	IS FOR MANY OF US THE GATE OF HELL; BUT WE ARE	INSIDE	ON THE WAY OUT, NOT OUTSIDE ON THE WAY IN. THEREFORE
3PLA PREFACE(R28)	FUSS ABOUT NIETZSCHE AND HIS GOOD AND EVIL TURNED	INSIDE	OUT? MR ROBERT BUCHANAN HAS ACTUALLY WRITTEN A LONG
APPL I (201)	BEEN TOO CLEVER FOR THEM. HE'LL TURN BOANERGES	INSIDE	OUT AFTER LETTING HIM ROAR THE PALACE DOWN. BOANERGES
ARMS I (7)	LEAVES DREAMILY; FINDS HER PAGE; TURNS THE BOOK	INSIDE	OUT AT IT; AND, WITH A HAPPY SIGH, GETS INTO BED AND
SUPR III (129)	NOTHING BUT WORDS WHICH I OR ANYONE ELSE CAN TURN	INSIDE	OUT LIKE A GLOVE. WERE THEY REALITIES, YOU WOULD HAVE
DOCT PREFACE(3)	RECEIVES A FEW SHILLINGS: HE WHO CUTS YOUR	INSIDE	OUT RECEIVES HUNDREDS OF GUINEAS, EXCEPT WHEN HE DOES
BUOY II (19)	ON THE STOEP. /THE NATIVE/ (CALLING TO THE LADY	INSIDE	) AHAIYA! MISSY'S RATIONS. PINK PERSON LOAFING
PRES (163)	THE DOOR OF GENERAL SANDSTONE'S ROOM ON THE	INSIDE	; AN' SHE'S SITTIN ON HIS ED TIL HE SIGNS A
MRS II SD(198)	ACT II.	INSIDE	THE COTTAGE AFTER NIGHTFALL. LOOKING EASTWARD FROM
SIM II SD(54)	SOME YEARS LATER. THE GARDEN IS UNCHANGED; BUT	INSIDE	THE DISTANT BREAKWATER THE HARBOR IS CROWDED WITH
MTH2 SD(46)	FOLLOWED BY HASLAM, WHO REMAINS TIMIDLY JUST	INSIDE	THE DOOR. /SAVVY/ (RUNNING TO FRANKLYN) I SAY! WHO
ROCK II SD(247)	ANGRY, AND RESOLUTE, THEY GROUP THEMSELVES JUST	INSIDE	THE DOOR, GLOWERING AT THE PRIME MINISTER AND HIS
MIS. SD(157)	BUT HAS MADE NO OTHER CHANGE. SHE STOPS JUST	INSIDE	THE DOOR, HOLDING IT OPEN, EVIDENTLY NOT INTENDING TO
LION I (111)	ENTERING ROME. YOU WILL INSTRUCT THEM THAT ONCE	INSIDE	THE GATES OF ROME THEY ARE IN THE PRESENCE OF THE
BARB II (274)	WORKERS, FOURTH, I'M FLY ENOUGH TO KNOW WOTS	INSIDE	THE LAW AND WOTS OUTSIDE IT; AND INSIDE IT I DO AS
DEVL III (74)	THAT HE IS TOO LATE) HOW IS THIS? WHY IS SHE	INSIDE	THE LINES? /SERGEANT/ (GUILTILY) I DUNNO, SIR.
DEVL III (74)	TAKING HER HAND) HERE, MADAM: YOU HAD BETTER KEEP	INSIDE	THE LINES; BUT STAND HERE BEHIND US; AND DONT LOOK.
CLEO III (150)	AND HIS MERCHANDIZE. IF HE DRAWS HIS SWORD AGAIN	INSIDE	THE LINES, KILL HIM. TO YOUR POSTS. MARCH. HE GOES
KING I SD(161)	MAKING THE ROOM ACCESSIBLE FROM THE GARDEN.	INSIDE	THE ROOM THE WALLS ARE LINED WITH CUPBOARDS BELOW AND
LION PREFACE(92)	THEN WE CAN BE AS WICKED AS WE LIKE WITH IMPUNITY	INSIDE	THE SECULAR LAW, EVEN FROM SELF-REPROACH, WHICH
DEVL III (71)	HUSTLING THE PERSONS WHO FIND THEMSELVES	INSIDE	THE SQUARE OUT AT THE CORNERS). NOW THEN! OUT OF IT
MTH4 III SD(194)	ACT III.	INSIDE	THE TEMPLE. A GALLERY OVERHANGING AN ABYSS. DEAD
LION PREFACE(84)	OWN CONGREGATIONS, AND TO A CONSIDERABLE EXTENT	INSIDE	THEM, HEARTILY DETESTED. NOW NOBODY DETESTS JESUS,

MRS II (207) MIND ALL THE TIME IVE BEEN WALKING WITH THAT FOOL INSIDE THERE. /MRS WARREN/ (REVOLTED) YES: IT'S THE SORT OF
ARMS I (19) TWO ROWS OF WINDOWS. THERE IS A FLIGHT OF STAIRS INSIDE TO GET UP AND DOWN BY. /THE MAN/ STAIRS! HOW GRAND!
HART PREFACE(10) TO OVARIES AND APPENDICES UNTIL AT LAST NO ONE'S INSIDE WAS SAFE. THEY EXPLAINED THAT THE HUMAN INTESTINE WAS
LION II (133) THE BOX. THE CAPTAIN SHUTS THE DOOR, REMAINING INSIDE WITH THE EMPEROR. METELLUS AND THE REST OF THE SUITE
DEST (186) /NAPOLEON/ AND YOU HAVE NO DEVOURING DEVIL INSIDE YOU WHO MUST BE FED WITH ACTION AND VICTORY: GORGED
NEVR I (212) BE GOOD TO KEEP A LOT OF QUESTIONS BOTTLED UP INSIDE YOU. YOU DID IT, MAMMA; BUT SEE HOW AWFULLY IT'S
DEST (182) BE IRRECOVERABLY LOST. /LADY/ NONSENSE! THEY ARE INSIDE YOUR COAT. /NAPOLEON/ YOU WILL FIND IT HARD, I THINK,
MRS I (193) /FRANK/ THE MOTHER! IS SHE HERE? /PRAED/ YES: INSIDE , AT TEA. /MRS WARREN/ (CALLING FROM WITHIN)
ARMS III (72) SEVENTY. TWENTY-FOUR OF THEM WILL HOLD TWELVE INSIDE , BESIDES TWO ON THE BOX, WITHOUT COUNTING THE DRIVER
BULL III (120) BE PRAISED. WHERES YOUR FATHER? /AUNT JUDY/ HE'S INSIDE , IN THE OFFICE, MR HAFFIGAN, WITH BARNEY DOARN N
BARB III (329) IT AWAY. /BILTON/ THE TOP OF IT WAS RED HOT INSIDE , SIR. /LOMAX/ WELL, SUPPOSE IT WAS! I DIDN'T CHUCK
MRS PREFACE(160) THE NUPTIAL CHAMBER IS IN VIEW OF THE AUDIENCE. INSIDE , THE PRINCESS AWAITS HER BRIDEGROOM. A DUENNA IS IN
MIS. (123) A DUCHESS COULD HAVE ANYTHING SO COMMON AS AN INSIDE ! I SHOULDNT HAVE MINDED IF IT HAD BEEN CHILDREN'S
SIM PRO,1, (23) NEED THINGS TO MAKE YOU HAPPY. /THE E.O./ MY INSIDE ! OH LORD! /THE Y.W./ WELL, YOU CAN MAKE YOUR

INSIDE-OUT

ROCK I (233) AT THEIR OWN SILLY GAME. I'LL JUST TURN KARL MARX INSIDE-OUT FOR THEM. (THE HOUSEHOLD GONG SOUNDS). LUNCH!

INSIDES

MIS. (123) I SHOULDNT HAVE MINDED IF IT HAD BEEN CHILDREN'S INSIDES : WE HAVE TO TALK ABOUT THEM. BUT GROWN-UP PEOPLE!
DOCT I (101) YOU WANT IS A DAILY FAMILIARITY WITH PEOPLE'S INSIDES ; AND THAT YOU CAN ONLY GET AT THE OPERATING TABLE.
HART I (47) INDIAN TEA: THE STUFF THEY TAN THEIR OWN LEATHER INSIDES WITH. (HE SEIZES THE CUP AND THE TEA-POT AND
MTH1 II (27) OF BREATHING, YOU SNEEZE, OR COUGH UP YOUR INSIDES , AND WITHER AND PERISH. YOUR BOWELS BECOME ROTTEN;
PYGM III (246) SAFE! TO TALK ABOUT OUR HEALTH! ABOUT OUR INSIDES ! PERHAPS ABOUT OUR OUTSIDES! HOW COULD YOU BE SO

INSIDIOUS

6CAL PREFACE(89) YEAR OR SO I HURL AT THEM A LONG PLAY FULL OF INSIDIOUS PROPAGANDA, WITH A MORAL IN EVERY LINE. THEY NEVER

INSIGHT

CAND III (132) OF IT. (DREAMILY) A WOMAN LIKE THAT HAS DIVINE INSIGHT : SHE LOVES OUR SOULS, AND NOT OUR FOLLIES AND
MRS III (233) YOU SHOULDNT HAVE TO WAIT. I THINK I SHEWED GREAT INSIGHT INTO YOUR CHARACTER, CROFTS. /CROFTS/ FOR TWO PINS
PLES PREFACE(R11) BE OFTEN ASSOCIATED WITH EXCEPTIONAL CRITICAL INSIGHT . AS A RULE, BY THE TIME A MANAGER HAS EXPERIENCE
MIS. PREFACE(89) DECLARE THE TRUTH, BECAUSE THEIR SINCERITY AND INSIGHT REFLECTS ON OUR DELUSION AND BLINDNESS. WE ARE ALL
POSN PREFACE(399) BUT IT WOULD PRESUMABLY HAVE A FAR DEEPER INSIGHT TO AND CONCERN FOR THE REAL ETHICAL TENDENCY OF THE
SIM II (56) METHOD. WELL, IT HAS WORKED, UP TO A POINT. THE INSIGHT YOU OBTAINED INTO EASTERN MODES OF THOUGHT HAS

INSIGNIFICANCE

SUPR PREFACE(R21) FATHER HAS NO PART, DWARF HIM INTO THE MEANEST INSIGNIFICANCE : HE SLINKS OUT OF THE WAY OF THE HUMBLEST
DEVL I SD(24) POWER THAT INFLICTS THEM, AND OF HER OWN WORMLIKE INSIGNIFICANCE . FOR AT THIS TIME, REMEMBER, MARY

INSIGNIFICANT

OVER PREFACE(162) OF MARRIED WOMEN IS NOT SEX, ONLY THE MOST INSIGNIFICANT FRACTION OF THE GALLANTRIES OF MARRIED PEOPLE
BARB PREFACE(221) PRACTICALLY UNKNOWN, WHILST I, A COMPARATIVELY INSIGNIFICANT IRISH JOURNALIST, WAS LEADING THEM BY THE NOSE
POSN PREFACE(378) FAITH, WITHOUT A THOUGHT AS TO THESE APPARENTLY INSIGNIFICANT LITTLE BOOKS BEING OF ANY IMPORTANCE OR HAVING
MILL IV (202) YOU SIT BEFORE MY VERY EYES, SNUGGLING UP TO THAT INSIGNIFICANT LITTLE NOTHINGNESS WHO CANNOT AFFORD TO PAY
2TRU II SD(51) VIEW WITH THE LETTER IN HIS HAND. HE IS AN INSIGNIFICANT LOOKING PRIVATE SOLDIER, DUSTY AS TO HIS
2TRU II SD(79) MEEK RETURNS FROM THE HILL IN THE CHARACTER OF AN INSIGNIFICANT PRIVATE, FOLLOWED BY AUBREY, TO THE COLONEL'S
PLES PREFACE(R10) A WAY AS TO MAKE THE EXPENSES OF REPRESENTATION INSIGNIFICANT ; SO THAT, WITHOUT PRETENDING THAT I COULD
ARMS II SD(25) FOLLOWED BY NICOLA. HE IS A CHEERFUL, EXCITABLE, INSIGNIFICANT , UNPOLISHED MAN OF ABOUT 50, NATURALLY

INSINCERE

NEVR III (277) ART OF SHEWING WORTHLESS ATTENTIONS AND PAYING INSINCERE COMPLIMENTS IN A KINDLY CHARMING WAY. IF YOU LIVED
CAND III (132) SHE WOULD HAVE LOVED ME ANY THE BETTER FOR BEING INSINCERE IN MY PROFESSION? /MARCHBANKS/ (ON THE SOFA,
BARB I (266) HALLMARK IS TO SILVER. /BARBARA/ DOLLY: DONT BE INSINCERE . CHOLLY: FETCH YOUR CONCERTINA AND PLAY SOMETHING
ROCK II (255) BROLLIKINS, THAT NOBLEMEN ARE ALWAYS CYNICAL AND INSINCERE . I FIND YOU A MOST BRILLIANT AND DELIGHTFUL
BULL IV (153) I WOULD ALMOST RATHER BE INCONSISTENT THAN INSINCERE . /KEEGAN/ DO NOT BE OFFENDED, SIR: I KNOW THAT
PRES (153) /LADY CORINTHIA/ DEMORALIZING. /MRS BANGER/ INSINCERE . /LADY CORINTHIA/ THEY ARE MERELY EMBRACES IN
DEVL II (46) REPROACH AT HIM). YES, DEAR, NONSENSE IS ALWAYS INSINCERE ; AND MY DEAREST IS TALKING NONSENSE. JUST
CYMB FORWORD(135) STRING OF UNSURPRISING DENOUEMENTS SUGARED WITH INSINCERE SENTIMENTALITY AFTER A LUDICROUS STAGE BATTLE.
DEVL II (46) DONT SPEAK SO STRANGELY, MY LOVE. IT SOUNDS INSINCERE TO ME. (SHE LOOKS UNUTTERABLE REPROACH AT HIM).
PHIL II SD(94) BUT NOT CONSCIOUSLY UNHAPPY NOR INTENTIONALLY INSINCERE , AND HIGHLY SELF-SATISFIED INTELLECTUALLY. SYLVIA
GETT PREFACE(218) SOLEMN VOWS THAT IT SHALL NOT HAPPEN, ARE EITHER INSINCERE , INSANE, OR HOPELESSLY STUPID. THERE IS SOME

INSINUATE

SUPR II (59) IS FOR EVERYBODY TO LIE AND SLANDER AND INSINUATE AND PRETEND AS HARD AS THEY CAN. THAT IS WHAT
AUGS (266) MAJESTY'S GOVERNMENT? /THE CLERK/ I DONT MEAN TO INSINUATE ANYTHING UNTIL THE DEFENCE OF THE REALM ACT IS
PHIL II (123) YOUNG MAN. /JULIA/ WHAT DO YOU MEAN? DO YOU DARE INSINUATE -- /CHARTERIS/ SH-- SH-- SH! DONT DISTURB THEM.
AUGS (266) (SPRINGING TO HIS FEET) DO YOU MEAN TO INSINUATE THAT HELL IS PAVED WITH MY GOOD INTENTIONS -- WITH
DOCT III (138) (RISING IN IRREPRESSIBLE RAGE) DO YOU DARE INSINUATE THAT MRS DUBEDAT IS LIVING WITH YOU WITHOUT BEING

INSINUATED

CATH 1 (163) WHO HAS CREPT ROUND THE TABLE TO THE SCREEN, AND INSINUATED HIMSELF BETWEEN PATIOMKIN'S BACK AND VARINKA) DO

INSINUATING

NEVR IV (304) UNWISE TO LIVE; AND IT'S WISE TO DIE. /WAITER/ (INSINUATING HIMSELF BETWEEN CRAMPTON AND VALENTINE) THEN, IF
APPL I (219) HAS HAPPENED. IT MAY HAPPEN AGAIN. /CRASSUS/ (INSINUATING) AS DEMOCRATS, I THINK WE ARE BOUND TO PROCEED

INSINUATINGLY

WIDO III (63) THATS ENOUGH: A GENTLEMAN COULD SAY NO LESS. (INSINUATINGLY) NOW, WOULD YOU MIND ME AND COKANE AND THE

INSIPID

MTH3 (100) NOSES AND LITTLE LIPS! THEY ARE PHYSICALLY INSIPID : THEY HAVE NO BEAUTY: YOU CANNOT LOVE THEM; BUT HOW
SUPR PREFACE(R22) FIELD: THE WILDEST HOMINIST OR FEMINIST FARCE IS INSIPID AFTER THE MOST COMMONPLACE " SLICE OF LIFE." THE
3PLA PREFACE(R10) ALWAYS LADYLIKE AND GENTLEMANLIKE. JEJUNELY INSIPID , ALL THIS, TO THE STALLS, WHICH ARE PAID FOR (WHEN

INSIST

BULL III (140) SURE IT'D BE THROUBLIN YOUR HONOR. /BROADBENT/ I INSIST : IT WILL GIVE ME THE GREATEST PLEASURE, I ASSURE
LION PREFACE(18) THE TITLE OF GOD. ILLOGICALLY, SUCH DIVINE KINGS INSIST A GOOD DEAL ON THEIR ROYAL HUMAN ANCESTORS.
OVER (193) HIM) WELL, IF WE'RE NOT TO FIGHT, I MUST INSIST AT LEAST ON YOUR NEVER SPEAKING TO MY WIFE AGAIN.
DOCT PREFACE(46) SO CLEAR THAT IT WOULD BE WASTE OF TIME TO INSIST FURTHER ON IT. AS A MATTER OF FACT THE MAN WHO ONCE
MIS. PREFACE(10) TRUTHFULNESS. ON THESE VIRTUES, HE SAID, HE MUST INSIST . AS ONE OF THEM IS NOT A VIRTUE AT ALL, AND THE
GETT (293) TO IT. YOU HAVE ME AT YOUR MERCY: MARRY ME IF YOU INSIST . BUT TAKE NOTICE THAT I PROTEST. (HE SITS DOWN
INCA PROLOG (234) WELL, ELEGANCE IF YOU LIKE. LUXURY, IF YOU INSIST . CALL IT WHAT YOU PLEASE. A HOUSE THAT COSTS LESS
PHIL II (104) DOOR GOES FIRST. /CUTHBERTSON/ OH, WELL, IF YOU INSIST . COME, GENTLEMEN: LET US GO TO LUNCH IN THE IBSEN
CATH 2 (176) NO, NO. THIS IS CARRYING A JOKE TOO FAR. I MUST INSIST . LET ME DOWN! HANG IT, WILL YOU LET ME DOWN!
NEVR I (213) MOTHER. /MRS CLANDON/ (INDIGNANTLY) AH! YOU INSIST . /GLORIA/ DO YOU INTEND THAT WE SHALL NEVER KNOW?
MIS. (144) IVE NOT THE SLIGHTEST DOUBT OF IT. DONT INSIST . /HYPATIA/ IT'S NOT YOUR IDEAL, IS IT? /LORD
APPL I (236) YOU, BUT THAT YOUR SUCCESS IS CERTAIN IF YOU INSIST . /LYSISTRATA/ SPLENDID! /AMANDA/ YOU DID SPEAK THAT
MILL III (180) CONVINCED THAT YOU WILL PAY FIVE SHILLINGS IF I INSIST . /THE WOMAN/ OH, MAAM, HAVE SOME FEELING FOR US. YOU
CAND II (125) BUT, JAMES-- /MORELL/ (AUTHORITATIVELY) I INSIST . YOU DO NOT WANT TO COME; AND HE DOES NOT WANT TO
POSN PREFACE(425) BIGOTRY OF PEOPLE SO UNFIT FOR SOCIAL LIFE AS TO INSIST NOT ONLY THAT THEIR OWN PREJUDICES AND SUPERSTITIONS
NEVR II (228) IN SPITE OF YOUR SEX (MRS CLANDON NODS); TO INSIST ON A MARRIED WOMAN'S RIGHT TO HER OWN SEPARATE
NEVR IV (304) (NAILING VALENTINE TO THE POINT INSTANTLY) THEN INSIST ON A SETTLEMENT. THAT SHOCKS YOUR DELICACY: MOST
BULL PREFACE(36) OFFICIAL IRISH CHURCH. THE IRISH PARLIAMENT WOULD INSIST ON A VOICE IN THE PROMOTION OF CHURCHMEN: FEES AND
MIS. PREFACE(44) ANY KIND, OR WHAT IS CALLED BAD TASTE, AND MUST INSIST ON ALL PERSONS FACING SUCH SHOCKS AS THEY FACE FROSTY
WIDO II (39) NO MATTER! BUT IT DOES MATTER, SIR. I INSIST ON AN ANSWER. WHY DID YOU NOT SAY SO BEFORE?
JOAN EPILOG (162) IN THAT WAY: A TOUCH OF TRUE BREEDING. BUT I MUST INSIST ON APOLOGIZING VERY AMPLY. THE TRUTH IS, THESE

SUPR PREFACE(R29)	I PROCEED TO WRITE A DON JUAN PLAY. WELL, IF YOU	INSIST	ON ASKING ME WHY I BEHAVE IN THIS ABSURD WAY, I CAN
SUPR PREFACE(R11)	MADE THE MAINSPRING OF THE ACTION. THAT IS WHY WE	INSIST	ON BEAUTY IN OUR PERFORMERS, DIFFERING HEREIN FROM
BULL PREFACE(43)	FOOL, SOLELY BECAUSE WE HAVE LEARNT THAT NATIONS	INSIST	ON BEING GOVERNED BY THEIR OWN CONSENT-- OR, AS THEY
WIDO III (50)	AND HAVE NOTHING PREYING ON YOUR SPIRITS, I MUST	INSIST	ON BEING ILL AND HAVE SOMETHING PREYING ON MINE. AND
OVER (187)	I'M AS GUILTY AS IF I HAD ACTUALLY SINNED. AND I	INSIST	ON BEING TREATED AS A SINNER, AND NOT WALKED OVER AS
HART II (124)	AND WALKING ANGRILY UP AND DOWN THE ROOM) I	INSIST	ON BEING TREATED WITH A CERTAIN CONSIDERATION. I WILL
2TRU PREFACE(22)	THE CATHOLIC CHURCH AND OUR BOARD OF EDUCATION	INSIST	ON CELIBACY, THE ONE FOR PRIESTS AND THE OTHER FOR
DOCT III (133)	ISNT IT EXTRAORDINARILY KIND OF THEM, LOUIS, TO	INSIST	ON COMING? ALL OF THEM, TO CONSULT ABOUT YOU?
3PLA PREFACE(R36)	HIS NEW IDEAS HAVE MASTERED HIM SUFFICIENTLY TO	INSIST	ON CONSTANT EXPRESSION BY HIS ART. IN SUCH CASES YOU
APPL PREFACE(180)	HE BELIEVES IN IT. SO DO I. THAT IS WHY I	INSIST	ON EQUALITY OF INCOME. EQUAL CONSIDERATION FOR A
BULL PREFACE(24)	IRELAND THAT YOU WILL NEVER UNDERSTAND UNLESS I	INSIST	ON EXPLAINING IT TO YOU WITH THAT IRISH INSISTENCE ON
GETT PREFACE(183)	BE LED TO THE REGISTRY OR EVEN TO THE ALTAR, THEY	INSIST	ON FIRST ARRIVING AT AN EXPLICIT UNDERSTANDING THAT
MIS. (203)	THEREFORE I HOPE SHE'LL STAY TO DINNER, AND NOT	INSIST	ON FLYING AWAY IN THAT AEROPLANE. /PERCIVAL/ YOU
METH PREFACE(R59)	ROCK ON WHICH EQUALITY IS BUILT, HAD LED US TO	INSIST	ON GOD OFFERING US SPECIAL TERMS BY PLACING US APART
SUPR I (21)	ON THE BACK) MY DEAR ANNIE, NONSENSE. I	INSIST	ON GRANNY. I WONT ANSWER TO ANY OTHER NAME THAN
JOAN PREFACE(19)	MAD FATHER AND HIS WISE GRANDFATHER. WHY DID SHE	INSIST	ON HAVING A SOLDIER'S DRESS AND ARMS AND SWORD AND
ARMS II (28)	HE MARRIES RAINA. BESIDES, THE COUNTRY SHOULD	INSIST	ON HAVING AT LEAST ONE NATIVE GENERAL. /PETKOFF/ YES;
NEVR III (275)	WITH IRRELEVANT INTERJECTIONS. (VEHEMENTLY) I	INSIST	ON HAVING EARNEST MATTERS EARNESTLY AND REVERENTLY
BARB I (270)	WATCH) WELL, IF YOU ARE DETERMINED TO HAVE IT, I	INSIST	ON HAVING IT IN A PROPER AND RESPECTABLE WAY.
2TRU I (33)	MEASLES FROM A MICROBE? /THE DOCTOR/ PATIENTS	INSIST	ON HAVING MICROBES NOWADAYS. IF I TOLD HER THERE IS
BARB PREFACE(220)	ARE MONEY. THE FIRST DUTY OF EVERY CITIZEN IS TO	INSIST	ON HAVING MONEY ON REASONABLE TERMS; AND THIS DEMAND
JOAN PREFACE(26)	VICTORIAN; BUT BOTH OF THEM RECOGNIZE AND	INSIST	ON HER CAPACITY FOR LEADERSHIP, THOUGH THE SCOTS
JOAN 6 (128)	ISSUE OF HERESY, ON WHICH SHE SEEMS SO FAR TO	INSIST	ON HER OWN GUILT. I WILL ASK YOU, THEREFORE, TO SAY
MIS. PREFACE(40)	THE CALCULUS TO FALL BACK ON, UNLESS INDEED YOU	INSIST	ON HIS LEARNING MUSIC, AND PROCEED TO HIT HIM IF HE
LION PREFACE(30)	SUGGESTS THAT HE SHOULD RELEASE JESUS. BUT THEY	INSIST	ON HIS RELEASING A PRISONER NAMED BARABBAS INSTEAD,
LION PREFACE(89)	THE SMALLEST OF OUR SINS BRINGS ITS KARMA, ALSO	INSIST	ON INDIVIDUAL IMMORTALITY AND METEMPSYCHOSIS IN ORDER
GETT (317)	GRUDGE ME MY SELF-RESPECT AND INDEPENDENCE. I	INSIST	ON IT IN FAIRNESS TO YOU, CECIL, BECAUSE IN THIS WAY
DOCT PREFACE(42)	TO DEATH BECAUSE IT IS THE CUSTOM TO EAT VEAL AND	INSIST	ON ITS BEING WHITE; OR AS A GERMAN PURVEYOR NAILS A
MIS. PREFACE(96)	ALL LIKE THE STORY OF JONAH AND THE WHALE (THEY	INSIST	ON ITS BEING A WHALE IN SPITE OF DEMONSTRATIONS BY
NEVR IV (295)	ME, SIR: THIS IS SOMETHING REALLY SERIOUS. I	INSIST	ON KNOWING WHO MISS CLANDON SAID THAT TO. /DOLLY/
PHIL I (92)	CHARTERIS: WHAT HAS BEEN GOING ON HERE? I	INSIST	ON KNOWING. GRACE HAS NOT GONE TO BED: I HAVE SEEN
SUPR PREFACE(R10)	WHEN THEY OUGHT TO BE UNCOMFORTABLE; AND I	INSIST	ON MAKING THEM THINK IN ORDER TO BRING THEM TO
BULL PREFACE(11)	THE NOTION THAT THE WAY TO PROSPER IS TO	INSIST	ON MANAGING EVERYBODY ELSE'S AFFAIRS IS, ON THE FACE
GETT PREFACE(215)	WHOSE SOLE MEANS OF LIVELIHOOD WAS WIFEHOOD WOULD	INSIST	ON MARRIAGE: HENCE A TENDENCY WOULD SET IN TO MAKE
3PLA PREFACE(R14)	THE STALLS, FROM RACIAL PREJUDICE, WERE APT TO	INSIST	ON MORE REBECCA AND LESS ROWENA THAN THE PIT CARED
DEST (181)	YOU, DESPATCHES OR NO DESPATCHES. I HOPE YOU WONT	INSIST	ON MY STARTING OFF ON A WILD GOOSE CHASE AFTER THE
MIS. PREFACE(29)	THEM TO RESPECT OTHER PEOPLE'S OPINIONS, AND TO	INSIST	ON RESPECT FOR THEIR OWN IN THESE AS IN OTHER
BARB PREFACE(229)	AS WELL MIGHT WE ASSUME THAT THE POOR PEOPLE WHO	INSIST	ON SHEWING DISGUSTING ULCERS TO DISTRICT VISITORS ARE
GENV IV (99)	KIKKERONIAN IS AN INSULT TO MY OLD SCHOOL. I	INSIST	ON SISSERONIAN. /THE BETROTHED/ HEAR HEAR! /BBDE/
JOAN PREFACE(42)	THEIR CASES, OR AS CONSCIENTIOUS A JUDGE TO	INSIST	ON STRICT LEGALITY OF PROCEDURE AS JOAN HAD FROM THE
GETT PREFACE(243)	BY THE VICTIMS FOR ADOPTING THEIR TRADE, AND	INSIST	ON THE FACT THAT POVERTY IS NOT OFTEN ALLEGED. BUT
POSN PREFACE(398)	BETWEEN THE KING AND QUEEN. HE WOULD PROBABLY	INSIST	ON THE SUBSTITUTION OF SOME FICTITIOUS COUNTRY FOR
FABL PREFACE(86)	TO MAKE ROOM FOR SHEEP OR DEER. BOTH PARTIES	INSIST	ON THE SUPREME NECESSITY FOR INCREASED PRODUCTION;
WIDO III (59)	SEKKETERRY. DR TRENCH IS ONLY JOKING. /COKANE/ I	INSIST	ON THE WITHDRAWAL OF THAT EXPRESSION. I HAVE BEEN
SIM PREFACE(4)	HAVE THEIR CHILDREN BAPTIZED OR CIRCUMCIZED, AND	INSIST	ON THEIR BEING VACCINATED, IN THE TEETH OF
BARB PREFACE(221)	WILL BE DISCOVERED. MEANWHILE I RECOMMEND THEM TO	INSIST	ON THEIR OWN MERITS AS AN IMPORTANT PART OF THEIR OWN
ROCK II (251)	SPEECH, MISS BROLLIKINS! I REALLY MUST	INSIST	ON YOUR SHAKING HANDS WITH ME BEFORE WE PART.
BARB I (271)	ADOLPHUS, CAN BEHAVE YOURSELF IF YOU CHOOSE TO. I	INSIST	ON YOUR STAYING. /CUSINS/ MY DEAR LADY BRIT: THERE
FANY II (290)	MATTER. (KNOX HANDS HIM TWO SOVEREIGNS). IF YOU	INSIST	-- (HE POCKETS THEM). THANK YOU. /MARGARET/ I'M EVER
LION PREFACE(78)	THIS VIEW OF THE CASE INEVITABLY LED HIM TO	INSIST	THAT A WIFE SHOULD BE RATHER A SLAVE THAN A PARTNER,
BULL PREFACE(58)	AHMED HASSAN ZAKZOUK, AGED 26, WAS RASH ENOUGH TO	INSIST	THAT AFTER THE SHOT THAT STRUCK THE WOMAN, THE
GETT PREFACE(205)	COMES IN; AND THOUGH I AM DEMOCRAT ENOUGH TO	INSIST	THAT HE MUST FIRST CONVINCE A REPRESENTATIVE BODY OF
LION PREFACE(4)	RIGHT WITH RESPECTABLE SOCIETY; BUT I MUST STILL	INSIST	THAT IF JESUS COULD HAVE WORKED OUT THE PRACTICAL
MTH3 (107)	AND THE ACCOUNTANT GENERAL ARE GOING TO	INSIST	THAT IT'S TRUE. WE SHALL HAVE EITHER TO LOCK THEM UP
LION PREFACE(88)	VICARIOUS ATONEMENT SO STERNLY THAT THEY	INSIST	THAT THE SMALLEST OF OUR SINS BRINGS ITS KARMA, ALSO

INSISTED

3PLA PREFACE(R15)	AND THE DRUNKEN UNDERGRADUATE IN THE STALLS, THEY	INSISTED	ALL THE TIME ON THEIR VIRTUE AND PATRIOTISM AND
MILL PREFACE(131)	OF GOVERNORS AS THE CHURCHES WOULD BE IF THEY	INSISTED	ON ALL THEIR PARISH PRIESTS OR RECTORS BEING
O'FL PREFACE(201)	FROM THEIR OWN POINT OF VIEW. BUT THE WAR OFFICE	INSISTED	ON APPROACHING THEM FROM THE POINT OF VIEW OF
LION PREFACE(93)	THAT DIVINE SPARK WITHIN HIM WHICH JESUS	INSISTED	ON AS THE EVERYDAY REALITY OF WHAT THE ATHEIST
METH PREFACE(R41)	THE NATURAL MULTIPLICATION OF THEIR NUMBERS, AS	INSISTED	ON BY MALTHUS. SUPPOSE THE AVERAGE HEIGHT OF THE
JITT II (34)	AND EDITH) I WANTED TO COME ALONE; BUT EDITH	INSISTED	ON COMING WITH ME. /LENKHEIM/ SHE WAS QUITE RIGHT.
GETT PREFACE(251)	THE PRESENCE OF MIND TO ASK THE LADY WHETHER SHE	INSISTED	ON HAVING A DOCTOR, A NURSE, A DENTIST, AND EVEN A
BULL PREFACE(23)	APOLOGIST OF DOING NOTHING, AND, WHEN THE PEOPLE	INSISTED	ON HIS DOING SOMETHING, ONLY ROUSED HIMSELF TO
CAPT II (260)	AT WAYNFLETE WHEN HE WAS STAYING WITH US; AND I	INSISTED	ON HIS LOCKING THE POOR MAN UP, UNTIL THE POLICE
METH PREFACE(R9)	MONKEYS," I TRIED TO EXPLAIN THAT WHAT DARWIN HAD	INSISTED	ON IN THIS CONNECTION WAS THAT SOME MONKEYS HAVE NO
ARMS II (26)	REMEMBER THAT. THEY WANTED TO PUT THAT IN; BUT I	INSISTED	ON ITS BEING STRUCK OUT. WHAT MORE COULD I DO?
3PLA PREFACE(R21)	THE NEXT. IF THE CONVENTIONS OF ROMANCE ARE ONLY	INSISTED	ON LONG ENOUGH AND UNIFORMLY ENOUGH (A CONDITION
KING I (209)	IT THIS MORNING HAD NOT HER GRACE OF CLEVELAND	INSISTED	ON MY DRAWING HER INSTEAD. BUT HOW CAN AN
INCA PROLOG (233)	I WANTED TO; AND YOU WOULDNT LET ME. YOU	INSISTED	ON MY MARRYING ROOSENHONKERS-PIPSTEIN. /THE
DOCT I (95)	WOMAN, AND SHE SIMPLY A WHITED SEPULCHRE. SO SHE	INSISTED	ON MY OPERATING ON HER, TOO. AND BY GEORGE, SIR,
DOCT IV (170)	/WALPOLE/ GOODBYE. I BLAME MYSELF: I SHOULD HAVE	INSISTED	ON OPERATING. (HE GOES). /B.B./ I WILL SEND THE
DOCT PREFACE(38)	CALLOUS EXTERMINATION OF OUR FELLOW CREATURES. WE	INSISTED	ON OUR BUTCHERS SUPPLYING US WITH WHITE VEAL, AND
BUOY III (40)	THE COMMUNAL LIFE OF A UNIVERSITY GIVES. BUT HE	INSISTED	ON OUR LEAVING WITHOUT A DEGREE. /SIR F./ IN
MIS. PREFACE(42)	UNUSED TO HORSES AND VERY MUCH AFRAID OF THEM,	INSISTED	ON PUTTING ME ON A RATHER RUMBUSTIOUS PONY WITH
LION PREFACE(76)	CONTENT TO TAKE POLITICAL ECONOMY AS HE FOUND IT,	INSISTED	ON REBUILDING IT FROM THE BOTTOM UPWARDS IN HIS OWN
DOCT IV (158)	SIR RALPH: WHAT AM I TO DO? THAT MAN WHO	INSISTED	ON SEEING ME, AND SENT IN WORD THAT HIS BUSINESS
DOCT V (179)	THEY WILL NOT BE SOLD TO YOU. LOUIS' CREDITORS	INSISTED	ON SELLING THEM; BUT THIS IS MY BIRTHDAY; AND THEY
MILL PREFACE(131)	SYMPTOM OF SUPREME FITNESS FOR IT. BUT IF WE	INSISTED	ON THIS QUALIFICATION IN ALL CASES, WE SHOULD FIND
JOAN PREFACE(45)	A SWOOP ON PARIS SHE WAS LOST. THE FACT THAT SHE	INSISTED	ON THIS WHILST THE KING AND THE REST TIMIDLY AND
PYGM EPILOG (300)	THE ENDS MEET OVER AND OVER AGAIN, AT LAST GENTLY	INSISTED	; AND ELIZA, HUMBLED TO THE DUST BY HAVING TO BEG
METH PREFACE(R29)	IN PREHISTORIC TIME BY AGES AND AGES. WE	INSISTED	THAT EVOLUTION ADVANCED MORE SLOWLY THAN ANY SNAIL
MIS. PREFACE(32)	SKINNED ALIVE WITH A BIRCH ROD. IT MIGHT EVEN BE	INSISTED	THAT GIRLS WITH HIGH-CLASS BADGES SHOULD BE
LION PREFACE(79)	PUT IT ALL ON ME." HE SAID " SIN NO MORE," AND	INSISTED	THAT HE WAS PUTTING UP THE STANDARD OF CONDUCT, NOT
JOAN PREFACE(20)	AND THE REST TO THE RELIEF OF DUNOIS AT ORLEANS,	INSISTED	THAT SHE MUST GO HERSELF AND LEAD THE ASSAULT IN
METH PREFACE(R49)	BEYOND DENYING CONSCIOUSNESS TO TREES. WEISMANN	INSISTED	THAT THE CHICK BREAKS OUT OF ITS EGGSHELL
BARB III (316)	MY PARTNER LAZARUS HAS AT LAST MADE A STAND AND	INSISTED	THAT THE SUCCESSION MUST BE SETTLED ONE WAY OR THE
DOCT PREFACE(26)	NO SUCH EXPERIENCE, HAS ALWAYS CHANCED IT, AND	INSISTED	, WHEN HE WAS UNLUCKY, THAT THE RESULTS WERE NOT
POSN PREFACE(432)	MR YEATS NOT ONLY WOULD NOT YIELD AN INCH, BUT	INSISTED	, WITHIN THE DUE LIMITS OF GALLANT WARFARE, ON

INSISTENCE

BULL II SD(111)	REILLY AT THE ROUND TOWER. NOT THAT ANY SPECIAL	INSISTENCE	IS NEEDED; FOR THE ENGLISH INHIBITIVE INSTINCT
SUPR PREFACE(R35)	OF THE CHURCH AS THE SUPPLANTER OF RELIGION, HIS	INSISTENCE	ON COURAGE AS THE VIRTUE OF VIRTUES, HIS ESTIMATE
SHAK PREFACE(136)	SPLENDID STYLE OWES MUCH MORE TO HIS MOTHER'S	INSISTENCE	ON HIS LEARNING THE BIBLE BY HEART THAN TO HIS
MILL PREFACE(114)	TO MAKE A COURT FOR HIMSELF, HIS SILLY	INSISTENCE	ON IMPERIAL ETIQUETTE WHEN HE WAS A DETHRONED AND
BULL PREFACE(24)	I INSIST ON EXPLAINING IT TO YOU WITH THAT IRISH	INSISTENCE	ON INTELLECTUAL CLARITY TO WHICH MY ENGLISH
METH PREFACE(R65)	FOR EXAMPLE, THE QUINCY ADAMSES, WITH THEIR	INSISTENCE	ON MODERN DEMOCRATIC DEGRADATION AS AN INEVITABLE
UNPL PREFACE(R18)	LOATHING OF THE VERY WORD HOME), AND HER	INSISTENCE	ON QUALIFYING HERSELF FOR AN INDEPENDENT WORKING
3PLA PREFACE(R20)	THE OLD MAIDS OF ENGLAND?); RATHER, INDEED, AN	INSISTENCE	ON THE BLINDING AND NARROWING POWER OF
SIM PREFACE(6)	THE LATE MRS BRADLAUGH BONNER, NOR OF TOLSTOY'S	INSISTENCE	ON THE DAMNATION ON EARTH OF THE UNDETECTED,
METH PREFACE(R59)	SOCIALISTS WERE SPECIALLY ENCOURAGED BY DARWIN'S	INSISTENCE	ON THE INFLUENCE OF ENVIRONMENT. PERHAPS THE
FANY II (289)	I CAME IN AT YOUR INVITATION-- AT YOUR AMIABLE	INSISTENCE	, IN FACT, NOT AT MY OWN. BUT YOU NEED HAVE NO
ROCK II (238)	OF THE ADMIRALTY, AT MY PERSONAL SUGGESTION AND	INSISTENCE	, IN THIS SO-CALLED NATIONAL GOVERNMENT, WHICH

INSISTENT

ROCK I (200)	MORE EXPLICIT, MISS HANWAYS. /HILDA/ (GENTLY	INSISTENT	) NOT ANY PARTICULAR FAMILY. THE FAMILY. SOCIALISM

2TRU III SD(94)	THE PATH THROUGH THE GAP, THE LADY DISTRACTED AND	INSISTENT	, THE COLONEL ALMOST EQUALLY DISTRACTED: SHE

INSISTENTLY

NEVR IV (294)	(HE SITS DOWN IN TOKEN OF SUBMISSION). /DOLLY/ (	INSISTENTLY	) DO YOU LIKE IT? /CRAMPTON/ MY CHILD: HOW CAN
MTH1 II SD(20)	INTO THE GARDEN, IN POSE, VOICE, AND DRESS HE IS	INSISTENTLY	WARLIKE. HE IS EQUIPPED WITH HUGE SPEAR AND

INSISTING

DOCT IV (164)	/MRS DUBEDAT/ OH, HOW CAN YOU, LOUIS? /LOUIS/ (	INSISTING	CHILDISHLY) YES, BECAUSE PEOPLE WHO HAVE FOUND
LION PREFACE(14)	NOT, INSTEAD OF DRIVING OURSELVES TO DESPAIR BY	INSISTING	ON A SEPARATE ATONEMENT BY A SEPARATE REDEEMER FOR
MTH4 I (152)	I MADE MY FIRST STAND FOR CHILDREN'S RIGHTS BY	INSISTING	ON BEING CALLED AT LEAST JOE. AT FIFTEEN I REFUSED
SUPR IV (163)	SHE WILL DO JUST WHAT SHE LIKES HERSELF WHILST	INSISTING	ON EVERYBODY ELSE DOING WHAT THE CONVENTIONAL CODE
GETT PREFACE(242)	ADVISE A WOMAN TO KEEP HOUSE WITH A MAN WITHOUT	INSISTING	ON HIS MARRYING HER, UNLESS SHE IS INDEPENDENT OF
NEVR IV (286)	BOWS. BOHUN BOWS). MR CLANDON? /CRAMPTON/ (	INSISTING	ON HIS RIGHTFUL NAME AS ANGRILY AS HE DARES) MY
BULL III (136)	HUMANITY IS LOOKING FORWARD TO IT TOO, AND	INSISTING	ON IT WITH NO UNCERTAIN VOICE-- I LOOK FORWARD TO
ROCK II (236)	AND I DRANK NOTHING BUT BARLEY WATER. /BASHAM/ (	INSISTING	) BUT LOOK AT IT, MAN. (QUOTING THE HEADLINES)
GETT (276)	OH, DONT BEGIN BOTHERING ABOUT THOSE-- /LEO/ (	INSISTING	) HAVE? YOU? KEPT? YOUR? PROMISES? HAVE YOU
BULL I (92)	LOOK HERE, LARRY: DONT BE AN ASS. /DOYLE/ (	INSISTING	) I SAY A CATERPILLAR AND I MEAN A CATERPILLAR.
DEST (171)	(HURRIEDLY) TAKE CARE. TREASON! /LADY/ (	INSISTING	) YES, EMPEROR OF FRANCE; THEN OF EUROPE; PERHAPS
CAND II (117)	COME AND TALK TO ME. /MORELL/ BUT-- /CANDIDA/ (	INSISTING	) YES, I MUST BE TALKED TO. (SHE MAKES HIM SIT
JITT III (79)	BEEN SO VERY HARD ON YOU, HAVE I? /JITTA/ (	INSISTING	) YOU WILL NOT DESTROY THE BOOK? YOU WILL EDIT
ROCK PREFACE(177)	JOSHUA'S VICTORY AS A RELIGIOUS TRUTH INSTEAD OF	INSISTING	THAT IT DID NOT MAKE THE SMALLEST DIFFERENCE TO
OVER PREFACE(164)	UNCONVINCING CONVENTION: THE ACTORS RATHER	INSISTING	THAT IT SHALL BE IMPOSSIBLE FOR ANY SPECTATOR TO
LION PREFACE(80)	GOOD CONDUCT THE TEST OF SINCERE BELIEF, AND	INSISTING	THAT SINCERE BELIEF WAS NECESSARY TO SALVATION,

INSISTS

LION PREFACE(41)	THAT THOU, BEING A MAN, MAKEST THYSELF GOD." HE	INSISTS	(REFERRING TO THE 82ND PSALM) THAT IF IT IS PART OF
MIS. PREFACE(38)	IDEAS OR EXTENDING THE DOMAIN OF KNOWLEDGE, AND	INSISTS	ON A READY-MADE ROUTINE. IT MAY COME TO FORCING
BULL PREFACE(43)	HE IS ASSERTING A NATURAL RIGHT TO LIVE. WHEN HE	INSISTS	ON A VOTE IN ORDER THAT HIS COUNTRY MAY BE GOVERNED
BULL PREFACE(43)	ARE DEDUCED FROM NATURAL RIGHTS. WHEN A MAN	INSISTS	ON CERTAIN LIBERTIES WITHOUT THE SLIGHTEST REGARD TO
MTH2 (46)	HOUSE OF COMMONS AND HEAD A GROUP THERE. SO HE	INSISTS	ON COMING TO SEE ME. HE IS STAYING WITH SOME PEOPLE
METH PREFACE(R46)	DARWIN BECOMES TEDIOUS IN THE MANNER OF A MAN WHO	INSISTS	ON CONTINUING TO PROVE HIS INNOCENCE AFTER HE HAS
BULL II SD(111)	BED AND PERHAPS DREAM OF PROSAIC ENGLAND, THAT HE	INSISTS	ON GOING OUT TO SMOKE A CIGAR AND LOOK FOR NORA
BULL PREFACE(43)	A NATURAL RIGHT TO SELF-GOVERNMENT. WHEN HE	INSISTS	ON GUIDING HIMSELF AT 21 BY HIS OWN INEXPERIENCE AND
LIED (191)	TOLD YOU ALREADY THAT I HATE DIAMONDS; ONLY TEDDY	INSISTS	ON HANGING ME ALL OVER WITH THEM. YOU NEED NOT
LION PREFACE(63)	ORDER TO REMAIN ALIVE, PLUS THE THINGS THE STATE	INSISTS	ON HIS HAVING AND USING WHETHER HE WANTS TO OR NOT:
SIM II (56)	IMPERIAL ARMADA, IN WHICH EVERY PETTY PROVINCE	INSISTS	ON ITS SEPARATE FLEET, EVERY TRUMPERY ISLET ITS
BULL PREFACE(43)	RIGHT TO THAT LIBERTY. WHEN, FOR INSTANCE, HE	INSISTS	ON LIVING, IN SPITE OF THE IRREFUTABLE
HART II (122)	APPEARANCE IN THE DAYS OF MY VANITY; AND HESIONE	INSISTS	ON MY KEEPING IT UP. SHE MAKES ME WEAR THESE
SIM II (55)	ENGLAND WONT TOLERATE POLYGAMY ON ANY TERMS, AND	INSISTS	ON OUR PROSECUTING IDDY IF WE CANNOT WHITEWASH HIM.
MIS. PREFACE(95)	IS EDUCATING THE CHILD RELIGIOUSLY, EVEN IF HE	INSISTS	ON REPUDIATING THAT PIOUS ADVERB AND SUBSTITUTING
OVER PREFACE(160)	BLOOD FEUD OR VENDETTA . AS LONG AS HUMAN NATURE	INSISTS	ON REVENGE, THE OFFICIAL ORGANIZATION AND
DOCT IV (158)	HIM! /MRS DUBEDAT/ (STOPPING HIM) BUT LOUIS	INSISTS	ON SEEING HIM! HE ALMOST BEGAN TO CRY ABOUT IT. AND
2TRU PREFACE(7)	SAID, DO NOT KNOW HOW THE POOR LIVE; BUT NOBODY	INSISTS	ON THE MORE MISCHIEVOUS FACT THAT THE POOR DO NOT
MRS PREFACE(169)	REASONABLE BEINGS, AND THE MORE POWERFULLY HE	INSISTS	ON THE RUTHLESS INDIFFERENCE OF THEIR GREAT DRAMATIC
ROCK PREFACE(168)	THE EMINENT FRENCH STATESMAN, GOES TO RUSSIA AND	INSISTS	ON VISITING THE UKRAINE SO THAT HE MAY HAVE OCULAR
JOAN PREFACE(54)	THE THEATRE FOR THE SAKE OF THE PLAY SOLELY, AND	INSISTS	SO EFFECTIVELY ON A CERTAIN NUMBER OF HOURS'
CAND II (123)	WHAT BETTER DO THEY WANT? /LEXY/ BUT HE ALWAYS	INSISTS	SO POWERFULLY ON THE DIVORCE OF SOCIALISM FROM
DOCT PREFACE(49)	WHETHER HE IS A RASCAL OR NOT, HE NOT ONLY	INSISTS	THAT THE REAL POINT IS WHETHER SOME HOT-HEADED
SUPR HANDBOK(218)	IS THE EQUAL OF THE ASTRONOMER ROYAL; BUT HE	INSISTS	THAT THEY SHALL BOTH BE HANGED EQUALLY IF THEY

INSOFAR

CAND I (101)	FOR ME TO CONTROL MYSELF. MY TALENT IS LIKE YOURS	INSOFAR	AS IT HAS ANY REAL WORTH AT ALL. IT IS THE GIFT OF
GETT PREFACE(208)	BE REMEMBERED THAT URBAN CIVILIZATION ITSELF,	INSOFAR	AS IT IS A METHOD OF EVOLUTION (AND WHEN IT IS NOT

INSOLENCE

MTH3 (123)	THE ANXIETIES! THE HEARTBREAK! THE	INSOLENCE	AND TYRANNY THAT WERE THE DAILY LOT OF MANKIND
ROCK II (265)	MONEY. BUT TODAY YOUR HATRED, YOUR ENVY, YOUR	INSOLENCE	HAS BETRAYED ITSELF. I AM NIGGER. I AM BAD
CATH 2 (179)	OH! HE HAS DARED TO ADMIRE YOUR MAJESTY. SUCH	INSOLENCE	IS NOT TO BE ENDURED. /EDSTASTON/ ALL EUROPE IS A
CAPT II (250)	(POINTING TO DRINKWATER) IS SUBJECT TO FITS OF	INSOLENCE	. IF HE IS IMPERTINENT TO YOUR LADYSHIP, OR
6CAL (104)	HUSBAND. /THE QUEEN/ YOU SHALL SUFFER FOR THIS	INSOLENCE	. (TO THE KING) WILL YOU, MY LORD, STAND BY AND
2TRU II (75)	WAS WHITE AS SNOW." /TALLBOYS/ BUT THAT WAS	INSOLENCE	. /MEEK/ IT GOT HER OUT OF HER DIFFICULTY, SIR.
INCA SD(236)	WHICH SAILS VERY CLOSE TO THE EAST WIND OF	INSOLENCE	. /THE MANAGER/ I AM SORRY I AM UNABLE TO
GETT (329)	SITTING DOWN WITH AN OVERDONE ATTEMPT AT STUDIED	INSOLENCE	) AND PRAY WHAT IS YOUR WRETCHED HUSBAND'S VULGAR
PHIL III (137)	TO THE END OF THE COUCH). /JULIA/ (WITH STUDIED	INSOLENCE	) HAS THAT WOMAN TOLD YOU THAT SHE HAS GIVEN YOU
NEVR I (200)	OF FIVE SHILLINGS. /THE YOUNG LADY/ (WITH COOL	INSOLENCE	) WELL, SO YOU HAVE. (SHE GETS UP). WHY SHOULDNT
LADY PREFACE(216)	THE FLUNKEYISM TOWARDS SOCIAL SUPERIORS AND	INSOLENCE	TOWARDS SOCIAL INFERIORS, THE EASY WAYS WITH
LADY PREFACE(216)	BY THOSE WHO HAVE A TURN FOR THEM, BUT IN WHICH	INSOLENCE	, DERISION, PROFLIGACY, OBSCENE JESTING, DEBT
CATH 2 (179)	/EDSTASTON/ ALL EUROPE IS A PARTY TO THAT	INSOLENCE	, MADAM. /THE PRINCESS DASHKOFF/ ALL EUROPE IS
SUPR HANDBOK(205)	FOR MORE OF IT, CONSTANT AS THE CLAMOR FOR MORE	INSOLENCE	, MORE WAR, AND LOWER RATES, IS TOLERATED AND EVEN
CAPT III (295)	MY MOTHER, WITH HER COMMENTS ON THEIR COLD DRAWN	INSOLENCE	, THEIR TREACHERY AND CRUELTY, AND THE PITEOUS

INSOLENT

UNPL PREFACE(R14)	BUT I MUST SUBMIT IN ORDER TO OBTAIN FROM HIM AN	INSOLENT	AND INSUFFERABLE DOCUMENT, WHICH I CANNOT READ
SUPR IV (167)	/TANNER/ SO THAT SHE MAY MAKE HER TRIUMPH MORE	INSOLENT	BY PUBLICLY THROWING AWAY THE BAIT THE MOMENT THE
AUGS (279)	THE LOWER MIDDLE CLASSES. /THE LADY/ SERVE THE	INSOLENT	CREATURE RIGHT! LOOK! I HAVE FOUND YOU A
LADY (244)	DARK LADY/ WILL: FOR PITY'S SAKE-- /ELIZABETH/	INSOLENT	DOG-- /SHAKESPEAR/ (CUTTING THEM SHORT) HOW KNOW
MTH3 (130)	GOOD FOR IT? /BARNABAS/ HOLD YOUR TONGUE, YOU	INSOLENT	HEATHEN, BURGE! I SPOKE TO YOU. /BURGE-LUBIN/ WELL,
6CAL (94)	I WILL KICK IT TO MY DOGS TO EAT. I WILL CHOP HIS	INSOLENT	HERALD INTO FOUR QUARTERS-- /THE PRINCE/ (SHOCKED)
CLEO II (137)	MY OPINION HE NEEDS A LESSON. HIS MANNER IS MOST	INSOLENT	. /CAESAR/ WHERE IS HE? /BRITANNUS/ HE WAITS
ARMS I SD(6)	SO DEFIANT THAT HER SERVILITY TO RAINA IS ALMOST	INSOLENT	. SHE IS AFRAID OF CATHERINE, BUT EVEN WITH HER
AUGS (264)	YOU AT THE SAME TIME, CAN I? /AUGUSTUS/ DONT BE	INSOLENT	. WHERE IS THE GENTLEMAN I HAVE BEEN CORRESPONDING
6CAL (105)	QUEEN/ WILL YOU MOCK MY CONDITION BEFORE THIS	INSOLENT	MAN AND BEFORE THE WORLD? I WILL NOT ENDURE IT.
DEVL III (73)	BECAUSE YOURE PAID TO DO IT. /SWINDON/ YOU	INSOLENT	-- (HE SWALLOWS HIS RAGE). /BURGOYNE/ (WITH MUCH
KING I (175)	OUT OF PLACE IN IT. YOU GO OR I GO. /BARBARA/ YOU	INSOLENT	SLUT, I WILL HAVE YOU TAKEN TO THE BRIDEWELL AND
MIS. PREFACE(104)	ARE AS IMPUDENTLY SERVILE TO THE SUCCESSFUL, AND	INSOLENT	TO COMMON HONEST FOLK, AS THE FLATTERERS OF THE
DEVL III (60)	(WHITENING WITH ANGER) I ADVISE YOU NOT TO BE	INSOLENT	, PRISONER. /RICHARD/ YOU CANT HELP YOURSELF,

INSOLENTLY

ROCK PREFACE(161)	WITH IT THE PRIVILEGE OF TREATING THE PUBLIC	INSOLENTLY	AND EXTORTING BRIBES FROM IT, FOR EXAMPLE, WHEN
PHIL III SD(136)	CONSULTING ROOM. JULIA TURNS HER HEAD, AND STARES	INSOLENTLY	AT CHARTERIS. HIS NERVES PLAY HIM FALSE: HE IS
LADY PREFACE(215)	CLASS, NOT HUMBLY AND ENVIOUSLY FROM BELOW, BUT	INSOLENTLY	FROM ABOVE. MR HARRIS HIMSELF NOTES SHAKESPEAR'S
CLEO PRO2,SD(103)	IN THE PALACE, AND CONFRONTS THE GUARDSMEN	INSOLENTLY	. /FTATATEETA/ MAKE WAY FOR THE QUEEN'S CHIEF
BARB II (282)	FROM HIM TO BILL). WHATS YOUR NAME? /BILL/ (	INSOLENTLY	) WOTS THET TO YOU? /BARBARA/ (CALMLY MAKING A
CATH 4 (187)	TEARS) WELL, IT ISNT MY FAULT. (TO THE SOLDIERS,	INSOLENTLY	) YOU KNOW YOUR ORDERS? YOU REMEMBER WHAT YOU
CAPT II (245)	WHILST YOU ARE GETTING THE WATER? /DRINKWATER/ (	INSOLENTLY	) YR ROOM! OW! THIS YNT GOOD ENAF FR YR, YNT
MIS. (179)	WILL WRITE IT: YOU CAN SIGN IT. /BENTLEY/ (	INSOLENTLY	TO GUNNER) GET UP. (GUNNER OBEYS; AND BENTLEY,
ARMS I SD(12)	CURTAIN; THEN PURSES HER LIPS SECRETIVELY, LAUGHS	INSOLENTLY	, AND GOES OUT. RAINA, HIGHLY OFFENDED BY THIS
NEVR IV (301)	BY UPSETTING THEM PRETTY EASILY. /GLORIA/ (	INSOLENTLY	, FEELING THAT NOW SHE CAN DO AS SHE LIKES WITH
2TRU I (38)	ME? SHUT THAT WINDOW INSTANTLY. /THE NURSE/ (	INSOLENTLY	, IN HER COMMONEST DIALECT) OH GO TO-- TO SLEEP (
CLEO IV (166)	PROVOCATION. /CLEOPATRA/ CAN I-- /FTATATEETA/ (	INSOLENTLY	, TO THE PLAYER) PEACE, THOU! THE QUEEN SPEAKS.

INSOLUBLE

METH PREFACE(R36)	THE ULTIMATE PROBLEM OF EXISTENCE, BEING CLEARLY	INSOLUBLE	AND EVEN UNTHINKABLE ON CAUSATION LINES, COULD NOT
SUPR HANDBOK(218)	AND, BEING FINALLY BROUGHT BY THIS MEANS INTO	INSOLUBLE	CONFLICT WITH THE INSULAR BRITISH IMPERIALIST, "
JITT II (30)	THESE MORAL PROBLEMS ARE VERY DIFFICULT: IN FACT,	INSOLUBLE	. IS THERE ANY MAN WHO CAN SAY THAT HE HAS NEVER
MRS PREFACE(161)	OF MRS WARREN'S GROUP ARE IN MY PLAY, WITH THE	INSOLUBLE	PROBLEM OF THEIR OWN POSSIBLE CONSANGUINITY. IN
GETT SD(293)	EXACTING CONSCIENCE, AND JUST NOW DISTRACTED BY	INSOLUBLE	PROBLEMS OF CONDUCT. /COLLINS/ (ANNOUNCING) MR

GETT PREFACE(191)	TO AVOID DISTURBING ONE ANOTHER'S SLEEP, SEEMED	INSOLUBLE	QUESTIONS TO ME. BUT THE MEMBERS OF THE CONFERENCE
METH PREFACE(R33)	GIVEN UP THE RIDDLE OF THE GREAT FIRST CAUSE AS	INSOLUBLE	, AND WERE CALLING THEMSELVES, ACCORDINGLY,
PHIL II (117)	AND THEN AT THE BUST, GIVING THE PROBLEM UP AS	INSOLUBLE	, HE SHAKES HIS HEAD AND FOLLOWS THEM. NEAR THE
MILL I (140)	COMBINE AND MAKE TARTRATE OF POTASH. THIS, BEING	INSOLUBLE	, WILL BE PRECIPITATED TO THE BOTTOM OF THE GLASS;
		INSOLVENCIES	
SIM PREFACE(9)	FALSIFIES BOOKS AND ACCOUNTS TO PRODUCE	INSOLVENCIES	, LEAVES THE FIELDS UNSOWN OR THE HARVESTS TO
		INSOLVENT	
BULL IV (177)	THE PRIEST REBUKING SIN) WHEN THE HOTEL BECOMES	INSOLVENT	(BROADBENT TAKES HIS CIGAR OUT OF HIS MOUTH, A
		INSOUCIANCE	
FANY PROLOG (271)	SUCH DELICIOUS FUN OF THE SERIOUS PEOPLE. YOUR	INSOUCIANCE	-- /TROTTER/ (FRANTIC) STOP TALKING FRENCH TO
		INSPECT	
2TRU II (61)	IS, AFTER ALL. (RISING) AND NOW I AM OFF TO	INSPECT	STORES. THERE IS A SHORTAGE OF MAROONS THAT I DONT
6CAL (100)	/THE QUEEN/ (EVADING HIM AND PASSING ON TO	INSPECT	THE BURGESSES) BUT THESE GENTLEMEN. THEY ARE ALMOST
CATH 4 (198)	WE MUST NOT DETAIN THE QUEEN: SHE IS ANXIOUS TO	INSPECT	THE MODEL OF HER MUSEUM, TO WHICH I AM SURE WE WISH
SUPR II SD(63)	THINGS THAT INTEREST HER. RAMSDEN STROLLS OVER TO	INSPECT	THE MOTOR CAR. OCTAVIUS JOINS HECTOR. /ANN/ (
DEVL I (14)	HER ROUGHLY BY THE ARM AND PULLS HER ROUND TO	INSPECT	THE RESULTS OF HER ATTEMPT TO CLEAN AND TIDY
		INSPECTED	
BARB II (302)	ME SHEW YOU TO THIS GENTLEMAN (PRICE COMES TO BE	INSPECTED	). DO YOU REMEMBER THE WINDOW BREAKING? /PRICE/
NEVR II (227)	PLANTS HIMSELF WITH HIS HANDS ON HIS HIPS TO BE	INSPECTED	). /MRS CLANDON/ I BELIEVE YOU ARE. (SHE GIVES
VWOO 1 (115)	WHY. /A/ WITHIN THE LAST FORTNIGHT YOU HAVE	INSPECTED	THE PRICELESS ANTIQUITIES OF NAPLES, ATHENS,
2TRU II (76)	MAROONS! (TOGETHER) /TALLBOYS/ YES, MAROONS. I	INSPECTED	THE STORES THIS MORNING; AND THE MAROONS ARE
		INSPECTING	
HART II (90)	(GOING PAST THE NURSE TO MANGAN'S SIDE, AND	INSPECTING	HIM LESS CREDULOUSLY THAN MAZZINI) NONSENSE! HE
		INSPECTION	
SUPR HANDBOK(212)	SOMETHING OF THAT SORT) MIGHT WELL, UNDER PROPER	INSPECTION	AND REGULATION, PRODUCE BETTER RESULTS THAN OUR
APPL PREFACE(183)	ONLY BY STERN LAWS ENFORCED BY CONSTANT	INSPECTION	HAVE WE STOPPED THE MONSTROUS WASTE OF HUMAN LIFE
HART I SD(69)	AIR OF BEING YOUNG AND UNMARRIED, BUT ON CLOSE	INSPECTION	IS FOUND TO BE AT LEAST OVER FORTY. /THE
2TRU II SD(61)	CAP GALLANTLY AND BUSTLES OFF PAST THE HUT TO HIS	INSPECTION	. /THE PATIENT/ (RISING VENGEFULLY) YOU DARE
APPL PREFACE(172)	OF THE ELECTORATE, BUT THE MOST SUPERFICIAL	INSPECTION	OF ANY TWO SUCH FIGURES SHEWS THAT THEY ARE NOT
DEVL I SD(4)	BLACK HORSEHAIR SOFA STANDS AGAINST THE WALL. AN	INSPECTION	OF ITS STRIDULOUS SURFACE SHEWS THAT MRS DUDGEON
		INSPECTOR	
GETT PREFACE(254)	THE SCHOOL ATTENDANCE OFFICER, AND THE SANITARY	INSPECTOR	: " IS THIS CHILD MINE OR YOURS? " THE ANSWER IS
ROCK I (223)	KNOCKED ABOUT. HE SCREAMED TO THEM TO STAND. THE	INSPECTOR	COLLARED HIM. /SIR ARTHUR/ OF COURSE HE DID. QUITE
GETT PREFACE(254)	THE CHILD, UNLESS, INDEED, A HINT FROM A POLICE	INSPECTOR	CONVINCED THEM THAT BAD CHARACTERS CANNOT ALWAYS
WIDO II (25)	THE ST GILES PROPERTY? /LICKCHEESE/ THE SANITARY	INSPECTOR	HAS BEEN COMPLAINING AGAIN ABOUT NO. 13 ROBBINS'S
BULL PREFACE(62)	POPULATION OF NEARLY TEN MILLIONS, ONE IRRIGATION	INSPECTOR	IS STONED. THE DENSHAWAI EXECUTIONS ARE THEN
MILL III (179)	LOOK AT HER SHOES. /EPIFANIA/ I AM NOT AN	INSPECTOR	. AND WHAT IS THE MATTER WITH MY SHOES, PRAY?
MILL III (179)	THE MAN AND HOLDING HIM) TAKE CARE, JOE. SHE'S AN	INSPECTOR	. LOOK AT HER SHOES. /EPIFANIA/ I AM NOT AN
MILL III (181)	MUCH. /EPIFANIA/ I SEE. THEY MIGHT CALL IN THE	INSPECTOR	. /THE MAN/ CALL IN THE INSPECTOR! WHAT SORT OF
BULL PREFACE(61)	NATIVES STONED AND SEVERELY INJURED AN IRRIGATION	INSPECTOR	. TWO DAYS AGO THREE NATIVES KNOCKED A SOLDIER OFF
PYGM V (269)	SITS IN THE ELIZABETHAN CHAIR). /PICKERING/ THE	INSPECTOR	MADE A LOT OF DIFFICULTIES. I REALLY THINK HE
POSN PREFACE(389)	ATHEIST OR AN ANTI-VACCINATOR, JUST AS A SANITARY	INSPECTOR	MAY HAVE FORMED A CAREFUL OPINION THAT DRAINS ARE
MILL III (181)	WHAT SORT OF FOOL ARE YOU? THEY DREAD THE	INSPECTOR	MORE THAN I DO. /EPIFANIA/ WHY? DONT THEY WANT TO
POSN PREFACE(389)	DEMANDS ARE LAWFULLY MADE; AND IN CITIES THE	INSPECTOR	MUST COMPEL THE BUILDER TO MAKE DRAINS AND MUST
POSN PREFACE(401)	TO UNDERTAKE SUCH A TASK. THE ATTACHMENT OF AN	INSPECTOR	OF MORALS TO EACH MUSIC HALL WOULD HAVE MEANT AN
MILL III (180)	AND ANOTHER EVERY WEDNESDAY IF YOU KEEP THE	INSPECTOR	OFF ME. /EPIFANIA/ IT'S NO USE RINGING HALF CROWNS
POSN PREFACE(389)	BETWEEN A CENSOR AND A MAGISTRATE OR A SANITARY	INSPECTOR	; BUT IT IS IMPOSSIBLE TO IGNORE THE CARELESSNESS
PYGM V (269)	THE OTTOMAN). /HIGGINS/ WHAT DOES THAT ASS OF AN	INSPECTOR	SAY? HAVE YOU OFFERED A REWARD? /MRS HIGGINS/ (
ROCK I (223)	/SIR ARTHUR/ I HAVE A GREAT MIND TO HAVE THAT	INSPECTOR	SEVERELY REPRIMANDED FOR LETTING YOU GO. THREE
BASH III (125)	SERVICES ARE NOT FORGOT: IN FUTURE CALL THYSELF	INSPECTOR	SMITH. (RENEWED ACCLAMATION.) /POLICEMAN/ I THANK
MILL III (182)	ME TO PAY TRADE UNION WAGES AS DO ALL THAT THE	INSPECTOR	WANTS: I SHOULD BE OUT OF BUSINESS IN A WEEK.
ROCK I (223)	ARRESTED? WHO BAILED YOU? /DAVID/ I ASKED THE	INSPECTOR	WHO IN HELL HE THOUGHT HE WAS TALKING TO. THEN
MILL III (181)	DONT THEY WANT TO BE PROTECTED? /THE WOMAN/ THE	INSPECTOR	WOULDNT PROTECT THEM, MAAM: HE'D ONLY SHUT UP THE
MILL III (181)	CALL IN THE INSPECTOR. /THE MAN/ CALL IN THE	INSPECTOR	! WHAT SORT OF FOOL ARE YOU? THEY DREAD THE
		INSPECTOR'S	
ROCK PREFACE(159)	ANYBODY OF THE SOUNDNESS OF THE NEAREST POLICE	INSPECTOR'S	BELIEF THAT EVERY NORMAL HUMAN GROUP CONTAINS
DOCT PREFACE(29)	THE PRIVATE DOCTOR'S VISITS RARER, AND THE PUBLIC	INSPECTOR'S	FREQUENTER, WHILST THE ADVANCE OF SCIENTIFIC
		INSPECTORS	
POSN PREFACE(402)	MELTED AWAY. HAD IT BEEN PUSHED THROUGH, AND THE	INSPECTORS	APPOINTED, EACH OF THEM WOULD HAVE BECOME A
POSN PREFACE(405)	CODE AND THE PUBLIC HEALTH AND BUILDING ACTS, THE	INSPECTORS	APPOINTED TO CARRY OUT THESE ACTS NEVER GO TO A
DOCT PREFACE(72)	MIGHT DO MORE IN ONE YEAR THAN ALL THE SANITARY	INSPECTORS	IN IRELAND COULD DO IN TWENTY; AND THEY COULD
MILL III (182)	IS. THIS IS A RESPECTABLE BUSINESS, WHATEVER YOUR	INSPECTORS	MAY SAY. /EPIFANIA/ CAN A WOMAN LIVE ON TWELVE
POSN PREFACE(402)	UNDERSTAND HOW IMPOSSIBLE IT WOULD BE TO PROCURE	INSPECTORS	WHOSE CHARACTERS WOULD STAND THE STRAIN OF THEIR
POSN PREFACE(402)	WOULD HAVE BECOME A CENSOR, AND THE WHOLE BODY OF	INSPECTORS	WOULD HAVE BECOME A POLICE DES MOEURS. THOSE WHO
APPL PREFACE(183)	EMPLOYING A PRODIGIOUS ARMY OF POLICE,	INSPECTORS	, TEACHERS, AND OFFICIALS OF ALL GRADES IN
		INSPECTS	
HART I (66)	THINK THAT. (HE GOES TO THE BOOKSHELVES, AND	INSPECTS	THE TITLES OF THE VOLUMES). BOSS MANGAN COMES IN
		INSPIRATION	
MTH5 (229)	I DO NOT ADMIT THAT. THE ARTIST DIVINES BY	INSPIRATION	ALL THE TRUTHS THAT THE SO-CALLED SCIENTIST
JOAN PREFACE(50)	THE INQUISITION, THE FEUDAL SYSTEM, WITH DIVINE	INSPIRATION	ALWAYS BEATING AGAINST THEIR TOO INELASTIC
MILL PREFACE(136)	HAVE BEEN DISABLED, THE WAY WILL BE CLEAR FOR	INSPIRATION	AND ASPIRATION TO SAVE US FROM THE FATHEADED
JOAN PREFACE(15)	IN WHICH SHE WOULD BE MILDLY TAUGHT TO CONNECT	INSPIRATION	AND CONSCIENCE WITH ST CATHERINE AND ST MICHAEL
LADY (247)	THE MODEST COUGH OF A MINOR POET, BELITTLING MY	INSPIRATION	AND MAKING THE MIGHTIEST WONDER OF YOUR REIGN A
POSN PREFACE(390)	PLAYWRIGHT'S LIVELIHOOD, HIS REPUTATION, AND HIS	INSPIRATION	AND MISSION ARE AT THE PERSONAL MERCY OF THE
MIS. PREFACE(99)	THE WHOLE BODY OF GREAT LITERATURE IN WHICH THE	INSPIRATION	AND REVELATION OF HEBREW SCRIPTURE HAS BEEN
GENV IV (119)	CARE. YOU ARE WALKING ON A RAZOR'S EDGE BETWEEN	INSPIRATION	AND THE MADNESS OF THE BEGGAR ON HORSEBACK. WE
MIS. PREFACE(90)	CRUDE LUSTS, WHICH IS THE APPOINTED VEHICLE OF	INSPIRATION	AND THE METHOD OF THE COMMUNION OF SAINTS, IS
GETT PREFACE(235)	UP A RELIGION OF OUR OWN OUT OF OUR WESTERN	INSPIRATION	AND WESTERN SENTIMENT. THE RESULT IS THAT WE ALL
ROCK II (242)	PEOPLE. I DARENT SAY A WORD AGAINST IT. IT'S AN	INSPIRATION	AS FAR AS MY CONSTITUENTS ARE CONCERNED. THEYRE
MTH5 (225)	FASCINATES TO THE END. BUT HOW CAN SO NOBLE AN	INSPIRATION	BE SATISFIED WITH ANY IMAGE, EVEN AN IMAGE OF
MTH5 (224)	ARE THEY, MAN? WILL YOU BE TALKED OUT OF YOUR	INSPIRATION	BY ECRASIA AND THE FOOLS WHO IMAGINE SHE SPEAKS
BARB II (294)	AHA! BARBARA UNDERSHAFT WOULD BE. HER	INSPIRATION	COMES FROM WITHIN HERSELF. /CUSINS/ HOW DO YOU
APPL INTRLUD(249)	KINGS. /MAGNUS/ SUBLIME! NOTHING BUT GENUINE	INSPIRATION	COULD GIVE A WOMAN SUCH CHEEK. /ORINTHIA/ YES:
SUPR PREFACE(R32)	ALL THEIR FICTIONS THERE IS NO LEADING THOUGHT OR	INSPIRATION	FOR WHICH ANY MAN COULD CONCEIVABLY RISK THE
BARB PREFACE(208)	CONSCIOUSNESS OF THE FACT THAT LUNACY MAY BE	INSPIRATION	IN DISGUISE, SINCE A MAN WHO HAS MORE BRAINS
SUPR II (54)	ANN; AND AT THE END OF A WEEK YOULL FIND NO MORE	INSPIRATION	IN HER THAN IN A PLATE OF MUFFINS. /OCTAVIUS/
METH PREFACE(R65)	PRODUCES POETRY: JOHN DAVIDSON FOUND HIS HIGHEST	INSPIRATION	IN IT. EVEN ITS PESSIMISM AS IT FACES THE
SUPR II (54)	YOU DONT GET TIRED OF MUFFINS. BUT YOU DONT FIND	INSPIRATION	IN THEM; AND YOU WONT IN HER WHEN SHE CEASES TO
JOAN 6 (130)	HONESTLY AND SINCERELY THAT THEIR DIABOLICAL	INSPIRATION	IS DIVINE. THEREFORE YOU MUST BE ON YOUR GUARD
MILL PREFACE(112)	OF COMMON SENSE, HE MUST PERSUADE THEM THAT HIS	INSPIRATION	IS THE RESULT OF DIRECT AND MIRACULOUS
SUPR II (54)	HAS NOTHING. /OCTAVIUS/ I CANNOT WRITE WITHOUT	INSPIRATION	. AND NOBODY CAN GIVE ME THAT EXCEPT ANN.
SIM PREFACE(6)	BETWEEN HIM AND ALLAH, THE FOUNTAIN OF ALL	INSPIRATION	. EXCEPT IN THIS WAY HE COULD NOT HAVE MADE THEM
JITT I (17)	/JITTA/ BRUNO: THAT MUST BE RIGHT. IT IS AN	INSPIRATION	. IT TAKES HOLD OF MY HEART WITH BOTH HANDS. YOU
PPP (200)	AND WILL NOT. /MAGNESIA/ I HAVE A THOUGHT-- AN	INSPIRATION	. MY BUST. (SHE SNATCHES IT FROM ITS PEDESTAL
BULL I (89)	YOU HIT THE MARK THERE, TOM, WITH TRUE BRITISH	INSPIRATION	. /BROADBENT/ COMMON SENSE, YOU MEAN. /DOYLE/ (

DOCT I	(86)	ISNT IT? /RIDGEON/ MY DEAR LOONY, IT WAS AN	INSPIRATION	. WAS IT ON THE BRASS PLATE? /SCHUTZMACHER/
GENV IV	(111)	MUST CHOOSE THEMSELVES: THAT IS PART OF THEIR	INSPIRATION	. WHEN THEY HAVE DARED TO DO THIS, WHAT
JITT I	(22)	DISCARD WITHOUT UNFAITHFULNESS. THIS IS SUCH AN	INSPIRATION	. WILL YOU BE UNFAITHFUL TO IT? /JITTA/ BRUNO:
JOAN 4	(98)	OTHER COURTS, HOWEVER SACRED THEIR FUNCTION AND	INSPIRATION	MAY BE. AND IF THE MEN ARE FRENCHMEN, AS THE
CAND III	(142)	/MORELL/ THAT FOOLISH BOY CAN SPEAK WITH THE	INSPIRATION	OF A CHILD AND THE CUNNING OF A SERPENT. HE HAS
MRS II	(212)	CONVENTIONAL MANNERS GONE, AND AN OVERWHELMING	INSPIRATION	OF TRUE CONVICTION AND SCORN IN HER) OH, I WONT
SIM PREFACE	(6)	IF THEY DID, AND AS THEY COULD NOT UNDERSTAND HIS	INSPIRATION	OTHERWISE THAN AS A SPOKEN COMMUNICATION BY A
BULL IV	(178)	THE PRIEST IS AN OLD FINANCIAL HAND, MUST BE	INSPIRATION	); YOU WILL GET RID OF ITS ORIGINAL SHAREHOLDERS
FABL PREFACE	(66)	OF THE LIFE FORCE, WRITING BY WHAT IS CALLED	INSPIRATION	; BUT AS THE LIFE FORCE PROCEEDS EXPERIMENTALLY
MTH4 I	(165)	TO BE CONTINUALLY PONTIFICATING. OUR FLASHES OF	INSPIRATION	SHEW THAT OUR HEARTS ARE IN THE RIGHT PLACE.
MIS. PREFACE	(99)	WAGNER. THERE IS NOTHING IN THE BIBLE GREATER IN	INSPIRATION	THAN BEETHOVEN'S NINTH SYMPHONY; AND THE POWER
MIS. PREFACE	(99)	AND THE POWER OF MODERN MUSIC TO CONVEY THAT	INSPIRATION	TO A MODERN MAN IS FAR GREATER THAN THAT OF
MTH4 III	(200)	THE SAME ANSWER. THE ANSWER TO EASTWIND WAS AN	INSPIRATION	TO OUR PARTY FOR YEARS. IT WON US THE ELECTION.
METH PREFACE	(R84)	GIFTS, THE FACT REMAINS THAT HE NEVER FOUND THE	INSPIRATION	TO WRITE AN ORIGINAL PLAY. HE FURBISHED UP OLD
DOCT I	(112)	AT THE BEGINNING-- TO ENABLE HIM TO FOLLOW HIS	INSPIRATION	UNTIL HIS GENIUS WAS RECOGNIZED. AND I WAS
JOAN PREFACE	(15)	OF THE HALLUCINATED ADULT ABOUT THE FOUNTAIN OF	INSPIRATION	WHICH IS CONTINUALLY FLOWING IN THE UNIVERSE, OR
LION PREFACE	(36)	HIM WITH THAT HOPE UNTIL PETER HAS THE SUDDEN	INSPIRATION	WHICH PRODUCES SO STARTLING AN EFFECT ON JESUS.
BULL PREFACE	(37)	OF THE LUTHERAN MINISTERS GLAD TO CLAIM A COMMON	INSPIRATION	WITH HIM. UNFORTUNATELY VOLTAIRE HAD AN
3PLA PREFACE	(R38)	THIS COUNTRY, CARLYLE, WITH HIS VEIN OF PEASANT	INSPIRATION	, APPREHENDED THE SORT OF GREATNESS THAT PLACES
SUPR PREFACE	(R17)	UNINTELLIGIBLE TO HIMSELF EXCEPT IN FLASHES OF	INSPIRATION	, FROM THE PERFORMER WHO HAS TO TALK AT ANY COST
GENV IV	(118)	HIM! /JUDGE/ I UNDERSTAND YOU TO PLEAD DIVINE	INSPIRATION	, MR BATTLER. /BATTLER/ I SAY THAT MY POWER IS
APPL INTRLUD	(249)	COULD GIVE A WOMAN SUCH CHEEK. /ORINTHIA/ YES:	INSPIRATION	, NOT CHEEK. (SITTING AS BEFORE) MAGNUS: WHEN
DOCT IV	(158)	ARE HIS BEST PHYSICIAN AFTER ALL, DEAR LADY. AN	INSPIRATION	! CORNWALL: OF COURSE, YES, YES, YES. /MRS
			INSPIRATIONS	
JOAN PREFACE	(11)	OF REVELATIONS ARE NOT ALWAYS CRIMINALS. THE	INSPIRATIONS	AND INTUITIONS AND UNCONSCIOUSLY REASONED
SIM PREFACE	(5)	GIVING VERY RESPECTFUL CONSIDERATION TO THE	INSPIRATIONS	AND REVELATIONS OF THE PROPHETS AND POETS. FOR
JITT I	(22)	ARE NOT ALWAYS CHILDREN OF FLESH AND BLOOD, BUT	INSPIRATIONS	, INTUITIONS, CONVICTIONS THAT THEY CANNOT
JOAN 6	(130)	REJECT MARRIAGE AND EXALT THEIR LUSTS INTO DIVINE	INSPIRATIONS	, THEN, AS SURELY AS THE SUMMER FOLLOWS THE
			INSPIRE	
MTH5	(227)	VERY BEST WORKMANSHIP. LET ME ADD THAT THEY WILL	INSPIRE	A LOATHING THAT WILL CURE YOU OF THE LUNACY OF ART
DOCT I	(102)	A WRETCHED DIGESTION; AND I LOOK IT. HOW AM I TO	INSPIRE	CONFIDENCE? (HE SITS DISCONSOLATELY ON THE COUCH).
MILL II	(171)	ATTEND TO ME. YOU ARE ABOMINABLY RUDE; BUT YOU	INSPIRE	CONFIDENCE AS A DOCTOR. /THE DOCTOR/ IF I ATTENDED
MILL II	(171)	/THE DOCTOR/ IF I ATTENDED ALL THOSE IN WHOM I	INSPIRE	CONFIDENCE I SHOULD BE WORN OUT IN A WEEK. I HAVE TO
HART II	(94)	ON EARTH IS THE MATTER WITH YOU? WHY DONT YOU	INSPIRE	EVERYBODY WITH CONFIDENCE? WITH RESPECT? /MAZZINI/
MIS.	(159)	CHORDS. YOU APPEAL TO THE POETRY IN A MAN. YOU	INSPIRE	HIM. COME NOW! YOURE A WOMAN OF THE WORLD: YOURE
PRES	(147)	HER TO THE POET LAUREATE, THINKIN SHE'D	INSPIRE	HIM. /MITCHENER/ DID SHE? /MRS FARRELL/ FAITH, I
SUPR I	(24)	TO MAKE HIM SEE VISIONS AND DREAM DREAMS, TO	INSPIRE	HIM, AS HE CALLS IT. HE PERSUADES WOMEN THAT THEY
PHIL III	(132)	IT! IT'S THE SORT OF ATTACHMENT I SEEM ALWAYS TO	INSPIRE	, (IRONICALLY) YOU CANT THINK HOW FLATTERING IT IS.
2TRU III	(112)	OF REVELATION THE SPIRIT WILL DESCEND ON ME AND	INSPIRE	ME WITH A MESSAGE THE SOUND WHEREOF SHALL GO OUT
MIS.	(196)	WHAT ABOUT THE MONEY? /TARLETON/ YOU DONT	INSPIRE	ME WITH GENEROSITY, YOUNG MAN. /HYPATIA/ (LAUGHING
BULL PREFACE	(8)	RELATIONS, NATURAL PASSION CANNOT PRETEND TO	INSPIRE	MORE INTENSE DEVOTION THAN PERVERTED PASSION. BUT
SUPR III SD	(96)	HIS ADVANCES ARE NOT RECIPROCATED. HE DOES NOT	INSPIRE	MUCH CONFIDENCE IN HIS POWERS OF HARD WORK OR
BULL PREFACE	(14)	SUCCEED WHERE THEY WOULD FAIL; THAT HE COULD	INSPIRE	STRONG AFFECTION AND LOYALTY IN AN IRISHMAN WHO KNEW
FABL VI	(127)	EVERYTHING THAT OPPOSES IT. THE DISEMBODIED MUST	INSPIRE	THE SOLDIER AND THE HUNTER AS WELL AS THE PACIFIST
LADY	(247)	YOUR PLAYS FOR YOU! /SHAKESPEAR/ YOU ARE HERE TO	INSPIRE	THEM, MADAM. FOR THIS, AMONG THE REST, WERE YOU
			INSPIRED	
GETT	(343)	BREAK IN SILENCE. /SOAMES/ (WHISPERING) IS SHE	INSPIRED	? /THE BISHOP/ MARVELLOUS. HUSH. /MRS GEORGE/ I
MIS.	(203)	THOUGH SHE HAS BEEN SO SHORT A TIME WITH US, HAS	INSPIRED	A GOOD DEAL OF ATTACHMENT IN-- I MAY SAY IN ALMOST
CAND III	(136)	YOU, (GRASPING HIS HAND) WHAT A NOBLE, SPLENDID,	INSPIRED	ADDRESS YOU GAVE US! YOU SURPASSED YOURSELF.
SUPR HANDBOK	(198)	JEWS, WHO, FROM MOSES TO MARX AND LASSALLE, HAVE	INSPIRED	ALL THE REVOLUTIONS, HAVE HAD TO CONFESS THAT,
NEVR III	(271)	WITH INTENSE SCORN) ASK THIS MAN WHOM YOU HAVE	INSPIRED	AND MADE BRAVE, HOW MANY WOMEN HAVE INSPIRED HIM
ROCK I SD	(208)	THE MASKED DOOR). SIR ARTHUR, LEFT ALONE, LOOKS	INSPIRED	AND TRIUMPHANT. HE ADDRESSES AN IMAGINARY ASSEMBLY.
GENV PREFACE	(16)	WHEN I AM NOT WRITING PLAYS AS A MORE OR LESS	INSPIRED	ARTIST I WRITE POLITICAL SCHOOLBOOKS IN WHICH I SAY
MIS. PREFACE	(20)	WORLD'S BOOKSHELVES LOADED WITH FASCINATING AND	INSPIRED	BOOKS, THE VERY MANNA SENT DOWN FROM HEAVEN TO FEED
FOUN	(214)	OF OUR TIME HAS SUCCEEDED IN TEMPERING THE AWE	INSPIRED	BY A COMMANDING STATURE AND MAJESTIC PRESENCE WITH
LADY PREFACE	(216)	THEIR VALETS, BUT IN THE AFFECTION AND RESPECT	INSPIRED	BY A GREAT SERVANT LIKE ADAM: ALL THESE ARE THE
DOCT PREFACE	(63)	AND " RESCUE WORK." BUT THE TRUE DOCTOR IS	INSPIRED	BY A HATRED OF ILL-HEALTH, AND A DIVINE IMPATIENCE
JOAN PREFACE	(5)	FEAR WILL DRIVE MEN TO ANY EXTREME; AND THE FEAR	INSPIRED	BY A SUPERIOR BEING IS A MYSTERY WHICH CANNOT BE
JOAN 6	(150)	OF ANOTHER'S DANGER IN SUCH A MOMENT WAS NOT	INSPIRED	BY THE DEVIL. WHEN I HAD TO SNATCH THE CROSS FROM
ROCK PREFACE	(159)	NO DOUBT MANY PRIVATE AMIABILITIES HAVE BEEN	INSPIRED	BY THIS TEACHING; BUT POLITICALLY IT HAS RECEIVED
BULL I	(87)	ALL IMAGINATION. HE CANT BE RELIGIOUS. THE	INSPIRED	CHURCHMAN THAT TEACHES HIM THE SANCTITY OF LIFE AND
PYGM II	(223)	IDEA GROWS ON HIM) WHAT IS LIFE BUT A SERIES OF	INSPIRED	FOLLIES? THE DIFFICULTY IS TO FIND THEM TO DO.
JOAN 4	(103)	WITH THE MONSTROUS SELF-CONCEIT OF BEING DIRECTLY	INSPIRED	FROM HEAVEN? IT WILL BE A WORLD OF BLOOD, OF FURY,
PLES PREFACE	(R18)	THE POLITICAL AND RELIGIOUS IDEALISM WHICH HAD	INSPIRED	GLADSTONE TO CALL FOR THE RESCUE OF THESE BALKAN
MIS. PREFACE	(44)	THESE PROCESSES IN A SINGLE BRAIN THAT WE GET THE	INSPIRED	GUESS OF THE MAN OF GENIUS AND THE FANATICAL
NEVR III	(271)	HAVE INSPIRED AND MADE BRAVE, HOW MANY WOMEN HAVE	INSPIRED	HIM BEFORE (GLORIA LOOKS UP SUDDENLY WITH A FLASH
MTH2	(78)	THE ONE IS CLASSROOM JARGON: THE OTHER IS	INSPIRED	HUMAN LANGUAGE. /LUBIN/ (CALMLY REMINISCENT) ONE
BULL IV	(164)	BE FRANK, TO BE EXPLICIT. MISS REILLY: YOU HAVE	INSPIRED	IN ME A VERY STRONG ATTACHMENT. PERHAPS, WITH A
JOAN 6	(136)	PROMOTER HERE, WILL YOU SUBMIT YOUR CASE TO THE	INSPIRED	INTERPRETATION OF THE CHURCH MILITANT? /JOAN/ I AM
GETT	(341)	SHOULD NEVER HAVE MARRIED. /SOAMES/ THIS WOMAN IS	INSPIRED	. LISTEN TO HER, MY LORD. /THE BISHOP/ (TAKEN
JOAN 4	(100)	SEE THIS GIRL. SHE IS INSPIRED, BUT DIABOLICALLY	INSPIRED	. /THE CHAPLAIN/ I TOLD YOU SHE WAS A WITCH.
JOAN PREFACE	(38)	CARDINALS PRAY EFFECTIVELY THAT ITS CHOICE MAY BE	INSPIRED	. THE CONSCIOUS PRAYER OF THE INFERIOR MAY BE THAT
ARMS II	(33)	DEAREST: ALL MY DEEDS HAVE BEEN YOURS. YOU	INSPIRED	ME. I HAVE GONE THROUGH THE WAR LIKE A KNIGHT IN A
HART PREFACE	(38)	WAS IN PERISHING FROM THE EARTH BEFORE HIS	INSPIRED	MESSAGES BECAME SCRAPS OF PAPER. HE KNOWS HELL THAT
GLIM	(177)	/FERRUCCIO/ I TAKE IT THAT EITHER SAINT BARBARA	INSPIRED	ME, OR ELSE THAT YOU ARE A GREAT FOOL. /GIULIA/
CAPT NOTES	(300)	IN STUPIDITY, DID NOT UNDERSTAND HIM UNTIL IN AN	INSPIRED	MOMENT HE VOICED A UNIVERSAL IMPULSE BY BLUNTLY
LADY PREFACE	(224)	A GRIEVANCE? EVEN IN THAT MOST THOROUGHGOING AND	INSPIRED	OF ALL SHAKESPEAR'S LOVES: HIS LOVE OF MUSIC (
MTH2	(79)	DECLARE HE IS THE GREATEST POLITICIAN, THE MOST	INSPIRED	PARTY LEADER, IN THE KINGDOM. I TAKE OFF MY HAT TO
FABL PREFACE	(75)	BY THE NECESSITY FOR ADAPTING THEIR ORIGINAL	INSPIRED	PHILOSOPHIC CREEDS TO THE NARROW INTELLIGENCES OF
MILL PREFACE	(120)	PIE. MUSSOLINI DID NOT MAKE THAT MISTAKE, WITH	INSPIRED	PRECISION HE DENOUNCED LIBERTY AS A PUTREFYING
METH PREFACE	(R62)	AND THE BASEST OF ALL ROBBERIES, HE BECAME AN	INSPIRED	PROPHET IN THE MIND OF EVERY GENEROUS SOUL WHOM HIS
MIS. PREFACE	(97)	BODY OF FINE ART: THAT IS, TO THE WHOLE BODY OF	INSPIRED	REVELATION, THAT WE CAN BUILD UP THAT CONCEPTION OF
GETT	(320)	I DREW UP AS A SOLICITOR NO LESS THAN FROM	INSPIRED	REVELATION. YOU HAVE SET YOURSELVES HERE TO PUT
ROCK PREFACE	(176)	THE HEBREW SCRIPTURES AND THE GREEK TESTAMENT AS	INSPIRED	REVELATIONS, COULD STAND THE SHOCK OF THE DISCOVERY
SIM II	(77)	WAR WITH HEAVEN FOR MANY A LONG YEAR. /VASHTI/ (	INSPIRED	) THE MOST SPLENDID OF ALL HER WARS! /KANCHIN/ THE
KING I	(205)	THEM SO. BUT YOUR HUGUENOT RANTERS PRETEND TO BE	INSPIRED	; AND FOOLISH PEOPLE ARE DELUDED BY THEM. AND WHAT
BARB PREFACE	(246)	OF MINE, MAJOR BARBARA, IS, I HOPE, BOTH TRUE AND	INSPIRED	; BUT WHOEVER SAYS THAT IT ALL HAPPENED, AND THAT
POSN PREFACE	(432)	OF SUCCESS, AND PROVOKED NO MURMUR, THOUGH IT	INSPIRED	SEVERAL APPROVING SERMONS. LATER ON, LADY GREGORY
SUPR PREFACE	(R36)	RECTOR CAN AGREE WITH THE PROPHET MICAH AS TO HIS	INSPIRED	STYLE WITHOUT BEING COMMITTED TO ANY COMPLICITY IN
BARB PREFACE	(225)	INSTEAD OF THE CROSS, HE WAS PERHAPS BETTER	INSPIRED	THAN HE KNEW: SUCH KNOWLEDGE, FOR THE DAUGHTER OF
2TRU PREFACE	(13)	PROTESTANT IMPOSTURES ON ENGLISH HISTORY WHICH	INSPIRED	THE VIGOROUS LIBERALISM OF HIS SALAD DAYS, HAS
KING I	(216)	IMAGES OF GOD AND REVEAL THE SOUL IN THEM, AND IS	INSPIRED	TO DO THIS AND NOTHING ELSE EVEN IF HE STARVES AND
FABL VI	(128)	BY DISEMBODIED THOUGHT. THE MONGOOSE MUST BE	INSPIRED	TO KILL THE COBRA, THE CHEMIST TO DISTIL POISONS,
METH PREFACE	(R89)	IS NOW COMPARATIVELY RARE. I NOW FIND MYSELF	INSPIRED	TO MAKE A SECOND LEGEND OF CREATIVE EVOLUTION
GETT	(342)	RING. (HE DOES SO. HER EYES CLOSE). /SOAMES/ (	INSPIRED	TO PROPHESY) THERE WAS A CERTAIN WOMAN, THE WIFE OF
ROCK I	(227)	ARE THE GLORIES OF OUR LITERATURE, AND THE	INSPIRED	VOICES OF OUR RELIGION, OUR PATRIOTISM, AND-- OF
LION PREFACE	(95)	QUITE LEGITIMATELY MAY, THAT ALL PROPHETS ARE	INSPIRED	, AND ALL MEN WITH A MISSION, CHRISTS. THE TEACHER
JOAN 4	(100)	OF THAT DESIGN THAT I SEE THIS GIRL. SHE IS	INSPIRED	, BUT DIABOLICALLY INSPIRED. /THE CHAPLAIN/ I TOLD
			INSPIRES	
SIM PRO,3,	(33)	THE MAN ISNT A DOG, IS HE? /THE PRIESTESS/ HE	INSPIRES	A DOGLIKE DEVOTION IN WOMEN. HE ONCE DID IN ME; SO
SUPR I SD	(16)	HER POSE IS FASHIONABLY FRANK AND IMPULSIVE. SHE	INSPIRES	CONFIDENCE AS A PERSON WHO WILL DO NOTHING SHE DOES
JOAN PREFACE	(5)	THE STRANGE SUPERIORITY OF CHRIST AND THE FEAR IT	INSPIRES	ELICIT A SHRIEK OF CRUCIFY HIM FROM ALL WHO CANNOT
JOAN PREFACE	(5)	OF HEROD AND PILATE, AND OF ANNAS AND CAIAPHAS,	INSPIRES	FEAR; BUT THE FEAR, BEING A REASONABLE FEAR OF

SUPR IV SD(143)	STRAKER, BEING A VERY OBVIOUS COCKNEY,	INSPIRES	HIM WITH IMPLACABLE CONTEMPT, AS A STUPID
LADY (249)	WORD THAT COMETH FROM THE MOUTH OF THOSE WHOM GOD	INSPIRES	. BY THAT TIME YOU AND I WILL BE DUST BENEATH THE
MTH4 I (160)	COULD ONLY INCREASE THE DISGUST WITH WHICH HE	INSPIRES	ME, AND MAKE ME MORE DETERMINED THAN EVER NOT TO
MILL PREFACE(109)	LESS, WHO MAKES LARGER AND LARGER PROFITS, AND	INSPIRES	MORE AND MORE CONFIDENCE IN HIS BANKER, UNTIL HE
CATH PREFACE(158)	FOR IT MUST BE SAID THAT THE ACTOR OR ACTRESS WHO	INSPIRES	OR COMMISSIONS A PLAY AS OFTEN AS NOT REGARDS IT AS
GETT PREFACE(196)	BROUGHT-UP" GIRLS IS SO EASY, AND THE DEVOTION HE	INSPIRES	SO EXTRAVAGANT, THAT IT IS IMPOSSIBLE NOT TO SEE
CAND I (99)	THAT OF HER! YOU THINK THAT WAY OF THE LOVE SHE	INSPIRES	! IT IS AN INSULT TO HER! /MORELL/ (RISING
		INSPIRING	
NEVR II (255)	INSPIRING. /GLORIA/ (WITH A SLIGHT LAUGH) AM I	INSPIRING	? /VALENTINE/ YES. STRENGTH'S INFECTIOUS.
BARB PREFACE(219)	ORDER THAT YOU MAY BECOME CRANKS" IS NOT A VERY	INSPIRING	CALL TO ARMS; NOR IS IT REALLY IMPROVED BY
METH PREFACE(R51)	WITH WHICH BUTLER'S MIND MOVED TO HUMANE AND	INSPIRING	CONCLUSIONS WITH THE GROTESQUE STUPIDITIES AND
NEVR II (255)	SENTIMENT. /VALENTINE/ THATS WHAT MAKES YOU SO	INSPIRING	. /GLORIA/ (WITH A SLIGHT LAUGH) AM I INSPIRING?
METH PREFACE(R59)	EVOLUTION NOT ONLY A CONCEIVABLE THEORY, BUT AN	INSPIRING	ONE. ST ANTHONY WAS RIPE FOR THE EVOLUTION THEORY
MIS. (160)	ENOUGH FOR THAT. BUT WHEN IT BECOMES SO GRAND, SO	INSPIRING	THAT I FEEL THAT EVERYTHING MUST BE AN ANTI-CLIMAX
FANY III (324)	THINK OF YOUR GREAT WELLINGTON: THINK OF HIS	INSPIRING	WORDS, WHEN THE LADY ASKED HIM WHETHER BRITISH
		INSPIRITING	
POSN PREFACE(431)	WILLIAM BUTLER YEATS, ROSE TO THE OCCASION WITH	INSPIRITING	COURAGE. I AM A CONCILIATORY PERSON, AND WAS
		INSTABILITY	
BULL PREFACE(21)	AS A COMMON SYMPTOM OF WORTHLESSNESS, VICE, AND	INSTABILITY	. NOW IN THIS HE IS MOST DANGEROUSLY WRONG.
		INSTAL	
DOCT PREFACE(56)	HEALTH AUTHORITIES FREQUENTLY COMPEL THEM TO	INSTAL	COSTLY SANITARY APPLIANCES WHICH ARE CONDEMNED A FEW
		INSTALLATION	
MTH3 SD(133)	OF A STEAM YACHT IN GLORIOUS SEA WEATHER. THE	INSTALLATION	WITH WHICH SHE IS COMMUNICATING IS BESIDE THE
		INSTALLED	
GENV IV (90)	LONDON, WHEREVER THE LATEST TYPE OF RECEIVER IS	INSTALLED	. /BEGONIA/ HEARD! YOU MEAN OVERHEARD. /THE
MRS IV (236)	TOLD HER I HADNT A FARTHING IN THE WORLD. SO I	INSTALLED	MYSELF AND PACKED HER OFF FOR A FORTNIGHT'S
APPL PREFACE(187)	WE ELECT HIM TRIUMPHANTLY; AND HE IS DULY	INSTALLED	, UNIFORMED, PROVIDED WITH A RED BICYCLE, AND EVEN
		INSTALMENTS	
BULL I (89)	IF HE HADNT TAKEN TO COLLECTING THE NEW PURCHASE	INSTALMENTS	INSTEAD OF THE OLD RENTS. I DOUBT IF HE'S BEEN
MIS. PREFACE(39)	UNTIL YOU HIT ON THE PLAN OF MAKING IT LEARN	INSTALMENTS	OF BIBLE VERSES, PREFERABLY FROM THE BOOK OF
		INSTANCE	
DOCT II (129)	HIM IN OTHER HANDS. /RIDGEON/ IN B.B.'S, FOR	INSTANCE	: EH? (LOOKING AT HIM SIGNIFICANTLY). /SIR
SUPR III (91)	FOR YOU, PERHAPS, THERE ARE CONSOLATIONS. FOR	INSTANCE	: HOW OLD WERE YOU WHEN YOU CHANGED FROM TIME TO
CLEO III (151)	THEM. /CLEOPATRA/ NOT INTO THAT MAN'S BOAT, FOR	INSTANCE	? (POINTING TO THE BOATMAN). /APOLLODORUS/ NO.
CAPT II (262)	IF YOU COULD ONLY RECOLLECT THEM. WITH GORDON FOR	INSTANCE	? NOBODY CAN BELITTLE THAT. HE LOOKS UP AT HER FOR
WIDO I (20)	UP ANY POINT ON WHICH YOU ARE NOT INFORMED, FOR	INSTANCE	? OR EVEN, IF I MAY SO FAR PRESUME ON MY YEARS,
MIS. (119)	SUMMERHAYS/ NOT AT ALL ASHAMED OF YOURSELF, FOR	INSTANCE	? /BENTLEY/ IF I STARTED BEING ASHAMED OF MYSELF I
GENV IV (110)	WHAT ABOUT THE UNLOVABLES? JUDAS ISCARIOT, FOR	INSTANCE	? /DEACONESS/ IF HE HAD LOVED THE MASTER HE WOULD
MILL II (175)	INTELLECT. AND WHAT DO YOU WANT AT PRESENT, FOR	INSTANCE	? /EPIFANIA/ THAT IS THE DEVIL OF IT. THERE IS
BARB III (315)	WILL SEE TO IT. ANYTHING ELSE? FOR YOURSELF, FOR	INSTANCE	? /LADY BRITOMART/ I WANT TO TALK TO YOU ABOUT
DEST (178)	MANY INTERESTING THINGS IN IT. /NAPOLEON/ FOR	INSTANCE	? /LADY/ FOR INSTANCE, A DUEL WITH BARRAS, A
CURE (233)	OH, ALL THE VERY BEST MUSIC. /STREGA/ FOR	INSTANCE	? /REGINALD/ I WISH YOU BELONGED TO ME. /STREGA/ (
GLIM (174)	AMIABLE SIN. WHAT SIN WERE YOU THINKING OF, FOR	INSTANCE	? /THE GIRL/ THERE IS A YOUNG COUNT FERRUCCIO (
METH PREFACE(R21)	THE ENVIRONMENT THEORY MUCH FURTHER, POINTING OUT	INSTANCE	AFTER INSTANCE OF MODIFICATIONS MADE IN SPECIES
2TRU PREFACE(17)	OF THE PRIESTLY VOCATION VERIFIED IN THE FIRST	INSTANCE	BY THE GROUP OF PEASANTS OR INDUSTRIAL WORKERS WITH
FABL PREFACE(66)	OF THE FORCE'S FORMER HIGHEST ACHIEVEMENTS. FOR	INSTANCE	I AM MUCH LESS MENTALLY GIFTED THAN, SAY, LEIBNIZ,
LION PREFACE(27)	THE STORY IS; AND IT IS BY NO MEANS THE ONLY	INSTANCE	IN WHICH MATTHEW REPORTS JESUS, IN SPITE OF THE
DEVL EPILOG (82)	ENGLISH ATTITUDE TOWARDS THE BURGOYNE TYPE. EVERY	INSTANCE	IN WHICH THE CRITICAL GENIUS IS DEFEATED, AND THE
UNPL PREFACE(R22)	WOULD REDUCE THEM TO ABSURDITY. THE EXTREME	INSTANCE	IS A PURE PANTOMIME, LIKE L' ENFANT PRODIGUE, IN
DOCT PREFACE(63)	AND CORRUPT HIM, HIS SELECTION IN THE FIRST	INSTANCE	IS NOT A SELECTION OF A BASE CHARACTER. THE
POSN PREFACE(395)	MATTER WHAT ITS MORAL ASPECT MAY BE. A BRILLIANT	INSTANCE	IS THE DIVORCONS OF THE LATE VICTORIEN SARDOU,
GETT PREFACE(185)	OF THE PERSON OF ANOTHER HUMAN BEING, FOR	INSTANCE	. AND HE NEVER TELLS THE TRUTH ABOUT HIS OWN
PRES (155)	ALL THE FEMININE WEAKNESSES. QUEEN ELIZABETH, FOR	INSTANCE	. HER VANITY, HER LEVITY-- /MRS BANGER/ NOBODY WHO
PYGM I (210)	THE NOTE TAKER AND THE GENTLEMAN) PARK LANE, FOR	INSTANCE	. I'D LIKE TO GO INTO THE HOUSING QUESTION WITH
SUPR II (53)	I OUGHT TO HAVE SPOKEN TO YOU BOTH IN THE FIRST	INSTANCE	. OF COURSE SHE IS RIGHT; BUT SOMEHOW IT SEEMS
ROCK II (274)	NO BOTHER ABOUT YOUR CLOTHES AT THE LAUNDRY, FOR	INSTANCE	. /ALOYSIA/ THANK YOU, SIR ARTHUR: THATS A
MIS. (113)	SOMETHING SOLID: SOME DECENT CHAP'S FIST, FOR	INSTANCE	. /BENTLEY/ I HOPE YOUR BEASTLY FIST MAY COME UP
APPL I (213)	A STRONG MAN. /NICOBAR/ (SNEERING) YOURSELF, FOR	INSTANCE	. /BOANERGES/ I SHOULD STAND A BETTER CHANCE THAN
PYGM II (241)	HER BEFORE YOU GO, DOOLITTLE? YOUR BLESSING, FOR	INSTANCE	. /DOOLITTLE/ NO, GOVERNOR: I AINT SUCH A MUG AS TO
CATH 4 (188)	SOMETIMES LEARN THROUGH SUFFERING. MANNERS, FOR	INSTANCE	. /EDSTASTON/ OH, WELL, OF COURSE, IF YOURE AN
MRS I (195)	SPEAKING OF HIGHER THINGS. SOCIAL POSITION, FOR	INSTANCE	. /FRANK/ I DONT CARE A RAP ABOUT THAT. /REV. S./
GENV II (60)	YOU KNOW, THAT IS PLAIN ENGLISH. OIL, FOR	INSTANCE	. /JUDGE/ CASTOR OIL? /SIR O./ NO NO: MOTOR OIL.
PRES (157)	WOMAN-- /MITCHENER/ (GALLANTLY) YOURSELF, FOR	INSTANCE	. /LADY CORINTHIA/ (SNATCHING UP HIS REVOLVER)
BUOY IV (50)	ONE CAN TAKE. /JUNIUS/ A JOINT ANNUITY, FOR	INSTANCE	. /OLD BILL/ YOUR SENSE OF MONEY IS VERY CLEAR,
BULL PREFACE(19)	TO YOUR POINT, LET ME FIND YOU A MORE DRAMATIC	INSTANCE	. THINK OF THE FAMOUS MEETING BETWEEN THE DUKE OF
LION PREFACE(63)	INDIVIDUAL INCOMES. FOREIGN TRAVEL IS AN OBVIOUS	INSTANCE	. WE ARE SO FAR FROM EVEN NATIONAL COMMUNISM STILL,
DOCT I (95)	I'M ONE OF THE FIVE PER CENT. I'LL GIVE YOU AN	INSTANCE	. YOU KNOW MRS JACK FOLJAMBE: THE SMART MRS
3PLA PREFACE(R20)	WRITTEN IN THE SENSUOUSLY ECSTATIC STYLE. AT THE	INSTANCE	OF MARTIN LUTHER WE LONG AGO GAVE UP IMPOSING
METH PREFACE(R21)	THEORY MUCH FURTHER, POINTING OUT INSTANCE AFTER	INSTANCE	OF MODIFICATIONS MADE IN SPECIES APPARENTLY TO
HART PREFACE(12)	IT, MAY BE ESTABLISHED BY ONE CONCLUSIVE	INSTANCE	OF THE GENERAL CRAZINESS. MEN WERE SEIZED WITH THE
LION PREFACE(99)	WHICH PROVES THE RULE; FOR IRELAND, THE STANDING	INSTANCE	OF THE INABILITY OF THE ENGLISH TO COLONIZE WITHOUT
GETT PREFACE(246)	OF THE STREETS. AND THIS IS ONLY THE EXTREME	INSTANCE	OF THE OUTLAWRY WHICH OUR MARRIAGE LAWS EFFECT. IN
BARB PREFACE(224)	SHOCK TO EARNEST YOUNG SOULS WHEN SOME DRAMATIC	INSTANCE	OF THE TAINT FIRST MAKES THEM CONSCIOUS OF IT. WHEN
MIS. PREFACE(81)	THEM. OUR ABANDONED MOTHERS. TAKE A VERY COMMON	INSTANCE	OF THIS AGONIZING INCOMPATIBILITY. A WIDOW BRINGS
DOCT PREFACE(56)	DISCARDED MISTAKES ARE ALWAYS MADE IN THE FIRST	INSTANCE	ON THE STRENGTH OF A DEMONSTRATION THAT THEIR
CLEO NOTES (211)	OF TRUTH, MONEY, OR SUCCESS IN ANY PARTICULAR	INSTANCE	QUITE INDEPENDENTLY OF CONVENTION AND MORAL
NEVR II (251)	WHAT IS DUE TO ME AS YOUR FATHER? /GLORIA/ FOR	INSTANCE	--? /CRAMPTON/ (RISING AS IF TO COMBAT A MONSTER)
BULL I (91)	CANNOT EXCUSE ANY COMPROMISE OR LAXITY. FOR	INSTANCE	-- /DOYLE/ (IMPATIENTLY SPRINGING UP AND WALKING
APPL II (269)	AN ABDICATION. THE EMPEROR CHARLES THE FIFTH, FOR	INSTANCE	-- /LYSISTRATA/ OH, CHARLES THE FIFTH BE -- BE
MTH2 (69)	YOU READ THE RECENT BIOGRAPHIES-- DILKE'S, FOR	INSTANCE	-- WHICH REVEALED THE TRUTH ABOUT THEM? /LUBIN/ I
DOCT PREFACE(72)	A POETIC BLESSING OF THE THRESHOLD, FOR	INSTANCE	-- WOULD BE MUCH BETTER; BUT UNFORTUNATELY OUR
MIS. PREFACE(73)	WHO HAVE REALLY WORKED (HERBERT SPENCER FOR	INSTANCE	) WARN US AGAINST WORK AS EARNESTLY AS SOME PEOPLE
2TRU PREFACE(15)	WE CALL DEMOCRATIC. ITS MEMBERS WERE IN THE FIRST	INSTANCE	SELF-ELECTED: THAT IS, THEY VOLUNTARILY LIVED HOLY
DOCT I SD(85)	CHISELLING OF FEATURE, REVEAL THE JEW: IN THIS	INSTANCE	THE HANDSOME GENTLEMANLY JEW, GONE A LITTLE
BARB PREFACE(242)	NAIVELY SET THE EXAMPLE OF VIOLATING IT. IN THIS	INSTANCE	THE MAN LAGS BEHIND THE LAW; BUT WHEN THE LAW LAGS
SUPR HANDBOK(199)	THE PERIOD COVERED BY HISTORY; AND IN EVERY	INSTANCE	THE TURNING POINT HAS BEEN REACHED LONG BEFORE THE
WIDO I (9)	IS WHAT THEY OCCASIONALLY FAIL IN. BUT IN THIS	INSTANCE	THEY ARE NOT TO BLAME. THE WATER IS CALLED AFTER
DOCT PREFACE(50)	MAY ACCIDENTALLY TEACH US A GOOD DEAL MORE: FOR	INSTANCE	, A CUTTHROAT LEARNS (AND PERHAPS TEACHES) THE
DEST (178)	IN IT. /NAPOLEON/ FOR INSTANCE? /LADY/ FOR	INSTANCE	, A DUEL WITH BARRAS, A DOMESTIC SCENE, A BROKEN
METH PREFACE(R51)	COULD POSSIBLY ESTABLISH A HABIT: THAT, FOR	INSTANCE	, A FAMILY COULD ACQUIRE A HABIT OF BEING KILLED IN
METH PREFACE(R46)	NATURALLY (IN DARWIN'S SENSE) TOO; THAT, FOR	INSTANCE	, A HARD WINTER WILL KILL OFF A WEAKLY CHILD AS THE
POSN PREFACE(396)	CONSEQUENCES OF ADULTERY AND PROSTITUTION-- FOR	INSTANCE	, AN UNSUCCESSFUL ILLEGAL OPERATION (SUCCESSFUL
MTH5 (235)	YOU THINK OF WHAT YOU SEE AROUND YOU? OF US, FOR	INSTANCE	, AND OUR WAYS AND DOINGS? /THE MALE FIGURE/ I
OVER PREFACE(157)	ANYONE UNDER ANY CIRCUMSTANCES (MANY WOMEN, FOR	INSTANCE	, ARE MUCH MORE JEALOUS OF THEIR HUSBANDS' MOTHERS
APPL PREFACE(181)	POLITICS FROM THEM. MOST GENERAL ELECTIONS, FOR	INSTANCE	, ARE NOTHING BUT STAMPEDES. OUR LAST BUT ONE WAS A
JOAN PREFACE(10)	MIGHT HAVE SAID THE SAME. MARIE ANTOINETTE, FOR	INSTANCE	, AT JOAN'S AGE COULD NOT SPELL HER OWN NAME
MTH2 (77)	THAT STEP ONLY: HE FELL DOWN A WHOLE FLIGHT, FOR	INSTANCE	, BEFORE HE INVENTED BIRTH HE DARED NOT HAVE LOST
ROCK PREFACE(172)	ETERNAL, FINAL, AND ABSOLUTE TRUTHS. I, FOR	INSTANCE	, BEING THE SON OF AN IRISH PROTESTANT GENTLEMAN,
BARB PREFACE(243)	HIDEOUS; BUT WHAT IS TO BE DONE? HERE AM I, FOR	INSTANCE	, BY CLASS A RESPECTABLE MAN, BY COMMON SENSE A

KING PREFACE(153)	THE SITUATION BECOMES INTERESTING AND FRESH. FOR	INSTANCE	, CHARLES MIGHT HAVE MET THAT HUMAN PRODIGY ISAAC
DOCT PREFACE(55)	TO THE LAST MAN. OR, TO TAKE ANOTHER COMMON	INSTANCE	, COMPARISONS WHICH ARE REALLY COMPARISONS BETWEEN
POSN PREFACE(390)	THE LAW HAS FORGOTTEN SOME ATROCIOUS SIN-- FOR	INSTANCE	, CONTRACTING MARRIAGE WHILST SUFFERING FROM
APPL I (204)	MUST SIGN: THERE IS NOTHING ELSE TO BE DONE. FOR	INSTANCE	, DEATH WARRANTS. NOT ONLY HAVE I TO SIGN THE DEATH
MIS. (158)	NEVER CONDESCEND TO DO AS COMMON PEOPLE DO? FOR	INSTANCE	, DO YOU NOT PRAY AS COMMON PEOPLE PRAY? /LINA/
SUPR PREFACE(R15)	THE DON JUAN PLAY ARE DILAPIDATED PAST USE: FOR	INSTANCE	, DON JUAN'S SUPERNATURAL ANTAGONIST HURLED THOSE
NEVR II (251)	A MONSTER) FOR INSTANCE! FOR INSTANCE! ! FOR	INSTANCE	, DUTY, AFFECTION, RESPECT, OBEDIENCE-- /GLORIA/ (
MILL PREFACE(117)	THAT WE WERE A LIBERTY LOVING PEOPLE: THAT, FOR	INSTANCE	, ENGLISHMEN WOULD NEVER TOLERATE COMPULSORY
POSN PREFACE(399)	FOR THE REAL ETHICAL TENDENCY OF THE PLAY. FOR	INSTANCE	, HAD IT BEEN IN EXISTENCE DURING THE LAST QUARTER
POSN PREFACE(366)	MR FORBES ROBERTSON AND SIR HERBERT TREE, FOR	INSTANCE	, HAD NEVER FELT THE REAL DISADVANTAGE OF WHICH
BULL PREFACE(43)	CLAIM A NATURAL RIGHT TO THAT LIBERTY. WHEN, FOR	INSTANCE	, HE INSISTS ON LIVING, IN SPITE OF THE IRREFUTABLE
BULL I (91)	(IMPATIENTLY SPRINGING UP AND WALKING ABOUT) FOR	INSTANCE	, HOME RULE, SOUTH AFRICA, FREE TRADE, AND PUTTING
MTH5 (228)	ALL THESE FORCES CAN BE USED BY US. FOR	INSTANCE	, I USE THE FORCE OF GRAVITATION WHEN I PUT A STONE
BULL PREFACE(45)	BE OBEYED WITHOUT REGARD TO CONSEQUENCES: FOR	INSTANCE	, IF HE CALLS HIS MEN DOGS, AND PERVERTS A MUSKETRY
LION PREFACE(11)	THE RELIGIOUS PEOPLE UP TO A CERTAIN POINT: FOR	INSTANCE	, IF SAVONAROLA ONLY TELLS THE LADIES OF FLORENCE
ROCK PREFACE(161)	AND CERTAIN PENALTIES IN THE OLD FASHION: AS, FOR	INSTANCE	, IF YOU HOARD MONEY YOU WILL BE SHOT; IF YOU
MIS. PREFACE(70)	TO ADULTS, DOES NOT PRESS VERY HARDLY, AS, FOR	INSTANCE	, IN THE HOUSES OF THE VERY POOR, WHO CAN SEND
PLES PREFACE(R15)	NOT ONLY OBSOLETE, BUT FUNDAMENTALLY WRONG: FOR	INSTANCE	, IN THE SIMPLE CASE OF LAUGHTER AND TEARS, IN
PLES PREFACE(R8)	CHRISTIAN SOCIALISM WITH VULGAR UNSOCIALISM: FOR	INSTANCE	, IN WIDOWERS' HOUSES, THE CLERGYMAN, WHO DOES NOT
SUPR PREFACE(R35)	NEW IN THESE MATTERS EXCEPT THEIR NOVELTIES: FOR	INSTANCE	, IT IS A NOVELTY TO CALL JUSTIFICATION BY FAITH "
POSN PREFACE(423)	BE SET UP AND USED FOR CERTAIN PURPOSES, FOR	INSTANCE	, IT MIGHT BE MADE A CONDITION OF THE INTERVENTION
BULL PREFACE(57)	PRACTICES. THIS IS A FAR-REACHING ARGUMENT: FOR	INSTANCE	, IT SUGGESTS THAT CHURCH OF ENGLAND MISSIONARIES
2TRU PREFACE(25)	VOCATIONAL INCENTIVE; FOR SUCCESS, IN THE FIRST	INSTANCE	, MEANS, NOT RELEASE FROM THE DAY'S ORDINARY WORK,
POSN PREFACE(376)	THEY DID NOT ALL WANT TO PART WITH THE BOOKS. FOR	INSTANCE	, MR HUGH LAW, BEING AN IRISHMAN, WITH AN
SUPR PREFACE(R34)	THE ARTIST-PHILOSOPHERS. YOU CANNOT SAY IT, FOR	INSTANCE	, OF THE PILGRIM'S PROGRESS. PUT YOUR SHAKESPEARIAN
LADY PREFACE(227)	REPLY. IN THE CASE OF MICHEL ANGELO, FOR	INSTANCE	, ONE MUST ADMIT THAT IF HIS WORKS ARE SET BESIDE
BULL PREFACE(46)	OFFICERS. COMPARE WITH THIS THE POSITION OF, FOR	INSTANCE	, OUR RAILWAY MANAGERS OR OUR HEADS OF EXPLOSIVES
METH PREFACE(R26)	CHARACTERISTIC OF THE EVOLUTIONARY PROCESS. FOR	INSTANCE	, RAPHAEL, THOUGH DESCENDED FROM EIGHT
DOCT I SD(84)	DEAL LINED; HIS MOVEMENTS ARE SLOWER THAN, FOR	INSTANCE	, REDPENNY'S; AND HIS FLAXEN HAIR HAS LOST ITS
DOCT I (99)	THE DISEASE EXISTING WITHOUT THEM? CAN YOU, FOR	INSTANCE	, SHEW ME A CASE OF DIPHTHERIA WITHOUT THE
METH PREFACE(R54)	PERIODS AND UNDER CERTAIN CIRCUMSTANCES. FOR	INSTANCE	, SINCE IT IS THE UNGOVERNABLE GLUTTONS WHO STRIVE
BASH PREFACE(90)	WERE STEEPED IN MODERN LITERARY SOB STUFF. FOR	INSTANCE	, SUCH BALD STATEMENTS ABOUT BARABBAS AS THAT HE
APPL I (228)	ON THE OTHER SIDE? I HAVE NOTICED, FOR	INSTANCE	, THAT IN A CERTAIN NEWSPAPER WHICH LOSES NO
METH PREFACE(R21)	TO ADAPT IT TO CIRCUMSTANCES AND ENVIRONMENT: FOR	INSTANCE	, THAT THE BRILLIANT COLOURS OF THE LEOPARD, WHICH
LION PREFACE(32)	MORE CLEARLY BEFORE THE READER. HE SAYS, FOR	INSTANCE	, THAT WHEN JESUS WALKED ON THE WAVES TO THE BOAT,
DOCT PREFACE(41)	OF INVESTIGATION WHICH WOULD FINALLY MAKE, FOR	INSTANCE	, THE ASCERTAINMENT OF THE GUILT OR INNOCENCE OF AN
FABL PREFACE(88)	LEAST THIRTY YEARS OUT OF DATE: IN ECONOMICS, FOR	INSTANCE	, THE CANDIDATE WHO HAS BEEN TAUGHT THAT THE LATEST
3PLA PREFACE(R25)	FOR NOVELTY IN MY PLAYS AND OPINIONS. TAKE, FOR	INSTANCE	, THE FIRST PLAY IN THIS VOLUME, ENTITLED THE
KING PREFACE(158)	WOMEN HAS BECOME INDISPENSABLE IN CABINETS. FOR	INSTANCE	, THE HOUSE OF LORDS IS MORE REPRESENTATIVE THAN
JOAN 6 (127)	POINTS HAVE BEEN REDUCED ALMOST TO NOTHING. FOR	INSTANCE	, THE MAID HAS ACTUALLY DECLARED THAT THE BLESSED
MRS PREFACE(178)	PLAY DID NOT END THE MATTER. IN KANSAS CITY, FOR	INSTANCE	, THE MUNICIPALITY, FINDING ITSELF RESTRAINED BY
POSN PREFACE(393)	TO THE SUSCEPTIBILITIES OF FOREIGN COURTS. FOR	INSTANCE	, THE NOTION THAT THE MIKADO OF JAPAN SHOULD BE AS
3PLA PREFACE(R17)	GENTILITY WHICH GOVERNS OUR THEATRES TODAY. FOR	INSTANCE	, THE OBJECTION TO IBSEN IS NOT REALLY AN OBJECTION
BUOY PREFACE(3)	MAY BE RAISED AGAINST ANY FAMOUS SCRIPTURE. FOR	INSTANCE	, THE PECULIARS KNOWN AS BACONIANS BELIEVE, WITH
UNPL PREFACE(R26)	BUT WE HAVE GREAT PROSTITUTE CLASSES OF MEN: FOR	INSTANCE	, THE PLAYWRIGHTS AND JOURNALISTS, TO WHOM I MYSELF
FABL PREFACE(85)	AFFAIRS THE TIME LAG EXTENDS TO CENTURIES. FOR	INSTANCE	, THE PRACTICE OF EARTH BURIAL, WITH ITS CEMETERIES
2TRU PREFACE(14)	PROBLEMS TO DIFFERENT PEOPLE. TO THE THIEF, FOR	INSTANCE	, THE PROBLEM IS HOW TO EVADE HIS SHARE IN THE
METH PREFACE(R24)	TRANSMITTED WITHOUT ANY PERCEPTIBLE RELAPSE. FOR	INSTANCE	, THE VERY FIRST ACT OF YOUR SON WHEN HE ENTERS THE
DOCT PREFACE(43)	OF PREPARING LECTURES IN MEDICAL SCHOOLS. FOR	INSTANCE	, THERE ARE TWO WAYS OF MAKING THE ACTION OF THE
DOCT III (146)	BETTER DEAD. THERE ARE EXCEPTIONS, NO DOUBT. FOR	INSTANCE	, THERE IS THE COURT, AN ESSENTIALLY
GETT PREFACE(229)	MEN MAY BE VICIOUS WITH IMPUNITY. ADULTERY, FOR	INSTANCE	, THOUGH IT IS SOMETIMES FIERCELY PUNISHED BY
LION PREFACE(45)	FASHIONS IN BELIEF AND MODERN FASHIONS. FOR	INSTANCE	, THOUGH WE ARE MORE CREDULOUS THAN MEN WERE IN THE
KING I (184)	WITH YOU? /NEWTON/ MANY OTHER THINGS. FOR	INSTANCE	, TO ASCERTAIN THE EXACT DISTANCE OF THE SUN FROM
DOCT PREFACE(54)	OF THE PASTEUR TREATMENT OF HYDROPHOBIA, FOR	INSTANCE	, WAS DUE TO THE ASSUMPTION BY THE PUBLIC THAT
BARB PREFACE(214)	MAKE PEOPLE REALIZE THAT AN EVIL IS AN EVIL. FOR	INSTANCE	, WE SEIZE A MAN AND DELIBERATELY DO HIM A
JOAN PREFACE(41)	SOCIETY IS MAINTAINING ITS COHESION. IN WAR, FOR	INSTANCE	, WE SUPPRESS THE GOSPELS AND PUT QUAKERS IN
BARB II (287)	A WHILE. /BARBARA/ ALL RIGHT. /UNDERSHAFT/ FOR	INSTANCE	, WHATS THE MATTER WITH THAT OUT-PATIENT OVER
ROCK PREFACE(171)	WHAT COMPROMISE IS POSSIBLE BETWEEN MYSELF, FOR	INSTANCE	, WHO BELIEVE IN THE RELIGION OF CREATIVE
MIS. PREFACE(19)	MORE CRUEL THAN A PRISON. IN A PRISON, FOR	INSTANCE	, YOU ARE NOT FORCED TO READ BOOKS WRITTEN BY THE
GETT PREFACE(253)	ONE OF THE PARTIES PETITIONS FOR IT. IF, FOR	INSTANCE	, YOU HAVE A THOROUGHLY RASCALLY COUPLE MAKING A
PHIL II (121)	ISNT IT? /PARAMORE/ NO DOUBT. /CHARTERIS/ FOR	INSTANCE	, YOU HAVE A THEORY ABOUT CRAVEN'S LIVER, EH?
BULL IV (164)	SHE WOULD ALWAYS UNDERSTAND MY JOKES. FOR	INSTANCE	, YOU WOULD UNDERSTAND THEM, EH? /NORA/ (
APPL INTRLUD(252)	ONLY INDIVIDUALS, BUT WHOLE SORTS OF PEOPLE. FOR	INSTANCE	, YOUR SORT. MY WIFE DOESNT LIKE YOUR SORT, DOESNT
GETT PREFACE(186)	ON WHICH AMERICAN WIVES OBTAIN DIVORCES (FOR	INSTANCE	, " MENTAL ANGUISH" CAUSED BY THE HUSBAND'S NEGLECT
BARB III (328)	BREAK UP HOME LIFE. LOOK AT THE CONTINENT, FOR	INSTANCE	! ARE YOU SURE SO MUCH PAMPERING IS REALLY GOOD
NEVR II (251)	(RISING AS IF TO COMBAT A MONSTER) FOR	INSTANCE	! FOR INSTANCE! ! FOR INSTANCE, DUTY, AFFECTION,
LADY PREFACE(233)	PRODUCE POPULAR WORK. TAKE WAGNER AND IBSEN FOR	INSTANCE	! THEIR EARLIER WORKS ARE NO DOUBT MUCH CHEAPER
NEVR II (251)	AS IF TO COMBAT A MONSTER) FOR INSTANCE! FOR	INSTANCE	! ! FOR INSTANCE, DUTY, AFFECTION, RESPECT,

INSTANCES

METH PREFACE(R46)	BEFORE WE HAVE COME TO THE END OF THE INNUMERABLE	INSTANCES	AND ILLUSTRATIONS OF WHICH THE BOOK MAINLY
CYMB FORWORD(138)	VOICE DESTROYING ORGY. I MAY BE ASKED WHY ALL MY	INSTANCES	ARE MUSICAL INSTEAD OF LITERARY. IS IT A PLOT TO
ROCK PREFACE(149)	THE POINT. THE NOVELTY AND SIGNIFICANCE OF THESE	INSTANCES	CONSISTS IN THE EQUAL STATUS OF THE PARTIES. THE
JOAN PREFACE(41)	RUSSIAN BOLSHEVIK REVOLUTION AFTER 1917. THESE	INSTANCES	COULD EASILY BE MULTIPLIED; BUT THEY ARE ENOUGH TO
CLEO NOTES (205)	CONSCIOUSNESS THAT THE STRING OF CONTEMPTUOUS	INSTANCES	GIVEN MIGHT HAVE BEEN SAVED BY WRITING SIMPLY "
BULL PREFACE(62)	BEEN THE MOTIVE. MY OBJECT IN MENTIONING THESE	INSTANCES	IS TO SHEW THE RESULTS TO BE EXPECTED IF ONCE
DOCT PREFACE(49)	THE BURGLAR WITH MONEY TO SPEND, AND AS IN MANY	INSTANCES	IT HAS ACHIEVED THIS OBJECT, THEREFORE THE BURGLAR
DOCT PREFACE(9)	THAT DIAGNOSIS, THOUGH IT MEANS IN MANY	INSTANCES	(INCLUDING EVEN THE IDENTIFICATION OF PATHOGENIC
LION PREFACE(18)	CONSCIOUSNESS OF THE CONTRADICTION INVOLVED, MANY	INSTANCES	MIGHT BE GIVEN: A FAMILIAR ONE TO MY GENERATION
GETT PREFACE(195)	HIS SERVICES THAN THEY ARE WORTH. IN THE EXTREME	INSTANCES	OF REACTION AGAINST CONVENTION, FEMALE MURDERERS
SUPR PREFACE(R14)	OF A PHILOSOPHER AS PETER THE GREAT: BOTH WERE	INSTANCES	OF THAT RARE AND USEFUL, BUT UNEDIFYING VARIATION,
MTH2 (68)	/FRANKLYN/ I COULD RECALL TO YOU SEVERAL	INSTANCES	OF THE ADDITION TO YOUR PARTY PROGRAM OF MEASURES
MRS PREFACE(166)	ALL THE APPARENT INSTANCES TO THE CONTRARY ARE	INSTANCES	OF THE PERSONAL FASCINATION OF THE PERFORMERS. THE
MIS. PREFACE(17)	AND BEAR IN MIND THAT THEY ARE ONLY THE EXTREME	INSTANCES	OF WHAT IS COMMONLY CALLED NATURAL AFFECTION,
SUPR III (107)	DAILY WALK. I COULD GIVE YOU A THOUSAND	INSTANCES	; BUT THEY ALL COME TO THE SAME THING: THE POWER
MRS PREFACE(166)	DO LITTLE TO DELIGHT THE SENSES: ALL THE APPARENT	INSTANCES	TO THE CONTRARY ARE INSTANCES OF THE PERSONAL
LION PREFACE(89)	HE WILL STEAL YOUR WATCH. I COULD MULTIPLY THESE	INSTANCES	TO WEARINESS. THE MAIN DIFFERENCE THAT SET

INSTANT

CLEO II (124)	PTOLEMY, WHO SHRINKS FROM HER). GO THIS	INSTANT	AND SIT DOWN IN YOUR PLACE. /CAESAR/ GO, PTOLEMY.
KING I (162)	WALK INTO IT WITHOUT TAKING OFF HIS HAT? GO THIS	INSTANT	AND TELL HIM YOU WILL RAISE THE STREET AGAINST HIM
ROCK PREFACE(161)	AND SPECIFIC PENALTIES, COULD HAVE PROVIDED FOR	INSTANT	EXEMPLARY EXTERMINATIONS OF THIS KIND, ANY MORE THAN
MTH5 (248)	THINGS I HAD MODELLED, AND SAW THEM VANISH IN AN	INSTANT	INTO INOFFENSIVE DUST. /THE SHE-ANCIENT/ SPEAK,
SUPR I (34)	RACHEL ROSETREE? (ANN'S BROWS CONTRACT FOR AN	INSTANT	INVOLUNTARILY), I GOT UP A LOVE AFFAIR WITH HER; AND
BASH II,1, (105)	I BE, LET BUT MY MISTRESS GIVE ME THE WORD:	INSTANT	I'LL TAKE HIM ON HERE-- NOW-- AT CATCHWEIGHT. BETTER
PHIL II (130)	! NOW REALLY! ! ! I SHALL GO THIS	INSTANT	, COME ON, SYLVIA, CUTHBERTSON: I HOPE YOULL MARK
SIM II (67)	YOUR EARS, YOU ABOMINABLE IDOLATERS? GET UP THIS	INSTANT	. GO AND SCRUB THE FLOORS. DO ANYTHING THAT IS DIRTY
WIDO I (8)	HIM THE CUP, AND LOOKS MEANINGLY AT HIM FOR AN	INSTANT	. HE LOOKS DOWN HASTILY, AND GLANCES APPREHENSIVELY
BARB II (306)	TO THE GREAT MEETING AT ONCE. EXCUSE ME JUST AN	INSTANT	. (HE RUSHES INTO THE SHELTER. JENNY TAKES HER
INCA PROLOG (234)	WHAT! COME BACK, MISS. COME BACK THIS	INSTANT	. (THE LIGHTS ARE LOWERED). OH, VERY WELL: I HAVE
HART I (54)	ELSE. I WILL HAVE IT OUT WITH PAPA NOW, THIS	INSTANT	. (TO MAZZINI) EXCUSE ME. (SHE FOLLOWS THE CAPTAIN
CATH 1 (171)	GOING TO TAKE YOU TO THE EMPRESS NOW, THIS VERY	INSTANT	. /EDSTASTON/ IN THESE BOOTS? IMPOSSIBLE! I MUST
FANY II (296)	YOU YOUNG HUSSY; OR GO OUT OF MY HOUSE THIS	INSTANT	. /MARGARET/ I'M QUITE READY. (SHE TAKES HER HAT
DOCT I (112)	VANISHES. /MRS DUBEDAT/ (RISING) DOCTOR: ONE	INSTANT	ONLY BEFORE YOU GO-- /RIDGEON/ SIT DOWN/ IT'S
KING I (174)	NEWTON: EITHER THIS FEMALE LEAVES THE HOUSE THIS	INSTANT	OR I DO. /BARBARA/ DO YOU KNOW, WOMAN, THAT YOU ARE
GETT (327)	VAMPIRE. THERE IS ONLY ONE CHANCE FOR ME: FLIGHT.	INSTANT	PRECIPITATE FLIGHT, MAKE MY EXCUSES. FORGET ME.
CAND III (132)	WE ARE ROLLED UP IN. (HE REFLECTS ON THIS FOR AN	INSTANT	; THEN TURNS INTENTLY TO QUESTION MORELL). WHAT I

KING I (168)	YOU, PASTOR. NOTHING HAS EVER STOOD STILL FOR AN	INSTANT	SINCE THE CREATION OF THE WORLD: NEITHER THE SUN,
3PLA PREFACE(R34)	THERE WAS TIME FOR INSTEAD OF AS LITTLE. AND THE	INSTANT	SUCCESS OF THE EXPERIMENT PROBABLY ALTERED THEIR
GETT PREFACE(218)	QUITE USELESS AS A MAGIC SPELL FOR CHANGING IN AN	INSTANT	THE NATURE OF THE RELATIONS OF TWO HUMAN BEINGS TO
ARMS I SD(7)	DISAPPEAR, PULLED OPEN FROM WITHOUT; AND FOR AN	INSTANT	THE RECTANGLE OF SNOWY STARLIGHT FLASHES OUT WITH
SIM I (52)	ME THAT IS NOT A THROB FOR VASHTI: IF FOR EVEN AN	INSTANT	THERE ARE TWO WOMEN IN YOUR THOUGHTS INSTEAD OF ONE,
3PLA PREFACE(R29)	YOUNGER THAN HIMSELF, AND TURNS SOLDIER IN AN	INSTANT	TO SAVE THE MAN WHO HAS SAVED HIM, DICK LOOKS ROUND
KING I (195)	IN HIS HEAD COULD LOOK AT THE CREATURE FOR AN	INSTANT	WITHOUT SEEING THAT HE IS ONLY HALF HUMAN. /JAMES/
GETT (330)	IF YOU CAN TOUCH MY POOR DYING HEART EVEN FOR AN	INSTANT	, I'LL BLESS YOU, AND NEVER FORGET YOU. YOU MAY
LION I (124)	THAT? NOT PRAY! (SEIZING HIM AGAIN) PRAY THIS	INSTANT	, YOU DOG, YOU ROTTEN HOUND, YOU SLIMY SNAKE, YOU
PRES (152)	SITS DOWN DOGGEDLY). GET OUT OF THE ROOM THIS	INSTANT	, YOU FOOL; OR I'LL KICK YOU OUT. /THE ORDERLY/ (

INSTANTANEOUS

SIM PREFACE(16)	OF HIMSELF IF THE DOG'S DEATH HAD NOT BEEN	INSTANTANEOUS	AND UNANTICIPATED. AND THE IDEA OF PUNISHMENT
METH PREFACE(R27)	DIFFICULT OPERATIONS OF OUR MINDS MAY YET BECOME	INSTANTANEOUS	, OR, AS WE CALL IT, INSTINCTIVE. IT ALSO

INSTANTANEOUSLY

MILL I (140)	ARE SURE THAT THEY HAVE ALL DIED PAINLESSLY AND	INSTANTANEOUSLY	? /SAGAMORE/ NO. THEY ARE ALL ALIVE.
METH PREFACE(R27)	ENCYCLOPAEDIA BRITANNICA, IS SO COMPLETELY AND	INSTANTANEOUSLY	AT MY CALL THAT I HAVE NEVER HAD TO CONSULT
METH PREFACE(R28)	AND TO SIR EDWARD ELGAR AN ORCHESTRAL SCORE IS AS	INSTANTANEOUSLY	INTELLIGIBLE AT SIGHT AS A PAGE OF
LION PREFACE(25)	ME A MAN WITH ONLY ONE LEG AND MAKE ANOTHER GROW	INSTANTANEOUSLY	ON HIM BEFORE MY EYES, AND I WILL BE REALLY
DEST (156)	MOMENT HE COMES BACK, SEND HIM TO ME. /GIUSEPPE/	INSTANTANEOUSLY	, YOUR EXCELLENCY. /A LADY'S VOICE/ (

INSTANTANEOUSNESS

GENV PREFACE(10)	IF THIS DISINTEGRATION COULD BE SPEEDED UP TO	INSTANTANEOUSNESS	IT WOULD MAKE A HEAT SO PRODIGIOUS THAT A

INSTANTLY

MIS. PREFACE(105)	YOU MUST DO THIS" OR " YOU MUST NOT DO THAT," HE	INSTANTLY	ASKS WHAT WILL HAPPEN TO HIM IF HE DOES (OR DOES
DEST SD(172)	IN THE ATTITUDE OF A MARTYR. THE GESTURE AND POSE	INSTANTLY	AWAKEN HIS THEATRICAL INSTINCT: HE FORGETS HIS
PYGM V SD(289)	HIGGINS RETURNS, DRESSED FOR THE WEDDING. ELIZA	INSTANTLY	BECOMES COOL AND ELEGANT. /MRS HIGGINS/ THE
SUPR II (66)	VIOLET: I WISH YOUD LET ME OWN UP. /VIOLET/ (	INSTANTLY	BECOMING SERIOUS AND RESOLUTE) NO, NO, HECTOR: YOU
ARMS II (33)	I HAVE A WORD OR TWO TO SAY TO PAUL. (SERGIUS	INSTANTLY	BOWS AND STEPS BACK). NOW, DEAR (TAKING PETKOFF'S
2TRU III SD(81)	ONE OF THEM APPRECIATIVELY WITH HIS FIST. SHE	INSTANTLY	BRIGHTENS UP; CLIMBS TO THE MOUTH OF THE GROTTO
PYGM I (206)	HANDS. A BLINDING FLASH OF LIGHTNING, FOLLOWED	INSTANTLY	BY A RATTLING PEAL OF THUNDER, ORCHESTRATES THE
MRS PREFACE(174)	RESPECTABLE GENTLEMEN LIKE THEMSELVES, WHO WOULD	INSTANTLY	CALL THE POLICE TO REMOVE MRS WARREN IF SHE
NEVR II (255)	SELF-RESPECTING WOMAN CAN ACCEPT. /VALENTINE/ (	INSTANTLY	CHANGING HIS TONE FOR ONE OF CORDIAL SINCERITY, AS
WIDO III SD(51)	UP. LICKCHEESE, WHO HAS BEEN WAITING AT THE DOOR,	INSTANTLY	COMES IN. THE CHANGE IN HIS APPEARANCE IS
CAND III (136)	TO EUGENE) YOU BEGAN IT: THIS MORNING. (CANDIDA,	INSTANTLY	CONNECTING THIS WITH HIS MYSTERIOUS ALLUSION IN
LION PREFACE(73)	SOCIOLOGISTS AND OUR LEGISLATORS. THIS WILL NOT	INSTANTLY	CURE ALL THE EVILS OF MARRIAGE, NOR ROOT UP AT ONE
DOCT PREFACE(46)	CONVULSIONS, HE EXPERIMENTED ON A RABBIT, WHICH	INSTANTLY	DROPPED DEAD. IT WAS THEN, AND NOT UNTIL THEN,
BULL III (138)	ALL. COME IN AN WET THE BARGAIN. /MATTHEW/ (	INSTANTLY	DROPPING INTO THE OLD WHINE OF THE TENANT) I'M
NEVR IV (291)	MORE QUIETLY. /VALENTINE/ NONSENSE. /BOHUN/ (	INSTANTLY	FLINGING HIMSELF BACK IN HIS CHAIR, OUTRAGED BY
CAPT III (277)	FAMILY WILL BE FURIOUS. (SIR HOWARD QUAILS. SHE	INSTANTLY	FOLLOWS UP HER ADVANTAGE WITH) THINK OF PAPA!
NEVR I (213)	HER MOTHER'S FOR THE FIRST TIME. THE TWINS	INSTANTLY	GO OVER TO THE ENEMY). /MRS CLANDON/ (WOUNDED) IN
WIDO III SD(55)	SPRINGS UP. THE PARLORMAID LOOKS AT HER FACE, AND	INSTANTLY	HURRIES OUT OF THE ROOM ON TIPTOE WITH HER TRAY.
ANNA (299)	ADOPTING HIS VIEWS ON THE SINGLE TAX AND BEING	INSTANTLY	INVADED AND ANNIHILATED. A THIRD ORDERS ME TO GO
BARB III (341)	/LADY BRITOMART/ (RISING) CHILDREN: COME HOME	INSTANTLY	. ANDREW: I AM EXCEEDINGLY SORRY I ALLOWED YOU TO
INCA (240)	QUALITY? TAKE AWAY YOUR COLD TEA AND COLD CAKE	INSTANTLY	. GIVE THEM TO THE CHAMBERMAID YOU WERE FLIRTING
LION PREFACE(46)	AND THE PATIENT BELIEVES HIM ABJECTLY AND	INSTANTLY	. HAD A BISHOP TOLD WILLIAM THE CONQUEROR THAT THE
DEVL I (25)	HER GRATEFUL EYES. HIS MOCKING EXPRESSION RETURNS	INSTANTLY	. HE PUTS DOWN THE GLASS; DELIBERATELY WINDS HIS
MILL II (170)	BODY IT IS NO MORE THAN HE DESERVES. COME BACK	INSTANTLY	. I WANT YOU. COME BACK. COME BACK. /THE DOCTOR/ (
LION II (144)	SORCERER: I COMMAND YOU TO PUT THAT LION TO DEATH	INSTANTLY	. IT IS GUILTY OF HIGH TREASON. YOUR CONDUCT IS
PPP (201)	IT IN A JUG OF HOT WATER; AND BRING IT BACK	INSTANTLY	. MR BASTABLE'S LIFE DEPENDS ON YOUR HASTE.
GENV II (49)	PRESENT USING. /THE SECRETARY/ YES: SEND HER UP	INSTANTLY	. REMIND ME OF HER NAME. WHAT? ! . . . AMMONIA?
MILL IV (196)	AT ALL: YOU ARE RE-ENGAGED. THROW THEM BOTH OUT,	INSTANTLY	. /ALASTAIR/ HA HA HA! /SAGAMORE/ YOUR MANAGER
NEVR IV SD(294)	DOLLY WITH THE HIGHEST APPROVAL, IS DOWN ON HIM	INSTANTLY	. /BOHUN/ NO: DONT INTERRUPT, M'COMAS. THE YOUNG
MIS. (187)	THAT INFERNAL NOISE, SIR: DO YOU HEAR? STOP IT	INSTANTLY	. /JOHNNY/ THATS THE GAME HE TRIED ON ME. THERE
DEST (163)	YOU ARE UNDER ARREST. PUT DOWN YOUR SWORD, SIR,	INSTANTLY	. /LIEUTENANT/ GENERAL: I TELL YOU HE'S AN
MILL IV (193)	ME OUT OF THIS. PACK UP, SEEDY. MY BILL, PLEASE,	INSTANTLY	. /THE MANAGER/ CERTAINLY, SIR. BUT MAY I SAY THAT
2TRU I (38)	TO SIT THERE NEGLECTING ME? SHUT THAT WINDOW	INSTANTLY	. /THE NURSE/ (INSOLENTLY, IN HER COMMONEST
2TRU I (42)	TO BE OUR MOST GLORIOUS ACHIEVEMENT. OBEY ME	INSTANTLY	. /THE NURSE/ (RESIGNEDLY) OH, VERY WELL. (SHE
2TRU II (56)	SHEEP AND SIX TURKEYS. /TALLBOYS/ SEND THEM BACK	INSTANTLY	. TAKE THEM BACK ON YOUR DAMNED BICYCLE. INFORM
MILL I (155)	I AM IMPULSIVE: I KEPT MY WORD AND MARRIED HIM	INSTANTLY	. THEN, TOO LATE, I FOUND OUT HOW HE HAD MADE IT.
DEST (181)	BUSTLING HIM). /GIUSEPPE/ INSTANTLY, LIEUTENANT,	INSTANTLY	(HE DISAPPEARS IN THE VINEYARD, WHERE THE LIGHT
METH PREFACE(R49)	UP ON THE DINNER TABLE, AND YOU PUT IT DOWN, IT	INSTANTLY	JUMPS UP AGAIN, AND FINALLY ESTABLISHES ITS RIGHT
CAPT NOTES (302)	I WAS WALKING WITH MY MOTHER. HER INTEREST WAS	INSTANTLY	KINDLED; AND THE FOLLOWING CONVERSATION ENSUED. "
MIS. PREFACE(13)	ITSELF. TO ALLOW THE CHILD TO MISBEHAVE WITHOUT	INSTANTLY	MAKING IT UNPLEASANTLY CONSCIOUS OF THE FACT WOULD
METH PREFACE(R27)	TO WHOM THE ANSWER TO SUCH SUMS AS I CAN DO IS	INSTANTLY	OBVIOUS WITHOUT ANY CONSCIOUS CALCULATION AT ALL;
GENV PREFACE(24)	OF CYPHERING (IF I COULD SOLVE THEM AT ALL) ARE	INSTANTLY	OBVIOUS. IN GRAMMAR AND SCRIPTURE I AM PRACTICALLY
BUOY 1 (13)	BUT WITH CHARLEMAGNE IT WAS EMBRACE CHRISTIANITY	INSTANTLY	OR DIE; WITH MAHOMET THE SLAYING OF THE INFIDEL
NEVR IV (289)	WHAT D'Y' MEAN? I'M HER HUSBAND. /BOHUN/ (	INSTANTLY	POUNCING ON THE INCONSISTENCY BETWEEN THIS AND HIS
CAND II SD(122)	TO MORELL, GREATLY AMUSED). EUGENE LOOKS, AND	INSTANTLY	PRESSES HIS HAND ON HIS HEART, AS IF SOME PAIN HAD
MRS PREFACE(175)	PROFESSION IN NEW YORK. THE PRESS OF THAT CITY	INSTANTLY	RAISED A CRY THAT SUCH PERSONS AS MRS WARREN ARE "
HART PREFACE(26)	AND THE ELECTORATE, DISGUSTED AT ITS OWN WORK,	INSTANTLY	RECOILED TO THE OPPOSITE EXTREME, AND CAST OUT ALL
BULL IV (153)	MR KEEGAN'S PECULIAR VEIN OF HUMOR. /BROADBENT/ (	INSTANTLY	RECOVERING HIS CONFIDENCE) AH! IT WAS ONLY YOUR
WIDO II SD(33)	TEETH ON EDGE. COKANE IS TAKEN ABACK, BUT	INSTANTLY	RECOVERS HIMSELF. /COKANE/ HA! HA! HA! HO!
CLEO II (132)	FTATATEETA. (CALLING) FTATATEETA. (FTATATEETA	INSTANTLY	RISES AND COMES TO CLEOPATRA). /CAESAR/ (
DEVL II (37)	PUTS HIS HAND ENCOURAGINGLY ON HER SHOULDER. SHE	INSTANTLY	RISES HAUGHTILY, AND STARES AT HIM DEFIANTLY. HE
DOCT I (112)	TELEPHONED FROM THE HOSPITAL THAT YOURE TO COME	INSTANTLY	-- A PATIENT ON THE POINT OF DEATH. THE CARRIAGE
PHIL III (133)	ALL THAT, MISS CRAVEN. /JULIA/ (RAISING HER HEAD	INSTANTLY	) IF HE SAYS THAT, HE LIES. IF EVER YOU HEAR IT
NEVR IV (304)	A RAP. /BOHUN/ (NAILING VALENTINE TO THE POINT	INSTANTLY	) THEN INSIST ON A SETTLEMENT. THAT SHOCKS YOUR
ARMS I (21)	BED WITH A FINAL EFFORT; AND FALLS FAST ASLEEP	INSTANTLY	). CATHERINE COMES IN, FOLLOWED BY RAINA. /RAINA/
SIM PRO,3, (34)	NO: I-- (HE LOOKS AT HER. HIS TONE CHANGES	INSTANTLY	). WELL, YES, IF YOU WILL BE SO GOOD. CERTAINLY.
ARMS I (8)	ON THE BED) WHO'S THERE? (THE MATCH IS OUT	INSTANTLY	). WHO'S THERE? WHO IS THAT? /A MAN'S VOICE/ (
PYGM I (214)	WOMAN: CEASE THIS DETESTABLE BOOHOOING	INSTANTLY	; OR ELSE SEEK THE SHELTER OF SOME OTHER PLACE OF
WIDO I (11)	FILM ON HER EYES). BLANCHE. (SHE BRISTLES	INSTANTLY	; OVERDOES IT; AND FRIGHTENS HIM). I BEG YOUR
SIM PREFACE(12)	DOG, GROWING OLD, MADE A MISTAKE: ITS FIRST. HE	INSTANTLY	SHOT IT. I LEARNT THAT HE ALWAYS SHOT HIS SPORTING
NEVR I SD(219)	LOOK AWAY FROM THEM AT ONE ANOTHER, AND ARE	INSTANTLY	SO DISCONCERTED BY CATCHING ONE ANOTHER'S EYE,
SUPR IV (172)	YOU ARE PREPARING TO HEAP UPON US, WILL BE	INSTANTLY	SOLD, AND THE PROCEEDS DEVOTED TO CIRCULATING FREE
MILL III SD(179)	A FARTHER COMPARTMENT. A BELL TINKLES. THE WOMAN	INSTANTLY	STOPS SEWING AND CONCEALS THE PILES OF COATS UNDER
BARB II (278)	TO HIM TO SCOLD HIM) OH, YOU GREAT BRUTE-- (HE	INSTANTLY	SWINGS HIS LEFT HAND BACK AGAINST HER FACE. SHE
ARMS III (58)	YES. /SERGIUS/ SHALL I CURE IT? /LOUKA/ (	INSTANTLY	WITHDRAWING HERSELF PROUDLY, BUT STILL NOT LOOKING
DEST (178)	HOW YOU CAN VERY WELL AVOID DOING SO NOW. (HE	INSTANTLY	WITHDRAWS HIS HAND). OH, DONT BE AFRAID. YOU WILL
ARMS I (9)	(SHE TURNS TO THE OTTOMAN. HE RAISES HIS PISTOL	INSTANTLY	, AND CRIES) STOP! (SHE STOPS). WHERE ARE YOU
METH PREFACE(R47)	A STUPENDOUS ISSUE, BECAUSE, THOUGH IT AROSE	INSTANTLY	, IT WAS NOT HIS BUSINESS. HE WAS CONSCIOUS OF
DEST (181)	MARCH. OFF WITH YOU (BUSTLING HIM). /GIUSEPPE/	INSTANTLY	, LIEUTENANT, INSTANTLY (HE DISAPPEARS IN THE
6CAL (100)	YOU, MADAM, TO WITHDRAW AT ONCE? /THE QUEEN/	INSTANTLY	, MY DEAR LORD. (TO EUSTACHE) SIR: WHEN HIS
HART III (132)	THE FLUTE REPLIES PERTLY) HOW VULGAR! GO TO BED	INSTANTLY	, RANDALL: HOW DARE YOU? (THE WINDOW IS SLAMMED
AUGS (271)	THE LATEST POPULAR LOVE BALLAD). STOP WHISTLING	INSTANTLY	, SIR. THIS IS NOT A CASINO. /THE CLERK/ AINT IT?
PRES (132)	/MITCHENER/ (PEPPERILY, RISING) OBEY YOUR ORDERS	INSTANTLY	, SIR; AND DONT PRESUME TO ARGUE. EVEN IF SHE

INSTANT'S

DEVL III SD(71)	AND LET ME STAY? THE SERGEANT, WITHOUT AN	INSTANT'S	HESITATION, LOOKS QUICKLY AND FURTIVELY ROUND AS

INSTEAD

JOAN PREFACE(18)	IT, AND DELIBERATELY AND EXPLICITLY CHOSE BURNING	INSTEAD	: A DECISION WHICH SHEWED NOT ONLY THE EXTRAORDINARY
MIS. (161)	HE CRUMPLES INTO THE NEAREST CHAIR). /LINA/ PRAY	INSTEAD	: DONT CRY. WHY SHOULD YOU CRY? YOURE NOT THE FIRST
MIS. PREFACE(57)	A WHIP WOULD HAVE INVENTED THE EXPLOSION ENGINE	INSTEAD	COULD HE HAVE FORESEEN THE CURSE HE WAS LAYING ON

SUPR III (100)	AWAY FROM THEM AND GO TO THE CLASSICAL CONCERTS	INSTEAD	IF THEY LIKE: THERE IS NO LAW AGAINST IT; FOR
POSN (460)	DONT HANG THAT MAN: OH DONT. YOU MAY HANG ME	INSTEAD	IF YOU LIKE: IVE NOTHING TO LIVE FOR NOW. YOU DARENT
MIS. PREFACE(96)	IS TO MAKE CHILDREN GOOD. IF IT MAKES THEM SICK	INSTEAD	ITS PLACE IS THE WASTE-PAPER BASKET. AND IF IT IS TO
GETT (287)	GET MARRIED AND WENT IN FOR MARRIAGE SETTLEMENTS	INSTEAD	. A FEW OF THE OLDEST FAMILIES STUCK TO THE MARRIAGE
KING I (209)	HER GRACE OF CLEVELAND INSISTED ON MY DRAWING HER	INSTEAD	. BUT HOW CAN AN INTERESTING HEAD CONTAIN NO BRAIN:
BULL PREFACE(61)	THE FOUR HANGED MEN OUGHT TO HAVE BEEN FLOGGED	INSTEAD	. BUT MR FINDLAY DOES NOT DRAW THAT CONCLUSION.
GETT PREFACE(202)	OUT OF THE QUESTION, AND DEAL WITH HUMAN NATURE	INSTEAD	. FOR EVEN IF THERE COULD BE ANY REAL PUBLIC OPINION
BARB II (283)	HIS GREAT SHAME AND TERROR, IN DANGER OF CRYING	INSTEAD	. HE SITS DOWN AGAIN SUDDENLY). WHATS HER NAME?
GETT (282)	HERE TO PREACH TO LEO. YOU ARE PREACHING AT ME	INSTEAD	. I AM NOT CONSCIOUS OF HAVING SAID OR DONE ANYTHING
BULL II (112)	NOT COME WITH YOU? /BROADBENT/ NO. IVE COME	INSTEAD	. I HOPE I AM NOT UNWELCOME. /NORA/ (DEEPLY
WIDO II (35)	AS POOR; BUT I'M GOING TO MAKE YOU TWICE AS RICH	INSTEAD	. (HE SHAKES HIS HEAD). HAS PAPA MADE ANY
CAND I (81)	THATLL DO: I'LL GO TO THE HOXTON GROUP OF FREEDOM	INSTEAD	. (SHE ENTERS THE ENGAGEMENT IN SILENCE, WITH
MTH1 II (30)	A BEAR WOULD NOT EAT A MAN IF IT COULD GET HONEY	INSTEAD	. /CAIN/ I DO NOT WANT TO BE A BEAR. I DO NOT WANT
PHIL II (98)	KNOW, SHE OFTEN SAID SHE WISHED SHE'D MARRIED YOU	INSTEAD	. /CRAVEN/ (SOBERED BY THE SUGGESTION) DEAR ME!
JITT II (35)	WE FIND OURSELVES AT THE BEGINNING OF EVERYTHING	INSTEAD	. /EDITH/ (IMPATIENT) YOU NEED NOT SPEAK TO ME LIKE
KING I (180)	GIVE IT UP AND TRY FOR THE PHILOSOPHER'S STONE	INSTEAD	. /FOX/ WOULD YOU ENDANGER YOUR SOULS BY DABBLING IN
SIM II (60)	SO FUNNY OR SO PITEOUS THAT I HAVE KISSED YOU	INSTEAD	. /IDDY/ YOU MAKE ME HAPPIER THAN I HAVE BEEN FOR
DEST (163)	YOU TO LEAVE THE ROOM. /LADY/ OH PRAY LET ME GO	INSTEAD	. /NAPOLEON/ (DRILY) EXCUSE ME, MADAM. WITH ALL
DEVL III (51)	WANTED HIM TO COME HERE AND SAVE YOU. HE RAN AWAY	INSTEAD	. /RICHARD/ WELL, THATS WHAT I MEANT HIM TO DO. WHAT
ROCK II (235)	HERE HE GAVE THEM A DOSE OF BOILING SOCIALISM	INSTEAD	. /SIR DEXTER/ (NERVOUSLY) BY THE WAY, BASHAM, I
AUGS (267)	BECAUSE A FRIEND ADVISED ME TO TAKE TO DRINK	INSTEAD	. THAT SAVED MY LIFE, THOUGH IT MAKES ME VERY POOR
MIS. PREFACE(106)	WHEN YOU HAVE SOLID CONSIDERATIONS TO OFFER HIM	INSTEAD	. THE CAMPAIGNS OF NAPOLEON, WITH THEIR ATMOSPHERE
PRES (149)	IF YOUD LET ME OFF THE DRILL AND LET ME SHAVE YOU	INSTEAD	. YOUD APPRECIATE MY QUALITIES THEN: YOU WOULD
PRES (165)	ME CARDS I COULD MARRY ANY GENERAL ON THE STAFF	INSTEAD	O DISGRACIN YOU BE BEIN A CHARWOMAN? (SHE LISTENS
BARB II (280)	ABOUT YOU MYSELF IF I HAD A WEEK'S FEEDIN IN ME	INSTEAD	O TWO MONTHS STARVATION. (HE TURNS HIS BACK ON HIM
BULL III (128)	LONDON AND PAY HIS OWN WAY UNTIL HOME RULE COMES,	INSTEAD	O WANTIN SUBSCRIPTIONS AND THE LIKE. /FATHER
MTH3 SD(113)	AWFUL, UNANSWERABLE. SHE WEARS A DIANESQUE TUNIC	INSTEAD	OF A BLOUSE, AND A SILVER CORONET INSTEAD OF A GOLD
BULL III (128)	OF PARLIAMENT OUGHT TO BE A HELP TO THE CHURCH	INSTEAD	OF A BURDEN ON IT. /LARRY/ HERES A CHANCE FOR YOU,
JOAN PREFACE(49)	CAUCHON WOULD HAVE BEEN A TYRANT AND A BULLY	INSTEAD	OF A CATHOLIC, AND THE INQUISITOR LEMAITRE WOULD
DOCT PREFACE(23)	MICROBE OF A DISEASE MIGHT BE A SYMPTOM	INSTEAD	OF A CAUSE. AN UNPUNCTUAL MAN IS ALWAYS IN A HURRY;
CAPT I SD(217)	SAND SHOES OF THE MODERN SCOTCH MISSIONARY; BUT	INSTEAD	OF A CHEAP TOURIST'S SUIT FROM GLASGOW, A GREY
CLEO PRO1 (92)	AND KNEW HER OWN MIND, AND HAD A MIND TO KNOW	INSTEAD	OF A CIRCULATION OF NEWSPAPERS. WHEREFORE LOOK TO
SUPR I (14)	ONE HORSE INSTEAD OF TWO AND A GROOM-GARDENER	INSTEAD	OF A COACHMAN AND FOOTMAN. THE MORE THINGS A MAN IS
MIS. PREFACE(23)	I HAD BEEN A BOARDER AT AN ENGLISH PUBLIC SCHOOL	INSTEAD	OF A DAY BOY AT AN IRISH ONE, I MIGHT HAVE HAD TO
SUPR PREFACE(R34)	ON THE SCRAP HEAP; THE BEING A FORCE OF NATURE	INSTEAD	OF A FEVERISH SELFISH LITTLE CLOD OF AILMENTS AND
DOCT PREFACE(72)	AT BETHANY WAS A COMMON PEASANT FARMER'S STABLE	INSTEAD	OF A FIRST-RATE RACING ONE, AND TOO SAVAGE TO
ROCK PREFACE(179)	ACCUSED MAN THREATENED WITH A HORRIBLE PENALTY,	INSTEAD	OF A GOD GOING THROUGH AN INEVITABLE ORDEAL AS A
MTH3 SD(113)	TUNIC INSTEAD OF A BLOUSE, AND A SILVER CORONET	INSTEAD	OF A GOLD FILLET. HER DRESS OTHERWISE IS NOT
BARB III (326)	IT ONLY NEEDS A CATHEDRAL TO BE A HEAVENLY CITY	INSTEAD	OF A HELLISH ONE. /BARBARA/ HAVE YOU FOUND OUT
6CAL (93)	THEY NEVER TELL ME ANYTHING. I MIGHT BE A DOG	INSTEAD	OF A KING. /THE PRINCE/ (ABOUT TO KNEEL) MAJESTY--
JOAN PREFACE(49)	THE INQUISITOR LEMAITRE WOULD HAVE BEEN A SADIST	INSTEAD	OF A LAWYER, WARWICK WOULD HAVE HAD NO MORE FEUDAL
SUPR PREFACE(R15)	HOUSE AND ASSERTING HERSELF AS AN INDIVIDUAL	INSTEAD	OF A MERE ITEM IN A MORAL PAGEANT. NOW IT IS ALL
OVER PREFACE(158)	OPINION, OUR ACTUAL CONDUCT AND OUR REAL THOUGHTS	INSTEAD	OF A MORAL FICTION WHICH WE AGREE TO CALL VIRTUOUS
3PLA PREFACE(R10)	MOMENT YOU MAKE HIS THEATRE A PLACE OF AMUSEMENT	INSTEAD	OF A PLACE OF EDIFICATION, YOU MAKE IT, NOT A REAL
ROCK PREFACE(183)	AS YOU DO. IF YOU WERE A RESPONSIBLE GOVERNOR	INSTEAD	OF A POETIC VAGRANT, YOU WOULD SOON DISCOVER THAT MY
LION PREFACE(73)	AS A REAL EVENT WHICH HAD REALLY HAPPENED,	INSTEAD	OF A PORTION OF THE CHURCH SERVICE. I CAN ONLY
MIS. PREFACE(29)	IT UP TO THE AGE AT WHICH IGNORANCE IS A DANGER	INSTEAD	OF A SAFEGUARD. EVEN AS IT IS, IT SEEMS UNDESIRABLE
HART II (107)	OFF MY HEAD. WHY DONT YOU HAVE A PROPER REVOLVER	INSTEAD	OF A THING LIKE THAT, THAT GOES OFF IF YOU AS MUCH
ROCK II (243)	THE HAPPIER WHEN IT HAS TEN SQUARE MILES OF DOCKS	INSTEAD	OF A TUPPENY-HAPENY FISHING HARBOR? WHAT HAVE I TO
ROCK I (227)	THAT YOU MAKE SPEECHES ABOUT PROGRESS AND LIBERTY	INSTEAD	OF ABOUT KING AND COUNTRY. /SIR ARTHUR/ OF COURSE I
SUPR I (26)	INCREASE, MULTIPLY, AND REPLENISH THE EARTH. AND	INSTEAD	OF ADMIRING HER COURAGE AND REJOICING IN HER
GLIM (179)	IS THAT WE SHALL HAVE THE HONOR TO EAT WITH YOU	INSTEAD	OF AFTER YOU. /FERRUCCIO/ DOG OF A BANDIT: YOU
BULL PREFACE(38)	A REVOLUTION AGAINST ENGLAND AND ENGLISH RULE	INSTEAD	OF AGAINST ARISTOCRACY AND ECCLESIASTICISM; AND ALL
2TRU PREFACE(18)	A SCALE THAT WHEN TORQUEMADA BEGAN BURNING JEWS	INSTEAD	OF ALLOWING THEM TO RANSOM THEIR BODIES BY PAYMENTS
MILL III (184)	I AM GOING TO SWEAT MR TIMOTHY GOODENOUGH	INSTEAD	OF ALLOWING MR SUPERFLEW TO SWEAT HIM. /THE MAN/ SEE
MRS PREFACE(168)	FOOL THAT I WAS NOT TO MAKE HIM A THEATRE CRITIC	INSTEAD	OF AN ARCHITECT!) BURLESQUES THEM BY EXPECTING ALL
BULL PREFACE(71)	OF; FOR IT HAS A BELFAST HOME RULE PARLIAMENT	INSTEAD	OF AN IRISH ONE. AND IT HAS ALLOWED CATHOLIC IRELAND
MIS. PREFACE(84)	AS TO COMPEL HIM TO CARRY A CLAYMORE AND TARGET	INSTEAD	OF AN UMBRELLA. THE CIVILIZED MAN HAS NO SPECIAL USE
BUOY III (45)	ASSOCIATION OF IDEAS, MOSTLY NONSENSICAL IDEAS.	INSTEAD	OF ANALYSIS, EVERYTHING IN TOTALITARIAN LUMPS.
MIS. PREFACE(9)	" DONT BE NAUGHTY," WHICH MEANS THAT THE CHILD,	INSTEAD	OF ANNOYING YOU BY A PERFECTLY HEALTHY AND NATURAL
LION PREFACE(37)	BY MAKING JESUS PUT THE QUESTION TO THE LAWYER	INSTEAD	OF ANSWERING IT. AS TO DOCTRINE, LUKE IS ONLY CLEAR
LION PREFACE(13)	WITH THE RINDERPEST: IT CALLS DOWN DIVINE WRATH	INSTEAD	OF APPEASING IT. IN DOING IT WE OFFER GOD AS A
SUPR III SD(71)	NEVADA. ROLLING SLOPES OF BROWN WITH OLIVE TREES	INSTEAD	OF APPLE TREES IN THE CULTIVATED PATCHES, AND
LION PREFACE(101)	A POPULATION OF SEVENTEENTH-CENTURY CHRISTIANS	INSTEAD	OF ARABS WHO WORSHIPPED STONES. AS IT IS, MEN DO NOT
GETT PREFACE(195)	FOR POMPOUS TALKING, IS REPRESENTED AS A CRIMINAL	INSTEAD	OF AS A VERY TYPICAL ENGLISH PATERFAMILIAS KEEPING A
MRS PREFACE(165)	WHICH TREAT SEX QUESTIONS AS PROBLEMS FOR THOUGHT	INSTEAD	OF AS APHRODISIACS WILL BE FREELY PERFORMED.
3PLA PREFACE(R34)	PLAYED AS MUCH OF HAMLET AS THERE WAS TIME FOR	INSTEAD	OF AS LITTLE. AND THE INSTANT SUCCESS OF THE
BULL PREFACE(31)	WILL THEN BE A NATIONAL IRISH GOVERNMENT	INSTEAD	OF AS NOW AN ENGLISH GOVERNMENT, THEIR DETERMINATION
BULL PREFACE(37)	HE THINKS OF VOLTAIRE AS A FRENCH " INFIDEL,"	INSTEAD	OF AS THE CHAMPION OF THE LAITY AGAINST THE OFFICIAL
MIS. PREFACE(69)	SHOULD BE TREATED AS IN GOETHE'S WILHELM MEISTER	INSTEAD	OF AS THEY ARE TREATED AT THE ELEMENTARY SCHOOL AT
METH PREFACE(R48)	SCIENCE TALKING OF AN UNKNOWN FACTOR AS A SPORT	INSTEAD	OF AS X!) AND LEFT THEM TO " ACCUMULATE" AND
BARB I (263)	THAT SARAH WILL WANT TO FEEL PROUD OF YOU	INSTEAD	OF ASHAMED OF YOU. /LOMAX/ OH I SAY! THERES NOTHING
JOAN PREFACE(40)	SHOULD HAVE WAITED FOR THE ALLEGED EVIL RESULTS	INSTEAD	OF ASSUMING THAT THEY WOULD OCCUR, AND WHAT THEY
LION PREFACE(80)	THE BURDEN OF THEIR SINS AND STOP COMMITTING THEM	INSTEAD	OF ASSURING THEM THAT THEY COULD NOT HELP IT, AS IT
SUPR III (129)	OF THAT CASTE AIMED AT MORE LIFE FOR THE WORLD	INSTEAD	OF AT MORE POWER AND LUXURY FOR OUR MISERABLE
HART PREFACE(26)	THE EUROPE WE HAVE WOUNDED ALMOST TO DEATH	INSTEAD	OF ATTEMPTING TO COMPLETE HER DESTRUCTION. THE YAHOO
PHIL II (107)	THE CLUB TODAY IN A BEAUTIFUL NEW COAT AND TIE	INSTEAD	OF ATTENDING TO HIS PATIENTS? THAT LUNCH WITH JULIA
ROCK PREFACE(161)	WHO HAD THROWN HIS TELEGRAMS INTO THE DUSTBIN	INSTEAD	OF ATTENDING TO THEM, SO THAT HE MIGHT THE MORE
LION PREFACE(57)	DEALING WITH US, EVEN IF WE PROVIDED WORK FOR HIM	INSTEAD	OF BASING, AS WE DO, OUR WHOLE INDUSTRIAL SYSTEM ON
MIS. (175)	SKUNKS AND COWARDS YOUD BE SUFFERING WITH THEM	INSTEAD	OF BATTENING HERE ON THE PLUNDER OF THE POOR. /MRS
MTH5 (255)	BUT YOU YOURSELF ARE MAKING STATUES OF ANCIENTS	INSTEAD	OF BEAUTIFUL NYMPHS AND SWAINS. AND ECRASIA IS RIGHT
KING I (206)	A PLAIN WOMAN. MY FACE WOULD BE FULL OF BRAINS	INSTEAD	OF BEAUTY. AND YOU WOULD SEND ME BACK TO FRANCE BY
JOAN PREFACE(53)	IN THE WORLD ENDED UNHAPPILY WITH HER EXECUTION,	INSTEAD	OF BEGINNING THERE. IT WAS NECESSARY BY HOOK OR
MTH2 SD(37)	AND HIS COLLAR, THOUGH IT BUTTONS IN FRONT	INSTEAD	OF BEHIND, COMBINE WITH THE PROSPERITY INDICATED BY
PHIL PREFACE(68)	INDEED I AM FAR FROM SURE THAT ITS IDEAS,	INSTEAD	OF BEING 36 YEARS BEHIND THE TIMES, ARE NOT FOR A
METH PREFACE(R66)	WORSE. IT DID NOT OCCUR TO US THAT OLD NOBODADDY,	INSTEAD	OF BEING A RIDICULOUS FICTION, MIGHT BE ONLY AN
MIS. PREFACE(46)	OF CLAMOROUS DEMANDS THAT HE SHOULD BE CANED	INSTEAD	OF BEING ALLOWED TO CANE OTHER PEOPLE. THE SIN OF
MIS. PREFACE(69)	REMEDYING IT. THE COSTER MAY RESENT THE INQUIRY	INSTEAD	OF BEING AMUSED BY IT; BUT HIS ANSWER, IF TRUE, WILL
DOCT PREFACE(78)	WHAT IS WRONG WITH PRIESTS AND POPES IS THAT	INSTEAD	OF BEING APOSTLES AND SAINTS, THEY ARE NOTHING BUT
MIS. PREFACE(96)	NOT BE CULTIVATED IN RATIONALLY SCIENTIFIC TERMS	INSTEAD	OF BEING ASSOCIATED WITH THE STORY OF JONAH AND THE
SUPR PREFACE(R23)	CONCLUSION, ASTONISHING TO THE VULGAR, THAT ART,	INSTEAD	OF BEING BEFORE ALL THINGS THE EXPRESSION OF THE
LION PREFACE(31)	BEEN TREATED IN THAT WAY WHEN HE ALSO WENT MAD,	INSTEAD	OF BEING CARED FOR AS AN INVALID. AND WE SHOULD HAVE
METH PREFACE(R74)	REEL AT THE IMPACT OF EVERY ADVANCE IN SCIENCE,	INSTEAD	OF BEING CLARIFIED BY IT. IF YOU TAKE AN ENGLISH
FANY EPILOG (331)	THE CHARACTERS ARE SECOND-RATE MIDDLE CLASS,	INSTEAD	OF BEING DUKES AND MILLIONAIRES. THE HEROINE GETS
MTH5 (222)	WITH THE BUSTS? /ECRASIA/ WRONG WITH THEM!	INSTEAD	OF BEING IDEALLY BEAUTIFUL NYMPHS AND YOUTHS, THEY
APPL I (215)	POWERMISTRESS GENERAL, CLOSETED WITH YOUR MAJESTY	INSTEAD	OF BEING IN THEIR PLACES TO CONFER WITH ME.
CAPT NOTES (302)	REPRESENT ABSTRACT PRINCIPLES OF JUSTICE	INSTEAD	OF BEING MERE SOCIAL SCAFFOLDING IS THAT PERSONS OF
LION PREFACE(22)	JESUS TELLS THEM THAT THEY SHOULD REJOICE IN HIM	INSTEAD	OF BEING MELANCHOLY, HE IS JOCULAR, AND TELLS THEM
LADY PREFACE(223)	HAVE BECOME ONE OF THE ABLEST MEN OF HIS TIME	INSTEAD	OF BEING MERELY ITS ABLEST PLAYWRIGHT, ONE MIGHT
MTH5 (233)	THE WOMAN HAD REPRODUCED IN SOME PREHISTORIC WAY	INSTEAD	OF BEING OVIPAROUS AS WE ARE? SHE COULDNT HAVE DONE
CAPT I (232)	WHY DO PEOPLE GET KILLED BY SAVAGES? BECAUSE	INSTEAD	OF BEING POLITE TO THEM, AND SAYING HOW DYE DO?
WIDO III (57)	I SUPPOSE I SHOULD HAVE BEEN DOWN ON HER LEVEL	INSTEAD	OF BEING RAISED ABOVE IT, AS I AM NOW. WOULD YOU
APPL PREFACE(193)	AN ENORMOUS SAVING OF LABOR AND SMASH. BUT	INSTEAD	OF BEING RECEIVED WITH OPEN ARMS AS A SOCIAL
GETT (341)	COME TO CARE UNSELFISHLY AND DILIGENTLY FOR MONEY	INSTEAD	OF BEING SELFISHLY AND LAZILY INDIFFERENT TO IT. FOR
MILL PREFACE(120)	HE CALLED FOR ACTION AND SILENCE. THE PEOPLE,	INSTEAD	OF BEING SHOCKED LIKE GOOD LIBERALS, ROSE TO HIM. HE
POSN PREFACE(430)	WHICH IS ABOVE OUR LAWS AND CONDITIONS OUR LAWS,	INSTEAD	OF BEING SUBJECT TO THEM, IS ANARCHIC AND ABHORRENT.
MIS. (143)	NEVER IMAGINE HOW DELIGHTED I WAS TO FIND THAT	INSTEAD	OF BEING THE CORRECT SORT OF BIG PANJANDRUM YOU WERE

DOCT PREFACE(70)	BUT ON HALF-CROWNS. IF THE VACCINATION ACTS,	INSTEAD	OF BEING WHOLLY REPEALED AS THEY ARE ALREADY HALF
MIS. PREFACE(38)	A YEAR FOR THE SAKE OF HAVING TO EARN IT.	INSTEAD	OF BEING WHAT WE ARE NOW, THE CHEAPEST AND NASTIEST
NEVR IV (290)	(INTERRUPTING HIM) IF YOU DID, YOU WOULD BE ME,	INSTEAD	OF BEING WHAT YOU ARE. /M'COMAS/ (FAWNING ON HIM)
LION PREFACE(97)	AFFIRMED. IN SHORT, THE ENGLISHMAN OF TODAY,	INSTEAD	OF BEING, LIKE THE FOREFATHERS WHOSE IDEAS HE CLINGS
SUPR HANDBOK(190)	WEALTHY, NOR WISE; AND THEY WOULD BE WORSE	INSTEAD	OF BETTER IF THEIR POPULAR MINISTERS WERE NOT
DOCT III (138)	GOOD PEOPLE AS YOU. WHY DONT YOU LEARN TO THINK,	INSTEAD	OF BLEATING AND BAAHING LIKE A LOT OF SHEEP WHEN YOU
SUPR PREFACE(R24)	OF LIFE TO BECOME DIVINELY CONSCIOUS OF ITSELF	INSTEAD	OF BLINDLY STUMBLING HITHER AND THITHER IN THE LINE
SIM PRO,1, (21)	WHY THE DEVIL DIDNT YOU TELL ME THAT AT FIRST,	INSTEAD	OF BLITHERING ABOUT HER AS IF SHE WAS A COMMON
KING I (213)	/NELL/ NOT WHEN YOU MAKE IT INTO BREECHES	INSTEAD	OF BOOTS, GEORGE. /BARBARA/ BE DECENT, WOMAN. ONE
MTH1 II (27)	MAN'S FLESH! IT GROWS LIKE A FUNGUS ON A TREE.	INSTEAD	OF BREATHING, YOU SNEEZE, OR COUGH UP YOUR INSIDES,
CAPT II (257)	PROPERTY NOW COSTS 150 POUNDS A YEAR TO KEEP UP	INSTEAD	OF BRINGING IN ANYTHING, I AM AFRAID IT WOULD NOT BE
MILL I (161)	I WAS FOUR HUNDRED AND THIRTY POUNDS TO THE BAD.	INSTEAD	OF BRINGING ME THE REVENUES OF A PRINCE AND A HERO
BULL PREFACE(27)	AS A SON OF THE CHURCH, CALLING HIS PRIEST FATHER	INSTEAD	OF BROTHER OR MISTER. TO REBEL POLITICALLY, HE MUST
GETT PREFACE(235)	FOR HAVING BORROWED OUR RELIGION FROM THE EAST,	INSTEAD	OF BUILDING UP A RELIGION OF OUR OWN OUT OF OUR
BULL III (137)	BE A MAN OF SOME MEANS, ABLE TO HELP THE LOCALITY	INSTEAD	OF BURDENING IT. AND IF HE WERE A COUNTRYMAN OF MY
LION PREFACE(24)	AND PUNISHMENT, THE COUNTERACTING OF EVIL BY GOOD	INSTEAD	OF BY A HOSTILE EVIL, AND AN ORGANIC CONCEPTION OF
BULL PREFACE(62)	FRIGHTENED SOLDIERS AND DENATURALIZED OFFICIALS	INSTEAD	OF BY COURAGEOUS HELPFULNESS AND MORAL SUPERIORITY.
SIM II (75)	OF BEING JUDGED BY A COMMISSION OF A FEW ANGELS	INSTEAD	OF BY DIRECT DIVINE AUTHORITY. SUCH A SLIGHT TO THE
BULL PREFACE(26)	AND CATHOLICS BY TEMPERAMENT AND ADULT CHOICE	INSTEAD	OF BY FAMILY TRADITION. THE PEASANT WHO SUPPOSED
KING I (195)	I MUST, SINCE ENGLAND IS GOVERNED BY ITS MOB	INSTEAD	OF BY ITS KING. BUT I TELL YOU, CHARLES, WHEN I AM
GENV PREFACE(17)	THEY HAD TO MAKE THEIR VICTIMS DIE OF ILLUSAGE	INSTEAD	OF BY MILITARY LAW. UNDER SUCH CIRCUMSTANCES ANY
BULL PREFACE(43)	BY HIS OWN INEXPERIENCE AND FOLLY AND IMMATURITY	INSTEAD	OF BY THE EXPERIENCE AND SAGACITY OF HIS FATHER, OR
FABL PREFACE(90)	HAD TO CALL HER DOCTRINE CHRISTIAN SCIENCE	INSTEAD	OF CALLING THE POPULAR FAITH IN PSEUDOSCIENTIFIC
POSN PREFACE(407)	IS EXPLOITING DRUNKENNESS AND PROSTITUTION	INSTEAD	OF CARRYING ON A LEGITIMATE DRAMATIC BUSINESS.
DOCT PREFACE(56)	OF LONDON CRUDE AND UNTREATED INTO THE THAMES,	INSTEAD	OF CARRYING IT, AFTER ELABORATE TREATMENT, FAR OUT
CAND I (85)	WHY DO YOU TUCK YOUR UMBRELLA UNDER YOUR LEFT ARM	INSTEAD	OF CARRYING IT IN YOUR HAND LIKE ANYONE ELSE? WHY
ROCK II (242)	DEXTER, WHEN YOU FORMED THIS NATIONAL GOVERNMENT,	INSTEAD	OF CARRYING THEM OUT YOU TOLD THE VOTERS TO TIGHTEN
GETT PREFACE(237)	TO THINK OUT WHAT THEY REALLY HAD TO FACE	INSTEAD	OF CHOPPING LOGIC IN A UNIVERSITY CLASS-ROOM,
LION PREFACE(23)	WOULD BE IN RELIGION A JEW INITIATED BY BAPTISM	INSTEAD	OF CIRCUMCISION, AND ACCEPTING JESUS AS THE MESSIAH,
KING II (228)	IS THE RESULT? PROTESTANTISM AND PARLIAMENTS	INSTEAD	OF CITIZENSHIP. /CATHERINE/ IN PORTUGAL, GOD BE
FABL PREFACE(84)	CANNIBAL TRIBES FIGHTING AND EATING ONE ANOTHER	INSTEAD	OF CIVILIZED MEN DRIVEN BY SHEER PRESSURE OF FACTS
AUGS (268)	FROM THE MINISTER OF MUNITIONS IS TO USE GAS	INSTEAD	OF COAL, BECAUSE IT SAVES MATERIAL. WHICH IS IT TO
NEVR IV (288)	MAAM. /GLORIA/ OH WELL, I'LL HAVE CLARET CUP	INSTEAD	OF COFFEE. PUT SOME CUCUMBER IN IT. /WAITER/ (
LION PREFACE(41)	ALSO BE BECAUSE HE SAW AND HEARD WHAT HAPPENED	INSTEAD	OF COLLECTING TRADITIONS ABOUT IT. THE PALEOGRAPHERS
LIED (191)	ARE NOTHING TO YOU. WHAT WAS I SAYING? -- OH YES.	INSTEAD	OF COMING BACK HERE FROM THE THEATRE, YOU WILL COME
MILL IV (207)	HEART AS MONEY HAD NEVER REJOICED IT BEFORE. BUT	INSTEAD	OF COMING TO YOU WITH FIFTY THOUSAND POUNDS I AM IN
SUPR HANDBOK(181)	ARE), THE ERROR WILL BE CORRECTED BY EXPERIENCE	INSTEAD	OF CONFIRMED BY EVASION. ONE FACT MUST BE FACED
MTH3 (105)	TO PUT A CASE TO YOU, CONFUCIUS. SUPPOSE A MAN,	INSTEAD	OF CONFORMING TO THE OFFICIAL ESTIMATE OF HIS
MRS PREFACE(168)	WHICH MY CHARACTERS BEHAVE LIKE HUMAN BEINGS,	INSTEAD	OF CONFORMING TO THE ROMANTIC LOGIC OF THE STAGE.
BULL PREFACE(40)	MAY STOP THEIR ORDERS IF HE VOTES LIBERAL	INSTEAD	OF CONSERVATIVE. ENGLISH LADIES AND GENTLEMEN WHO
DOCT I (103)	DOCTOR'S STUFF; AND NOW THEY BUY IT AT THE STORES	INSTEAD	OF CONSULTING A MEDICAL MAN. /WALPOLE/ QUITE TRUE.
ROCK PREFACE(177)	WAS IDIOTIC TO TRY TO ADAPT NATURE TO THE CHURCH	INSTEAD	OF CONTINUALLY ADAPTING THE CHURCH TO NATURE BY
LION PREFACE(58)	PARASITISM. THEY CORRUPT CULTURE AND STATECRAFT	INSTEAD	OF CONTRIBUTING TO THEM, THEIR EXCESSIVE LEISURE
BULL PREFACE(38)	IN MERE ANTI-ANGLICISM AND NATIONALIST DITHYRAMBS	INSTEAD	OF CONTRIBUTING TO POLITICAL SCIENCE AND BROADENING
POSN PREFACE(405)	INFORM HIM THAT UNLESS HE MANUFACTURES WOOLLENS	INSTEAD	OF COTTONS, GINGER-BEER INSTEAD OF WHISKEY, BIBLES
SUPR I (26)	HER COURAGE AND REJOICING IN HER INSTINCT;	INSTEAD	OF CROWNING THE COMPLETED WOMANHOOD AND RAISING THE
MIS. PREFACE(91)	WHICH ART IMPOSES ON APPETITE ARE WAIVED:	INSTEAD	OF CULTIVATED MEN AND WOMEN RESTRAINED BY A THOUSAND
DOCT I (89)	TO CURE HER WITH KOCH'S TUBERCULIN. /RIDGEON/ AND	INSTEAD	OF CURING HER, IT ROTTED HER ARM RIGHT OFF. YES: I
MTH1 II (30)	CLOTHES, SO THAT MEN MAY GLORIFY AND HONOR HIM	INSTEAD	OF CURSING HIM AS MURDERER AND THIEF. ALL YOU MEN,
METH PREFACE(R55)	OUT THE GREAT CENTRAL TRUTH OF THE WILL TO POWER	INSTEAD	OF CUTTING OFF MOUSE-TAILS, HAD NO DIFFICULTY IN
MIS. PREFACE(20)	STILL AGONIZING OVER HIS DETESTABLE SHAM BOOKS	INSTEAD	OF DARING TO LIVE, AND YOUR CHILDISH HATRED OF YOUR
METH PREFACE(R15)	THE POISONOUS ILLUSION THAT IT ENLIGHTENS	INSTEAD	OF DARKENING. THE SUGGESTION MAY, HOWEVER, EXPLAIN
ROCK PREFACE(175)	SAY EVERYTHING HE HAD TO SAY IN HIS DEFENCE; BUT	INSTEAD	OF DEFENDING HIS RIGHT TO CRITICIZE HE INFURIATED
LION PREFACE(7)	EVIDENTLY WILLING ENOUGH TO BE CONCILIATED. BUT	INSTEAD	OF DENYING THE CHARGE, JESUS REPEATED THE OFFENCE.
SUPR I (29)	FATHER OF VIOLET'S CHILD, I SHOULD BOAST OF IT	INSTEAD	OF DENYING IT. SO BE EASY: OUR FRIENDSHIP IS NOT IN
VWOO 3 (139)	BECAUSE I AM ALWAYS GETTING AGREEABLE SURPRISES	INSTEAD	OF DESOLATING DISAPPOINTMENTS. /Z/ WELL, YOUR SECOND
GETT PREFACE(249)	ASKED MORE MONEY FOR VIRGINITY, THE CHURCH,	INSTEAD	OF DETECTING THE MONEY-CHANGER AND DRIVING HIM OUT
GENV PREFACE(26)	FIXED AT ALL. IF WE MASTER THE ART OF LIVING	INSTEAD	OF DIGGING OUR GRAVES WITH OUR TEETH AS WE DO AT
ROCK PREFACE(152)	LIKE RABBITS; AND FOR THE MOMENT POPULATION GROWS	INSTEAD	OF DIMINISHING. BUT SOON MACHINES COME ALONG AND
UNPL PREFACE(R15)	NICE LITTLE PLACES TO JOB NICE LITTLE PEOPLE INTO	INSTEAD	OF DOING AWAY WITH THEM. NAY, I MYSELF, THOUGH I
DOCT PREFACE(57)	ALL OUR EXPERTS. YET IF CROMWELL HAD DONE THAT	INSTEAD	OF DOING NOTHING, THERE WOULD PROBABLY HAVE BEEN NO
LION PREFACE(67)	WIFE, AND A MARRIED WOMAN TO PLEASE HER HUSBAND,	INSTEAD	OF DOING THE WORK OF GOD. THIS IS ANOTHER VERSION OF
BULL IV (176)	CALL IT-- IN DOING THE WILL OF HIS GREEDY MASTERS	INSTEAD	OF DOING THE WILL OF HEAVEN THAT IS IN HIMSELF. HE
SUPR III (128)	WILL, OR RATHER DRIFTING WITH YOUR WANT OF WILL,	INSTEAD	OF DOING THEIR OWN, THAT MAKES THEM THE
MTH1 II (32)	SLEEPING. THEY HAVE NOT WILL ENOUGH TO CREATE	INSTEAD	OF DREAMING; BUT THE SERPENT SAID THAT EVERY DREAM
METH PREFACE(R14)	FROM BEING DASHED ON THE ROCKS OF FALSE DOCTRINE	INSTEAD	OF DRIFTING DOWN THE MIDSTREAM OF MERE IGNORANCE.
BULL PREFACE(33)	CHANGES INTELLIGENTLY AND PROVIDENTIALLY	INSTEAD	OF DRIFTING ALONG HELPLESSLY UNTIL PUBLIC DISASTERS
LION PREFACE(14)	OUR IMAGINATION MUST COME TO OUR RESCUE. WHY NOT,	INSTEAD	OF DRIVING OURSELVES TO DESPAIR BY INSISTING ON A
2TRU III (110)	THE MASK STRUCK FROM HER SOUL AND REVELLED IN IT	INSTEAD	OF DYING OF IT-- I SHRANK FROM THE REVELATION AS
LION PREFACE(94)	TO BEG FOR AND ACCEPT ETERNAL LIFE AS A PRESENT	INSTEAD	OF EARNING IT, WOULD BE MEAN ENOUGH EVEN IF WE
MILL PREFACE(118)	THE DONKEY HAD OVERTAKEN THE CARROTS AT LAST; AND	INSTEAD	OF EATING THEM HE ALLOWED THEM TO BE SNATCHED AWAY
PYGM EPILOG (291)	A PASSION FOR PHONETICS AND IDEALIZE HIS MOTHER	INSTEAD	OF ELIZA, WOULD SEEM TO THEM ABSURD AND UNNATURAL.
ROCK I (215)	PLEASANT AIR OF BEGINNING THE BUSINESS	INSTEAD	OF ENDING IT) YES: NOW WE CAN TALK A BIT. I BEEN AT
FABL PREFACE(95)	CONVICTION THAT HIS SPECIALTY WAS AN ABSURDITY.	INSTEAD	OF ENLIGHTENING ME HE LAUGHED (HE HAD AN ENGAGING
PHIL I SD(92)	(THE OUTSIDE DOOR SHUTS), CUTHBERTSON RETURNS.	INSTEAD	OF ENTERING, HE STANDS IMPRESSIVELY IN THE DOORWAY
APPL I (230)	OUT LONG AGO THAT DEMOCRACY IS HUMBUG, AND THAT	INSTEAD	OF ESTABLISHING RESPONSIBLE GOVERNMENT IT HAS
SUPR PREFACE(R36)	I CANNOT ENDURE THEIR MORAL TIRADES. AND YET,	INSTEAD	OF EXCLAIMING " SEND THIS INCONCEIVABLE SATANIST TO
BULL PREFACE(23)	AND SUPPORT ENGLISH SHAMS AND HYPOCRISIES	INSTEAD	OF EXPOSING AND DENOUNCING THEM; IF HE CONSTITUTED
BULL PREFACE(49)	TO IGNORE HUMAN NATURE AND CRY FOR THE MOON	INSTEAD	OF FACING MODERN SOCIAL FACTS AND ACCEPTING MODERN
HART PREFACE(30)	I WAS MADE TO SIT WITH MY BACK TO THE SINGERS	INSTEAD	OF FACING THEM. WHEN THE CURTAIN WENT UP, MY
GETT (355)	THROUGH HIS OWN RELIGION AND NOT THROUGH YOURS.	INSTEAD	OF FACING THAT FACT, YOU PERSIST IN TRYING TO
BUOY III (45)	ANY ADVICE. /SECONDBORN/ WHAT HAVE YOU GIVEN US?	INSTEAD	OF FACTS, ESCAPIST ROMANCE FROM THE CINEMAS. INSTEAD
DOCT PREFACE(23)	BY THE PLAGUE LONG AGO, AND THAT EVERY EPIDEMIC,	INSTEAD	OF FADING OUT AS MYSTERIOUSLY AS IT RUSHED IN, WOULD
MIS. PREFACE(83)	ALL EUROPE (EXCEPT SCOTLAND, WHICH HAS CLANS	INSTEAD	OF FAMILIES) DRAWS THE LINE AT SECOND COUSINS.
FABL IV (116)	CRAFTSMEN, PHYSICISTS, AND MATHEMATICIANS,	INSTEAD	OF FARMERS, MILLERS, BAKERS, BUTCHERS, BAR TENDERS,
HART II (117)	SHIP WHERE THEY WERE TAUGHT TO FEAR THE CANE	INSTEAD	OF FEARING GOD; AND THOUGHT THEYD MADE MEN AND
METH PREFACE(R78)	THEM LITERALLY MADE HIM A MADMAN WHO SLEW LAMBS	INSTEAD	OF FEEDING THEM. IN ENGLAND TODAY GOOD BOOKS OF
BUOY 1 (12)	THAT IS A QUIBBLE. IT IS ALWAYS POSSIBLE TO VOTE	INSTEAD	OF FIGHTING. ALL THE BLOOD SHED IN REVOLUTIONS HAS
BUOY 1 (11)	ALL POSSIBLE POLITICAL CHANGES. /SON/ VOTING	INSTEAD	OF FIGHTING. NO USE. THE DEFEATED PARTY ALWAYS
MIS. PREFACE(28)	THAT FIRST TEACHES ITS CHILDREN THAT TRUTH,	INSTEAD	OF FLOGGING THEM IF THEY DISCOVER IT FOR THEMSELVES,
LADY (249)	THERE BE ANY HORSES THEN, AND MEN BE STILL RIDING	INSTEAD	OF FLYING. NOW IT MAY BE THAT BY THEN YOUR WORKS
CLEO III (145)	A PATRICIAN! A PATRICIAN KEEPING A SHOP	INSTEAD	OF FOLLOWING ARMS! /APOLLODORUS/ I DO NOT KEEP A
SUPR III (105)	DOG COULD HAVE INVENTED IF IT HAD WANTED MONEY	INSTEAD	OF FOOD. I KNOW HIS CLUMSY TYPEWRITERS AND BUNGLING
ARMS II (31)	IF ONLY I HAD BOUGHT THE HORSES FOR MY REGIMENT	INSTEAD	OF FOOLISHLY LEADING IT INTO DANGER, I SHOULD HAVE
SUPR PREFACE(R17)	AND IS CONCERNED FOR THE FUTURE OF THE RACE	INSTEAD	OF FOR THE FREEDOM OF HIS OWN INSTINCTS. THUS HIS
GENV PREFACE(5)	II OF THE GERMAN REICH FRIGHTENED HER. BUT	INSTEAD	OF FRIGHTENING THE WITS OUT OF HER THEY FRIGHTENED
UNPL PREFACE(R11)	DRAMA OF THE DAY BEING WRITTEN FOR THE THEATRES	INSTEAD	OF FROM ITS OWN INNER NECESSITY. STILL, A THING THAT
2TRU I (45)	AND ENJOY EVERYTHING THAT IS TO BE ENJOYED	INSTEAD	OF FROWSTING HERE AND BEING MESSED ABOUT BY YOUR
BULL PREFACE(46)	REPRIMANDED, WHILST THE LEADER OF THE MUTINY,	INSTEAD	OF GETTING THE VICTORIA CROSS AND A PUBLIC
BUOY III (47)	AND RESTORE ITS PEACE LEST IT KILL FATHER BUOYANT	INSTEAD	OF GIVING HIM A FORETASTE OF HEAVEN. GO NOW: YOU
JITT III (55)	YOU BUT SYMPATHY, AS IF YOU WERE ONLY A VISITOR	INSTEAD	OF GOING TO MARRY MY DAUGHTER. /FESSLER/ YOU SEE,
SIM II (71)	OF HEAVEN. THEY GO MOTORING OR GOLFING ON SUNDAYS	INSTEAD	OF GOING TO CHURCH; AND THEY NEVER OPEN A BIBLE.
POSN (440)	HORSE DID THE SAME, AS ANY SENSIBLE HORSE WOULD.	INSTEAD	OF GOING TO LOOK FOR THE HORSE, YOU WENT LOOKING FOR
PYGM V (268)	USUAL, TO TURN OUT THE LIGHTS AND ALL THAT; AND	INSTEAD	OF GOING TO BED SHE CHANGED HER CLOTHES AND WENT
DEVL I (15)	FAMILY; AND HE WRESTLES AND PLAYS GAMES ON SUNDAY	INSTEAD	OF GOING TO CHURCH. NEVER LET HIM INTO YOUR
SUPR III SD(71)	CULTIVATED PATCHES, AND OCCASIONAL PRICKLY PEARS	INSTEAD	OF GORSE AND BRACKEN IN THE WILDS. HIGHER UP, TALL
GETT PREFACE(216)	WHAT ACTUAL MARRIAGE IS, ONE WOULD LIKE EVIDENCE	INSTEAD	OF GUESSES; BUT AS ALL DEPARTURES FROM THE IDEAL ARE

NEVR III (279) AT NINE, WILLIAM. CAN WE HAVE DINNER AT SEVEN INSTEAD OF HALF PAST? /WAITER/ (AT THE DOOR) SEVEN, MAAM?
GETT (300) BUT ONLY SUCCEEDED IN DISFIGURING HIMSELF. INSTEAD OF HANGING HIM, THEY SENT HIM TO PENAL SERVITUDE FOR
DEVL III (62) ME AS A PRISONER OF WAR, AND SHOOT ME LIKE A MAN INSTEAD OF HANGING ME LIKE A DOG. /BURGOYNE/ (
3PLA PREFACE(R27) MOTHER'S INDOMITABLE SELFFULNESS, BUT WITH PITY INSTEAD OF HATRED AS HIS MASTER PASSION, HE PITIES THE
CLEO NOTES (204) AT ONCE AS AN UNACCOUNTABLE FACT THAT THE WORLD, INSTEAD OF HAVING BEEN IMPROVED IN 67 GENERATIONS OUT OF ALL
GENV I (40) DIFFICULTY IN PUTTING DOWN THESE REVOLUTIONS; BUT INSTEAD OF HAVING HIS OPPONENT SHOT IN THE PROPER AND
HART PREFACE(31) INTENSITY AND STALE THINGS NOVELTY. THE ACTOR, INSTEAD OF HAVING TO COAX HIS AUDIENCES OUT OF THE BOREDOM
MTH3 (94) FORTY-THREE, IF ONLY THEY WERE ASKED AS A FAVOR INSTEAD OF HAVING TO. /BARNABAS/ THANK YOU: I NEED NO
LION PROLOG (106) TO THE GODS AS ALL RESPECTABLE PEOPLE DO, INSTEAD OF HAVING US HUNTED OUT OF HOUSE AND HOME FOR BEING
3PLA PREFACE(R16) HE BEEN ENTHRALLED BY THE PLAY, EVEN WITH HORROR, INSTEAD OF HIMSELF ENTHRALLING WITH THE DREAD OF HIS
CAND II (118) HARDER THAN EVER! YOU POSITIVELY HELP THEM AT IT INSTEAD OF HINDERING THEM. /MORELL/ (WITH ENERGETIC
MILL I (161) /EPIFANIA/ AT ALL EVENTS, THE NET RESULT WAS THAT INSTEAD OF HIS BEING FIFTY THOUSAND POUNDS TO THE GOOD I WAS
BARB III (332) CANNONS ANY THE BETTER FOR BEING HIS OWN COUSIN INSTEAD OF HIS PROPER SELF (SHE SITS DOWN ON THE RUG WITH A
MIS. (125) AN ANSWER; AND I WAS ONLY TOO GLAD TO BE HIS WIFE INSTEAD OF HIS SHOP-GIRL. STILL, IT'S CURIOUS; BUT I HAD
HART PREFACE(29) HAIG HAS POINTED OUT, ITS WATERLOOS LASTED MONTHS INSTEAD OF HOURS, BUT THERE WOULD HAVE BEEN NOTHING
DOCT I SD(81) OVER THEM THAT AGE INCREASES HER QUALIFICATION INSTEAD OF IMPAIRING IT. BEING AN INDUSTRIOUS, AGREEABLE,
LION PREFACE(70) THAT THIS DANGEROUS PREPOSTEROUSNESS IN MARRIAGE, INSTEAD OF IMPROVING AS THE GENERAL CONDUCT OF MARRIED
LADY PREFACE(211) LIKE MYSELF: IN FACT, IF I HAD BEEN BORN IN 1556 INSTEAD OF IN 1856, I SHOULD HAVE TAKEN TO BLANK VERSE AND
LION PREFACE(80) AND BY RIDING ON THE CLOUDS OF HEAVEN IN GLORY INSTEAD OF IN A THOUSAND-GUINEA MOTOR CAR. THAT WAS
CLEO NOTES (205) LODGINGS ON A SALARY OF FIFTEEN SHILLINGS A WEEK INSTEAD OF IN CASTLES ON PRINCELY REVENUES, DO NOT
CAND III (132) MY BLACK COAT; AND MY COLLAR WAS BUTTONED BEHIND INSTEAD OF IN FRONT. DO YOU THINK SHE WOULD HAVE LOVED ME
CAND III (131) YOU BY MERELY BUTTONING YOUR COLLAR AT THE BACK INSTEAD OF IN FRONT. /MORELL/ (BOLDLY AND STEADILY) WHEN
MIS. PREFACE(25) ARE LIKE ANGELS FORCED TO WORK IN PRISONS INSTEAD OF IN HEAVEN; AND EVEN AT THAT THEY ARE MOSTLY
BUOY II (21) MARX WHEN I WAS FIFTEEN. THAT IS WHY I AM HERE INSTEAD OF IN LONDON LOOKING FOR A RICH HUSBAND. /HE/ WE ARE
JITT I (24) HIS GESTURE) MIGHT HAPPEN WHEN YOU WERE ALONE INSTEAD OF IN MY ARMS. DOES THAT SOUND AS IF I CARED WHAT
CAPT NOTES (301) HIM SEEMS TO HAVE HAPPENED IN PARAGUAY OR TEXAS INSTEAD OF IN SPAIN OR SCOTLAND. HE IS, I REGRET TO ADD, AN
BUOY PREFACE(4) YEARS OF UNRELIEVED MARKET FAILURE, IN WRITING INSTEAD OF IN STOCKBROKING OR TURF BOOKMAKING OR PEDDLING, I
BARB III (321) ARE VALUED FOR YOUR MONEY AND DEFERRED TO FOR IT, INSTEAD OF IN THE DOUBTLESS VERY OLD-FASHIONED AND
MTH2 (48) IN SHARPLY) THEN WHY ARE YOU IN THE OPPOSITION INSTEAD OF IN THE GOVERNMENT? /BURGE/ (SHEWING SIGNS OF
O'FL (212) BE, HAVING TEA AT THE SAME TABLE AS YOU, SIR, INSTEAD OF IN THE KITCHEN. SHE'LL BE AFTER DRESSING IN THE
ARMS II (42) STUPID PEOPLE OF MINE THOUGHT I WAS OUT HERE, INSTEAD OF IN THE-- HAW! -- LIBRARY (HE CANNOT MENTION THE
ARMS I (4) HEAVENS, CHILD! ARE YOU OUT IN THE NIGHT AIR INSTEAD OF IN YOUR BED? YOULL CATCH YOUR DEATH. LOUKA TOLD
DOCT PREFACE(53) HAS REDUCED THE PERCENTAGE BY EIGHTY PER CENT INSTEAD OF INCREASING IT BY FIVE, BECAUSE THE PUBLIC, LEFT
HART PREFACE(15) AND INTENSITY OF TOIL REDUCES PRODUCTION HEAVILY INSTEAD OF INCREASING IT, THE FACTORY LAWS WERE SUSPENDED,
MTH4 I (159) INFALLIBLE AND OMNISCIENT. THUS OUR DISCOVERIES, INSTEAD OF INCREASING OUR WISDOM, ONLY DESTROYED THE LITTLE
MIS. PREFACE(37) TRAINING; TO BECOME CITIZENS OF THE WORLD INSTEAD OF INMATES OF THE ENLARGED RABBIT HUTCHES WE CALL
GENV III (69) ARE MAKING SPEECHES OUTSIDE YOUR PARLIAMENT HOUSE INSTEAD OF INSIDE IT. BUT TO ME THE PERSECUTION IS A MATTER
ROCK PREFACE(177) LEGEND OF JOSHUA'S VICTORY AS A RELIGIOUS TRUTH INSTEAD OF INSISTING THAT IT DID NOT MAKE THE SMALLEST
POSN PREFACE(418) WILL BE THE RESULT? THE MANAGERS WILL FIND THAT INSTEAD OF INSURING THEM AS THE LORD CHAMBERLAIN DOES, HE
ARMS III (71) HOME TWICE WHEN I WAS A BOY. I WENT INTO THE ARMY INSTEAD OF INTO MY FATHER'S BUSINESS. I CLIMBED THE BALCONY
APPL PREFACE(176) WORK, MADE TO FIT INTO THE TWENTIETH CENTURY INSTEAD OF INTO THE SIXTEENTH. UNTIL WE FACE THIS TASK AND
BULL PREFACE(16) INTOLERABLE HE FINDS IT TO BE RULED BY ENGLISH INSTEAD OF IRISH FOLLY. A " LOYAL" IRISHMAN IS AN ABHORRENT
UNPL PREFACE(R24) WRITING THEM DOWN. EVEN THE USE OF SPACED LETTERS INSTEAD OF ITALICS FOR UNDERLINING, THOUGH FAMILIAR TO
BUOY 1 (9) COULD HAVE IF YOU HAD CHOSEN TO WORK FOR HONORS INSTEAD OF JOINING RATHER DISREPUTABLE CLUBS AND WORKING ON
JOAN PREFACE(30) THEMSELVES PARTICULARLY AGREEABLE IN FRANCE INSTEAD OF JUST THE CONTRARY) AGAINST A FRENCHWOMAN WHO HAD
MIS. PREFACE(87) GOOD DEAL OF SOCIAL INTERCOURSE, AND THE FAMILY, INSTEAD OF KEEPING ITSELF TO ITSELF, AS THE EVIL OLD SAYING
POSN (455) LOOKING AT A RAINBOW LIKE A DAMNED SILLY FOOL INSTEAD OF KEEPING YOUR WITS ABOUT YOU; AND WE STOLE UP ON
GETT PREFACE(249) DOCTRINE TO MEET THIS OR THAT PRACTICAL EMERGENCY INSTEAD OF KEEPING IT ADJUSTED TO THE WHOLE SCHEME OF LIFE,
GETT SD(259) LAVISH ON A HOUSE BUILT FOR THE GLORY OF GOD, INSTEAD OF KEEPING A COMPETITIVE EYE ON THE ADVANTAGE OF
DOCT III (139) /LOUIS/ NO; BUT YOU WERE SMELLING OUT A SCANDAL INSTEAD OF KEEPING YOUR MIND CLEAN AND WHOLESOME. I CAN JUST
NEVR IV (285) SEEMS THAT EVERYBODY HAS GONE TO THIS FANCY BALL INSTEAD OF KEEPING TO OUR APPOINTMENT HERE. /VALENTINE/ OH,
VWOO 2 (130) CONCEAL. YOU PLAY WITH YOUR CARDS ON THE TABLE INSTEAD OF KEEPING THEM WHERE A LADY SHOULD KEEP THEM: UP
SUPR I (14) TO RIDE IN AN OMNIBUS, ASHAMED TO HIRE A HANSOM INSTEAD OF KEEPING A CARRIAGE, ASHAMED OF KEEPING ONE HORSE
HART I (53) SIT DOWN (SHE PUSHES HER BACK INTO THE CHAIR INSTEAD OF KISSING HER, AND POSTS HERSELF BEHIND IT). YOU DO
BULL PREFACE(37) BY THE IGNORANCE OF THE ORDINARY ENGLISHMAN, WHO, INSTEAD OF KNOWING THE DISTINCTIVE TENETS OF HIS CHURCH OR
MIS. (137) COULD ONLY PUT BACK HIS EARS OR WAG HIS TAIL INSTEAD OF LAYING DOWN THE LAW, HOW MUCH BETTER IT WOULD
POSN (442) ME, YOUD BE A FREE AND RESPECTABLE MAN THIS DAY INSTEAD OF LAYING THERE WITH A ROPE ROUND YOUR NECK.
MTH3 (123) LOT OF MANKIND WHEN I WAS LEARNING TO SUFFER INSTEAD OF LEARNING TO LIVE! WHEN I SEE HOW LIGHTLY YOU
INCA (242) DO THE WORK OF TEACHING YOU YOUR PLACE HERSELF, INSTEAD OF LEAVING IT TO HER MAID. /THE MANAGER/ OH PLEASE,
MRS PREFACE(155) ITS BRAINS WITH IT WHEN IT GOES TO THE THEATRE, INSTEAD OF LEAVING THEM AT HOME WITH ITS PRAYER-BOOK AS IT
BUOY III (30) FOR NOT HAVING THRASHED THE LIFE OUT OF ME INSTEAD OF LEAVING ME TO LEARN LIFE'S LESSONS BY BREAKING MY
GETT PREFACE(257) ALL THE CONSEQUENCES OF THESE ACTS OF JUSTICE INSTEAD OF LETTING YOURSELF BE FRIGHTENED OUT OF REASON AND
ROCK I (222) IF YOU WILL TALK TO EVERYBODY FOR HALF AN HOUR INSTEAD OF LETTING ME GET RID OF THEM FOR YOU IN TWO
6CAL PREFACE(89) HUMAN BEING IN A VERY TRYING SITUATION INSTEAD OF LIKE A MODERN CONSTITUTIONAL MONARCH ON PARADE
2TRU PREFACE(14) THAT IT MAY PROTECT AND GLORIFY HIS CHICANERIES INSTEAD OF LIQUIDATING HIM. TO MR CHESTERTON THE
CYMB FORWORD(138) I MAY BE ASKED WHY ALL MY INSTANCES ARE MUSICAL INSTEAD OF LITERARY. IS IT A PLOT TO TAKE THE LITERARY
ROCK II (264) WITH EYES IN HER HEAD THAT MIRROR THE UNIVERSE INSTEAD OF LITTLE PEEPHOLES FILLED WITH FADED PEBBLES. SET
MRS IV (249) HIMSELF IN HIS OWN WAY AND MAKE PLENTY OF MONEY INSTEAD OF LIVING THE USUAL SHOOTING, HUNTING, DINING-OUT,
LION PREFACE(33) PREDETERMINED RITUAL, LIKE THE WORKS OF A CLOCK, INSTEAD OF LIVING. FINALLY MARK REPORTS CHRIST AS SAYING,
BUOY III (45) A THREE DIMENSIONAL TIMELESS UNIVERSE. INSTEAD OF LOGIC, ASSOCIATION OF IDEAS, MOSTLY NONSENSICAL
JOAN 4 (94) PICTURES CUNNINGLY INSET. BUT NOWADAYS, INSTEAD OF LOOKING AT BOOKS, PEOPLE READ THEM. A BOOK MIGHT
LION II (133) I ASK YOU WHETHER IT IS FAIR FOR THE RETIARIUS, INSTEAD OF MAKING A FAIR THROW OF HIS NET AT ME, TO SWISH IT
BULL IV (175) IRELAND TAKE CARE THAT IT DOESNT SHARE HIS FATE, INSTEAD OF MAKING ANOTHER EMPTY GRIEVANCE OF IT. LET YOUR
DEVL III (77) I SHOULD HAVE DONE FOR YOU WHAT YOU DID FOR ME, INSTEAD OF MAKING A VAIN SACRIFICE. /ANDERSON/ NOT VAIN, MY
MILL PREFACE(115) IT WAS TOO LATE TO DO ANYTHING BUT RUN AWAY. INSTEAD OF MAKING FOR AMERICA AT ALL HAZARDS HE THREW
BULL PREFACE(23) BEGAN TO USE HIS POWERS TO MAKE HIMSELF AGREEABLE INSTEAD OF MAKING HIMSELF RECKONED WITH BY THE ENEMY; IF HE
SUPR I SD(16) COMELY, WITH ENSNARING EYES AND HAIR. BESIDES, INSTEAD OF MAKING HERSELF AN EYESORE, LIKE HER MOTHER, SHE
OVER PREFACE(160) OFFHAND. IN MANY CASES IT MAY SAVE MISCHIEF INSTEAD OF MAKING IT: FOR EXAMPLE, THOUGH THE HANGING OF A
SUPR II (55) OUR WORK, AND WE ATE THEIR CHILDREN'S BREAD INSTEAD OF MAKING IT, THEY WOULD KILL US AS THE SPIDER KILLS
ANNA (302) NOT STAND TO YOUR GUNS AND JUSTIFY WHAT YOU DID, INSTEAD OF MAKING SILLY EXCUSES. DO YOU SUPPOSE I THINK
MIS. PREFACE(42) AND CRAMPING AND DELAYING PROGRESS AND GROWTH INSTEAD OF MAKING THE DANGEROUS PLACES AS SAFE AS POSSIBLE
ROCK II (258) WHO WILL DISCIPLINE THEM AND MAKE THEM DO IT INSTEAD OF MAKING THEM DO THE OTHER THING. THEY ARE READY TO
MTH2 (51) JEALOUS OF THE NOBILITY, AND HAVE SHIPPING SHARES INSTEAD OF MANUFACTURING BUSINESSES IN THE MIDLANDS? I CAN
PHIL I (80) OF FEELING FROM EITHER SIDE. YOU CHOSE FRIENDSHIP INSTEAD OF MARRIAGE. NOW DO YOUR DUTY, AND ACCEPT YOUR
BUOY III (45) OF FACTS, ESCAPIST ROMANCE FROM THE CINEMAS. INSTEAD OF MATHEMATICAL AND RELATIVE MEASUREMENTS, A THREE
MRS IV (250) PART. IT WILL NOT MAKE MUCH DIFFERENCE TO US: INSTEAD OF MEETING ONE ANOTHER FOR PERHAPS A FEW MONTHS IN
ARMS II (39) IS YOUR PET. I SOMETIMES WISH YOU COULD MARRY HIM INSTEAD OF ME. YOU WOULD JUST SUIT HIM. YOU WOULD PET HIM,
CAND I (84) TO BE A MAN AND HAVE A FINE PENETRATING INTELLECT INSTEAD OF MERE EMOTIONS LIKE US, AND TO KNOW THAT THE
SUPR III (112) IN PARTICULAR, JUAN. STILL, SINCE IN THIS PLACE, INSTEAD OF MERELY KILLING TIME WE HAVE TO KILL ETERNITY, GO
BARB PREFACE(225) DIVINE THAT THEY MUST ACTUALLY FIGHT THE DEVIL INSTEAD OF MERELY PRAYING AT HIM? AT PRESENT, IT IS TRUE,
2TRU III (86) WHEN YOU HAVE HAD FOUR YEARS OF THE REAL THING INSTEAD OF MERELY READING ABOUT IT? NO: DAMN IT, WE'RE
JITT I (16) THEN I COULD REALLY BEGIN A NEW LIFE WITH YOU INSTEAD OF MERELY THINKING AND DREAMING ABOUT IT. /JITTA/ I
UNPL PREFACE(R21) HAVE HAD ALL THIS AND MUCH MORE IF SHAKESPEAR, INSTEAD OF MERELY WRITING OUT HIS LINES, HAD PREPARED THE
GETT (342) IMPORTANT THINGS THAT MAKE MEN WORK AND STRIVE INSTEAD OF MOONING AND NURSING THEIR SALVATION. /SOAMES/ IN
ROCK PREFACE(156) A WOMAN'S SEX WAS MADE AN EXCUSE FOR BURNING HER INSTEAD OF MORE MERCIFULLY HANGING HER, MALE CRIMINALS WERE
MIS. (137) INDIARUBBER EXPANDER; BUT I WASNT STRONG ENOUGH: INSTEAD OF MY EXPANDING IT, IT CRUMPLED ME UP. COME ALONG,
MRS PREFACE(172) FOR DEDUCING CHARACTER LOGICALLY FROM OCCUPATION INSTEAD OF OBSERVING IT ACCURATELY IN SOCIETY. ONE CRITIC IS
MTH1 I (5) YOU SHOULD TRY TO HAVE AN EXISTENCE OF YOUR OWN, INSTEAD OF OCCUPYING YOURSELF WITH MY EXISTENCE. /EVE/ I
GENV IV (103) AM I TO CROSS THE RIVER ON A TIGHT ROPE INSTEAD OF ON A BRIDGE? AM I TO BEHAVE LIKE A FOOL OR A MAN
PLES PREFACE(R19) OUR IMAGINATIONS BY OUR HALF-SATISFIED PASSIONS, INSTEAD OF ON A GENUINELY SCIENTIFIC NATURAL HISTORY. AND
FABL PREFACE(91) BUT IF DR INGE HAD BEEN BROUGHT UP ON BEETHOVEN INSTEAD OF ON JACKSON'S TE DEUM, HE MIGHT HAVE PREFERRED
BULL I (94) POST-OFFICES WITH THE STRESS ON OFFICES, INSTEAD OF ON POST). /BROADBENT/ YOU ANSWER THE LETTERS?
GENV PREFACE(10) ON THE JET PROPULSION OF PILOTLESS AEROPLANES INSTEAD OF ON THE ATOMIC BOMB, THEY MIGHT HAVE CONTRIVED IT
APPL I (237) AND SENDING IT TO THEIR REPAIR SHOPS ONCE A WEEK INSTEAD OF ONCE A YEAR, OUR NATIONAL REPAIR BILL RUNS UP TO
JOAN PREFACE(4) ONE OF THE MOST ODIOUS PERSONS KNOWN TO HISTORY INSTEAD OF ONE OF THE MOST ATTRACTIVE. IF SHE HAD BEEN OLD
BARB I (269) A DOZEN MORALITIES AND RELIGIONS TO CHOOSE FROM, INSTEAD OF ONE TRUE MORALITY AND ONE TRUE RELIGION.
MTH1 I (10) WILL. THEN I TOO WILLED TO RENEW MYSELF AS TWO INSTEAD OF ONE; AND AFTER MANY DAYS THE MIRACLE HAPPENED,

SIM I (52)	AN INSTANT THERE ARE TWO WOMEN IN YOUR THOUGHTS	INSTEAD	OF ONE, THEN YOU DO NOT KNOW WHAT LOVE CAN BE.
ARMS III (57)	MIGHT COME TO BE ONE OF MY GRANDEST CUSTOMERS,	INSTEAD	OF ONLY BEING MY WIFE AND COSTING ME MONEY. /LOUKA/
CAND II (118)	BUT IF IT WERE THAT, THEYD DO WHAT YOU TELL THEM	INSTEAD	OF ONLY COMING TO LOOK AT YOU. THEY ALL HAVE
PYGM V (288)	PICKERING WILL BE THREE OLD BACHELORS TOGETHER	INSTEAD	OF ONLY TWO MEN AND A SILLY GIRL. MRS HIGGINS
APPL PREFACE(190)	WORKING ON OUR MUNICIPAL COMMITTEE SYSTEM	INSTEAD	OF OUR PARLIAMENTARY PARTY SYSTEM. WE NEED A CENTRAL
FABL V (118)	KEYBOARDS HAD ONLY TWELVE NOTES IN THE OCTAVE	INSTEAD	OF OUR SIXTY-FOUR. ONE WOULD THINK THEY MIGHT AT
MIS. PREFACE(106)	WHILST WELLINGTON WAS AN ORIGINAL SOLDIER WHO,	INSTEAD	OF OUTDOING THE TERRIBLE ACADEMIC COLUMNS WITH STILL
MRS PREFACE(175)	THE IMPRESSION THAT THEY WERE UPHOLDING VIRTUE	INSTEAD	OF OUTRAGING IT, THEY INFECTED EACH OTHER WITH THEIR
MIS. PREFACE(21)	HAD BEEN REALLY ENGAGED IN EDUCATING ME	INSTEAD	OF PAINFULLY EARNING THEIR BREAD BY KEEPING ME FROM
BULL PREFACE(7)	A ROMAN CATHOLIC LEADER ON THE HOME RULE MOVEMENT	INSTEAD	OF PARNELL? SIMPLY BECAUSE PARNELL WAS SO PROUD OF
CAPT I (233)	IF YOU WOULD ONLY TALK TO THEM IN A FRIENDLY WAY	INSTEAD	OF PASSING CRUEL SENTENCES ON THEM, YOU WOULD FIND
MIS. PREFACE(7)	TO INDUCE PARENTS TO KEEP THEIR CHILDREN AT HOME	INSTEAD	OF PAYING SCHOOLMASTERS TO TAKE THEM OFF THEIR
GENV PREFACE(25)	THEY ARE LUCKY ENOUGH TO GET PAID FOR THEIR WORK	INSTEAD	OF PERSECUTED. WE CAN AND MUST LIVE LONGER.
LIED PREFACE(185)	IF ONLY HE WILL LOOK ABOUT HIM FOR HIS MATERIAL	INSTEAD	OF PLAGIARIZING OTHELLO AND THE THOUSAND PLAYS THAT
CLEO III (158)	BRITON WEARS CLOTHES OF MANY COLORS AS YOU DO,	INSTEAD	OF PLAIN BLUE, AS ALL SOLID, WELL ESTEEMED MEN
SUPR III (103)	AS I PICTURE IT, DEAR LADY, YOU LIVE AND WORK	INSTEAD	OF PLAYING AND PRETENDING. YOU FACE THINGS AS THEY
POSN PREFACE(405)	COTTONS, GINGER-BEER INSTEAD OF WHISKEY, BIBLES	INSTEAD	OF PLAYING-CARDS, HE WILL BE FORBIDDEN TO PLACE HIS
PRES (154)	WOULD BE KIND ENOUGH TO PLACE IT IN SOME MUSEUM	INSTEAD	OF POINTING IT AT MY HEAD, I SHOULD BE OBLIGED TO
BUOY 1 (11)	IN A SOCIAL CIRCLE WHERE RICH MEN BECOME RICHER	INSTEAD	OF POORER IF THEY ARE SENSIBLE AND WELL CONDUCTED.
CYMB FORWORD(136)	IT IF HE HAD BEEN POST-IBSEN AND POST-SHAW	INSTEAD	OF POST-MARLOWE. IN DOING SO I HAD TO FOLLOW THE
FABL PREFACE(74)	TRIED TO SUBSTITUTE HIS GOSPEL FOR THAT OF MOSES	INSTEAD	OF POURING THE NEW WINE INTO THE OLD BOTTLES (
SIM II (78)	EXCEPT HOW TO WORK FOR THEIR DAILY BREAD	INSTEAD	OF PRAYING FOR IT. /PROLA/ IT IS DANGEROUS TO
SUPR PREFACE(R16)	ACKNOWLEDGED POSITION AS THE FOUNDER OF A SCHOOL.	INSTEAD	OF PRETENDING TO READ OVID HE DOES ACTUALLY READ
BULL PREFACE(19)	OF DOYLE'S AFFECTION FOR TOM. NELSON'S GENIUS,	INSTEAD	OF PRODUCING INTELLECTUAL KEENNESS AND
SUPR HANDBOK(198)	WHICH BUILT THE CIVILIZATION BECOME FATAL	INSTEAD	OF PRODUCTIVE, JUST AS THE SAME QUALITIES WHICH MAKE
DOCT PREFACE(41)	VERY FALLIBLE METHODS OF OUR CRIMINAL COURTS. BUT	INSTEAD	OF PROPOSING SUCH AN INVESTIGATION, OUR VIVISECTORS
DOCT PREFACE(29)	TYPHOID RALLIES OUR POWERS TO RESIST THE DISEASE	INSTEAD	OF PROSTRATING US WITH IT. BUT HAHNEMANN AND HIS
INCA PREFACE(231)	BUT I SHOULD CERTAINLY PUT THE PLAY IN THE FIRE	INSTEAD	OF PUBLISHING IT IF IT CONTAINED A WORD AGAINST OUR
GETT PREFACE(254)	CHILDREN TO THEIR TRADE, THE KING'S PROCTOR,	INSTEAD	OF PURSUING HIS PRESENT PURELY MISCHIEVOUS FUNCTION
CATH PREFACE(157)	THE CONSEQUENCE IS THAT THE GREAT ACTOR,	INSTEAD	OF PUTTING PRESSURE ON CONTEMPORARY AUTHORS TO
ARMS III (70)	IT APPEARS THAT SERGIUS IS GOING TO MARRY LOUKA	INSTEAD	OF RAINA. (SHE IS ABOUT TO BREAK OUT INDIGNANTLY AT
GENV I (40)	ELECTION BY THE MAN HE HAD SO FOOLISHLY SPARED.	INSTEAD	OF RAISING AN ARMY TO AVENGE THIS OUTRAGE, MY
APPL PREFACE(181)	LOST AND TERRIFIED ANIMALS, AND THINGS LIKE THAT.	INSTEAD	OF READING BOOKS AND NEWSPAPER ARTICLES, YOU WILL
APPL II (263)	REAL ENGLISH PEOPLE WHO TAKE THINGS AS THEY COME	INSTEAD	OF READING BOOKS ABOUT THEM, WILL BE MORE AT HOME
MIS. (201)	HONEST PEOPLE'S EYES WITH CONJURING TRICKS	INSTEAD	OF REAL FEATS OF STRENGTH AND SKILL. I WOULD BE A
ARMS II (28)	YES; SO THAT HE COULD THROW AWAY WHOLE BRIGADES	INSTEAD	OF REGIMENTS. IT'S NO USE, MY DEAR: HE HASNT THE
CATH 4 (196)	FAREWELL. /EDSTASTON/ (KISSING HER HAND, WHICH,	INSTEAD	OF RELEASING, HE HOLDS CARESSINGLY AND RATHER
DOCT III (153)	AM I OFFENDING YOU BY CALLING YOU DOCTOR	INSTEAD	OF REMEMBERING YOUR TITLE? /RIDGEON/ NONSENSE. I AM
BUOY PREFACE(6)	TIMES (AS THEY ALL ASSUME), THEY INFURIATE ME.	INSTEAD	OF REMINDING THEM CALMLY THAT, LIKE NEWTON, ALL I
LION PREFACE(32)	PREACHES HIS OWN DOCTRINE AS AN ORIGINAL MORALIST	INSTEAD	OF REPEATING WHAT THE BOOKS SAY. HE DESCRIBES THE
GENV IV (103)	WONDERFUL MAN IF YOU COULD WALK ON A TIGHT ROPE	INSTEAD	OF REQUIRING SEVERAL FEET OF SOLID PAVEMENT, COSTING
HART II (120)	LIFE GOES, THE HAPPINESS OF YIELDING AND DREAMING	INSTEAD	OF RESISTING AND DOING, THE SWEETNESS OF THE FRUIT
MTH3 (94)	FOR THEM, AND WOULD BE ONLY TOO GLAD TO STICK ON	INSTEAD	OF RETIRING AT FORTY-THREE, IF ONLY THEY WERE ASKED
MIS. PREFACE(106)	UNDERSTOOD THE NATURE OF WELLINGTON'S STRENGTH	INSTEAD	OF RETURNING WELLINGTON'S SNOBBISH CONTEMPT FOR HIM
GENV III (67)	SHOOT ME UNLESS I STAY IN THIS GHASTLY EUROPE	INSTEAD	OF RETURNING TO MY BELOVED EARTHLY PARADISE. /SIR
MRS PREFACE(162)	GIVEN ABOVE, THREW HIS PLEDGE TO THE WINDS, AND,	INSTEAD	OF RETURNING THE ARTICLE, PRINTED IT WITH THE
BULL PREFACE(45)	IS POLITICALLY AND SOCIALLY A CHILD, WITH RATIONS	INSTEAD	OF RIGHTS, TREATED LIKE A CHILD, PUNISHED LIKE A
GENV IV (120)	OF THE WORLD BY TEACHING IT TO FEED ITS PEOPLE	INSTEAD	OF ROBBING THEM. /FLANCO/ DID YOUR LANDLORDS EVER
HART PREFACE(40)	HIS ORDERS ON THAT OCCASION, AND FIGHTING	INSTEAD	OF RUNNING AWAY AS HE OUGHT TO HAVE DONE. AN
KING I (206)	WHAT YOU SAY, WHY DO YOU NOT MAKE MONEY YOURSELF	INSTEAD	OF RUNNING AFTER WOMEN? /CHARLES/ BECAUSE THERE IS
LION PREFACE(19)	REASONS FOR GOING " LIKE A LAMB TO THE SLAUGHTER"	INSTEAD	OF SAVING HIMSELF AS MAHOMET DID, BECOME QUITE
BARB PREFACE(215)	SHILLINGS A WEEK ON HIS BEER AND HIS FAMILY	INSTEAD	OF SAVING IT UP FOR HIS OLD AGE, LET HIM BE POOR.
BARB PREFACE(214)	EFFECTUAL PRECAUTIONS AGAINST DETECTION; SO THAT	INSTEAD	OF SAVING OUR WIVES' DIAMONDS FROM BURGLARY WE ONLY
SUPR II (60)	AND LEARN TO ENJOY A FAST RIDE IN A MOTOR CAR	INSTEAD	OF SEEING NOTHING IN IT BUT AN EXCUSE FOR A
WIDO III (62)	GET TWO HUNDRED AND FIFTY POUNDS A YEAR FOR IT	INSTEAD	OF SEVEN HUNDRED. TRENCH, COMPLETELY OUT WITTED,
2TRU I (28)	THERMOMETER: THEYVE LEFT IT FOR THE DOCTOR TO SEE	INSTEAD	OF SHAKING IT DOWN. IF IT'S OVER A HUNDRED I'M DONE
SUPR I (34)	GOT SOMETHING THAT I WANTED TO KEEP ALL TO MYSELF	INSTEAD	OF SHARING IT WITH YOU. /ANN/ I AM SURE I SHOULDNT
VWOO 2,SD(123)	BUT WEARS WELL CUT BREECHES (NOT PLUS FOURS)	INSTEAD	OF SHORTS. SEEING NOBODY TO ATTEND TO HIM HE RAPS
HART III (142)	DRESSING-GOWN AT DINNER. YOU COMPLICATE LIFE	INSTEAD	OF SIMPLIFYING IT BY DOING THESE RIDICULOUS THINGS.
SIM II (66)	CANT YOU FOUR DARLINGS DO SOMETHING USEFUL	INSTEAD	OF SITTING THERE DEAFENING US WITH YOUR SLOGANS?
ROCK PREFACE(180)	OF THE MOB, WHICH BECOME UNBEARABLE INTERRUPTIONS	INSTEAD	OF SKILFUL DIVERSIONS. FOR MY PART, WHEN I READ THE
MILL III (186)	A PENNY IS TO ME. WHY SHOULDNT I TRY THEIR GAME	INSTEAD	OF SLAVING HERE FOR PENCE AND HAPENCE? /THE WOMAN/
APPL PREFACE(176)	A POLITICAL SYSTEM FOR RAPID POSITIVE WORK	INSTEAD	OF SLOW NUGATORY WORK, MADE TO FIT INTO THE
ARMS III (56)	UP YOUR SHOP YOU WILL ONLY BE EVERYBODY'S SERVANT	INSTEAD	OF SOMEBODY'S SERVANT. (SHE GOES MOODILY TO THE
PYGM V (272)	TO LEARN TO SPEAK MIDDLE CLASS LANGUAGE FROM YOU,	INSTEAD	OF SPEAKING PROPER ENGLISH. THATS WHERE YOULL COME
3PLA PREFACE(R34)	COINCIDED WITH THE MOVEMENT FOR GIVING GENUINE	INSTEAD	OF SPURIOUS AND SILLY REPRESENTATIONS OF HIS PLAYS.
KING I (197)	WAS THAT JACK BOUGHT AN ANNUITY WITH THE MONEY	INSTEAD	OF SQUANDERING IT AS ANY OTHER MAN OF HIS AGE WOULD
BARB PREFACE(246)	AND PUNISHMENT, VIRTUOUS INDIGNATION AND PARDON,	INSTEAD	OF STANDING UP TO THE FACTS WITHOUT EITHER MALICE OR
MRS II (215)	TRADE IN THEM OURSELVES AND GET ALL THE PROFITS	INSTEAD	OF STARVATION WAGES? NOT LIKELY. /VIVIE/ YOU WERE
AUGS (272)	SAY SO! /AUGUSTUS/ HOW ELSE SHOULD I BE HERE	INSTEAD	OF STARVING TO DEATH IN RUHLEBEN? YES, MADAM: THE
DEVL I (6)	THE PUBLIC GALLOWS AS A REBEL; AND YOUR FATHER,	INSTEAD	OF STAYING AT HOME WHERE HIS DUTY WAS, WITH HIS OWN
GENV I (35)	SAID THE DEFEATED MINORITY MUST STEP DOWN AND OUT	INSTEAD	OF STAYING THERE TO OBSTRUCT AND DELAY AND ANNOY
DOCT PREFACE(26)	AT THE WRONG MOMENT, AND REINFORCING THE DISEASE	INSTEAD	OF STIMULATING THE RESISTANCE TO IT. TO ASCERTAIN
DEVL I (13)	TO GIVE HER A SELF-ASSURANCE WHICH SERVES HER	INSTEAD	OF STRENGTH. SHE HAS A PRETTY TASTE IN DRESS, AND IN
FOUN (212)	THEN WHY THE DICKENS DONT YOU OPEN THE DOOR	INSTEAD	OF STRIKING MELODRAMATIC ATTITUDES? HOW DARE YOU
SUPR III SD(73)	DOING HIS BEST TO GET A PENSION OR A SINECURE	INSTEAD	OF SWEEPING A CROSSING, NOBODY WOULD BLAME HIM FOR
GETT (299)	I THINK YOU SHEW GREAT WEAKNESS OF CHARACTER; AND	INSTEAD	OF TAKING ADVANTAGE OF IT I SHALL SET YOU A BETTER
HART I (69)	GLAD INDEED TO MAKE YOUR ACQUAINTANCE, HESIONE. (	INSTEAD	OF TAKING HER HAND HE KISSES HER. AT THE SAME MOMENT
MIS. (175)	NEVER ASKED TO BE LET OFF. I'M ASHAMED TO BE FREE	INSTEAD	OF TAKING MY PART WITH THE REST. WOMEN-- BEAUTIFUL
CYMB FORWORD(136)	SHAKESPEAR NEVER COULD INVENT ONE. UNFORTUNATELY,	INSTEAD	OF TAKING NATURE'S HINT AND DISCARDING PLOTS, HE
MIS. PREFACE(50)	OF READING AND STUDYING FOR THE SAKE OF STUDYING,	INSTEAD	OF TAKING SOME TROUBLE TO FIND OUT WHAT THEY REALLY
SUPR HANDBOK(186)	HIS SOLDIERS TO KILL THEIR ENEMIES IN THE FIELD	INSTEAD	OF TAKING THEM PRISONERS TO BE SPARED BY CAESAR; AND
ROCK I (205)	THEM BRING THEMSELVES UP IN THE POST-WAR FASHION	INSTEAD	OF TEACHING THEM TO BE LADIES AND GENTLEMEN.
ROCK PREFACE(176)	UP FROM HELL THROUGH A TRAP IN THE FLOOR. BUT IF	INSTEAD	OF TELLING ME THAT JESUS WAS TAKEN UP INTO THE
HART I (58)	MAN, THAT THEY LET HIM OFF AT SIX-AND-EIGHTPENCE	INSTEAD	OF TEN SHILLINGS. THEN MR MANGAN STARTED A COMPANY
DOCT PREFACE(8)	DIPHTHERIA, HAD BEEN PLACED UNDER HIS TREATMENT	INSTEAD	OF THAT OF ST JAMES, IT WOULD NOT HAVE DIED. AND HE
LION PREFACE(64)	INTO THE WORLD TO LIVE THE LIFE OF AN HONEST MAN	INSTEAD	OF THAT OF A CRUEL IDOL. THERE HAS ALSO BEEN A
LION PREFACE(61)	OUR COUNTRY BECAUSE OUR COUNTRY TAKES CARE OF US,	INSTEAD	OF THE COMMERCIALIZED CADS WE ARE, DOING EVERYTHING
BARB PREFACE(225)	CHOSE BLOOD AND FIRE FOR THE EMBLEM OF SALVATION	INSTEAD	OF THE CROSS, HE WAS PERHAPS BETTER INSPIRED THAN HE
CAPT II (256)	SPEECH OF THE JUDGE WHO IS SENTENCING YOU,	INSTEAD	OF THE DESPAIR IN THE WHITE FACE OF THE WRETCH YOU
KING II (230)	TO MY OWN BEAUTIFUL COUNTRY AND SMELL THE TAGUS	INSTEAD	OF THE DIRTY THAMES, AND RULE PORTUGAL AS MY MOTHER
SUPR PREFACE(R21)	MAN BY THE WOMAN; AND MY DON JUAN IS THE QUARRY	INSTEAD	OF THE HUNTSMAN. YET HE IS A TRUE DON JUAN, WITH A
MIS. PREFACE(75)	ALL THE NOVELTY WE NEED IS TO ORGANIZE IT SO THAT	INSTEAD	OF THE INDIVIDUAL CHILD FASTENING LIKE A PARASITE ON
JOAN 4 (105)	AND MAKE THE KING SOLE AND ABSOLUTE AUTOCRAT.	INSTEAD	OF THE KING BEING MERELY THE FIRST AMONG HIS PEERS,
BULL PREFACE(38)	OF THREE GENERATIONS OF ENGLISH IGNORAMUSES,	INSTEAD	OF THE LEGITIMATE SUCCESSOR OF MARTIN LUTHER AND
ROCK PREFACE(164)	MY PRESENT SUBJECT, WILL BECOME A HUMANE SCIENCE	INSTEAD	OF THE MISERABLE MIXTURE OF PIRACY, CRUELTY,
LION PREFACE(60)	OF ARTISTS AND THE ADVERTISEMENTS OF QUACKS	INSTEAD	OF THE NORMAL CONDITIONS OF LIFE. SOCIETY IS NOT
GETT PREFACE(215)	HAVE EVERY INDUCEMENT TO ADOPT THE NEW CONDITIONS	INSTEAD	OF THE OLD ONES. ONLY THE WOMEN WHOSE SOLE MEANS OF
BULL I (89)	TAKEN TO COLLECTING THE NEW PURCHASE INSTALMENTS	INSTEAD	OF THE OLD RENTS. I DOUBT IF HE'S BEEN FURTHER FROM
ARMS I (12)	FOR YOUR SAKE I HAD JOINED THE BULGARIAN ARMY	INSTEAD	OF THE OTHER ONE. I AM NOT A NATIVE SERB. /RAINA/ (
SIM I (41)	YOU WERE ALIVE AND I COULD KISS YOUR LIVING LIPS	INSTEAD	OF THE PAINT ON A HARD WOODEN IMAGE. I WONDER IS IT
MILL I (144)	WITH FIFTY THOUSAND POUNDS IN HIS POCKET	INSTEAD	OF THE PENAL SERVITUDE HE RICHLY DESERVED. THAT
MIS. PREFACE(72)	TO MEAN THE PURSUIT OF LEARNING BY THE CHILD	INSTEAD	OF THE PURSUIT OF THE CHILD BY LEARNING, CANE IN
2TRU II (60)	THE UMBRELLA)! ! ! /TALLBOYS/ (SURPRISED) NO.	INSTEAD	OF THE RANSOM. /THE COUNTESS/ (RECOLLECTING
METH PREFACE(R59)	EARTHLY KINGSHIP, A SUPREME CLASS DISTINCTION	INSTEAD	OF THE ROCK ON WHICH EQUALITY IS BUILT, HAD LED US
GETT PREFACE(255)	AS POVERTY AND IGNORANCE BECOME THE EXCEPTION	INSTEAD	OF THE RULE, GIVE WAY TO THE SYSTEM OF SIMPLY
BULL IV (171)	PAYS LIKE A GOLFING HOTEL, IF YOU HOLD THE LAND	INSTEAD	OF THE SHARES, AND IF THE FURNITURE PEOPLE STAND IN

SUPR III SD(86)	THE SKY SEEMS TO STEAL AWAY OUT OF THE UNIVERSE.	INSTEAD	OF THE SIERRA THERE IS NOTHING: OMNIPRESENT NOTHING.
BULL I (89)	VERY WELL THAT IF I HAD BEEN THE SON OF A LABORER	INSTEAD	OF THE SON OF A COUNTRY LANDAGENT, I SHOULD HAVE
KING I (213)	TO DISCOVER THAT THE EARTH GOES ROUND THE SUN	INSTEAD	OF THE SUN GOING ROUND THE EARTH. SIR: COPERNICUS
MIS. (146)	THE DAY SCHOOL AND THE BUSINESS TRAINING	INSTEAD	OF THE UNIVERSITY. I BELIEVE IN THE DAY SCHOOL PART
SUPR HANDBOK(196)	DEMOCRACY. AT THE PRESENT TIME WE HAVE,	INSTEAD	OF THE UTILITARIANS, THE FABIAN SOCIETY, WITH ITS
JOAN PREFACE(16)	THAT THE ETERNAL SOUL IN NATURE LOATHES,	INSTEAD	OF THE VIRTUES OF WHICH ST CATHERINE WAS THE FIGURE
BULL PREFACE(43)	MAY BE GOVERNED ACCORDING TO HIS IGNORANCE	INSTEAD	OF THE WISDOM OF THE PRIVY COUNCIL, HE IS ASSERTING
SUPR PREFACE(R11)	WHENEVER I TAKE HOLD OF A STICK BY THE RIGHT	INSTEAD	OF THE WRONG END. WHY ARE OUR OCCASIONAL ATTEMPTS TO
METH PREFACE(R53)	FORBADE THE SMALLEST EFFORT TO USE THEIR MINDS	INSTEAD	OF THEIR KNIVES AND EYES, AND ESTABLISHED AN
MTH1 II (26)	MEN WHO ARE CONTENT TO BE THEIR BROTHERS' KEEPERS	INSTEAD	OF THEIR MASTERS, ARE DESPISED AND REJECTED, AND
HART PREFACE(6)	HAD SPENT THEIR LIVES FURNISHING THEIR POCKETS	INSTEAD	OF THEIR MINDS. BOTH, HOWEVER, WERE PRACTISED IN
VWOO 2 (130)	YOU CAN SAY TH-REEE FIV-V-V-V-E NI-N-N-N	INSTEAD	OF THEREE FAUV NAWN. BUT YOU HAVE NOT ACQUIRED ANY
ROCK II (266)	ARTHUR, WHY DIDNT YOU PLAY GOLF ON YOUR HOLIDAY	INSTEAD	OF THINKING? DIDNT YOU KNOW THAT ENGLISH POLITICS
MRS II (208)	SHOULDER). AH, IF YOU HAD ONLY BEEN MY FATHER	INSTEAD	OF THIS UNWORTHY OLD MAN! (HE PUTS HIS OTHER HAND
APPL PREFACE(176)	THE CANDIDATES WHO WERE AT THE FOOT OF THE POLL	INSTEAD	OF THOSE WHO WERE AT THE HEAD OF IT THERE IS NO
ARMS I (20)	UNDERSTAND THAT NOTION, AS YOU CALL IT. AND IF	INSTEAD	OF THREATENING ME WITH YOUR PISTOL AS YOU DID YOU
UNPL PREFACE(R20)	FEELINGS OPERATING THROUGH A ROMANTIC INTELLECT	INSTEAD	OF THROUGH AN ENTIRELY COMMERCIAL ONE; BUT PRAY DONT
KING I (206)	ONE WEEK MAKING MONEY OR EVEN THINKING ABOUT IT	INSTEAD	OF THROWING IT AWAY WITH BOTH HANDS ALL MY CHARM
SUPR III (114)	ENABLE THE INDIVIDUAL TO WORK FOR THAT PURPOSE	INSTEAD	OF THWARTING AND BAFFLING IT BY SETTING UP
HART PREFACE(17)	SACRIFICED TO REDEEM THE LIBERTY OF MANKIND,	INSTEAD	OF TO EXPIATE THE HEEDLESSNESS AND FOLLY OF THEIR
METH PREFACE(R68)	HE DEALT WITH THEM ACCORDING TO THEIR BLINDNESS	INSTEAD	OF TO HIS OWN WISDOM. BUT THOUGH THERE IS NO
DEST (174)	/NAPOLEON/ THEN WHY NOT SEND IT TO HER HUSBAND	INSTEAD	OF TO ME? /LADY/ (COMPLETELY TAKEN ABACK) OH! (
DEVL III (56)	SUPPOSE THE REPORTS HAVE BEEN TAKEN TO YOU, SIR,	INSTEAD	OF TO ME. IS THERE ANYTHING SERIOUS? /BURGOYNE/ (
SIM PRO,3, (31)	KIND TO TREAT THEM ACCORDING TO THEIR FOLLY	INSTEAD	OF TO OUR WISDOM? /THE Y.W./ HERE! STEADY ON, YOU.
SUPR HANDBOK(185)	PERSON WHO PROPOSES TO ENRICH THE COMMON FUND	INSTEAD	OF TO SPUNGE ON IT) IS SUPERIOR TO AN ORDINARY JOINT
POSN PREFACE(389)	THE MAGISTRATE MUST ALLOW THE ATHEIST TO AFFIRM	INSTEAD	OF TO SWEAR, AND MUST GRANT THE ANTI-VACCINATOR AN
SUPR HANDBOK(218)	PARLIAMENT SENDING ITS MEASURES TO THE THRONE	INSTEAD	OF TO THE COLONIAL OFFICE, AND, BEING FINALLY
HART PREFACE(19)	WORK TO A STANDARD OF INEVITABLE EVIL	INSTEAD	OF TO THE IDEAL OF LIFE MORE ABUNDANT. I CAN ANSWER
PYGM IV (267)	THEM INTO HIS HANDS). IF THESE BELONGED TO ME	INSTEAD	OF TO THE JEWELLER. I'D RAM THEM DOWN YOUR
BULL PREFACE(40)	OF HIS COTTAGE IF HE GOES TO A METHODIST CHAPEL	INSTEAD	OF TO THE PARISH CHURCH. HIS CUSTOMERS MAY STOP
GENV PREFACE(13)	EXCEPT THAT THE PLUNDER GOES TO THE TRADE UNIONS	INSTEAD	OF TO THE PLUTOCRATS. THIS MAY BE A CONSIDERABLE
SUPR PREFACE(R40)	RENEGADE BECAUSE I WOULD HAVE MY MOB ALL CAESARS	INSTEAD	OF TOMS, DICKS, AND HARRYS. WORST OF ALL, I HAVE
PHIL II (125)	FORM: REASONABLE AND IMPULSIVELY GOODNATURED	INSTEAD	OF TRAGIC) I KNOW I WAS WRONG TO ACT AS I DID LAST
CLEO IV (167)	ALL TO CHATTER IMPERTINENTLY JUST AS YOU PLEASE,	INSTEAD	OF TREATING YOU AS FTATATEETA WOULD TREAT YOU IF SHE
O'FL (210)	FILL UP MINE TOO. IT'S KEPT IRELAND POOR, BECAUSE	INSTEAD	OF TRYING TO BETTER OURSELVES WE THOUGHT WE WAS THE
ROCK II (275)	DO YOU PART. IF HE TELLS YOU TO GO TO HELL TODAY	INSTEAD	OF TRYING TO ARGUE WITH YOU, HE WILL DO THE SAME ON
SUPR I (14)	KEEPING A CARRIAGE, ASHAMED OF KEEPING ONE HORSE	INSTEAD	OF TWO AND A GROOM-GARDENER INSTEAD OF A COACHMAN
HART PREFACE(39)	BE ASKED, DID I NOT WRITE TWO PLAYS ABOUT THE WAR	INSTEAD	OF TWO PAMPHLETS ON IT? THE ANSWER IS SIGNIFICANT.
MTH4 I (170)	OF PRIDE IN US, AND KEEP US LOOKING DOWN AT YOU	INSTEAD	OF UP TO SOMETHING HIGHER THAN OURSELVES. /THE
JOAN PREFACE(19)	SHE PRESENTED HERSELF IN HER MAN'S DRESS, AND	INSTEAD	OF URGING CHARLES, LIKE QUEEN VICTORIA URGING THE
UNPL PREFACE(R19)	PERFORMING SHAKESPEAR'S PLAYS AS HE WROTE THEM,	INSTEAD	OF USING THEM AS A CUCKOO USES A SPARROW'S NEST. IN
MRS PREFACE(171)	THE TALENTS OF ITS PROFESSORS, NO CONTENTION THAT	INSTEAD	OF VIOLATING MORALS IT ONLY VIOLATES A LEGAL
SUPR HANDBOK(175)	OR PLEBISCITE IN WHICH THE PEOPLE FIGHT	INSTEAD	OF VOTING. THE FRENCH REVOLUTION OVERTHREW ONE SET
CAPT III (280)	TOO. I SAID, WHY DID YOU OBEY THAT LADY'S ORDERS	INSTEAD	OF WAITING FOR MINE? THEY SAID THEY DIDNT SEE
JITT II (34)	HIS OWN HANDS": THAT IS WHY I HAVE COME TODAY	INSTEAD	OF WAITING FOR MRS LENKHEIM TO CALL. /LENKHEIM/ DEAR
APPL II (257)	THEM: IT TEACHES THEM HOW TO USE THEIR STRENGTH	INSTEAD	OF WASTING IT IN MAKING FOOLS OF THEMSELVES. SO MUCH
CLEO IV (176)	WHY NOT? YOU HAVE BEEN GUARDING THIS MAN	INSTEAD	OF WATCHING THE ENEMY. HAVE I NOT TOLD YOU ALWAYS TO
MRS II SD(198)	AFTER NIGHTFALL. LOOKING EASTWARD FROM WITHIN	INSTEAD	OF WESTWARD FROM WITHOUT, THE LATTICED WINDOW, WITH
MTH2 (39)	SIXTY YEARS I COULD MAKE MYSELF A REAL BIOLOGIST,	INSTEAD	OF WHAT I AM NOW: A CHILD TRYING TO WALK. ARE YOU
JOAN 2 (78)	LIVES, IF THEY KNEW WHAT IS REALLY HAPPENING	INSTEAD	OF WHAT SEEMS TO THEM TO BE HAPPENING? /LA
NEVR I (206)	AND TOLD MY PATIENTS THE BRUTE TRUTH	INSTEAD	OF WHAT THEY WANTED TO BE TOLD. RESULT, RUIN. NOW
MILL PREFACE(128)	BY WIRELESS, AS AUTHENTIC POLITICAL ECONOMY	INSTEAD	OF WHAT THEY REALLY ARE: THAT IS, THE SPECIAL
FABL IV (116)	THEIR ASPIRATIONS TO BE FREE TO DO WHAT THEY LIKE	INSTEAD	OF WHAT THEY MUST. THE WORLD BECAME A WORLD OF
MRS PREFACE(151)	THE LARGE SOCIAL SCALE WE GET WHAT WE CALL VICE	INSTEAD	OF WHAT WE CALL VIRTUE IT IS SIMPLY BECAUSE WE ARE
MTH1 II (21)	I DESPISED MYSELF FOR NOT DOING AS HE DID	INSTEAD	OF WHAT YOU DID. HE BECAME SO HAPPY THAT HE SHARED
POSN PREFACE(405)	WOOLLENS INSTEAD OF COTTONS, GINGER-BEER	INSTEAD	OF WHISKEY, BIBLES INSTEAD OF PLAYING-CARDS, HE WILL
KING II (225)	A COURT WHERE BAWDY STORIES ARE TOLD OUT LOUD	INSTEAD	OF WHISPERED-- IS MORE TEDIOUS THAN A RESPECTABLE
ROCK PREFACE(177)	NEVER BEEN BURNT FOR WEARING BLACK UNDERCLOTHES	INSTEAD	OF WHITE; AND THE NOTION THAT PREACHING A SERMON OR
BULL PREFACE(63)	IT AND FOUGHT IT BRAVELY BY HONORABLE MEANS,	INSTEAD	OF WILDLY LASHING AND STRANGLING A HANDFUL OF POOR
SUPR PREFACE(R26)	BOBBIES, THESE CRICKETERS TO WHOM AGE BRINGS GOLF	INSTEAD	OF WISDOM, THESE PLUTOCRATIC PRODUCTS OF " THE NAIL
BUOY PREFACE(5)	THEM AT THE RISK OF BEING CLASSED WITH CAGLIOSTRO	INSTEAD	OF WITH CLERK-MAXWELL AND EINSTEIN, GALILEO AND
LIED PREFACE(185)	IT IN WITH AN OBSERVED TOUCH OF ACTUAL HUMANITY	INSTEAD	OF WITH DOCTRINAIRE ROMANTICISM. NOTHING IN THE
SUPR PREFACE(R32)	ARE CONCERNED WITH THE DIVERSITIES OF THE WORLD	INSTEAD	OF WITH ITS UNITIES: THEY ARE SO IRRELIGIOUS THAT
NEVR I SD(209)	SEA WITH HER THOUGHTS FAR AWAY. THE PARLORMAID,	INSTEAD	OF WITHDRAWING, SHUTS THE DOOR AND WAITS AT IT. /MRS
MIS. (143)	PHRASE IS. /HYPATIA/ LIVING ANY LIFE. LIVING,	INSTEAD	OF WITHERING WITHOUT EVEN A GARDENER TO SNIP YOU OFF
PYGM II (242)	HE'S A DISGRACE TO ME, HE IS, COLLECTING DUST,	INSTEAD	OF WORKING AT HIS TRADE. /PICKERING/ WHAT IS HIS
MTH4 I (158)	INSTRUMENTS AND APPARATUS AS THE WONDER WORKERS,	INSTEAD	OF WORSHIPPING THE GREATNESS AND WISDOM OF THE
VWOO 1 (122)	EARN MORE MONEY AS NAVVIES. I WISH I WAS A NAVVY	INSTEAD	OF WRITING GUIDE BOOKS. /Z/ WELL, WHATS TO PREVENT
WIDO I (21)	(COKANE, NOW FULLY ENLIGHTENED, STARES AT HIM	INSTEAD	OF WRITING). HAVE YOU WRITTEN THAT? /COKANE/ (
SUPR III (132)	BE ABLE TO CHOOSE THE LINE OF GREATEST ADVANTAGE	INSTEAD	OF YIELDING IN THE DIRECTION OF THE LEAST
MILL IV (203)	NOT FAIR TO ALASTAIR. WHY IS HE TO BE DIVORCED	INSTEAD	OF YOU? /EPIFANIA/ MR SAGAMORE: TAKE AN ACTION
O'FL (219)	ME, AND MAKE OUT THAT I OUGHT TO PAY YOU MONEY	INSTEAD	OF YOU PAYING ME." " THERES A FALLACY IN YOUR
MTH4 II (186)	AGAIN; BUT NOW I WISH HE WOULD TAKE CHARGE OF US	INSTEAD	OF ZOO, SHE WAS CHARMING AT FIRST: QUITE CHARMING;
LION PREFACE(23)	CURING A LAME MAN, SAYS " THY SINS ARE FORGIVEN"	INSTEAD	OF " ARISE AND WALK," SUBSEQUENTLY MAINTAINING, WHEN
DOCT PREFACE(78)	THEY ARE NOTHING BUT EMPIRICS WHO SAY " I KNOW"	INSTEAD	OF " I AM LEARNING," AND PRAY FOR CREDULITY AND
LIED (194)	PIECES, YOU WOULD BE THANKFUL THAT YOU ARE ALIVE	INSTEAD	OF-- OF-- OF HOWLING ABOUT FIVESHILLINGSWORTH OF
MIS. PREFACE(71)	CROPS TO BE DAMAGED NOR BULLS TO BE ENCOUNTERED,	INSTEAD	OF, AS AT PRESENT, IMPRISONING THE HUMAN RACE IN
GENV PREFACE(26)	INTO COMPETENT RULERS OF GREAT MODERN STATES	INSTEAD	OF, AS AT PRESENT, TRYING VAINLY TO GOVERN EMPIRES
SHAK PREFACE(135)	NOT MOVE A MUSCLE NOR CHANGE THEIR EXPRESSION,	INSTEAD	OF, AS BEGINNERS MOSTLY DO, PLAYING TO THEM AND
HART PREFACE(35)	THAT THIS WAS THE WORK OF WICKED GODLESS RIOTERS,	INSTEAD	OF, AS IT WAS, THE WORK PARTLY OF ZEALOTS BENT ON
JOAN PREFACE(13)	WHICH AMOUNTS TO JOAN BEING MENTALLY DEFECTIVE	INSTEAD	OF, AS SHE OBVIOUSLY WAS, MENTALLY EXCESSIVE, WILL
BARB I (250)	YOUR PARDON. (HE FIDDLES WITH HIS WATCH CHAIN	INSTEAD	). /LADY BRITOMART/ NOW ARE YOU ATTENDING TO ME,
ARMS I (13)	CARTRIDGES IN BATTLE? I ALWAYS CARRY CHOCOLATE	INSTEAD	; AND I FINISHED THE LAST CAKE OF THAT HOURS AGO.
SIM PREFACE(8)	AWAY FROM OUR CAPITALIST UTOPIA AND ADOPTING	INSTEAD	THE VIEWS OF THE BOLSHEVIST PROPHETS WHOSE
MILL IV SD(188)	THE STUFFED FISH, THE SIGNBOARDS ARE NO MORE:	INSTEAD	THERE IS AN ELEGANT DOUBLE WRITING DESK FOR TWO
ANNA (302)	IF THE TRUTH DOES NOT SUIT THEM THEY SPREAD LIES	INSTEAD	, AND MAKE IT A CRIME TO TELL THE TRUTH. /THE GRAND
LION PREFACE(30)	INSIST ON HIS RELEASING A PRISONER NAMED BARABBAS	INSTEAD	, AND ON HAVING JESUS CRUCIFIED. MATTHEW GIVES NO
DEVL I (12)	AT THE FIRE) YOUD BETTER PUT THE INKSTAND	INSTEAD	, FOR THE LAWYER. /MRS DUDGEON/ THATS NO ANSWER TO
MIS. PREFACE(23)	ITALIAN; BUT THESE I WAS NEVER TAUGHT AT SCHOOL.	INSTEAD	, I WAS TAUGHT LYING, DISHONORABLE SUBMISSION TO
POSN PREFACE(370)	BEEN ADDED. THIS EXPECTATION WAS NOT FULFILLED.	INSTEAD	, LORD WILLOUGHBY DE BROKE, WHO HAD DISTINGUISHED
BARB PREFACE(240)	HIM BACK TO THE PURSUING WOLVES-- GIVES HIM,	INSTEAD	, WHAT HELP HE CAN TO ESCAPE, AND SENDS HIM OFF
KING II (228)	IT, AND NOBODY TEACHES THEM HOW NECESSARY IT IS.	INSTEAD	, WHEN WE TEACH THEM ANYTHING WE TEACH THEM GRAMMAR
CAPT II (247)	CICELY/ (REASSURINGLY) YES: YOU CAN HAVE MY ROOM	INSTEAD	, WHEREVER IT MAY BE: I'M SURE YOU CHOSE ME A NICE
2TRU PREFACE(10)	OR STEAL YOUR DINNER AND THE PRICE OF YOUR BED.	INSTEAD	, YOU HAVE THE DAILY QUESTION " WHAT SHALL I DO?
		INSTEP	
JOAN 1 (63)	HE HOOKS THE STOOL FROM UNDER THE TABLE WITH HIS	INSTEP	). POULENGEY, RELAXING, COMES INTO THE ROOM; PLACES
2TRU II (52)	SARCASM) THANK YOU. (HE SURVEYS HIM FROM HIS	INSTEP	TO HIS NOSE). WHAT IS YOUR NAME? /THE RIDER/ MEEK,
		INSTEPS	
NEVR II SD(225)	AN HOUR AFTER NOON, IS TOASTING HIS PROTENDED	INSTEPS	. AT THE HOTEL SIDE OF THE TERRACE, THERE IS A
		INSTHRUCTED	
BULL III (139)	A YEOMAN. /MATTHEW/ (HUFFILY) I DONT NEED TO BE	INSTHRUCTED	BE YOU, LARRY DOYLE. SOME PEOPLE THINK NO ONE
		INSTIGATE	
UNPL PREFACE(R15)	AS AN ORDINARY CITIZEN, TO PROSECUTE ME, OR	INSTIGATE	SOME OTHER CITIZEN TO PROSECUTE ME, FOR AN OUTRAGE

INSTINC

CAND I (91)	IT'S HONLY TO STOP YOUR MOUTH. YOU AD THE RIGHT	INSTINC	ARTER ALL, JAMES: THE LINE YOU TOOK IS THE PAYIN

INSTINCT

DEST SD(172)	GESTURE AND POSE INSTANTLY AWAKEN HIS THEATRICAL	INSTINCT	: HE FORGETS HIS RAGE IN THE DESIRE TO SHEW HER
DOCT PREFACE(33)	OF FOLLY, WE CONTINUE LIVING AND LEARNING BY	INSTINCT	: THAT IS, AS OF RIGHT. WE LEGISLATE ON THE
MTH4 II (179)	MY SUPERIOR: HAVE I NOT BOWED MY KNEE TO YOU BY	INSTINCT	? YET I CHALLENGE YOU TO A TEST OF OUR RESPECTIVE
BUOY IV (50)	SEEN MEN RUINED BY TAKING RISKS. I HAVE A SORT OF	INSTINCT	ABOUT THEM WHICH BRINGS ME OUT ALL RIGHT. FOR OLD
BULL I (85)	A MOMENT BITTERLY; THEN BURSTS OUT) I HAVE AN	INSTINCT	AGAINST GOING BACK TO IRELAND: AN INSTINCT SO
MIS. (125)	MAKE A PERFECT SLAVE OF YOU. THERES A SORT OF	INSTINCT	AGAINST IT, I THINK, THATS JUST AS STRONG AS THE
BULL PREFACE(8)	LINE AT PROMOTING A SPY, HE FOLLOWED A UNIVERSAL	INSTINCT	AND A SOUND ONE. WHEN THE IRISH CATHOLIC WHO,
CAND III (139)	COLDLY, OFFENDED BY HIS YIELDING TO HIS ORATOR'S	INSTINCT	AND TREATING HER AS IF SHE WERE THE AUDIENCE AT THE
ROCK I (232)	A WOMAN MAY BE ALL THAT AND YET HAVE THE RIGHT	INSTINCT	AS TO HOW TO FLIRT INTELLECTUALLY WITH A TIRED
BULL II SD(111)	INSISTENCE IS NEEDED; FOR THE ENGLISH INHIBITIVE	INSTINCT	DOES NOT SEEM TO EXIST IN ROSSCULLEN. JUST AS
3PLA PREFACE(R18)	THAN THE EXTENT TO WHICH, IN REAL LIFE, THE SEX	INSTINCT	DOES SO PROCEED, EVEN WHEN THE CONSEQUENCE IS ITS
METH PREFACE(R49)	WHAT HAS HAPPENED BEING SIMPLY THAT A FLIGHT	INSTINCT	EVOLVED BY CIRCUMSTANTIAL SELECTION REACTS PROMPTLY
MIS. PREFACE(65)	MOST TRUSTWORTHY MAN IN THE COUNTY. DICKENS'S	INSTINCT	FOR DETECTING SOCIAL CANKERS NEVER SERVED HIM
CLEO NOTES (212)	THAT WHAT HAS BEEN CALLED HIS AMBITION WAS AN	INSTINCT	FOR EXPLORATION. HE HAD MUCH MORE OF COLUMBUS AND
HART PREFACE(18)	BOMB, FORCING THEMSELVES TO PERVERT THEIR DIVINE	INSTINCT	FOR PERFECT ARTISTIC EXECUTION TO THE EFFECTIVE
LION PREFACE(41)	DRAMATIC ART IS THE OPERATION OF A DIVINATORY	INSTINCT	FOR TRUTH. BE THAT AS IT MAY, JOHN WAS CERTAINLY
PYGM EPILOG (292)	IMPETUOUS BULLYING, AND YOU WILL SEE THAT ELIZA'S	INSTINCT	HAD GOOD GROUNDS FOR WARNING HER NOT TO MARRY HER
PLES PREFACE(R16)	I WISH MY PLAYS TO BE PERFORMED, AS A MATTER OF	INSTINCT	I FIGHT AGAINST THE INEVITABLE MISREPRESENTATION OF
GETT (309)	EXPERIENCE, AND A WONDERFUL TEMPERAMENT AND	INSTINCT	IN AFFAIRS OF THE HEART. /HOTCHKISS/ EXCUSE ME, MR
LION PREFACE(42)	DRIVING AT, THEY APPEAL TO SOME SUB-INTELLECTUAL	INSTINCT	IN HIM THAT MAKES HIM STICK THEM IN, LIKE A CHILD
SUPR III (128)	THE WORLD AND SAW THAT IT WAS GOOD, AGAINST THE	INSTINCT	IN ME THAT LOOKED THROUGH MY EYES AT THE WORLD AND
GETT PREFACE(223)	PREVALENCE OF THE SUPERSTITION THAT THE SEXUAL	INSTINCT	IN MEN IS UTTERLY PROMISCUOUS AND THAT THE LEAST
PYGM EPILOG (289)	SENSE OF HUMAN NATURE IN GENERAL, AND OF FEMININE	INSTINCT	IN PARTICULAR. ELIZA, IN TELLING HIGGINS SHE WOULD
PYGM EPILOG (289)	PICK AND CHOOSE. SHE IS THEREFORE GUIDED BY HER	INSTINCT	IN THE MATTER. ELIZA'S INSTINCT TELLS HER NOT TO
BASH II,1, (108)	MUSCLE AND UNTIRING HEART? DID I IMPLANT THE	INSTINCT	IN THE RACE THAT FOUND A USE FOR THESE, AND SAID TO
BULL I (85)	STRONGEST PATRIOTISM! THE MOST INVETERATE HOMING	INSTINCT	IN THE WORLD! AND YOU PRETEND YOUD RATHER GO
SUPR HANDBOK(189)	NORMAL MEN AND WOMEN. IN SHORT, THE INDIVIDUAL	INSTINCT	IN THIS MATTER, OVERWHELMING AS IT IS THOUGHTLESSLY
SUPR III (128)	SO DEADLY TO ME. IT IS THE ABSENCE OF THIS	INSTINCT	IN YOU THAT MAKES YOU THAT STRANGE MONSTER CALLED A
MILL PREFACE(126)	A DANGEROUS ONE, AS IT REVIVES A PRIMITIVE	INSTINCT	INCOMPATIBLE WITH CIVILIZATION: INDEED CIVILIZATION
CAND I (96)	NEVER MIND HER, MARCHBANKS. THE OVERPAYING	INSTINCT	IS A GENEROUS ONE: BETTER THAN THE UNDERPAYING
GETT PREFACE(224)	PORTRAIT ON THE GROUND THAT SINCE THE SEXUAL	INSTINCT	IS PROMISCUOUS, ONE PORTRAIT IS AS PLEASING AS
DEVL II (44)	ON THE CHAIR AT THE FIRE, SOBBING SILENTLY). MY	INSTINCT	IS THE SAME AS HERS-- TO SAVE HIM ABOVE ALL THINGS,
DOCT PREFACE(33)	WHICH HAS AN AIR OF BEING SCIENTIFIC, THEIR FIRST	INSTINCT	IS TO RALLY TO THE DEFENCE OF THAT METHOD WITHOUT
MILL I (145)	THAT HE ALWAYS COUNTERED THAT WAY, BY	INSTINCT	, BUT THAT DOES NOT PREVENT HIM FROM THREATENING TO
LION PREFACE(69)	GOOD CHRISTIAN SEXUALLY. INCONSISTENCY OF THE SEX	INSTINCT	. BUT THE QUESTION IS NOT SO SIMPLE AS THAT. SEX IS
BUOY III (37)	OF PROPERTY IS STRONGER THAN YOUR BIOLOGICAL	INSTINCT	. I AM YOUR PROPERTY. THEREFORE YOU ARE DAMNABLY
MIS. PREFACE(60)	HABIT LONG AFTER IT HAS CEASED TO BE A BENEFICIAL	INSTINCT	. IF YOU CATCH A CHILD WHEN IT IS YOUNG ENOUGH TO
MIS. (125)	IT, I THINK, THATS JUST AS STRONG AS THE OTHER	INSTINCT	. ONE OF THEM, TO MY CERTAIN KNOWLEDGE, REFUSED A
SUPR PREFACE(R28)	OUR FINGERS GO UP TO THE BRIMS OF OUR HATS BY	INSTINCT	. OUR IDEAL PROSPERITY IS NOT THE PROSPERITY OF THE
CLEO IV (172)	CAESAR! HOW COULD YOU? (PROUDLY) I DO-- BY	INSTINCT	. /POTHINUS/ (DEFERENTIALLY, AFTER A MOMENT'S
DOCT I (95)	HAD THE RIGHT SPIRIT-- THE GENUINE HYGIENIC	INSTINCT	. SHE COULDNT STAND HER SISTER-IN-LAW BEING A
MTH4 I (168)	HERE. WE DO IT EVEN AGAINST OUR OWN WILLS BY	INSTINCT	. TAKE CARE. /THE ELDERLY GENTLEMAN/ (RISING WITH
SIM PRO,3, (33)	ON HER LEFT). /THE PRIESTESS/ NO: YOU DO IT BY	INSTINCT	. THAT, ALSO, IS RATHER DOGLIKE. /THE PRIEST/ NO
CLEO IV (190)	HARM BY KILLING: I DO IT AS A DOG KILLS A CAT, BY	INSTINCT	. WE ARE ALL DOGS AT YOUR HEELS; BUT WE HAVE SERVED
BASH I (94)	WHO KNOWS? WE SHALL. THAT MUCH I KNOW BY	INSTINCT	. WHATS YOUR NAME? /LYDIA/ LYDIA CAREW. /CASHEL/
SUPR IV (163)	SOMEBODY. /TANNER/ AHA! THERE SPEAKS THE LIFE	INSTINCT	. YOU DETEST HER; BUT YOU FEEL THAT YOU MUST GET
SUPR HANDBOK(220)	ARE CONDEMNED TO CELIBACY BY IT; FOR THE MATERNAL	INSTINCT	LEADS A WOMAN TO PREFER A TENTH SHARE IN A FIRST
MTH5 (230)	BIRTH. WHY, THE NEWLY BORN THERE ALREADY KNOWS BY	INSTINCT	MANY THINGS THAT THEIR GREATEST PHYSICISTS COULD
3PLA PREFACE(R18)	GENTEEL PLAYS, FIT FOR CHURCHGOERS. THE SEX	INSTINCT	MUST THEREFORE PROCEED UPON GENTEEL ASSUMPTIONS.
MIS. PREFACE(59)	NATURE HAS PROVIDED FOR THIS BY EVOLVING THE	INSTINCT	OF DOCILITY. CHILDREN ARE VERY DOCILE: THEY HAVE A
SUPR HANDBOK(188)	PREVAIL WITH THOSE DEGENERATES ONLY IN WHOM THE	INSTINCT	OF FERTILITY HAS FADED INTO A MERE ITCHING FOR
MRS II (217)	LIZ WAS SUCH A PERFECT LADY! SHE HAD THE TRUE	INSTINCT	OF IT; WHILE I WAS ALWAYS A BIT OF A VULGARIAN. I
3PLA PREFACE(R24)	THIS NOT AT ALL AS A RELUCTANT SACRIFICE OF MY	INSTINCT	OF PRIVACY TO POLITICAL NECESSITY, BUT BECAUSE,
DEST SD(152)	ONE GIRL OF BAD CHARACTER, IN WHOM AN	INSTINCT	OF PRIVILEGE WITH SOLDIERS IS ALREADY STIRRING,
3PLA PREFACE(R17)	ON THE PRINCIPLE OF APPEALING EXCLUSIVELY TO THE	INSTINCT	OF SELF-GRATIFICATION IN PEOPLE WITHOUT POWER OF
3PLA PREFACE(R14)	INEVITABLY FLUNG THE MANAGERS BACK ON THE	INSTINCT	OF SEX AS THE AVENUE TO ALL HEARTS. OF COURSE THE
MTH2 (48)	YOU OLD ARISTOCRAT, YOU! BUT BELIEVE ME, THE	INSTINCT	OF THE PEOPLE IS SOUND-- /CONRAD/ (CUTTING IN
DOCT PREFACE(62)	PRETTY BAD STATE OF THINGS, AND THE MELODRAMATIC	INSTINCT	OF THE PUBLIC, ALWAYS DEMANDING THAT EVERY WRONG
APPL I (235)	GULLIBILITY AND PRUDERY, THE HATING AND HUNTING	INSTINCT	OF THE VOTING MOB, AND CAST YOU DOWN FROM POWER IF
MRS PREFACE(172)	AND UNNATURAL, NO POSSIBLE PLEA THAT THE	INSTINCT	ON WHICH IT IS FOUNDED IS A VITAL ONE. PROSTITUTION
SUPR III SD(72)	DO THIS IS BECAUSE WE WORK LIKE BEES OR ANTS, BY	INSTINCT	OR HABIT, NOT REASONING ABOUT THE MATTER AT ALL.
LION PREFACE(15)	BETTER THAN KNOWLEDGE COULD HAVE DONE; FOR IT WAS	INSTINCT	RATHER THAN THEOLOGICAL CASUISTRY THAT MADE HIM
LION PREFACE(69)	SEX IS AN EXCEEDINGLY SUBTLE AND COMPLICATED	INSTINCT	; AND THE MASS OF MANKIND NEITHER KNOW NOR CARE
3PLA PREFACE(R18)	FOR THEIR DRAMATIC FORCE ON APPEALS TO THE SEX	INSTINCT	; AND YET HE OWES IT TO HIS OWN NEWLY CONQUERED
SUPR I (26)	OF ADMIRING HER COURAGE AND REJOICING IN HER	INSTINCT	; INSTEAD OF CROWNING THE COMPLETED WOMANHOOD AND
SUPR I (44)	NOT SAY SO, THAT YOU WERE RIGHT TO FOLLOW YOUR	INSTINCT	; THAT VITALITY AND BRAVERY ARE THE GREATEST
LION PREFACE(15)	SOCIOLOGICAL WAY IN WHICH WE KNOW IT; BUT HIS	INSTINCT	SERVED HIM BETTER THAN KNOWLEDGE COULD HAVE DONE;
BULL I (85)	AN INSTINCT AGAINST GOING BACK TO IRELAND: AN	INSTINCT	SO STRONG THAT I'D RATHER GO WITH YOU TO THE SOUTH
PYGM EPILOG (289)	GUIDED BY HER INSTINCT IN THE MATTER. ELIZA'S	INSTINCT	TELLS HER NOT TO MARRY HIGGINS. IT DOES NOT TELL
SUPR I (38)	GET LOOSE FROM YOU. EVEN THEN YOU HAD ACQUIRED BY	INSTINCT	THAT DAMNABLE WOMAN'S TRICK OF HEAPING OBLIGATIONS
SUPR III (110)	BEHEST IN THE MOST ECONOMICAL WAY. SHE KNOWS BY	INSTINCT	THAT FAR BACK IN THE EVOLUTIONAL PROCESS SHE
PLES PREFACE(R9)	HIMSELF CONSCIOUS OF THE RAY: IT IS BY A BLIND	INSTINCT	THAT HE KEEPS ON BUILDING UP HIS MASTERPIECES UNTIL
GETT PREFACE(200)	OR REMARKABLE; AND IT IS A PERFECTLY SOUND	INSTINCT	THAT LEADS US TO MISTRUST THE GOOD MAN AS MUCH AS
SUPR I (37)	AND BOREDOM FROM HER FACE). IT WAS THE CREATIVE	INSTINCT	THAT LED YOU TO ATTACH ME TO YOU BY BONDS THAT HAVE
DOCT III (152)	I CANT EXPLAIN; BUT I HAD SUCH A STRONG	INSTINCT	THAT YOU WOULD CURE HIM. I DONT-- I CANT FEEL THE
GETT PREFACE(251)	OF THEM BETRAY THE COMMERCIAL AND PROPRIETARY	INSTINCT	THE MOMENT THEY LOSE THEIR TEMPERS. " I FOUND YOU,"
MTH4 I (168)	THEY WERE STONES, MEANING TO HURT ME. IT WAS THE	INSTINCT	TO KILL THAT YOU ROUSED IN ME. I DID NOT KNOW IT
DEST (176)	CANNOT HELP LOVING HER-- CANNOT HELP HIS MAN'S	INSTINCT	TO MAKE USE OF HER FOR HIS OWN ADVANCEMENT WITH
DEST (169)	IS ONLY THROUGH LOVE, THROUGH PITY, THROUGH THE	INSTINCT	TO SAVE AND PROTECT SOMEONE ELSE, THAT I CAN DO THE
DOCT III (139)	I'D HAVE HAD THE GENTLEMANLY FEELING AND ARTISTIC	INSTINCT	TO SAY THAT SHE CARRIED HER MARRIAGE CERTIFICATE IN
WIDO I (15)	CONDESCENDING TO TRENCH'S HUMILITY FROM THE MERE	INSTINCT	TO SEIZE AN ADVANTAGE, AND YET DEFERRING TO LADY
MTH4 II (180)	THEIR SHAME OF BEING BRANDED AS DASTARDS, THEIR	INSTINCT	TO TEST THEMSELVES IN TERRIBLE TRIALS, THEIR FEAR
MIS. PREFACE(54)	AND MISERABLY, WITH JUST ENOUGH GREGARIOUS	INSTINCT	TO TURN FURIOUSLY ON ANY INTELLIGENT PERSON WHO
SUPR III (126)	I WAS CRUEL AS WHEN I WAS KIND. WHEN THE LADY'S	INSTINCT	WAS SET ON ME, THERE WAS NOTHING FOR IT BUT
SUPR III (126)	OF FIGURES. BESIDES, I SAID " WHEN THE LADY'S	INSTINCT	WAS SET ON ME." IT WAS NOT ALWAYS SO; AND THEN,
LADY PREFACE(220)	WILDE. WE ALL DREADED TO READ DE PROFUNDIS: OUR	INSTINCT	WAS TO STOP OUR EARS, OR RUN AWAY FROM THE WAIL OF
2TRU III (97)	WANT IT TOO. FLORENCE NIGHTINGALE HAD THE SAME	INSTINCT	WHEN SHE WENT TO CLEAN UP THE CRIMEAN WAR. SHE
GENV PREFACE(12)	DEMOCRACY. MANKIND, THOUGH PUGNACIOUS, YET HAS AN	INSTINCT	WHICH CHECKS IT ON THE BRINK OF SELFDESTRUCTION. WE
BARB I SD(260)	CRUELTY OR COARSENESS. BY THE OPERATION OF SOME	INSTINCT	WHICH IS NOT MERCIFUL ENOUGH TO BLIND HIM WITH THE
LION EPILOG (147)	ORGANIZATION, AND ARMING OF THAT HERD	INSTINCT	WHICH MAKES MEN ABHOR ALL DEPARTURES FROM CUSTOM,
DOCT PREFACE(32)	OF CURIOSITY, HERE WE HAVE NO DECAYING TRIBAL	INSTINCT	WHICH MEN STRIVE TO ROOT OUT OF THEMSELVES AS THEY
MTH1 II (32)	TO YOU. /CAIN/ FOR ALL THAT, MOTHER, I HAVE AN	INSTINCT	WHICH TELLS ME THAT DEATH PLAYS ITS PART IN LIFE.
CAPT II (252)	MUST KEEP TOGETHER ALL: SIDI EL ASSIF'S NATURAL	INSTINCT	WILL BE TO CUT EVERY CHRISTIAN THROAT HERE.
ARMS III (52)	(PROMPTLY) INSTINCT, DEAR YOUNG LADY.	INSTINCT	, AND EXPERIENCE OF THE WORLD. /RAINA/ (
CAND I (96)	IS A GENEROUS ONE: BETTER THAN THE UNDERPAYING	INSTINCT	, AND NOT SO COMMON. /MARCHBANKS/ (RELAPSING INTO
BUOY III (32)	DOES NOT UNDERSTAND IT HIMSELF. HE MAKES MONEY BY	INSTINCT	, AS BEAVERS BUILD DAMS. /SECONDBORN/ WHENEVER I
ARMS III (52)	DID YOU FIND ME OUT? /BLUNTSCHLI/ (PROMPTLY)	INSTINCT	, DEAR YOUNG LADY. INSTINCT, AND EXPERIENCE OF THE
GENV PREFACE(12)	THE MAGNITUDE OF THE NEW PERIL ROUSES THAT OTHER	INSTINCT	, STRONGER FINALLY THAN PUGNACITY, THAT THE RACE
UNPL PREFACE(R21)	AND WIN THE SYMPATHY OF THE AUTHOR'S HISTRIONIC	INSTINCT	, UNLESS HE WERE A REALIST OF FANATICAL INTEGRITY.
BASH II,1, (104)	THEN FLED TO BAR YOUR DOOR. /LYDIA/ O LOVER'S	INSTINCT	! HE FELT MY PRESENCE. WELL, LET HIM COME IN. WE

INSTINCTIVE

METH PREFACE(R28)	PROCESS OF ACQUIREMENT HAS BEEN CONDENSED INTO AN	INSTINCTIVE	AND UNCONSCIOUS INBORN ONE. FACTORS WHICH
SUPR PREFACE(R17)	WILL GET A TRUE PROMETHEAN FOE OF THE GODS, WHOSE	INSTINCTIVE	ATTITUDE TOWARDS WOMEN MUCH RESEMBLES THAT TO
MTH3 SD(114)	RISE AS SHE ENTERS, AND INCLINE THEIR HEADS WITH	INSTINCTIVE	AWE. SHE COMES TO THE VACANT CHAIR BETWEEN
BARB PREFACE(225)	OF BODGER. IT IS A VERY SIGNIFICANT THING, THIS	INSTINCTIVE	CHOICE OF THE MILITARY FORM OF ORGANIZATION,
SUPR III (115)	/DON JUAN/ YES, PARTLY. FOR WITH A WONDERFUL	INSTINCTIVE	CUNNING, SHE KEPT SILENT AND ALLOWED ME TO
LION I (124)	DISEASE. (FERROVIUS TAKES HIS HAND FROM HIM WITH	INSTINCTIVE	DISGUST). IVE DRUNK ALL MY NERVES AWAY. I SHALL
SUPR IV (149)	OF TWO OUTCASTS). /VIOLET/ (SNUBBING HIM WITH AN	INSTINCTIVE	DISLIKE FOR SCENE MAKING) DONT BE UNREASONABLE,
GETT PREFACE(250)	CALVIN, AND HAILED WITH RELIEF BY LUTHER. BUT THE	INSTINCTIVE	DOCTRINE THAT THERE IS SOMETHING HOLY AND MYSTIC
GETT PREFACE(220)	THAN THE EXAGGERATION AND GLORIFICATION OF AN	INSTINCTIVE	FUNCTION WHICH CLOUDS THE REASON AND UPSETS THE
DEVL I (19)	(QUICKLY SLIPPING DOWN FROM THE TABLE WITH	INSTINCTIVE	GOOD MANNERS) YOUR SERVANT, MADAM: NO OFFENCE. (
MRS III (232)	AND THE OLD CROFTS BREED COMES OUT IN A SORT OF	INSTINCTIVE	HATRED OF ANYTHING LOW, IN WHICH I'M SURE YOULL
MTH3 (105)	MR CHIEF SECRETARY. /BURGE-LUBIN/ (RISING IN	INSTINCTIVE	IMITATION OF THE ARCHBISHOP) HONOR US BY TAKING
METH PREFACE(R27)	MAY YET BECOME INSTANTANEOUS, OR, AS WE CALL IT,	INSTINCTIVE	. IT ALSO DIRECTED OUR ATTENTION TO EXAMPLES OF
BULL IV (150)	OF LIBERTY (A CHEERY VOICE " HEAR HEAR"), THAT	INSTINCTIVE	MISTRUST OF THE GOVERNMENT (A SMALL PIOUS
BULL PREFACE(15)	PIECE OF MY MIND HERE, AS AN IRISHMAN, FULL OF AN	INSTINCTIVE	PITY FOR THOSE OF MY FELLOW-CREATURES WHO ARE
SUPR PREFACE(R23)	UP AN INTELLECTUAL CONSCIOUSNESS OF HER OWN	INSTINCTIVE	PURPOSE. ACCORDINGLY, WE OBSERVE IN THE MAN OF
GETT PREFACE(190)	THEREFORE NO LONGER ANY POPULATION QUESTION. HIS	INSTINCTIVE	RECOIL FROM ITS WORST ASPECT AS A SLAVERY TO
JOAN 2,SD(83)	HEM OF HIS ROBE FERVENTLY. HE SHAKES HIS HEAD IN	INSTINCTIVE	REMONSTRANCE; GATHERS THE ROBE FROM HER; AND
METH PREFACE(R74)	AND PRIESTS OF THEIR DISTRICT STOOD FOR THEIR	INSTINCTIVE	RIGHTEOUSNESS, WHO HAVE KEPT SWEET THE TRADITION
GETT PREFACE(197)	DASHED A HANDFUL OF SALT INTO IT WITH AN	INSTINCTIVE	SENSE THAT IT WAS HIS DUTY AS A FATHER TO
SIM PREFACE(17)	RECONCILED TO IT, WE HAVE ALSO TO RECKON WITH THE	INSTINCTIVE	SHRINKING FROM OUTRIGHT KILLING WHICH MAKES SO
MIS. PREFACE(30)	PEOPLE. THE DOGMATIC OBJECTION, THE SHEER	INSTINCTIVE	TABOO WHICH RULES THE SUBJECT OUT ALTOGETHER AS
SUPR PREFACE(R33)	CORIOLANUS, LEONTES ARE ADMIRABLE DESCRIPTIONS OF	INSTINCTIVE	TEMPERAMENTS: INDEED THE PLAY OF CORIOLANUS IS
GENV I (32)	PEOPLE. THEY ARE DISLIKED EVERYWHERE. IT'S	INSTINCTIVE	, SOMEHOW. HAVNT YOU NOTICED IT? /THE JEW/ ALL

INSTINCTIVELY

BULL II (99)	NOT YET FULLY FILLED OUT, WITH BLUE EYES AND AN	INSTINCTIVELY	ACQUIRED AIR OF HELPLESSNESS AND SILLINESS,
DEVL I (18)	THE OTHER SIDE OF THE KITCHEN, HOLDING HER SKIRT	INSTINCTIVELY	AS IF TO SAVE IT FROM CONTAMINATION. UNCLE
DOCT I SD(109)	IS EXTREMELY SUSCEPTIBLE TO THE BEAUTY OF WOMEN,	INSTINCTIVELY	ASSUMES THE DEFENSIVE AT ONCE, AND HARDENS HIS
DOCT V (175)	THERE IS FORGIVENESS. I TRUSTED IN YOUR STRENGTH	INSTINCTIVELY	AT FIRST; THEN I THOUGHT I HAD MISTAKEN
DOCT PREFACE(22)	THE CITY THAN THIRTY MILES ABOVE IT. BUT DOCTORS	INSTINCTIVELY	AVOID ALL FACTS THAT ARE REASSURING, AND
PYGM EPILOG (291)	PROSTRATED FREDDY AT THE FIRST GLANCE, SHE WAS	INSTINCTIVELY	AWARE THAT SHE COULD NEVER OBTAIN A COMPLETE
SUPR HANDBOK(205)	ANIMALS FOR NO REASON AT ALL EXCEPT TO FOLLOW AN	INSTINCTIVELY	CRUEL FASHION; AND WE CONNIVE AT THE MOST
METH PREFACE(R17)	SECRET OF PREVIOUS COLLAPSES), THAT THE RICH ARE	INSTINCTIVELY	CRYING " LET US EAT AND DRINK; FOR TOMORROW WE
PYGM IV (263)	/LIZA/ (GIVES A SUFFOCATED SCREAM OF FURY, AND	INSTINCTIVELY	DARTS HER NAILS AT HIS FACE)! ! /HIGGINS/ (
GETT SD(259)	THE BUILDERS, ANTICIPATING OUR MODERN IDEAS AND	INSTINCTIVELY	DEFYING THEM, HAD RESOLVED TO SHEW HOW MUCH
CAPT II SD(266)	THIRTY, WITH FINE EYES, BRONZED COMPLEXION, AND	INSTINCTIVELY	DIGNIFIED CARRIAGE. HE PLACES HIMSELF BETWEEN
SUPR PREFACE(R19)	TEACH IRISHMEN TO BE PROUD. FOR THE IRISHMAN	INSTINCTIVELY	DISPARAGES THE QUALITY WHICH MAKES THE
MIS. PREFACE(60)	YOU CATCH A CHILD WHEN IT IS YOUNG ENOUGH TO BE	INSTINCTIVELY	DOCILE, AND KEEP IT IN A CONDITION OF
SUPR PREFACE(R19)	ENGLISHMAN DANGEROUS TO HIM; AND THE ENGLISHMAN	INSTINCTIVELY	FLATTERS THE FAULT THAT MAKES THE IRISHMAN
BARB PREFACE(230)	BE A RUFFIAN. IN DOING THIS, THE SALVATION ARMY	INSTINCTIVELY	GRASPS THE CENTRAL TRUTH OF CHRISTIANITY AND
FANY III (327)	JUGGINS SINCE THE FIRST DAY I BEHELD HIM. I FELT	INSTINCTIVELY	HE HAD BEEN IN THE GUARDS. MAY HE WALK OUT
SUPR I SD(42)	AND LOOKS AS UNCONCERNED AS POSSIBLE. OCTAVIUS	INSTINCTIVELY	IMITATES HER. /THE MAID/ THE CAB IS AT THE
SUPR III (139)	CAPABLE OF REASONABLE CONVERSATION; AND YOU ALL	INSTINCTIVELY	INSULT HIM. EVEN THE NEW MAN IS AS BAD AS ANY
MTH5 (246)	JUST SO. YOU HAVE NO SENSE OF ART; AND YOU	INSTINCTIVELY	INSULT IT. /THE HE-ANCIENT/ CHILDREN HAVE BEEN
WIDO I (12)	MEAN THAT YOU DID IT ON PURPOSE, OF COURSE. ONLY	INSTINCTIVELY	. /BLANCHE/ (STILL A LITTLE ANXIOUS) BUT YOU
MRS II SD(219)	SHE EMBRACES HER DAUGHTER PROTECTINGLY,	INSTINCTIVELY	LOOKING UPWARD FOR DIVINE SANCTION.
CAPT I SD(225)	COMES DOWN THE SIDE OF THE GARDEN NEXT THE HOUSE,	INSTINCTIVELY	MAINTAINING A DISTANCE BETWEEN HIMSELF AND THE
BULL I (93)	THE ENGLISHMAN DOES WHAT THE CATERPILLAR DOES. HE	INSTINCTIVELY	MAKES HIMSELF LOOK LIKE A FOOL, AND EATS UP
BULL I (92)	BUT DOES NOT PRESS IT) WHEN IT GETS INTO A TREE,	INSTINCTIVELY	MAKES ITSELF LOOK EXACTLY LIKE A LEAF; SO THAT
MTH1 I (18)	TO HIM AND NOT TO ANY OTHER MAN IS WIFE. /ADAM/ (	INSTINCTIVELY	MOVING HIS HAND TOWARDS HER) HUSBAND AND WIFE.
JOAN 2,SD(87)	QUICKLY PUTS HER HAND ON CHARLES'S SHOULDER AS HE	INSTINCTIVELY	RECOILS. CHARLES, WITH A GROTESQUE EFFORT
ROCK PREFACE(147)	ANY OTHER CONVENIENT VERBAL WHITEWASH FOR WHAT WE	INSTINCTIVELY	RECOIL FROM AS FROM A DIRTY JOB. THESE
DEVL II (39)	OF MY CLOTH BEFORE, SERGEANT? /THE SERGEANT/ (	INSTINCTIVELY	RESPECTFUL, HALF TO THE BLACK COAT, HALF TO
CYMB V (142)	BY BRITISH SOLDIERS. /BELARIUS/ (TAKING COMMAND	INSTINCTIVELY	) PART THEM THERE. MAKE FAST THE ROMAN.
SUPR PREFACE(R12)	WITH WHICH THE EXPERIENCED POPULAR AUTHOR	INSTINCTIVELY	SAVES HIMSELF FROM FAILURE. BUT WHAT DID YOU
OVER (189)	TAKE MUCH NOTICE OF MY INTENTIONS. (GREGORY	INSTINCTIVELY	SEEKS HER HAND AND PRESSES IT). AND I REALLY
MTH3 (127)	SHE WALKS STRAIGHT AT THE ACCOUNTANT GENERAL, WHO	INSTINCTIVELY	SHRINKS OUT OF HER WAY AS SHE LEAVES THE
ARMS I (9)	(RAINA, SUDDENLY CONSCIOUS OF HER NIGHTGOWN,	INSTINCTIVELY	SHRINKS, AND GATHERS IT MORE CLOSELY ABOUT HER
DEVL EPILOG (82)	TYPICALLY STUPID IN VALUING AND INTERPRETING IT,	INSTINCTIVELY	SNEERED AT HIM AND EXULTED IN HIS DEFEAT. THAT
LION PREFACE(28)	AND NOT DOMINATION; BUT HE HIMSELF, ALWAYS	INSTINCTIVELY	SOMEWHAT HAUGHTY, NOW BECOMES ARROGANT,
DOCT PREFACE(42)	TO BE BEATEN. THE ILL-TEMPERED VULGARITY THAT	INSTINCTIVELY	STRIKES AT AND HURTS A THING THAT ANNOYS IT (
LION PREFACE(36)	THE ONLY TOUCH OF REALISM WHICH LUKE DOES NOT	INSTINCTIVELY	SUPPRESS FOR THE SAKE OF PRODUCING THIS KIND
MTH2 SD(41)	SHE TURNS QUICKLY AND SEES THE RECTOR. SHE	INSTINCTIVELY	SWITCHES AT HER GOZZOLI FRINGE WITH HER
DOCT PREFACE(61)	HE IS A RUINED MAN; AND THE RESULT IS THAT HE	INSTINCTIVELY	TAKES CARE NOT TO GET AHEAD OF THEM. THAT IS
GETT PREFACE(186)	WORTH COUNTING BELIEVES DIRECTLY, FRANKLY, AND	INSTINCTIVELY	THAT WHEN A PERSON COMMITS A MURDER AND IS PUT
ARMS III (55)	THE DOCUMENTS IN HIS HAND). /LOUKA/ (KNOWING	INSTINCTIVELY	THAT SHE CAN ANNOY RAINA BY DISPARAGING
2TRU II (63)	SUBTLE AND EXQUISITELY PUT TOGETHER. I MAY FEEL	INSTINCTIVELY	THAT IT IS THE ROTTENEST NONSENSE. STILL, IF I
WIDO II (43)	ADMIRABLE, MY DEAR SIR, EXCELLENT! I FELT	INSTINCTIVELY	THAT TRENCH WAS TALKING UNPRACTICAL NONSENSE.
BARB II SD(301)	OTHER NINETY-NINE. BILL, DAZED BY SUCH OPULENCE,	INSTINCTIVELY	TOUCHES HIS CAP. /BARBARA/ OH, YOURE TOO
CAND I (103)	THINK SOMEBODY HAD BEEN THROTTLING YOU. (EUGENE	INSTINCTIVELY	TRIES TO LOOK ROUND AT MORELL; BUT SHE PULLS
CAND I SD(91)	THEIR AFFECTION, AND WHO DOES SO FRANKLY AND	INSTINCTIVELY	WITHOUT THE SMALLEST SCRUPLE. SO FAR, SHE IS

INSTINCTS

SUPR PREFACE(R33)	HIS MOTIVES ARE HIS OWN APPETITES AND	INSTINCTS	AND HUMORS. RICHARD III, TOO, IS DELIGHTFUL AS THE
MRS PREFACE(168)	PROFESSION IS NO MERE THEOREM, BUT A PLAY OF	INSTINCTS	AND TEMPERAMENTS IN CONFLICT WITH EACH OTHER AND
GETT PREFACE(210)	TO THE DEPENDENT WOMAN. THE WOMAN WHOSE	INSTINCTS	ARE MATERNAL, WHO DESIRES SUPERIOR CHILDREN MORE
PYGM EPILOG (289)	TO YOUTH, DID NOT EXIST BETWEEN THEM. AS OUR	INSTINCTS	ARE NOT APPEALED TO BY HER CONCLUSION, LET US SEE
ARMS I (6)	/CATHERINE/ (BUSINESSLIKE, HER HOUSEKEEPING	INSTINCTS	AROUSED) I MUST SEE THAT EVERYTHING IS MADE SAFE
LION PREFACE(71)	FOR A HUSBAND WHEN ALL HER HEALTHY SOCIAL	INSTINCTS	CALL HER TO ACQUIRE A PROFESSION AND WORK. IT IS
MRS PREFACE(158)	AND THE REST: IN SHORT, FOR BANISHING THE SEXUAL	INSTINCTS	FROM THE STAGE ALTOGETHER. THOSE WHO THINK THIS
3PLA PREFACE(R18)	FEW OF US HAVE VITALITY ENOUGH TO MAKE ANY OF OUR	INSTINCTS	IMPERIOUS: WE CAN BE MADE TO LIVE ON PRETENCES, AS
CAPT III SD(279)	OF HIS HAIR, HIS CHEEKBONES, AND THE MANLIER	INSTINCTS	IN HIM WHICH THE SEA HAS RESCUED FROM
SUPR IV (159)	NICE WOMAN WOULD DELIBERATELY PRACTISE ON MEN'S	INSTINCTS	IN THAT WAY. /ANN/ (THROWING UP HER HANDS) OH,
GETT (355)	MORALITY OF THE MIDDLE CLASSES WITH ALL MY	INSTINCTS	. IF I WERE AN EIGHTEENTH CENTURY MARQUIS I COULD
GETT (291)	THEIR OWN CLASS. I AGREE WITH THEM. I SHARE THEIR	INSTINCTS	. IN MY UNDERGRADUATE DAYS I WAS A REPUBLICAN-- A
SUPR HANDBOK(228)	NOTIONS OF PROPRIETY ARE STRONGER THAN NATURAL	INSTINCTS	. IT IS EASIER TO RECRUIT FOR MONASTERIES AND
SUPR HANDBOK(189)	WOULD STILL SHATTER THE OPPOSITION OF INDIVIDUAL	INSTINCTS	. NOT ONLY DO THE BEES AND THE ANTS SATISFY THEIR
SUPR PREFACE(R17)	OF THE RACE INSTEAD OF FOR THE FREEDOM OF HIS OWN	INSTINCTS	. THUS HIS PROFLIGACY AND HIS DAREDEVIL AIRS HAVE
LION PREFACE(77)	TO THIS DAY, AND IS ONE OF THE STRONGEST OF OUR	INSTINCTS	. THUS PAUL'S POSTULATE OF ADAM AS THE NATURAL MAN
CLEO PRO1 (92)	TO THIS KIND OF KILLING; FOR THOU HAST IMPERIAL	INSTINCTS	. WILT THOU THEREFORE KILL THE LESSER DOG FOR
SUPR PREFACE(R12)	GAINING THE ARDENT SYMPATHY OF OUR REBELLIOUS	INSTINCTS	(WHICH ARE FLATTERED BY THE BRILLIANCIES WITH
2TRU III (97)	THERE IS NO SUCH THING AS A LADY. I HAVE THE	INSTINCTS	OF A GOOD HOUSEKEEPER: I WANT TO CLEAN UP THIS
2TRU III (97)	TO HAVE TO SAY IT, MOPS; BUT YOU HAVE NOT THE	INSTINCTS	OF A LADY. (HE SITS DOWN MOODILY ON A STONE A
CLEO NOTES (204)	AGES WERE FINALLY ENLIGHTENED BY THE PROTESTANT	INSTINCTS	OF THE ENGLISH RACE. THE WHOLE PROCESS IS SUMMED
METH PREFACE(R75)	UNTIL THE STATESMAN CAN APPEAL TO THE VITAL	INSTINCTS	OF THE PEOPLE IN TERMS OF A COMMON RELIGION. THE
CAPT III (288)	NO HAHND IN OFFERING ANY VIOLENCE TO THE PURE	INSTINCTS	OF WOMANHOOD. LADY WAYNFLETE: I THAHNK YOU FOR THE
GETT PREFACE(220)	AND UPSETS THE JUDGMENT MORE THAN ALL THE OTHER	INSTINCTS	PUT TOGETHER. THE PROCESS MAY BE PLEASANT AND
ROCK I (217)	WRONG-- WRONG IN FEELING-- CONTRARY TO ENGLISH	INSTINCTS	-- OUT OF CHARACTER, IF I MAY PUT IT THAT WAY,
OVER PREFACE(164)	A GREATER LICENSE IN APPEALING TO THE SEXUAL	INSTINCTS	THAN THE FRENCH STAGE ALLOWS THEM, LEARN ENGLISH
GETT PREFACE(213)	NOT THOSE WHO ARE SO ENSLAVED BY THEIR PRIMITIVE	INSTINCTS	THAT THEY WILL BEAR CHILDREN NO MATTER HOW HARD
BULL PREFACE(7)	MISFORTUNE OF BEING BORN WITH ONE'S NATURAL	INSTINCTS	TURNED AGAINST NATURE BY A FREAK OF NATURE IS A
SUPR HANDBOK(189)	THE ANTS SATISFY THEIR REPRODUCTIVE AND PARENTAL	INSTINCTS	VICARIOUSLY; BUT MARRIAGE ITSELF SUCCESSFULLY
MIS. PREFACE(7)	SPITE OF YOU AND SAVE ITS SOUL ALIVE; FOR ALL ITS	INSTINCTS	WILL RESIST YOU, AND POSSIBLY BE STRENGTHENED IN
SUPR PREFACE(R12)	BETWEEN GOOD AND EVIL, FOLLOWS HIS OWN	INSTINCTS	WITHOUT REGARD TO THE COMMON, STATUTE, OR CANON

MILL I (155)	BY YOUR OWN FOLLY, YOUR IGNORANCE, YOUR CRIMINAL	INSTINCTS	, AND THE LUCK THAT ATTENDS THE HALF-WITTED. YOU
BUOY IV (59)	OF FEELINGS, PASSIONS, EMOTIONS, INTUITIONS,	INSTINCTS	, AS WELL AS COLD QUANTITIES AND FIGURES AND
3PLA PREFACE(R20)	MOST TRANSIENT; MOST EASILY BAFFLED OF ALL	INSTINCTS	, IS INEXHAUSTIBLE, AND THAT THE FIELD OF THE
NEVR II (258)	YOU WISH ME TO BELIEVE MY EYES, MY HEART, MY	INSTINCTS	, MY IMAGINATION, WHICH ARE ALL TELLING ME THE
PYGM EPILOG (293)	TO A DEGREE THAT OVERWHELMS ALL HER OTHER	INSTINCTS	, SHE WILL, IF SHE MARRIES EITHER OF THEM, MARRY

INSTITUTE

MIS. PREFACE(24)	A SECONDHAND BRASS PLATE INSCRIBED PESTALOZZIAN	INSTITUTE	AND NAIL IT TO YOUR DOOR, THOUGH YOU HAVE NO MORE
DOCT PREFACE(54)	IN MY YOUTH BY DOCTORS IN DUBLIN BEFORE A PASTEUR	INSTITUTE	EXISTED, THE SUBJECT HAVING BEEN BROUGHT FORWARD
DOCT PREFACE(54)	THAN MIGHT HAVE BEEN EXPECTED HAD THERE BEEN NO	INSTITUTE	IN EXISTENCE. BUT TO THE PUBLIC EVERY PASTEUR
FABL V SD(117)	BUT THE BUILDING IS NOW LABELLED GENETIC	INSTITUTE	. ON THE TERRACE, SEATED ROUND A TABLE LOADED WITH
DOCT PREFACE(54)	THEREFORE, THE RESULTS PUBLISHED BY THE PASTEUR	INSTITUTE	PRODUCED NO SUCH EFFECT AS THEY DID ON THE
POSN PREFACE(397)	IT HAS NO DIRECT COERCIVE FORCES, NO FUNDS TO	INSTITUTE	PROSECUTIONS AND RECOVER THE LEGAL PENALTIES OF
BARB PREFACE(241)	MAY SECURE IMPUNITY TO THE PRINCIPAL. IF YOU	INSTITUTE	PUNISHMENT AS PART OF THE LAW, YOU MUST PUNISH
PYGM PREFACE(199)	OF PHONETICS, ONCE, IN THE DAYS WHEN THE IMPERIAL	INSTITUTE	ROSE IN SOUTH KENSINGTON, AND JOSEPH CHAMBERLAIN
CATH PREFACE(153)	ABOUT IT, AND PASS THEIR FLOGGING BILLS, AND	INSTITUTE	THEIR PROSECUTIONS FOR SEDITION AND BLASPHEMY AND
DOCT PREFACE(54)	OF DEATHS AMONG THE CASES TREATED AT THE	INSTITUTE	WAS RATHER HIGHER, IF ANYTHING, THAN MIGHT HAVE
DOCT I (104)	A SAMPLE OF HYDROPHOBIA SERUM FROM THE PASTEUR	INSTITUTE	, AND IT ANSWERED CAPITALLY. IT STIMULATED THE
MIS. PREFACE(24)	NEW BRASS PLATES ARE BEING INSCRIBED MONTESSORI	INSTITUTE	, AND WILL BE USED WHEN THE DOTTORESSA IS NO

INSTITUTED

JOAN EPILOG (163)	THE MAID, HAVING BEEN THE SUBJECT OF AN INQUIRY	INSTITUTED	BY THE BISHOP OF ORLEANS -- /JOAN/ (
DOCT PREFACE(44)	IN VIVISECTION, AS IN ALL THE OTHER TOLERATED AND	INSTITUTED	CRUELTIES, THIS ANTI-CLIMAX: THAT ONLY A

INSTITUTES

GETT PREFACE(227)	SHALL BE BROUGHT UP IN AN ATMOSPHERE OF LOVE, AND	INSTITUTES	A SYSTEM OF SEDULOUS ENDEARMENTS AND EXCHANGES OF
LION PREFACE(81)	IT TO ITS UTMOST CONCLUSIONS, AND DEVISING "	INSTITUTES	" FOR HARDHEADED ADULT SCOTS AND LITERAL SWISS,

INSTITUTION

GETT PREFACE(211)	THOUGH UNLIMITED, IS NOT REALLY A POPULAR	INSTITUTION	: IF YOU ARE A PERSON OF HIGH CASTE YOU PAY
MIS. PREFACE(85)	OF MARRIAGE, MARRIAGE IS NOT A SINGLE INVARIABLE	INSTITUTION	: IT CHANGES FROM CIVILIZATION TO CIVILIZATION,
POSN PREFACE(369)	BE AGREED THAT THE CENSORSHIP WAS AN ANTI-LIBERAL	INSTITUTION	AND AN ABOMINABLE NUISANCE TO BOOT, INDULGED HIM
BULL PREFACE(72)	WHICH WILL RECUR UNTIL THEY BECOME A PERMANENT	INSTITUTION	AND FINALLY DEVELOP INTO WHAT THE AMERICANS CALL
APPL PREFACE(179)	IN THE PARLIAMENT OF MAN WHEN THAT CELEBRATED	INSTITUTION	COMES INTO EXISTENCE. I DONT BELIEVE YOUR NAME
HART PREFACE(10)	CLAIMED. THE INQUISITION ITSELF WAS A LIBERAL	INSTITUTION	COMPARED TO THE GENERAL MEDICAL COUNCIL. THOSE
GETT PREFACE(253)	AS WE HAVE SEEN, IS NOT POSSIBLE AS A TYPICAL	INSTITUTION	IN A DEMOCRATIC COUNTRY WHERE THE NUMBERS OF THE
MRS PREFACE(162)	IS CONCERNED, THE CENSORSHIP IS THE MOST POPULAR	INSTITUTION	IN ENGLAND; AND THE PLAYWRIGHT WHO CRITICIZES IT
SUPR HANDBOK(175)	THEY CHOOSE. REVOLUTION IS THEREFORE A NATIONAL	INSTITUTION	IN ENGLAND; AND ITS ADVOCACY BY AN ENGLISHMAN
BULL PREFACE(40)	WITH ROPES ROUND THEIR NECKS. HE CAN ATTACK ANY	INSTITUTION	IN HIS COUNTRY WITHOUT BETRAYING IT TO FOREIGN
GETT PREFACE(243)	MRS WARREN'S PROFESSION, I HAVE SHEWN THAT THE	INSTITUTION	IN QUESTION IS AN ECONOMIC PHENOMENON, PRODUCED
SUPR HANDBOK(204)	IN SPITE OF THAT CHANGE, FLOGGING IS STILL AN	INSTITUTION	IN THE PUBLIC SCHOOL, IN THE MILITARY PRISON, ON
POSN PREFACE(398)	NO SCIENCE, NO ART, POSSIBLY NO ENGLAND. THE	INSTITUTION	IS AT ONCE ABSURDLY DESPOTIC AND ABJECTLY WEAK.
UNPL PREFACE(R18)	PORTS, IN PROPORTION AS THIS HORRIBLE DOMESTIC	INSTITUTION	IS BROKEN UP BY THE ACTIVE SOCIAL CIRCULATION OF
PHIL II (127)	MAY SOON SEE THE LAST OF THIS MOST OUTRAGEOUS	INSTITUTION	. CHARTERIS RETURNS. /CHARTERIS/ (AT THE DOOR)
APPL PREFACE(187)	BY THIS TIME THE BOY HAS GROWN UP AND BECOME AN	INSTITUTION	. HE PRESENTS HIMSELF TO THE NEW POSTMAN AS AN
CAPT II (249)	OUT, SHE MEANS TO MAKE HERSELF MATRON OF THIS	INSTITUTION	. I SPOSE ITS ALL RIGHT, ISN'T IT? /DRINKWATER/
BUOY III (38)	WIDOWER/ I HOLD THAT CONCUBINES ARE A NECESSARY	INSTITUTION	. IN A NATION WELLBRED BIOLOGICALLY THERE SHOULD
GENV IV (93)	FROM ALL THAT BY MY LEADERSHIP. I AM A DEMOCRATIC	INSTITUTION	. /NEWCOMER/ GOSH. YOU DEMOCRATIC! YOUVE
MIS. PREFACE(22)	TRUTH WAS, A BOY MEANT JUST SO MUCH A YEAR TO THE	INSTITUTION	. THAT WAS WHY HE WAS KEPT THERE AGAINST HIS
FOUN (217)	IN WHAT YOU MIGHT POLITELY CALL A SORT OF PUBLIC	INSTITUTION	. THEY FOUND ME ON THE DOORSTEP, YOU KNOW. MIGHT
GENV PREFACE(11)	IT HAS BECOME TOO RUINOUS TO BE TOLERATED AS AN	INSTITUTION	. WAR AND IMPERIALIST DIPLOMACY PERSIST NONE THE
GETT PREFACE(188)	OFFENCE WAS THAT HE ATTACKED MARRIAGE AS AN	INSTITUTION	. WE FEEL A STRANGE ANGUISH OF TERROR AND HATRED
BARB PREFACE(217)	SENTIMENTS WHICH LEAD TO IT AND SUPPORT IT AS AN	INSTITUTION	. WHAT ELSE CAN THEY DO? THEY KNOW, OF COURSE,
BUOY III (45)	/SIR F./ THEN MARRIAGE IS NOT A FAILURE AS AN	INSTITUTION	. WITH REASONABLE DIVORCE LAWS, NOT AT ALL. /HE/
BARB PREFACE(216)	GROW TO SOMETHING VALUABLE. ONE IS THE	INSTITUTION	OF A LEGAL MINIMUM WAGE. THE OTHER, OLD AGE
UNPL PREFACE(R24)	THEIR FULL CONTENT TO THE READER. THIS MEANS THE	INSTITUTION	OF A NEW ART; AND I DARESAY THAT BEFORE THESE
MILL IV (199)	AND SISTERHOOD, EVERY CHURCH AND CHAPEL, EVERY	INSTITUTION	OF EVERY KIND ON EARTH IS BUSY FROM MORNING TO
GETT PREFACE(194)	OF THAT SYSTEM WAS THE FAMILY AND THE	INSTITUTION	OF MARRIAGE AS WE HAVE IT TODAY IN ENGLAND.
GETT PREFACE(202)	CLUB OR IN A SET WHICH IS NOT HIS WIFE'S; AND THE	INSTITUTION	OF MARRIAGE ENJOYS THE CREDIT OF A DOMESTIC
GETT PREFACE(209)	AS HE HAS WIVES. THE NATURAL FOUNDATION OF THE	INSTITUTION	OF MONOGAMY IS NOT ANY INHERENT VICIOUSNESS IN
SUPR HANDBOK(220)	IN ENGLAND (WHERE THE QUOTIENT IS 1) BY THE	INSTITUTION	OF MONOGAMY. THE MODERN SENTIMENTAL TERM FOR THE
2TRU III (108)	OUT OF MISCHIEF. THEY WANT TO INTRODUCE THE ONLY	INSTITUTION	OF OURS THAT THEY ADMIRE. /THE ELDER/ AND PRAY
MIS. PREFACE(63)	IS INHUMAN AND UNNATURAL. WE MUST RECONSIDER OUR	INSTITUTION	OF THE COMING OF AGE, WHICH IS TOO LATE FOR SOME
MIS. PREFACE(83)	DRAWING IT AT SISTERS AND BROTHERS IS THAT THE	INSTITUTION	OF THE FAMILY COMPELS US TO SPEND OUR CHILDHOOD
3PLA PREFACE(R22)	KILLED FOR THE SAKE OF CONFERRING HIMSELF AS AN	INSTITUTION	ON OTHER COUNTRIES. IN THE COURTS CASES WILL BE
DEVL EPILOG (82)	THERE IS THE SAME RELUCTANCE TO DISCREDIT AN	INSTITUTION	OR TO " DO A MAN OUT OF HIS JOB." AT BOTTOM, OF
MTH3 (96)	I DO, OF COURSE; BUT DEMOCRACY-- /CONFUCIUS/ AN	INSTITUTION	PECULIAR TO CHINA, AND IT WAS NEVER REALLY A
MIS. PREFACE(34)	HUMAN SACRIFICE (A MUCH LESS SLAUGHTEROUS	INSTITUTION	). THERE IS EVERY REASON WHY A CHILD SHOULD NOT
POSN PREFACE(363)	MERE CAPRICE OF OPINION HAD TURNED AGAINST THE	INSTITUTION	; AND A REFORM WAS EXPECTED, EVIDENCE OR NO
BUOY III (38)	GOD OUT OF THE QUESTION. MARRIAGE IS A LEGAL	INSTITUTION	; AND GOD HAS NOTHING TO DO WITH LEGAL
SIM II (80)	THE DEAN PREACHING TO THE CHOIR, AT THE ROYAL	INSTITUTION	SIR RUTHLESS BONEHEAD, EGREGIOUS PROFESSOR OF
2TRU PREFACE(22)	IT STILL TAKES SOME CONVICTION TO REPUDIATE AN	INSTITUTION	SO WELL SPOKEN OF AS PRIVATE PROPERTY; BUT THE
GETT (287)	THE SITUATION; BUT IN ENGLAND WE ALWAYS LET AN	INSTITUTION	STRAIN ITSELF UNTIL IT BREAKS. IVE TOLD OUR LAST
MRS PREFACE(163)	AND NOT MERELY A CONSEQUENCE OF THE FORM THE	INSTITUTION	TAKES IN LONDON, NO DOUBT THERE IS A STAGGERING
LION PREFACE(72)	IT IS A FORM OF SUICIDE. NOW TO SAY OF ANY	INSTITUTION	THAT IT IS INCOMPATIBLE WITH BOTH THE
PYGM EPILOG (300)	A HUMBLE PERSONAL APPEAL TO THE DIRECTOR OF THAT	INSTITUTION	TO RECOMMEND A COURSE BEARING ON THE FLOWER
BARB PREFACE(234)	TO AMERICANS WHO HAVE MADE DIVORCE A PUBLIC	INSTITUTION	TURNING THE FACE OF EUROPE INTO ONE HUGE
POSN PREFACE(397)	IS MADE DELIGHTFUL AND VIRTUE BANNED BY THE VERY	INSTITUTION	WHICH IS SUPPORTED ON THE UNDERSTANDING THAT IT
MRS PREFACE(171)	OF VIOLATING MORALS IT ONLY VIOLATES A LEGAL	INSTITUTION	WHICH IS IN MANY RESPECTS OPPRESSIVE AND
GETT PREFACE(256)	EMPTY THE BABY OUT WITH THE BATH BY ABOLISHING AN	INSTITUTION	WHICH NEEDS NOTHING MORE THAN A LITTLE OBVIOUS
LION PREFACE(69)	YET CLING WITH FEROCITY TO THE SACREDNESS OF THE	INSTITUTION	WHICH PROVIDES A REFUGE FROM CELIBACY. FOR
UNPL PREFACE(R25)	TO SOME THAT WORST OF BLUNDERING ABOMINATIONS, AN	INSTITUTION	WHICH SOCIETY HAS OUTGROWN BUT NOT MODIFIED, AND
SIM I (49)	LAWS AND RELIGIOUS RITUALS, AND FINALLY A GREAT	INSTITUTION	WHICH THEY CALLED THE SUPERFAMILY. IT BEGAN BY
GETT PREFACE(215)	A STATESMAN HAS TO PAUSE BEFORE MEDDLING WITH AN	INSTITUTION	WHICH, UNENDURABLE AS ITS DRAWBACKS ARE,
SUPR HANDBOK(179)	ON PROPERTY. THE KNELL OF THAT OVERRATED	INSTITUTION	WILL NOT SOUND UNTIL IT IS FELT TO CONFLICT WITH
DOCT PREFACE(15)	BEEN TRAINED AS DOMESTIC SERVANTS IN SOME HUGE	INSTITUTION	WITH LIFTS, VACUUM CLEANERS, ELECTRIC LIGHTING,
POSN PREFACE(394)	IMMEDIATELY CONCERNED, THE INHERENT VICES OF THE	INSTITUTION	WOULD NOT BE APPRECIABLY LESS DISASTROUS. THEY
POSN PREFACE(419)	GAVE HIM A SALARY FOR DOING NOTHING? THE	INSTITUTION	WOULD NOT LAST A YEAR, EXCEPT AS A JOB FOR
DOCT PREFACE(27)	HIGHLY ORGANIZED AS A PUBLIC SERVICE IN A PUBLIC	INSTITUTION	, AND SUCH CHEAP, NASTY, DANGEROUS AND
2TRU PREFACE(7)	AND MAINTAIN THE TOTALISATOR AS A NATIONAL	INSTITUTION	, AND TO PRODUCE UNLIMITED DAYDREAMS OF BEQUESTS
GETT PREFACE(243)	ON HIM AFTER THE HIRING IS ENDED. AND SUCH AN	INSTITUTION	, AS WE KNOW, EXISTS AMONG US. IT IS COMMONLY
POSN PREFACE(392)	PRESENT ARRANGEMENT IS NOT ONLY CRITICIZED AS AN	INSTITUTION	, BUT RESENTED AS AN INSULT. THE DIPLOMATIC
POSN PREFACE(368)	KIND, DEMANDED, NOT THE ABOLITION OF THE	INSTITUTION	, BUT SUCH A REFORM AS MIGHT MAKE IT CONSISTENT
GENV I (47)	HOW WOULD YOU LIKE IT IF OUR CHIEF CULTURAL	INSTITUTION	, ENDOWED BY OUR GOVERNMENT, THE KOMINTERN, WERE
MRS PREFACE(171)	WELL. YET GAMBLING IS A VICE, AND BOOKMAKING AN	INSTITUTION	, FOR WHICH THERE IS ABSOLUTELY NOTHING TO BE
GENV PREFACE(5)	NOBODY NOTICED HOW COMPLETELY WAR, AS AN	INSTITUTION	, HAD REDUCED ITSELF TO ABSURDITY. WHEN GERMANY
NEVR II (254)	IS YOUR OBJECTION AN OBJECTION TO MARRIAGE AS AN	INSTITUTION	, OR MERELY AN OBJECTION TO MARRYING ME
POSN PREFACE(409)	AND MORALS, OR THAT THE THEATRE IS AN UNDESIRABLE	INSTITUTION	, OR THAT THERE ARE ALREADY AS MANY THEATRES AS
DOCT III (146)	IS THE COURT, AN ESSENTIALLY SOCIAL-DEMOCRATIC	INSTITUTION	, SUPPORTED OUT OF PUBLIC FUNDS BY THE PUBLIC
ROCK PREFACE(189)	HERETICAL, AND REVOLUTIONARY. THAT SOUND CATHOLIC	INSTITUTION	, THE DEVIL'S ADVOCATE, MUST BE PRIVILEGED AS

INSTITUTIONAL

MILL PREFACE(111)	DIFFICULT TO ATTACK A PERSONAL DESPOTISM THAN AN	INSTITUTIONAL	ONE. MONARCHS CAN BE ABOLISHED: THEY HAVE BEEN
MILL PREFACE(110)	REFORM ON THE GROUND THAT TO ABOLISH ALL THE	INSTITUTIONAL	TYRANNIES WOULD ONLY DELIVER THE COUNTRY

INSTITUTION'S

SUPR HANDBOK(183)	CONFIDENCE OF THE PUBLIC IN THE STABILITY OF THE	INSTITUTION'S	NAME, MAKES IT ALL THE EASIER TO ALTER ITS

INSTITUTIONS

BULL IV (176)	HERE: I SHALL RAISE WAGES: I SHALL FOUND PUBLIC	INSTITUTIONS	: A LIBRARY, A POLYTECHNIC (UNDENOMINATIONAL,
BARB I (256)	FACE THAT HISTORY TELLS US OF ONLY TWO SUCCESSFUL	INSTITUTIONS	: ONE THE UNDERSHAFT FIRM, AND THE OTHER THE
SUPR III (119)	DETERMINEDLY) I SAY THE MOST LICENTIOUS OF HUMAN	INSTITUTIONS	: THAT IS THE SECRET OF ITS POPULARITY. AND A
JOAN PREFACE(25)	EVERYTHING THAT VOLTAIRE RIGHTEOUSLY HATED IN THE	INSTITUTIONS	AND FASHIONS OF HIS OWN DAY. HE MADE JOAN
GENV I (45)	WOULD YOU IN YOUR BLIND HATRED OF BRITISH	INSTITUTIONS	AND OF ALL LIBERTY OF THOUGHT AND SPEECH, MAKE
SUPR HANDBOK(211)	IN THE REPUDIATED DIRECTION; SO THAT ALL SORTS OF	INSTITUTIONS	AND PUBLIC AUTHORITIES WILL UNDER SOME PRETEXT
GETT PREFACE(205)	WHICH ARE TO BE OBEYED: THAT IS, TO MAKING NEW	INSTITUTIONS	AND SCRAPPING OLD ONES, THEN YOU NEED
GETT PREFACE(194)	UNIVERSITY, DOES, IN SPITE OF THE FACT THAT THESE	INSTITUTIONS	ARE CLASS WARPED AND IN SOME RESPECTS QUITE
2TRU II (69)	GOES SHOUTING THEM ALL OVER THE PLACE, THE	INSTITUTIONS	ARE ROCKING AND SPLITTING AND SUNDERING. THEY
MIS. PREFACE(67)	COMPREHENSION AND MAINTENANCE OF SUCH CIVILIZED	INSTITUTIONS	AS HAVE BEEN INTRODUCED BY BENEVOLENT AND
LION EPILOG (149)	THOSE WHO ARE NOT GOOD ENOUGH FOR ESTABLISHED	INSTITUTIONS	AS WELL AS THOSE WHO ARE TOO GOOD FOR THEM. BUT
GETT PREFACE(183)	GIVE UP THE IDEA OF REFORMING OUR MARRIAGE	INSTITUTIONS	BY PRIVATE ENTERPRISE AND PERSONAL
GETT PREFACE(191)	CHOOSING AND MAINTAINING ITS RELIGIOUS AND MORAL	INSTITUTIONS	BY THEIR POWERS OF SOCIAL PERSECUTION, THEY
SUPR III (125)	ON THESE FLATTERIES. IS IT ANY WONDER THAT THE	INSTITUTIONS	DO NOT WORK SMOOTHLY? /THE STATUE/ WHAT USED
MIS. PREFACE(19)	BY ORGANIZED PROFESSIONAL ENTERPRISE IN LARGE	INSTITUTIONS	ESTABLISHED FOR THE PURPOSE. AND IT IS TO SUCH
GETT PREFACE(235)	WHEN IT IS DIFFICULT TO SEE ANYTHING IN OUR SEX	INSTITUTIONS	EXCEPT A POLICE DES MOEURS KEEPING THE FIELD
MIS. PREFACE(32)	ACQUAINTANCES; AND THE FIRST OBJECT OF ALL OUR	INSTITUTIONS	FOR CHILDREN IS SEGREGATION. IF, FOR EXAMPLE,
DOCT PREFACE(29)	ORGANIZED LABORATORIES, HOSPITALS, AND PUBLIC	INSTITUTIONS	GENERALLY, IT UNLUCKILY HAPPENS THAT THE
3PLA PREFACE(R23)	IF IT HAS TO DRAG DEMOCRACY DOWN WITH IT. FOR ALL	INSTITUTIONS	HAVE IN THE LONG RUN TO LIVE BY THE NATURE OF
2TRU II (69)	BEFORE-- TRUTHS THAT THE MAKERS OF OUR DOMESTIC	INSTITUTIONS	HAVE TRIED TO IGNORE. AND NOW THAT SWEETIE GOES
BARB PREFACE(243)	ONCE HE IS BROUGHT TO REPUDIATE THE LAWS AND	INSTITUTIONS	HE KNOWS, HE WILL REPUDIATE THE VERY CONCEPTION
JOAN 4 (105)	A MOMENT; AND REMEMBER THAT THERE ARE TEMPORAL	INSTITUTIONS	IN THE WORLD AS WELL AS SPIRITUAL ONES. I AND
MIS. PREFACE(55)	SUCH OBSCENITIES ARE MADE POINTS OF HONOR, OR OF	INSTITUTIONS	IN WHICH THEY ARE AN ACCEPTED PART OF THE DAILY
GETT PREFACE(206)	OF TAKING ADVANTAGE OF THIS POWER TO REFORM OUR	INSTITUTIONS	IS DEFEAT BY A VEHEMENT " SWING OF THE
MIS. PREFACE(103)	DIFFICULTY OF COMBINING LAW AND ORDER WITH FREE	INSTITUTIONS	IS NOT A NATURAL ONE. IT IS A MATTER OF
MRS PREFACE(164)	FROM CHALLENGING CURRENT CONCEPTIONS AND EXISTING	INSTITUTIONS	. ALL PROGRESS IS INITIATED BY CHALLENGING
APPL I (230)	WITH MUCH LESS HUMBUG ABOUT IT THAN MANY OLDER	INSTITUTIONS	. BUT IT MEANS, NOT THAT THE PEOPLE GOVERN, BUT
MRS PREFACE(164)	CONCEPTIONS, AND EXECUTED BY SUPPLANTING EXISTING	INSTITUTIONS	. CONSEQUENTLY THE FIRST CONDITION OF PROGRESS
GETT (355)	IN THE GRIP OF THIS WORLD, AT LEAST RESPECT ITS	INSTITUTIONS	. DO YOU BELIEVE IN MARRIAGE OR DO YOU NOT?
LION PREFACE(71)	THAT IT WILL CURE WHAT JESUS OBJECTED TO IN THESE	INSTITUTIONS	. HE MADE NO COMPREHENSIVE STUDY OF THEM: HE
ROCK PREFACE(158)	HIM WAS TO THROW OVER CIVILIZATION AND ALL ITS	INSTITUTIONS	. HISTORY HAS BORNE OUT THE CASE AGAINST HIM;
BULL IV (155)	REMEDIED BY FREEDOM, SELF-GOVERNMENT, AND ENGLISH	INSTITUTIONS	. I THINK SO, NOT BECAUSE I AM AN ENGLISHMAN,
SUPR HANDBOK(184)	TOOK PLACE IN A COMMUNITY WHICH DISCARDED BOTH	INSTITUTIONS	. III: THE PERFECTIONIST EXPERIMENT AT ONEIDA
MTH4 I (144)	IN A COUNTRY WHERE NOBODY UNDERSTANDS CIVILIZED	INSTITUTIONS	. (HE COLLAPSES ON THE BOLLARD, STRUGGLING
MTH4 I (164)	I HAVE SEEN THEIR WORK AND LIVED UNDER THEIR	INSTITUTIONS	. LIKE ALL YOUNG THINGS I REBELLED AGAINST
BUOY III (38)	INSTITUTION; AND GOD HAS NOTHING TO DO WITH LEGAL	INSTITUTIONS	. /MRS THIRDBORN/ GOD KEEPS BUTTING IN SOMEHOW.
SUPR HANDBOK(185)	IN SPITE OF THE INTERFERENCE OF MAN'S BLUNDERING	INSTITUTIONS	. THE EXISTENCE OF NOYES SIMPLIFIED THE
SUPR HANDBOK(185)	THAN ORDINARY FOLK UNDER THE HARROW OF BOTH THESE	INSTITUTIONS	. YET THEIR SUPERMAN HIMSELF ADMITTED THAT THIS
MRS PREFACE(151)	REVOLUTIONARY CRITIC OF OUR MOST RESPECTED SOCIAL	INSTITUTIONS	KEPT ME SO CONTINUALLY IN HOT WATER THAT THE
SUPR I (37)	SO USEFUL. CONSTRUCTION CUMBERS THE GROUND WITH	INSTITUTIONS	MADE BY BUSYBODIES. DESTRUCTION CLEARS IT AND
MILL PREFACE(135)	AS THEY ARE TO US UNDER POLITICAL AND ECONOMIC	INSTITUTIONS	MADE TO ENCOURAGE WILLIAM THE CONQUEROR TO SLAY
GETT PREFACE(204)	OF MEN WHOM HE CAN TRUST TO DEVIZE OR SUPPORT	INSTITUTIONS	MAKING FOR THE COMMON WELFARE. THIS IS HIGHLY
GETT PREFACE(214)	AT THEIR ESCAPE. OUR DEMOCRATIC AND MATRIMONIAL	INSTITUTIONS	MAY HAVE THEIR MERITS: AT ALL EVENTS THEY ARE
MIS. PREFACE(62)	EDUCATED TO CHALLENGE ALL THE MOST SACRED	INSTITUTIONS	OF HIS COUNTRY, THE HOUSEHOLDS THEY WERE
JOAN PREFACE(23)	STRUCTURES AS THE GREAT ECCLESIASTICAL AND SOCIAL	INSTITUTIONS	OF THE MIDDLE AGES. SHE HAD A HORROR OF
BARB PREFACE(234)	AS OUR PERSISTENT ATTEMPTS TO FOUND POLITICAL	INSTITUTIONS	ON A BASIS OF SOCIAL INEQUALITY HAVE ALWAYS
BARB PREFACE(234)	WILL AMERICANS PLEASE NOTE-- TO FOUND MORAL	INSTITUTIONS	ON A BASIS OF MORAL INEQUALITY CAN LEAD TO
SUPR HANDBOK(194)	ARE NOT RADICAL, BUT ARE MERE REACTIONS OF OUR	INSTITUTIONS	ON OUR VERY VIRTUES. THE ANARCHIST, THE FABIAN,
PLES PREFACE(R19)	OF OUR PERSISTENT ATTEMPTS TO FOUND OUR	INSTITUTIONS	ON THE IDEALS SUGGESTED TO OUR IMAGINATIONS BY
DEST SD(151)	THEIR AUSTRIAN CONQUERORS, AND CONFER REPUBLICAN	INSTITUTIONS	ON THEM; SO THAT IN INCIDENTALLY LOOTING THEM
SUPR III (125)	PREFERRED TO STAND UP TO THOSE FACTS AND BUILD	INSTITUTIONS	ON THEIR RECOGNITION. YOU PREFER TO PROPITIATE
SUPR III (125)	AND THEIR LOVING KINDNESS; AND TO BASE YOUR	INSTITUTIONS	ON THESE FLATTERIES. IS IT ANY WONDER THAT THE
BARB PREFACE(242)	CENTURIES, THROWS OUR LEGAL AND INDUSTRIAL	INSTITUTIONS	OUT OF DATE, ANARCHISM BECOMES ALMOST A
ROCK PREFACE(172)	THE WORLD AS OUR PSEUDO-DEMOCRATIC PARLIAMENTARY	INSTITUTIONS	REDUCE THEMSELVES MORE AND MORE DISASTROUSLY TO
CAPT NOTES (302)	ONE OF THE EVILS OF THE PRETENCE THAT OUR	INSTITUTIONS	REPRESENT ABSTRACT PRINCIPLES OF JUSTICE
SUPR III (119)	A RAP. MARRIAGE IS THE MOST LICENTIOUS OF HUMAN	INSTITUTIONS	-- /ANA/ JUAN! /THE STATUE/ (PROTESTING)
LION PREFACE(69)	IT IS USELESS TO LOOK FOR ANY CONSISTENCY IN SUCH	INSTITUTIONS	; AND IT IS ONLY BY CONTINUAL REFORM AND
PPP (196)	LAUGH AT MY MANNERS, AT MY BRAINS, AT MY NATIONAL	INSTITUTIONS	; BUT IF YOU LAUGH AT MY CLOTHES, ONE OF US
BARB PREFACE(232)	BY TAKING HIS OWN ADVICE; HE ENDOWS EDUCATIONAL	INSTITUTIONS	; HE SUPPORTS CHARITIES; HE DIES FINALLY IN THE
GETT PREFACE(185)	OF MARRIAGE MEAN ANY OF THESE WIDELY DIFFERENT	INSTITUTIONS	; SOMETIMES HE DOES NOT MEAN MARRIAGE AT ALL.
JOAN PREFACE(23)	AND WHERE SCHOLARSHIP WAS THE ONLY CLUE TO	INSTITUTIONS	SHE WAS IN THE DARK, AND BROKE HER SHINS
POSN PREFACE(394)	AS THE CHURCH, PRESS, OR PLATFORM, BUT THAT THESE	INSTITUTIONS	SHOULD BE CENSORED AS STRICTLY AS THE STAGE. IT
MILL PREFACE(133)	THE BEGINNING IN THE INTERESTS OF ESTABLISHED	INSTITUTIONS	SO EFFECTUALLY THAT HE REMAINS ALL HIS LIFE
HART PREFACE(28)	AT OUR ANCIENT PUBLIC SCHOOLS, AND THE CHEAPER	INSTITUTIONS	THAT APE THEM WILL BE QUITE SUFFICIENT TO KEEP
MIS. PREFACE(69)	ORGANIZED: NO PARENT, RICH OR POOR, CAN CHOOSE	INSTITUTIONS	THAT DO NOT EXIST; AND THE PRIVATE ENTERPRISE
MILL PREFACE(136)	MEANS DOMINATE: IT IS UP TO US TO SO ORDER OUR	INSTITUTIONS	THAT YOU SHALL NOT OPPRESS US, NOR BEQUEATH ANY
JOAN PREFACE(7)	THE INQUISITION. THE EASIEST WAY TO MAKE THESE	INSTITUTIONS	THE VILLAINS OF A MELODRAMA WAS TO MAKE THE
GETT PREFACE(257)	FEAR OF CONSEQUENCES. WE MUST FINALLY ADAPT OUR	INSTITUTIONS	TO HUMAN NATURE. IN THE LONG RUN OUR PRESENT
BULL PREFACE(62)	LESSONS OF THAT ADVERSITY WHICH COMES FINALLY TO	INSTITUTIONS	WHICH MAKE THEMSELVES ABHORRED BY THE ASPIRING
LION PREFACE(69)	OURSELVES, WE ARE THUS LED TO DEVISE MARRIAGE	INSTITUTIONS	WHICH WILL AT THE SAME TIME SECURE
MIS. PREFACE(78)	FOR NOBODY NOW ALIVE CAN IMAGINE WHAT CUSTOMS AND	INSTITUTIONS	WOULD GROW UP IN SOCIETIES OF FREE CHILDREN.
BARB III (313)	/CUSINS/ HE SAID ALL THE CHARITABLE	INSTITUTIONS	WOULD BE DOWN ON HIM LIKE KITES ON A BATTLE
SUPR HANDBOK(177)	THIS IS NO NEW CONCLUSION. THE DESPAIR OF	INSTITUTIONS	, AND THE INEXORABLE " YE MUST BE BORN AGAIN,"
SUPR PREFACE(R13)	FINDS HIMSELF IN MORTAL CONFLICT WITH EXISTING	INSTITUTIONS	, AND DEFENDS HIMSELF BY FRAUD AND FORCE AS
UNPL PREFACE(R16)	EXTOL HIM AS THE MOST SALUTARY OF ENGLISH	INSTITUTIONS	, AND SPREAD THEMSELVES WITH UNCTIOUS FLATTERY
METH PREFACE(R29)	TRADES AND CLASSES WERE THE BEST KNOWN OF SOCIAL	INSTITUTIONS	, AND IN SOME CASES OF PUBLIC NUISANCES.
MIS. PREFACE(30)	BELONG TO A BYGONE ORDER OF EDUCATIONAL IDEAS AND	INSTITUTIONS	, AND THAT SCHOOLS ARE NOT NOW A BIT LIKE MY
SUPR HANDBOK(177)	CHANGE THAT IS REAL. THE MERE TRANSFIGURATION OF	INSTITUTIONS	, AS FROM MILITARY AND PRIESTLY DOMINANCE TO
GETT PREFACE(213)	TRUSTS THEM, AS SCHOOLMISTRESSES AND MATRONS OF	INSTITUTIONS	, MORE THAN WOMEN OF ANY OTHER TYPE WHEN IT IS
BARB PREFACE(213)	CRITICISM OF OUR MORAL, RELIGIOUS AND JURIDICAL	INSTITUTIONS	, MUST NECESSARILY BE EITHER A FOREIGN IMPORT,
FANY III (323)	OUR NARROW IDEAS, OUR PREJUDICES, OUR OBSOLETE	INSTITUTIONS	, OUR INSUFFERABLE PEDANTRY ON THE WORLD BY
BARB PREFACE(243)	VERY CONCEPTION OF LAW AND THE VERY GROUNDWORK OF	INSTITUTIONS	, RIDICULING HUMAN RIGHTS, EXTOLLING BRAINLESS
MTH3 (131)	UNTIL THEY GROW UP TO BE CAPABLE OF ADOPTING OUR	INSTITUTIONS	, THAT RACE IS THE ENGLISH RACE. IT IS THE ONLY
ROCK PREFACE(163)	NOT PLANNED AND THOUGHT OUT AT LEISURE, THE TWO	INSTITUTIONS	, THE OGPU AND THE ORDINARY POLICE
MIS. (199)	LET THE HUMAN RACE BE BROUGHT UP IN	INSTITUTIONS	! /HYPATIA/ OH YES. HOW JOLLY! YOU AND I

INSTRUCT

CAPT NOTES (306)	BY MAL-ERR-ERR: NOT AT ALL A BAD MAKESHIFT TO	INSTRUCT	A LONDONER, BUT OUT OF THE QUESTION ELSEWHERE IN
MILL I (142)	YOU THAT IT IS THE LAW. MY FATHER ALWAYS HAD TO	INSTRUCT	HIS LAWYERS IN THE LAW WHENEVER HE DID ANYTHING
BUOY PREFACE(4)	BE BURNT RATHER THAN RECANT HIS " I DONT KNOW.	INSTRUCT	ME"? WHEN I WAS A SMALL BOY I SAW A PROFESSIONAL
SUPR IV (170)	FOLLOWING THEM UP, PAUSES FOR A MOMENT TO	INSTRUCT	TANNER). DONT LIFT ER ED, MR TANNER: LET IT GO FLAT
DOCT PREFACE(7)	TO ANSWER IT AT ALL. AND ON THIS THE JUDGE HAD TO	INSTRUCT	THE JURY THAT THEY MUST ACQUIT THE PRISONER. THUS A
FANY PROLOG (268)	ONE OF THOSE IN WHICH MEMBERS OF FABIAN SOCIETIES	INSTRUCT	THEIR GRANDMOTHERS IN THE ART OF MILKING DUCKS, AND
LION I (111)	THAT WE ARE NOW ENTERING ROME. YOU WILL	INSTRUCT	THEM THAT ONCE INSIDE THE GATES OF ROME THEY ARE IN
LION I (111)	OF THE MARCH CANNOT BE PERMITTED HERE. YOU WILL	INSTRUCT	THEM TO SHAVE EVERY DAY, NOT EVERY WEEK. YOU WILL
GENV IV (127)	IT KNOWS THE TRUTH AS GOD KNOWS IT, AND WILL	INSTRUCT	US ACCORDINGLY. ANYONE WHO QUESTIONS ITS DECISION
FABL PREFACE(75)	FAMILY BY A BRIBE OF ROAST MEAT. LATER ARTICLES	INSTRUCT	US TO LOVE OUR FELLOW-CREATURES, YET TO OBEY AN
MTH5 (219)	A CHILD. UNTIL THEN YOUR YOUNG COMPANIONS WILL	INSTRUCT	YOU IN WHATEVER IS NECESSARY. YOU ARE NOT FORBIDDEN
MILL I (142)	IT UP IN MY LAW BOOKS. /EPIFANIA/ YOU NEED NOT, I	INSTRUCT	YOU THAT IT IS THE LAW. MY FATHER ALWAYS HAD TO
LION I (111)	CHRISTIANS) SILENNNNCE! /THE CAPTAIN/ YOU ARE TO	INSTRUCT	YOUR MEN THAT ALL INTIMACY WITH CHRISTIAN PRISONERS

INSTRUCTED

GENV PREFACE(16)	THE NEED FOR CONFINING AUTHORITY TO THE	INSTRUCTED	AND CAPABLE HAS BEEN DEMONSTRATED BY TERRIBLE
FABL PREFACE(81)	DESCRIBES HOW THE ISRAELITES IN CAPTIVITY WERE	INSTRUCTED	BY A DEIFIED JONATHAN WILD TO STEAL THE JEWELRY
INCA (245)	JEWEL CASE, AND RELAPSING INTO SOLEMNITY) I AM	INSTRUCTED	BY THE ALLERHOCHST TO TAKE A CAREFUL NOTE OF YOUR

OVER PREFACE(159)	ABERRATIONS AND ABSURDITIES TO WHICH NO SANELY	INSTRUCTED	COMMUNITY WOULD CALL ANY ATTENTION. WE CREATE AN
DOCT PREFACE(73)	OF WELL-TO-DO, HIGHLY CULTIVATED, AND THOROUGHLY	INSTRUCTED	FREE PERSONS IN A POSITION TO TAKE CARE OF
LION PREFACE(74)	INTELLIGENT HEATHEN MAY STUDY, IF THEY WOULD BE	INSTRUCTED	IN IT BY MODERN BOOKS, IN SAMUEL BUTLER'S NOVEL,
MRS PREFACE(152)	OUR LEGISLATORS AND JOURNALISTS WERE NOT BETTER	INSTRUCTED	. IN 1902 THE STAGE SOCIETY, TECHNICALLY A CLUB
ARMS III (59)	(IRONICALLY) INDEED! I AM WILLING TO BE	INSTRUCTED	. (HE SITS ON THE OTTOMAN, SPRAWLING
FABL PREFACE(88)	PUBLIC SCHOOLMASTERS. EVEN POLICE CONSTABLES ARE	INSTRUCTED	. YET FOR THE MINISTERS WHO ARE SUPPORTED TO
MILL I (142)	YOU ARE WRONG. I NEVER UTTER A LIBEL. MY FATHER	INSTRUCTED	ME MOST CAREFULLY IN THE LAW OF LIBEL. IF I
BUOY IV (55)	YOU THAT I EXPLAINED TO YOUR SECOND FAMILY AS YOU	INSTRUCTED	ME, THAT THE SOURCE OF THEIR INCOMES WOULD DRY UP
CATH 1 (165)	I HAVE SERVED AGAINST THE REBELS; AND I AM	INSTRUCTED	TO PLACE MYSELF AT THE DISPOSAL OF HER MAJESTY,
BULL PREFACE(58)	FOR THEM TO OFFEND THE OCCUPATION WERE	INSTRUCTED	TO " DEFEND" THE PRISONERS. FAR FROM DEFENDING
		INSTRUCTING	
LION PREFACE(87)	WHICH ARE NOW OF PRESSING IMPORTANCE, AND	INSTRUCTING	HIS DISCIPLES TO CARRY THEM OUT IN THEIR DAILY
GENV IV (125)	TO HIS STOCKBROKER, GENTLEMEN. HE IS	INSTRUCTING	HIS STOCKBROKER TO SELL GILT-EDGED IN ANY
ROCK I (197)	KNOW HOW. IN THE SECOND, THEY ARE AFRAID. I AM	INSTRUCTING	MY AGENTS TO PRESS ALL THE TALKING SOCIETIES,
DEVL EPILOG (81)	ON HIS RETURN HOME." THESE WERE THE DISPATCHES	INSTRUCTING	SIR WILLIAM HOWE, WHO WAS IN NEW YORK, TO EFFECT
SIM PREFACE(4)	THAT NOTHING CAN FILL": HE PROPOSED TO FILL IT BY	INSTRUCTING	THE TRIBESMAN ON THE ASSUMPTION THAT THE
		INSTRUCTION	
LADY (248)	NAME FOR IT, A NATIONAL THEATRE, FOR THE BETTER	INSTRUCTION	AND GRACING OF YOUR MAJESTY'S SUBJECTS.
MILL PREFACE(113)	AND RULE FROM DAY TO DAY: HE MUST, BY SCHOOL	INSTRUCTION	AND PRINTED PROPAGANDA, CREATE AND MAINTAIN AN
GENV PREFACE(16)	IGNORANCE AND DELUSION IS CURABLE BY SIMPLE	INSTRUCTION	AS TO THE FACTS WITHOUT ANY INCREASE OF
MIS. PREFACE(96)	RELIGION IN ABSTRACT TERMS. THE OBJECT OF A MORAL	INSTRUCTION	BOOK IS NOT TO BE RATIONAL, SCIENTIFIC, EXACT,
MIS. PREFACE(96)	ELISHA AND THE BEARS. TO THE AUTHORS OF THE MORAL	INSTRUCTION	BOOKS IT IS IN THE LAST DEGREE REPREHENSIBLE. IT
MIS. PREFACE(96)	AND THAT NO CHILD ON EARTH CAN STAND MORAL	INSTRUCTION	BOOKS OR CATECHISMS OR ANY OTHER STATEMENT OF
JOAN PREFACE(13)	ILLUSIONPROOF GENIUS. THEY CAME TO JOAN AS AN	INSTRUCTION	FROM HER COUNSEL, AS SHE CALLED HER VISIONARY
MIS. PREFACE(25)	CERTAINLY HAVE PESTERED FOR INFORMATION AND	INSTRUCTION	IF I COULD HAVE GOT INTO ANY DECENT HUMAN
GETT PREFACE(251)	SHAMEFUL AND SINFUL WE SHALL HAVE NO SYSTEMATIC	INSTRUCTION	IN SEXUAL HYGIENE, BECAUSE SUCH LECTURES AS ARE
HART PREFACE(6)	KEEP FASHIONABLE SOCIETY GOING WITHOUT ANY	INSTRUCTION	IN SOCIOLOGY. THE CHERRY ORCHARD. THE HEARTBREAK
MIS. PREFACE(29)	CONSIDERATIONS OF MERE DECORUM, FOR GIVING PROPER	INSTRUCTION	IN THE FACTS OF SEX. THOSE WHO OBJECT TO IT (
MIS. (147)	LET THEIR CHILDREN GO OUT INTO THE WORLD WITHOUT	INSTRUCTION	IN THE DANGERS AND TEMPTATIONS THEY WERE GOING
METH PREFACE(R16)	OF HIGH EXPLOSIVES IS REWARDED AND DIGNIFIED:	INSTRUCTION	IN THE MANUFACTURE OF THE WEAPONS, BATTLESHIPS,
METH PREFACE(R15)	AND HERE COMES THE HORROR OF IT-- OUR TECHNICAL	INSTRUCTION	IS HONEST AND EFFICIENT. THE PUBLIC SCHOOLBOY
CLEO PRO1 (93)	AND NOW I LEAVE YOU; FOR YE ARE A DULL FOLK, AND	INSTRUCTION	IS WASTED ON YOU; AND I HAD NOT SPOKEN SO MUCH
SIM PREFACE(4)	I BELIEVE THEY ARE CAPABLE ENOUGH AND ONLY LACK	INSTRUCTION	. I WONDER HOW MANY OF THEM HAVE GIVEN SERIOUS
CLEO PRO2 (96)	/BELZANOR/ O BARBAROUS PERSIAN, HEAR MY	INSTRUCTION	. IN EGYPT THE BEARER OF GOOD TIDINGS IS
MIS. PREFACE(57)	BY A COMIC PAPER AS A CAPITAL JOKE. TECHNICAL	INSTRUCTION	. TECHNICAL INSTRUCTION TEMPTS TO VIOLENCE (AS
MIS. PREFACE(96)	LEAGUES. AND NOW THE VOICES OF OUR MORAL	INSTRUCTION	LEAGUES WILL BE LIFTED, ASKING WHETHER THERE IS
MIS. PREFACE(96)	AS DR WATTS AND IN FACT FATHOMS DEEPER. MORAL	INSTRUCTION	LEAGUES. AND NOW THE VOICES OF OUR MORAL
MILL PREFACE(134)	LONG AND PERILOUSLY OVERDUE. IN THE DIRECTION AND	INSTRUCTION	OF OUR CHILDREN'S MINDS POLITICALLY AND
HART PREFACE(29)	TO KEEP THE TWO GOING UNTIL THE NEXT WAR. FOR THE	INSTRUCTION	OF THAT GENERATION I LEAVE THESE PAGES AS A
JOAN 6 (139)	SEEKING YOUR SOUL'S PERDITION. DO YOU ACCEPT THE	INSTRUCTION	OF THE CHURCH? /JOAN/ I ACCEPT THE MESSENGER OF
LION PREFACE(100)	GOVERNMENT, IS DELIBERATELY LEAVING THE RELIGIOUS	INSTRUCTION	OF THESE NEGROES IN THE HANDS OF MISSIONS OF
BULL II (100)	NOT FOR THE LIKE OF YOU, PATSY, TO GO BEHIND THE	INSTRUCTION	OF YOUR PARISH PRIEST AND SET YOURSELF UP TO
HART PREFACE(8)	PRUSSIA THIS RELIGION; AND PRUSSIA BETTERED OUR	INSTRUCTION	SO EFFECTIVELY THAT WE PRESENTLY FOUND OURSELVES
GETT PREFACE(213)	THE WORK OF GOVERNING; AND YET WE HAVE TAKEN HIS	INSTRUCTION	SO LITTLE TO HEART THAT WE ARE AT PRESENT
MIS. PREFACE(57)	A CAPITAL JOKE. TECHNICAL INSTRUCTION. TECHNICAL	INSTRUCTION	TEMPTS TO VIOLENCE (AS A SHORT CUT) MORE THAN
SIM PREFACE(8)	METHOD CALLED SECULAR EDUCATION, BUT BY POSITIVE	INSTRUCTION	THAT THERE IS NO PERSONAL LIFE AFTER DEATH FOR
BUOY III (33)	ON TO ANOTHER MATTER. MR BUOYANT HAS ADDED TO HIS	INSTRUCTION	THIS SENTENCE. " MY ELDER DAUGHTER IS PROVIDED
GENV PREFACE(15)	ME IN SPITE OF POPE PIUS THE NINTH'S HUMANE	INSTRUCTION	TO THEM TO ABSOLVE ME ON THE PLEA OF INVINCIBLE
SUPR HANDBOK(219)	DO NOT GIVE YOUR CHILDREN MORAL AND RELIGIOUS	INSTRUCTION	UNLESS YOU ARE QUITE SURE THEY WILL NOT TAKE IT
MIS. PREFACE(74)	OF THEIR NATIVE COUNTRY, FOOD, CLOTHING, LODGING,	INSTRUCTION	, AND PARENTAL KINDNESS FOR THE ASKING. FOR THE
LADY (248)	LIKE, GOD KNOWS, IS NOT THEIR OWN BETTERMENT AND	INSTRUCTION	, AS WE WELL SEE BY THE EXAMPLE OF THE CHURCHES,
BASH II,1, (105)	(TO BASHVILLE) WHY DIDST THOU BETTER THY	INSTRUCTION	, MAN? HADST THOU BUT SAID, " SHE BADE ME TELL
POSN PREFACE(414)	SCHOOL, OR OTHER PLACE OF WORSHIP, EDIFICATION,	INSTRUCTION	, OR ENTERTAINMENT (INCLUDING ANOTHER THEATRE)
LION PREFACE(97)	I WAS TAUGHT IN MY CHILDHOOD, BY WAY OF RELIGIOUS	INSTRUCTION	, TO REGARD AS GROSS IDOLATERS CONSIGNED TO
		INSTRUCTIONS	
LION I (114)	AND THE ACTING MANAGER. YOU UNDERSTAND YOUR	INSTRUCTIONS	? /CENTURION/ YES, SIR. /THE CAPTAIN/ DISMISS.
BUOY III (27)	IN THIS HOLY PLACE. DID HE NOT MENTION IT IN YOUR	INSTRUCTIONS	? /SIR FERDINAND/ NO. THIS PLACE IS NOT HOLY.
AUGS (264)	ME. /AUGUSTUS/ IS THERE NOBODY ELSE TO TAKE MY	INSTRUCTIONS	? /THE CLERK/ IT'S ME OR NOBODY. AND FOR TWO
MILL I (163)	HERE FOR, MR SAGAMORE? /SAGAMORE/ TO GIVE ME	INSTRUCTIONS	ABOUT YOUR WILL. /ALASTAIR/ SHE MAKES A NEW
DOCT PREFACE(7)	SHALL BE FORGIVEN HIM. THE PECULIARS OBEY THESE	INSTRUCTIONS	AND DISPENSE WITH DOCTORS. THEY ARE THEREFORE
CATH 1 (168)	WAY I DO; THOUGH I DONT KNOW WHY I SHOULD. BUT MY	INSTRUCTIONS	ARE THAT I AM TO SEE THE EMPRESS; AND--
BUOY III (28)	ATMOSPHERE IS MENTALLY PARALYZING. MR BUOYANT'S	INSTRUCTIONS	ARE THAT YOUR ADVICE TO HIS FAMILY MUST BE
APPL I (201)	GEORGE! EVEN I DONT READ ORINTHIA'S LETTERS. MY	INSTRUCTIONS	ARE TO READ EVERYTHING; BUT I TAKE CARE TO
APPL I (202)	VISITOR'S CHAIR IN HIS HAND, READY FOR THE KING'S	INSTRUCTIONS	AS TO WHERE TO PLACE IT). PAMPHILIUS RISES.
JOAN PREFACE(52)	MOST GENEROUSLY ENTHUSIASTIC, FOR THEIR HEARTFELT	INSTRUCTIONS	AS TO HOW IT CAN BE IMPROVED. THEY POINT OUT
GETT (318)	/SOAMES/ (INEXORABLY) I'M WAITING FOR MY	INSTRUCTIONS	AS TO THE TERM OF THE AGREEMENT. /REGINALD/ (
DEVL EPILOG (79)	H.M.S. PINAFORE: IT IS TAKEN FROM THE CODE OF	INSTRUCTIONS	DRAWN UP BY HIMSELF FOR HIS OFFICERS WHEN HE
BUOY III (35)	/SIR F./ DID YOU SAY CLEMMY? THE NAME IN MY	INSTRUCTIONS	IS BABZY. /SHE/ BABZY IS MY VULGAR FATHER'S
2TRU II (54)	ME. TELL HIM TO BRING HIS NOTE OF COLONEL SAXBY'S	INSTRUCTIONS	. DO YOU HEAR? STOP MAKING IDIOTIC FACES; AND
MILL I (154)	CONSULTING ME; BUT NONE OF YOU HAS GIVEN ME ANY	INSTRUCTIONS	. HAD YOU NOT BETTER ALL BE DIVORCED?
2TRU I (35)	TO RECEIVE THE NEW NIGHT NURSE AND GIVE HER HER	INSTRUCTIONS	. HERE SHE IS. AND OH, DO COVER UP YOUR ARM,
PPP (204)	THIS CASE IS NOT PROVIDED FOR IN MY BOOK OF	INSTRUCTIONS	. IT DONT SEEM NO USE TRYING ARTIFICIAL
JOAN EPILOG (166)	CANONIZATION. I MUST RETURN TO ROME FOR FRESH	INSTRUCTIONS	. (HE BOWS FORMALLY, AND WITHDRAWS). /THE
WIDO II (33)	HAD TO DISMISS HIM FOR REPEATEDLY DISREGARDING MY	INSTRUCTIONS	. (TRENCH SAYS NOTHING, SARTORIUS THROWS OFF
DEVL III SD(67)	OUT A PAIR OF HANDCUFFS AND LOOKS TO BURGOYNE FOR	INSTRUCTIONS	. /BURGOYNE/ HAVE YOU ADDRESSED PROFANE
GETT (323)	OF UTTER DEADLOCK) I AM STILL AWAITING MY	INSTRUCTIONS	. /REGINALD/ WELL, WE DONT SEEM TO BE GETTING
GETT (313)	I DIDNT EXPECT YOU WOULD. WELL, I AWAIT YOUR	INSTRUCTIONS	. /REGINALD/ WE GOT STUCK ON THE FIRST CLAUSE.
MILL IV (209)	YOUR LIFE. /EPIFANIA/ MR SAGAMORE! YOU HAVE YOUR	INSTRUCTIONS	. /SAGAMORE/ (BOWS)! /PATRICIA/
GENV IV (128)	DID NOT INCLUDE SCIENCE. /COMMISSAR/ I AWAIT	INSTRUCTIONS	. THE MARXIAN DIALECTIC DOES NOT INCLUDE THE
GETT (321)	/SOAMES/ (IMPLACABLY) I'M STILL AWAITING MY	INSTRUCTIONS	. THEY LOOK AT ONE ANOTHER, EACH WAITING FOR
FABL IV (116)	FULL STOP. POSTSCRIPT. STOP TYPING AND LISTEN TO	INSTRUCTIONS	. WHAT I HAVE JUST DICTATED IS FOR THE TENTH
JOAN PREFACE(43)	THEY WILL UNHESITATINGLY ASK FOR AND ACCEPT THE	INSTRUCTIONS	OF A POLICEMAN OR THE ADVICE OF A TAILOR
JOAN 5 (119)	THROUGH SETTING YOUR PRIVATE JUDGMENT ABOVE THE	INSTRUCTIONS	OF YOUR SPIRITUAL DIRECTORS, THE CHURCH DISOWNS
PYGM II (219)	PEARCE, WHO IS WAITING AT THE DOOR FOR FURTHER	INSTRUCTIONS	) DID YOU TELL HIM I COME IN A TAXI? /MRS
DEVL I (13)	THE DOOR. SHE COMES AFTER HIM, PLYING HIM WITH	INSTRUCTIONS	). TELL THAT GIRL TO COME TO ME AS SOON AS
DEVL EPILOG (81)	BURGOYNE REALIZED WHAT HAD HAPPENED ABOUT THE	INSTRUCTIONS	TO HOWE (THE SCENE IN WHICH I HAVE REPRESENTED
CLEO II SD(119)	HIS PLACE BEFORE IT, HE LOOKS NERVOUSLY FOR	INSTRUCTIONS	TO POTHINUS, WHO PLACES HIMSELF AT HIS LEFT
MILL IV (200)	BUT THAT IS ALL: ABSOLUTELY ALL. MY STANDING	INSTRUCTIONS	TO YOU ARE TO DEFEND EVERY ACTION AND TO
JOAN PREFACE(14)	SPECTRES, ECHOES AND THE LIKE. SAINT CATHERINE'S	INSTRUCTIONS	WERE FAR TOO COGENT FOR THAT; AND THE SIMPLEST
BUOY IV (54)	AND ME? /SIR FERDINAND/ WELL, HARDLY YET. YOUR	INSTRUCTIONS	WERE RATIONAL ENOUGH. I PUT YOUR FINANCIAL CASE
DEST (158)	IN HAND) WELL, SIR, YOU HAVE COME AT LAST. YOUR	INSTRUCTIONS	WERE THAT I SHOULD ARRIVE HERE AT SIX, AND FIND
JOAN PREFACE(13)	CAME DOWN FROM HEAVEN AND GAVE HER CERTAIN	INSTRUCTIONS	WITH WHICH THEY WERE CHARGED BY GOD FOR HER.
DEST (180)	HE HAS HAD A GOOD DINNER, ACCORDING TO YOUR	INSTRUCTIONS	, EXCELLENCY, AND IS NOW DOING ME THE HONOR TO
		INSTRUCTIVE	
3PLA PREFACE(R19)	THE RESULT IS THAT THEY ARE INFINITELY MORE	INSTRUCTIVE	AND ENJOYABLE THAN OUR ROMANCES, BECAUSE LOVE IS
MIS. PREFACE(20)	AND BIRDS AND STREAMS AND FISHES AND ALL SORTS OF	INSTRUCTIVE	AND HEALTHY THINGS EASILY ACCESSIBLE, OR WITH
DOCT PREFACE(50)	BURNING OF ST JOAN OF ARC MUST HAVE BEEN A MOST	INSTRUCTIVE	AND INTERESTING EXPERIMENT TO A GOOD OBSERVER,
APPL I (218)	VARIETY OF OPINION IN THE CABINET IS ALWAYS MOST	INSTRUCTIVE	AND INTERESTING. WHO IS TO BE ITS SPOKESMAN
MILL III (183)	THE INFORMATION YOU HAVE GIVEN ME: IT HAS BEEN	INSTRUCTIVE	AND TO THE POINT. IS THAT A SUFFICIENT APOLOGY?
BULL PREFACE(3)	NOTHING BY MISSING THIS ONE EXCEPT A POSSIBLY	INSTRUCTIVE	EXAMPLE OF HOW OUR ETERNAL MARCH INTO THE FUTURE
NEVR IV (292)	MIND: VERY STIMULATING, VERY ENTERTAINING AND	INSTRUCTIVE	INDEED, MAAM. /BOHUN/ (RESUMING COMMAND OF THE
LION PREFACE(73)	WHAT HAPPENED AFTER THE DISAPPEARANCE OF JESUS IS	INSTRUCTIVE	. UNFORTUNATELY, THE CRUCIFIXION WAS A COMPLETE
CYMB FORWORD(137)	PASSES BEYOND THE SPHERE OF CRIME AND BECOMES AN	INSTRUCTIVE	JOKE. BUT WHAT OF THE MANY SUCCESSFUL AND AVOWED

HART III (130)	AND DESTROY US. /LADY UTTERWORD/ (IN A COOL	INSTRUCTIVE	MANNER, WALLOWING COMFORTABLY IN HER HAMMOCK) WE
APPL I (210)	A MOST INTERESTING CONVERSATION, AND TO ME A MOST	INSTRUCTIVE	ONE. IT'S NO USE OUR TRYING TO GO ON, MR
BARB PREFACE(226)	CAUSTIC CRITICISM, CONCLUSIVE ARGUMENT AND	INSTRUCTIVE	PAMPHLETEERING, EVEN WHEN DONE BY THE MOST
GENV II (60)	ME. SIR MIDLANDER: OUR INTERVIEW HAS BEEN MOST	INSTRUCTIVE	TO ME AS TO THE ATTITUDE OF YOUR COUNTRY. MR
MIS. PREFACE(7)	A CUFF OR A KICK; AND THE EXPERIENCE WILL BE AS	INSTRUCTIVE	TO THE CHILD AS A DIFFICULTY WITH A
DOCT PREFACE(43)	OTHER, AN ELEGANT, INGENIOUS, WELL-INFORMED, AND	INSTRUCTIVE	WAY, IS TO PUT A SPHYGMOGRAPH ON THE STUDENT'S
DOCT PREFACE(47)	THE MEN, BEING OF COURSE ENORMOUSLY MORE	INSTRUCTIVE	, AND COSTING NOTHING, WERE EXPERIMENTED ON
MIS. PREFACE(9)	IN WIDE USE WHICH IS NEITHER STRAIGHTFORWARD,	INSTRUCTIVE	, NOR HARMLESS. IN ITS SIMPLEST FORM IT
		INSTRUCTOR	
ARMS III (61)	NO HARM WILL BE DONE: IVE OFTEN ACTED AS SWORD	INSTRUCTOR	. HE WONT BE ABLE TO TOUCH ME; AND I'LL NOT HURT
FANY III (307)	EXAMPLE TO ALL EUROPE. (INDICATING BOBBY) YOUR	INSTRUCTOR	, NO DOUBT, MONSIEUR-- (HE BOWS). /BOBBY/ (
		INSTRUCTORS	
METH PREFACE(R16)	ARE APPLIED DESTRUCTIVELY, IS QUITE GENUINE: THE	INSTRUCTORS	KNOW THEIR BUSINESS, AND REALLY MEAN THE
		INSTRUCTS	
BUOY III (31)	IT. /SECONDBORN/ HE NOW ADVISES HIS DOCTORS AND	INSTRUCTS	HIS SOLICITORS. /SIR F./ IF SO, WHY DOES HE CALL
SUPR HANDBOK(209)	WRITES HIS DISPATCHES BY THE ELECTRIC LIGHT, AND	INSTRUCTS	HIS STOCKBROKER THROUGH THE TELEPHONE? ENOUGH,
JOAN 6 (139)	A MESSENGER FROM THE MOST HIGH? JOAN! THE CHURCH	INSTRUCTS	YOU THAT THESE APPARITIONS ARE DEMONS SEEKING YOUR
		INSTRUMENT	
LION PREFACE(62)	BEING PROVIDED AT ALL. WE HAVE IN THE INVALUABLE	INSTRUMENT	CALLED MONEY A MEANS OF ENABLING EVERY INDIVIDUAL
CLEO I SD(117)	AND THEIR BUCINATOR, A BURLY FELLOW WITH HIS	INSTRUMENT	COILED ROUND HIS BODY, ITS BRAZEN BELL SHAPED
MILL PREFACE(117)	OF THE DEMOCRATIC DREAM THAT PARLIAMENT WAS AN	INSTRUMENT	FOR CARRYING OUT THE WISHES OF THE VOTERS,
LION PREFACE(60)	JUSTICE AND LAW TO A FARCE: LAW BECOMES MERELY AN	INSTRUMENT	FOR KEEPING THE POOR IN SUBJECTION; AND ACCUSED
POSN PREFACE(390)	IMPORTANCE OF THE THEATRE AS A MOST POWERFUL	INSTRUMENT	FOR TEACHING THE NATION HOW AND WHAT TO THINK AND
BULL PREFACE(55)	WHAT HE CALLED THE LAW OF GOD, AND NOT SIMPLY AN	INSTRUMENT	FOR THE GRATIFICATION OF HIS OWN CRUELTY AND
MRS PREFACE(179)	THE LADY RIGHTLY CONCLUDED THAT MUCH THE BEST	INSTRUMENT	FOR WARNING THE MEN, AND MAKING KNOWN TO THE
BUOY II (20)	HOW TO PLAY THE SOPRANO SAXOPHONE. I HAVE THE	INSTRUMENT	HERE. TWENTY NOTES FROM IT WILL SURROUND YOU WITH
MTH2 (69)	IT HAD NOT BEEN FOR THE SENSE THAT I WAS ONLY AN	INSTRUMENT	IN THE HANDS OF A POWER ABOVE US. /CONRAD/ I'M
6CAL PREFACE(90)	OF LIFE IN ACTION, NOBLE OR IGNOBLE, FIND THEIR	INSTRUMENT	IN THE THEATRE; AND ALL THE ACADEMIC DEFINITIONS
WIDO III SD(49)	BEDSPREAD WHICH COVERS THE TOP, SHEWING THAT THE	INSTRUMENT	IS SELDOM, IF EVER, OPENED. THERE ARE TWO DOORS:
MTH2 (70)	PIOUSLY BROUGHT UP, AND REGARDED HERSELF AS AN	INSTRUMENT	. IF A STATESMAN REMEMBERS THAT HE IS ONLY AN
GENV IV (110)	JESUS WHO HAS DONE IT; AND YOU, SIR, ARE ONLY THE	INSTRUMENT	. /NEWCOMER/ (RISING) A POINT OF ORDER, MISTER.
INCA SD(236)	AND RECOILS AS FAR AS POSSIBLE FROM THE	INSTRUMENT	. /THE PRINCESS/ OH DEAR! (IT RINGS AGAIN. SHE
DOCT I (94)	YES: I GOT IT. IT'S A GOOD SAW: A USEFUL, HANDY	INSTRUMENT	. /WALPOLE/ (CONFIDENTLY) I KNEW YOUD SEE ITS
METH PREFACE(R38)	IN THE STRONGEST TERMS, AND SENDING HIM BACK HIS	INSTRUMENT	." TO DISCREDIT THE OPTICIAN'S SKILL WAS NOT TO
PHIL II (95)	/PARAMORE/ OH, MANY THANKS; BUT IT'S ONLY AN	INSTRUMENT	MAKER. /CUTHBERTSON/ ANY NEW MEDICAL DISCOVERIES,
PHIL II (97)	BETTER TO DO, WHEN YOUVE FINISHED WITH THE	INSTRUMENT	MAN. IF JULIA TURNS UP I'LL ASK HER TOO.
BARB PREFACE(220)	INDEED HIS CONSTANT SENSE THAT HE IS ONLY THE	INSTRUMENT	OF A WILL OR LIFE FORCE WHICH USES HIM FOR
MIS. PREFACE(91)	CULTIVATED THEIR HUMANITY BY THE ONLY EFFECTIVE	INSTRUMENT	OF CULTURE: ART. THE DEARTH IS ARTIFICIALLY
DOCT PREFACE(73)	FOR BEHAVING WELL, THE CHURCH WILL BECOME AN	INSTRUMENT	OF HIS CORRUPTION AND AN EXPLOITER OF HIS
MRS PREFACE(155)	SUBTLEST, THE MOST SEDUCTIVE, THE MOST EFFECTIVE	INSTRUMENT	OF MORAL PROPAGANDA IN THE WORLD, EXCEPTING ONLY
MTH4 II (181)	ORACLE/ WHAT IS THAT THING? /NAPOLEON/ IT IS AN	INSTRUMENT	OF MY PROFESSION, MADAM. I RAISE THIS HAMMER; I
MIS. PREFACE(10)	MYSTERY CALLED THE CHILD'S CONSCIENCE INTO AN	INSTRUMENT	OF OUR OWN CONVENIENCE, AND TO USE THAT WONDERFUL
POSN PREFACE(386)	IN SUPPORT OF ASSASSINATION AS AN INDISPENSABLE	INSTRUMENT	OF PROGRESS. NOW IT HAPPENS THAT WE HAVE IN THE
MIS. PREFACE(93)	YOU WILL GO TO HELL; FOR HELL IS PRESENTED AS THE	INSTRUMENT	OF SOMETHING ETERNAL, DIVINE, AND INEVITABLE: YOU
SUPR I (23)	WHOLE UNIVERSE, A MAN IS NOTHING TO THEM BUT AN	INSTRUMENT	OF THAT PURPOSE. /OCTAVIUS/ DONT BE UNGENEROUS,
FABL PREFACE(66)	THEY ARE NEEDED. I PRESENT MYSELF THEREFORE AS AN	INSTRUMENT	OF THE LIFE FORCE, WRITING BY WHAT IS CALLED
APPL PREFACE(174)	WHO CAN ALWAYS PLEAD THAT HE IS ONLY THE	INSTRUMENT	OF THE PEOPLE'S WILL, WHEREAS THE UNFORTUNATE
GENV III (75)	DECIDED AMONG THEMSELVES TO MAKE USE OF IT AS AN	INSTRUMENT	OF THEIR OLDFASHIONED DIPLOMACY. THAT IS TRUE, MR
DOCT PREFACE(64)	BY SEVERAL SUCCESSIVE NIGHTS DISTURBED BY THAT	INSTRUMENT	OF TORTURE, THE NIGHT BELL; BUT WHO EVER THINKS
MIS. PREFACE(39)	IS ONLY AN EXCUSE FOR IMPRISONMENT. IT IS AN	INSTRUMENT	OF TORTURE WHICH BECOMES MORE PAINFUL THE MORE
ROCK PREFACE(158)	CHURCHES EVER SINCE AS AN AID TO PIETY. THE CHIEF	INSTRUMENT	OF TORTURE IS THE SUBJECT OF A SPECIAL ADORATION.
SUPR III (111)	PART TO MAKE HIMSELF SOMETHING MORE THAN THE MERE	INSTRUMENT	OF WOMAN'S PURPOSE. SO FAR, THE RESULT OF LIFE'S
MILL I (152)	SEND MR BLENDERBLAND UP. (HE HANGS UP THE	INSTRUMENT	). /ALASTAIR/ (TO PATRICIA) YOU WILL NOW SEE THE
BARB I (266)	THEN I'LL GET IT. (HE GOES UPSTAIRS FOR THE	INSTRUMENT	). /UNDERSHAFT/ DO YOU PLAY, BARBARA? /BARBARA/
3PLA PREFACE(R25)	ME. THIS IS ALL VERY WELL; BUT THE TRUMPET IS AN	INSTRUMENT	THAT GROWS ON ONE; AND SOMETIMES MY BLASTS HAVE
BUOY II (26)	FOR IT IS TRUE THAT WHEN SHE PLAYS ON HER STRANGE	INSTRUMENT	THE SERPENTS OF THE BUSH AND THE MONSTERS OF THE
MIS. PREFACE(56)	TO BE FLOGGED TO THE UTMOST EXTREMITY WITH ANY	INSTRUMENT	USABLE FOR SUCH A PURPOSE THAT HE CARES TO
METH PREFACE(R38)	AND THAT " IF AN OPTICIAN TRIED TO SELL ME AN	INSTRUMENT	WHICH HAD ALL THESE DEFECTS I SHOULD THINK MYSELF
METH PREFACE(R38)	POSSIBLE DEFECT THAT CAN BE FOUND IN AN OPTICAL	INSTRUMENT	, AND EVEN SOME PECULIAR TO ITSELF," AND THAT "
MTH2 (70)	IF A STATESMAN REMEMBERS THAT HE IS ONLY AN	INSTRUMENT	, AND FEELS QUITE SURE THAT HE IS RIGHTLY
PYGM II (235)	/HIGGINS/ HOW MUCH LUGGAGE? /DOOLITTLE/ MUSICAL	INSTRUMENT	, GOVERNOR. A FEW PICTURES, A TRIFLE OF JEWLERY,
KING I (184)	SET ABOUT IT. I SHOULD LEARN TO PLAY SOME MUSICAL	INSTRUMENT	, OR BUY A NEW WIG. /LOUISE/ BUT YOU ARE AN
		INSTRUMENTALITY	
POSN PREFACE(432)	IT UNDER THE LORD CHAMBERLAIN'S NOSE, THROUGH THE	INSTRUMENTALITY	OF THE STAGE SOCIETY. AFTER THIS, THE PLAY
		INSTRUMENTS	
JOAN 6 (134)	THINK BEFORE YOU ANSWER. HAS SHE BEEN SHEWN THE	INSTRUMENTS	? /THE EXECUTIONER/ THEY ARE READY, MY LORD.
MTH4 I (158)	TO HAVE TIME TO STUDY THESE THINGS, AND TO INVENT	INSTRUMENTS	AND APPARATUS FOR RESEARCH. BUT WHAT IS THE
MTH4 I (158)	BUT ONLY WONDERS AND MIRACLES, WITH SCIENTIFIC	INSTRUMENTS	AND APPARATUS AS THE WONDER WORKERS. INSTEAD OF
GETT PREFACE(223)	IN WHICH WE ARE KEENLY INTERESTED PERSONAL	INSTRUMENTS	AND ASK US TO REGARD IT, AND FEEL ABOUT IT, AND
METH PREFACE(R74)	SECRET WAS THEIR CONCEPTION OF THEMSELVES AS THE	INSTRUMENTS	AND VEHICLES OF DIVINE POWER AND ASPIRATION: A
PPP PREFACE(192)	A HARP, A DRUM, AND A PAIR OF CYMBALS, THESE	INSTRUMENTS	BEING THE MOST USEFUL IN ENHANCING THE STAGE
BARB PREFACE(237)	AND AS THE POLICE AND THE MILITARY ARE THE	INSTRUMENTS	BY WHICH THE RICH ROB AND OPPRESS THE POOR (ON
FABL IV (115)	RATE OF RADIATION, AND THE SENSITIVENESS OF THE	INSTRUMENTS	FOR DETECTING AND MEASURING IT. AS TEMPERATURE
ROCK PREFACE(160)	TO COMMUNISM IT FOUND ITSELF WITHOUT ANY	INSTRUMENTS	FOR THE MAINTENANCE OF ORDER EXCEPT A LIST OF
NEVR I SD(199)	A CHAIR. ALSO A SOFA, FARTHER ALONG. A CABINET OF	INSTRUMENTS	IS HANDY TO THE OPERATING CHAIR. THE FURNITURE,
METH PREFACE(R12)	OF DIVINE JUSTICE OF WHICH THEY ARE THE ARDENT	INSTRUMENTS	. BUT IF MAN IS REALLY INCAPABLE OF ORGANIZING A
GENV PREFACE(25)	MUCH LESS CONCERTED FOR 30 DIFFERENT ORCHESTRAL	INSTRUMENTS	. IN PHILOSOPHY WE SPOT DESCARTES AND KANT,
NEVR I (200)	SECRETLY AS HE PROCEEDS TO CLEAN AND REPLACE HIS	INSTRUMENTS	. SHE SHAKES HER DRESS INTO ORDER: LOOKS
3PLA PREFACE(R22)	BUT IF I FOUND THAT THEY WERE BECOMING THE	INSTRUMENTS	OF A SYSTEMATIC IDOLATRY OF SENSUOUSNESS, I
SUPR HANDBOK(199)	AND EVOLUTION IN ONE EPOCH, BECOME RUINOUS	INSTRUMENTS	OF DEGENERATION IN THE NEXT. IN THE BREEDING OF
SUPR HANDBOK(198)	AND THE WIDE PURPOSE: WAR AND COMPETITION, POTENT	INSTRUMENTS	OF SELECTION AND EVOLUTION IN ONE EPOCH, BECOME
JOAN 4 (100)	STANDS EVER ON GUARD. AND IT IS AS ONE OF THE	INSTRUMENTS	OF THAT DESIGN THAT I SEE THIS GIRL. SHE IS
DOCT PREFACE(39)	EXCEPTIONALLY CRUEL AND AS DEVISERS OF HORRIBLE	INSTRUMENTS	OF TORTURE BY PEOPLE WHOSE MAIN NOTION OF
CATH 4 (189)	/NARYSHKIN/ LITTLE MOTHER: THEY HAVE BROUGHT SOME	INSTRUMENTS	OF TORTURE. WILL THEY BE NEEDED? /CATHERINE/ (
WIDO I (3)	A ZOO. NEXT DAY, NUREMBERG! FINEST COLLECTION OF	INSTRUMENTS	OF TORTURE IN THE WORLD. /TRENCH/ ALL RIGHT. YOU
MIS. PREFACE(64)	ANALOGUES THE LAWGIVER AND THE JUDGE, BECOME	INSTRUMENTS	OF TYRANNY IN THE HANDS OF THOSE WHO ARE TOO
GENV IV (89)	BEST CONGRATULATIONS. MAY I WARN YOU ALL THAT THE	INSTRUMENTS	ON THE TABLE ARE MICROPHONES AND TELEVISORS? I
CURE PREFACE(224)	FOR TWO PIANISTS, BUT CAN BE ADAPTED TO ANY	INSTRUMENTS	ON WHICH THE PERFORMERS HAPPEN TO BE PROFICIENT.
NEVR I (200)	(PUTTING IT DOWN ON THE LEDGE OF HIS CABINET OF	INSTRUMENTS	) THAT WAS MY FIRST TOOTH. /THE YOUNG LADY/ (
DOCT PREFACE(22)	IN THE FIRST FRENZY OF MICROBE KILLING, SURGICAL	INSTRUMENTS	WERE DIPPED IN CARBOLIC OIL, WHICH WAS A GREAT
GETT SD(260)	CRANE, AND A COLLECTION OF OLD IRON AND BRASS	INSTRUMENTS	WHICH PASS AS THE ORIGINAL FURNITURE OF THE
LADY PREFACE(222)	AND HURT NOT. SOMETIMES A THOUSAND TWANGLING	INSTRUMENTS	WILL HUM ABOUT MINE EARS; AND SOMETIMES VOICES,
FABL PREFACE(65)	NOT DEFEATED BY THE IMPERFECTION OF ITS MORTAL	INSTRUMENTS	, ALWAYS TAKES CARE THAT THE NECESSARY
DOCT I (100)	GERMS OVER THEIR PATIENTS FROM THEIR CLOTHES AND	INSTRUMENTS	, AND CONTRAST ALL THAT WITH THE SCIENTIFIC
BULL I SD(73)	WITH PLANS, ROLLS OF TRACING PAPER, MATHEMATICAL	INSTRUMENTS	, AND OTHER DRAUGHTSMAN'S ACCESSORIES ON IT. IN
HART I SD(43)	STRAIGHTEDGES, SET SQUARES, MATHEMATICAL	INSTRUMENTS	, SAUCERS OF WATER COLOR, A TUMBLER OF
SUPR III SD(86)	IT UP, EXTINGUISHED BY WAILINGS FROM UNCANNY WIND	INSTRUMENTS	, THUS:-- IT IS ALL VERY ODD. ONE RECOGNIZES THE
BUOY III (29)	FOR SCHOLARSHIP, PAINTING, PLAYING MUSICAL	INSTRUMENTS	, WRITING, AND TALKING. ONE BROTHER IS A
		INSUBORDINATE	
BARB PREFACE(217)	PAID TO POVERTY AND OBEDIENCE BY RICH AND	INSUBORDINATE	DO-NOTHINGS WHO WANT TO ROB THE POOR WITHOUT

PRES (139)	WAS REPRIMANDED. BESIDES, THE MAN WAS THOROUGHLY	INSUBORDINATE	. YOU CANT DENY THAT THE VERY FIRST THING HE
BULL PREFACE(61)	POLITICAL ANIMOSITY. IT IS, HOWEVER, DUE TO THE	INSUBORDINATE	SPIRIT WHICH HAS BEEN SEDULOUSLY FOSTERED
SUPR HANDBOK(228)	FOR AN OBJECTION TO POVERTY. THE COWARDLY, THE	INSUBORDINATE	, AND THE ENVIOUS SHARE YOUR OBJECTIONS. TAKE
		INSUBORDINATION	
AUGS (278)	NOW; AND LET ME HAVE NO MORE OF YOUR CIVILIAN	INSUBORDINATION	. ATTENTION! LEFT TURN! QUICK MARCH! /THE
BULL PREFACE(46)	HANDLE LARGE BODIES OF MEN WHOSE CARELESSNESS OR	INSUBORDINATION	MAY CAUSE WHOLESALE DESTRUCTION OF LIFE AND
		INSUBSTANTIAL	
DOCT IV (169)	LIFE'S FITFUL FEVER; THEY SLEEP WELL AND LIKE THIS	INSUBSTANTIAL	BOURNE FROM WHICH NO TRAVELLER RETURNS LEAVE
		INSUFFERABLE	
UNPL PREFACE(R14)	IN ORDER TO OBTAIN FROM HIM AN INSOLENT AND	INSUFFERABLE	DOCUMENT, WHICH I CANNOT READ WITHOUT BOILING
SUPR III (99)	SATISFY YOU? /DON JUAN/ IT IS A SOMEWHAT LESS	INSUFFERABLE	FORM OF CANT THAN THE OTHER. BUT IF YOULL ALLOW
NEVR I SD(202)	LESS STAGGERING TO HIS ELDERS, AND WOULD BE QUITE	INSUFFERABLE	IN A LESS PREPOSSESSING YOUTH. HE IS
DEST (156)	EARS. /NAPOLEON/ GIUSEPPE! YOUR FLATTERIES ARE	INSUFFERABLE	. GO AND TALK OUTSIDE. (HE SITS DOWN AGAIN AT
JITT III (75)	FUNNY, ISNT IT? /JITTA/ (RISING) DONT BE	INSUFFERABLE	. YOU OWE IT TO YOUR POSITION AS AN INJURED
BULL PREFACE(40)	WINDBAGS OF THE TWO RIVAL PLATFORMS ARE THE MOST	INSUFFERABLE	OF ALL WINDBAGS. IT REQUIRES NEITHER KNOWLEDGE,
FANY III (323)	OUR PREJUDICES, OUR OBSOLETE INSTITUTIONS, OUR	INSUFFERABLE	PEDANTRY ON THE WORLD BY BRUTE FORCE-- BY THAT
JOAN PREFACE(3)	BUT ESSENTIALLY FOR WHAT WE CALL UNWOMANLY AND	INSUFFERABLE	PRESUMPTION. AT EIGHTEEN JOAN'S PRETENSIONS
MIS. PREFACE(88)	WHAT WE CALL FAMILY FEELING. EVEN APART FROM ITS	INSUFFERABLE	PRETENSIONS, THE FAMILY NEEDS HEARTY
MIS. PREFACE(34)	MOST OF THIS LEGISLATION WILL BECOME AN	INSUFFERABLE	RESTRAINT UPON FREEDOM AND VARIETY OF ACTION
JOAN PREFACE(45)	SEEMED, TO ALL WHO WERE NOT INFATUATED BY HER, SO	INSUFFERABLE	THAT NOTHING BUT AN UNBROKEN CHAIN OF
3PLA PREFACE(R22)	HYSTERICAL. IS IT CLEAR NOW, WHY THE THEATRE WAS	INSUFFERABLE	TO ME; WHY IT LEFT ITS BLACK MARK ON MY BONES
POSN PREFACE(425)	OF THE PRIMROSE LEAGUE WOULD BE RESENTED AS AN	INSUFFERABLE	TYRANNY. BUT A LAW TO SHUT UP BOTH ST PAUL'S
GETT (296)	INTO THE FRONT OF EVERY DISCUSSION IN THE MOST	INSUFFERABLE	WAY. (REGINALD, WITH AN EXCLAMATION OF
MILL I (149)	I HAVE NEVER LOST MY DIGNITY EVEN UNDER THE MOST	INSUFFERABLE	WRONGS. /ALASTAIR/ YOU HADNT ANY WRONGS. YOU
MTH4 II (185)	/THE ELDERLY GENTLEMAN/ DO YOU MEAN THAT RATHER	INSUFFERABLE	YOUNG MAN WHOM YOU FOUND BORING ME ON THE
		INSUFFERABLY	
LADY PREFACE(223)	DARK LADY MOST LIKELY THOUGHT THIS SIDE OF HIM	INSUFFERABLY	CONCEITED; FOR THERE IS NO REASON TO SUPPOSE
BULL PREFACE(19)	WHICH IN AN IRISHMAN WOULD HAVE BEEN AN	INSUFFERABLY	VULGAR AFFECTATION, WAS QUITE NATURAL AND
		INSUFFICIENT	
LION PREFACE(21)	HAS DECLARED THAT THE RITE OF CIRCUMCISION IS	INSUFFICIENT	AS A DEDICATION OF THE INDIVIDUAL TO GOD, AND
FABL PREFACE(88)	BETTER THAN NO TEST AT ALL. BUT IT IS NOW QUITE	INSUFFICIENT	IN VIEW OF THE ENORMOUS INCREASE OF PUBLIC
GENV I (32)	ANY TIME YOU FOUND THAT YOUR EMOLUMENTS HERE WERE	INSUFFICIENT	. /SHE/ THEY ARE. BUT I MUSTNT TAKE BRIBES, YOU
		INSUFFICIENTLY	
DOCT PREFACE(52)	PUBLIC INTERFERENCE WITH THE INSANITARY, BECAUSE	INSUFFICIENTLY	FINANCED, PRIVATE HOUSE. WHAT THE PUBLIC
SIM I (47)	MAN. HERE, THEN, WE HAVE FOUR YOUNG ADULTS,	INSUFFICIENTLY	NITROGENIZED, AND THEREFORE DEFICIENT IN
		INSULAR	
SUPR HANDBOK(218)	BY THIS MEANS INTO INSOLUBLE CONFLICT WITH THE	INSULAR	BRITISH IMPERIALIST, " CUTS THE PAINTER" AND BREAKS
SIM PREFACE(18)	IT IS JUST AS WELL TO REMIND OUR WESTERN AND VERY	INSULAR	IMPERIALISTS THAT MARRIAGE IN THE BRITISH EMPIRE IS
LION PREFACE(97)	TURN TO FRANCE, A COUNTRY TEN TIMES MORE	INSULAR	IN ITS PREOCCUPATION WITH ITS OWN LANGUAGE, ITS OWN
METH PREFACE(R17)	IN DETAIL TO SOLDIERS AND TO PAROCHIAL AND	INSULAR	PATRIOTIC CIVILIANS. FLIMSINESS OF CIVILIZATION.
CATH PREFACE(155)	THAN ANY RUSSIAN, AND MY ENGLISH PEOPLE MORE	INSULAR	THAN ANY BRITON, I WILL NOT PLEAD, AS I HONESTLY
		INSULARITY	
SUPR HANDBOK(218)	ANTHROPOMETRIC METHOD. IMPERIALISM. EXCESS OF	INSULARITY	MAKES A BRITON AN IMPERIALIST. EXCESS OF LOCAL
O'FL PREFACE(202)	BE, FOR ENGLAND, KNOWING THAT THE IGNORANCE AND	INSULARITY	OF THE IRISHMAN IS A DANGER TO HIMSELF AND TO HIS
		INSULATING	
MTH4 II (177)	INTO ITS FIELD. IF I WERE NOT VEILED AND ROBED IN	INSULATING	MATERIAL YOU COULD NOT ENDURE MY PRESENCE; AND I
MTH4 III SD(195)	RISES SLOWLY FROM IT. SHE HAS DISCARDED THE	INSULATING	ROBE AND VEIL IN WHICH SHE CONVERSED WITH
		INSULIN	
JOAN PREFACE(16)	EXTRACT, ADRENALIN, THYMIN, PITUITRIN, AND	INSULIN	, WITH PICK-ME-UPS OF HORMONE STIMULANTS, THE BLOOD
		INSULT	
PHIL II (109)	THEN YOU OUGHT TO. UGH! IT WAS HIDEOUS: AN	INSULT	: AN OUTRAGE. A NICE END TO ALL MY PLANS FOR MAKING
ARMS III (60)	ME. /LOUKA/ (TURNING) WHAT DOES THAT MEAN? AN	INSULT	? /SERGIUS/ (COMMANDINGLY) IT MEANS THAT YOU LOVE
ROCK II (266)	HIM. HOW ARE WE TO HOLD THE EMPIRE TOGETHER IF WE	INSULT	A MAN WHO REPRESENTS NEARLY SEVENTY PER CENT OF ITS
POSN (447)	THREATENINGLY). YOURE NO TRUE AMERICAN MAN, TO	INSULT	A WOMAN LIKE THAT. /BLANCO/ A WOMAN! OH LORD! YOU
APPL PREFACE(178)	IN THE SEA. YOU WILL NOT TAKE THAT AS A PERSONAL	INSULT	AND ASK ME INDIGNANTLY IF I CONSIDER YOU INFERIOR TO
HART PREFACE(16)	GOVERNOR EXPELLING THE GERMAN PROFESSOR WITH	INSULT	AND BODILY VIOLENCE, AND DECLARING THAT NO ENGLISH
FOUN (209)	WANT TO? /BRABAZON/ THAT SPEECH WAS MEANT TO	INSULT	AND HUMILIATE ME. I MAKE IT A RULE TO FIGHT PEOPLE
FOUN (209)	I MAKE IT A RULE TO FIGHT PEOPLE WHO ATTEMPT TO	INSULT	AND HUMILIATE ME. (THROWING AWAY HIS STICK) PUT UP
SUPR I (45)	OUT THE TRUTH. BUT I WONT BEAR SUCH A HORRIBLE	INSULT	AS TO BE COMPLIMENTED BY JACK ON BEING ONE OF THE
FANY EPILOG (332)	HIS PLAYS AS PLAYS. ALL HE WANTS TO DO IS TO	INSULT	EVERYBODY ALL ROUND AND SET US TALKING ABOUT HIM.
JITT II (38)	WITH HER ON HER HUSBAND'S UNFAITHFULNESS. THEY	INSULT	GOD BY DECLARING THAT MY FATHER THREW HIMSELF INTO
SUPR III (139)	CONVERSATION; AND YOU ALL INSTINCTIVELY	INSULT	HIM. EVEN THE NEW MAN IS AS BAD AS ANY OF YOU. ENRY:
CLEO IV (188)	CAESAR THE DREAMER, WHO ALLOWS EVERY SLAVE TO	INSULT	HIM. RUFIO HAS SAID I DID WELL: NOW THE OTHERS SHALL
GETT (329)	IF YOU PROMISE TO AMUSE GEORGE. /HOTCHKISS/ I'LL	INSULT	HIM, SNEER AT HIM, WIPE MY BOOTS ON HIM. /MRS GEORGE/
PYGM IV (265)	DECISIVELY INTO THE GRATE) TOSH, ELIZA. DONT YOU	INSULT	HUMAN RELATIONS BY DRAGGING ALL THIS CANT ABOUT
ARMS III (60)	PERHAPS HAVE YOU THERE AGAIN. WHETHER THAT IS AN	INSULT	I NEITHER KNOW NOR CARE: TAKE IT AS YOU PLEASE. BUT (
OVER PREFACE(156)	MATTER OF REPUTATION IN THIS DEPARTMENT: EVERY	INSULT	IS A FLATTERY: EVERY TESTIMONIAL IS A DISPARAGEMENT:
SUPR II (57)	DOES SHE GIVE ANY REASON? /TANNER/ REASON! AN	INSULT	IS NOT A REASON. ANN FORBIDS HER TO BE ALONE WITH ME
POSN PREFACE(425)	IS TO INSULT THE UNIVERSE) I CLAIM THE RIGHT TO	INSULT	IT TO MY HEART'S CONTENT, IF I CHOOSE, PROVIDED I DO
ARMS II (35)	ENOUGH TO BETRAY THE HIGHER LOVE; BUT DO NOT YOU	INSULT	IT. /LOUKA/ (DEMURELY) NOT FOR THE WORLD, SIR, I'M
MTH5 (246)	YOU HAVE NO SENSE OF ART; AND YOU INSTINCTIVELY	INSULT	IT. /THE HE-ANCIENT/ CHILDREN HAVE BEEN KNOWN TO MAKE
FANY PROLOG (271)	THE CENSORSHIP IN THE FACE OF RIDICULE AND	INSULT	. AND NOW I'M TOLD THAT I'M A CENTRE OF IMMORALISM!
GENV IV (106)	IN ABRAHAM. /BATTLER/ THIS IS AN INTOLERABLE	INSULT	. I DEMAND SATISFACTION. I CANNOT PUNCH YOUR HEAD
DOCT III (144)	ANNOYED FOR THE FIRST TIME) IT'S AN INTELLECTUAL	INSULT	. I DONT BELIEVE THERES SUCH A THING AS SIN. /SIR
CURE (232)	PLAY IF YOU KEEP YOUR EARS STOPPED. IT IS AN	INSULT	. LEAVE THE ROOM. /REGINALD/ BUT I TELL YOU IT'S MY
GLIM (182)	PRESUME-- /GIULIA/ AND INSULT, AND INSULT, AND	INSULT	. /SQUARCIO/ UNTIL ONE DAY YOU FIND YOURSELF IN A
MTH4 I (144)	/THE GENTLEMAN/ THIS IS A GROSS IMPERTINENCE. AN	INSULT	. /THE WOMAN/ (REPLACING HER TUNING-FORK AND
MTH4 I (149)	THAT MY POSITION AS A GUEST WOULD PROTECT ME FROM	INSULT	. /ZOO/ PUTTING MY FRIEND IN HIS PLACE. THAT IS SOME
POSN PREFACE(392)	CRITICIZED AS AN INSTITUTION, BUT RESENTED AS AN	INSULT	. THE DIPLOMATIC OBJECTION TO THE LORD CHAMBERLAIN.
MTH5 (220)	ARE YOU MAD, ARJILLAX? THIS IS AN OUTRAGE. AN	INSULT	. YAH! ETC. ETC. ETC. (THE MALCONTENTS APPEAR ON
DOCT V (178)	(LAUGHING BITTERLY) HA! /JENNIFER/ DONT	INSULT	ME: DONT BLASPHEME. (SHE SNATCHES UP THE BOOK AND
MIS. (169)	WHAT DO YOU WANT? MONEY? /THE MAN/ HOW DARE YOU	INSULT	ME? /TARLETON/ WELL, WHAT DO YOU WANT? /THE MAN/
MIS. (187)	ENGAGED TO ME. /HYPATIA/ BENTLEY! IF YOU	INSULT	ME AGAIN: IF YOU SAY ANOTHER WORD, I'LL LEAVE THE
SUPR I (26)	TABLE WITH HIS FIST). /TANNER/ LOOK HERE! IF YOU	INSULT	ME AGAIN I'LL TAKE YOU AT YOUR WORD AND LEAVE YOUR
PYGM V (287)	YOU TWO; AND IT'S WICKED AND CRUEL OF YOU TO	INSULT	ME BY PRETENDING I COULD. YOU THINK I MUST GO BACK TO
MILL I (142)	A ROTTEN SOLICITOR. YOU ARE NOT A GENTLEMAN. YOU	INSULT	ME IN MY DISTRESS. YOU BACK UP MY HUSBAND AGAINST ME.
LIED (200)	YOU. /HE/ (MUCH TAKEN ABACK) THERE IS NO NEED TO	INSULT	ME LIKE THIS. I ASSURE YOU, ON MY HONOR AS A-- /HER
DEVL I (8)	WERE MARRIED: HE HAD TOO MUCH RESPECT FOR ME TO	INSULT	ME WITH SUCH A BROTHER. WOULD SUCH A SELFISH WRETCH
OVER (192)	IF YOU TELL ME IVE DONE SOMETHING WRONG YOU	INSULT	ME. BUT IF YOU SAY THAT SOMETHING THAT I DID IS WRONG
KING I (212)	TO BLASPHEME. AND NOW HE ENCOURAGES THEM TO	INSULT	ME. I WILL NOT BEAR IT. /CHARLES/ DO NOT BE AN IDIOT,
KING I (208)	CAN. /BARBARA/ LIKENESS! YOU HAVE BRIBED HIM TO	INSULT	ME. IT MAKES ME LOOK A HUNDRED. /CHARLES/ NONSENSE,
MILL IV (199)	FELT. IT SERVES YOU RIGHT. /EPIFANIA/ YES: GO ON.	INSULT	ME. THREATEN ME. BLACKMAIL ME. YOU CAN ALL DO IT WITH
LION PROLOG (107)	WERE GETTING TOO STOUT, DEARIE. /MEGAERA/ YES:	INSULT	ME, DO. (RISING) OH! I WONT BEAR IT ANOTHER MOMENT.
MIS. (164)	LIAR. /PERCIVAL/ OF COURSE IF YOURE GOING TO	INSULT	ME, I AM QUITE HELPLESS. YOURE A WOMAN: YOU CAN SAY
CAPT II (257)	VERY ANGRY, AND FULL OF THE CRUSTIEST PLUCK) YOU	INSULT	ME, SIR, YOU ARE A RASCAL. YOU ARE A RASCAL. JOHNSON,

GENV III	(74)	/THE WIDOW/ OH, SIR ORPHEUS! YOU, OF ALL MEN, TO	INSULT	MY FAITH! /SIR O./ NOT AT ALL, NOT AT ALL, I ASSURE
JITT II	(38)	PEOPLE WHO CALL ON US MISUNDERSTAND HIM. THEY	INSULT	MY MOTHER BY CONDOLING WITH HER ON HER HUSBAND'S
POSN PREFACE	(425)	IT CAN BE INSULTED (ANY MAN IS AS WELCOME TO	INSULT	MY RELIGION, IF HE CAN, AS HE IS TO INSULT THE
MIS.	(192)	LOOK HERE, MR PERCIVAL: YOURE NOT SUPPOSED TO	INSULT	MY SISTER. /HYPATIA/ OH, SHUT UP, JOHNNY. I CAN TAKE
LIED	(200)	YOU. BUT IF YOU THINK I'LL STAND HERE AND LET YOU	INSULT	MY WIFE IN HER OWN HOUSE, YOURE MISTAKEN. /HE/ (VERY
GENV I	(39)	ARE A HIGH SPIRITED RACE AND DO NOT SUBMIT TO THE	INSULT	OF DEFEAT AT THE POLLS. BUT MY HUSBAND WAS A MILITARY
DEVL II	(34)	HER HUSBAND TO SHARE AND EXPRESS FOR HER AT EVERY	INSULT	OF RICHARD'S) YOU ARE WELCOME FOR MY HUSBAND'S SAKE.
MIS. PREFACE	(61)	AND FOLLOW THE QUESTION WITH A BLOW OR AN	INSULT	OR SOME OTHER UNMISTAKEABLE EXPRESSION OF RESENTMENT,
GETT	(291)	MAJORITY OF THE ENGLISH PEOPLE ARE SNOBS. THEY	INSULT	POVERTY. THEY DESPISE VULGARITY. THEY LOVE NOBILITY.
SUPR PREFACE	(R26)	TO ITS UNIVERSAL APPLICATION MADE IT A CLASS	INSULT	; AND IT CERTAINLY WAS NOT FOR THE POT TO CALL THE
MTH4 I	(165)	YOUR MOUTH I FEEL THAT THE COMPLIMENT HIDES SOME	INSULT	; SO I DO NOT THANK YOU FOR IT. /ZOO/ ALL I MEANT WAS
6CAL	(103)	MADAM. HE DEFIED ME. HE SPAT AT ME. THERE IS NO	INSULT	THAT HE DID NOT HEAP ON ME. HE LOOKED ME IN THE FACE
POSN PREFACE	(425)	TO INSULT MY RELIGION, IF HE CAN, AS HE IS TO	INSULT	THE UNIVERSE) I CLAIM THE RIGHT TO INSULT IT TO MY
GETT	(335)	FOR HUSBANDS: THE MAN WHO CAN BULLY THEM CAN	INSULT	THEIR WIVES WITH IMPUNITY. TELL HIM IF YOU DARE. IF I
GETT	(282)	ARE POLYGAMISTS. I CANT AS A BRITISH BISHOP	INSULT	THEM BY SPEAKING DISRESPECTFULLY OF POLYGAMY. IT'S A
BULL PREFACE	(46)	OF LIFE AND PROPERTY; YET ANY OF THESE MEN MAY	INSULT	THEM, DEFY THEM, OR ASSAULT THEM WITHOUT SPECIAL
POSN	(454)	OF HER TELL THE TRUTH? /BABSY/ IT WOULD BE AN	INSULT	TO EVERY RESPECTABLE WOMAN HERE TO BELIEVE HER.
CAND I	(99)	THAT WAY OF THE LOVE SHE INSPIRES! IT IS AN	INSULT	TO HER! /MORELL/ (RISING QUICKLY, IN AN ALTERED
JOAN EPILOG	(153)	COULD NOT IMPOSE ON A PLOUGHBOY. YET OUT OF THIS	INSULT	TO JUSTICE, THIS DEFAMATION OF THE CHURCH, THIS ORGY
NEVR IV	(299)	/GLORIA/ NEVER MIND HIM, MOTHER. THIS IS A FRESH	INSULT	TO ME: THAT IS ALL. /MRS CLANDON/ (HARDLY ABLE TO
SUPR III	(118)	/ANA/ DON JUAN: A WORD AGAINST CHASTITY IS AN	INSULT	TO ME. /DON JUAN/ I SAY NOTHING AGAINST YOUR
GENV IV	(99)	MODERN MISPRONUNCIATIONS. KIKKERONIAN IS AN	INSULT	TO MY OLD SCHOOL. I INSIST ON SISSERONIAN. /THE
MTH4 II	(187)	SIR, THE SHOW, AS YOU CALL IT, BECOMES ALMOST AN	INSULT	TO OUR COMMON SENSE. /ZOZIM/ QUITE, I SHOULD SAY. YOU
DOCT PREFACE	(72)	TO TEACH THEIR FLOCKS THAT IT IS A DEADLY	INSULT	TO THE BLESSED VIRGIN TO PLACE HER IMAGE IN A COTTAGE
CAPT III	(289)	SHE NO LADY. /JOHNSON/ (REVOLTED BY THE SEEMING	INSULT	TO THE ENGLISH PEERAGE FROM A LOW ITALIAN) WHAT?
LADY PREFACE	(212)	DESCRIPTION IMPLIES; WHOSE VERY EXISTENCE IS AN	INSULT	TO THE IDEAL IT REALIZES; WHOSE EYE DISPARAGES, WHOSE
SIM II	(55)	ANY ATTEMPT TO PERSECUTE POLYGAMY WOULD BE AN	INSULT	TO THE RELIGIONS OF INDIA. /PRA/ THE CULTURAL
AUGS	(275)	HE IS JEALOUS OF YOUR INTELLECT. THE BET IS AN	INSULT	TO YOU: DONT YOU FEEL THAT? AFTER WHAT YOU HAVE DONE
CATH 2	(178)	DRUNK). /THE PRINCESS DASHKOFF/ SCANDALOUS! AN	INSULT	TO YOUR IMPERIAL MAJESTY! /CATHERINE/ DASHKOFF: YOU
SUPR IV	(153)	BOY. I'M SORRY FOR WHAT I SAID: I NEVER MEANT TO	INSULT	VIOLET: I TAKE IT ALL BACK. SHE'S JUST THE WIFE YOU
MIS. PREFACE	(52)	A STAGE COACH, AND CONCEIVED THE PHENOMENON AS AN	INSULT	WHICH REFLECTED ON HIMSELF. THIS EXCLAMATION OF SAM
CLEO III	(150)	DEFIANT ELEGANCE) I WILL MAKE AMENDS FOR THAT	INSULT	WITH MY SWORD AT FITTING TIME AND PLACE. WHO SAYS
BUOY II	(19)	YOU ARE A COMMERCIAL MINDED BRITISH SNOB. MUST I	INSULT	YOU BY OFFERING TO PAY FOR MY ENTERTAINMENT? OR
FANY III	(305)	YOU KNOW. /MARGARET/ DOES HIM CREDIT! TO	INSULT	YOU LIKE THAT! BOBBY: SAY THAT WASNT WHAT YOU MEANT.
GLIM	(182)	PRESUME, AND PRESUME-- /GIULIA/ AND INSULT, AND	INSULT	, AND INSULT. /SQUARCIO/ UNTIL ONE DAY YOU FIND
GLIM	(182)	PRESUME, AND PRESUME, AND PRESUME-- /GIULIA/ AND	INSULT	, AND INSULT, AND INSULT. /SQUARCIO/ UNTIL ONE DAY
DEVL I	(18)	VERY HUMBLE SERVANT. (WITH THIS COMPREHENSIVE	INSULT	, HE THROWS HIS HAT TO CHRISTY WITH A SUDDENNESS THAT
MRS III	(233)	CATCH HIM IN A TRAP. (CROFTS, UNDERSTANDING THE	INSULT	, MAKES A THREATENING MOVEMENT). CROFTS: THERE ARE
PHIL III	(141)	YOUD ANNOY ANYBODY: UPON MY SOUL YOU WOULD; BUT	INSULT	! NOW WHAT DO YOU MEAN BY THAT? /PARAMORE/ (VERY

INSULTED

FANY III	(326)	BUT ONLY MRS KNOX WILL UNDERSTAND. I ONCE	INSULTED	A SERVANT, RASHLY; FOR HE WAS A SINCERE CHRISTIAN.
SUPR IV	(168)	NOT HYPOCRITES GO ABOUT IN RATIONAL DRESS AND ARE	INSULTED	AND GET INTO ALL SORTS OF HOT WATER. AND THEN THEIR
HART I	(46)	WOMAN, THAT BECAUSE THIS YOUNG LADY HAS BEEN	INSULTED	AND NEGLECTED, YOU HAVE THE RIGHT TO ADDRESS HER AS
DOCT IV	(165)	MYSELF. IVE BEEN THREATENED AND BLACKMAILED AND	INSULTED	AND STARVED. BUT IVE PLAYED THE GAME. IVE FOUGHT
MIS. PREFACE	(67)	ANYBODY'S VIEWS BUT HIS OWN, HE FEELS PERSONALLY	INSULTED	AND WANTS TO RESIGN OR LEAVE THE ROOM UNLESS HE IS
JOAN 2	(74)	AND LEFT ME THE POOR FOOL I AM, BULLIED AND	INSULTED	BY ALL OF YOU. /THE ARCHBISHOP/ CONTROL YOURSELF,
ARMS III	(69)	(SUDDENLY BREAKING OUT AT SERGIUS) I HAVE BEEN	INSULTED	BY EVERYONE HERE. YOU SET THEM THE EXAMPLE. YOU OWE
O'FL	(218)	WORLD, AND THEN TO COME HOME AND BE SCOLDED AND	INSULTED	BY HIS OWN MOTHER. I'LL FIGHT FOR WHO I LIKE; AND
JOAN PREFACE	(28)	THE TRUTH IS THAT CAUCHON WAS THREATENED AND	INSULTED	BY THE ENGLISH FOR BEING TOO CONSIDERATE TO JOAN. A
MIS. PREFACE	(54)	CASE OF A SCHOOLMASTER WHO, CONCEIVING HIMSELF	INSULTED	BY THE SMOKING OF A CIGARET AGAINST HIS ORDERS BY A
PHIL II	(124)	/JULIA/ YOU WILL NOT LEAVE ME HERE TO BE	INSULTED	BY THIS WOMAN, MR CHARTERIS. (SHE TAKES HIS ARM AS
KING I	(176)	(TO CHARLES) WILL YOU STAND THERE AND LET ME BE	INSULTED	BY THIS WOMAN? /CHARLES/ (WITH CONVICTION)
PYGM V	(280)	(ALMOST SOBBING) I'LL DEMEAN MYSELF. AND GET	INSULTED	FOR MY PAINS, LIKE ENOUGH. /DOOLITTLE/ DONT BE
PHIL III	(141)	HASTILY. IT WAS MY FAULT. I ANNOYED MISS CRAVEN--	INSULTED	HER. HANG IT ALL, DONT GO AND SPOIL EVERYTHING LIKE
DEVL II	(31)	WITH HIM. HE INSULTED YOU: HE INSULTED ME: HE	INSULTED	HIS MOTHER. /ANDERSON/ (QUAINTLY) WELL, DEAR, LETS
POSN	(448)	/FEEMY/ MR KEMP: WILL YOU STAND BY AND HEAR ME	INSULTED	IN THAT LOW WAY? (TO BLANCO, SPITEFULLY) I'LL SEE
POSN PREFACE	(372)	OF THE COMMITTEE'S SUDDEN DISCOVERY THAT I HAD	INSULTED	IT, AND ITS SUSPENSION OF ITS INVESTIGATION FOR THE
CLEO IV	(189)	WHITE WITH TERROR). HEARKEN, YOU WHO MUST NOT BE	INSULTED	. GO NEAR ENOUGH TO CATCH THEIR WORDS: YOU WILL
BARB III	(320)	AND I WILL NOT HEAR THE GOVERNMENT OF MY COUNTRY	INSULTED	. (HE THRUSTS HIS HANDS IN HIS POCKETS, AND WALKS
SUPR I	(45)	NOW I CLAIM MY RIGHT AS A MARRIED WOMAN NOT TO BE	INSULTED	. /OCTAVIUS/ (RAISING HIS HEAD WITH INEXPRESSIBLE
MILL I	(147)	HIM PROMISE YOU? /ALASTAIR/ I WONT HAVE POLLY	INSULTED	. /SAGAMORE/ (GOODHUMOREDLY) YOU DONT MIND, MISS
GENV IV	(96)	I WONT SIT HERE AND LISTEN TO MY COUNTRY BEING	INSULTED	. /THE BETROTHED/ HEAR HEAR! UP, CAMBERWELL!
ROCK II	(265)	MY RACE BY REMAINING HERE WHERE BOTH HAVE BEEN	INSULTED	. UNTIL NOW I HAVE SUPPORTED THE CONNECTION BETWEEN
POSN PREFACE	(425)	ENOUGH TO HAVE A RELIGION SO PETTY THAT IT CAN BE	INSULTED	(ANY MAN IS AS WELCOME TO INSULT MY RELIGION, IF
PHIL III	(141)	INFERNALLY PERPLEXING. I CANT BELIEVE THAT YOU	INSULTED	JULIA, CHARTERIS. IVE NO DOUBT YOU ANNOYED HER:
DEVL II	(31)	HE WILL BRING HARM WITH HIM. HE INSULTED YOU: HE	INSULTED	ME: HE INSULTED HIS MOTHER. /ANDERSON/ (QUAINTLY)
DEST	(179)	BETWEEN THEM) TEN MINUTES AGO YOU HAD NOT	INSULTED	ME BEYOND ALL BEARING. /NAPOLEON/ I-- (SWALLOWING
MIS.	(190)	I AFFIRM IT IN YOUR PRESENCE. I TELL THAT MAN WHO	INSULTED	ME THAT I DONT GIVE A DAMN FOR HIM. AND NEITHER I
POSN	(461)	WASNT HIM. I ONLY SAID IT OUT OF SPITE BECAUSE HE	INSULTED	ME. MAY I BE STRUCK DEAD IF I EVER SAW HIM WITH THE
CLEO IV	(188)	OWN TREACHERY. I CAUGHT HIM IN THE ACT; AND HE	INSULTED	ME-- ME, THE QUEEN! TO MY FACE. CAESAR WOULD NOT
FANY II	(293)	KNEES; THEY TWISTED MY ARMS; THEY TAUNTED AND	INSULTED	ME; THEY CALLED ME VILE NAMES; AND I TOLD THEM WHAT
MILL IV	(197)	I NEVER HEARD. WHAT HAPPENED WAS THAT HE	INSULTED	MY FATHER GROSSLY, WITHOUT THE SLIGHTEST
MILL II	(174)	DID HE MAKE LOVE TO YOU? /EPIFANIA/ NO. HE	INSULTED	MY FATHER'S MEMORY BECAUSE HE WAS DISAPPOINTED WITH
SUPR IV	(152)	(OUTRAGED) THIS IS THE LAST STRAW. DAD: YOU HAVE	INSULTED	MY WIFE. /MALONE/ YOUR WIFE! /TANNER/ YOU THE
OVER PREFACE	(157)	AS BADLY AS IF HE REALLY FELT IT, IS DESPISED AND	INSULTED	; AND MANY A MAN HAS SHOT OR STABBED A FRIEND OR
GENV II	(51)	THE BRITISH FLAG. /BEGONIA/ (RISING IN A FURY)	INSULTED	THE BRITISH FLAG! ! ! /THE SECRETARY/ THEY HAVE
CATH 3	(186)	SPITEFULLY) TO THE EMPRESS, LITTLE BEAUTY. HE HAS	INSULTED	THE EMPRESS. HE WILL RECEIVE A HUNDRED AND ONE
MTH5	(222)	YOU FALLEN OUT WITH ARJILLAX? /ECRASIA/ HE HAS	INSULTED	US! OUTRAGED US! PROFANED HIS ART! YOU KNOW HOW
DEVL II	(31)	MY MIND: I KNOW HE WILL BRING HARM WITH HIM. HE	INSULTED	YOU: HE INSULTED ME: HE INSULTED HIS MOTHER.
METH PREFACE	(R15)	ABOUT HISTORY FOR THE SAKE OF BEING CONTRADICTED,	INSULTED	, AND REFUTED, WOULD CERTAINLY DO LESS HARM THAN
MRS PREFACE	(178)	AND DRAG ACTRESSES TO THE POLICE COURT TO BE	INSULTED	, BULLIED, AND THREATENED FOR FULFILLING THEIR
CAND I	(100)	THE WORTH OF HIS HAPPINESS. MORELL, DEEPLY	INSULTED	, CONTROLS HIMSELF WITH FINE FORBEARANCE, AND
PYGM I	(210)	A GIRL CANT SHELTER FROM THE RAIN WITHOUT BEING	INSULTED	, ETC., ETC., ETC. (SHE IS CONDUCTED BY THE MORE
MIS. PREFACE	(99)	HAVE TO SATISFY CRAVINGS WHICH, IF STARVED OR	INSULTED	, MAY BECOME MORBID AND SEEK DISGRACEFUL
MILL PREFACE	(134)	THE MISERABLE PLIGHT OF THE GREAT MEN NEGLECTED,	INSULTED	, STARVED, AND OCCASIONALLY PUT TO DEATH, SOMETIMES
LION PREFACE	(84)	PITY AND HORROR A DESCRIPTION OF THEIR BEING	INSULTED	, TORTURED, AND KILLED. AND THE SAME IS TRUE OF

INSULTING

NEVR IV	(299)	/VALENTINE/ MRS CLANDON: HAVE I SAID ANYTHING	INSULTING	? /GLORIA/ YOU HAVE IMPLIED THAT MY PAST HAS BEEN
PHIL III	(138)	HAVE YOU THE FACE TO TURN ROUND LIKE THIS AFTER	INSULTING	AND TORTURING ME? /CHARTERIS/ NEVER MIND.
LION PREFACE	(28)	ABUSIVE, NEVER REPLYING TO HIS CRITICS WITHOUT AN	INSULTING	EPITHET, AND EVEN CURSING A FIG-TREE WHICH
LION PREFACE	(34)	NEVER ADDRESSES A PHARISEE OR A SCRIBE WITHOUT AN	INSULTING	EPITHET, BECOMES A CONSIDERATE, GENTLE, SOCIABLE,
LADY PREFACE	(215)	WHICH CONSISTS IN MERCILESSLY LIBELLING AND	INSULTING	EVERY WRITER WHOSE OPINIONS ARE SUFFICIENTLY
FANY PROLOG	(264)	HUMOR; AND IF YOU JOKE WITH HIM HE'LL THINK YOURE	INSULTING	HIM ON PURPOSE. MIND: IT'S NOT THAT HE DOESNT SEE
DEVL II	(38)	BEEN VERY GOOD TO YOU. HE HAS FORGIVEN YOU FOR	INSULTING	HIM, AND IS TRYING TO SAVE YOU. CAN YOU NOT
ARMS III	(49)	ONE OF THEM IS MAN ENOUGH TO SPIT IN MY FACE FOR	INSULTING	HIM, I'LL BUY HIS DISCHARGE AND GIVE HIM A
ROCK I	(198)	UP ALL NIGHT IN BAD AIR LISTENING TO FOOLS	INSULTING	ME? I TELL YOU I SHOULD HAVE BEEN DEAD LONG AGO
ARMS III	(52)	HAUGHTILY AT HIM) DO YOU KNOW, SIR, THAT YOU ARE	INSULTING	ME? /BLUNTSCHLI/ I CANT HELP IT. WHEN YOU STRIKE
NEVR II	(246)	NOT CLANDON. DO YOU WISH TO JOIN THEM IN	INSULTING	ME? /VALENTINE/ (IGNORING HIM) I'M OVERWHELMED,
POSN PREFACE	(372)	ITS INVESTIGATION FOR THE PURPOSE OF ELABORATELY	INSULTING	ME BACK AGAIN, COMIC TO THE LOOKERS-ON, THAT IS;
PHIL I	(78)	AND INTOLERABLE JEALOUSY AND ILL TEMPER; OF	INSULTING	ME ON IMAGINARY PROVOCATION; OF POSITIVELY BEATING
GENV III	(78)	DOLORES. /THE WIDOW/ I SUPPOSE YOU THINK YOU ARE	INSULTING	ME. YOU ARE SIMPLY MAKING A FOOL OF YOURSELF. MY
SUPR IV	(152)	I'M DONE WITH YOU. I DONT SELL THE PRIVILEGE OF	INSULTING	MY WIFE FOR A THOUSAND DOLLARS. /MALONE/ (DEEPLY
SUPR III	(89)	AND HE TRIED TO ASSASSINATE ME AFTER CALLING ME	INSULTING	NAMES. /THE OLD WOMAN/ YOU WERE LIKE ALL MEN.
BULL PREFACE	(49)	OR HESITATION TO OBEY ORDERS, HOWEVER GROSSLY	INSULTING	OR DISASTROUS THOSE ORDERS MAY BE, WITH SENTENCES
GENV III	(79)	BLOOD IN MY VEINS, THOUGH I SHOULD NEVER DREAM OF	INSULTING	QUETZALCOATL BY SACRIFICING A JEW TO HIM. /THE

LION PREFACE(75)	AS HE, AND THEN REVILED THEM IN THE MOST	INSULTING TERMS AS " STIFFNECKED AND UNCIRCUMCIZED."
POSN (451)	FOR IT. /THE BOYS/ THATS SO. OF COURSE HE HAS.	INSULTING THE COURT! CHALLENGE BE JIGGERED! GAG HIM.
MILL IV (199)	THERE IS NO QUESTION OF BLACKMAILING OR	INSULTING YOU. I ONLY WANT TO SETTLE THIS BUSINESS OF MR
		INSULTINGLY
CATH 4 (187)	POLE. NARYSHKIN STOOPS OVER HIM AND ADDRESSES HIM	INSULTINGLY). WELL! ARE YOU READY TO BE TORTURED? THIS IS
		INSULTS
ARMS III (59)	ARE AFRAID OF THEIR OFFICERS; THEY PUT UP WITH	INSULTS AND BLOWS; THEY STAND BY AND SEE ONE ANOTHER
APPL PREFACE(195)	WAS EVIDENT THAT OFFICIALDOM, WRITHING UNDER HIS	INSULTS AND SHOCKED BY HIS UTTER LACK OF VENERATION FOR
NEVR III (280)	SAY THOSE THINGS TO ME. I FORBID YOU. THEY ARE	INSULTS . /VALENTINE/ NO: THEYRE ONLY FOLLIES. I CANT HELP
NEVR IV (299)	MY PAST HAS BEEN LIKE YOURS. THAT IS THE WORST OF	INSULTS . /VALENTINE/ I IMPLY NOTHING OF THE SORT. I DECLARE
KING I (189)	OF MY REPEATED REQUESTS. HE STAYED HERE TO HEAP	INSULTS ON THE IMMORTAL GALILEO, WHOSE SHOE LATCHET HE IS
PRES (158)	AND FUMING AWAY TO THE FIREPLACE) THOSE REPEATED	INSULTS TO A MAN OF BLAMELESS LIFE ARE AS DISGRACEFUL TO YOU
UNPL PREFACE(R14)	EXAMINER OF PLAYS, A GENTLEMAN WHO ROBS,	INSULTS , AND SUPPRESSES ME AS IRRESISTIBLY AS IF HE WERE
DEVL II (37)	BY BEING A WOMAN? HAS HE NOT RAISED YOU ABOVE MY	INSULTS , LIKE HIMSELF? (SHE STOPS CRYING, AND RECOVERS
		INSUPERABLE
KING PREFACE(156)	BECAUSE THE ENGLISH PEOPLE, HAVING AN	INSUPERABLE DISLIKE OF BEING GOVERNED AT ALL, WOULD NOT PAY
CATH PREFACE(156)	ALWAYS FOUND THAT THE DIFFICULTIES ARE NOT REALLY	INSUPERABLE , THE AUTHOR HAVING FORESEEN UNSUSPECTED
		INSURANCE
LION PREFACE(73)	IT AS AN ORDINARY EVENT LIKE HOME RULE OR THE	INSURANCE ACT: THAT IS (THOUGH THIS DID NOT OCCUR TO THE
POSN PREFACE(367)	OF TWO GUINEAS PER PLAY, WITH AN EFFECTIVE	INSURANCE AGAINST THE AUTHOR GETTING HIM INTO TROUBLE, AND A
MILL I (162)	/PATRICIA/ YOU SHALL, DEAR. I WILL SELL OUT MY	INSURANCE AND GIVE IT TO YOU. /EPIFANIA/ MAY I HAVE THAT IN
MRS I (185)	MAKE CALCULATIONS FOR ENGINEERS, ELECTRICIANS,	INSURANCE COMPANIES, AND SO ON; BUT I KNOW NEXT TO NOTHING
GETT (347)	TO THE CHURCH, WE WENT TO THE OFFICE OF THAT	INSURANCE COMPANY-- WHATS ITS NAME, CECIL? /SYKES/ THE
GETT (347)	ITS NAME, CECIL? /SYKES/ THE BRITISH FAMILY	INSURANCE CORPORATION. IT INSURES YOU AGAINST POOR RELATIONS
BARB III (327)	TOWN HALL! ? /STEPHEN/ HAVE YOU GONE INTO THE	INSURANCE FUND, THE PENSION FUND, THE BUILDING SOCIETY, THE
MRS I (185)	TO NOTHING ABOUT ENGINEERING OR ELECTRICITY OR	INSURANCE , I DONT EVEN KNOW ARITHMETIC WELL. OUTSIDE
ROCK II (246)	THE CHANCE OF EACH OF YOU GRABBING A SHARE OF THE	INSURANCE MONEY. BUT THE COUNTRY WILL DEAL WITH YOU. THE
POSN PREFACE(365)	SHEW LATER ON, THE CENSORSHIP AFFORDS A CHEAP	INSURANCE OF ENORMOUS VALUE. FOURTH, THERE WAS THE POWERFUL
GETT (347)	MAY WELL ASK. WHILE EDIE AND CECIL WERE AT THE	INSURANCE OFFICE I TOOK A TAXY AND WENT OFF TO YOUR
MILL I (154)	PLAYER IF HIS UNCLE HAD NOT PUSHED HIM INTO AN	INSURANCE OFFICE, WHERE HE WAS PERFECTLY USELESS. /ALASTAIR/
JITT III (56)	THATS NOT THE BOOK THAT HE SAID MIGHT BE MY BEST	INSURANCE POLICY. IT WAS PART OF HIS PROVISION FOR ME. HE
JITT III (78)	JUST TOLD ME THAT HE SAID THE BOOK WAS TO BE HER	INSURANCE POLICY. NO DOUBT I AM BRUNO'S INFERIOR; BUT I DRAW
POSN PREFACE(367)	THAT THE PLAY WAS A PROPER ONE. A TWO GUINEA	INSURANCE POLICY. THE CENSORSHIP, THEN, PROVIDES THE
		INSURE
GETT (347)	FAMILY CONTINGENCIES. /EDITH/ IT HAS CONSENTED TO	INSURE CECIL AGAINST LIBEL ACTIONS BROUGHT AGAINST HIM ON MY
DOCT PREFACE(16)	A THOUSAND A YEAR BEFORE HE CAN AFFORD EVEN TO	INSURE HIS LIFE, HIS HOUSE, HIS SERVANTS, AND HIS EQUIPAGE (
DOCT PREFACE(25)	APPEARED ON IT, BUT THE PRECAUTIONS NECESSARY TO	INSURE THAT THE INOCULATION SHALL CONSIST OF NOTHING ELSE
METH PREFACE(R69)	FOR RULERS WHO THINK IT POSSIBLE TAKE CARE TO	INSURE THE RISK BY RULING REASONABLY. THIS BRINGS ABOUT A
		INSURED
DOCT III (134)	WOULD SHE HAVE TO LIVE ON IF I DIED? I'M NOT	INSURED : CANT AFFORD THE PREMIUMS. (PICKING OUT ANOTHER
HART PREFACE(37)	HE HAS PAID HIS INCOME TAX AND SUPER TAX, AND	INSURED HIS LIFE FOR THE AMOUNT OF HIS DEATH DUTIES, HE IS
		INSURES
FABL PREFACE(64)	MORE SCEPTICAL OF THE DOGMA THAT A HEALTHY BODY	INSURES A HEALTHY MIND (MENS SANA IN CORPORE SANO) AND MORE
GETT (347)	THE BRITISH FAMILY INSURANCE CORPORATION. IT	INSURES YOU AGAINST POOR RELATIONS AND ALL SORTS OF FAMILY
		INSURGENT
HART PREFACE(35)	AND THE DEVIL OUT OF THE TEMPLE, AND PARTLY OF	INSURGENT MEN WHO HAD BECOME INTOLERABLY POOR BECAUSE THE
SUPR HANDBOK(196)	THE SOCIALIST AGITATION, HAVE DRAWN THE TEETH OF	INSURGENT POVERTY AND SAVED THE EXISTING ORDER FROM THE ONLY
		INSURING
POSN PREFACE(418)	RESULT? THE MANAGERS WILL FIND THAT INSTEAD OF	INSURING THEM AS THE LORD CHAMBERLAIN DOES, HE WILL WARN
BUOY 1 (16)	YOURSELF WHEN I AM GONE. /SON/ I HAVE THOUGHT OF	INSURING YOUR LIFE. /FATHER/ HOW ARE YOU TO PAY THE
		INSURRECTION
GETT PREFACE(256)	THAT THEY AT LAST PROVOKE A FURIOUS GENERAL	INSURRECTION AGAINST THEM AS THEY ALREADY PROVOKE MANY
LION PREFACE(17)	OF HEAVEN TO CONSOLE THE POOR AND KEEP THEM FROM	INSURRECTION ALSO CURBS THE VICIOUS BY THREATENING THEM WITH
LION PREFACE(33)	WITH THEM THAT MADE INSURRECTION, MEN WHO IN THE	INSURRECTION HAD COMMITTED MURDER." JOSEPH OF ARIMATHEA, WHO
LION PREFACE(99)	HOURS PROVOKE THE VILLAGE AT ITS GATES TO	INSURRECTION . THAT IS BECAUSE THE MONASTERY SELECTS ITS
LION PREFACE(30)	SIGNIFICANTLY, THAT HIS OFFENCE WAS SEDITION AND	INSURRECTION ; THAT HE WAS AN ADVOCATE OF PHYSICAL FORCE;
DOCT PREFACE(31)	CALAMITY: A CHOLERA EPIDEMIC, A WAR, OR AN	INSURRECTION , BEFORE WAKING US UP SUFFICIENTLY TO GET
LION PREFACE(33)	BARABBAS WAS " LYING BOUND WITH THEM THAT MADE	INSURRECTION , MEN WHO IN THE INSURRECTION HAD COMMITTED
		INSURRECTIONARY
BARB PREFACE(237)	BECOME A SORT OF AUXILIARY POLICE, TAKING OFF THE	INSURRECTIONARY EDGE OF POVERTY WITH COALS AND BLANKETS,
		INSUSCEPTIBLE
MILL I (145)	STRIPPED WELL, UNLIKE MANY HANDSOME MEN. I AM NOT	INSUSCEPTIBLE TO SEX APPEAL, VERY FAR FROM IT. /SAGAMORE/ (
DEST SD(157)	WITHOUT IMAGINATION, WITHOUT SENSE, HOPELESSLY	INSUSCEPTIBLE TO THE NAPOLEONIC OR ANY OTHER IDEA,
SUPR PREFACE(R39)	BUT HERE AND THERE OCCURS A SCRAP OF INTENSELY	INSUSCEPTIBLE , INTENSELY RESISTANT MATERIAL; AND THAT
		INT
CAND II (111)	ALONE, MR MORCHBANKS, LET ME GIVE YOU A FRIENDLY	INT THAT I WOULDNT GIVE TO HEVERYBODY. OW LONG AVE YOU KNOWN
		INTACT
JOAN PREFACE(6)	HER AUDACITY, BUT ON THE CONTRARY GOODHUMORED, AN	INTACT VIRGIN, VERY PIOUS, VERY TEMPERATE (WE SHOULD CALL
		INTEGRATED
METH PREFACE(R28)	HAD TO BE CONSIDERED ONE BY ONE IN SUCCESSION ARE	INTEGRATED INTO WHAT SEEMS A SINGLE SIMPLE FACTOR. CHAINS OF
		INTEGRATION
MIS. PREFACE(44)	DEDUCTION; OR EVEN INTO SO RAPID AND INTUITIVE AN	INTEGRATION OF ALL THESE PROCESSES IN A SINGLE BRAIN THAT WE
DOCT PREFACE(68)	THAT LARGE, SLOWLY ADVANCING, PETTISHLY RESISTED	INTEGRATION OF SOCIETY CALLED GENERALLY SOCIALISM. UNTIL THE
		INTEGRITY
LION PREFACE(89)	VIEW OF SUCH BELIEF AS A BREACH OF INTELLECTUAL	INTEGRITY : IT IS THE DIFFERENCE BETWEEN BELIEF IN THE
FABL PREFACE(67)	WHILST MANY SIMPLE CREDULOUS SOULS ARE MODELS OF	INTEGRITY AND PIETY, HIGH IN THE CALENDAR OF SAINTS. MENTAL
BUOY PREFACE(6)	CHRONOLOGY) DOES NOT INVALIDATE IN THE LEAST HIS	INTEGRITY AS A SCIENTIFIC INVESTIGATOR, NOR EXEMPLIFY HIS
CAPT III (284)	AND LOOKS AT RANKIN WITH A SUDDEN DOUBT OF HIS	INTEGRITY AS A WITNESS). /KEARNEY/ BUT I UNDERSTOOD FROM OUR
UNPL PREFACE(R21)	INSTINCT, UNLESS HE WERE A REALIST OF FANATICAL	INTEGRITY . AND THAT WOULD NOT SAVE HIM EITHER; FOR HIS
GENV I (39)	THE ELECTIONS WERE CONDUCTED WITH ABSOLUTE	INTEGRITY . THE BALLOT WAS SECRET. THE PEOPLE FELT FREE FOR
DOCT PREFACE(12)	RELATIVE IMPORTANCE OF PRESERVING THEIR BODILY	INTEGRITY (INCLUDING THE CAPACITY FOR PARENTAGE) AND THE
UNPL PREFACE(R25)	DESIRES TO FOUND ITSELF ON A HIGH STANDARD OF	INTEGRITY OF CHARACTER IN ITS UNITS SHOULD ORGANIZE ITSELF
FANY PREFACE(255)	THAT WILL COMBINE LOSS OF RESPECTABILITY WITH	INTEGRITY OF SELF-RESPECT AND REASONABLE CONSIDERATION FOR
POSN PREFACE(431)	WHY I TRUST LORD GORELL WHEN HE IS DEFENDING THE	INTEGRITY OF THE LAW AGAINST THE PROPOSAL TO MAKE IT IN ANY
LION PREFACE(67)	OF HOW WE ARE TO SECURE THE SPIRITUAL FREEDOM AND	INTEGRITY OF THE PRIEST AND THE NUN WITHOUT THEIR BARRENNESS
DEVL EPILOG (80)	THEMSELVES ENGAGED IN A CIVIL WAR FOR THE	INTEGRITY OF THEIR UNION. IN 1885 THE WHIGS WHO REPRESENTED
POSN PREFACE(391)	OF LIBERTY OF CONSCIENCE AND INTELLECTUAL	INTEGRITY -- SAY A MILTON, A CHESTERFIELD, A BENTHAM-- WOULD
LION PREFACE(67)	HE NEEDS ONLY COURAGE AND CONVICTION TO MAKE HIS	INTEGRITY UNASSAILABLE. BUT HE FORFEITS THAT RIGHT WHEN HE

APPL I (235)	ETERNAL AGAINST THE EXPEDIENT; FOR INTELLECTUAL	INTEGRITY	, FOR HUMANITY, FOR THE RESCUE OF INDUSTRY FROM
		INTELLECT	
MIS. (171)	LITTLE DEN COUNTING ANOTHER MAN'S MONEY. IVE AN	INTELLECT	: A MIND AND A BRAIN AND A SOUL; AND THE USE HE
NEVR III (270)	WAS NOTHING BUT COWARDICE. I DIDNT RESPECT YOUR	INTELLECT	: IVE A BETTER ONE MYSELF: IT'S A MASCULINE
3PLA PREFACE(R24)	ATTENTION TO THE DISTINCTION BETWEEN WILL AND	INTELLECT	? NOT SCHOPENHAUER, I THINK, BUT SHAW. AGAIN,
MIS. (117)	PLAIN IF POSSIBLE. HE HAS A HARD AND PENETRATING	INTELLECT	AND A REMARKABLE POWER OF LOOKING FACTS IN THE
MTH2 (71)	SET THE FASHION; AND THAT IS MERE ENERGY WITHOUT	INTELLECT	AND WITHOUT KNOWLEDGE. YOUR MIND IS NOT A TRAINED
CAND I (84)	SO NICE TO BE A MAN AND HAVE A FINE PENETRATING	INTELLECT	INSTEAD OF MERE EMOTIONS LIKE US, AND TO KNOW THAT
UNPL PREFACE(R20)	STRONG FEELINGS OPERATING THROUGH A ROMANTIC	INTELLECT	INSTEAD OF THROUGH AN ENTIRELY COMMERCIAL ONE; BUT
SUPR III (113)	UNPOPULAR. BUT TO LIFE, THE FORCE BEHIND THE MAN,	INTELLECT	IS A NECESSITY, BECAUSE WITHOUT IT HE BLUNDERS
FABL PREFACE(86)	NEVER SUPPLY THIS, ESPECIALLY IN ENGLAND, WHERE	INTELLECT	IS HATED AND DREADED, NOT WHOLLY WITHOUT REASON,
SUPR III (113)	DONT BEAR THINKING ABOUT. /DON JUAN/ THAT IS WHY	INTELLECT	IS SO UNPOPULAR. BUT TO LIFE, THE FORCE BEHIND THE
DOCT I (105)	FOLLOWED BY EMMY). /B.B./ (SADLY) WALPOLE HAS NO	INTELLECT	. A MERE SURGEON. WONDERFUL OPERATOR; BUT, AFTER
MILL II (175)	WHAT I CAN GET. /THE DOCTOR/ GOOD. A PRACTICAL	INTELLECT	, AND WHAT DO YOU WANT AT PRESENT, FOR INSTANCE..
GENV IV (118)	ARE NOT TO BE STOPPED BY ACADEMIC TWADDLE ABOUT	INTELLECT	, BUT I WILL CONDESCEND TO TELL THIS FELLOW FROM
FANY III (317)	WITH YOU, GILBEY, IF YOU BEGIN TALKING ABOUT MY	INTELLECT	, GIVE US SOME TEA, MARIA. IVE SAID MY SAY; AND
MTH5 (229)	BUT IT IS SUCH A PITY THAT YOU ARTISTS HAVE NO	INTELLECT	. /ECRASIA/ (SENTENTIOUSLY) I DO NOT ADMIT THAT.
FOUN (221)	MANNERS. /MERCER/ MY LORD! THIS MAN HAS A GIANT	INTELLECT	. /THE LORD CHANCELLOR/ IT WILL AVAIL HIM AS
GENV IV (118)	OWN. YOU HAVE EMPLOYED PHYSICAL FORCE TO SUPPRESS	INTELLECT	. THAT IS THE SIN AGAINST THE HOLY GHOST. I ACCUSE
AUGS (275)	/THE LADY/ OH, IMPOSSIBLE! HE IS JEALOUS OF YOUR	INTELLECT	. THE BET IS AN INSULT TO YOU: DONT YOU FEEL
NEVR IV (285)	HIM, MISS CLANDON: HE'S THE VERY INCARNATION OF	INTELLECT	. YOU CAN HEAR HIS MIND WORKING. /GLORIA/ (
GENV I (34)	YOU WILL BE ACTING, NOT FOR YOURSELF, BUT FOR THE	INTELLECT	OF EUROPE. I ASSURE YOU IT IS THE CORRECT COURSE.
MRS PREFACE(166)	BECOME SO FLACCID IN ITS SENTIMENTALITY, AND THE	INTELLECT	OF ITS FREQUENTERS SO ATROPHIED BY DISUSE, THAT
SUPR III (84)	BY THIS TIME) IT WAS JUST SO WITH HER, SIR. HER	INTELLECT	REACHED FORWARD INTO THE TWENTIETH CENTURY: HER
SUPR III (81)	HEAD OF HAIR I EVER SAW. SHE HAD HUMOR; SHE HAD	INTELLECT	; SHE COULD COOK TO PERFECTION; AND HER HIGHLY
SIM II (83)	BUT OUTSIDE THAT ROUTINE THERE IS A LIFE OF THE	INTELLECT	THAT IS QUITE INDEPENDENT OF IT. WHAT HAVE I BEEN
NEVR III (278)	YOUR WEAKNESS, MISS CLANDON. I APPEAL FROM HER	INTELLECT	TO YOUR HEART. /GLORIA/ I HAVE LEARNT TO MISTRUST
MIS. PREFACE(72)	HAVE A SILLY HABIT OF TALKING AND THINKING AS IF	INTELLECT	WERE A MECHANICAL PROCESS AND NOT A PASSION; AND
SUPR III (125)	THINGS; THAT UNLESS THE LADY'S CHARACTER AND	INTELLECT	WERE EQUAL OR SUPERIOR TO MY OWN, HER CONVERSATION
FANY EPILOG (332)	OF THE NOTE OF PASSION. /BANNAL/ YES, I KNOW.	INTELLECT	WITHOUT EMOTION. THATS RIGHT. I ALWAYS SAY THAT
3PLA PREFACE(R24)	ME, AND PROCLAIM THAT I WRITE AS IF MANKIND HAD	INTELLECT	WITHOUT WILL, OR HEART, AS THEY CALL IT. INGRATES:
ROCK I (231)	OF THE HOUSE AS PRIME MINISTER. INTELLECT,	INTELLECT	, ALL THE TIME. /THE LADY/ AT HARROW YOU WROTE
NEVR I SD(208)	A JEALOUSLY ASSERTIVE ATTITUDE OF CHARACTER AND	INTELLECT	, AND IN BEING A WOMAN OF CULTIVATED INTERESTS
PLES PREFACE(R9)	ADDRESSED INTELLIGIBLY AND PROSAICALLY TO THE	INTELLECT	, CAN ONLY COME WHEN THE WORK IS DONE, AND INDEED
ROCK I (231)	THE LEADERSHIP OF THE HOUSE AS PRIME MINISTER.	INTELLECT	, INTELLECT, ALL THE TIME. /THE LADY/ AT HARROW
FANY III (317)	(REVERENTLY) I NEVER DENIED THAT YOUVE A GREAT	INTELLECT	, MRS KNOX-- /MRS KNOX/ OH, GET ALONG WITH YOU,
MIS. PREFACE(72)	CANE IN HAND, THE DANGER WILL BE PRECOCITY OF THE	INTELLECT	, WHICH IS JUST AS UNDESIRABLE AS PRECOCITY OF THE
SUPR III (112)	MAKING LONG SPEECHES? HOWEVER, IF I OVERTAX YOUR	INTELLECT	, YOU CAN LEAVE US AND SEEK THE SOCIETY OF LOVE
SUPR III (99)	FAILURE. /THE DEVIL/ NOT THAT WE DONT ADMIRE YOUR	INTELLECT	, YOU KNOW. WE DO. BUT I LOOK AT THE MATTER FROM
BARB III (334)	BY HUMANITY, NO CAPITAL? MY CHARACTER! MY	INTELLECT	! MY LIFE! MY CAREER! WHAT BARBARA CALLS MY
ARMS III (64)	SHOCKING SACRIFICE, ISNT IT? SUCH BEAUTY! SUCH	INTELLECT	! SUCH MODESTY! WASTED ON A MIDDLE-AGED SERVANT
		INTELLECTS	
INCA (250)	SURROUNDED WITH THE ABLEST AND MOST FAR-REACHING	INTELLECTS	IN THE WORLD? /THE INCA/ (EXPLOSIVELY) WHAT ON
		INTELLECTUAL	
FANY PROLOG (264)	ABOUT THAT: I SHOULDNT LIKE ANYONE TO CALL ME AN	INTELLECTUAL	: I DONT THINK ANY ENGLISHMAN WOULD! THEY DONT
VWOO 1 (119)	ARNT YOU? /A/ WHAT DO YOU THINK YOU MEAN BY AN	INTELLECTUAL	? /Z/ ONLY THAT YOU CONSIDER ME NO BETTER THAN
JOAN PREFACE(54)	I CANNOT ASSOCIATE PLEASURE WITH ANY SORT OF	INTELLECTUAL	ACTIVITY; AND I DONT BELIEVE ANYONE ELSE CAN
3PLA PREFACE(R23)	BUT THE SUBSTITUTION OF SENSUOUS ECSTASY FOR	INTELLECTUAL	ACTIVITY AND HONESTY IS THE VERY DEVIL. IT HAS
MILL PREFACE(124)	THAT THEY ARE SOMETIMES FORCED TO DO IT BECAUSE	INTELLECTUAL	ADVANCES MAY PRESENT THEMSELVES AS QUACKERY,
PYGM EPILOG (291)	WHICH PERSONS OF GENIUS ACHIEVE BY SHEER	INTELLECTUAL	ANALYSIS, IS SOMETIMES PRODUCED OR AIDED BY
UNPL PREFACE(R11)	OF LIFE IN LONDON FOR PERSONS OF SERIOUS	INTELLECTUAL	AND ARTISTIC INTERESTS IS THE WANT OF A
LADY PREFACE(223)	OF STATE HAD NOT CONFINED HIS OPPORTUNITIES OF	INTELLECTUAL	AND POLITICAL TRAINING TO PRIVATE CONVERSATION
MIS. PREFACE(85)	AND IF MEN WERE CUT OFF ARTIFICIALLY FROM	INTELLECTUAL	AND PUBLIC INTERESTS AS WOMEN ARE, THE
BULL PREFACE(38)	ARISTOCRACY AND ECCLESIASTICISM; AND ALL THE	INTELLECTUAL	AND SPIRITUAL FORCES IN FRANCE, FROM TURGOT TO
BARB I SD(259)	FORM OF LOMAX'S COMPLAINT. HIS SENSE OF HUMOR IS	INTELLECTUAL	AND SUBTLE, AND IS COMPLICATED BY AN APPALLING
SIM II (56)	THAT SHE REALLY COULD NOT UNDERSTAND ANY PURELY	INTELLECTUAL	APPEAL. YOUR OWN MIND, THANKS TO YOUR PUBLIC
MRS PREFACE(166)	I DO NOT FIND THOSE CRITICS WHO ARE GIFTED WITH	INTELLECTUAL	APPETITE AND POLITICAL CONSCIENCE COMPLAINING
2TRU PREFACE(24)	ECLECTIC DEMOCRACY. I THINK MY VIEWS ON	INTELLECTUAL	ARISTOCRACY AND DEMOCRACY AND ALL THE REST OF
MRS II (208)	WILL BE DELIGHTED TO SEE YOU. SHE'S A GENUINELY	INTELLECTUAL	ARTISTIC WOMAN; AND SHE SEES NOBODY HERE FROM
MIS. PREFACE(62)	CONTINUAL AND SHAMELESS ASSUMPTION OF MORAL AND	INTELLECTUAL	AUTHORITY. THUS THE SCHOOLBOY HEARS BOTH SIDES,
LADY PREFACE(218)	TO NERVOUS BREAKDOWN AND MADNESS." IN TIMON THE	INTELLECTUAL	BANKRUPTCY IS OBVIOUS ENOUGH: SHAKESPEAR TRIED
MILL I (150)	LIMITED. /ALASTAIR/ A CHAP THAT SETS UP TO BE AN	INTELLECTUAL	BECAUSE HIS FATHER WAS A PUBLISHER! HE MAKES
ROCK I (233)	HER AND HER RABBLE OF HALF-BAKED HALF-EDUCATED	INTELLECTUAL	BEGGARS-ON-HORSEBACK THAT ANY OXFORD MAN CAN
LION PREFACE(101)	ONLY AS THE CAT JUMPS, IS CLEARLY A POLITICAL AND	INTELLECTUAL	BRIGAND. THE RULE OF THE NEGATIVE MAN WHO HAS
GENV I (30)	A NEW CHAIR? /SHE/ IT CANT AFFORD ANYTHING. THE	INTELLECTUAL	BUDGET IS THE INTEREST ON TWO MILLION PAPER
GENV I (37)	REALLY NOTHING FOR THEM TO ATTEND TO. IT'S ONLY	INTELLECTUAL	BUSINESS, YOU KNOW. /THE WIDOW/ BUT DO THEY NOT
LADY PREFACE(222)	HAVE SEEMED CRUEL BEYOND DESCRIPTION: AN	INTELLECTUAL	CALIBAN. TRUE, A CALIBAN WHO COULD SAY " BE NOT
BULL PREFACE(24)	IT TO YOU WITH THAT IRISH INSISTENCE ON	INTELLECTUAL	CLARITY TO WHICH MY ENGLISH CRITICS ARE SO
METH PREFACE(R77)	EVERY DOGMA. THE REAL CLASS WAR WILL BE A WAR OF	INTELLECTUAL	CLASSES; AND ITS CONQUEST WILL BE THE SOULS OF
2TRU III (96)	DISGUSTING MENTAL PICTURES. I REALLY CANNOT STAND	INTELLECTUAL	COARSENESS. SWEETIE'S VULGARITY I CAN FORGIVE
GENV II (56)	I HAVE COMMUNICATED WITH ALL THE MEMBERS OF THE	INTELLECTUAL	COMMITTEE; AND EVERY ONE OF THEM DENIES ANY
GENV III (66)	ANY LAW IN GENEVA. THE HAGUE HAS ABOLISHED THE	INTELLECTUAL	COMMITTEE, LEAVING MY HUSBAND'S MURDER STILL
GENV IV (112)	ONLY TO SAY PECKHAM TO THE REPRESENTATIVE OF THE	INTELLECTUAL	COMMITTEE OF THE LEAGUE OF NATIONS TO REVEAL
LION PREFACE(9)	NOT LONG AGO I ASKED A WRITER OF DISTINGUISHED	INTELLECTUAL	COMPETENCE WHETHER HE HAD MADE A STUDY OF THE
FANY PREFACE(256)	DESIGNED TO COMPASS THEIR ETHICAL PERVERSION AND	INTELLECTUAL	CONFUSION. IF IT WERE POSSIBLE, I SHOULD PUT
METH PREFACE(R78)	EDUCATED PEOPLE NOT ONLY REFUSE TO OUTRAGE THEIR	INTELLECTUAL	CONSCIENCES BY READING THE LEGEND OF NOAH'S
METH PREFACE(R61)	ACTING ON INDIVIDUALS WITHOUT ANY CHARACTER OR	INTELLECTUAL	CONSCIOUSNESS WHATEVER, NO WONDER THE
LION PREFACE(82)	INTO THE PAGES OF NIETZSCHE, TORMENTED BY AN	INTELLECTUAL	CONSCIENCE THAT DEMANDED AN ARGUED CASE EVEN AT
3PLA PREFACE(R21)	EXPATIATION. THE WORST OF IT IS THAT SINCE MAN'S	INTELLECTUAL	CONSCIOUSNESS OF HIMSELF IS DERIVED FROM THE
MTH5 (225)	EVEN AN IMAGE OF THE TRUTH? IN THE END THE	INTELLECTUAL	CONSCIENCE THAT TORE YOU AWAY FROM THE FLEETING
SUPR PREFACE(R23)	BY NATURE TO CARRY ON THE WORK OF BUILDING UP AN	INTELLECTUAL	CONSCIOUSNESS OF HER OWN INSTINCTIVE PURPOSE.
FABL PREFACE(69)	AND FORGERIES MOST DISTRESSING TO THEIR	INTELLECTUAL	CONSCIENCES. WHEN THE PEOPLE DEMAND MIRACLES,
BARB PREFACE(243)	BY COMMON SENSE A HATER OF WASTE AND DISORDER, BY	INTELLECTUAL	CONSTITUTION LEGALLY MINDED TO THE VERGE OF
METH PREFACE(R54)	PREACHED THERE I MADE NO ATTEMPT TO CONCEAL MY	INTELLECTUAL	CONTEMPT FOR ITS BLIND COARSENESS AND SHALLOW
GENV I (37)	/THE WIDOW/ ARE YOU THE PRESIDENT OF THE	INTELLECTUAL	COOPERATION COMMITTEE OF THE LEAGUE OF
GENV I (30)	DO? /SHE/ OH NO. I TELL YOU I HAVE TO DO ALL THE	INTELLECTUAL	CO-OPERATION. I HAVE TO DO IT SINGLEHANDED TOO:
GENV I (30)	IT NEAR THE OFFICE TABLE; AND SITS DOWN). THE	INTELLECTUAL	CO-OPERATION OF SIXTY NATIONS MUST BE A VERY
GENV I (33)	OF NATIONS CAN ACT THROUGH ITS COMMITTEE FOR	INTELLECTUAL	CO-OPERATION. THE COMMITTEE CAN ACT THROUGH THE
GENV I (30)	THE OFFICE OF THE INTERNATIONAL COMMITTEE FOR	INTELLECTUAL	CO-OPERATION. /SHE/ YES: THATS QUITE ALL RIGHT.
GENV I (31)	TAKES UP HALF MY TIME. /HE/ AND DO THEY CALL THAT	INTELLECTUAL	CO-OPERATION? /SHE/ WELL, WHAT ELSE WOULD YOU
GENV I (33)	THE INITIATIVE MUST BE TAKEN BY ITS COMMITTEE FOR	INTELLECTUAL	CO-OPERATION: THAT IS, FOR THE MOMENT, BY YOU.
GENV I (30)	SECRETARIAT, I EXPECTED TO FIND THE COMMITTEE FOR	INTELLECTUAL	CO-OPERATION LODGED IN SOME IMPOSINGLY
GENV I (43)	HAPPENED? /HE/ YOU ARE IN THE OFFICE OF THE	INTELLECTUAL	CO-OPERATION COMMITTEE IN GENEVA. YOU HAVE HAD
GENV II SD(49)	THE RECEIVER AS BEGONIA ENTERS. SHE IS THE	INTELLECTUAL	CO-OPERATION TYPIST. SHE IS IN WALKING DRESS,
GENV I (47)	FLOOR? WHAT HAS HAPPENED? /HE/ YOU ARE IN THE	INTELLECTUAL	CO-OPERATION BUREAU IN GENEVA; AND YOU HAVE
GENV II (54)	I DIDNT DO IT. IT WAS DONE BY THE COMMITTEE FOR	INTELLECTUAL	CO-OPERATION. /SIR O./ THE WHAT? ? ! I NEVER
GENV III (65)	YES. THE INTERNATIONAL COURT HAS ABOLISHED	INTELLECTUAL	CO-OPERATION (HE SEATS HIMSELF AT THE NEXT
GENV II (60)	IS NO WRONG WITHOUT A REMEDY. YOUR COMMITTEE FOR	INTELLECTUAL	CO-OPERATION HAS BEEN APPEALED TO BY FOUR
GENV II (58)	LAWBREAKERS CAN BE BROUGHT TO JUSTICE. WELL, THE	INTELLECTUAL	CO-OPERATION COMMITTEE-- OF THE EXISTENCE OF
GENV II (59)	INTERNATIONAL COURT, MOVED BY THE COMMITTEE FOR	INTELLECTUAL	CO-OPERATION, WERE TO DELIVER AN ADVERSE
GENV IV (89)	DAME BEGONIA BROWN, REPRESENTS THE COMMITTEE FOR	INTELLECTUAL	CO-OPERATION. THE YOUNG GENTLEMAN IS THE
GENV IV (127)	NOT HAVE APPEALED TO ME BEFORE I REPRESENTED	INTELLECTUAL	CO-OPERATION. BUT I AM A DAME OF THE BRITISH
POSN PREFACE(375)	IMPATIENT AND CONTEMPTUOUS I MIGHT FEEL OF THE	INTELLECTUAL	COWARDICE SHEWN BY THE MAJORITY OF THE
MTH4 I (154)	AT THAT IMMORTAL MOMENT THE ENGLISH RACE HAD LOST	INTELLECTUAL	CREDIT TO SUCH AN EXTENT THAT THEY HABITUALLY

MIS. PREFACE(50)	TO DISCUSS THE IMPORTANCE OF ART, LEARNING, AND	INTELLECTUAL	CULTURE. THE FIRST THING WE HAVE TO RECOGNIZE
LADY PREFACE(230)	OF ADVENTURE, THAT PERSONAL REFINEMENT AND	INTELLECTUAL	CULTURE, THAT SCOPE OF ACTION, WHICH THE HIGHER
LION EPILOG (150)	BE AN ARTIST EXPRESSING RELIGIOUS EMOTION WITHOUT	INTELLECTUAL	DEFINITION BY MEANS OF POETRY, MUSIC,
BULL PREFACE(20)	PRODUCE A HERO SO UTTERLY DEVOID OF COMMON SENSE,	INTELLECTUAL	DELICACY, AND INTERNATIONAL CHIVALRY AS NELSON,
MTH3 (104)	VOICE/ YOU ARE SPEAKING TO HIM. /BURGE-LUBIN/ AN	INTELLECTUAL	DIFFICULTY, OLD MAN. SOMETHING WE DONT
MTH3 (104)	DEPARTMENTS. /BURGE-LUBIN/ SYNTHESIS! THIS IS AN	INTELLECTUAL	DIFFICULTY. THIS IS A JOB FOR CONFUCIUS. I
LION PREFACE(18)	THREE VIEWS ARE ACCEPTED SIMULTANEOUSLY WITHOUT	INTELLECTUAL	DISCOMFORT. WE CAN PROVISIONALLY ENTERTAIN HALF
APPL I (206)	THAN TEN MINUTES, YOU HAVE ALREADY LED ME INTO AN	INTELLECTUAL	DISCUSSION WHICH SHEWS THAT WE ARE SOMETHING
BUOY IV (60)	PROMISES A DEVELOPMENT IN WHICH LIFE WILL BE AN	INTELLECTUAL	ECSTASY SURPASSING THE ECSTASIES OF SAINTS.
GETT PREFACE(193)	EVEN THESE CREDULITIES INVOLVED TOO SEVERE AN	INTELLECTUAL	EFFORT FOR MANY OF THEM: IT WAS EASIER TO GRIN
PLES PREFACE(R16)	WITHOUT LONG AND ARDUOUS PRACTICE, AND AN	INTELLECTUAL	EFFORT WHICH MY PLAYS PROBABLY DO NOT SEEM
DEVL III (57)	/SWINDON/ I AM SORRY I CANNOT PRETEND TO YOUR	INTELLECTUAL	EMINENCE, SIR. I CAN ONLY DO MY BEST, AND RELY
LION PREFACE(26)	WOULD BE ADDED TO HIS DOCTRINE, AND YET THE	INTELLECTUAL	ENERGY OF SCEPTICS AND DIVINES HAS BEEN WASTED
MTH2 (39)	IS A CHAP LIKE ME TO GO? I'M AFRAID I'M NOT	INTELLECTUAL	ENOUGH TO SPLIT STRAWS WHEN THERES A JOB IN
2TRU II (65)	WOMAN: MADLY IN LOVE WITH HER. SHE WAS NOT MY	INTELLECTUAL	EQUAL; AND I HAD TO TEACH HER TABLE MANNERS.
FANY PROLOG (268)	/FANNY/ (ADORINGLY) BUT HOW FEW MEN ARE YOUR	INTELLECTUAL	EQUALS, MR TROTTER! /TROTTER/ I'M GETTING THE
FANY PROLOG (268)	CAMBRIDGE FABIAN VIRAGO, I'LL TREAT YOU AS MY	INTELLECTUAL	EQUAL, AS I WOULD TREAT A MAN. /FANNY/ (
GETT (182)	WHEN DRAMA REACHES A CERTAIN POINT IN POETIC AND	INTELLECTUAL	EVOLUTION, ITS ADOPTION WAS NOT, ON MY PART, A
WIDO I (22)	TIME AS HE GOES, WITH EVERY APPEARANCE OF SEVERE	INTELLECTUAL	EXERTION). /SARTORIUS/ (CALLING THROUGH THE
BULL PREFACE(32)	TO ANY CONSIDERATIONS WHICH REQUIRE A LITTLE	INTELLECTUAL	EXERTION AND SYMPATHETIC ALERTNESS-- IS
ROCK PREFACE(180)	AND CATASTROPHE FOR THEIR OWN SAKE AND HAVE NO	INTELLECTUAL	EXPECTATIONS TO BE DISAPPOINTED. DIFFERENCE
POSN PREFACE(367)	AND SECTARIAN CONTROVERSIES WHICH MAY FORM THE	INTELLECTUAL	FABRIC OF THE PLAY, AND MAY HONESTLY SEE
MIS. (152)	PERCIVAL, THE PROMISING SON OF THREE HIGHLY	INTELLECTUAL	FATHERS. /HYPATIA/ (STARTLED) BENTLEY'S
MTH2 SD(37)	NEITHER DEAN NOR BISHOP; HE IS RATHER TOO STARKLY	INTELLECTUAL	FOR A POPULAR FREE CHURCH ENTHUSIAST; AND HE IS
CLEO NOTES (208)	WIDE DIFFERENCE BETWEEN COMMON KNOWLEDGE AND THE	INTELLECTUAL	GAME CALLED SCIENCE. WE HAVE MEN OF EXACTLY THE
SUPR HANDBOK(229)	POLITICAL ECONOMY AND SOCIAL ECONOMY ARE AMUSING	INTELLECTUAL	GAMES; BUT VITAL ECONOMY IS THE PHILOSOPHER'S
GENV I (31)	IT? /HE/ IT IS MERE COMPILATION. HOW ARE THE	INTELLECTUAL	GIANTS WHO FORM YOUR COMMITTEE BRINGING THE
LIED (199)	(SHAKEN) APJOHN: PLAY FAIR. DONT ABUSE YOUR	INTELLECTUAL	GIFTS. DO YOU REALLY MEAN THAT I AM MAKING A
METH PREFACE(R89)	EMOTIONS. MY ANSWER TO THIS WAS TO PUT ALL MY	INTELLECTUAL	GOODS IN THE SHOP WINDOW UNDER THE SIGN OF MAN
UNPL PREFACE(R11)	A THEATRE WHICH SHOULD BE TO THE NEWLY GATHERED	INTELLECTUAL	HARVEST OF THE NINETEENTH CENTURY WHAT
3PLA PREFACE(R31)	BUT EVEN IN PESSIMISM THERE IS A CHOICE BETWEEN	INTELLECTUAL	HONESTY AND DISHONESTY. HOGARTH DREW THE RAKE
FABL PREFACE(76)	AT ALL HAZARDS IF IT IS TO BE CREDITED WITH THE	INTELLECTUAL	HONESTY NECESSARY TO ITS INFLUENCE AND
ROCK PREFACE(180)	ISSUE. SOME OF THEM REMAIN IN THIS CONDITION OF	INTELLECTUAL	INNOCENCE TO THE END OF THEIR LIVES, WHILST THE
DOCT III (144)	(SERIOUSLY ANNOYED FOR THE FIRST TIME) IT'S AN	INTELLECTUAL	INSULT. I DONT BELIEVE THERES SUCH A THING AS
LION PREFACE(89)	THE STERNEST VIEW OF SUCH BELIEF AS A BREACH OF	INTELLECTUAL	INTEGRITY: IT IS THE DIFFERENCE BETWEEN BELIEF
POSN PREFACE(391)	A BORN CHAMPION OF LIBERTY OF CONSCIENCE AND	INTELLECTUAL	INTEGRITY-- SAY A MILTON, A CHESTERFIELD, A
APPL I (235)	FOR THE ETERNAL AGAINST THE EXPEDIENT; FOR	INTELLECTUAL	INTEGRITY, FOR HUMANITY, FOR THE RESCUE OF
MRS PREFACE(165)	ARE BUILT TO INDUCE, NOT VOLUPTUOUS REVERIE BUT	INTELLECTUAL	INTEREST, NOT ROMANTIC RHAPSODY BUT HUMANE
GENV III (78)	OF THING; BUT PLEASE UNDERSTAND THAT I AM NOT AN	INTELLECTUAL	. A PLAIN ENGLISHMAN DOING MY DUTY TO MY
CURE (228)	MAGAZINE. /REGINALD/ BUT IT'S SO FRIGHTFULLY	INTELLECTUAL	. IT WOULD OVERTAX MY BRAIN. /THE DOCTOR/ OH,
MIS. (110)	IS SIMPLY BLUE-MOULDY. LETS ARGUE ABOUT SOMETHING	INTELLECTUAL	. (HE THROWS HIMSELF INTO THE WICKER CHAIR ON
MRS I (195)	OF COURSE NOT: SHE'S A THIRD WRANGLER. EVER SO	INTELLECTUAL	. TOOK A HIGHER DEGREE THAN YOU DID; SO WHY
2TRU PREFACE(3)	BY GOOD LOOKS AND AGREEABLE MANNERS, THE LESS	INTELLECTUAL	JOURNALIST CRITICS SULKED AS THEY ALWAYS DO
BULL PREFACE(19)	FOR TOM, NELSON'S GENIUS, INSTEAD OF PRODUCING	INTELLECTUAL	KEENNESS AND SCRUPULOUSNESS, PRODUCED MERE
BULL PREFACE(21)	THE ENGLISHMAN IS TOO LAZY INTELLECTUALLY (THE	INTELLECTUAL	LAZINESS AND SLOVENLINESS OF THE ENGLISH IS
BULL PREFACE(40)	AND DISHONOR. BUT THEY CANNOT MUZZLE HIS	INTELLECTUAL	LEADERS, THE ENGLISH PHILOSOPHER, THE ENGLISH
ROCK I (230)	AS A MATTER OF FACT MY LIFE HAS BEEN A COMPLETELY	INTELLECTUAL	LIFE, AND MY TRAINING THE FINEST INTELLECTUAL
BARB III (346)	MEN'S SOULS. AS A TEACHER OF GREEK I GAVE THE	INTELLECTUAL	MAN WEAPONS AGAINST THE COMMON MAN. I NOW WANT
BARB III (346)	WANT TO GIVE THE COMMON MAN WEAPONS AGAINST THE	INTELLECTUAL	MAN. I LOVE THE COMMON PEOPLE. I WANT TO ARM
UNPL PREFACE(R23)	BUT TO EXPECT THEM TO BE INTUITIVE AS TO	INTELLECTUAL	MEANING AND CIRCUMSTANTIAL CONDITIONS AS WELL,
MRS PREFACE(167)	BUT THIS WILL SOON PASS AWAY. WHEN THE	INTELLECTUAL	MUSCLE AND MORAL NERVE OF THE CRITICS HAS BEEN
LION PREFACE(39)	IS EDUCATED, SUBTLE, AND OBSESSED WITH ARTIFICIAL	INTELLECTUAL	MYSTIFICATIONS, THE DISCOVERY THAT HE IS STUPID
UNPL PREFACE(R23)	THOUGH IT MAY BE, IS PRODUCED AT THE COST OF	INTELLECTUAL	OBSCURITY? IBSEN, INTERROGATED AS TO HIS
BARB III (347)	COMMON MEN TO USE, YET STRONG ENOUGH TO FORCE THE	INTELLECTUAL	OLIGARCHY TO USE ITS GENIUS FOR THE GENERAL
MRS II (208)	IT PANS OUT FOR HER. (TO HIS FATHER) YOURE NOT	INTELLECTUAL	OR ARTISTIC: ARE YOU, PATER? SO TAKE PRAED
FABL VI (130)	4/ NO PASSIONS, THEN? /RAPHAEL/ ON THE CONTRARY:	INTELLECTUAL	PASSION, MATHEMATICAL PASSION, PASSION FOR
SUPR III (112)	FAIR, DON JUAN, AND NOT CIVIL. I AM ALSO ON THE	INTELLECTUAL	PLANE. NOBODY CAN APPRECIATE IT MORE THAN I DO.
METH PREFACE(R89)	CRITICAL EXPONENTS HAVE BEEN DRIVEN TO TAKE AN	INTELLECTUAL	POSE WHICH, THOUGH OFTEN MORE TRYING THAN THEIR
BARB III (346)	PIECES HAS NEVER BEEN SO HORRIBLY ABUSED AS THE	INTELLECTUAL	POWER, THE IMAGINATIVE POWER, THE POETIC,
FANY EPILOG (331)	AND THE OLD ENJOYMENT, AND A FEEBLE AIR OF	INTELLECTUAL	PRETENTIOUSNESS KEPT UP ALL THROUGH TO PERSUADE
ROCK PREFACE(165)	OF INTELLIGENTSIA TO THE HONORABLE ONE OF " THE	INTELLECTUAL	PROLETARIAT." EVEN LENIN AND HIS COLLEAGUES,
APPL II (269)	INTEREST IN PARLIAMENTARY POLITICS. HE PREFERS	INTELLECTUAL	PURSUITS. /NICOBAR/ DONT YOU BELIEVE IT. HE IS
POSN PREFACE(400)	THAT THE WORK INVOLVED WOULD DRIVE A MAN OF ANY	INTELLECTUAL	RANK MAD. CONSIDER, FOR EXAMPLE, THE CHRISTMAS
ROCK PREFACE(165)	WOULD NEVER HAVE SO ABSURDLY OVERESTIMATED THE	INTELLECTUAL	RESOURCES OF THE PROLETARIAT AND BEEN SO
MTH2 SD(54)	AND QUITE SELF-ASSURED IN CONTRAST TO THE	INTELLECTUAL	RESTLESSNESS OF FRANKLYN AND THE MESMERIC
MTH2 (80)	OF THE TWENTIETH CENTURY: A RELIGION THAT HAS ITS	INTELLECTUAL	ROOTS IN PHILOSOPHY AND SCIENCE JUST AS
MTH2 (80)	AND SCIENCE JUST AS MEDIEVAL CHRISTIANITY HAD ITS	INTELLECTUAL	ROOTS IN ARISTOTLE. /LUBIN/ BUT SURELY ANY
MIS. PREFACE(98)	ROMANTIC; SOME INTUITIONAL; SOME SOPHISTICAL AND	INTELLECTUAL	; NONE SUITED TO THE CHARACTER AND CONDITIONS
METH PREFACE(R89)	OF THE THEATRE CURRENT AT THAT TIME WAS THAT	INTELLECTUAL	SERIOUSNESS IS OUT OF PLACE ON THE STAGE; THAT
POSN PREFACE(369)	PRESENTING A KEEN AND JOYOUS FRONT TO ENGLISH	INTELLECTUAL	SLOTH. ABOVE ALL, THERE WAS COLONEL LOCKWOOD TO
SUPR II (51)	OF US SAY RUGBY! HARROW! ETON! IN THAT TONE OF	INTELLECTUAL	SNOBBERY? SHERBROOKE ROAD IS A PLACE WHERE
BULL PREFACE(22)	A PRIVATE GOVERNESS, WE SHOULD LAPSE INTO GROSS	INTELLECTUAL	SOTTISHNESS, AND PREFER LEADERS WHO ENCOURAGED
METH PREFACE(R33)	NATURALIST, OF THE MORE OR LESS MYSTICAL	INTELLECTUAL	SPECULATIONS OF THE DEISTS OF 1790-1830.
MIS. PREFACE(44)	ALONG THE LINE OF LEAST RESISTANCE TO CONSCIOUS	INTELLECTUAL	SPECULATION, WITH ITS ROUTINE OF HYPOTHESIS AND
METH PREFACE(R75)	CLASSES WHOSE RECREATION IS READING AND WHOSE	INTELLECTUAL	SPORT IS CONTROVERSY, THEY BANISH THE BIBLE
METH PREFACE(R89)	PEOPLE GO THERE TO BE SOOTHED AFTER THE ENORMOUS	INTELLECTUAL	STRAIN OF A DAY IN THE CITY: IN SHORT, THAT A
POSN PREFACE(370)	WAS THROWN IN TO MAKE UP FOR ANY SHORTCOMING IN	INTELLECTUAL	SUBTLETY THAT MIGHT ARISE IN THE CASE OF HIS
KING PREFACE(154)	SO I BRING THE THREE ON THE STAGE TO RELIEVE THE	INTELLECTUAL	TENSION. NEWTON'S RECTILINEAR UNIVERSE. THERE
FABL PREFACE(73)	IRRELIGIOUS ONES CAPABLE OF NOTHING MORE	INTELLECTUAL	THAN SPORT AND SEX, REACTED AGAINST THEIR
2TRU PREFACE(25)	RULER TO DO SOMETHING AND ANOTHER TO UNDO IT, ONE	INTELLECTUAL	TO RESTORE THE NATION AND ANOTHER TO RUIN THE
ROCK I (230)	INTELLECTUAL LIFE, AND MY TRAINING THE FINEST	INTELLECTUAL	TRAINING IN THE WORLD. FIRST RATE PREPARATORY
DEST (191)	DO. (WITH A LIVELY AIR OF ANTICIPATING AN	INTELLECTUAL	TREAT, SHE SITS DOWN ON THE COUCH AND COMPOSES
METH PREFACE(R65)	IN THE ICE. BUT THE PHYSICISTS FOUND THEIR	INTELLECTUAL	VISION OF THE WORLD INCOMMUNICABLE TO THOSE WHO
METH PREFACE(R84)	PRESENCE OF ERROR WHICH IS THE SUREST SYMPTOM OF	INTELLECTUAL	VITALITY, MEANWHILE THE NAME OF TRAGEDY WAS
BULL PREFACE(21)	GUARANTEES OF EFFICIENCY AND TRUSTWORTHINESS THAN	INTELLECTUAL	VIVACITY, WHICH HE MISTRUSTS AS A COMMON
DEVL EPILOG (83)	THE CLIMATE THERE IS NO DOUBT MORE FAVORABLE TO	INTELLECTUAL	VIVACITY. I HAVE DESCRIBED BURGOYNE'S
BARB PREFACE(213)	ASHAMED OF THEIR HABIT OF TREATING BRITAIN AS AN	INTELLECTUAL	VOID, AND ASSUMING THAT EVERY PHILOSOPHICAL
METH PREFACE(R89)	NOTICED THE NEW RELIGION IN THE CENTRE OF THE	INTELLECTUAL	WHIRLPOOL, NOW I PROTEST I DID NOT CUT THESE
VWOO 1 (119)	I AM NOT GETTING ON WITH MY WORK. /Z/ YOURE AN	INTELLECTUAL	, ARNT YOU? /A/ WHAT DO YOU THINK YOU MEAN BY
SUPR III (100)	ADMITTED TO BE A HIGHER, MORE CULTIVATED, POETIC,	INTELLECTUAL	, ENNOBLING PLACE THAN THE RACECOURSE, BUT DO
SUPR HANDBOK(181)	RANGE OF HIS CLASS, AND OF A CLEVER, IMAGINATIVE,	INTELLECTUAL	, HIGHLY CIVILIZED JEWESS, MIGHT BE VERY
DOCT PREFACE(30)	ANY INTEREST IN VIVISECTION, EITHER PECUNIARY OR	INTELLECTUAL	, OR WOULD TREAT HIS DOG CRUELLY OR ALLOW
JOAN PREFACE(11)	SHORT, MUCH MORE OF A YOUNG LADY, AND EVEN OF AN	INTELLECTUAL	, THAN MOST OF THE DAUGHTERS OF OUR PETTY

INTELLECTUALLY

LION PREFACE(76)	MOST AMAZING THING OF THE KIND KNOWN TO US. BEING	INTELLECTUALLY	AN INVETERATE ROMAN RATIONALIST, ALWAYS
BARB PREFACE(213)	I HAVE REPRESENTED A MAN WHO HAS BECOME	INTELLECTUALLY	AND SPIRITUALLY AS WELL AS PRACTICALLY
SUPR HANDBOK(225)	THE PERICLEAN ATHENIAN WAS A TYPE OF THE	INTELLECTUALLY	AND ARTISTICALLY CULTIVATED GENTLEMAN. BOTH
UNPL PREFACE(R25)	AND THE MARRIAGE WITH WHICH IT ENDS, ARE, FOR THE	INTELLECTUALLY	AND ARTISTICALLY CONSCIOUS CLASSES IN MODERN
MRS PREFACE(169)	ITS CLOTHES. I NOW COME TO THOSE CRITICS WHO,	INTELLECTUALLY	BAFFLED BY THE PROBLEM IN MRS WARREN'S
MIS. PREFACE(48)	IF NOT EXCOMMUNICATED, AND YET NO HONEST AND	INTELLECTUALLY	CAPABLE DOCTOR OR PARSON CAN SAY MORE.
UNPL PREFACE(R21)	HUMORIST, AND RHETORICIAN, HAS LEFT US NO	INTELLECTUALLY	COHERENT DRAMA, AND COULD NOT AFFORD TO
METH PREFACE(R37)	WITH FATHER ADDIS, BUT THEIR POSITION WAS NOT	INTELLECTUALLY	COMFORTABLE. A MEMBER OF PARLIAMENT EXPRESSED
PLES PREFACE(R13)	INVENTION IS THE FIRST EFFORT OF MAN TO BECOME	INTELLECTUALLY	CONSCIOUS. NO FRONTIER CAN BE MARKED BETWEEN
3PLA PREFACE(R23)	IS THAT THEY CANNOT WRITE THEM, THE BUSINESS OF	INTELLECTUALLY	CONSCIOUS PHILOSOPHER AND SKILLED CRITIC
MRS PREFACE(175)	FEW AMONG THEM WHO KEPT THEIR FEET MORALLY AND	INTELLECTUALLY	COULD DO NOTHING TO CHECK THE EPIDEMIC OF
MTH4 I (160)	AN OPINION OF MINE WHICH IS SO ADVANCED! SO	INTELLECTUALLY	DARING! THAT I HAVE NEVER VENTURED TO

METH PREFACE(R58)	DID NOT BELIEVE IT, BUT QUITE CONSCIOUSLY AND	INTELLECTUALLY	FORMED THE OPINION THAT THE DISTINCTION WAS
BARB PREFACE(246)	TO SCOFF AT ITS RELIGIONS. CREEDS MUST BECOME	INTELLECTUALLY	HONEST. AT PRESENT THERE IS NOT A SINGLE
MIS. PREFACE(94)	OF THAT ISLAND. BUT THIS OBJECTIVITY, THOUGH	INTELLECTUALLY	HONEST, TELLS THE CHILD ONLY WHAT OTHER
APPL II (270)	MAJESTY PROPOSES IS THE STRAIGHTFORWARD, LOGICAL,	INTELLECTUALLY	HONEST SOLUTION OF OUR DIFFICULTY.
MTH4 I (157)	BLINDNESS, YOUR IMBECILITY. HUMANLY I PITY YOU.	INTELLECTUALLY	I DESPISE YOU. /ZOO/ BRAVO, DADDY! YOU HAVE
GETT SD(275)	HAPPENS TO STRIKE HER IMAGINATION AS SOUNDING	INTELLECTUALLY	IMPORTANT. SHE HAS MORE THAN COMMON
PHIL I (80)	/CHARTERIS/ I WONT, MY DEAR. THATS FLAT. WE'RE	INTELLECTUALLY	INCOMPATIBLE. /JULIA/ BUT WHY? WE COULD BE
METH PREFACE(R48)	LIFE AND HOPE FROM DEATH AND DESPAIR. WE WERE	INTELLECTUALLY	INTOXICATED WITH THE IDEA THAT THE WORLD
PHIL II SD(94)	INSINCERE, AND HIGHLY SELF-SATISFIED	INTELLECTUALLY	. SYLVIA CRAVEN IS SITTING IN THE MIDDLE OF
BULL PREFACE(21)	A DISTINCTION WHICH THE ENGLISHMAN IS TOO LAZY	INTELLECTUALLY	(THE INTELLECTUAL LAZINESS AND SLOVENLINESS
MTH3 (124)	AS IT WAS CALLED, THAT THEY HAD BECOME THE MOST	INTELLECTUALLY	LAZY AND FAT-HEADED PEOPLE ON THE FACE OF THE
METH PREFACE(R89)	WHICH, THOUGH OFTEN MORE TRYING THAN THEIR OLD	INTELLECTUALLY	NIHILISTIC VULGARITY, AT LEAST CONCEDES THE
POSN PREFACE(385)	A BARELY THIRD-RATE POWER POLITICALLY, AND	INTELLECTUALLY	NO POWER AT ALL, IN THE EUROPE SHE HAD ONCE
SUPR II SD(62)	IS UNDENIABLY PLEASANT AND ENLIVENING, THERE IS	INTELLECTUALLY	NOTHING NEW TO BE GOT OUT OF HIM, ESPECIALLY
DEST (184)	HIMSELF TO YOU. YOU UNDERSTAND? /LIEUTENANT/ (	INTELLECTUALLY	OVERTAXED) WELL, IT'S A LITTLE COMPLICATED;
BULL PREFACE(21)	AND THE ENERGETIC INFATUATIONS THAT HAVE ENABLED	INTELLECTUALLY	RIDICULOUS MEN, WITHOUT WIT OR HUMOR, TO GO
MTH5 (229)	HERSELF ON ECRASIA, AND TRYING TO OUTDO HER	INTELLECTUALLY	) CLEARLY BECAUSE THEY WERE DEAD. /PYGMALION/
MRS III (232)	ME A BAD SORT: I DONT GO IN FOR BEING SUPERFINE	INTELLECTUALLY	; BUT IVE PLENTY OF HONEST HUMAN FEELING; AND
GETT SD(274)	(SOLICITOR-MANAGED) WHO HAVE NEVER DEVELOPED	INTELLECTUALLY	SINCE THEIR SCHOOLDAYS. HE IS A MUDDLED,
BULL PREFACE(39)	ENGLISHMAN, MORE DOCILE, LESS DANGEROUS, TOO LAZY	INTELLECTUALLY	TO USE SUCH POLITICAL AND LEGAL POWER AS LIES
LION PREFACE(88)	BEING AS IT IS A COMPARATIVELY MODERN FANCY OF	INTELLECTUALLY	UNTRAINED PEOPLE WHO KEEP THE BIBLE ON THE
ROCK I (232)	YET HAVE THE RIGHT INSTINCT AS TO HOW TO FLIRT	INTELLECTUALLY	WITH A TIRED THINKER. WILL YOU PROMISE TO
METH PREFACE(R44)	THAT WE COULD DO WITHOUT SHELLEY'S ALMIGHTY FIEND	INTELLECTUALLY	, HE WENT INTO THE GULF THAT SEEMED ONLY A
		INTELLECTUALS	
FANY PROLOG (264)	THE THING TO HAVE THEM. GUNN IS ONE OF THE YOUNG	INTELLECTUALS	: HE WRITES PLAYS HIMSELF. HE'S USEFUL BECAUSE
FANY PROLOG (264)	THE INTELLECTUALS. /THE COUNT/ BUT ARNT THEY ALL	INTELLECTUALS	? /SAVOYARD/ LORD! NO: HEAVEN FORBID! YOU
MIS. (189)	BECAUSE I'M ONLY A CLERK, THAT I'M NOT ONE OF THE	INTELLECTUALS	. I'M A READING MAN, A THINKING MAN. I READ IN
FANY PROLOG (264)	IF I MAY ASK? /SAVOYARD/ GUNN IS ONE OF THE	INTELLECTUALS	. /THE COUNT/ BUT ARNT THEY ALL
METH PREFACE(R47)	RUSHED DOWN A STEEP PLACE. NOT SO THE REST OF US	INTELLECTUALS	. WE ALL BEGAN GOING TO THE DEVIL WITH THE
FANY PROLOG (264)	HE'S USEFUL BECAUSE HE PITCHES INTO THE OLDER	INTELLECTUALS	WHO ARE STANDING IN HIS WAY. BUT YOU MAY TAKE
		INTELLIGENCE	
METH PREFACE(R48)	MAKE ITSELF WITHOUT DESIGN, PURPOSE, SKILL, OR	INTELLIGENCE	: IN SHORT, WITHOUT LIFE. WE COMPLETELY
METH PREFACE(R38)	WAS NO PURPOSE IN THIS, NO DESIGN, NO GUIDING	INTELLIGENCE	? THE THING WAS INCREDIBLE. IN VAIN DID
SUPR I SD(43)	NO MERCY EITHER: IF ANYTHING RESTRAINS HER, IT IS	INTELLIGENCE	AND PRIDE, NOT COMPASSION. HER VOICE MIGHT BE
METH PREFACE(R87)	IT MAY BE FOR AUDIENCES WHO READ THE POLICE	INTELLIGENCE	AND SKIP THE REVIEWS AND LEADING ARTICLES. I
FABL PREFACE(77)	ME TO THE CONCLUSION THAT EVERY GRADE OF HUMAN	INTELLIGENCE	CAN BE CIVILIZED BY PROVIDING IT WITH A FRAME
MIS. PREFACE(14)	AND YET PEOPLE OF HIGH CHARACTER AND	INTELLIGENCE	CANNOT BE PLAGUED WITH THE CARE OF CHILDREN. A
METH PREFACE(R41)	OF THE ANIMAL ITSELF OR ON THE PART OF A SUPERIOR	INTELLIGENCE	CONTROLLING ITS DESTINY. DARWIN POINTED OUT--
GENV III (79)	NOT STUPIDITY. SHE SPEAKS SEVERAL LANGUAGES. HER	INTELLIGENCE	IS REMARKABLE: SHE TAKES A POINT LIKE
MIS. PREFACE(14)	BE DISCHARGED BY PERSONS OF FEEBLE CHARACTER OR	INTELLIGENCE	. AND YET PEOPLE OF HIGH CHARACTER AND
SUPR PREFACE(R31)	OF TAPPERTITIAN ROMANCE WITH THE POLICE	INTELLIGENCE	. BUNYAN, BLAKE, HOGARTH, AND TURNER (THESE
BULL PREFACE(35)	FOR ANY ENGLISH GOVERNMENT IN DETERMINATION AND	INTELLIGENCE	. HERE, NO DOUBT, HE FLATTERS HIMSELF; FOR HIS
LION PREFACE(44)	HAVE BEEN BELIEVED AND DOUBTED BY MEN OF EQUAL	INTELLIGENCE	. MIRACLES, IN THE SENSE OF PHENOMENA WE CANNOT
SUPR III (104)	HAS ALL THE KNOWLEDGE, AND IMAGINATION ALL THE	INTELLIGENCE	. /THE DEVIL/ AND A PRETTY KETTLE OF FISH THEY
SUPR I (36)	GROTESQUE AND RIDICULOUS TO THE MATURE	INTELLIGENCE	. WHEN THEY SUDDENLY BEGAN TO SHINE LIKE NEWLY
BULL PREFACE(41)	THE LIGHT OF THE WORLD. NOBODY IN IRELAND OF ANY	INTELLIGENCE	LIKES NATIONALISM ANY MORE THAN A MAN WITH A
BARB PREFACE(239)	ONE MAN WHO STILL HAS FAITH IN THE KINDNESS AND	INTELLIGENCE	OF HUMAN NATURE IS THE FULMINATOR, NOW A HUNTED
2TRU III (108)	CANNOT BE TRUE, MEEK. IT INDICATES A DEGREE OF	INTELLIGENCE	OF WHICH NO GOVERNMENT IS CAPABLE. /MEEK/ IT'S
2TRU II (79)	INDEED! QUARTERMASTER'S CLERK, INTERPRETER,	INTELLIGENCE	ORDERLY. ANY FURTHER RANK OF WHICH I HAVE NOT
2TRU II (79)	DUTY OF THE INTELLIGENCE ORDERLY, SIR, I'M THE	INTELLIGENCE	ORDERLY. I HAD TO MAKE THE ENEMY BELIEVE THAT
2TRU II (79)	FACE OF THE ENEMY? /MEEK/ IT WAS THE DUTY OF THE	INTELLIGENCE	ORDERLY, SIR, I'M THE INTELLIGENCE ORDERLY. I
METH PREFACE(R28)	GENERAL INTELLIGENCE, NOR EVEN IN THE SPECIALIZED	INTELLIGENCE	PROPER TO THE FACULTY IN QUESTION: FOR EXAMPLE,
CAPT II (243)	IT SIFER NORT, DIDNT YR? /REDBROOK/ (WITH CRISP	INTELLIGENCE	) WHAT! YOURE RUNNING AWAY, ARE YOU? (HE
CLEO III (163)	CAESAR AND RUFIO TURN TO ONE ANOTHER WITH QUICK	INTELLIGENCE	). /CAESAR/ COME, RUFIO. /CLEOPATRA/ (
GETT PREFACE(208)	SHEWS A MUCH HIGHER DEVELOPMENT OF SOCIAL	INTELLIGENCE	THAN OUR MARRIAGE SYSTEM; BUT IF IT WERE
MTH5 (261)	FREED FROM MATTER, TO THE WHIRLPOOL IN PURE	INTELLIGENCE	THAT, WHEN THE WORLD BEGAN, WAS A WHIRLPOOL IN
KING I (216)	OF YOU, LOUISE. /BARBARA/ IT TAKES SOME	INTELLIGENCE	TO BE BOTH A FRENCH SPY AND A BLUESTOCKING. I
GETT (334)	NEITHER THE STRENGTH TO RESIST MARRIAGE NOR THE	INTELLIGENCE	TO UNDERSTAND ITS INFINITE DISHONOR WILL MAKE
PLES PREFACE(R15)	BUT I HAVE NOT HESITATED ON OCCASION TO TAX HIS	INTELLIGENCE	VERY SEVERELY, MAKING THE STAGE EFFECT DEPEND
BARB II (274)	BUT THE GENTEEL SORT. I'M TOO UPPISH, OWING TO MY	INTELLIGENCE	, AND MY FATHER BEING A CHARTIST AND A READING,
METH PREFACE(R56)	THAT PART OF EVOLUTION WHICH HAS NO PURPOSE, NO	INTELLIGENCE	, AND MIGHT MORE APPROPRIATELY BE CALLED
INCA (255)	FROM BANKRUPTCY THAN MYSELF, HAS NOT A RAY OF	INTELLIGENCE	, AND WILL GO ON FIGHTING UNTIL CIVILIZATION IS
JOAN PREFACE(12)	ESTABLISHED NEWTON'S REPUTATION FOR EXTRAORDINARY	INTELLIGENCE	, AND WOULD HAVE DONE SO NO MATTER HOW
OVER PREFACE(162)	THE LOWER MIDDLE CLASS WERE CRAMMED WITH POLICE	INTELLIGENCE	, AND MORE ESPECIALLY WITH DIVORCE AND MURDER
AUGS (280)	ALL VERY WELL; BUT UNLESS IT'S CARRIED OUT WITH	INTELLIGENCE	, BELIEVE ME, YOU MAY WASTE A POUND TO SAVE A
BUOY III (42)	WHAT SHE IS. I KNOW NOTHING OF HER TASTES, HER	INTELLIGENCE	, HER MANNERS, HER TEMPER: IN SHORT, OF
GENV IV (104)	THE JEW? BECAUSE YOU CANNOT COMPETE WITH HIS	INTELLIGENCE	, HIS PERSISTENCE, HIS FORESIGHT, HIS GRASP OF
NEVR IV (289)	I COULD NOT FIND OUT FOR MYSELF. YOU MISTRUST MY	INTELLIGENCE	, MR VALENTINE-- (STOPPING HIM AS HE IS ABOUT
MTH4 I (141)	DOWN) OH, THIS IS DREADFUL. NO UNDERSTANDING, NO	INTELLIGENCE	, NO SYMPATHY-- (HIS SOBS CHOKE HIM). /THE
METH PREFACE(R28)	AND HAVE NOTHING TO DO WITH VARIATIONS IN GENERAL	INTELLIGENCE	, NOR EVEN IN THE SPECIALIZED INTELLIGENCE
METH PREFACE(R42)	A GHASTLY AND DAMNABLE REDUCTION OF BEAUTY AND	INTELLIGENCE	, OF STRENGTH AND PURPOSE, OF HONOR AND
PYGM EPILOG (291)	BOY HAS A SUFFICIENTLY RICH MOTHER WHO HAS	INTELLIGENCE	, PERSONAL GRACE, DIGNITY OF CHARACTER WITHOUT
LION PREFACE(26)	OF CATARACT" WOULD HAVE BEEN, TO A MAN OF JESUS'S	INTELLIGENCE	, THE PROPOSITION OF AN IDIOT. IF IT COULD BE
LION PREFACE(6)	WHICH HAS NO REAL SIGNIFICANCE BECAUSE IT HAS NO	INTELLIGENCE	, THERE IS, AMONG PEOPLE WHO ARE REALLY FREE TO
ARMS II SD(23)	OF COOL TEMPERAMENT AND LOW BUT CLEAR AND KEEN	INTELLIGENCE	, WITH THE COMPLACENCY OF THE SERVANT WHO
INCA (254)	ANY PRINCESS THAT EVER WALKED COULD HAVE YOUR	INTELLIGENCE	! /ERMYNTRUDE/ HOW CLEVER OF YOU, SIR! BUT
		INTELLIGENCES	
FABL PREFACE(75)	INSPIRED PHILOSOPHIC CREEDS TO THE NARROW	INTELLIGENCES	OF ILLITERATE PEASANTS AND OF CHILDREN. EIGHT
		INTELLIGENT	
SUPR HANDBOK(182)	BEING MUCH NOTICED. TO THE MASS OF MEN, THE	INTELLIGENT	ABOLITION OF PROPERTY WOULD MEAN NOTHING EXCEPT
MIS. (190)	POLICEMAN THAT YOU ARE A TROUBLESOME PERSON. THE	INTELLIGENT	AND AMBITIOUS POLICEMAN WOULD TAKE AN EARLY
MIS. (190)	IN A DIFFICULTY OF ANY SORT. I SHOULD WARN AN	INTELLIGENT	AND AMBITIOUS POLICEMAN THAT YOU ARE A
LION EPILOG (152)	CHRISTIAN PRISONERS. NO ENGLISH IMPERIALIST WAS	INTELLIGENT	AND EARNEST ENOUGH TO DO THE SAME IN LONDON. IF
MTH4 II (188)	IN THE WORLD IN WHOSE ARTICLES OF FAITH ANY	INTELLIGENT	AND EDUCATED PERSON COULD BELIEVE. /THE ENVOY/
SIM PREFACE(17)	POLICE. BUT POLICE MEASURES ARE NOT ENOUGH. AN	INTELLIGENT	AND EXPERIENCED ADMINISTRATOR OF THE CRIMINAL
METH PREFACE(R56)	PUPPY, I ASK MYSELF WHAT SPELL HAS FALLEN ON	INTELLIGENT	AND HUMANE MEN THAT THEY ALLOW THEMSELVES TO BE
METH PREFACE(R44)	DISCUSSION; BUT WHEN I DESCRIBED DARWIN AS " AN	INTELLIGENT	AND INDUSTRIOUS PIGEON FANCIER," THAT
KING II (224)	HER ENOUGH, IT SEEMS. I HOLD HER BECAUSE SHE IS	INTELLIGENT	AND LADYLIKE AND KEEPS ME IN TOUCH WITH FRANCE
METH PREFACE(R72)	NIHILISM, AND ARE ATTEMPTING TO MOVE IN AN	INTELLIGENT	AND ORDERED MANNER, PRACTISING A VERY STRENUOUS
BULL PREFACE(63)	THE LIES OF FALSTAFF, SHOULD HAVE IMPOSED ON ANY	INTELLIGENT	AND POLITICALLY EXPERIENCED HUMAN BEING, IS
MIS. PREFACE(14)	BEYOND TOLERATION. CONSEQUENTLY THE HIGHLY	INTELLIGENT	AND SENSITIVE ADULT HANDS THE CHILD OVER TO A
MIS. PREFACE(14)	THE CHILD IS TO REMAIN IN THE ROOM WITH A HIGHLY	INTELLIGENT	AND SENSITIVE ADULT, IT MUST TO TOLD, AND IF
METH PREFACE(R48)	DESIGNED, LIKE PALEY'S WATCH, BY A CONSCIOUS AND	INTELLIGENT	ARTIFICER FOR THE PURPOSE. WE TOOK A PERVERSE
BARB II (274)	DONT LIKE A MAN THAT SEES THROUGH EM. SECOND, AN	INTELLIGENT	BEIN NEEDS A DOO SHARE OF APPINESS; SO I DRINK
AUGS (268)	IRRITATED) CAN YOU TELL ME WHERE I CAN FIND AN	INTELLIGENT	BEING TO TAKE MY ORDERS? /THE CLERK/ ONE OF THE
HART PREFACE(9)	AND DANGEROUS A CREED EVER CAME TO BE ACCEPTED BY	INTELLIGENT	BEINGS, I WILL ANSWER THAT QUESTION MORE FULLY
BARB II (274)	COLD HERE (HE DANCES A STEP OR TWO)-- YES:	INTELLIGENT	BEYOND THE STATION O LIFE INTO WHICH IT HAS
SUPR HANDBOK(213)	DUKE. LET THOSE WHO THINK THE WHOLE CONCEPTION OF	INTELLIGENT	BREEDING ABSURD AND SCANDALOUS ASK THEMSELVES
FABL PREFACE(72)	ARGUMENT COULD, OF THE WAY IN WHICH HIGHLY	INTELLIGENT	CHILDREN OF PIOUS FAMILIES, OR OF IRRELIGIOUS
LADY PREFACE(231)	ONE OF SHAKESPEAR'S DEFECTS IS HIS LACK OF AN	INTELLIGENT	COMPREHENSION OF FEUDALISM. HE HAD OF COURSE NO
METH PREFACE(R57)	APPEARANCE OF BEING ELABORATELY PLANNED BY SOME	INTELLIGENT	CONTRIVER ARE ONLY ACCIDENTS WITHOUT ANY MORAL
MIS. PREFACE(67)	AS HAVE BEEN INTRODUCED BY BENEVOLENT AND	INTELLIGENT	DESPOTS AND ARISTOCRATS. WE MUST REFORM SOCIETY
DOCT PREFACE(47)	AS HIGH-MINDED AS EVER, IN SPITE OF THE FEW	INTELLIGENT	DOCTORS WHO POINT OUT RIGHTLY THAT ALL

FABL PREFACE(65)	STOOD ROUND TIMIDLY AT A DISTANCE, A HANDSOME AND	INTELLIGENT	DONKEY CAME AND CONVERSED WITH ME AFTER ITS
BULL I (89)	NONSENSE THAT WOULD NOT TAKE IN ANY ORDINARILY	INTELLIGENT	DONKEY; BUT YOU CAN HIT ME IN THE EYE WITH THE
CAPT NOTES (300)	IN THE AUTHORSHIP OF THIS PLAY THAT I HAVE BEEN	INTELLIGENT	ENOUGH TO STEAL ITS SCENERY, ITS SURROUNDINGS,
ROCK PREFACE(181)	/JESUS/ YOU ARE THE FIRST PERSON I HAVE MET	INTELLIGENT	ENOUGH TO ASK ME THAT QUESTION. /PILATE/ COME
MILL I (151)	HIS HAIR CUT. /EPIFANIA/ SURELY THE CREATURE IS	INTELLIGENT	ENOUGH TO DO AT LEAST THAT MUCH FOR HIMSELF.
MILL IV (191)	I COULD NEVER HAVE MADE THE CHANGE MYSELF, I WAS	INTELLIGENT	ENOUGH TO SEE THAT SHE WAS RIGHT. I BACKED HER
MILL PREFACE(130)	SHOT AT DAWN. LET US TAKE FOR GRANTED ARMIES	INTELLIGENT	ENOUGH TO PRESENT THEIR OFFICERS AT ANY MOMENT
GENV I (44)	WE? I KNOW NOTHING OF YOUR FOOTMAN. IF HE IS	INTELLIGENT	ENOUGH TO BECOME A COMMUNIST, AS SO MANY FAMOUS
BULL III (132)	ARE YOU ONE? /LARRY/ NO. I AM A CATHOLIC	INTELLIGENT	ENOUGH TO SEE THAT THE PROTESTANTS ARE NEVER
MIS. PREFACE(102)	COMTE SAW, WOULD GIVE US ALL THAT MOST OF US ARE	INTELLIGENT	ENOUGH TO WANT. WHAT MAKES IT PRODUCE SUCH
INCA (255)	HOPELESSLY BANKRUPT; AND THE WORST OF IT IS, I AM	INTELLIGENT	ENOUGH TO KNOW IT. AND I SHALL BE BEATEN IN
LION PREFACE(83)	NOSING OUT OF THEIR SINS OF THE PEOPLE WHO, BEING	INTELLIGENT	ENOUGH TO BE INCAPABLE OF MERE DULL
GENV III (80)	A WORD AGAINST IT ALL. /THE JUDGE/ YOU ARE	INTELLIGENT	ENOUGH, WELL-MEANING ENOUGH, TO BE AGAINST SUCH
LION PREFACE(74)	IT HAS REMAINED EVER SINCE, AND THAT THING THE	INTELLIGENT	HEATHEN MAY STUDY, IF THEY WOULD BE INSTRUCTED
GENV PREFACE(21)	TOO SHORTSIGHTED AND JEALOUS TO DO ANYTHING SO	INTELLIGENT	. IT SHOOK HANDS WITH STALIN AND STABBED HITLER
MILL PREFACE(126)	FUSIONIST AS BETWEEN DUTCH AND BRITISH STOCK. THE	INTELLIGENT	JEW IS A FUSIONIST AS BETWEEN JEW AND GENTILE
HART I SD(44)	SHE IS A PRETTY GIRL, SLENDER, FAIR, AND	INTELLIGENT	LOOKING, NICELY BUT NOT EXPENSIVELY DRESSED,
BASH PREFACE(88)	IN THE THEATRE; FOR IT INCLUDES A LARGE BODY OF	INTELLIGENT	MANUAL AND OPEN AIR WORKERS AND SPORTSMEN WHO,
KING I (197)	HE HAS HIS PRICE ALL THE SAME. /CHARLES/ ALL	INTELLIGENT	MEN HAVE, JAMIE. /JAMES/ PSHA! DONT WASTE YOUR
BUOY III (40)	NEW HARE ARE YOU STARTING NOW? /THE YOUTH/ ALL	INTELLIGENT	MEN OF MY AGE ARE WORLD BETTERERS TODAY. /SIR
SUPR PREFACE(R19)	BRIMMING WITH CRUDE VITALITY, WHO ARE NEITHER	INTELLIGENT	NOR POLITICALLY EDUCATED ENOUGH TO BE
KING I (216)	THEM EQUALLY, MR NEWTON. /CHARLES/ THAT IS VERY	INTELLIGENT	OF YOU, LOUISE. /BARBARA/ IT TAKES SOME
CATH 4 (192)	I HAVE BEEN MENTIONED IN DISPATCHES AS A HIGHLY	INTELLIGENT	OFFICER. AND LET ME WARN YOUR MAJESTY THAT I AM
LION EPILOG (151)	DIANA OR CHRIST, OR COULD HAVE GIVEN YOU ANY	INTELLIGENT	OR CORRECT ACCOUNT OF THE THINGS DIANA AND
HART I (75)	ARE CERTAINLY VERY INCONVENIENT SOMETIMES. BUT	INTELLIGENT	PEOPLE CAN ALWAYS MANAGE, UNLESS THEY ARE
NEVR II (255)	SUCCESS OF HIS HUNTER'S GUILE) OF COURSE! TWO	INTELLIGENT	PEOPLE LIKE US! ISNT IT PLEASANT, IN THIS
SIM I (46)	HAD NOT VOLUNTARILY BROKEN UP. WE WANT TO SET THE	INTELLIGENT	PEOPLE TALKING, AND TO STRIKE THE STUPID PEOPLE
BARB III (340)	UP IN IT. /CUSINS/ THAT IS PERHAPS WHY, LIKE MOST	INTELLIGENT	PEOPLE, I NEVER VOTE. /UNDERSHAFT/ VOTE! BAH!
MIS. PREFACE(54)	GREGARIOUS INSTINCT TO TURN FURIOUSLY ON ANY	INTELLIGENT	PERSON WHO PROPOSES A CHANGE. IT WOULD BE QUITE
MILL PREFACE(126)	OR SOUTH SEA ISLANDERS LEFT. IN AFRICA THE	INTELLIGENT	PINK NATIVE IS A FUSIONIST AS BETWEEN DUTCH AND
BULL PREFACE(64)	OF MATERIAL WEALTH WITHOUT HAVING MADE ANY	INTELLIGENT	PROVISION FOR ITS PROPER DISTRIBUTION AND
MTH4 III (197)	QUESTION; BUT IT IS A PRACTICAL QUESTION, AN	INTELLIGENT	QUESTION. SHE ASKS WHY WE SEEK TO LIFT A CORNER
UNPL PREFACE(R11)	PLAYHOUSE. I AM FOND OF THE PLAY, AND AM, AS	INTELLIGENT	READERS OF THIS PREFACE WILL HAVE OBSERVED,
MIS. PREFACE(93)	WHAT CONFUSES THIS ISSUE AND LEADS EVEN HIGHLY	INTELLIGENT	RELIGIOUS PERSONS TO ADVOCATE SECULAR EDUCATION
2TRU PREFACE(8)	A CONSEQUENCE OF NOT WORKING. BUT, LIKE ALL THE	INTELLIGENT	RICH PEOPLE OF MY ACQUAINTANCE, I HAVE WORKED AS
BARB II (274)	GET IT? /THE MAN/ I'LL TELL YOU WHY. FUST: I'M	INTELLIGENT	-- FFFFF! IT'S ROTTEN COLD HERE (HE DANCES A
GENV I (33)	PRECISELY MY BUSINESS HERE TODAY. I FIND YOU MOST	INTELLIGENT	-- MOST SYMPATHETIC. /SHE/ COME NOW! NONE OF
CLEO II (133)	INTEREST, HALF REAL, HALF AFFECTED TO SHEW HOW	INTELLIGENT	SHE IS) YOU MUST NOT TALK TO ME NOW AS IF I WERE
SUPR IV SD(142)	WHICH, WITH THE ABSENCE OF GAMES, MIGHT LEAD AN	INTELLIGENT	SPECTATOR TO THE MOST FAR REACHING CONCLUSIONS
GETT PREFACE(253)	QUITE CONTENT IN THEM) WHICH WOULD JUSTIFY ANY	INTELLIGENT	STATE IN BREAKING UP THE HOME AND GIVING THE
MTH2 (58)	IS THE VERY MOST CHARMING AND PENETRATING AND	INTELLIGENT	THING THAT HAS EVER BEEN SAID TO ME. BARNABAS:
ROCK PREFACE(181)	I AM A ROMAN, AND NO DOUBT SEEM EXCEPTIONALLY	INTELLIGENT	TO A JEW. YOU JEWS ARE ALWAYS TALKING ABOUT
MILL PREFACE(131)	EVEN WHEN THEY LACK AMBITION AND ARE FAR TOO	INTELLIGENT	TO BELIEVE THAT EMINENCE AND ITS
METH PREFACE(R42)	CASE; BUT STILL, AS COMPARED TO THE OPEN-EYED	INTELLIGENT	WANTING AND TRYING OF LAMARCK, THE DARWINIAN
APPL PREFACE(175)	FARTHER THAN I HAVE ALREADY CARRIED IT IN MY	INTELLIGENT	WOMAN'S GUIDE TO SOCIALISM AND CAPITALISM. WE
BARB II (273)	ENOUGH FOR YOU, PRAPS; BUT WOT IS IT TO ME, AN	INTELLIGENT	WORKIN MAN. /THE WOMAN/ WORKIN MAN! WOT ARE
GENV III (79)	STUPID. /THE WIDOW/ I HARDLY FOLLOW YOU, HOWEVER	INTELLIGENT	YOU MAY THINK ME. BUT I AM PROUD OF HAVING AZTEC
DEST SD(161)	AND EXTRAORDINARILY GRACEFUL, WITH A DELICATELY	INTELLIGENT	, APPREHENSIVE, QUESTIONING FACE: PERCEPTION IN
DEVL III SD(55)	HIS EYES, LARGE, BRILLIANT, APPREHENSIVE, AND	INTELLIGENT	, ARE HIS MOST REMARKABLE FEATURE: WITHOUT THEM
BULL IV (157)	(ENTHUSIASTICALLY) WHAT A NICE CHAP! WHAT AN	INTELLIGENT	, BROADMINDED CHARACTER, CONSIDERING HIS CLOTH!
FABL PREFACE(64)	MRS EDDY PRACTISING CHRISTIAN SCIENCE. THE MORE	INTELLIGENT	, OBSERVANT, AND OPEN-MINDED APOTHECARIES AND
SUPR III (129)	GREGARIOUS; NOT CONSIDERATE, ONLY POLITE; NOT	INTELLIGENT	, ONLY OPINIONATED; NOT PROGRESSIVE, ONLY
CAPT I SD(225)	AND FORTY, TALL, VERY GOODLOOKING, SYMPATHETIC,	INTELLIGENT	, TENDER AND HUMOROUS, DRESSED WITH CUNNING
		INTELLIGENTLY	
FANY III (323)	IS THERE ANY FUTURE FOR THE RAT? WE NEVER FIGHT	INTELLIGENTLY	: WHEN WE LOSE BATTLES, IT IS BECAUSE WE HAVE
CATH PREFACE(153)	WAS THAT WHEREAS SHE TALKED AND WROTE QUITE	INTELLIGENTLY	ABOUT LIBERAL PRINCIPLES BEFORE SHE WAS
SUPR HANDBOK(190)	OR EVEN FOR DOING ORDINARY PAROCHIAL WORK	INTELLIGENTLY	AND ECONOMICALLY. ONLY UNDER DESPOTISMS AND
LION PROLOG (109)	SEE? (HE LICKS HIS OWN HAND. THE LION NODS	INTELLIGENTLY	AND LICKS HIS PAW INDUSTRIOUSLY). CLEVER
BULL PREFACE(33)	POSSIBLE TO CONDUCT SOCIAL AND POLITICAL CHANGES	INTELLIGENTLY	AND PROVIDENTIALLY INSTEAD OF DRIFTING ALONG
ROCK PREFACE(154)	CONTRARY, IT MIGHT CONTINUE MUCH MORE OPENLY AND	INTELLIGENTLY	AND SCIENTIFICALLY THAN AT PRESENT, BECAUSE
APPL I (208)	DO"; AND I TELL THEM, I SAY " EXERCISE YOUR VOTE	INTELLIGENTLY	BY VOTING FOR ME," AND THEY DO. THAT'S
SUPR HANDBOK(189)	INEVITABLE, ALMOST UNCONSCIOUS FERTILITY BY AN	INTELLIGENTLY	CONTROLLED, CONSCIOUS FERTILITY, AND THE
METH PREFACE(R43)	MOST CERTAINLY THE WAY IN WHICH MANY APPARENTLY	INTELLIGENTLY	DESIGNED TRANSFORMATIONS HAD ACTUALLY COME TO
SUPR HANDBOK(188)	AT WORK; AND THE CONSEQUENT SURVIVAL OF THE	INTELLIGENTLY	FERTILE MEANS THE SURVIVAL OF THE PARTIZANS OF
DOCT I (95)	A HEALTHY CIRCULATION. I TELL YOU THIS: IN AN	INTELLIGENTLY	GOVERNED COUNTRY PEOPLE WOULDNT BE ALLOWED TO
MIS. PREFACE(3)	EVEN WANT TO LIVE FOR EVER THEMSELVES. BUT THE	INTELLIGENTLY	IMAGINATIVE MAN KNOWS VERY WELL THAT IT IS
SUPR III SD(71)	OF THEM IS NOT WHOLLY CONTEMPTUOUS. WHOEVER HAS	INTELLIGENTLY	OBSERVED THE TRAMP, OR VISITED THE ABLEBODIED
BULL I (87)	HIM OUT OF THE PENNIES OF THE POOR. HE CANT BE	INTELLIGENTLY	POLITICAL: HE DREAMS OF WHAT THE SHAN VAN
MIS. PREFACE(102)	TO BE THERE, AND NOBODY UNDERSTANDS IT. AN	INTELLIGENTLY	WORKED CAPITALIST SYSTEM, AS COMTE SAW, WOULD
METH PREFACE(R71)	SELECTED THEIR ALLIES IN THE LAMARCKIAN MANNER	INTELLIGENTLY	, PURPOSELY, AND VITALLY, AD MAJOREM DEI
METH PREFACE(R29)	READY-MADE AS SOON AS HE CAN CONTROL HIS HANDS	INTELLIGENTLY	, WE ARE FORCED TO SUSPECT EITHER THAT
FABL PREFACE(92)	BEVERAGE" OR SIMPLY " WATER HAS NO TASTE," OR,	INTELLIGENTLY	, " WATER HAS NO TASTE FOR ME, BECAUSE IT IS
		INTELLIGENTSIA	
ROCK II (257)	AS A SPECIAL INTERVIEW: YOU KNOW THAT WE LABOR	INTELLIGENTSIA	HAVE TO LIVE BY OUR BRAINS. AU REVOIR. (SHE
PHIL PREFACE(68)	LIBERAL MORALS WITH THE GREAT NORWEGIAN, EVEN THE	INTELLIGENTSIA	HAVE FORGOTTEN THAT THE LESSON THAT MIGHT
PHIL PREFACE(68)	IBSEN CLUB IN THIS PLAY WAS FAMILIAR THEN TO OUR	INTELLIGENTSIA	. THAT FAR MORE NUMEROUS BODY WHICH MAY BE
ROCK PREFACE(165)	AND TRANSFERRED FROM THE INFAMOUS CATEGORY OF	INTELLIGENTSIA	TO THE HONORABLE ONE OF " THE INTELLECTUAL
ROCK PREFACE(164)	EXTERMINATE THE BOURGEOISIE BY CLASSING THEM AS	INTELLIGENTSIA	, RESTRICTING THEIR RATIONS, AND PUTTING
		INTELLIGIBILITY	
LION PREFACE(9)	HAVE BEEN INTRODUCED PERFORCE TO SAVE ITS BARE	INTELLIGIBILITY	. IT IS QUITE EASY TODAY TO FIND CULTIVATED
		INTELLIGIBLE	
CATH 4 (193)	IT WITH THE TRAIN IN HIS MOUTH IT IS NOT VERY	INTELLIGIBLE	:) /CLAIRE/ LET GO. YOU ARE UNDIGNIFIED AND
LION PREFACE(19)	THEY ARE FAIRLY PLAIN SAILING. JESUS BECOMES AN	INTELLIGIBLE	AND CONSISTENT PERSON. HIS REASONS FOR GOING "
LION PREFACE(9)	AND THE CONDUCT AND ULTIMATE FATE OF JESUS	INTELLIGIBLE	AND INTERESTING. WORLDLINESS OF THE MAJORITY.
MRS PREFACE(155)	BY EXHIBITING EXAMPLES OF PERSONAL CONDUCT MADE	INTELLIGIBLE	AND MOVING TO CROWDS OF UNOBSERVANT
6CAL PREFACE(90)	THE HIGH-BROWED DRAMATIC POET WANTS TO MAKE IT	INTELLIGIBLE	AND SUBLIME. THE FARCE WRITER WANTS TO MAKE IT
SUPR PREFACE(R30)	THE ARTIST, AMUSING TO THE AMATEUR, AND AT LEAST	INTELLIGIBLE	AND THEREFORE POSSIBLY SUGGESTIVE TO THE
METH PREFACE(R28)	ELGAR AN ORCHESTRAL SCORE IS AS INSTANTANEOUSLY	INTELLIGIBLE	AT SIGHT AS A PAGE OF SHAKESPEAR IS TO ME. ONE
GENV IV (124)	THIS? WHY IS HUMANITY DOOMED? /SECRETARY/ IT IS	INTELLIGIBLE	ENOUGH, AND VERY SERIOUS INDEED. /JUDGE/ IT IS
LION PREFACE(15)	WE NOW SEE OUR RELIGION AS A QUAINT BUT QUITE	INTELLIGIBLE	EVOLUTION FROM CRUDE ATTEMPTS TO PROPITIATE THE
MTH3 (101)	SUCH A METHOD. FOR SOME REASON WHICH IS NOT	INTELLIGIBLE	IN CHINA, ENGLISHMEN ALWAYS BELIEVE ANY
JOAN PREFACE(29)	SUCH MORAL COWARDS CAPABLE OF PLEADING TO AN	INTELLIGIBLE	INDICTMENT, THE POINT NEED BE NO FURTHER
SIM PREFACE(14)	THE SPECIAL INQUISITIONARY WORK OF THE TCHEKA	INTELLIGIBLE	. FOR THE TCHEKA WAS SIMPLY CARRYING OUT THE
MTH5 (256)	PUT THINGS VERY CRUDELY TO YOU TO MAKE OURSELVES	INTELLIGIBLE	. /THE HE-ANCIENT/ AND I AM AFRAID WE DO NOT
6CAL PREFACE(90)	HOW THEY ACTUALLY OCCUR) THAT IT CAN BE MADE	INTELLIGIBLE	. THE HIGH-BROWED DRAMATIC POET WANTS TO MAKE
METH PREFACE(R79)	OF RELIGION WOULD FOR THE MULTITUDE BE NEITHER	INTELLIGIBLE	NOR EVEN APPREHENSIBLE; AND THE PROPHETS WOULD
JOAN PREFACE(52)	IN THIS CASE CAUCHON AND LEMAITRE HAVE TO MAKE	INTELLIGIBLE	NOT ONLY THEMSELVES BUT THE CHURCH AND THE
GETT (307)	/COLLINS/ (SNATCHING AT THIS, THE FIRST	INTELLIGIBLE	PROPOSITION HE HAS HEARD) OH, THE WORLD WILL GO
MIS. PREFACE(49)	EXPERIMENTING ON ONE ANOTHER WOULD NOT PRODUCE	INTELLIGIBLE	RESULTS. I ADMIT, HOWEVER, THAT IF MY
BASH PREFACE(88)	MORE EUPHUISTIC BLANK VERSE IS HARDLY MORE	INTELLIGIBLE	THAN CLASSICAL GREEK. EVEN ACTORS MAY BE HEARD
DOCT PREFACE(28)	A CORRUPT AND MISCHIEVOUS SUPERSTITION, BECOMES	INTELLIGIBLE	THE MOMENT THE TRAGEDY OF MEDICAL POVERTY AND
UNPL PREFACE(R22)	A PANTOMIME, IT IS CLEAR THAT HE COULD MAKE IT	INTELLIGIBLE	TO A READER ONLY BY GIVING HIM THE WORDS WHICH
UNPL PREFACE(R22)	BY DIALOGUE ALONE, THAN TO MAKE A PANTOMIME	INTELLIGIBLE	TO A READER WITHOUT IT. OBVIOUS AS THIS IS, THE

HART PREFACE(21)	OF LANE. I EVEN FOUND A GRIM SATISFACTION, VERY	INTELLIGIBLE	TO ALL SOLDIERS, IN THE FACT THAT THE CIVILIANS
UNPL PREFACE(R22)	IMPOSSIBLE TO MAKE A MODERN PRACTICAL STAGE PLAY	INTELLIGIBLE	TO AN AUDIENCE BY DIALOGUE ALONE, THAN TO MAKE
CAPT NOTES (301)	THE TWO THINGS AT THE SAME TIME IS NO MORE	INTELLIGIBLE	TO ME THAN THE FACT THAT EVERYTHING THAT HAS
GENV IV (124)	AND VERY SERIOUS INDEED. /JUDGE/ IT IS NOT	INTELLIGIBLE	TO ME. WILL YOU KINDLY EXPLAIN? /SECRETARY/
JOAN PREFACE(51)	BUSINESS OF THE STAGE TO MAKE ITS FIGURES MORE	INTELLIGIBLE	TO THEMSELVES THAN THEY WOULD BE IN REAL LIFE;
JOAN PREFACE(52)	REAL LIFE; FOR BY NO OTHER MEANS CAN THEY BE MADE	INTELLIGIBLE	TO THE AUDIENCE. AND IN THIS CASE CAUCHON AND
GENV PREFACE(7)	HISTORY CANNOT BE ASCERTAINED. NO EPOCH IS	INTELLIGIBLE	UNTIL IT IS COMPLETED AND CAN BE SEEN IN THE
LION PREFACE(90)	OF A PSYCHOPATHIC DELUSION, ARE QUITE CREDIBLE,	INTELLIGIBLE	, AND INTERESTING TO MODERN THINKERS. IN ANY
BARB PREFACE(220)	TO THEM UNDERSHAFT THE MYSTIC WILL BE QUITE	INTELLIGIBLE	, AND HIS PERFECT COMPREHENSION OF HIS DAUGHTER
MIS. PREFACE(28)	ECONOMIC KNOWLEDGE, DISASTROUS AS IT IS, IS QUITE	INTELLIGIBLE	, ITS CORRUPT MOTIVE BEING AS CLEAR AS THE
LION PREFACE(90)	IN ANY OTHER LIGHT THEY ARE NEITHER CREDIBLE,	INTELLIGIBLE	, NOR INTERESTING EXCEPT TO PEOPLE UPON WHOM
JOAN PREFACE(52)	JUST AS WARWICK HAS TO MAKE THE FEUDAL SYSTEM	INTELLIGIBLE	, THE THREE BETWEEN THEM HAVING THUS TO MAKE A
		INTELLIGIBLY	
PLES PREFACE(R9)	EXPLANATION OF ANY SUCH REVOLT, ADDRESSED	INTELLIGIBLY	AND PROSAICALLY TO THE INTELLECT, CAN ONLY COME
MTH4 I (142)	IF IT IS POSSIBLE FOR YOU TO EXPRESS YOURSELF	INTELLIGIBLY	-- /THE ELDERLY GENTLEMAN/ (SNORTS
		INTEMPERANCE	
GETT PREFACE(191)	THERE WAS NOTHING IN THEIR CIRCUMSTANCES TO CHECK	INTEMPERANCE	. THEY WERE MEN OF BUSINESS; THAT IS, MEN FOR
GETT PREFACE(190)	HIS PARISH ARE VISIBLY SUFFERING MUCH LESS FROM	INTEMPERANCE	THAN MANY OF THE MARRIED PEOPLE WHO STIGMATIZE
		INTEMPERANCES	
APPL PREFACE(173)	KICKINGS: IN SHORT, THE COMMONER VIOLENCES AND	INTEMPERANCES	OF AUTHORITY. HIS MINISTERS HAVE MUCH LAXER
DOCT PREFACE(70)	TOO MUCH (TO GO NO FURTHER IN THE LIST OF	INTEMPERANCES	THAT MAKE UP SO MUCH OF FAMILY LIFE) WOULD
		INTEMPERATE	
BULL PREFACE(43)	WERE AS UNHEALTHY AS AN ENGLISHMAN'S EATING, AS	INTEMPERATE	AS HIS DRINKING, AS FILTHY AS HIS SMOKING, AS
CATH 1,SD(161)	A RUSSIAN BUT A GERMAN, BY NO MEANS BARBAROUS OR	INTEMPERATE	IN HER PERSONAL HABITS. SHE NOT ONLY DISPUTES
		INTEND	
BUOY PREFACE(4)	PATMOS. WHEN I WRITE A PLAY I DO NOT FORESEE NOR	INTEND	A PAGE OF IT FROM ONE END TO THE OTHER: THE PLAY
POSN (459)	DELICACY. /THE FOREMAN/ NO WE DONT; AND WE DONT	INTEND	HE SHALL. NOT WHILE I AM FOREMAN OF THIS JURY.
GETT (282)	OF US AFTER ALL. PERHAPS THATS WHAT MOST OF US	INTEND	HIM TO DO. /THE GENERAL/ ALFRED: WE ASKED YOU HERE TO
CATH 2 (180)	GOOD. I HAVE BEEN VERY AWKWARD; BUT I DID NOT	INTEND	IT. I AM RATHER STUPID, I AM AFRAID. /CATHERINE/
SUPR I (14)	SOME WISHES IN THIS MATTER? /RAMSDEN/ I QUITE	INTEND	THAT ANNIE'S WISHES SHALL BE CONSULTED IN EVERY
NEVR I (213)	(INDIGNANTLY) AH! YOU INSIST. /GLORIA/ DO YOU	INTEND	THAT WE SHALL NEVER KNOW? /DOLLY/ OH GLORIA, DONT.
MIS. (178)	SHOULD I GO OUT WITH YOU? /PERCIVAL/ BECAUSE I	INTEND	THAT YOU SHALL. /GUNNER/ I WONT BE BULLIED BY YOU. (
VWOO 3 (138)	AN INCONSIDERATE REMARK WHICH HURT YOU. I DID NOT	INTEND	THAT. I SHOULD HAVE TOLD YOU SERIOUSLY THAT I PAY YOU
JITT III (65)	MY HUSBAND WHEN HE DIED. /JITTA/ SHE DID NOT	INTEND	THAT. YOU MAY FORGIVE HER THAT, AT LEAST. /AGNES/ OH,
GENV IV (99)	OF NO IMPORTANCE WHATEVER. /SIR O./ I DID NOT	INTEND	THAT, I ASSURE YOU, AND I CANNOT ADMIT THAT THE
NEVR III (279)	FINCH: I DONT WANT COUNSEL'S OPINION, BECAUSE I	INTEND	TO BE GUIDED BY MY OWN OPINION. I DONT WANT TO MEET
NEVR IV (303)	GENTLEMAN? /GLORIA/ (RESOLUTELY) YES, DO YOU	INTEND	TO BE OUR FRIEND OR-- /DOLLY/-- OR OUR FATHER?
JITT II (36)	HIMSELF THE DAY WE BURIED POOR PAPA. BUT I DONT	INTEND	TO BE TAKEN AS A LEGACY, SACRED OR NOT. /JITTA/
OVER (189)	BEHAVE AS I THOUGHT I SHOULD BEHAVE. I DIDNT	INTEND	TO BE WICKED; BUT SOMEHOW OR OTHER, NATURE, OR
JOAN 6 (142)	EARL OF WARWICK WILL DO WHEN HE LEARNS THAT YOU	INTEND	TO BETRAY HIM. THERE ARE EIGHT HUNDRED MEN AT THE
ROCK I (198)	FACE TO FACE, AND EXPLAIN TO THEM THAT I	INTEND	TO CALL A CONFERENCE IN MARCH NEXT ON THE PROSPECTS
SUPR I (18)	ME, GRANNY? /TANNER/ (STARTING) GRANNY! DO YOU	INTEND	TO CALL YOUR GUARDIANS GRANNY? /ANN/ DONT BE
PYGM V (281)	TREATED YOU. I CANT CHANGE MY NATURE; AND I DONT	INTEND	TO CHANGE MY MANNERS. MY MANNERS ARE EXACTLY THE SAME
2TRU I (46)	COME WITH US? /THE PATIENT/ (CALMLY) I FULLY	INTEND	TO COME WITH YOU. I'M GOING TO MAKE THE MOST OF THIS
BARB III (318)	NO CAPACITY FOR BUSINESS AND NO TASTE FOR IT. I	INTEND	TO DEVOTE MYSELF TO POLITICS. /UNDERSHAFT/ (RISING)
MILL PREFACE(111)	IV USURPED THE ENGLISH CROWN HE CERTAINLY DID NOT	INTEND	TO DIE OF POLITICAL OVERWORK; BUT THAT IS WHAT
SUPR I (31)	GO UP TO THE DRAWING ROOM AND TELL THEM WHAT WE	INTEND	TO DO? /RAMSDEN/ (LOOKING POINTEDLY AT TANNER) I
SUPR I (13)	BETWEEN US. (HE SITS DOWN AGAIN). WHAT DO YOU	INTEND	TO DO ABOUT THIS WILL? /OCTAVIUS/ MAY I MAKE A
CAPT II (256)	I CALL ON YOU TO OBEY THE LAW. /BRASSBOUND/ I	INTEND	TO DO SO. THE LAW OF THE ATLAS MOUNTAINS IS
2TRU II (77)	WELL, WHAT OF IT? /TALLBOYS/ THAT IS WHAT I	INTEND	TO FIND OUT. YOU ARE NOT A NATIVE. /THE PATIENT/ YES,
ARMS I (8)	THAT? /RAINA/ YES. /THE MAN/ WELL, I DONT	INTEND	TO GET KILLED IF I CAN HELP IT. (STILL MORE
DOCT III (137)	OUT OF HIS LAST HALF-CROWN WAS DAMNABLE. I	INTEND	TO GIVE HIM THAT HALF-CROWN AND TO BE IN A POSITION
MIS. (176)	FOR THE POLICE. /GUNNER/ I'LL GO WITH HIM. I	INTEND	TO GIVE MYSELF UP. I'M GOING TO EXPOSE WHAT IVE SEEN
OVER (194)	THE MOST HORRIBLE IMMORALITY. /MRS LUNN/ I DONT	INTEND	TO GIVE UP MEETING YOU, MR JUNO. YOU AMUSE ME VERY
WIDO II (36)	WE SHALL LIVE ALWAYS ON SEVEN HUNDRED A YEAR. I	INTEND	TO GO AT MY PROFESSION IN EARNEST, AND WORK MY
GETT (314)	MARRY FOR CHILDREN. THERES THE PEOPLE THAT DONT	INTEND	TO HAVE CHILDREN AND THAT ARNT FIT TO HAVE THEM.
MIS. PREFACE(61)	HIM AS BY A PHYSICAL CRIPPLE; AND AS YOU DO NOT	INTEND	TO HAVE HIM ON YOUR HANDS ALL YOUR LIFE, AND ARE
JITT III (75)	IT. I HAVE NOT EXCUSED MYSELF. BUT I DO NOT	INTEND	TO HAVE IT THROWN IN MY TEETH EVERY TIME WE MEET. (
FANY III (322)	MINDS ARE SO-- HOW DO YOU SAY? -- WHOLESOME. I	INTEND	TO HAVE MY DAUGHTERS EDUCATED IN ENGLAND. NOWHERE
MRS II (202)	SCAMP! /FRANK/ (CONTINUING) AND AS YOU NO DOUBT	INTEND	TO HOLD OUT OTHER PROSPECTS TO HER, I SHALL LOSE NO
INCA (240)	I VENTURE TO ASK YOU TO LET ME KNOW HOW LONG YOU	INTEND	TO HONOR US WITH YOUR PRESENCE. /THE PRINCESS/ (
JOAN PREFACE(5)	SO EASY FOR MENTAL GIANTS WHO NEITHER HATE NOR	INTEND	TO INJURE THEIR FELLOWS TO REALIZE THAT NEVERTHELESS
CATH 4 (190)	/EDSTASTON/ FOR HEAVEN'S SAKE, MADAM, DO YOU	INTEND	TO LEAVE ME TIED UP LIKE THIS WHILE YOU DISCUSS THE
BUOY IV (50)	OF MY LIFE. /JUNIUS/ NOT ALWAYS. HOW LONG DO YOU	INTEND	TO LIVE, OLD MAN? /OLD BILL/ NOT FOR EVER: GOD
PHIL II (122)	/CHARTERIS/ (TAKING IT) IT DOESNT MATTER: I DONT	INTEND	TO MAKE ANY. (HE RETIRES TO THE RECESS ON IBSEN'S
VWOO 3 (142)	REAL GENTLEMEN OF THEIR HUSBANDS. WHAT DO YOU	INTEND	TO MAKE OF ME, I WONDER? /Z/ WELL, I HAVE MADE A
CLEO NOTES (211)	THINGS YOU DO NOT WANT TO PEOPLE OF WHOM YOU	INTEND	TO MAKE USE. THIS DISTINCTION BETWEEN VIRTUE AND
HART II (97)	THAT, HESIONE? I DO WANT TO MARRY HIM. I FULLY	INTEND	TO MARRY HIM. /MAZZINI/ ARE YOU QUITE SURE, ELLIE?
JITT I (23)	TODAY WITHOUT DARING TO TELL YOU THAT I DO NOT	INTEND	TO MEET YOU AGAIN. /JITTA/ (STRUCK TO THE HEART) NOT
HART PREFACE(28)	BECAUSE WE HAVE NO FIGURES FOR IT AND DO NOT	INTEND	TO PAY IT. A BLOCKADE THAT CUTS OFF " THE GRACE OF
MRS II (210)	MY SOCIAL STANDING, AND THE PROFESSION I	INTEND	TO PURSUE. I KNOW NOTHING ABOUT YOU. WHAT IS THAT WAY
BARB I (250)	AGGRESSIVELY) STEPHEN: MAY I ASK HOW SOON YOU	INTEND	TO REALIZE THAT YOU ARE A GROWN-UP MAN, AND THAT I AM
MTH2 (64)	NEW POLITICAL NAMES MAY COME INTO VOGUE. I DO NOT	INTEND	TO RESIST THE TRANSITION TO SOCIALISM. YOU MAY DEPEND
HART II (92)	MR DUNN, LOOK. JUST LOOK. LOOK HARD. DO YOU STILL	INTEND	TO SACRIFICE YOUR DAUGHTER TO THAT THING? /MAZZINI/
MRS IV (237)	/FRANK/ (LOOKING ROUND DISPARAGINGLY) DO YOU	INTEND	TO STICK IN THIS CONFOUNDED PLACE? /VIVIE/ (BLOWING
PHIL II (125)	(GETTING UP AND LOOKING DARKLY AT HER) YOU	INTEND	TO TAKE HIM FROM ME, THEN? /GRACE/ DO YOU EXPECT ME
NEVR II (231)	BALD HEADED. /M'COMAS/ (NETTLED) I HOPE YOU	INTEND	TO TAKE WHAT I HAVE TO SAY SERIOUSLY. /PHILIP/ (WITH
JITT III (74)	/EDITH/ (SLOWLY) I SUPPOSE NOT. /JITTA/ DID YOU	INTEND	TO TELL EVERYBODY? /EDITH/ NO, OF COURSE NOT: I AM
LIED (196)	THAT IVE NOT HAD TIME TO READ THEM ALL; THOUGH I	INTEND	TO THE VERY FIRST MOMENT I CAN GET: I PROMISE YOU
MIS. PREFACE(67)	AT THE WORK HAVE NO PATIENCE WITH HIM AND DO NOT	INTEND	TO TREAT HIM AS INFALLIBLE, ARE PITIABLE AS FAR AS
CATH 4 (191)	MY TOES AND YOURS. /CATHERINE/ DO YOU STILL	INTEND	TO WRITE TO THE LONDON GAZETTE ABOUT ME? /EDSTASTON/
HART I (67)	YOU KNOW? /MANGAN/ (PLAYING THE STRONG MAN) I	INTEND	TO. I MEAN TO. SEE? I NEVER MADE UP MY MIND TO DO A
GETT (321)	MY DEEPEST OBJECTION TO MARRIAGE; AND I DONT	INTEND	TO. THERE ARE CERTAIN RIGHTS I WILL NOT GIVE ANY
POSN PREFACE(432)	NOT AVAILED MYSELF OF THIS LICENCE, AND DO NOT	INTEND	TO. THERE IS ENOUGH LICENSED DARKNESS IN OUR THEATRES
BARB II (288)	DO ELSE IS IT? /BARBARA/ SOMEBODY THAT DOESNT	INTEND	YOU TO SMASH WOMEN'S FACES, I SUPPOSE. SOMEBODY OR
ARMS III (69)	BEEN NO MORE THAN HER CONFIDENTIAL SERVANT. I	INTEND	, AS YOU KNOW, SIR, TO SET UP A SHOP LATER ON IN
		INTENDED	
SUPR PREFACE(R13)	HIMSELF TO HIS HEART'S CONTENT. BUT THE LESSON	INTENDED	BY AN AUTHOR IS HARDLY EVER THE LESSON THE WORLD
PYGM EPILOG (295)	UNHAPPINESS TO FREDDY HIMSELF, WHO WAS OBVIOUSLY	INTENDED	BY NATURE FOR SUCH LIGHT WORK AS AMUSING ELIZA,
FOUN (214)	A HAPPY ONE, MADAM; BUT I BELIEVE I AM THE PERSON	INTENDED	BY THE WRITER. /MERCER/ (PRODUCING ANOTHER PAPER)
ARMS III (53)	ONLY A PHOTOGRAPH: HOW CAN HE TELL WHO IT WAS	INTENDED	FOR? TELL HIM HE PUT IT THERE HIMSELF. /RAINA/ (
GETT PREFACE(245)	MENTIONED IN MY PRESENCE OR IN ANY BOOK THAT IS	INTENDED	FOR FAMILY READING." WICKED AND FOOLISH AS THE
POSN PREFACE(371)	PRESS BECAUSE NO EDITOR OF A PAPER OR MAGAZINE	INTENDED	FOR GENERAL FAMILY READING COULD ADMIT INTO HIS
MIS. PREFACE(19)	AND THERE IS, ON THE WHOLE, NOTHING ON EARTH	INTENDED	FOR INNOCENT PEOPLE SO HORRIBLE AS A SCHOOL. TO
CURE (233)	DO YOU LIKE THAT? /STREGA/ WHAT IS IT? IS IT	INTENDED	FOR MUSIC? /REGINALD/ OH, YOU BEAUTIFUL DOLL.
DEVL II (40)	TO DISTRESS HERSELF. STILL-- (IN A LOWER VOICE,	INTENDED	FOR RICHARD ALONE) YOUR LAST CHANCE, SIR. THEY LOOK
MRS II (218)	GOT COMPLETELY THE BETTER OF ME TONIGHT, THOUGH I	INTENDED	IT TO BE THE OTHER WAY. LET US BE GOOD FRIENDS NOW.
SUPR I (41)	THIS CONVERSATION HAS ALREADY GONE FURTHER THAN I	INTENDED	. RAMSDEN AND OCTAVIUS COME BACK WITH MISS RAMSDEN,
HART I (76)	EFFECT, YOU GOT YOUR CLAWS DEEPER INTO ME THAN I	INTENDED	. /MRS HUSHABYE/ (COMING IN FROM THE GARDEN) DONT
AUGS (266)	IS PERFECTLY MONSTROUS. NOT IN THE LEAST WHAT I	INTENDED	. /THE CLERK/ HELL -- /AUGUSTUS/ SIR! /THE CLERK/
POSN (457)	CARE. THAT WOMAN WILL MAKE YOU DO WHAT YOU NEVER	INTENDED	. THATS THE RAINBOW WOMAN. THATS THE WOMAN THAT

PHIL II (99)	/CHARTERIS/ THATS RIGHT. I'M EARLIER THAN I	INTENDED	. THE FACT IS, I HAVE SOMETHING RATHER PRESSING TO
2TRU III (111)	AND RESTORED HIS BOOTY TO ITS OWNER. NATURE NEVER	INTENDED	ME FOR SOLDIERING OR THIEVING: I AM BY NATURE AND
FOUN (211)	BETTER. NO! THE CHURCH IS NOT IN MY LINE. NATURE	INTENDED	ME FOR THE STAGE. THE UNREAL MOCKERY HERE WAS
MIS. PREFACE(13)	THEIR WORKPEOPLE; BUT THIS IS NOT A JUSTIFIED AND	INTENDED	PART OF THE SITUATION: IT IS AN ABUSE OF CAPITALISM
MRS III (231)	ME IN WITH. /CROFTS/ (QUITE SINCERELY) I NEVER	INTENDED	THAT. ON MY WORD AS A GENTLEMAN I DIDNT. VIVIE
GETT (324)	OUT OF PLACE IN YOUR CELLAR, AS NATURE EVIDENTLY	INTENDED	THEM FOR THE ROOF? /HOTCHKISS/ I REMEMBER THAT
SIM II (85)	OUR WARS WILL MAKE WILL NEVER BE THE CHANGES WE	INTENDED	THEM TO MAKE. WE SHALL CLAMOR FOR SECURITY LIKE
BULL IV (159)	YOU LAST FEBRUARY? /LARRY/ OH YES; AND I REALLY	INTENDED	TO ANSWER IT. BUT I HAVNT HAD A MOMENT; AND I KNEW
JOAN PREFACE(25)	ON HER ASSAILANTS, CAN BE LAUGHED AT AS THEY ARE	INTENDED	TO BE WITHOUT SCRUPLE; FOR NO SANE PERSON COULD
FANY III (322)	YOU ARE TO US, WITHOUT WANTING TO KNOW WHETHER HE	INTENDED	TO BEHAVE HONORABLY? /DUVALLET/ AH, MADAM, MY
PYGM II (231)	/HIGGINS/ (GOING TO HER SOLEMNLY) JUST SO. I	INTENDED	TO CALL YOUR ATTENTION TO THAT. (HE PASSES ON TO
LIED SD(187)	IT IS AS LIKE A SHOP WINDOW AS POSSIBLE, AND IS	INTENDED	TO DEMONSTRATE THE SOCIAL POSITION AND SPENDING
BARB PREFACE(246)	BUT THEY HAVE NEVER DONE MISCHIEF UNLESS THEY	INTENDED	TO DO IT. THAT IS WHY GREAT SCOUNDRELS HAVE BEEN
SUPR HANDBOK(194)	SYSTEM, AND THAT MAN, FAULTY AS HE IS, NO MORE	INTENDED	TO ESTABLISH ANY SUCH ORDERED DISORDER THAN A MOTH
DOCT III (132)	HE ASKED ME THE OTHER DAY WHETHER YOU REALLY	INTENDED	TO FINISH THEM. /LOUIS/ CONFOUND HIS IMPUDENCE!
MIS. PREFACE(55)	TO WHAT HE CALLED HIS HONOR AND AUTHORITY. I HAD	INTENDED	TO GIVE THE PARTICULARS OF THIS CASE, BUT FIND THE
SUPR IV (145)	SON HECTOR. /VIOLET/ (CONVERSATIONALLY) YES. WE	INTENDED	TO GO TO NICE; BUT WE HAD TO FOLLOW A RATHER
DOCT PREFACE(25)	THAT THE PARTICULAR PATHOGENIC GERM WHICH THEY	INTENDED	TO INTRODUCE INTO THE PATIENT'S SYSTEM MAY BE QUITE
BARB PREFACE(210)	IT IS NEITHER POLITE NOR PROFOUND, WAS PROBABLY	INTENDED	TO KNOCK THIS NONSENSE VIOLENTLY ON THE HEAD. A
MTH5 (233)	WOULD HAVE BEEN INTERESTING. /PYGMALION/ I	INTENDED	TO MAKE A WOMAN; BUT AFTER MY EXPERIENCE WITH THE
HART III (137)	YOU SATISFIED NOW? /ELLIE/ NO. I NEVER REALLY	INTENDED	TO MAKE YOU MARRY ME, MR MANGAN. NEVER IN THE
CAND I (92)	FORTH HIS REMORSEFUL REGRETS ALL THE TIME) I	INTENDED	TO MEET YOU AT THE TRAIN. I LET THE TIME SLIP. (
CATH 1,SD(163)	AND HURRIES OUT, DIVINING THAT PATIOMKIN HAS	INTENDED	TO SEE THE ENGLISH CAPTAIN ALL ALONG, AND HAS
BARB III (327)	/CUSINS/ I WANTED TO SEE EVERYTHING I WAS NOT	INTENDED	TO SEE; AND BARBARA WANTED TO MAKE THE MEN TALK.
MRS PREFACE(174)	HIM " WONDERING WHAT USEFUL PURPOSE THE PLAY WAS	INTENDED	TO SERVE." THE BALANCE HAS TO BE REDRESSED BY THE
PYGM II (235)	BUT WHY DID YOU BRING HER LUGGAGE IF YOU	INTENDED	TO TAKE HER AWAY? /DOOLITTLE/ HAVE I SAID A WORD
SUPR I (5)	AS TO ME. AND HIS DEATH WAS SO SUDDEN! I ALWAYS	INTENDED	TO THANK HIM-- TO LET HIM KNOW THAT I HAD NOT TAKEN
HART II (106)	TO THE CHAIR). I HOPE YOU WONT BELIEVE I REALLY	INTENDED	TO. HECTOR COMES IN, MARCHING AN OLD AND VILLAINOUS
DOCT V (177)	DIFFERENCE AT ALL. /RIDGEON/ PERHAPS NOT. BUT I	INTENDED	TO. /JENNIFER/ (LOOKING AT HIM AMAZEDLY: NOT
2TRU I (41)	BUT OH, MY SWEETIE-WEETIE, NATURE NEVER	INTENDED	US TO BE BURGLARS. OUR FIRST ATTEMPT HAS BEEN A
WIDO I (12)	HE GOES INTO THE HOTEL). /SARTORIUS/ (GRAVELY) I	INTENDED	YOU TO ACCOMPANY US, BLANCHE. /BLANCHE/ YES, PAPA.
JOAN PREFACE(37)	IS TOO HARD A SAYING TELLS ME THAT IT WAS NOT SO	INTENDED	, I SHALL REMIND HIM THAT THE CHURCH IS IN THE
GETT PREFACE(215)	MAN IN IT WOULD BE NO HOME AT ALL, AND WHO FULLY	INTENDED	, IF THE MAN TURNED OUT TO BE THE RIGHT ONE, TO
DOCT I (89)	/SIR PATRICK/ STILL, THAT WASNT QUITE WHAT YOU	INTENDED	, WAS IT? /RIDGEON/ I TOOK MY CHANCE OF IT. /SIR
POSN (461)	CRY-BABY! LANDED LIKE ME! DOING WHAT YOU NEVER	INTENDED	! (TAKING UP HIS HAT AND SPEAKING IN HIS ORDINARY

INTENDING

SUPR IV SD(143)	ALARM WHEN THE OLD GENTLEMAN SHEWS SIGNS OF	INTENDING	HIS IRISH NONSENSE TO BE TAKEN SERIOUSLY.
MIS. PREFACE(78)	CHILDREN. CHILDREN ARE EXTREMELY CRUEL WITHOUT	INTENDING	IT; AND IN NINETY-NINE CASES OUT OF A HUNDRED THE
NEVR II (240)	HE SMILES. SHE PASSES ON AND CONFRONTS CRAMPTON,	INTENDING	TO ADDRESS HIM WITH COMPLETE COMPOSURE; BUT HIS
SUPR I SD(25)	PART, OF WORRY. HE COMES BETWEEN THE TWO MEN,	INTENDING	TO ADDRESS OCTAVIUS, BUT PULLS HIMSELF UP ABRUPTLY
DOCT II (123)	GET IT, WITHOUT IN THE LEAST UNDERSTANDING IT, OR	INTENDING	TO CARRY OUT THE AGREEMENT IF IT TURNS OUT BADLY
MRS IV (247)	A CUNNING GLEAM IN HER EYE) I'LL DOUBLE IT: I WAS	INTENDING	TO DOUBLE IT. ONLY LET ME KNOW HOW MUCH YOU WANT.
BULL II (107)	MR DOYLE ARRIVED, TO MEET US AT ATHENMULLET,	INTENDING	TO GET HERE LONG BEFORE ME. /AUNT JUDY/ LORD SAVE
MIS. SD(157)	INSIDE THE DOOR, HOLDING IT OPEN, EVIDENTLY NOT	INTENDING	TO STAY. /LINA/ OH, MRS TARLETON, SHALL I BE

INTENDS

GENV IV (96)	WITH US? I DONT KNOW. BUT THEY KNOW WHAT ENGLAND	INTENDS	. THEY KNOW WHAT TO EXPECT FROM US. WE HAVE NO
MTH2 (49)	IN BEFORE BURGE CAN PROCEED-- AS HE EVIDENTLY	INTENDS	-- TO ANSWER HIS OWN QUESTION) I WILL TELL YOU. HE
BULL II (99)	THINK HIM HALF-WITTED, WHICH IS EXACTLY WHAT HE	INTENDS	THEM TO THINK. HE IS CLAD IN CORDUROY TROUSERS,
SUPR HANDBOK(194)	ESTABLISH ANY SUCH ORDERED DISORDER THAN A MOTH	INTENDS	TO BE BURNT WHEN IT FLIES INTO A CANDLE FLAME. HE
NEVR IV (297)	HER NOT BEARING HER FATHER'S NAME. THE OTHER LADY	INTENDS	TO GET MARRIED. /GLORIA/ (FLUSHING) MR BOHUN!
SUPR I (42)	DOORS. BUT WHEN A WOMAN IS NOT ONLY WICKED, BUT	INTENDS	TO GO ON BEING WICKED, SHE AND I PART COMPANY. /ANN/
SUPR IV (156)	HE HAS BEEN URGING ME NOT TO MARRY YOU BECAUSE HE	INTENDS	TO MARRY YOU HIMSELF? /ANN/ (ALARMED) NO, NO: YOU
SUPR I (14)	DOWN FROM THE DRAWING ROOM AND ASK HER WHAT SHE	INTENDS	US TO DO. OFF WITH YOU, TAVY, AND FETCH HER. (TAVY

INTENSE

MTH1 II (28)	OF ANOTHER LIFE: A LIFE INFINITELY SPLENDID AND	INTENSE	: A LIFE OF THE SOUL ALONE: A LIFE WITHOUT CLODS OR
ROCK PREFACE(170)	EVEN ONE AND THE SAME PERSON MAY HAVE SPELLS OF	INTENSE	ACTIVITY AND SLACKNESS VARYING FROM WEEKS TO YEARS.
ARMS II SD(28)	ACUTE CRITICAL FACULTY WHICH HAS BEEN THROWN INTO	INTENSE	ACTIVITY BY THE ARRIVAL OF WESTERN CIVILIZATION IN
GETT PREFACE(226)	HUSBAND AND WIFE AND PARENT AND CHILD IS ONE OF	INTENSE	AFFECTION, AND THAT TO FEEL ANY OTHER SENTIMENT
BUOY PREFACE(5)	THIS APPETITE, IS AS YET FAR FROM BEING AS	INTENSE	AS THE SEXUAL ORGASM OR THE ECSTASY OF A SAINT,
MRS II (205)	LOT, FRANK! /FRANK/ WHAT A CREW! /VIVIE/ (WITH	INTENSE	CONTEMPT FOR THEM) IF I THOUGHT THAT I WAS LIKE
ROCK I (215)	BRIGHTENING) INDEED? WHAT IS IT? /BLEE/ (WITH	INTENSE	CONTEMPT) YOUR MEASURE. (HE GOES OUT). THE PRIME
JOAN 2 (75)	I CAN READ, YOU KNOW. /LA TREMOUILLE/ (WITH	INTENSE	CONTEMPT, NOT AT ALL STUNG BY THE TAUNT) YES:
BARB III (324)	TURNED BACK TO DRUNKENNESS AND DERISION. (WITH	INTENSE	CONVICTION) I WILL NEVER FORGIVE YOU THAT. IF I HAD
BARB II (285)	AND ADDRESSING HIM IN A SUBDUED VOICE, BUT WITH	INTENSE	CONVICTION) I'D AV THE LOR OF YOU, YOU FLAT EARED
MTH2 (85)	MUCH BY VISIONS OF THE FUTURE. /BURGE/ (WITH	INTENSE	CONVICTION) THE FUTURE DOES NOT EXIST FOR HENRY
BULL II (101)	DONT KNEEL TO ME: I'M NOT A SAINT. /PATSY/ (WITH	INTENSE	CONVICTION) OH IN THROTH YAR, SIR. (THE GRASSHOPPER
SUPR IV (172)	BE IN ORDINARY WALKING DRESS-- /VIOLET/ (WITH	INTENSE	CONVICTION) YOU ARE A BRUTE, JACK. /ANN/ (LOOKING
CAND II (110)	MISS GARNETT MEANT ANYTHING. /PROSERPINE/ (WITH	INTENSE	CONVICTION) OH, DIDNT I THOUGH, JUST! /BURGESS/ I
ROCK PREFACE(169)	FALLOWS, OR AT LEAST LIGHT CROPPINGS, BETWEEN THE	INTENSE	CULTIVATIONS; FOR WE CANNOT EXPECT THE VERY
PHIL I (77)	HAVE YOU NO FEELING FOR ME? /CHARTERIS/ ONLY AN	INTENSE	DESIRE TO GET YOU SAFELY OUT OF THIS. /JULIA/ (
BULL PREFACE(8)	NATURAL PASSION CANNOT PRETEND TO INSPIRE MORE	INTENSE	DEVOTION THAN PERVERTED PASSION. BUT WHEN ALL IS
BULL III (142)	WRONGS AN DISTHRESS AN SUFFERIN? /HODSON/ (WITH	INTENSE	DISGUST AND CONTEMPT) OW, CHACK IT, PADDY. CHEESE
CLEO IV (182)	CAESAR. BRING ME MY BARLEY WATER. /RUFIO/ (WITH	INTENSE	DISGUST) UGH! BRING ME MY FALERNIAN. (THE
ROCK II (247)	GROUP AND FLINGS HIMSELF INTO HILDA'S CHAIR WITH	INTENSE	DISGUST). /SIR ARTHUR/ (SURPRISED) AM I TO
POSN SD(438)	ON HIS BROW, PROCLAIM THE DANDY IN SPITE OF HIS	INTENSE	DISREPUTABLENESS. HE CARRIES HIS HEAD HIGH, AND HAS
CAPT III (288)	THAT SORT OF READING, MY MAN. /DRINKWATER/ (IN	INTENSE	DISTRESS, APPEALING TO LADY CICELY) DOWNT LET EM
DOCT PREFACE(5)	MISTAKE FOR THESE IS SENTIMENTALITY AND AN	INTENSE	DREAD OF DOING ANYTHING THAT EVERYBODY ELSE DOES NOT
BULL I (88)	YOU BETTER THAN THEM. /BROADBENT/ (ROUSED TO	INTENSE	EARNESTNESS BY DOYLE'S ELOQUENCE) NEVER DESPAIR,
DEVL III (52)	SHE GIVES HIM HER HAND, AND ADDS, WITH	INTENSE	EARNESTNESS) IF I COULD SAVE YOU AS YOU SAVED HIM, I
WIDO II (34)	PASSIONATELY. THEN, LOOKING INTO HER EYES WITH	INTENSE	EARNESTNESS, HE SAYS) BLANCHE: ARE YOU FOND OF
BULL IV (148)	TOWN ABLE TO SPEAK FOR LAUGHIN-- /KEEGAN/ (WITH	INTENSE	EMPHASIS) IT IS HELL: IT IS HELL. NOWHERE ELSE COULD
NEVR II (253)	/GLORIA/ (SPRINGING UP) YOU WRETCH! (WITH	INTENSE	EMPHASIS) YOU WRETCH! ! YOU DARE CURSE MY MOTHER!
UNPL PREFACE(R11)	ACCUSTOMED TO DO WITHOUT, COULD NEVER PROVIDE THE	INTENSE	ENERGY NECESSARY FOR THE ESTABLISHMENT OF THE NEW
AUGS (282)	CLERK/ (LAUGHING SLOWLY AND LABORIOUSLY, WITH	INTENSE	ENJOYMENT) HA HA! HA HA HA! HA! (AUGUSTUS RUSHES
FABL IV (116)	NOT WEAKEN THEM WHEN THEIR SPIRITUAL ACTIVITY WAS	INTENSE	ENOUGH TO PRODUCE A STATE OF ECSTASY. FULL STOP! NEW
HART III SD(148)	HIM? OUR TURN NEXT. THEY WAIT IN SILENCE AND	INTENSE	EXPECTATION. HESIONE AND ELLIE HOLD EACH OTHER'S
CATH 4 (191)	/EDSTASTON/ IT'S AGREEABLE ENOUGH; ONLY (WITH	INTENSE	EXPRESSION) FOR HEAVEN'S SAKE DONT TOUCH ME IN THE
POSN (459)	WHILE I AM FOREMAN OF THIS JURY. /BLANCO/ (WITH	INTENSE	EXPRESSION) A ROTTEN FOREMAN! OH, WHAT A ROTTEN
GETT (300)	UNCLE REJJY? /REGINALD/ (AT HOTCHKISS, WITH	INTENSE	EXPRESSION) YES. /LEO/ REJJY! /REGINALD/ I SAID
BARB II (290)	STOP ER JAWR; OR YOULL DOY AFOAH YOUR TAWM (WITH	INTENSE	EXPRESSION) WORE AHT: THETS WOT YOULL BE: WORE AHT.
NEVR II (260)	IS THE MATTER WITH YOU? /GLORIA/ (WITH THE MOST	INTENSE	EXPRESSION) ONLY SHAME! SHAME! ! SHAME! ! ! (
BULL IV (150)	OF THE GOVERNMENT (A SMALL PIOUS VOICE, WITH	INTENSE	EXPRESSION, " GOD BLESS YOU, SIR! "), THAT LOVE OF
NEVR I SD(208)	OF HER PASSION WITH HER OBSTINATE PRIDE AND	INTENSE	FASTIDIOUSNESS RESULTS IN A FREEZING COLDNESS OF
POSN SD(457)	STRAPPER RETURNS WITH A WOMAN. HER EXPRESSION OF	INTENSE	GRIEF SILENCES THEM AS THEY CRANE OVER ONE ANOTHER'S
DEVL I (20)	(THEY LOOK AT ONE ANOTHER FOR A MOMENT WITH	INTENSE	HATRED; AND THEN SHE SINKS, CHECKMATED, INTO HER
DEST SD(173)	OF PAPERS FROM HER BOSOM. FOR A MOMENT SHE HAS AN	INTENSE	IMPULSE TO DASH THEM IN HIS FACE. BUT HER GOOD
MTH1 I SD(19)	WHISPERING TO HER). EVE'S FACE LIGHTS UP WITH	INTENSE	INTEREST, WHICH INCREASES UNTIL AN EXPRESSION OF
VWOO 3 (142)	AND NOTHING ELSE. AN EXTRAORDINARY DELIGHT AND AN	INTENSE	LOVE WILL SEIZE US. IT WILL LAST HARDLY LONGER THAN
BARB II (283)	O YOUR TANGUE. (SUDDENLY TURNING ON HER WITH	INTENSE	MALICE) AND IF AW DOWNT FAWND MOG THERE, AW'LL CAM
BULL II SD(97)	BACK, IS STANDING NEAR THE STONE IN A TRANCE OF	INTENSE	MELANCHOLY, LOOKING OVER THE HILLS AS IF BY MERE
MTH5 (230)	AND LABORIOUS CALCULATIONS REQUIRING SUCH	INTENSE	MENTAL APPLICATION THAT THEY FREQUENTLY FORGOT TO
DEVL II (33)	AT THE DOOR, WITH A START WHICH BETRAYS HER	INTENSE	NERVOUSNESS, SHE RETREATS TO THE FURTHER END OF THE
METH PREFACE(R56)	GET WEAKER AND DIE IF YOU GIVE THEM NO FOOD; THAT	INTENSE	PAIN MAKES MICE SWEAT; AND THAT IF YOU CUT OFF A
WIDO II SD(45)	IS THAT OF A STRONG AND DETERMINED WOMAN IN AN	INTENSE	PASSION. THE MAID LOOKS AT HER WITH ABJECT WOUNDED

CAND I (84)	HIS HEAD SADLY. SHE RISES AND COMES AT HIM WITH	INTENSE	PEPPERINESS). YOU DONT BELIEVE ME? YOU THINK I'M
NEVR I SD(208)	ONLY, ONE OBSERVES THAT THIS REASONABLENESS AND	INTENSE	PERSONAL PRIVACY, WHICH LEAVES HER RELATIONS WITH
DEVL I (9)	HE CHANGED HIS MIND. /MRS DUDGEON/ (WHITE WITH	INTENSE	RAGE) AND YOU LET HIM ROB ME? /ANDERSON/ I HAD NO
6CAL SD(97)	PLANTING HIMSELF STIFFLY ERECT IN AN ATTITUDE OF	INTENSE	RECALCITRANCE. THE KING, SCOWLING FIERCELY AT ST
METH PREFACE(R57)	DESIGNED DEVILRY. IN THIS WAY DARWIN BROUGHT	INTENSE	RELIEF AS WELL AS AN ENLARGED KNOWLEDGE OF FACTS TO
SUPR IV (171)	/VIOLET/ NO. /ANN/ AH! (WITH A SIGH OF	INTENSE	RELIEF SHE RELAPSES). /MRS WHITEFIELD/ OH, SHE'S
METH PREFACE(R44)	HE DIED, HE SAID THAT EUROPE WOULD EXPRESS ITS	INTENSE	RELIEF WITH A GREAT " OUF! " WELL, WHEN DARWIN
MRS IV (253)	HER BREATH GOES OUT IN A HALF SOB, HALF LAUGH OF	INTENSE	RELIEF, SHE GOES BUOYANTLY TO HER PLACE AT THE
MTH4 I (150)	LIKE IT. /THE ELDERLY GENTLEMAN/ (EXPANDING WITH	INTENSE	RELIEF) BLESS YOU FOR THOSE PROFANE BUT FAMILIAR
ARMS I (10)	OH, THANK YOU. (SHE WRAPS HERSELF UP WITH	INTENSE	RELIEF). /THE MAN/ (BETWEEN HIS TEETH) DONT MENTION
JOAN PREFACE(44)	AN INCARNATE ANGEL AGAINST THOSE WHO ADDED TO AN	INTENSE	RESENTMENT OF HER PRESUMPTION A BIGOTED ABHORRENCE
LION II SD(127)	THEM, HIS EYES BLAZING, HIS FIGURE STIFF WITH	INTENSE	RESOLUTION. AT THE FOOT OF THE STEPS CROUCHES
NEVR I (211)	AND PRIVACY (HER EMPHASIS ON " PRIVACY" IS	INTENSE	) IN THEIR PERSONAL CONCERNS, AND BECAUSE YOU HAVE
MTH2 (69)	GOD COUNTS FOREIGNERS, YOU KNOW. /SAVVY/ (WITH	INTENSE	SATISFACTION) WELL SAID, BILL. /FRANKLYN/ I AM NOT
BARB PREFACE(238)	EPISODE, WHICH HE DECLARED HE NEVER READ WITHOUT	INTENSE	SATISFACTION? WHY, THE YOUNG GENERAL BONAPART'S
NEVR III (271)	THE OPPOSITE SIDE. MRS CLANDON THEN BEGINS, WITH	INTENSE	SCORN) ASK THIS MAN WHOM YOU HAVE INSPIRED AND MADE
DEVL EPILOG (82)	LONG AFTER HIS DEATH, THACKERAY, WHO HAD AN	INTENSE	SENSE OF HUMAN CHARACTER, BUT WAS TYPICALLY STUPID
GETT (342)	UNUSUAL. (HE SITS BY HER, WATCHING HER WITH	INTENSE	SURPRISE AND INTEREST). /MRS GEORGE/ NO MUSIC?
GENV IV (103)	OF MY POSITION. I LIVE DANGEROUSLY. IT IS MORE	INTENSE	THAN LIVING SAFELY. /NEWCOMER/ YOUR WORSHIP: THESE

INTENSELY

BARB II (293)	WAY ABOUT BARBARA. I DONT LIKE MARRIAGE! I FEEL	INTENSELY	AFRAID OF IT; AND I DONT KNOW WHAT I SHALL DO WITH
SUPR III (104)	OF ORGANIZATION YET ATTAINED BY LIFE, THE MOST	INTENSELY	ALIVE THING THAT EXISTS, THE MOST CONSCIOUS OF ALL
GETT SD(323)	FIRST GLANCE AS THE TRIUMPHANT, PAMPERED, WILFUL,	INTENSELY	ALIVE WOMAN WHO HAS ALWAYS BEEN RICH AMONG POOR
JITT II (41)	READS A BIT, AND MAKES A WRY FACE. HE DISAGREES	INTENSELY	AND CONTEMPTUOUSLY WITH EVERY PASSAGE HE READS,
PYGM PREFACE(202)	AND NORTH AMERICA AS WELL AS AT HOME. IT IS SO	INTENSELY	AND DELIBERATELY DIDACTIC, AND ITS SUBJECT IS
GENV PREFACE(7)	BETTER NOT TO THINK AT ALL THAN TO THINK	INTENSELY	AND THINK WRONG. STATESMEN WHO KNOW NO PAST
JITT III (78)	AND EVERYTHING I WAS TAUGHT MYSELF. /JITTA/ (	INTENSELY	ANGRY) DOES THAT PROVE IT TO BE TOMMY-ROT, OR DOES
NEVR II SD(232)	HE LIVES IN THIS TOWN. MRS CLANDON RISES,	INTENSELY	ANGRY, BUT SITS DOWN AGAIN, SPEECHLESS: GLORIA
CAND II (113)	PREACHING! WORDS! WORDS! WORDS! /BURGESS/ (	INTENSELY	APPRECIATING THIS RETORT) HAR, HAR! DEVIL A
NEVR III (273)	/GLORIA/ (RISING TO LEVEL THE DECLARATION MORE	INTENSELY	AT HIM) NEVER! WHILE GRASS GROWS OR WATER RUNS,
CYMB FORWORD(138)	FROM THE CHANGE TO SIX-FOUR ONWARD, THOUGH	INTENSELY	BEETHOVENISH, IS IN PERFORMANCE USUALLY A
ARMS I SD(3)	ALSO STAND OPEN. ON THE BALCONY A YOUNG LADY,	INTENSELY	CONSCIOUS OF THE ROMANTIC BEAUTY OF THE NIGHT, AND
NEVR IV SD(286)	INEXORABLE MANNER, AND A TERRIFYING POWER OF	INTENSELY	CRITICAL LISTENING, RAISE THE IMPRESSION PRODUCED
FANY EPILOG (331)	PLAIN WHO WROTE THAT PLAY. TO BEGIN WITH, IT'S	INTENSELY	DISAGREEABLE. THEREFORE IT'S NOT BY BARRIE. IN
BULL PREFACE(19)	THAT INTENSELY IRISH IRISHMAN, AND NELSON, THAT	INTENSELY	ENGLISH ENGLISHMAN. WELLINGTON'S CONTEMPTUOUS
NEVR II (239)	JUST SENSIBLE ENOUGH OF HIS OWN CALLOUSNESS TO	INTENSELY	ENJOY THE HUMOR AND ADROITNESS OF IT, PROCEEDS
HART PREFACE(30)	GYMNASTIC FEATS, HE NOT ONLY UNDERSTOOD BUT	INTENSELY	ENJOYED AN ARTIST WHO IMITATED COCKS CROWING AND
OVER PREFACE(165)	AND ILLUSION. THIS WAS TOLERATED, AND EVEN	INTENSELY	ENJOYED, BUT NOT IN THE LEAST BECAUSE NOTHING
WIDO III SD(51)	AT HIM, HE STANDS, SMILING, TO BE ADMIRED,	INTENSELY	ENJOYING THE EFFECT HE IS PRODUCING. THE
DEVL III SD(75)	AM ANTHONY ANDERSON, THE MAN YOU WANT. THE CROWD,	INTENSELY	EXCITED, LISTENS WITH ALL ITS EARS. JUDITH, HALF
NEVR II (242)	/WAITER/ (TACTFULLY) TURBOT, SIR? /M'COMAS/ (	INTENSELY	GRATEFUL FOR THE INTERRUPTION) THANK YOU, WAITER:
KING I SD(166)	VERY JUSTLY. I THANK YOU (HE PASSES IN). SALLY,	INTENSELY	IMPRESSED BY MR ROWLEY, GOES OUT. /FOX/ AM I
MTH5 (250)	IN ART THAT REAL LIFE HAS NEVER GIVEN ME. I AM	INTENSELY	IN EARNEST ABOUT ART. THERE IS A MAGIC AND MYSTERY
SUPR II (51)	AT THE BOTTOM OF WHAT HE SAYS. I BELIEVE MOST	INTENSELY	IN THE DIGNITY OF LABOR. /STRAKER/ (UNIMPRESSED)
SUPR PREFACE(R39)	WHATEVER. BUT HERE AND THERE OCCURS A SCRAP OF	INTENSELY	INSUSCEPTIBLE, INTENSELY RESISTANT MATERIAL; AND
DOCT I (104)	BLENKINSOP: ATTEND ONE MOMENT. YOU WILL ALL BE	INTENSELY	INTERESTED IN THIS. I WAS PUT ON THE TRACK BY
MRS II (215)	OUT OLD DRUDGE BEFORE I WAS FORTY? /VIVIE/ (	INTENSELY	INTERESTED BY THIS TIME) NO; BUT WHY DID YOU
MTH5 (231)	SUSCEPTIBLE TO A HIGHER POTENTIAL. /ARJILLAX/ (	INTENSELY	INTERESTED) YES; AND THEN? /PYGMALION/ THEN THE
MTH2 (43)	SCIENCE, HAVE COME ALIVE IN OUR HANDS, ALIVE AND	INTENSELY	INTERESTING, WE MAY JUST AS WELL GO OUT AND DIG
METH PREFACE(R82)	AND THERE ARE ALWAYS CERTAIN RARE BUT	INTENSELY	INTERESTING ANTICIPATIONS. MICHAEL ANGELO COULD
OVER PREFACE(161)	THAT THOUGH THEY WERE RIGHT IN RANKING SEX AS AN	INTENSELY	INTERESTING SUBJECT, THEY WERE WRONG IN ASSUMING
MTH5 (228)	/PYGMALION/ I ASSURE YOU THAT THESE DETAILS ARE	INTENSELY	INTERESTING. (CRIES OF NO! THEY ARE NOT! COME
MTH5 (209)	ARE TURNING OUT TO BE GREAT THINGS, AND BECOMING	INTENSELY	INTERESTING. HAVE YOU EVER THOUGHT ABOUT THE
MTH5 SD(214)	BALD, AND EQUALLY WITHOUT SEXUAL CHARM, BUT	INTENSELY	INTERESTING AND RATHER TERRIFYING. HER SEX IS
ROCK I (215)	ON A MORE HOPEFUL NOTE. I ASSURE YOU IT HAS BEEN	INTENSELY	INTERESTING TO ME; AND I MAY TELL YOU THAT SIGNS
BULL PREFACE(19)	MEETING BETWEEN THE DUKE OF WELLINGTON, THAT	INTENSELY	IRISH IRISHMAN, AND NELSON, THAT INTENSELY ENGLISH
AUGS (268)	TELL YOU WHY YOU CANT HAVE NO ROLLS. /AUGUSTUS/ (	INTENSELY	IRRITATED) CAN YOU TELL ME WHERE I CAN FIND AN
HART II (119)	AND DEATH, THAT I MIGHT FEEL THE LIFE IN ME MORE	INTENSELY	. I DID NOT LET THE FEAR OF DEATH GOVERN MY LIFE;
MTH5 (248)	FROM IMITATING THE LIGHTLY LIVING CHILD TO THE	INTENSELY	LIVING ANCIENT. IS IT TRUE, SO FAR? /ARJILLAX/ IT
BULL III (128)	PITEOUSLY FROM ONE SPEAKER TO ANOTHER IN AN	INTENSELY	MISTRUSTFUL EFFORT TO UNDERSTAND THEM). GO ON, MR
BULL PREFACE(20)	ITS MOST EXPLOSIVE CRISES OF DISTENTION. NELSON,	INTENSELY	NERVOUS AND THEATRICAL, MADE AN ENORMOUS FUSS
HART PREFACE(4)	DID NOT STRIKE ME IN THAT WAY. JUST AS IBSEN'S	INTENSELY	NORWEGIAN PLAYS EXACTLY FITTED EVERY MIDDLE AND
PYGM PREFACE(200)	WHICH HE NEVERTHELESS CLUNG BY DIVINE RIGHT IN AN	INTENSELY	OXONIAN WAY. I DARESAY HIS PAPERS, IF HE HAS LEFT
KING PREFACE(157)	TO AN INCREASING SEPARATION OF THE UNIQUE AND	INTENSELY	PERSONAL AND PERMANENT MARRIAGE RELATION FROM THE
GETT PREFACE(220)	THE RELATION THEY ARE TEMPTED TO CONTRACT IS SO	INTENSELY	PERSONAL, AND THE VOWS MADE UNDER THE INFLUENCE OF
JOAN PREFACE(49)	CATHOLIC BY FAMILY TRADITION, HIS FIGURES ARE ALL	INTENSELY	PROTESTANT, INDIVIDUALIST, SCEPTICAL,
SUPR HANDBOK(185)	FOR A GENUINE COMMUNIST (ROUGHLY DEFINABLE AS AN	INTENSELY	PROUD PERSON WHO PROPOSES TO ENRICH THE COMMON
OVER PREFACE(165)	STAGEY AS HIS COSTUMES. IN OUR DAY CALVE'S	INTENSELY	REAL CARMEN NEVER PLEASED THE MOB AS MUCH AS THE
DEVL I (8)	HAND VERY HEAVILY UPON YOU. /MRS DUDGEON/ (WITH	INTENSELY	RECALCITRANT RESIGNATION) IT'S HIS WILL, I
BULL PREFACE(24)	CLARITY TO WHICH MY ENGLISH CRITICS ARE SO	INTENSELY	RECALCITRANT. FIRST, LET ME TELL YOU THAT IN
SUPR PREFACE(R39)	BUT A LUMINOUS AUTHOR, I MUST ALSO BE A MOST	INTENSELY	REFRACTORY PERSON, LIABLE TO GO OUT AND TO GO
GENV IV (96)	EXISTS. /SIR O./ YOU ALARM ME, MY LORD. I AM	INTENSELY	RELUCTANT TO LOSE MY GRIP OF THE REALITIES OF THE
WIDO III (51)	I SUPPOSE, COME TO BEG? /THE PARLORMAID/ (	INTENSELY	REPUDIATING THE IDEA) O-O-O-O-H NO, SIR, QUITE THE
SUPR PREFACE(R39)	THERE OCCURS A SCRAP OF INTENSELY INSUSCEPTIBLE,	INTENSELY	RESISTANT MATERIAL; AND THAT STUBBORN SCRAP
HART PREFACE(4)	AND PROFESSIONAL CLASS SUBURB IN EUROPE, THESE	INTENSELY	RUSSIAN PLAYS FITTED ALL THE COUNTRY HOUSES IN
GENV I (44)	THAT OF THE BRITISH FOREIGN SECRETARY. /BISHOP/ (	INTENSELY	) NEVER, NEVER. /SHE/ (AIRILY) AND WHAT CAN WE DO
SIM II (61)	AND DREADFULLY BAD FOR THEM. I LOVE YOU ALL HERE	INTENSELY	; AND I ENJOY LOVING YOU. I LOVE VASHTI; I LOVE
GETT (343)	GIVE US YOUR MESSAGE. /MRS GEORGE/ (WITH	INTENSELY	SAD REPROACH) WHEN YOU LOVED ME I GAVE YOU THE
DOCT I (97)	ARE, SO YOU ARE. /WALPOLE/ (IN A TRAGIC WHISPER,	INTENSELY	SERIOUS) BLOOD-POISONING. I SEE, I SEE. (HE SITS
GETT PREFACE(212)	GRANDCHILDREN; BUT THIS FASHION OF A SMALL AND	INTENSELY	SNOBBISH CLASS IS NEGLIGIBLE AS A GENERAL
SIM II (84)	IN THEIR INFANCY. THEY GREW UP TO BORE ME MORE	INTENSELY	THAN I HAVE EVER BEEN BORED BY ANY OTHER SET OF
SIM II (60)	IDDY, I CAN ASSURE YOU THAT I ALREADY HATE YOU SO	INTENSELY	THAT IF IT WERE IN MY NATURE TO KILL ANYTHING I
OVER PREFACE(165)	RIGHT WHEN HE REPRESENTED PARTRIDGE AS ENJOYING	INTENSELY	THE PERFORMANCE OF THE KING IN HAMLET BECAUSE
CAPT III (291)	SCANDALIZED SOBRIETY, EXCEPT REDBROOK, WHO IS	INTENSELY	TICKLED BY THEIR PRUDERY). /DRINKWATER/ NAOW, LOOK

INTENSER

SUPR III (127)	ASPIRATION TO HIGHER ORGANIZATION, WIDER, DEEPER,	INTENSER	SELF-CONSCIOUSNESS, AND CLEARER SELF-UNDERSTANDING.
ARMS III (63)	SHE GOES CLOSER TO HIM, AND SAYS, IN A LOWER,	INTENSER	TONE) DO YOU KNOW THAT I LOOKED OUT OF THE WINDOW

INTENSEST

MTH5 (224)	WHOSE MAJESTY WAS THAT OF THE MIND ALONE AT ITS	INTENSEST	. AND THIS PAINTING WAS ACKNOWLEDGED THROUGH AGES
JOAN PREFACE(50)	THE REACTION AGAINST MEDIEVALISM AT ITS	INTENSEST	) AS IF THEY WERE BEINGS IN THE AIR, WITHOUT

INTENSIFICATION

LION PREFACE(83)	ENLARGEMENT OF KNOWLEDGE, AND THE ENRICHMENT AND	INTENSIFICATION	OF LIFE (" THAT YE MAY HAVE LIFE MORE

INTENSIFIED

DOCT PREFACE(55)	A PROPHYLACTIC ENFORCED BY LAW, THIS ILLUSION IS	INTENSIFIED	GROTESQUELY, BECAUSE ONLY VAGRANTS CAN EVADE IT.
METH PREFACE(R17)	A BALANCE OF POWER THROUGH COMMAND OF THE SEA IS	INTENSIFIED	INTO A TERROR THAT SEES SECURITY IN NOTHING
JOAN PREFACE(44)	AGES THE GENERAL BELIEF IN WITCHCRAFT GREATLY	INTENSIFIED	THIS CONTRAST, BECAUSE WHEN AN APPARENT MIRACLE

INTENSIFIES

SUPR HANDBOK(224)	ESCAPE FROM UGLINESS AND UNHAPPINESS THE RICH MAN	INTENSIFIES	BOTH. EVERY NEW YARD OF WEST END CREATES A NEW
MIS. PREFACE(7)	IN ADULT POLITICAL RELATIONS, IT SOMETIMES	INTENSIFIES	IT, SOMETIMES MITIGATES IT; BUT ON THE WHOLE
MILL II (172)	IF IT IS THE WRONG SORT OF REVOLUTION, IT	INTENSIFIES	THE DISEASE. I CAN DO NOTHING FOR YOU. I MUST GO

INTENSIFY

MIS. PREFACE(35)	PUNISHMENT; AND EVERYTHING POSSIBLE IS DONE TO	INTENSIFY	THE PRISONER'S INCULCATED AND UNNATURAL NOTION
ROCK PREFACE(153)	BY ENGAGING IN SUICIDAL WARS, ARE FORCED TO	INTENSIFY	THEIR ECONOMIES, AND THE RATE OF EXTERMINATION

INTENSITY

3PLA PREFACE(R11)	MEN BECOME RICH IN COMMERCE IN PROPORTION TO THE	INTENSITY	AND EXCLUSIVENESS OF THEIR DESIRE FOR MONEY. IT
HART PREFACE(31)	VALUES WERE ALTERED. TRIVIAL THINGS GAINED	INTENSITY	AND STALE THINGS NOVELTY. THE ACTOR, INSTEAD OF
2TRU III SD(100)	THEIR EARS FROM AFAR. IT INCREASES TO SHATTERING	INTENSITY	AS IT APPROACHES. THEY ALL PUT THEIR FINGERS TO
OVER PREFACE(157)	JEALOUSY IS INDEPENDENT OF SEX IS SHEWN BY ITS	INTENSITY	IN CHILDREN, AND BY THE FACT THAT VERY JEALOUS
MTH4 III SD(194)	BEYOND IS A VAST GLOOM, CONTINUALLY CHANGING IN	INTENSITY	. A SHAFT OF VIOLET LIGHT SHOOTS UPWARD; AND A
LION PREFACE(72)	PEER, THE MISCHIEF HE DOES DO IS OF EXTRAORDINARY	INTENSITY	. CELIBACY NO REMEDY. WE MUST, I THINK, REGARD THE
MTH3 SD(133)	NATURALLY, THE PRESIDENT WITH VISIBLE EFFORT AND	INTENSITY	. HE IS POSITIVELY GLARING INTO THE FUTURE WHEN
BULL III SD(123)	THEN COMES TO LARRY AND ADDRESSES HIM WITH SUDDEN	INTENSITY	. /BROADBENT/ LARRY. /LARRY/ WHAT IS IT?
CLEO II SD(123)	AND SITS THERE, WATCHING THE SCENE WITH SIBYLLINE	INTENSITY	. /PTOLEMY/ (MORTIFIED, AND STRUGGLING WITH HIS
2TRU III SD(87)	THE ELDER CONTINUES TO DECLAIM WITH FANATICAL	INTENSITY	. /THE ELDER/ YES, SIR: THE UNIVERSE OF ISAAC
2TRU III SD(112)	OF THOSE STRONG ENOUGH TO BEAR ITS TERRIBLE	INTENSITY	. THEY WILL NOT FORGET THAT IT IS ACCOMPANIED BY A
DOCT PREFACE(17)	AT ANY TIME. MEN DO NOT RESIST PRESSURE OF THIS	INTENSITY	. WHEN THEY COME UNDER IT AS DOCTORS THEY PAY
SHAK PREFACE(135)	THEY CALL IT) FROM PUPPETS. THEIR UNVARYING	INTENSITY	OF FACIAL EXPRESSION, IMPOSSIBLE FOR LIVING
BULL II SD(97)	MELANCHOLY, LOOKING OVER THE HILLS AS IF BY MERE	INTENSITY	OF GAZE HE COULD PIERCE THE GLORIES OF THE SUNSET
JOAN PREFACE(21)	AND SCOPE OF HER MIND AND CHARACTER, AND THE	INTENSITY	OF HER VITAL ENERGY. SHE WAS ACCUSED OF A SUICIDAL
OVER PREFACE(155)	OTHERS WITH AN EARNESTNESS PROPORTIONATE TO THE	INTENSITY	OF HIS OWN REMORSE. HE (OR SHE) MAY BE A LIAR AND
OVER PREFACE(166)	THE STAGE SHALL BE A MIRROR OF SUCH ACCURACY AND	INTENSITY	OF ILLUMINATION THAT THEY SHALL BE ABLE TO GET
MTH5 (222)	UNTIL YOU RECEIVE THE FULL IMPRESSION OF THE	INTENSITY	OF MIND THAT IS STAMPED ON THEM; AND THEN GO BACK
OVER PREFACE(165)	FOR COLLEY CIBBER AND GARRICK, EXCEPT THE	INTENSITY	OF OUR ARTIFICIAL LIGHT. WHEN GARRICK PLAYED
GETT (285)	SPELL. I LIKE THAT WOMAN'S LETTERS. THERES AN	INTENSITY	OF PASSION IN THEM THAT FASCINATES ME. /MRS
2TRU PREFACE(3)	BEEN ACCUSTOMED I THOUGHT I DETECTED AN UNUSUAL	INTENSITY	OF RESENTMENT, AS IF I HAD HIT THEM IN SOME NEW
DEVL I SD(17)	AT THE DOOR. THE REST ARE PETRIFIED WITH THE	INTENSITY	OF THEIR SENSE OF VIRTUE MENACED WITH OUTRAGE BY
HART PREFACE(15)	ESTABLISHED THAN THAT EXCESSIVE DURATION AND	INTENSITY	OF TOIL REDUCES PRODUCTION HEAVILY INSTEAD OF
MILL PREFACE(109)	OR SHE MAY BE A TYRANT RULING VIOLENTLY BY	INTENSITY	OF WILL AND RUTHLESS EGOTISM. SHE MAY BE A
CAPT II (253)	OF RANSOM? /BRASSBOUND/ (WITH UNACCOUNTABLE	INTENSITY	) ALL THE WEALTH OF ENGLAND SHALL NOT RANSOM YOU.
ROCK II (280)	ALOYSIA, ALOYSIA, WAIT A MOMENT. (WITH ANGUISHED	INTENSITY	) ALOYSIA. (HIS CRIES RECEDE IN THE DISTANCE).
DEST (161)	LITTLE HOUND. (LOWERING HIS VOICE WITH THRILLING	INTENSITY	) BUT MARK MY WORDS, GENERAL. IF EVER-- /THE
DEVL III (56)	AT HIM FOR A MOMENT, AND THEN ADDS, WITH GRIM	INTENSITY	) I AM GLAD YOU TAKE THAT VIEW OF THEM. /SWINDON/
MIS. (166)	IN MY NEW TURKISH BATH? /THE MAN/ (WITH TRAGIC	INTENSITY	) I AM THE SON OF LUCINDA TITMUS. /TARLETON/ (THE
DEST (182)	CLEVER: IT WAS YOU WHO RUINED HIM. (WITH SAVAGE	INTENSITY	) I HATE A BAD SOLDIER. HE GOES OUT DETERMINEDLY
SUPR III (81)	HENCE, PERHAPS, MY COSMOPOLITANISM. (WITH SUDDEN	INTENSITY	) SHALL I TELL YOU THE STORY OF MY LIFE?
DEVL I (21)	DUBIOUS GLANCE AT THE WINE, AND ADDS, WITH QUAINT	INTENSITY	) WILL ANYONE OBLIGE ME WITH A GLASS OF WATER?
BULL IV (179)	AS YOU CALL IT, EH? /KEEGAN/ (WITH FIERCE	INTENSITY	) YES, PERHAPS, EVEN ON THIS HOLY GROUND WHICH
CAND II (119)	NOT AT ALL. (LOOKING AT HER WITH TROUBLED	INTENSITY	) YOU KNOW THAT I HAVE PERFECT CONFIDENCE IN YOU,
DEST (191)	THE VOICE COMING THROUGH THE GLOOM WITH STARTLING	INTENSITY	). /NAPOLEON/ THERE ARE THREE SORTS OF PEOPLE IN
METH PREFACE(R18)	DO ANYTHING CAN AND DOES, AT A CERTAIN PITCH OF	INTENSITY	SET UP BY CONVICTION OF ITS NECESSITY, CREATE AND
DEVL II (35)	AND LOOKS IMPLORINGLY AT HIM, DOING BOTH WITH AN	INTENSITY	THAT CHECKS HIM AT ONCE). WELL, WELL, I MUSTNT
SUPR IV (152)	AMERICAN PRONUNCIATION IMPARTS AN OVERWHELMING	INTENSITY	TO THIS SIMPLE AND UNPOPULAR WORD). I START TO
CATH PREFACE(157)	PRODUCED A GROUP OF HEROIC PLAYS COMPARABLE IN	INTENSITY	TO THOSE OF AESCHYLUS, SOPHOCLES, AND EURIPIDES;
CAND I SD(93)	RUN AWAY INTO SOLITUDE IF HE DARED; BUT THE VERY	INTENSITY	WITH WHICH HE FEELS A PERFECTLY COMMONPLACE
PYGM EPILOG (301)	TASK OF TEACHING HER WITH A COMBINATION OF STORMY	INTENSITY	, CONCENTRATED PATIENCE, AND OCCASIONAL BURSTS OF
ARMS II SD(37)	HER AGAIN; HESITATES; AND THEN, WITH SHUDDERING	INTENSITY	, EXCLAIMS NEVER! AND GETS AWAY AS FAR AS
METH PREFACE(R52)	DESIRE TO LOSE THEIR TAILS WITH A LIFE-OR-DEATH	INTENSITY	, HE WOULD VERY SOON HAVE SEEN A FEW MICE BORN
DOCT PREFACE(13)	BE PRODUCED IN PRACTICALLY UNLIMITED QUANTITY AND	INTENSITY	, WITHOUT OBSERVATION OR REASONING, AND EVEN IN

INTENT

DOCT V (173)	THE DESK, AND FINDS HIMSELF FACE TO FACE WITH HER	INTENT	GAZE). I BEG YOUR PARDON. I THOUGHT I WAS ALONE.
HART II SD(114)	ELLIE ALONE WITH THE CAPTAIN). THE CAPTAIN IS	INTENT	ON HIS DRAWING. ELLIE, STANDING SENTRY OVER HIS
CLEO PRO2,SD(95)	IS INVADING HIS COUNTRY, NOT KNOWING THIS, IS	INTENT	ON HIS GAME WITH THE PERSIAN, WHOM, AS A FOREIGNER,
DEST (153)	/GIUSEPPE/ WILL YOUR EXCELLENCY-- /NAPOLEON/ (	INTENT	ON HIS MAP, BUT CRAMMING HIMSELF MECHANICALLY WITH
CLEO PRO2,SD(95)	AND THE MAHDI. THEY ARE IN TWO GROUPS: ONE	INTENT	ON THE GAMBLING OF THEIR CAPTAIN BELZANOR, A WARRIOR
SIM I SD(36)	ALMOST CRUDE BESIDE THEM. THEIR EXPRESSIONS ARE	INTENT	, GRAVE, AND INSCRUTABLE. THEY FACE SOUTH WITH THEIR

INTENTION

CAND III (146)	HIS FACE IN HER HANDS; AND AS HE DIVINES HER	INTENTION	AND FALLS ON HIS KNEES, SHE KISSES HIS FOREHEAD.
CATH 1 (167)	NONSENSE, I'M YOUR FRIEND. YOU MISTOOK MY	INTENTION	BECAUSE I WAS DRUNK. NOW THAT I AM SOBER -- IN
POSN PREFACE(380)	THAT THE REPRESENTATION WAS LAWFUL AND THE	INTENTION	INNOCENT, SINCE WHEN IT HAS BEEN REPEATEDLY
2TRU II (58)	HUMAN BEING. /TALLBOYS/ MOST CERTAINLY NOT. YOUR	INTENTION	IS NATURAL AND KINDLY; BUT IF YOU TREAT A PRIVATE
OVER (188)	/GREGORY/ PARDON ME. I'M NOT GUILTY. /JUNO/ IN	INTENTION	. DONT QUIBBLE. YOU WERE GUILTY IN INTENTION, AS I
OVER (187)	HAS HE TO ANY SUCH HONOR? /JUNO/ I SINNED IN	INTENTION	. (MRS JUNO ABANDONS HIM AND RESUMES HER SEAT,
OVER (188)	MYSELF AS BEING GUILTY IN FACT, BUT NOT IN	INTENTION	. RISING AND EXCLAIMING SIMULTANEOUSLY /JUNO/
MRS IV (249)	THE IMPLIED INDIFFERENCE TOWARDS HER AFFECTIONATE	INTENTION	. VIVIE, NEITHER UNDERSTANDING THIS NOR CONCERNING
UNPL PREFACE(R21)	OF US IN THIS FORTUNATE MISREPRESENTATION OF MY	INTENTION	." EVEN IF THE AUTHOR HAD NOTHING TO GAIN
MRS PREFACE(160)	WHEN SHE MET CAPTAIN ARDALE SHE SINNED " BUT IN	INTENTION	." PLAY NUMBER ONE. A PRINCE IS COMPELLED BY HIS
2TRU III (101)	MET. /THE ELDER/ AND MAY I ASK, SIR, IS IT YOUR	INTENTION	NOT ONLY TO CONDONE MY SON'S FRAUDS, BUT TO TAKE
BULL PREFACE(58)	STAND ANYTHING. THE TRIBUNAL HAD CERTAINLY NO	INTENTION	OF ALLOWING WITNESSES TO TESTIFY AGAINST BRITISH
BARB III (318)	STEPHEN. THEY ARE ENTERPRISE. /STEPHEN/ I HAVE NO	INTENTION	OF BECOMING A MAN OF BUSINESS IN ANY SENSE. I HAVE
MIS. (164)	THE FACE. YOU WERE THE NEXT. /PERCIVAL/ I HAD NO	INTENTION	OF BEING OFFENSIVE. SURELY THERE IS NOTHING THAT
ROCK II (266)	I'LL JUST GO AND ASSURE HIM THAT WE HAVE NO	INTENTION	OF BREAKING WITH HIM. TA TA. GOOD MORNING, DUKE. (
CLEO NOTES (213)	PUNISHMENT, AND THE REST OF IT, THAT BAFFLED ITS	INTENTION	OF CHANGING THE WORLD. BUT THESE ARE BOUND UP IN
ROCK II (257)	THINK THAT. /SIR ARTHUR/ AS YOU HAVE NO MORE	INTENTION	OF CONSULTING THE PEOPLE OF ENGLAND THAN I HAVE,
JITT III (74)	HAS APPARENTLY BEEN OFFERING YOU. BUT I HAVE NO	INTENTION	OF DIVORCING HER AT PRESENT. /EDITH/ (NOT KNOWING
MILL I (162)	CANNOT AFFORD TO DIVORCE ME, AND I HAVE NO	INTENTION	OF DIVORCING HIM, THE QUESTION DOES NOT ARISE.
BULL PREFACE(3)	THE ENGLISH PEOPLE ANXIOUSLY THAT IT HAD NO	INTENTION	OF DOING ANYTHING FOR ENGLAND (ITS OBJECT BEING
MTH4 I (157)	/THE ELDERLY GENTLEMAN/ I HAVE NOT THE SMALLEST	INTENTION	OF DOING SO, MADAM. I AM NO LONGER YOUNG; AND I
SUPR IV (163)	DARE; WE ALL BID FOR ADMIRATION WITHOUT THE LEAST	INTENTION	OF EARNING IT; WE ALL GET AS MUCH RENT AS WE CAN
NEVR II (254)	IN A SENSIBLE AND WHOLESOME WAY. I HAVE NO	INTENTION	OF GETTING MARRIED; AND UNLESS YOU ARE CONTENT TO
NEVR IV (296)	A QUESTION STRAIGHT AT DOLLY) HAVE YOU ANY	INTENTION	OF GETTING MARRIED? /DOLLY/ I! WELL, FINCH CALLS
VWOO 2 (131)	RUSHED. PRECIPITATED. CARRIED TO LENGTHS I HAD NO	INTENTION	OF GOING TO. /Z/ WELL, IT GETS YOU SOMEWHERE:
SUPR IV (162)	AS A WOMAN WHO ROUSES PASSIONS SHE HAS NO	INTENTION	OF GRATIFYING, AND AS SHE HAS NOW REDUCED YOU TO
JOAN PREFACE(38)	ON A GREATER THAN HIMSELF; BUT THE SUB-CONSCIOUS	INTENTION	OF HIS SELF-PRESERVING INDIVIDUALITY MUST BE TO
NEVR I (215)	STRUCK YOU PURPOSELY, DELIBERATELY, WITH THE	INTENTION	OF HURTING YOU, WITH A WHIP BOUGHT FOR THE
CAND I (86)	ME AND MR MORELL. /LEXY/ (HUFFILY) I HAVE NO	INTENTION	OF INTRUDING, I AM SURE, MR BURGESS. GOOD MORNING.
KING I (188)	ON A ROYAL PERSONAGE. /NEWTON/ SIR: I HAD NO	INTENTION	OF KNOCKING YOUR ROYAL BROTHER DOWN. HE FELL AND
MIS. PREFACE(21)	I WAS THOROUGHLY DISLOYAL TO IT; THAT I HAD NO	INTENTION	OF LEARNING; THAT I WAS MOCKING AND DISTRACTING
SUPR IV (162)	TAVY HEAD OVER EARS IN LOVE WITH HER WITHOUT ANY	INTENTION	OF MARRYING HIM, SHE IS A COQUETTE, ACCORDING TO
SUPR IV (162)	/TANNER/ (EMPHATICALLY) I HAVNT THE SLIGHTEST	INTENTION	OF MARRYING HER. /MRS WHITEFIELD/ (SLYLY) SHE'D
2TRU I (39)	HAPPEN TO MEET AGAIN. /THE PATIENT/ I HAVE NO	INTENTION	OF MEETING YOU AGAIN. SO YOU MAY JUST AS WELL TAKE
SUPR I SD(10)	WALKS STRAIGHT UP TO RAMSDEN AS IF WITH THE FIXED	INTENTION	OF SHOOTING HIM ON HIS OWN HEARTHRUG. BUT WHAT HE
SUPR HANDBOK(196)	NOT BECAUSE THE ENGLISH HAVE THE SMALLEST	INTENTION	OF STUDYING OR ADOPTING THE FABIAN POLICY, BUT
CAPT NOTES (303)	I MUST, HOWEVER, MOST VEHEMENTLY DISCLAIM ANY	INTENTION	OF SUGGESTING THAT ENGLISH PRONUNCIATION IS
SUPR III (80)	EXCEPT TWO OR THREE FADDISTS. /TANNER/ I HAD NO	INTENTION	OF SUGGESTING ANYTHING DISCREDITABLE. IN FACT, I
LION PREFACE(76)	LIFE BECAME A DENIAL OF LIFE. PAUL HAD NO	INTENTION	OF SURRENDERING EITHER HIS JUDAISM OR HIS ROMAN
BARB PREFACE(226)	WAGES, DO NOT TAKE, AND HAVE NOT THE SLIGHTEST	INTENTION	OF TAKING, ANY EFFECTIVE STEP TO ORGANIZE SOCIETY
INCA (244)	CARELESSLY TO THE TABLE) I HADNT THE SLIGHTEST	INTENTION	OF TREATING YOU WITH CEREMONY. (SHE SITS DOWN: A
ARMS I (8)	OF THE HUMOR OF IT, WITHOUT, HOWEVER, THE LEAST	INTENTION	OF TRIFLING WITH IT OR THROWING AWAY A CHANCE.
PYGM II (224)	MY DEAR PICKERING, I NEVER HAD THE SLIGHTEST	INTENTION	OF WALKING OVER ANYONE. ALL I PROPOSE IS THAT WE
APPL II (272)	WE ARE NOT TAKING LEAVE OF ONE ANOTHER, I HAVE NO	INTENTION	OF WITHDRAWING FROM AN ACTIVE PART IN POLITICS.
MTH4 I (169)	NO, NO, NO. I HAD MUCH RATHER DISCUSS YOUR	INTENTION	OF WITHDRAWING FROM THE CONSERVATIVE PARTY. HOW
PRES (158)	YOU? /LADY CORINTHIA/ I HAVE NOT THE SLIGHTEST	INTENTION	OF YIELDING TO THEM; BUT TO MAKE THEM WOULD BE A
CATH 1 (170)	(IN ASTONISHMENT) I HAVNT THE SLIGHTEST	INTENTION	-- /PATIOMKIN/ NOT NOW; BUT YOU WILL HAVE: TAKE MY

MIS. PREFACE(30)	OF EDUCATION, A FRIEND TO WHOM I MENTIONED MY	INTENTION	SAID, " YOU KNOW NOTHING OF MODERN EDUCATION:
APPL II (273)	HOUSE OF COMMONS! /MAGNUS/ (BLANDLY) IT IS MY	INTENTION	TO OFFER MYSELF TO THE ROYAL BOROUGH OF WINDSOR AS
GETT (274)	/REGINALD/ YOU ARE, I HOPE. (HE EMPHASIZES HIS	INTENTION	TO STAY BY SITTING DOWN). /THE GENERAL/ ALICE!
KING I (189)	BROTHER DOWN. HE FELL AND DRAGGED ME DOWN. MY	INTENTION	WAS ONLY TO THROW HIM OUT OF THE WINDOW. /CHARLES/
JOAN PREFACE(39)	THAT WERE ALL THE MORE RUTHLESS BECAUSE THEIR	INTENTION	WAS SO EXCELLENT. TODAY, WHEN THE DOCTOR HAS
FABL PREFACE(84)	WITH ALL THIS STARING THEM IN THE FACE, AND NO	INTENTION	WHATEVER OF GOING BACK TO TURNPIKE ROADS, TOLL
WIDO I (16)	YOU TO WRITE TO YOUR RELATIVES EXPLAINING YOUR	INTENTION	, AND ADDING WHAT YOU THINK PROPER AS TO MY
SUPR HANDBOK(177)	MAN HAS PLAYED THE GOD, SUBDUING NATURE TO HIS	INTENTION	, AND ENNOBLING OR DEBASING LIFE FOR A SET
LADY PREFACE(211)	WHILST MR HARRIS'S PLAY IS SERIOUS BOTH IN SIZE,	INTENTION	, AND QUALITY. BUT THERE COULD NOT IN THE NATURE
OVER (188)	IN INTENTION. DONT QUIBBLE. YOU WERE GUILTY IN	INTENTION	, AS I WAS. /GREGORY/ NO. I SHOULD RATHER DESCRIBE
SUPR III (88)	AT ALL EVENTS, SENORA, WHETHER BY OVERSIGHT OR	INTENTION	, YOU ARE CERTAINLY DAMNED, LIKE MYSELF; AND THERE
		INTENTIONAL	
KING I (164)	THAN FIVE THOUSAND MILLIONS OF CONSIDERED AND	INTENTIONAL	ACTIONS IN HER LIFETIME. HOW MANY OF THEM CAN
SUPR HANDBOK(180)	IS TO COME, HE MUST BE BORN OF WOMAN BY MAN'S	INTENTIONAL	AND WELL-CONSIDERED CONTRIVANCE. CONVICTION OF
3PLA PREFACE(R13)	RESULT); BUT IN BOTH THERE WAS THE SAME	INTENTIONAL	BRAINLESSNESS, FOUNDED ON THE SAME THEORY THAT
NEVR II (254)	FOR A MOMENT; THEN ANSWERING HIM WITH POLITE BUT	INTENTIONAL	CONTEMPT) THAT SEEMS TO BE AN ATTEMPT AT WHAT IS
SUPR PREFACE(R30)	ENRY STRAKER, MOTOR ENGINEER AND NEW MAN, IS AN	INTENTIONAL	DRAMATIC SKETCH OF THE CONTEMPORARY EMBRYO OF MR
APPL PREFACE(173)	BLOOD OPPOSE TO THE KING'S PERFECT BEHAVIOR AN	INTENTIONAL	MISBEHAVIOR AND APPARENTLY CHILDISH PETULANCE
METH PREFACE(R30)	IN HEREDITY LED NATURALLY TO THE PRACTICE OF	INTENTIONAL	SELECTION. GOOD BLOOD AND BREEDING WERE EAGERLY
METH PREFACE(R41)	WITH AN ABNORMALLY LONG NECK WAS EVOLVED BY	INTENTIONAL	SELECTION, JUST AS THE RACE-HORSE OR THE FANTAIL
METH PREFACE(R72)	AND ORDERED MANNER, PRACTISING A VERY STRENUOUS	INTENTIONAL	SELECTION OF WORKERS AS FITTER TO SURVIVE THAN
		INTENTIONALLY	
POSN PREFACE(381)	ON RELIGION, AND ON VIRTUE. A CENSOR IS NEVER	INTENTIONALLY	A PROTECTOR OF IMMORALITY. HE ALWAYS AIMS AT
CAPT II (253)	AND THAT OF THE WORST OF YOUR MEN HAS CHANGED--	INTENTIONALLY	CHANGED, I THINK. /BRASSBOUND/ (STOPPING
SUPR III (89)	/DON JUAN/ OH, THEN THERE IS NO MISTAKE: YOU ARE	INTENTIONALLY	DAMNED. /THE OLD WOMAN/ WHY DO YOU SAY THAT..
PHIL II SD(94)	OR FRANK MAN, BUT NOT CONSCIOUSLY UNHAPPY NOR	INTENTIONALLY	INSINCERE, AND HIGHLY SELF-SATISFIED
HART II (85)	I RUINED YOUR FATHER, DIDNT I? /ELLIE/ OH, NOT	INTENTIONALLY	. /MANGAN/ YES I DID. RUINED HIM ON PURPOSE.
DOCT II SD(117)	MEN AS MOST MEN MOVE AMONG THINGS, THOUGH HE IS	INTENTIONALLY	MAKING HIMSELF AGREEABLE TO THEM ON THIS
GETT PREFACE(193)	EVER ASCRIBED TO HIS DEITY, THOUGH THEY WERE NOT	INTENTIONALLY	MALICIOUS, THEY PRACTISED THE MOST APPALLING
2TRU PREFACE(4)	I DOUBT WHETHER THIS STATE OF THINGS IS EVER	INTENTIONALLY	PRODUCED. WE SEE A MAN APPARENTLY SLAVING TO
BULL III (120)	MATT HAFFIGAN? DO YOU REMEMBER ME? /MATTHEW/ (	INTENTIONALLY	RUDE AND BLUNT) NO. WHO ARE YOU? /NORA/ OH,
POSN PREFACE(412)	CENSORSHIP OF THE LORD CHAMBERLAIN DOES NOT ONLY	INTENTIONALLY	SUPPRESS HERESY AND CHALLENGES TO MORALITY IN
KING I (164)	/NEWTON/ YOU CAN DO, QUITE DELIBERATELY AND	INTENTIONALLY	, SEVEN DISTINCT ACTIONS IN A SECOND. HOW DO
		INTENTIONED	
SIM PREFACE(11)	INTO WHICH THE ORIGINAL TCHEKA, AS A BODY OF WELL	INTENTIONED	AMATEURS, NO DOUBT FELL BEFORE IT HAD LEARNT THE
FABL VI (127)	OLD EXPERIMENTS OF THE LIFE FORCE. THEY WERE WELL	INTENTIONED	AND PERHAPS NECESSARY AT THE TIME. BUT THEY ARE
JOAN PREFACE(53)	MY BUSINESS SO LITTLE AS TO LISTEN TO THESE WELL	INTENTIONED	BUT DISASTROUS COUNSELLORS: INDEED IT PROBABLY
CAND I (81)	HIS UNIVERSITY TRAINING. HE IS A CONCEITEDLY WELL	INTENTIONED	, ENTHUSIASTIC, IMMATURE NOVICE, WITH NOTHING
		INTENTIONS	
FANY III (322)	KNOWLEDGE OF ENGLISH IS NOT ENOUGH TO UNDERSTAND.	INTENTIONS	? HOW? /MARGARET/ HE WANTS TO KNOW WILL YOU
VWOO 2 (128)	/A/ ARE YOU MARRIED? /Z/ NO. WHY? HAVE YOU ANY	INTENTIONS	? /A/ DONT BE IN A HURRY. WEVE KNOWN EACH OTHER
MIS. (193)	GENTLEMAN OR NO GENTLEMAN, PATSY: WHAT ARE YOUR	INTENTIONS	? /HYPATIA/ MY INTENTIONS! SURELY IT'S THE
PRES (157)	COMPLIMENT WITHOUT SUSPECTING ME OF DISHONORABLE	INTENTIONS	? /LADY CORINTHIA/ LOVE-- REAL LOVE-- MAKES ALL
JITT III (78)	PROFIT. /JITTA/ THEN YOU REFUSE TO CARRY OUT HIS	INTENTIONS	? /LENKHEIM/ I CANT CARRY OUT HIS INTENTIONS.
NEVR III (264)	TO HIM ABOUT THIS. /PHILIP/ TO ASK HIM HIS	INTENTIONS	? WHAT A VIOLATION OF TWENTIETH CENTURY
2TRU PREFACE(24)	AS TO THE EVIL DONE BY THE CHURCH WITH THE BEST	INTENTIONS	AND THE GOOD DONE BY THE EMPIRE WITH THE WORST, I
GENV I (31)	RESPECTABLE. /HE/ I PLEDGE YOU MY WORD THAT MY	INTENTIONS	ARE COMPLETELY HONORABLE. /SHE/ WELL, WHAT ABOUT
PYGM II (237)	YOU OUGHT TO KNOW, DOOLITTLE, THAT MR HIGGINS'S	INTENTIONS	ARE ENTIRELY HONORABLE. /DOOLITTLE/ COURSE THEY
MRS II (199)	MY DEAR MRS WARREN: DONT YOU BE ALARMED. MY	INTENTIONS	ARE HONORABLE: EVER SO HONORABLE; AND YOUR LITTLE
GENV IV (96)	MY COMMONPLACENESS. BUT IF YOU ASK ME WHAT THEIR	INTENTIONS	ARE I MUST FRANKLY SAY THAT I DONT KNOW. WHERE DO
GENV III (81)	WHICH IS THAT DAME BEGONIA'S SYMPATHIES AND	INTENTIONS	ARE JUST THE SAME AS YOURS. /BEGONIA/ OH! I
GETT (328)	ANYTHING ELSE? /HOTCHKISS/ THIS. I LOVE YOU. MY	INTENTIONS	ARE NOT HONORABLE. (SHE SHEWS NO DISMAY).
BULL II (115)	THAT. I DONT ADMIT THAT, I AM SINCERE; AND MY	INTENTIONS	ARE PERFECTLY HONORABLE. I THINK YOU WILL ACCEPT
FANY III (321)	FATHER. /KNOX/ I ASK MR DOOVALLEY WHAT HIS	INTENTIONS	ARE. /MARGARET/ OH FATHER: HOW CAN YOU?
GETT SD(262)	BE PATIENT WITH HIM WHEN HIS UNQUESTIONABLY GOOD	INTENTIONS	BECOME ACTIVELY MISCHIEVOUS; BUT ONE BLAMES
FANY III (321)	YOU AND YOUR SON, GILBEY: HE KNOWS HIS OWN	INTENTIONS	BEST, NO DOUBT, AND PERHAPS HAS TOLD THEM TO YOU.
METH PREFACE(R12)	CAPACITY TO SATISFY THAT APPETITE? GOOD	INTENTIONS	DO NOT CARRY WITH THEM A GRAIN OF POLITICAL
BARB III (318)	HURT AND OFFENDED. ANY FURTHER DISCUSSION OF MY	INTENTIONS	HAD BETTER TAKE PLACE WITH MY FATHER, AS BETWEEN
PHIL III (137)	MARRY YOU, DO YOU? /CHARTERIS/ I AM AFRAID YOUR	INTENTIONS	HAVE BEEN HONORABLE, JULIA. /JULIA/ YOU CAD!
JOAN PREFACE(37)	SO IF HE ANSWERS TOO CONFIDENTLY FOR GOD'S	INTENTIONS	HE MAY BE ASKED " HAST THOU ENTERED INTO THE
PRES (157)	/LADY CORINTHIA/ LOVE-- REAL LOVE-- MAKES ALL	INTENTIONS	HONORABLE. BUT YOU COULD NEVER UNDERSTAND THAT.
MRS PREFACE(180)	PRODUCED GRATUITOUSLY BY CENSORS WITH THE BEST	INTENTIONS	.
SUPR HANDBOK(226)	MARX CONVICTED THE BOURGEOISIE OF THEFT. GOOD	INTENTIONS	. HELL IS PAVED WITH GOOD INTENTIONS, NOT WITH
OVER (189)	CHOOSE TO CALL IT, DIDNT TAKE MUCH NOTICE OF MY	INTENTIONS	. (GREGORY INSTINCTIVELY SEEKS HER HAND AND
AUGS (266)	(EXPLAINING) HELL, THEY SAYS, IS PAVED WITH GOOD	INTENTIONS	. /AUGUSTUS/ (SPRINGING TO HIS FEET) DO YOU MEAN
NEVR IV (297)	STOP, I WARN YOU, MR BOHUN, NOT TO ANSWER FOR MY	INTENTIONS	. /BOHUN/ (RISING) IT'S NO USE, MISS CLANDON:
JITT III (78)	HIS INTENTIONS? /LENKHEIM/ I CANT CARRY OUT HIS	INTENTIONS	. /JITTA/ YOU MEAN YOU WONT. /LENKHEIM/ I MEAN
MIS. (193)	SURELY IT'S THE GENTLEMAN WHO SHOULD BE ASKED HIS	INTENTIONS	. /TARLETON/ COME NOW, PATSY! NONE OF THAT
AUGS (266)	IS PAVED WITH MY GOOD INTENTIONS -- WITH THE GOOD	INTENTIONS	OF HIS MAJESTY'S GOVERNMENT? /THE CLERK/ I DONT
2TRU PREFACE(24)	REST OF IT ARE NOW PLAIN ENOUGH, AS BETWEEN THE	INTENTIONS	OF THE CHURCH AND INTENTIONS OF THE EMPIRE (
2TRU PREFACE(24)	AS BETWEEN THE INTENTIONS OF THE CHURCH AND	INTENTIONS	OF THE EMPIRE (UNREALIZED IDEALS BOTH) I AM ON
OVER (188)	YES: I MAINTAIN THAT I AM RESPONSIBLE FOR MY	INTENTIONS	ONLY, AND NOT FOR REFLEX ACTIONS OVER WHICH I
BULL I (95)	WAIT UNTIL SHE DIED OF OLD AGE SOONER THAN ASK MY	INTENTIONS	OR CONDESCEND TO HINT AT THE POSSIBILITY OF MY
AUGS (266)	MEAN TO INSINUATE THAT HELL IS PAVED WITH MY GOOD	INTENTIONS	-- WITH THE GOOD INTENTIONS OF HIS MAJESTY'S
GENV II (53)	HE WAS A BIT OF A SUCKER; AND I THOUGHT HE HAD	INTENTIONS	; AND OF COURSE HE WOULD HAVE BEEN A JOLLY GOOD
SUPR I (27)	TANNER) HOW DARE YOU, SIR, IMPUTE SUCH MONSTROUS	INTENTIONS	TO ME? I PROTEST AGAINST IT. I AM READY TO PUT
GENV IV (100)	HIGH SEAS TO SLAUGHTER INNOCENT TRAVELLERS WHOSE	INTENTIONS	TOWARDS YOURSELF, YOUR WIFE, AND YOUR DAUGHTERS,
JOAN 6 (124)	THE MAID. /WARWICK/ DEAR ME! AT ALL EVENTS THEIR	INTENTIONS	WERE FRIENDLY TO YOU, MY LORD. /CAUCHON/ (
OVER (188)	BEAR ME OUT WHEN I SAY THAT FROM THAT MOMENT MY	INTENTIONS	WERE STRICTLY AND RESOLUTELY HONORABLE; THOUGH MY
GETT PREFACE(222)	CELIBACY AND INDIGENCE. TO ASK A YOUNG MAN HIS	INTENTIONS	WHEN YOU KNOW HE HAS NO INTENTIONS, BUT IS UNABLE
BULL IV (153)	QUOTE IT ACCURATELY. /LARRY/ TOM: WITH THE BEST	INTENTIONS	YOURE MAKING AN ASS OF YOURSELF. YOU DONT
JOAN PREFACE(50)	IT. IT IS WHAT MEN DO AT THEIR BEST, WITH GOOD	INTENTIONS	, AND WHAT NORMAL MEN AND WOMEN FIND THAT THEY
GENV IV (100)	YOUR WIFE, AND YOUR DAUGHTERS, IF THEY HAVE ANY	INTENTIONS	, ARE ENTIRELY FRIENDLY? WHAT HAS IT TO DO WITH
GETT PREFACE(222)	YOUNG MAN HIS INTENTIONS WHEN YOU KNOW HE HAS NO	INTENTIONS	, BUT IS UNABLE TO DENY THAT HE HAS PAID
FABL PREFACE(80)	TRIAL-AND-ERROR, AND MAKES MISTAKES WITH THE BEST	INTENTIONS	, IS NOT IN EFFECT IRRECONCILABLE WITH BELIEF IN
SUPR HANDBOK(226)	THEFT. GOOD INTENTIONS. HELL IS PAVED WITH GOOD	INTENTIONS	, NOT WITH BAD ONES. ALL MEN MEAN WELL. NATURAL
CLEO NOTES (212)	OF US THAT THE CHRISTIAN ERA, SO EXCELLENT IN ITS	INTENTIONS	, SHOULD HAVE BEEN PRACTICALLY SUCH A VERY
JOAN PREFACE(50)	FIND THAT THEY MUST AND WILL DO IN SPITE OF THEIR	INTENTIONS	, THAT REALLY CONCERN US. THE RASCALLY BISHOP AND
SUPR HANDBOK(191)	HAPPENS IN THE PROCESS, WHICH, WITH THE BEST	INTENTIONS	, THEY DO ALL IN THEIR POWER TO PREVENT. FINALLY,
MIS. (193)	PATSY: WHAT ARE YOUR INTENTIONS? /HYPATIA/ MY	INTENTIONS	! SURELY IT'S THE GENTLEMAN WHO SHOULD BE ASKED
		INTENTLY	
GETT (324)	(GOING TO HER PAST THE BISHOP, AND GAZING	INTENTLY	AT HER) ARE YOU HIS WIFE? /MRS BRIDGENORTH/ THE
DEVL III (53)	(SHE PUTS HER HANDS ON HIS SHOULDERS AND LOOKS	INTENTLY	AT HIM). /RICHARD/ (AMAZED-- DIVINING THE TRUTH)
PHIL III (134)	UNDERSTOOD BY THOSE ABOUT YOU. /JULIA/ (LOOKING	INTENTLY	AT HIM, AND YET BEGINNING TO BE DERISIVELY
CAND III SD(127)	IS UPRIGHT IN HER HAND. LEANING BACK AND LOOKING	INTENTLY	AT THE POINT OF IT, WITH HER FEET STRETCHED TOWARDS
WIDO II (46)	THEYRE STAYING TO LUNCH. /BLANCHE/ (LOOKING	INTENTLY	INTO HER FACE) HE? /THE PARLORMAID/ (WHISPERING
LION I (120)	BUT LAVINIA HOLDS HIM DOWN, WATCHING FERROVIUS	INTENTLY	. FERROVIUS, WITHOUT FLINCHING, TURNS THE OTHER
WIDO III SD(64)	IT SOFTLY AND STEALS OVER TO HIM, WATCHING HIM	INTENTLY	. HE RISES FROM HIS LEANING ATTITUDE, AND TAKES THE
PHIL III SD(140)	FROM HER. SHE RISES AND FOLLOWS HIM UP SLOWLY AND	INTENTLY	. /JULIA/ (DELIBERATELY) I HAVE SEEN YOU VERY MUCH
DEST SD(153)	THE RISOTTO WHEN HE FORGETS IT AND LEANS MORE	INTENTLY	OVER THE MAP. /GIUSEPPE/ WILL YOUR EXCELLENCY--
ARMS I (21)	KEEPS ME AWAKE EXCEPT DANGER: REMEMBER THAT: (	INTENTLY	) DANGER, DANGER, DANGER, DAN-- (TRAILING OFF
SIM I (52)	MAYA, WHO HAS STOLEN IN AND LISTENED GRAVELY AND	INTENTLY	TO HIS EXHORTATION). /IDDY/ (COLLAPSING IN DESPAIR

CAND III (132)	(HE REFLECTS ON THIS FOR AN INSTANT; THEN TURNS	INTENTLY	TO QUESTION MORELL). WHAT I WANT TO KNOW IS HOW YOU
SUPR II SD(48)	FROM BENEATH THE MACHINE. HE IS WATCHING THEM	INTENTLY	WITH BENT BACK AND HANDS SUPPORTED ON HIS KNEES.
		INTENTS	
BULL IV (173)	FOR YOUR HOTEL? /BROADBENT/ MY DEAR SIR! TO ALL	INTENTS	AND PURPOSES THE SYNDICATE I REPRESENT ALREADY OWNS
PRES (164)	OF HIS LIFE; AND THE BRITISH ARMY IS NOW TO ALL	INTENTS	AND PURPOSES COMMANDED BY MRS BANGER. WHEN I
PRES (138)	OF THE TIMES BOOK CLUB, YOU HAVE BECOME TO ALL	INTENTS	AND PURPOSES HIS SENIOR. HE LOST GROUND BY SAYING
SIM PRO,3, (32)	HIS SKIN AND BONES. YOU MAY REGARD ME AS TO ALL	INTENTS	AND PURPOSES BORN AGAIN. /THE PRIEST/ DO YOU STILL
		INTER	
VWOO 2,SD(123)	MILK CHOCOLATE, GLASS JARS OF SWEETS CONTAINING (	INTER	ALIA) SUGARED ALMONDS, ALL ON THE COUNTER; CHEESE,
CAPT I (219)	MAWT WORNT TO TIKE A WALK CROST MOROCKER-- A RAWD	INTER	THE MAHNTNS OR SECH LAWK. WEOLL, AS YOU KNAOW, GAVNER,
		INTERACTION	
JOAN PREFACE(37)	SAINTS IN THE KINGDOM OF GOD, BUT THEIR FRUITFUL	INTERACTION	IN A COSTLY BUT NOBLE STATE OF TENSION." THE
		INTERBRED	
ROCK PREFACE(149)	RACE. AS BOTH THESE LINGUAL STOCKS ARE HOPELESSLY	INTERBRED	BY THIS TIME, SUCH A SACRIFICE TO ETHNOLOGICAL
		INTERCEDE	
CATH 1 (163)	KNOWS IT IS YOUR DUTY TO SEE HIM! (TO VARINKA)	INTERCEDE	FOR HIM AND FOR ME, BEAUTIFUL LITTLE DARLING. HE
JOAN 1 (62)	WHO SPEAK TO ME EVERY DAY (HE GAPES) , WILL	INTERCEDE	FOR YOU. YOU WILL GO TO PARADISE; AND YOUR NAME
		INTERCEPT	
PHIL I (76)	INQUIRINGLY AT CHARTERIS AS JULIA SPRINGS UP TO	INTERCEPT	HER. HE ADVANCES A STEP TO GUARD THE WAY TO THE
6CAL (100)	THEY TELL ME? /THE KING/ (HURRYING ACROSS TO	INTERCEPT	HER) MADAM: THIS IS NO PLACE FOR YOU. I PRAY YOU,
SUPR III (76)	THE SUNNY SHORES OF THE MEDITERRANEAN. WE	INTERCEPT	THAT WEALTH. WE RESTORE IT TO CIRCULATION AMONG
DEST (174)	THAT HE HAS BEEN BETRAYED, AND HAS SENT YOU TO	INTERCEPT	THE INFORMATION AT ALL HAZARDS. AS IF THAT COULD
		INTERCEPTED	
HART I SD(48)	BY THE DOOR, AND IS HURRYING OUT WHEN SHE IS	INTERCEPTED	BY LADY UTTERWORD, WHO BURSTS IN MUCH FLUSTERED.
		INTERCEPTING	
PYGM II (225)	(DEFTLY RETRIEVING THE HANDKERCHIEF AND	INTERCEPTING	HER ON HER RELUCTANT WAY TO THE DOOR) YOURE AN
2TRU I (38)	I DONT (SHE REACHES FOR THE BELL). /THE NURSE/ (	INTERCEPTING	HER QUICKLY) NO YOU DONT. (SHE THROWS THE BELL
JITT II (45)	(SHE ATTEMPTS TO LEAVE THE ROOM). /LENKHEIM/ (	INTERCEPTING	HER) YOU SHANT RUN AWAY. IF YOU DONT TELL ME
PHIL I (91)	AND BOLT. (HE STARTS FOR THE DOOR). /CRAVEN/ (	INTERCEPTING	HIM) STOP! DONT LEAVE ME LIKE THIS: I SHALL
MIS. (132)	TAUGHT HIM EVERYTHING ELSE FIRST? /JOHNNY/ (	INTERCEPTING	HIS FATHER'S REPLY BY COMING OUT OF THE SWING
AUGS (278)	BREAKFAST-TABLE THIS MORNING. /THE LADY/ (	INTERCEPTING	IT) IT IS THE LIST. GOOD HEAVENS! /THE CLERK/
CAND III (139)	HANDS. BURGESS GOES TO THE DOOR). /CANDIDA/ (	INTERCEPTING	MORELL, WHO IS FOLLOWING BURGESS) STAY HERE,
SUPR IV (170)	GARDEN. OCTAVIUS REMAINS PETRIFIED). /MENDOZA/ (	INTERCEPTING	MRS WHITEFIELD, WHO COMES FROM THE VILLA WITH A
		INTERCEPTS	
DEST (171)	(HE PASSES SWIFTLY UP THE MIDDLE OF THE ROOM AND	INTERCEPTS	HER AS SHE MAKES FOR THE VINEYARD). /LADY/ (AT
BARB II SD(277)	THE NEWCOMER MOVES QUICKLY UP TO THE DOOR AND	INTERCEPTS	HER. HIS MANNER IS SO THREATENING THAT SHE
MTH4 I SD(145)	NUMBER ONE ON HIS CAP, WHO COMES UP THE STEPS AND	INTERCEPTS	HIM. HE IS DRESSED LIKE THE WOMAN, BUT A SLIGHT
MIS. SD(162)	A DASH FOR THE PAVILION DOOR. SHE FLIES BACK AND	INTERCEPTS	HIM. /HYPATIA/ AHA! ARNT YOU GLAD IVE CAUGHT
DEST SD(182)	ROAD. HE IS CROSSING TO THE OUTER DOOR WHEN SHE	INTERCEPTS	HIM. /LADY/ LIEUTENANT. /LIEUTENANT/ (
SUPR IV SD(149)	WHEN VIOLET, GREATLY DISMAYED, SPRINGS UP AND	INTERCEPTS	HIM. STRAKER DOES NOT WAIT; AT LEAST HE DOES NOT
		INTERCESSION	
SIM II (79)	A SINGLE GUEST. FRESH DISAPPEARANCES. CROWDED	INTERCESSION	SERVICE AT WESTMINSTER ABBEY BROUGHT TO A CLOSE
JOAN PREFACE(29)	AND THE LIE IT IMPLIES, THEY WILL NEED EDITH'S	INTERCESSION	WHEN THEY ARE THEMSELVES BROUGHT TO JUDGMENT,
JOAN 4 (103)	THE MOTHER OF GOD NOW TO WHOM WE MUST LOOK FOR	INTERCESSION	, BUT TO JOAN THE MAID. WHAT WILL THE WORLD BE
BULL PREFACE(65)	BE CELEBRATED IN EGYPT BY THE RETIREMENT, AT HIS	INTERCESSION	, OF ABD-EL-NEBI AND THE REST FROM PENAL
		INTERCESSORS	
BARB PREFACE(245)	HUMAN SAVIORS, AND PRAY TO MIRACULOUS VIRGIN	INTERCESSORS	. WE ATTRIBUTE MERCY TO THE INEXORABLE; SOOTHE
		INTERCOURSE	
UNPL PREFACE(R18)	WORSE: THEY ARE POSITIVELY UNFIT FOR CIVILIZED	INTERCOURSE	: GRACELESS, IGNORANT, NARROW-MINDED TO A QUITE
HART I (46)	IN IGNORANCE OF THE COMMONEST DECENCIES OF SOCIAL	INTERCOURSE	? /NURSE GUINNESS/ NEVER MIND HIM, DOTY. (
JITT I (22)	ANOTHER AS WE STAND, THE CHILDREN BORN FROM THEIR	INTERCOURSE	ARE NOT ALWAYS CHILDREN OF FLESH AND BLOOD, BUT
KING PREFACE(157)	AND PERMANENT MARRIAGE RELATION FROM THE CARNAL	INTERCOURSE	DESCRIBED IN SHAKESPEAR'S SONNET. THIS, BEING A
BULL PREFACE(29)	AND HEARTILY; NOWHERE IS ACTUAL PERSONAL	INTERCOURSE	FOUND COMPATIBLE FOR LONG WITH THE INTOLERABLE
GETT PREFACE(227)	SPECIAL FEELINGS WHICH ALTER THE NATURE OF HUMAN	INTERCOURSE	IS A MISCHIEVOUS ONE. THE WHOLE DIFFICULTY OF
GETT (295)	THE VERY FIRST QUALIFICATION FOR TOLERABLE SOCIAL	INTERCOURSE	. /THE GENERAL/ (MARKEDLY) I HOPE YOU WILL
MTH4 I (147)	TO THE ELEMENTARY DECENCIES OF HUMAN	INTERCOURSE	. /THE MAN/ WHAT ARE DECENCIES? /THE ELDERLY
LION PREFACE(27)	OF HIS PREACHING, AS EXTREMELY UNCIVIL IN PRIVATE	INTERCOURSE	. THE GREAT CHANGE. SO FAR THE HISTORY IS THAT
MIS. PREFACE(87)	BY OUT-OF-DOOR HABITS, AND BY FRANK NEIGHBORLY	INTERCOURSE	THROUGH DANCES AND CONCERTS AND THEATRICALS AND
SUPR II SD(62)	TO INTOLERABLE COARSENESS; AND ENGLISH	INTERCOURSE	TO NEED ENLIVENING BY GAMES AND STORIES AND
WIDO I (16)	SPARE ME THE NECESSITY OF HAVING TO RESTRAIN AN	INTERCOURSE	WHICH PROMISES TO BE VERY PLEASANT TO US ALL?
DOCT I SD(81)	FOR UNSPECIFIED ADVANTAGES INVOLVED BY INTIMATE	INTERCOURSE	WITH A LEADER OF HIS PROFESSION, AND AMOUNTING
DOCT I SD(84)	SENSITIVE MAN ACQUIRES IN BREAKING HIMSELF IN TO	INTERCOURSE	WITH ALL SORTS AND CONDITIONS OF MEN. HIS FACE
MTH2 (71)	WITH THE BEST INFORMATION, NOR CULTIVATED BY	INTERCOURSE	WITH EDUCATED MINDS AT ANY OF OUR GREAT SEATS OF
BULL PREFACE(29)	AND BE KIND, HOSPITABLE, AND SERVICEABLE IN HIS	INTERCOURSE	WITH ENGLISHMEN, WHILST BEING PERFECTLY PREPARED
JOAN 6 (139)	CRIMES WHICH SHE DOES NOT DENY. FIRST, SHE HAS	INTERCOURSE	WITH EVIL SPIRITS, AND IS THEREFORE A SORCERESS.
SUPR III (125)	TO CUT ME OFF FROM ALL NATURAL AND UNCONSTRAINED	INTERCOURSE	WITH HALF MY FELLOW-CREATURES WOULD NARROW AND
APPL PREFACE(173)	GOOD MANNERS AS AN INDISPENSABLE CONDITION OF HIS	INTERCOURSE	WITH HIS SUBJECTS, AND TO LEAVE TO THE LESS
MTH4 I (140)	PEOPLE HAVE TO TAKE VERY STRICT PRECAUTIONS.	INTERCOURSE	WITH US PUTS TOO GREAT A STRAIN ON THEM. /THE
MIS. PREFACE(87)	SUBURB, WHERE THERE IS A GOOD DEAL OF SOCIAL	INTERCOURSE	, AND THE FAMILY, INSTEAD OF KEEPING ITSELF TO
HART PREFACE(20)	I NOTICED EITHER IN THE PAPERS, OR IN GENERAL	INTERCOURSE	, ANY FEELING BEYOND THE USUAL ONE THAT THE
JITT I (22)	ON MYSELF. THIS SACRIFICE IS NO CHILD BORN OF OUR	INTERCOURSE	, BRUNO: YOU MAY BE ITS FATHER; BUT I AM NOT ITS
SUPR HANDBOK(190)	BY THE SAME VARIETY AND INTIMACY OF INTERNATIONAL	INTERCOURSE	, THERE MIGHT BE LITTLE TO CHOOSE BETWEEN THEM.
		INTEREST	
DEVL III (54)	AS I DO FOR MYSELF. I HAD NO MOTIVE AND NO	INTEREST	: ALL I CAN TELL YOU IS THAT WHEN IT CAME TO THE
WIDO II (42)	IS DERIVED FROM? /TRENCH/ (DEFIANTLY) FROM	INTEREST	: NOT FROM HOUSES. MY HANDS ARE CLEAN AS FAR AS
BULL PREFACE(33)	TO DEMOCRACY IS THE REPRESENTATION OF EVERY	INTEREST	: THE INDISPENSABLE PRELIMINARY TO JUSTICE IS THE
GETT (296)	GIVES ME A CERTAIN RIGHT TO BE PRESENT IN CECIL'S	INTEREST	? /THE GENERAL/ (GRAVELY) THERE IS SUCH A THING
LION PREFACE(35)	IS A DISTINCT ATTEMPT TO INCREASE THE FEMININE	INTEREST	ALL THROUGH. THE SLIGHT LEAD GIVEN BY MARK IS TAKEN
POSN PREFACE(392)	(1909), AN ENGLISHMAN'S HOME, HAS FOR ITS MAIN	INTEREST	AN INVASION OF ENGLAND BY A FICTITIOUS POWER WHICH
SUPR I (37)	IN BIRD AND BEAST, EVEN IN YOU. (A FLUSH OF	INTEREST	AND DELIGHT SUDDENLY CHASES THE GROWING PERPLEXITY
DOCT I (103)	(SUDDENLY RISING TO THE NEW IDEA WITH IMMENSE	INTEREST	AND EXCITEMENT) WHAT! RIDGEON! DID YOU HEAR THAT?
DOCT PREFACE(69)	WHICH WILL PRESENTLY TAKE THE PLACE IN GENERAL	INTEREST	AND HONOR NOW OCCUPIED BY OUR MILITARY AND NAVAL
BARB I (267)	EH? /BARBARA/ (LOOKING AT HIM WITH QUICK	INTEREST	AND NODDING) JUST SO. HOW DID YOU COME TO
MILL PREFACE(128)	THAT THE DECISIONS SHALL BE MADE IN THE GENERAL	INTEREST	AND NOT SOLELY IN THE IMMEDIATE PERSONAL INTEREST
HART I (63)	SEE, ONLY SOMETHING TO THINK ABOUT-- TO GIVE SOME	INTEREST	AND PLEASURE TO LIFE. /ELLIE/ JUST SO. THATS ALL,
ROCK II (263)	AS FAST AS WE FILL OUR POCKETS WITH RENT AND	INTEREST	AND PROFITS THEYRE EMPTIED AGAIN BY WEST END
MTH2 (61)	STUDY OF THE LABOR QUESTION. /FRANKLYN/ (WITH	INTEREST	AND SOME SURPRISE) INDEED? /LUBIN/ YES. IT
CAND II (106)	HER MACHINE WHEN HE ADDRESSES HER WITH AWAKENED	INTEREST	AND SYMPATHY). /MARCHBANKS/ REALLY! OH, THEN YOU
APPL PREFACE(186)	LEAVES ME IS INVESTED WHERE I CAN GET THE HIGHEST	INTEREST	AND THE BEST SECURITY, AS THEREBY I CAN MAKE SURE
BASH PREFACE(90)	A CERTAIN MAN IN A SEDITION, QUITE FAILED TO	INTEREST	ANYONE IN HIM; BUT WHEN MARIE CORELLI EXPANDED THIS
UNPL PREFACE(R18)	SO INCREDIBLY ILL-MANNERED, THAT NOT EVEN THEIR	INTEREST	AS MEN OF BUSINESS IN WELCOMING A POSSIBLE CUSTOMER
FABL PREFACE(86)	THE MARXIST CLASS WAR, THE CONFLICT OF ECONOMIC	INTEREST	BETWEEN PROPRIETORS AND PROLETARIANS WAS DESCRIBED
DEVL I SD(17)	LOOK ROUND SOCIABLY. ESSIE, WITH A GLEAM OF	INTEREST	BREAKING THROUGH HER MISERY, LOOKS UP. CHRISTY
MTH5 (222)	PROCEEDING? /ARJILLAX/ IF YOU COME TO THAT, WHAT	INTEREST	CAN YOU FIND IN THE STATUES OF SMIRKING NYMPHS AND

MIS. PREFACE(81)	CONCEIVE THAT ITS BLAME OR CONTEMPT OR WANT OF	INTEREST	COULD POSSIBLY HURT ITS PARENT, AND THEREFORE
APPL I (203)	MR BOANERGES. I HAVE FOLLOWED YOUR CAREER WITH	INTEREST	EVER SINCE YOU CONTESTED NORTHAMPTON TWENTY-FIVE
MIS. (171)	NOT ONE OF THOSE TRANSACTIONS HAS THE SMALLEST	INTEREST	FOR ME OR ANYONE ELSE IN THE WORLD BUT HIM; AND
KING PREFACE(153)	CASTLEMAINE RAGING IN THE BACKGROUND, HAS NO	INTEREST	FOR ME, IF IT EVER HAD FOR ANY GROWN-UP PERSON. BUT
MTH5 SD(226)	INTEREST IN EVERYTHING, AND EXPECTATION OF EQUAL	INTEREST	FROM EVERYBODY ELSE, COMES FROM THE TEMPLE TO THE
WIDO II (42)	THROUGH THE POVERTY OF MY TENANTS THAT YOU EXACT	INTEREST	FROM ME AT THE MONSTROUS AND EXORBITANT RATE OF
APPL I (224)	THREE EMPERORS, AND A SULTAN. /MAGNUS/ BUT WHAT	INTEREST	HAS A KING IN FLATTERING A SUBJECT? /AMANDA/
POSN PREFACE(365)	BUT FOR SATIRICAL POLEMICS. AND SINCE EVERY	INTEREST	HAS ITS OPPOSITION, ALL THESE INFLUENCES HAD
2TRU III SD(81)	AND BORED. ON THE BEACH SHE FINDS NOTHING TO	INTEREST	HER UNTIL THE SERGEANT UNCONSCIOUSLY ATTRACTS HER
SUPR II SD(63)	LET ALONE OR LET PRATTLE ABOUT THE THINGS THAT	INTEREST	HER. RAMSDEN STROLLS OVER TO INSPECT THE MOTOR CAR.
CATH 4 (192)	TO GO MAD WITH LOVE WHEN AN EMPRESS DEIGNS TO	INTEREST	HERSELF IN YOU . WHEN AN EMPRESS ALLOWS YOU TO SEE
NEVR III (273)	ENTERTAINING MY ADDRESSES, OR CONDESCENDING TO	INTEREST	HERSELF IN ME IN ANY WAY. (GLORIA, SATISFIED,
BULL I (87)	VAN VOCHT SAID IN NINETYEIGHT. IF YOU WANT TO	INTEREST	HIM IN IRELAND YOUVE GOT TO CALL THE UNFORTUNATE
ROCK II (279)	FIND HIM A JOB AND SEE THAT HE DOES IT. I WILL	INTEREST	HIM IN IT. /SIR ARTHUR/ SPLENDID! /ALOYSIA/ (
LION PREFACE(29)	SELLERS OUT OF THE TEMPLE IN A RIOT; REFUSES TO	INTEREST	HIMSELF IN THE BEAUTIES AND WONDERS OF THE TEMPLE
SIM PREFACE(17)	OF EVEN THE WORST MURDERERS, AND TAKE NO FURTHER	INTEREST	IF A REPRIEVE DECREES THAT THEIR LIVES SHALL BE
ROCK II (279)	THAT I CANNOT BRING MYSELF TO TAKE THE SMALLEST	INTEREST	IN: PARLIAMENTARY AFFAIRS AND LOVE AFFAIRS. THEY
MRS II (206)	THAN YOU HAVE. /CROFTS/ MAYNT A MAN TAKE AN	INTEREST	IN A GIRL? /MRS WARREN/ NOT A MAN LIKE YOU.
JOAN PREFACE(25)	NONSENSE MISSED. TYPICAL PRODUCTS OF THAT	INTEREST	IN AMERICA AND ENGLAND ARE THE HISTORIES OF JOAN BY
POSN PREFACE(376)	EACH OF MY STATEMENT, AND THAT ONE NOT FROM ANY	INTEREST	IN AN UNDESIRABLE DOCUMENT BY AN IRREVERENT AUTHOR,
FABL PREFACE(91)	THEIR KNOWLEDGE OF THE BEST MUSIC AND THEIR	INTEREST	IN AND ENJOYMENT OF IT, IF ANY. I WOULD HAVE THEM
DOCT PREFACE(3)	THE SUPPLY OF BREAD BY GIVING BAKERS A PECUNIARY	INTEREST	IN BAKING FOR YOU, SHOULD GO ON TO GIVE A SURGEON A
DOCT PREFACE(13)	THE SIMPLE DESIRE TO BELIEVE FOUNDED ON A STRONG	INTEREST	IN BELIEVING. EVERYBODY RECOGNIZES THIS IN THE CASE
BULL I (77)	THERE IS NO COUNTRY LEFT TO ME TO TAKE AN	INTEREST	IN BUT IRELAND. MIND: I DONT SAY THAT AN ENGLISHMAN
BULL PREFACE(33)	OF THEM, WHEREAS IT IS ONLY BY HAVING EVERY	INTEREST	IN COMMON WITH BOTH OF THEM THAT HE CAN GOVERN THEM
BULL PREFACE(33)	TWO LITIGANTS, AND THAT IS THAT HE SHALL HAVE NO	INTEREST	IN COMMON WITH EITHER OF THEM, WHEREAS IT IS ONLY
DOCT PREFACE(3)	YOU, SHOULD GO ON TO GIVE A SURGEON A PECUNIARY	INTEREST	IN CUTTING OFF YOUR LEG, IS ENOUGH TO MAKE ONE
METH PREFACE(R58)	MAKES THE WHOLE WORLD KIN, ANOTHER HUMANITARIAN	INTEREST	IN DARWINISM WAS THAT DARWIN POPULARIZED EVOLUTION
ROCK II (279)	/ALOYSIA/ (TO SIR ARTHUR) WELL, DONT YOU TAKE AN	INTEREST	IN DAVID? /SIR ARTHUR/ DAVID IS AT THE AGE AT
DOCT PREFACE(62)	CONDITION OF MEDICAL PRACTICE. NOT THAT THE	INTEREST	IN DISEASE AND ABERRATIONS WHICH TURNS SOME MEN AND
JOAN PREFACE(54)	AT HOME; IN SHORT, FOR ANY OR EVERY REASON EXCEPT	INTEREST	IN DRAMATIC ART AS SUCH, IN FASHIONABLE CENTRES THE
JITT III (74)	HER HUSBAND CONTRASTING STRONGLY WITH HER WARM	INTEREST	IN EDITH) SHE GUESSED. SHE KNEW. IT IS NO USE
HART PREFACE(8)	OR AN UNLUCKY ONE, IT LEFT HIM A FAIRLY STRONG	INTEREST	IN ENCOURAGING HIS HOPES OF SALVATION AND ALLAYING
MTH5 SD(226)	BLOCKS, AND A PERPETUAL SMILE OF EAGER BENEVOLENT	INTEREST	IN EVERYTHING, AND EXPECTATION OF EQUAL INTEREST
MTH5 (224)	MY DESIRE TO MODEL LIMBS, AND RETAINED ONLY MY	INTEREST	IN HEADS AND FACES. I, TOO, MADE BUSTS OF ANCIENTS;
PYGM EPILOG (292)	SHE WOULD STILL HAVE REFUSED TO ACCEPT AN	INTEREST	IN HERSELF THAT WAS SECONDARY TO PHILOSOPHIC
PYGM EPILOG (298)	TACK WITH DISASTROUS RESULTS, SUDDENLY TOOK AN	INTEREST	IN HER, AND REVEALED A HOSTILITY TO CONVENTIONAL
ROCK II (279)	WITH AT THAT AGE. HE WOULD REGARD MY TAKING AN	INTEREST	IN HIM AS PARENTAL TYRANNY. THEREFORE I AM
ROCK II (279)	I AM PARTICULARLY CAREFUL NOT TO TAKE ANY	INTEREST	IN HIM. /ALOYSIA/ (RISING) WELL, YOU PREACH AT ME
DOCT PREFACE(40)	A HOPELESS FOOL THAT IT IS IMPOSSIBLE TO TAKE ANY	INTEREST	IN HIM. WHY NOT TEST THE DIAGNOSIS SCIENTIFICALLY?
DEST (170)	IN FRANCE. /LADY/ (AFFECTING A MARKED ACCESS OF	INTEREST	IN HIM) YOU WERE NOT BORN A SUBJECT AT ALL, I
HART II (118)	IN THE WORLD IS ONLY THE OVERFLOW FROM HIS	INTEREST	IN HIMSELF. WHEN YOU ARE A CHILD YOUR VESSEL IS NOT
JITT III (57)	A SUDDEN CHANGE. UP TO THAT TIME HE WAS FULL OF	INTEREST	IN HIS HOME, IN EDITH'S EDUCATION, IN OUR PLANS,
DOCT PREFACE(79)	VESTED INTERESTS THE WORST IS THE VESTED	INTEREST	IN ILL-HEALTH. 3, REMEMBER THAT AN ILLNESS IS A
APPL PREFACE(177)	THEY CAN AFFORD IT AND HAVE A FANCY FOR IT OR AN	INTEREST	IN IT. LAST OCTOBER (1929) I WAS ASKED TO ADDRESS
PYGM II (219)	SIR, REALLY, I DONT KNOW HOW YOU CAN TAKE AN	INTEREST	IN IT. /HIGGINS/ (TO PICKERING) LETS HAVE HER UP.
JOAN PREFACE(25)	ENTIRELY REALISTIC DOCUMENTS CREATED A LIVING	INTEREST	IN JOAN WHICH VOLTAIRE'S MOCK HOMERICS AND
FOUN (218)	SOMEWHAT FLIGHTY GIRL; I REQUIRE SOME SERIOUS	INTEREST	IN LIFE TO STEADY ME. AS I HAD AN UNGOVERNABLE
ROCK PREFACE(162)	POWER OF LIFE AND DEATH WAS THAT THE CHEKA HAD NO	INTEREST	IN LIQUIDATING ANYBODY WHO COULD BE MADE PUBLICLY
JITT III (66)	WANTED TO SHAKE HIM FOR NOT TAKING A LITTLE MORE	INTEREST	IN ME OCCASIONALLY? HIS CONSCIENCE WAS NEVER EASY
BULL II (113)	I DID REALLY. I WISH YOU HAD TAKEN HALF AS MUCH	INTEREST	IN ME. /NORA/ OH, I WAS DYING TO SEE YOU, OF
DOCT PREFACE(63)	AND SURGERY IS NOT SOMETIMES AS MORBID AS THE	INTEREST	IN MISERY AND VICE WHICH TURNS SOME OTHERS TO
GETT PREFACE(239)	FOR THE FIRST TIME THAT THEY HAVE LONG SINCE LOST	INTEREST	IN ONE ANOTHER, AND HAVE BEEN UNITED ONLY BY A
JOAN PREFACE(39)	BECAUSE THE PRIEST HAD NO SUCH DIRECT PECUNIARY	INTEREST	IN OUR SINS AS THE DOCTOR HAS IN OUR DISEASES: HE
GENV PREFACE(27)	NEXT GREAT INVENTION MAY CREATE AN OVERWHELMING	INTEREST	IN PACIFIC CIVILIZATION AND WIPE OUT WAR. YOU NEVER
APPL II (269)	I HAVE NEVER BEEN ABLE TO INDUCE HIM TO TAKE ANY	INTEREST	IN PARLIAMENTARY POLITICS. HE PREFERS INTELLECTUAL
LADY PREFACE(214)	DESIRED TO PLEASE, AND WHO TOOK A MOTHERLY	INTEREST	IN PEMBROKE. THERE IS A FURTHER TEMPTATION IN THE
ROCK I SD(205)	OF APOLOGY FOR BEING NOT ONLY UNABLE TO TAKE AN	INTEREST	IN PEOPLE, BUT EVEN TO PRETEND THAT SHE DOES. /LADY
HART PREFACE(9)	AS IT HAPPENED, BY DISCOVERIES OF EXTRAORDINARY	INTEREST	IN PHYSICS, CHEMISTRY, AND THAT LIFELESS METHOD OF
MTH4 III (197)	I AM ALWAYS GLAD TO SEE THE YOUNG TAKING AN	INTEREST	IN POLITICS. IT IS AN IMPATIENT QUESTION; BUT IT IS
MTH3 (95)	I WISH THE PEOPLE WOULD TAKE A SERIOUS	INTEREST	IN POLITICS. /CONFUCIUS/ I DO NOT AGREE. THE
OVER PREFACE(162)	STORIES SUITED TO PEOPLE WHO ARE INCAPABLE OF ANY	INTEREST	IN PSYCHOLOGY, BUT THE FINE ARTIST MUST KEEP THE
JOAN PREFACE(10)	HAD A DIVINE REVELATION. THIS KNOWLEDGE OF AND	INTEREST	IN PUBLIC AFFAIRS WAS NOTHING EXTRAORDINARY AMONG
DOCT I (88)	TO ME NOW, COLLY. /RIDGEON/ YOU KEEP UP YOUR	INTEREST	IN SCIENCE, DO YOU? /SIR PATRICK/ LORD! YES.
MTH5 (229)	I AM BORING YOU. NOT ONE OF YOU TAKES THE LEAST	INTEREST	IN SCIENCE. GOODBYE. (HE DESCENDS FROM THE ALTAR
OVER PREFACE(162)	ESSENTIAL DULNESS OF THEIR TOPICS, AND YET THE	INTEREST	IN SEX IS STRONGER THAN EVER: IN FACT, THE
SHAK PREFACE(136)	LET REFORMERS BEWARE. NOTHING CAN EXTINGUISH MY	INTEREST	IN SHAKESPEAR. IT BEGAN WHEN I WAS A SMALL BOY, AND
POSN PREFACE(381)	MENTION THESE FACTS TO SHEW THAT I HAVE A SPECIAL	INTEREST	IN THE ACHIEVEMENT BY MY PROFESSION OF THOSE RIGHTS
DOCT PREFACE(19)	WITH THAT ARRANGEMENT. THE PUBLIC ACTUALLY HAS AN	INTEREST	IN THE ARTIST'S VICES, IT HAS NO SUCH INTEREST IN
DOCT III (132)	HE TAKE ME FOR? NOW THAT JUST DESTROYS ALL MY	INTEREST	IN THE BEASTLY JOB. IVE A GOOD MIND TO THROW UP THE
KING I (181)	CALLED AN INFIDEL. YOU YOURSELF, IN SPITE OF YOUR	INTEREST	IN THE BOOK OF DANIEL, HAVE BEEN SUSPECTED OF
SUPR I (6)	CALL POSITION; AND I CANT BRING MYSELF TO TAKE AN	INTEREST	IN THE BUSINESS OF STRUGGLING FOR THEM. WELL, ANN
GENV I (43)	ACQUAINTANCE LAST NIGHT AT MY HOTEL. HIS	INTEREST	IN THE CHURCH OF ENGLAND KEPT US UP TALKING LONG
PHIL III (133)	IS THE WAY CLEAR FOR ME THEN? /JULIA/ (LOSING	INTEREST	IN THE CONVERSATION, AND LOOKING CROSSLY AWAY FROM
SUPR III SD(136)	MAKING IT A POINT OF HONOR NOT TO SHEW ANY UNDUE	INTEREST	IN THE EXCITEMENT OF THE BANDITS. MENDOZA GIVES A
ROCK I (204)	YOU MIGHT FOR ONCE IN A WAY TAKE SOME SLIGHT	INTEREST	IN THE FAMILY. /SIR ARTHUR/ MY DEAR BOY, AT THIS
CLEO PRO2,SD(95)	ARE MOSTLY HANDSOME YOUNG FELLOWS WHOSE	INTEREST	IN THE GAME AND THE STORY SYMBOLIZE WITH TOLERABLE
DOCT PREFACE(28)	PERSECUTION TO LEGAL PENALTIES, CAN HAVE NO	INTEREST	IN THE MATTER EXCEPT THE INTEREST OF A REFORMER IN
BULL PREFACE(66)	VILLAGERS DENSHAVIANS; BUT THEY SHEWED NO OTHER	INTEREST	IN THE MATTER: ANOTHER ILLUSTRATION OF HOW HOPELESS
PYGM I SD(211)	TAKER/ (PROMPTLY) HOXTON. TITTERINGS. POPULAR	INTEREST	IN THE NOTE TAKER'S PERFORMANCE INCREASES. /THE
DOCT PREFACE(19)	AN INTEREST IN THE ARTIST'S VICES. IT HAS NO SUCH	INTEREST	IN THE SURGEON'S VICES. THE SURGEON'S ART IS
CATH 1,SD(163)	OF FURY AND EXHAUSTED IMPATIENCE TO CONCEAL HIS	INTEREST	IN THE VISITOR. /VARINKA/ HAVE YOU NO SHAME? YOU
BULL PREFACE(66)	IS WITH ITS OWN AFFAIRS, TO TAKE ANY REAL	INTEREST	IN THE WELFARE OF ANOTHER, EVEN WHEN IT PROFESSES
HART II (93)	OF THEM. I NEVER CAN GET HIM TO TAKE THE LEAST	INTEREST	IN THE WORKS: HE HARDLY KNOWS MORE ABOUT THEM THAN
HART II (118)	HAPPEN TO THEMSELVES. /CAPTAIN SHOTOVER/ A MAN'S	INTEREST	IN THE WORLD IS ONLY THE OVERFLOW FROM HIS INTEREST
GETT PREFACE(239)	ANOTHER, AND HAVE BEEN UNITED ONLY BY A COMMON	INTEREST	IN THEIR CHILDREN. WE MAY EXPECT, THEN, THAT
BULL PREFACE(4)	WHO MIGHT ASTONISH THEM BY SEEMING TO TAKE AN	INTEREST	IN THEIR ROUTINE OF BLEEDING CANDIDATES FOR
NEVR I SD(209)	AVOIDS ENCOURAGING THE TWINS BY BETRAYING ANY	INTEREST	IN THEM, WANDERS TO THE WINDOW AND LOOKS OUT TO SEA
2TRU III (84)	USING ME AS A SORT OF BAIT TO DRAW YOU TO TAKE AN	INTEREST	IN THINGS OF THE MIND. NATURE MAY BE USING YOUR
HART III (129)	IT SEEMS MADE FOR US. /HECTOR/ THE NIGHT TAKES NO	INTEREST	IN US. WHAT ARE WE TO THE NIGHT? (HE SITS DOWN
DOCT PREFACE(30)	DOCTOR IN A THOUSAND IS A VIVISECTOR, OR HAS ANY	INTEREST	IN VIVISECTION, EITHER PECUNIARY OR INTELLECTUAL,
BUOY III (37)	TASTES, WHICH YOU OCCASIONALLY GRATIFY, I TAKE AN	INTEREST	IN YOUNG MEN; BUT I DO NOT MISCONDUCT MYSELF WITH
ROCK I (207)	THATS WHY I CANT BE A GOOD WIFE AND TAKE AN	INTEREST	IN YOUR CAREER. /SIR ARTHUR/ STUFF! POLITICS ARE
MTH5 (211)	BEGAN TO CHANGE BIT BY BIT. I KEPT A SORT OF	INTEREST	IN YOUR HEAD AND ARMS LONG AFTER I LOST INTEREST IN
MTH2 (66)	THEN, AS A BIOLOGIST, I DONT TAKE THE SLIGHTEST	INTEREST	IN YOUR POLITICS; AND I SHALL NOT WALK ACROSS THE
MTH5 (211)	INTEREST IN YOUR HEAD AND ARMS LONG AFTER I LOST	INTEREST	IN YOUR WHOLE BODY, AND NOW THAT HAS GONE.
MRS PREFACE(161)	HAVE A MONOPOLY OF THE THEATRE AS FAR AS SEXUAL	INTEREST	IS CONCERNED. WHAT IS MORE, THE REPULSIVENESS OF
3PLA PREFACE(R20)	STORY, NOT TO BE LAID DOWN UNTIL FINISHED. LOVE	INTEREST	IS IMPOSSIBLE ON ITS SCIENTIFIC PLANE: NOTHING
DEST (193)	LETS ITS DUTY GET ON THE OPPOSITE SIDE TO ITS	INTEREST	IS LOST, HE-- /LADY/ W-W-W-W-W-WH! DO STOP A
SUPR PREFACE(R20)	PLAYS AND HIS POPULAR PLAYS ALIKE THE LOVE	INTEREST	IS THE INTEREST OF SEEING THE WOMAN HUNT THE MAN
MTH3 (101)	FOR SOMETHING TO DO? /BURGE-LUBIN/ WHAT EARTHLY	INTEREST	IS THERE IN LOOKING AT A MOVING PICTURE OF A LOT OF
MRS PREFACE(164)	WHAT THEY LIKE, WITHOUT REGARD TO THE PUBLIC	INTEREST	. BUT THAT IS NOT THE ALTERNATIVE. THE MANAGERS OF
HART PREFACE(11)	MATTERS LYING OUTSIDE THEIR LITTLE CIRCLE OF	INTEREST	. BUT THE ORDINARY WAR-CONSCIOUS CIVILIAN WENT MAD,
MIS. PREFACE(29)	THEY DISCUSS NOTHING ELSE WITH FULLY-AWAKENED	INTEREST	. COMMONER AND LESS CULTIVATED PEOPLE, EVEN WHEN
PYGM EPILOG (291)	SHE WOULD BE HIS NEAREST AND FONDEST AND WARMEST	INTEREST	. EVEN HAD THERE BEEN NO MOTHER-RIVAL, SHE WOULD
LADY PREFACE(209)	THE PESSIMISM OF SHAKESPEAR AND SWIFT WITH KEEN	INTEREST	. HE DELIGHTED IN A HIDEOUS CONCEPTION WHICH HE
JITT III SD(52)	AS THEY PROVE ONE AFTER ANOTHER TO BE OF NO	INTEREST	. HER SIGHS AND EXCLAMATIONS OF DISAPPOINTMENT AND

BULL I (84)	THE PROPERTY. /BROADBENT/ BUT HE WOULDNT PAY THE	INTEREST	. I HAD TO FORECLOSE ON BEHALF OF THE SYNDICATE. SO
BULL IV (173)	IS WORTH; SO THEY WILL BE ABLE TO PAY YOU THE	INTEREST	. /BROADBENT/ AH, YOU ARE A POET, MR KEEGAN, NOT A
BULL II SD(106)	BEAMING AT THE STONE AND THE TOWER WITH FATUOUS	INTEREST	. /CORNELIUS/ OH, BE THE HOKEY, THE SAMMIN'S BROKE
SIM II (63)	HAVE BEEN NO DISTURBANCES AND LITTLE POPULAR	INTEREST	. /KANCHIN/ THE VARIOUS INTERNATIONAL BOARDS ARE
APPL INTRLUD(245)	HER DEVOTION TO IT GIVES US A TOPIC OF ENDLESS	INTEREST	. /ORINTHIA/ WELL, GO TO HER: I AM NOT DETAINING
JOAN 2 (73)	HOWEVER, I CAN GET ON VERY WELL WITHOUT YOUR	INTEREST	. /THE ARCHBISHOP/ YOUR HIGHNESS IS TAKING OFFENCE
VWOO 1 (117)	IF YOU CARED; OR IF IT WAS OF THE SMALLEST	INTEREST	. /Z/ OH, I'D NEVER THINK OF YOU AS A STRANGER.
3PLA PREFACE(R23)	OF THE MAN OF THOUGHT WHOM SHAMS CANNOT ILLUDE OR	INTEREST	. THAT COMBINATION WILL BE ON ONE SIDE; AND
MILL IV (191)	AND WAS AT HIS WITS' END TO PAY THE MORTGAGE	INTEREST	. THE NEXT THING WE KNEW, THE GIRL HAD PAID OFF THE
GENV IV (88)	OCCASION ONLY, YOU ARE NOT THE CENTRE OF EUROPEAN	INTEREST	. THE STUPENDOUS AND COLOSSAL JOKE OF THE PRESENT
BULL PREFACE(33)	TO JUSTICE IS THE ELIMINATION OF EVERY	INTEREST	. WHEN WE WANT AN ARBITRATOR OR AN UMPIRE, WE TURN
CAPT III (278)	OF HIS VICTORY) OH, MY DEAR, YOU MUSTNT ACT IN MY	INTEREST	. YOU MUST GIVE YOUR EVIDENCE WITH ABSOLUTE
SUPR I (41)	A DEVILISH CHARM-- OR NO: NOT A CHARM, A SUBTLE	INTEREST	(SHE LAUGHS)-- JUST SO: YOU KNOW IT; AND YOU
SHAK PREFACE(136)	PROFESSIONAL SCHOLAR OF HIM. THESE CIRCUMSTANCES	INTEREST	ME BECAUSE THEY ARE JUST LIKE MY OWN. THEY WERE A
SUPR III (81)	YOU HAVE NO ROMANCE IN YOU. (TO MENDOZA) YOU	INTEREST	ME EXTREMELY, PRESIDENT. NEVER MIND HENRY: HE CAN
OVER PREFACE(167)	MY DEAR SIR: SUCH MANUFACTURED CEREMONIES DO NOT	INTEREST	ME IN THE LEAST. I KNOW HOW A MAN IS TRIED, AND HOW
MTH5 (207)	AND A WOMAN. /THE ANCIENT/ IT HAS LONG CEASED TO	INTEREST	ME IN THE WAY IT INTERESTS YOU. AND WHEN ANYTHING
GENV III (69)	A PRESIDENT? /THE JEW/ NO, MADAM. BUT IT WOULD	INTEREST	ME TO HEAR IT. /THE WIDOW/ I WOULD SHOOT EVERY JEW
BARB III (315)	DOESNT INTEREST ME. /LADY BRITOMART/ HE DOES	INTEREST	ME. HE IS OUR SON. /UNDERSHAFT/ DO YOU REALLY THINK
MTH4 II (176)	ON A TRIPOD AND PRETENDING TO BE DRUNK DO NOT	INTEREST	ME. HER WORDS ARE PUT INTO HER MOUTH, NOT BY A GOD,
MTH3 (98)	TEACH YOU MARINE GOLF? /CONFUCIUS/ IT DOES NOT	INTEREST	ME. I AM NOT A BARBARIAN. /BURGE-LUBIN/ YOU MEAN
GETT (330)	AND VERY GOOD, AND VERY REAL, IF YOU ARE TO	INTEREST	ME. IF GEORGE TAKES A FANCY TO YOU, AND YOU AMUSE
CATH PREFACE(153)	CATHERINE'S DIPLOMACY AND HER CONQUESTS DO NOT	INTEREST	ME. IT IS CLEAR TO ME THAT NEITHER SHE NOR THE
BARB III (315)	(RATHER WEARILY) DONT, MY DEAR. STEPHEN DOESNT	INTEREST	ME. /LADY BRITOMART/ HE DOES INTEREST ME. HE IS OUR
2TRU I (44)	SWEETIE OUT, POPS. HER AMOROUS EMOTIONS DO NOT	INTEREST	ME. /THE BURGLAR/ YOU MISUNDERSTAND. SWEETIE'S
MTH5 (207)	OH, I WAS NOT LOOKING AT YOU. YOUR LOOKS DO NOT	INTEREST	ME. /THE MAIDEN/ THANK YOU. THEY ALL LAUGH. /THE
MTH2 (51)	THAT SATISFY YOU? /FRANKLYN/ IT DOES NOT EVEN	INTEREST	ME. SUPPOSE YOUR FRIENDS DO COMMIT THEMSELVES TO
3PLA PREFACE(R29)	STRANGER-- THAT THE LAW OF HIS OWN NATURE, AND NO	INTEREST	NOR LUST WHATSOEVER, FORBAD HIM TO CRY OUT THAT THE
UNPL PREFACE(R7)	THIS INSANE GIFT, I MUST HAVE CONJURED SO AS TO	INTEREST	NOT ONLY MY OWN IMAGINATION, BUT THAT OF AT LEAST
3PLA PREFACE(R14)	NOT EITHER OF THEM HAVE STAKED A FARTHING ON THE	INTEREST	OF A GENUINE PROBLEM. IN FACT THESE SO-CALLED
DOCT PREFACE(28)	CAN HAVE NO INTEREST IN THE MATTER EXCEPT THE	INTEREST	OF A REFORMER IN ABOLISHING A CORRUPT AND
VWOO 1 (115)	ARE GOING EAST. /Z/ I ALWAYS THINK IT ADDS TO THE	INTEREST	OF A VOYAGE HAVING TO PUT ON YOUR WATCH. /A/ I AM
CLEO II SD(120)	IN HAND IS IN MARKED CONTRAST TO THE KINDLY	INTEREST	OF CAESAR, WHO LOOKS AT THE SCENE, WHICH IS NEW TO
FABL PREFACE(82)	VENTRILOQUIST, DEMOCRACY MEANS GOVERNMENT IN THE	INTEREST	OF EVERYBODY. IT MOST EMPHATICALLY DOES NOT MEAN
FABL VI (124)	YES: THAT IS THE STORY. BUT WHERE IS THE	INTEREST	OF IT FOR YOU? /MAIDEN 5/ WELL, A STORY IS A
LION PREFACE(27)	NOT SAFE TO REJECT THE STORY AS INVENTED IN THE	INTEREST	OF MATTHEW'S DETERMINATION THAT JESUS SHALL HAVE
KING PREFACE(154)	AND FREQUENT WORSE PLACES. STILL, THOUGH THE	INTEREST	OF MY PLAY LIES MAINLY IN THE CLASH OF CHARLES,
SUPR PREFACE(R20)	HIS POPULAR PLAYS ALIKE THE LOVE INTEREST IS THE	INTEREST	OF SEEING THE WOMAN HUNT THE MAN DOWN. SHE MAY DO
BULL IV (159)	DULL FOR YOU. /LARRY/ NO: I HAVNT EXHAUSTED THE	INTEREST	OF STROLLING ABOUT THE OLD PLACES AND REMEMBERING
NEVR II SD(225)	AS TREASON TO THE ABOUNDING SUFFICIENCY AND	INTEREST	OF THE ACTUAL. HE HAS A CERTAIN EXPRESSION PECULIAR
GETT PREFACE(253)	ALL CAUSES. BUT IT MUST NOT BE FORGOTTEN THAT THE	INTEREST	OF THE CHILDREN FORMS ONE OF THE MOST POWERFUL
MIS. PREFACE(28)	SAID ABOUT THE OPPOSITION TO REFORM OF THE VESTED	INTEREST	OF THE CLASSICAL AND COERCIVE SCHOOLMASTER. HE,
MIS. PREFACE(70)	THE QUESTION FROM THE POINT OF VIEW OF THE TOTAL	INTEREST	OF THE COMMUNITY, WHICH MUST ALWAYS CONSIST OF
MILL PREFACE(128)	INTEREST AND NOT SOLELY IN THE IMMEDIATE PERSONAL	INTEREST	OF THE DECIDER. IT WAS ARGUED BY OUR CLASSICAL
SUPR HANDBOK(182)	PUBLIC OR COLLECTIVE CONDITIONS, IMPOSED IN THE	INTEREST	OF THE GENERAL WELFARE WITHOUT ANY REGARD FOR
BARB PREFACE(229)	THE IMPULSE TO MAKE THEM WAS PIOUS OR THAT THE	INTEREST	OF THE HEARERS IS WHOLESOME. AS WELL MIGHT WE
METH PREFACE(R89)	OF THE GARDEN OF EDEN. I EXPLOIT THE ETERNAL	INTEREST	OF THE PHILOSOPHER'S STONE WHICH ENABLES MEN TO
CAND I (87)	(IN A PAROXYSM OF PUBLIC SPIRIT) I HACTED IN THE	INTEREST	OF THE RATEPAYERS, JAMES. IT WAS THE LOWEST TENDER:
LION PREFACE(83)	AND HIGHLY SUSCEPTIBLE TO THE BEAUTY AND	INTEREST	OF THE REAL WORKINGS OF THE HOLY GHOST, TRY TO LIVE
BARB III (329)	LIKE A BIT OF PAPER. (WARMING TO THE SCIENTIFIC	INTEREST	OF THE SUBJECT) DID YOU KNOW THAT, UNDERSHAFT?
POSN PREFACE(365)	OTHER DIRECTIONS. THIRD, THERE WAS THE COMMERCIAL	INTEREST	OF THE THEATRICAL MANAGERS AND THEIR SYNDICATES OF
POSN PREFACE(365)	OF ENORMOUS VALUE. FOURTH, THERE WAS THE POWERFUL	INTEREST	OF THE TRADE IN INTOXICATING LIQUORS, FIERCELY
ROCK PREFACE(153)	INTO OR SUPERSEDED BY A GOVERNMENT ACTING IN THE	INTEREST	OF THE WHOLE PEOPLE, THAT GOVERNMENT WILL NOT
3PLA PREFACE(R20)	TALES EXPOSE, FURTHER, THE DELUSION THAT THE	INTEREST	OF THIS MOST CAPRICIOUS, MOST TRANSIENT, MOST
WIDO II (42)	HOUSES. MY HANDS ARE CLEAN AS FAR AS THAT GOES.	INTEREST	ON A MORTGAGE. /SARTORIUS/ (FORCIBLY) YES: A
CATH PREFACE(154)	ATROCITIES, NOT FORGETTING THE INDISPENSABLE LOVE	INTEREST	ON AN ENORMOUS AND UTTERLY INDECOROUS SCALE.
3PLA PREFACE(R14)	PLAYS INVARIABLY DEPENDED FOR THEIR DRAMATIC	INTEREST	ON FOREGONE CONCLUSIONS OF THE MOST HEARTWEARYING
DEVL I SD(22)	HERSELF CONVULSIVELY RIGID) TO BE PAID OUT OF THE	INTEREST	ON HER OWN MONEY"-- THERE'S A WAY TO PUT IT, MR
SUPR I SD(43)	COMES TO HER WITHOUT ANY COMPULSION OR EVEN	INTEREST	ON HER PART; BESIDES, THERE IS SOME FUN IN ANN, BUT
MRS III (231)	SHOULDNT I INVEST MY MONEY THAT WAY? I TAKE THE	INTEREST	ON MY CAPITAL LIKE OTHER PEOPLE: I HOPE YOU DONT
DOCT PREFACE(4)	BE IMPARTIAL WHERE THEY HAVE A STRONG PECUNIARY	INTEREST	ON ONE SIDE? NOBODY SUPPOSES THAT DOCTORS ARE LESS
MIS. PREFACE(19)	TO TURNKEYS DISCOURSING WITHOUT CHARM OR	INTEREST	ON SUBJECTS THAT THEY DONT UNDERSTAND AND DONT CARE
ROCK II (241)	WILLING TO CALL IT A QUARTER OF A MILLION AND PAY	INTEREST	ON THAT SUM. BUT WHAT GOOD IS THAT TO A MAN IN THE
APPL II (259)	CONCERNS THAT AFTER PAYING YOURSELVES THE	INTEREST	ON THE DEBT YOU HAVE TO SEND US TWO THOUSAND
GETT (319)	INTO THE WORLD: SAY A THOUSAND POUNDS APIECE. THE	INTEREST	ON THIS COULD GO TOWARDS THE SUPPORT OF THE CHILD
GENV I (30)	AFFORD ANYTHING. THE INTELLECTUAL BUDGET IS THE	INTEREST	ON TWO MILLION PAPER FRANCS THAT ONE IS GLAD TO GET
SUPR HANDBOK(201)	AND NOT TO MONEY, TO STATESMANSHIP AND NOT TO	INTEREST	OR MUTINY, WE ARE DISILLUSIONED. FOR EXAMPLE, WE
GETT (317)	I SAY, YOU CAN PAY THE DAMAGES AND STOP THE	INTEREST	OUT OF MY SALARY. /SOAMES/ YOU FORGET THAT UNDER
3PLA PREFACE(R12)	WAS DOOMED TO ATTEND THEM. ON THE OTHER HAND, TO	INTEREST	PEOPLE OF DIVERS AGES, CLASSES, AND TEMPERAMENTS BY
SUPR IV (156)	ME-- THOUGH I KNOW I AM SPEAKING IN MY OWN	INTEREST	-- THERE IS ANOTHER SIDE TO THIS QUESTION. IS IT
CLEO PRO2 (103)	GODS. /FTATATEETA/ (RETORTING HIS ARROGANCE WITH	INTEREST	) BELZANOR: I AM FTATATEETA, THE QUEEN'S CHIEF
MTH4 I (143)	WOMAN/ (TAKING IT AND EXAMINING IT WITHOUT MUCH	INTEREST	) I DO NOT UNDERSTAND A SINGLE WORD OF WHAT YOU
HART II (96)	LOOK. /ELLIE/ (CONTEMPLATING MANGAN WITHOUT	INTEREST	) I KNOW. HE IS ONLY ASLEEP. WE HAD A TALK AFTER
ARMS III (66)	(FACING HER AND RETORTING HER CONTEMPT WITH	INTEREST	) MY LOVE, STRONGER THAN ANYTHING YOU CAN FEEL,
BULL III (139)	BAD CESS TO THEM! /BROADBENT/ (WITH SYMPATHETIC	INTEREST	) THEN YOU ARE NOT THE FIRST MARTYR OF YOUR FAMILY,
CLEO II (127)	/POTHINUS/ (RETORTING THE DEFIANCE WITH	INTEREST	) WELL SAID, RUFIO. WHY NOT? /RUFIO/ TRY,
PYGM I (209)	COPPER'S NARK, SIR. /THE NOTE TAKER/ (WITH QUICK	INTEREST	) WHATS A COPPER'S NARK? /THE BYSTANDER/ (INAPT
HART I (71)	LADY UTTERWORD. /LADY UTTERWORD/ (WITH MARKED	INTEREST	) WHO IS THAT GENTLEMAN WALKING IN THE GARDEN WITH
SIM PRO,3, (32)	MEANWHILE READING THE TITLE WITH A POLITE SHOW OF	INTEREST	) " WHERE WILL YOU SPEND ETERNITY? " /THE L.T./ (
DEST (170)	(TURNING TO HER QUICKLY WITH A FLASH OF STRONG	INTEREST	), /LADY/ (EARNESTLY, WITH RISING ENTHUSIASM) WHAT
MTH2 (57)	ALREADY TALKING CALMLY, BUT WITHOUT A PRETENCE OF	INTEREST	), /LUBIN/ THE LABOR PARTY! OH NO, MR BARNABAS.
GETT (342)	BY HER, WATCHING HER WITH INTENSE SURPRISE AND	INTEREST	), /MRS GEORGE/ NO MUSIC? /SOAMES/ NO. (HE STEALS
METH PREFACE(R83)	EVEN HIS DESIGN WOULD HAVE HAD ONLY AN ACADEMIC	INTEREST	; BUT AS A PAINTER OF PROPHETS AND SIBYLS HE IS
POSN PREFACE(405)	THEATRES, FACTORIES ARE REGULATED IN THE PUBLIC	INTEREST	; BUT THERE IS NO CENSORSHIP OF FACTORIES, FOR
SIM I SD(36)	THE RAISED FLOWER GARDEN IS THE CENTRE OF	INTEREST	; FOR IN IT ARE FOUR SHRINES MARKING THE CORNERS OF
HART PREFACE(13)	FROM THE POINT OF VIEW OF THEIR OWN PERSONAL	INTEREST	; FOR THEY WERE PERSECUTED WITH SAVAGE LOGICALITY
MTH2 (60)	SOME EXTENT POLITICAL, WE SHOULD HEAR WITH GREAT	INTEREST	SOMETHING ABOUT YOUR POLITICAL AIMS, MR LUBIN.
BULL PREFACE(71)	THOUGH ITS FREEDOM HAS DESTROYED ALL THE ROMANTIC	INTEREST	THAT USED TO ATTACH TO IT, HAS BECOME AT LAST
MTH2 (82)	QUITE SO. MY IDEA IS THAT WHILST WE SHOULD	INTEREST	THE ELECTORATE IN THIS AS A SORT OF RELIGIOUS
APPL PREFACE(194)	PROCEEDED TO DISCUSS WHAT COULD BE DONE TO	INTEREST	THE PROPER PEOPLE IN IT. TO MY AMAZEMENT GATTIE
APPL PREFACE(194)	OF TRADE TO DEAL WITH AN INVENTOR WHO WISHED TO	INTEREST	THEM, NOT IN HIS NEW MACHINES, BUT IN THE
MTH5 (219)	AS MOST OF THEM HAVE LONG AGO EXHAUSTED ALL THE	INTEREST	THERE IS IN OBSERVING CHILDREN AND CONVERSING WITH
MTH2 (73)	MAN. BUT WILL YOU TELL ME WHAT EARTHLY USE OR	INTEREST	THERE IS IN A CONCLUSION THAT CANNOT BE REALIZED..
APPL PREFACE(185)	AND INCOME TAX AND DEATH DUTIES WOULD SAVE THE	INTEREST	THEY NOW HAVE TO PAY ON IT: THAT IS ALL. I SHOULD
3PLA PREFACE(R16)	WHEN THEIR ATTENTION IS ENTIRELY CAPTURED, THEIR	INTEREST	THOROUGHLY AROUSED, THEIR SYMPATHIES RAISED TO THE
INCA (250)	HOW COULD A HUMBLE PERSON LIKE MYSELF BE OF ANY	INTEREST	TO A PRINCE WHO IS SURROUNDED WITH THE ABLEST AND
GETT (182)	1908. N.B.-- THERE IS A POINT OF SOME TECHNICAL	INTEREST	TO BE NOTED IN THIS PLAY. THE CUSTOMARY DIVISION
NEVR II (226)	WITH A GENTLE MELODY IN IT THAT GIVES SYMPATHETIC	INTEREST	TO HIS MOST COMMONPLACE REMARK; AND HE SPEAKS WITH
CAPT NOTES (302)	REGENT ST. WHEN I WAS WALKING WITH MY MOTHER, HER	INTEREST	WAS INSTANTLY KINDLED; AND THE FOLLOWING
GETT PREFACE(253)	OBSTACLE TO DIVORCE: THEY GIVE PARENTS A COMMON	INTEREST	WHICH KEEPS TOGETHER MANY A COUPLE WHO, IF
OVER PREFACE(157)	NAME OF LOVE OF A GENEROUS NATURAL ATTRACTION AND	INTEREST	WITH THE MURDEROUS JEALOUSY THAT FASTENS ON AND
MTH4 I (141)	ON ME, MADAM. I FEAR MY CONVERSATION DOES NOT	INTEREST	YOU. IF NOT, THE REMEDY IS IN YOUR OWN HANDS. /THE
MTH2 (67)	PROGRAM WILL BE THROWN AWAY ON YOU. IT WOULD NOT	INTEREST	YOU. /BURGE/ (WITH CHALLENGING AUDACITY) TRY.
BULL IV (177)	IT WILL NOT STOP THE SYNDICATE; AND IT WILL NOT	INTEREST	YOUNG IRELAND SO MUCH AS MY FRIEND'S GOSPEL OF
MTH5 (231)	KEEP OFF THE PRIMITIVE TRIBES, PYGMALION. THEY	INTEREST	YOU; BUT THEY BORE THESE YOUNG THINGS. /PYGMALION/
DOCT III (145)	INTERESTING. /LOUIS/ OH, WELL, IF IT WOULD	INTEREST	YOU, AND IF IT WONT HURT, THATS ANOTHER MATTER. HOW
MRS III (234)	I'LL JUST TELL YOU THIS BEFORE I GO. IT MAY	INTEREST	YOU, SINCE YOURE SO FOND OF ONE ANOTHER. ALLOW ME,

FABL PREFACE(66)	FABLES WHICH, HOWEVER FARFETCHED, CAN AT LEAST	INTEREST	, AMUSE, AND PERHAPS ENLIGHTEN THOSE CAPABLE OF
2TRU II (68)	ONLY A BEGINNER; AND WHAT YOU THINK IS LOVE, AND	INTEREST	, AND ALL THAT, IS NOT REAL LOVE AT ALL: THREE
KING PREFACE(156)	HE IS REPRESENTED AS HAVING PRACTICALLY NO OTHER	INTEREST	, AND BEING A DISGRACEFULLY UNFAITHFUL HUSBAND. IT
BARB PREFACE(224)	MONEY IN THE COUNTRY CONSISTS OF A MASS OF RENT,	INTEREST	, AND PROFIT, EVERY PENNY OF WHICH IS BOUND UP WITH
GENV PREFACE(16)	IN PURSUIT OF SURPLUS VALUE, AS MARX CALLED RENT,	INTEREST	, AND PROFIT, THEY GROUP THEMSELVES IN POLITICAL
ARMS III (53)	NO. (HE SITS DOWN BESIDE HER, WITH RENEWED	INTEREST	, AND SAYS, WITH SOME COMPLACENCY) WHEN DID YOU
SUPR PREFACE(R25)	CONDUCT, WHOSE POWER OF ATTENTION AND SCOPE OF	INTEREST	, ARE MEASURED BY THE BRITISH THEATRE AS YOU KNOW
BULL PREFACE(35)	OF CHARACTER, BUT OF COMPARATIVE DIRECTNESS OF	INTEREST	, CONCENTRATION OF FORCE ON ONE NARROW ISSUE,
ROCK PREFACE(174)	COMMUNISM FOR OURSELVES OR NOT, IT IS OUR CLEAR	INTEREST	, EVEN FROM THE POINT OF VIEW OF OUR CRUDEST AND
SUPR PREFACE(R11)	PREOCCUPATION WITH SEX, IS REALLY VOID OF SEXUAL	INTEREST	, GOOD LOOKS ARE MORE DESIRED THAN HISTRIONIC
CLEO II (133)	KNEELING BESIDE HIM AND LOOKING AT HIM WITH EAGER	INTEREST	, HALF REAL, HALF AFFECTED TO SHEW HOW INTELLIGENT
CAND II (119)	SO EUGENE SAYS. /CANDIDA/ (WITH LIVELY	INTEREST	, LEANING OVER TO HIM WITH HER ARMS ON HIS KNEE)
BULL PREFACE(35)	THAN IN IRELAND. HE HAS NO RESPONSIBILITY, NO	INTEREST	, NO STATUS OUTSIDE HIS OWN COUNTRY AND HIS OWN
MRS PREFACE(165)	INDUCE, NOT VOLUPTUOUS REVERIE BUT INTELLECTUAL	INTEREST	, NOT ROMANTIC RHAPSODY BUT HUMANE CONCERN.
CATH PREFACE(154)	THERE WAS NO ROMANCE, NO SCIENTIFIC POLITICAL	INTEREST	, NOTHING THAT A SANE MIND CAN NOW RETAIN EVEN IF
MTH1 I SD(19)	TO HER). EVE'S FACE LIGHTS UP WITH INTENSE	INTEREST	, WHICH INCREASES UNTIL AN EXPRESSION OF
SUPR PREFACE(R12)	OF TOTAL FAILURE TO EDIFY AND PARTIAL FAILURE TO	INTEREST	, WHICH IS AS FAMILIAR TO YOU IN THE THEATRES AS IT
GENV IV (95)	COUNTRY WOULD DO IN THE EVENT OF A CONFLICT OF	INTEREST	, YOU SAID FRANKLY YOU DID NOT KNOW. /SIR O./ WELL,
3PLA PREFACE(R20)	ACCEPT A STORY OR PRODUCE A PLAY WITHOUT " LOVE	INTEREST	" IN IT. TAKE, FOR A RECENT EXAMPLE, MR H.G.

INTERESTED

2TRU II (63)	THINGS; AND IT IS IN SPIRITUAL THINGS THAT I AM	INTERESTED	: THEY ALONE CALL MY GIFT INTO FULL PLAY. /THE
BULL PREFACE(61)	FOSTERED DURING THE LAST YEAR BY UNSCRUPULOUS AND	INTERESTED	AGITATORS." AGAIN, " IT IS MY DUTY TO WARN YOU OF
MTH5 (217)	YOU. YOU WILL NOT BE VERY HAPPY; BUT YOU WILL BE	INTERESTED	AND AMUSED BY THE NOVELTY OF THE WORLD; AND YOUR
MILL II SD(166)	AND BISCUITS ARE STILL ON THE TABLE. SHE LOOKS	INTERESTED	AND HAPPY. HE IS IN THE WORST OF TEMPERS.
2TRU III SD(87)	SOMETHING NOBLER THAN KISSING THEM. THE SERGEANT,	INTERESTED	AND OVERAWED, SITS DOWN QUIETLY AND MAKES SWEETIE
JITT I (17)	WOMAN CAN LOVE THE CHILD OF THE MAN SHE HAS	INTERESTED	AND SAVED. I AM NOT CLEVER ENOUGH TO SHARE THE
MRS II (215)	DRUDGE BEFORE I WAS FORTY? /VIVIE/ (INTENSELY	INTERESTED	BY THIS TIME) NO; BUT WHY DID YOU CHOOSE THAT
SUPR PREFACE(R34)	ONLY KNOW WHAT HAS HAPPENED TO DAVID, AND ARE NOT	INTERESTED	ENOUGH IN HIM TO WONDER WHAT HIS POLITICS OR
LION PREFACE(42)	SCRAPS WHICH HE HAS PICKED UP; HE IS FAR MORE	INTERESTED	IN A NOTION OF HIS OWN THAT MEN CAN ESCAPE DEATH
SUPR II SD(48)	OF THE HOUSE ON HIS LEFT WERE HE NOT FAR TOO MUCH	INTERESTED	IN A PAIR OF SUPINE LEGS IN DUNGAREE OVERALLS
LADY PREFACE(217)	DICKS, AND HARRYS OF HIS TIME TO BE ANY MORE	INTERESTED	IN DRAMATIC POETRY THAN NEWTON, LATER ON,
HART I (74)	LIES I HAVE TO TELL HER! /LADY UTTERWORD/ (NOT	INTERESTED	IN ELLIE) WHEN YOU SAW ME WHAT DID YOU MEAN BY
PYGM II SD(218)	SCIENTIFIC TYPE, HEARTILY, EVEN VIOLENTLY	INTERESTED	IN EVERYTHING THAT CAN BE STUDIED AS A SCIENTIFIC
MTH5 (206)	A CREATURE ON EARTH CALLED A DOG. THOSE WHO ARE	INTERESTED	IN EXTINCT FORMS OF LIFE WILL TELL YOU THAT IT
LADY PREFACE(217)	POETRY THAN NEWTON, LATER ON, EXPECTED THEM TO BE	INTERESTED	IN FLUXIONS. AND WHEN WE COME TO THE QUESTION
KING I (220)	WILL YOU TAKE HER GRACE OF CLEVELAND, AS YOU ARE	INTERESTED	IN HER CURVES? /BARBARA/ (VIOLENTLY) NO. I AM
APPL INTRLUD(245)	COULD TALK OF NOTHING ELSE. BUT I AM VERY MUCH	INTERESTED	IN HER DEPARTMENT. HER DEVOTION TO IT GIVES US A
APPL INTRLUD(245)	IF LYSISTRATA HAD A LOVER I SHOULD NOT BE	INTERESTED	IN HIM IN THE LEAST; AND SHE WOULD BORE ME TO
BULL PREFACE(28)	HAS FOUND IN HIS NURSE A FOSTER-MOTHER MORE	INTERESTED	IN HIM THAN HIS ACTUAL MOTHER. THEY LOVE THE
PYGM EPILOG (302)	INFATUATION OF COMMONER SOULS. SHE IS IMMENSELY	INTERESTED	IN HIM. SHE HAS EVEN SECRET MISCHIEVOUS MOMENTS
GETT SD(281)	AND THE WAYS OF A SUCCESSFUL MAN WHO IS ALWAYS	INTERESTED	IN HIMSELF AND GENERALLY RATHER WELL PLEASED WITH
CYMB FORWORD(136)	CANNOT SHARE THESE INFANTILE JOYS. HAVING BECOME	INTERESTED	IN IACHIMO, IN IMOGEN, AND EVEN IN THE TWO LONG
DOCT PREFACE(20)	DOCTORS (PROBABLY A LARGE MAJORITY) WHO ARE NOT	INTERESTED	IN IT, AND PRACTISE ONLY TO EARN THEIR BREAD.
KING I (174)	OF LIFE. MR ROWLEY: YOU ARE WELL KNOWN TO BE AS	INTERESTED	IN LADIES AS I AM INTERESTED IN THE SCRIPTURES;
KING PREFACE(154)	ARE NOT MEANT FOR SUCH. AND ANYONE WHO IS MORE	INTERESTED	IN LADY CASTLEMAINE'S HIPS THAN IN FOX'S
PYGM EPILOG (289)	BACHELOR'S WIFE, ESPECIALLY IF HE IS SO LITTLE	INTERESTED	IN MARRIAGE THAT A DETERMINED AND DEVOTED WOMAN
HART II (95)	(RELAXING HER CONTEMPTUOUS ATTITUDE, QUITE	INTERESTED	IN MAZZINI NOW) YOU KNOW, I REALLY THINK YOU MUST
DOCT II (129)	FOR THAT SORT OF THING. I KNOW WHEN A WOMAN IS	INTERESTED	IN ME. SHE IS. /SIR PATRICK/ WELL, SOMETIMES A
SUPR II (65)	NAME. IT IS ONLY RIGHT TO TELL YOU, SINCE YOU ARE	INTERESTED	IN MISS-- ER-- IN VIOLET. /OCTAVIUS/ (
WIDO III (55)	I MAY TAKE IT AWAY? (NO ANSWER). OH, YOU ARE	INTERESTED	IN MR LICKCHEESE'S BOOK, MISS. BLANCHE SPRINGS
MTH2 (58)	THAT ALL THE DEAD PEOPLE WE FEEL ESPECIALLY	INTERESTED	IN MUST HAVE BEEN OURSELVES. YOU MUST BE HORACE'S
GETT (296)	IS IT EDITH? /HOTCHKISS/ I'M SO SORRY. I GET SO	INTERESTED	IN MYSELF THAT I THRUST MYSELF INTO THE FRONT OF
MILL I (151)	/PATRICIA/ YOU DONT UNDERSTAND MEN; THEY GET	INTERESTED	IN OTHER THINGS AND NEGLECT THEMSELVES UNLESS
PYGM II (228)	MEAN HER ANY HARM; BUT WHEN YOU GET WHAT YOU CALL	INTERESTED	IN PEOPLE'S ACCENTS, YOU NEVER THINK OR CARE WHAT
MTH2 (49)	OF IT. I WANT TO CULTIVATE MY GARDEN. I AM NOT	INTERESTED	IN POLITICS: I AM INTERESTED IN ROSES. I HAVNT A
FABL PREFACE(65)	WAS LIVING IN AN IMAGINARY WORLD. DEEPLY AS I WAS	INTERESTED	IN POLITICS, HAMLET AND FALSTAFF WERE MORE ALIVE
2TRU II (67)	LUMP IT. YOU MAY BE IN LOVE WITH POPSY; BUT YOURE	INTERESTED	IN PRIVATE MEEK, THOUGH WHAT YOU SEE IN THAT DRY
LION PREFACE(10)	PEOPLE, AND A SMALL PERCENTAGE OF PERSONS DEEPLY	INTERESTED	IN RELIGION AND CONCERNED ABOUT THEIR OWN SOULS
MTH2 (47)	DEVOTED MYSELF TO BIOLOGY! I HAVE ALWAYS BEEN	INTERESTED	IN ROCKS AND STRATA AND VOLCANOES AND SO FORTH:
MTH2 (49)	MY GARDEN. I AM NOT INTERESTED IN POLITICS: I AM	INTERESTED	IN ROSES. I HAVNT A SCRAP OF AMBITION. I WENT
DOCT PREFACE(20)	IS AN ART, NOT A SCIENCE: ANY LAYMAN WHO IS	INTERESTED	IN SCIENCE SUFFICIENTLY TO TAKE IN ONE OF THE
ROCK I (215)	AT THIS GAME NOW FOR FIFTY YEAR. /SIR ARTHUR/ (	INTERESTED	IN SPITE OF HIMSELF) WHAT GAME? DEPUTATIONS?
METH PREFACE(R79)	THE WORLD, AND BE VERY GLAD TO FIND HIS LADDIE AS	INTERESTED	IN SUCH THINGS AS IN MARBLES OR POLICE AND
MTH4 I (157)	IT IS ALSO A GREAT SCIENTIFIC FACT. I AM NOT	INTERESTED	IN THE CHEMICALS AND THE MICROBES: I LEAVE THEM
GENV I (44)	YESTERDAY AS A CULTIVATED AND HUMANE GENTLEMAN,	INTERESTED	IN THE CHURCH OF ENGLAND, AND NOW IT TURNS OUT
PRES (144)	ALL IN THE SAME FIX AS WE ARE. I'M MUCH MORE	INTERESTED	IN THE DEATH-RATE IN LAMBETH THAN IN THE GERMAN
MTH2 (59)	MR BURGE. YOU KNOW, MR LUBIN, I AM FRIGHTFULLY	INTERESTED	IN THE LABOR MOVEMENT, AND IN THEOSOPHY, AND IN
GENV II (52)	SO UNEXPECTEDLY IN YOUR HANDS? /BEGONIA/ WAS I	INTERESTED	IN THE LEAGUE? LET ME SEE. YOU KNOW THAT THERE
GENV II (52)	ASK YOU A PERSONAL QUESTION? HOW DID YOU BECOME	INTERESTED	IN THE LEAGUE OF NATIONS? HOW DID YOU GET THIS
JOAN 2 (73)	/THE ARCHBISHOP/ (CONTEMPTUOUSLY) I AM NOT	INTERESTED	IN THE NEWEST TOYS. /CHARLES/ (INDIGNANTLY) IT
DOCT III SD(131)	ABOUT HIS WIFE. SHE IS SITTING ON THE THRONE, NOT	INTERESTED	IN THE PAINTING, AND APPEALING TO HIM VERY
BARB I (267)	/UNDERSHAFT/ ONE MOMENT, MR LOMAX. I AM RATHER	INTERESTED	IN THE SALVATION ARMY. ITS MOTTO MIGHT BE MY OWN:
PYGM PREFACE(199)	THE WILDERNESS FOR MANY YEARS PAST. WHEN I BECAME	INTERESTED	IN THE SUBJECT TOWARDS THE END OF THE
KING I (174)	WELL KNOWN TO BE AS INTERESTED IN LADIES AS I AM	INTERESTED	IN THE SCRIPTURES; AND I THANK YOU FOR BRINGING
BARB II (290)	I AM IMPOSING ON BARBARA. I AM QUITE GENUINELY	INTERESTED	IN THE VIEWS OF THE SALVATION ARMY. THE FACT IS,
MTH3 (128)	BARNABAS! WHAT HARM ARE THEY DOING? ARNT YOU	INTERESTED	IN THEM? DONT YOU LIKE THEM? /BARNABAS/ LIKE
FABL PREFACE(91)	ANYTHING TO SAY ABOUT THEM, OR ARE IN ANY WAY	INTERESTED	IN THEM, THEY SHOULD THEN BE TAKEN INTO A MUSIC
DOCT I (104)	ATTEND ONE MOMENT. YOU WILL ALL BE INTENSELY	INTERESTED	IN THIS. I WAS PUT ON THE TRACK BY ACCIDENT. I
APPL II (270)	THE PRINCE; BUT SOMEHOW I DO NOT FEEL THAT HE IS	INTERESTED	IN WHAT I AM DOING. /BALBUS/ HE ISNT. HE WONT
HART II (118)	ELSE MATTERED TO OLD MEN. THEY CANT BE VERY	INTERESTED	IN WHAT IS GOING TO HAPPEN TO THEMSELVES.
HART I (55)	US. /MAZZINI/ (SMILING) I'M AFRAID ELLIE IS NOT	INTERESTED	IN YOUNG MEN, MRS HUSHABYE. HER TASTE IS ON THE
JOAN 1 (63)	NOTHING. /ROBERT/ IT'S ABOUT THIS GIRL YOU ARE	INTERESTED	IN. NOW, I HAVE SEEN HER. I HAVE TALKED TO HER.
UNPL PREFACE(R11)	TO THE HARVEST OF THE RENASCENCE, I WAS WARMLY	INTERESTED	. BUT IT SOON APPEARED THAT THE LANGUID DEMAND OF
BULL I (78)	FOR THE LAND DEVELOPMENT SYNDICATE, IN WHICH I AM	INTERESTED	. I AM CONVINCED THAT ALL IT NEEDS TO MAKE IT PAY
MTH2 (68)	DREAMT. BUT I UNDERSTAND THAT YOU ARE NOT REALLY	INTERESTED	. I WILL SPARE YOU, AND DROP THE SUBJECT. /LUBIN/
MTH2 (41)	TONE) YOU NEEDNT GO, YOU KNOW, IF YOU ARE REALLY	INTERESTED	. /HASLAM/ (FED UP) WELL, I'M AFRAID I OUGHT
WIDO I SD(6)	TELLS IMMEDIATELY. THE GENTLEMAN IS PERCEPTIBLY	INTERESTED	. /TRENCH/ MY MOTHER'S, OF COURSE. WHAT PUT THAT
MTH4 II (183)	DAUGHTER/ (COPYING HER MOTHER) WE SHOULD BE SO	INTERESTED	. /ZOO/ NONSENSE! ALL I CAN TELL YOU ABOUT IT IS
MTH5 (229)	PAIR. WE WILL LISTEN. WE ARE TREMENDOUSLY	INTERESTED	. TELL US ALL ABOUT IT. /PYGMALION/ (RELENTING)
PYGM II (223)	YOU RIGHT, MR HIGGINS. /PICKERING/ HIGGINS: I'M	INTERESTED	. WHAT ABOUT THE AMBASSADOR'S GARDEN PARTY? I'LL
VWOO 1 (115)	ON YOUR WATCH. /A/ I AM GLAD YOU ARE SO EASILY	INTERESTED	(HE RESUMES HIS WRITING POINTEDLY). /Z/ THE
MIS. PREFACE(25)	SCHOOLMASTERS I CAN RECOLLECT A FEW WHOSE CLASSES	INTERESTED	ME, AND WHOM I SHOULD CERTAINLY HAVE PESTERED FOR
GETT PREFACE(223)	TO TAKE A VITAL PROCESS IN WHICH WE ARE KEENLY	INTERESTED	PERSONAL INSTRUMENTS AND ASK US TO REGARD IT, AND
NEVR II (255)	WOMEN WERE CAPABLE OF NOTHING BETTER! /GLORIA/ (	INTERESTED	) AH, NOW YOU ARE BEGINNING TO TALK HUMANLY AND
2TRU II (65)	MAN THAT KEPT IT UP TIL HE DIED. /THE PATIENT/ (	INTERESTED	) AH! THEN THE THING IS POSSIBLE? /THE
DOCT II (126)	WITH HIM? /RIDGEON/ TUBERCULOSIS. /BLENKINSOP/ (	INTERESTED	) AND CAN YOU CURE THAT? /RIDGEON/ I BELIEVE SO.
BULL I (93)	RATHER. NORA HAS A FORTUNE. /BROADBENT/ (KEENLY	INTERESTED	) EH? HOW MUCH? /DOYLE/ FORTY PER ANNUM.
KING I (165)	BREECHES, HAD THE IMPUDENCE TO CALL. /NEWTON/ (	INTERESTED	) GEORGE FOX? IF HE CALLS AGAIN I WILL SEE HIM.
BULL II (106)	ANTIQUITY WORTH LOOKIN AT. /BROADBENT/ (DEEPLY	INTERESTED	) HAVE YOU ANY THEORY AS TO WHAT THE ROUND TOWERS
MTH4 I (169)	FOR YOU AND YOUR LIKE. /THE ELDERLY GENTLEMAN/ (	INTERESTED	) INDEED? PRAY, MAY I ASK WHAT IT IS? I AM A
DEVL III (59)	PRESBYTERIAN MINISTER IN THIS TOWN. /BURGOYNE/ (	INTERESTED	) INDEED! PRAY, MR ANDERSON, WHAT DO YOU
DOCT IV (160)	HE MAY DIE AT ANY MOMENT. /THE NEWSPAPER MAN/ (	INTERESTED	) IS HE AS BAD AS THAT? I SAY: I AM IN LUCK
AUGS (277)	I CANT MAKE OUT THE WORD. /AUGUSTUS/ (GREATLY	INTERESTED	) IS IT BLIGHTER? THAT IS A FAVORITE EXPRESSION
MTH5 (246)	IS THE DEAREST OF ALL. /THE NEWLY BORN/ (EAGERLY	INTERESTED	) OH! HAVE YOU GOT IT STILL? /THE SHE-ANCIENT/
JOAN 4 (105)	AND THEN REIGN AS GOD'S BAILIFFS. /CAUCHON/ (NOT	INTERESTED	) QUITE SOUND THEOLOGICALLY, MY LORD. BUT THE
BARB II (290)	MONEY AND GUNPOWDER. /CUSINS/ (SURPRISED, BUT	INTERESTED	) THAT IS THE GENERAL OPINION OF OUR GOVERNING

HART II (84)	TO ME ABOUT YOU. YOU AND ME, YOU KNOW. /ELLIE/ (	INTERESTED	) THE CAPTAIN! WHAT DID HE SAY? /MANGAN/ WELL,
DEST (166)	VIOLENCE: DANGER MAKES ME MISERABLE. /NAPOLEON/ (	INTERESTED	) THEN WHY HAVE YOU THRUST YOURSELF INTO DANGER?
DOCT I (102)	ME TO SYMPATHIZE WITH MY PATIENTS. /WALPOLE/ (	INTERESTED	) WHAT? YOURE NEVER ILL? /B.B./ NEVER.
SUPR III (79)	ONE WE CAPTURED CURED US OF THAT. /STRAKER/ (	INTERESTED	) WHAT DID IT DO? /MENDOZA/ IT CARRIED THREE
ROCK II (237)	DEXTER/ OUR PROMISE! WHOSE PROMISE? /BASHAM/ (	INTERESTED	) WHAT WAS THAT YOU SAID? ARE YOU GOING TO PUT
MTH5 (231)	TO A HIGHER POTENTIAL. /ARJILLAX/ (INTENSELY	INTERESTED	) YES; AND THEN? /PYGMALION/ THEN THE EYES AND
GETT (342)	END OF THE TABLE AND SITS ON HER RIGHT, EQUALLY	INTERESTED	). /MRS GEORGE/ DO YOU SEE NOTHING-- NOT A GREAT
MTH1 II (31)	AND I HAVE TO PRETEND TO BE SURPRISED, DELIGHTED,	INTERESTED	; THOUGH THE LAST CHILD IS LIKE THE FIRST, AND
WIDO III (54)	NO MATTER HOW DARK THEYRE KEPT. /SARTORIUS/ (	INTERESTED	, BUT CAUTIOUS) WELL? /LICKCHEESE/ IS THAT ALL
MIS. (167)	AND LOOKS FROM ONE TO THE OTHER, PLEASED AND	INTERESTED	, BUT WITHOUT ANY SIGN OF RECOGNITION) WHAT A
GENV IV (88)	THE PUBLIC? /THE SECRETARY/ THE PUBLIC IS NOT	INTERESTED	, IT SEEMS. /BEGONIA/ ONE FREE LANCE JOURNALIST
PHIL III (134)	NOT MERELY YOUR BEAUTY THAT ATTRACTS ME (JULIA,	INTERESTED	, LOOKS UP AT HIM QUICKLY): I KNOW OTHER
FANY III (301)	TO SAY I DONT BELIEVE HER. /BOBBY/ (CURIOUS AND	INTERESTED	, RESUMING HIS SEAT ON THE TABLE BESIDE HER) WHAT
DOCT I (95)	NOT A RUDIMENT! ! I WAS SO TAKEN ABACK-- SO	INTERESTED	, THAT I FORGOT TO TAKE THE SPONGES OUT, AND WAS

INTERESTING

JOAN PREFACE(50)	IN THE PIECE. CRIME, LIKE DISEASE, IS NOT	INTERESTING	: IT IS SOMETHING TO BE DONE AWAY WITH BY
GETT PREFACE(224)	FIVE TIMES BECAUSE SHE IS WISE, ATTRACTIVE, AND	INTERESTING	? PROBABLY SOME OF THE TRUTH LIES BOTH WAYS. I
MILL II (172)	SHAMMING-- LYING: WHY? IS IT TO MAKE YOURSELF	INTERESTING	? /EPIFANIA/ MAKE MYSELF INTERESTING! MAN! I
SUPR III (124)	THOUGH UNIVERSALLY CONDEMNED, HAVE MADE ME SO	INTERESTING	A HERO OF LEGEND, I WAS NOT INFREQUENTLY MET IN
PYGM II (219)	OH, THATS ALL RIGHT, MRS PEARCE. HAS SHE AN	INTERESTING	ACCENT? /MRS PEARCE/ OH, SOMETHING DREADFUL,
FABL PREFACE(65)	I STILL HAVE THE PHOTOGRAPH I TOOK OF THIS	INTERESTING	ACQUAINTANCE. THE WORD ASS WOULD HAVE RECALLED
MTH2 (78)	MAKE OUT THAT I AM AN INFIDEL? /LUBIN/ IT'S VERY	INTERESTING	AND AMUSING, BURGE; AND I THINK I SEE A CASE IN
MILL II (173)	ONCE AND HAVE AN AFTERNOON ON THE RIVER WITH AN	INTERESTING	AND ATTRACTIVE WOMAN? /THE DOCTOR/ WOMEN ARE
ROCK I (207)	REST YOU; AND I THINK YOU WOULD FIND HER A RATHER	INTERESTING	AND ATTRACTIVE WOMAN. /SIR ARTHUR/ HAS SHE A
SUPR HANDBOK(193)	THE SUBJECTS WHICH IT TABOOS REMAIN THE MOST	INTERESTING	AND EARNEST OF SUBJECTS IN SPITE OF IT. VII:
OVER (193)	AND SACRED FEELINGS, AND WHICH LEAD TO SUCH	INTERESTING	AND EXCITING ADVENTURES, END IN VULGAR SQUABBLES
DOCT II (123)	IN A JEW TO ME, WHEREAS THERE IS ALWAYS SOMETHING	INTERESTING	AND FOREIGN IN AN ENGLISHMAN. BUT IN MONEY
KING PREFACE(153)	TO HIM BUT DID NOT, THE SITUATION BECOMES	INTERESTING	AND FRESH. FOR INSTANCE, CHARLES MIGHT HAVE MET
LION PREFACE(87)	OPINIONS OF JESUS, AS GUIDES TO CONDUCT, ARE	INTERESTING	AND IMPORTANT: THE REST IS MERE PSYCHOPATHY AND
DOCT PREFACE(41)	SYMPTOMS? SUCH EXPERIMENTS WOULD BE QUITE AS	INTERESTING	AND IMPORTANT AS ANY YET UNDERTAKEN BY THE
KING I (167)	SAY TO ONEANOTHER. I FIND YOU TWO GENTLEMEN MORE	INTERESTING	AND INFINITELY MORE IMPORTANT. /MRS BASHAM/ (
POSN PREFACE(394)	AN UNMIXED EVIL. GREAT RELIGIOUS LEADERS ARE MORE	INTERESTING	AND MORE IMPORTANT SUBJECTS FOR THE DRAMATIST
BARB PREFACE(223)	THINK OF RELIGIOUS PEOPLE AS PEOPLE WHO ARE NOT	INTERESTING	AND NOT AMUSING. AND SO, WHEN BARBARA CUTS THE
MTH5 SD(214)	AND EQUALLY WITHOUT SEXUAL CHARM, BUT INTENSELY	INTERESTING	AND RATHER TERRIFYING. HER SEX IS DISCOVERABLE
JITT II (38)	HAS FALLEN ON HER. SHE THINKS IT MAKES HER	INTERESTING	AND REVENGES HER. SHE POSITIVELY WALLOWS IN IT.
HART III (134)	IN THE GOVERNMENT. /LADY UTTERWORD/ THIS IS MOST	INTERESTING	AND UNEXPECTED, MR MANGAN. AND WHAT HAVE YOUR
METH PREFACE(R82)	AND THERE ARE ALWAYS CERTAIN RARE BUT INTENSELY	INTERESTING	ANTICIPATIONS, MICHAEL ANGELO COULD NOT VERY
LION PREFACE(27)	SO FAR THE HISTORY IS THAT OF A MAN SANE AND	INTERESTING	APART FROM HIS SPECIAL GIFTS AS ORATOR, HEALER,
SIM I (40)	BUT I AM NOT MAD. /PRA/ I HAVE READ SOME VERY	INTERESTING	ARTICLES ABOUT THIS BY AN ENGLISH CHEMIST NAMED
JITT III (76)	EVERYTHING THAT HAPPENS TO YOU IS EXTRAORDINARILY	INTERESTING	BECAUSE IT HAPPENS TO YOU. AND YOU THINK THAT
GETT PREFACE(224)	THE QUESTION IS, IS SHE WISE, ATTRACTIVE, AND	INTERESTING	BECAUSE SHE HAS BEEN MARRIED FIVE TIMES, OR HAS
OVER PREFACE(167)	THE MORE MOMENTOUS THE CONSEQUENCES, THE MORE	INTERESTING	BECOME THE IMPULSES AND IMAGINATIONS AND
MTH3 (126)	WELL, WHAT OF IT, MADAM? HAVE YOU READ A VERY	INTERESTING	BOOK BY THE LIBRARIAN OF THE BIOLOGICAL SOCIETY
HART I (63)	LIFE TRANSFIGURED! NO MORE WISHING ONE HAD AN	INTERESTING	BOOK TO READ, BECAUSE LIFE IS SO MUCH HAPPIER
MILL PREFACE(125)	CHAMBERLAIN'S FOUNDATIONS OF THE XIX CENTURY, AN	INTERESTING	BOOK WHICH AT THE TIME OF ITS APPEARANCE I
PHIL II (123)	SUPPRESSED FURY) YOU SEEM TO HAVE FOUND A VERY	INTERESTING	BOOK, DR PARAMORE. (THEY LOOK UP, ASTONISHED).
BULL PREFACE(68)	AND BRITISH COURTS WERE BOYCOTTED. UPON THIS	INTERESTING	BUT HOPELESS ATTEMPT TO IGNORE BRITISH RULE THE
DOCT IV (157)	COURSE. /RIDGEON/ YES. /B.B./ IT'S AN ENORMOUSLY	INTERESTING	CASE. YOU KNOW, COLLY, BY JUPITER, IF I DIDNT
DOCT II (118)	OUTLINES! PERFECT EVENING! GREAT SUCCESS!	INTERESTING	CASE! GLORIOUS NIGHT! EXQUISITE SCENERY!
3PLA PREFACE(R34)	NAIVE SURPRISE THAT POLONIUS IS A COMPLETE AND	INTERESTING	CHARACTER. IT WAS THE AGE OF GROSS IGNORANCE OF
SUPR III (133)	YOU WELL, DON JUAN. I SHALL OFTEN THINK OF OUR	INTERESTING	CHATS ABOUT THINGS IN GENERAL. I WISH YOU EVERY
MTH4 I (140)	A THOUSAND YEARS AGO. FEW PEOPLE KNOW THIS	INTERESTING	CIRCUMSTANCE NOW; BUT I ASSURE YOU IT IS TRUE. I
SUPR HANDBOK(181)	LIKELY THAT THE JEWESS WOULD FIND THE SQUIRE AN	INTERESTING	COMPANION, OR HIS HABITS, HIS FRIENDS, HIS PLACE
APPL I (210)	ALICE) WELL, MY DEAR, YOU HAVE BROKEN UP A MOST	INTERESTING	CONVERSATION, AND TO ME A MOST INSTRUCTIVE ONE.
HART III (139)	IT'S IMPOSSIBLE TO GO TO SLEEP WITH SUCH AN	INTERESTING	CONVERSATION GOING ON UNDER ONE'S WINDOW, AND ON
2TRU PREFACE(13)	AND NOT IN THE LEAST TERRIFIED, AND WHOSE VERY	INTERESTING	CONVERSION TO ROMAN CATHOLICISM HAS OBLIGED HIM
LION PREFACE(36)	HIS HANDS; AND THAT IS RETAINED BECAUSE AN	INTERESTING	DISCOURSE HANGS ON IT. WAITING FOR THE MESSIAH.
PYGM EPILOG (301)	CONCENTRATED PATIENCE, AND OCCASIONAL BURSTS OF	INTERESTING	DISQUISITION ON THE BEAUTY AND NOBILITY, THE
PYGM IV (261)	ALL THESE MONTHS THAT HAS TOLD ON ME. IT WAS	INTERESTING	ENOUGH AT FIRST, WHILE WE WERE AT THE PHONETICS;
LION PREFACE(51)	INTERESTING PROPOSITIONS; AND THEY BECOME MORE	INTERESTING	EVERY DAY, AS EXPERIENCE AND SCIENCE DRIVE US
LION PREFACE(90)	THEY ARE NEITHER CREDIBLE, INTELLIGIBLE, NOR	INTERESTING	EXCEPT TO PEOPLE UPON WHOM THE DELUSION IMPOSES.
MTH5 (255)	BY BEING A BORE. NOTHING REMAINS BEAUTIFUL AND	INTERESTING	EXCEPT THOUGHT, BECAUSE THE THOUGHT IS THE LIFE.
BUOY III (34)	UP BY HERSELF AND A FEW NATIVES. /SECONDBORN/ AN	INTERESTING	EXPERIENCE. WHEN I FEEL THAT I CAN NO LONGER
DOCT PREFACE(50)	JOAN OF ARC MUST HAVE BEEN A MOST INSTRUCTIVE AND	INTERESTING	EXPERIMENT TO A GOOD OBSERVER, AND COULD HAVE
DOCT PREFACE(50)	FEASTS BY BURNING HUMAN BEINGS ALIVE (ANOTHER	INTERESTING	EXPERIMENT) TO THE SIMPLEST ACT OF KINDNESS. AND
DOCT PREFACE(50)	ACQUIRING KNOWLEDGE ALL THE TIME FROM HIS HIGHLY	INTERESTING	EXPERIMENT. THERE IS MORE DANGER IN ONE
PYGM II SD(233)	NECK AND SHOULDERS. HE HAS WELL MARKED AND RATHER	INTERESTING	FEATURES, AND SEEMS EQUALLY FREE FROM FEAR AND
GENV I (32)	SHOULD KEEP IT. BUT I THINK I CAN MAKE IT MORE	INTERESTING	FOR YOU. AND I SHOULD OF COURSE MAKE YOU A
SUPR PREFACE(R14)	OUR VAGABOND LIBERTINES ARE NO MORE	INTERESTING	FROM THAT POINT OF VIEW THAN THE SAILOR WHO HAS
MTH2 (60)	BRIDGE THAN ABOUT ELECTIONEERING! IT IS THE MORE	INTERESTING	GAME OF THE TWO. /BURGE/ HE WANTS TO DISCUSS
MIS. (140)	THAT WAS THE FIRST TIME THAT ANYTHING REALLY	INTERESTING	HAPPENED TO ME. /LORD SUMMERHAYS/ DO YOU MEAN TO
KING I (209)	HIS PICTURE IF YOUR MAJESTY SO DESIRES. HE HAS AN	INTERESTING	HEAD: I SHOULD HAVE DRAWN IT THIS MORNING HAD
KING I (209)	ON MY DRAWING HER INSTEAD. BUT HOW CAN AN	INTERESTING	HEAD CONTAIN NO BRAIN! THAT IS THE QUESTION.
JOAN PREFACE(34)	JOAN WAS BURNT JUST AS DOZENS OF LESS	INTERESTING	HERETICS WERE BURNT IN HER TIME. CHRIST, BEING
MIS. (129)	(IMPRESSED) THATS AN IDEA. THATS A MOST	INTERESTING	IDEA: A MOST IMPORTANT IDEA. /MRS TARLETON/ YOU
MTH2 (69)	NEEDED FOR THEIR OWN GOVERNMENT. /LUBIN/ QUITE AN	INTERESTING	IDEA, DOCTOR. EXTRAVAGANT. FANTASTIC. BUT QUITE
DOCT II (123)	NATURAL, BECAUSE, AS I AM A JEW, THERES NOTHING	INTERESTING	IN A JEW TO ME, WHEREAS THERE IS ALWAYS
MILL II (172)	/THE DOCTOR/ NOT IN THE LEAST, MEDICALLY. ARE YOU	INTERESTING	IN ANY OTHER WAY? /EPIFANIA/ I AM THE MOST
LION PREFACE(91)	IS A GOOD DEAL OF JERRY-BUILDING IN THE BIBLE IS	INTERESTING	IN ITS WAY, BECAUSE EVERYTHING ABOUT THE BIBLE
MTH5 (228)	/PYGMALION/ YES. BUT THAT IS A MERE FACT. WHAT IS	INTERESTING	IS THE EXPLANATION OF THE FACT. FORGIVE MY
POSN PREFACE(361)	ELSE. THE NUMBER OF THE BLUEBOOK IS 214. HOW	INTERESTING	IT IS MAY BE JUDGED FROM THE FACT THAT IT
PYGM III (256)	MOTHER. BUT YOU HAVE NO IDEA HOW FRIGHTFULLY	INTERESTING	IT IS TO TAKE A HUMAN BEING AND CHANGE HER INTO
SUPR I (33)	I WANTED TO BRAG TO YOU, TO MAKE MYSELF	INTERESTING	. AND I FOUND MYSELF DOING ALL SORTS OF
MTH5 (209)	OUT TO BE GREAT THINGS, AND BECOMING INTENSELY	INTERESTING	. HAVE YOU EVER THOUGHT ABOUT THE PROPERTIES OF
SUPR III SD(96)	AND NOT AT ALL UNLIKE MENDOZA, THOUGH NOT SO	INTERESTING	. HE LOOKS OLDER; IS GETTING PREMATURELY BALD;
2TRU I (44)	HERSELF." /THE PATIENT/ OH! THIS IS GETTING	INTERESTING	. HOW COULD I STEAL MY OWN NECKLACE? /THE
MTH5 (218)	CAPACITY, YOU WILL NO DOUBT FIND LIFE INFINITELY	INTERESTING	. HOWEVER, ALL YOU HAVE TO DO NOW IS TO PLAY
SIM PRO,3, (34)	HER) NO THANK YOU, NO, NO. /THE PRIESTESS/ IT IS	INTERESTING	. I AM NOT A PROFESSIONAL GUIDE: I AM A
SIM II (60)	/IDDY/ SHUT UP, YOU TWO. THIS IS SOMETHING REALLY	INTERESTING	. I AM WRITING A SECOND SERMON. /ALL THE REST/ (
MTH2 (84)	OF ALL THE CRANKS; BUT YOU ARE MUCH THE MOST	INTERESTING	. I AM CONSCIOUS OF A VERY CURIOUS MIXTURE OF
PYGM III (256)	BENDING OVER TO HER EAGERLY) YES: IT'S ENORMOUSLY	INTERESTING	. I ASSURE YOU, MRS HIGGINS, WE TAKE ELIZA VERY
DOCT I (102)	YOURE NEVER ILL? /B.B./ NEVER. /WALPOLE/ THATS	INTERESTING	. I BELIEVE YOU HAVE NO NUCIFORM SAC. IF YOU
BARB III (322)	SARAH AND UNDERSHAFT) YOULL FIND IT AWFULLY	INTERESTING	. IVE BEEN THROUGH THE WOOLWICH ARSENAL; AND IT
MTH5 (228)	I ASSURE YOU THAT THESE DETAILS ARE INTENSELY	INTERESTING	. (CRIES OF NO! THEY ARE NOT! COME TO THE
FANY III (308)	THESE ENGLISH DOMESTIC INTERIORS ARE VERY	INTERESTING	. (HE GOES OUT, FOLLOWED BY JUGGINS). PRESENTLY
PHIL I (74)	BUT COME! LET US TALK ABOUT SOMETHING REALLY	INTERESTING	. (HE TAKES HER IN HIS ARMS). DO YOU LOVE ME
ROCK I (213)	UP AND DO SOMETHING. /SIR ARTHUR/ INDEED? THATS	INTERESTING	. MAY I ASK WHAT? /OXFORD YOUTH/ BREAK YOUR
BUOY 1 (15)	IN OUR SPARE TIME WILL MAKE LIFE ENORMOUSLY MORE	INTERESTING	. NO MORE DOUBT AS TO WHETHER LIFE IS WORTH
HART II (86)	CANT THINK HOW LITTLE IT MATTERS. BUT IT'S QUITE	INTERESTING	. ONLY, YOU MUST EXPLAIN IT TO ME. I DONT
MILL II (176)	AHA! YOU ARE A PSYCHOLOGIST. THIS IS VERY	INTERESTING	. /EPIFANIA/ NONSENSE! I KNOW HOW TO BUY AND
DOCT III (145)	OF COURSE. AND IT WILL BE EXTRAORDINARILY	INTERESTING	. /LOUIS/ OH, WELL, IF IT WOULD INTEREST YOU,
MTH5 (233)	MAN AND A WOMAN? THEIR CHILDREN WOULD HAVE BEEN	INTERESTING	. /PYGMALION/ I INTENDED TO MAKE A WOMAN; BUT
DOCT I (88)	BEEN DEAD NOW OVER FORTY YEARS. OH, IT'S VERY	INTERESTING	. /RIDGEON/ WELL, THERES NOTHING LIKE PROGRESS,
MILL II (172)	/EPIFANIA/ MAKE MYSELF INTERESTING! MAN! I AM	INTERESTING	. /THE DOCTOR/ NOT IN THE LEAST, MEDICALLY. ARE
GENV I (39)	WHO HE MURDERED. MURDER STORIES ARE THRILLINGLY	INTERESTING	. /THE WIDOW/ YOU WOULD NOT THINK SO IF YOU
BULL I (95)	AGREEABLY) YOU KNOW, ALL THIS SOUNDS RATHER	INTERESTING	. THERES THE IRISH CHARM ABOUT IT. THATS THE

DOCT I	(88)	I BELIEVE SO. /SIR PATRICK/ AH YES. IT'S VERY	INTERESTING	. WHAT IS IT THE OLD CARDINAL SAYS IN BROWNING'S
MTH2	(69)	IDEA, DOCTOR, EXTRAVAGANT, FANTASTIC, BUT QUITE	INTERESTING	. WHEN I WAS YOUNG I USED TO FEEL MY HUMAN
APPL I	(218)	IN THE CABINET IS ALWAYS MOST INSTRUCTIVE AND	INTERESTING	. WHO IS TO BE ITS SPOKESMAN TODAY? /PROTEUS/ I
LION PREFACE	(9)	AND ULTIMATE FATE OF JESUS INTELLIGIBLE AND	INTERESTING	. WORLDLINESS OF THE MAJORITY. THE FIRST COMMON
GENV I	(31)	PLACE. OH, IT IS DULL. /HE/ SHALL I GIVE YOU AN	INTERESTING	JOB, MADEMOISELLE? ONE THAT WOULD GET YOU
DOCT I	(99)	MY DEAR SIR PATRICK, THAT EVERY ONE OF THESE	INTERESTING	LITTLE CREATURES HAS AN IMITATOR. JUST AS MEN
BULL PREFACE	(60)	DOUBT BELIEVES WHAT HE SAYS; BUT HIS OPINION IS	INTERESTING	MAINLY AS AN EXAMPLE OF THE STATE OF HIS MIND,
BULL IV	(156)	/KEEGAN/ YES, I ASSURE YOU, YOU ARE AN EXTREMELY	INTERESTING	MAN. (HE GOES OUT). /BROADBENT/ (
NEVR II	(237)	INFERNAL WIFE. /VALENTINE/ (COOLLY) OH INDEED!	INTERESTING	MEETING! (HE RESUMES HIS STUDY OF THE MENU).
GETT	(282)	IT'S A VERY INTERESTING QUESTION. MANY VERY	INTERESTING	MEN HAVE BEEN POLYGAMISTS: SOLOMON, MAHOMET, AND
GETT	(283)	AND I STICK TO IT: I STILL WANT TO HAVE A LOT OF	INTERESTING	MEN TO KNOW QUITE INTIMATELY-- TO SAY EVERYTHING
MILL II	(173)	ATTRACTIVE WOMAN? /THE DOCTOR/ WOMEN ARE NEITHER	INTERESTING	NOR ATTRACTIVE TO ME EXCEPT WHEN THEY ARE ILL. I
MIS. PREFACE	(39)	GAUL IS DIVIDED INTO THREE PARTS, THOUGH NEITHER	INTERESTING	NOR TRUE, WAS THE ONLY LATIN SENTENCE I COULD
BULL PREFACE	(61)	NOTHING TO DESERVE BLAME"? MR FINDLAY IS ANOTHER	INTERESTING	OFFICIAL CORRESPONDENT OF SIR EDWARD. EVEN AFTER
APPL PREFACE	(194)	AS HE DECLARED, THAN HIS TRUCKS. HE WAS VERY	INTERESTING	ON THAT OCCASION. HE BEGAN BY GIVING ME A VIVID
CAPT I	(229)	HISTORY OF THAT PROPERTY IS A VERY CURIOUS AND	INTERESTING	ONE-- AT LEAST IT IS SO TO A LAWYER LIKE MYSELF.
JOAN PREFACE	(51)	BUT BOTH EQUALLY MECHANICAL, AND THEREFORE	INTERESTING	ONLY AS MECHANISM. IT IS, I REPEAT, WHAT
LION PREFACE	(87)	OF A PROPHET WHO, AFTER EXPRESSING SEVERAL VERY	INTERESTING	OPINIONS AS TO PRACTICAL CONDUCT, BOTH PERSONAL
MTH3	(123)	ABOUT YOUR WORK; THAT UNLESS IT IS MADE EITHER	INTERESTING	OR DELIGHTFUL TO YOU YOU LEAVE IT TO NEGRESSES
PYGM II	(233)	NOT I WITH HIM. AND WE ARE SURE TO GET SOMETHING	INTERESTING	OUT OF HIM. /PICKERING/ ABOUT THE GIRL?
DOCT II	(127)	AFFECTIONATELY). DONT LET US LOSE SIGHT OF YOUR	INTERESTING	PATIENT AND HIS VERY CHARMING WIFE. WE MUST NOT
JOAN PREFACE	(50)	THEY REDUCE JOAN TO THE LEVEL OF THE EVEN LESS	INTERESTING	PERSON WHOSE POCKET IS PICKED, I HAVE
DOCT PREFACE	(48)	OF THE SENSATION OF EXTREME PAIN (THE MUCH MORE	INTERESTING	PHYSIOLOGY OF PLEASURE REMAINS UNINVESTIGATED)
WIDO I	(8)	/COKANE/ ROLANDSECK APPEARS TO BE AN EXTREMELY	INTERESTING	PLACE. (HE READS) " IT IS ONE OF THE MOST
LION PREFACE	(51)	THE PERSON YOU ARE MARRIED TO. NOW THESE ARE VERY	INTERESTING	PROPOSITIONS; AND THEY BECOME MORE INTERESTING
GETT	(282)	SPEAKING DISRESPECTFULLY OF POLYGAMY. IT'S A VERY	INTERESTING	QUESTION. MANY VERY INTERESTING MEN HAVE BEEN
CLEO NOTES	(212)	POSSESS ALL QUALITIES IN SOME DEGREE. THE REALLY	INTERESTING	QUESTION IS WHETHER I AM RIGHT IN ASSUMING THAT
MTH4 I	(155)	AND WHO OWED THEIR POSITION AS THE MOST	INTERESTING	RACE ON EARTH SOLELY TO THEIR SUFFERINGS! THE
BUOY III	(36)	WITHOUT MAKING THE LEAST IMPRESSION ON YOUR VERY	INTERESTING	RELATIVES, I REALLY DO NOT KNOW WHY I AM
APPL I	(227)	HURRY. HIS MAJESTY'S SPEECHES ARE VERY WISE AND	INTERESTING	; AND YOUR BACK CHAT AMUSES BOTH YOU AND HIM.
MTH2	(55)	TO BE LEADER. /LUBIN/ HAVE YOU NOW? THATS VERY	INTERESTING	; FOR I THOUGHT I WAS THE LEADER OF THE LIBERAL
HART PREFACE	(18)	THE PROSTITUTION NOT ONLY EFFECTIVE, BUT EVEN	INTERESTING	; SO THAT SOME OF THEM WERE RAPIDLY PROMOTED,
LADY PREFACE	(225)	BARDOLATERS TO GIVE US A CREDIBLE OR EVEN	INTERESTING	SHAKESPEAR, AND THE EASY TRIUMPH OF MR HARRIS IN
OVER PREFACE	(161)	THEY WERE RIGHT IN RANKING SEX AS AN INTENSELY	INTERESTING	SUBJECT, THEY WERE WRONG IN ASSUMING THAT SEX IS
MTH4 I	(166)	YOU. /ZOO/ GOOD. NOW LET US GO BACK TO THE REALLY	INTERESTING	SUBJECT OF OUR DISCUSSION. YOU REMEMBER? THE
MTH5	(245)	TO THE CONCLUSION THAT YOU ANCIENTS ARE THE MOST	INTERESTING	SUBJECTS AFTER ALL. /MARTELLUS/ WHAT! HAVE
SUPR III	(110)	HOWEVER, I CONFESS IT IS FOR ME THE ONE SUPREMELY	INTERESTING	SUBJECT. /DON JUAN/ TO A WOMAN, SENORA, MAN'S
SIM PREFACE	(15)	THAT AN UP-TO-DATE VISION OF JUDGMENT IS NOT AN	INTERESTING	SUBJECT FOR A PLAY, ESPECIALLY AS EVENTS IN
MTH2	(82)	TO SAY THAT YOUR THEORY IS LIKELY TO PROVE MORE	INTERESTING	THAN EVER WELSH DISESTABLISHMENT WAS. BUT AS A
MTH5	(257)	SLEPT FOR WEEKS. AND SHE FOUND MATHEMATICS MORE	INTERESTING	THAN ME. /MARTELLUS/ THERE IS A PREHISTORIC
2TRU III	(87)	ELDER/ SIR: WOMEN ARE NOT, AS THEY SUPPOSE, MORE	INTERESTING	THAN THE UNIVERSE. WHEN THE UNIVERSE IS
DOCT PREFACE	(34)	DEGREES FAHRENHEIT, NO MATTER HOW IMPORTANT OR	INTERESTING	THAT PARTICULAR ADDITION TO THE STORE OF HUMAN
OVER PREFACE	(162)	UTTERLY UNSATISFYING AS SEX PLAYS, HOWEVER	INTERESTING	THEY MAY BE AS PLAYS OF INTRIGUE AND PLOT
2TRU III	(85)	MEN WOULD JUST ORDER YOU OFF; BUT TO ME THE MOST	INTERESTING	THING IN THE WORLD IS THE EXPERIENCE OF A WOMAN
DEST	(178)	HIS HAND). OH, DONT BE AFRAID. YOU WILL FIND MANY	INTERESTING	THINGS IN IT. /NAPOLEON/ FOR INSTANCE? /LADY/
MTH2	(59)	PLACE, WITH MISS SAVVY TELLING ME ALL SORTS OF	INTERESTING	THINGS. /SAVVY/ (WHO HAS BEEN GROWING MORE AND
DOCT I	(89)	MUCH AS A ROOF OVER HIS HEAD. OH, IT'S VERY VERY	INTERESTING	TO AN OLD MAN. /RIDGEON/ YOU OLD CYNIC, YOU DONT
2TRU II	(70)	POLICEMAN BECAUSE HE CAN THINK OF NOTHING MORE	INTERESTING	TO DO. QUITE RIGHT TO HANG HIM, AND ALL THE
DOCT I	(88)	YOU THE SAME ANSWER; BUT THE WORLD'S GROWING VERY	INTERESTING	TO ME NOW, COLLY. /RIDGEON/ YOU KEEP UP YOUR
ROCK I	(215)	HOPEFUL NOTE. I ASSURE YOU IT HAS BEEN INTENSELY	INTERESTING	TO ME; AND I MAY TELL YOU THAT SIGNS OF A
LION PREFACE	(90)	DELUSION, ARE QUITE CREDIBLE, INTELLIGIBLE, AND	INTERESTING	TO MODERN THINKERS. IN ANY OTHER LIGHT THEY ARE
3PLA PREFACE	(R11)	THERE IS NOTHING ROMANTIC, AND LITTLE THAT IS	INTERESTING	TO MOST OF THE MASQUERADERS EXCEPT THE
LION PREFACE	(96)	ELAPSED (THE POINT AT ISSUE, THOUGH TECHNICALLY	INTERESTING	TO PALEOGRAPHERS AND HISTORIANS, HAVING NO MORE
LION PREFACE	(90)	BUT THESE DISINTEGRATIONS, THOUGH TECHNICALLY	INTERESTING	TO SCHOLARS, AND GRATIFYING OR EXASPERATING, AS
BULL II	(112)	STRANGER AND AN ENGLISHMAN, I THOUGHT IT WOULD BE	INTERESTING	TO SEE THE ROUND TOWER BY MOONLIGHT. /NORA/ OH,
VWOO 1	(116)	IT? OH, THAT REMINDS ME: I HAVE SOMETHING REALLY	INTERESTING	TO TELL YOU. I BELIEVE THE MAN IN THE CABIN NEXT
BULL PREFACE	(71)	USED TO ATTACH TO IT, HAS BECOME AT LAST HIGHLY	INTERESTING	TO THE STUDENT OF POLITICAL SCIENCE AS AN
SUPR III	(129)	MORAL GAME ENOUGH TO PLAY IT FAIRLY, IT WOULD BE	INTERESTING	TO WATCH; BUT YOU DONT: YOU CHEAT AT EVERY
PYGM II	(238)	OF HIS BROW UNTIL SHE'S GROWED BIG ENOUGH TO BE	INTERESTING	TO YOU TWO GENTLEMEN? IS FIVE POUNDS
SUPR PREFACE	(R30)	A SUFFICIENT BODY OF FACT AND EXPERIENCE TO BE	INTERESTING	TO YOU, IF NOT TO THE PLAYGOING PUBLIC OF
KING I	(208)	BARBARA. A WOMAN'S FACE DOES NOT BEGIN TO BE	INTERESTING	UNTIL SHE IS OUR AGE. /BARBARA/ OUR AGE! YOU
LION PREFACE	(82)	IN IT AS VERY COMMONPLACE REVIVALISTS,	INTERESTING	US BY THEIR ADVENTURES MORE THAN BY ANY
PRES	(158)	YOU MAY NOT BELIEVE ME, I FIND YOU ARE MORE	INTERESTING	WHEN YOU TALK ABOUT MUSIC THAN WHEN YOU ARE
MILL II	(172)	IN ANY OTHER WAY? /EPIFANIA/ I AM THE MOST	INTERESTING	WOMAN IN ENGLAND. I AM EPIFANIA OGNISANTI DI
GETT PREFACE	(224)	IS, AS MIGHT BE EXPECTED, A WISE, ATTRACTIVE, AND	INTERESTING	WOMAN. THE QUESTION IS, IS SHE WISE, ATTRACTIVE,
DEST	(171)	BIT. COME: YOU ARE A VERY CLEVER AND SENSIBLE AND	INTERESTING	WOMAN. (HE PATS HER ON THE CHEEK). SHALL WE BE
BUOY III	(37)	I HAD TO INVITE AND ENTERTAIN A SUCCESSION OF	INTERESTING	YOUNG MEN TO KEEP HER SUPPLIED WITH WHAT I CALL
SUPR PREFACE	(R14)	MOCKING EXQUISITELY AT SLAVERY TO THEM, AND	INTERESTING	YOU, ATTRACTING YOU, TEMPTING YOU, INEXPLICABLY
CAPT I SD	(235)	GESTURES, AND MUCH SIGNIFICANCE. ON THE WHOLE,	INTERESTING	, AND EVEN ATTRACTIVE, BUT NOT FRIENDLY. HE
MTH2	(56)	I SHOULD BE DEAD LONG BEFORE I CAME TO IT. MOST	INTERESTING	, AND QUITE TRUE. HE WAS INTRODUCED TO ME AT A
GENV I	(31)	WHEN I TOOK THE JOB I THOUGHT IT WAS GOING TO BE	INTERESTING	, AND THAT I'D SEE ALL THE GREAT MEN. I AM
LION PREFACE	(91)	IN ITS WAY, BECAUSE EVERYTHING ABOUT THE BIBLE IS	INTERESTING	, IT DOES NOT ALTER THE SYNTHESIS VERY
KING I	(214)	APPLY TO THEM TOO? /CHARLES/ THEIR QUARRELS ARE	INTERESTING	, LOUISE. /NELL/ ARE THEY? THEY BORE ME TO
BARB II	(294)	TO BRING HIM DOWN TO EARTH) THIS IS EXTREMELY	INTERESTING	, MR UNDERSHAFT. OF COURSE YOU KNOW THAT YOU ARE
ROCK PREFACE	(189)	ONLY FOR PROPOSITIONS WHICH, HOWEVER NOVEL, SEEM	INTERESTING	, STATESMANLIKE, AND RESPECTABLE, BUT FOR
BULL IV	(178)	AND PENNY-IN-THE-SLOT MUTOSCOPES TO MAKE IT	INTERESTING	, THEN NO DOUBT YOUR ENGLISH AND AMERICAN
MTH2	(44)	HAVE COME ALIVE IN OUR HANDS, ALIVE AND INTENSELY	INTERESTING	, WE MAY JUST AS WELL GO OUT AND DIG THE GARDEN
MILL II	(172)	YOURSELF INTERESTING? /EPIFANIA/ MAKE MYSELF	INTERESTING	! MAN: I AM INTERESTING. /THE DOCTOR/ NOT IN
JITT III	(56)	MUST READ IT, FESSLER. /FESSLER/ (EAGERLY) HOW	INTERESTING	! MAY I LOOK? (TAKING IT FROM MRS
BASH II,1,	(106)	/LUCIAN/ HOW HORRIBLE! /LYDIA/ NAY, NAY: HOW	INTERESTING	! /CASHEL/ A THOUSAND VICTORIES CANNOT WIPE OUT

INTERESTINGLY

OVER	(172)	CONVERSATION. WHAT IS A MAN TO DO? SHE CANT TALK	INTERESTINGLY	; AND IF HE TALKS THAT WAY HIMSELF SHE DOESNT

INTERESTING-TO-EXPERIMENT-ON

DOCT PREFACE	(46)	A MORE HIGHLY DEVELOPED, AND CONSEQUENTLY MORE	INTERESTING-TO-EXPERIMENT-ON	VERTEBRATE THAN THE DOG.

INTERESTS

APPL I	(238)	INTO THE CABINET TO RUN MY DEPARTMENT IN THEIR	INTERESTS	; THAT IS, TO MAKE SUCH A FAILURE OF IT THAT JOE
MIS. PREFACE	(97)	BUT IT IS A CAPITAL STORY FOR A CHILD. IT	INTERESTS	A CHILD BECAUSE IT IS ABOUT BEARS; AND IT LEAVES
2TRU PREFACE	(21)	THAT THE STRAINS SET UP BY SUCH A DIVISION OF	INTERESTS	ALSO DESTROY PEACE, JUSTICE, RELIGION, GOOD
MIS. PREFACE	(97)	IT GIVES US OF THE TEMPER OF GOD (WHICH IS WHAT	INTERESTS	AN ADULT READER) IS SHOCKING AND BLASPHEMOUS. BUT
SUPR HANDBOK	(175)	OF RULERS AND SUBSTITUTED ANOTHER WITH DIFFERENT	INTERESTS	AND DIFFERENT VIEWS. THAT IS WHAT A GENERAL
SUPR III	(114)	UNIVERSALLY RESPECTED AMONG ALL THE CONFLICTS OF	INTERESTS	AND ILLUSIONS. /THE STATUE/ YOU MEAN THE MILITARY
METH PREFACE	(R67)	HAD NO SENSE OF ANYTHING BEYOND HIS OWN BUSINESS	INTERESTS	AND PERSONAL APPETITES AND AMBITIONS. AS A RESULT,
APPL PREFACE	(186)	OUR PASSIONS, OUR PRIVATE AND IMMEDIATE	INTERESTS	ARE CONSTANTLY IN CONFLICT WITH THE KNOWLEDGE, THE
GENV IV	(95)	WHEN YOU ASK ME WHAT WILL HAPPEN IF BRITISH	INTERESTS	ARE SERIOUSLY MENACED YOU ASK ME TO FORD THE
MIS. PREFACE	(85)	CUT OFF ARTIFICIALLY FROM INTELLECTUAL AND PUBLIC	INTERESTS	AS WOMEN ARE, THE FATHER-IN-LAW WOULD BE AS
3PLA PREFACE	(R12)	SAME INTERESTS; AND THAT MOST PLAYGOERS HAVE NO	INTERESTS	AT ALL. THIS BEING PRECISELY CONTRARY TO THE
O'FL	(210)	NO KNOWLEDGE OF THE CAUSES OF THE WAR? OF THE	INTERESTS	AT STAKE? OF THE IMPORTANCE -- I MAY ALMOST SAY
BULL PREFACE	(34)	TO, MY OWN. FINALLY, I AM IMPARTIAL AS TO YOUR	INTERESTS	BECAUSE THEY ARE BOTH EQUALLY OPPOSED TO MINE,
MILL PREFACE	(112)	IT, AND THE PEOPLE WITH WIDER AND MORE GENEROUS	INTERESTS	BECOME OR REMAIN POOR WITH EQUAL CERTAINTY,
HART PREFACE	(24)	MEN WHO HAD BECOME RICH BY PLACING THEIR PERSONAL	INTERESTS	BEFORE THOSE OF THE COUNTRY, AND MEASURING THE
ROCK PREFACE	(162)	WHO COULD BE MADE PUBLICLY USEFUL, ALL ITS	INTERESTS	BEING IN THE OPPOSITE DIRECTION, LIMITED LIABILITY
DOCT PREFACE	(19)	HORROR AND SUFFER THIS MUTILATION SHOULD HAVE NO	INTERESTS	BUT OUR OWN TO THINK OF; SHOULD JUDGE OUR CASES
APPL I	(227)	NOT INSERT A SINGLE PARAGRAPH AGAINST THEIR OWN	INTERESTS	EVEN IF IT WERE SIGNED BY MY OWN HAND AND SENT TO
BULL PREFACE	(35)	MANY HINDERING AND HAMPERING RESPONSIBILITIES AND	INTERESTS	IN DEALING WITH HIM, GETS BULLIED AND DRIVEN BY

APPL PREFACE(191)	OF PRIVATE CAPITALISM IN SETTING UP HUGE VESTED	INTERESTS	IN DESTRUCTION, WASTE, AND DISEASE. THE ARMAMENT
PYGM EPILOG (289)	AS TO HIS REMAINING ONE OF THE STRONGEST PERSONAL	INTERESTS	IN HER LIFE. IT WOULD BE VERY SORELY STRAINED IF
GENV III (82)	FIVE THOUSAND BEHIND IT. IN THE WEST THE VESTED	INTERESTS	IN IGNORANCE AND SUPERSTITION ARE SO OVERWHELMING
CLEO PRO2,SD(96)	SYMBOLIZE WITH TOLERABLE COMPLETENESS THE MAIN	INTERESTS	IN LIFE OF WHICH THEY ARE CONSCIOUS. THEIR SPEARS
GETT PREFACE(223)	CAPABLE OF RESPONDING TO. WE ALL HAVE PERSONAL	INTERESTS	IN MARRIAGE WHICH WE ARE NOT PREPARED TO SINK. IT
LION EPILOG (147)	SUPPRESS A PROPAGANDA THAT SEEMED TO THREATEN THE	INTERESTS	INVOLVED IN THE ESTABLISHED LAW AND ORDER,
UNPL PREFACE(R11)	FOR PERSONS OF SERIOUS INTELLECTUAL AND ARTISTIC	INTERESTS	IS THE WANT OF A SUITABLE PLAYHOUSE. I AM FOND OF
JOAN EPILOG (166)	A MASTER IN MY PROFESSION I HAVE TO CONSIDER ITS	INTERESTS	, AND, AFTER ALL, MY FIRST DUTY IS TO MY WIFE AND
PYGM EPILOG (292)	IN HERSELF THAT WAS SECONDARY TO PHILOSOPHIC	INTERESTS	, HAD MRS HIGGINS DIED, THERE WOULD STILL HAVE
MILL PREFACE(129)	EXCUSE FOR BELIEVING IN THE ALLEGED HARMONY OF	INTERESTS	, NOTHING MORE DIABOLICAL CAN BE CONCEIVED THAN
JOAN 4 (101)	ONE WHO IS NOT WHOLLY DEVOTED TO OUR ENGLISH	INTERESTS	. /CAUCHON/ I AM SORRY: I DID NOT UNDERSTAND. (HE
SUPR III (103)	SO WOULD I ENJOY THE CONTEMPLATION OF THAT WHICH	INTERESTS	ME ABOVE ALL THINGS: NAMELY, LIFE: THE FORCE THAT
WIDO III (62)	DR TRENCH, I HOPED FOR SOME TIME THAT OUR	INTERESTS	MIGHT BE JOINED BY CLOSER TIES EVEN THAN THOSE OF
HART PREFACE(10)	WAS SO IMPORTANT THAT NO CONSIDERATION FOR THE	INTERESTS	OF ANY INDIVIDUAL CREATURE, WHETHER FROG OR
GETT PREFACE(220)	PURPOSE SO COMPLETELY TRANSCENDS THE PERSONAL	INTERESTS	OF ANY INDIVIDUAL OR EVEN OF ANY TEN GENERATIONS
APPL PREFACE(195)	ALL OUR GOVERNMENT DEPARTMENTS ARE BY THE VESTED	INTERESTS	OF BREAKAGES, LIMITED, WOULD DO NOTHING FOR HIM. I
MILL PREFACE(133)	HE IS PROSELYTIZED FROM THE BEGINNING IN THE	INTERESTS	OF ESTABLISHED INSTITUTIONS SO EFFECTUALLY THAT HE
GETT PREFACE(213)	HAVE ANY CONDITIONS ATTACHED TO IT EXCEPT IN THE	INTERESTS	OF RACE WELFARE, THERE ARE MANY WOMEN OF ADMIRABLE
LION I (112)	YOU TO THE LIONS HE WILL BE UPHOLDING THE	INTERESTS	OF RELIGION IN ROME. IF YOU WERE TO THROW HIM TO
MILL PREFACE(128)	THAT THERE IS A DIVINE HARMONY BETWEEN THESE TWO	INTERESTS	OF SUCH A NATURE THAT IF EVERY DECIDER DOES THE
GENV IV (113)	WORLD EXISTS ONLY AS A MEANS OF FURTHERING THE	INTERESTS	OF THAT GEOGRAPHICAL EXPRESSION. /SIR O./ SURELY
PRES (142)	NEVER WILL RECOGNIZE, THE PLAIN FACT THAT THE	INTERESTS	OF THE BRITISH EMPIRE ARE PARAMOUNT, AND THAT THE
GENV IV (94)	EVER LEAD YOU TO ANY STEPS CONTRARY TO THE	INTERESTS	OF THE BRITISH EMPIRE WE SHALL HAVE TO COME DOWN
GETT (311)	HAVING BISHOPS OF THIS SORT IS THAT THE SPIRITUAL	INTERESTS	OF THE CHURCH, AND ITS INFLUENCE ON THE SOULS AND
POSN PREFACE(374)	THE AVOWED PREJUDICES OF THE FREE CHURCHES OR THE	INTERESTS	OF THE MANAGERS OR THEATRICAL SPECULATORS ON THE
SUPR HANDBOK(191)	PROFESSES (AND FAILS) TO READJUST MATTERS IN THE	INTERESTS	OF THE MAJORITY OF THE ELECTORS, YET STEREOTYPES
MILL PREFACE(113)	THEIR OWN IMMEDIATE INTERESTS TO THE PERMANENT	INTERESTS	OF THE NATION OR THE WORLD. IN SHORT, A RULER MUST
METH PREFACE(R68)	HIS PERSONAL AMBITION AND THE COMMERCIAL	INTERESTS	OF THE PLUTOCRATS WHO OWN THE NEWSPAPERS AND
BULL PREFACE(30)	IT IS SIMPLY EXPLOITATION OF ENGLISH RULE IN THE	INTERESTS	OF THE PROPERTY, POWER, AND PROMOTION OF THE IRISH
BULL PREFACE(16)	DOUBT ENGLISH RULE IS VIGOROUSLY EXPLOITED IN THE	INTERESTS	OF THE PROPERTY, POWER, AND PROMOTION OF THE IRISH
ROCK PREFACE(155)	OF A HANDFUL OF PRIVATE PERSONS AGAINST THE	INTERESTS	OF THE RACE IS PERMITTED AND PRACTISED. THE OLD
FANY PREFACE(255)	CONSIDERATION FOR OTHER PEOPLES' FEELINGS AND	INTERESTS	ON EVERY POINT EXCEPT THEIR DREAD OF LOSING THEIR
SUPR IV SD(141)	US ON OUR RIGHT) WE FIND EVIDENCE OF LITERARY	INTERESTS	ON THE PART OF THE TENANTS IN THE FACT THAT THERE
POSN PREFACE(364)	ENQUIRY ARE MORE OR LESS INTIMIDATED BOTH BY THE	INTERESTS	ON WHICH THEY HAVE TO SIT IN JUDGMENT AND, WHEN
APPL PREFACE(175)	THEM FROM ABUSING THEIR AUTHORITY IN THEIR OWN	INTERESTS	OR THOSE OF THEIR CLASS OR RELIGION. OUR SOLUTION
LION PREFACE(4)	ON IT FROM HEAVEN LIKE HAILSTONES. CHRISTIANITY	INTERESTS	PRACTICAL STATESMEN NOW BECAUSE OF THE DOCTRINES
NEVR I SD(208)	AND INTELLECT, AND IN BEING A WOMAN OF CULTIVATED	INTERESTS	RATHER THAN PASSIONATELY DEVELOPED PERSONAL
CAPT III (278)	/LADY CICELY/ (PROMPTLY WASHING HER HANDS OF HIS	INTERESTS	) OH, VERY WELL. TELL THE STORY YOURSELF, IN YOUR
3PLA PREFACE(R12)	QUALITIES OF PASSION; THAT NO TWO HAVE THE SAME	INTERESTS	; AND THAT MOST PLAYGOERS HAVE NO INTERESTS AT
SUPR HANDBOK(186)	ALTER THE BALANCE OF CLASSES AND THEIR	INTERESTS	; AND, AS A RESULT OF THE TINKERING, THERE MAY BE
POSN PREFACE(364)	POLITICIANS, BY THE VOTES AT THE BACK OF THOSE	INTERESTS	; BUT THIS UNFORTUNATE COMMITTEE SAT UNDER A QUITE
MILL PREFACE(128)	PROPERTY OWNERS IN WHOSE GROSSLY ANTISOCIAL	INTERESTS	THE COUNTRY IS MISGOVERNED. SINCE KARL MARX AND
DOCT PREFACE(79)	A POOR LANDLORD. 2. OF ALL THE ANTI-SOCIAL VESTED	INTERESTS	THE WORST IS THE VESTED INTEREST IN ILL-HEALTH. 3.
DEVL EPILOG (82)	APPARENTLY SHAMELESS SACRIFICE OF GREAT PUBLIC	INTERESTS	TO PETTY PERSONAL ONES, IS SIMPLY THE PREFERENCE
MILL PREFACE(113)	THEY DID, WOULD NOT SACRIFICE THEIR OWN IMMEDIATE	INTERESTS	TO THE PERMANENT INTERESTS OF THE NATION OR THE
LION PREFACE(21)	HER CHILDREN: IN FACT, HE SAYS SO. NOTHING THAT	INTERESTS	US NOWADAYS TURNS ON THE CREDIBILITY OF THE
MTH5 (207)	WAY IT INTERESTS YOU. AND WHEN ANYTHING NO LONGER	INTERESTS	US WE NO LONGER KNOW IT. /THE MAIDEN/ YOU HAVNT
POSN PREFACE(368)	ALL WITH A QUESTION IN WHICH SO MANY CONFLICTING	INTERESTS	WERE INVOLVED, AND WHICH HAD PROBABLY NO ELECTORAL
2TRU PREFACE(4)	YOU FIND RICH LADIES TAKING UP OCCUPATIONS AND	INTERESTS	WHICH KEEP THEM SO BUSY DOING PROFESSIONAL OR
KING I (222)	OR CARE ABOUT THE PERRY HEALING OF MERCURY THAT	INTERESTS	YOU SO MUCH? WE SHALL NEVER GET THESE PEOPLE OUT
MTH5 (207)	IT HAS LONG CEASED TO INTEREST ME IN THE WAY IT	INTERESTS	YOU. AND WHEN ANYTHING NO LONGER INTERESTS US WE
FANY PROLOG (258)	PERHAPS I HAD BETTER EXPLAIN THE POSITION, IF IT	INTERESTS	YOU. /SAVOYARD/ CERTAINLY. /THE COUNT/ WELL, YOU
PYGM EPILOG (289)	A WELL-CONSIDERED DECISION. WHEN A BACHELOR	INTERESTS	, AND DOMINATES, AND TEACHES, AND BECOMES
ROCK PREFACE(157)	TO ENTER THE KINGDOM OF HEAVEN), AGAINST ALL THE	INTERESTS	, CLASSES, PRINCIPALITIES AND POWERS, INVITING
MIS. PREFACE(18)	FOR ADULTS WITHOUT THE SMALLEST REGARD FOR THE	INTERESTS	, EITHER REMOTE OR IMMEDIATE, OF THE CHILDREN.
APPL INTRLUD(245)	THAT IS A RATHER DESIRABLE EXTENSION OF THEIR	INTERESTS	, IN MY OPINION, IF LYSISTRATA HAD A LOVER I
LION EPILOG (147)	AND HARDWON PUBLIC LIBERTIES AND PRIVATE	INTERESTS	, IN THE IRRESISTIBLE SURGE OF THEIR PUGNACITY AND
MIS. PREFACE(85)	IS NOT. WOE TO THE OLD IF THEY HAVE NO IMPERSONAL	INTERESTS	, NO CONVICTIONS, NO PUBLIC CAUSES TO ADVANCE, NO
GETT PREFACE(257)	OF EXISTING ABUSES, SUPERSTITIONS, AND CORRUPT	INTERESTS	, PRODUCES THE EXPLOSIVE FORCES THAT WRECK
GETT PREFACE(203)	IT WOULD BE AT BEST A JUMBLE OF SUPERSTITIONS AND	INTERESTS	, TABOOS AND HYPOCRISIES, WHICH COULD NOT BE
BARB II (296)	UNSELFISH-- /UNDERSHAFT/ INDIFFERENT TO THEIR OWN	INTERESTS	, WHICH SUITS ME EXACTLY. /CUSINS/ -- WITH THEIR
3PLA PREFACE(R17)	IN PEOPLE WITHOUT POWER OF ATTENTION, WITHOUT	INTERESTS	, WITHOUT SYMPATHY: IN SHORT, WITHOUT BRAINS OR
LION EPILOG (150)	INDULGED THEIR CLASS PREJUDICES AND COMMERCIAL	INTERESTS	, WITHOUT TROUBLING THEMSELVES FOR A MOMENT AS TO
NEVR II (255)	DESIGNS OF THAT KIND? AS IF THERE WERE NO OTHER	INTERESTS	! NO OTHER SUBJECTS OF CONVERSATION! AS IF WOMEN

INTERFERE

DEST (168)	BY A MOB IN PARIS BECAUSE I WAS AFRAID TO	INTERFERE	: I FELT MYSELF A COWARD TO THE TIPS OF MY TOES AS
LION II (128)	LADIES OF RANK. /LAVINIA/ DOES THE EMPEROR EVER	INTERFERE	? /THE EDITOR/ OH, YES: HE TURNS HIS THUMB UP
FANY III (316)	OVER THE PLACE? (TO KNOX) I WAS NEVER ONE TO	INTERFERE	BETWEEN MAN AND WIFE, KNOX; BUT IF MARIA STARTED
MIS. (116)	LET HIM ALONE -- /JOHNNY/ (FIERCELY) DONT YOU	INTERFERE	BETWEEN MY MOTHER AND ME: D'Y' HEAR? /HYPATIA/
FANY III (321)	WHATS TO BE THE END OF THIS? IT'S NOT FOR ME TO	INTERFERE	BETWEEN YOU AND YOUR SON, GILBEY: HE KNOWS HIS OWN
WIDO II (26)	AM AN ENGLISHMAN; AND I WILL SUFFER NO PRIEST TO	INTERFERE	IN MY BUSINESS. (HE TURNS SUDDENLY ON
ROCK II (239)	FOR A MOMENT THAT THE NAVY WOULD BE ALLOWED TO	INTERFERE	IN POLITICS? /SIR BEMROSE/ WHO'S TO STOP IT?
CAND I SD(79)	WITHOUT HUMILIATING THEM, AND, ON OCCASION, TO	INTERFERE	IN THEIR BUSINESS WITHOUT IMPERTINENCE. HIS
MIS. PREFACE(43)	WE ARE TOO LAZY TO FIND OUT THE PROPER WAY TO	INTERFERE	, BUT THE INTERFERENCE MUST BE REGULATED BY SOME
2TRU III (104)	JUST LET ME ALONE, WILL YOU? NOBODY ASKED YOU TO	INTERFERE	. GET AWAY WITH YOU. GENERAL AWE AND DISMAY. MRS
WIDO II (29)	YOU SEE, MR LICKCHEESE, I DONT SEE HOW I CAN	INTERFERE	. I'M VERY SORRY, OF COURSE. /COKANE/ CERTAINLY
WIDO II (29)	SORRY, OF COURSE. /COKANE/ CERTAINLY YOU CANNOT	INTERFERE	. IT WOULD BE IN THE MOST EXECRABLE TASTE.
PYGM V (281)	YOU TWO GETTING THE BETTER OF ELIZA. I SHANT	INTERFERE	. IT'S TIME FOR US TO GO, COLONEL. SO LONG, HENRY.
PYGM II (228)	/PICKERING/ EXCUSE ME, HIGGINS; BUT I REALLY MUST	INTERFERE	. MRS PEARCE IS QUITE RIGHT. IF THIS GIRL IS TO
MIS. (192)	UP, JOHNNY. I CAN TAKE CARE OF MYSELF. DONT YOU	INTERFERE	. /JOHNNY/ OH, VERY WELL. IF YOU CHOOSE TO GIVE
MTH4 I (172)	NEEDS WEEDING? BUT IT IS NOT NECESSARY FOR US TO	INTERFERE	. WE ARE NATURALLY RATHER PARTICULAR AS TO THE
BARB I (251)	FAMILY AFFAIRS. /LADY BRITOMART/ WELL, YOU MUST	INTERFERE	NOW; FOR THEY ARE GETTING QUITE BEYOND ME.
O'FL (225)	THING TO ME? (TERESA RETORTS FURIOUSLY; THE MEN	INTERFERE	; AND THE SOLO BECOMES A QUARTET, FORTISSIMO). IVE
LION I (119)	ANDROCLES MAKES A WILD MOVEMENT TO RISE AND	INTERFERE	; BUT LAVINIA HOLDS HIM DOWN, WATCHING FERROVIUS
MIS. PREFACE(12)	A HOUSE TO KEEP AND AN INCOME TO EARN, CAN STILL	INTERFERE	TO A DISASTROUS EXTENT WITH THE RIGHTS AND
PYGM I (212)	THE REACTION) HE'S NO GENTLEMAN, HE AINT, TO	INTERFERE	WITH A POOR GIRL. /THE DAUGHTER/ (OUT OF
APPL II (270)	HE WONT INTERFERE WITH YOU AS LONG AS YOU DONT	INTERFERE	WITH HIM. JUST THE RIGHT KING FOR US. NOT
SIM PRO?2, (29)	WE NEVER OFFER VIOLENCE TO THE UNHAPPY. DO NOT	INTERFERE	WITH HIS DESTINY. /THE E.O./ (PLANTING HIMSELF ON
GETT (287)	CLASSES, WHERE NO GOVERNMENT WOULD DARE TO	INTERFERE	WITH IT. /REGINALD/ WHAT DID THEY SAY TO THAT?
BARB II (279)	AND TELL HER IF SHE WANTS ONE LAWK IT TO CAM AND	INTERFERE	WITH ME. (JENNY, CRYING WITH PAIN, GOES INTO THE
KING I (196)	THE ANTI-POPE YOU MIGHT CALL HIM, DARED TO	INTERFERE	WITH ME, A CATHOLIC KING, THE POPE COULD TAKE HIS
SIM I (49)	THEY SAID IT WAS VULGAR NONSENSE AND MADE THEM	INTERFERE	WITH ONEANOTHER AND HATE ONEANOTHER. THEN THEY HIT
KING I (197)	WHO ARE SO FRIGHTFULLY CRUEL THAT I DARE NOT	INTERFERE	WITH PROTESTANT JUDGES WHO ARE MERCILESS. THE
MIS. PREFACE(17)	BITTERLY JEALOUS OF ALLOWING ANYONE ELSE TO	INTERFERE	WITH THEIR CHILDREN, WHOM THEY MAY NONE THE LESS
MTH3 (127)	IT. THERE IS NO LAW THAT GIVES YOU POWER TO	INTERFERE	WITH THEM. /BARNABAS/ IF THEY FORCE ME TO IT I
MILL III (186)	THERE! HOLD YOUR NOISE: I'M NOT GOING TO LET HER	INTERFERE	WITH US. I'LL PUT HER OUT ALL RIGHT. (HE GOES TO
APPL II (270)	IN WHAT I AM DOING. /BALBUS/ HE ISNT. HE WONT	INTERFERE	WITH YOU AS LONG AS YOU DONT INTERFERE WITH HIM.
BARB III (318)	YES, YES, YES: THATS ALL RIGHT, STEPHEN. SHE WONT	INTERFERE	WITH YOU ANY MORE: YOUR INDEPENDENCE IS ACHIEVED:
FANY III (310)	DAY ONCE A MONTH; AND NO OTHER MANSERVANT TO	INTERFERE	WITH YOU. IT MAY BE A BIT QUIET PERHAPS; BUT YOURE
CAPT II (249)	AND DRINKWATER) DO PLEASE TELL ME, CAPTAIN, IF I	INTERFERE	WITH YOUR ARRANGEMENTS IN ANY WAY. IF I DISTURB
DEVL I (25)	/RICHARD/ BY YOUR LEAVE, MINISTER: I DO NOT	INTERFERE	WITH YOUR SERMONS: DO NOT YOU INTERRUPT MINE. (TO
ARMS III (61)	I DONT KNOW: HE HASNT TOLD ME. BETTER NOT	INTERFERE	, DEAR YOUNG LADY. NO HARM WILL BE DONE: IVE OFTEN
MRS I (190)	OF THEM, AND A GOOD DEAL MORE BESIDES. DONT YOU	INTERFERE	, PRADDY: I KNOW HOW TO TREAT MY OWN CHILD AS WELL

INTERFERED

MIS. (192)	OF PROTECTING ME. I'M NOT YOUR BABY. IF I	INTERFERED	BETWEEN YOU AND A WOMAN, YOU WOULD SOON TELL ME

BARB I (251)	/STEPHEN/ (MUCH PERPLEXED) YOU KNOW I HAVE NEVER	INTERFERED	IN THE HOUSEHOLD-- /LADY BRITOMART/ NO: I SHOULD
POSN PREFACE(368)	KINDS IS INHERENTLY SINFUL. WHY THE GOVERNMENT	INTERFERED	. IT MAY NOW BE ASKED HOW A LIBERAL GOVERNMENT
2TRU II (80)	HITHERTO THE WORK OF COMMANDING MY REGIMENT HAS	INTERFERED	VERY SERIOUSLY WITH ITS GRATIFICATION. HENCEFORTH
ROCK II (279)	FATHERS. THEY ARE VERY SENSITIVE ABOUT BEING	INTERFERED	WITH AT THAT AGE. HE WOULD REGARD MY TAKING AN
ROCK PREFACE(177)	THAT SELFREGARDING ACTIONS SHOULD NOT BE	INTERFERED	WITH BY THE AUTHORITIES CARRIES VERY LITTLE
MIS. (192)	BUT I WONT BE PROTECTED. I'LL NOT HAVE MY AFFAIRS	INTERFERED	WITH BY MEN ON PRETENCE OF PROTECTING ME. I'M NOT
BULL PREFACE(51)	AS IF OUR IMAGINARY CHINESE OFFICERS, ON BEING	INTERFERED	WITH IN THEIR SLAUGHTER OF TURKEYS, HAD KILLED AN
CAPT III (279)	CAWNDOOCE TO THE COMFORT OF THE MEN, I HAVE NOT	INTERFERED	WITH THEM. /LADY CICELY/ HOW CLEVER OF YOU TO
ROCK II (280)	AS I TAKE MYSELF OFF THEIR HANDS, AND I WONT BE	INTERFERED	WITH. DO YOU HEAR? I WONT BE INTERFERED WITH.
MIS. (130)	DONT FUSS. YOUR PRECIOUS JOHNNY SHANT BE	INTERFERED	WITH. (BOUNCING UP, TOO ENERGETIC TO SIT STILL)
ROCK II (280)	WONT BE INTERFERED WITH. DO YOU HEAR? I WONT BE	INTERFERED	WITH. /ALOYSIA/ YOUR PARENTS ARE TOO GOOD FOR
DEVL EPILOG (81)	FACT THAT LORD GEORGE'S TRIP TO KENT HAD NOT BEEN	INTERFERED	WITH, AND THAT NOBODY KNEW ABOUT THE OVERSIGHT OF

INTERFERENCE

APPL PREFACE(186)	THIS IS THE BEST I CAN DO WITHOUT GOVERNMENT	INTERFERENCE	: INDEED ANY OTHER WAY OF DEALING WITH MY SPARE
METH PREFACE(R64)	" DOING THE OTHER FELLOW DOWN" WITH IMPUNITY, ALL	INTERFERENCE	BY A GUIDING GOVERNMENT, ALL ORGANIZATION
GENV IV (93)	TO MAKE ITSELF SUPREME AND ROB THE PEOPLE WITHOUT	INTERFERENCE	FROM KING OR PRIEST; BUT THE PEOPLE ALWAYS
GETT PREFACE(246)	OURSELVES AS WE PLEASE WITHOUT REPROACH OR	INTERFERENCE	FROM LAW, RELIGION, OR EVEN CONSCIENCE (AND
POSN PREFACE(426)	A PLAY INCITING THE COUNTRY TO THAT WAR WITHOUT	INTERFERENCE	FROM THE AMBASSADORS OF THE MENACED COUNTRY. I
CAPT I (237)	THAT I TAKE MY OWN WAY WITH THEM AND SUFFER NO	INTERFERENCE	. /LADY CICELY/ CAPTAIN BRASSBOUND: I DONT WANT
POSN PREFACE(384)	OF HUMAN ACTIVITY ENTIRELY FREE FROM LEGAL	INTERFERENCE	. THIS HAS NOTHING TO DO WITH ANY SYMPATHY
MIS. PREFACE(43)	TO FIND OUT THE PROPER WAY TO INTERFERE. BUT THE	INTERFERENCE	MUST BE REGULATED BY SOME THEORY OF THE
DOCT PREFACE(8)	PROVED EXCEPT THAT HIS CHILD DIED WITHOUT THE	INTERFERENCE	OF A DOCTOR AS EFFECTUALLY AS ANY OF THE
SUPR HANDBOK(185)	WHICH OCCUR FROM TIME TO TIME IN SPITE OF THE	INTERFERENCE	OF MAN'S BLUNDERING INSTITUTIONS. THE EXISTENCE
JOAN 4 (107)	IS THE PROTEST OF THE INDIVIDUAL SOUL AGAINST THE	INTERFERENCE	OF PRIEST OR PEER BETWEEN THE PRIVATE MAN AND
POSN PREFACE(396)	AT WHICH A STEP FURTHER WOULD HAVE INVOLVED THE	INTERFERENCE	OF THE POLICE. PROVIDED THE TREATMENT OF THE
GENV PREFACE(14)	CHANGE OF HABITS AND THE SAME DREAD OF GOVERNMENT	INTERFERENCE	SURVIVING IN THE ADULT VOTER LIKE THE CHILD'S
POSN PREFACE(365)	GIVEN TO ANY PUBLIC BODY WITHOUT TOO SERIOUS AN	INTERFERENCE	WITH CERTAIN LIBERAL TRADITIONS OF LIBERTY
METH PREFACE(R44)	TABLE BY CHLOROFORM WAS OBJECTED TO AS AN	INTERFERENCE	WITH HIS ARRANGEMENTS WHICH HE WOULD PROBABLY
ROCK PREFACE(161)	ACTUALLY PASSED THE MOST SEVERE LAWS AGAINST ANY	INTERFERENCE	WITH HIS IDLING. IT WAS THE BUSINESS OF THE
SUPR HANDBOK(188)	ARISE FROM THE GENERAL FEAR OF MANKIND THAT ANY	INTERFERENCE	WITH OUR CONJUGAL CUSTOMS WILL BE AN
SUPR HANDBOK(188)	INTERFERENCE WITH OUR CONJUGAL CUSTOMS WILL BE AN	INTERFERENCE	WITH OUR PLEASURES AND OUR ROMANCE. THIS FEAR,
DOCT PREFACE(52)	TOWARDS A RISE IN THE RATES AND MORE PUBLIC	INTERFERENCE	WITH THE INSANITARY, BECAUSE INSUFFICIENTLY
DOCT PREFACE(71)	BY DOING HIS BUSINESS WITH THE LEAST POSSIBLE	INTERFERENCE	WITH THE PRIVATE CITIZEN. THE MAN PAID BY THE
SUPR PREFACE(R25)	CEASED TO MEAN A VERY LIMITED AND OCCASIONAL	INTERFERENCE	, MOSTLY BY WAY OF JOBBING PUBLIC APPOINTMENTS,

INTERFERENCES

METH PREFACE(R35)	TO THE ABSURDITY OF THE BELIEF IN THESE VIOLENT	INTERFERENCES	WITH THE ORDER OF NATURE BY A SHORT-TEMPERED
MILL PREFACE(118)	AND SWEATING WERE JEALOUSLY RESISTED AS	INTERFERENCES	WITH THE LIBERTY OF FREE BRITONS. IF THERE WAS

INTERFERES

APPL I (238)	I CHOOSE? I TELL YOU, BREAKAGES, LIMITED, NEVER	INTERFERES	IN MY DEPARTMENT. I'D LIKE TO CATCH THEM AT IT.
ROCK I (203)	PAPA: I WILL NOT STAND MAMMA ANY LONGER. SHE	INTERFERES	WITH ME IN EVERY POSSIBLE WAY OUT OF SHEER

INTERFERING

FABL PREFACE(77)	HAVING CEASED TO BELIEVE IN THE BENEFICENTLY	INTERFERING	AND OVERRULING GOD OF ADAM SMITH AND VOLTAIRE,
GENV II (54)	POLITICS: I SEE. BUT WE CANT HAVE LITERARY PEOPLE	INTERFERING	IN FOREIGN AFFAIRS. AND THEY MUST HAVE HELD
POSN PREFACE(427)	OF FREEDOM BY OUR BLACKGUARDS AN EXCUSE FOR	INTERFERING	WITH ANY DISQUIETING USE OF IT BY MYSELF, THEN I
GETT PREFACE(205)	HER HEART WAS IS THE RIGHT PLACE: A STATESMAN	INTERFERING	WITH HER ON THE GROUND THAT HE DID NOT WANT THE
BULL II (114)	YOU OUGHT TO KNOW BETTER THAN ME WHETHER YOURE	INTERFERING	WITH HIM. YOUVE SEEN HIM OFTENER THAN I HAVE.
BULL II (114)	SEE YOU AGAIN. THATS ON MY HONOR: I WILL. AM I	INTERFERING	WITH HIM? /NORA/ (ANSWERING IN SPITE OF
ROCK PREFACE(177)	SUN STAND STILL. THE CHURCH'S MISTAKE WAS NOT IN	INTERFERING	WITH HIS LIBERTY, BUT IN IMAGINING THAT THE
BULL II (114)	I'M DESPERATELY SERIOUS. TELL ME THAT I'M	INTERFERING	WITH LARRY; AND I'LL GO STRAIGHT FROM THIS SPOT
CURE (236)	WOULD NEVER MEDDLE IN POLITICS OR ANNOY YOU BY	INTERFERING	WITH YOUR PROFESSION? IS THERE ANY HOPE FOR

INTERIM

BULL PREFACE(3)	THE HOME RULE EDITION OF 1912. (I REPRINT THIS	INTERIM	PREFACE AFTER MUCH HESITATION. IT IS BASED ON TWO

INTERIOR

KING I SD(161)	MAID IN MORNING DESHABILLE COMES IN THROUGH THE	INTERIOR	DOOR, WHICH IS IN THE SIDE WALL TO THE LEFT OF THE
BUOY 1 SD(9)	BILLIONS. ACT I: THE WORLD BETTERER. A MODERN	INTERIOR	. A WELL FURNISHED STUDY. MORNING LIGHT. A FATHER
CAPT I (233)	ESCORTS PARTIES OF MERCHANTS ON JOURNEYS INTO THE	INTERIOR	. I UNDERSTAND THAT HE SERVED UNDER GORDON IN THE
CAPT II (263)	A HEAD FOR EVERY PARTY I ESCORT THROUGH TO THE	INTERIOR	. IN RETURN HE PROTECTS ME AND LETS MY CARAVANS
MIS. SD(109)	TWO DOORS: ONE NEAR THE HAT STAND, LEADING TO THE	INTERIOR	OF THE HOUSE, THE OTHER ON THE OPPOSITE SIDE AND AT
BULL IV SD(145)	A MAHOGANY SIDEBOARD. A DOOR LEADING TO THE	INTERIOR	OF THE HOUSE IS NEAR THE FIREPLACE, BEHIND AUNT
ARMS I SD(3)	AT HAND, THOUGH IT IS REALLY MILES AWAY. THE	INTERIOR	OF THE ROOM IS NOT LIKE ANYTHING TO BE SEEN IN THE

INTERIORS

FANY III (308)	IT IS WHAT I THOUGHT. THESE ENGLISH DOMESTIC	INTERIORS	ARE VERY INTERESTING. (HE GOES OUT, FOLLOWED BY
GETT PREFACE(253)	MANY THINGS THAT MAKE SOME OF OUR DOMESTIC	INTERIORS	LITTLE PRIVATE HELLS FOR CHILDREN (ESPECIALLY

INTERJECT

ROCK PREFACE(148)	LIKE A LION IN A SHOW. HERE SOMEBODY IS SURE TO	INTERJECT	THAT THERE IS THE ALTERNATIVE OF TEACHING HIM

INTERJECTIONS

NEVR III (275)	THIS VERY SERIOUS CONVERSATION WITH IRRELEVANT	INTERJECTIONS	. (VEHEMENTLY) I INSIST ON HAVING EARNEST

INTERJECTS

CLEO V (200)	I MIGHT HAVE REVENGED POTHINUS ON IT. /CAESAR/ (	INTERJECTS	) POTHINUS! /RUFIO/ (CONTINUING) I MIGHT HAVE
ROCK II (254)	FRENCH FORM OF YOUR CHARMING NAME. /ALOYSIA/ (	INTERJECTS	) THE CHEEK! /THE DUKE/ (CONTINUING) I WAS

INTERLACED

SIM I SD(53)	IS THE KINGDOM OF LOVE. THE THREE EMBRACE WITH	INTERLACED	ARMS AND VANISH IN BLACK DARKNESS.
MTH1 I (10)	AND I BURST FROM MY SKIN WITH ANOTHER SNAKE	INTERLACED	WITH ME; AND NOW THERE ARE TWO IMAGINATIONS, TWO

INTERLACING

CAND II SD(121)	LEANING FORWARD TO HIDE HIS FACE, AND	INTERLACING	HIS FINGERS RIGIDLY TO KEEP THEM STEADY.

INTERLOCUTORS

BARB I SD(249)	OUTSPOKEN AND INDIFFERENT TO THE OPINION OF HER	INTERLOCUTORS	, AMIABLE AND YET PEREMPTORY, ARBITRARY, AND

INTERLUDE

POSN PREFACE(372)	TO AT ONCE, AND THE CENSORSHIP SAVED. A COMIC	INTERLUDE	. IT WAS PART OF THIS NERVOUS DISLIKE OF THE
APPL INTRLUD(243)	AN	INTERLUDE	. ORINTHIA'S BOUDOIR AT HALF-PAST FIFTEEN ON THE

INTERLUDES

LADY (250)	LAWS; AND THE SAME MAY WELL BE TRUE OF PLAYS AND	INTERLUDES	. (THE CLOCK CHIMES THE FIRST QUARTER. THE

INTERMARRIAGEABILITY

GENV PREFACE(23)	A CHOICE. EQUALITY, WHICH IN PRACTICE MEANS	INTERMARRIAGEABILITY	, IS BASED ON THE HARD FACTS THAT THE
FABL PREFACE(68)	NO LONGER MATTER; FOR THE EUGENIC TEST IS GENERAL	INTERMARRIAGEABILITY	; AND THOUGH THE DIFFERENCE BETWEEN 5

INTERMARRIAGEABLE

ROCK PREFACE(170)	WITHOUT GREAT DISCOMFORT, AND ARE PRACTICALLY NOT	INTERMARRIAGEABLE	. IT IS POSSIBLE TO GET RID OF THEIR
GENV PREFACE(23)	MENTAL DOMAIN IS THE UNIVERSE. THEIR CHILDREN ARE	INTERMARRIAGEABLE	WITHOUT MISALLIANCE. BUT WHEN WE FACE THE

INTERMARRY

BARB PREFACE(234)	WHO MUST NOT BE INTRODUCED TO ONE ANOTHER OR	INTERMARRY	. NAPOLEON CONSTRUCTING A GALAXY OF GENERALS AND

INTERMEDIARIES

WIDO II (42)	DID FOR ME, I DO FOR YOU. HE AND I ARE ALIKE	INTERMEDIARIES	: YOU ARE THE PRINCIPAL. IT IS BECAUSE OF THE

INTERMEDIATE

ROCK II (245)	BECOME THE ROBBED. I WISH YOU WOULD CREATE SOME	INTERMEDIATE	CLASS OF HONEST FOLK. I DISLIKE YOUR CALLING ME

INTERNAL

APPL PREFACE(190)	CO-ORDINATE THE FEDERAL WORK. OUR OBSOLETE LITTLE	INTERNAL	FRONTIERS MUST BE OBLITERATED, AND OUR UNITS OF
MTH5 (233)	PRODUCTS AND A REPRODUCTIVE SYSTEM CAPABLE OF	INTERNAL	NOURISHMENT AND INCUBATION. /ECRASIA/ WHY DID YOU
DOCT PREFACE(5)	THROAT AND KILLS THE PATIENT, OR EXTIRPATES AN	INTERNAL	ORGAN AND KEEPS THE WHOLE NATION PALPITATING FOR
BULL IV SD(151)	SPIRITS PRESENT, A QUESTION OF VOCIFERATION OR	INTERNAL	RUPTURE. /BROADBENT/ THANK YOU FROM THE BOTTOM OF
LIED (199)	OWN UP. YOU WROTE THOSE POEMS TO MY WIFE. (AN	INTERNAL	STRUGGLE PREVENTS HENRY FROM ANSWERING). OF COURSE

INTERNATIONAL

DOCT PREFACE(74)	PRACTICE AND BIOLOGICAL RESEARCH, WHICH ARE	INTERNATIONAL	ACTIVITIES, THAT THE PLAY WHICH FURNISHES THE
APPL II (263)	BY THE SYNTHETIC BUILDING MATERIALS TRUST, AN	INTERNATIONAL	AFFAIR. BELIEVE ME, THE ENGLISH PEOPLE, THE
APPL I (221)	OR THE ENGLISH PARLORMAID? SHE WINS AT ALL THE	INTERNATIONAL	BEAUTY SHOWS. /PLINY/ NOW MANDY, MANDY! NONE
SIM II (63)	LITTLE POPULAR INTEREST. /KANCHIN/ THE VARIOUS	INTERNATIONAL	BOARDS ARE CARRYING ON AS USUAL. /JANGA/
BULL PREFACE(21)	OF COMMON SENSE, INTELLECTUAL DELICACY, AND	INTERNATIONAL	CHIVALRY AS NELSON, IT MAY BE CONTENDED THAT
MRS PREFACE(151)	MISTRESS, BUT ORGANIZED AND EXPLOITED AS A BIG	INTERNATIONAL	COMMERCE FOR THE PROFIT OF CAPITALISTS LIKE
GENV I (29)	PARDON, MADEMOISELLE: I SEEK THE OFFICE OF THE	INTERNATIONAL	COMMITTEE FOR INTELLECTUAL CO-OPERATION. /SHE/
SUPR PREFACE(R25)	OF BRITAIN, THE CONSTRUCTION OF A PRACTICALLY	INTERNATIONAL	COMMONWEALTH, AND THE PARTITION OF THE WHOLE
APPL PREFACE(184)	BEING FORCED ON US BY THE GROWTH OF NATIONAL AND	INTERNATIONAL	CORPORATE ACTION. NOW CORPORATE ACTION IS
JOAN PREFACE(29)	OF THE TWO) WERE COURTS CHRISTIAN: THAT IS,	INTERNATIONAL	COURTS; AND SHE WAS TRIED, NOT AS A TRAITRESS,
GENV I (34)	MADEMOISELLE. WHAT YOU MUST DO IS TO WRITE TO THE	INTERNATIONAL	COURT, CALLING ON IT TO ISSUE A WARRANT FOR
GENV I (37)	DID YOU BY ANY CHANCE WANT A WARRANT FROM THE	INTERNATIONAL	COURT AT THE HAGUE? /THE WIDOW/ YES: THAT IS
GENV I (36)	HIM? /SHE/ QUITE SIMPLE. I SHALL APPLY TO THE	INTERNATIONAL	COURT AT THE HAGUE FOR A WARRANT FOR HIS
GENV I (43)	MOST OFFICIAL AIR) SURELY THIS IS A CASE FOR THE	INTERNATIONAL	COURT AT THE HAGUE, MY LORD. /BISHOP/ YES,
GENV II (59)	SIR MIDLANDER, YOU WOULD NOT LIKE IT. AND IF THE	INTERNATIONAL	COURT, MOVED BY THE COMMITTEE FOR INTELLECTUAL
GENV II (60)	WRONGS. IT HAS VERY PROPERLY REFERRED THEM TO THE	INTERNATIONAL	COURT. AS PRESIDENT OF THAT COURT IT IS MY
GENV III (65)	FRESH FROM THE HAGUE? /THE JOURNALIST/ YES. THE	INTERNATIONAL	COURT HAS ABOLISHED INTELLECTUAL CO-OPERATION
GENV IV (90)	OF DESTINY. /BOMBARDONE/ IS THIS THE SO-CALLED	INTERNATIONAL	COURT? /THE JUDGE/ IT IS. /BBDE/ MY NAME IS
GENV IV (89)	I'M SORRY. YOU SHOULD HAVE BEEN WARNED. IN THE	INTERNATIONAL	COURT NO WALLS CAN HIDE YOU, AND NO DISTANCE
GENV III (75)	I HAVE SAID I HAVE SAID. /THE JUDGE/ WHEN THE	INTERNATIONAL	COURT WAS MOVED TO ACTION BY THE ENTERPRISE OF
GENV IV (115)	QUITE CONVENTIONAL. /FLANCO/ PARDON. IS THIS THE	INTERNATIONAL	COURT? /JUDGE/ IT IS. /FLANCO/ MY NAME IS
VWOO 3 (133)	YOU? /A/ MRS WARD SHOULD HAVE GONE TO GENEVA.	INTERNATIONAL	FINANCE WOULD HAVE COME NATURALLY TO HER. /Z/
2TRU PREFACE(24)	HIERARCHY. PANEL A WOULD BE FOR DIPLOMACY AND	INTERNATIONAL	FINANCE, PANEL B FOR NATIONAL AFFAIRS, PANEL C
SUPR HANDBOK(190)	EDUCATED BY THE SAME VARIETY AND INTIMACY OF	INTERNATIONAL	INTERCOURSE, THERE MIGHT BE LITTLE TO CHOOSE
BULL I (91)	CHEMISTRY MAY BE, IT'S NOT NATIONAL. IT'S	INTERNATIONAL	. AND MY BUSINESS AND YOURS AS CIVIL ENGINEERS
JOAN PREFACE(23)	WITH CATHOLICISM AND FEUDALISM, BOTH ESSENTIALLY	INTERNATIONAL	, SHE WORKED BY COMMONSENSE; AND WHERE
GENV III (86)	TRIAL OF THE DICTATORS BY THE PERMANENT COURT OF	INTERNATIONAL	JUSTICE HAS BEEN FIXED FOR THIS DAY FORTNIGHT.
GENV IV (92)	IS THIS THE SITTING OF THE DEPARTMENT OF	INTERNATIONAL	JUSTICE? /BBDE/ (SPRINGING UP) BATTLER, BY
GENV II (57)	WELL, SIR MIDLANDER, THE JUDGES OF THE COURT OF	INTERNATIONAL	JUSTICE ARE NOT NONENTITIES. WE HAVE WAITED A
GENV II (55)	(TO SIR O.) THE SENIOR JUDGE OF THE COURT OF	INTERNATIONAL	JUSTICE AT THE HAGUE IS DOWNSTAIRS. HADNT YOU
GENV II (52)	THOSE LETTERS THAT YOU SENT TO THE COURT OF	INTERNATIONAL	JUSTICE AT THE HAGUE-- /BEGONIA/ OH, OF
GENV I (33)	COMMITTEE CAN ACT THROUGH THE PERMANENT COURT OF	INTERNATIONAL	JUSTICE AT THE HAGUE, WHICH IS ALSO AN ORGAN
GENV I (30)	THAT AFTER VISITING THE MAGNIFICENT PALACE OF THE	INTERNATIONAL	LABOR OFFICE AND THE NEW QUARTERS OF THE
GENV II (60)	SHOULD FORM THE BEGINNING OF A NEW CODE OF	INTERNATIONAL	LAW AND BE QUITE UNPRECEDENTED. /SIR O./ BUT,
GENV IV (121)	SO FAR, MY WORK OF BUILDING UP A BODY OF	INTERNATIONAL	LAW BY JUDICIAL PRECEDENT WOULD SEEM TO BE
BULL PREFACE(12)	TRADE BY TARIFFS, IT HAD BETTER BE DONE BY	INTERNATIONAL	LAW THAN BY ARBITRARY NATIONAL FORCE AS AT
FABL PREFACE(84)	COMMUNISM, WHICH IS MORE THAN TROTSKY CLAIMED FOR	INTERNATIONAL	MARXISM. WITH ALL THIS STARING THEM IN THE
SUPR HANDBOK(191)	SOCIAL AGGREGATION ARRIVES AT A POINT DEMANDING	INTERNATIONAL	ORGANIZATION BEFORE THE DEMAGOGUES AND
SUPR HANDBOK(179)	BUT WE HAVE NOW REACHED THE STATE OF	INTERNATIONAL	ORGANIZATION. MAN'S POLITICAL CAPACITY AND
BULL PREFACE(10)	POCKET; AND RUN AWAY, WAS, IN THE ABSENCE OF ANY	INTERNATIONAL	POLICE, A PROFITABLE BIT OF SPORT, IF A
BULL PREFACE(34)	IDEA OF FOREIGN RULE BY A SPIRITUALLY SUPERIOR	INTERNATIONAL	POWER, AND IS TRAINED TO SUBMISSION AND
HART PREFACE(7)	SCIENCE WAS IN THE DAYS OF CHARLES THE SECOND. IN	INTERNATIONAL	RELATIONS DIPLOMACY HAS BEEN A BOYISHLY
BULL PREFACE(11)	TIBET IF TIBET PERSIST IN REFUSING ME MY	INTERNATIONAL	RIGHTS. IF THE MOORS AND ARABS CANNOT OR WILL
BULL PREFACE(11)	LENDS ITSELF, I AM NOT FORGETTING THAT THERE ARE	INTERNATIONAL	RIGHTS AS WELL AS NATIONAL ONES. WE ARE NOT
BULL PREFACE(12)	FROM AMERICA AND AUSTRALIA IS A VIOLATION OF	INTERNATIONAL	RIGHT WHICH THE CHINESE WILL BE PERFECTLY
GENV III (68)	PEOPLE GOD'S CHOSEN RACE. YOU ARE SUPPOSED TO BE	INTERNATIONAL	STATESMEN; BUT NONE OF YOU COULD KEEP A COFFEE
ROCK I (218)	IT. FIFTY YEARS AFTER HE FOUNDED HIS RED	INTERNATIONAL	THE WORKING CLASSES OF EUROPE ROSE UP AND SHOT
BULL PREFACE(12)	INTER-MARRIAGE WITH FOREIGNERS, AND EVEN	INTERNATIONAL	TRADE BY TARIFFS, IT HAD BETTER BE DONE BY
MTH4 I (161)	THAN THE COLLECTOR OF USED POSTAGE STAMPS ABOUT	INTERNATIONAL	TRADE OR LITERATURE. THE SCIENTIFIC TERRORIST
2TRU PREFACE(25)	OTHERS TO ABSORB ITS UNEMPLOYED BY A REVIVAL OF	INTERNATIONAL	TRADE. MR CHESTERTON SAYS TRULY THAT A
FABL PREFACE(98)	FOLLOWED BY MASSACRES, WITCH HUNTS, CIVIL AND	INTERNATIONAL	WARS OF RELIGION, AND ALL FORMS OF

INTERNATIONALISM

GENV II (61)	OH, I SEE. INTERNATIONALISM. /THE SECRETARY/ NO.	INTERNATIONALISM	IS NONSENSE. PUSHING ALL THE NATIONS INTO
GENV II (61)	NO. SUPERNATIONALISM. /SIR O./ OH, I SEE.	INTERNATIONALISM	. /THE SECRETARY/ NO. INTERNATIONALISM IS
GENV IV (91)	PART, AS IT HAPPENS. THE WORLD MOVES TOWARDS	INTERNATIONALISM	. WITHOUT THIS MOVEMENT TO NERVE YOU YOU

INTERNATIONALIST

GENV IV (91)	HOW CAN YOU BE AT ONCE A NATIONALIST AND AN	INTERNATIONALIST	? /BBDE/ HOW CAN I BE ANYTHING ELSE? HOW
GENV III (75)	THE ATMOSPHERE OF GENEVA CHANGED ME. I AM NOW AN	INTERNATIONALIST	. I AM THE RUTHLESS ENEMY OF EVERY NATION,
2TRU PREFACE(14)	LEFT COMMUNIST) AND CATHOLIC (OR EQUALITARIAN	INTERNATIONALIST	) IT IS HOW TO SELECT RULERS WHO WILL

INTERNATIONALIZE

SUPR HANDBOK(191)	MANAGE EVEN A COUNTRY PARISH PROPERLY MUCH LESS	INTERNATIONALIZE	CONSTANTINOPLE, THE WHOLE POLITICAL

INTERNED

AUGS (267)	BAKER THAT BAKED ROLLS WAS A HUN; AND HE'S BEEN	INTERNED	. /AUGUSTUS/ QUITE RIGHT, TOO. AND WAS THERE NO
GENV PREFACE(4)	GERMAN ONE INTO THE RIVER PLATE, RATHER THAN BE	INTERNED	WITH HIS CREW THE GERMAN CAPTAIN PUT TO SEA AGAIN

INTERPOLATED

LADY PREFACE(225)	ARE EITHER STROKES OF CHARACTER-DRAWING OR GAGS	INTERPOLATED	BY THE ACTORS. THIS IDEAL SHAKESPEAR WAS TOO
CAPT NOTES (306)	SPEECH DWELL TOO DERISIVELY ON THE DROPPED OR	INTERPOLATED	H. AMERICAN WRITERS HAVE APPARENTLY NOT NOTICED
CAPT NOTES (306)	HE WHO RIDICULES A DROPPED H A SNOB. AS TO THE	INTERPOLATED	H, MY EXPERIENCE AS A LONDON VESTRYMAN HAS

INTERPOLATION

LION PREFACE(18)	HELD THAT THE STORY OF THE HOLY GHOST IS A LATER	INTERPOLATION	BORROWED FROM THE GREEK AND ROMAN IMPERIAL
LION PREFACE(18)	UNCONSCIOUS OF IT. A BETTER GROUND FOR SUSPECTING	INTERPOLATION	IS THAT ST PAUL KNEW NOTHING OF THE DIVINE
CAPT NOTES (302)	RECOVERY OF THE ESTATE BY THE NEXT HEIR, IS AN	INTERPOLATION	OF MY OWN. IT IS NOT, HOWEVER, AN INVENTION.

INTERPOLATIONS

LION PREFACE(40)	ASSUME AS A MATTER OF COMMON SENSE THAT,	INTERPOLATIONS	APART, THE GOSPELS ARE DERIVED FROM
LION PREFACE(5)	AND HOW FAR THEY CONSIST OF GREEK AND CHINESE	INTERPOLATIONS	. THE RECORD THAT JESUS SAID CERTAIN THINGS
LION PREFACE(91)	NOTHING BUT DISPUTES AS TO WHETHER THEY ARE	INTERPOLATIONS	OR NOT, IN WHICH PAUL IS ONLY THE MAN WHO

INTERPOLATORS

LION PREFACE(18)	BEEN UNCONSCIOUS OF THE CONTRADICTION: INDEED THE	INTERPOLATORS	THEMSELVES MUST HAVE BEEN UNCONSCIOUS OF IT. A

INTERPOSED

METH PREFACE(R35)	UNDER SENTENCE OF EXTERMINATION IN FIVE MINUTES,	INTERPOSED	AND FORBADE THE EXPERIMENT, PLEADING AT THE SAME

INTERPOSES

NEVR III (273)	WITH JOY. (SOME QUICK TAUNT IS ON HER LIPS: HE	INTERPOSES	SWIFTLY) NO: I NEVER SAID THAT BEFORE: THATS NEW.
DEVL III (74)	IS STRIDING TO THE CART WHEN JUDITH ADVANCES AND	INTERPOSES	WITH HER ARMS STRETCHED OUT TO HIM. RICHARD,

INTERPOSING

NEVR III (275)	MR VALENTINE WISHES TO MARRY YOU-- /VALENTINE/ (	INTERPOSING	ADROITLY) I DO. /M'COMAS/ (HUFFILY) IN THAT
NEVR III (266)	WELL, YES: I'M IN LOVE WITH GLORIA. (	INTERPOSING	AS SHE IS ABOUT TO SPEAK) I KNOW WHAT YOURE
DEVL I (23)	EXCELLENT DISPOSAL OF HIS PROPERTY. /ANDERSON/ (	INTERPOSING	BEFORE MRS DUDGEON CAN RETORT) THAT IS NOT WHAT
NEVR IV (305)	THE BEST OF IT) MAY I HAVE A DANCE-- /BOHUN/ (	INTERPOSING	IN HIS GRANDEST DIAPASON) EXCUSE ME: I CLAIM
LION II (129)	SPRINGS FORWARD. /LAVINIA/ (RISING QUICKLY AND	INTERPOSING	) BROTHER, BROTHER: YOU FORGET. /FERROVIUS/ (
CYMB V (143)	UP AND STANDS ON THE DEFENSIVE). /PISANIO/ (	INTERPOSING	) HANDS OFF MY MASTER! HE IS KIN TO THE KING.
JOAN 4 (98)	ORLEANS! /CAUCHON/ LET ME REMIND -- /WARWICK/ (	INTERPOSING	) I KNOW WHAT YOU ARE GOING TO SAY, MY LORD.
PYGM III (252)	HAVE I SAID ANYTHING I OUGHTNT? /MRS HIGGINS/ (	INTERPOSING	) NOT AT ALL, MISS DOOLITTLE. /LIZA/ WELL, THATS
SUPR III (83)	EXASPERATED) HERE-- /TANNER/ (RISING QUICKLY AND	INTERPOSING	) OH COME, HENRY: EVEN IF YOU COULD FIGHT THE
BARB III (318)	HANDS WITH HIM). /LADY BRITOMART/ (RISING AND	INTERPOSING	) STEPHEN: I CANNOT ALLOW YOU TO THROW AWAY AN
JOAN 6 (134)	IF YOU WILL BE REASONABLE. /THE INQUISITOR/ (	INTERPOSING	) THIS IS NOT YET IN ORDER. YOU FORGET, MASTER
JOAN 5 (119)	THE COUNSELS OF YOUR COMMANDERS -- /DUNOIS/ (	INTERPOSING	) TO PUT IT QUITE EXACTLY, IF YOU ATTEMPT TO
LION II (137)	BOY MAKE A MOVEMENT TOWARDS THEM. /FERROVIUS/ (	INTERPOSING	) TOUCH THEM, DOGS; AND WE DIE HERE, AND CHEAT
WIDO I (5)	(THE PORTER DOES NOT UNDERSTAND). /WAITER/ (	INTERPOSING	) ZESE ZHENTELLMEN ARE USING ZIS TABLE, ZARE.
NEVR II (241)	ASK A BLESSING IN THIS HOUSEHOLD? /PHILIP/ (	INTERPOSING	SMARTLY) LET US FIRST SETTLE WHAT WE ARE ABOUT
JOAN 6 (125)	POLITICAL NECESSITY, MY LORD. /THE INQUISITOR/ (	INTERPOSING	SMOOTHLY) YOU NEED HAVE NO ANXIETY ABOUT THE

INTERPRET

JOAN 5 (113)	WITH THE NAME OF GOD AS YOU ARE, IT BECAUSE I	INTERPRET	HIS WILL WITH THE AUTHORITY OF THE CHURCH AND OF
SUPR PREFACE(R27)	OMNISCIENCE CAN DEVISE FOR THEM, AND THEY WILL	INTERPRET	IT INTO MERE FASHIONABLE FOLLY OR CANTING CHARITY
BULL PREFACE(12)	BURDEN, AS MOST OF MR KIPLING'S READERS SEEM TO	INTERPRET	IT. TRIBES MUST MAKE THEMSELVES INTO NATIONS
FANY III (309)	GREATLY DISTRESSED IF YOU OR MRS GILBEY WERE TO	INTERPRET	MY NOTICE AS AN EXPRESSION OF DISSATISFACTION.
MTH4 I (171)	MAKE NO DIFFERENCE, BECAUSE THE SHORTLIVED CANNOT	INTERPRET	THE PLAINEST WRITINGS. YOUR SCRIPTURES COMMAND YOU
MTH1 II (34)	IT TOOK ENOCH TWO HUNDRED YEARS TO LEARN TO	INTERPRET	THE WILL OF THE VOICE. WHEN HE WAS A MERE CHILD OF
2TRU II (54)	WELL. IF YOU ARE THE INTERPRETER YOU HAD BETTER	INTERPRET	THIS FOR ME. (HE PROFFERS THE LETTER). /MEEK/ (

INTERPRETATION

KING I (213)	TRIFLES BESIDE OUR GREAT LABOR OF CREATION AND	INTERPRETATION	. /JAMES/ I HAD A BOATSWAIN ONCE IN MY
JOAN PREFACE(30)	LUXURIES, BUT CALLING ON HER TO ACCEPT ITS	INTERPRETATION	OF GOD'S WILL, AND TO SACRIFICE HER OWN, SHE
CLEO NOTES (212)	THIS STORY, OR ACCEPT THE TRADITIONAL SENTIMENTAL	INTERPRETATION	OF IT, THERE IS STILL ABUNDANT EVIDENCE OF
JOAN 6 (136)	HERE, WILL YOU SUBMIT YOUR CASE TO THE INSPIRED	INTERPRETATION	OF THE CHURCH MILITANT? /JOAN/ I AM A
METH PREFACE(R40)	IGNORAMUSES CLAIMING INFALLIBILITY FOR THEIR	INTERPRETATION	OF THE BIBLE, WHICH WAS REGARDED, NOT AS
BUOY PREFACE(6)	NO HIGHER THAN A SCHOOLBOY'S CRIB, AND THE	INTERPRETATION	OF THE BIBLE AS FAR MORE IMPORTANT. IN THIS
GETT PREFACE(240)	WHICH DIVORCE CAN BE GRANTED ADMIT OF SO WIDE AN	INTERPRETATION	THAT ALL UNHAPPY MARRIAGES CAN BE DISSOLVED
LADY PREFACE(225)	EVERY CONSIDERATION OF FACT, TRADITION, OR	INTERPRETATION	, THAT POINTED TO ANY HUMAN IMPERFECTION IN

INTERPRETATIONS

METH PREFACE(R81)	AND NOT ACCORDING TO HIS OWN PERSONAL	INTERPRETATIONS	IF THESE HAPPEN TO BE HETERODOX. IT WILL BE
FABL PREFACE(82)	THE FACE OF THESE HARD FACTS MOST OF THE CURRENT	INTERPRETATIONS	OF THE WORD DEMOCRACY ARE DANGEROUS
UNPL PREFACE(R20)	LATELY SEEN SOME REMARKABLY SYMPATHETIC STAGE	INTERPRETATIONS	OF POETIC DRAMA, FROM THE EXPERIMENTS OF

INTERPRETED

SUPR III (117)	ALL HER DEFECTS. /DON JUAN/ SHE DID MORE: SHE	INTERPRETED	ALL THE OTHER TEACHING FOR ME. AH, MY FRIENDS,
SUPR III (92)	PLACE. /DON JUAN/ PROVIDED MY STAYING BE NOT	INTERPRETED	AS PURSUIT. /ANA/ (RELEASING HIM) YOU MAY WELL
MRS III (227)	(A LITTLE TAKEN ABACK AT BEING SO PRECISELY	INTERPRETED	) OH, IT'S NOT THAT. BUT WHILE WE'RE IN THIS
LION PREFACE(50)	THAT SURROUNDS HIS HEAD IN THE PICTURES MAY BE	INTERPRETED	SOME DAY AS A LIGHT OF SCIENCE RATHER THAN A
ROCK PREFACE(161)	WERE COMMUNIZED, SOME OF THE LOCAL STATIONMASTERS	INTERPRETED	THE CHANGE AS MEANING THAT THEY MIGHT NOW BE AS

INTERPRETER

JITT PREFACE(3)	ASKED TO SEE ME WITH A VIEW TO HIS BECOMING MY	INTERPRETER	AND APOSTLE IN CENTRAL EUROPE. I ATTEMPTED TO
BULL PREFACE(51)	TO SHOOT; BUT THE OMDEH WAS AWAY; AND ALL THE	INTERPRETER	COULD GET FROM THE OMDEH'S DEPUTY, WHO KNEW
2TRU II (74)	(TO MEEK) HERE, YOU. YOU SAY YOURE THE	INTERPRETER	. DID YOU UNDERSTAND WHAT THAT GIRL SAID TO ME?
2TRU II (53)	DID YOU HEAR ME GIVE YOU AN ORDER? SEND ME THE	INTERPRETER	. /MEEK/ THE FACT IS, COLONEL-- /TALLBOYS/ (
2TRU II (53)	YOUR TONGUE. /MEEK/ YESSIR. SORRY, SIR. I AM THE	INTERPRETER	. TALLBOYS BOUNDS TO HIS FEET; TOWERS OVER MEEK,
JITT PREFACE(4)	SHOPS AND RAILWAY STATIONS, WITHOUT THE AID OF AN	INTERPRETER	. THE PROVERBIAL BITS OF GOETHE AND WAGNER AND
FABL PREFACE(65)	BUT MACBETH. HIGHWAY OR STILE PRODUCED AUTOLYCUS,	INTERPRETER	THE PILGRIM'S PROGRESS, BLACKSMITH JOE GARGERY.
2TRU II (52)	PUZZLES OVER IT. /TALLBOYS/ IN DIALECT. SEND THE	INTERPRETER	TO ME. /MEEK/ IT'S OF NO CONSEQUENCE, SIR. IT
2TRU II (53)	ARMY. /MEEK/ YESSIR. /TALLBOYS/ GO AND SEND THE	INTERPRETER	TO ME. AND DONT COME BACK WITH HIM. KEEP OUT OF
2TRU II (54)	AND QUITE GENTLY) VERY WELL. IF YOU ARE THE	INTERPRETER	YOU HAD BETTER INTERPRET THIS FOR ME. (HE
2TRU II (79)	THEM. /TALLBOYS/ INDEED! QUARTERMASTER'S CLERK,	INTERPRETER	, INTELLIGENCE ORDERLY. ANY FURTHER RANK OF

INTERPRETERS

DOCT PREFACE(54)	VITIATED BY THE UNRECORDED ASSUMPTIONS OF THEIR	INTERPRETERS	. THEIR ATTENTION IS TOO MUCH OCCUPIED WITH THE
SIM PREFACE(12)	THE CONCLUSIONS OF OUR PRIVATE JUDGMENTS AS THE	INTERPRETERS	OF GOD'S WILL, WHETHER WE BELIEVE IN A TRIUNE
JOAN 6 (130)	CHURCH, AND TAKING IT UPON THEMSELVES TO BE THE	INTERPRETERS	OF GOD'S WILL. YOU MUST NOT FALL INTO THE
6CAL PREFACE(90)	THE PORNOGRAPHER WANTS TO MAKE IT SALACIOUS. ALL	INTERPRETERS	OF LIFE IN ACTION, NOBLE OR IGNOBLE, FIND THEIR

INTERPRETING

DEVL EPILOG (82)	BUT WAS TYPICALLY STUPID IN VALUING AND	INTERPRETING	IT, INSTINCTIVELY SNEERED AT HIM AND EXULTED IN
BUOY PREFACE(5)	AND NEWTON, WHO, BY THE WAY, WORKED HARD AT	INTERPRETING	THE BIBLE, AND WAS ASHAMED OF HIS INVENTION OF
DEST SD(162)	CAN SEE A THING WHEN IT IS PAINTED RED FOR HIM.	INTERPRETING	THE BLUSH AS THE INVOLUNTARY CONFESSION OF
MTH2 (70)	AND FEELS QUITE SURE THAT HE IS RIGHTLY	INTERPRETING	THE DIVINE PURPOSE, HE WILL COME OUT ALL RIGHT,
KING I (211)	FUTURE I SHALL DO NOTHING BUT MY PROPER WORK OF	INTERPRETING	THE SCRIPTURES. LEAVE ME TO THAT WORK AND TO MY

INTERPRETS

SUPR I (40)	NOT MISUNDERSTAND IT, I HOPE. /TANNER/ MY BLOOD	INTERPRETS	FOR ME, ANN. POOR RICKY TICKY TAVY! /ANN/ (

INTERRED

DOCT IV (169)	THAT MOST MEN DO LIVES AFTER THEM: THE EVIL LIES	INTERRED	WITH THEIR BONES. YES: INTERRED WITH THEIR BONES.
DOCT IV (169)	THE EVIL LIES INTERRED WITH THEIR BONES. YES:	INTERRED	WITH THEIR BONES. BELIEVE ME, PADDY, WE ARE ALL

INTERREGNUM

LION PREFACE(14)	GRATUITOUS RELIGION OF THE POOR THERE COMES AN	INTERREGNUM	IN WHICH THE REDEEMER, THOUGH CONCEIVED BY THE

INTERROGATED

UNPL PREFACE(R23)	AT THE COST OF INTELLECTUAL OBSCURITY? IBSEN,	INTERROGATED	AS TO HIS MEANING, REPLIED " WHAT I HAVE SAID,
GETT PREFACE(243)	ALL SORTS OF PRIVATIONS. WHEN A GIRL, SIMILARLY	INTERROGATED	, SAYS SHE WANTED FINE CLOTHES, OR MORE FUN, OR

INTERROGATION

FABL VI (125)	BEYOND KNOWLEDGE. ALL THE WHYS LEAD TO THE GREAT	INTERROGATION	MARK THAT SHINES FOR EVER ACROSS THE SKY LIKE

INTERROGATIVE

ARMS II SD(28)	TYPE. THE RIDGES OF HIS EYEBROWS, CURVING WITH AN	INTERROGATIVE	TWIST ROUND THE PROJECTIONS AT THE OUTER

INTERROGATIVELY

BULL III (126)	/CORNELIUS/ NO: I DONT KNOW THAT HE IS. /LARRY/ (	INTERROGATIVELY	) WELL? THEN? /MATTHEW/ (BREAKING OUT
ROCK I SD(224)	ORATOR IN HIM. HE RAISES HIS HEAD AND REPEATS IT	INTERROGATIVELY	; THEN TRIES ITS EFFECT SWEETLY AND SOLEMNLY

INTERRUPT

POSN (456)	SHERIFF'S COURT OR IS IT A SALOON? /BLANCO/ DONT	INTERRUPT	A LADY IN THE ACT OF HANGING A GENTLEMAN. WHERES
LIED (193)	THATS ALL VERY WELL; MR APJOHN (HE IS ABOUT TO	INTERRUPT	AGAIN: BUT SHE WONT HAVE IT): NO: IT'S NO USE: IVE

BASH II,1,	(103)	TO KNOW THERE'S LAW IN ENGLAND. /LUCIAN/ DO NOT	INTERRUPT	HIM: MINE EARS ARE THIRSTING. FINISH, MAN. WHAT
MTH5	(228)	BEINGS! CONSPUEZ VOLTAIRE! CUT IT SHORT, PYG!	INTERRUPT	HIM FROM ALL SIDES). YOU WILL SEE THEIR BEARING
ROCK I	(200)	SUBJECT ARE WE ON? (TESTILY) I WISH YOU WOULDNT	INTERRUPT	ME: I HAD THE WHOLE SPEECH IN MY HEAD BEAUTIFULLY;
NEVR IV	(297)	LADY. (M'COMAS IS ABOUT TO PROTEST). NO! DONT	INTERRUPT	ME: IF SHE DOESNT MARRY YOU SHE WILL MARRY
MIS. PREFACE	(50)	SOME GOOD AT. SOME SILLY PERSON WILL PROBABLY	INTERRUPT	ME HERE WITH THE REMARK THAT MANY CHILDREN HAVE NO
BASH III	(123)	A BROKEN-HEARTED MOTHER'S GRIEF, AND DO NOT	INTERRUPT	ME IN MY SCENE. TEN YEARS AGO MY DARLING
MIS.	(127)	HAVE YOU HAD TEA, JOHN? /TARLETON/ YES. DONT	INTERRUPT	ME WHEN I'M IMPROVING THE BOY'S MIND. WHERE WAS
MILL I	(144)	THE THIRTY MILLIONS. PRECISELY. /EPIFANIA/ DONT	INTERRUPT	ME. HE MADE ME PROMISE THAT WHENEVER A MAN ASKED
NEVR IV	(289)	THINK OVER IT WHEN YOU FEEL YOUR NEXT IMPULSE TO	INTERRUPT	ME. /VALENTINE/ (DAZED) THIS IS SIMPLY BREAKING A
VWOO 2	(123)	CHEDDAR CHEESE-- /Z/ THANKS VERY MUCH. /A/ DONT	INTERRUPT	ME. YOU CAN EXPRESS YOUR GRATITUDE FOR THE ORDER
NEVR IV	(295)	MR VALENTINE-- /VALENTINE/ (PEPPERILY) DONT YOU	INTERRUPT	ME, SIR! THIS IS SOMETHING REALLY SERIOUS. I
DEVL I	(25)	I DO NOT INTERFERE WITH YOUR SERMONS: DO NOT YOU	INTERRUPT	MINE. (TO ESSIE) DO YOU KNOW WHAT THEY CALL ME,
NEVR II	(231)	/MRS CLANDON/ (SOFTLY) DEAR DOLLY! DONT LET US	INTERRUPT	MR M'COMAS. /M'COMAS/ (EMPHATICALLY) THANK YOU,
AUGS	(278)	AND DID YOU DARE TO KNOCK AT MY DOOR AND	INTERRUPT	MY BUSINESS WITH THIS LADY TO REPEAT THIS MAN'S
KING I	(172)	GWYNN HAS CALLED TO TAKE YOU AWAY, NOT TO	INTERRUPT	MY WORK ON FLUXIONS, AND IF YOU WILL CONDESCEND TO
2TRU II	(60)	SLAP ON THE MOUTH) SILENCE, GIRL. HOW DARE YOU	INTERRUPT	THE COLONEL? GO BACK TO YOUR PLACE AND HOLD YOUR
NEVR III	(275)	I MUST REALLY ASK YOU, MISS CLANDON, NOT TO	INTERRUPT	THIS VERY SERIOUS CONVERSATION WITH IRRELEVANT
PRES	(140)	/MITCHENER/ (ANGRILY) WHAT IS IT? HOW DARE YOU	INTERRUPT	US LIKE THIS? /THE ORDERLY/ DIDNT YOU HEAR THE
SUPR III	(104)	FLAT WITH THEM, COMMANDER. /ANA/ OH, DO NOT	INTERRUPT	WITH THESE FRIVOLITIES, FATHER. IS THERE NOTHING
ROCK I	(223)	ARE WE TO DO? MAMMA SENDS US IN ON PURPOSE TO	INTERRUPT	YOU WHEN SHE THINKS YOU HAVE DONE ENOUGH. /DAVID/
VWOO 1	(122)	/Z/ THATS WHAT I MEAN. WELL, I SUPPOSE I MUSTNT	INTERRUPT	YOUR WORK. /A/ YOU MEAN THAT THE STEWARD IS COMING
BULL I	(91)	DEMPSEY. /BROADBENT/ (SHREWDLY) I DONT WANT TO	INTERRUPT	YOU, LARRY; BUT YOU KNOW THIS IS ALL GAMMON. THESE
MTH5	(223)	KEEP SILENT, LET HER ALONE. /ECRASIA/ I SHALL NOT	INTERRUPT	, ACIS. WHY SHOULD I NOT PREFER YOUTH AND BEAUTY
NEVR IV	(294)	IS DOWN ON HIM INSTANTLY. /BOHUN/ NO! DONT	INTERRUPT	, M'COMAS. THE YOUNG LADY'S METHOD IS RIGHT. (TO

INTERRUPTED

PYGM III	(248)	COME FOR? /HIGGINS/ (OVER HIS SHOULDER) WE WERE	INTERRUPTED	: DAMN IT! /MRS HIGGINS/ OH HENRY, HENRY,
PHIL I	(75)	THE DOOR, RAGING). OH, THIS IS CHARMING. I HAVE	INTERRUPTED	A PRETTY TETE-A-TETE. OH, YOU VILLAIN! (SHE
BUOY IV	(54)	AMERICA OF THE LADY WHO HAS JUST LEFT US. I WAS	INTERRUPTED	AGAIN BY THE ARRIVAL OF A YOUNG MAN WHO PROPOSED
CAND III	(132)	STOPPED ME. /MORELL/ PERHAPS BECAUSE I WAS NOT	INTERRUPTED	AT THE END OF TEN MINUTES. /MARCHBANKS/ (TAKEN
HART PREFACE	(21)	AT BREAKFAST IN A WEEK-END MARINE HOTEL HAD BEEN	INTERRUPTED	BY A BOMB DROPPING INTO HIS EGG-CUP, THEIR WRATH
MRS I	SD(194)	COME IN. ON THEIR WAY TO THE PORCH THEY ARE	INTERRUPTED	BY A CALL FROM THE GATE. TURNING, THEY SEE AN
AUGS	(277)	B. (READING) " WHAT A FORGETFUL OLD" -- (SHE IS	INTERRUPTED	BY A KNOCK AT THE DOOR). /AUGUSTUS/ (
SIM II	(85)	I SHALL NOT FEAR THE DAY OF JUDGMENT. (SHE IS	INTERRUPTED	BY A ROLL OF THUNDER). BE SILENT: YOU CANNOT
6CAL	SD(96)	NOW, SIR SONNY, TELL ME ALL YOUR NEWS. I-- SHE IS	INTERRUPTED	BY A SHRILL TRUMPET CALL. /THE KING/ WHAT IS
FABL II	(107)	THE CLOSING OF ALL WINDOWS. WE MUST-- (HE IS	INTERRUPTED	BY A SIREN ALARM, FOLLOWED BY AN ARTILLERY
SUPR HANDBOK	(217)	BY ARTIFICIAL HALLUCINATION. WHEN THE PROCESS IS	INTERRUPTED	BY ADVERSITY AT A CRITICAL AGE, AS IN THE CASE
CLEO II	SD(138)	AND (ANXIOUSLY) HURRY THEM AS MUCH AS-- HE IS	INTERRUPTED	BY AN OUTCRY AS OF AN OLD MAN IN THE EXTREMITY
GENV IV	(110)	A COURT OF JUSTICE OR IS IT NOT? ARE WE TO BE	INTERRUPTED	BY EVERY DOTTY FEMALE WHO STARTS PREACHING AT
MIS.	SD(148)	YES, HA HA! AWFUL HYPOCRITES, AINT WE? THEY ARE	INTERRUPTED	BY EXCITED CRIES FROM THE GROUNDS. /HYPATIA/
ARMS I	SD(4)	TIMES THE FURNITURE OF HER ROOM. HER REVERIE IS	INTERRUPTED	BY HER MOTHER, CATHERINE PETKOFF, A WOMAN OVER
JITT III	SD(56)	RISES AND GOES MOODILY TO THE CONSOLE). THEY ARE	INTERRUPTED	BY LENKHEIM, WHO OPENS THE DOOR OF THE STUDY AND
HART I	SD(55)	MY FATHER SELFISH! HOW LITTLE YOU KNOW-- SHE IS	INTERRUPTED	BY MAZZINI, WHO RETURNS, EXCITED AND PERSPIRING.
KING I	SD(166)	PHILOSOPHY? CAN THEY MAKE A MAN GREAT? HE IS	INTERRUPTED	BY SALLY, WHO THROWS OPEN THE DOOR AND ANNOUNCES
ARMS I	SD(6)	WHAT UNSPEAKABLE FULFILMENT! THEY ARE	INTERRUPTED	BY THE ENTRY OF LOUKA, A HANDSOME PROUD GIRL IN
CAND II	SD(121)	DONT TOUCH ME. /CANDIDA/ JAMES! ! ! THEY ARE	INTERRUPTED	BY THE ENTRANCE OF MARCHBANKS WITH BURGESS, WHO
DEST	SD(182)	HIM A FEW STEPS WITH AN APPEALING GESTURE, BUT IS	INTERRUPTED	BY THE RETURN OF THE LIEUTENANT, GLOVED AND
NEVR II	SD(229)	I CANNOT BRING MYSELF TO TELL THEM. I-- SHE IS	INTERRUPTED	BY THE TWINS AND GLORIA. DOLLY COMES TEARING UP
NEVR I	(220)	MOTHER AND HE HATES HIS DAUGHTER AND-- (SHE IS	INTERRUPTED	BY THE RETURN OF VALENTINE). /VALENTINE/ MISS
SUPR II	SD(61)	DO WE START? /TANNER/ BUT-- THE CONVERSATION IS	INTERRUPTED	BY THE ARRIVAL OF MRS WHITEFIELD FROM THE HOUSE.
BUOY IV	(54)	CASE BEFORE YOUR SONS AS YOU DESIRED. I WAS	INTERRUPTED	BY THE ARRIVAL FROM AMERICA OF THE LADY WHO HAS
SIM II	(76)	ANTHEM AT THE MANSION HOUSE THE PROCEEDINGS WERE	INTERRUPTED	BY THE APPEARANCE OF AN ANGEL WITH A FLAMING
KING I	SD(177)	GENTLE SPEECH. YOU MUST CONTROL YOURSELF-- HE IS	INTERRUPTED	BY THE CLANGOR OF A CHURCH BELL, WHICH HAS A
BULL I	(80)	MUST BE KEP DOWN WID A STHRONG HAND; AN-- (HE IS	INTERRUPTED	BY THE ARRIVAL OF BROADBENT'S PARTNER). MR
DOCT I	SD(81)	THE UNTIDY BOY TO THE TIDY DOCTOR. REDPENNY IS	INTERRUPTED	BY THE ENTRANCE OF AN OLD SERVING-WOMAN WHO HAS
HART I	(53)	/LADY UTTERWORD/ OH! YOU UNFEELING-- (SHE IS	INTERRUPTED	BY THE RETURN OF THE CAPTAIN). /THE CAPTAIN/ (
HART III	(131)	IT INTO MY HOUSE, IF HE WOULD ONLY-- (SHE IS	INTERRUPTED	BY THE MELANCHOLY STRAINS OF A FLUTE COMING FROM
PYGM III	SD(247)	WHAT SHE PRONOUNCES; AND THATS WHERE-- THEY ARE	INTERRUPTED	BY THE PARLOR-MAID, ANNOUNCING GUESTS. /THE
GENV I	SD(43)	IN ENGLAND. IT IS IN THE TREATIES. HE IS	INTERRUPTED	BY THE ENTRANCE OF A VERY SMART RUSSIAN
HART I	SD(43)	THE WINDOWS PROVIDES AN UNUPHOLSTERED WINDOW-SEAT	INTERRUPTED	BY TWIN GLASS DOORS, RESPECTIVELY HALFWAY
DOCT III	(136)	FOR HIM BY BLACKMAILING HIS WIFE; AND YOUVE JUST	INTERRUPTED	HIM IN THE ACT OF SUGGESTING THAT I SHOULD
SUPR III	(97)	ME THAT HE WAS TALKING EXCELLENT SENSE WHEN YOU	INTERRUPTED	HIM. /THE DEVIL/ (WARMLY PATTING THE STATUE'S
GENV IV	(113)	THAT POINT I AM A REPRESENTATIVE WOMAN. SORRY I	INTERRUPTED	. CARRY ON, OLD MAN. /SECRETARY/ I THANK YOU,
NEVR IV	(295)	/VALENTINE/ (VERY RED) EXCUSE ME: I AM SORRY I	INTERRUPTED	. I SHALL INTRUDE NO FURTHER, MRS CLANDON. (HE
JOAN 6	(122)	/WARWICK/ GET OUT; AND SEE THAT WE ARE NOT	INTERRUPTED	. /THE PAGE/ RIGHT, MY LORD (HE VANISHES
MTH2	(38)	THE VERY LAST WORDS I WROTE WHEN YOU	INTERRUPTED	ME WERE " AT LEAST THREE CENTURIES." (HE
SUPR I	(13)	VIEWS. I WAS ABOUT TO DISPOSE OF IT WHEN OCTAVIUS	INTERRUPTED	ME. I SHALL DO SO NOW, WITH YOUR PERMISSION. (
SUPR III	(122)	ITSELF. I HAD NOT FINISHED WHEN HIS EXCELLENCY	INTERRUPTED	ME. /THE STATUE/ I BEGIN TO DOUBT WHETHER YOU
GENV I	(46)	A CONDITION WHICH SHE DESCRIBED AS " SAVED," AND	INTERRUPTED	MY WORK CONTINUALLY WITH ATTEMPTS TO SAVE ME.
LION I	SD(122)	THE CENTURION RETURNS TO HIS SEAT TO RESUME HIS	INTERRUPTED	NAP. THE DEEPEST AWE HAS SETTLED ON THE
BULL IV	(161)	EIGHTEEN MONTHS, WE SHOULD BE ABLE TO PICK UP THE	INTERRUPTED	THREAD, AND CHATTER LIKE TWO MAGPIES. BUT AS IT
PHIL I	(85)	(POLITELY) I BEG YOUR PARDON, MR CHARTERIS: I	INTERRUPTED	YOU. /CHARTERIS/ NOT AT ALL, MISS CRAVEN. (AN
SUPR III	(103)	I BEG YOUR PARDON. /THE DEVIL/ NOT AT ALL. I	INTERRUPTED	YOU. /THE STATUE/ YOU WERE GOING TO SAY
NEVR IV	(287)	ALL, MAAM. YOULL EXCUSE ME, I'M SURE, HAVING	INTERRUPTED	YOUR BUSINESS. (HE BEGINS TO MAKE HIS WAY ALONG
WIDO I	(16)	I MEAN BETWEEN YOU AND MISS SARTORIUS. WHEN I	INTERRUPTED	YOUR CONVERSATION HERE SOME TIME AGO, YOU AND
NEVR IV	(292)	PEACE REIGNS). /MRS CLANDON/ I AM AFRAID WE	INTERRUPTED	YOU, MR BOHUN. /BOHUN/ (CALMLY) YOU DID. (TO
NEVR I	(205)	YES, SO WE ARE. /PHILIP/ (APOLOGETIC) WE	INTERRUPTED	YOU, MR VALENTINE. /DOLLY/ YOU WERE GOING TO

INTERRUPTING

DEST	(184)	THEN YOU WILL PRODUCE MY BROTHER-- /LIEUTENANT/ (	INTERRUPTING	AS HE MASTERS THE PLOT) AND HAVE THE LAUGH AT
ARMS III	(70)	(STARTING AS IF A NEEDLE HAD PRICKED HIM AND	INTERRUPTING	BLUNTSCHLI IN INCREDULOUS AMAZEMENT) EXCUSE ME,
NEVR II	(238)	BUT RECOILS ON SEEING CRAMPTON. /WAITER/ (SOFTLY	INTERRUPTING	CRAMPTON) STEADY, SIR. HERE THEY COME, SIR. (
JOAN 6	(125)	ERRING BUT BELOVED CHILD? HAVE WE -- /CAUCHON/ (	INTERRUPTING	DRILY) TAKE CARE, CANON. ALL THAT YOU SAY IS
MTH2	(48)	YOU WHETHER WE LIKE IT OR NOT. WE-- /FRANKLYN/ (	INTERRUPTING	FIRMLY) I NEVER MEDDLE IN PARTY POLITICS NOW.
NEVR IV	(304)	/VALENTINE/ THE POINT IS, MR BOHUN-- /M'COMAS/ (	INTERRUPTING	FROM THE HEARTHRUG) EXCUSE ME, SIR: THE POINT
MTH5	(253)	HILLS AND ENCHANTED VALLEYS, NO-- /ACIS/ (	INTERRUPTING	HER DISGUSTEDLY) WHAT AN INHUMAN MIND YOU HAVE,
INCA	(251)	DESCENDED FROM BEDROCK THE GREAT -- /THE INCA/ (	INTERRUPTING	HER IMPATIENTLY) MADAM: IF YOU ASK ME, I
JOAN 5	(111)	TELL BEFOREHAND. THEN, OH THEN -- /DUNOIS/ (	INTERRUPTING	HER KINDLY BUT NOT SYMPATHETICALLY) THEN, JOAN,
CATH 4	(189)	A NECESSARY AND SALUTARY SEVERITY-- /EDSTASTON/ (	INTERRUPTING	HER PETULANTLY) QUACK! QUACK! QUACK!
WIDO II	(37)	ENTERS AND SHUTS IT BEHIND HIM). /SARTORIUS/ (	INTERRUPTING	HER SEVERELY) HUSH, PRAY, BLANCHE: YOU ARE
ARMS III	(66)	MEAN? /LOUKA/ (FIERCELY) IT MEANS-- /SERGIUS/ (	INTERRUPTING	HER SLIGHTINGLY) OH, I REMEMBER: THE ICE
AUGS	(273)	CERTAIN LIST OF GUN EMPLACEMENTS -- /AUGUSTUS/ (	INTERRUPTING	HER SOMEWHAT LOFTILY) ALL THAT IS PERFECTLY
DEVL II	(36)	MUST I-- /ANDERSON/ (TAKING HER HANDS AND	INTERRUPTING	HER TO COVER HER AGITATION) MY DEAR: I CAN
PHIL I	(73)	PUZZLED) OF COURSE YOU HAVE; BUT-- /CHARTERIS/ (	INTERRUPTING	HER TRIUMPHANTLY) THEN HOW CAN YOU STEAL ME
DEVL I	(6)	HAVING YOUR UNCLE'S BASTARDS-- /CHRISTY/ (	INTERRUPTING	HER WITH AN APPREHENSIVE GLANCE AT THE DOOR BY
CLEO IV	(179)	HER) PEACE, CHILD: BE COMFORTED-- /CLEOPATRA/ (	INTERRUPTING	HER) CAN THEY HEAR US? /FTATATEETA/ NO, DEAR
CLEO IV	(170)	THAT THE QUEEN REMAIN ALONE WITH-- /CLEOPATRA/ (	INTERRUPTING	HER) FTATATEETA: MUST I SACRIFICE YOU TO YOUR
CAPT II	(271)	/LADY CICELY/ BUT I ASSURE YOU-- /BRASSBOUND/ (	INTERRUPTING	HER) WHAT HAVE YOU TO ASSURE HIM OF? YOU
OVER	(175)	ABOUT PROMISES TO HIS MOTHER! -- /GREGORY/ (	INTERRUPTING	HER) YES, YES: I KNOW ALL ABOUT THAT. IT'S NOT
DEVL I	(18)	BE ASHAMED OF YOURSELF, SIR-- /RICHARD/ (	INTERRUPTING	HIM AND SHAKING HIS HAND IN SPITE OF HIM) I AM:
MRS I	(195)	NO, OF COURSE NOT: THERES THE MONEY-- /REV. S./ (	INTERRUPTING	HIM AUSTERELY) I WAS NOT THINKING OF MONEY,
JOAN EPILOG	(159)	SILLIEST THING YOU EVER HEARD OF. I -- /JOAN/ (	INTERRUPTING	HIM BY STROLLING ACROSS TO THE BED, WHERE SHE
MTH2	(64)	PEOPLE-- FOR I AM A MAN OF THE PEOPLE-- /LUBIN/ (	INTERRUPTING	HIM CONTEMPTUOUSLY) DONT BE RIDICULOUS, BURGE.
NEVR IV	(300)	THE SUICIDES, THE-- THE-- THE-- /GLORIA/ (	INTERRUPTING	HIM CONTEMPTUOUSLY) MOTHER: THIS MAN IS A
ROCK I	(219)	LAWS OF POLITICAL ECONOMY. I-- /HIPNEY/ (	INTERRUPTING	HIM CONFIDENTIALLY) NO USE, SRARTHUR. THAT GAME
JITT III	(75)	TO ME, YOU MEANT IT, DIDNT YOU? /JITTA/ (	INTERRUPTING	HIM CURTLY) YOU NEED NOT REMIND ME OF THAT
CAPT II	(256)	/BRASSBOUND/ YOUR DEFENCE-- /SIR HOWARD/ (	INTERRUPTING	HIM DETERMINEDLY) I DO NOT DEFEND MYSELF. I

MTH4 II	(184)	READING BOOKS; BUT-- /THE ELDERLY GENTLEMAN/ (	INTERRUPTING	HIM ENCOURAGINGLY) YOU MAKE HISTORY, AMBROSE.
MTH2	(78)	WHO WAS A SORT OF DEIST LIKE BURGE-- /BURGE/ (	INTERRUPTING	HIM FORCIBLY) LUBIN: HAS THIS STUPENDOUSLY
CURE	(225)	WORLD IF YOU DID BUY A FEW SHARES-- /REGINALD/ (	INTERRUPTING	HIM FRANTICALLY) I NEVER MEANT ANY HARM IN
DEVL II	(34)	WHO ARE IN DANGER. I WARNED YOU-- /ANDERSON/ (	INTERRUPTING	HIM GOODHUMOREDLY BUT AUTHORITATIVELY) YES,
GLIM	(173)	HIM UNLESS HIS BRIDE HAS A DOWRY-- /THE GIRL/ (	INTERRUPTING	HIM IMPETUOUSLY) YES, YES: OH BLESSED BE SAINT
NEVR III	(271)	TRUE? /VALENTINE/ DONT BE ANGRY-- /GLORIA/ (	INTERRUPTING	HIM IMPLACABLY) IS IT TRUE? DID YOU EVER SAY
MTH4 III	(196)	I THROW MYSELF UPON YOUR INDULGENCE-- /ZOO/ (	INTERRUPTING	HIM INTOLERANTLY) DONT THROW YOURSELF ON
WIDO II	(27)	WORK HARDLY; AND NOW YOU TURN ME-- /SARTORIUS/ (	INTERRUPTING	HIM MENACINGLY) WHAT DO YOU MEAN BY DIRTYING
WIDO II	(38)	/SARTORIUS/ (AGGRESSIVELY) SIR-- /TRENCH/ (	INTERRUPTING	HIM MORE AGGRESSIVELY) WELL, SIR? /COKANE/ (
ARMS III	(62)	IN HER OWN ROOM, LATE AT NIGHT-- /BLUNTSCHLI/ (	INTERRUPTING	HIM PEPPERILY) YES, YOU BLOCKHEAD! SHE
APPL I	(217)	THIS IS NOT A SUBJECT FOR JESTING -- /MAGNUS/ (	INTERRUPTING	HIM QUICKLY) I AM NOT JESTING, MR NICOBAR. BUT
GENV II	(57)	YOU CANT. YOUR EXPERIENCE AT THE BAR-- /JUDGE/ (	INTERRUPTING	HIM SHARPLY) I HAVE HAD NO EXPERIENCE AT THE
WIDO II	(38)	(VEHEMENTLY) I DECLARE I NEVER-- /BLANCHE/ (	INTERRUPTING	HIM STILL MORE VEHEMENTLY) YOU DID. YOU DID.
NEVR II	(233)	CLANDON, THAT YOU ARE TOO YOUNG TO-- /DOLLY/ (	INTERRUPTING	HIM SUDDENLY AND EAGERLY) STOP: I FORGOT! HAS
BULL I	(84)	TO BE IN THE OLD HOME AGAIN? TO-- /DOYLE/ (	INTERRUPTING	HIM VERY IMPATIENTLY) YES, YES: I KNOW ALL THAT
NEVR II	(248)	IT'S STRENGTH, CERTAINTY, PARADISE! /CRAMPTON/ (	INTERRUPTING	HIM WITH ACRID CONTEMPT) RUBBISH, MAN! WHAT
CLEO III	(150)	(ANGRY) APOLLODORUS-- /APOLLODORUS/ (	INTERRUPTING	HIM WITH DEFIANT ELEGANCE) I WILL MAKE AMENDS
MTH2	(60)	(IMPATIENTLY) GREAT HEAVENS! -- /LUBIN/ (	INTERRUPTING	HIM WITH QUIET AUTHORITY) ONE MOMENT, DR
BULL III	(132)	TO PUT THE TITHES ON US AGAIN. HE-- /LARRY/ (	INTERRUPTING	HIM WITH OVERBEARING CONTEMPT) PUT THE TITHES
CLEO IV	(173)	I SET MYSELF AGAINST IT-- /FTATATEETA/ (	INTERRUPTING	HIM-- WRANGLING) AY; THAT IT MIGHT BE RULED BY
CLEO II	(124)	BESIDE CAESAR. /CAESAR/ POTHINUS-- /CLEOPATRA/ (	INTERRUPTING	HIM) ARE YOU NOT GOING TO SPEAK TO ME?
CLEO IV	(178)	/CAESAR/ (ORATORICALLY) POTHINUS-- /RUFIO/ (	INTERRUPTING	HIM) CAESAR: THE DINNER WILL SPOIL IF YOU BEGIN
PYGM III	(255)	(DEEPLY INJURED) WELL I MUST SAY-- /PICKERING/ (	INTERRUPTING	HIM) COME, HIGGINS: YOU MUST LEARN TO KNOW
ARMS III	(48)	(EAGERLY) YOUR BEST CHAR-- /CATHERINE/ (HASTILY	INTERRUPTING	HIM) DONT BE FOOLISH, PAUL. AN ARABIAN MARE
PHIL II	(99)	NO CONSCIENTIOUS OBJECTION-- /CRAVEN/ (TESTILY	INTERRUPTING	HIM) I OBJECT TO THE EXISTENCE OF THE PLACE ON
NEVR IV	(290)	/M'COMAS/ (FLATTERINGLY) IF I DID-- /BOHUN/ (	INTERRUPTING	HIM) IF YOU DID, YOU WOULD BE ME, INSTEAD OF
FANY EPILOG	(331)	ON A WINTER MORNING. /THE COUNT/ BUT-- /GUNN/ (	INTERRUPTING	HIM) I KNOW WHAT YOURE GOING TO SAY, COUNT.
NEVR IV	(290)	COURSE, BOHUN, YOUR SPECIALITY-- /BOHUN/ (AGAIN	INTERRUPTING	HIM) MY SPECIALITY IS BEING RIGHT WHEN OTHER
ARMS II	(43)	ORDERS, MAJOR. LOUKA TOLD ME THAT-- /CATHERINE/ (	INTERRUPTING	HIM) MY ORDERS! WHY SHOULD I ORDER YOU TO
NEVR IV	(295)	WONT: NEVER. SHE THINKS SHE WILL; BUT-- /DOLLY/ (	INTERRUPTING	HIM) NO I DONT. (RESOLUTELY) I'LL NEVER GIVE
NEVR IV	(296)	TO BULLY US, MR BOHUN. /BOHUN/ I-- /DOLLY/ (	INTERRUPTING	HIM) OH YES YOU ARE: YOU THINK YOURE NOT; BUT
SUPR I	(30)	(RISING) NO, SIR-- /TANNER/ (RISING ALSO AND	INTERRUPTING	HIM) OH, WE UNDERSTAND: IT'S AGAINST YOUR
MTH1 II	(32)	I AM NOT, PERHAPS, VERY CLEVER; BUT-- /EVE/ (	INTERRUPTING	HIM) PERHAPS NOT; BUT DO NOT BEGIN TO BOAST OF
MTH3	(108)	TO LIVE THREE HUNDRED YEARS! I-- /CONFUCIUS/ (	INTERRUPTING	HIM) PARDON ME. SUCH A DISCOVERY WAS
FANY II	(286)	RESPECTABLE HOME-- EVERYTHING-- /MRS KNOX/ (	INTERRUPTING	HIM) THERES NO USE GOING OVER IT ALL AGAIN, JO.
GETT	(291)	YOU BACK TO YOUR PLACE IN SOCIETY-- /HOTCHKISS/ (	INTERRUPTING	HIM) THANK YOU: I HAVNT LOST IT. MY MOTIVES
SUPR III	(81)	IF IT AINT TOO LONG, OLD CHAP-- /TANNER/ (	INTERRUPTING	HIM) TSH-SH: YOU ARE A PHILISTINE, HENRY: YOU
CLEO III	(146)	AM HERE BY ORDER OF THE QUEEN TO-- /CENTURION/ (	INTERRUPTING	HIM) THE QUEEN! YES, YES: (TO THE SENTINEL)
BULL I	(90)	THE ARTS OF A POLITICAL CHARLATAN WHO-- /DOYLE/ (	INTERRUPTING	HIM) YOU MEAN THAT YOU KEEP CLEAR OF YOUR
CAPT III	(286)	THIS MAN TOLD ME-- /LADY CICELY/ (SWIFTLY	INTERRUPTING	HIM) YOU MUSTNT SAY WHAT PEOPLE TOLD YOU: IT'S
NEVR II	(235)	VEXED AND HURT, MR CLANDON-- /PHILIP/ (	INTERRUPTING	HIM) YOU WILL GET USED TO US. COME, DOLLY. (
MRS II	(206)	IS AS GOOD AS EVER IT WAS-- /MRS WARREN/ (	INTERRUPTING	HIM) YES; BECAUSE YOURE AS STINGY AS YOURE
GETT	(293)	TO MARRY EDITH. HE SAID THE SOONER I STOPPED	INTERRUPTING	HIM, THE SOONER HE'D BE READY. THEN HE STUFFED
GENV III	(79)	AH WELL, NEVER MIND, SENORA, NEVER MIND. WE ARE	INTERRUPTING	HIS HONOR THE JUDGE. (TO THE JUDGE) YOU WERE
MTH4 II	(188)	/THE ELDERLY GENTLEMAN/ (DIPLOMATICALLY	INTERRUPTING	HIS SCANDALIZED SON-IN-LAW) THERE CAN BE NO
ARMS III	(47)	IN ANY WAY, BLUNTSCHLI? /BLUNTSCHLI/ (WITHOUT	INTERRUPTING	HIS WRITING OR LOOKING UP) QUITE SURE, THANK
FANY PROLOG	(263)	AND TOLD HIM YOUR DAUGHTER-- /THE COUNT/ (	INTERRUPTING	IN ALARM) YOU DID NOT SAY THAT THE PLAY WAS BY
GENV I	(34)	(LOOKING AT THE JEWISH GENTLEMAN) I'M AFRAID I'M	INTERRUPTING	. /THE JEW/ NOT AT ALL: MY BUSINESS IS
DEVL III	(68)	MR DUDGEON. GOOD MORNING, MADAM. /RICHARD/ (	INTERRUPTING	JUDITH ALMOST FIERCELY AS SHE IS ABOUT TO MAKE
DOCT I	(112)	GET OUT. (GREATLY ANNOYED) WHAT DO YOU MEAN BY	INTERRUPTING	ME LIKE THIS? /REDPENNY/ BUT-- /RIDGEON/
ROCK I	(201)	ANYTHING? IT IS YOU WHO HAVE WASTED THE MORNING	INTERRUPTING	ME WITH YOUR SILLY REMARKS ABOUT YOUR NECKLACE.
BARB I	(255)	DREAMT OF SUCH A THING. THIS IS WHAT COMES OF	INTERRUPTING	ME. /STEPHEN/ BUT YOU SAID-- /LADY BRITOMART/ (
VWOO 3	(140)	DAMN THAT WOMAN: SHE WONT STOP TALKING TO ME AND	INTERRUPTING	MY WORK." /Z/ WELL, I TELL YOU WE WERE MADE FOR
MTH5	(246)	YOU HAVE LIVED AS LONG AS I HAVE-- /ECRASIA/ (	INTERRUPTING	RUDELY) I SHALL WORSHIP RAG DOLLS, PERHAPS.
JOAN EPILOG	(163)	INSTITUTED BY THE BISHOP OF ORLEANS -- /JOAN/ (	INTERRUPTING	) AH! THEY REMEMBER ME STILL IN ORLEANS. /THE
WIDO I	(15)	THAT I HAVE, EXCEPT THAT I LOVE-- /SARTORIUS/ (	INTERRUPTING	) ANYTHING ABOUT YOUR FAMILY, FOR EXAMPLE? YOU
JOAN EPILOG	(163)	ARC TO BE CANONIZED AS A SAINT -- /JOAN/ (AGAIN	INTERRUPTING	) BUT I NEVER MADE ANY SUCH CLAIM. /THE
ARMS III	(64)	BEING IN MY ROOM? /SERGIUS/ NO: BUT-- /RAINA/ (	INTERRUPTING	) DO YOU DENY THAT YOU WERE MAKING LOVE TO HER
WIDO I	(21)	IS IN EVERY ESSENTIAL PARTICULAR--" /COKANE/ (	INTERRUPTING	) EXCUSE THE REMARK; BUT DONT YOU THINK THIS IS
CLEO IV	(181)	FIELDFARES WITH ASPARAGUS-- /CLEOPATRA/ (	INTERRUPTING	) FATTENED FOWLS! HAVE SOME FATTENED FOWLS,
HART II	(98)	I AM POOR AND RESPECTABLE-- /MRS HUSHABYE/ (	INTERRUPTING	) HO! RESPECTABLE! HOW DID YOU PICK UP
MTH2	(67)	A LITTLE PROGRAM OF OUR OWN WHICH-- /CONRAD/ (	INTERRUPTING	) IT'S NOT A LITTLE PROGRAM: IT'S AN ALMIGHTY
JOAN 2	(75)	SOME CRACKED COUNTRY LASS HERE -- /CHARLES/ (	INTERRUPTING	) NO: HE IS SENDING A SAINT: AN ANGEL. AND SHE
BULL I	(96)	HER IN THE LOWER MIDDLE CLASS-- /DOYLE/ (	INTERRUPTING	) NOW LOOK HERE, TOM. THAT REMINDS ME. WHEN YOU
INCA	(249)	EMMANUEL ALBERT THEODORE WILSON -- /ERMYNTRUDE/ (	INTERRUPTING	) OH, PLEASE, PLEASE, MAYNT I HAVE ONE WITH A
SUPR IV	(143)	IT IS OF MINE, MISS ROBINSON-- /THE IRISHMAN/ (	INTERRUPTING	) OH, HER NAME IS ROBINSON, IS IT? THANK YOU.
GETT	(268)	LESBIA, FOR THE TENTH AND LAST TIME-- /LESBIA/ (	INTERRUPTING	) ON FLORENCE'S WEDDING MORNING, TWO YEARS AGO,
PHIL I	(92)	TO APOLOGIZE FOR JULIA, JO. SHE-- /CHARTERIS/ (	INTERRUPTING	) SHE SAID SHE WAS QUITE SURE THAT IF WE DIDNT
MILL II	(176)	TO MY FATHER ON HIS DEATHBED-- /THE DOCTOR/ (	INTERRUPTING	) STOP. I HAD BETTER TELL YOU THAT I MADE A
MTH3	(93)	ON THE DURATION OF HUMAN LIFE; AND-- /BARNABAS/ (	INTERRUPTING	) THE AMERICAN THINKS! WHAT DO YOU MEAN? I AM
INCA	(242)	OH YES. YOU ARE QUITE RIGHT -- /ERMYNTRUDE/ (	INTERRUPTING	) THERE! HER HIGHNESS FORGIVES YOU; BUT DONT
MTH4 I	(174)	ROAD CROSSES THE THAMES, IT-- /ZOO/ (CURTLY	INTERRUPTING	) THERE IS NOTHING THERE NOW. WHY SHOULD
MILL IV	(192)	OF ENTERTAINING THE CELEBRATED-- /ALASTAIR/ (	INTERRUPTING	) YES: IT'S ALL RIGHT: I AM THE TENNIS CHAMPION
MTH4 I	(164)	ARE MISTAKES, AND THAT THE GOLDEN RULE-- /ZOO/ (	INTERRUPTING	) YES, YES, YES, DADDY: WE LONGLIVED PEOPLE
MILL I	(153)	(SITTING DOWN) THANK YOU. I HOPE I AM NOT	INTERRUPTING	THIS LADY. /PATRICIA/ NOT AT ALL. DONT MIND ME.
FANY I	(278)	TO GIVE IT TO ME. /GILBEY/ MARIA: IF YOU KEEP	INTERRUPTING	WITH SILLY QUESTIONS, I SHALL GO OUT OF MY
GETT	(268)	ONLY, GETS INDELIBLY-- /LESBIA/ YES. EXCUSE MY	INTERRUPTING	YOU SO OFTEN; BUT YOUR SENTIMENTS ARE SO
SIM I	(49)	ME IDDY. NOW GO ON, LADY FARWATERS. EXCUSE ME FOR	INTERRUPTING	YOU SO LONG. /LADY FARWATERS/ YOU SEE, IDDY--
GENV I	(43)	/RUSSIAN/ QUITE WELL, THANK YOU, MY LORD. AM I	INTERRUPTING	YOUR BUSINESS? /BISHOP/ NO NO NO NO: I BEG YOU
VWOO 2	(127)	(SITTING DOWN) THANKS VERY MUCH. /A/ I AM NOT	INTERRUPTING	YOUR WORK, I HOPE. THERE IS NOTHING SO
ARMS III	(47)	/CATHERINE/ (IN A LOW WARNING TONE) YOU CAN STOP	INTERRUPTING	, PAUL. /PETKOFF/ (STARTING AND LOOKING ROUND

INTERRUPTION

2TRU II	(79)	INTERRUPTION. /TALLBOYS/ OH! YOU CALL THIS AN	INTERRUPTION	? /MEEK/ YESSIR: THERES NOTHING IN IT TO
JOAN 4	(99)	I KNEW YOUR LORDSHIP WOULD NOT FAIL US. PARDON MY	INTERRUPTION	. PROCEED. /CAUCHON/ IF IT BE SO, THE DEVIL HAS
2TRU II	(79)	RESPECTIVELY. /MEEK/ THATS ALL RIGHT, SIR. EXCUSE	INTERRUPTION	. /TALLBOYS/ OH! YOU CALL THIS AN
APPL I	(229)	EXPERIENCE AS I HAVE YOU WILL BE VERY GLAD OF AN	INTERRUPTION	OCCASIONALLY. MAY I PROCEED? SILENCE.
DOCT I SD	(96)	ENVELOPS ITS SUBJECT AND ITS AUDIENCE, AND MAKES	INTERRUPTION	OR INATTENTION IMPOSSIBLE, AND IMPOSES
MTH4 I	(149)	(VEHEMENTLY) NO. /THE MAN/ (IGNORING THE	INTERRUPTION	) BLESS YOU FOR TAKING HIM OFF MY HANDS! I
JITT III	(59)	MORNING, PROFESSOR. /LENKHEIM/ (RELIEVED BY THE	INTERRUPTION	) GOOD MORNING. WILL YOU EXCUSE ME, MRS
GENV IV	(109)	(WITHOUT TAKING THE SLIGHTEST NOTICE OF THE	INTERRUPTION	) IT IS SO SIMPLE! AND THE HAPPINESS IT BRINGS
JOAN EPILOG	(163)	(EMPHATICALLY, TO MARK HIS INDIGNATION AT THE	INTERRUPTION	) -- BY THE BISHOP OF ORLEANS INTO THE CLAIM OF
NEVR II	(242)	SIR? /M'COMAS/ (INTENSELY GRATEFUL FOR THE	INTERRUPTION	) THANK YOU, WAITER: THANK YOU. /WAITER/ (
BULL I	(89)	MENTIONED YOUR FATHER. /DOYLE/ (NOT HEEDING THE	INTERRUPTION	) THERE HE IS IN ROSSCULLEN, A LANDAGENT WHO'S
JOAN 4	(97)	AN ARRANT WITCH. /WARWICK/ (GENTLY REPROVING THE	INTERRUPTION	) WE ARE ASKING FOR THE BISHOP'S OPINION,
DOCT I	(82)	TO SEE THE DOCTOR. /REDPENNY/ (DISTRACTED BY THE	INTERRUPTION	) WELL, SHE CANT SEE THE DOCTOR. LOOK HERE:
NEVR IV	(291)	HIMSELF BACK IN HIS CHAIR, OUTRAGED BY THE	INTERRUPTION	) WHEN YOU ARE DONE, MR VALENTINE: WHEN YOU ARE
MTH2	(44)	PARLOR MAID RETURNS. FRANKLYN IS IMPATIENT AT THE	INTERRUPTION	), WELL? WHAT IS IT NOW? /THE PARLOR MAID/ MR
CAPT I	(218)	AND TURNS, RESIGNING HIMSELF DUTIFULLY TO THE	INTERRUPTION	), YR HONOR'S EOLTH. /RANKIN/ (RESERVEDLY)
POSN	(448)	NOT AS DRUNK AS THAT. /BLANCO/ (IGNORING THE	INTERRUPTION	)-- AND YOU FOUND A MAN WITHOUT A HORSE, IS A
2TRU II SD	(51)	IRRITATED BY THE RACKET OF THE BICYCLE AND THE	INTERRUPTION	TO HIS NEWSPAPER, CONTEMPLATES HIM WITH STERN
WIDO III SD	(54)	THE COFFEE CUPS. SARTORIUS, IMPATIENT AT THE	INTERRUPTION	, RISES AND MOTIONS LICKCHEESE TO THE DOOR OF

INTERRUPTIONS

ROCK PREFACE	(180)	THE BAWLING OF THE MOB, WHICH BECOME UNBEARABLE	INTERRUPTIONS	INSTEAD OF SKILFUL DIVERSIONS. FOR MY PART,
MTH4 III	(197)	WOMAN, TO BE ALLOWED TO PROCEED WITHOUT UNSEEMLY	INTERRUPTIONS	. A LOW ROLL OF THUNDER COMES FROM THE ABYSS.

INTERRUPTS

MTH4 I (162) AND YET ANOTHER; AND LO! A MOUNTAIN. I-- /ZOO/ (INTERRUPTS HIM BY LAUGHING HEARTILY AT HIM) ! ! ! ! !
CLEO PRO2 (102) IS TRUE. (AN AFFRIGHTED UPROAR IN THE PALACE INTERRUPTS HIM). QUICK: THE FLIGHT HAS BEGUN: GUARD THE
ARMS II (32) GOING TO BEGIN A LONG SPEECH WHEN THE MAJOR INTERRUPTS HIM). /PETKOFF/ STUFF AND NONSENSE, SERGIUS!
SIM II (58) /SIR CHARLES/ GOOD. (THE BOOM OF A CANNON INTERRUPTS HIM). THERE GOES THE NOONDAY CANNON! /HYERING/ I
VWOO 1 (115) HAVE TO WAIT AN HOUR. /A/ I NEVER TAKE IT. IT INTERRUPTS MY WORK. /Z/ WHY DO YOU WORK ALL THE TIME? IT'S
GETT SD(342) HAND AWAY. MRS GEORGE'S EYES OPEN VIVIDLY AS SHE INTERRUPTS SOAMES) /MRS GEORGE/ YOU PROPHESY FALSELY,
CATH 2 (178) SO I NATURALLY APPLIED TO HIM. /PATIOMKIN/ (INTERRUPTS THE CONVERSATION BY AN AGONIZED WHEEZING GROAN,

INTER-MARRIAGE

BULL PREFACE(12) ENOUGH. IF NATIONS ARE TO LIMIT IMMIGRATION, INTER-MARRIAGE WITH FOREIGNERS, AND EVEN INTERNATIONAL TRADE

INTERVAL

BASH PREFACE(88) FOR THE INDOOR SCENES, AND WITH ONLY ONE INTERVAL AFTER THE SECOND ACT. ON READING OVER THE ABOVE
BULL PREFACE(3) IN POWER, AND HAD BEEN IN POWER WITH ONE BRIEF INTERVAL FOR TWENTY YEARS. THE REASON FOR THIS APPARENT
JOAN PREFACE(55) PRACTICALLY CONTINUOUS PLAYING, BARRING THE ONE INTERVAL IMPOSED BY CONSIDERATIONS WHICH HAVE NOTHING TO DO
ARMS I (12) I MUST TAKE MY CHANCE TO GET OFF IN A QUIET INTERVAL . (PLEASANTLY) YOU DONT MIND MY WAITING JUST A
2TRU III (90) TO HEAR THE NAME FROM YOUR LIPS AFTER SO LONG AN INTERVAL . /SWEETIE/ I ALWAYS ASK A MAN WHAT HIS MOTHER
GENV PREFACE(21) WAY, THAN THAT OF NAPOLEON, WHO, WITH AN INTERVAL OF ONE YEAR, WAS EMPEROR FOR FOURTEEN YEARS.
SUPR I (14) BETWEEN MYSELF AND RAMSDEN WILL MAKE THE INTERVAL RATHER PAINFUL. (RAMSDEN COMPRESSES HIS LIPS, BUT
DEST (156) FINAL NOTES NOW MAKING A PEREMPTORY DESCENDING INTERVAL) GIUSEPPE! /NAPOLEON/ (RISING TO LISTEN) THATS
DEST (156) AND THE TWO FINAL NOTES MAKE AN ASCENDING INTERVAL). /NAPOLEON/ (STARTLED) WHO'S THAT? /GIUSEPPE/
APPL II SD(265) THE STEPS. BOANERGES HAS TAKEN ADVANTAGE OF THE INTERVAL TO PROCURE A BRILLIANT UNIFORM AND CHANGE INTO IT.

INTERVALS

GENV PREFACE(14) WHICH HAD TO PROVIDE LAW AND ORDER DURING THE INTERVALS BETWEEN DOMINATING PERSONALITIES, WHEN ORDINARY
FABL PREFACE(83) REPRESENTATION, RESTRICTED FRANCHISE, INTERVALS BETWEEN GENERAL ELECTIONS, OR OTHER " CHECKS AND
MIS. PREFACE(18) OF ADULTS FOR CHILDREN IN THE LONG PROSAIC INTERVALS BETWEEN THE MOMENTS OF AFFECTIONATE IMPULSE IS
METH PREFACE(R82) THE ARTIST SUPPLIED WITH SUBJECT MATTER IN THE INTERVALS BETWEEN THE AGES OF FAITH; SO THAT YOUR SCEPTICAL
JOAN PREFACE(53) IS BURNT, AND PEOPLE CAN PAY TO SEE IT DONE. THE INTERVALS BETWEEN THE ACTS WHILST THESE SPLENDORS WERE BEING
FABL PREFACE(66) ADAM SMITH AND KARL MARX ARRIVE ONLY ONCE AT INTERVALS OF HUNDREDS OF YEARS, WHILST CARPENTERS AND
JOAN PREFACE(54) ENDURE MORE THAN TWO HOURS OF IT (WITH TWO LONG INTERVALS OF RELIEF) IS AN INTOLERABLE IMPOSITION. NOBODY
MIS. SD(109) THE HOT-WATER PIPES WHICH SKIRT THE GLASS. AT INTERVALS ROUND THE PAVILION ARE MARBLE PILLARS WITH
GENV PREFACE(23) AND, IF THEY WILL, CHANGE THEM AT SUFFICIENT INTERVALS ; BUT THE CHOICE MUST BE LIMITED TO THE PUBLIC

INTERVENE

GETT PREFACE(254) PROVING THAT THEY BOTH DESIRE IT, MIGHT VERY WELL INTERVENE AND DIVORCE THESE CHILDREN FROM THEIR PARENTS. AT
GETT PREFACE(254) OF CHILDREN HAS ALREADY COMPELLED THE STATE TO INTERVENE BETWEEN PARENT AND CHILD MORE THAN BETWEEN HUSBAND
GETT PREFACE(257) WHO MAY, HOWEVER, BE MOVED BY EITHER PARTY TO INTERVENE IN ORDINARY REQUEST CASES, NOT TO PREVENT THE
GENV IV (112) TOOL OF THAT ACCURSED RACE. /COMMISSAR/ I MUST INTERVENE , ARE WE HERE TO DISCUSS THE JEWISH PROBLEM? IF
SIM II (55) SUGGESTION, I SUPPOSE? /PRA/ THE UNITED STATES INTERVENE WITH A FRIENDLY SUGGESTION THAT THE PARTIES SHOULD

INTERVENED

MILL I (160) TO TURN THE WILD BEASTS LOOSE AND RUN AWAY WHEN I INTERVENED . I WAS DOWN FOUR HUNDRED AND THIRTY POUNDS

INTERVENES

BULL IV (179) AN IRISHMAN PITYING ENGLAND; BUT AS LARRY INTERVENES ANGRILY, HE GIVES IT UP AND TAKES TO THE HILL AND
NEVR I SD(213) FOLLOWING THE ALTERCATION ATTENTIVELY, SUDDENLY INTERVENES . /GLORIA/ (ADVANCING) MOTHER: WE HAVE A RIGHT
ARMS II (33) IS ABOUT TO FOLLOW HIM WHEN CATHERINE RISES AND INTERVENES). /CATHERINE/ OH, PAUL, CANT YOU SPARE SERGIUS

INTERVENTION

BULL PREFACE(49) AND HIS FELLOW-OFFICERS HAVE POWER, WITHOUT THE INTERVENTION OF A JURY, TO PUNISH THE SLIGHTEST
METH PREFACE(R42) IN THE MOON, AND THIS, MARK YOU, WITHOUT THE INTERVENTION OF ANY STOCK-BREEDER, HUMAN OR DIVINE, AND
METH PREFACE(R24) CYCLIST INTO A PIANIST OR VIOLINIST, WITHOUT THE INTERVENTION OF CIRCUMSTANTIAL SELECTION, YOU CAN TURN AN
METH PREFACE(R24) OF ORGANIZED LIFE ON LAMARCKIAN LINES WITHOUT THE INTERVENTION OF CIRCUMSTANTIAL SELECTION AT ALL. IF YOU CAN
POSN PREFACE(423) FOR INSTANCE, IT MIGHT BE MADE A CONDITION OF THE INTERVENTION OF THE ATTORNEY-GENERAL OR THE DIRECTOR OF

INTERVIEW

ROCK II (257) AN ACCOUNT OF WHAT HAPPENS AS A SPECIAL INTERVIEW ; YOU KNOW THAT WE LABOR INTELLIGENTSIA HAVE TO
DOCT IV (167) MRS DUBEDAT IS NOT IN A POSITION TO CARRY THE INTERVIEW ANY FURTHER. NEITHER ARE WE. /SIR PATRICK/ GOOD
GENV II (60) I MUST ASK YOU TO EXCUSE ME, SIR MIDLANDER: OUR INTERVIEW HAS BEEN MOST INSTRUCTIVE TO ME AS TO THE ATTITUDE
DOCT IV (158) LOUIS IS SERIOUSLY ILL; AND THIS MAN WANTS TO INTERVIEW HIM ABOUT IT. HOW CAN PEOPLE BE SO BRUTALLY
MTH4 II (186) I FEEL FAR FROM COMFORTABLE ABOUT THE APPROACHING INTERVIEW ; AND THATS THE HONEST TRUTH. /THE ELDERLY
NEVR I (210) RENT; AND IVE HAD NO PATIENTS UNTIL TODAY. MY INTERVIEW WITH MY LANDLORD WILL BE CONSIDERABLY SMOOTHED BY
NEVR III (266) KNOW THAT A MAN WHO COULD MAKE AS MUCH WAY IN ONE INTERVIEW WITH SUCH A WOMAN AS MY DAUGHTER, CAN HARDLY BE A
MTH3 (94) RESPECTFULLY SOLICITS THE PRIVILEGE OF AN INTERVIEW WITH THE CHIEF SECRETARY, AND HOLDS HIMSELF

INTERVIEWED

FABL II (107) SORT OF FELLOW WAS THIS VOLATILE GAS MAN? YOU INTERVIEWED HIM. WHAT DID YOU MAKE OF HIM? /C.-IN-C./ OH, A
PPP (199) CLOTHES. I DARNED HIS SOCKS. I BOUGHT HIS FOOD. I INTERVIEWED HIS CREDITORS. I STOOD BETWEEN HIM AND THE
SIM II (76) ATHEISM. THE FIRST LORD OF THE ADMIRALTY, INTERVIEWED LAST NIGHT, SAID THAT HE COULD NOT MAKE HEAD OR
NEVR III (266) VERY DIFFERENT TO ALL THE OTHER MOTHERS WHO HAVE INTERVIEWED ME. /MRS CLANDON/ AH, NOW WE ARE COMING TO IT,

INTERVIEWING

GENV II SD(49) THE WRITING TABLE FOR THE CONVENIENCE OF PEOPLE INTERVIEWING THE SECRETARY. HE IS A DISILLUSIONED OFFICIAL

INTERVIEWS

POSN PREFACE(361) IT CONTAINS VERBATIM REPORTS OF LONG AND ANIMATED INTERVIEWS BETWEEN THE COMMITTEE AND SUCH WITNESSES AS MR
NEVR II SD(236) TO UNBUTTON HIS OVERCOAT. MEANWHILE VALENTINE INTERVIEWS THE WAITER. /VALENTINE/ WAITER! /WAITER/ (
GENV II SD(49) OF DOGGED PATIENCE ACQUIRED IN THE COURSE OF INTERVIEWS WITH DISTINGUISHED STATESMEN OF DIFFERENT

INTERWEAVING

LION PREFACE(16) AND SAVE YOU AND RENEW YOUR LIFE. AND FROM THE INTERWEAVING OF THESE TWO TRADITIONS WITH THE CRAVING FOR

INTESTATE

LION PREFACE(101) WAITS TO MAKE AN ENTIRELY REASONABLE WILL DIES INTESTATE , A MAN SO REASONABLE AS TO HAVE AN OPEN MIND

INTESTINE

HART PREFACE(10) THE PYLORUS BY CUTTING A LENGTH OUT OF THE LOWER INTESTINE AND FASTENING IT DIRECTLY TO THE STOMACH. AS THEIR
HART PREFACE(10) INSIDE WAS SAFE. THEY EXPLAINED THAT THE HUMAN INTESTINE WAS TOO LONG, AND THAT NOTHING COULD MAKE A CHILD

INTHROJOOCED

PRES (147) WHAT ELSE WOULD A YOUNG FOOL LIKE HER DO? HE INTHROJOOCED HER TO THE POET LAUREATE, THINKIN SHE'D INSPIRE

INTIMACY

GETT PREFACE(219) MARRIAGE IS A SHORT CUT TO PERFECT AND PERMANENT INTIMACY AND AFFECTION. BUT THERE IS A STILL MORE UNWORKABLE
OVER PREFACE(162) OCCUPIED WITH SEX TO AN EXTENT AND WITH AN INTIMACY AND FRANKNESS THAT WOULD HAVE SEEMED UTTERLY
FANY I (276) HOUSE. /DORA/ (PLUNGING AT ONCE INTO PRIVILEGED INTIMACY AND INTO THE MIDDLE OF THE ROOM) HOW D'YE DO, BOTH.
SUPR IV (145) IMPLY A VERY CONSIDERABLE DEGREE OF AFFECTIONATE INTIMACY BETWEEN THE PARTIES. /VIOLET/ YES: I KNOW YOUR SON
LADY PREFACE(223) THE CONSOLIDATION OF A PASSION INTO AN ENDURING INTIMACY GENERALLY PUTS AN END TO SONNETS. THAT THE DARK
MIS. PREFACE(83) OBLIGATION TO LIKE THEM AND TO ADMIT THEM TO OUR INTIMACY , BUT TO HAVE A PERSON IMPOSED ON US AS A BROTHER
SUPR HANDBOK(190) AND A POPULATION EDUCATED BY THE SAME VARIETY AND INTIMACY OF INTERNATIONAL INTERCOURSE, THERE MIGHT BE LITTLE
SUPR I (8) THAT SHE MUST, OUT OF REGARD FOR YOU, SUFFER THE INTIMACY OF THIS FELLOW TANNER. IT'S NOT FAIR: IT'S NOT
PYGM IV (267) KNOWLEDGE AND THE TREASURE OF MY REGARD AND INTIMACY ON A HEARTLESS GUTTERSNIPE. (HE GOES OUT WITH
CAND II (120) TO HIM AGAIN, SO AS TO EXPLAIN WITH THE FONDEST INTIMACY), I MEAN, WILL HE FORGIVE ME FOR NOT TEACHING HIM
LION I (111) CAPTAIN/ YOU ARE TO INSTRUCT YOUR MEN THAT ALL INTIMACY WITH CHRISTIAN PRISONERS MUST NOW CEASE. THE MEN

LION PREFACE(39) TIL I COME." NO OTHER EVANGELIST CLAIMS PERSONAL INTIMACY WITH CHRIST, OR EVEN PRETENDS TO BE HIS
MILL I SD(137) IS FENCED OFF BY HIS WRITING TABLE FROM EXCESSIVE INTIMACY WITH EMOTIONAL CLIENTS OR POSSIBLE ASSAULT BY
GETT SD(276) MRS BRIDGENORTH IS. BUT LEO AFFECTS A SPECIAL INTIMACY WITH LESBIA, AS OF TWO THINKERS AMONG THE
APPL INTRLUD(249) WOULD NOT THINK IT RIGHT TO KEEP UP HER PRESENT INTIMACY WITH ME IF I WERE MARRIED TO YOU. /ORINTHIA/ WHAT A

INTIMATE

GETT PREFACE(232) FAILURE: ONE OF THE TWO RIVALS FOR THE REALLY INTIMATE AFFECTION OF THE THIRD INEVITABLY DRIVES OUT THE
UNPL PREFACE(R20) FOUNDED ON THE CONCERT ROOM ALONE, A REALLY INTIMATE AND ACCURATE ONE. THE VERY ORIGINALITY AND GENIUS
2TRU PREFACE(25) COMMONS THEY MUST DEPEND ON THE VOTES OF THEIR INTIMATE AND EQUAL NEIGHBORS AND WORKMATES. THEY HAVE NO
GETT PREFACE(219) AUTHORIZES BETWEEN THE PARTIES IS THE MOST INTIMATE AND PERSONAL OF HUMAN RELATIONS, AND EMBRACES ALL
GETT PREFACE(231) SET UP BY A COMFORTABLE MARRIAGE IS SO INTIMATE AND SO PERVASIVE OF THE WHOLE LIFE OF THE PARTIES
MIS. PREFACE(16) THAN THEY CAN HELP, LIVING MEANWHILE IN DAILY AND INTIMATE CONTACT WITH THEIR VALETS AND LADY'S-MAIDS, WHOSE
BASH PREFACE(90) PRODUCE AN UNINTELLIGENT REVERENCE IT BROUGHT NO INTIMATE CONVICTION TO THE READER. SOMETIMES, HOWEVER, THE
PYGM EPILOG (294) NIETZSCHEAN TRANSCENDENCE OF GOOD AND EVIL. AT INTIMATE DUCAL DINNERS HE SAT ON THE RIGHT HAND OF THE
AUGS (274) CHARMING). /THE LADY/ QUITE SO. WELL, SHE IS AN INTIMATE FRIEND OF YOUR BROTHER AT THE WAR OFFICE,
MILL I (153) MIND ME. /SAGAMORE/ (INTRODUCING) MISS SMITH, AN INTIMATE FRIEND OF MR FITZFASSENDEN. /PATRICIA/ PLEASED TO
DEVL III (60) GENTLEMANLY JOHNNY, SIR, AT YOUR SERVICE. MY MORE INTIMATE FRIENDS CALL ME GENERAL BURGOYNE. (RICHARD BOWS
MTH4 I (152) MY OPINION. I THEN BECAME POPHAM TO MY FAMILY AND INTIMATE FRIENDS, AND MISTER BARLOW TO THE REST OF THE
MRS IV (242) AS AN ARTIST, AND BELIEVING THAT THE MOST INTIMATE HUMAN RELATIONSHIPS ARE FAR BEYOND AND ABOVE THE
DOCT I SD(81) IN RETURN FOR UNSPECIFIED ADVANTAGES INVOLVED BY INTIMATE INTERCOURSE WITH A LEADER OF HIS PROFESSION, AND
BULL PREFACE(65) PERSONAL AND SOCIAL CREDENTIALS, AND AN INTIMATE KNOWLEDGE OF EGYPT AND THE EGYPTIANS, CAN FIND IT
BULL PREFACE(29) ADJUSTED TO YOUR TAXABLE CAPACITY BY AN INTIMATE KNOWLEDGE OF YOUR AFFAIRS VERIFIED IN THE
BULL PREFACE(22) CAN POSSIBLY BE. NOBODY DARES TO PUBLISH REALLY INTIMATE MEMOIRS OF HIM OR REALLY PRIVATE LETTERS OF HIS
FABL PREFACE(71) AS IT IS. PARENTAL DILEMMAS. THE FIRST AND MOST INTIMATE OF THE MORAL DILEMMAS THAT ARISE FROM DIFFERENCES
GETT PREFACE(233) THERE IS NOT ROOM FOR TWO WOMEN IN THAT SACREDLY INTIMATE RELATION OF SENTIMENTAL DOMESTICITY WHICH IS WHAT
SUPR I (24) HE IS HALF VIVISECTOR, HALF VAMPIRE. HE GETS INTO INTIMATE RELATIONS WITH THEM TO STUDY THEM, TO STRIP THE
NEVR II (232) AND NOW YOU WISH TO THRUST INTO THE MOST INTIMATE RELATIONSHIP WITH US A MAN WHOM WE DONT KNOW--
GENV III (84) IF YOU HINT AT THE POSSIBILITY OF A MORE INTIMATE RELATION, YOU ARE A DEAD MAN. /THE JEW/ YOU NEED
2TRU II (80) MEEK. AND SINCE YOU ALL SEEM TO BE ON MORE INTIMATE TERMS WITH HIM THAN I CAN CLAIM, WILL YOU BE GOOD
HART II (121) BROTHER. /RANDALL/ BUT YOU SEEM TO BE ON INTIMATE TERMS WITH HER. /HECTOR/ SO DO YOU. /RANDALL/ YES;
HART II (121) /HECTOR/ SO DO YOU. /RANDALL/ YES; BUT I AM ON INTIMATE TERMS WITH HER. I HAVE KNOWN HER FOR YEARS.
METH PREFACE(R58) THAT OUR DOG AND OUR PARROT, WITH WHOM I WAS ON INTIMATE TERMS, WERE NOT CREATURES LIKE MYSELF, BUT WERE
GETT PREFACE(202) CREDIT OF A DOMESTIC PEACE WHICH IS HARDLY MORE INTIMATE THAN THE RELATIONS OF PRISONERS IN THE SAME GAOL OR
PHIL II (119) IN THE NEAREST EASY CHAIR, READING HIS JOURNAL TO INTIMATE THAT HE DOES NOT WISH TO PURSUE THE CONVERSATION).
MTH4 III SD(195) ENVOY AND HIS FAMILY, BY SHUDDERING NEGATIVELY, INTIMATE THAT IT IS IMPOSSIBLE. THE ELDERLY GENTLEMAN
BULL I (94) GRAVE, AND THROWING HIMSELF BACK IN HIS CHAIR TO INTIMATE THAT THE CROSS-EXAMINATION IS OVER, AND THE RESULT
MIS. PREFACE(13) THE AFFECTIONS OF THE INDIVIDUAL SCHOLAR IN THE INTIMATE WAY THAT, FOR EXAMPLE, THE MOTHER OF A SINGLE CHILD
JITT II (28) WITH HIM, YOU KNOW. /LENKHEIM/ WAS I REALLY INTIMATE WITH HIM? CERTAINLY WE WERE FRIENDS AT COLLEGE;
JITT II (28) THAT IS, UNLESS YOU KNOW ANYTHING. YOU WERE SO INTIMATE WITH HIM, YOU KNOW. /LENKHEIM/ WAS I REALLY
GETT PREFACE(201) MOMENTS CAN THEY EVER BE TOGETHER. A MAN AS INTIMATE WITH HIS OWN WIFE AS A MAGISTRATE IS WITH HIS

INTIMATED

INCA (245) IMITATION: A FAILURE, I ADMIT. /ERMYNTRUDE/ YOU INTIMATED THAT YOU HAD SOME BUSINESS? /THE INCA/ (
POSN PREFACE(374) TO THE PRESS; AND AFTER THE SITTING IT WAS INTIMATED TO ME THAT YET MORE COPIES WERE DESIRED FOR THE

INTIMATELY

MTH4 I (142) CONTRACTING IT. I AM QUITE ACCUSTOMED TO CONVERSE INTIMATELY AND AT THE GREATEST LENGTH WITH THE MOST
HART I (61) YOU DONT KNOW HIM; AND YOU KNOW HIM ALMOST INTIMATELY . HOW LUCID! /ELLIE/ I MEAN THAT HE DOES NOT
HART I (61) EH? /ELLIE/ NO; NO: I KNOW HIM QUITE-- ALMOST INTIMATELY . /MRS HUSHABYE/ YOU DONT KNOW HIM; AND YOU KNOW
2TRU II (60) AND SAID " DEAR AUBREY BAGOT! I KNOW HIS SISTER INTIMATELY . WE WERE ALL THREE CHILDREN TOGETHER." /THE
GETT (283) TO HAVE A LOT OF INTERESTING MEN TO KNOW QUITE INTIMATELY -- TO SAY EVERYTHING I THINK OF TO THEM, AND HAVE
JITT I (19) WE ARE PROFESSIONAL COLLEAGUES. HE KNOWS ME INTIMATELY ; AND IF HE WERE NOT SUCH A CONFOUNDEDLY BAD
JOAN PREFACE(8) CHURCH, AND THE HOLY ROMAN EMPIRE MUCH MORE INTIMATELY THAN OUR WHIG HISTORIANS HAVE EVER UNDERSTOOD
HART I (61) BUT YOU WANT TO KNOW HIM EVER SO MUCH MORE INTIMATELY , EH? /ELLIE/ NO NO: I KNOW HIM QUITE-- ALMOST
MRS II (200) HE KNOWS THE DUKE PERSONALLY. /FRANK/ OH, EVER SO INTIMATELY ! WE CAN STICK HIM IN GEORGINA'S OLD ROOM. /MRS

INTIMATES

CATH 4,SD(194) DARLING. CATHERINE RESUMES HER SEAT AS PATIOMKIN INTIMATES BY A GROTESQUE BOW THAT HE IS AT EDSTASTON'S
ROCK II SD(246) THINK IT OVER. SIR JAFNA SHRUGS HIS SHOULDERS AND INTIMATES THAT IT IS HOPELESS. THE DUKE RESIGNS HIMSELF TO
KING I (213) BORN TWENTYONE YEARS BEFORE HIM, WHO TOLD ALL HIS INTIMATES THAT THE EARTH IS A MOON OF THE SUN. /NEWTON/ DID
CAPT III SD(281) VERRY GOOD. I'M WAITING. THE BLUEJACKET TURNS AND INTIMATES THIS TO THOSE WITHOUT. THE OFFICERS OF THE

INTIMATING

APPL PREFACE(192) PLATFORM WITH HIS HAND HOVERING OVER THE BUTTONS. INTIMATING THAT THE MIRACLE WOULD TAKE PLACE WHEN MY TRUCK

INTIMATION

METH PREFACE(R89) GARRULITY OF 1920; AND THE WAR HAS BEEN A STERN INTIMATION THAT THE MATTER IS NOT ONE TO BE TRIFLED WITH. I
POSN PREFACE(364) (IN THEIR SENSE OF THE WORD) BY THE SLIGHTEST INTIMATION THAT THE KING WOULD PREFER NOT TO MEET THEM; AND
POSN PREFACE(364) RETAINER THREATENED, NOTHING BUT AN EXPRESS ROYAL INTIMATION TO THE CONTRARY, WHICH IS A CONSTITUTIONAL

INTIMIDATE

BULL PREFACE(58) WITHOUT RUDELY CALLING THIS A USE OF TORTURE TO INTIMIDATE ANTI-BRITISH WITNESSES, I MAY COUNT ON THE ASSENT
MIS. PREFACE(106) REASON FOR REFRAINING. IN SHORT, THOUGH YOU CAN INTIMIDATE HIM, YOU CANNOT BLUFF HIM. BUT YOU CAN ALWAYS
ARMS I SD(10) HIM, AND DROPS THE MANNER HE HAS BEEN ASSUMING TO INTIMIDATE RAINA. /THE MAN/ (SINCERELY AND KINDLY) NO USE,
GENV PREFACE(18) BY CLAUSE BY ANYONE WITH A BIG ENOUGH ARMY TO INTIMIDATE THE PLUNDERERS; AND THAT EUROPE WAS DOMINATED
HART PREFACE(23) USING THE IRRESISTIBLE POWERS OF THE STATE TO INTIMIDATE THE SENSIBLE PEOPLE, THUS ENABLING A DESPICABLE
APPL I (239) BY PAYING FOR IT. NO USE TRYING TO COAX THAT LOT. INTIMIDATE THEM: THATS THE WAY TO HANDLE THEM. /LYSISTRATA/
SUPR HANDBOK(222) SPOILED CHILDREN OF THEIR MASTERS, ARE FORCED TO INTIMIDATE THEM IN ORDER TO BE ABLE TO LIVE WITH THEM. IN A
SIM PREFACE(6) CONSCIENTIOUS PEOPLE WHO NEED NO HELL TO INTIMIDATE THEM INTO CONSIDERATE SOCIAL BEHAVIOR, AND WHO
MIS. PREFACE(19) WHEN THEY CANNOT FIND ANYBODY BRAVE ENOUGH TO INTIMIDATE THEM THEY INTIMIDATE THEMSELVES AND LIVE IN A
APPL I (239) (HER VOICE STILL BROKEN) I WISH I COULD INTIMIDATE THEM. /MAGNUS/ BUT WHAT CAN AMANDA DO THAT YOU
MIS. PREFACE(19) FIND ANYBODY BRAVE ENOUGH TO INTIMIDATE THEM THEY INTIMIDATE THEMSELVES AND LIVE IN A CONTINUAL MORAL AND

INTIMIDATED

2TRU III (111) HIM). I AM IGNORANT: I HAVE LOST MY NERVE AND AM INTIMIDATED : ALL I KNOW IS THAT I MUST FIND THE WAY OF
MTH4 II (177) EXACTLY. /NAPOLEON/ (FOLDING HIS ARMS) I AM NOT INTIMIDATED : NO WOMAN ALIVE, OLD OR YOUNG, CAN PUT ME OUT
PYGM V (273) CLASS; AND I HAVNT THE NERVE FOR THE WORKHOUSE. INTIMIDATED : THATS WHAT I AM. BROKE. BOUGHT UP. HAPPIER MEN
POSN PREFACE(364) COMMISSIONS OF PUBLIC ENQUIRY ARE MORE OR LESS INTIMIDATED BOTH BY THE INTERESTS ON WHICH THEY HAVE TO SIT
JOAN 2 (76) DAUPHIN) DO YOU DARE SAY SHE SHALL? /CHARLES/ (INTIMIDATED BUT SULKY) OH, IF YOU MAKE IT AN EXCOMMUNICATION
CATH 1,SD(162) MAN TO BE RECKONED WITH EVEN BY THOSE WHO ARE NOT INTIMIDATED BY HIS TEMPER, BODILY STRENGTH, AND EXALTED
MTH4 II (176) DISCOURAGEMENT FOR PEOPLE CREDULOUS ENOUGH TO BE INTIMIDATED BY IT, MADAM. I DO NOT BELIEVE IN METAPHYSICAL
MTH3 (132) AN ADULT. WHEN I WAS A CHILD I WAS DOMINATED AND INTIMIDATED BY PEOPLE WHOM I NOW KNOW TO HAVE BEEN WEAKER
APPL I (223) HOME OFFICE TO A BULLY LIKE BALBUS -- /BALBUS/ (INTIMIDATED BY THE FATE OF CRASSUS, BUT UNABLE TO FORBEAR A
METH PREFACE(R17) WANT OF ANY OTHER SCHOOLS. THE RULERS ARE EQUALLY INTIMIDATED BY THE IMMENSE EXTENSION AND CHEAPENING OF THE
DOCT PREFACE(31) HE MADE IN RUSSIA IF HE HAD NOT FASCINATED AND INTIMIDATED HIS PEOPLE BY HIS MONSTROUS CRUELTIES AND
OVER (188) I REGARD THIS AS A GREAT OCCASION; AND I WONT BE INTIMIDATED INTO BREAKING MY PROMISE. I SOLEMNLY DECLARE
SIM PREFACE(11) THE HERETICS ARE EITHER LIQUIDATED, CONVERTED, OR INTIMIDATED . BUT IT WAS INDISPENSABLE IN ITS PRIME. THE
BARB III (344) HATRED IS THE COWARD'S REVENGE FOR BEING INTIMIDATED . DARE YOU MAKE WAR ON WAR? HERE ARE THE MEANS:
CATH 4 (188) VERY HANDSOME; BUT I CANT SEE YOU; AND I AM NOT INTIMIDATED . I AM AN ENGLISHMAN; AND YOU CAN KIDNAP ME; BUT
PYGM V (273) I HAVNT THE NERVE. WHICH OF US HAS? WE'RE ALL INTIMIDATED . INTIMIDATED, MAAM: THATS WHAT WE ARE. WHAT IS
PYGM V (280) /DOOLITTLE/ (SADLY) INTIMIDATED, GOVERNOR. INTIMIDATED . MIDDLE CLASS MORALITY CLAIMS ITS VICTIM. WONT
INCA (241) HIGHNESS DISSATISFIED WITH ME? /THE PRINCESS/ (INTIMIDATED . OH NO: PLEASE DONT THINK THAT. I ONLY MEANT --
JOAN 6,SD(129) AT A TIME. COURCELLES COLLAPSES INTO HIS CHAIR, INTIMIDATED . /THE CHAPLAIN/ (SULKILY RESUMING HIS SEAT)
GENV IV (102) PEACE; BUT IT MUST BE A VOLUNTARY PEACE, NOT AN INTIMIDATED ONE. NOT UNTIL I AM ARMED TO THE TEETH AND READY
CAPT II (264) TO SIDI OR TO THE DEVIL IF I CHOOSE. I'LL NOT BE INTIMIDATED OR TALKED BACK TO. IS THAT UNDERSTOOD?
SUPR HANDBOK(188) PUTTING ON AIRS OF OFFENDED MORALITY, HAS ALWAYS INTIMIDATED PEOPLE WHO HAVE NOT MEASURED ITS ESSENTIAL
BARB II (278) PRICE) EV YOU ENNYTHING TO SY AGEN IT? /PRICE/ (INTIMIDATED) NO, MATEY: SHE AINT ANYTHING TO DO WITH ME.

CLEO III (152)	(THEY MUTTER FEROCIOUSLY; BUT HE IS NOT AT ALL	INTIMIDATED	). LISTEN: WERE YOU SET HERE TO WATCH ME, OR TO
SUPR PREFACE(R40)	WELL. THE STRONG CRITICS ARE IMPRESSED; THE WEAK	INTIMIDATED	; THE CONNOISSEURS TICKLED BY MY LITERARY
BULL PREFACE(48)	THE EXTERNAL STIMULUS OF A SHOUTED ORDER, AND IS	INTIMIDATED	TO THE PITCH OF BEING AFRAID TO RUN AWAY FROM A
CAND II (123)	AN ATTACK OF BAD CONSCIENCE TOMORROW. /LEXY/ (	INTIMIDATED	, BUT URGENT) I KNOW, OF COURSE, THAT THEY MAKE
KING I SD(208)	I TELL YOU I AM TIRED OF YOUR TANTRUMS, BARBARA.	INTIMIDATED	, BUT WITH A DEFIANT FINAL STAMP ON THE DRAWING,
PYGM V (280)	HAS SHE CHANGED HER MIND? /DOOLITTLE/ (SADLY)	INTIMIDATED	, GOVERNOR. INTIMIDATED. MIDDLE CLASS MORALITY
LION I (122)	/CENTURION/ TAKE HIM HOME. (THE SERVANTS,	INTIMIDATED	, HASTILY CARRY HIM OUT. METELLUS IS ABOUT TO
PYGM V (285)	TWOPENCE WHAT HAPPENS TO EITHER OF US. I AM NOT	INTIMIDATED	, LIKE YOUR FATHER AND YOUR STEPMOTHER. SO YOU
PYGM V (273)	NERVE. WHICH OF US HAS? WE'RE ALL INTIMIDATED.	INTIMIDATED	, MAAM: THATS WHAT WE ARE. WHAT IS THERE FOR ME
		INTIMIDATES	
MIS. PREFACE(9)	AND TORTURE AND OVERWORK THEIR CHILDREN, AND	INTIMIDATES	A GOOD MANY MORE. WHEN PARENTS OF THIS TYPE ARE
MIS. PREFACE(23)	ALL THE BLACKGUARD'S SHIFTS BY WHICH THE COWARD	INTIMIDATES	OTHER COWARDS. AND IF I HAD BEEN A BOARDER AT AN
		INTIMIDATING	
GENV PREFACE(3)	MADE PRE-ATOMIC AIR RAIDING FUTILE AS A MEANS OF	INTIMIDATING	A NATION, AND ENABLED THE GOVERNMENT OF THE
MIS. PREFACE(4)	SORT OF HELL, HOWEVER CONVENIENT AS A MEANS OF	INTIMIDATING	PERSONS WHO HAVE PRACTICALLY NO HONOR AND NO
HART PREFACE(23)	THE SUN WITH ITS DUST. IT WAS ALSO UNFORTUNATELY	INTIMIDATING	THE GOVERNMENT BY ITS BLUSTERINGS INTO USING
SUPR HANDBOK(196)	BY THE PEOPLE WHO WANT IT KILLING, COERCING, AND	INTIMIDATING	THE PEOPLE WHO DONT WANT IT, IS DENOUNCED AS A
		INTIMIDATION	
SIM PREFACE(6)	WHO ARE CAPABLE OF NO RESTRAINT EXCEPT THAT OF	INTIMIDATION	? MUST THEY NOT BE EITHER RESTRAINED OR, AS
SUPR HANDBOK(196)	THAT THE FABIANS, BY ELIMINATING THE ELEMENT OF	INTIMIDATION	FROM THE SOCIALIST AGITATION, HAVE DRAWN THE
MIS. PREFACE(104)	UNDERSTAND HOW BALEFUL IS THIS CONDITION OF	INTIMIDATION	IN WHICH WE LIVE, IT IS NECESSARY TO CLEAR UP
BULL PREFACE(32)	IRISH WELL KNOW, BY AN ABSURD SUSCEPTIBILITY TO	INTIMIDATION	. FOR LET ME HALT A MOMENT HERE TO IMPRESS ON
DOCT III (142)	WHEN THEYRE BEATEN IN ARGUMENT THEY FALL BACK ON	INTIMIDATION	. I NEVER KNEW A LAWYER YET WHO DIDNT THREATEN
DOCT III (143)	YOUVE ONLY ONE REAL TRUMP IN YOUR HAND, AND THATS	INTIMIDATION	. WELL, I'M NOT A COWARD; SO IT'S NO USE WITH
SUPR HANDBOK(205)	RELIGION, MORALITY, ARE ONLY FINE NAMES FOR	INTIMIDATION	; AND CRUELTY, GLUTTONY, AND CREDULITY KEEP
MIS. PREFACE(44)	AND SO ON UNTIL OUR WHOLE SYSTEM OF ABORTION,	INTIMIDATION	, TYRANNY, CRUELTY AND THE REST IS IN FULL
MIS. PREFACE(18)	AFRAID TO ENJOY IT. THEIR CIVILIZATIONS REST ON	INTIMIDATION	, WHICH IS SO NECESSARY TO THEM THAT WHEN THEY
		INTIMIDATIONS	
LION PREFACE(65)	SUCH OF OUR LAWS AS ARE NOT MERELY THE	INTIMIDATIONS	BY WHICH TYRANNIES ARE MAINTAINED UNDER
		INTINDIN	
BULL IV (146)	GRANMOTHER HADNT COTCH HIM IN HER APERN WIDHOUT	INTINDIN	TO. (IMMENSE MERRIMENT). /AUNT JUDY/ AH, FOR
		INTIRELY	
BULL I (78)	NEVER BE LESS! FOR YOURE THE BROTH OF A BOY	INTIRELY	. AN HOW CAN I HELP YOU? COMMAND ME TO THE LAST
		INTOLERABLE	
GETT PREFACE(202)	IT CAN AFFORD ONLY A SINGLE ROOM, THE STRAIN IS	INTOLERABLE	: VIOLENT QUARRELLING IS THE RESULT. VERY FEW
BULL PREFACE(41)	ARE MAFFICKINGS. ENGLISH RULE IS SUCH AN	INTOLERABLE	ABOMINATION THAT NO OTHER SUBJECT CAN REACH THE
HART PREFACE(12)	AND CULTURE AND THE LIKE MUST BE FLUNG OFF AS AN	INTOLERABLE	AFFECTATION; AND THE PICTURE GALLERIES AND
LION PREFACE(73)	DOES MARRIAGE, ITSELF INTOLERABLE, THRUST US UPON	INTOLERABLE	ALTERNATIVES. THE PRACTICAL SOLUTION IS TO MAKE
BARB PREFACE(213)	" THE RESPECTABLE POOR," AND SUCH PHRASES ARE AS	INTOLERABLE	AND AS IMMORAL AS " DRUNKEN BUT AMIABLE," "
CATH 1,SD(161)	BRUTAL BARBARIAN, AN UPSTART DESPOT OF THE MOST	INTOLERABLE	AND DANGEROUS TYPE, UGLY, LAZY, AND DISGUSTING
APPL INTRLUD(253)	AND WITHOUT GOOD MANNERS HUMAN SOCIETY IS	INTOLERABLE	AND IMPOSSIBLE. /ORINTHIA/ WOULD ANY OTHER WOMAN
MIS. PREFACE(14)	WHAT IS MORE, THE NUISANCE BECOMES MORE AND MORE	INTOLERABLE	AS THE GROWN-UP PERSON BECOMES MORE CULTIVATED,
HART PREFACE(24)	ITS FEROCITIES, ITS PANICS, AND ITS ENDLESS AND	INTOLERABLE	BLARINGS OF ALLIED NATIONAL ANTHEMS IN SEASON
LION PREFACE(85)	DID NOT MATTER; AND THIS, TO THE JEWS, WAS AN	INTOLERABLE	BLASPHEMY. TO GENTILES LIKE OURSELVES, A GOOD
BUOY III (37)	HUSBAND WHO MAY BE ANYTHING FROM A CRIMINAL TO AN	INTOLERABLE	BORE. SO I HAVE RUN AWAY AND PUT THE SEAS
OVER PREFACE(161)	DUMAS FILS. THE ROMANTIC ADULTERERS HAVE ALL BEEN	INTOLERABLE	BORES. THE PSEUDO SEX PLAY. LATER ON, I HAD
MTH4 I (155)	THEY HAD HELPED TO SET FREE BOYCOTTED THEM AS	INTOLERABLE	BORES. THE COMMUNITIES WHICH HAD ONCE IDOLIZED
MIS. PREFACE(74)	AND HAVE THEIR NEEDS SATISFIED. THE PARENTS'	INTOLERABLE	BURDEN. THERE IS NOTHING NEW IN THIS: IT IS HOW
APPL PREFACE(182)	RATES AND TAXES AND RENTS AND DEATH DUTIES AS	INTOLERABLE	BURDENS. WHAT WE WANT TO KNOW IS HOW LITTLE
GETT PREFACE(213)	RIGHTS TO ANY PERSON UNDER ANY CONDITIONS	INTOLERABLE	BY THEIR SELF-RESPECT, YET THE GENERAL SENSE OF
SUPR II SD(62)	TO AN EXTENT WHICH STRETCHES OCCASIONALLY TO	INTOLERABLE	COARSENESS; AND ENGLISH INTERCOURSE TO NEED
BARB PREFACE(230)	LASS, PRESENTLY FINDS HIMSELF OVERWHELMED WITH AN	INTOLERABLE	CONVICTION OF SIN UNDER THE SKILLED TREATMENT OF
2TRU PREFACE(21)	OF VERY INCOMPETENT OFFICIAL GOVERNMENT WITH AN	INTOLERABLE	DEAL OF VERY COMPETENT PRIVATE TYRANNY.
CAND III (142)	AND KEEP A SECRET FROM YOU. I WILL NOT SUFFER THE	INTOLERABLE	DEGRADATION OF JEALOUSY. WE HAVE AGREED-- HE AND
POSN PREFACE(406)	ARE IS MUCH TO THEIR CREDIT; BUT IT IS STILL AN	INTOLERABLE	EVIL THAT RESPECTABLE MANAGERS SHOULD HAVE TO
SIM II (68)	GARDEN). /VASHTI/ OBEDIENCE IS FREEDOM FROM THE	INTOLERABLE	FATIGUE OF THOUGHT. (SHE MAKES HER OBEISANCE
JOAN 6 (142)	IN A FRENCHMAN! DID YOU HEAR THAT? THIS IS AN	INTOLERABLE	FELLOW. WHO IS HE? IS THIS WHAT ENGLISH
BULL PREFACE(29)	INTERCOURSE FOUND COMPATIBLE FOR LONG WITH THE	INTOLERABLE	FRICTION OF HATRED AND MALICE. BUT PEOPLE WHO
PYGM II (219)	DISAPPOINTMENT, AND AT ONCE, BABYLIKE, MAKING AN	INTOLERABLE	GRIEVANCE OF IT) WHY, THIS IS THE GIRL I JOTTED
2TRU PREFACE(8)	OF DAILY TOIL AND SERVITUDE, THAT THE MOST	INTOLERABLE	HARDSHIPS AND DISCOMFORTS AND FATIGUES IN
BULL PREFACE(16)	IT FLATTERS YOU TO HAVE IT PUT THAT WAY, THE MORE	INTOLERABLE	HE FINDS IT TO BE RULED BY ENGLISH INSTEAD OF
JOAN PREFACE(54)	OF IT (WITH TWO LONG INTERVALS OF RELIEF) IS AN	INTOLERABLE	IMPOSITION. NOBODY SAYS " I HATE CLASSICAL
GETT PREFACE(255)	LAW THAT WOULD BE QUITE UNNECESSARY AND INDEED	INTOLERABLE	IN A PROSPEROUS COMMUNITY. BUT, HOWEVER WE
UNPL PREFACE(R14)	UPON THE OBSTACLE THAT MAKES DRAMATIC AUTHORSHIP	INTOLERABLE	IN ENGLAND TO WRITERS ACCUSTOMED TO THE FREEDOM
BASH I (93)	FROM THE WELL OF NATURE IN OUR HEARTS THAW THE	INTOLERABLE	INCH OF ICE THAT BEARS THE WEIGHT OF ALL THE
GETT PREFACE(190)	CELIBATES WHOSE OBJECTION TO MARRIAGE IS THE	INTOLERABLE	INDIGNITY OF BEING SUPPOSED TO DESIRE OR LIVE
PHIL II (113)	FEEL WHAT I FEEL NOW. (WRITHING UNDER A SENSE OF	INTOLERABLE	INJUSTICE) IT'S THE FAULT OF THE WICKEDLY
GENV IV (106)	HAS HIS SHARE IN ABRAHAM. /BATTLER/ THIS IS AN	INTOLERABLE	INSULT. I DEMAND SATISFACTION. I CANNOT PUNCH
MTH5 (256)	BLOOD AND BONE AND ALL THE REST OF IT, THAT IS	INTOLERABLE	. EVEN PREHISTORIC MAN DREAMED OF WHAT HE CALLED
NEVR II (252)	ME MAD? (SHE FROWNS, FINDING SUCH PETULANCE	INTOLERABLE	. HE ADDS HASTILY) NO! I'M NOT ANGRY: INDEED I'M
APPL I (215)	AM I INTRUDING? /PROTEUS/ I PROTEST. IT IS	INTOLERABLE	. I CALL A CONFERENCE OF MY CABINET TO CONSIDER
JOAN PREFACE(29)	RIGHTLY OR WRONGLY, BETWEEN THE TOLERABLE AND THE	INTOLERABLE	. JOAN NOT TRIED AS A POLITICAL OFFENDER.
METH PREFACE(R87)	AS A PLAYWRIGHT I FOUND THIS STATE OF THINGS	INTOLERABLE	. THE FASHIONABLE THEATRE PRESCRIBED ONE SERIOUS
SUPR III (99)	BLUNTNESS; BUT THE STRAIN OF LIVING IN HEAVEN IS	INTOLERABLE	. THERE IS A NOTION THAT I WAS TURNED OUT OF IT;
MTH2 (70)	TOGETHER WHEN THEIR TEMPERS AND QUARRELS BECAME	INTOLERABLE	. WITHIN THIRTEEN YEARS OF HER DEATH EUROPE
PHIL I (78)	YOU CAN UNDERSTAND. I ACCUSE YOU OF HABITUAL AND	INTOLERABLE	JEALOUSY AND ILL TEMPER; OF INSULTING ME ON
GETT PREFACE(243)	REALLY ONE ANSWER-- THAT POVERTY MEANS HUNGER, AN	INTOLERABLE	LACK OF VARIETY AND PLEASURE, AND, IN SHORT, ALL
SUPR III (112)	AND EVASIONS AND SOPHISTRIES, NOT TO MENTION THE	INTOLERABLE	LENGTH OF YOUR SPEECHES. /DON JUAN/ OH, COME!
MTH4 I (166)	AND REDUCED ME TO DESPAIR AND SILENCE BY YOUR	INTOLERABLE	LOQUACITY, YOU ACTUALLY PROPOSE TO BEGIN ALL
ROCK PREFACE(160)	AND TO PRIVILEGE THE LARGE RANGE OF	INTOLERABLE	MISCONDUCT THAT LIES OUTSIDE THEM, BUT TO DIVERT
PYGM III (257)	BY THIS TIME SHOUTING ONE ANOTHER DOWN WITH AN	INTOLERABLE	NOISE) SH-SH-SH-- SH! (THEY STOP). /PICKERING/
LION PREFACE(70)	HOLD BACK THE SWIFT), THAT MARRIAGE BECOMES AN	INTOLERABLE	OBSTACLE TO INDIVIDUAL EVOLUTION. AND THAT IS
SUPR HANDBOK(224)	BY KEEPING HIS MOUTH ALWAYS FULL OF IT. THE MOST	INTOLERABLE	PAIN IS PRODUCED BY PROLONGING THE KEENEST
3PLA PREFACE(R19)	THE AUDIENCE. THE RESULT IS, TO ME AT LEAST, AN	INTOLERABLE	PERVERSION OF HUMAN CONDUCT. THERE ARE TWO
OVER PREFACE(163)	WERE TO STAB MACBETH, THE SPECTACLE WOULD BE	INTOLERABLE	; AND EVEN THE PRETENCE WHICH WE ALLOW ON OUR
SUPR HANDBOK(193)	ITS DESECRATION BY VILE LANGUAGE AND COARSE HUMOR	INTOLERABLE	; SO THAT AT LAST WE CANNOT BEAR TO HAVE IT
MRS PREFACE(158)	WILL, I HOPE, ADMIT THAT THIS STATE OF THINGS IS	INTOLERABLE	; THAT THE SUBJECT OF MRS WARREN'S PROFESSION
GETT PREFACE(226)	THAT THE INDISSOLUBILITY OF MARRIAGE CREATES SUCH	INTOLERABLE	SITUATIONS THAT ONLY BY BEGLAMORING THE HUMAN
LION PREFACE(29)	ANOTHER; REVILES THE HIGH PRIESTS AND ELDERS IN	INTOLERABLE	TERMS; AND IS ARRESTED BY NIGHT IN A GARDEN TO
FABL PREFACE(90)	COUNTRIES. THE PERSONAL OUTRAGE INVOLVED IS SO	INTOLERABLE	THAT IT WILL NOT BE IN THE LEAST SURPRISING IF
CAPT III (292)	(THE IMPLICATION THAT HE IS SUCH A PERSON IS SO	INTOLERABLE	THAT THEY RECEIVE IT WITH A PROLONGED BURST OF
MTH4 II (178)	BECAUSE I AM SO SUPERIOR TO OTHER MEN THAT IT IS	INTOLERABLE	TO ME TO BE MISRULED BY THEM. YET ONLY AS A
INCA PROLOG (234)	THAN A HUNDRED THOUSAND DOLLARS A YEAR TO RUN IS	INTOLERABLE	TO ME. /THE ARCHDEACON/ THEN, MY DEAR, YOU HAD
BULL PREFACE(48)	AND ATTRACTIVE AS THEY ARE ABHORRENT AND	INTOLERABLE	TO THE WILLIAM TELL TEMPERAMENT. JUST AS THE
3PLA PREFACE(R30)	ANTONY AND CLEOPATRA MUST NEEDS BE AS	INTOLERABLE	TO THE TRUE PURITAN AS IT IS VAGUELY DISTRESSING
MTH3 (122)	IN THIS MATTER OF SEX THAN IN ANY OTHER, YOU ARE	INTOLERABLE	TO US IN THAT RELATION? /BURGE-LUBIN/ DO YOU
METH PREFACE(R39)	THAT BROUGHT IT LOW. WHAT MADE IT SCIENTIFICALLY	INTOLERABLE	WAS THAT IT WAS READY AT A MOMENT'S NOTICE TO
GETT PREFACE(247)	SHOULD NOT BE CONDEMNED TO EXPOSE THEMSELVES TO	INTOLERABLE	WRONGS. BESIDES, PEOPLE OUGHT NOT TO BE CONTENT
LION PREFACE(75)	SECT WHICH THE APOSTLES WERE NOW FORMING. A QUITE	INTOLERABLE	YOUNG SPEAKER NAMED STEPHEN DELIVERED AN ORATION
JOAN PREFACE(17)	IT IS NO LONGER OUR ACADEMY PICTURES THAT ARE	INTOLERABLE	, BUT OUR CREDULITIES THAT HAVE NOT THE EXCUSE

LION PREFACE(73)	IS A REFORMED RAKE. THUS DOES MARRIAGE, ITSELF	INTOLERABLE	, THRUST US UPON INTOLERABLE ALTERNATIVES. THE
		INTOLERABLY	
JOAN PREFACE(53)	CURSE ME FOR WRITING SUCH INORDINATELY LONG AND	INTOLERABLY	DREARY AND MEANINGLESS PLAYS. BUT THE APPLAUSE
POSN PREFACE(392)	SURVIVAL OF THE OLD OSTRACISM IN THE ACT OF 1843	INTOLERABLY	GALLING; AND THOUGH IT EXPLAINS THE APPARENTLY
LION PREFACE(72)	FREE FROM THEM BECAUSE THEY HAMPER HIS OWN WORK	INTOLERABLY	. WHEN HE SAID THAT IF WE ARE TO FOLLOW HIM IN
HART PREFACE(9)	AGAINST A BARBAROUS PSEUDO-EVANGELICAL TELEOLOGY	INTOLERABLY	OBSTRUCTIVE TO ALL SCIENTIFIC PROGRESS, BUT WAS
METH PREFACE(R57)	THEY ARE IN THE FIRST HAPPINESS OF ESCAPE FROM AN	INTOLERABLY	OPPRESSIVE SITUATION. LIKE BUNYAN'S PILGRIM THEY
BULL II SD(106)	THE EARLY CHURCH, POINTING US ALL TO GOD. PATSY,	INTOLERABLY	OVERBURDENED, LOSES HIS BALANCE, AND SITS DOWN
HART PREFACE(35)	AND PARTLY OF INSURGENT MEN WHO HAD BECOME	INTOLERABLY	POOR BECAUSE THE TEMPLE HAD BECOME A DEN OF
KING PREFACE(153)	TO PUT ON THE STAGE. AS TO THE ROMANCE, IT IS	INTOLERABLY	STALE; THE SPECTACLE OF A CHARLES SITTING WITH
SUPR III (125)	COMPANIONSHIP MIGHT, FOR ALL I KNEW, BECOME	INTOLERABLY	TEDIOUS TO ME; THAT I COULD NOT ANSWER FOR MY
APPL PREFACE(181)	IN A HUGE MAJORITY WE CAN, IF RULERS OPPRESS US	INTOLERABLY	, BURN THEIR HOUSES AND TEAR THEM TO PIECES.
		INTOLERANCE	
POSN PREFACE(389)	OF THE COMMUNITY; BUT IT IS A DEFINED AND LIMITED	INTOLERANCE	. THE LIMITATION IS SOMETIMES CARRIED SO FAR
JOAN PREFACE(40)	WE MUST FACE THE FACT THAT SOCIETY IS FOUNDED ON	INTOLERANCE	. THERE ARE GLARING CASES OF THE ABUSE OF
POSN PREFACE(402)	AUTHORITY. THIS PLAN WOULD COMBINE THE INEVITABLE	INTOLERANCE	OF AN ENLIGHTENED CENSORSHIP WITH THE POPULAR
BULL III SD(125)	AND SENSELESS FUN, AND A VIOLENT AND IMPETUOUS	INTOLERANCE	OF OTHER TEMPERAMENTS AND OTHER OPINIONS, ALL
SIM PREFACE(17)	THESE PREJUDICES WE NEED A GREATLY INCREASED	INTOLERANCE	OF SOCIALLY INJURIOUS CONDUCT AND AN
POSN PREFACE(389)	IF HE MAKES CESSPOOLS. THE LAW MAY BE ONLY THE	INTOLERANCE	OF THE COMMUNITY; BUT IT IS A DEFINED AND
JOAN PREFACE(40)	THERE ARE GLARING CASES OF THE ABUSE OF	INTOLERANCE	; BUT THEY ARE QUITE AS CHARACTERISTIC OF OUR
GETT PREFACE(245)	MINDS, AND THEIR SELF-RIGHTEOUS INDIFFERENCE AND	INTOLERANCE	SOON CHANGE INTO LIVELY CONCERN FOR THEMSELVES
LION PREFACE(98)	AND EVEN THAT IS A CONCESSION TO A MISCHIEVOUS	INTOLERANCE	WHICH AN EMPIRE SHOULD USE ITS CONTROL OF
JOAN PREFACE(38)	IN SHORT, THOUGH ALL SOCIETY IS FOUNDED ON	INTOLERANCE	, ALL IMPROVEMENT IS FOUNDED ON TOLERANCE, OR
MIS. PREFACE(104)	THERE HAS BEEN AS MUCH BRUTE COERCION AND SAVAGE	INTOLERANCE	, AS MUCH FLOGGING AND HANGING, AS MUCH IMPUDENT
SUPR HANDBOK(191)	ELECTORS, YET STEREOTYPES MEDIOCRITY, ORGANIZES	INTOLERANCE	, DISPARAGES EXHIBITIONS OF UNCOMMON QUALITIES,
JOAN PREFACE(29)	A GOOD OPPORTUNITY FOR LECTURING THE ENEMY ON HIS	INTOLERANCE	, PUT UP A STATUE TO HER, BUT TOOK PARTICULAR
		INTOLERANCES	
ROCK PREFACE(175)	OF BRITISH AND AMERICAN ATTENTION ON THE	INTOLERANCES	OF FASCISM AND COMMUNISM CREATES AN ILLUSION
		INTOLERANT	
JOAN PREFACE(40)	SUCCEED IN DOING SO; AND THAT WILL BE JUST AS	INTOLERANT	AS MAKING IT COMPULSORY. NEITHER THE PASTEURIANS
LADY (244)	OF HARRY THE EIGHTH. /SHAKESPEAR/ (SWELLING WITH	INTOLERANT	IMPORTANCE) NAME NOT THAT INORDINATE MAN IN THE
BARB I SD(259)	HE IS A MOST IMPLACABLE, DETERMINED, TENACIOUS,	INTOLERANT	PERSON WHO BY MERE FORCE OF CHARACTER PRESENTS
DOCT III (144)	ANY OTHER MAN STRIVES TOWARDS HIS IDEAL. /B.B./ (	INTOLERANT	) DONT TROUBLE TO EXPLAIN. I NOW UNDERSTAND YOU
JOAN PREFACE(41)	MAXIMUM OF INDULGENT TOLERATION AND A RUTHLESSLY	INTOLERANT	TERRORISM THERE IS A SCALE THROUGH WHICH
SUPR HANDBOK(195)	BEEN ATTAINED BY PUBLIC SPIRIT, BUT ALWAYS BY	INTOLERANT	WILFULNESS AND BRUTE FORCE. TAKE THE REFORM BILL
		INTOLERANTLY	
PRES (141)	I THINK I MAY SAY YES. /MITCHENER/ (RISING	INTOLERANTLY	AND GOING TO THE HEARTHRUG) THAT WONT DO FOR
INCA (250)	IS ADMIRAL VON COCKPITS -- /THE INCA/ (RISING	INTOLERANTLY	AND STRIDING ABOUT THE ROOM) VON COCKPITS!
PYGM V (271)	OF MIDDLE CLASS MORALITY. /HIGGINS/ (RISING	INTOLERANTLY	AND STANDING OVER DOOLITTLE) YOURE RAVING.
GETT (270)	AND VERY DULL. (SHE SHAKES HER SHOULDERS	INTOLERANTLY	AND WALKS ACROSS TO THE OTHER SIDE OF THE
3PLA PREFACE(R15)	DISGUSTED ME, NOT BECAUSE I WAS PHARISAICAL, OR	INTOLERANTLY	REFINED, BUT BECAUSE I WAS BORED; AND BOREDOM
MTH4 III (196)	UPON YOUR INDULGENCE-- /ZOO/ (INTERRUPTING HIM	INTOLERANTLY	) DONT THROW YOURSELF ON ANYTHING BELONGING TO
PYGM V (284)	ME. /HIGGINS/ (JUMPING UP AND WALKING ABOUT	INTOLERANTLY	) ELIZA: YOURE AN IDIOT. I WASTE THE TREASURES
PRES (135)	MIND. /BALSQUITH/ BUT HANG IT ALL-- /MITCHENER/ (	INTOLERANTLY	) NO I WONT HANG IT ALL. IT'S NO USE COMING TO
LADY (238)	SIR. DECENT BODIES, MANY OF THEM. /THE MAN/ (	INTOLERANTLY	) NO. ALL FALSE. ALL. IF THOU DENY IT, THOU
DOCT I (112)	OF DEATH. THE CARRIAGE IS WAITING. /RIDGEON/ (	INTOLERANTLY	) OH, NONSENSE: GET OUT. (GREATLY ANNOYED)
OVER (190)	UP, OUT OF PATIENCE, AND PACING ROUND THE LOUNGE	INTOLERANTLY	) WELL, REALLY, I MUST HAVE MY DINNER. THESE
NEVR IV (283)	BUT SURELY I HAVE A RIGHT-- /M'COMAS/ (	INTOLERANTLY	) YOU WONT GET YOUR RIGHTS. NOW, ONCE FOR ALL,
HART I (59)	COMPLETING THE SENTENCE AND PRANCING AWAY	INTOLERANTLY	TO STARBOARD)-- GRATEFUL TO HIM FOR HIS
CAND I (100)	YOU WILL BE A HAPPY MAN LIKE ME. (EUGENE CHAFES	INTOLERANTLY	, REPUDIATING THE WORTH OF HIS HAPPINESS.
		INTONATION	
SUPR IV SD(142)	IT IS CLEAR THAT HE IS AN IRISHMAN WHOSE NATIVE	INTONATION	HAS CLUNG TO HIM THROUGH MANY CHANGES OF PLACE
SUPR III SD(94)	HIS VOICE, SAVE FOR A MUCH MORE DISTINGUISHED	INTONATION	, IS SO LIKE THE VOICE OF ROEBUCK RAMSDEN THAT IT
		INTONE	
BARB II (306)	MR UNDERSHAFT IS A GIFTED TROMBONIST: HE SHALL	INTONE	AN OLYMPIAN DIAPASON TO THE WEST HAM SALVATION MARCH.
JOAN 6,SD(146)	NODS AFFIRMATIVELY. THEY RISE SOLEMNLY, AND	INTONE	THE SENTENCE ANTIPHONALLY. /CAUCHON/ WE DECREE THAT
		INTONES	
MTH4 I (145)	AFTER TAKING OUT HER TUNING-FORK AND SOUNDING IT,	INTONES	AS BEFORE) BURRIN PIER. WASH OUT. (SHE PUTS UP THE
		INTONING	
MTH4 I (144)	SPEAKING INTO SPACE ON ONE NOTE, LIKE A CHORISTER	INTONING	A PSALM) BURRIN PIER GALWAY PLEASE SEND SOMEONE TO
CAND I SD(85)	EASILY TO HIS VOICE BY HIS HABIT OF POMPOUSLY	INTONING	HIS SENTENCES. /BURGESS/ (STOPPING ON THE
MTH4 II (183)	/ZOO/ (WHIPPING OUT HER TUNING-FORK AND	INTONING	) HALLO GALWAY CENTRAL. (THE WHISTLING CONTINUES).
SHAK (142)	BEAUTY. /SHOTOVER/ (RAISING HIS HAND AND	INTONING	) I BUILDED A HOUSE FOR MY DAUGHTERS AND OPENED THE
MTH4 II (183)	CURIOUS STATUE OF A FAT OLD MAN. /ZOO/ (QUICKLY,	INTONING	) ISOLATE THE FALSTAFF MONUMENT ISOLATE HARD.
MTH4 I (166)	GENTLEMAN/ (IS HEARD TO YELL) OH! /ZOO/ (STILL	INTONING	) THANKS. . . . OH NOTHING SERIOUS I AM NURSING A
		INTOXICATED	
WIDO I (23)	LET US BREAK IT OFF HERE AND NOW. /TRENCH/ (	INTOXICATED	WITH AFFECTION) BLANCHE: ON MY MOST SACRED
LION PREFACE(83)	THE MOST IGNORANT MAN HAS ONLY TO BECOME	INTOXICATED	WITH HIS OWN VANITY, AND MISTAKE HIS
METH PREFACE(R48)	FROM DEATH AND DESPAIR. WE WERE INTELLECTUALLY	INTOXICATED	WITH THE IDEA THAT THE WORLD COULD MAKE ITSELF
MTH3 (120)	/MRS LUTESTRING/ YOU, MR PRESIDENT, WERE BORN	INTOXICATED	WITH YOUR OWN WELL-FED NATURAL EXUBERANCE. YOU
		INTOXICATING	
MTH4 II (175)	CLASSICAL ONE OF THE PYTHONESS ON HER TRIPOD, THE	INTOXICATING	FUMES ARISING FROM THE ABYSS, THE CONVULSIONS
POSN PREFACE(365)	THERE WAS THE POWERFUL INTEREST OF THE TRADE IN	INTOXICATING	LIQUORS, FIERCELY DETERMINED TO RESIST ANY
		INTOXICATION	
OVER (178)	DOING: MY CONSCIENCE IS AWAKE. OH, WHERE IS THE	INTOXICATION	OF LOVE? THE DELIRIUM? THE MADNESS THAT MAKES
SUPR III (117)	I HAD BEEN PREPARED FOR INFATUATION, FOR	INTOXICATION	, FOR ALL THE ILLUSIONS OF LOVE'S YOUNG DREAM;
		INTRACTABLE	
MIS. PREFACE(61)	NOT ALLOW FAIR PLAY BETWEEN THEM. THE REBELLIOUS,	INTRACTABLE	, AGGRESSIVE, SELFISH SET PROVOKE A CORRECTIVE
		INTRANSIGENT	
MILL PREFACE(119)	BENCH. PARLIAMENT TOOK THESE MEN, WHO HAD BEEN	INTRANSIGENT	SOCIALISTS AND REVOLUTIONISTS ALL THEIR LIVES,
		INTREPID	
CAPT II SD(254)	AND HIS HANDS TREMBLE; BUT HIS EYES AND MOUTH ARE	INTREPID	, RESOLUTE, AND ANGRY. /LADY CICELY/ UNCLE! WHAT
		INTRIGUE	
CATH PREFACE(153)	FOR ALL THE REST OF HER CONTEMPORARIES. IN SUCH	INTRIGUE	AND DIPLOMACY, HOWEVER, THERE WAS NO ROMANCE. NO
CATH PREFACE(153)	BUT IN THE LITTLE WORLD OF EUROPEAN COURT	INTRIGUE	AND DYNASTIC DIPLOMACY WHICH WAS THE ONLY WORLD SHE
OVER PREFACE(162)	HOWEVER INTERESTING THEY MAY BE AS PLAYS OF	INTRIGUE	AND PLOT PUZZLES, THE WORLD IS FINDING THIS OUT
SUPR II (60)	NOTHING IN IT BUT AN EXCUSE FOR A DETESTABLE	INTRIGUE	. COME WITH ME TO MARSEILLES AND ACROSS TO ALGIERS
APPL I (234)	OF A FEW FANCIERS OF PUBLIC SPEAKING AND PARTY	INTRIGUE	WHO FIND ALL THE OTHER AVENUES TO DISTINCTION
GENV I (40)	I FOUND OUT THE REASON. HE WAS CARRYING ON AN	INTRIGUE	WITH HIS OPPONENT'S WIFE, MY BEST FRIEND. I HAD TO

INTRIGUERS

APPL INTRLUD(251) WIFE AND THE RABBLE OF DOWDIES AND UPSTARTS AND INTRIGUERS AND CLOWNS THAT THINK THEY ARE GOVERNING THE

INTRIGUES

SUPR PREFACE(R16) GALLANTRY, AFTER BECOMING, AT MOST, TWO IMMATURE INTRIGUES LEADING TO SORDID AND PROLONGED COMPLICATIONS AND
UNPL PREFACE(R26) SLUMS WITH DECENT DWELLINGS, CHARTERIS'S INTRIGUES WITH REASONABLE MARRIAGE CONTRACTS, AND MRS
HART PREFACE(7) HAS BEEN A BOYISHLY LAWLESS AFFAIR OF FAMILY INTRIGUES , COMMERCIAL AND TERRITORIAL BRIGANDAGE, TORPORS

INTRIGUING

SUPR III (116) BECAME ANXIOUS, PREOCCUPIED WITH ME, ALWAYS INTRIGUING , CONSPIRING, PURSUING, WATCHING, WAITING, BENT

INTRODOOCE

CAPT II (247) PEOPLE ARE ALWAYS SO GENTLE. /JOHNSON/ LET ME INTRODOOCE MR REDBROOK. YOUR LADYSHIP MAY KNOW HIS FATHER,

INTRODUCE

NEVR I (218) WHICH HE IS SECRETLY GRATEFUL. /VALENTINE/ MAY I INTRODUCE ? THIS IS MR CRAMPTON: MISS DOROTHY CLANDON, MR
BULL IV (150) IN PARLIAMENT, IT SHALL BE MY FIRST CARE TO INTRODUCE A BILL LEGALIZING SUCH AN OPERATION. I BELIEVE A
BARB II (289) A BIG DRUM). OH! THERE YOU ARE, DOLLY. LET ME INTRODUCE A NEW FRIEND OF MINE, MR BILL WALKER. THIS IS MY
HART PREFACE(29) NEARLY TWENTY YEARS SINCE I WAS LAST OBLIGED TO INTRODUCE A PLAY IN THE FORM OF A BOOK FOR LACK OF AN
DOCT PREFACE(72) LIKE MAHOMET, HAD BEEN ENLIGHTENED ENOUGH TO INTRODUCE AS RELIGIOUS DUTIES SUCH SANITARY MEASURES AS
GENV III (70) TABLE, YOUR HONOR. /THE JUDGE/ THANK YOU. MAY I INTRODUCE COMMISSAR POSKY. (HE SEATS HIMSELF ON THE
SUPR I (28) OUR IGNORANCE WE ARE TO SHAKE HIM BY THE HAND; TO INTRODUCE HIM INTO OUR HOMES; TO TRUST OUR DAUGHTERS WITH
NEVR I (204) IMPROVED. /PHILIP/ IN THAT CASE WE SHALL HAVE TO INTRODUCE HIM TO THE OTHER MEMBER OF THE FAMILY: THE WOMAN
METH PREFACE(R64) FRAUD AGAINST FISTICUFFS, ALL ATTEMPT TO INTRODUCE HUMAN PURPOSE AND DESIGN AND FORETHOUGHT INTO THE
DOCT PREFACE(25) PARTICULAR PATHOGENIC GERM WHICH THEY INTENDED TO INTRODUCE INTO THE PATIENT'S SYSTEM MAY BE QUITE INNOCENT OF
BULL PREFACE(8) POLAND, PERSIANS WHO ARE RISKING THEIR LIVES TO INTRODUCE IT IN PERSIA, INDIANS AND EGYPTIANS WHO ARE READY
GETT PREFACE(208) SYSTEM; BUT IF IT WERE PHYSICALLY POSSIBLE TO INTRODUCE IT INTO HUMAN SOCIETY IT WOULD BE WRECKED BY AN
FANY III (320) PERFECTLY. KNOX FOLLOWS. /MARGARET/ OH-- LET ME INTRODUCE . MY FRIEND LIEUTENANT DUVALLET. MRS GILBEY. MR
FANY III (321) PLACING A CHAIR FOR HIM. /DORA/ NOW, BOBBY: INTRODUCE ME: THERES A DEAR. /BOBBY/ (A LITTLE NERVOUS
GETT (306) GOWN) IVE NOT HAD THE PLEASURE. WILL YOU INTRODUCE ME? /COLLINS/ (CONFIDENTIALLY) ALL RIGHT, SIR.
MIS. PREFACE(80) I REALIZED THAT I KNEW VERY LITTLE ABOUT HER. INTRODUCE ME TO A STRANGE WOMAN WHO WAS A CHILD WHEN I WAS A
MILL I (147) LETTING YOURSELF GO IF YOU ARE BUILT THAT WAY. INTRODUCE ME TO THE GENTLEMAN, ALLY. /ALASTAIR/ OH, I
FANY III (304) THE OTHER END OF THE TABLE). I SUPPOSE YOU WONT INTRODUCE ME TO THE CLERGYMAN'S DAUGHTER. /BOBBY/ I DONT
MTH2 (56) MY MEMORY NEVER DECEIVES ME. THANK YOU. WILL YOU INTRODUCE ME TO THIS GENTLEMAN, BARNABAS? /CONRAD/ (NOT AT
OVER (186) BEFORE PEOPLE NOW, PRAY? /MRS LUNN/ WONT YOU INTRODUCE ME TO YOUR WIFE, MR JUNO? /MRS JUNO/ HOW DO YOU
MILL I (139) INDEED WORTH KNOWING. I SHALL CERTAINLY MAKE HIM INTRODUCE ME. /EPIFANIA/ YOU ARE HARDLY TACTFUL, JULIUS
HART I (52) ATTENTION). OH! YOUVE BROUGHT SOMEONE WITH YOU. INTRODUCE ME. /LADY UTTERWORD/ HESIONE: IS IT POSSIBLE THAT
ROCK II (249) JAFNA/ MAY I SPEAK TO THIS GENTLEMAN? WILL YOU INTRODUCE ME, ARTHUR? /SIR ARTHUR/ (INTRODUCING) SIR JAFNA
BARB I (264) /UNDERSHAFT/ PERHAPS YOU WILL BE GOOD ENOUGH TO INTRODUCE ME, MY DEAR. /LADY BRITOMART/ THAT IS CHARLES
NEVR I (203) MR VALENTINE'S JUDGMENT. HE IS RIGHT. LET ME INTRODUCE MISS DOROTHY CLANDON, COMMONLY CALLED DOLLY. (
GENV I (42) A NUDIST! I WAS GRACIOUSLY ALLOWED TO INTRODUCE MY DAUGHTERS TO GOOD QUEEN VICTORIA. IF SHE COULD
WIDO I (7) DR TRENCH. (THEY BOW). /TRENCH/ PERHAPS I SHOULD INTRODUCE MY FRIEND COKANE TO YOU, MR SARTORIUS: MR WILLIAM
SUPR III (77) DO YOU? /MENDOZA/ (WITH DIGNITY) ALLOW ME TO INTRODUCE MYSELF: MENDOZA, PRESIDENT OF THE LEAGUE OF THE
JOAN 4 (96) BISHOP, HOW GOOD OF YOU TO COME! ALLOW ME TO INTRODUCE MYSELF: RICHARD DE BEAUCHAMP, EARL OF WARWICK, AT
MIS. (151) EVIDENT REFINEMENT AND DISTINCTION. ALLOW ME TO INTRODUCE MYSELF: TARLETON: JOHN TARLETON (SEEING
GENV I (43) HIS SEAT) THANK YOU. THANK YOU. /RUSSIAN/ LET ME INTRODUCE MYSELF. I AM COMMISSAR POSKY OF THE SOVNARKOM AND
GETT (289) AS YOU ARE IN THE SERVICE, ALLOW ME TO INTRODUCE MYSELF. READ MY CARD, PLEASE. (HE PRESENTS HIS
FABL VI (122) BUILDING AND TAKES HER PLACE. /TEACHER/ LET ME INTRODUCE MYSELF. YOU HAVE JUST BEEN PROMOTED TO THE SIXTH
BULL II (112) GOT! /BROADBENT/ (RISING INTO VIEW) I MUST INTRODUCE MYSELF-- /NORA/ (VIOLENTLY STARTLED, RETREATING)
CYMB FORWORD(134) A BALLET USED TO BE DE RIGUEUR. GOUNOD HAD TO INTRODUCE ONE INTO HIS FAUST, AND WAGNER INTO HIS
DEST (175) PARDON YOU. IN FUTURE, DO NOT PERMIT YOURSELF TO INTRODUCE REAL PERSONS IN YOUR ROMANCES. /LADY/ (POLITELY
MRS I (197) THE CLERGYMAN. /VIVIE/ (CONTINUING) LET ME INTRODUCE -- /MRS WARREN/ (SWOOPING ON THE REVEREND SAMUEL)
LADY PREFACE(207) HAD I WISHED TO BE UP TO DATE. WHY, THEN, DID I INTRODUCE THE DARK LADY AS MISTRESS FITTON? WELL, I HAD TWO
MILL I (147) (TO SAGAMORE) WHY DIDNT YOU TELL ME? /EPIFANIA/ INTRODUCE THE FEMALE. /PATRICIA/ PATRICIA SMITH IS MY NAME,
2TRU III (108) TO KEEP THEM OUT OF MISCHIEF. THEY WANT TO INTRODUCE THE ONLY INSTITUTION OF OURS THAT THEY ADMIRE.
MIS. PREFACE(74) I HAVE MORE THAN ONCE THOUGHT OF TRYING TO INTRODUCE THE SHOOTING OF CHILDREN AS A SPORT, AS THE
ANNA (290) THE COLONEL ACTUALLY FORCED TO TAKE THE CHAIR AND INTRODUCE THE SPEAKER, I MYSELF AM MADE COMMANDER-IN-CHIEF
ROCK I (209) DOING SOMETHING TO THE REFRIGERATOR. I'D BETTER INTRODUCE THEM. /SIR ARTHUR/ OH, BUNDLE THEM IN ANYHOW. AND
MRS PREFACE(158) AS TO PROMISE THE EXAMINER MY SUPPORT IF HE WILL INTRODUCE THIS LIMITATION FOR PART OF THE YEAR, SAY DURING
HART I (72) IS MY HUSBAND. /HECTOR/ WE HAVE MET, DEAR. DONT INTRODUCE US ANY MORE. (HE MOVES AWAY TO THE BIG CHAIR, AND
PRES (152) TO WHAT AM I INDEBTED-- /MRS BANGER/ LET ME INTRODUCE US. I AM ROSA CARMINA BANGER: MRS BANGER,
FANY PREFACE(256) PERSONAL APPEARANCE. THE CRITICS WHOM I DID NOT INTRODUCE WERE SOMEWHAT HURT, AS I SHOULD HAVE BEEN MYSELF
BARB II (286) PAPA, WHAT IS YOUR RELIGION? IN CASE I HAVE TO INTRODUCE YOU AGAIN. /UNDERSHAFT/ MY RELIGION? WELL, MY
MRS I (195) HIS FATHER WITH IT INTO THE GARDEN). I WANT TO INTRODUCE YOU TO HER. DO YOU REMEMBER THE ADVICE YOU GAVE ME
PHIL I (85) AND SITS THERE). /CUTHBERTSON/ CRAVEN: LET ME INTRODUCE YOU TO MR LEONARD CHARTERIS, THE FAMOUS IBSENIST
PHIL III (144) MRS TRANFIELD: CUTHBERTSON: ALLOW ME TO INTRODUCE YOU TO MY FUTURE WIFE. /CUTHBERTSON/ (COMING
SIM I (43) ATTRACTIVE MATRON. /PRA/ MR HAMMINGTAP: LET ME INTRODUCE YOU TO THE GOVERNOR OF THE UNEXPECTED ISLES, SIR
CAND I (91) THEYLL MAKE ME A BISHOP; BUT IF THEY DO, I'LL INTRODUCE YOU TO THE BIGGEST JOBBERS I CAN GET TO COME TO MY
MRS III (234) FOND OF ONE ANOTHER. ALLOW ME, MISTER FRANK, TO INTRODUCE YOU TO YOUR HALF-SISTER, THE ELDEST DAUGHTER OF
WIDO I (7) TRENCH RISE). TRENCH, MY DEAR FELLOW, ALLOW ME TO INTRODUCE YOU TO-- ER--? (HE LOOKS INQUIRINGLY AT THE
MRS III (232) EVERYBODY GUESSES. IN THE CLASS OF PEOPLE I CAN INTRODUCE YOU TO, NO LADY OR GENTLEMAN WOULD SO FAR FORGET
MRS IV (249) KNOW PLENTY OF THEM. I KNOW THEM TO SPEAK TO, TO INTRODUCE YOU TO, TO MAKE FRIENDS OF FOR YOU. I DONT MEAN
SUPR II (50) EASY UNDER FIFTEEN. /TANNER/ BY THE WAY, LET ME INTRODUCE YOU. MR OCTAVIUS ROBINSON: MR ENRY STRAKER.
BUOY III (42) ALONE. /SHE/ THE BUOYANTS ARE NEVER ALONE. LET ME INTRODUCE YOU. MY STEPBROTHERS, TOM AND DICK. MRS DICK AND
MRS I (189) HAT ON, DEAR: YOULL GET SUNBURNT. OH, I FORGOT TO INTRODUCE YOU. SIR GEORGE CROFTS: MY LITTLE VIVIE. CROFTS
SUPR IV (150) WE HAVE NOT ALL MET BEFORE. MR MALONE: WONT YOU INTRODUCE YOUR FATHER? /HECTOR/ (WITH ROMAN FIRMNESS) NO,
ROCK I (211) YOU ARE ALL MOST WELCOME. PERHAPS, TOM, YOU WILL INTRODUCE YOUR YOUNG FRIENDS. /THE MAYOR/ (INTRODUCING)
ROCK I (225) CHAIR). /SIR ARTHUR/ WILL YOU BE SO GOOD AS TO INTRODUCE YOURSELF? WHO ARE YOU? /THE LADY/ A MESSENGER.
NEVR I (209) HIM WITH CHILLING ATTENTION. /PHILIP/ LET ME INTRODUCE YOU. MR VALENTINE, MY MOTHER, MRS LANFREY CLANDON.
NEVR I (223) WATER INTO THE TUMBLER). /CRAMPTON/ SORRY I CANT INTRODUCE YOU, SIR. I'M HAPPY TO SAY THAT I DONT KNOW WHERE

INTRODUCED

JOAN PREFACE(24) OF ENGLISH TROOPS, AND THAT UNLESS HE AT ONCE INTRODUCED ALL THE OLD CHARGES AGAINST JOAN OF BEING A
DOCT PREFACE(75) THE VARIOUS SERUMS THAT WERE FROM TIME TO TIME INTRODUCED AS HAVING EFFECTED MARVELLOUS CURES, PRESENTLY
APPL PREFACE(177) ON A RANGE OF POLITICAL AND CULTURAL TOPICS INTRODUCED BY A PREVIOUS SPEAKER UNDER THE GENERAL HEADING
MIS. PREFACE(67) OF SUCH CIVILIZED INSTITUTIONS AS HAVE BEEN INTRODUCED BY BENEVOLENT AND INTELLIGENT DESPOTS AND
GENV I (39) ADVANCED MEMBER OF THE LEAGUE OF NATIONS, WERE INTRODUCED BY MY LATE HUSBAND THE SIXTH PRESIDENT. HE
MIS. (127) ROOM FOR THE FRESH SUPPLIES, AND SO DEATH WAS INTRODUCED BY NATURAL SELECTION. YOU GET IT OUT OF YOUR
LION PREFACE(35) TO ACCOUNT FOR THEIR PRESENCE AT HIS TOMB, IS INTRODUCED EARLIER; AND SOME OF THE WOMEN ARE NAMED; SO THAT
2TRU II (62) FROM EVERY QUARTER OF THE GLOBE. IF SWEETIE HAD INTRODUCED HERSELF AS WHAT SHE OBVIOUSLY IS: THAT IS, AN
HART I (58) SO TAKEN ABACK AS HE WAS WHEN I TOOK HIM HOME AND INTRODUCED HIM TO MY FATHER: HIS OWN MANAGER. IT WAS THEN
SUPR IV (161) /TANNER/ WELL, IVE DISPOSED OF OLD MALONE. IVE INTRODUCED HIM TO MENDOZA, LIMITED; AND LEFT THE TWO
KING PREFACE(159) DOUBLES THE RESISTANCE TO ANY CHANGE. WHEN IT WAS INTRODUCED IN ENGLAND NOT A SINGLE WOMAN WAS RETURNED AT THE
BULL PREFACE(56) HIS REASONS. IT APPEARS THAT THE BOASTED JUSTICE INTRODUCED INTO EGYPT BY THE ENGLISH IN 1882 WAS IMAGINARY,
SIM PREFACE(18) MYSELF AGAINST THE ASSUMPTION THAT BECAUSE I HAVE INTRODUCED INTO MY FABLE A EUGENIC EXPERIMENT IN GROUP
SIM PREFACE(18) FROM MARRIAGE IN THE BRITISH ISLES; BUT I HAVE INTRODUCED IT ONLY TO BRING INTO THE STORY THE FOUR LOVELY
KING I (219) IT. /CHARLES/ NOBODY BUT BARBARA WOULD HAVE INTRODUCED IT. I FORBID IT ABSOLUTELY. MRS BASHAM RETURNS.
ROCK II (269) TOWN, AS YOU MIGHT SAY, THOUGH WEVE NEVER BEEN INTRODUCED . /THE DUKE/ VERY MUCH HONORED, MR HIPNEY.
DEVL EPILOG (79) DRAWN UP BY HIMSELF FOR HIS OFFICERS WHEN HE INTRODUCED LIGHT HORSE INTO THE ENGLISH ARMY. HIS OPINION
SUPR III (118) THE HAPPIER, NO: THE WISER, YES. THAT MOMENT INTRODUCED ME FOR THE FIRST TIME TO MYSELF, AND, THROUGH
LION PREFACE(9) RE-TRANSLATIONS INTO MODERN ENGLISH HAVE BEEN INTRODUCED PERFORCE TO SAVE ITS BARE INTELLIGIBILITY. IT IS
ROCK PREFACE(150) IT WAS, BY THE WAY, THE ENGLISH REVOLUTION WHICH INTRODUCED THE CATEGORY OF MALIGNANT OR MAN OF BLOOD, AND
CYMB FORWORD(133) DESPERATE EXPERIMENTS BY THE LATE WILLIAM POEL, INTRODUCED THE STARTLING INNOVATION OF PERFORMING THE PLAYS
KING PREFACE(153) CHARACTERS OF THE STAGE. MANY OF THESE PLAYS HAVE INTRODUCED THEIR HEROINES AS NELL GWYNN, AND NELL'S
LION PREFACE(35) AND SOME OF THE WOMEN ARE NAMED; SO THAT WE ARE INTRODUCED TO JOANNA THE WIFE OF CHUZA, HEROD'S STEWARD, AND
MTH2 (56) TO IT. MOST INTERESTING, AND QUITE TRUE. HE WAS INTRODUCED TO ME AT A MEETING WHERE THE SUFFRAGETTES KEPT

KING I (170) /CHARLES/ NELLY! MR NEWTON: WOULD YOU LIKE TO BE INTRODUCED TO MISTRESS GWYNN, THE FAMOUS DRURY LANE
BARB PREFACE(234) CASTE REPRESENT DISTINCT ANIMALS WHO MUST NOT BE INTRODUCED TO ONE ANOTHER OR INTERMARRY. NAPOLEON
METH PREFACE(R18) AN ETERNAL CONDITION OF LIFE, BUT AN EXPEDIENT INTRODUCED TO PROVIDE FOR CONTINUAL RENEWAL WITHOUT
CAND II (125) I'M SORRY. I THOUGHT YOU MIGHT LIKE TO BE INTRODUCED TO THE CHAIRMAN. HE'S ON THE WORKS COMMITTEE OF
MRS I (182) AND THAT I WAS TO COME OVER FROM HORSHAM TO BE INTRODUCED TO YOU. /VIVIE/ (NOT AT ALL PLEASED) DID SHE?
CLEO II (133) YOU HAVE BEEN GROWING UP SINCE THE SPHINX INTRODUCED US THE OTHER NIGHT; AND YOU THINK YOU KNOW MORE
DOCT PREFACE(25) OF THE CATASTROPHE, AND THAT THE CASUAL DIRT INTRODUCED WITH IT MAY BE AT FAULT. WHEN, AS IN THE CASE OF
WIDO I (13) I OBTAINED THE PRIVILEGE OF HIS ACQUAINTANCE: I INTRODUCED YOU: I ALLOWED HIM TO BELIEVE THAT HE MIGHT LEAVE
CYMB FORWORD(134) WITH JUPITER AS DEUS EX MACHINA, EAGLE AND ALL, INTRODUCED , LIKE THE CERES SCENE IN THE TEMPEST, TO PLEASE
UNPL PREFACE(R18) HABIT OF TREATING EVERYBODY WHO HAS NOT BEEN " INTRODUCED " AS A STRANGER AND INTRUDER. THE WOMEN, WHO HAVE

INTRODUCES

PYGM III (247) FOR THE DOOR; BUT BEFORE HE REACHES IT HIS MOTHER INTRODUCES HIM). MRS AND MISS EYNSFORD HILL ARE THE MOTHER
MTH2 (47) TO SEE YOU. (HE SHAKES BURGE'S HAND, AND INTRODUCES SAVVY) MY DAUGHTER. /SAVVY/ (NOT DARING TO
BUOY III SD(28) AN IRREVERENT YOUTH OF 17, ENTERS. THE WIDOWER INTRODUCES THEM. /THE WIDOWER/ GOOD MORNING, SIR FERDINAND.

INTRODUCING

LIED (201) I'D FLATTEN YOUR NOSE IN TO TEACH YOU MANNERS. INTRODUCING A FINE WOMAN TO YOU IS CASTING PEARLS BEFORE
DOCT PREFACE(44) THE TORMENTS OF VIVISECTION DRAMATICALLY WITHOUT INTRODUCING A SINGLE VIVISECTOR WHO HAD NOT FELT SICK AT HIS
FANY PROLOG (269) POSSIBLY, THOUGH A LITTLE DECENT RETICENCE AS TO INTRODUCING ACTUAL PERSONS, AND THUS VIOLATING THE SANCTITY
BULL III (125) TO BE SURE, BARNEY: I FORGOT. (TO BROADBENT, INTRODUCING BARNEY) MR DORAN. HE OWNS THAT FINE MILL YOU
HART PREFACE(13) AS CRIMINAL OR UNCHRISTIAN. THE ACT OF PARLIAMENT INTRODUCING COMPULSORY MILITARY SERVICE THOUGHTLESSLY
HART I (50) SAILOR WHO ROBBED YOU? /THE CAPTAIN/ (INTRODUCING ELLIE) HIS DAUGHTER. (HE SITS DOWN ON THE
INCA PREFACE(231) CAESAR'S FOIBLES BY LAUGHING AT THEM, WHILST INTRODUCING ENOUGH OBVIOUS AND OUTRAGEOUS FICTION TO RELIEVE
MILL PREFACE(124) SCIENCE BY DENYING THE INFALLIBILITY OF NEWTON, INTRODUCING FANTASTIC FACTORS INTO MATHEMATICS, DESTROYING
GETT PREFACE(238) BY PUTTING THE WOMAN DOWN AS A HOUSEKEEPER AND INTRODUCING HER TO AN EMPLOYER WITHOUT MAKING MARRIAGE A
MTH5 (237) THIS (TAKING THE HAND OF THE FEMALE FIGURE AND INTRODUCING HER) IS CLEOPATRA-SEMIRAMIS, CONSORT OF THE KING
CAPT I (226) IF YOU WILL HAVE US, MR RANKIN. /SIR HOWARD/ (INTRODUCING HER) MY SISTER-IN-LAW, LADY CICELY WAYNFLETE, MR
MTH2 (57) HEARD OF HIM. IS HE ANY GOOD? /FRANKLYN/ I WAS INTRODUCING HIM. THIS IS MR HASLAM. /HASLAM/ HOW D'YE DO?
GETT (324) THAN HE HAS, HAVNT YOU? /MRS BRIDGENORTH/ (INTRODUCING HOTCHKISS) MR ST JOHN HOTCHKISS. HOTCHKISS,
GETT (324) IN IT BY MISS GRANTHAM. /MRS BRIDGENORTH/ (INTRODUCING LEO) MRS REGINALD BRIDGENORTH. /REGINALD/ THE
ARMS III (68) /RAINA/ TO NEITHER OF THEM. THIS YOUNG LADY (INTRODUCING LOUKA, WHO FACES THEM ALL PROUDLY) IS THE OBJECT
BUOY II (19) TO PAY FOR MY ENTERTAINMENT? OR IMPRESS YOU BY INTRODUCING MYSELF AS A GRADUATE OF OXFORD UNIVERSITY?
METH PREFACE(R85) TO SEEK ONE BY THE QUAINT PROFESSIONAL METHOD OF INTRODUCING PHILOSOPHERS AS CHARACTERS INTO HIS PLAYS, AND
ROCK II (250) PAGES OF WORKING CLASS HISTORY. /SIR ARTHUR/ (INTRODUCING) ALDERWOMAN ALOYSIA BROLLIKINS. THE DUKE OF
ROCK I (211) WILL INTRODUCE YOUR YOUNG FRIENDS. /THE MAYOR/ (INTRODUCING) ALDERWOMAN ALOYSIA BROLLIKINS. /SIR ARTHUR/ (
PYGM III (248) /MRS HIGGINS/ VERY GOOD OF YOU TO COME. (INTRODUCING) COLONEL PICKERING. /FREDDY/ (BOWING) AHDEDO?
ROCK II (268) THIS IS WHAT IT ENDS IN. /SIR ARTHUR/ (INTRODUCING) HIS GRACE THE DUKE OF DOMESDAY, MR HIPNEY.
MILL I (153) /PATRICIA/ NOT AT ALL. DONT MIND ME. /SAGAMORE/ (INTRODUCING) MISS SMITH, AN INTIMATE FRIEND OF MR
FANY III (307) TO CALL FOR ME HERE; AND I FORGOT TO TELL YOU. (INTRODUCING) MONSIEUR DUVALLET: MISS FOUR HUNDRED AND
ROCK II (249) AGAIN. DO YOU TAKE US FOR FOOLS? /SIR ARTHUR/ (INTRODUCING) MR ALDERMAN BLEE. /THE DUKE/ ENCHANTED. I
HART I (72) BETWEEN MANGAN AND MRS HUSHABYE. /MRS HUSHABYE/ (INTRODUCING) MR MAZZINI DUNN, LADY UT-- OH, I FORGOT: YOUVE
NEVR II (240) ONE ANOTHER ALREADY TODAY. OH NO: EXCUSE ME. (INTRODUCING) MR VALENTINE: MR M'COMAS. (SHE GOES TO THE
SIM I (43) HUGO? /HYERING/ (SHAKING HANDS) NOT SIR HUGO. (INTRODUCING) MRS HYERING. /MRS HYERING/ (SHAKING HANDS)
PYGM III (250) LEFT VACANT BY HIGGINS). /MRS EYNSFORD HILL/ (INTRODUCING) MY DAUGHTER CLARA. /LIZA/ HOW DO YOU DO?
SUPR III (78) /STRAKER/ ERE! WHERE DO I COME IN? /TANNER/ (INTRODUCING) MY FRIEND AND CHAUFFEUR. /THE SULKY
PYGM III (250) CERTAINLY HAD THE PLEASURE. /MRS EYNSFORD HILL/ (INTRODUCING) MY SON FREDDY. /LIZA/ HOW DO YOU DO? FREDDY
PYGM III (247) HOW D' YOU DO? (SHE SHAKES). /MRS HIGGINS/ (INTRODUCING) MY SON HENRY. /MRS EYNSFORD HILL/ YOUR
ROCK II (249) WILL YOU INTRODUCE ME, ARTHUR? /SIR ARTHUR/ (INTRODUCING) SIR JAFNA PANDRANATH. THE MAYOR OF THE ISLE OF
JOAN 6 (123) RESERVES OF AUTHORITY AND FIRMNESS. /CAUCHON/ (INTRODUCING THE CANON, WHO IS ON HIS LEFT) THIS GENTLEMAN IS
CAPT I (226) THE BUST WORKER IN THE WUST COWST VAWNYARD. (INTRODUCING THE JUDGE) MR RENKIN: IS LAWDSHIP SIR AHRD
JOAN 6 (123) YOUR FRIENDS BEFORE? I THINK NOT. /CAUCHON/ (INTRODUCING THE MONK, WHO IS ON HIS RIGHT) THIS, MY LORD, IS
HART I (66) THEM. /CAPTAIN SHOTOVER/ (TO MRS HUSHABYE, INTRODUCING THE NEW COMER) SAYS HIS NAME IS MANGAN. NOT
LION PREFACE(82) NO POWER OVER JESUS. AS WE HAVE SEEN, IT WAS BY INTRODUCING THIS BONDAGE AND TERROR OF HIS INTO THE
JITT PREFACE(3) OUT THE HEAVY ADDITIONAL TASK OF TRANSLATING AND INTRODUCING TO THE GERMAN-SPEAKING PUBLIC AND TO THE GERMAN

INTRODUCTION

MTH4 I (146) I CANNOT FOLLOW. WHAT IS A SHILLING? WHAT IS AN INTRODUCTION ? IMPROPER FEMALE DOESNT MAKE SENSE. /THE
UNPL PREFACE(R13) THE TEXT OF THE PLAY WAS PUBLISHED WITH AN INTRODUCTION BY MR GREIN, AN AMUSING ACCOUNT BY ARCHER OF
MTH4 II (190) ONE PRESUMES TO SPEAK TO ANYONE ELSE WITHOUT AN INTRODUCTION FOLLOWING A STRICT EXAMINATION OF SOCIAL
DOCT PREFACE(56) ON THE STRENGTH OF A DEMONSTRATION THAT THEIR INTRODUCTION HAS REDUCED THE DEATH-RATE. THE EXPLANATION IS
GENV IV (115) NO, BUT I HAVE SEEN MANY CARICATURES OF THEM. NO INTRODUCTION IS NECESSARY. /THE JUDGE/ YOU RECOGNIZE ALSO
VWOO 3 (135) YOUR CLASS AND WANTED TO SPEAK TO YOU WITHOUT AN INTRODUCTION . NOW IT'S A PLEASURE TO HEAR YOU SAY " GOOD
WIDO I (10) YOU WERE READY ENOUGH TO SPEAK TO ME WITHOUT ANY INTRODUCTION . /TRENCH/ I DIDNT PARTICULARLY WANT TO TALK TO
DOCT PREFACE(29) AS THE BEST CARPENTER OR MASON WILL RESIST THE INTRODUCTION OF A MACHINE THAT IS LIKELY TO THROW HIM OUT OF
DOCT PREFACE(44) IMPRISONMENT IS SHEWN AT ITS WORST WITHOUT THE INTRODUCTION OF A SINGLE CRUEL PERSON INTO THE DRAMA, SO IT
FABL PREFACE(89) OF DEATHS FROM A SPECIFIC DISEASE FOLLOWING THE INTRODUCTION OF AN ALLEGED PROPHYLACTIC PROVES THAT THE
ROCK II (262) FOR IT. TO CARRY OUT THE PROGRAM WILL INVOLVE THE INTRODUCTION OF AT LEAST TWELVE BILLS. THEY ARE HIGHLY
BULL PREFACE(4) ONE OF THEIR ARGUMENTS WAS EQUALLY VALID FOR THE INTRODUCTION OF CHINESE LABOR INTO LANCASHIRE, AND AS THE
DOCT PREFACE(72) (THE SANDWICH ISLANDS, FOR EXAMPLE) MADE THE INTRODUCTION OF CHRISTIANITY ALSO THE INTRODUCTION OF
GETT PREFACE(187) AND SOCIALLY INOPERATIVE ECCENTRICITY BY THE INTRODUCTION OF CIVIL MARRIAGE AND DIVORCE. THEORETICALLY,
DOCT PREFACE(72) MADE THE INTRODUCTION OF CHRISTIANITY ALSO THE INTRODUCTION OF DISEASE, BECAUSE THE FORMULATORS OF THE
MIS. PREFACE(67) MIND IS INCOMPATIBLE NOT ONLY WITH THE DEMOCRATIC INTRODUCTION OF HIGH CIVILIZATION, BUT WITH THE
ROCK II SD(250) AN ACCUSING FINGER AT HIM. AT THE MOMENT OF HIS INTRODUCTION OF HIMSELF AS A DUKE, HER EYES LIGHTED UP; AND
LADY PREFACE(210) MALL GAZETTE I ATTRIBUTE, RIGHTLY OR WRONGLY, THE INTRODUCTION OF MARY FITTON TO MR FRANK HARRIS. MY REASON
LION PREFACE(82) WHERE THE STONING OF STEPHEN WAS FOLLOWED BY THE INTRODUCTION OF PAUL. THE AUTHOR OF THE ACTS, THOUGH A GOOD
SUPR HANDBOK(196) GOVERNED US THEN BY PRIVILEGE, AND WHO, SINCE THE INTRODUCTION OF PRACTICALLY MANHOOD SUFFRAGE IN 1884, NOW
GETT (287) ESPECIALLY THEY WILL. IN OTHER COUNTRIES THE INTRODUCTION OF REASONABLE DIVORCE LAWS WILL SAVE THE
MRS PREFACE(167) DRAMA ENDS EXACTLY WHERE RESISTANCE ENDS. YET THE INTRODUCTION OF THIS RESISTANCE PRODUCES SO STRONG AN
DOCT PREFACE(53) ALLUDED TO THIS IMAGINARY PHENOMENON BEFORE THE INTRODUCTION OF VACCINATION, AND ATTRIBUTED IT TO THE OLDER
DOCT PREFACE(53) ALL THIS DISFIGUREMENT HAS VANISHED SINCE THE INTRODUCTION OF VACCINATION, JENNER HIMSELF ALLUDED TO THIS
GETT (325) (SHE COMES TOWARDS THE STUDY DOOR TO MAKE THE INTRODUCTION). /MRS GEORGE/ THE BRIDE! (LOOKING AT
FANY III (321) (KNOX, AS HE RESUMES HIS SEAT, ACKNOWLEDGES THE INTRODUCTION SUSPICIOUSLY, MRS KNOX BOWS GRAVELY, LOOKING
NEVR II (243) THAT WOULD HAVE BEEN! PERHAPS HE'LL GIVE US AN INTRODUCTION TO HIS SON AND GET US INTO LONDON SOCIETY. THE
MTH2 SD(47) BUT HE SCREWS UP HIS CHEEKS INTO A SMILE AT EACH INTRODUCTION , AND MAKES HIS EYES SHINE IN A VERY WINNING
BULL I (83) AND PREVENTS HIS TOPPLING OVER). /DOYLE/ A NICE INTRODUCTION , BY GEORGE! DO YOU SUPPOSE THE WHOLE
MTH4 I (145) BEEN OF NO USE TO ME. SHE SPOKE TO ME WITHOUT ANY INTRODUCTION , LIKE ANY IMPROPER FEMALE. AND SHE HAS MADE

INTRODUCTIONS

SUPR III (82) AND DISAPPOINTED MAN. HE GAVE ME SOME VALUABLE INTRODUCTIONS TO CAPITALISTS OF THE RIGHT SORT. I FORMED A

INTROJOOCING

BULL IV (168) EVERYBODY THAT WE'RE GOING TO BE MARRIED, AND INTROJOOCING ME TO THE LOWEST OF THE LOW, AND LETTING THEM

INTROJOOSHA

BULL IV (152) OH, I FORGOT. YOUVE NOT MET MR KEEGAN. LET ME INTROJOOSHA . /BROADBENT/ (SHAKING HANDS EFFUSIVELY) MOST

INTROSPECTION

MIS. (144) MY HEAD. BESIDES, WHY SHOULD I GIVE WAY TO MORBID INTROSPECTION ? IT'S A SIGN OF MADNESS. READ LOMBROSO. (TO

INTROSPECTIVE

OVER PREFACE(167) SAME CONDITION, THOUGH THEY WERE NOT VIGILANTLY INTROSPECTIVE ENOUGH TO FIND THAT OUT, AND WERE APT TO BLAME

INTRUDE

2TRU I (40) BOTH HAD THEM, DEAR INVALID. I AM AFRAID WE MUST INTRUDE A LITTLE LONGER. (TO THE NURSE) HAVE YOU FOUND OUT
SIM I (38) REALLY SORRY? /THE CLERGYMAN/ I DID NOT MEAN TO INTRUDE . I APOLOGIZE MOST SINCERELY. /PROLA/ I DID NOT ASK
SUPR IV (144) ALL RIGHT, MISS: YOU WANT TO TALK TO HIM: I SHANT INTRUDE . (HE NODS AFFABLY TO MALONE AND GOES OUT THROUGH

SUPR II (69)	KNOW HOW TO KEEP MY PROPER DISTANCE, AND NOT	INTRUDE	MY PRIVATE AFFAIRS ON YOU. EVEN OUR BUSINESS
NEVR IV (295)	RED) EXCUSE ME: I AM SORRY I INTERRUPTED. I SHALL	INTRUDE	NO FURTHER, MRS CLANDON. (HE BOWS TO MRS CLANDON
WIDO I (14)	SEE HIM BRING A HORSEWHIP WITH HIM. I SHALL NOT	INTRUDE	ON THE PAINFUL SCENE. /TRENCH/ DONT GO, CONFOUND IT.
WIDO III (65)	IN YOUR WAY, DR TRENCH. (SHE RISES). I SHALL NOT	INTRUDE	ON YOU ANY LONGER. YOU SEEM SO PERFECTLY AT HOME
DEVL I (13)	INDEED IT IS. PERHAPS YOU HAD RATHER I DID NOT	INTRUDE	ON YOU JUST NOW. /MRS DUDGEON/ OH, ONE MORE OR LESS
DEVL II (36)	NATURE OF YOUR SENTIMENTS TOWARDS ME. I SHALL NOT	INTRUDE	ON YOU, GOOD EVENING. (AGAIN HE STARTS FOR THE
CAPT I (226)	HOUSE). /SIR HOWARD/ (TO RANKIN) I AM SORRY TO	INTRUDE	ON YOU, MR RANKIN; BUT IN THE ABSENCE OF A HOTEL
ARMS I (11)	GOOD EVENING, GRACIOUS LADY. I AM SORRY TO	INTRUDE	; BUT THERE IS A SERB HIDING ON THE BALCONY. WILL
ROCK II (245)	DUKE/ (SURPRISED TO SEE SO MANY PEOPLE) DO I	INTRUDE	, ARTHUR? I THOUGHT YOU WERE DISENGAGED. /SIR

INTRUDED

MIS. (113)	CARE. (TRYING TO RECOVER HIMSELF) I'M SORRY I	INTRUDED	: I DIDNT KNOW. (BREAKING DOWN AGAIN) OH YOU
CATH 4 (193)	HAVE AS MUCH MORE OF IT AS HE WANTS. I AM SORRY I	INTRUDED	. (SHE RISES TO GO). /EDSTASTON/ (CATCHING HER
UNPL PREFACE(R12)	SILLY AND IRRITATING BEYOND ALL ENDURANCE WHEN	INTRUDED	UPON A SUBJECT OF SUCH DEPTH, REALITY, AND FORCE AS

INTRUDER

DEVL I SD(24)	RISE AND CHAT WITH HAWKINS. MRS DUDGEON, NOW AN	INTRUDER	IN HER OWN HOUSE, STANDS INERT, CRUSHED BY THE
UNPL PREFACE(R18)	WHO HAS NOT BEEN " INTRODUCED" AS A STRANGER AND	INTRUDER	. THE WOMEN, WHO HAVE NOT EVEN THE CITY TO EDUCATE
BUOY II SD(19)	THE DOOR BEFORE, AFTER AN ANGRY GLANCE AT THE	INTRUDER	, LEAVING THE MEAL ON THE STOEP. /HE/ (TO THE
MTH2 SD(38)	TO RISE; AND THE TWO BROTHERS STARE AT THE	INTRUDER	, QUITE UNABLE TO CONCEAL THEIR DISMAY. HASLAM, WHO

INTRUDERS

MRS PREFACE(167)	IT IS THEY AND NOT THE DRAMATISTS WHO ARE THE	INTRUDERS	, HE HAS TO FACE THE ACCUSATION THAT HIS PLAYS

INTRUDING

BUOY III (42)	AFTER LOOKING AT THE COMPANY IN DISMAY) AM I	INTRUDING	? I HAD HOPED TO FIND YOU ALONE. /SHE/ THE
APPL I (215)	EARLY. (NOTING THE PRIME MINISTER'S SCOWL) AM I	INTRUDING	? /PROTEUS/ I PROTEST. IT IS INTOLERABLE. I CALL
HART I (69)	BE AT LEAST OVER FORTY. /THE GENTLEMAN/ EXCUSE MY	INTRUDING	IN THIS FASHION; BUT THERE IS NO KNOCKER ON THE
JOAN 6 (148)	COMES IN, MEETING THEM. /WARWICK/ OH, I AM	INTRUDING	. I THOUGHT IT WAS ALL OVER. (HE MAKES A FEINT OF
SUPR IV SD(150)	WHERE THEY CAN ENJOY THE DISTURBANCE WITHOUT	INTRUDING	. ON THEIR WAY TO THE STEPS ANN SENDS A LITTLE
WIDO II (47)	BREAST). /TRENCH/ (NERVOUSLY) I HOPE WE ARE NOT	INTRUDING	. /SARTORIUS/ (FORMIDABLY) DR TRENCH: MY DAUGHTER
SIM I (37)	THE FIGURES) BUT I ASSURE YOU I HAD NO IDEA I WAS	INTRUDING	ON CONSECRATED GROUND. /PRA/ YOU ARE NOT ON
CAND I (86)	MORELL. /LEXY/ (HUFFILY) I HAVE NO INTENTION OF	INTRUDING	, I AM SURE, MR BURGESS. GOOD MORNING. /BURGESS/ (

INTRUDUCED

BUOY III SD(28)	FREDERICK. THEY BOW TO SIR FERDINAND AS THEY ARE	INTRUDUCED	, AND SEAT THEMSELVES ON THE DIVAN, THE HUSBANDS

INTRUSION

MTH4 II (190)	THEIR OWN, AND PROTECT THEMSELVES ABSOLUTELY FROM	INTRUSION	BY COMMON PERSONS. I THINK I MAY CLAIM THAT OUR
KING I (179)	ME THAT WE ARE MAKING A MOST UNWARRANTABLE	INTRUSION	ON OUR HOST'S VALUABLE TIME. MR NEWTON: ON MY
CATH 4 (188)	SPEAKING. /CATHERINE/ (VIOLENTLY, FURIOUS AT HIS	INTRUSION	) REMEMBER THAT DOGS SHOULD BE DUMB. (HE
BASH III (119)	ASKING YOUR LADYSHIP TO PARDON ME FOR THIS	INTRUSION	, MIGHT I BE SO BOLD AS ASK A QUESTION OF YOUR

INTRUSIVE

FABL I (101)	YOU SIT. /YOUNG MAN/ I HOPE YOU DONT THINK ME	INTRUSIVE	? /YOUNG WOMAN/ I AM NOT THINKING ABOUT YOU AT
2TRU I (48)	THE GIRL'S PRISON AND THE WOMAN'S WORKHOUSE. THE	INTRUSIVE	CARE OF HER ANXIOUS PARENTS, THE OFFICIOUS CONCERN
MRS I (181)	(DAUNTED AND CONCILIATORY) I'M AFRAID I APPEAR	INTRUSIVE	. MY NAME IS PRAED. (VIVIE AT ONCE THROWS HER
BARB I (265)	OF A FATHER, I SHALL PRODUCE THE EFFECT OF AN	INTRUSIVE	STRANGER; AND IF I PLAY THE PART OF A DISCREET

INTUITION

DOCT I (99)	STAGERS DID MARVELS THROUGH SHEER PROFESSIONAL	INTUITION	AND CLINICAL EXPERIENCE; BUT WHEN I THINK OF THE
MIS. PREFACE(52)	CHRISTIANITY, CHRIST STANDS IN THE WORLD FOR THAT	INTUITION	OF THE HIGHEST HUMANITY THAT WE, BEING MEMBERS ONE
MIS. PREFACE(59)	CHILDREN ARE VERY DOCILE: THEY HAVE A SOUND	INTUITION	THAT THEY MUST DO WHAT THEY ARE TOLD OR PERISH.
FANY PROL,SD(266)	NEGATIVELY BY A COMFORTABLE IGNORANCE AND LACK OF	INTUITION	WHICH HIDES FROM HIM ALL THE DANGERS AND DISGRACES
MIS. PREFACE(59)	WHAT THEY ARE TOLD OR PERISH. AND ADULTS HAVE AN	INTUITION	, EQUALLY SOUND, THAT THEY MUST TAKE ADVANTAGE OF
BULL IV (164)	A VERY STRONG ATTACHMENT. PERHAPS, WITH A WOMAN'S	INTUITION	, YOU HAVE ALREADY GUESSED THAT. /NORA/ (RISING

INTUITIONAL

MIS. PREFACE(98)	PESSIMISTIC; SOME AMORISTIC AND ROMANTIC; SOME	INTUITIONAL	; SOME SOPHISTICAL AND INTELLECTUAL; NONE SUITED

INTUITIONS

JOAN PREFACE(11)	ARE NOT ALWAYS CRIMINALS. THE INSPIRATIONS AND	INTUITIONS	AND UNCONSCIOUSLY REASONED CONCLUSIONS OF GENIUS
JITT I (22)	CHILDREN OF FLESH AND BLOOD, BUT INSPIRATIONS,	INTUITIONS	, CONVICTIONS THAT THEY CANNOT DISCARD WITHOUT
BUOY IV (59)	TAKE ACCOUNT OF FEELINGS, PASSIONS, EMOTIONS,	INTUITIONS	, INSTINCTS, AS WELL AS COLD QUANTITIES AND

INTUITIVE

MIS. PREFACE(44)	AND DEDUCTION; OR EVEN INTO SO RAPID AND	INTUITIVE	AN INTEGRATION OF ALL THESE PROCESSES IN A SINGLE
UNPL PREFACE(R23)	THEIR PARTS INTUITIVELY. BUT TO EXPECT THEM TO BE	INTUITIVE	AS TO INTELLECTUAL MEANING AND CIRCUMSTANTIAL
ARMS III (65)	COOLLY. /RAINA/ (QUAINTLY TO BLUNTSCHLI, WITH AN	INTUITIVE	GUESS AT HIS STATE OF MIND) I DARESAY YOU THINK US

INTUITIVELY

UNPL PREFACE(R23)	ENABLES THEM TO SEIZE THE MOODS OF THEIR PARTS	INTUITIVELY	. BUT TO EXPECT THEM TO BE INTUITIVE AS TO

INURED

MIS. PREFACE(88)	STUDIED BY PSYCHOPATHOLOGISTS. YET WE ARE SO	INURED	TO IT IN SCHOOL, WHERE PRACTICALLY ALL THE TEACHERS
GLIM (177)	MEN ARE DANGEROUS, YOUR EXCELLENCY: THEY ARE	INURED	TO TOIL AND ENDURANCE. BESIDES, I KNOW ALL THE

INVADE

GENV PREFACE(21)	A LEGITIMATE TITLE TO THE TERRITORIES THEY	INVADE	. WHEN MUSSOLINI INVADED ABYSSINIA AND MADE IT
PRES (142)	/BALSQUITH/ AFTER ALL, WHY SHOULD THE GERMANS	INVADE	US? /MITCHENER/ WHY SHOULDNT THEY? WHAT ELSE HAS

INVADED

GENV PREFACE(21)	TO THE TERRITORIES THEY INVADE. WHEN MUSSOLINI	INVADED	ABYSSINIA AND MADE IT POSSIBLE FOR A STRANGER TO
ANNA (299)	HIS VIEWS ON THE SINGLE TAX AND BEING INSTANTLY	INVADED	AND ANNIHILATED. A THIRD ORDERS ME TO GO TO A DAMNED
BULL PREFACE(59)	THAT DEFENCE WAS OBVIOUS ENOUGH: THE VILLAGE WAS	INVADED	BY FIVE ARMED FOREIGNERS WHO ATTEMPTED FOR THE
PRES (142)	/MITCHENER/ THINK OF WHAT IT WOULD COST TO BE	INVADED	BY GERMANY AND FORCED TO PAY AN INDEMNITY OF FIVE
GETT PREFACE(233)	AND SENSIBLE MAN DOES WHEN HIS HOUSEHOLD IS	INVADED	IS WHAT THE REVEREND JAMES MAVOR MORELL DOES IN MY
GENV IV (122)	GRAVE PIECE OF NEWS. MR BATTLER'S TROOPS HAVE	INVADED	RURITANIA. GENERAL CONSTERNATION. ALL RISE TO THEIR

INVADER

PRES (143)	NOT ALWAYS LOOKING UNDER THE NATION'S BED FOR AN	INVADER	, AND IF IT COMES TO FIGHTING, I'M QUITE WILLING TO
O'FL (213)	COLLAR OF GOLD THAT MALACHI WON FROM THE PROUD	INVADER	. OH, SHE'S THE ROMANTIC WOMAN IS MY MOTHER, AND NO
CLEO IV (189)	BE SLAIN IN MY TURN BY THEIR COUNTRYMEN AS THE	INVADER	OF THEIR FATHERLAND? CAN ROME DO LESS THEN THAN
GENV PREFACE(5)	BE TAKEN DOWN AND HIDDEN LEST THEY SHOULD HELP AN	INVADER	TO FIND HIS WAY. IT WAS A CRIME TO GIVE AN ADDRESS
DEVL EPILOG (83)	IN AMERICA, WHERE BURGOYNE WAS AN ENEMY AND AN	INVADER	, HE WAS ADMIRED AND PRAISED. THE CLIMATE THERE IS

INVADERS

BULL PREFACE(59)	VILLAGERS HAD LOST THEIR TEMPERS AND KNOCKED THE	INVADERS	ABOUT; AND THE OLDER MEN AND WATCHMEN HAD FINALLY
BULL I (86)	WAS; AND ITS BREED WAS CROSSED BY JUST THE SAME	INVADERS	. /BROADBENT/ TRUE. ALL THE CAPABLE PEOPLE IN

INVADING

GENV PREFACE(6)	THEM THERE AS PART OF THE BAGGAGE OF THE ALLIED	INVADING	ARMIES, WAS A FEAT WHICH STILL SEEMS INCREDIBLE
DOCT III (147)	ME YOU ARE SIMPLY A FIELD OF BATTLE IN WHICH AN	INVADING	ARMY OF TUBERCLE BACILLI STRUGGLES WITH A PATRIOTIC
PRES (144)	SAY IT THE DAY AFTER YOU PUBLISH YOUR SCHEME FOR	INVADING	GERMANY AND REPEALING ALL THE REFORM ACTS. THE
PRES (142)	A NAVY FOR? /BALSQUITH/ WELL, WE NEVER THINK OF	INVADING	GERMANY. /MITCHENER/ YES, WE DO. I HAVE THOUGHT OF
CLEO PRO2,SD(95)	NOW IN VIEW OF THE FACT THAT JULIUS CAESAR IS	INVADING	HIS COUNTRY. NOT KNOWING THIS, IS INTENT ON HIS

INVALID

2TRU I (41) ME THAT THIS HEAVYWEIGHT CHAMPION WAS A HELPLESS INVALID ? /THE NURSE/ SHUT UP. GET THE PEARLS. /THE
2TRU I (43) SEIZES THE HANDLE OF THE BELL) AND BE A MISERABLE INVALID AGAIN FOR THE REST OF YOUR LIFE. (SHE DROPS THE
WIDO III (50) PLAN TO TAKE ME ABROAD? SINCE I WILL NOT BE THE INVALID AND ALLOW YOU TO BE THE NURSE, YOU ARE TO BE THE
WIDO III (50) AND ALLOW YOU TO BE THE NURSE, YOU ARE TO BE THE INVALID AND I AM TO BE THE NURSE. /SARTORIUS/ WELL, BLANCHE,
KING PREFACE(159) AND ADVOCATE THE COUPLED VOTE, MAKING ALL VOTES INVALID EXCEPT THOSE FOR A BISEXED COUPLE, AND THUS ENSURING
MILL IV (193) YOUR FRIEND MR SAGAMORE, SIR, COMING UP WITH THE INVALID GENTLEMAN. (HE HOLDS THE DOOR OPEN FOR SAGAMORE AND
LION PREFACE(31) ALSO WENT MAD, INSTEAD OF BEING CARED FOR AS AN INVALID . AND WE SHOULD HAVE HAD NO CLEAR PERCEPTION OF ANY
2TRU I (40) /THE BURGLAR/ WE HAVE BOTH HAD THEM, DEAR INVALID . I AM AFRAID WE MUST INTRUDE A LITTLE LONGER. (TO
2TRU I SD(28) ON TIPTOE, FULL OF THE DEEPEST CONCERN FOR THE INVALID . THE DOCTOR IS INDIFFERENT, BUT KEEPS UP HIS
2TRU I SD(27) THAT THE BED IS A SICK BED AND THE YOUNG LADY AN INVALID . THE FURNITURE INCLUDES A VERY HANDSOME DRESSING
2TRU I (44) THE PRICE. SEE LIFE. LIVE. YOU DONT CALL BEING AN INVALID LIVING, DO YOU? /THE PATIENT/ WHY SHOULDNT I CALL
DOCT PREFACE(16) WHO CAN BE PERSUADED THAT HE OR SHE IS A LIFELONG INVALID MEANS ANYTHING FROM FIFTY TO FIVE HUNDRED POUNDS A
MIS. PREFACE(28) PLAY CAN BEAT AN INVALID WHO HAS TO CARRY ANOTHER INVALID ON HIS BACK. THIS, HOWEVER, IS NOT AN EVIL PRODUCED
LION PREFACE(66) HIM TO HIS CONSCIENCE, OR TO TREAT HIM AS AN INVALID OR A LUNATIC IS NOW TREATED (IT IS ONLY OF LATE
JITT III (53) WAY. /AGNES/ DOCTOR FESSLER: A WIDOW IS NOT AN INVALID ; AND IT DOESNT HELP HER TO BE TREATED AS ONE WHEN
MIS. PREFACE(28) WITH ALL HIS ENERGIES IN FULL PLAY CAN BEAT AN INVALID WHO HAS TO CARRY ANOTHER INVALID ON HIS BACK. THIS,
BULL II SD(101) CENTURY, HELPLESS, USELESS, ALMOST SEXLESS, AN INVALID WITHOUT THE EXCUSE OF DISEASE, AN INCARNATION OF
JITT II (43) QUITE UNNECESSARILY. /JITTA/ THE WHIM OF AN INVALID , I SUPPOSE. /LENKHEIM/ (OUT OF PATIENCE) WHIM! HE
PHIL I (89) TO BE AN UNWOMANLY WOMAN! IF I WERENT AN INVALID , I'D KICK HIM. /CHARTERIS/ OH DONT SAY THAT. IT WAS
MILL IV (192) TO ANYBODY. THEN THERE IS ANOTHER GENTLEMAN, AN INVALID , ONLY JUST DISCHARGED FROM THE COTTAGE HOSPITAL.
MIS. (142) POSSIBLY THINK OF ME AS HALF AN ANGEL AND HALF AN INVALID , WE SHOULD GET ON MUCH BETTER TOGETHER. /HYPATIA/

INVALIDATE

LION PREFACE(26) OF JESUS ACTUALLY OCCURRED, THAT PROOF WOULD NOT INVALIDATE A SINGLE ONE OF HIS DIDACTIC UTTERANCES; AND
BUOY PREFACE(6) THE ENGLISH LANGUAGE (HIS CHRONOLOGY) DOES NOT INVALIDATE IN THE LEAST HIS INTEGRITY AS A SCIENTIFIC
POSN PREFACE(387) OF THE CENSORIAL PRINCIPLE, IT DOES NOT INVALIDATE THE ARGUMENT. TAKE ANOTHER ACTUAL CASE. A MODERN
LION PREFACE(8) ACCEPTED AS SUCH BY ALL WESTERN NATIONS, DOES NOT INVALIDATE THE PROCEEDINGS, NOR GIVE US THE RIGHT TO REGARD

INVALIDATED

LION PREFACE(5) THE RECORD THAT JESUS SAID CERTAIN THINGS IS NOT INVALIDATED BY A DEMONSTRATION THAT CONFUCIUS SAID THEM
JOAN PREFACE(11) APPLES WERE FALLING. SUCH AN ILLUSION WOULD HAVE INVALIDATED NEITHER THE THEORY OF GRAVITATION NOR NEWTON'S

INVALIDED

CATH 1 (166) FIELD AT THE GLORIOUS BATTLE OF BUNKER'S HILL. INVALIDED HOME FROM AMERICA AT THE REQUEST OF AUNT FANNY,

INVALID'S

DOCT IV SD(160) SITS DOWN ON THE PIANO STOOL AS DUBEDAT, IN AN INVALID'S CHAIR, IS WHEELED IN BY MRS DUBEDAT AND SIR RALPH.
2TRU I SD(28) AS THE LADY DOES, SHE COMES TO THE BEDSIDE ON THE INVALID'S LEFT, HE COMES TO THE OTHER SIDE OF THE BED AND

INVALIDS

BARB PREFACE(215) CELL AND ON THE PLANK BED, AND FLOGGING, ON MORAL INVALIDS AND ENERGETIC REBELS, IS AS NOTHING COMPARED TO THE
PHIL II (113) TO THINK ONLY OF YOURSELF. I DONT BLAME YOU: ALL INVALIDS ARE SELFISH. ONLY A SCIENTIFIC MAN CAN FEEL WHAT I
MILL II (172) IN THE WORLD BESIDES ATTENDING RICH IMAGINARY INVALIDS . /EPIFANIA/ BUT IF YOU ARE WELL PAID? /THE
JOAN 5 (119) WILL BRING YOU THEIR LITTLE CHILDREN AND THEIR INVALIDS TO HEAL: THEY WILL KISS YOUR HANDS AND FEET, AND DO
DOCT PREFACE(79) ORGANIZATION, PROCEED ON THE PRINCIPLE THAT INVALIDS , MEANING PERSONS WHO CANNOT KEEP THEMSELVES ALIVE

INVALUABLE

DOCT PREFACE(50) THE EARTHQUAKE IN SAN FRANCISCO PROVED INVALUABLE AS AN EXPERIMENT IN THE STABILITY OF GIANT STEEL
2TRU I (42) PUNCH IS ANYTHING LIKE HER KICK SHE WILL BE AN INVALUABLE BODYGUARD FOR US TWO WEAKLINGS-- IF I CAN
LION PREFACE(62) TO THEIR BEING PROVIDED AT ALL. WE HAVE IN THE INVALUABLE INSTRUMENT CALLED MONEY A MEANS OF ENABLING EVERY
WIDO I (20) /COKANE/ (MURMURING AS HE WRITES) INVALUABLE. INVALUABLE . THE VERY THING. "-- MY FRIEND MR COKANE UP THE
ARMS II (42) I CAN SHEW YOU HOW TO MANAGE THAT. /SERGIUS/ INVALUABLE MAN! COME ALONG! (TOWERING OVER BLUNTSCHLI, HE
BARB II (296) THEIR SHOP. /CUSINS/ -- HAPPY-- /UNDERSHAFT/ AN INVALUABLE SAFEGUARD AGAINST REVOLUTION. /CUSINS/ --
GENV I (43) AT THE HAGUE, MY LORD. /BISHOP/ YES, YES. AN INVALUABLE SUGGESTION. THE COURT MUST STOP THE BOLSHIES FROM
KING I (167) HAVE NO BUSINESS HERE EXCEPT TO WASTE OUR HOST'S INVALUABLE TIME AND TO IMPROVE MY OWN, IF HE WILL BE GOOD
GENV I (42) YOU, MY LORD? /BISHOP/ YOUR ADVICE WOULD BE INVALUABLE TO ME; FOR I REALLY DONT KNOW WHAT TO DO OR WHERE
NEVR II (238) HIS WAY OUT) IVE BROKE IT TO HIM, SIR. /PHILIP/ INVALUABLE WILLIAM! (HE PASSES ON TO THE TABLE). /DOLLY/ (
WIDO I (20) THE RHINE--" /COKANE/ (MURMURING AS HE WRITES) INVALUABLE , INVALUABLE. THE VERY THING. "-- MY FRIEND MR

INVARIABLE

METH PREFACE(R26) RELAPSING FROM GENERATION TO GENERATION IS AN INVARIABLE CHARACTERISTIC OF THE EVOLUTIONARY PROCESS. FOR
MIS. PREFACE(85) DISCUSSIONS OF MARRIAGE. MARRIAGE IS NOT A SINGLE INVARIABLE INSTITUTION: IT CHANGES FROM CIVILIZATION TO
GETT PREFACE(252) VICTIMS, DIRECT AND INDIRECT, ARISES WITH ITS INVARIABLE REFRAIN: " WHY DID NOBODY WARN ME? " WHAT IS TO
MILL IV (198) /EPIFANIA/ AN ACTION! VERY WELL: YOU KNOW MY INVARIABLE RULE. FIGHT HIM TO THE LAST DITCH, NO MATTER WHAT

INVARIABLY

METH PREFACE(R54) VALUE WHICH CIRCUMSTANTIAL SELECTION MUST INVARIABLY AND INEVITABLY DEVELOP IN THE LONG RUN.
3PLA PREFACE(R15) AS IT OFTEN DID TO THE VERY FIBRES, IT WAS INVARIABLY AT THE NAUSEOUS COMPLIANCES OF THE THEATRE WITH
APPL I (228) THE LAST SENTENCE OF THE LEADING ARTICLE ALMOST INVARIABLY BEGINS WITH THE WORDS " ONCE FOR ALL." WHOSE
APPL I (231) HAVNT FOUND OUT BY THIS TIME THAT JOE'S RAGES ARE INVARIABLY CALCULATED, THEN NOTHING WILL EVER TEACH YOU
JOAN 4 (96) THE MEN WHO WANT SOMETHING FOR NOTHING ARE INVARIABLY CHRISTIANS. A PAGE APPEARS. /THE PAGE/ THE RIGHT
3PLA PREFACE(R14) PROBLEM. IN FACT THESE SO-CALLED PROBLEM PLAYS INVARIABLY DEPENDED FOR THEIR DRAMATIC INTEREST ON FOREGONE
3PLA PREFACE(R23) THIS THOUGHTLESS COMPARISON IS THAT THE PAINTER INVARIABLY DOES SO LABEL HIS PICTURE. WHAT IS A ROYAL
GETT (356) SO ALL LIBERTINES, BOTH MALE AND FEMALE, ARE INVARIABLY PEOPLE OVERFLOWING WITH DOMESTIC SENTIMENTALITY
MTH4 I (167) NOT OBSERVE IT. BUT WHAT THE NATIVES TELL HIM IS INVARIABLY PURE FICTION. /ZOO/ NOT HERE, DADDY. WITH US LIFE
GETT (320) OF JOSEPH PURSUED BY THE WIFE OF POTIPHAR, I AM INVARIABLY REPELLED AND TERRIFIED. /HOTCHKISS/ ARE YOU NOW
SUPR III (125) EXTRAORDINARY IRRELEVANCE THAT PROSTRATED ME. I INVARIABLY REPLIED WITH PERFECT FRANKNESS THAT I HAD NEVER
BULL PREFACE(28) PEASANTS AND COUNTRY PARSONS IN ENGLAND ARE NOT INVARIABLY UNKINDLY; IN THE SOUTHERN STATES OF AMERICA
INCA (250) WITH PROFESSIONALS HIRED FOR THAT PURPOSE. HE IS INVARIABLY VICTORIOUS. YES: THEY ALL HAVE THEIR DIFFERENT

INVASION

METH PREFACE(R16) TO MILITARIST IMPERIALISTS IN CHRONIC TERROR OF INVASION AND SUBJUGATION, POMPOUS TUFTHUNTING FOOLS,
POSN PREFACE(393) THE LESSON TAUGHT BY THE PLAY IS THE DANGER OF INVASION AND THE NEED FOR EVERY ENGLISH CITIZEN TO BE A
HART PREFACE(28) BECOME THE KINGDOM OF THIS WORLD. HIS ATTEMPTS AT INVASION HAVE BEEN RESISTED FAR MORE FIERCELY THAN THE
BULL PREFACE(54) FALSE WITNESS; AND HIS RESISTANCE TO THE BRITISH INVASION IS THE ONLY OFFICIALLY RECORDED INCIDENT OF HIS
JOAN PREFACE(9) SO AS TO OCCUPY IT WHEN THERE WAS ANY DANGER OF INVASION . AS A CHILD, JOAN COULD PLEASE HERSELF AT TIMES
PRES (142) SERVICE THERE WOULD BE AN END OF THE DANGER OF INVASION . /MITCHENER/ ON THE CONTRARY, MY DEAR FELLOW, IT
SUPR HANDBOK(203) DID IN SOUTH AFRICA. THE INCIDENTS OF THE WHITE INVASION OF AFRICA IN SEARCH OF IVORY, GOLD, DIAMONDS, AND
POSN PREFACE(392) ENGLISHMAN'S HOME, HAS FOR ITS MAIN INTEREST AN INVASION OF ENGLAND BY A FICTITIOUS POWER WHICH IS
2TRU I (48) COUSINS WHO WILL NOT KEEP THEIR DISTANCE. THE INVASION OF HER PRIVACY AND INDEPENDENCE AT EVERY TURN BY
3PLA PREFACE(R20) MR H.G. WELLS'S WAR OF TWO WORLDS, A TALE OF THE INVASION OF THE EARTH BY THE INHABITANTS OF THE PLANET MARS:
APPL I (233) THE REMAINING HUNDREDTH IS RESENTED BY THEM AS AN INVASION OF THEIR LIBERTY OR AN INCREASE IN THEIR TAXATION.
KING I (179) MY HONOR I HAD NO PART IN BRINGING UPON YOU THIS INVASION OF WOMANHOOD. I HASTEN TO TAKE THEM AWAY, AND WILL
JOAN PREFACE(41) TO SHEW A LIGHT AT NIGHT. UNDER THE STRAIN OF INVASION THE FRENCH GOVERNMENT IN 1792 STRUCK OFF 4000
GENV PREFACE(4) WOULD HAVE OVERHEARD AND RUSHED THE THREATENED INVASION THEY WERE BLUFFED INTO ABANDONING. FAR FROM
POSN PREFACE(393) ANOTHER PLAY IN WHICH THE FEAR OF A GERMAN INVASION WAS RIDICULED, THE GERMAN PRESS DREW THE INEVITABLE
BULL PREFACE(49) AND BE HELPLESSLY CONQUERED IN THE GERMAN INVASION WHICH HE CONFIDENTLY EXPECTS TO OCCUR IN THE COURSE
PRES (143) DO THE INHABITANTS SLEEP WITH THE POSSIBILITY OF INVASION , OF BOMBARDMENT, CONTINUALLY PRESENT TO THEIR

INVASION-SCAREMONGER

BULL PREFACE(31) THEY KNOW THAT THE IRISH COAST IS FOR THE ENGLISH INVASION-SCAREMONGER THE HEEL OF ACHILLES, AND THAT THEY CAN

INVASIONS

BULL PREFACE(16) NORMAN, CROMWELLIAN, AND (OF COURSE) SCOTCH INVASIONS . I AM VIOLENTLY AND ARROGANTLY PROTESTANT BY
PRES (143) YOUR LIVES IN AN ECSTASY OF TERROR OF IMAGINARY INVASIONS . I DONT BELIEVE YOU EVER GO TO BED WITHOUT

BULL PREFACE(17)	HIS PEDIGREE TO THE CONQUEST OR ONE OF THE	INVASIONS	, IS EQUALLY CONVINCED THAT IF THIS SUPERIORITY
		INVECTIVE	
METH PREFACE(R55)	SELECTION WORKS, A SAMPLE OF LAMARCKO-SHAVIAN	INVECTIVE	. THE VITALIST PHILOSOPHERS MADE NO SUCH MISTAKES.
METH PREFACE(R62)	LITERARY GIFT, WITH TERRIBLE POWERS OF HATRED,	INVECTIVE	, IRONY, AND ALL THE BITTER QUALITIES BRED, FIRST
FABL PREFACE(97)	WAS BY NO MEANS SILENT ON THE SUBJECT. MARX'S	INVECTIVE	, THOUGH IT RIVALLED JEREMIAH'S, WAS PALE BESIDE
		INVECTIVES	
SIM PREFACE(8)	THE VIEWS OF THE BOLSHEVIST PROPHETS WHOSE	INVECTIVES	AND WARNINGS FILL THE LAST BOOKS OF THE OLD
METH PREFACE(R55)	IN THE YEAR 1906 I INDULGED MY TEMPER BY HURLING	INVECTIVES	AT THE NEO-DARWINIANS IN THE FOLLOWING TERMS. " I
		INVENT	
2TRU II (78)	IS NO LARK. ANSWER ME. DONT STAND THERE TRYING TO	INVENT	A LIE. WHY DID YOU PRETEND TO BE A SERVANT? /THE
DOCT PREFACE(78)	WORDS FOR IT, AND ARE THEREFORE COMPELLED TO	INVENT	A NEW LANGUAGE OF NONSENSE FOR EVERY BOOK THEY WRITE.
BARB III (316)	PROBABLY AN ITALIAN OR A GERMAN-- WOULD	INVENT	A NEW METHOD AND CUT HIM OUT. /LADY BRITOMART/ THERE
APPL PREFACE(187)	THEM AND CHANGE THEM IF THEY DO NOT SUIT? LET ME	INVENT	A PRIMITIVE EXAMPLE OF DEMOCRATIC CHOICE. IT IS
SUPR III (110)	THE HEARTH. BUT HOW RASH AND DANGEROUS IT WAS TO	INVENT	A SEPARATE CREATURE WHOSE SOLE FUNCTION WAS HER OWN
DOCT PREFACE(75)	WILL BE FOUND IN MY PLAY. BUT IT IS ONE THING TO	INVENT	A TECHNIQUE: IT IS QUITE ANOTHER TO PERSUADE THE
PYGM V (271)	ALL OVER THE WORLD, AND THAT WANTED YOU TO	INVENT	A UNIVERSAL LANGUAGE FOR HIM? /HIGGINS/ WHAT! EZRA
LIED (196)	BECAUSE MY NAME WAS AURORA TOO. SO YOUVE GOT TO	INVENT	ANOTHER AURORA FOR THE OCCASION. /HE/ (VERY COLDLY)
SUPR I (21)	ELSE? /TANNER/ OH, FOR HEAVEN'S SAKE DONT TRY TO	INVENT	ANYTHING WORSE. I CAPITULATE. I CONSENT TO JACK. I
JOAN PREFACE(49)	AND HAVE TO DO AGAIN IN THE PLAY, I CAN ONLY	INVENT	APPROPRIATE CHARACTERS FOR THEM IN SHAKESPEAR'S
2TRU III (109)	HOWEVER RECKLESS A LIAR, WOULD DARE TO	INVENT	FIGURES SO IMPROBABLE AS MEN AND WOMEN WITH THEIR
SUPR HANDBOK(177)	CENTURY DEIST, IF WOULD BE NECESSARY TO	INVENT	HIM. NOW THIS XVIII CENTURY GOD WAS DEUS EX MACHINA,
METH PREFACE(R66)	IF GOD DID NOT EXIST IT WOULD BE NECESSARY TO	INVENT	HIM, AND THE OTHER THAT AFTER AN HONEST ATTEMPT TO
MTH4 I (158)	ENOUGH TO HAVE TIME TO STUDY THESE THINGS, AND TO	INVENT	INSTRUMENTS AND APPARATUS FOR RESEARCH. BUT WHAT IS
CAND I (84)	WHERE DID YOU HEAR MORELL SAY THAT? YOU DIDNT	INVENT	IT YOURSELF: YOURE NOT CLEVER ENOUGH. /LEXY THATS
ROCK PREFACE(150)	HAD NO NOTION OF SOCIAL CRITICISM AND NO TIME TO	INVENT	IT. KING CHARLES'S HEAD. IT WAS, BY THE WAY, THE
SUPR III (121)	THAT THE HUMAN WILL SHALL SAY TO THE HUMAN BRAIN:	INVENT	ME A MEANS BY WHICH I CAN HAVE LOVE, BEAUTY, ROMANCE,
MTH2 (75)	WORK TO A NEW PAIR. CONSEQUENTLY, THEY HAD TO	INVENT	NATURAL BIRTH AND NATURAL DEATH, WHICH ARE, AFTER
2TRU I (33)	LOSE MY PATIENT. WHEN THERE IS NO MICROBE I	INVENT	ONE. AM I TO UNDERSTAND THAT YOU ARE THE MISSING
CYMB FORWORD(136)	SO OUT-OF-PLACE THERE THAT SHAKESPEAR NEVER COULD	INVENT	ONE. UNFORTUNATELY, INSTEAD OF TAKING NATURE'S HINT
KING II (232)	ARE NOT. DO YOU THINK GOD SO STUPID THAT HE COULD	INVENT	ONLY ONE SORT OF CONSCIENCE? /CATHERINE/ (SHOCKED)
SUPR PREFACE(R33)	THAT THEY HAD A PUPPET ON THEIR HANDS, AND HAD TO	INVENT	SOME ARTIFICIAL EXTERNAL STIMULUS TO MAKE IT WORK.
PHIL I (84)	WE'RE AT THE TOP OF THE HOUSE. NO, NO: YOU MUST	INVENT	SOME THUMPING LIE. I CANT THINK OF ONE: YOU CAN.
HART I (81)	IT DID WHEN I WAS A BOY. WHY DOESNT YOUR HUSBAND	INVENT	SOMETHING? HE DOES NOTHING BUT TELL LIES TO WOMEN.
APPL INTRLUD(244)	MY BELOVED". /ORINTHIA/ THE NAME YOU PRETENDED TO	INVENT	SPECIALLY FOR ME, THE ONLY WOMAN IN THE WORLD FOR
SIM II (66)	IN THE WORLD, OVER THE AGE OF SIX, EXCEPT IDDY,	INVENT	SUCH A RIDICULOUS EXCUSE FOR GOING TO HIS ROOM TO
BARB PREFACE(245)	WE FRANTICALLY SCATTER CONSCIENCE MONEY AND	INVENT	SYSTEMS OF CONSCIENCE BANKING, WITH EXPIATORY
MTH5 (232)	OH, IT WAS NOT HIS SHAPE. YOU SEE I DID NOT	INVENT	THAT. I TOOK ACTUAL MEASUREMENTS AND MOULDS FROM MY
FABL V (118)	BECAUSE THEY HAD ONLY TEN FINGERS AND COULD NOT	INVENT	THE TWO MISSING FIGURES. THEY COULD NOT CHANGE THEIR
VWOO 1 (117)	IT? /A/ NO, I TELL YOU. WHEN I WANT ROMANCES I	INVENT	THEM FOR MYSELF. /Z/ OH, WELL, PERHAPS YOU WOULDNT
MTH1 I (14)	SOMETHING NEW. HE HAS INVENTED TOMORROW. YOU WILL	INVENT	THINGS EVERY DAY NOW THAT THE BURDEN OF IMMORTALITY
		INVENTED	
DOCT I (94)	I SENT YOU A PAPER LATELY ABOUT A LITTLE THING I	INVENTED	: A NEW SAW, FOR SHOULDER BLADES. /SIR PATRICK/ (
HART I (81)	ALL THE MONEY YOU HAD FOR THAT PATENT LIFEBOAT I	INVENTED	? /MRS HUSHABYE/ FIVE HUNDRED POUNDS; AND I HAVE
KING PREFACE(154)	THE ARTIST AND THE PHYSICIST. I HAVE THEREFORE	INVENTED	A COLLISION BETWEEN NEWTON AND A PERSONAGE WHOM I
FABL VI (123)	YOURS ARE ONLY IN YOUR HEAD. HAVE YOU EVER	INVENTED	A MACHINE AND CONSTRUCTED IT? /TEACHER/ NO. HAVE
GENV PREFACE(24)	AM PRACTICALLY NEVER AT A LOSS; BUT I HAVE NEVER	INVENTED	A MACHINE, THOUGH I AM BUILT LIKE ENGINEERS WHO,
MTH3 (101)	YOU ARE SPEAKING OF IS THE AMERICAN WHO HAS	INVENTED	A MEANS OF BREATHING UNDER WATER. /CONFUCIUS/ HE
MTH3 (92)	DONT SWITCH OFF. LISTEN. THIS AMERICAN HAS	INVENTED	A METHOD OF BREATHING UNDER WATER. /BARNABAS/ WHAT,
JOAN EPILOG (163)	/WARWICK/ I CONGRATULATE YOU ON HAVING	INVENTED	A MOST EXTRAORDINARILY COMIC DRESS. /THE GENTLEMAN/
SUPR III (135)	WAGNER ONCE DRIFTED INTO LIFE FORCE WORSHIP, AND	INVENTED	A SUPERMAN CALLED SIEGFRIED. BUT HE CAME TO HIS
DOCT PREFACE(75)	AND PRODUCE JUST THE OPPOSITE RESULT. AND HE	INVENTED	A TECHNIQUE FOR ASCERTAINING IN WHICH PHASE THE
MTH1 I (17)	BLESSED. /THE SERPENT/ WHAT IS WICKED? YOU HAVE	INVENTED	A WORD. /ADAM/ WHATEVER I FEAR TO DO IS WICKED.
MTH4 II (185)	WHY, WE MUST DRESS-UP FOR YOU. IT WAS YOU WHO	INVENTED	ALL THIS NONSENSE, NOT WE. /THE ELDERLY GENTLEMAN/
BARB PREFACE(212)	REGARDED THE SLAVE-MORALITY AS HAVING BEEN	INVENTED	AND IMPOSED ON THE WORLD BY SLAVES MAKING A VIRTUE
SIM PREFACE(5)	HAVE THEIR SOCIAL USES. THEY HAVE BEEN	INVENTED	AND IMPOSED ON US TO SECURE CERTAIN LINES OF
GENV IV (98)	LIKE THAT OF MY FORERUNNER OPPOSITE, WAS	INVENTED	AND PERFECTED WITH THAT OBJECT. YOU MUST ADMIT THAT
MTH3 (101)	AMERICAN INVENTOR, ESPECIALLY ONE WHO HAS NEVER	INVENTED	ANYTHING. THEREFORE YOU BELIEVE THIS PERSON AND
METH PREFACE(R28)	ANOTHER WILL TAKE UP A FLUTE WITH A NEWLY	INVENTED	ARRANGEMENT OF KEYS ON IT, AND PLAY IT AT ONCE WITH
MTH2 (77)	FELL DOWN A WHOLE FLIGHT. FOR INSTANCE, BEFORE HE	INVENTED	BIRTH HE DARED NOT HAVE LOST HIS TEMPER; FOR IF HE
MTH2 (77)	LONELY AND BARREN TO ALL ETERNITY. BUT WHEN HE	INVENTED	BIRTH, AND ANYONE WHO WAS KILLED COULD BE REPLACED,
DEVL EPILOG (86)	MAY HAVE ACTUALLY OCCURRED, LIKE MOST STORIES	INVENTED	BY DRAMATISTS; BUT I CANNOT PRODUCE ANY DOCUMENTS.
GENV PREFACE(23)	OF IDEAS, OR, TO CALL IT BY THE NEW NAME	INVENTED	BY ITS MONSTROUS PRODUCT PAVLOV, CONDITIONAL
LION PREFACE(14)	HAVE TO DO WHEN THE REDEEMER IS ONCE FOUND (OR	INVENTED	BY THE IMAGINATION) IS TO BELIEVE IN THE EFFICACY
VWOO 3 (142)	WHAT YOU HAVE SEEN AND NOT GABBLE CATCHWORDS	INVENTED	BY THE WASTED VIRGINS THAT WALK IN DARKNESS. IT IS
MTH1 II (33)	DEATH PLAYS ITS PART IN LIFE. TELL ME THIS: WHO	INVENTED	DEATH? ADAM SPRINGS TO HIS FEET. EVE DROPS HER
MTH1 II (33)	I SHALL DIE. WHO PUT THIS UPON ME? I SAY, WHO	INVENTED	DEATH? /ADAM/ BE REASONABLE, BOY. COULD YOU BEAR
MTH1 II (33)	WON FOR YOU AN ETERNAL REST; FOR IT WAS WE WHO	INVENTED	DEATH. /CAIN/ (RISING) YOU DID WELL: I, TOO, DO
MTH2 (76)	DESIRABLE COUNTRY RESIDENCE. BUT THE MOMENT HE	INVENTED	DEATH, AND BECAME A TENANT FOR LIFE ONLY, THE PLACE
MTH1 II (33)	I, TOO, DO NOT WANT TO LIVE FOR EVER, BUT IF YOU	INVENTED	DEATH, WHY DO YOU BLAME ME, WHO AM A MINISTER OF
SUPR PREFACE(R13)	MEANS AGAINST VERMIN. THE PROTOTYPIC DON JUAN,	INVENTED	EARLY IN THE XVI CENTURY BY A SPANISH MONK, WAS
MTH2 (62)	THAT SOCIALISM IS BAD ECONOMICS AND THAT DARWIN	INVENTED	EVOLUTION. ASK PAPA. ASK UNCLE. ASK THE FIRST
JOAN PREFACE(28)	AND THAT THE INQUISITION WAS A CHAMBER OF HORRORS	INVENTED	EXPRESSLY AND EXCLUSIVELY FOR SUCH BURNINGS.
SIM I (49)	THE TIME WHEN AS TINY TOTS THEY COULD SPEAK, THEY	INVENTED	FAIRY STORIES. I THOUGHT IT SILLY AND DANGEROUS,
BULL PREFACE(20)	AND HAD IT NOT BEEN FOR THE NELSONIC ANECDOTES	INVENTED	FOR HIM-- " UP GUARDS, AND AT EM" AND SO FORTH--
KING I (212)	THEM FROM FIGURES WHICH THEY CALL EQUATIONS,	INVENTED	FOR THAT DISHONEST PURPOSE. THIS MAN TALKS OF
CYMB V (148)	TRAIN OF FLATTERERS, COMPELLED TO WORSHIP PRIEST	INVENTED	GODS, NOT FREE TO WED THE WOMAN OF MY CHOICE, BEING
SUPR III (110)	THAT FAR BACK IN THE EVOLUTIONAL PROCESS SHE	INVENTED	HIM, DIFFERENTIATED HIM, CREATED HIM IN ORDER TO
FABL PREFACE(79)	DISGUSTING HELL TO KEEP THEM IN ORDER, WHETHER HE	INVENTED	HIS CONVERSATIONS WITH THE ARCHANGEL GABRIEL, OR,
SUPR III (105)	LIKE, WITH MACHINERY THAT A GREEDY DOG COULD HAVE	INVENTED	IF IT HAD WANTED MONEY INSTEAD OF FOOD. I KNOW HIS
LION PREFACE(27)	CHARACTER, IT IS NOT SAFE TO REJECT THE STORY AS	INVENTED	IN THE INTEREST OF MATTHEW'S DETERMINATION THAT
MTH1 II (33)	ABEL? WHO INVENTED KILLING? DID I? NO: HE	INVENTED	IT HIMSELF. I FOLLOWED YOUR TEACHING. I DUG AND DUG
APPL INTRLUD(244)	OF MAGIC FOR ME. IT COULD NOT BE THAT IF I HAD	INVENTED	IT MYSELF. I HEARD IT AT A CONCERT OF ANCIENT MUSIC
KING I (198)	IS SO ABOMINABLE THAT ONLY A DIVVLE COULD HAVE	INVENTED	IT, AND A NATION OF DIVVLES CROWD TO SEE IT DONE.
METH PREFACE(R20)	BOTANIST. IN THE MEANTIME THE MICROSCOPE HAD BEEN	INVENTED	. IT REVEALED A NEW WORLD OF HITHERTO INVISIBLE
MIS. (171)	RICHER THAN HE'D BE IF BOOKKEEPING HAD NEVER BEEN	INVENTED	. OF ALL THE DAMNABLE WASTE OF HUMAN LIFE THAT EVER
MTH4 II (192)	CURSED THE DAY WHEN ETERNAL LIFE WAS	INVENTED	. /ZOZIM/ POOH! YOU COULD LIVE THREE CENTURIES IF
DOCT PREFACE(53)	AS A MATTER OF COURSE BEFORE VACCINATION WAS	INVENTED	, THAT DOCTORS GET INFECTED WITH THESE DELUSIONS,
MTH3 (101)	LOST THEIR LIVES BY DROWNING SINCE THE CINEMA WAS	INVENTED	. WHY NOT GO TO SEE IT IF YOU ARE AT A LOSS FOR
MTH1 II (21)	WHOSE FAULT WAS IT THAT I KILLED ABEL? WHO	INVENTED	KILLING? DID I? NO: HE INVENTED IT HIMSELF. I
MTH5 (260)	DO YOU MAKE OF IT, CAIN, MY FIRST-BORN? /CAIN/ I	INVENTED	KILLING AND CONQUEST AND MASTERY AND THE WINNOWING
GETT (328)	NAME IS ASHTORETH-- DURGA-- THERE IS NO NAME YET	INVENTED	MALIGN ENOUGH FOR YOU. /MRS GEORGE/ (SITTING DOWN
MTH1 I (18)	MAN UNTIL HE DIES. /THE SERPENT/ YOU HAVE BOTH	INVENTED	MARRIAGE. AND WHAT HE WILL BE TO YOU AND NOT TO ANY
MTH2 (77)	AND THAT WAS ANOTHER STEP DOWN. ONE OF HIS SONS	INVENTED	MEAT-EATING. THE OTHER WAS HORRIFIED AT THE
GETT (267)	CLAIRVOYANT. /LESBIA/ I WONDER WHETHER HE REALLY	INVENTED	MRS GEORGE, OR STOLE HER OUT OF SOME BOOK. /MRS
MTH1 II (33)	YOU HAVE ASKED US A TERRIBLE QUESTION. /EVE/ YOU	INVENTED	MURDER. LET THAT BE ENOUGH FOR YOU. /CAIN/ MURDER
MTH2 (77)	HE SLEW HIS BEEFSTEAK-EATING BROTHER, AND THUS	INVENTED	MURDER. THAT WAS A VERY STEEP STEP) IT WAS SO
MTH1 II (22)	MADE THE BEASTS AFRAID OF US; AND THE SNAKE HAS	INVENTED	POISON TO PROTECT HERSELF AGAINST YOU. I FEAR YOU
BASH PREFACE(90)	(A RIDICULOUS BUT CONVENIENT NAME NOT THEN	INVENTED	), YET IT WAS IN THE UNITED STATES THAT THE
DEVL EPILOG (86)	PRODUCE ANY DOCUMENTS. MAJOR SWINDON'S NAME IS	INVENTED	; BUT THE MAN, OF COURSE, IS REAL. THERE ARE DOZENS
SUPR PREFACE(R31)	EVEN PLATO AND BOSWELL, AS THE DRAMATISTS WHO	INVENTED	SOCRATES AND DR JOHNSON, IMPRESS ME MORE DEEPLY
FABL VI (130)	WAIT A BIT, RAPHAEL. /YOUTH 3/ NO USE. HE HAS	INVENTED	SOME TRICK OF VANISHING BEFORE HE IS FOUND OUT. HE
MTH1 I (14)	WHY DO YOU MAKE IT AGAIN? /THE SERPENT/ ADAM HAS	INVENTED	SOMETHING NEW. HE HAS INVENTED TOMORROW. YOU WILL
MTH3 (101)	BREATHING UNDER WATER. /CONFUCIUS/ HE SAYS HE HAS	INVENTED	SUCH A METHOD. FOR SOME REASON WHICH IS NOT

DOCT II (123)	SOVEREIGNS. /B.B./ NO, NO, MR SCHUTZMACHER. YOU	INVENTED	THAT LAST TOUCH. SERIOUSLY, NOW? /SCHUTZMACHER/
MTH4 III (200)	ROTTERJACKS LOOK TO IT." /THE ENVOY/ THE OLD MAN	INVENTED	THAT. I SEE IT ALL. HE WAS A DODDERING OLD ASS WHEN
MTH1 II (21)	OF THE SUN COULD BE BROUGHT DOWN BY A DEWDROP. HE	INVENTED	THE ALTAR TO KEEP THE FIRE ALIVE. HE CHANGED THE
2TRU III (101)	I HAD NOTHING WHATEVER TO DO WITH IT. /AUBREY/ I	INVENTED	THE BRIGANDS AND THE BRITISH LADY. (TO TALLBOYS)
MTH4 I (167)	ONLY AN AMUSING BARBARIAN. HE IS SAID TO HAVE	INVENTED	THE ELECTRIC HEDGE. I CONSIDER THAT IN USING IT ON
MIS. PREFACE(57)	AND " BROKE IN" AN ANIMAL WITH A WHIP WOULD HAVE	INVENTED	THE EXPLOSION ENGINE INSTEAD COULD HE HAVE FORESEEN
HART I (78)	OVER THEM BOTH. I REFUSE TO DIE UNTIL I HAVE	INVENTED	THE MEANS. /HECTOR/ WHO ARE WE THAT WE SHOULD JUDGE
FABL PREFACE(83)	BOURBONIC BOSSES. THE RUSSIAN BOLSHEVIKS, HAVING	INVENTED	THE SOVIET SYSTEM, AND BROUGHT THEIR COUNTRY TO THE
PYGM PREFACE(199)	SPEECH, HAD EMIGRATED TO CANADA, WHERE HIS SON	INVENTED	THE TELEPHONE; BUT ALEXANDER J. ELLIS WAS STILL A
APPL PREFACE(196)	IN A MAN WHO, HAVING NOT ONLY IMAGINED THEM BUT	INVENTED	THEIR MACHINERY, COULD, FAR FROM BEING CRUSHED BY
ROCK PREFACE(155)	COULD CONCEIVE AT ITS VILEST WAS SPECIALLY	INVENTED	TO PUNISH HIM FOR BEING A TRAITOR (OR " LARN HIM
BULL PREFACE(57)	THE NATURE OF A COURT-MARTIAL HAD THEREFORE TO BE	INVENTED	TO REPLACE THE BRIGANDAGE COMMISSIONS; BUT SIMPLE
MTH1 I (14)	SERPENT/ ADAM HAS INVENTED SOMETHING NEW. HE HAS	INVENTED	TOMORROW. YOU WILL INVENT THINGS EVERY DAY NOW THAT
LADY PREFACE(210)	MARY INTO HIS HEAD, BELIEVED, I THINK, THAT I HAD	INVENTED	TYLER EXPRESSLY FOR HIS DISCOMFITURE; FOR THE
MTH2 (77)	BEGAN TO KILL ONE ANOTHER FOR SPORT, AND THUS	INVENTED	WAR, THE STEEPEST STEP OF ALL. THEY EVEN TOOK TO
MTH2 (77)	HE COULD AFFORD TO LET HIMSELF GO. HE UNDOUBTEDLY	INVENTED	WIFE-BEATING; AND THAT WAS ANOTHER STEP DOWN. ONE
2TRU PREFACE(25)	WAS OBLIGED TO CONFESS THAT THEY HAD NOT YET BEEN	INVENTED	, AND THAT SUCH EXISTING ATTEMPTS AT THEM AS
MIS. (171)	THE DAMNABLE WASTE OF HUMAN LIFE THAT EVER WAS	INVENTED	, CLERKING IS THE VERY WORST. /TARLETON/ WHY NOT
MTH4 II (192)	REALIZATION. I CURSE THE DAY WHEN LONG LIFE WAS	INVENTED	, JUST AS THE VICTIMS OF JONHOBSNOXIUS CURSED THE
SUPR HANDBOK(189)	EVEN IF THIS SELECTIVE AGENCY HAD NOT BEEN	INVENTED	, THE PURPOSE OF THE RACE WOULD STILL SHATTER THE

INVENTING

FABL PREFACE(79)	FOUND THAT HE COULD NOT GOVERN THE ARABS WITHOUT	INVENTING	A VERY SENSUAL PARADISE AND A VERY DISGUSTING HELL
HART I (62)	HUSHABYE/ OF COURSE I DONT BELIEVE YOU. YOURE	INVENTING	EVERY WORD OF IT. DO YOU TAKE ME FOR A FOOL?
MRS PREFACE(157)	WOMEN. IF HE MADE HIS PLAY FALSE TO LIFE BY	INVENTING	FICTITIOUS DISADVANTAGES FOR HER, HE WOULD BE
PYGM III (257)	DRESSING ELIZA. /MRS HIGGINS/ WHAT! /HIGGINS/	INVENTING	NEW ELIZAS. SPEAKING TOGETHER /HIGGINS/ YOU KNOW,
MIS. PREFACE(38)	THE MENTAL TOIL AND ADVENTURE OF MAKING WORK BY	INVENTING	NEW IDEAS OR EXTENDING THE DOMAIN OF KNOWLEDGE,
MTH3 (95)	ENGLAND ONCE SAVED THE LIBERTIES OF THE WORLD BY	INVENTING	PARLIAMENTARY GOVERNMENT, WHICH WAS HER PECULIAR
METH PREFACE(R10)	WRITTEN BADMAN. SCHOPENHAUER WAS CREDITED WITH	INVENTING	THE DISTINCTION BETWEEN THE COVENANT OF GRACE AND
LADY PREFACE(226)	THE GREATEST OF TEETOTALERS. NOW THIS SYSTEM OF	INVENTING	YOUR GREAT MAN TO START WITH, AND THEN REJECTING

INVENTION

MTH2 (75)	A PART OF LIFE, BUT A LATER AND QUITE SEPARATE	INVENTION	? /BURGE/ NOW YOU MENTION IT, THATS TRUE. DEATH
METH PREFACE(R88)	EVOLUTION. BUT BEING THEN AT THE HEIGHT OF MY	INVENTION	AND COMEDIC TALENT, I DECORATED IT TOO BRILLIANTLY
HART I (81)	FOR THAT LIFEBOAT! I GOT TWELVE THOUSAND FOR THE	INVENTION	BEFORE THAT. /MRS HUSHABYE/ YES, DEAR; BUT THAT
CAPT NOTES (302)	I AM EQUALLY GUILTLESS OF ANY EXERCISE OF	INVENTION	CONCERNING THE STORY OF THE WEST INDIAN ESTATE
ROCK PREFACE(171)	DETAILS OF WHICH HE MUST HAVE KNOWN TO BE HIS OWN	INVENTION	EVEN IF HE DID BELIEVE GENERALLY IN A POST MORTEM
APPL PREFACE(191)	HIM I CONSENTED TO INVESTIGATE THE ALLEGED GREAT	INVENTION	IN PERSON ON GATTIE'S PROMISING TO BEHAVE LIKE A
APPL I (237)	AS MUCH AS IT SHOULD. WHY? BECAUSE EVERY NEW	INVENTION	IS BOUGHT UP AND SUPPRESSED BY BREAKAGES, LIMITED.
PLES PREFACE(R13)	CHEAP, AND VULGAR. THE TRUTH IS THAT DRAMATIC	INVENTION	IS THE FIRST EFFORT OF MAN TO BECOME
SIM PREFACE(5)	CREDULITY FROM RELIGIOUS DIVINATION TO SCIENTIFIC	INVENTION	IS VERY OFTEN A RELAPSE FROM COMPARATIVELY
CAPT NOTES (302)	INTERPOLATION OF MY OWN. IT IS NOT, HOWEVER, AN	INVENTION	, ONE OF THE EVILS OF THE PRETENCE THAT OUR
BUOY IV (58)	/OLD BILL/ NO. EARTHLY PROVIDENCE. DARKIE'S	INVENTION	, /SIR FERDINAND/ AH! PRECISELY. THE YOUTH FIFFY
MTH1 I (14)	TOMORROW; FOR THAT SURELY IS A GREAT AND BLESSED	INVENTION	, /THE SERPENT/ PROCRASTINATION. /EVE/ THAT IS A
BASH II,2, (116)	THE UPPER CUT, AND THIS A HOOK-HIT OF MINE OWN	INVENTION	. THE HOLLOW REGION WHERE I PLANT THIS BLOW IS
SIM II (76)	THE CHERUBS HAD DISAPPEARED." /HYERING/ OH, AN	INVENTION	. WE CANT SWALLOW THOSE CHERUBS, REALLY. /SIR
BASH II,2, (114)	THESE TWO CONJOINED BECOME THE GRISLY PARENTS OF	INVENTION	. WHY DOES THE TREMBLING WHITE WITH FRANTIC TOIL
GENV PREFACE(27)	IT IS CONCEIVABLE EVEN THAT THE NEXT GREAT	INVENTION	MAY CREATE AN OVERWHELMING INTEREST IN PACIFIC
MTH3 (92)	DAY YOU WILL WALK INTO THE SERPENTINE. THIS MAN'S	INVENTION	MAY SAVE YOUR LIFE. /BARNABAS/ (ANGRILY) WILL YOU
MTH3 (93)	DURING THE LAST TWO CENTURIES, AND THAT WHEN THIS	INVENTION	OF BREATHING UNDER WATER TAKES EFFECT, YOUR
APPL PREFACE(191)	FOR SOME YEARS, I WAS TOLD THAT HE HAD MADE AN	INVENTION	OF FIRST-RATE IMPORTANCE, I WAS INCREDULOUS, AND
DEST SD(149)	AND HAS PERCEIVED, FOR THE FIRST TIME SINCE THE	INVENTION	OF GUNPOWDER, THAT A CANNON BALL, IF IT STRIKES A
GETT (267)	YOU WERE JUST LATE FOR A PARTICULARLY THRILLING	INVENTION	OF HIS. /LESBIA/ ABOUT MRS GEORGE? /MRS
3PLA PREFACE(R27)	NOVELTY IN IT. ONLY, THAT NOVELTY IS NOT ANY	INVENTION	OF MY OWN, BUT SIMPLY THE NOVELTY OF THE ADVANCED
MIS. (128)	THE REPULSIVE MASK. THAT, MY BOY, IS ANOTHER	INVENTION	OF NATURAL SELECTION TO DISGUST YOUNG WOMEN WITH
POSN PREFACE(427)	BUT IT IS CERTAIN THAT SOMEBODY WILL. THE	INVENTION	OF PRINTING AND THE FREEDOM OF THE PRESS HAVE
FABL PREFACE(69)	TO HIS CREDIT AS THE BEGINNING OF WISDOM. THE	INVENTION	OF SATAN IS A HEROIC ADVANCE ON JAHVISM. IT IS AN
LION PREFACE(49)	AS A FORCE LIKE ELECTRICITY, ONLY NEEDING THE	INVENTION	OF SUITABLE POLITICAL MACHINERY TO BE APPLIED TO
MRS PREFACE(179)	DESCRIBING THIS I MUST EXPLAIN THAT WITH THE	INVENTION	OF THE CINEMATOGRAPH A NEW CENSORSHIP HAS COME
BUOY PREFACE(5)	AT INTERPRETING THE BIBLE, AND WAS ASHAMED OF HIS	INVENTION	OF THE INFINITESIMAL CALCULUS UNTIL LEIBNIZ MADE
METH PREFACE(R10)	THEORY OF GRAVITATION, SIR HUMPHRY DAVY'S	INVENTION	OF THE SAFETY-LAMP, THE DISCOVERY OF ELECTRICITY,
BARB PREFACE(212)	STUART-GLENNIE REGARDED THE SLAVE-MORALITY AS AN	INVENTION	OF THE SUPERIOR WHITE RACE TO SUBJUGATE THE MINDS
SUPR HANDBOK(220)	ITS ESSENTIAL ONE. THE MOST REVOLUTIONARY	INVENTION	OF THE XIX CENTURY WAS THE ARTIFICIAL
APPL PREFACE(177)	ADDRESS THE ENORMOUS AUDIENCE CREATED BY THE NEW	INVENTION	OF WIRELESS BROADCAST ON A RANGE OF POLITICAL AND
DOCT PREFACE(52)	VACCINATION WITH IRRESISTIBLE FAITH, SWEEPING THE	INVENTION	OUT OF JENNER'S HANDS AND ESTABLISHING IT IN A
APPL PREFACE(194)	IT CONTAINED NOT A WORD DESCRIPTIVE OF HIS	INVENTION	; AND IT BEGAN SOMEWHAT IN THIS FASHION: " SIR: IF
SUPR III (114)	TO DISCOVER THE INNER WILL OF THE WORLD, IN	INVENTION	TO DISCOVER THE MEANS OF FULFILLING THAT WILL, AND
FABL II (107)	WHAT SECURITY HAVE WE THAT AFTER SELLING HIS	INVENTION	TO KETCHEWAYO IN AFRICA HE DID NOT SELL IT OVER
FABL II (106)	IS TO HANG THIS TRAITOR WHO HAS SOLD HIS ACCURSED	INVENTION	TO THE ENEMY. /C.-IN-C./ WHAT! DONT YOU KNOW THAT
APPL PREFACE(191)	I WAS INCREDULOUS, AND CONCLUDED THAT THE	INVENTION	WAS ONLY A UTOPIAN PROJECT, OUR FRIEND HENRY
LION PREFACE(24)	TO A BAD END LIKE PUNCH OR TIL EULENSPIEGEL: AN	INVENTION	WHICH COST THEM DEAR WHEN THE CHRISTIANS GOT THE
DOCT PREFACE(75)	THE DRAMATIC POSSIBILITIES OF THIS DISCOVERY AND	INVENTION	WILL BE FOUND IN MY PLAY. BUT IT IS ONE THING TO
3PLA PREFACE(R38)	FOR MY OWN PART, I CAN AVOUCH THAT SUCH POWERS OF	INVENTION	, HUMOR AND STAGE INGENUITY AS I HAVE BEEN ABLE TO
HART I (81)	LIES TO WOMEN. /HECTOR/ WELL, THAT IS A FORM OF	INVENTION	, IS IT NOT? HOWEVER, YOU ARE RIGHT: I OUGHT TO
LION PREFACE(7)	JESUS, MEEK AND MILD" IS A SNIVELLING MODERN	INVENTION	, WITH NO WARRANT IN THE GOSPELS. ST MATTHEW WOULD

INVENTIONS

SUPR III (118)	ILLUSION; BUT THEY NOW SEEMED THE EMPTIEST OF	INVENTIONS	: MY JUDGMENT WAS NOT TO BE CORRUPTED: MY BRAIN
BUOY PREFACE(4)	CLEARLY WERE THEY AS MUCH HER OWN STORY-TELLING	INVENTIONS	AS THE WAVERLEY NOVELS WERE SCOTT'S. BUT WHY DID
FABL II (106)	THAT THE GAS WAS ANY GOOD? I GET DOZENS OF SUCH	INVENTIONS	EVERY WEEK, ALL GUARANTEED TO MAKE AN END OF WAR
2TRU PREFACE(21)	PROPERTY AS THE VERY WORST OF ALL THE DEVIL'S	INVENTIONS	FOR THE DEMORALIZATION AND DAMNATION OF MANKIND.
GENV PREFACE(24)	ARE YET SO UNABLE TO PUT DESCRIPTIONS OF THEIR	INVENTIONS	INTO WORDS THAT THEY HAVE TO BE HELPED OUT BY
SUPR III (105)	I HAVE; AND I HAVE EXAMINED MAN'S WONDERFUL	INVENTIONS	. AND I TELL YOU THAT IN THE ARTS OF LIFE MAN
HART I (81)	AT THE RATE WE DO, YOU CANNOT AFFORD LIFE-SAVING	INVENTIONS	. CANT YOU THINK OF SOMETHING THAT WILL MURDER
FABL PREFACE(77)	SO BIGOTED AS TO DISMISS THEIR EXPERIENCES AS THE	INVENTIONS	OF LIARS AND THE FANCIES OF NOODLES. THEY ARE
LION PREFACE(87)	AND THE MORE INCREDIBLE MIRACLES ARE REJECTED AS	INVENTIONS	; AND SUCH EPISODES AS THE CONVERSATION WITH THE
METH PREFACE(R29)	EITHER THAT KEYBOARDS AND SHORTHAND ARE OLDER	INVENTIONS	THAN WE SUPPOSE, OR ELSE THAT ACQUIREMENTS CAN BE
MTH1 II (21)	MEAL WITH THE VOICE THAT HAD WHISPERED ALL HIS	INVENTIONS	TO HIM. HE SAID THAT THE VOICE WAS THE VOICE OF
APPL I (237)	TO HUNDREDS OF MILLIONS. I COULD NAME YOU A DOZEN	INVENTIONS	WITHIN MY OWN TERM OF OFFICE WHICH WOULD HAVE

INVENTIVENESS

DOCT PREFACE(18)	THEY EXPEND MORE THOUGHT, LABOR, SKILL,	INVENTIVENESS	, TASTE AND ENDURANCE ON MAKING THEMSELVES

INVENTOR

APPL I (237)	THEY HAVE BOUGHT IT THEY SMOTHER IT. WHEN THE	INVENTOR	IS POOR AND NOT GOOD AT DEFENDING HIMSELF THEY MAKE
APPL PREFACE(193)	MISSED THE REAL POINT, WHICH WAS THAT HE WAS AN	INVENTOR	. LIKE MANY MEN OF GENIUS HE COULD NOT UNDERSTAND
APPL I (237)	BREAKDOWNS; BUT THESE PEOPLE CAN AFFORD TO PAY AN	INVENTOR	MORE FOR HIS MACHINE OR HIS PROCESS OR WHATEVER IT
MTH1 II (21)	HE WAS THE DISCOVERER OF BLOOD. HE WAS THE	INVENTOR	OF KILLING. HE FOUND OUT THAT THE FIRE OF THE SUN
SUPR III (107)	WAS NEEDED; AND THAT SOMETHING WAS MAN, THE	INVENTOR	OF THE RACK, THE STAKE, THE GALLOWS, THE ELECTRIC
BARB PREFACE(211)	METAPHYSICAL SYSTEM CALLED COMPREHENSIONISM, AND	INVENTOR	OF THE TERM " CROSSTIANITY" TO DISTINGUISH THE
PYGM PREFACE(199)	THE ILLUSTRIOUS ALEXANDER MELVILLE BELL, THE	INVENTOR	OF VISIBLE SPEECH, HAD EMIGRATED TO CANADA, WHERE
KING I (213)	LEONARDO AS AN ENGINEER? OF MICHAEL ANGELO AS AN	INVENTOR	OR A SONNETEER? OF ME AS A SCHOLAR AND A
APPL PREFACE(193)	GATTIE, BEING, I SUPPOSE, BY NATURAL GENIUS AN	INVENTOR	THOUGH BY MISTAKEN VOCATION A PLAYWRIGHT, SOLVED
APPL PREFACE(194)	NOT EASY FOR THE BOARD OF TRADE TO DEAL WITH AN	INVENTOR	WHO WISHED TO INTEREST THEM, NOT IN HIS NEW
APPL PREFACE(192)	AND HAD TAKEN HIM TO BE THE USUAL AMATEUR	INVENTOR	WITH NO PROFESSIONAL TRAINING, HE TOLD ME THAT THIS
MTH3 (101)	ALWAYS BELIEVE ANY STATEMENT MADE BY AN AMERICAN	INVENTOR	, ESPECIALLY ONE WHO HAS NEVER INVENTED ANYTHING.
SUPR HANDBOK(194)	THE GYMNAST, THE SOLDIER, THE SPORTSMAN, THE	INVENTOR	, THE POLITICAL PROGRAM-MAKER, ALL HAVE SOME

INVENTOR'S
2TRU PREFACE(11) OUR LATEST MODEL AUTOMOBILE: WE HAVE CHANGED THE INVENTOR'S DESIGN FOR-BETTER-FOR-WORSE SOLELY TO GIVE YOU AN

INVENTORS
LION PREFACE(58) FOR THE TRIUMPHANT SOLUTION OF THE FIRST BY OUR INVENTORS AND CHEMISTS HAS BEEN OFFSET BY THE DISASTROUS
APPL I (237) THAT IT IS NO USE. I HAVE BEEN SHOT AT TWICE BY INVENTORS DRIVEN CRAZY BY THIS SORT OF THING: THEY BLAMED ME

INVENTS
FABL VI (124) WRITE EVEN A SPECIFICATION OF THE MACHINES HE INVENTS . IF YOU ASK HIM TO, HE CAN ONLY TWIDDLE HIS FINGERS
SUPR III (105) AND I TELL YOU THAT IN THE ARTS OF LIFE MAN INVENTS NOTHING; BUT IN THE ARTS OF DEATH HE OUTDOES NATURE

INVERSE
METH PREFACE(R79) DOGMAS ARE MORE COMPREHENSIBLE. THE LAW OF INVERSE SQUARES IS AS INCOMPREHENSIBLE TO THE COMMON MAN AS
METH PREFACE(R80) SHOUTING EUREKA, EUREKA, OR THAT THE LAW OF INVERSE SQUARES MUST BE DISCARDED IF ANYONE CAN PROVE THAT

INVERTED
JOAN PREFACE(9) THE SOMEWHAT SIMILAR CASE OF SHAKESPEAR A WHOLE INVERTED PYRAMID OF WASTED RESEARCH HAS BEEN BASED ON THE
MRS PREFACE(168) ENCLOSE A SPACE. THEY DO NOT SEE HOW COMPLETELY INVERTED THEIR VISION HAS BECOME EVEN WHEN I THROW ITS

INVEST
BUOY 1 (13) NOT LAST. INDEED IT HAS COLLAPSED ALREADY. I NOW INVEST ALL MY SAVINGS IN RUSSIAN GOVERNMENT STOCK. MY
LADY (242) WORLD IS, AND WORMS AS WE ARE, YOU HAVE BUT TO INVEST ALL THIS VILENESS WITH A MAGICAL GARMENT OF WORDS TO
PRES (138) WITH WHICH IT WAS ABSOLUTELY NECESSARY TO INVEST HIM. /MITCHENER/ QUITE RIGHT. /BALSQUITH/ THAT
MILL I (156) I GIVE YOU MY HUNDRED AND FIFTY POUNDS, WILL YOU INVEST IT FOR ME? /EPIFANIA/ IT IS NOT WORTH INVESTING. YOU
PLES PREFACE(R12) WONDER. ONLY, AUTHORS MUST NOT EXPECT MANAGERS TO INVEST MANY THOUSANDS OF POUNDS IN PLAYS, HOWEVER FINE (OR
MRS III (228) PROPERTY. IVE USED MY KNOWLEDGE OF THE WORLD TO INVEST MY MONEY IN WAYS THAT OTHER MEN HAVE OVERLOOKED; AND
MRS III (231) ME AND IT AMUSES YOU. WHY THE DEVIL SHOULDNT I INVEST MY MONEY THAT WAY? I TAKE THE INTEREST ON MY CAPITAL
FABL PREFACE(96) LUXURY THEY HAVE STILL A SURPLUS WHICH THEY CAN INVEST WITHOUT PRIVATION. IN THE NINETEENTH CENTURY THIS
WIDO III (62) SINCE YOU ARE RESOLVED TO RUN NO RISKS, YOU CAN INVEST YOUR TEN THOUSAND POUNDS IN CONSOLS AND GET TWO

INVESTED
OVER PREFACE(159) WIFE FOR A MODERN BRITISH BISHOP, HAS BEEN INVESTED BY THE POPULAR HISTORICAL IMAGINATION WITH ALL THE
HART I (57) I DONT MEAN THAT HE LENT IT TO HIM, OR THAT HE INVESTED IT IN HIS BUSINESS. HE JUST SIMPLY MADE HIM A
MRS III (229) THAT THE BUSINESS IS WOUND UP, AND THE MONEY INVESTED . /CROFTS/ (STOPPING SHORT, AMAZED) WOUND UP!
APPL II (259) DOES THAT MATTER, NOW THAT OUR CAPITALISTS HAVE INVESTED SO HEAVILY IN AMERICAN CONCERNS THAT AFTER PAYING
APPL PREFACE(186) ANY SPARE MONEY THAT THE GOVERNMENT LEAVES ME IS INVESTED WHERE I CAN GET THE HIGHEST INTEREST AND THE BEST
APPL PREFACE(182) OF HIM. BUT WHEN THESE TWO POOR FELLOWS WERE INVESTED WITH ABSOLUTE POWERS OVER THEIR FELLOW-CREATURES
SUPR HANDBOK(221) WORST FORM OF ASSASSINATION, BECAUSE THERE IT IS INVESTED WITH THE APPROVAL OF SOCIETY. IT IS THE DEED THAT
DEVL EPILOG (83) DESTROYED, THEIR RETREAT CUT OFF, AND THEIR CAMP INVESTED , THEY CAN ONLY BE ALLOWED TO SURRENDER AS

INVESTIGATE
GENV IV (101) THEY WERE BROUGHT TO TRIAL. WHAT WE ARE HERE TO INVESTIGATE IS WHY THEY ARE NOT BROUGHT TO TRIAL. /SIR O./
LION PREFACE(101) CONCLUSION, WE STILL, WHEN WE CAN REASON AND INVESTIGATE NO MORE, MUST CLOSE OUR MINDS FOR THE MOMENT
BUOY 1 (16) AND THE LOCUST, I WANT TO GO ROUND THE WORLD TO INVESTIGATE THAT, ESPECIALLY THROUGH THE PANAMA CANAL. WILL
APPL PREFACE(191) BY MY ATTITUDE THAT TO APPEASE HIM I CONSENTED TO INVESTIGATE THE ALLEGED GREAT INVENTION IN PERSON ON
GETT PREFACE(239) TO APPOINT THE COMMISSION NOW SITTING TO INVESTIGATE THE MARRIAGE QUESTION: THE SCANDAL, THAT IS, OF
METH PREFACE(R51) IN RAILWAY ACCIDENTS, AND YET WEISMANN BEGAN TO INVESTIGATE THE POINT BY BEHAVING LIKE THE BUTCHER'S WIFE IN
POSN PREFACE(369) APPOINTING A SELECT COMMITTEE OF BOTH HOUSES TO INVESTIGATE THE SUBJECT. THE THEN CHANCELLOR OF THE DUCHY OF

INVESTIGATION
BUOY III (42) BY PROFESSION A WORLD BETTERER. I NEED MONEY FOR INVESTIGATION AND EXPERIMENT. I SAW MISS BUOYANT ONE NIGHT
MTH4 I (159) /THE ELDERLY GENTLEMAN/ CERTAINLY NOT. ANY SUCH INVESTIGATION COULD ONLY INCREASE THE DISGUST WITH WHICH HE
POSN PREFACE(372) THAT I HAD INSULTED IT, AND ITS SUSPENSION OF ITS INVESTIGATION FOR THE PURPOSE OF ELABORATELY INSULTING ME
DOCT PREFACE(37) IS NOT UNATTAINABLE. CONSEQUENTLY NO METHOD OF INVESTIGATION IS THE ONLY METHOD; AND NO LAW FORBIDDING ANY
DOCT PREFACE(39) OF THE ARMY AND NAVY STORES. THE SCIENTIFIC INVESTIGATION OF CRUELTY. THERE IS IN MAN A SPECIFIC LUST
SIM PREFACE(16) PRESSING NEED FOR BRINGING US TO THE BAR FOR AN INVESTIGATION OF OUR PERSONAL SOCIAL VALUES IS NOT A
BULL PREFACE(15) SCOTCHMAN OR IRISHMAN, OFTEN TURNS OUT ON INVESTIGATION TO BE, IF NOT AN AMERICAN, AN ITALIAN, OR A
OVER PREFACE(159) FATE OF LUCREZIA BORGIA, WHO, THOUGH SHE SEEMS ON INVESTIGATION TO HAVE BEEN QUITE A SUITABLE WIFE FOR A
APPL PREFACE(192) WITH WHOM WE WERE THEN AT WAR. I APPROACHED THE INVESTIGATION VERY SCEPTICALLY. OUR FRIEND SPOKE OF "-THE
METH PREFACE(R53) DID NOT THINK OF THIS. THEIR ONLY IDEA OF INVESTIGATION WAS TO IMITATE " NATURE" BY PERPETRATING
2TRU PREFACE(4) POSITION OF MY THREE ADVENTURERS; BUT ON CLOSER INVESTIGATION WE GENERALLY FIND THAT HE DOES NOT CARE
DOCT PREFACE(41) BY THE VIVISECTORS. THEY MIGHT OPEN A LINE OF INVESTIGATION WHICH WOULD FINALLY MAKE, FOR INSTANCE, THE
DOCT PREFACE(41) CRIMINAL COURTS, BUT INSTEAD OF PROPOSING SUCH AN INVESTIGATION , OUR VIVISECTORS OFFER US ALL THE PIOUS
SHAK PREFACE(136) AND PRIVATE ENTERTAINERS OF THE PLAYERS. THIS, ON INVESTIGATION , PROVES TO BE EXACTLY WHAT SHAKESPEAR WAS.

INVESTIGATOR
DOCT PREFACE(40) FOR A DISEASE-RIDDEN WORLD. THE REALLY SCIENTIFIC INVESTIGATOR ANSWERS THAT THE QUESTION CANNOT BE SETTLED BY
DOCT PREFACE(39) ITS EXCUSES, CAN BE REGARDED AS A SCIENTIFIC INVESTIGATOR OF IT, THOSE WHO ACCUSE VIVISECTORS OF
BUOY PREFACE(6) IN THE LEAST HIS INTEGRITY AS A SCIENTIFIC INVESTIGATOR , NOR EXEMPLIFY HIS EXTRAORDINARY MENTAL GIFTS

INVESTIGATORS
HART PREFACE(9) AND THAT LIFELESS METHOD OF EVOLUTION WHICH ITS INVESTIGATORS CALLED NATURAL SELECTION. HOWBEIT, THERE WAS
DOCT PREFACE(49) IS A DESERTER FROM THE ARMY OF HONORABLE INVESTIGATORS , BUT THE VIVISECTOR DOES NOT SEE THIS. HE NOT
JOAN PREFACE(18) JOAN WAS WHAT FRANCIS GALTON AND OTHER MODERN INVESTIGATORS OF HUMAN FACULTY CALL A VISUALIZER. SHE SAW

INVESTING
GETT PREFACE(252) AND ALL THE TIME WE SHALL KEEP ENTHUSIASTICALLY INVESTING HER TRADE WITH EVERY ALLUREMENT THAT THE ART OF
MILL I (157) YOU INVEST IT FOR ME? /EPIFANIA/ IT IS NOT WORTH INVESTING , YOU CANNOT MAKE MONEY ON THE STOCK EXCHANGE

INVESTMENT
MILL IV (207) MAY BE SAID TO HAVE MADE A RETROSPECTIVE INVESTMENT IN THE DISCOVERY, AND HE HAS SHEWN THE GREATEST
MIS. PREFACE(86) TO LEND A HAND TO THE FAMILY INDUSTRY, IS AN INVESTMENT IN WHICH THE ONLY DANGER IS THAT OF TEMPORARY
BUOY 1 (13) ME THAT IT IS THE ONLY PERFECTLY SAFE FOREIGN INVESTMENT . THE RUSSIANS PAY IN THEIR OWN GOLD. /SON/ AND
BARB PREFACE(228) ENDURING A VERY BAD TIME ON EARTH AS AN INVESTMENT WHICH WILL BRING THEM IN DIVIDENDS LATER ON IN
METH PREFACE(R12) THAT THE KICKING IS NOT ONLY A SOUND COMMERCIAL INVESTMENT , BUT AN ACT OF DIVINE JUSTICE OF WHICH THEY ARE
WIDO III (61) THERE IS A CERTAIN RISK IN THIS COMPENSATION INVESTMENT , DR TRENCH. THE COUNTY COUNCIL MAY ALTER THE

INVESTMENTS
MTH2 (85) /FRANKLYN/ THE MONEY MAY NOT WAIT FOR THEM. FEW INVESTMENTS FLOURISH FOR THREE HUNDRED YEARS. /SAVVY/ AND
BUOY III (32) MY BANK PASSBOOK AS CASH OR DIVIDENDS ON THE FEW INVESTMENTS MY STOCKBROKER HAS ADVISED. /SIR F./ DOES THAT

INVETERACY
FABL PREFACE(79) I, BEING IRISH, KNOW BETTER. TO RETURN TO THE INVETERACY OF IDOLATRY. TEN YEARS AGO DISCIPLES OF A RIVAL

INVETERATE
MIS. PREFACE(50) BROKE DOWN IN DISGUST AT WHAT SEEMED TO ME THEIR INVETERATE CROOKEDNESS OF MIND. IF THERE HAD BEEN A SCHOOL
GETT PREFACE(226) COMPLAIN: THERE ARE MEN WHO GRUMBLE AND NAG FROM INVETERATE HABIT EVEN WHEN THEY ARE COMFORTABLE. BUT THEIR
BULL I (85) A NATION WITH THE STRONGEST PATRIOTISM! THE MOST INVETERATE HOMING INSTINCT IN THE WORLD! AND YOU PRETEND
METH PREFACE(R81) OF DEALING WITH THEM AROSE FROM THEIR BEING INVETERATE LIARS, BUT THEY WOULD NOT VOTE A SECOND TIME FOR
GENV PREFACE(12) PEOPLE FOR THE COMMON GOOD IN SPITE OF PEOPLE'S INVETERATE OBJECTION TO BE GOVERNED AT ALL. LAW HAS BEEN
PYGM EPILOG (291) RIVAL IN HIS MOTHER, HE GAVE THE CLUE TO HIS INVETERATE OLD-BACHELORDOM. THE CASE IS UNCOMMON ONLY TO THE
BULL PREFACE(16) ON MY ALLEGIANCE: I AM ENGLISH ENOUGH TO BE AN INVETERATE REPUBLICAN AND HOME RULER. IT IS TRUE THAT ONE OF
LION PREFACE(76) OF THE KIND KNOWN TO US. BEING INTELLECTUALLY AN INVETERATE ROMAN RATIONALIST, ALWAYS DISCARDING THE
LION PREFACE(22) MEANING EVIDENTLY TO CLEAR HIMSELF OF THE INVETERATE SUPERSTITION THAT SUFFERING IS GRATIFYING TO GOD.
HART PREFACE(25) FOR THOUGH THE GREAT MEN OF ACTION ARE ALWAYS INVETERATE TALKERS AND OFTEN VERY CLEVER WRITERS, AND

INVETERATELY

ROCK I	(233)	UNDERWORKED, THE THOUGHTLESS AND BRAINLESS, THE	INVETERATELY LAZY AND FRIVOLOUS. YES: THE FRIVOLOUS: YOUR

INVIDIOUS

POSN PREFACE	(422)	(C) TO REPRESENT ON THE STAGE IN AN	INVIDIOUS MANNER A LIVING PERSON, OR ANY PERSON RECENTLY
SIM I	(47)	/PRA/ NOT AT ALL. THEY WOULD REGARD THAT AS AN	INVIDIOUS PROCEEDING. /THE CLERGYMAN/ INVIDIOUS! I DONT
SIM I	(47)	THAT AS AN INVIDIOUS PROCEEDING. /THE CLERGYMAN/	INVIDIOUS ! I DONT UNDERSTAND. /LADY FARWATERS/ (

INVIDIOUSLY

SUPR III	(101)	THAT SEPARATES MY FRIENDS HERE FROM THOSE WHO ARE	INVIDIOUSLY CALLED THE BLEST. /ANA/ I SHALL GO TO HEAVEN AT

INVIGORATING

NEVR III	(263)	ON A FINE AFTERNOON LIKE THIS: VERY PLEASANT AND	INVIGORATING INDEED. (HE TAKES THE TRAY FROM THE CENTRE

INVINCIBLE

JOAN 6	(125)	NO ANXIETY ABOUT THE RESULT, MY LORD. YOU HAVE AN	INVINCIBLE ALLY IN THE MATTER: ONE IS FAR MORE DETERMINED
BULL PREFACE	(9)	WITHOUT THE LORD OF HOSTS, WHO SCATTERED THAT	INVINCIBLE ARMADA FOR LITTLE ENGLAND. THE MODERN IMPERIALIST
GENV PREFACE	(6)	AT CLIVEDEN SHE HAD ANNIHILATED PHILIP'S	INVINCIBLE ARMADA TO THE MUSIC OF THE WINDS AND WAVES, AND,
BULL PREFACE	(9)	SHE DREAMS OF NOTHING BUT THE OLD BEGINNING: AN	INVINCIBLE ARMADA. SPAIN RECKONED WITHOUT THE LORD OF HOSTS,
JOAN 2	(77)	BRAVE DUNOIS, THE HANDSOME DUNOIS, THE WONDERFUL	INVINCIBLE DUNOIS, THE DARLING OF ALL THE LADIES, THE
MIS. PREFACE	(79)	BEING A SIMPLE SOUL, REALLY BELIEVED ME TO BE AN	INVINCIBLE HERO. I CANNOT REMEMBER WHETHER THIS PLEASED ME
JOAN 4	(104)	YOU, MESSIRE DE STOGUMBER, ON THE GROUND OF	INVINCIBLE IGNORANCE. THE THICK AIR OF YOUR COUNTRY DOES NOT
JOAN PREFACE	(31)	OF THEM AS HERETICS. SHE WAS IN A STATE OF	INVINCIBLE IGNORANCE AS TO THE CHURCH'S VIEW; AND THE CHURCH
GENV PREFACE	(15)	INSTRUCTION TO THEM TO ABSOLVE ME ON THE PLEA OF	INVINCIBLE IGNORANCE. WE WERE BOTH TAUGHT TO WORSHIP " A
GENV II SD	(49)	OF DIFFERENT NATIONS, ALL IN A CONDITION OF	INVINCIBLE IGNORANCE AS TO THE SPIRIT OF GENEVA AND THE
MILL PREFACE	(116)	HAVE WON THE BATTLE OF PHARSALIA. CROMWELL PROVED	INVINCIBLE IN THE FIELD-- SUCH AS IT WAS. IT IS NOT,
MTH4 II	(181)	TRAGIC DILEMMA? VICTORY I CAN GUARANTEE! I AM	INVINCIBLE . BUT THE COST OF VICTORY IS THE DEMORALIZATION,
INCA	(251)	MARKET GARDENS. AMONG MARKET GARDENS HE IS	INVINCIBLE . BUT WHAT IS THE GOOD OF THAT? THE WORLD DOES
JITT PREFACE	(4)	UNDERTAKING; BUT HIS FAITH IN MY DESTINY WAS	INVINCIBLE . I SURRENDERED AT DISCRETION; AND THE RESULT WAS
AUGS	(263)	THE GREATEST KNOWN TO HISTORY. OUR GENERALS ARE	INVINCIBLE . OUR ARMY IS THE ADMIRATION OF THE WORLD. (
GETT PREFACE	(188)	FOR ALL THEIR NUMERICAL WEIGHT AND APPARENTLY	INVINCIBLE PREJUDICES, ACCEPT SOCIAL CHANGES TODAY AS TAMELY
BULL I	(90)	IT DOESNT SUIT YOU TO UNDERSTAND. /BROADBENT/ (	INVINCIBLE) UNMITIGATED ROT, LARRY, I ASSURE YOU. /DOYLE/
CATH 3	(186)	END , LITTLE DARLING. /CLAIRE/ (SUSTAINED BY AN	INVINCIBLE SNOBBERY) THEY DARE NOT TOUCH AN ENGLISH OFFICER.
JOAN 5	(117)	SHE IS AS VULNERABLE AS I AM AND NOT A BIT MORE	INVINCIBLE , SHE WILL NOT BE WORTH THE LIFE OF A SINGLE

INVIOLABLE

GETT PREFACE	(186)	IS ALWAYS SOME POINT AT WHICH THE THEORY OF THE	INVIOLABLE BETTER-FOR-WORSE MARRIAGE BREAKS DOWN IN
GETT PREFACE	(256)	THAT THERE IS OR EVER CAN BE ANYTHING MAGICAL AND	INVIOLABLE IN THE LEGAL RELATIONS OF DOMESTICITY, AND THE
BULL PREFACE	(10)	THAT FEELING IN OTHER MEN AS SOMETHING HOLY AND	INVIOLABLE , SPITS OUT OF HIS MOUTH WITH ENORMOUS CONTEMPT.

INVIOLATE

HART PREFACE	(14)	SHOULDERS AND SAYING " C'EST LA GUERRE," ENGLAND,	INVIOLATE FOR SO MANY CENTURIES THAT THE SWOOP OF WAR ON HER
GENV PREFACE	(5)	COMMONWEALTH, HAVING BOUND ITSELF TO MAINTAIN	INVIOLATE THE FRONTIERS OF POLAND AS THEY WERE LEFT AFTER

INVISIBLE

BULL IV	(174)	POOR LOST SOUL, SO CUNNINGLY FENCED IN WITH	INVISIBLE BARS! /LARRY/ HAFFIGAN DOESNT MATTER MUCH. HE'LL
CLEO I	(107)	THAT CHASE YOUR SANDS IN FORBIDDEN PLAY-- OUR	INVISIBLE CHILDREN, O SPHINX, LAUGHING IN WHISPERS. MY WAY
2TRU I SD	(27)	OF THE DRESSING TABLE. THE ROOM IS LIGHTED BY	INVISIBLE CORNICE LIGHTS, AND BY TWO MIRROR LIGHTS ON THE
METH PREFACE	(R21)	INVENTED, IT REVEALED A NEW WORLD OF HITHERTO	INVISIBLE CREATURES CALLED INFUSORIANS, AS COMMON WATER WAS
MTH5	(250)	ART IS THE MAGIC MIRROR YOU MAKE TO REFLECT YOUR	INVISIBLE DREAMS IN VISIBLE PICTURES. YOU USE A GLASS MIRROR
SIM PRO,2,SD	(28)	CLIFF. BUT THERE IS A PATH DOWN THE CLIFF FACE,	INVISIBLE FROM THE SEAT. A NATIVE PRIEST, A HANDSOME MAN IN
MTH4 II	(176)	EVERY MASS OF MATTER IN MOTION CARRIES WITH IT AN	INVISIBLE GRAVITATIONAL FIELD, EVERY MAGNET AN INVISIBLE
DOCT I	(98)	DEAR SIR PATRICK, THOUGH THE GERM IS THERE, IT'S	INVISIBLE . NATURE HAS GIVEN IT NO DANGER SIGNAL FOR US.
FABL PREFACE	(81)	THE HYMNS WERE ASPIRATIONS TO " JOIN THE CHOIR	INVISIBLE ." LATER ON, WHEN I ATTENDED A CHURCH SERVICE IN
MTH4 II	(176)	AN INVISIBLE GRAVITATIONAL FIELD, EVERY MAGNET AN	INVISIBLE MAGNETIC FIELD, AND EVERY LIVING ORGANISM A
MTH4 I	(160)	AND EVERYONE ELSE OUT OF THEIR WITS WITH THE	INVISIBLE MONSTERS THEY SAW: POOR HARMLESS LITTLE THINGS
LION PREFACE	(11)	SOMEBODY ELSE DOING THE EVIL, OR THAT ARMIES OF	INVISIBLE PERSONS, BENEFICENT AND MALEVOLENT, ARE DOING IT;
2TRU II	(78)	SERGEANT? HOW FAR OFF? /SERGEANT FIELDING/ (	INVISIBLE) FORTY HORSE. NINE HUNDRED YARDS, ABOUT, I MAKE
VWOO 2	(123)	SOME STRING BAGS HANGING FROM THE RAFTERS. /Z/ (	INVISIBLE) TH-REEE NI-NNN. SORRY: NO SUCH NUMBER. WHOO-MMM
2TRU II SD	(52)	THERE IS AN IMPRESCRIPTIBLE JOKE SOMEWHERE BY AN	INVISIBLE SMILE WHICH UNHAPPILY PRODUCES AT TIMES AN
MTH4 III SD	(199)	HER HAND TO COMMAND SILENCE. /ALL/ SH-SH-SH!	INVISIBLE TROMBONES UTTER THREE SOLEMN BLASTS IN THE MANNER
SHAK PREFACE	(135)	LIVING ACTORS HAVE TO LEARN THAT THEY TOO MUST BE	INVISIBLE WHILE THE PROTAGONISTS ARE CONVERSING, AND
HART PREFACE	(23)	ALL THE EFFICIENCY OF ENGLAND WAS SILENT AND	INVISIBLE , ALL ITS IMBECILITY WAS DEAFENING THE HEAVENS
SHAK PREFACE	(135)	REST LEFT ASIDE, THESE, THOUGH IN FULL VIEW, ARE	INVISIBLE , AS THEY SHOULD BE. LIVING ACTORS HAVE TO LEARN
SIM I	(43)	GIRLS AWAY THROUGH THE SHRUBBERIES. /VASHTI/ (	INVISIBLE , CALLING) I WILL RETURN IN DREAMS. /MAYA/ (
BUOY IV	(59)	DISCOVERED IT; BUT IT IS THERE, UNDISCOVERED AND	INVISIBLE , POURING INTO OUR BRAINS, CONTROLLED BY OUR

INVITATION

MRS I	(194)	ALL RIGHT. (TO FRANK) WILL YOU ACCEPT THE	INVITATION ? /FRANK/ (INCREDULOUS, BUT IMMENSELY AMUSED)
JITT PREFACE	(4)	FOR THE JOB, THE HUNDRED WOULD HAVE FLED FROM MY	INVITATION AS ONE MAN. IT IS NOT FOR ME TO SAY HOW FAR
MRS I	(186)	THAT WASNT THE BEGINNING. I WENT UP TO TOWN ON AN	INVITATION FROM SOME ARTISTIC PEOPLE IN FITZJOHN'S AVENUE:
MIS.	(154)	FOR THE REST OF THE WEEK. FORTUNATELY I HAD AN	INVITATION FROM THE AERIAL LEAGUE TO SEE THIS GENTLEMAN TRY
HART I	(68)	MY POSITION HERE. I CAME HERE ON YOUR DAUGHTER'S	INVITATION . AM I IN HER HOUSE OR IN YOURS? /CAPTAIN
MRS III	(221)	WITH DESPAIRING VEHEMENCE) I NEVER GAVE ANY SUCH	INVITATION . I NEVER THOUGHT OF SUCH A THING. /FRANK/ (
KING PREFACE	(154)	IN, BUT I MUST MAKE AN EXCEPTION TO THIS GENERAL	INVITATION . IF BY ANY CHANCE YOU ARE A GREAT MATHEMATICIAN
PYGM V	(277)	PUT, INDEED, HENRY. NO WOMAN COULD RESIST SUCH AN	INVITATION . /HIGGINS/ YOU LET HER ALONE, MOTHER. LET HER
DEVL II	(33)	IN ITS PLACE). /RICHARD/ I COME, SIR, ON YOUR OWN	INVITATION . YOU LEFT WORD YOU HAD SOMETHING IMPORTANT TO
FANY II	(289)	COME IN, MAY I ASK? /DUVALLET/ I CAME IN AT YOUR	INVITATION -- AT YOUR AMIABLE INSISTENCE, IN FACT, NOT AT MY
MRS I	(183)	/VIVIE/ SO DO I. SIT DOWN, MR PRAED. (THIS	INVITATION SHE GIVES WITH GENIAL PEREMPTORINESS, HIS ANXIETY
MIS. PREFACE	(87)	ON THE SUBJECT OF THE CONVENTIONAL FAMILY WAS AN	INVITATION TO ALL OF US TO LEAVE OUR FAMILIES AND FOLLOW
PHIL II	(128)	HIS HOUSE, SHE IS SIMPLY TAKING ADVANTAGE OF HIS	INVITATION TO EXTRICATE HERSELF FROM A VERY EMBARRASSING
NEVR I	(213)	CONSIDERABLE DIFFICULTIES ABOUT ACCEPTING OUR	INVITATION TO LUNCH, ALTHOUGH I DOUBT IF HE HAS HAD ANYTHING
NEVR I	(206)	IT WILL BE IMPOSSIBLE FOR ME TO ACCEPT YOUR KIND	INVITATION TO LUNCH. (HE RISES WITH AN AIR OF FINALITY, AND
AUGS PREFACE	(261)	OF WAR IN FLANDERS BY THE COMMANDER-IN-CHIEF: AN	INVITATION WHICH WAS, UNDER THE CIRCUMSTANCES, A SUMMONS TO

INVITATIONS

HART I	(45)	NO PARENTS, TO WARN HER AGAINST MY DAUGHTER'S	INVITATIONS ? THIS IS A PRETTY SORT OF HOUSE, BY HEAVENS!
WIDO I	(17)	AND HE WONT CONSENT UNLESS THEY SEND LETTERS AND	INVITATIONS AND CONGRATULATIONS AND THE DEUCE KNOWS WHAT
PRES	(139)	HEARTRENDING GROANS); AND THEY ALL ADORE HIM. THE	INVITATIONS FOR SIX GARDEN PARTIES AND FOURTEEN DANCES HAVE
ARMS III	(61)	SIR. IT IS NOT OUR CUSTOM IN BULGARIA TO ALLOW	INVITATIONS OF THAT KIND TO BE TRIFLED WITH. /BLUNTSCHLI/ (
FANY III	(312)	IN PRISON, AND SHE HASNT TIME TO GO TO ALL THE	INVITATIONS SHE'S HAD FROM PEOPLE THAT NEVER ASKED HER
GENV IV	(88)	THIS MIGHT HAPPEN. I TOLD HIM TO SEND SPECIAL	INVITATIONS TO THE PRESS, AND CARDS TO ALL THE LEADING

INVITE

BUOY III	(37)	TO KEEP HER IN GOOD HUMOR AND HEALTH I HAD TO	INVITE AND ENTERTAIN A SUCCESSION OF INTERESTING YOUNG MEN
NEVR I	(218)	LUNCH, I'LL NOD TO DOLLY; AND IF SHE NODS TO YOU,	INVITE HIM STRAIGHT AWAY. VALENTINE COMES BACK WITH HIS
APPL PREFACE	(185)	WAR BONDS TO THE CHANCELLOR OF THE EXCHEQUER AND	INVITE HIM TO CANCEL THE PART OF THE NATIONAL DEBT THAT THEY
PLES PREFACE	(R17)	EVEN A GOOD COMIC OPERA CAN BE PRODUCED BY IT, I	INVITE HIM TO TRY HIS HAND, AND SEE WHETHER ANYTHING
POSN PREFACE	(378)	QUESTION, AS IT PRESUMABLY WILL BEFORE LONG, I	INVITE IT TO BE GUIDED BY THE CHAIRMAN, THE MINORITY, AND BY
MRS III	(230)	REMAIN SO. /VIVIE/ AND THIS IS THE BUSINESS YOU	INVITE ME TO JOIN YOU IN? /CROFTS/ OH NO. MY WIFE SHANT BE
MRS II	(210)	ABOUT YOU. WHAT IS THAT WAY OF LIFE WHICH YOU	INVITE ME TO SHARE WITH YOU AND SIR GEORGE CROFTS, PRAY?
FANY PROLOG	(266)	DO: YOU ARE INFLUENCING ME VERY SHOCKINGLY. YOU	INVITE ME TO THIS CHARMING HOUSE, WHERE I'M ABOUT TO ENJOY A
FOUN	(221)	YOU SHOULD MARRY ONE OF MY FRIENDS. YOU CAN THEN	INVITE ME TO YOUR HOUSE, AND PUT ON YOUR BEST COMPANY
BARB I	(261)	THANK YOU. HAVE I YOUR PERMISSION, ADOLPHUS, TO	INVITE MY OWN HUSBAND TO MY OWN HOUSE? /CUSINS/ (
PRES	(162)	THAT IF THEY ARE DEFEATED ON THEIR RESOLUTION TO	INVITE TENDERS FROM PRIVATE CONTRACTORS FOR CARRYING ON THE
PRES	(158)	UNDESERVED BY ME, LADY CORINTHIA. SUCH SUSPICIONS	INVITE THE CONDUCT THEY IMPUTE. (SHE RAISES THE PISTOL).

PHIL II (122)	TO SAY ANYTHING MORE. IF I WERE YOU I SHOULD	INVITE	THE CRAVENS TO TEA IN HONOR OF THE COLONEL'S ESCAPE
MIS. (155)	STAY HERE QUIETLY WITH LORD SUMMERHAYS. YOUD	INVITE	THEM ALL TO DINNER. COME, BUNNY. (SHE GOES OUT,
HART I (75)	SCHOOLFELLOWS. /LADY UTTERWORD/ I SHALL	INVITE	THEM FOR CHRISTMAS. /HECTOR/ THEIR ABSENCE LEAVES US
MRS III (221)	MRS WARREN AND VIVIE OVER HERE TODAY, AND TO	INVITE	THEM TO MAKE THIS HOUSE THEIR HOME. MY MOTHER THEN
FANY III (325)	AMELIA KNOX, I WANT NO MORE OF IT. WOULD YOU	INVITE	THEM TO YOUR HOUSE IF HE MARRIED HER? /MRS KNOX/ HE
2TRU PREFACE(18)	A HOPELESS FAILURE, DO YOU GO BACK TO IT, AND	INVITE	US TO GO BACK TO IT? " WHY THE CHRISTIAN SYSTEM
CAPT III (290)	HOSPITAHLITY YOU HAVE EXTENDED TO US TODAY; AND I	INVITE	YOU TO ACCOMPANY ME BAHCK TO MY SHIP WITH A VIEW TO
MTH2 (67)	TO GATHER YOUR OPINIONS AND REPRESENT THEM. I	INVITE	YOU TO PUT YOUR VIEWS BEFORE ME. I OFFER MYSELF TO BE
VWOO 1 (117)	RACKETS, THE SWIMMING POOL, THE GYMNASIUM ALL	INVITE	YOU. /Z/ I AM NO GOOD AT GAMES: BESIDES, THEYRE
MIS. (130)	/HYPATIA/ (THOUGHTFUL) BENTLEY: COULDNT YOU	INVITE	YOUR FRIEND MR PERCIVAL DOWN HERE? /BENTLEY/ NOT IF
		INVITED	
HART I (77)	TO GRUDGE IT TO YOU OR ANYONE ELSE SINCE. I HAVE	INVITED	ALL SORTS OF PRETTY WOMEN TO THE HOUSE ON THE CHANCE
UNPL PREFACE(R16)	LORD CHAMBERLAIN. THE AUDIENCE WOULD HAVE TO BE	INVITED	AS GUESTS ONLY; SO THAT THE SUPPORT OF THE PUBLIC
INCA (253)	HIS FIRST REAL CHANCE. HE WILL BE UNANIMOUSLY	INVITED	BY THOSE REPUBLICS TO RETURN FROM HIS EXILE AND ACT
PYGM III (246)	I PICKED HER OFF THE KERBSTONE. /MRS HIGGINS/ AND	INVITED	HER TO MY AT-HOME! /HIGGINS/ (RISING AND COMING TO
HART I (45)	BY HEAVENS! A YOUNG AND ATTRACTIVE LADY IS	INVITED	HERE. HER LUGGAGE IS LEFT ON THE STEPS FOR HOURS;
HART I (44)	TO SHEW SOME SIGNS OF KNOWING THAT I HAVE BEEN	INVITED	HERE. /THE WOMANSERVANT/ OH, YOURE INVITED, ARE
HART I (54)	SHE WOULD HAVE HAD NO HOLIDAY IF YOU HAD NOT	INVITED	HER. /MRS HUSHABYE/ NOT AT ALL. VERY NICE OF HER TO
HART I (45)	YOUNG LADY? /NURSE GUINNESS/ SHE SAYS MISS HESSY	INVITED	HER, SIR. /THE CAPTAIN/ AND HAD SHE NO FRIEND, NO
CAPT II (252)	WE LOOK TO YOU, CAPTAIN, TO SQUARE HIM, SINCE YOU	INVITED	HIM OVER. /BRASSBOUND/ YOU CAN DEPEND ON ME; AND YOU
GENV IV (88)	DOORS ARE OPEN ALL RIGHT. ALL ARE AFFECTIONATELY	INVITED	. /SIR ORPHEUS/ (SEATING HIMSELF NEXT BEGONIA). BUT
HART I (71)	TO COME BOTHERING YOU AND PAPA WITHOUT BEING	INVITED	(SHE GOES TO THE WINDOW-SEAT AND SITS DOWN, TURNING
3PLA PREFACE(R16)	FRANKNESS AS A SLAVE DEALER CATERS FOR A PASHA,	INVITED	ME TO FORGET THE COMMON BOND OF HUMANITY BETWEEN ME
PHIL II (130)	LEAVE YOU. /GRACE/ (RISING) NOT AT ALL. PARAMORE	INVITED	ME, TOO. /CHARTERIS/ (AGHAST) YOU DONT MEAN TO SAY
NEVR II (233)	DO YOU UNDERSTAND THAT MY CHILDREN HAVE	INVITED	THAT MAN TO LUNCH, AND THAT HE WILL BE HERE IN A FEW
PHIL II (126)	THAT DOZENS OF MEN WOULD MAKE LOVE TO YOU IF YOU	INVITED	THEM? /JULIA/ (SULLENLY) I SUPPOSE IT'S BETTER TO
MIS. (155)	PEOPLE HAVE NO RIGHT TO DO SUCH THINGS. AND YOU	INVITED	THEM TO DINNER TOO! WHAT SORT OF WOMAN IS THAT TO
POSN PREFACE(372)	PREPARE AND READ WRITTEN STATEMENTS, AND FORMALLY	INVITED	THEM TO READ THEM TO THE COMMITTEE BEFORE BEING
FABL PREFACE(80)	OPEN A POLITICAL MEETING WITH PRAYER. WHEN I WAS	INVITED	TO ADDRESS THE MOST IMPORTANT SECULAR SOCIETY IN
MIS. PREFACE(67)	MERELY CRITICIZED OR OPPOSED IN COMMITTEE, OR	INVITED	TO CONSIDER ANYBODY'S VIEWS BUT HIS OWN, HE FEELS
CAND I (81)	28TH GONE TOO? /PROSERPINE/ CITY DINNER. YOURE	INVITED	TO DINE WITH THE FOUNDERS' COMPANY. /MORELL/ THATLL
APPL PREFACE(179)	DOWN TO EARTH EVERY FIVE YEARS OR SO YOU ARE	INVITED	TO GET INTO THE BASKET IF YOU CAN THROW OUT ONE OF
FABL PREFACE(91)	STORIES. IF THE ANSWER BE YES, THEY CAN BE	INVITED	TO INDICATE THE BOOKS THEY KNOW. I AM QUITE AWARE OF
METH PREFACE(R35)	OF ITS MANUFACTURER. WE DID THEN. WE WERE	INVITED	TO PITY THE DELUSION OF CERTAIN HEATHENS WHO HELD
DOCT PREFACE(38)	WITH SOME VERY UGLY TRUTHS. ON ONE OCCASION I WAS	INVITED	TO SPEAK AT A LARGE ANTI-VIVISECTION MEETING IN THE
AUGS PREFACE(261)	SECURED FOR ME IN JANUARY 1917. I HAD BEEN	INVITED	TO VISIT THE THEATRE OF WAR IN FLANDERS BY THE
PHIL II (128)	I ASSURE YOU, MRS TRANFIELD, DR PARAMORE HAS JUST	INVITED	US ALL TO TAKE AFTERNOON TEA WITH HIM; AND IF MY
HART I (46)	DAUGHTERS. ONE OF THEM IS HESIONE HUSHABYE, WHO	INVITED	YOU HERE. I KEEP THIS HOUSE: SHE UPSETS IT. I DESIRE
HART I (45)	ELSE. I SUPPOSE IT WAS MRS HUSHABYE THAT	INVITED	YOU, DUCKY? /THE YOUNG LADY/ I UNDERSTOOD HER TO DO
HART I (44)	BEEN INVITED HERE! /THE WOMANSERVANT/ OH, YOURE	INVITED	, ARE YOU? AND HAS NOBODY COME? DEAR! DEAR! /THE
PHIL II (103)	BUT THE THIRD PLACE IS FOR PARAMORE, WHOM I HAVE	INVITED	, NOT FOR YOU. (HE GOES OUT THROUGH THE DINING ROOM
		INVITES	
CLEO IV (175)	CAN WE BE OVERHEARD HERE? /CAESAR/ OUR PRIVACY	INVITES	EAVESDROPPING. I CAN REMEDY THAT. (HE CLAPS HIS
DOCT I SD(108)	PROFESSIONAL MANNER, TURNS TO THE LADY, AND	INVITES	HER, BY A GESTURE, TO SIT DOWN ON THE COUCH. MRS
DEVL III SD(50)	DOOR OF A LITTLE EMPTY PANELLED WAITING ROOM, AND	INVITES	JUDITH TO ENTER. SHE HAS HAD A BAD NIGHT, PROBABLY A
BASH I (96)	/CASHEL/ THE PUTRID BAG ENGIRDLED BY THY BELT	INVITES	MY FIST. /MELLISH/ (WEEPING) INGRATE! O WRETCHED
HART I (46)	ATTAIN THE SEVENTH DEGREE OF CONCENTRATION: SHE	INVITES	VISITORS AND LEAVES ME TO ENTERTAIN THEM. (NURSE
		INVITING	
DOCT I (113)	OH YES. WHY? /RIDGEON/ I'LL TELL YOU. I AM	INVITING	ALL MY OLD FRIENDS TO A DINNER TO CELEBRATE MY
ROCK PREFACE(157)	INTERESTS, CLASSES, PRINCIPALITIES AND POWERS,	INVITING	EVERYBODY TO ABANDON ALL THESE AND FOLLOW HIM. BY
BUOY IV SD(54)	PASSES OUT, THEN CLOSES THE DOOR, AND, AFTER AN	INVITING	GESTURE FROM OLD BILL, SITS DOWN IN THE CHAIR
CLEO V SD(200)	IT. RUFIO, SATISFIED, NODS AT CLEOPATRA, MUTELY	INVITING	HER TO MARK THAT. /CLEOPATRA/ (PETTISH AND
APPL I (200)	BUT IF I MISSED A NOTE FROM ONE OF HIS AUNTS	INVITING	HERSELF TO TEA, OR A LITTLE LINE FROM ORINTHIA THE
JITT II (34)	IN HERE? (HE RISES AND CROSSES THE ROOM,	INVITING	HER, BY A GESTURE, TO COME WITH HIM THROUGH THE
WIDO III (64)	SHE PROVOCATIVE, TAUNTING, HALF DEFYING, HALF	INVITING	HIM TO ADVANCE, IN A FLUSH OF UNDISGUISED ANIMAL
LIED SD(198)	AT THEM REFLECTIVELY; THEN LOOKS AT HENRY, MUTELY	INVITING	HIS ATTENTION. HENRY REFUSES TO UNDERSTAND, DOING
CAND I SD(78)	IN TITIAN'S ASSUMPTION OF THE VIRGIN, IS VERY	INVITING	. ALTOGETHER THE ROOM IS THE ROOM OF A GOOD
CAPT III (283)	AND JOHNSON. KEARNEY SITS DOWN AGAIN, AFTER	INVITING	LADY CICELY, WITH A SOLEMN GESTURE, TO TAKE THE
POSN PREFACE(378)	I TURNED EXPECTANTLY TO HIS COLLEAGUES, MUTELY	INVITING	THEM TO FOLLOW HIS EXAMPLE. BUT THERE WAS ONLY ONE
POSN PREFACE(430)	AND THAT I HAD BEEN RIGHT ALL THROUGH, AND	INVITING	THEM TO SCRAP HALF THEIR WORK AND ADOPT MY
LADY PREFACE(222)	ALWAYS EXCHANGING GRINS WITH YORICK'S SKULL, AND	INVITING	" MY LADY" TO LAUGH AT THE SEPULCHRAL HUMOR OF THE
		INVITINGLY	
LION I (117)	GOT A FIGURE. (HE WALKS PAST HER, STARING AT HER	INVITINGLY	; BUT SHE IS PREOCCUPIED AND IS NOT CONSCIOUS OF
		INVOCATION	
GETT PREFACE(196)	OMAR KHAYYAM CLUBS AND VIBRATES TO SWINBURNE'S	INVOCATION	OF DOLORES TO " COME DOWN AND REDEEM US FROM
HART II (128)	WOMEN! WOMEN! WOMEN! (HE LIFTS HIS FISTS IN	INVOCATION	TO HEAVEN) FALL. FALL AND CRUSH. (HE GOES OUT
		INVOKE	
MTH4 III (201)	HIS HANDS IN ENTREATY OVER THE ABYSS). I	INVOKE	THE ORACLE. I CANNOT GO BACK AND CONNIVE AT A
HART PREFACE(38)	EDICT ON WHICH HE WILL BE ABLE, LIKE LINCOLN, TO	INVOKE	" THE CONSIDERATE JUDGMENT OF MANKIND, AND THE
		INVOKED	
BULL PREFACE(54)	HAVE SAID). HASSAN, HOWEVER, " IN A LOUD VOICE	INVOKED	RUIN UPON THE HOUSES OF THOSE WHO HAD GIVEN EVIDENCE
CLEO V (196)	WHAT SAID THE CHIEF PRIEST? /APOLLODORUS/ HE	INVOKED	THE MERCY OF APIS, AND ASKED FOR FIVE. /BELZANOR/
		INVOKING	
JOAN 6 (143)	OF HUMAN BLOOD, INCITING MEN TO SLAY EACH OTHER,	INVOKING	EVIL SPIRITS TO DELUDE THEM, AND STUBBORNLY AND
		INVOLUNTARILY	
GETT SD(325)	AS WELL? HE'S A MARRIED MAN. THEY ALL TURN	INVOLUNTARILY	AND CONTEMPLATE THE BEADLE, WHO SUSTAINS THEIR
MRS III (233)	HER HAND. IT CLANGS HARSHLY; AND HE STARTS BACK	INVOLUNTARILY	. ALMOST IMMEDIATELY FRANK APPEARS AT THE
BULL II SD(106)	OVERBURDENED, LOSES HIS BALANCE, AND SITS DOWN	INVOLUNTARILY	. HIS BURDENS ARE SCATTERED OVER THE HILLSIDE.
NEVR II (253)	HAS NEVER MENTIONED YOUR NAME TO ME. (HE GROANS	INVOLUNTARILY	. SHE LOOKS AT HIM RATHER CONTEMPTUOUSLY, AND
MTH2 (67)	(SITTING DOWN RESIGNEDLY ON THE SETTEE, BUT	INVOLUNTARILY	MAKING A MOVEMENT WHICH LOOKS LIKE THE
MIS. (142)	LIKE THAT TOO. SPARE IT: BE GENTLE WITH IT (HE	INVOLUNTARILY	PUTS OUT HIS HANDS TO PLEAD; SHE TAKES THEM
DEST (164)	OUT HIS HAND FOR THEM). /LADY/ GENERAL! (SHE	INVOLUNTARILY	PUTS HER HANDS ON HER FICHU AS IF TO PROTECT
CLEO I (109)	HIS NOSE IS LIKE AN ELEPHANT'S TRUNK. (CAESAR	INVOLUNTARILY	RUBS HIS NOSE). THEY ALL HAVE LONG NOSES, AND
CAND III (130)	ABOUT LEAVING ME HERE WITH CANDIDA-- /MORELL/ (	INVOLUNTARILY	) CANDIDA! /MARCHBANKS/ OH YES: IVE GOT THAT
CAPT III (285)	ONLY TELL YOU THE EXACT TRUTH-- /DRINKWATER/ (	INVOLUNTARILY	) NAOW, DOWNT DO THET, LIDY-- /REDBROOK/ (AS
BULL IV (170)	THING I WAS GOING TO ADVISE YOU TO DO. /NORA/ (	INVOLUNTARILY	) OH YOU BRUTE! TO TELL ME THAT TO ME FACE!
OVER (189)	SERAPHITA: I PROMISED MY MOTHER-- /MRS JUNO/ (	INVOLUNTARILY	) OH, BOTHER YOUR MOTHER! (RECOVERING
DOCT IV (165)	I'M SORE ABOUT IT. I FORGIVE YOU. /WALPOLE/ (	INVOLUNTARILY	) WELL, DAMN ME! (ASHAMED) I BEG YOUR
DEVL II (49)	(RISING AND STRETCHING OUT HER ARMS AFTER HIM	INVOLUNTARILY	) WONT YOU SAY GOODBYE? /ANDERSON/ AND WASTE
BULL IV (154)	HIMSELF FOR A SERIOUS UTTERANCE: THEY ATTEND	INVOLUNTARILY	). I HEARD THAT A BLACK MAN WAS DYING, AND
SUPR I (34)	ROSETREE? (ANN'S BROWS CONTRACT FOR AN INSTANT	INVOLUNTARILY	). I GOT UP A LOVE AFFAIR WITH HER; AND WE MET
HART II (94)	BEEN QUITE RESIGNED-- /MRS HUSHABYE/ (SHUDDERING	INVOLUNTARILY	)! ! /MAZZINI/ THERE! YOU SEE, MRS
DEST (173)	(QUICKLY) WHAT? (THE HAND UNFOLDING THE PAPER	INVOLUNTARILY	STOPS. THE LADY LOOKS AT HIM ENIGMATICALLY, IN
DEVL III (75)	TOWN CLOCK STRIKES THE FIRST STROKE OF TWELVE.	INVOLUNTARILY	THE PEOPLE FLINCH AT THE SOUND, AND A SUBDUED
		INVOLUNTARY	
MRS PREFACE(152)	HYSTERICAL TUMULT OF PROTEST, OF MORAL PANIC, OF	INVOLUNTARY	AND FRANTIC CONFESSION OF SIN, OF A HORROR OF
DEST SD(162)	RED FOR HIM. INTERPRETING THE BLUSH AS THE	INVOLUNTARY	CONFESSION OF BLACK DEceIT CONFRONTED WITH ITS

LION PREFACE(50) A PREJUDICE AGAINST JESUS ON THE SCORE OF HIS INVOLUNTARY CONNECTION WITH IT, WE ENGAGE ON A PURELY
CAND I (102) TURNS SUDDENLY ON HIM. HE FLIES TO THE DOOR IN INVOLUNTARY DREAD). LET ME ALONE, I SAY. I'M GOING. /MORELL/
CLEO IV (191) SMILE AS IT ALWAYS HAS ON CAESAR. /CAESAR/ (WITH INVOLUNTARY HAUGHTINESS) DO YOU PRESUME TO ENCOURAGE ME?
MTH4 II (177) BUT I WARN YOU NOT TO JUDGE MY QUALITY BY THESE INVOLUNTARY MOMENTS. /THE ORACLE/ I HAVE NO OCCASION TO
METH PREFACE(R51) UNTIL IT HAS BECOME MORE OR LESS AUTOMATIC AND INVOLUNTARY ; AND IT WOULD NEVER HAVE OCCURRED TO HIM THAT

INVOLVE
2TRU II (57) WILL IT BE A LOT OF TROUBLE? /MEEK/ IT WILL INVOLVE A CAMEL. /THE COUNTESS/ OH, STRINGS OF CAMELS IF
FANY I (274) BOBBY OUGHT TO BE MADE TO FEEL THAT SUCH SCRAPES INVOLVE A CERTAIN DEGREE OF REPROBATION." " AS YOU MAY
MRS PREFACE(161) NOT BY THE EXAMINER, BUT BY THE POLICE, DO NOT INVOLVE ADULTERY, NOR ANY ALLUSION TO MRS WARREN'S
PHIL I (80) WITH YOU WHEN I PLEASE. ADVANCED VIEWS, JULIA, INVOLVE ADVANCED DUTIES: YOU CANNOT BE AN ADVANCED WOMAN
METH PREFACE(R34) THE EXPRESSION OF ATHEISTIC OPINIONS REALLY DID INVOLVE ANY PERSONAL RISK, IT WAS CERTAINLY THE METHOD
3PLA PREFACE(R37) (OUR OWN) ON THE PAIR. THIS DID NOT IN THE LEAST INVOLVE ANY PRETENCE ON SHAKESPEAR'S PART TO BE A GREATER
FANY PREFACE(256) IF A SECRET DE POLICHINELLE CAN BE SAID TO INVOLVE CONCEALMENT, WAS A NECESSARY PART OF THE PLAY. IN SO
METH PREFACE(R41) BOTH THESE EXPLANATIONS, YOU WILL OBSERVE, INVOLVE CONSCIOUSNESS, WILL, DESIGN, PURPOSE, EITHER ON THE
MIS. PREFACE(43) AT MARRIAGES OR FINANCIAL SPECULATIONS THAT MAY INVOLVE FAR WORSE CONSEQUENCES THAN BURNT FINGERS, AND JUST
DOCT PREFACE(29) IS IN THE DIRECTION OF TREATMENTS THAT INVOLVE HIGHLY ORGANIZED LABORATORIES, HOSPITALS, AND PUBLIC
METH PREFACE(R38) OWN CONSCIOUSNESS. YET TO ADMIT IT SEEMED TO INVOLVE LETTING THE BOGEY COME BACK, SO INEXTRICABLY HAD WE
SUPR HANDBOK(181) BUT MATING SUCH COUPLES MUST CLEARLY NOT INVOLVE MARRYING THEM. IN CONJUGATION TWO COMPLEMENTARY
POSN PREFACE(407) TAKE IT FOR GRANTED THAT MUNICIPAL CONTROL MUST INVOLVE MUNICIPAL CENSORSHIP OF PLAYS, SO THAT PLAYS MIGHT
MRS PREFACE(161) STAGE. I REPLIED THAT SUCH AN ARTICLE WOULD INVOLVE PASSAGES TOO DISAGREEABLE FOR PUBLICATION IN A
MIS PREFACE(76) TO THE CONDITIONS OF THAT ORGANIZATION, WHICH MAY INVOLVE SUCH PORTIONS OF ADULT RESPONSIBILITY AND DUTY AS A
APPL II (269) (HE SITS DOWN). /MAGNUS/ MY ABDICATION DOES NOT INVOLVE THAT, MR BOANERGES. I AM ABDICATING TO SAVE THE
POSN PREFACE(388) THE ABOLITION OF THE CENSORSHIP DOES NOT INVOLVE THE ABOLITION OF THE MAGISTRATE AND OF THE WHOLE
ROCK II (262) TIMETABLE FOR IT. TO CARRY OUT THE PROGRAM WILL INVOLVE THE INTRODUCTION OF AT LEAST TWELVE BILLS. THEY ARE
JITT I (19) HAVE TO SPEAK OF IT AGAIN. GOD KNOWS IT IS NOT TO INVOLVE YOU IN MY STRUGGLES WITH MYSELF, NOR TO WHITEWASH

INVOLVED
MIS. PREFACE(9) IS THE SAME: THERE ARE NO FALSE PRETENCES INVOLVED : THE CHILD LEARNS IN A STRAIGHTFORWARD WAY THAT IT
JOAN PREFACE(40) OF DAMNATION AND ANARCHY, ITS TOLERATION INVOLVED A GREATER STRAIN ON FAITH IN FREEDOM THAN POLITICAL
GETT PREFACE(208) AND CONSCIENCE INDICATED BY SUCH PAYMENTS INVOLVED ALSO THE OPENING UP OF OTHER MEANS OF LIVELIHOOD TO
METH PREFACE(R29) A MIRACULOUSLY SHORTENED TIME. THE TIME PHENOMENA INVOLVED ARE CURIOUS, AND SUGGEST THAT WE ARE EITHER WRONG
JOAN PREFACE(39) IS A BURNING QUESTION STILL, THOUGH THE PENALTIES INVOLVED ARE NOT SO SENSATIONAL. THAT IS WHY I AM PROBING
DOCT I SD(81) GENERALLY, IN RETURN FOR UNSPECIFIED ADVANTAGES INVOLVED BY INTIMATE INTERCOURSE WITH A LEADER OF HIS
FABL PREFACE(88) VIEW OF THE ENORMOUS INCREASE OF PUBLIC FUNCTIONS INVOLVED BY MODERN SOCIALISM. WE ALREADY HAVE IN OUR
APPL PREFACE(193) THE PRODIGIOUS NUMBER OF BREAKAGES OF GLASS BULBS INVOLVED BY THE HANDLING OF THE CRATES IN WHICH THEY WERE
PLES PREFACE(R12) HEAVY LOSS, AND THE INITIAL EXPENSE AND THOUGHT, INVOLVED BY THE PRODUCTION OF A PLAY, THE EASE WITH WHICH
GETT PREFACE(221) OF MOST MEN TO HIMSELF, IS THAT THE SEX SLAVERY INVOLVED HAS BECOME COMPLICATED BY ECONOMIC SLAVERY; SO THAT
LION PREFACE(4) (THAT IS, TO THE SYRIAN LIFE OF HIS PERIOD) INVOLVED HIS BELIEF IN MANY THINGS, TRUE AND FALSE, THAT IN
APPL PREFACE(173) HAD A ROYAL TRAINING, WILL, IF HE FINDS HIMSELF INVOLVED IN A DUEL WITH HIS KING, BE CAREFUL NOT TO CHOOSE
METH PREFACE(R28) A MAN ONCE, WILL, WITHOUT MORE STRAIN THAN IS INVOLVED IN EATING A SANDWICH, DRAW HIM TO THE LIFE. THE
CLEO NOTES (207) HAD, WE ARE ALSO TO ACCEPT THE CONCLUSION, INVOLVED IN HIS FORMER ONE, THAT HUMANITY HAS PROGRESSED
DOCT PREFACE(66) IS THE PRACTITIONER EXPECTED TO DO ALL THE WORK INVOLVED IN IT FROM THE FIRST DAY OF HIS PROFESSIONAL CAREER
OVER PREFACE(161) DROWN HERSELF, OR THE CONVENTION THAT PERSONS INVOLVED IN SCENES OF RECRIMINATION OR CONFESSION BY THESE
LION EPILOG (147) PROPAGANDA THAT SEEMED TO THREATEN THE INTERESTS INVOLVED IN THE ESTABLISHED LAW AND ORDER, ORGANIZED AND
BULL PREFACE(18) DISTINCTION, WE BOTH FEEL A CERTAIN DISPARAGEMENT INVOLVED IN THE MISAPPREHENSION. MACAULAY, SEEING THAT THE
MIS. PREFACE(35) AND HUNGRY IN THE EVENING. WHEN THEY ARE NOT INVOLVED IN WHAT THEY CALL SPORT, THEY ARE DOING AIMLESSLY
FABL PREFACE(90) SIMILARLY DELUDED COUNTRIES, THE PERSONAL OUTRAGE INVOLVED IS SO INTOLERABLE THAT IT WILL NOT BE IN THE LEAST
LION PREFACE(18) UNEASINESS OR CONSCIOUSNESS OF THE CONTRADICTION INVOLVED . MANY INSTANCES MIGHT BE GIVEN: A FAMILIAR ONE TO
BULL III (124) THERE IS RATHER A DELICATE MORAL QUESTION INVOLVED . THE POINT IS, WAS I DRUNK ENOUGH NOT TO BE
2TRU PREFACE(14) DAY AND THE JUST SHARING OF THE LABOR AND LEISURE INVOLVED . THUS THE INDIVIDUAL CITIZEN HAS TO BE COMPELLED
ROCK PREFACE(173) GO TO HELL WHEN THEY DIE, A CONVICTION WHICH INVOLVED NOT ONLY A BELIEF IN THE EXISTENCE OF HELL BUT A
METH PREFACE(R30) HE BELIEVED THAT EVOLUTION WAS A HERESY WHICH INVOLVED THE DESTRUCTION OF CHRISTIANITY, OF WHICH, AS A
POSN PREFACE(396) TO A POINT AT WHICH A STEP FURTHER WOULD HAVE INVOLVED THE INTERFERENCE OF THE POLICE. PROVIDED THE
HART PREFACE(23) ENGLAND ALL THIS TIME WAS CONDUCTING A WAR WHICH INVOLVED THE ORGANIZATION OF SEVERAL MILLIONS OF FIGHTING
GETT PREFACE(193) BY DRINKING SOUR MILK. EVEN THESE CREDULITIES INVOLVED TOO SEVERE AN INTELLECTUAL EFFORT FOR MANY OF THEM:
JITT PREFACE(5) VIENNA INTO LONDON AND NEW YORK, AND THIS INVOLVED TRANSLATING ONE THEATRICAL EPOCH INTO ANOTHER.
FABL II (106) NATAL, AND RHODESIA WENT TO WAR WITH HIM AND INVOLVED US IN IT. THAT MADE IT YOUR JOB, DIDNT IT?
LION PREFACE(15) IT MUST BE SAID FOR THE EARLIER FORMS THAT THEY INVOLVED VERY REAL SACRIFICES. THE SACRIFICE WAS NOT ALWAYS
POSN PREFACE(400) IT IS NOT TOO MUCH TO SAY THAT THE WORK INVOLVED WOULD DRIVE A MAN OF ANY INTELLECTUAL RANK MAD.
POSN PREFACE(368) IN WHICH SO MANY CONFLICTING INTERESTS WERE INVOLVED , AND WHICH HAD PROBABLY NO ELECTORAL VALUE
JOAN PREFACE(33) CASE IN WHICH HIS PARTY AND CLASS PREJUDICES ARE INVOLVED , THE HUMAN FACT REMAINS THAT THE BURNING OF JOAN
DOCT PREFACE(71) AS TO ANY TECHNICAL MEDICAL PROBLEM SPECIALLY INVOLVED , THERE IS NONE. IF THERE WERE, I SHOULD NOT BE

INVOLVES
2TRU PREFACE(23) IN THE ROYAL NAVY EVERY MISHAP TO A SHIP INVOLVES A COURT MARTIAL ON THE RESPONSIBLE OFFICER: IF THE
ROCK PREFACE(168) SORT OF CIVILIZATION THAT IS DESIRABLE, AND THIS INVOLVES A DECISION AS TO THE SORT OF PEOPLE THAT ARE
MIS. PREFACE(14) AND THE ADULT HAD BETTER NOT FORGET THIS; FOR IT INVOLVES A HEAVY RESPONSIBILITY, AND NOW COMES OUR
2TRU PREFACE(13) GOVERNMENT IS THAT AS THE GOOD OF THE COMMUNITY INVOLVES A MAXIMUM OF INDIVIDUAL LIBERTY FOR ALL ITS MEMBERS
POSN PREFACE(405) SUPPRESSED, BECAUSE EVERY MOMENT OF ITS DURATION INVOLVES A MEASURABLE PECUNIARY LOSS TO THE PROPRIETOR,
SIM PREFACE(18) INVOLVES A NEW SOCIAL CREED. A NEW SOCIAL CREED INVOLVES A NEW HERESY. A NEW HERESY INVOLVES AN INQUISITION.
SIM PREFACE(18) THAN THE PRESENT VERY IMPERFECT BARGAIN. THIS INVOLVES A NEW SOCIAL CREED. A NEW SOCIAL CREED INVOLVES A
KING I (170) OCCUR EARLIER. YOU WILL SEE AT ONCE THAT THIS INVOLVES A RETROGRADE MOTION OF THE EQUINOCTIAL POINTS ALONG
2TRU PREFACE(19) THAT THE WORK OF ROBBING THE POOR ALL THE TIME INVOLVES A VERY ELABORATE SYSTEM OF GOVERNMENT TO ENSURE
SIM PREFACE(18) SOCIAL CREED INVOLVES A NEW HERESY. A NEW HERESY INVOLVES AN INQUISITION. THE PRECEDENTS ESTABLISHED BY THE
DOCT PREFACE(26) AS A CRAZE OR A FAD, OBVIOUSLY DO SO BECAUSE IT INVOLVES AN OPERATION WHICH THEY HAVE NEITHER THE MEANS NOR
MIS. PREFACE(5) ME THAT THEY HAVE NOT THE FAINTEST NOTION THAT IT INVOLVES ANYTHING MORE THAN CALLING THE HELPLESS CHILD
2TRU PREFACE(6) OF THE LIVES OF THE RICH. POVERTY, WHEN IT INVOLVES CONTINUAL PRIVATION AND ANXIETY, IS, LIKE A
MIS. PREFACE(7) CHILDREN FROM THE SLAVERY THAT DENIAL OF RIGHTS INVOLVES IN ADULT POLITICAL RELATIONS. IT SOMETIMES
METH PREFACE(R42) BECAUSE YOU DO NOT AT FIRST REALIZE ALL THAT IT INVOLVES . BUT WHEN ITS WHOLE SIGNIFICANCE DAWNS ON YOU,
MRS I (185) BUT I KNOW NOTHING EXCEPT THE MATHEMATICS IT INVOLVES . I CAN MAKE CALCULATIONS FOR ENGINEERS,
APPL PREFACE(183) NOT INDIVIDUAL ACTION; AND CORPORATE ACTION INVOLVES MORE GOVERNMENT THAN INDIVIDUAL ACTION. THUS
DOCT PREFACE(37) NEED NOT HURT THE PATIENT; AND SPECTRUM ANALYSIS INVOLVES NO DESTRUCTION. AFTER SUCH TRIUMPHS OF HUMANE
GETT PREFACE(205) OBEY THE WAVE OF HIS HAND. ALL CONCERTED ACTION INVOLVES SUBORDINATION AND THE APPOINTMENT OF DIRECTORS AT
POSN PREFACE(405) THE UNCOMPROMISING ABOLITION OF ALL CENSORSHIP INVOLVES THE ABANDONMENT OF ALL CONTROL AND REGULATION OF
DOCT PREFACE(69) IT MUST NOT BE HASTILY CONCLUDED THAT THIS INVOLVES THE EXTINCTION OF THE PRIVATE PRACTITIONER. WHAT IT
GETT PREFACE(245) OF MARRIAGE. THE PATHOLOGY OF MARRIAGE INVOLVES THE POSSIBILITY OF THE MOST HORRIBLE CRIME
3PLA PREFACE(R34) HOWEVER, THAT THE RIGHT TO CRITICIZE SHAKESPEAR INVOLVES THE POWER OF WRITING BETTER PLAYS. AND IN FACT-- DO
MIS. PREFACE(43) US ARE MORAL OR PHYSICAL, OUR RIGHT TO LIBERTY INVOLVES THE RIGHT TO RUN THEM, A MAN WHO IS NOT FREE TO
MTH4 II (178) TO TELL YOU THAT? /NAPOLEON/ WAIT. THIS TALENT INVOLVES THE SHEDDING OF HUMAN BLOOD. /THE ORACLE/ ARE YOU A
FABL VI (127) YES; FOR THE PURSUIT OF KNOWLEDGE AND POWER INVOLVES THE SLAUGHTER AND DESTRUCTION OF EVERYTHING THAT
LION EPILOG (148) THEY ACCEPT AS THE SAME RELIGION ONLY BECAUSE IT INVOLVES THEM IN A COMMON OPPOSITION TO THE OFFICIAL

INVOLVING
APPL PREFACE(173) HIS WAY FROM OBSCURITY TO CELEBRITY: A PROCESS INVOLVING A CONSIDERABLE USE OF THE SHORTER AND MORE SELFISH
PYGM EPILOG (295) WOULD HAVE THE TROUBLE OF UNDOING IT: A PROCEDURE INVOLVING A NET LOSS TO THE COMMUNITY, AND GREAT UNHAPPINESS
METH PREFACE(R54) THEMSELVES, BUT A CHANGE OF CIRCUMSTANCES INVOLVING A PLENTIFUL SUPPLY OF FOOD WOULD DESTROY THEM. WE
MIS. PREFACE(63) AND PASS AN EXAMINATION IN GOING A SIMPLE ERRAND INVOLVING A PURCHASE AND A JOURNEY BY RAIL OR OTHER PUBLIC
DOCT PREFACE(39) OTHER EXHIBITIONS OF SUFFERING, ESPECIALLY THOSE INVOLVING BLOODSHED, BLOWS, AND LACERATION. A CRAZE FOR
METH PREFACE(R27) " PROVING" THE SUM BY A FURTHER CALCULATION INVOLVING MORE CIPHERING, BUT THERE ARE MEN WHO CAN NEITHER
METH PREFACE(R41) FAMOUS DISCOVERY-- THAT A THIRD EXPLANATION, INVOLVING NEITHER WILL NOR PURPOSE NOR DESIGN EITHER IN THE
GETT PREFACE(184) IT THEN THAT WHEN A JOINT DOMESTIC ESTABLISHMENT, INVOLVING QUESTIONS OF CHILDREN OR PROPERTY, IS
MILL PREFACE(132) AND DICTATION OF SCIENTIFIC BUSINESS METHODS, INVOLVING SUCH AN EXPOSURE OF THE OBSOLESCENCE AND
HART PREFACE(8) IN A FAVORABLE CONDITION, A PROCESS INCIDENTALLY INVOLVING THE RUTHLESS DESTRUCTION OR SUBJECTION OF ITS

INVULNERABILITY
CLEO NOTES (211) ENCHANTED SWORD, SUPEREQUINE HORSE AND MAGICAL INVULNERABILITY , THE POSSESSION OF WHICH, FROM THE VULGAR

INVULNERABLE
LADY PREFACE(225) PICTURE OF A WRITHING WORM SUBSTITUTED FOR THE INVULNERABLE GIANT. BUT IT IS NONE THE LESS PROBABLE THAT IN

INWARD
GETT PREFACE(250) DIVORCE A DUTY WHEN THE MARRIAGE HAS LOST THE INWARD AND SPIRITUAL GRACE OF WHICH THE MARRIAGE CEREMONY IS

INWARDLY
CAPT I (239) (OUTWARDLY DETERMINED NOT TO BE TRIFLED WITH: INWARDLY PUZZLED AND RATHER DAUNTED) MADAM: IF YOU WANT AN
DEVL I (22) /MRS DUDGEON/ AND THIS IS MY REWARD! (RAGING INWARDLY) YOU KNOW WHAT I THINK, MR ANDERSON: YOU KNOW THE

IONS
MTH5 (255) A VORTEX WITHOUT GAS, OR MOLECULES OR ATOMS OR IONS OR ELECTRONS OR SOMETHING, NOT NOTHING. /THE

IPECACUANHA
ROCK PREFACE(184) MAKE ME VIOLENTLY SICK. SALUTARY SEVERITY IS IPECACUANHA TO ME. I HAVE SPOKEN TO YOU AS ONE MAN TO

IPHIGENIA
CYMB FORWORD(137) LIKE WAGNER DEALING WITH GLUCK'S OVERTURE TO IPHIGENIA IN AULIS I HAVE MADE A NEW ENDING FOR ITS OWN

IRAN
MILL PREFACE(116) OF THESE COMMANDERS MADE HIMSELF SHAH OF IRAN . JULIUS CAESAR AND CROMWELL ALSO MOUNTED ON THE DEBRIS
GENV IV (95) /BATTLER/ THERE ARE RIVALS IN RUSSIA, ARABIA, AND IRAN . /BBDE/ AND THERE IS ERNEST THE GREAT. WHY OMIT HIM..
GENV PREFACE(22) OF RUSSIA, OUR JAMES THE SECOND, RIZA KHAN IN IRAN , AND SOME OF THE SMALL FRY OF DEGENERATE HEREDITARY

IRAS
CLEO IV SD(166) AND NEATLY FINISHED AT THE HANDS AND FEET. IRAS IS A PLUMP, GOODNATURED CREATURE, RATHER FATUOUS, WITH
CLEO IV (168) THINGS. (THEY LAUGH. SHE TURNS FIERCELY ON IRAS). AT WHOM ARE YOU LAUGHING-- AT ME OR AT CAESAR?
CLEO IV SD(166) YOUNG, THE MOST CONSPICUOUS BEING CHARMIAN AND IRAS , HER FAVORITES. CHARMIAN IS A HATCHET FACED, TERRA

IRASCIBLE
ROCK PREFACE(159) WRONG; THAT WE SHOULD CONCEIVE GOD, NOT AS AN IRASCIBLE AND VINDICTIVE TYRANT BUT AS AN AFFECTIONATE
PHIL I SD(84) EXCEPT AS A MEANS OF RECUPERATION. HIS VIGILANT, IRASCIBLE EYE, PILED-UP HAIR, AND THE HONORABLE SERIOUSNESS
ROCK PREFACE(155) US IN OUR CHILDHOOD BY BARBAROUS SCRIPTURISTS, IRASCIBLE OR SADIST PARENTS, AND A HIDEOUS CRIMINAL CODE.

IRELAND
BULL I (85) OUT) I HAVE AN INSTINCT AGAINST GOING BACK TO IRELAND : AN INSTINCT SO STRONG THAT I'D RATHER GO WITH YOU
BULL PREFACE(37) ON. HOLY AND BEAUTIFUL IS THE SOUL OF CATHOLIC IRELAND : HER PRAYERS ARE LOVELIER THAN THE TEETH AND CLAWS
BULL III (133) CHURCH. I WANT THE CATHOLIC CHURCH ESTABLISHED IN IRELAND : THATS WHAT I WANT. DO YOU THINK THAT I, BROUGHT UP
BULL IV (180) WITH ME. FINE MANNERS AND FINE WORDS ARE CHEAP IN IRELAND : YOU CAN KEEP BOTH FOR MY FRIEND HERE, WHO IS STILL
O'FL (223) YOU ARE! WITH ALL YOUR FINE TALK ABOUT IRELAND : YOU THAT NEVER STEPPED BEYOND THE FEW ACRES OF IT
O'FL (210) BOSHES. AND WHAT GOOD HAS IT EVER DONE HERE IN IRELAND ? IT'S KEPT ME IGNORANT BECAUSE IT FILLED UP MY
MTH2 (65) IN THE SCHOOL? /CONRAD/ NO. /BURGE/ IS IT ABOUT IRELAND ? /CONRAD/ NO. /BURGE/ IS IT ABOUT GERMANY?
BULL I (74) SIR. I'LL RISK IT, SIR. /BROADBENT/ EVER BEEN IN IRELAND ? /HODSON/ NO SIR. I UNDERSTAND IT'S A VERY WET
BULL I (78) WHAT I SAY IS, WHY NOT START A GARDEN CITY IN IRELAND ? /TIM/ (WITH ENTHUSIASM) THATS JUST WHAT WAS ON
BULL I (77) THAT AN ENGLISHMAN'S FIRST DUTY IS HIS DUTY TO IRELAND ? UNFORTUNATELY, WE HAVE POLITICIANS HERE MORE
BULL PREFACE(25) PROVIDED IT IS PROTESTANTISM. THERE IS ALSO IN IRELAND A CHARACTERISTICALLY PROTESTANT REFUSAL TO TAKE
BULL PREFACE(13) MOVEMENT, WHICH IS BENT ON CREATING A NEW IRELAND AFTER ITS OWN IDEAL, WHEREAS MY PLAY IS A VERY
BULL PREFACE(31) ASSET THAT CAN BE EXPLOITED FOR THE PROTECTION OF IRELAND AGAINST FOREIGN AGGRESSION OR THE SHARING OF
BULL PREFACE(68) LAST RESORT REPUDIATE THE CONSTITUTION AND HOLD IRELAND AGAINST THE IRISH BY PHYSICAL FORCE, AND HAD BEEN
BULL PREFACE(71) ULSTER IS INDUSTRIAL IRELAND AND CATHOLIC IRELAND AGRICULTURAL IRELAND, AND THROUGHOUT THE WORLD FOR A
BULL PREFACE(41) A DETERMINED CALL FOR THE POLICE. WELL, IN IRELAND ALL POLITICAL ORATORY IS JINGO ORATORY; AND ALL
BULL PREFACE(24) TO TEACH THAT ALL METHODISTS INCUR DAMNATION. IN IRELAND ALL THAT THE MEMBER OF THE IRISH PROTESTANT CHURCH
SUPR IV (144) WHAT COMES O LIVIN IN PROVINCIAL PLACES LIKE IRELAND AND AMERICA. OVER HERE YOURE ECTOR: IF YOU AVNT
BULL PREFACE(71) IT HAPPENS THAT PROTESTANT ULSTER IS INDUSTRIAL IRELAND AND CATHOLIC IRELAND AGRICULTURAL IRELAND. AND
BULL PREFACE(71) ULSTER, WHICH ARMED AGAINST THE REST OF IRELAND AND DEFIED THE BRITISH PARLIAMENT TO THE CRY OF " WE
O'FL PREFACE(202) STIMULATE HIS LOYALTY, AND HE WILL STAY IN IRELAND AND DIE FOR HER; FOR, INCOMPREHENSIBLE AS IT SEEMS
BULL PREFACE(70) BEFORE INDIA IS LEFT TO GOVERN ITSELF AS MUCH AS IRELAND AND EGYPT NOW ARE I AM IN THE DARK UNTIL THE EVENT
BULL II (113) MUSTNT CHAFF ME, I'M VERY MUCH IN EARNEST ABOUT IRELAND AND EVERYTHING IRISH. I'M VERY MUCH IN EARNEST ABOUT
BULL I (94) TO LEARN TO DO SOMETHING; AND THEN TO GET OUT OF IRELAND AND HAVE A CHANCE OF DOING IT. SHE DIDNT COUNT. I
ROCK PREFACE(174) SUPPRESSED AND EDITORS SWEPT AWAY, NOT ONLY IN IRELAND AND INDIA BUT IN LONDON IN MY TIME, TO BE TAKEN IN
SHAK (139) THIS CAITIFF. FACE TO FACE SET BUT THIS FIEND OF IRELAND AND MYSELF; AND LEAVE THE REST TO ME. (SHAV
LION PREFACE(92) THE RANK AND FILE! IT HAS FLED TO THOSE PARTS OF IRELAND AND SCOTLAND WHICH ARE STILL IN THE SEVENTEENTH
BULL II (102) THE MONASTERY OF MOUNT ATHOS. FROM THAT I CAME TO IRELAND AND SETTLED DOWN AS A PARISH PRIEST UNTIL I WENT
BULL I (78) /TIM/ BEDAD I DO, SIR. TAKE ALL YOU CAN OUT OF IRELAND AND SPEND IT IN ENGLAND: THATS IT. /BROADBENT/ (NOT
BULL PREFACE(41) CAN REACH THE PEOPLE. NATIONALISM STANDS BETWEEN IRELAND AND THE LIGHT OF THE WORLD. NOBODY IN IRELAND OF ANY
BULL II (114) AGAIN I SHANT ANSWER FOR MYSELF: ALL THE HARPS OF IRELAND ARE IN YOUR VOICE. (SHE LAUGHS AT HIM. HE SUDDENLY
BULL I (86) /BROADBENT/ TRUE. ALL THE CAPABLE PEOPLE IN IRELAND ARE OF ENGLISH EXTRACTION. IT HAS OFTEN STRUCK ME AS
BULL PREFACE(30) POPULAR, AND DEMOCRATIC. THE OLIGARCHY GOVERNS IRELAND AS A BUREAUCRACY DERIVING AUTHORITY FROM THE KING OF
O'FL (214) SIR. WHAT CALL WOULD HE HAVE TO MEDDLE WITH IRELAND AS HE DID IF HE WASNT? /SIR PEARCE/ WHAT NONSENSE!
BULL PREFACE(11) INHERITORS OF THE EARTH, ENGLAND HAS RIGHTS IN IRELAND AS IRELAND HAS RIGHTS IN ENGLAND. I DEMAND OF EVERY
BULL PREFACE(36) WILL MAKE AS SHORT WORK OF SACERDOTAL TYRANNY IN IRELAND AS IT HAS DONE IN FRANCE AND ITALY. AND IN DOING SO
BULL I (79) DAMN IT! CALL ME TIM. A MAN THAT TALKS ABOUT IRELAND AS YOU DO MAY CALL ME ANYTHING. GIMMY A HOWLT O THAT
BULL PREFACE(32) TO HIS OWN COUNTRY, WITH A WHOLLY PROTESTANT IRELAND AT HIS BACK HE MIGHT HAVE BULLIED ENGLAND INTO
BULL PREFACE(42) IS NOT A SENSIBLE ONE. TO TAKE THE GOVERNMENT OF IRELAND AWAY FROM THE IRISH AND HAND IT OVER TO THE ENGLISH
BULL PREFACE(7) BEEN ALL THE MORE POWERFUL BECAUSE THEY LOVED IRELAND BETTER, NOT ONLY THAN ROME, BUT THAN ENGLAND. WHY
BULL PREFACE(39) LAITY IN ENGLAND. SHE GETS NOTHING OUT OF IRELAND BUT INFINITE TROUBLE, INFINITE CONFUSION AND
BULL PREFACE(8) TO ENGLAND. IF CATHOLICISM IS TO BE LIMITED IN IRELAND BY ANY GEOGRAPHICAL EXPRESSION (IN WHICH CASE IT
POSN PREFACE(431) WAS MADE TO PREVENT EVEN ITS PERFORMANCE IN IRELAND BY SOME INDISCREET CASTLE OFFICIALS IN THE ABSENCE
BULL PREFACE(28) THE ENGLISH, AS EVERY ENGLISHMAN WHO TRAVELS IN IRELAND CAN TESTIFY, PLEASE DO NOT SUPPOSE THAT I SPEAK
SIM II (63) RESCUE! /JANGA/ FREE STATE PRESIDENT DECLARES IRELAND CANNOT PERMIT ENGLAND TO BREAK THE UNITY OF THE
BULL III (133) WORLDLY PRIDE OR AMBITION, AYE; AND I WOULD HAVE IRELAND COMPETE WITH ROME ITSELF FOR THE CHAIR OF ST PETER
BULL I (83) GEORGE! DO YOU SUPPOSE THE WHOLE POPULATION OF IRELAND CONSISTS OF DRUNKEN BEGGING LETTER WRITERS, OR THAT
DOCT PREFACE(72) IN ONE YEAR THAN ALL THE SANITARY INSPECTORS IN IRELAND COULD DO IN TWENTY; AND THEY COULD HARDLY DOUBT THAT
DOCT PREFACE(72) TAKEN BY LAZINESS AND NEGLECT. IF THE PRIESTS OF IRELAND COULD ONLY BE PERSUADED TO TEACH THEIR FLOCKS THAT
BULL PREFACE(38) REPLY TO THE SHALLOW PEOPLE WHO IMAGINE THAT IRELAND DELIVERED UP TO THE IRISH DEMOCRACY-- THAT IS, TO
BULL PREFACE(39) A COUNTRY, WHO DO NOT LOATHE ENGLISH RULE. FOR IN IRELAND ENGLAND IS NOTHING BUT THE POPE'S POLICEMAN. SHE
BULL IV (159) AT SUNSET, WHEN ONE GOT MAUDLIN AND CALLED IRELAND ERIN, AND IMAGINED ONE WAS REMEMBERING THE DAYS OF
BULL PREFACE(40) STRENGTHENING THE HANDS OF ANY COMMON ENEMY. IN IRELAND EVERY SUCH ATTACK, EVERY SUCH EXPOSURE, IS A SERVICE
BULL I (77) SORT O MAN YAR. AN SO YOURE THINKIN O COMIN TO IRELAND FOR A BIT? /BROADBENT/ WHERE ELSE CAN I GO? I AM
BULL PREFACE(18) SEE THAT HE HAS NOT, AND UNLESS HE SETTLES IN IRELAND FOR A FEW YEARS WILL ALWAYS REMAIN CONSTITUTIONALLY
O'FL (223) A YEAR AGO, AND THAT I WOULDNT TAKE NOW WITH ALL IRELAND FOR HER FORTUNE? I TELL YOU THE WORLD'S CREATION IS
BULL III (142) ANGER) D'YE HAVE THE FACE TO SET UP ENGLAND AGEN IRELAND FOR INJUSTICES AN WRONGS AN DISTHRESS AN SUFFERIN..
SUPR HANDBOK(197) BETTER FOR THE WRECK OF CLERKENWELL PRISON, OR IRELAND FOR THE DISESTABLISHMENT OF THE IRISH CHURCH? IS
DEVL EPILOG (81) HE WAS AFTERWARDS MADE COMMANDER OF THE FORCES IN IRELAND FOR THE PURPOSE OF BANISHING HIM FROM PARLIAMENT.
O'FL (222) THAT SIR PEARCE HIMSELF MIGHT GO BEGGING THROUGH IRELAND FOR, AND NEVER SEE THE LIKE OF. I'LL HAVE A FRENCH
BULL IV (150) POWER TO PATSY! "). GENTLEMEN: I FELT AT HOME IN IRELAND FROM THE FIRST (RISING EXCITEMENT AMONG HIS
BULL PREFACE(66) A SCHOOLMASTER NAMED PEARSE, AS PRESIDENT. IF ALL IRELAND HAD RISEN AT THIS GESTURE IT WOULD HAVE BEEN A
BULL PREFACE(44) FINALLY, SOME WORDS OF WARNING TO BOTH NATIONS. IRELAND HAS BEEN DELIBERATELY RUINED AGAIN AND AGAIN BY
BULL PREFACE(65) FORBEARANCE; AND WHEN I ADD THAT ENGLISH RULE IN IRELAND HAS BEEN " ANIMATED BY THE SAME SPIRIT" (I THANK
BULL III (144) I DIVINED IT, LARRY: I SAW IT IN THEIR FACES. IRELAND HAS NEVER SMILED SINCE HER HOPES WERE BURIED IN THE
BULL PREFACE(11) OF THE EARTH, ENGLAND HAS RIGHTS IN IRELAND AS IRELAND HAS RIGHTS IN ENGLAND. I DEMAND OF EVERY NATION
BULL I (85) HOW MANY OF ALL THOSE MILLIONS THAT HAVE LEFT IRELAND HAVE EVER COME BACK OR WANTED TO COME BACK? BUT
BULL II (108) THE DRIVER TOLD ME THERE WAS THE FINEST HOTEL IN IRELAND HERE. (THEY REGARD HIM JOYLESSLY). /AUNT JUDY/ ARRA
BULL II (103) NEVER SEEN IN IRELAND. BUT WHEN I CAME BACK TO IRELAND I FOUND ALL THE WONDERS THERE WAITING FOR ME. YOU
BULL I (78) THERE ARE DIFFICULTIES. WHEN I FIRST ARRIVE IN IRELAND I SHALL BE HATED AS AN ENGLISHMAN, AS A PROTESTANT,
BULL PREFACE(34) TAKE ITS ORDERS FROM ENGLAND AND LET HER RULE IRELAND IF ENGLAND WERE ROMAN CATHOLIC. THE PROTESTANT

BULL IV (175)	OF RESPONSIBLE MEN OF GOOD POSITION. WE'LL TAKE	IRELAND	IN HAND, AND BY STRAIGHTFORWARD BUSINESS HABITS
BULL I (83)	UPRIGHT). /DOYLE/ BORN IN GLASGOW. NEVER WAS IN	IRELAND	IN HIS LIFE. I KNOW ALL ABOUT HIM. /BROADBENT/ BUT
SUPR IV (147)	TALKING ABOUT. ME FATHER DIED OF STARVATION IN	IRELAND	IN THE BLACK 47. MAYBE YOUVE HEARD OF IT. /VIOLET/
BARB PREFACE(242)	HIS POWER OFFICIALLY, AND BY THE RIBBON LODGES OF	IRELAND	IN THEIR LONG STRUGGLE WITH THE LANDLORDS. UNDER
BULL PREFACE(5)	THAT THE EFFECT OF HOME RULE WOULD BE TO DELIVER	IRELAND	INTO THE HANDS OF THE ROMAN CATHOLIC CHURCH, WHICH
BULL PREFACE(6)	PRIEST CAN BE KEPT WITHIN ITS PROPER LIMITS IN	IRELAND	IS BY SETTING THE IRISH PEOPLE FREE TO TAKE IT IN
DOCT PREFACE(72)	WOULD BE DELIGHTED. PERHAPS THEY DO NOWADAYS; FOR	IRELAND	IS CERTAINLY A TRANSFIGURED COUNTRY SINCE MY YOUTH
BULL PREFACE(37)	GENIUS IS ONE OF OUR NATIONAL PRODUCTS; AND	IRELAND	IS NO BAD ROCK TO BUILD A CHURCH ON. HOLY AND
BULL I (77)	ABDUL THE DAMNED; AND IT IS UNDER THEIR HEEL THAT	IRELAND	IS NOW WRITHING. /TIM/ FAITH, THEYVE RECKONED UP
BULL IV (156)	TO NORA) WHEN I LOOK AT YOU, I THINK THAT PERHAPS	IRELAND	IS ONLY PURGATORY, AFTER ALL. (HE PASSES ON TO THE
BULL PREFACE(29)	PRIEST. REALIZE, THEN, THAT THE POPULAR PARTY IN	IRELAND	IS SEETHING WITH REBELLION AGAINST THE TYRANNY OF
BULL PREFACE(36)	ANGLICIZED. BUT THE CATHOLIC CHURCH IN	IRELAND	IS STILL ROMAN. HOME RULE WILL HERALD THE DAY WHEN
LION PREFACE(99)	INDIFFERENCE TO THE SALVATION OF OUR SUBJECTS.	IRELAND	IS THE EXCEPTION WHICH PROVES THE RULE; FOR IRELAND,
BULL PREFACE(14)	RATIONAL CONDUCT. BUT THE NEED FOR THIS LESSON IN	IRELAND	IS THE MEASURE OF ITS DEMORALIZING SUPERFLUOUSNESS
BULL PREFACE(16)	THE IDOLATER OF EVERY NUMSKULL, I PERCEIVE THAT	IRELAND	IS THE ONLY SPOT ON EARTH WHICH STILL PRODUCES THE
BULL PREFACE(32)	THE IRISH PROTESTANT TEMPER. THE NOTION THAT	IRELAND	IS THE ONLY COUNTRY IN THE WORLD NOT WORTH SHEDDING
BULL PREFACE(30)	PHENOMENON, BECAUSE HE IS AN UNNATURAL ONE. IN	IRELAND	IT IS NOT " LOYALTY" TO DRINK THE ENGLISH KING'S
BULL IV (159)	COUNTRIES I MEANT TO GET TO WHEN I ESCAPED FROM	IRELAND	, AMERICA AND LONDON, AND SOMETIMES ROME AND THE
BULL III (131)	OF THE WORLD THAT WE DROVE ENGLAND TO RUIN	IRELAND	, AND SHE'LL RUIN US AGAIN THE MOMENT WE LIFT OUR
BULL PREFACE(71)	IRELAND AND CATHOLIC IRELAND AGRICULTURAL	IRELAND	, AND THROUGHOUT THE WORLD FOR A CENTURY PAST THE
BULL I (94)	COURSE I KNOW THAT THE MORAL CODE IS DIFFERENT IN	IRELAND	, BUT IN ENGLAND IT'S NOT CONSIDERED FAIR TO TRIFLE
BULL I (80)	I'LL HAVE TO SIND FIVE TIMMY POOR OUL MOTHER IN	IRELAND	, BUT NO MATTER: I SAID A HUNDHERD; AND WHAT I SAID
BULL II (103)	GREAT CITIES I SAW WONDERS I HAD NEVER SEEN IN	IRELAND	. BUT WHEN I CAME BACK TO IRELAND I FOUND ALL THE
BULL IV (181)	I AM RIGHT IN DEVOTING MY LIFE TO THE CAUSE OF	IRELAND	. COME ALONG AND HELP ME TO CHOOSE THE SITE FOR THE
O'FL (216)	HIS EYES FOR A PATTERN OF THE FINEST SOLDIER IN	IRELAND	. COME AND KISS YOUR OLD MOTHER, DINNY DARLINT. (
BULL IV (174)	OH, I'M NOT AFRAID OF THAT. I HAVE FAITH IN	IRELAND	. GREAT FAITH, MR KEEGAN. /KEEGAN/ AND WE HAVE NONE:
BULL PREFACE(35)	THE PRESSURE OF CAPITAL ANYWHERE RATHER THAN IN	IRELAND	, HE HAS NO RESPONSIBILITY, NO INTEREST, NO STATUS
BULL I (88)	DESPAIR, LARRY. THERE ARE GREAT POSSIBILITIES FOR	IRELAND	. HOME RULE WILL WORK WONDERS UNDER ENGLISH
BULL IV (159)	RESUMES) I HAD A SORT OF DREAD OF RETURNING TO	IRELAND	. I FELT SOMEHOW THAT MY LUCK WOULD TURN IF I CAME
BULL PREFACE(30)	A FORECAST. NOW LET US HAVE A LOOK AT PROTESTANT	IRELAND	. I HAVE ALREADY SAID THAT A " LOYAL" IRISHMAN IS AN
BULL I (84)	FROM HIS FATHER, WHO CAME FROM MY PART OF	IRELAND	. I KNEW HIS UNCLES, MATT AND ANDY HAFFIGAN OF
BULL PREFACE(40)	EXPOSURE, IS A SERVICE TO ENGLAND AND A STAB TO	IRELAND	. IF YOU EXPOSE THE TYRANNY AND RAPACITY OF THE
SUPR IV (148)	ME AND MINE OUT OF IRELAND. WELL, YOU CAN KEEP	IRELAND	. ME AND ME LIKE ARE COMING BACK TO BUY ENGLAND; AND
BULL I (77)	NO COUNTRY LEFT TO ME TO TAKE AN INTEREST IN BUT	IRELAND	. MIND: I DONT SAY THAT AN ENGLISHMAN HAS NOT OTHER
GENV PREFACE(15)	THEN ESTABLISHED PROTESTANT EPISCOPAL CHURCH IN	IRELAND	. MY RELIGIOUS EDUCATION LEFT ME CONVINCED THAT I
BULL PREFACE(4)	AND THAT IT CARED FOR NOTHING BUT HOME RULE IN	IRELAND	. NOW AS THE ENGLISH ELECTORS, BEING MOSTLY WORSE
DEVL EPILOG (80)	IN DEFENCE OF THE UNION BETWEEN ENGLAND AND	IRELAND	. ONLY THE OTHER DAY ENGLAND SENT 200,000 MEN INTO
BULL PREFACE(30)	IS, ROUGHLY, THE PREDICAMENT OF ROMAN CATHOLIC	IRELAND	. PROTESTANT LOYALTY: A FORECAST. NOW LET US HAVE A
BULL IV (151)	EPISODES IN THE HISTORY OF ENGLAND AND	IRELAND	. /AUNT JUDY/ SURE HE WOULDNT MAKE A FOOL OF HIMSELF
BULL I (94)	AT QUEENSTOWN AND COME BACK TO LONDON THROUGH	IRELAND	. /BROADBENT/ BUT DID YOU EVER SAY ANYTHING THAT
BULL I (74)	PERHAPS IT MIGHT BE AS WELL. I'M GOING TO	IRELAND	. /HODSON/ (REASSURED) YES SIR. /BROADBENT/ YOU
BULL II (113)	TO MEETING YOU MORE THAN TO ANYTHING ELSE IN	IRELAND	. /NORA/ (IRONICALLY) DEAR ME! DID YOU NOW?
BULL I (78)	A LITTLE MONEY OUT OF ENGLAND AND SPEND IT IN	IRELAND	. /TIM/ MORE POWER TO YOUR ELBOW! AN MAY YOUR
O'FL PREFACE(202)	TURN ON HIS OPPORTUNITIES OF GETTING OUT OF	IRELAND	. STIMULATE HIS LOYALTY, AND HE WILL STAY IN IRELAND
BULL PREFACE(13)	A VERY UNCOMPROMISING PRESENTMENT OF THE REAL OLD	IRELAND	. THE NEXT THING THAT HAPPENED WAS THE PRODUCTION OF
BULL PREFACE(22)	AFFORD THAT SORT OF ENCOURAGEMENT AND FLATTERY IN	IRELAND	. THE ODDS AGAINST WHICH OUR LEADERS HAVE TO FIGHT
BULL PREFACE(30)	THERE IS NO SUCH THING AS GENUINE LOYALTY IN	IRELAND	. THERE IS A SEPARATION OF THE IRISH PEOPLE INTO TWO
BULL PREFACE(71)	PART IN A SINGLE PARLIAMENT RULING AN UNDIVIDED	IRELAND	. THEY DID NOT TAKE MY ADVICE. PROBABLY THEY DID NOT
APPL II (263)	SHOULD NOT BE ALLOWED TO GO FROM ENGLAND TO	IRELAND	. THEY NEVER COME BACK. /VANHATTAN/ WELL, CAN YOU
BUOY 1 (12)	WE DONT DO THEM HERE. /SON/ WE DO. WE DID IT IN	IRELAND	. WE DID IT IN INDIA. IT HAS ALWAYS BEEN SO. WE
SUPR IV (148)	ARMS. ENGLISH RULE DROVE ME AND MINE OUT OF	IRELAND	. WELL, YOU CAN KEEP IRELAND. ME AND ME LIKE ARE
BULL I (85)	YOU PRETEND YOUD RATHER GO ANYWHERE THAN BACK TO	IRELAND	. YOU DONT SUPPOSE I BELIEVE YOU, DO YOU? IN YOUR
BULL I (88)	YOU WERE ONLY A YOUNG FELLOW WHEN YOU WERE IN	IRELAND	. YOULL FIND ALL THAT CHAFFING AND DRINKING AND NOT
BULL PREFACE(9)	THE SLAYING OF AN IRISHMAN BY AN IRISHMAN FOR	IRELAND	MAY BE A TRAGEDY-- MAY BE EVEN A CRIME TO THOSE WHO
BULL PREFACE(44)	OF DEMOCRATIC ELECTION. AND THE FINAL REASON WHY	IRELAND	MUST HAVE HOME RULE IS THAT SHE HAS A NATURAL RIGHT
BULL PREFACE(3)	IT WAS EVIDENT IT MUST COME, THE PROTESTANTS OF	IRELAND	MUST STAND TOGETHER AND MAKE THE BEST OF IT. THE
BULL PREFACE(68)	IMMEDIATELY THE BRITISH OFFICERS ON SERVICE IN	IRELAND	MUTINIED, REFUSING TO ENFORCE THE ACT OR OPERATE
BULL III (131)	THEN LET THEM MAKE ROOM FOR THOSE WHO CAN. IS	IRELAND	NEVER TO HAVE A CHANCE? FIRST SHE WAS GIVEN TO THE
BULL II (115)	BROADBENT; SO PERHAPS YOU DONT MEAN ANY HARM. IN	IRELAND	NOBODY'D MIND WHAT A MAN'D SAY IN FUN, NOR TAKE
BULL IV (180)	FORGET THAT I AM A CATHOLIC. MY COUNTRY IS NOT	IRELAND	NOR ENGLAND, BUT THE WHOLE MIGHTY REALM OF MY
METH PREFACE(R17)	THE BRITISH GOVERNMENT IS MORE AFRAID OF	IRELAND	NOW THAT SUBMARINES, BOMBS, AND POISON-GAS ARE CHEAP
APPL II (263)	WITH A SIGH) OUR OWN BEST FAMILIES GO SO MUCH TO	IRELAND	NOWADAYS, PEOPLE SHOULD NOT BE ALLOWED TO GO FROM
BULL PREFACE(41)	IRELAND AND THE LIGHT OF THE WORLD. NOBODY IN	IRELAND	OF ANY INTELLIGENCE LIKES NATIONALISM ANY MORE THAN
APPL II (267)	/AMANDA/ ALL THEIR PEOPLE CAME FROM SCOTLAND OR	IRELAND	OR WALES OR JERUSALEM OR SOMEWHERE, SIR. IT IS NO
BULL PREFACE(41)	THAT IS WHY EVERYTHING IS IN ABEYANCE IN	IRELAND	PENDING THE ACHIEVEMENT OF HOME RULE. THE GREAT
O'FL (210)	THOUGHT IT OUGHT TO FILL UP MINE TOO. IT'S KEPT	IRELAND	POOR, BECAUSE INSTEAD OF TRYING TO BETTER OURSELVES
BULL PREFACE(24)	RECALCITRANT. FIRST, LET ME TELL YOU THAT IN	IRELAND	PROTESTANTISM IS REALLY PROTESTANT. IT IS TRUE THAT
BULL PREFACE(12)	DO THEIR OWN GOVERNING WORK THEMSELVES, THAT IF	IRELAND	REFUSED HOME RULE NOW, IT WOULD SOONER OR LATER BE
BULL II (103)	CURIOSITY. I WANTED TO KNOW WHETHER YOU FOUND	IRELAND	-- I MEAN THE COUNTRY PART OF IRELAND, OF COURSE--
SIM II (71)	AUSTRALASIA NEXT DAY, SCOTLAND NEXT, THEN	IRELAND	-- /LADY FARWATERS/ BUT EXCUSE ME: THEY DO NOT SPEAK
O'FL (217)	TAKE THE HAND OF A TYRANT RED WITH THE BLOOD OF	IRELAND	-- /O'FLAHERTY/ ARRA HOLD YOUR NONSENSE, MOTHER:
BULL PREFACE(6)	THEIR LOST SUPREMACY (THAT SURVIVES ONLY IN	IRELAND	), BUT FOR THEIR HOUSES, THEIR PROPERTY, THEIR RIGHT
POSN PREFACE(427)	OF PRESS LAWS (ESPECIALLY IN EGYPT, INDIA, AND	IRELAND	), EXACTLY AS THEY SHRIEK FOR A CENSORSHIP OF THE
BULL PREFACE(4)	BUT BECAUSE IT CARED MORE FOR ENGLAND THAN FOR	IRELAND	), EXCEPT ON ONE OCCASION IN 1893, WHEN THE LIBERALS
JOAN PREFACE(46)	(YOU CAN SEE PLENTY OF THE BURNT HOUSES STILL IN	IRELAND	), WITH THE RESULT THAT JOAN HAS REMAINED THE
BULL PREFACE(7)	COULD HOLD ITS OWN ONLY TOO WELL IN A FREE	IRELAND	; AND EVEN IF HE HAD NOT KNOWN IT HE WOULD HAVE
BULL I (88)	IVE LISTENED CAREFULLY TO ALL YOUVE SAID ABOUT	IRELAND	; AND I CAN SEE NOTHING WHATEVER TO PREVENT YOUR
BULL IV (169)	I GET ENGAGED TO THE MOST DELIGHTFUL WOMAN IN	IRELAND	; AND IT TURNS OUT THAT I COULDNT HAVE DONE A
BULL PREFACE(39)	HAVE HAPPENED IN FRANCE IS WHAT HAS HAPPENED IN	IRELAND	; AND THAT IS WHY IT IS ONLY THE SMALL-MINDED IRISH,
BULL PREFACE(9)	A DISHONOR. BOTH PARTIES WOULD BE FIGHTING FOR	IRELAND	; AND THOUGH THE SLAYING OF AN IRISHMAN BY AN
BULL III (136)	FAITH OF THE GREAT MAJORITY OF THE PEOPLE OF	IRELAND	; BUT I SHALL CONTENT MYSELF WITH SAYING THAT IN MY
BULL PREFACE(5)	RULE AGITATIONS IN EGYPT AND INDIA MORE THAN IN	IRELAND	; FOR THE IRISH, NOW CONFIDENT THAT THEIR BATTLE IS
DEVL EPILOG (80)	THE AMERICAN UNIONIST IS OFTEN A SEPARATIST AS TO	IRELAND	; THE ENGLISH UNIONIST OFTEN SYMPATHIZES WITH THE
GENV III (73)	SUPPRESSED NEWSPAPERS IN ENGLAND AS WELL AS IN	IRELAND	; THEY DISMISSED EDITORS WHO WERE TOO INDEPENDENT
FABL PREFACE(95)	WORKMEN. SENIOR WRANGLERS AND DOUBLE-FIRSTS AND	IRELAND	SCHOLARS SEE NO MORE THAN COSTERMONGERS IN THE FACT
BULL IV (177)	THE SYNDICATE; AND IT WILL NOT INTEREST YOUNG	IRELAND	SO MUCH AS MY FRIEND'S GOSPEL OF EFFICIENCY.
BULL IV (175)	LET US HAVE NO MORE OF HIS LIKE. AND LET YOUNG	IRELAND	TAKE CARE THAT IT DOESNT SHARE HIS FATE, INSTEAD OF
BULL PREFACE(69)	MORE COMPLETE CONCESSION OF SELF-GOVERNMENT TO	IRELAND	THAN THAT DECREED BY THE REPUDIATED HOME RULE ACT,
BULL II SD(101)	OF DISEASE, AN INCARNATION OF EVERYTHING IN	IRELAND	THAT DROVE HIM OUT OF IT. THESE JUDGMENTS HAVE
BULL PREFACE(31)	TO HOLD EVERY INCH OF THE GOVERNMENT OF	IRELAND	THAT THEY CAN GRASP; BUT AS THAT GOVERNMENT WILL
BULL PREFACE(24)	TO A PART OF THE RELATION BETWEEN ENGLAND AND	IRELAND	THAT YOU WILL NEVER UNDERSTAND UNLESS I INSIST ON
BULL PREFACE(26)	WITH ALL THE ANGLICAN CONTEMPT FOR CHAPEL; BUT IN	IRELAND	THE CHAPEL MEANS THE ROMAN CATHOLIC CHURCH, FOR
BULL PREFACE(25)	NO PLACE IN THE COUNTY COUNCIL CURRICULUM. BUT IN	IRELAND	THE CHURCH PARENT SENDS HIS SON TO A WESLEYAN SCHOOL
SIM PREFACE(6)	IS SUCH A PLACE AS HELL, ANYWHERE ELSE THAN IN	IRELAND	THE OBSOLESCENCE OF THIS EXPLANATION WOULD HAVE BEEN
BULL III (133)	MARTYRS, IS PAGAN AT HEART TO THIS DAY, WHILE IN	IRELAND	THE PEOPLE IS THE CHURCH AND THE CHURCH THE PEOPLE.
BULL PREFACE(39)	THAN THE AVERAGE ENGLISHMAN. IT IS TRUE THAT IN	IRELAND	THE POOR MAN IS ROBBED AND STARVED AND OPPRESSED
BULL PREFACE(27)	FROM THE ATMOSPHERE IN WHICH IT IS BROUGHT UP. IN	IRELAND	THE ROMAN CATHOLIC PEASANT CANNOT ESCAPE THE
O'FL (207)	MORNING TO ST PATRICK TO CLEAR THE ENGLISH OUT OF	IRELAND	THE SAME AS HE CLEARED THE SNAKES, YOULL BE
BULL III (122)	THERLL SOON BE NOTHING ELSE; AND THE LORD HELP	IRELAND	THEN! /AUNT JUDY/ AH, YOURE NEVER SATISFIED, LARRY.
BULL I (91)	3 HOURS OF COLCHESTER AND 24 OF NEW YORK. I WANT	IRELAND	TO BE THE BRAINS AND IMAGINATION OF A BIG
BULL I (83)	HE'S EVIDENTLY THE VERY MAN TO TAKE WITH ME TO	IRELAND	TO BREAK THE ICE FOR ME. HE CAN GAIN THE CONFIDENCE
BULL PREFACE(50)	WITNESS WHEREOF, LET ME SHIFT THE SCENE FROM	IRELAND	TO EGYPT, AND TELL THE STORY OF THE DENSHAWAI AFFAIR
BULL IV (179)	HAVE FOR SO MANY GENERATIONS TAKEN MONEY FROM	IRELAND	TO ENGLAND. HAS THAT SAVED ENGLAND FROM POVERTY AND
BULL PREFACE(25)	DOES NOT EXIST. NOBODY IS SURPRISED IN	IRELAND	TO FIND THAT THE SQUIRE WHO IS THE LOCAL PILLAR OF
JOAN PREFACE(41)	THE BRITISH GOVERNMENT SLAUGHTERED AND BURNT IN	IRELAND	TO PERSECUTE THE ADVOCATES OF A CONSTITUTIONAL
BULL PREFACE(71)	OF AN IRISH ONE. AND IT HAS ALLOWED CATHOLIC	IRELAND	TO SECURE THE IRISH PARLIAMENT. THUS, OF THE TWO
BULL PREFACE(6)	THE ATTENTION OF MY NERVOUS FELLOW PROTESTANTS IN	IRELAND	TO THE FACT THAT IN ITALY, THE CENTRE OF ROMAN

SIM II (63)	ENGLAND; AND TO HELL WITH THE EMPIRE! /KANCHIN/	IRELAND	TO THE RESCUE! /JANGA/ FREE STATE PRESIDENT
FABL PREFACE(85)	OF 50 YEARS TO MAKE THEM EFFECTIVE. HOME RULE FOR	IRELAND	TOOK THIRTY YEARS TO GET THROUGH PARLIAMENT, AND WAS
BULL PREFACE(5)	HANDS OF THE ROMAN CATHOLIC CHURCH AS THEY ARE IN	IRELAND	UNDER ENGLISH RULE AND BECAUSE OF ENGLISH RULE. IN
BULL PREFACE(12)	AND THAT THERE WILL NO DOUBT BE ABUSES IN	IRELAND	UNDER HOME RULE WHICH DO NOT EXIST UNDER ENGLISH
MIS. PREFACE(17)	PRETEXTS. NOT VERY LONG AGO A SCHOOLMASTER IN	IRELAND	WAS MURDERED BY HIS BOYS; AND FOR REASONS WHICH WERE
BULL I (85)	CELT TO FEEL MELANCHOLY IN ROSSCULLEN? WHY, MAN,	IRELAND	WAS PEOPLED JUST AS ENGLAND WAS; AND ITS BREED WAS
BULL PREFACE(3)	AGAINST IT. THE SECOND ASSUMPTION WAS THAT	IRELAND	WAS POLITICALLY ONE AND INDIVISIBLE, AND,
GENV PREFACE(11)	GERMANS AND JAPANESE MUST BE TREATED AS CATHOLIC	IRELAND	WAS TREATED BY ENGLAND IN THE SEVENTEENTH CENTURY.
BULL PREFACE(9)	IN SPITE OF ENGLAND'S INDIFFERENCE TO IT. IN	IRELAND	WE ARE STILL SANE: WE DO NOT SNEER AT OUR COUNTRY AS
ROCK II (262)	AUXILIARY FORCES: I WAS IN COMMAND OF THEM IN	IRELAND	WHEN YOU TRIED THAT GAME ON THE IRISH, WHO WERE ONLY
O'FL (224)	ME! /O'FLAHERTY/ AND WOULD YOU ASK ME TO LIVE IN	IRELAND	WHERE IVE BEEN IMPOSED ON AND KEPT IN IGNORANCE, AND
BULL PREFACE(6)	IF I MAY PUT IT ELLIPTICALLY, THE ONLY PEOPLE IN	IRELAND	WHO CAN AFFORD MORE THAN SIXPENCE ARE THOSE WHO LIVE
SIM II (63)	PERMIT ENGLAND TO BREAK THE UNITY OF THE EMPIRE.	IRELAND	WILL LEAD THE ATTACK ON TREASON AND DISRUPTION.
BULL I (89)	JUST THE SAME AS IN DONNYBROOK. YOU LOOKED AT	IRELAND	WITH A BOY'S EYES AND SAW ONLY BOYISH THINGS. COME
BULL I (92)	HAS NOTHING TO DO WITH YOUR RELUCTANCE TO COME TO	IRELAND	WITH ME? /DOYLE/ (SITTING DOWN AGAIN, VANQUISHED)
BULL I (96)	CALL, SIR? /DOYLE/ PACK FOR ME TOO. I'M GOING TO	IRELAND	WITH MR BROADBENT. /HODSON/ RIGHT, SIR. (HE RETIRES
BULL I (96)	MIDDLE CLASS AND BRAGGING OF BELONGING TO IT. IN	IRELAND	YOURE EITHER A GENTLEMAN OR YOURE NOT. IF YOU WANT
BULL I (87)	IN NINETYEIGHT. IF YOU WANT TO INTEREST HIM IN	IRELAND	YOUVE GOT TO CALL THE UNFORTUNATE ISLAND KATHLEEN NI
MTH4 I SD(139)	BURRIN PIER ON THE SOUTH SHORE OF GALWAY BAY IN	IRELAND	, A REGION OF STONE-CAPPED HILLS AND GRANITE FIELDS.
CLEO NOTES (209)	THE SAME LANGUAGE, GROWING IN GREAT BRITAIN, IN	IRELAND	, AND IN AMERICA. THE RESULT IS THREE OF THE MOST
ROCK II (269)	DIFFERENCE. THEY PUT DOWN THE PEOPLE IN EGYPT, IN	IRELAND	, AND IN INDIA WITH FIRE AND SWORD, WITH FLOGGINGS
BULL PREFACE(15)	THAT I AM AN IRISHMAN I MEAN THAT I WAS BORN IN	IRELAND	, AND THAT MY NATIVE LANGUAGE IS THE ENGLISH OF
MTH4 I (143)	YOU DO NOT KNOW THAT YOU ARE ON THE WEST COAST OF	IRELAND	, AND THAT IT IS THE PRACTICE AMONG NATIVES OF THE
BULL PREFACE(65)	WHY HOME RULE IS A NECESSITY NOT ONLY FOR	IRELAND	, BUT FOR ALL CONSTITUENTS OF THOSE FEDERATIONS OF
MTH4 I (155)	DOWN AND PASSIONATELY KISSED THE SOIL OF	IRELAND	, CALLING ON THE YOUNG TO EMBRACE THE EARTH THAT HAD
MTH4 I (154)	OF MAN ON THIS SIDE OF THE ATLANTIC: THIS	IRELAND	, DESCRIBED BY THE EARLIEST BARDS AS AN EMERALD GEM
BULL PREFACE(32)	CHEAP A FLUID COULD HAVE PURCHASED THE HONOR OF	IRELAND	, HE GREATLY MISTAKES THE IRISH PROTESTANT TEMPER.
O'FL PREFACE(202)	FOR CHANGE AND ADVENTURE, AND, TO ESCAPE FROM	IRELAND	, HE WILL GO ABROAD TO RISK HIS LIFE FOR FRANCE, FOR
BULL IV (177)	KEEGAN: IF YOU ARE GOING TO BE SENTIMENTAL ABOUT	IRELAND	, I SHALL BID YOU GOOD EVENING. WE HAVE HAD ENOUGH
BULL PREFACE(9)	IS STILL MORE IMPORTANT FOR ENGLAND THAN FOR	IRELAND	, IN SPITE OF ENGLAND'S INDIFFERENCE TO IT. IN
O'FL (224)	SENSE. /MRS O'FLAHERTY/ ASK ME TO DIE OUT OF	IRELAND	, IS IT? AND THE ANGELS NOT TO FIND ME WHEN THEY
BULL II (97)	(LOUDLY) X.X.X. /THE MAN/ THREE CHEERS FOR OULD	IRELAND	, IS IT? THAT HELPS YOU TO FACE OUT THE MISERY AND
BULL PREFACE(34)	IS SUFFICIENT TO ENSURE THE WELFARE OF INDIA OR	IRELAND	, IT OUGHT TO SUFFICE EQUALLY FOR ENGLAND. BUT THE
BULL I (96)	LOOK HERE, TOM, THAT REMINDS ME. WHEN YOU GO TO	IRELAND	, JUST DROP TALKING ABOUT THE MIDDLE CLASS AND
BULL PREFACE(31)	AS AN ESSENTIALLY NATIONALIST FORCE IN	IRELAND	, LET HIM ASK HIMSELF WHICH LEADER HE, IF HE WERE AN
BULL II (113)	TO HIM. (GENTEELLY) AN WHAT DO YOU THINK OF	IRELAND	, MR BROADBENT? HAVE YOU EVER BEEN HERE BEFORE?
ROCK PREFACE(174)	CRIME TO HAVE " DANGEROUS THOUGHTS," IN MY NATIVE	IRELAND	, NOW NOMINALLY A FREE STATE, ONE OF MY BOOKS IS ON
BULL II (103)	YOU FOUND IRELAND-- I MEAN THE COUNTRY PART OF	IRELAND	, OF COURSE-- VERY SMALL AND BACKWARDLIKE WHEN YOU
BULL I (83)	IRISH MUSIC? NO IRISHMAN EVER TALKS LIKE THAT IN	IRELAND	, OR EVER DID, OR EVER WILL. BUT WHEN A THOROUGHLY
PYGM V (287)	OF INDIA OR THE LORD-LIEUTENANT OF	IRELAND	, OR SOMEBODY WHO WANTS A DEPUTY-QUEEN. I'M NOT
BULL IV (177)	THAT THE SOIL HIS HOOF TOUCHES IS HOLY GROUND.	IRELAND	, SIR, FOR GOOD OR EVIL, IS LIKE NO OTHER PLACE
BULL PREFACE(14)	SUCCESS. NO DOUBT, WHEN THE PLAY IS PERFORMED IN	IRELAND	, THE DUBLIN CRITICS WILL REGARD IT AS SELF-EVIDENT
LION PREFACE(99)	IS THE EXCEPTION WHICH PROVES THE RULE; FOR	IRELAND	, THE STANDING INSTANCE OF THE INABILITY OF THE
BULL I (78)	WOULDNT; AND I HONOR YOU FOR IT. YOURE GOIN TO	IRELAND	, THEN, OUT O SYMPITHY: IS IT? /BROADBENT/ I'M
BULL III (142)	WHICH PRACTICALLY RHYMES WITH BONNET IN	IRELAND	, THOUGH IN HODSON'S DIALECT IT RHYMES WITH
JOAN 4 (100)	COMPARE SIR JOHN TALBOT, THREE TIMES GOVERNOR OF	IRELAND	, TO A MAD BULL? ! ! ! /WARWICK/ IT WOULD NOT BE
BULL PREFACE(3)	CATHOLIC HOME RULE GOVERNMENT OF THE REST OF	IRELAND	, WAS UNDREAMT OF. HOW BOTH THESE THINGS
MTH4 I (155)	DEVOTED IRISHMEN, NOT ONE OF WHOM HAD EVER SEEN	IRELAND	, WERE COUNSELLED BY AN ENGLISH ARCHBISHOP, THE
BULL PREFACE(6)	STILL MORE NEEDED IS THIS CHEAP EDITION IN	IRELAND	, WHERE NOBODY CAN WELL AFFORD TO PAY MORE THAN
GETT PREFACE(200)	WITH THE RESULT THAT THEY COME TO ENGLAND AND	IRELAND	, WHERE THEY ARE PARTLY UNNOTICED AND PARTLY
BULL IV (176)	AS THE CLEANEST AND MOST ORDERLY PLACE I KNOW IN	IRELAND	, WHICH IS OUR POETICALLY NAMED MOUNTJOY PRISON.
O'FL PREFACE(201)	ON THE SIDE OF FRANCE AND SEE THE WORLD OUTSIDE	IRELAND	, WHICH IS A DULL PLACE TO LIVE IN. IT WAS QUITE
JOAN PREFACE(41)	DID EVERYTHING THAT THE BLACK AND TANS DID IN	IRELAND	, WITH SOME GROTESQUELY FEROCIOUS VARIATIONS, UNDER
BULL PREFACE(9)	SANE: WE DO NOT SNEER AT OUR COUNTRY AS " LITTLE	IRELAND	," AND CHEER FOR A DOUBTFUL COMMERCIAL SPECULATION
BULL PREFACE(36)	SCRAWL ON EVERY BLANK WALL IN THE NORTH OF	IRELAND	" TO HELL WITH THE POPE! " MAY REAPPEAR IN THE
BULL IV (179)	ALL, THE IDLERS WILL BRING MONEY FROM ENGLAND TO	IRELAND	! /KEEGAN/ JUST AS OUR IDLERS HAVE FOR SO MANY
MTH4 I (156)	THING TO CALL PEOPLE IRISH BECAUSE THEY LIVE IN	IRELAND	! YOU MIGHT AS WELL CALL THEM AIRISH BECAUSE THEY

IRELAND'S

BULL PREFACE(43)	AS HIS PRISONS, AND AS MERCILESS AS HIS STREETS,	IRELAND'S	CLAIM TO SELF-GOVERNMENT WOULD STILL BE AS GOOD AS
BULL PREFACE(39)	IN MONEY, IN POWER, IN PRIDE, AND IN POPULARITY.	IRELAND'S	REAL GRIEVANCE. BUT IT IS NOT THE SPOILS THAT
CYMB FORWORD(137)	IT COMES TO COMPLETE FORGERY, AS IN THE CASE OF	IRELAND'S	VORTIGERN, WHICH WAS MUCH ADMIRED AND AT LAST

IRELAN'S

BULL III (134)	ELSE'S; AND HWEN IT WAS NOBODY ELSE'S IT WAS OULD	IRELAN'S	. HOW THE DIVIL ARE WE TO LIVE ON WAN ANODHER'S

IRENE

PPP PREFACE(192)	ACTORS' ORPHANAGE, ON THE 14TH JULY 1905, BY MISS	IRENE	VANBRUGH, MISS NANCY PRICE, MR G. P. HUNTLEY, MR CYRIL

IRI

BULL IV (171)	IRISH BOTH OF US TO THE BACKBONE: IRISH! IRISH!	IRI	-- BROADBENT ARRIVES, CONVERSING ENERGETICALLY WITH

IRIS

MRS PREFACE(157)	IS IN NO WAY BOUND TO SUPPRESS THE FACT THAT HIS	IRIS	IS A PERSON TO BE ENVIED BY MILLIONS OF BETTER WOMEN.
MRS PREFACE(158)	A SINGLE SCENE OF MRS WARREN'S PROFESSION OR	IRIS	. NONE OF OUR PLAYS ROUSE THE SYMPATHY OF THE AUDIENCE
MRS PREFACE(161)	THE GAY LORD QUEX, MRS DANE'S DEFENCE, AND	IRIS	WOULD BE SWEPT FROM THE STAGE, AND PLACED UNDER THE
FANY EPILOG (331)	INEVITABLE IMPROPER FEMALE: THE MRS TANQUERAY,	IRIS	, AND SO FORTH. WELL, IF YOU CANT RECOGNIZE THE AUTHOR
MRS PREFACE(157)	WANTON'S TRAGEDIES, FROM ANTONY AND CLEOPATRA TO	IRIS	, ARE SNARES TO POOR GIRLS, AND ARE OBJECTED TO ON THAT

IRISES

MRS PREFACE(157)	IF SOCIETY CHOOSES TO PROVIDE FOR ITS	IRISES	BETTER THAN FOR ITS WORKING WOMEN, IT MUST NOT EXPECT

IRISH

BULL PREFACE(15)	NORTH SPANISH STRAIN WHICH PASSES FOR ABORIGINAL	IRISH	: I AM A GENUINE TYPICAL IRISHMAN OF THE DANISH,
FANY PROLOG (258)	WORD. I'M NOT REALLY AN ENGLISHMAN: MY FAMILY IS	IRISH	: IVE LIVED ALL MY LIFE IN ITALY-- IN VENICE MOSTLY--
NEVR IV (288)	UP) CLARET CUP, SYPHON, ONE SCOTCH AND ONE	IRISH	? /MRS CLANDON/ I THINK THATS RIGHT. /WAITER/ (
BULL PREFACE(68)	FOR SAYING SO, WAS JUSTIFIED. THE CATHOLIC	IRISH	ACCORDINGLY ARMED THEMSELVES AND DRILLED AS VOLUNTEERS
MTH3 (134)	/THE NEGRESS/ THERE IS A LIGHTNING EXPRESS ON THE	IRISH	AIR SERVICE AT HALF-PAST SIXTEEN. THEY WILL DROP YOU
MTH3 (135)	I HAVE SOME IMPORTANT BUSINESS AT FISHGUARD. THE	IRISH	AIR SERVICE CAN DROP ME IN THE BAY BY PARACHUTE. I
BULL PREFACE(20)	THIS TIME. NOW THAT CONTRAST IS ENGLISH AGAINST	IRISH	ALL OVER, AND IS THE MORE DELICIOUS BECAUSE THE REAL
CAPT NOTES (306)	ENGLISH H IS NOT THE SAME AS THE NEVER-DROPPED	IRISH	AND AMERICAN H, AND THAT TO RIDICULE AN ENGLISHMAN FOR
BULL PREFACE(18)	TO EXPLODE THOSE TWO HOLLOWEST OF FICTIONS, THE	IRISH	AND ENGLISH " RACES," THERE IS NO IRISH RACE ANY MORE
BULL PREFACE(42)	TO TAKE THE GOVERNMENT OF IRELAND AWAY FROM THE	IRISH	AND HAND IT OVER TO THE ENGLISH ON THE GROUND THAT
BULL PREFACE(16)	GOD'S ENGLISHMAN." ENGLAND CANNOT DO WITHOUT ITS	IRISH	AND ITS SCOTS TODAY, BECAUSE IT CANNOT DO WITHOUT AT
BULL PREFACE(13)	DEAL MORE TO SAY ABOUT THE RELATIONS BETWEEN THE	IRISH	AND THE ENGLISH THAN WILL BE FOUND IN MY PLAY. WRITING
MTH3 (125)	WITH US IS THAT WE ARE A NON-ADULT RACE; AND THE	IRISH	AND THE SCOTS, AND THE NIGGERS AND CHINKS, AS YOU CALL
MTH4 I (154)	TO YOURSELVES; AND MUCH GOOD MAY IT DO YOU," THE	IRISH	AS ONE MAN UTTERED THE HISTORIC SHOUT " NO: WE'LL BE
BULL I (79)	SOLID ENGLISH FOOTING, THOUGH THE REST CAN BE AS	IRISH	AS YOU PLEASE. YOU MUST COME AS MY-- MY-- WELL, I
BULL PREFACE(13)	WILL BE FOUND IN MY PLAY. WRITING THE PLAY FOR AN	IRISH	AUDIENCE, I THOUGHT IT WOULD BE GOOD FOR THEM TO BE
MTH4 I (156)	I DO. AND WHAT A RIDICULOUS THING TO CALL PEOPLE	IRISH	BECAUSE THEY LIVE IN IRELAND! YOU MIGHT AS WELL CALL
BULL PREFACE(23)	OF ANY MYSTERIOUS IRISH PLUCK, IRISH HONESTY,	IRISH	BIAS ON THE PART OF PROVIDENCE, OR STERLING IRISH
BULL PREFACE(7)	SIMPLY BECAUSE PARNELL WAS SO PROUD OF HIS	IRISH	BIRTHRIGHT THAT HE WOULD RATHER HAVE BEEN ONE OF EVEN
BULL PREFACE(23)	IRISH SOLIDITY OF CHARACTER, THAT WILL ENABLE AN	IRISH	BLOCKHEAD TO HOLD HIS OWN AGAINST ENGLAND. BLOCKHEADS
SUPR IV (149)	AND FACES HIS FATHER, WHOSE CHEEKS DARKEN AS HIS	IRISH	BLOOD BEGINS TO SIMMER). DAD: YOUVE NOT PLAYED THIS
BULL I (86)	TO BE AS BIG A FOOL AS I AM MYSELF. IF ALL MY	IRISH	BLOOD WERE POURED INTO YOUR VEINS, YOU WOULDNT TURN A
BULL IV (171)	SHE GOES) GOODBYE. GOODBYE. OH, THATS SO IRISH!	IRISH	BOTH OF US TO THE BACKBONE: IRISH! IRISH! IRI--
BULL IV (150)	(RISING EXCITEMENT AMONG HIS HEARERS). IN EVERY	IRISH	BREAST I HAVE FOUND THAT SPIRIT OF LIBERTY (A CHEERY

BULL PREFACE(35)	OF WORLD-POLITICS. THE BUSINESS IS	IRISH	BUSINESS, NOT ENGLISH; AND HE IS IRISH. AND HIS
BULL PREFACE(19)	OF ILLUSTRATING THE CONTRAST BETWEEN ENGLISH AND	IRISH	BY MOORE AND MR KIPLING, OR EVEN BY PARNELL AND
BULL PREFACE(68)	THE CONSTITUTION AND HOLD IRELAND AGAINST THE	IRISH	BY PHYSICAL FORCE, AND HAD BEEN REBUKED, LECTURED, AND
BULL II SD(104)	ALL IN OVERCOATS AND AS STIFF AS ONLY AN	IRISH	CAR COULD MAKE THEM. THE PRIEST, STOUT AND FATHERLY,
BULL PREFACE(29)	FREEDOM COULD BE OBTAINED AT THAT PRICE; SO AN	IRISH	CATHOLIC MAY LIKE HIS PRIEST AS A MAN AND REVERE HIM
BULL PREFACE(36)	CATHOLIC PARTY MUST OF NECESSITY BECOME AN	IRISH	CATHOLIC PARTY. THE HOLY ROMAN EMPIRE, LIKE THE OTHER
BULL PREFACE(8)	A UNIVERSAL INSTINCT AND A SOUND ONE. WHEN THE	IRISH	CATHOLIC WHO, FEELING BITTERLY THAT THE DOMINATION OF
BULL PREFACE(35)	EXPERIENCE OF THE TYRANNY OF THE ORANGE PARTY.	IRISH	CATHOLICISM FORECAST. LET US SUPPOSE THAT THE
BULL PREFACE(8)	IN WHICH CASE IT CEASES TO BE CATHOLIC) LET IT BE	IRISH	CATHOLICISM, NOT ITALIAN CATHOLICISM. LET US MAINTAIN
BULL III (129)	AN BE LESS AFEERD TO SPAKE OUT ABOUT IT, DHAN AN	IRISH	CATHOLIC. /CORNELIUS/ BUT SURE LARRY'S AS GOOD AS
BULL PREFACE(36)	QUIT OF THE PRELIMINARY DEAD LIFT THAT AWAITS THE	IRISH	CATHOLIC, THEIR CHURCH HAS THROWN OFF THE YOKE OF
BULL PREFACE(9)	CASE AS IN THE OTHER, A FREE PARTNERSHIP. BUT THE	IRISH	CATHOLICS ARE NOT ITALIAN IN THEIR POLITICS. THEY DO
POSN PREFACE(369)	THERE WAS MR HUGH LAW, AN IRISH MEMBER, SON OF AN	IRISH	CHANCELLOR, PRESENTING A KEEN AND JOYOUS FRONT TO
O'FL (217)	THREATENINGLY TO HER SON WITH ONE OF THOSE SUDDEN	IRISH	CHANGES OF MANNER WHICH AMAZE AND SCANDALIZE LESS
BULL IV (149)	HAS BROUGHT OUT THE KINDNESS AND SYMPATHY OF THE	IRISH	CHARACTER TO AN EXTENT I HAD NO CONCEPTION OF.
BULL III (135)	MR DOYLE, THERES A STRONG DASH OF TORYISM IN THE	IRISH	CHARACTER. LARRY HIMSELF SAYS THAT THE GREAT DUKE OF
BULL I (95)	ALL THIS SOUNDS RATHER INTERESTING. THERES THE	IRISH	CHARM ABOUT IT. THATS THE WORST OF YOU: THE IRISH
BULL I (95)	IRISH CHARM ABOUT IT. THATS THE WORST OF YOU: THE	IRISH	CHARM DOESNT EXIST FOR YOU. /DOYLE/ OH YES IT DOES.
PRES SD(146)	MRS FARRELL, A LEAN, HIGHLY RESPECTABLE	IRISH	CHARWOMAN OF ABOUT FIFTY, COMES IN. /MITCHENER/ MRS
BASH PREFACE(91)	LITERATURE MAY BE POSSIBLE. IF I, AS AN	IRISH	CHILD IN THE EIGHTEEN-SIXTIES, COULD WITHOUT ENFORCED
SUPR HANDBOK(197)	OR IRELAND FOR THE DISESTABLISHMENT OF THE	IRISH	CHURCH? IS THERE THE SMALLEST REASON TO SUPPOSE THAT
BULL PREFACE(24)	RITUALISTIC AND POPISH. I MYSELF ENTERED THE	IRISH	CHURCH BY BAPTISM, A CEREMONY PERFORMED BY MY UNCLE IN
BULL III (132)	FROM ALL ALLIANCES WITH THE STATE. THE SO-CALLED	IRISH	CHURCH IS STRONGER TODAY THAN EVER IT WAS. /MATTHEW/
METH PREFACE(R30)	OF CHRISTIANITY, OF WHICH, AS A MEMBER OF THE	IRISH	CHURCH (THE PSEUDO-PROTESTANT ONE), HE CONCEIVED
SUPR HANDBOK(197)	PHYSICAL FORCE? DID NOT GLADSTONE ADMIT THAT THE	IRISH	CHURCH WAS DISESTABLISHED, NOT BY THE SPIRIT OF
BULL PREFACE(33)	SERVICE, AND A GUNPOWDER PLOT TO DISESTABLISH THE	IRISH	CHURCH. IT WAS BY THE LIGHT, NOT OF REASON, BUT OF THE
BULL III (132)	TO REPEAL THE DISESTABLISHMENT OF THE SO-CALLED	IRISH	CHURCH. /LARRY/ YES: WHY NOT? (SENSATION). /MATTHEW/
BULL PREFACE(35)	ROMAN CATHOLIC CHURCH WOULD BECOME THE OFFICIAL	IRISH	CHURCH. THE IRISH PARLIAMENT WOULD INSIST ON A VOICE
MTH4 I (155)	A PESTILENCE. TO REGAIN THEIR LOST PRESTIGE, THE	IRISH	CLAIMED THE CITY OF JERUSALEM, ON THE GROUND THAT THEY
BULL PREFACE(30)	OF THE PROPERTY, POWER, AND PROMOTION OF THE	IRISH	CLASSES AS AGAINST THE IRISH MASSES. FROM ANY OTHER
BULL PREFACE(16)	OF THE PROPERTY, POWER, AND PROMOTION OF THE	IRISH	CLASSES AS AGAINST THE IRISH MASSES. OUR DELICACY IS
BULL I (86)	/DOYLE/ ME DEAR TOM, YOU ONLY NEED A TOUCH OF THE	IRISH	CLIMATE TO BE AS BIG A FOOL AS I AM MYSELF. IF ALL MY
BULL PREFACE(18)	IS AN ENGLISH RACE OR A YANKEE RACE. THERE IS AN	IRISH	CLIMATE, WHICH WILL STAMP AN IMMIGRANT MORE DEEPLY AND
BULL PREFACE(41)	SWEEP IN WAVES OVER EUROPE ARE STOPPED ON THE	IRISH	COAST BY THE ENGLISH GUNS OF THE PIGEON HOUSE FORT.
BULL PREFACE(31)	WITH THE BRITISH TAXPAYER. THEY KNOW THAT THE	IRISH	COAST IS FOR THE ENGLISH INVASION-SCAREMONGER THE HEEL
O'FL PREFACE(203)	WHY I DID NOT ENDOW O'FLAHERTY V.C. WITH AN IDEAL	IRISH	COLLEEN FOR HIS SWEETHEART, AND GAVE HIM FOR HIS
MILL PREFACE(124)	BE IMPROVED. I AM TOLD THAT CHILDREN BRED FROM	IRISH	COLLEENS AND CHINESE LAUNDRYMEN ARE FAR SUPERIOR TO
O'FL PREFACE(203)	MOMENT BY THE ROUT OF THE FIFTH ARMY, ORDAINED	IRISH	CONSCRIPTION, AND THEN DID NOT DARE TO GO THROUGH WITH
BULL IV (150)	AND IF EVER IT BE MY GOOD FORTUNE TO REPRESENT AN	IRISH	CONSTITUENCY IN PARLIAMENT, IT SHALL BE MY FIRST CARE
O'FL SD(205)	AT THE DOOR OF AN	IRISH	COUNTRY HOUSE IN A PARK. FINE SUMMER WEATHER: THE
BULL PREFACE(68)	THEY MUST STOP SHORT OF RAPINE. THEY WRECKED THE	IRISH	COURTS AND PRODUCED A STATE OF ANARCHY. THEY STRUCK AT
BULL PREFACE(68)	DUBLIN AND CLAIMED TO BE THE NATIONAL GOVERNMENT.	IRISH	COURTS WERE SET UP FOR THE ADMINISTRATION OF IRISH
BUOY IV (59)	AND THE ROMANCE OF BEATRICE AND FRANCESCA, OF	IRISH	DEIRDRE, THE GREATEST BORES IN LITERATURE, MERE NAMES
BULL IV (165)	WHAT A FOOL! WHAT A BRUTE I AM! IT'S ONLY YOUR	IRISH	DELICACY: OF COURSE, OF COURSE. YOU MEAN YES, EH?
BULL PREFACE(38)	WHO IMAGINE THAT IRELAND DELIVERED UP TO THE	IRISH	DEMOCRACY-- THAT IS, TO THE CATHOLIC LAITY-- WOULD BE
ROCK PREFACE(156)	IRISH NATIONALISTS. ALAS! THE FIRST THING THE	IRISH	DID WHEN THEY AT LAST ENJOYED SELF-GOVERNMENT WAS TO
O'FL SD(220)	HER AND KISSES HER). TERESA, WITHOUT LOSING HER	IRISH	DIGNITY, TAKES THE KISS AS APPRECIATIVELY AS A
BULL III (141)	SUFFER FROM INJUSTICE AND STARVATION? DHATS THE	IRISH	DISEASE. IT'S AISY FOR YOU TO TALK O SUFFERIN, AN YOU
BULL PREFACE(14)	IN BUSINESS OF MESSRS ENGLISH BROADBENT AND	IRISH	DOYLE MIGHT POSSIBLY HAVE BEEN DUE TO SOME EXTENT TO
METH PREFACE(R88)	AND LEFT LITERATE CHRISTENDOM FAITHLESS. MY OWN	IRISH	EIGHTEENTH-CENTURYISM MADE IT IMPOSSIBLE FOR ME TO
BULL I (85)	TO YOU? THREE VERSES OF TWADDLE ABOUT THE	IRISH	EMIGRANT " SITTING ON THE STILE, MARY," OR THREE HOURS
O'FL PREFACE(202)	ANYONE MIGHT HAVE INFERRED FROM THE RECORDS OF	IRISH	EMIGRATION, THAT ALL AN IRISHMAN'S HOPES AND AMBITIONS
CAPT NOTES (303)	NEITHER AMERICAN ENGLISH NOR ENGLISH ENGLISH, BUT	IRISH	ENGLISH; SO I AM AS NEARLY IMPARTIAL IN THE MATTER AS
BULL PREFACE(13)	THE RESOURCES OF THE NEW ABBEY THEATRE, WHICH THE	IRISH	ENTERPRISE OWED TO THE PUBLIC SPIRIT OF MISS A.E.F.
BULL PREFACE(67)	FROM A BATTERY PLANTED AT TRINITY COLLEGE (THE	IRISH	EQUIVALENT OF OXFORD UNIVERSITY), AND FROM A WARSHIP
BULL PREFACE(17)	AGREEABLE, AND ENGLISH HOUSES VERY COMFORTABLE,	IRISH	ESTABLISHMENTS BEING GENERALLY STRAITENED BY AN
BULL IV (175)	A SIMPLE THING SIMPLY, LARRY, WITHOUT ALL THAT	IRISH	EXAGGERATION AND TALKY-TALKY? THE SYNDICATE IS A
BULL II SD(101)	HER BEST), SHE IS A FIGURE COMMONPLACE ENOUGH TO	IRISH	EYES; BUT ON THE INHABITANTS OF FATTER-FED, CROWDED,
2TRU PREFACE(6)	TEN THOUSAND A YEAR; AND THIS, TO ANY RESIDENT	IRISH	FAMILY IN MY BOYHOOD, REPRESENTED AN OPULENCE BEYOND
BULL PREFACE(31)	FANATICS. THEY CANNOT AFFORD TO RETIRE INTO AN	IRISH	FAUBOURG ST GERMAIN, THEY WILL TAKE AN ENERGETIC PART
BULL PREFACE(16)	HE FINDS IT TO BE RULED BY ENGLISH INSTEAD OF	IRISH	FOLLY. A " LOYAL" IRISHMAN IS AN ABHORRENT PHENOMENON,
BULL PREFACE(34)	PREFERRING DEMOCRACY. THEY CAN HARDLY BLAME THE	IRISH	FOR TAKING THE SAME VIEW. IN SHORT, DEAR ENGLISH
NEVR IV (292)	CRAMPTON, SETTING A TUMBLER APART ON THE TABLE)	IRISH	FOR YOU, SIR. (CRAMPTON SITS DOWN A LITTLE
NEVR IV (288)	SCOTCH. /WAITER/ RIGHT, SIR. (TO CRAMPTON/	IRISH	FOR YOU, SIR, I THINK, SIR? (CRAMPTON ASSENTS WITH A
SIM II (54)	TO DO NOTHING UNTIL THEN BUT SING HYMNS. THE	IRISH	FREE STATE ADMIRAL THREATENS TO SINK THEM IF THEY DONT
SIM II (56)	THAT THE PARTIES SHOULD BE DIVORCED. BUT THE	IRISH	FREE STATE WILL NOT HEAR OF DIVORCE, AND POINTS OUT
BULL PREFACE(67)	MARTYRS WHOSE BLOOD WAS THE SEED OF THE PRESENT	IRISH	FREE STATE. AMONG THOSE WHO ESCAPED WAS ITS FIRST
APPL II (261)	VISIT TO OUR SHORES OF THE PRESIDENT OF THE	IRISH	FREE STATE. I CANNOT PRONOUNCE HIS NAME IN ITS
BULL PREFACE(29)	TO MAKE THE SHANNON RUN RED WITH ENGLISH BLOOD IF	IRISH	FREEDOM COULD BE OBTAINED AT THAT PRICE; SO AN IRISH
BULL PREFACE(67)	INTO A HEROIC EPISODE IN THE STRUGGLE FOR	IRISH	FREEDOM. THE VICTORIOUS ARTILLERISTS PROCEEDED TO KILL
BULL I (80)	MY PARTNER, MR DOYLE. (TO DOYLE) THIS IS A NEW	IRISH	FRIEND OF MINE, MR TIM HAFFIGAN. /TIM/ (RISING WITH
BULL III SD(117)	THOUGH APPARENTLY WORKS OF ART, GROW NATURALLY IN	IRISH	GARDENS. THEIR GERMINATION IS A MYSTERY TO THE OLDEST
DEST (193)	I FORGOT THE IRISH. AN ENGLISH ARMY LED BY AN	IRISH	GENERAL: THAT MIGHT BE A MATCH FOR A FRENCH ARMY LED
DOCT PREFACE(14)	MATTERS WORSE, DOCTORS ARE HIDEOUSLY POOR. THE	IRISH	GENTLEMAN DOCTOR OF MY BOYHOOD, WHO TOOK NOTHING LESS
BULL PREFACE(28)	VATICAN. THEY LOVE THEIR LANDLORDS TOO: MANY AN	IRISH	GENTLEMAN HAS FOUND IN HIS NURSE A FOSTER-MOTHER MORE
BULL PREFACE(17)	IN THE DEEPER ASPECTS OF HUMAN CHARACTER, AS THE	IRISH	GENTLEMAN, TRACING HIS PEDIGREE TO THE CONQUEST OR ONE
BULL PREFACE(17)	IS AN ENTIRE LACK OF GALL IN THE FEELING OF THE	IRISH	GENTRY TOWARDS THE ENGLISH, IT IS BECAUSE THE
SUPR IV (147)	WAS HE? /MALONE/ HIS GRANMOTHER WAS A BAREFOOTED	IRISH	GIRL THAT NURSED ME BY A TURF FIRE. LET HIM MARRY
BULL PREFACE(31)	BUT AS THAT GOVERNMENT WILL THEN BE A NATIONAL	IRISH	GOVERNMENT INSTEAD OF AS NOW AN ENGLISH GOVERNMENT,
METH PREFACE(R64)	AND POTENCY OF LIFE, AND WITH HIS	IRISH	GRAPHIC LUCIDITY MADE A PICTURE OF A WORLD OF MAGNETIC
BULL II (97)	(SADLY) X.X. /THE MAN/ AYE, YOURE A THRUE	IRISH	GRASSHOPPER. /THE GRASSHOPPER/ (LOUDLY) X.X.X. /THE
BULL PREFACE(18)	IN THE MISAPPREHENSION, MACAULAY, SEEING THAT THE	IRISH	HAD IN SWIFT AN AUTHOR WORTH STEALING, TRIED TO ANNEX
BULL II SD(104)	TO EARLIER GENERATIONS AS BEEYANKINY CARS, THE	IRISH	HAVING LAID VIOLENT TONGUES ON THE NAME OF THEIR
BULL III (143)	THE PIG'S THE THING: THE PIG WILL WIN OVER EVERY	IRISH	HEART TO ME. WE'LL TAKE THE PIG HOME TO HAFFIGAN'S
BULL IV (175)	WICKEDNESS AND TYRANNY, AND TO CRACK UP YOUR OWN	IRISH	HEROISM, JUST AS HAFFIGAN ONCE PAID A WITCH A PENNY TO
BULL PREFACE(68)	PARLIAMENT, HAD CARRIED AN ACT TO ESTABLISH	IRISH	HOME RULE, AS IT WAS THEN CALLED, WHICH DULY RECEIVED
BULL PREFACE(23)	TO THE EXISTENCE OF ANY MYSTERIOUS IRISH PLUCK,	IRISH	HONESTY, IRISH BIAS ON THE PART OF PROVIDENCE, OR
KING II (233)	ENGLISH BIRDS AND ENGLISH TREES, ENGLISH DOGS AND	IRISH	HORSES, ENGLISH RIVERS AND ENGLISH SHIPS; BUT ENGLISH
BULL IV (150)	SUBJECTS; AND WE MUST NOT ABUSE THE WARMHEARTED	IRISH	HOSPITALITY OF MISS DOYLE BY TURNING HER SITTING ROOM
BULL II SD(111)	GUEST AS THE WHIMSICAL AFFECTATION OF A SHREWD	IRISH	HUMORIST AND INCORRIGIBLE SPENDTHRIFT. AUNT JUDY SEEMS
BULL IV (153)	HIS CONFIDENCE) AH! IT WAS ONLY YOUR DELIGHTFUL	IRISH	HUMOR, MR KEEGAN. OF COURSE, OF COURSE. HOW STUPID OF
BULL PREFACE(21)	WITH THE CONTRAST BETWEEN THE ENGLISH AND	IRISH	IDIOSYNCRASIES. THE IRISHMAN MAKES A DISTINCTION WHICH
NEVR II (241)	M'COMAS. /WAITER/ YES, SIR. /DOLLY/ HAVE A SIX OF	IRISH	IN IT, FINCH? /M'COMAS/ (SCANDALIZED) NO. NO. THANK
BULL PREFACE(21)	IV AND BYRON, CONTRASTED WITH GLADSTONE, SEEM	IRISH	IN RESPECT OF A CERTAIN HUMOROUS BLACKGUARDISM, AND A
BULL PREFACE(24)	UNLESS I INSIST ON EXPLAINING IT TO YOU WITH THAT	IRISH	INSISTENCE ON INTELLECTUAL CLARITY TO WHICH MY ENGLISH
BULL PREFACE(19)	BETWEEN THE DUKE OF WELLINGTON, THAT INTENSELY	IRISH	IRISHMAN, AND NELSON, THAT INTENSELY ENGLISH
DEST (193)	IRISH! (THOUGHTFULLY) YES! I FORGOT THE	IRISH	. AN ENGLISH ARMY LED BY AN IRISH GENERAL: THAT MIGHT
BULL PREFACE(35)	IS IRISH BUSINESS, NOT ENGLISH; AND HE IS	IRISH	. AND HIS OBJECT, WHICH IS SIMPLY TO SECURE THE
BULL IV (174)	IT DONT MATTER WHETHER THEYRE ENGLISH OR	IRISH	. I SHALL COLLAR THIS PLACE, NOT BECAUSE I'M AN
MILL PREFACE(124)	DEMONSTRATE THE SAME OF THE ENGLISH, ALSO OF THE	IRISH	. IF HERR HITLER WOULD ONLY CONSULT THE FRENCH AND
BULL II (113)	VERY MUCH IN EARNEST ABOUT IRELAND AND EVERYTHING	IRISH	. I'M VERY MUCH IN EARNEST ABOUT YOU AND ABOUT LARRY.
BULL I (75)	/HODSON/ YES SIR: I NOTICED THAT HE WAS RATHER	IRISH	. /BROADBENT/ IF HE CALLS AGAIN LET HIM COME UP.
O'FL (215)	OF USE, SIR. SHE SAYS ALL THE ENGLISH GENERALS IS	IRISH	. SHE SAYS ALL THE ENGLISH POETS AND GREAT MEN WAS
O'FL (215)	SHE SAYS ALL THE ENGLISH POETS AND GREAT MEN WAS	IRISH	. SHE SAYS THE ENGLISH NEVER KNEW HOW TO READ THEIR
BULL II SD(111)	WHEN HE IS IN LONDON, SEEMS TO HIM DELIGHTFULLY	IRISH	. THE ALMOST TOTAL ATROPHY OF ANY SENSE OF ENJOYMENT
ROCK PREFACE(149)	SAID CROMWELL WHEN HE TRIED TO EXTERMINATE THE	IRISH	. " THE ONLY GOOD NIGGER IS A DEAD NIGGER" SAY THE
FABL II (105)	(SEATING HIMSELF) IS THIS A TIME FOR YOUR	IRISH	JOKES? WHAT THE DEVIL ARE WE TO DO? HOW MUCH DO YOU

BARB PREFACE(221)	UNKNOWN, WHILST I, A COMPARATIVELY INSIGNIFICANT	IRISH	JOURNALIST, WAS LEADING THEM BY THE NOSE INTO AN
BULL PREFACE(68)	COURTS WERE SET UP FOR THE ADMINISTRATION OF	IRISH	JUSTICE; IRISH ORDER WAS KEPT BY IRISH POLICE; IRISH
BULL PREFACE(33)	THAT THE NEED FOR PAYING SERIOUS ATTENTION TO THE	IRISH	LAND QUESTION WAS SEEN IN ENGLAND. IT COST THE
MTH4 I (156)	THINGS DO NOT HAPPEN REALLY. THAT SCENE OF THE	IRISH	LANDING HERE AND KISSING THE GROUND MIGHT HAVE
BULL III (127)	FARRLL AN DHE LIKE O HIM? /BROADBENT/ BUT SURELY	IRISH	LANDLORDISM WAS ACCOUNTABLE FOR WHAT MR HAFFIGAN
BULL IV (160)	YES, YES. (HE GAZES THROUGH THE DOORWAY AT THE	IRISH	LANDSCAPE, AND SINGS, ALMOST UNCONSCIOUSLY, BUT VERY
BULL III (136)	VOICE-- I LOOK FORWARD TO THE TIME WHEN AN	IRISH	LEGISLATURE SHALL ARISE ONCE MORE ON THE EMERALD
BULL PREFACE(13)	MACHINERY OR TAX THE SPECIAL RESOURCES OF THE	IRISH	LITERARY THEATRE FOR ITS PRODUCTION. HOW TOM BROADBENT
BULL PREFACE(13)	A PATRIOTIC CONTRIBUTION TO THE REPERTORY OF THE	IRISH	LITERARY THEATRE. LIKE MOST PEOPLE WHO HAVE ASKED ME
BULL PREFACE(12)	RULE, JUST AS THINGS HAVE BEEN DONE UNDER THE	IRISH	LOCAL GOVERNMENT ACT THAT THE OLD OLIGARCHICAL GRAND
O'FL (221)	HER FOREHEAD, IN A FRINGE LIKE. AND SHE HAS AN	IRISH	LOOK ABOUT HER EYEBROWS, AND SHE DIDNT KNOW WHAT TO
BULL PREFACE(28)	SPIRITUAL FATHERS. I AM PERFECTLY AWARE THAT THE	IRISH	LOVE THEIR PRIESTS AS DEVOTEDLY AS THE FRENCH LOVED
BULL IV (170)	/LARRY/ (NERVOUSLY RELAPSING INTO HIS MOST	IRISH	MANNER) NORA, DEAR, DONT YOU UNDERSTAND THAT I'M AN
GETT PREFACE(185)	MARRIAGE OF DIVORCED PERSONS, SCOTCH MARRIAGE,	IRISH	MARRIAGE, FRENCH, GERMAN, TURKISH, OR SOUTH DAKOTAN
BULL PREFACE(30)	AND PROMOTION OF THE IRISH CLASSES AS AGAINST THE	IRISH	MASSES. FROM ANY OTHER POINT OF VIEW IT IS COWARDICE
BULL PREFACE(16)	AND PROMOTION OF THE IRISH CLASSES AS AGAINST THE	IRISH	MASSES. OUR DELICACY IS PART OF A KEEN SENSE OF
BULL II SD(101)	HER NOVEL ACCENT, WITH THE CARESSING PLAINTIVE	IRISH	MELODY OF HER SPEECH, GIVE HER A CHARM WHICH IS ALL
BULL II SD(112)	RESIGNEDLY TO WAIT, AND HUMS A SONG-- NOT AN	IRISH	MELODY, BUT A HACKNEYED ENGLISH DRAWING ROOM BALLAD OF
POSN PREFACE(369)	IN THE ADVANCED DRAMA. THERE WAS MR HUGH LAW, AN	IRISH	MEMBER, SON OF AN IRISH CHANCELLOR, PRESENTING A KEEN
BULL II SD(111)	MOONLIGHT. THE ROUND TOWER STANDS ABOUT HALF AN	IRISH	MILE FROM ROSSCULLEN, SOME FIFTY YARDS SOUTH OF THE
BULL PREFACE(21)	WITTY FASHION WHICH SUITS THE FLEXIBILITY OF THE	IRISH	MIND VERY WELL; AND THE CONTRAST BETWEEN THIS FASHION
BULL I (83)	TO FOOL YOU, LIKE THE ALBERT HALL CONCERTS OF	IRISH	MUSIC? NO IRISHMAN EVER TALKS LIKE THAT IN IRELAND,
BULL PREFACE(22)	I DO NOT CLAIM IT AS A NATURAL SUPERIORITY IN THE	IRISH	NATION THAT IT DISLIKES AND MISTRUSTS FOOLS, AND
POSN PREFACE(431)	AUDIENCE IN THE KINGDOM, THE DIRECTORS OF THE	IRISH	NATIONAL THEATRE, LADY GREGORY AND MR WILLIAM BUTLER
BULL PREFACE(31)	DETERMINATION WILL MAKE THEM THE VANGUARD OF	IRISH	NATIONALISM AND DEMOCRACY AS AGAINST ROMANISM AND
ROCK PREFACE(156)	LEAGUE, AND VOICED IN PARLIAMENT BY THE	IRISH	NATIONALISTS. ALAS! THE FIRST THING THE IRISH DID
BULL PREFACE(68)	GOVERNMENT THROUGHOUT THE WORLD. THE	IRISH	NATIONALISTS, AFTER THIRTY YEARS OF CONSTITUTIONAL
BULL I (89)	UNFORTUNATELY I'M NOT GOING BACK TO VISIT THE	IRISH	NATION, BUT TO VISIT MY FATHER AND AUNT JUDY AND NORA
SUPR IV SD(143)	THE OLD GENTLEMAN SHEWS SIGNS OF INTENDING HIS	IRISH	NONSENSE TO BE TAKEN SERIOUSLY. /STRAKER/ I'LL GO TELL
BULL PREFACE(21)	WOULD HARDLY BE POSSIBLE IN THE WORKS OF AN	IRISH	NOVELIST, EVEN DICKENS, THOUGH TOO VITAL A GENIUS AND
BARB PREFACE(207)	WITH MODERN IDEAS. ABOUT HALF A CENTURY AGO, AN	IRISH	NOVELIST, CHARLES LEVER, WROTE A STORY ENTITLED A
BULL III (138)	HAVE PLENTY OF SHREWDNESS IN SPITE OF THEIR	IRISH	ODDITY. (HODSON COMES FROM THE HOUSE. LARRY SITS IN
BULL PREFACE(68)	BY IRISH POLICE; IRISH TAXES WERE COLLECTED BY	IRISH	OFFICIALS; AND BRITISH COURTS WERE BOYCOTTED. UPON
BULL PREFACE(19)	FORMULA FOR THAT KIND OF THING WAS A WELL-KNOWN	IRISH	ONE: " SIR: DONT BE A DAMNED FOOL." IT IS THE FORMULA
BULL PREFACE(71)	HAS A BELFAST HOME RULE PARLIAMENT INSTEAD OF AN	IRISH	ONE. AND IT HAS ALLOWED CATHOLIC IRELAND TO SECURE THE
MIS. PREFACE(23)	ENGLISH PUBLIC SCHOOL INSTEAD OF A DAY BOY AT AN	IRISH	ONE, I MIGHT HAVE HAD TO ADD TO THESE, DEEPER SHAMES
MILL PREFACE(125)	AND CHINESE LAUNDRYMEN ARE FAR SUPERIOR TO INBRED	IRISH	OR CHINESE. HERR HITLER IS NOT A TYPICAL GERMAN. I
BULL PREFACE(68)	SET UP FOR THE ADMINISTRATION OF IRISH JUSTICE;	IRISH	ORDER WAS KEPT BY IRISH POLICE; IRISH TAXES WERE
BULL PREFACE(68)	TO THE PARALLEL PREPARATIONS OF THE ORANGEMEN. AN	IRISH	PARLIAMENT (OR DAIL) SAT IN DUBLIN AND CLAIMED TO BE
BULL PREFACE(33)	AND THE IRISH VOLUNTEER MOVEMENT TO OBTAIN THE	IRISH	PARLIAMENT OF 1782, THE CONSTITUTION OF WHICH FAR
BULL PREFACE(42)	NOT MORE CAUSE TO HAND OVER THEIR AFFAIRS TO AN	IRISH	PARLIAMENT THAN TO CLAMOR FOR ANOTHER NATION'S CITIES
BULL PREFACE(7)	HAVE BEEN ONE OF EVEN A PERSECUTED MINORITY IN AN	IRISH	PARLIAMENT THAN THE PREMIER OF AN ENGLISH CABINET. HE
PRES (136)	ON PROPERTY? PARLIAMENT MUST ABOLISH ITSELF. THE	IRISH	PARLIAMENT VOTED FOR ITS OWN EXTINCTION. THE ENGLISH
BULL PREFACE(35)	WOULD BECOME THE OFFICIAL IRISH CHURCH. THE	IRISH	PARLIAMENT WOULD INSIST ON A VOICE IN THE PROMOTION OF
BULL PREFACE(71)	AND IT HAS ALLOWED CATHOLIC IRELAND TO SECURE THE	IRISH	PARLIAMENT. THUS, OF THE TWO REGIONAL PARLIAMENTS
BULL III (137)	GAS A BIT, AN CHIVY THE GOVERMENT, AN VOTE WI DH	IRISH	PARTY? /CORNELIUS/ (RUMINATIVELY) HE'S THE QUEEREST
BULL I (86)	GENUINE OLD ENGLISH CHARACTER AND SPIRIT IS THE	IRISH	PARTY. LOOK AT ITS INDEPENDENCE, ITS DETERMINATION,
BULL PREFACE(63)	HANGINGS. YET MR DILLON, REPRESENTING THE	IRISH	PARTY, WHICH WELL KNOWS WHAT BRITISH OCCUPATIONS AND
O'FL PREFACE(202)	INCOMPREHENSIBLE AS IT SEEMS TO AN ENGLISHMAN,	IRISH	PATRIOTISM DOES NOT TAKE THE FORM OF DEVOTION TO
BULL I (85)	" SITTING ON THE STILE, MARY," OR THREE HOURS OF	IRISH	PATRIOTISM IN BERMONDSEY OR THE SCOTLAND DIVISION OF
BULL PREFACE(9)	BY SUCH AN OVERWHELMING MAJORITY OF WHAT AN	IRISH	PEASANT WOULD CALL " BLACK HEATHENS," THAT THEY FORCE
BULL PREFACE(28)	HAVE WITNESSED THE CHARMING RELATIONS BETWEEN THE	IRISH	PEASANTRY AND THEIR SPIRITUAL FATHERS. I AM PERFECTLY
BULL III (121)	TO MAKE ME SICK, EVEN AS A BOY. I TELL YOU, AN	IRISH	PEASANT'S INDUSTRY IS NOT HUMAN: IT'S WORSE THAN THE
BULL IV (167)	MUCH MORE COMFORTABLE FOR YOU. /NORA/ (WITH	IRISH	PEEVISHNESS) AH, YOU MUSTNT GO ON LIKE THAT. I DONT
BULL I (93)	LARRY, THAT WOULD NEVER HAVE OCCURRED TO ME. YOU	IRISH	PEOPLE ARE AMAZINGLY CLEVER. OF COURSE IT'S ALL TOMMY
BULL PREFACE(6)	ITS PROPER LIMITS IN IRELAND IS BY SETTING THE	IRISH	PEOPLE FREE TO TAKE IT IN HAND THEMSELVES WITHOUT
BULL PREFACE(39)	TO ALTER THE CONSTITUTION, AS THE MAJORITY OF THE	IRISH	PEOPLE HAVE MADE UP THEIR MINDS TO OBTAIN HOME RULE,
BULL PREFACE(30)	LOYALTY IN IRELAND. THERE IS A SEPARATION OF THE	IRISH	PEOPLE INTO TWO HOSTILE CAMPS: ONE PROTESTANT,
CAPT NOTES (305)	WARD AND OTHER AMERICAN DIALECT WRITERS CAUSES	IRISH	PEOPLE TO MISREAD THEM GROTESQUELY. I ONCE SAW THE
BULL II (113)	AN ENGLISHMAN LIKE YOU WOULD MAKE AMONG US POOR	IRISH	PEOPLE. /BROADBENT/ AH, NOW YOURE CHAFFING ME, MISS
BULL PREFACE(28)	LIGHT OF THAT VERY ENGLISH CHARACTERISTIC OF THE	IRISH	PEOPLE, THEIR POLITICAL HATRED OF PRIESTS. DO NOT BE
BULL PREFACE(41)	ITSELF AS AN ATTACK ON THE NATIVE LANGUAGE OF THE	IRISH	PEOPLE, WHICH IS MOST FORTUNATELY ALSO THE NATIVE
MTH4 I SD(139)	FLAGS, SUGGEST THAT THE PIER, UNLIKE MANY REMOTE	IRISH	PIERS, IS OCCASIONALLY USEFUL AS WELL AS ROMANTIC. ON
MILL PREFACE(117)	HAVE NO MORE CHANCE NOWADAYS THAN THE RAGGED	IRISH	PIKEMEN ON VINEGAR HILL; AND WELLINGTON'S THIN RED
BULL PREFACE(13)	RECALCITRANT LONDON PLAYGOER, AND GAVE A THIRD	IRISH	PLAYWRIGHT, DR JOHN TODHUNTER, AN OPPORTUNITY WHICH
BULL PREFACE(23)	ILLUSIONS AS TO THE EXISTENCE OF ANY MYSTERIOUS	IRISH	PLUCK, IRISH HONESTY, IRISH BIAS ON THE PART OF
BULL PREFACE(68)	OF IRISH JUSTICE; IRISH ORDER WAS KEPT BY	IRISH	POLICE; IRISH TAXES WERE COLLECTED BY IRISH OFFICIALS;
BULL III (126)	/DORAN/ THERES TOO MUCH BLATHERUMSKITE IN	IRISH	POLITICS: A DALE TOO MUCH. /LARRY/ BUT WHAT ABOUT YOUR
BULL PREFACE(28)	BITE IT, THE UNNATURALLY COMBINED ELEMENTS IN	IRISH	POLITICS WOULD FLY ASUNDER AND RECOMBINE ACCORDING TO
BULL I (95)	POSSIBILITY OF MY HAVING ANY. YOU DONT KNOW WHAT	IRISH	PRIDE IS. ENGLAND MAY HAVE KNOCKED A GOOD DEAL OF IT
BULL II (105)	(SOMEWHAT INDIGNANTLY; FOR TO BE REBUKED BY AN	IRISH	PRIEST FOR SUPERSTITION IS MORE THAN HE CAN STAND) YOU
BULL PREFACE(34)	MAY BUY A COMMON AND NOT INEFFECTIVE VARIETY OF	IRISH	PROTESTANT BY DELEGATING YOUR POWERS TO HIM, AND IN
BULL PREFACE(26)	HE BECOMES HORRIFICALLY INCOMPREHENSIBLE TO THE	IRISH	PROTESTANT CHURCHMAN, WHO, ON HIS PART, PUZZLES THE
BULL PREFACE(24)	DAMNATION. IN IRELAND ALL THAT THE MEMBER OF THE	IRISH	PROTESTANT CHURCH KNOWS IS THAT HE IS NOT A ROMAN
BULL PREFACE(24)	IS REALLY PROTESTANT. IT IS TRUE THAT THERE IS AN	IRISH	PROTESTANT CHURCH (DISESTABLISHED SOME 35 YEARS AGO)
BULL PREFACE(16)	ENGLISHMEN TODAY, AND SEE THEM BULLIED BY THE	IRISH	PROTESTANT GARRISON AS NO BENGALEE NOW LETS HIMSELF BE
ROCK PREFACE(172)	TRUTHS. I, FOR INSTANCE, BEING THE SON OF AN	IRISH	PROTESTANT GENTLEMAN, FOUND MYSELF, AT THE DAWN OF MY
BULL PREFACE(26)	MEANS THE ROMAN CATHOLIC CHURCH, FOR WHICH THE	IRISH	PROTESTANT RESERVES ALL THE CLASS RANCOR, THE
BULL PREFACE(8)	NOT SUPPOSE FOR A MOMENT THAT I PROPOSE THAT THE	IRISH	PROTESTANT SHOULD SUBMIT TO THE IRISH ROMAN CATHOLIC.
BULL PREFACE(26)	PROTESTANT ORGANIZATIONS. WHEN A VULGAR	IRISH	PROTESTANT SPEAKS OF A " PAPIST" HE FEELS EXACTLY AS A
BULL PREFACE(34)	THE SAME VIEW. IN SHORT, DEAR ENGLISH READER, THE	IRISH	PROTESTANT STANDS OUTSIDE THAT ENGLISH MUTUAL
BULL PREFACE(32)	THE HONOR OF IRELAND, HE GREATLY MISTAKES THE	IRISH	PROTESTANT TEMPER. THE NOTION THAT IRELAND IS THE ONLY
BULL PREFACE(35)	DO NOT SHAKE THE STURDY CONVICTION OF THE	IRISH	PROTESTANT THAT HE IS MORE THAN A MATCH FOR ANY
BULL PREFACE(9)	THAT GIVES THEM THE RIGHT TO THE SUPPORT OF EVERY	IRISH	PROTESTANT UNTIL HOME RULE IS ACHIEVED. AFTER THAT,
BULL PREFACE(24)	THAT I AM AN IRISHMAN AND YOU AN ENGLISHMAN.	IRISH	PROTESTANTISM REALLY PROTESTANT. WHEN I REPEAT THAT I
BULL PREFACE(31)	AT THEIR DISCOVERY OF THE TRUE VALUE OF AN	IRISH	PROTESTANT'S LOYALTY. BUT THERE WILL BE NO OPEN BREAK
MIS. PREFACE(46)	THAT SCOURGE OF HUMANITY, THE AMATEUR POPE. AS AN	IRISH	PROTESTANT, I RAISE THE CRY OF NO POPERY WITH
BULL PREFACE(24)	REALLY PROTESTANT. WHEN I REPEAT THAT I AM AN	IRISH	PROTESTANT, I COME TO A PART OF THE RELATION BETWEEN
LION PREFACE(100)	TO ACCEPT FELLOW-CITIZENSHIP WITH THE OTHER	IRISH	PROVINCES BECAUSE THE SOUTH BELIEVES IN ST PETER AND
POSN PREFACE(431)	EVERY POSSIBLE EFFORT WAS MADE TO PERSUADE THE	IRISH	PUBLIC THAT THE PERFORMANCE WOULD BE AN OUTRAGE TO
BULL PREFACE(69)	BLACK AND TAN TERRORISM, AND SO WE SETTLED THE	IRISH	QUESTION, NOT AS CIVILIZED AND REASONABLE MEN SHOULD
FABL PREFACE(94)	HAD BETTER REMEMBER. DR INGE, COMMENTING ON THE	IRISH	QUESTION, POINTED OUT HOW DIFFICULT IS THE COMMON
MTH2 (51)	AND TO DOING SOMETHING OR OTHER TO KEEP THE	IRISH	QUIET. DOES THAT SATISFY YOU? /FRANKLYN/ IT DOES NOT
BULL IV (146)	(GENERAL DELIGHT AT THIS TYPICAL STROKE OF	IRISH	RABELAISIANISM). /NORA/ IT'S WELL MR DOYLE WASNT
BULL PREFACE(18)	THE IRISH AND ENGLISH " RACES." THERE IS NO	IRISH	RACE ANY MORE THAN THERE IS AN ENGLISH RACE OR A
MTH4 I (156)	SO THAT WHEN THAT GENERATION PASSED AWAY THE	IRISH	RACE VANISHED FROM HUMAN KNOWLEDGE. AND THE DISPERSED
MTH4 I (154)	ITS SEAT TO THE EAST, AND SAID TO THE TURBULENT	IRISH	RACE WHICH IT HAD OPPRESSED BUT NEVER CONQUERED, " AT
O'FL PREFACE(201)	MORE DEVILMENT THAN PRUDENCE. UNFORTUNATELY,	IRISH	RECRUITING WAS BADLY BUNGLED IN 1915. THE IRISH WERE
O'FL PREFACE(203)	OFFENCE BY KEEPING MY HEAD IN THIS MATTER OF	IRISH	RECRUITING. WHAT CAN I DO BUT APOLOGIZE, AND PUBLISH
BULL III (123)	? ? (HE SCREAMS WITH LAUGHTER IN THE FALSETTO	IRISH	REGISTER UNUSED FOR THAT PURPOSE IN ENGLAND).
BULL PREFACE(66)	SEIZED THE DUBLIN POST OFFICE AND PROCLAIMED AN	IRISH	REPUBLIC, WITH ONE OF THEIR NUMBER, A SCHOOLMASTER
BULL PREFACE(8)	TO THE IRISH ROMAN CATHOLIC. I REPROACH THE	IRISH	ROMAN CATHOLIC FOR HIS SUBMISSION TO ROME EXACTLY AS I
BULL PREFACE(8)	THAT THE IRISH PROTESTANT SHOULD SUBMIT TO THE	IRISH	ROMAN CATHOLIC. I REPROACH THE IRISH ROMAN CATHOLIC
BULL PREFACE(57)	AND BULLY ENGLAND EXACTLY AS THE " LOYAL"	IRISH	RULE THE GARRISON AND BULLY THE UNIONISTS NEARER HOME.
DOCT I SD(87)	HIS YOUTH, AND AN OCCASIONAL TURN OF SPEECH, ARE	IRISH	; BUT HE HAS LIVED ALL HIS LIFE IN ENGLAND AND IS
BULL II (113)	TO SAY HOW MUCH I LIKE IT, THE MAGIC OF THIS	IRISH	SCENE, AND-- I REALLY DONT WANT TO BE PERSONAL, MISS
MIS. PREFACE(25)	KNOWLEDGE OF CLASSICAL LITERATURE BY AN	IRISH	SCHOOLMASTER WHOM YOU WOULD CALL A HEDGE SCHOOLMASTER

BULL III (144)	ON, YOU OLD CROAKER! I'LL SHEW YOU HOW TO WIN AN	IRISH	SEAT. /PATSY/ (MEDITATIVELY) BEDAD, IF DHAT PIG GETS
BULL PREFACE(35)	ORDERS THE ENGLISH GOVERNMENT TO REMOVE AN	IRISH	SECRETARY WHO HAS DARED TO APPLY ENGLISH IDEAS TO THE
BULL I (82)	VERY AMUSING-- ABOUT THE HOME SECRETARY AND THE	IRISH	SECRETARY. AT ALL EVENTS, HE'S EVIDENTLY THE VERY MAN
BULL I (79)	THEN WE'LL CALL HIM THE HOME SECRETARY AND ME THE	IRISH	SECRETARY. EH? /BROADBENT/ (LAUGHING INDUSTRIOUSLY)
BULL III (144)	SERIOUS! I! ! ! /LARRY/ YES, YOU. YOU SAY THE	IRISH	SENSE OF HUMOR IS IN ABEYANCE. WELL, IF YOU DRIVE
BULL IV (178)	ENGLISH SENTIMENT SO MUCH MORE EFFICIENT THAN OUR	IRISH	SENTIMENT, AFTER ALL? MR BROADBENT SPENDS HIS LIFE
BULL II SD(97)	THERE ARE GREAT BREADTHS OF SILKEN GREEN IN THE	IRISH	SKY. THE SUN IS SETTING. A MAN WITH THE FACE OF A
BULL PREFACE(17)	AND EVEN, ON OCCASION, A VERY COARSE PEOPLE. THE	IRISH	SOLDIER TAKES THE KING'S SHILLING AND DRINKS THE
O'FL PREFACE(201)	AND AT LEAST TO SET A PERILOUS PACE FOR HIM.	IRISH	SOLDIERS GIVE IMPETUS TO THOSE MILITARY OPERATIONS
O'FL PREFACE(201)	IN DISGUISE. THE BRITISH OFFICER SELDOM LIKES	IRISH	SOLDIERS; BUT HE ALWAYS TRIES TO HAVE A CERTAIN
BULL PREFACE(23)	IRISH BIAS ON THE PART OF PROVIDENCE, OR STERLING	IRISH	SOLIDITY OF CHARACTER, THAT WILL ENABLE AN IRISH
BULL PREFACE(17)	SHILLING AND DRINKS THE KING'S HEALTH; AND THE	IRISH	SQUIRE TAKES THE TITLE DEEDS OF THE ENGLISH SETTLEMENT
SIM PREFACE(6)	STILL. A FRIEND OF MINE LATELY ASKED A LEADING	IRISH	STATESMAN WHY HE DID NOT RESORT TO A RATHER SOULLESS
2TRU PREFACE(8)	IN AUSTRALIA OR A LUCKY TICKET IN THE CALCUTTA OR	IRISH	SWEEPS. TRYING IT FOR AN HOUR. BESIDES, EVEN QUITE
BULL PREFACE(34)	TOLERATE A PROPOSAL TO ESTABLISH THE INDIAN OR	IRISH	SYSTEM IN GREAT BRITAIN, YET IF THE JUSTICE OF THE
DOCT PREFACE(17)	ARE AS ABSURD AS THE RUB OF CHALK WITH WHICH AN	IRISH	TAILOR ONCE CHARMED AWAY A WART FROM MY FATHER'S
BULL PREFACE(68)	JUSTICE; IRISH ORDER WAS KEPT BY IRISH POLICE;	IRISH	TAXES WERE COLLECTED BY IRISH OFFICIALS; AND BRITISH
BULL PREFACE(69)	PRODUCED A STATE OF ANARCHY, THEY STRUCK AT THE	IRISH	THROUGH THE POPULAR CO-OPERATIVE STORES AND
BULL PREFACE(40)	YOU ARE DEMONSTRATING THE UNFITNESS OF THE	IRISH	TO GOVERN THEMSELVES, AND THE SUPERIORITY OF THE OLD
BULL PREFACE(67)	NEEDED RECRUITS, TO COVER WITH APPEALS TO THE	IRISH	TO REMEMBER BELGIUM LEST THE FATE OF LOUVAIN SHOULD
BULL PREFACE(21)	CENTURY ARISTOCRATIC TYPE, THAN A SPECIFICALLY	IRISH	TYPE. GEORGE IV AND BYRON, CONTRASTED WITH GLADSTONE,
O'FL PREFACE(201)	TO ROMAN CATHOLIC OFFICERS, OR TO ALLOW DISTINCT	IRISH	UNITS TO BE FORMED, TO ATTRACT THEM, THE WALLS WERE
BULL II (102)	IF YOU DONT MIND, /KEEGAN/ (DROPPING THE BROAD	IRISH	VERNACULAR OF HIS SPEECH TO PATSY) AN HOUR IF YOU
BULL I (75)	BROADBENT. /BROADBENT/ (DELIGHTED WITH HIS	IRISH	VISITOR) GOOD AFTERNOON, MR HAFFIGAN. /TIM/ AN IS IT
BULL II (113)	BE PERSONAL, MISS REILLY; BUT THE CHARM OF YOUR	IRISH	VOICE-- /NORA/ (QUITE ACCUSTOMED TO GALLANTRY, AND
BULL III (124)	VOICE HAS A MOST EXTRAORDINARY EFFECT ON ME. THAT	IRISH	VOICE! /LARRY/ (SYMPATHETICALLY) YES, I KNOW. WHEN I
BULL PREFACE(33)	IT COST THE AMERICAN WAR OF INDEPENDENCE AND THE	IRISH	VOLUNTEER MOVEMENT TO OBTAIN THE IRISH PARLIAMENT OF
BULL I (79)	ME FACE. BUT I CONFESS TO THE GOODNATURE: IT'S AN	IRISH	WAKENESS. I'D SHARE ME LAST SHILLIN WITH A FRIEND.
BULL PREFACE(32)	AND SYMPATHETIC ALERTNESS-- IS TEMPERED, AS WE	IRISH	WELL KNOW, BY AN ABSURD SUSCEPTIBILITY TO
O'FL PREFACE(201)	IRISH RECRUITING WAS BADLY BUNGLED IN 1915. THE	IRISH	WERE FOR THE MOST PART ROMAN CATHOLICS AND LOYAL
BULL I (79)	(LAUGHING INDUSTRIOUSLY) CAPITAL. YOUR	IRISH	WIT HAS SETTLED THE FIRST DIFFICULTY. NOW ABOUT YOUR
BULL IV (180)	/KEEGAN/ SIR: WHEN YOU SPEAK TO ME OF ENGLISH AND	IRISH	YOU FORGET THAT I AM A CATHOLIC. MY COUNTRY IS NOT
BULL I (91)	NOT EVEN HOME RULE. WE OWE HOME RULE NOT TO THE	IRISH	, BUT TO OUR ENGLISH GLADSTONE. NO, LARRY: I CANT HELP
MTH4 I (155)	AND NO IRISHMAN EVER AGAIN CONFESSED TO BEING	IRISH	, EVEN TO HIS OWN CHILDREN; SO THAT WHEN THAT
MTH4 I (156)	SINCE THEN THE WORLD, BEREFT OF ITS JEWS AND ITS	IRISH	, HAS BEEN A TAME DULL PLACE. IS THERE NO PATHOS FOR
BULL III (118)	STILL, IT'S NO END OF A JOKE. HOW DO YOU LIKE THE	IRISH	, HODSON? /HODSON/ WELL, SIR, THEYRE ALL RIGHT
BULL PREFACE(39)	AND THAT IS WHY IT IS ONLY THE SMALL-MINDED	IRISH	, INCAPABLE OF CONCEIVING WHAT RELIGIOUS FREEDOM MEANS
FABL PREFACE(79)	ALL OTHER COUNTRIES " POLICE STATES." I, BEING	IRISH	, KNOW BETTER. TO RETURN TO THE INVETERACY OF
BULL PREFACE(5)	IN EGYPT AND INDIA MORE THAN IN IRELAND; FOR THE	IRISH	, NOW CONFIDENT THAT THEIR BATTLE IS WON, ARE KEEPING
CAPT NOTES (305)	DIPHTHONGAL OI, WHICH MR CHEVALIER STILL USES.	IRISH	, SCOTCH, AND NORTH COUNTRY READERS MUST REMEMBER THAT
BULL I (76)	NOT A WORD, SURE ITLL DO TOMORROW. BESIDES, I'M	IRISH	, SIR: A POOR AITHER, BUT A POWERFUL DHRINKER.
NEVR II (242)	LAGER FOR YOU, SIR. (TO CRAMPTON) SELTZER AND	IRISH	, SIR. (TO M'COMAS) APOLLINARIS, SIR. (TO DOLLY)
NEVR II (249)	NOTICED THAT YOU HADNT TOUCHED THAT SELTZER AND	IRISH	, SIR. WHEN THE PARTY BROKE UP. (HE TAKES THE TUMBLER
BULL PREFACE(4)	ENGLISH ELECTORS, BEING MOSTLY WORSE OFF THAN THE	IRISH	, WERE ANXIOUS TO HAVE SOMETHING DONE TO ALLEVIATE
MTH4 I (155)	A NATIONAL MOVEMENT. THINK OF THE POSITION OF THE	IRISH	, WHO HAD LOST ALL THEIR POLITICAL FACULTIES BY DISUSE
ROCK II (262)	THEM IN IRELAND WHEN YOU TRIED THAT GAME ON THE	IRISH	, WHO WERE ONLY A LITTLE HANDFUL OF PEASANTS IN THEIR
BULL IV (171)	IRISH! IRISH BOTH OF US TO THE BACKBONE: IRISH!	IRISH	! IRI-- BROADBENT ARRIVES, CONVERSING ENERGETICALLY
BULL IV (171)	HER AS SHE GOES) GOODBYE. GOODBYE. OH, THATS SO	IRISH	! IRISH BOTH OF US TO THE BACKBONE: IRISH! IRISH!
BULL IV (171)	SO IRISH! IRISH BOTH OF US TO THE BACKBONE:	IRISH	! IRISH! IRI-- BROADBENT ARRIVES, CONVERSING
DEST (193)	OH NO. AN IRISHWOMAN. /NAPOLEON/ (QUICKLY)	IRISH	! (THOUGHTFULLY) YES: I FORGOT THE IRISH. AN ENGLISH

IRISHMAN

O'FL (215)	WHAT NONSENSE! DOES SHE SUPPOSE MR ASQUITH IS AN	IRISHMAN	? /O'FLAHERTY/ SHE WONT GIVE HIM ANY CREDIT FOR
BULL PREFACE(15)	FELLOW-CREATURES WHO ARE ONLY ENGLISH. WHAT IS AN	IRISHMAN	? WHEN I SAY THAT I AM AN IRISHMAN I MEAN THAT I
BULL PREFACE(24)	GENERALS, THE EXPLANATION IS SIMPLY THAT I AM AN	IRISHMAN	AND YOU AN ENGLISHMAN. IRISH PROTESTANTISM REALLY
BULL PREFACE(17)	THE ENGLISHMAN IS ALWAYS GAPING ADMIRINGLY AT THE	IRISHMAN	AS AT SOME CLEVER CHILD PRODIGY. HE OVERRATES HIM
BULL I (83)	PUBLIC HOUSES ON THE WAY. SECOND, HE'S NOT AN	IRISHMAN	AT ALL. /BROADBENT/ NOT AN IRISHMAN! (HE IS SO
BULL PREFACE(9)	IT IS NOT UNNATURAL CRIME, LIKE THE SLAYING OF AN	IRISHMAN	BY AN IRISHMAN FOR ENGLAND'S SAKE. THERE WILL, OF
BULL PREFACE(9)	FOR IRELAND; AND THOUGH THE SLAYING OF AN	IRISHMAN	BY AN IRISHMAN FOR IRELAND MAY BE A TRAGEDY-- MAY
BULL I (83)	OR EVER WILL. BUT WHEN A THOROUGHLY WORTHLESS	IRISHMAN	COMES TO ENGLAND, AND FINDS THE WHOLE PLACE FULL OF
BULL II (116)	IS SENTIMENTAL HE BEHAVES VERY MUCH AS AN	IRISHMAN	DOES WHEN HE IS DRUNK).
MTH4 I (155)	THEY ALL LEFT FOR ENGLAND NEXT DAY; AND NO	IRISHMAN	EVER AGAIN CONFESSED TO BEING IRISH, EVEN TO HIS
BULL I (83)	LIKE THE ALBERT HALL CONCERTS OF IRISH MUSIC? NO	IRISHMAN	EVER TALKS LIKE THAT IN IRELAND, OR EVER DID, OR
BULL PREFACE(16)	BE BULLIED BY AN ENGLISHMAN; WHEN I SEE THE	IRISHMAN	EVERYWHERE STANDING CLEARHEADED, SANE, HARDILY
O'FL PREFACE(201)	AND PARTLY BECAUSE EVEN THE MOST COWARDLY	IRISHMAN	FEELS OBLIGED TO OUTDO AN ENGLISHMAN IN BRAVERY IF
BULL PREFACE(9)	CRIME, LIKE THE SLAYING OF AN IRISHMAN BY AN	IRISHMAN	FOR ENGLAND'S SAKE, THERE WILL, OF COURSE, BE NO
BULL PREFACE(9)	AND THOUGH THE SLAYING OF AN IRISHMAN BY AN	IRISHMAN	FOR IRELAND MAY BE A TRAGEDY-- MAY BE EVEN A CRIME
BULL PREFACE(21)	IN THIS HE IS MOST DANGEROUSLY WRONG. WHETHER THE	IRISHMAN	GRASPS THE TRUTH AS FIRMLY AS THE ENGLISHMAN MAY BE
SUPR PREFACE(R19)	INSTINCTIVELY FLATTERS THE FAULT THAT MAKES THE	IRISHMAN	HARMLESS AND AMUSING TO HIM. WHAT IS WRONG WITH THE
BULL PREFACE(39)	FAR AS MONEY OR COMFORT IS CONCERNED, THE AVERAGE	IRISHMAN	HAS A MORE TOLERABLE LIFE-- ESPECIALLY NOW THAT THE
UNPL PREFACE(R7)	NO ADMIRATION FOR POPULAR HEROICS. AS AN	IRISHMAN	I COULD PRETEND TO PATRIOTISM NEITHER FOR THE
BULL PREFACE(15)	WHAT IS AN IRISHMAN? WHEN I SAY THAT I AM AN	IRISHMAN	I MEAN THAT I WAS BORN IN IRELAND, AND THAT MY
BULL PREFACE(20)	OVER, AND IS THE MORE DELICIOUS BECAUSE THE REAL	IRISHMAN	IN IT IS THE ENGLISHMAN OF TRADITION, WHILST THE
SUPR PREFACE(R19)	ENGLISHMEN TEACH IRISHMEN TO BE PROUD. FOR THE	IRISHMAN	INSTINCTIVELY DISPARAGES THE QUALITY WHICH MAKES
O'FL PREFACE(202)	KNOWING THAT THE IGNORANCE AND INSULARITY OF THE	IRISHMAN	IS A DANGER TO HIMSELF AND TO HIS NEIGHBORS, I HAD
BULL PREFACE(30)	IRELAND. I HAVE ALREADY SAID THAT A " LOYAL"	IRISHMAN	IS AN ABHORRENT PHENOMENON, BECAUSE HE IS AN
BULL PREFACE(16)	BY ENGLISH INSTEAD OF IRISH FOLLY. A " LOYAL"	IRISHMAN	IS AN ABHORRENT PHENOMENON, BECAUSE IT IS AN
BULL IV (177)	OF CLEVERLY PROVING THAT EVERYBODY WHO IS NOT AN	IRISHMAN	IS AN ASS. IT IS NEITHER GOOD SENSE NOR GOOD
BULL PREFACE(40)	BE A VICTORY FOR THE NATIONALIST ENEMY. EVERY	IRISHMAN	IS IN LANCELOT'S POSITION: HIS HONOR ROOTED IN
BULL PREFACE(27)	DIFFER VERY VEHEMENTLY AS TO WHOSE SUBJECT THE	IRISHMAN	IS TO BE; BUT THEY ARE QUITE AGREED AS TO THE
BULL PREFACE(41)	STATION; EVERY CHURCH IS A BARRACK; AND EVERY	IRISHMAN	IS UNSPEAKABLY TIRED OF THE WHOLE MISERABLE
BULL PREFACE(16)	THE PROTESTANT GARRISON. THE MORE PROTESTANT AN	IRISHMAN	IS-- THE MORE ENGLISH HE IS, IF IT FLATTERS YOU TO
SUPR IV (160)	TO ITS OWNER) I MET ROEBUCK AND THAT AWFUL OLD	IRISHMAN	. ARE YOU SURE YOURE NOT ILL? WHATS THE MATTER?
BULL I (83)	/BROADBENT/ POOH! NONSENSE! HE'S ONLY AN	IRISHMAN	. BESIDES, YOU DONT SERIOUSLY SUPPOSE THAT HAFFIGAN
BULL PREFACE(39)	MORE AND MAKES LESS FUSS ABOUT IT THAN THE	IRISHMAN	. BUT AT LEAST HE HAS NOBODY TO BLAME BUT HIMSELF
BULL I (81)	BY PLUNGING AGAIN INTO HIS ROLE OF DAREDEVIL	IRISHMAN	. HE RUSHES TO BROADBENT; PLUCKS AT HIS SLEEVE WITH
BULL IV (151)	FROM THE DOORWAY) OH NO HE WONT: HE'S NOT AN	IRISHMAN	. HE'LL NEVER KNOW THEYRE LAUGHING AT HIM; AND
BULL III (140)	WITH A PIG IN THE CAR: I SHALL FEEL QUITE LIKE AN	IRISHMAN	. HODSON: STAY WITH MR HAFFIGAN; AND GIVE HIM A
BULL I (90)	AN IMAGINARY ONE. I OWE MORE TO YOU THAN TO ANY	IRISHMAN	. /BROADBENT/ (SHAKING HIS HEAD WITH A TWINKLE IN
BULL I (83)	BUT HE SPOKE-- HE BEHAVED JUST LIKE AN	IRISHMAN	. /DOYLE/ LIKE AN IRISHMAN! ! MAN ALIVE, DONT YOU
BULL IV (180)	BUT AT LEAST HE CAN FORGIVE YOU FOR BEING AN	IRISHMAN	. /KEEGAN/ SIR: WHEN YOU SPEAK TO ME OF ENGLISH AND
BULL III (121)	INDUSTRIOUS? THATS REMARKABLE, YOU KNOW, IN AN	IRISHMAN	. /LARRY/ INDUSTRIOUS! THAT MAN'S INDUSTRY USED TO
BULL III (123)	DEAD) I DONT KNOW, THATS THE SORT OF THING AN	IRISHMAN	LAUGHS AT. HAS SHE ACCEPTED YOU? /BROADBENT/ I
BULL PREFACE(21)	BETWEEN THE ENGLISH AND IRISH IDIOSYNCRASIES. THE	IRISHMAN	MAKES A DISTINCTION WHICH THE ENGLISHMAN IS TOO
BULL PREFACE(16)	UNPARALLELED POLITICAL TRAITOR: ALL THESE YOUR	IRISHMAN	MAY EASILY BE, JUST AS HE MAY BE A GENTLEMAN (A
BULL PREFACE(29)	OF STATE ARE TO BE DISCUSSED, JUST AS AN	IRISHMAN	MAY HAVE ENGLISH FRIENDS WHOM HE MAY PREFER TO ANY
BULL PREFACE(29)	HAVE ENGLISH FRIENDS WHOM HE MAY PREFER TO ANY	IRISHMAN	OF HIS ACQUAINTANCE, AND BE KIND, HOSPITABLE, AND
3PLA PREFACE(R39)	THAT MARKS THE WORK OF EVERY LITERARY	IRISHMAN	OF MY GENERATION WILL SEEM ANTIQUATED AND SILLY. IT
BULL PREFACE(6)	RULE YEAR, BECAUSE ITS PREFACE WAS WRITTEN BY AN	IRISHMAN	OF PROTESTANT FAMILY AND PROTESTANT PREJUDICES, AND
BULL PREFACE(15)	FOR ABORIGINAL IRISH: I AM A GENUINE TYPICAL	IRISHMAN	OF THE DANISH, NORMAN, CROMWELLIAN, AND (OF
BULL PREFACE(41)	HAS GIVEN RISE TO THE PROVERB THAT IF YOU PUT AN	IRISHMAN	ON A SPIT YOU CAN ALWAYS GET ANOTHER IRISHMAN TO
PYGM I (213)	CAN MAKE A LIVING BY HIS HOBBY! YOU CAN SPOT AN	IRISHMAN	OR A YORKSHIREMAN BY HIS BROGUE. I CAN PLACE ANY
BULL IV (179)	NOW I PITY IT. (BROADBENT CAN HARDLY CONCEIVE AN	IRISHMAN	PITYING ENGLAND; BUT AS LARRY INTERVENES ANGRILY,
BULL IV (150)	LEGALLY POSSIBLE I SHOULD BECOME A NATURALIZED	IRISHMAN	; AND IF EVER IT BE MY GOOD FORTUNE TO REPRESENT AN
BULL I (91)	YOU ABOUT THEM. /BROADBENT/ YES; BUT YOU ARE AN	IRISHMAN	; AND THESE THINGS ARE NOT SERIOUS TO YOU AS THEY
BULL I (92)	BROADBENT: I SURRENDER. THE POOR SILLY-CLEVER	IRISHMAN	TAKES OFF HIS HAT TO GOD'S ENGLISHMAN. THE MAN WHO
BULL III (135)	THE GREAT DUKE OF WELLINGTON WAS THE MOST TYPICAL	IRISHMAN	THAT EVER LIVED. OF COURSE THATS AN ABSURD PARADOX;

BULL PREFACE(41) AN IRISHMAN ON A SPIT YOU CAN ALWAYS GET ANOTHER IRISHMAN TO BASTE HIM. JINGO ORATORY IN ENGLAND IS SICKENING
O'FL PREFACE(201) HEADED REMEMBER BELGIUM. THE FOLLY OF ASKING AN IRISHMAN TO REMEMBER ANYTHING WHEN YOU WANT HIM TO FIGHT FOR
BULL PREFACE(14) COULD INSPIRE STRONG AFFECTION AND LOYALTY IN AN IRISHMAN WHO KNEW THE WORLD AND WAS MOVED ONLY TO DISLIKE,
BULL PREFACE(26) BY REGARDING A METHODIST AS TOLERANTLY AS AN IRISHMAN WHO LIKES GROG REGARDS AN IRISHMAN WHO PREFERS
BULL PREFACE(26) AS AN IRISHMAN WHO LIKES GROG REGARDS AN IRISHMAN WHO PREFERS PUNCH, A FUNDAMENTAL ANOMALY. NOW
SUPR IV SD(142) THAT FALLS FROM HIM IT IS CLEAR THAT HE IS AN IRISHMAN WHOSE NATIVE INTONATION HAS CLUNG TO HIM THROUGH
BULL III (121) TO GET HIM TO DO THAT WITHOUT SCAMPING IT; BUT AN IRISHMAN WILL WORK AS IF HE'D DIE THE MOMENT HE STOPPED.
BULL PREFACE(19) AND RHAPSODE, A THEATRICALITY WHICH IN AN IRISHMAN WOULD HAVE BEEN AN INSUFFERABLY VULGAR AFFECTATION,
BULL PREFACE(22) HAROLD SKIMPOLE. ON THE OTHER HAND, IT TAKES AN IRISHMAN YEARS OF RESIDENCE IN ENGLAND TO LEARN TO RESPECT
BULL I (82) THERE YOU GO! WHY ARE YOU SO DOWN ON EVERY IRISHMAN YOU MEET, ESPECIALLY IF HE'S A BIT SHABBY? POOR
SIM PREFACE(11) THEM HAD TO BE FIERCELY IN EARNEST. I, AN OLD IRISHMAN , AM TOO USED TO COERCION ACTS, SUSPENSIONS OF THE
BULL IV (170) NORA, DEAR, DONT YOU UNDERSTAND THAT I'M AN IRISHMAN , AND HE'S AN ENGLISHMAN. HE WANTS YOU; AND HE
BULL PREFACE(19) THE DUKE OF WELLINGTON, THAT INTENSELY IRISH IRISHMAN , AND NELSON, THAT INTENSELY ENGLISH ENGLISHMAN.
BULL I (75) HIM, SIR. /BROADBENT/ OH, HE'S ALL RIGHT. HE'S AN IRISHMAN , AND NOT VERY PARTICULAR ABOUT HIS APPEARANCE.
BULL IV (150) I AM GLAD TO SAY THAT PATSY TOOK IT LIKE AN IRISHMAN , AND, FAR FROM EXPRESSING ANY VINDICTIVE FEELING,
BULL PREFACE(64) AND INADEQUATELY, BECAUSE I AM HAMPERED, AS AN IRISHMAN , BY MY IMPLACABLE HOSTILITY TO ENGLISH DOMINATION.
MILL PREFACE(124) WORLD IF THE JEWS HAD NEVER EXISTED. BUT I, AS AN IRISHMAN , CAN, WITH PATRIOTIC RELISH, DEMONSTRATE THE SAME
BULL IV (154) NOT AT ALL, NOT AT ALL. ONLY A WHIMSICAL IRISHMAN , EH? /LARRY/ ARE YOU REALLY MAD, MR KEEGAN?
BULL PREFACE(15) TO GIVE HIM A PIECE OF MY MIND HERE, AS AN IRISHMAN , FULL OF AN INSTINCTIVE PITY FOR THOSE OF MY
GENV III (83) /THE JUDGE/ AT LEAST YOU ARE NOT A SCOT, NOR AN IRISHMAN , NOR A MAN OF KENT, NOR A MAN OF DEVON, NOR A
BULL PREFACE(18) THE IDOLATROUS ENGLISHMAN AND THE FACT-FACING IRISHMAN , OF THE SAME EXTRACTION THOUGH THEY BE, REMAINS TO
BULL PREFACE(15) TODAY, WHEN HE IS NOT A TRANSPLANTED SCOTCHMAN OR IRISHMAN , OFTEN TURNS OUT ON INVESTIGATION TO BE, IF NOT AN
O'FL (214) (OVER HIS SHOULDER) SHE SAYS GLADSTONE WAS AN IRISHMAN , SIR. WHAT CALL WOULD HE HAVE TO MEDDLE WITH
BULL IV (180) SO CLEVER IN YOUR FOOLISHNESS, AND THIS IRISHMAN , SO FOOLISH IN HIS CLEVERNESS, I CANNOT IN MY
BULL IV (163) MAKE AS MUCH DIFFERENCE IN YOU AS IT WOULD IN AN IRISHMAN , SOMEHOW. /BROADBENT/ PERHAPS NOT. PERHAPS NOT. I
BULL PREFACE(18) HAVING NO SENSE OF REALITY TO CHECK IT. THE IRISHMAN , WITH A FAR SUBTLER AND MORE FASTIDIOUS
BULL I (79) WAY? THAT I SAW AT ONCE THAT YOU ARE A THOROUGH IRISHMAN , WITH ALL THE FAULTS AND ALL THE QUALITIES OF YOUR
POSN PREFACE(376) THE BOOKS. FOR INSTANCE, MR HUGH LAW, BEING AN IRISHMAN , WITH AN IRISHMAN'S SENSE OF HOW TO BEHAVE LIKE A
BULL PREFACE(31) HIM ASK HIMSELF WHICH LEADER HE, IF HE WERE AN IRISHMAN , WOULD RATHER HAVE BACK FROM THE GRAVE TO FIGHT
BULL I (83) HE'S NOT AN IRISHMAN AT ALL. /BROADBENT/ NOT AN IRISHMAN ! (HE IS SO AMAZED BY THE STATEMENT THAT HE
BULL I (83) HE BEHAVED JUST LIKE AN IRISHMAN. /DOYLE/ LIKE AN IRISHMAN ! ! MAN ALIVE, DONT YOU KNOW THAT ALL THIS

IRISHMAN'S

BULL I (85) IN YOUR HEART-- /DOYLE/ NEVER MIND MY HEART: AN IRISHMAN'S HEART IS NOTHING BUT HIS IMAGINATION. HOW MANY OF
O'FL PREFACE(202) FROM THE RECORDS OF IRISH EMIGRATION, THAT ALL AN IRISHMAN'S HOPES AND AMBITIONS TURN ON HIS OPPORTUNITIES OF
BULL I (87) AND USEFULNESS OUT OF HIM LIKE THAT DREAMING. AN IRISHMAN'S IMAGINATION NEVER LETS HIM ALONE, NEVER CONVINCES
SUPR PREFACE(R19) FUNDAMENTAL CONSTITUTION OF LONDON SOCIETY AS AN IRISHMAN'S REPROACH TO YOUR NATION. FROM THE DAY I FIRST SET
POSN PREFACE(376) INSTANCE, MR HUGH LAW, BEING AN IRISHMAN, WITH AN IRISHMAN'S SENSE OF HOW TO BEHAVE LIKE A GALLANT GENTLEMAN

IRISHMEN

O'FL PREFACE(202) WERE PRESENTLY SUPPLEMENTED BY A FRESH APPEAL. IRISHMEN : DO YOU WISH TO HAVE THE HORRORS OF WAR BROUGHT TO
BULL IV (179) EVEN A LAND DEVELOPMENT SYNDICATE OF ANGLICIZED IRISHMEN AND GLADSTONIZED ENGLISHMEN. /LARRY/ OH, IN HEAVEN,
BULL PREFACE(52) PLUNDER WAS NOT GONE INTO. THE OFFICERS, TWO IRISHMEN AND THREE ENGLISHMEN, HAVING MADE A HOPELESS MESS
BULL PREFACE(17) BEING EQUAL. SUCH CONSIDERATIONS PRODUCE LOYAL IRISHMEN AS THEY PRODUCE LOYAL POLES AND FINS, LOYAL
BULL IV (179) YES, PERHAPS, EVEN ON THIS HOLY GROUND WHICH SUCH IRISHMEN AS YOU HAVE TURNED INTO A LAND OF DERISION.
BULL I (76) A FAIR HALF. THANKYA. /BROADBENT/ (LAUGHING) YOU IRISHMEN CERTAINLY DO KNOW HOW TO DRINK. (POURING SOME
BULL PREFACE(19) DONT BE A DAMNED FOOL." IT IS THE FORMULA OF ALL IRISHMEN FOR ALL ENGLISHMEN TO THIS DAY. IT IS THE FORMULA
BULL PREFACE(52) BUT THE THIRD, THE YOUNGEST, SEEING THE TWO IRISHMEN HARD PUT TO IT, WENT BACK AND STOOD BY THEM. OF THE
BULL PREFACE(7) TO BE GOVERNED FROM LONDON? THE GREAT PROTESTANT IRISHMEN HAVE BEEN ALL THE MORE POWERFUL BECAUSE THEY LOVED
SUPR HANDBOK(197) TO THE FENIAN WHO COLLECTS MONEY FROM THOUGHTLESS IRISHMEN IN AMERICA TO BLOW UP DUBLIN CASTLE; TO THE
BULL PREFACE(52) SHOULD RUN AWAY TO CAMP AND BRING HELP TO THE IRISHMEN . THEY BOLTED ACCORDINGLY; BUT THE THIRD, THE
BULL IV (165) THAT SORT OF THING TO YOUR DAMNED SENTIMENTAL IRISHMEN . YOU THINK I HAVE NO FEELING BECAUSE I AM A PLAIN
BULL PREFACE(17) PERSONALLY I LIKE ENGLISHMEN MUCH BETTER THAN IRISHMEN (NO DOUBT BECAUSE THEY MAKE MORE OF ME) JUST AS
BULL PREFACE(66) I HAD NO PREVISION. AT EASTER 1916 A HANDFUL OF IRISHMEN SEIZED THE DUBLIN POST OFFICE AND PROCLAIMED AN
SUPR PREFACE(R19) KNEW THE VALUE OF THE PROSAIC QUALITIES OF WHICH IRISHMEN TEACH ENGLISHMEN TO BE ASHAMED AS WELL AS I KNEW
SUPR PREFACE(R19) OF THE POETIC QUALITIES OF WHICH ENGLISHMEN TEACH IRISHMEN TO BE PROUD. FOR THE IRISHMAN INSTINCTIVELY
O'FL PREFACE(201) REMEMBERING BELGIUM AND ITS BROKEN TREATY LED IRISHMEN TO REMEMBER LIMERICK AND ITS BROKEN TREATY; AND THE
BULL III (132) TO HAS GONE PAST YOU AND LEFT YOU. ANYHOW, WE IRISHMEN WERE NEVER MADE TO BE FARMERS; AND WE'LL NEVER DO
BULL IV (174) BECAUSE I'M AN ENGLISHMAN AND HAFFIGAN AND CO ARE IRISHMEN , BUT BECAUSE THEYRE DUFFERS, AND I KNOW MY WAY
MTH4 I (155) THROUGHOUT EUROPE. IT WAS THEN THAT THESE DEVOTED IRISHMEN , NOT ONE OF WHOM HAD EVER SEEN IRELAND, WERE
O'FL PREFACE(201) WERE FOR THE MOST PART ROMAN CATHOLICS AND LOYAL IRISHMEN , WHICH MEANS THAT FROM THE ENGLISH POINT OF VIEW
BULL IV (179) CARE! YOU WILL BE QUARRELLING PRESENTLY. OH, YOU IRISHMEN , YOU IRISHMEN! TOUJOURS BALLYHOOLY, EH? (LARRY,
BULL IV (179) BE QUARRELLING PRESENTLY. OH, YOU IRISHMEN, YOU IRISHMEN ! TOUJOURS BALLYHOOLY, EH? (LARRY, WITH A SHRUG,

IRISHWOMAN

DEST (193) WAS-- WHAT? A FRENCHWOMAN? /LADY/ OH NO. AN IRISHWOMAN . /NAPOLEON/ (QUICKLY) IRISH! (THOUGHTFULLY)
BULL IV (164) I HAVE ALWAYS THOUGHT I SHOULD LIKE TO MARRY AN IRISHWOMAN . SHE WOULD ALWAYS UNDERSTAND MY JOKES. FOR

IRISHWOMEN

BULL II SD(101) DRAMATIZING AND EXPLOITING IT, AS THE IRISHWOMEN IN ENGLAND DO. FOR TOM BROADBENT THEREFORE, AN

IRKSOME

HART PREFACE(19) III AND THE MADNESS OF DON QUIXOTE EXTREMELY IRKSOME . BUT THAT CHANGE HAD TO BE MADE; AND WE ARE ALL THE
GETT PREFACE(239) IS ALMOST THE ONLY DISCOMFORT SUFFICIENTLY IRKSOME TO INDUCE A WOMAN TO BREAK UP HER HOME, AND ECONOMIC
O'FL PREFACE(202) AND SHREWS, NONE OF WHOM ARE ANY THE LESS IRKSOME WHEN THEY HAPPEN BY ILL-LUCK TO BE ALSO OUR FATHERS,

IRON

LADY (243) THEM. YOU HOLD ME AS THE LODESTAR HOLDS THE IRON : I CANNOT BUT CLING TO YOU. WE ARE LOST, YOU AND I:
FANY II (295) ME WAITING, AMELIA? DO YOU THINK I'M MADE OF IRON ? WHATS THE GIRL DONE? WHAT ARE WE GOING TO DO? /MRS
LION I (117) A ROMAN SOLDIER? /THE CAPTAIN/ IT WILL SOON BE IRON AGAIN. I HAVE SEEN MANY WOMEN DIE, AND FORGOTTEN THEM
LION PREFACE(55) TAXGATHERER, TO THE MEN FROM WHOM HE BOUGHT THE IRON AND ANVIL AND THE COALS, LEAVING ONLY A SCRAP OF ITS
GETT SD(260) SPIT LIKE A BABY CRANE, AND A COLLECTION OF OLD IRON AND BRASS INSTRUMENTS WHICH PASS AS THE ORIGINAL
ROCK PREFACE(188) THE RULE OF GOD: FAITH IN NOTHING BUT BLOOD AND IRON AND GOLD. YOU, STANDING FOR ROME, ARE THE UNIVERSAL
KING I SD(161) FIRST FLOOR THROUGH A LARGE WINDOW WHICH HAS AN IRON BALCONY OUTSIDE, WITH AN IRON STAIRCASE DOWN TO THE
LION II (146) FROM THE PASSAGE WITH OTHER KEEPERS ARMED WITH IRON BARS AND TRIDENTS). TAKE THOSE THINGS AWAY. I HAVE
ROCK PREFACE(156) ON THE WHEEL: THAT IS, BATTERED TO DEATH WITH IRON BARS, UNTIL WELL INTO THE NINETEENTH CENTURY. THIS WAS
ARMS I SD(3) THE OTTOMAN AND WINDOW, CONSISTS OF AN ENAMELLED IRON BASIN WITH A PAIL BENEATH IT IN A PAINTED METAL FRAME,
HART II (92) FOR HIM: A MAN ACCUSTOMED TO HAVE GREAT MASSES OF IRON BEATEN INTO SHAPE FOR HIM BY STEAM-HAMMERS! TO FIGHT
DOCT II (118) WELL UP. DONT THINK YOUR LUNGS ARE MADE OF IRON BECAUSE THEYRE BETTER THAN HIS. GOODNIGHT. /MRS
LION I (117) KNOWLEDGE. /LAVINIA/ SOMETHING STIRS, EVEN IN THE IRON BREAST OF A ROMAN SOLDIER? /THE CAPTAIN/ IT WILL SOON
JOAN 3 (89) TRYING TO TRAP THEM, AND I WILL PUT YOU IN THE IRON CAGE FOR A MONTH TO TEACH YOU WHAT A CAGE FEELS LIKE.
GENV IV SD(122) TO THEIR FEET EXCEPT BATTLER, WHO PRESERVES AN IRON CALM. /JUDGE/ IS THIS TRUE, MR BATTLER? /BATTLER/ I AM
CYMB V SD(140) BUT WEARING A ROMAN SWORD AND A SOLDIER'S IRON CAP. HE HAS IN HIS HAND A BLOODSTAINED HANDKERCHIEF.
MRS III (229) TO SUPPORT HERSELF. THEN SHE GETS QUICKLY TO THE IRON CHAIR AND SITS DOWN). WHAT BUSINESS ARE YOU TALKING
O'FL SD(205) UNDER THE WINDOW IS A GARDEN SEAT WITH AN IRON CHAIR AT EACH END OF IT. THE LAST FOUR BARS OF GOD SAVE
MRS III SD(220) AND THERE IS A SUNDIAL ON THE TURF, WITH AN IRON CHAIR NEAR IT. A LITTLE PATH LEADS OFF THROUGH THE BOX
O'FL SD(226) LONG TIME NOTHING IS SAID. SIR PEARCE SITS ON AN IRON CHAIR. O'FLAHERTY SITS ON THE GARDEN SEAT. THE THRUSH
O'FL (206) ENJOY YOUR HOLIDAY (HE SITS DOWN ON ONE OF THE IRON CHAIRS: THE ONE AT THE DOORLESS SIDE OF THE PORCH).
NEVR II SD(236) GOT OVER THAT INFERNAL GAS YET. HE GOES TO THE IRON CHAIR, SO THAT HE CAN LEAN HIS ELBOWS ON THE LITTLE
CAND II (121) THE MATTER? /MORELL/ (DEADLY WHITE, PUTTING AN IRON CONSTRAINT ON HIMSELF) NOTHING BUT THIS: THAT EITHER
BULL IV SD(149) MUST LAUGH OR BURST, HURRIES OUT. BARNEY PUTS AN IRON CONSTRAINT ON HIS FEATURES. /BROADBENT/ ALL I CAN SAY
3PLA PREFACE(R20) NATURALLY AS ANY OTHER PASSION. THERE IS NO CAST IRON CONVENTION AS TO ITS EFFECTS; NO FALSE ASSOCIATION OF
GENV PREFACE(18) HE HAD ACHIEVED NO MORE AS A SOLDIER THAN THE IRON CROSS AND THE RANK OF CORPORAL. HE WAS POOR AND WHAT WE
2TRU PREFACE(19) PIRATE SHIP NEEDS A HIERARCHY OF OFFICERS AND AN IRON DISCIPLINE EVEN MORE THAN POLICE BOATS, AND THAT THE
MRS I (196) SIR; AND I DONT WANT TO HEAR IT. /FRANK/ THE OLD IRON DUKE DIDNT THROW AWAY 50 POUNDS: NOT HE. HE JUST WROTE:
MIS. PREFACE(56) RESULT (AMONG OTHERS LESS MENTIONABLE) THAT THE IRON DUKE OF WELLINGTON COMPLAINED THAT IT WAS IMPOSSIBLE TO
BULL PREFACE(20) EYES OF THE WHOLE WORLD TO THE CATASTROPHE, THE IRON DUKE WOULD HAVE BEEN ALMOST FORGOTTEN BY THIS TIME. NOW

APPL I SD(213)	AND OF BOANERGES, WHO SQUARES HIMSELF WITH AN	IRON	FACE. /PLINY/ NO: DONT DO THAT, JOE. /BALBUS/ WHAT!
MRS PREFACE(166)	OF PROBLEM, WITH ITS REMORSELESS LOGIC AND	IRON	FRAMEWORK OF FACT, INEVITABLY PRODUCES AT FIRST AN
PRES SD(156)	AT ONCE. THE ORDERLY FORLORNLY CONTEMPLATES THE	IRON	FRONT PRESENTED BY MRS BANGER. /THE ORDERLY/ (
SUPR IV SD(141)	SET OF CROQUET HOOPS, BUT, ON OUR LEFT, A LITTLE	IRON	GARDEN TABLE WITH BOOKS ON IT, MOSTLY YELLOW-BACKED,
DEVL II SD(28)	WITH BOILER, TOASTER HANGING ON THE BARS, MOVABLE	IRON	GRIDDLE SOCKETED TO THE HOB, HOOK ABOVE FOR ROASTING,
JOAN PREFACE(22)	PROPORTION OF SOCIAL FORCES. SHE KNEW NOTHING OF	IRON	HANDS IN VELVET GLOVES: SHE JUST USED HER FISTS. SHE
BULL PREFACE(15)	THEY ARE THE VIRTUES OF THE MONEY THAT COAL AND	IRON	HAVE PRODUCED. BUT AS THE MINERAL VIRTUES ARE BEING
CAND II (121)	VOICE) I HAD RATHER YOU HAD PLUNGED A GRAPPLING	IRON	INTO MY HEART THAN GIVEN ME THAT KISS. /CANDIDA/ (
JOAN 5 (114)	CAN TELL YOU: THAT YOU MUST STRIKE WHILE THE	IRON	IS HOT? I TELL YOU WE MUST MAKE A DASH AT COMPIEGNE
MTH5 (230)	TO BE ABLE TO DISTINGUISH BETWEEN WOOD AND SOFT	IRON	. IN THOSE DAYS THEY WERE VERY IGNORANT OF THE
GETT (335)	FOUGHT SEVEN DUELS WITH SABRES. IVE MUSCLES OF	IRON	. NOTHING HURTS ME: NOT EVEN BROKEN BONES. FIGHTING IS
DEVL II (39)	(HE LOOKS UP QUICKLY AT HER, WITH A FACE OF	IRON	. SHE STOPS HER MOUTH HASTILY WITH THE HAND SHE HAS
2TRU II (77)	SHE CAN RUN LIKE A DEER. AND SHE HAS MUSCLES OF	IRON	. YOU HAD BETTER TURN OUT THE GUARD BEFORE YOU TACKLE
6CAL SD(97)	AND HALTERS, EACH CARRYING A BUNCH OF MASSIVE	IRON	KEYS. THEIR LEADER, EUSTACHE DE ST PIERRE, KNEELS AT
NEVR II SD(225)	A MIDDLE AGED GENTLEMAN SITTING ON A CHAIR OF	IRON	LATHS AT A LITTLE IRON TABLE WITH A BOWL OF LUMP SUGAR
DEVL I SD(4)	OVER HER HEAD, AND HER FEET ON A BROAD FENDER OF	IRON	LATHS, THE STEP OF THE DOMESTIC ALTAR OF THE FIREPLACE,
FABL PREFACE(97)	HAD ALREADY DEMONSTRATED THE INJUSTICE OF ITS "	IRON	LAW OF WAGES." ENGLAND'S SHAMEFACED LEADERSHIP. ENGLAND
2TRU III (110)	ENABLE THEM TO BEAR ONE ANOTHER'S COMPANY? THE	IRON	LIGHTNING OF WAR HAS BURNT GREAT RENTS IN THESE ANGELIC
LION PREFACE(93)	THEN, TOO, THERE IS THE ATTITUDE OF IBSEN: THAT	IRON	MORALIST TO WHOM THE WHOLE SCHEME OF SALVATION WAS ONLY
GETT SD(262)	UP MAN OF FIFTY, WITH LARGE BRAVE NOSTRILS, AN	IRON	MOUTH, FAITHFUL DOG'S EYES, AND MUCH NATURAL SIMPLICITY
GENV I SD(29)	THE WALL NEAR THE DOOR. THE STOVE, AN UNDECORATED	IRON	ONE OF THE PLAINEST SORT, DESIGNED RATHER FOR CENTRAL
2TRU PREFACE(12)	ADDITION THAT THEI GOLD CHAINS ARE AS BAD AS THE	IRON	ONES, CANNOT SILENCE THEM, BECAUSE THEY THINK THEY ARE
2TRU PREFACE(11)	A NEW ONE AND SELLING YOUR OLD ONE AT SCRAP	IRON	PRICES. COME AND BUY OUR LATEST FASHIONS IN DRESS: YOU
APPL I (238)	HAVE TO SELL IT TO BREAKAGES, LIMITED, AT SCRAP	IRON	PRICES. I -- I -- OH, IT IS BEYOND BEARING (SHE BREAKS
CAND I SD(77)	MILES AND MILES OF UNLOVELY BRICK HOUSES, BLACK	IRON	RAILINGS, STONY PAVEMENTS, SLATED ROOFS, AND
JITT I (24)	(HE KISSES HER LIPS). WHAT A FOOL I WAS WITH MY	IRON	RESOLUTIONS! ONE THROB OF YOUR BREAST, ONE TOUCH OF
DEST (169)	AND HAD BECOME STRENGTH, PENETRATION, VIGILANCE,	IRON	RESOLUTION! HOW WOULD YOU ANSWER THEN IF YOU WERE
ROCK II (273)	/BARKING/ (BARRING HER WAY WITH AN ARM OF	IRON	) LADIES BE DAMNED! YOURE NO LADY. (HE COMES PAST THE
LION I (124)	THROAT). /FERROVIUS/ (HOLDING HIM IN A GRASP OF	IRON	) WHATS THIS, BROTHER? ANGER! VIOLENCE! RAISING YOUR
FANY I SD(275)	OR MORE, OF GOOD APPEARANCE AND ADDRESS, AND	IRON	SELF-COMMAND. /JUGGINS/ (PRESENTING THE SALVER TO MR
CLEO III SD(144)	IS A STOUT WOODEN SHAFT 4 1-2 FEET LONG, WITH AN	IRON	SPIT ABOUT THREE FEET LONG FIXED IN IT. THE SENTINEL IS
KING I SD(161)	WINDOW WHICH HAS AN IRON BALCONY OUTSIDE, WITH AN	IRON	STAIRCASE DOWN TO THE GARDEN LEVEL. THE DIVISION OF THE
LION I (115)	-- WHEN THESEI MEN DRAG ME TO THE FOOT OF AN	IRON	STATUE THAT HAS BECOME THE SYMBOL OF THE TERROR AND
NEVR II (257)	YOUVE DONE WITHI ME FOR EVER. (HE GOES TO THE	IRON	TABLE AND TAKES UP HIS HAT). /GLORIA/ (WITH ELABORATE
NEVR II SD(225)	ARE UNTOUCHED BY ENVY. THE GENTLEMAN AT THE	IRON	TABLE IS NOT DRESSED FOR THE SEASIDE. HE WEARS HIS
SUPR IV (145)	DOWN, EXAMINING HER CURIOUSLY AS SHE GOES TO THE	IRON	TABLE TO PUT DOWN THE BOOKS. WHEN SHE TURNS TO HIM
NEVR II SD(225)	SITTING ON A CHAIR OF IRON LATHS AT A LITTLE	IRON	TABLE WITH A BOWL OF LUMP SUGAR ON IT, READING AN
NEVR II (235)	THE COMMUNICATION, PHIL SEATS HIMSELF ON THE	IRON	TABLE WITH A SPRING, AND LOOKS AT THE WAITER WITH HIS
NEVR II (255)	(HE TAKES OFF HIS HAT AND THROWS IT GAILY ON THE	IRON	TABLE). NO: WHAT I WANT IS TO GET RID OF ALL THAT
NEVR II (249)	EARNINGS COME TO. (HE CROSSES THE TERRACE TO THE	IRON	TABLE, AND SITS DOWN). /WAITER/ (PHILOSOPHICALLY)
NEVR II (246)	THEN TAKES HIS HAT AND UMBRELLA FROM THE LITTLE	IRON	TABLE, AND TURNS TOWARDS THE STEPS. MEANWHILE THE
CAND I SD(77)	MYRIAD-POPULATED; WELL SERVED WITH UGLY	IRON	URINALS, RADICAL CLUBS, AND TRAM LINES CARRYING A
DEVL I SD(4)	ON A NAIL, WITH ITS WHITE WOODEN DIAL, BLACK	IRON	WEIGHTS, AND BRASS PENDULUM. BETWEEN THE CLOCK AND THE
CLEO PRO1 (91)	THE IMPOSSIBLE CAME TO PASS; THE BLOOD AND	IRON	YE PIN YOUR FAITH ON FELL BEFORE THE SPIRIT OF MAN; FOR
PRES (155)	THIS QUESTION MUST BE SOLVED BY BLOOD AND	IRON	, AS WAS WELL SAID BY BISMARCK, WHOM I HAVE REASON TO
ARMS II SD(36)	SHE HAD STABBED HIM. THEN, SETTING HIS FACE LIKE	IRON	, HE STRIDES GRIMLY TO HER, AND GRIPS HER ABOVE THE
BULL PREFACE(15)	NOT LESS REAL BECAUSE THEY CONSIST OF COAL AND	IRON	, NOT OF METAPHYSICAL SOURCES OF CHARACTER. THE VIRTUES
BUOY II SD(18)	VERANDAH TO THE GROUND. THE ROOF IS OF CORRUGATED	IRON	, PAINTED GREEN. THE SON, DRESSED IN FLANNEL SLACKS, A
HART II (98)	ALL THE STRENGTH I CAN GET TO LEAN ON: SOMETHING	IRON	, SOMETHING STONY, I DONT CARE HOW CRUEL IT IS, YOU GO

IRONCLAD

DOCT PREFACE(32)	THAN THE TRADITIONAL CEREMONY OF CHRISTENING AN	IRONCLAD	HAS TO DO WITH THE EFFECTIVENESS OF ITS ARMAMENT.
SUPR I (11)	THE LATEST GAME. ANI ORPHAN! IT'S LIKE HEARING AN	IRONCLAD	TALK ABOUT BEING AT THE MERCY OF THE WINDS AND

IRONIC

ARMS II SD(29)	HE HAS ACQUIRED THE HALF TRAGIC, HALF	IRONIC	AIR, THE MYSTERIOUS MOODINESS, THE SUGGESTION OF A
BARB III (329)	FOREMAN) ANYTHING WRONG, BILTON? /BILTON/ (WITH	IRONIC	CALM) GENTLEMAN WALKED INTO THE HIGH EXPLOSIVES SHED
LADY PREFACE(211)	WORLD OF LONDON THERE WAS A SHARP STROKE OF	IRONIC	COMEDY IN THE IRRESISTIBLE VERDICT IN ITS FAVOR. IN
BARB PREFACE(237)	HE IS KILLED BY A CAUTIOUS MATADOR. BUT THE	IRONIC	CONTRAST BETWEEN THE BULLFIGHT AND THE SACRAMENT OF
SUPR III (103)	THERE ARE NO HARD FACTS TO CONTRADICT YOU, NO	IRONIC	CONTRAST OF YOUR NEEDS WITH YOUR PRETENSIONS, NO
DEVL EPILOG (82)	BY STUPID PEOPLE BECAUSE OF THEIR DREAD OF	IRONIC	CRITICISM, LONG AFTER HIS DEATH, THACKERAY, WHO HAD
HART PREFACE(18)	CONTRIVING OF RUINI AND SLAUGHTER, FOR IT GAVE AN	IRONIC	EDGE TO THEIR TRAGEDY THAT THE VERY TALENTS THEY WERE
FANY III (314)	HAS BEEN: NOT IN EITHER OF YOU. /GILBEY/ (WITH	IRONIC	HUMILITY) I'M SURE I'M OBLIGED TO YOU FOR YOUR GOOD
BARB II (293)	BUT YOU APPEAL VERY STRONGLY TO MY SENSE OF	IRONIC	HUMOR. UNDERSHAFT MUTELY OFFERS HIS HAND. THEY SHAKE.
CAPT I (237)	ON THE WEST COAST. /DRINKWATER/ (AFFECTING AN	IRONIC	INDIFFERENCE) GOW ORN, GOW ORN. SR AHRD EZ ERD
FOUN (211)	MACDUFF: A CHAIRI. /THE LORD CHANCELLOR/ (WITH	IRONIC	POLITENESS) YOU ARE TOO GOOD. (HE SITS DOWN).

IRONICAL

DEVL II (34)	WHOEVER IT BELONGS TO. (RICHARD MAKES HIM AN	IRONICAL	BOW. ANDERSON RETURNS THE BOW HUMOROUSLY). COME:
APPL I (230)	(WITH PLACID BUT FORMIDABLE OBSTINACY AND	IRONICAL	EXPLICITNESS) I SAID WHICH? YOU SAID THAT IF TWO
DEST (185)	I CATCH THAT FELLOW FOR YOU! /NAPOLEON/ (WITH	IRONICAL	GRAVITY) YOU WILL NOT CATCH HIM, MY FRIEND.
AUGS (269)	KNOW THAT WE AREI AT WAR? /THE CLERK/ (FEEBLY	IRONICAL	) I HAVE NOTICED SOMETHING ABOUT IT IN THE PAPERS.
OVER (180)	PRESENCE HERE IS A ROMANCE. /MRS LUNN/ (FAINTLY	IRONICAL	) INDEED? /JUNO/ YES. YOUVE GUESSED, OF COURSE,
BARB II (305)	REASONABLENESS WHICH CUSINS ALONE PERCEIVES TO BE	IRONICAL	) MY DEAR BARBARA: ALCOHOL IS A VERY NECESSARY
JOAN 4 (104)	VIEWS OF THE SAME THING. /CAUCHON/ (BITTERLY	IRONICAL	) ONLY EAST AND WEST! ONLY! ! /WARWICK/ OH, MY
3PLA PREFACE(R14)	PLEASING EVERYBODY INTO PRACTICE, NECESSITY, EVER	IRONICAL	TOWARDS FOLLY, HAD DRIVEN THEM TO SEEK A UNIVERSAL

IRONICALLY

POSN (450)	PLACE IS AT THE BARI THERE. TAKE IT. (BLANCO BOWS	IRONICALLY	AND GOES TO THE BAR). MISS EVANS: YOUD BEST SIT
BARB PREFACE(222)	OF SOCIETY. INDEED NOTHING COULD BE MORE	IRONICALLY	CURIOUS THAN THE CONFRONTATION MAJOR BARBARA
POSN (458)	(MOPPING HIS DABBLED RED CREST AND TRYING TO BE	IRONICALLY	GAY) STORY SIMPLY WONT WASH, MY ANGEL. YOU GOT IT
CATH 1 (170)	BECOME TSAR, I SHALL MURDER YOU. /EDSTASTON/ (	IRONICALLY	RETURNING THE CARESS) THANK YOU. THE OCCASION
BULL II (113)	MORE THAN TO ANYTHING ELSE IN IRELAND. /NORA/ (	IRONICALLY	) DEAR ME! DID YOU NOW? /BROADBENT/ I DID
ARMS III (59)	YOU DONT KNOW WHAT TRUE COURAGE IS. /SERGIUS/ (	IRONICALLY	) INDEED! I AM WILLING TO BE INSTRUCTED. (HE
ARMS I (14)	I NEVER SAW ANYTHING SO UNPROFESSIONAL. /RAINA/ (	IRONICALLY	) OH! WAS IT UNPROFESSIONAL TO BEAT YOU? /THE
BULL IV (179)	HEAVEN: IT MAY BE NO FARTHER OFF. /LARRY/ (	IRONICALLY	) ON THIS HOLY GROUND, AS YOU CALL IT, EH?
CAND II (122)	MAKE ANOTHER SUFFER. /CANDIDA/ (PETTING HIM	IRONICALLY	) POOR BOY! HAVE I BEEN CRUEL? DID I MAKE IT
GETT (316)	SEEING NOBODY BUT HIS FRIENDS' WIVES! /LESBIA/ (	IRONICALLY	) POOR FELLOW! /HOTCHKISS/ THE FRIENDS' WIVES
PYGM V (275)	HIS SHOULDERS) THAT WAS ALL. /MRS HIGGINS/ (	IRONICALLY	) QUITE SURE? /PICKERING/ ABSOLUTELY. REALLY,
JITT III (75)	JITTA: WHEN I SWORE THAT, I MEANT IT. /JITTA/ (	IRONICALLY	) SO IT APPEARS. /LENKHEIM/ WHEN YOU SWORE TO BE
SUPR III (108)	WE SWEPT THEM BACK TO AFRICA. /THE DEVIL/ (	IRONICALLY	) WHAT! YOU A CATHOLIC, SENOR DON JUAN! A
DEVL II (36)	I DISOBEYED HIM AND DROVE YOU AWAY. /RICHARD/ (	IRONICALLY	) WHEREAS, OF COURSE, YOU HAVE REALLY BEEN SO
KING I (184)	LOVE CHARMS TO THE KING'S LADIES. /LOUISE/ (	IRONICALLY	) YES: TO ENTERTAIN THE DUCHESS OF CLEVELAND AND
PHIL III (133)	SORT OF ATTACHMENT I SEEM ALWAYS TO INSPIRE. (	IRONICALLY	) YOU CANT THINK HOW FLATTERING IT IS. /PARAMORE/
DEVL III (59)	/BURGOYNE/ (COMPLETING THE SENTENCE FOR HIM	IRONICALLY	) YOU THOUGHT IT WOULD BE A PLEASURE FOR HER.
MTH4 I (149)	STEPS AND DISAPPEARS). /THE ELDERLY GENTLEMAN/ (	IRONICALLY	TAKING OFF HIS HAT AND MAKING A SWEEPING BOW FROM
ROCK PREFACE(158)	THORNS AND, WHEN THEY BUFFETED HIM, CHALLENGE HIM	IRONICALLY	TO GUESS WHICH OF THEM HAD STRUCK THE BLOW. "
MIS. PREFACE(64)	PARENT AND CHILD WHICH RECUR TO OUR MEMORY SO	IRONICALLY	WHEN WE HEAR PEOPLE SENTIMENTALIZING ABOUT
CATH 4 (197)	I MUST SAY IT -- IT IS NOT PROPER. /CATHERINE/ (	IRONICALLY	, IN GERMAN) SO! /EDSTASTON/ NOT THAT I CANNOT
CURE (233)	OH! I CAN STAND THAT, YOU KNOW. /STREGA/ (	IRONICALLY	, STILL PRELUDING) THANK YOU. /REGINALD/ THE FACT

IRONMONGER

SUPR HANDBOK(197)	YOUNG WORKMEN TO ORDER BOMBS FROM THE NEAREST	IRONMONGER	AND THEN DELIVERS THEM UP TO PENAL SERVITUDE; TO

IRON-GREY

SUPR I SD(3)	A MAYORI AMONG ALDERMEN. FOUR TUFTS OF	IRON-GREY	HAIR, WHICH WILL SOON BE AS WHITE AS ISINGLASS,

IRON-HARD

CLEO II SD(120) HOWEVER, LIKE THE REST OF HIS FLESH, ARE IN IRON-HARD CONDITION. /RUFIO/ (FROM THE STEPS) PEACE, HO! (

IRON-WILLED

CAPT II (261) DIDNT MEAN THAT. FIRM! UNALTERABLE! RESOLUTE! IRON-WILLED ! STONEWALL JACKSON! THATS THE IDEA, ISNT IT?

IRONS

LION II (140) WHIP). IF THAT WILL NOT MOVE THEM, BRING THE HOT IRONS . THE MAN IS LIKE A MOUNTAIN. (HE RETURNS ANGRILY
MIS. PREFACE(67) TO CONSIDER OTHERS OR ELSE GO OVERBOARD OR INTO IRONS , AND THE HABIT OR WORKING ON COMMITTEES AND CEASING

IRONSIDES

GENV PREFACE(7) NOR THE RED ROSES ON BOSWORTH FIELD AND THE IRONSIDES AT NASEBY KNOW THAT THEY WERE EXCHANGING IT FOR

IRONY

BARB PREFACE(240) HUMAN CIRCUMSTANCES. THEN COMES THE CLIMAX OF IRONY AND BLIND STUPIDITY. THE WOLVES, BALKED OF THEIR MEAL
LADY PREFACE(224) NOT SHAKESPEAR BECAUSE I MISS THE SHAKESPEARIAN IRONY AND THE SHAKESPEARIAN GAIETY. TAKE THESE AWAY AND
BARB PREFACE(241) THE OTHER IS CRIMINAL FELONY. CONNOISSEURS IN IRONY ARE WELL AWARE OF THE FACT THAT THE ONLY EDITOR IN
APPL PREFACE(174) WHEN THEY ATTAIN TO WHAT IS WITH UNINTENTIONAL IRONY CALLED POWER (MEANING THE DRUDGERY OF CARRYING ON FOR
BARB III (325) BE SOME TRUTH OR OTHER BEHIND ALL THIS FRIGHTFUL IRONY . COME, DOLLY. (SHE GOES OUT). /CUSINS/ MY GUARDIAN
2TRU II SD(52) UNHAPPILY PRODUCES AT TIMES AN IMPRESSION OF IRONY . HE SALUTES; HANDS THE LETTER TO THE COLONEL; AND
LADY PREFACE(225) A BOOK ON SHAKESPEAR WITH THE SHAKESPEARIAN IRONY LEFT OUT OF ACCOUNT. I DO NOT SAY THAT THE MISSING
PPP (196) US MUST DIE. THUNDER. /FITZ/ I LAUGHED BUT AT THE IRONY OF FATE (HE TAKES A GAZOGENE FROM THE CUPBOARD).
SUPR III (97) TO THE STATUE) YOU HEAR, SIR! OH, BY WHAT IRONY OF FATE WAS THIS COLD SELFISH EGOTIST SENT TO MY
MRS III SD(231) I DIDNT. VIVIE WONDERS AT HIM. HER SENSE OF THE IRONY OF HIS PROTEST COOLS AND BRACES HER. SHE REPLIES WITH
SUPR I (11) IT'S ALL MY OWN DOING: THATS THE HORRIBLE IRONY OF IT. HE TOLD ME ONE DAY THAT YOU WERE TO BE ANN'S
LADY PREFACE(224) AND THE BANK OF VIOLETS, I LAY STRESS ON THIS IRONY OF SHAKESPEAR'S, THIS IMPISH REJOICING IN PESSIMISM,
BARB PREFACE(207) IS IT THAT WHEN I ALSO DEAL IN THE TRAGI-COMIC IRONY OF THE CONFLICT BETWEEN REAL LIFE AND THE ROMANTIC
METH PREFACE(R86) MUD, OR AT BEST FINDING AN ACID ENJOYMENT IN THE IRONY OF THEIR PREDICAMENT. GOETHE IS OLYMPIAN: THE OTHER
HART PREFACE(29) AT WHICH BOTH WERE BLUFFED. AND, WITH THE USUAL IRONY OF WAR, IT REMAINS DOUBTFUL WHETHER GERMANY AND
CAND III (145) A MOMENT AGO HOW IT CAME TO BE SO. (WITH SWEET IRONY) AND WHEN HE THOUGHT I MIGHT GO AWAY WITH YOU, HIS
CAND I (95) VERY NICE OLD GENTLEMAN. /CANDIDA/ (WITH GENTLE IRONY) AND YOULL GO TO THE FREEMAN FOUNDERS TO DINE WITH
BARB II (298) THAN BEG FOR MYSELF. /UNDERSHAFT/ (IN PROFOUND IRONY) GENUINE UNSELFISHNESS IS CAPABLE OF ANYTHING, MY
NEVR II (250) SIR, THE BETTER FOR US. /CRAMPTON/ (IN POIGNANT IRONY) HOME! /WAITER/ (REFLECTIVELY) WELL, YES, SIR:
HART I (72) TAKE ELLIE'S HAND, AND BEAMING AT HIS OWN NAUGHTY IRONY) I HAVE MET MISS DUNN ALSO. SHE IS MY DAUGHTER. (HE
BULL IV (177) TO THE EFFICIENT. /KEEGAN/ (WITH POLISHED IRONY) I STAND REBUKED, GENTLEMEN. BUT BELIEVE ME, I DO
PHIL II (118) COUNTRY WITH THE HOUNDS. /PARAMORE/ (WITH BITTER IRONY) ISNT THAT RATHER CRUEL? A PACK OF DOGS RIPPING UP A
BARB II (306) IT ALL IS! /CUSINS/ (IN A CONVULSION OF IRONY) LET US SEIZE THIS UNSPEAKABLE MOMENT. LET US MARCH
ARMS II (29) CAVALRY CHARGE. /SERGIUS/ (WITH GRAVE IRONY) MADAM: IT WAS THE CRADLE AND THE GRAVE OF MY
NEVR I (223) MARRIED MYSELF. /CRAMPTON/ (WITH GRUMBLING IRONY) NATURALLY, SIR, NATURALLY. WHEN A YOUNG MAN HAS COME
MTH2 (63) I MAY BE WRONG. /BURGE/ (IN A BURST OF IRONY) OH NO. IMPOSSIBLE! IMPOSSIBLE! /LUBIN/ YES, MR
ARMS II (32) BEING HID BY TWO WOMEN. /SERGIUS/ (WITH BITTER IRONY) OH YES: QUITE A ROMANCE! HE WAS SERVING IN THE VERY
BULL III (132) THE WORMS ALONE. /FATHER DEMPSEY/ (WITH GENTLE IRONY) OH! IS IT JEWS YOU WANT TO MAKE OF US? I MUST
NEVR II (229) WANTED TO SEE YOU-- /M'COMAS/ (WITH GOOD-HUMORED IRONY) THANKS, /MRS CLANDON/-- AND PARTLY BECAUSE I WANT
JITT II (48) MY HOUSE. /JITTA/ (WITH FAINT SURPRISE AND SOME IRONY) YOU CAN BRING YOURSELF TO THAT? YOU CAN STILL BEAR
MRS III (228) FOR GOOD ON THE WHOLE. /VIVIE/ (WITH BITING IRONY) " A POWER, NOT OURSELVES, THAT MAKES FOR
METH PREFACE(R62) GIFT, WITH TERRIBLE POWERS OF HATRED, INVECTIVE, IRONY , AND ALL THE BITTER QUALITIES BRED, FIRST IN THE
BULL IV (177) PLUMBERS, WHICH I RATHER DOUBT. (DROPPING HIS IRONY , AND BEGINNING TO FALL INTO THE ATTITUDE OF THE
CATH 4 (190) A SINGLE TAX ON LAND! HOW HE WITHERS IT WITH HIS IRONY ! HOW HE MAKES YOU LAUGH WHILST HE IS CONVINCING YOU
BASH II,1, (113) AS SHE; AND NOW! AND NOW! A PRIZEFIGHTER! O IRONY ! O BATHOS! TO HAVE MADE WAY FOR THIS! OH,
GLIM (188) WHO WOULD HAVE THOUGHT SAINT BARBARA SO FULL OF IRONY ! /SANDRO/ AND IF THE OFFER YOUR EXCELLENCY WAS GOOD

IRRADIATING

JOAN 2 (82) (RISING, WITH A SUNFLUSH OF RECKLESS HAPPINESS IRRADIATING HER FACE) THERE IS ALWAYS DANGER, EXCEPT IN

IRRATIONAL

JOAN PREFACE(33) IMPORTANT THINGS HAS BECOME BOUND UP WITH A QUITE IRRATIONAL FAITH IN THE CHRONICLE OF JOSHUA'S CAMPAIGNS AS A
GETT PREFACE(218) OWN IRRATIONAL SURPRISE AND HIS WIFE'S EQUALLY IRRATIONAL INDIGNATION, THAT HIS WIFE IS A STRANGER TO HIM,
LION PREFACE(76) ROMAN RATIONALIST, ALWAYS DISCARDING THE IRRATIONAL REAL THING FOR THE UNREAL BUT RATIOCINABLE
GETT PREFACE(218) FOR TWENTY YEARS, HE FINDS, SOMETIMES TO HIS OWN IRRATIONAL SURPRISE AND HIS WIFE'S EQUALLY IRRATIONAL

IRRECLAIMABLE

ROCK PREFACE(160) A PERCENTAGE OF SAINTS BUT ALSO A PERCENTAGE OF IRRECLAIMABLE SCOUNDRELS AND GOOD-FOR-NOUGHTS WHO WILL WRECK

IRRECONCILABLE

GENV IV (112) OF THE LEAGUE OF NATIONS TO REVEAL HER AS AN IRRECONCILABLE BELLIGERENT. YOU HAVE-- /BEGONIA/ WHATS THAT
OVER PREFACE(156) THE SUBJECT ALTOGETHER. THERE IS A CONTINUAL AND IRRECONCILABLE CONFLICT BETWEEN THE NATURAL AND CONVENTIONAL
FABL PREFACE(76) ARE PRACTICALLY ALL INDEPENDENTS. COMMON TO THESE IRRECONCILABLE FAITHS IS THE PRETENSION THAT EACH IS THE
GENV IV (97) PEACE BETWEEN THE POWERS OF EUROPE ON A BASIS OF IRRECONCILABLE HOSTILITY BETWEEN CAMBERWELL AND PECKHAM:
JOAN PREFACE(54) OVER, THE BETTER. THIS WOULD SEEM TO PLACE HIM IN IRRECONCILABLE OPPOSITION TO THE PAYING PLAYGOER, FROM WHOSE
MIS. PREFACE(49) CITIZENS, ETC. ETC. ETC." I AM SORRY TO SEEM IRRECONCILABLE ; BUT IT IS THE LIFE FORCE THAT HAS TO MAKE
LION PREFACE(39) OF CHRIST'S CAREER AND CHARACTER IS HOPELESSLY IRRECONCILABLE WITH MATTHEW'S. HE IS ALMOST AS BAD AS
2TRU III (89) SILVER MEDAL FOR COMMITTING ATROCITIES WHICH WERE IRRECONCILABLE WITH THE PROFESSION OF A CHRISTIAN CLERGYMAN.
FABL PREFACE(73) WAS TRUE. IF JEHOVAH WAS A BARBAROUS TRIBAL IDOL, IRRECONCILABLE WITH THE GOD OF MICAH, THEN THERE WAS NO GOD
FABL PREFACE(80) WITH THE BEST INTENTIONS, IS NOT IN EFFECT IRRECONCILABLE WITH BELIEF IN A SUPERNATURAL BENIGNANT

IRRECONCILABLES

MILL PREFACE(130) PAPIST RIOTERS OF BELFAST, THE MOSLEM AND HINDU IRRECONCILABLES OF THE EAST AND THE KU-KLUX-KLANS AND

IRRECONCILABLY

MTH2 (52) IN SHORT, OF MEN DIFFERING FIERCELY AND IRRECONCILABLY ON EVERY PRINCIPLE THAT GOES TO THE ROOT OF

IRRECOVERABLY

DEST (182) NO SUCH PERSON. /NAPOLEON/ THE DESPATCHES WILL BE IRRECOVERABLY LOST. /LADY/ NONSENSE! THEY ARE INSIDE YOUR

IRREDEEMABLE

JOAN PREFACE(17) TO IT, IS TO PROVE THAT WE ARE NOT ONLY LOST BUT IRREDEEMABLE . LET US THEN ONCE FOR ALL DROP ALL NONSENSE

IRREDUCIBLE

JOAN PREFACE(56) THE EPILOGUE BY NOT WAITING FOR IT. AND IF THE IRREDUCIBLE MINIMUM THUS ATTAINED IS STILL TOO PAINFUL, THEY
MIS. PREFACE(42) BOLDLY TAKING AND ALLOWING OTHERS TO TAKE THE IRREDUCIBLE MINIMUM OF RISK, ENGLISH PHYSICAL HARDIHOOD AND
POSN PREFACE(423) FOR PARTY, CLASS, OR SECTARIAN ENDS BEYOND THAT IRREDUCIBLE MINIMUM OF ABUSE WHICH A POPULAR JURY WOULD

IRREFUTABLE

BULL PREFACE(43) INSTANCE, HE INSISTS ON LIVING, IN SPITE OF THE IRREFUTABLE DEMONSTRATIONS OF MANY ABLE PESSIMISTS, FROM THE
SUPR HANDBOK(179) UTOPIA), THE DEMONSTRATIONS OF SOCIALISTS, THOUGH IRREFUTABLE , WILL NEVER MAKE ANY SERIOUS IMPRESSION ON

IRREGULAR

DEVL I (19) PASTOR, BY THE WAY, WHAT HAS BECOME OF THE IRREGULAR CHILD? /ANDERSON/ (POINTING TO ESSIE) THERE,
DEVL I (19) WAS A FATHER? /UNCLE TITUS/ HE HAD ONLY ONE IRREGULAR CHILD, SIR. /RICHARD/ ONLY ONE! HE THINKS ONE A
MRS PREFACE(159) BE DURING THEIR LIFETIME: THAT IS, A LICENTIOUSLY IRREGULAR GROUP TO BE KEPT IN ORDER IN A ROUGH AND READY WAY
JOAN 6 (135) JUSTIFIED. /COURCELLES/ BUT THIS IS UNUSUAL AND IRREGULAR , SHE REFUSES TO TAKE THE OATH. /LADVENU/ (
JOAN 6 (147) AGAIN IN THE ACT OF SITTING DOWN) NO, NO: THIS IS IRREGULAR . THE REPRESENTATIVE OF THE SECULAR ARM SHOULD BE
BASH II,2, (117) RING IS SWEPT AWAY.) /LUCIAN/ FORBEAR THESE MOST IRREGULAR PROCEEDINGS. POLICE! POLICE! (HE ENGAGES
GETT (350) OF THEIR DRESSES, AND THOUGHT IT ALL RATHER IRREGULAR ; BUT THEYVE AGREED TO COME TO THE BREAKFAST. THE

SUPR II SD(48)	WITH SHORT WELL BRUSHED BLACK HAIR AND RATHER	IRREGULAR	SCEPTICALLY TURNED EYEBROWS. WHEN HE IS
ROCK I (229)	OVERDRIVEN MAN, SUFFERING FROM LATE HOURS,	IRREGULAR	SNATCHED MEALS, NO TIME FOR DIGESTION NOR FOR
MTH5 SD(205)	AND HIS FEET FEELING AUTOMATICALLY FOR THE ROUGH	IRREGULAR	STEPS AS HE SLOWLY DESCENDS THEM. EXCEPT FOR A
		IRREGULARITIES	
GETT PREFACE(184)	NO SUCH ESTABLISHMENT IS DESIRED. CLANDESTINE	IRREGULARITIES	ARE NEGLIGIBLE AS AN ALTERNATIVE TO MARRIAGE.
		IRREGULARLY	
DEVL I (23)	ALL TO ME. /HAWKINS/ THIS IS A VERY WRONGLY AND	IRREGULARLY	WORDED WILL, MRS DUDGEON; THOUGH (TURNING
		IRRELEVANCE	
MIS. PREFACE(99)	OF A BEWILDERED SOUL CANNOT DISGUISE THE IGNOBLE	IRRELEVANCE	OF THE RETORT OF GOD WITH WHICH IT CLOSES, NOR
LION PREFACE(26)	ANNOYANCE ARISING FROM THE MIRACLES WOULD BE THE	IRRELEVANCE	OF THE ISSUE RAISED BY THEM. JESUS'S TEACHING
SUPR III (125)	AND INHUMAN: IT WAS THEIR EXTRAORDINARY	IRRELEVANCE	THAT PROSTRATED ME. I INVARIABLY REPLIED WITH
SUPR PREFACE(R12)	OF EVASION, OF DISSATISFACTION, OF FUNDAMENTAL	IRRELEVANCE	, OF SHALLOWNESS, OF USELESS DISAGREEABLENESS,
		IRRELEVANCIES	
OVER PREFACE(163)	OF SIN AND NOTIONS OF PROPRIETY AND ALL THE OTHER	IRRELEVANCIES	WHICH PROVIDE HACKNEYED AND BLOODLESS MATERIAL
		IRRELEVANT	
2TRU PREFACE(25)	AT THEM AS COMPETITIVE EXAMINATIONS ARE SO	IRRELEVANT	AND MISLEADING AS TO BE WORSE THAN USELESS AS
GETT PREFACE(221)	OF SEXUAL RELATIONS FROM A MASS OF EXORBITANT AND	IRRELEVANT	CONDITIONS IMPOSED ON THEM ON FALSE PRETENCES TO
SUPR HANDBOK(184)	EQUALITY AND THUS HAMPERING SEXUAL SELECTION WITH	IRRELEVANT	CONDITIONS, ARE HOSTILE TO THE EVOLUTION OF THE
NEVR III (275)	TO INTERRUPT THIS VERY SERIOUS CONVERSATION WITH	IRRELEVANT	INTERJECTIONS. (VEHEMENTLY) I INSIST ON HAVING
LION PREFACE(25)	FROM HIS DOCTRINE BY RAISING AN ENTIRELY	IRRELEVANT	ISSUE BETWEEN HIS DISCIPLES AND HIS OPPONENTS.
SUPR HANDBOK(179)	OF ITS UNITS, AND FINALLY THE MAINTENANCE OF SOME	IRRELEVANT	POLITICAL FORM OR OTHER, SUCH AS A NATION, AN
UNPL PREFACE(R16)	WITH UNCTIOUS FLATTERY ON THE PERFECTLY	IRRELEVANT	QUESTION OF HIS ESTIMABLE PERSONAL CHARACTER, I
GENV PREFACE(16)	AND ILLITERATES BECAUSE ON THE STRENGTH OF THEIR	IRRELEVANT	SCHOOLING THEY BELIEVE THEMSELVES POLITICALLY
UNPL PREFACE(R24)	EVENTS, I HAVE TRIED TO PUT DOWN NOTHING THAT IS	IRRELEVANT	TO THE ACTOR'S PERFORMANCE, AND, THROUGH IT, TO
		IRRELEVANTLY	
LION PREFACE(95)	AND HUXLEYS SHOULD NO LONGER WASTE THEIR TIME	IRRELEVANTLY	AND RIDICULOUSLY WRANGLING ABOUT THE GADARENE
		IRRELIGION	
METH PREFACE(R76)	ELECTION SHEWS US VERY TERRIFYINGLY HOW A COMMON	IRRELIGION	CAN BE USED BY MYOPIC DEMAGOGY; AND COMMON
GETT (355)	ME: THAT WHICH MY SOUL KNOWS TO BE TRUE; BUT EVEN	IRRELIGION	HAS ONE TENET; AND THAT IS THE SACREDNESS OF
GENV IV (117)	I STAND FOR THE RELIGION OF GENTLEMEN AGAINST THE	IRRELIGION	OF CADS. FOR ME THERE ARE ONLY TWO CLASSES,
METH PREFACE(R86)	BUT THEIR VERACITY AND THEIR REPUDIATION OF THE	IRRELIGION	OF THEIR TIME: THAT IS, THEY ARE BITTER AND
METH PREFACE(R76)	CAN BE USED BY MYOPIC DEMAGOGY; AND COMMON	IRRELIGION	WILL DESTROY CIVILIZATION UNLESS IT IS COUNTERED
FABL PREFACE(82)	THUS GIVE SOCIALISM A REPUTATION FOR ANARCHISM,	IRRELIGION	, AND SEXUAL PROMISCUITY WHICH IS ASSOCIATION OF
		IRRELIGIOUS	
METH PREFACE(R45)	AND LAMARCKIANS. THE AVERAGE CITIZEN IS	IRRELIGIOUS	AND UNSCIENTIFIC: YOU TALK TO HIM ABOUT CRICKET
METH PREFACE(R76)	ONLY CRUDE ENOUGH TO BELIEVE THESE THINGS, BUT	IRRELIGIOUS	ENOUGH TO BELIEVE THAT SUCH BELIEF CONSTITUTES A
METH PREFACE(R12)	HE CALLS IT, HIS CIVILIZATION. COWARDICE OF THE	IRRELIGIOUS	. ANOTHER OBSERVATION I HAD MADE WAS THAT
FABL PREFACE(72)	INTELLIGENT CHILDREN OF PIOUS FAMILIES, OR OF	IRRELIGIOUS	ONES CAPABLE OF NOTHING MORE INTELLECTUAL THAN
JOAN PREFACE(54)	ART AS SUCH. IN FASHIONABLE CENTRES THE NUMBER OF	IRRELIGIOUS	PEOPLE WHO GO TO CHURCH, OF UNMUSICAL PEOPLE WHO
FABL PREFACE(79)	BY LENIN. AS A PLAYWRIGHT I WAS HELD UP AS AN	IRRELIGIOUS	PORNOGRAPHER, AND AS SUCH A PUBLIC ENEMY, NOT TO
GETT PREFACE(206)	A CIPHER EXCEPT FOR THE PURPOSES OF A PETULANTLY	IRRELIGIOUS	SOCIAL AND POLITICAL CLUB. DEMOCRACY AS TO THE
MIS. PREFACE(104)	TRUE ALSO OF POPULAR RELIGION: IT IS SO HORRIBLY	IRRELIGIOUS	THAT NOBODY WITH THE SMALLEST PRETENCE TO
METH PREFACE(R37)	BENEATH THEM. THEY REVEAL A CONDITION SO UTTERLY	IRRELIGIOUS	THAT RELIGION MEANS NOTHING BUT BELIEF IN A
SUPR PREFACE(R32)	WORLD INSTEAD OF WITH ITS UNITIES: THEY ARE SO	IRRELIGIOUS	THAT THEY EXPLOIT POPULAR RELIGION FOR
LION PREFACE(17)	AND WHO ARE HORRIFIED AT THE INDIFFERENCE OF THE	IRRELIGIOUS	TO THE APPROACHING DOOM. AND REVIVALIST
METH PREFACE(R69)	TERROR OF ONE ANOTHER, THAT COWARDICE OF THE	IRRELIGIOUS	, WHICH, MASKED IN THE BRAVADO OF MILITARIST
		IRREMOVABLE	
FABL PREFACE(88)	ARE TESTED, THEY ARE THERE FOR LIFE, PRACTICALLY	IRREMOVABLE	. AND SO GOVERNMENT GOES ON. UNFORTUNATELY THE
		IRREPARABLE	
MIS. PREFACE(30)	IN THE DISCOVERY THAT THE MARRIAGE HAS BEEN AN	IRREPARABLE	MISTAKE. NOTHING CAN JUSTIFY SUCH A RISK. THERE
MILL PREFACE(120)	A RUSH. THIS GAVE HIM THE CHANCE OF MAKING AN	IRREPARABLE	MISTAKE AND SPENDING THE NEXT FIFTEEN YEARS IN
CLEO II (138)	WORSE THAN THE DEATH OF TEN THOUSAND MEN! LOSS	IRREPARABLE	TO MANKIND! /RUFIO/ WHAT HAS HAPPENED, MAN?
SIM II (80)	THERE IS GENERAL AGREEMENT THAT OUR LOSSES ARE	IRREPARABLE	, THOUGH THEIR BAD EFFECTS ARE AS YET UNFELT.
		IRREPRESSIBLE	
LADY PREFACE(220)	OF A HEART BROKEN BY THE DARK LADY. THERE IS AN	IRREPRESSIBLE	GAIETY OF GENIUS WHICH ENABLES IT TO BEAR THE
SUPR III SD(140)	WITH A MEPHISTOPHELEAN SMILE, BOWS PROFOUNDLY. AN	IRREPRESSIBLE	GRIN RUNS FROM FACE TO FACE AMONG THE
JOAN 2,SD(73)	DOG ACCUSTOMED TO BE KICKED, YET INCORRIGIBLE AND	IRREPRESSIBLE	, BUT HE IS NEITHER VULGAR NOR STUPID; AND HE
APPL I (226)	US, IN ANY CASE. /AMANDA/ (SPLUTTERS INTO AN	IRREPRESSIBLE	LAUGH)! ! /MAGNUS/ (LOOKS REPROACHFULLY AT
DOCT III (138)	HAVE YOU SEEN JENNIFER'S? /RIDGEON/ (RISING IN	IRREPRESSIBLE	RAGE) DO YOU DARE INSINUATE THAT MRS DUBEDAT
BULL I (96)	WOMAN, HEAVEN HELP YOU! /BROADBENT/ (	IRREPRESSIBLE	) NEVER FEAR. YOURE ALL DESCENDED FROM THE
BULL PREFACE(37)	WITH HIM. UNFORTUNATELY VOLTAIRE HAD AN	IRREPRESSIBLE	SENSE OF HUMOR. HE JOKED ABOUT HABAKKUK; AND
		IRREPRESSIBLY	
BULL III (118)	OUT FOR SOME OTHER ARRANGEMENT. (CHEERING UP	IRREPRESSIBLY	) STILL, IT'S NO END OF A JOKE. HOW DO YOU
		IRRESISTIBLE	
MILL IV (209)	I HAD FORGOTTEN THE PULSE. ONE, TWO, THREE: IT IS	IRRESISTIBLE	: IT IS A PULSE IN A HUNDRED THOUSAND. I LOVE
MILL PREFACE(114)	HAD ALL THE QUALITIES THAT MAKE AN INDIVIDUAL	IRRESISTIBLE	: THE PHYSICAL STRENGTH AND FEROCITY OF A KING
ROCK I (204)	EFFECT OF SOCIALISM ON FAMILY LIFE. /FLAVIA/ (	IRRESISTIBLE	AMUSEMENT STRUGGLING WITH HYSTERICS AND GETTING
2TRU PREFACE(4)	GAMES IT IS ENJOYABLE ONLY BY PEOPLE WITH AN	IRRESISTIBLE	AND VIRTUALLY EXCLUSIVE FANCY FOR IT, AND
GENV PREFACE(19)	THAT ALL SHE NEEDS TO ESTABLISH HER RULE IS AN	IRRESISTIBLE	ARMY. THESE DELUSIONS WERE HIGHLY FLATTERING TO
KING PREFACE(154)	BUT I FIND THE PERIHELION OF MERCURY SO	IRRESISTIBLE	AS A LAUGH CATCHER (LIKE WESTON-SUPER-MARE)
SUPR PREFACE(R23)	HERE WOMAN MEETS A PURPOSE AS IMPERSONAL, AS	IRRESISTIBLE	AS HER OWN; AND THE CLASH IS SOMETIMES TRAGIC.
MILL I (145)	I MADE A VERY COMMON MISTAKE. I THOUGHT THAT THIS	IRRESISTIBLE	ATHLETE WOULD BE AN ARDENT LOVER. HE WAS
CAND II (119)	YOU VAIN THING! ARE YOU SO SURE OF YOUR	IRRESISTIBLE	ATTRACTIONS? /MORELL/ CANDIDA: YOU ARE
MILL II (167)	THIS AND SAY " HOW JOLLY! " THERE MUST BE SOME	IRRESISTIBLE	ATTRACTION PRESENT; AND I CAN SEE NOTHING THAT
LION PREFACE(69)	NOTHING. IN OUR SEXUAL NATURES WE ARE TORN BY AN	IRRESISTIBLE	ATTRACTION AND AN OVERWHELMING REPUGNANCE AND
2TRU II SD(78)	THERE FIRST AND TAKES THE WORD OF COMMAND WITH	IRRESISTIBLE	AUTHORITY, LEAVING HIM STUPENT. AUBREY, WHO HAS
MILL PREFACE(115)	HAD BEEN BEHIND THE TIMES, BUT HE WAS FOR A TIME	IRRESISTIBLE	BECAUSE, THOUGH HE COULD FIGHT BATTLES ON
OVER PREFACE(158)	A SERIES OF REACTIONS AND REVULSIONS IN WHICH THE	IRRESISTIBLE	BECOMES THE UNBEARABLE, AND THE UNBEARABLE THE
POSN PREFACE(395)	COMEDY WITH A STRONGLY POLYGAMOUS MORAL WAS FOUND	IRRESISTIBLE	BY THE LORD CHAMBERLAIN. PLENTY OF FUN AND A
METH PREFACE(R38)	IN THE EXISTENCE OF DESIGN IN THE UNIVERSE. THE	IRRESISTIBLE	CRY OF ORDER, ORDER! OUR SCORNFUL YOUNG
DOCT PREFACE(52)	MEDICAL PROFESSION THAT TOOK UP VACCINATION WITH	IRRESISTIBLE	FAITH, SWEEPING THE INVENTION OUT OF JENNER'S
CYMB FORWORD(134)	TEMPEST, TO PLEASE KING JAMIE, OR ELSE BECAUSE AN	IRRESISTIBLE	FASHION HAD SET IN, JUST AS AT ALL THE GREAT
JOAN PREFACE(31)	AND IN HER TEENS, WHICH WAS UNTHINKABLE. THUS AN	IRRESISTIBLE	FORCE MET AN IMMOVABLE OBSTACLE, AND DEVELOPED
SUPR III (118)	IT IS TO ATTEMPT TO IMPOSE CONDITIONS ON THE	IRRESISTIBLE	FORCE OF LIFE; TO PREACH PRUDENCE, CAREFUL
SUPR III (104)	IGNORANCE AND BLINDNESS. IT NEEDS A BRAIN, THIS	IRRESISTIBLE	FORCE, LEST IN ITS IGNORANCE IT SHOULD RESIST
DOCT IV (157)	BUT IT'S BLOOD-POISONING. /B.B./ (RECOVERING HIS	IRRESISTIBLE	GOOD NATURE) MY DEAR WALPOLE, EVERYTHING IS
LION PREFACE(5)	DOGGED INCREDULITY AND RECALCITRANCE, PRODUCED AN	IRRESISTIBLE	IMPRESSION THAT CHRIST, THOUGH REJECTED BY HIS
METH PREFACE(R83)	BUT IN THE EIGHTEENTH CENTURY PASSION MEANT	IRRESISTIBLE	IMPULSE OF THE LOFTIEST KIND: FOR EXAMPLE A
OVER SD(171)	WITH THE LADY, AND IS, IN FACT, YIELDING TO AN	IRRESISTIBLE	IMPULSE TO THROW HIS ARMS ROUND HER. /THE LADY/
GETT SD(323)	HER IN A MOMENT, AND MAKES HER COMPANY	IRRESISTIBLE	. ALL RISE EXCEPT SOAMES, WHO SITS DOWN. LEO
PYGM EPILOG (299)	FROM HIS TOPMOST HAIR TO HIS TIPMOST TOE, PROVED	IRRESISTIBLE	. CLARA TALKED OF NOTHING FOR WEEKS AND WEEKS
BUOY III (36)	IMPULSES THAT WERE UTTERLY UNREASONABLE AND	IRRESISTIBLE	. DESIRES IN WHICH MY BODY WAS TAKING COMMAND
INCA (247)	ORDER YOU TO CUT OFF THAT MOUSTACHE. IT IS TOO	IRRESISTIBLE	. DOESNT IT FASCINATE EVERYONE IN PERUSALEM?
BARB II (304)	(SARDONICALLY GALLANT) MRS BAINES: YOU ARE	IRRESISTIBLE	. I CANT DISAPPOINT YOU; AND I CANT DENY MYSELF

PYGM II (239)	COMING BETWEEN DOOLITTLE AND THE PIANO) THIS IS	IRRESISTIBLE	. LETS GIVE HIM TEN. (HE OFFERS TWO NOTES TO
DEST (192)	WHO POSSESS THE THING HE WANTS. THEN HE BECOMES	IRRESISTIBLE	. LIKE THE ARISTOCRAT, HE DOES WHAT PLEASES HIM
JITT I (24)	NOTHING: THIS IS LOVE; AND LOVE IS LIFE MADE	IRRESISTIBLE	. /BRUNO/ (CARRIED AWAY) LIFE: YES: THIS IS
SUPR III (126)	ME AND MY FATHER; THAT EVERY WOMAN FOUND YOU	IRRESISTIBLE	. /DON JUAN/ AM I BOASTING? IT SEEMS TO ME
OVER (172)	BUT THE IMPULSE TO COMMIT SUICIDE IS SOMETIMES	IRRESISTIBLE	. /GREGORY/ NOT WITH YOU. /MRS JUNO/ WHAT!
PYGM II (223)	/HIGGINS/ (TEMPTED, LOOKING AT HER) IT'S ALMOST	IRRESISTIBLE	. SHE'S SO DELICIOUSLY LOW-- SO HORRIBLY
DOCT PREFACE(14)	TO REVIVE AND COMMUNICATE WITH THEM BECOMES	IRRESISTIBLE	. THE COBBLER BELIEVES THAT THERE IS NOTHING
CYMB FORWORD(136)	SOMETIMES THE CIRCUMSTANCES WHICH DEMAND IT, ARE	IRRESISTIBLE	. THE RESULTS ARE VERY VARIOUS. WHEN A MEDIOCRE
GENV II (55)	IN SINGAPORE, WHERE THE NATIVE DANCING GIRLS ARE	IRRESISTIBLE	. THE TELEPHONE RINGS. /THE SECRETARY/ EXCUSE
BUOY III (44)	TO GO ON. /HE/ OUR FANCIES COME FIRST: THEY ARE	IRRESISTIBLE	. THEY MUST HAVE A MEANING AND A PURPOSE. WELL,
BARB PREFACE(227)	IS NOTHING, AND CAN BE NOTHING, BUT EVIL MADE	IRRESISTIBLE	. WEAKNESSES OF THE SALVATION ARMY. FOR THE
GENV IV (109)	SAY THAT? JESUS IS STRONGER THAN EVER. JESUS IS	IRRESISTIBLE	. YOU CAN PERHAPS UNIFY YOUR COUNTRYMEN IN LOVE
BARB PREFACE(213)	AS WELL AS PRACTICALLY CONSCIOUS OF THE	IRRESISTIBLE	NATURAL TRUTH WHICH WE ALL ABHOR AND REPUDIATE:
MIS. PREFACE(17)	FANCIERS (LIKE BIRD FANCIERS OR DOG FANCIERS) BY	IRRESISTIBLE	NATURAL PREDILECTION, NEVER HAPPY UNLESS THEY
NEVR II (257)	CHEMICAL AFFINITY, CHEMICAL COMBINATION: THE MOST	IRRESISTIBLE	OF ALL NATURAL FORCES. WELL, YOURE ATTRACTING
MTH2 (69)	DESTRUCTION, OUR SYSTEMS OF COERCION MANNED BY AN	IRRESISTIBLE	POLICE, YOU WERE CALLED ON TO CONTROL POWERS SO
METH PREFACE(R16)	WORSE THAN GOVERNMENT BY DEFECTIVES WHO WIELD	IRRESISTIBLE	POWERS OF PHYSICAL COERCION. THE COMMONPLACE
HART PREFACE(23)	THE GOVERNMENT BY ITS BLUSTERINGS INTO USING THE	IRRESISTIBLE	POWERS OF THE STATE TO INTIMIDATE THE SENSIBLE
SUPR HANDBOK(213)	NEED SHEWS HOW NEGLIGIBLE ALL THESE APPARENTLY	IRRESISTIBLE	PREJUDICES ARE WHEN THEY COME INTO CONFLICT
VWOO 3 (142)	PURPOSELESS VILLAGE EXISTENCE WILL BECOME ONE	IRRESISTIBLE	PURPOSE AND NOTHING ELSE. AN EXTRAORDINARY
ROCK I (209)	TO MY POOR ELOQUENCE, BUT THE SPONTANEOUS AND	IRRESISTIBLE	RECOGNITION OF THE GREAT NATURAL TRUTH THAT OUR
2TRU PREFACE(15)	TO BE CORRUPTED BY THEM UNLESS THEY HAVE AN	IRRESISTIBLE	RELIGIOUS VOCATION FOR PUBLIC WORK AND A FAITH
PYGM EPILOG (289)	TO YOUNG WOMEN ON THE GROUND THAT THEY HAD AN	IRRESISTIBLE	RIVAL IN HIS MOTHER, HE GAVE THE CLUE TO HIS
MTH1 I (12)	IMAGINATION; INFLAME YOUR DESIRES; MAKE YOUR WILL	IRRESISTIBLE	; AND CREATE OUT OF NOTHING. /EVE/ (
DOCT PREFACE(68)	AND THE SURGERY OF ACCIDENTS, HIS CLAIMS ARE	IRRESISTIBLE	; AND THIS IS THE IDEAL AT WHICH EVERY M.O.H.
SUPR III (119)	WHEN YOU WERE FORTY, YOU WOULD STILL HAVE BEEN	IRRESISTIBLE	; AND A WOMAN WHO MARRIES THICE MARRIES THREE
BULL PREFACE(11)	IN SHORT, TO COMMONWEALTHS, IN EXPRESSING THIS	IRRESISTIBLE	SENTIMENT OF NATIONALITY WITH ALL THE RHETORIC
BULL I (88)	YOU SELECT MY MOST TRAGIC MOMENTS FOR YOUR MOST	IRRESISTIBLE	STROKES OF HUMOR? /BROADBENT/ HUMOR! I WAS
LION EPILOG (147)	PUBLIC LIBERTIES AND PRIVATE INTERESTS, IN THE	IRRESISTIBLE	SURGE OF THEIR PUGNACITY AND THE TENSE
MILL PREFACE(110)	ABILITY OR MILITARY GENIUS OR BOTH? THEY ARE	IRRESISTIBLE	UNLESS THEY ARE RESTRAINED BY LAW; FOR ORDINARY
LADY PREFACE(211)	THERE WAS A SHARP STROKE OF IRONIC COMEDY IN THE	IRRESISTIBLE	VERDICT IN ITS FAVOR. IN CRITICAL LITERATURE
FABL PREFACE(75)	I ONCE HELD LIGHTLY THAT CANDIDATES OF	IRRESISTIBLE	VOCATION MIGHT SWEAR THIS BLAMELESSLY BECAUSE
FABL PREFACE(74)	AFTER MISTAKE, BUT STILL WINNING ITS FINALLY	IRRESISTIBLE	WAY. WHERE IN THE WORLD IS THERE A CHURCH THAT
DEST SD(151)	SOCIETY, NAPOLEON FINDS IT POSSIBLE TO BE	IRRESISTIBLE	WITHOUT WORKING HEROIC MIRACLES. THE WORLD,
CLEO IV (177)	WATER FROM THEM, WE HAVE KNOWN THAT YOUR GODS ARE	IRRESISTIBLE	, AND THAT YOU ARE A WORKER OF MIRACLES. I NO
BUOY 1 (14)	REPUBLICS EVERYWHERE; AND THEIR GOVERNMENTS ARE	IRRESISTIBLE	, BECAUSE THEY ALONE CAN AFFORD TO MAKE ATOMIC
SUPR III (132)	FOR ME. AS TO YOUR LIFE FORCE, WHICH YOU THINK	IRRESISTIBLE	, IT IS THE MOST RESISTIBLE THING IN THE WORLD
BULL PREFACE(18)	ONE; BUT THE GEOGRAPHIC CLIMATE IS ETERNAL AND	IRRESISTIBLE	, MAKING A MANKIND AND A WOMANKIND THAT KENT,
BULL I SD(74)	SOMETIMES JOLLY AND IMPETUOUS, ALWAYS BUOYANT AND	IRRESISTIBLE	, MOSTLY LIKEABLE, AND ENORMOUSLY ABSURD IN HIS
BULL PREFACE(61)	THE SO-CALLED PATRIOTIC PARTY," I FIND MR FINDLAY	IRRESISTIBLE	, SO EXQUISITELY DOES HE GIVE US THE MEASURE
MTH5 (237)	OF CAUSE AND EFFECT. WE ARE THE UNALTERABLE, THE	IRRESISTIBLE	, THE IRRESPONSIBLE, THE INEVITABLE. MY NAME IS
OVER PREFACE(158)	BECOMES THE UNBEARABLE, AND THE UNBEARABLE THE	IRRESISTIBLE	, UNTIL NONE OF US CAN SAY WHAT OUR CHARACTERS
		IRRESISTIBLY	
PHIL II (98)	/CRAVEN/ (TAKEN ABACK) SEPARATED! (HE IS	IRRESISTIBLY	AMUSED). OH! THAT WAS THE END OF THE HEARTH
POSN PREFACE(395)	CENSOR DOES-- STAND OUT AGAINST IT. IF A PLAY IS	IRRESISTIBLY	AMUSING, IT GETS LICENSED NO MATTER WHAT ITS
GENV PREFACE(17)	CIRCUMSTANCES ANY MISCELLANEOUS COLLECTION OF	IRRESISTIBLY	ARMED MEN WOULD BE DEMORALIZED; AND THE NATURAL
UNPL PREFACE(R14)	GENTLEMAN WHO ROBS, INSULTS, AND SUPPRESSES ME AS	IRRESISTIBLY	AS IF HE WERE THE TSAR OF RUSSIA AND I THE
BUOY III (37)	CALAMITY. YET I REPEATEDLY FOUND MYSELF	IRRESISTIBLY	ATTRACTED BIOLOGICALLY BY FEMALES WITH WHOM I
FABL I (101)	SEEN YOU BEFORE. BUT AT FIRST SIGHT I FIND YOU	IRRESISTIBLY	ATTRACTIVE. /YOUNG WOMAN/ LOTS OF MEN DO. WHAT
KING PREFACE(157)	DECREE THAT THE WORLD MUST BE PEOPLED, MAY ARISE	IRRESISTIBLY	BETWEEN PERSONS WHO COULD NOT LIVE TOGETHER
METH PREFACE(R61)	RUSSIA) THAT CIVILIZATION IS AN ORGANISM EVOLVING	IRRESISTIBLY	BY CIRCUMSTANTIAL SELECTION; AND HE PUBLISHED
LADY PREFACE(212)	THE STORY, AS HE TELLS IT, INEVITABLY AND	IRRESISTIBLY	DISPLACES ALL THE VULGAR, MEAN, PURBLIND,
BARB PREFACE(208)	HAD A VILLAGE IDIOT EXHIBITED TO ME AS SOMETHING	IRRESISTIBLY	FUNNY. ON THE STAGE THE MADMAN WAS ONCE A
MILL I (149)	I HAVE NO SENSE OF HUMOR; BUT THIS STRIKES ME AS	IRRESISTIBLY	FUNNY. YOU ACTUALLY LEFT ME TO SPEND THE NIGHT
NEVR II (257)	OF ALL NATURAL FORCES. WELL, YOURE ATTRACTING ME	IRRESISTIBLY	. CHEMICALLY. /GLORIA/ (CONTEMPTUOUSLY)
JOAN PREFACE(21)	TWO ABNORMALITIES WERE THE ONLY ONES THAT WERE	IRRESISTIBLY	PREPOTENT IN JOAN; AND THEY BROUGHT HER TO THE
DOCT I (98)	HEAVENS, B.B., NO, NO, NO. /B.B./ (SWEEPING ON	IRRESISTIBLY	) YES, YES, YES, COLLY. THE PROOF OF THE
HART PREFACE(24)	AND OUT. THE ESOTERIC ENGLAND WAS PROCEEDING	IRRESISTIBLY	TO THE CONQUEST OF EUROPE. THE PRACTICAL
		IRRESOLUTE	
ROCK II (278)	RESOLUTE AND SUCCESSFUL YOUNG WOMAN. DAVID IS AN	IRRESOLUTE	AND UNSUCCESSFUL YOUNG MAN. IF SHE HAS MADE UP
MIS. (182)	(SNATCHING THE PHOTOGRAPHS FROM GUNNER'S	IRRESOLUTE	FINGERS, AND RECOGNIZING THEM AT A GLANCE) LUCY
CATH 1,SD(165)	THE FLOOR, SOMEWHAT SOBERED. THE SOLDIERS STAND	IRRESOLUTE	. /EDSTASTON/ STAND OFF. (TO PATIOMKIN) ORDER
SUPR IV SD(165)	WITH TANNER, WATCHES HIM AND WAITS. HE MAKES AN	IRRESOLUTE	MOVEMENT TOWARDS THE GATE; BUT SOME MAGNETISM IN
CAND I SD(93)	HAS GROWN TO ITS FULL STRENGTH. MISERABLY	IRRESOLUTE	, HE DOES NOT KNOW WHERE TO STAND OR WHAT TO DO.
		IRRESOLUTELY	
MIS. (179)	AND TAKE THAT PEN IN YOUR HAND. (GUNNER LOOKS	IRRESOLUTELY	A LITTLE WAY ROUND; THEN OBEYS). NOW WRITE. "
CAND I (95)	A START, AND COMES EAGERLY TOWARDS HER, BUT STOPS	IRRESOLUTELY	AS HE MEETS HER AMUSED LOOK). WHAT DO YOU THINK
GETT (327)	SYKES. (HE GOES INTO THE STUDY). /SYKES/ (LOOKS	IRRESOLUTELY	AT HOTCHKISS)--? /HOTCHKISS/ TOO LATE: YOU
WIDO I SD(6)	BREEDING, AND CALLS TO TRENCH, WHO IS PROWLING	IRRESOLUTELY	IN THE BACKGROUND. /COKANE/ TRENCH, MY DEAR
6CAL SD(100)	CONCERN. THE MEN-AT-ARMS RELEASE THE BURGESSES	IRRESOLUTELY	. IT IS EVIDENT THAT THE QUEEN'S ARRIVAL WASHES
MRS III SD(221)	DISCONSOLATELY TOWARDS THE GATE; THEN COMES BACK	IRRESOLUTELY	. /REV. S./ ER-- FRANK. /FRANK/ YES. /REV. S./
DEVL III (74)	BACK OF THE SQUARE TO PULL HER BACK, AND STOPPED	IRRESOLUTELY	ON FINDING THAT HE IS TOO LATE) HOW IS THIS?
NEVR II SD(239)	SNATCHES THE WINE LIST RUDELY FROM HIM AND	IRRESOLUTELY	PRETENDS TO READ IT. PHILIP ABANDONS IT TO HIM
CATH 3 (184)	KNOWS WE GET BUT LITTLE TO DRINK. /EDSTASTON/ (	IRRESOLUTELY	) BUT I CANT TAKE THESE VALUABLE THINGS. BY
LION I (118)	WHAT DO YOU TAKE ME FOR? /LENTULUS/ (	IRRESOLUTELY	) LOOK HERE, YOU KNOW: I -- YOU-- I --
CAND II (112)	/MORELL/ YOUD BETTER NOT. (MARCHBANKS STOPS	IRRESOLUTELY	). SHE'D ONLY SET YOU TO CLEAN MY BOOTS, TO
JITT II (51)	POCKETS LIKE A CLEANED-OUT GAMBLER; TROTS BACK	IRRESOLUTELY	TO HIS WRITING-TABLE; TAKES UP THE MS.; STARES
SUPR I (42)	VIOLET AWAY, MISS RAMSDEN, I WILL. (HE TURNS	IRRESOLUTELY	TO THE DOOR). /RAMSDEN/ NO, NO-- /MISS RAMSDEN/
BARB II (278)	HER UP AGAIN). /PRICE/ (RISING, AND VENTURING	IRRESOLUTELY	TOWARDS BILL) EASY THERE, MATE. SHE AINT DOIN
JITT I SD(11)	SITS UP, STRAIGHTENING HIS COLLAR AND COAT RATHER	IRRESOLUTELY	, AND LOOKING VERY CAREWORN INDEED. HE IS WELL
MIS. (173)	A MAN OF YOURSELF. (THE MAN IS ABOUT TO RISE	IRRESOLUTELY	, FROM THE MERE HABIT OF DOING WHAT HE IS TOLD,
LION II (135)	TSHA! YOU OBSTINATE FOOL! (HE BITES HIS LIPS	IRRESOLUTELY	, NOT KNOWING EXACTLY WHAT TO DO). /ANDROCLES/
		IRRESOLUTENESS	
JOAN 1 (65)	THE SANE ONES HAVE LANDED US! /ROBERT/ (HIS	IRRESOLUTENESS	NOW OPENLY SWAMPING HIS AFFECTED
MRS III (222)	UNITES TO MANY ADMIRABLE DOMESTIC QUALITIES THE	IRRESOLUTENESS	OF A SHEEP AND THE POMPOUSNESS AND
		IRRESOLUTION	
SUPR PREFACE(R33)	THEY DECLARE THAT THE PLAY IS THE TRAGEDY OF	IRRESOLUTION	; BUT ALL SHAKESPEAR'S PROJECTIONS OF THE
MILL III SD(185)	TIM. SHE GOES OUT. THE MAN, AFTER A MOMENT OF	IRRESOLUTION	, SITS DOWN HELPLESSLY. /THE WOMAN/ (CRYING)
		IRRESPECTIVE	
ROCK II (237)	ROT. /BASHAM/ COMPULSORY PUBLIC SERVICE FOR ALL,	IRRESPECTIVE	OF INCOME, AS IN WAR TIME. /SIR DEXTER/
		IRRESPONSIBILITY	
APPL PREFACE(172)	AND CONSEQUENTLY OF THE LIMITS OF THEIR	IRRESPONSIBILITY	: IN SHORT, IN THE AUTHORITY AND PRACTICAL
SIM PREFACE(15)	EXULTANT IMPULSE TO ABUSE IT. THE SUBSTITUTION OF	IRRESPONSIBILITY	FOR RESPONSIBILITY MAY PRESENT ITSELF AS AN
GETT PREFACE(192)	PARTISANERIES, AS IGNORANCE CAN UNDERSTAND AND	IRRESPONSIBILITY	RELISH. WHAT THEY CALLED PATRIOTISM WAS A
		IRRESPONSIBLE	
JOAN PREFACE(50)	TO OUR MIDDLE CLASSES, WHO ARE COMFORTABLE AND	IRRESPONSIBLE	AT OTHER PEOPLE'S EXPENSE, AND ARE NEITHER
GENV PREFACE(17)	WOULD WALLOW IN CRUELTY AND IN THE EXERCISE OF	IRRESPONSIBLE	AUTHORITY FOR ITS OWN SAKE. MAN BEATING IS
FABL PREFACE(79)	TO SAY A THOROUGHPACED CAD, FOR MANY YEARS BY AN	IRRESPONSIBLE	CENSORSHIP WHICH COULD NOT BE CHALLENGED IN
APPL PREFACE(188)	POWERFUL AND EFFECTIVE PART OF OUR GOVERNMENT AN	IRRESPONSIBLE	CLASS GOVERNMENT. NOW, WHAT CONTROL HAVE YOU

GETT PREFACE(255) THE NATION CANNOT AFFORD TO LEAVE IT AT THE IRRESPONSIBLE DISPOSAL OF ANY INDIVIDUAL OR COUPLE OF
POSN PREFACE(371) PLAYS WHICH WERE MERELY LIGHTMINDED AND IRRESPONSIBLE IN THEIR VICIOUSNESS WERE REPEATEDLY MENTIONED
FABL III (112) EVERYBODY. IF YOU REFUSE YOU MAY BE CLASSED AS IRRESPONSIBLE . THAT MEANS THAT YOULL BE ENLISTED IN THE
POSN PREFACE(403) IN TO SETTLE A SINGLE CASE, HE WOULD BE VIRTUALLY IRRESPONSIBLE . WORSE STILL, HE WOULD TAKE ALL
TRFL (83) IF IT AMUSES THEM AND THEIR AUDIENCES HARMLESSLY. IRRESPONSIBLE LAUGHTER IS SALUTARY IN SMALL QUANTITIES. ONE
2TRU II (54) WORM! IF MY LETTER WAS SENT BY THE HANDS OF AN IRRESPONSIBLE MESSENGER IT SHOULD HAVE CONTAINED A STATEMENT
2TRU PREFACE(12) THE COUNTRY REMAINS THE PRIVATE PROPERTY OF IRRESPONSIBLE OWNERS MAINTAINING A PARLIAMENT TO MAKE ANY
SIM II (76) AS A RIGHT OF PUBLIC MEETING BY UNDISCIPLINED AND IRRESPONSIBLE PERSONS, DECLARED THAT THE MANSION HOUSE
FABL PREFACE(83) DEVISED TO PREVENT GLARING ABUSES OF VIRTUALLY IRRESPONSIBLE POWER. NONE OF THEM HAS EVER MADE VOLTAIRE'S
ROCK PREFACE(153) THESE FACTS IS THAT THE PRIVATE PROPRIETORS HAVE IRRESPONSIBLE POWERS OF LIFE AND DEATH IN THE STATE. SUCH
MIS. PREFACE(96) AND TEACH THE CHILD TO REGARD ITSELF AS THE IRRESPONSIBLE PREY OF ITS CIRCUMSTANCES AND APPETITES (OR
APPL PREFACE(175) DOING ANYTHING, AND THUS LEAVING EVERYTHING TO IRRESPONSIBLE PRIVATE ENTERPRISE. BUT AS PRIVATE ENTERPRISE
POSN PREFACE(363) TO BE RESCUED FROM THEIR PRESENT SUBJECTION TO AN IRRESPONSIBLE SECRET TRIBUNAL WHICH CAN CONDEMN THEIR PLAYS
FABL PREFACE(78) BOTH PLATFORM AND PRESS ARE GAGGED BY SUCH AN IRRESPONSIBLE TYRANNY OF PARTISAN NEWSPAPER PROPRIETORS AND
GENV I (37) I AM NOT PREPARED TO DISCUSS IT WITH AN IRRESPONSIBLE YOUNG WOMAN. /SHE/ I AM AFRAID I DONT LOOK THE
FANY PROLOG (271) WE REGARD YOU AS A BEL ESPRIT, A WIT, AN IRRESPONSIBLE , A PARISIAN IMMORALIST, TRES CHIC. /TROTTER/
DOCT PREFACE(65) PRACTITIONER HAS A PRECARIOUS, SHABBY-GENTEEL, IRRESPONSIBLE , SERVILE POSITION, BASED WHOLLY ON THE
MTH5 (237) WE ARE THE UNALTERABLE, THE IRRESISTIBLE, THE IRRESPONSIBLE , THE INEVITABLE. MY NAME IS OZYMANDIAS, KING
FOUN (221) WILL TELL YOU THAT YOU ARE TOO YOUNG, TOO IRRESPONSIBLE , TOO IMPULSIVE TO BE ANYTHING MORE TO ME THAN

IRRESPONSIBLY
BULL PREFACE(11) OF MONEY, LEISURE, AND POWER OVER OTHERS, TO USE IRRESPONSIBLY FOR HIS OWN AMUSEMENT. IN SHORT, THEN, THE
KING PREFACE(158) WOMEN EXERCISE SO MUCH INFLUENCE PRIVATELY AND IRRESPONSIBLY THAT THE CLEVEREST OF THEM ARE FOR GIVING ALL

IRRESPONSIVE
DOCT IV (159) WHERE HE HAS HIS MODELS, EH? /WALPOLE/ (GRIMLY IRRESPONSIVE) NO DOUBT. /THE NEWSPAPER MAN/ CUBICLE, YOU

IRRETRIEVABLE
MTH5 (238) IN ONE AND ONE IN TWO, LEST BY ERROR YE FALL INTO IRRETRIEVABLE DAMNATION. /THE FEMALE FIGURE/ AND IF ANY SAY

IRRETRIEVABLY
MIS. PREFACE(4) TO LIVE FOR EVER YOU MUST BE WICKED ENOUGH TO BE IRRETRIEVABLY DAMNED, SINCE THE SAVED ARE NO LONGER WHAT

IRREVERENCE
JOAN PREFACE(25) SOBER HISTORY; AND IT MAY BE THAT THEIR RIBALD IRREVERENCE IS MORE WHOLESOME THAN THE BEGLAMORED
SUPR II SD(62) AT BOTTOM, HE FIRST LEADS THE UNWARY, BY HUMOROUS IRREVERENCE , TO LEAVE POPULAR THEOLOGY OUT OF ACCOUNT IN

IRREVERENT
POSN PREFACE(376) ANY INTEREST IN AN UNDESIRABLE DOCUMENT BY AN IRREVERENT AUTHOR, BUT IN THE RELUCTANT DISCHARGE OF ITS
NEVR I SD(208) BY THE CONSTANT DANGER OF RIDICULE FROM HER IRREVERENT JUNIORS. UNLIKE HER MOTHER, SHE IS ALL PASSION;
BUOY III SD(28) MARRIED LADIES, AN UNMARRIED GIRL OF 20, AND AN IRREVERENT YOUTH OF 17, ENTERS. THE WIDOWER INTRODUCES THEM.

IRREVOCABILITY
SUPR HANDBOK(184) TO REVIVE ALL THE OLD INHUMAN STRINGENCY AND IRREVOCABILITY OF MARRIAGE, TO ABOLISH DIVORCE, TO CONFIRM

IRREVOCABLE
BARB PREFACE(245) AS IF ONE HOUR OF IMPRISONMENT WERE NOT AS IRREVOCABLE AS ANY EXECUTION! IF A MAN CANNOT LOOK EVIL IN
SUPR HANDBOK(221) WHOSE MONEY HE DESIRES, IMPRISONMENT IS AS IRREVOCABLE AS DEATH. CRIMINALS DO NOT DIE BY THE HANDS OF
BARB PREFACE(245) WE ARE FORCED TO ADMIT THAT IT, AT LEAST, IS IRREVOCABLE -- AS IF ONE HOUR OF IMPRISONMENT WERE NOT AS
SUPR HANDBOK(183) WILL BE CONTINUED UNTIL IT IS NO MORE ONEROUS NOR IRREVOCABLE THAN ANY ORDINARY COMMERCIAL DEED OF
BARB PREFACE(245) UNTIL EVERYONE KNOWS THAT HIS DEEDS ARE IRREVOCABLE , AND THAT HIS LIFE DEPENDS ON HIS USEFULNESS.

IRREVOCABLY
JITT I (21) /BRUNO/ NO-- EXCEPT THIS. WHEN I FINALLY AND IRREVOCABLY SEALED MY RESOLUTION YESTERDAY BY BURNING THE

IRRIGATE
MTH4 II (188) IS SAID. FIVE-EIGHTHS OF IT IS DESERT. THEY DONT IRRIGATE AS WE DO. BESIDES-- NOW I AM SURE THIS WILL APPEAL

IRRIGATION
BULL PREFACE(61) SOME NATIVES STONED AND SEVERELY INJURED AN IRRIGATION INSPECTOR. TWO DAYS AGO THREE NATIVES KNOCKED A
BULL PREFACE(62) IT! IN A POPULATION OF NEARLY TEN MILLIONS, ONE IRRIGATION INSPECTOR IS STONED. THE DENSHAWAI EXECUTIONS ARE

IRRITABLE
CAPT II (259) /LADY CICELY/ I'M SO SORRY. ALL THE HALLAMS ARE IRRITABLE . /BRASSBOUND/ (PENNING UP HIS FURY WITH
2TRU I (36) BLANKETS AND AN EIDERDOWN! NO WONDER YOU FEEL IRRITABLE . /THE PATIENT/ (SCREAMING) DONT TOUCH ME. GO
SUPR PREFACE(R39) I SOMETIMES DISLIKE MYSELF SO MUCH THAT WHEN SOME IRRITABLE REVIEWER CHANCES AT THAT MOMENT TO PITCH INTO ME
NEVR IV (284) SUPPOSE IT IS. I'M AFRAID I'M SOMETIMES A LITTLE IRRITABLE ; BUT I KNOW WHATS RIGHT AND REASONABLE ALL THE
GETT (332) I GAVE IT UP, I SHOULD BECOME SO MELANCHOLY AND IRRITABLE THAT YOU WOULD BE THE FIRST TO IMPLORE ME TO TAKE
JITT III (58) SYMPTOMS? /AGNES/ WELL, HE WAS SOMETIMES VERY IRRITABLE , THOUGH HE USED TO BE A PERFECT LAMB. I THOUGHT

IRRITABLY
DEST (177) HIM, HIS FINGERS TWITCHING, AND SAYS, AS HE WALKS IRRITABLY AWAY FROM HER TO THE FIREPLACE) THIS WOMAN WILL
CAPT II (248) UP) WEOLL, BLIMEY! /BRASSBOUND/ (TURNING IRRITABLY ON HIM) WHAT DID YOU SAY? /DRINKWATER/ WEOLL, WOT
DEST (160) /NAPOLEON/ (TURNING ON HIS HEEL IN DISGUST AND IRRITABLY RESUMING HIS MARCH TO AND FRO) YES: YOU HAVE SAID
ARMS I (13) HORSE TO THE OTHER SIDE OF THE ROOM. /THE MAN/ (IRRITABLY) DONT FRIGHTEN ME LIKE THAT. WHAT IS IT? /RAINA/
NEVR I (224) THE CHAIR IS RAISED AND LOWERED). /CRAMPTON/ (IRRITABLY) I ADVISE YOU TO GET MY TOOTH OUT AND HAVE DONE
JITT II (44) TO BE AFRAID OF ME. DONT BE CHILDISH. /JITTA/ (IRRITABLY) I AM LIKE YOURSELF: I AM ONLY TRYING TO GUESS
CAPT II (259) MAKE IT A LITTLE EASIER FOR YOU. /BRASSBOUND/ (IRRITABLY) LET MY COAT ALONE. IT WILL DO VERY WELL AS IT
PHIL II (111) WONT MY PET TELL HER OWN DADDY WHAT-- (IRRITABLY) WHAT THE DEVIL IS WRONG WITH EVERYBODY. DO PULL
SUPR I (20) ME INTO A PAINFUL DILEMMA, JACK. /RAMSDEN/ (IRRITABLY) YES, YES, ANNIE: THIS IS ALL VERY WELL, AND, AS
HART II (112) ENJOY THEMSELVES IMMENSELY. /LADY UTTERWORD/ (IRRITABLY) YOU ARE NOT MARRIED; AND YOU KNOW NOTHING ABOUT
DEST (189) WOULD YOU LIKE TO DO IT YOURSELF? /NAPOLEON/ (IRRITABLY) YOU REFUSE TO OBEY MY ORDER? /LIEUTENANT/ (

IRRITATE
LADY PREFACE(218) NOT ONLY IDOLATRY, BUT IDOLATRY FULSOME ENOUGH TO IRRITATE JONSON INTO AN EXPRESS DISAVOWAL OF IT? JONSON,
NEVR II (241) YOU PLEASE REMEMBER THAT YOUR JOKES ARE APT TO IRRITATE PEOPLE WHO ARE NOT ACCUSTOMED TO US, AND THAT YOUR
MIS. PREFACE(8) MAY STRIKE THE CHILD AS BEING RATHER AMUSING TO IRRITATE YOU; ALSO THE CHILD, HAVING COMPARATIVELY NO

IRRITATED
LION PREFACE(25) HIS POWERS AS A SIGN OF HIS MISSION, HE WAS IRRITATED BEYOND MEASURE, AND REFUSED WITH AN INDIGNATION
MILL PREFACE(123) RESCUE AND RESTORE, WHEREAS MUSSOLINI HAD ONLY AN IRRITATED BUT VICTORIOUS ONE. HE CARRIED OUT A PERSECUTION
MIS. PREFACE(22) ABLEST AND MOST IMPATIENT OF THEM WERE OFTEN SO IRRITATED BY THE AWKWARD, SLOW-WITTED, SLOVENLY BOYS: THAT
2TRU II SD(51) SPEECH READY AND RAPID. YET THE COLONEL, ALREADY IRRITATED BY THE RACKET OF THE BICYCLE AND THE INTERRUPTION
BULL PREFACE(52) THEIR WAY OUT, AS THERE IS NO USE ARGUING WITH AN IRRITATED MOB, ESPECIALLY IF YOU DO NOT KNOW ITS LANGUAGE.
AUGS (268) YOU CANT HAVE NO ROLLS. /AUGUSTUS/ (INTENSELY IRRITATED) CAN YOU TELL ME WHERE I CAN FIND AN INTELLIGENT
JITT III (59) WELL, OF COURSE, DARLING, I WANT YOU. /EDITH/ (IRRITATED) NO, NOT OF COURSE, NOT IN THE WAY YOU THINK. HAS
HART I (68) EMPTY TEA-CUPS ON THE CHINESE TRAY). /MANGAN/ (IRRITATED) SEE HERE, CAPTAIN SHOTOVER. I DONT QUITE
PYGM V (281) /LIZA/ AMEN. YOU ARE A BORN PREACHER. /HIGGINS/ (IRRITATED) THE QUESTION IS NOT WHETHER I TREAT YOU RUDELY,
PYGM EPILOG (297) PICK UP AND PRACTISE ARTISTIC AND LITERARY TALK IRRITATED THEM. SHE WAS, IN SHORT, AN UTTER FAILURE, AN
DEST (176) TAKING NO ACCOUNT OF THE REBUKE, MORE AND MORE IRRITATED , HE DROPS HIS HAUGHTY MANNER, OF WHICH HE IS

IRRITATES
MIS. PREFACE(8) ANSWERS IN USE. THE SIMPLEST: " BECAUSE IT IRRITATES ME," MAY FAIL; FOR IT MAY STRIKE THE CHILD AS

IRRITATING

UNPL PREFACE(R12) THE FASHION OF THE TIMES BECAME SILLY AND IRRITATING BEYOND ALL ENDURANCE WHEN INTRUDED UPON A SUBJECT
JOAN PREFACE(44) AS WE HAVE SEEN. THIS WOULD HAVE BEEN UNBEARABLY IRRITATING EVEN IF HER ORDERS HAD BEEN OFFERED AS RATIONAL
GETT (338) BLAME FOR THIS SCENE. I'M AFRAID IVE BEEN RATHER IRRITATING . /THE BISHOP/ I CAN QUITE BELIEVE IT, SINJON.
3PLA PREFACE(R20) PLANE: NOTHING COULD BE MORE IMPERTINENT AND IRRITATING . YET MR WELLS HAS HAD TO PRETEND THAT THE HERO
OVER PREFACE(168) OUT, THEY NECESSARILY DISGRACE THEMSELVES BY IRRITATING LIES AND TRANSPARENT SUBTERFUGES. MY PLAYLET,
LION PREFACE(65) SEIZE THEIR WIVES AND CAST THEM UNDER DRAYS AT AN IRRITATING WORD. WE HAVE NOT ONLY PEOPLE WHO CANNOT RESIST

IRRITATION

3PLA PREFACE(R15) WHICH MAKES MEN AS SUSCEPTIBLE TO DISGUST AND IRRITATION AS HEADACHE MAKES THEM TO NOISE AND GLARE. BEING
ARMS III SD(46) BUSINESSLIKE PROGRESS WITH A MIXTURE OF ENVIOUS IRRITATION AT HIS OWN INCAPACITY AND AWESTRUCK WONDER AT AN
SUPR I SD(17) A BRUSQUE GESTURE, SUBSEQUENTLY RELIEVING HIS IRRITATION BY SITTING DOWN ON THE CORNER OF THE WRITING
GETT (326) INFERIOR TO THE FAMILY SILKSTONE; AND IN THE IRRITATION INTO WHICH THE FIRST SCUTTLE THREW ME, I CALLED
PYGM IV (264) GOING TO HER; LISTEN TO ME, ELIZA. ALL THIS IRRITATION IS PURELY SUBJECTIVE. /LIZA/ I DONT UNDERSTAND.
INCA PROL,SD(233) COMES THROUGH THEM IN A CONDITION OF EXTREME IRRITATION . HE SPEAKS THROUGH THE CURTAINS TO SOMEONE
SUPR HANDBOK(201) WE HAD HARDLY RECOVERED FROM THE FRUITLESS IRRITATION OF THIS DISCOVERY WHEN IT TRANSPIRED THAT THE
JOAN PREFACE(44) WITCH. TO THIS ABHORRENCE WE MUST ADD THE EXTREME IRRITATION OF THOSE WHO DID NOT BELIEVE IN THE VOICES, AND
MIS. PREFACE(22) AND PATIENT TREATMENT, THAT THEY VENTED THEIR IRRITATION ON THEM RUTHLESSLY, NOTHING BEING EASIER THAN TO
DEST (164) /NAPOLEON/ (LOOKING AFTER THEM WITH CONCENTRATED IRRITATION) IDIOT! THE STRANGE LADY SMILES
BULL I (84) BETWEEN CONNEMARA AND RATHMINES. (WITH VIOLENT IRRITATION) OH, DAMN TIM HAFFIGAN! LETS DROP THE SUBJECT:
MIS. PREFACE(8) THEREFORE HAVE TO EXPLAIN THAT THE EFFECT OF THE IRRITATION WILL BE THAT YOU WILL DO SOMETHING UNPLEASANT IF

IRRUPTION

GENV II SD(61) THE CONVERSATION IS ABRUPTLY BROKEN BY THE IRRUPTION OF BEGONIA HERSELF IN A STATE OF UNGOVERNABLE
DEST SD(152) AND EXCURSIONS OF THE PAST FEW DAYS, AND BY AN IRRUPTION OF FRENCH TROOPS AT SIX O' CLOCK, KNOW THAT THE

IRVING

CYMB FORWORD(133) AND THE CRITICS AS SHAKESPEAR'S PLAYS BY HENRY IRVING AND AUGUSTIN DALY AT THE END OF THE LAST CENTURY, IS
POSN PREFACE(372) SUIT MEMBERS TO PUT TO THEM, ALLOWED SIR HENRY IRVING AND SIR JOHN HARE TO PREPARE AND READ WRITTEN
PHIL I SD(69) MACREADY AS WERNER (AFTER MACLISE), SIR HENRY IRVING AS RICHARD III (AFTER LONG), ELLEN TERRY, MRS
UNPL PREFACE(R20) IMAGINE SHAKESPEAR CONFRONTED WITH SIR HENRY IRVING AT A REHEARSAL OF THE MERCHANT OF VENICE, OR SHERIDAN
3PLA PREFACE(R34) TOO GOOD A SHAKESPEAREAN EVER TO FORGIVE HENRY IRVING FOR PRODUCING A VERSION OF KING LEAR SO MUTILATED
MRS PREFACE(163) MORALS OF THE NATION, AND TO RESTRAIN SIR HENRY IRVING FROM PRESUMING TO IMPERSONATE SAMSON OR DAVID ON THE
POSN PREFACE(415) WHO KNEW LEAST ABOUT THE THEATRE WAS HENRY IRVING . YET A MOMENT'S CONSIDERATION WOULD HAVE SHEWN THAT
3PLA PREFACE(R13) DISLIKE AND DISTRUST OF RITUALISM. NO DOUBT THE IRVING RITUAL APPEALED TO A FAR MORE CULTIVATED SENSUOUSNESS
CATH PREFACE(157) BELONGED TO A DIFFERENT SOLAR SYSTEM AS FAR AS IRVING WAS CONCERNED; AND THE SAME WAS TRUE OF THEIR
POSN PREFACE(415) WAS A PLATITUDE. FOR ABOUT QUARTER OF A CENTURY IRVING WAS CONFINED NIGHT AFTER NIGHT TO HIS OWN THEATRE AND
3PLA PREFACE(R13) WITH HIS BRAINS CUT OUT. IN 1896, WHEN SIR HENRY IRVING WAS DISABLED BY AN ACCIDENT AT A MOMENT WHEN MISS
POSN PREFACE(388) IT WAS BROKEN DOWN BY THE LATE SIR HENRY IRVING WHEN HE FINALLY SHAMED THE GOVERNMENT INTO EXTENDING
CYMB FORWORD(134) OF THE PLAY AT THE OLD LYCEUM THEATRE, WHEN IRVING , AS IACHIMO, A STATUE OF ROMANTIC MELANCHOLY, STOOD
FABL PREFACE(82) THE PEOPLE? WERE GENERAL ROBERTS AND HENRY IRVING , NOMINATED BY GALLUP POLL AS IDEAL RULERS, THE
CATH PREFACE(157) CAREERS OF KEAN, MACREADY, BARRY SULLIVAN, AND IRVING , OUGHT TO HAVE PRODUCED A GROUP OF HEROIC PLAYS
POSN PREFACE(415) FOR ALL THAT. NOW IF THIS WAS TRUE OF SIR HENRY IRVING , WHO DID NOT BECOME A LONDON MANAGER UNTIL HE HAD

IRVING'S

LADY PREFACE(233) OF GARRICK'S RICHARD, AND KEAN'S OTHELLO, AND IRVING'S SHYLOCK, AND FORBES ROBERTSON'S HAMLET WITHOUT

I-AM-THY-HELP

JOAN 5 (110) AT THE THREE-QUARTERS THEY WILL SAY " I-AM-THY-HELP ." BUT IT IS AT THE HOUR, WHEN THE GREAT BELL

I'VE

DOCT II (129) (WITH A SELF-ASSURED SHAKE OF THE HEAD) I'VE A PRETTY GOOD FLAIR FOR THAT SORT OF THING. I KNOW WHEN
O'FL (206) YES: I KNOW. I KNOW. ONE DOES GET FED UP WITH IT: I'VE BEEN DOG TIRED MYSELF ON PARADE MANY A TIME. BUT STILL,
BULL IV (158) OH, THAT! NO: IT SEEMS HARDLY MORE THAN A WEEK. I'VE BEEN SO BUSY-- HAD SO LITTLE TIME TO THINK. /NORA/ IVE
CYMB V (141) AND DREST MYSELF AS DOES A BRITON PEASANT; SO I'VE FOUGHT AGAINST THE PART I CAME WITH; SO I'LL DIE FOR
O'FL (209) WHEN I WAS OLD ENOUGH TO UNDERSTAND THEM, I'VE HARDLY TOLD MY MOTHER THE TRUTH TWICE A YEAR SINCE I
DOCT II (121) I LENT IT TO HIM. AND HE'S FORGOTTEN TO PAY ME. I'VE JUST TWOPENCE TO GET BACK WITH. /RIDGEON/ OH, NEVER
CYMB V (146) THY SONS; AND LET IT BE CONFISCATE ALL SO SOON AS I'VE RECEIVED IT. /CYMBELINE/ NURSING OF MY SONS!
CAND II (110) MACHINE SO CROSSLY THAT IT TEARS). THERE! NOW I'VE SPOILED THIS LETTER! HAVE TO BE DONE ALL OVER AGAIN!
HART II (94) COULDNT: WE SHOULD RUIN THE BUSINESS IN A YEAR. I'VE TRIED; AND I KNOW. WE SHOULD SPEND TOO MUCH ON

ISAAC

KING I (168) I LONG TO HEAR WHAT YOU HAVE TO SAY TO HIM. /FOX/ ISAAC NEWTON: I HAVE FRIENDS WHO BELONG TO THE NEW SO-CALLED
KING I (166) GOES OUT. /FOX/ AM I ADDRESSING THE PHILOSOPHER ISAAC NEWTON? /NEWTON/ YOU ARE, SIR. (RISING) WILL YOUR
MIS. PREFACE(14) CHILD AT PLAY IS NOISY AND OUGHT TO BE NOISY: SIR ISAAC NEWTON AT WORK IS QUIET AND OUGHT TO BE QUIET. AND THE
KING PREFACE(154) OF SWEET NELL OF OLD DRURY MORE ATTRACTIVE THAN ISAAC NEWTON HAD BETTER AVOID MY PLAYS: THEY ARE NOT MEANT
KING I SD(161) GOLDEN DAYS". ACT I. THE LIBRARY IN THE HOUSE OF ISAAC NEWTON IN CAMBRIDGE IN THE YEAR 1680. IT IS A CHEERFUL
KING I (211) WORLD-- WHICH WOULD HAVE COST ANY OTHER MAN THAN ISAAC NEWTON TWENTY YEARS HARD LABOR. /CHARLES/ I HAVE SEEN
KING PREFACE(153) CHARLES MIGHT HAVE MET THAT HUMAN PRODIGY ISAAC NEWTON. AND NEWTON MIGHT HAVE MET THAT PRODIGY OF
KING I (170) PRECESSION OF THE EQUINOXES. /FOX/ I THANK YOU, ISAAC NEWTON. I AM AS WISE AS I WAS BEFORE. /MRS BASHAM/ YOU
KING I (168) PASTOR: ENOUGH OF ME. YOU ARE FACE TO FACE WITH ISAAC NEWTON. I LONG TO HEAR WHAT YOU HAVE TO SAY TO HIM.
CLEO NOTES (208) IV BY A TYPE FOUNDED ON THE ATTAINMENTS OF SIR ISAAC NEWTON. IT IS TRUE THAT AN ORDINARILY WELL EDUCATED
KING I (167) TO HEAR WHAT GEORGE FOX CAN HAVE TO SAY TO ISAAC NEWTON. IT IS NOT ALTOGETHER AN IMPERTINENT CURIOSITY.
KING I (194) A KING, CANNOT GET RID OF HIM. THIS HOUSE IS ISAAC NEWTON'S; AND HE CAN ORDER YOU OUT AND THROW YOU OUT
KING I (168) OF YESTERDAY? IF WHAT HAS BEEN REVEALED TO YOU, ISAAC NEWTON, BE TRUE, THERE IS NO HEAVEN ABOVE US AND NO
KING I (181) HIS WORD BEFORE THE WORD OF GOD! SHAME ON YOU, ISAAC NEWTON, FOR MAKING AN IDOL OF AN ARCHBISHOP! THERE IS
LION PREFACE(56) BOTTOMLEY, SHAKESPEAR, MR JACK JOHNSON, SIR ISAAC NEWTON, PALESTRINA, OFFENBACH, SIR THOMAS LIPTON, MR
KING I (187) DUKE OF YORK, THE KING'S BROTHER. /NEWTON/ I AM ISAAC NEWTON, THE PHILOSOPHER. I AM ALSO AN ENGLISHMAN; AND
2TRU III (87) INTENSITY. /THE ELDER/ YES, SIR: THE UNIVERSE OF ISAAC NEWTON, WHICH HAS BEEN AN IMPREGNABLE CITADEL OF
KING PREFACE(154) LIES MAINLY IN THE CLASH OF CHARLES, GEORGE, AND ISAAC , THERE IS SOME FUN IN THE CLASH BETWEEN ALL THREE AND

ISABELLA

LION PREFACE(66) OF JUSTICE. WHICH, I TAKE IT, IS WHY SHAKESPEAR'S ISABELLA GAVE SUCH A DRESSING-DOWN TO JUDGE ANGELO, AND WHY
LADY PREFACE(219) NOTION OF RELIGION. I SAY ALMOST, BECAUSE ISABELLA IN MEASURE FOR MEASURE HAS RELIGIOUS CHARM, IN

ISAIAH

LION PREFACE(15) WE HAVE ONLY TO TAKE UP THE BIBLE AND READ ISAIAH AT ONE END OF SUCH A PERIOD AND LUKE AND JOHN AT THE
KING I (169) WHO WAS DYING OF A BOIL UNTIL THE PROPHET ISAIAH MADE THEM PUT A LUMP OF FIGS ON IT. /MRS BASHAM/

ISANDHLANA

BASH II,2, (117) SURGES BOILING UP AND BIDS ME JOIN THE MELLAY. ISANDHLANA AND VICTORY! (HE FALLS ON THE BYSTANDERS.) /THE
BASH II,2, (117) ON THE BYSTANDERS.) /THE CHIEFS/ VICTORY AND ISANDHLANA ! (THEY RUN AMOK. GENERAL PANIC AND STAMPEDE.

ISCARIOT

LION PREFACE(56) OF THE VIRTUES OF JESUS AS 100, AND OF JUDAS ISCARIOT AS ZERO, GIVE THE CORRECT FIGURES FOR,
SIM PREFACE(15) NOT TROUBLED TO ASK. WE ARE CLEAR ABOUT JUDAS ISCARIOT GOING TO HELL AND FLORENCE NIGHTINGALE TO HEAVEN;
GENV IV (110) HEAR! /SIR O./ WHAT ABOUT THE UNLOVABLES? JUDAS ISCARIOT , FOR INSTANCE? /DEACONESS/ IF HE HAD LOVED THE
LION II (129) I'LL SACRIFICE. /FERROVIUS/ DOG OF AN APOSTATE. ISCARIOT ! /SPINTHO/ I'LL REPENT AFTERWARDS. I FULLY MEAN

ISINGLASS

SUPR I SD(3) OF IRON-GREY HAIR, WHICH WILL SOON BE AS WHITE AS ISINGLASS , AND ARE IN OTHER RESPECTS NOT AT ALL UNLIKE IT.

ISIS

CLEO III (147) LOOKING MALIGNANTLY AFTER HIM) WE SHALL SEE WHOM ISIS LOVES BEST: HER SERVANT FTATATEETA OR A DOG OF A ROMAN.

ISLAM

CAPT NOTES (302)	WHO RIGHTLY HELD THAT THERE WAS MORE DANGER TO	ISLAM	IN ONE CUNNINGHAME GRAHAM THAN IN A THOUSAND
BULL PREFACE(63)	STRANGLING A HANDFUL OF POOR PEASANTS TO SCARE	ISLAM	INTO TERRIFIED SUBMISSION. WERE I ABJECT ENOUGH TO
SIM II (55)	HEARD OF, CALLING HIMSELF THE CALIPH OF BRITISH	ISLAM	. HE DEMANDS THAT IDDY SHALL PUT AWAY ALL HIS WIVES
SUPR III (108)	OF MEN WHO FOUGHT, NOT FOR THEMSELVES, BUT FOR	ISLAM	. THEY TOOK SPAIN FROM US, THOUGH WE WERE FIGHTING FOR
LION PREFACE(77)	POLYTHEISM IN INDIA, MONOTHEISM THROUGHOUT	ISLAM	, AND PRAGMATISM, OR NO-ISM, IN ENGLAND. PAUL'S
CLEO NOTES (212)	PUBLIC EXECUTIONS FOR THE PASSION OF HUMANITY.	ISLAM	, SUBSTITUTING VOLUPTUOUSNESS FOR TORMENT (A MERELY
SUPR III (109)	THIS IDEA OF A CATHOLIC CHURCH WILL SURVIVE	ISLAM	, WILL SURVIVE THE CROSS, WILL SURVIVE EVEN THAT

ISLAND

FABL III (111)	TO SPARE? /THE MATRON/ HOW DID YOU GET INTO THIS	ISLAND	? WHY WERE YOU ALLOWED TO LAND? /HE/ I WAS A
INCA (247)	HIS SON TO MARRY YOU IF THE BOY WERE ON A DESERT	ISLAND	AND YOU WERE THE ONLY OTHER HUMAN BEING ON IT (HE
CLEO II (125)	AND THINKS THAT THE CUSTOMS OF HIS TRIBE AND	ISLAND	ARE THE LAWS OF NATURE. /BRITANNUS/ ON THE CONTRARY,
MIS. PREFACE(99)	SUBSTITUTE THE IMITATION OF CHRIST FOR TREASURE	ISLAND	AS A PRESENT FOR A BOY OR GIRL, OR FOR BYRON'S DON
SIM II (57)	INFORMED YOU THAT THE IMPERIAL PROVINCE OF HOLY	ISLAND	DEMANDS THE IMMEDIATE AND EXEMPLARY COMBUSTION OF THE
SUPR PREFACE(R40)	IN FRANCE, CONFIDENTLY UTTERING THEIR OWN	ISLAND	DIPHTHONGS AS GOOD FRENCH VOWELS, MANY OF THEM OFFER,
MIS. PREFACE(94)	MAJORITY OF THE FELLOW SUBJECTS OF THE GOVERNING	ISLAND	DO NOT PROFESS THE RELIGION OF THAT ISLAND. BUT THIS
SIM II (57)	AS PHOSFOR HAMMINGTAP. THE PATIENCE OF THE HOLY	ISLAND	FLEET WILL BE EXHAUSTED AT NOON ON THE 13TH" TODAY "
SIM II (54)	/SIR CHARLES/ WHAT IS IT? /HYERING/ THE PITCAIRN	ISLAND	FLEET. THEY ARE SEVENTH DAY ADVENTISTS, AND ARE QUITE
BARB III (332)	MY FATHER'S DECEASED WIFE'S SISTER; AND IN THIS	ISLAND	I AM CONSEQUENTLY A FOUNDLING. (SENSATION).
LADY (245)	THE IMPREGNABLE ROCK OF YOUR PROUD HEART, A STONY	ISLAND	IN A SEA OF DESIRE. THERE, MADAM, IS SOME WHOLESOME
BUOY PREFACE(5)	GREAT BAYS BETWEEN HOWTH AND BRAY, WITH DALKEY	ISLAND	IN THE MIDDLE. I HAD ALREADY HAD A GLIMPSE OF THEM,
SIM I SD(36)	A STATELY HOUSE ON THE NORTH COAST OF A TROPICAL	ISLAND	IN THE PACIFIC COMMANDS A FINE VIEW OF THE OCEAN AND
CLEO III SD(144)	TO THE TOP, ON WHICH STANDS A CRESSET BEACON. THE	ISLAND	IS JOINED TO THE MAIN LAND BY THE HEPTASTADIUM, A
BULL (1)	JOHN BULL'S OTHER	ISLAND	. 1904.
APPL I (199)	AND HE MANAGED TO SWIM TO AN UNINHABITED	ISLAND	. ALL THE REST WERE DROWNED; AND HE WAS NOT TAKEN OFF
MIS. PREFACE(94)	ISLAND DO NOT PROFESS THE RELIGION OF THAT	ISLAND	. BUT THIS OBJECTIVITY, THOUGH INTELLECTUALLY HONEST,
VWOO 3 (133)	AND DISADVANTAGES OF BEING CAST AWAY ON A DESERT	ISLAND	. I AM CAST AWAY IN A VILLAGE ON THE WILTSHIRE DOWNS.
CLEO III (156)	MESSENGERS COMING ALONG THE MOLE TO US FROM THE	ISLAND	. I MUST SEE WHAT THEIR BUSINESS IS. (HE HURRIES OUT
BULL PREFACE(13)	FOR CHANGING THE DESTINATION OF JOHN BULL'S OTHER	ISLAND	. IT WAS UNCONGENIAL TO THE WHOLE SPIRIT OF THE
FABL III (109)	DOING HERE? /THE TOURIST/ ONLY HIKING ROUND THE	ISLAND	. MAY I TAKE A SNAPSHOT? /THE GIRL/ YOU HAVE NO
APPL I (199)	MY DEAR SEM: ONE ISNT ALONE ON AN UNINHABITED	ISLAND	. MY MOTHER USED TO STAND ME ON THE TABLE AND MAKE ME
BULL PREFACE(72)	CALL CONGRESS, OR FEDERAL GOVERNMENT OF THE WHOLE	ISLAND	. NO DOUBT THIS WILL BE RECEIVED IN BELFAST (IF
CYMB V (147)	MARK. THERE SPAKE THE FUTURE KING OF THIS RUDE	ISLAND	. /GUIDERIUS/ WITH YOU, SIR THIEF, TO TUTOR ME? NO,
SIM II (62)	STREET DECLARES FOR A RIGHT LITTLE TIGHT LITTLE	ISLAND	. /KANCHIN/ THE BRITISH PRIME MINISTER CUTS THE CABLE
SIM II (68)	THERE IS NOT SUCH A THING AS A TRUMPET IN THE	ISLAND	. THE FOUR COME RUSHING BACK INTO THE GARDEN, WILDLY
BULL I (91)	OF A BIG COMMONWEALTH, NOT A ROBINSON CRUSOE	ISLAND	. THEN THERES THE RELIGIOUS DIFFICULTY. MY
BULL I (87)	HIM IN IRELAND YOUVE GOT TO CALL THE UNFORTUNATE	ISLAND	KATHLEEN NI HOOLIHAN AND PRETEND SHE'S A LITTLE OLD
LION PREFACE(96)	FRENCH REPUBLIC AND THE TIGHT LITTLE	ISLAND	OF BRITAIN, INTO EMPIRES WHICH OVERFLOW THE FRONTIERS
BULL IV (174)	SEEMS DEAD, AND OUR HEARTS COLD AND COWED. AN	ISLAND	OF DREAMERS WHO WAKE UP IN YOUR JAILS, OF CRITICS AND
BULL IV (172)	OVER THE DEAD HEART AND BLINDED SOUL OF THE	ISLAND	OF THE SAINTS, YOU WILL COMFORT ME WITH THE BUSTLE OF
BULL IV (177)	PERFECTION: SAINTS AND TRAITORS. IT IS CALLED THE	ISLAND	OF THE SAINTS; BUT INDEED IN THESE LATER YEARS IT
BULL PREFACE(36)	VATICAN WILL GO THE WAY OF DUBLIN CASTLE, AND THE	ISLAND	OF THE SAINTS ASSUME THE HEADSHIP OF HER OWN CHURCH.
BULL PREFACE(37)	AND IMMORTAL MEMORY); BUT IT MAY HAPPEN SO. " THE	ISLAND	OF THE SAINTS" IS NO IDLE PHRASE. RELIGIOUS GENIUS IS
BULL IV (177)	LATER YEARS IT MIGHT BE MORE FITLY CALLED THE	ISLAND	OF THE TRAITORS; FOR OUR HARVEST OF THESE IS THE FINE
ROCK II (264)	VASTER THAN A MILLION DOGHOLES LIKE THIS	ISLAND	OF YOURS. THEY FOUNDED A CIVILIZATION COMPARED TO
JOAN 4 (102)	HIM GOD'S COMMAND THROUGH HER TO RETURN TO HIS	ISLAND	ON PAIN OF GOD'S VENGEANCE, WHICH SHE WILL EXECUTE.
MTH4 I (154)	OF THE WISE MEN OF THE WEST. CONSIDER THIS	ISLAND	ON WHICH WE STAND, THE LAST FOOTHOLD OF MAN ON THIS
GENV IV (111)	THE SCRUFF OF THE NECK AND FLINGS HIM INTO SOME	ISLAND	OR CAMP WHERE HE AND HIS LIKE CAN TRIFLE AND TWADDLE
BULL III (136)	BE REPLACED BY A FLAG AS GREEN AS THE	ISLAND	OVER WHICH IT WAVES: A FLAG ON WHICH WE SHALL ASK FOR
APPL II (261)	EMPEROR. KING MAY BE GOOD ENOUGH FOR THIS LITTLE	ISLAND	; BUT IF WE COME IN WE SHALL REQUIRE SOMETHING
NEVR II (230)	IT IMPOSSIBLE TO TAKE THE INHABITANTS OF THIS	ISLAND	SERIOUSLY. /M'COMAS/ I PRESUME, SIR, YOU ARE MASTER
DEST (192)	MARKET AS A REWARD FROM HEAVEN. IN DEFENCE OF HIS	ISLAND	SHORES, HE PUTS A CHAPLAIN ON BOARD HIS SHIP; NAILS A
BULL PREFACE(6)	TO ISSUE THIS CHEAP EDITION OF JOHN BULL'S OTHER	ISLAND	THIS HOME RULE YEAR, BECAUSE ITS PREFACE WAS WRITTEN
APPL I (200)	COUNTRY HOUSES. THINK OF THE HORROR OF THAT	ISLAND	TO HIM! A VOID! A PLACE WHERE HE WAS DEAF AND DUMB
MTH4 I (143)	IT IS THE PRACTICE AMONG NATIVES OF THE EASTERN	ISLAND	TO SPEND SOME YEARS HERE TO ACQUIRE MENTAL
CAPT I (229)	AGENT. CONSEQUENTLY THERE WAS NO SOLICITOR IN THE	ISLAND	TO TAKE UP THE CASE AGAINST HIM. /RANKIN/ IS SUCH A
BULL PREFACE(3)	GUESSED RIGHTLY). JOHN BULL'S OTHER	ISLAND	WAS WRITTEN WHEN A UNIONIST GOVERNMENT WAS IN POWER,
BULL PREFACE(13)	TO THE FIRST EDITION IN 1906). JOHN BULL'S OTHER	ISLAND	WAS WRITTEN IN 1904 AT THE REQUEST OF MR WILLIAM
LION PREFACE(99)	EMPIRE. THE STUARTS WRECKED EVEN THE TIGHT LITTLE	ISLAND	WHICH WAS THE NUCLEUS OF THE EMPIRE BY THEIR SCOTTISH
DOCT PREFACE(45)	WHO DARED TO APPEAR IN THE STREETS OF THIS RAINY	ISLAND	WITH AN UMBRELLA. THE OLD LINE BETWEEN MAN AND BEAST.
CLEO II (136)	IN THE EAST HARBOR, AND SEIZE THE PHAROS-- THAT	ISLAND	WITH THE LIGHTHOUSE. LEAVE HALF OUR MEN BEHIND TO
CAPT I (230)	HE HAD FORMERLY FORCED ME INTO. NOBODY IN THE	ISLAND	WOULD ACT AGAINST ME, LEAST OF ALL THE ATTORNEY AND
LION PREFACE(97)	FAITH IS NOW THE FAITH? THE INHABITANTS OF THIS	ISLAND	WOULD, WITHIN THE MEMORY OF PERSONS STILL LIVING,
CAPT I (230)	I FOUND THAT THIS DISHONEST AGENT HAD LEFT THE	ISLAND	, AND PLACED THE ESTATE IN THE HANDS OF AN AGENT OF
PYGM EPILOG (303)	SHE WISHES SHE COULD GET HIM ALONE, ON A DESERT	ISLAND	, AWAY FROM ALL TIES AND WITH NOBODY ELSE IN THE
BULL I (86)	THEM ENGLISH, THEY DONT BELONG TO THE DEAR OLD	ISLAND	, BUT TO THEIR CONFOUNDED NEW EMPIRE; AND BY GEORGE!
MTH4 I (143)	(HAUGHTILY) I WAS BORN, NOT IN THE EASTERN	ISLAND	, BUT, THANK GOD, IN DEAR OLD BRITISH BAGHDAD; AND I
CAPT I (229)	THE LAW? /SIR HOWARD/ THE LAW, SIR, IN THAT	ISLAND	, CONSISTED PRACTICALLY OF THE ATTORNEY GENERAL AND
MIS. (130)	MAN. READ BROWNING. NATURAL THEOLOGY ON AN	ISLAND	, EH? CALIBAN WAS AFRAID TO TEMPT PROVIDENCE: THAT
CLEO III SD(144)	WEST OVER THE EAST HARBOR OF ALEXANDRIA TO PHAROS	ISLAND	, JUST OFF THE END OF WHICH, AND CONNECTED WITH IT BY
BULL PREFACE(71)	SWING AS I WRITE. MEANWHILE, JOHN BULL'S OTHER	ISLAND	, THOUGH ITS FREEDOM HAS DESTROYED ALL THE ROMANTIC
BULL PREFACE(4)	SWING OF THE PENDULUM WAS THAT JOHN BULL'S OTHER	ISLAND	, WHICH HAD UP TO THAT MOMENT BEEN A TOPICAL PLAY,
SUPR PREFACE(R25)	THE MISMANAGEMENT OF A TIGHT BUT PAROCHIAL LITTLE	ISLAND	, WITH OCCASIONAL MEANINGLESS PROSECUTION OF DYNASTIC
CLEO II (141)	IS IT TRUE THAT WHEN CAESAR CAUGHT YOU ON THAT	ISLAND	, YOU WERE PAINTED ALL OVER BLUE? /BRITANNUS/ BLUE
BULL PREFACE(9)	LITTLE ENGLAND," THE " RIGHT LITTLE, TIGHT LITTLE	ISLAND	," DESPISED SPAIN FOR HER IMPERIAL POLICY, AND SAW
APPL II (261)	REQUIRE SOMETHING GRANDER. /MAGNUS/ THIS LITTLE	ISLAND	! " THIS LITTLE GEM SET IN A SILVER SEA! " HAS IT

ISLANDER

CLEO III (157)	WAS-- THAN CATO'S IS. O INCORRIGIBLE BRITISH	ISLANDER	: AM I A BULL DOG, TO SEEK QUARRELS MERELY TO SHEW
GENV III (83)	HEART OF ENGLAND. /THE JUDGE/ YOU MEAN A BRITISH	ISLANDER	FROM BIRMINGHAM, THE CHOICEST BREED OF MONGRELS IN
CLEO II (122)	THIS IS BRITANNUS, MY SECRETARY. HE IS AN	ISLANDER	FROM THE WESTERN END OF THE WORLD, A DAY'S VOYAGE
CLEO III (157)	OF A PARADOX? /RUFIO/ (RISING) CAESAR: WHEN THE	ISLANDER	HAS FINISHED PREACHING, CALL ME AGAIN. I AM GOING
CLEO II (140)	AN HOUR AGO. (CALLING) BRITANNICUS, THOU BRITISH	ISLANDER	. BRITANNICUS! CLEOPATRA RUNS IN THROUGH THE
CLEO III (155)	OF THE LIGHTHOUSE DOOR. /RUFIO/ WELL, MY BRITISH	ISLANDER	. HAVE YOU BEEN UP TO THE TOP? /BRITANNUS/ I HAVE.
ROCK II (265)	WASHED IN HIS PERSON OR HIS GARMENTS, A BRITISH	ISLANDER	. I WILL NO LONGER BEAR IT. THE VEIL OF YOUR
CLEO V (197)	RECOVER HIMSELF). /CAESAR/ WHERE IS THAT BRITISH	ISLANDER	OF MINE? /BRITANNUS/ (COMING FORWARD ON CAESAR'S
CLEO II (141)	HE BUCKLES THE CUIRASS). /CLEOPATRA/ PEACE, THOU:	ISLANDER	! (TO CAESAR) YOU SHOULD RUB YOUR HEAD WITH

ISLANDERS

LION PREFACE(97)	OF GOD, AND THAT ALL OTHERS ARE HEATHEN. BUT WE	ISLANDERS	ARE ONLY FORTY-FIVE MILLIONS; AND IF WE COUNT
CAPT NOTES (304)	INTO HIS NATIVE LANGUAGE FOR THE USE OF BRITISH	ISLANDERS	AS A PRIMER OF SPOKEN ENGLISH, IS THE MOST
CLEO PRO1 (89)	BE SILENT AND HEARKEN UNTO ME, YE QUAINT LITTLE	ISLANDERS	. GIVE EAR, YE MEN WITH WHITE PAPER ON YOUR
MILL PREFACE(126)	ARE HARDLY ANY PURE-BRED MAORIES OR SOUTH SEA	ISLANDERS	LEFT. IN AFRICA THE INTELLIGENT PINK NATIVE IS A
JOAN PREFACE(33)	SIDE IS IMPLIED IN THE REFUSAL OF THE MARQUESAS	ISLANDERS	TO BE PERSUADED THAT THE ENGLISH DID NOT EAT JOAN.
SIM II (69)	POSSIBLY. /HYERING/ DO YOU MEAN THAT THE PITCAIRN	ISLANDERS	WERE RIGHT AFTER ALL? ! /THE ANGEL/ YES. YOU ARE
SIM II (68)	WILL GET TIRED OF LAZY PEOPLE; AND THE PITCAIRN	ISLANDERS	WILL SEE THEIR DAY OF JUDGMENT AT LAST. A DISTANT

ISLANDS

MTH4 I (170)	AND DIGNITY OF ONE WHO HAS VISITED THE HOLY	ISLANDS	AND SPOKEN FACE TO FACE WITH THE INEFFABLE ONES. HE
MTH4 II (192)	BY THIS DREAM TO WHICH THE EXISTENCE OF THESE	ISLANDS	AND THEIR ORACLES GIVES A DELUSIVE POSSIBILITY OF
FABL II (106)	JUST AS WE SELECTED HIROSHIMA IN 1945. HE THINKS	ISLANDS	ARE OUT-OF-THE-WAY LITTLE PLACES THAT DONT MATTER TO
MTH3 (94)	WON. /BARNABAS/ THEY WOULD HAVE MADE THE BRITISH	ISLANDS	BANKRUPT IF THEYD WON. BUT YOU DONT CARE FOR THAT:
MTH4 II (191)	TO REPRODUCE IT IN THE NORTHERN PART OF THESE	ISLANDS	BY JONHOBSNOXIUS, CALLED THE LEVIATHAN? THOSE
SIM II (81)	AND I HAVE STILL OUR DUTIES: THE UNEXPECTED	ISLANDS	HAVE TO BE GOVERNED TODAY JUST AS THEY HAD TO BE
PYGM III (251)	THE SHALLOW DEPRESSION IN THE WEST OF THESE	ISLANDS	IS LIKELY TO MOVE SLOWLY IN AN EASTERLY DIRECTION.

MTH3 SD(91)	OFFICIAL PARLOR OF THE PRESIDENT OF THE BRITISH	ISLANDS	. A BOARD TABLE, LONG ENOUGH FOR THREE CHAIRS AT
MTH4 I (154)	MAJESTIC SPIRIT. WELL, THEY WERE BORN IN THESE	ISLANDS	. I REPEAT, THESE ISLANDS WERE THEN, INCREDIBLE AS
CAPT I (229)	DIED, HE LEFT AN ESTATE IN ONE OF THE WEST INDIAN	ISLANDS	. IT WAS IN CHARGE OF AN AGENT WHO WAS A SHARPISH
MTH4 II (190)	SOON REVERTED TO THE ORIGINAL WHITE OF THESE	ISLANDS	. /THE ELDERLY GENTLEMAN/ BUT HAVE YOU CONSIDERED
SIM II (57)	13TH" TODAY " AND THE CAPITAL OF THE UNEXPECTED	ISLANDS	MUST TAKE THE CONSEQUENCES." NUMBER FOUR-- /SIR
FANY III (323)	COUNCIL IS UNKNOWN TO YOU; EVERYWHERE IN THESE	ISLANDS	ONE CAN ENJOY THE EXHILARATING, THE SOUL-LIBERATING
BULL IV (177)	CROP OF INFAMY, BUT THE DAY MAY COME WHEN THESE	ISLANDS	SHALL LIVE BY THE QUALITY OF THEIR MEN RATHER THAN
BARB PREFACE(207)	THAT LIFE AND LITERATURE ARE SO POOR IN THESE	ISLANDS	THAT WE MUST GO ABROAD FOR ALL DRAMATIC MATERIAL
APPL PREFACE(190)	THE WORK OF AN ATLANTIC LINER. WE NEED IN THESE	ISLANDS	TWO OR THREE ADDITIONAL FEDERAL LEGISLATURES,
HART PREFACE(7)	ACTIVITY PRODUCED BY TERROR. BUT IN THESE	ISLANDS	WE MUDDLED THROUGH. NATURE GAVE US A LONGER CREDIT
MTH4 I (154)	CRADLE OF HIS RACE IN MESOPOTAMIA, THE WESTERN	ISLANDS	WERE CAST OFF, AS THEY HAD BEEN BEFORE BY THE ROMAN
GENV PREFACE(3)	ONLY FROM TEN TO FIFTEEN INHABITANTS OF THESE	ISLANDS	WERE KILLED BY AIR RAIDS EVERY DAY; AND A DOZEN OR
MTH4 I (140)	YES, YOU MAY NOT BE AWARE, MADAM, THAT THESE	ISLANDS	WERE ONCE THE CENTRE OF THE BRITISH COMMONWEALTH,
MTH4 I (154)	THEY WERE BORN IN THESE ISLANDS. I REPEAT, THESE	ISLANDS	WERE THEN, INCREDIBLE AS IT NOW SEEMS, THE CENTRE OF
MTH4 I (162)	BE INSECTS; BUT LIKE THE CORAL INSECT WE BUILD	ISLANDS	WHICH BECOME CONTINENTS: LIKE THE BEE WE STORE
MTH4 I (149)	ELDERLY GENTLEMAN/ PRAY, IS THERE NO ONE IN THESE	ISLANDS	WHO UNDERSTANDS PLAIN ENGLISH? /ZOO/ WELL, NOBODY
MTH4 II (181)	WERE YOU NOT RASH TO VENTURE INTO THESE SACRED	ISLANDS	WITH SUCH A QUESTION ON YOUR LIPS? WARRIORS ARE NOT
MTH4 I (169)	THAT WE SHOULD STAY AS WE ARE, CONFINED TO THESE	ISLANDS	, A RACE APART, WRAPPED UP IN THE MAJESTY OF OUR
DOCT PREFACE(72)	PIETY, AND IN SOME UNLUCKY PLACES (THE SANDWICH	ISLANDS	, FOR EXAMPLE) MADE THE INTRODUCTION OF CHRISTIANITY
MTH4 I (154)	BUT IT WAS TO THE BRITISH RACE, AND IN THESE	ISLANDS	, THAT THE GREATEST MIRACLE IN HISTORY OCCURRED.
MTH4 I (154)	HEART, TO THE MYSTERY AND BEAUTY OF THESE HAUNTED	ISLANDS	, THRONGED WITH SPECTRES FROM A MAGIC PAST, MADE
MTH4 I (153)	THE EASTERN EMPIRE TO ITS ANCIENT SEAT IN THESE	ISLANDS	, TO A TIME WHEN TWO OF MY ANCESTORS, JOYCE BOLGE

ISLE

LADY PREFACE(222)	A CALIBAN WHO COULD SAY " BE NOT AFEARD: THE	ISLE	IS FULL OF NOISES, SOUNDS AND SWEET AIRS THAT GIVE
ROCK I (215)	OUT OF THIS. WE DONT RUN TO SPANISH IN THE	ISLE	. (RESIGNEDLY) GOOD MORNING. (HE GOES OUT). /SIR
ROCK I (218)	AND YOU CALL THAT DEBATING. IF I DID THAT IN THE	ISLE	NOT A MAN WOULD STOP TO LISTEN TO ME. MIND YOU, I KNOW
ROCK II (255)	DROP COMPENSATION OR NEVER SHEW YOUR FACE IN THE	ISLE	OF CATS AGAIN. (HE GOES OUT RESOLUTELY). /BLEE/ TAKE
ROCK I (217)	I COULD WIN THE SEAT. PUT UP OLD HIPNEY FOR THE	ISLE	OF CATS AND YOUR BEST MAN WOULDNT HAVE A CHANCE AGAINST
ROCK I (222)	I HATE TO SAY ANYTHING; BUT REALLY, WHEN THOSE	ISLE	OF CATS PEOPLE TOOK THEMSELVES OFF YOUR HANDS ALMOST
ROCK II (252)	I'M TELLING YOU THAT THE LABOR PARTY OF THE	ISLE	OF CATS PUTS DOWN ITS FOOT AND SAYS NO COMPENSATION. IS
ROCK II (249)	LOSE EVERY VOTE IN THE ISLE OF CATS, AND WHAT THE	ISLE	OF CATS THINKS TODAY, ALL ENGLAND THINKS TOMORROW. /SIR
ROCK I (209)	YOU SAY YOU WOULD RECEIVE A DEPUTATION FROM THE	ISLE	OF CATS THIS MORNING? I HAVE NO NOTE OF IT. /SIR
ROCK II (249)	SILLY NEW PROGRAM HE'LL LOSE EVERY VOTE IN THE	ISLE	OF CATS, AND WHAT THE ISLE OF CATS THINKS TODAY, ALL
ROCK I (213)	OF THAT CLASS I APOLOGIZE FOR HIM TO THE	ISLE	OF CATS. I APOLOGIZE FOR HIS DRESS, FOR HIS MANNERS,
ROCK I (210)	THAT YOU REPRESENT THE UPPER CLASSES IN THE	ISLE	OF CATS. /OXFORD YOUTH/ THERE ARE NO UPPER CLASSES IN
ROCK I (211)	/OXFORD YOUTH/ THERE ARE NO UPPER CLASSES IN THE	ISLE	OF CATS. /SIR ARTHUR/ IN THAT CASE, SINCE IT IS AGREED
ROCK II (249)	SIR JAFNA PANDRANATH. THE MAYOR OF THE	ISLE	OF CATS. /SIR JAFNA/ YOU HAVE HEARD OF ME, MR MAYOR.
ROCK I (221)	WHOLE MORNING IS GONE WITH THOSE PEOPLE FROM THE	ISLE	OF CATS. /SIR ARTHUR/ BUT I HAVE MOUNTAINS OF WORK TO
ROCK I (210)	BEING MAYOR OF-- OF-- /HILDA/ (PROMPTING) THE	ISLE	OF CATS. /THE YOUNG WOMAN/ (BRIGHTLY, HELPING HER OUT)
ROCK I (209)	THE DOOR OPEN) THE WORSHIPFUL THE MAYOR OF THE	ISLE	OF CATS. THE MAYOR, THICK AND ELDERLY, ENTERS, A LITTLE
ROCK II (247)	(BEAMING) GENTLEMEN: A LABOR DEPUTATION FROM THE	ISLE	OF CATS. THE ONE ELEMENT THAT WAS LACKING IN OUR
POSN PREFACE(416)	WORLD AS THE KING'S NAVAL CAREER FROM THE	ISLE	OF DOGS? THE MOMENT WE COME TO THAT NECESSARY PART OF
METH PREFACE(R52)	SEEMS TO HAVE CONVINCED THE CATS OF THE	ISLE	OF MAN. HAVING THUS MADE THE MICE DESIRE TO LOSE THEIR
FABL IV SD(114)	FOURTH FABLE. THE SAME PLACE IN THE	ISLE	OF WIGHT: BUT THE BUILDING IS NOW INSCRIBED DIET
FABL II (106)	WHAT! DONT YOU KNOW THAT HE WENT TO LIVE IN THE	ISLE	OF WIGHT AS THE SAFEST CIVILIZED PLACE IN THE WORLD,
FABL III (109)	/THE GIRL/ YOU HAVE NO BUSINESS TO BE ON THE	ISLE	OF WIGHT AT ALL. WHO LET YOU LAND? /THE TOURIST/ I
FABL II (106)	THAT THE WORLD WAS AT HIS MERCY. HE SELECTED THE	ISLE	OF WIGHT BECAUSE IT'S A SAFE DISTANCE FROM HIS OWN
FABL II (106)	TO WAR WITH ANYBODY. HE DROPPED HIS BOMBS ON THE	ISLE	OF WIGHT JUST TO SHEW CAPETOWN AND THE REST THAT THE
FABL III SD(109)	THIRD FABLE. A PLEASANT SPOT IN THE	ISLE	OF WIGHT. A BUILDING OF STEEL AND GLASS IS INSCRIBED
FABL II (105)	IS NOT ONE OF GOD'S CREATURES LEFT ALIVE IN THE	ISLE	OF WIGHT. I SHALL HAVE TO SEND EVERY SOLDIER IN ENGLAND
SUPR PREFACE(R28)	THE INDUSTRIAL NORTH, BUT THE PROSPERITY OF THE	ISLE	OF WIGHT, OF FOLKESTONE AND RAMSGATE, OF NICE AND MONTE
OVER (185)	FOR MY SAKE, AND COME WITH ME TO SOME SOUTHERN	ISLE	-- OR SAY SOUTH AMERICA-- WHERE WE CAN BE ALL IN ALL TO

ISLES

SIM (1)	THE SIMPLETON OF THE UNEXPECTED	ISLES	: 1934.
CLEO NOTES (209)	DIFFERENCE IN THE HUMAN FAUNA OF THESE	ISLES	? CERTAINLY I DO NOT, JULIUS CAESAR, AS TO CAESAR
LION PREF,FN(43)	ALL THE WHITE INHABITANTS OF THE BRITISH	ISLES	
SIM II (84)	IN THE UNEXPECTED ISLES; AND IN THE UNEXPECTED	ISLES	ALL PLANS FAIL. SO MUCH THE BETTER: PLANS ARE ONLY
SIM II (84)	CYNICS AND PESSIMISTS BECAUSE IN THE UNEXPECTED	ISLES	ALL THEIR LITTLE PLANS FAIL: WOMEN WILL NEVER LET GO
SIM II (63)	IS ALL. WE HAD BETTER PROCLAIM THE UNEXPECTED	ISLES	AN INDEPENDENT REPUBLIC AND SECURE THE NEW JOBS FOR
SIM II (84)	IS NO COUNTRY OF THE EXPECTED. THE UNEXPECTED	ISLES	ARE THE WHOLE WORLD. /PROLA/ YES, IF OUR FOOLS ONLY
CAPT NOTES (306)	BUT OUT OF THE QUESTION ELSEWHERE IN THE BRITISH	ISLES	. IN AMERICA, REPRESENTATIONS OF ENGLISH SPEECH DWELL
SIM PREFACE(16)	THE FABLE OF THE SIMPLETON OF THE UNEXPECTED	ISLES	. IN IT I STILL RETAIN THE ANCIENT FANCY THAT THE RACE
MILL PREFACE(121)	THE SHRIEKERS AND TRANSPORTED THEM TO THE LIPARI	ISLES	. PARLIAMENT, OPENLY FLOUTED, CHASTISED, AND
SIM PRO,1, (21)	THE SIMPLETON OF THE UNEXPECTED	ISLES	. PROLOGUE. THE EMIGRATION OFFICE AT A TROPICAL PORT
SIM II (64)	/KANCHIN/ WE SHALL MAKE YOU THE EMPRESS OF THE	ISLES	. /JANGA/ PROLA THE FIRST. /VASHTI/ HOMAGE, PROLA.
2TRU II (54)	HIM, SIR. HE ADDRESSED ME AS LORD OF THE WESTERN	ISLES	. /TALLBOYS/ YOU! YOU WORM! IF MY LETTER WAS SENT BY
SIM I (43)	IS MR HUGO HYERING, POLITICAL SECRETARY TO THE	ISLES	. /THE CLERGYMAN/ HOW DO YOU DO, SIR HUGO? /HYERING/
SIM II (85)	OUR PLANS WILL STILL LEAD US TO THE UNEXPECTED	ISLES	. WE SHALL MAKE WARS BECAUSE ONLY UNDER THE STRAIN OF
SIM I (38)	VERY HARD TO BELIEVE. /PROLA/ IN THE UNEXPECTED	ISLES	NOTHING IS UNBELIEVABLE. HOW DID YOU GET IN HERE?
SIM II (84)	OF THE WORLD. REMEMBER: WE ARE IN THE UNEXPECTED	ISLES	; AND IN THE UNEXPECTED ISLES ALL PLANS FAIL. SO MUCH
SIM PREFACE(18)	IN THE EAST FROM MARRIAGE IN THE BRITISH	ISLES	; BUT I HAVE INTRODUCED IT ONLY TO BRING INTO THE
SIM I (37)	BRITISH EMPIRE. /THE CLERGYMAN/ DO YOU MEAN THE	ISLES	THAT CAME UP OUT OF THE SEA WHEN I WAS A BABY. /PRA/
SIM II (85)	LIKE FRIGHTENED CHILDREN; BUT IN THE UNEXPECTED	ISLES	THERE IS NO SECURITY; AND THE FUTURE IS TO THOSE WHO
SIM I (37)	COUNTRY I AM IN. /PRA/ YOU ARE IN THE UNEXPECTED	ISLES	, A CROWN COLONY OF THE BRITISH EMPIRE. /THE
KING I (192)	ARE NOT A FIGHTING MAN; AND I AM. IN THE BRITISH	ISLES	, CHARLES, NOTHING IS MORE POPULAR THAN THE NAVY; AND
GENV I (45)	AT WORK IN RUSSIA, FINANCED FROM THE BRITISH	ISLES	, HAVING FOR ITS OBJECT THE OVERTHROW OF THE SOVIET
SIM I (43)	INTRODUCE YOU TO THE GOVERNOR OF THE UNEXPECTED	ISLES	, SIR CHARLES FARWATERS. /SIR CHARLES/ (OFFERING HIS

ISLET

SIM II (56)	INSISTS ON ITS SEPARATE FLEET, EVERY TRUMPERY	ISLET	ITS BATTLESHIP, ITS CRUISER, OR AT LEAST ITS SLOOP OR

ISLINGTON

BASH II,1, (112)	AS YET BUT HALF BEGUN, MUST ENDED BE IN MERRIE	ISLINGTON	. (EXEUNT LYDIA AND CASHEL.) /BASHVILLE/ GODS!
BASH II,1, (110)	I MUST MEET A MONARCH THIS VERY AFTERNOON AT	ISLINGTON	. /LYDIA/ AT ISLINGTON! YOU MUST BE MAD. /CASHEL/
ROCK II (267)	LENIN LEARNT HIS LESSON IN HOLFORD SQUARE,	ISLINGTON	. WHY CAN WE NEVER THINK OUT ANYTHING, NOR LEARN
FOUN (221)	/MERCER/ I MOVED ALL THE WAY FROM GOSPEL OAK TO	ISLINGTON	TO ESCAPE; BUT IT WAS NO USE. /THE LORD
BASH II,2,SD(113)	THE AGRICULTURAL HALL IN	ISLINGTON	, CROWDED WITH SPECTATORS. IN THE ARENA A THRONE,
BASH III (125)	HIS GLORIOUS VICTORY OVER OUR COUNTRY'S FOES AT	ISLINGTON	, THE FLAG OF ENGLAND SHALL FOR EVER BEAR ON AZURE
BASH II,1, (110)	THIS VERY AFTERNOON AT ISLINGTON. /LYDIA/ AT	ISLINGTON	! YOU MUST BE MAD. /CASHEL/ A CAB! GO CALL A

ISM

GENV PREFACE(16)	OF THE PRINCIPLES OF SOCIALISM OR ANY OTHER	ISM	(I DISPOSED OF ALL THAT LONG AGO), AND TRY TO OPEN MY

ISMS

SUPR III (107)	OF JUSTICE, DUTY, PATRIOTISM, AND ALL THE OTHER	ISMS	BY WHICH EVEN THOSE WHO ARE CLEVER ENOUGH TO BE

ISN'T

CAPT II (249)	OF THIS INSTITUTION. I SPOSE ITS ALL RIGHT,	ISN'T	IT? /DRINKWATER/ YUSS, AN HORDER HUZ ABAHT AS IF WE

ISOLATE

MTH4 I (166)	STILL A LITTLE MORE. . . . GOT YOU: RIGHT.	ISOLATE	BURRIN PIER QUICK. /THE ELDERLY GENTLEMAN/ (IS
MTH4 II (183)	QUICKLY, INTONING) ISOLATE THE FALSTAFF MONUMENT	ISOLATE	HARD. PARALYZE-- (THE WHISTLING STOPS). THANK YOU.
METH PREFACE(R45)	LEARN HOW COMPLETELY EVEN A MAN OF GENIUS COULD	ISOLATE	HIMSELF BY ANTAGONIZING DARWIN ON THE ONE HAND AND
MTH4 II (183)	CENTRAL. (THE WHISTLING CONTINUES). STAND BY TO	ISOLATE	. (TO THE ELDERLY GENTLEMAN, WHO IS STARING AFTER
MTH4 II (183)	OF A FAT OLD MAN. /ZOO/ (QUICKLY, INTONING)	ISOLATE	THE FALSTAFF MONUMENT ISOLATE HARD. PARALYZE-- (THE

ISOLATED
METH PREFACE(R73) SCIENTIFICALLY INADMISSIBLE, BECAUSE IT CANNOT BE ISOLATED AND EXPERIMENTED WITH IN THE LABORATORY. SECOND,

ISOLATION
UNPL PREFACE(R18) UPPER CLASSES IN THEIR OWN ORBIT, OR ITS STAGNANT ISOLATION MADE IMPOSSIBLE BY THE CONDITIONS OF WORKING CLASS

ISOLATIONIST
GENV III (76) POSE IS THAT OF THE RUGGED INDIVIDUALIST, THE ISOLATIONIST , AT BOTTOM AN ANARCHIST. /THE NEWCOMER/

ISOLDE
OVER PREFACE(166) GIOVANNI AND ZERLINA ARE NOT GROSS: TRISTAN AND ISOLDE ARE NOT EXTRAVAGANT OR SENTIMENTAL. THEY SAY AND DO
MRS PREFACE(166) IN COMPARISON WITH WAGNER'S TRISTAN, EVEN THOUGH ISOLDE BE BOTH FOURTEEN STONE AND FORTY, AS SHE OFTEN IS IN
HART II (113) IS A MOON: IT'S LIKE THE NIGHT IN TRISTAN AND ISOLDE . (SHE CARESSES HIS ARM AND DRAWS HIM TO THE PORT
OVER PREFACE(163) ON THE STAGE IN THE SAME WAY. IN TRISTAN AND ISOLDE , THE CURTAIN DOES NOT, AS IN ROMEO AND JULIET, RISE

ISOLDES
SUPR PREFACE(R11) TO OUR CHILDISH THEATRES. THERE THE JULIETS AND ISOLDES , THE ROMEOS AND TRISTANS, MIGHT BE OUR MOTHERS AND

ISOTOPE
FABL II (106) NOT A LABORATORY BLOKE. DO YOU KNOW WHAT AN ISOTOPE IS? DO YOU KNOW WHAT A MESON IS? I DONT: NEITHER

ISRAEL
O'FL (215) SHE SAYS WE'RE THE LOST TRIBES OF THE HOUSE OF ISRAEL AND THE CHOSEN PEOPLE OF GOD. SHE SAYS THAT THE
MILL PREFACE(125) CANNOT GET OVER THE FACT THAT THE LOST TRIBES OF ISRAEL EXPOSE US ALL TO THE SUSPICION (SOMETIMES, AS IN
LION PREFACE(27) EXCLUSIVELY TO " THE LOST SHEEP OF THE HOUSE OF ISRAEL ." WHEN A WOMAN OF CANAAN BEGGED JESUS TO CURE HER
UNPL PREFACE(R20) I LOOK AT YOUR PLAYING, SIR HENRY, I SEEM TO SEE ISRAEL MOURNING THE CAPTIVITY AND CRYING, ' HOW LONG, O
MTH4 I (155) ON THE GROUND THAT THEY WERE THE LOST TRIBES OF ISRAEL ; BUT ON THEIR APPROACH THE JEWS ABANDONED THE CITY
POSN PREFACE(361) THE BISHOP OF SOUTHWARK, MR HALL CAINE, MR ISRAEL ZANGWILL, SIR SQUIRE BANCROFT, SIR ARTHUR PINERO, AND
LION PREFACE(75) ON THEM A TEDIOUS SKETCH OF THE HISTORY OF ISRAEL , WITH WHICH THEY WERE PRESUMABLY AS WELL ACQUAINTED

ISRAELITES
FABL PREFACE(81) CHAPTER FROM THE BIBLE WHICH DESCRIBES HOW THE ISRAELITES IN CAPTIVITY WERE INSTRUCTED BY A DEIFIED
FABL V (119) /ROSE/ TRUE. ANOTHER SET OF THEM, CALLED JEWS OR ISRAELITES , TORTURED A YOUNG MAN TO DEATH FOR TRYING TO

ISSELF
BARB II (274) I KNOW. EVERY LOAFER THAT CANT DO NOTHINK CALLS ISSELF A PAINTER. WELL, I'M A REAL PAINTER: GRAINER,

ISSEOLF
CAPT I (222) (OFFICIOUSLY) BRARSBAHND, GAVNER. AWLUS CALLS ISSEOLF BRARSBAHND. /RANKIN/ WELL, BRASSBOUND THEN. WHAT IS

ISSUE
CYMB V (147) AND BLOOD OF YOUR BEGETTING. /CYMBELINE/ HOW? MY ISSUE ? /BELARIUS/ SO SURE AS YOU YOUR FATHER'S. THESE YOUR
POSN PREFACE(429) COURT THAT HE HAD INDUCED THE LORD CHAMBERLAIN TO ISSUE A CERTIFICATE THAT THE PROSPECTUS CONTAINED NOTHING
GENV I (34) TO THE INTERNATIONAL COURT, CALLING ON IT TO ISSUE A WARRANT FOR THE ARREST OF MY OPPRESSOR ON A CHARGE
GENV II (58) NAPOLEON AND THE DUC D'ENGHIEN. BUT IF YOU ISSUE A WARRANT OR PRONOUNCE A SENTENCE AGAINST ONE OF THEM
NEVR II SD(240) TABLE AND BECKONS TO THE KITCHEN ENTRANCE, WHENCE ISSUE A YOUNG WAITER WITH SOUP PLATES, AND A COOK, IN WHITE
ROCK PREFACE(183) NEVER HAD TO PASS A SENTENCE NOR LEVY A TAX NOR ISSUE AN EDICT! WHAT HAVE YOU TO SAY THAT I SHOULD NOT HAVE
MIS. PREFACE(93) SCHOOLMASTER'S BACK IS TURNED. WHAT CONFUSES THIS ISSUE AND LEADS EVEN HIGHLY INTELLIGENT RELIGIOUS PERSONS TO
ROCK PREFACE(178) TRIALS, NO DOUBT GALILEO MISSED THE REAL POINT AT ISSUE AS COMPLETELY AS SOCRATES OR JESUS. FOR THIS WE NEED
ROCK PREFACE(176) THE POINT BECAUSE THEY THINK THAT THE QUESTION AT ISSUE AT HIS TRIAL WAS WHETHER THE EARTH WENT ROUND THE SUN
DOCT PREFACE(49) OF THE METHOD AND TEMPER OF SCIENCE. THE POINT AT ISSUE BEING PLAINLY WHETHER HE IS A RASCAL OR NOT, HE NOT
LION PREFACE(25) HIS DOCTRINE BY RAISING AN ENTIRELY IRRELEVANT ISSUE BETWEEN HIS DISCIPLES AND HIS OPPONENTS. POSSIBLY MY
PLES PREFACE(R18) FROM SLAVERY. BUT IT HAD NO BEARING ON THE REAL ISSUE BETWEEN MY CRITIC AND MYSELF, WHICH WAS, WHETHER THE
SUPR I (24) WOMAN. WHICH SHALL USE UP THE OTHER? THAT IS THE ISSUE BETWEEN THEM. AND IT IS ALL THE DEADLIER BECAUSE, IN
PLES PREFACE(R18) IT WAS NOT REALLY MERE MATTER OF FACT THAT WAS AT ISSUE BETWEEN US. ONE STRONGLY LIBERAL CRITIC, THE LATE MOY
APPL I (205) OUGHT NOT TO BE KILLED; BUT I MAY NOT EVEN ISSUE DEATH WARRANTS FOR A GREAT MANY PEOPLE WHO IN MY
CLEO II (123) NO. /CAESAR/ YOU SAY THE MATTER HAS BEEN AT ISSUE FOR A YEAR, POTHINUS. MAY I HAVE TEN MINUTES AT IT?
ROCK PREFACE(175) EITHER CASE THE QUESTION OF TOLERATION WAS NOT AT ISSUE FOR HIM; THEREFORE HE DID NOT RAISE IT. THE CASE OF
LION PREFACE(91) YOU HAVE TO JUDGE BROUGHT TO AN APPREHENSIBLE ISSUE FOR YOU. EVEN IF YOU HAVE LITTLE MORE RESPECT FOR
MTH5 SD(220) TO THE STEPS OF THE TEMPLE). THE TWO SCULPTORS ISSUE FROM THE TEMPLE. ONE HAS A BEARD TWO FEET LONG: THE
6CAL SD(96) AND THE LORDS DERBY, NORTHAMPTON, AND ARUNDEL, ISSUE FROM THEIR TENTS AND ASSEMBLE BEHIND THE CHAIR OF
LADY PREFACE(229) NOT OF DEMOCRACY, WHICH WAS NOT A LIVE POLITICAL ISSUE IN SHAKESPEAR'S TIME, BUT OF IMPARTIALITY IN JUDGING
APPL I (232) WITH ME IN PRIVATE TO A POINT AT WHICH THE ISSUE IS NOW CLEAR. IF I DO NOT ACCEPT THE ULTIMATUM I SHALL
HART PREFACE(40) BE MILITARILY EXPEDIENT TO REVEAL THEM WHILST THE ISSUE IS STILL IN THE BALANCE. TRUTH TELLING IS NOT
DOCT PREFACE(25) AND BOTH PARTIES ASSUME THAT WHAT IS AT ISSUE IS THE SCIENTIFIC SOUNDNESS OF THE PROPHYLAXIS. IT
SUPR III (118) TO BE CORRUPTED: MY BRAIN STILL SAID NO ON EVERY ISSUE . AND WHILST I WAS IN THE ACT OF FRAMING MY EXCUSE TO
BULL PREFACE(12) I COULD RIDE OFF IF I WISHED TO SHIRK THE MAIN ISSUE . BUT WHEN ALL IS SAID, IT IS SO CERTAIN THAT IN THE
ROCK PREFACE(180) NOTHING OF THE CONSTITUTIONAL QUESTIONS AT ISSUE . SOME OF THEM REMAIN IN THIS CONDITION OF
ROCK PREFACE(176) ROUND WHICH THE SUN CIRCLED. NOW THAT WAS NOT THE ISSUE . TAKEN BY ITSELF IT WAS A MERE QUESTION OF PHYSICAL
DOCT PREFACE(33) PRESENTLY FIND THEMSELVES FIGHTING ON A FALSE ISSUE . THE FLAW IN THE ARGUMENT. I MAY AS WELL PAUSE HERE
DOCT PREFACE(65) AS EVERY INCREASE IN HIS SALARY DEPENDS ON THE ISSUE OF A PUBLIC DEBATE AS TO THE HEALTH OF THE
FABL PREFACE(76) CLERGY OF THE ESTABLISHED CHURCH ON THE POLITICAL ISSUE OF EPISCOPAL OR LAY CHURCH GOVERNMENT. THE UNITARIANS
MILL IV (207) THEY WERE RICH AND GENEROUS: THEY MADE A SPECIAL ISSUE OF FOUNDERS' SHARES FOR HER, WORTH THREE HUNDRED A
POSN PREFACE(407) HOWEVER, QUITE ARGUABLE THAT THE INDISCRIMINATE ISSUE OF FREE ADMISSIONS, THOUGH AN APPARENTLY INNOCENT AND
POSN PREFACE(406) IS STRIPPED BY THE VIRTUALLY INDISCRIMINATE ISSUE OF FREE TICKETS TO THE MEN. ACCESS TO THE STAGE IS
JOAN 6 (128) HER INNOCENT, SHE MAY ESCAPE US ON THE GREAT MAIN ISSUE OF HERESY, ON WHICH SHE SEEMS SO FAR TO INSIST ON HER
CYMB V (147) THEY ARE MY SONS, ARE NONE OF MINE. THEY ARE THE ISSUE OF YOUR LOINS, MY LIEGE, AND BLOOD OF YOUR BEGETTING.
APPL I (232) CABINET GOVERNMENT AND MONARCHICAL GOVERNMENT: AN ISSUE ON WHICH I FRANKLY SAY THAT I SHOULD BE VERY SORRY TO
LION PREFACE(26) FROM THE MIRACLES WOULD BE THE IRRELEVANCE OF THE ISSUE RAISED BY THEM. JESUS'S TEACHING HAS NOTHING TO DO
BASH II,1, (103) ON WINNING OUT OF HAND, SENT IN HIS RIGHT. THE ISSUE SEEMED A CERT, WHEN CASHEL, DUCKING SMARTLY TO HIS
LION PREFACE(59) ECONOMIC EQUALITY BETWEEN CABIN BOYS. WHAT IS AT ISSUE STILL IS WHETHER THERE SHALL BE ECONOMIC EQUALITY
LION PREFACE(92) MAKES DIFFERENT SORTS OF TARTS, THE PRACTICAL ISSUE STILL LIES AS PLAINLY BEFORE YOU AS BEFORE THE MOST
GENV IV (94) SNAPPED MY FINGERS IN ENGLAND'S FACE ON EVERY ISSUE THAT HAS RISEN BETWEEN US. EUROPE LOOKS TO ME, NOT TO
BULL PREFACE(6) VOLUMES. THEREFORE, I THINK IT OPPORTUNE TO ISSUE THIS CHEAP EDITION OF JOHN BULL'S OTHER ISLAND THIS
APPL II (267) ARE YOU INEXORABLY DETERMINED TO FORCE THIS ISSUE TO ITS LOGICAL END? YOU KNOW HOW UNENGLISH IT IS TO
METH PREFACE(R72) AS FAR AS THE CASTING OUT WAS CONCERNED; BUT THE ISSUE WAS CONFUSED BY THE PHYSIOLOGISTS, WHO WERE DIVIDED ON
LION EPILOG (148) THE OFFICERS OF HIS STAFF TOWARDS THE OPINIONS AT ISSUE WERE MUCH THE SAME AS THOSE OF A MODERN BRITISH HOME
ROCK PREFACE(178) A POLITICIAN; AND TO HIM THE ONLY QUESTIONS AT ISSUE WERE WHETHER THE EARTH MOVED OR NOT, AND WHETHER A TEN
METH PREFACE(R34) ACCORDINGLY I SAID THAT IF THE QUESTION AT ISSUE WERE WHETHER THE PENALTY OF QUESTIONING THE THEOLOGY
MRS PREFACE(172) IS A VITAL ONE. PROSTITUTION CAN CONFUSE THE ISSUE WITH ALL THESE EXCUSES: GAMBLING HAS NONE OF THEM.
METH PREFACE(R46) WAS NOT CONSCIOUS OF HAVING RAISED A STUPENDOUS ISSUE , BECAUSE, THOUGH IT AROSE INSTANTLY, IT WAS NOT HIS
BULL PREFACE(35) OF INTEREST, CONCENTRATION OF FORCE ON ONE NARROW ISSUE , SIMPLICITY OF AIM, WITH FREEDOM FROM THE SCRUPLES
JOAN EPILOG (153) TO THEIR LIGHTS, COWARDLY EVASION OF THE ISSUE , TESTIMONY MADE OF IDLE TALES THAT COULD NOT IMPOSE
LION PREFACE(96) EIGHT CENTURIES ELAPSED (THE POINT AT ISSUE , THOUGH TECHNICALLY INTERESTING TO PALEOGRAPHERS AND

ISSUED
GENV IV (87) ANY NOTICE HAS BEEN TAKEN OF THE SUMMONSES ISSUED BY THE COURT. /THE BETROTHED/ THE JUDGE HIMSELF HASNT
BULL PREFACE(60) PARTY. IT SAYS: THAT " ORDERS WILL SHORTLY BE ISSUED BY THE GENERAL PROHIBITING OFFICERS IN THE ARMY FROM
MRS PREFACE(156) REPORT ON HOME INDUSTRIES (SACRED WORD, HOME!) ISSUED BY THE WOMEN'S INDUSTRIAL COUNCIL (HOME INDUSTRIES
POSN PREFACE(429) AND THAT ON THE STRENGTH OF THAT CERTIFICATE HE ISSUED IT; ALSO, THAT BY LAW THE COURT COULD DO NOTHING TO
POSN PREFACE(402) THE PIONEERS, WHILST THE EXAMINER OF PLAYS ISSUED TWO GUINEA CERTIFICATES FOR THE VULGAR AND VICIOUS
ARMS II (26) AND THE DECREE FOR OUR ARMY TO DEMOBILIZE WAS ISSUED YESTERDAY. /CATHERINE/ (SPRINGING ERECT, WITH
POSN PREFACE(394) FOR THE KING TO ALLOW THE LICENCE TO BE ISSUED , AS HE WOULD THEREBY BE MADE RESPONSIBLE FOR THE

ISSUES
GENV II (58) UGLY THING. IF ANY OF THESE DEMAGOGUE DICTATORS ISSUES A WARRANT FOR YOUR ARREST OR EVEN AN ORDER FOR YOUR

POSN PREFACE(399)	OF THE PLAY, THIS INDIFFERENCE TO THE LARGER	ISSUES	OF A THEATRICAL PERFORMANCE COULD NOT BE SAFELY
JOAN 6 (128)	THAT IF WE PERSIST IN TRYING THE MAID ON TRUMPERY	ISSUES	ON WHICH WE MAY HAVE TO DECLARE HER INNOCENT, SHE MAY
JOAN 6 (138)	GENTLEMEN, GENTLEMEN: IN CLINGING TO THESE SMALL	ISSUES	YOU ARE THE MAID'S BEST ADVOCATES. I AM NOT SURPRISED

ISSUING

POSN PREFACE(406)	IS NO LAW TO PREVENT THE THEATRE PROPRIETOR FROM	ISSUING	FREE PASSES BROADCAST AND RECOUPING HIMSELF BY THE
LION II (142)	THING: HE WILL DO VERY WELL. /THE CALL BOY/ (	ISSUING	FROM THE PASSAGE) NUMBER TWELVE. THE CHRISTIAN FOR

ISTRIA

2TRU I (47)	WE SHALL HIDE HER IN THE MOUNTAINS OF CORSICA OR	ISTRIA	OR DALMATIA OR GREECE OR IN THE ATLAS OR WHERE YOU

ITALIAN

CAPT I (240)	IF YOU PLEASE, CAPTAIN, NEVER MIND ABOUT THE	ITALIAN	: I HAVE A BIG BOX OF CLOTHES WITH ME FOR MY BROTHER
POSN PREFACE(392)	THE ENGLISH STAGE WITHOUT BEING PELTED OFF AS THE	ITALIAN	ACTRESSES WERE, THE THEATRICAL PROFESSION WAS
SUPR III (106)	TWO OF THE GREATEST FOOLS THAT EVER LIVED, AN	ITALIAN	AND AN ENGLISHMAN. THE ITALIAN DESCRIBED IT AS A
FANY PROLOG (261)	TO THE GRACEFUL AND CHARMING FANTASIES OF THE	ITALIAN	AND FRENCH STAGES OF THE SEVENTEENTH AND EIGHTEENTH
MILL II (172)	DI PARERGA. /THE DOCTOR/ NEVER HEARD OF HER.	ITALIAN	ARISTOCRAT, I PRESUME. /EPIFANIA/ ARISTOCRAT! DO
MTH3 (125)	MY EARLY DAYS BY JEWISH BRAINS, SCOTTISH BRAINS,	ITALIAN	BRAINS, GERMAN BRAINS. THE ONLY WHITE MEN WHO STILL
MILL PREFACE(122)	HIS OWN PEOPLE BY THE SPECTACLE OF A GREAT	ITALIAN	BULLYING THE WORLD, AND GETTING AWAY WITH IT
BULL PREFACE(8)	TO BE CATHOLIC) LET IT BE IRISH CATHOLICISM, NOT	ITALIAN	CATHOLICISM. LET US MAINTAIN OUR PARTNERSHIP WITH
GENV PREFACE(8)	FRENCH CITIES, DUTCH CITIES, BELGIAN CITIES,	ITALIAN	CITIES: THAT IS, THEY WERE DESTROYING THEM EXACTLY
PLES PREFACE(R8)	THE WHOLE, BIRMINGHAM WAS MORE HOPEFUL THAN THE	ITALIAN	CITIES; FOR THE ART IT HAD TO SHEW ME WAS THE WORK
MIS. PREFACE(89)	NEVER HISS WHEN IT IS MURDERED. I HAVE HEARD AN	ITALIAN	CONDUCTOR (NO LONGER LIVING) TAKE THE ADAGIO OF
SUPR III (106)	EVER LIVED, AN ITALIAN AND AN ENGLISHMAN. THE	ITALIAN	DESCRIBED IT AS A PLACE OF MUD, FROST, FILTH, FIRE,
CAPT I SD(234)	YOURS. DRINKWATER COMES FROM THE HOUSE WITH AN	ITALIAN	DRESSED IN A MUCH WORN SUIT OF BLUE SERGE, A
PHIL II (122)	THE JOURNAL FROM THE BOOKSTAND). I ADMIT THAT THE	ITALIAN	EXPERIMENTS APPARENTLY UPSET MY THEORY. BUT PLEASE
DEST (193)	THAT MIGHT BE A MATCH FOR A FRENCH ARMY LED BY AN	ITALIAN	GENERAL. (HE PAUSES, AND ADDS, HALF JESTINGLY, HALF
CYMB V (141)	ME BLEST TO OBEY! I AM BROUGHT HITHER AMONG THE	ITALIAN	GENTRY, AND TO FIGHT AGAINST MY LADY'S KINGDOM: 'TIS
CAPT I (239)	I SEE THAT YOU DONT NOTICE THINGS. THAT POOR	ITALIAN	HAD ONLY ONE PROPER BOOTLACE: THE OTHER WAS A BIT OF
PYGM EPILOG (301)	AND WHO HIMSELF WROTE A MOST BEAUTIFUL	ITALIAN	HAND, THAT HE WOULD TEACH HER TO WRITE. HE DECLARED
BULL PREFACE(9)	FREE PARTNERSHIP. BUT THE IRISH CATHOLICS ARE NOT	ITALIAN	IN THEIR POLITICS, THEY DO NOT OPPOSE HOME RULE; AND
DEST SD(152)	MONSTROUS AND HORRIBLE TO THE CONTEMPORARY NORTH	ITALIAN	INFANT, TO WHOM NOTHING WOULD SEEM MORE NATURAL THAN
CAPT I (237)	PROPERLY TREATED. /DRINKWATER/ (CHUCKLING: THE	ITALIAN	IS ALSO GRINNING) NAH, KEPN, NAH! OWP YR PRAHD O
DOCT PREFACE(40)	FAILING HIM, TO ANY SANE PERSON IN EUROPE. THE	ITALIAN	IS DIAGNOSED AS A CRUEL VOLUPTUARY: THE DOG-STARVER
FANY PROLOG (259)	KEEP OUT OF HEARING OF IT AND SPEAK AND LISTEN TO	ITALIAN	. I FIND BEETHOVEN'S MUSIC COARSE AND RESTLESS, AND
PHIL II (113)	DESPERATE RESOLUTION) BUT I WONT BE BEATEN BY ANY	ITALIAN	. I'LL GO TO ITALY MYSELF. I'LL REDISCOVER MY
BULL II SD(104)	OF THEIR PROJECTOR, ONE BIANCONI, AN ENTERPRISING	ITALIAN	. THE THREE PASSENGERS ARE THE PARISH PRIEST, FATHER
GLIM SD(171)	CENTURY A. D. GLOAMING. AN INN ON THE EDGE OF AN	ITALIAN	LAKE. A STONE CROSS WITH A PEDESTAL OF STEPS. A VERY
MILL PREFACE(121)	FOR EVERYTHING THAT HAS HAPPENED." WHEN THE	ITALIAN	LIBERALS JOINED IN THE SHRIEKING HE SEIZED THE
CAPT NOTES (306)	IS AS ABSURD AS TO RIDICULE THE WHOLE FRENCH AND	ITALIAN	NATION FOR DOING THE SAME. THE AMERICAN H. HELPED
PLES PREFACE(R15)	IN LONDON FOR TWO HUNDRED YEARS IN SUPPORT OF	ITALIAN	OPERA. RETURNING NOW TO THE ACTUAL STATE OF THINGS,
JITT PREFACE(6)	NOWADAYS, SUCH ROMANCE IS PRIVILEGED ONLY IN	ITALIAN	OPERA, AND IS NOT TOLERATED WITHOUT THE MUSIC. THE
BARB III (316)	MOMENTUM UNTIL THE REAL UNDERSHAFT-- PROBABLY AN	ITALIAN	OR A GERMAN-- WOULD INVENT A NEW METHOD AND CUT HIM
DEST (170)	COUNTRY, GENERAL BU-- SHALL I PRONOUNCE IT IN	ITALIAN	OR FRENCH? /NAPOLEON/ YOU ARE PRESUMING ON MY
BARB III (316)	OUT. /LADY BRITOMART/ THERE IS NOTHING THAT ANY	ITALIAN	OR GERMAN COULD DO THAT STEPHEN COULD NOT DO. AND
KING I (213)	EASIER. BUT HIS DISCOVERY WAS MADE BY THE GREAT	ITALIAN	PAINTER LEONARDO, BORN TWENTYONE YEARS BEFORE HIM,
METH PREFACE(R81)	AFTER THE RELIGION HAD BECOME A SUPERSTITION.	ITALIAN	PAINTING FROM GIOTTO TO CARPACCIO IS ALL RELIGIOUS
SUPR HANDBOK(204)	CREED THAT OUR RULERS PRIVATELY SMILE AT AS THE	ITALIAN	PATRICIANS OF THE FIFTH CENTURY SMILED AT JUPITER
SUPR HANDBOK(204)	THE PEOPLE BELIEVE IN IT AS DEVOUTLY AS THE	ITALIAN	PEASANT BELIEVES IN THE LIQUEFACTION OF THE BLOOD OF
DOCT PREFACE(73)	THE GOVERNMENT ITSELF FREE OF SUPERSTITION. IF	ITALIAN	PEASANTS ARE SO IGNORANT THAT THE CHURCH CAN GET NO
MIS. (129)	MOTHER WAS AN ITALIAN PRINCESS; AND SHE HAD AN	ITALIAN	PRIEST ALWAYS ABOUT. HE WAS SUPPOSED TO TAKE CHARGE
2TRU PREFACE(18)	SO PRODIGIOUSLY RICH THAT THE POPE WAS A SECULAR	ITALIAN	PRINCE WITH ARMIES AND FRONTIERS, ENJOYING NOT ONLY
MIS. (129)	WAS THE SECOND FATHER. THEN HIS MOTHER WAS AN	ITALIAN	PRINCESS; AND SHE HAD AN ITALIAN PRIEST ALWAYS
DEST (165)	GENERAL BUONAPARTE. (SHE GIVES THE NAME A MARKED	ITALIAN	PRONUNCIATION: BWAWNA-PARR-TE). /NAPOLEON/ (
DEST (167)	MAN? /LADY/ (AMAZED) YOU! GENERAL BUONAPARTE (	ITALIAN	PRONUNCIATION). /NAPOLEON/ YES, I, GENERAL BONAPARTE
CAPT I (234)	CICELY. /DRINKWATER/ YR HONOR'S SERVANT. (TO THE	ITALIAN	) MAWTZOW: IS LAWDSHIP SR AHRD ELLAM (MARZO TOUCHES
CAPT III (289)	SEEMING INSULT TO THE ENGLISH PEERAGE FROM A LOW	ITALIAN	) WHAT? WHATS THAT YOU SAY? /MARZO/ NO LADY NURSE
CAPT I (238)	FOR HIS LIFE INTO THE HOUSE, FOLLOWED BY THE	ITALIAN	). /BRASSBOUND/ YOUR LADYSHIP SEES, THESE MEN SERVE
CLEO III (160)	HIS MANNER IS FRIVOLOUS BECAUSE HE IS AN	ITALIAN	; BUT HE MEANS WHAT HE SAYS. /APOLLODORUS/ SERIOUS
MIS. PREFACE(23)	SOME SCRAPS OF GERMAN AND A LITTLE OPERATIC	ITALIAN	; BUT THESE I WAS NEVER TAUGHT AT SCHOOL. INSTEAD, I
MILL PREFACE(121)	HEEL OF A RUTHLESS DICTATOR MERELY BECAUSE THE	ITALIAN	TRAINS WERE RUNNING PUNCTUALLY AND TRAVELLERS IN
CYMB V (149)	/IMOGEN/ NO, NOT QUITE, NOR YET A WORM, SUBTLE	ITALIAN	VILLAIN! I WOULD THAT CHEST HAD SMOTHERED YOU.
CYMB V (141)	GIVE NO WOUND TO THEE. I HAVE DISROBED ME OF MY	ITALIAN	WEEDS, AND DREST MYSELF AS DOES A BRITON PEASANT; SO
GENV PREFACE(25)	FACULTIES AS ATTAINMENTS OF MANKIND, AS IF EVERY	ITALIAN	WERE MICHAEL ANGELO AND RAPHAEL AND DANTE AND
PHIL II (113)	DEGREES BELOW ZERO. AND NOW COMES THIS CURSED	ITALIAN	WHO HAS RUINED ME. HE HAS A GOVERNMENT GRANT TO BUY
DOCT PREFACE(40)	EMOTIONS. TAKE THE HACKNEYED CASE OF THE	ITALIAN	WHO TORTURED MICE, OSTENSIBLY TO FIND OUT ABOUT THE
MTH2 SD(41)	HAZEL HAIR CUT TO THE LEVEL OF HER NECK, LIKE AN	ITALIAN	YOUTH IN A GOZZOLI PICTURE, COMES IN IMPETUOUSLY.
FANY III (324)	IS NOT REALLY STRONGER THAN A GERMAN, THAN AN	ITALIAN	, EVEN THAN AN ENGLISHMAN, SIR: IF ALL FRENCHWOMEN
KING II (228)	GOVERN THEM. /CHARLES/ YOU ARE PORTUGUESE. I AM	ITALIAN	, FRENCH, SCOTTISH, HARDLY AT ALL ENGLISH. WHEN I
BULL PREFACE(15)	ON INVESTIGATION TO BE, IF NOT AN AMERICAN, AN	ITALIAN	, OR A JEW, AT LEAST TO BE DEPENDING ON THE BRAINS,

ITALIAN'S

SUPR III (128)	BE DRAGGED THROUGH ALL THE CIRCLES OF THE FOOLISH	ITALIAN'S	INFERNO THAN THROUGH THE PLEASURES OF EUROPE. THAT

ITALIANS

ROCK I (216)	PROVIDED THEYRE THE CHEAPEST. THEY TELL ME THE	ITALIANS	ARE TAPPING THEIR VOLCANOES FOR CHEAP POWER. WE
GENV PREFACE(21)	AND HE WAS SCANDALOUSLY LYNCHED IN MILAN. THE	ITALIANS	HAD HAD ENOUGH OF HIM; FOR HE, TOO, WAS NEITHER A
DEST SD(151)	THAT THE FRENCH ARMY DOES NOT MAKE WAR ON THE	ITALIANS	. IT IS THERE TO RESCUE THEM FROM THE TYRANNY OF
BULL PREFACE(28)	FRENCH LOVED THEM BEFORE THE REVOLUTION OR AS THE	ITALIANS	LOVED THEM BEFORE THEY IMPRISONED THE POPE IN THE
CLEO NOTES (208)	ANCESTORS OF MR PODSNAP TO IMPRESS THE CULTIVATED	ITALIANS	OF THEIR TIME. I AM TOLD THAT IT IS NOT SCIENTIFIC
BULL PREFACE(11)	QUITE PREPARED TO CO-OPERATE WITH THE FRENCH, THE	ITALIANS	, AND THE SPANIARDS IN MOROCCO, ALGERIA, TUNISIA,
JOAN 4 (107)	FRENCH, ENGLAND FOR THE ENGLISH, ITALY FOR THE	ITALIANS	, SPAIN FOR THE SPANISH, AND SO FORTH. IT IS

ITALICS

UNPL PREFACE(R24)	DOWN. EVEN THE USE OF SPACED LETTERS INSTEAD OF	ITALICS	FOR UNDERLINING, THOUGH FAMILIAR TO FOREIGN READERS,

ITALY

GETT (290)	WORD. IVE FOUGHT SEVEN DUELS WITH THE SABRE IN	ITALY	AND AUSTRIA, AND ONE WITH PISTOLS IN FRANCE, WITHOUT
GENV PREFACE(21)	FIGHT, BACKED BY HIS FELLOW ADVENTURERS IN	ITALY	AND SPAIN; BUT, BEING NEITHER A JULIUS CAESAR NOR A
MRS IV (239)	WHOE'ER HE BE! /VIVIE/ IT'S PRAED. HE'S GOING TO	ITALY	AND WANTS TO SAY GOODBYE. I ASKED HIM TO CALL THIS
MILL PREFACE(121)	SICK. IT WAS EVIDENT THAT MUSSOLINI WAS MASTER OF	ITALY	AS FAR AS SUCH MASTERSHIP IS POSSIBLE; BUT WHAT WAS
DEST SD(151)	HAS ENTIRELY JUSTIFIED HIM. THE ARMY CONQUERS	ITALY	AS THE LOCUSTS CONQUERED CYPRUS. THEY FIGHT ALL DAY
MILL PREFACE(121)	TRAINS WERE RUNNING PUNCTUALLY AND TRAVELLERS IN	ITALY	COULD DEPEND ON THEIR LUGGAGE NOT BEING STOLEN WITHOUT
JOAN PREFACE(41)	TO EFFECT ITSELF. LATER ON THE FASCISTI IN	ITALY	DID EVERYTHING THAT THE BLACK AND TANS DID IN IRELAND,
JOAN 4 (107)	FRANCE FOR THE FRENCH, ENGLAND FOR THE ENGLISH,	ITALY	FOR THE ITALIANS, SPAIN FOR THE SPANISH, AND SO FORTH.
PLES PREFACE(R8)	TO APPRECIATE. WHEN MY SUBSEQUENT VISIT TO	ITALY	FOUND ME PRACTISING THE PLAYWRIGHT'S CRAFT, THE TIME
PLES PREFACE(R8)	ME WAS THE WORK OF LIVING MEN, WHEREAS MODERN	ITALY	HAD, AS FAR AS I COULD SEE, NO MORE CONNECTION WITH
DEST (181)	I'LL FIND THAT HORSE IF IT'S ALIVE ANYWHERE IN	ITALY	. AND I SHANT FORGET THE DESPATCHES: NEVER FEAR.
BULL PREFACE(36)	TYRANNY IN IRELAND AS IT HAS DONE IN FRANCE AND	ITALY	. AND IN DOING SO IT WILL BE FORCED TO FACE THE OLD
MRS IV (239)	CONTINUE OUR CONVERSATION AFTER HIS DEPARTURE FOR	ITALY	. I'LL STAY HIM OUT. (HE GOES TO THE DOOR AND OPENS
PHIL II (113)	BESIDES HAVING THE RUN OF THE LARGEST HOSPITAL IN	ITALY	. (WITH DESPERATE RESOLUTION) BUT I WONT BE BEATEN BY
MILL PREFACE(121)	WITH HORROR AS IF NOTHING ELSE WAS HAPPENING IN	ITALY	. MUSSOLINI REFUSED TO BE TURNED ASIDE FROM HIS WORK
MRS IV (239)	VIADUCT. I WISH I COULD PERSUADE YOU TO TRY	ITALY	. /VIVIE/ WHAT FOR? /PRAED/ WHY, TO SATURATE YOURSELF
CAPT I (234)	(NODDING AFFABLY TO MARZO) HOWDYE DO? I LOVE	ITALY	. WHAT PART OF IT WERE YOU BORN IN? /DRINKWATER/
PHIL II (113)	BUT I WONT BE BEATEN BY ANY ITALIAN. I'LL GO TO	ITALY	MYSELF. I'LL REDISCOVER MY DISEASE: I KNOW IT EXISTS;
PLES PREFACE(R8)	BY THE RENASCENCE. FROM A FORMER VISIT TO	ITALY	ON THE SAME BUSINESS I HAD HURRIED BACK TO BIRMINGHAM
FANY PROLOG (258)	MY FAMILY IS IRISH: IVE LIVED ALL MY LIFE IN	ITALY	-- IN VENICE MOSTLY-- MY VERY TITLE IS A FOREIGN ONE:

CYMB V (144) NO BETTER, MADAM. WE MADE A WAGER, HE AND I, IN ITALY THAT I SHOULD SPEND A NIGHT IN YOUR BEDCHAMBER.
DEST SD(151) MONEY, NO CLOTHES, AND HARDLY ANYTHING TO EAT. IN ITALY THERE ARE ALL THESE THINGS, AND GLORY AS WELL, TO BE
DOCT IV (162) EYES THAT YOU WERE MARRIED TO ME. THE PEOPLE IN ITALY USED TO POINT AT DANTE AND SAY " THERE GOES THE MAN
ROCK PREFACE(175) NOT WITH RIDICULOUS HOTHEADED ATTACKS ON GERMANY, ITALY , AND RUSSIA, BUT BY A RESTATEMENT OF THE CASE FOR
DEST SD(149) DESTINY. 1896. THE TWELFTH OF MAY, 1796, IN NORTH ITALY , AT TAVAZZANO, ON THE ROAD FROM LODI TO MILAN. THE
DEST (154) /NAPOLEON/ YOU WOULD MAKE YOURSELF EMPEROR OF ITALY , EH? /GIUSEPPE/ TOO TROUBLESOME, EXCELLENCY: I LEAVE
ROCK PREFACE(174) AND THE UNITED STATES OF NORTH AMERICA THAN IN ITALY , GERMANY, AND RUSSIA. I HAVE SEEN TOO MANY NEWSPAPERS
LION EPILOG (150) EMPIRE, THE FRENCH REPUBLIC, AND THE KINGDOMS OF ITALY , JAPAN, AND SERBIA) ACTUALLY SUCCEEDED IN CLOSING A
BUOY 1 (11) IN RUSSIA, IN PERSIA, IN MEXICO, IN TURKEY, IN ITALY , SPAIN, GERMANY, AUSTRIA, EVERYWHERE IF YOU COUNT
BULL PREFACE(6) FELLOW PROTESTANTS IN IRELAND TO THE FACT THAT IN ITALY , THE CENTRE OF ROMAN CATHOLICISM, THE POPE IS IN A
METH PREFACE(R15) IF HE CAN. BYRON AND SHELLEY HAD TO FLY TO ITALY , WHILST CASTLEREAGH AND ELDON RULED THE ROOST AT

ITCHING
SUPR HANDBOK(188) THE INSTINCT OF FERTILITY HAS FADED INTO A MERE ITCHING FOR PLEASURE. THE MODERN DEVICES FOR COMBINING
ARMS II (39) /CATHERINE/ (LOOKING AFTER HER, HER FINGERS ITCHING) OH, IF YOU WERE ONLY TEN YEARS YOUNGER! (LOUKA
BULL III (121) HONOR THERE, WHEN ALL THE TIME THEIR FINGERS WERE ITCHING TO BE AT HIS THROAT. /AUNT JUDY/ DEEDN WHY SHOULD

ITEM
VWOO 3 (134) LISTEN. (HE TAKES UP HIS MANUSCRIPT AND READS). ITEM : I HAVE SHARPENED MY FACULTIES, AND GREATLY IMPROVED
SUPR PREFACE(R15) HERSELF AS AN INDIVIDUAL INSTEAD OF A MERE ITEM IN A MORAL PAGEANT. NOW IT IS ALL VERY WELL FOR YOU AT
GENV II (50) MY LIVING. /THE SECRETARY/ NO DOUBT. A FURTHER ITEM IS THAT THE BRITISH EMPIRE HAS DECLARED WAR ON RUSSIA.
HART PREFACE(21) MEETINGS, PROLONGED INTO THE NIGHT, OVER AN ITEM OF SEVEN SHILLINGS FOR REFRESHMENTS? LITTLE MINDS AND
ROCK I (214) ALL NIGHT SITTING OF THE BOROUGH COUNCIL ABOUT AN ITEM OF THREE-AND-SIX FOR REFRESHMENTS. IF YOU, SIR ARTHUR,
POSN PREFACE(401) OF VARIETY PERFORMANCES, AND PUTTING EACH ITEM TO THE VOTE, POSSIBLY AFTER A PROLONGED DISCUSSION

ITEMS
JOAN 4 (102) COUNTRYSIDES BURNT OVER AND OVER AGAIN AS MERE ITEMS IN MILITARY ROUTINE, ONE HAS TO GROW A VERY THICK
GENV PREFACE(12) THE RATES AND TAXES THEY PAY THAN FOR MOST OTHER ITEMS IN THEIR EXPENDITURE NEVER OCCURS TO THEM. THEY WILL
ROCK II (241) SAME HERE, SIR DEXTER. I CLAIM AT LEAST TWO ITEMS . /SIR DEXTER/ MUCH GOOD MAY THEY DO YOU. ARTHUR'S
CATH 1 (166) OF TRUTH. NOW LISTEN TO ME. (HE MARKS OFF THE ITEMS OF HIS STATEMENT WITH RIDICULOUS STIFF GESTURES OF HIS
GENV II (50) I ASSURE YOU. /THE SECRETARY/ THERE ARE OTHER ITEMS OF NEWS, MISS BROWN. GERMANY HAS WITHDRAWN FROM THE

ITINERANT
LION PREFACE(22) TO MATTHEW, THOUGH, LIKE JOHN, HE BECAME AN ITINERANT PREACHER, HE DEPARTED WIDELY FROM JOHN'S MANNER OF

ITIS
DOCT I (101) AND ARTHRITIS, AND APPENDICITIS, AND EVERY OTHER ITIS , WHEN ANY REALLY EXPERIENCED SURGEON CAN SEE THAT IT'S

ITLL
NEVR IV (303) I SHANT COMMIT SUICIDE: I SHANT EVEN BE UNHAPPY. ITLL BE A RELIEF TO ME: I-- I'M FRIGHTENED, I'M POSITIVELY
SIM II (82) GOES INTO THE HOUSE). /MRS HYERING/ J'YOU THINK ITLL BE ALL RIGHT IF I GO AND DO SOME CROSSWORD PUZZLES? IT
NEVR IV (283) HIS HANDS). /M'COMAS/ (RELENTING) THERE, THERE: ITLL BE ALL RIGHT, IF YOU WILL ONLY BEAR AND FORBEAR. COME:
BULL II (110) BROADBENT: I LEFT THE TEA ON THE HOB TO DRAW; AND ITLL BE BLACK IF WE DONT GO IN AN DRINK IT. THEY GO UP THE
MIS. (147) ALLUDE TO IT, DEPEND ON IT, IN A THOUSAND YEARS ITLL BE CONSIDERED BAD FORM TO KNOW WHO YOUR FATHER AND
FANY III (300) THE TRANSACTION MAY LEAVE MUCH TO BE DESIRED; BUT ITLL BE LESS CAMBERWELLIAN THAN IF YOU SAY YOURE NOT WORTHY.
FANY III (327) SPARE ME. /GILBEY/ (IN A GUST OF ENVY, TO BOBBY) ITLL BE LONG ENOUGH BEFORE YOULL MARRY THE SISTER OF A DUKE,
BULL II (109) ACCURATELY THAN HIS SISTER DOES) THATS ALL RIGHT: ITLL BE NO TROUBLE AT ALL. WHERES NORA? /AUNT JUDY/ OH, HOW
POSN (450) TO BUY THEM. THEY MAY AS WELL HAVE THEIR FUN; AND ITLL BE SHORTER FOR HIM. /STRAPPER/ YOUNG JACK HAS BROUGHT A
BARB II (278) KNAOW WOT THET MEANS; AND IF SHE KEEPS ME WITIN ITLL BE WORSE. YOU STOP TO JAWR BECK AT ME; AND AW'LL STAWT
CAND III (139) GIVE YOU A NIGHTLIGHT BY YOUR BED, MR MORCHBANKS: ITLL COMFORT YOU IF YOU WAKE UP IN THE NIGHT WITH A TOUCH OF
MIS. (155) THING TO HAPPEN! AND LOOK AT THE GREENHOUSE! ITLL COST THIRTY POUNDS TO MEND IT. PEOPLE HAVE NO RIGHT TO
BULL I (76) BUT-- /TIM/ NOT A WORD, SIR, NOT A WORD. SURE ITLL DO TOMORROW. BESIDES, I'M IRISH, SIR: A POOR AITHER,
GETT (322) AND SETTLE THE RIGHT AND WRONG OF IT AFTERWARDS. ITLL EASE YOUR MINDS, BELIEVE ME: I SPEAK FROM EXPERIENCE.
ROCK I (217) THAT HIS LIFE DEPENDS ON. TURN A CAT LOOSE AND ITLL FEED ITSELF. TURN AN ENGLISH WORKING MAN LOOSE AND
LION I (110) THE GLADIATORS PRESENTLY. THINK OF THAT; AND ITLL HELP YOU TO BEHAVE PROPERLY BEFORE THE CAPTAIN. (THE
MIS. (117) ANOTHER FREE LIBRARY LAST WEEK. IT'S RUINOUS. ITLL HIT YOU AS WELL AS ME WHEN BUNNY MARRIES HYPATIA. WHEN
MTH5 (215) THE SPONGE IN IT. /THE MAIDEN/ SHUT YOUR EYES. ITLL HURT IF YOU DONT. /ANOTHER MAIDEN/ DONT BE SILLY. ONE
GENV II (63) /BEGONIA/ (TAKING IT) THANKS EVER SO MUCH! ITLL JUST SEE ME THROUGH. AND NOW I MUST TODDLE OFF TO MY
MILL III (186) AND CHANGE OUR WAYS I CANT GO ON: I CANT GO ON: ITLL KILL ME. GO UP AND STOP HER, JOE. DONT LET HER TALK:
FANY II (295) THEN I DONT KNOW WHAT I SHALL DO: I DONT INDEED: ITLL KILL ME. /MARGARET/ YOU SHOULDNT HAVE PRAYED FOR ME TO
DOCT III (142) EVER. ITLL PUT THE GIRL IN PRISON AND RUIN HER: ITLL LAY HIS WIFE'S LIFE WASTE. YOU MAY PUT THE CRIMINAL LAW
FOUN (209) MAKING IT ON PURPOSE. I WANT YOU TO FIGHT BECAUSE ITLL MAKE MORE NOISE THAN ANYTHING ELSE. THE LORD CHANCELLOR
BULL IV (171) THROW IT IN ME FACE: IF IT IS TRUE-- AT ALL EVENTS ITLL MAKE US INDEPENDENT; FOR IF THE WORST COMES TO THE
BULL IV (167) TO HUG OCCASIONALLY. BESIDES, IT'S GOOD FOR YOU: ITLL PLUMP OUT YOUR MUSCLES AND MAKE EM ELASTIC AND SET UP
DOCT III (142) LEAST IT WILL PUNISH HIM. /SIR PATRICK/ OH YES: ITLL PUNISH HIM. ITLL PUNISH NOT ONLY HIM BUT EVERYBODY
DOCT III (142) HIM. /SIR PATRICK/ OH YES: ITLL PUNISH HIM. ITLL PUNISH NOT ONLY HIM BUT EVERYBODY CONNECTED WITH HIM,
DOCT III (142) ON US A MORE DANGEROUS BLACKGUARD THAN EVER. ITLL PUT THE GIRL IN PRISON AND RUIN HER: ITLL LAY HIS
FANY EPILOG (334) STUFF NAUGHTY PLAYS DOWN MY THROAT? /FANNY/ YES: ITLL TEACH YOU WHAT IT FEELS LIKE TO BE FORCIBLY FED. /THE
DOCT III (142) CONNECTED WITH HIM, INNOCENT AND GUILTY ALIKE. ITLL THROW HIS BOARD AND LODGING ON OUR RATES AND TAXES FOR
O'FL (214) AND BE THE SAME AS EVER. IT'S LIKE THE VERMIN: ITLL WASH OFF AFTER A WHILE. /SIR PEARCE/ (RISING AND

IT'D
BULL IV (165) WITH YOUR STRENGTH. AN I NEVER THOUGHT O WHETHER IT'D BE A GOOD THING FOR US OR NOT. BUT WHEN YOU FOUND ME
MRS II (199) TEMPTATION). /FRANK/ DO COME TO VIENNA WITH ME? IT'D BE EVER SUCH LARKS. /MRS WARREN/ NO, THANK YOU. VIENNA
PHIL I (90) GO UNTIL YOUVE SAID GOODNIGHT TO MRS TRANFIELD. IT'D BE HORRIBLY RUDE. /JULIA/ YOU CAN STAY IF YOU LIKE,
FANY III (304) SEE WHAT FUN IT WOULD BE FOR YOU. /MARGARET/ OH, IT'D BE NO FUN. IF I WANTED WHAT YOU CALL FUN, I SHOULD ASK
BULL III (140) ALLOW ME TO DRIVE YOU HOME? /MATTHEW/ OH SURE IT'D BE THROUBLIN YOUR HONOR. /BROADBENT/ I INSIST: IT WILL
PRES (150) COUNTRY DIDNT KNOW YOU WERE GOING TO DO THAT OR IT'D NEVER AVE STOOD IT. IS AN ENGLISHMAN TO BE MADE A
BULL III (142) WITHAHT SICH THINGS. /MATTHEW/ BEDAD YOURE RIGHT. IT'D ONY BE WASTE O TIME TO MUZZLE A SHEEP. HERE! WHERES ME
FANY PROLOG (269) AS TO STRAUSS, IF HE HEARD THREE BARS OF ELEKTRA, IT'D PART US FOR EVER. NOW WHAT I WANT YOU TO DO IS THIS. IF

IT'LL
MRS II (218) GOT THE WORST OF IT FROM LIZ; AND NOW I SUPPOSE IT'LL BE THE SAME WITH YOU. /VIVIE/ WELL, NEVER MIND. COME:
MIS. (202) MENTION OUR LITTLE CONVERSATION, MISS SHEPANOSKA. IT'LL DO NO GOOD; AND I'D RATHER YOU DIDNT. /TARLETON/ WEVE

ITT
BARB II (300) AN E'S BIN FAWND FIFTEEN BOB. E ED A RAWT TO ITT ER CAUSE THEY WAS GOWIN TO BE MERRID; BUT AW EDNT NAO
BARB II (289) BECK AND SHAOW IT TO ER. EE'LL ITT ME ARDERN AW ITT ER. THATLL MIKE US SQUARE. (TO ADOLPHUS) IS THET FAIR
BARB II (279) YOU. THERE WAS A YANG MENN EAH. DID AW OFFER TO ITT HIM OR DID AW NOT? /SHIRLEY/ WAS HE STARVIN OR WAS HE
BARB II (289) BESHED AND CAM BECK AND SHAOW IT TO ER. EE'LL ITT ME ARDERN AW ITT ER. THATLL MIKE US SQUARE. (TO
BARB II (308) DONT YOU HIT HER WHEN SHE'S DOWN. /BILL/ SHE ITT ME WEN AW WIZ DAHN. WAW SHOULDNT AW GIT A BIT O ME AOWN
BARB II (300) WAS GOWIN TO BE MERRID; BUT AW EDNT NAO RAWT TO ITT YOU; SAO PUT ANATHER FAWV BOB ON AN CALL IT A PAHND'S

ITTIN
BARB II (309) AOLD MACKER YOU? /RUMMY/ TO SERVE YOU AHT FOR ITTIN ME ACROST THE FICE. IT'S COST Y'PAHND, THAT AZ. (

IV
SUPR HANDBOK(188) NATIONS IS THE ONLY REAL CHANGE POSSIBLE TO US. IV : MAN'S OBJECTION TO HIS OWN IMPROVEMENT. BUT WOULD SUCH
BUOY IV (48) ACT IV : THE END. WHEN THE TEMPLE REAPPEARS THE CENSER IS ON THE
MTH4 (137) PART IV : TRAGEDY OF AN ELDERLY GENTLEMAN.
BULL PREFACE(21) TYPE, THAN A SPECIFICALLY IRISH TYPE. GEORGE IV AND BYRON, CONTRASTED WITH GLADSTONE, SEEM IRISH IN
GETT PREFACE(229) THE QUESTION BY CLASSING SHELLEY WITH GEORGE IV AS A BAD MAN; AND SHELLEY IS NOT LIKELY TO HAVE CALLED
CLEO NOTES (208) TYPE WOULD BE AS ABSURD AS TO REPRESENT GEORGE IV BY A TYPE FOUNDED ON THE ATTAINMENTS OF SIR ISAAC NEWTON.
LION PREFACE(86) IN ENLISTING THE EMPERORS ON THEIR SIDE. IN THE IV CENTURY THEY BEGAN TO BURN ONE ANOTHER FOR DIFFERENCES OF
GENV IV (87) ACT IV . A SALON IN THE OLD PALACE OF THE HAGUE. ON A SPACIOUS
JOAN 4 (94) SCENE IV . A TENT IN THE ENGLISH CAMP. A BULLNECKED ENGLISH
CLEO IV (166) ACT IV . CLEOPATRA'S SOUSING IN THE EAST HARBOR OF ALEXANDRIA

MRS IV (235) ACT IV . HONORIA FRASER'S CHAMBERS IN CHANCERY LANE. AN OFFICE
MILL IV (188) ACT IV . THE COFFEE ROOM OF THE PIG AND WHISTLE, NOW
SUPR IV (141) ACT IV . THE GARDEN OF A VILLA IN GRANADA. WHOEVER WISHES TO
BULL IV (145) ACT IV . THE PARLOR IN CORNELIUS DOYLE'S HOUSE. IT COMMUNICATES
NEVR IV (282) ACT IV . THE SAME ROOM. NINE O' CLOCK. NOBODY PRESENT. THE LAMPS
DOCT IV (156) ACT IV . THE STUDIO. THE EASEL IS PUSHED BACK TO THE WALL.
BULL I (80) NOT OFTEN I MEET TWO SUCH SPLENDID SPECIMENTS IV THE ANGLO-SAXON RACE. /BROADBENT/ (CHUCKLING) WRONG FOR
MILL PREFACE(111) A RUTHLESSNESS GREATER THAN HIS OWN. WHEN HENRY IV USURPED THE ENGLISH CROWN HE CERTAINLY DID NOT INTEND TO
SUPR HANDBOK(213) ABSURD AND SCANDALOUS ASK THEMSELVES WHY GEORGE IV WAS NOT ALLOWED TO CHOOSE HIS OWN WIFE WHILST ANY TINKER
SUPR HANDBOK(213) NO MORE FREE TO MARRY THE DAIRYMAID THAN GEORGE IV WAS TO MARRY MRS FITZHERBERT; AND SUCH A MARRIAGE COULD
MRS PREFACE(161) THE BIANCA EPISODE), TROILUS AND CRESSIDA, HENRY IV , MEASURE FOR MEASURE, TIMON OF ATHENS, LA DAME AUX

IVANHOE
MIS. PREFACE(100) ECSTASY; BUT FOR THE PURPOSES OF A BOY OF FIFTEEN IVANHOE AND THE TEMPLAR MAKE A MUCH BETTER SAINT AND DEVIL.

IVOR
BUOY PREFACE(5) AND THEY HAD GIVEN ME THE MAGIC DELIGHT MR IVOR BROWN HAS DESCRIBED AS THE EFFECT ON HIM OF NATURAL

IVORY
NEVR I (212) /PHILIP/ DENTIST IS AN UGLY WORD. THE MAN OF IVORY AND GOLD ASKED US WHETHER WE WERE THE CHILDREN OF MR
BARB PREFACE(232) THE EXPLOITATION OF AFRICAN GOLD, DIAMONDS, IVORY AND RUBBER, OUTDOES IN VILLAINY THE WORST THAT HAS
ROCK PREFACE(158) ADORATION. LITTLE MODELS OF IT IN GOLD AND IVORY ARE WORN AS PERSONAL ORNAMENTS; AND BIG REPRODUCTIONS
CAND II (114) LIKE TO PRESENT ME WITH A NICE NEW ONE, WITH AN IVORY BACK INLAID WITH MOTHER-OF-PEARL? /MARCHBANKS/ (
PRES (146) MEDDLES N ORDHERS N THE CROOKED SWORD WIDH THE IVORY HANDLE N YOUR FULL DRESS UNIFORM IS IN THE WAXWORKS IN
ARMS I SD(3) A PAINTED WOODEN SHRINE, BLUE AND GOLD, WITH AN IVORY IMAGE OF CHRIST, AND A LIGHT HANGING BEFORE IT IN A
FANY I (278) CONCERTINA. THERES ONE IN A SHOP IN GREEN STREET, IVORY INLAID, WITH GOLD KEYS AND RUSSIA LEATHER BELLOWS; AND
LIED (194) OF-- OF-- OF HOWLING ABOUT FIVESHILLINGSWORTH OF IVORY . DAMN YOUR FAN! /SHE/ OH! DONT YOU DARE SWEAR IN MY
BASH II,1, (102) AT LONG SHOTS, DID NOT GET FAIRLY HOME UPON THE IVORY ; AND BYRON HAD THE BEST OF THE EXCHANGE." /LYDIA/ I
NEVR I (207) THE OPERATING CHAIR) THAT WRETCHED BANKRUPT IVORY SNATCHER MAKES A COMPLIMENT OF ALLOWING US TO STAND
NEVR I (212) THE QUESTION IS A SIMPLE ONE. WHEN THE IVORY SNATCHER-- /MRS CLANDON/ (REMONSTRATING) PHIL!
CLEO I (109) RUBS HIS NOSE), THEY ALL HAVE LONG NOSES, AND IVORY TUSKS, AND LITTLE TAILS, AND SEVEN ARMS WITH A HUNDRED
CLEO V (195) WORTH LOOKING AT WAS APIS: A MIRACLE OF GOLD AND IVORY WORK. BY MY ADVICE HE OFFERED THE CHIEF PRIEST TWO
SUPR III (118) WITH A DEATHLESS, AGELESS CREATURE OF CORAL AND IVORY , DESERTED ME IN THAT SUPREME HOUR. I REMEMBERED THEM
SUPR HANDBOK(203) OF THE WHITE INVASION OF AFRICA IN SEARCH OF IVORY , GOLD, DIAMONDS, AND SPORT, HAVE PROVED THAT THE

IVORY-HANDLED
PRES (153) ANY DESCRIPTION. /LADY CORINTHIA/ (PRODUCING AN IVORY-HANDLED REVOLVER AND

IX
SUPR HANDBOK(208) OF THE ONE AND THE LONELINESS OF THE OTHER. IX : THE VERDICT OF HISTORY. IT MAY BE SAID THAT THOUGH THE

IZ
BARB II (300) NEGGIN AN JAWRIN THAT MIKES A MENN THET SORE THAT IZ LAWF'S A BURDN TO IM. AW WOWNT EV IT, AW TELL YOU; SAO
PRES (149) IN FUTURE YOU ATTEND TO MY ORDERS AND NOT TO IZ , E SAYS: WHAT DOES E KNOW ABOUT IT? E SAYS. YOU DIDNT

J
BUOY PREFACE(5) THE MOMENTS OF INEXPLICABLE HAPPINESS OF WHICH MR J . B. PRIESTLEY SPOKE IN A RECENT BROADCAST AS PART OF HIS
FABL PREFACE(64) AND BY THE ABLE SCOTCH DOCTOR SCOTT HALDANE (J . B. S. HALDANE'S FATHER), BECOME MORE AND MORE SCEPTICAL
PYGM PREFACE(199) HIS SON INVENTED THE TELEPHONE; BUT ALEXANDER J . ELLIS WAS STILL A LONDON PATRIARCH, WITH AN IMPRESSIVE
AUGS (260) 1917, WITH LALLA VANDERVELDE AS THE LADY, F. B. J . SHARP AS LORD AUGUSTUS HIGHCASTLE, AND CHARLES ROCK AS

JA
WIDO I (5) RAPS ON ANOTHER TABLE, NEARER THE GATE). /PORTER/ JA WOHL, GNAD'G' HERR. (HE PUTS DOWN THE PARCELS). /THE

JAB
GETT (335) DO THAT AGAIN, YOU YOUNG BLACKGUARD; AND I'LL JAB ONE OF THESE CHAIRS IN YOUR FACE (SHE SEIZES ONE AND

JABBERERS
SUPR PREFACE(R31) CLASS WHICH WILL, HE HOPES, FINALLY SWEEP THE JABBERERS OUT OF THE WAY OF CIVILIZATION. MR BARRIE HAS

JABBERING
JOAN 1 (58) MOST INCOMPETENT, DRIVELLING SNIVELLING JIBBERING JABBERING IDIOT OF A STEWARD IN FRANCE. (HE STRIDES BACK TO

JABS
CLEO I (110) SEE, SEE. (SHE PLUCKS A PIN FROM HER HAIR AND JABS IT REPEATEDLY INTO HIS ARM). /CAESAR/ FFFF-- STOP. (

JACK
SUPR I (37) OUGHT TO BE! WHERE ARE YOUR PRINCIPLES? /ANN/ JACK : ARE YOU SERIOUS OR ARE YOU NOT? /TANNER/ DO YOU MEAN
SUPR IV (170) /TAVY/ (ASIDE TO TANNER, GRASPING HIS HAND) JACK : BE VERY HAPPY. /TANNER/ (ASIDE TO TAVY) I NEVER
JOAN 5 (113) HANDLING. WE DID NOT BEGIN IT. /JOAN/ (SUDDENLY) JACK : BEFORE I GO HOME, LET US TAKE PARIS. /CHARLES/ (
KING I (197) GREATEST GENERAL. YOUR CROWN MAY DEPEND ON JACK : BY THE TIME I DIE HE WILL BE AS OLD A SOLDIER AS
JOAN 5 (112) I KNOW IT SOMEHOW. /DUNOIS/ NONSENSE! /JOAN/ JACK : DO YOU THINK YOU WILL BE ABLE TO DRIVE THEM OUT?
JOAN EPILOG (158) HERE BY YOURS. /JOAN/ AND YOU FOUGHT THEM MY WAY, JACK : EH? NOT THE OLD WAY, CHAFFERING FOR RANSOMS; BUT THE
BASH II,1, (101) CORNER. THE FLYING DUTCHMAN WORE THE UNION JACK : HIS COLORS FREELY SOLD AMID THE CROWD' BUT CASHEL'S
CAPT II (245) AND DISGRICE IT, AWK YOU. /JOHNSON/ BRANDYFACED JACK : I NAME YOU FOR CONDUCT AND LANGUAGE UNBECOMING TO A
SUPR I (31) KNOW MUST PAIN ME? I DO MY BEST TO PLEASE YOU, JACK : I SUPPOSE I MAY TELL YOU SO NOW THAT YOU ARE MY
JOAN 5 (109) YOUR FOOD AND DRINK, MY LITTLE SAINT, /JOAN/ DEAR JACK : I THINK YOU LIKE ME AS A SOLDIER LIKES HIS COMRADE.
SUPR I (10) HER THAN A COUPLE OF MICE OVER A CAT. /OCTAVIUS/ JACK : I WISH YOU WOULDNT TALK LIKE THAT ABOUT ANN. /TANNER/
SUPR IV (169) HEART AS WELL AS A MOTHER'S? /ANN/ TAKE CARE, JACK : IF ANYONE COMES WHILE WE ARE LIKE THIS, YOU WILL HAVE
SUPR II (52) MAUDLIN IDIOT? /OCTAVIUS/ YES, I AM AN IDIOT. JACK : IF YOU HAD HEARD HER VOICE! IF YOU HAD SEEN HER
SUPR I (39) (PLACIDLY) I AM SO GLAD YOU UNDERSTAND POLITICS, JACK : IT WILL BE MOST USEFUL TO YOU IF YOU GO INTO
SUPR IV (169) PANTING, FAILING MORE AND MORE UNDER THE STRAIN) JACK : LET ME GO. I HAVE DARED SO FRIGHTFULLY-- IT IS
JOAN 5 (110) /JOAN/ YOU ARE THE PICK OF THE BASKET HERE, JACK : THE ONLY FRIEND I HAVE AMONG ALL THESE NOBLES. I'LL
JOAN 5 (110) PARIS TOOK YOU, I THINK, SO TAKE CARE. /JOAN/ JACK : THE WORLD IS TOO WICKED FOR ME. IF THE GODDAMS AND
SUPR II (52) WHAT DO YOU MEAN? /OCTAVIUS/ (DITHYRAMBICALLY) JACK : WE MEN ARE ALL COARSE: WE NEVER UNDERSTAND HOW
JOAN 5 (117) AS A COMPANION-IN-ARMS. /JOAN/ I DONT BLAME YOU, JACK : YOU ARE RIGHT. I AM NOT WORTH ONE SOLDIER'S LIFE IF
SUPR I (29) I THINK HE SUSPECTS ME JUST A LITTLE. /OCTAVIUS/ JACK : YOU COULDNT-- YOU WOULDNT-- /TANNER/ WHY NOT?
SUPR I (22) YOU GO. /OCTAVIUS/ SHE IS THE SAME TO EVERYBODY, JACK : YOU KNOW HER WAYS. /TANNER/ YES: SHE BREAKS
CAPT III (291) COLLAR AND THE FRONT OF HIS SHIRT) BRANDYFACED JACK : YOURE LOOKING AT THESE STUDS. I KNOW WHATS IN YOUR
JOAN 5 (109) AND DIED TOO: SOME OF US. /JOAN/ ISNT IT STRANGE, JACK ? I AM SUCH A COWARD: I AM FRIGHTENED BEYOND WORDS
JOAN EPILOG (158) GOD BUT FRANCE FREE AND FRENCH. WAS IT MY WAY, JACK ? /DUNOIS/ FAITH, IT WAS ANY WAY THAT WOULD WIN. BUT
JOAN 5 (113) THEM AGAIN. /JOAN/ YOU WILL NOT BE CRUEL TO THEM, JACK ? /DUNOIS/ THE GODDAMS WILL NOT YIELD TO TENDER
SUPR IV (160) HASTILY) DOES ANN SAY THAT I WANT HER TO MARRY JACK ? /OCTAVIUS/ YES: SHE HAS TOLD ME. /MRS WHITEFIELD/ (
SUPR I (39) ROUND HIS NECK). DOESNT IT FEEL NICE AND SOFT, JACK ? /TANNER/ (IN THE TOILS) YOU SCANDALOUS WOMAN, WILL
SUPR I (20) WHITEFIELD/ WHY? WHAT'S THE MATTER WITH POOR JACK ? /TANNER/ MY VIEWS ARE TOO ADVANCED FOR HIM.
SUPR I (31) ABOUT WITH HIM) BUT ISNT THAT ONLY NATURAL, JACK ? WE HAVE KNOWN EACH OTHER SINCE WE WERE CHILDREN. DO
JOAN 1 (63) (COMING OFF THE TABLE) BUT SHE SAYS YOU AND JACK AND DICK HAVE OFFERED TO GO WITH HER. WHAT FOR? YOU
JOAN 1 (61) ME. THEY HAVE PROMISED TO COME WITH ME. POLLY AND JACK AND -- /ROBERT/ POLLY! ! YOU IMPUDENT BAGGAGE, DO YOU
ROCK II (271) ARE THEY TO TELL THE DIFFERENCE BETWEEN ANY CHEAP JACK AND SOLOMON OR MOSES? THE JEWS DIDNT ELECT MOSES: HE
O'FL PREFACE(202) HAD TO FIGHT UNLESS IT MEANT TO COME UNDER THE JACK BOOT OF THE GERMAN VERSION OF DUBLIN CASTLE. THERE WAS
KING I (197) HUMOR, WHAT STRUCK ME MOST IN THE AFFAIR WAS THAT JACK BOUGHT AN ANNUITY WITH THE MONEY INSTEAD OF SQUANDERING
LADY PREFACE(230) CROMWELL IS WRITTEN DOWN TO A POINT AT WHICH THE JACK CADE OF HENRY VI BECOMES A HERO IN COMPARISON; AND THEN
LADY PREFACE(230) GENTLEMAN ALEXANDER IDEN AND THE STAGE RADICAL JACK CADE. WE GET THE SHEPHERD IN AS YOU LIKE IT, AND MANY
GENV PREFACE(19) HITLER FOUND HIMSELF A BORN LEADER, AND, LIKE JACK CADE, WAT TYLER, ESSEX UNDER ELIZABETH TUDOR, EMMET
KING I (196) SINCE WE CAME BACK. I SOMETIMES WONDER WHETHER JACK CHURCHILL HAS ANY MILITARY STUFF IN HIM. /JAMES/ WHAT!
KING II (229) HEREDITY IS NO USE. LEARNING LATIN IS NO USE: JACK CHURCHILL, WHO IS AN IGNORAMUS, IS WORTH FIFTY
JOAN 2 (77) BETWEEN THE ARCHBISHOP AND CHARLES) YOU HAVE JACK DUNOIS AT THE HEAD OF YOUR TROOPS IN ORLEANS: THE BRAVE

JOAN EPILOG	(167)	AT TWELVE O'CLOCK. AND WHAT CAN I DO BUT FOLLOW	JACK	DUNOIS' EXAMPLE, AND GO BACK TO BED TOO? (HE DOES
CAPT III	(296)	SHUT MINE. I'M A STUPIDER MAN THAN BRANDYFACED	JACK	EVEN; FOR HE GOT HIS ROMANTIC NONSENSE OUT OF HIS PENNY
DOCT I	(95)	PER CENT. I'LL GIVE YOU AN INSTANCE. YOU KNOW MRS	JACK	FOLJAMBE? THE SMART MRS FOLJAMBE? I OPERATED AT EASTER
MIS.	(115)	A TURNSPIT. IF YOUR FATHER HADNT MADE A ROASTING	JACK	FOR YOU TO TURN, YOUD BE EARNING TWENTY-FOUR SHILLINGS
KING I	(197)	NEVER HAD A PENNY TO BLESS THEMSELVES WITH.	JACK	GOT NO MORE EDUCATION THAN MY GROOM. /CHARLES/ LATIN
BULL I	(77)	AND A HOUSE IN PARK LANE, I SHOULD CARRY A UNION	JACK	HANDKERCHIEF AND A PENNY TRUMPET, AND TAX THE FOOD OF
SUPR IV	(156)	WITH GROWING RESENTMENT) DO YOU MEAN TO SAY THAT	JACK	HAS BEEN PLAYING WITH ME ALL THIS TIME? THAT HE HAS
POSN	(450)	AND ITLL BE SHORTER FOR HIM. /STRAPPER/ YOUNG	JACK	HAS BROUGHT A BOXFUL UP. THEYRE ALL READY. /THE
SUPR IV	(157)	SELF-CONTROL) I KNOW YOU MEAN TO BE KIND, ANN.	JACK	HAS PERSUADED YOU THAT CYNICISM IS A GOOD TONIC FOR ME.
SUPR I	(20)	IS MORE ADVANCED THAN GRANNY. I AM SURE IT IS	JACK	HIMSELF WHO HAS MADE ALL THE DIFFICULTY. COME, JACK!
KING I	(163)	BASHAM/ (CALLING AFTER HER) AND MIND YOU ASK	JACK	HOW MUCH THREE TIMES SEVEN IS. /SALLY/ (OUTSIDE)
KING I	(197)	HE'S WORTH IT. /CHARLES/ OR IF YOU ARE WORTH IT.	JACK	IS A GOOD JUDGE OF A WINNER. /JAMES/ HE HAS HIS PRICE
SUPR II	(63)	MOTHER JOYOUSLY) OH, MAMMA, WHAT DO YOU THINK!	JACK	IS GOING TO TAKE ME TO NICE IN HIS MOTOR CAR. ISNT IT
SUPR I	(29)	PARTICULARLY KIND TO HER. /ANN/ I HAVE SEEN HER,	JACK	. AND I AM SORRY TO SAY I AM AFRAID SHE IS GOING TO BE
SUPR IV	(156)	FROM MY FATHER'S WILL THAT HE WISHED ME TO MARRY	JACK	. AND MY MOTHER IS SET ON IT. /OCTAVIUS/ BUT YOU ARE
SUPR II	(57)	/OCTAVIUS/ SURELY YOU CANNOT MISUNDERSTAND,	JACK	. ANN IS SHEWING YOU THE KINDEST CONSIDERATION, EVEN AT
SUPR I	(39)	/ANN/ I AM NEVER HYPOCRITICAL WITH YOU,	JACK	. ARE YOU ANGRY? (SHE WITHDRAWS THE BOA AND THROWS IT
SUPR I	(40)	AWAY WITH PERFECT DIGNITY) YOU ARE INCORRIGIBLE,	JACK	. BUT YOU SHOULD NOT JEST ABOUT OUR AFFECTION FOR ONE
SUPR II	(52)	/OCTAVIUS/ (IMPATIENTLY) OH, DONT BE A FOOL,	JACK	. DO YOU SUPPOSE THIS ETERNAL SHALLOW CYNICISM OF YOURS
SUPR I	(35)	STILL? /ANN/ OUR MORAL SENSE CONTROLS PASSION,	JACK	. DONT BE STUPID. /TANNER/ OUR MORAL SENSE! AND IS
SUPR I	(25)	GUARDIAN (HE GOES TOWARDS THE DOOR). /ANN/ STOP,	JACK	. GRANNY: HE MUST KNOW, SOONER OR LATER. /RAMSDEN/
SUPR I	(12)	MR RAMSDEN: I THINK YOU ARE PREJUDICED AGAINST	JACK	. HE IS A MAN OF HONOR, AND INCAPABLE OF ABUSING--
SUPR I	(21)	WORSE. I CAPITULATE. I CONSENT TO JACK. I EMBRACE	JACK	. HERE ENDETH MY FIRST AND LAST ATTEMPT TO ASSERT MY
SUPR I	(39)	I WONT BE CUT TO IT. /ANN/ NOBODY WANTS YOU TO,	JACK	. I ASSURE YOU-- REALLY ON MY WORD-- I DONT MIND YOUR
SUPR II	(58)	LIAR YOU ARE. /ANN/ YOU MISUNDERSTAND,	JACK	. I DIDNT DARE TELL TAVY THE TRUTH. /TANNER/ NO: YOUR
SUPR I	(21)	INVENT ANYTHING WORSE. I CAPITULATE. I CONSENT TO	JACK	. I EMBRACE JACK. HERE ENDETH MY FIRST AND LAST ATTEMPT
SUPR II	(57)	COMING BETWEEN OCTAVIUS AND TANNER) GOOD MORNING,	JACK	. I HAVE COME TO TELL YOU THAT POOR RHODA HAS GOT ONE
SUPR IV	(164)	WHITEFIELD/ YOU SHOULDNT SAY THINGS LIKE THAT,	JACK	. I HOPE YOU WONT TELL ANN THAT I HAVE BEEN SPEAKING TO
SUPR II	(58)	HOUR. I AM OFF FOR A TURN IN THE CAR. /ANN/ NO,	JACK	. I MUST SPEAK TO YOU ABOUT RHODA. RICKY: WILL YOU GO
SUPR I	(33)	FLASHING OUT) OH, THATS NOT TRUE: IT'S NOT TRUE,	JACK	. I NEVER WANTED YOU TO DO THOSE DULL, DISAPPOINTING,
SUPR IV	(162)	BETTER THAN TAVY. SHE'D MEET HER MATCH IN YOU,	JACK	. I'D LIKE TO SEE HER MEET HER MATCH. /TANNER/ NO MAN
SUPR II	(61)	WOULD BE DELIGHTFUL: THANK YOU A THOUSAND TIMES,	JACK	. I'LL COME. /TANNER/ (AGHAST) YOULL COME! ! !
JOAN 5	(110)	AFTER THE CORONATION. I'LL TELL YOU SOMETHING,	JACK	. IT IS IN THE BELLS I HEAR MY VOICES. NOT TO-DAY, WHEN
SUPR IV	(161)	(WITH SNIVELLING GRATITUDE) THANK YOU,	JACK	. (SHE SITS DOWN. TANNER BRINGS THE OTHER CHAIR FROM
SUPR IV	(170)	WITH A SUPREME EFFORT) I HAVE PROMISED TO MARRY	JACK	. (SHE SWOONS. VIOLET KNEELS BY HER AND CHAFES HER
SUPR IV	(171)	BACK TO ME. /ANN/ (COMPLYING) YOU ARE ABSURD,	JACK	. (SHE TAKES HIS PROFFERED ARM). /TANNER/ (
SUPR IV	(161)	IT'S ONLY HER WAY OF SAYING SHE WANTS TO MARRY	JACK	. LITTLE SHE CARES WHAT I SAY OR WHAT I WANT!
SUPR I	(29)	NOT IN THE DRAWING ROOM? /ANN/ DONT BE ABSURD,	JACK	. MISS RAMSDEN IS IN THE DRAWING ROOM WITH MY MOTHER,
SUPR I	(18)	YOUR GUARDIANS GRANNY? /ANN/ DONT BE FOOLISH,	JACK	. MR RAMSDEN HAS ALWAYS BEEN GRANDPAPA ROEBUCK TO ME: I
SUPR I	(37)	BREATHING SPACE AND LIBERTY. /ANN/ IT'S NO USE,	JACK	. NO WOMAN WILL AGREE WITH YOU THERE. /TANNER/ THATS
POSN	(465)	SPEAKS FIRST? WHO'LL MARRY FEEMY? COME ALONG,	JACK	. NOWS YOUR CHANCE, PETER. PASS ALONG A HUSBAND FOR
SUPR I	(27)	I THINK YOU ARE ALL MAD. /ANN/ DONT BE ABSURD,	JACK	. OF COURSE YOU ARE QUITE RIGHT, TAVY; BUT WE DONT KNOW
SUPR IV	(157)	/OCTAVIUS/ YOU DO NOT DREAD DISILLUSIONIZING	JACK	. /ANN/ (HER FACE LIGHTING UP WITH MISCHIEVOUS
SUPR IV	(172)	(WITH INTENSE CONVICTION) YOU ARE A BRUTE,	JACK	. /ANN/ (LOOKING AT HIM WITH FOND PRIDE AND CARESSING
CAPT I	(237)	MADAM: HE IS ACCUSTOMED TO BE CALLED BRANDYFACED	JACK	. /DRINKWATER/ (INDIGNANTLY) EAH, AW SY! NAH LOOK
SUPR IV	(156)	THAT MY MOTHER IS DETERMINED THAT I SHALL MARRY	JACK	. /OCTAVIUS/ (AMAZED) JACK! /ANN/ IT SEEMS ABSURD,
SUPR I	(25)	/OCTAVIUS/ (TURNING PALE) I HAVE NO SECRETS FROM	JACK	. /RAMSDEN/ BEFORE YOU DECIDE THAT FINALLY, LET ME SAY
SUPR I	(20)	NEVER PURPOSELY FORCE ME INTO A PAINFUL DILEMMA,	JACK	. /RAMSDEN/ (IRRITABLY) YES, YES, ANNIE: THIS IS ALL
SUPR I	(26)	OF SYMPATHY? /OCTAVIUS/ DONT BE BRUTAL,	JACK	. /TANNER/ BRUTAL! GOOD HEAVENS, MAN, WHAT ARE YOU
SUPR IV	(165)	DRIES HER EYES, AND SUBSIDES). /VIOLET/ GOODBYE,	JACK	. /TANNER/ GOODBYE, VIOLET. /VIOLET/ THE SOONER YOU GET
SUPR IV	(163)	EXPOSTULATION) WELL, YOU CANT EXPECT PERFECTION,	JACK	. /TANNER/ I DONT. BUT WHAT ANNOYS ME IS THAT ANN DOES.
SUPR I	(19)	AND I WILL. /ANN/ BUT I HAVNT READ YOUR BOOK,	JACK	. /TANNER/ (DIVING AT THE WASTE-PAPER BASKET AND
SUPR II	(60)	YOU WILL GO IN SERIOUSLY FOR POLITICS SOME DAY,	JACK	. /TANNER/ (HEAVILY LET DOWN) EH? WHAT? WH--? (
SUPR I	(12)	/OCTAVIUS/ THIS SORT OF TALK IS NOT KIND TO ME,	JACK	. /TANNER/ (RISING AND GOING TO OCTAVIUS TO CONSOLE
SUPR II	(59)	YOUR MOTHER COMES TO. /ANN/ I LOVE MY MOTHER,	JACK	. /TANNER/ (WORKING HIMSELF UP INTO A SOCIOLOGICAL
SUPR I	(33)	AND THEREFORE UNREAL. /ANN/ I NEVER TOLD OF YOU,	JACK	. /TANNER/ NO; BUT IF YOU HAD WANTED TO STOP ME YOU
SUPR I	(24)	TAVY. /OCTAVIUS/ I MEANT WHERE THERE IS LOVE,	JACK	; /TANNER/ OH, THE TIGER WILL LOVE YOU. THERE IS NO
SUPR I	(35)	PASSION. /ANN/ ALL PASSIONS OUGHT TO BE MORAL,	JACK	. /TANNER/ OUGHT! DO YOU THINK THAT ANYTHING IS STRONG
SUPR I	(21)	/ANN/ (GRATEFULLY) YOU ALL SPOIL ME, EXCEPT	JACK	. /TANNER/ OVER HIS SHOULDER, FROM THE BOOKCASE) I
SUPR II	(57)	OF GIRLS. /OCTAVIUS/ ANN DOESNT SAY THAT,	JACK	. /TANNER/ WHAT ELSE DOES SHE MEAN? /STRAKER/ (
SUPR I	(14)	TO SEE HER-- /OCTAVIUS/ (SHYLY) I AM NOT,	JACK	. /TANNER/ YOU LIE, TAVY: YOU ARE. SO LETS HAVE HER
SUPR I	(11)	THE WINDS AND WAVES. /OCTAVIUS/ THIS IS NOT FAIR,	JACK	. SHE IS AN ORPHAN. AND YOU OUGHT TO STAND BY HER.
SUPR I	(27)	ME. WHERE IS SHE? /ANN/ DONT BE SO HEADSTRONG,	JACK	. SHE'S UPSTAIRS. /TANNER/ WHAT! UNDER RAMSDEN'S
SUPR IV	(161)	TO KNOW TOO LITTLE, LIKE YOU, OR TOO MUCH, LIKE	JACK	. TANNER RETURNS. /TANNER/ WELL, IVE DISPOSED OF OLD
JOAN 5	(115)	OF US, GENERAL JOAN. /JOAN/ NEVER MIND THAT,	JACK	. TELL THEM WHAT YOU THINK OF ME. /DUNOIS/ I THINK THAT
SUPR I	(21)	CALL ME MR TANNER. /ANN/ (GENTLY) NO YOU DONT,	JACK	. THATS LIKE THE THINGS YOU SAY ON PURPOSE TO SHOCK
SUPR I	(41)	(OFFENDED) YOU HAVE NO RIGHT TO SAY SUCH THINGS,	JACK	. THEY ARE NOT TRUE, AND NOT DELICATE. IF YOU AND TAVY
SUPR I	(23)	OF THAT PURPOSE. /OCTAVIUS/ DONT BE UNGENEROUS,	JACK	. THEY TAKE THE TENDEREST CARE OF US. /TANNER/ YES, AS
SUPR I	(36)	CHILD INTO A MAN. /ANN/ THERE ARE OTHER PASSIONS,	JACK	. VERY STRONG ONES. /TANNER/ ALL THE OTHER PASSIONS
JOAN EPILOG	(158)	IN HEAVEN. TELL ME ALL ABOUT THE FIGHTING,	JACK	. WAS IT THOU THAT LED THEM? WERT THOU GOD'S CAPTAIN
SUPR IV	(164)	YOU SEEM TO BE HAVING A DELIGHTFUL CHAT WITH	JACK	. WE CAN HEAR YOU ALL OVER THE PLACE. /MRS WHITEFIELD/
SUPR IV	(168)	YOU HAD BETTER MARRY WHAT YOU CALL A HYPOCRITE,	JACK	. WOMEN WHO ARE NOT HYPOCRITES GO ABOUT IN RATIONAL
SUPR II	(61)	I DONT THINK THERE WOULD BE ANY HARM IN THAT,	JACK	. YOU ARE MY GUARDIAN: YOU STAND IN MY FATHER'S PLACE,
SUPR II	(54)	BE A ROW. /OCTAVIUS/ THIS SORT OF TALK IS NO USE,	JACK	. YOU DONT UNDERSTAND. YOU HAVE NEVER BEEN IN LOVE.
SUPR I	(35)	/TANNER/ MY SOUL. /ANN/ OH, DO BE SENSIBLE,	JACK	. YOU KNOW YOURE TALKING NONSENSE. /TANNER/ THE MOST
SUPR I	(40)	I KNOW YOU HAVE. /ANN/ (EARNESTLY) TAKE CARE,	JACK	. YOU MAY MAKE TAVY VERY UNHAPPY IF YOU MISLEAD HIM
SUPR I	(32)	ANYTHING. /ANN/ YOU DIDNT WANT TO TALK ABOUT ME,	JACK	. YOU WANTED TO TALK ABOUT YOURSELF. /TANNER/ AH, TRUE,
SUPR I	(31)	GOES TO HIM AND SPEAKS ALMOST INTO HIS EAR. /ANN/	JACK	(HE TURNS WITH A START): ARE YOU GLAD THAT YOU ARE MY
INCA	(249)	AND PONGO AND THE CORSAIR AND THE PIFFLER AND	JACK	JOHNSON THE SECOND, ALL UNMARRIED. AT LEAST NOT
INCA	(250)	PIFFLER WRITES PLAYS, AND PAINTS MOST ABOMINABLY.	JACK	JOHNSON TRIMS LADIES' HATS, AND BOXES WITH
INCA	(252)	TO THE ABILITIES OF CHIPS AND THE PIFFLER AND	JACK	JOHNSON. I BELIEVE IN INDIVIDUAL GENIUS. THAT IS THE
LION PREFACE	(56)	POOR-BOX, MR HORATIO BOTTOMLEY, SHAKESPEAR, MR	JACK	JOHNSON, SIR ISAAC NEWTON, PALESTRINA, OFFENBACH, SIR
SUPR IV	(156)	THAT I SAID THAT. I DONT FOR A MOMENT THINK THAT	JACK	KNOWS HIS OWN MIND. BUT IT'S CLEAR FROM MY FATHER'S
SUPR I	(12)	I WAS RIGHT. YOU KNOW I LOVE HER, MR RAMSDEN; AND	JACK	KNOWS IT TOO. IF JACK LOVED A WOMAN, I WOULD NOT
SUPR I	(12)	I LOVE HER, MR RAMSDEN; AND JACK KNOWS IT TOO. IF	JACK	LOVED A WOMAN, I WOULD NOT COMPARE HER TO A BOA
ROCK II	(261)	OF CONSTABLES BUT MILLIONS. /SIR DEXTER/ MY UNION	JACK	MEN WOULD KEEP ORDER, OR THEYD KNOW THE REASON WHY.
BUOY 1	(15)	NOTHING. /FATHER/ I HOPE NOT. FOR IF EVERY MAN	JACK	OF US CAN BLOW THE WORLD TO PIECES THERE WILL BE AN END
SUPR I	(45)	SUCH A HORRIBLE INSULT AS TO BE COMPLIMENTED BY	JACK	ON BEING ONE OF THE WRETCHES OF WHOM HE APPROVES. I
APPL PREFACE	(188)	AN ARTICLE IN THE MORNING POST, AND HAS A UNION	JACK	ON IT. ANOTHER IS LIKE THE DAILY NEWS OR MANCHESTER
BARB II	(297)	AND VERSE BY VERSE, WAS A CAUTION. NOT A CHEAP	JACK	ON MILE END WASTE COULD TOUCH YOU AT IT. /BARBARA/ YES;
GENV II	(50)	HAVE HEARD THE NEWS, NO DOUBT? /BEGONIA/ OH YES.	JACK	PALAMEDES HAS WON THE DANCING TOURNAMENT. I HAD TEN
KING II	(233)	HAVE HER OUT OF THE KINGDOM BEFORE SHE COULD SAY	JACK	ROBINSON. SO NOW SHE HAS THROWN OVER SHAFTESBURY; AND
GENV PREFACE	(10)	THEM VANISHED BEFORE THE EXPERIMENTERS COULD SAY	JACK	ROBINSON. THERE IS NO GETTING AWAY FROM THE FACT THAT
SUPR I	(7)	OF THE IDLE RICH CLASS. /OCTAVIUS/ (SMILING) BUT	JACK	-- /RAMSDEN/ (TESTILY) FOR GOODNESS' SAKE, DONT CALL
JOAN 1	(61)	SO, SQUIRE: I DID NOT KNOW HE HAD ANY OTHER NAME.	JACK	-- /ROBERT/ THAT IS MONSIEUR JOHN OF METZ, I SUPPOSE..
BULL III	(136)	EMERALD PASTURE OF COLLEGE GREEN, AND THE UNION	JACK	-- THAT DETESTABLE SYMBOL OF A DECADENT IMPERIALISM--
JOAN 5	(116)	GOD DEFEND THE RIGHT! YOU MAY SHAKE YOUR HEAD,	JACK	; AND BLUEBEARD MAY TWIRL HIS BILLYGOAT'S BEARD AND
SUPR II	(58)	RIGHT-- QUITE RIGHT. ANN WAS ONLY DOING HER DUTY,	JACK	; AND YOU KNOW IT, DOING IT IN THE KINDEST WAY, TOO.
SUPR I	(33)	HEROIC AT LAST. (RECOVERING HERSELF) EXCUSE ME,	JACK	; BUT THE THINGS YOU DID WERE NEVER A BIT LIKE THE
SUPR IV	(171)	EAR, CLUTCHING HER ROUND THE NECK) VIOLET: DID	JACK	SAY ANYTHING WHEN I FAINTED? /VIOLET/ NO. /ANN/ AH! (
KING I	(163)	IT DOWN AS-- SALLY RETURNS. /SALLY/ PLEASE, MAAM,	JACK	SAYS IT'S TWENTYONE. /NEWTON/ EXTRAORDINARY! HERE WAS
ROCK II	(260)	THOUSAND PATRIOTIC YOUNG LONDONERS INTO UNION	JACK	SHIRTS. YOU SAY THEY WANT DISCIPLINE AND ACTION. THEY
SUPR IV	(158)	THAN LIVING UP TO AN IDEAL. OH, I SHALL ENRAPTURE	JACK	SOMETIMES! /OCTAVIUS/ (RESUMING THE CALM PHASE OF
SUPR IV	(171)	BETWEEN MALONE AND TANNER) YOU ARE A HAPPY MAN,	JACK	TANNER. I ENVY YOU. /MENDOZA/ (ADVANCING BETWEEN
SUPR II	(67)	ABOUT THAT; AND-- /VIOLET/ THE BEAST! I HATE	JACK	TANNER. /HECTOR/ (MAGNANIMOUSLY) OH, HEE'S ALL RIGHT:
SUPR IV	(158)	FOR MORE OF IT? /ANN/ YOU HAVE OFFERED TO TELL	JACK	THAT I LOVE HIM. THATS SELF-SACRIFICE, I SUPPOSE; BUT
SUPR I	(8)	DO ABOUT IT? /OCTAVIUS/ BUT ANN HERSELF HAS TOLD	JACK	THAT WHATEVER HIS OPINIONS ARE, HE WILL ALWAYS BE

KING I	(167)	BASHAM. HE MUST NOT BE QUESTIONED AS IF HE WERE	JACK THE FISH HAWKER. HIS BUSINESS IS HIS FATHER'S BUSINESS.
KING I	(167)	FOR I AM FAR LESS IMPORTANT NOW IN ENGLAND THAN	JACK THE FISH HAWKER. /MRS BASHAM/ BUT HOW DO YOU LIVE,
KING I	(162)	NEWTON. HE'LL KNOW, IF ANYBODY WILL. OR STOP. ASK	JACK THE FISH HAWKER. HE'S PAUNCHING THE RABBIT IN THE
KING I	(200)	WILL HAVE TO BE CONTENT WITH A PROTESTANT DINNER.	JACK THE FISH HAWKER IS GONE. BUT HE LEFT US A NICE PIECE OF
SUPP I	(21)	CASTS A GLANCE AT TANNER OVER HER SHOULDER). AND	JACK THE GIANT KILLER. (SHE GOES PAST HER MOTHER TO
ROCK PREFACE	(178)	TO RELIGION WHETHER JOSHUA WAS ANY MORE REAL THAN	JACK THE GIANT KILLER, AND THAT GALILEO MIGHT PLAY SKITTLES
SUPR IV	(158)	HE HAS NO ILLUSIONS ABOUT ME. I SHALL SURPRISE	JACK THE OTHER WAY. GETTING OVER AN UNFAVORABLE IMPRESSION
SUPR IV	(156)	IS ANOTHER SIDE TO THIS QUESTION. IS IT FAIR TO	JACK TO MARRY HIM IF YOU DO NOT LOVE HIM? IS IT FAIR TO
SUPR IV	(160)	YOU GUESS? I DARESAY YOU ARE RIGHT TO PREFER	JACK TO ME AS A HUSBAND FOR ANN; BUT I LOVE ANN; AND IT
CAPT III	(292)	ANCHOR; AND MAKE ALL READY FOR SEA. THEN SEND	JACK TO WAIT FOR ME AT THE SLIP WITH A BOAT; AND GIVE ME A
SUPR I	(7)	(TESTILY) FOR GOODNESS' SAKE, DONT CALL HIM	JACK UNDER MY ROOF (HE THROWS THE BOOK VIOLENTLY DOWN ON
SUPR I	(21)	I CERTAINLY WONT CALL YOU THAT. MAY I CALL YOU	JACK UNTIL I CAN THINK OF SOMETHING ELSE? /TANNER/ OH, FOR
KING I	(197)	THE BATTLEFIELD, AS WE FOUND OUT. TURENNE FOUND	JACK USEFUL ENOUGH IN SPAIN; AND TURENNE WAS SUPPOSED TO BE
KING II	(229)	BILLY DIES AND ONE OF MY NIECES SUCCEEDS HIM	JACK WILL BE KING OF ENGLAND. /CATHERINE/ PERHAPS THE CHURCH
JOAN 1	(62)	JOHN OF METZ, I SUPPOSE? /JOAN/ YES, SQUIRE.	JACK WILL COME WILLINGLY: HE IS A VERY KIND GENTLEMAN, AND
JOAN 1	(66)	JOAN COMES IN, FULL OF GOOD NEWS. /JOAN/	JACK WILL GO HALVES FOR THE HORSE. /ROBERT/ WELL! ! (HE
BULL PREFACE	(31)	CALLED THE EMPIRE. THEY WILL PULL DOWN THE UNION	JACK WITHOUT THE SMALLEST SCRUPLE; BUT THEY KNOW THE VALUE
SUPR IV	(171)	STRONG ENOUGH NOW. BUT YOU VERY NEARLY KILLED ME,	JACK , FOR ALL THAT. /MALONE/ A ROUGH WOOER, EH? THEYRE THE
SUPR I	(25)	A NICELY UNDERDONE CHOP. /OCTAVIUS/ YOU KNOW,	JACK , I SHOULD HAVE TO RUN AWAY FROM YOU IF I DID NOT MAKE
SUPR I	(40)	HAPPEN TO POOR TAVY. /ANN/ I SHOULD LAUGH AT YOU,	JACK , IF IT WERE NOT FOR POOR PAPA'S DEATH. MIND! TAVY
SUPR IV	(167)	FLATTERER. WHY ARE YOU TRYING TO FASCINATE ME,	JACK , IF YOU DONT WANT TO MARRY ME? /TANNER/ THE LIFE
SUPR I	(46)	OF US. /VIOLET/ IT WAS NO BUSINESS OF YOURS,	JACK , IN ANY CASE. /TANNER/ NO BUSINESS OF MINE! WHY,
SUPR I	(42)	OUT OF OCTAVIUS'S MOUTH) THE DIFFICULTY, MR	JACK , IS THAT WHEN I OFFERED TO HELP HER I DIDNT OFFER TO
SUPR IV	(167)	IN THE STREET. /ANN/ YES, I KNOW. ALL THE SAME,	JACK , MEN LIKE THAT ALWAYS LIVE IN COMFORTABLE BACHELOR
SUPR I	(9)	WORDS. /OCTAVIUS/ (GRINNING) THATS VERY LIKE	JACK , MR RAMSDEN. YOU MUST SEE HIM, EVEN IF IT'S ONLY TO
SUPR II	(59)	WOMEN ARE CONVENTIONAL: WE MUST BE CONVENTIONAL,	JACK , OR WE ARE SO CRUELLY, SO VILELY MISUNDERSTOOD. EVEN
SUPR II	(61)	(WITH SIMPLE EARNESTNESS) YES, I WILL COME,	JACK , SINCE YOU WISH IT. YOU ARE MY GUARDIAN; AND I THINK
SUPR IV	(161)	YOU WISH. (TO TANNER) YOU MAY TAKE IT FROM ME,	JACK , THAT ANN APPROVES OF IT. /TANNER/ (PUZZLED BY HIS
SUPR II	(61)	IT'S VERY THOUGHTFUL AND VERY KIND OF YOU,	JACK , TO OFFER ME THIS LOVELY HOLIDAY, ESPECIALLY AFTER
SUPR I	(38)	SHALL EVER ENSLAVE ME IN THAT WAY. /ANN/ BUT,	JACK , YOU CANNOT GET THROUGH LIFE WITHOUT CONSIDERING OTHER
SUPR I	(13)	MY HEART ON SAVING YOU FROM HER! /OCTAVIUS/ OH,	JACK , YOU TALK OF SAVING ME FROM MY HIGHEST HAPPINESS.
SUPR I	(36)	STUFF! I WAS ONLY MISCHIEVOUS. /ANN/ OH,	JACK , YOU WERE VERY DESTRUCTIVE. YOU RUINED ALL THE YOUNG
SUPR IV	(157)	COULD DO THAT IF WE WERE MARRIED. BUT IF I MARRY	JACK , YOULL NEVER BE DISILLUSIONED-- AT LEAST NOT UNTIL I
SUPR I	(20)	HIMSELF WHO HAS MADE ALL THE DIFFICULTY. COME,	JACK ! BE KIND TO ME IN MY SORROW. YOU DONT REFUSE TO
SUPR IV	(168)	QUIETLY AND SHAKING HER FINGER AT HIM) NOW,	JACK ! BEHAVE YOURSELF. /TANNER/ INFAMOUS, ABANDONED
SUPR IV	(156)	THAT I SHALL MARRY JACK. /OCTAVIUS/ (AMAZED)	JACK ! /ANN/ IT SEEMS ABSURD, DOESNT IT? /OCTAVIUS/ (WITH
SUPR I	(44)	SHAME. /ANN/ (PLEADING TO TANNER TO BE SENSIBLE)	JACK ! /MISS RAMSDEN/ (OUTRAGED) WELL, I MUST SAY!
SUPR I	(8)	TO SEE YOU, SIR. /RAMSDEN/ MR TANNER! /OCTAVIUS/	JACK ! /RAMSDEN/ HOW DARE MR TANNER CALL ON ME! SAY I
SUPR I	(29)	BEFORE HER JUDGES. THE OLD CATS! /ANN/ OH,	JACK ! /RAMSDEN/ YOU ARE AT PRESENT A GUEST BENEATH THE
SUPR I	(41)	IN IT! /ANN/ WHAT A SHOCKING FLIRT YOU ARE,	JACK ! /TANNER/ A FLIRT! ! I! ! ! /ANN/ YES, A FLIRT.
SUPR III	(138)	ON HIS LEFT, SUPPORTING HIM IN FLANK. /ANN/ IT'S	JACK ! /TANNER/ CAUGHT! /HECTOR/ WHY, CERTAINLY IT IS. I
SUPR I	(37)	US WAS AN UNCONSCIOUS LOVE COMPACT-- /ANN/	JACK ! /TANNER/ OH, DONT BE ALARMED-- /ANN/ I AM NOT
SUPR I	(22)	MARRY YOU. /OCTAVIUS/ (SIGHING) NO SUCH LUCK,	JACK ! /TANNER/ WHY, MAN, YOUR HEAD IS IN THE LIONESS'S
SUPR I	(37)	YOU HATED TO BE TREATED AS A BOY ANY LONGER. POOR	JACK ! /TANNER/ YES, BECAUSE TO BE TREATED AS A BOY WAS TO
SUPR I	(32)	REASON YOU NEVER TEMPTED TAVY. /ANN/ TEMPTED!	JACK ! /TANNER/ YES, MY DEAR LADY MEPHISTOPHELES, TEMPTED.
SUPR IV	(164)	WHY, OF COURSE I DO. WHAT QUEER THINGS YOU SAY,	JACK ! WE CANT HELP LOVING OUR OWN BLOOD RELATIONS.

JACKAL

CLEO II	(131)	NOT THE LION I FEAR, BUT (LOOKING AT RUFIO) THE	JACKAL . (HE GOES OUT THROUGH THE LOGGIA). /CAESAR/ (

JACKANAPES

KING I	(189)	JAMIE, AND NOT SIT ON THE FLOOR GRINNING LIKE A	JACKANAPES . GET UP, I TELL YOU. /JAMES/ (RISING) YOU SEE

JACKASS

MTH3	(129)	HAD BETTER GO AND WRITE THE AUTOBIOGRAPHY OF A	JACKASS . I AM GOING TO RAISE THE COUNTRY AGAINST THIS
DEVL III	(65)	DICK. /RICHARD/ ANSWER PROPERLY, YOU JUMPING	JACKASS . WHAT DO THEY KNOW ABOUT DICK? /CHRISTY/ WELL, YOU
DEST	(171)	ON ME; AND I HAVE BEEN AS GROSS A GULL AS MY	JACKASS OF A LIEUTENANT. (MENACINGLY) COME: THE DESPATCHES.
MRS III	(222)	SHEEP AND THE POMPOUSNESS AND AGGRESSIVENESS OF A	JACKASS -- /PRAED/ NO, PRAY, PRAY, MY DEAR FRANK, REMEMBER!

JACKBOOTS

O'FL	(208)	PALACE THIS DAY, AND KING GEORGE POLISHING HIS	JACKBOOTS FOR HIM IN THE SCULLERY. /SIR PEARCE/ BUT I DONT

JACKDAW

ROCK II	(265)	SNEERING AT MY COLOR BECAUSE YOU HAVE NONE. THE	JACKDAW HAS LOST HIS TAIL AND WOULD PERSUADE THE WORLD THAT

JACKET

CAPT III	SD(293)	THEN HE TAKES FROM THE BREAST POCKET OF HIS	JACKET A LEATHER CASE, FROM WHICH HE EXTRACTS A SCRAPPY
PHIL II	SD(94)	TRIM, WEARING A MOUNTAINEERING SUIT OF NORFOLK	JACKET AND BREECHES WITH NEAT TOWN STOCKINGS AND SHOES. A
PHIL I	SD(69)	UNCONVENTIONALLY BUT SMARTLY DRESSED IN A VELVET	JACKET AND CASHMERE TROUSERS. HIS COLLAR, DYED WOTAN BLUE,
MRS IV	(235)	FOR A CUP OF TEA. (SHE TAKES OFF HER HAT AND	JACKET AND HANGS THEM UP BEHIND THE SCREEN). HOW DID YOU GET
CAPT III	(292)	(RETURNING IN HIS OWN CLOTHES, GETTING INTO HIS	JACKET AS HE COMES). STAND BY, ALL. (THEY START ASUNDER
NEVR IV	SD(293)	ORANGE AND POPPY CRIMSON, WITH A TINY VELVET	JACKET FOR THE POPPY STAMENS. THEY PASS, AN EXQUISITE AND
ARMS II	SD(38)	THE HOUSE WHEN RAINA RETURNS, WEARING A HAT AND	JACKET IN THE HEIGHT OF THE VIENNA FASHION OF THE PREVIOUS
WIDO I	(4)	FOR DINNER; AND YOU HAVE NOTHING BUT THAT NORFOLK	JACKET . HOW ARE THEY TO KNOW THAT YOU ARE WELL CONNECTED IF
MRS IV	SD(235)	IT'S NOT LOCKED. VIVIE COMES IN, IN HER HAT AND	JACKET . SHE STOPS AND STARES AT HIM. /VIVIE/ (STERNLY)
BARB II	(299)	JAW? /BILL/ NAO E AINT. /BARBARA/ I THOUGHT YOUR	JACKET LOOKED A BIT SNOWY. /BILL/ SAO IT IS SNAOWY. YOU WANT
CAND III	SD(136)	HIM. MISS GARNETT, WITH HER SMARTEST HAT AND	JACKET ON, FOLLOWS THEM; BUT THOUGH HER EYES ARE BRIGHTER
PYGM IV	SD(260)	OF HIS COAT IN THE SAME WAY; PUTS ON THE SMOKING	JACKET ; AND THROWS HIMSELF WEARILY INTO THE EASY-CHAIR AT
HART I	SD(54)	EARNEST MANNERS. HE IS DRESSED IN A BLUE SERGE	JACKET SUIT WITH AN UNBUTTONED MACKINTOSH OVER IT, AND
PYGM IV	SD(260)	OVERCOAT AND HAT, COMES IN, CARRYING A SMOKING	JACKET WHICH HE HAS PICKED UP DOWNSTAIRS. HE TAKES OFF THE
HART I	(45)	MAN WITH AN IMMENSE WHITE BEARD, IN A REEFER	JACKET WITH A WHISTLE HANGING FROM HIS NECK) NURSE: THERE IS
ARMS II	SD(23)	NO ILLUSIONS. HE WEARS A WHITE BULGARIAN COSTUME:	JACKET WITH EMBROIDERED BORDER, SASH, WIDE KNICKERBOCKERS,
DEST	SD(162)	FOR TRAVELLING. AT ALL EVENTS SHE WEARS NO	JACKET WITH EXTRAVAGANT LAPPELS, NO GRECO-TALLIEN SHAM
CAND I	SD(94)	HANDKERCHIEF FOR A CRAVAT, TROUSERS MATCHING THE	JACKET , AND BROWN CANVAS SHOES. IN THESE GARMENTS HE HAS
BARB II	SD(298)	BACK TO JOIN US. BILL WALKER, WITH FROST ON HIS	JACKET , COMES THROUGH THE GATE, HIS HANDS DEEP IN HIS
CAPT II	(262)	POOR MARZO, SAY THANK YOU TO ME FOR MENDING YOUR	JACKET , LIKE A NICE POLITE SAILOR. /BRASSBOUND/ (SITTING
CAND I	SD(93)	HIS DRESS IS ANARCHIC. HE WEARS AN OLD BLUE SERGE	JACKET , UNBUTTONED, OVER A WOOLLEN LAWN TENNIS SHIRT, WITH
NEVR II	SD(236)	EXTENUATING THE UNFASHIONABLENESS OF HIS REEFER	JACKET , WEARS A LIGHT OVERCOAT. HE STOPS AT THE CHAIR LEFT

JACKETS

DOCT PREFACE	(42)	WHOLESALE MASSACRE BECAUSE LADIES WANT SEALSKIN	JACKETS ; OR AS FANCIERS BLIND SINGING BIRDS WITH HOT

JACK'S

SUPR I	(21)	(SHE GOES PAST HER MOTHER TO OCTAVIUS) AND	JACK'S INSEPARABLE FRIEND RICKY-TICKY-TAVY (HE BLUSHES AND
SUPR IV	(145)	AND HAVE THE GARDEN ALL TO MYSELF. JUMP INTO	JACK'S MOTOR: STRAKER WILL RATTLE YOU HERE IN A JIFFY.
CAPT II	(243)	LOOK ALIVE, JOHNNIES: THERE'S DANGER. BRANDYFACED	JACK'S ON THE RUN. (THEY SPRING UP HASTILY, GRASPING THEIR

JACKSON

APPL	(170)	WAS PRODUCED IN ENGLAND BY SIR BARRY	JACKSON AT THE MALVERN FESTIVAL ON THE 19TH AUGUST, 1929,
MIS. PREFACE	(90)	AND CAN THEREBY BE LED TO THE DISCOVERY THAT	JACKSON IN F AND HYMNS ANCIENT AND MODERN ARE NOT PERHAPS
CAPT NOTES	(302)	A PEG TO HANG CAPTAIN BRASSBOUND. TO MR FREDERICK	JACKSON OF HINDHEAD, WHO, AGAINST ALL HIS PRINCIPLES,
FANY III	(313)	HYGIENIC CORSET ADVERTISEMENTS THAT VINES AND	JACKSON WANT US TO PUT IN THE WINDOW? I TOLD VINES THEY
CAPT II	(261)	UNALTERABLE! RESOLUTE! IRON-WILLED! STONEWALL	JACKSON ! THATS THE IDEA, ISNT IT? /BRASSBOUND/ (

JACKSON'S

POSN	(458)	SHERIFF/ WHERES THE CHILD? /STRAPPER/ ON PUG	JACKSON'S BENCH IN HIS SHED. HE'S MAKIN A COFFIN FOR IT.

POSN (460) GOOD YOUR CHILD IS TO YOU NOW, LYING THERE ON PUG JACKSON'S BENCH! /BLANCO/ (RUSHING AT HER WITH A SHRIEK)
FABL PREFACE(91) HAD BEEN BROUGHT UP ON BEETHOVEN INSTEAD OF ON JACKSON'S TE DEUM, HE MIGHT HAVE PREFERRED WAGNER TO

JACKSONSLAND
GENV II (51) ONE OTHER TRIFLE OF NEWS. THE LITTLE DOMINION OF JACKSONSLAND HAS DECLARED ITSELF AN INDEPENDENT REPUBLIC.
GENV IV (104) WHY AM I LOCKED OUT OF THE PARLIAMENT OF JACKSONSLAND , TO WHICH I HAVE BEEN LAWFULLY ELECTED: TELL

JACOBEAN
BUOY PREFACE(4) OUR GREATEST MASTERPIECE OF LITERATURE IS THE JACOBEAN TRANSLATION OF THE BIBLE; AND THIS THE CHRISTIAN

JACOBINS
SUPR HANDBOK(198) LIMIT OF HUMAN ENDURANCE, BOTH ON GIRONDINS AND JACOBINS . FOUQUIER TINVILLE FOLLOWED MARIE ANTOINETTE TO

JACOBITE
KING PREFACE(153) OF ALL PARTIES, FROM THE WHIG MACAULAY TO THE JACOBITE HILAIRE BELLOC, THAT THERE IS NO NOVELTY LEFT FOR

JACOB'S
MTH2 (77) AS THEY CAME CRASHING DOWN ALL THE STEPS OF THIS JACOB'S LADDER THAT REACHED FROM PARADISE TO A HELL ON EARTH

JACOBUS
APPL I (209) THE MULTITUDE! /BOANERGES/ YOURE THINKING OF IKY JACOBUS ? HE IS ONLY A TALKER. (SNAPPING HIS FINGERS) I
APPL I (209) THAT FOR HIM. /MAGNUS/ I NEVER EVEN HEARD OF MR JACOBUS . BUT WHY DO YOU SAY " ONLY A TALKER." TALKERS ARE

JACQUES
MIS. PREFACE(23) BEST OF ALL AS I THINK, THE EURYTHMICS SCHOOL OF JACQUES DALCROZE AT HELLERAU NEAR DRESDEN. JACQUES DALCROZE,
MIS. PREFACE(23) OF JACQUES DALCROZE AT HELLERAU NEAR DRESDEN. JACQUES DALCROZE, LIKE PLATO, BELIEVES IN SATURATING HIS
MIS. PREFACE(24) TO DO ALL THESE THINGS TO. STRANGER STILL, THOUGH JACQUES DALCROZE, LIKE ALL THESE GREAT TEACHERS, IS THE
6CAL SD(97) FOUR OF HIS FELLOW VICTIMS, PIERS DE WISSANT, JACQUES DE WISSANT, JEAN D'AIRE, AND GILLES D'OUDEBOLLE,

JADE
CLEO III SD(144) OF BRONZE, OXYDIZED SILVER, AND STONES OF JADE AND AGATE. HIS SWORD, DESIGNED AS CAREFULLY AS A
POSN (457) TO FEEMY) AND WHAT DO YOU MEAN, YOU LYING JADE , BY PUTTING UP THIS STORY ON US ABOUT BLANCO? /FEEMY/

JADED
MRS PREFACE(153) WHAT A TRIUMPH FOR THE ACTOR, THUS TO REDUCE A JADED LONDON JOURNALIST TO THE CONDITION OF THE SIMPLE

JADES
LADY (243) QUOTHA! AND WHO IN THE NAME OF ALL THE SLUTS AND JADES AND LIGHT-O'-LOVES AND FLY-BY-NIGHTS THAT INFEST THIS

JADGE
CAPT I (219) COMPOSES HIMSELF FOR CONVERSATION). HEVER EAR O JADGE ELLAM? /RANKIN/ SIR HOWRRD HALLAM? /DRINKWATER/
CAPT I (220) IS CREW, INCLOODIN MAWSEOLF, WILL SEE THE LIDY AN JADGE ELLAM THROUGH HENNY LITTLE EXCURSION IN REASON. YR
CAPT I (219) HOWRRD HALLAM? /DRINKWATER/ THETS IM-- ENGINEST JADGE IN HINGLAND! -- AWLUS GIVES THE KET WEN ITS ROBBRY

JAFNA
ROCK II (243) END CHAIR TO THE VISITOR) YOU ARE WELCOME, SIR JAFNA : MOST WELCOME. YOU REPRESENT MONEY; AND MONEY BRINGS
ROCK II (244) THIS QUESTION NOT AS AN EMOTIONAL ORIENTAL (SIR JAFNA CHOKES CONVULSIVELY) BUT AS A SANE MAN OF BUSINESS. IF
ROCK II (245) /SIR DEXTER/ YOU COME IN THE NICK OF TIME. SIR JAFNA HERE HAS JUST BEEN QUALIFYING YOU AS A BLOODSUCKER, A
ROCK II (266) THE DOOR). /SIR ARTHUR/ MAKE MY APOLOGIES TO SIR JAFNA IF YOU OVERTAKE HIM. HOW ARE WE TO HOLD THE EMPIRE
ROCK II SD(242) RISE AS IF TO RECEIVE A ROYAL PERSONAGE. SIR JAFNA IS AN ELDERLY CINGALESE PLUTOCRAT, SMALL AND SLENDER
ROCK II (245) ME VERMIN, ARTHUR. /SIR ARTHUR/ I DIDNT. IT WAS JAFNA . /THE DUKE/ UNGRATEFUL JAFNA! HE IS BUYING UP MY
ROCK II (254) I, A CONSERVATIVE DUKE, EMBRACE IT. SIR JAFNA PANDRANATH HERE, A LIBERAL CAPITALIST WHOSE BILLIONS
ROCK II (242) ARTHUR ALL THE TIME. /HILDA/ (ANNOUNCING) SIR JAFNA PANDRANATH. (SHE WITHDRAWS). THIS ANNOUNCEMENT
ROCK II (249) ME, ARTHUR? /SIR ARTHUR/ (INTRODUCING) SIR JAFNA PANDRANATH, THE MAYOR OF THE ISLE OF CATS. /SIR JAFNA/
ROCK II SD(246) DUKE/ NOT BY AEROPLANE. DO THINK IT OVER. SIR JAFNA SHRUGS HIS SHOULDERS AND INTIMATES THAT IT IS
ROCK II (250) TELL YOU? HEAR HEAR! /ALOYSIA/ I THANK YOU, SIR JAFNA , FOR SHEWING THIS MAN THAT EVEN HARDENED CAPITALIST
ROCK II (246) I DONT PRETEND TO UNDERSTAND IT. BY THE WAY, SIR JAFNA , I WISH YOU WOULD TAKE DOMESDAY TOWERS OFF MY HANDS
ROCK II (243) SIT DOWN). /SIR BEMROSE/ I HAPPEN TO KNOW, SIR JAFNA , THAT YOUR ENTERPRISES STAND AT TWENTY MILLIONS TODAY
ROCK II (245) I DIDNT. IT WAS JAFNA. /THE DUKE/ UNGRATEFUL JAFNA ! HE IS BUYING UP MY BLAYPORT ESTATE FOR NEXT TO

JAFNA'S
ROCK II (245) AND A HALF I SHALL BE INCOME-TAXED AND SURTAXED. JAFNA'S GRANDSONS WILL GO TO ETON. MINE WILL GO TO A

JAGGEDLY
MTH1 II SD(20) AND GRACE; AND ADAM HAS AN UNKEMPT BEARD AND JAGGEDLY CUT HAIR; BUT THEY ARE STRONG AND IN THE PRIME OF

JAGGINSES
CAPT I (227) I HAVE EVER MET. /DRINKWATER/ LAWD, SR AHRD, WOT JAGGINSES THEM JURYMEN WAS! YOU AN ME KNAOWED IT TOO, DIDNT

JAHRE
JITT (1) MUTTERSOHN, DER TOD UND DIE LIEBE, GEFAHRLICHE JAHRE , SPATES LICHT, DIE FRAU OHNE DIENSTAG, DER GELIEBTE,

JAHVISM
FABL PREFACE(69) THE INVENTION OF SATAN IS A HEROIC ADVANCE ON JAHVISM . IT IS AN ATTEMPT TO SOLVE THE PROBLEM OF EVIL, AND

JAIL
DOCT III (142) THE FAMILY SOLICITOR TO KEEP SOME RASCAL OUT OF JAIL AND SOME FAMILY OUT OF DISGRACE? /B.B./ BUT AT LEAST
CAPT III (284) AN HOUR, AND LODGED YOU AND YOUR MEN IN MOGADOR JAIL AT MY DISPOSAL. THE CADI THEN WENT BACK TO HIS MOUNTAIN
O'FL (206) HE'D THINK ME THE FINEST ORNAMENT FOR THE COUNTY JAIL HE EVER SENT THERE FOR POACHING." /SIR PEARCE/ (
WIDO II (41) MONEY? PEOPLE MUST LIVE SOMEWHERE, OR ELSE GO TO JAIL . ADVANTAGE IS TAKEN OF THAT TO MAKE THEM PAY FOR
FANY III (312) RESPECTABLE TO HAVE YOUR CHILDREN IN AND OUT OF JAIL . /KNOX/ OH COME, GILBEY! WE'RE NOT TRAMPS BECAUSE
MIS. (173) WITH THAT LADY. BUT YOULL BE MORE COMFORTABLE IN JAIL . /LINA/ (GREATLY AMUSED) WAS THAT WHY YOU WENT AWAY,
CAPT III (279) THE PRISONERS? /BLUEJACKET/ PARTY GAWN TO THE JAIL TO FETCH EM, MARM. /LADY CICELY/ THANK YOU. I SHOULD
LION EPILOG (152) LONGER SEE A MAN HANGED, WE ASSEMBLE OUTSIDE THE JAIL TO SEE THE BLACK FLAG RUN UP. THAT IS OUR DULLER METHOD

JAILERS
DEVL II (32) ONE ANOTHER OUT OF SIGHT FOR A DAY, ARE MORE LIKE JAILERS AND SLAVE-OWNERS THAN LOVERS. THINK OF THOSE VERY

JAILOR
CYMB FORWORD(138) BY LEAVING OUT THE MASQUE AND THE COMIC JAILOR AND MUTILATING THE REST, AS THEIR MANNER IS, I
CYMB FORWORD(135) WITH THE VERY SHAKESPEAREAN FEATURE OF A COMIC JAILOR WHICH PRECEDES IT, JUST THE THING TO SAVE THE LAST

JAILS
BULL IV (174) COWED, AN ISLAND OF DREAMERS WHO WAKE UP IN YOUR JAILS , OF CRITICS AND COWARDS WHOM YOU BUY AND TAME FOR

JAIN
FABL PREFACE(77) SECTS, CHRISTIAN OR MOSLEM, BUDDHIST OR SHINTO, JAIN OR JEW, CALL ME TO REPENTANCE, AND ASK ME FOR
ROCK II (264) CAME FROM THE EAST; YET NO HINDU, NO PARSEE, NO JAIN , WOULD STOOP TO ITS CRUDITIES. IS THERE A MIRROR

JAINIST
FABL PREFACE(75) ELEPHANT IDOLS AND WHAT NOT? THE STATUES OF THE JAINIST SAGES AND SAINTS, FAR FROM BEING CONTEMPLATED AS
FABL PREFACE(75) TEMPLES THEY BUILT FOR THEIR FAITH, BUT GO INTO A JAINIST TEMPLE TODAY: WHAT DO YOU FIND? IDOLS EVERYWHERE.

JAINISTS
FABL PREFACE(75) THE UTMOST REACH OF THE HUMAN MIND BY THE INDIAN JAINISTS , WHO RENOUNCED IDOLATRY AND BLOOD SACRIFICE LONG

			JAINS	
LION PREFACE	(97)	ADD TO THESE THE HINDOOS AND BUDDHISTS, SIKHS AND	JAINS	, WHOM I WAS TAUGHT IN MY CHILDHOOD, BY WAY OF
			JAM	
BARB III	(328)	HOW THEY GAVE US ALL THAT LUXURY AND CAKE AND	JAM	AND CREAM FOR THREEPENCE I REALLY CANNOT IMAGINE! --
PYGM II	(232)	YOU NEARLY CHOKED YOURSELF WITH A FISHBONE IN THE	JAM	ONLY LAST WEEK. /HIGGINS/ (ROUTED FROM THE HEARTHRUG
			JAMAICA	
HART II	(120)	HAND TO MOUTH. AND I HAVE A WIFE SOMEWHERE IN	JAMAICA	: A BLACK ONE. MY FIRST WIFE. UNLESS SHE'S DEAD.
FANY I	(279)	ALONG, SINGING AND ALL THAT. WHEN WE CAME INTO	JAMAICA	SQUARE, THERE WAS A YOUNG COPPER ON POINT DUTY AT
FANY III	(312)	/GILBEY/ SAN FRANCISCO! /MRS GILBEY/	JAMAICA	! /KNOX/ MARTINIQUE! /GILBEY/ MESSINA! /MRS
			JAMAICAN	
MILL PREFACE	(126)	BLACK NATIVES FOR POSSESSION OF THE LAND, AND OUR	JAMAICAN	MISCEGENATION SHOCKS PUBLIC SENTIMENT, THE SUN
			JAMAIS	
SUPR III	(78)	WHAT HE SAY. HE SAY BOURGEOIS. HE SAY COMPROMISE.	JAMAIS	DE LA VIE! MISERABLE MENTEUR-- /STRAKER/ SEE HERE,
			JAMES	
CAND II	(119)	THING TO SAY TO ME! OH, YOU ARE A CLERGYMAN,	JAMES	: A THOROUGH CLERGYMAN! /MORELL/ (TURNING AWAY FROM
CAND I	(89)	BAD TERMS WITH MY HOWN DAUGHRTER'S USBAN. COME,	JAMES	: BE A KERISCHIN, AND SHAKE ANDS. (HE PUTS HIS HAND
CAND III	(141)	IN HIS MEANING SHE TURNS TO MORELL, SHOCKED). OH,	JAMES	: DID YOU-- (SHE STOPS)? /MORELL/ (ASHAMED) YOU
CAND II	(115)	LIKE THAT. IT'S GOIN TOO FUR WITH IT. LOOKEE ERE,	JAMES	: DO E OFTEN GIT TAKEN QUEER LIKE THAT? /MORELL/ (
CAND III	(143)	(RETREATING, CHILLED) I BEG YOUR PARDON,	JAMES	: I DID NOT MEAN TO TOUCH YOU. I AM WAITING TO HEAR
CAND III	(145)	HAPPINESS: LIFE IS NOBLER THAN THAT. PARSON	JAMES	: I GIVE YOU MY HAPPINESS WITH BOTH HANDS: I LOVE YOU
CAND I	(88)	IN THE EASY CHAIR). IT'S HALL VERY WELL FOR YOU,	JAMES	: IT GITS YOU HINTO THE PAPERS AND MAKES A GREAT MAN
CAND III	(138)	HUSETER. (BUSTLING ACROSS TO THE HEARTH) WELL,	JAMES	: IT'S TIME TO LOCK UP. MR MORCHBANKS: SHALL I AVE THE
CAND II	(118)	TO GET IN A CITY OFFICE? SHE'S IN LOVE WITH YOU,	JAMES	: THATS THE REASON. THEYRE ALL IN LOVE WITH YOU. AND
CAND I	(91)	YOUR MOUTH, YOU AD THE RIGHT INSTINC ARTER ALL,	JAMES	: THE LINE YOU TOOK IS THE PAYIN LINE IN THE LONG RUN
CAND I	(87)	BECOMING VERY SOLEMN, AND APPROACHING MORELL)	JAMES	: THREE YEARS AGO, YOU DONE ME A HIL TURN. YOU DONE ME
CAND II	(112)	A NICE BOOK TO READ OVER THE FIRE, WILL YOU,	JAMES	: THUR'S A GOOD CHAP. /MORELL/ WHAT SORT OF BOOK? A
CAND II	(114)	TO SEE HOW YOU DO IT FIRST. (TURNING TO MORELL)	JAMES	: YOUVE NOT BEEN LOOKING AFTER THE HOUSE PROPERLY.
CAND I	(87)	IS THAT BECOMIN LANGUAGE FOR A CLORGYMAN,	JAMES	? AND YOU SO PARTICLAR, TOO! /MORELL/ (HOTLY) NO,
CAND II	(126)	MISGIVING) BUT-- BUT-- IS ANYTHING THE MATTER,	JAMES	? (GREATLY TROUBLED) I CANT UNDERSTAND-- /MORELL/ (
CAND II	(123)	TELEGRAM. /CANDIDA/ WHAT DID YOU TELEGRAPH ABOUT,	JAMES	? /LEXY/ (TO CANDIDA) HE WAS TO HAVE SPOKEN FOR THEM
CAND II	(123)	I ANSWERED IT. I CANT GO. /CANDIDA/ BUT WHY,	JAMES	? /MORELL/ (ALMOST FIERCELY) BECAUSE I DONT CHOOSE.
CAND II	(124)	PROSSY'S COMPLAINT! WHAT ARE YOU TALKIN ABOUT,	JAMES	? /MORELL/ (NOT HEEDING HIM, RISES; GOES TO THE
CAND III	(142)	I AM UP FOR AUCTION, IT SEEMS. WHAT DO YOU BID,	JAMES	? /MORELL/ (REPROACHFULLY) CAND-- (HE BREAKS DOWN:
CAND I	(92)	NUNNERSTANNIN. A HONORABLE UNNERSTANNIN. AIN WE,	JAMES	? /MORELL/ (IMPETUOUSLY) OH BOTHER YOUR
CAND II	(112)	SICKLY CIVILITY OF A HUNGRY MAN) WHEN'S DINNER,	JAMES	? /MORELL/ NOT FOR A COUPLE OF HOURS YET. /BURGESS/ (
CAND II	(113)	GRAVE DISAPPROVAL) DONT YOU KEEP A SERVANT NOW,	JAMES	? /MORELL/ YES; BUT SHE ISNT A SLAVE; AND THE HOUSE
SUPR II	(55)	HE CAN. /TANNER/ TAVY: DO YOU REMEMBER MY UNCLE	JAMES	? /OCTAVIUS/ YES. WHY? /TANNER/ UNCLE JAMES HAD A
CAND III	(139)	TO BED LIKE A GOOD LITTLE BOY: I WANT TO TALK TO	JAMES	ABOUT YOU. /MARCHBANKS/ (RISING IN GREAT
CAND III	(134)	EARTH ARE YOU AT, EUGENE? /MARCHBANKS/ (ODDLY)	JAMES	AND I ARE HAVING A PREACHING MATCH; AND HE IS GETTING
LION PREFACE	(37)	WHEN JESUS IS ILL RECEIVED IN A SAMARITAN VILLAGE	JAMES	AND JOHN PROPOSE TO CALL DOWN FIRE FROM HEAVEN AND
CAND I	(92)	ARMS, OFFERS HIM HER CHEEK, WHICH HE KISSES).	JAMES	AND ME IS COME TO A NUNNERSTANNIN. A HONORABLE
CAND III	(144)	THE ONIONS. ASK THE TRADESMEN WHO WANT TO WORRY	JAMES	AND SPOIL HIS BEAUTIFUL SERMONS WHO IT IS THAT PUTS
KING I	(195)	KING JAMES THE SECOND AND KING TITUS OATES. AND	JAMES	AND THE CHURCH-- AND THERE IS ONLY ONE REAL CHURCH OF
KING II	(230)	CROWN AND SAVE ALL THIS KILLING OF MONMOUTH AND	JAMES	AND THE HANDING OVER OF YOUR KINGDOM TO THE HOLLANDER.
CAND III	(144)	SEE THE PICTURES OF THE HERO OF THAT HOUSEHOLD.	JAMES	AS A BABY! THE MOST WONDERFUL OF ALL BABIES. JAMES
CAND III	(144)	SCHOOL PRIZE, WON AT THE RIPE AGE OF EIGHT!	JAMES	AS THE CAPTAIN OF HIS ELEVEN! JAMES IN HIS FIRST
APPL	(170)	AS ORINTHIA, BARBARA EVEREST AS QUEEN JEMIMA, AND	JAMES	CAREW AS THE AMERICAN AMBASSADOR.
CAND I	(93)	ME, CANDY: IT'S A 'IGH CHURCH PICTURE; AND	JAMES	CHOSE IT HISSELF. /CANDIDA/ GUESS AGAIN. EUGENE ISNT A
CAND I	(96)	WHICH HAVE COME BY THE MIDDAY POST. /CANDIDA/ OH,	JAMES	DEAR, HE WAS GOING TO GIVE THE CABMAN TEN SHILLINGS!
CAND II	(118)	WERE, THEY DARENT BE SEEN GOING TO THEM. BESIDES,	JAMES	DEAR, YOU PREACH SO SPLENDIDLY THAT IT'S AS GOOD AS A
CAND II	(111)	HEVERYBODY. OW LONG AVE YOU KNOWN MY SON-IN-LAW	JAMES	ERE? /MARCHBANKS/ I DONT KNOW. I NEVER CAN REMEMBER
CAND I	(96)	UP HER HAND-BAG). AND NOW I MUST LEAVE YOU TO	JAMES	FOR THE PRESENT. I SUPPOSE YOU ARE TOO MUCH OF A POET
CAND I	(93)	A SEVEN DAY BILL FOR 55 POUNDS IN HIS POCKET WHEN	JAMES	FOUND HIM ON THE EMBANKMENT, HE THOUGHT HE COULDNT GET
SUPR II	(55)	JAMES? /OCTAVIUS/ YES. WHY? /TANNER/ UNCLE	JAMES	HAD A FIRST RATE COOK: HE COULDNT DIGEST ANYTHING
CAND III	(141)	TERRIFIED) NO. /CANDIDA/ (ALMOST FIERCELY) THEN	JAMES	HAS JUST TOLD ME A FALSEHOOD. IS THAT WHAT YOU MEAN..
BASH PREFACE	(90)	REPUDIATION OF THE NAME OF GENTLEMAN, AND	JAMES	HEARN'S LAMENTATION OVER THE TRAGEDY OF CETEWAYO CAME
CAND III	(144)	AS A BABY! THE MOST WONDERFUL OF ALL BABIES.	JAMES	HOLDING HIS FIRST SCHOOL PRIZE, WON AT THE RIPE AGE OF
KING I	SD(187)	HIGHNESS THE DUKE OF YORK, THE DUKE, AFTERWARDS	JAMES	II, COMES IN PRECIPITATELY. /JAMES/ (IMPERIOUSLY)
CAND III	(144)	OF EIGHT! JAMES AS THE CAPTAIN OF HIS ELEVEN!	JAMES	IN HIS FIRST FROCK COAT! JAMES UNDER ALL SORTS OF
KING II	(226)	CARE WHAT BECOMES OF ME WHEN YOU ARE GONE. BUT	JAMES	IS A CATHOLIC. WHEN HE IS KING WHAT HAVE I TO FEAR?
CAND III	(140)	DIDNT YOU HEAR JAMES SAY HE WISHED YOU TO STAY?	JAMES	IS MASTER HERE. DONT YOU KNOW THAT? /MARCHBANKS/ (
CAND II	(109)	IN CONSTERNATION, WHICH IS QUITE LOST ON HIM).	JAMES	IS RECEIVIN A DEPPITATION IN THE DININ ROOM; AND CANDY
CAND II	(125)	/BURGESS/ (WITH ENTHUSIASM) CAWRSE I'LL COME,	JAMES	. AINT IT AWLUS A PLEASURE TO EAR YOU! /MORELL/ (
KING I	(190)	OF HANOVER HAS THE SAME HOOK ON TO GRANDFATHER	JAMES	. BOTH OF THEM ARE RANK PROTESTANTS AND HARDENED
CAND III	(140)	/CANDIDA/ (WITH EMPHATIC WARNING) TAKE CARE,	JAMES	. EUGENE: I ASKED YOU TO GO. ARE YOU GOING? /MORELL/
CAND I	(86)	OUT. /BURGESS/ SPOILIN YOUR KORATES AS USUAL,	JAMES	. GOOD MORNIN. WHEN I PAY A MAN, AN' 'IS LIVIN DEPENS
CAND I	(89)	BEFORE YOU LOST THAT CONTRACT? /BURGESS/ I DO,	JAMES	. I DO-- HONEST. /MORELL/ THEN WHY DONT YOU BEHAVE AS
CAND III	(140)	(WITH QUIET ANGER) EUGENE IS VERY QUICK-WITTED,	JAMES	. I HOPE I AM GOING TO LAUGH; BUT I AM NOT SURE THAT I
CAND I	(89)	FOOL THEN. /BURGESS/ (COAXINGLY) NO I DIDNT,	JAMES	. I-- /MORELL/ (CUTTING HIM SHORT) YES, YOU DID. AND
CAND III	(136)	YOU SURPASSED YOURSELF. /BURGESS/ SO YOU DID,	JAMES	. IT FAIR KEP ME AWAKE TO THE LARS' WORD. DIDNT IT,
CAND I	(87)	I HACTED IN THE INTEREST OF THE RATEPAYERS,	JAMES	. IT WAS THE LOWEST TENDER: YOU CARNT DENY THAT.
CAND II	(125)	TO COME. /BURGESS/ OH, DONT PUT IT LIKE THAT,	JAMES	. IT'S ONY THAT IT AINT SUNDAY, YOU KNOW. /MORELL/ I'M
CAND II	(112)	AND OFFERS IT. HE ACCEPTS IT HUMBLY). THANK YER,	JAMES	. (HE GOES BACK TO THE BIG CHAIR AT THE FIRE, AND
CAND III	(139)	/BURGESS/ OH WELL, I'LL SAY GOODNIGHT. SO LONG,	JAMES	. (HE SHAKES HANDS WITH MORELL, AND GOES OVER TO
CAND I	(89)	HEXPECT TO FIND A HUNFORGIVIN SPIRIT IN YOU,	JAMES	. (MORELL STILL NOT RESPONDING, HE TAKES A FEW MORE
FABL PREFACE	(90)	VIVISECTOR AND QUACK IMMUNIZER ABOVE JESUS AND ST	JAMES	, MRS EDDY, A MUCH SOUNDER HYGIENIST THAN JENNER,
CAND I	(89)	SELF-ACCUSATION ON MORELL'S PART) NO YOU DIDNT,	JAMES	. NOW YOU DO YOURSELF A HINJUSTICE. /MORELL/ (YES I
CAND I	(91)	THE HAND OF FRIENDSHIP) YOU WILL AVE YOUR JOKE,	JAMES	. OUR QUARREL'S MADE UP NOW, AIN IT? /A WOMAN'S
CAND III	(135)	(STOPPING HIM) SH! -- NO: LET ME DEAL WITH HIM,	JAMES	. /MARCHBANKS/ OH, YOURE NOT ANGRY WITH ME, ARE YOU..
CAND III	(140)	IS HE MASTER? /CANDIDA/ (QUIETLY) TELL HIM,	JAMES	. /MORELL/ (TAKEN ABACK) MY DEAR: I DONT KNOW OF ANY
CAND II	(116)	GOIN FOR A TURN IN THE GORDING TO SMOKE,	JAMES	. /MORELL/ (BRUSQUELY) OH, ALL RIGHT, ALL RIGHT. (
CAND I	(87)	A KERISCHIN. (OFFERING HIS HAND) I FORGIVE YOU,	JAMES	. /MORELL/ (STARTING UP) CONFOUND YOUR IMPUDENCE!
CAND I	(95)	BYE, CANDY. I'LL LOOK IN AGAIN LATER ON. SO LONG,	JAMES	. /MORELL/ MUST YOU GO? /BURGESS/ DONT STIR. (HE
CAND II	(125)	/LEXY/ CERTAINLY. /CANDIDA/ WE'RE ALL COMING,	JAMES	. /MORELL/ NO: YOU ARE NOT COMING; AND EUGENE IS NOT
CAND I	(91)	MADE UP NOW, AIN IT? /A WOMAN'S VOICE/ SAY YES,	JAMES	. STARTLED, THEY TURN QUICKLY AND FIND THAT CANDIDA
KING I	SD(188)	A WRESTLING MATCH? NEWTON HASTILY ROLLS OFF	JAMES	. THE TWO COMBATANTS REMAIN SITTING ON THE FLOOR,
CAND II	(124)	BURGESS). /CANDIDA/ (COAXINGLY) OH, DO GO,	JAMES	. WE'LL ALL GO. /BURGESS/ (GRUMBLINGLY) LOOK 'ERE,
DOCT PREFACE	(8)	HIS OWN PATIENT, OR FOR PERJURY IN THE CASE OF ST	JAMES	. YET NO BARRISTER, APPARENTLY, DREAMS OF ASKING FOR
GETT PREFACE	(233)	HIS HOUSEHOLD IS INVADED IS WHAT THE REVEREND	JAMES	MAVOR MORELL DOES IN MY PLAY. HE RECOGNIZES THAT JUST
CAND I	SD(79)	TO BE WASTED ON SNOBBISH TRIMMINGS. THE REVEREND	JAMES	MAVOR MORELL IS A CHRISTIAN SOCIALIST CLERGYMAN OF THE
CAND I	(89)	RISING THREATENINGLY) DONT SAY THAT TO ME AGAIN,	JAMES	MAVOR MORELL. /MORELL/ (UNMOVED) I'LL SAY IT JUST AS
CAND I	SD(78)	AND THE FAMILY MEALS, THE PARSON, THE REVEREND	JAMES	MAVOR MORELL, DOES HIS WORK. HE IS SITTING IN A STRONG
CAND III	(131)	MEAN ME? /MARCHBANKS/ I DONT MEAN THE REVEREND	JAMES	MAVOR MORELL, MORALIST AND WINDBAG. I MEAN THE REAL
BASH PREFACE	(90)	SUCH VIVID AND UNAFFECTED MODERN VERSIONS AS DR	JAMES	MOFFATT'S NEW TRANSLATION OF THE NEW TESTAMENT I AT
CAND III	(131)	WINDBAG. I MEAN THE REAL MAN THAT THE REVEREND	JAMES	MUST HAVE HIDDEN SOMEWHERE INSIDE HIS BLACK COAT: THE
KING I	(220)	NOT GET AT IT FIRST. LET US HURRY. (SHE HURRIES	JAMES	OUT). /MRS BASHAM/ WILL YOU TAKE THE PLAYER WOMAN, MR
CAND I	(94)	FIND YORESELF THIS WEATHER? OPE YOU AINT LETTIN	JAMES	PUT NO FOOLISH IDEAS INTO YOUR ED? /MARCHBANKS/
CAND II	(125)	HOME. (EUGENE RISES, BREATHLESS). /CANDIDA/ BUT,	JAMES	-- /MORELL/ (AUTHORITATIVELY) I INSIST. YOU DO NOT
KING I	(208)	DO YOU SAY, JAMIE? (HE HANDS THE DRAWING TO	JAMES	). /JAMES/ IT'S YOU, DUCHESS. HE HAS GOT YOU WRINKLE
CAND II	(120)	RESTRAIN ME. PUT YOUR TRUST IN MY LOVE FOR YOU,	JAMES	; FOR IF THAT WENT, I SHOULD CARE VERY LITTLE FOR YOUR
CAND III	(140)	/CANDIDA/ STOP! (HE OBEYS). DIDNT YOU HEAR	JAMES	SAY HE WISHED YOU TO STAY? JAMES IS MASTER HERE. DONT

LION EPILOG (151)	PRISON FOR BEING SO VERY PECULIAR AS TO TAKE ST	JAMES	SERIOUSLY. IN SHORT, A CHRISTIAN MARTYR WAS THROWN TO
DEVL I (23)	HE SHOULD HAVE WRITTEN JAMES, SIR. /RICHARD/	JAMES	SHALL LIVE IN CLOVER. GO ON. /HAWKINS/-- " AND KEEP MY
KING I SD(189)	CHARLES TAKES THE ARMCHAIR. WHEN HE IS SEATED	JAMES	TAKES NEWTON'S CHAIR AT THE TABLE. /JAMES/ THAT FELLOW
CAND II (121)	MORCHBANKS THINK OF YOU? /CANDIDA/ THIS COMES OF	JAMES	TEACHING ME TO THINK FOR MYSELF, AND NEVER TO HOLD
BULL PREFACE(43)	WOULD STILL BE AS GOOD AS ENGLAND'S. KING	JAMES	THE FIRST PROVED SO CLEVERLY AND CONCLUSIVELY THAT THE
BARB I (255)	IN THE CITY. THAT WAS LONG AGO, IN THE REIGN OF	JAMES	THE FIRST. WELL, THIS FOUNDLING WAS ADOPTED BY AN
KING I (195)	OF ENGLAND WILL HAVE TO CHOOSE BETWEEN KING	JAMES	THE SECOND AND KING TITUS OATES. AND JAMES AND THE
GENV PREFACE(22)	ORDINARY MORTALS LIKE NERO, PAUL OF RUSSIA, OUR	JAMES	THE SECOND, RIZA KHAN IN IRAN, AND SOME OF THE SMALL
CAND III (144)	MOTHER AND HIS THREE SISTERS WHAT IT COST TO SAVE	JAMES	THE TROUBLE OF DOING ANYTHING BUT BE STRONG AND CLEVER
CAND II (124)	DONT BE AFRAID. THEYLL BE TOO BUSY LOOKING AT	JAMES	TO NOTICE YOU. /MORELL/ PROSSY'S COMPLAINT, CANDIDA!
KING I SD(208)	FINAL STAMP ON THE DRAWING, FLINGS AWAY BEHIND	JAMES	TO ONE OF THE CHAIRS AGAINST THE CUPBOARDS, AND SITS
CAND III (144)	OF HIS ELEVEN! JAMES IN HIS FIRST FROCK COAT!	JAMES	UNDER ALL SORTS OF GLORIOUS CIRCUMSTANCES! YOU KNOW
SUPR II (56)	KNOW HIS PLACE. I AM ENRY'S SLAVE, JUST AS UNCLE	JAMES	WAS HIS COOK'S SLAVE. /STRAKER/ (EXASPERATED) GARN!
LION EPILOG (151)	PERSECUTE A POOR FREETHINKER FOR SAYING THAT ST	JAMES	WAS NOT INFALLIBLE, AND TO SEND ONE OF THE PECULIAR
ARMS (2)	THE RUSSIAN OFFICER, ORLANDO BARNETT AS NICOLA,	JAMES	WELCH AS PETKOFF, AND BERNARD GOULD (SIR BERNARD
CAND III (128)	READING TO ME FOR MORE THAN TWO HOURS, EVER SINCE	JAMES	WENT OUT. I WANT TO TALK. /MARCHBANKS/ (RISING,
LION PREFACE(37)	STORIES. HE CANNOT ALLOW THE CALLING OF PETER,	JAMES	, AND JOHN FROM THEIR BOATS TO PASS WITHOUT A COMIC
CAND I (90)	IN SPITE OF HIMSELF) WELL, YOU ORR A QUEER BIRD,	JAMES	, AND NO MISTAKE. BUT (ALMOST ENTHUSIASTICALLY) ONE
DOCT PREFACE(7)	AS TO THE TREATMENT OF ILLNESS. THE EPISTLE OF	JAMES	, CHAPTER V., CONTAINS THE FOLLOWING EXPLICIT
CAND III (135)	CANT BE TRUE. (TO MORELL) YOU DIDNT BEGIN IT,	JAMES	, DID YOU? /MORELL/ (CONTEMPTUOUSLY) NO.
CAND II (120)	MY GOODNESS, OF MY PURITY, AS YOU CALL IT? AH,	JAMES	, HOW LITTLE YOU UNDERSTAND ME, TO TALK OF YOUR
CAND III (129)	ANKLES, ALSO QUITE UNEMBARRASSED. /CANDIDA/ OH,	JAMES	, HOW YOU STARTLED ME! I WAS SO TAKEN UP WITH EUGENE
CAND III (136)	YOU NEED NOT UNDERSTAND, MY DEAR. /CANDIDA/ BUT	JAMES	, I (THE STREET BELL RINGS)-- OH BOTHER! HERE THEY
CAND I (103)	ADVANCE TO THE CONTRARY. /CANDIDA/ SHALL HE STAY,	JAMES	, IF HE PROMISES TO BE A GOOD BOY AND HELP ME LAY THE
DOCT PREFACE(8)	PLACED UNDER HIS TREATMENT INSTEAD OF THAT OF ST	JAMES	, IT WOULD NOT HAVE DIED, AND HE DOES SO NOT ONLY WITH
DEVL I (23)	(AGAIN SHAKING HIS HEAD) HE SHOULD HAVE WRITTEN	JAMES	, SIR. /RICHARD/ JAMES SHALL LIVE IN CLOVER. GO ON.
CAND II (113)	HA! DEVIL A BETTER! (RADIANTLY) AD YOU THERE,	JAMES	, STRAIGHT. CANDIDA COMES IN, WELL APRONED, WITH A
CAND II (119)	OF HIM ALL THE TIME I WAS AWAY. DO YOU KNOW,	JAMES	, THAT THOUGH HE HAS NOT THE LEAST SUSPICION OF IT
CAND II (111)	ON IM AND SEE. (RISING MOMENTOUSLY) I'M SORRY,	JAMES	, TO AVE TO MAKE A COMPLAINT TO YOU. I DONT WANT TO DO
CAND II (122)	A TRAGEDY. /BURGESS/ (ON THE HEARTHRUG) WELL,	JAMES	, YOU CERTNLY HAINT AS HIMPRESSIVE LOOKIN AS USU'L.
CAND II (123)	HIS EXPRESSION REMAINS UNCHANGED. /CANDIDA/ OH,	JAMES	, YOU MUSNT MIND WHAT I SAID ABOUT THAT. AND IF YOU
LADY PREFACE(230)	MYSTERIOUS RESTRAINT THAT KEPT " ELIZA AND OUR	JAMES	" FROM TEACHING SHAKESPEAR TO BE CIVIL TO CROWNED
CAND I (87)	TALK ABOUT YOUR DAUGHTER, AND-- /BURGESS/ HEASY,	JAMES	! HEASY! HEASY! DONT GIT HINTO A FLUSTER ABOUT
CAND II (114)	SELFISH, AND USELESS. /CANDIDA/ (JARRED) OH,	JAMES	! HOW COULD YOU SPOIL IT ALL? /MARCHBANKS/ (FIRING
CAND I (103)	STATE! YOU ARE A POET, CERTAINLY. LOOK AT HIM,	JAMES	! (SHE TAKES HIM BY THE COAT, AND BRINGS HIM
CAND III (140)	INFINITE REPROACH) YOU DONT KNOW! OH, JAMES!	JAMES	! (TO EUGENE, MUSINGLY) I WONDER DO YOU UNDERSTAND,
CAND III (140)	(WITH INFINITE REPROACH) YOU DONT KNOW! OH,	JAMES	! JAMES! (TO EUGENE, MUSINGLY) I WONDER DO YOU
CAND II (122)	AND LAUGH. /CANDIDA/ (INCREDULOUSLY) I TORTURE	JAMES	! NONSENSE, EUGENE! HOW YOU EXAGGERATE! SILLY! (
CAND I (86)	(WITHOUT MOVING) JUST THE SAME AS HEVER,	JAMES	! /MORELL/ WHEN YOU LAST CALLED-- IT WAS ABOUT THREE
CAND III (146)	TO MORELL, HOLDING OUT HER ARMS TO HIM). AH,	JAMES	! THEY EMBRACE. BUT THEY DO NOT KNOW THE SECRET IN
CAND III (140)	THE HEARTH AND PLACES HERSELF BETWEEN THEM). NOW,	JAMES	! WHATS THE MATTER? COME: TELL ME. /MARCHBANKS/ (
CAND II (121)	WAVING HER OFF) DONT TOUCH ME. /CANDIDA/	JAMES	! ! ! THEY ARE INTERRUPTED BY THE ENTRANCE OF
CAND I (86)	WORDS THEN WERE! " JUST AS BIG A FOOL AS EVER,	JAMES	! " /BURGESS/ (SOOTHINGLY) WELL, PRAPS I DID; BUT (

JAMESON

ROCK I (200)	MISS HANWAYS. A FULL DRESS DEBATE ON WHETHER	JAMESON	OR THOMPSON WAS RIGHT ABOUT WHAT JOHNSON SAID IN THE
ROCK I (200)	MATTER? THE REAL QUESTION: THE QUESTION WHETHER	JAMESON	OR THOMPSON IS A LIAR, IS A VITAL QUESTION OF THE

JAMES'S

CAND I (92)	COME WITH YOU? /CANDIDA/ OH, EUGENE'S ONE OF	JAMES'S	DISCOVERIES. HE FOUND HIM SLEEPING ON THE EMBANKMENT
MRS PREFACE(171)	WOMEN THAT HAS EVER BEEN PENNED." HAPPILY THE ST	JAMES'S	GAZETTE HERE SPEAKS IN ITS HASTE. MRS WARREN'S
MRS PREFACE(170)	IS SO OVERWHELMING THAT IT PROVOKES THE ST	JAMES'S	GAZETTE TO DECLARE THAT " THE TENDENCY OF THE PLAY
CAND III (144)	AND CLEVER AND HAPPY. ASK ME WHAT IT COSTS TO BE	JAMES'S	MOTHER AND THREE SISTERS AND WIFE AND MOTHER TO HIS
CAND III (144)	HE IS: HOW HAPPY. (WITH DEEPENING GRAVITY) ASK	JAMES'S	MOTHER AND HIS THREE SISTERS WHAT IT COST TO SAVE
POSN PREFACE(393)	WERE A REFLECTION OF THOSE PREVAILING IN ST.	JAMES'S	PALACE. IMMEDIATELY AFTER THIS, THE LORD CHAMBERLAIN
APPL I (235)	A SENTENCE OF SOCIAL DEATH WITHIN RANGE OF ST	JAMES'S	PALACE. THINK OF THE THINGS YOU DARE NOT DO! THE
SUPR HANDBOK(195)	TO CUT THE THROATS OF THE GENTLEMEN OF ST.	JAMES'S	PARISH IN DUE MILITARY FORM. IT WOULD NOT HAVE BEEN
KING I (168)	FOR SUPPOSING THAT REVELATION CEASED WHEN KING	JAMES'S	PRINTERS FINISHED WITH THE BIBLE? /FOX/ I DO NOT
CAND I SD(77)	MILES AWAY FROM THE LONDON OF MAYFAIR AND ST	JAMES'S	, AND MUCH LESS NARROW, SQUALID, FETID AND AIRLESS

JAMIE

KING I (194)	OF THEM. /CHARLES/ LET ME TELL YOU A SECRET,	JAMIE	: A KING'S SECRET. PETER THE FISHERMAN DID NOT KNOW
KING I (191)	YOU ARE JEALOUS OF MY POPULARITY. /CHARLES/ NO,	JAMIE	: I CAN BEAT YOU AT THAT GAME. I AM AN AGREEABLE SORT
KING I (196)	I HAVE NEVER BEEN BEATEN AT SEA. /CHARLES/ JAMIE,	JAMIE	: NOTHING FRIGHTENS ME SO MUCH AS YOUR SIMPLE STUPID
KING I (193)	FIND IF EVER HE FALLS INTO MY HAND. /CHARLES/	JAMIE	: THIS IS A DREADFUL SUSPICION TO PUT INTO MY MIND. I
KING I (200)	OF COD; AND THATS ALL YOULL GET, SIR. /CHARLES/	JAMIE	: WE MUST CLEAR OUT AND TAKE THE OTHERS WITH US. IT
KING I (208)	DEAR. IT IS YOU TO THE LIFE. WHAT DO YOU SAY,	JAMIE	? (HE HANDS THE DRAWING TO JAMES). /JAMES/ IT'S YOU,
KING I (188)	/CHARLES/ AND WHAT THE DIVVLE ARE YOU DOING HERE,	JAMIE	? WHY ARNT YOU IN HOLLAND? /JAMES/ I AM HERE WHERE I
KING I (201)	CLASSICAL. (GOING TO THE DUKE) AND WHAT IS MY	JAMIE	DOING HERE? /LOUISE/ (TAKING A CHAIR FROM THE WALL
KING II (226)	THEM! THEY ARE GREAT KILLERS, THESE PROTESTANTS.	JAMIE	HAS JUST ONE CHANCE. THEY MAY CALL IN ORANGE BILLY
KING I (195)	REVEL IN HIS ROARINGS. /CHARLES/ THAT WILL COME,	JAMIE	. I AM HUNTING OUT HIS RECORD; AND YOUR MAN JEFFRIES
KING I (193)	OF THE NORTH SEA. KEEP YOUR EYE ON THE ORANGEMAN,	JAMIE	. /JAMES/ I SHALL KEEP MY EYE ON YOUR PROTESTANT
KING I (197)	ALL THE SAME. /CHARLES/ ALL INTELLIGENT MEN HAVE,	JAMIE	. /JAMES/ PSHA! DONT WASTE YOUR WITTICISMS ON ME:
KING I (193)	THIS IS A DEUCED FOGGY CLIMATE FOR SUN KINGS,	JAMIE	. /JAMES/ SO YOU THINK, CHARLES. BUT THE BRITISH
KING I (193)	NOT DEEP ENOUGH TO BE AT THE BOTTOM OF ANYTHING,	JAMIE	. /JAMES/ THEN HE IS AT THE TOP. I FORGIVE HIM FOR
KING II (228)	THEN I TELL IT TO CHIFFINCH. THEN I TELL IT TO	JAMIE	. WHEN I HAVE THE RESPONSES OF BARBARA, CHIFFINCH, AND
KING II (226)	WAS NOTHING. THEN THE PROTESTANTS WILL KILL	JAMIE	; AND THE DUTCH LAD WILL SEE HIS CHANCE AND TAKE IT.
KING II (226)	KILL HIS WIFE'S FATHER. BUT THEY WILL GET RID OF	JAMIE	SOMEHOW; SO YOU MUST MAKE FOR HOME THE MOMENT I HAVE
KING II (226)	KING? /CHARLES/ NO. HE WILL TRY, POOR BOY; BUT	JAMIE	WILL KILL HIM. HE IS HIS MOTHER'S SON; AND HIS MOTHER
KING I (189)	THE KING WITH DIGNITY. /CHARLES/ WILL YOU GET UP,	JAMIE	, AND NOT SIT ON THE FLOOR GRINNING LIKE A JACKANAPES.
KING I (195)	NOTHING TO DO WITH IT. THE REAL LEVELLERS TODAY,	JAMIE	, ARE THE LORDS AND THE RICH SQUIRES-- CROMWELL'S
KING I (192)	HAVE TO TAKE YOUR MONEY WHERE YOU CAN GET IT,	JAMIE	, AS I DO. FRENCH MONEY IS AS GOOD AS ENGLISH. KING
KING I (191)	FINISHED MY EDUCATION IN THAT RESPECT. NOW YOU,	JAMIE	, BECAME THAT VERY DISAGREEABLE CHARACTER A MAN OF
KING I (207)	DEAD ALL THE SAME. THE PROTESTANTS WILL HAVE YOU,	JAMIE	, BY HOOK OR CROOK; I FORESEE THAT: THEY ARE THE REAL
KING I (199)	ARE FAITHFUL TO THE ELDERLY KING. I AM FIFTY,	JAMIE	, FIFTY: DONT FORGET THAT. AND WOMEN GOT HOLD OF ME
KING I (200)	BEFORE A KING? " YOUR FAST WILL BE A REAL FAST,	JAMIE	, FOR THE FIRST TIME IN YOUR LIFE. /JAMES/ YOU LIE. MY
KING II (228)	I HAVE THE RESPONSES OF BARBARA, CHIFFINCH, AND	JAMIE	, I KNOW HOW TOM, DICK AND HARRY WILL TAKE IT. AND IT
KING I (198)	THE ONE REDEEMING POINT IN YOUR CHARACTER,	JAMIE	, IS THAT YOU ARE NOT A MAN OF PRINCIPLE IN THE MATTER
KING I (196)	I HAVE NEVER BEEN BEATEN AT SEA. /CHARLES/	JAMIE	, JAMIE: NOTHING FRIGHTENS ME SO MUCH AS YOUR SIMPLE
KING I (202)	HIMSELF TO PLEASE THE QUAKER. /CHARLES/ FORGIVE	JAMIE	, LADIES AND GENTLEMEN. HE WILL GIVE YOU HIS OWN
CYMB FORWORD(134)	THE CERES SCENE IN THE TEMPEST, TO PLEASE KING	JAMIE	, OR ELSE BECAUSE AN IRRESISTIBLE FASHION HAD SET IN,
KING I (190)	IN A CANDLE FLAME. /CHARLES/ IT IS A FUNNY THING,	JAMIE	, THAT YOU, WHO ARE CLEVER ENOUGH TO SEE THAT THE

JANE

DOCT I (89)	/RIDGEON/ I TOOK MY CHANCE OF IT. /SIR PATRICK/	JANE	DID, YOU MEAN. /RIDGEON/ WELL, IT'S ALWAYS THE PATIENT
MRS II (215)	FOR A WOMAN TO BE IN THAN THE FACTORY WHERE ANNE	JANE	GOT POISONED. NONE OF OUR GIRLS WERE EVER TREATED AS I
DOCT I (89)	OH, YOUR WASHERWOMAN'S DAUGHTER. WAS HER NAME	JANE	MARSH? I FORGOT. /SIR PATRICK/ PERHAPS YOUVE FORGOTTEN
DOCT I (89)	BUT STILL, YOU REMEMBER JANE MARSH? /RIDGEON/	JANE	MARSH? NO. /SIR PATRICK/ YOU DONT! /RIDGEON/ NO. /SIR
DOCT I (89)	SO FAR AS THAT, COLLY. BUT STILL, YOU REMEMBER	JANE	MARSH? /RIDGEON/ JANE MARSH? NO. /SIR PATRICK/ YOU
DOCT I (90)	DOWNS, AS THE CASE MAY BE. IF WE HAD INOCULATED	JANE	MARSH WHEN HER BUTTER FACTORY WAS ON THE UP-GRADE, WE
DOCT IV (156)	WHAT HAS HAPPENED? /SIR PATRICK/ DO YOU REMEMBER	JANE	MARSH'S ARM? /RIDGEON/ IS THAT WHATS HAPPENED? /SIR
DEVL EPILOG (85)	HALF BURGOYNE'S FORCE, I MAY CITE THE CASE OF	JANE	MCCREA, BETROTHED TO ONE OF BURGOYNE'S OFFICERS. A
MRS PREFACE(154)	THAT THOUGH " THE WHITE-LEAD FACTORY WHERE ANNE	JANE	WAS POISONED" MAY BE A FAR MORE TERRIBLE PLACE THAN MRS
GETT (288)	SEEN ONE OF OUR DAUGHTERS AFTER ANOTHER-- ETHEL,	JANE	, FANNY, AND CHRISTINA AND FLORENCE-- GO OUT AT THAT
LIED (188)	NAME. OH, IF I HAD ONLY BEEN CHRISTENED MARY	JANE	, OR GLADYS MURIEL, OR BEATRICE, OR FRANCESCA, OR
DOCT I (89)	ROTTED HER ARM RIGHT OFF. YES: I REMEMBER. POOR	JANE	! HOWEVER, SHE MAKES A GOOD LIVING OUT OF THAT ARM NOW

		JANE'S	
DOCT IV (156)	THATS WHATS HAPPENED. HIS LUNG HAS GONE LIKE	JANE'S	ARM. I NEVER SAW SUCH A CASE. HE HAS GOT THROUGH
DOCT I (89)	/SIR PATRICK/ WHAT DID YOU FIND OUT FROM	JANE'S	CASE? /RIDGEON/ I FOUND OUT THAT THE INOCULATION
		JANET	
CYMB FORWORD(135)	THE LATE CHARLES CHARRINGTON, WHO WITH HIS WIFE	JANET	ACHURCH BROKE THE ICE FOR IBSEN IN ENGLAND, USED TO
UNPL PREFACE(R12)	OF A DOLL'S HOUSE BY CHARLES CHARRINGTON AND	JANET	ACHURCH. WHILST THEY WERE TAKING THAT EPOCH MAKING
		JANGA	
SIM II (63)	AS USUAL. /JANGA/ TODAY'S FOOTBALL-- /PROLA/ NO,	JANGA	: CERTAINLY NOT. /SIR CHARLES/ BUT WHAT BECOMES OF OUR
SIM II SD(62)	THE DEPTHS OF HELL HE WILL FIND US. KANCHIN AND	JANGA	ENTER PROCESSIONALLY, READING NEWSPAPERS. /KANCHIN/
SIM I (41)	THE SIMPLE ONES! /THE ELDER YOUTH/ BEWARE. I,	JANGA	, WARN THEE. /THE YOUNGER YOUTH/ ON GUARD. I, KANCHIN,
		JANGLING	
JOAN 5 (110)	TO-DAY, WHEN THEY ALL RANG: THAT WAS NOTHING BUT	JANGLING	. BUT HERE IN THIS CORNER, WHERE THE BELLS COME
		JANISSARIES	
ROCK II (253)	WE KNOW TOO WELL WHAT WE HAVE TO EXPECT FROM YOUR	JANISSARIES	. /BLEE/ YOUR BLUDGEONING BASHI-BAZOUKS.
		JANUARIUS	
FABL PREFACE(71)	EQUIVALENT TO LIQUEFYING THE BLOOD OF SAINT	JANUARIUS	. SOME TWENTY YEARS LATER I WROTE A PLAY CALLED
DOCT PREFACE(73)	WHY, MIRACLES THERE MUST BE. THE BLOOD OF ST	JANUARIUS	MUST LIQUEFY WHETHER THE SAINT IS IN THE HUMOR OR
SUPR HANDBOK(204)	BELIEVES IN THE LIQUEFACTION OF THE BLOOD OF ST	JANUARIUS	; AND STRAIGHTFORWARD PUBLIC LYING HAS REACHED
LION PREFACE(45)	MIRACLE OF THE LIQUEFACTION OF THE BLOOD OF ST	JANUARIUS	, AND REJECT IT AS A TRICK OF PRIESTCRAFT. I
FABL PREFACE(69)	THEIR FAITH BY LIQUEFYING THE BLOOD OF SAINT	JANUARIUS	, AND SAYING MASS OVER A JAWBONE LABELLED AS THAT
		JANUARY	
LADY PREFACE(209)	IT IN THE PALL MALL GAZETTE ON THE 7TH OF	JANUARY	1886, AND THEREBY LET LOOSE THE FITTON THEORY IN A
MRS PREFACE(179)	BE TOO CAREFULLY EXAMINED. PICCARD'S COTTAGE,	JANUARY	1902. P.S. (1930) ON READING THE ABOVE AFTER A
MRS (150)	OF THE NEW LYRIC CLUB, LONDON, ON THE 5TH AND 6TH	JANUARY	1902, WITH MADGE MCINTOSH AS VIVIE, JULIUS KNIGHT AS
BARB I SD(249)	ACT I. IT IS AFTER DINNER IN	JANUARY	1906, IN THE LIBRARY IN LADY BRITOMART UNDERSHAFT'S
BULL PREFACE(12)	SLIDE AND MUDDLING THROUGH IS PAST. LONDON, 19TH	JANUARY	1912. PREFACE FOR POLITICIANS (TO THE FIRST EDITION
CURE (238)	MARCH. SHE PLAYS THE BASS. AYOT ST LAWRENCE, 21ST	JANUARY	1914. THE END.
AUGS PREFACE(261)	GOOD OFFICES WHICH AUGUSTUS SECURED FOR ME IN	JANUARY	1917. I HAD BEEN INVITED TO VISIT THE THEATRE OF WAR
AUGS (260)	IN LONDON BY THE STAGE SOCIETY ON THE 21ST	JANUARY	1917, WITH LALLA VANDERVELDE AS THE LADY, F. B. J.
ANNA (286)	AT THE COLISEUM THEATRE IN LONDON ON THE 21ST	JANUARY	1918, WITH LILLAH MCCARTHY AS THE GRAND DUCHESS,
JITT PREFACE(7)	AT THE SHUBERT THEATRE, NEW YORK CITY, ON THE 6TH	JANUARY	1923, WHEN JITTA WAS PLAYED BY BERTHA KALICH.
VWOO 3 (143)	THE CURTAIN FALLS. IN THE SUNDA STRAIT, 27TH	JANUARY	1933.
BARB II SD(273)	AND MISERABLE; FOR IT IS A GRINDINGLY COLD RAW	JANUARY	DAY; AND A GLANCE AT THE BACKGROUND OF GRIMY
MTH4 I (146)	A SECONDARY, AS I SHALL BE NINETY-FIVE NEXT	JANUARY	. THE TERTIARIES ARE IN THEIR THIRD CENTURY. DID YOU
VWOO 2 (125)	YOU WILL BELIEVE ME WHEN I TELL YOU THAT IN	JANUARY	LAST I WAS SITTING ON THE DECK OF A SHIP NAMED THE
BARB II SD(273)	OF THE SALVATION ARMY IS A COLD PLACE ON A	JANUARY	MORNING. THE BUILDING ITSELF, AN OLD WAREHOUSE, IS
VWOO 2 (125)	THE SORT OF THING. MISSING FROM HIS HOME SINCE	JANUARY	THE FIRST. LAST SEEN IN A DECK CHAIR ON THE EMPRESS
		JAP	
BARB II (288)	SALVATION HARDER THAN HE EVER WRESTLED WITH THE	JAP	AT THE MUSIC HALL. HE GAVE IN TO THE JAP WHEN HIS ARM
GENV III (68)	LOOK AT THE AMERICANS! WILL THEY LET A	JAP	INTO CALIFORNIA? SEE WHAT HAPPENED TO THE BRITISH
BARB II (288)	WITH THE JAP AT THE MUSIC HALL. HE GAVE IN TO THE	JAP	WHEN HIS ARM WAS GOING TO BREAK. BUT HE DIDNT GIVE IN TO
		JAPAN	
GENV II (50)	THOSE SOVIETS. /THE SECRETARY/ IN CONSEQUENCE	JAPAN	HAS DECLARED WAR ON RUSSIA AND IS THEREFORE IN
MIS. PREFACE(55)	OF HIGH CHARACTER, AND HAD HIS CLAIM ALLOWED. IN	JAPAN	HE WOULD HARDLY HAVE BEEN ALLOWED THE PRIVILEGE OF
BUOY 1 (15)	HIROSHIMA AND NAGASAKI ARE ALREADY REBUILT; AND	JAPAN	IS ALL THE BETTER FOR THE CHANGE. WHEN ATOM SPLITTING
ROCK PREFACE(174)	OF LIBERTY IN IMPERIALIST JAPAN, THOUGH IN	JAPAN	IT IS A CRIME TO HAVE " DANGEROUS THOUGHTS." IN MY
ROCK II (239)	AEROPLANE-CARRYING BATTLESHIPS. I HAVE MY EYE ON	JAPAN	. AND THERES AMERICA. AND, OF COURSE, RUSSIA. /SIR
ROCK I (199)	JOURNEYS AND THE CHANGE. AND I LOOK FORWARD TO	JAPAN	. I SHALL BE ABLE TO PICK UP SOME NICE OLD BRIC-A-BRAC
BARB I (250)	AT HARROW AND CAMBRIDGE. YOUVE BEEN TO INDIA AND	JAPAN	. YOU MUST KNOW A LOT OF THINGS, NOW; UNLESS YOU HAVE
POSN PREFACE(393)	FOR INSTANCE, THE NOTION THAT THE MIKADO OF	JAPAN	SHOULD BE AS SACRED TO THE ENGLISH PLAYWRIGHT AS HE IS
GETT PREFACE(240)	LESS THAN ONE PER CENT OF DOMESTIC FAILURES. IN	JAPAN	THE RATE IS 215, WHICH IS SAID TO BE THE HIGHEST ON
GENV PREFACE(9)	STATES OF NORTH AMERICA GOT AHEAD OF GERMANY AND	JAPAN	WITH THIS TERRIFIC WEAPON ALL THEIR OPPONENTS AT ONCE
LION EPILOG (150)	THE FRENCH REPUBLIC, AND THE KINGDOMS OF ITALY,	JAPAN	, AND SERBIA) ACTUALLY SUCCEEDED IN CLOSING A CHURCH
ROCK PREFACE(174)	ABOUT THE SUPPRESSION OF LIBERTY IN IMPERIALIST	JAPAN	, THOUGH IN JAPAN IT IS A CRIME TO HAVE " DANGEROUS
GENV PREFACE(9)	WE PLAYED IT THE WAR, WHICH STILL LINGERED IN	JAPAN	, WAS BROUGHT TO AN ABRUPT STOP BY AN ANGLO-AMERICAN
ROCK I (198)	ONE IN PARIS! TWO IN GENEVA! ONE IN	JAPAN	! YOU CANT POSSIBLY DO IT: YOU WILL BREAK DOWN. /SIR
		JAPANESE	
BARB III (343)	RYOT, THE UNDERDOG EVERYWHERE. DO YOU LOVE THE	JAPANESE	? DO YOU LOVE THE FRENCH? DO YOU LOVE THE
ROCK I (226)	FILL THAT IN WITH WHATEVER NUMBER OF SHIPS THE	JAPANESE	ARE STANDING OUT FOR. BY THE WAY, DO YOU THINK
ROCK PREFACE(174)	STATE, EITHER INDEPENDENTLY OR AS PART OF A	JAPANESE	ASIATIC HEGEMONY, ALL THE WESTERN STATES WOULD HAVE
GENV PREFACE(10)	OF A SECOND. THE EXPERIMENT WAS TRIED ON TWO	JAPANESE	CITIES. FOUR SQUARE MILES OF THEM VANISHED BEFORE
PYGM II (232)	/MRS PEARCE/ NO, SIR. MIGHT SHE USE SOME OF THOSE	JAPANESE	DRESSES YOU BROUGHT FROM ABROAD? I REALLY CANT PUT
ARMS II SD(23)	HEAD IS SHAVED UP TO THE CROWN, GIVING HIM A HIGH	JAPANESE	FOREHEAD. HIS NAME IS NICOLA. /NICOLA/ BE WARNED IN
BULL PREFACE(33)	THIS IS HUMAN NATURE AND NOT CLASS WEAKNESS. THE	JAPANESE	HAVE PROVED THAT IT IS POSSIBLE TO CONDUCT SOCIAL
GENV IV (104)	IN AUSTRALIA, AS THE AMERICANS EXCLUDE THE	JAPANESE	IN CALIFORNIA. /JEW/ WHY DO THE BRITISH EXCLUDE THE
PYGM II (240)	WITH A DAINTY AND EXQUISITELY CLEAN YOUNG	JAPANESE	LADY IN A SIMPLE BLUE COTTON KIMONO PRINTED
POSN PREFACE(393)	SACRED TO THE ENGLISH PLAYWRIGHT AS HE IS TO THE	JAPANESE	LORD CHAMBERLAIN WOULD HAVE SEEMED GROTESQUE A
GENV PREFACE(11)	ALLIES AGREE IN DEMANDING THAT GERMANS AND	JAPANESE	MUST BE TREATED AS CATHOLIC IRELAND WAS TREATED BY
BARB III (327)	GOOD NEWS FROM MANCHURIA. /STEPHEN/ ANOTHER	JAPANESE	VICTORY? /UNDERSHAFT/ OH, I DONT KNOW. WHICH SIDE
BARB II (280)	O BALLS POND. HIM THAT WON 20 POUNDS OFF THE	JAPANESE	WRASTLER AT THE MUSIC HALL BY STANDIN OUT 17
		JAPANNED	
DEST SD(152)	HIS NECK, EXCEPT WHERE IT HAS DRIED IN STIFF	JAPANNED	FLAKES AND HAD ITS SWEEPING OUTLINE CHIPPED OFF IN
CAND I SD(78)	HEARTH, WITH A COMFORTABLE ARMCHAIR AND A BLACK	JAPANNED	FLOWER-PAINTED COAL SCUTTLE AT ONE SIDE, A
BULL III SD(117)	IS CROWDED UPON A LARGE SQUARE BLACK TRAY OF	JAPANNED	METAL. THE TEAPOT IS OF BROWN DELFT WARE. THERE IS
DEVL II SD(28)	ENOUGH TO CONTAIN NEARLY A QUART, ON A BLACK	JAPANNED	TRAY, AND, IN THE MIDDLE OF THE TABLE, A WOODEN
		JAPS	
BARB III (329)	IT'S YOUR BUSINESS TO BLOW UP THE RUSSIANS AND	JAPS	; BUT YOU MIGHT REALLY STOP SHORT OF BLOWING UP POOR
		JAQUES	
6CAL PREFACE(90)	OF THE SENTENTIOUS FUTILITY OF THE MELANCHOLY	JAQUES	; AND MILLAMANT, IMPOSSIBLE AS SHE IS, STILL PRODUCES
		JAR	
CAPT II (251)	I MUST BE OFF TO MY PATIENT. (SHE TAKES UP HER	JAR	AND GOES OUT BY THE LITTLE DOOR, LEAVING BRASSBOUND AND
CAPT II SD(249)	CICELY RETURNS WITH REDBROOK. SHE CARRIES THE	JAR	FULL OF WATER. /LADY CICELY/ (PUTTING DOWN THE JAR, AND
CAPT II SD(248)	RETURNS WITH JOHNSON AND REDBROOK. SHE CARRIES A	JAR	. /LADY CICELY/ (STOPPING BETWEEN THE DOOR AND THE
2TRU III (83)	SOLDIERS DO: TO THEM A WOMAN IS NO MORE THAN A	JAR	OF MARMALADE, TO BE CONSUMED AND PUT AWAY. I DONT TAKE
BUOY II SD(19)	SLAMS THE DOOR). AN ELDERLY NATIVE ARRIVES WITH A	JAR	OF MILK AND A BASKET OF BREAD AND FRUIT. HE DEPOSITS
MTH2 (42)	AND DOWN THE ROOM DISCONTENTEDLY) SAVVY'S MANNERS	JAR	ON ME. THEY WOULD HAVE HORRIFIED HER GRANDMOTHER.
MTH5 (238)	LOOK TO YOUR WORDS; FOR IF THEY ENTER MY EAR AND	JAR	TOO REPUGNANTLY ON MY SENSORIUM, WHO KNOWS THAT THE
CAPT II (249)	FULL OF WATER. /LADY CICELY/ (PUTTING DOWN THE	JAR	, AND COMING BETWEEN BRASSBOUND AND DRINKWATER AS
NEVR III (278)	WAY! PEOPLE WHOSE TOUCH HURTS, WHOSE VOICES	JAR	, WHOSE TEMPERS PLAY THEM FALSE, WHO WOUND AND WORRY THE
		JARGEAU	
JOAN 4 (94)	AND SORCERY. BUT WE ARE STILL BEING DEFEATED.	JARGEAU	, MEUNG, BEAUGENCY, JUST LIKE ORLEANS. AND NOW WE

JARGON
MTH2 (78) OTHER IS SCIENCE. /FRANKLYN/ THE ONE IS CLASSROOM JARGON : THE OTHER IS INSPIRED HUMAN LANGUAGE. /LUBIN/ (
FABL PREFACE(66) LEIBNIZ'S ALGEBRAIC SYMBOLS AND HIS PHILOSOPHIC JARGON . HERE I MUST WARN YOU THAT YOU CAN MAKE NO GREATER
BULL PREFACE(15) IS THE ENGLISH OF SWIFT AND NOT THE UNSPEAKABLE JARGON OF THE MID-XIX CENTURY LONDON NEWSPAPERS. MY
DOCT PREFACE(78) TO BELIEVE ANYTHING UNLESS IT IS WORDED IN THE JARGON OF THOSE WRITERS WHO, BECAUSE THEY NEVER REALLY
MIS. PREFACE(96) YOU WILL, IN SPITE OF YOUR PSEUDO-SCIENTIFIC JARGON , FIND YOURSELF BACK IN THE OLD-FASHIONED RELIGIOUS

JARRED
MRS IV (251) REFUSE TO DO YOUR DUTY AS A DAUGHTER. /VIVIE/ (JARRED AND ANTAGONIZED BY THE ECHO OF THE SLUMS IN HER
MTH1 I (11) /THE SERPENT/ (LAUGHS) ! ! ! /EVE/ (JARRED AND STARTLED) WHAT A HATEFUL NOISE! WHAT IS THE
POSN (458) HE BREAKS INTO HIDEOUS LAUGHTER). /THE SHERIFF/ (JARRED BEYOND ENDURANCE BY THE SOUND) HOLD YOUR NOISE, WILL
SUPR II SD(57) SURPRISED BY THIS BURST OF LARKLIKE MELODY, AND JARRED BY A SARDONIC NOTE IN ITS CHEERFULNESS, THEY TURN AND
MTH4 III (194) HER BACK TO THE ABYSS). /THE ELDERLY GENTLEMAN/ (JARRED BY HER CALLOUSNESS) WE DESIRE TO BEHAVE IN A BECOMING
MTH3 (103) /THE ARCHBISHOP/ (LOOKING CURIOUSLY AT HIM, JARRED BY HIS UNCIVIL TONE) CERTAINLY. WHAT IS IT?
LIED (189) SISTERS-IN-LAW THINK OF THEM? /HE/ (PAINFULLY JARRED) HAVE YOU GOT SISTERS-IN-LAW? /SHE/ YES, OF COURSE
CAND II (114) BUT TO BE IDLE, SELFISH, AND USELESS. /CANDIDA/ (JARRED) OH, JAMES! HOW COULD YOU SPOIL IT ALL?

JARRING
WIDO II (33) ANY CIRCUMSTANCES, AND JUST NOW ALMOST UNBEARABLY JARRING). BLANCHE WILL BE DOWN PRESENTLY, HARRY (TRENCH

JARROWFIELDS
MTH2 (38) IS MY BROTHER CONRAD, PROFESSOR OF BIOLOGY AT JARROWFIELDS UNIVERSITY: DR CONRAD BARNABAS. MY NAME IS

JARS
CAND I (97) WHY, YOU DUFFER-- (BUT THIS BOISTEROUSNESS JARS HIMSELF AS WELL AS EUGENE. HE CHECKS HIMSELF). NO: I
SUPR PREFACE(R17) FOR ALI BABA. HE SIMPLY THRUSTS A FEW OIL JARS INTO THE VALLEY OF DIAMONDS, AND SO FULFILS THE PROMISE
DOCT III SD(131) THE WALL IS A BARE WOODEN TABLE WITH BOTTLES AND JARS OF OIL AND MEDIUM, PAINT-SMUDGED RAGS, TUBES OF COLOR,
VWOO 2,SD(123) STONE BOTTLES, TABLETS OF MILK CHOCOLATE, GLASS JARS OF SWEETS CONTAINING (INTER ALIA) SUGARED ALMONDS, ALL
DEVL III (54) ME? (THE SERGEANT KNOCKS. THE BLOW ON THE DOOR JARS ON HER HEART). OH, ONE MOMENT MORE. (SHE THROWS
MRS IV (239) A CERTAIN SENTIMENTALITY IN HIS HIGH SPIRITS JARS ON HER). I START IN AN HOUR FROM HOLBORN VIADUCT. I
PPP (203) DETESTABLE VULGARIAN! YOUR PRONUNCIATION JARS ON THE FINEST CHORDS OF MY NATURE. BEGONE! /THE
DEVL I SD(16) WITH WHICH CHRISTY NAMES THE REPROBATE JARS ON THE MORAL SENSE OF THE FAMILY. UNCLE WILLIAM SHAKES

JASMINE
PYGM II (240) COTTON KIMONO PRINTED CUNNINGLY WITH SMALL WHITE JASMINE BLOSSOMS. MRS PEARCE IS WITH HER. HE GETS OUT OF HER

JAST
BULL III (141) AND TIKE AND THE ROTTEN PLICES YOULL SLEEP IN, I JAST FEEL THAT I COULD TIKE THE AOWL BLOOMIN BRITISH AWLAND
BULL III (141) DAR YOU CALL ME PADDY? /HODSON/ (UNMOVED) YOU JAST KEEP YOUR AIR ON AND LISTEN TO ME. YOU AWRISH PEOPLE
CAPT I (225) NITRE IS THE SIME EVERYWHERES. THEM EATHENS IS JAST LAWK YOU AN' ME, GAVNER. A LADY AND GENTLEMAN, BOTH
BARB II (299) WAS ME MATHER WORSHIN ME A SETTERDA NAWT. AW EDNT JAST NAO SHAOW WIV IM AT ALL. ARF THE STREET PRYED; AN THE
BULL III (142) AS GOOD AOWLD ENGLISH CRAMWELL SAID. I'M JAST SICK OF AWRLAND. LET IT GOW. CAT THE CAIBLE. MIKE IT A
BULL III (142) BRITISH AWLAND AND MIKE YOU A PRESENT OF IT, JAST TO LET YOU FAWND AHT WOT REEL AWDSHIP'S LAWK. /MATTHEW/
WIDO III (53) BUT I'LL TELL YOU WHAT I DID. I KEP IT BACK, JAST TO OBLIGE ONE OR TWO PEOPLE WHOSE FEELINS WOULD 'A BIN

JASTICE
PRES (149) YOU WOULD INDEED, SIR. I SHANT NEVER DO MYSELF JASTICE AT SOLJERIN, SIR. I CANT BRING MYSELF TO THINK OF IT
BARB II (281) TO THE CORNER OF THE PENTHOUSE) GAWD? THERES NO JASTICE IN THIS CANTRY. TO THINK WOT THEM PEOPLE CAN DO!

JAUNDICE
MIS. (157) EAT SO MANY ORANGES? ARNT YOU AFRAID OF GETTING JAUNDICE ? /LINA/ NOT IN THE LEAST. BUT BILLIARD BALLS WILL

JAUNT
PYGM II (235) THE GIRL TOOK A BOY IN THE TAXI TO GIVE HIM A JAUNT . SON OF HER LANDLADY, HE IS. HE HUNG ABOUT ON THE

JAUNTING
BULL II SD(104) ROAD AT THE FOOT OF THE HILL. IT IS A MONSTER JAUNTING CAR, BLACK AND DILAPIDATED, ONE OF THE LAST

JAUNTY
SUPR III SD(94) BUT FOR ITS SPANISH DIGNITY, WOULD BE CALLED JAUNTY . HE IS ON THE PLEASANTEST TERMS WITH DON JUAN. HIS

JAURES
HART PREFACE(13) COUPLE OF DAYS IN BED. THE SLAYER OF JAURES WAS RECKLESSLY ACQUITTED: THE WOULD-BE SLAYER OF M.
HART PREFACE(13) THE GREATEST SOCIALIST STATESMAN IN EUROPE, JAURES , WAS SHOT AND KILLED BY A GENTLEMAN WHO RESENTED HIS

JAVELIN
CLEO PRO2 (99) AND BREASTPLATES. EVERY MAN OF THEM FLUNG HIS JAVELIN : THE ONE THAT CAME MY WAY DROVE THROUGH MY SHIELD
CLEO PRO2 (100) /THE SENTINEL/ WOE, ALAS! (HE THROWS DOWN HIS JAVELIN AND FLIES INTO THE PALACE.) /BELZANOR/ NAIL HIM TO
CLEO PRO2 (96) AM NOT IN THE VEIN. /THE SENTINEL/ (POISING HIS JAVELIN AS HE PEERS OVER THE WALL) STAND. WHO GOES THERE?
CLEO PRO2 (96) SENTRY) PASS HIM. /THE SENTINEL/ (GROUNDING HIS JAVELIN) DRAW NEAR, O BEARER OF EVIL TIDINGS. /BELZANOR/ (
CLEO PRO2 (97) IN THE HOUSE OF THE QUEEN. /VOICE/ GO ANOINT THY JAVELIN WITH FAT OF SWINE, O BLACKAMOOR; FOR BEFORE MORNING
SUPR III (105) ALL THE HIDDEN MOLECULAR ENERGIES, AND LEAVES THE JAVELIN , THE ARROW, THE BLOWPIPE OF HIS FATHERS FAR BEHIND.

JAVELINS
CLEO PRO2 (99) UPON US WITH SHORT SWORDS ALMOST AS SOON AS THEIR JAVELINS . WHEN A MAN IS CLOSE TO YOU WITH SUCH A SWORD, YOU

JAW
BARB II (299) WELL, HAS TODGER PAID YOU OUT FOR POOR JENNY'S JAW ? /BILL/ NAO E AINT. /BARBARA/ I THOUGHT YOUR JACKET
LION I (121) YES; BUT I SAVED HIS SOUL. WHAT MATTERS A BROKEN JAW ? /LENTULUS/ DONT TOUCH ME, DO YOU HEAR? THE LAW --
BASH II,2, (117) WITH MY RIGHT AIMING BESIDE THE ANGLE OF THE JAW AND LANDING WITH A CERTAIN DELICATE SCREW I WITHOUT
BARB II (280) LUMP OF CONCEIT AND IGNORANCE. HIT A GIRL IN THE JAW AND ONY MAKE HER CRY! IF TODGER FAIRMILE'D DONE IT, SHE
DEST (159) HIS CONFIDENCE IN ME, OF COURSE. (NAPOLEON'S JAW DOES NOT EXACTLY DROP; BUT ITS HINGES BECOME NERVELESS).
JITT I SD(25) BUT THE BACK OF HIS HEAD REMAINS HANGING AND HIS JAW DROPS. WITH A GASP OF HORROR SHE REPLACES THE HEAD AND
CLEO I (116) A SHRIEK. THE WOMEN FLY AFTER HIM. FTATATEETA'S JAW EXPRESSES SAVAGE RESOLUTION: SHE DOES NOT BUDGE.
CLEO PRO2 (99) FIST AND SMOTE MY ROMAN ON THE SHARPNESS OF HIS JAW . HE WAS BUT MORTAL AFTER ALL: HE LAY DOWN IN A STUPOR;
LION I (121) EASY, FERROVIUS, EASY: YOU BROKE THE LAST MAN'S JAW . LENTULUS, WITH A MOAN OF TERROR, ATTEMPTS TO FLY; BUT
PRES (139) WAS TO WALK UP TO CHUBBS-JENKINSON AND BREAK HIS JAW . THAT SHEWED THERE WAS NO USE FLOGGING HIM; SO NOW HE
MILL I (145) IT DOES NOT PUT YOU TO SLEEP LIKE A PUNCH ON THE JAW . WHEN HE SAW MY FACE DISTORTED WITH AGONY AND MY BODY
PYGM I (215) AT THE CARLTON. COME WITH ME NOW AND LETS HAVE A JAW OVER SOME SUPPER. /HIGGINS/ RIGHT YOU ARE. /THE FLOWER
DOCT PREFACE(40) WHEN HE WAS TOLD THAT HE COULD NOT MOVE HIS UPPER JAW); BUT SCIENCE HAS TO CONSIDER ONLY THE TRUTH OF THE
BASH II,1, (103) BET WAS BOOKED, WHEN, AT THE REELING CHAMPION'S JAW THE SAILOR, BENT ON WINNING OUT OF HAND, SENT IN HIS
SUPR HANDBOK(206) EVEN THE HORSE, WITH HIS DOCKED TAIL AND BITTED JAW , FINDS HIS SLAVERY MITIGATED BY THE FACT THAT A TOTAL

JAWBONE
FABL PREFACE(69) BLOOD OF SAINT JANUARIUS, AND SAYING MASS OVER A JAWBONE LABELLED AS THAT OF SAINT ANTHONY OF PADUA. WHEN THE

JAWR
BARB II (278) IF SHE KEEPS ME WITIN ITLL BE WORSE. YOU STOP TO JAWR BECK AT ME; AND AW'LL STAWT ON YOU: D'YE EAH? THERES
BARB II (300) WOT AW DID AW'LL PY FOR. AW TRAWD TO GAT ME AOWN JAWR BROWK TO SETTISFAW YOU-- /JENNY/ (DISTRESSED) OH NO--
BARB II (283) AW CAM TO TIKE HER AHT O THIS AND TO BRIKE ER JAWR FOR ER. /BARBARA/ (COMPLACENTLY) YOU SEE I WAS RIGHT
BARB II (282) /BILL/ (SULLENLY) I WANT NAN O YOUR KENTIN JAWR . I SPOWSE YOU THINK AW CAM EAH TO BEG FROM YOU, LIKE
BARB II (300) FOR ME: YOUVE NO CALL. LISTEN EAH. AW BROWK YOUR JAWR . /JENNY/ NO, IT DIDNT HURT ME: INDEED IT DIDNT, EXCEPT
BARB II (289) (TO ADOLPHUS) YOU TIKE MAW TIP, MITE. STOP ER JAWR ; OR YOULL DOY AFOAH YOUR TAWM (WITH INTENSE
BARB II (278) AGAIN AN AW'LL GAWD FORGIVE YOU ONE ON THE JAWR THETLL STOP YOU PRYIN FOR A WEEK. (HOLDING HER AND

JAWRIN

BARB II (276)	THE FIRST CHANGE? /PRICE/ (CHEERFULLY) NO GOOD	JAWRIN	ABOUT IT. YOURE ONY A JUMPED-UP, JERKED-OFF,
BARB II (300)	NO MORE O YOUR FORGIVIN AN PRYIN AND YOUR MIJOR	JAWRIN	ME. LET WOT AW DAN BE DAN AN PIDE FOR; AND LET THERE
BARB II (300)	PLYED AGEN ME: THIS BLOOMIN FORGIVIN AN NEGGIN AN	JAWRIN	THAT MIKES A MENN THET SORE THAT IZ LAWF'S A BURDN TO

JAWS

BUOY II (20)	YOU WITH HISSING RATTLING THINGS, WITH GAPING	JAWS	AND SLASHING TAILS. I AM FAR BETTER PROTECTED AGAINST
CLEO III (157)	TO SEEK QUARRELS MERELY TO SHEW HOW STUBBORN MY	JAWS	ARE? /BRITANNUS/ BUT YOUR HONOR-- THE HONOR OF ROME--
GENV PREFACE(5)	IN 1939, HALF OF IT WAS SNATCHED OUT OF HER	JAWS	BY SOVIET RUSSIA. THE BRITISH COMMONWEALTH, HAVING
DEST (156)	(HE SITS DOWN AGAIN AT THE TABLE, WITH HIS	JAWS	IN HIS HANDS, AND HIS ELBOWS PROPPED ON THE MAP, PORING
SUPR I SD(3)	ABOVE HIS EARS AND AT THE ANGLES OF HIS SPREADING	JAWS	. HE WEARS A BLACK FROCK COAT, A WHITE WAISTCOAT (IT
DOCT I SD(93)	THREE TRIMLY TURNED CORNERS MADE BY HIS CHIN AND	JAWS	. IN COMPARISON WITH RIDGEON'S DELICATE BROKEN LINES,
CLEO III (147)	AND I WILL GIVE YOU THIS (THE PILUM) IN YOUR	JAWS	. /CLEOPATRA/ (CALLING FROM THE PALACE) FTATATEETA,
CLEO PRO2,SD(102)	STRONG; WITH THE MOUTH OF A BLOODHOUND AND THE	JAWS	OF A BULLDOG, APPEARS ON THE THRESHOLD. SHE IS DRESSED
JOAN 5 (115)	OF IT HE WILL SOMETIMES SNATCH YOU OUT OF THE	JAWS	OF DEATH AND SET YOU ON YOUR FEET AGAIN; BUT THAT IS
SUPR PREFACE(R20)	BUNSBY DROPPING LIKE A FASCINATED BIRD INTO THE	JAWS	OF MRS MACSTINGER IS BY COMPARISON A TRUE TRAGIC OBJECT
LION II (138)	OF YOUR FELLOWS BOLTED, AND RAN RIGHT INTO THE	JAWS	OF THE LION. I LAUGHED. I STILL LAUGH. /LAVINIA/ THEN
LION II (129)	WHEN YOU SMELL THE BEAST'S BREATH AND SEE HIS	JAWS	OPENING TO TEAR OUT YOUR THROAT? /SPINTHO/ (RISING
HART I SD(43)	A CARPENTER'S BENCH. THE VICE HAS A BOARD IN ITS	JAWS	; AND THE FLOOR IS LITTERED WITH SHAVINGS, OVERFLOWING
FANY II SD(285)	SKIN, WHILST KNOX HAS COARSE BLACK HAIR, AND BLUE	JAWS	WHICH NO DILIGENCE IN SHAVING CAN WHITEN. MRS KNOX IS A
LION PROLOG (109)	THORN ANOTHER PULL. THE LION ROARS AND SNAPS HIS	JAWS	WITH A TERRIFYING CLASH). OH, MUSTNT FRIGHTEN UM'S GOOD
MRS I SD(188)	FROM HIS STRONG FRAME. CLEAN-SHAVEN BULLDOG	JAWS	, LARGE FLAT EARS, AND THICK NECK: GENTLEMANLY

JAY

O'FL SD(227)	THE GENERAL STRIKES A MATCH. THE THRUSH SINGS. A	JAY	LAUGHS. THE CONVERSATION DROPS.

JAZZ

2TRU II (62)	ON WHICH YOU CAN PLAY ALL SORTS OF MUSIC, FROM	JAZZ	TO MOZART. (RELAXING) BUT THE OLD MAN NEVER COULD BE
MTH2 SD(87)	SEIZE EACH OTHER IN AN ECSTASY OF AMUSEMENT, AND	JAZZ	TO THE SETTEE, WHERE THEY SIT DOWN AGAIN SIDE BY SIDE.

JE

SUPR III (75)	IT'S A LIE. I NEVER SAID SO. BE FAIR, MENDOZA. 3.	JE	DEMANDE LA PAROLE. C'EST ABSOLUMENT FAUX. C'EST FAUX!
FOUN (218)	TONE-- /MERCER/ ADDRESS-- /THE LORD CHANCELLOR/ A	JE	NE SAIS QUOI-- /MERCER/ A TOUT ENSEMBLE-- /ANASTASIA/ YOU
WIDO III (61)	CENT AS USUAL. /TRENCH/ A MAN MUST LIVE. /COKANE/	JE	N'EN VOIS PAS LA NECESSITE. /TRENCH/ SHUT UP, BILLY; OR

JEALOUS

CAND I (84)	PEPPERINESS). YOU DONT BELIEVE ME? YOU THINK I'M	JEALOUS	? OH, WHAT A KNOWLEDGE OF THE HUMAN HEART YOU HAVE,
CAND II (119)	ARE YOU JESTING? OR-- CAN IT BE? -- ARE YOU	JEALOUS	? /CANDIDA/ (WITH CURIOUS THOUGHTFULNESS) YES, I
HART II (123)	A CONSPIRACY TO MAKE ME OUT TO BE PETTISH AND	JEALOUS	AND CHILDISH AND EVERYTHING I AM NOT. EVERYONE KNOWS
METH PREFACE(R44)	ACT OF AN ARBITRARY PERSONAL GOD OF DANGEROUSLY	JEALOUS	AND CRUEL PERSONAL CHARACTER, SO THAT EVEN THE
PHIL III (139)	YES, MY DEAR. THAT MEANS THAT WHENEVER YOU GOT	JEALOUS	AND FLEW INTO A TEARING RAGE, I COULD ALWAYS DEPEND
GETT PREFACE(217)	BEING ORGANIZED IN A DEFENCE OF ITS IDEAL SO	JEALOUS	AND IMPLACABLE THAT THE LEAST STEP FROM THE STRAIGHT
APPL INTRLUD(249)	AS YOU LIKE WHEN WE ARE MARRIED. I SHALL NOT BE	JEALOUS	AND MAKE SCENES. /MAGNUS/ THAT IS VERY MANGANIMOUS
NEVR III (271)	BEFORE (GLORIA LOOKS UP SUDDENLY WITH A FLASH OF	JEALOUS	ANGER AND AMAZEMENT); HOW MANY TIMES HE HAS LAID THE
SHAK (143)	THESE WORDS ARE MINE, NOT THINE. /SHAV/ PEACE,	JEALOUS	BARD. WE BOTH ARE MORTAL. FOR A MOMENT SUFFER MY
GETT PREFACE(236)	CREDIT. STILL LESS SHOULD PEOPLE WHO ARE NOT	JEALOUS	BE URGED TO BEHAVE AS IF THEY WERE JEALOUS, AND TO
APPL I (211)	(CONCILIATORY) NEVER MIND THEM, BILL: THEYRE	JEALOUS	BECAUSE THEY DIDNT THINK OF IT THEMSELVES. HOW DID
KING I (208)	/BARBARA/ WHO ASKED YOU FOR YOUR OPINION, YOU	JEALOUS	CAT? /CHARLES/ SIT DOWN; AND DONT BE SILLY,
GETT PREFACE(195)	VIEWS, ITS UNNATURALLY SUSTAINED AND SPITEFULLY	JEALOUS	CONCUPISCENCES, ITS PETTY TYRANNIES, ITS FALSE
GETT (269)	AND ORDER. I AM PROUD OF MY INDEPENDENCE AND	JEALOUS	FOR IT. I HAVE A SUFFICIENTLY WELL-STOCKED MIND TO
LION PREFACE(84)	THE RITE OF CIRCUMCISION; AND THEY WERE FIERCELY	JEALOUS	FOR IT, BECAUSE IT MARKED THEM AS THE CHOSEN PEOPLE
CAND II (119)	LAUGHING) NO, NO, NO, NO. NOT JEALOUS OF ANYBODY.	JEALOUS	FOR SOMEBODY ELSE, WHO IS NOT LOVED AS HE OUGHT TO
DOCT PREFACE(33)	PALATABLE TO VULGAR PEOPLE, MAKES THEM SORELY	JEALOUS	FOR THAT RIGHT; AND WHEN THEY HEAR A POPULAR OUTCRY
SUPR II (59)	FIENDS WHO HIDE THEIR SELFISH AMBITIONS, THEIR	JEALOUS	HATREDS OF THE YOUNG RIVALS WHO HAVE SUPPLANTED
JOAN PREFACE(43)	A MAN IS TOO ACCREDITED AUTHORITY THE MORE	JEALOUS	HE IS OF ALLOWING ANY UNAUTHORIZED PERSON TO ORDER
OVER PREFACE(158)	IN SUCH MATTERS. IN AN ELEGANT PLUTOCRACY, A	JEALOUS	HUSBAND IS REGARDED AS A BOOR. AMONG THE TRADESMEN
HART II (124)	IS YOUR HUSBAND. /LADY UTTERWORD/ I KNOW. HE IS	JEALOUS	, AS IF HE HAD ANY RIGHT TO BE! HE COMPROMISES ME
CLEO IV (171)	WOMEN? /CLEOPATRA/ BECAUSE I CANNOT MAKE HIM	JEALOUS	. I HAVE TRIED. /POTHINUS/ HM! PERHAPS I SHOULD
DOCT IV (164)	MARRIAGE HAPPY ALWAYS MARRY AGAIN. AH, I SHANT BE	JEALOUS	. (SLYLY) BUT DONT TALK TO THE OTHER FELLOW TOO
DEST (184)	YOU ARE. /LIEUTENANT/ I UNDERSTAND. HE'D BE	JEALOUS	. /LADY/ DONT TELL HIM ANYTHING EXCEPT THAT YOU ARE
BUOY III (37)	I AM YOUR PROPERTY. THEREFORE YOU ARE DAMNABLY	JEALOUS	. /MRS SECONDBORN/ I DENY IT. I AM NOT JEALOUS. /THE
SUPR IV (165)	SOOTHING HER) THERE, THERE: SO I AM. ANN WILL BE	JEALOUS	. /MRS WHITEFIELD/ ANN DOESNT CARE A BIT FOR ME.
BUOY III (37)	JEALOUS. /MRS SECONDBORN/ I DENY IT. I AM NOT	JEALOUS	. /THE WIDOWER/ I THINK SIR FERDINAND'S MIND WOULD
DOCT I (94)	BE-- /RIDGEON/ NEVER MIND HIM, WALPOLE. HE'S	JEALOUS	. /WALPOLE/ BY THE WAY, I HOPE I'M NOT DISTURBING
KING II (227)	I KNOW, I KNOW: IT WAS THE ONLY TIME I EVER WAS	JEALOUS	. WELL, I FORGIVE YOU: WHY SHOULD A GREAT MAN LIKE
KING I (199)	TO LOOK THROUGH MR NEWTON'S TELESCOPE; AND THE	JEALOUS	LADY WOULDNT LEAVE UNTIL THE FRENCH LADY LEFT; AND
JOAN 5 (120)	STRENGTH: WHAT WOULD HE BE IF HE LISTENED TO YOUR	JEALOUS	LITTLE COUNSELS? WELL, MY LONELINESS SHALL BE MY
GETT PREFACE(225)	FORTH IS ONLY POSSIBLE TO A WRETCHEDLY NARROW AND	JEALOUS	NATURE; AND NEITHER HISTORY NOR CONTEMPORARY SOCIETY
MIS. PREFACE(17)	WHICH OFTEN MAKES MOTHERS AND FATHERS BITTERLY	JEALOUS	OF ALLOWING ANYONE ELSE TO INTERFERE WITH THEIR
CAND II (119)	/CANDIDA/ (LAUGHING) NO, NO, NO, NO. NOT	JEALOUS	OF ANYBODY. JEALOUS FOR SOMEBODY ELSE, WHO IS NOT
OVER PREFACE(157)	OF IT, AND BY CLASS FEELING, THAT A WILL BE	JEALOUS	OF B AND NOT OF C, AND WILL TOLERATE INFIDELITIES ON
CLEO II (132)	(LAUGHING APPROVINGLY) BRAVE BOY! /CLEOPATRA/ (	JEALOUS	OF CAESAR'S APPROBATION, CALLING AFTER PTOLEMY)
OVER PREFACE(157)	AND BY THE FACT THAT VERY JEALOUS PEOPLE ARE	JEALOUS	OF EVERYBODY WITHOUT REGARD TO RELATIONSHIP OR SEX,
PHIL II (108)	I AM GOING TO SPEAK AS A PHILOSOPHER. JULIA IS	JEALOUS	OF EVERYBODY: EVERYBODY. IF SHE SAW YOU FLIRTING
PHIL II (106)	(SPEAKING TO HER OVER HIS SHOULDER) NO.	JEALOUS	OF GRACE. /SYLVIA/ SERVE YOU RIGHT. YOU ARE AN AWFUL
MILL II (176)	YOU CAN HAVE SCIENCE AS WELL: I SHALL NOT BE	JEALOUS	OF HER. BUT I MADE A SOLEMN PROMISE TO MY FATHER ON
ARMS III (59)	ABOVE YOU AS HEAVEN IS ABOVE EARTH. AND YOU ARE	JEALOUS	OF HER. /LOUKA/ I HAVE NO REASON TO BE. SHE WILL
BULL III (130)	NICK WAS TOO HIGH ABOVE PATSY FARRELL TO BE	JEALOUS	OF HIM; BUT YOU, THAT ARE ONLY ONE LITTLE STEP ABOVE
MTH2 (64)	FROM THE PEOPLE, MORE FOREIGN TO THEM, MORE	JEALOUS	OF LETTING THEM UP TO YOUR LEVEL, THAN ANY DUKE OR
KING I (191)	MY CATHOLIC UNPOPULARITY. THE TRUTH IS YOU ARE	JEALOUS	OF MY POPULARITY. /CHARLES/ NO, JAMIE: I CAN BEAT
CAND I (84)	SHARE YOUR AMOROUS DELUSIONS IS THAT WE'RE ALL	JEALOUS	OF ONE ANOTHER! (SHE ABANDONS HIM WITH A TOSS OF
DEVL II (32)	FRIENDS WORRY ONE ANOTHER, TAX ONE ANOTHER, ARE	JEALOUS	OF ONE ANOTHER, CANT BEAR TO LET ONE ANOTHER OUT OF
SUPR I (40)	NEW LIGHT) SURELY YOU ARE NOT SO ABSURD AS TO BE	JEALOUS	OF TAVY. /TANNER/ JEALOUS! WHY SHOULD I BE? BUT I
MTH2 (51)	CHURCH AND HATE THE LANDED GENTRY; THAT THEY ARE	JEALOUS	OF THE NOBILITY, AND HAVE SHIPPING SHARES INSTEAD OF
OVER PREFACE(157)	(MANY WOMEN, FOR INSTANCE, ARE MUCH MORE	JEALOUS	OF THEIR HUSBANDS' MOTHERS AND SISTERS THAN OF
SUPR HANDBOK(221)	GREAT MEN REFUSE TITLES BECAUSE THEY ARE	JEALOUS	OF THEM. HONOR. THERE ARE NO PERFECTLY HONORABLE
LIED (200)	/HER HUSBAND/ JEALOUSY! DO YOU SUPPOSE I'M	JEALOUS	OF YOU? NO, NOR OF TEN LIKE YOU. BUT IF YOU THINK
BULL II (100)	KNEW MORE LATN THAN FATHER DEMPSEY THAT HE WAS	JEALOUS	OF YOU? /KEEGAN/ (SCOLDING HIM TO KEEP HIMSELF
JOAN 5 (110)	OWN ALTARS, EVEN BY SAINTS? WHY, I SHOULD BE	JEALOUS	OF YOU MYSELF IF I WERE AMBITIOUS ENOUGH. /JOAN/ YOU
MTH5 (257)	HAVE FINISHED WITH THE DOLLS; AND I AM NO LONGER	JEALOUS	OF YOU, THAT LOOKS LIKE THE END. TWO HOURS SLEEP IS
ROCK II (275)	HIM THAT HE WAS IN LOVE WITH HIS MOTHER AND WAS	JEALOUS	OF YOU. THE EDIPUS COMPLEX, YOU KNOW. /SIR ARTHUR/
JITT III (66)	HAD BEEN THAT SORT OF WOMAN, I MIGHT HAVE BEEN	JEALOUS	OF YOU. YOU ARE CLEVER IN HIS WAY; AND YOU COULD
AUGS (275)	ME FOR A FOOL? /THE LADY/ OH, IMPOSSIBLE! HE IS	JEALOUS	OF YOUR INTELLECT. THE BET IS AN INSULT TO YOU: DONT
OVER PREFACE(157)	INTENSITY IN CHILDREN, AND BY THE FACT THAT VERY	JEALOUS	PEOPLE ARE JEALOUS OF EVERYBODY WITHOUT REGARD TO
SUPR III (117)	CLEARER, NOR MY CRITICISM MORE RUTHLESS. THE MOST	JEALOUS	RIVAL OF MY MISTRESS NEVER SAW EVERY BLEMISH IN HER
JITT I (17)	IS SOMEBODY ELSE WORKING AT IT WITH ME. /JITTA/ (	JEALOUS	) SOMEBODY ELSE! /BRUNO/ YOU WOULD NEVER GUESS WHO.
CATH 3 (184)	NOT A PATCH ON YOU, DEAREST. /CLAIRE/ (	JEALOUS	) THEN YOU DID SEE HER CLOSE? /EDSTASTON/ FAIRLY
MTH5 (237)	(THE MALE FIGURE LOOKS OFFENDED, AND THE FEMALE	JEALOUS	). OH, I THOUGHT THEY COULDNT UNDERSTAND. HAVE THEY
2TRU III (91)	THEY COULD NOT STAND SWEETIE. /SWEETIE/ THEY WERE	JEALOUS	; AND YOU KNOW IT. /AUBREY/ I DARESAY THEY WERE.
LADY (246)	EYE) HA! IS IT SO? /SHAKESPEAR/ MADAM: SHE IS	JEALOUS	; AND, HEAVEN HELP ME! NOT WITHOUT REASON. OH, YOU
SUPR I (37)	PASSION MADE OUR CHILDISH RELATIONS IMPOSSIBLE. A	JEALOUS	SENSE OF MY NEW INDIVIDUALITY AROSE IN ME-- /ANN/
CAND II (119)	WITH CURIOUS THOUGHTFULNESS) YES, I FEEL A LITTLE	JEALOUS	SOMETIMES. /MORELL/ (INCREDULOUSLY) OF PROSSY?
PHIL I (80)	IS INFINITELY WORSE THAN ALL THREE TOGETHER: A	JEALOUS	TERMAGANT. /JULIA/ (SHAKING HER HEAD BITTERLY) YES:
MILL IV (208)	THAT IS DEVILISH: THE THORN IN HIS FLESH, THE	JEALOUS	TERMAGANT, THE DETECTIVE DOGGING ALL HIS MOVEMENTS,
MIS. PREFACE(82)	CALLED A PURE LOVE MAY EASILY BE MORE SELFISH AND	JEALOUS	THAN A CARNAL ONE. ANYHOW, IT IS PLAIN MATTER OF
BASH II,1, (113)	BY LOWERING MINE, AND OF HER DIGNITY TO BE SO	JEALOUS	THAT MY CHEEK HAS FLAMED EVEN AT THE THOUGHT OF SUCH

GENV PREFACE(21)	THE CAPITALIST WEST WAS MUCH TOO SHORTSIGHTED AND	JEALOUS	TO DO ANYTHING SO INTELLIGENT. IT SHOOK HANDS WITH
PHIL I (78)	ON ME COMPARED TO WHICH THE CLAIMS OF THE MOST	JEALOUS	WIFE WOULD HAVE BEEN TRIFLES? HAVE I A SINGLE WOMAN
GETT PREFACE(207)	OF MULTITUDES OF THE ELECTORATE NARROW, PERSONAL,	JEALOUS	, AND CORRUPT. UNDER SUCH CIRCUMSTANCES, IT IS NOT
OVER PREFACE(158)	PLUTOCRACY WITH ITS MEALS, A HUSBAND WHO IS NOT	JEALOUS	, AND REFRAINS FROM ASSAILING HIS RIVAL WITH HIS
GENV PREFACE(15)	TENTH RATE TRIBAL DEITY" OF THE MOST VINDICTIVE,	JEALOUS	, AND RUTHLESS PUGNACITY, EQUALLY WITH HIS
GETT PREFACE(236)	NOT JEALOUS BE URGED TO BEHAVE AS IF THEY WERE	JEALOUS	, AND TO ENTER UPON DUELS AND DIVORCE SUITS IN WHICH
PHIL III (134)	DO YOU REALLY BELIEVE THAT I AM NOT THE SHALLOW,	JEALOUS	, DEVILISH TEMPERED CREATURE THEY ALL PRETEND I AM?
BUOY IV (50)	MY DAUGHTER ON A YOUNG LUNATIC. /JUNIUS/ YOU ARE	JEALOUS	, EH? LET ME REMIND YOU THAT ALL PARENTS MUST SEE
PYGM II (229)	I LET A WOMAN MAKE FRIENDS WITH ME, SHE BECOMES	JEALOUS	, EXACTING, SUSPICIOUS, AND A DAMNED NUISANCE. I
ARMS II (36)	DEEP BITTERNESS) AND ONE, AT LEAST, IS A COWARD:	JEALOUS	, LIKE ALL COWARDS. (HE GOES TO THE TABLE). LOUKA.
GENV IV (114)	I WAS NOT AN AMIABLE LADY. I WAS A PERFECT FIEND,	JEALOUS	, QUARRELSOME, FULL OF IMAGINARY AILMENTS, AS TOUCHY
CLEO II SD(124)	BOY'S HAND TO ENCOURAGE HIM. CLEOPATRA, FURIOUSLY	JEALOUS	, RISES AND GLARES AT THEM. /CLEOPATRA/ (WITH
METH PREFACE(R39)	CHARACTER AND UNLIMITED POWER, SPITEFUL, CRUEL,	JEALOUS	, VINDICTIVE, AND PHYSICALLY VIOLENT. THE MOST
HART I (59)	OTHELLO. /MRS HUSHABYE/ DO YOU INDEED? HE WAS	JEALOUS	, WASNT HE? /ELLIE/ OH, NOT THAT. I THINK ALL THE
HART II (123)	MUCH FROM THIS JEALOUSY? /RANDALL/ JEALOUSY! I	JEALOUS	! MY DEAR FELLOW, HAVNT I TOLD YOU THAT THERE IS
MTH5 (247)	THAN SHE COULD EVER HAVE BEEN. /STREPHON/ PSHA!	JEALOUS	! /THE NEWLY BORN/ OH NO. I HAVE GROWN OUT OF THAT.
SUPR I (40)	NOT SO ABSURD AS TO BE JEALOUS OF TAVY. /TANNER/	JEALOUS	! WHY SHOULD I BE? BUT I DONT WONDER AT YOUR GRIP
		JEALOUSIES	
GETT (356)	YOU KNOW ALL ITS SCANDALS AND HYPOCRISIES, ITS	JEALOUSIES	AND SQUABBLES, ITS HUNDREDS OF DIVORCE CASES THAT
MRS PREFACE(172)	AS THE RICH MAN'S NOTION THAT THERE ARE NO SOCIAL	JEALOUSIES	OR SNOBBERIES AMONG THE VERY POOR. NO: HAD I
DOCT I SD(81)	CARES, THE PREOCCUPATIONS, THE RESPONSIBILITIES,	JEALOUSIES	, AND ANXIETIES OF PERSONAL BEAUTY. SHE HAS THE
		JEALOUSLY	
POSN PREFACE(381)	IMPORTANCE THAT IMMORALITY SHOULD BE PROTECTED	JEALOUSLY	AGAINST THE ATTACKS OF THOSE WHO HAVE NO STANDARD
NEVR I SD(208)	FOREFRONT OF HER OWN PERIOD (SAY 1860-80) IN A	JEALOUSLY	ASSERTIVE ATTITUDE OF CHARACTER AND INTELLECT, AND
POSN PREFACE(364)	RETINUE; AND AS A KING'S RETINUE HAS TO BE	JEALOUSLY	GUARDED TO AVOID CURTAILMENT OF THE ROYAL STATE NO
MTH4 II (190)	IN WHICH THE PRIVACY OF PRIVATE LIFE IS VERY	JEALOUSLY	GUARDED, AND IN WHICH NO ONE PRESUMES TO SPEAK TO
LADY SD(243)	SHE RISES ANGRILY TO HER FULL HEIGHT, AND LISTENS	JEALOUSLY	. /THE MAN/ (UNAWARE OF THE DARK LADY) THEN CEASE
ARMS II SD(28)	ROUND THE PROJECTIONS AT THE OUTER CORNERS; HIS	JEALOUSLY	OBSERVANT EYE; HIS NOSE, THIN, KEEN, AND
MILL PREFACE(118)	AND LAWS AGAINST ADULTERATION AND SWEATING WERE	JEALOUSLY	RESISTED AS INTERFERENCES WITH THE LIBERTY OF FREE
FABL PREFACE(84)	THE BUREAUCRACY BOTH IN NUMBERS AND POWER WHILST	JEALOUSLY	RESTRICTING OFFICIAL SALARIES MORE GRUDGINGLY WITH
NEVR I (223)	(POLITELY) DAMN THEM? EH? /CRAMPTON/ (	JEALOUSLY	) NO, SIR: THE CHILDREN ARE AS MUCH MINE AS HERS.
PHIL II (123)	(HE POINTS TO THE PAIR IN THE RECESS). /JULIA/ (	JEALOUSLY	) THAT WOMAN! /CHARTERIS/ MY YOUNG WOMAN,
SUPR III (102)	I THINK, ANA, YOU HAD BETTER STAY HERE. /ANA/ (	JEALOUSLY	) YOU DO NOT WANT ME TO GO WITH YOU. /DON JUAN/
CATH 4 (194)	(SHE STOOPS TO LOOSEN THE STRAPS). /CLAIRE/ (	JEALOUSLY	) YOU NEEDNT TROUBLE, THANK YOU. (SHE POUNCES ON
OVER PREFACE(156)	WHO KNOW MOST ABOUT IT KEEP THEIR KNOWLEDGE VERY	JEALOUSLY	TO THEMSELVES. WHICH IS HARDLY FAIR TO THE
PHIL II (127)	YOU UNDERSTAND? (JULIA, WATCHING THEM	JEALOUSLY	, LEAVES HER FATHER AND GETS CLOSE TO CHARTERIS.
CLEO III (162)	THE COMPANIONSHIP OF SOME MATRON. /CLEOPATRA/ (	JEALOUSLY	, TO CAESAR, WHO IS OBVIOUSLY PERPLEXED) ARNT YOU
		JEALOUSY	
AUGS (272)	INITIATIVE? I SAY NOTHING OF PROFESSIONAL	JEALOUSY	: IT EXISTS IN THE ARMY AS ELSEWHERE; BUT IT IS A
OVER PREFACE(157)	NEIGHBORS. THE SAME THING IS TRUE OF MATRIMONIAL	JEALOUSY	: THE MAN WHO DOES NOT AT LEAST PRETEND TO FEEL IT,
HART II (123)	BE CAREFUL. /HECTOR/ DO YOU SUFFER MUCH FROM THIS	JEALOUSY	? /RANDALL/ JEALOUSY! I JEALOUS! MY DEAR FELLOW,
PHIL I (78)	I ACCUSE YOU OF HABITUAL AND INTOLERABLE	JEALOUSY	AND ILL TEMPER; OF INSULTING ME ON IMAGINARY
GETT PREFACE(219)	AND CONTEMPT ARE NOT INCOMPATIBLE WITH IT; AND	JEALOUSY	AND MURDER ARE AS NEAR TO IT AS AFFECTIONATE
CATH 4 (193)	OF UNBUCKLING THE STRAPS AND TURNING SICK WITH	JEALOUSY	AS SHE GRASPS THE SITUATION) WAS THAT WHAT I
LADY PREFACE(207)	AND IT WAS SHE WHO SUGGESTED A SCENE OF	JEALOUSY	BETWEEN QUEEN ELIZABETH AND THE DARK LADY AT THE
HART II (123)	THAT SUPPLANTS US ALL IN THE LONG RUN. BESIDES,	JEALOUSY	DOES NOT BELONG TO YOUR EASY MAN-OF-THE-WORLD POSE,
PHIL III (139)	HAD HAD YOUR FLING, AND CALLED THE OBJECT OF YOUR	JEALOUSY	EVERY NAME YOU COULD LAY YOUR TONGUE TO, AND ABUSED
HART II (122)	I ASSURE YOU, MY DEAR FELLOW, I HAVNT AN ATOM OF	JEALOUSY	IN MY COMPOSITION; BUT SHE MAKES HERSELF THE TALK
HART II (122)	OLD CHAP. NOW, I ASSURE YOU I HAVE NOT AN ATOM OF	JEALOUSY	IN MY DISPOSITION-- /HECTOR/ THE QUESTION WOULD
BULL PREFACE(54)	THE ROOF, AND LEST THIS PRIVILEGE SHOULD EXCITE	JEALOUSY	IN OTHER HOUSEHOLDS, THREE OTHER DENSHAVIANS WERE
OVER PREFACE(157)	THE TWO PASSIONS IN PRACTICE. BESIDES,	JEALOUSY	IS AN INCULCATED PASSION, FORCED BY SOCIETY ON
HART I (59)	/ELLIE/ OH, NOT THAT. I THINK ALL THE PART ABOUT	JEALOUSY	IS HORRIBLE. BUT DONT YOU THINK IT MUST HAVE BEEN A
OVER PREFACE(157)	COMMITTED BY E. THE CONVENTION OF JEALOUSY, THAT	JEALOUSY	IS INDEPENDENT OF SEX IS SHEWN BY ITS INTENSITY IN
SHAK PREFACE(137)	THE SHALLOW MISTAKING OF IT FOR MERE PROFESSIONAL	JEALOUSY	. AYOT SAINT LAWRENCE, 1949.
MTH1 I (17)	NAME FOR THAT KNOWLEDGE? /THE SERPENT/ JEALOUSY.	JEALOUSY	. JEALOUSY. /ADAM/ A HIDEOUS WORD. /EVE/ (SHAKING
MTH1 I (17)	FIND A NAME FOR THAT KNOWLEDGE. /THE SERPENT/	JEALOUSY	. JEALOUSY. JEALOUSY. /ADAM/ A HIDEOUS WORD. /EVE/
GENV IV (107)	BE HERE? /WIDOW/ MY NAME IS REVENGE. MY NAME IS	JEALOUSY	. MY NAME IS THE UNWRITTEN LAW THAT IS NO LAW.
MTH1 I (17)	KNOWLEDGE? /THE SERPENT/ JEALOUSY. JEALOUSY.	JEALOUSY	. /ADAM/ A HIDEOUS WORD. /EVE/ (SHAKING HIM) ADAM:
OVER PREFACE(157)	WHEN THEY ARE COMMITTED BY E. THE CONVENTION OF	JEALOUSY	. THAT JEALOUSY IS INDEPENDENT OF SEX IS SHEWN BY
CAND III (142)	I WILL NOT SUFFER THE INTOLERABLE DEGRADATION OF	JEALOUSY	. WE HAVE AGREED-- HE AND I-- THAT YOU SHALL CHOOSE
HART PREFACE(32)	ALL THREE INHABITED BY COUPLES CONSUMED WITH	JEALOUSY	. WHEN THESE PEOPLE CAME HOME DRUNK AT NIGHT;
PPP (197)	WHAT DROVE YOU TO THIS WICKED DEED? /FITZ/	JEALOUSY	. YOU ADMIRED HIS CLOTHES: YOU DID NOT ADMIRE MINE.
LADY (245)	THAT YOU STRIKE BLINDLY AT YOUR SOVEREIGN IN YOUR	JEALOUSY	OF HIM. /THE DARK LADY/ MADAM: AS I LIVE AND HOPE
PRES (142)	THE DANGER TENFOLD, BECAUSE IT INCREASES GERMAN	JEALOUSY	OF OUR MILITARY SUPREMACY. /BALSQUITH/ AFTER ALL,
BULL PREFACE(57)	OFFICIAL LYNCH LAW, WERE MADE IMPOSSIBLE BY THE	JEALOUSY	OF THE " LOYAL" (TO ENGLAND) EGYPTIANS, WHO, IT
HART II (123)	WASTE YOUR JEALOUSY ON MY MOUSTACHE. NEVER WASTE	JEALOUSY	ON A REAL MAN: IT IS THE IMAGINARY HERO THAT
HART II (123)	ME SHE NEVER MADE SCENES. WELL, DONT WASTE YOUR	JEALOUSY	ON MY MOUSTACHE. NEVER WASTE JEALOUSY ON A REAL
SUPR PREFACE(R20)	WHO PURSUE WOMEN WITH APPEALS TO THEIR PITY OR	JEALOUSY	OR VANITY, OR CLING TO THEM IN A ROMANTICALLY
LIED (200)	/HE/ MR BOMPAS: I CAN MAKE ALLOWANCES FOR YOUR	JEALOUSY	-- /HER HUSBAND/ JEALOUSY! DO YOU SUPPOSE I'M
CATH 3 (183)	ALL THE MORNING. /CLAIRE/ (WITH A FLASH OF	JEALOUSY	) BY WHOM? /EDSTASTON/ BY EVERYBODY. BY THE MOST
CATH 4 (198)	FOR MY -- FOR MY -- /PATIOMKIN/ (IN A GROWL OF	JEALOUSY	) FOR YOUR LOVER? /CATHERINE/ (WITH AN INEFFABLE
SUPR IV (153)	(IMPULSIVELY) OR ON ME. /MALONE/ (WITH FIERCE	JEALOUSY	) WHO WANTS YOUR DURTY MONEY? WHO SHOULD HE DRAW
PRES (138)	WRECKING WAS GOT UP BY THE BOOKSELLERS. IT SHEWED	JEALOUSY	; AND THE PUBLIC FELT IT. /MITCHENER/ BUT I CRACKED
PHIL I (81)	I'LL READ; I'LL TRY TO THINK; I'LL CONQUER MY	JEALOUSY	; I'LL-- (SHE BREAKS DOWN, ROCKING HER HEAD
NEVR IV (302)	YEARS EXPERIENCE IS NOT ENOUGH. (IN A GUST OF	JEALOUSY	SHE THROWS HIM AWAY FROM HER; AND HE REELS BACK
OVER PREFACE(157)	ATTRACTION AND INTEREST WITH THE MURDEROUS	JEALOUSY	THAT FASTENS ON AND CLINGS TO ITS MATE (ESPECIALLY
DOCT V (176)	TO TELL ME THAT IT WAS TO GRATIFY A MISERABLE	JEALOUSY	THAT YOU DELIBERATELY-- OH! OH! YOU MURDERED HIM.
MIS. PREFACE(82)	NAIVELY SELFISH PEOPLE SOMETIMES TRY WITH FIERCE	JEALOUSY	TO PREVENT THEIR CHILDREN MARRYING. FAMILY
MIS. PREFACE(82)	FEELING FROM IT DOES NOT EXCLUDE THE BITTERNESS,	JEALOUSY	, AND DESPAIR AT LOSS WHICH CHARACTERIZE SEXUAL
JITT II (28)	AND DAUGHTER NEVER GOT ON VERY WELL TOGETHER--	JEALOUSY	, I SUPPOSE, AS USUAL-- BUT I THOUGHT THIS AWFUL
GETT PREFACE(233)	OF MATRIMONIAL RIGHTS, OR TO CONDESCEND TO	JEALOUSY	, SOMETIMES MAKE THE THREATENED HUSBAND OR WIFE
NEVR I (212)	OF PUNISHMENTS AND LIES, COERCION AND REBELLION,	JEALOUSY	, SUSPICION, RECRIMINATION-- OH! I CANNOT DESCRIBE
MTH5 (245)	NOW, /THE HE-ANCIENT/ GOOD. THAT HATRED IS CALLED	JEALOUSY	, THE WORST OF OUR CHILDISH COMPLAINTS. MARTELLUS,
GETT PREFACE(236)	SHOULD THEY BE ENCOURAGED TO PETITION IN A FIT OF	JEALOUSY	, WHICH IS CERTAINLY THE MOST DETESTABLE AND
3PLA PREFACE(R21)	WILL BECOME THE LAWS OF PERSONAL HONOR.	JEALOUSY	, WHICH IS EITHER AN EGOTISTICAL MEANNESS OR A
LIED (200)	MAKE ALLOWANCES FOR YOUR JEALOUSY-- /HER HUSBAND/	JEALOUSY	! DO YOU SUPPOSE I'M JEALOUS OF YOU? NO, NOR OF
HART II (123)	DO YOU SUFFER MUCH FROM THIS JEALOUSY? /RANDALL/	JEALOUSY	! I JEALOUS! MY DEAR FELLOW, HAVNT I TOLD YOU
		JEAN	
6CAL SD(97)	VICTIMS, PIERS DE WISSANT, JACQUES DE WISSANT,	JEAN	D'AIRE, AND GILLES D'OUDEBOLLE, KNEEL IN PAIRS BEHIND
		JEANNE	
JOAN PREFACE(51)	FACTS. IT GOES ALMOST WITHOUT SAYING THAT THE OLD	JEANNE	D'ARC MELODRAMAS, REDUCING EVERYTHING TO A CONFLICT
		JEER	
MILL IV (202)	WAIST). /EPIFANIA/ ALASTAIR: HOW CAN YOU	JEER	AT ME? IS IT JUST THAT I, BECAUSE I AM A
KING I (195)	I AM KING THERE SHALL BE NO SUCH NONSENSE. YOU	JEER	AT ME AND SAY THAT I AM THE PROTECTOR OF YOUR LIFE,
		JEERING	
DEVL III SD(78)	PRESS IN BEHIND, AND FOLLOW THEM UP THE MARKET,	JEERING	AT THEM; AND THE TOWN BAND, A VERY PRIMITIVE AFFAIR,
		JEFFERSON	
MIS. (131)	DEMOCRACY'S ALL RIGHT, YOU KNOW. READ MILL. READ	JEFFERSON	. /LORD SUMMERHAYS/ YES. DEMOCRACY READS WELL; BUT

		JEFFRIES	
KING I (195)	JAMIE. I AM HUNTING OUT HIS RECORD; AND YOUR MAN	JEFFRIES	WILL SEE TO IT THAT THE POOR DIVVLE SHALL HAVE NO
KING I (198)	FIRES OF SMITHFIELD AGAIN IF I WERE YOU. YOUR PET	JEFFRIES	WOULD DO IT FOR YOU AND ENJOY IT; BUT PROTESTANTS
		JEHOVAH	
SUPR HANDBOK(227)	USELESSNESS. STRAY SAYINGS. WE ARE TOLD THAT WHEN	JEHOVAH	CREATED THE WORLD HE SAW THAT IT WAS GOOD. WHAT
METH PREFACE(R44)	YET IT WAS SO. IN 1906 I MIGHT HAVE VITUPERATED	JEHOVAH	MORE HEARTILY THAN EVER SHELLEY DID WITHOUT
LION PREFACE(98)	OR THAT THE CHRIST IS MORE THAN THE BUDDHA, OR	JEHOVAH	MORE THAN KRISHNA, OR JESUS MORE OR LESS HUMAN THAN
FABL PREFACE(74)	JEHOVAH'S WITNESS WITH WILLIAM BLAKE, WHO CALLED	JEHOVAH	OLD NOBODADDY. NAPOLEON, WHO POINTED TO THE STARRY
FABL PREFACE(73)	ITS BELLY, THEN NOTHING IN THE BIBLE WAS TRUE. IF	JEHOVAH	WAS A BARBAROUS TRIBAL IDOL, IRRECONCILABLE WITH THE
		JEHOVAH'S	
FABL PREFACE(74)	CAN RECONCILE AND ASSOCIATE IN COMMON WORSHIP A	JEHOVAH'S	WITNESS WITH WILLIAM BLAKE, WHO CALLED JEHOVAH OLD
FABL PREFACE(76)	TO LIST THEM. THEY RANGE FROM PILLARS OF FIRE,	JEHOVAH'S	WITNESSES, PLYMOUTH BROTHERS, AND GLASITES, TO
		JEJUNE	
ARMS II SD(28)	HIS CONSEQUENT CYNICAL SCORN FOR HUMANITY; BY HIS	JEJUNE	CREDULITY AS TO THE ABSOLUTE VALIDITY OF HIS CONCEPTS
ROCK PREFACE(174)	THE EXTRAVAGANCES OF CENSORSHIP INDULGED IN BY	JEJUNE	GOVERNMENTS OF REVOLUTIONISTS, AND BY CHURCHES WHO
		JEJUNELY	
3PLA PREFACE(R10)	ROMANTICALLY; ALWAYS LADYLIKE AND GENTLEMANLIKE.	JEJUNELY	INSIPID. ALL THIS, TO THE STALLS, WHICH ARE PAID
		JELLY	
DOCT PREFACE(27)	TO CORNWALL, AND THE ORDERS GIVEN FOR CHAMPAGNE	JELLY	AND OLD PORT IN HOUSEHOLDS WHERE SUCH LUXURIES MUST
SIM II (60)	I HAVE BEEN ON THE POINT OF BEATING YOU TO A	JELLY	FOR EVER SO LONG PAST; BUT JUST AS MY FISTS WERE
GLIM (175)	OUT AND BE KILLED. COME OUT AND BE BEATEN TO A	JELLY	. COME OUT, DOG, SWINE, ANIMAL, MANGY HOUND, LOUSY-- (
APPL INTRLUD(254)	MAN YOU WOULD JUST DELIGHT IN BEATING HIM TO A	JELLY	. /MAGNUS/ A REAL MAN WOULD NEVER DO AS A KING. I AM
2TRU II (74)	AND I SHALL JUST KICK YOU AND BEAT YOU TO A	JELLY	. SHE RUSHES AT HIM. HE DODGES HER AND RUNS OFF PAST
DOCT I (101)	RECOMMEND HORSE EXERCISE OR MOTORING OR CHAMPAGNE	JELLY	OR COMPLETE CHANGE AND REST FOR SIX MONTHS. I MIGHT AS
DOCT PREFACE(69)	WATER TO TEETOTALLERS AND BRANDY OR CHAMPAGNE	JELLY	TO DRUNKARDS; BEEFSTEAKS AND STOUT IN ONE HOUSE, AND "
2TRU I SD(28)	IN SUBSTANCE IT SEEMS TO BE MADE OF A LUMINOUS	JELLY	WITH A VISIBLE SKELETON OF SHORT BLACK RODS. IT DROOPS
CURE (237)	FORCE ME TO CONFESS IT? -- I SHOULD BEAT IT TO A	JELLY	, AND THEN CAST MYSELF IN TRANSPORTS OF REMORSE ON ITS
GLIM (175)	VIOLENCE. I'LL RELIEVE IT NOW BY POUNDING YOU TO	JELLY	, ASSASSIN THAT YOU ARE. /SQUARCIO/ (SHRUGGING HIS
		JELLYFISH	
HART III (144)	BUT IN POLITICS, I ASSURE YOU, THEY ONLY RUN INTO	JELLYFISH	. NOTHING HAPPENS. /CAPTAIN SHOTOVER/ AT SEA
		JEMIMA	
APPL II (261)	FRIENDS AS MICK O'RAFFERTY. /MAGNUS/ THE RASCAL!	JEMIMA	: WE SHALL HAVE TO LIVE IN DUBLIN. THIS IS THE END OF
APPL INTRLUD(249)	THE QUEEN? WHAT IS TO BECOME OF MY POOR DEAR	JEMIMA	? /ORINTHIA/ OH, DROWN HER: SHOOT HER: TELL YOUR
APPL INTRLUD(254)	GIVE YOU YOUR TEA. /MAGNUS/ IMPOSSIBLE, BELOVED.	JEMIMA	DOES NOT LIKE TO BE KEPT WAITING. /ORINTHIA/ OH,
APPL INTRLUD(252)	THAT IT IS IMPOSSIBLE EVER TO GET TIRED OF THEM.	JEMIMA	HAS HER LIMITATIONS, AS YOU HAVE OBSERVED. AND I HAVE
APPL INTRLUD(249)	BUT I CANT IMAGINE WHAT I SHOULD DO WITHOUT	JEMIMA	. /ORINTHIA/ NOBODY ELSE CAN IMAGINE WHAT YOU DO WITH
APPL INTRLUD(254)	BOTHER JEMIMA! YOU SHALL NOT LEAVE ME TO GO TO	JEMIMA	(SHE PULLS HIM BACK SO VIGOROUSLY THAT HE FALLS INTO
APPL II (277)	SEVEN O'CLOCK. /MAGNUS/ (WORRIED) BUT REALLY,	JEMIMA	-- /THE QUEEN/ (GOING TO HIM AND TAKING HIS ARM)
APPL INTRLUD(249)	I AM AFRAID IT DOES NOT SETTLE THE DIFFICULTY.	JEMIMA	WOULD NOT THINK IT RIGHT TO KEEP UP HER PRESENT
APPL (170)	EDITH EVANS AS ORINTHIA, BARBARA EVEREST AS QUEEN	JEMIMA	, AND JAMES CAREW AS THE AMERICAN AMBASSADOR.
APPL INTRLUD(254)	LIKE TO BE KEPT WAITING. /ORINTHIA/ OH, BOTHER	JEMIMA	! YOU SHALL NOT LEAVE ME TO GO TO JEMIMA (SHE PULLS
		JEMIMA'S	
APPL INTRLUD(250)	QUITE DIFFERENT. THE SMALLEST DEROGATION TO	JEMIMA'S	DIGNITY WOULD HIT ME LIKE THE LASH OF A WHIP ACROSS
		JEMMY	
HART II (109)	YOU HAVE YOUR BURGLING KIT. /THE BURGLAR/ WHATS A	JEMMY	AND A CENTREBIT AND AN ACETYLENE WELDING PLANT AND A
MIS. PREFACE(28)	AS THE MOTIVE OF A BURGLAR FOR CONCEALING HIS	JEMMY	FROM A POLICEMAN. BUT THE OTHER GREAT SUPPRESSION IN
		JENKINS	
OVER (181)	I WAS BORN IN GIBRALTAR. MY FATHER WAS CAPTAIN	JENKINS	. IN THE ARTILLERY. /JUNO/ (ARDENTLY) IT IS CLIMATE
		JENKINSES	
OVER (183)	NO USE, MR JUNO: I'M HOPELESSLY RESPECTABLE: THE	JENKINSES	ALWAYS WERE. DONT YOU REALIZE THAT UNLESS MOST
		JENNER	
FABL PREFACE(74)	ANY COMPETENT STATISTICIAN, AND WAS PICKED UP BY	JENNER	FROM A DAIRY FARMER AND HIS MILKMAIDS. CATHOLICISM
DOCT PREFACE(53)	VANISHED SINCE THE INTRODUCTION OF VACCINATION.	JENNER	HIMSELF ALLUDED TO THIS IMAGINARY PHENOMENON BEFORE
DOCT PREFACE(52)	BECAUSE THE PUBLIC WOULD HAVE IT SO IN SPITE OF	JENNER	. ALL THE GROSSEST LIES AND SUPERSTITIONS WHICH HAVE
DOCT PREFACE(52)	IT IN A FORM WHICH HE HIMSELF REPUDIATED.	JENNER	WAS NOT A MAN OF SCIENCE; BUT HE WAS NOT A FOOL; AND
DOCT PREFACE(53)	TO SEE THE DISEASE MADE HARMLESS. IT WAS NOT	JENNER	WHO SET PEOPLE DECLARING THAT SMALLPOX, IF NOT
METH PREFACE(R80)	BACTERIOLOGIST READS THE PAMPHLETS OF	JENNER	, AND DISCOVERS THAT THEY MIGHT HAVE BEEN WRITTEN BY
FABL PREFACE(89)	FAULTY CHAIR LEGS AND LEAKING PIPES. HE MAY, LIKE	JENNER	, BE SO IGNORANT OF THE RUDIMENTS OF STATISTICS AS TO
DOCT PREFACE(53)	CONSIDERED THEMSELVES AS SERIOUSLY ILL. NEITHER	JENNER	, NOR ANY OTHER DOCTOR EVER, AS FAR AS I KNOW,
FABL PREFACE(90)	ST JAMES. MRS EDDY, A MUCH SOUNDER HYGIENIST THAN	JENNER	, PASTEUR, LISTER, AND THEIR DISCIPLES, HAD TO CALL
		JENNERIAN	
DOCT PREFACE(52)	TERMS; AND TO THIS DAY THE LAW WHICH PRESCRIBES	JENNERIAN	VACCINATION IS CARRIED OUT WITH AN ANTI-JENNERIAN
		JENNER'S	
DOCT PREFACE(52)	IRRESISTIBLE FAITH, SWEEPING THE INVENTION OUT OF	JENNER'S	HANDS AND ESTABLISHING IT IN A FORM WHICH HE
		JENNIFER	
DOCT I (112)	EYES) THATS A WONDERFUL DRAWING. WHY IS IT CALLED	JENNIFER	? /MRS DUBEDAT/ MY NAME IS JENNIFER. /RIDGEON/ A
DOCT IV SD(160)	B.B. TAKES THE EASEL CHAIR AND PLACES IT FOR	JENNIFER	AT DUBEDAT'S SIDE, NEXT THE DAIS, FROM WHICH THE
DOCT V SD(172)	WITH HIS SURVEY, HE DISAPPEARS BEHIND THE SCREEN.	JENNIFER	COMES BACK WITH HER BOOK. A LOOK ROUND SATISFIES
DOCT III (149)	THE MAN WHO COULD PUT ME OUT OF COUNTENANCE. (	JENNIFER	COMES IN). AH, MRS DUBEDAT! AND HOW ARE WE TODAY?
DOCT III (149)	I'M A MAN AND CAN TAKE CARE OF MYSELF. BUT WHEN	JENNIFER	COMES IN, PLEASE REMEMBER THAT SHE'S A LADY, AND
DOCT III (134)	LUNGS BUT BILLS. IT DOESNT MATTER ABOUT ME; BUT	JENNIFER	HAS ACTUALLY TO ECONOMIZE IN THE MATTER OF FOOD.
DOCT III (134)	/RIDGEON/ NO. /LOUIS/ THATS ALL RIGHT. POOR	JENNIFER	HAS BEEN LOOKING FORWARD TO YOUR VISIT MORE THAN
DOCT III (139)	SOFA). /LOUIS/ JUST SO. AND YET YOU BELIEVE THAT	JENNIFER	IS A BAD LOT BECAUSE YOU THINK I TOLD YOU SO.
DOCT III (139)	IN HER CHARACTER. BUT YOU ARE ALL MORAL MEN; AND	JENNIFER	IS ONLY AN ARTIST'S WIFE-- PROBABLY A MODEL; AND
DOCT III (149)	HELP IT. BEFORE YOU GO, SIR PATRICK, LET ME FETCH	JENNIFER	. I KNOW SHE'D LIKE TO SEE YOU, IF YOU DONT MIND. (
DOCT IV (165)	IN HEAVEN, IMMORTAL IN THE HEART OF MY BEAUTIFUL	JENNIFER	. I'M NOT AFRAID, AND NOT ASHAMED. (REFLECTIVELY,
DOCT I (112)	NAMES WITH A CERTAIN PLEASURE IN THEM) GUINEVERE.	JENNIFER	. (LOOKING AGAIN AT THE DRAWING) YES: IT'S REALLY
DOCT II (117)	/MRS DUBEDAT/ OH, ON GRAND OCCASIONS I AM	JENNIFER	. /B.B./ YOU ARE A BACHELOR: YOU DO NOT UNDERSTAND
DOCT III (133)	LIVING HERE. BUT WE PIG ALONG SOMEHOW, THANKS TO	JENNIFER	. /MRS DUBEDAT/ NOW I'LL RUN AWAY. PERHAPS LATER
DOCT IV (161)	YOU MAY STAY HERE AS LONG AS YOU LIKE. /LOUIS/	JENNIFER	. /MRS DUBEDAT/ YES, MY DARLING. /LOUIS/ IS THE
DOCT IV (163)	PATRICK/ YES, YES. THANK YOU. ALL RIGHT. /LOUIS/	JENNIFER	. /MRS DUBEDAT/ YES, DEAR. /LOUIS/ (WITH A STRANGE
DOCT IV (161)	DONT SET HIM COUGHING. /LOUIS/ (AFTER DRINKING)	JENNIFER	. /MRS DUBEDAT/ YES, DEAR. /LOUIS/ IF THERES ONE
DOCT IV (164)	ART IS TOO LARGE FOR THAT. YOU WILL MARRY AGAIN,	JENNIFER	. /MRS DUBEDAT/ OH, HOW CAN YOU, LOUIS? /LOUIS/ (
DOCT IV (164)	COME I HAVE NO FEAR; AND I'M PERFECTLY HAPPY.	JENNIFER	. /MRS DUBEDAT/ YES, DEAR? /LOUIS/ I'LL TELL YOU A
DOCT I (112)	IS IT CALLED JENNIFER? /MRS DUBEDAT/ MY NAME IS	JENNIFER	. /RIDGEON/ A STRANGE NAME. /MRS DUBEDAT/ NOT IN
DOCT IV (162)	OF IMMORTALITY I WANT. YOU CAN MAKE THAT FOR ME,	JENNIFER	. THERE ARE LOTS OF THINGS YOU DONT UNDERSTAND THAT
DOCT III (150)	SO FOR TODAY, GOODBYE. (HE GOES OUT, LEAVING	JENNIFER	MUCH PUZZLED BY HIS UNEXPECTED WITHDRAWAL AND
DOCT II SD(117)	HE IS NOT IN THE LEAST SHY. HE IS YOUNGER THAN	JENNIFER	; BUT HE PATRONIZES HER AS A MATTER OF COURSE. THE
DOCT IV SD(161)	ARTIST. B.B. THEN RETURNS TO DUBEDAT'S LEFT.	JENNIFER	SITS. WALPOLE SITS DOWN ON THE EDGE OF THE DAIS.
DOCT III (139)	ONLY AN IMMORAL ARTIST; BUT IF YOUD TOLD ME THAT	JENNIFER	WASNT MARRIED, I'D HAVE HAD THE GENTLEMANLY FEELING

Work	Location	Preceding context	Keyword	Following context
DOCT III	(141)	PUT MINNIE IN PRISON. PUT ME IN PRISON. KILL	JENNIFER	WITH THE DISGRACE OF IT ALL. AND THEN, WHEN YOUVE
DOCT III	(135)	RUBBISH OF THAT SORT. THEN YOU CAN TAKE IT TO	JENNIFER	, AND HINT THAT IF THE CHEQUE ISNT TAKEN UP AT ONCE
DOCT V	SD(171)	NEAR THE CORNERS RIGHT AND LEFT OF THE ENTRANCE.	JENNIFER	, BEAUTIFULLY DRESSED AND APPARENTLY VERY HAPPY AND
DOCT III	(140)	BACK TO SERVICE, AND I BACK TO MY STUDIO AND MY	JENNIFER	, BOTH THE BETTER AND HAPPIER FOR OUR HOLIDAY.
DOCT IV	(165)	GLEE) I HEARD THAT, RIDGEON. THAT WAS GOOD.	JENNIFER	, DEAR: BE KIND TO RIDGEON ALWAYS; BECAUSE HE WAS
DOCT IV	(163)	IN THE BURNING BUSH. WHENEVER YOU SEE THE FLAME,	JENNIFER	, THAT WILL BE ME. PROMISE ME THAT I SHALL BE
DOCT IV	SD(157)	RIDGEON HAS COOKED OUR YOUNG FRIEND'S GOOSE.	JENNIFER	, WORRIED AND DISTRESSED, BUT ALWAYS GENTLE, COMES
DOCT III	(139)	PRAY? /LOUIS/ WELL, YOU SET UP TO APPRECIATE	JENNIFER	, YOU KNOW. AND YOU DESPISE ME, DONT YOU?
			JENNIFER'S	
DOCT III	(138)	LINES. /LOUIS/ (COOLLY) INDEED? HAVE YOU SEEN	JENNIFER'S	? /RIDGEON/ (RISING IN IRREPRESSIBLE RAGE) DO
DOCT IV	(164)	ARNT YOU? I'M TOO WEAK TO SEE ANYTHING BUT	JENNIFER'S	BOSOM, THAT PROMISES REST. /RIDGEON/ WE ARE ALL
DOCT III	(135)	I'LL POSTDATE THE CHEQUE NEXT OCTOBER. IN OCTOBER	JENNIFER'S	DIVIDENDS COME IN. WELL, YOU PRESENT THE CHEQUE
DOCT III	(139)	PEOPLE LIKE YOU. I ONLY ASKED YOU HAD YOU SEEN	JENNIFER'S	MARRIAGE LINES; AND YOU CONCLUDED STRAIGHT AWAY
			JENNY	
BARB II	(304)	THE CHEQUE TO SHEW AT THE MEETING, WONT YOU?	JENNY	: GO IN AND FETCH A PEN AND INK. (JENNY RUNS TO THE
BARB II	(303)	OF LABOR, MRS BAINES. /MRS BAINES/ BARBARA:	JENNY	: I HAVE GOOD NEWS: MOST WONDERFUL NEWS. (JENNY RUNS
MRS I	(196)	AWAY 50 POUNDS: NOT HE. HE JUST WROTE: " DEAR	JENNY	: PUBLISH AND BE DAMNED! YOURS AFFECTIONATELY,
BARB II	(308)	BE ALL RIGHT TOMORROW. WE'LL NEVER LOSE YOU. NOW	JENNY	: STEP OUT WITH THE OLD FLAG. BLOOD AND FIRE! (SHE
BARB II	(297)	STRIGHT. /BARBARA/ SO IT WILL, SNOBBY. HOW MUCH,	JENNY	? /JENNY/ FOUR AND TENPENCE, MAJOR. /BARBARA/ OH
BARB II	(307)	CUSINS RECKLESSLY TOSSES THE TAMBOURINE BACK TO	JENNY	AND GOES TO THE GATE) I CANT COME. /JENNY/ NOT COME!
BARB II	SD(296)	FROM THE SHELTER AND GO TO THE DRUM, ON WHICH	JENNY	BEGINS TO COUNT THE MONEY. /UNDERSHAFT/ (REPLYING TO
BARB II	SD(285)	THE SHELTER) RUMMY: THE MAJOR SAYS YOU MUST COME.	JENNY	COMES TO BARBARA, PURPOSELY KEEPING ON THE SIDE NEXT
POSN	PREFACE(424)	TAKEN OUT OF THE HANDS OF THE PUBLIC. AT PRESENT	JENNY	GEDDES MAY THROW HER STOOL AT THE HEAD OF A PLAYWRIGHT
BARB II	(304)	DO NOT DISTURB MISS HILL: I HAVE A FOUNTAIN PEN (	JENNY	HALTS. HE SITS AT THE TABLE AND WRITES THE CHEQUE.
BARB II	(288)	I SUPPOSE. BUT WHY DID HE LET YOU HIT POOR LITTLE	JENNY	HILL? THAT WASNT VERY MANLY OF HIM, WAS IT? /BILL/ (
BARB III	(313)	MEETING. MRS BAINES ALMOST DIED OF EMOTION.	JENNY	HILL SIMPLY GIBBERED WITH HYSTERIA. THE PRINCE OF
BARB II	(282)	(RECOLLECTING) OH, I KNOW: YOURE THE MAN THAT	JENNY	HILL WAS PRAYING FOR INSIDE JUST NOW. (SHE ENTERS HIS
BARB II	(283)	AS (WRITING) THE MAN WHO-- STRUCK-- POOR LITTLE	JENNY	HILL-- IN THE MOUTH. /BILL/ (RISING THREATENINGLY)
BARB II	SD(276)	TO DRINK IF I CAN GET FUN ENOUGH ANY OTHER WAY.	JENNY	HILL, A PALE, OVERWROUGHT, PRETTY SALVATION LASS OF
BARB III	(320)	THATS EVERYBODY'S BIRTHRIGHT. LOOK AT POOR LITTLE	JENNY	HILL, THE SALVATION LASSIE! SHE WOULD THINK YOU WERE
BARB II	SD(296)	SNOBBY PRICE, BEAMING SANCTIMONIOUSLY, AND	JENNY	HILL, WITH A TAMBOURINE FULL OF COPPERS, COME FROM THE
BARB II	(276)	HURRY UP WITH THE FOOD, MISS: E'S FAIR DONE. (	JENNY	HURRIES INTO THE SHELTER). ERE, BUCK UP, DADDY! SHE'S
BARB II	(282)	ENTERS HIS NAME IN HER NOTE BOOK). /BILL/ OO'S	JENNY	ILL? AND WOT CALL AS SHE TO PRY FOR ME? /BARBARA/ I
BARB II	(288)	WIV IT, AW TELL YOU. CHACK IT. AW'M SICK O YOUR	JENNY	ILL AND ER SILLY LITTLE FICE. /BARBARA/ THEN WHY DO
BARB II	(309)	TOOK IT SAMMUN ELSE: EZ. WERES IT GORN? BLY ME IF	JENNY	ILL DIDNT TIKE IT ARTER ALL! /RUMMY/ (SCREAMING AT
BARB II	(289)	TO SPIT IN TODGER FAIRMAWL'S EYE. AW BESHED	JENNY	ILL'S FICE; AN NAR AW'LL GIT ME AOWN FICE BESHED AND
JOAN	1 (66)	NAME? /JOAN/ (CHATTILY) THEY ALWAYS CALL ME	JENNY	IN LORRAINE. HERE IN FRANCE I AM JOAN. THE SOLDIERS
BARB II	SD(277)	AT THE YARD GATE AND LOOKS MALEVOLENTLY AT	JENNY	. /JENNY/ THAT MAKES ME SO HAPPY. WHEN YOU SAY THAT, I
BARB II	(276)	MANY A ONE FROM YOU, GET A BIT O YOUR OWN BACK. (	JENNY	RETURNS WITH THE USUAL MEAL). THERE YOU ARE, BROTHER.
BARB II	(303)	JENNY: I HAVE GOOD NEWS: MOST WONDERFUL NEWS. (	JENNY	RUNS TO HER). MY PRAYERS HAVE BEEN ANSWERED. I TOLD
BARB II	(304)	YOU? JENNY: GO IN AND FETCH A PEN AND INK. (	JENNY	RUNS TO THE SHELTER DOOR). /UNDERSHAFT/ DO NOT DISTURB
BARB II	(278)	YOU WITH ONE FINGER ARTER, YOU STAWVED CUR. (TO	JENNY	) NAH ARE YOU GOWIN TO FETCH AHT MOG EBBIJEM; OR EM AW
BARB II	(301)	A BABY. (SHE LEAVES THEM TOGETHER AND CHATS WITH	JENNY	). /MRS BAINES/ HAVE YOU BEEN SHEWN OVER THE SHELTER,
BARB II	(306)	ME JUST AN INSTANT. (HE RUSHES INTO THE SHELTER.	JENNY	TAKES HER TAMBOURINE FROM THE DRUM HEAD). /MRS BAINES/
BARB II	(279)	WANTS ONE LAWK IT TO CAM AND INTERFERE WITH ME. (	JENNY	, CRYING WITH PAIN, GOES INTO THE SHED. HE GOES TO THE
BARB II	(303)	HAVE BEEN ANSWERED. I TOLD YOU THEY WOULD,	JENNY	, DIDNT I? /JENNY/ YES, YES. /BARBARA/ (MOVING
BARB II	(277)	FED MY BODY AND SAVED MY SOUL, HAVNT YOU? (	JENNY	, TOUCHED, KISSES HER). SIT DOWN AND REST A BIT: YOU
BARB II	(285)	FROM HIM OR BORE MALICE. /BARBARA/ POOR LITTLE	JENNY	! ARE YOU TIRED? (LOOKING AT THE WOUNDED CHEEK)
BARB II	(284)	NOT. (HE RESUMES HIS SEAT). /BARBARA/ (CALLING)	JENNY	! /JENNY/ (APPEARING AT THE SHELTER DOOR WITH A
			JENNY'S	
BARB II	(288)	MAN WITH A HEART WOULDNT HAVE BASHED POOR LITTLE	JENNY'S	FACE, WOULD HE? /BILL/ (ALMOST CRYING) AW, WILL
BARB II	(307)	/CUSINS/ (SNATCHES THE TAMBOURINE OUT OF	JENNY'S	HAND AND MUTELY OFFERS IT TO BARBARA). /BARBARA/ (
BARB II	(276)	AND HURRYING OFFICIOUSLY TO TAKE THE OLD MAN OFF	JENNY'S	HANDS) POOR OLD MAN! CHEER UP, BROTHER: YOULL FIND
BARB II	(299)	NEARLY. WELL, HAS TODGER PAID YOU OUT FOR POOR	JENNY'S	JAW? /BILL/ NAO E AINT. /BARBARA/ I THOUGHT YOUR
			JENSEITS	
BARB	PREFACE(211)	SAW WHAT I HAD BEEN READING: NAMELY, NIETZSCHE'S	JENSEITS	VON GUT UND BOSE, WHICH I PROTEST I HAD NEVER SEEN,
			JEPHTHAH	
BARB	PREFACE(228)	THE ORIGIN OF SPECIES, AND THAT THE GOD TO WHOM	JEPHTHAH	SACRIFICED HIS DAUGHTER IS ANY LESS OBVIOUSLY A
			JEREMIAH	
LADY	PREFACE(231)	AND LORDS AND GENTLEMEN! WOULD EVEN JOHN BALL OR	JEREMIAH	COMPLAIN THAT THEY ARE FLATTERED? SURELY A MORE
SIM	PREFACE(8)	ALLOWS THE SMALLEST AUTHORITY TO JESUS OR PETER,	JEREMIAH	OR MICAH THE MORASTHITE. THEY CALL THEIR ECONOMIC
SIM	PREFACE(3)	EVEN IF THE TWO ARE PESSIMISTS WHO AGREE WITH	JEREMIAH	THAT THE HEART OF MAN IS DECEITFUL ABOVE ALL THINGS
			JEREMIAH'S	
LION	PREFACE(20)	HOSEA'S " OUT OF EGYPT HAVE I CALLED MY SON," AND	JEREMIAH'S	RACHEL WEEPING FOR HER CHILDREN: IN FACT, HE SAYS
FABL	PREFACE(97)	THE SUBJECT. MARX'S INVECTIVE, THOUGH IT RIVALLED	JEREMIAH'S	, WAS PALE BESIDE THE FIERCE DIATRIBES OF RUSKIN,
			JEREMY	
KING I	(205)	BEFORE. AGAIN YOU UNSETTLE MY MIND. THERE IS ONE	JEREMY	COLLIER WHO SWEARS HE WILL WRITE SUCH A BOOK ON THE
			JERICHO	
2TRU III	(87)	HUNDRED YEARS, HAS CRUMBLED LIKE THE WALLS OF	JERICHO	BEFORE THE CRITICISM OF EINSTEIN. NEWTON'S UNIVERSE
ROCK II	(275)	HE SAY TO THAT? /ALOYSIA/ HE TOLD ME TO GO TO	JERICHO	, BUT I SHALL TEACH HIM MANNERS. /SIR ARTHUR/ DO,
KING I	(198)	FACE OF GOD. /CHARLES/ OH, GO TO SCOTLAND: GO TO	JERICHO	, YOU SICKEN ME. GO. /JAMES/ CHARLES! WE MUST NOT
			JERICHOWISE	
JOAN	PREFACE(21)	DO. SHE DID NOT EXPECT BESIEGED CITIES TO FALL	JERICHOWISE	AT THE SOUND OF HER TRUMPET, BUT, LIKE
			JERK	
APPL I	(203)	/BOANERGES/ (INDICATING THE SECRETARIES WITH A	JERK	OF HIS HEAD) WHAT ABOUT THESE TWO? ARE THEY TO
CAND I	(95)	HAND). /MARCHBANKS/ (TAKING IT WITH A NERVOUS	JERK	) NOT AT ALL. /BURGESS/ BYE, BYE, CANDY. I'LL LOOK IN
MTH5	(234)	GIVE THEM A CLIP BELOW THE KNEE, AND THEY WILL	JERK	THEIR FOOT FORWARD. GIVE THEM A CLIP IN THEIR APPETITES
2TRU I	SD(37)	FROM THE BED, LETTING THE PATIENT DOWN WITH A	JERK	, AND ARRANGES THEM COMFORTABLY IN THE BEDSIDE CHAIR.
CATH	2,SD(181)	DOORS. HE RETURNS EACH OBEISANCE WITH A NERVOUS	JERK	, AND TURNS AWAY FROM IT, ONLY TO FIND ANOTHER COURTIER
			JERKED	
DOCT I	(104)	ANTI-TETANUS SERUM. BUT THE MISSIONARY	JERKED	ALL MY THINGS OFF THE TABLE IN ONE OF HIS PAROXYSMS;
			JERKED-OFF	
POSN	(463)	BE BAD MEN OR YOU WOULDNT BE IN THIS JUMPED-UP,	JERKED-OFF	, HOSPITAL-TURNED-OUT CAMP THAT CALLS ITSELF A
BARB II	(276)	NO GOOD JAWRIN ABOUT IT. YOURE ONY A JUMPED-UP,	JERKED-OFF	, ORSPITTLE-TURNED-OUT INCURABLE OF AN OLE WORKIN
			JERKILY	
SIM I	(43)	HOW DO YOU DO, MR HAMMINGTAP? /THE CLERGYMAN/ (	JERKILY	NERVOUS) VERY PLEASED. (THEY SHAKE HANDS). SIR
BARB I	(264)	HAND WITH PATERNAL KINDNESS TO LOMAX). /LOMAX/ (	JERKILY	SHAKING HIS HAND) AHDEDOO. /UNDERSHAFT/ I CAN SEE
			JERKING	
GETT	(346)	GENERAL/ MARRIED! WHO GAVE YOU AWAY? /SYKES/ (	JERKING	HIS HEAD TOWARDS THE TOWER) THIS GENTLEMAN DID. (
CLEO IV	(176)	I HAVE BROUGHT HIM WITH ME. HE IS WAITING THERE (	JERKING	HIS THUMB OVER HIS SHOULDER) UNDER GUARD. /CAESAR/

JERKS

LION PROLOG (109)	THE THORN. THE LION, WITH AN ANGRY YELL OF PAIN,	JERKS	BACK HIS PAW SO ABRUPTLY THAT ANDROCLES IS THROWN ON

JEROME

LION PREFACE(96)	HIS HISTORY OF THE REFORMATION, OR THAT ST	JEROME	WROTE THE PASSAGE ABOUT THE THREE WITNESSES IN THE

JERRY

JOAN PREFACE(29)	NO DISTINCTION BEFORE CHRIST BETWEEN TOMMY AND	JERRY	AND PITOU THE POILU. WELL MIGHT EDITH HAVE WISHED THAT
MIS. (125)	ARE TOO SMALL, LIKE BUNNY, OR TOO SILLY, LIKE	JERRY	. OF COURSE ONE CAN GET INTO A STATE ABOUT ANY MAN:
MIS. (124)	REASON I NEVER SAID A WORD WHEN YOU JILTED POOR	JERRY	MACKINTOSH. /HYPATIA/ (EXCUSING HERSELF) I REALLY
MIS. (124)	WITH FATHER, IVE GOT ACCUSTOMED TO CLEVERNESS.	JERRY	WOULD DRIVE ME MAD: YOU KNOW VERY WELL HES A FOOL:
MIS. (124)	HERSELF) I REALLY COULDNT STICK IT OUT WITH	JERRY	, MOTHER. I KNOW YOU LIKED HIM; AND NOBODY CAN DENY

JERRY-BUILDING

LION PREFACE(91)	PETERBOROUGH CATHEDRAL WAS FOUND TO BE FLAGRANT	JERRY-BUILDING	AS A CRITICISM OF THE DEAN'S SERMONS. FOR
LION PREFACE(91)	THOUGH THE DISCOVERY THAT THERE IS A GOOD DEAL OF	JERRY-BUILDING	IN THE BIBLE IS INTERESTING IN ITS WAY,

JERSEY

CAPT II (251)	IT ON THE TABLE, STANDING AT HIS EASE IN HIS BLUE	JERSEY	). /SIR HOWARD/ (AFTER A MOMENTARY FLUSH OF ANGER,
APPL II (263)	OF WHICH FROM THE COUNTY OF CAMBRIDGE TO NEW	JERSEY	WAS MY DEAR OLD FATHER'S FIRST BIG PROFESSIONAL JOB.
CAPT III (292)	(HE PULLS OFF THE SHIRT AND STANDS IN HIS BLUE	JERSEY	, WITH HIS HAIR RUFFLED. HE PASSES HIS HAND THROUGH

JERSEYS

CAPT II SD(242)	AT THE THROAT FOR GREATER COOLNESS. SOME HAVE	JERSEYS	. ALL WEAR BOOTS AND BELTS, AND HAVE GUNS READY TO

JERUSALEM

LION PREFACE(31)	CUNNING AND PENETRATION WHICH JESUS DISPLAYED IN	JERUSALEM	AFTER HIS DELUSION HAD TAKEN COMPLETE HOLD OF HIM.
LION PREFACE(29)	IN THIS NEW FRAME OF MIND HE AT LAST ENTERS	JERUSALEM	AMID GREAT POPULAR CURIOSITY; DRIVES THE
LION PREFACE(53)	THE COMMON STOCK. ONE CAN HEAR THE PHARISEES OF	JERUSALEM	AND CHORAZIN AND BETHSAIDA SAYING, " MY GOOD
LION PREFACE(24)	RISING FLOOD OF CHRISTIANITY AFTER THE CAPTURE OF	JERUSALEM	AND THE DESTRUCTION OF THE TEMPLE, SET UP WHAT WAS
LION PREFACE(29)	DURING THE LIFETIME OF PERSONS THEN PRESENT.	JERUSALEM	AND THE MYSTICAL SACRIFICE. IN THIS NEW FRAME OF
ROCK PREFACE(158)	AND IN THE ABSENCE OF ANY DEFENCE, THE	JERUSALEM	COMMUNITY AND THE ROMAN GOVERNMENT DECIDED TO
LION PREFACE(52)	THE PART OF THE SEPARATE UNITS OF THE POPULATION.	JERUSALEM	COULD NOT HAVE DONE WHAT EVEN A VILLAGE COMMUNITY
BULL II (102)	JERUSALEM TO WALK THE OXFORD FEELING OFF ME. FROM	JERUSALEM	I CAME BACK TO PATMOS, AND SPENT SIX MONTHS AT THE
GENV III (82)	RACE WHOSE BRAINS WILL GUIDE THE WORLD TO THE NEW	JERUSALEM	IS THE RACE THAT PRODUCED KARL MARX, WHO PRODUCED
LION PREFACE(38)	PREACHER WHO AT THE END OF HIS LIFE CAME TO	JERUSALEM	. JOHN DESCRIBES A PREACHER WHO SPENT PRACTICALLY
GENV III (68)	BEEN BORN THERE. YOU OUGHT TO HAVE BEEN BORN IN	JERUSALEM	. /THE JEW/ AND YOU, MY FRIEND, OUGHT NEVER TO
LION PREFACE(35)	HE MAKES THEM A SPEECH BEGINNING " DAUGHTERS OF	JERUSALEM	," SLIGHT AS THESE CHANGES MAY SEEM, THEY MAKE A
LION PREFACE(37)	PILATE SENDS JESUS TO HEROD, WHO HAPPENS TO BE IN	JERUSALEM	JUST THEN, BECAUSE HEROD HAD EXPRESSED SOME
LION PREFACE(53)	SATISFACTIONS. AND WHAT CANNOT BE DONE IN	JERUSALEM	OR JUAN FERNANDEZ CANNOT BE DONE IN LONDON, NEW
LION PREFACE(38)	VIEW OF THE KINGDOM AS A LOCALITY AS DEFINITE AS	JERUSALEM	OR MADAGASCAR. JOHN. A NEW STORY AND A NEW
APPL II (267)	PEOPLE CAME FROM SCOTLAND OR IRELAND OR WALES OR	JERUSALEM	OR SOMEWHERE, SIR. IT IS NO USE APPEALING TO
LION PREFACE(28)	ANNOUNCING THAT HE WILL BE KILLED WHEN HE GOES TO	JERUSALEM	; FOR IF HE IS REALLY THE CHRIST, IT IS A
LION PREFACE(30)	IN IT, WHEREUPON JESUS ROSE AND RETURNED FROM	JERUSALEM	TO GALILEE AND RESUMED HIS PREACHING WITH HIS
BULL II (102)	THE SEA. AFTER A YEAR OF OXFORD I HAD TO WALK TO	JERUSALEM	TO WALK THE OXFORD FEELING OFF ME. FROM JERUSALEM
JOAN 4 (103)	CAMEL DRIVER DROVE CHRIST AND HIS CHURCH OUT OF	JERUSALEM	, AND RAVAGED HIS WAY WEST LIKE A WILD BEAST UNTIL
LION PREFACE(32)	THE NEWS THAT MANY WOMEN HAD COME WITH JESUS TO	JERUSALEM	, INCLUDING MARY MAGDALENE, OUT OF WHOM HE HAD
MTH4 I (155)	LOST PRESTIGE, THE IRISH CLAIMED THE CITY OF	JERUSALEM	, ON THE GROUND THAT THEY WERE THE LOST TRIBES OF
FABL I (104)	HIGH EXPLOSIVE CHEAPLY HE MADE HIM A PRESENT OF	JERUSALEM	, WHICH DIDNT BELONG TO US. /YOUNG MAN/ (
ROCK I (215)	AGAIN REACHED THE 1913 LEVEL. /OXFORD YOUTH/ HOLY	JERUSALEM	! SPANISH ONIONS! COME ON, BROLLY. (HE GOES

JESCHU

LION PREFACE(24)	AND TO THEIR LIST OF THE ACCURSED ADDED ONE	JESCHU	, A BASTARD MAGICIAN, WHOSE COMIC ROGUERIES BROUGHT

JESSICA'S

DOCT (2)	I AM GRATEFUL TO HESBA STRETTON, THE AUTHORESS OF	JESSICA'S	FIRST PRAYER, FOR PERMISSION TO CALL MY PLAY BY.

JESSIE

POSN (436)	TO HANG. /EMMA/ (A SNEAK WHO SIDES WITH BABSY OR	JESSIE	, ACCORDING TO THE FORTUNE OF WAR) WELL, I MUST SAY
POSN SD(450)	THE CROWD COMES IN AND FILLS THE COURT. BABSY,	JESSIE	, AND EMMA COME TO THE SHERIFF'S RIGHT; HANNAH AND
POSN SD(438)	PLEASE, PLEASE. THEY RISE RELUCTANTLY. HANNAH,	JESSIE	, AND LOTTIE RETREAT TO THE SHERIFF'S BENCH,

JEST

CAND III (142)	FOOLISH BOY, BECAUSE I SAID SOMETHING LIKE IT IN	JEST	? /MORELL/ THAT FOOLISH BOY CAN SPEAK WITH THE
JOAN 1 (57)	I CANNOT LAY EGGS. /ROBERT/ (SARCASTIC) HA! YOU	JEST	ABOUT IT. /STEWARD/ NO, SIR, GOD KNOWS. WE ALL HAVE TO
SUPR I (40)	YOU ARE INCORRIGIBLE, JACK. BUT YOU SHOULD NOT	JEST	ABOUT OUR AFFECTION FOR ONE ANOTHER. NOBODY COULD
DEST (188)	HIMSELF) OH, NO, NO, NO. IT IS NOT SAFE TO	JEST	ABOUT SUCH THINGS. I CANNOT HAVE IT IN MY HOUSE,
PHIL II (119)	EXCUSE ME: THIS IS A SUBJECT I DO NOT CARE TO	JEST	ABOUT. (HE WALKS AWAY FROM CHARTERIS, AND SITS DOWN IN
CAPT III (285)	FOUND HIM OUT. /DRINKWATER/ RAWT, GAVNER. THETS	JEST	AH IT WORS. THE KEPN-- /REDBROOK/ (AGAIN SUPPRESSING
CAPT II (262)	RECOVERS HIMSELF QUICKLY). EAHS THE BLOOMIN SHIKE	JEST	APPEAHD ON THE ORAWZN WIV ABAHT FIFTY MEN. THYLL BE EAH
MIS. PREFACE(58)	THE WHOLE CONCEPTION OF CHILDREN'S RIGHTS WITH A	JEST	AT THE EXPENSE OF BACHELORS' AND OLD MAIDS' CHILDREN.
GLIM (187)	HAS GOT THAT IN HER NET TOO. SHE HAS TURNED YOUR	JEST	INTO EARNEST. /SANDRO/ IT IS INDEED TRUE, SIR. THAT
BULL IV (181)	THE LAST TIME) EVERY DREAM IS A PROPHECY: EVERY	JEST	IS AN EARNEST IN THE WOMB OF TIME. /BROADBENT/ (
ARMS II (38)	OF HERSELF) FORGIVE ME, DEAR: IT WAS ONLY A	JEST	. I AM SO HAPPY TODAY. HE GOES QUICKLY TO HER, AND
NEVR IV (303)	/GLORIA/ NO. I WILL HAVE NO SUCH THING, EVEN IN	JEST	. WHEN I NEED A BLESSING, I SHALL ASK MY MOTHER'S.
DEVL II (32)	OH, DONT SAY THAT: DONT SAY THAT, TONY, EVEN IN	JEST	. YOU DONT KNOW WHAT A HORRIBLE FEELING IT GIVES ME.
PHIL III (145)	USE HE CAN FIND FOR SACRED THINGS IS TO MAKE A	JEST	OF THEM. THATS THE NEW ORDER, THANK HEAVEN, WE BELONG
PHIL III (145)	AND SYLVIA) NOW YOU REALLY SHOULDNT MAKE A	JEST	OF THESE THINGS: UPON MY LIFE AND SOUL YOU SHOULDNT,
6CAL (94)	FAULT: IT IS YOURS. /THE KING/ WOULD YOU MAKE A	JEST	OF THIS? IF IT IS NOT THEIR FAULT IT SHALL BE THEIR
DEVL I (9)	THEIR OWN LIKINGS AND DISLIKINGS, AND MAKE A	JEST	OF US AND OF THEIR MAKER'S WORD? /ANDERSON/ WELL,
LADY (245)	DISCOURSE WITH HIM. HE HATH EVER SOME LEWD	JEST	ON HIS TONGUE. YOU HEAR HOW HE USETH ME! CALLING ME
PPP (205)	CHACK IT. (HE TRIPS THE DOCTOR UP. BOTH FALL).	JEST	OWLD THIS LEOONATIC, WILL YOU, MISTER HORFICER? /THE
CAPT I (223)	BE BLAOWED! -- AWSKINK YR PAWDN, GAVNER. NAH,	JEST	TO SHAOW YOU AH LITTLE THET THERE STRITEFORARD MAN Y'
OVER PREFACE(160)	FOR THE TRUTH. WE ARE PERMITTED TO DISCUSS IN	JEST	WHAT WE MAY NOT DISCUSS IN EARNEST. A SERIOUS COMEDY
NEVR IV (301)	WAS IN DEADLY EARNEST WITH ME WHEN I WAS IN	JEST	WITH HER. WHEN THE GREAT MOMENT CAME, WHO WAS
WIDO I (9)	TO THE GATE) THERE IS MANY A TRUE WORD SPOKEN IN	JEST	, MR COKANE. /COKANE/ (ACCOMPANYING HIM) HOW TRUE!
DEVL III (52)	TO TOUCH HIS LIPS WITH IT) DONT (MEANING " DONT	JEST	"). NO: BY TELLING THE COURT WHO YOU REALLY ARE.

JESTER

3PLA PREFACE(R21)	A TRUE MIRROR AS THE WORK OF A FOOL, MADMAN, OR	JESTER	. NAY, I BELIEVE WE SHOULD, BY LAMARCKIAN ADAPTATION,
UNPL PREFACE(R9)	THAT THE CRITIC ADDS THE PRIVILEGES OF THE COURT	JESTER	TO THOSE OF THE CONFESSOR. GARRICK, HAD HE CALLED DR

JESTICE

PPP (203)	LANDLORD/ (APPEALING TO THE HEAVENS) OW, IS THIS	JESTICE	! AH COULD AW TELL E WIZ GOWIN TE EAT MOY CEILIN..

JESTING

CAND II (118)	WHAT SOUL-DESTROYING CYNICISM! ARE YOU	JESTING	? OR-- CAN IT BE? -- ARE YOU JEALOUS? /CANDIDA/ (
APPL I (217)	A MOMENT? /NICOBAR/ THIS IS NOT A SUBJECT FOR	JESTING	-- /MAGNUS/ (INTERRUPTING HIM QUICKLY) I AM NOT
OVER PREFACE(160)	BY SUCH AFFAIRS FOR CENTURIES, NOT ONLY IN THE	JESTING	VEIN OF RESTORATION COMEDY AND PALAIS ROYAL FARCE,
LADY PREFACE(216)	IN WHICH INSOLENCE, DERISION, PROFLIGACY, OBSCENE	JESTING	, DEBT CONTRACTING, AND ROWDY MISCHIEVOUSNESS, GIVE
APPL I (217)	-- /MAGNUS/ (INTERRUPTING HIM QUICKLY) I AM NOT	JESTING	, MR NICOBAR. BUT I AM CERTAINLY TRYING TO DISCUSS

JESTINGLY

DEST (193)	AN ITALIAN GENERAL. (HE PAUSES, AND ADDS, HALF	JESTINGLY	, HALF MOODILY) AT ALL EVENTS, YOU HAVE BEATEN ME;

JESTS

DEVL III (61) DREAD AND HORROR DEEPENING AT EVERY ONE OF THESE JESTS AND COMPLIMENTS) HOW CAN YOU? /RICHARD/ YOU PROMISED
3PLA PREFACE(R39) MY STAGE TRICKS AND SUSPENSES AND THRILLS AND JESTS ARE THE ONES IN VOGUE WHEN I WAS A BOY, BY WHICH TIME
MIS. PREFACE(81) ENFANT TERRIBLE (A TRAGIC TERM IN SPITE OF THE JESTS CONNECTED WITH IT); WHILST THE PARENT CAN SUFFER FROM
SUPR PREFACE(R16) VIEW IS HEAPING RESPONSIBILITY ON HIM. HIS FORMER JESTS HE HAS HAD TO TAKE AS SERIOUSLY AS I HAVE HAD TO TAKE
POSN PREFACE(395) THE CRITICS IN LONDON BY THE LIBERTINAGE OF ITS JESTS IS PLAYED TO THE RESPECTABLE DRESS CIRCLE OF
MIS. PREFACE(30) BY OTHER CHILDREN IN GUILTY SECRETS AND UNCLEAN JESTS . AND THAT SETTLES THE QUESTION FOR ALL SENSIBLE
SUPR PREFACE(R16) AS SERIOUSLY AS I HAVE HAD TO TAKE SOME OF THE JESTS OF MR W.S. GILBERT. HIS SCEPTICISM, ONCE HIS LEAST
POSN PREFACE(395) DRESS CIRCLE OF NORTHAMPTON WITH THESE SAME JESTS SLURRED OVER SO AS TO BE IMPERCEPTIBLE BY EVEN THE

JESUISM

LION PREFACE(76) (AS ROBERT OWEN CALLED IT) OF COMMUNISM AND JESUISM . JUST AS IN OUR OWN TIME KARL MARX, NOT CONTENT TO

JESUIST

LION PREFACE(82) IT PRACTICABLE BY DESTROYING THE SPECIFICALLY JESUIST SIDE OF IT. HE WOULD HAVE BEEN QUITE IN HIS PLACE IN
LION PREFACE(95) OR LAO TSE, AND MAY THEREFORE CALL YOURSELF A JESUIST , OR EVEN A CHRISTIAN, IF YOU HOLD, AS THE STRICTEST

JESUIT

BULL PREFACE(38) WAS A ROMAN CATHOLIC LAYMAN, EDUCATED AT A JESUIT COLLEGE, IS THE CONCLUSIVE REPLY TO THE SHALLOW
BARB III (342) LOMAX: YOU ARE A FOOL. ADOLPHUS CUSINS: YOU ARE A JESUIT . STEPHEN: YOU ARE A PRIG. BARBARA: YOU ARE A
GENV III (79) THE SELFLESS DEVOTION TO DIVINE PURPOSES OF THE JESUIT MISSIONARIES, AND THE READINESS OF THEM ALL TO FACE

JESUITS

BULL PREFACE(71) AN UNDERGROUND CONSPIRACY ENTITLED BY THEM " THE JESUITS ." IT IS A PITY THEY DID NOT BEGIN THEIR POLITICAL
METH PREFACE(R14) IT SOMETIMES DOES. VOLTAIRE WAS A PUPIL OF THE JESUITS ; SAMUEL BUTLER WAS THE PUPIL OF A HOPELESSLY
JOAN PREFACE(35) PRIESTLY LAZINESS AND LAODICEANISM, THAT OF THE JESUITS WITH PRIESTLY APATHY AND IGNORANCE AND INDISCIPLINE.
GENV I (32) DISLIKE ONEANOTHER. SO ARE THE CATHOLICS, THE JESUITS , THE FREEMASONS. YOU TELL ME THAT THE INHABITANTS

JESU'S

GENV IV (109) MOTHER TAUGHT YOU TO SAY " ALL HAIL THE POWER OF JESU'S NAME." /THE BETROTHED/ " LET ANGELS PROSTRATE FALL."

JESUS

LION PREFACE(48) THERE WILL BE ANYTHING LEFT OF THE MISSION OF JESUS : WHETHER, IN SHORT, WE MAY NOT THROW THE GOSPELS INTO
LION PREFACE(85) VIRGIN THE MOTHER OF GOD OR ONLY THE MOTHER OF JESUS ? ARIAN SCHISMS AND NESTORIAN SCHISMS AROSE ON THESE
LION PREFACE(86) THEY WOULD HAVE BEEN REPUDIATED WITH HORROR BY JESUS ? OUR OWN NOTION THAT THE MASSACRE OF ST
LION PREFACE(6) MADMAN, WAS GREATER THAN HIS JUDGES. WAS JESUS A COWARD? I KNOW QUITE WELL THAT THIS IMPRESSION OF
LION PREFACE(7) DO NOT WISH TO SHARE HIS DEFEAT AND DISGRACE. WAS JESUS A MARTYR? IT IS IMPORTANT THEREFORE THAT WE SHOULD
LION PREFACE(8) BLASPHEMY. THE FACT THAT THE BLASPHEMY WAS TO JESUS A SIMPLE STATEMENT OF FACT, AND THAT IT HAS SINCE BEEN
LION PREFACE(32) IN ANY CIVILIZED COMMUNITY; BUT IT DOES NOT PLACE JESUS ABOVE CONFUCIUS OR PLATO, NOT TO MENTION MORE MODERN
LION PREFACE(26) BE PROVED TODAY THAT NOT ONE OF THE MIRACLES OF JESUS ACTUALLY OCCURRED, THAT PROOF WOULD NOT INVALIDATE A
LION PREFACE(52) TO US. IF WE ASK OUR STOCKBROKER TO ACT SIMPLY AS JESUS ADVISED HIS DISCIPLES TO ACT, HE WILL REPLY, VERY
LION PREFACE(37) TO DESTROY LIVES BUT TO SAVE THEM. THE BIAS OF JESUS AGAINST LAWYERS IS EMPHASIZED, AND ALSO HIS RESOLUTION
LION PREFACE(72) REMEDY. WE MUST, I THINK, REGARD THE PROTEST OF JESUS AGAINST MARRIAGE AND FAMILY TIES AS THE CLAIM OF A
LION PREFACE(74) OF STEPHEN. TAKE, FOR EXAMPLE, THE MIRACLES. OF JESUS ALONE OF ALL THE CHRISTIAN MIRACLE WORKERS THERE IS NO
LION PREFACE(84) EFFECT OF DROPPING THE PECULIAR DOCTRINES OF JESUS AND GOING BACK TO JOHN THE BAPTIST, WAS TO MAKE IT
LION PREFACE(22) THAN THEMSELVES, ARE DISAPPOINTED AT FINDING THAT JESUS AND HIS TWELVE FRIENDS DO NOT FAST; AND JESUS TELLS
LION PREFACE(36) EVENT WITH WHICH LUKE BEGINS HIS STORY. WHILST JESUS AND JOHN ARE STILL IN THEIR MOTHERS' WOMBS, JOHN LEAPS
LION PREFACE(6) ON THE SUBJECT, A GREAT DEAL OF HEARTY DISLIKE OF JESUS AND OF CONTEMPT FOR HIS FAILURE TO SAVE HIMSELF AND
HART PREFACE(19) PERSON WHO FOUND THE CHANGE FROM THE WISDOM OF JESUS AND ST FRANCIS TO THE MORALS OF RICHARD III AND THE
FABL PREFACE(90) LABORATORY VIVISECTOR AND QUACK IMMUNIZER ABOVE JESUS AND ST JAMES. MRS EDDY, A MUCH SOUNDER HYGIENIST THAN
BARB PREFACE(226) BEAUMARCHAIS, SWIFT, GOETHE, IBSEN, TOLSTOY, JESUS AND THE PROPHETS ALL THROWN IN (AS INDEED IN SOME
LION PREFACE(72) RECONCILE OUR SOULS TO ITS SLAVERY. THE UNMARRIED JESUS AND THE UNMARRIED BEETHOVEN, THE UNMARRIED JOAN OF
LION PREFACE(37) HIS LOGIC IS WEAK; FOR SOME OF THE SAYINGS OF JESUS ARE PIECED TOGETHER WRONGLY, AS ANYONE WHO HAS READ
ROCK PREFACE(175) PERSECUTION MADE NO VALID DEFENCE. SOCRATES AND JESUS ARE THE MOST TALKED OF IN CHRISTIAN COUNTRIES.
LION PREFACE(38) MADE IN THE TEMPLE AT A MUCH EARLIER PERIOD. JESUS ARGUES MUCH MORE; COMPLAINS A GOOD DEAL OF THE
LION PREFACE(56) AS, " TAKING THE MONEY VALUE OF THE VIRTUES OF JESUS AS 100, AND OF JUDAS ISCARIOT AS ZERO, GIVE THE
LION PREFACE(27) HE DRAWS THE LINE AT THE GENTILE, AND REPRESENTS JESUS AS A BIGOTED JEW WHO REGARDS HIS MISSION AS ADDRESSED
LION PREFACE(6) SECULARIST IS OFTEN SO DETERMINED TO REGARD JESUS AS A MAN LIKE HIMSELF AND NOTHING MORE, THAT HE SLIPS
LION PREFACE(68) FACTS ARE FLATLY CONTRARY. THE MERE THOUGHT OF JESUS AS A MARRIED MAN IS FELT TO BE BLASPHEMOUS BY THE MOST
LION PREFACE(32) HIS ADULT BAPTISM BY JOHN. HE APPARENTLY REGARDS JESUS AS A NATIVE OF NAZARETH, AS JOHN DOES, AND NOT OF
LION PREFACE(49) OF THIS IS THAT IF YOU SPEAK OR WRITE OF JESUS AS A REAL LIVE PERSON, OR EVEN AS A STILL ACTIVE GOD,
LION PREFACE(8) IN A VERY DANGEROUS WAY. THAT WAS WHY HE TREATED JESUS AS AN IMPOSTOR AND A BLASPHEMER WHERE WE SHOULD HAVE
LION PREFACE(61) THAT HE WAS A FIRST-RATE POLITICAL ECONOMIST. JESUS AS BIOLOGIST. HE WAS ALSO, AS WE NOW SEE, A FIRST-RATE
LION PREFACE(61) PEOPLE BETWEEN WHOM THERE IS EQUALITY OF INCOME. JESUS AS ECONOMIST. IT SEEMS THEREFORE THAT WE MUST BEGIN BY
LION PREFACE(94) THERE IS THE SAME EVIDENCE FOR THE EXISTENCE OF JESUS AS FOR THAT OF ANY OTHER PERSON OF HIS TIME; AND THE
LION PREFACE(95) THE CHILD IS BUILT LIKE GLADSTONE. HE WILL ACCEPT JESUS AS HIS SAVIOR, AND PETER AND JOHN THE BAPTIST AS THE
LION PREFACE(19) MAKES IT CLEAR THAT HE IS TELLING THE STORY OF JESUS AS HOLINSHED TOLD THE STORY OF MACBETH, EXCEPT THAT,
ROCK PREFACE(179) THAT I MUST ENDEAVOR TO DRAMATIZE THE TRIAL OF JESUS AS IT MIGHT HAVE PROCEEDED HAD IT TAKEN PLACE BEFORE
LION PREFACE(74) DID NOT CONTAIN A RAY OF THAT LIGHT WHICH REVEALS JESUS AS ONE OF THE REDEEMERS OF MEN FROM FOLLY AND ERROR.
LION PREFACE(42) CHRIST HIMSELF: IN FACT, HE ACTUALLY REPRESENTS JESUS AS PROMISING THIS EXPLICITLY, AND IS FINALLY LED INTO
ROCK PREFACE(181) JOHN, THE ONLY ONE OF THE FOUR WHICH REPRESENTS JESUS AS SAYING ANYTHING MORE THAN ANY CRAZY PERSON MIGHT IN
LION PREFACE(23) BY BAPTISM INSTEAD OF CIRCUMCISION, AND ACCEPTING JESUS AS THE MESSIAH, AND HIS TEACHINGS AS OF HIGHER
LION PREFACE(88) THAN HUXLEY DID; AND YOU MAY UTTERLY REPUDIATE JESUS AS THE SAVIOR AND YET CITE HIM AS A HISTORICAL WITNESS
LION PREFACE(27) OF HIS HERO WITH HIS OWN. ALTHOUGH HE DESCRIBES JESUS AS TOLERANT EVEN TO CARELESSNESS, HE DRAWS THE LINE AT
FABL PREFACE(78) OF SUCCESS FOR ANY ENTERPRISE, MY AGE THAT OF JESUS AT HIS DEATH, AND THE ENTIRE PRESS AT MY COMMAND,
LION PREFACE(39) AND THAT HE ACTUALLY LEANED ON THE BOSOM OF JESUS AT THE LAST SUPPER AND ASKED IN A WHISPER WHICH OF
LION PREFACE(6) FOR BELIEVING THAT JESUS EVER EXISTED) THAT JESUS AT THE TIME OF HIS DEATH BELIEVED HIMSELF TO BE THE
LION PREFACE(31) CLASSES, HE MENTIONS LATER ON THAT WHEN JESUS ATTEMPTED TO PREACH IN HIS OWN COUNTRY, AND HAD NO
LION PREFACE(19) WITH THE CLUES, THEY ARE FAIRLY PLAIN SAILING. JESUS BECOMES AN INTELLIGIBLE AND CONSISTENT PERSON. HIS
LION PREFACE(19) IN THE BELIEF THAT THE STRANGE DEMEANOR OF JESUS BEFORE PILATE WAS MEANT AS AN EXAMPLE OF NORMAL HUMAN
LION PREFACE(36) HOPE OF A MESSIAH BEGIN TO STIR AGAIN; AND AS JESUS BEGINS AS A DISCIPLE OF JOHN, AND IS BAPTIZED BY HIM,
LION PREFACE(31) BEGINS HIS STORY IN SUCH A WAY AS TO SUGGEST THAT JESUS BELONGED TO THE PRIVILEGED CLASSES, HE MENTIONS LATER
LION PREFACE(42) THE POINT IS OBSCURED BY THE DISTINCTION MADE BY JESUS BETWEEN HIMSELF AND OTHER MEN. HE SAYS, IN EFFECT, "
LION PREFACE(19) AFFIRMED THE MIRACULOUS CONCEPTION NOT ONLY OF JESUS BUT OF HIS MOTHER. WITH NO MORE SCHOLARLY EQUIPMENT
LION PREFACE(84) AND A DOZEN PETERS. ONE FEELS AT LAST THAT WHEN JESUS CALLED PETER FROM HIS BOAT, HE SPOILED AN HONEST
LION PREFACE(68) ROUND HIM. WE ARE NOT SURPRISED THAT WHEN JESUS CALLED THE SONS OF ZEBEDEE TO FOLLOW HIM, HE DID NOT
LION PREFACE(76) DECLARED, STRUCK HIM BLIND FOR DAYS. HE HEARD JESUS CALLING TO HIM FROM THE CLOUDS, " WHY PERSECUTE ME? "
LION PREFACE(18) KNEW NOTHING OF THE DIVINE BIRTH, AND TAUGHT THAT JESUS CAME INTO THE WORLD AT HIS BIRTH AS THE SON OF JOSEPH,
GENV IV (109) CAN YOU MAKE BETTER MEN AND WOMEN OF THEM AS JESUS CAN? CAN-- /BATTLER/ I HAVE MADE BETTER MEN AND WOMEN
LION PREFACE(15) MUST BE CONNED AND DIGESTED BEFORE THE CAREER OF JESUS CAN BE FULLY UNDERSTOOD. PEOPLE WHO CAN READ LONG
GENV IV (109) UNIFY YOUR COUNTRYMEN IN LOVE OF YOURSELF. BUT JESUS CAN UNITE THE WHOLE WORLD IN LOVE OF HIM. HE WILL LIVE
LION PREFACE(102) RESTORE SOME SENSE OF PROPORTION IN THE MATTER. JESUS CERTAINLY DID NOT CONSIDER THE OVERTHROW OF THE ROMAN
LION PREFACE(76) HIS FANCIES: THE FANCY FOR ATTACHING THE NAME OF JESUS CHRIST TO THE GREAT IDEA WHICH FLASHED UPON HIM ON THE
ROCK PREFACE(157) AND PROBABLY ENJOY THE JOB. LEADING CASE OF JESUS CHRIST. I DISLIKE CRUELTY, EVEN CRUELTY TO OTHER
ROCK PREFACE(157) TAKE THE CASE OF THE EXTERMINATION OF JESUS CHRIST. NO DOUBT THERE WAS A STRONG CASE FOR IT. JESUS
LION PREFACE(25) " AND THE WHOLE WORLD WILL FALL AT THE FEET OF JESUS CHRIST." HE POINTS OUT THAT MIRACLES OFFERED AS
LION PREFACE(36) THE ADVENT OF THE CHRIST. IN MATTHEW AND MARK, JESUS COMES INTO A NORMAL PHILISTINE WORLD LIKE OUR OWN OF
LION PREFACE(66) I PRESUME, IS THE FORM IN WHICH THE TEACHING OF JESUS COULD HAVE BEEN PUT INTO PRACTICE. JESUS ON MARRIAGE
LION PREFACE(79) IS NOT ONE OF THE SAYINGS IN THE GOSPELS. IF JESUS COULD HAVE BEEN CONSULTED ON BUNYAN'S ALLEGORY AS TO
LION PREFACE(4) SOCIETY; BUT I MUST STILL INSIST THAT IF JESUS COULD HAVE WORKED OUT THE PRACTICAL PROBLEMS OF A
LION PREFACE(30) A PRISONER NAMED BARABBAS INSTEAD, AND ON HAVING JESUS CRUCIFIED. MATTHEW GIVES NO CLUE TO THE POPULARITY OF
LION PREFACE(33) EYES. HE REPRESENTS THE FATHER OF THE BOY WHOM JESUS CURED OF EPILEPSY AFTER THE TRANSFIGURATION AS A
LION PREFACE(27) FOR THE MIRACLES! MATTHEW TELLS US FURTHER, THAT JESUS DECLARED THAT HIS DOCTRINES WOULD BE ATTACKED BY
LION PREFACE(42) OR LUKE, THAT QUESTION IS, WHY ON EARTH DID NOT JESUS DEFEND HIMSELF, AND MAKE THE PEOPLE RESCUE HIM FROM
LION PREFACE(39) OR EXCITING ANY COMMENT, IT ALSO IMPLIES THAT JESUS DELIBERATELY BEWITCHED JUDAS IN ORDER TO BRING ABOUT
LION PREFACE(86) ALL THESE PERVERSIONS OF THE DOCTRINE OF JESUS DERIVED THEIR MORAL FORCE FROM HIS CREDIT, AND SO HAD

LION PREFACE(68)	CELIBACY WAS A WORSE FAILURE THAN MARRIAGE. WHY	JESUS	DID NOT MARRY. TO ALL APPEARANCE THE PROBLEM OPPRESSES
LION PREFACE(58)	AN INDEPENDENT INCOME. WE ALL KNOW AS WELL AS	JESUS	DID THAT IF WE HAVE TO TAKE THOUGHT FOR THE MORROW AS
LION PREFACE(4)	GREAT DEAL MORE ABOUT ECONOMICS AND POLITICS THAN	JESUS	DID, AND CAN DO THINGS HE COULD NOT DO. I AM BY ALL
LION PREFACE(7)	THAT WE SHOULD CLEAR OUR MINDS OF THE NOTION THAT	JESUS	DIED, AS SOME OF US ARE IN THE HABIT OF DECLARING, FOR
LION PREFACE(31)	THE ARGUMENTATIVE CUNNING AND PENETRATION WHICH	JESUS	DISPLAYED IN JERUSALEM AFTER HIS DELUSION HAD TAKEN
GENV IV (109)	IN THE FACES OF THEIR OPPRESSORS. /DEACONESS/	JESUS	DOES NOT SPIT IN PEOPLE'S FACES. IF YOUR PEOPLE ARE
LION PREFACE(21)	OF THE XVI CENTURY. JESUS JOINS THE BAPTISTS.	JESUS	ENTERED AS A MAN OF THIRTY (LUKE SAYS) INTO THE
LION PREFACE(20)	ALL THE MALE CHILDREN TO BE SLAUGHTERED; AND	JESUS	ESCAPES BY THE FLIGHT OF HIS PARENTS INTO EGYPT,
LION PREFACE(44)	I CANNOT TELL WHY MEN WHO WILL NOT BELIEVE THAT	JESUS	EVER EXISTED YET BELIEVE FIRMLY THAT SHAKESPEAR WAS
LION PREFACE(6)	(THE CHIEF AUTHORITIES FOR BELIEVING THAT	JESUS	EVER EXISTED) THAT JESUS AT THE TIME OF HIS DEATH
LION PREFACE(47)	QUITE ARBITRARY ONES. ST JOHN TELLS US THAT WHEN	JESUS	EXPLICITLY CLAIMED DIVINE HONORS BY THE SACRAMENT OF
LION PREFACE(81)	IS NOW EASY TO UNDERSTAND WHY THE CHRISTIANITY OF	JESUS	FAILED COMPLETELY TO ESTABLISH ITSELF POLITICALLY AND
ROCK PREFACE(158)	MATTERS WORSE BY TRYING TO APPEASE THEM BY HAVING	JESUS	FLOGGED. THE SOLDIERS, TOO, HAD TO HAVE THEIR BIT OF
LION PREFACE(36)	THIS KIND OF AMENITY IS THE REPROACH ADDRESSED TO	JESUS	FOR SITTING DOWN TO TABLE WITHOUT WASHING HIS HANDS;
LION PREFACE(25)	CREDENTIALS OF DIVINE MISSION. ROUSSEAU SHEWS, AS	JESUS	FORESAW, THAT THE MIRACLES ARE THE MAIN OBSTACLE TO
LION PREFACE(89)	NOT, THAT WHILST MANY OF US CANNOT BELIEVE THAT	JESUS	GOT HAS CURIOUS GRIP OF OUR SOULS BY MERE
LION PREFACE(50)	OF OUR OWN NUMBERS, HAVE ALWAYS KNOWN THAT	JESUS	HAD A REAL MESSAGE, AND HAVE FELT THE FASCINATION OF
ROCK PREFACE(159)	SOCRATES, ONE IS FORCED TO THE CONCLUSION THAT IF	JESUS	HAD BEEN HUMANELY EXTERMINATED HIS MEMORY WOULD HAVE
LION PREFACE(8)	OF CANTERBURY AND THE HEAD MASTER OF ETON. IF	JESUS	HAD BEEN INDICTED IN A MODERN COURT, HE WOULD HAVE
LION PREFACE(58)	THEY WERE HANDSOMELY PENSIONED OFF AS INCURABLES.	JESUS	HAD MORE SENSE THAN TO PROPOSE ANYTHING OF THE SORT.
LION PREFACE(5)	IS INDEPENDENT OF ANY INDIVIDUAL PREACHER. IF	JESUS	HAD NEVER EXISTED (AND THAT HE EVER EXISTED IN ANY
FABL PREFACE(64)	TALES EVER EXISTED? HE PLEADED THAT	JESUS	HAD TAUGHT BY PARABLES; BUT THIS MADE MATTERS WORSE;
LION PREFACE(76)	RECONSTRUCTED THE OLD SALVATIONISM FROM WHICH	JESUS	HAD VAINLY TRIED TO REDEEM HIM, AND PRODUCED A
LION PREFACE(43)	THAT ALL THESE INQUIRIES ARE IDLE, BECAUSE IF	JESUS	HAD WISHED TO ESCAPE, HE COULD HAVE SAVED HIMSELF ALL
LION PREFACE(95)	HOW, IN A WORLD SATURATED WITH THIS TRADITION,	JESUS	HAS BEEN LARGELY ACCEPTED AS THE LONG EXPECTED AND
LION PREFACE(3)	THE CRUCIFIXION; AND THE SPECIFIC DOCTRINE OF	JESUS	HAS NOT IN ALL THAT TIME BEEN PUT INTO POLITICAL OR
LION PREFACE(59)	BETWEEN CAPTAINS AND CABIN BOYS. WHAT WOULD	JESUS	HAVE SAID? PRESUMABLY HE WOULD HAVE SAID THAT IF YOUR
LION PREFACE(74)	IT WAS TOO EARLY IN THE DAY TO GET DRUNK; BUT OF	JESUS	HE HAD NOTHING TO SAY EXCEPT THAT HE WAS THE CHRIST
LION PREF,FN(43)	NOT TO SAVE HIMSELF " LIKE ONE OF THE PRINCES."	JESUS	HIMSELF HAD REFERRED TO THAT PSALM (LXXXII) IN WHICH
LION PREFACE(98)	AND SAINTS DECLARE, SOME OF THEM IN THE NAME OF	JESUS	HIMSELF, THAT THIS WORLD IS A VALE OF TEARS, AND THAT
LION PREFACE(68)	CALL THEIR FATHER, AND THAT THE DISCIPLES, LIKE	JESUS	HIMSELF, WERE ALL MEN WITHOUT FAMILY ENTANGLEMENTS. IT
LION PREFACE(52)	POLITICAL MEASURES. EVEN IN SYRIA IN THE TIME OF	JESUS	HIS TEACHINGS COULD NOT POSSIBLY HAVE BEEN REALIZED BY
LION PREFACE(36)	HE REALLY THE CHRIST. THIS IS NOTEWORTHY BECAUSE	JESUS	IMMEDIATELY GIVES THEM A DELIBERATE EXHIBITION OF
LION PREFACE(33)	MURDER." JOSEPH OF ARIMATHEA, WHO BURIED	JESUS	IN HIS OWN TOMB, AND WHO IS DESCRIBED BY MATTHEW AS A
LION PREFACE(30)	JOSEPH, A RICH MAN OF ARIMATHEA, WHO HAD BURIED	JESUS	IN IT, WHEREUPON JESUS ROSE AND RETURNED FROM
LION PREFACE(86)	BUT THEY INCIDENTALLY LET LOOSE THE SAYINGS OF	JESUS	IN OPEN COMPETITION WITH THE SAYINGS OF PAUL AND
LION PREFACE(68)	NOT ONLY DEMUR VEHEMENTLY TO THE TEACHINGS OF	JESUS	IN THIS MATTER, BUT OBJECT STRONGLY TO HIS NOT HAVING
ROCK PREFACE(175)	RAISE IT. THE CASE OF GALILEO IN THE EPOCH WHICH	JESUS	INAUGURATED, OR AT LEAST IN WHICH HIS NAME WAS
LION PREFACE(93)	BY DEVELOPING THAT DIVINE SPARK WITHIN HIM WHICH	JESUS	INSISTED ON AS THE EVERYDAY REALITY OF WHAT THE
LION PREFACE(9)	THE GOSPELS AND THE CONDUCT AND ULTIMATE FATE OF	JESUS	INTELLIGIBLE AND INTERESTING. WORLDLINESS OF THE
GENV IV (110)	TO ANY FRUITFUL CONCLUSIONS HERE. I RULE THAT	JESUS	IS A PARTY IN THIS CASE. /NEWCOMER/ YOU ARE AS DOTTY
LION PREFACE(28)	THE CHRIST, THE SON OF THE LIVING GOD." AT THIS	JESUS	IS EXTRAORDINARILY PLEASED AND EXCITED. HE DECLARES
LION PREFACE(36)	DISCIPLE'S CAREER HE SENDS TWO YOUNG MEN TO ASK	JESUS	IS HE REALLY THE CHRIST. THIS IS NOTEWORTHY BECAUSE
LION PREFACE(37)	OF IT: THE PRISONER WILL NOT SPEAK TO HIM. WHEN	JESUS	IS ILL RECEIVED IN A SAMARITAN VILLAGE JAMES AND JOHN
LION PREFACE(73)	FOR WHAT HAPPENED AFTER THE DISAPPEARANCE OF	JESUS	IS INSTRUCTIVE. UNFORTUNATELY, THE CRUCIFIXION WAS A
GENV IV (109)	CAN YOU SAY THAT? JESUS IS STRONGER THAN EVER.	JESUS	IS IRRESISTIBLE. YOU CAN PERHAPS UNIFY YOUR COUNTRYMEN
LION PREFACE(68)	BELIEVERS; AND EVEN THOSE OF US TO WHOM	JESUS	IS NO SUPERNATURAL PERSONAGE, BUT A PROPHET ONLY AS
LION PREFACE(41)	ONE"; THAT " GOD IS A SPIRIT"; THAT THE AIM OF	JESUS	IS NOT ONLY THAT THE PEOPLE SHOULD HAVE LIFE, BUT THAT
LION PREFACE(92)	THE PERILS OF SALVATIONISM. THE SECULAR VIEW OF	JESUS	IS POWERFULLY REINFORCED BY THE INCREASE IN OUR DAY OF
LION PREFACE(34)	OF THE ECSTASY OF THE BRIDE OF THE HOLY GHOST.	JESUS	IS REFINED AND SOFTENED ALMOST OUT OF RECOGNITION: THE
LION PREFACE(36)	WHICH NOW HANG IN MANY LADIES' CHAMBERS, IN WHICH	JESUS	IS REPRESENTED EXACTLY AS HE IS REPRESENTED TO THE
LION PREFACE(32)	DO, BETHLEHEM BEING THE CITY OF DAVID, FROM WHOM	JESUS	IS SAID BY MATTHEW AND LUKE TO BE DESCENDED. HE
GENV IV (109)	JESUS. /DEACONESS/ HOW CAN YOU SAY THAT?	JESUS	IS STRONGER THAN EVER. JESUS IS IRRESISTIBLE. YOU CAN
LION PREFACE(20)	ANY COMMENT. AN ANGEL ANNOUNCES TO JOSEPH THAT	JESUS	IS THE SON OF THE HOLY GHOST, AND THAT HE MUST NOT
LION PREFACE(63)	THE MODERN PRACTICAL FORM OF THE COMMUNISM OF	JESUS	IS THEREFORE, FOR THE PRESENT, EQUAL DISTRIBUTION OF
LION PREFACE(50)	OR A LABEL OF IDOLATRY. THE DOCTRINES IN WHICH	JESUS	IS THUS CONFIRMED ARE, ROUGHLY, THE FOLLOWING: 1. THE
LION PREFACE(19)	WITHIN THE LIFETIME OF PERSONS CONTEMPORARY WITH	JESUS	. ALLOWANCE MUST ALSO BE MADE FOR THE FACT THAT THE
LION PREFACE(82)	OF SIN, DEATH, AND LOGIC, WHICH HAD NO POWER OVER	JESUS	. AS WE HAVE SEEN, IT WAS BY INTRODUCING THIS BONDAGE
SIM II (79)	AND MY LITTLE TREASURE OF WORDS SPOKEN BY MY LORD	JESUS	. BLESSED BE THE NAME OF THE LORD: I SHALL NOT FORGET
LION PREFACE(36)	WHICH PRODUCES SO STARTLING AN EFFECT ON	JESUS	. BUT IN LUKE'S GOSPEL MEN'S MINDS, AND ESPECIALLY
LION PREFACE(84)	TORTURED, AND KILLED. AND THE SAME IS TRUE OF	JESUS	. BUT IT REQUIRES THE MOST STRENUOUS EFFORT OF
LION PREFACE(30)	AT THAT TIME, AND SUGGESTS THAT HE SHOULD RELEASE	JESUS	. BUT THEY INSIST ON HIS RELEASING A PRISONER NAMED
FABL PREFACE(76)	UNITARIANS REJECT THE TRINITY AND DENY DEITY TO	JESUS	. CALVINISTS DENY UNIVERSAL ATONEMENT, PREACHED BY OUR
ROCK PREFACE(178)	REAL POINT AT ISSUE AS COMPLETELY AS SOCRATES OR	JESUS	. FOR THIS WE NEED NOT BLAME HIM: HE WAS A PHYSICIST
GENV IV (113)	TEMPERS. ALL YOU HAVE TO DO IS TO BRING THEM TO	JESUS	. HE WILL RELIEVE YOU OF THEM. HE WILL SHEW YOU THAT
GENV IV (109)	YOU SPEAK? /DEACONESS/ HIS BELOVED NAME, SIR, IS	JESUS	. I AM SURE THAT WHEN YOU WERE A CHILD YOUR MOTHER
LION PREFACE(60)	WHICH HAVE HEAPED THEMSELVES UP SINCE THE TIME OF	JESUS	. IN POLITICS IT DEFEATS EVERY FORM OF GOVERNMENT
LION PREFACE(41)	AT THE PROMISED TIME. THE PECULIAR THEOLOGY OF	JESUS	. IN SPITE OF THE SUSPICIONS ROUSED BY JOHN'S
ROCK PREFACE(175)	IN GENERAL. LEADING CASES: SOCRATES AND	JESUS	. IT IS A HISTORICAL MISFORTUNE THAT THE MOST
LION PREFACE(18)	NOT JOSEPH BUT THE HOLY GHOST WAS THE FATHER OF	JESUS	. IT IS THEREFORE NOW HELD THAT THE STORY OF THE HOLY
GENV IV (110)	YOU? YOU CAN EASILY GET RID OF IT. BRING IT TO	JESUS	. IT WILL FALL FROM YOU LIKE A HEAVY BURDEN; AND YOUR
LION PREFACE(22)	BEYOND THIS. THE SAVAGE JOHN AND THE CIVILIZED	JESUS	. JESUS WENT BEYOND IT VERY RAPIDLY, ACCORDING TO
LION PREFACE(21)	NARRATIVE, WHICH SKIPS AT ONCE TO THE MANHOOD OF	JESUS	. JOHN THE BAPTIST. AT THIS MOMENT, A SALVATIONIST
LION EPILOG (149)	WHEN THE TRUMPET SOUNDS, THAT HE CANNOT FOLLOW	JESUS	. MANY YEARS EARLIER, IN THE DEVIL'S DISCIPLE, I
LION PREFACE(27)	AS SHEEP AMONG WOLVES. MATTHEW IMPUTES BIGOTRY TO	JESUS	. MATTHEW, LIKE MOST BIOGRAPHERS, STRIVES TO IDENTIFY
LION PREFACE(86)	AND IGNATIUS LOYOLA MEN AFTER THE VERY HEART OF	JESUS	. NEITHER THEY NOR THEIR EXPLOITS HAD ANYTHING TO DO
FABL PREFACE(75)	HOLY AS A MEMORIAL OF THE LAST RECORDED SUPPER OF	JESUS	. NO MAN CAN BE ORDAINED A MINISTER OF THE CHURCH OF
LION PREFACE(31)	OF HEAVEN ON EARTH. CLASS TYPE OF MATTHEW'S	JESUS	. ONE MORE CIRCUMSTANCE MUST BE NOTED AS GATHERED FROM
GENV IV (109)	MADAM, THEY SAY HEIL BATTLER. HE HAS ABOLISHED	JESUS	. /DEACONESS/ HOW CAN YOU SAY THAT? JESUS IS STRONGER
GENV IV (114)	TO GOVERN MYSELF, SIR. AND I AM NOW GOVERNED BY	JESUS	. /JUDGE/ ALLOW THE LADY THE LAST WORD, MR LEADER.
LION PREFACE(24)	WITHOUT CEASING TO BE A JEW. THE TEACHINGS OF	JESUS	. SO MUCH FOR HIS PERSONAL LIFE AND TEMPERAMENT. HIS
LION PREFACE(79)	BOLDLY SET IT ON ITS LEGS AGAIN IN THE NAME OF	JESUS	. THE CONFUSION OF CHRISTENDOM. NOW IT IS EVIDENT THAT
LION PREFACE(83)	TO DO WITH THE CHARACTERISTIC DOCTRINES OF	JESUS	. THE HOLY GHOST MAY BE AT WORK ALL ROUND PRODUCING
LION PREFACE(80)	THE LIMITATIONS OF PAUL'S SOUL UPON THE SOUL OF	JESUS	. THE SECRET OF PAUL'S SUCCESS. PAUL MUST SOON HAVE
GENV IV (126)	/DEACONESS/ BUT IN HEAVEN I SHALL LOSE MY	JESUS	. THERE HE WILL BE A KING; AND THERE WILL BE NO MORE
ROCK PREFACE(158)	AND THE ROMAN GOVERNMENT DECIDED TO EXTERMINATE	JESUS	. THEY HAD JUST AS MUCH RIGHT TO DO SO AS TO
2TRU PREFACE(15)	THE FAMILY INFLUENCES SO BITTERLY DEPRECATED BY	JESUS	. THIS NATURAL " CALLED" MINORITY WAS NEVER ELECTED IN
SIM PREFACE(10)	SCEPTICAL JOKES ABOUT THE PARTHENOGENESIS OF	JESUS	. THUS THE INQUISITION CAME TO BE REMEMBERED IN
LION PREFACE(79)	CHRISTIANITY IN THE CHARACTERISTIC UTTERANCES OF	JESUS	. WHEN SAUL WATCHED THE CLOTHES OF THE MEN WHO STONED
LION PREFACE(63)	HAVE THROWN NO FRESH LIGHT ON THE VIEWS OF	JESUS	. WHEN SWIFT HAD OCCASION TO ILLUSTRATE THE CORRUPTION
LION PREFACE(81)	AND REACTION. IT IS ONLY IN COMPARISON WITH	JESUS	(TO WHOM MANY PREFER HIM) THAT HE APPEARS COMMON AND
LION PREFACE(26)	WHEREAS IT IS CLEAR FROM MATTHEW'S STORY THAT	JESUS	(UNFORTUNATELY FOR HIMSELF, AS HE THOUGHT) HAD SOME
LION PREFACE(21)	THE MASS WAS TO THE CATHOLICS OF THE XVI CENTURY.	JESUS	JOINS THE BAPTISTS. JESUS ENTERED AS A MAN OF THIRTY (
LION PREFACE(95)	FURTHER THAN THIS. YOU CAN BECOME A FOLLOWER OF	JESUS	JUST AS YOU CAN BECOME A FOLLOWER OF CONFUCIUS OR LAO
LION PREFACE(79)	SACRIFICE OF THE CROSS. IN FACT, NO SOONER HAD	JESUS	KNOCKED OVER THE DRAGON OF SUPERSTITION THAN PAUL
LION PREFACE(85)	SLAUGHTER, HATRED, AND EVERYTHING THAT	JESUS	LOATHED, ON A MONSTROUS SCALE. BUT LONG BEFORE THAT,
LION PREFACE(39)	HE DECLARES THAT HE IS " THE DISCIPLE WHOM	JESUS	LOVED," AND THAT HE ACTUALLY LEANED ON THE BOSOM OF
ROCK PREFACE(175)	AND BLAMELESS RECORD AS CITIZEN AND SOLDIER.	JESUS	MADE NO DEFENCE AT ALL. HE DID NOT REGARD HIMSELF AS A
LION PREFACE(66)	WHEN WE COME TO MARRIAGE AND THE FAMILY, WE FIND	JESUS	MAKING THE SAME OBJECTION TO THAT INDIVIDUAL
LION PREFACE(90)	(FOR THE MOMENT) THAT THE DATE OF THE BIRTH OF	JESUS	MAY BE PLACED AT ABOUT 7 B.C.; BUT THEY DO NOT
LION PREFACE(98)	THAN THE BUDDHA, OR JEHOVAH MORE THAN KRISHNA, OR	JESUS	MORE OR LESS HUMAN THAN MAHOMET OR ZOROASTER OR
LION PREFACE(5)	BARABBASQUES GENERALLY, INCLUDING OURSELVES. WHY	JESUS	MORE THAN ANOTHER? I DO NOT IMPLY, HOWEVER, THAT
LION PREFACE(20)	TRADITIONS AND THE ACTUAL UTTERANCES OF	JESUS	MUST HAVE BEEN IN ARAMAIC, THE DIALECT OF PALESTINE.
LION PREFACE(26)	ARE FALSE OR TRUE, ACCORDING TO MATTHEW HIMSELF,	JESUS	MUST HAVE KNOWN THIS ONLY TOO WELL; FOR WHEREVER HE
LION PREFACE(102)	WHO LENDS HIM A HUGE PAIR OF SLIPPERS); AND	JESUS	NEVER SUGGESTED THAT HIS DISCIPLES SHOULD SEPARATE
LION PREFACE(23)	AN ARTIST AND A BOHEMIAN IN HIS MANNER OF LIFE.	JESUS	NOT A PROSELYTIST. A POINT OF CONSIDERABLE PRACTICAL
LION PREFACE(28)	ON HIM AND CRIES, " GET THEE BEHIND ME, SATAN."	JESUS	NOW BECOMES OBSESSED WITH A CONVICTION OF HIS

LION PREFACE(71)	YET IT CAN BE SAID THAT IT WILL CURE WHAT	JESUS	OBJECTED TO IN THESE INSTITUTIONS. HE MADE NO
LION PREFACE(31)	THE BAPTIST MAY HAVE BEEN A KEIR HARDIE; BUT THE	JESUS	OF MATTHEW IS OF THE RUSKIN-MORRIS CLASS. THIS HAUGHTY
LION PREFACE(5)	THE IMAGINATION OF WHITE MANKIND HAS PICKED OUT	JESUS	OF NAZARETH AS THE CHRIST, AND ATTRIBUTED ALL THE
LION PREFACE(101)	COMES IN THE IMPORTANCE OF THE REPUDIATION BY	JESUS	OF PROSELYTISM. HIS RULE " DONT PULL UP THE TARES: SOW
LION PREFACE(76)	HIS TWO TERRORS, BUT THAT THE MOVEMENT STARTED BY	JESUS	OFFERED HIM THE NUCLEUS FOR HIS NEW CHURCH. IT WAS A
LION PREFACE(66)	OF JESUS COULD HAVE BEEN PUT INTO PRACTICE.	JESUS	ON MARRIAGE AND THE FAMILY. WHEN WE COME TO MARRIAGE
LION PREFACE(69)	HERE I AM CONCERNED ONLY WITH THE VIEWS OF	JESUS	ON THE QUESTION; AND IT IS NECESSARY, IN ORDER TO
LION PREFACE(50)	AND EVEN CONTRACTED A PREJUDICE AGAINST	JESUS	ON THE SCORE OF HIS INVOLUNTARY CONNECTION WITH IT. WE
LION PREFACE(81)	THAN JESUS WAS A BAPTIST: HE IS A DISCIPLE OF	JESUS	ONLY AS JESUS WAS A DISCIPLE OF JOHN. HE DOES NOTHING
LION PREFACE(39)	IS MORE NATURAL THAN THE OTHER ACCOUNTS, IN WHICH	JESUS	OPENLY INDICATES JUDAS WITHOUT ELICITING ANY PROTEST
LION PREFACE(53)	NOT TO HAVE THEIR PROPERTY MEDDLED WITH BY	JESUS	OR ANY OTHER REFORMER. MODERN COMMUNISM. NOW LET US
FABL PREFACE(74)	OF METAPHOR) NOTHING WOULD BE LEFT OF EITHER	JESUS	OR MOSES. AS I PUT IT, THE CONVERSION OF SAVAGERY TO
LION PREFACE(94)	AS TO WHETHER THERE WAS EVER SUCH A PERSON AS	JESUS	OR NOT. WHEN HUME SAID THAT JOSHUA'S CAMPAIGNS WERE
SIM PREFACE(8)	SOVIET REPUBLIC ALLOWS THE SMALLEST AUTHORITY TO	JESUS	OR PETER, JEREMIAH OR MICAH THE MORASTHITE. THEY CALL
METH PREFACE(R50)	TO FIT THEM TO THE EVOLUTION OF AN AUTOMATIC	JESUS	OR SHAKESPEAR? WHEN A MAN TELLS YOU THAT YOU ARE A
LION PREFACE(36)	MOTHERS VISIT ONE ANOTHER. AT THE CIRCUMCISION OF	JESUS	PIOUS MEN AND WOMEN HAIL THE INFANT AS THE CHRIST. THE
LION PREFACE(7)	AS TO JESUS; AND EVEN ST LUKE, WHO MAKES	JESUS	POLITE AND GRACIOUS, DOES NOT MAKE HIM MEEK. THE
LION PREFACE(37)	THE TWO CHIEF COMMANDMENTS IS CHANGED BY MAKING	JESUS	PUT THE QUESTION TO THE LAWYER INSTEAD OF ANSWERING
LION PREFACE(32)	WHAT THE BOOKS SAY. HE DESCRIBES THE MIRACLE OF	JESUS	REACHING THE BOAT BY WALKING ACROSS THE SEA, BUT SAYS
LION PREFACE(29)	AND CUTS OFF THE EAR OF ONE OF HIS CAPTORS.	JESUS	REBUKES HIM, BUT DOES NOT ATTEMPT TO HEAL THE WOUND,
LION PREFACE(57)	HIS DESERTS, AND WHO SHALL SCAPE WHIPPING? "	JESUS	REMAINS UNSHAKEN AS THE PRACTICAL MAN; AND WE STAND
LION PREFACE(7)	CONCILIATED. BUT INSTEAD OF DENYING THE CHARGE,	JESUS	REPEATED THE OFFENCE. HE KNEW WHAT HE WAS DOING: HE
LION PREFACE(37)	TO CALL DOWN FIRE FROM HEAVEN AND DESTROY IT; AND	JESUS	REPLIES THAT HE IS COME NOT TO DESTROY LIVES BUT TO
LION PREFACE(35)	HIM WHEN HE COMES INTO HIS KINGDOM. TO WHICH	JESUS	REPLIES, " THIS DAY SHALT THOU BE WITH ME IN
LION PREFACE(30)	ARIMATHEA, WHO HAD BURIED JESUS IN IT, WHEREUPON	JESUS	ROSE AND RETURNED FROM JERUSALEM TO GALILEE AND
LION PREFACE(7)	APPLYING SUCH ADJECTIVES TO JUDAS MACCABEUS AS TO	JESUS	; AND EVEN ST LUKE, WHO MAKES JESUS POLITE AND
GENV IV (114)	AND YOU WILL UNDERSTAND. I BROUGHT IT ALL TO	JESUS	; AND NOW I AM HAPPY: I AM WHAT THE GENTLEMAN IS KIND
GENV IV (126)	/THE SECRETARY/ YES, MAAM. TAKE YOUR TROUBLE TO	JESUS	; AND SET ALL THE WOMEN A GOOD EXAMPLE. /DEACONESS/
LION PREFACE(95)	AS TO THE SOUNDNESS OF THE SECULAR DOCTRINES OF	JESUS	; FOR IT IS ABOUT THESE THAT THEY MAY COME TO BLOWS IN
FABL PREFACE(70)	DISCIPLE OF THE UNBORN ADAM SMITH RATHER THAN OF	JESUS	; SO THEY LET THE NARRATIVE STAND, BUT TAUGHT THAT
LION PREFACE(49)	TO SUPPER WITH HIM. YOU MAY DENY THE DIVINITY OF	JESUS	; YOU MAY DOUBT WHETHER HE EVER EXISTED; YOU MAY
LION PREFACE(5)	GREEK AND CHINESE INTERPOLATIONS. THE RECORD THAT	JESUS	SAID CERTAIN THINGS IS NOT INVALIDATED BY A
LION PREFACE(69)	ALMOST TO OBSESSION WITH SEX, AS TO WHICH	JESUS	SAID NOTHING. IN OUR SEXUAL NATURES WE ARE TORN BY AN
LION PREFACE(98)	THEMSELVES OF RELIGION, OR EVEN OF DOGMA. WHEN	JESUS	SAID THAT PEOPLE SHOULD NOT ONLY LIVE BUT LIVE MORE
LION PREFACE(39)	ABOUT HIS OWN BETRAYAL. LATER ON JOHN CLAIMS THAT	JESUS	SAID TO PETER " IF I WILL THAT JOHN TARRY TIL I COME,
LION PREFACE(66)	OF HIS HELL FOR JUDGES. ALSO, OF COURSE, WHY	JESUS	SAID " JUDGE NOT THAT YE BE NOT JUDGED" AND " IF ANY
LION PREFACE(30)	DEATH OF THE LAST PERSON WHO HAD BEEN ALIVE WHEN	JESUS	SAID " THERE BE SOME OF THEM THAT STAND HERE THAT
LION PREFACE(61)	IN THEIR POCKETS AND SAFES AND AT THEIR BANKERS.	JESUS	SAID, WHERE YOUR TREASURE IS, THERE WILL YOUR HEART BE
LION PREFACE(22)	MARTYRDOM, AND MET IT AT THE HANDS OF HEROD.	JESUS	SAW NO MERIT EITHER IN ASCETICISM OR MARTYRDOM. IN
LION PREFACE(86)	OF JOB AND THE PENTATEUCH; AND, AS WE HAVE SEEN,	JESUS	SEEMS TO BE THE WINNING NAME. THE GLARING
LION PREFACE(27)	IN THE INTEREST OF MATTHEW'S DETERMINATION THAT	JESUS	SHALL HAVE NOTHING TO DO WITH THE GENTILES. AT ALL
LION PREFACE(6)	UNCONSCIOUSLY INTO THE ERROR OF ASSUMING THAT	JESUS	SHARED THAT VIEW. BUT IT IS QUITE CLEAR FROM THE NEW
ROCK PREFACE(176)	OF HEAVEN, AND A BASEMENT WHICH WAS HELL. THAT	JESUS	SHOULD BE TAKEN UP INTO THE CLOUDS AS THE SHORTEST WAY
ROCK PREFACE(159)	CLEARNESS OF VISION ON THIS VERY POINT THAT SET	JESUS	SO HIGH ABOVE HIS PERSECUTORS. HE TAUGHT THAT TWO
LION PREFACE(22)	JESUS AND HIS TWELVE FRIENDS DO NOT FAST; AND	JESUS	TELLS THEM THAT THEY SHOULD REJOICE IN HIM INSTEAD OF
LION PREFACE(102)	WAYS IT IS EASIER TO RECONCILE A MAHOMETAN TO	JESUS	THAN A BRITISH PARSON, BECAUSE THE IDEA OF A
LION PREFACE(68)	SOMETHING MORE DIGNIFIED IN THE BACHELORDOM OF	JESUS	THAN IN THE SPECTACLE OF MAHOMET LYING DISTRACTED ON
LION PREFACE(94)	TELLS YOU NO MORE DISPROVES THE EXISTENCE OF	JESUS	THAN THE FACT THAT YOU DO NOT BELIEVE EVERYTHING
LION PREFACE(31)	THAT IF WE HAD NO OTHER DOCUMENTS CONCERNING	JESUS	THAN THE GOSPEL OF MATTHEW, WE SHOULD NOT FEEL AS WE
LION PREFACE(102)	A STATESMAN. THERE IS NOTHING IN THE TEACHING OF	JESUS	THAT CANNOT BE ASSENTED TO BY A BRAHMAN, A MAHOMETAN,
ROCK PREFACE(190)	PRIESTS: IF IT IS TO SUBSTITUTE THE DOCTRINE OF	JESUS	THAT PUNISHMENT IS ONLY A SENSELESS ATTEMPT TO MAKE A
LION PREFACE(53)	AND SOCIOLOGY HAVE TO SAY TO THE SUGGESTION OF	JESUS	THAT YOU SHOULD GET RID OF YOUR PROPERTY BY THROWING
LION PREFACE(88)	THAUMATURGICAL POWERS. " CHRIST SCIENTIST" AND	JESUS	THE MAHATMA ARE PREACHED BY PEOPLE WHOM PETER WOULD
LION PREFACE(18)	TWO ARE DIFFERENT) ESTABLISHING THE DESCENT OF	JESUS	THROUGH JOSEPH FROM THE ROYAL HOUSE OF DAVID, AND YET
LION PREFACE(3)	READER; AND YET, LIKE PILATE, I GREATLY PREFER	JESUS	TO ANNAS AND CAIAPHAS; AND I AM READY TO ADMIT THAT
LION PREFACE(30)	MATTHEW'S NARRATIVE. ONE EFFECT OF THE PROMISE OF	JESUS	TO COME AGAIN IN GLORY DURING THE LIFETIME OF SOME OF
LION PREFACE(27)	HOUSE OF ISRAEL." WHEN A WOMAN OF CANAAN BEGGED	JESUS	TO CURE HER DAUGHTER, HE FIRST REFUSED TO SPEAK TO
LION PREFACE(40)	THE SECOND COMING WHICH THEY AGREE IN DECLARING	JESUS	TO HAVE POSITIVELY AND UNEQUIVOCALLY PROMISED WITHIN
LION PREFACE(37)	OTHER NOVELTIES IN LUKE'S VERSION. PILATE SENDS	JESUS	TO HEROD, WHO HAPPENS TO BE IN JERUSALEM JUST THEN,
LION PREFACE(32)	AND THE NEWS THAT MANY WOMEN HAD COME WITH	JESUS	TO JERUSALEM, INCLUDING MARY MAGDALENE, OUT OF WHOM HE
MILL PREFACE(135)	FACT THAT IT IS ALWAYS THE GREATEST SPIRITS, FROM	JESUS	TO LENIN, FROM ST THOMAS MORE TO WILLIAM MORRIS, WHO
LION PREFACE(67)	WAS THE BEGINNING AND THE END OF THE OBJECTION OF	JESUS	TO MARRIAGE AND FAMILY TIES, AND THE EXPLANATION OF
LION PREFACE(52)	MUST REDUCE THE ETHICAL COUNSELS AND PROPOSALS OF	JESUS	TO MODERN PRACTICE IF THEY ARE TO BE OF ANY USE TO US.
ROCK PREFACE(180)	THE EVANGELISTS CAN SWITCH OFF OUR ATTENTION FROM	JESUS	TO PETER HEARING THE COCK CROW (OR THE BUGLE BLOW) OR
LION PREFACE(69)	ATTRIBUTE THE GENERAL APPROVAL OF THE DECISION OF	JESUS	TO REMAIN UNMARRIED AS AN ENDORSEMENT OF HIS VIEWS. WE
LION PREFACE(35)	THIS; AND HE IS REBUKED BY THE OTHER, WHO BEGS	JESUS	TO REMEMBER HIM WHEN HE COMES INTO HIS KINGDOM. TO
LION PREFACE(35)	TO CHARLES SURFACE AND DES GRIEUX. WOMEN FOLLOW	JESUS	TO THE CROSS; AND HE MAKES THEM A SPEECH BEGINNING "
LION PREFACE(66)	WE HAVE BEEN JUDGING AND PUNISHING EVER SINCE	JESUS	TOLD US NOT TO; AND I DEFY ANYONE TO MAKE OUT A
LION PREFACE(82)	ADAPTED IT TO THE CHURCH AND STATE SYSTEMS WHICH	JESUS	TRANSCENDED, AND MADE IT PRACTICABLE BY DESTROYING THE
LION PREFACE(28)	HIM FOR WHAT SEEMS MERE CRAVEN MELANCHOLY; AND	JESUS	TURNS FIERCELY ON HIM AND CRIES, " GET THEE BEHIND ME,
SIM PREFACE(15)	I MAY DO THEM THE MISCHIEF AGAINST WHICH	JESUS	VAINLY WARNED OUR MISSIONARIES. I MAY ROOT OUT OF
LION PREFACE(32)	THE READER. HE SAYS, FOR INSTANCE, THAT WHEN	JESUS	WALKED ON THE WAVES TO THE BOAT, HE WAS PASSING IT BY
LION PREFACE(8)	CALLED THE PROPER SPIRIT TO READ THE BIBLE IN.	JESUS	WAS A BABY; AND HE WAS OLDER THAN CREATION. HE WAS A
LION PREFACE(81)	BY FLASHES ONLY. HE IS NO MORE A CHRISTIAN THAN	JESUS	WAS A BAPTIST: HE IS A DISCIPLE OF JESUS ONLY AS JESUS
LION PREFACE(69)	OF THE CONFUSION THAT WE SHOULD CONCLUDE THAT	JESUS	WAS A CELIBATE, AND SHRINK EVEN FROM THE IDEA THAT HIS
LION PREFACE(81)	WAS A BAPTIST: HE IS A DISCIPLE OF JESUS ONLY AS	JESUS	WAS A DISCIPLE OF JOHN. HE DOES NOTHING THAT JESUS
LION PREFACE(70)	THAT IS WHY THE REVOLT AGAINST MARRIAGE OF WHICH	JESUS	WAS AN EXPONENT ALWAYS RECURS WHEN CIVILIZATION RAISES
LION PREFACE(20)	TO THE TEST. MATTHEW TELLS US THAT THE MOTHER OF	JESUS	WAS BETROTHED TO A MAN OF ROYAL PEDIGREE NAMED JOSEPH,
LION PREFACE(87)	THAT THOUGH NINETEEN CENTURIES HAVE PASSED SINCE	JESUS	WAS BORN (THE DATE OF HIS BIRTH IS NOW QUAINTLY GIVEN
LION PREFACE(40)	WERE THE KEENEST CRITICS OF THE CHRISTIANS, THAT	JESUS	WAS EITHER AN IMPOSTOR OR THE VICTIM OF A DELUSION.
ROCK PREFACE(157)	CHRIST. NO DOUBT THERE WAS A STRONG CASE FOR IT.	JESUS	WAS FROM THE POINT OF VIEW OF THE HIGH PRIEST A
LION PREFACE(61)	OVER THE PRICE. DECIDEDLY, WHETHER YOU THINK	JESUS	WAS GOD OR NOT, YOU MUST ADMIT THAT HE WAS A
LION PREFACE(22)	WAS A TEETOTALLER AND VEGETARIAN, WHILST, BECAUSE	JESUS	WAS NEITHER ONE NOR THE OTHER, THEY REVILED HIM AS A
ROCK PREFACE(176)	IN THE FLOOR. BUT IF INSTEAD OF TELLING ME THAT	JESUS	WAS TAKEN UP INTO THE CLOUDS AND THAT THE DISCIPLES
LION PREFACE(89)	MORE OUR REASON AND STUDY LEAD US TO BELIEVE THAT	JESUS	WAS TALKING THE MOST PENETRATING GOOD SENSE WHEN HE
LION PREFACE(37)	THINKS THAT THE WHOLE POINT OF IT IS THAT	JESUS	WAS THE LONG EXPECTED CHRIST, AND THAT HE WILL
LION PREFACE(69)	MUCH ABOUT FREEDOM OF CONSCIENCE, WHICH IS WHAT	JESUS	WAS THINKING ABOUT, AND ARE CONCERNED ALMOST TO
LION PREFACE(8)	JUST SO, THE CLAIM TO DIVINITY MADE BY	JESUS	WAS TO THE HIGH PRIEST, WHO LOOKED FORWARD TO THE
LION PREFACE(57)	YOUR EXAMINATION PAPER WILL READ " THE TIME OF	JESUS	WAS WORTH NOTHING (HE COMPLAINED THAT THE FOXES HAD
LION PREFACE(22)	THIS. THE SAVAGE JOHN AND THE CIVILIZED JESUS.	JESUS	WENT BEYOND IT VERY RAPIDLY, ACCORDING TO MATTHEW.
LION PREFACE(32)	THAT IS, A FORM OF SALVATIONISM. HE TELLS US THAT	JESUS	WENT INTO THE SYNAGOGUES AND TAUGHT, NOT AS THE
GETT PREFACE(250)	OF FIFTY YEARS AGO BY PLEADING THAT THE WORDS OF	JESUS	WERE IN AN OBSCURE ARAMAIC DIALECT, AND WERE PROBABLY
POSN PREFACE(382)	OF ONE GOD; THE STILL MORE STARTLING BLASPHEMY OF	JESUS	WHEN HE DECLARED GOD TO BE THE SON OF MAN AND HIMSELF
LION PREFACE(36)	MOTHERS' WOMBS, JOHN LEAPS AT THE APPROACH OF	JESUS	WHEN THE TWO MOTHERS VISIT ONE ANOTHER. AT THE
LION PREFACE(73)	DISPOSES OF ALL THE OPINIONS AND TEACHINGS OF	JESUS	WHICH ARE STILL MATTERS OF CONTROVERSY. THEY ARE ALL
LION PREFACE(39)	WHICH OF THEM IT WAS THAT SHOULD BETRAY HIM.	JESUS	WHISPERED THAT HE WOULD GIVE A SOP TO THE TRAITOR, AND
GENV IV (110)	PEOPLE ARE REALLY RAISED UP, REALLY SAVED. IT IS	JESUS	WHO HAS DONE IT; AND YOU, SIR, ARE ONLY THE
LION PREFACE(35)	AS SUPERIOR TO HUMAN SUFFERING. IT IS LUKE'S	JESUS	WHO HAS WON OUR HEARTS. THE TOUCH OF PARISIAN ROMANCE.
LION PREFACE(35)	MONEY AND THE POOR. THE WOMAN WASHES THE FEET OF	JESUS	WITH HER TEARS AND DRIES THEM WITH HER HAIR; AND HE IS
LION PREFACE(24)	NEVER DREAMT OF SUCH THINGS, AND COULD FOLLOW	JESUS	WITHOUT CEASING TO BE A JEW. THE TEACHINGS OF JESUS,
ROCK PREFACE(158)	ARRANGED PRIVATELY BETWEEN PILATE AND CAIAPHAS	JESUS	WOULD HAVE BEEN DISPATCHED AS QUICKLY AND SUDDENLY AS
LION PREFACE(81)	WAS A DISCIPLE OF JOHN. HE DOES NOTHING THAT	JESUS	WOULD HAVE DONE, AND SAYS NOTHING THAT JESUS WOULD
LION PREFACE(81)	THAT JESUS WOULD HAVE DONE, AND SAYS NOTHING THAT	JESUS	WOULD HAVE SAID, THOUGH MUCH, LIKE THE FAMOUS ODE TO
ROCK PREFACE(179)	OF TIME AND SPACE TO BE A THRILLING PLAY. BUT	JESUS	WOULD NOT DEFEND HIMSELF. IT WAS NOT THAT HE HAD NOT A
LION PREFACE(85)	OR BY A SPRINKLING OF WATER: MERE RITES ON WHICH	JESUS	WOULD NOT HAVE WASTED TWENTY WORDS. LATER ON, WHEN THE
LION PREFACE(56)	RIGHT AS AN ALTERNATIVE TO TAKING THE ADVICE OF	JESUS	WOULD NOT WORK. IN PRACTICE NOTHING WAS POSSIBLE IN
LION PREFACE(25)	ELSE THAN DESIRE TO HELP AND POWER TO CURE.	JESUS	, ACCORDING TO MATTHEW, AGREED SO ENTIRELY WITH

LION PREFACE(6) WHO ARE, LIKE THEIR PROPHET, VERY CIVIL TO JESUS , AND ALLOW HIM A PLACE IN THEIR ESTEEM AND VENERATION
LION PREFACE(32) OTHER HAND MARK SAYS NOTHING ABOUT THE BIRTH OF JESUS , AND DOES NOT TOUCH HIS CAREER UNTIL HIS ADULT
LION PREFACE(81) SPURIOUS ASSOCIATION WITH THE PERSONAL CHARM OF JESUS , AND EXISTS ONLY FOR UNTRAINED MINDS. IN THE HANDS OF
LION PREFACE(52) BEAR IN MIND THAT WHEREAS, IN THE TIME OF JESUS , AND IN THE AGES WHICH GREW DARKER AND DARKER AFTER
LION PREFACE(87) THE POLITICAL, ECONOMIC, AND MORAL OPINIONS OF JESUS , AS GUIDES TO CONDUCT, ARE INTERESTING AND IMPORTANT:
LION PREFACE(45) KINGS BRINGING COSTLY GIFTS TO THE CRADLE OF JESUS , BELIEVE LUKE'S STORY OF THE SHEPHERDS AND THE
LION PREFACE(64) DONE THIS NOT AS A RESTATEMENT OF THE DOCTRINE OF JESUS , BUT AS THE OUTCOME OF HIS OWN OBSERVATION AND
LION PREFACE(36) OF A CHRIST NOT ONLY BEFORE THE BIRTH OF JESUS , BUT BEFORE THE BIRTH OF JOHN THE BAPTIST, THE EVENT
FABL PREFACE(79) ENGLAND. ONE OF THE PUZZLES OF HISTORY IS WHETHER JESUS , DENOUNCED BY THE LADIES AND GENTLEMEN OF HIS TIME AS
LION PREFACE(24) THE UPPER HAND OF THEM POLITICALLY. THE JEW AS JESUS , HIMSELF A JEW, KNEW HIM, NEVER DREAMT OF SUCH
LION PREFACE(70) A REFUGE FROM CELIBACY, FOR BETTER FOR WORSE. JESUS , HOWEVER, DID NOT EXPRESS A COMPLICATED VIEW OF
LION PREFACE(27) MEANS THE ONLY INSTANCE IN WHICH MATTHEW REPORTS JESUS , IN SPITE OF THE CHARM OF HIS PREACHING, AS EXTREMELY
LION PREFACE(82) PLACE IN ANY MODERN PROTESTANT STATE; AND HE, NOT JESUS , IS THE TRUE HEAD AND FOUNDER OF OUR REFORMED CHURCH,
LION PREFACE(72) TAKES US INTO THE MATTER FAR MORE RESOLUTELY THAN JESUS , IS UNABLE TO FIND ANY GOLDEN RULE: BOTH BRAND AND
BUOY 1 (10) PLATO'S PROFESSION. CONFUCIUS, GAUTAMA, JESUS , MAHOMET, LUTHER, WILLIAM MORRIS. THE PROFESSION OF
LION PREFACE(6) THE MONEY-CHANGERS OUT OF THE TEMPLE. " GENTLE JESUS , MEEK AND MILD" IS A SNIVELLING MODERN INVENTION,
LION PREFACE(20) THERE IS NO RECORD OF ITS HAVING BEEN TOLD TO JESUS , NOR ANY INDICATION OF HIS HAVING ANY KNOWLEDGE OF
FABL PREFACE(82) AM I THE PEOPLE? WAS RUSKIN? WERE MOSES, JESUS , PETER AND PAUL, MAHOMET, BRIGHAM YOUNG? IF THEIR
SIM PREFACE(8) OLD TESTAMENT, AND THE COMMUNIST PRINCIPLES OF JESUS , PETER, AND PAUL. NOT THAT THE SOVIET REPUBLIC ALLOWS
LION PREFACE(74) AS A SPECIFIC DOCTRINE WAS SLAIN WITH JESUS , SUDDENLY AND UTTERLY. HE WAS HARDLY COLD IN HIS
LION PREFACE(67) YEARS LATER WE FIND A VERY DIFFERENT PERSON FROM JESUS , TALLEYRAND TO WIT, SAYING THE SAME THING. A MARRIED
FABL PREFACE(98) THE PRECEPTS OF THE BUDDHA, THE PARABLES OF JESUS , THE THESES OF LUTHER, THE JEUX D'ESPRIT OF ERASMUS
GETT PREFACE(250) DIALECT, AND WERE PROBABLY MISUNDERSTOOD, AS JESUS , THEY THINK, COULD NOT HAVE SAID ANYTHING A BISHOP
LION PREFACE(38) THEIR BEING FISHERMEN. HE SAYS EXPRESSLY THAT JESUS , THOUGH BAPTIZED BY JOHN, DID NOT HIMSELF PRACTISE
LION PREFACE(84) THEM, HEARTILY DETESTED. NOW NOBODY DETESTS JESUS , THOUGH MANY WHO HAVE BEEN TORMENTED IN THEIR
LION PREFACE(102) FOR BRITISH CITIZENS AND STATESMEN TO FOLLOW JESUS , THOUGH THEY CANNOT POSSIBLY FOLLOW EITHER TWEEDLEDUM
LION PREFACE(62) MERE AUTOMATISM HAVE NOT TOUCHED THE DOCTRINE OF JESUS , THOUGH THEY HAVE MADE SHORT WORK OF THE THEOLOGIANS
LION PREFACE(50) OUR PRACTICAL CONCLUSIONS ARE VIRTUALLY THOSE OF JESUS , WE ARE DISTINCTLY PLEASED AND ENCOURAGED TO FIND
FABL PREFACE(73) REACTION BY TRANSLATING EMIL STRAUSS'S LIFE OF JESUS , WHICH DIVESTED THE WORSHIPPED REDEEMER OF
LION PREFACE(70) ON ONE ANOTHER. THE COMMUNISM ADVOCATED BY JESUS , WHICH WE HAVE SEEN TO BE ENTIRELY PRACTICABLE, AND
LION PREFACE(88) IS ROUND HIS NECK, FLIES STRAIGHT TO THE ARMS OF JESUS , WHILST TOM PAINE AND SHELLEY FALL INTO THE
ROCK PREFACE(178) OF CONDUCT, BOTH PERSONAL AND POLITICAL, AND JESUS , WHO HAD SPENT HIS LIFE IN PROPOUNDING THE MOST
LION PREFACE(83) ENOUGH; BUT IT IS TOTALLY UNLIKE THE PREACHING OF JESUS , WHO NEVER TALKED ABOUT HIS PERSONAL HISTORY, AND
LION PREFACE(75) OF A TENTMAKER. THIS TEMPERAMENTAL HATRED OF JESUS , WHOM HE HAS NEVER SEEN, IS A PATHOLOGICAL SYMPTOM OF
LION PREFACE(56) ACCORDING TO MERIT? " HERE ONE IMAGINES JESUS , WHOSE SMILE HAS BEEN BROADENING DOWN THE AGES AS
LION PREFACE(75) THE TERROR OF SEX AND THE TERROR OF LIFE. NOW JESUS , WITH HIS HEALTHY CONSCIENCE ON HIS HIGHER PLANE, WAS
JOAN 6 (149) ME! SHE CRIED TO THEE IN THE MIDST OF IT: JESUS ! JESUS! JESUS! SHE IS IN THY BOSOM; AND I AM IN
JOAN 6 (149) SHE CRIED TO THEE IN THE MIDST OF IT: JESUS! JESUS ! JESUS! SHE IS IN THY BOSOM; AND I AM IN HELL FOR
JOAN 6 (149) CRIED TO THEE IN THE MIDST OF IT: JESUS! JESUS! JESUS ! SHE IS IN THY BOSOM; AND I AM IN HELL FOR EVERMORE.

JESUSES

GENV PREFACE(25) RUSKIN AND MORRIS, WITH DOZENS OF UNCRUCIFIED JESUSES AND SAINTLY WOMEN IN EVERY GENERATION, LOOK LIKE
FABL PREFACE(83) THAN I WAS. POLITICAL ADVENTURERS AND " TIN JESUSES " ROSE LIKE ROCKETS TO DICTATORSHIPS AND FELL TO

JESUS'S

LION PREFACE(30) IT MUST HAVE BEEN WRITTEN DURING THE LIFETIME OF JESUS'S CONTEMPORARIES: THAT IS, WHILST IT WAS STILL
LION PREFACE(43) BECAUSE IT PROVES THE ABSOLUTE SINCERITY OF JESUS'S DECLARATION THAT HE WAS A GOD. NO IMPOSTOR WOULD
LION PREFACE(26) OF CATARACT" WOULD HAVE BEEN, TO A MAN OF JESUS'S INTELLIGENCE, THE PROPOSITION OF AN IDIOT. IF IT
LION PREFACE(31) SAID, " IS NOT THIS THE CARPENTER'S SON? " BUT JESUS'S MANNER THROUGHOUT IS THAT OF AN ARISTOCRAT, OR AT
LION PREFACE(35) IS TAKEN UP AND DEVELOPED. MORE IS SAID ABOUT JESUS'S MOTHER AND HER FEELINGS. CHRIST'S FOLLOWING OF
LION PREFACE(42) ALTHOUGH JOHN, FOLLOWING HIS PRACTICE OF SHEWING JESUS'S SKILL AS A DEBATER, MAKES HIM PLAY A LESS PASSIVE
LION PREFACE(26) BE THE IRRELEVANCE OF THE ISSUE RAISED BY THEM. JESUS'S TEACHING HAS NOTHING TO DO WITH MIRACLES. IF HIS
LION PREFACE(33) CALLED OUT TO HIM. HE SEEMS TO FEEL THAT JESUS'S TREATMENT OF THE WOMAN OF CANAAN REQUIRES SOME
FABL PREFACE(74) THE WHEAT. I THEREFORE APPRECIATE THE WISDOM OF JESUS'S WARNING TO HIS MISSIONARIES THAT IF THEY TORE UP THE

JET

GENV PREFACE(13) SUBJUGATION, AND NOWADAYS EXTINCTION BY BOMBS, JET PROPELLED OR ATOMIC, IS ANY SUBSTANTIAL ADVANCE MADE OR
GENV PREFACE(10) FOR HAD THE GERMANS NOT CONCENTRATED ON THE JET PROPULSION OF PILOTLESS AEROPLANES INSTEAD OF ON THE

JEU

CYMB FORWORD(133) AND DO IT TOO, NOT WHOLLY AS A LITERARY JEU D'ESPRIT, BUT IN RESPONSE TO AN ACTUAL EMERGENCY IN THE
FANY PROLOG (271) OF A GOOD CAUSE! OH, MR TROTTER! THATS VIEUX JEU . /TROTTER/ (SHOUTING AT HER) DONT TALK FRENCH. I WILL

JEUCE

BULL II (105) MATCH WITH THE DEVIL. /CORNELIUS/ (DUBIOUSLY) JEUCE A WORD I EVER HEARD OF IT! /FATHER DEMPSEY/ (VERY

JEUNE

SUPR I SD(4) LOOKING YOUNG FELLOW. HE MUST, ONE THINKS, BE THE JEUNE PREMIER; FOR IT IS NOT IN REASON TO SUPPOSE THAT A

JEUX

FABL PREFACE(98) THE PARABLES OF JESUS, THE THESES OF LUTHER, THE JEUX D'ESPRIT OF ERASMUS AND MONTAIGNE, THE UTOPIAS OF MORE

JEVER

BULL IV (159) (HE WHISTLES LET ERIN REMEMBER). /NORA/ DID JEVER GET A LETTER I WROTE YOU LAST FEBRUARY? /LARRY/ OH

JEVONS

FABL PREFACE(89) UP THE SUBJECT AND RETURN TO THE CHARGE. STANLEY JEVONS WOULD PASS IT, THOUGH AFTER HE HAD KNOCKED OUT

JEW

DOCT I SD(85) YET FOREIGN CHISELLING OF FEATURE, REVEAL THE JEW : IN THIS INSTANCE THE HANDSOME GENTLEMANLY JEW, GONE A
GENV IV (104) A YELLOW ONE WITHIN REACH. WHY DO YOU EXCLUDE THE JEW ? BECAUSE YOU CANNOT COMPETE WITH HIS INTELLIGENCE, HIS
GENV III (70) WOULD FIND ME GUILTY FOR RIDDING THE WORLD OF A JEW ? /THE JEW/ ONE CAN NEVER BE QUITE CERTAIN, MADAM. IF
GENV III (70) FOR CARRYING ARMS. /THE WIDOW/ THREE MEN AND A JEW AGAINST ONE DISARMED WOMAN! COWARDS. /THE JEW/
JOAN 4 (96) TIME MONEY CHANGES HANDS. I WOULD NOT LEAVE A JEW ALIVE IN CHRISTENDOM IF I HAD MY WAY. /THE NOBLEMAN/ WHY
SUPR III (82) ENTERPRISE IS THE RESULT. I BECAME LEADER, AS THE JEW ALWAYS BECOMES LEADER, BY HIS BRAINS AND IMAGINATION.
MILL PREFACE(126) BALTIC CELT, THAN THERE IS BETWEEN A FRANKFORT JEW AND A FRANKFORT GENTILE. EVEN IN AFRICA, WHERE PINK
CLEO NOTES (209) QUITE ANOTHER MATTER. THE DIFFERENCE BETWEEN A JEW AND A GENTILE HAS NOTHING TO DO WITH THE DIFFERENCE
NEVR I (206) DRINKING ON CREDIT; MY LANDLORD IS AS RICH AS A JEW AND AS HARD AS NAILS; AND IVE MADE FIVE SHILLINGS IN SIX
MILL PREFACE(126) THE INTELLIGENT JEW IS A FUSIONIST AS BETWEEN JEW AND GENTILE STOCK, EVEN WHEN HE IS ALSO A BIT OF A
UNPL PREFACE(R23) AND THE STATESMAN. EVEN AS IT IS, SHYLOCK AS A JEW AND USURER, OTHELLO AS A MOOR AND A SOLDIER, CAESAR,
LION PREFACE(24) GOT THE UPPER HAND OF THEM POLITICALLY. THE JEW AS JESUS, HIMSELF A JEW, KNEW HIM, NEVER DREAMT OF SUCH
ROCK PREFACE(149) BUT ACTUALLY ATTEMPTED. THE EXTIRPATION OF THE JEW AS SUCH FIGURED FOR A FEW MAD MOMENTS IN THE PROGRAM OF
MILL PREFACE(124) ANY GENTILE HAS THE SAME REASON FOR KILLING ANY JEW AT SIGHT AS THE ROMAN SOLDIER HAD FOR KILLING
ROCK II (258) TO MAKE THEM DO ANYTHING, EVEN IF IT IS ONLY JEW BAITING, PROVIDED IT'S SOMETHING TYRANNICAL, SOMETHING
LION PREFACE(34) ALMOST URBANE PERSON; AND THE CHAUVINIST JEW BECOMES A PRO-GENTILE WHO IS THROWN OUT OF THE SYNAGOGUE
SIM PRO,1, (25) THAT NOBODY NEEDNT BE IN THE OFFICE, AND THAT ANY JEW BOY COULD DO ALL I DO HERE AND DO IT BETTER. BUT I
GENV III (84) WITH YOU! DINE WITH A JEW! /THE JEW/ ONLY A JEW CAN APPRECIATE YOUR MAGNIFICENT TYPE OF BEAUTY, SENORA.
SUPR III (82) NO: SHE WAS A FREETHINKER. SHE SAID THAT EVERY JEW CONSIDERS IN HIS HEART THAT ENGLISH PEOPLE ARE DIRTY IN
MILL PREFACE(124) BUT TO SET THE POLICE ON HIM BECAUSE HE WAS A JEW COULD BE JUSTIFIED ONLY ON THE GROUND THAT THE JEWS ARE
GENV III (70) WIDOW/ WOMEN ON JURIES ARE AN ABOMINATION. ONLY A JEW COULD MENTION SUCH A THING TO A LADY (SHE GIVES UP THE
GENV III (84) DOLLS AND WOMEN WHO ARE COWS. BUT WHEREVER THE JEW DOMINATES THE THEATRE AND THE PICTURE GALLERY-- AND HE
GENV III SD(68) AND AM GOING TO RESIGN; BUT THE MOOD PASSES. THE JEW ENTERS, IN ANIMATED CONVERSATION WITH THE QUONDAM
GENV III (84) WHAT A GOOD DINNER IS. COME! TRY DINING WITH A JEW FOR THE FIRST TIME IN YOUR LIFE. /THE WIDOW/ (
ROCK PREFACE(187) WHEREAS I UNDERSTAND THAT YOU HAVE ONLY RAISED A JEW FROM THE DEAD. SO FOR THE LAST TIME SET YOUR WITS TO
DOCT II (123) HIM, I MIGHT HAVE LENT IT TO HIM IF HE HAD BEEN A JEW HIMSELF. /SIR PATRICK/ (WITH A GRUNT) AND WHAT DID HE
GENV III (84) END TO YOUR IMPUDENCE? I HAVE NEVER DINED WITH A JEW IN MY LIFE. /THE JEW/ THEN YOU DO NOT KNOW WHAT A GOOD
GENV III (69) ME TO HEAR IT. /THE WIDOW/ I WOULD SHOOT EVERY JEW IN THE COUNTRY: THAT IS WHAT I WOULD DO. /THE JEW/ PRAY

LION PREFACE(23)	TO THIS DAY A CHRISTIAN WOULD BE IN RELIGION A	JEW	INITIATED BY BAPTISM INSTEAD OF CIRCUMCISION, AND
MILL PREFACE(126)	BETWEEN DUTCH AND BRITISH STOCK. THE INTELLIGENT	JEW	IS A FUSIONIST AS BETWEEN JEW AND GENTILE STOCK, EVEN
GENV IV (105)	BE NORDIC, NOT HITTITE: THAT IS ALL. /JEW/ A	JEW	IS A HUMAN BEING. HAS HE NOT A RIGHT OF WAY AND
GENV IV (105)	HIMSELF BACK INTO HIS SEAT). /BATTLER/ LIAR. NO	JEW	IS EVER SATISFIED. ENOUGH. YOU HAVE YOUR WARNING. KEEP
ROCK PREFACE(184)	THE DIFFERENCE. THE DIFFERENCE BETWEEN ROMAN AND	JEW	IS ONLY A WORD. /PILATE/ IT IS A FACT. /JESUS/ A FACT
GENV III (69)	CHRISTIANS YOU WOULD HELP ME TO KILL THIS DIRTY	JEW	. DID YOU HEAR WHAT HE SAID? /SIR O./ YES, YES, SENORA:
LADY PREFACE(220)	THEM, AND NOT THE VINDICTIVENESS OF A STAGE	JEW	. GAIETY OF GENIUS. IN VIEW OF THESE FACTS, IT IS
DOCT II (126)	DUBEDAT. HOWEVER, PERHAPS THATS BECAUSE I'M A	JEW	. GOODNIGHT, DR BLENKINSOP (SHAKING HANDS).
GENV IV (104)	/BATTLER/ WHAT DO YOU MEAN? /THE JEW/ I AM A	JEW	. /BATTLER/ THEN WHAT RIGHT HAVE YOU IN MY COUNTRY? I
GENV IV (118)	OF HISTORY AS A CATHOLIC: THAT IS, NINE TENTHS A	JEW	. /BBDE/ THE BEE IN YOUR BONNET BUZZES TOO MUCH, ERNEST.
GENV I (32)	/THE JEW/ I MUST BEGIN BY EXPLAINING THAT I AM A	JEW	. /SHE/ I DONT BELIEVE YOU. YOU DONT LOOK LIKE ONE. /THE
SUPR III (82)	I BE HERE IF SHE DID? SHE OBJECTED TO MARRY A	JEW	. /TANNER/ ON RELIGIOUS GROUNDS? /MENDOZA/ NO: SHE WAS
GENV III (72)	AND SPRINKLE ITS BLOOD ON HIS THRESHOLD. HE IS A	JEW	. /THE COMMISSAR/ COME TO RUSSIA. JEWS DO NOT DO SUCH
GENV III (76)	YOU THE JEW THERE: I HATE YOU BECAUSE YOU ARE A	JEW	. /THE JEW/ A GERMAN JEW. /THE SECRETARY/ WORSE AND
GENV III (76)	YOU BECAUSE YOU ARE A JEW. /THE JEW/ A GERMAN	JEW	. /THE SECRETARY/ WORSE AND WORSE. TWO NATIONALITIES ARE
GENV III (69)	/THE JEW/ AFTER ALL, MADAM, YOUR SAVIOR WAS A	JEW	. /THE WIDOW/ OH, WHAT A HORRIBLE BLASPHEMY! (SHE
LION PREFACE(24)	AND COULD FOLLOW JESUS WITHOUT CEASING TO BE A	JEW	. THE TEACHINGS OF JESUS. SO MUCH FOR HIS PERSONAL LIFE
ROCK PREFACE(181)	AND NO DOUBT SEEM EXCEPTIONALLY INTELLIGENT TO A	JEW	. YOU JEWS ARE ALWAYS TALKING ABOUT TRUTH AND
MTH3 (110)	WAS OVER AGE. THEY BEGAN TO CALL ME THE WANDERING	JEW	. YOU SEE HOW IMPOSSIBLE MY POSITION WAS. I FORESAW THAT
DOCT II (123)	LIKE THE MERCHANT OF VENICE, YOU KNOW. BUT IF A	JEW	MAKES AN AGREEMENT, HE MEANS TO KEEP IT AND EXPECTS YOU
ROCK I (233)	THE BOOKS YOU CAN FIND BY A REVOLUTIONARY GERMAN	JEW	NAMED HARRY MARKS-- /HILDA/ DONT YOU MEAN KARL MARX?
DOCT II (122)	WELL, HE MADE A VERY UNCALLED-FOR REMARK ABOUT A	JEW	NOT UNDERSTANDING THE FEELINGS OF A GENTLEMAN. I MUST
LION PREFACE(27)	FALL FROM THEIR MASTER'S TABLE," SHE MELTED THE	JEW	OUT OF HIM AND MADE CHRIST A CHRISTIAN. TO THE WOMAN
GENV III (69)	NOT A MATTER OF PRINCIPLE. /THE WIDOW/ (TO THE	JEW	) DO YOU KNOW WHAT I WOULD DO IF I WERE A PRESIDENT?
GENV I (34)	HER UNAFFECTED DEFERENCE TO THE GENTLEMANLIKE	JEW	) I AM SORRY, OUR CHIEFS ARE SCATTERED OVER EUROPE, VERY
SUPR III (135)	WROTE A PAMPHLET TO PROVE THAT NIETZSCHE WAS A	JEW	; AND IT ENDED IN NIETZSCHE'S GOING TO HEAVEN IN A HUFF.
SUPR III (75)	RULES. IT IS TRUE THAT I HAVE THE HONOR TO BE A	JEW	; AND WHEN THE ZIONISTS NEED A LEADER TO REASSEMBLE OUR
LION PREFACE(85)	AS AN EXCELLENT THING IN ITS WAY FOR A	JEW	; BUT IF IT HAS NO EFFICACY TOWARDS SALVATION, AND IF
GENV III (72)	ONE EXCUSE IS AS GOOD AS ANOTHER. I AM NOT A	JEW	; BUT THE LADY MAY SHOOT ME BECAUSE I AM A COMMUNIST.
LION PREFACE(11)	OF HIS CRUDE CREED; BUT NEITHER SARACEN NOR	JEW	SEES ANY ADVANTAGE IN IT OVER HIS OWN VERSION. THE
GENV III (76)	OTHERS/ OH! /THE SECRETARY/ YES I DO. YOU THE	JEW	THERE: I HATE YOU BECAUSE YOU ARE A JEW. /THE JEW/ A
ROCK PREFACE(184)	A ROMAN WORDS MEAN SOMETHING: IN THE MOUTH OF A	JEW	THEY ARE A CHEAP SUBSTITUTE FOR STRONG DRINK. IF WE
GENV IV (112)	TO GET ANY FURTHER. YOU HAVE ONLY TO SAY THE WORD	JEW	TO HERR BATTLER OR THE WORD BOLSHEVIST TO SIGNOR
GENV III (79)	DREAM OF INSULTING QUETZALCOATL BY SACRIFICING A	JEW	TO HIM. /THE JUDGE/ AS TO THE JEWISH GENTLEMAN HIMSELF,
DOCT II (123)	AS I AM A JEW, THERES NOTHING INTERESTING IN A	JEW	TO ME, WHEREAS THERE IS ALWAYS SOMETHING INTERESTING AND
MILL II (172)	DI PARERGA CAN JUST WALK ROUND THE CLEVEREST	JEW	WHEN IT COMES TO MONEYMAKING. WE ARE THE ONLY REAL
BARB III (335)	SAY? /UNDERSHAFT/ LAZARUS IS A GENTLE ROMANTIC	JEW	WHO CARES FOR NOTHING BUT STRING QUARTETS AND STALLS AT
LION PREFACE(27)	AT THE GENTILE, AND REPRESENTS JESUS AS A BIGOTED	JEW	WHO REGARDS HIS MISSION AS ADDRESSED EXCLUSIVELY TO "
ROCK PREFACE(186)	TO HAVE YOU CRUCIFIED; FOR THOUGH YOU ARE ONLY A	JEW	, AND A HALF BAKED YOUNG ONE AT THAT, YET I PERCEIVE
GENV III (69)	I OUGHT TO BE HANGED FOR IT. BUT IF I VOTE FOR A	JEW	, AS I OFTEN HAVE, AND HE IS ELECTED AND THEN NOT LET
BULL PREFACE(15)	TO BE, IF NOT AN AMERICAN, AN ITALIAN, OR A	JEW	, AT LEAST TO BE DEPENDING ON THE BRAINS, THE NERVOUS
GENV IV (112)	ALL KINGS AND KAISERS. FOR MY SUPPORT IS NO DEAD	JEW	, BUT A MIGHTY MOVEMENT IN THE HISTORY OF THE WORLD.
FABL PREFACE(77)	CHRISTIAN OR MOSLEM, BUDDHIST OR SHINTO, JAIN OR	JEW	, CALL ME TO REPENTANCE, AND ASK ME FOR SUBSCRIPTIONS. I
DOCT I SD(85)	JEW: IN THIS INSTANCE THE HANDSOME GENTLEMANLY	JEW	, GONE A LITTLE PIGEON-BREASTED AND STALE AFTER THIRTY,
GENV I (34)	DRAFT THE LETTER FOR YOU. /SHE/ OH I SAY, MISTER	JEW	, I DONT LIKE THIS. /THE JEW/ THEN WRITE THE LETTER
GENV III (70)	YOU WILL BE TELLING ME NEXT THAT KING DAVID WAS A	JEW	, I SUPPOSE. /SIR O./ WELL, ETHNOLOGICALLY-- /THE WIDOW/
GENV IV (110)	PARTY IN WHAT CAPACITY, MAY I ASK? I SPEAK AS A	JEW	, IF MR BATTLER WILL PERMIT ME. /THE JUDGE/ IN THE
LION PREFACE(24)	OF THEM POLITICALLY. THE JEW AS JESUS, HIMSELF A	JEW	, KNEW HIM, NEVER DREAMT OF SUCH THINGS, AND COULD
BULL IV (161)	OH, IT DOESNT MEAN ANYTHING: IT'S BY A GERMAN	JEW	, LIKE MOST ENGLISH PATRIOTIC SENTIMENT. NEVER MIND ME,
JOAN PREFACE(53)	AS MR MATHESON LANG ALWAYS IS IN THE WANDERING	JEW	, ON THE PRINCIPLE THAT IT DOES NOT MATTER IN THE LEAST
GETT (302)	COME! YOU ARE NO MORE A CHILD OF SIN THAN ANY	JEW	, OR MAHOMETAN, OR NONCONFORMIST, OR ANYONE ELSE BORN
ANNA (290)	AM MADE COMMANDER-IN-CHIEF BY MY OWN SOLICITOR: A	JEW	, SCHNEIDEKIND! A HEBREW JEW! IT SEEMS ONLY YESTERDAY
ROCK PREFACE(181)	PUT IT INTO YOUR HEAD TO ASK ME? /PILATE/ AM I A	JEW	, THAT I SHOULD TROUBLE MYSELF ABOUT YOU? YOUR OWN
GENV III (69)	PARLIAMENT ON DEMOCRATIC PRINCIPLES. IF I SHOOT A	JEW	, THATS MURDER; AND I OUGHT TO BE HANGED FOR IT. BUT IF
GENV IV SD(87)	BEHIND HIM, IN THE FRONT ROW OF CHAIRS ARE THE	JEW	, THE COMMISSAR AND THE WIDOW. IN THE OPPOSITE FRONT ROW
DOCT II (123)	WITH THEM. THATS ONLY NATURAL, BECAUSE, AS I AM A	JEW	, THERES NOTHING INTERESTING IN A JEW TO ME, WHEREAS
LION PREFACE(102)	TO BY A BRAHMAN, A MAHOMETAN, A BUDDHIST OR A	JEW	, WITHOUT ANY QUESTION OF THEIR CONVERSION TO
ANNA (290)	MY OWN SOLICITOR: A JEW, SCHNEIDEKIND! A HEBREW	JEW	! IT SEEMS ONLY YESTERDAY THAT THESE THINGS WOULD HAVE
GENV III (83)	WITH ME? /THE WIDOW/ DINE WITH YOU! DINE WITH A	JEW	! /THE JEW/ ONLY A JEW CAN APPRECIATE YOUR MAGNIFICENT
GENV III (71)	SOVIET. /THE WIDOW/ (EXPLODING AGAIN) ANOTHER	JEW	! ! ! /THE SECRETARY/ NO, NO. YOU HAVE JEWS ON THE
		JEWEL	
WIDO II SD(45)	WITH ANOTHER SOB. BLANCHE COMES IN, WITH A	JEWEL	BOX IN HER HANDS. HER EXPRESSION IS THAT OF A STRONG
2TRU I SD(27)	A DAINTY PINCUSHION, A STAND OF RINGS, A	JEWEL	BOX OF BLACK STEEL WITH THE LID OPEN AND A ROPE OF
INCA (245)	THEM SATISFACTORY. ALLOW ME (HE OPENS THE	JEWEL	CASE AND PRESENTS IT)! /ERMYNTRUDE/ (STARING AT THE
INCA SD(244)	AT THE MIRROR, BEFORE THE MANAGER, WITH A LARGE	JEWEL	CASE IN HIS HAND, RETURNS, USHERING IN THE INCA. /THE
INCA SD(244)	THE TREMBLING MANAGER BY A GESTURE TO PLACE THE	JEWEL	CASE ON THE TABLE; DISMISSES HIM WITH A FROWN; TOUCHES
2TRU I (40)	BACK TO THE DRESSING TABLE AS A BULWARK FOR THE	JEWEL	CASE) NOT IF I KNOW IT, YOU SHANT. /THE BURGLAR/ (
2TRU I (41)	NOW? /THE BURGLAR/ YOU SHALL SEE. (HANDLING THE	JEWEL	CASE) ONE OF THESE SAFES THAT OPEN BY A SECRET
INCA (245)	BUSINESS? /THE INCA/ (PRODUCING A VERY LARGE	JEWEL	CASE, AND RELAPSING INTO SOLEMNITY) I AM INSTRUCTED BY
CATH 4 (195)	WILD DUCK! LITTLE STAR! LITTLE GLORY! LITTLE	JEWEL	IN THE CROWN OF HEAVEN! /CLAIRE/ THIS IS PERFECTLY
KING I (184)	OF THE GUTTER; BUT THE GOOD GOD SOMETIMES DROPS A	JEWEL	THERE: MY NURSE, A PEASANT WOMAN, WAS WORTH A THOUSAND
		JEWELLED	
MTH4 I SD(139)	LAVENDER TROUSERS, A BRILLIANT SILK CRAVAT WITH A	JEWELLED	PIN STUCK IN IT, A TALL HAT OF GREY FELT, AND
MRS PREFACE(156)	WERE YOUR LOT IN LIFE, YOU WOULD NOT RATHER BE A	JEWELLED	VAMP. IF YOU CAN GO DEEP ENOUGH INTO THINGS TO BE
		JEWELLER	
PYGM IV (267)	HANDS). IF THESE BELONGED TO ME INSTEAD OF TO THE	JEWELLER	. I'D RAM THEM DOWN YOUR UNGRATEFUL THROAT. (HE
O'FL (220)	/TERESA/ DO YOU THINK I MIGHT TAKE IT TO THE	JEWELLER	NEXT MARKET DAY AND ASK HIM? /O'FLAHERTY/ (
		JEWELLER'S	
PYGM IV (267)	/LIZA/ (TAKING A RING OFF) THIS RING ISNT THE	JEWELLER'S	: IT'S THE ONE YOU BOUGHT ME IN BRIGHTON. I DONT
		JEWELLERY	
SUPR III (130)	ABSOLUTELY NONE. ALL DOWDIES. NOT TWO PENNORTH OF	JEWELLERY	AMONG A DOZEN OF THEM. THEY MIGHT BE MEN OF FIFTY.
WIDO II (45)	PAPER. IT CONTAINS A PACKET OF LETTERS AND SOME	JEWELLERY	. SHE PLUCKS A RING FROM HER FINGER AND THROWS IT
ARMS III (48)	YES, PAUL? /PETKOFF/ I BET YOU ANY PIECE OF	JEWELLERY	YOU LIKE TO ORDER FROM SOFIA AGAINST A WEEK'S
ARMS III (48)	REALLY, MOTHER, IF YOU ARE GOING TO TAKE THE	JEWELLERY	, I DONT SEE WHY YOU SHOULD GRUDGE ME MY ARAB.
PYGM IV (265)	WEARING TODAY; AND THAT, WITH THE HIRE OF THE	JEWELLERY	, WILL MAKE A BIG HOLE IN TWO HUNDRED POUNDS. WHY,
		JEWELRY	
O'FL (221)	BROOCHES IN HER EARS, THOUGH SHE HADNT HALF THE	JEWELRY	OF MRS SULLIVAN THAT KEEPS THE POPSHOP IN DRUMPOGUE.
FABL PREFACE(81)	BY A DEIFIED JONATHAN WILD TO STEAL THE	JEWELRY	OF THE EGYPTIANS BEFORE THEIR FLIGHT INTO THE
		JEWELS	
LION PREFACE(11)	OF FLORENCE THAT THEY OUGHT TO TEAR OFF THEIR	JEWELS	AND FINERY AND SACRIFICE THEM TO GOD, THEY OFFER HIM
CLEO I (110)	OH DO, DO, DO. I WILL STEAL FTATATEETA'S	JEWELS	AND GIVE THEM TO YOU. I WILL MAKE THE RIVER NILE
CLEO IV SD(185)	HER REPEATEDLY AND SAVAGELY; AND TEARS OFF HER	JEWELS	AND HEAPS THEM ON HER. THE TWO MEN TURN FROM THE
INCA (238)	YOUR HIGHNESS. /THE PRINCESS/ WELL, SHE WORE MY	JEWELS	AND ONE OF MY DRESSES AT A RATHER IMPROPER BALL WITH
APPL I (200)	THE LOVELINESS OF WOMEN THE DAZZLE OF THEIR	JEWELS	AND ROBES, THE CHARM OF THE COUNTRYSIDE NOT IN ITS
2TRU I (47)	SO HAVE YOU, NO MORE MEASLES: THAT SCRAP FOR THE	JEWELS	CURED YOU AND CURED ME. HA HA! I AM WELL, I AM WELL,
2TRU I (50)	(SHE RUSHES TO THE DRESSING TABLE; BUNDLES THE	JEWELS	INTO THEIR CASE; AND CARRIES IT OUT). /THE MONSTER/ (
2TRU I (44)	IT CONTAINED AN ILLUSTRATED ACCOUNT OF YOUR	JEWELS	. CAN YOU GUESS WHAT SWEETIE SAID TO ME AS SHE GAZED
2TRU I (41)	TO THE ZOO, NO: I AM NOT GOING TO STEAL THOSE	JEWELS	. HONESTY IS THE BEST POLICY. I HAVE ANOTHER IDEA,
2TRU II (76)	A DOUBT OF IT. SHE'S A FRAUD: TAKE CARE OF YOUR	JEWELS	. OR ELSE-- AND THIS IS WHAT I SUSPECT-- SHE'S A SPY.
PYGM IV (266)	THE WHOLE DAMNED HOUSEFUL IF YOU LIKE. EXCEPT THE	JEWELS	. THEYRE HIRED. WILL THAT SATISFY YOU? (HE TURNS ON

DOCT IV (162)	ALWAYS WEAR BEAUTIFUL DRESSES AND SPLENDID MAGIC	JEWELS	. THINK OF ALL THE WONDERFUL PICTURES I SHALL NEVER
LADY PREFACE(235)	AS TREASURING AND USING (AS I DO MYSELF) THE	JEWELS	OF UNCONSCIOUSLY MUSICAL SPEECH WHICH COMMON PEOPLE
PYGM IV (267)	FURTHER SUPPLY) STOP, PLEASE. (SHE TAKES OFF HER	JEWELS	). WILL YOU TAKE THESE TO YOUR ROOM AND KEEP THEM
CATH 1,SD(161)	ENORMOUS SLIPPERS, WORTH, WITH THEIR CRUST OF	JEWELS	, SEVERAL THOUSAND ROUBLES APIECE. SUPERFICIALLY
		JEWESS	
MIS. PREFACE(83)	MUCH LONGER IN THE SEXUAL ARENA. THE CULTIVATED	JEWESS	NO LONGER CUTS OFF HER HAIR AT HER MARRIAGE. THE
SUPR HANDBOK(181)	BOTH HIS PARENTS; BUT IT IS NOT LIKELY THAT THE	JEWESS	WOULD FIND THE SQUIRE AN INTERESTING COMPANION, OR
MILL II (172)	WE ARE NOW BANKERS TO ALL THE WORLD. /THE DOCTOR/	JEWESS	, EH? /EPIFANIA/ CHRISTIAN, TO THE LAST DROP OF MY
SUPR HANDBOK(181)	IMAGINATIVE, INTELLECTUAL, HIGHLY CIVILIZED	JEWESS	, MIGHT BE VERY SUPERIOR TO BOTH HIS PARENTS; BUT IT
		JEWISH	
GENV IV (112)	I HAVE SNAPPED MY FINGERS IN THE FACE OF ALL YOUR	JEWISH	BELIEFS AND ROMAN TRADITIONS, YOUR FUTILE TREATIES
MTH3 (125)	BRAINS, JUST AS IT WAS DONE IN MY EARLY DAYS BY	JEWISH	BRAINS, SCOTTISH BRAINS, ITALIAN BRAINS, GERMAN
LION PREFACE(101)	THEOLOGY AS OURS IN EXCHANGE FOR HIS OWN, OR OUR	JEWISH	CANONICAL LITERATURE AS AN IMPROVEMENT ON HINDOO
FABL I (104)	WONT PAY TWOPENCE FOR A WASHING MACHINE. WHEN A	JEWISH	CHEMIST FOUND OUT HOW TO MAKE HIGH EXPLOSIVE CHEAPLY
LION PREFACE(102)	OF A NEW ECCLESIASTICAL ORGANIZATION FOR THE	JEWISH	CHURCH OR FOR THE PRIESTHOOD OF THE ROMAN GODS AS
SUPR III (82)	IVE HEARD MY SISTER SAY SO. SHE WAS COOK IN A	JEWISH	FAMILY ONCE. /MENDOZA/ I COULD NOT DENY IT; NEITHER
ROCK PREFACE(186)	EXCEPT BY DEALING WITH JEWISH FOOLS ACCORDING TO	JEWISH	FOLLY. BUT SEDITION CONCERNS ME AND MY OFFICE VERY
ROCK PREFACE(186)	CANNOT KEEP ORDER IN JEWRY EXCEPT BY DEALING WITH	JEWISH	FOOLS ACCORDING TO JEWISH FOLLY. BUT SEDITION
GENV IV (125)	RACE, WILL PROFIT BY OUR DESPAIR. WHY HAS OUR	JEWISH	FRIEND JUST LEFT US? TO TELEPHONE, HE SAID. YES; BUT
GENV III (79)	HER TO PREVENT HER FROM SACRIFICING THIS HARMLESS	JEWISH	GENTLEMAN AS HER ANCESTORS WOULD HAVE SACRIFICED HIM
GENV III (79)	SACRIFICING A JEW TO HIM. /THE JUDGE/ AS TO THE	JEWISH	GENTLEMAN HIMSELF, I NEED NOT DWELL ON HIS CASE, AS
GENV IV (118)	TO ANSWER AN ACCUSATION MADE AGAINST YOU BY A	JEWISH	GENTLEMAN OF UNLAWFUL ARREST AND IMPRISONMENT,
GENV I (34)	CAN I DO ANYTHING? /NEWCOMER/ (LOOKING AT THE	JEWISH	GENTLEMAN) I'M AFRAID I'M INTERRUPTING. /THE JEW/ NOT
ROCK PREFACE(182)	AND ALL THE WORLD KNOWS WHAT THE PEACE OF YOUR	JEWISH	GOD MEANS. HAVE I NOT READ IT IN THE CAMPAIGNS OF
LION PREFACE(36)	THAN HIMSELF SHALL COME AFTER HIM DOES THE OLD	JEWISH	HOPE OF A MESSIAH BEGIN TO STIR AGAIN; AND AS JESUS
3PLA PREFACE(R11)	JEWS. ALL THAT CAN FAIRLY BE SAID OF THE	JEWISH	INFLUENCE ON THE THEATRE IS THAT IT IS EXOTIC, AND IS
LION PREFACE(43)	IN THE TEMPLE, AND JUSTIFIED HIMSELF BOTH TO THE	JEWISH	LAW AND TO CAESAR. AND HE HAD PHYSICAL FORCE AT HIS
GENV IV (118)	THAT YOU HAVE NO DEFENCE. YOU CANNOT EVEN FIND A	JEWISH	LAWYER TO DEFEND YOU, BECAUSE YOU HAVE DRIVEN THEM
METH PREFACE(R62)	WHAT DARWIN HAD NOT: IMPLACABILITY AND A FINE	JEWISH	LITERARY GIFT, WITH TERRIBLE POWERS OF HATRED,
3PLA PREFACE(R11)	AND HIS FAMILY, AND THE PRESENCE OF THE RICH	JEWISH	MERCHANT AND HIS FAMILY. I CAN SEE NO VALIDITY
LION PREFACE(24)	THAN THOSE OF MOSES, BUT FOR THE ACTION OF THE	JEWISH	PRIESTS, WHO TO SAVE JEWRY FROM BEING SUBMERGED IN
GENV IV (112)	I MUST INTERVENE. ARE WE HERE TO DISCUSS THE	JEWISH	PROBLEM? IF SO, I HAVE NO BUSINESS HERE: MY COUNTRY
LION PREFACE(20)	AS MERE RECORDS OF THE FULFILMENT OF ANCIENT	JEWISH	PROPHECIES. THIS CRAZE NO DOUBT LED HIM TO SEEK FOR
ROCK PREFACE(186)	QUALITY TO THE MOB, EVEN IF HIS QUALITY BE ONLY A	JEWISH	QUALITY. FOR I AM A PATRICIAN AND THEREFORE MYSELF A
GENV IV (105)	IF YOU ALLOW ERNEST TO EXPATIATE ON THE	JEWISH	QUESTION WE SHALL GET NO FURTHER BEFORE BED-TIME. HE
CLEO V (196)	THINK YOU? /APOLLODORUS/ HE WAS SETTLING THE	JEWISH	QUESTION WHEN I LEFT. A FLOURISH OF TRUMPETS FROM THE
ROCK PREFACE(186)	YOUR BLASPHEMY IS NOTHING TO ME: THE WHOLE	JEWISH	RELIGION IS BLASPHEMY FROM BEGINNING TO END FROM MY
SUPR HANDBOK(197)	PURITANS, INFLAMED BY THE MASTERPIECES OF	JEWISH	REVOLUTIONARY LITERATURE, CUT OFF THE HEADS OF THE
GENV IV (112)	MIND THAT HAS BEEN FORMED IN ITS INFANCY BY THE	JEWISH	SCRIPTURES. THAT OBSTACLE I MUST SMASH THROUGH AT ALL
3PLA PREFACE(R11)	AND THOSE PERFORMERS THAT APPEAL SPECIALLY TO THE	JEWISH	TASTE. ENGLISH INFLUENCE ON THE THEATRE, AS FAR AS
LION PREFACE(81)	CHARITY, THAT HE WOULD HAVE ADMIRED. HE IS MORE	JEWISH	THAN THE JEWS, MORE ROMAN THAN THE ROMANS, PROUD BOTH
ROCK PREFACE(186)	ONE AT THAT, YET I PERCEIVE THAT YOU ARE IN YOUR	JEWISH	WAY A MAN OF QUALITY; AND IT MAKES ME UNEASY TO THROW
		JEWLERY	
PYGM II (235)	INSTRUMENT, GOVERNOR. A FEW PICTURES, A TRIFLE OF	JEWLERY	, AND A BIRD-CAGE. SHE SAID SHE DIDNT WANT NO
		JEWRY	
ROCK PREFACE(186)	TO THE HIGH PRIEST; AND I CANNOT KEEP ORDER IN	JEWRY	EXCEPT BY DEALING WITH JEWISH FOOLS ACCORDING TO
LION PREFACE(24)	FOR THE ACTION OF THE JEWISH PRIESTS, WHO TO SAVE	JEWRY	FROM BEING SUBMERGED IN THE RISING FLOOD OF
LION PREFACE(21)	" JOINED THE SOCIALISTS." AS FAR AS ESTABLISHED	JEWRY	WAS CONCERNED, HE BURNT HIS BOATS BY THIS ACTION, AND
		JEW'S	
SUPR HANDBOK(201)	PEOPLE WHO ONCE, AS " THE UNSOAPED," PLAYED THE	JEW'S	HARP OR THE ACCORDION IN MOLESKINS AND BELCHERS. SOME
		JEWS	
BULL III (132)	AND WE'LL NEVER DO ANY GOOD AT IT. WE'RE LIKE THE	JEWS	: THE ALMIGHTY GAVE US BRAINS, AND BID US FARM THEM,
POSN PREFACE(384)	NEEDED NO TOLERATION FROM CATHOLICS AND	JEWS	: THE TOLERATION THEY NEEDED WAS THAT OF THE PEOPLE WHO
JOAN 4 (96)	MONSTROUS. IT IS ALL THOSE SCOUNDRELS OF	JEWS	: THEY GET IN EVERY TIME MONEY CHANGES HANDS. I WOULD
MILL PREFACE(124)	GLASS HOUSES. IS IT WISE TO THROW STONES AT THE	JEWS	? IS IT WISE TO THROW STONES AT ALL? HERR HITLER IS
GENV I (33)	I DENY THAT THERE ARE GOOD REASONS FOR DISLIKING	JEWS	? ON THE CONTRARY, I DISLIKE MOST OF THEM MYSELF.
ROCK PREFACE(181)	CIRCUMSTANCES. /PILATE/ ARE YOU THE KING OF THE	JEWS	? /JESUS/ DO YOU REALLY WANT TO KNOW? OR HAVE THOSE
MTH4 I (155)	LOST TRIBES OF ISRAEL; BUT ON THEIR APPROACH THE	JEWS	ABANDONED THE CITY AND REDISTRIBUTED THEMSELVES
ROCK PREFACE(188)	THE RICH, FEAR OF THE HIGH PRIESTS, FEAR OF THE	JEWS	AND GREEKS WHO ARE LEARNED, FEAR OF THE GAULS AND GOTHS
MTH4 I (156)	TO PALESTINE. SINCE THEN THE WORLD, BEREFT OF ITS	JEWS	AND ITS IRISH, HAS BEEN A TAME DULL PLACE. IS THERE NO
ROCK PREFACE(159)	WHICH CONSISTED OF GREAT PUBLIC SHOWS AT WHICH	JEWS	AND PROTESTANTS OR CATHOLICS, AND ANYONE ELSE WHO COULD
LION PREFACE(4)	THE DOCTRINES THAT DISTINGUISHED CHRIST FROM THE	JEWS	AND THE BARABBASQUES GENERALLY, INCLUDING OURSELVES.
CAPT II (263)	BUT I HAVE SWORN AN OATH TO HIM TO TAKE ONLY	JEWS	AND TRUE BELIEVERS-- NO CHRISTIANS, YOU UNDERSTAND.
ROCK PREFACE(182)	THE PROTESTS OF MY SHRINKING FLESH? /PILATE/ YOU	JEWS	ARE A SIMPLE FOLK. YOU HAVE FOUND ONLY ONE GOD. WE
ROCK PREFACE(181)	SEEM EXCEPTIONALLY INTELLIGENT TO A JEW. YOU	JEWS	ARE ALWAYS TALKING ABOUT TRUTH AND RIGHTEOUSNESS AND
GENV PREFACE(19)	SUCH AS THAT ALL PLUTOCRATS ARE JEWS; THAT THE	JEWS	ARE AN ACCURSED RACE WHO SHOULD BE EXTERMINATED AS
MILL PREFACE(124)	SOLDIER HAD FOR KILLING ARCHIMEDES. NOW NO DOUBT	JEWS	ARE MOST OBNOXIOUS CREATURES. ANY COMPETENT HISTORIAN
DOCT II (123)	/RIDGEON/ COME, LOONY! DO YOU MEAN TO SAY THAT	JEWS	ARE NEVER ROGUES AND THIEVES? /SCHUTZMACHER/ OH, NOT
MILL PREFACE(124)	COULD BE JUSTIFIED ONLY ON THE GROUND THAT THE	JEWS	ARE THE NATURAL ENEMIES OF THE REST OF THE HUMAN RACE,
LION PREFACE(21)	DISCARDING OF CIRCUMCISION FOR BAPTISM WAS TO THE	JEWS	AS STARTLING A HERESY AS THE DISCARDING OF
GENV III (71)	TO SHOOT ME. /THE COMMISSAR/ WE DO NOT SHOOT	JEWS	AS SUCH: WE CIVILIZE THEM. YOU SEE, A COMMUNIST STATE
ROCK PREFACE(150)	ENEMIES OF GOD, JUST AS TORQUEMADA REGARDED THE	JEWS	AS THE MURDERERS OF GOD. ALL THAT IS AN OLD STORY: WHAT
LION PREFACE(23)	OR OBSTRUCTIVE; AND OUTRAGES THE FEELINGS OF THE	JEWS	BY BREACHES OF IT. HE IS APT TO ACCUSE PEOPLE WHO FEEL
MTH4 I (156)	VANISHED FROM HUMAN KNOWLEDGE. AND THE DISPERSED	JEWS	DID THE SAME LEST THEY SHOULD BE SENT BACK TO
ROCK II (271)	BETWEEN ANY CHEAP JACK AND SOLOMON OR MOSES? THE	JEWS	DIDNT ELECT MOSES: HE JUST TOLD THEM WHAT TO DO AND
GENV III (72)	HE IS A JEW. /THE COMMISSAR/ COME TO RUSSIA.	JEWS	DO NOT DO SUCH THINGS THERE. NO DOUBT THEY ARE CAPABLE
LION PREFACE(22)	HE POINTED OUT THE CONTRAST HIMSELF, CHAFFING THE	JEWS	FOR COMPLAINING THAT JOHN MUST BE POSSESSED BY THE
LION PREFACE(74)	APOSTLES ADDED INCESSANT DENUNCIATIONS OF THE	JEWS	FOR HAVING CRUCIFIED HIM, AND THREATS OF THE
LION PREFACE(7)	THAN GALILEO DID. HE WAS EXECUTED BY THE	JEWS	FOR THE BLASPHEMY OF CLAIMING TO BE A GOD; AND PILATE
JOAN 4 (96)	IF I HAD MY WAY. /THE NOBLEMAN/ WHY NOT? THE	JEWS	GENERALLY GIVE VALUE. THEY MAKE YOU PAY; BUT THEY
MILL PREFACE(124)	IT WOULD HAVE BEEN BETTER FOR THE WORLD IF THE	JEWS	HAD NEVER EXISTED. BUT I, AS AN IRISHMAN, CAN, WITH
LION PREFACE(84)	THAT PAUL BECAME THE APOSTLE TO THE GENTILES. THE	JEWS	HAD THEIR OWN RITE OF INITIATION: THE RITE OF
ROCK PREFACE(182)	MANY; AND ONE OF THEM IS A GOD OF LIES. EVEN YOU	JEWS	HAVE TO ADMIT A FATHER OF LIES WHOM YOU CALL THE DEVIL.
SUPR HANDBOK(204)	REHOBOAM: INDEED, THE COMPARISON IS UNFAIR TO THE	JEWS	IN VIEW OF THE FACTS THAT THE MOSAIC LAW FORBADE MORE
2TRU PREFACE(18)	SUCH A SCALE THAT WHEN TORQUEMADA BEGAN BURNING	JEWS	INSTEAD OF ALLOWING THEM TO RANSOM THEIR BODIES BY
LION PREFACE(21)	EFFECT OF SUCH A HERESY AS THIS ON THE	JEWS	IS NOT APPARENT: IT SEEMS TO US AS NATURAL THAT JOHN
2TRU III (86)	AND THOUGH IT MAY HAVE GONE DOWN WITH THOSE OLD	JEWS	IT ISNT RELIGION. AND, IF IT ISNT, WHERE ARE WE? THATS
3PLA PREFACE(R11)	CHRISTIANS THAN WHEN THEY KNOW THEMSELVES	JEWS	. ALL THAT CAN FAIRLY BE SAID OF THE JEWISH INFLUENCE
LION PREFACE(30)	AND BORE OUT THE INCREDULITY OF PILATE AND THE	JEWS	. AND AS MATTHEW WRITES AS ONE BELIEVING IN THAT SECOND
POSN PREFACE(394)	IN A CITY OCCUPIED LARGELY AND INFLUENTIALLY BY	JEWS	. COURT ETIQUET IS NO DOUBT AN EXCELLENT THING FOR
GENV III (71)	WIDOW/ HE IS A BOLSHEVIST. ALL BOLSHEVISTS ARE	JEWS	. DO YOU REALIZE THAT IF I LIVED UNDER THE HORRIBLE
GENV III (68)	PEOPLE VOTED TEN TO ONE FOR GETTING RID OF THE	JEWS	. HADNT THEY THE RIGHT TO CHOOSE THE SORT OF PEOPLE
LION PREFACE(7)	ROME BY SAYING THAT HE WAS THE KING OF THE	JEWS	. HE WAS NOT FALSELY ACCUSED, NOR DENIED FULL
LION PREFACE(34)	THE PROPHETS HAD SOMETIMES PREFERRED GENTILES TO	JEWS	. IN FACT THEY TRY TO THROW HIM DOWN FROM A SORT OF
DOCT II (123)	I WAS COMPARING HONEST ENGLISHMEN WITH HONEST	JEWS	. ONE OF THE HOTEL MAIDS, A PRETTY, FAIR-HAIRED WOMAN
CLEO II SD(118)	DARKER, FROM UPPER EGYPT; WITH A FEW GREEKS AND	JEWS	. PROMINENT IN A GROUP ON PTOLEMY'S RIGHT HAND IS
MILL PREFACE(124)	WAY, THOUGH EXCEPTIONALLY DESIRABLE GERMANS, WERE	JEWS	. SURELY THE AVERAGE GERMAN CAN BE IMPROVED. I AM TOLD
LION PREFACE(11)	WITH GREAT EASE, BUT CANNOT CONVERT MAHOMETANS OR	JEWS	. THE NEGRO FINDS IN CIVILIZED SALVATIONISM AN
DOCT II (122)	WITH MY KNOWLEDGE, AND THAT SHE ALWAYS ADMIRED	JEWS	. THEN HE ASKED ME TO ADVANCE HIM 50 POUNDS ON THE
MILL PREFACE(125)	CROSSFERTILIZED ALIENS, POSSIBLY BY COSMOPOLITAN	JEWS	. THERE IS MORE DIFFERENCE BETWEEN A CATHOLIC BAVARIAN

DOCT PREFACE(59) DECLARING CERTAIN KINDS OF FLESH UNCLEAN BY THE JEWS . TO ADVERTIZE ANY REMEDY OR OPERATION, YOU HAVE ONLY
GENV I (33) OH, DONT SAY THAT. IVE KNOWN LOTS OF QUITE NICE JEWS . WHAT I SAY IS WHY PICK ON THE JEWS, AS IF THEY WERE
GENV III (84) /THE WIDOW/ IT IS TRUE. YOU HAVE TASTE, YOU JEWS . YOU HAVE APPETITES, YOU ARE VITAL, IN YOUR ORIENTAL
LION PREFACE(70) THE EFFECT OF MARRIAGE AS IT EXISTED AMONG THE JEWS (AND AS IT STILL EXISTS AMONG OURSELVES) WAS TO MAKE
ROCK PREFACE(150) IS THAT ARISTOCRATS (LAVOISIER'S CLASS) AND JEWS (EINSTEIN'S RACE) ARE UNFIT TO ENJOY THE PRIVILEGE OF
GENV IV (105) MEDDLING WITH IT, AND FORCING ME TO BANISH THE JEWS LEST MY PEOPLE SHOULD BE SWAMPED BY THE MULTITUDES HE
LION PREFACE(85) -- HIS PLEAS IN MITIGATION ONLY MADE THE JEWS MORE DETERMINED TO STONE HIM. THUS FROM THE VERY
DOCT I SD(85) AND STALE AFTER THIRTY, AS HANDSOME YOUNG JEWS OFTEN DO, BUT STILL DECIDEDLY GOOD-LOOKING. /THE
GENV III (71) JEW! ! ! /THE SECRETARY/ NO, NO. YOU HAVE JEWS ON THE BRAIN. /THE WIDOW/ HE IS A BOLSHEVIST. ALL
3PLA PREFACE(R11) IN THE VIEW THAT THE INFLUENCE OF THE RICH JEWS ON THE THEATRE IS ANY WORSE THAN THE INFLUENCE OF THE
FABL V (119) PUNS. /ROSE/ TRUE. ANOTHER SET OF THEM, CALLED JEWS OR ISRAELITES, TORTURED A YOUNG MAN TO DEATH FOR TRYING
JOAN PREFACE(28) THAT ALL HERETICS WERE ALBIGENSIANS OR HUSITES OR JEWS OR PROTESTANTS OF THE HIGHEST CHARACTER; AND THAT THE
ROCK PREFACE(185) IS WITHIN YOU. IT WAS WHEN I SAID THIS THAT THE JEWS -- MY OWN PEOPLE-- BEGAN PICKING UP STONES. BUT WHY
LION PREFACE(84) TO MAKE IT MUCH EASIER TO CONVERT GENTILES THAN JEWS ; AND IT WAS BY FOLLOWING THE LINE OF LEAST RESISTANCE
GENV PREFACE(19) UP WITH FANCIES SUCH AS THAT ALL PLUTOCRATS ARE JEWS ; THAT THE JEWS ARE AN ACCURSED RACE WHO SHOULD BE
LION PREFACE(38) URBANE EASY-MINDED CHARMER OF LUKE. INDEED, THE JEWS SAY OF HIM " HOW KNOWETH THIS MAN LETTERS, HAVING NEVER
LION PREFACE(41) THE DOING OF THE MERCY AND JUSTICE OF GOD. THE JEWS STONED HIM FOR SAYING THESE THINGS, AND, WHEN HE
MILL II (172) CHRISTIAN, TO THE LAST DROP OF MY BLOOD. JEWS THROW HALF THEIR MONEY AWAY ON CHARITIES AND FANCIES
POSN PREFACE(384) CATHOLIC EMANCIPATION AND THE ADMISSION OF JEWS TO PARLIAMENT NEEDED NO TOLERATION FROM CATHOLICS AND
DOCT II (122) CONVERSATION WITH MR WALPOLE, HE SAID THAT THE JEWS WERE THE ONLY PEOPLE WHO KNEW ANYTHING ABOUT ART, AND
MILL PREFACE(123) ONE. HE CARRIED OUT A PERSECUTION OF THE JEWS WHICH WENT TO THE SCANDALOUS LENGTH OF OUTLAWING,
MILL PREFACE(125) FUSION OF RACES DOES NOT ALWAYS BLEND THEM. THE JEWS WILL OFTEN THROW UP AN APPARENTLY PURE-BRED HITTITE OR
BULL III (132) /FATHER DEMPSEY/ (WITH GENTLE IRONY) OH! IS IT JEWS YOU WANT TO MAKE OF US? I MUST CATECHIZE YOU A BIT
DOCT II (123) AT ALL. PERSONALLY, I LIKE ENGLISHMEN BETTER THAN JEWS , AND ALWAYS ASSOCIATE WITH THEM. THATS ONLY NATURAL,
SIM PREFACE(10) WHICH CLASSED RESPECTABLE PROTESTANTS WITH JEWS , AND BURNED BOTH. CONCEIVE, THEN, OUR HORROR WHEN THE
GENV PREFACE(20) UP OF SCRAPS OF SOCIALISM, MORTAL HATRED OF THE JEWS , AND COMPLETE CONTEMPT FOR PSEUDO-DEMOCRATIC
GENV I (33) OF QUITE NICE JEWS. WHAT I SAY IS WHY PICK ON THE JEWS , AS IF THEY WERE ANY WORSE THAN OTHER PEOPLE? /THE
LION PREFACE(85) MADE WAY FASTER AMONG THE GENTILES THAN AMONG THE JEWS , AS IT ENABLED THEM TO PLEAD THAT THEY TOO WERE
BUOY 1 (13) FOR HITLERS WHO CALL ON THEM TO EXTERMINATE JEWS , FOR MUSSOLINIS WHO RALLY THEM TO NATIONALIST DREAMS
LION PREFACE(81) HE WOULD HAVE ADMIRED. HE IS MORE JEWISH THAN THE JEWS , MORE ROMAN THAN THE ROMANS, PROUD BOTH WAYS, FULL OF
LION PREFACE(85) CIRCUMCISION DID NOT MATTER; AND THIS, TO THE JEWS , WAS AN INTOLERABLE BLASPHEMY. TO GENTILES LIKE
SIM PREFACE(12) WHETHER WE ACCEPT THE DIVINITY OF CHRIST OR ARE JEWS , WHETHER WE BELIEVE IN TRANSUBSTANTIATION OR MERELY IN
LION PREFACE(40) BEEN MADE, OR ELSE HAVE HAD TO CONFESS TO THE JEWS , WHO WERE THE KEENEST CRITICS OF THE CHRISTIANS, THAT
SUPR HANDBOK(198) BY ENTHUSIASTIC CRIMINALS AND LUNATICS. EVEN THE JEWS , WHO, FROM MOSES TO MARX AND LASSALLE, HAVE INSPIRED
GENV IV (125) THROW OFF ALL DECENCY, ALL PRUDENCE. ONLY THE JEWS , WITH THE BUSINESS FACULTY PECULIAR TO THEIR RACE,
BULL I (86) MONOPOLIZE ENGLAND. HYPOCRITES, HUMBUGS, GERMANS, JEWS , YANKEES, FOREIGNERS, PARK LANERS, COSMOPOLITAN
GENV III (70) MADAM. IF THERE WERE WOMEN ON THE JURY, OR SOME JEWS , YOUR GOOD LOOKS MIGHT NOT SAVE YOU. /THE WIDOW/ WOMEN
GENV III (75) DANGEROUS IN GENEVA, BUT THE PEOPLE. /THE WIDOW/ JEWS ! BOLSHEVIKS! GUNMEN! /THE JEW/ WHAT ABOUT

JIBBERING
JOAN 1 (58) WORST, MOST INCOMPETENT, DRIVELLING SNIVELLING JIBBERING JABBERING IDIOT OF A STEWARD IN FRANCE. (HE

JIBE
SUPR PREFACE(R10) I NEVER DO ANYTHING ELSE: IT IS YOUR FAVORITE JIBE AT ME THAT WHAT I CALL DRAMA IS NOTHING BUT
CAPT NOTES (304) PHONETICIAN. THIS IS NO MERE RASH AND IGNORANT JIBE OF MY OWN AT THE EXPENSE OF MY ENGLISH NEIGHBORS.
NEVR IV (285) HEAR HIS MIND WORKING. /GLORIA/ (IGNORING THE JIBE) WHERE IS HE? /VALENTINE/ BOUGHT A FALSE NOSE AND
JOAN 5 (111) YOU TO HEAVY DRESSING. /CHARLES/ YES: THE OLD JIBE ! WELL, I AM NOT GOING TO WEAR ARMOR: FIGHTING IS NOT

JIBES
GETT (328) SOCIETY SMALL TALK? /HOTCHKISS/ (RECKLESSLY) JIBES ARE USELESS: THE FORCE THAT IS SWEEPING ME AWAY WILL
METH PREFACE(R74) THE SCEPTICAL CITY PROLETARIAT, THEN, WHEN THE JIBES OF HIS MATES SET HIM THINKING, AND HE SEES THAT THESE

JIFFY
SUPR IV (145) JACK'S MOTOR: STRAKER WILL RATTLE YOU HERE IN A JIFFY . QUICK, QUICK, QUICK. YOUR LOVING VIOLET." (HE LOOKS

JIGGERED
POSN (451) COURSE HE HAS. INSULTING THE COURT! CHALLENGE BE JIGGERED ! GAG HIM. /NESTOR/ (A JURYMAN WITH A LONG WHITE
POSN (462) IS THIS A MOTHERS' MEETING? WELL, I'LL BE JIGGERED ! WHERE DOES THE SPORT COME IN? /THE SHERIFF/ (

JIGSAW
SIM II (84) UTOPIAS AND THE MILLENNIUMS AND THE REST OF THE JIGSAW PUZZLES: I AM A WOMAN AND I KNOW IT. LET MEN DESPAIR
SIM II (84) PLANS FAIL. SO MUCH THE BETTER: PLANS ARE ONLY JIGSAW PUZZLES: ONE GETS TIRED OF THEM LONG BEFORE ONE CAN
SIM II (84) I TELL YOU THIS IS A WORLD OF MIRACLES, NOT OF JIGSAW PUZZLES. FOR ME EVERY DAY MUST HAVE ITS MIRACLE, AND

JILT
FANY III (299) IF YOU TELL THE YOUNG LADY THAT YOU WANT TO JILT HER, AND SHE CALLS YOU A PIG, THE TONE OF THE
SUPR I (10) THATS ANOTHER COMPLICATION. WELL, SHE'LL EITHER JILT HIM AND SAY I DIDNT APPROVE OF HIM, OR MARRY HIM AND

JILTED
PHIL II (110) MEAN? /GRACE/ WHAT I SAY, LEONARD. /CHARTERIS/ JILTED AGAIN: THE FICKLENESS OF THE WOMEN I LOVE IS ONLY
LADY PREFACE(232) AND A VERY SERIOUS ONE. HE MIGHT HAVE BEEN JILTED BY TEN DARK LADIES AND BEEN NONE THE WORSE FOR IT;
JITT III (71) YOU MEAN. /JITTA/ DOCTOR FESSLER SAYS YOU HAVE JILTED HIM. /EDITH/ DID HE CALL IT JILTING HIM? /JITTA/ NO.
MIS. (124) THATS THE REASON I NEVER SAID A WORD WHEN YOU JILTED POOR JERRY MACKINTOSH. /HYPATIA/ (EXCUSING HERSELF)

JILTING
JITT III (71) SAYS YOU HAVE JILTED HIM. /EDITH/ DID HE CALL IT JILTING HIM? /JITTA/ NO. I CALL IT THAT. /EDITH/ BUT YOU
FANY III (299) I ASSURE YOU, SIR, THERES NO CORRECT WAY OF JILTING . IT'S NOT CORRECT IN ITSELF. /BOBBY/ (HOPEFULLY)

JIM
MTH2 (87) UP. I FORGOT ABOUT IT TOO; AND I WAS VERY FOND OF JIM . /HASLAM/ I DIDNT FORGET IT, BECAUSE I'M OF MILITARY
DEVL I (22) THAT HE SHALL BE A GOOD FRIEND TO MY OLD HORSE JIM "-- (AGAIN SHAKING HIS HEAD) HE SHOULD HAVE WRITTEN

JIMINY
ROCK II (260) THATS THE STUFF, DEXY. NOW YOU ARE TALKING. BY JIMINY . /BASHAM/ (TAKING COMMAND OF THE DISCUSSION COOLLY)
POSN (465) MORE GOOD AND BAD. THERES NO GOOD AND BAD; BUT BY JIMINY , GENTS, THERES A ROTTEN GAME, AND THERES A GREAT
CATH 3 (184) BUT I CANT TAKE THESE VALUABLE THINGS. BY JIMINY , THOUGH, THEYRE BEAUTIFUL! LOOK AT THEM, CLAIRE. AS

JIMMINY
JITT II (27) UP LAST NIGHT, WERE YOU? /FESSLER/ NO. BUT, BY JIMMINY , LENKHEIM, I HAVE GONE THROUGH A LOT THIS LAST

JIMMY
CAND I (82) /LEXY/ (ANXIOUSLY) BUT, MY DEAR MORELL, IF WHAT JIMMY AND FLUFFY HAD WAS SCARLATINA, DO YOU THINK IT WISE--
DOCT I (94) /SIR PATRICK/ IT WAS CALLED A CABINETMAKER'S JIMMY THEN. /WALPOLE/ GET OUT! NONSENSE! CABINETMAKER BE--
CAND I (82) UP FOR TWO DAYS, TO GET SOME FLANNEL THINGS FOR JIMMY , AND TO SEE HOW WE'RE GETTING ON WITHOUT HER. /LEXY/

JIM'S
MTH2 (87) SONS WERE KILLED IN IT. /SAVVY/ (SOBERED) YES. JIM'S DEATH KILLED MOTHER. /HASLAM/ AND THEY NEVER SAID A

JINGHISKAHN
MIS. (190) SUMMERHAYS: DID YOU HAVE CHAPS OF THIS SORT IN JINGHISKAHN ? /LORD SUMMERHAYS/ OH YES: THEY EXIST
MIS. (190) HERE IN ENGLAND. WHAT WOULD YOU DO WITH ME IN JINGHISKAHN IF YOU HAD ME THERE? /LORD SUMMERHAYS/ WELL,
MIS. (157) SUMMERHAYS/ IT DOESNT MATTER, MRS TARLETON: IN JINGHISKAHN IT WAS A PUNISHABLE OFFENCE TO EXPOSE A BIBLE
MIS. (147) ABOUT IT. /TARLETON/ (RESTLESS AGAIN) YOU MEAN JINGHISKAHN . AH YES. GOOD THING THE EMPIRE. EDUCATES US.
MIS. (131) FOR GOVERNMENT. YOU LEARNT YOUR JOB OUT THERE IN JINGHISKAHN . WELL, WE WANT TO BE GOVERNED HERE IN ENGLAND.
MIS. (199) WHAT TO DO. /LORD SUMMERHAYS/ WHEN MY COUNCIL IN JINGHISKAHN REACHED THE POINT OF COMING TO BLOWS, I USED TO

MIS. (136) NOT AT ALL. I HAD FIVE KINGS TO MANAGE IN JINGHISKAHN ; AND I THINK YOU DO YOUR HUSBAND SOME
MIS. (131) US. /LORD SUMMERHAYS/ AH YES, MY FRIEND; BUT IN JINGHISKAHN YOU HAVE TO GOVERN THE RIGHT WAY. IF YOU DONT,

JINGHISKAHNS
MIS. (148) NO; BUT I WISH YOUD TELL THE CHICKABIDDY THAT THE JINGHISKAHNS EAT NO END OF TOASTED CHEESE, AND THAT IT'S THE

JINGLE
LADY (241) FAILING HIM). YET TELL ME WHICH WAS THE VILE JINGLE ? YOU SAID VERY JUSTLY: MINE OWN EAR CAUGHT IT EVEN
LADY (241) ADMIRATION FOR A SPACE--" /THE LADY/ A VERY VILE JINGLE OF ESSES. I SAID " SEASON YOUR-- /THE MAN/ (HASTILY)
WIDO II (46) NOW YOUVE SET MY HANDS ALL TREMBLING; AND I SHALL JINGLE THE THINGS ON THE TRAY AT LUNCH SO THAT EVERYBODY

JINGLES
MTH5 (210) THE BEAUTY OF A FEW PILLARS AND ARCHES; MAKING JINGLES WITH WORDS; LYING ABOUT WITH YOUR ARMS ROUND ME,

JINGLING
PYGM III (245) BE CHANGED. (RISING ABRUPTLY AND WALKING ABOUT, JINGLING HIS MONEY AND HIS KEYS IN HIS TROUSER POCKETS)
NEVR IV SD(292) JUST COME BACK FROM THE BAR IN THE GARDEN, AND IS JINGLING HIS TRAY AS HE COMES SOFTLY TO THE TABLE WITH IT.
WIDO II (48) GOES OUT, VERY ANGRY. THE PARLORMAID, WITH A TRAY JINGLING IN HER HANDS, PASSES OUTSIDE). YOU HAVE
CLEO III (151) IN A BOWL OF WINE? (HE TAKES OUT HIS PURSE, JINGLING THE COINS IN IT). THE QUEEN HAS PRESENTS FOR YOU

JINGO
PRES (143) /MITCHENER/ THESE ARE THE ROMANTIC RAVINGS OF A JINGO CIVILIAN, BALSQUITH. AT LEAST YOULL NOT DENY THAT THE
MTH2 (52) OF A RABBLE OF SOCIALISTS AND ANTI-SOCIALISTS, OF JINGO IMPERIALISTS AND LITTLE ENGLANDERS, OF CAST-IRON
APPL I (213) CORRUPT LEGISLATION. /BOANERGES/ SO IT IS, BY JINGO . WHAT OTHER DEFENCE IS THERE? DEMOCRACY? YAH! WE
BULL PREFACE(41) YOU CAN ALWAYS GET ANOTHER IRISHMAN TO BASTE HIM. JINGO ORATORY IN ENGLAND IS SICKENING ENOUGH TO SERIOUS
BULL PREFACE(41) POLICE. WELL, IN IRELAND ALL POLITICAL ORATORY IS JINGO ORATORY; AND ALL POLITICAL DEMONSTRATIONS ARE
JOAN PREFACE(7) HER IN ITS CONCLUDING SCENES IN DEFERENCE TO JINGO PATRIOTISM. THE MUD THAT WAS THROWN AT HER HAS DROPPED
LADY PREFACE(230) BESIDE THE INEVITABLE COMIC ONES. EVEN IN THE JINGO PLAY, HENRY V, WE GET BATES AND WILLIAMS DRAWN WITH
BULL PREFACE(62) OF OUR ARISTOCRATIC-MILITARY CASTE AND TO OUR JINGO PLUTOCRATS-- THEN THERE CAN BE NO MORE SACRED AND
JOAN PREFACE(7) WHICH DISFIGURES HER BEYOND RECOGNITION. WHEN JINGO SCURRILITY HAD DONE ITS WORST TO HER, SECTARIAN
MTH3 (132) TRUE. BUT SOME DAY WE'LL GROW UP; AND THEN, BY JINGO , WE'LL SHEW EM. /CONFUCIUS/ THE ARCHBISHOP IS AN
APPL I (205) PERHAPS. BUT NOT WHEN I AM HOME SECRETARY, BY JINGO ! NOBODY WILL MAKE AN INDIARUBBER STAMP OF BILL

JINGOISM
JOAN PREFACE(25) BELIEVED THE ILIAD TO BE A BURLESQUE OF GREEK JINGOISM AND GREEK RELIGION, WRITTEN BY A HOSTAGE OR A

JINNY
DOCT IV (166) HALF RETURN OF HIS NORMAL STRENGTH AND COMFORT) JINNY GWINNY: I THINK I SHALL RECOVER AFTER ALL. (SIR

JINNY-GWINNY
DOCT II (117) ON HIS GLOVES BEHIND RIDGEON'S CHAIR) NOW, JINNY-GWINNY : THE MOTOR HAS COME ROUND. /RIDGEON/ WHY DO

JIST
CAPT I (221) THE WEST INDIES. /DRINKWATER/ THE WUST HINDIES! JIST ACROST THERE, TATHER SAWD THET HOWCEAN (POINTING
CAPT I (225) INTO THE HOUSE WITH THE KROOBOYS). /DRINKWATER/ JIST THORT EED TRAH IT ORN, E DID. HOOMAN NITRE IS THE SIME

JITTA
JITT II (42) (SCORNFULLY) A KEEPSAKE! DONT TALK NONSENSE, JITTA : A MAN DOES NOT GIVE AWAY HIS BIGGEST WORK AS IF IT
JITT III (72) KNOW. YOUR MOTHER COULD NEVER UNDERSTAND. /EDITH/ JITTA : DO YOU KNOW? /JITTA/ YES. /EDITH/ JITTA! ! !
JITT I (16) HAPPY, ONE IS RUTHLESS AND SHAMELESS. /BRUNO/ JITTA : DO YOU KNOW THAT YOU BELONGED TO ME BEFORE WE EVER
JITT II (32) HAVE TOLD IT TO YOU. (SHE SITS DOWN AGAIN). JITTA : HAVE YOU REALLY NO SUSPICION? /JITTA/ OF WHAT?
JITT II (51) (DESPERATELY PERPLEXED; YIELDING) BUT, JITTA : I DONT REALLY BELIEVE THAT. IT'S NOT LIKE YOU: YOU
JITT III (79) NOT, BEING ONLY A CHUMP, BE A LITTLE AMIABLE, JITTA : I HAVNT BEEN SO VERY HARD ON YOU, HAVE I? /JITTA/ (
JITT II (31) FULL OF EXCITEMENT AND CURIOSITY. /LENKHEIM/ JITTA : OLD AGNES IS COMING TO SEE US. BRUNO HAS MADE ME HIS
JITT III (75) PRESENT TO TALK TO. /LENKHEIM/ MAKE NO MISTAKE, JITTA : WHEN I SWORE THAT, I MEANT IT. /JITTA/ (IRONICALLY)
JITT II (44) THAT WAS WHAT HE WANTED TO PREVENT. /LENKHEIM/ JITTA : YOU ARE SIMPLY DRIVELLING. BRUNO WAS TOO JOLLY
JITT II (48) SIGHS WEARILY)! ! /LENKHEIM/ (UNAGGRESSIVELY) JITTA ? HER NAME AND THE CHANGE IN HIS TONE GIVE HER A
JITT II SD(40) THROWS THE DOOR OPEN: HE IS RETURNING WITH AGNES. JITTA AND EDITH MOVE ASUNDER AND RISE HASTILY. AGNES COMES
JITT II (34) OPPOSITE THE WINDOW). /AGNES/ (PAUSING BETWEEN JITTA AND EDITH) I WANTED TO COME ALONE; BUT EDITH INSISTED
JITT III SD(64) BEST PROFESSIONAL BEDSIDE MANNER. EDITH RUSHES TO JITTA AND EMBRACES HER. /EDITH/ OH, HOW GOOD OF YOU TO
JITT III SD(69) THAT SHE IS NOT ENJOYING THE JOKE IN GOOD FAITH. JITTA AT LAST RECOVERS HER SELF-CONTROL WITH A DESPERATE
JITT III SD(64) I HOPE YOU MAY, DARLING. DOES THAT PLEASE YOU? JITTA COMES IN FROM THE CORRIDOR. FESSLER PULLS HIMSELF
JITT II SD(31) GOES OUT FOR A MOMENT THROUGH THE INNER DOOR. JITTA COMES IN, LANGUID, AND DRESSED AS LENKHEIM HAS
JITT III (59) I HAVE A FEW WORDS TO SAY TO FESSLER BEFORE JITTA COMES. /AGNES/ YOU HAVE BEEN SO GOOD. I WILL THINK
JITT II SD(41) GOES OUT WITH HER MOTHER LEANING HEAVILY ON HER. JITTA GOES OUT WITH THEM. /LENKHEIM/ (RELIEVED AT BEING RID
JITT III SD(69) MORE THAN EVER). /JITTA/ OH NO! OF COURSE NOT. JITTA HAS A PAROXYSM OF AGONIZING LAUGHTER; AND AGNES
JITT II SD(27) AND HIS DEATH FROM NATURAL CAUSES DULY CERTIFIED. JITTA HAS TAKEN REFUGE IN AN ILLNESS, AND IS KEEPING HER
JITT II SD(33) IN LOW TONES AND UNNATURALLY BOOKISH SENTENCES. JITTA HAS TO DRAW THE GIRL TO HER, AND KISS HER ON THE BROW.
JITT II (30) FORGOT TO ASK HOW MRS LENKHEIM IS. /LENKHEIM/ OH, JITTA IS GETTING OVER IT. SHE HOPES TO BE ABLE TO GET UP FOR
JITT I (14) THEIR CHARACTERS AND CIRCUMSTANCES MAY BE. JITTA IS NOTHING MORE EXTRAORDINARY THAN THE WIFE OF A
JITT I (14) DREAMLAND. (NOW THAT HER HAT AND VEIL ARE OFF JITTA IS REVEALED AS ONE OF THOSE ATTRACTIVELY REFINED WOMEN
JITT I (17) STRANGEST FANCIES. /BRUNO/ THIS IS NOT A FANCY, JITTA . IT IS A HARD SCIENTIFIC FACT: I WORKED OUT ITS
JITT III SD(70) JOYFUL SURPRISE AND RELIEF. SHE RUNS EAGERLY TO JITTA . /EDITH/ WHAT ON EARTH HAVE YOU DONE TO MOTHER? SHE
JITT I (20) DEEPEST WISH. IT IS MY MOST URGENT PRAYER TO YOU, JITTA . /JITTA/ (GASPING) YOU ASK ME TO DO THAT! TO
JITT III (79) I SUPPOSE. OH, YOU CAN BE NASTY WHEN YOU WANT TO, JITTA . /JITTA/ OH, NO, NO. WILL YOU NEVER UNDERSTAND?
JITT II (44) WHERE IS THE SENSE IN IT? I BELIEVE YOU KNOW, JITTA . /JITTA/ REALLY, ALFRED--! I MUST GO BACK TO BED.
JITT I (24) ARE THEY? NOTHING MATTERS BUT JITTA, JITTA, JITTA (HE KISSES HER AGAIN AND AGAIN). I AM NEITHER WEAK
JITT II SD(33) SITS DOWN. HE SITS ON THE WINDOW-SEAT NEAR HER. JITTA LEADS EDITH TO THE CHAIR SHE HAS JUST VACATED, AND
JITT PREFACE(6) AS WELL CONFESS AT ONCE THAT IN THE ORIGINAL PLAY JITTA LIVES MISERABLY EVER AFTER, AND THAT HER HUSBAND BEARS
JITT III (74) POLITENESS). /EDITH/ (TO LENKHEIM, AFTER KISSING JITTA RATHER DEFIANTLY) MRS LENKHEIM DID NOT SAY A SINGLE
JITT II (42) ONLY TO BE STILL MORE DISGUSTED WITH THE NEXT. JITTA RETURNS; SEES WHAT HE IS DOING; AND HALTS BETWEEN HIM
JITT III (80) NOW, MAY I TAKE MY GOOD ANGEL HOME? /AGNES/ (TO JITTA) OH, MUST YOU GO, DEAR? /JITTA/ (SWEETLY, TO AGNES)
JITT II (36) WAS: HE WAS THROWN AWAY AMONG US. (TURNING ON JITTA) WHY DID HE NOT DIE WITH US? WHY HAD HE NO LAST WORD
JITT II SD(33) DISPATCH CASE. SHE IS NOT REALLY MUCH OLDER THAN JITTA ; BUT SHE HAS RETIRED SO COMPLETELY FROM THE
JITT III (65) AND GOES OUT). /AGNES/ SIT DOWN, WONT YOU? (JITTA SITS ON THE COUCH. AGNES SITS DOWN WOEFULLY BESIDE
JITT II (37) SILENT FOR A MOMENT, AND A LITTLE BREATHLESS. JITTA SMILES, AND SITS DOWN IN THE WRITING-TABLE CHAIR). AND
JITT II (34) STAY AWAY. /AGNES/ (NOT AT ALL DISPOSED TO ALLOW JITTA SO PROMINENT A SHARE IN HER GRIEF, BUT CONVENTIONALLY
JITT III (74) THATS VERY KIND OF YOU, EDITH, AND VERY KIND OF JITTA TO INCLUDE ME IN THE NUMBER OF HUSBANDS SHE HAS
JITT III (69) FOR AWHILE. I-- /AGNES/ (RISING TO MAKE ROOM FOR JITTA TO RECLINE) YES, YES; OF COURSE YOU SHALL, DEAR. MAKE
JITT PREFACE(7) NEW YORK CITY, ON THE 6TH JANUARY 1923, WHEN JITTA WAS PLAYED BY BERTHA KALICH.
JITT PREFACE(5) GUESS, AND CO-INVENT THE STORY OF GITTA, OR JITTA , AS I HAVE HAD TO SPELL HER TO AVERT HAVING HER NAME
JITT I (22) YOUR LOVE TO THE CRUELLEST TEST; BUT OH, JITTA, JITTA , DO NOT FAIL ME. /JITTA/ SO BE IT. (HE SNATCHES HER
JITT I (24) AND WHERE ARE THEY? NOTHING MATTERS BUT JITTA, JITTA , JITTA (HE KISSES HER AGAIN AND AGAIN). I AM NEITHER
JITT I (22) PUTTING YOUR LOVE TO THE CRUELLEST TEST; BUT OH, JITTA , JITTA, DO NOT FAIL ME. /JITTA/ SO BE IT. (HE
JITT I (24) LIPS; AND WHERE ARE THEY? NOTHING MATTERS BUT JITTA , JITTA, JITTA (HE KISSES HER AGAIN AND AGAIN). I AM
JITT III SD(70) HAPPY, DEAR! (SHE GOES OUT INTO THE CORRIDOR). JITTA , LEFT ALONE, BEGINS TO LAUGH AGAIN HYSTERICALLY, AND
JITT II (42) /ALFRED/ (AFTER A STIFLED EXCLAMATION) JITTA! JITTA ! (HE TURNS, HALF RISING, AND SEES HER). OH, YOURE
JITT II (42) /ALFRED/ (AFTER A STIFLED EXCLAMATION) JITTA ! JITTA! (HE TURNS, HALF RISING, AND SEES HER). OH,
JITT III (76) A LITTLE) HOW YOU ENJOY BEING MISERABLE, JITTA ! /JITTA/ ENJOY! ! /LENKHEIM/ YOU JUST REVEL IN IT.
JITT I (25) /BRUNO/ (WITH A GRIM CHANGE OF COUNTENANCE) POOR JITTA ! THAT LIFT BROKE THE MAINSPRING. (HE STAGGERS
JITT III (73) /EDITH/ JITTA: DO YOU KNOW? /JITTA/ YES. /EDITH/ JITTA ! ! ! /JITTA/ YES. I KNOW THAT POOR CRIMINAL. I

JITTA'S
JITT III (73) ONLY ME, DEAR. /EDITH/ (FLINGING HERSELF INTO JITTA'S ARMS) ONLY YOU! WHO BETTER COULD IT BE? OF COURSE
JITT PREFACE(7) BURGTHEATER OF VIENNA ON THE 3RD FEBRUARY 1920. JITTA'S ATONEMENT WAS PERFORMED FOR THE FIRST TIME AT THE
JITT I (9) JITTA'S ATONEMENT. ACT I. 1920. THE DRAWING ROOM IN A FLAT
JITT (1) JITTA'S ATONEMENT. BY SIEGFRIED TREBITSCH. AUTHOR OF

JITT III (80) KISS HIM. /FESSLER/ (HASTILY) TCHUT! (TAKING JITTA'S HAND, AND KISSING IT) I OWE YOU MY LIFE'S HAPPINESS,

J.B

MIS (179) GET ANY LETTERS: I'M ONLY A CLERK. I CAN SHEW YOU J.B . ON MY HANDKERCHIEF. (HE TAKES OUT A NOT VERY CLEAN

J.E.H.A.N.E

JOAN 6 (144) THEY BEGIN TO WRITE, USING THE BOOK AS A DESK) J.E.H.A.N.E . SO. NOW MAKE YOUR MARK BY YOURSELF. /JOAN/ (

J.M

DOCT III (146) THE MAJORITY OF THEM WOULD BE, AS MY FRIEND MR J.M . BARRIE HAS TERSELY PHRASED IT, BETTER DEAD. BETTER
POSN PREFACE(361) AS MR WILLIAM ARCHER, MR GRANVILLE BARKER, MR J.M . BARRIE, MR FORBES ROBERTSON, MR CECIL RALEIGH, MR JOHN

JO

PHIL I (92) I'M REALLY ASHAMED-- /CRAVEN/ DONT MENTION IT, JO : DONT MENTION IT. SHE'S WAITING FOR ME BELOW. (GOING)
PHIL II (98) YES: YOU ALWAYS BELIEVED IN HEARTH AND HOME, JO : IN A TRUE ENGLISH WIFE, AND A HAPPY WHOLESOME FIRESIDE.
FANY III (317) GILBEY WASNT GOOD ENOUGH FOR YOU? /MRS KNOX/ NO, JO : YOU KNOW I'M NOT. WHAT BETTER WERE MY PEOPLE THAN
FANY III (313) AT SEVEN TO THE TICK! /MRS KNOX/ YOU HEAR THAT, JO ? (TO MRS GILBEY) HE'S TAKEN TO WHISKY AND SODA. A PINT
PHIL II (100) SUSPECT THAT? /CRAVEN/ CERTAINLY NOT. DID YOU, JO ? /CUTHBERTSON/ NOT AT THE MOMENT. /CRAVEN/ WHATS MORE,
PHIL II (127) SOME DAY, JULIA. /CRAVEN/ DO YOU KNOW THIS LADY, JO ? /CUTHBERTSON/ THIS IS MY DAUGHTER, MRS TRANFIELD, DAN.
PHIL III (146) PLAIN BEFORE YOU. (TO CUTHBERTSON) AM I RIGHT, JO ? /CUTHBERTSON/ (FIRMLY) YOU ARE, DAN. /CRAVEN/ (TO
PHIL I (89) MANLY SENTIMENT IN LONDON. /CRAVEN/ THAT DIDNT DO JO ANY HARM; BUT IT TOOK AWAY MY JULIA'S CHARACTER. /JULIA/
PHIL I (86) DAN CRAVEN! /CRAVEN/ JUST IMAGINE YOU BEING JO CUTHBERTSON, THOUGH! THATS A FAR MORE EXTRAORDINARY
SIM PRO71, (26) THIS MONTH. (HE GOES TO THE DOOR). HALLO THERE, JO . BRING ALONG THE STRETCHER AND TWO OR THREE WITH YOU. MR
PHIL II (98) SINCERE FEELING) I GOT TO BE VERY FOND OF HER, JO . I HAD A HOME UNTIL SHE DIED. NOW EVERYTHING'S CHANGED.
FANY III (315) /MRS KNOX/ (GENTLY) OH, WELL, SAY NO MORE, JO . I WONT PLAGUE YOU ABOUT IT. (HE SITS DOWN). YOU NEVER
FANY II (286) HIM) THERES NO USE GOING OVER IT ALL AGAIN, JO . IF A GIRL HASNT HAPPINESS IN HERSELF, SHE WONT BE HAPPY
PHIL III (146) THERE I FLATLY CONTRADICT YOU, AND STAND UP FOR JO . I'D NO MORE HAVE BEHAVED AS YOU DO WHEN I WAS A YOUNG
NEVR II (244) MOTIONING HIM TO SERVE GLORIA) THIS SIDE, JO . (HE TAKES A SPECIAL PORTION OF SALAD FROM THE SERVICE
PHIL III (144) AS WELL AS MINE, I HOPE. /CRAVEN/ SHE WILL, JO . (PEREMPTORILY) NOW, JULIA. JULIA SLOWLY RISES.
NEVR II (244) WAITER, ADMONISHING HIM TO SERVE DOLLY AFRESH) JO . (RESUMING) MOSTLY MEMBERS OF THE CHURCH OF ENGLAND,
PHIL II (114) /CRAVEN/ (WARMLY) I MADE A VIRTUE OF NECESSITY, JO . NO ONE CAN BLAME ME. /JULIA/ (SOOTHING HIM) WELL,
PHIL II (129) WITHOUT MORAL RESPONSIBILITY. /CRAVEN/ QUITE SO, JO . OF COURSE. /CUTHBERTSON/ THEREFORE, THOUGH I HAVE NO
PHIL I (85) ALREADY. CHARTERIS IS QUITE AT HOME IN OUR HOUSE, JO . /CUTHBERTSON/ I BEG BOTH YOUR PARDONS. HE'S QUITE AT
PHIL III (143) MRS TRANFIELD SEES YOU. SHE'S COMING ALONG WITH JO . /JULIA/ (RISING) THAT WOMAN AGAIN! /SYLVIA/ ANOTHER
FANY II (289) KNOX/ YOU OUGHT TO PAY THE GENTLEMAN THE FINE, JO . /KNOX/ (REDDENING) OH, CERTAINLY. (HE TAKES OUT SOME
FANY II (290) (BOW)-- (HE GOES OUT). /MRS KNOX/ DONT RING, JO . SEE THE GENTLEMAN OUT YOURSELF. KNOX HASTILY SEES
PHIL I (92) IT IS I WHO HAVE TO APOLOGIZE FOR JULIA, JO . SHE-- /CHARTERIS/ (INTERRUPTING) SHE SAID SHE WAS
PHIL I (88) NEVER HAVE THOUGHT IT FROM HEARING YOU TALK, JO . WHY, YOU SAID THE WHOLE MODERN MOVEMENT WAS ABHORRENT
FANY III (316) /MRS KNOX/ WELL, YOU GAVE ME ALL YOU COULD, JO ; AND IF IT WASNT WHAT I WANTED, THAT WASNT YOUR FAULT.
PHIL II (112) (PETTISHLY) OH YES, THATS ALL VERY WELL, JO ; BUT IT'S NOT GOOD MANNERS AT TABLE: HE SHOULD SHUT UP
POSN (457) THE HORSE. (HE COMES IN, FOLLOWED BY WAGGONER JO , AN ELDERLY CARTER, WHO CROSSES THE COURT TO THE JURY
FANY II (296) GOING TO DO? /MRS KNOX/ SHE'S BEYOND MY CONTROL, JO , AND BEYOND YOURS. I CANT EVEN PRAY FOR HER NOW; FOR I
PHIL I (87) MAY LONG BE SPARED, DAN. /CRAVEN/ TO OBLIGE ME, JO , CHANGE THE SUBJECT. (HE GETS UP, AND AGAIN POSTS
FANY III (315) MY MAN HERE. HE'S A BITTER HARD HEATHEN, IS MY JO , GOD HELP ME! (SHE BEGINS TO CRY QUIETLY). /KNOX/ NOW,
PHIL III (144) WHILST HER FATHER JOINS THE OTHERS. /CRAVEN/ AH, JO , HERE YOU ARE. NOW, PARAMORE: TELL EM THE NEWS.
PHIL II (98) OH YES: WE ALL HEARD OF IT. /CRAVEN/ WELL, JO , I MAY AS WELL MAKE A CLEAN BREAST OF IT: EVERYBODY KNEW
PHIL II (130) BACK). /CRAVEN/ (DEEPLY DISAPPOINTED) OH WELL, JO , IF THAT IS YOUR DECISION, I MUST KEEP MY WORD AND ABIDE
FANY II (287) /MRS KNOX/ (SUDDENLY POINTING TO THE STREET) JO , LOOK! /KNOX/ MARGARET! WITH A MAN! /MRS KNOX/ RUN
FANY II (287) MARGARET! WITH A MAN! /MRS KNOX/ RUN DOWN, JO , QUICK. CATCH HER! SAVE HER. /KNOX/ (LINGERING) SHE'S
FANY II (287) ALL KNEW AND DIDNT CARE. /MRS KNOX/ IF THEY KNEW, JO , THERED BE A CROWD ROUND THE HOUSE LOOKING UP AT US. YOU
FANY II (286) TO HIM AND DRAWING HER ARM THROUGH HIS) THERE, JO , THERE! I'M SURE I'D HAVE YOU HERE ALWAYS IF I COULD.
FANY III (314) NEW NAME HE'S GOT FOR ME. (TO KNOX) I TELL YOU, JO , THIS DOESNT SIT WELL ON YOU. YOU MAY CALL IT PREACHING
PHIL II (98) NOT NATURAL TO HER SEX. /CRAVEN/ (SIGHING) AH, JO , TIMES HAVE CHANGED SINCE WE BOTH COURTED MOLLY EBDEN
PHIL II (98) OH! THAT WAS THE END OF THE HEARTH AND HOME, JO , WAS IT? /CUTHBERTSON/ (WARMLY) IT WAS NOT MY FAULT,
FANY II (296) /MRS KNOX/ (RISING) YOU MUSTNT TURN HER OUT, JO ! I'LL GO WITH HER IF SHE GOES. /KNOX/ WHO WANTS TO TURN
FANY II (286) WITH HER AUNT. /MRS KNOX/ (REPROACHFULLY) JO ! (SHE TAKES HER HANDKERCHIEF FROM THE WRITING-TABLE
PHIL II (116) GIRL! (HE PINCHES HER EAR). SHALL WE COME, JO ! YOULL BE THE BETTER FOR A PICK-ME-UP AFTER ALL THIS

JOACHIM

PLES PREFACE(R17) THEM; BUT I CAN NO MORE WRITE WHAT THEY WANT THAN JOACHIM CAN PUT ASIDE HIS FIDDLE AND OBLIGE A HAPPY COMPANY

JOAN

JOAN (1) SAINT JOAN : A CHRONICLE PLAY IN SIX SCENES AND AN EPILOGUE. SAINT
JOAN PREFACE(30) HUS NOR WYCLIFFE WAS AS BLUNTLY DEFIANT AS JOAN : BOTH WERE REFORMERS OF THE CHURCH LIKE LUTHER; WHILST
JOAN 6 (139) ME I MUST DRESS AS A SOLDIER. /LADVE54/ JOAN, JOAN : DOES NOT THAT PROVE TO YOU THAT THE VOICES ARE THE
JOAN 6 (136) /CAUCHON/ COME! WE ARE WASTING TIME ON TRIFLES. JOAN : I AM GOING TO PUT A MOST SOLEMN QUESTION TO YOU. TAKE
JOAN 3 (91) ME. /DUNOIS/ YOU MUST NOT DARE A STAFF OFFICER, JOAN : ONLY COMPANY OFFICERS ARE ALLOWED TO INDULGE IN
JOAN 6 (139) TO TAKE HIM FOR A MESSENGER FROM THE MOST HIGH? JOAN : THE CHURCH INSTRUCTS YOU THAT THESE APPARITIONS ARE
JOAN 6 (140) FOR TRYING TO SAVE HER, BROTHER MARTIN. /LADVENU/ JOAN : WE ARE ALL TRYING TO SAVE YOU. HIS LORDSHIP IS TRYING
JOAN 6 (141) THE WISDOM OF SCHOLARS. /LADVENU/ WE KNOW THAT, JOAN : WE ARE NOT SO FOOLISH AS YOU THINK US. TRY TO RESIST
JOAN EPILOG (166) (HE GOES OUT AS HE CAME). /DUNOIS/ FORGIVE US, JOAN : WE ARE NOT YET GOOD ENOUGH FOR YOU. I SHALL GO BACK
JOAN 5 (109) /DUNOIS/ HE ONLY SPOILS THE SHOW, POOR DEVIL. NO, JOAN : YOU HAVE CROWNED HIM; AND YOU MUST GO THROUGH WITH
JOAN EPILOG (155) /CHARLES/ (PEEPING OUT) JOAN! ARE YOU A GHOST, JOAN ? /JOAN/ HARDLY EVEN THAT, LAD. CAN A POOR BURNT-UP
JOAN 6 (144) /THE INQUISITOR/ YOU UNDERSTAND THIS, JOAN ? /JOAN/ (LISTLESS) IT IS PLAIN ENOUGH, SIR. /THE
JOAN 5 (111) MAY CHOOSE TO BELIEVE. /DUNOIS/ ARE YOU ANGRY, JOAN ? /JOAN/ YES. (SMILING) NO: NOT WITH YOU. I WISH YOU
JOAN EPILOG (167) MY ONE FAITHFUL? WHAT COMFORT HAVE YOU FOR SAINT JOAN ? /THE SOLDIER/ WELL, WHAT DO THEY ALL AMOUNT TO,
JOAN 6 (134) BE PUT TO THE TORTURE. /THE INQUISITOR/ YOU HEAR, JOAN ? THAT IS WHAT HAPPENS TO THE OBDURATE. THINK BEFORE
JOAN PREFACE(16) AS TO THE NEW RITES, WHICH WOULD BE THE SANER JOAN ? THE ONE WHO CARRIED LITTLE CHILDREN TO BE BAPTIZED
JOAN PREFACE(24) PLAYWRIGHT, HAVING BEGUN BY AN ATTEMPT TO MAKE JOAN A BEAUTIFUL AND ROMANTIC FIGURE, WAS TOLD BY HIS
JOAN PREFACE(26) AND MARK TWAIN ARE EQUALLY DETERMINED TO MAKE JOAN A BEAUTIFUL AND MOST LADYLIKE VICTORIAN; BUT BOTH OF
JOAN PREFACE(18) HER RELAPSE AS DICTATED TO HER BY HER VOICES. JOAN A GALTONIC VISUALIZER. THE MOST SCEPTICAL SCIENTIFIC
JOAN PREFACE(51) THE CHARACTERS, MAKING CAUCHON A SCOUNDREL, JOAN A PRIMA DONNA, AND DUNOIS A LOVER. BUT THE WRITER OF
JOAN PREFACE(36) IT MAKES THESE APPALLING BLUNDERS ABOUT JOAN AND BRUNO AND GALILEO AND THE REST WHICH MAKE IT SO
JOAN 4 (103) WHAT WILL IT BE WHEN EVERY GIRL THINKS HERSELF A JOAN AND EVERY MAN A MAHOMET? I SHUDDER TO THE VERY MARROW
JOAN PREFACE(17) US, AND WILL DESTROY US IF WE DISREGARD IT? TO JOAN AND HER CONTEMPORARIES WE SHOULD APPEAR AS A DROVE OF
JOAN PREFACE(4) MIRACULOUS: THE OTHER THAT SHE WAS UNBEARABLE. JOAN AND SOCRATES. IF JOAN HAD BEEN MALICIOUS, SELFISH,
JOAN PREFACE(33) TOO OFTEN. STILL, THERE WAS A GREAT WRONG DONE TO JOAN AND TO THE CONSCIENCE OF THE WORLD BY HER BURNING. TOUT
JOAN 1,SD(60) A SWORD! ACTUALLY! (HE STEALS BEHIND ROBERT). JOAN APPEARS IN THE TURRET DOORWAY. SHE IS AN ABLEBODIED
JOAN PREFACE(24) ACCOUNTING FOR THE SYMPATHETIC REPRESENTATION OF JOAN AS A HEROINE CULMINATING IN HER ELOQUENT APPEAL TO THE
JOAN PREFACE(30) MIGHT ALMOST HAVE BEEN DIRECTLY CHARGED AGAINST JOAN AS AN ADDITIONAL HERESY, YET IT WAS NOT SO CHARGED; AND
JOAN PREFACE(13) OR ANY OTHER ILLUSIONPROOF GENIUS. THEY CAME TO JOAN AS AN INSTRUCTION FROM HER COUNSEL, AS SHE CALLED HER
JOAN PREFACE(4) WAS NEVER " I SAY SO," BUT ALWAYS " GOD SAYS SO." JOAN AS THEOCRAT. LEADERS WHO TAKE THAT LINE HAVE NO TROUBLE
JOAN PREFACE(53) NECESSARY BY HOOK OR CROOK TO SHEW THE CANONIZED JOAN AS WELL AS THE INCINERATED ONE; FOR MANY A WOMAN HAS
JOAN PREFACE(24) TO BE SAID OF HIS PLAY BUT THAT IT IS NOT ABOUT JOAN AT ALL, AND CAN HARDLY BE SAID TO PRETEND TO BE; FOR HE
JOAN PREFACE(17) LET US THEN ONCE FOR ALL DROP ALL NONSENSE ABOUT JOAN BEING CRACKED, AND ACCEPT HER AS AT LEAST AS SANE AS
JOAN PREFACE(13) IS RIGHT, BECAUSE AN EXPLANATION WHICH AMOUNTS TO JOAN BEING MENTALLY DEFECTIVE INSTEAD OF, AS SHE OBVIOUSLY
JOAN PREFACE(25) IN AMERICA AND ENGLAND ARE THE HISTORIES OF JOAN BY MARK TWAIN AND ANDREW LANG. MARK TWAIN WAS CONVERTED
JOAN 1,SD(66) STANDING TO INFLATE HIMSELF MORE IMPOSINGLY. JOAN COMES IN, FULL OF GOOD NEWS. /JOAN/ JACK WILL GO HALVES
JOAN PREFACE(42) OR THAT SUCH AN EVENT AS THE EXECUTION OF JOAN COULD NOT POSSIBLY OCCUR IN WHAT WE CALL OUR OWN MORE
JOAN PREFACE(9) THERE WAS ANY DANGER OF INVASION. AS A CHILD, JOAN COULD PLEASE HERSELF AT TIMES WITH BEING THE YOUNG LADY
JOAN 1,SD(66) TO ROBERT) MAY I? /ROBERT/ DO WHAT YOU ARE TOLD. JOAN CURTSIES AND SITS DOWN ON THE STOOL BETWEEN THEM.
ROCK PREFACE(177) MUOVE," FIGMENT OF THE SELFREGARDING ACTION. ST JOAN DID NOT CLAIM TOLERATION: SHE WAS SO FAR FROM BELIEVING
JOAN PREFACE(11) AND HEARD VOICES JUST AS SAINT FRANCIS AND SAINT JOAN DID. IF NEWTON'S IMAGINATION HAD BEEN OF THE SAME
JOAN PREFACE(13) COULD I EXPECT ALL MY READERS TO BELIEVE, AS JOAN DID, THAT THREE OCULARLY VISIBLE WELL DRESSED PERSONS,
JOAN PREFACE(26) MARK TWAIN WAS CONVERTED TO DOWNRIGHT WORSHIP OF JOAN DIRECTLY BY QUICHERAT. LATER ON, ANOTHER MAN OF GENIUS,
JOAN PREFACE(15) AS THE CASE MAY BE. THE MODERN EDUCATION WHICH JOAN ESCAPED. IT IS IMPORTANT TO EVERYONE NOWADAYS TO
JOAN PREFACE(32) THE VERDICT AT THE FIRST TRIAL WHEN IT CANONIZED JOAN FIVE HUNDRED YEARS LATER? THE CHURCH UNCOMPROMISED BY

JOAN PREFACE(7)	THAT MELODRAMA MAY BE DISMISSED AS RUBBISH.	JOAN	GOT A FAR FAIRER TRIAL FROM THE CHURCH AND THE
JOAN PREFACE(4)	THAT SHE WAS UNBEARABLE. JOAN AND SOCRATES. IF	JOAN	HAD BEEN MALICIOUS, SELFISH, COWARDLY OR STUPID, SHE
JOAN PREFACE(42)	TO INSIST ON STRICT LEGALITY OF PROCEDURE AS	JOAN	HAD FROM THE INQUISITION AND FROM THE SPIRIT OF THE
JOAN PREFACE(51)	INNOCENT PEOPLE DO THAT CONCERNS US; AND IF	JOAN	HAD NOT BEEN BURNT BY NORMALLY INNOCENT PEOPLE IN THE
JOAN PREFACE(32)	OUTRAGE ON THE THRONE AND ON THE PATRIOTISM WHICH	JOAN	HAD SET ON FOOT. WE HAVE NONE OF THESE OVERWHELMING
ROCK PREFACE(175)	THEIR EXISTENCE. IN AUSTRIA MY CHRONICLE PLAY ST	JOAN	HAD TO BE ALTERED TO PLEASE CATHOLIC AUTHORITIES WHO
JOAN PREFACE(29)	AND WE MAY CHARGE OUR CONSCIENCES ACCORDINGLY. IF	JOAN	HAD TO BE DEALT WITH BY US IN LONDON SHE WOULD BE
JOAN PREFACE(44)	WITH THE DEVIL TO THE SCEPTICAL. ALL THROUGH,	JOAN	HAD TO DEPEND ON THOSE WHO ACCEPTED HER AS AN INCARNATE
JOAN PREFACE(11)	OF SORDID POVERTY, AND NO REASON TO BELIEVE THAT	JOAN	HAD TO WORK AS A HIRED SERVANT WORKS, OR INDEED TO WORK
JOAN PREFACE(46)	BECAME OBSOLETE. THE REFORMATION, WHICH	JOAN	HAD UNCONSCIOUSLY ANTICIPATED, KEPT THE QUESTIONS WHICH
JOAN PREFACE(24)	A WITCH'S CALDRON OF RAGING ROMANCE. SCHILLER'S	JOAN	HAS NOT A SINGLE POINT OF CONTACT WITH THE REAL JOAN.
JOAN PREFACE(46)	HOUSES STILL IN IRELAND), WITH THE RESULT THAT	JOAN	HAS REMAINED THE SUBJECT OF ANTI-CLERICAL LIES, OF
JOAN PREFACE(34)	DID OUT OF THEIR STAKES AND WHEELS AND GIBBETS.	JOAN	HERSELF JUDGED THIS MATTER WHEN SHE HAD TO CHOOSE
JOAN PREFACE(55)	HOUSE OF COMMONS, AND MUCH MORE USEFUL. BUT IN ST	JOAN	I HAVE DONE MY BEST BY GOING TO THE WELL-ESTABLISHED
JOAN PREFACE(48)	OF HISTORICAL REPRESENTATION. FOR THE STORY OF	JOAN	I REFER THE READER TO THE PLAY WHICH FOLLOWS. IT
JOAN PREFACE(27)	YOU MUST UNDERSTAND HER ENVIRONMENT AS WELL.	JOAN	IN A NINETEENTH-TWENTIETH CENTURY ENVIRONMENT IS AS
JOAN PREFACE(26)	WAVE OF ENTHUSIASM, AND WROTE A LIFE OF	JOAN	IN WHICH HE ATTRIBUTED JOAN'S IDEAS TO CLERICAL
FABL PREFACE(71)	TWENTY YEARS LATER I WROTE A PLAY CALLED SAINT	JOAN	IN WHICH I MADE AN ARCHBISHOP EXPLAIN THAT A MIRACLE IS
JOAN PREFACE(6)	LOIRE, WERE EQUALLY GLAD TO BE RID OF HER. WAS	JOAN	INNOCENT OR GUILTY? AS THIS RESULT COULD HAVE BEEN
JOAN PREFACE(10)	PRETENSIONS. THERE IS THE SAME TENDENCY TO DRIVE	JOAN	INTO THE POSITION OF A HIRED SHEPHERD GIRL, THOUGH A
JOAN PREFACE(48)	OF ELECTRONS (WHATEVER THEY MAY BE). THE FATE OF	JOAN	IS A WARNING TO ME AGAINST SUCH HERESY. BUT WHY THE MEN
JOAN 5,SD(109)	THE PEOPLE OUT OF THE NAVE AFTER THE CORONATION.	JOAN	IS KNEELING IN PRAYER BEFORE THE STATION. SHE IS
JOAN PREFACE(23)	ONE OF THE LEADING CHARACTERS. THIS PORTRAIT OF	JOAN	IS NOT MORE AUTHENTIC THAN THE DESCRIPTIONS IN THE
JOAN PREFACE(23)	TRILOGY OF HENRY VI, IN WHICH	JOAN	IS ONE OF THE LEADING CHARACTERS. THIS PORTRAIT OF JOAN
JOAN PREFACE(47)	BUT EVEN IN ITS SIMPLICITY, THE FAITH DEMANDED BY	JOAN	IS ONE WHICH THE ANTI-METAPHYSICAL TEMPER OF NINETEENTH
JOAN 6,SD(147)	AT HER, AND HELPS THE SOLDIERS TO PUSH HER OUT).	JOAN	IS TAKEN AWAY THROUGH THE COURTYARD. THE ASSESSORS RISE
JOAN PREFACE(28)	BY THE ENGLISH FOR BEING TOO CONSIDERATE TO	JOAN	. A RECENT FRENCH WRITER DENIES THAT JOAN WAS BURNT,
JOAN PREFACE(38)	OR RANK, ARE ALWAYS REALLY SELF-SELECTED, LIKE	JOAN	. AND SINCE NEITHER CHURCH NOR STATE, BY THE SECULAR
ROCK PREFACE(179)	ADMIRERS OF MY DRAMATIZATION OF THE TRIAL OF ST	JOAN	. BUT THE TRIAL OF A DUMB PRISONER, AT WHICH THE JUDGE
JOAN PREFACE(28)	WAS NOT A PRETENDER BUT THE REAL AUTHENTIC	JOAN	. HE IS ABLE TO CITE CAUCHON'S PRO-JOAN PARTIALITY IN
JOAN 5 (120)	MERCY ON YOUR SOUL. /DUNOIS/ THAT IS THE TRUTH,	JOAN	. HEED IT. /JOAN/ WHERE WOULD YOU ALL HAVE BEEN NOW IF
JOAN PREFACE(30)	CHURCH WAS ONE IN WHICH THE POPE WAS POPE	JOAN	. HOW COULD THE CHURCH TOLERATE THAT, WHEN IT HAD JUST
JOAN 6 (133)	/THE INQUISITOR/ (KINDLY/ SIT DOWN,	JOAN	. (SHE SITS ON THE PRISONER'S STOOL). YOU LOOK VERY
JOAN PREFACE(3)	PREFACE TO SAINT	JOAN	. JOAN THE ORIGINAL AND PRESUMPTUOUS. JOAN OF ARC, A
JOAN PREFACE(31)	AND DEVELOPED THE HEAT THAT CONSUMED POOR	JOAN	. MARK AND ANDREW WOULD HAVE SHARED HER INNOCENCE AND
JOAN PREFACE(26)	THAT THERE EVER WAS ANY SUCH PERSON AS THE REAL	JOAN	. MARK TWAIN'S JOAN, SKIRTED TO THE GROUND, AND WITH AS
JOAN EPIL,SD(159)	THE CURTAINS AND MARCHES BETWEEN DUNOIS AND	JOAN	. /DUNOIS/ WHAT VILLAINOUS TROUBADOUR TAUGHT YOU THAT
JOAN 1 (66)	SITS, DEFLATED). /POULENGEY/ (GRAVELY) SIT DOWN,	JOAN	. /JOAN/ (CHECKED A LITTLE AND LOOKING TO ROBERT) MAY
JOAN EPILOG (163)	THE COMMUNION OF THE CHURCH TRIUMPHANT AS SAINT	JOAN	. /JOAN/ (RAPT) SAINT JOAN! /THE GENTLEMAN/ ON EVERY
JOAN 5 (115)	/DUNOIS/ I KNOW WHAT YOU THINK OF US, GENERAL	JOAN	. /JOAN/ NEVER MIND THAT, JACK. TELL THEM WHAT YOU
JOAN 5 (116)	AS WELL. /THE ARCHBISHOP/ PRIDE WILL HAVE A FALL,	JOAN	. /JOAN/ OH, NEVER MIND WHETHER IT IS PRIDE OR NOT: IS
JOAN 6 (129)	HER SIMPLICITY? MANY SAINTS HAVE SAID AS MUCH AS	JOAN	. /THE INQUISITOR/ (DROPPING HIS BLANDNESS AND
JOAN 6 (139)	IS AGAINST COURCELLES. /LADVENU/ WELL ANSWERED,	JOAN	. /THE INQUISITOR/ IT IS, IN EFFECT, WELL ANSWERED. BUT
JOAN EPIL,SD(161)	BUT BENEVOLENT SMILE, COMES IN AND TROTS OVER TO	JOAN	. /THE NEWCOMER/ EXCUSE ME, GENTLE LORDS AND LADIES. DO
JOAN PREFACE(43)	WITH ALL THIS IN MIND, CONSIDER THE CAREER OF	JOAN	. SHE WAS A VILLAGE GIRL, IN AUTHORITY OVER SHEEP AND
JOAN 6 (141)	FOR RESCUE) OH GOD! /LADVENU/ DO NOT DESPAIR,	JOAN	. THE CHURCH IS MERCIFUL. YOU CAN SAVE YOURSELF. /JOAN/
JOAN EPIL,SD(167)	LIGHT GATHER INTO A WHITE RADIANCE DESCENDING ON	JOAN	. THE HOUR CONTINUES TO STRIKE. /JOAN/ O GOD THAT
JOAN 1 (66)	CALL ME JENNY IN LORRAINE. HERE IN FRANCE I AM	JOAN	. THE SOLDIERS CALL ME THE MAID. /ROBERT/ WHAT IS YOUR
JOAN PREFACE(23)	THE BOOKS THEY ARE MOST FAMILIAR WITH ABOUT	JOAN	. THERE IS THE FIRST PART OF THE SHAKESPEAREAN, OR
JOAN PREFACE(33)	TO BE PERSUADED THAT THE ENGLISH DID NOT EAT	JOAN	. WHY, THEY ASK, SHOULD ANYONE TAKE THE TROUBLE TO
JOAN 6 (136)	/THE INQUISITOR/ THIS IS NOT A TIME FOR VANITY,	JOAN	. YOU STAND IN GREAT PERIL. /JOAN/ I KNOW IT: HAVE I
JOAN 3 (93)	TEARS. SET MY FOOT ON THE LADDER, AND SAY " UP,	JOAN	." /DUNOIS/ (DRAGGING HER OUT) NEVER MIND THE TEARS:
JOAN 2,SD(81)	YOU ARE IN THE PRESENCE OF THE DAUPHIN.	JOAN	LOOKS AT HIM SCEPTICALLY FOR A MOMENT, SCANNING HIM
JOAN PREFACE(17)	CONDITION AS A STANDARD OF SANITY, AND DECLARE	JOAN	MAD BECAUSE SHE NEVER CONDESCENDED TO IT, IS TO PROVE
JOAN PREFACE(37)	HIM." THE LAW OF CHANGE IS THE LAW OF GOD. WHEN	JOAN	MAINTAINED HER OWN WAYS SHE CLAIMED, LIKE JOB, THAT
JOAN PREFACE(12)	DIAGNOSE NEWTON AS A MADMAN? IN THE SAME WAY	JOAN	MUST BE JUDGED A SANE WOMAN IN SPITE OF HER VOICES
JOAN PREFACE(19)	YOUNG ENOUGH TO IMAGINE THAT HE WAS IN EARNEST.	JOAN	MUST THEREFORE AS A CHILD HAVE WANTED TO RUN AWAY AND
JOAN PREFACE(21)	TO CAPTIVITY, HAS BEEN ACCUSED OF SUICIDAL MANIA.	JOAN	NEED NOT BE SUSPECTED OF IT. IN THE BEAUREVOIR AFFAIR
JOAN 5 (117)	IS WORTH THE COST I MAKE IT AND PAY THE COST. BUT	JOAN	NEVER COUNTS THE COST AT ALL: SHE GOES AHEAD AND TRUSTS
JOAN PREFACE(25)	AGNES SOREL, THE DAUPHIN'S MISTRESS, WHOM	JOAN	NEVER MET, AS A WOMAN WITH A CONSUMING PASSION FOR THE
JOAN PREFACE(20)	MUSSETS TO LIVE WOMEN'S LIVES TO AMUSE HER. HAD	JOAN	NOT BEEN ONE OF THOSE " UNWOMANLY WOMEN," SHE MIGHT
JOAN PREFACE(47)	WE TAKE IT WITHOUT ANY SAUCE AT ALL. THE REAL	JOAN	NOT MARVELLOUS ENOUGH FOR US. BUT EVEN IN ITS
JOAN PREFACE(29)	BETWEEN THE TOLERABLE AND THE INTOLERABLE.	JOAN	NOT TRIED AS A POLITICAL OFFENDER. BESIDES, JOAN'S
ROCK PREFACE(175)	HIS NAME WAS HABITUALLY TAKEN IN VAIN. WE HAVE	JOAN	OF ARC AND JOHN OF LEYDEN, GIORDANO BRUNO AND GALILEO,
DOCT PREFACE(50)	THERE CAN BE NO QUESTION THAT THE BURNING OF ST	JOAN	OF ARC MUST HAVE BEEN A MOST INSTRUCTIVE AND
JOAN EPILOG (163)	THE BISHOP OF ORLEANS INTO THE CLAIM OF THE SAID	JOAN	OF ARC TO BE CANONIZED AS A SAINT -- /JOAN/ (AGAIN
JOAN PREFACE(33)	THE HUMAN FACT REMAINS THAT THE BURNING OF	JOAN	OF ARC WAS A HORROR, AND THAT A HISTORIAN WHO WOULD
GETT PREFACE(199)	IT WAS FOOLISH TO POISON SOCRATES AND BURN ST	JOAN	OF ARC. BUT IT IS NONE THE LESS NECESSARY TO TAKE A
2TRU III (98)	HERE I HAVE BEEN WANTING TO JOIN THE ARMY, LIKE	JOAN	OF ARC. IT'S A BROTHERHOOD, OF A SORT. /THE SERGEANT/
JOAN PREFACE(3)	SAINT JOAN. JOAN THE ORIGINAL AND PRESUMPTUOUS.	JOAN	OF ARC, A VILLAGE GIRL FROM THE VOSGES, WAS BORN ABOUT
LION PREFACE(72)	JESUS AND THE UNMARRIED BEETHOVEN, THE UNMARRIED	JOAN	OF ARC, CLARE, TERESA, FLORENCE NIGHTINGALE SEEM AS
ROCK PREFACE(156)	OFFICIALLY OBLIGED TO WITNESS IT DIED OF HORROR.	JOAN	OF ARC, FOR WEARING MEN'S CLOTHES AND BEING A
JOAN EPILOG (163)	MANNER). I AM SENT TO ANNOUNCE TO YOU THAT	JOAN	OF ARC, FORMERLY KNOWN AS THE MAID, HAVING BEEN THE
FABL PREFACE(79)	WITH THE ARCHANGEL GABRIEL, OR, LIKE	JOAN	OF ARC, REALLY HEARD VOICES WHEN HE LISTENED FOR THE
CLEO NOTES (210)	WITHOUT BEING WISER THAN CHARLES XII OR NELSON OR	JOAN	OF ARC, WHO WERE, LIKE MOST MODERN " SELF-MADE"
JOAN PREFACE(24)	HE AT ONCE INTRODUCED ALL THE OLD CHARGES AGAINST	JOAN	OF BEING A SORCERESS AND A HARLOT, AND ASSUMED HER TO
JOAN PREFACE(7)	THEREFORE BE WASTE OF TIME NOW TO PROVE THAT THE	JOAN	OF THE FIRST PART OF THE ELIZABETHAN CHRONICLE PLAY OF
JOAN PREFACE(25)	VERY UNCHASTE INDEED, HE MAY BE SAID TO HAVE LET	JOAN	OFF VERY EASILY. BUT INDEED THE PERSONAL ADVENTURES OF
JOAN PREFACE(53)	OF IT, WITH THE VICTORIOUS FRENCH LED BY	JOAN	ON A REAL HORSE. THE CORONATION WOULD ECLIPSE ALL
JOAN 5 (117)	OF YOU, WHICH OF YOU WILL LIFT A FINGER TO SAVE	JOAN	ONCE THE ENGLISH HAVE GOT HER? I SPEAK FIRST, FOR THE
JOAN 2,SD(87)	CHARLES) WHAT IS THIS? I COMMAND THE ARMY.	JOAN	QUICKLY PUTS HER HAND ON CHARLES'S SHOULDER AS HE
JOAN PREFACE(48)	FREE. THEREFORE THE READER MUST NOT SUPPOSE THAT	JOAN	REALLY PUT ROBERT DE BAUDRICOURT IN HER POCKET IN
JOAN PREFACE(14)	LUNATICS. IT IS ONE THING TO SAY THAT THE FIGURE	JOAN	RECOGNIZED AS ST CATHERINE WAS NOT REALLY ST CATHERINE,
JOAN PREFACE(25)	WORST EXTREMITIES OF RAPINE. THE COMBATS IN WHICH	JOAN	RIDES A FLYING DONKEY, OR IN WHICH, TAKEN UNAWARE WITH
JOAN PREFACE(25)	INSTITUTIONS AND FASHIONS OF HIS OWN DAY. HE MADE	JOAN	RIDICULOUS, BUT NOT CONTEMPTIBLE NOR (COMPARATIVELY)
JOAN 5,SD(112)	OH, ARE YOU? WELL, THAT WILL BE VERY NICE.	JOAN	RISES, DEEPLY DISCOURAGED. /CHARLES/ (CONTINUING
JOAN 2 (81)	DARE SAY NOW THAT I AM NOT MY FATHER'S SON (TO	JOAN	) BUT IF YOU WANT ME TO BE CROWNED AT RHEIMS YOU MUST
JOAN EPILOG (164)	NINETEEN HUNDRED AND TWENTY. /DUNOIS/ (RAISING	JOAN	) HALF AN HOUR TO BURN YOU, DEAR SAINT; AND FOUR
JOAN 1 (69)	SOMETHING ABOUT THE GIRL -- /ROBERT/ (TURNING TO	JOAN	) NOW LISTEN YOU TO ME; AND (DESPERATELY) DONT CUT IN
JOAN 1 (67)	/POULENGEY/ CHECKMATE. /ROBERT/ NO FEAR! (TO	JOAN	) SO GOD SAYS YOU ARE TO RAISE THE SIEGE OF ORLEANS?
JOAN 1 (68)	CAN SHE, BY SAINT DENNIS! WE SHALL SEE. (TO	JOAN	) WE ARE NOT TALKING ABOUT GOD: WE ARE TALKING ABOUT
JOAN 3 (93)	HAS SPOKEN. (KNEELING AND HANDING HIS BATON TO	JOAN	) YOU COMMAND THE KING'S ARMY. I AM YOUR SOLDIER. /THE
JOAN 1 (62)	DE POULENGEY TO ME, WILL YOU? (HE TURNS TO	JOAN	). GET OUT; AND WAIT IN THE YARD. /JOAN/ (SMILING
JOAN 5 (117)	NUMBERS ON HER SIDE; AND SHE HAS WON. BUT I KNOW	JOAN	; AND I SEE THAT SOME DAY SHE WILL GO AHEAD WHEN SHE
JOAN PREFACE(21)	THE ONLY ONES THAT WERE IRRESISTIBLY PREPOTENT IN	JOAN	; AND THEY BROUGHT HER TO THE STAKE. NEITHER OF THEM
JOAN PREFACE(19)	MISSION FROM HEAVEN TO THE DAUPHIN (THIS WAS HOW	JOAN	SAW HER VERY ABLE PLAN FOR RETRIEVING THE DESPERATE
JOAN PREFACE(9)	REAL WOMAN ONE HAS EVER SEEN. IT IS SURMISED THAT	JOAN	SERVED UNCONSCIOUSLY AS THE SCULPTOR'S MODEL. THERE IS
JOAN PREFACE(39)	AT FIRST SIGHT WE ARE DISPOSED TO REPEAT THAT	JOAN	SHOULD HAVE BEEN EXCOMMUNICATED AND THEN LEFT TO GO HER
JOAN 5,SD(111)	FROM THE VESTRY, WHERE HE HAS BEEN DISROBING.	JOAN	SHRINKS AWAY BEHIND THE PILLAR. DUNOIS IS LEFT BETWEEN
JOAN PREFACE(48)	FOR THE DUC D'ALENCON. BOTH LEFT DESCRIPTIONS OF	JOAN	SO SIMILAR THAT, AS A MAN ALWAYS DESCRIBES HIMSELF
JOAN 2,SD(83)	PARDON, MAAM, I AM SURE. THE DUCHESS PASSES ON.	JOAN	STARES AFTER HER; THEN WHISPERS TO THE DAUPHIN. /JOAN/
JOAN EPILOG (163)	THE USUAL COURSE, AND, HAVING ADMITTED THE SAID	JOAN	SUCCESSIVELY TO THE RANKS OF VENERABLE AND BLESSED, --
JOAN PREFACE(21)	DISPENSABLE, AND ARE SACRIFICED ACCORDINGLY. WAS	JOAN	SUICIDAL? THESE TWO ABNORMALITIES WERE THE ONLY ONES
JOAN PREFACE(21)	BUT FORGAVE HER AFTERWARDS FOR HER DISOBEDIENCE.	JOAN	SUMMED UP. WE MAY ACCEPT AND ADMIRE JOAN, THEN, AS A
ROCK PREFACE(179)	OF COLONIAL GOVERNORS, IS NOT A HEROIC FIGURE.	JOAN	TACKLED HER JUDGES VALIANTLY AND WITTILY: HER TRIAL WAS
JOAN PREFACE(14)	MORTALS IS NEARER TO THE SCIENTIFIC TRUTH ABOUT	JOAN	THAN THE RATIONALIST AND MATERIALIST HISTORIANS AND
JOAN 3 (89)	TO HIS SHIELD) YOU SEE THE BEND SINISTER. ARE YOU	JOAN	THE MAID? /JOAN/ SURE. /DUNOIS/ WHERE ARE YOUR

JOAN 2 (80)	TO THE MAN-AT-ARMS). THE DUKE OF VENDOME PRESENTS	JOAN	THE MAID TO HIS MAJESTY. /CHARLES/ (PUTTING HIS FINGER
JOAN 4 (103)	NOW TO WHOM WE MUST LOOK FOR INTERCESSION, BUT TO	JOAN	THE MAID. WHAT WILL THE WORLD BE LIKE WHEN THE CHURCH'S
JOAN PREFACE(3)	PREFACE TO SAINT JOAN.	JOAN	THE ORIGINAL AND PRESUMPTUOUS. JOAN OF ARC, A VILLAGE
JOAN PREFACE(33)	BUT EXCEPTIONALLY MERCIFUL IN RESPECT OF SPARING	JOAN	THE TORTURE WHICH WAS CUSTOMARY WHEN SHE WAS OBDURATE
JOAN EPIL,SD(160)	IN THE FRENCH WARS. HELL WAS A TREAT AFTER THAT.	JOAN	THROWS UP HER ARMS, AND TAKES REFUGE FROM DESPAIR OF
JOAN PREFACE(6)	THE HEMLOCK, CHRIST TO HANG ON THE CROSS, AND	JOAN	TO BURN AT THE STAKE, WHILST NAPOLEON, THOUGH HE ENDS
JOAN 3,SD(89)	THE LANCE; BUT DUNOIS IS TOO MUCH OCCUPIED WITH	JOAN	TO NOTICE IT. /JOAN/ (BLUNTLY) BE YOU BASTARD OF
JOAN EPILOG (163)	AND CALLS THE SAID VENERABLE AND BLESSED	JOAN	TO THE COMMUNION OF THE CHURCH TRIUMPHANT AS SAINT
JOAN PREFACE(50)	LANG ARE AS DULL AS PICKPOCKETS; AND THEY REDUCE	JOAN	TO THE LEVEL OF THE EVEN LESS INTERESTING PERSON WHOSE
JOAN PREFACE(28)	CAUCHON, BISHOP OF BEAUVAIS, THE JUDGE WHO SENT	JOAN	TO THE STAKE, AS AN UNCONSCIONABLE SCOUNDREL, AND ALL
JOAN PREFACE(36)	TO GO A STEP FURTHER, A STEP ACROSS THE RUBICON.	JOAN	VIRTUALLY TOOK THAT STEP, CATHOLICISM NOT YET CATHOLIC
JOAN PREFACE(36)	SO, IF WE ADMIT, AS WE MUST, THAT THE BURNING OF	JOAN	WAS A MISTAKE, WE MUST BROADEN CATHOLICISM SUFFICIENTLY
JOAN PREFACE(48)	BELIEVE, WITH THE ROUEN ASSESSORS OF 1431, THAT	JOAN	WAS A WITCH, IT IS NOT BECAUSE THAT EXPLANATION IS TOO
JOAN PREFACE(5)	SLOWLY AND PEACEFULLY ON MEN'S MINDS, WHEREAS	JOAN	WAS A WOMAN OF ACTION, OPERATING WITH IMPETUOUS
JOAN PREFACE(10)	THAT IS, FOR PRACTICAL PURPOSES, NONE AT ALL.	JOAN	WAS ABSOLUTELY ILLITERATE. " I DO NOT KNOW A FROM B"
JOAN PREFACE(10)	OWN NAME CORRECTLY. BUT THIS DOES NOT MEAN THAT	JOAN	WAS AN IGNORANT PERSON, OR THAT SHE SUFFERED FROM THE
JOAN PREFACE(5)	AGE OF SEVENTY, IT MAY BE IMAGINED HOW INNOCENT	JOAN	WAS AT THE AGE OF SEVENTEEN. NOW SOCRATES WAS A MAN OF
JOAN PREFACE(34)	OF THE BURNING HAS ANY SPECIAL SIGNIFICANCE.	JOAN	WAS BURNT JUST AS DOZENS OF LESS INTERESTING HERETICS
JOAN PREFACE(34)	AGONIES OF SO-CALLED NATURAL DEATH AT ITS WORST.	JOAN	WAS BURNT MORE THAN FIVE HUNDRED YEARS AGO. MORE THAN
JOAN PREFACE(6)	AND THAT DEFEAT AND CAPTURE MEAN MARTYRDOM.	JOAN	WAS BURNT WITHOUT A HAND LIFTED ON HER OWN SIDE TO SAVE
JOAN PREFACE(28)	TO JOAN. A RECENT FRENCH WRITER DENIES THAT	JOAN	WAS BURNT, AND HOLDS THAT CAUCHON SPIRITED HER AWAY AND
JOAN PREFACE(27)	JOAN'S TIME, THEN YOU WILL NEVER UNDERSTAND WHY	JOAN	WAS BURNT, MUCH LESS FEEL THAT YOU MIGHT HAVE VOTED FOR
JOAN PREFACE(36)	SACERDOTAL, AND PROPHETICAL POWERS, IN WHICH	JOAN	WAS CRUSHED, TO ME IT IS NOT THE VICTORY OF ANY ONE OF
JOAN PREFACE(5)	OF SOCRATES ENDURED HIM SO LONG, AND WHY	JOAN	WAS DESTROYED BEFORE SHE WAS FULLY GROWN. BUT BOTH OF
JOAN PREFACE(14)	TALKING TO HER AS EITHER CRAZY OR MENDACIOUS. IF	JOAN	WAS MAD, ALL CHRISTENDOM WAS MAD TOO; FOR PEOPLE WHO
JOAN PREFACE(6)	ENOUGH TO SATISFY ALL REASONABLE CRITICS THAT	JOAN	WAS NOT A COMMON TERMAGANT, NOT A HARLOT, NOT A WITCH,
JOAN (2)	PLAY IN SIX SCENES AND AN EPILOGUE. SAINT	JOAN	WAS PERFORMED FOR THE FIRST TIME BY THE THEATRE GUILD
JOAN PREFACE(29)	INDICTMENT. THE POINT NEED BE NO FURTHER LABORED.	JOAN	WAS PERSECUTED ESSENTIALLY AS SHE WOULD BE PERSECUTED
JOAN PREFACE(9)	CASE AND WON IT. JOAN'S SOCIAL POSITION. BY CLASS	JOAN	WAS THE DAUGHTER OF A WORKING FARMER WHO WAS ONE OF THE
JOAN PREFACE(9)	BE FINALLY CHILLED BY THE PROSAIC FACT THAT	JOAN	WAS THE DEFENDANT IN A SUIT FOR BREACH OF PROMISE OF
JOAN PREFACE(42)	DANGEROUS AND TERRIFYING TO OUR GOVERNMENTS THAN	JOAN	WAS TO THE GOVERNMENT OF HER DAY, HAVE WITHIN THE LAST
JOAN PREFACE(29)	COURTS AND THE COURTS OF THE INQUISITION (	JOAN	WAS TRIED BY A COMBINATION OF THE TWO) WERE COURTS
JOAN PREFACE(18)	NO IMPLICATION OF UNSOUNDNESS OF MIND, THAT	JOAN	WAS WHAT FRANCIS GALTON AND OTHER MODERN INVESTIGATORS
JOAN PREFACE(15)	VITAL IMPORTANCE OF THE THINGS THEY SYMBOLIZE. IF	JOAN	WERE REBORN TODAY SHE WOULD BE SENT, FIRST TO A CONVENT
JOAN PREFACE(31)	A VULGAR VILLAIN, AND THAT THE QUESTIONS PUT TO	JOAN	WERE TRAPS, IS THAT IT HAS THE SUPPORT OF THE INQUIRY
JOAN PREFACE(8)	TO PUT THE LAST POINT ROUGHLY, ANY BOOK ABOUT	JOAN	WHICH BEGINS BY DESCRIBING HER AS A BEAUTY MAY BE AT
JOAN PREFACE(25)	REALISTIC DOCUMENTS CREATED A LIVING INTEREST IN	JOAN	WHICH VOLTAIRE'S MOCK HOMERICS AND SCHILLER'S ROMANTIC
JOAN 1 (65)	AT A DILATORY STEP WITH AN UNCONSCIOUS HOPE THAT	JOAN	WILL MAKE UP HIS MIND FOR HIM) DO YOU THINK I OUGHT TO
JOAN PREFACE(33)	MIGHT DO WORSE. BUT IT HAS BEEN ABLE TO CANONIZE	JOAN	WITHOUT ANY COMPROMISE AT ALL. SHE NEVER DOUBTED THAT
JOAN PREFACE(10)	ON IN THE FEUDAL WORLD. THEY WERE NOT RICH; AND	JOAN	WORKED ON THE FARM AS HER FATHER DID, DRIVING THE SHEEP
JOAN PREFACE(53)	CATHEDRAL, WITH SPECIAL MUSIC WRITTEN FOR BOTH.	JOAN	WOULD BE BURNT ON THE STAGE, AS MR MATHESON LANG ALWAYS
JOAN EPILOG (153)	SHALL NOT FUSS ABOUT HOW THE TRICK HAS BEEN DONE.	JOAN	WOULD NOT HAVE FUSSED ABOUT IT IF IT CAME ALL RIGHT IN
JOAN 2,SD(81)	JUMPS DOWN FROM THE DAIS BESIDE LA TREMOUILLE.	JOAN	, ALSO ON THE BROAD GRIN, TURNS BACK, SEARCHING ALONG
JOAN PREFACE(46)	AND SIXTEENTH CENTURIES THEY WERE TOLD LIES ABOUT	JOAN	, AND BY THIS TIME MIGHT VERY WELL BE TOLD THE TRUTH
KING PREFACE(153)	HISTORICAL PLAYS, CAESAR AND CLEOPATRA AND ST	JOAN	, ARE FULLY DOCUMENTED CHRONICLE PLAYS OF THIS TYPE.
JOAN 2 (86)	AND SHOUTING) HALLO! COME BACK, EVERYBODY. (TO	JOAN	, AS HE RUNS BACK TO THE ARCH OPPOSITE) MIND YOU STAND
JOAN PREFACE(12)	BY THE PROPHET DANIEL HE WAS MORE FANTASTIC THAN	JOAN	, BECAUSE HIS IMAGINATION WAS NOT DRAMATIC BUT
JOAN PREFACE(24)	INDECORUM. BUT ITS PURPOSE WAS NOT TO DEPICT	JOAN	, BUT TO KILL WITH RIDICULE EVERYTHING THAT VOLTAIRE
JOAN 6,SD(132)	(CALLING) THE ACCUSED. LET HER BE BROUGHT IN.	JOAN	, CHAINED BY THE ANKLES, IS BROUGHT IN THROUGH THE
JOAN 6 (143)	ALL BE SILENT. /LADVENU/ (READING QUIETLY) " I,	JOAN	, COMMONLY CALLED THE MAID, A MISERABLE SINNER, DO
JOAN 2,SD(80)	(MAJESTICALLY) LET HER APPROACH THE THRONE.	JOAN	, DRESSED AS A SOLDIER, WITH HER HAIR BOBBED AND
JOAN PREFACE(6)	THOSE WHO HAVE BEEN BOTH, LIKE MAHOMET AND	JOAN	, HAVE FOUND THAT IT IS THE CONQUEROR WHO MUST SAVE THE
JOAN PREFACE(35)	BUT CRUELTY FOR THE SALVATION OF JOAN'S SOUL.	JOAN	, HOWEVER, BELIEVED THAT THE SAVING OF HER SOUL WAS HER
JOAN 3,SD(89)	/DUNOIS/ LET HER PASS. HITHER, MAID! TO ME!	JOAN	, IN SPLENDID ARMOR, RUSHES IN IN A BLAZING RAGE. THE
JOAN 6 (139)	TELL ME I MUST DRESS AS A SOLDIER. /LADVE54/	JOAN	, JOAN: DOES NOT THAT PROVE TO YOU THAT THE VOICES ARE
JOAN PREFACE(30)	THEM. THE TRAGIC PART OF THE TRIAL WAS THAT	JOAN	, LIKE MOST PRISONERS TRIED FOR ANYTHING BUT THE
JOAN PREFACE(31)	WERE REFORMERS OF THE CHURCH LIKE LUTHER; WHILST	JOAN	, LIKE MRS EDDY, WAS QUITE PREPARED TO SUPERSEDE ST
JOAN PREFACE(24)	HAS NOT A SINGLE POINT OF CONTACT WITH THE REAL	JOAN	, NOR INDEED WITH ANY MORTAL WOMAN THAT EVER WALKED
JOAN PREFACE(51)	SEVERITY IN HIS JUDICIAL RELATIONS WITH	JOAN	, OR OF AS MUCH ANTI-PRISONER, PRO-POLICE, CLASS AND
MILL PREFACE(135)	TO REPLACE THEM, BUT STILL AS DOMINANT AS SAINT	JOAN	, SAINT CLARE, AND SAINT TERESA. THE MOST COMPLETE
JOAN 2,SD(83)	AND LA TREMOUILLE. AS THE ARCHBISHOP PASSES	JOAN	, SHE FALLS ON HER KNEES, AND KISSES THE HEM OF HIS
JOAN PREFACE(26)	ANY SUCH PERSON AS THE REAL JOAN. MARK TWAIN'S	JOAN	, SKIRTED TO THE GROUND, AND WITH AS MANY PETTICOATS AS
JOAN 6 (134)	INDIGNANTLY). /CAUCHON/ I HAVE WARNED YOU BEFORE,	JOAN	, THAT YOU ARE DOING YOURSELF NO GOOD BY THESE PERT
JOAN PREFACE(21)	JOAN SUMMED UP. WE MAY ACCEPT AND ADMIRE	JOAN	, THEN, AS A SANE AND SHREWD COUNTRY GIRL OF
JOAN PREFACE(28)	NEUTRAL TRIBUNALS WERE NOT AVAILABLE. EDITH, LIKE	JOAN	, WAS AN ARCH HERETIC: IN THE MIDDLE OF THE WAR SHE
JOAN PREFACE(6)	YEARS LATER, IN FORM A REHABILITATION OF	JOAN	, WAS REALLY ONLY A CONFIRMATION OF THE VALIDITY OF THE
JOAN 5 (111)	HER KINDLY BUT NOT SYMPATHETICALLY) THEN,	JOAN	, WE SHALL HEAR WHATEVER WE FANCY IN THE BOOMING OF THE
JOAN PREFACE(9)	SO POWERFULLY THE QUESTION " IF THIS WOMAN BE NOT	JOAN	, WHO IS SHE? " THAT I DISPENSE WITH FURTHER EVIDENCE,
JOAN PREFACE(8)	DEPARTMENTS, HE WILL NEVER MAKE ANYTHING OF	JOAN	, WHOSE GENIUS WAS TURNED TO PRACTICAL ACCOUNT MAINLY
JOAN 1 (61)	/STEWARD/ (ABJECTLY) YES, SIR. /ROBERT/ (TO	JOAN	, WITH A SOUR LOSS OF CONFIDENCE) SO YOU ARE PRESUMING
JOAN 5 (116)	(OFFENDED) NOT CONTENT WITH BEING POPE	JOAN	, YOU MUST BE CAESAR AND ALEXANDER AS WELL. /THE
JOAN EPILOG (155)	LIGHT BY THE BEDSIDE). /CHARLES/ (PEEPING OUT)	JOAN	! ARE YOU A GHOST, JOAN? /JOAN/ HARDLY EVEN THAT,
JOAN 6 (145)	A RAT IN A HOLE? MY VOICES WERE RIGHT. /LADVENU/	JOAN	! JOAN! /JOAN/ YES: THEY TOLD ME YOU WERE FOOLS (THE
JOAN 1 (65)	(RISING) YES. (HE GOES TO THE WINDOW AND CALLS)	JOAN	! /JOAN'S VOICE/ WILL HE LET US GO, POLLY?
JOAN 6 (145)	A HOLE? MY VOICES WERE RIGHT. /LADVENU/ JOAN!	JOAN	! /JOAN/ YES: THEY TOLD ME YOU WERE FOOLS (THE WORD
JOAN EPILOG (163)	TRIUMPHANT AS SAINT JOAN. /JOAN/ (RAPT) SAINT	JOAN	! /THE GENTLEMAN/ ON EVERY THIRTIETH DAY OF MAY, BEING
JOAN EPILOG (166)	THINK OVER THIS. (HE GOES). /CHARLES/ POOR OLD	JOAN	! THEY HAVE ALL RUN AWAY FROM YOU EXCEPT THIS
JOAN 5 (109)	THE AMBULATORY FROM THE VESTRY. /DUNOIS/ COME,	JOAN	! YOU HAVE HAD ENOUGH PRAYING. AFTER THAT FIT OF

JOANESQUE

JOAN PREFACE(32)	NO WRONG WITHOUT A REMEDY. IT DOES NOT DEFER TO	JOANESQUE	PRIVATE JUDGMENT AS SUCH, THE SUPREMACY OF PRIVATE

JOANNA

LION PREFACE(35)	THE WOMEN ARE NAMED; SO THAT WE ARE INTRODUCED TO	JOANNA	THE WIFE OF CHUZA, HEROD'S STEWARD, AND SUSANNA.

JOAN'S

JOAN PREFACE(26)	THE OTHER. LANG HAD NO DIFFICULTY IN SHEWING THAT	JOAN'S	ABILITY WAS NOT AN UNNATURAL FICTION TO BE EXPLAINED
JOAN PREFACE(10)	SAID THE SAME. MARIE ANTOINETTE, FOR INSTANCE, AT	JOAN'S	AGE COULD NOT SPELL HER OWN NAME CORRECTLY. BUT THIS
JOAN PREFACE(44)	NOR WERE THEY OFFERED AS THE EXPRESSION OF	JOAN'S	ARBITRARY WILL. IT WAS NEVER " I SAY SO," BUT ALWAYS
JOAN PREFACE(39)	AS SPIRITUALLY. THEREFORE THE QUESTION RAISED BY	JOAN'S	BURNING IS A BURNING QUESTION STILL, THOUGH THE
JOAN PREFACE(12)	SO MANY OF OUR WOMEN INTO MILITARY LIFE, THAT	JOAN'S	CAMPAIGNING COULD NOT HAVE BEEN CARRIED ON IN
JOAN PREFACE(45)	THAT WE CAN NOW PRETEND TO SAY ABOUT THE PROSE OF	JOAN'S	CAREER. THE ROMANCE OF HER RISE, THE TRAGEDY OF HER
JOAN PREFACE(23)	AND ODDITY, FULLY ACCOUNTS FOR ALL THE FACTS IN	JOAN'S	CAREER, AND MAKES HER A CREDIBLE HISTORICAL AND HUMAN
JOAN PREFACE(51)	HERE THEN WE HAVE A REASON WHY MY DRAMA OF SAINT	JOAN'S	CAREER, THOUGH IT MAY GIVE THE ESSENTIAL TRUTH OF IT,
JOAN PREFACE(10)	YOUNG LADY OF THE FARM. THE DIFFERENCE BETWEEN	JOAN'S	CASE AND SHAKESPEAR'S IS THAT SHAKESPEAR WAS NOT
JOAN PREFACE(6)	THE QUESTION WHICH OF THE TWO WAS OPERATIVE IN	JOAN'S	CASE HAS TO BE FACED. IT WAS DECIDED AGAINST HER BY
JOAN PREFACE(51)	TO A CONFLICT OF VILLAIN AND HERO, OR IN	JOAN'S	CASE VILLAIN AND HEROINE, NOT ONLY MISS THE POINT
JOAN PREFACE(8)	MAY BE AT ONCE CLASSED AS A ROMANCE. NOT ONE OF	JOAN'S	COMRADES, IN VILLAGE, COURT, OR CAMP, EVEN WHEN THEY
JOAN PREFACE(48)	NEITHER DO I CLAIM MORE FOR MY DRAMATIZATIONS OF	JOAN'S	CONTEMPORARIES THAN THAT SOME OF THEM ARE PROBABLY
JOAN EPIL,SD(152)	KING CHARLES THE SEVENTH OF FRANCE, FORMERLY	JOAN'S	DAUPHIN, NOW CHARLES THE VICTORIOUS, AGED 51, IS IN
JOAN PREFACE(28)	BUT THAT THEY WERE POLITICAL PARTISANS OF	JOAN'S	ENEMIES. THIS IS A VALID OBJECTION TO ALL SUCH
JOAN PREFACE(32)	THE MASS OF SINCERE TESTIMONY IT PRODUCED AS TO	JOAN'S	ENGAGING PERSONAL CHARACTER. THE QUESTION THEN
JOAN PREFACE(25)	CERTAINLY VOLTAIRE SHOULD NOT HAVE ASSERTED THAT	JOAN'S	FATHER WAS A PRIEST; BUT WHEN HE WAS OUT TO ECRASER
JOAN PREFACE(28)	TRIBUNALS THEY ARE UNAVOIDABLE. A TRIAL BY	JOAN'S	FRENCH PARTISANS WOULD HAVE BEEN AS UNFAIR AS THE
JOAN PREFACE(8)	WITH SPECIFIC CHARMS AND SPECIFIC IMBECILITIES.	JOAN'S	GOOD LOOKS. TO PUT THE LAST POINT ROUGHLY, ANY BOOK
JOAN PREFACE(53)	BE EXPECTED TO STULTIFY MYSELF BY IMPLYING THAT	JOAN'S	HISTORY IN THE WORLD ENDED UNHAPPILY WITH HER
JOAN PREFACE(27)	HOWEVER, ONE DISABILITY IN COMMON, TO UNDERSTAND	JOAN'S	HISTORY IT IS NOT ENOUGH TO UNDERSTAND HER CHARACTER:

JOAN PREFACE(45)	HAD TO RETIRE TO CAPRERA. MODERN DISTORTIONS OF	JOAN'S	HISTORY. THIS, I THINK, IS ALL THAT WE CAN NOW
JOAN PREFACE(26)	AND WROTE A LIFE OF JOAN IN WHICH HE ATTRIBUTED	JOAN'S	IDEAS TO CLERICAL PROMPTING AND HER MILITARY SUCCESS
JOAN PREFACE(14)	NOT REALLY ST CATHERINE, BUT THE DRAMATIZATION BY	JOAN'S	IMAGINATION OF THAT PRESSURE UPON HER OF THE DRIVING
JOAN PREFACE(22)	A SHARP EDGE. SHE WAS VERY CAPABLE: A BORN BOSS.	JOAN'S	IMMATURITY AND IGNORANCE. ALL THIS, HOWEVER, MUST BE
JOAN EPILOG (162)	THE BED CURTAINS ON THE OTHER SIDE, AND COMING TO	JOAN'S	LEFT HAND) MADAM: MY CONGRATULATIONS ON YOUR
JOAN EPILOG (158)	GONE? /DUNOIS/ (COMING THROUGH THE TAPESTRY ON	JOAN'S	LEFT, THE CANDLES RELIGHTING THEMSELVES AT THE SAME
JOAN PREFACE(37)	TO RELIEVE IT BY BURNING THE THREAD. THIS IS	JOAN'S	LESSON TO THE CHURCH; AND ITS FORMULATION BY THE HAND
JOAN PREFACE(8)	BY CONSCIOUS RATIOCINATION, HE WILL NEVER CATCH	JOAN'S	LIKENESS. HER IDEAL BIOGRAPHER MUST BE FREE FROM
JOAN PREFACE(18)	NORMAL PERMANENT EQUIPMENT OF ALL HUMAN BEINGS.	JOAN'S	MANLINESS AND MILITARISM. JOAN'S OTHER ABNORMALITY,
JOAN PREFACE(31)	THE PATRIOTIC NATIONALIST POPULACE, WHO IDOLIZED	JOAN'S	MEMORY. THE ENGLISH WERE GONE; AND A VERDICT IN THEIR
JOAN PREFACE(42)	WE MAY NOW CONSIDER THE SPECIAL FEATURE OF	JOAN'S	MENTAL CONSTITUTION WHICH MADE HER SO UNMANAGEABLE.
JOAN PREFACE(40)	NECESSARIES OF LIFE TO HER. SUCH A SPIRIT AS	JOAN'S	MIGHT HAVE GOT OVER THAT DIFFICULTY AS THE CHURCH OF
JOAN PREFACE(18)	HUMAN BEINGS. JOAN'S MANLINESS AND MILITARISM.	JOAN'S	OTHER ABNORMALITY, TOO COMMON AMONG UNCOMMON THINGS
JOAN PREFACE(37)	THOU WALKED IN THE RECESSES OF THE DEEP? " AND	JOAN'S	OWN ANSWER IS ALSO THE ANSWER OF OLD: " THOUGH HE
JOAN PREFACE(17)	AND VISIONS WERE ILLUSORY, AND THEIR WISDOM ALL	JOAN'S	OWN, IS SHEWN BY THE OCCASIONS ON WHICH THEY FAILED
JOAN PREFACE(10)	DOOR TOO OFTEN SWORD IN HAND TO BE DISREGARDED:	JOAN'S	PEOPLE COULD NOT AFFORD TO BE IGNORANT OF WHAT WAS
JOAN PREFACE(31)	QUESTION AND FIT EVERY OCCASION. THE ENORMITY OF	JOAN'S	PRETENSION WAS PROVED BY HER OWN UNCONSCIOUSNESS OF
JOAN PREFACE(3)	AND INSUFFERABLE PRESUMPTION. AT EIGHTEEN	JOAN'S	PRETENSIONS WERE BEYOND THOSE OF THE PROUDEST POPE OR
JOAN PREFACE(9)	AND THAT SHE CONDUCTED HER OWN CASE AND WON IT.	JOAN'S	SOCIAL POSITION. BY CLASS JOAN WAS THE DAUGHTER OF A
JOAN PREFACE(35)	CRUELTY'S SAKE, BUT CRUELTY FOR THE SALVATION OF	JOAN'S	SOUL. JOAN, HOWEVER, BELIEVED THAT THE SAVING OF HER
JOAN PREFACE(44)	AMBITION OF THE BASER NATURES EXACERBATED BY	JOAN'S	SUCCESS, BUT AMONG THE FRIENDLY ONES THAT WERE CLEVER
JOAN PREFACE(27)	ENORMOUSLY, BOTH MORALLY AND MECHANICALLY, SINCE	JOAN'S	TIME, THEN YOU WILL NEVER UNDERSTAND WHY JOAN WAS
JOAN PREFACE(29)	JOAN NOT TRIED AS A POLITICAL OFFENDER. BESIDES,	JOAN'S	TRIAL WAS NOT, LIKE CASEMENT'S, A NATIONAL POLITICAL
JOAN PREFACE(28)	A DIFFERENT HEADDRESS. COMPARATIVE FAIRNESS OF	JOAN'S	TRIAL. THE TRUTH IS THAT CAUCHON WAS THREATENED AND
JOAN PREFACE(13)	ATTACH ANY SUCH OBJECTIVE VALIDITY TO THE FORM OF	JOAN'S	VISIONS, BUT THAT THERE ARE FORCES AT WORK WHICH USE
JOAN PREFACE(13)	APPETITE. WHAT THEN IS THE MODERN VIEW OF	JOAN'S	VOICES AND VISIONS AND MESSAGES FROM GOD? THE
JOAN PREFACE(11)	MOST OF THE DAUGHTERS OF OUR PETTY BOURGEOISIE.	JOAN'S	VOICES AND VISIONS. JOAN'S VOICES AND VISIONS HAVE
JOAN PREFACE(11)	OUR PETTY BOURGEOISIE. JOAN'S VOICES AND VISIONS.	JOAN'S	VOICES AND VISIONS HAVE PLAYED MANY TRICKS WITH HER
JOAN EPILOG (157)	GOOD, NOR CHARLES THE WISE, NOR CHARLES THE BOLD.	JOAN'S	WORSHIPPERS MAY EVEN CALL ME CHARLES THE COWARD

JOB

ROCK PREFACE(161)	OF ANY OTHER PUBLIC SERVICE, IS A WHOLE TIME	JOB	: IT CANNOT BE PERMANENTLY COMBINED WITH THAT OF AMATEUR
APPL PREFACE(186)	BESIDES, MODERN GOVERNMENT IS NOT A ONE-MAN	JOB	: IT IS TOO BIG FOR THAT. IF WE RESORT TO A COMMITTEE OR
SUPR III (100)	GO BACK THERE. HAVE YOU NEVER READ THE BOOK OF	JOB	? HAVE YOU ANY CANONICAL AUTHORITY FOR ASSUMING THAT
JOAN 2 (83)	IS THE DUKE DE LA TREMOUILLE. /JOAN/ WHAT BE HIS	JOB	? /CHARLES/ HE PRETENDS TO COMMAND THE ARMY. AND
JOAN 1 (67)	OF A MEADOW. YOU THINK SOLDIERING IS ANYBODY'S	JOB	? /JOAN/ I DO NOT THINK IT CAN BE VERY DIFFICULT IF GOD
FANY PROLOG (265)	THE VERY OUTSIDE, MYSELF. IT'S NOT AN OLD MAN'S	JOB	AFTER ALL, IS IT? BANNAL MAY NOT RIDE THE LITERARY HIGH
FABL II (107)	AND I THINK YOULL ADMIT THAT I KNOW MY	JOB	AFTER MY FIFTEEN YEARS IN THE FOREIGN OFFICE. YOU KNOW
ROCK II (262)	HAVE TO WAIT TWO YEARS AND GO THROUGH THE WHOLE	JOB	AGAIN BEFORE YOU CAN GET YOUR BILL ON THE STATUTE BOOK
VWOO 3 (138)	THAT A WOMAN WANTS SOMETHING MORE IN LIFE THAN A	JOB	AND A SALARY. /A/ I KNOW THAT PERFECTLY WELL. THERE IS
MIS. PREFACE(4)	BACK OF HIS CONSCIENCE THAT HE IS RATHER A POOR	JOB	AND HAD BETTER BE REMANUFACTURED. HE KNOWS THAT HIS
MIS. PREFACE(99)	PLEASURE WE GET FROM THE RHETORIC OF THE BOOK OF	JOB	AND ITS TRAGIC PICTURE OF A BEWILDERED SOUL CANNOT
APPL I (212)	FACTS AND LOOK THEM IN THE FACE, OR ELSE TAKE MY	JOB	AND LEAD THE PARTY YOURSELF. /NICOBAR/ THE WORST OF YOU
PRES (142)	I DONT KNOW. THAT IS THE DIFFERENCE BETWEEN YOUR	JOB	AND MINE, MITCHENER. AFTER TWENTY YEARS IN THE ARMY A
FABL VI (131)	IT WAS AN ARGUMENT BETWEEN AN OLD JOSSER NAMED	JOB	AND ONE OF THE OLD GODS, WHO PRETENDED HE HAD MADE THE
ROCK I (216)	ENGLISH WORKING MAN WHEN NOBODY WILL GIVE HIM A	JOB	AND PAY HIM TO DO IT. AND WHEN HE GETS IT WHAT DOES HE
ROCK II (279)	DONT KNOW DAVID YET. /ALOYSIA/ I WILL FIND HIM A	JOB	AND SEE THAT HE DOES IT. I WILL INTEREST HIM IN IT. /SIR
LION PREFACE(86)	KOHELETH AND DAVID AND SOLOMON AND THE AUTHORS OF	JOB	AND THE PENTATEUCH; AND, AS WE HAVE SEEN, JESUS SEEMS TO
METH PREFACE(R82)	TOLD PARRY THE BLUDGEONING TRUTH ABOUT HIS	JOB	AND WOKE HIM TO CONVICTION OF SIN. COMPARE FLAXMAN AND
PYGM V (273)	AGE? I HAVE TO DYE MY HAIR ALREADY TO KEEP MY	JOB	AS A DUSTMAN. IF I WAS ONE OF THE DESERVING POOR, AND
MILL IV (190)	MADAM. ONE DAY A WOMAN CAME HERE AND ASKED FOR A	JOB	AS A SCULLERY MAID. MY POOR OLD FATHER HADNT THE NERVE
APPL I (208)	(CONTINUING) NO KING ON EARTH IS AS SAFE IN HIS	JOB	AS A TRADE UNION OFFICIAL. THERE IS ONLY ONE THING THAT
BARB III (326)	PETER SHIRLEY? /CUSINS/ THEY HAVE FOUND HIM A	JOB	AS GATEKEEPER AND TIMEKEEPER. HE'S FRIGHTFULLY
FABL III (109)	OF ANY SORT? /THE TOURIST/ NO. THEY OFFERED ME A	JOB	AS HOSPITAL PORTER BECAUSE I'M PHYSICALLY STRONG. HOW
JOAN PREFACE(6)	NEVERTHELESS THE REHABILITATION OF 1456, CORRUPT	JOB	AS IT WAS, REALLY DID PRODUCE EVIDENCE ENOUGH TO SATISFY
FABL VI (131)	PUT TEN TIMES AS MANY UNANSWERABLE QUESTIONS TO	JOB	AS JOB COULD PUT TO HIM. IT WILL TEACH YOU THAT I CAN DO
MILL III (186)	IT ALL IN HALF A DAY EVERY WEEK. I SHALL TAKE A	JOB	AS SCULLERY MAID AT A HOTEL TO FILL UP MY TIME. BUT
PYGM II (241)	GOVERNOR. NOT JUST THIS WEEK, BECAUSE I HAVE A	JOB	AT A DISTANCE. BUT LATER ON YOU MAY DEPEND ON ME.
BARB II (279)	ANY FAT YOUNG SOAKER OF YOUR AGE. GO AND TAKE MY	JOB	AT HORROCKSES, WHERE I WORKED FOR TEN YEAR. THEY WANT
SIM PRO,3, (30)	WAS A TEACHER; BUT WHEN SHE MARRIED THEY TOOK HER	JOB	AWAY FROM HER AND WOULDNT LET HER TEACH ANY MORE. /THE
DOCT PREFACE(19)	FOUND WHO EARN GOOD WAGES AND ARE NEVER OUT OF A	JOB	BECAUSE THEY ARE STRONG, INDEFATIGABLE, AND SKILFUL, AND
DOCT IV SD(159)	IN ANY HAND, HE GENERALLY GIVES IT UP AS A BAD	JOB	BEFORE HE SUCCEEDS IN FINISHING A SENTENCE. /THE
BARB II (281)	STEADY? /SHIRLEY/ TEETOTALLER. NEVER OUT OF A	JOB	BEFORE. GOOD WORKER. AND SENT TO THE KNACKERS LIKE AN
FABL VI (131)	THE OLD GOD MADE NO SUCH PRETENCE, AND CRUSHED	JOB	BY SHEWING THAT HE COULD PUT TEN TIMES AS MANY
FABL VI (131)	TIMES AS MANY UNANSWERABLE QUESTIONS TO JOB AS	JOB	COULD PUT TO HIM. IT WILL TEACH YOU THAT I CAN DO THE
MIS. (173)	HIM) ALL RIGHT: I'M DONE. COULDNT EVEN DO THAT	JOB	DECENTLY. THATS A CLERK ALL OVER. VERY WELL: SEND FOR
ROCK I (206)	AS MUCH AS YOU DO. IT MAKES A PRIME MINISTER'S	JOB	EASY BECAUSE IT BRINGS EVERY DOG TO HEEL; BUT IT
DOCT I (92)	AND YOU HAD TO SET YOUR TEETH AND FINISH THE	JOB	FAST. NOWADAYS YOU WORK AT YOUR EASE; AND THE PAIN
BARB II (282)	OF YOU. SO BUCK UP, PETER! WE CAN ALWAYS FIND A	JOB	FOR A STEADY MAN LIKE YOU. (SHIRLEY, DISARMED AND A
2TRU PREFACE(22)	DISCOVERY IS THAT GOVERNMENT IS NOT A WHOLE-TIME	JOB	FOR ALL ITS AGENTS. A COUNCIL OF PEASANTS DERIVES ITS
MTH3 (104)	THIS IS AN INTELLECTUAL DIFFICULTY. THIS IS A	JOB	FOR CONFUCIUS. I HEARD HIM USE THAT VERY WORD THE OTHER
HART II (85)	YOU KNOW. AND YOULL ADMIT THAT I KEPT A	JOB	FOR HIM WHEN I HAD FINISHED WITH HIM. BUT BUSINESS IS
APPL I (219)	A WEEK NOW, AND A BIG DOLE WHEN THERE IS NO	JOB	FOR HIM. AND WHAT ENGLISHMAN WILL GIVE HIS MIND TO
BARB II (274)	AND DO AS LITTLE AS I CAN SO'S TO LEAVE ARF THE	JOB	FOR ME FELLOW WORKERS. FOURTH, I'M FLY ENOUGH TO KNOW
POSN (464)	RIPS LIKE FEEMY. HE MADE ME BECAUSE HE HAD A	JOB	FOR ME. HE LET ME RUN LOOSE TIL THE JOB WAS READY; AND
APPL II (275)	ME INTO IT; AND I DARESAY THEYLL FIND ANOTHER	JOB	FOR ME. (HE GOES). /PLINY/ (CHEERFUL TO THE LAST AS
POSN PREFACE(419)	INSTITUTION WOULD NOT LAST A YEAR, EXCEPT AS A	JOB	FOR SOMEBODY, COUNSEL'S OPINION. THE PROPOSAL IS STILL
MIS. (148)	THE OTHER CHAPS. LOOK AT THE SPANISH EMPIRE! BAD	JOB	FOR SPAIN, BUT SPLENDID FOR SOUTH AMERICA. LOOK AT WHAT
GETT (280)	IS! /THE GENERAL/ (DECISIVELY) ALICE: THIS IS A	JOB	FOR THE BARMECIDE. HE'S A BISHOP: IT'S HIS DUTY TO TALK
APPL I (237)	EVERY ACCIDENT, EVERY SMASH AND CRASH, IS A	JOB	FOR THEM. BUT FOR THEM WE SHOULD HAVE UNBREAKABLE GLASS,
APPL INTRLUD(250)	TO ONE OF THEM. BEING YOUR HUSBAND IS ONLY A	JOB	FOR WHICH ONE MAN WILL DO AS WELL AS ANOTHER, AND WHICH
CAND I (91)	I KNOW A CLORGYMAN WHAT 'AS BIN KEP HOUT OF HIS	JOB	FOR YORRS BY THE BISHOP O LONDON, ALTHOUGH THE PORE
PYGM III (245)	DEAR, YOU MUSTNT STAY. /HIGGINS/ I MUST. IVE A	JOB	FOR YOU. A PHONETIC JOB. /MRS HIGGINS/ NO USE, DEAR. I'M
SUPR II (70)	WHAT YOU ARE AND NO MISTAKE; AND A JOLLY GOOD	JOB	FOR YOU, TOO, I SHOULD SAY. /TANNER/ (MOMENTOUSLY)
BARB II (278)	SHE AINT ANYTHING TO DO WITH ME. /BILL/ GOOD	JOB	FOR YOU! AW'D PAT TWO MEALS INTO YOU AND FAWT YOU WITH
MILL III (181)	HE'D ONLY SHUT UP THE PLACE AND TAKE AWAY THEIR	JOB	FROM THEM. IF THEY THOUGHT YOUD BE SO CRUEL AS TO REPORT
BARB II (276)	AND NOW AM I TO BE THROWN INTO THE GUTTER AND MY	JOB	GIVEN TO A YOUNG MAN THAT CAN DO IT NO BETTER THAN ME
AUGS (267)	EVERYTHING'S CHANGED. BESIDES, I SHOULD LOSE MY	JOB	HERE IF I STOOD DRINKING AT THE BAR. I'M A RESPECTABLE
APPL I (197)	THE LAST TWO CORONATIONS. THAT WAS HOW I GOT MY	JOB	HERE IN THE PALACE. ALL OUR ROYAL PEOPLE KNEW HIM QUITE
GENV III (77)	! ! /THE SECRETARY/ I CANNOT AFFORD TO LOSE MY	JOB	HERE. DO NOT FORCE ME TO FIGHT YOU WITH YOUR OWN WEAPONS
GENV II (53)	OFF FOR A TOUR ROUND THE EMPIRE, AND GOT ME THIS	JOB	HERE-- TO KEEP ME OUT OF HIS WAY, I SUPPOSE. ANYHOW HERE
APPL I (224)	MAN. THERE IS NOT A MAN OR WOMAN HERE WHOSE	JOB	I COULD DO AS WELL AS THEY DO IT. I AM PRIME MINISTER
PYGM III (256)	YOUR LIVE DOLL. /HIGGINS/ PLAYING! THE HARDEST	JOB	I EVER TACKLED: MAKE NO MISTAKE ABOUT THAT, MOTHER. BUT
GENV IV (114)	HAVE SAID ENOUGH. YOU KNOW NOW WHAT AN IMPOSSIBLE	JOB	I HAVE HERE AS SECRETARY TO THE LEAGUE OF NATIONS. TO ME
GENV I (31)	SAY IT'S AS DULL AS DITCHWATER. WHEN I TOOK THE	JOB	I THOUGHT IT WAS GOING TO BE INTERESTING, AND THAT I'D
GETT (325)	WRITE ADVERTISEMENTS, AND THAT I COULD TAKE THE	JOB	IF I LIKED. /MRS GEORGE/ IT'S STILL OPEN. (SHE TURNS TO
ROCK II (270)	TO EXIST ON THE EARTH, OR TO FIRE YOU OUT OF YOUR	JOB	IF YOU STAND UP TO HIM AS A MAN AND AN EQUAL. YOU CANT
MIS. (183)	YOURE A FOOL; BUT YOUVE JUST PUT THE LID ON THIS	JOB	IN A MASTERLY MANNER. I KNEW YOU WOULD. I TOLD YOU ALL
GENV II (56)	ONE TENTH OF IT. THE ABYSSINIAN WAR WAS A HOLIDAY	JOB	IN COMPARISON. WEVE NEVER HAD ANYTHING LIKE IT BEFORE.
MTH2 (39)	INTELLECTUAL ENOUGH TO SPLIT STRAWS WHEN THERES A	JOB	IN FRONT OF ME, AND NOTHING BETTER FOR ME TO DO. I
JITT PREFACE(4)	HOW GREAT I NEVER REALIZED UNTIL I TOOK THE	JOB	IN HAND. AT FIRST I WAS PREOCCUPIED WITH A QUITE MINOR
CAPT II (260)	RETURN TO A LIFE OF CRIME UNLESS I GAVE HIM A	JOB	IN THE GARDEN; AND I DID. IT WAS MUCH MORE SENSIBLE THAN
FANY PROLOG (259)	I WAS QUITE A LAD, OF COURSE. BUT I HAD A	JOB	IN THE ORIGINAL PRODUCTION OF OUR BOYS. /THE COUNT/ MY
BULL III (141)	RAN AP FOUR WEEKS IN LEMBETH WEN OI WAS AHT OF A	JOB	IN WINTER. THEY TOOK THE DOOR OFF ITS INGES AND THE
2TRU II (63)	NO CONSCIENCE ABOUT WHAT YOU PREACH, YOUR PROPER	JOB	IS AT THE BAR. BUT AS YOU HAVE NO CONSCIENCE ABOUT WHAT
ROCK PREFACE(170)	MORE COMPLETELY THAN HUMAN NATURE WHEN THE	JOB	IS TAKEN IN HAND EARLY ENOUGH. SUCH ARTIFICIAL PRODUCTS
ROCK II (259)	THAT, AND I WILL PREVENT YOU. /SIR ARTHUR/ YOUR	JOB	IS TO PREVENT ME OR ANYBODY ELSE FROM DOING ANYTHING.

ROCK II (259)	ME OR ANYBODY ELSE FROM DOING ANYTHING. YOUR	JOB	IS TO PREVENT THE WORLD FROM MOVING. WELL, IT IS MOVING;
ROCK II (259)	THE COUNTRY AND DESTROYING THE EMPIRE? MY	JOB	IS TO PREVENT YOU FROM DOING THAT. AND I WILL PREVENT
ROCK II (259)	ARTHUR/ NOTHING, IF YOU ARE WILLING TO TAKE ON MY	JOB	. ARE YOU? /SIR DEXTER/ THE JOB OF RUINING THE COUNTRY
WIDO III (59)	IS THIS. DONT LETS HAVE ANY NONSENSE ABOUT THIS	JOB	. AS I UNDERSTAND IT, ROBBINS'S ROW IS TO BE PULLED DOWN
2TRU PREFACE(24)	WITH WHOM GOVERNING IS NECESSARILY A WHOLE-TIME	JOB	. BUT HE IS NO RICHER THAN HIS NEIGHBORS, AND CAN "
GENV II (53)	AND ALL THAT, AND THAT I WAS LOOKING OUT FOR A	JOB	. HIS PEOPLE FIXED ME UP FOR GENEVA ALL RIGHT. A PERFECT
BASH II,2, (116)	AM TO BE HEARD OF ANY DAY BY SUCH AS LIKES THE	JOB	. I DONT KNOW, GOVERNOR, AS ENNYTHINK REMAINS FOR ME TO
BUOY III (36)	I BEG YOUR PARDON. /SHE/ NO. IT'S NOT A DOCTOR'S	JOB	. I FOUND MYSELF WHAT IS CALLED FALLING IN LOVE. I HAD
VWOO 1 (122)	WHEN YOU HAVE BEEN ACCUSTOMED TO A CLEAN DECENT	JOB	. I HAVE SEEN SO MANY BRIGHT JOLLY GIRLS TURN INTO DIRTY
VWOO 3 (136)	TO THAT, WHAT BECOMES OF ME? YOU CAN GET ANOTHER	JOB	. I VERY GREATLY DOUBT WHETHER ANYONE WOULD GIVE ME ONE.
BARB III (339)	SOUND HOUSE IN A HANDSOME STREET, AND A PERMANENT	JOB	. IN THREE WEEKS HE WILL HAVE A FANCY WAISTCOAT; IN
GETT (316)	THAT THE DOCTOR IS TO HAVE NO SAY IN THE	JOB	. IT'S BAD ENOUGH FOR THE TWO PEOPLE TO BE MARRIED TO
DOCT III (132)	THAT JUST DESTROYS ALL MY INTEREST IN THE BEASTLY	JOB	. IVE A GOOD MIND TO THROW UP THE COMMISSION, AND PAY
SIM II (82)	DEAR: GARDENING IS THE ONLY UNQUESTIONABLY USEFUL	JOB	. (HE FOLLOWS HYERING INTO THE HOUSE). /LADY FARWATERS/
LION II (137)	ALL BE THROWN TO THE LIONS? IT'S NOT A MAN'S	JOB	. (HE THROWS HIMSELF MOODILY INTO HIS CHAIR). THE
2TRU I (42)	OF THE BELL AS DESIRED). I WASH MY HANDS OF THIS	JOB	. (SHE SITS DOWN DOGGEDLY). /THE BURGLAR/ (COMING TO
FANY II (290)	(SHORTLY AND STERNLY) AMELIA: THIS IS YOUR	JOB	. (TO MARGARET) I LEAVE YOU TO YOUR MOTHER. I SHALL
ROCK PREFACE(157)	DO IT FOR HALF A CROWN, AND PROBABLY ENJOY THE	JOB	. LEADING CASE OF JESUS CHRIST. I DISLIKE CRUELTY, EVEN
POSN (445)	KEMP SHALL NEVER HAVE THE LAUGH ON ME OVER THAT	JOB	. LET THEM HANG ME. LET THEM SHOOT. SO LONG AS THEY ARE
2TRU PREFACE(10)	PEOPLE ARE THOSE WHO WILL NOT WORK AT THEIR	JOB	. MISERIES OF THE VAGRANT ROOTLESS RICH. BUT THE NEW
MILL I (159)	WE KITED THEM ALL. BUT IT WAS A HEARTBREAKING	JOB	. /ADRIAN/ I DONT UNDERSTAND. WHAT DOES KITING MEAN?
GETT (350)	EXCEPT THE PEW OPENER AND THE CURATE WHO DID THE	JOB	. /EDITH/ THEY HAD ALL GONE HOME. /MRS BRIDGENORTH/ BUT
GENV I (32)	CHANCY. YOU DONT KNOW WHAT IT IS TO BE OUT OF A	JOB	. /HE/ I SHALL NOT ASK YOU TO GIVE UP YOUR POST HERE. ON
PYGM V (284)	ME? /HIGGINS/ (HEARTILY) WHY, BECAUSE IT WAS MY	JOB	. /LIZA/ YOU NEVER THOUGHT OF THE TROUBLE IT WOULD MAKE
PYGM III (245)	/HIGGINS/ I MUST. IVE A JOB FOR YOU. A PHONETIC	JOB	. /MRS HIGGINS/ NO USE, DEAR. I'M SORRY; BUT I CANT GET
PYGM III (245)	SEND ME. /HIGGINS/ WELL, THIS ISNT A PHONETIC	JOB	. /MRS HIGGINS/ YOU SAID IT WAS. /HIGGINS/ NOT YOUR PART
APPL INTRLUD(250)	RATHER MARRY THE DEVIL. BEING A WIFE IS NOT YOUR	JOB	. /ORINTHIA/ YOU THINK SO BECAUSE YOU HAVE NO
PYGM II (243)	/HIGGINS/ PICKERING: WE HAVE TAKEN ON A STIFF	JOB	. /PICKERING/ (WITH CONVICTION) HIGGINS: WE HAVE.
ARMS I (16)	BUSINESS SOMEHOW, AND KNEW IT WAS A SAFE	JOB	. /RAINA/ THAT IS TO SAY, HE WAS A PRETENDER AND A
HART II (111)	IN THE END I HAVE HAD TO WALK OUT AND LEAVE THE	JOB	. /RANDALL/ WHEN THAT HAPPENS, DO YOU PUT BACK THE
MTH2 (88)	ARE LAUGHING. LAUGHING MAY EVEN LUBRICATE ITS	JOB	. /SAVVY/ WHAT DOES THAT MEAN? /CONRAD/ IT MEANS THAT
APPL I (200)	FOR HIM AT 12 O'CLOCK, A SECRETARY LOSES HIS	JOB	. /SEMPRONIUS/ (HASTILY RESUMING HIS WORK) YES, DEVIL
BARB II (310)	PETER: I'M LIKE YOU NOW. CLEANED OUT, AND LOST MY	JOB	. /SHIRLEY/ YOUVE YOUTH AN HOPE. THATS TWO BETTER THAN
ROCK II (267)	IT. /THE DUKE/ OF COURSE NOT. NOT A GENTLEMAN'S	JOB	. /SIR ARTHUR/ IT MIGHT BE A DUKE'S JOB, THOUGH. WHY NOT
MTH5 SD(217)	HER WITH AN AIR OF HAVING FINISHED HER	JOB	. /THE SHE-ANCIENT/ SHE WILL DO. SHE MAY LIVE. THEY ALL
GETT (281)	THEM! WHY, MAN, THE WHOLE DIVORCE WAS A PUT-UP	JOB	. SHE WANTS TO MARRY SOME FELLOW NAMED HOTCHKISS.
APPL II (263)	WAS MY DEAR OLD FATHER'S FIRST BIG PROFESSIONAL	JOB	. THE BUILDING WHICH STANDS ON ITS FORMER SITE IS A VERY
CAPT II (263)	LOOKOUT. LOOK HERE, CAPN: WE DONT HALF LIKE THIS	JOB	. THE GENTLEMAN HAS BEEN TALKING TO US A BIT; AND WE
APPL I (234)	ANYONE ELSE WHO COULD BE PERSUADED TO TAKE ON THE	JOB	. THEN BEGAN THAT ABANDONMENT OF POLITICS BY THE OLD
FANY PROLOG (262)	YEARS SOMETIMES; BUT THATS NO RULE FOR A SINGLE	JOB	. THEN THERES SUCH A LOT OF THEM: ON FIRST NIGHTS THEY
VWOO 2 (126)	TO LIVE IN THE SAME PLACE AND STICK AT THE SAME	JOB	. THEN YOU NEVER HAVE TO THINK ABOUT IT. THATS THE WAY
ROCK PREFACE(147)	WHAT WE INSTINCTIVELY RECOIL FROM AS FROM A DIRTY	JOB	. THESE CHILDISH EVASIONS ARE REVOLTING. WE MUST STRIP
CYMB V (140)	MUST HAVE BEEN RECALLED. THAT FELLOW KNEW HIS	JOB	. THESE FAT CIVILIANS WHEN WE'RE AT PEACE, ROB US OF OUR
BARB II (279)	YEARS-- SURE A STEADY MAN WONT BE LONG OUT OF A	JOB	. WELL, LET EM TRY YOU. THEYLL FIND THE DIFFER. WHAT DO
FABL PREFACE(65)	FUNCTIONARIES ARE BORN SPECIALIZED FOR THEIR	JOB	. WHEN NO SPECIALIZATION BEYOND THAT OF COMMON MENTAL
JOAN 5 (111)	I AM NOT GOING TO WEAR ARMOR: FIGHTING IS NOT MY	JOB	. WHERE IS THE MAID? /JOAN/ (COMING FORWARD BETWEEN
POSN (459)	STRAPPER; BUT YOURE NOT SHERIFF YET. THIS IS MY	JOB	. YOU JUST WAIT. I SUBMIT THAT WE'RE IN A DIFFICULTY
FABL VI (131)	COUNTER COPIES OF AN OLD POEM CALLED THE BOOK OF	JOB	. YOU WILL READ IT THROUGH; AND-- /YOUTH 2/ I READ IT
DEVL EPILOG (82)	AN INSTITUTION OR TO " DO A MAN OUT OF HIS	JOB	." AT BOTTOM, OF COURSE, THIS APPARENTLY SHAMELESS
ROCK I SD(210)	ANYTHING FROM A WORKING MAN WITH A VERY SEDENTARY	JOB	(SAY A WATCHMAN) TO A CITY MISSIONARY OF HUMBLE
GENV I (31)	WELL, WHAT ABOUT THE PAY? AND HOW LONG WILL THE	JOB	LAST? THE WORK HERE MAY BE DULL; AND THE PAY IS JUST
2TRU II (72)	ITS DAM AND BRING UP ITS FAMILY. I WANT MY LITTLE	JOB	LIKE THE BEAVER. IF I DO NOTHING BUT CONTEMPLATE THE
DOCT PREFACE(71)	WITH THE PRIVATE CITIZEN. THE MAN PAID BY THE	JOB	LOSES MONEY BY NOT FORCING HIS JOB ON THE PUBLIC AS
LION PREFACE(56)	AND TO WHOM THEY SHOULD BELONG BY MAKER'S RIGHT,	JOB	MUST SCRATCH HIS PUZZLED HEAD WITH A POTSHERD AND BE
ROCK II (267)	IT THAT IVE LOST ALL MY SELF-RESPECT. THIS	JOB	NEEDS A MAN WITH NOTHING TO LOSE, PLENTY OF HARD DRIVING
UNPL PREFACE(R15)	TO INDIVIDUALS, MAKES NICE LITTLE PLACES TO	JOB	NICE LITTLE PEOPLE INTO INSTEAD OF DOING AWAY WITH THEM.
SUPR PREFACE(R38)	DARWIN HAS NO MORE DESTROYED THE STYLE OF	JOB	NOR OF HANDEL THAN MARTIN LUTHER DESTROYED THE STYLE OF
FABL III (109)	I'M A GENIUS. /THE MATRON/ INDEED! HAVE YOU A	JOB	OF ANY SORT? /THE TOURIST/ NO. THEY OFFERED ME A JOB AS
MIS. PREFACE(12)	GETTING TIRED OF THE THANKLESS AND MISCHIEVOUS	JOB	OF BRINGING UP THEIR CHILDREN IN THE WAY THEY THINK THEY
MILL PREFACE(115)	HIS DESCENDANTS STILL HOLD IT), MADE A FAR BETTER	JOB	OF HIS AFFAIRS. WHEN FOR THE FIRST TIME NAPOLEON CAME UP
HART PREFACE(6)	OF POLITICS, AND WOULD HAVE MADE A VERY POOR	JOB	OF IT IF THEY HAD CHANGED THEIR MINDS. NOT THAT THEY
6CAL PREFACE(91)	ROBBER WAS AT LEAST A BARON. HE MADE A VERY POOR	JOB	OF IT IN MY OPINION. ON THE HIGH SEAS, 28TH MAY 1935.
MILL IV (189)	IT. /ALASTAIR/ WELL, YOU HAVE MADE A FIRST RATE	JOB	OF IT NOW. /THE MANAGER/ OH, IT WAS NOT MY DOING, SIR: I
GENV III (82)	WHICH HEAVEN FORBID, IT WILL MAKE A FIRST-RATE	JOB	OF IT. DOWNING STREET WILL NOT TAKE ITS ORDERS FROM
ROCK PREFACE(189)	UNTIL A BETTER MAN THAN I MAKES A BETTER	JOB	OF IT. PUT SHORTLY AND UNDRAMATICALLY THE CASE IS THAT A
ROCK II (270)	MANY KICKS AS MAY BE NEEDFUL TO MAKE A THOROUGH	JOB	OF IT. /BASHAM/ A DICTATOR: EH? THATS WHAT YOU WANT.
JOAN 5 (117)	THOSE WHO KNOW LEAST ABOUT IT OFTEN MAKE THE BEST	JOB	OF IT. /DUNOIS/ I KNOW ALL THAT. I DO NOT FIGHT IN THE
SIM II (84)	FACT THAT WE TWO HAVE MADE A PRECIOUS MESS OF OUR	JOB	OF PRODUCING THE COMING RACE BY A MIXTURE OF EAST AND
APPL I (238)	MOB; AND THAT BREAKAGES, LIMITED, WOULD GET THE	JOB	OF PUTTING IN NEW GLASS. AND IT IS TRUE. IT IS INFAMOUS;
2TRU III (109)	NAPOLEON ALEXANDER TROTSKY MEEK TO HIS	JOB	OF REPATRIATING THE EXPEDITION (MEEK TAKES TO FLIGHT UP
MILL PREFACE(116)	IT WAS EASY FOR NAPOLEON TO MAKE A BETTER	JOB	OF RESTORING ORDER AFTER THE FRENCH REVOLUTION THAN
ROCK II (259)	TO TAKE ON MY JOB. ARE YOU? /SIR DEXTER/ THE	JOB	OF RUINING THE COUNTRY AND DESTROYING THE EMPIRE? MY
ROCK I (217)	YOU AND YOUR LIKE HAVE TAKEN ON YOURSELVES THE	JOB	OF SETTING IT RIGHT. I HAVNT: I'M ONLY A POOR MAN: A
BULL PREFACE(57)	HAS TO BE PURCHASED; AND THE PRICE IS AN OFFICIAL	JOB	OF SOME SORT WITH A POSITION AND A SALARY ATTACHED.
SUPR HANDBOK(185)	HINDOO CASTE OR SUTTEE, MIGHT MAKE A MUCH BETTER	JOB	OF THEIR LIVES THAN ORDINARY FOLK UNDER THE HARROW OF
POSN (440)	A CHANCE TO KEEP YOU OUT OF HELL, I'D TAKE THE	JOB	OF TWISTING YOUR NECK OFF THE HANDS OF THE VIGILANCE
CYMB FORWORD(137)	I HAVE NOT CONFINED MYSELF TO THE JOURNEYMAN'S	JOB	OF WRITING " ADDITIONAL ACCOMPANIMENTS": I HAVE
APPL I (204)	TO THEM FOR TAKING A VERY DIFFICULT AND THANKLESS	JOB	OFF MY HANDS. /BAONERGES/ BUT IT'S NOT ON YOUR HANDS.
POSN (452)	KNOW. THERES PLENTY OF WILLING HANDS TO TAKE THAT	JOB	OFF YOUR CONSCIENCE. SO RIP AHEAD, OLD SON. /STRAPPER/
MTH3 (92)	WOULD GIVE ME GREATER PLEASURE THAN TO TAKE THE	JOB	OFF YOUR HANDS-- /BARNABAS/ THEN DO IT. THATS ALL I WANT
FANY PROLOG (265)	FOR HIM TO EARN TEN GUINEAS: HE'S DONE THE SAME	JOB	OFTEN ENOUGH FOR HALF A QUID, I EXPECT. FANNY O'DOWDA
ROCK I (217)	DID THE MATERIAL THAT HE DOES HIS LITTLE BIT OF A	JOB	ON COME FROM? HE DONT KNOW. WHAT WILL HAPPEN TO IT WHEN
PYGM EPILOG (299)	SELL PRETTY THINGS TO HIM, SHE OFFERED CLARA A	JOB	ON THE CHANCE OF ACHIEVING THAT END THROUGH HER. AND SO
DOCT PREFACE(71)	PAID BY THE JOB LOSES MONEY BY NOT FORCING HIS	JOB	ON THE PUBLIC AS OFTEN AS POSSIBLE WITHOUT REFERENCE TO
FANY II (290)	SUFFRAGET SAID TO ME IN HOLLOWAY. HE THROWS THE	JOB	ON YOU. /MRS KNOX/ (REPROACHFULLY) MARGARET!
MILL PREFACE(121)	OF HIS OWN CHOICE, WHO HAD TO DO THEIR	JOB	OR GET OUT. THE EDITORS HAD FINALLY TO ACCORD HIM A SORT
BUOY PREFACE(4)	AS BROWNING'S MR SLUDGE OR DUNGLAS HOME, OR AS	JOB	OR JOHN OF PATMOS. WHEN I WRITE A PLAY I DO NOT FORESEE
MIS. (131)	YOU HAVE A GENIUS FOR GOVERNMENT. YOU LEARNT YOUR	JOB	OUT THERE IN JINGHISKAHN. WELL, WE WANT TO BE GOVERNED
MTH5 (245)	BEST AS FAR AS HANDWORK IS CONCERNED. BUT THIS	JOB	REQUIRED BRAINS. THAT IS WHERE I SHOULD HAVE COME IN.
MTH2 (41)	/CONRAD/ (GRUFFLY, GIVING HIM UP AS A BAD	JOB	) GOODBYE. /HASLAM/ GOODBYE. SORRY-- ER-- AS THE RECTOR
NEVR II (226)	(YAWNING AND GIVING UP THE PAPER AS A BAD	JOB	) WAITER! /WAITER/ SIR? (COMING TO HIM). /THE
PYGM PREFACE(199)	(HE WAS, I THINK, THE BEST OF THEM ALL AT HIS	JOB	) WOULD HAVE ENTITLED HIM TO HIGH OFFICIAL RECOGNITION,
FABL IV SD(116)	SIGHS WITH RELIEF AT HAVING DONE A TEDIOUS	JOB	; AND GOES INTO THE BUILDING.
DOCT V (179)	TURNS TO SAY SOMETHING MORE; GIVES IT UP AS A BAD	JOB	; AND GOES).
ROCK I (196)	DEALING WITH THE UNEMPLOYED IS NOT A SOLDIER'S	JOB	; AND I WAS A SOLDIER. IF YOU WANT THESE CROWDS SETTLED
POSN (454)	/THE SHERIFF/ SILENCE. THIS TRIAL IS A MAN'S	JOB	; AND IF THE WOMEN FORGET THEIR SEX THEY CAN GO OUT OR
MIS. (133)	A FACT THAT WE'RE INFERIOR TO THEM: IT'S A PUT-UP	JOB	; AND IT'S THEY THAT HAVE PUT THE JOB UP. IT'S WE THAT
GETT PREFACE(238)	THAT OF A WIFE AND MOTHER; THAT SHE IS OUT OF A	JOB	; AND THAT SHE WANTS AN EMPLOYER? IF THE EXCHANGES
VWOO 1 (122)	/A/ DONT BE AFRAID OF DIRT. MINE IS A CLEAN	JOB	; BUT I OFTEN WISH I HAD A DIRTY ONE TO EXERCISE ME AND
MIS. (144)	SUMMERHAYS/ I HOPE NOT. /HYPATIA/ IT'S A DIRTY	JOB	; BUT JOHNNY AND I WERE VULGAR ENOUGH TO LIKE IT. I LIKE
FABL PREFACE(71)	IT IS NONE THE WORSE WHEN IT DOES A NECESSARY	JOB	; FOR I MYSELF HAVE BEEN A FAKER OF MIRACLES. LET ME
APPL PREFACE(172)	CANNOT BE IMPOSED ON A KING WHO WORKS AT HIS	JOB	; FOR THE KING WORKS CONTINUOUSLY WHILST HIS MINISTERS
FABL VI (131)	OLD GODS, WHO PRETENDED HE HAD MADE THE UNIVERSE.	JOB	SAID IF SO HE HAD MADE IT VERY UNFAIRLY. BUT WHAT USE IS
FABL PREFACE(70)	FOR IT BUT TO ALTER THE WORD OF GOD, MAKING	JOB	SAY THAT THOUGH WORMS WOULD DESTROY HIS BODY YET IN HIS
GETT (355)	ANY OF THE OTHER JOHNNIES WHO HAVE BEEN ON THIS	JOB	SINCE THE WORLD EXISTED? /MRS GEORGE/ (ADMIRING HIS
CLEO NOTES (206)	MUST BE MUCH LESS CHANGED FROM THE SERVANTS OF	JOB	THAN THE PROLETARIAT OF MODERN LONDON FROM THE
FABL III (110)	HERE FOR YOU TO PAINT; BUT WE CAN OFFER YOU A	JOB	THAT WILL ENABLE YOU TO SUPPORT YOURSELF AND HAVE ENOUGH

GENV I	(31)	A LONDON COUNTY COUNCIL SCHOLARSHIP. I WANTED A	JOB	THAT WOULD DRAW OUT MY FACULTIES, IF YOU UNDERSTAND ME.
POSN	(437)	DOING? WELL, IT IS TIRESOME. LET THEM FINISH THE	JOB	THEMSELVES. OH DEAR, OH DEAR! WE CANT HAVE A MINUTE TO
O'FL	(224)	LANGUAGE NOR THEM OF MINE? /O'FLAHERTY/ A GOOD	JOB	THEY DONT: MAY BE THEYLL THINK YOURE TALKING SENSE. /MRS
ROCK II	(255)	THE BRIDGE FOR THEM. IF I ASKED MY MEN TO DO MY	JOB	THEYD CHUCK ME OVERBOARD; AND SERVE ME JOLLY WELL
GENV I	(31)	THROUGH IT. JUST LOOK HERE AT THIS NICE LITTLE	JOB	THEYVE GIVEN ME! A CARD INDEX OF ALL THE UNIVERSITIES
PYGM IV	(261)	BE ALL RIGHT. NO: IT'S THE STRAIN OF PUTTING THE	JOB	THROUGH ALL THESE MONTHS THAT HAS TOLD ON ME. IT WAS
AUGS	(273)	REMAINS ENGLAND, WHEREVER THERE IS A PUBLIC	JOB	TO BE DONE YOU WILL FIND A HIGHCASTLE STICKING TO IT.
WIDO III	(63)	HAS HER FATHER'S EYE FOR BUSINESS. EXPLAIN THIS	JOB	TO HER; AND SHE'LL MAKE IT UP WITH DR TRENCH. WHY NOT
MILL PREFACE	(119)	ITS RECIPIENTS TO PREFER EVEN THE POORLIEST PAID	JOB	TO ITS HUMILIATIONS. THE ONLY WAY OF ESCAPE WAS FOR THE
MTH3	(125)	OF THE LABOR OF THE NATION TO THEM, AND A GOOD	JOB	TOO: WHY SHOULD WE DRUDGE AT IT? BUT THINK OF THE
FABL II	(107)	YEARS IN THE FOREIGN OFFICE. YOU KNOW YOUR	JOB	TOO AS A SOLDIER: I DONT QUESTION IT. THAT GIVES US ONE
6CAL PREFACE	(89)	HAVING BEEN MISERABLY KILLED FOR TAKING HIS	JOB	TOO LIGHTLY. BUT THE JOURNALIST CRITICS KNEW NOTHING OF
PRES	(148)	/MRS FARRELL/ (GRUMBLING TO HERSELF) A GOOD	JOB	TOO. IF I COULD HAVE MADE FARRELL BLUSH I WOULDNT HAVE
POSN	(447)	IT'S NO GOOD: WE HANG MADMEN HERE; AND A GOOD	JOB	TOO! /BLANCO/ I FEEL SAFE WITH YOU, STRAPPER. YOURE ONE
MIS.	(133)	A PUT-UP JOB; AND IT'S THEY THAT HAVE PUT THE	JOB	UP. IT'S WE THAT RUN THE COUNTRY FOR THEM; AND ALL THE
POSN	(464)	HE HAD A JOB FOR ME. HE LET ME RUN LOOSE TIL THE	JOB	WAS READY; AND THEN I HAD TO COME ALONG AND DO IT.
SUPR HANDBOK	(191)	EXHIBITIONS OF COMMON ONES. HE MANAGES A SMALL	JOB	WELL; HE MUDDLES RHETORICALLY THROUGH A LARGE ONE. WHEN
DEST	(186)	BE ANY SORT OF RIFF-RAFF IF HE UNDERSTANDS HIS	JOB	WELL ENOUGH. A LIEUTENANT IS A GENTLEMAN: ALL THE REST
AUGS	(278)	SAY? /THE CLERK/ HE SAID THAT NOW YOU WAS ON THE	JOB	WE'D WANT ANOTHER MILLION MEN, AND HE WAS GOING TO TAKE
GENV PREFACE	(22)	OF AUTHORITY IS NOT A HEAVY AND RESPONSIBLE	JOB	WHICH STRAINS THEIR MENTAL CAPACITY AND INDUSTRY TO THE
LION PREFACE	(55)	ONE HAND AND A STEEL PEN IN THE OTHER, AND ASKS	JOB	WHO MADE THEM, AND TO WHOM THEY SHOULD BELONG BY MAKER'S
METH PREFACE	(R47)	BUT AN HONEST NATURALIST WORKING AWAY AT HIS	JOB	WITH SO LITTLE PREOCCUPATION WITH THEOLOGICAL
APPL I	(233)	WORK THAT NEVER ENDS BECAUSE WE CANNOT FINISH ONE	JOB	WITHOUT CREATING TEN FRESH ONES. WE GET NO THANKS FOR IT
BARB II	(277)	WHY SHOULD YOU BE? BESIDES, WHEN WE FIND YOU A	JOB	YOU CAN PAY US FOR IT IF YOU LIKE. /SHIRLEY/ (EAGERLY)
BULL III	(129)	WHY COULDNT YOU SAY SO AT ONCE? IT'S A GOOD	JOB	YOUVE MADE UP YOUR MIND AT LAST. /DORAN/ (SUSPICIOUSLY)
ROCK I	(219)	THEM ON? ALL THEY WANTED WAS TO BE GIVEN THEIR	JOB	, AND FED AND MADE COMFORTABLE ACCORDING TO THEIR NOTION
MILL PREFACE	(111)	A NATION, THE MAGNITUDE AND DIFFICULTY OF HIS	JOB	, AND THE KNOWLEDGE THAT IF HE MAKES A MESS OF IT HE
MIS.	(133)	BE JOLLY GLAD TO FORGET. AS HE HAS A MUCH SOFTER	JOB	, AND WANTS TO KEEP HIMSELF BEFORE THE PUBLIC, HIS CRY
MIS. PREFACE	(96)	MUCH NICER CHILD AND YOU WILL HAVE A MUCH EASIER	JOB	, AT WHICH POINT YOU WILL, IN SPITE OF YOUR
MTH2	(61)	THING AT THE MOMENT. IT WAS RATHER A TROUBLESOME	JOB	, BECAUSE I HAD NOT GONE INTO POLITICAL ECONOMY AT THE
MIS.	(171)	AYE, ENVIED FOR THE VARIETY AND LIVELINESS OF MY	JOB	, BY THE POOR DEVIL OF A BOOKKEEPER THAT HAS TO COPY ALL
ROCK II	(283)	AGAINST IT ALL? BECAUSE I'M NOT THE MAN FOR THE	JOB	, DARLING; AND NOBODY KNOWS THAT BETTER THAN YOU. AND I
FABL II	(106)	WITH HIM AND INVOLVED US IN IT. THAT MADE IT YOUR	JOB	, DIDNT IT? /C.-IN-C./ NOT A BIT OF IT. KETCH IS FAR
HART II	(122)	THERE IS PLENTY OF COMPETITION FOR THE	JOB	, EH? /RANDALL/ (ANGRILY) SHE ENCOURAGES THEM. HER
FABL PREFACE	(70)	PRESENTLY STAGGERED BY A PASSAGE IN THE BOOK OF	JOB	, IN WHICH THAT PROPHET DECLARED THAT AS WORMS WOULD
ROCK II	(282)	AND RATHER THAN GO BACK TO THE OLD WHITEWASHING	JOB	, I'D SEIZE YOU TIGHT ROUND THE WAIST AND MAKE A HOLE IN
MILL I	(159)	EVEN. /ALASTAIR/ IF YOU THINK THAT WAS AN EASY	JOB	, JUST TRY IT YOURSELF: THATS ALL. I DREAM OF IT
BUOY III	(30)	/THE YOUTH/ HE PICKS UP HIS SOLICITOR FOR THE	JOB	, LIKE PICKING UP A TAXI. /THE WIDOWER/ THERE IS
GENV I	(31)	IT IS DULL. /HE/ SHALL I GIVE YOU AN INTERESTING	JOB	, MADEMOISELLE? ONE THAT WOULD GET YOU APPRECIATED AND
APPL I	(214)	/PROTEUS/ RIGHT YOU ARE. PERFECTLY TRUE. TAKE MY	JOB	, NICK. IT'S VACANT FOR YOU, BILL. I WISH YOU JOY OF IT.
ROCK II	(239)	BEMROSE/ I LEAVE THE SPEAKING TO ARTHUR: IT'S HIS	JOB	, NOT MINE. BUT IF THERE IS ANY FURTHER ATTEMPT TO
2TRU III	(86)	WITH OUR RELIGIOUS DUTIES. IT'S THE CHAPLAIN'S	JOB	, NOT MINE; BUT WHEN YOU GET A REAL RELIGIOUS CHAPLAIN
FABL II	(106)	STILL TECHNICALLY AT PEACE. THAT MAKES IT YOUR	JOB	, NOT MINE, THOUGH AS USUAL WHEN THERE IS ANYTHING TO BE
APPL I	(201)	SUPPOSITION ON THAT SUBJECT, YOU WILL LOSE YOUR	JOB	, OLD CHAP. SO STOW IT. /PAMPHILIUS/ DONT CRY OUT BEFORE
BARB II	(310)	TWO BETTER THAN ME. /BARBARA/ I'LL GET YOU A	JOB	, PETER. THATS HOPE FOR YOU: THE YOUTH WILL HAVE TO BE
BARB II	(275)	ARE. /PRICE/ THIEVIN SWINE! WISH I AD THEIR	JOB	, RUMMY, ALL THE SAME. WOT DOES RUMMY STAND FOR? PET
JOAN PREFACE	(37)	JOAN MAINTAINED HER OWN WAYS SHE CLAIMED, LIKE	JOB	, THAT THERE WAS NOT ONLY GOD AND THE CHURCH TO BE
JITT PREFACE	(4)	TRANSLATORS. WHEN TREBITSCH VOLUNTEERED FOR THE	JOB	, THE HUNDRED WOULD HAVE FLED FROM MY INVITATION AS ONE
ROCK II	(267)	JOB. /SIR ARTHUR/ IT MIGHT BE A DUKE'S	JOB	, THOUGH. WHY NOT HAVE A TRY AT IT? /THE DUKE/ FOR
SIM PREFACE	(10)	CATHOLIC CHURCH, WHICH HAD PERHAPS THE TOUGHEST	JOB	, WAS COMPELLED TO DEVELOP A NEW JUDICIAL ORGAN, CALLED
LIED	(201)	YOU HAVE SOME BLOOD IN YOUR BODY AFTER ALL! GOOD	JOB	! /HE/ THIS IS RIDICULOUS. I ASSURE YOU MRS BOMPAS IS

JOBBER

APPL I	(223)	AND CROSS THE TS. YOU WILL SAY THAT CRASSUS IS A	JOBBER	. /CRASSUS/ (SPRINGING UP) I -- /PROTEUS/ (FIERCELY
APPL I	(226)	MATTER WHAT FOOL THROWS THEM. CALL A MINISTER A	JOBBER	-- /BALBUS/ OR A BUNGLER. /CRASSUS/ YES, OR A
APPL I	(224)	KICK A MAN WHEN HE'S DOWN. /CRASSUS/ I MAY BE A	JOBBER	; BUT NOBODY SHALL SAY THAT I AM AN UNGENEROUS
APPL I	(223)	SIT DOWN. LEAVE THIS TO ME. /CRASSUS/ (SITS) I A	JOBBER	! WELL! /PROTEUS/ (CONTINUING) YOU WILL SAY THAT I

JOBBERIES

SIM II	(63)	THE WORLD IS TIRED OF REPUBLICS AND THEIR	JOBBERIES	, PROCLAIM A KINGDOM. /MAYA/ OR A QUEENDOM. /IDDY/

JOBBERS

CAND I	(91)	BUT IF THEY DO, I'LL INTRODUCE YOU TO THE BIGGEST	JOBBERS	I CAN GET TO COME TO MY DINNER PARTIES. /BURGESS/ (

JOBBERY

APPL I	(226)	YES, OR A BUNGLER, AND EVERYBODY BELIEVES IT.	JOBBERY	AND INCOMPETENCE ARE THE TWO SORTS OF MUD THAT STICK
DEVL III	(69)	IN LONDON! WHAT ENEMIES? /BURGOYNE/ (FORCIBLY)	JOBBERY	AND SNOBBERY, INCOMPETENCE AND RED TAPE. (HE HOLDS
BULL PREFACE	(40)	ASCENDENCY. IF YOU DENOUNCE THE NEPOTISM AND	JOBBERY	OF THE NEW LOCAL AUTHORITIES, YOU ARE DEMONSTRATING
UNPL PREFACE	(R12)	REALISTIC EXPOSURE OF SLUM LANDLORDISM, MUNICIPAL	JOBBERY	, AND THE PECUNIARY AND MATRIMONIAL TIES BETWEEN

JOBBING

SUPR PREFACE	(R25)	AND OCCASIONAL INTERFERENCE, MOSTLY BY WAY OF	JOBBING	PUBLIC APPOINTMENTS, IN THE MISMANAGEMENT OF A TIGHT

JOB'S

MTH5	(245)	OUF! (HE SITS DOWN NEXT THE NEWLY BORN) THAT	JOB'S	FINISHED. /ARJILLAX/ ANCIENTS: I SHOULD LIKE TO MAKE A
CLEO NOTES	(206)	ALIVE. THIS DOES NOT SEEM AS IF THE CHANGE SINCE	JOB'S	TIME WERE PROGRESS IN THE POPULAR SENSE: QUITE THE

JOBS

2TRU PREFACE	(23)	THEIR ACTIVITIES OF MANY OF THE MOST NECESSARY	JOBS	AS BENEATH THEIR DIGNITY. ANOTHER STIPULATION MADE BY
OVER PREFACE	(162)	AND THAT SUCH FACTITIOUS CONSEQUENCES AND PUT-UP	JOBS	AS DIVORCES AND EXECUTIONS AND THE DETECTIVE OPERATIONS
SIM II	(63)	NOT. /SIR CHARLES/ BUT WHAT BECOMES OF OUR	JOBS	AS GOVERNOR AND POLITICAL SECRETARY, HYERING? WILL
SIM II	(63)	ISLES AN INDEPENDENT REPUBLIC AND SECURE THE NEW	JOBS	FOR OURSELVES. /VASHTI/ THE WORLD IS TIRED OF REPUBLICS
ROCK I	(194)	PRIME MINISTER I'M DIVINE PROVIDENCE AND CAN FIND	JOBS	FOR THEM BEFORE TRADE REVIVES. (HE SITS DOWN AND
ROCK II	(247)	AND YOUR LABOR. /BLEE/ WE KNOW. KEEP ALL THE SOFT	JOBS	FOR YOUR LOT AND THE HARD ONES FOR US. DO YOU TAKE US
APPL I	(217)	THEM TO GO TO SEA. I COULD HAVE FOUND THEM BETTER	JOBS	IN THE POST OFFICE. /MAGNUS/ APART FROM AMANDA'S FAMILY
FANY III	(309)	UP YOUR FINGER TO GET THE PICK OF HALF A DOZEN	JOBS	. BUT YOU WONT BE TREATED EVERYWHERE AS YOURE TREATED
APPL I	(228)	IN OUR PARTY PROGRAM ARE MADE TO LOOK LIKE CITY	JOBS	. /MAGNUS/ AM I SUPPOSED TO WRITE THESE ARTICLES?
BUOY 1	(14)	THERE ARE ENOUGH SELFSEEKERS FOR ALL THE PAYING	JOBS	. STILL, SOME OF THE WORLD BETTERERS MANAGE TO SURVIVE.
DOCT PREFACE	(66)	THE TIME OF HIGHLY QUALIFIED EXPERTS ON TRIVIAL	JOBS	. THE INDIVIDUALISM OF PRIVATE PRACTICE LEADS TO AN
BUOY 1	(14)	THEY MARRY RICH WOMEN. THEY TAKE COMMERCIAL	JOBS	. THEY SPUNGE ON DISCIPLES FROM WHOM THEY BEG OR
ROCK I	(217)	AND HIS LIKE HAVE ALL DONE THEIR LITTLE BITS OF	JOBS	ON IT? HE DONT KNOW, WHERE COULD HE BUY IT IF IT
BUOY IV	(55)	GAME IS UP. THE NEW LABOR GOVERNMENT GIVES SUCH	JOBS	TO SUPERANNUATED TRADE UNION SECRETARIES. /SIR

JOCK

LION II	(130)	MARTYRED ALL RIGHT ENOUGH. GOOD OLD LION! OLD	JOCK	DOESNT LIKE THAT: LOOK AT HIS FACE. DEVIL A BETTER!
MIS.	(144)	OH! MY DESTINY. GAD, I FORGOT ALL ABOUT IT:	JOCK	STARTED A RABBIT AND PUT IT CLEAN OUT OF MY HEAD.

JOCKEYS

ROCK II	(263)	AND GARDENERS, VALETS AND GAMEKEEPERS AND	JOCKEYS	, BUTLERS AND HOUSEKEEPERS AND LADIES' MAIDS AND

JOCOSE

WIDO II	(33)	THROWS OFF HIS EMBARRASSMENT, AND ASSUMES A	JOCOSE	, RALLYING AIR, UNBECOMING TO HIM UNDER ANY

JOCOSELY

CAND I	(98)	THEY CANT HELP IT. I LIKE IT. BUT (LOOKING UP	JOCOSELY	AT HIM) I SAY, EUGENE: DO YOU THINK YOURS IS A CASE

WIDO III	SD(66)	EXEUNT OMNES: BLANCHE ON COKANE'S ARM; LICKCHEESE	JOCOSELY	TAKING SARTORIUS ON ONE ARM, AND TRENCH ON THE

JOCULAR

BULL II	SD(97)	ADDRESSING THE INSECT IN A BROGUE WHICH IS THE	JOCULAR	ASSUMPTION OF A GENTLEMAN AND NOT THE NATURAL SPEECH
CAPT II	(243)	VISITORS. DRINKWATER TURNS AND RECEIVES THEM WITH	JOCULAR	CEREMONY). WEOLCOME TO BRARSBAHND CAWSTL, SR AHRD AN
GETT	(293)	NO SENSE OF HUMOR, AND IVE NEVER SEEN A MAN IN A	JOCULAR	MOOD ON HIS WEDDING MORNING. COLLINS APPEARS IN THE
LION PREFACE	(22)	REJOICE IN HIM INSTEAD OF BEING MELANCHOLY. HE IS	JOCULAR	, AND TELLS THEM THEY WILL ALL HAVE AS MUCH FASTING
CYMB FORWORD	(134)	THE APPLAUSE, LIKE THE PROPOSAL, WAS NOT WHOLLY	JOCULAR	, THE FANCY BEGAN TO HAUNT ME, AND PERSISTED UNTIL I

JOCULARLY

DOCT I	SD(87)	RIDGEON'S HAND AND BEAMS AT HIM CORDIALLY AND	JOCULARLY	, /SIR PATRICK/ WELL, YOUNG CHAP, IS YOUR HAT TOO
NEVR II	(227)	(HE SHUTS THE UMBRELLA; PUTS IT ASIDE; AND	JOCULARLY	PLANTS HIMSELF WITH HIS HANDS ON HIS HIPS TO BE
MRS III	(232)	WHAT HARM DOES IT DO AFTER ALL? (RALLYING HER	JOCULARLY	) SO YOU DONT THINK ME SUCH A SCOUNDREL NOW YOU
MTH3	(94)	OF A CHINESE SAGE, ENTERS. /BURGE-LUBIN/ (	JOCULARLY	) WELL, ILLUSTRIOUS SAGE-AND-ONIONS, HOW ARE YOUR

JOE

MILL III	(180)	WHOLE BLOODY BASEMENT. /THE WOMAN/ HUSH, HUSH,	JOE	: DONT SPEAK TO THE LADY LIKE THAT. YOU SEE, MAAM:
APPL I	(226)	COULD MENTION. /AMANDA/ THANKS, DEAREST BILL. NOW	JOE	: DONT YOU THINK YOU HAVE LET US RUN LOOSE LONG ENOUGH?
APPL I	(241)	LIKE OLD QUEEN ELIZABETH, EH? DONT GRIEVE,	JOE	: I'LL LUNCH WITH YOU SINCE YOURE SO PRESSING. /CRASSUS/
MILL III	(186)	AND BE REFUSED A WEEK'S CREDIT IN THE SHOPS?	JOE	: IVE GONE ON IN OUR NATURAL WAYS ALL THESE YEARS
APPL II	(270)	NOTHING WE DO MATTERS A RAP. WHAT DO YOU SAY,	JOE	? /PROTEUS/ AFTER ALL, WHY NOT? IF YOUR MAJESTY IS IN
APPL I	(216)	UNDOUBTEDLY YOU HAVE. /LYSISTRATA/ YOU HEAR THAT,	JOE	? /PROTEUS/ I -- /BALBUS/ OH FOR HEAVEN'S SAKE DONT
APPL I	(230)	WHICH MAN MUST RIDE BEHIND? /AMANDA/ GOT IT,	JOE	? /PROTEUS/ THAT IS EXACTLY THE QUESTION THAT HAS TO BE
APPL I	(232)	WITH THE KING BEHIND OUR BACKS. THAT IS WHAT	JOE	ALWAYS CONTRIVES TO DO, BY HOOK OR CROOK. /PLINY/ YOU
APPL I	(215)	OURSELVES AND RESPECT THE THRONE. ALL THIS	JOE	AND BILL AND NICK AND LIZZIE: WE MIGHT AS WELL BE
APPL I	(232)	/AMANDA/ THERE WASNT ANY NEED TO ARRANGE IT.	JOE	CAN ALWAYS DEPEND ON ONE OR OTHER OF US SAYING SOMETHING
APPL I	(232)	MY ADVICE IS THAT WE JUST SIT HERE QUIETLY UNTIL	JOE	COMES BACK AND TELLS US WHATS BEEN SETTLED. PERHAPS
FANY I	(279)	/MRS GILBEY/ DID A WHAT? /DORA/ A BUNK. HOLY	JOE	DID ONE TOO ALL RIGHT: HE SPRINTED FASTER THAN HE EVER
APPL I	(228)	IS THE JOKE NOW? I AM SURPRISED AT YOU. /AMANDA/	JOE	FRANK! WHEN I WANT TO FIND OUT WHAT HE IS UP TO HAVE TO
FABL PREFACE	(65)	INTERPRETER THE PILGRIM'S PROGRESS, BLACKSMITH	JOE	GARGERY. I WAS LIVING IN AN IMAGINARY WORLD. DEEPLY AS I
FANY I	(277)	ONLY FANCY! YOU SEE IT WAS LIKE THIS. HOLY	JOE	GOT TALKING ABOUT HOW HE'D BEEN A CHAMPION SPRINTER AT
APPL II	(270)	AND FORWARD FROM ONE MIND TO ANOTHER WHENEVER	JOE	HOLDS UP HIS FINGER IS DISGUSTING. THIS IS A CABINET OF
APPL I	(215)	BUSINESS IS NOBODY'S BUSINESS, WHICH IS JUST WHAT	JOE	IS FIT FOR. (SHE TAKES A CHAIR FROM THE WALL WITH A
FANY I	(278)	WELL, WHAT WOULD HE CALL HIM? AFTER ALL, HOLY	JOE	IS HOLY JOE; AND BOYS WILL BE BOYS. /MRS GILBEY/ WHATS A
MTH4 I	(152)	RIGHTS BY INSISTING ON BEING CALLED AT LEAST	JOE	. AT FIFTEEN I REFUSED TO ANSWER TO ANYTHING SHORTER
MILL III	(186)	I CANT GO ON: IT'LL KILL ME. GO UP AND STOP HER,	JOE	. DONT LET HER TALK: JUST PUT HER OUT. BE A MAN,
FANY I	(281)	OUT; AND IF YOU WONT FORK OUT, I'LL HUNT UP HOLY	JOE	. HE MIGHT GET IT OFF HIS BROTHER, THE MONSIGNOR.
APPL I	(232)	WE HAVE DONE OUR BIT, AND MAY LEAVE THE REST TO	JOE	. MATTERS HAD REACHED A POINT AT WHICH IT WAS YES OR NO
APPL I	(214)	COMES IN. YOU HAVE SOMETHING IN YOUR POCKET,	JOE	. OUT WITH IT. READ IT TO THEM. /PROTEUS/ (TAKING A
APPL II	(270)	TO YOU. /CRASSUS/ I NEVER SAID I WAS AGAINST IT,	JOE	. /BALBUS/ NEITHER DID I. /NICOBAR/ I THINK THERES A
APPL I	(240)	HAVE DONE WITH IT? /NICOBAR/ NOW YOURE TALKING,	JOE	. /BALBUS/ THATS THE STUFF TO GIVE HIM. /PLINY/ GULP IT
APPL I	(213)	WITH AN IRON FACE. /PLINY/ NO: DONT DO THAT,	JOE	. /BALBUS/ WHAT! NOW! YOU CANT. YOU MUSTNT. /CRASSUS/
MILL III	(185)	FOR THE LIKES OF US. DONT LET HER TEMPT YOU,	JOE	. /EPIFANIA/ WHEN HAD YOU LAST A HOLIDAY? /THE WOMAN/
APPL I	(224)	(DELIGHTED) HEAR HEAR! YOURE GETTING IT NOW,	JOE	. /MAGNUS/ (CONTINUING) BUT WHEN THE DECISIVE MOMENT
APPL I	(215)	WITH ME. /LYSISTRATA/ YOU MIND YOUR OWN BUSINESS,	JOE	. /MAGNUS/ OH NO: REALLY, REALLY, MY DEAR LYSISTRATA,
APPL I	(217)	NO, YOUR MAJESTY. WE GET ENOUGH OF THAT FROM	JOE	. /PROTEUS/ I PRO -- /MAGNUS/ (HIS HAND PERSUASIVELY ON
MILL III	(179)	(HURRYING TO THE MAN AND HOLDING HIM) TAKE CARE,	JOE	. SHE'S AN INSPECTOR. LOOK AT HER SHOES. /EPIFANIA/ I AM
APPL I	(215)	THE PRIME MINISTER IS THE PRIME MINISTER: HE ISNT	JOE	. THE POWERMISTRESS ISNT LIZZIE: SHE'S LYSIS TRAITOR.
APPL II	(272)	REIGN -- /AMANDA/ YOULL BE THE VICAR OF BRAY,	JOE	. UPROAR. PROTEUS FLINGS HIMSELF INTO HIS CHAIR
MILL III	(186)	/THE WOMAN/ CAUSE YOU DONT UNDERSTAND IT,	JOE	. WE KNOW OUR OWN WAYS; AND THOUGH WE'RE POOR OUR WAYS
APPL I	(216)	OH FOR HEAVEN'S SAKE DONT CONTRADICT HER,	JOE	. WE SHALL NEVER GET ANYWHERE AT THIS RATE. COME TO THE
MILL III	(187)	EPIFANIA'S ALLUSION TO HER) DO WHAT SHE TELLS US,	JOE	. WE'RE LIKE CHILDREN-- (SHE BEGINS CRYING AGAIN
APPL I	(211)	GET ON WITH THE KING? /BOANERGES/ RIGHT AS RAIN,	JOE	. YOU LEAVE THE KING TO ME. I KNOW HOW TO HANDLE HIM. IF
APPL II	(271)	QUARRELS? /PLINY/ (WIPING HIS EYES) YOU MAY,	JOE	. YOU MAY. /PROTEUS/ MY FRIENDS, WE CAME HERE TO A
APPL I	(231)	/CRASSUS/ (THOUGHTFUL) TAKE IT EASY, FRIENDS.	JOE	KNOWS WHAT HE IS ABOUT. /LYSISTRATA/ OF COURSE HE DOES.
FANY I	(277)	HALLS? /DORA/ NO: BOBBY TAKES HIM. BUT HOLY	JOE	LIKES IT: FAIRLY LAPS IT UP LIKE A KITTEN, POOR OLD
APPL I	(223)	BUT UNABLE TO FORBEAR A PROTEST) LOOK HERE,	JOE	-- /PROTEUS/ YOU SHUT UP, BERT. IT'S TRUE. /BALBUS/ (
FANY I	(278)	WOULD HE CALL HIM? AFTER ALL, HOLY JOE IS HOLY	JOE	; AND BOYS WILL BE BOYS. /MRS GILBEY/ WHATS A SQUIFFER?
FANY I	(279)	BOY: IS IT A BARGAIN ABOUT THE SQUIFFER IF I MAKE	JOE	SPRINT FOR YOU? " " ANYTHING YOU LIKE, DARLING," SAYS
FANY I	(278)	KEYS." /MRS GILBEY/ DOES HE CALL HIS TUTOR HOLY	JOE	TO HIS FACE? GILBEY CLUTCHES AT HIS HAIR IN HIS
FANY I	(278)	WELL, HE SAYS, " DARLING, IF YOU CAN GET HOLY	JOE	TO SPRINT A HUNDRED YARDS, I'LL STAND YOU THAT SQUIFFER
APPL I	(238)	THAT IS, TO MAKE SUCH A FAILURE OF IT THAT	JOE	WILL HAVE TO SELL IT TO BREAKAGES, LIMITED, AT SCRAP
FANY I	(276)	HERE; BUT THEN WHAT WAS I TO DO? YOU KNOW HOLY	JOE	, BOBBY'S TUTOR, DONT YOU? BUT OF COURSE YOU DO.
MILL III	(181)	TWO HALF CROWNS ON THE TABLE). /THE WOMAN/ OH,	JOE	, DONT BE SO HASTY. /THE MAN/ YOU SHUT UP. YOU THINK YOU
MILL III	(185)	SITS DOWN HELPLESSLY. /THE WOMAN/ (CRYING) OH,	JOE	, DONT LISTEN TO HER: DONT LET HER MEDDLE WITH US. THAT
MILL III	(185)	YOUR BUSINESS. /THE WOMAN/ (TERRIFIED) OH,	JOE	, DONT TRUST YOUR MONEY IN A BANK. NO GOOD EVER COMES
APPL I	(215)	/AMANDA/ (GOING TO HIM AND PETTING HIM) COME,	JOE	! DONT MAKE A SCENE. YOU ASKED FOR IT, YOU KNOW.
APPL I	(223)	MORALS. /MAGNUS/ (STARTS) WHAT! /BALBUS/ GOOD,	JOE	! /CRASSUS/ (ASIDE TO AMANDA) THATS GOT HIM. /MAGNUS/
APPL I	(218)	NOT GET IT FROM MY PARTY. /BALBUS/ HEAR HEAR,	JOE	! /MAGNUS/ HEAVEN FORBID! THE VARIETY OF OPINION IN

JOE'S

APPL I	(215)	MY TEMPER. BUT I AM NOT GOING TO STAND ANY OF	JOE'S	NONSENSE; AND THE SOONER HE MAKES UP HIS MIND TO THAT
APPL I	(231)	THE REST OF YOU HAVNT FOUND OUT BY THIS TIME THAT	JOE'S	RAGES ARE INVARIABLY CALCULATED, THEN NOTHING WILL

JOEY

MIS.	(184)	/BENTLEY/ (SUDDENLY BREAKING OUT LAMENTABLY)	JOEY	: HAVE YOU TAKEN HYPATIA AWAY FROM ME? /LORD
MIS.	(197)	HER AFFAIR, NOT MINE. /HYPATIA/ DONT ANSWER HIM,	JOEY	: IT WONT LAST. LORD SUMMERHAYS, I'M SORRY ABOUT
MIS.	(174)	WITH ME; AND I CANT FIND HER ANYWHERE. AND WHERES	JOEY	? /GUNNER/ SUDDENLY BREAKING OUT AGGRESSIVELY, BEING
MIS.	(199)	HOW JOLLY! YOU AND I MIGHT BE FRIENDS THEN; AND	JOEY	COULD STAY TO DINNER. /TARLETON/ LET HIM STAY TO
MIS.	(129)	WHATEVER PAID HIM BEST. BETWEEN THE LOT OF THEM	JOEY	GOT CULTIVATED NO END. HE SAID IF HE COULD ONLY HAVE
MIS.	(175)	SET! ONE OF THE JOHNNIES I SLAVE FOR! WELL,	JOEY	HAS MORE DECENCY THAN YOUR DAUGHTER, ANYHOW. THE WOMEN
MIS.	(175)	TO TARLETON) OH! IS HYPATIA YOUR DAUGHTER? AND	JOEY	IS MISTER PERCIVAL, IS HE? ONE OF YOUR SET, I SUPPOSE.
MIS.	(174)	TELL YOU WHERE HYPATIA IS, I CAN TELL YOU WHERE	JOEY	IS. AND I SAY IT'S A SCANDAL AND AN INFAMY. IF PEOPLE
MIS.	(198)	YOU SEE WHAT LIVING WITH ONE'S PARENTS MEANS,	JOEY	. IT MEANS LIVING IN A HOUSE WHERE YOU CAN BE ORDERED
MIS.	(184)	I WOULDNT HAVE PLAYED YOU SUCH A DIRTY TRICK,	JOEY	. (STRUGGLING WITH A SOB) YOU BEAST. /LORD SUMMERHAYS/
MIS.	(165)	MISS TARLETON-- /HYPATIA/ (CARESSINGLY) HYPATIA,	JOEY	. PATSY, IF YOU LIKE. /PERCIVAL/ LOOK HERE: THIS IS NO
MIS.	(196)	WITH GENUINE AMUSEMENT) HE HAD YOU THERE,	JOEY	. /TARLETON/ I HAVNT BEEN A BAD FATHER TO YOU, PATSY.
MIS.	(199)	BENTLEY! OF COURSE YOU GUESSED I WANTED TO MARRY	JOEY	. WHAT DID THE POLISH LADY DO TO YOU? /BENTLEY/ (
MIS.	(131)	THANK YOU. I SHALL TAKE JOLLY GOOD CARE TO KEEP	JOEY	OUT OF THIS UNTIL HYPATIA IS PAST PRAYING FOR. JOHNNY
MIS.	(128)	YES. THATS AN IDEA OF MINE. I KNEW A CHAP NAMED	JOEY	PERCIVAL AT OXFORD (YOU KNOW I WAS TWO MONTHS AT
MIS.	(150)	YOURE REALLY MORE THAN KIND. /BENTLEY/ WHY, IT'S	JOEY	PERCIVAL. /PERCIVAL/ HALLO, BEN! THAT YOU? /TARLETON/
MIS.	(176)	CRYING WITH ANXIETY) YOU BEASTLY ROTTER, I'LL GET	JOEY	TO GIVE YOU SUCH A HIDING-- /TARLETON/ YOU CANT LEAVE
MIS.	(129)	I JUST LET HIM WANT; AND SERVE HIM RIGHT!) WELL,	JOEY	WAS A MOST AWFULLY CLEVER FELLOW, AND SO NICE! I ASKED

JOEY'S

MIS.	(129)	OF HIS. THE WHOLE THREE OF THEM TOOK CHARGE OF	JOEY'S	CONSCIENCE. HE USED TO HEAR THEM ARGUING LIKE MAD
MIS.	(197)	LORD SUMMERHAYS, I'M SORRY ABOUT BENTLEY; BUT	JOEY'S	THE ONLY MAN FOR ME. /LORD SUMMERHAYS/ IT MAY--

JOG

FABL III	(112)	GIVE ME A MEAL OR THE PRICE OF ONE, AND LET ME	JOG	ON THE FOOTPATH WAY. MY NAME'S NOT PROSPERO: IT'S

JOHANNESBURG

APPL II	(267)	WE'LL SEE IT SHIFTED TO MELBOURNE OR MONTREAL OR	JOHANNESBURG	FIRST. /MAGNUS/ IT WOULD NOT STAY THERE. IT

JOHANNIS

WIDO I	(9)	DR TRENCH? (WITH A GRIMACE) I'M SURE THE	JOHANNIS	CHURCH WILL BE A TREAT FOR YOU. /COKANE/ (LAUGHING
WIDO I	(9)	DO YOU KNOW, MISS SARTORIUS, THERE ACTUALLY ARE	JOHANNIS	CHURCHES HERE-- SEVERAL OF THEM-- AS WELL AS

		JOHN	
MIS. (149)	SHRIEKS. /MRS TARLETON/ OH, ARE THEY KILLED?	JOHN	: ARE THEY KILLED? /LORD SUMMERHAYS/ ARE YOU HURT? IS
BUOY II (23)	NATIVE/ (CRIES) AHAIYA! MISSY'S MEAL. /HE/ SAY,	JOHN	: CAN YOU DIRECT ME TO THE NEAREST WITCH DOCTOR? SPELL
MIS. (156)	THE INNER DOOR. /MRS TARLETON/ WELL I NEVER!	JOHN	: I DONT THINK THAT YOUNG WOMAN'S RIGHT IN HER HEAD. DO
MIS. (128)	WITH ME, AND GIVE THE LADS A TURN. /MRS TARLETON/	JOHN	: I WONT HAVE IT. THATS A FORBIDDEN SUBJECT. /TARLETON/
MIS. (186)	HE-- /MRS TARLETON/ NOW STOP JOKING THE POOR LAD.	JOHN	: I WONT HAVE IT. HE'S BEEN WORRIED TO DEATH BETWEEN
GETT PREFACE(217)	EARLY FREETHINKER SLIPPED INTO THE GOSPEL OF ST	JOHN	: NAMELY, THAT WE ALL LIVE IN GLASS HOUSES. WE MAY TAKE
JOAN 6 (123)	INTO THE EVIL OF HERESY IN FRANCE. BROTHER	JOHN	: THE EARL OF WARWICK. /WARWICK/ YOUR REVERENCE IS MOST
2TRU III (85)	A LOT OF THEM LANDED UP IN THE OTHER PLACE. NO,	JOHN	: YOU COULD TELL A STORY WELL; AND THEY SAY YOU WERE A
MIS. (130)	SCENTING A PLOT AGAINST HER BELOVED JOHNNY) NOW,	JOHN	: YOU PROMISED-- /TARLETON/ YES, YES. ALL RIGHT,
MIS. (188)	MAN DOUBTS IT, I'M READY FOR HIM. /MRS TARLETON/	JOHN	: YOU SHOULDNT HAVE GIVEN HIM THAT SLOE GIN. IT'S GONE
JOAN 4 (99)	-- /WARWICK/ (REASSURED) AH! YOU HEAR, MESSIRE	JOHN	? I KNEW YOUR LORDSHIP WOULD NOT FAIL US. PARDON MY
MIS. (174)	TARLETON/ (ON THE STEPS) IS ANYTHING THE MATTER,	JOHN	? NURSE SAYS SHE HEARD YOU CALLING ME A QUARTER OF AN
MIS. (127)	ABOUT SOLOMON. /MRS TARLETON/ HAVE YOU HAD TEA,	JOHN	? /TARLETON/ YES. DONT INTERRUPT ME WHEN I'M IMPROVING
JOAN 6 (148)	PATTING HIM ON THE SHOULDER) WHAT IS IT, MASTER	JOHN	? WHAT IS THE MATTER? /THE CHAPLAIN/ (CLUTCHING AT
MIS. (182)	HAND AND STOPS HIM). /MRS TARLETON/ WHATS THIS,	JOHN	? WHAT WERE YOU DOING WITH HIS MOTHER'S PHOTOGRAPHS..
MIS. PREFACE(62)	THAT RUSKIN'S PARENTS WERE WISE PEOPLE WHO GAVE	JOHN	A FULL SHARE IN THEIR OWN LIFE, AND PUT UP WITH HIS
LION PREFACE(42)	CAREER, AT THE CALL OF THE SONS OF ZEBEDEE.	JOHN	AGREED AS TO THE TRIAL AND CRUCIFIXION. ALTHOUGH JOHN,
MIS. (121)	GETTING OLD, I'M DROPPING BACK INTO ALL THE WAYS	JOHN	AND I HAD WHEN WE HAD BARELY A HUNDRED A YEAR. YOU
LION PREFACE(22)	NO RECORD OF JOHN GOING BEYOND THIS. THE SAVAGE	JOHN	AND THE CIVILIZED JESUS. JESUS WENT BEYOND IT VERY
LION PREFACE(36)	WHICH LUKE BEGINS HIS STORY. WHILST JESUS AND	JOHN	ARE STILL IN THEIR MOTHERS' WOMBS, JOHN LEAPS AT THE
LION PREFACE(15)	ISAIAH AT ONE END OF SUCH A PERIOD AND LUKE AND	JOHN	AT THE OTHER. COMPLETION OF THE SCHEME BY LUTHER AND
LADY PREFACE(231)	KINGS AND LORDS AND GENTLEMEN! WOULD EVEN	JOHN	BALL OR JEREMIAH COMPLAIN THAT THEY ARE FLATTERED?
CAND I SD(78)	PROGRESS AND POVERTY, FABIAN ESSAYS, A DREAM OF	JOHN	BALL, MARX'S CAPITAL, AND HALF A DOZEN OTHER LITERARY
LION PREFACE(16)	AND DRINKING HIS BLOOD, AND FROM THE SONG OF	JOHN	BARLEYCORN YOU MAY LEARN HOW THE MIRACLE OF THE SEED,
LION PREFACE(16)	FOR EVER AND EVER. YOU MAY, AND INDEED MUST, USE	JOHN	BARLEYCORN " RIGHT BARBAROUSLEE," CUTTING HIM " OFF AT
LION PREFACE(15)	HAD ADVOCATED THIS; BUT LUTHER AND CALVIN DID IT.	JOHN	BARLEYCORN. THERE IS YET ANOTHER PAGE IN THE HISTORY OF
LION PREFACE(89)	NEITHER CAN WE BELIEVE THAT HE WAS	JOHN	BARLEYCORN. THE MORE OUR REASON AND STUDY LEAD US TO
LION PREFACE(28)	OF THE FOLK-LORE GODS, AND ANNOUNCES THAT, LIKE	JOHN	BARLEYCORN, HE WILL BE BARBAROUSLY SLAIN AND BURIED,
LION PREFACE(16)	FOLK WILL FIND IT IN THE PEASANT'S SONG OF	JOHN	BARLEYCORN, NOW MADE ACCESSIBLE TO OUR DRAWING ROOM
LION PREFACE(95)	TO MAKE KNOWN TO THE CHILD, FIRST THE SONG OF	JOHN	BARLEYCORN, WITH THE FIELDS AND SEASONS AS WITNESS TO
JOAN 4 (96)	JOHN DE STOGUMBER. /THE CHAPLAIN/ (GLIBLY)	JOHN	BOWYER SPENSER NEVILLE DE STOGUMBER, AT YOUR SERVICE,
SUPR I SD(4)	ARE TWO BUSTS ON PILLARS: ONE, TO HIS LEFT, OF	JOHN	BRIGHT; THE OTHER, TO HIS RIGHT, OF MR HERBERT SPENCER.
SUPR I (8)	STARTS OFF LIKE A GOADED OX IN THE DIRECTION OF	JOHN	BRIGHT, IN WHOSE EXPRESSION THERE IS NO SYMPATHY FOR
MIS. (181)	A HARDLY AUDIBLE VOICE, LIKE A VERY SICK MAN) I	JOHN	BROWN OF 4 CHESTERFIELD PARADE KENTISH TOWN DO HEREBY
MIS. (179)	(WITH DISGUST) OH, PUT IT UP AGAIN. LET IT GO AT	JOHN	BROWN. /PERCIVAL/ WHERE DO YOU LIVE? /GUNNER/ 4
MIS. (179)	TO WRITE). /PERCIVAL/ WHATS YOUR NAME? /GUNNER/	JOHN	BROWN. /TARLETON/ OH COME! COULDNT YOU MAKE IT HORACE
MIS. (188)	LIKELY! NOT ME! /TARLETON/ SO YOU THOUGHT OF	JOHN	BROWN, THAT WAS CLEVER OF YOU. /GUNNER/ CLEVER! YES:
MIS. (179)	ROBINSON? /GUNNER/ (AGITATEDLY) BUT MY NAME IS	JOHN	BROWN. THERE ARE REALLY JOHN BROWNS. HOW CAN I HELP IT
MIS. (179)	BUT MY NAME IS JOHN BROWN. THERE ARE REALLY	JOHN	BROWNS. HOW CAN I HELP IT IF MY NAME'S A COMMON ONE?
MIS. (179)	KENTISH TOWN, N.W. /PERCIVAL/ (DICTATING) I,	JOHN	BROWN, OF 4 CHESTERFIELD PARADE, KENTISH TOWN, DO
O'FL PREFACE(201)	IT WAS ONLY THE USUAL CHILDISH PETULANCE IN WHICH	JOHN	BULL DOES THINGS IN A WEEK THAT DISGRACE HIM FOR A
APPL II (276)	FATHER. HE IS NO MORE UNCLE JONATHAN THAN YOU ARE	JOHN	BULL. /MAGNUS/ YES: WE LIVE IN A WORLD OF WOPS, ALL
BULL PREFACE(71)	ARE IN FULL SWING AS I WRITE. MEANWHILE,	JOHN	BULL'S OTHER ISLAND, THOUGH ITS FREEDOM HAS DESTROYED
BULL PREFACE(13)	FOR POLITICIANS (TO THE FIRST EDITION IN 1906).	JOHN	BULL'S OTHER ISLAND WAS WRITTEN IN 1904 AT THE REQUEST
BULL PREFACE(13)	ANOTHER REASON FOR CHANGING THE DESTINATION OF	JOHN	BULL'S OTHER ISLAND. IT WAS UNCONGENIAL TO THE WHOLE
BULL PREFACE(6)	THINK IT OPPORTUNE TO ISSUE THIS CHEAP EDITION OF	JOHN	BULL'S OTHER ISLAND THIS HOME RULE YEAR, BECAUSE ITS
BULL PREFACE(4)	OF THIS POLITICAL SWING OF THE PENDULUM WAS THAT	JOHN	BULL'S OTHER ISLAND, WHICH HAD UP TO THAT MOMENT BEEN A
BULL (1)		JOHN	BULL'S OTHER ISLAND. 1904.
BULL PREFACE(3)	MORE IGNORANT FELLOW-PILGRIMS GUESSED RIGHTLY).	JOHN	BULL'S OTHER ISLAND WAS WRITTEN WHEN A UNIONIST
BULL IV (153)	SORRY. (HE PATS KEEGAN CONSOLINGLY ON THE BACK).	JOHN	BULL'S WITS ARE STILL SLOW, YOU SEE. BESIDES, CALLING
3PLA PREFACE(R27)	AGO OUR GREATEST ENGLISH DRAMATIZER OF LIFE,	JOHN	BUNYAN, ENDED ONE OF HIS STORIES WITH THE REMARK THAT
DEVL EPILOG (79)	NOTES TO THE DEVIL'S DISCIPLE: BURGOYNE. GENERAL	JOHN	BURGOYNE, WHO IS PRESENTED IN THIS PLAY FOR THE FIRST
BULL PREFACE(22)	TOO HASTILY THE SUPERIORITY OF MR MEAGLES TO SIR	JOHN	CHESTER AND HAROLD SKIMPOLE. ON THE OTHER HAND, IT
MTH3 (131)	MIND IS NOT AN ADULT MIND. /BURGE-LUBIN/ STOW IT,	JOHN	CHINAMAN. IF EVER THERE WAS A RACE DIVINELY APPOINTED
LION PREFACE(39)	ORDER TO BRING ABOUT HIS OWN BETRAYAL. LATER ON	JOHN	CLAIMS THAT JESUS SAID TO PETER " IF I WILL THAT JOHN
METH PREFACE(R65)	THERE IS A NOBILITY WHICH PRODUCES POETRY:	JOHN	DAVIDSON FOUND HIS HIGHEST INSPIRATION IN IT. EVEN ITS
JOAN 4 (97)	I BELIEVE. OUR KING'S UNCLE. /CAUCHON/ MESSIRE	JOHN	DE STOGUMBER: I AM ALWAYS THE VERY GOOD FRIEND OF HIS
JOAN 4 (96)	TO ME. /WARWICK/ THIS REVEREND CLERIC IS MASTER	JOHN	DE STOGUMBER. /THE CHAPLAIN/ (GLIBLY) JOHN BOWYER
JOAN 4 (101)	I APOLOGIZE TO YOU FOR THE WORD USED BY MESSIRE	JOHN	DE STOGUMBER. IT DOES NOT MEAN IN ENGLAND WHAT IT DOES
JOAN EPILOG (161)	TO THE CARDINAL: TO MY LORD OF WINCHESTER.	JOHN	DE STOGUMBER, AT YOUR SERVICE. (HE LOOKS AT THEM
LION PREFACE(74)	ON SENTIENT SUBJECTS WAS AN ACT OF KINDNESS.	JOHN	DECLARES THAT HE HEALED THE WOUND OF THE MAN WHOSE EAR
LION PREFACE(38)	WHO AT THE END OF HIS LIFE CAME TO JERUSALEM.	JOHN	DESCRIBES A PREACHER WHO SPENT PRACTICALLY HIS WHOLE
LION PREFACE(43)	HAVE SAVED HIMSELF ALL THAT TROUBLE BY DOING WHAT	JOHN	DESCRIBES HIM AS DOING: THAT IS, CASTING HIS CAPTORS TO
LION PREFACE(42)	DISCIPLES. IT IS ON ONE OF THESE OCCASIONS THAT	JOHN	DESCRIBES THE MIRACULOUS DRAUGHT OF FISHES WHICH LUKE
LION PREFACE(42)	STICKING TINSEL STARS ON THE ROBE OF A TOY ANGEL.	JOHN	DOES NOT MENTION THE ASCENSION; AND THE END OF HIS
MIS. (121)	TURN! YOURE A HUMBUG, YOU KNOW, LORD SUMMERHAYS.	JOHN	DOESNT KNOW IT; AND JOHNNY DOESNT KNOW IT; BUT YOU AND
LION PREFACE(32)	REGARDS JESUS AS A NATIVE OF NAZARETH, AS	JOHN	DOES, AND NOT OF BETHLEHEM, AS MATTHEW AND LUKE DO,
HART PREFACE(34)	HOUSMAN, ARNOLD BENNETT, JOHN GALSWORTHY,	JOHN	DRINKWATER, AND OTHERS WHICH WOULD IN THE XIX CENTURY
KING I (201)	THE GREATEST POET OF THE AGE: THE POET LAUREATE,	JOHN	DRYDEN. /FOX/ IF HE HAS GIVEN TO THE PLAYHOUSE TALENTS
JOAN 6 (123)	WHO IS ON HIS LEFT) THIS GENTLEMAN IS CANON	JOHN	D'ESTIVET, OF THE CHAPTER OF BAYEUX. HE IS ACTING AS
MIS. (175)	/MRS TARLETON/ (WITH A SCREAM) OH! AND	JOHN	ENCOURAGING HIM, I'LL BE BOUND! BUNNY: YOU GO FOR THE
MRS PREFACE(173)	VIEW SUBALTERN IAGO IS AN ATTACK ON THE ARMY, SIR	JOHN	FALSTAFF AN ATTACK ON KNIGHTHOOD, AND KING CLAUDIUS AN
BULL PREFACE(64)	IS WORTHLESS WITHOUT HONOR? IT IS TRUE THAT SIR	JOHN	FALSTAFF DID NOT THINK SO; BUT SIR JOHN IS HARDLY A
MTH4 II (184)	PREACHER, AN ANCIENT AND VERY FAT SAGE CALLED SIR	JOHN	FALSTAFF. WELL (POINTING), THATS FALSTAFF. /THE
SHAK PREFACE(136)	MOTHER WAS OF EQUAL RANK AND SOCIAL PRETENSION,	JOHN	FINALLY FAILED COMMERCIALLY, HAVING NO DOUBT LET HIS
LION PREFACE(37)	HE CANNOT ALLOW THE CALLING OF PETER, JAMES, AND	JOHN	FROM THEIR BOATS TO PASS WITHOUT A COMIC MIRACULOUS
HART PREFACE(34)	ST JOHN HANKIN, LAURENCE HOUSMAN, ARNOLD BENNETT,	JOHN	GALSWORTHY, JOHN DRINKWATER, AND OTHERS WHICH WOULD IN
POSN PREFACE(361)	BARRIE, MR FORBES ROBERTSON, MR CECIL RALEIGH, MR	JOHN	GALSWORTHY, MR LAURENCE HOUSMAN, SIR HERBERT BEERBOHM
HART PREFACE(5)	BY MR H. G. WELLS, MR ARNOLD BENNETT, AND MR	JOHN	GALSWORTHY, THE HOUSE WOULD HAVE BEEN OUT OF THE
MIS. (135)	FATHER HAD ASKED FOR HIS USUAL FIVE POUNDS; AND	JOHN	GAVE HIM A HUNDRED IN HIS BIG WAY. JUST LIKE A KING.
JOAN 1 (62)	AND GIVES ME MONEY TO GIVE TO THE POOR. I THINK	JOHN	GODSAVE WILL COME, AND DICK THE ARCHER, AND THEIR
LION PREFACE(21)	OR LAY FALSE ACCUSATIONS. THERE IS NO RECORD OF	JOHN	GOING BEYOND THIS. THE SAVAGE JOHN AND THE CIVILIZED
MIS. (125)	HAVE HAD MORE OF A PICK, AS YOU MIGHT SAY, IF	JOHN	HADNT SUITED ME. /HYPATIA/ I CAN IMAGINE ALL SORTS OF
JITT PREFACE(6)	UTTERLY UNHAPPY ONE. IT IS TRUE, AS THE LATE ST	JOHN	HANKIN POINTED OUT AND ILLUSTRATED BY HIS PLAYS WITH
HART PREFACE(34)	BARKER, GILBERT MURRAY, JOHN MASEFIELD, ST	JOHN	HANKIN, LAURENCE HOUSMAN, ARNOLD BENNETT, JOHN
POSN PREFACE(372)	TO PUT TO THEM, ALLOWED SIR HENRY IRVING AND SIR	JOHN	HARE TO PREPARE AND READ WRITTEN STATEMENTS, AND
LION PREFACE(21)	NAMED JOHN IS STIRRING THE PEOPLE VERY STRONGLY.	JOHN	HAS DECLARED THAT THE RITE OF CIRCUMCISION IS
MIS. (128)	INTO THE GROUNDS FOR A WALK: THERES A GOOD BOY.	JOHN	HAS GOT ONE OF HIS NAUGHTY FITS THIS EVENING. /HYPATIA/
LION PREFACE(42)	TO THE PEOPLE " YE ARE THE LIGHT OF THE WORLD."	JOHN	HAS NO GRIP OF THE SIGNIFICANCE OF THESE SCRAPS WHICH
LION PREFACE(22)	EITHER IN ASCETICISM OR MARTYRDOM. IN CONTRAST TO	JOHN	HE WAS ESSENTIALLY A HIGHLY-CIVILIZED, CULTIVATED
GETT SD(289)	THAT EDITH SHOULD BE ONE OF THE COMBATANTS! ST	JOHN	HOTCHKISS COMES INTO THE TOWER USHERED BY COLLINS. HE
GETT (324)	/MRS BRIDGENORTH/ (INTRODUCING HOTCHKISS) MR ST	JOHN	HOTCHKISS, HOTCHKISS, STILL FAR ALOOF BY THE STUDY
GETT (289)	GENERAL). /THE GENERAL/ (READING) " MR ST	JOHN	HOTCHKISS, THE CELEBRATED COWARD, LATE LIEUTENANT IN
ROCK PREFACE(175)	LEYDEN, GIORDANO BRUNO AND GALILEO, SERVETUS AND	JOHN	HUS AND THE HEROES OF FOXE'S BOOK OF MARTYRS STANDING
BUOY PREFACE(4)	INEXPLICABLE. WHAT LESS COULD MR SLUDGE SAY? OR	JOHN	HUS, WHO LET HIMSELF BE BURNT RATHER THAN RECANT HIS "
MIS. (135)	BUT AT LAST ONE DAY HE SAID TO ME, "	JOHN	IS A KING," /BENTLEY/ HOW MUCH DID HE BORROW ON THAT
LION PREFACE(38)	A NEW STORY AND A NEW CHARACTER. THE GOSPEL OF	JOHN	IS A SURPRISE AFTER THE OTHERS. MATTHEW, MARK AND LUKE
LION PREFACE(40)	THE SECOND COMING, THE CONCLUSION BEING THAT	JOHN	IS ALIVE AT THIS MOMENT, I CANNOT BELIEVE THAT A
BULL PREFACE(64)	THAT SIR JOHN FALSTAFF DID NOT THINK SO; BUT SIR	JOHN	IS HARDLY A MODEL FOR SIR EDWARD. YET EVEN SIR JOHN
MIS. (135)	PARTIALITY, LORD SUMMERHAYS; BUT I DO THINK	JOHN	IS REALLY GREAT. I'M SURE HE WAS MEANT TO BE A KING. MY
LION PREFACE(21)	AT THIS MOMENT, A SALVATIONIST PROPHET NAMED	JOHN	IS STIRRING THE PEOPLE VERY STRONGLY. JOHN HAS DECLARED
LION PREFACE(39)	THE PUBLICAN WITH MATTHEW THE EVANGELIST); AND	JOHN	IS THE ONLY EVANGELIST WHOSE ACCOUNT OF CHRIST'S CAREER
LION PREFACE(38)	LOCALITY AS DEFINITE AS JERUSALEM OR MADAGASCAR.	JOHN	. A NEW STORY AND A NEW CHARACTER. THE GOSPEL OF JOHN
MIS. (124)	ME I WASNT GOING TO LOSE ANOTHER CHILD NOR TRUST	JOHN	. AND I DONT WANT MY GRANDCHILDREN TO DIE ANY MORE THAN
MIS. (119)	HES TOO MODEST FOR IT. HE CALLS HIMSELF PLAIN	JOHN	. BUT YOU CANT CALL HIM THAT IN HIS OWN OFFICE:

MIS. (130)	MATTER WHAT I GO INTO. /MRS TARLETON/ DONT BOAST,	JOHN	. DONT TEMPT PROVIDENCE. /TARLETON/ RATS! YOU DONT
LION PREFACE(32)	NOT TOUCH HIS CAREER UNTIL HIS ADULT BAPTISM BY	JOHN	. HE APPARENTLY REGARDS JESUS AS A NATIVE OF NAZARETH,
LION PREFACE(81)	DISCIPLE OF JESUS ONLY AS JESUS WAS A DISCIPLE OF	JOHN	. HE DOES NOTHING THAT JESUS WOULD HAVE DONE, AND SAYS
MIS. (122)	THEYD PUT ME ON TO GET A BIG SUBSCRIPTION OUT OF	JOHN	. I'D NEVER HEARD SUCH TALK IN MY LIFE. THE THINGS THEY
JOAN 4 (99)	INDEED? IN WHAT WAY? LISTEN TO THIS, MESSIRE	JOHN	. /CAUCHON/ IF THE DEVIL WANTED TO DAMN A COUNTRY GIRL,
JOAN 4 (98)	WE ARE ASKING FOR THE BISHOP'S OPINION, MESSIRE	JOHN	. /CAUCHON/ WE SHALL HAVE TO CONSIDER NOT MERELY OUR
MIS. (157)	DONT TALK LIKE THAT BEFORE LORD SUMMERHAYS,	JOHN	. /LORD SUMMERHAYS/ IT DOESNT MATTER, MRS TARLETON: IN
MIS. (129)	/MRS TARLETON/ YOU ALWAYS WERE ONE FOR IDEAS,	JOHN	. /TARLETON/ YOURE RIGHT, CHICKABIDDY. WHAT DO I TELL
GETT (305)	CECIL. /LEO/ (RISING) AND I WITH REJJY AND ST	JOHN	. /THE GENERAL/ (AGHAST) AN ALLIANCE! DO YOU MEAN A--
MIS. (154)	WELL AS THE LADY. /MRS TARLETON/ DONT BE SILLY,	JOHN	. THE LADY IS ONLY JOKING, I'M SURE. (TO LINA) I
MIS. (121)	LOT, AND THAT THEY WERE LAUGHING AT ME AND	JOHN	. THEYRE ALWAYS GIGGLING AND PRETENDING NOT TO CARE
BUOY II (24)	DWELLS WITHIN IS ONE OF THEM. /HE/ LISTEN TO ME,	JOHN	. WE WHITE MEN HAVE A GOD MUCH MUCH GREATER THAN
MIS. (203)	GOING ON? DONT YOU HOLD ANYTHING BACK FROM ME,	JOHN	. WHAT HAVE YOU BEEN DOING? /TARLETON/ PATSY ISNT
POSN PREFACE(420)	COMPREHENSION NOR POLITICAL VIRTUE THAN KING	JOHN	. WHEN HENRY VII CALMLY PROCEEDED TO TEAR UP MAGNA
MIS. (135)	DOWN ON JOHN, BECAUSE HE WAS A RATE COLLECTOR AND	JOHN	KEPT A SHOP. IT HURT HIS PRIDE TO HAVE TO BORROW MONEY
LADY PREFACE(212)	TO MRS PROUDIE A DON JUAN, TO ASPASIA A	JOHN	KNOX: IN SHORT, TO EVERYONE HIS COMPLEMENT RATHER THAN
BULL PREFACE(38)	OF THE LEGITIMATE SUCCESSOR OF MARTIN LUTHER AND	JOHN	KNOX. NOWADAYS, HOWEVER, VOLTAIRE'S JOKES ARE EITHER
LION PREFACE(36)	JESUS AND JOHN ARE STILL IN THEIR MOTHERS' WOMBS,	JOHN	LEAPS AT THE APPROACH OF JESUS WHEN THE TWO MOTHERS
JOAN 6 (123)	WHO IS ON HIS RIGHT) THIS, MY LORD, IS BROTHER	JOHN	LEMAITRE, OF THE ORDER OF ST DOMINIC. HE IS ACTING AS
MIS. (175)	GOOD GRACIOUS! HE'S MAD. (TO LINA) DID	JOHN	MAKE HIM TAKE A TURKISH BATH? /LINA/ NO. HE DOESNT
LION PREFACE(42)	" IF YOU ARE GODS, THEN, A FORTIORI, I AM A GOD."	JOHN	MAKES HIM SAY THIS, JUST AS HE MAKES HIM SAY " I AM THE
HART PREFACE(34)	BY THE PLAYS OF GRANVILLE BARKER, GILBERT MURRAY,	JOHN	MASEFIELD, ST JOHN HANKIN, LAURENCE HOUSMAN, ARNOLD
METH PREFACE(R39)	COULD BE INDUCED TO ADOPT THAT ARTICLE. ST	JOHN	MIGHT SAY THAT " GOD IS SPIRIT" AS POINTEDLY AS HE
LION PREFACE(22)	HIMSELF, CHAFFING THE JEWS FOR COMPLAINING THAT	JOHN	MUST BE POSSESSED BY THE DEVIL BECAUSE HE WAS A
JOAN PREFACE(49)	ATMOSPHERE IN SHAKESPEAR'S HISTORIES. HIS	JOHN	OF GAUNT IS LIKE A STUDY OF THE OLD AGE OF DRAKE.
6CAL SD(98)	HIS MOUTH WITH IT. HE BARKS TO THE LAST MOMENT.	JOHN	OF GAUNT LAUGHS ECSTATICALLY AT THIS PERFORMANCE, AND
6CAL SD(97)	AT THE KING'S RIGHT HAND AND TAKES CHARGE OF	JOHN	OF GAUNT. /THE KING/ NOW FOR THESE SWINE, THESE
6CAL SD(93)	SCREAM IS HEARD FROM THE ROYAL PAVILION; AND	JOHN	OF GAUNT, AGED 7, DASHES OUT AND IS MAKING FOR HIS
6CAL SD(96)	CALL. /THE KING/ WHAT IS THAT? WHAT NOW?	JOHN	OF GAUNT, WHO HAS BEEN UP TO THE TOWN GATES TO SEE THE
JOAN 1 (62)	COME, AND DICK THE ARCHER, AND THEIR SERVANTS	JOHN	OF HONECOURT AND JULIAN. THERE WILL BE NO TROUBLE FOR
LION PREFACE(4)	NO DEFENCE OF SUCH CHRISTIANS AS SAVONAROLA AND	JOHN	OF LEYDEN: THEY WERE SCUTTLING THE SHIP BEFORE THEY HAD
GETT PREFACE(199)	BAD MAN: THAT IS WHY SAVONAROLA WAS BURNT AND	JOHN	OF LEYDEN TORN TO PIECES WITH RED-HOT PINCERS WHILST
ROCK PREFACE(156)	OUT, WITHIN THE MEMORY OF PERSONS NOW LIVING.	JOHN	OF LEYDEN, FOR BEING A COMMUNIST, WAS TORTURED SO
ROCK PREFACE(175)	HABITUALLY TAKEN IN VAIN, WE HAVE JOAN OF ARC AND	JOHN	OF LEYDEN, GIORDANO BRUNO AND GALILEO, SERVETUS AND
JOAN 1 (61)	ANY OTHER NAME. JACK -- /ROBERT/ THAT IS MONSIEUR	JOHN	OF METZ, I SUPPOSE? /JOAN/ YES, SQUIRE. JACK WILL COME
SIM II (59)	NEVER BEEN ABLE TO IMAGINE ETERNITY PROPERLY. ST	JOHN	OF PATMOS STARTED THE NOTION OF PLAYING HARPS AND
BUOY PREFACE(4)	MR SLUDGE OR DUNGLAS HOME, OR AS JOB OR	JOHN	OF PATMOS. WHEN I WRITE A PLAY I DO NOT FORESEE NOR
BUOY PREFACE(6)	WHO SOLVES THE PROBLEM OF THE PROPHET DANIEL AND	JOHN	OF PATMOS, AND INCIDENTALLY OF SHAKESPEAR AND MYSELF,
LION PREFACE(37)	IS ILL RECEIVED IN A SAMARITAN VILLAGE JAMES AND	JOHN	PROPOSE TO CALL DOWN FIRE FROM HEAVEN AND DESTROY IT;
LION PREFACE(88)	TO THE SECULARIST VIEW. WE HAVE SEEN LUKE AND	JOHN	REJECT MATTHEW'S STORY OF THE MASSACRE OF THE INNOCENTS
PLES PREFACE(R9)	FIRST TO MAKE THAT EPIGRAM AT HIS OWN EXPENSE.	JOHN	RUSKIN HAS TOLD US CLEARLY ENOUGH WHAT IS IN THE
GENV III (82)	HAS TOLD YOU. MY GRANDFATHER BOUGHT SHERRY FROM	JOHN	RUSKIN'S FATHER; AND VERY GOOD SHERRY IT WAS. AND JOHN
GENV III (82)	RUSKIN'S FATHER; AND VERY GOOD SHERRY IT WAS. AND	JOHN	RUSKIN'S GOSPEL COMPARED WITH KARL MARX'S WAS LIKE
MIS. PREFACE(62)	HE COMES TO HATE BOOKS AND LANGUAGES. IN THE END,	JOHN	RUSKIN, TIED SO CLOSELY TO HIS MOTHER'S APRON-STRING
MIS. (135)	HIS PRIDE TO HAVE TO BORROW MONEY SO OFTEN FROM	JOHN	; AND HE USED TO CONSOLE HIMSELF BY SAYING, " AFTER
LION PREFACE(74)	OF THE MAN WHOSE EAR WAS CUT OFF (BY PETER,	JOHN	SAYS) AT THE ARREST IN THE GARDEN. ONE OF THE FIRST
BUOY 1 (14)	DEAL OVER THIS. I HAVE TRIED TO IMAGINE WHAT OLD	JOHN	SHAKESPEAR OF STRATFORD-UPON-AVON, MAYOR AND ALDERMAN
LADY (244)	SAME BREATH WITH STRATFORD'S WORTHIEST ALDERMAN.	JOHN	SHAKESPEAR WEDDED BUT ONCE: HARRY TUDOR WAS MARRIED SIX
SHAK PREFACE(136)	TO BE EXACTLY WHAT SHAKESPEAR WAS. HIS FATHER,	JOHN	SHAKESPEAR, GENT, WAS AN ALDERMAN WHO DEMANDED A COAT
LION PREFACE(21)	IS NOT APPARENT: IT SEEMS TO US AS NATURAL THAT	JOHN	SHOULD HAVE BAPTIZED PEOPLE AS THAT THE RECTOR OF OUR
MIS. PREFACE(3)	PROVOKE. WITH ALL OUR PERVERSE NONSENSE AS TO	JOHN	SMITH LIVING FOR A THOUSAND MILLION EONS AND FOR EVER
GETT PREFACE(256)	GOD MEANS THE DISTRICT REGISTRAR OR THE REVEREND	JOHN	SMITH OR WILLIAM JONES, MUST BE GOT RID OF. MEANS OF
LION PREFACE(88)	BESET ALL EARTHLY CHRONICLERS, WOULD HAVE MADE	JOHN	STARE, BEING AS IT IS A COMPARATIVELY MODERN FANCY OF
METH PREFACE(R81)	AND COLERIDGE DID NOT REMAIN SOLDIERS, NOR COULD	JOHN	STUART MILL REMAIN THE REPRESENTATIVE OF WESTMINSTER IN
LADY PREFACE(229)	THEY ARE MERELY A RECORD OF OBSERVED FACT.	JOHN	STUART MILL TOLD OUR BRITISH WORKMEN THAT THEY WERE
FABL PREFACE(73)	IT WAS SIMPLY TRANSFERRED TO HERBERT SPENCER AND	JOHN	STUART MILL, THE TRANSFER WAS OFTEN FOR THE WORSE, AS
MILL PREFACE(121)	AND WROTE SYMPATHETIC ARTICLES PARAPHRASING	JOHN	STUART MILL'S ESSAY ON LIBERTY. MUSSOLINI, NOW IL DUCE,
NEVR II (228)	DARWIN'S VIEW OF THE ORIGIN OF SPECIES AND	JOHN	STUART MILL'S ESSAY ON LIBERTY (NOD); TO READ HUXLEY,
NEVR I (207)	WOMEN'S RIGHTS MOVEMENT WHICH HAD FOR ITS BIBLE	JOHN	STUART MILL'S TREATISE ON THE SUBJECTION OF WOMEN. SHE
MIS. PREFACE(62)	DID NOT ESCAPE EVEN WHEN HE WHEN TO OXFORD, AND	JOHN	STUART MILL, WHOSE FATHER OUGHT TO HAVE BEEN PROSECUTED
JOAN 4 (98)	/THE CHAPLAIN/ WHAT! NOT WHEN THE FAMOUS SIR	JOHN	TALBOT HIMSELF HAS BEEN DEFEATED AND ACTUALLY TAKEN
JOAN 4 (94)	AND NOW WE HAVE BEEN BUTCHERED AT PATAY, AND SIR	JOHN	TALBOT TAKEN PRISONER. (HE THROWS DOWN HIS PEN, ALMOST
JOAN 4 (100)	BELIEVE HIS EARS) DOES YOUR LORDSHIP COMPARE SIR	JOHN	TALBOT, THREE TIMES GOVERNOR OF IRELAND, TO A MAD
JOAN 4 (98)	DRAB FROM THE DITCHES OF LORRAINE! /CAUCHON/ SIR	JOHN	TALBOT, WE ALL KNOW, IS A FIERCE AND FORMIDABLE
SUPR I SD(9)	OF ANN. THERE MUST BE SOMETHING THE MATTER. MR	JOHN	TANNER SUDDENLY OPENS THE DOOR AND ENTERS. HE IS TOO
SUPR I (8)	WONT HAVE IT: I WILL NOT HAVE IT. SHE MUST FORBID	JOHN	TANNER THE HOUSE; AND SO MUST YOU. THE PARLORMAID
SUPR HANDBOK(175)	THEY HAVE ONLY SHIFTED IT TO ANOTHER SHOULDER.	JOHN	TANNER. I: ON GOOD BREEDING. IF THERE WERE NO GOD, SAID
SUPR III SD(87)	EVEN AN IDENTITY, THE NAME TOO: DON JUAN TENORIO,	JOHN	TANNER. WHERE ON EARTH-- OR ELSEWHERE-- HAVE WE GOT TO
SUPR HANDBOK(173)	REVOLUTIONIST'S HANDBOOK AND POCKET COMPANION: BY	JOHN	TANNER, M.I.R.C. (MEMBER OF THE IDLE RICH CLASS).
SUPR I (7)	REVOLUTIONIST'S HANDBOOK AND POCKET COMPANION. BY	JOHN	TANNER, M.I.R.C., MEMBER OF THE IDLE RICH CLASS.
MIS. (181)	WHICH I THREATENED TO TAKE THE LIFE OF THE SAID	JOHN	TARLETON AND WAS PREVENTED FROM DOING SO ONLY BY THE
MIS. (179)	(DICTATING) -- I TRESPASSED ON THE LAND OF	JOHN	TARLETON AT HINDHEAD, AND EFFECTED AN UNLAWFUL ENTRY
MIS. (181)	ON THE 31ST MAY 1909 I TRESPASSED ON THE LAND OF	JOHN	TARLETON AT HINDHEAD AND EFFECTED AN UNLAWFUL ENTRY
MIS. (151)	ALLOW ME TO INTRODUCE MYSELF: TARLETON:	JOHN	TARLETON (SEEING CONJECTURE IN THE PASSENGER'S EYE)--
MIS. (160)	NAME WAS? /TARLETON/ JOHN TARLETON. THE GREAT	JOHN	TARLETON OF TARLETON'S UNDERWEAR. /LINA/ (WRITING)
MIS. (160)	IT) WHAT DID YOU SAY YOUR NAME WAS? /TARLETON/	JOHN	TARLETON. THE GREAT JOHN TARLETON OF TARLETON'S
MIS. (179)	WHICH I THREATENED TO TAKE THE LIFE OF THE SAID	JOHN	TARLETON-- /MRS TARLETON/ OH, JOHN! YOU MIGHT HAVE
MIS. SD(109)	FRIDAY TO TUESDAY IN THE HOUSE OF HIS FATHER,	JOHN	TARLETON, WHO HAS MADE A GREAT DEAL OF MONEY OUT OF
LION PREFACE(39)	CLAIMS THAT JESUS SAID TO PETER " IF I WILL THAT	JOHN	TARRY TIL I COME, WHAT IS THAT TO THEE? "; AND JOHN,
LION PREFACE(47)	AT ALL, THEY WILL BE QUITE ARBITRARY ONES. ST	JOHN	TELLS US THAT WHEN JESUS EXPLICITLY CLAIMED DIVINE
JOAN 6 (129)	MAN WHO THROWS OFF HIS FUR GOWN AND DRESSES LIKE	JOHN	THE BAPTIST: THEY ARE FOLLOWED, AS SURELY AS THE NIGHT
LION PREFACE(74)	THEY CANCELLED HIM, AND WENT BACK STRAIGHT TO	JOHN	THE BAPTIST AND HIS FORMULA OF SECURING REMISSION OF
LION PREFACE(21)	INTO THE RELIGIOUS LIFE OF HIS TIME BY GOING TO	JOHN	THE BAPTIST AND DEMANDING BAPTISM FROM HIM, MUCH AS
LION PREFACE(95)	HE WILL ACCEPT JESUS AS HIS SAVIOR, AND PETER AND	JOHN	THE BAPTIST AS THE SAVIOR'S REVEALER AND FORERUNNER
LION PREFACE(31)	BUT AS A MASTER CRAFTSMAN OF ROYAL DESCENT.	JOHN	THE BAPTIST MAY HAVE BEEN A KEIR HARDIE; BUT THE JESUS
SIM PREFACE(5)	HAS EVER BEEN A PENNY THE WORSE FOR BAPTISM SINCE	JOHN	THE BAPTIST RECOMMENDED IT. RELIGION IS THE MOTHER OF
LION PREFACE(21)	WHICH SKIPS AT ONCE TO THE MANHOOD OF JESUS.	JOHN	THE BAPTIST. AT THIS MOMENT, A SALVATIONIST PROPHET
ROCK PREFACE(158)	HAVE BEEN DISPATCHED AS QUICKLY AND SUDDENLY AS	JOHN	THE BAPTIST, BUT THE MOB WANTED THE HORRIBLE FUN OF
LION PREFACE(6)	AND VENERATION AT LEAST AS HIGH AS WE ACCORD TO	JOHN	THE BAPTIST. BUT THIS BRITISH BULLDOG CONTEMPT IS
LION PREFACE(24)	A POPULAR PREACHER CARRIES HIM EQUALLY FAR BEYOND	JOHN	THE BAPTIST, HE LAYS NO STRESS ON BAPTISM OR VOWS, AND
LION PREFACE(17)	AND REVIVALIST PREACHERS, NOW AS IN THE DAYS OF	JOHN	THE BAPTIST, SELDOM FAIL TO WARN THEIR FLOCKS TO WATCH
LION PREFACE(36)	THE BIRTH OF JESUS, BUT BEFORE THE BIRTH OF	JOHN	THE BAPTIST, THE EVENT WITH WHICH LUKE BEGINS HIS
LION PREFACE(34)	OF RECOGNITION: THE STERN PEREMPTORY DISCIPLE OF	JOHN	THE BAPTIST, WHO NEVER ADDRESSES A PHARISEE OR A SCRIBE
LION PREFACE(22)	BEFORE SITTING DOWN TO TABLE. THE FOLLOWERS OF	JOHN	THE BAPTIST, WHO FAST, AND WHO EXPECT TO FIND THE
LION PREFACE(84)	THE PECULIAR DOCTRINES OF JESUS AND GOING BACK TO	JOHN	THE BAPTIST, WAS TO MAKE IT MUCH EASIER TO CONVERT
LION PREFACE(39)	OF SAMARIA. THIS PERHAPS IS WHY HIS CLAIM TO BE	JOHN	THE DISCIPLE, OR TO BE A CONTEMPORARY OF CHRIST'S
LION PREFACE(39)	KNOWETH THIS MAN LETTERS, HAVING NEVER LEARNT? "	JOHN	THE IMMORTAL EYE-WITNESS. JOHN, MOREOVER, CLAIMS TO BE
BULL PREFACE(13)	PLAYGOER, AND GAVE A THIRD IRISH PLAYWRIGHT, DR	JOHN	TODHUNTER, AN OPPORTUNITY WHICH THE COMMERCIAL THEATRES
PLES PREFACE(R7)	INDEPENDENT THEATRE (AT MY OWN SUGGESTION); DR	JOHN	TODHUNTER, WHO HAD BEEN DISCOVERED BEFORE (HIS PLAY
LION PREFACE(41)	DIVINATORY INSTINCT FOR TRUTH, BE THAT AS IT MAY,	JOHN	WAS CERTAINLY NOT THE MAN TO BELIEVE IN THE SECOND
LION PREFACE(41)	OF LUKE. THIS MAY BE BECAUSE	JOHN	WAS OBVIOUSLY MORE A MAN OF THE WORLD THAN THE OTHERS,
LION PREFACE(22)	HE DEPARTED WIDELY FROM JOHN'S MANNER OF LIFE.	JOHN	WENT INTO THE WILDERNESS, NOT INTO THE SYNAGOGUES; AND
LION PREFACE(86)	WITH HIM. IT IS PROBABLE THAT ARCHBISHOP LAUD AND	JOHN	WESLEY DIED EQUALLY PERSUADED THAT HE IN WHOSE NAME
DOCT III (144)	LEARNT THE DOCTRINE OF DELIVERANCE FROM SIN FROM	JOHN	WESLEY'S OWN LIPS BEFORE YOU OR MR SHAW WERE BORN. IT
LION PREFACE(36)	EXHIBITION OF MIRACLES, AND BIDS THEM TELL	JOHN	WHAT THEY HAVE SEEN, AND ASK HIM WHAT HE THINKS NOW.
LION PREFACE(41)	GOSPELS FOR A CREDIBLE MODERN RELIGION, FOR IT IS	JOHN	WHO ADDS TO THE OTHER RECORDS SUCH SAYINGS AS THAT " I
LION PREFACE(43)	AN EXERTION OF HIS MIRACULOUS POWER. IF YOU ASKED	JOHN	WHY HE LET THEM GET UP AGAIN AND TORMENT AND EXECUTE

JOAN 4 (107)	THOUGH PERHAPS I SHALL NOT CARRY MESSIRE	JOHN	WITH ME THERE. ENGLAND FOR THE ENGLISH WILL APPEAL TO
BULL PREFACE(64)	IS HARDLY A MODEL FOR SIR EDWARD. YET EVEN SIR	JOHN	WOULD HAVE HAD ENOUGH GUMPTION TO SEE THAT THE
LION PREFACE(43)	THEM GET UP AGAIN AND TORMENT AND EXECUTE HIM.	JOHN	WOULD HAVE REPLIED THAT IT WAS PART OF THE DESTINY OF
LION PREFACE(36)	STIR AGAIN; AND AS JESUS BEGINS AS A DISCIPLE OF	JOHN	, AND IS BAPTIZED BY HIM, NOBODY CONNECTS HIM WITH THAT
JOAN 4 (100)	IT WOULD NOT BE SEEMLY FOR YOU TO DO SO, MESSIRE	JOHN	, AS YOU ARE STILL SIX REMOVES FROM A BARONY. BUT AS I
MIS. (135)	WAS MEANT TO BE A KING. MY FATHER LOOKED DOWN ON	JOHN	, BECAUSE HE WAS A RATE COLLECTOR AND JOHN KEPT A SHOP.
LION PREFACE(40)	WRITTEN IN THE FIRST CENTURY A. D. I INCLUDE	JOHN	, BECAUSE THOUGH IT MAY BE CLAIMED THAT HE HEDGED HIS
LION PREFACE(38)	HE SAYS EXPRESSLY THAT JESUS, THOUGH BAPTIZED BY	JOHN	, DID NOT HIMSELF PRACTISE BAPTISM, AND THAT HIS
LION PREFACE(42)	AGREED AS TO THE TRIAL AND CRUCIFIXION. ALTHOUGH	JOHN	, FOLLOWING HIS PRACTICE OF SHEWING JESUS'S SKILL AS A
LION PREFACE(22)	VERY RAPIDLY, ACCORDING TO MATTHEW. THOUGH, LIKE	JOHN	, HE BECAME AN ITINERANT PREACHER, HE DEPARTED WIDELY
JOAN 4 (102)	MAY I SPEAK, MY LORD? /WARWICK/ REALLY, MESSIRE	JOHN	, I HAD RATHER YOU DID NOT, UNLESS YOU CAN KEEP YOUR
LION PREFACE(42)	IS FINALLY LED INTO THE AUDACIOUS HINT THAT HE,	JOHN	, IS HIMSELF IMMORTAL IN THE FLESH. STILL, HE DOES NOT
MIS. (182)	RECOGNIZING THEM AT A GLANCE) LUCY TITMUS! OH	JOHN	, JOHN! /TARLETON/ (GRIMLY, TO GUNNER) YOUNG MAN:
MIS. (176)	TELL HIM SO? /MRS TARLETON/ I DO WONDER AT YOU,	JOHN	, LETTING HIM TALK LIKE THIS BEFORE EVERYBODY. (
LION PREFACE(39)	NEVER LEARNT? " JOHN THE IMMORTAL EYE-WITNESS.	JOHN	, MOREOVER, CLAIMS TO BE NOT ONLY A CHRONICLER BUT A
ROCK PREFACE(181)	DISCORD. I BEGIN WITH THE NARRATIVE OF ST	JOHN	, THE ONLY ONE OF THE FOUR WHICH REPRESENTS JESUS AS
LION PREFACE(39)	THE IMPRESSION IS MORE UNPLEASANT, BECAUSE, AS	JOHN	, UNLIKE MATTHEW, IS EDUCATED, SUBTLE, AND OBSESSED
BUOY II (26)	BY SPEAKING PIDGIN TO ME. YOU ADDRESSED ME AS	JOHN	, WHICH IS NOT MY NAME. IN COURTESY I SPOKE AS YOU
LION PREFACE(20)	ACCEPTS THIS STORY, AS NONE OF THEM EXCEPT	JOHN	, WHO THROWS OVER MATTHEW ALTOGETHER, SHARES HIS CRAZE
LION PREFACE(39)	TARRY TIL I COME, WHAT IS THAT TO THEE? "; AND	JOHN	, WITH A RATHER OBVIOUS MOCK MODESTY, ADDS THAT HE MUST
MIS. (127)	(EXPLOSIVELY) WHAT IS DEATH? /MRS TARLETON/	JOHN	! /HYPATIA/ DEATH IS A RATHER UNPLEASANT SUBJECT,
MIS. (182)	THEM AT A GLANCE) LUCY TITMUS! OH JOHN,	JOHN	! /TARLETON/ (GRIMLY, TO GUNNER) YOUNG MAN: YOURE A
MIS. (127)	A DRINK OF LEMONADE). /MRS TARLETON/ FOR SHAME,	JOHN	! TELL HIM TO READ HIS BIBLE. /TARLETON/ (
JOAN EPILOG (161)	YOU SEE; AND THEY INDULGE ME. /JOAN/ POOR OLD	JOHN	! WHAT BROUGHT THEE TO THIS STATE? /DE STOGUMBER/ I
MIS. (133)	ALLOWED TO OTHER MEN? /MRS TARLETON/ YOU SEE,	JOHN	! WHAT HAVE I ALWAYS TOLD YOU? JOHNNY HAS AS MUCH TO
MIS. (179)	OF THE SAID JOHN TARLETON-- /MRS TARLETON/ OH,	JOHN	! YOU MIGHT HAVE BEEN KILLED. /TARLETON/ -- AND WAS

JOHNNIES

CAPT II (243)	ARE YOU? (HE SPRINGS UP, CRYING) LOOK ALIVE,	JOHNNIES	: THERE'S DANGER. BRANDYFACED JACK'S ON THE RUN. (
MIS. (175)	EIGHTY-HORSE-POWER, WEEK-ENDER SET! ONE OF THE	JOHNNIES	I SLAVE FOR! WELL, JOEY HAS MORE DECENCY THAN YOUR
GETT (355)	THAN MAHOMET OR CONFUCIUS OR ANY OF THE OTHER	JOHNNIES	WHO HAVE BEEN ON THIS JOB SINCE THE WORLD EXISTED?
ROCK II (252)	OR MINE. WHATS THE GOOD OF TUBTHUMPING AT THESE	JOHNNIES	, BROLLY? THEYVE BEEN DOING IT THEMSELVES ALL

JOHNNY

MIS. (119)	AFTERNOON. /BENTLEY/ RIGHT O! I SHANT PRESS	JOHNNY	: HES HAD ENOUGH OF ME FOR ONE WEEK-END. (HE GOES
MIS. (116)	TO DEFEND MYSELF AGAINST JOHNNY. /MRS TARLETON/	JOHNNY	: HOW OFTEN HAVE I TOLD YOU THAT YOU MUST NOT BULLY
MIS. (154)	(IMPATIENTLY) OH, IT'S ALL RIGHT, MAMMA.	JOHNNY	: LOOK AFTER MR PERCIVAL. (TO LINA, RISING) COME
MIS. (151)	REMOVE THE GOGGLES. /TARLETON/ DO. HAVE A WASH.	JOHNNY	: TAKE THE GENTLEMAN TO YOUR ROOM: I'LL LOOK AFTER MR
MIS. (136)	SPECIAL OCCASIONS. (SHE GOES TO THE INNER DOOR).	JOHNNY	: WHEN HE COMES BACK ASK HIM WHERE WE'RE TO PUT THAT
MIS. (132)	JOHNNY? /JOHNNY/ IF YOU ASK ME, NO. /TARLETON/	JOHNNY	: YOU DONT CULTIVATE YOUR MIND. YOU DONT READ.
MIS. (186)	THATS NOT BAD. /MRS TARLETON/ NOW DONT BE RUDE,	JOHNNY	: YOU KNOW I DONT LIKE IT. (TO GUNNER) A CUP OF TEA
MIS. (203)	AND WHAT DO YOU CONCLUDE FROM THAT, MISTER	JOHNNY	? /JOHNNY/ WELL, OBVIOUSLY, THAT INDEPENDENCE FOR
MIS. (132)	MORE IMPROVING CONVERSATION. WOULDNT YOU RATHER,	JOHNNY	? /JOHNNY/ IF YOU ASK ME, NO. /TARLETON/ JOHNNY: YOU
MIS. (115)	TO MAKE IT WELL. /HYPATIA/ WHAT HAS HAPPENED,	JOHNNY	? /MRS TARLETON/ WAS IT A WASP? /BENTLEY/ (
6CAL (93)	WHEN THE PRINCE SEIZES HIM. /THE PRINCE/ HOW NOW,	JOHNNY	? WHATS THE MATTER? /JOHN/ (STRUGGLING) LET ME GO.
MIS. (193)	ASHAMED OF YOU. /HYPATIA/ I'LL MAKE IT UP WITH	JOHNNY	AFTERWARDS; BUT I REALLY CANT HAVE HIM HERE STICKING
MIS. (124)	/MRS TARLETON/ DONT BE CROSS, DEARIE. YOU LET	JOHNNY	ALONE; AND I'LL LET BUNNY ALONE. I'M JUST AS BAD AS
MIS. (134)	THATS A NEW IDEA. I BELIEVE I OUGHT TO HAVE MADE	JOHNNY	AN AUTHOR. IVE NEVER SAID SO BEFORE FOR FEAR OF
MIS. SD(152)	POLISH. WONT YOU SIT DOWN? THE GROUP BREAKS UP.	JOHNNY	AND BENTLEY HURRY TO THE PAVILION AND FETCH THE TWO
MIS. (144)	I HOPE NOT. /HYPATIA/ IT'S A DIRTY JOB; BUT	JOHNNY	AND I WERE VULGAR ENOUGH TO LIKE IT. I LIKE YOUNG
MIS. SD(131)	OUT OF THIS UNTIL HYPATIA IS PAST PRAYING FOR.	JOHNNY	AND LORD SUMMERHAYS RETURN THROUGH THE PAVILION FROM
MIS. (138)	CANT GET OFF THAT SUBJECT, YOUD BETTER SEND FOR	JOHNNY	AND PAPA AND BEGIN IT ALL OVER AGAIN. /LORD
MIS. (201)	ALL THESE I BORE IN SILENCE. BUT NOW COMES YOUR	JOHNNY	AND TELLS ME I'M A RIPPING FINE WOMAN, AND ASKS TO ME
MIS. SD(150)	BEGOGGLED, COMES IN THROUGH THE PAVILION WITH	JOHNNY	AND THE TWO LADIES. THE PASSENGER COMES BETWEEN
MIS. (145)	SO SURPRISED IN MY LIFE AS WHEN I CAME TO KNOW	JOHNNY	AS A MAN OF BUSINESS AND FOUND OUT WHAT HE WAS REALLY
MIS. SD(116)	TURNS DERISIVELY AT THE DOOR TO COCK A SNOOK AT	JOHNNY	AS HE GOES OUT. JOHNNY, LEFT ALONE, CLENCHES HIS
MIS. (123)	IT CAN GET ANY GOOD OUT OF THE THING. THEYRE WHAT	JOHNNY	CALLS CYNICAL-LIKE. AND OF COURSE NOBODY CAN SAY A
MIS. SD(181)	BUT THAT YOU ARE SORRY. LORD SUMMERHAYS AND	JOHNNY	COME IN THROUGH THE PAVILION DOOR. /MRS TARLETON/
MIS. (137)	DUMB. HOW I ENVY THE ANIMALS! THEY CANT TALK. IF	JOHNNY	COULD ONLY PUT BACK HIS EARS OR WAG HIS TAIL INSTEAD
MIS. (121)	KNOW, LORD SUMMERHAYS, JOHN DOESNT KNOW IT; AND	JOHNNY	DOESNT KNOW IT; BUT YOU AND I KNOW IT, DONT WE? NOW
MIS. (116)	TARLETON/ YES: THAT WILL BE BEST. (TO BENTLEY)	JOHNNY	DOESNT MEAN ANY HARM, DEAR: HE'LL BE HIMSELF
MIS. (115)	EXTRICATES HIMSELF FROM THEM). THATS ALL RIGHT.	JOHNNY	FRIGHTENED ME. YOU KNOW HOW EASY IT IS TO HURT ME;
MIS. SD(152)	TO THE PAVILION AND FETCH THE TWO WICKER CHAIRS.	JOHNNY	GIVES HIS TO LINA. HYPATIA AND PERCIVAL TAKE THE
MIS. SD(116)	HE REACHES IT, AND LORD SUMMERHAYS COMES IN.	JOHNNY	GLARES AT HIM, SPEECHLESS. LORD SUMMERHAYS TAKES IN
MIS. (133)	YOU SEE, JOHN! WHAT HAVE I ALWAYS TOLD YOU?	JOHNNY	HAS AS MUCH TO SAY FOR HIMSELF AS ANYBODY WHEN HE
DEVL III SD(55)	A SUBDUED MANNER WHICH SUGGESTS THAT GENTLEMANLY	JOHNNY	HAS BEEN MAKING HIS PRESENCE FELT RATHER HEAVILY.
MIS. (186)	DINNERTIME. /MRS TARLETON/ OH, YOUVE NO SENSE,	JOHNNY	. HE CALLS HIS LUNCH HIS DINNER, AND HAS HIS TEA AT
MIS. (192)	TO INSULT MY SISTER. /HYPATIA/ OH, SHUT UP,	JOHNNY	. I CAN TAKE CARE OF MYSELF. DONT YOU INTERFERE.
MIS. (147)	ANY MORE THAN I'D BEEN ABLE TO DO IT MYSELF TO	JOHNNY	. I HAD TO LEAVE BOOKS IN HIS WAY; AND I FELT JUST
MIS. (185)	LEAVE IT AT THAT. ENOUGH SAID. YOU KEEP QUIET,	JOHNNY	. MR PERCIVAL: YOURE WHITEWASHED. SO ARE YOU, PATSY.
MIS. SD(121)	GOES OUT THROUGH THE VESTIBULE DOOR, FOLLOWED BY	JOHNNY	. MRS TARLETON SITS DOWN AT THE WORKTABLE AND TAKES
MIS. (137)	MY EXPANDING IT, IT CRUMPLED ME UP. COME ALONG,	JOHNNY	. /JOHNNY/ DO YOU NO END OF GOOD, YOUNG CHAP. (HE
MIS. (202)	YOU DIDNT. /TARLETON/ WEVE JUST HEARD ABOUT IT,	JOHNNY	. /JOHNNY/ (SHORTLY, BUT WITHOUT ILL-TEMPER) OH: IS
MIS. (147)	FACE AND TALK TO HIM AS MAN TO MAN. YOU CAN HAVE	JOHNNY	. /LORD SUMMERHAYS/ THANK YOU. IVE LIVED SO LONG IN A
MIS. SD(116)	THE PUNCHBOWL FROM THE SIDEBOARD AND OFFERS IT TO	JOHNNY	. /LORD SUMMERHAYS/ SMASH IT. DONT HESITATE: IT'S AN
MIS. (116)	ME; AND I'M TOO SMALL TO DEFEND MYSELF AGAINST	JOHNNY	. /MRS TARLETON/ JOHNNY: HOW OFTEN HAVE I TOLD YOU
MIS. SD(154)	LINA GOES OUT WITH HYPATIA, AND PERCIVAL WITH	JOHNNY	. /MRS TARLETON/ WELL, THIS IS A NICE THING TO
DEVL III (60)	THOUGHT I HAD THE HONOR OF ADDRESSING GENTLEMANLY	JOHNNY	. SENSATION AMONG THE OFFICERS. THE SERGEANT HAS A
MIS. (125)	IF THEY WERENT THE SONS OF THEIR FATHERS, LIKE	JOHNNY	. WHAT'S A GIRL TO DO? I NEVER MET ANYBODY LIKE
MIS. (124)	IN DEFENCE OF HER BOY) NOW DONT BEGIN ABOUT MY	JOHNNY	. YOU KNOW IT ANNOYS ME. JOHNNY'S AS CLEVER AS
MIS. (137)	MORE OF IT) BENTLEY: DO GO AND PLAY TENNIS WITH	JOHNNY	. YOU MUST TAKE EXERCISE. /LORD SUMMERHAYS/ DO, MY
GENV IV (89)	WE HERE FOR? /THE BETROTHED/ TO SEE THE FUN WHEN	JOHNNY	JUDGE COMES AND FINDS NOTHING DOING, I SUPPOSE. /THE
GENV IV (88)	HAVE BEEN SUMMONED AND THAT THEY WONT COME. YOUNG	JOHNNY	JUDGE HAS NO MORE AUTHORITY OVER THEM THAN HIS CAT.
MIS. (117)	AND THAT PERSON IS MY SON BENTLEY. WAS IT HE? (	JOHNNY	NODS AGAIN, NOT YET ABLE TO SPEAK). AS THE CAR
MIS. (116)	SITS DOWN AND MOPS HIS BROW). FEEL BETTER NOW? (	JOHNNY	NODS). I KNOW ONLY ONE PERSON ALIVE WHO COULD DRIVE
MIS. (121)	I WAS FORTY! I TALKED LIKE A DUCHESS; AND IF	JOHNNY	OR HYPATIA LET SLIP A WORD THAT WAS LIKE OLD TIMES, I
MIS. (138)	BUT JUST WHEN IT SEEMS TO BE COMING TO A POINT,	JOHNNY	OR PAPA JUST STARTS ANOTHER HARE; AND IT ALL BEGINS
MIS. (141)	IT ALL: HE AND I. WE GOT PAPA AND MAMMA AND	JOHNNY	OUT OF THE WAY SPLENDIDLY; AND THEN BENTLEY TOOK
MIS. (192)	CHAIR, ON HER RIGHT. PERCIVAL TAKES THE CHAIR	JOHNNY	PLACED FOR LINA ON HER ARRIVAL. TARLETON SITS DOWN AT
MIS. SD(110)	ELABORATE PATENT SWING SEAT AND AWNING IN WHICH	JOHNNY	RECLINES WITH HIS NOVEL. THERE ARE TWO WICKER CHAIRS
MIS. (192)	SITS DOWN AT THE END OF THE WRITING TABLE.	JOHNNY	REMAINS STANDING. LORD SUMMERHAYS CONTINUES, WITH A
MIS. SD(153)	WITH A WICKER CHAIR, WHICH LORD SUMMERHAYS TAKES.	JOHNNY	REMAINS STANDING BEHIND THE WORKTABLE, BENTLEY BEHIND
MIS. (131)	HAT AND HANGS IT UP BESIDE HIS OWN). THANK YOU. (	JOHNNY	RETURNS TO HIS SWING AND HIS NOVEL. LORD SUMMERHAYS
MIS. (130)	TARLETON/ (SCENTING A PLOT AGAINST HER BELOVED	JOHNNY	) NOW, JOHN: YOU PROMISED-- /TARLETON/ YES, YES. ALL
MIS. (137)	EXERCISE. /LORD SUMMERHAYS/ DO, MY BOY, DO. (TO	JOHNNY	) TAKE HIM OUT AND MAKE HIM SKIP ABOUT. /BENTLEY/ (
MIS. (130)	ALL RIGHT, CHICKABIDDY: DONT FUSS. YOUR PRECIOUS	JOHNNY	SHANT BE INTERFERED WITH. (BOUNCING UP, TOO
MIS. (112)	HEAR? (BENTLEY ATTEMPTS TO GO WITH DIGNITY.	JOHNNY	SLINGS HIM INTO A CHAIR AT THE WRITING TABLE, WHERE
MIS. SD(110)	THE PAVILION, HE IS UNMISTAKABLY A GRADE ABOVE	JOHNNY	SOCIALLY; AND THOUGH HE LOOKS SENSITIVE ENOUGH, HIS
MIS. SD(181)	IS, COMES FORWARD BETWEEN PERCIVAL AND LINA.	JOHNNY	STOPS BESIDE HYPATIA. /PERCIVAL/ CERTAINLY.
MIS. (131)	SOONER, BUT I'M STILL RATHER LOST IN ENGLAND. (	JOHNNY	TAKES HIS HAT AND HANGS IT UP BESIDE HIS OWN). THANK
MIS. (137)	AND WHEN PAPA STOPS FOR A BREATH I LISTEN TO	JOHNNY	TALKING. /LORD SUMMERHAYS/ YOU MAKE ME FEEL VERY
MIS. SD(109)	MISALLIANCE.	JOHNNY	TARLETON, AN ORDINARY YOUNG BUSINESS MAN OF THIRTY OR
MIS. (124)	DRIVE ME MAD: YOU KNOW VERY WELL HES A FOOL: EVEN	JOHNNY	THINKS HIM A FOOL. /MRS TARLETON/ (UP IN ARMS AT
MIS. (191)	CONSEQUENCES OF THIS DEFIANCE, WHICH HAS PROVOKED	JOHNNY	TO AN IMPATIENT MOVEMENT TOWARDS HIM). /HYPATIA/
MIS. SD(150)	HYPATIA BETWEEN PERCIVAL AND BENTLEY, AND	JOHNNY	TO BENTLEY'S RIGHT. /TARLETON/ JUST DISCUSSING YOUR
MIS. (202)	OF MY BODY AND SOUL. AND SO YOU MAY TELL YOUR	JOHNNY	TO BUY AN ENGLISHWOMAN: HE SHALL NOT BUY LINA
MIS. (119)	SOME YELLING -- /BENTLEY/ I SHOULD THINK YOU DID.	JOHNNY	WAS RATHER ROUGH ON ME, THOUGH. HE TOLD ME NOBODY

DEVL III	(50)	GENERAL BURGOYNE'S JUST ARRIVED-- GENTLEMANLY	JOHNNY	WE CALL HIM, SIR-- AND HE WONT HAVE DONE FINDING
MIS.	(129)	YOURE RIGHT, CHICKABIDDY. WHAT DO I TELL	JOHNNY	WHEN HE BRAGS ABOUT TARLETON'S UNDERWEAR? IT'S NOT
MIS.	(115)	PUT HIM INTO A CHAIR): THERE! THERE! THERE!	JOHNNY	WILL GO FOR THE DOCTOR; AND HE'LL GIVE YOU SOMETHING
MIS.	(134)	ALL, THE LAD CANT HELP IT; BUT IVE NEVER THOUGHT	JOHNNY	WORTH TUPPENCE AS A MAN OF BUSINESS. /JOHNNY/ (
MIS.	(202)	IS THAT SO? /HYPATIA/ THE CAT'S OUT OF THE BAG,	JOHNNY	, ABOUT EVERYBODY. THEY WERE ALL BEFOREHAND WITH YOU:
CAPT II	(251)	ME HER HAND. /JOHNSON/ YES; AND YOU TOOK IT TOO,	JOHNNY	, DIDNT YOU? /BRASSBOUND/ TAKE HORSE, THEN; AND RIDE
MIS.	(111)	THOUGH IT'S QUITE NATURAL TO HEAR ME CALLING YOU	JOHNNY	, IT SOUNDS RIDICULOUS AND UNBECOMING FOR YOU TO CALL
MIS.	SD(116)	DOOR TO COCK A SNOOK AT JOHNNY AS HE GOES OUT.	JOHNNY	, LEFT ALONE, CLENCHES HIS FISTS AND GRINDS HIS
MIS.	(119)	SILLY ASS OF MYSELF HERE. I'M AWFULLY SORRY,	JOHNNY	, OLD CHAP; I BEG YOUR PARDON. WHY DONT YOU KICK ME
MIS.	SD(109)	HOUSE IS IN SURREY, ON THE SLOPE OF HINDHEAD; AND	JOHNNY	, RECLINING, NOVEL IN HAND, IN A SWINGING CHAIR WITH
MIS.	(184)	TO THE PAVILION, AND EXCHANGES GRIMACES WITH	JOHNNY	, SHAMELESSLY ENJOYING PERCIVAL'S SUDDEN REVERSE.
DEVL III	(60)	WITH EXTREME SUAVITY) I BELIEVE I AM GENTLEMANLY	JOHNNY	, SIR, AT YOUR SERVICE. MY MORE INTIMATE FRIENDS CALL
CAPT II	(264)	/BRASSBOUND/ WELL, REDBROOK. /REDBROOK/ NOT THIS	JOHNNY	, THANK YOU. HAVNT CHARACTER ENOUGH. /BRASSBOUND/
MIS.	(202)	TO GO, BUT IS FACED IN THE PAVILION DOORWAY BY	JOHNNY	, WHO COMES IN SLOWLY, HIS HANDS IN HIS POCKETS,
MIS.	(116)	HESITATE: IT'S AN UGLY THING. SMASH IT: HARD. (	JOHNNY	, WITH A STIFLED YELL, DASHES IT IN PIECES, AND THEN
MIS.	(117)	OF THE PUNCHBOWL IN THE WASTEPAPER BASKET WHILST	JOHNNY	, WITH DIMINISHING DIFFICULTY, COLLECTS HIMSELF).
MIS.	(134)	HEAR! /MRS TARLETON/ FANCY YOU WRITING A BOOK,	JOHNNY	! DO YOU THINK HE COULD, LORD SUMMERHAYS? /LORD
MIS.	(201)	THE HEALTH; BUT IT IS NOT DISHONORABLE. BUT YOUR	JOHNNY	! OH, YOUR JOHNNY! WITH HIS MARRIAGE. HE WILL DO
MIS.	(201)	IS NOT DISHONORABLE. BUT YOUR JOHNNY! OH, YOUR	JOHNNY	! WITH HIS MARRIAGE. HE WILL DO THE STRAIGHT THING
			JOHNNY'S	
MIS.	(135)	THAN LAST YEAR, I COULD ASK HER TO LET ME CHANCE	JOHNNY'S	AND HYPATIA'S FUTURE BY GOING INTO LITERATURE. BUT
MIS.	(124)	BEGIN ABOUT MY JOHNNY. YOU KNOW IT ANNOYS ME.	JOHNNY'S	AS CLEVER AS ANYBODY ELSE IN HIS OWN WAY. I DONT
MIS.	(115)	YOU AS GOOD A HIDING AS EVER -- /BENTLEY/ HELP!	JOHNNY'S	BEATING ME! OH! MURDER! (HE THROWS HIMSELF ON
MIS.	(157)	VERSION BIBLE, AND THE DOVES PRESS BIBLE, AND	JOHNNY'S	BIBLE AND BOBBY'S BIBLE AND PATSY'S BIBLE AND THE
MIS.	(116)	/HYPATIA/ (ANGRILY) I DO DECLARE, MAMMA, THAT	JOHNNY'S	BRUTALITY MAKES IT IMPOSSIBLE TO LIVE IN THE HOUSE
MIS.	(116)	BETWEEN MY MOTHER AND ME; D'Y' HEAR? /HYPATIA/	JOHNNY'S	LOST HIS TEMPER, MOTHER. WE'D BETTER GO. COME,
MIS.	(124)	I SAY NOTHING AGAINST YOUR DARLING: WE ALL KNOW	JOHNNY'S	PERFECTION. /MRS TARLETON/ DONT BE CROSS, DEARIE.
MIS.	SD(109)	IN THE CENTRE OF THE WALL. THERE IS MORE WALL TO	JOHNNY'S	RIGHT THAN TO HIS LEFT; AND THIS SPACE IS OCCUPIED
MIS.	(110)	(HE THROWS HIMSELF INTO THE WICKER CHAIR ON	JOHNNY'S	RIGHT). /JOHNNY/ (STRAIGHTENING UP IN THE SWING
			JOHN'S	
LION PREFACE	(41)	OF FIRST QUOTATIONS MAY SAY WHAT THEY PLEASE:	JOHN'S	CLAIM TO GIVE EVIDENCE AS AN EYEWITNESS WHILST THE
LION PREFACE	(32)	BY MATTHEW AND LUKE; TO BE DESCENDED. HE DESCRIBES	JOHN'S	DOCTRINE AS " BAPTISM OF REPENTANCE UNTO REMISSION OF
LION PREFACE	(48)	EXCEPT AS SIGHTSEERS, WILL REVEL IN PARTS OF	JOHN'S	GOSPEL WHICH MEAN NOTHING TO A PIOUS MATTER-OF-FACT
LION PREFACE	(21)	AND ORTHODOXY. HE THEN BEGAN PREACHING	JOHN'S	GOSPEL, WHICH, APART FROM THE HERESY OF BAPTISM, THE
LION PREFACE	(41)	OF JESUS. IN SPITE OF THE SUSPICIONS ROUSED BY	JOHN'S	IDIOSYNCRASIES, HIS NARRATIVE IS OF ENORMOUS
FANY I	(282)	OF MY OWN; AND I CANT GET IT AT PERRY AND	JOHN'S	. /DORA/ KNAGG AND PANTLE'S: ONE AND FOURPENCE. IT'S
LION PREFACE	(22)	AN ITINERANT PREACHER, HE DEPARTED WIDELY FROM	JOHN'S	MANNER OF LIFE. JOHN WENT INTO THE WILDERNESS, NOT
LION PREFACE	(40)	SITUATION BY SO OUTRAGEOUS A PRETENSION. ALSO,	JOHN'S	NARRATIVE IS IN MANY PASSAGES NEARER TO THE REALITIES
JOAN 4	(99)	WITCHCRAFT? /WARWICK/ YOU WILL FORGIVE MESSIRE	JOHN'S	VEHEMENCE, MY LORD; BUT HE HAS PUT OUR CASE. DUNOIS
			JOHNSON	
CAPT II	(252)	TELL HIM WHAT YOU HAVE SEEN HERE. THAT IS ALL.	JOHNSON	: GIVE HIM A DOLLAR; AND NOTE THE HOUR OF HIS GOING,
CAPT III	(292)	PORTMANTEAU, AND PUT IT ABOARD THE YACHT FOR HER.	JOHNSON	: YOU TAKE ALL HANDS ABOARD THE THANKSGIVING; LOOK
CAPT II	(249)	WHAT HAS SHE BEEN FIXING UP IN THERE,	JOHNSON	? /JOHNSON/ WELL: MARZO'S IN YOUR BED. LADY WANTS
CAPT II	(247)	CAREFULLY. WHERE IS THAT TRULY GENTLEMANLY MR	JOHNSON	? -- OH, THERE YOU ARE, MR JOHNSON. (SHE RUNS TO
MIS. PREFACE	(21)	I ESCAPED SQUEERS AND CREAKLE JUST AS I ESCAPED	JOHNSON	AND CARLYLE. AND THIS IS WHAT HAPPENS TO MOST OF US.
CAPT II	(247)	GOES TOO). NOW, COUNT MARZO. (MARZO GROANS AS	JOHNSON	AND REDBROOK RAISE HIM). /LADY CICELY/ NOW THEYRE
CAPT II	SD(248)	/DRINKWATER/ EAH, EAH! LADY CICELY RETURNS WITH	JOHNSON	AND REDBROOK. SHE CARRIES A JAR. /LADY CICELY/ (
CAPT II	SD(257)	SIR HOWARD GOES OUT THROUGH THE ARCH BETWEEN	JOHNSON	AND REDBROOK, MUTTERING WRATHFULLY. THE REST, EXCEPT
CAPT II	(265)	NOW THEN, DO YOU UNDERSTAND PLAIN ENGLISH?	JOHNSON	AND REDBROOK: TAKE WHAT MEN YOU WANT AND OPEN THE
DOCT PREFACE	(31)	ASSURING YOU THAT PEOPLE LIKE SHAKESPEAR AND DR	JOHNSON	AND RUSKIN AND MARK TWAIN ARE IGNORANT
3PLA PREFACE	(R33)	LIMITED AS NOT TO INCLUDE EVEN THE PREFACES OF DR	JOHNSON	AND THE UTTERANCES OF NAPOLEON. I HAVE MERELY
CAPT II	(251)	(GRIMLY) MUCH GOOD MAY IT DO YOU! (	JOHNSON	COMES IN THROUGH THE ARCH). WHERE IS OSMAN, THE
MIS. PREFACE	(21)	LIFE TRIFLING WITH LITERARY FOOLS IN TAVERNS AS	JOHNSON	DID WHEN HE SHOULD HAVE BEEN SHAKING ENGLAND WITH
CAPT II	(252)	MASTER'S WORD ERE I GO OUT FROM HIS PRESENCE, O	JOHNSON	EL HULL. /JOHNSON/ HE WANTS THE DOLLAR. BRASSBOUND
CAPT II	SD(246)	TO A GENLMN. BRASSBOUND IS ABOUT TO ASK	JOHNSON	FOR AN EXPLANATION, WHEN LADY CICELY RETURNS THROUGH
CAPT II	(245)	O WUST COWST CAZHLS (CASUAL WARD PAUPERS)? (	JOHNSON	IS SCANDALIZED; AND THERE IS A GENERAL THRILL OF
INCA	(252)	THE ABILITIES OF CHIPS AND THE PIFFLER AND JACK	JOHNSON	, I BELIEVE IN INDIVIDUAL GENIUS. THAT IS THE INCA'S
CAPT II	(253)	IS A CASE OF SEWING MATERIALS. /LADY CICELY/ MR	JOHNSON	. (HE TURNS). IVE GOT MARZO TO SLEEP. WOULD YOU
CAPT II	(247)	GENTLEMANLY MR JOHNSON? -- OH, THERE YOU ARE, MR	JOHNSON	. (SHE RUNS TO JOHNSON, PAST BRASSBOUND, WHO HAS TO
CAPT III	(283)	WITH THE REST. (BRASSBOUND JOINS REDBROOK AND	JOHNSON	. KEARNEY SITS DOWN AGAIN, AFTER INVITING LADY
CAPT II	(243)	NAMED-- AS IT AFTERWARDS APPEARS--	JOHNSON	. LADY CICELY WALKS BESIDE MARZO. REDBROOK, A LITTLE
CAPT II	(264)	/BRASSBOUND/ YOURE WASTING YOUR FIVE MINUTES. TRY	JOHNSON	. /JOHNSON/ NO. I HAVNT THE HEAD FOR IT.
CAPT II	(251)	HIM) I WILL ATTEND TO YOU PRESENTLY. (CALLING)	JOHNSON	. SEND ME JOHNSON THERE. AND OSMAN. (HE PULLS OFF
CAPT II	(263)	TALKS STRAIGHT SENSE. /REDBROOK/ RIGHTO, BROTHER	JOHNSON	(TO BRASSBOUND) WONT DO, GOVERNOR. NOT GOOD ENOUGH.
ANNA PREFACE	(287)	AS MRS SIDDONS, SIR JOSHUA REYNOLDS, AND DR	JOHNSON	MIGHT HAVE UNBENT, TO DEVISE A " TURN" FOR THE
CAPT II	SD(252)	KNOWS IT HIMSELF. I SHALL NOT LOSE SIGHT OF IT.	JOHNSON	NODS GRAVELY, AND IS GOING OUT WHEN LADY CICELY
CAPT II	(245)	WITH ALL SORTS. MY FATHER, SIR, WAS CAPN	JOHNSON	O HULL-- OWNED HIS OWN SCHOONER, SIR. WE'RE MOSTLY
CAPT II	SD(244)	THE WALL CLOSE TO THE LITTLE DOOR. HE GROANS.	JOHNSON	PHLEGMATICALLY LEAVES HIM AND JOINS REDBROOK. /LADY
UNPL PREFACE	(R9)	THOSE OF THE CONFESSOR. GARRICK, HAD HE CALLED DR	JOHNSON	PUNCH, WOULD HAVE SPOKEN PROFOUNDLY AND WITTILY;
CAPT II	(251)	ALI (OSMAN COMES FORWARD BETWEEN BRASSBOUND AND	JOHNSON	): YOU HAVE SEEN THIS UNBELIEVER (INDICATING SIR
CAPT II	(252)	HE GOES OUT THROUGH THE ARCH). /BRASSBOUND/ (TO	JOHNSON	) KEEP THE MEN OUT OF THIS UNTIL THE SHEIKH COMES. I
ROCK I	(200)	WHETHER JAMESON OR THOMPSON WAS RIGHT ABOUT WHAT	JOHNSON	SAID IN THE CABINET! /HILDA/ TEN YEARS AGO. /SIR
CAPT III	SD(282)	SMIRK A CHEERFUL CONFIDENCE IN HIS INNOCENCE.	JOHNSON	SOLID AND INEXPRESSIVE, REDBROOK UNCONCERNED AND
INCA	(249)	PONGO AND THE CORSAIR AND THE PIFFLER AND JACK	JOHNSON	THE SECOND, ALL UNMARRIED, AT LEAST NOT SERIOUSLY
CAPT II	(251)	TO YOU PRESENTLY. (CALLING) JOHNSON. SEND ME	JOHNSON	THERE. AND OSMAN. (HE PULLS OFF HIS COAT AND THROWS
3PLA PREFACE	(R33)	LEARNT TO READ. HIS GENUINE CRITICS, FROM BEN	JOHNSON	TO MR FRANK HARRIS, HAVE ALWAYS KEPT AS FAR ON THIS
DOCT PREFACE	(30)	ITS CRUDE RASCALITY. FROM SHAKESPEAR AND DR	JOHNSON	TO RUSKIN AND MARK TWAIN, THE NATURAL ABHORRENCE OF
CAPT II	(247)	QUESTION) CARDS AND DRINK, LADY SIS. (HE FOLLOWS	JOHNSON	TO THE PATIENT. LADY CICELY GOES TOO). NOW, COUNT
INCA	(250)	WRITES PLAYS, AND PAINTS MOST ABOMINABLY. JACK	JOHNSON	TRIMS LADIES' HATS, AND BOXES WITH PROFESSIONALS
MIS. PREFACE	(20)	WRATH. NO WONDER MEN OF DOWNRIGHT SENSE, LIKE DR	JOHNSON	, ADMIT THAT UNDER SUCH CIRCUMSTANCES CHILDREN WILL
PRES PREFACE	(130)	ADDRESSED AND DESCRIBED AS GENERAL BONES AND MR	JOHNSON	, AND BY NO MEANS AS GENERAL MITCHENER AND MR
CAPT III	(292)	OWN TROUSERS). /REDBROOK/ (SOFTLY) LOOK HERE,	JOHNSON	, AND GENTS GENERALLY. (THEY GATHER ABOUT HIM).
DOCT PREFACE	(35)	A GOOD FRIEND, MAY SAY YES, THOUGH SHAKESPEAR, DR	JOHNSON	, AND THEIR LIKE MAY SAY NO. BUT EVEN THOSE WHO SAY
CAPT II	(252)	HOWARD SPEAKS). /SIR HOWARD/ YOU KNOW ALSO, MR	JOHNSON	, I HOPE, THAT YOU CAN DEPEND ON ME. /JOHNSON/ (
SUPR PREFACE	(R31)	AS THE DRAMATISTS WHO INVENTED SOCRATES AND DR	JOHNSON	, IMPRESS ME MORE DEEPLY THAN THE ROMANTIC
UNPL PREFACE	(R9)	HAVE SPOKEN PROFOUNDLY AND WITTILY; WHEREAS DR	JOHNSON	, IN HURLING THAT EPITHET AT HIM, WAS BUT PICKING UP
CAPT II	(247)	OH, THERE YOU ARE, MR JOHNSON. (SHE RUNS TO	JOHNSON	, PAST BRASSBOUND, WHO HAS TO STEP BACK HASTILY OUT
CAPT II	SD(257)	ME, SIR. YOU ARE A RASCAL. YOU ARE A RASCAL.	JOHNSON	, REDBROOK, AND A FEW OTHERS COME IN THROUGH THE
CAPT II	(263)	EVENTS. (SHE GOES OUT THROUGH THE LITTLE DOOR.	JOHNSON	, REDBROOK, AND THE REST COME IN THROUGH THE ARCH,
CAPT II	SD(266)	IN MOGADOR AWBR, AWD PUT A BIT ON IT, AW WOULD.	JOHNSON	, REDBROOK, AND THE OTHERS RETURN, RATHER
LION PREFACE	(56)	MR HORATIO BOTTOMLEY, SHAKESPEAR, MR JACK	JOHNSON	, SIR ISAAC NEWTON, PALESTRINA, OFFENBACH, SIR
CAPT II	(263)	VERY CRUSTY AND DETERMINED. HE KEEPS CLOSE TO	JOHNSON	, WHO COMES TO BRASSBOUND'S RIGHT, REDBROOK TAKING
CAPT II	(245)	QUIETLY, AND TAKING REFUGE BETWEEN REDBROOK AND	JOHNSON	, WHOM HE ADDRESSES) CAN YOU FIND ME A MORE PRIVATE
CAPT II	(257)	BE PAID IN FALSE COIN. (CALLING) HALLO THERE!	JOHNSON	! REDBROOK! SOME OF YOU THERE! (TO SIR HOWARD)
			JOHNSON'S	
MIS. PREFACE	(68)	OFF, CREATES AN IMPRESSION THAT IF WE ONLY TAKE	JOHNSON'S	ADVICE TO FREE OUR MINDS FROM CANT, WE CAN ACHIEVE
MIS. PREFACE	(21)	ENOUGH TO FORCE HIM TO LAME HIS MIND -- FOR	JOHNSON'S	GREAT MIND WAS LAMED -- BY LEARNING HIS LESSONS,
METH PREFACE	(R84)	" CHASTENING MORALS BY RIDICULE," BUT, IN	JOHNSON'S	PHRASE, CLEARING OUR MINDS OF CANT, AND THEREBY
MIS. PREFACE	(20)	BUT THEN I DID NOT LEARN ANYTHING AT SCHOOL. DR	JOHNSON'S	SCHOOLMASTER PRESUMABLY DID CARE ENOUGH WHETHER
MILL PREFACE	(132)	IS NOT ONLY THE LAST REFUGE OF A SCOUNDREL IN DR	JOHNSON'S	SENSE, IT IS FAR MORE DANGEROUSLY THE EVERYDAY
			JOHNSWORT	
MTH1 I	SD(3)	NEAR HER HEAD A LOW ROCK SHEWS ABOVE THE	JOHNSWORT	. THE ROCK AND TREE ARE ON THE BORDER OF A GLADE

MTH1 I SD(3)	SLEEPING WITH HER HEAD BURIED IN A THICK BED OF	JOHNSWORT	, AND HER BODY COILED IN APPARENTLY ENDLESS RINGS
MTH1 I SD(6)	COLORS. SHE REARS HER HEAD SLOWLY FROM THE BED OF	JOHNSWORT	, AND SPEAKS INTO EVE'S EAR IN A STRANGE

JOIN

PHIL II (99)	TO CONSULT YOU ABOUT. DO YOU THINK I OUGHT TO	JOIN	? /CUTHBERTSON/ WELL, IF YOU HAVE NO CONSCIENTIOUS
PHIL I (89)	US, CRAVEN. LET ME PUT YOU UP. /CRAVEN/ WHAT!	JOIN	A CLUB WHERE THERES SOME SCOUNDREL WHO GUARANTEED MY
WIDO I (19)	PRAY DO SO. (HE GRACIOUSLY WAVES HIM OFF TO	JOIN	BLANCHE. TRENCH HURRIES AFTER HER THROUGH THE GATE. THE
BULL I (91)	MY BUSINESS AND YOURS AS CIVIL ENGINEERS IS TO	JOIN	COUNTRIES, NOT TO SEPARATE THEM. THE ONE REAL POLITICAL
NEVR III SD(274)	LOOKS ROUND TO SEE WHERE SHE IS, AND IS GOING TO	JOIN	HER AT THE WINDOW WHEN GLORIA COMES DOWN TO MEET HER
APPL I SD(225)	KEEP HIS COUNTENANCE. THE OTHERS ARE BEGINNING TO	JOIN	IN THE CHORUS WHEN PROTEUS RISES IN A FURY. /PROTEUS/
GENV IV (91)	IS A LEAGUE OF FOOLS; THEREFORE THE WISE MUST	JOIN	IT TO WATCH THEM. THAT IS WHY ALL THE EFFECTIVE POWERS
BULL IV (180)	A FEW MEN LIKE MR KEEGAN, I SHOULD CERTAINLY	JOIN	IT. /KEEGAN/ YOU DO ME TOO MUCH HONOR, SIR. (WITH
JOAN PREFACE(36)	WHICH MAKE IT SO DIFFICULT FOR A FREETHINKER TO	JOIN	IT; AND A CHURCH WHICH HAS NO PLACE FOR FREETHINKERS:
GENV III (85)	EVENING? IF NOT, I SHOULD BE GLAD IF YOU WOULD	JOIN	ME AT DINNER. I WANT TO TALK TO YOU ABOUT THIS FUNNY
MTH3 (134)	/THE NEGRESS/ FISHGUARD BAY. WHY NOT RUN OVER AND	JOIN	ME FOR THE AFTERNOON? I AM DISPOSED TO BE APPROACHABLE
SIM II (83)	NOBODY BUT A FOOL WOULD BE FRIVOLOUS ENOUGH TO	JOIN	ME IN DOING ALL THE MAD THINGS I WANTED TO DO. AND NO
WIDO III (58)	YES. AND REMEMBER, BLANCHE: IF HE CONSENTS TO	JOIN	ME IN THE SCHEME, I SHALL HAVE TO BE FRIENDS WITH HIM.
SUPR III (101)	/THE DEVIL/ YES: THE SOUTHERNERS GIVE IT UP AND	JOIN	ME JUST AS YOU HAVE DONE. BUT THE ENGLISH REALLY DO NOT
MIS. (198)	(COMING BETWEEN THEM) LORD SUMMERHAYS: YOULL	JOIN	ME, I'M SURE, IN POINTING OUT TO BOTH FATHER AND
PHIL I (87)	BACK TO THE FIRE). /CHARTERIS/ PERSUADE HIM TO	JOIN	OUR CLUB, CUTHBERTSON. HE MOPES. /JULIA/ IT'S NO USE.
PHIL I (87)	IT'S NO USE. SYLVIA AND I ARE ALWAYS AT HIM TO	JOIN	; BUT HE WONT. /CRAVEN/ MY CHILD: I HAVE MY OWN CLUB.
BASH III (119)	A SIMPLE MAID; AND BOTH HAVE CRAVED A HOLIDAY TO	JOIN	SOME LOCAL FESTIVAL. BUT, SIR, YOUR HELMET PROCLAIMS
BULL PREFACE(50)	REFUSE OF POLITICAL AND DIPLOMATIC LIFE, WHO	JOIN	THE ARMY AND PAY FOR THEIR POSITIONS IN THE MORE OR
2TRU III (98)	SINCE I CAME HERE I HAVE BEEN WANTING TO	JOIN	THE ARMY, LIKE JOAN OF ARC. IT'S A BROTHERHOOD, OF A
FABL PREFACE(81)	FROM BROWNING AND THE HYMNS WERE ASPIRATIONS TO "	JOIN	THE CHOIR INVISIBLE." LATER ON, WHEN I ATTENDED A
PHIL II (99)	ME TO BE ALWAYS HERE. THEYRE AT ME EVERY DAY TO	JOIN	THE CLUB. TO STOP MY GRUMBLING, I SUPPOSE. THATS WHAT I
BARB III (339)	WITH A DUCHESS AT A PRIMROSE LEAGUE MEETING, AND	JOIN	THE CONSERVATIVE PARTY. /BARBARA/ AND WILL HE BE THE
JOAN 1 (64)	COMMONSENSE? IF WE HAD ANY COMMONSENSE WE SHOULD	JOIN	THE DUKE OF BURGUNDY AND THE ENGLISH KING. THEY HOLD
HART III (133)	THE PRIME MINISTER OF THIS COUNTRY ASKED ME TO	JOIN	THE GOVERNMENT WITHOUT EVEN GOING THROUGH THE NONSENSE
MTH4 II (190)	WE SHALL ARRANGE ALL THAT. NEVER MIND HOW. LET US	JOIN	THE LADIES. /THE ELDERLY GENTLEMAN/ (THROWING OFF HIS
BASH II,2, (117)	THE JOY OF BATTLE SURGES BOILING UP AND BIDS ME	JOIN	THE MELLAY. ISANDHLANA AND VICTORY! (HE FALLS ON THE
FANY II (292)	I WOULD GIVE ANYTHING FOR A DANCE. I LONGED TO	JOIN	THE PEOPLE ON THE STAGE AND DANCE WITH THEM: ONE OF
CLEO PRO2 (96)	DESIRE TO BRING THEMSELVES INTO NOTICE. (THEY	JOIN	THE REST AT THE GATE.) /THE SENTINEL/ PASS, O YOUNG
LION PREFACE(75)	IF THEY DID NOT REPENT: THAT IS, IF THEY DID NOT	JOIN	THE SECT WHICH THE APOSTLES WERE NOW FORMING. A QUITE
MIS. (171)	CLERKING IS THE VERY WORST. /TARLETON/ WHY NOT	JOIN	THE TERRITORIALS? /THE MAN/ BECAUSE THE BOSS WONT LET
O'FL (218)	/O'FLAHERTY/ (SARCASTIC) MAYBE YOUD HAVE ME	JOIN	THE TURKISH ARMY, AND WORSHIP THE HEATHEN MAHOMET THAT
GENV II (50)	OF THE NEW BRITISH FEDERATION. SOUTH AFRICA MAY	JOIN	THEM AT ANY MOMENT. /BEGONIA/ (FLUSHING WITH
NEVR II (246)	MR VALENTINE, NOT CLANDON. DO YOU WISH TO	JOIN	THEM IN INSULTING ME? /VALENTINE/ (IGNORING HIM) I'M
ROCK II (284)	HYSTERICAL) OH, MY GOD! I WILL GO OUT AND	JOIN	THEM (SHE RUSHES OUT THROUGH THE MAIN DOOR). /LADY
APPL I (221)	LAUGH UPROARIOUSLY AT THIS. /BOANERGES/ I MUST	JOIN	THEM THERE, SIR. I AM AS MUCH AGAINST CHOCOLATE CREAMS
2TRU III (97)	BELIEVE. WOMEN HAVE TO SET THEMSELVES APART TO	JOIN	THEM. I DONT WANT TO SET MYSELF APART. I WANT TO HAVE
FANY EPIL,SD(335)	THE COUNT, SAVOYARD, THE CRITICS, AND FANNY	JOIN	THEM, SHAKING HANDS AND CONGRATULATING. /THE COUNT/
FABL PREFACE(73)	SNAPPED WE DID NOT PICK UP THE SOUND LINKS AND	JOIN	THEM, WE THREW THE CHAIN AWAY AS IF ALL ITS LINKS HAD
GETT (325)	WHAT WE ARE DISCUSSING. WILL YOU BE SO GOOD AS TO	JOIN	US AND ALLOW US THE BENEFIT OF YOUR WISDOM AND
PHIL II (104)	MISS CRAVEN. (THEY SHAKE HANDS). WONT YOU	JOIN	US AT LUNCH? PARAMORE'S COMING TOO. /JULIA/ THANKS: I
WIDO II (38)	THE DOOR, AND CALLS) MR COKANE: WILL YOU KINDLY	JOIN	US HERE. /COKANE/ (IN THE CONSERVATORY) COMING, MY
PHIL II (97)	COMING TO LUNCH WITH ME AND CHARTERIS. YOU MIGHT	JOIN	US IF YOUVE NOTHING BETTER TO DO, WHEN YOUVE FINISHED
LION I (114)	/LAVINIA/ CAPTAIN: IS THIS MAN WHO IS TO	JOIN	US THE FAMOUS FERROVIUS, WHO HAS MADE SUCH WONDERFUL
BARB II (298)	MAN THAT HIT ME. OH, I HOPE HE'S COMING BACK TO	JOIN	US. BILL WALKER, WITH FROST ON HIS JACKET, COMES
LION I (121)	DEAL IN WHAT YOU SAY. /FERROVIUS/ (RADIANT)	JOIN	US. COME TO THE LIONS. COME TO SUFFERING AND DEATH.
PHIL I (89)	(RISING) NO: HE'S ENGAGED TO ME. BUT YOU CAN	JOIN	US. /CHARTERIS/ WHAT HOUR? /CUTHBERTSON/ ANY TIME
2TRU I (42)	FOR US TWO WEAKLINGS-- IF I CAN PERSUADE HER TO	JOIN	US. /THE NURSE/ JOIN US! WHAT DO YOU MEAN? /THE
SUPR III (98)	SENT TO HEAVEN. /THE DEVIL/ WHY, SIR, DO YOU NOT	JOIN	US, AND LEAVE A SPHERE FOR WHICH YOUR TEMPERAMENT IS
GETT (340)	AT THE STUDY DOOR). MRS COLLINS WISHES YOU TO	JOIN	US, ANTHONY. SOAMES LOOKS PUZZLED. /MRS GEORGE/ YOU
PHIL I (89)	FOR ALL THE SHADY CHARACTERS IN LONDON. BETTER	JOIN	US, CRAVEN. LET ME PUT YOU UP. /CRAVEN/ WHAT! JOIN A
BUOY III (42)	SOUL. /SIR F./ IN WHAT CAPACITY DO YOU CLAIM TO	JOIN	US, MAY I ASK? /HE/ ONLY IN PURSUIT OF OLD BILL
GETT (311)	STUDY). /THE BISHOP/ (TO HIS WIFE) COAX HIM TO	JOIN	US, MY LOVE. (MRS BRIDGENORTH GOES INTO THE STUDY).
2TRU I (42)	IF I CAN PERSUADE HER TO JOIN US. /THE NURSE/	JOIN	US! WHAT DO YOU MEAN? /THE BURGLAR/ SHSHSHSHSH. NOT
SUPR III (139)	TAKES HIS ARM AND COAXES HIM AWAY TO THE HILL TO	JOIN	VIOLET AND HECTOR. OCTAVIUS FOLLOWS HER, DOG-LIKE).
HART III (139)	BEAUTIFUL NIGHT TOO. I JUST HAD TO COME DOWN AND	JOIN	YOU ALL. WHAT HAS IT ALL BEEN ABOUT? /MRS HUSHABYE/
MRS I (194)	LOOK HERE, PRAED: YOUD BETTER GO IN TO TEA. I'LL	JOIN	YOU DIRECTLY. /PRAED/ VERY GOOD. (HE GOES INTO THE
MRS III (230)	/VIVIE/ AND THIS IS THE BUSINESS YOU INVITE ME TO	JOIN	YOU IN? /CROFTS/ OH NO. MY WIFE SHANT BE TROUBLED WITH
SUPR IV (153)	YOU A ROOM OVERLOOKING THE GARDEN FOR ME? I'LL	JOIN	YOU IN HALF AN HOUR. /HECTOR/ VERY WELL. YOULL DINE
HART II (105)	SEND ME ITS LATITUDE AND LONGITUDE; AND I WILL	JOIN	YOU THERE. /LADY UTTERWORD/ YOU WILL CERTAINLY NOT BE
MTH4 I (173)	COME. IT IS JUST SIXTEEN O'CLOCK; AND YOU HAVE TO	JOIN	YOUR PARTY AT HALF-PAST IN THE TEMPLE IN GALWAY. /THE
PHIL II (99)	(RISING) DO YOU KNOW, IVE A GREAT MIND TO	JOIN	, JUST TO SEE WHAT IT'S LIKE. /CHARTERIS/ (COMING
BARB PREFACE(239)	FACE OF THE EARTH; AND IF ANY STATE REFUSES TO	JOIN	, MAKE WAR ON IT. THIS TIME THE LEADING LONDON

JOINED

GENV PREFACE(18)	CELLAR ORATOR WHO COULD HOLD HIS AUDIENCE. HE	JOINED	A CELLAR DEBATING SOCIETY (LIKE OUR OLD COGER'S
GENV I (42)	IN MY HOUSEHOLD! AND MY GRANDSON AT OXFORD HAS	JOINED	A COMMUNIST CLUB. THE UNION-- THE OXFORD UNION-- HAS
WIDO III (62)	I HOPED FOR SOME TIME THAT OUR INTERESTS MIGHT BE	JOINED	BY CLOSER TIES EVEN THAN THOSE OF FRIENDSHIP.
MTH2 SD(55)	SLIP AWAY TO THE SETTEE, WHERE SHE IS STEALTHILY	JOINED	BY HASLAM, WHO SITS DOWN ON HER LEFT. /LUBIN/ (
GETT (303)	THE HISTORY OF ANCIENT ROME REPEATED. WE SHALL BE	JOINED	BY OUR SOLICITORS FOR SEVEN, FOURTEEN, OR TWENTY-ONE
MTH2 SD(47)	WINDOW SEAT AT THE OTHER SIDE OF THE ROOM, AND IS	JOINED	BY SAVVY. THEY SIT THERE, SIDE BY SIDE, HUNCHED UP
SUPR IV (153)	(HE WAVES HIS HAND TO ANN, WHO HAS NOW BEEN	JOINED	BY TANNER, OCTAVIUS, AND RAMSDEN IN THE GARDEN, AND
6CAL SD(96)	BEHIND THE CHAIR OF STATE, WHERE THEY ARE	JOINED	BY THE BLACK PRINCE, WHO STANDS AT THE KING'S RIGHT
GENV PREFACE(21)	THE NEAR WEST ROSE UP AGAINST HIM, AND WAS	JOINED	BY THE MIGHTY FAR WEST OF AMERICA. AFTER TWELVE YEARS
GENV PREFACE(20)	AGAINST SOVIET COMMUNISM HE WOULD FINALLY BE	JOINED	BY THE WHOLE CAPITALIST WEST. BUT THE CAPITALIST WEST
DOCT II (122)	YOU? /SCHUTZMACHER/ WELL, THE FACT IS, WHEN I	JOINED	DUBEDAT AFTER HIS CONVERSATION WITH MR WALPOLE, HE
BULL PREFACE(52)	OTHER OFFICERS, SEEING THEIR FRIEND IN TROUBLE,	JOINED	HIM. ABD-EL-NEBI HIT THE SUPPOSED MURDERER OF HIS
HART III (144)	KNEW MORE THAN MANGAN, MOST OF THEM WOULDNT HAVE	JOINED	IF THEY HAD KNOWN AS MUCH . YOU SEE THEY HAD NEVER
BARB III (313)	EVER REALLY IN EARNEST ABOUT IT? WOULD YOU HAVE	JOINED	IF YOU HAD NEVER SEEN ME? /CUSINS/ (DISINGENUOUSLY)
METH PREFACE(R70)	AND THE OTHER STATES EITHER DID THE SAME OR	JOINED	IN THE FRAY THROUGH COMPULSION, BRIBERY, OR THEIR
APPL PREFACE(181)	EVERYONE WHO SAW THEM DOING IT IMMEDIATELY	JOINED	IN THE RUSH. THEY RAN SIMPLY BECAUSE EVERYONE ELSE
MILL PREFACE(121)	THAT HAS HAPPENED." WHEN THE ITALIAN LIBERALS	JOINED	IN THE SHRIEKING HE SEIZED THE SHRIEKERS AND
FANY II (292)	BUT WE DANCED AND DANCED UNTIL A LOT OF THEM	JOINED	IN. WE GOT QUITE RECKLESS; AND WE HAD CHAMPAGNE AFTER
GENV III (67)	CARRIED OUT. WITH WHAT OTHER OBJECT WOULD WE HAVE	JOINED	IT? /THE SECRETARY/ (DESPERATELY) OH, THERE IS NO
BARB III (336)	THAT I NEVER KNEW WHAT TO DO WITH MYSELF. WHEN I	JOINED	IT, I HAD NOT TIME ENOUGH FOR ALL THE THINGS I HAD TO
AUGS (265)	SPEECH I EVER MADE IN MY LIFE; AND NOT A MAN	JOINED	. /THE CLERK/ WHAT DID YOU EXPECT? YOU TOLD THEM OUR
PHIL II (127)	I'M NOT A WOMANLY WOMAN. I WAS GUARANTEED WHEN I	JOINED	JUST AS YOU WERE. /GRACE/ BY MR CHARTERIS, I THINK.
CLEO PRO2 (100)	LOSE MY BREATH AND BE STABBED IN THE BACK; SO I	JOINED	OUR CAPTAIN AND STOOD. THEN THE ROMANS TREATED US
HART III (144)	DIDNT YOU DO SOMETHING? /MAZZINI/ BUT I DID. I	JOINED	SOCIETIES AND MADE SPEECHES AND WROTE PAMPHLETS. THAT
O'FL PREFACE(202)	AT PRESENT. NO ONE WILL EVER KNOW HOW MANY MEN	JOINED	THE ARMY IN 1914 AND 1915 TO ESCAPE FROM TYRANTS AND
ARMS I (12)	SERVANT TO THE DEATH. I WISH FOR YOUR SAKE I HAD	JOINED	THE BULGARIAN ARMY INSTEAD OF THE OTHER ONE. I AM NOT
PHIL I (87)	CHARTERIS. YOU KNOW VERY WELL THAT THOUGH I	JOINED	THE CLUB ON GRACE'S ACCOUNT, THINKING THAT HER
GENV II (56)	PROCEDURE WAS NEVER CONTEMPLATED WHEN THE POWERS	JOINED	THE LEAGUE? /JUDGE/ I DO NOT THINK ANYTHING WAS
GENV II (56)	THINK ANYTHING WAS CONTEMPLATED WHEN THE POWERS	JOINED	THE LEAGUE. THEY SIGNED THE COVENANT WITHOUT READING
LION EPILOG (150)	DISLIKE HIM, AND SAY THAT HE OUGHT TO HAVE	JOINED	THE METHODISTS, OR HE MAY BE AN ARTIST EXPRESSING
NEVR IV (285)	FIVE SHILLINGS FROM HIM AND GO IN WITH HIM; SO I	JOINED	THE MOB AND LOOKED THROUGH THE RAILINGS UNTIL MISS
ANNA (292)	DASH IT, SIR, OUT WITH IT. /STRAMMFEST/ SHE HAS	JOINED	THE REVOLUTION. /SCHNEIDEKIND/ BUT SO HAVE YOU, SIR.
ANNA (292)	/SCHNEIDEKIND/ BUT SO HAVE YOU, SIR. WEVE ALL	JOINED	THE REVOLUTION. SHE DOESNT MEAN IT ANY MORE THAN WE
BARB III (336)	REALLY MEANS. /BARBARA/ (HYPNOTIZED) BEFORE I	JOINED	THE SALVATION ARMY, I WAS IN MY OWN POWER; AND THE
ARMS I (12)	FIGHTING MERELY AS A PROFESSIONAL SOLDIER. I	JOINED	THE SERBS BECAUSE THEY CAME FIRST ON THE ROAD FROM
LION PREFACE(21)	WELL-TO-DO YOUNG GENTLEMEN FORTY YEARS AGO "	JOINED	THE SOCIALISTS," AS FAR AS ESTABLISHED JEWRY WAS
FANY II (288)	/KNOX AND MRS KNOX/ HOLLOWAY GAOL! /KNOX/ YOUVE	JOINED	THE SUFFRAGETS! /MARGARET/ NO. I WISH I HAD. I COULD
BULL I (90)	GONE MAD? YOU NEVER TOLD ME. /BROADBENT/ HE HAS	JOINED	THE TARIFF REFORM LEAGUE. HE WOULD NEVER HAVE DONE

ANNA (301)	MY FIRST GLIMPSE OF HEAVEN. I RAN AWAY AND	JOINED	THE TROUPE. THEY CAUGHT ME AND DRAGGED ME BACK TO MY
2TRU PREFACE(15)	AND IN DUE TIME THE LAST OF THE CHESTERTONS	JOINED	THIS CATHOLIC CHURCH, LIKE A VERY LARGE SHIP ENTERING
SIM I (45)	YEARS AGO MY WIFE AND I, WITH MR AND MRS HYERING,	JOINED	THIS EASTERN GENTLEMAN AND HIS COLLEAGUE IN A EUGENIC
MTH5 SD(205)	FROM IT INTO THE FOREGROUND; BUT THEY ARE NOT	JOINED	TO IT: THERE IS PLENTY OF SPACE TO PASS BETWEEN THE
CLEO III SD(144)	ON WHICH STANDS A CRESSET BEACON. THE ISLAND IS	JOINED	TO THE MAIN LAND BY THE HEPTASTADIUM, A GREAT MOLE OR
GETT (283)	CLEVER AND MOCK AT YOUR RELIGION. " WHAT GOD HATH	JOINED	TOGETHER LET NOT MAN PUT ASUNDER." REMEMBER THAT.
GETT (283)	/THE BISHOP/ DONT BE AFRAID, BOXER. WHAT GOD HATH	JOINED	TOGETHER NO MAN EVER SHALL PUT ASUNDER: GOD WILL TAKE
MTH4 II (190)	OF LONG LIFE HAVE OCCURRED IN NORTH AMERICA. THEY	JOINED	US HERE; AND THEIR STOCK SOON REVERTED TO THE
GETT (283)	OF THAT. (TO LEO) BY THE WAY, WHO WAS IT THAT	JOINED	YOU AND REGINALD, MY DEAR? /LEO/ IT WAS THAT AWFUL
ANNA (296)	STRAMMFEST CONTINUES IN A FORENSIC MANNER) HE	JOINED	YOU AT THE GOLDEN ANCHOR IN HAKONSBURG. YOU GAVE US
DOCT II (120)	BUT-- WHEN WAS THIS, MAY I ASK? /WALPOLE/ WHEN I	JOINED	YOU THAT TIME DOWN BY THE RIVER. /B.B./ BUT, MY DEAR
GETT (283)	/THE BISHOP/ WELL, WHOM EGERTON FOTHERINGAY HATH	JOINED	, LET SIR GORELL BARNES PUT ASUNDER BY ALL MEANS.
GETT PREFACE(256)	IMAGINE THAT IN THE PHRASE " WHOM GOD HATH	JOINED	," THE WORD GOD MEANS THE DISTRICT REGISTRAR OR THE
BUOY III (38)	SANE. YET WE CAN SAY HONESTLY " WHOM GOD HATH	JOINED	"-- /SIR F./ OH, DO PLEASE LEAVE GOD OUT OF THE

JOINERS

CLEO NOTES (207)	WHETHER SHAKESPEAR THOUGHT THAT ANCIENT ATHENIAN	JOINERS	, WEAVERS, OR BELLOWS MENDERS WERE ANY DIFFERENT

JOINING

ROCK II (234)	HER. /HILDA/ SIR DEXTER RIGHTSIDE. /SIR DEXTER/ (	JOINING	BASHAM ON THE HEARTH) AH! THAT YOU, BASHAM? HAVE
ROCK II (283)	OFFICE AND RUNS TO THE WINDOW. /LADY CHAVENDER/ (	JOINING	HER) WHAT IS GOING ON, HILDA? /HILDA/ THE
MTH1 I (6)	THERE IS SOMETHING UNCANNY ABOUT IT. /EVE/ (	JOINING	HIM) OH! IT IS CHANGING INTO LITTLE WHITE WORMS.
GENV IV (115)	SOLDIERS. /BBDE/ I CANNOT PREVENT HONEST MEN FROM	JOINING	IN A CRUSADE, AS VOLUNTEERS, AGAINST SCOUNDRELS AND
BULL PREFACE(38)	IF HE HAD PLAYED THE GAME OF ENGLAND BY	JOINING	IN ITS CAMPAIGN AGAINST HIS OWN AND HIS COUNTRY'S
OVER PREFACE(155)	TO CONFESS HIS PURSUITS , OR TO REFRAIN FROM	JOINING	IN THE CRY OF STOP THIEF WHEN THE POLICE GET ON THE
HART PREFACE(16)	AS THE ILLITERATE. THE CHRISTIAN PRIEST	JOINING	IN THE WAR DANCE WITHOUT EVEN THROWING OFF HIS
CATH 2 (176)	BABY, BABY, LIT-TLE BA-BY BUMPKINS. /VARINKA/ (	JOINING	IN TO THE SAME DOGGEREL IN CANON, A THIRD ABOVE)
BUOY 1 (9)	IF YOU HAD CHOSEN TO WORK FOR HONORS INSTEAD OF	JOINING	RATHER DISREPUTABLE CLUBS AND WORKING ON YOUR OWN
BARB III (331)	IS TRUE. YOU ACCUSED ME YOURSELF, LADY BRIT, OF	JOINING	THE ARMY TO WORSHIP BARBARA; AND SO I DID. SHE
MIS. PREFACE(94)	CHURCHES IN THE NAME OF CHRIST, A TURKISH CHILD	JOINING	THE CHURCH OF ENGLAND OR AN ENGLISH CHILD FOLLOWING
BUOY 1 (15)	ONLY BLEW UP A FEW OF THEIR OWN PEOPLE FOR NOT	JOINING	THE UNIONS. NO: MANKIND HAS NOT THE NERVE TO GO
HART I (71)	MY HUSBAND BE A HANDSOME MAN? /RANDALL/ (	JOINING	THEM AT THE WINDOW) ONE'S HUSBAND NEVER IS, ARIADNE
JOAN 3 (92)	(HE LOOKS EAGERLY FOR IT UP THE RIVER). /JOAN/ (	JOINING	THEM) OH, A KINGFISHER! WHERE? /THE PAGE/ NO: THE
KING II (232)	OFTEN HAVE YOU ASKED ME TO DO SOME BIG THING LIKE	JOINING	YOUR CHURCH, OR SOME LITTLE THING LIKE PARDONING A

JOINS

CLEO III (163)	STANDING IN TOWARDS US ALREADY. (CAESAR QUICKLY	JOINS	BRITANNUS AT THE PARAPET). /RUFIO/ (TO APOLLODORUS,
CAND I (94)	TO HIM WITH GREAT HEARTINESS, WHILST MORELL	JOINS	CANDIDA AT THE FIRE) GLAD TO MEET YOU, I'M SHORE, MR
SUPR II SD(63)	STROLLS OVER TO INSPECT THE MOTOR CAR. OCTAVIUS	JOINS	HECTOR. /ANN/ (POUNCING ON HER MOTHER JOYOUSLY) OH,
GETT (285)	(RISING) HA! YOU HEAR THAT, LESBIA? (HE	JOINS	HER AT THE GARDEN DOOR). /LESBIA/ THATS ONLY AN
PYGM I (208)	/THE MOTHER/ OH DEAR! (SHE RETIRES SADLY AND	JOINS	HER DAUGHTER). /THE FLOWER GIRL/ (TAKING ADVANTAGE OF
PYGM I (212)	TAKER PRODUCES A WHISTLE). OH, THANK YOU. (SHE	JOINS	HER DAUGHTER). THE NOTE TAKER BLOWS A PIERCING BLAST.
PYGM V SD(281)	TO AVOID BEING ALONE WITH HIGGINS. HE RISES AND	JOINS	HER THERE. SHE IMMEDIATELY COMES BACK INTO THE ROOM
PYGM V SD(281)	THE CENTRE WINDOW AND THE OTTOMAN. PICKERING	JOINS	HER. /DOOLITTLE/ BRIDEGROOM! WHAT A WORD! IT MAKES A
PYGM III (254)	THIS IS NOT MEANT FOR HIM TO HEAR, DISCREETLY	JOINS	HIGGINS AT THE WINDOW). WE'RE SO POOR! AND SHE GETS
MRS II SD(203)	THE SETTLE AND PULLS HIMSELF TOGETHER AS PRAED	JOINS	HIM AT THE FIREPLACE. MRS WARREN LOSES HER EASE OF
DEVL II (40)	(THE SERGEANT RETIRES DELICATELY AND	JOINS	HIS MEN NEAR THE DOOR). HE IS TRYING TO SPARE YOU THE
JOAN 2,SD(81)	OUT AS GILLES, WITH A GESTURE OF SURRENDER,	JOINS	IN THE LAUGH, AND JUMPS DOWN FROM THE DAIS BESIDE LA
HART I (70)	AT HIM PAST MRS HUSHABYE, WHO RETREATS AND	JOINS	MANGAN NEAR THE SOFA). /RANDALL/ HOW DARE I WHAT? I
MRS II (207)	(THE CLERGYMAN TAKES HIS HAT FROM THE TABLE, AND	JOINS	MRS WARREN AT THE FIRESIDE. MEANWHILE VIVIE COMES IN,
GETT PREFACE(196)	SAVIOR. AS TO THE RESPECTABLE VOLUPTUARY, WHO	JOINS	OMAR KHAYYAM CLUBS AND VIBRATES TO SWINBURNE'S
CAPT III (283)	CAN TAKE YOUR PLACE WITH THE REST. (BRASSBOUND	JOINS	REDBROOK AND JOHNSON. KEARNEY SITS DOWN AGAIN. AFTER
CAPT II SD(244)	HE GROANS. JOHNSON PHLEGMATICALLY LEAVES HIM AND	JOINS	REDBROOK. /LADY CICELY/ BUT YOU CANT LEAVE HIM THERE
GETT SD(323)	ALL RISE EXCEPT SOAMES, WHO SITS DOWN. LEO	JOINS	REGINALD AT THE GARDEN DOOR. MRS BRIDGENORTH HURRIES
LION PREFACE(21)	WAS TO THE CATHOLICS OF THE XVI CENTURY. JESUS	JOINS	THE BAPTISTS. JESUS ENTERED AS A MAN OF THIRTY (LUKE
CATH 2,SD(177)	AND STAGGERS PAST IT TO THE CABINET DOOR. VARINKA	JOINS	THE COURTIERS AT THE OPPOSITE SIDE OF THE ROOM.
JOAN 5,SD(113)	OIL! THE ARCHBISHOP COMES FROM THE VESTRY, AND	JOINS	THE GROUP BETWEEN CHARLES AND BLUEBEARD. /CHARLES/
PHIL III SD(144)	WHO REMAINS NEAR THE DOOR WHILST HER FATHER	JOINS	THE OTHERS. /CRAVEN/ AH, JO, HERE YOU ARE. NOW,
SUPR III (77)	AUTOMOBILE! (HE RUSHES DOWN THE HILL AND	JOINS	THE REST, WHO ALL SCRAMBLE TO THEIR FEET). /MENDOZA/ (
BARB I (251)	CAREER OF ALL OF YOU. AND WHAT DOES SHE DO?	JOINS	THE SALVATION ARMY; DISCHARGES HER MAID; LIVES ON A
CLEO IV SD(177)	TO CAESAR. HER RETINUE, HEADED BY FTATATEETA,	JOINS	THE STAFF AT THE TABLE. CAESAR GIVES CLEOPATRA HIS
SUPR IV (170)	HAS ALREADY BECOME CONSCIOUS OF HIS USELESSNESS,	JOINS	THEM. STRAKER, FOLLOWING THEM UP, PAUSES FOR A MOMENT
CLEO II SD(130)	BY ACHILLAS, WHO MOVES HAUGHTILY AWAY AND	JOINS	THEODOTUS ON THE OTHER SIDE. LUCIUS SEPTIMIUS GOES OUT
DEVL I SD(24)	PARTY. ANDERSON TAKES HIS HAT FROM THE RACK AND	JOINS	UNCLE WILLIAM AT THE FIRE. TITUS FETCHES JUDITH HER

JOINT

BUOY IV (50)	ARE CERTAIN PRECAUTIONS ONE CAN TAKE. /JUNIUS/ A	JOINT	ANNUITY, FOR INSTANCE. /OLD BILL/ YOUR SENSE OF MONEY
SUPR I (18)	FOR I FEAR IT IS IMPOSSIBLE FOR US TO UNDERTAKE A	JOINT	ARRANGEMENT. /ANN/ (IN A LOW MUSICAL VOICE) MAMMA--
DOCT PREFACE(58)	TOP JOINT OF THE LITTLE FINGER; AND THAT IF THIS	JOINT	BE AMPUTATED IMMEDIATELY AFTER BIRTH, TYPHUS FEVER
MRS PREFACE(154)	QUITE CONTENT TO HAVE MY PLAY JUDGED BY, SAY, A	JOINT	COMMITTEE OF THE CENTRAL VIGILANCE SOCIETY AND THE
MIS. PREFACE(44)	COMPACT TREATISE ON IT WHICH I PREPARED FOR THE	JOINT	COMMITTEE ON THE CENSORSHIP OF STAGE PLAYS, AND
GETT PREFACE(184)	WORST LEGAL ONE, WE MAY TAKE IT THEN THAT WHEN A	JOINT	DOMESTIC ESTABLISHMENT, INVOLVING QUESTIONS OF
APPL II (259)	IS SOMEWHAT MORE EXPENSIVELY DEFENDED AT OUR	JOINT	EXPENSE BY THE LEAGUE OF NATIONS. /VANHATTAN/ (RISING
BARB II (284)	OF JOINT, BILL. /BILL/ AW'LL PUT HIS NOWSE AHT O	JOINT	FOR HIM. NOT THAT AW CARE A CARSE FOR ER, MAWND THET.
SUPR I (17)	SAY I AM SURPRISED TO FIND MR TANNER NAMED AS	JOINT	GUARDIAN AND TRUSTEE WITH MYSELF OF YOU AND RHODA. (A
SUPR I (11)	AFTER THAT CONVERSATION-- APPOINTING ME AS	JOINT	GUARDIAN WITH YOU! /RAMSDEN/ (PALE AND DETERMINED) I
NEVR II (242)	A LITTLE MORE FISH, MISS? YOU WONT CARE FOR THE	JOINT	IN THE MIDDLE OF THE DAY. /GLORIA/ NO, THANK YOU. THE
MIS. (173)	AT PUTTING A MAN ON THE RACK. IF YOU WANT EVERY	JOINT	IN YOUR BODY STRETCHED UNTIL IT'S AN AGONY TO LIVE--
HART II (113)	I'M FORGOTTEN. THE BURGLAR HAS PUT MY NOSE OUT OF	JOINT	. SHOVE ME INTO A CORNER AND HAVE DONE WITH ME. /MRS
DOCT PREFACE(58)	THEORY THAT TYPHUS FEVER ALWAYS BEGINS AT THE TOP	JOINT	OF THE LITTLE FINGER; AND THAT IF THIS JOINT BE
POSN PREFACE(361)	THIS COMMITTEE. ITS FULL TITLE IS REPORT FROM THE	JOINT	SELECT COMMITTEE OF THE HOUSE OF LORDS AND THE HOUSE
POSN PREFACE(362)	MATTERS EXACTLY AS THEY ARE. THE REPORT OF THE	JOINT	SELECT COMMITTEE IS A CAPITAL ILLUSTRATION OF THIS
POSN PREFACE(365)	WAS NOT REMOVED BY THE EVIDENCE GIVEN BEFORE THE	JOINT	SELECT COMMITTEE. THE MANAGERS DID NOT MAKE THEIR CASE
POSN PREFACE(364)	OF DICKENS IS TO BE JUSTIFIED. THE STORY OF THE	JOINT	SELECT COMMITTEE. LET ME NOW TELL THE STORY OF THE
POSN PREFACE(369)	THE SCENT OF CARNATIONS) FAINT. THE PEERS ON THE	JOINT	SELECT COMMITTEE. THE HOUSE OF LORDS THEN PROCEEDED TO
POSN PREFACE(421)	GUARANTEE THAT ANY MEMBER OF THE MAJORITY OF THE	JOINT	SELECT COMMITTEE EVER HEARD OF THE STAR CHAMBER OR OF
POSN PREFACE(420)	CHAMBER AGAIN, LET HIM READ THE REPORT OF THE	JOINT	SELECT COMMITTEE, ON WHICH I NOW VENTURE TO OFFER A
POSN PREFACE(415)	STATEMENT, AND IN MY EVIDENCE BEFORE THE	JOINT	SELECT COMMITTEE, NO CONTROVERSY AROSE EXCEPT ON ONE
POSN PREFACE(431)	MY ADVICE WHEREVER IT CONFLICTS WITH THAT OF THE	JOINT	SELECT COMMITTEE. IT IS, I THINK, OBVIOUSLY MORE
POSN PREFACE(428)	THE VOLUNTARY SYSTEM MUST INEVITABLY WORK. THE	JOINT	SELECT COMMITTEE EXPRESSLY URGES THAT THE LORD
POSN PREFACE(428)	TO ME, AND UNCOVER FOR HIM THE PITFALLS WHICH THE	JOINT	SELECT COMMITTEE HAVE DUG (AND CONCEALED) IN HIS
POSN PREFACE(427)	WHEN HE GIVES HIM A LATCHKEY. THE MEMBERS OF THE	JOINT	SELECT COMMITTEE RISKED MY PRODUCING A REVOLVER AND
SUPR HANDBOK(185)	OF TO SPUNGE ON IT) IS SUPERIOR TO AN ORDINARY	JOINT	STOCK CAPITALIST PRECISELY AS AN ORDINARY JOINT STOCK
SUPR HANDBOK(185)	JOINT STOCK CAPITALIST PRECISELY AS AN ORDINARY	JOINT	STOCK CAPITALIST IS SUPERIOR TO A PIRATE. FURTHER, THE
2TRU PREFACE(12)	IT BEFORE A CERTAIN MORE OR LESS REMOTE DAY. WHEN	JOINT	STOCK COMPANIES WERE FORMED TO RUN BIG INDUSTRIAL
SUPR HANDBOK(212)	BIRTH AS IT NOW PAYS FOR DEATH, BE EXPLOITED BY	JOINT	STOCK COMPANIES FOR DIVIDENDS, JUST AS THEY ARE IN
MTH3 (124)	NOTHING LIKE IT. I KNOW ALL ABOUT THE OLD	JOINT	STOCK COMPANIES. THE SHAREHOLDERS DID NO WORK. /THE
APPL PREFACE(184)	COMPANY, OR OF A TRUST MADE BY COMBINING SEVERAL	JOINT	STOCK COMPANIES. SUCH BOARDS, ELECTED BY THE VOTES OF
MTH3 (124)	IS THAT THE ENGLISH PEOPLE HAVE BECOME A	JOINT	STOCK COMPANY ADMITTING ASIATICS AND AFRICANS AS
SUPR HANDBOK(185)	CHILDREN AND DONE AND SUFFERED LESS EVIL THAN ANY	JOINT	STOCK COMPANY ON RECORD. IT WAS, HOWEVER, A HIGHLY
APPL PREFACE(184)	COUNCIL. IT MAY BE THE BOARD OF DIRECTORS OF A	JOINT	STOCK COMPANY, OR OF A TRUST MADE BY COMBINING SEVERAL
MIS. PREFACE(86)	CAN HELP; THE TRAM CONDUCTOR, WHEN EMPLOYED BY A	JOINT	STOCK COMPANY, SOMETIMES NEVER SEES THEM AT ALL. UNDER
SUPR HANDBOK(212)	JUST AS THEY ARE IN ORDINARY INDUSTRIES, EVEN A	JOINT	STOCK HUMAN STUD FARM (PIOUSLY DISGUISED AS A
LION PREFACE(54)	THEMSELVES HAVE ORGANIZED COMMUNISM IN CAPITAL.	JOINT	STOCK IS THE ORDER OF THE DAY. AN ATTEMPT TO RETURN TO
CATH PREFACE(155)	NO OTHER QUEEN CAPABLE OF STANDING UP TO OUR	JOINT	TALENTS. IN COMPOSING SUCH BRAVURA PIECES, THE AUTHOR
BARB II (284)	TOO LATE. THE NEW BLOKE HAS PUT YOUR NOSE OUT OF	JOINT	, BILL. /BILL/ AW'LL PUT HIS NOWSE AHT O JOINT FOR
MILL II (167)	TOMATO TEA CALLED SOUP, THE REMAINS OF SUNDAY'S	JOINT	, SPROUTS, POTATOES, APPLE TART AND STALE AMERICAN

			JOINTLY	
CLEO II	(125)	THERE. /CAESAR/ PTOLEMY AND CLEOPATRA SHALL REIGN	JOINTLY	IN EGYPT. /ACHILLAS/ WHAT OF THE KING'S YOUNGER
SUPR I	(11)	GUARDIANSHIP. I SHALL CERTAINLY REFUSE TO HOLD IT	JOINTLY	WITH YOU. /TANNER/ YES; AND WHAT WILL SHE SAY TO
			JOINTURE	
PYGM EPILOG	(293)	HAD NO MONEY AND NO OCCUPATION. HIS MOTHER'S	JOINTURE	, A LAST RELIC OF THE OPULENCE OF LARGELADY PARK,
			JOKE	
FANY PROLOG	(264)	ON PURPOSE. MIND: IT'S NOT THAT HE DOESNT SEE A	JOKE	: HE DOES; AND IT HURTS HIM. A COMEDY SCENE MAKES HIM
APPL I	(226)	SETTING ME OFF, YOU ARE. /BOANERGES/ WHERE IS THE	JOKE	? I DONT SEE IT. /AMANDA/ IF YOU COULD SEE A JOKE,
ANNA	(296)	DONT YOU APPRECIATE HER IMPERIAL HIGHNESS'S	JOKE	? /SCHNEIDEKIND/ (SUDDENLY BECOMING SOLEMN) I DONT
MTH5	(220)	SHAMEFUL. DISGRACEFUL. WHAT FILTH! IS THIS A	JOKE	? WHY, THEYRE ANCIENTS! SS-S-S-SSS! ARE YOU MAD,
O'FL	(207)	UP BY MY MOTHER, SIR, YOUD KNOW BETTER THAN TO	JOKE	ABOUT HER. WHAT I'M TELLING YOU IS THE TRUTH; AND I
WIDO I	(12)	BUT SERIOUSLY. THIS IS SERIOUS, HARRY: YOU MUSNT	JOKE	ABOUT IT. /TRENCH/ (LOOKING SUDDENLY ROUND TO THE
GETT	(261)	BOWS IN ACKNOWLEDGMENT OF THE COMPLIMENT). THEY	JOKE	ABOUT THE GREENGROCER, JUST AS THEY JOKE ABOUT THE
GETT	(261)	THEY JOKE ABOUT THE GREENGROCER, JUST AS THEY	JOKE	ABOUT THE MOTHER-IN-LAW. BUT THEY CANT GET ON WITHOUT
JOAN 2	(72)	ARCHBISHOP AND LA TREMOUILLE) THIS IS NOTHING TO	JOKE	ABOUT, IT IS WORSE THAN WE THOUGHT. IT WAS NOT A
LION I	SD(110)	AND DETERMINED TO TREAT THEIR HARDSHIPS AS A	JOKE	AND ENCOURAGE ONE ANOTHER. A BUGLE IS HEARD FAR BEHIND
BULL I	(82)	DONT SEE THE JOKE. /BROADBENT/ YOU CAN SPOIL ANY	JOKE	BY BEING COLD BLOODED ABOUT IT. I SAW IT ALL RIGHT WHEN
LION I	(126)	WITH A LOUDER LAUGH BY ALL THE REST AS THE	JOKE	CATCHES ON). /CENTURION/ (SCANDALIZED) SILENCE! HAVE
METH PREFACE	(R53)	WEISMANN'S EXPERIMENT UPON THE MICE WAS A MERE	JOKE	COMPARED TO THE ATROCITIES COMMITTED BY OTHER
NEVR II	(237)	HIS HEAD AS HE STOOD THERE, THINKING WHAT NEW	JOKE	HE'D HAVE WITH ME. YES, SIR: THATS THE SORT HE IS: VERY
JITT III	SD(69)	WITHOUT A SUSPICION THAT SHE IS NOT ENJOYING THE	JOKE	IN GOOD FAITH. JITTA AT LAST RECOVERS HER SELF-CONTROL
BULL II	(103)	OF JOKING IS TO TELL THE TRUTH. IT'S THE FUNNIEST	JOKE	IN THE WORLD. /NORA/ (INCREDULOUS) GALONG WITH YOU!
JOAN 6,	SD(139)	ASSESSORS CANNOT HELP SMILING, ESPECIALLY AS THE	JOKE	IS AGAINST COURCELLES. /LADVENU/ WELL ANSWERED, JOAN.
OVER	(178)	FEELING; AND YOU THINK OF NOTHING BUT A SILLY	JOKE	. A QUIP LIKE THAT MAKES YOU FORGET ME. /GREGORY/ (
MTH3	(109)	LIKE ALL REVOLUTIONARY TRUTHS, IT BEGAN AS A	JOKE	. AS I SHEWED NO SIGNS OF AGEING AFTER FORTY-FIVE, MY
CYMB FORWORD	(137)	THE SPHERE OF CRIME AND BECOMES AN INSTRUCTIVE	JOKE	. BUT WHAT OF THE MANY SUCCESSFUL AND AVOWED
OVER	(183)	THAT BECAME RIDICULOUS. THATS MY ONE LITTLE PET	JOKE	. CALL ME MRS LUNN FOR SHORT. AND CHANGE THE SUBJECT,
MTH3	(116)	AND EIGHTY-THREE, HE SAYS. THAT IS HIS LITTLE	JOKE	. DO YOU KNOW, MRS LUTESTRING, HE HAD ALMOST TALKED US
BULL III	(118)	UP IRREPRESSIBLY) STILL, IT'S NO END OF A	JOKE	. HOW DO YOU LIKE THE IRISH, HODSON? /HODSON/ WELL,
PHIL II	(124)	(HASTILY) NOTHING. MY FAULT: A STUPID PRACTICAL	JOKE	. I BEG YOUR PARDON AND MRS TRANFIELD'S. /GRACE/ (
CAND I	(95)	ILL AT EASE WITH STRANGERS; AND I NEVER CAN SEE A	JOKE	. I'M VERY SORRY. (HE SITS DOWN ON THE SOFA, HIS
PYGM V	(271)	/DOOLITTLE/ AH! YOU MAY WELL CALL IT A SILLY	JOKE	. IT PUT THE LID ON ME RIGHT ENOUGH. JUST GIVE HIM THE
INCA	(253)	INCA/ QUITE SAFE, MADAM: THEY WOULD TAKE IT AS A	JOKE	. (HE RISES). AND NOW, PREPARE YOURSELF FOR A
BULL IV	(146)	A PIG THAT IN ENGLAND. THATS THEIR NOTION OF A	JOKE	. /AUNT JUDY/ MUSHA GOD HELP THEM IF THEY CAN JOKE NO
FANY III	(301)	DAUGHTER, DO YOU, YOU SILLY BOY? IT'S A STOCK	JOKE	. /BOBBY/ DO YOU MEAN TO SAY YOU DONT BELIEVE ME?
BULL I	(82)	HE VERY WITTILY CALLED IT. /DOYLE/ I DONT SEE THE	JOKE	. /BROADBENT/ YOU CAN SPOIL ANY JOKE BY BEING COLD
NEVR II	(230)	THEY THINK EVERY ENGLISHMAN THEY MEET IS A	JOKE	. /DOLLY/ WELL, SO HE IS: IT'S NOT OUR FAULT. /PHILIP/
FABL VI	(125)	IF YOU ASK ME I SHOULD SAY THE UNIVERSE IS A BIG	JOKE	. /MAIDEN 4/ I DO NOT SEE ANY FUN IN IT. I SHOULD SAY
MIS. PREFACE	(57)	FIRST FORMULATED BY A COMIC PAPER AS A CAPITAL	JOKE	. TECHNICAL INSTRUCTION. TECHNICAL INSTRUCTION TEMPTS
FABL VI	(126)	AS WE KEEP OUR PETS. I TOLD YOU THE UNIVERSE IS A	JOKE	. THAT IS MY THEORY. /MAIDEN 5/ BUT WHERE DO OUR
ROCK PREFACE	(176)	THE EXALTING VISION HAS SUDDENLY BECOME A RIBALD	JOKE	. THAT IS WHAT THE CHURCH FEARED; AND THAT IS WHAT HAS
BULL II	SD(111)	SPENDTHRIFT, AUNT JUDY SEEMS TO HIM AN INCARNATE	JOKE	. THE LIKELIHOOD THAT THE JOKE WILL PALL AFTER A MONTH
GETT	(293)	YOU. /REGINALD/ THIS LOOKS TO ME LIKE A PRACTICAL	JOKE	. THEYVE ARRANGED IT BETWEEN THEM. /THE BISHOP/ NO.
ROCK I	(204)	THE BEST-- HA HA HA! /SIR ARTHUR/ I DONT SEE THE	JOKE	. WHY THIS HILARITY? /DAVID/ TREAT THE HOUSE TO A
NEVR II	(236)	WHAT! /WAITER/ ONLY HIS JOKE, SIR, HIS FAVORITE	JOKE	. YESTERDAY, I WAS TO BE HIS FATHER. TODAY, AS SOON AS
LION I	(126)	THE ROAST BOAR. /FERROVIUS/ (HEAVILY) I SEE THE	JOKE	. YES, YES: I SHALL BE THE ROAST BOAR. HA! HA! (HE
FABL VI	(125)	IT. I SHOULD SAY IT IS A BIG MISTAKE. /YOUTH 2/ A	JOKE	MUST HAVE A JOKER. A MISTAKE MUST HAVE A BLUNDERER. IF
BULL IV	(146)	JOKE. /AUNT JUDY/ MUSHA GOD HELP THEM IF THEY CAN	JOKE	NO BETTER THAN THAT! /DORAN/ (WITH RENEWED SYMPTOMS)
APPL I	(228)	(GENTLY REPROACHFUL) AMANDA: WHAT IS THE	JOKE	NOW? I AM SURPRISED AT YOU. /AMANDA/ JOE FRANK! WHEN
WIDO II	(34)	TO GIVE ME ANY? /TRENCH/ (WINCING) DONT MAKE A	JOKE	OF IT: I'M SERIOUS. DO YOU KNOW THAT WE SHALL BE VERY
PYGM V	(271)	YOUR LAST VISIT I REMEMBER MAKING SOME SILLY	JOKE	OF THE KIND. /DOOLITTLE/ AH! YOU MAY WELL CALL IT A
GENV IV	(88)	OF EUROPEAN INTEREST. THE STUPENDOUS AND COLOSSAL	JOKE	OF THE PRESENT PROCEEDINGS IS THAT THIS COURT HAS
SUPR I	(31)	OF SCAPEGOATS, EH? /ANN/ OH, THAT STUPID OLD	JOKE	OF YOURS ABOUT ME! DO PLEASE DROP IT. WHY DO YOU SAY
2TRU II	(72)	ALONE: D'Y'HEAR? I HAVE HAD ENOUGH OF THAT	JOKE	ON ME. /THE PATIENT/ (RISING AND TAKING HER BY THE
JOAN 2,	SD(80)	THE KING, AND, LIKE THE COURTIERS, ENJOYING THE	JOKE	RATHER OBVIOUSLY. THERE IS A CURTAINED ARCH IN THE WALL
DEST	(167)	EYE. HE BEGINS LIKE A MAN ENJOYING SOME SECRET	JOKE	). HOW DO YOU KNOW I AM A BRAVE MAN? /LADY/ (AMAZED)
DEST	(185)	HIMSELF ECSTATICALLY ON THE COUCH TO ENJOY THE	JOKE	). /NAPOLEON/ (LAUGHING AND PINCHING GIUSEPPE'S EAR)
BARB PREFACE	(227)	NOISE CALLED " SACRED MUSIC" IS A STANDING	JOKE	; A FLAG WITH BLOOD AND FIRE ON IT IS UNFURLED, NOT IN
APPL II	(272)	/NICOBAR/ SHUT UP, YOU B -- /PLINY/ A JOKE'S A	JOKE	; BUT REALLY -- /CRASSUS/ TOO BAD, AMANDA! BEHAVE
ROCK PREFACE	(165)	THE SOIL. THE PRETENCE HAS NOW BECOME A STANDING	JOKE	; BUT YOU WILL STILL COME UP AGAINST IT IF YOU ACCUSE
MTH4 II	(184)	OUT OF EXISTENCE. IT SEEMS TO HAVE BEEN A GREAT	JOKE	; FOR THE STATESMEN WHO THOUGHT THEY HAD SENT TEN
BARB PREFACE	(239)	IN " THE WHIFF OF DYNAMITE" (THE FLAVOR OF THE	JOKE	SEEMS TO EVAPORATE A LITTLE, DOES IT NOT?) BECAUSE IT
2TRU II	SD(52)	SOMEHOW SUGGESTS THAT THERE IS AN IMPRESCRIPTIBLE	JOKE	SOMEWHERE BY AN INVISIBLE SMILE WHICH UNHAPPILY
PYGM EPILOG	(300)	THE NOTION OF FREDDY SUCCEEDING AT ANYTHING WAS A	JOKE	THAT NEVER PALLED, GRASPED THE FACT THAT BUSINESS, LIKE
SUPR IV	SD(143)	HAND, REGARDS THE OLD GENTLEMAN'S ACCENT AS A	JOKE	THOUGHTFULLY PROVIDED BY PROVIDENCE EXPRESSLY FOR THE
PHIL II	(102)	ON THE OTHERS) OH, STUFF! DO YOU SUPPOSE IT'S A	JOKE	TO BE SITUATED AS I AM? YOUVE GOT YOUR HEAD SO STUFFED
GENV III	(65)	HALL, SOME BLACKSHIRT THOUGHT IT WOULD BE A GOOD	JOKE	TO PRETEND TO FORGET HER NAME AND CALL HER MONGOLIA
BULL IV	(154)	BESIDES, CALLING ME A HYPOCRITE WAS TOO BIG A	JOKE	TO SWALLOW ALL AT ONCE, YOU KNOW. /KEEGAN/ YOU MUST
CATH 1	(172)	(TO EDSTASTON) COME! YOU SHALL TELL THE	JOKE	TO THE EMPRESS: SHE IS BY WAY OF BEING A HUMORIST (HE
NEVR I	(212)	ONLY KNEW HOW GLAD I AM THAT IT IS NOTHING BUT A	JOKE	TO YOU, THOUGH IT IS SUCH BITTER EARNEST TO ME. (MORE
CATH 2	(176)	TO MAKE HIMSELF HEARD) NO, NO. THIS IS CARRYING A	JOKE	TOO FAR. I MUST INSIST. LET ME DOWN! HANG IT, WILL YOU
BULL II	SD(111)	TO HIM AN INCARNATE JOKE. THE LIKELIHOOD THAT THE	JOKE	WILL PALL AFTER A MONTH OR SO, AND IS PROBABLY NOT
FANY PROLOG	(264)	WELL, VAUGHAN HAS NO SENSE OF HUMOR; AND IF YOU	JOKE	WITH HIM HE'LL THINK YOURE INSULTING HIM ON PURPOSE.
MTH3	(116)	BUT IT'S GETTING ON MY NERVES. THE BEST	JOKE	WONT BEAR BEING PUSHED BEYOND A CERTAIN POINT. THAT
GETT	(261)	/COLLINS/ LORD BLESS YOU, NO, MAAM. IT WOULD BE A	JOKE	, AFTER MARRYING FIVE OF YOUR DAUGHTERS, IF I WAS TO
NEVR II	(237)	HIS LAY). EVEN THE SOLICITOR TOOK UP THE	JOKE	, ALTHOUGH HE WAS IN A MANNER OF SPEAKING IN MY
APPL I	(226)	JOKE? I DONT SEE IT. /AMANDA/ IF YOU COULD SEE A	JOKE	, BILL, YOU WOULDNT BE THE GREAT POPULAR ORATOR YOU
MILL I	(154)	HE KNOWS WHAT I MEAN. /EPIFANIA/ SOME SILLY	JOKE	, I SUPPOSE. /ADRIAN/ DONT BE ABSURD, FITZFASSENDEN.
CAND I	(91)	THE HAND OF FRIENDSHIP) YOU WILL AVE YOUR	JOKE	, JAMES. OUR QUARREL'S MADE UP NOW, AIN IT? /A WOMAN'S
ARMS III	(67)	THAT TO ME, FATHER? /PETKOFF/ WELL, WELL, ONLY A	JOKE	, LITTLE ONE. COME: GIVE ME A KISS. (SHE KISSES HIM).
FANY I	(279)	THE COPPER! HE THOUGHT THE COPPER WOULD SEE THE	JOKE	, POOR LAMB. HE WAS ARGUING ABOUT IT WHEN THE TWO THAT
NEVR II	(236)	FATHER, SIR. /CRAMPTON/ WHAT! /WAITER/ ONLY HIS	JOKE	, SIR, HIS FAVORITE JOKE. YESTERDAY, I WAS TO BE HIS
2TRU II	(72)	HER BY THE CHIN TO TURN HER FACE UP) IT IS NO	JOKE	, SWEETIEST: IT IS THE DEAD SOLEMN EARNEST. I CALLED
			JOKED	
BULL PREFACE	(37)	VOLTAIRE HAD AN IRREPRESSIBLE SENSE OF HUMOR. HE	JOKED	ABOUT HABAKKUK; AND JOKES ABOUT HABAKKUK SMELT TOO
HART II	(94)	THEYVE BEEN PROUD OF MY POVERTY. THEYVE EVEN	JOKED	ABOUT IT QUITE OFTEN. BUT MY WIFE HAS HAD A VERY POOR
			JOKER	
MIS.	(168)	AND SAY IT ELSEWHERE. /THE MAN/ WHAT SORT OF A	JOKER	ARE YOU? ARE YOU TRYING TO PUT ME IN THE WRONG, WHEN
FABL VI	(125)	IT IS A BIG MISTAKE. /YOUTH 2/ A JOKE MUST HAVE A	JOKER	. A MISTAKE MUST HAVE A BLUNDERER. IF THE WORLD EXISTS
			JOKE'S	
APPL II	(272)	SHAME! /NICOBAR/ SHUT UP, YOU B -- /PLINY/ A	JOKE'S	A JOKE; BUT REALLY -- /CRASSUS/ TOO BAD, AMANDA!
			JOKES	
MILL II	(178)	AND GLORIOUS, IS THIS ANOTHER OF THY TERRIBLE	JOKES	?
FANY III	(320)	TELL ME THAT MY DAUGHTER LAUGHS AT A FRENCHMAN'S	JOKES	? /GILBEY/ WE ALL KNOW WHAT FRENCH JOKES ARE.
FABL II	(105)	(SEATING HIMSELF) IS THIS A TIME FOR YOUR IRISH	JOKES	? WHAT THE DEVIL ARE WE TO DO? HOW MUCH DO YOU
BUOY IV	(50)	OR LATER. MOTHERS-IN-LAW ARE STOCK JOKES. NOBODY	JOKES	ABOUT FATHERS-IN-LAW; BUT THEY ARE TROUBLESOME ENOUGH
BULL PREFACE	(37)	SENSE OF HUMOR. HE JOKED ABOUT HABAKKUK; AND	JOKES	ABOUT HABAKKUK SMELT TOO STRONGLY OF BRIMSTONE TO BE
SIM PREFACE	(10)	OR IMPRISONING POOR MEN FOR MAKING SCEPTICAL	JOKES	ABOUT THE PARTHENOGENESIS OF JESUS. THUS THE
NEVR II	(241)	CLANDON/ PHIL: WILL YOU PLEASE REMEMBER THAT YOUR	JOKES	ARE APT TO IRRITATE PEOPLE WHO ARE NOT ACCUSTOMED TO
BULL PREFACE	(38)	AND JOHN KNOX. NOWADAYS, HOWEVER, VOLTAIRE'S	JOKES	ARE EITHER FORGOTTEN OR ELSE FALL FLAT ON A WORLD

LION I (113)	REALLY COMMITTED SUICIDE. /LAVINIA/ CAPTAIN! YOUR	JOKES	ARE TOO GRIM. DO NOT THINK IT IS EASY FOR US TO DIE.
FANY III (320)	JOKES? /GILBEY/ WE ALL KNOW WHAT FRENCH	JOKES	ARE. /JUGGINS/ BELIEVE ME! YOU DO NOT, SIR. THE NOISE
METH PREFACE(R66)	OPINIONS WERE QUOTED AT ALL, THEY WERE QUOTED AS	JOKES	AT THE EXPENSE OF NOBODADDY. WE WERE QUITE SURE FOR
METH PREFACE(R84)	DESPAIR BY DISGUISING THE CRUELTIES OF NATURE AS	JOKES	. BUT WITH ALL HIS GIFTS, THE FACT REMAINS THAT HE
BULL IV (164)	AN IRISHWOMAN. SHE WOULD ALWAYS UNDERSTAND MY	JOKES	. FOR INSTANCE, YOU WOULD UNDERSTAND THEM, EH? /NORA/
LADY PREFACE(215)	AND HIS INCORRIGIBLE ADDICTION TO SMUTTY	JOKES	. HE DOES US THE PUBLIC SERVICE OF SWEEPING AWAY THE
CLEO II (140)	OF HIS SECRETARY'S NAME IS ONE OF CAESAR'S	JOKES	. IN LATER YEARS IT WOULD HAVE MEANT, QUITE SERIOUSLY
BUOY IV (50)	OUT SOONER OR LATER. MOTHERS-IN-LAW ARE STOCK	JOKES	. NOBODY JOKES ABOUT FATHERS-IN-LAW; BUT THEY ARE
FANY EPILOG (334)	MISS O'DOWDA. KEEP SERIOUS. GIVE UP MAKING SILLY	JOKES	. SUSTAIN THE NOTE OF PASSION, AND YOULL DO GREAT
BARB III (330)	ME OFF THE SUBJECT OF THE INHERITANCE BY PROFANE	JOKES	. WELL, YOU SHANT. I DONT ASK IT ANY LONGER FOR
NEVR IV (299)	SURELY DO NOT BELIEVE THAT THESE AFFAIRS-- MERE	JOKES	OF THE CHILDREN'S-- WERE SERIOUS, MR VALENTINE?
GENV III (73)	THEY PERSECUTED POOR MEN FOR MAKING PROFANE	JOKES	; THEY SUPPRESSED NEWSPAPERS IN ENGLAND AS WELL AS IN
LIED (189)	THEY ALWAYS HAVE A LOT OF STUPID LOW FAMILY	JOKES	THAT NOBODY UNDERSTANDS BUT THEMSELVES. HALF THE TIME
LION I (112)	CAPTAIN: THERE WILL BE NOBODY TO APPRECIATE YOUR	JOKES	WHEN WE ARE GONE. /THE CAPTAIN/ (UNSHAKEN IN HIS
BARB PREFACE(223)	SO, WHEN BARBARA CUTS THE REGULAR SALVATION ARMY	JOKES	, AND SNATCHES A KISS FROM HER LOVER ACROSS HIS DRUM,
HART PREFACE(31)	TO HIS OWN ASTONISHMENT, THIRSTING FOR SILLY	JOKES	, DANCES, AND BRAINLESSLY SENSUOUS EXHIBITIONS OF
MIS. PREFACE(23)	HABIT OF TREATING LOVE AND MATERNITY AS OBSCENE	JOKES	, HOPELESSNESS, EVASION, DERISION, COWARDICE, AND ALL
		JOKING	
PHIL II (119)	WHY ON EARTH DO YOU ALWAYS SUSPECT ME OF	JOKING	? I NEVER WAS MORE SERIOUS IN MY LIFE. /PARAMORE/ (
NEVR III (264)	CLANDON/ (INCREDULOUSLY) PHIL! DOLLY! ARE YOU	JOKING	? (THEY SHAKE THEIR HEADS). DID SHE ALLOW IT?
PHIL II (127)	AND DR PARAMORE'S. /CRAVEN/ CUTHBERTSON: ARE THEY	JOKING	? OR AM I DREAMING? /CUTHBERTSON/ (GRIMLY) IT'S
GETT (302)	HAS? I NEVER SUSPECTED-- I NEVER KNEW-- ARE YOU	JOKING	? OR HAVE WE ALL GONE MAD? /THE BISHOP/ DONT BE
PHIL II (119)	SURPRISE) CHARTERIS! I-- (SUSPICIOUSLY) ARE YOU	JOKING	? /CHARTERIS/ WHY ON EARTH DO YOU ALWAYS SUSPECT ME
O'FL (207)	(TURNING AND FACING HIM) ARE YOU -- ARE YOU	JOKING	? /O'FLAHERTY/ IF YOUD BEEN BROUGHT UP BY MY MOTHER,
MTH2 (68)	/CONRAD/ NO. WE ARE NOT MAD. /SAVVY/ THEYRE NOT	JOKING	EITHER. THEY MEAN IT. /LUBIN/ (CAUTIOUSLY) ASSUMING
BULL II (103)	MR KEEGAN: I'M SURE YAR. /KEEGAN/ MY WAY OF	JOKING	IS TO TELL THE TRUTH. IT'S THE FUNNIEST JOKE IN THE
VWOO 3 (138)	OH, I DIDNT KNOW: I DIDNT INDEED. I WAS ONLY	JOKING	. (SHE SITS AGAIN) I WOULDNT HAVE SAID IT FOR THE
WIDO III (59)	STEADY! MR SEKKETERRY. DR TRENCH IS ONLY	JOKING	. /COKANE/ I INSIST ON THE WITHDRAWAL OF THAT
HART II (88)	(BOUNCING ANGRILY OUT OF HIS CHAIR) I'M NOT	JOKING	. /ELLIE/ WHO TOLD YOU I WAS? /MANGAN/ I TELL YOU
DEST (188)	RUBBISH; BUT STILL IT'S NOT A PROPER SUBJECT FOR	JOKING	. /LADY/ BUT THIS IS VERY SERIOUS. MY SISTER HAS
DOCT I (85)	/RIDGEON/ (APOLOGETIC) OF COURSE NOT. I WAS ONLY	JOKING	. /SCHUTZMACHER/ MY TWO WORDS WERE SIMPLY CURE
SIM PRO;1, (23)	THE TICKET. YOU WONT HAVE TO GO BACK: WE WAS ONLY	JOKING	. /THE Y.W./ BUT I WANT TO GO BACK. IF THIS PLACE IS
DOCT II (123)	HE DIDNT REALLY WANT 50 POUNDS; THAT HE WAS ONLY	JOKING	; THAT ALL HE WANTED WAS A COUPLE OF SOVEREIGNS.
LION I (111)	EVERY DAY, SIR. THEYRE ALWAYS LAUGHING AND	JOKING	SOMETHING SCANDALOUS. THEYVE NO RELIGION: THATS HOW
MIS. (186)	A DISTURBED STATE. HE-- /MRS TARLETON/ NOW STOP	JOKING	THE POOR LAD, JOHN! I WONT HAVE IT. HE'S BEEN WORRIED
CAND I (83)	FOR THREE YEARS. ARE YOU SURE, LEXY? YOURE NOT	JOKING	, ARE YOU? /LEXY/ (EARNESTLY) NO SIR, REALLY.
BARB III (312)	MADE ANY ADDITION SUPERFLUOUS. /BARBARA/ ARE YOU	JOKING	, DOLLY? /CUSINS/ (PATIENTLY) NO. I HAVE BEEN
PYGM V (271)	IN WHICH, HENRY HIGGINS, THANKS TO YOUR SILLY	JOKING	, HE LEAVES ME A SHARE IN HIS PRE-DIGESTED CHEESE
MIS. (154)	TARLETON/ DONT BE SILLY, JOHN. THE LADY IS ONLY	JOKING	, I'M SURE. (TO LINA) I SUPPOSE YOUR LUGGAGE IS IN
BULL II (103)	AFTERWARDS. /NORA/ (BLUSHING WITH DELIGHT) YOURE	JOKING	, MR KEEGAN: I'M SURE YAR. /KEEGAN/ MY WAY OF JOKING
MIS. (156)	LORD, YES! YES, YES, YES, YES, YES, I WAS ONLY	JOKING	, OF COURSE. MRS TARLETON COMES BACK THROUGH THE
BARB PREFACE(222)	YET ALWAYS IN THE WILDEST SPIRITS, LAUGHING,	JOKING	, SINGING, REJOICING, DRUMMING, AND TAMBOURINING: HIS
		JOLLIER	
MTH3 (125)	OF THE ACTIVITIES OF OUR LEISURE! IS THERE A	JOLLIER	PLACE ON EARTH TO LIVE IN THAN ENGLAND OUT OF OFFICE
BARB I SD(259)	SLENDER, BORED, AND MUNDANE. BARBARA IS ROBUSTER,	JOLLIER	, MUCH MORE ENERGETIC. SARAH IS FASHIONABLY DRESSED:
		JOLLITY	
LADY PREFACE(234)	MAN IN THE FACE OF THE PASSAGES OF RECKLESS	JOLLITY	AND SERENELY HAPPY POETRY IN HIS LATEST PLAYS, YET
BULL I SD(80)	THAT CONTRASTS STRONGLY WITH BROADBENT'S EUPEPTIC	JOLLITY	. HE COMES IN AS A MAN AT HOME THERE, BUT ON SEEING
MTH3 (122)	WHEN YOUR LEVITY, YOUR INGRATITUDE, YOUR SHALLOW	JOLLITY	, MAKE MY GORGE RISE SO AGAINST YOU THAT IF I COULD
		JOLLY	
MILL IV (188)	PARADISE. /ALASTAIR/ I SAY, SEEDY, ISNT THIS	JOLLY	? /PATRICIA/ YES, DARLING: IT'S LOVELY. /ALASTAIR/
BULL I SD(74)	OF LIFE, SOMETIMES PORTENTOUSLY SOLEMN, SOMETIMES	JOLLY	AND IMPETUOUS, ALWAYS BUOYANT AND IRRESISTIBLE, MOSTLY
WIDO I (16)	TO MY PEOPLE. BUT I ASSURE YOU YOULL FIND THEM AS	JOLLY	AS POSSIBLE OVER IT. I'LL MAKE THEM WRITE BY RETURN.
GENV IV (88)	BUT THE POINT-- THE STAGGERING, PARALYZING,	JOLLY	BALLY BREATH-BEREAVING POINT OF OUR ASSEMBLY TODAY IS
DEST (184)	PLOT) AND HAVE THE LAUGH AT HIM! I SAY: WHAT A	JOLLY	CLEVER WOMAN YOU ARE! (SHOUTING) GIUSEPPE! /LADY/
DOCT III (141)	I HOPE IT WILL BE A LESSON TO YOU NOT TO BE SO	JOLLY	COCKSURE NEXT TIME. /WALPOLE/ ROT! YOU WERE MARRIED
JITT II (44)	JITTA: YOU ARE SIMPLY DRIVELLING. BRUNO WAS TOO	JOLLY	CONCEITED TO BE AFRAID OF ME. DONT BE CHILDISH.
MRS II (208)	EXCEPT THE GOV'NOR; SO YOU CAN IMAGINE HOW	JOLLY	DULL IT PANS OUT FOR HER. (TO HIS FATHER) YOURE NOT
GETT (274)	YOU GOT MY ANSWER, REJJY. /REGINALD/ IT'S SO	JOLLY	EASY TO SAY NO IN A LETTER. WONT YOU LET ME STAY?
KING II (229)	TO SELECT A DECENT POPE. ALEXANDER BORGIA WAS A	JOLLY	FELLOW; AND I AM THE LAST MAN ALIVE TO THROW STONES AT
MTH2 (38)	HAVE HEARD SUCH A LOT ABOUT YOU; AND THERE ARE SO	JOLLY	FEW PEOPLE TO TALK TO. I THOUGHT YOU PERHAPS WOULDNT
PRES (135)	YOU SHOOT THEM DOWN. /BALSQUITH/ OH YES; IT'S ALL	JOLLY	FINE FOR YOU AND OLD RED. YOU DONT DEPEND ON VOTES FOR
SIM II (62)	AND THAT IS ENOUGH FOR ME. AND NOW YOU SEE WHAT A	JOLLY	FINE SERMON IT WILL BE, AND WHY I SHALL BE SO HAPPY
DOCT III (138)	LIKE TO DRAW THE LOT OF YOU NOW: YOU DO LOOK	JOLLY	FOOLISH. ESPECIALLY YOU, RIDGEON. I HAD YOU THAT TIME,
MRS I (193)	WHAT! DO YOU KNOW VIVIE? ISNT SHE A	JOLLY	GIRL? I'M TEACHING HER TO SHOOT WITH THIS (PUTTING
VWOO 1 (122)	TO A CLEAN DECENT JOB. I HAVE SEEN SO MANY BRIGHT	JOLLY	GIRLS TURN INTO DIRTY OLD DRUDGES THROUGH GETTING
MIS. (132)	IF HE HAD TO RUN TARLETON'S UNDERWEAR, HE'D BE	JOLLY	GLAD TO FORGET. AS HE HAS A MUCH SOFTER JOB, AND WANTS
PYGM III (256)	ON WITH HER? /HIGGINS/ MRS PEARCE? OH, SHE'S	JOLLY	GLAD TO GET SO MUCH TAKEN OFF HER HANDS; FOR BEFORE
MIS. (194)	CANT THEY? WHEN I MARRIED, I SHOULD HAVE BEEN	JOLLY	GLAD TO HAVE FELT SURE OF THE QUARTER OF IT.
DOCT I (83)	RIDGEON IS TO BE HIS NAME NOW. /REDPENNY/ I'M	JOLLY	GLAD. /EMMY/ I NEVER WAS SO TAKEN ABACK. I ALWAYS
FANY PROLOG (265)	FIFTY. AFTER ALL, WHAT IS HE? ONLY A PRESSMAN.	JOLLY	GOOD BUSINESS FOR HIM TO EARN TEN GUINEAS: HE'S DONE
MILL I (163)	WILL EVERY TIME SHE LOSES HER TEMPER, SAGAMORE.	JOLLY	GOOD BUSINESS FOR YOU. /EPIFANIA/ DO BE QUIET,
HART I (82)	SORT OF DINNER FOR THEM. THE SERVANTS ALWAYS TAKE	JOLLY	GOOD CARE THAT THERE IS FOOD IN THE HOUSE. /CAPTAIN
MIS. (131)	A FULL-SIZED BODY? NO, THANK YOU. I SHALL TAKE	JOLLY	GOOD CARE TO KEEP JOEY OUT OF THIS UNTIL HYPATIA IS
BARB III (329)	MATCH? /LOMAX/ OH COME! I'M NOT A FOOL. I TOOK	JOLLY	GOOD CARE TO BLOW IT OUT BEFORE I CHUCKED IT AWAY.
GENV II (53)	INTENTIONS; AND OF COURSE HE WOULD HAVE BEEN A	JOLLY	GOOD CATCH FOR ME. BUT WHEN HIS PEOPLE GOT WIND OF IT
APPL II (272)	SINGING) -- HE'S A JOLLY GOOD FEL-LOW FOR HE'S A	JOLLY	GOOD FEL-LOW FOR HE'S -- /MAGNUS/ (PEREMPTORILY)
APPL II (272)	EXCEPT PROTEUS/ (RISING AND SINGING) -- HE'S A	JOLLY	GOOD FEL-LOW FOR HE'S A JOLLY GOOD FEL-LOW FOR HE'S --
SUPR II (70)	VICTIM, THATS WHAT YOU ARE AND NO MISTAKE; AND A	JOLLY	GOOD JOB FOR YOU, TOO, I SHOULD SAY. /TANNER/ (
MIS. (114)	PITY YOUR FATHER DIDNT GIVE YOUR THIN SKIN A	JOLLY	GOOD LACING WITH A CANE! /BENTLEY/ PITY YOU HAVNT GOT
MIS. (112)	IT TOO. YOURE A SPOILT YOUNG PUP; AND YOU NEED A	JOLLY	GOOD LICKING. AND IF YOURE NOT CAREFUL YOULL GET IT:
FANY EPILOG (334)	KNOW. /BANNAL/ (COMING TO HER ENCOURAGINGLY) A	JOLLY	GOOD LITTLE PLAY, MISS O'DOWDA. MIND: I DONT SAY IT'S
SIM PRO;2, (28)	/THE Y.W./ HE'S REAL. AND, MY WORD! ISNT HE	JOLLY	GOOD LOOKING? (TO THE PRIEST) YOULL EXCUSE THIS
ROCK II (267)	YOU ARE A MAN OF ACTION. /BASHAM/ I HAVE A	JOLLY	GOOD MIND TO GO TO THE KING AND MAKE HIM TAKE THE BIT
BULL IV (168)	LIKE THIS SPOT. I LIKE THIS VIEW. THIS WOULD BE A	JOLLY	GOOD PLACE FOR A HOTEL AND A GOLF LINKS. FRIDAY TO
JITT III (79)	ARE CHUMPS, DEAR, AFTER THE FIRST MONTH OR SO.	JOLLY	GOOD THING FOR THEIR WIVES TOO, SOMETIMES. /JITTA/
MIS. (114)	WHICH IS YOUR IDEA OF A MAN, I SUPPOSE. /JOHNNY/	JOLLY	GOOD THING FOR YOU THAT MY FATHER MADE YOU COME INTO
MTH2 (59)	AT ALL, MY DEAR. YOU ARE ONLY DISTRACTING BURGE.	JOLLY	GOOD THING FOR HIM TO BE DISTRACTED BY A PRETTY GIRL.
GETT (321)	ANY PERSON OVER ME. /REGINALD/ WELL, I THINK IT	JOLLY	HARD THAT A MAN SHOULD SUPPORT HIS WIFE FOR YEARS, AND
PHIL I (91)	SAY SO! NOW REALLY, WHO'D HAVE THOUGHT IT! HOW	JOLLY	IT MUST BE TO BE ABLE TO GO TO THE THEATRE FOR
ROCK I (228)	OR NOT; BUT IT'S ELECTRIC, AND VERY SOOTHING AND	JOLLY	. AH-A-A-AH! (A DEEP SIGHING BREATH). AND NOW, MY
MRS II (204)	REALLY AND TRULY. /FRANK/ WELL, SHE'S EVER SO	JOLLY	. BUT SHE'S RATHER A CAUTION, ISNT SHE? AND CROFTS!
JOAN EPILOG (160)	/THE SOLDIER/ YOU WONT FIND IT SO BAD, SIR.	JOLLY	. LIKE AS IF YOU WERE ALWAYS DRUNK WITHOUT THE TROUBLE
MIS. (144)	WOULD JUST SHRIVEL YOU UP THAT I THINK RATHER	JOLLY	. NOW! /LORD SUMMERHAYS/ IVE NOT THE SLIGHTEST DOUBT
BULL IV (169)	WITHOUT DISTINCTION OF CLASS. I TELL YOU I'M A	JOLLY	LUCKY MAN, NORA CRYNA. I GET ENGAGED TO THE MOST
APPL INTRLUD(251)	IS THERE FOR YOU IN YOUR COMMON HEALTHY	JOLLY	LUMPS OF CHILDREN AND YOUR COMMON HOUSEKEEPER WIFE AND
APPL INTRLUD(252)	WHEN MY STUPID WIFE HAS BEEN WORRYING ME, OR	JOLLY	LUMPS OF CHILDREN BOTHERING ME, OR MY TURBULENT
GETT (301)	MEAN YES. THERE WAS ONE NIGHT, HOTCHKISS, WHEN I	JOLLY	NEARLY SHOT YOU AND LEO AND FINISHED UP WITH MYSELF;
MIS. (126)	(VEHEMENTLY) I ASK YOU, WHAT IS IT? /BENTLEY/	JOLLY	NICE AND VENERABLE, OLD MAN. DONT BE DISCOURAGED.
MIS. (119)	IT RELIEVES MY WRETCHED NERVES. I FEEL PERFECTLY	JOLLY	NOW. /LORD SUMMERHAYS/ NOT AT ALL ASHAMED OF YOURSELF,
BULL IV (155)	FIND THE WORLD QUITE GOOD ENOUGH FOR ME: RATHER A	JOLLY	PLACE, IN FACT. /KEEGAN/ (LOOKING AT HIM WITH QUIET
LADY PREFACE(215)	ALL THIS CRUEL BLACKGUARDISM BUT AN UPROARIOUSLY	JOLLY	RAG, ALTHOUGH THEY ARE BY NO MEANS WITHOUT GENUINE

JITT III	(76) YOU JUST REVEL IN IT. YOU THINK YOURSELF SUCH A	JOLLY	ROMANTIC FIGURE, YOU THINK THAT EVERYTHING THAT
FANY II	(293) IT WAS HIDEOUS; BUT THE POLICE WERE QUITE	JOLLY	; AND EVERYBODY SAID IT WAS A BIT OF ENGLISH FUN, AND
ROCK II	(282) OR WINNING A GOLF CHAMPIONSHIP. IT WAS ALL VERY	JOLLY	; AND I'M STILL A LITTLE PROUD OF IT. BUT EVEN IF I
MILL I	(150) THINGS ON YOU THAT YOU WONT TAKE. YOURE A	JOLLY	SIGHT MORE CAREFUL OF MY MONEY THAN I AM MYSELF.
PRES	(151) I'M SAYING TO YOU IS THE VOICE OF OLD ENGLAND A	JOLLY	SIGHT MORE THAN ALL THIS ROT THAT YOU GET OUT OF
MTH1 I	(18) NOISE IS GOOD! IT LIGHTENS MY HEART. YOU ARE A	JOLLY	SNAKE. BUT YOU HAVE NOT MADE A VOW YET. WHAT VOW DO
PYGM V	(274) /HIGGINS/ (AMAZED) UPSTAIRS! ! ! THEN I SHALL	JOLLY	SOON FETCH HER DOWNSTAIRS. (HE MAKES RESOLUTELY FOR
PYGM V	(277) MOTHER. LET HER SPEAK FOR HERSELF. YOU WILL	JOLLY	SOON SEE WHETHER SHE HAS AN IDEA THAT I HAVNT PUT INTO
ANNA	(293) MOMENT. WASH OUT; AND SEND THE GIRL ALONG. WE'LL	JOLLY	SOON TEACH HER TO BEHAVE HERSELF HERE. . . . OH, YOUVE
LIED	(200) WHO ARE YOU, PRAY, THAT YOU SHOULD BE SO	JOLLY	SUPERIOR? /HE/ MR BOMPAS: I CAN MAKE ALLOWANCES FOR
MRS IV	(236) YOU SAY TO RICHMOND, AND THEN A MUSIC HALL, AND A	JOLLY	SUPPER? /VIVIE/ CANT AFFORD IT. I SHALL PUT IN
MTH2	(84) THIS ROOM. /HASLAM/ IT WONT HAPPEN TO ME: THATS	JOLLY	SURE. /CONRAD/ IT MIGHT HAPPEN TO ANYONE. IT MIGHT
2TRU II	(71) PATIENT/ SWEETIE; ARE YOU REALLY HAVING SUCH A	JOLLY	TIME AFTER ALL? YOU BEGAN BY THREATENING TO GIVE UP
2TRU II	(72) I WANT SOMETHING SENSIBLE TO DO. A BEAVER HAS A	JOLLY	TIME BECAUSE IT HAS TO BUILD ITS DAM AND BRING UP ITS
MIS.	(173) MACHINES AND PEEPSHOWS OF ROWDY GIRLS HAVING A	JOLLY	TIME. I SPENT A PENNY ON THE LIFT AND FOURPENCE ON
OVER	(178) MYSELF. /MRS JUNO/ I GLORY IN MYSELF. IT'S SO	JOLLY	TO BE RECKLESS. CAN A MAN BE RECKLESS, I WONDER?
MRS I	(193) TO A SINGING TONE AS HE EXCLAIMS) IT'S EVER SO	JOLLY	TO FIND YOU HERE, PRAED. /PRAED/ I'M AN OLD FRIEND OF
PYGM EPILOG	(296) BUT HE AGREED THAT IT WOULD BE EXTRAORDINARILY	JOLLY	TO GO EARLY EVERY MORNING WITH ELIZA TO COVENT GARDEN
BARB II	SD(273) TO WHICH THEIR MEAL HAS JUST NOW GIVEN AN ALMOST	JOLLY	TURN. THE MAN TAKES A PULL AT HIS MUG, AND THEN GETS
MRS II	(199) EVER SO HONORABLE; AND YOUR LITTLE GIRL IS	JOLLY	WELL ABLE TO TAKE CARE OF HERSELF. SHE DONT NEED
FANY III	(306) IF YOU DONT TAKE CARE, YOULL GET YOUR FAT HEAD	JOLLY	WELL CLOUTED. /MARGARET/ IF YOU DONT TAKE CARE, THE
MTH3	(98) YOU; AND IF YOU THINK I'M AFRAID OF YOU, YOU	JOLLY	WELL DONT KNOW BURGE-LUBIN: THATS ALL. /CONFUCIUS/ YOU
MTH3	(110) WELL, I'M HANGED IF I SEE IT. I SHOULD	JOLLY	WELL LIVE FOR EVER IF I COULD. /THE ARCHBISHOP/ IT IS
MTH2	(40) OUR FAULT, MR HASLAM? /HASLAM/ NOT A BIT. SHE IS	JOLLY	WELL OFF HERE. /THE PARLOR MAID/ (REDDENING) I HAVE
MIS.	(181) DUSTING; BUT THEY WONT BEAR SCOURING. PATSY IS	JOLLY	WELL OUT OF IT. WHAT DOES IT MATTER, ANYHOW?
BULL IV	(167) YOU HAVE. NO, MY DEAR: TAKE MY WORD FOR IT, YOURE	JOLLY	WELL OUT OF THAT. THERE! (SWINGING HER ROUND AGAINST
OVER	(185) ANOTHER. OR YOU CAN TELL YOUR HUSBAND AND LET HIM	JOLLY	WELL PUNCH MY HEAD IF HE CAN. BUT I'M DAMNED IF I'M
HART III	(134) I DONT KNOW WHAT YOU CALL ACHIEVEMENTS; BUT IVE	JOLLY	WELL PUT A STOP TO THE GAMES OF THE OTHER FELLOWS IN
ROCK II	(255) DO MY JOB THEYD CHUCK ME OVERBOARD; AND SERVE ME	JOLLY	WELL RIGHT! YOU JUST KNOW NOTHING ABOUT IT, BECAUSE
OVER	(190) /GREGORY/ OH YES! IF, IF, IF. YOU KNOW	JOLLY	WELL THAT SELF-SACRIFICE DOESNT WORK EITHER WHEN YOU
MIS.	(128) WOMAN WHO WAS HEAD OF THAT SILLY COLLEGE WHAT I	JOLLY	WELL THOUGHT OF HIM. HE WOULD HAVE BEEN GLAD TO HAVE
MIS.	(129) CONSCIENCE; BUT FROM WHAT I COULD MAKE OUT SHE	JOLLY	WELL TOOK CHARGE OF HIS. THE WHOLE THREE OF THEM TOOK
O'FL PREFACE	(202) WHY THE SURVIVORS OF HIS WRATH DO NOT FEEL AS	JOLLY	WITH HIM AS HE DOES WITH THEM. ON THE SMOULDERING
APPL INTRLUD	(252) IS NO WIFE ON EARTH SO PRECIOUS, NO CHILDREN SO	JOLLY	, NO CABINET SO TACTFUL THAT IT IS IMPOSSIBLE EVER TO
JOAN 3	(88) AFRAID, KNOWING HIS MAN) IT LOOKED FRIGHTFULLY	JOLLY	, THAT FLASH OF BLUE. LOOK! THERE GOES THE OTHER!
FANY I	(279) GET A CAB ON THE NOD; SO WE STARTED TO WALK, VERY	JOLLY	, YOU KNOW: ARM IN ARM, AND DANCING ALONG, SINGING AND
MILL II	(166) HE IS IN THE WORST OF TEMPERS. /EPIFANIA/ HOW	JOLLY	! /ADRIAN/ (LOOKING ROUND DISPARAGINGLY) I MUST BE A
SUPR II	(67) TO NICE; AND I'M GOING TO TAKE YOU. /VIOLET/ HOW	JOLLY	! /HECTOR/ YES; BUT HOW ARE WE GOING TO MANAGE? YOU
MTH5	(220) THEM AND DANCE ROUND THEM. /THE NEWLY BORN/ HOW	JOLLY	! WHAT IS A SCULPTOR? /ACIS/ LISTEN HERE, YOUNG ONE.
MIS.	(199) UP IN INSTITUTIONS! /HYPATIA/ OH YES. HOW	JOLLY	! YOU AND I MIGHT BE FRIENDS THEN; AND JOEY COULD
MILL II	(166) WHAT I HAVE JUST SAID? /ADRIAN/ YOU SAID " HOW	JOLLY	! " I LOOK ROUND AT THIS ROTTEN OLD INN TRYING TO
MILL II	(167) CHEESE. IF YOU CAN SUFFER THIS AND SAY " HOW	JOLLY	! " THERE MUST BE SOME IRRESISTIBLE ATTRACTION
MILL II	(167) YET YOU CHOOSE THIS FILTHY OLD INN AND SAY " HOW	JOLLY	! " WHAT IS THE USE OF BEING A MILLIONAIRESS ON SUCH
		JOLT	
HART PREFACE	(38) EXTENT. WE HAVE ALL HAD A TREMENDOUS	JOLT	; AND ALTHOUGH THE WIDESPREAD NOTION THAT THE SHOCK OF
		JOLTED	
GENV III	(73) IN ENGLAND. THEY NEVER WILL BE. THE WORLD MAY BE	JOLTED	OUT OF ITS TRACKS FOR A MOMENT BY THE SHOCK OF A WAR
		JONAH	
MIS. PREFACE	(96) INSTEAD OF BEING ASSOCIATED WITH THE STORY OF	JONAH	AND THE GREAT FISH AND THE THOUSAND OTHER TALES THAT
GETT PREFACE	(193) STATESMAN. THOSE WHO DID NOT BELIEVE THE STORY OF	JONAH	AND THE GREAT FISH WERE ALL THE READIER TO BELIEVE
MIS. PREFACE	(96) OF THEM IS THAT CHILDREN ALL LIKE THE STORY OF	JONAH	AND THE WHALE (THEY INSIST ON ITS BEING A WHALE IN
LION PREFACE	(23) AND CLAIMS TO BE GREATER THAN SOLOMON OR	JONAH	. WHEN REPROACHED, AS BUNYAN WAS, FOR RESORTING TO THE
SIM I	(45) THROWN YOU ON THIS SHORE FOR THE PURPOSE, LIKE	JONAH	. WILL YOU UNDERTAKE IT? /THE CLERGYMAN/ I SHOULD
FABL PREFACE	(73) AJALON, IF THE BIG FISH COULD NOT HAVE SWALLOWED	JONAH	NOR HE SURVIVE IN ITS BELLY, THEN NOTHING IN THE BIBLE
MIS. PREFACE	(96) BY BIBLE SMASHERS WITHOUT ANY SENSE OF HUMOR THAT	JONAH	WOULD NOT HAVE FITTED INTO A WHALE'S GULLET -- AS IF
		JONAS	
DOCT PREFACE	(45) NO MATTER HOW SENSIBLE IT MAY BE, THE NAME OF	JONAS	HANWAY LIVES AS THAT OF A BRAVE MAN BECAUSE HE WAS THE
		JONATHAN	
APPL II	(276) TO BE A PILGRIM FATHER. HE IS NO MORE UNCLE	JONATHAN	THAN YOU ARE JOHN BULL. /MAGNUS/ YES: WE LIVE IN A
FABL PREFACE	(81) IN CAPTIVITY WERE INSTRUCTED BY A DEIFIED	JONATHAN	WILD TO STEAL THE JEWELRY OF THE EGYPTIANS BEFORE
		JONES	
FANY EPILOG	(330) UNTIL YOU KNEW WHICH WAS PINERO AND WHICH WAS	JONES	? BESIDES, WHAT SORT OF PLAY IS THIS? THATS WHAT I
GETT PREFACE	(195) UP IN WHICH THE LIBERTINE AND PROFLIGATE-- TOM	JONES	AND CHARLES SURFACE-- ARE THE HEROES, AND DECOROUS,
BARB III	(323) THANK YOU, SIR." AND THATS ALL. /CUSINS/ BUT	JONES	HAS TO BE KEPT IN ORDER. HOW DO YOU MAINTAIN
PYGM III	SD(244) CHAIR ROUGHLY CARVED IN THE TASTE OF INIGO	JONES	, ON THE SAME SIDE A PIANO IN A DECORATED CASE. THE
BARB III	(323) WELL, JONES, IS THE BABY DOING WELL? AND HAS MRS	JONES	MADE A GOOD RECOVERY? " " NICELY, THANK YOU, SIR." AND
PYGM III	SD(244) MRS HIGGINS WAS BROUGHT UP ON MORRIS AND BURNE	JONES	; AND HER ROOM, WHICH IS VERY UNLIKE HER SON'S ROOM IN
BARB III	(324) I DONT, THEY DO. YOU SEE, THE ONE THING	JONES	WONT STAND IS ANY REBELLION FROM THE MAN UNDER HIM, OR
METH PREFACE	(R48) IS UNCHALLENGED, AND HIS BIOGRAPHER, MR FESTING	JONES	, IS ENJOYING A VOGUE LIKE THAT OF BOSWELL OR
BARB III	(323) ORDERS. WHEN I SPEAK TO ONE OF THEM IT IS " WELL,	JONES	, IS THE BABY DOING WELL? AND HAS MRS JONES MADE A
GETT PREFACE	(256) REGISTRAR OR THE REVEREND JOHN SMITH OR WILLIAM	JONES	, MUST BE GOT RID OF. MEANS OF BREAKING UP UNDESIRABLE
PYGM III	SD(244) GROSVENOR GALLERY THIRTY YEARS AGO (THE BURNE	JONES	, NOT THE WHISTLER SIDE OF THEM) ARE ON THE WALLS. THE
PHIL I	SD(69) KENDAL, ADA REHAN, SARAH BERNHARDT, HENRY ARTHUR	JONES	, SIR ARTHUR PINERO, SYDNEY GRUNDY, AND SO ON, BUT NOT
BARB III	(324) 4 SHILLINGS A WEEK LESS THAN HIMSELF, AND MRS	JONES	! OF COURSE THEY ALL REBEL AGAINST ME, THEORETICALLY.
FANY EPILOG	(329) HAD TO WRITE ABOUT A PLAY BY PINERO AND ONE BY	JONES	! WOULD YOU SAY EXACTLY THE SAME THING ABOUT THEM?
		JONES'S	
METH PREFACE	(R44) NINETEENTH CENTURY HAS ONLY TO READ MR FESTING	JONES'S	MEMOIR OF SAMUEL BUTLER TO LEARN HOW COMPLETELY EVEN
		JONHOBSNOXIUS	
MTH4 II	(192) LONG LIFE WAS INVENTED, JUST AS THE VICTIMS OF	JONHOBSNOXIUS	CURSED THE DAY WHEN ETERNAL LIFE WAS INVENTED.
MTH4 II	(191) IT IN THE NORTHERN PART OF THESE ISLANDS BY	JONHOBSNOXIUS	, CALLED THE LEVIATHAN? THOSE MISGUIDED
		JONSON	
LADY PREFACE	(226) HIS DEATH WAS HASTENED BY A DRINKING BOUT WITH	JONSON	AND DRAYTON MUST BE REJECTED, AND THE REMORSE OF
LADY PREFACE	(226) HE GOT DRUNK WHEN HE MADE A NIGHT OF IT WITH	JONSON	AND DRAYTON, THE SONNETS RAISE AN UNPLEASANT QUESTION
LADY PREFACE	(218) STOP " THIS SIDE IDOLATRY," IF, THEREFORE, EVEN	JONSON	FELT HIMSELF FORCED TO CLEAR HIMSELF OF EXTRAVAGANCE
LADY PREFACE	(218) IDOLATRY, BUT IDOLATRY FULSOME ENOUGH TO IRRITATE	JONSON	INTO AN EXPRESS DISAVOWAL OF IT? JONSON, THE
MILL PREFACE	(109) AND CURIOUS CONTEMPORARY CHARACTERS SUCH AS BEN	JONSON	MIGHT WRITE WERE HE ALIVE NOW, YET IT RAISES A
LADY PREFACE	(232) MATTER. THE IDOLATRY WHICH EXASPERATED BEN	JONSON	WAS BY NO MEANS A POPULAR MOVEMENT; AND, LIKE ALL
LADY PREFACE	(214) COUNTESS OF ROUSILLON, I PREFER THAT ONE OF WHOM	JONSON	WROTE " SIDNEY'S SISTER: PEMBROKE'S MOTHER: DEATH ERE
LADY PREFACE	(218) IRRITATE JONSON INTO AN EXPRESS DISAVOWAL OF IT?	JONSON	, THE BRICKLAYER, MUST HAVE FELT SORE SOMETIMES WHEN
BASH PREFACE	(89) WROTE ALL HIS STAGE DIRECTIONS IN LATIN, OR BEN	JONSON	, WHO DEPLORED THE SLENDERNESS OF SHAKESPEAR'S
		JONSON'S	
PHIL PREFACE	(68) TO DATE. I SHOULD AS SOON THINK OF BRINGING BEN	JONSON'S	BARTHOLOMEW FAIR UP TO DATE BY CHANGING THE FAIR
LADY PREFACE	(217) BY HIS OWN GENERATION," HE EVEN DESCRIBES	JONSON'S	DESCRIPTION OF HIS " LITTLE LATIN AND LESS GREEK"
LADY PREFACE	(217) OF THEIR GENERATION THAT THEY WERE GREAT MEN, BEN	JONSON'S	EVIDENCE DISPOSES OF SO IMPROBABLE A NOTION AT ONCE
		JONSONS	
LADY PREFACE	(224) WRETCHED AND BROKEN AMONG A ROBUST CROWD OF	JONSONS	AND ELIZABETHS; BUT TO ME HE IS NOT SHAKESPEAR

			JOOK	
PRES	(146)	SHE'S GOT AN OFFER OF MARRIAGE FROM A YOUNG	JOOK	. /MITCHENER/ IS IT POSSIBLE? WHAT DID YOU DO? /MRS
			JOOTY	
PRES	(147)	RUN TO BLOW DHEM OUT OF IT. A MOTHER'S RISK IS	JOOTY	: A SOLDIER'S IS NOTHIN BUT DIVILMINT. /MITCHENER/ (
			JORDAN	
LION PREFACE	(22)	SYNAGOGUES; AND HIS BAPTISMAL FONT WAS THE RIVER	JORDAN	. HE WAS AN ASCETIC, CLOTHED IN SKINS AND LIVING ON
HART III	(145)	HE DRANK NOTHING BUT THE WATERS OF THE RIVER	JORDAN	. /ELLIE/ SPLENDID! AND YOU HAVNT HAD A DROP FOR AN
			JORJY	
GETT	(330)	CALL HIM GEORGE. /HOTCHKISS/ DO YOU LOVE YOUR	JORJY	PORJY? /MRS GEORGE/ OH, I DONT KNOW THAT I LOVE HIM.
			JORN'S	
CAPT I	(237)	KEPN: MAW NIME IS DRINKWORTER. YOU AWSK EM ET SIN	JORN'S	IN THE WORTERLEOO ROWD. ORN MAW GRENFAWTHER'S
			JORNSN	
CAPT II	(249)	AND DISILLUSION) DOWNT AWSK ME, MISTE	JORNSN	. THE KEPN'S NAOW CLAWSS ARTER ALL. /BRASSBOUND/ (A
CAPT II	(245)	EH? /DRINKWATER/ (CHAPFALLEN) NO OFFENCE, MISTE	JORNSN	-- /JOHNSON/ (OMINOUSLY) AY; BUT THERE IS OFFENCE.
			JORNSON	
CAPT II	(265)	UNS. (TO THE OTHERS) YNT YER SPOWK TO IM, MISTE	JORNSON	-- MISTE REDBROOK-- /BRASSBOUND/ (CUTTING HIM
			JOSEF	
INCA	(249)	PRINCE EITEL WILLIAM FREDERICK GEORGE FRANZ	JOSEF	ALEXANDER NICHOLAS VICTOR EMMANUEL ALBERT THEODORE
			JOSEPH	
GETT	(325)	GOT EM ALL ON TOO. GO AND HUNT UP A DRINK FOR	JOSEPH	: THERES A DEAR. (COLLINS GOES OUT. SHE LOOKS AT
LION PREFACE	(18)	ROYAL HOUSE OF DAVID, AND YET DECLARE THAT NOT	JOSEPH	BUT THE HOLY GHOST WAS THE FATHER OF JESUS. IT IS
MTH2	(71)	INFLUENCE AND POPULARITY IN THIS COUNTRY SINCE	JOSEPH	CHAMBERLAIN SET THE FASHION; AND THAT IS MERE ENERGY
PYGM PREFACE	(199)	IMPERIAL INSTITUTE ROSE IN SOUTH KENSINGTON, AND	JOSEPH	CHAMBERLAIN WAS BOOMING THE EMPIRE, I INDUCED THE
BULL PREFACE	(5)	IS NO LONGER UP-TO-DATE. HIS BETE NOIR, MR	JOSEPH	CHAMBERLAIN, HAS RETIRED FROM PUBLIC LIFE. THE
PHIL I	SD(84)	PROCEEDINGS OF HIS CHILDREN. HIS COMPANION, MR	JOSEPH	CUTHBERTSON, GRACE'S FATHER, HAS NONE OF THE
LION PREFACE	(18)	ESTABLISHING THE DESCENT OF JESUS THROUGH	JOSEPH	FROM THE ROYAL HOUSE OF DAVID, AND YET DECLARE THAT
FANY I	(276)	COURSE YOU DO. /GILBEY/ (WITH DIGNITY) I KNOW MR	JOSEPH	GRENFELL, THE BROTHER OF MONSIGNOR GRENFELL, IF IT IS
OVER PREFACE	(156)	A FLATTERY: EVERY TESTIMONIAL IS A DISPARAGEMENT:	JOSEPH	IS DESPISED AND PROMOTED, POTIPHAR'S WIFE ADMIRED AND
MTH4 I	(152)	I REFUSED TO ANSWER TO ANYTHING SHORTER THAN	JOSEPH	. AT EIGHTEEN I DISCOVERED THAT THE NAME JOSEPH WAS
GETT	(325)	AND ADDRESSES THE BEADLE) TAKE AWAY THAT BAUBLE,	JOSEPH	. WAIT FOR ME WHEREVER YOU FIND YOURSELF MOST
LION PREFACE	(33)	WHO IN THE INSURRECTION HAD COMMITTED MURDER,"	JOSEPH	OF ARIMATHEA, WHO BURIED JESUS IN HIS OWN TOMB, AND
MIS.	(152)	WAVES. HIS SON BENTLEY, ENGAGED TO HYPATIA. MR	JOSEPH	PERCIVAL, THE PROMISING SON OF THREE HIGHLY
MTH4 I	(152)	STIMULATED BY INDIGNATION) MY NAME, I REPEAT, IS	JOSEPH	POPHAM BOLGE BLUEBIN BARLOW, O.M. /ZOO/ WHAT A
MTH4 I	(147)	WAS DADDY. /THE ELDERLY GENTLEMAN/ MY NAME IS	JOSEPH	POPHAM BOLGE BLUEBIN BARLOW, O.M. /THE MAN/ THAT IS
APPL PREFACE	(174)	IN THE SCRAP BETWEEN KING MAGNUS AND MR	JOSEPH	PROTEUS IS SEEN TO BE A PLAIN DEDUCTION FROM THEIR
APPL I	(218)	ASHAMED OF YOURSELVES? BUT I AM NOT SURPRISED,	JOSEPH	PROTEUS. I OWN I LIKE A PRIME MINISTER THAT KNOWS HOW
GETT	(320)	TERRIBLE CURSE OF THE PRIEST'S LOT, THE CURSE OF	JOSEPH	PURSUED BY THE WIFE OF POTIPHAR, I AM INVARIABLY
MILL PREFACE	(112)	WITH THEIR DEITY. MOSES AND MAHOMET AND	JOSEPH	SMITH THE MORMON HAD TO PLEAD DIVINE REVELATIONS TO
GETT PREFACE	(195)	AND DECOROUS, LAW-ABIDING PERSONS-- BLIFIL AND	JOSEPH	SURFACE-- ARE THE VILLAINS AND BUTTS. PEOPLE LIKE TO
LION PREFACE	(20)	PROVOKING ANY COMMENT. AN ANGEL ANNOUNCES TO	JOSEPH	THAT JESUS IS THE SON OF THE HOLY GHOST, AND THAT HE
FABL PREFACE	(68)	AS PETER THE FISHERMAN, LUKE THE PAINTER,	JOSEPH	THE CARPENTER, SAINT CECILIA THE MUSICIAN, AND THE
MTH4 I	(152)	JOSEPH. AT EIGHTEEN I DISCOVERED THAT THE NAME	JOSEPH	WAS SUPPOSED TO INDICATE AN UNMANLY PRUDERY BECAUSE
MTH4 I	(152)	UNMANLY PRUDERY BECAUSE OF SOME OLD STORY ABOUT A	JOSEPH	WHO REJECTED THE ADVANCES OF HIS EMPLOYER'S WIFE:
LION PREFACE	(30)	DAYS AN ANGEL OPENED THE FAMILY VAULT OF ONE	JOSEPH	, A RICH MAN OF ARIMATHEA, WHO HAD BURIED JESUS IN
LION PREFACE	(34)	ANNUNCIATION, AS DESCRIBED BY MATTHEW, IS MADE TO	JOSEPH	, AND IS SIMPLY A WARNING TO HIM NOT TO DIVORCE HIS
LION PREFACE	(18)	CAME INTO THE WORLD AT HIS BIRTH AS THE SON OF	JOSEPH	, BUT ROSE FROM THE DEAD AFTER THREE DAYS AS THE SON
LION PREFACE	(31)	AT THAT. WE MUST BE CAREFUL THEREFORE TO CONCEIVE	JOSEPH	, NOT AS A MODERN PROLETARIAN CARPENTER WORKING FOR
LION PREFACE	(20)	WAS BETROTHED TO A MAN OF ROYAL PEDIGREE NAMED	JOSEPH	, WHO WAS RICH ENOUGH TO LIVE IN A HOUSE IN BETHLEHEM
			JOSHUA	
ROCK PREFACE	(183)	GOD MEANS. HAVE I NOT READ IT IN THE CAMPAIGNS OF	JOSHUA	? WE ROMANS HAVE PURCHASED THE PAX ROMANA WITH OUR
JOAN PREFACE	(33)	THE INFALLIBILITY CLAIMED FOR THE BOOK OF	JOSHUA	BY SIMPLE SOULS WHOSE RATIONAL FAITH IN MORE
FABL PREFACE	(73)	IF THE STORY OF NOAH'S ARK WAS A FABLE, IF	JOSHUA	COULD NOT HAVE DELAYED THE SUNSET IN THE VALLEY OF
FABL PREFACE	(70)	COLLAPSE, AND CIVILIZATION PERISH IN ANARCHY. IF	JOSHUA	COULD NOT MAKE THE SUN STAND STILL, THERE IS A
ROCK PREFACE	(176)	THAT MANY OF ITS TALES, FROM THE TACTICS OF	JOSHUA	IN THE BATTLE OF GIBEON TO THE ASCENSION, MUST HAVE
ANNA PREFACE	(287)	FOR US. WE THREE UNBENT AS MRS SIDDONS, SIR	JOSHUA	REYNOLDS, AND DR JOHNSON MIGHT HAVE UNBENT, TO DEVISE
KING I	(169)	WAS WHEN THE SUN STOOD STILL ON GIBEON TO GIVE	JOSHUA	TIME TO SLAUGHTER THE AMORITES. THE SECOND WAS WHEN
KING I	(169)	SEE NOTHING BUT THE DAILY ROUND, THE COMMON TASK.	JOSHUA	WAS AN IGNORANT SOLDIER. HAD HE BEEN A PHILOSOPHER HE
ROCK PREFACE	(177)	MAKE THE SMALLEST DIFFERENCE TO RELIGION WHETHER	JOSHUA	WAS ANY MORE REAL THAN JACK THE GIANT KILLER, AND
FABL PREFACE	(73)	IF GALILEO, THE MAN OF SCIENCE, KNEW BETTER THAN	JOSHUA	, AND LINNEUS AND DARWIN BETTER THAN MOSES, THEN
			JOSHUA'S	
JOAN PREFACE	(33)	WITH A QUITE IRRATIONAL FAITH IN THE CHRONICLE OF	JOSHUA'S	CAMPAIGNS AS A TREATISE ON PHYSICS. THEREFORE THE
LION PREFACE	(94)	A PERSON AS JESUS OR NOT. WHEN HUME SAID THAT	JOSHUA'S	CAMPAIGNS WERE IMPOSSIBLE, WHATELY DID NOT WRANGLE
ROCK PREFACE	(177)	OF SETTING THE EARTH ROLLING WAS AS STARTLING AS	JOSHUA'S	FEAT OF MAKING THE SUN STAND STILL. THE CHURCH'S
SIM PREFACE	(4)	LOST THEIR SIMPLE FAITH IN A FLAT EARTH AND IN	JOSHUA'S	FEAT OF STOPPING THE SUN UNTIL HE HAD FINISHED HIS
ROCK PREFACE	(177)	KNOWLEDGE OF NATURE. IN TREATING THE LEGEND OF	JOSHUA'S	VICTORY AS A RELIGIOUS TRUTH INSTEAD OF INSISTING
			JOSSER	
GETT	(310)	DIGNITY). /REGINALD/ BOXER IS RATHER A FINE OLD	JOSSER	IN HIS WAY. /HOTCHKISS/ HIS UNIFORM GIVES HIM AN
MIS.	(126)	BECAUSE I'M A YOUNG CUB AND YOURE AN OLD	JOSSER	. (HE THROWS A CUSHION AT HYPATIA'S FEET AND SITS
FABL VI	(131)	I WAS THIRTEEN, IT WAS AN ARGUMENT BETWEEN AN OLD	JOSSER	NAMED JOB AND ONE OF THE OLD GODS, WHO PRETENDED HE
			JOSTLED	
MTH5	SD(206)	REST STOP. THE MUSIC STOPS. THE YOUTH WHOM HE HAS	JOSTLED	ACCOSTS HIM WITHOUT MALICE BUT WITHOUT ANYTHING THAT
MTH2	(52)	YOUR PEOPLE ARE A MOB IN WHICH ATHEISTS ARE	JOSTLED	BY PLYMOUTH BRETHREN, AND POSITIVISTS BY PILLARS OF
			JOSTLES	
LADY PREFACE	(212)	RESONANT VOICE DENOUNCES, WHOSE COLD SHOULDER	JOSTLES	EVERY DECENCY, EVERY DELICACY, EVERY AMENITY, EVERY
			JOSTLING	
SUPR PREFACE	(R26)	CONTINENTS AS THEY DRIVE A FOUR-IN-HAND; TURN A	JOSTLING	ANARCHY OF CASUAL TRADE AND SPECULATION INTO AN
MTH4 II	(183)	FETCH THE POLICE (HE GOES OUT PAST ZOO, ALMOST	JOSTLING	HER, AND BLOWING PIERCING BLASTS ON HIS WHISTLE).
PPP	SD(205)	AS THE THREE VICTIMS, AFTER REELING,	JOSTLING	, CANNONING THROUGH A GHASTLY QUADRILLE, AT LAST
			JOT	
SUPR HANDBOK	(208)	AS HAVE COME DOWN TO US, AND YOU WILL FIND NO	JOT	OF GROUND FOR THE BELIEF THAT ANY MORAL PROGRESS
GETT	(292)	EQUALITY OF OUR PROFESSION BY PUTTING A SINGLE	JOT	OF HIS DUTY OR HIS RISK ON THE SHOULDERS OF THE HUMBLEST
PYGM EPILOG	(295)	OF TEACHING PHONETICS, HIGGINS ABATED NOT A	JOT	OF HIS VIOLENT OPPOSITION TO IT. HE SAID SHE WAS NOT
LION PREFACE	(26)	MIRACLES A THOUSAND TIMES MORE WONDERFUL, NOT A	JOT	OF WEIGHT WOULD BE ADDED TO HIS DOCTRINE. AND YET THE
ROCK I	(199)	ABOUT THE FAMILY ALWAYS GOES DOWN WELL. JUST	JOT	THIS DOWN FOR ME. (DICTATING) FAMILY, FOUNDATION OF
SUPR I	(24)	THIS KNOWLEDGE OF OURSELVES; AND HE WHO ADDS A	JOT	TO SUCH KNOWLEDGE CREATES NEW MIND AS SURELY AS ANY
			JOTTED	
PYGM II	(219)	GRIEVANCE OF IT) WHY, THIS IS THE GIRL I	JOTTED	DOWN LAST NIGHT. SHE'S NO USE: IVE GOT ALL THE
			JOUNCE	
POSN	(440)	IN YOUR MAMMY'S LAP. /STRAPPER/ (FURIOUS) YOU	JOUNCE	ME ANY MORE ABOUT THAT HORSE, BLANCO POSNET; AND

JOURDAIN

TRFL (83)	ELSE INDEED ARE THE PASSAGES BETWEEN MONSIEUR	JOURDAIN	AND HIS PHILOSOPHERS AND FENCING MASTERS IN

JOURNAL

SUPR PREFACE(R9)	EVEN AS YOUR DAYS DO GROW, NO MERE PIONEERING	JOURNAL	DARES MEDDLE WITH THEM NOW: THE STATELY TIMES ITSELF
UNPL PREFACE(R9)	A PROMINENT PLACE RESERVED FOR ME ON A PROMINENT	JOURNAL	EVERY WEEK TO SAY MY SAY AS IF I WERE THE MOST
PHIL II (122)	YOU WISH IT. I HAVE NO OBJECTION. (HE TAKES THE	JOURNAL	FROM THE BOOKSTAND). I ADMIT THAT THE ITALIAN
FOUN (215)	LORD CHANCELLOR/ I TAKE IT THAT THE EXCELLENT	JOURNAL	FROM WHICH YOU FIRST QUOTED HAS PUT ALL
PHIL II (108)	PARTICULAR ORDERS, MISS. THE BRITISH MEDICAL	JOURNAL	HAS ALWAYS TO BE BROUGHT TO HIM DRECKLY IT COMES.
PHIL II SD(112)	IN THE UTMOST DISORDER, WITH THE BRITISH MEDICAL	JOURNAL	IN HIS CLENCHED HAND. THEY RISE IN ALARM. HE TRIES
DOCT PREFACE(59)	I TURN OVER THE PAGES OF BIOMETRIKA, A QUARTERLY	JOURNAL	IN WHICH IS RECORDED THE WORK DONE IN THE FIELD OF
PHIL II SD(94)	ON IBSEN'S RIGHT, READING THE BRITISH MEDICAL	JOURNAL	. HE IS YOUNG AS AGE IS COUNTED IN THE PROFESSIONS:
PHIL II SD(108)	THE PAGE ENTERS, CARRYING THE BRITISH MEDICAL	JOURNAL	, /CHARTERIS/ (CALLING TO THE PAGE) DR PARAMORE IS
PHIL II (114)	FOR LOST TIME NOW. (BITTERLY, SHEWING CRAVEN THE	JOURNAL	) THERE! YOU CAN READ FOR YOURSELF. THE CAMEL WAS
PHIL II (122)	EXPERIMENTS ON ANIMALS. (HE HANDS CHARTERIS THE	JOURNAL	). /CHARTERIS/ (TAKING IT) IT DOESNT MATTER: I DONT
2TRU I SD(37)	DOWN; TAKES OUT A LEAF CUT FROM AN ILLUSTRATED	JOURNAL	; AND PROCEEDS TO STUDY IT ATTENTIVELY. /THE
PHIL II (111)	HE'S PRETENDING TO READ THE BRITISH MEDICAL	JOURNAL	; BUT HE MUST BE MAKING UP HIS MIND FOR THE PLUNGE:
PHIL II (119)	SITS DOWN IN THE NEAREST EASY CHAIR, READING HIS	JOURNAL	TO INTIMATE THAT HE DOES NOT WISH TO PURSUE THE
PHIL II (113)	WORK OF MY LIFE! LOOK HERE (HE POINTS TO THE	JOURNAL	WITH A GHASTLY EXPRESSION OF HORROR)! IF THIS IS
PHIL II (115)	SUPPRESSED SOB, BENDING OVER THE BRITISH MEDICAL	JOURNAL	WITH HIS HEAD ON HIS HANDS AND HIS ELBOWS ON HIS
PHIL II (120)	MOMENT I READ THE NEWS IN THIS. (HE SHEWS THE	JOURNAL	, AND PUTS IT DOWN ON THE BOOKSTAND). /CHARTERIS/
PHIL II (122)	THE WAY, IF YOUVE DONE WITH THAT BRITISH MEDICAL	JOURNAL	, I SHOULD LIKE TO SEE HOW THEYVE SMASHED YOUR

JOURNALESE

BASH PREFACE(90)	TO PRODUCE VERSIONS IN MODERN VERNACULAR AND	JOURNALESE	UNDER STRESS OF THE FLAT FACT THAT THEIR FLOCKS

JOURNALISM

GENV IV (99)	TO PARALYZE ACTION, OUT OF THE RAGBAG OF STALE	JOURNALISM	AND KIKKERONIAN LATIN-- /SIR O./ I PROTEST. I
MILL PREFACE(116)	BY VICTORIES; AND HE COULD USE ALL THE DEVICES OF	JOURNALISM	AND PAGEANTRY AND PATRIOTIC BRAGGADOCIO TO MAKE
SUPR PREFACE(R13)	FOR A WHOLE CENTURY, THUS TREATING HIM AS ENGLISH	JOURNALISM	HAS TREATED THAT COMIC FOE OF THE GODS, PUNCH.
LADY PREFACE(215)	SURVEY FOR A MOMENT THE FIELD OF CONTEMPORARY	JOURNALISM	. HE WILL SEE THERE SOME MEN WHO HAVE THE VERY
ROCK I (207)	HIS WIFE WENT INTO PARLIAMENT AND MADE MONEY BY	JOURNALISM	. THAT WAS THE END OF HIM. /LADY CHAVENDER/ AND I
DOCT IV SD(159)	IN WHICH THESE DEFECTS DO NOT MATTER IS	JOURNALISM	(FOR A NEWSPAPER, NOT HAVING TO ACT ON ITS
SUPR PREFACE(R9)	FIFTEEN YEARS SINCE, AS TWIN PIONEERS OF THE NEW	JOURNALISM	OF THAT TIME, WE TWO, CRADLED IN THE SAME NEW
OVER PREFACE(162)	IN FACT, THE LITERATURE THAT HAS DRIVEN OUT THE	JOURNALISM	OF THE DIVORCE COURTS IS A LITERATURE OCCUPIED
POSN PREFACE(419)	NO CHANCES. AND AS FAR AS THE LAW IS CONCERNED,	JOURNALISM	, LITERATURE, AND THE DRAMA EXIST ONLY BY CUSTOM

JOURNALIST

DOCT PREFACE(62)	IN 1907 BECAUSE I MADE THE ARTIST A RASCAL, THE	JOURNALIST	AN ILLITERATE INCAPABLE, AND ALL THE DOCTORS "
FABL PREFACE(78)	WITH SUCH COMPLAINTS. HERE IN ENGLAND I, AN OLD	JOURNALIST	AND AGITATOR, KNOW ONLY TOO WELL THAT BOTH
FABL PREFACE(78)	ONLY A SUPERANNUATED (NOT SUPERNATURAL)	JOURNALIST	AND PLAYWRIGHT DOES NOT SHAKE THE FAITH OF MY
SIM PREFACE(3)	WITHOUT A SUITABLE CIVILIZATION. IF AUTHOR AND	JOURNALIST	ARE BOTH PLACID PANGLOSSIANS, CONVINCED THAT
SIM PREFACE(3)	NOT COVER THE CASES IN WHICH THE AUTHOR AND THE	JOURNALIST	ARE NOT WRITING AGAINST THE SAME BACKGROUND. THE
DOCT IV (160)	(HE SHUTS THE BOOK WITH A SNAP WHICH MAKES THE	JOURNALIST	BLINK, AND RETURNS IT TO HIM). MR DUBEDAT WILL BE
MILL PREFACE(120)	A MAN WAS MUSSOLINI. HE HAD BECOME KNOWN AS A	JOURNALIST	BY CHAMPIONING THE DEMOBILIZED SOLDIERS, WHO,
GENV III SD(65)	CENTRE TABLE, READING A MAGAZINE. THE AMERICAN	JOURNALIST	COMES IN FLOURISHING A CABLEGRAM. /THE
2TRU PREFACE(3)	AND AGREEABLE MANNERS, THE LESS INTELLECTUAL	JOURNALIST	CRITICS SULKED AS THEY ALWAYS DO WHEN THEIR
SIM PREFACE(3)	OF JUDGMENT, THE INCREASING BEWILDERMENT OF MY	JOURNALIST	CRITICS AS TO WHY I SHOULD WRITE SUCH PLAYS AS
6CAL PREFACE(89)	KILLED FOR TAKING HIS JOB TOO LIGHTLY, BUT THE	JOURNALIST	CRITICS KNEW NOTHING OF THIS. A KING EDWARD WHO
SIM PREFACE(3)	BACKGROUND, THE SIMPLEST ARE THOSE IN WHICH THE	JOURNALIST	IS IGNORANT AND UNCULTIVATED, AND THE AUTHOR IS
BARB III (321)	IVE FOUND YOUR PROFESSION FOR YOU. YOURE A BORN	JOURNALIST	. I'LL START YOU WITH A HIGH-TONED WEEKLY REVIEW.
GENV I (34)	HERE, I HAVE A PARTICULAR FRIEND, AN AMERICAN	JOURNALIST	. WOULD YOU MIND IF I SHEWED HIM YOUR DRAFT
BASH PREFACE(91)	FAMILIAR WITH IT THAT I HAD SOME DIFFICULTY AS A	JOURNALIST	LATER ON IN GETTING RID OF IT, IT MUST BE
GENV IV (88)	INTERESTED, IT SEEMS. /BEGONIA/ ONE FREE LANCE	JOURNALIST	LOOKED IN; BUT SHE WENT AWAY WHEN SHE FOUND THERE
3PLA PREFACE(R26)	COURSE OF HYPNOTIC SUGGESTION BY WHICH G.B.S. THE	JOURNALIST	MANUFACTURED AN UNCONVENTIONAL REPUTATION FOR
POSN PREFACE(388)	OF THE PRESS OR OF POLITICAL MEETINGS. ANY	JOURNALIST	MAY PUBLISH AN ARTICLE, ANY DEMAGOGUE MAY DELIVER
MRS PREFACE(153)	FOR THE ACTOR, THUS TO REDUCE A JADED LONDON	JOURNALIST	TO THE CONDITION OF THE SIMPLE SAILOR IN THE
GETT (288)	LET EVERY SNOB AND EVERY CAD AND EVERY HALFPENNY	JOURNALIST	WALK OVER US. WHY, THERES NOT A NEWSPAPER IN
DOCT IV SD(159)	AND UNVERACITY), HE HAS PERFORCE BECOME A	JOURNALIST	, AND HAS TO KEEP UP AN AIR OF HIGH SPIRITS
BARB PREFACE(221)	WHILST I, A COMPARATIVELY INSIGNIFICANT IRISH	JOURNALIST	, WAS LEADING THEM BY THE NOSE INTO AN
SUPR HANDBOK(192)	CAN ALSO THINK DECENTLY. BUT THE ORDINARY MODERN	JOURNALIST	, WHO HAS NEVER DISCUSSED SUCH MATTERS EXCEPT IN
GENV I (34)	BEFORE I SEND IT OFF? /THE JEW/ AN AMERICAN	JOURNALIST	! EXCELLENT, EXCELLENT. BY ALL MEANS SUBMIT MY

JOURNALISTIC

LION PREFACE(73)	NATIVE TOWN, THE DUBLIN DAILY EXPRESS, BECAUSE MY	JOURNALISTIC	PHRASE SHEWED THAT I WAS TREATING IT AS AN

JOURNALIST-CRITIC

CYMB FORWORD(133)	THAT SUPERSTITION IN THE DAYS WHEN I WAS A	JOURNALIST-CRITIC	, SHOULD PERPETRATE A SPURIOUS FIFTH ACT

JOURNALIST-PATIENT

DOCT PREFACE(11)	CENTURY A LONDON EVENING PAPER SENT ROUND A	JOURNALIST-PATIENT	TO ALL THE GREAT CONSULTANTS OF THAT DAY,

JOURNALISTS

MRS PREFACE(175)	BY THE WHOLE LONDON AND NEW YORK PRESS, GAVE THE	JOURNALISTS	A PIECE OF HIS MIND AS TO THEIR MORAL TASTE IN
GETT PREFACE(241)	WHOLE SOCIAL FABRIC WAS TUMBLING TO PIECES, WHEN	JOURNALISTS	AND BISHOPS AND AMERICAN PRESIDENTS AND OTHER
HART PREFACE(16)	AND GERMAN DYNASTIC AMBITION SHOULD BE PAINTED BY	JOURNALISTS	AND RECRUITERS IN BLACK AND RED AS EUROPEAN
GETT PREFACE(257)	IS, IN OTHER WORDS, DO NOT ASK YOUR NEWSPAPER.	JOURNALISTS	ARE TOO POORLY PAID IN THIS COUNTRY TO KNOW
MRS PREFACE(173)	OBSERVATION AND KNOWLEDGE ARE LEFT BEHIND WHEN	JOURNALISTS	GO TO THE THEATRE. ONCE IN THEIR STALLS, THEY
MILL PREFACE(120)	SHAMBLES, OF THIS CHANGE OUR PARLIAMENTARIANS AND	JOURNALISTS	HAD NO SUSPICION. CREATURES OF HABIT, THEY WENT
MRS PREFACE(154)	OF THE COMMITTEE WERE, THE BETTER. SOME OF THE	JOURNALISTS	I HAVE SHOCKED REASON SO UNRIPELY THAT THEY WILL
6CAL PREFACE(89)	OF THE QUAINT ILLITERACY OF OUR MODERN LONDON	JOURNALISTS	. THEIR ONLY NOTION OF A KING WAS A PLEASANT AND
BARB PREFACE(222)	AND DR STANTON COIT, AND STRENUOUS NONCONFORMIST	JOURNALISTS	LIKE WILLIAM STEAD, WHO NOT ONLY UNDERSTOOD THE
MRS PREFACE(175)	CONSCIENCE SO TOOK POSSESSION OF THE NEW YORK	JOURNALISTS	THAT THE FEW AMONG THEM WHO KEPT THEIR FEET
APPL PREFACE(180)	STATESMEN TO MAKE SPEECHES ABOUT DEMOCRACY, OR	JOURNALISTS	TO REPORT THEM, WITHOUT OBSCURING IT IN A CLOUD
MRS PREFACE(152)	FAULT OF THE CENSORSHIP THAT OUR LEGISLATORS AND	JOURNALISTS	WERE NOT BETTER INSTRUCTED. IN 1902 THE STAGE
MRS PREFACE(176)	FINANCIAL DISASTROUSNESS OF MORAL DISCREDIT, THE	JOURNALISTS	WHO HAD DONE ALL THE MISCHIEF KEPT PAYING VICE
PRES (142)	IT MANUFACTURED IN OUR PAPERS BY POOR DEVILS OF	JOURNALISTS	WHO WILL SELL THEIR SOULS FOR FIVE SHILLINGS.
MIS. PREFACE(45)	ORATIONS AND ARTICLES OF OUR POLITICIANS AND	JOURNALISTS	, MUST ALL BE TOLERATED NOT ONLY BECAUSE ANY OF
UNPL PREFACE(R26)	CLASSES OF MEN: FOR INSTANCE, THE PLAYWRIGHTS AND	JOURNALISTS	, TO WHOM I MYSELF BELONG, NOT TO MENTION THE

JOURNALISTS-ON-THE-MAKE

ROCK II (235)	OF LABOR MEN AND SOCIALISTS AND LAWYERS AND	JOURNALISTS-ON-THE-MAKE	AND USED-UP TRADE UNION SECRETARIES,

JOURNALS

DOCT PREFACE(20)	SUFFICIENTLY TO TAKE IN ONE OF THE SCIENTIFIC	JOURNALS	AND FOLLOW THE LITERATURE OF THE SCIENTIFIC
PHIL II SD(94)	AND TOUCHING IT, IS A GREEN TABLE, LITTERED WITH	JOURNALS	, IBSEN, LOOKING DOWN THE ROOM, HAS THE DINING ROOM
MRS PREFACE(169)	MEN; AND WHEN THEY PROCEEDED TO EXPLAIN THAT THE	JOURNALS	THEY REPRESENTED COULD NOT POSSIBLY DEMORALIZE THE
CAND I SD(78)	THE LARGE TABLE IS LITTERED WITH PAMPHLETS,	JOURNALS	, LETTERS, NESTS OF DRAWERS, AN OFFICE DIARY,

JOURNEY

HART III (133)	ANY OF US BUT TRAVELLING EXPENSES FOR OUR LIFE'S	JOURNEY	? /MRS HUSHABYE/ BUT YOU HAVE FACTORIES AND CAPITAL
CAPT III (273)	HANDS. (LOOKING REPROACHFULLY AT HER) ON YOUR	JOURNEY	BACK HERE, YE SEEM TO HAVE FRIGHTENED THE POOR MAN
MIS. PREFACE(63)	GOING A SIMPLE ERRAND INVOLVING A PURCHASE AND A	JOURNEY	BY RAIL OR OTHER PUBLIC METHOD OF LOCOMOTION, IT
PYGM III SD(250)	IMPRECATIONS; AND FINISHING HIS DISASTROUS	JOURNEY	BY THROWING HIMSELF SO IMPATIENTLY ON THE DIVAN THAT
SUPR III (139)	/TANNER/ THERE! I HAVE FOUND ONE MAN ON MY	JOURNEY	CAPABLE OF REASONABLE CONVERSATION; AND YOU ALL
HART I (67)	ELLIE) I HOPE, MISS ELLIE, YOU HAVE NOT FOUND THE	JOURNEY	DOWN TOO FATIGUING. (THEY SHAKE HANDS). /MRS

2TRU PREFACE(9) OF WHAT HE CALLS WITH GOOD REASON " THE WORST JOURNEY IN THE WORLD" THROUGH THE ANTARCTIC WINTER, WAS NO
OVER (180) NOT. BUT, YOU KNOW, PART OF THE ROMANCE OF A JOURNEY IS THAT A MAN KEEPS IMAGINING THAT SOMETHING MIGHT
AUGS PREFACE(261) PASSPORTS AND OTHER OFFICIAL FACILITIES FOR MY JOURNEY , IT HAPPENED JUST THEN THAT THE STAGE SOCIETY GAVE
MTH4 I (140) TO A MACHINE, BUT TO A-- A-- A-- SENTIMENTAL JOURNEY , /THE WOMAN/ I AM AFRAID I AM AS MUCH IN THE DARK
CLEO PRO2 (99) IS ALREADY COME; FOR WE HAD NOT MADE HALF A DAY'S JOURNEY ON OUR WAY BACK WHEN WE CAME UPON A CITY RABBLE
GENV I (42) I MUST BE CAREFUL NOT TO OVERSTRAIN MY HEART. THE JOURNEY TO GENEVA IS A TERRIBLE ONE FOR A MAN OF MY YEARS.
CLEO PRO2 (99) PTOLEMY, BUT ONLY THE HIGH GODS. WE WENT A JOURNEY TO INQUIRE OF PTOLEMY WHY HE HAD DRIVEN CLEOPATRA
WIDO I (9) THINK IT SENSIBLE TO TAKE A LONG AND EXPENSIVE JOURNEY TO SEE WHAT THERE IS TO BE SEEN, AND THEN GO AWAY
MRS III (223) SITS DOWN TO READ IT). /FRANK/ I DONT KNOW. HER JOURNEY TO TOWN LOOKS AS IF SHE DID. NOT THAT MY MOTHER
CAPT I (226) YOU WILL BE WISHING TO HAVE SOME TEA AFTER YOUR JOURNEY , I'M THINKING. /LADY CICELY/ THOUGHTFUL MAN THAT
POSN PREFACE(418) MAY VENTURE ON AN EDITION OF STERNE'S SENTIMENTAL JOURNEY , OR A MANAGER WHETHER HE MAY PRODUCE KING LEAR

JOURNEYMAN
CAND I (100) MAY BE A MASTER BUILDER WHERE I AM ONLY A HUMBLE JOURNEYMAN ; FOR DONT THINK, MY BOY, THAT I CANNOT SEE IN

JOURNEYMAN'S
CYMB FORWORD(137) LIKE MOZART, I HAVE NOT CONFINED MYSELF TO THE JOURNEYMAN'S JOB OF WRITING " ADDITIONAL ACCOMPANIMENTS": I

JOURNEYS
ROCK I (198) AGO BUT FOR THE RELIEF OF THESE CONFERENCES: THE JOURNEYS AND THE CHANGE. AND I LOOK FORWARD TO JAPAN. I
CAPT I (233) AND OCCASIONALLY ESCORTS PARTIES OF MERCHANTS ON JOURNEYS INTO THE INTERIOR. I UNDERSTAND THAT HE SERVED

JOVE
DOCT III (148) (RISING AND COMING OVER TO LOOK) NO, BY JOVE : I MUST HAVE THIS. /LOUIS/ I WISH I COULD AFFORD TO
HART PREFACE(27) MEN, SAYING THAT " COULD GREAT MEN THUNDER AS JOVE HIMSELF DOES JOVE WOULD NE'ER BE QUIET; FOR EVERY
MTH5 (228) COME DOWN TO US IN SEVERAL FORMS. ONE OF THEM IS JOVE . ANOTHER IS VOLTAIRE. /ECRASIA/ YOU ARE BORING US TO
HART PREFACE(27) ANGRY APE ENDOWED WITH POWERS OF DESTRUCTION THAT JOVE NEVER PRETENDED TO, HAVE BEGGARED EVEN HIS COMMAND OF
HART PREFACE(27) " COULD GREAT MEN THUNDER AS JOVE HIMSELF DOES JOVE WOULD NE'ER BE QUIET; FOR EVERY PELTING PETTY OFFICER
BULL I (92) IS THAT POSSIBLE? (SPRINGING TO HIS FEET) BY JOVE , I SEE IT ALL NOW. I'LL WRITE AN ARTICLE ABOUT IT, AND
CLEO IV (190) BLAZE. /RUFIO/ (GREATLY ALARMED) NOW, BY GREAT JOVE , YOU FILTHY LITTLE EGYPTIAN RAT, THAT IS THE VERY WORD
2TRU I (41) NOBODY EVER LOCKS THEM. HERE IS THE NECKLACE. BY JOVE ! IF THEY ARE ALL REAL, IT MUST BE WORTH ABOUT TWENTY
ROCK II (238) MEETING OF PARLIAMENT? /SIR BEMROSE/ WONT IT, BY JOVE ! IT'S SAFE FOR THE NEXT FIVE YEARS, WHAT THE COUNTRY
LION I (117) SKINNED, NOT A TALKER. /LENTULUS/ CHRISTIANS, BY JOVE ! LETS CHAFF THEM. /METELLUS/ AWFUL BRUTES. IF YOU
PYGM II (240) /HIGGINS/ WHATS THAT! THIS! /PICKERING/ BY JOVE ! /LIZA/ DONT I LOOK SILLY? /HIGGINS/ SILLY? /MRS
MRS I (194) IS THAT VIVIE'S MOTHER? /PRAED/ YES. /FRANK/ BY JOVE ! WHAT A LARK! DO YOU THINK SHE'LL LIKE ME? /PRAED/
2TRU II (80) AND TROTS SMARTLY OUT PAST THE HUT. /AUBREY/ BY JOVE ! ! /THE COUNTESS/ WELL I NE-- (CORRECTING HERSELF)

JOVE'S
HART PREFACE(27) HAVE SEEN A STRATFORD COTTAGE STRUCK BY ONE OF JOVE'S THUNDERBOLTS, AND HAVE HELPED TO EXTINGUISH THE

JOVIALLY
BULL IV (149) BUT THE SHOCK HAS QUITE PASSED OFF. /DORAN/ (JOVIALLY) NEVER MIND. COME ALONG ALL THE SAME AND TELL US

JOY
PHIL III (139) ME WISDOM: I BROKE YOUR HEART; AND YOU BROUGHT ME JOY : I MADE YOU CURSE YOUR WOMANHOOD; AND YOU REVEALED MY
CYMB V (143) OH, YOU GODS, WHAT SACRIFICE CAN PAY YOU FOR THIS JOY ? /IMOGEN/ YOU DARE PRETEND YOU LOVE ME. /POSTHUMUS/
MTH4 II (178) CHAINS. /THE ORACLE/ AND YOU? DO YOU SHARE THEIR JOY ? /NAPOLEON/ NOT AT ALL. WHAT SATISFACTION IS IT TO ME
DOCT V (177) PAINT THOSE PICTURES WHICH ARE MY IMPERISHABLE JOY AND PRIDE: YOU DID NOT SPEAK THE WORDS THAT WILL ALWAYS
DOCT V (177) YOU ARE WELL. HIS WORKS ARE AN IMPERISHABLE JOY AND PRIDE FOR YOU. /JENNIFER/ AND YOU THINK THAT IS YOUR
JITT II (35) YOUR FATHER BROUGHT YOU. HE WAS RADIANT WITH JOY AND PRIDE IN YOU. WE WERE ALL SO HAPPY. /EDITH/ (
BULL IV (147) MAKE US MERRY? GO ON, BARNEY: THE LAST DROPS OF JOY ARE NOT SQUEEZED FROM THE STORY YET. TELL US AGAIN HOW
SIM PREFACE(18) NOT BE PUT OUT OF THEIR PAIN, OR OUT OF THEIR JOY AS THE CASE MAY BE. THE COMMUNITY MUST DRIVE A MUCH
NEVR IV (298) AND GRACE). /PHILIP/ " ON WITH THE DANCE: LET JOY BE UNCONFINED." WILLIAM. /WAITER/ YES, SIR. /PHILIP/ CAN
PHIL I (78) SUCH SUFFERING IN MY HAPPINESS THAT I HARDLY KNEW JOY FROM PAIN. (SHE SINKS ON THE PIANO STOOL, AND ADDS, AS
MTH5 (248) WHOLE PATH. /MARTELLUS/ IT IS TRUE. WITH FIERCE JOY I TURNED A TEMPERATURE OF A MILLION DEGREES ON THOSE TWO
CATH PREFACE(158) OF HIS BUSINESS: THERE IS A KEEN AND WHIMSICAL JOY IN DIVINING AND REVEALING A SIDE OF AN ACTOR'S GENIUS
CAND I (88) (OVERWHELMED) IS IT POSSIBLE! WELL, THERES MORE JOY IN HEAVEN OVER ONE SINNER THAT REPENTETH! -- (GOING TO
PRES (161) ARE ONE OF THOSE UNSEXED CREATURES WHO HAVE NO JOY IN LIFE, NO SENSE OF BEAUTY, NO HIGH NOTES. /MITCHENER/
SUPR PREFACE(R34) SKILL TO HIM THAT CAN GET IT." THIS IS THE TRUE JOY IN LIFE, THE BEING USED FOR A PURPOSE RECOGNIZED BY
SUPR III (116) BUT IT WAS NOT MUSIC, PAINTING, POETRY, AND JOY INCARNATED IN A BEAUTIFUL WOMAN. I RAN AWAY FROM IT. I
BARB II (297) SHE'D BE SORRY I DIDNT. BUT I'M GLAD. OH WHAT A JOY IT WILL BE TO HER WHEN SHE HEARS I'M SAVED!
BUOY III (28) SUNDAY CLOTHES AND POKER FACES. NO PEACE, NO JOY . BUT FOR THE MUSIC THEY WOULD ALL GO MAD. THAT IS,
SUPR III (104) JUAN? /DON JUAN/ IN THE HEAVEN I SEEK, NO OTHER JOY . BUT THERE IS THE WORK OF HELPING LIFE IN ITS STRUGGLE
PHIL III (142) I DID IT. I GAVE HER UP, AND WISHED CUTHBERTSON JOY . HE TOLD ME THIS MORNING, WHEN WE MET AFTER MANY YEARS,
NEVR III (273) THE THOUGHT OF YOU WILL ALWAYS MAKE ME WILD WITH JOY . (SOME QUICK TAUNT IS ON HER LIPS: HE INTERPOSES
ARMS I (6) (HER EMOTION COMES BACK FOR A MOMENT). WISH ME JOY . (THEY KISS). THIS IS THE HAPPIEST NIGHT OF MY LIFE--
JOAN EPILOG (152) (SOLEMNLY) I BRING YOU GLAD TIDINGS OF GREAT JOY . REJOICE, O KING; FOR THE TAINT IS REMOVED FROM YOUR
FANY III (308) DESCRIBED IN YOUR NATIVE IDIOM AS A DAUGHTER OF JOY . /DUVALLET/ IT IS WHAT I THOUGHT. THESE ENGLISH
DEVL II (38) AGAIN). I SEE THERE IS ANOTHER SIDE TO DOMESTIC JOY . /JUDITH/ (ANGRILY) I WOULD RATHER HAVE A HUSBAND WHOM
MTH5 SD(217) MAY LIVE. THEY ALL WAVE THEIR HANDS AND SHOUT FOR JOY . /THE NEWLY BORN/ (INDIGNANT) I MAY LIVE! SUPPOSE
DOCT IV (163) IT NOW! /LOUIS/ DOES IT? IT FILLS ME WITH JOY . TELL THEM ABOUT IT. /MRS DUBEDAT/ IT WAS NOTHING--
POSN PREFACE(365) PLAYS A CHERISHED PRIVILEGE AND AN INEXHAUSTIBLE JOY . THIS ERROR WAS NOT REMOVED BY THE EVIDENCE GIVEN
BASH III (123) OUT. /CASHEL/ NEVER. I DO EMBRACE MY DOOM WITH JOY . WITH PARADISE IN PENTONVILLE OR PORTLAND I SHALL FEEL
MTH1 II (22) SHIELD TO SHIELD. IT IS TERRIBLE; BUT THERE IS NO JOY LIKE IT. I CALL IT FIGHTING. HE WHO HAS NEVER FOUGHT HAS
BASH II,2, (117) /THE CROWD/ UNFAIR! THE RULES! /CETEWAYO/ THE JOY OF BATTLE SURGES BOILING UP AND BIDS ME JOIN THE MELLAY.
BULL I (86) BY GEORGE! THEYRE WORTHY OF IT; AND I WISH THEM JOY OF IT. /DOYLE/ (UNMOVED BY THIS OUTBURST) THERE! YOU
APPL I (214) JOB, NICK. IT'S VACANT FOR YOU, BILL. I WISH YOU JOY OF IT. /PLINY/ NOW BOYS, BOYS! BE GOOD. WE CANT MAKE A
FABL III (111) A TRAMP. I MUST LIVE FROM HAND TO MOUTH. ALL THE JOY OF LIFE GOES WHEN YOU HAVE FIVE GUINEAS IN YOUR POCKET.
MIS. (130) BEEF TODAY, OLD MAN. /TARLETON/ BEEF BE BLOWED! JOY OF LIFE. READ IBSEN. (HE GOES INTO THE PAVILION TO
SIM II (62) HERE WITH YOU FROM THIS DAY ON. FOR I HAVE THE JOY OF LOVING YOU ALL WITHOUT THE BURDEN OF BEING LOVED IN
LION PROLOG (107) /MEGAERA/ SERVE YOU RIGHT! I WISH THE LIONS JOY OF YOU. (SCREAMING) ARE YOU GOING TO GET OUT OF MY WAY
MIS. (197) FIFTEEN HUNDRED A YEAR. TAKE IT. AND I WISH YOU JOY OF YOUR BARGAIN. /PERCIVAL/ IF YOU WISH TO KNOW WHO I
ROCK II (272) GOES TO THE DOOR). /BASHAM/ GOODBYE. I WISH YOU JOY OF YOUR HOST. /THE DUKE/ YOU DONT APPRECIATE HIM. HE IS
SUPR III (97) SINCERITY, THE BOND OF SYMPATHY WITH LOVE AND JOY --/DON JUAN/ YOU ARE MAKING ME ILL. /THE DEVIL/ THERE!
BARB II (284) TODGER FAIRMILE! /SHIRLEY/ (RISING WITH GRIM JOY) I'LL GO WITH HIM, MISS. I WANT TO SEE THEM TWO MEET.
PYGM IV (267) ME TO THE HEART. /LIZA/ (THRILLING WITH HIDDEN JOY) I'M GLAD. IVE GOT A LITTLE OF MY OWN BACK, ANYHOW.
LADY PREFACE(221) AN INCORRIGIBLE DIVINE LEVITY, AN INEXHAUSTIBLE JOY THAT DERIDED SORROW? THINK OF THE POOR DARK LADY HAVING
SUPR I (20) WILL IS TO BE CARRIED OUT. YOU DONT KNOW WHAT A JOY THAT IS TO ME AND TO MY MOTHER! (SHE GOES TO RAMSDEN
SUPR III (94) D MINOR AND ITS DOMINANT: A SOUND OF DREADFUL JOY TO ALL MUSICIANS). HA! MOZART'S STATUE MUSIC. IT IS
MTH4 II (178) THIS SLAUGHTER; TO GIVE MANKIND THIS TERRIBLE JOY WHICH THEY CALL GLORY; TO LET LOOSE THE DEVIL IN THEM
NEVR II (254) GONE. (VALENTINE'S FACE LIGHTS UP WITH SUDDEN JOY , DREAD, AND MISCHIEF AS HE REALIZES THAT HE IS ALONE
BARB II (291) UNDERSTAND THE SALVATION ARMY. IT IS THE ARMY OF JOY , OF LOVE, OF COURAGE: IT HAS BANISHED THE FEAR AND
OVER (178) PUSHED OVER A PRECIPICE. I'M INNOCENT. THIS WILD JOY , THIS EXQUISITE TENDERNESS, THIS ASCENT INTO HEAVEN CAN
SUPR III (97) AND OF THE HEART. I CALL ON IT TO SYMPATHIZE WITH JOY , WITH LOVE, WITH HAPPINESS, WITH BEAUTY-- /DON JUAN/ (
FABL PREFACE(98) MOZART'S MAGIC FLUTE AND BEETHOVEN'S ODE TO JOY , WITH THE MUSIC DRAMAS OF WAGNER, TO SAY NOTHING OF

JOYCE
MTH4 I (153) ISLANDS, TO A TIME WHEN TWO OF MY ANCESTORS, JOYCE BOLGE AND HENGIST HORSA BLUEBIN, WRESTLED WITH ONE
MTH2 (46) CAN TELL THINGS ONLY TO PEOPLE WHO CAN LISTEN. JOYCE BURGE HAS TALKED SO MUCH THAT HE HAS LOST THE POWER OF
MTH2 (68) IMMEDIATE REACH OF YOUR SEVENTIETH YEAR. MR JOYCE BURGE IS YOUR JUNIOR BY ABOUT ELEVEN YEARS. YOU WILL
MTH2 (44) WELL? WHAT IS IT NOW? /THE PARLOR MAID/ MR JOYCE BURGE ON THE TELEPHONE, SIR. HE WANTS TO SPEAK TO YOU.
MTH2 (70) AMAZED) OH! /FRANKLYN/ MR LUBIN: DO YOU CONSIDER JOYCE BURGE QUALIFIED TO GOVERN ENGLAND? /LUBIN/ (WITH
MTH2 SD(47) NOT DARING TO APPROACH) VERY KIND OF YOU TO COME. JOYCE BURGE STANDS FAST AND SAYS NOTHING; BUT HE SCREWS UP
MTH2 (45) PARLOR MAID GOES OUT. /CONRAD/ WELL, WHAT DOES JOYCE BURGE WANT? /FRANKLYN/ OH, A SILLY MISUNDERSTANDING.
MTH2 (46) WAIT HERE, BOTH OF YOU. WHEN YOU START YAWNING, JOYCE BURGE WILL TAKE THE HINT, PERHAPS. /SAVVY/ (TO
MTH2 (47) /THE PARLOR MAID/ (ENTERING AND ANNOUNCING) MR JOYCE BURGE. (HASLAM HASTILY MOVES TO THE FIREPLACE; AND
MTH2 (60) I SAY THAT SINCE THE OBJECT OF YOUR VISIT AND MR JOYCE BURGE'S IS TO SOME EXTENT POLITICAL, WE SHOULD HEAR

MTH2 (79) IN THE KINGDOM. I TAKE OFF MY HAT TO HIM. I, JOYCE BURGE, GIVE HIM BEST. AND YOU SIT THERE PURRING LIKE
MTH2 (46) HAS JUST DRIVEN UP IN A BIG CAR? /FRANKLYN/ MR JOYCE BURGE, PERHAPS. /SAVVY/ (DISAPPOINTED) OH, THEY KNOW,
MTH2 (49) /FRANKLYN/ I DO. /BURGE/ I AM, IF I MISTAKE NOT, JOYCE BURGE, PRETTY WELL KNOWN THROUGHOUT EUROPE, AND INDEED
MTH3 SD(91) GOLD FILLET ROUND HIS BROWS, COMES IN. HE IS LIKE JOYCE BURGE, YET ALSO LIKE LUBIN, AS IF NATURE HAD MADE A
MTH2 (44) TO SPEAK TO YOU. /FRANKLYN/ (ASTONISHED) MR JOYCE BURGE! /THE PARLOR MAID/ YES, SIR. /FRANKLYN/ TO

JOYFUL
DEVL I (18) THEM) WHO COULD LOOK AT THEM AND NOT BE PROUD AND JOYFUL ? (UNCLE TITUS, OVERBORNE, RESUMES HIS SEAT ON THE
PHIL II (119) BUSINESS SOMEHOW. I FULLY EXPECTED TO FIND YOU A JOYFUL ACCEPTED SUITOR. /PARAMORE/ (ANGRILY) YES, YOU HAVE
LION II SD(133) TAKE THE SUMMONS AS BEST THEY CAN, SOME JOYFUL AND BRAVE, SOME PATIENT AND DIGNIFIED, SOME TEARFUL
JITT III SD(70) HER EYES ARE WIDE OPEN AND HER EXPRESSION ONE OF JOYFUL SURPRISE AND RELIEF. SHE RUNS EAGERLY TO JITTA.
BARB II (306) THE UNSELFISHNESS OF UNDERSHAFT AND BODGER. OH BE JOYFUL ! (HE TAKES THE DRUMSTICKS FROM HIS POCKETS AND

JOYFULLY
CATH 4 (195) HIM! I PARDON HIM! /PATIOMKIN/ (SPRINGING UP JOYFULLY AND GOING BEHIND CLAIRE, WHOM HE RAISES IN HIS
CATH 1,SD(163) TO HAVE A MOMENT'S PEACE? THE SERGEANT SALUTES JOYFULLY AND HURRIES OUT, DIVINING THAT PATIOMKIN HAS
APPL PREFACE(171) THAT THE PRIME MINISTER MUST AT ONCE ACCEPT IT JOYFULLY AS SUCH. HE KNOWS BETTER. THE CHANGE WOULD RALLY
FOUN (215) EMPTY AWAY, I WOULD GIVE IT TO YOU, MISS, MOST JOYFULLY . /ANASTASIA/ I ASK, NOT CHARITY, BUT JUSTICE. /THE
CATH 3 (186) IF I CAN SPEAK TO THE EMPRESS. /THE SERGEANT/ (JOYFULLY) I PRAISE HEAVEN FOR YOU, LITTLE MOTHER. COME. (HE
MTH3 (133) /THE NEGRESS/ MR PRESIDENT. /BURGE-LUBIN/ (JOYFULLY) YES. (TAKING UP A PEG) ARE YOU AT HOME? /THE
LION II (143) OF CHRISTIANITY. (THE CHRISTIANS PRESS TO HIM JOYFULLY). THIS CHRISTIAN SORCERER -- (WITH A YELL, HE
PRES (162) WOMAN THAT I AM AT LAST CONVINCED-- /BALSQUITH/ (JOYFULLY)-- THAT THE SUFFRAGETS MUST BE SUPPORTED?
POSN (458) MET ME. I THOUGHT GOD SENT HIM TO ME. I RODE HERE JOYFULLY THINKING SO ALL THE TIME TO MYSELF. THEN I NOTICED

JOYLESS
SUPR PREFACE(R11) KEPT FREE, CANNOT PRETEND TO RELISH THESE JOYLESS ATTEMPTS AT SOCIAL SANITATION? IS IT NOT BECAUSE AT
MTH5 (213) TO DECAY INTO UNNATURAL, HEARTLESS, LOVELESS, JOYLESS MONSTERS IN FOUR SHORT YEARS? WHAT USE ARE THE
BARB PREFACE(222) THE PLAYGOER DESPISING THE SALVATIONIST AS A JOYLESS PERSON, SHUT OUT FROM THE HEAVEN OF THE THEATRE,
CAPT I SD(235) THE HOUSE. AGE ABOUT 36. HANDSOME FEATURES, BUT JOYLESS ; DARK EYEBROWS DRAWN TOWARDS ONE ANOTHER; MOUTH SET

JOYLESSLY
BULL II (108) FINEST HOTEL IN IRELAND HERE. (THEY REGARD HIM JOYLESSLY). /AUNT JUDY/ ARRA WOULD YOU MIND WHAT THE LIKE
WIDO III (49) EXCITEMENT! YOU NEED EXCITEMENT! (SHE LAUGHS JOYLESSLY , AND SITS DOWN ON THE RUG AT HIS FEET). HOW IS

JOYOUS
BASH I (93) BOUGHS! MOCK ME-- POOR MAID! -- DERIDE WITH JOYOUS COMFORTABLE CHATTER THESE STOLEN FEATHERS. LAUGH AT
MRS IV (253) HER GRAVE EXPRESSION BREAKS UP INTO ONE OF JOYOUS CONTENT; HER BREATH GOES OUT IN A HALF SOB, HALF
POSN PREFACE(369) SON OF AN IRISH CHANCELLOR, PRESENTING A KEEN AND JOYOUS FRONT TO ENGLISH INTELLECTUAL SLOTH. ABOVE ALL, THERE
MTH5 SD(214) QUICKLY INTO THE TEMPLE) ALL READY. COME ALONG. JOYOUS PROCESSIONAL MUSIC STRIKES UP IN THE TEMPLE. /THE
PHIL III (138) NIGHT BEFORE AT CUTHBERTSON'S: HE FACES THEM WITH JOYOUS RECKLESSNESS). NO USE TO THREATEN ME NOW: I AM NOT

JOYOUSLY
CLEO III (148) BUY MY CARPETS THROUGH YOU. (APOLLODORUS BOWS JOYOUSLY . AN OAR APPEARS ABOVE THE QUAY; AND THE BOATMAN, A
MTH3 (98) I SEEM TO SEE A GREAT DOG WAG HIS TAIL AND BARK JOYOUSLY . BUT IF HE LEAVES MY HEEL HE IS LOST.
SUPR II (63) JOINS HECTOR. /ANN/ (POUNCING ON HER MOTHER JOYOUSLY) OH, MAMMA, WHAT DO YOU THINK! JACK IS GOING TO
2TRU III (100) HONORS LIST BY WIRELESS. /TALLBOYS/ (RISING JOYOUSLY TO TAKE THE PAPER) AH! CONGRATULATE ME, MY

JOYOUSNESS
SUPR III SD(94) IN HIS WAR WORN VISAGE BRIM OVER WITH HOLIDAY JOYOUSNESS . TO HIS SCULPTOR HE OWES A PERFECTLY TRAINED
BARB PREFACE(227) VITALITY SUDDENLY BEGINS TO GERMINATE AGAIN. JOYOUSNESS , A SACRED GIFT LONG DETHRONED BY THE HELLISH
JOAN 2,SD(72) TO MAKE HIMSELF AGREEABLE, BUT LACKS NATURAL JOYOUSNESS , AND IS NOT REALLY PLEASANT. IN FACT WHEN HE

JOYS
BULL IV (170) REAL LIFE AND REAL WORK AND REAL CARES AND REAL JOYS AMONG REAL PEOPLE: SOLID ENGLISH LIFE IN LONDON. THE
MTH4 II (192) ATTAINING. I HAVE BEEN CHEATED OUT OF THE NATURAL JOYS AND FREEDOMS OF MY LIFE BY THIS DREAM TO WHICH THE
CYMB FORWORD(136) DOCILITY. I CANNOT SHARE THESE INFANTILE JOYS . HAVING BECOME INTERESTED IN IACHIMO, IN IMOGEN, AND

J'YOU
SIM II (82) BASKET. (SHE GOES INTO THE HOUSE). /MRS HYERING/ J'YOU THINK ITLL BE ALL RIGHT IF I GO AND DO SOME CROSSWORD

JUAN
SUPR III (118) SELECTION, VIRTUE, HONOR, CHASTITY-- /ANA/ DON JUAN : A WORD AGAINST CHASTITY IS AN INSULT TO ME. /DON
SUPR III (93) I BEG YOUR PARDON. /ANA/ (ALMOST TENDERLY) JUAN : DID YOU REALLY LOVE ME WHEN YOU BEHAVED SO
SUPR III (124) STATUE/ (IMPRESSED) A VERY CLEVER POINT THAT, JUAN : I MUST THINK IT OVER. YOU ARE REALLY FULL OF IDEAS.
OVER (175) ALL ABOUT THAT. IT'S NOT ROMANTIC: IT'S NOT DON JUAN : IT'S NOT ADVANCED; BUT WE FEEL IT ALL THE SAME. IT'S
SUPR III (130) WALKS PAST THEM. /DON JUAN/ I GO. /THE DEVIL/ DON JUAN : SHALL I BE FRANK WITH YOU? /DON JUAN/ WERE YOU NOT
SUPR III (124) FALL IN LOVE WITH AND MARRY HIM! /ANA/ YES, JUAN : WE KNOW THE LIBERTINE'S PHILOSOPHY. ALWAYS IGNORE THE
SUPR III (118) WHICH I REPLENISHED. /THE STATUE/ BRAVO ANA! JUAN : YOU ARE FLOORED, QUELLED, ANNIHILATED. /DON JUAN/ NO;
SUPR III (128) THEY ARE. /THE DEVIL/ (MORTIFIED) SENOR DON JUAN : YOU ARE UNCIVIL TO MY FRIENDS. /DON JUAN/ POOH! WHY
SUPR III (109) GLADIATORS WHICH YOU CALL THE ARMY. /THE STATUE/ JUAN : YOU WILL FORCE ME TO CALL YOU TO ACCOUNT FOR THIS.
SUPR III (94) /ANA/ HAS EVEN DEATH FAILED TO REFINE YOUR SOUL, JUAN ? HAS THE TERRIBLE JUDGMENT OF WHICH MY FATHER'S
SUPR III (97) OF MINE. /THE STATUE/ WHAT HARM IS HE DOING YOU, JUAN ? IT SEEMS TO ME THAT HE WAS TALKING EXCELLENT SENSE
SUPR III (104) IS THERE NOTHING IN HEAVEN BUT CONTEMPLATION, JUAN ? /DON JUAN/ IN THE HEAVEN I SEEK, NO OTHER JOY. BUT
SUPR III (118) YOU NOT THE HAPPIER FOR THE EXPERIENCE, SENOR DON JUAN ? /DON JUAN/ THE HAPPIER, NO: THE WISER, YES. THAT
SUPR III (125) /THE STATUE/ WHAT USED THE LADIES TO SAY, JUAN ? /DON JUAN/ OH, COME! CONFIDENCE FOR CONFIDENCE.
SUPR III (133) MY FRIENDLY FAREWELL BACK IN MY TEETH, THEN, DON JUAN ? /DON JUAN/ BY NO MEANS. BUT THOUGH THERE IS MUCH TO
SUPR PREFACE(R12) THEN, I HAVE HAD TO ASK MYSELF, WHAT IS A DON JUAN ? VULGARLY, A LIBERTINE. BUT YOUR DISLIKE OF VULGARITY
SUPR PREFACE(R29) JUAN COMEDY. I HAVE NOT. I HAVE ONLY MADE MY DON JUAN A POLITICAL PAMPHLETEER, AND GIVEN YOU HIS PAMPHLET IN
SUPR III SD(103) MUST HEAVEN BE! THE DEVIL, THE STATUE, AND DON JUAN ALL BEGIN TO SPEAK AT ONCE IN VIOLENT PROTEST; THEN
BUOY IV (59) GREAT PASSION THE VULGAR CONCUPISCENCES OF DON JUAN AND CASANOVA, AND THE ROMANCE OF BEATRICE AND
MIS. PREFACE(99) A PRESENT FOR A BOY OR GIRL, OR FOR BYRON'S DON JUAN AS A PRESENT FOR A SWAIN OR LASS. PICKWICK IS THE
SUPR PREFACE(R13) ARE FLATTERED BY THE BRILLIANCIES WITH WHICH DON JUAN ASSOCIATES THEM) FINDS HIMSELF IN MORTAL CONFLICT WITH
SUPR PREFACE(R14) TELL HIS OWN STORY. IN FACT HE IS NOT A TRUE DON JUAN AT ALL; FOR HE IS NO MORE AN ENEMY OF GOD THAN ANY
SUPR PREFACE(R13) SUCH ENEMIES HAVE ALWAYS BEEN POPULAR. DON JUAN BECAME SUCH A PET THAT THE WORLD COULD NOT BEAR HIS
SUPR PREFACE(R13) THAT COMIC FOE OF THE GODS, PUNCH, MOLIERE'S DON JUAN CASTS BACK TO THE ORIGINAL IN POINT OF IMPENITENCE; BUT
SUPR PREFACE(R29) ACTUALLY PUT ALL THIS TUB THUMPING INTO A DON JUAN COMEDY. I HAVE NOT. I HAVE ONLY MADE MY DON JUAN A
LION PREFACE(53) AND WHAT CANNOT BE DONE IN JERUSALEM OR JUAN FERNANDEZ CANNOT BE DONE IN LONDON, NEW YORK, PARIS,
SUPR PREFACE(R15) BY SUCH PENS AS IBSEN'S AND TOLSTOY'S, DON JUAN HAD CHANGED HIS SEX AND BECOME DONA JUANA, BREAKING OUT
SUPR PREFACE(R20) DID IN THE PLAYS OF SHAKESPEAR. AND SO YOUR DON JUAN HAS COME TO BIRTH AS A STAGE PROJECTION OF THE
SUPR III (122) I AM SORRY TO SHOCK YOU, MY LOVE; BUT SINCE JUAN HAS STRIPPED EVERY RAG OF DECENCY FROM THE DISCUSSION I
SUPR PREFACE(R17) NO LONGER MISUNDERSTOOD AS MERE CASANOVISM. DON JUAN HIMSELF IS ALMOST ASCETIC IN HIS DESIRE TO AVOID THAT
METH PREFACE(R88) ACCORDINGLY, IN 1901, I TOOK THE LEGEND OF DON JUAN IN ITS MOZARTIAN FORM AND MADE IT A DRAMATIC PARABLE OF
LADY PREFACE(219) MORE BY WHAT THEY DO THAN BY WHAT THEY ARE. DON JUAN IN MUCH ADO IS A TRUE VILLAIN: A MAN WITH A MALICIOUS
SUPR PREFACE(R12) ME, SO I TOOK IT THAT YOU DEMANDED A DON JUAN IN THE PHILOSOPHIC SENSE. PHILOSOPHICALLY, DON JUAN IS
SUPR PREFACE(R30) THIS EPISTLE DEDICATORY NOR THE DREAM OF DON JUAN IN THE THIRD ACT OF THE ENSUING COMEDY IS SUITABLE FOR
SUPR PREFACE(R15) YOU WILL SEE FROM THE FOREGOING SURVEY THAT DON JUAN IS A FULL CENTURY OUT OF DATE FOR YOU AND FOR ME; AND
SUPR PREFACE(R12) IN THE PHILOSOPHIC SENSE. PHILOSOPHICALLY, DON JUAN IS A MAN WHO, THOUGH GIFTED ENOUGH TO BE EXCEPTIONALLY
SUPR III (95) YOU SPEAK AS THIS VILLAIN SPEAKS. /THE STATUE/ JUAN IS A SOUND THINKER, ANA. A BAD FENCER, BUT A SOUND
SUPR PREFACE(R17) TOWARDS WOMEN MUCH RESEMBLES THAT TO WHICH DON JUAN IS NOW DRIVEN. FROM THIS POINT OF VIEW HAMLET WAS A
SUPR PREFACE(R13) LATE. THIS IS REALLY THE ONLY POINT ON WHICH DON JUAN IS SCEPTICAL; FOR HE IS A DEVOUT BELIEVER IN AN
SUPR PREFACE(R21) LOVE CHASE OF THE MAN BY THE WOMAN; AND MY DON JUAN IS THE QUARRY INSTEAD OF THE HUNTSMAN. YET HE IS A TRUE
SUPR III (120) CHURCH UNITED HIM TO YOU? /ANA/ YOU ARE A FOOL, JUAN . A YOUNG MARRIED WOMAN HAS SOMETHING ELSE TO DO THAN
SUPR III (118) AND NO CHILDREN: THATS WHAT I COULD HAVE DONE, JUAN . AND LET ME TELL YOU THAT THAT WOULD HAVE MADE ALL THE
SUPR III SD(94) JAUNTY. HE IS ON THE PLEASANTEST TERMS WITH DON JUAN . HIS VOICE, SAVE FOR A MUCH MORE DISTINGUISHED
SUPR III (129) STATUE/ YOUR FLOW OF WORDS IS SIMPLY AMAZING, JUAN . HOW I WISH I COULD HAVE TALKED LIKE THAT TO MY

SUPR III (132)	/THE DEVIL/ WELL WELL, GO YOUR WAY, SENOR DON	JUAN	. I PREFER TO BE MY OWN MASTER AND NOT THE TOOL OF ANY
SUPR III (133)	SATAN. /THE DEVIL/ (AMIABLY) FARE YOU WELL, DON	JUAN	. I SHALL OFTEN THINK OF OUR INTERESTING CHATS ABOUT
SUPR III (117)	THIS IS EXTREMELY ABSTRACT AND METAPHYSICAL,	JUAN	. IF YOU WOULD STICK TO THE CONCRETE, AND PUT YOUR
SUPR III (115)	HIS HEAD) YOU SHOULDNT REPEAT WHAT A WOMAN SAYS,	JUAN	. /ANA/ (SEVERELY) IT SHOULD BE SACRED TO YOU. /THE
SUPR II (55)	AND THAT YOU ARE THE REAL DESCENDANT OF DON	JUAN	. /OCTAVIUS/ I BEG YOU NOT TO SAY ANYTHING LIKE THAT TO
SUPR I (21)	I'LL CALL YOU AFTER YOUR FAMOUS ANCESTOR DON	JUAN	. /RAMSDEN/ DON JUAN! /ANN/ (INNOCENTLY) OH, IS THERE
SUPR III (112)	OF YOUR COMING TO ANY POINT IN PARTICULAR,	JUAN	. STILL, SINCE IN THIS PLACE, INSTEAD OF MERELY KILLING
SUPR III (127)	FOR AN ACCIDENT. /THE STATUE/ I WAS EXPECTED TO,	JUAN	. THAT IS HOW THINGS WERE ARRANGED ON EARTH. I WAS NOT
JITT III (77)	NOW DONT BEGIN IMAGINING THAT I AM A DON	JUAN	. TO BE PRECISE, I HAVE KISSED OTHER WOMEN TWICE. I WAS
SUPR III (113)	/THE STATUE/ THIS IS METAPHYSICS,	JUAN	. WHY THE DEVIL SHOULD-- (TO THE DEVIL) I BEG YOUR
SUPR III (118)	HAVE GONE WITHOUT THINKING SUCH A LOT ABOUT IT,	JUAN	. YOU ARE LIKE ALL THE CLEVER MEN: YOU HAVE MORE BRAINS
SUPR PREFACE(R13)	FATHER SEEKS PRIVATE REDRESS WITH THE SWORD, DON	JUAN	KILLS HIM WITHOUT AN EFFORT. NOT UNTIL THE SLAIN FATHER
SUPR PREFACE(R14)	LIKE SHELLEY. LET US, THEN, LEAVE BYRON'S DON	JUAN	OUT OF ACCOUNT. MOZART'S IS THE LAST OF THE TRUE DON
SUPR PREFACE(R15)	GIOVANNI. EVEN THE MORE ABSTRACT PARTS OF THE DON	JUAN	PLAY ARE DILAPIDATED PAST USE: FOR INSTANCE, DON JUAN'S
SUPR PREFACE(R10)	IS, WILL YOU NOT BE DISAPPOINTED WITH A DON	JUAN	PLAY IN WHICH NOT ONE OF THAT HERO'S MILLE ETRE
SUPR PREFACE(R10)	NATURE. YOUR SUGGESTION THAT I SHOULD WRITE A DON	JUAN	PLAY WAS VIRTUALLY A CHALLENGE TO ME TO TREAT THIS
SUPR PREFACE(R12)	IBSEN. I TAKE IT THAT WHEN YOU ASKED ME FOR A DON	JUAN	PLAY YOU DID NOT WANT THAT SORT OF THING. NOBODY DOES:
SUPR PREFACE(R9)	YOU ONCE ASKED ME WHY I DID NOT WRITE A DON	JUAN	PLAY. THE LEVITY WITH WHICH YOU ASSUMED THIS FRIGHTFUL
SUPR PREFACE(R29)	BE MISLEADING; AND THEN I PROCEED TO WRITE A DON	JUAN	PLAY. WELL, IF YOU INSIST ON ASKING ME WHY I BEHAVE IN
SUPR PREFACE(R15)	BEGINNING OF THE XX CENTURY TO ASK ME FOR A DON	JUAN	PLAY; BUT YOU WILL SEE FROM THE FOREGOING SURVEY THAT
SUPR PREFACE(R19)	TO HIM IN IMAGINATION AND CUNNING. THE DON	JUAN	PLAY, HOWEVER, IS TO DEAL WITH SEXUAL ATTRACTION, AND
SUPR PREFACE(R16)	THE NONCONFORMIST CONSCIENCE BY THE BEARD AS DON	JUAN	PLUCKED THE BEARD OF THE COMMANDANT'S STATUE IN THE
SUPR III (122)	YOU ARE GOING BACK FROM YOUR WORD! (TO DON	JUAN	) AND ALL YOUR PHILOSOPHIZING HAS BEEN NOTHING BUT A
SUPR III (122)	WHICH I AM OFFERING YOU A REFUGE HERE? (TO DON	JUAN	) AND DOES YOUR DEMONSTRATION OF THE APPROACHING
SUPR III (103)	JUAN/ AFTER YOU, GENTLEMEN. /THE DEVIL/ (TO DON	JUAN	) YOU HAVE BEEN SO ELOQUENT ON THE ADVANTAGES OF MY
SUPR III (96)	(DON JUAN SIGHS DEEPLY). YOU SIGH, FRIEND	JUAN	; BUT IF YOU DWELT IN HEAVEN, AS I DO, YOU WOULD
SUPR PREFACE(R17)	IN FACT, HE IS NOW MORE HAMLET THAN DON	JUAN	; FOR THOUGH THE LINES PUT INTO THE ACTOR'S MOUTH TO
SUPR III (96)	YOU HAVE NOTHING TO DO BUT AMUSE YOURSELF. (DON	JUAN	SIGHS DEEPLY). YOU SIGH, FRIEND JUAN; BUT IF YOU DWELT
SUPR III SD(87)	RESEMBLANCE, EVEN AN IDENTITY. THE NAME TOO: DON	JUAN	TENORIO, JOHN TANNER, WHERE ON EARTH-- OR ELSEWHERE--
SUPR III (92)	I CANNOT SEE YOUR FACE. (HE RAISES HIS HAT). DON	JUAN	TENORIO! MONSTER! YOU WHO SLEW MY FATHER! EVEN HERE
SUPR III (134)	TOO, ALSO OUTSIDE THE MORAL WORLD. THIS DON	JUAN	WAS KIND TO WOMEN AND COURTEOUS TO MEN AS YOUR DAUGHTER
LION PREFACE(49)	GOD, SUCH WORSHIPPERS ARE MORE HORRIFIED THAN DON	JUAN	WAS WHEN THE STATUE STEPPED FROM ITS PEDESTAL AND CAME
SUPR III (113)	HABITS OF SPEECH. WHAT I WAS GOING TO ASK	JUAN	WAS WHY LIFE SHOULD BOTHER ITSELF ABOUT GETTING A
SUPR PREFACE(R15)	IN THE UNIVERSE. GOETHE'S FAUST AND MOZART'S DON	JUAN	WERE THE LAST WORDS OF THE XVIII CENTURY ON THE
SUPR PREFACE(R17)	THIS POINT OF VIEW HAMLET WAS A DEVELOPED DON	JUAN	WHOM SHAKESPEAR PALMED OFF AS A REPUTABLE MAN JUST AS
METH PREFACE(R89)	TO BE TRIFLED WITH. I ABANDON THE LEGEND OF DON	JUAN	WITH ITS EROTIC ASSOCIATIONS, AND GO BACK TO THE LEGEND
GETT PREFACE(190)	SHOCKED; BYRON WOULD HAVE BEEN HORRIFIED; DON	JUAN	WOULD HAVE FLED FROM THE CONFERENCE INTO A MONASTERY.
SUPR III (100)	TASTES: THERE ARE PEOPLE WHO LIKE IT. I THINK DON	JUAN	WOULD LIKE IT. /DON JUAN/ BUT-- PARDON MY FRANKNESS--
SUPR III (112)	DEVIL/ (MUCH OFFENDED) THIS IS NOT FAIR, DON	JUAN	, AND NOT CIVIL. I AM ALSO ON THE INTELLECTUAL PLANE.
SUPR PREFACE(R15)	A SPANISH NOBLEMAN IN THE DAYS OF THE FIRST DON	JUAN	, ARE NOW TRIUMPHANT EVERYWHERE. CIVILIZED SOCIETY IS
SUPR III (113)	ARE? /ANA/ ARISTOPHANES WAS A HEATHEN; AND YOU,	JUAN	, I AM AFRAID, ARE VERY LITTLE BETTER. /THE DEVIL/ YOU
SUPR PREFACE(R13)	THE SAME MEANS AGAINST VERMIN. THE PROTOTYPIC DON	JUAN	, INVENTED EARLY IN THE XVI CENTURY BY A SPANISH MONK,
SUPR III (121)	SCHOOLMASTERS. /THE DEVIL/ ALL THIS, SENOR DON	JUAN	, IS REALIZED HERE IN MY REALM. /DON JUAN/ YES, AT THE
SUPR III (111)	/THE STATUE/ (VERY SERIOUSLY) MOST TRUE,	JUAN	, MOST TRUE. SOME DONKEYS HAVE AMAZING LUCK. /DON JUAN/
SUPR III SD(87)	OF A SPANISH NOBLEMAN OF THE XV-XVI CENTURY. DON	JUAN	, OF COURSE; BUT WHERE? WHY? HOW? BESIDES, IN THE
SUPR III (127)	/THE DEVIL/ I STILL FAIL TO SEE, SENOR DON	JUAN	, THAT THESE EPISODES IN YOUR EARTHLY CAREER AND IN
LADY PREFACE(212)	KLOOTZ A WASHINGTON, TO MRS PROUDIE A DON	JUAN	, TO ASPASIA A JOHN KNOX; IN SHORT, TO EVERYONE HIS
SUPR PREFACE(R16)	CENTURY. AS A RESULT, MAN IS NO LONGER, LIKE DON	JUAN	, VICTOR IN THE DUEL OF SEX. WHETHER HE HAS EVER REALLY
SUPR PREFACE(R21)	INSTEAD OF THE HUNTSMAN. YET HE IS A TRUE DON	JUAN	, WITH A SENSE OF REALITY THAT DISABLES CONVENTION,
SUPR III (97)	COMMANDER OF CALATRAVA? (COLDLY) DON	JUAN	, YOUR SERVANT. (POLITELY) AND A STRANGE LADY? MY
SUPR III (108)	(IRONICALLY) WHAT! YOU A CATHOLIC, SENOR DON	JUAN	! A DEVOTEE! MY CONGRATULATIONS. /THE STATUE (
SUPR III (134)	/THE STATUE/ (CALLING AFTER HIM) BON VOYAGE,	JUAN	! (HE WAFTS A FINAL BLAST OF HIS GREAT ROLLING CHORDS
SUPR I (21)	YOUR FAMOUS ANCESTOR DON JUAN. /RAMSDEN/ DON	JUAN	! /ANN/ (INNOCENTLY) OH, IS THERE HARM IN IT? I
SUPR III (115)	LED ME AT LAST INTO THE WORSHIP OF WOMAN. /ANA/	JUAN	! /DON JUAN/ YES: I CAME TO BELIEVE THAT IN HER VOICE
SUPR III (99)	HERE, HAVE TURNED OUT SOCIAL FAILURES, LIKE DON	JUAN	! /DON JUAN/ I AM REALLY VERY SORRY TO BE A SOCIAL
SUPR III (119)	THE MOST LICENTIOUS OF HUMAN INSTITUTIONS-- /ANA/	JUAN	! /THE STATUE/ (PROTESTING) REALLY! -- /DON JUAN/ (

JUANA

SUPR PREFACE(R15)	DON JUAN HAD CHANGED HIS SEX AND BECOME DONA	JUANA	, BREAKING OUT OF THE DOLL'S HOUSE AND ASSERTING

JUANISM

SUPR PREFACE(R17)	(AT LEAST ON YOUR PLANE AND MINE) BECAUSE DON	JUANISM	IS NO LONGER MISUNDERSTOOD AS MERE CASANOVISM. DON

JUAN'S

SUPR PREFACE(R13)	MINUTE TO MINUTE. NO ANXIETY IS CAUSED ON DON	JUAN'S	ACCOUNT BY ANY MINOR ANTAGONIST: HE EASILY ELUDES THE
SUPR PREFACE(R29)	POLITICS OF THE SEX QUESTION AS I CONCEIVE DON	JUAN'S	DESCENDANT TO UNDERSTAND THEM. NOT THAT I DISCLAIM
SUPR PREFACE(R16)	IT TO A HERO WITH ANY MIND, BESIDES, IT IS DON	JUAN'S	OWN BEARD THAT IS IN DANGER OF PLUCKING. FAR FROM
SUPR PREFACE(R15)	PLAY ARE DILAPIDATED PAST USE: FOR INSTANCE, DON	JUAN'S	SUPERNATURAL ANTAGONIST HURLED THOSE WHO REFUSE TO

JUANS

SUPR PREFACE(R14)	OF ACCOUNT. MOZART'S IS THE LAST OF THE TRUE DON	JUANS	; FOR BY THE TIME HE WAS OF AGE, HIS COUSIN FAUST HAD,

JUBA

CLEO II (126)	HE MAY BE FLYING FOR HIS LIFE BEFORE CATO AND	JUBA	OF NUMIDIA, THE AFRICAN KING. /ACHILLAS/ (FOLLOWING UP

JUBILANT

ROCK II SD(246)	BRILLIANTLY DRESSED, AND QUITE TRANSFIGURED, IS	JUBILANT	. ALOYSIA GLOWS INDIGNATION. BLEE AND THE MAYOR,
ROCK II SD(281)	I-- BARKING ENTERS THROUGH THE MASKED DOOR,	JUBILANT	. HE COMES BETWEEN THE PAIR AS THEY RISE, AND CLAPS
FABL VI SD(131)	QUESTIONS OR WRITE ESSAYS BEFORE NEXT FRIDAY. A	JUBILANT	MARCH IS HEARD. /TEACHER/ LUNCH. MARCH. (BEATING
NEVR II (259)	THE AGONIZED VOICE NOW SOLID, RINGING, AND	JUBILANT	) AH, IT'S COME AT LAST: MY MOMENT OF COURAGE. (HE

JUBILATION

DEVL III SD(78)	TO THEM) THEYRE COMING BACK. THEY WANT YOU.	JUBILATION	IN THE MARKET. THE TOWNSFOLK SURGE BACK AGAIN IN

JUDAISM

LION PREFACE(76)	PAUL HAD NO INTENTION OF SURRENDERING EITHER HIS	JUDAISM	OR HIS ROMAN CITIZENSHIP TO THE NEW MORAL WORLD (AS
LION PREFACE(23)	HIMSELF, AND DOES NOT CONVERT HIS DISCIPLES FROM	JUDAISM	TO CHRISTIANITY. TO THIS DAY A CHRISTIAN WOULD BE IN
SIM PREFACE(10)	NEW HISTORICALLY. THE CHANGE FROM PAGANISM AND	JUDAISM	TO CHRISTIANITY, FROM THE WORSHIP OF CONSECRATED
LION PREFACE(49)	HE EVER EXISTED; YOU MAY REJECT CHRISTIANITY FOR	JUDAISM	, MAHOMETANISM, SHINTOISM, OR FIRE WORSHIP; AND THE

JUDAS

JOAN 6 (150)	WILL GO PRAY AMONG HER ASHES. I AM NO BETTER THAN	JUDAS	: I WILL HANG MYSELF. /WARWICK/ QUICK, BROTHER MARTIN:
LION PREFACE(39)	IT ALSO IMPLIES THAT JESUS DELIBERATELY BEWITCHED	JUDAS	IN ORDER TO BRING ABOUT HIS OWN BETRAYAL. LATER ON
LION PREFACE(56)	VALUE OF THE VIRTUES OF JESUS AS 100, AND OF	JUDAS	ISCARIOT AS ZERO, GIVE THE CORRECT FIGURES FOR,
SIM PREFACE(15)	WE HAVE NOT TROUBLED TO ASK. WE ARE CLEAR ABOUT	JUDAS	ISCARIOT GOING TO HELL AND FLORENCE NIGHTINGALE TO
GENV IV (110)	HEAR HEAR! /SIR O./ WHAT ABOUT THE UNLOVABLES?	JUDAS	ISCARIOT, FOR INSTANCE? /DEACONESS/ IF HE HAD LOVED
POSN (459)	ITS HEAD WITH THE FEVER. HE SAID IT WAS A LITTLE	JUDAS	KID, AND THAT IT WAS BETRAYING HIM WITH A KISS, AND
POSN (458)	OF THE THROAT-- FRANTICALLY) DEAD! THE LITTLE	JUDAS	KID! THE CHILD I GAVE MY LIFE FOR! (HE BREAKS INTO
LION PREFACE(7)	SOON HAVE THOUGHT OF APPLYING SUCH ADJECTIVES TO	JUDAS	MACCABEUS AS TO JESUS; AND EVEN ST LUKE, WHO MAKES
LION PREFACE(39)	OTHER ACCOUNTS, IN WHICH JESUS OPENLY INDICATES	JUDAS	WITHOUT ELICITING ANY PROTEST OR EXCITING ANY COMMENT.
JOAN 2 (86)	LAWFUL HOMES IN PEACE. WILT BE A POOR LITTLE	JUDAS	, AND BETRAY ME AND HIM THAT SENT ME? /CHARLES/ (
LION PREFACE(39)	A SOP TO THE TRAITOR, AND THEREUPON HANDED ONE TO	JUDAS	, WHO ATE IT AND IMMEDIATELY BECAME POSSESSED BY THE
LADY (239)	TURNS AWAY, OVERCOME). TWO GENTLEMEN OF VERONA!	JUDAS	! JUDAS! ! /THE BEEFEATER/ IS HE SO BAD AS THAT,
LADY (239)	OVERCOME). TWO GENTLEMEN OF VERONA! JUDAS!	JUDAS	! ! /THE BEEFEATER/ IS HE SO BAD AS THAT, SIR? /THE

JUDASES

METH PREFACE(R78)	ADMIRATION, WONDER, AND WORSHIP, AND THEIR	JUDASES	AND DEVILS TO ENABLE THEM TO BE ANGRY AND YET FEEL

JUDEA

LION PREFACE(53)	FELLOW, IF YOU WERE TO DIVIDE UP THE WEALTH OF	JUDEA	EQUALLY TODAY, BEFORE THE END OF THE YEAR YOU WOULD
BARB I (253)	AND DESTRUCTION DEALERS: ADDRESS, CHRISTENDOM AND	JUDEA	." BUT THAT WAS NOT SO BAD AS THE WAY I WAS KOWTOWED

JUDEECIAL

CAPT III (272)	AND CANNOT COME. I MISDOUBT ME IT WILL NOT LOOK	JUDEECIAL	TO HAVE CAPTAIN KEARNEY'S OFFICERS SQUATTING ON

JUDGE

GENV IV (100)	IT IS A DANGER TO IT. /COMMISSAR/ COME, COMRADE	JUDGE	: HAVE YOU NEVER SENTENCED A CRIMINAL TO DEATH? HAS
GENV II SD(56)	HE IS A DUTCHMAN, MUCH YOUNGER THAN A BRITISH	JUDGE	: UNDER FORTY, IN FACT, BUT VERY GRAVE AND EVERY INCH
GENV III (77)	HE MAY BE, IS NO GENTLEMAN. /THE SECRETARY/	JUDGE	: YOU HEAR WHAT WE HAVE TO CONTEND WITH HERE.
JOAN 6 (138)	AND YOU, AND NOT THE CHURCH, ARE TO BE THE	JUDGE	? /JOAN/ WHAT OTHER JUDGMENT CAN I JUDGE BY BUT MY
POSN PREFACE(430)	ALLOWED TO MEDDLE WITH POLITICAL RIGHTS. NOW TO A	JUDGE	A POLITICAL RIGHT, THAT IS, A DOGMA WHICH IS ABOVE OUR
GENV IV SD(115)	SEATED. THE SECRETARY PLACES A CHAIR BETWEEN THE	JUDGE	AND BOMBARDONE. FLANCO CROSSES TO IT. /JUDGE/ (BEFORE
FABL PREFACE(67)	AND SCAVENGER, FOR ADMIRAL AND CABIN BOY, FOR	JUDGE	AND EXECUTIONER, FOR FIELD MARSHAL AND DRUMMER BOY,
BULL PREFACE(33)	CONFUSION OF THE MUTUALLY EXCLUSIVE FUNCTIONS OF	JUDGE	AND LEGISLATOR. FOR THERE IS ONLY ONE CONDITION ON
GENV III SD(86)	MAY FIND YOURSELVES CROWDED OUT. ALL EXCEPT THE	JUDGE	AND THE SECRETARY RISE HASTILY AND DISAPPEAR IN THE
PHIL II (128)	I'M ON THE COMMITTEE MYSELF: I CANT ACT AS	JUDGE	AND WITNESS TOO. YOU MUST APPLY TO PARAMORE: HE SAW IT
LION PREFACE(66)	ISABELLA GAVE SUCH A DRESSING-DOWN TO	JUDGE	ANGELO, AND WHY SWIFT RESERVED THE HOTTEST CORNER OF
POSN PREFACE(389)	OF GUILT TO THE JURY: THE CENSOR IS JURY AND	JUDGE	AS WELL AS LAW-GIVER. A MAGISTRATE MAY BE STRONGLY
POSN PREFACE(396)	COARSE AND VICIOUS PLAYS. IT IS NOT LONG SINCE A	JUDGE	BEFORE WHOM A LICENSED PLAY CAME IN THE COURSE OF A
BULL II (116)	DRUNK? /NORA/ (SOOTHINGLY) YOULL BE ABLE TO	JUDGE	BETTER IN THE MORNING. COME ON NOW BACK WITH ME, AN
KING I (209)	HE IS BLINDED BY HIS MONSTROUS CONCEIT. YOU SHALL	JUDGE	BETWEEN US, SIR. AM I OR AM I NOT THE GREATEST
3PLA PREFACE(R18)	OF HER DISCUSSIONS OF A MENAGE A TROIS WITH	JUDGE	BRACK. A LITTLE EXPERIENCE OF POPULAR PLAYS WOULD SOON
LION PREFACE(91)	IS WHAT YOU WANT: IT IS THE CASE YOU HAVE TO	JUDGE	BROUGHT TO AN APPREHENSIBLE ISSUE FOR YOU. EVEN IF YOU
JOAN 6 (138)	BE THE JUDGE? /JOAN/ WHAT OTHER JUDGMENT CAN I	JUDGE	BY BUT MY OWN? /THE ASSESSORS/ (SCANDALIZED) OH! (
GENV III (85)	PERSON WITH ABSOLUTELY NO MIND AT ALL. THE	JUDGE	CAN HAVE HIS PICK OF A HUNDRED CLEVER WOMEN IN GENEVA;
ROCK PREFACE(187)	THAT NEITHER YOU NOR THE PRISONER WHOM YOU	JUDGE	CAN PROVE THAT HE IS IN THE RIGHT; THEREFORE YOU MUST
MIS. PREFACE(56)	OF CANTERBURY, AND PASSED AN ACT UNDER WHICH A	JUDGE	CAN SENTENCE A MAN TO BE FLOGGED TO THE UTMOST
POSN PREFACE(389)	THE LIMITATION IS SOMETIMES CARRIED SO FAR THAT A	JUDGE	CANNOT INFLICT THE PENALTY FOR HOUSEBREAKING ON A
GENV IV (89)	FOR? /THE BETROTHED/ TO SEE THE FUN WHEN JOHNNY	JUDGE	COMES AND FINDS NOTHING DOING, I SUPPOSE. /THE WIDOW/
CAPT II (264)	MYSELF AND LADY CICELY. /BRASSBOUND/ WHAT! A	JUDGE	COMPOUND A FELONY! YOU GREENHORNS, HE IS MORE LIKELY
GENV II SD(56)	NEVER HAD ANYTHING LIKE IT BEFORE. THE SENIOR	JUDGE	ENTERS. HE IS A DUTCHMAN, MUCH YOUNGER THAN A BRITISH
JOAN PREFACE(33)	BOTH AS PRIEST AND LAWYER THAN ANY ENGLISH	JUDGE	EVER DREAMS OF BEING IN A POLITICAL CASE IN WHICH HIS
LION PREFACE(59)	GIVE A CARPENTER A HUNDRED POUNDS A YEAR AND A	JUDGE	FIVE THOUSAND; BUT THE WAGE FOR ONE CARPENTER IS THE
SUPR II (59)	TO SUCH TREATMENT BEFORE SHE IS OLD ENOUGH TO	JUDGE	FOR HERSELF? /TANNER/ IN SHORT, THE WAY TO AVOID
BULL PREFACE(48)	NO SOLDIER IS ASKED TO THINK FOR HIMSELF, TO	JUDGE	FOR HIMSELF, TO CONSULT HIS OWN HONOR AND MANHOOD, TO
FANY II (288)	PLACE. /KNOX/ WILL YOU TELL ME WHAT PLACE? I CAN	JUDGE	FOR MYSELF HOW SAFE IT WAS. /MARGARET/ HOLLOWAY GAOL.
BARB PREFACE(212)	THEIR SUBJUGATION BY EUROPEAN CAPITALISM, WE CAN	JUDGE	FOR OURSELVES WHETHER THE INITIATIVE CAME FROM ABOVE
DOCT PREFACE(7)	TO BE ABLE TO ANSWER IT AT ALL. AND ON THIS THE	JUDGE	HAD TO INSTRUCT THE JURY THAT THEY MUST ACQUIT THE
GENV IV (88)	SUMMONED AND THAT THEY WONT COME. YOUNG JOHNNY	JUDGE	HAS NO MORE AUTHORITY OVER THEM THAN HIS CAT. /THE
CAPT III (276)	NEPHEW, YOU KNOW. /SIR HOWARD/ CICELY: AN ENGLISH	JUDGE	HAS NO NEPHEWS, NO SONS EVEN, WHEN HE HAS TO CARRY OUT
SUPR HANDBOK(202)	WHILST THESE PAGES ARE BEING WRITTEN AN ENGLISH	JUDGE	HAS SENTENCED A FORGER TO TWENTY YEARS PENAL SERVITUDE
DOCT PREFACE(67)	ONE. IF THE PRACTICE OF LAW NOT ONLY LED TO A	JUDGE	HAVING TO HANG, BUT THE HANGMAN TO JUDGE, OR IF IN THE
ARMS III (66)	SILENT. /BLUNTSCHLI/ (SHAKING HIS HEAD) I MUSNT	JUDGE	HER. I ONCE LISTENED MYSELF OUTSIDE A TENT WHEN THERE
ARMS III (65)	FLINGS VIOLENTLY AGAINST THE TABLE, EXCLAIMING)	JUDGE	HER, BLUNTSCHLI. YOU, THE COOL IMPARTIAL MAN: JUDGE
LION PREFACE(66)	AND " IF ANY MAN HEAR MY WORDS AND BELIEVE NOT, I	JUDGE	HIM NOT" BECAUSE " HE HATH ONE THAT JUDGETH HIM":
DOCT II (127)	PATIENT AND HIS VERY CHARMING WIFE. WE MUST NOT	JUDGE	HIM TOO HASTILY, YOU KNOW. (WITH UNCTION)
GENV IV (87)	ISSUED BY THE COURT. /THE BETROTHED/ THE	JUDGE	HIMSELF HASNT TURNED UP. /THE SECRETARY/ (LOOKING AT
POSN PREFACE(402)	MIGHT BE BIASED AGAINST THE THEATRE ALTOGETHER, A	JUDGE	IN CHAMBERS WOULD BE THE PROPER AUTHORITY. THIS PLAN
GENV II SD(56)	HANDS WHILST THE SECRETARY PLACES A CHAIR FOR THE	JUDGE	IN THE MIDDLE OF THE ROOM, BETWEEN HIS TABLE AND SIR
LION PREFACE(59)	AS A DEVICE FOR PERSUADING A CARPENTER THAT A	JUDGE	IS A CREATURE OF SUPERIOR NATURE TO HIMSELF, TO BE
BULL PREFACE(41)	APPOINTMENT IS MADE ON NATIONALIST GROUNDS; EVERY	JUDGE	IS A PARTISAN IN THE NATIONALIST CONFLICT; EVERY
DEVL I (9)	FATHER HAS BEEN MERCIFUL TO HIM; AND HIS HEAVENLY	JUDGE	IS THE FATHER OF US ALL. /MRS DUDGEON/ (FORGETTING
LION PREFACE(59)	WAGE FOR ALL THE CARPENTERS: THE SALARY FOR ONE	JUDGE	IS THE SALARY FOR ALL THE JUDGES. THE CAPTAIN AND THE
ROCK PREFACE(179)	UNANSWERED, CANNOT BE DRAMATIZED UNLESS THE	JUDGE	IS TO BE THE HERO OF THE PLAY. NOW PILATE, THOUGH
GETT PREFACE(257)	DO NOT ASK SOMEBODY WHO DOES NOT KNOW WHAT A	JUDGE	IS, OR WHAT A BISHOP IS, OR WHAT THE LAW IS, OR WHAT
CLEO V (200)	IT HAS ALREADY EATEN. /CAESAR/ NO. /RUFIO/ NOR	JUDGE	IT FOR ITS GUILTINESS. /CAESAR/ NO. /RUFIO/ WHAT,
APPL II (258)	LIKE A CRAZY MAN. BUT YOU SHALL HEAR. YOU SHALL	JUDGE	. AND THEN YOU SHALL SAY WHETHER I EXAGGERATE THE
GENV IV (108)	OBEYED: THAT IS ALL. /BBDE/ THAT IS TRUE, SIGNOR	JUDGE	. AUTHORITY IS A SORT OF GENIUS: EITHER YOU HAVE IT OR
DOCT IV (167)	AS OTHER MEN. NO MATTER: IT'S NOT FOR US TO	JUDGE	. HE'S IN ANOTHER WORLD NOW. /WALPOLE/ BORROWING HIS
GENV III (83)	BEEN MAKING NOTES OF THE DISCUSSION). YOU SEE,	JUDGE	. IF YOU KNOCK ALL THIS NONSENSE OF BELONGING TO
MILL I SD(137)	HIM. IT IS SURMOUNTED BY A DINGY PORTRAIT OF A	JUDGE	. IN THE WALL ON HIS RIGHT, NEAR THE CORNER FARTHEST
NEVR III (264)	APPEARED TO LIKE IT. /DOLLY/ AS FAR AS WE COULD	JUDGE	. (STOPPING PHIL, WHO IS ABOUT TO POUR OUT ANOTHER
GENV III (79)	NEVER MIND. WE ARE INTERRUPTING HIS HONOR THE	JUDGE	. (TO THE JUDGE) YOU WERE ABOUT TO SAY--? /THE
WIDO I SD(13)	CONTEMPLATES TRENCH WITH THE SEVERITY OF A	JUDGE	. /COKANE/ (WITH REPROBATION) NO, MY DEAR BOY. NO.
CAPT I (221)	HONEST, STRAIGHTFORWARD MAN, AS FAR AS I COULD	JUDGE	. /DRINKWATER/ (EMBRACING THE IMPLICATION) COURSE E
INCA (245)	INCA/ I -- ER. ER -- I. I -- ER. I AM NOT A GOOD	JUDGE	. /ERMYNTRUDE/ THEY SAY HE TAKES HIMSELF VERY
GENV II (58)	WE SHOULD HAVE HAD NO TROUBLE WITH A BRITISH	JUDGE	. /JUDGE/ WHY SHOULD YOU HAVE ANY TROUBLE WITH ME? I
GENV II SD(56)	FORTY, IN FACT, BUT VERY GRAVE AND EVERY INCH A	JUDGE	. /THE SECRETARY/ I AM DESOLATE AT HAVING BROUGHT YOUR
MILL I SD(137)	A CLEFT PEDIMENT ENSHRINING A BUST OF SOME OTHER	JUDGE	. THE REST OF THIS WALL IS OCCUPIED BY SHELVES OF
BARB III (335)	HAVE THE RIGHT TO FIGHT: NONE HAVE THE RIGHT TO	JUDGE	. THE THIRD WROTE UP TO MAN THE WEAPON: TO HEAVEN THE
CAPT III (288)	REAL FLESH AND BLOOD BENEATH THE ERMINE OF THE	JUDGE	. WE WILL NOW DROP A SUBJECT THAT SHOULD NEVER HAVE
CAPT II (254)	TRUST, AS BECOMES AN INNOCENT MAN AND AN UPRIGHT	JUDGE	. WHAT DO YOU CHARGE AGAINST ME? /BRASSBOUND/ I
GENV II (58)	NECESSARILY, JUSTICE IS AN IDEAL; AND I AM A	JUDGE	. WHAT, MAY I ASK, ARE YOU? /SIR O./ OH, ONLY A MUCH
POSN PREFACE(389)	A CENSOR HAS NOTHING BUT HIS OWN OPINION. A	JUDGE	LEAVES THE QUESTION OF GUILT TO THE JURY: THE CENSOR
BULL PREFACE(59)	PITIABLE AS THE VIRTUOUS INDIGNATION WITH WHICH	JUDGE	LYNCH, HIMSELF PROVABLE BY HIS OWN JUDGMENT TO BE A
BULL PREFACE(59)	WHEN LORD CROMER, IN HIS OFFICIAL APOLOGY FOR	JUDGE	LYNCH, SAYS THAT " THE PRISONERS HAD A PERFECTLY FAIR
BULL PREFACE(55)	AND HAD ALREADY HAD SEVERAL FITS IN THE COURT OF	JUDGE	LYNCH, THE DOCTOR SAID BETTER NOT; AND HE ESCAPED.
GENV IV (118)	/BATTLER/ WHAT DO YOU MEAN? DO YOU PRESUME TO	JUDGE	ME? /BBDE/ JUDGE ME IF YOU DARE. /FLANCO/ GIVE
SUPR I (14)	IT: THE ONLY THING YOURE NOT ASHAMED OF IS TO	JUDGE	ME FOR IT WITHOUT HAVING READ IT; AND EVEN THAT ONLY
GENV IV (118)	DO YOU MEAN? DO YOU PRESUME TO JUDGE ME? /BBDE/	JUDGE	ME IF YOU DARE. /FLANCO/ GIVE JUDGMENT AGAINST ME AND
ROCK PREFACE(187)	THAT HE IS IN THE RIGHT; THEREFORE YOU MUST NOT	JUDGE	ME LEST YOU BE YOURSELF JUDGED, WITHOUT SEDITION AND
CLEO IV (188)	RUFIO HAS SAID I DID WELL: NOW THE OTHERS SHALL	JUDGE	ME TOO. (SHE TURNS TO THE OTHERS). THIS POTHINUS
CAPT III (277)	BUT A JUDGE, IT WOULDNT MATTER SO MUCH. BUT A	JUDGE	MUSTNT EVEN BE MISUNDERSTOOD. (DESPAIRINGLY) OH, IT'S
MTH4 II (177)	BEHAVED LIKE A POLTROON. BUT I WARN YOU NOT TO	JUDGE	MY QUALITY BY THESE INVOLUNTARY MOMENTS. /THE ORACLE/
LION PREFACE(66)	FOR JUDGES. ALSO, OF COURSE, WHY JESUS SAID "	JUDGE	NOT THAT YE BE NOT JUDGED" AND " IF ANY MAN HEAR MY
LION PREFACE(63)	INCOME THAT IS NOT ABSORBED BY SIMPLE COMMUNISM.	JUDGE	NOT. IN DEALING WITH CRIME AND THE FAMILY, MODERN
SIM II (81)	CHARLES/ I SEEM TO REMEMBER SOMEBODY SAYING "	JUDGE	NOT, THAT YE BE NOT JUDGED." /PROLA/ THAT MEANS "
KING I (197)	/CHARLES/ OR IF YOU ARE WORTH IT. JACK IS A GOOD	JUDGE	OF A WINNER. /JAMES/ HE HAS HIS PRICE ALL THE SAME.
FABL III (110)	WILL SUIT ME DOWN TO THE GROUND. I'M A FIRST-RATE	JUDGE	OF CHARACTER. /THE MATRON/ SPLENDID. TAKE THIS IN TO
POSN PREFACE(391)	OF RELATIONSHIP TO DRAMATIC LITERATURE. A GREAT	JUDGE	OF LITERATURE, A FAR-SEEING STATESMAN, A BORN CHAMPION
BASH III (123)	AGED; FOR I AM YOUNGER FAR THAN I APPEAR).	JUDGE	OF MY ANGUISH WHEN TODAY I SAW STRIPPED TO THE WAIST,
GETT (326)	AT THAT, YES. BUT THERE WAS SOMETHING WORSE.	JUDGE	OF MY HORROR WHEN, CALLING ON THE COAL MERCHANT TO
PLES PREFACE(R11)	HAS EXPERIENCE ENOUGH TO MAKE HIM AS SAFE A	JUDGE	OF PLAYS AS A BOND STREET DEALER IS OF PICTURES, HE
MTH5 (222)	ACIS IS LEANING OVER IT). /ACIS/ I AM NO GREAT	JUDGE	OF SCULPTURE. ART IS NOT MY LINE. WHAT IS WRONG WITH
WIDO I (21)	(QUICKLY) BY NO MEANS: LADY ROXDALE MUST	JUDGE	OF THAT FOR HERSELF. LET IT STAND AS I SAID. " I HAVE
GENV IV (128)	WHAT AN ACTOR! /SECRETARY/ YOU SHOULD BE A GOOD	JUDGE	OF THAT. YOU HAVE DONE A GOOD DEAL IN THAT LINE
GETT (316)	FOR HIS HEALTH. /THE BISHOP/ WHO IS TO BE THE	JUDGE	OF THAT, MY DEAR? YOU OR HE? /EDITH/ NEITHER OF US.
WIDO II (29)	FAIR AND GENEROUS; AND I BELIEVE HE IS A BETTER	JUDGE	OF THE CIRCUMSTANCES THAN I AM. /COKANE/ (
GENV II (55)	. . . HOLD ON A MOMENT. (TO SIR O.) THE SENIOR	JUDGE	OF THE COURT OF INTERNATIONAL JUSTICE AT THE HAGUE IS
POSN PREFACE(400)	FOR EXAMPLE, THE CHRISTMAS PANTOMIMES. IMAGINE A	JUDGE	OF THE HIGH COURT, OR AN ARCHBISHOP, OR A CABINET
JITT III (60)	ON ME. SURELY, CHILD, NOBODY CAN BE A BETTER	JUDGE	OF WHAT IS BEST FOR YOU THAN YOUR OWN MOTHER. HERE I
MTH4 II (177)	MOMENTS. /THE ORACLE/ I HAVE NO OCCASION TO	JUDGE	OF YOUR QUALITY. YOU WANT MY ADVICE. SPEAK QUICKLY; OR
CAPT III (273)	IS JUST LIKE YOU: HE THINKS WE HAVE NO RIGHT TO	JUDGE	ONE ANOTHER; AND AS SIR HOWARD GETS 5,000 POUNDS A
GETT PREFACE(257)	OR RELIGION. IF YOU DOUBT THIS, ASK ANY DECENT	JUDGE	OR BISHOP. DO NOT ASK SOMEBODY WHO DOES NOT KNOW WHAT

MIS. PREFACE(53)	PARENTS OR HIS SCHOOLMASTER OR HIS BISHOP OR HIS	JUDGE	OR HIS ARMY OR HIS NAVY WILL DO SOMETHING TO FRIGHTEN
PHIL III (139)	/CHARTERIS/ YES, IF YOU ARE TO BE JUDGED AS YOU	JUDGE	OTHERS. FROM THE CONVENTIONAL POINT OF VIEW, THERES
DOCT PREFACE(19)	HAVE NO INTERESTS BUT OUR OWN TO THINK OF; SHOULD	JUDGE	OUR CASES SCIENTIFICALLY; AND SHOULD FEEL ABOUT THEM
DOCT PREFACE(66)	CAREER TO THE LAST AS THE DOCTOR IS. THE	JUDGE	PASSES SENTENCE OF DEATH; BUT HE IS NOT EXPECTED TO
CAPT I (226)	IN THE WUST COWST VAWNYARD. (INTRODUCING THE	JUDGE	) MR RENKIN: IS LAWDSHIP SIR AHRD ELLAM. (HE
GENV IV (91)	I DONT UNDERSTAND. /BBDE/ (CONTEMPTUOUSLY TO THE	JUDGE	) TELL HIM THAT THIS IS A COURT OF PEOPLE WHO
GENV IV (108)	FOOL. /BBDE/ (HUGELY AMUSED) HA HA! (TO THE	JUDGE	) THE INCIDENT IS CLOSED. AN ATTRACTIVE AND VERY
GENV IV (118)	IN YOUR BONNET BUZZES TOO MUCH, ERNEST. (TO THE	JUDGE	) WHAT IS THE LAW? /JUDGE/ UNFORTUNATELY THERE IS NO
GENV III (79)	WE ARE INTERRUPTING HIS HONOR THE JUDGE. (TO THE	JUDGE	) YOU WERE ABOUT TO SAY--? /THE JUDGE/ I WAS ABOUT TO
GENV IV (105)	NOT GOD ALMIGHTY, AS YOU PRETEND TO BE. (TO THE	JUDGE	) YOUR HONOR: I AM SATISFIED. HE HAS ADMITTED HIS
LION PREFACE(11)	LAW WITHIN YOU MAKES YOU CONCEIVE YOUR GOD AS A	JUDGE	; AND STRAIGHTWAY YOU TRY TO CORRUPT HIM, ALSO WITH
CAPT II (260)	PEOPLE. OF COURSE HE DOES DREADFUL THINGS AS A	JUDGE	; BUT THEN IF YOU TAKE A MAN AND PAY HIM 5,000 POUNDS
JOAN PREFACE(42)	OF THE REALM ACT SUSPENDING ALL LAW; AND THE	JUDGE	SHE WOULD HAVE HAD, AT BEST, A BOTHERED MAJOR, AND AT
POSN PREFACE(430)	JUDGMENT ON ALL POINTS. IT IS INEVITABLE THAT A	JUDGE	SHOULD BE DEEPLY IMPRESSED BY HIS PROFESSIONAL
POSN PREFACE(390)	THE TWO DO NOT STAND, AS THE CRIMINAL AND THE	JUDGE	STAND, IN THE PRESENCE OF A LAW THAT BINDS THEM BOTH
DEST (155)	SEE WITH YOUR EXCELLENCY'S EYES: EVERY MAN MUST	JUDGE	THAT FOR HIMSELF. IN MY OPINION, EXCELLENCY, A FINE
ARMS III (65)	HER. BLUNTSCHLI. YOU, THE COOL IMPARTIAL MAN:	JUDGE	THE EAVESDROPPER. LOUKA STANDS HER GROUND, PROUD AND
HART I (78)	THE MEANS. /HECTOR/ WHO ARE WE THAT WE SHOULD	JUDGE	THEM? /CAPTAIN SHOTOVER/ WHAT ARE THEY THAT THEY
SIM II (81)	FEAR THE JUDGMENT OF GOD, THEY MUST LEARN TO	JUDGE	THEMSELVES. /SIR CHARLES/ I SEEM TO REMEMBER SOMEBODY
UNPL PREFACE(R8)	I WAS NOT SPLENETIC OVER OUR VARIANCE.	JUDGE	THEN, HOW IMPOSSIBLE IT WAS FOR ME TO WRITE FICTION
POSN PREFACE(381)	BETWEEN THE POWERS OF A MAGISTRATE OR	JUDGE	TO ADMINISTER A CODE, AND THOSE OF A CENSOR TO PLEASE
JOAN PREFACE(42)	LAW TO GOVERN THEIR CASES, OR AS CONSCIENTIOUS A	JUDGE	TO INSIST ON STRICT LEGALITY OF PROCEDURE AS JOAN HAD
GENV II (60)	NECESSARY APPLICATIONS. IT IS THE BUSINESS OF A	JUDGE	TO SEE THAT THERE IS NO WRONG WITHOUT A REMEDY. YOUR
LION PREFACE(66)	TO THE MISERY OF CRIME, AND THE CRUELTY OF THE	JUDGE	TO THE CRUELTY OF THE CRIMINAL. WE HAVE TAKEN THE BAD
LADY (238)	IF THOU DENY IT, THOU LIEST. /THE BEEFEATER/ YOU	JUDGE	TOO MUCH BY THE COURT, SIR. THERE, INDEED, YOU MAY SAY
HART I (78)	/CAPTAIN SHOTOVER/ WHAT ARE THEY THAT THEY SHOULD	JUDGE	US? YET THEY DO, UNHESITATINGLY. THERE IS ENMITY
SUPR HANDBOK(207)	AND OTHER MOMENTARY OUTBURSTS OF SOCIAL DISORDER.	JUDGE	US BY THE ADMITTED AND RESPECTED PRACTICE OF OUR MOST
SIM II (74)	FARWATERS/ HE ACTUALLY WENT AWAY AND FORGOT TO	JUDGE	US. /PRA/ I AM NOT SO SURE OF THAT. /IDDY/ WELL, ARE
SIM II (74)	GET OVER IS THEIR SENDING ALONG JUST ONE ANGEL TO	JUDGE	US, AS IF WE DIDNT MATTER. /LADY FARWATERS/ HE
BULL PREFACE(61)	OF WHICH THE BEST ENGLISH AND THE BEST NATIVE	JUDGE	WERE MEMBERS. THIS FACT WILL, MOREOVER, SUPPLY THE
POSN PREFACE(366)	WORLD) IS BY NO MEANS EQUALLY QUALIFIED TO	JUDGE	WHETHER A PLAY IS SAFE FROM PROSECUTION OR NOT. HE MAY
APPL I (237)	LIMITED! JUST SO! LISTEN TO ME, SIR; AND	JUDGE	WHETHER I HAVE NOT REASON TO FEEL EVERYTHING YOU HAVE
ROCK PREFACE(182)	AND CRUCIFIXIONS OF INNOCENT MEN, HOW AM I TO	JUDGE	WHETHER IT IS HE WHO IS DRIVING YOU TO SACRIFICE
HART I (64)	MISS DUNN, IS HECTOR HUSHABYE. I LEAVE YOU TO	JUDGE	WHETHER THAT IS A NAME ANY SENSITIVE MAN WOULD CARE TO
BULL II (100)	OF YOUR PARISH PRIEST AND SET YOURSELF UP TO	JUDGE	WHETHER YOUR CHURCH IS RIGHT OR WRONG. /PATSY/ SURE I
CAPT II (256)	THE HYPOCRISY IN THE SANCTIMONIOUS SPEECH OF THE	JUDGE	WHO IS SENTENCING YOU, INSTEAD OF THE DESPAIR IN THE
ROCK PREFACE(179)	BUT THE TRIAL OF A DUMB PRISONER, AT WHICH THE	JUDGE	WHO PUTS THE CRUCIAL QUESTION TO HIM REMAINS
JOAN PREFACE(28)	PETER CAUCHON, BISHOP OF BEAUVAIS, THE	JUDGE	WHO SENT JOAN TO THE STAKE, AS AN UNCONSCIONABLE
ROCK PREFACE(159)	THE HANGING OF A CRUCIFIX ABOVE THE SEAT OF THE	JUDGE	WHO WAS SENTENCING EVILDOERS TO BE BROKEN ON THE
DOCT PREFACE(4)	THAT DOCTORS ARE LESS VIRTUOUS THAN JUDGES; BUT A	JUDGE	WHOSE SALARY AND REPUTATION DEPENDED ON WHETHER THE
LION PREFACE(64)	GILBERT CHESTERTON'S STORIES HAS FOR ITS HERO A	JUDGE	WHO, WHILST TRYING A CRIMINAL CASE, IS SO OVERWHELMED
DOCT PREFACE(7)	JURY THAT THEY MUST ACQUIT THE PRISONER. THUS A	JUDGE	WITH A KEEN SENSE OF LAW (A VERY RARE PHENOMENON ON
ROCK PREFACE(164)	MEDICINES; AND IT WILL BECOME POSSIBLE TO BE A	JUDGE	WITHOUT CEASING TO BE A CHRISTIAN. AND EXTERMINATION,
POSN PREFACE(402)	THE POPULAR LAXITY OF THE LORD CHAMBERLAIN. THE	JUDGE	WOULD SUPPRESS THE PIONEERS, WHILST THE EXAMINER OF
LION PREFACE(66)	THAN IT WOULD HAVE BEEN IF THERE HAD NEVER BEEN A	JUDGE	, A PRISON, OR A GALLOWS IN IT ALL THAT TIME. WE HAVE
DOCT PREFACE(8)	UNERRING SKILL. HE HAS TAUGHT THE JURY AND THE	JUDGE	, AND EVEN HIS OWN COUNSEL, TO BELIEVE THAT EVERY
DOCT PREFACE(3)	MAN'S HOUSE STABLE. BUT WE DO MAKE THE DOCTOR THE	JUDGE	, AND FINE HIM ANYTHING FROM SIXPENCE TO SEVERAL
DOCT PREFACE(4)	THE PAY OF THE ENEMY. TO OFFER ME A DOCTOR AS MY	JUDGE	, AND THEN WEIGHT HIS DECISION WITH A BRIBE OF A LARGE
CLEO V (200)	RUFIO: HAD YOU SET YOURSELF IN THE SEAT OF THE	JUDGE	, AND WITH HATEFUL CEREMONIES AND APPEALS TO THE GODS
GETT PREFACE(193)	ANARCHIST AS A	JUDGE	, ANY DESPOT AS A WHIG, ANY SENTIMENTAL SOCIALIST AS A
MIS. PREFACE(64)	OF THEIR PUBLIC ANALOGUES THE LAWGIVER AND THE	JUDGE	, BECOME INSTRUMENTS OF TYRANNY IN THE HANDS OF THOSE
GENV III (70)	ORPHEUS. YOU REMEMBER ME, SENORA. YOU KNOW THE	JUDGE	, BOSS. /THE SECRETARY/ DO ME THE HONOR TO SHARE MY
BULL PREFACE(16)	BEGGAR, BACKBITER, VENAL FUNCTIONARY, CORRUPT	JUDGE	, ENVIOUS FRIEND, VINDICTIVE OPPONENT, UNPARALLELED
GENV II (58)	YOU HAVE ANY TROUBLE WITH ME? I AM SIMPLY A	JUDGE	, FIRST AND LAST. TO ME IT IS A CONTINUAL TROUBLE AND
JOAN 5 (120)	DO WITH SUCH A CHARACTER? /DUNOIS/ AS GOD IS MY	JUDGE	, IF SHE FELL INTO THE LOIRE I WOULD JUMP IN IN FULL
GENV IV SD(89)	HE IS DUE NOW, IT IS ON THE STROKE OF TEN. THE	JUDGE	, IN HIS JUDICIAL ROBE, ENTERS. THEY ALL RISE. HE IS
DOCT II (127)	ARTIST, EH? /RIDGEON/ IT'S NOT AN EASY CASE TO	JUDGE	, IS IT? BLENKINSOP'S AN HONEST DECENT MAN; BUT IS HE
CAPT III (277)	HELP IT. /LADY CICELY/ IF YOU WERE ANYBODY BUT A	JUDGE	, IT WOULDNT MATTER SO MUCH. BUT A JUDGE MUSTNT EVEN
MIS. PREFACE(13)	THE PERSON WHOM HE HAS INJURED ALLOWED TO ACT AS	JUDGE	, JURY, AND EXECUTIONER. IT IS TRUE THAT EMPLOYERS DO
CAPT II (256)	EL ASSIF. HE WILL BE HERE WITHIN AN HOUR. HE IS A	JUDGE	, LIKE YOURSELF. YOU CAN TALK LAW TO HIM. HE WILL GIVE
GENV III SD(70)	THE COMMISSAR COMES IN WITH BEGONIA AND THE	JUDGE	, OF WHOM SHE HAS EVIDENTLY MADE A CONQUEST. /BEGONIA/
FANY PROLOG (267)	GOD FORBID THAT I SHOULD SET UP TO BE A	JUDGE	, OR DO MORE THAN RECORD AN IMPRESSION; BUT MY
DOCT PREFACE(67)	LED TO A JUDGE HAVING TO HANG, BUT THE HANGMAN TO	JUDGE	, OR IF IN THE ARMY MATTERS WERE SO ARRANGED THAT IT
SUPR HANDBOK(210)	A MAN AS HARNESS IS PUT ON A HORSE, ERMINE ON A	JUDGE	, PIPECLAY ON A SOLDIER, OR A WIG ON AN ACTOR, AND
GENV III (78)	WORD HAS NO MEANING. /SIR O./ THANK YOU, MY DEAR	JUDGE	, THANK YOU. BUT FOR HEAVEN'S SAKE DONT CALL ME CLEVER
MIS. PREFACE(25)	IF DIFFICULT, TO FIND A SOLICITOR, OR EVEN A	JUDGE	, WHO HAS SOME NOTION OF WHAT LAW MEANS, A DOCTOR WITH
GENV IV (92)	ORPHEUS, AND MOUNTS THE DAIS TO THE RIGHT OF THE	JUDGE	, WHO NOW HAS A DICTATOR ON EACH SIDE OF HIM) BY YOUR
BULL PREFACE(56)	DO WITH OUR DIVORCE COURT. EVENTUALLY A BELGIAN	JUDGE	, WHO WAS APPOINTED PROCUREUR-GENERAL, EXPOSED THE
CAPT III (284)	SHE BREAKS OUT AGAIN). YOU LOOK SO NICE AS A	JUDGE	! A GENERAL SMILE. DRINKWATER SPLUTTERS INTO A HALF
GENV IV (88)	BUT WHAT A DREADFUL FIASCO FOR OUR FRIEND THE	JUDGE	! I WARNED HIM THAT THIS MIGHT HAPPEN. I TOLD HIM TO

JUDGED

JOAN PREFACE(12)	NEWTON AS A MADMAN? IN THE SAME WAY JOAN MUST BE	JUDGED	A SANE WOMAN IN SPITE OF HER VOICES BECAUSE THEY
SIM PREFACE(14)	OF LAW WILL GOVERN THE JUDGMENT AND CLASSIFY THE	JUDGED	AS SHEEP OR GOATS AS THE CASE MAY BE, WE HAVE NOT
PHIL III (139)	IS THAT IT? /CHARTERIS/ YES, IF YOU ARE TO BE	JUDGED	AS YOU JUDGE OTHERS. FROM THE CONVENTIONAL POINT OF
SIM II (75)	EMPIRE TO BE PLACED IN THE POSITION OF BEING	JUDGED	BY A COMMISSION OF A FEW ANGELS INSTEAD OF BY DIRECT
POSN PREFACE(428)	FOR THE BENEFIT OF THOSE WHO PREFER TO BE	JUDGED	BY HIM. BUT I AM NOT SO SURE THAT THE LORD
WIDO II SD(25)	A NERVOUS, WIRY, PERTINACIOUS HUMAN TERRIER,	JUDGED	BY HIS MOUTH AND EYES, BUT MISERABLY APPREHENSIVE AND
POSN PREFACE(400)	MATERIAL DIFFICULTY IS THAT NO PLAY CAN BE	JUDGED	BY MERELY READING THE DIALOGUE. TO BE FULLY EFFECTIVE
2TRU PREFACE(16)	OF THE VOCATION OF THE NEW RECRUITS WERE	JUDGED	BY THE CHURCH. IF THE JUDGMENT WAS FAVORABLE, AND THE
LADY PREFACE(218)	SHAKESPEAR'S PERCEPTION OF THE FACT THAT ALL MEN,	JUDGED	BY THE MORAL STANDARD WHICH THEY APPLY TO OTHERS AND
BULL PREFACE(57)	OFFICIALISM. AND WHAT THAT BEST IS MAY BE	JUDGED	BY THE SENTENCES ON THE DENSHAWAI VILLAGERS. LORD
SUPR PREFACE(R33)	THE AUTHOR NOR REVEALS HIM. HE MUST BE	JUDGED	BY THOSE CHARACTERS INTO WHICH HE PUTS WHAT HE KNOWS
CLEO IV (188)	SLANDERER. /CLEOPATRA/ (PASSIONATELY) I WILL BE	JUDGED	BY YOUR VERY SLAVE, CAESAR. BRITANNUS: SPEAK. WAS I
MRS PREFACE(154)	BUT I SHOULD BE QUITE CONTENT TO HAVE MY PLAY	JUDGED	BY, SAY, A JOINT COMMITTEE OF THE CENTRAL VIGILANCE
POSN PREFACE(361)	THE BLUEBOOK IS 214. HOW INTERESTING IT IS MAY BE	JUDGED	FROM THE FACT THAT IT CONTAINS VERBATIM REPORTS OF
MILL PREFACE(128)	MAD. THAT IS A PLAIN FACT OF POLITICAL PATHOLOGY.	JUDGED	IN THIS LIGHT OUR PRESENT PREDICAMENT IS LAMENTABLE.
CLEO V (200)	POTHINUS! /RUFIO/ (CONTINUING) I MIGHT HAVE	JUDGED	IT. BUT I PUT ALL THESE FOLLIES BEHIND ME; AND,
LION PREFACE(64)	JUDGES A CONSPICUOUS PLACE ALONGSIDE OF THEM THEY	JUDGED	. AND HE SEEMS TO HAVE DONE THIS NOT AS A RESTATEMENT
PHIL II (130)	WHEN THERES A DIFFICULT SITUATION TO BE	JUDGED	. (HE SITS DOWN ON THE SETTEE BACK). /CRAVEN/ (
MTH5 (240)	IS NEVER A TRIFLE. I HAD RATHER HAVE THE CASE	JUDGED	. THE HE-ANCIENT EMERGES FROM THE GROVE. THE FIGURES
LION PREFACE(74)	WITHOUT REMORSE, JUDGING BECAUSE THEY HAD BEEN	JUDGED	. THEY HEALED THE SICK AND RAISED THE DEAD APPARENTLY
ROCK PREFACE(187)	YOU MUST NOT JUDGE ME LEST YOU BE YOURSELF	JUDGED	." WITHOUT SEDITION AND BLASPHEMY THE WORLD WOULD
SIM II (81)	SOMEBODY SAYING " JUDGE NOT, THAT YE BE NOT	JUDGED	." /PROLA/ THAT MEANS " PUNISH NOT, THAT YE BE NOT
FANY EPILOG (330)	NAME. THE AUTHOR DESIRES THAT THE PLAY SHOULD BE	JUDGED	ON ITS MERITS. /BANNAL/ BUT WHAT MERITS CAN IT HAVE
NEVR II (256)	LETTING US BELONG TO OURSELVES AND DO WHAT WE	JUDGED	RIGHT AND REASONABLE FOR ALL THESE YEARS, WERE
JOAN PREFACE(34)	THEIR STAKES AND WHEELS AND GIBBETS. JOAN HERSELF	JUDGED	THIS MATTER WHEN SHE HAD TO CHOOSE BETWEEN
LION PREF,FN(43)		JUDGED	UNJUSTLY AND ACCEPTED THE PERSONS OF THE WICKED (
DOCT PREFACE(65)	BUT ON THE NUMBER OF PEOPLE WHO ARE WELL. HE IS	JUDGED	, AS ALL DOCTORS AND TREATMENTS SHOULD BE JUDGED, BY
DOCT PREFACE(65)	JUDGED, AS ALL DOCTORS AND TREATMENTS SHOULD BE	JUDGED	, BY THE VITAL STATISTICS OF HIS DISTRICT. WHEN THE
LION PREFACE(66)	COURSE, WHY JESUS SAID " JUDGE NOT THAT YE BE NOT	JUDGED	" AND " IF ANY MAN HEAR MY WORDS AND BELIEVE NOT, I

JUDGEMADE

GENV II (57)	TO MAKE IT. YOU ARE FAMILIAR WITH WHAT YOU CALL	JUDGEMADE	LAW IN ENGLAND. WELL, SIR MIDLANDER, THE JUDGES OF

JUDGE'S

GENV IV SD(90)	A PARLIAMENTARY FACT. A TELEPHONE RINGS ON THE	JUDGE'S	DESK. HE HOLDS DOWN A BUTTON AND LISTENS. /THE

SUPR I (28)	TO US ALL. IT'S A SORT OF MUD THAT STICKS TO THE	JUDGE'S	ERMINE OR THE CARDINAL'S ROBE AS FAST AS TO THE RAGS.
GENV IV (90)	CHAIR WITH A POWERFUL HAND AND PLACES IT ON THE	JUDGE'S	LEFT; THEN FLINGS HIMSELF MASSIVELY INTO IT) DO NOT

JUDGES

POSN PREFACE(430)	PROPOSALS WOULD NEVER HAVE COME INTO EXISTENCE.	JUDGES	: THEIR PROFESSIONAL LIMITATIONS. I DO NOT, HOWEVER,
LION PREFACE(64)	TYPES OF SCOUNDRELS IT PRODUCES. HE ALWAYS GAVE	JUDGES	A CONSPICUOUS PLACE ALONGSIDE OF THEM THEY JUDGED.
GENV I (39)	BY ADULT SUFFRAGE EVERY TWO YEARS. SO ARE ALL THE	JUDGES	AND ALL THE OFFICIALS, EVEN THE ROAD SWEEPERS. ALL
GENV IV (124)	OF LAW, OF LEADERS AND FOREIGN SECRETARIES, OF	JUDGES	AND GENERALS. A MOMENT AGO WE WERE IMPORTANT PERSONS:
POSN PREFACE(430)	EXPERIENCE WITH A SENSE OF THE IMPOTENCE OF	JUDGES	AND LAWS AND COURTS TO DEAL SATISFACTORILY WITH EVILS
HART PREFACE(12)	INDICTMENTS FOR WILFUL MURDER, UNTIL AT LAST THE	JUDGES	AND MAGISTRATES HAD TO ANNOUNCE THAT WHAT WAS CALLED
ROCK PREFACE(190)	AND UNDONE BY A WORSE WRONG DONE TO HIM BY	JUDGES	AND PRIESTS: IF IT IS TO SUBSTITUTE THE DOCTRINE OF
LION PREFACE(51)	SERVE TWO MASTERS: GOD AND MAMMON. 3. GET RID OF	JUDGES	AND PUNISHMENT AND REVENGE. LOVE YOUR NEIGHBOR AS
BULL PREFACE(34)	PENSIONS TO MYSELF AND MY FELLOW ENGLISHMEN AS	JUDGES	AND RULERS OVER YOU. IN RETURN FOR WHICH YOU GET THE
ROCK PREFACE(176)	IT IS QUITE CREDIBLE THAT BOTH HIS IMMEDIATE	JUDGES	AND THE POPE BELIEVED WITH AT LEAST HALF THEIR MINDS
GETT PREFACE(257)	8. NEVER FORGET THAT IF YOU LEAVE YOUR LAW TO	JUDGES	AND YOUR RELIGION TO BISHOPS YOU WILL PRESENTLY FIND
JOAN EPILOG (154)	/CHARLES/ NEVER MIND THE FALSEHOODS: HER	JUDGES	ARE DEAD. /LADVENU/ THE SENTENCE ON HER IS BROKEN,
GENV II (57)	REMEMBER THAT YOU ARE NOT NOW IN ENGLAND, WHERE	JUDGES	ARE ONLY WORN-OUT BARRISTERS, MOST OF WHOM HAVE
POSN PREFACE(398)	FURTHER THAN THE PUBLIC WILL LET IT. IF OUR	JUDGES	HAD SO LITTLE POWER THERE WOULD BE NO LAW IN ENGLAND.
JOAN EPILOG (165)	/THE INQUISITOR/ (KNEELING TO HER) THE	JUDGES	IN THE BLINDNESS AND BONDAGE OF THE LAW PRAISE THEE,
JOAN PREFACE(29)	TO THE SERVICE OF GOD, TO SUPPORT TWO SKILLED	JUDGES	IN TRYING HER CASE ACCORDING TO THE CATHOLIC LAW OF
LION PREFACE(66)	SWIFT RESERVED THE HOTTEST CORNER OF HIS HELL FOR	JUDGES	. ALSO, OF COURSE, WHY JESUS SAID " JUDGE NOT THAT YE
ROCK PREFACE(155)	IN THE MOST PAINLESS MANNER KNOWN TO THEIR	JUDGES	. BUT FROM THAT SUMMIT THERE WAS A SPEEDY RELAPSE
ROCK PREFACE(149)	BELOVED BY OUR PRISON COMMISSIONERS AND	JUDGES	. IT DISPOSES OF THE DOGMA OF THE UNCONDITIONAL
JOAN 6,SD(122)	SIDE BY SIDE FOR THE BISHOP AND THE INQUISITOR AS	JUDGES	. ROWS OF CHAIRS RADIATING FROM THEM AT AN OBTUSE
CAPT I (235)	WILL BE WELL KNOWN TO YE AS ONE OF HER MAJESTY'S	JUDGES	. /BRASSBOUND/ (TURNING THE SINGULAR LOOK AGAIN ON
LION PREFACE(59)	SALARY FOR ONE JUDGE IS THE SALARY FOR ALL THE	JUDGES	. THE CAPTAIN AND THE CABIN BOY. NOTHING, THEREFORE,
SUPR I (29)	THE PRISONER IS WAITING TO BE BROUGHT BEFORE HER	JUDGES	. THE OLD CATS! /ANN/ OH, JACK! /RAMSDEN/ YOU ARE
LION PREFACE(6)	AND BLASPHEMOUS MADMAN, WAS GREATER THAN HIS	JUDGES	. WAS JESUS A COWARD? I KNOW QUITE WELL THAT THIS
JOAN 6 (141)	OF EXCOMMUNICATION HAS PASSED THE LIPS OF YOUR	JUDGES	. YOU ARE WITHIN A FEW SHORT MOMENTS OF THAT DOOM.
GETT PREFACE(193)	DOING WHAT EVERYBODY ELSE DID), AND BY BEING GOOD	JUDGES	OF HATS, TIES, DOGS, PIPES, CRICKET, GARDENS,
DOCT PREFACE(3)	NOT TO MAKE THE HANGMAN AND THE HOUSEBREAKER THE	JUDGES	OF THAT. IF WE DID, NO MAN'S NECK WOULD BE SAFE AND
GENV II (57)	LAW IN ENGLAND. WELL, SIR MIDLANDER, THE	JUDGES	OF THE COURT OF INTERNATIONAL JUSTICE ARE NOT
ROCK PREFACE(190)	WE SHALL NEED CRITICS EDUCATED OTHERWISE THAN OUR	JUDGES	OF TODAY; BUT THE SAME MAY BE SAID OF ALL WHOSE
JOAN PREFACE(6)	HAS QUASHED THE ORIGINAL PROCEEDINGS, AND PUT HER	JUDGES	ON THEIR TRIAL, WHICH, SO FAR, HAS BEEN MUCH MORE
ROCK PREFACE(157)	AN APOLOGIST OF SINNERS, AND A DISPARAGER OF	JUDGES	; AND HIS DAILY COMPANIONS WERE TRAMPS WHOM HE HAD
LION PREFACE(12)	THAT LITIGANTS SHOULD GIVE PRESENTS TO HUMAN	JUDGES	; AND THE BUYING OFF OF DIVINE WRATH BY ACTUAL MONEY
DOCT PREFACE(4)	SUPPOSES THAT DOCTORS ARE LESS VIRTUOUS THAN	JUDGES	; BUT A JUDGE WHOSE SALARY AND REPUTATION DEPENDED ON
JOAN 6,SD(151)	THE EXECUTIONER COMES IN BY THE DOOR BEHIND THE	JUDGES	' CHAIRS; AND WARWICK, RETURNING, FINDS HIMSELF FACE
JOAN 6,SD(122)	COMES IN THROUGH THE ARCHED DOORWAY ON THE	JUDGES	' SIDE, FOLLOWED BY HIS PAGE. /THE PAGE/ (PERTLY) I
ROCK PREFACE(163)	BUT QUITE EASY TO CONVINCE ANY REASONABLE BODY OF	JUDGES	THAT HE IS WHAT THE PEOPLE CALL " A WRONG ONE." IN
ROCK PREFACE(179)	IS NOT A HEROIC FIGURE. JOAN TACKLED HER	JUDGES	VALIANTLY AND WITTILY: HER TRIAL WAS A DRAMA READY
JOAN EPILOG (154)	IT. /LADVENU/ IT IS SOLEMNLY DECLARED THAT HER	JUDGES	WERE FULL OF CORRUPTION, COZENAGE, FRAUD, AND MALICE.
JOAN EPILOG (156)	AGAIN. AND THE COURTS HAVE DECLARED THAT YOUR	JUDGES	WERE FULL OF CORRUPTION AND COZENAGE, FRAUD AND
BULL PREFACE(58)	ZAKZOUK, ON BEING ASKED BY ONE OF THE ENGLISH	JUDGES	WHETHER HE WAS NOT AFRAID TO SAY SUCH A THING,
KING I (197)	CRUEL THAT I DARE NOT INTERFERE WITH PROTESTANT	JUDGES	WHO ARE MERCILESS. THE PENALTY FOR HIGH TREASON IS SO
SUPR HANDBOK(207)	MORE MERCIFUL THAN THE AMERICAN LEGISLATORS AND	JUDGES	WHO NOT SO LONG AGO CONDEMNED MEN TO SOLITARY
LION EPILOG (148)	MEANS HYPOCRISY. THE HOME SECRETARY AND THE	JUDGES	WHO TRY THE CASE ARE USUALLY FAR MORE SCEPTICAL AND
FABL PREFACE(91)	BAFFLING AT PRESENT ARE THE CASES IN WHICH THE	JUDGES	WILL BE FACED WITH APPARENTLY VACANT MINDS, AND MET,
GENV IV (118)	SAID, ERNEST, SAME HERE. /JUDGE/ AS YOU ARE NOT	JUDGES	YOUR PRECEDENTS HAVE NO AUTHORITY OUTSIDE THE
JOAN PREFACE(32)	OUR INFALLIBLE ASTRONOMERS, OUR INFALLIBLE	JUDGES	, AND OUR INFALLIBLE PARLIAMENTS. THE POPE IS ON HIS
3PLA PREFACE(R22)	DESTROY THE VERY SENSE OF LAW. KAISERS, GENERALS,	JUDGES	, AND PRIME MINISTERS WILL SET THE EXAMPLE OF PLAYING
JOAN PREFACE(7)	GET RID OF IS THE MUD THAT IS BEING THROWN AT HER	JUDGES	, AND THE WHITEWASH WHICH DISFIGURES HER BEYOND
LION PREFACE(7)	WHOM THE APPEAL LAY, FAVORED HIM AND DESPISED HIS	JUDGES	, AND WAS EVIDENTLY WILLING ENOUGH TO BE CONCILIATED.
POSN PREFACE(398)	THE LORD CHAMBERLAIN'S. CLEARLY A CENSORSHIP OF	JUDGES	, BISHOPS, OR STATESMEN WOULD NOT BE IN THIS ABJECT
FABL PREFACE(84)	ELECTRIC LIGHTING, CADIS UNDER PALM TREES FOR	JUDGES	, CONDOTTIERI AND PRIVATEERS FOR NATIONAL DEFENCE,
FABL VI (128)	NUCLEAR BOMBS, OTHERS TO BE BIG GAME HUNTERS,	JUDGES	, EXECUTIONERS, AND KILLERS OF ALL SORTS, OFTEN THE
POSN PREFACE(400)	UNDER A COLLEGE OF CARDINALS, OR BISHOPS, OR	JUDGES	, OR ANY OTHER CONCEIVABLE FORM OF EXPERTS IN MORALS,
POSN PREFACE(431)	MISTRUST HIM, AS I MISTRUST ALL PROFESSIONAL	JUDGES	, WHEN POLITICAL RIGHTS ARE IN DANGER. CONCLUSION. I

JUDGETH

LION PREFACE(66)	NOT, I JUDGE HIM NOT" BECAUSE " HE HATH ONE THAT	JUDGETH	HIM": NAMELY, THE FATHER WHO IS ONE WITH HIM. WHEN

JUDGING

LION PREFACE(66)	I HAVE ONLY TO POINT OUT THAT WE HAVE BEEN	JUDGING	AND PUNISHING EVER SINCE JESUS TOLD US NOT TO; AND I
LION PREFACE(74)	THEY STRUCK PEOPLE BLIND OR DEAD WITHOUT REMORSE,	JUDGING	BECAUSE THEY HAD BEEN JUDGED. THEY HEALED THE SICK
DEST SD(162)	THE SECRET OF HER SIZE AND STRENGTH. SHE IS NOT,	JUDGING	BY HER DRESS, AN ADMIRER OF THE LATEST FASHIONS OF
GETT (356)	YOU MUST HAVE NOTICED THAT JUST AS ALL MURDERERS,	JUDGING	BY THEIR EDIFYING REMARKS ON THE SCAFFOLD, SEEM TO
LADY PREFACE(229)	IN SHAKESPEAR'S TIME, BUT OF IMPARTIALITY IN	JUDGING	CLASSES, WHICH IS WHAT ONE DEMANDS FROM A GREAT
3PLA PREFACE(R31)	TO CONTINUE LIVING) OR ADMIT THAT THEIR WAY OF	JUDGING	CONDUCT IS ABSURD, BUT WHEN YOUR SHAKESPEARS AND
POSN PREFACE(366)	ARE HIGHLY CULTIVATED ARTISTS, QUITE CAPABLE OF	JUDGING	FOR THEMSELVES ANYTHING THAT THE MOST ABSTRUSE
POSN PREFACE(390)	SELLING UNHEALTHY OR POISONOUS SUBSTANCES, OR	JUDGING	FOR THEMSELVES WHAT SUBSTANCES ARE UNHEALTHY AND
NEVR I (211)	OVER THINGS A GOOD DEAL LATELY; AND I DONT THINK,	JUDGING	FROM MY KNOWLEDGE OF HUMAN NATURE-- WE DONT THINK
MIS. PREFACE(87)	CUSTOM OF MOURNING IS CARRIED IN FRANCE; BUT	JUDGING	FROM THE APPEARANCE OF THE FRENCH PEOPLE I SHOULD
MIS. (169)	ABLE TO LAY YOUR HAND ON FORTY-TWO SHILLINGS.	JUDGING	FROM YOUR CONVERSATIONAL STYLE, I SHOULD THINK YOU
CAPT III (273)	YOU. YOU SAID JUST NOW, HEAVEN FORGIVE YOU FOR	JUDGING	HIM! WELL, THATS JUST WHAT THE WHOLE QUARREL IS
CAPT III (273)	THAT THIS BRASSBOUND IS-- HEAVEN FORGIVE ME FOR	JUDGING	HIM! -- A PRECIOUS SCOUNDREL? DID YE NOT HEAR WHAT
JITT III (71)	YOU HAVE TO LEAVE ALL THAT OUT WHEN YOU ARE	JUDGING	MEN. HE THINKS A WOMAN DOESNT MATTER. I CANT FORGIVE
JITT III (62)	TO HUMAN NATURE THAT MUST JUST BE RULED OUT IN	JUDGING	PEOPLE'S CHARACTERS. EVEN THE BEST MEN ARE SUBJECT
CAPT III (273)	5,000 POUNDS A YEAR FOR DOING NOTHING ELSE BUT	JUDGING	PEOPLE. HE THINKS POOR CAPTAIN BRASSBOUND A REGULAR

JUDGMENT

GENV IV (118)	GETTING ON, GENTLEMEN, HAD WE NOT BETTER COME TO	JUDGMENT	? /BATTLER/ JUDGMENT! /BBDE/ JUDGMENT! /BATTLER/
BULL IV (152)	FOR OUR PRINCIPLES TO GET THE BETTER OF YOUR	JUDGMENT	? /KEEGAN/ I HAVE NO ENTHUSIASM FOR YOUR
SIM II (81)	NOT PUNISHMENT, BUT JUDGMENT. /HYERING/ WHAT IS	JUDGMENT	? /PRA/ JUDGMENT IS VALUATION. CIVILIZATIONS LIVE
JOAN 5 (119)	IF YOU PERISH THROUGH SETTING YOUR PRIVATE	JUDGMENT	ABOVE THE INSTRUCTIONS OF YOUR SPIRITUAL DIRECTORS,
GENV IV (118)	ME? /BBDE/ JUDGE ME IF YOU DARE. /FLANCO/ GIVE	JUDGMENT	AGAINST ME AND YOU PASS OUT OF HISTORY AS A CAD.
JOAN 6 (130)	BY VAIN AND IGNORANT PERSONS SETTING UP THEIR OWN	JUDGMENT	AGAINST THE CHURCH, AND TAKING IT UPON THEMSELVES
POSN (452)	WAS, TOO. /THE SHERIFF/ ELDER DANIEL IS COME TO	JUDGMENT	ALL RIGHT, MY LAD. ELDER: THE FLOOR IS YOURS. (THE
DEVL I (23)	(TURNING POLITELY TO RICHARD) IT CONTAINS IN MY	JUDGMENT	AN EXCELLENT DISPOSAL OF HIS PROPERTY. /ANDERSON/ (
SIM PREFACE(14)	HELL; BUT AS TO WHAT CODE OF LAW WILL GOVERN THE	JUDGMENT	AND CLASSIFY THE JUDGED AS SHEEP OR GOATS AS THE
SIM II (83)	WONDERFUL CHILDREN. AND WHO ARE NOW BROUGHT TO	JUDGMENT	AND CONVICTED OF HAVING CREATED NOTHING. WE HAVE
SUPR HANDBOK(219)	IS POSTPONED UNTIL ITS AUTHOR ATTAINS IMPARTIAL	JUDGMENT	AND PERFECT KNOWLEDGE. IF A HORSE COULD WAIT AS
POSN PREFACE(364)	BY THE INTERESTS ON WHICH THEY HAVE TO SIT IN	JUDGMENT	AND, WHEN THEIR MEMBERS ARE PARTY POLITICIANS, BY
JOAN PREFACE(32)	A REMEDY. IT DOES NOT DEFER TO JOANESQUE PRIVATE	JUDGMENT	AS SUCH, THE SUPREMACY OF PRIVATE JUDGMENT FOR THE
METH PREFACE(R70)	IN THE FRAY THROUGH COMPULSION, BRIBERY, OR THEIR	JUDGMENT	AS TO WHICH SIDE THEIR BREAD WAS BUTTERED. AND AT
SIM II (68)	AND THE PITCAIRN ISLANDERS WILL SEE THEIR DAY OF	JUDGMENT	AT LAST. A DISTANT FUSILLADE OF SHOTGUNS ANSWERS
SIM PREFACE(16)	TRIBUNAL IMMEDIATELY CALLS UP VISIONS NOT ONLY OF	JUDGMENT	BUT OF PUNISHMENT AND CRUELTY. NOW THERE NEED BE NO
SIM PREFACE(16)	ANCIENT FANCY THAT THE RACE WILL BE BROUGHT TO	JUDGMENT	BY A SUPERNATURAL BEING, COMING LITERALLY OUT OF
JOAN 6 (138)	CHURCH, ARE TO BE THE JUDGE? /JOAN/ WHAT OTHER	JUDGMENT	CAN I JUDGE BY BUT MY OWN? /THE ASSESSORS/ (
SIM II (70)	IT IS THE JUDGMENT DAY IN ENGLAND IT MUST BE THE	JUDGMENT	DAY EVERYWHERE. /THE ANGEL/ WHY? /HYERING/ (
SIM II (70)	THATS IT: AN ANGEL. . . . WELL, AFTER ALL, THE	JUDGMENT	DAY HAD TO COME SOME DAY, HADNT IT? WHY NOT THIS
SIM II (70)	HOW DO YOU ACCOUNT FOR THAT? IF IT IS THE	JUDGMENT	DAY IN ENGLAND IT MUST BE THE JUDGMENT DAY
SIM II (70)	HAS BEEN ON ALL OVER EUROPE. LONDON REPORTS THE	JUDGMENT	DAY IN FULL SWING; BUT PARIS KNOWS NOTHING ABOUT
SIM II (54)	SEVENTH DAY ADVENTISTS, AND ARE QUITE SURE THE	JUDGMENT	DAY IS FIXED FOR FIVE O'CLOCK THIS AFTERNOON. THEY
SIM II (74)	SITTING IN HIS FORMER PLACE) WELL, MY DEARS: THE	JUDGMENT	DAY IS OVER, IT SEEMS. /IDDY/ I CANT BELIEVE IT WAS
SIM II (71)	SEE HERE, ANGEL. THIS ISNT A PROPER SORT OF	JUDGMENT	DAY. IT'S A FINE DAY. IT'S LIKE BANK HOLIDAY. /THE
SIM II (69)	HAVE YOU NOT HEARD THE TRUMPET? THIS IS THE	JUDGMENT	DAY. /ALL THE REST/ THE WHAT? ? ? ! ! ! /THE

SIM II (74)	IT SEEMS. /IDDY/ I CANT BELIEVE IT WAS REALLY THE	JUDGMENT	DAY. /PRA/ WHY? /IDDY/ WELL, I THOUGHT SOME
SIM II (69)	REST/ THE WHAT? ? ? ! ! ! /THE ANGEL/ THE	JUDGMENT	DAY. THE DAY OF JUDGMENT. /SIR CHARLES/ WELL I'LL
SIM II (75)	LETS HAVE IT. /SIR CHARLES/ (READING) "	JUDGMENT	DAY. WIDESPREAD INCREDULITY AS TO ANYTHING HAVING
GETT PREFACE(248)	TO LAST, REALLY DO BELIEVE THAT THERE WILL BE A	JUDGMENT	DAY, AND THAT IT MIGHT EVEN BE IN THEIR OWN TIME. A
FANY EPILOG (329)	FOR THE YOUNGEST OFFICER PRESENT TO DELIVER HIS	JUDGMENT	FIRST; SO THAT HE MAY NOT BE INFLUENCED BY THE
JOAN PREFACE(32)	JUDGMENT AS SUCH, THE SUPREMACY OF PRIVATE	JUDGMENT	FOR THE INDIVIDUAL BEING THE QUINTESSENCE OF
HART III (147)	NOT BE READY IN TIME. /CAPTAIN SHOTOVER/ THE	JUDGMENT	HAS COME. COURAGE WILL NOT SAVE YOU; BUT IT WILL
SIM II (83)	REGRETS ON THAT SCORE. /PRA/ NO. WE ARE AWAITING	JUDGMENT	HERE QUITE SIMPLY AS A UNION OF A MADWOMAN WITH A
BULL PREFACE(53)	AMIABLE BUT DISASTROUS WANT OF DETERMINATION AND	JUDGMENT	IN DEALING WITH THE RIOT THEY PROVOKED. THEY SHOULD
JOAN PREFACE(32)	NEVERTHELESS IT FINDS A PLACE FOR PRIVATE	JUDGMENT	IN EXCELSIS BY ADMITTING THAT THE HIGHEST WISDOM
SIM PREFACE(15)	IT IS NO USE MY TELLING THEM THAT THEIR VISION OF	JUDGMENT	IS A SILLY SUPERSTITION, AND THAT THERE NEVER WILL
VWOO 3 (141)	IF SHE HAD NOT BECOME PERSUADED THAT THE DAY OF	JUDGMENT	IS FIXED FOR THE SEVENTH OF AUGUST NEXT. /Z/ I DONT
SIM PREFACE(15)	WHO SHALL SAY, THEN, THAT AN UP-TO-DATE VISION OF	JUDGMENT	IS NOT AN INTERESTING SUBJECT FOR A PLAY,
SIM II (81)	WHAT WE HAVE LEARNT HERE TODAY IS THAT THE DAY OF	JUDGMENT	IS NOT THE END OF THE WORLD BUT THE BEGINNING OF
SIM II (73)	END OF THE WORLD COME IN? /THE ANGEL/ THE DAY OF	JUDGMENT	IS NOT THE END OF THE WORLD, BUT THE END OF ITS
JOAN PREFACE(32)	AS A PERSON OF HEROIC VIRTUE WHOSE PRIVATE	JUDGMENT	IS PRIVILEGED. MANY INNOVATING SAINTS, NOTABLY
SIM II (81)	BUT JUDGMENT. /HYERING/ WHAT IS JUDGMENT? /PRA/	JUDGMENT	IS VALUATION. CIVILIZATIONS LIVE BY THEIR
BULL PREFACE(34)	TO SUBMISSION AND ABNEGATION OF HIS PRIVATE	JUDGMENT	. A ROMAN CATHOLIC GARRISON WOULD TAKE ITS ORDERS
2TRU III (88)	AND THE PROTESTANT WITH HIS PRETENCE OF PRIVATE	JUDGMENT	. AND NOW-- NOW-- WHAT IS LEFT OF IT? THE ORBIT OF
FABL PREFACE(70)	BODIES WOULD BE RESURRECTED ON A GREAT DAY OF	JUDGMENT	. BUT THE OFFICIAL TRANSLATORS OF THE BIBLE IN
NEVR I (203)	KNOWLEDGE OF HUMAN NATURE CONFIRMS MR VALENTINE'S	JUDGMENT	. HE IS RIGHT. LET ME INTRODUCE MISS DOROTHY
SIM II (61)	ME: HER HATRED IS A PROOF OF HER BEAUTIFUL CLEAR	JUDGMENT	. I LOVE MAYA FOR BEING OUT OF ALL PATIENCE WITH
NEVR III (276)	ADVICE. YOU KNOW I HAVE ALWAYS TRUSTED YOUR	JUDGMENT	. I PROMISE YOU THE CHILDREN WILL BE QUIET.
SIM II (72)	DAY OF WRATH SHINES TODAY OVER HEAVEN'S DAY OF	JUDGMENT	. IT WILL CONTINUE TO LIGHT US AND WARM US; AND
SIM II (85)	OF WONDER FOR ME AND I SHALL NOT FEAR THE DAY OF	JUDGMENT	. (SHE IS INTERRUPTED BY A ROLL OF THUNDER). BE
CLEO PRO1 (89)	YE HOLD THEM IN YOUR HEARTS AS CHILDREN WITHOUT	JUDGMENT	. LOOK UPON MY HAWK'S HEAD; AND KNOW THAT I AM RA,
LION PREFACE(64)	BUT AS THE OUTCOME OF HIS OWN OBSERVATION AND	JUDGMENT	. ONE OF MR GILBERT CHESTERTON'S STORIES HAS FOR
CLEO V (199)	WITHOUT PUNISHMENT. WITHOUT REVENGE. WITHOUT	JUDGMENT	. /CAESAR/ (APPROVINGLY) AY: THAT IS THE RIGHT
SIM II (81)	YE BE NOT PUNISHED." THIS IS NOT PUNISHMENT, BUT	JUDGMENT	. /HYERING/ WHAT IS JUDGMENT? /PRA/ JUDGMENT IS
SIM II (77)	/VASHTI/ PROLA HAS FAILED US IN THE GREAT DAY OF	JUDGMENT	. /KANCHIN/ OUR SOULS HAVE BEEN CALLED TO THEIR
SIM II (79)	SHE AND THEY WERE ONE: I FOUND NOTHING. IT IS THE	JUDGMENT	. /PROLA/ HAS SHE LEFT A GREAT VOID IN YOUR HEART,
SIM II (69)	! ! ! /THE ANGEL/ THE JUDGMENT DAY. THE DAY OF	JUDGMENT	. /SIR CHARLES/ WELL I'LL BE DAMNED! /THE ANGEL/
DOCT II (129)	YOU? MIND: IT'S NOT CLEAR TO ME. SHE TROUBLES MY	JUDGMENT	. /SIR PATRICK/ TO ME, IT'S A PLAIN CHOICE BETWEEN
JOAN EPILOG (165)	THOU ART A SHIELD OF GLORY BETWEEN THEM AND THE	JUDGMENT	. /THE ARCHBISHOP/ (KNEELING TO HER) THE PRINCES
HART III (146)	GET US. (HE RISES). STAND BY, ALL HANDS, FOR	JUDGMENT	. /THE BURGLAR/ OH MY LORDY GOD! (HE RUSHES AWAY
SIM PREFACE(3)	PREFACE ON DAYS OF	JUDGMENT	. THE INCREASING BEWILDERMENT OF MY JOURNALIST
SIM II (72)	CHILD THROWING STONES. WE ANGELS ARE EXECUTING A	JUDGMENT	. THE LIVES WHICH HAVE NO USE, NO MEANING, NO
ROCK PREFACE(181)	AND THEIR PRIESTS HAVE BROUGHT YOU TO ME FOR	JUDGMENT	. WHAT HAVE YOU DONE? /JESUS/ MY KINGDOM IS NOT OF
POSN (452)	AS THE ACTOR SAYS IN THE PLAY, " A DANIEL COME TO	JUDGMENT	." ROTTEN ACTOR HE WAS, TOO. /THE SHERIFF/ ELDER
GETT PREFACE(220)	FUNCTION WHICH CLOUDS THE REASON AND UPSETS THE	JUDGMENT	MORE THAN ALL THE OTHER INSTINCTS PUT TOGETHER. THE
JOAN PREFACE(32)	COME BY WAY OF AN ENLIGHTENMENT OF THE PRIVATE	JUDGMENT	NO LESS THAN BY THE WORDS OF A CELESTIAL PERSONAGE
SIM II (71)	/THE ANGEL/ AND PRAY WHY SHOULD THE DAY OF	JUDGMENT	NOT BE A FINE DAY? /MRS HYERING/ WELL, IT'S HARDLY
SIM PREFACE(19)	IDEALS OF OUR CULTURED SUBURBS, ON THE DAY OF	JUDGMENT	NOT MERELY DO THEY CEASE TO EXIST LIKE THE USELESS
GENV IV (124)	TELL US THAT NOTHING MATTERS. TEN MINUTES AGO THE	JUDGMENT	OF GOD SEEMED FAR OFF: NOW WE STAND AT THE GATES OF
JOAN 6 (136)	HAVE SAID AND DONE, BE IT GOOD OR BAD, ACCEPT THE	JUDGMENT	OF GOD'S CHURCH ON EARTH? MORE ESPECIALLY AS TO
SIM II (81)	NOT COME OUT ALIVE. WHEN MEN NO LONGER FEAR THE	JUDGMENT	OF GOD, THEY MUST LEARN TO JUDGE THEMSELVES. /SIR
KING I (200)	HAS HIS POSITION TO KEEP UP. /CHARLES/ IT IS THE	JUDGMENT	OF HEAVEN ON YOU FOR TURNING AWAY MY PRETTY
FANY PREFACE(255)	MOUTH OF MRS KNOX I HAVE DELIVERED ON THEM THE	JUDGMENT	OF HER GOD. THE CRITICS WHOM I HAVE LAMPOONED IN
HART PREFACE(38)	ABLE, LIKE LINCOLN, TO INVOKE " THE CONSIDERATE	JUDGMENT	OF MANKIND, AND THE GRACIOUS FAVOR OF ALMIGHTY
JOAN PREFACE(36)	PRETEND TO BE), CAN KEEP PACE WITH THE PRIVATE	JUDGMENT	OF PERSONS OF GENIUS EXCEPT WHEN, BY A VERY RARE
POSN PREFACE(414)	THE VALIDITY OF WHICH SHALL BE SUBJECT TO THE	JUDGMENT	OF THE HIGH COURTS. E. THE ANNUAL LICENCE, ONCE
JOAN 6 (132)	OF THE FLESH; BUT IT, TOO, SETS UP THE PRIVATE	JUDGMENT	OF THE SINGLE ERRING MORTAL AGAINST THE CONSIDERED
JOAN 6 (146)	THE SAME SECULAR POWER THAT IT MODERATE ITS	JUDGMENT	OF THEE IN RESPECT OF DEATH AND DIVISION OF THE
MIS. PREFACE(36)	PRISONERS. UNDER SUCH ABSURD CIRCUMSTANCES OUR	JUDGMENT	OF THINGS BECOMES AS PERVERTED AS OUR HABITS. IF WE
SUPR III (94)	TO REFINE YOUR SOUL, JUAN? HAS THE TERRIBLE	JUDGMENT	OF WHICH MY FATHER'S STATUE WAS THE MINISTER TAUGHT
POSN PREFACE(430)	I DO NOT, HOWEVER, APPEAL TO LORD GORELL'S	JUDGMENT	ON ALL POINTS. IT IS INEVITABLE THAT A JUDGE SHOULD
SUPR PREFACE(R26)	POPULAR ELOQUENCE. THE MULTITUDE THUS PRONOUNCES	JUDGMENT	ON ITS OWN UNITS: IT ADMITS ITSELF UNFIT TO GOVERN,
KING I (203)	TRADES! SUCH WICKEDNESS WILL BRING A BLACK	JUDGMENT	ON THE NATION. CHARLES STUART: HAVE YOU NO REGARD
GETT (308)	MY LORD AND LADIES AND GENTLEMEN: I DONT TRUST MY	JUDGMENT	ON THIS SUBJECT. THERES A CERTAIN LADY THAT I
GENV IV (129)	IT IS USELESS NOW: GOD WILL EXECUTE HIS OWN	JUDGMENT	ON US ALL. (SHE THROWS IT INTO THE WASTE PAPER
GENV II (59)	CO-OPERATION, WERE TO DELIVER AN ADVERSE	JUDGMENT	ON YOU, YOU WOULD NOT LIKE IT. THE MAN WHOM THE
DOCT PREFACE(43)	GENEROUS, BUT SIMPLY INCAPABLE OF ETHICAL	JUDGMENT	OR INDEPENDENT ACTION. JUST SO DO WE FIND A CROWD
BULL PREFACE(58)	" WAS ABOVE EQUITY," THE TRIBUNAL IN DELIVERING	JUDGMENT	REMARKED THAT " THE COUNSEL FOR THE DEFENCE HAD A
LADY PREFACE(225)	THAT DOES NOT DISABLE THE BOOK AS (IN MY	JUDGMENT	) IT DISABLED THE HERO OF THE PLAY, BECAUSE MR
MIS. PREFACE(92)	NOON TOMORROW (SAY AS A PRELIMINARY TO THE GREAT	JUDGMENT	), THE ARTISTIC PEOPLE WOULD NOT TURN A HAIR; BUT
MIS. PREFACE(64)	TOO NARROW-MINDED TO UNDERSTAND LAW AND EXERCISE	JUDGMENT	; AND IN THEIR HANDS (WITH US THEY MOSTLY FALL
SIM PREFACE(16)	IN A LIVING SOCIETY EVERY DAY IS A DAY OF	JUDGMENT	; AND ITS RECOGNITION AS SUCH IS NOT THE END OF ALL
BASH I (98)	HIS AGE AND MINE. NOW FROM THE RING TO THE HIGH	JUDGMENT	SEAT I STEP AT YOUR BEHEST. BEAR YOU ME WITNESS
GENV IV (101)	A TIME WHEN I MIGHT HAVE ANSWERED " BEFORE THE	JUDGMENT	SEAT OF GOD". BUT SINCE PEOPLE NO LONGER BELIEVE
GENV IV (101)	PEOPLE NO LONGER BELIEVE THAT THERE IS ANY SUCH	JUDGMENT	SEAT, MUST WE NOT CREATE ONE BEFORE WE ARE
ROCK I (227)	LIKE SPEECHES? /THE LADY/ ON THE GREAT DAY OF	JUDGMENT	THE SPEECHMAKERS WILL STAND WITH THE SEDUCERS AND
APPL PREFACE(177)	BY THE LIGHT OF HEAVEN. BY CHANCE RATHER THAN BY	JUDGMENT	THEY FIND THEMSELVES REPRESENTED IN PARLIAMENT BY A
BULL PREFACE(59)	WHICH JUDGE LYNCH, HIMSELF PROVABLE BY HIS OWN	JUDGMENT	TO BE A PREVARICATOR, HYPOCRITE, TYRANT, AND COWARD
JOAN 5 (121)	HER LIKE THAT. /THE ARCHBISHOP/ SHE DISTURBS MY	JUDGMENT	TOO: THERE IS A DANGEROUS POWER IN HER OUTBURSTS.
WIDO II (41)	FOR A MOMENT OR SO. MAY I ASK YOU TO SUSPEND YOUR	JUDGMENT	UNTIL WE HAVE HAD A LITTLE QUIET DISCUSSION OF THIS
MIS. PREFACE(94)	WHICH SAYS TO A CHILD " YOU MUST SUSPEND YOUR	JUDGMENT	UNTIL YOU ARE OLD ENOUGH TO CHOOSE YOUR RELIGION"
2TRU PREFACE(16)	NEW RECRUITS WERE JUDGED BY THE CHURCH. IF THE	JUDGMENT	WAS FAVORABLE, AND THE CANDIDATES TOOK CERTAIN
SUPR III (118)	THEY NOW SEEMED THE EMPTIEST OF INVENTIONS: MY	JUDGMENT	WAS NOT TO BE CORRUPTED: MY BRAIN STILL SAID NO ON
JITT III (68)	LITTLE WE CAN TRUST OUR OWN FEELINGS AND OUR OWN	JUDGMENT	WHEN SUCH TROUBLES COME TO US. THE WEIGHT YOU HAVE
SUPR PREFACE(R32)	WHICH IS AT BOTTOM A COMBINATION OF SOUND MORAL	JUDGMENT	WITH LIGHTHEARTED GOOD HUMOR. BUT THEY ARE
JOAN PREFACE(4)	QUITE UNCONCEALED CONTEMPT FOR OFFICIAL OPINION,	JUDGMENT	, AND AUTHORITY, AND FOR WAR OFFICE TACTICS AND
BULL PREFACE(65)	PERHAPS FORGIVE ME FOR ACCUSING HIM OF FAILING	JUDGMENT	, AND FOR SUGGESTING THAT HIS RETIREMENT FROM
SIM PREFACE(18)	IT IS TIME FOR US TO RECONSIDER OUR VISIONS OF	JUDGMENT	, AND SEE WHETHER WE CANNOT CHANGE THEM FROM OLD
POSN PREFACE(381)	OF PERSONS WHO ARE INCAPABLE OF ORIGINAL ETHICAL	JUDGMENT	, AND WHO WOULD BE QUITE LOST IF THEY WERE NOT IN
JOAN PREFACE(29)	INTERCESSION WHEN THEY ARE THEMSELVES BROUGHT TO	JUDGMENT	, IF ANY HEAVENLY POWER THINKS SUCH MORAL COWARDS
SIM II (69)	ALL? ! /THE ANGEL/ YES. YOU ARE ALL NOW UNDER	JUDGMENT	, IN COMMON WITH THE REST OF THE ENGLISH SPEAKING
FANY III (324)	OF SEEING THINGS AS THEY REALLY ARE, THE CALM	JUDGMENT	, THE OPEN MIND, THE PHILOSOPHIC GRASP, THE
SIM II (71)	OR CAIN AND ABEL, TO SAY NOTHING OF THE DAY OF	JUDGMENT	, THEY DONT KNOW WHAT YOU ARE TALKING ABOUT. THE
MRS PREFACE(159)	OF A PARTIAL TAPU, APPLIED, TO THE BEST OF HIS	JUDGMENT	, WITH A CAREFUL RESPECT TO PERSONS AND TO PUBLIC
2TRU PREFACE(19)	OF INDIVIDUALISM, OR THE RIGHT OF PRIVATE	JUDGMENT	, WITH MOST OF THE ECCLESIASTICAL CORRUPTIONS
GENV IV (118)	COME TO JUDGMENT? /BATTLER/ JUDGMENT! /BBDE/	JUDGMENT	! /BATTLER/ WHAT DO YOU MEAN? DO YOU PRESUME TO
GENV IV (118)	HAD WE NOT BETTER COME TO JUDGMENT? /BATTLER/	JUDGMENT	! /BBDE/ JUDGMENT! /BATTLER/ WHAT DO YOU MEAN?

JUDGMENT-SEAT

INCA (256)	DOING! LET THEM SAY IT, IF THEY DARE, BEFORE THE	JUDGMENT-SEAT	AT WHICH THEY AND I SHALL ANSWER AT LAST FOR
METH PREFACE(R54)	ALL EQUAL AND MEMBERS ONE OF ANOTHER BEFORE THE	JUDGMENT-SEAT	OF OUR COMMON FATHER. DARWINISM PROCLAIMED

JUDGMENTS

SUPR I (31)	GO BEGGING FOR MY REGARD. HOW UNREAL OUR MORAL	JUDGMENTS	ARE! YOU SEEM TO ME TO HAVE ABSOLUTELY NO
SIM PREFACE(12)	OF THE CHURCH OR THE CONCLUSIONS OF OUR PRIVATE	JUDGMENTS	AS THE INTERPRETERS OF GOD'S WILL, WHETHER WE
BULL II SD(101)	IN IRELAND THAT DROVE HIM OUT OF IT. THESE	JUDGMENTS	HAVE LITTLE VALUE AND NO FINALITY; BUT THEY ARE
BARB PREFACE(233)	OF CIRCUMSTANCES, CONDUCT IS NOT; AND OUR MORAL	JUDGMENTS	OF CHARACTER ARE NOT: BOTH ARE CIRCUMSTANTIAL.
GENV IV (107)	WILL. /JUDGE/ BUT DO YOU NOT UNDERSTAND THAT THE	JUDGMENTS	OF THIS COURT ARE FOLLOWED BY NO EXECUTIONS? THEY
BULL II SD(101)	LITTLE VALUE AND NO FINALITY; BUT THEY ARE THE	JUDGMENTS	ON WHICH HER FATE HANGS JUST AT PRESENT. KEEGAN
GENV IV (107)	ARE FOLLOWED BY NO EXECUTIONS? THEY ARE MORAL	JUDGMENTS	ONLY. /WIDOW/ I UNDERSTAND PERFECTLY. YOU CAN

		JUDICIAL	
NEVR I (205)	PLACES IT BETWEEN THEM; AND SITS DOWN WITH A	JUDICIAL	AIR. THEY ATTEND TO HIM WITH EXTREME GRAVITY. HE
PYGM II (231)	HE ADDS, HIDING AN UNEASY CONSCIENCE WITH A	JUDICIAL	AIR) EXCEPT PERHAPS IN A MOMENT OF EXTREME AND
BULL PREFACE(57)	WITHOUT APPEAL. THEY REPRESENT THE BEST OF OUR	JUDICIAL	AND MILITARY OFFICIALISM, AND WHAT THAT BEST IS MAY
CAPT III SD(272)	THE SAME WAY AS THE PRESIDENTIAL CHAIR, GIVE A	JUDICIAL	ASPECT TO THE ARRANGEMENT. RANKIN IS PLACING A
MRS PREFACE(177)	IT (YOU FIND SUCH PEOPLE EVERYWHERE, EVEN ON THE	JUDICIAL	BENCH AND IN THE HIGHEST PLACES IN CHURCH AND
BULL PREFACE(38)	VICEROY THROUGH A HUGUENOT BUREAUCRACY AND A	JUDICIAL	BENCH APPOINTED ON THE UNDERSTANDING THAT LOYALTY
GENV II (58)	HOW VERY ODD! I OWN I WAS SURPRISED TO FIND THE	JUDICIAL	BENCH REPRESENTED BY SO YOUNG A MAN; AND I AM
BARB PREFACE(233)	OF BILL WALKER. WE MEET BILL EVERYWHERE: ON THE	JUDICIAL	BENCH, ON THE EPISCOPAL BENCH, IN THE PRIVY
JOAN 6 (126)	NOBLES ARE! /THE INQUISITOR/ (TAKING THE OTHER	JUDICIAL	CHAIR ON CAUCHON'S LEFT) ALL SECULAR POWER MAKES
JOAN 6,SD(122)	GREAT HALL FROM THE MIDDLE OF THE INNER END, THE	JUDICIAL	CHAIRS AND SCRIBES' TABLE ARE TO THE RIGHT. THE
JOAN 6 (124)	TO TRIAL THIS MORNING. (HE MOVES TOWARDS THE	JUDICIAL	CHAIRS). /CAUCHON/ THIS MOMENT, IF YOUR LORDSHIP'S
GENV IV (89)	MORNING, SIR MIDLANDER. (HE PASSES ON TO THE	JUDICIAL	CHAIR, GREETING THEM AS HE GOES) GOOD MORNING,
WIDO II (40)	(COKANE'S FEATURES ARE CONTORTED BY AN AIR OF	JUDICIAL	CONSIDERATION; BUT HE SAYS NOTHING; AND TRENCH
MRS PREFACE(178)	THEIR ENGAGEMENTS. FOR PLEASE OBSERVE THAT THE	JUDICIAL	DECISION IN NEW YORK STATE IN FAVOR OF THE PLAY DID
BULL PREFACE(39)	MAN IS ROBBED AND STARVED AND OPPRESSED UNDER	JUDICIAL	FORMS WHICH CONFER THE IMPOSING TITLE OF JUSTICE ON
MIS. PREFACE(13)	IT IS INEVITABLE. YOU CANNOT HOLD AN IMPARTIAL	JUDICIAL	INQUIRY EVERY TIME A CHILD MISBEHAVES ITSELF. TO
CAPT III (281)	/SIR HOWARD/ (RISING AND BOBBING TO THEM IN A	JUDICIAL	MANNER) GOOD MORNING, GENTLEMEN. THEY ACKNOWLEDGE
JOAN PREFACE(51)	THEY ARE NOT COMMITTED BY MURDERERS. THEY ARE	JUDICIAL	MURDERS, PIOUS MURDERS; AND THIS CONTRADICTION AT
SIM PREFACE(10)	THE TOUGHEST JOB, WAS COMPELLED TO DEVELOP A NEW	JUDICIAL	ORGAN, CALLED THE INQUISITION OR HOLY OFFICE, TO
GENV IV (121)	OF BUILDING UP A BODY OF INTERNATIONAL LAW BY	JUDICIAL	PRECEDENT WOULD SEEM TO BE SIMPLE ENOUGH.
GENV IV (118)	I SHALL HAVE TO CREATE IT AS I GO ALONG, BY	JUDICIAL	PRECEDENTS. /BATTLER/ IN MY COUNTRY I CREATE THE
GENV II (58)	ME. I HAVE SPENT YEARS IN TRYING TO DEVISE SOME	JUDICIAL	PROCEDURE BY WHICH THESE LAWBREAKERS CAN BE BROUGHT
BARB PREFACE(231)	BARBARA'S CHRISTIANITY AS AGAINST OUR SYSTEM OF	JUDICIAL	PUNISHMENT AND THE VINDICTIVE VILLAIN-THRASHINGS
BULL PREFACE(61)	IS THEREFORE MUCH TO BE SAID FOR FLOGGING AS A	JUDICIAL	PUNISHMENT IN EGYPT." LOGICALLY, THEN, THE FOUR
POSN PREFACE(420)	TO SANCTION ITS SALE. THE MAGISTRATE MUST GIVE A	JUDICIAL	REASON FOR HIS REFUSAL, MEANING REALLY A
POSN PREFACE(363)	LICENCE OF HIS THEATRE, NOR MAY IT BE GIVEN AS A	JUDICIAL	REASON FOR CANCELLING THAT LICENCE. 3. AUTHORS AND
JOAN PREFACE(51)	HIM OF BAD FAITH OR EXCEPTIONAL SEVERITY IN HIS	JUDICIAL	RELATIONS WITH JOAN, OR OF AS MUCH ANTI-PRISONER,
GENV IV SD(89)	IT IS ON THE STROKE OF TEN. THE JUDGE, IN HIS	JUDICIAL	ROBE, ENTERS. THEY ALL RISE. HE IS IN HIGH SPIRITS
SUPR PREFACE(R12)	ALL OTHER HUMAN CONFLICTS: BUT THEY ARE PURELY	JUDICIAL	; AND THE FACT THAT WE ARE MUCH MORE CURIOUS ABOUT
JOAN 6,SD(126)	THROUGH THE COURTYARD. CAUCHON TAKES ONE OF THE	JUDICIAL	SEATS; AND D'ESTIVET SITS AT THE SCRIBES' TABLE,
NEVR III (277)	THE MATTER PUBLIC BY APPLYING TO THE COURTS FOR A	JUDICIAL	SEPARATION. SUPPOSE HE HAD HAD THAT POWER OVER YOU,
LADY PREFACE(232)	AND ABOUT THE IDOLATRY AND HYPOCRISY OF OUR	JUDICIAL	SYSTEM; BUT HIS IMPLIED REMEDY WAS PERSONAL
DOCT PREFACE(38)	ONLY TOLERATED BY THE LAW ON CONDITION THAT, LIKE	JUDICIAL	TORTURE, IT SHALL BE DONE AS MERCIFULLY AS THE
SUPR HANDBOK(202)	AS CAN BE COUNTED ON BY ANY LADY CRIMINAL. THE	JUDICIAL	USE OF TORTURE TO EXTORT CONFESSION IS SUPPOSED TO
		JUDICIALLY	
SUPR HANDBOK(205)	OR ASSASSINATION; AND THE ASSASSIN IS STILL	JUDICIALLY	ASSASSINATED ON THE PRINCIPLE THAT TWO BLACKS
JOAN PREFACE(3)	OF THEM), IT IS HARDLY SURPRISING THAT SHE WAS	JUDICIALLY	BURNT, OSTENSIBLY FOR A NUMBER OF CAPITAL CRIMES
WIDO II (41)	AND LISTEN; AND CONSIDER THE MATTER CALMLY AND	JUDICIALLY	. DONT BE HEADSTRONG. /TRENCH/ I HAVE NO
SIM PREFACE(17)	MASS OF PEOPLE WHO THINK THAT MURDERERS SHOULD BE	JUDICIALLY	KILLED, BUT THAT THE LIVES OF THE MOST
GETT PREFACE(225)	PEOPLE. THE IMPERSONAL RELATION OF SEX MAY BE	JUDICIALLY	RESERVED FOR ONE PERSON; BUT ANY SUCH RESERVATION
CATH 4 (196)	(FOLLOWING THE EMPRESS AND RESUMING KINDLY BUT	JUDICIALLY	) AFTER ALL, THOUGH YOUR MAJESTY IS OF COURSE A
BULL IV (157)	SO FOR HEAVEN'S SAKE BE PRUDENT. /CORNELIUS/ (	JUDICIALLY	) ALL RIGHT, ALL RIGHT, ME SON: I'LL BE CAREFUL.
BULL III (134)	TO THE PRIEST TO ANSWER HIM. /FATHER DEMPSEY/ (	JUDICIALLY	) YOUNG MAN: YOULL NOT BE THE MEMBER FOR
PYGM II (237)	TO ME? (HE RETURNS TO HIS CHAIR AND SITS DOWN	JUDICIALLY	). /PICKERING/ I THINK YOU OUGHT TO KNOW,
		JUDICIAL-MINDED	
DOCT PREFACE(67)	THAT OUR HANGMEN WERE THEREBY MADE A LITTLE MORE	JUDICIAL-MINDED	, AND OUR DRUMMERS MORE RESPONSIBLE, THAN IN
		JUDICIARY	
ROCK PREFACE(157)	HE WAS AGAINST THE PRIESTS, AGAINST THE	JUDICIARY	, AGAINST THE MILITARY, AGAINST THE CITY (HE
		JUDICIOUS	
DOCT PREFACE(21)	QUESTION AS TO WHETHER THE DOSE OF DIGITALIS WAS	JUDICIOUS	OR NOT: THE POINT IS, THAT A FARM LABORER
		JUDICIOUSLY	
MTH2 (80)	ANYTHING THE ELECTORATE WILL NOT SWALLOW IF IT IS	JUDICIOUSLY	PUT TO THEM? BUT WE MUST MAKE SURE OF OUR
		JUDITH	
DEVL II (34)	SIR, I WILL ACCEPT YOUR ENMITY OR ANY MAN'S.	JUDITH	: MR DUDGEON WILL STAY TO TEA. SIT DOWN: IT WILL TAKE
DEVL II (33)	A WHILE: MY WIFE WILL EXCUSE YOUR SHIRTSLEEVES.	JUDITH	: PUT IN ANOTHER SPOONFUL OF TEA FOR MR DUDGEON.
DEVL II (36)	YOU WILL LET ME BRING YOU THE NEWS MYSELF.	JUDITH	: WILL YOU GIVE MR DUDGEON HIS TEA, AND KEEP HIM HERE
DEVL II (35)	(GRATIFIED, PATTING HER HAND) YOU HEAR THAT,	JUDITH	? MR DUDGEON KNOWS HOW TO TURN A COMPLIMENT. THE
DEVL III (74)	(HE TURNS AWAY, AND IS STRIDING TO THE CART WHEN	JUDITH	ADVANCES AND INTERPOSES WITH HER ARMS STRETCHED OUT
DEVL III (68)	GOOD MORNING, MADAM. /RICHARD/ (INTERRUPTING	JUDITH	ALMOST FIERCELY AS SHE IS ABOUT TO MAKE SOME WILD
DEVL III (77)	THE MARKET PLACE TOWARDS THE TOWN HALL, LEAVING	JUDITH	AND RICHARD TOGETHER. BURGOYNE FOLLOWS HIM A STEP OR
DEVL III (76)	AND ADDS)-- A CLERGYMAN. /ANDERSON/ (BETWEEN	JUDITH	AND RICHARD) SIR: IT IS IN THE HOUR OF TRIAL THAT A
DEVL III (74)	WANT A WOMAN NEAR ME NOW? /BURGOYNE/ (GOING TO	JUDITH	AND TAKING HER HAND) HERE, MADAM: YOU HAD BETTER KEEP
DEVL I (13)	SHE TURNS AND CRIES INHOSPITABLY) COME IN. (	JUDITH	ANDERSON, THE MINISTER'S WIFE, COMES IN. JUDITH IS
DEVL I SD(17)	ESPECIALLY FUNERAL ONES, IS NOT IN HIS NATURE.	JUDITH	APPEARS AT THE BEDROOM DOOR. /JUDITH/ (WITH GENTLE
DEVL II SD(29)	OF RAIN. AS THE TOWN CLOCK STRIKES THE QUARTER,	JUDITH	COMES IN WITH A COUPLE OF CANDLES IN EARTHENWARE
DEVL I (26)	WANT TO. (SHE SHRINKS BACK, LEAVING RICHARD AND	JUDITH	FACE TO FACE). /RICHARD/ (TO JUDITH) ACTUALLY DOESNT
DEVL III (61)	MR ANDERSON, IF YOU ARE DETERMINED TO BE HANGED (	JUDITH	FLINCHES) THERE'S NOTHING MORE TO BE SAID. AN UNUSUAL
DEVL II (43)	TAKEN. /ANDERSON/ I! (BEWILDERED, HE TURNS TO	JUDITH	FOR AN EXPLANATION). /JUDITH/ (COAXINGLY) ALL RIGHT,
DEVL II (48)	AM NOT GOD; AND I MUST GO TO WORK ANOTHER WAY. (	JUDITH	GASPS AT THE BLASPHEMY. HE THROWS THE PURSE ON THE
DEVL II SD(38)	(OUTSIDE) HALT! FOUR OUTSIDE: TWO IN WITH ME.	JUDITH	HALF RISES, LISTENING AND LOOKING WITH DILATED EYES
DEVL I SD(24)	JOINS UNCLE WILLIAM AT THE FIRE. TITUS FETCHES	JUDITH	HER THINGS FROM THE RACK. THE THREE ON THE SOFA RISE
DEVL III (77)	AT YOUR SERVICE, SIR. (TO RICHARD) SEE	JUDITH	HOME FOR ME, WILL YOU, MY BOY. (HE HANDS HER OVER TO
DEVL III (77)	TOLD ME, RICHARD, THAT I SHOULD NEVER HAVE CHOSEN	JUDITH	IF I'D BEEN BORN FOR THE MINISTRY. I AM AFRAID SHE
DEVL II (35)	NEED LEAVE US WORSE FRIEND-- ENEMIES, I MEAN.	JUDITH	IS A GREAT ENEMY OF YOURS. /RICHARD/ IF ALL MY
DEVL I (13)	(JUDITH ANDERSON, THE MINISTER'S WIFE, COMES IN.	JUDITH	IS MORE THAN TWENTY YEARS YOUNGER THAN HER HUSBAND,
DEVL II (48)	TO THE DEATH. /ANDERSON/ YOURE A FOOL, A FOOL,	JUDITH	. (FOR A MOMENT CHECKING THE TORRENT OF HIS HASTE,
DEVL II (46)	HIM DIE LIKE A CHRISTIAN. I'M ASHAMED OF YOU,	JUDITH	. /JUDITH/ HE WILL BE STEADFAST IN HIS RELIGION AS
DEVL II (41)	TO HER AND STOOPS BESIDE HER, LIFTING HER HEAD).	JUDITH	. /JUDITH/ (WAKING; FOR HER SWOON HAS PASSED INTO
DEVL II (44)	BE GOOD. /ANDERSON/ I MUST GO TO HIM AT ONCE,	JUDITH	. /JUDITH/ (SPRINGING UP) OH NO. YOU MUST GO AWAY--
DEVL III (54)	A LITTLE WAY FROM HIM, LOOKING STEADILY AT HER)	JUDITH	. /JUDITH/ (BREATHLESS-- DELIGHTED AT THE NAME) YES.
DEVL I SD(16)	HANGS UP HIS HAT AND WAITS FOR A WORD WITH	JUDITH	. /JUDITH/ SHE WILL BE HERE IN A MOMENT. ASK THEM TO
DEVL II SD(40)	RICHARD EXHALES A DEEP BREATH AND TURNS TOWARDS	JUDITH	. /RICHARD/ (VERY DISTINCTLY) MY LOVE. (SHE LOOKS
DEVL II (43)	THAT? /ANDERSON/ TELL HER THE TRUTH IF IT IS SO,	JUDITH	. SHE WILL LEARN IT FROM THE FIRST NEIGHBOR SHE MEETS
DEVL II (33)	HIS NOSE AT THE MEZZOTINTED DIVINE ON THE WALL.	JUDITH	KEEPS HER EYES ON THE TEA CADDY). IS IT STILL
DEVL II (41)	THE FLOOR FOR THE FIRST TIME; AND THERE HE SEES	JUDITH	LYING MOTIONLESS WITH HER EYES CLOSED. HE RUNS TO HER
DEVL II (43)	I SEE IT ALL NOW! THEY HAVE ARRESTED RICHARD. (	JUDITH	MAKES A GESTURE OF DESPAIR). /ESSIE/ NO. I ASKED THE
DEVL II (48)	WITH A WRENCH) I'LL GO TO THEM, SO I WILL. (TO	JUDITH	PEREMPTORILY) GET ME THE PISTOLS: I WANT THEM. AND
DEVL I (18)	AS USUAL? THATS RIGHT, THATS RIGHT. (	JUDITH	POINTEDLY MOVES AWAY FROM HIS NEIGHBORHOOD TO THE
DEVL II (41)	ME, I LEFT YOU ALONE WITH THAT SCOUNDREL. (	JUDITH	REMEMBERS, WITH AN AGONIZED CRY, SHE CLUTCHES HIS
DEVL I (19)	SIR: YOU ARE IN THE PRESENCE OF MY WIFE. (	JUDITH	RISES AND STANDS WITH STONY PROPRIETY). /RICHARD/ (
DEVL II (47)	THE FASTEST AND STRONGEST HORSE THEY HAVE (	JUDITH	RISES BREATHLESS, AND STARES AT HIM INCREDULOUSLY)--
DEVL I (26)	RICHARD AND JUDITH FACE TO FACE). /RICHARD/ (TO	JUDITH	) ACTUALLY DOESNT WANT TO, MOST VIRTUOUS LADY!
DEVL II (49)	OUT LIKE AN AVALANCHE). /ESSIE/ (HURRYING TO	JUDITH	) HE HAS GONE TO SAVE RICHARD, HASNT HE? /JUDITH/ TO
DEVL I (19)	OF GOOD LOOKS. /ANDERSON/ (QUIETLY INDICATING	JUDITH	) SIR: YOU ARE IN THE PRESENCE OF MY WIFE. (JUDITH
DEVL III (59)	NEAR HER. /BURGOYNE/ (LOOKING UP AND SEEING	JUDITH	) WHO IS THAT WOMAN? /SERGEANT/ PRISONER'S WIFE,
DEVL III (62)	(SICK WITH HORROR) MY GOD! /RICHARD/ (TO	JUDITH	) YOUR PROMISE! (TO BURGOYNE) THANK YOU, GENERAL:
DEVL III (76)	HE SHAKES HEARTILY, THE RIGHT BEING OCCUPIED BY	JUDITH	). BY THE WAY, MR ANDERSON, I DO NOT QUITE
DEVL I (25)	HER IN THIS WAY) YES. (SHE LOOKS DOUBTFULLY AT	JUDITH	). I THINK SO. I MEAN I-- I HOPE SO. /RICHARD/ ESSIE:
DEVL II (30)	AND AT LAST TURNS WITH HIS HANDS OUTSTRETCHED TO	JUDITH	). NOW! (SHE FLIES INTO HIS ARMS). I AM NOT LATE,

DEVL II (45)	A GOOD GIRL. (HE CLOSES THE DOOR, AND RETURNS TO	JUDITH	). /JUDITH/ (SEATED-- RIGID) YOU ARE GOING TO YOUR
DEVL II (44)	WHAT WILL THEY DO TO HIM? WILL THEY HANG HIM? (	JUDITH	SHUDDERS CONVULSIVELY, AND THROWS HERSELF INTO THE
DEVL I (18)	FORTH. (HE COMES UPON HIM HOLDING THE CHAIR AS	JUDITH	SITS DOWN). AS USUAL, LOOKING AFTER THE LADIES!
DEVL I (13)	STAY. IF YOU WOULDNT MIND SHUTTING THE DOOR! (	JUDITH	SMILES, IMPLYING " HOW STUPID OF ME! " AND SHUTS IT
DEVL III SD(59)	ARM, AND POSTS HIMSELF BEHIND HIM, AT HIS ELBOW.	JUDITH	STANDS TIMIDLY AT THE WALL. THE FOUR SOLDIERS PLACE
DEVL II (37)	LAID THERE. THE OTHER PLATE IS LAID NEAR IT: BUT	JUDITH	STAYS AT THE OPPOSITE END OF THE TABLE, NEXT THE
DEVL II (43)	OF ANXIETY. THE SURPRISE IS SO DISAGREEABLE TO	JUDITH	THAT IT BRINGS HER TO HER SENSES. HER TONE IS SHARP
DEVL II SD(33)	NOW THAT I HAVE SUCCEEDED TO MY FATHER'S ESTATE?	JUDITH	THROWS DOWN THE SPOON INDIGNANTLY. /ANDERSON/ (QUITE
DEVL III SD(50)	A LITTLE EMPTY PANELLED WAITING ROOM, AND INVITES	JUDITH	TO ENTER. SHE HAS HAD A BAD NIGHT, PROBABLY A RATHER
DEVL II (43)	THE FIRST NEIGHBOR SHE MEETS IN THE STREET. (	JUDITH	TURNS AWAY AND COVERS HER EYES WITH HER HANDS).
DEVL III SD(59)	AND SWINDON'S USELESSNESS. RICHARD IS BROUGHT IN.	JUDITH	WALKS BESIDE HIM. TWO SOLDIERS PRECEDE AND TWO FOLLOW
DEVL III (51)	IMMEDIATELY DROPS HIS RAFFISH MANNER AND TURNS TO	JUDITH	WITH CONSIDERATE SINCERITY). /RICHARD/ MRS ANDERSON:
DEVL II (40)	A MOMENT, AND THEN, TURNING ROGUISHLY TO	JUDITH	WITH SOMETHING OF A SMILE BREAKING THROUGH HIS
3PLA PREFACE(R30)	NIGHT CONFIRMED THE CRITIC BY STEALING BEHIND	JUDITH	, AND MUTELY ATTESTING HIS PASSION BY SURREPTITIOUSLY
DEVL I (26)	ON NOTHING WOULDNT HELP THEM. BUT A MINISTER! (	JUDITH	, DISMAYED, CLINGS TO ANDERSON) OR A LAWYER! (
DEVL III SD(75)	INTENSELY EXCITED, LISTENS WITH ALL ITS EARS.	JUDITH	, HALF RISING, STARES AT HIM; THEN LIFTS HER HANDS
DEVL II (46)	SAID GOODBYE TO HIM IN ALL KINDNESS AND CHARITY,	JUDITH	, I HOPE. /JUDITH/ I KISSED HIM. /ANDERSON/ WHAT!
DEVL II (41)	/ANDERSON/ WHY, WHAT ON EARTH--? (CALLING)	JUDITH	, JUDITH! (HE LISTENS: THERE IS NO ANSWER). HM! (
DEVL III (71)	THAT. GET OUT OF IT, WILL YOU. (HE COMES UPON	JUDITH	, STANDING NEAR THE GALLOWS). NOW THEN: YOUVE NO CALL
DEVL II SD(37)	WANT TO GO AWAY OUT OF MERE CONTRARINESS, EH?	JUDITH	, UNABLE TO BEAR IT, SINKS ON THE CHAIR AND BURSTS
DEVL III SD(72)	BACK OF THE SQUARE, AND FINISHES THE DEAD MARCH.	JUDITH	, WATCHING RICHARD PAINFULLY, STEALS DOWN TO THE
DEVL I SD(17)	(EXCEPT ESSIE) AMEN. THEY ALL SIT DOWN, EXCEPT	JUDITH	, WHO STANDS BEHIND MRS DUDGEON'S CHAIR. /JUDITH/ (
DEVL II (39)	BLACK SLEEVE ON HIS ARM, AND THEN SMILES SLYLY AT	JUDITH	, WHOSE WHITE FACE SHEWS HIM THAT WHAT SHE IS
DEVL II SD(40)	OF COMPASSION FOR HER DISTRESS) MY POOR GIRL!	JUDITH	, WITH A SUDDEN EFFORT, THROWS HER ARMS ROUND HIM;
DEVL III (61)	YOU PROMISED TO BE SILENT. /BURGOYNE/ (TO	JUDITH	, WITH STUDIED COURTESY) BELIEVE ME, MADAM, YOUR
DEVL II SD(49)	TERROR AND FALLS ON HER KNEES, HIDING HER FACE.	JUDITH	, WITHOUT HEEDING HER, LOOKS RIGIDLY STRAIGHT IN
DEVL II (41)	WHY, WHAT ON EARTH--? (CALLING) JUDITH,	JUDITH	! (HE LISTENS: THERE IS NO ANSWER). HM! (HE GOES
DEVL II (44)	DO I CARE ABOUT MY DUTY? /ANDERSON/ (SHOCKED)	JUDITH	! /JUDITH/ I AM DOING MY DUTY. I AM CLINGING TO MY
DEVL II (46)	I HOPE. /JUDITH/ I KISSED HIM. /ANDERSON/ WHAT!	JUDITH	! /JUDITH/ ARE YOU ANGRY? /ANDERSON/ NO, NO. YOU

JUDITH'S

DEVL II (33)	/RICHARD/ RAINING LIKE THE VERY (HIS EYE CATCHES	JUDITH'S	AS SHE LOOKS QUICKLY AND HAUGHTILY UP)-- I BEG YOUR
DEVL I (25)	AT THIS MOMENT HE CHANCES TO CATCH SIGHT OF	JUDITH'S	FACE, WHICH EXPRESSES THE MOST PRUDISH DISAPPROVAL
DEVL III (74)	(ANGRILY TO THE SERGEANT, WHO, ALARMED AT	JUDITH'S	MOVEMENT, HAS COME FROM THE BACK OF THE SQUARE TO
DEVL III SD(63)	SAID. BURGOYNE, WHO HAS BEEN VISIBLY SHAKEN BY	JUDITH'S	REPROACH, RECOVERS HIMSELF PROMPTLY AT THIS NEW

JUDY

2TRU III (86)	A MAN, EH? (HE KISSES HER) HOW DOES THAT FEEL,	JUDY	? /SWEETIE/ (STRUGGLING, BUT NOT VERY RESOLUTELY) YOU
BULL IV (151)	ARE YOU SURE HE'S SUCH A FOOL AFTER ALL, AUNT	JUDY	? SUPPOSE YOU HAD A VOTE! WHICH WOULD YOU RATHER GIVE
BULL I (89)	THE IRISH NATION, BUT TO VISIT MY FATHER AND AUNT	JUDY	AND NORA REILLY AND FATHER DEMPSEY AND THE REST OF
BULL II SD(111)	OR THAT HE HIMSELF UNCONSCIOUSLY ENTERTAINS AUNT	JUDY	BY HIS FANTASTIC ENGLISH PERSONALITY AND ENGLISH
BULL II SD(107)	IN DISGRACE, WITH FATHER DEMPSEY'S HAMPER). AUNT	JUDY	COMES DOWN THE HILL, A WOMAN OF 50, IN NO WAY
BARB II (300)	LEFT. A MITE O MAWN LAST WEEK ED WORDS WITH THE	JUDY	E'S GOWIN TO MERRY. E GIVE ER WOT-FOR; AN E'S BIN FAWND
BULL III (121)	HELPS TO TAKE OFF THE CLOTH, WHICH SHE AND AUNT	JUDY	FOLD UP BETWEEN THEM). /AUNT JUDY/ I WONDER WHAT HE
BULL III SD(119)	TRIALS. THEN HE GOES IN. BROADBENT RISES. AUNT	JUDY	GOES TO THE TABLE AND COLLECTS THE PLATES AND CUPS ON
BULL IV SD(145)	COULD POSSIBLY MAKE A MAN'S FACE SO GRIM. AUNT	JUDY	IS QUIETLY BUSY. NORA IS TRYING TO IGNORE DORAN AND
BARB II (310)	YOU KNAOW. NATHINK PASNL. NAOW MELLICE. SAO LONG,	JUDY	. (HE GOES). /BARBARA/ NO MALICE. SO LONG, BILL.
BULL II (107)	(BUSTLING HIM UP THE HILL) WHISHT! HERES ANT	JUDY	. (PATSY GOES GRUMBLING IN DISGRACE, WITH FATHER
BULL II (107)	HIS FRIEND, MR BROADBENT. MR BROADBENT: ME SISTER	JUDY	. /AUNT JUDY/ (HOSPITABLY: GOING TO BROADBENT AND
BULL IV SD(145)	OF THE HOUSE IS NEAR THE FIREPLACE, BEHIND AUNT	JUDY	. THERE ARE CHAIRS AGAINST THE WALL, ONE AT EACH END OF
BARB II (284)	WAS DIRT. AND AW'LL TEACH HIM TO MEDDLE WITH MAW	JUDY	. WOTS IS BLEEDIN NIME? /BARBARA/ SERGEANT TODGER
BULL III SD(119)	WHEN HE OPENS THE DOOR HE FINDS NORA AND AUNT	JUDY	ON THE THRESHOLD. HE STANDS ASIDE TO LET THEM PASS,
BULL III (119)	D'YE CALL THIS AIRLY, GOD HELP YOU? /LARRY/ AUNT	JUDY	PROBABLY BREAKFASTED ABOUT HALF PAST SIX. /AUNT JUDY/
BULL II (109)	THATS A GOOD LAD (GOING). /PATSY/ (TO AUNT	JUDY	) FADHER KEEGAN SEZ-- /FATHER DEMPSEY/ (TURNING
BULL II (109)	YOU, SIR. /FATHER DEMPSEY/ (PASSING ON TO AUNT	JUDY	) GOOD-NIGHT, MISS DOYLE. /AUNT JUDY/ WONT YOU STAY TO
BULL II SD(111)	IRISH HUMORIST AND INCORRIGIBLE SPENDTHRIFT. AUNT	JUDY	SEEMS TO HIM AN INCARNATE JOKE. THE LIKELIHOOD THAT THE
BULL II (106)	YOU BUTTHER-FINGERED OMADHAUN. WAITLL ANT	JUDY	SEES THE STATE OF THAT SAMMIN: SHE'LL TALK TO YOU.
JOAN EPILOG (160)	ALL SORTS. THEY CHIP ME ABOUT GIVING THAT YOUNG	JUDY	THE CROSS; BUT I DONT CARE: I STAND UP TO THEM PROPER,
BULL II SD(111)	HOSPITABLE REMONSTRANCE NOR SURPRISE. INDEED AUNT	JUDY	WANTS TO GET RID OF HIM WHILST SHE MAKES A BED FOR HIM
BULL III SD(123)	DOYLE! REALLY, REALLY-- NORA, FOLLOWING AUNT	JUDY	WITH THE ROLLED-UP CLOTH IN HER HANDS, LOOKS AT HIM AND
BULL IV SD(145)	ITS CORNER WITH HIM, ON HIS LEFT HAND. AUNT	JUDY	, A LITTLE FURTHER BACK, SITS FACING THE FIRE KNITTING,
BULL IV SD(151)	KNOWN TO PARLIAMENTARY CANDIDATES. NORA, AUNT	JUDY	, KEEGAN, LARRY, AND CORNELIUS ARE LEFT IN THE PARLOR.

JUDY'S

BULL II SD(110)	DOES NOT FARE SO BADLY AFTER ALL AT AUNT	JUDY'S	BOARD. HE GETS NOT ONLY TEA AND BREAD-AND-BUTTER, BUT
BULL IV SD(158)	WITH A CATCH IN HER THROAT SHE TAKES UP AUNT	JUDY'S	KNITTING, AND MAKES A PRETENCE OF GOING ON WITH IT.
BULL II SD(111)	SIGNS OF SLEEPINESS. THE CONTRAST BETWEEN AUNT	JUDY'S	TABLE SERVICE AND THAT OF THE SOUTH AND EAST COAST

JUG

DEVL II SD(28)	CUPS AND SAUCERS OF THE PLAINEST WARE, WITH MILK	JUG	AND BOWL TO MATCH, EACH LARGE ENOUGH TO CONTAIN NEARLY A
NEVR I (223)	WATER. /VALENTINE/ THANK YOU. (SHE GIVES HIM THE	JUG	AND GOES OUT. HE BRINGS IT TO THE CABINET, CONTINUING IN
DEVL I SD(21)	THE BEDROOM DOOR, RETURNING PRESENTLY WITH A	JUG	AND GOING OUT OF THE HOUSE AS QUIETLY AS POSSIBLE.
CAPT III SD(272)	RANKIN IS PLACING A LITTLE TRAY WITH A	JUG	AND SOME GLASSES NEAR THE INKSTAND WHEN LADY CICELY'S
NEVR IV (292)	HAND IMPATIENTLY. THE WAITER PLACES A LARGE GLASS	JUG	AND THREE TUMBLERS IN THE MIDDLE). AND CLARET CUP. (ALL
JITT I SD(10)	FILLS IT WITH WATER. MRS BILLITER TAKES THE	JUG	BACK INTO THE BEDROOM; AND THE GIRL STEALS AFTER HER TO
NEVR III (263)	DONT TAKE ALL THE MILK (HE DEFTLY TAKES THE	JUG	FROM HER). YES: IN THE SPRING-- /DOLLY/-- A YOUNG MAN'S
JITT I SD(10)	STOPS FASCINATED. MRS BILLITER RETURNS WITH A	JUG	FROM THE BEDROOM WASHSTAND: A VERY PRETTY JUG IN ROSE
DEVL I SD(24)	FROM HER APATHY BY ESSIE, WHO COMES BACK WITH THE	JUG	FULL OF WATER. SHE IS TAKING IT TO RICHARD WHEN MRS
JITT I SD(10)	A JUG FROM THE BEDROOM WASHSTAND: A VERY PRETTY	JUG	IN ROSE COLOR AND GOLD. THE FLOWER GIRL PUTS THE ROSES
NEVR IV (288)	ER-- OH YES! IT'S SO HOT, I THINK WE MIGHT HAVE A	JUG	OF CLARET CUP. /WAITER/ (BEAMING) CLARET CUP, MAAM!
CAND III SD(137)	CANDIDA COMES IN WITH GLASSES, LEMONS, AND A	JUG	OF HOT WATER ON A TRAY. /CANDIDA/ WHO WILL HAVE SOME
NEVR I SD(223)	AS MUCH MINE AS HERS. THE PARLORMAID BRINGS IN A	JUG	OF HOT WATER. /VALENTINE/ THANK YOU. (SHE GIVES HIM THE
PPP (201)	THIS (GIVING HER THE BUST); DISSOLVE IT IN A	JUG	OF HOT WATER; AND BRING IT BACK INSTANTLY. MR BASTABLE'S
MIS. SD(110)	IS A TANTALUS, LIQUEUR BOTTLES, A SYPHON, A GLASS	JUG	OF LEMONADE, TUMBLERS, AND EVERY CONVENIENCE FOR CASUAL
SIM PREFACE(8)	HAS EVER SEEN A LADY OR GENTLEMAN CARRYING A	JUG	OF MILK DOWN BOND STREET OR THE RUE DE LA PAIX. A WHITE
ROCK I (209)	RINGS THE TELEPHONE BELL; AND SEIZES THE MILK	JUG	, WHICH HE EMPTIES AT A SINGLE DRAUGHT). HILDA APPEARS

JUGFUL

MRS PREFACE(152)	IN HOT WATER THAT THE ADDITION OF ANOTHER	JUGFUL	OF BOILING FLUID BY THE LORD CHAMBERLAIN TROUBLED ME

JUGGINS

FANY I (276)	(LOOKING APPREHENSIVELY AT JUGGINS). TCH-- !	JUGGINS	: A CHAIR. /DORA/ OH, IVE LET IT OUT, HAVE I! (
FANY I (275)	GILBEY/ YOU MUSTNT MIND WHAT YOUR MASTER SAYS,	JUGGINS	: HE DOESNT MEAN IT. (SHE TAKES THE CARD AND READS
FANY III (310)	WHY YOU SHOULD BE DEPENDENT ON HIM? DONT DO IT,	JUGGINS	: PAY YOUR OWN WAY LIKE AN HONEST LAD; AND DONT EAT
FANY III (308)	WE CANT HAVE ANY FUN WITH THE MAR HERE. I SAY,	JUGGINS	: YOU CAN GIVE US TEA IN THE PANTRY, CANT YOU?
FANY I (275)	LIKE THAT-- IN BRACKETS. WHAT SORT OF PERSON,	JUGGINS	? /GILBEY/ WHATS HER ADDRESS? /MRS GILBEY/ THE
FANY I (275)	CIRCULAR ROAD. IS THAT A RESPECTABLE ADDRESS,	JUGGINS	? /JUGGINS/ A GREAT MANY MOST RESPECTABLE PEOPLE
FANY I (283)	/MRS GILBEY/ IT DOESNT SEEM JUSTICE, DOES IT,	JUGGINS	? /JUGGINS/ NO, MADAM. /MRS GILBEY/ (TO DORA,
FANY I (283)	GILBEY/ HAVE YOU EVER BEEN IN A POLICE COURT,	JUGGINS	? /JUGGINS/ YES, MADAM. /MRS GILBEY/ (RATHER
FANY III (319)	KNOW. /MRS GILBEY/ PERHAPS SHE DOES. DOES SHE, MR	JUGGINS	? /JUGGINS/ THE OTHER LADY SUSPECTS ME, MADAM. THEY
FANY I (275)	HOW DO YOU KNOW? (TO JUGGINS) IS SHE A LADY,	JUGGINS	? YOU KNOW WHAT I MEAN. /JUGGINS/ IN THE SENSE IN
FANY III (325)	A DUKE. WOULD-- /BOBBY/ WHATS THAT? /MARGARET/	JUGGINS	A DUKE! /DUVALLET/ COMMENT! /DORA/ WHAT DID I TELL
FANY III SD(297)	UP TO RING THE BELL; THEN RESUMES HIS CROUCH.	JUGGINS	ANSWERS THE BELL. /BOBBY/ JUGGINS. /JUGGINS/ SIR?
FANY III SD(305)	HIS NECK). /BOBBY/ NO. STOP. LEAVE GO, WILL YOU.	JUGGINS	APPEARS AT THE DOOR. /JUGGINS/ MISS DELANEY, SIR. (
FANY III (309)	BUT I'M NOT GOING TO ASK; AND DONT YOU EITHER. (	JUGGINS	APPEARS AT THE DOOR). YOU SAID YOU WANTED TO SAY
FANY I (276)	OH, IVE LET IT OUT, HAVE I! (CONTEMPLATING	JUGGINS	APPROVINGLY AS HE PLACES A CHAIR FOR HER BETWEEN THE
FANY III SD(318)	/KNOX/ IS IT HIM THAT YOU SAID WAS BROTHER TO A--	JUGGINS	COMES IN WITH THE TEA-TRAY. ALL RISE. HE TAKES THE

FANY III	SD(308)	NO CALL TO BE STIFF WITH ONE ANOTHER, HAVE WE?	JUGGINS	COMES IN. /JUGGINS/ BEG PARDON, SIR. MR AND MRS
FANY I	SD(283)	(OVERCOME) EXCUSE ME! I CANT HELP SMILING.	JUGGINS	ENTERS. /JUGGINS/ MR GILBEY HAS GONE TO WORMWOOD
FANY III	(305)	/JUGGINS/ MISS DELANEY, SIR. (DORA COMES IN.	JUGGINS	GOES OUT. MARGARET HASTILY RELEASES BOBBY, AND GOES
FANY I	SD(275)	(HE RISES AND PLANTS HIMSELF ON THE HEARTH-RUG).	JUGGINS	GOES OUT. /MRS GILBEY/ I WONDER WHAT SHE WANTS.
FANY III	(319)	HEIR. /MRS GILBEY/ IT'S A MUCH NICER NAME THAN	JUGGINS	. I THINK I'LL CALL YOU BY IT, IF YOU DONT MIND.
FANY III	(318)	/GILBEY/ I DIDNT MEAN TO ASK YOU TO DO THIS, MR	JUGGINS	. I WASNT THINKING WHEN I RANG. /MRS GILBEY/ (
FANY III	(309)	/GILBEY/ (PATERNALLY) NOW YOU LISTEN TO ME,	JUGGINS	. I'M AN OLDER MAN THAN YOU. DONT YOU THROW OUT
FANY I	(284)	LISTEN HERE, DEAR BOY. YOUR NAME ISNT	JUGGINS	. NOBODY'S NAME IS JUGGINS. /JUGGINS/ MY ORDERS ARE,
FANY III	(304)	FUN, I SHOULD ASK THE FRENCHMAN TO KISS ME-- OR	JUGGINS	. /BOBBY/ (RISING AND RETREATING TO THE HEARTH) OH,
FANY III	(297)	HIS CROUCH. JUGGINS ANSWERS THE BELL. /BOBBY/	JUGGINS	. /JUGGINS/ SIR? /BOBBY/ (MOROSELY SARCASTIC) SIR
FANY I	(284)	BOY. YOUR NAME ISNT JUGGINS. NOBODY'S NAME IS	JUGGINS	. /JUGGINS/ MY ORDERS ARE, MISS DELANEY, THAT YOU
FANY I	(283)	SHOCKED) I HOPE YOU HAD NOT BEEN EXCEEDING,	JUGGINS	. /JUGGINS/ YES, MADAM, I HAD. I EXCEEDED THE LEGAL
FANY III	(318)	(TRYING TO TAKE THE TRAY FROM HIM) LET ME,	JUGGINS	. /JUGGINS/ PLEASE SIT DOWN, MADAM. ALLOW ME TO
FANY III	(300)	WORTHY. /BOBBY/ OH, I CANT MAKE YOU UNDERSTAND,	JUGGINS	. THE GIRL ISNT A SCULLERY-MAID. I WANT TO DO IT
FANY III	(307)	NOW WHERE ARE YOU? /DORA/ (CALLING) JUGGINS,	JUGGINS	. THEYLL MURDER ONE ANOTHER. /JUGGINS/ (THROWING
FANY III	(303)	ROW YOU GOT INTO FOR LETTING OUT THAT YOU ADMIRED	JUGGINS	(SHE TURNS HER BACK ON HIM QUICKLY)-- A FOOTMAN!
FANY III	SD(324)	TO MARGARET'S HANDSHAKE WITH ENTHUSIASM, KISSES	JUGGINS	ON BOTH CHEEKS, AND SINKS INTO HIS CHAIR, WIPING HIS
FANY III	(321)	WITHOUT PREJUDICE). /DORA/ PLEASED TO MEET YOU. (	JUGGINS	PLACES THE BABY ROCKING-CHAIR FOR HER ON GILBEY'S
FANY III	SD(321)	DUVALLET BOWS AND SITS DOWN ON MR KNOX'S LEFT,	JUGGINS	PLACING A CHAIR FOR HIM. /DORA/ NOW, BOBBY:
FANY I	(275)	SHE MAY TELL US SOMETHING ABOUT THE LAD, I'D HAVE	JUGGINS	PUT THE HUSSY INTO THE STREET. /JUGGINS/ (RETURNING
FANY III	SD(318)	/GILBEY/ GOOD LORD! I NEVER THOUGHT OF THAT.	JUGGINS	RETURNS WITH THE CAKES. THEY REGARD HIM WITH
FANY III	SD(300)	RELUCTANTLY TO HIS BOOKS, AND SITS DOWN TO WRITE.	JUGGINS	RETURNS. /JUGGINS/ (ANNOUNCING) MISS KNOX. MARGARET
FANY III	(327)	BE VULGAR, GIRL. REMEMBER YOUR NEW POSITION. (TO	JUGGINS	) I SUPPOSE YOURE SERIOUS ABOUT THIS, MR-- MR
FANY I	(275)	JUMP TO CONCLUSIONS, ROB. HOW DO YOU KNOW? (TO	JUGGINS	) IS SHE A LADY, JUGGINS? YOU KNOW WHAT I MEAN.
FANY I	(275)	I'D BETTER TRY WHAT I CAN GET OUT OF HER. (TO	JUGGINS	) SHEW HER UP. YOU DONT MIND, DO YOU, ROB? /GILBEY/
FANY III	(318)	CLINCH IT, GILBEY. YOU LEAVE IT TO ME. (TO	JUGGINS	) WAS YOUR MOTHER THE DUCHESS? /JUGGINS/ YES, SIR.
FANY III	(310)	FOLK NOW. WEVE BEEN IN THE POLICE COURT. (TO	JUGGINS	) WELL, I SUPPOSE YOU KNOW YOUR OWN BUSINESS BEST. I
FANY III	(325)	THE BROTHER OF A DUKE: THATS WHAT HE IS. (TO	JUGGINS	) WELL, WOULD YOU MARRY HER? /JUGGINS/ I WAS ABOUT
FANY III	(305)	/DORA/ (THROUGH THE DOOR, TO THE DEPARTING	JUGGINS	) WELL, YOU ARE A JUGGINS TO SHEW ME UP WHEN THERES
FANY III	(309)	/GILBEY/ HE KNOWS THAT. (HE SITS DOWN. THEN, TO	JUGGINS	) WHAT IS IT? /JUGGINS/ (ADVANCING TO THE MIDDLE
FANY III	(308)	ARE VERY INTERESTING. (HE GOES OUT, FOLLOWED BY	JUGGINS	). PRESENTLY MR AND MRS GILBEY COME IN. THEY TAKE
FANY I	(276)	COURT? /MRS GILBEY/ (LOOKING APPREHENSIVELY AT	JUGGINS	). TCH-- ! JUGGINS: A CHAIR. /DORA/ OH, IVE LET IT
FANY III	(309)	GOING TO ASK? /GILBEY/ NO, I'M NOT GOING TO ASK.	JUGGINS	SAID THIS MORNING HE WANTED TO SPEAK TO ME. IF HE
FANY III	(327)	(SLIPPING HER ARM THROUGH HIS) I HAVE LOVED	JUGGINS	SINCE THE FIRST DAY I BEHELD HIM. I FELT
FANY III	SD(311)	ANNOUNCING) MR AND MRS KNOX. THE KNOXES COME IN.	JUGGINS	TAKES TWO CHAIRS FROM THE WALL AND PLACES THEM AT
FANY III	(305)	DOOR, TO THE DEPARTING JUGGINS) WELL, YOU ARE A	JUGGINS	TO SHEW ME UP WHEN THERES COMPANY. (TO MARGARET AND
FANY III	(304)	WAY TO THE DOOR) RING THE BELL, BOBBY; AND TELL	JUGGINS	TO SHEW ME OUT. /BOBBY/ (REDDENING) I'M NOT A CAD,
FANY III	(317)	/MRS GILBEY/ RING, ROB. (GILBEY RINGS). STOP.	JUGGINS	WILL THINK WE'RE RINGING FOR HIM. /GILBEY/ (
FANY III	SD(307)	SEPARATE BY THE WHOLE WIDTH OF THE ROOM.	JUGGINS	WITHDRAWS. /DUVALLET/ I FEAR I DERANGE YOU.
FANY III	SD(300)	(ANNOUNCING) MISS KNOX. MARGARET COMES IN.	JUGGINS	WITHDRAWS. /MARGARET/ STILL GRINDING AWAY FOR THAT
FANY III	(298)	HER THAN I CAN EVER BE OF ANYONE ELSE. YOU SEE,	JUGGINS	, A GENTLEMAN HAS TO THINK OF A GIRL'S FEELINGS.
FANY III	(297)	SIR? /BOBBY/ YES. DORA SAYS YOUR NAME CANT BE	JUGGINS	, AND THAT YOU HAVE THE MANNERS OF A GENTLEMAN. I
FANY III	(308)	ARE. COME ALONG. (AT THE DOOR) OH, BY THE WAY,	JUGGINS	, FETCH DOWN THAT CONCERTINA FROM MY ROOM, WILL
FANY III	(307)	THE TABLE). NOW WHERE ARE YOU? /DORA/ (CALLING)	JUGGINS	, JUGGINS. THEYLL MURDER ONE ANOTHER. /JUGGINS/ (
FANY III	(311)	DO YOU MEAN? DONT YOU BEGIN TO TAKE LIBERTIES,	JUGGINS	, NOW THAT YOU KNOW WE'RE LOTH TO PART WITH YOU.
FANY I	SD(274)	ANY OTHER LAD: BUT HE'D NEVER DO ANYTHING LOW.	JUGGINS	, THE FOOTMAN, COMES IN WITH A CARD ON A SALVER. HE
FANY III	(309)	SIR. /GILBEY/ WELL, WHAT IS IT? /MRS GILBEY/ OH,	JUGGINS	, WE'RE EXPECTING MR AND MRS KNOX TO TEA. /GILBEY/
FANY III	(299)	NEVER SUPPOSED YOU WERE, SIR. /BOBBY/ OH, I SAY,	JUGGINS	, YOU ARE A PESSIMIST. /JUGGINS/ (PREPARING TO GO)
FANY III	(299)	A NUISANCE! I DONT KNOW WHAT TO DO, YOU KNOW,	JUGGINS	, YOUR COOL SIMPLE-MINDED WAY OF DOING IT WOULDNT GO
FANY III	(311)	HE IS, SIR. TOGETHER /GILBEY/ WHAT! /MRS GILBEY/	JUGGINS	! /JUGGINS/ EXCUSE ME, SIR: THE BELL. /GILBEY/ (
			JUGGINS'S	
FANY III	(305)	ALL RIGHT, DEAR: ALL RIGHT, OLD MAN: I'LL WAIT IN	JUGGINS'S	PANTRY TIL YOURE DISENGAGED. /MARGARET/ DONT YOU
			JUGGLER	
MIS.	(157)	EM, CHICKABIDDY. I UNDERSTAND. (HE IMITATES A	JUGGLER	TOSSING UP BALLS). EH? /LINA/ (GOING TO HIM, PAST
			JUGS	
FANY III	(318)	THAT IS THE MILK, MADAM. (SHE HAS MISTAKEN THE	JUGS	). THIS IS THE WATER. THEY STARE AT HIM IN PITIABLE
			JUGULAR	
DOCT PREFACE	(50)	TEACHES) THE ANATOMY OF THE CAROTID ARTERY AND	JUGULAR	VEIN; AND THERE CAN BE NO QUESTION THAT THE BURNING
			JUJITSU	
FANY III	(307)	THINK I'M ALWAYS FIGHTING. /DUVALLET/ PRACTISING	JUJITSU	OR THE NEW ICELAND WRESTLING. ADMIRABLE, MISS KNOX.
			JULIA	
PHIL III	(146)	QUIVER SHALL BETRAY THE CONFLICT WITHIN. /CRAVEN/	JULIA	: CHARTERIS HAS NOT CONGRATULATED YOU YET. HE'S COMING
PHIL II	(116)	/SYLVIA/ HALLO! /CRAVEN/ TELL HER THE NEWS,	JULIA	: IT WOULD SOUND RIDICULOUS FROM ME. (HE GOES TO THE
PHIL III	(141)	I UTTERLY DESPISE HIM. /CRAVEN/ DONT RUB IT IN,	JULIA	: IT'S NOT KIND. NO MAN IS QUITE HIMSELF WHEN HE'S
PHIL I	(90)	SIGHING) WELL, WELL! (BRACING HIMSELF UP) NOW,	JULIA	: IT'S TIME FOR US TO BE OFF. (JULIA RISES).
PHIL III	(139)	POINT OF VIEW, THERES NOTHING TO BE SAID FOR YOU,	JULIA	: NOTHING. THATS WHY I HAVE TO FIND SOME OTHER POINT
PHIL III	(143)	NOW! NOW! MY DEAR CHILDREN, REALLY NOW! COME,	JULIA	: PUT UP YOUR HANDKERCHIEF BEFORE MRS TRANFIELD SEES
PHIL I	(83)	REAPPEARS, IN THE UTMOST DISMAY, EXCLAIMING)	JULIA	: WE'RE DONE. CUTHBERTSON'S COMING UPSTAIRS WITH YOUR
PHIL I	(83)	SOBBING ON HIS BREAST). COME! DONT CRY, MY DEAR	JULIA	: YOU DONT LOOK HALF SO BEAUTIFUL AS WHEN YOURE HAPPY;
PHIL III	(142)	WITH HIS HANDS IN HIS POCKETS). /CRAVEN/ (HURT)	JULIA	: YOU DONT TREAT ME RESPECTFULLY. I DONT WISH TO
PHIL I	(80)	IN THE EYE OF-- THE EYE OF-- /CHARTERIS/ YES,	JULIA	? CANT YOU GET IT OUT? IN THE EYE OF SOMETHING THAT
PHIL III	(146)	CHANCE IT. (HE WALKS CONFIDENTLY UP TO JULIA).	JULIA	? (HE PROFFERS HIS HAND). /JULIA/ (EXHAUSTED,
PHIL II	(123)	/CHARTERIS/ (IN A LOW VOICE) LOOKING FOR ME,	JULIA	? /JULIA/ (STARTING VIOLENTLY) OH, HOW YOU STARTLED
PHIL II	(121)	THEORY THAT IT WOULD BE PLEASANT TO BE MARRIED TO	JULIA	? /PARAMORE/ I SUPPOSE SO. IN A SENSE. /CHARTERIS/
PHIL I	(90)	DOOR). /CRAVEN/ (HORRIFIED) WHAT ARE YOU DOING,	JULIA	? YOU CANT GO UNTIL YOUVE SAID GOODNIGHT TO MRS
PHIL III	(144)	OTHER SIDE). /GRACE/ (SPEAKING IN A LOW VOICE TO	JULIA	ALONE) SO YOU HAVE SHEWN HIM THAT YOU CAN DO WITHOUT
PHIL I	(72)	/CHARTERIS/ SHE DID WHAT A WOMAN LIKE	JULIA	ALWAYS DOES. WHEN I EXPLAINED PERSONALLY, SHE SAID IT
PHIL I	(90)	BUT JUST FOR A MOMENT, TO SAY GOODNIGHT. (	JULIA	AND CHARTERIS LOOK AT ONE ANOTHER IN DISMAY.
PHIL II	SD(103)	IT'S PRIVATE BUSINESS. A CHASE BEGINS BETWEEN	JULIA	AND CHARTERIS, ALL THE MORE EXCITING TO THEM BECAUSE
PHIL II	(127)	AND PLACES HIMSELF WITH EVIDENT MISGIVING BETWEEN	JULIA	AND GRACE). IT'S A BAD CASE OF WOMANLINESS. /GRACE/ (
PHIL I	(87)	CLUB: I DONT. IT'S BAD ENOUGH TO HAVE	JULIA	AND HER SISTER-- A GIRL UNDER TWENTY! -- SPENDING HALF
PHIL II	SD(103)	IT'S NOT FAR OFF NOW. (HIS HEAD DROOPS AGAIN).	JULIA	AND PARAMORE COME IN FROM THE STAIRCASE. JULIA STOPS
PHIL II	(124)	GRACE VERY DETERMINED). /CHARTERIS/ (ASIDE TO	JULIA	AS HE GETS OUT OF THE EASY CHAIR) IDIOT! SHE'LL HAVE
PHIL II	(115)	/CUTHBERTSON/ (WHO HAS BEEN REJOICING WITH	JULIA	AT THE OTHER SIDE OF THE ROOM) WELL, LETS SAY NO MORE
PHIL II	(106)	OVER THE BACK OF IT) WHATS UP, CHARTERIS?	JULIA	BEEN MAKING LOVE TO YOU? /CHARTERIS/ (SPEAKING TO
PHIL II	SD(112)	HIS RIGHT SHOULDER, CUTHBERTSON ON HIS LEFT, AND	JULIA	BEHIND. /CRAVEN/ WHATS THE MATTER, PARAMORE? /JULIA/
PHIL II	(129)	CRAVEN'S FUTURE, EVERYBODY'S FUTURE DEPENDS ON	JULIA	BEING PARAMORE'S AFFIANCED BRIDE WHEN WE ARRIVE. HE'S
PHIL I	(73)	ADVANCED WOMAN, MIND! AS AN ADVANCED WOMAN, DOES	JULIA	BELONG TO ME? AM I HER OWNER-- HER MASTER? /GRACE/
PHIL II	(116)	SENSATION. THE GROUP OF CUTHBERTSON, CRAVEN, AND	JULIA	BREAKS UP AS THEY TURN IN DISMAY). /PARAMORE/ (
PHIL II	SD(104)	THE RETURN OF CUTHBERTSON. TURNING BACK, HE SEES	JULIA	CLOSE UPON HIM. THERE BEING NOTHING ELSE FOR IT, HE
PHIL I	(71)	HOW OFTEN? /CHARTERIS/ WELL, ONCE. /GRACE/	JULIA	CRAVEN? /CHARTERIS/ (RECOILING) WHO TOLD YOU THAT..
PHIL I	(71)	HICKORY. THAT IS WHAT COMES OF REMINDING ME OF	JULIA	CRAVEN. (BROODING, WITH HIS CHIN ON HIS RIGHT HAND
PHIL II	SD(103)	IT WHIRLING AS HE MAKES FOR THE OTHER DOOR.	JULIA	CROSSING IN PURSUIT OF HIM. HE IS ABOUT TO ESCAPE WHEN
PHIL II	(105)	HAVE YOU SEEN GRACE TRANFIELD THIS MORNING? (	JULIA	DROPS THE PAPER, AND COMES A STEP NEARER TO LISTEN).
PHIL I	SD(76)	PAST THE SOFA. GRACE GOES OUT. CHARTERIS, HOLDING	JULIA	FAST, LOOKS ROUND TO THE DOOR TO SEE WHETHER GRACE IS
PHIL III	(144)	I SAID, WILL YOU SHAKE HANDS WITH ME? (	JULIA	GIVES HER HAND PAINFULLY, WITH HER FACE AVERTED). THEY
PHIL II	(116)	/JULIA/ DEAR OLD DADDY! /CRAVEN/ AH, IS	JULIA	GLAD THAT THE OLD DAD IS LET OFF FOR A FEW YEARS
PHIL II	SD(128)	NUMBER IN SAVILE ROW? /CHARTERIS/ SEVENTY-NINE.	JULIA	GOES OUT QUICKLY BY THE STAIRCASE DOOR, TO THEIR
PHIL I	(74)	IT FLATTERED ME-- DELIGHTED ME-- THAT WAS HOW	JULIA	GOT ME, BECAUSE SHE WAS THE FIRST WOMAN WHO HAD THE
PHIL II	(130)	I CANT HELP IT: I'M TOO RESTLESS. THE FACT IS,	JULIA	HAS MADE ME SO NERVOUS THAT I CANT ANSWER FOR MYSELF
PHIL I	(73)	HER TRIUMPHANTLY) THEN HOW CAN YOU STEAL ME FROM	JULIA	IF I DONT BELONG TO HER? (HE CATCHES HER BY THE

PHIL II	SD(103)	CHARTERIS FIRST MAKES FOR THE STAIRCASE DOOR.	JULIA	IMMEDIATELY RETREATS TO IT, BARRING HIS PATH. HE
PHIL II	(116)	ANY ONE ELSE'S? (HE PATS HER CHEEK, MOLLIFIED.	JULIA	IMPATIENTLY TURNS AWAY FROM THEM). COME TO THE SMOKING
PHIL II	SD(106)	OF THE TABLE) YOUR LUNCH WILL BE COLD, JULIA.	JULIA	IS ABOUT TO RETORT FURIOUSLY WHEN SHE IS CHECKED BY
PHIL II	(108)	TO ME: I AM GOING TO SPEAK AS A PHILOSOPHER.	JULIA	IS JEALOUS OF EVERYBODY: EVERYBODY. IF SHE SAW YOU
PHIL I	(88)	SOMEBODY HAD THE AUDACITY TO GUARANTEE THAT MY	JULIA	IS NOT A WOMANLY WOMAN? /CHARTERIS/ (DARKLY) IT
PHIL II	(121)	AMIABLE AND HUMAN TO HOPE THAT YOUR THEORY ABOUT	JULIA	IS RIGHT, BECAUSE IT AMOUNTS TO HOPING THAT SHE MAY
PHIL I	(93)	I CAME HERE TONIGHT TO SWEETHEART GRACE. ENTER	JULIA	. ALARUMS AND EXCURSIONS. EXIT GRACE. ENTER YOU AND
PHIL III	(146)	(TO CHARTERIS) GO STRAIGHT UP AND CONGRATULATE	JULIA	. AND DO IT LIKE A GENTLEMAN, SMILING. /CHARTERIS/
PHIL I	(93)	SUBTERFUGES AND EXCUSES. EXEUNT CRAVEN AND	JULIA	. AND HERE WE ARE. THATS THE WHOLE STORY. SLEEP OVER
PHIL III	SD(141)	ASK JULIA. PARAMORE AND CRAVEN TURN TO	JULIA	. CHARTERIS REMAINS DOGGEDLY LOOKING STRAIGHT BEFORE
PHIL I	(84)	SOME THUMPING LIE. I CANT THINK OF ONE: YOU CAN,	JULIA	. EXERCISE ALL YOUR GENIUS. I'LL BACK YOU UP. /JULIA/
BUOY III	(35)	HOME FOR GOOD? /SHE/ THAT WONT MATTER TO YOU,	JULIA	. FOR MY HOME IS HERE, IN DADDY'S HOUSE, NOT IN YOURS.
PHIL I	(81)	ANXIOUSLY TO THE BOOK) DONT DAMAGE PROPERTY,	JULIA	. (HE PICKS IT UP AND DUSTS IT). MAKING SCENES IS AN
PHIL II	(104)	ARNT YOU COMING? /CHARTERIS/ NO. UNHAND ME,	JULIA	. (HE TRIES TO GET AWAY: SHE HOLDS HIM). IF YOU DONT
PHIL I	(83)	MUCH. NO: I'M DASHED IF I WILL. HERE! LET ME GO,	JULIA	. (SHE CLINGS TO HIM). WILL YOU COME WITHOUT ANOTHER
PHIL II	(123)	CHARTERIS CATCHES HER SLEEVE). STOP: BE CAREFUL,	JULIA	. (SHE FREES HERSELF BY GIVING HIM A PUSH WHICH
PHIL III	(138)	MY DEAR JULIA, (KISSING THE OTHER) MY BEAUTIFUL	JULIA	. (SHE TEARS HER HANDS AWAY AND RAISES THEM AS IF TO
PHIL II	(102)	CRAVEN AND PREPARING TO READ THE LETTER) NOW FOR	JULIA	. (THE COLONEL TURNS AWAY TO HIDE HIS FACE FROM
PHIL II	(105)	THE EDGE OF THE TABLE) YOUR LUNCH WILL BE COLD,	JULIA	. JULIA IS ABOUT TO RETORT FURIOUSLY WHEN SHE IS
PHIL III	(144)	HOPE. /CRAVEN/ SHE WILL, JO. (PEREMPTORILY) NOW,	JULIA	. JULIA SLOWLY RISES. /CUTHBERTSON/ NOW, GRACE. (HE
PHIL I	(73)	COAXING HER) IT WAS NOTHING BUT A PHILANDER WITH	JULIA	. NOTHING ELSE IN THE WORLD, I ASSURE YOU. /GRACE/ (
PHIL III	(136)	IT, DODGING HER. /CHARTERIS/ (NERVOUSLY) DONT,	JULIA	. NOW DONT ABUSE YOUR ADVANTAGE. YOUVE GOT ME HERE AT
PHIL III	(141)	US, WERENT YOU? /CHARTERIS/ (ENIGMATICALLY) ASK	JULIA	. PARAMORE AND CRAVEN TURN TO JULIA. CHARTERIS REMAINS
PHIL III	(140)	QUALITIES. /CHARTERIS/ (RETREATING) KEEP OFF,	JULIA	. REMEMBER YOUR NEW OBLIGATIONS TO PARAMORE. /JULIA/ (
PHIL III	(143)	(HE TURNS COMMANDINGLY TO JULIA). NOW LOOK HERE,	JULIA	. /CHARTERIS/ HALLO! A REVOLT OF THE FATHERS!
PHIL III	SD(146)	A MOMENT. GRACE SOFTLY RISES AND GETS CLOSE TO	JULIA	. /CHARTERIS/ (WHISPERING OVER HIS SHOULDER TO
PHIL II	(107)	OUT OF PARAMORE. I BELIEVE HE'S IN LOVE WITH	JULIA	. /CHARTERIS/ (STARTING UP EXCITEDLY) IN LOVE WITH
PHIL I	(90)	SAY PLUMP OUT BEFORE US ALL: THAT ABOUT YOU AND	JULIA	. /CHARTERIS/ I'LL EXPLAIN IT ALL TOMORROW. JUST AT
PHIL II	(100)	YOUR EXPLANATION WAS IN SHOCKING BAD TASTE BEFORE	JULIA	. /CHARTERIS/ NEVER MIND. IT WAS A GOOD, FAT, HEALTHY,
PHIL II	(127)	/SYLVIA/ I KNEW YOUD OVERDO IT SOME DAY,	JULIA	. /CRAVEN/ DO YOU KNOW THIS LADY, JO? /CUTHBERTSON/
PHIL I	(87)	I'M A SOLDIER. (A SOB FROM JULIA). DONT CRY,	JULIA	. /CUTHBERTSON/ (HUSKILY) I HOPE YOU MAY LONG BE
PHIL I	(73)	LOVE. YES: IT IS YOUR MISSION TO RESCUE ME FROM	JULIA	. /GRACE/ (RISING) THEN, IF YOU PLEASE, I DECLINE TO
PHIL I	(75)	I THINK YOU HAD BETTER LET ME TAKE YOU HOME,	JULIA	. /JULIA/ I WILL NOT. I AM NOT GOING HOME: I AM GOING
PHIL II	(104)	LAST). /CRAVEN/ (AT THE DOOR, GRAVELY) COME,	JULIA	. /JULIA/ (WITH PATRONIZING AFFECTION) YES, DADDY
PHIL III	(140)	WONDERFUL THING. DONT LET US DISPARAGE ANIMALS,	JULIA	. /JULIA/ THAT IS WHAT YOU REALLY THINK ME.
PHIL III	(137)	I AM AFRAID YOUR INTENTIONS HAVE BEEN HONORABLE,	JULIA	. /JULIA/ YOU CAD! /CHARTERIS/ (WITH A SIGH) I
PHIL III	(134)	I HAVE BEEN ALONE IN THE WORLD; AND I NEED YOU,	JULIA	. THAT IS HOW I HAVE DIVINED THAT YOU, ALSO, ARE ALONE
PHIL II	(129)	YOURE MAD. PARAMORE'S GOING TO PROPOSE TO	JULIA	. WE MUST GIVE HIM TIME: HE'S NOT THE MAN TO COME TO
PHIL III	(137)	SOMETHING EITHER MORE OR LESS THAN A GENTLEMAN,	JULIA	. YOU ONCE GAVE ME THE BENEFIT OF THE DOUBT. /JULIA/
PHIL I	(79)	CRIMINAL. /CHARTERIS/ YOU DONT SEE THE POINT YET,	JULIA	. YOU SEEM TO FORGET THAT IN RESERVING YOUR FREEDOM TO
PHIL II	(102)	THE SORT OF THING--" EVER AND ALWAYS YOUR LOVING	JULIA	." (THE COLONEL SINKS ON THE CHAIR, AND COVERS HIS
PHIL II	SD(113)	THERE IS NO SUCH DISEASE. CUTHBERTSON AND	JULIA	LOOK AT ONE ANOTHER, HARDLY DARING TO BELIEVE THE GOOD
PHIL II	(127)	SUCCEED IN ESTABLISHING YOUR COMPLAINT, AND THAT	JULIA	MAY SOON SEE THE LAST OF THIS MOST OUTRAGEOUS
PHIL II	(121)	/CHARTERIS/ I'LL TELL YOU. YOU THINK I'M FOND OF	JULIA	MYSELF. SO I AM; BUT THEN I'M FOND OF EVERYBODY; SO I
PHIL II	(120)	HIM ON HAVING HIS LIFE SAVED. CONGRATULATE	JULIA	ON HAVING HER FATHER SPARED, SWEAR THAT YOUR DISCOVERY
PHIL II	(106)	THE RESPECT DUE TO THEIR SEX. /CHARTERIS/ AH, IF	JULIA	ONLY HAD YOUR WISDOM, CRAVEN! (HE GETS OFF THE TABLE
PHIL III	SD(140)	(SHOUTING, UTTERLY SCANDALIZED) JULIA! !	JULIA	RELEASES CHARTERIS, BUT STANDS HER GROUND DISDAINFULLY
PHIL II	(123)	A DOCTOR! THEY CAN SAY WHAT THEY LIKE TO HIM. (	JULIA	RETURNS, BUT DOES NOT LOOK HIS WAY. HE TAKES HIS FEET
PHIL III	(134)	HEART, YOUR SINCERITY, YOUR STERLING REALITY, (	JULIA	RISES AND GAZES AT HIM, BREATHLESS WITH A NEW HOPE)
PHIL I	(90)	UP) NOW, JULIA: IT'S TIME FOR US TO BE OFF. (	JULIA	RISES). /CUTHBERTSON/ BUT WHERE ON EARTH IS GRACE? I
PHIL III	SD(146)	NOT CONGRATULATED YOU YET. HE'S COMING TO DO IT.	JULIA	RISES, AND FIXES A DANGEROUS LOOK ON CHARTERIS.
PHIL III	(143)	FIRE). SYLVIA ARRIVES. /SYLVIA/ (CONTEMPLATING	JULIA	) CRYING AGAIN! WELL, YOU ARE A WOMANLY ONE!
PHIL I	(76)	(QUIETLY, WITHOUT RELAXING HIS WATCH ON	JULIA	) MRS TRANFIELD: I THINK YOU HAD BETTER GO INTO
PHIL II	(103)	BEDSIDE MANNER IN FULL PLAY. /CHARTERIS/ (SEEING	JULIA	) OH, LORD! (HE RETREATS UNDER THE LEE OF THE
PHIL I	(87)	WHEN MY TIME COMES. I'M A SOLDIER. (A SOB FROM	JULIA	). DONT CRY, JULIA. /CUTHBERTSON/ (HUSKILY) I HOPE
PHIL III	(146)	I'LL CHANCE IT. (HE WALKS CONFIDENTLY UP TO	JULIA	). JULIA? (HE PROFFERS HIS HAND). /JULIA/ (
PHIL III	(143)	YOUR TONGUE, SYLVIA. (HE TURNS COMMANDINGLY TO	JULIA	). NOW LOOK HERE, JULIA. /CHARTERIS/ HALLO! A REVOLT
PHIL II	(118)	I'M OFF. (HE GOES GOODHUMOREDLY, PUSHED OUT BY	JULIA	). /JULIA/ (TURNING AT THE DOOR WITH HER UTMOST
PHIL I	(73)	EXACTLY MY OPINION. NOW TELL ME, DO I BELONG TO	JULIA	; OR HAVE I A RIGHT TO BELONG TO MYSELF? /GRACE/ (
PHIL III	SD(132)	ROUND-BACKED CHAIR ON CASTORS, POURING OUT TEA.	JULIA	SITS OPPOSITE HIM, WITH HER BACK TO THE FIRE. HE IS IN
PHIL III	SD(144)	SHE WILL, JO. (PEREMPTORILY) NOW, JULIA.	JULIA	SLOWLY RISES. /CUTHBERTSON/ NOW, GRACE. (HE CONDUCTS
PHIL III	(138)	BUT I SHOULD HAVE MADE GRACE UNHAPPY. (	JULIA	SNEERS). HOWEVER, NOW I COME TO THINK OF IT, YOULL
PHIL I	(76)	BUT STOPS AND LOOKS INQUIRINGLY AT CHARTERIS AS	JULIA	SPRINGS UP TO INTERCEPT HER. HE ADVANCES A STEP TO
PHIL II	SD(103)	JULIA AND PARAMORE COME IN FROM THE STAIRCASE.	JULIA	STOPS AS SHE CATCHES SIGHT OF CHARTERIS, HER FACE
PHIL I	SD(84)	AS IF ABOUT TO SING. TWO ELDERLY GENTLEMEN ENTER.	JULIA	STOPS PLAYING. THE ELDER OF THE TWO NEWCOMERS, COLONEL
PHIL I	SD(77)	HEAVES A LONG SIGH). THEY SIT SILENT FOR A WHILE:	JULIA	STRIVING, NOT TO REGAIN HER SELF-CONTROL, BUT TO
PHIL II	(124)	DO NOT WISH TO BREAK THAT RULE, MISS CRAVEN. (	JULIA	SULLENLY DROPS CHARTERIS'S ARM. GRACE TURNS TO
PHIL I	(84)	HERE THEY ARE. SIT DOWN AND LOOK AT HOME. (	JULIA	TEARS OFF HER TOQUE AND MANTLE; THROWS THEM ON THE
PHIL II	(101)	LETTER-CARDS: THE BLUE COLOR MAKES IT SO EASY FOR	JULIA	TO PICK THE BITS OUT OF MY WASTE PAPER BASKET AND
PHIL III	SD(140)	TO ADMIRE YOU FOR YOUR MORAL QUALITIES, DO YOU?	JULIA	TURNS AND LOOKS HARD AT HIM. HE STARTS UP
PHIL II	(105)	TO GO, BUT IS STOPPED BY THE RETURN OF SYLVIA.	JULIA	TURNS AWAY AND STANDS PRETENDING TO READ A PAPER WHICH
PHIL II	SD(105)	DID YOU GET MY LETTER? /CHARTERIS/ BURNT IT--	JULIA	TURNS AWAY, STRUCK TO THE HEART, AND BURIES HER FACE
PHIL III	SD(136)	CRAVEN AND PARAMORE GO INTO THE CONSULTING ROOM.	JULIA	TURNS HER HEAD, AND STARES INSOLENTLY AT CHARTERIS.
PHIL III	(141)	THAT YOU HELPED ME TO WIN HER, CHARTERIS. (	JULIA	TURNS QUICKLY, A SPASM OF FURY IN HER FACE).
PHIL II	(97)	WHEN YOUVE FINISHED WITH THE INSTRUMENT MAN. IF	JULIA	TURNS UP I'LL ASK HER TOO. /PARAMORE/ (FLUSHING WITH
PHIL II	(123)	HIS FEET FROM THE LADDER AND SITS UP). WHEW! (	JULIA	WANDERS ALONG HIS SIDE OF THE ROOM, APPARENTLY LOOKING
PHIL II	(100)	WAIT A BIT, CRAVEN: YOURE CONCERNED IN THIS.	JULIA	WANTS TO MARRY ME TOO. /CRAVEN/ (IN A TONE OF THE
PHIL I	(93)	I TELL YOU, SERIOUSLY, I'M THE MATTER.	JULIA	WANTS TO MARRY ME! I WANT TO MARRY GRACE. I CAME HERE
PHIL II	(100)	TO HAVE TO SAY SUCH A THING; BUT YOU FORGET THAT	JULIA	WAS PRESENT, AND DIDNT CONTRADICT YOU. /CHARTERIS/ SHE
PHIL II	(107)	OF ATTENDING TO HIS PATIENTS? THAT LUNCH WITH	JULIA	WILL FINISH HIM. HE'LL ASK DADDY'S CONSENT BEFORE THEY
PHIL III	SD(147)	SHAKES HIS HEAD LAUGHINGLY. THE REST LOOK AT	JULIA	WITH CONCERN, AND EVEN A LITTLE AWE, FEELING FOR THE
PHIL III	(143)	DONT CRY. /PARAMORE/ (TO CHARTERIS, LOOKING AT	JULIA	WITH DELIGHT) HOW BEAUTIFUL SHE IS! /CHARTERIS/ (
PHIL II	(111)	PAPER, AND NOT ANSWERING WHEN HE'S SPOKEN TO? (	JULIA	WRITHES IMPATIENTLY). COME, COME: (TENDERLY): WONT MY
PHIL II	(101)	AS LAST NIGHT'S. YOU HAD MUCH BETTER GO BACK TO	JULIA	, AND FORGET ME. YOURS SINCERELY, GRACE TRANFIELD."
PHIL I	SD(76)	THE SOFA TOWARDS THE DOOR. CHARTERIS SEIZES	JULIA	, AND PREVENTS HER FROM GETTING PAST THE SOFA. GRACE
PHIL II	SD(111)	LIBRARY REMAINS UNOCCUPIED FOR TEN MINUTES. THEN	JULIA	, ANGRY AND MISERABLE, COMES IN FROM THE DINING ROOM,
PHIL II	(111)	WRONG WITH EVERYBODY. DO PULL YOURSELF TOGETHER,	JULIA	, BEFORE CUTHBERTSON COMES. HE'S ONLY PAYING THE BILL:
PHIL III	(141)	PERPLEXING. I CANT BELIEVE THAT YOU INSULTED	JULIA	, CHARTERIS. IVE NO DOUBT YOU ANNOYED HER: YOUD ANNOY
PHIL I	(77)	WOMAN. /CHARTERIS/ (JUMPING UP) NO, NO. HANG IT,	JULIA	, DONT LETS HAVE ANOTHER WRESTLING MATCH. REMEMBER:
PHIL I	(75)	BUT RETREATS QUIETLY TO THE PIANO.	JULIA	, FINDING CHARTERIS TOO STRONG FOR HER, GIVES UP HER
PHIL II	(105)	/JULIA/ DONT BE A FOOL, SILLY. /SYLVIA/ REMEMBER,	JULIA	, IF YOU PLEASE, THAT HERE WE ARE MEMBERS OF THE CLUB,
PHIL III	(134)	IT IS NOT MERELY YOUR BEAUTY THAT ATTRACTS ME (	JULIA	, INTERESTED, LOOKS UP AT HIM QUICKLY): I KNOW OTHER
PHIL I	(80)	BREAKING WITH YOU WHEN I PLEASE. ADVANCED VIEWS,	JULIA	, INVOLVE ADVANCED DUTIES: YOU CANNOT BE AN ADVANCED
PHIL III	(138)	IN THE HAPPINESS OF (KISSING HER HAND) MY DEAR	JULIA	, (KISSING THE OTHER) MY BEAUTIFUL JULIA. (SHE TEARS
PHIL I	(92)	(EMBARRASSED) IT IS I WHO HAVE TO APOLOGIZE FOR	JULIA	, JO. SHE-- /CHARTERIS/ (INTERRUPTING) SHE SAID SHE
PHIL I	(75)	AS SHE FREES HERSELF). /CHARTERIS/ (SHOCKED) OH,	JULIA	, JULIA! THIS IS TOO BAD. /JULIA/ IS IT, INDEED, TOO
PHIL III	SD(146)	KNOW HER. CHARTERIS STOPS AND LOOKS CAUTIOUSLY AT	JULIA	, MEASURING THE SITUATION. THEY REGARD ONE ANOTHER
PHIL I	(77)	OH, LEONARD! /CHARTERIS/ LET ME REMIND YOU,	JULIA	, THAT WHEN FIRST WE BECAME ACQUAINTED, THE POSITION
PHIL III	(144)	FACE AVERTED). THEY THINK THIS A HAPPY ENDING,	JULIA	, THESE MEN: OUR LORDS AND MASTERS! THE TWO STAND
PHIL III	(140)	GET USED TO THIS, PARAMORE. /CRAVEN/ NOW REALLY,	JULIA	, THIS IS A VERY EXTRAORDINARY WAY TO BEHAVE. IT'S NOT
PHIL III	(143)	THE FATHERS! /CRAVEN/ SILENCE, CHARTERIS. (TO	JULIA	, UNANSWERABLY) THE TEST OF A MAN'S OR WOMAN'S
PHIL II	(127)	ASIDE TO HIM, SIGNIFICANTLY) YOU UNDERSTAND? (	JULIA	, WATCHING THEM JEALOUSLY, LEAVES HER FATHER AND GETS
PHIL II	(126)	FOLLOWED BY CUTHBERTSON AND CRAVEN, WHO COME TO	JULIA	, WHILST SYLVIA CROSSES TO GRACE). /SYLVIA/ HERE I AM,
PHIL I	SD(76)	GOING) GET HER AWAY AS SOON AS YOU CAN, LEONARD.	JULIA	, WITH A STIFLED CRY OF RAGE, RUSHES AT GRACE, WHO IS
PHIL II	(123)	/CHARTERIS/ PROBABLY A DIAGRAM OF THE LIVER. (	JULIA	, WITH AN EXCLAMATION OF DISGUST, MAKES FOR THE
PHIL II	(124)	HE FOLLOWS PARAMORE IGNOMINIOUSLY). /GRACE/ (TO	JULIA	, WITH QUIET PEREMPTORINESS) NOW: WHAT HAVE YOU TO SAY
PHIL II	(107)	/CHARTERIS/ (STARTING UP EXCITEDLY) IN LOVE WITH	JULIA	! A RAY OF HOPE ON THE HORIZON! DO YOU REALLY MEAN

PHIL II (96)	SISTER. /CUTHBERTSON/ (HIS EYE LIGHTING UP) AH,	JULIA	! I BELIEVE YOU. A SPLENDID FINE CREATURE: EVERY INCH
PHIL III (137)	TO DR PARAMORE. /CHARTERIS/ (ENRAPTURED) MY OWN	JULIA	! (HE ATTEMPTS TO EMBRACE HER). /JULIA/ (RECOILING:
PHIL III (143)	THAT WOMAN AGAIN! /SYLVIA/ ANOTHER ROW! GO IT,	JULIA	! /CRAVEN/ HOLD YOUR TONGUE, SYLVIA. (HE TURNS
PHIL I (75)	MR CHARTERIS HERE? /CHARTERIS/ (SPRINGING UP)	JULIA	! THE DEVIL! (HE STANDS AT THE END OF THE SOFA WITH
PHIL I (75)	FREES HERSELF). /CHARTERIS/ (SHOCKED) OH, JULIA,	JULIA	! THIS IS TOO BAD. /JULIA/ IS IT, INDEED, TOO BAD?
PHIL III (140)	IS WHAT YOU REALLY THINK ME. /CHARTERIS/ COME,	JULIA	! YOU DONT EXPECT ME TO ADMIRE YOU FOR YOUR MORAL
PHIL III (140)	/CRAVEN/ (SHOUTING, UTTERLY SCANDALIZED)	JULIA	! ! JULIA RELEASES CHARTERIS, BUT STANDS HER GROUND

JULIAN

APPL (170)	CLIFFORD MARQUAND AS THE FOREIGN SECRETARY,	JULIAN	D'ALBIE AS THE COLONIAL SECRETARY, AUBREY MALLALIEU
SIM PREFACE(19)	TROUNCER, VIVIENNE BENNETT, ELSPETH DUXBURY,	JULIAN	D'ALBIE, STEPHEN MURRAY, DONALD ECCLES, NORRIS
JOAN 1 (62)	ARCHER, AND THEIR SERVANTS JOHN OF HONECOURT AND	JULIAN	. THERE WILL BE NO TROUBLE FOR YOU, SQUIRE: I HAVE

JULIA'S

PHIL II (99)	A HOME UNTIL SHE DIED. NOW EVERYTHING'S CHANGED.	JULIA'S	ALWAYS HERE. SYLVIA'S OF A DIFFERENT NATURE; BUT
PHIL I (89)	THAT DIDNT DO JO ANY HARM; BUT IT TOOK AWAY MY	JULIA'S	CHARACTER. /JULIA/ (OUTRAGED) DADDY! /CHARTERIS/
PHIL I (91)	(PACING UP AND DOWN) I'M EXCESSIVELY VEXED ABOUT	JULIA'S	CONDUCT: I AM INDEED. SHE CANT BEAR TO BE CROSSED IN
PHIL I (91)	JUST AT PRESENT WE'D REALLY BETTER FOLLOW	JULIA'S	EXAMPLE AND BOLT. (HE STARTS FOR THE DOOR).
PHIL II (115)	HAND). NO, DAN: YOUR DAUGHTER FIRST. (HE TAKES	JULIA'S	HAND GENTLY AND HANDS HER ACROSS TO CRAVEN, INTO
PHIL III (139)	MANHOOD TO ME. BLESSINGS FOR EVER AND EVER ON MY	JULIA'S	NAME! (WITH GENUINE EMOTION, HE TAKES HER HAND TO
PHIL III (135)	REMBRANDT PHOTOGRAPH, SO AS TO BE AS FAR OUT OF	JULIA'S	REACH AS POSSIBLE). /CRAVEN/ YES; AND CHARTERIS HAS
PHIL II (130)	WILL TELL YOU WHAT A TIME IVE HAD LATELY.	JULIA'S	REALLY A MOST DETERMINED WOMAN, YOU KNOW. /CRAVEN/ (
PHIL III (144)	/CUTHBERTSON/ NOW, GRACE. (HE CONDUCTS HER TO	JULIA'S	RIGHT; THEN POSTS HIMSELF ON THE HEARTHRUG, WITH HIS
PHIL I (92)	I MUST APOLOGIZE TO YOU AND MISS-- (HE TURNS TO	JULIA'S	SEAT, AND STOPS ON SEEING IT VACANT). /CRAVEN/ (
PHIL II (128)	NOT HAD A MOMENT TO HIMSELF ALL DAY. /CRAVEN/ BUT	JULIA'S	WITH HIM. /CHARTERIS/ WELL, NO MATTER: SHE'S ONLY

JULIET

CYMB FORWORD(133)	IN THE TOMB OF THE CAPULETS BETWEEN ROMEO AND	JULIET	BEFORE THE POISON TAKES EFFECT, AND HAD CULMINATED IN
OVER PREFACE(161)	OF SEX: ONE MIGHT AS WELL SAY THAT ROMEO AND	JULIET	IS A DRAMATIC STUDY OF PHARMACY BECAUSE THE
MRS PREFACE(166)	AND TAME. ROMEO AND JULIET WITH THE LOVELIEST	JULIET	IS DRY, TEDIOUS, AND RHETORICAL IN COMPARISON WITH
HART II (85)	WE? IT'S NO USE PRETENDING THAT WE ARE ROMEO AND	JULIET	. BUT WE CAN GET ON VERY WELL TOGETHER IF WE CHOOSE
NEVR III (263)	/DOLLY/ (SITTING DOWN ON HER RIGHT)-- AND	JULIET	. /PHILIP/ (TAKING HIS CUP OF TEA FROM MRS CLANDON)
LADY PREFACE(231)	THE POVERTY OF THE APOTHECARY IN ROMEO AND	JULIET	PRODUCES A GREAT EFFECT, AND EVEN POINTS THE SOUND
MRS PREFACE(166)	ALL THE VERBAL ARTS SEEM COLD AND TAME. ROMEO AND	JULIET	WITH THE LOVELIEST JULIET IS DRY, TEDIOUS, AND
3PLA PREFACE(R15)	WOMEN, DOES NOT SHOCK ME. I ADMIT THAT ROMEO AND	JULIET	WOULD BE A DULLER PLAY IF IT WERE ROBBED OF THE
OVER PREFACE(163)	AND ISOLDE, THE CURTAIN DOES NOT, AS IN ROMEO AND	JULIET	, RISE WITH THE LARK: THE WHOLE NIGHT OF LOVE IS

JULIET'S

3PLA PREFACE(R15)	FOR US OF THE CONVERSATION OF THE HUSBAND OF	JULIET'S	NURSE. NO: MY DISGUST WAS NOT MERE THINSKINNED

JULIETS

SUPR PREFACE(R11)	SERIOUSNESS TO OUR CHILDISH THEATRES. THERE THE	JULIETS	AND ISOLDES, THE ROMEOS AND TRISTANS, MIGHT BE OUR

JULIUS

MIS. (188)	ADVANCES TO THE WRITING TABLE). MY NAME'S BAKER:	JULIUS	BAKER. MISTER BAKER. IF ANY MAN DOUBTS IT, I'M READY
MILL PREFACE(116)	OF THESE COMMANDERS MADE HIMSELF SHAH OF IRAN.	JULIUS	CAESAR AND CROMWELL ALSO MOUNTED ON THE DEBRIS OF
BARB PREFACE(234)	OUT OF HIS COLLECTION OF SOCIAL NOBODIES;	JULIUS	CAESAR APPOINTING AS GOVERNOR OF EGYPT THE SON OF A
POSN PREFACE(386)	THE NOTION OF PROHIBITING THE PERFORMANCES OF	JULIUS	CAESAR AT HIS MAJESTY'S THEATRE IN LONDON LAST YEAR,
CLEO PRO2,SD(95)	TO BE PITIED JUST NOW IN VIEW OF THE FACT THAT	JULIUS	CAESAR IS INVADING HIS COUNTRY. NOT KNOWING THIS, IS
GENV PREFACE(21)	IN ITALY AND SPAIN; BUT, BEING NEITHER A	JULIUS	CAESAR NOR A MAHOMET, HE FAILED TO MAKE HIS INITIAL
POSN PREFACE(386)	OF PROGRESS. NOW IT HAPPENS THAT WE HAVE IN THE	JULIUS	CAESAR OF SHAKESPEAR A PLAY WHICH THE TSAR OF RUSSIA
CLEO IV (188)	SLAIN BY ORDER OF THE QUEEN OF EGYPT. I AM NOT	JULIUS	CAESAR THE DREAMER, WHO ALLOWS EVERY SLAVE TO INSULT
CLEO II (120)	FTATATEETA SHE HATH CAST A SPELL ON THE ROMAN	JULIUS	CAESAR TO MAKE HIM UPHOLD HER FALSE PRETENCE TO RULE
CLEO PRO1 (90)	COULD BECOME WHAT HE WOULD. AND POMPEY'S FRIEND	JULIUS	CAESAR WAS ON THE SIDE OF THE GODS; FOR HE SAW THAT
CLEO NOTES (209)	HUMAN FAUNA OF THESE ISLES? CERTAINLY I DO NOT.	JULIUS	CAESAR. AS TO CAESAR HIMSELF, I HAVE PURPOSELY
3PLA PREFACE(R32)	LITERARY GENTLEMEN; BUT IT WILL NOT GIVE YOU A	JULIUS	CAESAR. CAESAR WAS NOT IN SHAKESPEAR, NOR IN THE
SUPR HANDBOK(186)	BEAT OLIVER CROMWELL, FRANCE NAPOLEON, OR ROME	JULIUS	CAESAR. CROMWELL LEARNT BY BITTER EXPERIENCE THAT GOD
CLEO I (109)	US. THEY ARE BARBARIANS. THEIR CHIEF IS CALLED	JULIUS	CAESAR. HIS FATHER WAS A TIGER AND HIS MOTHER A
DEST SD(150)	LOST IN NOT BEING CONQUERED BY HIM AS WELL AS BY	JULIUS	CAESAR. HOWEVER, ON THIS MAY AFTERNOON IN 1796, IT IS
3PLA PREFACE(R37)	KNIGHT VERCINGETORIX AND HIS GREAT CONQUEROR	JULIUS	CAESAR. IN THIS COUNTRY, CARLYLE, WITH HIS VEIN OF
CLEO I (111)	NOT BITE ME, NOR PREVENT ME CARRYING YOU OFF TO	JULIUS	CAESAR. /CLEOPATRA/ (IN PLEADING MURMURINGS) YOU
APPL PREFACE(190)	IT CAN NO MORE DO THE WORK OF A MODERN STATE THAN	JULIUS	CAESAR'S GALLEY COULD DO THE WORK OF AN ATLANTIC
CLEO NOTES (212)	I HAVE ATTRIBUTED TO HIM. ALL MEN, MUCH MORE	JULIUS	CAESARS, POSSESS ALL QUALITIES IN SOME DEGREE. THE
3PLA PREFACE(R30)	OF MY TITLE IS LESS OBVIOUS, SINCE NEITHER	JULIUS	CAESAR, CLEOPATRA, NOR LADY CICELY WAYNFLETE HAVE ANY
MRS PREFACE(158)	AMONG THEM LEAR, HAMLET, MACBETH, CORIOLANUS,	JULIUS	CAESAR, HAVE NO SEX COMPLICATIONS: THE THREAD OF
3PLA PREFACE(R37)	SHAKESPEAR IN TURN CAME TO DEAL WITH HENRY V AND	JULIUS	CAESAR, HE DID SO ACCORDING TO HIS OWN ESSENTIALLY
CLEO II (129)	THE MASTERY OF THE WORLD, OF OUR MAKING? AM I	JULIUS	CAESAR, OR AM I A WOLF, THAT YOU FLING TO ME THE GREY
LADY PREFACE(230)	RESPECT AND HONOR AS NORMAL RANK AND FILE MEN. IN	JULIUS	CAESAR, SHAKESPEAR WENT TO WORK WITH A WILL WHEN HE
CLEO PRO2 (97)	TOLD YOU? /BELZANOR/ HE SAYS THAT THE ROMAN	JULIUS	CAESAR, WHO HAS LANDED ON OUR SHORES WITH A HANDFUL
CLEO I (106)	SHOULDER. /THE MAN/ HAIL, SPHINX: SALUTATION FROM	JULIUS	CAESAR! I HAVE WANDERED IN MANY LANDS, SEEKING THE
CLEO I (107)	" OLD GENTLEMAN: DONT RUN AWAY"! ! I THIS! TO	JULIUS	CAESAR! /THE GIRL/ (URGENTLY) OLD GENTLEMAN.
METH PREFACE(R82)	MICHAEL ANGELO COULD NOT VERY WELL BELIEVE IN	JULIUS	II OR LEO X, OR IN MUCH THAT THEY BELIEVED IN; BUT HE
MRS (150)	6TH JANUARY 1902, WITH MADGE MCINTOSH AS VIVIE,	JULIUS	KNIGHT AS PRAED, FANNY BROUGH AS MRS WARREN, CHARLES
MIS. (189)	EH? I SHOULD THINK SO. /MRS TARLETON/ COME NOW,	JULIUS	-- /GUNNER/ (REASSURING HER GRAVELY) DONT YOU BE
MILL I (156)	SO VERY EXPLICIT, MRS FITZFASSENDEN? /EPIFANIA/	JULIUS	SAGAMORE: YOU MAY BE MADE OF SAWDUST; BUT I AM MADE
MILL I (141)	ABOUT IT? /EPIFANIA/ YOU ARE AN UNMITIGATED HOG,	JULIUS	SAGAMORE. /SAGAMORE/ WHY WORRY ABOUT ME? THE
MILL I (140)	INTRODUCE ME. /EPIFANIA/ YOU ARE HARDLY TACTFUL,	JULIUS	SAGAMORE. /SAGAMORE/ THAT WILL NOT MATTER WHEN YOU
MILL I SD(137)	THE MILLIONAIRESS. ACT I. MR	JULIUS	SAGAMORE, A SMART YOUNG SOLICITOR, IS IN HIS OFFICE
MILL I (147)	TO THE GENTLEMAN, ALLY. /ALASTAIR/ OH, I FORGOT.	JULIUS	SAGAMORE, MY SOLICITOR. AN OLD PAL. MISS SMITH.
MILL I (137)	ROOM. HE RISES OBSEQUIOUSLY. /THE LADY/ ARE YOU	JULIUS	SAGAMORE, THE WORTHLESS NEPHEW OF MY LATE SOLICITOR

JULY

PPP PREFACE(192)	THE BENEFIT OF THE ACTORS' ORPHANAGE, ON THE 14TH	JULY	1905, BY MISS IRENE VANBRUGH, MISS NANCY PRICE, MR G.
POSN PREFACE(432)	WITHOUT MY ADDING TO IT. AYOT ST LAWRENCE, 14TH	JULY	1910. POSTSCRIPT.-- SINCE THE ABOVE WAS WRITTEN THE
TRFL (83)	IN THE WINDOW WITH THE REST. AYOT ST LAWRENCE,	JULY	1926.
6CAL PREFACE(91)	THEATRE, IN REGENT'S PARK, LONDON, ON THE 17TH	JULY	1934, WITH PHYLLIS NEILSON TERRY, CHARLES CARSON,
BUOY PREFACE(7)	I SWITCH OFF THE WIRELESS. AYOT SAINT LAWRENCE,	JULY	1947.
2TRU I (43)	PICTURE TO YOURSELF A HEAVENLY AFTERNOON IN	JULY	: A SCOTTISH LOCH SURROUNDED BY MIRRORED MOUNTAINS, AND
MRS I (193)	THE SAKE OF ECONOMY. THINGS CAME TO A CRISIS IN	JULY	: THE ROMAN FATHER HAD TO PAY MY DEBTS. HE'S STONY
SIM PREFACE(19)	THE SIMPLETON IN ENGLAND TOOK PLACE ON THE 29TH	JULY	AT THE MALVERN FESTIVAL OF 1935 WHEN THE PARTS (IN
PHIL III (142)	TODAY WHERE CUTHBERTSON AND I STOOD ON A CERTAIN	JULY	EVENING THIRTY-FIVE YEARS AGO. HOW ARE YOU GOING TO
MRS II (202)	HAD HIS PATRIMONY; AND HE SPENT THE LAST OF IT IN	JULY	. (MRS WARREN'S FACE FALLS). /CROFTS/ (WATCHING HER)
PLES PREFACE(R7)	AND IT RAN FROM THE 21ST OF APRIL TO THE 7TH OF	JULY	. TO WITNESS IT THE PUBLIC PAID 1777 POUNDS 5 SHILLINGS
METH PREFACE(R32)	LET ME REPEAT THE STORY TOLD BY WEISMANN OF THE	JULY	REVOLUTION IN PARIS IN 1830, WHEN THE FRENCH GOT RID OF
MRS I (195)	HER. DO YOU REMEMBER THE ADVICE YOU GAVE ME LAST	JULY	, GOV'NOR? /REV. S./ (SEVERELY) YES. I ADVISED YOU TO

JUMBLE

GETT PREFACE(202)	OWN HABITS AND PREJUDICES, IT WOULD BE AT BEST A	JUMBLE	OF SUPERSTITIONS AND INTERESTS, TABOOS AND

JUMBLED

LION PREFACE(96)	THAN THREE DIFFERENT ACCOUNTS OF THE CREATION	JUMBLED	TOGETHER IN THE BOOK OF GENESIS. NOW THE MADDEST

JUMBO

GLIM (187)	PRETTY STORIES, AND SHELTERED MYSELF BEHIND MUMBO	JUMBO	, AS A SOLDIER WILL SHELTER HIMSELF FROM ARROWS BEHIND

JUMP

CLEO III (165)	ME. WHAT ELSE IS THERE TO DO? AND MIND WHERE YOU	JUMP	: I DO NOT WANT TO GET YOUR FOURTEEN STONE IN THE SMALL

BULL II	(97)	IT'S NO USE, ME POOR LITTLE FRIEND. IF YOU COULD	JUMP	AS FAR AS A KANGAROO YOU COULDNT JUMP AWAY FROM YOUR
ROCK II	(242)	IS GOOD BUSINESS FOR THEM: THEYLL JUST	JUMP	AT IT, /SIR DEXTER/ IN SHORT, YOU WILL MAKE UTOPIAN
GENV I	(31)	PERHAPS A LITTLE TALKED ABOUT? /SHE/ I'LL JUST	JUMP	AT IT-- IF IT IS ALL RIGHT. /HE/ HOW ALL RIGHT? /SHE/
BULL II	(97)	YOU COULD JUMP AS FAR AS A KANGAROO YOU COULDNT	JUMP	AWAY FROM YOUR OWN HEART AN ITS PUNISHMENT. YOU CAN
METH PREFACE	(R76)	INTO THE FIRE; AND WE ARE JUST AS LIKELY TO	JUMP	BACK AGAIN, NOW THAT WE FEEL HOTTER THAN EVER. HISTORY
ARMS II	(40)	/CATHERINE/ (WITH A BOUND THAT MAKES LOUKA	JUMP	BACK) SWISS! WHAT IS HE LIKE? /LOUKA/ (TIMIDLY) HE
GENV IV	(124)	CHANGE THEY DONT CHANGE GRADUALLY. THEY SUDDENLY	JUMP	BY DISTANCES CALLED QUANTUMS OR QUANTA. NOBODY KNOWS
JOAN 6	(133)	ME QUESTIONS ABOUT IT. /D'ESTIVET/ WHY DID YOU	JUMP	FROM THE TOWER? /JOAN/ HOW DO YOU KNOW THAT I JUMPED?
BULL IV	(146)	REILLY, LARRY CLEARED SIX YARDS SIDEWAYS AT WAN	JUMP	IF HE CLEARED AN INCH; AND HE'D A CLEARED SEVEN IF
JOAN 5	(120)	IS MY JUDGE, IF SHE FELL INTO THE LOIRE I WOULD	JUMP	IN IN FULL ARMOR TO FISH HER OUT. BUT IF SHE PLAYS THE
SUPR IV	(145)	HEADACHE AND HAVE THE GARDEN ALL TO MYSELF.	JUMP	INTO JACK'S MOTOR: STRAKER WILL RATTLE YOU HERE IN A
GLIM	(181)	DOOR TO FETCH HER MANDOLINE. /FERRUCCIO/ I SHALL	JUMP	INTO THE LAKE, SQUARCIO, IF YOUR CAT BEGINS TO MIAOWL.
KING I	(190)	YOUR HEAD OFF INSIDE OF FIVE YEARS UNLESS YOU	JUMP	INTO THE NEAREST FISHING SMACK AND LAND IN FRANCE.
LADY	(240)	HER GRAVE. I FEAR HER NOT: THESE CATS THAT DARE	JUMP	INTO THRONES THOUGH THEY BE FIT ONLY FOR MEN'S LAPS
MTH2	(81)	TO JUMP; BUT WHEN SHE MAKES IT UP AT LAST, THE	JUMP	IS BIG ENOUGH TO TAKE US INTO A NEW AGE. /LUBIN/ (
SUPR IV	(169)	EDGE OF A PRECIPICE, I WOULD HOLD YOU TIGHT AND	JUMP	. /ANN/ (PANTING, FAILING MORE AND MORE UNDER THE
DOCT PREFACE	(43)	RABBIT'S HEART AND LET THE STUDENT SEE THE FLAGS	JUMP	. THE OTHER, AN ELEGANT, INGENIOUS, WELL-INFORMED, AND
DEVL I	(18)	HAT TO CHRISTY WITH A SUDDENNESS THAT MAKES HIM	JUMP	LIKE A NEGLIGENT WICKET KEEPER, AND COMES INTO THE
DOCT III	(155)	AND DIE. I COULD SHOW YOU THE VERY CLIFF I SHOULD	JUMP	OFF. YOU MUST CURE HIM; YOU MUST MAKE HIM QUITE WELL
CAPT III	(291)	TALL HAT. (HE PUTS THE HAT DOWN AND PREPARES TO	JUMP	ON IT. THE EFFECT IS STARTLING, AND TAKES HIM
CAPT III	(291)	FEEL LIKE A MAN AGAIN. STAND BY, ALL HANDS, TO	JUMP	ON THE CAPTAIN'S TALL HAT. (HE PUTS THE HAT DOWN AND
2TRU I	(47)	BED BESIDE THE PATIENT). /THE NURSE/ IF YOU COULD	JUMP	OUT OF BED TO KNOCK OUT POPSY AND ME YOU CAN JUMP OUT
2TRU I	(47)	JUMP OUT OF BED TO KNOCK OUT POPSY AND ME YOU CAN	JUMP	OUT TO DRESS YOURSELF AND HOP IT FROM HERE. WRAP
JOAN PREFACE	(24)	GLAMOR ON THE FIGURE OF THE MAID. WHEN WE	JUMP	OVER TWO CENTURIES TO SCHILLER, WE FIND DIE JUNGFRAU
MTH5	(226)	YOU ARE WILLING TO CLASP ME ROUND THE WAIST AND	JUMP	OVERBOARD WITH ME. /ACIS/ OH, STOP SQUABBLING. THAT IS
MTH2	(81)	SPEND TWENTY THOUSAND YEARS MAKING UP HER MIND TO	JUMP	; BUT WHEN SHE MAKES IT UP AT LAST, THE JUMP IS BIG
BULL PREFACE	(21)	THING. IN THIS HE IS RIGHT. BUT HE OVERDOES HIS	JUMP	SO FAR AS TO CONCLUDE ALSO THAT STUPIDITY AND
FANY I	(275)	COME TO THAT WITH HIM, HAS IT? /MRS GILBEY/ DONT	JUMP	TO CONCLUSIONS, ROB. HOW DO YOU KNOW? (TO JUGGINS) IS
METH PREFACE	(R49)	THAT IF YOU PUT IT DOWN A HUNDRED TIMES IT WILL	JUMP	UP A HUNDRED AND ONE TIMES; SO THAT IF YOU DESIRE ITS
APPL PREFACE	(189)	ARE ASKED; AND WHEN HE IS COMPLETELY FLOORED THEY	JUMP	UP AND CRY " LET ME ANSWER THAT, MR CHAIRMAN! " AND
BARB I	(258)	EVENING. (STEPHEN BOUNDS FROM HIS SEAT) DONT	JUMP	, STEPHEN: IT FIDGETS ME. /STEPHEN/ (IN UTTER
HART II	(94)	OF HOW TO SAVE SIXPENCE. WONT ELLIE MAKE HIM	JUMP	, THOUGH, WHEN SHE TAKES HIS HOUSE IN HAND! /MRS

JUMPED

JOAN 6	(133)	FROM THE TOWER? /JOAN/ HOW DO YOU KNOW THAT I	JUMPED	? /D'ESTIVET/ YOU WERE FOUND LYING IN THE MOAT. WHY
METH PREFACE	(R44)	WHICH HE WOULD PROBABLY RESENT, THAT WE JUST	JUMPED	AT DARWIN. WHEN NAPOLEON WAS ASKED WHAT WOULD HAPPEN
ROCK II	(273)	WAY. /SIR ARTHUR/ DID HE OBJECT? HE SHOULD HAVE	JUMPED	AT IT. /ALOYSIA/ IT'S VERY NICE OF YOU TO SAY SO IF
MTH4 I	(155)	TO PREVENT THEM AND NOBODY TO FORBID THEM. THEY	JUMPED	AT THE SUGGESTION. THEY LANDED HERE: HERE IN GALWAY
BULL IV	(147)	JUMPIN FROM THE BACK SEAT INTO THE FRONT WAN, HE	JUMPED	FROM THE FRONT WAN INTO THE ROAD IN FRONT OF THE CAR.
ARMS III	(58)	HIS ATTITUDE) YES: I AM A BRAVE MAN. MY HEART	JUMPED	LIKE A WOMAN'S AT THE FIRST SHOT; BUT IN THE CHARGE I
DEST	(187)	/GIUSEPPE/ (WITH EAGER ADMIRATION) THEY SAY YOU	JUMPED	OFF YOUR HORSE AND WORKED THE BIG GUNS WITH YOUR OWN
METH PREFACE	(R80)	GRAVITY CONSISTS IN THE BELIEF THAT ARCHIMEDES	JUMPED	OUT OF HIS BATH AND RAN NAKED THROUGH THE STREETS OF
CLEO I	(108)	WAY FROM THE CITY A BLACK CAT CALLED HIM, AND HE	JUMPED	OUT OF MY ARMS AND RAN AWAY TO IT. DO YOU THINK THAT
METH PREFACE	(R76)	RUN BACK IN TERROR TO OUR OLD SUPERSTITIONS. WE	JUMPED	OUT OF THE FRYING-PAN INTO THE FIRE; AND WE ARE JUST
METH PREFACE	(R21)	NOT BE POSSIBLE. THEN CAME THE GREAT POET WHO	JUMPED	OVER THE FACTS TO THE CONCLUSION. GOETHE SAID THAT
MILL I	(158)	THAT I HAD ONLY A HUNDRED POUNDS IN THE WORLD. HE	JUMPED	UP AND SAID " WHY, MAN ALIVE, IF YOU HAVE A HUNDRED
POSN PREFACE	(377)	CLUE AS TO THE TEMPER OF THE MAJORITY; WHEN I HAD	JUMPED	UP WITH THE PROPER AIR OF RELIEF AND GRATITUDE; WHEN

JUMPED-UP

BARB II	(276)	CHEERFULLY) NO GOOD JAWRIN ABOUT IT. YOURE ONY A	JUMPED-UP	, JERKED-OFF, ORSPITTLE-TURNED-OUT INCURABLE OF AN
POSN	(463)	IN TO BE BAD MEN OR YOU WOULDNT BE IN THIS	JUMPED-UP	, JERKED-OFF, HOSPITAL-TURNED-OUT CAMP THAT CALLS

JUMPIN

BULL IV	(147)	WI DHAT AMBITIOUS BASTE; FOR NOT CONTENT WID	JUMPIN	FROM THE BACK SEAT INTO THE FRONT WAN, HE JUMPED FROM
BULL II	(98)	TO BRING THAT CURSE ON YOU? HERE! WHERE ARE YOU	JUMPIN	TO? WHERES YOUR MANNERS TO GO SKYROCKETIN LIKE THAT

JUMPING

NEVR I	(224)	YOUNG MAN. DONT YOU GAMMON ME. /VALENTINE/ (	JUMPING	AT THE BET AND SENDING HIM ALOFT VIGOROUSLY) DONE!
MTH5	(224)	SECRET, AND HID THEM FROM YOU ALL. /ARJILLAX/ (	JUMPING	DOWN FROM THE ALTAR BEHIND MARTELLUS IN HIS SURPRISE
SUPR IV	(153)	YOUR OWN HOME: I'LL SEE YOU THROUGH. /OCTAVIUS/ (	JUMPING	DOWN FROM THE GARDEN TO THE LAWN AND RUNNING TO
NEVR IV	(294)	TO HER AND TAKING HER HANDS) MY CHILD! /DOLLY/ (	JUMPING	DOWN, WITH HIS HELP) THANKS: SO NICE OF YOU. (PHIL
JOAN 6	(133)	WERE LEFT UNCHAINED, DID YOU NOT TRY TO ESCAPE BY	JUMPING	FROM A TOWER SIXTY FEET HIGH? IF YOU CANNOT FLY
JOAN PREFACE	(21)	SHE ATTEMPTED TO ESCAPE FROM BEAUREVOIR CASTLE BY	JUMPING	FROM A TOWER SAID TO BE SIXTY FEET HIGH, SHE TOOK A
MILL I	(140)	THAT YOU CAN DIE WITHOUT WASTING A LOT OF GAS OR	JUMPING	INTO THE SERPENTINE. SIX AND EIGHTPENCE I SHALL
DEVL III	(65)	/CHRISTY/ DICK. /RICHARD/ ANSWER PROPERLY, YOU	JUMPING	JACKASS. WHAT DO THEY KNOW ABOUT DICK? /CHRISTY/
METH PREFACE	(R59)	EXPRESSLY FOR THE FOOD OF FLEAS, DESTROYS THE	JUMPING	LORD OF CREATION WITH HIS SHARP AND ENORMOUS
MRS II	(214)	WAS ALWAYS WARNING ME THAT LIZZIE'D END BY	JUMPING	OFF WATERLOO BRIDGE. POOR FOOL: THAT WAS ALL HE KNEW
KING I	(196)	THAT THE POOR LAD RISKED BREAKING HIS BONES BY	JUMPING	OUT OF BARBARA'S WINDOW WHEN SHE WAS SEDUCING HIM
GENV IV	(124)	OR QUANTA. NOBODY KNOWS WHY. IF THE EARTH IS	JUMPING	TO A WIDER ORBIT IT IS TAKING US MILLIONS OF MILES
GENV IV	(123)	ASTRONOMERS REPORT THAT THE ORBIT OF THE EARTH IS	JUMPING	TO ITS NEXT QUANTUM. MESSAGE RECEIVED AT GREENWICH
GENV IV	(124)	KNOW THAT. BUT THE MESSAGE SAYS THAT THE ORBIT IS	JUMPING	TO ITS NEXT QUANTUM. WHAT DOES QUANTUM MEAN?
DOCT I	(96)	TO TELL THAT LADY-- (EMMY VANISHES). /WALPOLE/ (	JUMPING	UP AGAIN) OH, BY THE WAY, RIDGEON, THAT REMINDS ME.
CAPT III	(282)	BRITISH LADY, SIR. SHALL I ASK HER-- /KEARNEY/ (	JUMPING	UP AND EXPLODING IN STORM PIERCING TONES) BRING IN
DOCT I	(83)	AND IS DOWN ON IT IMMEDIATELY. /REDPENNY/ (	JUMPING	UP AND FOLLOWING HER) WHAT? /EMMY/ HE'S BEEN MADE A
CATH 1	(171)	TO WISH YOUR HIGHNESS GOOD MORNING. /PATIOMKIN/ (	JUMPING	UP AND STOPPING HIM ON HIS WAY TO THE DOOR) TUT
PYGM V	(284)	I NOTICE THAT YOU DONT NOTICE ME. /HIGGINS/ (	JUMPING	UP AND WALKING ABOUT INTOLERANTLY) ELIZA: YOURE AN
PRES	(143)	IS GOING TO SHOOT, NOT TO BE SHOT. /BALSQUITH/ (	JUMPING	UP AND WALKING ABOUT SULKILY) OH COME! I LIKE TO
LIED	(195)	ALL QUITE SIMPLE. /HE/ IT SEEMS SO TO ME. /SHE/ (	JUMPING	UP DISTRACTEDLY) IF YOU SAY THAT AGAIN I SHALL DO
2TRU II	(60)	REWARD FOR INFORMATION. /THE COUNTESS/ (	JUMPING	UP EXCITEDLY) WOTJESOY? A REWARD ON TOP OF THE
ARMS III	(62)	RECEIVED FAVORS I NEVER ENJOYED. /BLUNTSCHLI/ (	JUMPING	UP INDIGNANTLY) STUFF! RUBBISH! I HAVE RECEIVED NO
HART II	(113)	A CORNER AND HAVE DONE WITH ME. /MRS HUSHABYE/ (	JUMPING	UP MISCHIEVOUSLY, AND GOING TO HIM) WOULD YOU LIKE A
PHIL II	(106)	MORE NEURASTHENIA! (HE FOLLOWS HER). /SYLVIA/ (	JUMPING	UP ON HER KNEES ON THE SETTEE, AND SPEAKING OVER THE
POSN	(462)	(SUDDENLY RUSHING FROM THE BAR TO THE TABLE AND	JUMPING	UP ON IT) BOYS, I'M GOING TO PREACH YOU A SERMON ON
PRES	(139)	(THROWING DOWN HIS PEN AND HIS LETTERS AND	JUMPING	UP TO CONFRONT BALSQUITH) HIS DUTY WAS PERFECTLY
CATH 2	(181)	EXCEPT NARYSHKIN. /EDSTASTON/ OUF! /PATIOMKIN/ (	JUMPING	UP VIGOROUSLY) YOU HAVE DONE IT, DARLING. SUPERBLY!
MILL I	(148)	REALLY WAS YOU CAN SEE FOR YOURSELF. /ALASTAIR/ (	JUMPING	UP WITH HIS FISTS CLENCHED AND HIS FACE RED) I AM
DEVL III	(66)	AND I MAY KEEP THE CHINA PEACOCKS? /RICHARD/ (	JUMPING	UP) GET OUT. GET OUT, YOU BLITHERING BABOON, YOU. (
MRS III	(234)	GOODBYE. (SHE MAKES FOR THE GATE). /FRANK/ (	JUMPING	UP) HALLO! STOP! VIV! VIV! (SHE TURNS IN THE
NEVR III	(270)	AT THE FURTHER END OF THE TABLE). /VALENTINE/ (	JUMPING	UP) LOOK HERE-- /MRS CLANDON/ (SEVERELY) MR VA--
JITT II	(48)	LIFE. (SHE RISES). /LENKHEIM/ (OUT OF PATIENCE,	JUMPING	UP) LOOK HERE: SINCE YOU WONT TALK SENSE AND BE
MTH3	(116)	I MISS THE NOTE OF CONVICTION. /BURGE-LUBIN/ (	JUMPING	UP) LOOK HERE. LET US STOP TALKING DAMNED NONSENSE.
PYGM V	(273)	NOW, OUT OF THREE THOUSAND A YEAR. /HIGGINS/ (	JUMPING	UP) NONSENSE! HE CANT PROVIDE FOR HER. HE SHANT
PHIL I	(77)	I AM GOING TO SPEAK TO THAT WOMAN. /CHARTERIS/ (	JUMPING	UP) NO, NO. HANG IT, JULIA, DONT LETS HAVE ANOTHER
DEST	(190)	IN THE VINEYARD TEN MINUTES AGO. /LADY/ OH! (	JUMPING	UP) OH, GENERAL: IVE NOT BEATEN YOU AFTER ALL. I DO
BULL I	(95)	A GREAT CHANGE AFTER THE NEXT ELECTION. /DOYLE/ (	JUMPING	UP) OH, GET OUT, YOU IDIOT! /BROADBENT/ (RISING
FANY III	(298)	HER, SIR, OR TAKE THE CONSEQUENCES. /BOBBY/ (	JUMPING	UP) WELL, I WONT MARRY HER: THATS FLAT. WHAT WOULD
GETT	(278)	THAT MUSHROOM-FACED SERPENT--! /THE GENERAL/ (	JUMPING	UP) WHAT RIGHT HAD HE TO BE MADE ROOM FOR? ARE YOU
ARMS III	(49)	A PAPER) THATS THE LAST ORDER. /PETKOFF/ (	JUMPING	UP) WHAT! FINISHED? /BLUNTSCHLI/ FINISHED.
WIDO III	(62)	EVEN THAN THOSE OF FRIENDSHIP. /LICKCHEESE/ (	JUMPING	UP, RELIEVED) THERE! NOW THE MURDER'S OUT. EXCUSE
FANY III	(302)	GROSSLY. I ONLY LAUGHED AT HIM. /MARGARET/ (	JUMPING	UP, TRIUMPHANT) IVE BEATEN YOU HOLLOW. I KNOCKED OUT
GETT	(272)	OR IN YOUR CIVIC ROBES IS NOT A GENTLEMAN, BUT A	JUMPING	, BOUNDING, SNORTING CAD? /COLLINS/ WELL, STRICTLY
GETT	(291)	SIR, THOSE CLUBS CONSIST OF SNOBS; AND YOU ARE A	JUMPING	, BOUNDING, PRANCING, SNORTING SNOB YOURSELF. /THE

JUMPING-OFF

APPL I	(234)	WOOLSACK EVEN TO THE STOOL OF AN OFFICE BOY AS A	JUMPING-OFF	PLACE FOR HIS AMBITION. OUR WORK IS NO LONGER

JUMPS

LADY PREFACE(224)	HER, THOUGH HE IS SORRY HE FORGOT HIMSELF, AND	JUMPS	AT THE PROPOSAL OF A FENCING MATCH TO FINISH THE DAY
JOAN 2,SD(81)	A GESTURE OF SURRENDER, JOINS IN THE LAUGH, AND	JUMPS	DOWN FROM THE DAIS BESIDE LA TREMOUILLE. JOAN, ALSO ON
POSN (466)	ADJOURN TO THE SALOON. I STAND THE DRINKS. (HE	JUMPS	DOWN FROM THE TABLE). /THE BOYS/ RIGHT YOU ARE,
PHIL I (91)	THEYRE UNDER SOME SORT OF DECENT RESTRAINT? (HE	JUMPS	DOWN FROM THE PIANO, AND GOES TO THE WINDOW).
DEVL III (76)	I AM HUMANE ENOUGH TO BE GLAD OF IT. (RICHARD	JUMPS	DOWN FROM THE CART, BRUDENELL OFFERING HIS HAND TO
CLEO I (114)	SHE TURNS AND LOOKS AT HIM EXULTANTLY. THEN SHE	JUMPS	DOWN FROM THE STEPS, RUNS TO HIM, AND FLINGS HER ARMS
BARB III (331)	THE FOUNDLING DIFFICULTY CAN BE GOT OVER. (HE	JUMPS	DOWN TO THE EMPLACEMENT). /UNDERSHAFT/ (COMING BACK
GENV PREFACE(26)	YEARS TO ACQUIRE. THE OLD AXIOM THAT NATURE NEVER	JUMPS	HAS GIVEN WAY TO A DOUBT WHETHER NATURE IS NOT AN
JOAN EPILOG (155)	WHO IS THAT? HELP! MURDER! (THUNDER. HE	JUMPS	INTO BED, AND HIDES UNDER THE CLOTHES). /JOAN'S VOICE/
MTH2 (81)	THE NOTION THAT NATURE DOES NOT PROCEED BY	JUMPS	IS ONLY ONE OF THE BUDGET OF PLAUSIBLE LIES THAT WE
MTH2 (81)	CLASSICAL EDUCATION. NATURE ALWAYS PROCEEDS BY	JUMPS	. SHE MAY SPEND TWENTY THOUSAND YEARS MAKING UP HER
CLEO I (114)	AND VANISHES. SHE THROWS THE SNAKE-SKIN AWAY AND	JUMPS	ON THE STEP OF THE THRONE WITH HER ARMS WAVING,
BULL PREFACE(21)	THE PATRIOTIC, RELIGIOUS, AND REVOLUTIONARY WARS,	JUMPS	TO THE CONCLUSION THAT WILFULNESS IS THE MAIN THING.
METH PREFACE(R49)	DINNER TABLE, AND YOU PUT IT DOWN, IT INSTANTLY	JUMPS	UP AGAIN, AND FINALLY ESTABLISHES ITS RIGHT TO A PLACE
2TRU III SD(109)	ARE SEATED RISE IN ALARM, EXCEPT THE PATIENT, WHO	JUMPS	UP AND CLAPS HER HANDS IN MISCHIEVOUS ENCOURAGEMENT TO
MTH2 (87)	THE STREETS IN MY BEST CLOTHES; AND-- HSH! (SHE	JUMPS	UP AND PRETENDS TO BE LOOKING FOR A BOOK ON THE
JITT II (32)	BED. /LENKHEIM/ WHO'S NAGGING? (SHE RISES. HE	JUMPS	UP APPREHENSIVELY). THERE NOW: FOR GOD'S SAKE DONT
BARB I (266)	CONCERTINA AND PLAY SOMETHING FOR US. /LOMAX/ (	JUMPS	UP EAGERLY, BUT CHECKS HIMSELF TO REMARK DOUBTFULLY TO
METH PREFACE(R49)	ESCAPED SO CURIOUS AN OBSERVER THAT WHEN THE CAT	JUMPS	UP ON THE DINNER TABLE, AND YOU PUT IT DOWN, IT
ARMS I SD(13)	DOWN. UNFORTUNATELY SHE SITS ON THE PISTOL, AND	JUMPS	UP WITH A SHRIEK. THE MAN, ALL NERVES, SHIES LIKE A
O'FL SD(216)	SIR, FOR GOD'S SAKE: HERE SHE IS. THE GENERAL	JUMPS	UP. MRS O'FLAHERTY ARRIVES, AND COMES BETWEEN THE TWO
GENV I SD(29)	DOOR. SHE HASTILY TAKES HER HEELS OFF THE TABLE;	JUMPS	UP; THROWS HER CIGARETTE INTO THE STOVE; SNATCHES THE
LIED (190)	YOU DONT SEEM TO THINK A BIT ABOUT TEDDY. (SHE	JUMPS	UP, MORE AND MORE AGITATED). /HE/ (SUPINE ON THE
LION PREFACE(101)	THE WILL OF THE PEOPLE, AND MOVES ONLY AS THE CAT	JUMPS	, IS CLEARLY A POLITICAL AND INTELLECTUAL BRIGAND. THE

JUMPY

MIS. (153)	BAD THING TO AEROPLANE ON, I SHOULD IMAGINE. TOO	JUMPY	. BEEN UP MUCH? /LINA/ NOT IN AN AEROPLANE. IVE

JUNCTION

DEVL EPILOG (81)	WILLIAM HOWE, WHO WAS IN NEW YORK, TO EFFECT A	JUNCTION	AT ALBANY WITH BURGOYNE, WHO HAD MARCHED FROM
DEVL III (69)	HAS MARCHED NORTH FROM NEW YORK TO DO: EFFECT A	JUNCTION	AT ALBANY AND WIPE OUT THE REBEL ARMY WITH OUR

JUNE

JOAN EPIL,SD(152)	EPILOGUE. A RESTLESS FITFULLY WINDY NIGHT IN	JUNE	1456, FULL OF SUMMER LIGHTNING AFTER MANY DAYS OF HEAT.
DOCT I SD(81)	ACT I. ON THE 15TH	JUNE	1903, IN THE EARLY FORENOON, A MEDICAL STUDENT, SURNAME
BULL PREFACE(50)	AND TELL THE STORY OF THE DENSHAWAI AFFAIR OF	JUNE	1906 BY WAY OF OBJECT-LESSON. THE DENSHAWAI HORROR.
BARB PREFACE(247)	SUCH BY ME, THE AUTHOR, TO ALL POSTERITY. LONDON,	JUNE	1906.
LADY (251)	GATE NEAREST BLACKFRIARS. AYOT ST LAWRENCE, 20TH	JUNE	1910.
HART PREFACE(41)	EVEN THEN MIGHT NOT HAVE WAITED FOR THEIR CUES.	JUNE	1919.
CAND I (92)	HE FOUND HIM SLEEPING ON THE EMBANKMENT LAST	JUNE	. HAVNT YOU NOTICED OUR NEW PICTURE (POINTING TO THE
BARB I (250)	BRITOMART/ YES, YOU, OF COURSE. YOU WERE 24 LAST	JUNE	. YOUVE BEEN AT HARROW AND CAMBRIDGE. YOUVE BEEN TO
BULL PREFACE(51)	THE FEELINGS OF DENSHAWAI WHEN ON THE 13TH OF	JUNE	LAST THERE DROVE TO THE VILLAGE FOUR KHAKI-CLAD BRITISH

JUNGFRAU

JOAN PREFACE(24)	JUMP OVER TWO CENTURIES TO SCHILLER, WE FIND DIE	JUNGFRAU	VON ORLEANS DROWNED IN A WITCH'S CALDRON OF RAGING

JUNGLE

LION PROLOG (108)	WHAT A WIFE YOUVE LOST. (SHE DASHES INTO THE	JUNGLE	AND NEARLY FALLS OVER THE SLEEPING LION). OH! OH!
METH PREFACE(R21)	IN REGENT'S PARK, CONCEAL IT IN A TROPICAL	JUNGLE	. FINALLY HE WROTE, AS HIS DECLARATION OF FAITH, "
LION PROL,SD(105)	ROAR, A MELANCHOLY SUFFERING ROAR, COMES FROM THE	JUNGLE	. IT IS REPEATED NEARER. THE LION LIMPS FROM THE
LION PROLOG (107)	YOUR OWN WIFE, YOU CAN LIVE WITH THEM HERE IN THE	JUNGLE	. IVE HAD ENOUGH OF THEM AND ENOUGH OF YOU. I'M GOING
LION PROL,SD(108)	THE LION IS HEARD GROANING HEAVILY IN THE	JUNGLE	. /ANDROCLES/ (WHISPERING) DID YOU SEE? A LION.
LION PROL,SD(105)	IT IS REPEATED NEARER. THE LION LIMPS FROM THE	JUNGLE	ON THREE LEGS, HOLDING UP HIS RIGHT FOREPAW, IN WHICH
LION PROL,SD(105)	ROARING OF LIONS, CHRISTIAN HYMN FAINTLY. A	JUNGLE	PATH. A LION'S ROAR, A MELANCHOLY SUFFERING ROAR,
LION PROLOG (109)	COWARD! (SHE RUSHES OFF AFTER THEM INTO THE	JUNGLE	).
LION PROLOG (109)	ROUND AND ROUND AND FINALLY AWAY THROUGH THE	JUNGLE	). /MEGAERA/ (WHO HAS REVIVED DURING THE WALTZ) OH,
SUPR HANDBOK(191)	THE PROBLEM AS AN ELEPHANT BREAKS THROUGH A	JUNGLE	; AND THE POLITICIANS MAKE SPEECHES ABOUT WHATEVER

JUNIOR

BULL PREFACE(52)	AND THE SENIOR OFFICER ACTUALLY COLLARED THE	JUNIOR	AND PRETENDED TO ARREST HIM FOR THE MURDER OF THE
PHIL I (87)	OWN CLUB. /CHARTERIS/ (CONTEMPTUOUSLY) YES: THE	JUNIOR	ARMY AND NAVY! DO YOU CALL THAT A CLUB? WHY, THEY
MTH2 (68)	OF YOUR SEVENTIETH YEAR. MR JOYCE BURGE IS YOUR	JUNIOR	BY ABOUT ELEVEN YEARS. YOU WILL GO DOWN TO POSTERITY
BARB III (334)	TO A UNIVERSITY DON WHO IS OBVIOUSLY NOT WORTH A	JUNIOR	CLERK'S WAGES! -- WELL! WHAT WILL LAZARUS SAY?
PYGM EPILOG (300)	BOOKKEEPING AND TYPEWRITING WITH INCIPIENT	JUNIOR	CLERKS, MALE AND FEMALE, FROM THE ELEMENTARY SCHOOLS,
KING I (220)	HIS ARM) THE DUKE OF YORK WILL FOLLOW WITH THE	JUNIOR	DUCHESS. HAPPY MAN! ALL RISE, EXCEPT FOX. /BARBARA/
SUPR III (95)	IN MY 64TH YEAR, AND AM CONSIDERABLY YOUR	JUNIOR	IN CONSEQUENCE. BESIDES, MY CHILD, IN THIS PLACE,
FABL III SD(109)	A COMELY MATRON IN A PURPLE ACADEMIC GOWN, AND A	JUNIOR	IN SHORT-SKIRTED OVERALL AND BLUE SLACKS. A TOURIST
DEVL I SD(16)	ANXIOUS WIFE THE WIFE, OF A PROSPEROUS MAN. THE	JUNIOR	UNCLE, TITUS DUDGEON, IS A WIRY LITTLE TERRIER OF A

JUNIORS

BUOY III SD(29)	ON OPPOSITE SIDES FROM THEIR WIVES. THE TWO	JUNIORS	ALSO PLANT THEMSELVES ON OPPOSITE SIDES WELL TO THE
NEVR I SD(208)	CONSTANT DANGER OF RIDICULE FROM HER IRREVERENT	JUNIORS	. UNLIKE HER MOTHER, SHE IS ALL PASSION; AND THE
BULL PREFACE(52)	ARRANGEMENT BEING THAT THE ENGLISHMEN, BEING THE	JUNIORS	, SHOULD RUN AWAY TO CAMP AND BRING HELP TO THE

JUNIUS

BUOY IV SD(60)	QUALIFY AS A DOCTOR AND LOOK FOR THAT HORMONE.	JUNIUS	COMES IN WITH THE LICENCE IN HIS HAND. /JUNIUS/ WELL,
BUOY IV (49)	YOUR NAME? /HE/ SMITH. ONLY SMITH. CHRISTENED	JUNIUS	. /OLD BILL/ HAVE YOU NOTHING ELSE TO SAY FOR
BUOY IV (49)	NOT MEAN TO BE ANY MAN'S SLAVE. /OLD BILL/ (TO	JUNIUS	) WHAT ABOUT YOU? DO YOU WANT TO BE ANY WOMAN'S KEPT
DEVL EPILOG (79)	THOUGH HE WAS FINED 1000 POUNDS, AND DENOUNCED BY	JUNIUS	, FOR THE PISTOLS. IT IS ONLY WITHIN QUITE RECENT
BUOY 1 (9)	SMART, BUT ARTISTICALLY UNCONVENTIONAL. /FATHER/	JUNIUS	, MY BOY, YOU MUST MAKE UP YOUR MIND. I HAD A LONG

JUNK

GENV PREFACE(15)	INTO WHICH ALL SORTS OF ROMANTIC ANTIQUARIAN	JUNK	AND CAST-OFF PRIMITIVE RELIGION RUSHES. I HAVE TO

JUNO

OVER (194)	LOVE YOUR WIFE; AND THATS ALL ABOUT IT. /GREGORY/	JUNO	: I LOVE YOURS. WHAT THEN? /JUNO/ CLEARLY SHE MUST
OVER (183)	BY AN AMOROUS DEMONSTRATION). IT'S NO USE, MR	JUNO	: I'M HOPELESSLY RESPECTABLE: THE JENKINSES ALWAYS
OVER (193)	NO. /MRS LUNN/ NEITHER CAN MINE. /GREGORY/ MRS	JUNO	: I'M VERY SORRY I LET YOU IN FOR ALL THIS. I DONT KNOW
OVER (180)	ABOUT AND IT SIMPLY CANT HAPPEN. /MRS LUNN/ MR	JUNO	: ROMANCE IS ALL VERY WELL ON BOARD SHIP; BUT WHEN YOUR
OVER (186)	/MRS LUNN/ BUT WHATS THE GOOD OF SAYING THAT, MR	JUNO	? I'M MARRIED TO HIM; AND THERES AN END OF IT. /JUNO/
OVER (191)	TO DO? /MRS LUNN/ WHAT WOULD YOU ADVISE, MR	JUNO	? /JUNO/ I SHOULD ADVISE YOU TO DIVORCE YOUR HUSBAND.
OVER (193)	AND ARE YOU NEVER GOING TO SPEAK TO ME AGAIN, MR	JUNO	? /JUNO/ I'M PREPARED TO PROMISE NEVER TO DO SO. I
OVER (186)	/MRS LUNN/ WONT YOU INTRODUCE ME TO YOUR WIFE, MR	JUNO	? /MRS JUNO/ HOW DO YOU DO? (THEY SHAKE HANDS; AND
OVER (193)	MRS JUNO) CAN YOUR HUSBAND AFFORD A SCANDAL, MRS	JUNO	? /MRS JUNO/ NO. /MRS LUNN/ NEITHER CAN MINE.
OVER (187)	/MRS LUNN/ DONT YOU THINK YOUVE SAID ENOUGH, MR	JUNO	? THIS IS A MATTER FOR TWO WOMEN TO SETTLE. WONT YOU
OVER (187)	SUCH HONOR? /JUNO/ I SINNED IN INTENTION. (MRS	JUNO	ABANDONS HIM AND RESUMES HER SEAT, CHILLED). I'M AS
OVER (183)	YOU. /MRS LUNN/ NO: IT SENDS ME TO SLEEP. (	JUNO	APPEALS AGAINST THIS BY AN AMOROUS DEMONSTRATION). IT'S
OVER (179)	IT ALL. WE-- (THE DOOR OPENS; AND SIBTHORPE	JUNO	APPEARS IN THE ROSEATE GLOW OF THE CORRIDOR (WHICH
OVER (189)	TO SAY YOURE SORRY, AND TO MAKE FRIENDS WITH MR	JUNO	BEFORE WE ALL DINE TOGETHER. /GREGORY/ SERAPHITA: I
OVER (190)	LUNN/ OH, A GREAT DEAL, GREGORY. DONT BE RUDE. MR	JUNO	IS A VERY NICE MAN: HE HAS BEEN MOST ATTENTIVE TO ME ON
OVER (195)	GUEST, AND NOT MY OWN WIFE. /MRS LUNN/ WELL, MRS	JUNO	IS NOT YOUR WIFE, IS SHE? /GREGORY/ OH, OF COURSE: I
OVER (171)	HORRID. /GREGORY LUNN/ I'M NOT BEING HORRID, MRS	JUNO	. I'M NOT GOING TO BE HORRID. I LOVE YOU: THATS ALL.
OVER (191)	AND GIVES UP THE CONUNDRUM. GREGORY LOOKS AT	JUNO	. JUNO TURNS AWAY HIS HEAD HUFFILY). I MEAN, WHAT ARE
OVER (195)	LETS GO INTO DINNER, GREGORY: TAKE IN MRS	JUNO	. /GREGORY/ BUT SURELY I OUGHT TO TAKE IN OUR GUEST,
OVER (187)	US NOW THAT YOU AND GREGORY ARE SUCH FRIENDS, MRS	JUNO	. /JUNO/ THIS INSANE MAGNANIMITY-- /MRS LUNN/ DONT YOU

OVER	(185)	HE DISENGAGES HIMSELF FROM HER EMBRACE, AND FACES	JUNO	. SHE SITS DOWN PLACIDLY). YOU CALL ME A
OVER	(172)	CAN DO AS YOU PLEASE WITHOUT INJURING ANYONE, MRS	JUNO	. THAT IS THE WHOLE SECRET OF YOUR EXTRAORDINARY CHARM
OVER	(190)	CALL INNOCENT THINGS BY OFFENSIVE NAMES, MR	JUNO	. WHAT DO YOU CALL YOUR OWN CONDUCT? /JUNO/ (RISING)
OVER	(194)	LUNN/ I DONT INTEND TO GIVE UP MEETING YOU, MR	JUNO	. YOU AMUSE ME VERY MUCH. I DONT LIKE BEING LOVED: IT
OVER	(193)	STEPS AS MAY SEEM ADVISABLE. /MRS LUNN/ (TO MRS	JUNO	) CAN YOUR HUSBAND AFFORD A SCANDAL, MRS JUNO? /MRS
OVER	(187)	FURIOUS) I WONT BE BELITTLED. /MRS LUNN/ (TO MRS	JUNO	) I HOPE YOULL COME AND STAY WITH US NOW THAT YOU AND
OVER	(190)	OVER THE BACK OF THE CHESTERFIELD TO ADDRESS MRS	JUNO	) IF YOU WILL BE SO VERY GOOD, MY DEAR, AS TO TAKE MY
OVER	(195)	AFTER HIM) YES, DEAR. SHE'S A DARLING. (TO	JUNO	) NOW, SIBTHORPE. /JUNO/ (GIVING HER HIS ARM
OVER	(188)	RIGHT. IF YOU COME TO THAT -- (HE CROSSES TO MRS	JUNO	; PLANTS A CHAIR BY HER SIDE; AND SITS DOWN WITH EQUAL
OVER	(186)	JUNO/ HOW DO YOU DO? (THEY SHAKE HANDS; AND MRS	JUNO	SITS DOWN BESIDE MRS LUNN, ON HER LEFT). /MRS LUNN/ I'M
OVER	(188)	ACTIONS OVER WHICH I HAVE NO CONTROL. (MRS	JUNO	SITS DOWN, ASHAMED). I PROMISED MY MOTHER THAT I WOULD
OVER	(195)	VOICE TO THE OTHER COUPLE) I HAVE SAID TO MRS	JUNO	THAT I SIMPLY ADORE HER. (HE TAKES HER OUT DEFIANTLY).
OVER	(191)	GIVES UP THE CONUNDRUM. GREGORY LOOKS AT JUNO.	JUNO	TURNS AWAY HIS HEAD HUFFILY). I MEAN, WHAT ARE WE GOING
OVER	(188)	THAT I DID NOT KNOW UNTIL THIS EVENING THAT MRS	JUNO	WAS MARRIED. SHE WILL BEAR ME OUT WHEN I SAY THAT FROM
OVER	(191)	REALLY MIND, MRS LUNN? /MRS LUNN/ MY DEAR MRS	JUNO	, GREGORY IS ONE OF THOSE TERRIBLY UXORIOUS MEN WHO
OVER	(195)	HOPELESSLY CONFUSED. (HE OFFERS HIS ARM TO MRS	JUNO	, RATHER APPREHENSIVELY). /MRS JUNO/ YOU SEEM QUITE
OVER	(191)	WE HAD BETTER LET BYGONES BY BYGONES. (TO MRS	JUNO	, VERY TENDERLY) YOU WILL FORGIVE ME, WONT YOU? WHY
			JUNO'S	
OVER	(190)	ATTENTIVE TO ME ON THE VOYAGE. /GREGORY/ AND MRS	JUNO'S	A VERY NICE WOMAN. SHE OUGHTNT TO BE; BUT SHE IS.
OVER	PREFACE(168)	WITHOUT SHOCK. I MAY JUST ADD THAT MR SIBTHORPE	JUNO'S	VIEW THAT MORALITY DEMANDS, NOT THAT WE SHOULD BEHAVE
			JUPITER	
LION II	(128)	YOU CAN CHOOSE YOUR OWN ALTAR. SACRIFICE TO	JUPITER	: HE LIKES ANIMALS: HE TURNS HIMSELF INTO AN ANIMAL
SIM	PREFACE(14)	OF A CATHOLIC CONSTITUTION WHICH HAD ABOLISHED	JUPITER	AND DIANA AND VENUS AND APOLLO. SIMPLE ENOUGH; AND
LION II	(138)	FAIRY STORIES ANY TRUER THAN OUR STORIES ABOUT	JUPITER	AND DIANA, IN WHICH, I MAY TELL YOU, I BELIEVE NO
LADY	PREFACE(223)	MODEST NOT TO SEE AT LAST THAT IT WAS A CASE OF	JUPITER	AND SEMELE? SHAKESPEAR WAS MOST CERTAINLY NOT
LADY	PREFACE(222)	FALSTAFF, AND HIS POEMS BY CLOTEN AND TOUCHSTONE.	JUPITER	AND SEMELE. THIS DOES NOT MEAN THAT SHAKESPEAR WAS
LADY	(247)	I AM NOT CRUEL, MADAM; BUT YOU KNOW THE FABLE OF	JUPITER	AND SEMELE. I COULD NOT HELP MY LIGHTNINGS SCORCHING
SUPR	HANDBOK(204)	ITALIAN PATRICIANS OF THE FIFTH CENTURY SMILED AT	JUPITER	AND VENUS. SPORT IS, AS IT HAS ALWAYS BEEN,
CYMB	FORWORD(134)	CARELESS WOODNOTES WILD, COMPLETE WITH	JUPITER	AS DEUS EX MACHINA, EAGLE AND ALL, INTRODUCED, LIKE
LION I	(115)	TRUE GOD. WHAT DOES HIS NAME MATTER? WE CALL HIM	JUPITER	. THE GREEKS CALL HIM ZEUS. CALL HIM WHAT YOU WILL
CLEO IV	(174)	(HE SNIFFS AT RUFIO'S BEARD). YES, PERFUMED, BY	JUPITER	OLYMPUS! /RUFIO/ (GROWLING) WELL: IS IT TO PLEASE
CYMB V	(150)	LUD'S TOWN MARCH, AND IN THE TEMPLE OF GREAT	JUPITER	OUR PEACE WE'LL RATIFY; SEAL IT WITH FEASTS. SET ON
SUPR I	SD(9)	IS THROWN BACK FROM AN IMPOSING BROW, SUGGEST	JUPITER	RATHER THAN APOLLO. HE IS PRODIGIOUSLY FLUENT OF
LADY	PREFACE(222)	HE WAS NOT; BUT IT WAS NOT CRUELTY THAT MADE	JUPITER	REDUCE SEMELE TO ASHES: IT WAS THE FACT THAT HE
CLEO III	(164)	BRAVO, BRAVO! (THROWING OFF HIS CLOAK) BY	JUPITER	, I WILL DO THAT TOO. /RUFIO/ (SEIZING HIM) YOU ARE
DOCT IV	(157)	ENORMOUSLY INTERESTING CASE. YOU KNOW, COLLY, BY	JUPITER	, IF I DIDNT KNOW AS A MATTER OF SCIENTIFIC FACT
DOCT III	(149)	I AM NOT OUT OF COUNTENANCE. I SHOULD LIKE, BY	JUPITER	, TO SEE THE MAN WHO COULD PUT ME OUT OF
			JURIDICAL	
3PLA	PREFACE(R22)	IN THE COURTS CASES WILL BE ARGUED, NOT ON	JURIDICAL	BUT ON ROMANTIC PRINCIPLES; AND VINDICTIVE DAMAGES
BARB	PREFACE(213)	EVERY CRITICISM OF OUR MORAL, RELIGIOUS AND	JURIDICAL	INSTITUTIONS, MUST NECESSARILY BE EITHER A FOREIGN
			JURIES	
HART	PREFACE(12)	INDULGENCE. UNFORTUNATELY THE INSANITY OF THE	JURIES	AND MAGISTRATES DID NOT ALWAYS MANIFEST ITSELF IN
KING	PREFACE(158)	OUR CRUDE LEGISLATION IT MATTERS LITTLE WHETHER	JURIES	AND PARLIAMENTS ARE PACKED WITH MEN OR WOMEN; BUT NOW
GENV III	(70)	LOOKS MIGHT NOT SAVE YOU. /THE WIDOW/ WOMEN ON	JURIES	ARE AN ABOMINATION. ONLY A JEW COULD MENTION SUCH A
DOCT	PREFACE(65)	FAMOUS PICTURES, AND BY THE VERDICTS IN WHICH	JURIES	FROM TIME TO TIME EXPRESS THEIR CONVICTION THAT THE
BULL	PREFACE(40)	AND THE SUPERIORITY OF THE OLD OLIGARCHICAL GRAND	JURIES	. AND THERE IS THE SAME PRESSURE ON THE OTHER SIDE.
SUPR	PREFACE(R12)	BETWEEN BOTH AND OUR COURTS OF LAW AND PRIVATE	JURIES	OF MATRONS, PRODUCES THAT SENSATION OF EVASION, OF
ROCK	PREFACE(155)	THEREFORE CLEARLY ONE OF WILFUL MURDER, CORONERS'	JURIES	PERSIST IN TREATING IT AS A HARMLESS AND NECESSARY
DOCT	PREFACE(9)	TO PERSUADE THE JURY THAT THESE FACTS ARE FACTS.	JURIES	SELDOM NOTICE FACTS; AND THEY HAVE BEEN TAUGHT TO
CAPT II	(260)	IT, AND HAVE POLICEMEN AND COURTS AND LAWS AND	JURIES	TO DRIVE HIM INTO IT SO THAT HE CANT HELP DOING IT,
DOCT	PREFACE(51)	ARE DOING: NAMELY, MORE KNOWLEDGE. THE	JURIES	WHICH SEND THE POOR PECULIARS TO PRISON, AND GIVE
BULL	PREFACE(12)	GOVERNMENT ACT THAT THE OLD OLIGARCHICAL GRAND	JURIES	WOULD NOT HAVE TOLERATED. THERE ARE, INDEED, A
			JURISDICTION	
GENV II	(57)	HAVE NO JURISDICTION. /JUDGE/ YOU MEAN THAT OUR	JURISDICTION	IS UNDEFINED. THAT MEANS THAT OUR JURISDICTION
GENV II	(57)	JURISDICTION IS UNDEFINED. THAT MEANS THAT OUR	JURISDICTION	IS WHAT WE CHOOSE TO MAKE IT. YOU ARE FAMILIAR
CAPT II	(270)	HALLAM AND LADY CICELY WAYNFLETE, IN THE CADI'S	JURISDICTION	. AS THE SEARCH WILL BE CONDUCTED WITH MACHINE
GENV II	(57)	/SIR O./ POOH! YOU CANT BE SERIOUS. YOU HAVE NO	JURISDICTION	. /JUDGE/ YOU MEAN THAT OUR JURISDICTION IS
GENV IV	(99)	IMPORTANCE, SIR MIDLANDER; BUT IT IS OUTSIDE THE	JURISDICTION	OF THIS COURT; AND WE MUST NOT ALLOW IT TO
MRS	PREFACE(152)	AND THEREFORE EXEMPT FROM THE LORD CHAMBERLAIN'S	JURISDICTION	, RESOLVED TO PERFORM THE PLAY. NONE OF THE
			JURISPRUDENCE	
POSN	PREFACE(389)	PROPER TO THE SUPPORT OF A MAGISTRACY AND BODY OF	JURISPRUDENCE	APPLY EQUALLY TO A CENSORSHIP. A MAGISTRATE
BARB	PREFACE(210)	PUBLIC OPINION, AND CONSEQUENTLY LEGISLATION AND	JURISPRUDENCE	, IS CORRUPTED BY FEMINIST SENTIMENT. BELFORT
DOCT	PREFACE(32)	BY ANY GENERAL COMPREHENSION OF LAW OR STUDY OF	JURISPRUDENCE	, NOT EVEN BY SIMPLE VINDICTIVENESS, BUT BY
			JURIST	
LION	PREFACE(50)	ATTACHES TO AN EDUCATED MODERN PHILOSOPHER AND	JURIST	. BUT WHEN, HAVING ENTIRELY GOT RID OF SALVATIONIST
			JURISTS	
BARB	PREFACE(218)	TO THE CONTRARY MADE BY THE ECONOMISTS,	JURISTS	, MORALISTS AND SENTIMENTALISTS HIRED BY THE RICH TO
			JURORS	
POSN	PREFACE(426)	TO THE IGNORANCE AND PREJUDICES OF COMMON	JURORS	, THEN I WELCOME IT; BUT IS THAT REALLY THE OBJECT OF
			JURY	
POSN	PREFACE(389)	A JUDGE LEAVES THE QUESTION OF GUILT TO THE	JURY	: THE CENSOR IS JURY AND JUDGE AS WELL AS LAW-GIVER. A
MTH3	(96)	THE SLIGHTEST USE. /BURGE-LUBIN/ WELL, TRIAL BY	JURY	: YOU CANT DENY THAT WE ESTABLISHED THAT? /CONFUCIUS/
POSN	PREFACE(423)	HIM AT LAW, AND OBTAINED THE VERDICT OF A	JURY	AGAINST HIM, WERE SUFFICIENTLY GUARDED, THE PROPOSED
POSN	PREFACE(389)	THE QUESTION OF GUILT TO THE JURY; THE CENSOR IS	JURY	AND JUDGE AS WELL AS LAW-GIVER. A MAGISTRATE MAY BE
DOCT	PREFACE(8)	KNOWLEDGE AND UNERRING SKILL. HE HAS TAUGHT THE	JURY	AND THE JUDGE, AND EVEN HIS OWN COUNSEL, TO BELIEVE
BULL	PREFACE(57)	UNLIMITED POWERS OF PUNISHMENT WITHOUT A	JURY	AND WITHOUT APPEAL. THEY REPRESENT THE BEST OF OUR
BULL	PREFACE(58)	IN FUTURE. NOT ONLY WAS THERE OF COURSE NO	JURY	AT THE TRIAL, BUT CONSIDERABLY LESS THAN NO DEFENCE.
HART	PREFACE(13)	WILFUL MURDER HAD THE PREJUDICE OF THE CORONER'S	JURY	BEEN ON THE OTHER SIDE, THEIR TORMENTORS WERE
MILL IV	(195)	TAKE HER INTO COURT. /ADRIAN/ STUFF! WOULD ANY	JURY	BELIEVE THAT SHE AND I WERE LOVERS ON THE STRENGTH OF A
POSN	SD(435)	RAISED FLOORING A SEAT FOR THE SHERIFF, A ROUGH	JURY	BOX ON HIS RIGHT, AND A BAR TO PUT PRISONERS TO ON HIS
POSN	(444)	DANIELS, TO THE TABLE, WHERE HE SITS FACING THE	JURY	BOX). /ELDER DANIELS/ DONT DARE TO PUT YOUR THEFT ON
POSN	(448)	AND SITS AT THE TABLE WITH HIS BACK TO THE	JURY	BOX). /FEEMY/ (FOLLOWING HIM) I'LL HANG YOU, YOU DIRTY
POSN	(437)	PUTS IT OUT OF THE WAY AGAINST THE PANELS OF THE	JURY	BOX). /THE WOMEN/ (MURMURING) THATS ALWAYS THE WAY.
POSN	(449)	I SUPPOSE, THAT IF YOUVE STOLE A HORSE AND THE	JURY	FIND AGAINST YOU, YOU WONT HAVE ANY TIME TO SETTLE YOUR
MRS III	(233)	ACCIDENT, WITH A REPRIMAND FROM THE CORONER'S	JURY	FOR MY NEGLIGENCE. /VIVIE/ PUT THE RIFLE AWAY, FRANK:
POSN	(451)	A HORSE IN ANOTHER TOWN; FOR THIS IS ALL THE	JURY	HE'LL GET HERE. /THE FOREMAN/ THATS SO, BLANCO POSNET.
POSN	(451)	THIS IS ROT. HOW CAN YOU GET AN UNPREJUDICED	JURY	IF THE PRISONER STARTS BY TELLING THEM THEYRE ALL
MIS.	(118)	TO DESERVING CHARITIES, AND EVEN SERVE ON A	JURY	IN MY TURN; AND NO MAN CAN SAY I EVER REFUSED TO HELP A
POSN	(451)	AGAINST A HORSE-THIEF IS NOT FIT TO SIT ON A	JURY	IN THIS TOWN. /THE BOYS/ RIGHT. BULLY FOR YOU, NESTOR!
POSN	(451)	BRINGING DOWN HIS FIST ON THE BAR) SWEAR THE	JURY	. A ROTTEN SHERIFF YOU ARE NOT TO KNOW THAT THE JURY'S
POSN	(450)	/BLANCO/ ON THE GENERAL GROUND THAT IT'S A ROTTEN	JURY	. (LAUGHTER). /THE SHERIFF/ THATS NOT A LAWFUL GROUND
POSN	(459)	INTEND HE SHALL. NOT WHILE I AM FOREMAN OF THIS	JURY	. /BLANCO/ (WITH INTENSE EXPRESSION) A ROTTEN
APPL	PREFACE(178)	AND FREE SPEECH, AND PUBLIC MEETING, AND TRIAL BY	JURY	. STILL LESS MUST YOU RISE IN YOUR PLACES AND GIVE ME
KING	PREFACE(157)	OR PICKED UP IN THE STREET LIKE A CORONER'S	JURY	. THE COUPLED VOTE. IN THE CASE OF ELECTED BODIES THE
POSN	PREFACE(421)	ON THE MOTION OF THE ATTORNEY-GENERAL, WITHOUT A	JURY	. THE MEMBERS OF THE COMMITTEE WILL, OF COURSE, BE MEN
2TRU	PREFACE(16)	ON ANY POINT BEYOND THE CAPACITY OF A CORONER'S	JURY	. THE POPE MUST NOT BE AN ECCENTRIC GENIUS PRESIDING
MILL IV	(194)	A PENNY LESS. /SAGAMORE/ TOO MUCH. RIDICULOUS. A	JURY	MIGHT GIVE FIVE HUNDRED IF THERE WAS A CLEAR

LION PREFACE	(60)	AND ACCUSED WORKMEN ARE TRIED, NOT BY A	JURY	OF THEIR PEERS, BUT BY CONSPIRACIES OF THEIR
HART PREFACE	(15)	AND SHOT WITHOUT ANY PRETENCE OF TRIAL BY	JURY	OR PUBLICITY OF PROCEDURE OR EVIDENCE, THOUGH IT WAS
POSN PREFACE	(420)	OF A COMMITTEE OF THE PRIVY COUNCIL WITHOUT A	JURY	) NOBODY OBJECTED UNTIL, ABOUT A CENTURY AND A HALF
POSN	(459)	AT BLANCO, AND THEN AT THE SHERIFF AND AT THE	JURY	) NO. /THE FOREMAN/ YOU LIE. /THE SHERIFF/ YOUVE GOT TO
LADY PREFACE	(215)	INCOME BY AN APPEAL TO A PREJUDICED ORTHODOX	JURY	; AND THEY SEE NOTHING IN ALL THIS CRUEL BLACKGUARDISM
MILL IV	(201)	A MAN WHO HAS BEEN CALLED A SKUNK. IT MAKES THE	JURY	SEE YOU IN THAT LIGHT FROM THE START. IT IS ALSO VERY
POSN	(457)	AN ELDERLY CARTER, WHO CROSSES THE COURT TO THE	JURY	SIDE. STRAPPER PUSHES HIS WAY TO THE SHERIFF AND SPEAKS
DOCT PREFACE	(9)	USUALLY IT IS IMPOSSIBLE TO PERSUADE THE	JURY	THAT THESE FACTS ARE FACTS. JURIES SELDOM NOTICE FACTS;
DOCT PREFACE	(7)	AT ALL. AND ON THIS THE JUDGE HAD TO INSTRUCT THE	JURY	THAT THEY MUST ACQUIT THE PRISONER. THUS A JUDGE WITH A
MILL IV	(195)	WAS IT QUITE UNPROVOKED? YOU WILL NOT GET A	JURY	TO SWALLOW THAT WITHOUT A PECK OF SALT? /ADRIAN/ I
DOCT PREFACE	(9)	HE CAN ONLY DO SO BY OPENING THE EYES OF THE	JURY	TO THE FACTS THAT MEDICAL SCIENCE IS AS YET VERY
MILL IV	(195)	REMEMBER: NO MAN CAN GET DAMAGES OUT OF A BRITISH	JURY	UNLESS HE GOES INTO COURT AS A MORAL MAN. /ADRIAN/ DO
POSN PREFACE	(410)	LAW, AND TRY TO GET FROM THE PREJUDICES OF A	JURY	WHAT THEY ARE DEBARRED FROM GETTING FROM THE PREJUDICES
POSN	(450)	TO HIS LEFT. /THE SHERIFF/ SILENCE THERE. THE	JURY	WILL TAKE THEIR PLACES AS USUAL. (THEY DO SO).
POSN PREFACE	(423)	THAT IRREDUCIBLE MINIMUM OF ABUSE WHICH A POPULAR	JURY	WOULD ENDORSE, FOR WHICH MINIMUM THERE IS NO REMEDY.
GENV III	(70)	A CADAVER. /THE WIDOW/ DO YOU BELIEVE THAT ANY	JURY	WOULD FIND ME GUILTY FOR RIDDING THE WORLD OF A JEW?
POSN	(461)	I CALL THAT TO THE NOTICE OF THE FOREMAN OF THE	JURY	, AND ALSO TO THE NOTICE OF YOUNG STRAPPER. I AM ALSO
MIS. PREFACE	(13)	WHOM HE HAS INJURED ALLOWED TO ACT AS JUDGE,	JURY	, AND EXECUTIONER. IT IS TRUE THAT EMPLOYERS DO ACT IN
POSN	(451)	GO RIGHT AHEAD. IF THE PRISONER DONT LIKE THIS	JURY	, HE SHOULD HAVE STOLE A HORSE IN ANOTHER TOWN: FOR
POSN PREFACE	(422)	TAKE THEIR CHANCE WITH A STAR CHAMBER THAN WITH A	JURY	, JUST AS SOME SOLDIERS WOULD RATHER TAKE THEIR CHANCE
DOCT PREFACE	(7)	INTO PRISON FOR SIX MONTHS BY ASSURING THE	JURY	, ON OATH, THAT IF THE PRISONER'S CHILD, DEAD OF
GENV III	(70)	QUITE CERTAIN, MADAM. IF THERE WERE WOMEN ON THE	JURY	, OR SOME JEWS, YOUR GOOD LOOKS MIGHT NOT SAVE YOU.
POSN	(450)	USUAL. (THEY DO SO). /BLANCO/ I CHALLENGE THIS	JURY	, SHERIFF. /THE FOREMAN/ DO YOU, BY GOSH? /THE
POSN PREFACE	(423)	THOSE WHOM IT PURSUES THE ALTERNATIVE OF TRIAL BY	JURY	, THE EXPEDIENT STILL REMAINS A VERY QUESTIONABLE ONE,
BULL PREFACE	(49)	HAVE POWER, WITHOUT THE INTERVENTION OF A	JURY	, TO PUNISH THE SLIGHTEST SELF-ASSERTION OR HESITATION
			JURYMAN	
POSN	(451)	CHALLENGE BE JIGGERED! GAG HIM. /NESTOR/ (A	JURYMAN	WITH A LONG WHITE BEARD, DRUNK, THE OLDEST MAN
			JURYMEN	
POSN	(462)	SPITS DISGUSTEDLY, AND FOLLOWS STRAPPER OUT. THE	JURYMEN	LEAVE THE BOX, EXCEPT NESTOR, WHO COLLAPSES IN A
HART PREFACE	(28)	BY FEEBLE MIND AND MUCH AFRAID, AND BY ALL THE	JURYMEN	OF VANITY FAIR. ANOTHER GENERATION OF " SECONDARY
CAPT I	(227)	/DRINKWATER/ LAWD, SR AHRD, WOT JAGGINSES THEM	JURYMEN	WAS! YOU AN ME KNAOWED IT TOO, DIDNT WE? /SIR
			JURY'S	
POSN	(451)	A ROTTEN SHERIFF YOU ARE NOT TO KNOW THAT THE	JURY'S	GOT TO BE SWORN. /THE FOREMAN/ (GALLED) BE SWORE FOR
			JUS	
BULL IV	(146)	/DORAN/ FAITH IT WASNT O LARRY WE WERE THINKIN	JUS	DHEN, WI DHE PIG TAKIN THE MAIN STHREET O ROSSCULLEN ON
			JUST	
JOAN EPILOG	(157)	AS THEY THINK OF ME. YET GOD IS MY WITNESS I WAS	JUST	: I WAS MERCIFUL: I WAS FAITHFUL TO MY LIGHT: I COULD
BULL III	(128)	REMEMBERS MATTHEW AND TURNS TO HIM, GIVING HIM	JUST	A CRUMB OF GRACIOUSNESS). SIT DOWN, MATT (MATTHEW,
BULL I	(76)	POURS A LITTLE MORE, AND AGAIN STOPS AND LOOKS).	JUST	A DHRAIN MORE: THE LOWER HALF O THE TUMBLER DOESNT HOLD
BARB III	(337)	A NEW GUN OR AN AERIAL BATTLESHIP THAT TURNS OUT	JUST	A HAIRSBREADTH WRONG AFTER ALL? SCRAP IT. SCRAP IT
FABL VI	(129)	AND I DONT BELIEVE IT. YOUR CORRESPONDENT IS	JUST	A LIAR. /MAIDEN 4/ WHAT RUBBISH YOU TALK, NUMBER TWO!
FANY PROLOG	(272)	THIS TIME? /TROTTER/ I'M SO SORRY. I MUST HAVE	JUST	A LITTLE BRUSH UP: I-- (HE HURRIES OUT). /THE COUNT/
ARMS III	(56)	THAT IF RAINA WERE OUT OF THE WAY, AND YOU	JUST	A LITTLE LESS OF A FOOL AND SERGIUS JUST A LITTLE MORE
ARMS III	(56)	AND YOU JUST A LITTLE LESS OF A FOOL AND SERGIUS	JUST	A LITTLE MORE OF ONE, YOU MIGHT COME TO BE ONE OF MY
SUPR II	(54)	NOT DISCUSSING LITERATURE AT PRESENT. /TANNER/ BE	JUST	A LITTLE PATIENT WITH ME. I AM NOT DISCUSSING
FANY I	(274)	/GILBEY/ " I THINK MY BROTHER MUST HAVE BEEN	JUST	A LITTLE TO BLAME HIMSELF; SO, BETWEEN OURSELVES, I
SUPR I	(28)	MOMENT. /TANNER/ (DRILY) I THINK HE SUSPECTS ME	JUST	A LITTLE. /OCTAVIUS/ JACK: YOU COULDNT-- YOU WOULDNT--
MTH5	(243)	EVEN THE ANCIENTS ARE SMILING. /THE NEWLY BORN/	JUST	A LITTLE. /THE SHE-ANCIENT/ (QUICKLY RECOVERING HER
JOAN EPILOG	(162)	PERHAPS A LITTLE UNFORTUNATE. /JOAN/ AY, PERHAPS	JUST	A LITTLE, YOU FUNNY MAN. /WARWICK/ STILL, WHEN THEY
MTH3	(132)	THOUGHT OF THAT. THAT EXPLAINS EVERYTHING. WE ARE	JUST	A LOT OF SCHOOLBOYS: THERES NO DENYING IT. TALK TO AN
WIDO III	(64)	MORE TO SAY. /LICKCHEESE/ NO: DONT GO. ONLY	JUST	A MINUTE: ME AND COKANE WILL BE BACK IN NO TIME TO SEE
ARMS I	(12)	INTERVAL. (PLEASANTLY) YOU DONT MIND MY WAITING	JUST	A MINUTE OR TWO, DO YOU? /RAINA/ (PUTTING ON HER MOST
JITT I	(11)	THANK YOU, MRS BILLITER. I-- I-- I-- (GASPING)	JUST	A MOMENT. WHEW! (AS THE COAT COMES OFF HE PLUNGES TO
MIS.	(179)	TURKISH BATH-- /BENTLEY/ GO SLOW, OLD MAN.	JUST	A MOMENT. " TURKISH BATH"-- YES? /TARLETON/ (
MTH3	(135)	GONE? /BURGE-LUBIN/ YES, YES: IT'S ALL RIGHT.	JUST	A MOMENT, IF-- (CONFUCIUS RETURNS) CONFUCIUS: I HAVE
BULL II	(105)	(STOPPING TO EXAMINE THE GREAT STONE)	JUST	A MOMENT, MR DOYLE: I WANT TO LOOK AT THIS STONE. IT
POSN	(449)	/STRAPPER/ SHALL I CALL IN THE BOYS? /BLANCO/	JUST	A MOMENT, SHERIFF. A GOOD APPEARANCE IS EVERYTHING IN A
APPL II	(265)	US AS A MERE TRIBE OF REDSKINS. ENGLAND WILL BE	JUST	A RESERVATION. /THE QUEEN/ NONSENSE, DEAR! THEY KNOW
MTH4 I	(166)	YOU UP NOW BUT YOU ARE FLAT TO MY PITCH. . . .	JUST	A SHADE SHARPER. . . . THATS BETTER: STILL A LITTLE
JITT I	(15)	KNOW; BUT GREY AS I AM, I AM STILL A HOBBLEDEHOY:	JUST	A STUDENT WAITING FOR HIS GIRL AT THE CORNER OF THE
APPL PREFACE	(179)	YOUR ADDRESS IS THAT YOU HAVE NO ADDRESS, AND ARE	JUST	A TRAMP -- IF INDEED YOU EXIST AT ALL." YOU WILL NOTICE
GENV II	(62)	ARE CONTESTING THE SEAT AS WELL. IT WILL BE	JUST	A WALK-OVER FOR ME. /SIR O./ BUT MY NEPHEW IS THE
FANY PROLOG	(267)	DELIGHTFUL, WITTY, CHARMING BABY; BUT STILL	JUST	A WEE LAMB IN A WORLD OF WOLVES. CAMBRIDGE IS NOT WHAT
FANY III	(318)	TO KNOX) YOU ASK HIM. /KNOX/ (TO JUGGINS/	JUST	A WORD WITH YOU, MY MAN. WAS YOUR MOTHER MARRIED TO
WIDO II	(33)	A WORD FOR ME! (SUDDENLY CRINGING TO TRENCH)	JUST	A WORD, SIR. IT WOULD COST YOU NOTHING. (SARTORIUS
SUPR IV	(152)	HUMBUGGED US, SIR! /HECTOR/ HERE! I HAVE HAD	JUST	ABOUT ENOUGH OF BEING BADGERED. VIOLET AND I ARE
BULL I	(76)	BUT A POWERFUL DHRINKER. /BROADBENT/ I WAS	JUST	ABOUT TO RING FOR TEA WHEN YOU CAME. SIT DOWN, MR
WIDO I	(12)	US, BLANCHE. /BLANCHE/ YES, PAPA. WE WERE	JUST	ABOUT TO START. /SARTORIUS/ WE ARE RATHER DUSTY: WE
MTH5	(211)	SLEEP BECAUSE OUR WEIGHT STOPPED OUR CIRCULATIONS	JUST	ABOVE THE ELBOWS. THEN SOMEHOW MY FEELING BEGAN TO
SUPR II	(67)	SHE HAS NO HANDLE TO HER NAME. OF COURSE IT'S	JUST	ABSURD. BUT I TELL YOU, VIOLET, I DONT LIKE DECEIVING
OVER PREFACE	(168)	MAY NOW, I HOPE, BE READ WITHOUT SHOCK. I MAY	JUST	ADD THAT MR SIBTHORPE JUNO'S VIEW THAT MORALITY
SUPR HANDBOK	(197)	EASY FOR THE DYNAMITARD TO SAY " HAVE YOU NOT	JUST	ADMITTED THAT NOTHING IS EVER CONCEDED EXCEPT TO
DOCT I	SD(81)	IS THE MANNER OF AN OLD FAMILY NURSE TO A CHILD	JUST	AFTER IT HAS LEARNT TO WALK. SHE HAS USED HER UGLINESS
SUPR III	(85)	AND SAYS PLEADINGLY TO TANNER-- /MENDOZA/	JUST	ALLOW ME TO READ A FEW LINES BEFORE YOU GO TO SLEEP. I
MILL I	(148)	LONG NAME. IN MY LITTLE CIRCLE EVERYONE CALLS HIM	JUST	ALLY. /EPIFANIA/ (HER TEETH ON EDGE) YOU HEAR THIS, MR
PYGM II	(238)	THE DESERVING. WHAT IS MIDDLE CLASS MORALITY?	JUST	AN EXCUSE FOR NEVER GIVING ME ANYTHING. THEREFORE, I
BARB II	(306)	US MARCH TO THE GREAT MEETING AT ONCE. EXCUSE ME	JUST	AN INSTANT. (HE RUSHES INTO THE SHELTER. JENNY TAKES
JITT II	SD(27)	HIS AGE IS BETWEEN FORTY AND FIFTY. FESSLER IS	JUST	AN ORDINARY NICE-LOOKING YOUNG DOCTOR. THE ROOM HAS TWO
DOCT IV	(166)	SHALL. /LOUIS/ BECAUSE I SUDDENLY WANT TO SLEEP.	JUST	AN ORDINARY SLEEP. /MRS DUBEDAT/ (ROCKING HIM) YES,
NEVR IV	(301)	YOU WERE ONLY OFFENDED-- SHOCKED. YOU ARE	JUST	AN ORDINARY YOUNG LADY, TOO ORDINARY TO ALLOW TAME
BUOY II	(25)	TO THE EXTENT TO WHICH YOU AND I AND OUR LIKE ARE	JUST	AND BENEVOLENT THERE IS NO JUSTICE AND NO BENEVOLENCE.
MILL IV	(207)	ONE HUNDRED AND FIFTY POUNDS WIDE. HE WHO IS	JUST	AND EXACT SUPPLIED THAT SUM BY YOUR CHAUFFEUR'S HANDS
BULL PREFACE	(56)	CROMER CERTIFIES THAT THESE PROCEEDINGS WERE "	JUST	AND NECESSARY." HE ALSO GIVES HIS REASONS. IT APPEARS
BULL PREFACE	(60)	GUARANTEES FEROCIOUS SENTENCES OF FLOGGING AS "	JUST	AND NECESSARY," AND CAN SEE " NOTHING REPREHENSIBLE IN
BULL PREFACE	(62)	DESERVE THE WORST THAT LORD CROMER CAN CONSIDER "	JUST	AND NECESSARY" FOR HIM, THAT IS WHAT YOU GET BY
HART II	(108)	FOR THE POLICE AND HAVE DONE WITH IT. IT'S ONLY	JUST	AND RIGHT YOU SHOULD. /RANDALL/ (WHO HAS RELAXED HIS
METH PREFACE	(R60)	ON THEIR UMBRELLAS, AND HAPPENED ALIKE TO THE	JUST	AND UNJUST. NOTHING COULD BE MORE FLATTERING AND
SUPR I	(15)	ME A PIECE OF YOUR MIND, YOU ASK YOURSELF, AS A	JUST	AND UPRIGHT MAN, WHAT IS THE WORST YOU CAN FAIRLY SAY
WIDO III	SD(66)	(HE SHAKES SARTORIUS'S HAND). THE PARLORMAID HAS	JUST	APPEARED AT THE DOOR. /THE PARLORMAID/ SUPPER IS READY,
DEVL III	SD(67)	WHEN HE IS ANTICIPATED BY BURGOYNE, WHO HAS	JUST	APPEARED AT THE DOOR WITH TWO PAPERS IN HIS HAND: A
HART II	(105)	AND BRUSHES, YOUR PYJAMAS-- /HECTOR/ (WHO HAS	JUST	APPEARED IN THE PORT DOORWAY IN A HANDSOME ARAB
MRS I	SD(193)	WHEN HE IS HAILED BY A YOUNG GENTLEMAN WHO HAS	JUST	APPEARED ON THE COMMON, AND IS MAKING FOR THE GATE. HE
MTH4 II	SD(192)	HERE COME THE LADIES. TO HIS RELIEF, THEY HAVE	JUST	APPEARED ON THE THRESHOLD OF THE TEMPLE. /THE ELDERLY
NEVR II	(240)	TO THE HOTEL ENTRANCE, WHERE THE WAITER HAS	JUST	APPEARED) ORDER BEFORE WILLIAM! /DOLLY/ (TOUCHING
DOCT III	(143)	A SCOUNDREL? I AM. WHAT AM I? A SCOUNDREL. IT'S	JUST	ARGUING IN A CIRCLE. AND YOU IMAGINE YOURE A MAN OF
CATH 2	(181)	IS IN ENGLAND, ISNT SHE? /EDSTASTON/ NO. SHE HAS	JUST	ARRIVED IN ST PETERSBURG. /THE PRINCESS DASHKOFF/ (
DEVL III	(50)	HAS, SIR; BUT THERE'S A DELAY. GENERAL BURGOYNE'S	JUST	ARRIVED-- GENTLEMANLY JOHNNY WE CALL HIM, SIR-- AND HE
HART I	(51)	DONT ASK ME. YOU CAN SEE FOR YOURSELF THAT IVE	JUST	ARRIVED; HER ONLY SISTER, AFTER TWENTY-THREE YEARS
MIS. PREFACE	(93)	KNOWLEDGE OF ALL THE CREEDS AND CHURCHES.	JUST	AS A CHILD, NO MATTER WHAT ITS RACE AND COLOR MAY BE,
DOCT PREFACE	(39)	LACERATION. A CRAZE FOR CRUELTY CAN BE DEVELOPED	JUST	AS A CRAZE FOR DRINK CAN; AND NOBODY WHO ATTEMPTS TO
HART PREFACE	(5)	TO " RECOGNIZE" SOME POWERFUL TRADE UNION,	JUST	AS A GONDOLA MIGHT REFUSE TO RECOGNIZE A 20,000-TON
MIS. PREFACE	(103)	THAT IS FREE AT TWENTYONE IS NOT FREE AT ALL;	JUST	AS A MAN FIRST ENRICHED AT FIFTY REMAINS POOR ALL HIS

MTH3 (132)	YOU ARE NOT HUMAN. /CONFUCIUS/ I AM STAGGERED,	JUST	AS A MAN MAY BE STAGGERED BY AN EXPLOSION FOR WHICH HE
GETT PREFACE(256)	THE PURPOSES OF A FAMILY IT SHOULD BE DISSOLVED	JUST	AS A MARRIAGE SHOULD WHEN IT, TOO, IS NOT ACHIEVING THE
VWOO 1 (122)	AMONG THE NAVVIES. I AM ONLY A WRITING MACHINE,	JUST	AS A NAVVY IS A DIGGING MACHINE. /Z/ I DONT THINK THE
POSN PREFACE(389)	AGAINST AN ATHEIST OR AN ANTI-VACCINATOR,	JUST	AS A SANITARY INSPECTOR MAY HAVE FORMED A CAREFUL
BARB III (347)	YES; BUT THAT POWER CAN DESTROY THE HIGHER POWERS	JUST	AS A TIGER CAN DESTROY A MAN: THEREFORE MAN MUST MASTER
OVER PREFACE(156)	CONFESSES MAY BE BOTH UNIVERSAL AND UNSUSPECTED,	JUST	AS A VIRTUE WHICH EVERYBODY IS EXPECTED, UNDER HEAVY
GETT (356)	GOOD. /HOTCHKISS/ THEN YOU MUST HAVE NOTICED THAT	JUST	AS ALL MURDERERS, JUDGING BY THEIR EDIFYING REMARKS ON
OVER (183)	PEOPLE WHO GET INTO TROUBLE GO TO YOU,	JUST	AS ALL THE SICK PEOPLE GO TO THE DOCTORS; BUT MOST
BULL PREFACE(50)	ARE PIGEON-HOUSES; FOR THE VILLAGERS KEEP PIGEONS	JUST	AS AN ENGLISH FARMER KEEPS POULTRY. TRY TO IMAGINE THE
BULL PREFACE(29)	ROOM WHEN QUESTIONS OF STATE ARE TO BE DISCUSSED.	JUST	AS AN IRISHMAN MAY HAVE ENGLISH FRIENDS WHOM HE MAY
DOCT III (144)	BUT STILL, IT'S AN IDEAL THAT I STRIVE TOWARDS	JUST	AS ANY OTHER MAN STRIVES TOWARDS HIS IDEAL. /B.B./ (
CYMB FORWORD(134)	ELSE BECAUSE AN IRRESISTIBLE FASHION HAD SET IN,	JUST	AS AT ALL THE GREAT CONTINENTAL OPERA HOUSES A BALLET
MTH2 (87)	AND EVERYTHING ELSE EXCEPT YOU. /SAVVY/ OH, I WAS	JUST	AS BAD AS ANY OF THEM. I SOLD FLAGS IN THE STREETS IN
WIDO II (43)	MR COKANE. (TO TRENCH) IF, WHEN YOU SAY YOU ARE	JUST	AS BAD AS I AM, YOU MEAN THAT YOU ARE JUST AS POWERLESS
MIS. (122)	BUT NOT A BIT OF IT, IF YOU PLEASE. THEY WERE ALL	JUST	AS BAD AS SHE. THEY ALL HAD SYSTEMS; AND EACH OF THEM
WIDO II (43)	/TRENCH/ (DAZED) DO YOU MEAN TO SAY THAT I AM	JUST	AS BAD AS YOU ARE? /COKANE/ SHAME, HARRY, SHAME!
MIS. (124)	LET JOHNNY ALONE; AND I'LL LET BUNNY ALONE. I'M	JUST	AS BAD AS YOU. THERE! /HYPATIA/ OH, I DONT MIND YOUR
MRS III (232)	WHERE THE MONEY I SPENT CAME FROM. I BELIEVE I AM	JUST	AS BAD AS YOU. /CROFTS/ (GREATLY REASSURED) OF COURSE
JITT III (61)	I KNOW WHAT YOU ARE. JUST AS BAD AS YOUR FATHER!	JUST	AS BAD AS YOUR FATHER! /FESSLER/ WHAT ON EARTH IS THE
JITT III (61)	(TO EDITH, RISING) OH, NOW I KNOW WHAT YOU ARE.	JUST	AS BAD AS YOUR FATHER! JUST AS BAD AS YOUR FATHER!
2TRU II (67)	I'D RATHER BE DEAD. /THE PATIENT/ WELL, IT'S	JUST	AS BAD FOR ME. /THE COUNTESS/ NO IT ISNT. YOURE A REAL
GETT PREFACE(200)	THERE. AS A MATTER OF FACT, ETHICAL STRAIN IS	JUST	AS BAD FOR US AS PHYSICAL STRAIN. IT IS DESIRABLE THAT
NEVR II (241)	IT'S EMBARRASSING, ISNT IT? IT'S	JUST	AS BAD FOR US, YOU KNOW. /PHILIP/ SH! DOLLY: WE ARE
VWOO 1 (119)	YOU ALL THE TIME WHEN YOU DONT WANT TO. BUT IT'S	JUST	AS BAD WHEN YOU WANT TO TALK, AND THE OTHER PERSON
KING II (225)	AND REPEAT THEMSELVES ENDLESSLY. AND I AM	JUST	AS BAD WITH MY OLD STORIES ABOUT MY FLIGHT AFTER THE
HART I (71)	DONT BE VULGAR, RANDALL. AND YOU, HESIONE, ARE	JUST	AS BAD. ELLIE AND HECTOR COME IN FROM THE GARDEN BY THE
JOAN 6 (126)	NOT THE APOSTOLIC SUCCESSION. OUR OWN NOBLES ARE	JUST	AS BAD. THE BISHOP'S ASSESSORS HURRY INTO THE HALL,
2TRU II (66)	SO. /THE COUNTESS/ WELL, THE TRAVELLERS WERE	JUST	AS BAD, YOU KNOW. /AUBREY/ JUST AS BAD! SAY JUST AS
2TRU II (66)	TRAVELLERS WERE JUST AS BAD, YOU KNOW. /AUBREY/	JUST	AS BAD! SAY JUST AS GOOD. FICKLENESS MEANS SIMPLY
BULL II (113)	TWO MINUTES IN THE DARK. /BROADBENT/ THE VOICE IS	JUST	AS BEAUTIFUL IN THE DARK, YOU KNOW. BESIDES, IVE HEARD
CAND I (86)	LITTLE MORE FRANKLY. YOUR EXACT WORDS THEN WERE "	JUST	AS BIG A FOOL AS EVER, JAMES! " /BURGESS/ (SOOTHINGLY)
BARB II (275)	WHATS SO UNFAIR TO US WOMEN. YOUR CONFESSIONS IS	JUST	AS BIG LIES AS OURS: YOU DONT TELL WHAT YOU REALLY DONE
HART PREFACE(6)	OLD ROUTINE WITHOUT NECESSARILY UNDERSTANDING IT,	JUST	AS BOND STREET TRADESMEN AND DOMESTIC SERVANTS KEEP
DOCT PREFACE(78)	OF LIFE AND THE PHILOSOPHER'S STONE, AND IS	JUST	AS BUSY AFTER THEM TODAY AS EVER IT WAS IN THE DAYS OF
GETT PREFACE(199)	WHAT PEOPLE CALL GOODNESS HAS TO BE KEPT IN CHECK	JUST	AS CAREFULLY AS WHAT THEY CALL BADNESS; FOR THE HUMAN
POSN PREFACE(427)	STAGE. THE FREEDOM OF THE STAGE WILL BE ABUSED	JUST	AS CERTAINLY AS THE COMPLAISANCE AND INNOCENCE OF THE
BUOY 1 (12)	LISTEN TO REASON? /SON/ YES; BUT REASON LEADS	JUST	AS CLEARLY TO A CATHOLIC MONARCHY AS TO AN AMERICAN
ARMS I (5)	ON YOU! THE SERBS HAVE AUSTRIAN OFFICERS WHO ARE	JUST	AS CLEVER AS THE RUSSIANS; BUT WE HAVE BEATEN THEM IN
FABL PREFACE(77)	WITH DAS KAPITAL AS ITS BIBLE AND GOSPEL,	JUST	AS COBDENIST PLUTOCRACY USED TO MAKE A BIBLE OF ADAM
CAND II (124)	MORE 'N A COUPLE-O-HOUR AWAY. /CANDIDA/ YOULL BE	JUST	AS COMFORTABLE AT THE MEETING. WE'LL ALL SIT ON THE
LION PREFACE(72)	WHICH IS JUST AS SUICIDAL, JUST AS WEAK,	JUST	AS COWARDLY AS SELF-DENIAL. IBSEN, WHO TAKES US INTO
DOCT PREFACE(23)	TO BE OF SOME USE. BUT THE FACT REMAINS THAT	JUST	AS DOCTORS PERFORM FOR HALF-A-CROWN, WITHOUT THE LEAST
JOAN PREFACE(34)	HAS ANY SPECIAL SIGNIFICANCE. JOAN WAS BURNT	JUST	AS DOZENS OF LESS INTERESTING HERETICS WERE BURNT IN
GETT PREFACE(218)	QUARRELSOME. QUARREL WITH THEIR HUSBANDS AND WIVES	JUST	AS EASILY AS WITH THEIR SERVANTS AND RELATIVES AND
MRS PREFACE(158)	IN IT, AND SHE QUITE HEARTWHOLE; AND I COULD	JUST	AS EASILY WRITE A PLAY WITHOUT A WOMAN IN IT AT ALL. I
METH PREFACE(R33)	WERE BEING TAUGHT FROM THE BOOK OF GENESIS;	JUST	AS EDWARD VI WAS (AND EDWARD VII TOO, FOR THAT
SUPR HANDBOK(182)	AND WILL BE MODIFIED BY THE IMPULSE TOWARDS HIM	JUST	AS EFFECTUALLY. THE PRACTICAL ABROGATION OF PROPERTY
MIS. PREFACE(94)	BY WHICH GOD IS KNOWN TO TURKS AND ARABS, WHO ARE	JUST	AS ELIGIBLE FOR SALVATION AS ANY CHRISTIAN. FURTHER,
BULL I (85)	IN ROSSCULLEN? WHY, MAN, IRELAND WAS PEOPLED	JUST	AS ENGLAND WAS; AND ITS BREED WAS CROSSED BY JUST THE
DOCT PREFACE(35)	PURSUIT OF KNOWLEDGE YOU MAY DO AS YOU PLEASE."	JUST	AS EVEN THE STUPIDEST PEOPLE SAY IN EFFECT " IF YOU
ROCK PREFACE(178)	FALL TWICE AS FAST AS A FIVE POUND ONE OR ONLY	JUST	AS FAST AND NO FASTER, BUT SOCRATES WAS BY VOCATION AND
WIDO III (63)	A DAUGHTER TOO; AND MY FEELINS IN THAT MATTER IS	JUST	AS FINE AS YOURS. I PROPOSE NOTHING BUT WHAT IS FOR
OVER (177)	WAS NOT UP. /MRS JUNO/ BOTHER THE BOARD! I AM	JUST	AS FOND OF SIBTHORPE AS-- /GREGORY/ SIBTHORPE! /MRS
MTH2 (58)	OF THE 39 ARTICLES; AND THE CHURCH OF ENGLAND IS	JUST	AS GOOD AS ANY OTHER CHURCH; AND I DONT CARE WHO HEARS
FANY EPILOG (331)	OF THE PURITAN MIDDLE CLASS IN ENGLAND: PEOPLE	JUST	AS GOOD AS THE AUTHOR, ANYHOW. WITH, OF COURSE, THE
NEVR I (221)	WELL, YOUR TEETH ARE GOOD, I ADMIT. BUT IVE SEEN	JUST	AS GOOD IN VERY SELF-INDULGENT MOUTHS. (HE GOES TO THE
MRS II (217)	A FIRST-RATE EDUCATION, WHEN OTHER WOMEN THAT HAD	JUST	AS GOOD OPPORTUNITIES ARE IN THE GUTTER? BECAUSE I
DOCT III (138)	/LOUIS/ YES, WHY NOT? LOTS OF PEOPLE DO IT:	JUST	AS GOOD PEOPLE AS YOU. WHY DONT YOU LEARN TO THINK,
CLEO IV (171)	TO ROME? ASK HIS SLAVE, BRITANNUS: HE HAS BEEN	JUST	AS GOOD TO HIM. NAY, ASK HIS VERY HORSE! HIS KINDNESS
2TRU II (66)	JUST AS BAD, YOU KNOW. /AUBREY/ JUST AS BAD! SAY	JUST	AS GOOD. FICKLENESS MEANS SIMPLY MOBILITY, AND MOBILITY
BULL IV (175)	TYRANNY, AND TO CRACK UP YOUR OWN IRISH HEROISM,	JUST	AS HAFFIGAN ONCE PAID A WITCH A PENNY TO PUT A SPELL ON
SUPR HANDBOK(206)	BY THE BOMB; BUT RAVACHOL'S HEART BURNS	JUST	AS HAMILTON'S DID. THE WORLD WILL NOT BEAR THINKING OF
MTH5 (254)	EGG. /ACIS/ NOT A BIT OF IT. YOU AND ARJILLAX ARE	JUST	AS HARD AS TWO STONES. /ECRASIA/ YOU DID NOT ALWAYS
2TRU II (65)	HE BEAT HER ON THEIR WEDDING DAY; AND HE BEAT HER	JUST	AS HARD EVERY DAY AFTERWARDS. I MADE HER GET A
SUPR III (126)	DEVILISH COLDNESS THAT DREW TEARS. BUT I FOUND IT	JUST	AS HARD TO ESCAPE WHEN I WAS CRUEL AS WHEN I WAS KIND.
POSN PREFACE(366)	PHILOSOPHY, OR LAW. HE CALLS IN A PLAYWRIGHT	JUST	AS HE CALLS IN A DOCTOR, OR CONSULTS A LAWYER, OR
MIS. PREFACE(62)	WHEN HE DISOBEYS. HE LOSES HIS MORAL COURAGE	JUST	AS HE COMES TO HATE BOOKS AND LANGUAGES. IN THE END,
DOCT PREFACE(31)	AND MARK TWAIN ARE IGNORANT SENTIMENTALISTS,	JUST	AS HE COMPLIES WITH ANY OTHER SILLY FASHION: THE
DOCT PREFACE(76)	AS HE IS CALLED IN OUR HOMES) IS GOING ON	JUST	AS HE DID BEFORE, AND COULD NOT AFFORD TO LEARN OR
SUPR HANDBOK(195)	WOULD LIKE TO BE A BETTER MAN GOES ON BEHAVING	JUST	AS HE DID BEFORE. AND THE TRAMP WHO WOULD LIKE THE
BARB I (256)	WITH YOUR CAPACITY. ANDREW DID IT ON PRINCIPLE,	JUST	AS HE DID EVERY PERVERSE AND WICKED THING ON PRINCIPLE.
METH PREFACE(R63)	FROM THE TREATISE OF MALTHUS ON POPULATION,	JUST	AS HE GOT HIS OTHER POSTULATE OF A PRACTICALLY
NEVR III (268)	HIMSELF SCIENTIFICALLY AND BEAT HER AT THAT GAME	JUST	AS HE HAD BEATEN HER AT THE OLD GAME. I LEARNT HOW TO
MTH3 (132)	AND HE LISTENS TO YOU CURIOUSLY FOR A MOMENT	JUST	AS HE LISTENS TO A CHAP PLAYING CLASSICAL MUSIC. THEN
MIS. SD(162)	TRAIL; TURNS AT THE SAME SPOT; AND DISCOVERS HIM	JUST	AS HE MAKES A DASH FOR THE PAVILION DOOR. SHE FLIES
LION PREFACE(42)	A FORTIORI, I AM A GOD." JOHN MAKES HIM SAY THIS,	JUST	AS HE MAKES HIM SAY " I AM THE LIGHT OF THE WORLD." BUT
BULL PREFACE(16)	TRAITOR: ALL THESE YOUR IRISHMAN MAY EASILY BE,	JUST	AS HE MAY BE A GENTLEMAN (A SPECIES EXTINCT IN
SUPR PREFACE(R17)	WHOM SHAKESPEAR PALMED OFF AS A REPUTABLE MAN	JUST	AS HE PALMED POOR MACBETH OFF AS A MURDERER. TODAY THE
MIS. PREFACE(105)	FAILING AN UNROMANTIC CONVINCING ANSWER, HE DOES	JUST	AS HE PLEASES UNLESS HE CAN FIND FOR HIMSELF A REAL
LION PREFACE(37)	OF THAUMATURGIC POWERS. HE REVELS IN MIRACLES	JUST	AS HE REVELS IN PARABLES: THEY MAKE SUCH CAPITAL
GLIM (185)	PAINTER IN A VISION, AND ORDER HIM TO PAINT HER	JUST	AS HE SEES HER IF SHE REALLY WISHES TO BE PAINTED.
LADY PREFACE(214)	SUBMITTED TO ME TO SEE WHAT I WOULD SAY ABOUT IT,	JUST	AS HE USED TO SUBMIT DIFFICULT LINES FROM THE SONNETS.
ARMS I (5)	I'M PROMISING. /RAINA/ WELL, IT CAME INTO MY HEAD	JUST	AS HE WAS HOLDING ME IN HIS ARMS AND LOOKING INTO MY
FANY I (279)	I BET, THE OLD DEAR. HE GOT CLEAN OFF, TOO.	JUST	AS HE WAS OVERTAKING ME HALF-WAY DOWN THE SQUARE, WE
POSN (445)	IT? /BLANCO/ BECAUSE HE'D BE TOO CLEVER FOR YOU,	JUST	AS HE WAS TOO CLEVER FOR ME. /ELDER DANIELS/ MAKE YOUR
APPL I (198)	ALL RITUAL: HE WENT TO THE RIVIERA EVERY WINTER	JUST	AS HE WENT TO CHURCH. /PAMPHILIUS/ BY THE WAY, IS HE
PYGM EPILOG (302)	THIS. SHE KNOWS THAT HIGGINS DOES NOT NEED HER,	JUST	AS HER FATHER DID NOT NEED HER. THE VERY SCRUPULOUSNESS
MIS. (195)	CHILD LIKE LOTTERY NUMBERS, THERE WOULD BE	JUST	AS HIGH A PERCENTAGE OF HAPPY MARRIAGES AS WE HAVE HERE
MIS. PREFACE(94)	AND SO FORTH, AND THAT THEY ARE ON THE AVERAGE	JUST	AS HONEST AND WELL-BEHAVED AS ITS OWN FATHER. FOR
DOCT PREFACE(38)	THE CRUELTIES OF VIVISECTION. WE ALL DO	JUST	AS HORRIBLE THINGS, WITH EVEN LESS EXCUSE. BUT IN
PHIL I (71)	HIS ELBOW ON HIS KNEE) I HAVE SAT ALONE WITH HER	JUST	AS I AM SITTING WITH YOU-- /GRACE/ (SHRINKING FROM
INCA (249)	TONGUE AND HIS MOUSTACHE. WHILE HE TALKED: TALKED	JUST	AS I AM TALKING NOW TO YOU, SIMPLY, QUIETLY, SENSIBLY,
JOAN 1 (66)	BUT YOU ACTUALLY SEE THEM; AND THEY TALK TO YOU	JUST	AS I AM TALKING TO YOU? /JOAN/ NO: IT IS QUITE
MIS. (132)	CHASING ITS OWN TAIL. I CAN STAND A LITTLE OF IT,	JUST	AS I CAN STAND WATCHING THE CAT FOR TWO MINUTES, SAY,
JITT II (50)	(CONTINUING CALMLY) YOU CANNOT BELIEVE IT,	JUST	AS I CANNOT BELIEVE THAT YOU WILL NEVER SPEAK TO ME
BULL I (91)	FROM MY FATHER ON EVERY ONE OF THEM, PROBABLY,	JUST	AS I DIFFER FROM YOU ABOUT THEM. /BROADBENT/ YES; BUT
MIS. PREFACE(26)	WORKED BY ANGELS. I DO NOT ADMIT IT EVEN AT THAT,	JUST	AS I DO NOT ADMIT THAT IF THE SKY FELL WE SHOULD ALL
APPL I (239)	HO! YOU WILL, WILL YOU? HOW? /AMANDA/	JUST	AS I DROVE THE CHAIRMAN OF BREAKAGES OUT OF MY OWN
MIS. PREFACE(21)	THE DIRT; BUT I ESCAPED SQUEERS AND CREAKLE	JUST	AS I ESCAPED JOHNSON AND CARLYLE. AND THIS IS WHAT
GLIM (186)	NO: DEATH IS NOTHING. I CAN FACE A STAB	JUST	AS I FACED HAVING MY TOOTH PULLED OUT AT FAENZA.
PYGM V (281)	NOT ABOUT ME. IF YOU COME BACK I SHALL TREAT YOU	JUST	AS I HAVE ALWAYS TREATED YOU. I CANT CHANGE MY NATURE;
NEVR III (270)	HER MOTHER. I KNOW I HAVE LOST YOUR CONFIDENCE,	JUST	AS I HAVE LOST THIS MAN'S RESPECT;-- (SHE STOPS TO
KING I (165)	A GREAT HONOR TO US. BUT I MUST WARN YOU THAT	JUST	AS I HAVE MY TERRIBLE WEAKNESS FOR FIGURES MR ROWLEY
WIDO III (55)	IF ONLY A GIRL COULD HAVE NO FATHER, NO FAMILY,	JUST	AS I HAVE NO MOTHER! CLERGYMAN! BEAST! " THE WORST
2TRU II (72)	I INCLUDED YOU WITH THE ANIMALS AND THEIR WAYS,	JUST	AS I INCLUDED SWEETIE AND THE SERGEANT. /THE COUNTESS/
JITT III (60)	VERY WELL HOW TIDY YOU KEPT HIS HOUSE FOR HIM,	JUST	AS I KEEP MY ROOM. YOU DID YOUR DUTY: NOBODY CAN BLAME
MIS. (126)	BE IN LOVE WITH BUNNY? I LIKE HIM TO KISS ME	JUST	AS I LIKE A BABY TO KISS ME. I'M FOND OF HIM; AND HE

PHIL I (70)	I AM IN LOVE WITH YOU, YOU WILL LIKE ME FOR IT	JUST	AS I LIKED TRANFIELD. /CHARTERIS/ MY DEAR: IT IS
CAPT I (237)	SHALL BE YOUR ESCORT. I MAY REQUIRE A DOZEN MEN,	JUST	AS I MAY REQUIRE A DOZEN HORSES. SOME OF THE HORSES
SIM PREFACE(6)	OUTGROWN THE DEVIL WITH HIS BARBED TAIL AND HORNS	JUST	AS I OUTGREW THE COCK IN THE CHIMNEY. BUT WHAT OF THE
BARB III (338)	AND THEIR SOULS? /UNDERSHAFT/ I SAVE THEIR SOULS	JUST	AS I SAVED YOURS. /BARBARA/ (REVOLTED) YOU SAVED MY
SUPR III (81)	HAVE ALL HAD THEIR TURN AT THE BROILED RABBIT,	JUST	AS I SHALL HAVE MY TURN AT THE SAVOY. INDEED, I HAVE
PRES (155)	WILL AVAIL YOU JUST AS LITTLE. I SWEEP THEM AWAY,	JUST	AS I SWEEP YOUR PLANS OF CAMPAIGN " MADE IN GERMANY"--
MTH5 (209)	AND SAW; AND I WANTED ALL THAT FOR MYSELF,	JUST	AS I WANTED THE MOON TO PLAY WITH. NOW THE WORLD IS
BULL I (94)	IT. SHE DIDNT COUNT. I WAS ROMANTIC ABOUT HER,	JUST	AS I WAS ROMANTIC ABOUT BYRON'S HEROINES OR THE OLD
HART PREFACE(3)	RUSSIAN! " THEY DID NOT STRIKE ME IN THAT WAY,	JUST	AS IBSEN'S INTENSELY NORWEGIAN PLAYS EXACTLY FITTED
FANY II (292)	MARGARET! /MARGARET/ (CONTINUING) HE DID,	JUST	AS IF HE HAD KNOWN ME FOR YEARS. WE GOT ON TOGETHER
POSN PREFACE(367)	IF HE PRODUCES THE PLAY HE IS LEGALLY RESPONSIBLE	JUST	AS IF HE HAD WRITTEN IT HIMSELF. WITHOUT PROTECTION HE
ARMS I (14)	IF YOU WOULD, ALL YOU HAVE TO DO IS TO SCOLD ME	JUST	AS IF I WERE A LITTLE BOY AND YOU MY NURSE. IF I WERE
ROCK I (214)	DOING. AND HERE WE ARE ARGUING AND TALKING	JUST	AS IF IT WAS AN ALL NIGHT SITTING OF THE BOROUGH
JITT III (53)	MY BUSINESS AND RESPONSIBILITIES AND DUTIES GO ON	JUST	AS IF NOTHING HAD HAPPENED. /FESSLER/ I'M SO GLAD YOU
DEVL I (5)	GOES OUT). SHE'D HAVE GONE TO BED LAST NIGHT	JUST	AS IF NOTHING HAD HAPPENED IF I'D LET HER. /CHRISTY/ (
FANY II (290)	EVEN KNOW THAT I KNEW, COMING OUT OF MY MOUTH	JUST	AS IF SOMEBODY ELSE HAD SPOKEN THEM. THE POLICEMAN
CAPT I (226)	WITH YOUR SERVANTS; SO YOU MUST GO ON GARDENING	JUST	AS IF WE WERE NOT HERE. /SIR HOWARD/ I AM SORRY TO HAVE
ROCK II (277)	COULDNT BEAR HIS BEING DISTANT WITH ME. HE TALKS	JUST	AS IF WE WERE MARRIED ALREADY. /SIR ARTHUR/ QUITE. BUT
MIS. PREFACE(61)	ON YOUR KNOWING BETTER THAN YOUR ELDERS, ARE	JUST	AS IMPORTANT AS THOSE OF THE SERMON ON THE MOUNT; BUT
LION PREFACE(78)	RELIEVING THE MAN OF ALL PREOCCUPATION WITH SEX	JUST	AS IN HER CAPACITY OF HOUSEKEEPER AND COOK SHE RELIEVES
DOCT PREFACE(29)	SYMPTOMS, COUNTERACT THEM IN VERY SMALL DOSES,	JUST	AS IN MORE MODERN PRACTICE IT IS FOUND THAT A
LION PREFACE(76)	ROBERT OWEN CALLED IT) OF COMMUNISM AND JESUISM.	JUST	AS IN OUR OWN TIME KARL MARX, NOT CONTENT TO TAKE
JOAN PREFACE(40)	PROBABLY SUCCEED IN DOING SO; AND THAT WILL BE	JUST	AS INTOLERANT AS MAKING IT COMPULSORY, NEITHER THE
MTH1 II (30)	CHILD-EATING! FOR THAT IS WHAT IT WOULD COME TO,	JUST	AS IT CAME TO LAMBS AND KIDS WHEN ABEL BEGAN WITH SHEEP
2TRU III (110)	WAR HAS BURNT GREAT RENTS IN THESE ANGELIC VEILS,	JUST	AS IT HAS SMASHED GREAT HOLES IN OUR CATHEDRAL ROOFS
BARB PREFACE(211)	OF SELFISH BULLYING AS THE RULE OF LIFE,	JUST	AS IT IS ASSUMED, ON THE STRENGTH OF THE SINGLE WORD
MIS. PREFACE(43)	FAR WORSE CONSEQUENCES THAN BURNT FINGERS. AND	JUST	AS IT IS PART OF THE BUSINESS OF ADULTS TO PROTECT
BULL PREFACE(48)	MILITARY AND NAVAL CODES SIMPLIFY LIFE FOR THEM	JUST	AS IT IS SIMPLIFIED FOR CHILDREN. NO SOLDIER IS ASKED
SUPR PREFACE(R14)	THOUGHT MADE BYRON A BOLDER POET THAN WORDSWORTH	JUST	AS IT MADE PETER A BOLDER KING THAN GEORGE III; BUT AS
SUPR I (28)	MIGHT HAVE BEEN ME: IT MIGHT HAVE BEEN RAMSDEN;	JUST	AS IT MIGHT HAVE BEEN ANYBODY. IF IT HAD, WHAT COULD WE
MTH4 III SD(198)	THE ENVOY'S HAT IS BLOWN OFF; BUT HE SEIZES IT	JUST	AS IT QUITS HIS TEMPLES, AND HOLDS IT ON WITH BOTH
INCA (237)	QUITE EASY. I HAD NO IDEA -- AM I TO HANG IT UP	JUST	AS IT WAS? THANK YOU. (SHE HANGS IT UP). ERMYNTRUDE
MTH3 (125)	BY YELLOW BRAINS, BROWN BRAINS, AND BLACK BRAINS,	JUST	AS IT WAS DONE IN MY EARLY DAYS BY JEWISH BRAINS,
CLEO V (200)	(PROMPTLY) KILL IT, MAN, WITHOUT MALICE,	JUST	AS IT WOULD KILL ME. WHAT DOES THIS PARABLE OF THE LION
ROCK II (265)	OF BRAHMA IT MUST END IN INDIA RULING ENGLAND	JUST	AS I, BY MY WEALTH AND MY BRAINS, GOVERN THIS ROOMFUL
BUOY IV (50)	BE AS KEEN IF THERE WERE NO BILLIONS? /JUNIUS/	JUST	AS KEEN. HOW OFTEN MUST I TELL YOU THAT I AM MAD ABOUT
MIS. PREFACE(73)	BY PERSUADING CHILDREN THAT HE IS NOT HUMAN,	JUST	AS LADIES USED TO PERSUADE THEM THAT THEY HAVE NO LEGS.
SUPR III (113)	BECAUSE WITHOUT IT HE BLUNDERS INTO DEATH.	JUST	AS LIFE, AFTER AGES OF STRUGGLE, EVOLVED THAT WONDERFUL
METH PREFACE(R76)	OUT OF THE FRYING-PAN INTO THE FIRE; AND WE ARE	JUST	AS LIKELY TO JUMP BACK AGAIN, NOW THAT WE FEEL HOTTER
LION PREFACE(46)	WAS THE PROPER DISTANCE. THE KAISER, KNOWING	JUST	AS LITTLE ABOUT IT AS THE CONQUEROR, WOULD SEND THAT
SUPR III (108)	IT'S AS UNIVERSAL AS SEA SICKNESS, AND MATTERS	JUST	AS LITTLE. BUT THAT ABOUT PUTTING AN IDEA INTO A MAN'S
PRES (155)	A MAN'S LAST RESOURCE-- WILL AVAIL YOU	JUST	AS LITTLE. I SWEEP THEM AWAY, JUST AS I SWEEP YOUR
DOCT I SD(96)	BEING THAT, THOUGH HE KNOWS JUST AS MUCH (AND	JUST	AS LITTLE) AS HIS CONTEMPORARIES, THE QUALIFICATIONS
ROCK II (261)	THINK A MASSACRE WOULD LAST IN ENGLAND TODAY?	JUST	AS LONG AS IT TAKES A DRUNKEN MAN TO GET SICK AND
GETT (313)	CAN GET DIVORCED. /REGINALD/ IT OUGHT TO BE FOR	JUST	AS LONG AS THE TWO PEOPLE LIKE. THATS WHAT I SAY.
HART PREFACE(25)	VICTORY EXCEPT THE HOPE THAT THE ENEMY MIGHT BE	JUST	AS MAD. ONLY BY VERY RESOLUTE REFLECTION AND REASONING
FABL PREFACE(79)	HE COULD NOT MAKE CONVERTS ON ANY OTHER TERMS,	JUST	AS MAHOMET FOUND THAT HE COULD NOT GOVERN THE ARABS
HART III (142)	WITH HIS FLUTE HOWLS WHEN SHE TWISTS HIS HEART,	JUST	AS MANGAN HOWLS WHEN MY WIFE TWISTS HIS. /LADY
BULL PREFACE(17)	IRISHMEN (NO DOUBT BECAUSE THEY MAKE MORE OF ME)	JUST	AS MANY ENGLISHMEN LIKE FRENCHMEN BETTER THAN
ROCK PREFACE(183)	IF IT IS YOUR WILL TO SPARE ME I CAN FIND YOU	JUST	AS MANY REASONS FOR THAT; AND MY DISCIPLES WILL SUPPLY
MTH2 (80)	ITS INTELLECTUAL ROOTS IN PHILOSOPHY AND SCIENCE	JUST	AS MEDIEVAL CHRISTIANITY HAD ITS INTELLECTUAL ROOTS IN
OVER PREFACE(156)	NAPOLEON SAID, BE THE OCCUPATION OF THE IDLE MAN	JUST	AS MEN ARE THE PREOCCUPATION OF THE IDLE WOMAN; BUT THE
DOCT I (99)	INTERESTING LITTLE CREATURES HAS AN IMITATOR.	JUST	AS MEN IMITATE EACH OTHER, GERMS IMITATE EACH OTHER.
MILL I (165)	MAKING PEOPLE HAPPY. UNHAPPY PEOPLE COME TO ME	JUST	AS MONEY COMES TO HER. /SAGAMORE/ (SHAKING HIS HEAD) I
BUOY IV (50)	FATHER AND DAUGHTER ON EARTH THE UPSHOT WOULD BE	JUST	AS MUCH A TOSS-UP AS IF WE WERE THE TWO DAMNDEST FOOLS.
ROCK II (255)	NONE OF YOU HAS MENTIONED YET: A DEMOCRAT. I AM	JUST	AS MUCH AGAINST CABINET DICTATORSHIP AS INDIVIDUAL
MIS. PREFACE(97)	WHICH IS A HIGHLY DESIRABLE IMPRESSION, AND	JUST	AS MUCH AS A CHILD IS CAPABLE OF RECEIVING FROM THE
BARB III (317)	DUTY TO MAKE STEPHEN YOUR SUCCESSOR. /UNDERSHAFT/	JUST	AS MUCH AS IT IS YOUR DUTY TO SUBMIT TO YOUR HUSBAND.
DOCT III (141)	FOR HER SAKE. I COULD HAVE BEEN HAD UP FOR IT	JUST	AS MUCH AS SHE. BUT WHEN A MAN MAKES A SACRIFICE OF
DOCT PREFACE(6)	THEM; BUT HE HAD TO DIE UNDER THEIR TREATMENT	JUST	AS MUCH AS THE MOST CREDULOUS IGNORAMUS THAT EVER PAID
PYGM II (240)	EASY TO CLEAN UP HERE. HOT AND COLD WATER ON TAP,	JUST	AS MUCH AS YOU LIKE, THERE IS. WOOLLY TOWELS, THERE IS;
SIM PREFACE(4)	POINTED OUT ON A FORMER OCCASION THAT THERE IS	JUST	AS MUCH EVIDENCE FOR A LAW OF THE CONSERVATION OF
MILL I (156)	YOU MAY SAY WHAT YOU LIKE; BUT YOU WERE	JUST	AS MUCH IN LOVE WITH ME AS I WAS WITH YOU. /EPIFANIA/
DOCT I SD(96)	HUMBUG: THE FACT BEING THAT, THOUGH HE KNOWS	JUST	AS MUCH (AND JUST AS LITTLE) AS HIS CONTEMPORARIES,
MIS. PREFACE(15)	NO REASON WHY CHILDREN AND ADULTS SHOULD NOT SEE	JUST	AS MUCH OF ONE ANOTHER AS IS GOOD FOR THEM, NO MORE AND
ROCK PREFACE(150)	GOVERNMENT DECIDED TO EXTERMINATE JESUS. THEY HAD	JUST	AS MUCH RIGHT TO DO SO AS TO EXTERMINATE THE TWO
LADY PREFACE(224)	THUS, THEY WOULD HAVE HANGED HIM." THERE IS	JUST	AS MUCH SHAKESPEAR HERE AS IN THE INEVITABLE QUOTATION
LION EPILOG (152)	OF DOCTORS GOES BY. BUT THE LIONS WILL HURT THEM	JUST	AS MUCH, AND THE SPECTATORS WILL ENJOY THEMSELVES JUST
LION EPILOG (152)	AS MUCH, AND THE SPECTATORS WILL ENJOY THEMSELVES	JUST	AS MUCH, AS THE ROMAN LIONS AND SPECTATORS USED TO DO.
MTH3 (123)	MINDS FOR YOU AND TELL YOU WHAT ORDERS TO GIVE,	JUST	AS MY BROTHER, WHO WAS A SERGEANT IN THE GUARDS, USED
SIM II (60)	BEATING YOU TO A JELLY FOR EVER SO LONG PAST; BUT	JUST	AS MY FISTS WERE CLENCHED TO DO IT YOU ALWAYS MANAGED
BARB PREFACE(231)	IMITATES CHRIST, BILL'S CONSCIENCE REACTS TO THIS	JUST	AS NATURALLY AS IT DOES TO THE OLD WOMAN'S THREATS. HE
KING I (194)	SHAFTESBURY, I SUPPOSE. HE IS THE PROTESTANT HERO	JUST	AS NELLY IS THE PROTESTANT WHOOR. I TELL YOU
CAPT NOTES (303)	ONE: IN ENGLAND EVERY COUNTY HAS ITS CATCHWORDS,	JUST	AS NO DOUBT EVERY STATE IN THE UNION HAS. I CANNOT
CAND I (99)	YOU CAN SEE THAT I AM A FOOL ABOUT YOUR WIFE;	JUST	AS NO DOUBT THAT OLD MAN WHO WAS HERE JUST NOW IS VERY
BULL II SD(111)	INSTINCT DOES NOT SEEM TO EXIST IN ROSSCULLEN.	JUST	AS NORA'S LIKING TO MISS A MEAL AND STAY OUT AT THE
POSN PREFACE(411)	AND RUINING A HERETIC. HE IS UNFORTUNATELY	JUST	AS OFTEN A BLACKMAILER, WHO HAS STUDIED HIS POWERS AS A
CAND I (89)	MAVOR MORELL. /MORELL/ (UNMOVED) I'LL SAY IT	JUST	AS OFTEN AS MAY BE NECESSARY TO CONVINCE YOU THAT IT'S
JITT III (55)	AND WORST PEOPLE HAVE TO CALL IN DOCTORS	JUST	AS OFTEN AS RESPECTABLE PEOPLE; AND A DOCTOR CANT HAVE
BARB I (256)	HE REALLY HAD A SORT OF RELIGION OF WRONGNESS.	JUST	AS ONE DOESNT MIND MEN PRACTISING IMMORALITY SO LONG AS
LADY PREFACE(230)	TEACHING SHAKESPEAR TO BE CIVIL TO CROWNED HEADS,	JUST	AS ONE WONDERS WHY TOLSTOY WAS ALLOWED TO GO FREE WHEN
JOAN 4 (95)	GASCONS BEGINNING TO CALL THEMSELVES FRENCHMEN,	JUST	AS OUR FELLOWS ARE BEGINNING TO CALL THEMSELVES
BULL IV (179)	BRING MONEY FROM ENGLAND TO IRELAND! /KEEGAN/	JUST	AS OUR IDLERS HAVE FOR SO MANY GENERATIONS TAKEN MONEY
MIS. PREFACE(47)	IT; BUT UNFORTUNATELY QUITE THE CONTRARY HAPPENS,	JUST	AS OUR ILL HEALTH DELIVERS US INTO THE HANDS OF MEDICAL
ARMS II (31)	THE SERBIAN ARMY? /PETKOFF/ NO. ALL AUSTRIANS,	JUST	AS OUR OFFICERS WERE ALL RUSSIANS. THIS WAS THE ONLY
FANY III (317)	WE WERE BROUGHT UP; AND WE GO TO CHURCH OR CHAPEL	JUST	AS OUR PARENTS DID; AND WE SAY WHAT EVERYBODY SAYS; AND
BARB PREFACE(234)	NATURALLY DIVIDED IN THE SAME WAY SOCIALLY. AND	JUST	AS OUR PERSISTENT ATTEMPTS TO FOUND POLITICAL
MTH2 (72)	EXACTLY LIKE US; AND EVERY ONE OF THEM FAILED	JUST	AS OURS IS FAILING. THEY FAILED BECAUSE THE CITIZENS
GENV PREFACE(5)	GREAT. NATIONS SHOULD ALWAYS BE PREPARED FOR WAR,	JUST	AS PEOPLE WITH ANY PROPERTY TO LEAVE SHOULD ALWAYS HAVE
SUPR HANDBOK(198)	AND MARIE ANTOINETTE MIGHT HAVE ASKED THE CROWD,	JUST	AS POINTEDLY AS FOUQUIER DID, WHETHER THEIR BREAD WOULD
GETT PREFACE(210)	ENABLES THE BEST WOMEN TO MONOPOLIZE ALL THE MEN,	JUST	AS POLYGYNY ENABLES THE BEST MEN TO MONOPOLIZE ALL THE
WIDO II (43)	ARE JUST AS BAD AS I AM. YOU MEAN THAT YOU ARE	JUST	AS POWERLESS TO ALTER THE STATE OF SOCIETY, THEN YOU
MIS. (113)	YOUR HEAD. I'LL STAND NONE OF YOUR SNOBBERY. I'M	JUST	AS PROUD OF TARLETON'S UNDERWEAR AS YOU ARE OF YOUR
CAPT II (259)	WHEN IT COMES TO THE POINT, REALLY BAD MEN ARE	JUST	AS RARE AS REALLY GOOD ONES. /BRASSBOUND/ YOU FORGET
DOCT I SD(81)	SERMON ON THE VANITY OF FEMININE PRETTINESS.	JUST	AS REDPENNY HAS NO DISCOVERED CHRISTIAN NAME, SHE HAS
GETT PREFACE(186)	ARE UNCOMFORTABLE IT MUST BE THEIR OWN FAULT,	JUST	AS RICH PEOPLE ARE APT TO IMAGINE THAT IF OTHER PEOPLE
FANY II (293)	WHO WERE NOT DOING ANYTHING, AND TREATED THEM	JUST	AS ROUGHLY AS THEY HAD TREATED THE STUDENTS. DUVALLET
JOAN PREFACE(11)	SWEDENBORG, BLAKE SAW VISIONS AND HEARD VOICES	JUST	AS SAINT FRANCIS AND SAINT JOAN DID. IF NEWTON'S
SUPR PREFACE(R32)	OFTEN SANER AND SHREWDER THAN THE PHILOSOPHERS	JUST	AS SANCHO PANZA WAS OFTEN SANER AND SHREWDER THAN DON
CAND III (132)	SOFA, HUGGING HIS ANKLES) OH, SHE FORGAVE YOU,	JUST	AS SHE FORGIVES ME FOR BEING A COWARD, AND A WEAKLING,
PPP (201)	BUT FITZTOLLEMACHE SEIZES HER BY THE NIGHT-GOWN	JUST	AS SHE IS ESCAPING). UNHAND ME, VILLAIN! /FITZ/ THIS
NEVR IV (282)	SIR, YOUD FIND THAT SIMPLE FAITH WOULD LEAVE YOU	JUST	AS SHORT AS NORMAN BLOOD. I FIND IT BEST TO SPELL
METH PREFACE(R52)	WORLD DEPENDED ON THE DISAPPEARANCE OF ITS TAIL,	JUST	AS SOME ANCIENT AND FORGOTTEN EXPERIMENTER SEEMS TO
JOAN PREFACE(18)	CALL A VISUALIZER. SHE SAW IMAGINARY SAINTS	JUST	AS SOME OTHER PEOPLE SEE IMAGINARY DIAGRAMS AND
POSN PREFACE(422)	CHANCE WITH A STAR CHAMBER THAN WITH A JURY,	JUST	AS SOME SOLDIERS WOULD RATHER TAKE THEIR CHANCE WITH A
POSN PREFACE(399)	FALLING BEHIND THE NATIONS WHICH TOLERATED HIM	JUST	AS SPAIN FELL BEHIND ENGLAND; BUT THE PROPER ACTION TO
ARMS I (5)	TO THINK THAT IT WAS ALL TRUE! THAT SERGIUS IS	JUST	AS SPLENDID AND NOBLE AS HE LOOKS! THAT THE WORLD IS

SUPR HANDBOK(210) TO SMITH AND BROWN FOR THE SAKE OF PREACHING, JUST AS ST FRANCIS PREACHED TO THE BIRDS AND ST ANTHONY TO
METH PREFACE(R30) ORCHIDS, AND HAD ACTUALLY PRODUCED FLOWERS JUST AS STRANGE TO EVE. HIS QUARREL WITH THE EVOLUTIONISTS
MIS. (125) A SORT OF INSTINCT AGAINST IT, I THINK, THATS JUST AS STRONG AS THE OTHER INSTINCT. ONE OF THEM, TO MY
LION PREFACE(72) AT ALL COSTS IS LARGELY SELF-INDULGENCE, WHICH IS JUST AS SUICIDAL, JUST AS WEAK, JUST AS COWARDLY AS
MILL III (186) THAT WE SEND THEM OUR STUFF DIRECT AND COLLECT JUST AS SUPERFLEW DID. WHEN I HAVE ARRANGED EVERYTHING WITH
PRES (143) BUT IF YOU FIRE A RIFLE INTO A GERMAN HE DROPS JUST AS SURELY AS A RABBIT DOES. /BALSQUITH/ BUT DASH IT
SUPR HANDBOK(203) OFFICER INDULGES IN TORTURE IN THE PHILIPPINES JUST AS THE ARISTOCRATIC ENGLISH OFFICER DID IN SOUTH
UNPL PREFACE(R11) COME INTO EXISTENCE BUT FOR THE PLAYS OF IBSEN, JUST AS THE BAYREUTH FESTIVAL PLAYHOUSE WOULD NEVER HAVE
2TRU PREFACE(8) ELSE OF AN ACCEPTED KIND THAT I CAN IMAGINE. FOR, JUST AS THE BEAN-FEASTER CAN LIVE LIKE A LORD FOR AN
DOCT PREFACE(29) HAVE THEIR USES, REAL AS WELL AS IMAGINARY. BUT JUST AS THE BEST CARPENTER OR MASON WILL RESIST THE
O'FL (211) HAVE ME HUMBUG YOU AND TELL YOU LIES AS I USED, JUST AS THE BOYS HERE, GOD HELP THEM, WOULD RATHER HAVE ME
SUPR HANDBOK(196) RIGHTS, THE FABIAN SOCIETY IS PATTED ON THE BACK JUST AS THE CHRISTIAN SOCIAL UNION IS, WHILST THE SOCIALIST
MTH3 (131) OUT: THAT THE ENGLISH FACE IS NOT AN ADULT FACE, JUST AS THE ENGLISH MIND IS NOT AN ADULT MIND. /BURGE-LUBIN/
DOCT PREFACE(31) WHAT NOT, IS BY NO MEANS CONFINED TO BARBARIANS. JUST AS THE MANIFOLD WICKEDNESS AND STUPIDITIES OF OUR
POSN PREFACE(409) A DIFFICULT ONE. THE MUNICIPALITY CAN BE LIMITED JUST AS THE MONARCHY IS LIMITED. THE ACT TRANSFERRING
BULL PREFACE(48) AND INTOLERABLE TO THE WILLIAM TELL TEMPERAMENT. JUST AS THE MOST INCORRIGIBLE CRIMINAL IS ALWAYS, WE ARE
METH PREFACE(R63) OF THE INEXORABLE LAWS OF POLITICAL ECONOMY, JUST AS THE NEO-DARWINIANS WERE PRESENTLY ASSURING US THAT
DOCT PREFACE(29) AND HOMEOPATHY ARE TYPICAL OF ALL THE REST. JUST AS THE OBJECT OF A TRADE UNION UNDER EXISTING
SUPR III (91) LOOK WAS ONLY AN ILLUSION. YOUR WRINKLES LIED, JUST AS THE PLUMP SMOOTH SKIN OF MANY A STUPID GIRL OF 17,
METH PREFACE(R41) LONG NECK WAS EVOLVED BY INTENTIONAL SELECTION, JUST AS THE RACE-HORSE OR THE FANTAIL PIGEON HAS BEEN
2TRU PREFACE(21) NATURAL FACT WE SHALL ALWAYS HAVE TO COME BACK, JUST AS THE RUSSIAN REVOLUTIONISTS, WHO WERE REEKING WITH
BARB PREFACE(224) SAVE HIS OWN. THIS IS WHAT ALL THE CHURCHES FIND JUST AS THE SALVATION ARMY AND BARBARA FIND IT IN THE PLAY.
SUPR HANDBOK(198) CIVILIZATION BECOME FATAL INSTEAD OF PRODUCTIVE, JUST AS THE SAME QUALITIES WHICH MAKE THE LION KING IN THE
PRES (144) ENGLAND WILL BE SECURE WHEN ENGLAND IS DEAD, JUST AS THE STREETS OF LONDON WILL BE SAFE WHEN THERES NO
FABL PREFACE(84) AS TO BE PRE-MARX. FORTUNATELY IT CAN BE TAUGHT, JUST AS THE THEORIES OF RENT AND VALUE CAN BE TAUGHT; AND
METH PREFACE(R49) IF NO HUMAN BEING HAD EVER BEEN CONSCIOUS, JUST AS THE TREES STAND IN THE FOREST DOING WONDERFUL THINGS
MIS. SD(120) HAT STAND). MRS TARLETON AND HYPATIA COME BACK JUST AS THE TWO MEN ARE GOING OUT. HYPATIA SALUTES
MRS PREFACE(153) CHAMPIONS OF TEN YEARS AGO REMONSTRATE WITH ME JUST AS THE VETERANS OF THOSE BRAVE DAYS REMONSTRATED WITH
MTH4 II (192) I CURSE THE DAY WHEN LONG LIFE WAS INVENTED, JUST AS THE VICTIMS OF JONHOBSNOXIUS CURSED THE DAY WHEN
CLEO NOTES (209) IS DISPUTED. THEY REVEAL SOME OF HIS QUALITIES JUST AS THE VOYAGE OF A NATURALIST ROUND THE WORLD REVEALS
MIS. PREFACE(76) AS IT WERE. FOR THERE ARE FROWSTY CHILDREN, JUST AS THERE ARE FROWSTY ADULTS, WHO DONT WANT FREEDOM.
SUPR III SD(73) FRIENDLY AND FRANK MANNER; FOR THERE ARE BIPEDS, JUST AS THERE ARE QUADRUPEDS, WHO ARE TOO DANGEROUS TO BE
GETT PREFACE(233) MAYOR MORELL DOES IN MY PLAY. HE RECOGNIZES THAT JUST AS THERE IS NOT ROOM FOR TWO WOMEN IN THAT SACREDLY
CLEO II (124) PTOLEMY AND CLEOPATRA ARE BORN KING AND CONSORT JUST AS THEY ARE BORN BROTHER AND SISTER. /BRITANNUS/ (
KING I (221) NOT BEGIN TALKING ABOUT THE STARS TO PEOPLE JUST AS THEY ARE GOING AWAY QUIETLY. IT IS A HABIT THAT IS
SUPR HANDBOK(212) EXPLOITED BY JOINT STOCK COMPANIES FOR DIVIDENDS, JUST AS THEY ARE IN ORDINARY INDUSTRIES. EVEN A JOINT STOCK
SUPR HANDBOK(196) INTO PRISON, AND IN THE LAST RESORT " EXECUTED" JUST AS THEY ARE WHEN THEY BREAK THE PRESENT LAW. BUT AS OUR
GENV PREFACE(6) TO ENGLISHMEN THAT THEY ARE UNCONSCIOUS OF IT, JUST AS THEY CANNOT TASTE WATER BECAUSE IT IS ALWAYS IN
LION PREFACE(22) THE SYNAGOGUES AND IN THE OPEN AIR INDIFFERENTLY, JUST AS THEY COME. HE REPEATEDLY SAYS, " I DESIRE MERCY AND
DOCT PREFACE(36) JUST AS WELL HAVE BEEN SPARED: THINGS WENT ON JUST AS THEY DID BEFORE. IN THE SAME WAY, THE LIST OF
MTH1 II (21) AS HE KILLED THE BEASTS? I STRUCK; AND HE DIED, JUST AS THEY DID. THEN I GAVE UP YOUR OLD SILLY DRUDGING
HART PREFACE(40) HIDE UNDER THE MANTLE OF THE IDEALS ON THE STAGE JUST AS THEY DO IN REAL LIFE. AND THOUGH THERE MAY BE BETTER
GENV PREFACE(15) SAW VISIONS AND THEIR YOUNG MEN DREAMED DREAMS JUST AS THEY DO NOW. BUT THEY WERE NOT ALL SUCH FOOLS AS TO
LION PREFACE(45) ARITHMETICAL NUMBERS APPEALED TO THE MIDDLE AGES JUST AS THEY DO TO US, BECAUSE THEY ARE DIFFICULT TO DEAL
2TRU PREFACE(11) TOURISTS IN THE PALACE HOTELS AND LUXURY LINERS JUST AS THEY DO TO THE TRAMPS ON THE HIGHROAD. THEY COME UP
MIS. PREFACE(89) AND OPERA GLASSES AT THE MISCREANT, BEHAVED JUST AS THEY DO WHEN RICHTER CONDUCTS IT. THE MASS OF
DOCT PREFACE(26) AT " POPULAR PRICES" IN PRIVATE ENTERPRISE SHOPS JUST AS THEY EXPECT TO FIND OUNCES OF TOBACCO AND PAPERS OF
LION EPILOG (150) GOOD OR BAD. THEY SIMPLY INDULGED THEIR PASSIONS, JUST AS THEY HAD ALWAYS INDULGED THEIR CLASS PREJUDICES AND
BULL PREFACE(66) OF BOTH PARTIES IDOLIZED HIM WITHOUT KNOWING WHY, JUST AS THEY HAD FORMERLY IDOLIZED LORD CROMER AND LORD
SIM II (81) THE UNEXPECTED ISLANDS HAVE TO BE GOVERNED TODAY JUST AS THEY HAD TO BE YESTERDAY. SALLY: IF YOU HAVE GIVEN
GETT (261) THE COMPLIMENT). THEY JOKE ABOUT THE GREENGROCER, JUST AS THEY JOKE ABOUT THE MOTHER-IN-LAW. BUT THEY CANT GET
3PLA PREFACE(R33) SINCE HIS OWN TIME, HAVE DELIGHTED IN HIS PLAYS JUST AS THEY MIGHT HAVE DELIGHTED IN A PARTICULAR BREED OF
MRS PREFACE(168) IN A POPULAR SENTIMENTAL PLAY. THEY SAY THIS JUST AS THEY MIGHT SAY THAT NO TWO STRAIGHT LINES WOULD
DOCT PREFACE(60) ON THE WHOLE, WHAT THEIR PATIENTS BELIEVE, JUST AS THEY MUST WEAR THE SORT OF HAT THEIR PATIENTS WEAR.
LION EPILOG (151) AMIABLE AS WE, CROWDED TO SEE THE LIONS EAT HIM JUST AS THEY NOW CROWD THE LION-HOUSE IN THE ZOO AT
PRES (148) WASNT FOR THAT, THE MEN'D PUT THE FIGHTIN ON US JUST AS THEY PUT ALL THE OTHER DHRUDGERY. WHAT WOULD YOU DO
KING I (191) RIGHT: THEY TAKE THEIR CHOICE AND SEND FOR YOU, JUST AS THEY SENT FOR ME. /JAMES/ YES, IF YOU LOOK AT IT IN
GETT PREFACE(192) ROUTINE OF THE KITCHEN, NURSERY, AND DRAWING-ROOM JUST AS THEY WENT THROUGH THE ROUTINE OF THE OFFICE. THEY
JITT III (62) COMMONNESSES, IN THEIR RELATIONS WITH WOMEN, JUST AS THEY WILL EAT ROTTEN CHEESE, AND HALF-PUTRID
MIS. PREFACE(89) OF BEETHOVEN'S NINTH SYMPHONY OR OF WAGNER'S RING JUST AS THEY WILL SIT THROUGH A DULL SERMON OR A FRONT BENCH
BULL PREFACE(12) HOME RULE WHICH DO NOT EXIST UNDER ENGLISH RULE, JUST AS THINGS HAVE BEEN DONE UNDER THE IRISH LOCAL
JOAN EPILOG (162) MAKE YOU A SAINT, YOU WILL OWE YOUR HALO TO ME, JUST AS THIS LUCKY MONARCH OWES HIS CROWN TO YOU. /JOAN/ (
CAND I SD(93) THERE IS SOMETHING NOXIOUS IN THIS UNEARTHLINESS, JUST AS TO POETIC PEOPLE THERE IS SOMETHING ANGELIC IN IT.
ROCK PREFACE(150) REGARDED THE ALBIGENSES AS THE ENEMIES OF GOD, JUST AS TORQUEMADA REGARDED THE JEWS AS THE MURDERERS OF
SUPR II (56) HIS HAT AND KNOW HIS PLACE. I AM ENRY'S SLAVE, JUST AS UNCLE JAMES WAS HIS COOK'S SLAVE. /STRAKER/ (
MIS. PREFACE(72) WILL BE PRECOCITY OF THE INTELLECT, WHICH IS JUST AS UNDESIRABLE AS PRECOCITY OF THE EMOTIONS. WE STILL
GETT (272) FOR THE GREENGROCER, NOT FOR THE ALDERMAN. IT'S JUST AS UNPLEASANT TO GET MORE THAN YOU BARGAIN FOR AS TO
FANY III (318) SIT DOWN, MADAM. ALLOW ME TO DISCHARGE MY DUTIES JUST AS USUAL, SIR. I ASSURE YOU THAT IS THE CORRECT THING.
JOAN PREFACE(52) THEMSELVES BUT THE CHURCH AND THE INQUISITION, JUST AS WARWICK HAS TO MAKE THE FEUDAL SYSTEM INTELLIGIBLE,
METH PREFACE(R25) AND DISCARD AN ORGAN WHEN WE NO LONGER NEED THEM, JUST AS WE ACQUIRED THEM; BUT THIS PROCESS IS SLOW AND
SUPR I (14) OUR ACCENTS, OF OUR OPINIONS, OF OUR EXPERIENCE, JUST AS WE ARE ASHAMED OF OUR NAKED SKINS. GOOD LORD, MY
SUPR HANDBOK(180) OF MUCH OF IT WE ARE NOT EVEN CONSCIOUS, JUST AS WE ARE NOT NORMALLY CONSCIOUS OF KEEPING UP OUR
GENV I (45) OF PROPAGANDA IS RECIPROCAL. YOU ARE BOUND BY IT JUST AS WE ARE. /HE/ BUT WHAT IS THIS SEDITIOUS ORGANIZATION
NEVR II (233) CLANDON/ MY DEAR: WE CANNOT SIT DOWN TO LUNCH JUST AS WE ARE. WE SHALL COME BACK AGAIN. WE MUST HAVE NO
LION PREFACE(61) THE RIGHT TO AN INCOME AS SACRED AND EQUAL, JUST AS WE NOW BEGIN BY HOLDING THE RIGHT TO LIFE AS SACRED
FABL II (106) BECAUSE IT'S A SAFE DISTANCE FROM HIS OWN PEOPLE, JUST AS WE SELECTED HIROSHIMA IN 1945. HE THINKS ISLANDS ARE
GETT PREFACE(253) ARGUING WITH, WE SHALL DEAL WITH THE CHILDREN JUST AS WE SHOULD DEAL WITH THEM IF THEIR HOMES WERE BROKEN
LION PREFACE(31) AT THE SCOURGING AND MOCKING AND CRUCIFIXION JUST AS WE SHOULD IF RUSKIN HAD BEEN TREATED IN THAT WAY
MIS. PREFACE(3) AND AGAIN. WE SHOULD LIKE TO LIVE A LITTLE LONGER JUST AS WE SHOULD LIKE 50 POUNDS: THAT IS, WE SHOULD TAKE IT
POSN PREFACE(388) CORPUS ACT, OR A PROCLAMATION OF MARTIAL LAW, JUST AS WE STOP THE TRAFFIC IN A STREET DURING A FIRE, OR
METH PREFACE(R25) OPERATIONS, WE WANT TO BE UNCONSCIOUS OF THEM JUST AS WE WANTED TO ACQUIRE THEM; AND WE FINALLY WIN WHAT
FANY III (317) THE WAY THEY ALWAYS DID. WE BRING OUR CHILDREN UP JUST AS WE WERE BROUGHT UP; AND WE GO TO CHURCH OR CHAPEL
LION PREFACE(72) SELF-INDULGENCE, WHICH IS JUST AS SUICIDAL, JUST AS WEAK, JUST AS COWARDLY AS SELF-DENIAL. IBSEN, WHO
BARB III (315) THAT STEPHEN COULD NOT CARRY ON THE FOUNDRY JUST AS WELL AS ALL THE OTHER SONS OF THE BIG BUSINESS
MTH5 (252) BE SO FUNNY. /THE HE-ANCIENT/ MY CHILD: I AM JUST AS WELL AS I AM. I WOULD NOT LIFT MY FINGER NOW TO HAVE
NEVR IV (284) WHATS RIGHT AND DIGNIFIED AND STRONG AND NOBLE, JUST AS WELL AS SHE DOES; BUT OH, THE THINGS I DO! THE
LION PREFACE(101) ABOUT THE NEED FOR FOOD AND REPRODUCTION, MIGHT JUST AS WELL BE A FOOL AND A SCOUNDREL FOR ANY USE HE COULD
ROCK I (201) FIFTY THOUSAND OTHER THINGS EVERY DAY THAT MIGHT JUST AS WELL BE DONE BY THE BEADLE OF BURLINGTON ARCADE.
2TRU I (46) I, BECAUSE I AM RESPECTABLE AND A LADY, MIGHT JUST AS WELL BE IN PRISON. /THE BURGLAR/ DONT YOU WISH YOU
BULL III (132) /LARRY/ FOR MODERN INDUSTRIAL PURPOSES YOU MIGHT JUST AS WELL BE, BARNEY. YOURE ALL CHILDREN: THE BIG WORLD
MIS. PREFACE(4) CONCEIVE I CANNOT REMEMBER); SO THAT YOU MAY JUST AS WELL GIVE ME A NEW NAME AND FACE THE FACT THAT I AM
MTH2 (44) HANDS, ALIVE AND INTENSELY INTERESTING, WE MAY JUST AS WELL GO OUT AND DIG THE GARDEN UNTIL IT IS TIME TO
MIS. PREFACE(50) LITERARY EXERCISES HAS LEFT ON THEM THEY MIGHT JUST AS WELL HAVE BEEN PUT ON THE TREADMILL. IN FACT THEY
DOCT PREFACE(36) EXACTLY THAT THE MISERY CAUSED BY THE FLOOD MIGHT JUST AS WELL HAVE BEEN SPARED: THINGS WENT ON JUST AS THEY
FANY PROLOG (262) TO GIVE IT, BECAUSE IF WE HADNT HAD HIM WE MIGHT JUST AS WELL HAVE HAD NOBODY AT ALL. /THE COUNT/ BUT WHAT
SUPR I (33) BOYS. I DIDNT HATE; I LIED ABOUT THINGS I MIGHT JUST AS WELL HAVE TOLD THE TRUTH ABOUT; I STOLE THINGS I
2TRU I (39) NO INTENTION OF MEETING YOU AGAIN, SO YOU MAY JUST AS WELL TAKE IT OFF. /THE NURSE/ I HAVNT BROKEN TO HER
SUPR III SD(73) HEIGHTENED QUALIFICATIONS FOR MISCHIEF, IT IS JUST AS WELL THAT THEY ARE AT LARGE IN THE SIERRA, AND IN
BARB I (259) ANYHOW, BARBARA SHANT BULLY ME; BUT STILL IT'S JUST AS WELL THAT YOUR FATHER SHOULD BE HERE BEFORE SHE HAS
SIM PREFACE(18) IS A FORM OF MARRIAGE LIKE ANY OTHER; AND IT IS JUST AS WELL TO REMIND OUR WESTERN AND VERY INSULAR
CURE PREFACE(224) WAS CONFINED TO THE ENGLISH CONCERTINA. THAT DID JUST AS WELL. AS A LAST DESPERATE RESORT A PIANOLA BEHIND
FANY III (313) ABOUT WHAT A DOG HE IS; AND IT PLEASES PEOPLE JUST AS WELL. WHAT A WORLD IT IS! /KNOX/ IT TURNED MY BLOOD
MTH3 (125) WONDER OF THE WORLD. THEY ALWAYS WERE, AND IT IS JUST AS WELL; FOR OTHERWISE THEIR SENSUALITY WOULD BECOME
POSN (437) /THE WOMEN/ (MURMURING) THATS ALWAYS THE WAY. JUST AS WE'D SETTLED DOWN TO WORK. WHAT HARM ARE WE DOING..
SUPR II (68) WHAT ABOUT THE LADY'S VIEWS? /TANNER/ SHE IS JUST AS WILLING TO BE LEFT TO MR ROBINSON AS MR ROBINSON IS
SUPR PREFACE(R20) REAL CONTROL THAN I HAVE OVER MY WIFE), BEHAVES JUST AS WOMAN DID IN THE PLAYS OF SHAKESPEAR. AND SO YOUR
DOCT PREFACE(15) CASES UNDER POVERTY-STRICKEN DOMESTIC CONDITIONS, JUST AS WOMEN WHO HAVE BEEN TRAINED AS DOMESTIC SERVANTS IN

BULL IV	(170)	TONE) WHEN I LEFT YOU THAT TIME, I WAS	JUST	AS WRETCHED AS YOU. I DIDNT RIGHTLY KNOW WHAT I WANTED
MTH5	(206)	OWN VOICE AND BOUNDED ABOUT WHEN IT WAS HAPPY,	JUST	AS YOU ARE DOING HERE. IT IS YOU, MY CHILDREN, WHO ARE
JOAN 5	(109)	/DUNOIS/ YOU MUST LEARN TO BE ABSTEMIOUS IN WAR,	JUST	AS YOU ARE IN YOUR FOOD AND DRINK, MY LITTLE SAINT.
JITT I	(22)	YOU DEMAND, AND TAKE ALL THE GHASTLY CONSEQUENCES	JUST	AS YOU ARE MAD ENOUGH TO MEAN THEM. ARE YOU SATISFIED
ARMS I	(20)	GREAT SCENE WHERE ERNANI, FLYING FROM HIS FOES	JUST	AS YOU ARE TONIGHT, TAKES REFUGE IN THE CASTLE OF HIS
CATH 1	(171)	CHANGE. /PATIOMKIN/ NONSENSE! YOU SHALL COME	JUST	AS YOU ARE. YOU SHALL SHEW HER YOUR CALVES LATER ON.
LION PREFACE	(95)	THAN THIS, YOU CAN BECOME A FOLLOWER OF JESUS	JUST	AS YOU CAN BECOME A FOLLOWER OF CONFUCIUS OR LAO TSE,
MIS. PREFACE	(22)	HATED THE SCHOOL MUCH MORE THAN THE BOYS DID.	JUST	AS YOU CANNOT IMPRISON A MAN WITHOUT IMPRISONING A
OVER PREFACE	(163)	IN WHICH YOU CANNOT PRESENT SEX ON THE STAGE,	JUST	AS YOU CANNOT PRESENT MURDER. MACBETH MUST NO MORE
SUPR III	(102)	YOUR SENTIMENTS HEROISM, YOUR ASPIRATIONS VIRTUE,	JUST	AS YOU DID ON EARTH; BUT HERE THERE ARE NO HARD FACTS
PHIL II	(106)	ABOUT THEIR BEING ONLY WOMEN! YOU TALK TO THEM	JUST	AS YOU DO TO ME OR ANY OTHER FELLOW. THATS THE SECRET
JITT III	(77)	ME SO. WHEN YOU LET OUT ABOUT HALDENSTEDT I FELT	JUST	AS YOU FEEL NOW. TOMORROW YOU WILL THINK BETTER OF IT.
MTH4 III	(194)	IN A BECOMING MANNER. /ZOO/ VERY WELL. BEHAVE	JUST	AS YOU FEEL. IT DOESNT MATTER HOW YOU BEHAVE. BUT KEEP
MILL III	(181)	TELL ME WHY YOU CANNOT GIVE ME WORK TO LIVE BY	JUST	AS YOU GIVE IT, I SUPPOSE, TO THE WOMEN I SAW IN THERE.
SUPR III	(101)	YES: THE SOUTHERNERS GIVE IT UP AND JOIN ME	JUST	AS YOU HAVE DONE. BUT THE ENGLISH REALLY DO NOT SEEM TO
CLEO NOTES	(206)	OF THE TRUTH (ALL OTHERS DAMNABLE HERESIES),	JUST	AS YOU HAVE THEM TODAY, FLOURISHING IN COUNTRIES EACH
LION PREFACE	(53)	WOULD HAVE RICH AND POOR, POVERTY AND AFFLUENCE,	JUST	AS YOU HAVE TODAY; FOR THERE WILL ALWAYS BE THE IDLE
JOAN 1	(57)	SIR, GOD KNOWS. WE ALL HAVE TO GO WITHOUT EGGS	JUST	AS YOU HAVE, SIR. THE HENS WILL NOT LAY. /ROBERT/ (
PHIL III	(142)	NOBLE OF YOU TO MAKE A VIRTUE OF GIVING HER UP,	JUST	AS YOU MADE A VIRTUE OF BEING A TEETOTALLER WHEN PERCY
NEVR IV	(284)	ABOVE US. IS THAT AGREED? /CRAMPTON/ YES, YES.	JUST	AS YOU PLEASE, MY DEAR. /GLORIA/ (NOT SATISFIED,
CLEO II	(132)	RED CHEEKS AND CLENCHED FISTS) YOU ARE FREE TO DO	JUST	AS YOU PLEASE, CLEOPATRA. /CLEOPATRA/ THEN YOU DO NOT
CLEO IV	(167)	KNOW WHY I ALLOW YOU ALL TO CHATTER IMPERTINENTLY	JUST	AS YOU PLEASE, INSTEAD OF TREATING YOU AS FTATATEETA
ARMS III	(62)	YOU ALLOW HIM TO MAKE LOVE TO YOU BEHIND MY BACK,	JUST	AS YOU TREAT ME AS YOUR AFFIANCED HUSBAND BEHIND HIS.
CAPT II	(258)	YOU RULE YOUR MEN; AND IN REVENGE AND PUNISHMENT,	JUST	AS YOU WANT TO REVENGE YOUR MOTHER? DIDNT YOU
NEVR II	(230)	HIM) I WAS MASTER PHILIP: WAS SO FOR MANY YEARS;	JUST	AS YOU WERE ONCE MASTER FINCH. (HE GIVES THE HAND A
PHIL II	(127)	A WOMANLY WOMAN. I WAS GUARANTEED WHEN I JOINED	JUST	AS YOU WERE. /GRACE/ BY MR CHARTERIS, I THINK, AT YOUR
BARB I	(255)	SONS? /LADY BRITOMART/ OH YES: THEY MARRIED	JUST	AS YOUR FATHER DID; AND THEY WERE RICH ENOUGH TO BUY
DEVL II	(38)	I DARESAY YOUR LOVE HELPS HIM TO BE A GOOD MAN,	JUST	AS YOUR HATE HELPS ME TO BE A BAD ONE. /JUDITH/ MY
FANY PROLOG	(258)	I SHUT OUT WILL ALWAYS BE THE NINETEENTH CENTURY,	JUST	AS YOUR NATIONAL ANTHEM WILL ALWAYS BE GOD SAVE THE
MIS.	(156)	WOMAN'S RIGHT IN HER HEAD. DO YOU KNOW WHAT SHE'S	JUST	ASKED FOR? /TARLETON/ CHAMPAGNE? /MRS TARLETON/ NO.
CAPT III	(281)	TO YOUR MEN. /LADY CICELY/ I DIDNT GIVE ORDERS: I	JUST	ASKED HIM. HE HAS SUCH A NICE FACE! DONT YOU THINK SO,
ARMS II	(42)	/CATHERINE/ OH, QUITE AS A FRIEND, PAUL. I WAS	JUST	ASKING CAPTAIN BLUNTSCHLI TO STAY TO LUNCH; BUT HE
WIDO II	(39)	NEVER MENTIONING A WORD OF MY REASONS, BUT	JUST	ASKING HER TO BE CONTENT TO LIVE ON MY OWN LITTLE
BARB PREFACE	(217)	WOULD HAVE BEEN THE SHORTEST WAY TO THE GALLOWS,	JUST	AS, IF WE WERE ALL AS RESOLUTE AND CLEARSIGHTED AS
METH PREFACE	(R84)	IN WHICH EVERYONE WAS KILLED IN THE LAST ACT,	JUST	AS, IN SPITE OF MOLIERE, PLAYS IN WHICH EVERYONE WAS
JOAN 2,SD	(73)	ENABLES HIM TO HOLD HIS OWN IN CONVERSATION.	JUST	AT PRESENT HE IS EXCITED, LIKE A CHILD WITH A NEW TOY.
NEVR II SD	(226)	AVERAGE PROFESSIONAL CAPACITY AND RESPONSIBILITY.	JUST	AT PRESENT HE IS ENJOYING THE WEATHER AND THE SEA TOO
MIS. PREFACE	(100)	RESTRICTED TO WHAT ADULTS THINK GOOD FOR THEM.	JUST	AT PRESENT OUR YOUNG PEOPLE ARE GOING MAD OVER
DOCT PREFACE	(26)	DEPENDS NOT ONLY ON ITS COST, FOR EXAMPLE,	JUST	AT PRESENT THE WORLD HAS RUN RAVING MAD ON THE SUBJECT
DOCT I SD	(84)	CURIOSITY AND APPETITE, RATHER THAN THAT OF AGE.	JUST	AT PRESENT THE ANNOUNCEMENT OF HIS KNIGHTHOOD IN THE
SUPR I SD	(10)	WHO WOULD BE LOST WITHOUT A SENSE OF HUMOR.	JUST	AT PRESENT THE SENSE OF HUMOR IS IN ABEYANCE. TO SAY
SUPR III	(92)	WE HAVE A RAGE FOR 17; BUT IT DOES NOT LAST LONG.	JUST	AT PRESENT THE FASHIONABLE AGE IS 40-- OR SAY 37; BUT
PHIL I	(90)	JULIA. /CHARTERIS/ I'LL EXPLAIN IT ALL TOMORROW.	JUST	AT PRESENT WE'D REALLY BETTER FOLLOW JULIA'S EXAMPLE
BULL II SD	(101)	THEY ARE THE JUDGMENTS ON WHICH HER FATE HANGS	JUST	AT PRESENT. KEEGAN TOUCHES HIS HAT TO HER: HE DOES NOT
LIED	(195)	IT: INDEED I DO; BUT IT'S NOT SEASONABLE	JUST	AT PRESENT, NOW JUST LISTEN TO ME. I SUPPOSE YOU KNOW
CAND III	(144)	AND AT LAST I MET YOU. /CANDIDA/ NEVER MIND THAT	JUST	AT PRESENT. NOW I WANT YOU TO LOOK AT THIS OTHER BOY
METH PREFACE	(R22)	ON" BY A MYSTERIOUS FINGER. BUT NEVER MIND THAT	JUST	AT PRESENT. THE ADVENT OF THE NEO-LAMARCKIANS. I CALL
DOCT III	(138)	POCKET EMPTY) OH, I SAY, I HAVNT ANY MONEY ON ME	JUST	AT PRESENT. WALPOLE: WOULD YOU MIND LENDING ME
JOAN 1	(67)	SARCASTIC) ANYTHING ELSE? /JOAN/ (CHARMING) NOT	JUST	AT PRESENT, THANK YOU, SQUIRE. /ROBERT/ I SUPPOSE YOU
GETT	(287)	A CHAPTER IN MY HISTORY OF MARRIAGE. I'M	JUST	AT THE ROMAN BUSINESS, YOU KNOW. /THE GENERAL/ (COMING
MIS.	(154)	USUALLY SEVERAL OF US DO IT; BUT IT HAPPENS THAT	JUST	AT THIS MOMENT IT IS BEING KEPT UP BY ONE OF MY
MIS.	(168)	STONES AT HER. I DONT RECALL HER FEATURES	JUST	AT THIS MOMENT; BUT IVE NO DOUBT SHE WAS KIND TO ME AND
SIM PRO,1,	(22)	LOOK! YOU COULD WRITE YOUR NAME IN IT. AND IT'S	JUST	AWFUL TO SEE A YOUNG MAN DRINKING BEFORE ELEVEN IN THE
MIS.	(147)	I HAD TO LEAVE BOOKS IN HIS WAY; AND I FELT	JUST	AWFUL WHEN I DID IT. BELIEVE ME, SUMMERHAYS, THE
2TRU II	(68)	HE WONT BE WHEN I GET HIM UNDER MY THUMB. BUT YOU	JUST	BE CAREFUL. TAKE THIS TIP FROM ME: ONE MAN AT A TIME. I
JITT III	(62)	THERE IS A CERTAIN SIDE TO HUMAN NATURE THAT MUST	JUST	BE RULED OUT IN JUDGING PEOPLE'S CHARACTERS. EVEN THE
LIED	(199)	DONT OVERDO IT, OLD CHAP. HOWEVER, I WILL	JUST	BE SO FAR EXPLICIT AS TO SAY THAT IF YOU THINK THESE
ARMS I	(14)	SMELT POWDER BEFORE. WHY, HOW IS IT THAT YOUVE	JUST	BEATEN US? SHEER IGNORANCE OF THE ART OF WAR, NOTHING
INCA	(251)	HIS VANITY. VANITY! WHY DO THEY CALL HIM VAIN?	JUST	BECAUSE HE IS ONE OF THE FEW MEN WHO ARE NOT AFRAID TO
HART III	(131)	VALET TO STAY WITH HIM LONGER THAN A FEW MONTHS?	JUST	BECAUSE HE IS TOO LAZY AND PLEASURE-LOVING TO HUNT AND
HART II	(92)	SWEET, HELPLESS CHILD INTO SUCH A BEAST'S CLAWS	JUST	BECAUSE HE WILL KEEP HER IN AN EXPENSIVE HOUSE AND MAKE
HART II	(93)	TO MANGAN: THEY THINK HE IS ALL RUGGED STRENGTH	JUST	BECAUSE HIS MANNERS ARE BAD. /MRS HUSHABYE/ DO YOU MEAN
GETT	(334)	YET THAT IS EXACTLY WHY I OUGHT TO BE MARRIED.	JUST	BECAUSE I HAVE THE QUALITIES MY COUNTRY WANTS MOST I
JITT I	(20)	LEFT THIS EVENING-- /BRUNO/ (RESOLUTELY) IT IS	JUST	BECAUSE I HAVE SO LITTLE TIME LEFT THAT I DARE NOT PUT
LION PROLOG	(106)	AS IF BUTTER WOULDNT MELT IN YOUR MOUTH, AND	JUST	BECAUSE I LOOK A BIG STRONG WOMAN, AND BECAUSE I'M
GETT	(331)	CANT YOU SEE THAT I MAYNT THROW LEO OVER	JUST	BECAUSE I SHOULD BE ONLY TOO GLAD TO. IT WOULD BE
HART II	(116)	BUT IT WILL NOT BE THROWN AWAY ON ME. IT IS	JUST	BECAUSE I WANT TO SAVE MY SOUL THAT I AM MARRYING FOR
PYGM II	(239)	SINFUL. I'M A SLAVE TO THAT WOMAN, GOVERNOR,	JUST	BECAUSE I'M NOT HER LAWFUL HUSBAND. AND SHE KNOWS IT
DOCT PREFACE	(51)	HAS RETAINED A PASSION OF CRUELTY IN MAN	JUST	BECAUSE IT IS INDISPENSABLE TO THE FULNESS OF HIS
VWOO 1	(121)	THE SEASIDE AND MAKE YOURSELF TIRED AND MISERABLE	JUST	BECAUSE IT'S A CHANGE; AND YOUD DO ANYTHING FOR A
SUPR I	(23)	HESITATE TO SACRIFICE YOU? /OCTAVIUS/ WHY, IT IS	JUST	BECAUSE SHE IS SELF-SACRIFICING THAT SHE WILL NOT
MTH2	(40)	HIM AND A LOT OF KIDS TUMBLING OVER ONE ANOTHER,	JUST	BECAUSE THE FELLOW HAS POETIC-LOOKING EYES AND A
BULL PREFACE	(8)	THE DREGS OF THE NATIONALIST MOVEMENTS, WHICH,	JUST	BECAUSE THEY ARE NATIONAL AND NORMAL, ARE MADE UP OF
CAND II	(118)	TALKING ABOUT CHRISTIANITY EVERY SUNDAY? WHY,	JUST	BECAUSE THEYVE BEEN SO FULL OF BUSINESS AND
ROCK II	(255)	THEY ARE OFFERED WHAT THEY WANT THEY WONT HAVE IT	JUST	BECAUSE YOU FELLOWS WANT IT TOO. THEY THINK THERE MUST
GENV IV	(128)	YOU CAN RELY ON NOTHING BUT THIS. THE NEWS HAS	JUST	BEEN BROADCAST TO ALL THE WORLD THROUGH THE
DEVL III	(50)	KEP HIM IN THE BRIDEWELL FOR THE NIGHT; AND HE'S	JUST	BEEN BROUGHT OVER HERE FOR THE COURT MARTIAL. DONT
HART PREFACE	(5)	TO READ IN THE DAILY PAPER THAT THE COUNTRY HAD	JUST	BEEN BROUGHT TO THE VERGE OF ANARCHY BECAUSE A NEW HOME
BUOY III	(29)	HIM A SALUTE. /SIR FERDINAND/ AS I HAVE ONLY	JUST	BEEN CALLED IN, AND AM A STRANGER TO YOU ALL, I AM
MTH2	(47)	TO HIS GUEST WITH THE FALSE CORDIALITY HE HAS	JUST	BEEN DENOUNCING) OH! HERE YOU ARE. DELIGHTED TO SEE
APPL II	(273)	ELECTION. /BOANERGES/ (DISMAYED) BUT IVE ONLY	JUST	BEEN ELECTED. DO YOU MEAN THAT I SHALL HAVE TO STAND
PHIL I	(78)	IS THIS YOUR GRATITUDE FOR THE WAY I HAVE	JUST	BEEN FLATTERING YOU? WHAT HAVE I NOT ENDURED FROM
CURE	(235)	YOURSELF GOING INTO BATTLE. IMAGINE THAT YOU HAVE	JUST	BEEN IN A BATTLE; AND THAT YOU HAVE SAVED YOUR COUNTRY
DOCT II	(118)	(HE SIGNS AND HANDS IT TO RIDGEON). IVE	JUST	BEEN MAKING A LITTLE NOTE OF THE RIVER TONIGHT: IT WILL
CAPT II	(251)	/SIR HOWARD/ (POLITELY BUT THREATENINGLY) I HAVE	JUST	BEEN NOTICING THAT YOU THINK SO. I DO NOT AGREE WITH
APPL II SD	(257)	NOT RANGED, BUT STANDING ABOUT AS IF THEY HAD	JUST	BEEN OCCUPIED. THE TERRACE IS ACCESSIBLE FROM THE LAWN
NEVR I	(210)	HOW TIRESOME OF YOU TO LET IT ALL OUT! AND WEVE	JUST	BEEN PRETENDING THAT YOU WERE A RESPECTABLE
FABL VI	(122)	/TEACHER/ LET ME INTRODUCE MYSELF. YOU HAVE	JUST	BEEN PROMOTED TO THE SIXTH FORM. I AM YOUR TEACHER.
FABL PREFACE	(64)	ON MENTAL ABNORMALITY BY DR MILLAIS CULPIN HAS	JUST	BEEN PUBLISHED. IT WOULD HAVE BEEN IMPOSSIBLE WHEN I
MTH2	(86)	TO DO WITH PRACTICAL POLITICS! THEY HAVE	JUST	BEEN PULLING OUR LEGS VERY WITTILY. COME ALONG. (HE
ROCK II	(245)	YOU COME IN THE NICK OF TIME. SIR JAFNA HERE HAS	JUST	BEEN QUALIFYING YOU AS A BLOODSUCKER, A PIRATE, A
SUPR III	(127)	THE HERO OF THOSE SCANDALOUS ADVENTURES YOU HAVE	JUST	BEEN RELATING TO US, YOU HAD THE EFFRONTERY TO POSE AS
PHIL II	(106)	WE'RE ALL WAITING FOR YOU. /JULIA/ SO I HAVE	JUST	BEEN REMINDED, THANK YOU. (SHE GOES OUT ANGRILY PAST
SUPR III	(138)	CERTAINLY IT IS. I SAID IT WAS YOU, TANNER. WEVE	JUST	BEEN STOPPED BY A PUNCTURE: THE ROAD IS FULL OF NAILS.
APPL I	(201)	YOU KNOW THAT THAT BULL-ROARER BOANERGES HAS	JUST	BEEN TAKEN INTO THE CABINET AS PRESIDENT OF THE BOARD
PHIL I	(85)	/CHARTERIS/ NO, THANK YOU. MISS CRAVEN HAS	JUST	BEEN TAKING ME THROUGH AN OLD SONG; AND IVE HAD ENOUGH
HART I	(66)	WHAT AN ESCAPE! ELLIE, MY LOVE: MR HUSHABYE HAS	JUST	BEEN TELLING ME THE MOST EXTRAORDINARY-- /ELLIE/ YES:
JOAN 2	(72)	AND PRONOUNCED CAMP ONES. /BLUEBEARD/ I HAVE	JUST	BEEN TELLING THE CHAMBERLAIN AND THE ARCHBISHOP. THE
SIM II	(78)	WAS NOTHING. DONT YOU UNDERSTAND? WHERE SHE HAD	JUST	BEEN THERE WAS NOTHING. THERE NEVER HAD BEEN ANYTHING.
SIM II	(64)	NOT DO THAT IF THEY UNDERSTOOD. /IDDY/ I HAVE	JUST	BEEN THINKING-- /MAYA/ SOLOMON HAS BEEN THINKING.
GENV I	(47)	CO-OPERATION BUREAU IN GENEVA; AND YOU HAVE	JUST	BEEN TOLD THAT THE RUSSIAN KOMINTERN IS ANALOGOUS TO
MILL I	(159)	BANKS HAVE CLOSED FOR THE DAY: IF ON SATURDAY OR	JUST	BEFORE A BANK HOLIDAY ALL THE BETTER. SAY THE CHEQUE IS
FANY III	(312)	/KNOX/ NO! /MRS KNOX/ WHATS THAT! /GILBEY/	JUST	BEFORE HE LET YOU IN, A DUKE! HERE HAS EVERYTHING BEEN
FANY PROLOG	(267)	WHERE I'M ABOUT TO ENJOY A CHARMING DINNER, AND	JUST	BEFORE THE DINNER I'M TAKEN ASIDE BY A CHARMING YOUNG
DOCT III	(153)	HE HAS GIVEN ME HIS PROMISE: HERE IN THIS ROOM	JUST	BEFORE YOU CAME; AND HE IS INCAPABLE OF BREAKING HIS
CAND II	(116)	A MARCH HARE. HE DID FRIGHTEN ME, I CAN TELL YOU,	JUST	BEFORE YOU CAME IN THAT TIME. HAVENT YOU NOTICED THE
NEVR II	(256)	WERE GOING TO HAPPEN. IT CAME OVER ME SUDDENLY	JUST	BEFORE YOU PROPOSED THAT WE SHOULD RUN AWAY TO THE

DEST (156)	(WITH A SHRUG) WHO KNOWS? SHE ARRIVED HERE	JUST	BEFORE YOUR EXCELLENCY IN A HIRED CARRIAGE BELONGING TO
ROCK PREFACE(173)	THE TRENCHES FROM PLATOON TO PLATOON SAYING SO	JUST	BEFORE ZERO HOUR, WITH OR WITHOUT THE ADDITION " SIRS,
GENV II (61)	THROWING ALL THE FISHES INTO THE SAME POND: THEY	JUST	BEGIN EATING ONEANOTHER. WE NEED SOMETHING HIGHER THAN
CAPT III (283)	BY YOUR LEAVE, LADY WAYNFLETE, I THINK I WILL	JUST	BEGIN WITH MYSELF. SAILOR FASHION WILL DO AS WELL HERE
MTH2 (69)	HUMAN MUSHROOMS WHO DECAY AND DIE WHEN THEY ARE	JUST	BEGINNING TO HAVE A GLIMMER OF THE WISDOM AND KNOWLEDGE
3PLA PREFACE(R17)	THE DRAMA, NEGLECTED IN THE STRUGGLE, IS ONLY	JUST	BEGINNING TO STIR FEEBLY AFTER STANDING STILL IN
MTH2 (74)	MILK? OR WHAT IS THE LATEST? /BURGE/ WE WERE	JUST	BEGINNING TO TALK SERIOUSLY; AND NOW YOU SNATCH AT THE
HART II (115)	ME. I'M NEARLY OUT OF IT. /ELLIE/ AND I'M ONLY	JUST	BEGINNING. /CAPTAIN SHOTOVER/ YES; SO LOOK AHEAD.
BARB II (277)	MINUTES; AND I WAS ABLE TO GO ON AS IF I HAD ONLY	JUST	BEGUN. (TO PRICE) DID YOU HAVE A PIECE OF BREAD?
JOAN 6 (150)	WE DO NOT <NOW, MY LORD. IT MAY HAVE ONLY	JUST	BEGUN. /WARWICK/ WHAT DOES THAT MEAN, EXACTLY?
APPL II (258)	ITS CAUSE. /VANHATTAN/ THAT IS TRUE, MAAM. I AM	JUST	BEHAVING LIKE A CRAZY MAN. BUT YOU SHALL HEAR. YOU
LIED SD(202)	BUT UNFORTUNATELY FORGETS THE STOOL WHICH IS	JUST	BEHIND HIM. HE FALLS BACKWARDS OVER IT, UNINTENTIONALLY
BARB III (324)	PRACTICALLY, EVERY MAN OF THEM KEEPS THE MAN	JUST	BELOW HIM IN HIS PLACE. I NEVER MEDDLE WITH THEM. I
BARB II SD(273)	STREET ON THEIR LEFT, WITH A STONE HORSE-TROUGH	JUST	BEYOND IT, AND, ON THE RIGHT, A PENTHOUSE SHIELDING A
BULL PREFACE(12)	WHO SET UP LITTLE HELLS OF ANARCHY AND INFAMY	JUST	BEYOND THE BORDER, AND THUS COMPEL US TO ADVANCE AND
DOCT II (120)	BY THE RIVER. /B.B./ BUT, MY DEAR WALPOLE, HE HAD	JUST	BORROWED TEN POUNDS FROM ME. /WALPOLE/ WHAT! /SIR
BULL III (140)	IF YOU WOULDNT MIND, WE COULD BRING THE PIG IVE	JUST	BOUGHT FROM CORNY-- /BROADBENT/ (WITH ENTHUSIASM)
BARB III (312)	(SITTING DOWN BESIDE HER) I'M SORRY. I HAVE ONLY	JUST	BREAKFASTED. /SARAH/ BUT WEVE JUST FINISHED LUNCH.
ROCK I (200)	LEADING THE HOUSE IF IT NEVER GOES ANYWHERE? IT	JUST	BREAKS MY HEART TO SEE THE STATE YOU COME HOME IN. YOU
JITT I (10)	ALL RIGHT, ISNT IT? /MRS BILLITER'S VOICE/ YES.	JUST	BRING THEM IN, AND PUT THEM IN THE VASE FOR ME, WILL
MTH2 (71)	TO JUSTIFY YOU IN THE AMAZING ACCUSATION YOU HAVE	JUST	BROUGHT AGAINST ME. DO YOU REALIZE THAT YOU SAID THAT I
WIDO III SD(49)	GLUMLY NEAR THE FIRE. THE PARLORMAID, WHO HAS	JUST	BROUGHT IN COFFEE, IS PLACING IT ON A SMALL TABLE
POSN (465)	I TELL YOU IT DIDNT FEEL ROTTEN: IT FELT BULLY,	JUST	BULLY. ANYHOW, I GOT THE ROTTEN FEEL OFF ME FOR A
BARB III (329)	PUT A MATCH TO THEM WITHOUT THE LEAST RISK: THEY	JUST	BURN QUIETLY LIKE A BIT OF PAPER. (WARMING TO THE
GETT (345)	REMEMBER IT NOW; BUT IT WAS SOMETHING THAT WAS	JUST	BURSTING TO BE SAID; AND SO IT LAID HOLD OF ME AND SAID
METH PREFACE(R23)	THE PERSONAL EXPERIENCE OF ALL OF US THAT IT IS	JUST	BY THIS PROCESS THAT A CHILD TUMBLING ABOUT THE FLOOR
LION PREFACE(27)	MADE CHRIST A CHRISTIAN. TO THE WOMAN WHOM HE HAD	JUST	CALLED A DOG HE SAID, " O WOMAN, GREAT IS THY FAITH: BE
MRS PREFACE(165)	PROFESSION EXPECTING TO FIND IT WHAT I HAVE	JUST	CALLED AN APHRODISIAC. THAT WAS NOT MY FAULT: IT WAS
DOCT I (97)	TYPHOID: THE HEAD GARDENER'S BOY HAD IT; SO I	JUST	CALLED AT ST ANNE'S ONE DAY AND GOT A TUBE OF YOUR VERY
JOAN PREFACE(14)	FORCE THAT IS BEHIND EVOLUTION WHICH I HAVE	JUST	CALLED THE EVOLUTIONARY APPETITE. IT IS QUITE ANOTHER
3PLA PREFACE(R10)	BUT IT MUST BE TOLD. AND, TO BEGIN, WHY HAVE I	JUST	CALLED THE THEATRE A PLAYHOUSE? THE WELL-FED
ARMS II (39)	BY HER SIDE). WELL? /LOUKA/ THERES A GENTLEMAN	JUST	CALLED, MADAM. A SERBIAN OFFICER. /CATHERINE/ (
ROCK II (268)	I BEEN LISTENING ON THE QUIET AS YOU MIGHT SAY. I	JUST	CAME IN TO TELL YOU NOT TO MIND THAT PARLIAMENTARY LOT.
GETT (334)	/MRS GEORGE/ (LOOKING AFTER HIM TRIUMPHANTLY)	JUST	CAUGHT THE DEAR OLD WARRIOR ON THE BOUNCE, EH?
BARB II (305)	BLOOD, NOT ONE DROP OF WHICH IS SHED IN A REALLY	JUST	CAUSE! THE RAVAGED CROPS! THE PEACEFUL PEASANTS
BARB I (269)	ARE NEITHER GOOD MEN NOR SCOUNDRELS: THERE ARE	JUST	CHILDREN OF ONE FATHER; AND THE SOONER THEY STOP
SIM PRO,1, (23)	HERE! I'LL GIVE YOU A LANDING TICKET; AND YOU	JUST	CLEAR OFF AND SAY NOTHING. (HE TAKES A TICKET FROM THE
CAND I SD(91)	SO FAR, SHE IS LIKE ANY OTHER PRETTY WOMAN WHO IS	JUST	CLEVER ENOUGH TO MAKE THE MOST OF HER SEXUAL
ARMS I (6)	(TO LOUKA) LEAVE THE SHUTTERS SO THAT I CAN	JUST	CLOSE THEM IF I HEAR ANY NOISE. /CATHERINE/ (
ROCK II (283)	THEIR HEADS? OH LOOK! THAT POLICEMAN HAS	JUST	CLUBBED A QUITE OLD MAN. /SIR ARTHUR/ COME AWAY: IT'S
DOCT IV (156)	TOO. /WALPOLE/ WEVE ALL BEEN SENT FOR. IVE ONLY	JUST	COME: I HAVNT SEEN HIM YET. THE CHARWOMAN SAYS THAT OLD
NEVR IV SD(292)	THEY TURN GUILTILY AND FIND THAT THE WAITER HAS	JUST	COME BACK FROM THE BAR IN THE GARDEN, AND IS JINGLING
NEVR III (262)	MEANWHILE). THE YOUNG LADY AND GENTLEMAN HAVE	JUST	COME BACK, MAAM: THEY HAVE BEEN OUT IN A BOAT, MAAM.
BARB II (296)	/UNDERSHAFT/ (INDICATING PETER SHIRLEY, WHO HAS	JUST	COME FROM THE SHELTER AND STROLLED DEJECTEDLY DOWN THE
CAND II (123)	QUITE WELL, THANKS. /LEXY/ (TO MORELL) IVE	JUST	COME FROM THE GUILD OF ST MATTHEW. THEY ARE IN THE
AUGS (270)	AGAIN. (THE CLERK RETURNS). SH-SH! SOMEBODY'S	JUST	COME IN: RING OFF. GOODBYE. (HE HANGS UP THE
DEVL II (41)	DID YOU CALL? WHATS THE MATTER? /ANDERSON/ IVE	JUST	COME IN AND FOUND YOU LYING HERE WITH THE CANDLES BURNT
HART PREFACE(32)	THE OLDEST PERFORMERS WHEN THE GENTLEMAN WHO HAD	JUST	COME IN DRUNK THROUGH THE WINDOW PRETENDED TO UNDRESS,
DOCT V (172)	UP ONE OF THE NEW BOOKS). /THE SECRETARY/ THATS	JUST	COME IN. AN ADVANCE COPY OF MRS DUBEDAT'S LIFE OF HER
WIDO II (27)	(TAKING BLANCHE'S CHAIR) NOT AT ALL. WEVE ONLY	JUST	COME IN. (HE TAKES OUT A PACKET OF LETTERS, AND BEGINS
CAND I SD(91)	THEY TURN QUICKLY AND FIND THAT CANDIDA HAS	JUST	COME IN, AND IS LOOKING AT THEM WITH AN AMUSED MATERNAL
DOCT IV SD(156)	OF SIR PATRICK AND BLOOMFIELD BONINGTON. WALPOLE,	JUST	COME IN, IS HANGING UP HIS BESIDE THEM. THERE IS A
GETT (287)	(HE SEATS HIMSELF ON THE EDGE OF THE TABLE). IVE	JUST	COME TO THE PERIOD WHEN THE PROPERTIED CLASSES REFUSED
JOAN EPILOG (153)	PITILESS FIRE. AT THIS INQUIRY FROM WHICH I HAVE	JUST	COME, THERE WAS SHAMELESS PERJURY, COURTLY CORRUPTION,
SIM II (79)	SENSIBLE REPORTS? . . . SPECIAL NEWS BROADCAST	JUST	COMING IN? . . . GOOD: PUT ME ON TO IT. (TO THE
MTH4 III (198)	/THE ELDERLY GENTLEMAN/ (TACTFULLY) YOU WERE	JUST	COMING TO THE ELECTION, I THINK. /THE ENVOY/ (
JITT II (27)	A LOT THIS LAST WEEK. /LENKHEIM/ HOW? /FESSLER/	JUST	CONSIDER. IMAGINE HAVING TO CONSOLE BRUNO'S WIDOW WHEN
DOCT III (146)	THE QUESTION OF THE VALUE OF THE LIVES WE SAVE.	JUST	CONSIDER, RIDGEON. LET ME PUT IT TO YOU, PADDY. CLEAR
PHIL III (146)	TO SEE WHETHER THE OTHERS ARE LISTENING) ONLY	JUST	CONSIDER! THE SPECTACLE OF A RIVAL'S HAPPINESS! THE--
APPL I (231)	HIMSELF BACK INTO HIS CHAIR). /BALBUS/ WE'D	JUST	CORNERED THE OLD FOX; AND THEN AMANDA MUST HAVE HER
JITT I (15)	AWAY FROM ME, I PLOD THROUGH MY HOUSEWORK, AND	JUST	COUNT THE DAYS UNTIL-- UNTIL THIS (SHE AGAIN PRESSES
HART II (103)	YOU RIGHT! DO YOU HEAR? SERVE YOU RIGHT! YOURE	JUST	CRUEL. CRUEL. /MRS HUSHABYE/ YES: CRUELTY WOULD BE
FABL PREFACE(63)	WHEN THESE SURGEONS FIND A TUMOR OR A CANCER THEY	JUST	CUT IT OUT. WHEN YOUR DIGESTION OR EXCRETION GOES WRONG
FABL V (118)	ORGANS WENT WRONG THEY DID NOT SET IT RIGHT: THEY	JUST	CUT IT OUT, AND LEFT THE PATIENT TO RECOVER FROM THE
MILL IV (190)	MAID TOLD THEM THE TRUTH ABOUT THEMSELVES; AND IT	JUST	CUT THEM TO PIECES; FOR IT WAS THE TRUTH; AND I COULDNT
ARMS I (16)	WE'D NO BAYONETS: NOTHING. OF COURSE, THEY	JUST	CUT US TO BITS. AND THERE WAS DON QUIXOTE FLOURISHING
SUPR II (66)	MEAN, LYING TO THOSE MEN, AND DENYING MY WIFE.	JUST	DASTARDLY. /VIOLET/ I WISH YOUR FATHER WERE NOT SO
JOAN 6 (124)	SOLELY, AND NOT OF THE HOLY OFFICE. I HAVE ONLY	JUST	DECIDED TO ASSOCIATE MYSELF -- THAT IS, TO ASSOCIATE
METH PREFACE(R27)	BY THE EXPLOITS OF A CHILD OF EIGHT, WHO HAS	JUST	DEFEATED TWENTY ADULT CHESS PLAYERS IN TWENTY GAMES
APPL INTRLUD(254)	A MOLLYCODDLE. IF YOU WERE A REAL MAN YOU WOULD	JUST	DELIGHT IN BEATING HIM TO A JELLY. /MAGNUS/ A REAL MAN
MTH5 (245)	WHAT! HAVE THOSE TWO HORRORS, WHOSE ASHES I HAVE	JUST	DEPOSITED WITH PECULIAR PLEASURE IN POOR PYGMALION'S
HART PREFACE(34)	STRUCK THIS FOUNDATION AWAY IN THE MANNER I HAVE	JUST	DESCRIBED. THE EXPENSES OF RUNNING THE CHEAPEST
JOAN PREFACE(30)	HOW COULD THE CHURCH TOLERATE THAT, WHEN IT HAD	JUST	DESTROYED HUS, AND HAD WATCHED THE CAREER OF WYCLIFFE
VWOO 2 (128)	THE MOSQUITOES! AND THE SMELLS! ! TRAVELLING	JUST	DESTROYED THE WORLD FOR ME AS I IMAGINED IT. GIVE ME
DOCT III (132)	WHAT THE DEVIL DOES HE TAKE ME FOR? NOW THAT	JUST	DESTROYS ALL MY INTEREST IN THE BEASTLY JOB. IVE A GOOD
FABL IV (116)	TYPING AND LISTEN TO INSTRUCTIONS. WHAT I HAVE	JUST	DICTATED IS FOR THE TENTH EDITION OF MY PRIMER FOR
KING I (215)	DAUBER. WHEN OUR DEAR PETER LILLY, WHO HAS	JUST	DIED, PAINTED ME AS I REALLY AM, DID I DESTROY HIS
MILL IV (192)	THEN THERE IS ANOTHER GENTLEMAN, AN INVALID, ONLY	JUST	DISCHARGED FROM THE COTTAGE HOSPITAL. THE EGYPTIAN
GENV I (45)	BUT WHAT IS THIS SEDITIOUS ORGANIZATION YOU HAVE	JUST	DISCOVERED? /COMMISSAR/ IT IS CALLED THE SOCIETY FOR
GENV I (45)	DIFFICULTY, COMRADE POSKY? /COMMISSAR/ WE HAVE	JUST	DISCOVERED THAT THERE IS A MOST DANGEROUS ORGANIZATION
MIS. (150)	AND JOHNNY TO BENTLEY'S RIGHT. /TARLETON/	JUST	DISCUSSING YOUR PROWESS, MY DEAR SIR. MAGNIFICENT.
MILL I (161)	HIM A FOOL; BUT HE'S A DEAR GOOD BOY; AND IT	JUST	DISGUSTS ME THE WAY YOU ALL TURN AGAINST HIM, AND THE
LION PREFACE(59)	THE LAZY DELUSION THAT IT IS POSSIBLE TO FIND A	JUST	DISTRIBUTION THAT WILL WORK AUTOMATICALLY ARE THOSE WHO
MTH4 III (196)	ON ANY TERMS. IF MY LEGS WOULD SUPPORT ME I'D	JUST	DO A BUNK STRAIGHT FOR THE SHIP. /THE ELDERLY
GETT (336)	THIS AFTERNOON. /MRS GEORGE/ AFTER WHAT YOUVE	JUST	DONE? NOT IF IT WAS TO SAVE MY LIFE. /HOTCHKISS/ I'LL
GETT (335)	WHAT HE'LL SAY TO YOU WHEN I TELL HIM WHAT YOUVE	JUST	DONE. /HOTCHKISS/ WHAT CAN HE SAY? WHAT DARE HE SAY..
ROCK II (256)	LISTENING TO THAT OLD BIRD BUTTERING YOU UP. YOU	JUST	DONT KNOW WHEN TO GO. /ALOYSIA/ (MOVING TO THE
MIS. (123)	DECENT OR INDECENT; AND IF IT'S INDECENT, WE	JUST	DONT MENTION IT OR PRETEND TO KNOW ABOUT IT; AND THERES
MIS. (142)	WANT TO BE GOOD; AND I DONT WANT TO BE BAD: I	JUST	DONT WANT TO BE BOTHERED ABOUT EITHER GOOD OR BAD: I
AUGS (269)	WELL, I WANT TO SACRIFICE MYSELF THAT WAY TOO.	JUST	DOUBLE NEXT SATURDAY: DOUBLE AND NOT A PENNY LESS; OR
PYGM EPILOG (303)	WITH NOBODY ELSE IN THE WORLD TO CONSIDER, AND	JUST	DRAG HIM OFF HIS PEDESTAL AND SEE HIM MAKING LOVE LIKE
MTH2 (46)	RUNNING TO FRANKLYN) I SAY! WHO DO YOU THINK HAS	JUST	DRIVEN UP IN A BIG CAR? /FRANKLYN/ MR JOYCE BURGE,
LIED (189)	TIME YOU CANT TELL WHAT THEYRE TALKING ABOUT: IT	JUST	DRIVES YOU WILD. THERE OUGHT TO BE A LAW AGAINST A
BULL I (96)	TOM. THAT REMINDS ME. WHEN YOU GO TO IRELAND,	JUST	DROP TALKING ABOUT THE MIDDLE CLASS AND BRAGGING OF
BULL PREFACE(10)	US ARE DROPPING THE PERSONAL PRONOUN, AS I HAVE	JUST	DROPPED IT LEST I SHOULD BE PROSECUTED FOR SUPERSTITION
BARB III (314)	IF YOU PLEASE, MY LADY, MR UNDERSHAFT HAS	JUST	DROVE UP TO THE DOOR. /LADY BRITOMART/ WELL, LET HIM
WIDO II (33)	LIFE HERE IS AN IDYLL-- A PERFECT IDYLL. WE WERE	JUST	DWELLING ON IT. /SARTORIUS/ (SLYLY) HARRY CAN FOLLOW
MTH5 (211)	TO ME. IT MEANS THAT YOU ARE DYING TO ME: YES,	JUST	DYING. LISTEN TO ME (HE PUTS HIS ARM AROUND HER). /THE
MILL I (151)	AGREEABLE; BUT IF YOU TRY TO LIVE WITH THEM THEY	JUST	EAT UP YOUR WHOLE LIFE RUNNING AFTER THEM OR
HART II (105)	IS STOPPED BY A HAIL FROM THE CAPTAIN, WHO HAS	JUST	EMERGED FROM HIS PANTRY). /CAPTAIN SHOTOVER/ WHITHER
PLES PREFACE(R18)	APINGS OF WESTERN CIVILIZATION BY SPIRITED RACES	JUST	EMERGING FROM SLAVERY. BUT IT HAD NO BEARING ON THE
BUOY IV (48)	TURN OUT WELL WHEN I SPEND AN HOUR HERE AND	JUST	EMPTY MY MIND. /PRIEST/ WHEN THE MIND IS EMPTY THE GODS
BUOY III (46)	HOME, DICK. I HAVE HAD ENOUGH OF THIS. IT WILL	JUST	END IN THEIR GETTING MARRIED LIKE OTHER PEOPLE. COME
DEVL I (10)	BUT TO THAT POOR WRETCHED BROTHER OF HIS THAT HAS	JUST	ENDED HIS DAYS WITH A ROPE ROUND HIS NECK-- AYE, TO
HART PREFACE(9)	TO PREVENT PRUSSIA DESTROYING US, AND THAT HAS	JUST	ENDED IN EACH DESTROYING THE OTHER TO AN EXTENT
GENV III (74)	CHURCH OF ENGLAND SO EASY TO DEAL WITH. NO TYPES.	JUST	ENGLISH GENTLEMEN, NOT LIKE CATHOLIC PRIESTS. /THE
BULL PREFACE(33)	LITTLE CIRCLE OF ARISTOCRATS AND PLUTOCRATS. THE	JUST	ENGLISHMAN. ENGLISH UNIONISTS, WHEN ASKED WHAT THEY

MIS. PREFACE(54)	AND DRUDGE ALONG STUPIDLY AND MISERABLY, WITH	JUST	ENOUGH GREGARIOUS INSTINCT TO TURN FURIOUSLY ON ANY
BARB II (310)	BE ENOUGH FOR ME. (SHE COUNTS HER MONEY). I HAVE	JUST	ENOUGH LEFT FOR TWO TEAS AT LOCKHARTS, A ROWTON DOSS
BUOY III SD(27)	TEMPLE ON A DOMESTIC SCALE, WITH WHITE WALLS	JUST	ENOUGH ROSE TINTED TO TAKE THE GLARE OFF, AND A
GENV III (79)	NEWCOMER/ I AM NO MILLIONAIRE, MIND YOU. I HAVE	JUST	ENOUGH TO DO MY BIT ON THE BOROUGH COUNCIL, AND FIGHT
HART II (126)	GOT NERVES AND WERE NAUGHTY, I SMACKED THEM	JUST	ENOUGH TO GIVE THEM A GOOD CRY AND A HEALTHY NERVOUS
GLIM (176)	THE WHEEL FOR IT: YOU, MOST LIKELY. TEN CROWNS IS	JUST	ENOUGH TO MAKE HIM BREAK YOU ON THE WHEEL IF YOU KILL
MILL I (140)	IT TO MAKE LEMONADE. PUT THE TWO SEPARATELY IN	JUST	ENOUGH WATER TO DISSOLVE THEM. WHEN YOU MIX THE TWO
3PLA PREFACE(R9)	AGO, MANY THINGS HAVE HAPPENED TO ME. I HAD THEN	JUST	ENTERED ON THE FOURTH YEAR OF MY ACTIVITY AS A CRITIC
NEVR III SD(269)	FINDS HIMSELF FACE TO FACE WITH GLORIA, WHO HAS	JUST	ENTERED. SHE LOOKS STEADFASTLY AT HIM. HE STARES
PHIL I (77)	WITH BITING EMPHASIS. /CHARTERIS/ I OWE YOU	JUST	EXACTLY NOTHING. /JULIA/ (REPROACHFULLY) NOTHING! YOU
SUPR I (14)	FEEL TOWARDS ME, MR TANNER. /TANNER/ ANN WILL DO	JUST	EXACTLY WHAT SHE LIKES. AND WHATS MORE, SHE'LL FORCE US
PHIL I (71)	(SITTING UPRIGHT AND FACING HER STEADILY)	JUST	EXACTLY. SHE HAS PUT HER HANDS IN MINE, AND LAID HER
NEVR I (207)	OF LINCOLN! THAT MAKES IT ALL RIGHT, OF COURSE.	JUST	EXCUSE ME WHILE I CHANGE MY COAT. (HE REACHES THE DOOR
JOAN 2 (72)	ON THE POINT OF DEATH? /BLUEBEARD/ YES: HE HAS	JUST	FALLEN INTO A WELL AND BEEN DROWNED. LA HIRE IS
CAND I (89)	SENTIMENT. /BURGESS/ (OBSTINATELY) YES I HAM:	JUST	FAMILY SENTIMENT AND NOTHINK HELSE. /MORELL/ (WITH
MTH5 (219)	FRAGMENTS OF THE EGG BACK INTO THE TEMPLE. /ACIS/	JUST	FANCY! THAT OLD GIRL HAS BEEN GOING FOR SEVEN HUNDRED
ANNA (293)	SO, YOU -- (HE HANGS UP THE TELEPHONE ANGRILY).	JUST	FANCY! THEY STARTED HER OFF THIS MORNING: AND ALL THIS
MILL IV (204)	FELT ANYTHING LIKE IT BEFORE. /PATRICIA/ WELL,	JUST	FANCY THAT! HE LOVES HER PULSE. /THE DOCTOR/ I AM A
JOAN EPILOG (155)	EVER IS, LADDIE, I AM OUT OF THE BODY. /CHARLES/	JUST	FANCY! DID IT HURT MUCH? /JOAN/ DID WHAT HURT MUCH..
HART I (62)	OF THE ABERDEEN DARNLEYS? /ELLIE/ NOBODY KNOWS.	JUST	FANCY! HE WAS FOUND IN AN ANTIQUE CHEST-- /MRS
MTH5 (209)	REPULSIVE. /THE MAIDEN/ THEY ARE FASCINATING.	JUST	FASCINATING. I WANT TO GET AWAY FROM OUR ETERNAL
PHIL III (132)	DOWNCAST. /PARAMORE/ (HANDING HER THE CUP HE HAS	JUST	FILLED) THERE! MAKING TEA IS ONE OF THE FEW THINGS I
MILL II SD(166)	OF THE TABLE FARTHEST FROM THE DOOR. THEY HAVE	JUST	FINISHED A MEAL. THE CHEESE AND BISCUITS ARE STILL ON
SUPR I (11)	! ! ! ! ! ! /TANNER/ TOTALLY. I HAD	JUST	FINISHED AN ESSAY CALLED DOWN WITH GOVERNMENT BY THE
DOCT III (134)	HOW TIME DOES FLY! I COULD HAVE SWORN I'D ONLY	JUST	FINISHED IT. IT'S HARD FOR HER HERE, SEEING ME PILING
BARB III (312)	I HAVE ONLY JUST BREAKFASTED. /SARAH/ BUT WEVE	JUST	FINISHED LUNCH. /BARBARA/ HAVE YOU HAD ONE OF YOUR BAD
CLEO PRO2,SD(95)	THE OTHER GATHERED ABOUT A GUARDSMAN WHO HAS	JUST	FINISHED TELLING A NAUGHTY STORY (STILL CURRENT IN
KING PREFACE(154)	A VICTORIOUS ANTAGONIST. IN POINT OF DATE KNELLER	JUST	FITTED IN, BUT I MUST MAKE AN EXCEPTION TO THIS GENERAL
ROCK II (239)	AND THE COMMANDER SENDS IN WORD THAT HE GIVES YOU	JUST	FIVE MINUTES BEFORE HE TORPEDOES THE WHOLE DAMNED FRONT
ARMS II (38)	WALK. /SERGIUS/ I SHALL NOT BE LONG. WAIT FOR ME	JUST	FIVE MINUTES. (HE RUNS UP THE STEPS TO THE DOOR).
FABL PREFACE(86)	G. WELLS AS PAST AND OBSOLETE WHEN IT HAD IN FACT	JUST	FLAMED UP IN SPAIN FROM A BANDYING OF STRIKES AND
SUPR I (28)	PURPOSES WITH NATURE. THE SUSPICION YOU HAVE	JUST	FLUNG AT ME CLINGS TO US ALL. IT'S A SORT OF MUD THAT
HART II (98)	YOU THINK YOURE BEING SYMPATHETIC. YOU ARE	JUST	FOOLISH AND STUPID AND SELFISH. YOU SEE ME GETTING A
2TRU III (83)	QUITE. BUT WHEN MEN AND WOMEN PICK ONE ANOTHER UP	JUST	FOR A BIT OF FUN, THEY FIND THEYVE PICKED UP MORE THAN
MIS. (176)	WOULD YOU MIND GOING AWAY TO THE DRAWING ROOM	JUST	FOR A FEW MINUTES, MISS CHIPENOSKA. THIS IS A PRIVATE
DOCT III (153)	ME. OH, WILL YOU PLEASE SIT DOWN AND LISTEN TO ME	JUST	FOR A FEW MINUTES. (HE ASSENTS WITH A GRAVE
CLEO I (113)	(CAJOLING) FTATATEETA, DEAR: YOU MUST GO AWAY--	JUST	FOR A LITTLE. /CAESAR/ YOU ARE NOT COMMANDING HER TO GO
MTH3 (134)	THE CHIEF SECRETARY. SAY I WANT TO SEE HIM AGAIN,	JUST	FOR A MOMENT. /CONFUCIUS'S VOICE/ IS THE WOMAN GONE?
PHIL I (90)	MR CUTHBERTSON. SHE'S SO TIRED. /CUTHBERTSON/ BUT	JUST	FOR A MOMENT, TO SAY GOODNIGHT. (JULIA AND CHARTERIS
FABL VI (129)	THE SMOKER TRIED THE EXPERIMENT OF LISTENING	JUST	FOR FUN; AND SOON HIS HEAD WAS FILLED WITH THE WORDS "
LION I (124)	TUNIC) DEAR BROTHER: IF YOU WOULDNT MIND --	JUST	FOR MY SAKE -- /FERROVIUS/ WELL? /ANDROCLES/ DONT CALL
2TRU II (70)	WAS TOO GREAT AND HE WENT OUT AND SHOT THE COP.	JUST	FOR NOTHING BUT THE FEELING THAT HE'D FIRED THE THING
NEVR IV (298)	/CRAMPTON/ YES, YES. WHAT HARM WILL IT DO,	JUST	FOR ONCE, M'COMAS? DONT LET US BE SPOIL-SPORTS.
ARMS III (67)	AHA! GOING TO BE VERY GOOD TO POOR OLD PAPA	JUST	FOR ONE DAY AFTER HIS RETURN FROM THE WARS, EH?
2TRU III (98)	INNOCENT MEN KILLING ONE ANOTHER. /THE PATIENT/	JUST	FOR THE FUN OF IT. /THE SERGEANT/ NO, MISS: IT WAS NO
2TRU II (70)	BEGUN AS A BOY: HE PICKED UP A LOT IN THE WAR.	JUST	FOR THE ROMANCE OF IT, YOU KNOW: HE MEANT NO HARM. BUT
JITT III (56)	SEE HERE! /AGNES/ THE BOOK! /LENKHEIM/ I HAVE	JUST	FOUND AN UNFINISHED LECTURE ON VARIETIES OF SLEEP.
ROCK I (223)	OUR BELOVED COUNTRY: A RISE IN PRICES." THE MOB	JUST	GAVE ONE HOWL AND WENT FOR HIM. THEN THE POLICE DREW
BULL III (138)	I THINK IVE DONE THE TRICK THIS TIME. I	JUST	GAVE THEM A BIT OF STRAIGHT TALK; AND IT WENT HOME.
2TRU II (69)	IF IT WASNT SO DULL. IF YOURE GOODNATURED, YOU	JUST	GET PUT UPON. WHO ARE THE GOOD WOMEN? THOSE THAT ENJOY
MTH5 (217)	DREADFUL OLD CREATURE. YOU FRIGHTEN ME. /ACIS/	JUST	GIVE HER ANOTHER MOMENT. SHE IS NOT QUITE REASONABLE
PYGM V (271)	A SILLY JOKE. IT PUT THE LID ON ME RIGHT ENOUGH.	JUST	GIVE HIM THE CHANCE HE WANTED TO SHEW THAT AMERICANS IS
GENV I (39)	KNOW ABOUT THE LEAGUE IS THAT IT PAYS MY SALARY.	JUST	GIVE ME THE GENTLEMAN'S NAME AND WHO HE MURDERED.
CURE (235)	FEEL MY SOUL SWELLING. /REGINALD/ I UNDERSTAND.	JUST	GIVE ME THOSE CHORDS AGAIN TO BUCK ME UP TO IT. (SHE
JITT II (41)	MALICIOUSLY) SINCE YOU ARE SO STRONG, CHILD,	JUST	GIVE ME YOUR ARM. /JITTA/ (SHAKING HANDS) GOODBYE.
MILL PREFACE(135)	WITH THE COMMONPLACERS ECONOMICALLY: YOU	JUST	GIVE ONE OF THEM HALF-A-CROWN AND THE OTHER
ARMS I (7)	TO RAINA) IF YOU WOULD LIKE THE SHUTTERS OPEN,	JUST	GIVE THEM A PUSH LIKE THIS (SHE PUSHES THEM: THEY
WIDO II (29)	YOU SAY A WORD IN MY FAVOR TO THE GUVNOR? HE'S	JUST	GIVEN ME THE SACK; AND I HAVE FOUR CHILDREN LOOKING TO
GETT PREFACE(240)	SHIFTS IMPOSED BY OUR LAW. YET THE FIGURES	JUST	GIVEN TO THE ROYAL COMMISSION SHEW THAT IN THE STATE OF
ROCK II (266)	WE MUST FACE IT: HE'S INDISPENSABLE. I'LL	JUST	GO AND ASSURE HIM THAT WE HAVE NO INTENTION OF BREAKING
BULL IV (169)	I WOULD FLATTER ANY MAN: DONT THINK THAT. I'LL	JUST	GO AND MEET HIM. (HE GOES DOWN THE HILL WITH THE EAGER
LIED (190)	THEM TO HIM FOR THE FIRST TIME, I FEEL I SHALL	JUST	GO DISTRACTED. /HE/ YES, YOU ARE RIGHT. IT WILL BE A
O'FL (217)	TO SAY TO DENNIS THAT DOESNT CONCERN ME. I'LL	JUST	GO IN AND ORDER TEA. /MRS O'FLAHERTY/ OH, WHY WOULD
2TRU II (72)	AND INCONCEIVABLE AND IMPOSSIBLE, THAT I SHALL	JUST	GO STARK RAVING MAD AND BE TAKEN BACK TO MY MOTHER WITH
MTH3 (113)	LIFE. I DONT KNOW HOW YOU FELLOWS FEEL; BUT I'M	JUST	GOING DOTTY. /CONFUCIUS/ (INTO THE TELEPHONE) THE
ARMS II (38)	THE LIBRARY. /RAINA/ (DISAPPOINTED) BUT WE ARE	JUST	GOING OUT FOR A WALK. /SERGIUS/ I SHALL NOT BE LONG.
DOCT V (172)	I'M SORRY THE CATALOGUES HAVE NOT COME: I'M	JUST	GOING TO SEE ABOUT THEM. HERES MY OWN LIST, IF YOU DONT
CLEO IV (177)	BESIDE HER, IN THE MOST AMIABLE OF TEMPERS)	JUST	GOING TO TELL ME SOMETHING ABOUT YOU. YOU SHALL HEAR
ROCK II (278)	IN THE NEAREST CHAIR). /ALOYSIA/ (MURMURS) I WAS	JUST	GOING. (SHE RESUMES HER SEAT). SIR ARTHUR ALSO SITS.
NEVR I (218)	CHAIR)? /GLORIA/ THANK YOU, MR CRAMPTON: WE ARE	JUST	GOING. /VALENTINE/ (BUSTLING HIM ACROSS TO THE CHAIR
PHIL II (128)	ALL. /GRACE/ WHERE IS DR PARAMORE? /CHARTERIS/	JUST	GONE HOME. /JULIA/ (WITH SUDDEN RESOLUTION) WHAT IS DR
ARMS II (25)	YES, SIR. THE MISTRESS AND MISS RAINA HAVE	JUST	GONE IN. /PETKOFF/ (SITTING DOWN AND TAKING A ROLL) GO
FANY II (293)	ME A SHOVE TO THE DOOR. THAT QUITE MADDENED ME. I	JUST	GOT IN ONE GOOD BANG ON THE MOUTH OF ONE OF THEM. ALL
MIS. (150)	A PASSENGER. THE CLUB SUPPLIED THE PASSENGER. HE	JUST	GOT IN; AND IVE BEEN TOO BUSY HANDLING THE AEROPLANE TO
LION II (131)	SAVED HIM! SAVED HIM FROM A LION THAT I'D	JUST	GOT MAD WITH HUNGER! A WILD ONE THAT CAME OUT OF THE
DOCT V (179)	WITH A PILE OF CATALOGUES. /THE SECRETARY/	JUST	GOT THE FIRST BATCH OF CATALOGUES IN TIME. THE DOORS
MILL II (167)	TO PRETEND THAT IT'S A RIVERSIDE HOTEL. WE HAVE	JUST	HAD A HORRIBLE MEAL OF TOMATO TEA CALLED SOUP, THE
FABL PREFACE(79)	FOR THE VOICE OF GOD, WE SHALL NEVER KNOW. I HAVE	JUST	HAD A LETTER FROM A MAN WHO, HAVING MADE REPEATED
BARB II (296)	EXCITED AND A LITTLE OVERWROUGHT). /BARBARA/ WEVE	JUST	HAD A SPLENDID EXPERIENCE MEETING AT THE OTHER GATE IN
WIDO I (14)	/SARTORIUS/ (IGNORING THE DIGRESSION) I HAVE	JUST	HAD A WORD WITH MY DAUGHTER, DR TRENCH; AND I FIND HER
SIM II (72)	IN SPITE OF YOU AND YOUR WINGS. IVE ONLY	JUST	HAD MY TEA; AND I CANT FEEL A BIT SERIOUS WITHOUT ANY
WIDO II (25)	FROM HIS BAG) NOT MUCH THIS MORNING, SIR. I HAVE	JUST	HAD THE HONOR OF MAKING DR TRENCH'S ACQUAINTANCE, SIR.
HART III (139)	WINDOW, AND ON SUCH A BEAUTIFUL NIGHT TOO. I	JUST	HAD TO COME DOWN AND JOIN YOU ALL. WHAT HAS IT ALL BEEN
ROCK I (217)	I MIGHT ALMOST SAY A HEARTBREAKING ONE. I HAVE	JUST	HAD TO PROMISE MY WIFE TO SEE A DOCTOR FOR BRAIN FAG.
ARMS I (10)	THE CURTAINS. /THE MAN/ (YIELDING TO HER) THERES	JUST	HALF A CHANCE, IF YOU KEEP YOUR HEAD. /RAINA/ (DRAWING
HART PREFACE(7)	OF CREDIT, WITH THE SAME RESULT. THIS IS WHAT HAS	JUST	HAPPENED IN OUR POLITICAL HYGIENE. POLITICAL SCIENCE
ROCK II (268)	IF HE HAD BLOWN THAT PARLIAMENT UP, THEY WOULD	JUST	HAVE ELECTED ANOTHER. /HIPNEY/ YES; BUT IT WAS A SORT
GENV PREFACE(26)	IF THE ATOMIC BOMB WIPES OUT OURS WE SHALL	JUST	HAVE TO BEGIN AGAIN. WE MAY AGREE ON PAPER NOT TO USE
MIS (202)	GOOD; AND I'D RATHER YOU DIDNT. /TARLETON/ WEVE	JUST	HEARD ABOUT IT, JOHNNY. /JOHNNY/ (SHORTLY, BUT WITHOUT
MRS II (218)	TO SEE THAT YOU WERE GROWING UP LIKE LIZ: YOUVE	JUST	HER LADYLIKE, DETERMINED WAY. BUT I CANT STAND SAYING
2TRU III (105)	YOU ARE OR WHAT YOU THINK YOU MEAN; BUT YOU HAVE	JUST	HIT IT: I DONT KNOW MY HEAD FROM MY HEELS. WHY DID THEY
MTH2 (66)	READ MY BOOK; AND YOU KNOW NOTHING ABOUT IT. YOU	JUST	HOLD YOUR TONGUE. /SAVVY/ I JUST WONT, NUNK. I SHALL
PYGM V (286)	FRIENDLY LIKE. /HIGGINS/ WELL, OF COURSE. THATS	JUST	HOW I FEEL. AND HOW PICKERING FEELS. ELIZA: YOURE A
MILL PREFACE(121)	NOTHING. THE PEOPLE WERE DELIGHTED; FOR THAT WAS	JUST	HOW THEY WANTED TO SEE PARLIAMENT TREATED. THE
MRS III (222)	THAT. (RISING AND FLINGING DOWN HIS PAPER) BUT	JUST	IMAGINE HIS TELLING CROFTS TO BRING THE WARRENS OVER
PHIL I (86)	JUST IMAGINE YOU BEING DAN CRAVEN! /CRAVEN/	JUST	IMAGINE YOU BEING JO CUTHBERTSON, THOUGH: THATS A FAR
PHIL I (86)	SOFA, LEANING AGAINST IT AND ADMIRING CRAVEN).	JUST	IMAGINE YOU BEING DAN CRAVEN! /CRAVEN/ JUST IMAGINE
VWOO 2 (126)	WORRY ABOUT WHAT HE'LL DO OR WHERE HE'LL GO. HE	JUST	IMAGINES AND IMAGINES. IT'S THE ONLY WAY TO BE HAPPY
MILL I (151)	THEYRE ALL RIGHT. BUT AS EVERYDAY PARTNERS THEYRE	JUST	IMPOSSIBLE. /EPIFANIA/ SO I AM THE SUNDAY WIFE. (TO
JITT II (30)	TO BE ABLE TO GET UP FOR A COUPLE OF HOURS TODAY.	JUST	IN A DRESSING-GOWN, YOU KNOW, TO SIT ABOUT A BIT.
2TRU II (75)	AND PUTTING THE CIGARET CASE BACK IN HIS POCKET)	JUST	IN THE NICK OF TIME. I WAS ABOUT TO SEND FOR YOU. I
2TRU I (41)	I DONT SEEM TO WANT ANY PEARLS. SHE GOT ME	JUST	IN THE WIND. I AM SORRY TO HAVE BEEN OF SO LITTLE
VWOO 3 (143)	. . . YES: WE HAVE SOME VERY FINE ARTICHOKES	JUST	IN THIS MORNING. . . . THANKS VERY MUCH: THEY SHALL BE
MIS. PREFACE(80)	CRUELTY OF CHILDREN TO THEIR ELDERS IS PRODUCED	JUST	IN THIS WAY. ELDERS CANNOT BE SUPERHUMAN BEINGS AND
WIDO I (17)	/TRENCH/ (EXCITEDLY) BILLY, OLD CHAP: YOURE	JUST	IN TIME TO DO ME A FAVOR. I WANT YOU TO DRAFT A LETTER
MIS. SD(162)	THE TURKISH BATH, WHICH HE CLOSES UPON HIMSELF	JUST	IN TIME TO ESCAPE BEING CAUGHT BY PERCIVAL, WHO RUNS IN
DEVL III (75)	HAS BEEN GRANTED. /SWINDON/ INDEED. THEN YOU ARE	JUST	IN TIME TO TAKE YOUR PLACE ON THE GALLOWS. ARREST HIM.

NEVR IV	(303)	WINDOW. /DOLLY/ (RUNNING TO CRAMPTON) OH, YOURE	JUST	IN TIME. (SHE KISSES HIM). NOW (LEADING HIM FORWARD)
NEVR II	(244)	SAYS SWEETLY) THANK YOU, DEAR WILLIAM. YOU WERE	JUST	IN TIME. (SHE DRINKS). /M'COMAS/ IF I MAY BE ALLOWED
MIS.	SD(157)	ROOM, BUT HAS MADE NO OTHER CHANGE. SHE STOPS	JUST	INSIDE THE DOOR, HOLDING IT OPEN, EVIDENTLY NOT
MTH2	SD(46)	FOLLOWED BY HASLAM, WHO REMAINS TIMIDLY	JUST	INSIDE THE DOOR. /SAVVY/ (RUNNING TO FRANKLYN) I SAY!
ROCK II	SD(247)	ANGRY, AND RESOLUTE. THEY GROUP THEMSELVES	JUST	INSIDE THE DOOR, GLOWERING AT THE PRIME MINISTER AND
DOCT III	(136)	MONEY FOR HIM BY BLACKMAILING HIS WIFE; AND YOUVE	JUST	INTERRUPTED HIM IN THE ACT OF SUGGESTING THAT I SHOULD
PHIL II	(128)	I ASSURE YOU, MRS TRANFIELD, DR PARAMORE HAS	JUST	INVITED US ALL TO TAKE AFTERNOON TEA WITH HIM; AND IF
BARB III	(316)	OBSTINATELY) THERE IS STEPHEN. /UNDERSHAFT/ THATS	JUST	IT: ALL THE FOUNDLINGS I CAN FIND ARE EXACTLY LIKE
MIS.	(171)	BEFORE I DIE. HAVNT YOU? /THE MAN/ NO. THATS	JUST	IT: IVE NO BUSINESS TO DO. DO YOU KNOW WHAT MY LIFE
GETT	(281)	AND SOMETIMES NOBODY AT ALL. /LEO/ YES: THATS	JUST	IT. HOW DID YOU KNOW? /THE BISHOP/ OH, I SHOULD SAY
MIS.	(142)	OF THE RANKEST BOHEMIANISM. /HYPATIA/ THATS	JUST	IT. I'M FED UP WITH-- /LORD SUMMERHAYS/ HORRIBLE
GETT	(289)	THE CEREMONY. /HOTCHKISS/ YES, I KNOW: THATS	JUST	IT. MAY I HAVE A WORD WITH YOU IN PRIVATE? REJJY OR
JOAN 1	(65)	YOU WHICHEVER WAY YOU DECIDE. /ROBERT/ YES: THATS	JUST	IT. WHICH WAY AM I TO DECIDE? YOU DONT SEE HOW AWKWARD
GETT	(294)	SIMMERING REGINALD AND THE BOILING GENERAL) THATS	JUST	IT, BISHOP. EDITH IS HER UNCLES' NIECE. SHE CANT
MTH2	(45)	AS LONG AS YOU, YOU KNOW. /THE PARLOR MAID/ THATS	JUST	IT, SIR. YOU SEE, HE MUST TAKE ME FOR BETTER FOR WORSE,
PHIL II	(128)	AS A MEMBER OF THE COMMITTEE, I THINK THATS ONLY	JUST	. BE REASONABLE, CRAVEN: GIVE HIM HALF AN HOUR.
WIDO II	(30)	WORD? /COKANE/ TRUE: TRUE. QUITE TRUE. HARRY: BE	JUST	. /LICKCHEESE/ MARK MY WORDS, GENTLEMEN: HE'LL FIND
LION I	(125)	SUFFER HERE. /FERROVIUS/ THATS TRUE. YES: THAT IS	JUST	. THEY WILL HAVE THEIR SHARE IN HEAVEN. /SPINTHO/ (WHO
INCA	(248)	HE STARTED IT, YOU KNOW. /THE INCA/ MADAM, BE	JUST	. WHEN THE HUNTERS SURROUND THE LION, THE LION WILL
FABL PREFACE	(77)	UNREPEALED DURING MY OWN LIFETIME; AND HAS ONLY	JUST	(1948) BEEN REPEALED IN SCOTLAND. SO FAR I HAVE NOT
ROCK I	(199)	SENTIMENT ABOUT THE FAMILY ALWAYS GOES DOWN WELL.	JUST	JOT THIS DOWN FOR ME. (DICTATING) FAMILY. FOUNDATION
ROCK II	(242)	NATIONALIZATION IS GOOD BUSINESS FOR THEM: THEYLL	JUST	JUMP AT IT. /SIR DEXTER/ IN SHORT, YOU WILL MAKE
GENV I	(31)	AND PERHAPS A LITTLE TALKED ABOUT? /SHE/ I'LL	JUST	JUMP AT IT-- IF IT IS ALL RIGHT. /HE/ HOW ALL RIGHT?
METH PREFACE	(R44)	WHICH HE WOULD PROBABLY RESENT, THAT WE	JUST	JUMPED AT DARWIN. WHEN NAPOLEON WAS ASKED WHAT WOULD
LION II	(135)	AND MY MASTER IS CRUCIFIED AFRESH. /ANDROCLES/	JUST	KEEP THINKING HOW CRUELLY YOU MIGHT HURT THE POOR
PYGM V	(288)	LIFT UP MY FINGER TO BE AS GOOD AS YOU, I COULD	JUST	KICK MYSELF. /HIGGINS/ (WONDERING AT HER) YOU DAMNED
2TRU II	(74)	YOURE MISERABLE; AND I'M MISERABLE; AND I SHALL	JUST	KICK YOU AND BEAT YOU TO A JELLY. SHE RUSHES AT HIM. HE
CATH 1	(165)	YOU WITH UNUSUAL CIVILITY, CAPTAIN. HE HAS	JUST	KICKED A GENERAL DOWNSTAIRS. /EDSTASTON/ A RUSSIAN
LIED	(192)	DO YOU THINK FOR A MOMENT HE'D STAND IT? HE'D	JUST	KILL YOU. /HE/ (COMING TO A SUDDEN STOP AND SPEAKING
ROCK II	(255)	ME OVERBOARD; AND SERVE ME JOLLY WELL RIGHT! YOU	JUST	KNOW NOTHING ABOUT IT, BECAUSE YOUVE NEVER HAD TO
SIM II	(70)	WIRELESS. WELL, THEYRE NOT FOOLING: AN ANGEL HAS	JUST	LANDED HERE TO TELL US THE SAME THING. . . . AN ANGEL.
CLEO III	(145)	HERE TO WATCH THE LAND BUT THE SEA. CAESAR HAS	JUST	LANDED ON THE PHAROS. (LOOKING AT FTATATEETA) WHAT
GETT	(267)	THIS MORNING? /MRS BRIDGENORTH/ YES. YOU WERE	JUST	LATE FOR A PARTICULARLY THRILLING INVENTION OF HIS.
GENV II	(58)	A SENTENCE AGAINST ONE OF THEM EUROPE WILL	JUST	LAUGH AT YOU, BECAUSE YOU HAVE NO POWER. IT WILL BE AS
JOAN EPILOG	(160)	CAN DO IS GNASH THEIR TEETH, HELL FASHION; AND I	JUST	LAUGH, AND GO OFF SINGING THE OLD CHANTY: RUM TUM
MTH3	(134)	THAT IT WAS NOT WORTH BOTHERING ABOUT, BUT I HAVE	JUST	LEARNT THAT I MAY LIVE-- WELL, MUCH LONGER THAN I
GENV IV	(129)	MONTHS AGO. AND NOW I MUST DIE WHEN I HAVE ONLY	JUST	LEARNT TO LIVE. EXCUSE ME: I CANNOT BEAR TO SPEAK OF IT
DEVL III	(69)	ADDS, WITH DESPAIR IN HIS FACE AND VOICE) I HAVE	JUST	LEARNT, SIR, THAT GENERAL HOWE IS STILL IN NEW YORK.
SIM PREFACE	(14)	YOU NEED NOT BOTHER ABOUT THIS: YOU CAN	JUST	LEAVE IT TO STARVE WHEN IT CEASES TO BE USEFUL TO ITS
DOCT IV	(158)	(MOVING VENGEFULLY TOWARDS THE DOOR) YOU	JUST	LEAVE ME TO DEAL WITH HIM! /MRS DUBEDAT/ (STOPPING
JOAN EPILOG	(167)	AND BISHOPS AND LAWYERS AND SUCH LIKE? THEY	JUST	LEAVE YOU IN THE DITCH TO BLEED TO DEATH; AND THE NEXT
GENV IV	(125)	PROFIT BY OUR DESPAIR. WHY HAS OUR JEWISH FRIEND	JUST	LEFT US? TO TELEPHONE, HE SAID. YES; BUT TO WHOM IS HE
MTH3	(128)	YOU GOING TO LET THEM DO WHAT THE TWO WHO HAVE	JUST	LEFT US MEAN TO DO, AND CROWD US OFF THE FACE OF THE
BUOY IV	(54)	BY THE ARRIVAL FROM AMERICA OF THE LADY WHO HAS	JUST	LEFT US. I WAS INTERRUPTED AGAIN BY THE ARRIVAL OF A
SIM PRO,3,	(34)	OH, I SAY! /THE E.O./ (RISING DEFERENTIALLY)	JUST	LEFT US, SIR CHARLES. /THE M.T./ HALLO! WEVE MET
PYGM III	(250)	SITS DOWN ON THE OTTOMAN GRACEFULLY IN THE PLACE	JUST	LEFT VACANT BY HIGGINS). /MRS EYNSFORD HILL/ (
HART I	(70)	TOLD YOU I WAS HERE? /RANDALL/ HASTINGS. YOU HAD	JUST	LEFT WHEN I CALLED ON YOU AT CLARIDGE'S; SO I FOLLOWED
MIS.	(159)	DOWN QUIETLY IN THE CHAIR LORD SUMMERHAYS HAS	JUST	LEFT. /TARLETON/ GOOD. WELL, DO YOU LIKE ME? DONT
CLEO II	(129)	THAT, CAESAR! THEY SAW IT FROM THE SHIP HE HAD	JUST	LEFT. WE HAVE GIVEN YOU A FULL AND SWEET MEASURE OF
CAND I	(90)	VERY MODESTLY, SITS DOWN IN THE CHAIR MORELL HAS	JUST	LEFT), THATS RIGHT. NOW OUT WITH IT. /BURGESS/ (
GETT	(287)	THE GARDEN DOOR TO THE CHAIR MRS BRIDGENORTH HAS	JUST	LEFT, AND SITTING DOWN) NOT MORE RITUALISM, I HOPE,
MTH2	(42)	BEFORE SHE HAS ANY SELF TO POSSESS. YOU	JUST	LET HER ALONE: SHE IS RIGHT ENOUGH FOR HER YEARS.
NEVR II	(248)	IN VERY BAD PART) NOW LOOK HERE, CRAMPTON: YOU	JUST	LET HER ALONE: SHE'S TREATED YOU VERY WELL. I HAD A
MIS.	(129)	AT THE END OF SIX MONTHS; BUT I WOULDNT GO: I	JUST	LET HIM WANT; AND SERVE HIM RIGHT!) WELL, JOEY WAS A
2TRU III	(104)	IS APPROACHING RAPIDLY. /MRS MOPPLY'S VOICE/ YOU	JUST	LET ME ALONE, WILL YOU? NOBODY ASKED YOU TO INTERFERE.
SUPR IV	(162)	BUT DONT PUT IT ON ME: THATS ALL I ASK. TAVY HAS	JUST	LET OUT THAT SHE'S BEEN SAYING THAT I AM MAKING HER
JITT III	(69)	DEAR. CAN I GET YOU ANYTHING? /JITTA/ IF I MIGHT	JUST	LIE DOWN HERE FOR AWHILE. I-- /AGNES/ (RISING TO MAKE
JITT III	(70)	ME IN SPITE OF YOUR ILLNESS. WORDS CAN NEVER SAY.	JUST	LIE QUIET WHERE YOU ARE; AND I WILL SEND EDITH TO YOU.
MTH3	(132)	MARINE GOLF, OR MOTORING, OR FLYING, OR WOMEN,	JUST	LIKE A BIT OF STRETCHED ELASTIC WHEN YOU LET IT GO. (
DOCT III	(155)	I TOLD HIM I HAD SOME, HE SAID " OH, ALL RIGHT",	JUST	LIKE A BOY. HE IS STILL LIKE THAT, QUITE UNSPOILED, A
LION II	(131)	THE LION WONT EAT ME NOW. /THE KEEPER/ YES: THATS	JUST	LIKE A CHRISTIAN: THINK ONLY OF YOURSELF! WHAT AM I TO
NEVR II	(244)	THIS OUTBURST, YOU MUST REMEMBER THAT DOLLY IS	JUST	LIKE A FOREIGNER HERE. PRAY SIT DOWN. /CRAMPTON/ (
MIS.	(135)	AND JOHN GAVE HIM A HUNDRED IN HIS BIG WAY.	JUST	LIKE A KING. /LORD SUMMERHAYS/ NOT AT ALL. I HAD FIVE
SUPR III	(139)	IS AS BAD AS ANY OF YOU. ENRY: YOU HAVE BEHAVED	JUST	LIKE A MISERABLE GENTLEMAN. /STRAKER/ GENTLEMAN! NOT
MRS II	(216)	DISAGREEABLES AND TAKE THE ROUGH WITH THE SMOOTH,	JUST	LIKE A NURSE IN A HOSPITAL OR ANYONE ELSE. IT'S NOT
PYGM III	(257)	YOU, MY DEAR MRS HIGGINS, THAT GIRL /HIGGINS/	JUST	LIKE A PARROT. IVE TRIED HER WITH EVERY /PICKERING/ IS
BULL I	(83)	ABOUT HIM. /BROADBENT/ BUT HE SPOKE-- HE BEHAVED	JUST	LIKE AN IRISHMAN. /DOYLE/ LIKE AN IRISHMAN! ! MAN
CAND I	(80)	COMMUNIST ANARCHISTS, I THINK. /MORELL/	JUST	LIKE ANARCHISTS NOT TO KNOW THAT THEY CANT HAVE A
MTH1 II	(31)	BOAST TO ME OF THE LAST FIGHT; AND ONE HARVEST IS	JUST	LIKE ANOTHER, AND THE LAST FIGHT ONLY A REPETITION OF
MILL IV	(193)	RIGHT TO BE IN HER HOTEL IF WE PAY OUR WAY	JUST	LIKE ANYBODY ELSE. /ALASTAIR/ VERY WELL: HAVE IT YOUR
BARB I	(253)	THE LORD CHAMBERLAIN TO TAKE IT UP. BUT IT WAS	JUST	LIKE ASKING THEM TO DECLARE WAR ON THE SULTAN. THEY
2TRU I	(44)	ME. SHE WAS THINKING ABOUT YOU. /THE PATIENT/	JUST	LIKE HER IMPUDENCE! HOW DID SHE KNOW ABOUT ME? /THE
PYGM V	(277)	HIGGINS ALWAYS BEFORE ME. I WAS BROUGHT UP TO BE	JUST	LIKE HIM, UNABLE TO CONTROL MYSELF, AND USING BAD
BULL II	(107)	HIMSELF IN A MOTOR AND WE ALL EXPECTN HIM!	JUST	LIKE HIM! HE'D NEVER DO ANYTHING LIKE ANYBODY ELSE.
MIS.	(197)	TIME HE KICKED HIS FATHER, AND FOUND THAT IT WAS	JUST	LIKE KICKING ANY OTHER MAN. HE LAUGHED AND SAID THAT IT
PYGM V	(278)	/HIGGINS/ DAMNATION! /LIZA/ (CONTINUING) IT WAS	JUST	LIKE LEARNING TO DANCE IN THE FASHIONABLE WAY: THERE
VWOO 1	(121)	WONT SPEAK TO ANYONE ANYHOW. AND LOTS OF THEM ARE	JUST	LIKE ME. /A/ WELL, HOW DO YOU LIKE LIVING AT THE RATE
SUPR I	(32)	SUCH THINGS INMOST SECRETS! BOYS' SECRETS ARE	JUST	LIKE MEN'S; AND YOU KNOW WHAT THEY ARE! /TANNER/ (
MTH1 I	(7)	BUT MY OLD SKIN WOULD LIE ON THE GROUND LOOKING	JUST	LIKE ME; AND ADAM WOULD SEE IT SHRIVEL UP AND-- /THE
MRS I	(182)	I HOPE IVE NOT MISTAKEN THE DAY. THAT WOULD BE	JUST	LIKE ME, YOU KNOW. YOUR MOTHER ARRANGED THAT SHE WAS TO
SHAK PREFACE	(136)	THESE CIRCUMSTANCES INTEREST ME BECAUSE THEY ARE	JUST	LIKE MY OWN. THEY WERE A CONSIDERABLE CUT ABOVE THOSE
DOCT II	(121)	YOU SEE) WITH ALL MY TROUBLES LEFT BEHIND,	JUST	LIKE OLD TIMES. /RIDGEON/ BUT WHAT HAS HAPPENED?
JOAN 4	(94)	STILL BEING DEFEATED. JARGEAU, MEUNG, BEAUGENCY,	JUST	LIKE ORLEANS. AND NOW WE HAVE BEEN BUTCHERED AT PATAY,
DOCT PREFACE	(5)	THE HONOR AND CONSCIENCE OF A DOCTOR. DOCTORS ARE	JUST	LIKE OTHER ENGLISHMEN: MOST OF THEM HAVE NO HONOR AND
SIM PRO,3,	(30)	MUST BE MAD. /THE Y.W./ OH NO. THEYRE ALL RIGHT;	JUST	LIKE OTHER PEOPLE. (TO THE PRIEST) I SAY, REVEREND.
MRS II	(216)	LIZ AND I HAD TO WORK AND SAVE AND CALCULATE	JUST	LIKE OTHER PEOPLE; ELSEWAYS WE SHOULD BE AS POOR AS ANY
WIDO II	(41)	POOR PEOPLE, WHO REQUIRE ROOFS TO SHELTER THEM	JUST	LIKE OTHER PEOPLE. DO YOU SUPPOSE I CAN KEEP UP THOSE
O'FL	(213)	AND THIEVES, AND BACKBITERS, AND DRUNKARDS,	JUST	LIKE OURSELVES OR ANY OTHER CHRISTIANS. OH, HER
FANY III	(317)	OUR HABITS; AND WHEN THEYRE UPSET, WHERE ARE WE?	JUST	LIKE PETER IN THE STORM TRYING TO WALK ON THE WATER AND
APPL PREFACE	(192)	HE TOLD ME THAT THIS WAS EXACTLY WHAT HE WAS:	JUST	LIKE SIR CHRISTOPHER WREN. HE HAD BEEN CONCERNED IN AN
HART I	(49)	TEA. HE IS VERY OLD AND VERY STRANGE: HE HAS BEEN	JUST	LIKE THAT TO ME. I KNOW HOW DREADFUL IT MUST BE: MY OWN
FANY I	(282)	YOURE EXTRAVAGANT BY NATURE. MY SISTER MARTHA WAS	JUST	LIKE THAT. PAY ANYTHING SHE WAS ASKED. /DORA/ WHATS
MILL I	(147)	(UNCONCERNED) OH, I DONT MIND. MY SISTER GOES ON	JUST	LIKE THAT. /EPIFANIA/ YOUR SISTER! YOU PRESUME TO
NEVR III	(267)	YOU AGAIN. AND SO ON. WELL, THE DUEL OF SEX IS	JUST	LIKE THAT. /MRS CLANDON/ THE DUEL OF SEX! /VALENTINE/
MTH2	(40)	" STICK IT OR CHUCK IT: STICK IT OR CHUCK IT"--	JUST	LIKE THAT-- FOR AN HOUR ON END IN THE SPRING. I WISH MY
FANY I	(275)	(READING) " MISS D. DELANEY. DARLING DORA."	JUST	LIKE THAT-- IN BRACKETS. WHAT SORT OF PERSON, JUGGINS?
ANNA	(291)	I WONT, OF COURSE: MY OWN FATHER GOES ON	JUST	LIKE THAT; BUT SUPPOSE I DID? /STRAMMFEST/ (
ROCK I	(204)	TALK. (HE RETURNS PLACIDLY TO HIS CHAIR). IT'S	JUST	LIKE THE HOUSE OF COMMONS, EXCEPT THAT THE SPEECHES ARE
DOCT II	(123)	ASK HIM TO CARRY IT OUT UNDER SUCH CIRCUMSTANCES,	JUST	LIKE THE MERCHANT OF VENICE, YOU KNOW. BUT IF A JEW
FANY PROLOG	(271)	TO TELL MY FATHER THAT LOTS OF PEOPLE WRITE PLAYS	JUST	LIKE THIS ONE-- THAT I HAVNT SELECTED IT OUT OF MERE
PHIL I	(72)	YOU CAN FIND ON THE PIANO; BUT TO HER EARS IT IS	JUST	LIKE THIS. (HE SITS DOWN ON THE BASS END OF THE
PYGM II	(242)	I DONT MIND; ONLY IT SOUNDED SO GENTEEL. I SHOULD	JUST	LIKE TO TAKE A TAXI TO THE CORNER OF TOTTENHAM COURT
MTH5	(233)	OF MEN AND WOMEN I COULD MAKE WERE MEN AND WOMEN	JUST	LIKE US AS FAR AS THEIR BODIES WERE CONCERNED. THAT WAS
JOAN 1	(67)	/JOAN/ THEY ARE ONLY MEN. GOD MADE THEM	JUST	LIKE US; BUT HE GAVE THEM THEIR OWN COUNTRY AND THEIR
LION PROLOG	(107)	ARE THE VERY LOWEST OF THE LOW. /ANDROCLES/	JUST	LIKE US, DEAR. /MEGAERA/ SPEAK FOR YOURSELF. DONT YOU
MRS I	(183)	(HE SITS DOWN). /VIVIE/ DO YOU KNOW, YOU ARE	JUST	LIKE WHAT I EXPECTED. I HOPE YOU ARE DISPOSED TO BE
KING I	(171)	ROWLEY. THEY ARE NOT LIKE WOMEN AT ALL. THEY ARE	JUST	LIKE WHAT THEY ARE; AND THEY SPOIL THE PLAY FOR ANYONE

CAPT III (273)	THE WHOLE QUARREL IS ABOUT. CAPTAIN BRASSBOUND IS	JUST	LIKE YOU: HE THINKS WE HAVE NO RIGHT TO JUDGE ONE
BARB II (287)	WHEN HE GETS ROUND PEOPLE THEY GET MISERABLE,	JUST	LIKE YOU. /BILL/ (WITH A HEARTBREAKING ATTEMPT AT
CAND II (106)	YOU AFRAID TO BE YOUR REAL SELF WITH ME? I AM	JUST	LIKE YOU. /PROSERPINE/ LIKE ME! PRAY ARE YOU
CAND III (130)	VERY SAME WAY. I HAVE BEEN PLAYING THE GOOD MAN.	JUST	LIKE YOU. WHEN YOU BEGAN YOUR HEROICS ABOUT LEAVING ME
VWOO 2 (124)	NO COMPENSATORY ADVANTAGE WHATEVER. /Z/ THATS	JUST	LIKE YOU. YOURE NOT A BIT CHANGED. /A/ WHAT DO YOU
DOCT V (178)	ALL. YOU NEVER COULD HAVE BELIEVED IN HIM. IT IS	JUST	LIKE YOUR NOT BELIEVING IN MY RELIGION: IT IS A SORT OF
CATH 2 (175)	VOLTAIRE ALSO HAS HEADACHES. HIS BRAIN IS	JUST	LIKE YOURS. /CATHERINE/ DASHKOFF: WHAT A LIAR YOU ARE!
HART II (86)	UNDERSTAND: WHAT DO YOU KNOW ABOUT BUSINESS? YOU	JUST	LISTEN AND LEARN. YOUR FATHER'S BUSINESS WAS A NEW
O'FL (226)	(LOUDER) MRS O'FLAHERTY! ! WILL YOU	JUST	LISTEN TO ME ONE MOMENT? PLEASE. (FURIOUSLY) DO YOU
LIED (195)	DO; BUT IT'S NOT SEASONABLE JUST AT PRESENT. NOW	JUST	LISTEN TO ME. I SUPPOSE YOU KNOW ALL THOSE POEMS BY
ARMS III (57)	FOR GREATER EMPHASIS) NEVER YOU MIND MY SOUL; BUT	JUST	LISTEN TO MY ADVICE. IF YOU WANT TO BE A LADY, YOUR
WIDO II (29)	WHAT HARM WOULD IT DO YOU TO HELP A POOR MAN?	JUST	LISTEN TO THE CIRCUMSTANCES, SIR. I ONLY-- /TRENCH/ (
WIDO II (30)	AMUSEMENT IN THE MIDST OF HIS ANXIETY)	JUST	LISTEN TO THIS! WELL, YOU ARE AN INNOCENT YOUNG
KING I (204)	MR DRYDEN DOES NOT UNDERSTAND HOW HARD THAT IS.	JUST	LISTEN TO THIS, THE LONGEST SPEECH I HAD. MAY I BELIEVE
POSN (462)	THE PROTECTION OF THE VIGILANCE COMMITTEE FOR	JUST	LONG ENOUGH TO GET YOU OUT OF THIS TOWN, WHICH IS NOT A
FANY I (278)	HE COULDNT AFFORD IT, POOR LAD, THOUGH I KNEW HE	JUST	LONGED TO GIVE IT TO ME. /GILBEY/ MARIA: IF YOU KEEP
2TRU III (106)	THE TIME THEY WERE PRETENDING TO SYMPATHIZE, WERE	JUST	LONGING TO BASH ME OVER THE HEAD WITH THEIR UMBRELLAS.
SUPR PREFACE(R11)	AND WORRY OUR MINDS. TO CONSOLE OURSELVES WE MUST	JUST	LOOK AT HER. WE DO SO; AND HER BEAUTY FEEDS OUR
MRS I (189)	/MRS WARREN/ (TO PRAED, LOOKING AT CROFTS)	JUST	LOOK AT HIM, PRADDY: HE LOOKS CHEERFUL, DONT HE? HE'S
INCA (246)	MAY I ASK WHY? /ERMYNTRUDE/ WELL, LOOK AT IT!	JUST	LOOK AT IT! I ASK YOU! /THE INCA/ (HIS MOUSTACHE
FANY II (286)	(WANDERING TO THE WINDOW ARM IN ARM WITH HER)	JUST	LOOK AT THE PEOPLE IN THE STREET, GOING UP AND DOWN AS
MTH5 (239)	AGAIN. /MARTELLUS/ (CONTEMPLATING THE FIGURES)	JUST	LOOK AT THESE TWO DEVILS. I MODELLED THEM OUT OF THE
CAND I (103)	(LOOKING MORE OBSERVANTLY AT HIM) WELL, DEAR ME,	JUST	LOOK AT YOU, GOING OUT INTO THE STREET IN THAT STATE!
GENV I (31)	NO HURRY ABOUT IT, I SHOULD NEVER GET THROUGH IT.	JUST	LOOK HERE AT THIS NICE LITTLE JOB THEYVE GIVEN ME! A
WIDO II (31)	HAS EM IN MARYLEBONE: HE HAS EM IN BETHNAL GREEN.	JUST	LOOK HOW HE LIVES HIMSELF, AND YOULL SEE THE GOOD OF IT
POSN (463)	WHEN THEY TALKED THE GOLDEN RULE TO ME, I	JUST	LOOKED AT THEM AS IF THEY WERENT THERE, AND SPAT. BUT
HART II (92)	TO THE FIGURE ON THE CHAIR) NOW, MR DUNN, LOOK.	JUST	LOOK. LOOK HARD. DO YOU STILL INTEND TO SACRIFICE YOUR
CAND II (121)	JUST THOUGHT SOMETHING DIFFERENT! LOOK AT HIM!	JUST	LOOK! (SHE POINTS TO MORELL, GREATLY AMUSED). EUGENE
GETT (329)	MERCHANT. /MRS GEORGE/ (APPRECIATIVELY) HE WOULD	JUST	LOVE TO HEAR YOU TALK. HE'S BEEN DULL LATELY FOR WANT
APPL I (200)	ON IT AND STICK IT INTO A PROCESSION AND HE	JUST	LOVED IT. THE SAME WITH MEN AND WOMEN: THEY WERE
JITT III SD(70)	WITH A PROUD GESTURE; GOES TO THE GLASS; AND HAS	JUST	MADE HERSELF PRESENTABLE WHEN EDITH APPEARS. HER EYES
MTH2 (78)	COMMUNICATION WHICH PROFESSOR BARNABAS HAS	JUST	MADE TO US: A COMMUNICATION FOR WHICH I SHALL BE
MTH3 (101)	BEEN NOTICED BEFORE; BUT THE RECORD OFFICE HAS	JUST	MADE TWO REMARKABLE DISCOVERIES ABOUT THE PUBLIC MEN
APPL INTRLUD(251)	ONE ELSE; AND YOU CAN SAY THINGS TO ME THAT WOULD	JUST	MAKE YOUR STUPID WIFE CRY. THERE IS MORE OF YOU IN ME
CAPT II (268)	IT IS SO. /SIDI/ BRASSBOUND ALI: THE OATH OF A	JUST	MAN FULFILS ITSELF WITHOUT MANY WORDS. THE INFIDEL
MIS. PREFACE(49)	PRECISE FORMULA FOR THE SUPERMAN, CI-DEVANT THE	JUST	MAN MADE PERFECT, HAS NOT YET BEEN DISCOVERED. UNTIL IT
MIS. PREFACE(7)	AN EXPERIMENT. A FRESH ATTEMPT TO PRODUCE THE	JUST	MAN MADE PERFECT: THAT IS, TO MAKE HUMANITY DIVINE. AND
SUPR PREFACE(R40)	NO OTHER, IN FACT, THAN OUR OLD FRIEND THE	JUST	MAN MADE PERFECT! THIS MISUNDERSTANDING IS SO GALLING
FABL V (119)	NOR HOW LONG THEY OUGHT TO LAST. WE ALL WANT THE	JUST	MAN MADE PERFECT; BUT WHEN OUR CHEMISTS ASK US FOR AN
JITT PREFACE(4)	IN GERMANY (MOSTLY IN BAYREUTH), AND HAVE	JUST	MANAGED TO ASK MY WAY, AND GET WHAT I WANTED IN THE
INCA (243)	IT'S A DREADFUL THING TO BE A PRINCESS: THEY	JUST	MARRY YOU TO ANYONE THEY LIKE. THE INCA IS TO COME AND
SUPR PREFACE(R37)	OF HER FAITH, I FEAR I SHALL BE DEFRAUDED OF MY	JUST	MARTYRDOM IN THE SAME WAY. HOWEVER, I AM DIGRESSING, AS
LION PREFACE(35)	AND HER FEELINGS. CHRIST'S FOLLOWING OF WOMEN,	JUST	MENTIONED BY MARK TO ACCOUNT FOR THEIR PRESENCE AT HIS
MRS I (193)	(CALLING) YES, MRS WARREN. IN A MOMENT. IVE	JUST	MET A FRIEND HERE. /MRS WARREN/ A WHAT? /PRAED/ (
MRS I (194)	MUCH MORE SERIOUS THAN THAT. YOU SAY YOUVE ONLY	JUST	MET VIVIE FOR THE FIRST TIME? /PRAED/ YES. /FRANK/ (
GENV I (40)	MY HUSBAND, CRUSHED BY THE LOSS OF HIS MISTRESS,	JUST	MOPED AT HOME UNTIL THEY CAME AND SHOT HIM. THEY HAD
FANY III (320)	HE PRETENDS IT'S A CAT BITING MY ANKLES; AND I	JUST	MUST SCREAM. BOBBY AND MARGARET ENTER RATHER MORE
DEVL II (46)	INSINCERE; AND MY DEAREST IS TALKING NONSENSE.	JUST	NONSENSE. (HER FACE DARKENS INTO DUMB OBSTINACY. SHE
HART II (108)	LIKE A WELL-FOLDED UMBRELLA) IT IS NEITHER	JUST	NOR RIGHT THAT WE SHOULD BE PUT TO A LOT OF
MTH4 I (157)	BREATH OF LIFE THAT PUFFS YOU UP SO EXALTEDLY?	JUST	NOTHING. SO LET US SHAKE HANDS AS CULTIVATED AGNOSTICS.
ROCK I (216)	WHEN HE GETS IT WHAT DOES HE UNDERSTAND OF IT?	JUST	NOTHING. WHERE DID THE MATERIAL THAT HE DOES HIS LITTLE
ARMS III (52)	NOT BELIEVE HER SENSES) DO YOU MEAN WHAT YOU SAID	JUST	NOW? DO YOU KNOW WHAT YOU SAID JUST NOW? /BLUNTSCHLI/
DEST (194)	TABLE) EXCELLENCY: WHAT WERE YOU LOOKING UP AT	JUST	NOW? OUT THERE! (HE POINTS ACROSS HIS SHOULDER TO
ARMS III (52)	YOU SAID JUST NOW? DO YOU KNOW WHAT YOU SAID	JUST	NOW? /BLUNTSCHLI/ I DO. /RAINA/ (GASPING) I! I! !
MTH4 II (183)	TO GO ABOUT HERE ALONE. WHAT WAS THAT NOISE	JUST	NOW? WHAT IS THAT IN YOUR HAND? NAPOLEON GLARES AT
KING I (194)	RUN AWAY FROM THEM? /CHARLES/ YOU WERE TALKING	JUST	NOW ABOUT YOUR POPULARITY. DO YOU KNOW WHO IS THE MOST
WIDO II (33)	UNBECOMING TO HIM UNDER ANY CIRCUMSTANCES, AND	JUST	NOW ALMOST UNBEARABLY JARRING). BLANCHE WILL BE DOWN
BARB I (268)	I FIND MYSELF IN A SPECIALLY AMIABLE HUMOR	JUST	NOW BECAUSE, THIS MORNING, DOWN AT THE FOUNDRY, WE BLEW
DEST SD(157)	WHICH BUSTLES HIM INTO THE THICK OF THINGS. HE IS	JUST	NOW BOILING WITH VEXATION, ATTRIBUTABLE BY A
LION PREFACE(5)	WAS MADE FOR ALEXANDER AND AUGUSTUS, AND I AM NOT	JUST	NOW CONCERNED WITH THE CREDIBILITY OF THE GOSPELS AS
GETT SD(293)	SOMEWHAT CAREWORN BY AN EXACTING CONSCIENCE, AND	JUST	NOW DISTRACTED BY INSOLUBLE PROBLEMS OF CONDUCT.
NEVR II (228)	HER MARRYING AN ARCHBISHOP. YOU REPROACHED ME	JUST	NOW FOR HAVING BECOME RESPECTABLE. YOU WERE WRONG: I
BARB II SD(273)	THEY STUNG INTO VIVACITY, TO WHICH THEIR MEAL HAS	JUST	NOW GIVEN AN ALMOST JOLLY TURN. THE MAN TAKES A PULL AT
PHIL I SD(69)	OF FEATURE, AND SENSITIVE IN EXPRESSION. SHE IS	JUST	NOW GIVEN UP TO THE EMOTION OF THE MOMENT; BUT HER WELL
ARMS II SD(35)	INCOME AND HIS IMPORTANCE IN LOCAL SOCIETY, BUT	JUST	NOW GREATLY PLEASED WITH THE MILITARY RANK WHICH THE
PHIL II (127)	AS A WITNESS TO YOUR THOROUGHLY WOMANLY CONDUCT	JUST	NOW IN HIS PRESENCE AND DR PARAMORE'S. /CRAVEN/
DOCT I SD(109)	IN HER SPEECH AND SWIFT IN HER MOVEMENTS; AND IS	JUST	NOW IN MORTAL ANXIETY. SHE CARRIES A PORTFOLIO. /MRS
CLEO PRO2,SD(95)	HIS SUCCESS IN THE FIRST. IS RATHER TO BE PITIED	JUST	NOW IN VIEW OF THE FACT THAT JULIUS CAESAR IS INVADING
DOCT IV (157)	WHAT MADE ME SO SENSITIVE ABOUT WHAT YOU SAID	JUST	NOW IS THAT, STRICTLY BETWEEN OURSELVES, RIDGEON HAS
CAND I (99)	WIFE; JUST AS NO DOUBT THAT OLD MAN WHO WAS HERE	JUST	NOW IS VERY WISE OVER YOUR SOCIALISM, BECAUSE HE SEES
KING I (195)	IT THAT THE POOR DIVVLE SHALL HAVE NO MERCY. BUT	JUST	NOW IT IS NOT OATES THAT WE HAVE TO KILL: THE PEOPLE
CYMB V (149)	HAPPY. /IACHIMO/ LADY: A WORD. WHEN YOU ARRIVED	JUST	NOW I, AS YOU SAW, WAS HOT ON KILLING HIM. LET HIM BEAR
MTH4 II (187)	BEEN TELLING ME SOMETHING ABOUT IT; AND HE HAS	JUST	NOW LET OUT THAT YOU WANT NOT ONLY TO COLONIZE US, BUT
ROCK II (257)	NEVER MIND MY INCOME TAX. IF WHAT YOU SAID	JUST	NOW MEANS ANYTHING IT MEANS THAT YOU ARE GOING TO PLAY
BULL II (113)	LET MYSELF FEEL THAT CHARM OF WHICH I SPOKE	JUST	NOW MORE DEEPLY THAN I-- THAN I-- /NORA/ IS IT MAKING
NEVR I SD(199)	AND FESTIVE, NOT FOR EVERYDAY USE. TWO PERSONS	JUST	NOW OCCUPY THE ROOM. ONE OF THEM, A VERY PRETTY WOMAN
ROCK II (284)	HARM. SHE'LL BE BACK FOR TEA. BUT WHAT SHE FELT	JUST	NOW OTHER GIRLS AND BOYS MAY FEEL TOMORROW. AND JUST
HART PREFACE(40)	COMPATIBLE WITH THE DEFENCE OF THE REALM. WE ARE	JUST	NOW READING THE REVELATIONS OF OUR GENERALS AND
ARMS III SD(46)	OF THREE LARGE WINDOWS SHEWS A MOUNTAIN PANORAMA,	JUST	NOW SEEN IN ONE OF ITS FRIENDLIEST ASPECTS IN THE
CAND I SD(91)	OR INDEED OF ANY CONCERN WITH THE ART OF TITIAN.	JUST	NOW SHE IS IN BONNET AND MANTLE, CARRYING A STRAPPED
APPL I (208)	/BOANERGES/ SECURITY, EH? YOU ADMITTED	JUST	NOW THAT EVEN A MODEST INDIVIDUAL LIKE MYSELF HAD GIVEN
GENV II (63)	IT. (TO THE SECRETARY) YOU WERE SO KIND TO ME	JUST	NOW THAT I THOUGHT YOU HAD A RIGHT TO KNOW BEFORE
MTH1 II (27)	TEMPTS ME TO DO ALREADY. /ADAM/ LIAR: YOU DENIED	JUST	NOW THAT IT CALLED ON YOU TO PAY FOR ABEL'S LIFE WITH
WIDO II (39)	TOMORROW. BUT I UNDERSTOOD FROM WHAT SHE SAID	JUST	NOW THAT YOU HAVE MADE SOME DIFFICULTY ON THE SCORE OF
2TRU III (91)	BOY: DO NOT DARE TO TRIFLE WITH ME. YOU SAID	JUST	NOW THAT YOU OWE NO MAN ANYTHING, AND THAT YOU ARE
VWOO 3 (139)	PUT UP WITH HIM." /A/ NOT AT ALL. YOU TOLD ME	JUST	NOW THAT YOU SAID SOMETHING QUITE DIFFERENT. I BELIEVE
DEVL III (54)	SAVE YOURSELF? I IMPLORE YOU-- LISTEN. YOU SAID	JUST	NOW THAT YOU SAVED HIM FOR MY SAKE-- YES (CLUTCHING
OVER (176)	ME OR LAUGH AT ME. YOU FEEL IT TOO. YOU SAID	JUST	NOW THAT YOUR OWN CONSCIENCE WAS UNEASY WHEN YOU
NEVR IV (289)	BETWEEN THIS AND HIS PREVIOUS STATEMENT) YOU SAID	JUST	NOW THAT YOUR NAME WAS CRAMPTON. /CRAMPTON/ SO IT IS.
DEVL III SD(56)	THAN GO TO THE MAKING OF A FIRST RATE GENERAL.	JUST	NOW THE EYES ARE ANGRY AND TRAGIC, AND THE MOUTH AND
ROCK I (195)	NUISANCES EVEN IN THE QUIETEST TIMES; BUT	JUST	NOW THEY ARE A PUBLIC DANGER. THE CHIEF COMMISSIONER OF
MRS III (232)	HAVE SHARED PROFITS WITH YOU; AND I ADMITTED YOU	JUST	NOW TO THE FAMILIARITY OF KNOWING WHAT I THINK OF YOU.
MIS. (159)	LISTEN TO ME. (SHE TURNS QUICKLY). WHAT YOU SAID	JUST	NOW WAS BEAUTIFUL. YOU TOUCH CHORDS. YOU APPEAL TO THE
MTH1 II (28)	ALL THIS EMPTY TALK OF YOURS, WHICH TEMPTED ADAM	JUST	NOW WHEN HE THREW DOWN HIS SPADE AND LISTENED TO YOU
BULL II (115)	YOUR VOICE HAD SUCH AN EXTRAORDINARY EFFECT ON ME	JUST	NOW WHEN YOU ASKED ME SO QUAINTLY WHETHER I WAS MAKING
MRS III (225)	WARNING, FRANK. YOU WERE MAKING FUN OF MY MOTHER	JUST	NOW WHEN YOU SAID THAT ABOUT THE RECTORY GARDEN. THAT
POSN PREFACE(419)	WITH TABOOED SUBJECTS. SUCH A DECLARATION IS NOT	JUST	NOW WITHIN THE SCOPE OF PRACTICAL POLITICS, ALTHOUGH WE
MTH1 I (15)	SHOULD I? ARE YOU EAGER TO BE RID OF ME? ONLY	JUST	NOW YOU WANTED ME TO SIT STILL AND NEVER MOVE LEST I
MRS I (191)	WAS? /PRAED/ (WITH A TOUCH OF TEMPER) I SAID NO	JUST	NOW. DID YOU NOT HEAR ME? /CROFTS/ LOOK HERE, PRAED. I
DEVL II (40)	YOU MUST FIND OUR FRIEND WHO WAS WITH US	JUST	NOW. DO YOU UNDERSTAND? (SHE SIGNIFIES YES). SEE THAT
CAPT I (233)	IT IS SUCH A NICE NAME. /RANKIN/ YOU SAW HIM HERE	JUST	NOW. HE IS A CONVERT OF MINE. /LADY CICELY/ (
HART II (87)	ME. HE'D THINK IT WAS MY MODESTY, AS YOU DID	JUST	NOW. HE'D THINK ANYTHING RATHER THAN THE TRUTH, WHICH
SUPR II (52)	CHAFFING HIM. BUT I DONT WANT TO TALK ABOUT HIM	JUST	NOW. I WANT TO SPEAK TO YOU ABOUT ANN. /TANNER/ STRAKER
POSN PREFACE(386)	HARDLY CARE TO SEE PERFORMED IN THEIR CAPITALS	JUST	NOW. IT IS AN ARTISTIC TREASURE; BUT IT GLORIFIES A
DOCT PREFACE(4)	IS THE CHARACTER THE MEDICAL PROFESSION HAS GOT	JUST	NOW. IT MAY BE DESERVED OR IT MAY NOT: THERE IT IS AT
BARB II (282)	THE MAN THAT JENNY HILL WAS PRAYING FOR INSIDE	JUST	NOW. (SHE ENTERS HIS NAME IN HER NOTE BOOK). /BILL/
DOCT PREFACE(3)	WOULD MAKE ALL THE DIFFERENCE IN THE WORLD TO ME	JUST	NOW. MY WIFE-- MY PRETTY ONES-- THE LEG MAY MORTIFY--

DOCT I	(98)	WAY. /RIDGEON/ IT'S NOTHING. I WAS A LITTLE GIDDY	JUST	NOW. OVERWORK, I SUPPOSE. /WALPOLE/ BLOOD-POISONING.
JITT I	(17)	HUSBAND; AND I DO NOT WANT TO BE REMINDED OF HIM	JUST	NOW. /BRUNO/ BUT IT IS YOUR HUSBAND I MEAN. I HAVE
WIDO I	(14)	GO, CONFOUND IT. I DONT WANT TO MEET HIM ALONE	JUST	NOW. /COKANE/ (SHAKING HIS HEAD) DELICACY, HARRY,
DEVL I	(13)	PERHAPS YOU HAD RATHER I DID NOT INTRUDE ON YOU	JUST	NOW. /MRS DUDGEON/ OH, ONE MORE OR LESS WILL MAKE NO
NEVR I	(217)	THING AS THAT ABOUT OUR FATHER? WHAT MOTHER SAID	JUST	NOW. /PHILIP/ OH, THERE ARE LOTS OF PEOPLE OF THAT
ARMS I	(14)	MEAN TO REVENGE YOURSELF BECAUSE I FRIGHTENED YOU	JUST	NOW. /RAINA/ (LOFTILY) FRIGHTEN ME! DO YOU KNOW, SIR,
DOCT I	(102)	THANK YOU, MY DEAR FELLOW; BUT I'M TOO BUSY	JUST	NOW. /RIDGEON/ I WAS JUST TELLING THEM WHEN YOU CAME
WIDO II	(33)	DIRECTLY. /TRENCH/ (HASTILY) NO. I CANT FACE HER	JUST	NOW. /SARTORIUS/ (RALLYING HIM) INDEED! HA, HA! THE
GETT	(349)	YOU TODAY. I FEEL IN PARTICULARLY GOOD HUMOR	JUST	NOW. /THE GENERAL/ MAY I ASK WHY, LESBIA? /LESBIA/ (
MTH4 II	(186)	VERY NEARLY KILLED ME. YOU HEARD WHAT SHE SAID	JUST	NOW. SHE BELONGS TO A PARTY HERE WHICH WANTS TO HAVE US
SUPR IV	(164)	WELL. WE WERE DISCUSSING THAT HABIT OF HERS	JUST	NOW. SHE HASNT HEARD A WORD. /MRS WHITEFIELD/ (
BARB PREFACE	(239)	A GLADIATOR SHOW, IF THAT HAPPENED TO BE THE MODE	JUST	NOW. STRANGELY ENOUGH, IN THE MIDST OF THIS RAGING FIRE
DEST	(186)	AS I AM: MEN LIKE ME ARE WANTED IN THE ARMY	JUST	NOW. THE FACT IS, THE REVOLUTION WAS ALL VERY WELL FOR
HART II	(125)	I-- /LADY UTTERWORD/ YES YOU DO: YOU SAID IT	JUST	NOW. WHY CANT YOU THINK OF SOMETHING ELSE THAN WOMEN..
MTH5	(225)	/MARTELLUS/ I DID. THAT IS WHY I LAUGHED AT YOU	JUST	NOW. YOU WILL SMASH YOURS BEFORE YOU HAVE COMPLETED A
BARB II	(274)	WHEN TRADE IS BAD-- AND IT'S ROTTEN BAD	JUST	NOW-- AND THE EMPLOYERS AZ TO SACK ARF THEIR MEN, THEY
SUPR II	(58)	OF COURSE. /TANNER/ THEN TELL HER WHAT YOU SAID	JUST	NOW; AND ADD THAT YOU ARRIVED ABOUT TWO MINUTES AFTER I
WIDO I	(20)	I WERE PUTTING OUR HEADS TOGETHER OVER THE LETTER	JUST	NOW; AND THERE CERTAINLY WERE ONE OR TWO POINTS ON
CLEO II	(139)	I CANNOT SPARE YOU A MAN OR A BUCKET OF WATER	JUST	NOW; BUT YOU SHALL PASS FREELY OUT OF THE PALACE. NOW,
CAPT III	(273)	MR RANKIN: ALL A MISTAKE, I ASSURE YOU. YOU SAID	JUST	NOW, HEAVEN FORGIVE YOU FOR JUDGING HIM! WELL, THATS
JITT I	(24)	LONG; BUT WHEN I CLIMBED THOSE TERRIBLE STAIRS	JUST	NOW, I KNEW, YOU WOULD HAVE TO GIVE YOUR NAME TO THE
DOCT V	(174)	FOR REPROACHES NOW. WHEN I TURNED AND SAW YOU	JUST	NOW, I WONDERED HOW YOU COULD COME HERE COOLLY TO LOOK
ROCK I	(219)	BE NO SUPPLY. /HIPNEY/ THERES A POWERFUL DEMAND	JUST	NOW, IF DEMAND IS WHAT YOU ARE LOOKING FOR. /SIR
GETT PREFACE	(227)	BUT THE SMALL FAMILIES, WHICH ARE THE RULE	JUST	NOW, SUCCUMB MORE EASILY; AND IN THE CASE OF A SINGLE
MILL I	(160)	TO ME THAN THE AIR I BREATHED. /SAGAMORE/ BUT	JUST	NOW, WHEN I SUGGESTED A DIVORCE, YOU ASKED HOW HE WAS
WIDO III	(66)	HARRY: WHAT WERE YOU DOING WITH MY PHOTOGRAPH	JUST	NOW, WHEN YOU THOUGHT YOU WERE ALONE? (HE OPENS HIS
LION I	(112)	YOU THAT AS THERE IS A SHORTAGE OF CHRISTIANS	JUST	NOW, YOU MAY EXPECT TO BE CALLED ON VERY SOON.
PYGM III	(258)	THE ADVANTAGES OF THAT POOR WOMAN WHO WAS HERE	JUST	NOW! THE MANNERS AND HABITS THAT DISQUALIFY A FINE
GETT	(281)	/THE BISHOP/ QUITE A NICE DISTINCTION, LEO. /LEO/	JUST	OCCASIONALLY, YOU KNOW. /THE BISHOP/ (SITTING DOWN
CLEO III SD	(144)	THE EAST HARBOR OF ALEXANDRIA TO PHAROS ISLAND,	JUST	OFF THE END OF WHICH, AND CONNECTED WITH IT BY A NARROW
MTH4 I	(150)	TO GIVE YOU IN CHARGE TO ZOZIM. YOU SEE HE IS	JUST	ON THE VERGE OF BECOMING A SECONDARY; AND THESE
CATH 4	(198)	GOODBYE, LITTLE MOTHER, IF I MAY CALL YOU THAT	JUST	ONCE. (VARINKA PUTS HER FACE UP TO BE KISSED). EH?
SIM II	(74)	WHAT I CANT GET OVER IS THEIR SENDING ALONG	JUST	ONE ANGEL TO JUDGE US, AS IF WE DIDNT MATTER. /LADY
KING II	(226)	ARE GREAT KILLERS, THESE PROTESTANTS. JAMIE HAS	JUST	ONE CHANCE. THEY MAY CALL IN ORANGE BILLY BEFORE THEY
NEVR IV	(298)	YOU LOOK QUITE LIKE A HUMAN BEING. MAYNT I HAVE	JUST	ONE DANCE WITH YOU? CAN YOU DANCE? PHIL, RESUMING HIS
PYGM II	(239)	I'D NEVER HAD IT. IT WONT PAUPERIZE ME, YOU BET.	JUST	ONE GOOD SPREE FOR MYSELF AND THE MISSUS, GIVING
PHIL II	(131)	DARLING. (HE SLIPS HIS ARM ROUND HER WAIST)	JUST	ONE KISS. TO SOOTHE ME. /GRACE/ (COMPLACENTLY OFFERING
LION PROLOG	(109)	ONE MORE LITTLE PULL AND IT WILL BE ALL OVER.	JUST	ONE LITTLE, LITTLE, LEETLE PULL; AND THEN UM WILL LIVE
MTH3	(134)	NO: STOP: LET ME EXPLAIN: HOLD THE LINE	JUST	ONE MOMENT. OH, PLEASE. /THE NEGRESS/ (WAITING WITH
LION II	(129)	BETTER. BESIDES, I'M TOO YOUNG: I WANT TO HAVE	JUST	ONE MORE GOOD TIME. (THE GLADIATORS LAUGH AT HIM). OH,
BARB II	(297)	OH SNOBBY, IF YOU HAD GIVEN YOUR POOR MOTHER	JUST	ONE MORE KICK, WE SHOULD HAVE GOT THE WHOLE FIVE
MIS. PREFACE	(30)	ALLEGED NOVELTIES IN MODERN SCHOOLS, THERE IS	JUST	ONE MORE NUISANCE TO BE DISPOSED OF BEFORE I COME TO
LION PROLOG	(109)	NURSEY. THAT DIDNT HURT AT ALL: NOT A BIT.	JUST	ONE MORE. JUST TO SHEW HOW THE BRAVE BIG LION CAN BEAR
GENV II	(60)	BUT IN ENGLAND THE CASTOR OIL BUSINESS IS	JUST	ONE OF THOSE THINGS THAT ARE NOT DONE. CASTOR OIL IS
MTH2	(85)	AND NOW, BEFORE DROPPING THE SUBJECT, MAY I PUT	JUST	ONE QUESTION TO YOU? AN IDLE QUESTION, SINCE NOTHING
FANY PROLOG	(272)	YES, LOVE, OF COURSE IT WILL. COME ALONG. /FANNY/	JUST	ONE THING, PAPA, WHILE WE'RE ALONE. WHO WAS THE
DEVL I	(11)	(HE FASTENS HIS CLOAK, AND IS NOW READY TO GO).	JUST	ONE WORD-- ON NECESSARY BUSINESS, MRS DUDGEON. THERE IS
SHAK	(141)	OF YOUR PIFFLING PLAYS. /SHAV/ QUOTE ONE.	JUST	ONE. I CHALLENGE THEE. ONE LINE. /SHAKES/ " THE
CYMB V	(141)	SERVANT DOES NOT ALL COMMANDS: NO BOND, BUT TO DO	JUST	ONES. GODS, IF YOU SHOULD HAVE TA'EN VENGEANCE ON MY
LION II	(128)	MEN KILLED. /ANDROCLES/ BUT DONT THEY EVER	JUST	ONLY PRETEND TO KILL ONE ANOTHER? WHY SHOULDNT YOU
BULL PREFACE	(34)	HIMSELF RIDICULOUS, COULD PRETEND TO BE PERFECTLY	JUST	OR DISINTERESTED IN ENGLISH AFFAIRS, OR WOULD TOLERATE
2TRU III	(85)	ME! YOU DONT KNOW ME, MY LASS. SOME MEN WOULD	JUST	ORDER YOU OFF; BUT TO ME THE MOST INTERESTING THING IN
LION PREFACE	(76)	GAVE A NEW LEASE OF LIFE TO THE ERRORS IT WAS	JUST	OUTGROWING, SO PAUL RECONSTRUCTED THE OLD SALVATIONISM
INCA PROLOG	(234)	ONES WERE NOT PAID UP; AND THE GILT-EDGED ONES	JUST	PAID THE CALLS ON THEM UNTIL THE WHOLE SHOW BURST UP.
GENV III	(73)	IN ANY OTHER COUNTRY. THE BRITISH GOVERNMENT HAS	JUST	PASSED A NEW LAW UNDER WHICH ANY PERSON OBNOXIOUS TO
WIDO I	(4)	COME ABROAD TO ENJOY MYSELF. SO WOULD YOU IF YOUD	JUST	PASSED AN EXAMINATION AFTER FOUR YEARS IN THE MEDICAL
DEVL III SD	(59)	THE WALL OPPOSITE THE DOOR; BUT WHEN RICHARD HAS	JUST	PASSED BEFORE THE CHAIR OF STATE THE SERGEANT STOPS HIM
MTH2	(71)	/LUBIN/ (RECOVERING HIMSELF) AFTER WHAT HAS	JUST	PASSED I SINCERELY WISH I COULD HONESTLY SAY YES,
JOAN 6	(144)	REJOICES IN HER MORE THAN IN NINETY AND NINE	JUST	PERSONS. (HE RETURNS TO HIS SEAT). /THE INQUISITOR/ (
DEST	(194)	SITS DOWN AT THE TABLE IN THE CHAIR WHICH HE HAS	JUST	PLACED). /LADY/ YES; BUT YOU KNOW YOU HAVE THE LETTER
DOCT III	(139)	OF KEEPING YOUR MIND CLEAN AND WHOLESOME. I CAN	JUST	PLAY WITH PEOPLE LIKE YOU. I ONLY ASKED YOU HAD YOU
GETT PREFACE	(245)	TO KNOW ANYTHING ABOUT THE DISEASES WHICH ARE THE	JUST	PUNISHMENT OF WRETCHES WHO SHOULD NOT BE MENTIONED IN
ARMS II	(43)	FOR THE ICE PUDDING; AND THAT STUPID NICOLA HAS	JUST	PUT DOWN A PILE OF PLATES ON IT AND SPOILT IT. (TO
MILL III	(186)	ME. GO UP AND STOP HER, JOE. DONT LET HER TALK:	JUST	PUT HER OUT. BE A MAN, DARLING: DONT BE AFRAID OF HER.
WIDO I	(17)	CONGRATULATIONS AND THE DEUCE KNOWS WHAT NOT. SO	JUST	PUT IT IN SUCH A WAY THAT AUNT MARIA WILL WRITE BY
CAPT III	(274)	OF GOLD, MR RANKIN. NOW, BEFORE YOU GO, SHALL WE	JUST	PUT OUR HEADS TOGETHER, AND CONSIDER HOW TO GIVE
MIS.	(183)	TO GUNNER) YOUNG MAN: YOURE A FOOL; BUT YOUVE	JUST	PUT THE LID ON THIS JOB IN A MASTERLY MANNER. I KNEW
NEVR III	(276)	LADY, YOU PICK ME UP VERY SHARPLY. BUT LET ME	JUST	PUT THIS TO YOU. WHEN A MAN MAKES AN UNSUITABLE
ROCK II	(234)	RINGING UP AND CALLING ALL THE MORNING; BUT SHE	JUST	PUTS HER BACK TO HIS DOOR AND SAYS THAT ANYONE WHO
HART II	(126)	TOO BIG; SO WHEN HE GETS NERVES AND IS NAUGHTY, I	JUST	RAG HIM TIL HE CRIES. HE WILL BE ALL RIGHT NOW. LOOK:
FANY PROLOG	(257)	WILL PROBABLY USE THE LIBRARY A GOOD DEAL, I	JUST	RAN IN TO UNLOCK EVERYTHING. /SAVOYARD/ OH, YOU MEAN
HART PREFACE	(32)	TO BE DESCRIED FROM TIME TO TIME. MEN WHO HAD	JUST	READ THE NEWS THAT CHARLES WYNDHAM WAS DYING, AND WERE
MIS.	(198)	WANT TO BEAT ME JUST TO RELIEVE YOUR FEELINGS--	JUST	REALLY AND TRULY FOR THE FUN OF IT AND THE SATISFACTION
AUGS	(270)	YOU MEAN AM I DISENGAGED. TELL THE LADY I HAVE	JUST	RECEIVED NEWS OF THE GREATEST IMPORTANCE WHICH WILL
BULL PREFACE	(28)	PROTESTANTISM. THE NATURE OF POLITICAL HATRED.	JUST	RECONSIDER THE HOME RULE QUESTION IN THE LIGHT OF THAT
2TRU I	(45)	A GOOD BUSINESS WOMAN IN HER. (TO THE PATIENT)	JUST	REFLECT, MOPS (LET US CALL ONE ANOTHER MOPS AND POPS
NEVR IV	(291)	UTTERLY DISMANTLED AND DESTROYED BY THIS	JUST	REMARK, TAKES REFUGE IN A FEEBLE SPEECHLESS SMILE.
MTH3	(114)	I OFTEN OPENED A DOOR FOR THE PERSON YOU HAVE	JUST	REMINDED ME OF. BUT HE HAS BEEN DEAD MANY YEARS. THE
CYMB V	(149)	DO NOT MAKE ME LAUGH. LAUGHTER DISSOLVES TOO MANY	JUST	RESENTMENTS, PARDONS TOO MANY SINS. /IACHIMO/ AND SAVES
2TRU II	(52)	COLONEL SAXBY, SIR. /TALLBOYS/ COLONEL SAXBY HAS	JUST	RETURNED TO THE BASE, SERIOUSLY ILL. I HAVE TAKEN OVER
ARMS II	(41)	ONCE. (HE RAISES HIS EYEBROWS). MY HUSBAND HAS	JUST	RETURNED WITH MY FUTURE SON-IN-LAW; AND THEY KNOW
JITT III	(76)	JITTA! /JITTA/ ENJOY! ! /LENKHEIM/ YOU	JUST	REVEL IN IT. YOU THINK YOURSELF SUCH A JOLLY ROMANTIC
CURE	(235)	PLAYS THE OCTAVE PASSAGE IN THE BASS). /REGINALD/	JUST	RIDDLE TIDDLE, RIDDLE TIDDLE, RIDDLE TIDDLE, RIDDLE
JITT I	(10)	AND FINDS THE GIRL AT THE DOOR. /THE FLOWER GIRL/	JUST	RIGHT FOR TWO, AINT IT? /MRS BILLITER/ (INCENSED)
JITT I	(10)	(INCENSED) WHAT DO YOU MEAN, WITH YOUR "	JUST	RIGHT FOR TWO"? /THE FLOWER GIRL/ (GRINNING) OH, IT'S
CAND II	(113)	THERES ANYTHING COARSE-GRAINED TO BE DONE, YOU	JUST	RING THE BELL AND THROW IT ON TO SOMEBODY ELSE, EH?
ROCK I	(207)	A POLITICAL WIFE. LOOK AT HIGGINBOTHAM! HE WAS	JUST	RIPE FOR THE CABINET WHEN HIS WIFE WENT INTO PARLIAMENT
DOCT I	(85)	DOWN IN MY MOTOR AT AN HOUR'S NOTICE. /RIDGEON/	JUST	ROLLING IN MONEY! I WISH YOU RICH G.P.'S WOULD TEACH
ARMS III	(50)	(GRINNING) NO: THEY WERE GLAD; BECAUSE THEYD ALL	JUST	RUN AWAY THEMSELVES. /RAINA/ (GOING TO THE TABLE, AND
NEVR III	(263)	HE HAS BEEN ROWING THE BOAT, MISS, AND HAS	JUST	RUN DOWN THE ROAD TO THE CHEMIST'S FOR SOMETHING TO PUT
DEVL III	(55)	SOBBING). /RICHARD/ (TAKING HER ARM TO LIFT HER)	JUST	-- HER OTHER ARM, SERGEANT. THEY GO OUT, SHE SOBBING
MILL II	(166)	IT; BUT WHAT HAS IT TO DO WITH WHAT I HAVE	JUST	SAID? /ADRIAN/ YOU SAID " HOW JOLLY! " I LOOK ROUND AT
ARMS I	(17)	THING. YOU CANNOT STAY HERE AFTER WHAT YOU HAVE	JUST	SAID ABOUT MY FUTURE HUSBAND; BUT I WILL GO OUT ON THE
BULL PREFACE	(47)	CHARACTER SEEMS TO CONTRADICT EVERYTHING I HAVE	JUST	SAID ABOUT THE MILITARY CHARACTER. YOU HAVE ONLY TO
MTH4 I	(160)	ANY GOOD IN HIM. BESIDES, MADAM, WHAT YOU HAVE	JUST	SAID ENCOURAGES ME TO UTTER AN OPINION OF MINE WHICH IS
2TRU III	(91)	ELDER/ COMPLETE YOUR CONFESSION, SIR. YOU HAVE	JUST	SAID THAT YOU AND THIS LADY TOOK THE SAME LODGING. AM I
APPL I	(237)	I HAVE NOT REASON TO FEEL EVERYTHING YOU HAVE	JUST	SAID TO THE VERY MARROW OF MY BONES. HERE AM I, THE
FANY PROLOG	(263)	/SAVOYARD/ NO: THATS BEEN KEPT A DEAD SECRET. I	JUST	SAID YOUR DAUGHTER HAS ASKED FOR A REAL PLAY WITH A
JITT III	(79)	SYMPATHETICALLY) NOT A BIT OF IT, DEAR. YOU HAVE	JUST	SAID YOURSELF THAT IF SECRETS DONT KEEP THEMSELVES,
BULL II	(100)	YOUR PRIEST? FOR TWO PINS I'D TELL HIM WHAT YOU	JUST	SAID. /PATSY/ (COAXING) SURE YOU WOULDNT-- /KEEGAN/
MTH4 I	(143)	DO NOT UNDERSTAND A SINGLE WORD OF WHAT YOU HAVE	JUST	SAID. /THE ELDERLY GENTLEMAN/ I AM SPEAKING THE
DOCT III	(140)	CHAPS TO LICK YOUR LIPS OVER AT BREAKFAST. WE	JUST	SAID, WELL, THE MONEY'S GONE: WEVE HAD A GOOD TIME THAT
FABL VI	(130)	HE DID NOT ASK US FOR ANYTHING. /MAIDEN 4/ HE WAS	JUST	SAMPLING US. /YOUTH 1/ HE TOLD US NOTHING. WE KNOW
HART I	(52)	FLOWERS AND THINGS IN YOUR ROOM; AND WHEN I	JUST	SAT DOWN FOR A MOMENT TO TRY HOW COMFORTABLE THE
MTH5	(240)	LIKE THE LIGHTNING. /THE FEMALE FIGURE/ YOU	JUST	SAY THAT AGAIN IF YOU DARE, YOU FILTHY CREATURE. /ACIS/
FANY EPILOG	(333)	AWAY THE CRITICS. /VAUGHAN/ NO, NO. WHY, I WAS	JUST	SAYING THAT IT MUST HAVE BEEN WRITTEN BY PINERO. DIDNT
DEVL II	(35)	HIDE A CONVULSIVE SWELLING OF HIS THROAT). I WAS	JUST	SAYING TO MY WIFE, MR DUDGEON, THAT ENMITY-- (SHE

FANY III	(311)	THE OTHER CHAIR). /GILBEY/ (SITTING DOWN) I WAS	JUST	SAYING, KNOX, WHAT IS THE WORLD COMING TO? /KNOX/ (
DOCT II	(121)	OH, NOTHING. IT'S TOO RIDICULOUS. I HAD	JUST	SCRAPED UP FOUR SHILLINGS FOR THIS LITTLE OUTING; AND
MIS.	(199)	HA! DROPPING IN. THE NEW SPORT OF AVIATION. YOU	JUST	SEE A NICE HOUSE; DROP IN; SCOOP UP THE MAN'S DAUGHTER;
DOCT I	(108)	WITH YOU, EMMY? /EMMY/ (COAXING) COME NOW:	JUST	SEE HER FOR A MINUTE TO PLEASE ME: THERES A GOOD BOY.
GENV II	(63)	/BEGONIA/ (TAKING IT) THANKS EVER SO MUCH! ITLL	JUST	SEE ME THROUGH. AND NOW I MUST TODDLE OFF TO MY LITTLE
ARMS III	(49)	(HE GOES OUT). /BLUNTSCHLI/ (CONFIDENTIALLY)	JUST	SEE THAT HE TALKS TO THEM PROPERLY, MAJOR, WILL YOU?
2TRU PREFACE	(6)	ASPIRE. THE SCALE HAS CHANGED SINCE THEN. I HAVE	JUST	SEEN IN THE PAPERS A PICTURE OF THE FUNERAL OF A
DEST	(160)	LIKE! HE WAS LIKE-- WELL, YOU OUGHT TO HAVE	JUST	SEEN THE FELLOW: THAT WILL GIVE YOU A NOTION OF WHAT HE
MRS IV	(244)	THATS SETTLED. I SHANT WORRY HER ABOUT IT: I'LL	JUST	SEND HER A LITTLE NOTE AFTER WE'RE GONE. SHE'LL
NEVR II	(239)	WET; AND HE STARES DUMBLY AT HIS SON, WHO,	JUST	SENSIBLE ENOUGH OF HIS OWN CALLOUSNESS TO INTENSELY
BARB II	(277)	O' CLOCK, I WAS SO TIRED; BUT MAJOR BARBARA	JUST	SENT ME TO PRAY FOR FIVE MINUTES; AND I WAS ABLE TO GO
WIDO II	(35)	YOU HAVE SEVEN HUNDRED A YEAR. WELL, I WILL TAKE	JUST	SEVEN HUNDRED A YEAR FROM PAPA AT FIRST; AND THEN WE
2TRU PREFACE	(14)	DISTRIBUTION OF WEALTH FROM DAY TO DAY AND THE	JUST	SHARING OF THE LABOR AND LEISURE INVOLVED. THUS THE
PYGM I	(209)	DO I KNOW WHETHER YOU TOOK ME DOWN RIGHT? YOU	JUST	SHEW ME WHAT YOUVE WROTE ABOUT ME. (THE NOTE TAKER
HART I	(57)	BUSINESS, AND MADE A MESS OF IT. /ELLIE/ OH, THAT	JUST	SHEWS HOW ENTIRELY YOU ARE MISTAKEN ABOUT HIM. THE
POSN	(442)	MONEY ENOUGH TO GET DRUNK. /ELDER DANIELS/ THAT	JUST	SHEWS THE WISDOM OF PROVIDENCE AND THE LORD'S MERCY.
2TRU III	(106)	ME BY PRETENDING TO BE MY DAUGHTER; BUT THAT	JUST	SHEWS WHAT A FOOL YOU ARE; FOR I HATE MY DAUGHTER AND
JOAN 2	(75)	WOULD YOUR WISE GRANDFATHER SAY? /CHARLES/ THAT	JUST	SHEWS YOUR IGNORANCE, BLUEBEARD. MY GRANDFATHER HAD A
PHIL III	(141)	MAKE A NASTY SNEERING SPEECH; AND SHE-- WELL, SHE	JUST	SHOOK ME A LITTLE, AS YOU SAW. /PARAMORE/ (
GENV I	(32)	LAST? THE WORK HERE MAY BE DULL; AND THE PAY IS	JUST	SHORT OF STARVATION; BUT I HAVE THE APPOINTMENT FOR 25
SIM II	(78)	TO LEAVE THEM UNEDUCATED. /MRS HYERING/ THERE	JUST	SHOULDNT BE ANY FOOLS. THEY WERNT BORN FOOLS: WE MADE
2TRU I	(38)	TO OPEN HER MOUTH. A NURSE WHO KNOWS HER BUSINESS	JUST	SHOVES A HANDFUL OF THIS INTO IT. COMMON KITCHEN SALT.
MIS.	(144)	AND THERE ARE LOTS OF THINGS THAT WOULD	JUST	SHRIVEL YOU UP THAT I THINK RATHER JOLLY. NOW! /LORD
DEVL I	(16)	/CHRISTY/ (AT THE HOUSE DOOR, WHICH HE HAS	JUST	SHUT) ALL EXCEPT DICK. THE CALLOUSNESS WITH WHICH
POSN	(462)	ON HIS WAY OUT) A MAN LIKE YOU MAKES ME SICK.	JUST	SICK. (BLANCO MAKES NO SIGN. THE FOREMAN SPITS
MIS.	(181)	ENOUGH TO WITNESS THE DECLARATION THIS MAN HAS	JUST	SIGNED? /GUNNER/ I HAVNT YET. AM I TO SIGN NOW?
APPL I	(205)	THAT WAS MONSTROUS -- /BOANERGES/ IT WAS SILLY:	JUST	SILLY. /MAGNUS/ BUT WAS IT HALF SO SILLY AS OUR
HART I	(57)	HIM, OR THAT HE INVESTED IT IN HIS BUSINESS. HE	JUST	SIMPLY MADE HIM A PRESENT OF IT. WASNT THAT SPLENDID OF
APPL I	(223)	CLEVER AS YOU ARE AT SETTING IT. CRASSUS WILL SAY	JUST	SIMPLY THAT YOU ARE A FREETHINKER, AND BALBUS WILL SAY
MTH5	(209)	GET AWAY FROM OUR ETERNAL DANCING AND MUSIC, AND	JUST	SIT DOWN BY MYSELF AND THINK ABOUT NUMBERS. /THE YOUTH/
APPL I	(232)	EIGHT ALL OVER THE SHOP. SO MY ADVICE IS THAT WE	JUST	SIT HERE QUIETLY UNTIL JOE COMES BACK AND TELLS US
DEVL III	(69)	NO: OUR EVACUATION OF THE TOWN. THEY OFFER US	JUST	SIX HOURS TO CLEAR OUT. /SWINDON/ WHAT MONSTROUS
MTH4 I	(173)	/ZOO/ (GLANCING UP AT THE SUN) COME. IT IS	JUST	SIXTEEN O'CLOCK; AND YOU HAVE TO JOIN YOUR PARTY AT
ROCK II	(270)	BY THE SCRUFFS OF THEIR SILLY NECKS AND	JUST	SLING THEM INTO THE WAY THEY SHOULD GO WITH AS MANY
ROCK I	(206)	COUNTRY, ARTHUR. THE COUNTRY ISNT GOVERNED: IT	JUST	SLUMMOCKS ALONG ANYHOW. /SIR ARTHUR/ I HAVE TO GOVERN
HART II	(85)	HANDS INTO HIS POCKETS AND SHEWS HIS TEETH). I	JUST	SMOKED THEM OUT LIKE A HIVE OF BEES. WHAT DO YOU SAY TO
SUPR IV	(151)	AND FORTUNATE ENOUGH TO GAIN YOUR CONSENT, THEN I	JUST	SNAP MY FINGERS AND GO MY OWN WAY. /TANNER/ MARRY
MIS.	(142)	SIGNIFIES TO BE, TO DO, OR TO SUFFER. /HYPATIA/	JUST	SO: HOW CLEVER OF YOU! I WANT TO BE; I WANT TO DO; AND
MTH4 II	(187)	ENVOY/ (SUDDENLY MAKING HIMSELF VERY AGREEABLE)	JUST	SO: JUST SO. WE CAN WAIT AS LONG AS YOU PLEASE. AND
CAND III	(138)	IN THE STREET, OR ANYTHING OF THAT SORT. /MORELL/	JUST	SO: SHE MAY. THATS WHY YOUD BETTER SEE HER SAFELY HOME.
KING II	(229)	UP; AND PEDRO ALSO IS MY FATHER'S SON. /CHARLES/	JUST	SO: SIX OF ONE AND HALF A DOZEN OF THE OTHER. HEREDITY
CLEO III	(159)	TRUMPERY? THE QUEEN IS ONLY A CHILD. /CAESAR/	JUST	SO: THAT IS WHY WE MUST NOT DISAPPOINT HER. WHAT IS THE
VWOO 2	(131)	WHAT. I WILL NOT COMMIT MYSELF. WE'LL SEE. /Z/	JUST	SO: WE'LL SEE. IT'S A BARGAIN THEN? /A/ NO: IT MOST
JITT II	(29)	/FESSLER/ THEN WHY DID HE DIE? /LENKHEIM/	JUST	SO: WHY DID HE DIE? HE WOULDNT HAVE DIED IF HE HAD
SUPR I	(41)	NOT A CHARM, A SUBTLE INTEREST (SHE LAUGHS)--	JUST	SO: YOU KNOW IT; AND YOU TRIUMPH IN IT. OPENLY AND
PHIL II	(101)	SHE SHOULD HAVE ANY SUCH AMBITION? /CHARTERIS/	JUST	SO: YOURE QUITE RIGHT: SHE COULDNT HAVE MADE A WORSE
MIS. PREFACE	(39)	WE STUCK AT CAESAR THE BETTER I WAS PLEASED.	JUST	SO DO LESS CLASSICALLY EDUCATED CHILDREN SEE NOTHING IN
DOCT PREFACE	(43)	OF ETHICAL JUDGMENT OR INDEPENDENT ACTION.	JUST	SO DO WE FIND A CROWD OF PETTY VIVISECTIONISTS DAILY
DOCT PREFACE	(34)	LIFE TO SAVE THE LIFE OF THE COMMUNITY, IT IS	JUST	SO IN THE CASE OF THE RIGHT TO KNOWLEDGE. IT IS A RIGHT
METH PREFACE	(R21)	TO BEGIN A TREATISE BY SAYING " THERE ARE	JUST	SO MANY SPECIES AS THERE WERE FORMS CREATED IN THE
MIS. PREFACE	(22)	OF EXPELLING ME. THE TRUTH WAS, A BOY MEANT	JUST	SO MUCH A YEAR TO THE INSTITUTION. THAT WAS WHY HE WAS
ROCK I	(200)	UNTIL THREE IN THE MORNING; AND MY BRAINS ARE	JUST	SO MUCH TRIPE. /HILDA/ WHY DID YOU SIT UP? THE
MIS. PREFACE	(24)	RIGHT AND THAT HE MUST AND WILL HAVE THE LESSON	JUST	SO OR ELSE BREAK HIS HEART (NOT SOMEBODY ELSE'S,
GENV PREFACE	(15)	PUGNACITY, EQUALLY WITH HIS CHRISTLIKE SON.	JUST	SO TODAY CONSERVATIVES KNOW NOTHING OF THE TORY CREED,
SUPR III	(84)	FOR ALL THE REST ARE ASLEEP BY THIS TIME) IT WAS	JUST	SO WITH HER, SIR. HER INTELLECT REACHED FORWARD INTO
FANY PROLOG	(262)	A FEW FIRST-RATE REPRESENTATIVE MEN. /SAVOYARD/	JUST	SO. ALL YOU WANT IS A FEW SAMPLE OPINIONS. OUT OF A
MTH4 I	(159)	AND NATURALISTS OF MY ACQUAINTANCE. /ZOO/	JUST	SO. AND THE GREATEST FOOL ON EARTH, BY MERELY LOOKING
BARB III	(336)	THINGS I HAD TO DO. /UNDERSHAFT/ (APPROVINGLY)	JUST	SO. AND WHY WAS THAT, DO YOU SUPPOSE? /BARBARA/
DOCT III	(139)	YOU. (HE SITS DOWN AGAIN ON THE SOFA). /LOUIS/	JUST	SO. AND YET YOU BELIEVE THAT JENNIFER IS A BAD LOT
PYGM V	(279)	/HIGGINS/ (WITH A CROW OF TRIUMPH) AHA!	JUST	SO. A-A-A-A-AHOWOOH! A-A-A-A-AHOWOOH!
JITT III	(52)	AND EVERYONE ELSE FROM READING THEM? /ALFRED/	JUST	SO. BUT WHY NOT LEAVE THE WORK TO US? WHY WORRY? CANT
2TRU I	(46)	YOUD BE AFRAID TO BE SO UNLADYLIKE. /THE BURGLAR/	JUST	SO. COME! CONFESS! WE ARE BETTER FUN THAN YOUR DEAR
MTH2	(76)	TO PAY AT THE END OF THEM. /FRANKLYN/	JUST	SO. CONSEQUENTLY, WHEN ADAM HAD THE GARDEN OF EDEN ON A
APPL II	(270)	IT. HE IS UP TO HIS NECK IN BUSINESS. /MAGNUS/	JUST	SO. HE ASKS ME WHY I WASTE MY TIME WITH YOU HERE
MRS III	(231)	/CROFTS/ (BLACK WITH RAGE) THE OLD-- /VIVIE/	JUST	SO. HE SWALLOWS THE EPITHET AND STANDS FOR A MOMENT
FANY III	(301)	THAN THE OTHER THING, DOESNT IT? /MARGARET/	JUST	SO. HOW DID YOU FIND OUT THE DIFFERENCE? /BOBBY/ (
BARB I	(267)	(LOOKING AT HIM WITH QUICK INTEREST AND NODDING)	JUST	SO. HOW DID YOU COME TO UNDERSTAND THAT? (LOMAX IS
PYGM II	(231)	THINGS ABOUT. /HIGGINS/ (GOING TO HER SOLEMNLY)	JUST	SO. I INTENDED TO CALL YOUR ATTENTION TO THAT. (HE
PHIL II	(108)	ANY OTHER WOMAN FROM GETTING HIM. /CHARTERIS/	JUST	SO. I UNDERSTAND. NOW LISTEN TO ME: I AM GOING TO SPEAK
ROCK I	(217)	/HIPNEY/ (SOOTHINGLY) JUST SO, SRARTHUR:	JUST	SO. IT TRIES YOU AND WORRIES YOU, AND BREAKS YOUR HEART
BULL IV	(172)	HALF ADMIRINGLY, HALF PITYINGLY). JUST SO,	JUST	SO. (COMING BACK TO BUSINESS) BY THE WAY, I BELIEVE I
JOAN 5	(114)	I KNOW I AM RIGHT. /BLUEBEARD/ HA HA! /CHARLES/	JUST	SO. (EXCLAIMING TOGETHER) /THE ARCHBISHOP/ HOW DO YOU
MTH2	(54)	NATURALLY IN SO LONG A TIME. /LUBIN/ JUST SO.	JUST	SO. (LOOKING ROUND AT SAVVY) THE YOUNG LADY IS--?
BARB II	(283)	SMARTING) THETS NAO CONCERN O YOURS. /BARBARA/	JUST	SO. (VERY BUSINESSLIKE) I'LL PUT YOU DOWN AS (
MTH2	(54)	OF HEALTH NATURALLY IN SO LONG A TIME. /LUBIN/	JUST	SO. JUST SO. (LOOKING ROUND AT SAVVY) THE YOUNG LADY
JOAN 4	(97)	(FEELING THAT THEY ARE GETTING ON CAPITALLY)	JUST	SO. NOW I SUPPOSE THERE CAN BE NO REASONABLE DOUBT THAT
JITT III	(53)	DOING NOTHING BUT GRIEVING, CAN I? /FESSLER/	JUST	SO. OF COURSE NOT. /AGNES/ LIFE GOES ON, DOESNT IT?
WIDO I	(21)	SO. (HE WRITES) " -- ENTIRELY FOR HIMSELF."	JUST	SO. PROCEED, SARTORIUS, PROCEED. VERY CLEARLY
JITT III	(57)	COURSE. /LENKHEIM/ (SITTING DOWN, RELIEVED) OH!	JUST	SO. /AGNES/ SHE WASNT WHAT YOU THINK SHE WAS.
BARB II	(291)	IS IN HEARING ANY MAN CONFESS IT. /UNDERSHAFT/	JUST	SO. /CUSINS/ EXCUSE ME: IS THERE ANY PLACE IN YOUR
PYGM V	(281)	THE WINDOW), THE SAME TO EVERYBODY. /HIGGINS/	JUST	SO. /LIZA/ LIKE FATHER. /HIGGINS/ (GRINNING, A LITTLE
MRS IV	(247)	OF HER ESCAPE FROM UTTERING IT). /VIVIE/	JUST	SO. /MRS WARREN/ HE OUGHT TO HAVE HIS TONGUE CUT OUT.
MIS.	(157)	EH? /LINA/ (GOING TO HIM, PAST HIS WIFE)	JUST	SO. /TARLETON/ BILLIARD BALLS AND CUES? PLATES,
PYGM V	(274)	MAAM, TAKES AFTER ME. /MRS HIGGINS/	JUST	SO. SHE HAD BECOME ATTACHED TO YOU BOTH. SHE WORKED
ROCK I	(218)	BECAUSE THE PEOPLE HAVE SENT ME HERE. /HIPNEY/	JUST	SO. THATS ALL THE USE THEY COULD MAKE OF THE VOTE WHEN
BARB III	(322)	MATTER IN A VERY PROPER SPIRIT, MY DEAR. /LOMAX/	JUST	SO. THATS ALL I MEANT, I ASSURE YOU. /SARAH/ ARE YOU
HART I	(63)	GIVE SOME INTEREST AND PLEASURE TO LIFE. /ELLIE/	JUST	SO. THATS ALL, REALLY. /MRS HUSHABYE/ IT MAKES THE
FANY PROLOG	(267)	TIME. /TROTTER/ WELL, I MUST SAY! /FANNY/	JUST	SO. THATS ONE OUR CLASSIFICATIONS IN THE CAMBRIDGE
MTH3	(131)	WOMAN'S FACE; AND YOU BELIEVED. /BURGE-LUBIN/	JUST	SO. THATS WHERE SHE HAD ME. I SHOULDNT HAVE BELIEVED
MTH4 III	(198)	THE ELECTION, I THINK. /THE ENVOY/ (REASSURED)	JUST	SO. THE ELECTION. NOW WHAT WE WANT TO KNOW IS THIS:
WIDO II	(28)	GODFATHER, MY DEAR SIR, HIS GODFATHER. /TRENCH/	JUST	SO. THE PLEASANTEST FELLOW FOR HIS AGE YOU EVER MET. HE
ROCK PREFACE	(185)	I AM SO ACCUSTOMED TO BE CONTRADICTED-- /PILATE/	JUST	SO. THERE ARE MANY SORTS OF WORDS; AND THEY ARE ALL
JOAN EPILOG	(162)	YOU. /JOAN/ I BEAR NO MALICE, MY LORD. /WARWICK/	JUST	SO. VERY KIND OF YOU TO MEET ME IN THAT WAY: A TOUCH OF
HART I	(79)	/CAPTAIN SHOTOVER/ THEY ARE MINE ALSO. /HECTOR/	JUST	SO. WE ARE MEMBERS ONE OF ANOTHER. (HE THROWS HIMSELF
MTH4 II	(187)	SUDDENLY MAKING HIMSELF VERY AGREEABLE) JUST SO:	JUST	SO. WE CAN WAIT AS LONG AS YOU PLEASE. AND NOW, IF I
MTH2	(88)	MIGHT, THEN I SAW HOW ABSURD IT WAS. /FRANKLYN/	JUST	SO. WE HAD BETTER HOLD OUR TONGUES ABOUT IT, CON. WE
APPL II	(264)	KNOW, SIR, PROGRESS, PROGRESS! /MAGNUS/ JUST SO.	JUST	SO. WE MAY SURVIVE ONLY AS ANOTHER STAR ON YOUR FLAG.
2TRU II	(61)	IN THE WAR TO WARN US OF AN AIR RAID? /TALLBOYS/	JUST	SO. WELL, AU REVOIR. /THE COUNTESS/ AU REVOIR. AU
JOAN 2	(79)	ALIVE, THEY WOULDNT BELIEVE IT. /THE ARCHBISHOP/	JUST	SO. WELL, THE CHURCH HAS TO RULE MEN FOR THE GOOD OF
MTH5	(223)	YOUTH AND BEAUTY TO AGE AND UGLINESS? /ARJILLAX/	JUST	SO. WELL, THE ARCHANGEL MICHAEL WAS OF MY OPINION. NOT
BARB III	(319)	MAKE NO SUCH RIDICULOUS PRETENSION. /UNDERSHAFT/	JUST	SO. WELL, THERE IS THE ARMY, THE NAVY, THE CHURCH, THE
FABL II	(107)	FOR MONEY AND NOTHING ELSE, BIG MONEY. /OLDHAND/	JUST	SO. WELL, WHAT SECURITY HAVE WE THAT AFTER SELLING HIS
DOCT III	(143)	/B.B./ YOU ARE A SCOUNDREL, SIR. /LOUIS/	JUST	SO. WHAT IS A SCOUNDREL? I AM. WHAT AM I? A
JITT II	(44)	AM ONLY TRYING TO GUESS WHY HE DID IT. /LENKHEIM/	JUST	SO. WHY DID HE DO IT? WHERE IS THE SENSE IN IT? I
MTH5	(246)	OF ART. IMAGES. WE CALL THEM DOLLS. /ARJILLAX/	JUST	SO. YOU HAVE NO SENSE OF ART; AND YOU INSTINCTIVELY
JOAN 4	(102)	SOUL, WHICH MAY SUFFER TO ALL ETERNITY. /WARWICK/	JUST	SO; AND GOD GRANT THAT HER SOUL MAY BE SAVED! BUT THE
JITT II	(51)	YES? /LENKHEIM/ I WILL THINK IT OVER. /JITTA/	JUST	SO, ALFRED. GOODNIGHT. (SHE GOES OUT, TRANQUILLY

2TRU III	(107)	TO DO. BUT ONLY ON TRIAL, MIND. /MRS MOPPLY/	JUST	SO, DARLING. WE'LL BOTH BE ON TRIAL. SO THATS SETTLED.
PYGM II	(235)	RELIEVED AT BEING SO WELL UNDERSTOOD)	JUST	SO, GOVERNOR. THATS RIGHT. /PICKERING/ BUT WHY DID YOU
BULL IV	(172)	THE SHOULDER, HALF ADMIRINGLY, HALF PITYINGLY).	JUST	SO, JUST SO. (COMING BACK TO BUSINESS) BY THE WAY, I
APPL II	(264)	YOU KNOW, SIR, PROGRESS, PROGRESS! /MAGNUS/	JUST	SO, JUST SO. WE MAY SURVIVE ONLY AS ANOTHER STAR ON
MTH5	(250)	NOT BELIEVE, AND THAT YOU DO NOT BELIEVE. /ACIS/	JUST	SO, MAM. ART IS NOT HONEST: THAT IS WHY I NEVER COULD
DEVL II	(39)	HANDCUFFS). I'M SORRY SIR; BUT DUTY-- /RICHARD/	JUST	SO, SERGEANT. WELL, I'M NOT ASHAMED OF THEM: THANK YOU
ROCK I	(217)	ABOUT THE MILLENNIUM. /HIPNEY/ (SOOTHINGLY)	JUST	SO, SRARTHUR: JUST SO. IT TRIES YOU AND WORRIES YOU.
LION PREFACE(8)		ASSERTION IS CREDIBLE AND THEREFORE MISLEADING.	JUST	SO, THE CLAIM TO DIVINITY MADE BY JESUS WAS TO THE HIGH
APPL I	(237)	THE COUNTRY. /LYSISTRATA/ (LETTING HERSELF GO)	JUST	SO! BREAKAGES, LIMITED! JUST SO! LISTEN TO ME, SIR;
APPL I	(237)	HERSELF GO) JUST SO! BREAKAGES, LIMITED!	JUST	SO! LISTEN TO ME, SIR; AND JUDGE WHETHER I HAVE NOT
SUPR IV	(149)	MY MONEY: DO YOU KNOW THAT? /HECTOR/ WELL, YOUVE	JUST	SPOILED IT ALL BY OPENING THAT LETTER. A LETTER FROM AN
BARB PREFACE(216)		SYSTEM? WELL, THERE ARE TWO MEASURES	JUST	SPROUTING IN THE POLITICAL SOIL, WHICH MAY CONCEIVABLY
BARB II	(287)	BUT GRIMMER THAN EVER). IT WOULD BE NICE TO	JUST	STAMP ON MOG HABBIJAM'S FACE, WOULDNT IT, BILL? /BILL/
DEVL III	(71)	YOU UNDER ARREST UNTIL THE EXECUTION'S OVER. YOU	JUST	STAND THERE; AND DONT LET ME SEE YOU AS MUCH AS MOVE
MIS.	(138)	IT SEEMS TO BE COMING TO A POINT, JOHNNY OR PAPA	JUST	STARTS ANOTHER HARE; AND IT ALL BEGINS OVER AGAIN; AND
MTH5	(239)	BUT HIS THUMB IS CLINCHED. /MARTELLUS/ NO: IT HAS	JUST	STRAIGHTENED OUT. SEE! HE HAS GONE. POOR PYGMALION!
LION I	(120)	FAITHFUL. THE FIRST MAN WHO STRUCK ME AS YOU HAVE	JUST	STRUCK ME WAS A STRONGER MAN THAN YOU: HE HIT ME HARDER
JITT I	(13)	ALWAYS LOOK AS IF YOU WERE RUNNING AWAY, AND HAD	JUST	STUMBLED INTO MY ARMS BY CHANCE? /THE LADY/ I ALWAYS
SUPR III	(90)	SUCH A WRETCH AS YOU, IN JUST SUCH A DUEL, FOR	JUST	SUCH A CAUSE. I SCREAMED: IT WAS MY DUTY. MY FATHER
SUPR III	(90)	FATHER WAS SLAIN BY JUST SUCH A WRETCH AS YOU, IN	JUST	SUCH A DUEL, FOR JUST SUCH A CAUSE. I SCREAMED: IT WAS
LION I	(121)	-- WROUGHT BY ME IN CAPPADOCIA? A YOUNG MAN --	JUST	SUCH A ONE AS YOU, WITH GOLDEN HAIR LIKE YOURS --
SUPR III	(90)	OLD WOMAN/ LISTEN TO ME. MY FATHER WAS SLAIN BY	JUST	SUCH A WRETCH AS YOU, IN JUST SUCH A DUEL, FOR JUST
CLEO PR01	(93)	THAT MEN TWENTY CENTURIES AGO WERE ALREADY	JUST	SUCH AS YOU, AND SPOKE AND LIVED AS YE SPEAK AND LIVE,
DOCT PREFACE(60)		FROM THEM, FALL INTO QUITE CRUDE ERRORS BY	JUST	SUCH POPULAR OVERSIGHTS AS I HAVE BEEN DESCRIBING.
ARMS II	(39)	WISH YOU COULD MARRY HIM INSTEAD OF ME. YOU WOULD	JUST	SUIT HIM. YOU WOULD PET HIM, AND SPOIL HIM, AND MOTHER
DOCT III	(144)	CHRISTIAN SCIENTISTS, I BELIEVE. THEYLL	JUST	SUIT YOUR COMPLAINT. WE CAN DO NOTHING FOR YOU. (HE
ROCK II	(284)	NOW OTHER GIRLS AND BOYS MAY FEEL TOMORROW. AND	JUST	SUPPOSE--! /LADY CHAVENDER/ WHAT? /SIR ARTHUR/
HART II	(114)	DOOR, BUT TURNS ASIDE TO THE BOOKSHELVES). I'LL	JUST	TAKE A BOOK (HE TAKES ONE). GOODNIGHT. (HE GOES OUT,
PHIL II	(100)	(RETIRING DISCREETLY TOWARDS THE TABLE) I'LL	JUST	TAKE A LOOK AT THE TIMES-- /CHARTERIS/ (STOPPING HIM)
MTH2	(75)	COULD BEAR NEITHER. THEY DECIDED THAT THEY WOULD	JUST	TAKE A SHORT TURN OF A THOUSAND YEARS, AND MEANWHILE
BULL II	(116)	IT WAS INDEED. /NORA/ YES, OF COURSE IT WAS.	JUST	TAKE MY ARM, MR BROADBENT, WHILE WE'RE GOIN DOWN THE
BULL I	(74)	IN THE BEDROOM) YES SIR. /BROADBENT/ DONT UNPACK.	JUST	TAKE OUT THE THINGS IVE WORN; AND PUT IN CLEAN THINGS.
SUPR IV	(152)	HERE IT IS (THRUSTING IT ON HIS FATHER). NOW YOU	JUST	TAKE YOUR REMITTANCE AND YOURSELF OUT OF MY LIFE. I'M
DEVL II	(32)	ON THE PRESS, AND REPLACES IT BY THE ONE HE HAS	JUST	TAKEN OFF) DID ANYONE CALL WHEN I WAS OUT? /JUDITH/
PYGM III	(252)	THEN IT MAKES HIM LOW-SPIRITED. A DROP OF BOOZE	JUST	TAKES THAT OFF AND MAKES HIM HAPPY. (TO FREDDY, WHO IS
GETT PREFACE(192)		OLD-FASHIONED NEWSPAPERS WITH EFFORT, AND WERE	JUST	TAKING WITH AVIDITY TO A NEW SORT OF PAPER, COSTING A
NEVR II	(236)	PRESENTLY, SIR. THE YOUNG LADY AND GENTLEMAN WERE	JUST	TALKING ABOUT YOUR FRIEND, SIR. /VALENTINE/ INDEED!
DOCT I	(112)	(ENTERING WITH EVERY SIGN OF ALARM) THEYVE	JUST	TELEPHONED FROM THE HOSPITAL THAT YOURE TO COME
2TRU II	(62)	AND APOLOGIZE, IT WILL BE THE WORSE FOR YOU. BUT	JUST	TELL A THUNDERING SILLY LIE THAT EVERYONE KNOWS IS A
WIDO I	(18)	WITH HER, AND SO FORTH. YOU KNOW WHAT I MEAN.	JUST	TELL HER ALL ABOUT IT IN A CHATTY WAY; AND-- /COKANE/ (
DEVL I	(14)	IS AND WHAT SHE IS. IF SHE GIVES YOU ANY TROUBLE,	JUST	TELL ME; AND I'LL SETTLE ACCOUNTS WITH HER. (MRS
MRS III	(234)	THE CIRCUMSTANCES! THANK YOU. /CROFTS/ I'LL	JUST	TELL YOU THIS BEFORE I GO. IT MAY INTEREST YOU, SINCE
GETT	(274)	/THE GENERAL/ (WITH CRUSHING STIFFNESS) I WAS	JUST	TELLING ALICE, SIR, THAT IF YOU ENTERED THIS HOUSE, I
2TRU II	(60)	AH, BAGOT! READY FOR YOUR DIP? I WAS	JUST	TELLING THE COUNTESS THAT I MET SOME FRIENDS OF YOURS
DOCT I	(102)	BUT I'M TOO BUSY JUST NOW. /RIDGEON/ I WAS	JUST	TELLING THEM WHEN YOU CAME IN, BLENKINSOP, THAT I HAVE
MIS.	(185)	I ASK YOU JUST TO SAY THAT I AM NOT TO BLAME.	JUST	THAT AND NOTHING MORE. /HYPATIA/ (GLOATING
HART II	(103)	OH NO; NOT WHAT I CALL A MAN. ONLY A BOSS:	JUST	THAT AND NOTHING ELSE. WHAT BUSINESS HAS A BOSS WITH A
METH PREFACE(R55)		LITTLE DULLARDS, WITH THEIR PRECARIOUS HOLD OF	JUST	THAT CORNER OF EVOLUTION THAT A BLACKBEETLE CAN
MIS. PREFACE(18)		BETWEEN THE MOMENTS OF AFFECTIONATE IMPULSE IS	JUST	THAT FEELING THAT LEADS THEM TO AVOID THEIR CARE AND
SUPR I	(12)	WILL SHE SAY TO THAT? WHAT DOES SHE SAY TO IT?	JUST	THAT HER FATHER'S WISHES ARE SACRED TO HER, AND THAT
MILL IV	(202)	ALASTAIR: HOW CAN YOU JEER AT ME? IS IT	JUST	THAT I, BECAUSE I AM A MILLIONAIRESS, CANNOT KEEP MY
HART II	(87)	OF COURSE, BUT TO US CHILDREN-- THAT YOU WERE	JUST	THAT SORT OF MAN. /MANGAN/ (SITTING UP, MUCH HURT)
ROCK II	(275)	/SIR ARTHUR/ YES, A HASTY BOY. /ALOYSIA/ HE IS,	JUST	THAT. BUT I SHALL CURE HIM OF IT. /SIR ARTHUR/ (
ROCK I	(220)	/SIR ARTHUR/ TURNED THEIR HEADS, EH? /HIPNEY/	JUST	THAT, SRARTHUR. TURNED THEIR HEADS. TURNED THEM RIGHT
HART II	(123)	NOT SAID A WORD AGAINST LADY UTTERWORD. THIS IS	JUST	THE CONSPIRACY OVER AGAIN. /HECTOR/ WHAT CONSPIRACY?
SIM I	(52)	YOU DO NOT KNOW WHAT LOVE CAN BE. /IDDY/ BUT IT'S	JUST	THE CONTRARY. I-- /VASHTI/ (WHO HAS ENTERED SILENTLY,
JOAN PREFACE(30)		PARTICULARLY AGREEABLE IN FRANCE INSTEAD OF	JUST	THE CONTRARY) AGAINST A FRENCHWOMAN WHO HAD VANQUISHED
SUPR HANDBOK(193)		DECENTLY ON THE SUBJECT: ON THE CONTRARY, IT IS	JUST	THE DEPTH AND SERIOUSNESS OF OUR FEELING THAT MAKES ITS
LIED	(189)	UNFIT FOR ANYBODY BUT A MARRIED WOMAN. THATS	JUST	THE DIFFICULTY. WHAT WILL MY SISTERS-IN-LAW THINK OF
MIS. PREFACE(93)		IN SHORT, WE ALL GROW UP STUPID AND MAD TO	JUST	THE EXTENT TO WHICH WE HAVE NOT BEEN ARTISTICALLY
DOCT I	(83)	THE POOR LADY. I THINK HE OUGHT TO SEE HER. SHE'S	JUST	THE KIND THAT PUTS HIM IN A GOOD TEMPER. (SHE DUSTS
GETT	SD(273)	HIMSELF) WELL, DASH MY BUTTONS! ! REGINALD IS	JUST	THE MAN LESBIA HAS DESCRIBED. HE IS HARDENED AND TOUGH
SUPR II	(68)	TOLD ME IN CAWNFIDNCE THAT YOURE MARRIED. THATS	JUST	THE MOST OVERWHELMING CAWNFIDNCE IVE EVER BEEN HONORED
GETT	(352)	WHY DIDNT YOU TELL ME THAT BEFORE? SONNY IS	JUST	THE NAME I WANTED FOR YOU. (SHE PATS HIS CHEEK
MILL PREFACE(120)		THE NEXT FIFTEEN YEARS IN PRISON. IT SEEMED	JUST	THE OCCASION FOR A GRAND APPEAL FOR LIBERTY, FOR
APPL II	(263)	AND OUR IDEAS. A POLITICAL UNION WITH US WILL BE	JUST	THE OFFICIAL RECOGNITION OF AN ALREADY ACCOMPLISHED
METH PREFACE(R54)		SUCH THING AS SELF-CONTROL. YET SELF-CONTROL IS	JUST	THE ONE QUALITY OF SURVIVAL VALUE WHICH CIRCUMSTANTIAL
BULL IV	(166)	THE IDEAL IS WHAT I LIKE. NOW LARRY'S TASTE IS	JUST	THE OPPOSITE: HE LIKES EM SOLID AND BOUNCING AND RATHER
2TRU III	(106)	AM I TO DO? HOW AM I TO BEHAVE IN A WORLD THATS	JUST	THE OPPOSITE OF EVERYTHING I WAS TOLD ABOUT IT? /THE
CAND II	(118)	USE OF THEIR AGREEING WITH YOU IF THEY GO AND DO	JUST	THE OPPOSITE OF WHAT YOU TELL THEM THE MOMENT YOUR BACK
ROCK II	(269)	PARLIAMENTARY LEADERS SAY ONE THING ON MONDAY AND	JUST	THE OPPOSITE ON WEDNESDAY; AND NOBODY NOTICES ANY
DOCT PREFACE(75)		IT TO STILL FURTHER EXERTIONS AND PRODUCE	JUST	THE OPPOSITE RESULT, AND HE INVENTED A TECHNIQUE FOR
DOCT PREFACE(76)		IN INFINITESIMALLY SMALL QUANTITIES, PROVOKE	JUST	THE OPPOSITE SYMPTOMS; SO THAT THE DRUG THAT GIVES YOU
GENV I	(36)	BUSINESS? /NEWCOMER/ OF COURSE THEYRE NOT.	JUST	THE OPPOSITE. YOU KNOW THAT, DONT YOU? /SHE/ OH,
JOAN 2	(72)	HIMSELF INTO A FIT, PERHAPS. /BLUEBEARD/ NO:	JUST	THE OPPOSITE. FOUL MOUTHED FRANK, THE ONLY MAN IN
HART II	(123)	AND EVERYTHING I AM NOT. EVERYONE KNOWS I AM	JUST	THE OPPOSITE. /HECTOR/ (RISING) SOMETHING IN THE AIR
PYGM V	(274)	DID YOU BULLY HER AFTER I WENT TO BED? /HIGGINS/	JUST	THE OTHER WAY ABOUT. SHE THREW MY SLIPPERS IN MY FACE.
GETT PREFACE(253)		ARE OFTEN SO GOOD FOR CHILDREN. BUT IT IS	JUST	THE POLYGAMOUS HOUSEHOLD WHICH OUR MARRIAGE LAW ALLOWS
DEVL EPILOG (82)		OF SENTIMENT, HIS FINE SPIRIT AND HUMANITY, WERE	JUST	THE QUALITIES TO MAKE HIM DISLIKED BY STUPID PEOPLE
DOCT III	(132)	IN ADVANCE. /MRS DUBEDAT/ BUT, DEAREST, THAT IS	JUST	THE REASON WHY YOU SHOULD FINISH THEM. HE ASKED ME THE
MTH2	(62)	I AM NOT GIVING YOU MY OWN IDEAS, MR LUBIN, BUT	JUST	THE REGULAR ORTHODOX SCIENCE OF TODAY, ONLY THE MOST
FANY PROLOG (262)		THAT SAY ANYTHING DIFFERENT. WELL, IVE GOT	JUST	THE RIGHT FOUR FOR YOU, AND WHAT DO YOU THINK IT HAS
APPL II	(270)	WITH YOU AS LONG AS YOU DONT INTERFERE WITH HIM.	JUST	THE RIGHT KING FOR US, NOT PIG-HEADED, NOT MEDDLESOME,
MRS I	(184)	SPLENDID, YOUR TIEING WITH THE THIRD WRANGLER.	JUST	THE RIGHT PLACE, YOU KNOW. THE FIRST WRANGLER IS ALWAYS
HART PREFACE(21)		FOR THEM TO GRASP, AND THE LITTLE ONE HAD BEEN	JUST	THE RIGHT SIZE FOR THEM . I WAS NOT SURPRISED. HAVE I
JITT III	(76)	VERY SENSIBLY. YOU KEPT YOUR HEAD, AND DID	JUST	THE RIGHT THING. YOU SAVED YOUR REPUTATION AND MY
GETT	(336)	A HOUSE OF CARDS. A WORD FROM ME TO GEORGE--	JUST	THE RIGHT WORD, SAID IN THE RIGHT WAY-- AND DOWN COMES
HART I	(48)	BACK TO IT AFTER TWENTY-THREE YEARS; AND IT IS	JUST	THE SAME: THE LUGGAGE LYING ON THE STEPS, THE SERVANTS
HART II	(99)	IS MARCUS AND A LOT OF OTHER MEN OF WHOM ONE IS	JUST	THE SAME AS ANOTHER. WELL, IF I CANT HAVE LOVE, THATS
DOCT III	(150)	WORSE, DO YOU? /SIR PATRICK/ NO: HE'S NOT WORSE.	JUST	THE SAME AS AT RICHMOND. /MRS DUBEDAT/ OH, THANK YOU:
CAND I	(86)	FROM HIS VISITOR. /BURGESS/ (WITHOUT MOVING)	JUST	THE SAME AS HEVER, JAMES! /MORELL/ WHEN YOU LAST
BULL I	(88)	DRINKING AND NOT KNOWING WHAT TO BE AT IN PECKHAM	JUST	THE SAME AS IN DONNYBROOK. YOU LOOKED AT IRELAND WITH A
BULL III	(129)	KNOW THAT YOUR FATHER'S BOUGHT HIS PLACE HERE,	JUST	THE SAME AS MATT'S FARM N BARNEY'S MILL. ALL WE ASK NOW
MTH4 I	(156)	AIRISH BECAUSE THEY LIVE IN AIR, THEY MUST BE	JUST	THE SAME AS OTHER PEOPLE. WHY DO YOU SHORTLIVERS
LION I	(125)	ANXIOUSLY PROTESTING) OH, BELIEVE ME, THEY HAVE.	JUST	THE SAME AS YOU AND ME. I REALLY DONT THINK I COULD
GENV III	(81)	THAT DAME BEGONIA'S SYMPATHIES AND INTENTIONS ARE	JUST	THE SAME AS YOURS. /BEGONIA/ OH! I NEVER SAID SO. I
PYGM II	(238)	AND A BAND WHEN I FEEL LOW. WELL, THEY CHARGE ME	JUST	THE SAME FOR EVERTHING AS THEY CHARGE THE DESERVING.
BULL I	(86)	THE USUAL THING IN THE COUNTRY, LARRY.	JUST	THE SAME HERE. /DOYLE/ (HASTILY) NO, NO: THE CLIMATE
METH PREFACE(R10)		INDUSTRIAL PURPOSES, AND THE PENNY POST. IT WAS	JUST	THE SAME IN OTHER SUBJECTS. THUS NIETZSCHE, BY THE TWO
PYGM V	(288)	AND THAT SHE'LL TEACH ANYBODY TO BE A DUCHESS	JUST	THE SAME IN SIX MONTHS FOR A THOUSAND GUINEAS. OH, WHEN
BULL I	(86)	JUST AS ENGLAND WAS; AND ITS BREED WAS CROSSED BY	JUST	THE SAME INVADERS. /BROADBENT/ TRUE. ALL THE CAPABLE
CAPT III	(296)	HIS PENNY NUMBERS AND SUCH LIKE TRASH; BUT I GOT	JUST	THE SAME NONSENSE OUT OF LIFE AND EXPERIENCE. (SHAKING
MILL III	(184)	A CROWN ADVANCE ON HIS PRESENT WAGES TO DRIVE IT	JUST	THE SAME OLD ROUND TO THE SAME PLACES. HE KNOWS THE
HART PREFACE(30)		IN 1915 I SAW IN THE THEATRES MEN IN KHAKI IN	JUST	THE SAME PREDICAMENT. TO EVERYONE WHO HAD MY CLUE TO
HART PREFACE(21)		NOT SURPRISED. HAVE I NOT SEEN A PUBLIC BODY FOR	JUST	THE SAME REASON PASS A VOTE FOR 30,000 POUNDS WITHOUT A
BARB I	(269)	COUNTY COUNCILLORS, ALL SORTS. THEYRE ALL	JUST	THE SAME SORT OF SINNER; AND THERES THE SAME SALVATION
PYGM V	(278)	THOUGH OF COURSE I KNOW YOU WOULD HAVE BEEN	JUST	THE SAME TO A SCULLERY-MAID IF SHE HAD BEEN LET INTO

3PLA PREFACE(R17)	AND UNIVERSITY SHOCK A BOARD OF GUARDIANS. IN	JUST	THE SAME WAY, THE PLAYS WHICH CONSTITUTE THE GENUINE
DOCT III (140)	NOT AFFECT THE FUNDAMENTAL TRUTH OF SCIENCE. IN	JUST	THE SAME WAY, IN MORAL CASES, A MAN'S BEHAVIOR MAY BE
OVER PREFACE(168)	IN ME. AND, IF SO, WHAT THAT QUALITY IS. IN	JUST	THE SAME WAY, I WANT THE UNFAITHFUL HUSBAND OR THE
APPL INTRLUD(247)	THE GREAT THINGS COME ALONG. BUT THEY ARE GREAT	JUST	THE SAME WHEN THE GREAT THINGS DO NOT COME ALONG. IF I
DOCT II (123)	LEND MONEY; AND WHEN WE REFUSE TO LEND IT YOU SAY	JUST	THE SAME. I DIDNT MEAN TO BEHAVE BADLY, AS I TOLD HIM,
DOCT PREFACE(6)	THROUGH THE DOCTORS; BUT HE HAD TO CALL THEM IN	JUST	THE SAME. NAPOLEON HAD NO ILLUSIONS ABOUT THEM; BUT HE
APPL II (270)	THINGS ARE LIKE THAT NOWADAYS. MY SON SAYS	JUST	THE SAME. /LYSISTRATA/ PERSONALLY I GET ON VERY WELL
JOAN EPILOG (154)	OF HER. AND YOU WOULD HOLD UP THE CROSS, TOO,	JUST	THE SAME. SO (CROSSING HIMSELF) LET HER REST; AND LET
LION I (117)	FUTURE WERE ONE OF TORMENT, I SHOULD HAVE TO GO	JUST	THE SAME. THE HAND OF GOD IS UPON ME. /THE CAPTAIN/
PRES (165)	FARRELL/ NO THANK YOU. I'D HAVE TO WORK FOR YOU	JUST	THE SAME; ONLY I SHOULDNT GET ANY WAGES FOR IT.
POSN PREFACE(401)	CONVERT ANY DIALOGUE, HOWEVER INNOCENT, INTO	JUST	THE SORT OF ENTERTAINMENT AGAINST WHICH THE CENSOR IS
MRS I (193)	DOWN THE RIFLE). I'M SO GLAD SHE KNOWS YOU: YOURE	JUST	THE SORT OF FELLOW SHE OUGHT TO KNOW. (HE SMILES, AND
PHIL I (91)	/CRAVEN/ (CUNNINGLY) AH, THATS IT, IS IT? HE'S	JUST	THE SORT OF FELLOW THAT WOULD HAVE NO CONTROL OVER HIS
POSN PREFACE(430)	HIMSELF DISAGREEABLE FOR THE SAKE OF A PRINCIPLE:	JUST	THE SORT OF MAN WHO SHOULD NEVER BE ALLOWED TO MEDDLE
NEVR III (274)	PLEASANTRY) NO: DONT SAY THINGS LIKE THAT. THATS	JUST	THE SORT OF THOUGHTLESS REMARK THAT MAKES A LOT OF
MILL I (159)	A QUEER FOREIGN VOICE AND A HOLLYWOOD ACCENT,	JUST	THE SORT THE PUBLIC LOVES. WE NEVER ASKED THE PRICE OF
GENV I (38)	AN ASSASSINATION. /THE WIDOW/ AND IS NOT THAT	JUST	THE STATE OF THINGS THE LEAGUE OF NATIONS IS HERE TO
DOCT I (92)	LOCK THEM UP. /RIDGEON/ YOU THINK I'M MAD! THATS	JUST	THE SUSPICION THAT HAS COME ACROSS ME ONCE OR TWICE.
ROCK II (242)	THAT ENOUGH OF IT STICKS TO THEIR OWN FINGERS, IS	JUST	THE THING FOR MY PEOPLE. I DARENT SAY A WORD AGAINST
SUPR IV (154)	/MALONE/ (EAGERLY) YES, YES, YES: THATS	JUST	THE THING (HE HANDS HER THE THOUSAND DOLLAR BILL, AND
CYMB FORWORD(135)	FEATURE OF A COMIC JAILOR WHICH PRECEDES IT,	JUST	THE THING TO SAVE THE LAST ACT. WITHOUT IT THE ACT IS A
SUPR I SD(9)	THE SNORTING NOSTRIL AND THE RESTLESS BLUE EYE,	JUST	THE THIRTY-SECONDTH OF AN INCH TOO WIDE OPEN), POSSIBLY
O'FL (210)	LIKE OF ME, IT MEANS TALKING ABOUT THE ENGLISH	JUST	THE WAY THE ENGLISH PAPERS TALK ABOUT THE BOSHES. AND
O'FL (206)	HANDS WITH ME AND SAYS THEYRE PROUD TO KNOW ME,	JUST	THE WAY THE KING SAID WHEN HE PINNED THE CROSS ON ME.
SUPR IV (153)	MEANT TO INSULT VIOLET: I TAKE IT ALL BACK. SHE'S	JUST	THE WIFE YOU WANT: THERE! /HECTOR/ (PATTING HIM ON
GETT SD(338)	WHO FLIES TO THE STUDY DOOR. THE BISHOP ENTERS	JUST	THEN AND FINDS HIMSELF BETWEEN THEM, NARROWLY ESCAPING
DOCT I SD(109)	NEST OR A PANTALOON'S WIG (FASHION WAVERING	JUST	THEN BETWEEN THESE TWO MODELS); HAS UNEXPECTEDLY
LADY (249)	MARTYRDOMS; AND SO THE CHURCH, WHICH ALSO WAS	JUST	THEN BROUGHT INTO STRAITS BY THE POLICY OF YOUR ROYAL
MRS I (184)	I WENT IN FOR IT IN EARNEST. THE PAPERS WERE FULL	JUST	THEN OF PHILLIPA SUMMERS BEATING THE SENIOR WRANGLER.
BULL PREFACE(70)	ASSASSINATED, WHEREUPON THE BRITISH GOVERNMENT,	JUST	THEN RATHER DRUNK AFTER A SWEEPING ELECTION VICTORY
SUPR I (34)	TO ME? /TANNER/ (ENIGMATICALLY) IT HAPPENED	JUST	THEN THAT I GOT SOMETHING THAT I WANTED TO KEEP ALL TO
AUGS PREFACE(261)	OFFICIAL FACILITIES FOR MY JOURNEY. IT HAPPENED	JUST	THEN THAT THE STAGE SOCIETY GAVE A PERFORMANCE OF THIS
FABL IV (115)	IN EMPTY SPACE. BUT A FAMOUS MATHEMATICIAN SHEWED	JUST	THEN THAT THERE IS NO SUCH THING AS NOTHING, AND THAT
BULL PREFACE(30)	BATON AND BREAK THE HEADS OF A PATRIOTIC FACTION	JUST	THEN UPSETTING THE PEACE OF THE TOWN, YET BACK OUT AT
3PLA PREFACE(R30)	HE UTTERED THE BARREN DENIAL. AS FOR ME, I WAS	JUST	THEN WANDERING ABOUT THE STREETS OF CONSTANTINOPLE,
METH PREFACE(R40)	NEGATION: WHAT WAS DESIRED BY IT ABOVE ALL THINGS	JUST	THEN WAS A DEMONSTRATION THAT THE EVIDENCES OF DESIGN
JOAN PREFACE(44)	IN WHICH HER SOCIAL SUPERIORS FOUND THEMSELVES	JUST	THEN. BUT THEY WERE NOT SO OFFERED. NOR WERE THEY
METH PREFACE(R33)	SCIENTIFIC WORKERS WERE VERY TIRED OF DEISM	JUST	THEN. THEY HAD GIVEN UP THE RIDDLE OF THE GREAT FIRST
LION PREFACE(37)	JESUS TO HEROD, WHO HAPPENS TO BE IN JERUSALEM	JUST	THEN, BECAUSE HEROD HAD EXPRESSED SOME CURIOSITY ABOUT
CAPT II SD(262)	SHE SEES DRINKWATER, COMING IN THROUGH THE ARCH	JUST	THEN, WITH A PRISMATIC HALO ROUND HIM, EVEN WHEN SHE
APPL PREFACE(195)	THE MONEY NOR THE ENTERPRISE WAS AVAILABLE	JUST	THEN, WITH THE WAR ON OUR HANDS. THE CLEARING HOUSE,
JOAN PREFACE(43)	MOSTLY BY THE GIVING AND OBEYING OF ORDERS UNDER	JUST	THESE CONDITIONS. " DONT ARGUE: DO AS YOU ARE TOLD" HAS
HART I (63)	NOT TO HAVE TO TALK TO ANYONE: TO BE ALONE AND	JUST	THINK ABOUT IT. /ELLIE/ (EMBRACING HER) HESIONE: YOU
MTH4 III (200)	YEARS AGO. YOU ASKED FOR IT; AND YOU GOT IT. AND	JUST	THINK OF ALL THE IMPORTANT QUESTIONS YOU MIGHT HAVE
MRS III (229)	MY MOTHER'S BUSINESS PARTNER? /CROFTS/ YES, NOW	JUST	THINK OF ALL THE TROUBLE AND THE EXPLANATIONS IT WOULD
MIS. (141)	MY FATHER. AND THEN, WHAT A SITUATION IT WAS!	JUST	THINK OF IT! I WAS ENGAGED TO YOUR SON; AND YOU KNEW
BULL PREFACE(62)	CONSIDERABLY INCREASING THE ARMY OF OCCUPATION."	JUST	THINK OF IT! IN A POPULATION OF NEARLY TEN MILLIONS,
BULL I (90)	OF MY WORK HAS BEEN DONE WITH MEN OF THAT SORT.	JUST	THINK OF ME AS I AM NOW GOING BACK TO ROSSCULLEN! TO
APPL I (203)	/BOANERGES/ (PLEASED AND CREDULOUS) I SHOULD	JUST	THINK YOU HAVE, KING MAGNUS. I HAVE MADE YOU SIT UP.
JITT III (65)	TIME IN MY IMAGINATION, WITH NO RELIEF BUT	JUST	THINKING HOW I CAN CATCH THAT WRETCH THAT STOLE FROM ME
WIDO I (6)	PUT THAT INTO YOUR HEAD? /COKANE/ NOTHING. I WAS	JUST	THINKING-- HM! SHE WILL EXPECT YOU TO MARRY, HARRY: A
JITT II (37)	LOOKED STRAIGHT AT YOU AND DID NOT SEE YOU.	JUST	THINK. HE WAS A DOCTOR: HE KNEW HIS DANGER BETTER THAN
MTH5 (210)	TOWARDS ALL THE TRIVIALITIES OF OUR LIFE HERE.	JUST	THINK. I HAVE HUNDREDS OF YEARS TO LIVE: PERHAPS
GENV II (62)	SO HE IS. IT'S ALL BEEN DONE BY CABLE. IVE	JUST	THIS MINUTE HEARD IT. YOU SEE, DEAR BILLIKINS IS NOT
DOCT II (119)	(RISING, VERY PALE) GONE! /RIDGEON/	JUST	THIS MOMENT-- /BLENKINSOP/ PERHAPS I COULD OVERTAKE
2TRU I (49)	FIRST (SHE HURRIES OUT). /THE BURGLAR/ WELL, FOR	JUST	THIS ONCE, SAFETY FIRST (HE MAKES FOR THE WINDOW).
NEVR II (254)	/VALENTINE/ (CAUTIOUSLY) I SEE. MAY I ASK	JUST	THIS ONE QUESTION? IS YOUR OBJECTION AN OBJECTION TO
GETT (295)	THEM TO FOLLOW). /SYKES/ THATS IT, YOU SEE. IT'S	JUST	THIS OUTSPOKENNESS THAT MAKES MY POSITION HARD, MUCH AS
PYGM II (241)	(EVASIVELY) CERTAINLY. I'LL COME, GOVERNOR. NOT	JUST	THIS WEEK, BECAUSE I HAVE A JOB AT A DISTANCE. BUT
KING II (229)	ARE CHOSEN. AND EVEN THEN THE PICKED ONES WILL BE	JUST	THOSE WHOM THE PEOPLE WILL NOT CHOOSE. WHO IS IT THAT
CAND II (121)	SAME THINGS AS HE DOES. BUT NOW! BECAUSE I HAVE	JUST	THOUGHT SOMETHING DIFFERENT! LOOK AT HIM! JUST LOOK!
2TRU II (73)	YOU. WHAT ARE WE, WE THREE GLORIOUS ADVENTURERS?	JUST	THREE INEFFICIENT FERTILIZERS. /AUBREY/ WHAT ON EARTH
METH PREFACE(R48)	ENVIRONMENT AND THE APPEARANCE OF NEW SPECIES: WE	JUST	THREW IN THE WORD " VARIATIONS" OR THE WORD " SPORTS" (
MIS. SD(109)	HATS, AND OTHER SUMMERY ARTICLES ARE BESTOWED.	JUST	THROUGH THE ARCH AT THIS CORNER STANDS A NEW PORTABLE
MTH2 (67)	THE FAMILY AND THE GOOD OF THEIR OWN SOULS. YOU	JUST	TIP THEM A CHAPTER FROM THE GOSPEL OF THE BROTHERS
ROCK I (208)	NO. ONLY A SOCIAL CALL, NOT A PROFESSIONAL VISIT.	JUST	TO AMUSE YOU, AND GRATIFY HER CURIOSITY. SHE WANTS TO
MTH3 (106)	DO CERTAIN THINGS EVERY DAY WHEN THEY ARE THREE.	JUST	TO BREAK THEM IN, YOU KNOW. BUT THEY BECOME
DOCT I (86)	DOWN. GOODBYE. YOU DONT MIND MY CALLING, DO YOU?	JUST	TO CONGRATULATE YOU. /RIDGEON/ DELIGHTED, MY DEAR
SUPR III (78)	WILL HONOR US BY ACCEPTING IT. /STRAKER/ I SEE.	JUST	TO ENCOURAGE ME TO COME THIS WAY AGAIN. WELL, I'LL
GENV IV (97)	YOU BELIEVE HIM, GENTLEMEN. HE IS SAYING THAT	JUST	TO GET A RISE OUT OF ME. THE PEOPLE IN CAMBERWELL ARE
BULL IV (169)	AN WOULD YOU LET ME DEMEAN MESELF LIKE THAT,	JUST	TO GET YOURSELF INTO PARLIAMENT? /BROADBENT/ (
POSN (442)	ANYTHING. SO AS YOU REFUSED ME MY DUE I TOOK IT,	JUST	TO GIVE YOU A LESSON. /ELDER DANIELS/ WHY DIDNT YOU
ROCK I (228)	WELL, I RECEIVE THEM ALL AS I AM RECEIVING YOU,	JUST	TO GRATIFY HER, OR RATHER TO PREVENT HER FROM MAKING MY
MILL I (151)	YOUR SOUL YOUR OWN. AS SUNDAY HUSBANDS AND WIVES,	JUST	TO HAVE A GOOD TEARING BIT OF LOVEMAKING WITH, OR A
DOCT I (111)	HE IS WORTH SAVING. OH, DOCTOR, I MARRIED HIM	JUST	TO HELP HIM TO BEGIN: I HAD MONEY ENOUGH TO TIDE HIM
FANY PROLOG (260)	SOME OF US MUST LIVE IN ENGLAND, YOU KNOW,	JUST	TO KEEP THE PLACE GOING. BESIDES-- THOUGH, MIND YOU, I
APPL II (265)	AND I SUPPOSE I SHALL END AS AMERICAN EMPEROR	JUST	TO KEEP YOU AMUSED. /THE QUEEN/ I NEVER DESIRE ANYTHING
FANY I (282)	DO YOU REAL CREDIT. BUT I CANT GIVE HIM UP	JUST	TO LET HIM FALL INTO THE HANDS OF PEOPLE I COULDNT
MRS III (228)	OF COURTSHIP: I'M IN NO HURRY. IT WAS ONLY	JUST	TO LET YOU KNOW IN CASE YOUNG GARDNER SHOULD TRY TO
PHIL I (86)	MADE UP HIS MIND NOT TO SURVIVE NEXT EASTER,	JUST	TO OBLIGE THEM. /CRAVEN/ (WITH MILITARY AFFECTATION)
PYGM II (235)	ME WITH IT, THE LITTLE SWINE. I BROUGHT IT TO HER	JUST	TO OBLIGE YOU LIKE, AND MAKE MYSELF AGREEABLE. THATS
CAND II (112)	A YELL OF REMONSTRANCE) NAH-OO! SUMMAT PLEASANT,	JUST	TO PASS THE TIME. (MORELL TAKES AN ILLUSTRATED PAPER
FANY PROLOG (263)	OWN. WOULDNT HEAR OF PAYMENT! OFFERED TO COME	JUST	TO PLEASE HER! QUITE HUMAN. I WAS SURPRISED. /THE
BULL II (100)	NOW SAY GOD BLESS YOU, FETHER, TO ME BEFORE I GO,	JUST	TO PRACTISE YOU A BIT. /PATSY/ SURE IT WOULDNT BE
FANY III (304)	TO USE FORCE) NOW, I'LL MAKE YOU KISS ME,	JUST	TO PUNISH YOU. (SHE SEIZES HIS WRIST; PULLS HIM OFF
2TRU II (64)	THAT I SOMETIMES FEEL I COULD ALMOST MARRY HIM,	JUST	TO PUT HIM ON THE LIST OF THE INEVITABLES THAT I MUST
PYGM II (242)	AND GET OUT THERE AND TELL IT TO WAIT FOR ME,	JUST	TO PUT THE GIRLS IN THEIR PLACE A BIT. I WOULDNT SPEAK
LION II (144)	STILL; AND SMILE; AND LET HIM SMELL YOU ALL OVER	JUST	TO REASSURE HIM; FOR, YOU SEE, HE'S AFRAID OF YOU; AND
MIS. (198)	WRITHING SHOULDERS) OH, IF YOU WANT TO BEAT ME	JUST	TO RELIEVE YOUR FEELINGS-- JUST REALLY AND TRULY FOR
MIS. (185)	I'M SUFFERING THIS FOR YOUR SAKE. I ASK YOU	JUST	TO SAY THAT I AM NOT TO BLAME, JUST THAT AND NOTHING
MIS. (141)	HIM OFF OR GIVE HIM A CHANCE OF PROPOSING,	JUST	TO SEE HOW HE'LL DO IT, AND REFUSE HIM BECAUSE HE DOES
BULL II (104)	THATS ALL THAT BRINGS HIM BACK TO LOOK AT US,	JUST	TO SEE HOW MUCH WEVE CHANGED. WELL, HE CAN WAIT AND SEE
2TRU III (104)	I DONT MIND KEEPING COMPANY FOR A WHILE, SUSAN,	JUST	TO SEE HOW WE GET ALONG TOGETHER. THE VOICE OF MRS
FANY III (300)	LIKE, BOBBY. SUPPOSE WE GET OFF DUTY FOR THE DAY,	JUST	TO SEE WHAT IT'S LIKE. /BOBBY/ OFF DUTY? WHAT DO YOU
PHIL II (99)	(RISING) DO YOU KNOW, IVE A GREAT MIND TO JOIN,	JUST	TO SEE WHAT IT'S LIKE. /CHARTERIS/ (COMING BETWEEN
PHIL I (70)	ONE IS YOUNG, ONE MARRIES OUT OF MERE CURIOSITY,	JUST	TO SEE WHAT IT'S LIKE. /GRACE/ WELL, SINCE YOU ASK ME,
FANY EPILOG (331)	REAL SENSE IN THEM WHEN YOU COME TO EXAMINE THEM,	JUST	TO SET ALL THE FOOLS IN THE HOUSE GIGGLING. THEN WHAT
DOCT III (138)	WALPOLE: WOULD YOU MIND LENDING ME HALF-A-CROWN	JUST	TO SETTLE THIS. /WALPOLE/ LEND YOU HALF-- (HIS VOICE
FABL II (106)	HE DROPPED HIS BOMBS ON THE ISLE OF WIGHT	JUST	TO SHEW CAPETOWN AND THE REST THAT THE WORLD WAS AT HIS
LION PROLOG (109)	THAT DIDNT HURT AT ALL: NOT A BIT. JUST ONE MORE.	JUST	TO SHEW HOW THE BRAVE BIG LION CAN BEAR PAIN, NOT LIKE
POSN (435)	TO YOU ON A SHUTTER, PERHAPS FOR NOTHING, OR ONLY	JUST	TO SHEW THAT THE MAN THAT KILLED HIM WASNT AFRAID OF
PYGM V (280)	SMILE FOR HIM THROUGH HER VEXATION) OH WELL,	JUST	TO SHEW THERES NO ILL FEELING. I'LL BE BACK IN A
CATH 4 (193)	BURSTS INTO TEARS). RELEASE ME. /CATHERINE/ WELL,	JUST	TO SHEW YOU HOW MUCH KINDER A RUSSIAN SAVAGE CAN BE
MTH4 II (188)	AS I DO THAT HE HAS IMPOSED HIMSELF ON MY PARTY	JUST	TO SPY ON ME. I DONT DENY THAT HE HAS THE WHIP HAND OF
MIS. (149)	YOU ALL RIGHT? SURE YOU WONT HAVE SOME BRANDY	JUST	TO TAKE OFF THE SHOCK. /THE AVIATOR/ NO, THANK YOU.
PHIL II (107)	BOOKSTAND). I SHOULD LIKE PAPA TO LIVE FOR EVER	JUST	TO TAKE THE CONCEIT OUT OF PARAMORE. I BELIEVE HE'S IN
DOCT I (108)	THEM OTHERS THINK NOTHING OF HALF-A-SOVEREIGN	JUST	TO TALK ABOUT THEMSELVES TO YOU, THE SLUTS! BESIDES,

HART I	(65)	ONE THIRD-FLOOR WINDOW AND COMING IN AT ANOTHER,	JUST	TO TEST HIS NERVE. HE HAS A WHOLE DRAWERFUL OF ALBERT
SUPR I	(40)	AUDACITY! (SHE LAUGHS AND PATS HIS CHEEKS). NOW	JUST	TO THINK THAT IF I MENTIONED THIS EPISODE NOT A SOUL
JOAN 6	(140)	TO SAVE YOU. THE INQUISITOR COULD NOT BE MORE	JUST	TO YOU IF YOU WERE HIS OWN DAUGHTER. BUT YOU ARE
CAPT III	(277)	AND WHEN YOU CAME HOME AND SAID, " MARY: IVE	JUST	TOLD ALL THE WORLD THAT YOUR SISTER-IN-LAW WAS A POLICE
CAND III	(141)	NO. /CANDIDA/ (ALMOST FIERCELY) THEN JAMES HAS	JUST	TOLD ME A FALSEHOOD. IS THAT WHAT YOU MEAN?
JITT II	(31)	ABOUT HIS DEATH? ABSOLUTELY NOTHING: FESSLER HAS	JUST	TOLD ME SO. /JITTA/ (SITTING DOWN AT THE TABLE,
DOCT I	(103)	SIR PATRICK: I AM MORE STRUCK BY WHAT YOU HAVE	JUST	TOLD ME THAN I CAN WELL EXPRESS. YOUR FATHER, SIR,
JITT III	(78)	/LENKHEIM/ I DIDNT. AND THE OLD WOMAN HAS	JUST	TOLD ME THAT HE SAID THE BOOK WAS TO BE HER INSURANCE
DOCT I	(84)	IN THE LETTERS IF YOU HAVNT. /REDPENNY/ EMMY HAS	JUST	TOLD ME. I'M AWFULLY GLAD. I-- /RIDGEON/ ENOUGH, YOUNG
DOCT III	(155)	WHEN I TELL YOU THAT I UNDERSTAND WHAT YOU HAVE	JUST	TOLD ME; THAT I HAVE NO DESIRE BUT TO SERVE YOU IN THE
PRES	(162)	BALSQUITH: WE MUST NOT YIELD TO CLAMOR. I HAVE	JUST	TOLD THAT WOMAN THAT I AM AT LAST CONVINCED--
ROCK II	(271)	SOLOMON OR MOSES? THE JEWS DIDNT ELECT MOSES: HE	JUST	TOLD THEM WHAT TO DO AND THEY DID IT. LOOK AT THE WAY
GETT	(330)	A FANCY TO YOU, AND YOU AMUSE HIM ENOUGH, I'LL	JUST	TOLERATE YOU COMING IN AND OUT OCCASIONALLY FOR-- WELL,
BULL III	(118)	DID YOU TRY THE POTTINE, HODSON? /HODSON/ I	JUST	TOOK A MOUTHFUL, SIR, IT TASTED OF PEAT: OH! SOMETHING
BULL IV	(148)	O THE POUND. (WITH ENORMOUS ENJOYMENT) BEGOB, IT	JUST	TORE THE TOWN IN TWO AND SENT THE WHOLE DAM MARKET TO
POSN	(448)	EVER GET A WORD OR A LOOK FROM ME AGAIN. YOURE	JUST	TRASH: THATS WHAT YOU ARE. WHITE TRASH. /BLANCO/ AND
GENV III	(71)	SHOULD WE SHOOT HER, COMRADE? /THE JEW/ SHE HAS	JUST	TRIED TO SHOOT ME. /THE COMMISSAR/ WE DO NOT SHOOT JEWS
FANY III	(306)	OF COURSE IT ISNT, OLD MAN. (TO MARGARET) I'LL	JUST	TROT OFF AND COME BACK IN HALF AN HOUR. YOU TWO CAN
MILL IV	(190)	THE NERVE TO TURN HER OUT: HE SAID SHE MIGHT	JUST	TRY FOR A DAY OR TWO, SO SHE STARTED IN. SHE WASHED TWO
HART II	(100)	FOR YOUR PLAYING THAT TRUMP AGAINST ME. WELL, YOU	JUST	TRY IT: THATS ALL. I SHOULD HAVE MADE A MAN OF MARCUS,
MILL I	(159)	/ALASTAIR/ IF YOU THINK THAT WAS AN EASY JOB,	JUST	TRY IT YOURSELF: THATS ALL. I DREAM OF IT SOMETIMES:
GETT	(305)	THE GREATEST POSSIBLE SERVICE TO MORALITY BY	JUST	TRYING HOW THE NEW SYSTEM WOULD WORK. /LESBIA/ (
ROCK I	(233)	MAN CAN BEAT THEM AT THEIR OWN SILLY GAME. I'LL	JUST	TURN KARL MARX INSIDE-OUT FOR THEM. (THE HOUSEHOLD
POSN	(460)	SICKLY FACE AWAY FROM IN FRONT OF ME. /STRAPPER/	JUST	TURN YOUR BACK ON HER THERE, WILL YOU? /THE WOMAN/ GOD
POSN	SD(439)	AND A FEW OTHERS WITH BLANCO. STRAPPER IS A LAD	JUST	TURNING INTO A MAN: STRONG, SELFISH, SULKY, AND
MTH5	(209)	TELL ME THE TRUTH: HOW OLD ARE YOU? /THE MAIDEN/	JUST	TWICE YOUR AGE, MY POOR BOY. /THE YOUTH/ TWICE MY AGE!
BARB II	(277)	CAN DO. I MUSTNT STOP. /RUMMY/ TRY A PRAYER FOR	JUST	TWO MINUTES. YOULL WORK ALL THE BETTER AFTER. /JENNY/ (
NEVR I	(210)	WHO IS IMPERTURBABLE). IF HE WOULDNT MIND WAITING	JUST	TWO MINUTES, I-- I'LL SLIP DOWN AND SEE HIM FOR A
DOCT I	(91)	(TO EMMY) EMMY: ASK MR WALPOLE TO WAIT	JUST	TWO MINUTES, WHILE I FINISH A CONSULTATION. /EMMY/ OH,
MIS.	(123)	BEFORE MY CHILDREN DIED OF DIPHTHERIA. THAT WAS	JUST	TWO MONTHS AFTER I'D BURIED POOR LITTLE BOBBY; AND THAT
MTH2	(83)	EIGHTEEN HUNDRED AND TWENTY-FIVE OUNCES A YEAR:	JUST	TWO OUNCES OVER THE HUNDREDWEIGHT. /BURGE/ TWO MILLION
DOCT I	(85)	THE SECRET? /SCHUTZMACHER/ WELL, THE SECRET WAS	JUST	TWO WORDS. /RIDGEON/ NOT CONSULTATION FREE, WAS IT?
DOCT II	(121)	IT TO HIM. AND HE'S FORGOTTEN TO PAY ME. I'VE	JUST	TWOPENCE TO GET BACK WITH. /RIDGEON/ OH, NEVER MIND
BARB PREFACE	(220)	THE ENDS OF THE EARTH AND FIX THEM ON THIS TRUTH	JUST	UNDER YOUR NOSE; AND ANDREW UNDERSHAFT'S VIEWS WILL NOT
MRS I	(183)	CHAIR FORWARD WITH ONE SWING). /PRAED/ (WHO HAS	JUST	UNFOLDED HIS CHAIR) OH, NOW DO LET ME TAKE THAT HARD
JITT I	(15)	HEAR YOUR RING, I SUDDENLY BECOME LIKE A FRESHMAN	JUST	UP FROM SCHOOL. (SHE LAUGHS, SMOOTHING HIS GREY HAIR).
JOAN PREFACE	(22)	KNEW NOTHING OF IRON HANDS IN VELVET GLOVES: SHE	JUST	USED HER FISTS. SHE THOUGHT POLITICAL CHANGES MUCH
PYGM II	(231)	WORD I MUST ASK YOU NOT TO USE. THE GIRL HAS	JUST	USED IT HERSELF BECAUSE THE BATH WAS TOO HOT. IT BEGINS
KING I	(205)	THEATRE OR SHAME IT INTO DECENCY; BUT THESE LINES	JUST	UTTERED BY ELEANOR GWYN ARE NOT PROFANE AND IMMORAL:
MTH3	SD(127)	OF THIS PAINFUL EPISODE, MOVES TO THE CHAIR	JUST	VACATED BY THE ARCHBISHOP AND STANDS BEHIND IT WITH
JITT II	SD(33)	NEAR HER. JITTA LEADS EDITH TO THE CHAIR SHE HAS	JUST	VACATED, AND GOES TO THE SOFA, WHERE SHE SEATS HERSELF
CLEO III	SD(149)	STEPS OUT OF HARM'S WAY, BUT STOPS, WITH HIS HEAD	JUST	VISIBLE ABOVE THE EDGE OF THE QUAY, TO WATCH THE FIGHT.
DEST	(159)	I SAY IT AGAIN. JUST WAIT UNTIL I CATCH HIM.	JUST	WAIT: THATS ALL. (HE FOLDS HIS ARMS RESOLUTELY, AND
PRES	(165)	TO UNDERSTAND THAT YOU REFUSE ME? /MRS FARRELL/	JUST	WAIT A BIT. (SHE TAKES MITCHENER'S CHAIR AND RINGS UP
NEVR IV	(292)	YOU DID. (TO THE WAITER, WHO IS GOING OUT)	JUST	WAIT A BIT. /WAITER/ YES, SIR. CERTAINLY, SIR. (HE
BULL IV	(169)	AND I'M NOT FIT TO TALK TO THEM. /BROADBENT/	JUST	WAIT AND SAY SOMETHING NICE TO KEEGAN. THEY TELL ME HE
WIDO III	(55)	DOOR OPENS). /LICKCHEESE/ (IN THE STUDY) YOU	JUST	WAIT FIVE MINUTES: I'LL FETCH HIM. (BLANCHE SNATCHES A
MTH2	(46)	/HASLAM/ I'D BETTER GO, HADNT I? /CONRAD/ YOU	JUST	WAIT HERE, BOTH OF YOU. WHEN YOU START YAWNING, JOYCE
DEVL II	(45)	RISING AND DRYING HER EYES) YES? /ANDERSON/	JUST	WAIT OUTSIDE A MOMENT, LIKE A GOOD GIRL: MRS ANDERSON
AUGS	(271)	THIS IS NOT A CASINO. /THE CLERK/ AINT IT? YOU	JUST	WAIT TIL YOU SEE HER. (HE GOES OUT). AUGUSTUS PRODUCES
CAND II	(110)	GASPING)! HALL RIGHT, MY GURL! HALL RIGHT. YOU	JUST	WAIT TILL I TELL THAT TO YORE HEMPLOYER. YOULL SEE.
DEST	(159)	(DRAWING HIMSELF UPRIGHT) I SAY IT AGAIN.	JUST	WAIT UNTIL I CATCH HIM. JUST WAIT: THATS ALL. (HE
MTH4 III	(195)	BUT YOU ARE SPOILING THE EFFECT. /ZOO/ YOU	JUST	WAIT. ALL THIS BUSINESS WITH COLOURED LIGHTS AND CHORDS
POSN	(459)	BUT YOURE NOT SHERIFF YET. THIS IS MY JOB. YOU	JUST	WAIT. I SUBMIT THAT WE'RE IN A DIFFICULTY HERE. IF
DEST	(185)	/LIEUTENANT/ AHA! YOU THINK SO; BUT YOULL SEE.	JUST	WAIT. ONLY, IF I DO CATCH HIM AND HAND HIM OVER TO YOU,
OVER	(185)	(FONDLY) ARE YOU, DEAR? /GREGORY/ YOU	JUST	WAIT, MY PET. I'LL SETTLE THIS CHAP FOR YOU. (HE
MILL II	(172)	LIKE ZIONISM. THE STUPIDEST DI PARERGA CAN	JUST	WALK ROUND THE CLEVEREST JEW WHEN IT COMES TO
LION II	(130)	EDITOR/ SERVE THE ROTTER RIGHT! /THE GLADIATORS/	JUST	WALKED INTO IT, HE DID. HE'S MARTYRED ALL RIGHT ENOUGH.
2TRU II	(68)	I KNOW JUST WHAT HE'LL SAY AND WHAT HE'LL DO. I	JUST	WANT HIM TO DO IT. /THE PATIENT/ (RISING, REVOLTED)
BARB III	(345)	MUCH LESS DIFFICULT THAN GREEK. /STEPHEN/ WELL, I	JUST	WANT TO SAY THIS BEFORE I LEAVE YOU TO YOURSELVES. DONT
BARB II	(287)	HAS DEEPENED) OH, WE SHALL CURE HIM IN NO TIME.	JUST	WATCH. (SHE GOES OVER TO BILL AND WAITS. HE GLANCES UP
MILL I	(159)	LOVES. WE NEVER ASKED THE PRICE OF ANYTHING: WE	JUST	WENT IN UP TO OUR NECKS FOR THOUSANDS AND THOUSANDS.
GETT	(332)	NERVES WERE A LITTLE UPSET BY OUR CONVERSATION. I	JUST	WENT INTO THE GARDEN AND HAD A SMOKE. I'M ALL RIGHT NOW
BARB II	(281)	AW'M AS GOOD AS ER. /SHIRLEY/ TELL HER SO. IT'S	JUST	WHAT A FOOL LIKE YOU WOULD DO. BARBARA, BRISK AND
PYGM EPILOG	(293)	MARRIES EITHER OF THEM, MARRY FREDDY. AND THAT IS	JUST	WHAT ELIZA DID. COMPLICATIONS ENSUED; BUT THEY WERE
ROCK II	(266)	TO USE HIS MIND LIKE US IN SCOTLAND. BUT THAT IS	JUST	WHAT GIVES HIM SUCH A HOLD ON THE COUNTRY. WE MUST FACE
3PLA PREFACE	(R14)	TO PERFECTION IN THE LATEST FASHIONS. BUT THAT IS	JUST	WHAT HAPPENED TO ME IN THE THEATRE. I DID NOT FIND THAT
APPL INTRLUD	(247)	HER. I NEVER SAW A MAN SO CHANGED. /ORINTHIA/	JUST	WHAT HE IS FIT FOR. COMMONPLACE. BOURGEOISE. SHE TROTS
MTH2	(59)	THING FOR HIM TO BE DISTRACTED BY A PRETTY GIRL.	JUST	WHAT HE NEEDS. /BURGE/ I SOMETIMES ENVY YOU, LUBIN. THE
BARB III	(320)	THINK HE HAD BETTER DO, ANDREW? /UNDERSHAFT/ OH,	JUST	WHAT HE WANTS TO DO. HE KNOWS NOTHING; AND HE THINKS HE
APPL I	(212)	QUARRELLING AND SCOLDING AND BAWLING, WHICH IS	JUST	WHAT HE WANTS YOU TO DO, IT WILL END IN HIS HAVING HIS
DEVL II	(45)	ABOUT YOUR BEST COAT." EH? /JUDITH/ YES, THAT IS	JUST	WHAT HE WILL SAY TO YOU. (VACANTLY) IT DOESNT MATTER:
POSN	(459)	ME THE HORSE TO DISAPPOINT ME LIKE THAT. /BLANCO/	JUST	WHAT HE WOULD DO. /STRAPPER/ WE AINT GOT NOTHIN TO DO
2TRU II	(68)	LEAST CURIOSITY ABOUT MY LOVELY SERGEANT: I KNOW	JUST	WHAT HE'LL SAY AND WHAT HE'LL DO. I JUST WANT HIM TO DO
JOAN 2	(85)	YOU ALL HAVE YOUR HEADS FULL OF: I WANT TO BE	JUST	WHAT I AM. WHY CANT YOU MIND YOUR OWN BUSINESS, AND LET
SUPR IV	(147)	SOCIAL POSITION IN ENGLAND, MISS ROBINSON, IS	JUST	WHAT I CHOOSE TO BUY FOR HIM. I HAVE MADE HIM A FAIR
MRS PREFACE	(170)	TRAGEDY. I HAVE NO DOUBT THEY WOULD; BUT THAT IS	JUST	WHAT I DID NOT WANT TO DO. NOTHING WOULD PLEASE OUR
MTH1 I	(5)	I DO NOT KNOW HOW TO PREVENT IT. /EVE/ THAT IS	JUST	WHAT I FEEL; BUT IT IS VERY STRANGE THAT YOU SHOULD SAY
SUPR III	(128)	WITH WHICH I HAD TO STRIVE, I DID AGAIN	JUST	WHAT I HAD DONE AS A CHILD. I HAVE ENJOYED, TOO, MY
APPL I	(204)	HAND) YOU MEAN ABOUT THE CRISIS. WELL, FRANK IS	JUST	WHAT I HAVE COME HERE TO BE. AND THE FIRST THING I AM
GENV IV	(92)	OBEYED. YOU ARE HERE. WHY? /BATTLER/ THAT IS	JUST	WHAT I HAVE COME TO FIND OUT. WHY ARE YOU HERE, BARDO?
BUOY III	(30)	NO ACCOMPLISHMENTS, EXCEPT WHAT I PICKED UP DOING	JUST	WHAT I LIKED AND WAS GIVEN EVERYTHING I ASKED FOR. THAT
CLEO I	(108)	ME OUT OF IT. WHEN I AM OLD ENOUGH I SHALL DO	JUST	WHAT I LIKE. I SHALL BE ABLE TO POISON THE SLAVES AND
WIDO II	(35)	WE OUGHT TO BE SELF-SUPPORTING. /BLANCHE/ THATS	JUST	WHAT I MEAN TO BE, HARRY. IF I WERE TO EAT UP HALF YOUR
TRFL	(83)	IF IT ADDED DEFICIENCY TO FOLLY. I MEAN	JUST	WHAT I SAY: THEY ARE TOMFOOLERIES. ON THEIR TOPICAL
FANY III	(320)	CANT BE ALLOWED TO BEHAVE LIKE THIS. /KNOX/	JUST	WHAT I SAY. A CONCERTINA ADDS ITS MUSIC TO THE REVELRY.
BULL III	(127)	EVER SUFFER, I'D LIKE TO KNOW? /CORNELIUS/ THATS	JUST	WHAT I SAY. I WASNT COMPARIN YOU TO YOUR DISADVANTAGE.
ARMS III	(73)	TO THE EMPEROR OF SWITZERLAND. /BLUNTSCHLI/ THATS	JUST	WHAT I SAY. (HE CATCHES HER BY THE SHOULDERS AND TURNS
DEST	(158)	AND WHIP ON THE TABLE) AH! WHERE INDEED? THATS	JUST	WHAT I SHOULD LIKE TO KNOW, GENERAL. (WITH EMOTION)
NEVR III	(266)	WELL, HERE I AM, YOU SEE. /MRS CLANDON/ THIS IS	JUST	WHAT I SUSPECTED. (SEVERELY) MR VALENTINE: YOU ARE ONE
SUPR IV	(161)	WHAT AM I TO DO FOR YOU? /MRS WHITEFIELD/ THATS	JUST	WHAT I WANT TO TELL YOU. OF COURSE YOULL MARRY ANN
PRES	(166)	AT MY AGE. WHAT? (SHE LISTENS). WELL, THATS	JUST	WHAT I WAS THINKIN. /MITCHENER/ MAY I ASK WHAT YOU WERE
VWOO 3	(140)	MARRY ME IF SHE TOOK TROUBLE ENOUGH. /Z/ THATS	JUST	WHAT I'M AFRAID OF. IF I LET YOU OUT OF MY SIGHT FOR A
HART III	(130)	WHATS WRONG WITH MY HOUSE? /LADY UTTERWORD/	JUST	WHAT IS WRONG WITH A SHIP, PAPA. WASNT IT CLEVER OF
APPL I	(215)	BUSINESS IS NOBODY'S BUSINESS, WHICH IS	JUST	WHAT JOE IS FIT FOR. (SHE TAKES A CHAIR FROM THE WALL
ROCK II	(259)	WE GIVE THE PEOPLE AN HONEST GOOD TIME WE CAN DO	JUST	WHAT SEEMS GOOD TO US. THE PROOF OF THE PUDDING WILL BE
GENV II	(64)	NOT AT ALL. SHE WILL SAY PLUCKILY AND SINCERELY	JUST	WHAT SHE FEELS AND THINKS. YOU HEARD HER SAY THAT THERE
SUPR IV	(163)	ME, SHE'LL REFUSE TO KNOW A COQUETTE. SHE WILL DO	JUST	WHAT SHE LIKES HERSELF WHILST INSISTING ON EVERYBODY
KING I	(213)	THE ONLY PERFECT FIGURE IS THE CIRCLE. /KNELLER/	JUST	WHAT SUCH BLOCKHEADS WOULD BELIEVE. THE CIRCLE IS A
NEVR III	(268)	OF COURSE IT WAS. WELL, WHAT DID THE MAN DO?	JUST	WHAT THE ARTILLERY MAN DOES: WENT ONE BETTER THAN THE
INCA	(252)	TO ST HELENA. /THE INCA/ (TRIUMPHANTLY) THAT IS	JUST	WHAT THE INCA IS PLAYING FOR, MADAM. IT IS WHY HE
BULL PREFACE	(48)	OF THE MORAL MUSCLES. NO DOUBT THIS WEAKNESS IS	JUST	WHAT THE MILITARY SYSTEM AIMS AT, ITS IDEAL SOLDIER
DEVL EPILOG	(85)	BUT HIS OWN PROCLAMATIONS HAD THREATENED	JUST	WHAT THE SAVAGE CHIEF EXECUTED. BRUDENELL. BRUDENELL IS
FANY II	(290)	/MARGARET/ (WITH A BITTER LITTLE LAUGH)	JUST	WHAT THE SUFFRAGET SAID TO ME IN HOLLOWAY. HE THROWS
3PLA PREFACE	(R12)	LONGING ANOTHER AGE'S LOATHING? AND YET THAT IS	JUST	WHAT THE THEATRES KEPT TRYING TO DO ALMOST ALL THE TIME
CAPT III	(273)	HEAVEN FORGIVE YOU FOR JUDGING HIM! WELL, THATS	JUST	WHAT THE WHOLE QUARREL IS ABOUT. CAPTAIN BRASSBOUND IS
SUPR HANDBOK	(210)	AS HE WATCHES THEM: HE KNOWS THAT THEY WILL DO	JUST	WHAT THEIR FATHERS DID, AND THAT THE FEW VOICES WHICH

ROCK I (197)	DO I. IT'S ONLY A PHRASE THAT MEANS NOTHING:	JUST	WHAT THEY ARE SURE TO RISE AT. I MUST KEEP TRAFALGAR
MIS. PREFACE(37)	SHOPKEEPER IN THE HIGH STREET DOES, AND THIS IS	JUST	WHAT THEY DO NOT KNOW AT PRESENT. YOU MAY SAY OF THEM,
SUPR HANDBOK(203)	ANTONY, AND PIZARRO. PARLIAMENTS AND VESTRIES ARE	JUST	WHAT THEY WERE WHEN CROMWELL SUPPRESSED THEM AND
MTH5 (255)	BECAUSE THE THOUGHT IS THE LIFE. WHICH IS	JUST	WHAT THIS OLD GENTLEMAN AND THIS OLD LADY SEEM TO THINK
BULL I (78)	CITY IN IRELAND? /TIM/ (WITH ENTHUSIASM) THATS	JUST	WHAT WAS ON THE TIP O ME TONGUE TO ASK YOU. WHY NOT? (
GETT (325)	(COMING ROUND THE TABLE TO EDITH'S LEFT) THATS	JUST	WHAT WE ARE DISCUSSING. WILL YOU BE SO GOOD AS TO JOIN
DEVL III (60)	MR ANDERSON? /RICHARD/ I UNDERSTAND THAT THAT IS	JUST	WHAT WE ARE HERE TO FIND OUT. /SWINDON/ (SEVERELY) DO
METH PREFACE(R76)	THE DANGER THAT WHEN WE REALIZE THIS WE SHALL DO	JUST	WHAT WE DID HALF A CENTURY AGO, AND WHAT PLIABLE DID IN
SIM I (39)	LOOK SO INNOCENT AND RESPECTABLE" THEY SAID, "	JUST	WHAT WE WANT! " THEY TOOK ME ALL OVER THE WORLD, WHERE
PRES (134)	ATTACK OVER A CIRCULAR LINE TWELVE MILES LONG.	JUST	WHAT WELLINGTON WOULD HAVE DONE. /BALSQUITH/ BUT THE
MTH2 (55)	HIM STANDING UNEASILY IN THE CORNER) WELL,	JUST	WHAT YOU ARE DOING, IF YOU WANT TO KNOW. I AM TRYING TO
HART I (75)	TO SAY THE PERFECTLY CORRECT THING, YOU CAN DO	JUST	WHAT YOU LIKE. AN ILL-CONDUCTED, CARELESS WOMAN GETS
JOAN 5 (110)	BECOMES RAPT) DO YOU HEAR? " DEAR-CHILD-OF-GOD":	JUST	WHAT YOU SAID. AT THE HALF-HOUR THEY WILL SAY "
OVER (175)	WITHOUT GUILT. WHAT DO I SEE NOW? /MRS JUNO/	JUST	WHAT YOU SAW BEFORE. /GREGORY/ (DESPAIRINGLY) NO, NO.
JITT II (30)	I THINK. /LENKHEIM/ WHICH IS? /FESSLER/ WELL,	JUST	WHAT YOU THINK. AND WHEN SHE FINDS OUT WHAT THAT IS,
BULL III (127)	YOU DONT UNDERSTAND: CORNY DOYLE IS SAYING	JUST	WHAT YOU WANT TO HAVE SAID. (TO CORNELIUS) GO ON, MR
CLEO NOTES (211)	IN OTHER WORDS, WHEN ITS VALUE IS LEAST, WHICH IS	JUST	WHEN A COMMON MAN TRIES HARDEST TO GET IT. HE KNOWS
MIS. (138)	FOR IS SOME SIGN OF IT ENDING IN SOMETHING; BUT	JUST	WHEN IT SEEMS TO BE COMING TO A POINT, JOHNNY OR PAPA
JITT II? (60)	THAT LITTLE CHILDREN OUGHT NOT TO KNOW AND FEEL,	JUST	WHEN I, AS A WOMAN, MOST WANT THE COMPANIONSHIP OF
GETT (300)	UP HER CHILDREN BY HER OWN WORK, AND KNOWING THAT	JUST	WHEN THEY WERE GROWN UP AND BEGINNING LIFE, THIS
MTH5 (222)	(SHE SWEEPS TO THE CURVED SEAT, AND SITS DOWN	JUST	WHERE ACIS IS LEANING OVER IT). /ACIS/ I AM NO GREAT
POSN PREFACE(398)	THAT HE SHOULD BE TOLERANT, AND TOLERANT	JUST	WHERE HE COULD SCREW UP THE STANDARD A LITTLE BY BEING
MTH4 II SD(182)	BY HIS DAUGHTER. THE ELDERLY GENTLEMAN STOPS	JUST	WHERE HE ENTERED, TO SEE WHY ZOO HAS SWOOPED SO
POSN PREFACE(398)	HAS HIS POWERS SO ADJUSTED THAT HE IS TYRANNICAL	JUST	WHERE IT IS IMPORTANT THAT HE SHOULD BE TOLERANT, AND
CATH 4,SD(188)	IS IN FULL IMPERIAL REGALIA, AND STOPS STERNLY	JUST	WHERE SHE HAS ENTERED. THE SOLDIERS FALL ON THEIR
MTH4 I (174)	CITY OF ANTIQUITY. (RHETORICALLY) SITUATE	JUST	WHERE THE DOVER ROAD CROSSES THE THAMES, IT-- /ZOO/ (
SUPR IV (147)	SOMEONE. A MARRIAGE WITH YOU WOULD LEAVE THINGS	JUST	WHERE THEY ARE. /VIOLET/ MANY OF MY RELATIONS WOULD
APPL I (225)	YOU, MR BOANERGES. BUT IN TRUTH IT LEAVES MATTERS	JUST	WHERE THEY WERE; FOR I SHOULD NEVER HAVE DREAMT OF
CLEO PRO2 (98)	TIME: ALL WAS OVER IN A MOMENT. THE ATTACK CAME	JUST	WHERE WE LEAST EXPECTED IT. /BELZANOR/ THAT SHEWS THAT
JITT III (76)	AS ANY DECENT WOMAN WOULD. /LENKHEIM/ THAT IS	JUST	WHERE YOU ARE MISTAKEN, DARLING. WHEN YOU WERE BROUGHT
DEVL I (20)	SURE. I WILL NOT KEEP YOU ONE SECOND, MR DUDGEON,	JUST	WHILE I GET MY GLASSES-- (HE FUMBLES FOR THEM. THE
SUPR III (116)	AGAINST ROMANCE: INTO A FEW SENTENCES. THAT IS	JUST	WHY I TURNED MY BACK ON THE ROMANTIC MAN WITH THE
PHIL II (110)	THE ONLY THING THAT REALLY HURT ME. /CHARTERIS/	JUST	WHY SHE SAID IT. HOW ADORABLE OF YOU TO CARE! MY
PYGM II (230)	IS IT ALL RIGHT? /MRS PEARCE/ (AT THE DOOR) I	JUST	WISH TO TROUBLE YOU WITH A WORD, IF I MAY, MR HIGGINS.
HART II (99)	AM NEITHER COAXING AND KISSING NOR LAUGHING, I AM	JUST	WONDERING HOW MUCH LONGER I CAN STAND LIVING IN THIS
MTH2 (66)	ABOUT IT. YOU JUST HOLD YOUR TONGUE. /SAVVY/ I	JUST	WONT, NUNK. I SHALL HAVE A VOTE WHEN I AM THIRTY; AND I
MIS. (125)	IT WASNT MUCH FANCY WITH ME, DEAR: YOUR FATHER	JUST	WOULDNT TAKE NO FOR AN ANSWER; AND I WAS ONLY TOO GLAD
MRS I (196)	IRON DUKE DIDNT THROW AWAY 50 POUNDS: NOT HE. HE	JUST	WROTE: " DEAR JENNY: PUBLISH AND BE DAMNED! YOURS
DEST (184)	IS READY, LIEUTENANT, /LIEUTENANT/ I'M NOT GOING	JUST	YET. GO AND FIND THE GENERAL AND TELL HIM I WANT TO
CAND II (111)	/BURGESS/ (ASIDE TO MARCHBANKS) YORR HE IS.	JUST	YOU KEEP YOUR HEYE ON IM AND SEE. (RISING MOMENTOUSLY)
CAPT II (261)	AND CALL YOURSELF JUSTICE. I GIVE YOU UP. YOU ARE	JUST	YOUR UNCLE OVER AGAIN; ONLY HE GETS 5,000 POUNDS A YEAR
BARB III (335)	AND WEAPONS TO PEOPLE WHOSE CAUSE IS RIGHT AND	JUST	, AND REFUSE THEM TO FOREIGNERS AND CRIMINALS.
SUPR III (100)	/THE DEVIL/ OH, IT SUITS SOME PEOPLE. LET US BE	JUST	, COMMANDER: IT IS A QUESTION OF TEMPERAMENT. I DONT
BULL PREFACE(33)	PEOPLES, OFTEN REPLY THAT THE ENGLISHMAN IS	JUST	, LEAVING US DIVIDED BETWEEN OUR DERISION OF SO
CATH 1 (163)	KICK ME WHEN YOU KICK THEM. GOD KNOWS THAT IS NOT	JUST	, LITTLE FATHER! /PATIOMKIN/ (LAUGHS OGREISHLY; THEN
SUPR III (129)	NOT IMAGINATIVE, ONLY SUPERSTITIOUS; NOT	JUST	, ONLY VINDICTIVE; NOT GENEROUS, ONLY PROPITIATORY; NOT
SUPR II (53)	SHE DOES NOT THINK SO. /TANNER/ OH, DOESNT SHE!	JUST	! HOWEVER, SAY WHAT YOU WANT ME TO DO? /OCTAVIUS/ I
CAND II (110)	(WITH INTENSE CONVICTION) OH, DIDNT I THOUGH,	JUST	! /BURGESS/ I WOULDNT DEMEAN MYSELF TO TAKE NOTICE ON
PHIL I (71)	SITTING WITH YOU--- /GRACE/ (SHRINKING FROM HIM)	JUST	! /CHARTERIS/ (SITTING UPRIGHT AND FACING HER
2TRU III (106)	TOLD ME THAT? MY OWN CHILDREN! MURDERED THEM,	JUST	! /THE ELDER/ MEDEA! MEDEA! /MRS MOPPLY/ IT ISNT AN

JUSTICE

ROCK PREFACE(181)	ALWAYS TALKING ABOUT TRUTH AND RIGHTEOUSNESS AND	JUSTICE	: YOU FEED ON WORDS WHEN YOU ARE TIRED OF MAKING
HART II (109)	OF SPENDING A DAY AT THE SESSIONS? IS THAT	JUSTICE	? IS IT RIGHT? IS IT FAIR TO ME? /MAZZINI/ (
2TRU I (28)	AND SHE SAYS THAT I GAVE THEM TO HER. OH, IS THIS	JUSTICE	? OH, I FEEL SO ROTTEN. I WONDER WHAT MY
GENV IV (92)	THE SITTING OF THE DEPARTMENT OF INTERNATIONAL	JUSTICE	? /BBDE/ (SPRINGING UP) BATTLER, BY ALL THATS
CAPT II (261)	DO YOU FORGET THAT THERE IS SUCH A THING AS	JUSTICE	? /LADY CICELY/ (GAILY SHAKING OUT THE FINISHED
POSN (451)	JUSTICE; BUT IT IS JUSTICE. /BLANCO/ WHAT IS	JUSTICE	? /THE SHERIFF/ HANGING HORSE-THIEVES IS JUSTICE;
AUGS (263)	ME, GOT TWO AND SEVENPENCE. I GOT NOTHING. IS IT	JUSTICE	? THIS COUNTRY IS GOING TO THE DOGS, IF YOU ASK ME.
CAPT III (294)	NOT SELF-SEEKING: IT SEEMED TO ME THAT I HAD PUT	JUSTICE	ABOVE SELF. I TELL YOU LIFE MEANT SOMETHING TO ME
BUOY II (25)	NOT RECONCILE THE EXISTENCE OF EVIL WITH DIVINE	JUSTICE	AND BENEVOLENCE. HE THEREFORE BELIEVED NOT ONLY IN
BUOY II (25)	MY ANCESTORS BELIEVED. I BELIEVE AS THEY DID THAT	JUSTICE	AND BENEVOLENCE ARE MIGHTY POWERS IN THE WORLD, BUT
BARB PREFACE(238)	DAGGER NOR THE BOMB WITHOUT STRIPPING THE MASK OF	JUSTICE	AND HUMANITY FROM THEMSELVES ALSO, BE IT NOTED THAT
LION PREFACE(60)	IS AN IMPOSTURE AND A DELUSION. IT REDUCES	JUSTICE	AND LAW TO A FARCE: LAW BECOMES MERELY AN INSTRUMENT
LION PREFACE(80)	AWAY THE SINS OF THE WORLD BY GOOD GOVERNMENT, BY	JUSTICE	AND MERCY, BY SETTING THE WELFARE OF LITTLE CHILDREN
DUOY II (25)	AND OUR LIKE ARE JUST AND BENEVOLENT THERE IS NO	JUSTICE	AND NO BENEVOLENCE. /HE/ AND CONSEQUENTLY NO
GENV II (57)	USE IT? /JUDGE/ THEY COULD USE IT TO MAINTAIN	JUSTICE	AND ORDER BETWEEN THE NATIONS. /SIR O./ THERE IS
GENV II (57)	WE DESIRE MORE. THE BRITISH EMPIRE STANDS FOR	JUSTICE	AND ORDER. BUT I MUST TELL YOU THAT THE BRITISH
BARB III (320)	YOURE ALL READY TO HANDLE HONESTY AND TRUTH AND	JUSTICE	AND THE WHOLE DUTY OF MAN, AND KILL ONE ANOTHER AT
GENV II (57)	THE JUDGES OF THE COURT OF INTERNATIONAL	JUSTICE	ARE NOT NONENTITIES. WE HAVE WAITED A LONG TIME FOR
MILL IV (196)	YOU SEE MY CONDITION: YOU KNOW THAT RIGHT AND	JUSTICE	ARE ON MY SIDE. I SHALL NOT FORGET THIS. THE MANAGER
BULL PREFACE(34)	BENEFIT OF A GOVERNMENT THAT DOES ABSOLUTE	JUSTICE	AS BETWEEN INDIAN AND INDIAN, BEING WHOLLY
GETT PREFACE(233)	DEFEAT OF THE HUSBAND QUITE AS OFTEN AS IN POETIC	JUSTICE	AS CONCEIVED IN THE CONVENTIONAL NOVELET. WHAT AN
GENV III (66)	TOLERATE SUCH A MONSTROUS VIOLATION OF NATURAL	JUSTICE	AS LEAVING THE MURDER OF A FATHER UNAVENGED. IF OUR
GENV I (33)	ACT THROUGH THE PERMANENT COURT OF INTERNATIONAL	JUSTICE	AT THE HAGUE, WHICH IS ALSO AN ORGAN OF THE LEAGUE.
GENV II (55)	THE SENIOR JUDGE OF THE COURT OF INTERNATIONAL	JUSTICE	AT THE HAGUE IS DOWNSTAIRS. HADNT YOU BETTER SEE
GENV II (52)	THAT YOU SENT TO THE COURT OF INTERNATIONAL	JUSTICE	AT THE HAGUE-- /BEGONIA/ OH, OF COURSE. YES. FANCY
MIS. PREFACE(66)	HAT IN HAND, BUT LET THE MOST OBVIOUS MEASURE OF	JUSTICE	BE DEMANDED BY THE SECRETARY OF A TRADE UNION IN
CAPT III (278)	FIAT JUSTITIA: RUAT COELUM! /LADY CICELY/ LET	JUSTICE	BE DONE, THOUGH THE CEILING FALL! AN AMERICAN
INCA (254)	IF I MAY SAY SO, MY TALENTS, NEVER HAS SUCH	JUSTICE	BEEN DONE ME: NEVER HAVE I EXPERIENCED SUCH PERFECT
BULL PREFACE(33)	THERE IS ONLY ONE CONDITION ON WHICH A MAN CAN DO	JUSTICE	BETWEEN TWO LITIGANTS, AND THAT IS THAT HE SHALL
CAPT II (254)	DISGUISE-- THE VENGEANCE OF SOCIETY, DISGUISED AS	JUSTICE	BY ITS PASSIONS. NOW THE JUSTICE YOU HAVE OUTRAGED
LION EPILOG (147)	AND MAINTAINED IN THE NAME OF RELIGION AND	JUSTICE	BY POLITICIANS WHO ARE PURE OPPORTUNIST
CAPT II (254)	I THINK YOU MEAN VENGEANCE, DISGUISED AS	JUSTICE	BY YOUR PASSIONS. /BRASSBOUND/ TO MANY AND MANY A
JOAN EPILOG (157)	STILL DREAMING OF JUSTICE, PETER? SEE WHAT	JUSTICE	CAME TO WITH ME! BUT WHAT HAS HAPPENED TO THEE?
JOAN 6 (131)	BUT DO NOT CAST OUT MERCY. REMEMBER ONLY THAT	JUSTICE	COMES FIRST. HAVE YOU ANYTHING TO SAY, MY LORD,
JOAN EPILOG (156)	MIGHT SAY A WORD OF THANKS TO ME FOR HAVING HAD	JUSTICE	DONE AT LAST. /CAUCHON/ (APPEARING AT THE WINDOW
MILL IV (201)	HANDS, SHAKEN, ALMOST LACHRYMOSE) IS THERE ANY	JUSTICE	FOR A MAN AGAINST A WOMAN? /SAGAMORE/ (SITTING
SIM PREFACE(14)	TO THE OLD VISION OF A DAY OF RECKONING BY DIVINE	JUSTICE	FOR ALL MANKIND. NOW THE ORDINARY VISION OF THIS
ROCK II (239)	ORDERS, DISCIPLINE, CHARACTER, PLUCK, A BIG NAVY,	JUSTICE	FOR THE BRITISH SAILOR, NO SHAM DISARMAMENTS, AND
SIM PREFACE(15)	THAT THEY ARE ALL RESPONSIBLE TO DIVINE	JUSTICE	FOR THE USE THEY MAKE OF THEIR LIVES, AND PUT
BULL PREFACE(56)	COURTS SET UP TO FLATTER OUR SENSE OF IMPERIAL	JUSTICE	HAD, APPARENTLY, ABOUT AS MUCH TO DO WITH THE ACTUAL
GENV III (86)	DICTATORS BY THE PERMANENT COURT OF INTERNATIONAL	JUSTICE	HAS BEEN FIXED FOR THIS DAY FORTNIGHT. /THE REST/
GETT (312)	HIS FATHER DIED-- BY A CURIOUS STROKE OF POETIC	JUSTICE	HE DIED OF SCARLET FEVER, AND WAS FOUND TO HAVE HAD
MIS. (169)	YOUVE COME TO THE WRONG SHOP FOR IT: YOULL GET NO	JUSTICE	HERE: WE DONT KEEP IT. HUMAN NATURE IS WHAT WE
POSN (451)	(TO BLANCO) DONT YOU BE UNEASY. YOU WILL GET	JUSTICE	HERE. IT MAY BE ROUGH JUSTICE; BUT IT IS JUSTICE.
SUPR III (90)	YOU TELL ME: THAT IS THE REWARD OF DUTY. IS THERE	JUSTICE	IN HEAVEN? /DON JUAN/ NO; BUT THERE IS JUSTICE IN
SUPR III (90)	JUSTICE IN HEAVEN? /DON JUAN/ NO; BUT THERE IS	JUSTICE	IN HELL: HEAVEN IS FAR ABOVE SUCH IDLE HUMAN
PYGM II (237)	CHAP A FARTHING. AND YET I FEEL A SORT OF ROUGH	JUSTICE	IN HIS CLAIM. /DOOLITTLE/ THATS IT, GOVERNOR. THATS
BASH II,1, (112)	DAMN ME INTO OSTLERDOM. AND YET THERES AN ETERNAL	JUSTICE	IN IT; FOR BY SO MUCH AS THE NE'ER SUBDUED INDIAN
POSN (436)	LYNCHED THE WRONG MAN? NOT THEM. WHAT THEY CALL	JUSTICE	IN THIS PLACE IS NOTHING BUT A BREAKING OUT OF THE
CAPT NOTES (302)	OUR INSTITUTIONS REPRESENT ABSTRACT PRINCIPLES OF	JUSTICE	INSTEAD OF BEING MERE SOCIAL SCAFFOLDING IS THAT
GETT PREFACE(257)	DEAL WITH ALL THE CONSEQUENCES OF THESE ACTS OF	JUSTICE	INSTEAD OF LETTING YOURSELF BE FRIGHTENED OUT OF
BULL PREFACE(56)	GIVES HIS REASONS. IT APPEARS THAT THE BOASTED	JUSTICE	INTRODUCED INTO EGYPT BY THE ENGLISH IN 1882 WAS
GENV II (57)	CAN BE SET IN MOTION BY THE HUMBLEST INDIVIDUAL	JUSTICE	IS A MOCKERY. /SIR O./ OF COURSE I AGREE WITH THAT--
GENV II (58)	ARE A BIT OF AN IDEALIST. /JUDGE/ NECESSARILY.	JUSTICE	IS AN IDEAL; AND I AM A JUDGE. WHAT, MAY I ASK, ARE
ARMS II (29)	WOMEN ARE ON YOUR SIDE; AND THEY WILL SEE THAT	JUSTICE	IS DONE YOU. /SERGIUS/ IT IS TOO LATE. I HAVE ONLY

MTH3 (95) UNDERSTAND IT. WHY SHOULD IT BE SO? /CONFUCIUS/ JUSTICE IS IMPARTIALITY. ONLY STRANGERS ARE IMPARTIAL.
SUPR HANDBOK(221) IT FEROCITY. THE DISTINCTION BETWEEN CRIME AND JUSTICE IS NO GREATER. WHILST WE HAVE PRISONS IT MATTERS
2TRU III (101) OUT: MERIT IS REWARDED IN THE LONG RUN. JUSTICE IS NONE THE LESS JUSTICE THOUGH IT IS ALWAYS
LION PREFACE(12) ATONEMENT AND PUNISHMENT . THE PRIMITIVE IDEA OF JUSTICE IS PARTLY LEGALIZED REVENGE AND PARTLY EXPIATION BY
BULL PREFACE(33) EVERY INTEREST: THE INDISPENSABLE PRELIMINARY TO JUSTICE IS THE ELIMINATION OF EVERY INTEREST. WHEN WE WANT
MILL IV (201) NOT AGAINST A MILLIONAIRESS. /EPIFANIA/ AND WHAT JUSTICE IS THERE FOR A MILLIONAIRESS, I SHOULD LIKE TO
GENV IV (106) YOU ARE AT THE HAGUE, AND IN A COURT OF JUSTICE . DUELS ARE OUT OF DATE. AND YOUR LIVES ARE TOO
MTH1 II (27) AM NOT LYING! I DARE ALL TRUTHS. THERE IS DIVINE JUSTICE . FOR THE VOICE TELLS ME THAT I MUST OFFER MYSELF TO
SUPR III (88) BAD DEEDS, VICARIOUS ATONEMENT, MERCY WITHOUT JUSTICE . FOR YOUR GOOD DEEDS, JUSTICE WITHOUT MERCY. WE
JITT PREFACE(7) OF WHICH I HAVE BEEN SHAMEFULLY UNABLE TO DO JUSTICE . FRAU GITTA'S SUHNE WAS FIRST PERFORMED AT THE
PHIL I SD(69) TAKEN CARE THAT NATURE SHALL DO HIM THE FULLEST JUSTICE . HIS AMATIVE ENTHUSIASM, AT WHICH HE IS HIMSELF
BASH PREFACE(87) IN THE FINAL SCENE, THE TRIBUTE OF POETIC JUSTICE . I RESTORED TO PATRIOTISM ITS USUAL PLACE ON THE
MILL PREFACE(113) OF ETERNAL PEACE AND A MONUMENT OF RETRIBUTIVE JUSTICE . IN THIS WAY THE MOST HONEST RULER BECOMES A TYRANT
BULL IV (155) NOT FOR HOURS BUT FOR YEARS, IN THE NAME OF JUSTICE . IT IS A PLACE WHERE THE HARDEST TOIL IS A WELCOME
JOAN 6 (123) HANDSOME SUM, SOLELY THAT SHE MIGHT BE BROUGHT TO JUSTICE . IT IS VERY NEARLY THREE MONTHS SINCE I DELIVERED
GENV II (60) TO ANY OTHER SANCTION THAN THE SACREDNESS OF JUSTICE . IT WILL AFFIRM THIS SACREDNESS AND MAKE THE
KING PREFACE(156) YOURSELF ON ASSISTING AT AN ACT OF HISTORICAL JUSTICE . LET US THEREFORE DROP THE POPULAR SUBJECT OF THE
POSN (451) JUSTICE HERE. IT MAY BE ROUGH JUSTICE; BUT IT IS JUSTICE . /BLANCO/ WHAT IS JUSTICE? /THE SHERIFF/ HANGING
JITT III (61) I AM NOT UNJUST. IT IS MY FATHER WHO NEEDS JUSTICE . /FESSLER/ IT IS NOT MUCH USE, IS IT, GIVING
CAPT III (290) YOU HAVE MADE ME YOUR ACCOMPLICE IN DEFEATING JUSTICE . /LADY CICELY/ YES! ARNT YOU GLAD IT'S BEEN
DOCT III (143) NOT AN ORDINARY ONE, DUBEDAT. DO YOURSELF JUSTICE . /LOUIS/ WELL, YOURE ON THE WRONG TACK ALTOGETHER.
SIM II (64) BURDEN OF RIGHTEOUSNESS. /VASHTI/ THE BURDEN OF JUSTICE . /MAYA/ THE BURDEN OF MERCY. /PROLA/ CEASE, CEASE:
FOUN (215) OF LORDS ALWAYS GIVES CHARITY AND NEVER GIVES JUSTICE . /MERCER/ THE HOUSE OF LORDS WILL FIND ITSELF
CAPT II (254) GLANCE AT SIR HOWARD) I SHALL DO NO MORE THAN JUSTICE . /SIR HOWARD/ (RECOVERING HIS VOICE AND VIGOR)
CAPT II (254) WHO PUTS ON ERMINE AND SCARLET AND CALLS HIMSELF JUSTICE . /SIR HOWARD/ (ALMOST VOICELESS) YOU ARE THE SON
GLIM (175) ASSASSINATED, THE MURDERER WILL NOT BE BROUGHT TO JUSTICE . /SQUARCIO/ SO THAT IF I KILL YOU-- /FERRUCCIO/
MIS. (169) /TARLETON/ WELL, WHAT DO YOU WANT? /THE MAN/ JUSTICE . /TARLETON/ YOURE QUITE SURE THATS ALL? /THE MAN/
FOUN (215) JOYFULLY. /ANASTASIA/ I ASK, NOT CHARITY, BUT JUSTICE . /THE LORD CHANCELLOR/ MADAM: I MUST REQUEST YOU TO
LION PREFACE(13) A CRUEL DEATH TO BALANCE THE ACCOUNT WITH DIVINE JUSTICE . SALVATION AT FIRST A CLASS PRIVILEGE; AND THE
BARB PREFACE(241) OF VENGEANCE, OFTEN POLITELY CALLED PUNISHMENT OR JUSTICE . THE GIBBET PART OF CHRISTIANITY IS TOLERATED. THE
DOCT PREFACE(38) THE " YOURE ANOTHER" RETORT, AND USING IT WITH JUSTICE . WE MUST THEREFORE GIVE OURSELVES NO AIRS OF
GENV II (58) BY WHICH THESE LAWBREAKERS CAN BE BROUGHT TO JUSTICE . WELL, THE INTELLECTUAL CO-OPERATION COMMITTEE-- OF
LION PREFACE(66) THEY ARE LOATHSOME WHEN THEY ASSUME THE ROBES OF JUSTICE . WHICH, I TAKE IT, IS WHY SHAKESPEAR'S ISABELLA
BULL I (85) /BROADBENT/ OH, COME, LARRY! DO YOURSELF JUSTICE . YOURE VERY AMUSING AND AGREEABLE TO STRANGERS.
SIM PREFACE(7) WE KNOW THAT NAIVE ATTEMPTS TO BRIBE DIVINE JUSTICE LED TO A TRADE IN ABSOLUTIONS, PARDONS, AND
GENV I (41) DOES NOT BRING THE MURDERER OF MY HUSBAND TO JUSTICE MY SON WILL BE OBLIGED TO TAKE UP A BLOOD FEUD AND
SIM PREFACE(15) COMPLEXITY. IT IS EASY TO SAY THAT TO DIVINE JUSTICE NOTHING IS IMPOSSIBLE; BUT THE MORE DIVINE THE
ROCK II (265) I KNEW THAT IN THE COURSE OF NATURE AND BY THE JUSTICE OF BRAHMA IT MUST END IN INDIA RULING ENGLAND JUST
JOAN EPILOG (157) NONE. I ARRAIGN THE JUSTICE OF MAN. IT IS NOT THE JUSTICE OF GOD. /JOAN/ STILL DREAMING OF JUSTICE, PETER?
LION PREFACE(41) ARE RESPONSIBLE FOR THE DOING OF THE MERCY AND JUSTICE OF GOD. THE JEWS STONED HIM FOR SAYING THESE THINGS,
MILL IV (202) ARE IN THEMSELVES AN INJUSTICE. I SPEAK OF THE JUSTICE OF HEAVEN. /ALASTAIR/ OH LORD! NOW WE'RE FOR IT. (
METH PREFACE(R35) OF THEIR DEITY'S AIM WITH A THUNDERBOLT, AND THE JUSTICE OF HIS DISCRIMINATION BETWEEN THE INNOCENT AND THE
JOAN EPILOG (157) YOU BURNED ME? /CAUCHON/ NONE. I ARRAIGN THE JUSTICE OF MAN. IT IS NOT THE JUSTICE OF GOD. /JOAN/ STILL
JOAN 6 (124) THAT THE WOMAN SHALL HAVE A FAIR HEARING. THE JUSTICE OF THE CHURCH IS NOT A MOCKERY, MY LORD. /THE
JOAN 4 (108) I WILL NOT IMPERIL MY SOUL. I WILL UPHOLD THE JUSTICE OF THE CHURCH. I WILL STRIVE TO THE UTMOST FOR THIS
BULL PREFACE(34) OR IRISH SYSTEM IN GREAT BRITAIN. YET IF THE JUSTICE OF THE ENGLISHMAN IS SUFFICIENT TO ENSURE THE
MILL PREFACE(110) A KING, A PRELATE, A SQUIRE, A CAPITALIST, A JUSTICE OF THE PEACE MAY BE A GOOD KIND CHRISTIAN SOUL,
GENV IV (107) THE BRAND AS BEST HE CAN. /JUDGE/ THAT IS THE JUSTICE OF THIS COURT. I THANK YOU, SENORA, FOR YOUR
CAPT I (240) WRONGED A WOMAN, YOU MAY MEET HER SON THERE. THE JUSTICE OF THOSE HILLS IS THE JUSTICE OF VENGEANCE. /SIR
CAPT I (240) HER SON THERE. THE JUSTICE OF THOSE HILLS IS THE JUSTICE OF VENGEANCE. /SIR HOWARD/ (FAINTLY AMUSED) YOU ARE
METH PREFACE(R12) SOUND COMMERCIAL INVESTMENT, BUT AN ACT OF DIVINE JUSTICE OF WHICH THEY ARE THE ARDENT INSTRUMENTS. BUT IF MAN
CAPT I (240) IN THOSE HILLS THERE IS A JUSTICE THAT IS NOT THE JUSTICE OF YOUR COURTS IN ENGLAND. IF YOU HAVE WRONGED A
BULL PREFACE(39) JUDICIAL FORMS WHICH CONFER THE IMPOSING TITLE OF JUSTICE ON A CRUDE SYSTEM OF BLUDGEONING AND PERJURY. BUT SO
CAPT II (253) WHAT DO YOU EXPECT TO GAIN BY THIS? /BRASSBOUND/ JUSTICE ON A THIEF AND A MURDERER. LADY CICELY LAYS DOWN HER
ROCK PREFACE(147) DOING OR WHY WE ARE DOING IT; AND SO WE CALL IT JUSTICE OR CAPITAL PUNISHMENT OR OUR DUTY TO KING AND
GENV IV (110) A POINT OF ORDER, MISTER. IS THIS A COURT OF JUSTICE OR IS IT NOT? ARE WE TO BE INTERRUPTED BY EVERY
BARB PREFACE(214) AN EXPLANATION THAT THE OUTRAGE IS PUNISHMENT OR JUSTICE OR SOMETHING ELSE THAT IS ALL RIGHT, OR PERHAPS BY A
GETT PREFACE(230) AN UNBEARABLE TYRANNY, WITHOUT EVEN THE EXCUSE OF JUSTICE OR SOUND EUGENICS, THEY WILL RECONSIDER THEIR
POSN (451) YOU WILL GET JUSTICE HERE. IT MAY BE ROUGH JUSTICE ; BUT IT IS JUSTICE. /BLANCO/ WHAT IS JUSTICE? /THE
JOAN EPILOG (157) THIS THING THAT THEY HAVE DONE AGAINST ME HURTS JUSTICE ; DESTROYS FAITH; SAPS THE FOUNDATION OF THE CHURCH.
BULL PREFACE(68) WERE SET UP FOR THE ADMINISTRATION OF IRISH JUSTICE ; IRISH ORDER WAS KEPT BY IRISH POLICE; IRISH TAXES
2TRU III (86) EFFECT. SOME OF THIS SCRIPTURE IS ALL RIGHT. DO JUSTICE ; LOVE MERCY; AND WALK HUMBLY BEFORE YOUR GOD. THAT
POSN (451) JUSTICE? /THE SHERIFF/ HANGING HORSE-THIEVES IS JUSTICE ; SO NOW YOU KNOW. NOW THEN: WEVE WASTED ENOUGH
3PLA PREFACE(R14) WORD PROBLEM TO BE THE LATEST EUPHEMISM FOR WHAT JUSTICE SHALLOW CALLED A BONA ROBA, AND CERTAINLY WOULD NOT
LION PREFACE(14) AS A SUBSTITUTE FOR THAT. BAPTISM. OUR SENSE OF JUSTICE STILL DEMANDS AN EXPIATION, A SACRIFICE, A SUFFERER
DOCT PREFACE(73) ALL PRIESTHOODS ARE ACCUSED-- AND NONE WITH MORE JUSTICE THAN THE SCIENTIFIC PRIESTHOOD, AND HERE WE COME TO
CAPT I (240) SAFE HERE. I WARN YOU, IN THOSE HILLS THERE IS A JUSTICE THAT IS NOT THE JUSTICE OF YOUR COURTS IN ENGLAND.
SIM PREFACE(15) NOTHING IS IMPOSSIBLE; BUT THE MORE DIVINE THE JUSTICE THE MORE DIFFICULT IT IS TO CONCEIVE HOW IT COULD
DOCT PREFACE(44) OUT OF IT. AS IN MR GALSWORTHY'S PLAY JUSTICE THE USELESS AND DETESTABLE TORTURE OF SOLITARY
BULL PREFACE(34) ARE WISE ENOUGH TO REFUSE TO TRUST TO ENGLISH JUSTICE THEMSELVES, PREFERRING DEMOCRACY. THEY CAN HARDLY
MILL IV (202) I AM NOT THINKING OF THE COURTS: THERE IS LITTLE JUSTICE THERE FOR ANYBODY. MY MILLIONS ARE IN THEMSELVES AN
2TRU III (101) IN THE LONG RUN. JUSTICE IS NONE THE LESS JUSTICE THOUGH IT IS ALWAYS DELAYED, AND FINALLY DONE BY
SUPR III (123) EXPUNGED AS UNBEARABLE FRIVOLITIES. DO MY SEX THE JUSTICE TO ADMIT, SENORA, THAT WE HAVE ALWAYS RECOGNIZED
PYGM PREFACE(202) OBSCURITY, AND THE FAILURE OF OXFORD TO DO JUSTICE TO HIS EMINENCE, A PUZZLE TO FOREIGN SPECIALISTS IN
KING I (203) MAN WHO STOPS AT NOTHING, SEIZES ALL HE CAN. JUSTICE TO MERIT DOES WEAK AID AFFORD; SHE TRUSTS HER
JITT III (61) /FESSLER/ IT IS NOT MUCH USE, IS IT, GIVING JUSTICE TO THE DEAD AND WITHHOLDING IT FROM THE LIVING?
SUPR III (103) OF MY DOMINIONS THAT I LEAVE YOU TO DO EQUAL JUSTICE TO THE DRAWBACKS OF THE ALTERNATIVE ESTABLISHMENT.
BULL IV (177) REBUKED, GENTLEMEN. BUT BELIEVE ME, I DO EVERY JUSTICE TO THE EFFICIENCY OF YOU AND YOUR SYNDICATE. YOU ARE
MTH4 I (155) THEIR SUFFERINGS AND WRONGS. AND WHAT POEM CAN DO JUSTICE TO THE END, WHEN IT CAME AT LAST? HARDLY TWO
BULL PREFACE(65) WAS ALL THAT COULD BE DONE. I AM BOUND TO ADD, IN JUSTICE TO THE GOVERNMENT, THAT THIS WAS, AS FAR AS I COULD
INCA (249) MURDEROUS CANNONS. THE WORLD WILL ONE DAY DO JUSTICE TO THE INCA AS THE MAN WHO KEPT THE PEACE WITH
CYMB FORWORD(138) AS SHAKESPEAR LEFT IT, AND THE MEANS TO DO JUSTICE TO THE MASQUE. BUT IF THEY ARE HALFHEARTED ABOUT IT,
UNPL PREFACE(R18) OF A SINGLE CLEVER DAUGHTER (NOBODY HAS YET DONE JUSTICE TO THE MODERN CLEVER ENGLISHWOMAN'S LOATHING OF THE
BUOY III (30) HIS SOCIAL SUPERIORS. /MRS SECONDBORN/ IN JUSTICE TO THE OLD DEVIL I MUST SAY THAT, AS FAR AS I CAN
HART PREFACE(33) RUIN TO THE BOTTOM, I CAN ONLY SAY, " I CANNOT DO JUSTICE TO THIS SITUATION," AND LET IT PASS WITHOUT ANOTHER
SUPR III (84) A BRIGAND, AN OUTCAST. EVEN SHAKESPEAR CANNOT DO JUSTICE TO WHAT I FEEL FOR LOUISA. LET ME READ YOU SOME
LIED (199) WERE NEVER OUT OF BED IN YOUR LIFE. YOU HARDLY DO JUSTICE TO YOUR OWN LITERARY POWERS-- WHICH I ADMIRE AND
MIS. (190) AND YOU CALL THAT JUSTICE! /LORD SUMMERHAYS/ NO. JUSTICE WAS NOT MY BUSINESS. I HAD TO GOVERN A PROVINCE; AND
BASH II,2, (117) /PARADISE/ HOW CAN A BLOKE DO HISSELF PROPER JUSTICE WITH PILLOWS ON HIS FISTS? (HE TEARS OFF HIS
POSN (445) MYSELF THAT HE DESERVED IT AND THAT I WAS DOING JUSTICE WITH STRONG STERN MEN. WELL, MY TURN'S COME NOW. LET
SUPR III (88) MERCY WITHOUT JUSTICE. FOR YOUR GOOD DEEDS, JUSTICE WITHOUT MERCY. WE HAVE MANY GOOD PEOPLE HERE. /THE
CAPT II (254) DISGUISED AS JUSTICE BY ITS PASSIONS. NOW THE JUSTICE YOU HAVE OUTRAGED MEETS YOU DISGUISED AS VENGEANCE.
LION PREFACE(17) AWAY AND BE REPLACED BY A KINGDOM OF HAPPINESS, JUSTICE , AND BLISS IN WHICH THE RICH AND THE OPPRESSORS AND
LADY PREFACE(218) ACTUAL LAW AND ADMINISTRATION WITH ABSTRACT JUSTICE , AND SO FORTH, BUT SHAKESPEAR'S PERCEPTION OF THE
SUPR III (90) IN HELL, SENORA. HELL IS THE HOME OF HONOR, DUTY, JUSTICE , AND THE REST OF THE SEVEN DEADLY VIRTUES. ALL THE
GENV II (58) FRIEND-- IF YOU WILL ALLOW ME TO CALL YOU SO-- JUSTICE , AS YOU SAY, IS AN IDEAL, AND A VERY FINE IDEAL
BULL PREFACE(33) IN INDIA, FOR EXAMPLE, STANDS, A VERY STATUE OF JUSTICE , BETWEEN TWO NATIVES. HE SAYS, IN EFFECT, " I AM
MIS. (190) TO MAINTAIN ORDER IN IT. MEN ARE NOT GOVERNED BY JUSTICE , BUT BY LAW OR PERSUASION. WHEN THEY REFUSE TO BE
FANY I (283) THAT THEY DID, MADAM. /MRS GILBEY/ IT DOESNT SEEM JUSTICE , DOES IT, JUGGINS? /JUGGINS/ NO, MADAM. /MRS
SUPR III (107) OF SWORD AND GUN AND POISON GAS: ABOVE ALL, OF JUSTICE , DUTY, PATRIOTISM, AND ALL THE OTHER ISMS BY WHICH
GENV III (81) MONUMENTS TO THE GREAT SLAUGHTERERS THE CRY FOR JUSTICE , FOR MERCY, FOR FELLOWSHIP, FOR PEACE, HAS NEVER
BARB PREFACE(218) IN IT, THEY EVEN DEMAND ABSTRACT CONDITIONS: JUSTICE , HONOR, A NOBLE MORAL ATMOSPHERE, A MYSTIC NEXUS TO
CAPT II (261) TO DRESS YOURSELF IN ERMINE AND CALL YOURSELF JUSTICE , I GIVE YOU UP. YOU ARE JUST YOUR UNCLE OVER AGAIN;
JOAN EPILOG (152) FROM YOUR BLOOD, AND THE STAIN FROM YOUR CROWN. JUSTICE , LONG DELAYED, IS AT LAST TRIUMPHANT. /CHARLES/
METH PREFACE(R57) OR COULD RECONCILE IT WITH OUR IMPULSES TOWARDS JUSTICE , MERCY, AND A HIGHER LIFE. A COMPLETE DELIVERANCE
CLEO V (200) TO BE SLAIN BEFORE THE PEOPLE IN THE NAME OF JUSTICE , NEVER AGAIN WOULD I HAVE TOUCHED YOUR HAND WITHOUT
MTH4 I (170) OPERATIONS IN THE PAST, OUR WISDOM, OUR JUSTICE , OUR MERCY: STORIES IN WHICH WE OFTEN APPEAR AS

JOAN EPILOG (157)	NOT THE JUSTICE OF GOD. /JOAN/ STILL DREAMING OF	JUSTICE	, PETER? SEE WHAT JUSTICE CAME TO WITH ME! BUT
2TRU PREFACE(21)	SUCH A DIVISION OF INTERESTS ALSO DESTROY PEACE,	JUSTICE	, RELIGION, GOOD BREEDING, HONOR, REASONABLE
SUPR HANDBOK(188)	PRESENT TRUMPERY IDEALS OF RIGHT, DUTY, HONOR,	JUSTICE	, RELIGION, EVEN DECENCY, AND ACCEPT MORAL
MILL IV (205)	IS A CURSE; ONLY IN THE SERVICE OF ALLAH IS THERE	JUSTICE	, RIGHTEOUSNESS, AND HAPPINESS. BUT ALL THIS TALK IS
LION PREFACE(57)	THIS ARRANGEMENT; AND, IF YOU DISPUTE ITS	JUSTICE	, STATE IN POUNDS, DOLLARS, FRANCS AND MARKS, WHAT
BARB I (254)	ABACK BY THIS INFERENCE) OH NO. TO DO ANDREW	JUSTICE	, THAT WAS NOT THE SORT OF THING HE DID. BESIDES,
JOAN EPILOG (153)	IMPOSE ON A PLOUGHBOY. YET OUT OF THIS INSULT TO	JUSTICE	, THIS DEFAMATION OF THE CHURCH, THIS ORGY OF LYING
ROCK PREFACE(184)	IS NOT A CURE FOR PRESUMPTION, NOR IS IT	JUSTICE	, THOUGH YOU WILL PERHAPS CALL IT SO IN YOUR REPORT
GENV II (58)	REIGN OF LAW BASED ON THE ETERNAL PRINCIPLE OF	JUSTICE	, TO THE MAINTENANCE OF GOVERNMENTS SET UP BY
BARB PREFACE(238)	WHIFF OF GRAPESHOT," THOUGH NAPOLEON, TO DO HIM	JUSTICE	, TOOK A DEEPER VIEW OF IT, AND WOULD FAIN HAVE HAD
BARB II (291)	IS THERE ANY PLACE IN YOUR RELIGION FOR HONOR,	JUSTICE	, TRUTH, LOVE, MERCY AND SO FORTH? /UNDERSHAFT/
MTH1 II (26)	NO, /ADAM/ THEN THERE IS NO SUCH THING AS DIVINE	JUSTICE	, UNLESS YOU ARE LYING. /CAIN/ I AM NOT LYING: I
MTH4 II (192)	YEARS. IF THEY ARE FILLED WITH USEFULNESS, WITH	JUSTICE	, WITH MERCY, WITH GOOD-WILL: IF THEY ARE THE
BARB PREFACE(231)	THE VINDICTIVE VILLAIN-THRASHINGS AND " POETIC	JUSTICE	" OF THE ROMANTIC STAGE. FOR THE CREDIT OF
CAPT II (254)	/SIR HOWARD/ (RECOVERING HIS VOICE AND VIGOR)	JUSTICE	! I THINK YOU MEAN VENGEANCE, DISGUISED AS JUSTICE
LION II (130)	THE APOSTATE HAS PERISHED. PRAISE BE TO GOD'S	JUSTICE	! /ANDROCLES/ THE POOR BEAST WAS STARVING. IT
MIS. (190)	THINGS QUIETED DOWN. /GUNNER/ AND YOU CALL THAT	JUSTICE	! /LORD SUMMERHAYS/ NO. JUSTICE WAS NOT MY
SUPR III (90)	DUTY, TRAMPLED HONOR UNDERFOOT, AND LAUGHED AT	JUSTICE	! /THE OLD WOMAN/ OH, WHAT DO I CARE WHY YOU ARE
CLEO II (128)	/POTHINUS/ (BITTERLY) AND THIS IS ROMAN	JUSTICE	! /THEODOTUS/ BUT NOT ROMAN GRATITUDE, I HOPE.
		JUSTICES	
FABL PREFACE(88)	AS ASTRONOMERS ROYAL, ARCHBISHOPS, LORD CHIEF	JUSTICES	, AND PUBLIC SCHOOLMASTERS. EVEN POLICE CONSTABLES
		JUSTIFIABLE	
GENV PREFACE(11)	IT IS COMPLAINED THAT WAR IS NO LONGER	JUSTIFIABLE	AS A TEST OF HEROIC PERSONAL QUALITIES, AND
PYGM II (231)	AIR) EXCEPT PERHAPS IN A MOMENT OF EXTREME AND	JUSTIFIABLE	EXCITEMENT. /MRS PEARCE/ ONLY THIS MORNING, SIR,
DOCT PREFACE(65)	EXPRESSED IN HIS BOOKS), THE SCATHING AND QUITE	JUSTIFIABLE	EXPOSURE OF MEDICAL PRACTICE IN THE NOVEL BY MR
CAND I (103)	(TEMPORIZING) MARCHBANKS: IT IS SOMETIMES	JUSTIFIABLE	-- /MARCHBANKS/ (CUTTING HIM SHORT) I KNOW: TO
		JUSTIFIABLY	
MIS. PREFACE(9)	OF OUR EXISTING CIVILIZATIONS, DESCRIBED QUITE	JUSTIFIABLY	BY RUSKIN AS HEAPS OF AGONIZING HUMAN MAGGOTS,
		JUSTIFICATION	
DOCT V (178)	I WHO MADE HER A WIDOW. AND HER HAPPINESS IS MY	JUSTIFICATION	AND MY REWARD. NOW YOU KNOW WHAT I DID AND
LION PREFACE(15)	CASUISTRY THAT MADE HIM HOLD SO RESOLUTELY TO	JUSTIFICATION	BY FAITH AS THE TRUMP CARD BY WHICH HE SHOULD
SUPR PREFACE(R35)	NOVELTIES: FOR INSTANCE, IT IS A NOVELTY TO CALL	JUSTIFICATION	BY FAITH " WILLE," AND JUSTIFICATION BY WORKS
SUPR PREFACE(R35)	TO CALL JUSTIFICATION BY FAITH " WILLE," AND	JUSTIFICATION	BY WORKS " VORSTELLUNG." THE SOLE USE OF THE
ROCK PREFACE(160)	THEM, BUT TO DIVERT ATTENTION FROM THE ESSENTIAL	JUSTIFICATION	FOR EXTERMINATION, WHICH IS ALWAYS
BARB PREFACE(223)	THAT THE ARMY OUGHT NOT TO TAKE SUCH MONEY, ITS	JUSTIFICATION	IS OBVIOUS. IT MUST TAKE THE MONEY BECAUSE IT
CYMB FORWORD(134)	DOGGEREL. FOR THIS ESTIMATE I FOUND ABSOLUTELY NO	JUSTIFICATION	NOR EXCUSE. I MUST HAVE GOT IT FROM THE LAST
BARB PREFACE(231)	A MUG ON HER FACE. AND THAT IS THE TRIUMPHANT	JUSTIFICATION	OF BARBARA'S CHRISTIANITY AS AGAINST OUR
BARB PREFACE(236)	PAST, IS THE MORALITY OF MILITARISM; AND THE	JUSTIFICATION	OF MILITARISM IS THAT CIRCUMSTANCES MAY AT ANY
BULL PREFACE(57)	ON THE DENSHAWAI VILLAGERS. LORD CROMER'S	JUSTIFICATION	OF THE TRIBUNAL IS PRACTICALLY THAT, BAD AS IT
BARB III (338)	CLEANLINESS AND RESPECTABILITY DO NOT NEED	JUSTIFICATION	, BARBARA: THEY JUSTIFY THEMSELVES. I SEE NO
		JUSTIFIED	
MIS. PREFACE(13)	EVERY DAY TO THEIR WORKPEOPLE; BUT THIS IS NOT A	JUSTIFIED	AND INTENDED PART OF THE SITUATION: IT IS AN ABUSE
DOCT II (128)	PUT INTO BLENKINSOP'S SCALE ALL THE FAITH HE HAS	JUSTIFIED	AND THE HONOR HE HAS CREATED. /RIDGEON/ COME COME,
METH PREFACE(R64)	FOUNDED A HOPE ON HIM; EVERY BLACKGUARD FELT	JUSTIFIED	BY HIM; AND EVERY SAINT FELT ENCOURAGED BY HIM.
POSN PREFACE(387)	OTHER RESPECT, BUT MUZZLE IT POLITICALLY, BE	JUSTIFIED	BY THE PRACTICAL EXIGENCIES OF THE SITUATION? THE
DEST SD(151)	EN AVANT, MES ENFANTS! " THE RESULT HAS ENTIRELY	JUSTIFIED	HIM. THE ARMY CONQUERS ITALY AS THE LOCUSTS
LION PREFACE(43)	WITH THEM AS HE HAD OFTEN DONE IN THE TEMPLE, AND	JUSTIFIED	HIMSELF BOTH TO THE JEWISH LAW AND TO CAESAR. AND
METH PREFACE(R38)	HAD ALL THESE DEFECTS I SHOULD THINK MYSELF QUITE	JUSTIFIED	IN BLAMING HIS CARELESSNESS IN THE STRONGEST
MTH3 (105)	AND A HALF, WOULD THE ACCOUNTANT GENERAL BE	JUSTIFIED	IN CALLING HIM A THIEF? /CONFUCIUS/ NO. HE WOULD
MTH3 (105)	CALLING HIM A THIEF? /CONFUCIUS/ NO. HE WOULD BE	JUSTIFIED	IN CALLING HIM A LIAR. /THE ARCHBISHOP/ I THINK
ROCK PREFACE(178)	WITHOUT HAVING SATISFIED HIMSELF THAT HE WAS	JUSTIFIED	IN DOING SO. HE MUST HAVE BEEN TOLD AS FREQUENTLY
MIS. (134)	TO PRAY THAT I MIGHT FAIL, SO THAT I SHOULD BE	JUSTIFIED	IN GIVING UP BUSINESS AND DOING SOMETHING:
JOAN EPILOG (153)	GOD TO JUSTIFY HIS DAUGHTER ON EARTH AS SHE IS	JUSTIFIED	IN HEAVEN. /CHARLES/ (REASSURED, SITTING DOWN ON
WIDO III (60)	IS THE SAME AS HIS. I SHOULD HARDLY FEEL	JUSTIFIED	IN MAKING A LARGE CLAIM FOR COMPENSATION UNDER
DOCT PREFACE(50)	TO VIVISECTIONIST LOGIC OUR BUILDERS WOULD BE	JUSTIFIED	IN PRODUCING ARTIFICIAL EARTHQUAKES WITH DYNAMITE,
PHIL I (79)	SELFISH MONSTER OF A MAN. /JULIA/ (RISING) I WAS	JUSTIFIED	IN READING YOUR LETTERS. OUR PERFECT CONFIDENCE IN
DOCT PREFACE(13)	WOULD MEAN A MONTH'S ILLNESS, THEN HE IS CLEARLY	JUSTIFIED	IN RECOMMENDING THE OPERATION EVEN IF THE CURE
POSN PREFACE(397)	THE EVENT PROVED THAT THE MANAGER WAS	JUSTIFIED	IN REGARDING THE RISK AS NEGLIGIBLE; FOR THE LORD
POSN PREFACE(390)	LAWYER, IT WILL BE SEEN THAT THE PLAYWRIGHTS ARE	JUSTIFIED	IN REPROACHING THE FRAMERS OF THAT ACT FOR HAVING
BULL PREFACE(12)	RIGHT WHICH THE CHINESE WILL BE PERFECTLY	JUSTIFIED	IN RESISTING BY ARMS AS SOON AS THEY FEEL STRONG
JOAN PREFACE(22)	ARMY THAT, LIKE MOST OF HER POLICY, IT	JUSTIFIED	ITSELF AS SOUNDLY CALCULATED. SHE TALKED TO AND
UNPL PREFACE(R14)	A SOCIAL SUBJECT OF TREMENDOUS FORCE, THAT FORCE	JUSTIFIED	ITSELF IN SPITE OF THE INEXPERIENCE OF THE
SIM PRO,3, (35)	AGO. YOUR OFFENSIVE PERSONAL REMARKS WERE FULLY	JUSTIFIED	. BUT NOW THE TABLES ARE TURNED. I HAVNT GONE
SUPR IV (147)	PROFIT SOMEWHERE, I'LL REGARD MY EXPENDITURE AS	JUSTIFIED	, BUT THERE MUST BE A PROFIT FOR SOMEONE. A
MTH5 (260)	DO YOU MAKE OF IT, SNAKE? /THE SERPENT/ I AM	JUSTIFIED	, FOR I CHOSE WISDOM AND THE KNOWLEDGE OF GOOD AND
JOAN 6 (135)	WILL CONFESS VOLUNTARILY, THEN ITS USE CANNOT BE	JUSTIFIED	. /COURCELLES/ BUT THIS IS UNUSUAL AND IRREGULAR.
BULL PREFACE(68)	RULERS FOR A WHOLE GENERATION FOR SAYING SO, WAS	JUSTIFIED	. THE CATHOLIC IRISH ACCORDINGLY ARMED THEMSELVES
DOCT PREFACE(48)	BUT IN THE LINE OF ARGUMENT BY WHICH IT IS	JUSTIFIED	. THE MEDICAL CODE REGARDING IT IS SIMPLY CRIMINAL
POSN PREFACE(364)	TO BE SHIRKED. AND THE WORD OF DICKENS IS TO BE	JUSTIFIED	. THE STORY OF THE JOINT SELECT COMMITTEE. LET ME
BULL PREFACE(15)	THE ENGLISHMAN IN BROADBENT IS NOT FOR THE MOMENT	JUSTIFIED	. THE VIRTUES OF THE ENGLISH SOIL ARE NOT LESS
MILL PREFACE(124)	THE POLICE ON HIM BECAUSE HE WAS A JEW COULD BE	JUSTIFIED	ONLY ON THE GROUND THAT THE JEWS ARE THE NATURAL
METH PREFACE(R60)	OF ALL SUCH SELF-RIGHTEOUSNESS. IT MORE THAN	JUSTIFIED	ROBERT OWEN BY DISCOVERING IN THE ENVIRONMENT OF
MRS II (215)	NOT LIKELY. /VIVIE/ YOU WERE CERTAINLY QUITE	JUSTIFIED	-- FROM THE BUSINESS POINT OF VIEW. /MRS WARREN/
METH PREFACE(R59)	FAR FROM SURE THAT MY YOUTHFUL ARROGANCE WAS NOT	JUSTIFIED	; FOR THIS SENSE OF THE KINSHIP OF ALL FORMS OF
ANNA PREFACE(287)	THEATRE. WELL, MISS MCCARTHY AND MR RICKETTS	JUSTIFIED	THEMSELVES EASILY IN THE GLAMOR OF THE FOOTLIGHTS,
POSN PREFACE(393)	AS FAR AS THE LORD CHAMBERLAIN WAS CONCERNED, WAS	JUSTIFIED	, IS OF NO CONSEQUENCE. WHAT IS IMPORTANT IS THAT
		JUSTIFIES	
DOCT PREFACE(50)	OF KNOWLEDGE JUSTIFIES EVERY SORT OF CONDUCT, IT	JUSTIFIES	ANY SORT OF CONDUCT, FROM THE ILLUMINATION OF
FANY EPILOG (328)	IS SHOCKED). LOVE BEAUTIFIES EVERY ROMANCE AND	JUSTIFIES	EVERY AUDACITY. (BANNAL ASSENTS GRAVELY). BUT
DOCT PREFACE(50)	THE TRUTH IS, IF THE ACQUISITION OF KNOWLEDGE	JUSTIFIES	EVERY SORT OF CONDUCT, IT JUSTIFIES ANY SORT OF
LION PREFACE(23)	THE ART OF FICTION WHEN TEACHING IN PARABLES, HE	JUSTIFIES	HIMSELF ON THE GROUND THAT ART IS THE ONLY WAY IN
BARB PREFACE(242)	JUSTIFY HIM EXACTLY AS THE REGULAR GOVERNMENT	JUSTIFIES	ITS OFFICIAL EXECUTIONER, AND PARTLY BECAUSE THEY
LION PREFACE(79)	OF SATISFYING HIS APPETITE. THIS SLAVERY ALSO	JUSTIFIES	ITSELF PRAGMATICALLY BY WORKING EFFECTIVELY; BUT
OVER (195)	THANK YOU. I THINK LUNN'S CONDUCT FULLY	JUSTIFIES	ME IN ALLOWING YOU TO DO IT. /MRS LUNN/ YES: I
DOCT PREFACE(4)	CRUELTIES IN THE PURSUIT OF KNOWLEDGE, AND	JUSTIFIES	THEM ON GROUNDS WHICH WOULD EQUALLY JUSTIFY
		JUSTIFY	
FOUN (219)	PRINCIPLE. ON WHAT PRINCIPLE, MAY I ASK, DO YOU	JUSTIFY	AN ATTEMPT TO DEVOUR AN ESTIMABLE PUBLIC OFFICIAL..
BULL PREFACE(17)	A PARK AND A STABLE ON AN INCOME WHICH WOULD NOT	JUSTIFY	AN ENGLISHMAN IN VENTURING UPON A WHOLLY DETACHED
POSN PREFACE(386)	EXTREME FORM OF CENSORSHIP; AND IT SEEMS HARD TO	JUSTIFY	AN INCITEMENT TO IT ON ANTI-CENSORIAL PRINCIPLES.
GETT PREFACE(253)	CHILDREN ARE QUITE CONTENT IN THEM) WHICH WOULD	JUSTIFY	ANY INTELLIGENT STATE IN BREAKING UP THE HOME AND
SUPR I (10)	EVERY CRIME A RESPECTABLE WOMAN CAN; AND SHE'LL	JUSTIFY	EVERY ONE OF THEM BY SAYING THAT IT WAS THE WISH OF
BUOY III (41)	TAKEN A DEGREE OR NOT. /SIR F./ BUT THAT DOES NOT	JUSTIFY	FALSE PRETENCES. /THE YOUTH/ UNIVERSITY DEGREES ARE
SUPR III (124)	THE WOMAN. /DON JUAN/ THE CONSEQUENCES, YES: THEY	JUSTIFY	HER FIERCE GRIP OF THE MAN. BUT SURELY YOU DO NOT
BULL I (94)	BUT DID YOU EVER SAY ANYTHING THAT WOULD	JUSTIFY	HER IN WAITING FOR YOU? /DOYLE/ NO, NEVER. BUT SHE
CLEO II (133)	ALREADY. /CLEOPATRA/ (TAKEN DOWN, AND ANXIOUS TO	JUSTIFY	HERSELF) NO: THAT WOULD BE VERY SILLY OF ME: OF
BARB PREFACE(242)	DONE. THEY DO NOT BETRAY HIM, PARTLY BECAUSE THEY	JUSTIFY	HIM EXACTLY AS THE REGULAR GOVERNMENT JUSTIFIES ITS
ROCK PREFACE(179)	OF THIS PUNCHESQUE SCHADENFREUDE COULD	JUSTIFY	HIM IN HURTING ANYONE'S FEELINGS. WHAT, THEN, WOULD
SIM PREFACE(12)	MAY BE CHALLENGED AS A ROGUE AND A VAGABOND TO	JUSTIFY	HIMSELF BY DOING SOME HONEST WORK; BUT IF HE EARNS A
MILL PREFACE(123)	HIS MOST DANGEROUS OPPONENTS AT A BLOW AND THEN	JUSTIFY	HIMSELF COMPLETELY BEFORE AN ASSEMBLY FULLY AS
GETT PREFACE(255)	WE SETTLE THE QUESTION, WE MUST MAKE THE PARENT	JUSTIFY	HIS CUSTODY OF THE CHILD EXACTLY AS WE SHOULD MAKE A

JOAN EPILOG (153)	ON EVERY ONE OF THOSE DAYS I HAVE PRAYED GOD TO	JUSTIFY	HIS DAUGHTER ON EARTH AS SHE IS JUSTIFIED IN HEAVEN.
GETT PREFACE(255)	OF THE CHILD EXACTLY AS WE SHOULD MAKE A STRANGER	JUSTIFY	IT. IF A FAMILY IS NOT ACHIEVING THE PURPOSES OF A
APPL INTRLUD(247)	OF A GODDESS WITHOUT EVER DOING A THING TO	JUSTIFY	IT. /ORINTHIA/ GIVE ME A GODDESS'S WORK TO DO; AND I
CATH PREFACE(156)	AN ARTISTIC PRESENTMENT MUST NOT CONDESCEND TO	JUSTIFY	ITSELF BY A COMPARISON WITH CRUDE NATURE; AND I
SUPR PREFACE(R9)	ITS INFLUENCE ON THE YOUNG, ARE FOR YOU TO	JUSTIFY	. YOU WERE OF MATURE AGE WHEN YOU MADE THE
JOAN PREFACE(52)	IN THE ONLY POSSIBLE WAY SUFFICIENT VERACITY TO	JUSTIFY	ME IN CLAIMING THAT AS FAR AS I CAN GATHER FROM THE
GENV IV (101)	SLAUGHTERING INNOCENT PERSONS AT RANDOM. IT WOULD	JUSTIFY	ME IN SENTENCING THE YOUNG MEN TO DEATH IF THEY WERE
DOCT III (147)	ON MEDICAL ATTENDANCE REALLY WOULD NOT	JUSTIFY	ME IN WASTING MY TALENTS-- SUCH AS THEY ARE-- IN
SIM II (80)	NO PURPOSE, WILL FADE OUT. WE SHALL HAVE TO	JUSTIFY	OUR EXISTENCES OR PERISH. WE SHALL LIVE UNDER A
DOCT PREFACE(4)	AND JUSTIFIES THEM ON GROUNDS WHICH WOULD EQUALLY	JUSTIFY	PRACTISING THE SAME CRUELTIES ON YOURSELF OR YOUR
MIS. PREFACE(30)	HAS BEEN AN IRREPARABLE MISTAKE. NOTHING CAN	JUSTIFY	SUCH A RISK. THERE MAY BE PEOPLE INCAPABLE OF
FABL PREFACE(81)	ALL PROPORTION TO THEIR NUMBERS AND DESERTS. THEY	JUSTIFY	THEIR DELINQUENCIES AS ASSERTIONS OF PRINCIPLE, AND
LADY PREFACE(218)	WHICH THEY APPLY TO OTHERS AND BY WHICH THEY	JUSTIFY	THEIR PUNISHMENT OF OTHERS, ARE FOOLS AND
BARB III (338)	DO NOT NEED JUSTIFICATION, BARBARA: THEY	JUSTIFY	THEMSELVES. I SEE NO DARKNESS HERE, NO DREADFULNESS.
GENV IV (105)	THERE ARE NO FRONTIERS. LET THOSE WHO SET THEM	JUSTIFY	THEMSELVES. /BBDE/ MR PRESIDENT: IF YOU ALLOW ERNEST
ANNA (302)	KARL MARX? WHY DO YOU NOT STAND TO YOUR GUNS AND	JUSTIFY	WHAT YOU DID, INSTEAD OF MAKING SILLY EXCUSES. DO
MTH2 (71)	FOR YEARS; AND I HOPE I HAVE DONE NOTHING TO	JUSTIFY	YOU IN THE AMAZING ACCUSATION YOU HAVE JUST BROUGHT
GENV IV (101)	LEGAL ASSISTANCE AND PROTECTION. THIS DOES NOT	JUSTIFY	YOUNG MEN IN SLAUGHTERING INNOCENT PERSONS AT
SIM II (72)	NO PURPOSE, WILL FADE OUT. YOU WILL HAVE TO	JUSTIFY	YOUR EXISTENCE OR PERISH. ONLY THE ELECT SHALL
BARB III (337)	ONE. (TURNING ON HIM WITH SUDDEN VEHEMENCE).	JUSTIFY	YOURSELF: SHEW ME SOME LIGHT THROUGH THE DARKNESS OF

JUSTIFYING

CAND I (90)	A SELF-RESPECTING, THOROUGH, CONVINCED SCOUNDREL,	JUSTIFYING	YOUR SCOUNDRELISM AND PROUD OF IT, YOU ARE
FANY II (295)	THE LANGUAGE OF THIS WORLD. BUT WHEN I HEAR YOU	JUSTIFYING	YOUR WICKEDNESS IN THE WORDS OF GRACE, IT'S TOO

JUSTITIA

CAPT III (278)	ON IT). /SIR HOWARD/ (HOLDING HER HAND) FIAT	JUSTITIA	: RUAT COELUM! /LADY CICELY/ LET JUSTICE BE DONE,

JUSTLY

LADY (241)	TELL ME WHICH WAS THE VILE JINGLE? YOU SAID VERY	JUSTLY	: MINE OWN EAR CAUGHT IT EVEN AS MY FALSE TONGUE SAID
GENV IV (119)	ITS NORMAL, SOLID, EVERYDAY CHARACTER-- TO GOVERN	JUSTLY	AND PROSPEROUSLY, THEN I THINK I AGREE. /JUDGE/
LION EPILOG (152)	WHO LET THE LION LOOSE ON THE MAN, YOU WOULD BE	JUSTLY	INDIGNANT. NOW THAT WE MAY NO LONGER SEE A MAN
KING I (166)	/FOX/ YOU ARE VERY CIVIL, SIR; AND YOU SPEAK VERY	JUSTLY	. I THANK YOU (HE PASSES IN). SALLY, INTENSELY
LION PREFACE(53)	AND THE SOBER; AND, AS YOU YOURSELF HAVE VERY	JUSTLY	OBSERVED, THE POOR WE SHALL HAVE ALWAYS WITH US." AND
POSN PREFACE(393)	WHAT IS IMPORTANT IS THAT IT WAS SURE TO BE MADE,	JUSTLY	OR UNJUSTLY, AND EXTENDED FROM THE LORD CHAMBERLAIN
JITT II (38)	MY FATHER THREW HIMSELF INTO THE GUTTER, AND WAS	JUSTLY	PUNISHED FOR IT. /JITTA/ (SPRINGING UP) WHAT! THEY
2TRU II (59)	HAVE BEEN DONE; AND THE POOR LADY POINTS OUT VERY	JUSTLY	THAT I CANNOT REPLACE HER DAUGHTER'S EARS BY
LION PREFACE(10)	UPSIDE DOWN, AS ST PAUL WAS REPROACHED, QUITE	JUSTLY	, FOR WANTING TO DO. FEW PEOPLE CAN NUMBER AMONG
LION PREFACE(52)	ADVISED HIS DISCIPLES TO ACT, HE WILL REPLY, VERY	JUSTLY	, " YOU ARE ADVISING ME TO BECOME A TRAMP." IF WE

JUTIES

O'FL (222)	IT'S A SHAME FOR YOU TO KEEP THE GIRL FROM HER	JUTIES	, DINNY. YOU MIGHT GET HER INTO TROUBLE. /O'FLAHERTY/

JUTLAND

HART PREFACE(21)	WERE COLOSSAL TRAGEDIES, AND THE BATTLE OF	JUTLAND	A MERE BALLAD. THE WORDS " AFTER THOROUGH ARTILLERY

JUTY

O'FL (209)	TO LOVE YOUR ENEMIES? " HE SAYS. " I KNOW IT'S MY	JUTY	AS A SOLDIER TO KILL THEM" I SAYS. " THATS RIGHT,
O'FL (216)	YOUR WHISHT, AND LEARN BEHAVIOR WHILE I PAY MY	JUTY	TO HIS HONOR. (TO SIR PEARCE, HEARTILY) AND HOW IS

JUVENILE

MIS. PREFACE(59)	BE TO MOCK AND DESTROY IT. INFANTILE DOCILITY AND	JUVENILE	DEPENDENCE ARE, LIKE DEATH, A PRODUCT OF NATURAL
MIS. PREFACE(72)	WHETHER WE SHALL PRESENTLY BE DISCUSSING A	JUVENILE	MAGNA CHARTA OR DECLARATION OF RIGHTS BY WAY OF
GENV PREFACE(8)	CHANCELLORS OF THE EXCHEQUER WILL REPLY, LIKE THE	JUVENILE	SPENDTHRIFT EXHORTED TO PAY HIS DEBTS BY RICHELIEU

JUVENILITY

MIS PREFACE(60)	CONSEQUENTLY GOVERNING CLASSES: THEY PASS FROM	JUVENILITY	TO SENILITY WITHOUT EVER TOUCHING MATURITY EXCEPT

JUXTAPOSITION

JOAN PREFACE(5)	TO DESTROY THEM, NOT ONLY ENVIOUSLY BECAUSE THE	JUXTAPOSITION	OF A SUPERIOR WOUNDS THEIR VANITY, BUT QUITE

JYNT

BULL IV (148)	PIG DID TO HIS CLOES. PATSY HAD TWO FINGERS OUT O	JYNT	; BUT THE SMITH PULLED THEM STRAIGHT FOR HIM. OH, YOU

K

2TRU III (109)	THE COLONEL TO HIS WIFE, HIS WATERCOLORS, AND HIS	K	. C. B. (THE COLONEL HURRIES AWAY NOISELESSLY IN THE
2TRU II (80)	S. O. AND THAT WHAT I AM OUT FOR AT PRESENT IS A	K	. C. B. OR RATHER, TO BE STRICTLY ACCURATE, THAT IS WHAT
2TRU III (101)	AND POVERTY WHILST YOU ARE STRUTTING AS A	K	. C. B. /TALLBOYS/ HOW I ENVY HIM! LOOK AT ME AND LOOK AT
2TRU III (102)	WILLINGLY WOULD I EXCHANGE MY PAY, MY RANK, MY	K	. C. B., FOR MEEK'S POVERTY, HIS OBSCURITY! /MEEK/ BUT,
2TRU III (100)	TRAVEL FAST. /TALLBOYS/ FOR ME? /MEEK/ YOUR	K	. C. B., SIR. (PRESENTING A PAPER) HONORS LIST BY
2TRU II (52)	WHAT! /THE RIDER/ MEEK, SIR. M, DOUBLE E,	K	. THE COLONEL LOOKS AT HIM WITH LOATHING, AND TEARS OPEN

KAFFIR

GETT PREFACE(210)	WE SHOULD BE MET BY AN ECONOMIC DIFFICULTY. A	KAFFIR	IS RICH IN PROPORTION TO THE NUMBER OF HIS WIVES,

KAISER

O'FL (209)	I THINK THAT STORY ABOUT YOUR FIGHTING THE	KAISER	AND THE TWELVE GIANTS OF THE PRUSSIAN GUARD
METH PREFACE(R76)	OF A COMMON RELIGION. THE SUCCESS OF THE HANG THE	KAISER	CRY AT THE LAST GENERAL ELECTION SHEWS US VERY
MTH2 (70)	WILL COME OUT ALL RIGHT, YOU KNOW. /FRANKLYN/ THE	KAISER	FELT LIKE THAT. DID HE COME OUT ALL RIGHT? /BURGE/
MTH2 (70)	RIGHT? /BURGE/ WELL, LET US BE FAIR, EVEN TO THE	KAISER	. LET US BE FAIR. /FRANKLYN/ WERE YOU FAIR TO HIM
GENV PREFACE(6)	SHE WOKE UP AND SMASHED THEM ALL. IN VAIN DID THE	KAISER	SING DEUTSCHLAND UBER ALLES, AND HITLER CLAIM THAT
METH PREFACE(R69)	OF THE INDIVIDUAL STATESMEN CONCERNED MAY BE, A	KAISER	WHO IS A DEVOUT READER OF SERMONS, A PRIME MINISTER
O'FL (208)	GERMAN ARMY HAD BEEN BROUGHT UP BY MY MOTHER, THE	KAISER	WOULD BE DINING IN THE BANQUETING HALL AT BUCKINGHAM
PLES PREFACE(R13)	LIFE BECOME DAILY MORE THEATRICAL: THE MODERN	KAISER	, DICTATOR, PRESIDENT OR PRIME MINISTER IS NOTHING IF
LION PREFACE(46)	SEVENTY-SEVEN MILES WAS THE PROPER DISTANCE. THE	KAISER	, KNOWING JUST AS LITTLE ABOUT IT AS THE CONQUEROR,
ROCK II (269)	OR RALLY THEM BY PROMISING THEM TO HANG THE	KAISER	, OR LORD KNOWS WHAT SILLINESS THAT SHOULDNT HAVE
O'FL (211)	WOULD RATHER HAVE ME TELL THEM HOW I FOUGHT THE	KAISER	, THAT ALL THE WORLD KNOWS I NEVER SAW IN MY LIFE,

KAISER'S

HART PREFACE(28)	HAVE BEEN RESISTED FAR MORE FIERCELY THAN THE	KAISER'S	. SUCCESSFUL AS THAT RESISTANCE HAS BEEN, IT HAS
HART PREFACE(17)	OF THE BATTLE-FIELD. TEARING THE GARTER FROM THE	KAISER'S	LEG, STRIKING THE GERMAN DUKES FROM THE ROLL OF OUR

KAISERS

AUGS PREFACE(261)	AND CONTROLLERS, NOT TO MENTION EMPERORS,	KAISERS	AND TSARS, WERE SCRAPPED REMORSELESSLY AT HOME AND
GENV IV (112)	A NOBODY, AND NOW IN COMMAND ABOVE ALL KINGS AND	KAISERS	, FOR MY SUPPORT IS NO DEAD JEW, BUT A MIGHTY
3PLA PREFACE(R22)	TESTIMONY, WILL DESTROY THE VERY SENSE OF LAW.	KAISERS	, GENERALS, JUDGES, AND PRIME MINISTERS WILL SET THE

KALEIDOSCOPE

DOCT PREFACE(77)	BY THE TIME THIS PREFACE IS IN PRINT THE	KALEIDOSCOPE	MAY HAVE HAD ANOTHER SHAKE; AND OPSONIN MAY

KALICH

JITT PREFACE(7)	6TH JANUARY 1923, WHEN JITTA WAS PLAYED BY BERTHA	KALICH	

KAM

CAPT NOTES (304)	IN SOUTHERN ENGLAND PRONOUNCE THEM AS PLAM,	KAM	, HAMBAG, AP, GAN, ETC., EXACTLY AS FELIX DRINKWATER

		KAMERAD	
2TRU I (42)	HE FALLS ON HIS <NEES AND THROWS UP HIS HANDS).	KAMERAD	, MISS MOPPLY: KAMERAD! I AM UTTERLY AT YOUR MERCY.
2TRU I (42)	AND THROWS UP HIS HANDS). KAMERAD, MISS MOPPLY:	KAMERAD	! I AM UTTERLY AT YOUR MERCY. THE BELL IS ON YOUR
MTH4 II (181)	THE PISTOL AND COVERING HIS EYES) QUARTER!	KAMERAD	! TAKE IT, MADAM (HE KICKS IT TOWARDS HER): I
		KAMPF	
GENV PREFACE(20)	HESS, WROTE A BOOK ENTITLED MEIN	KAMPF	(MY STRUGGLE, MY PROGRAM, MY VIEWS OR WHAT YOU
		KANATT	
O'FL (207)	I TELL YOU THAT THAT OLD WOMAN IS THE BIGGEST	KANATT	FROM HERE TO THE CROSS OF MONASTERBOICE. SURE SHE'S
		KANCHIN	
SIM II SD(62)	/MAYA/ IN THE DEPTHS OF HELL HE WILL FIND US.	KANCHIN	AND JANGA ENTER PROCESSIONALLY, READING NEWSPAPERS.
SIM I (41)	WARN THEE. /THE YOUNGER YOUTH/ ON GUARD. I,	KANCHIN	, SHEW THEE THE RED LIGHT. /JANGA/ THEIR EYEBROWS
		KANGAROO	
GENV PREFACE(26)	TO A DOUBT WHETHER NATURE IS NOT AN INCORRIGIBLE	KANGAROO	. WHAT IS CERTAIN IS THAT NEW FACULTIES, HOWEVER
BULL II (97)	POOR LITTLE FRIEND. IF YOU COULD JUMP AS FAR AS A	KANGAROO	YOU COULDNT JUMP AWAY FROM YOUR OWN HEART AN ITS
		KANSAS	
MRS PREFACE(178)	IN FAVOR OF THE PLAY DID NOT END THE MATTER. IN	KANSAS	CITY, FOR INSTANCE, THE MUNICIPALITY, FINDING ITSELF
MRS PREFACE(178)	THIS. AT ALL EVENTS I DO NOT PROPOSE TO GIVE THE	KANSAS	COUNCILLORS THE BENEFIT OF THE DOUBT. I THEREFORE
		KANT	
GENV PREFACE(25)	INSTRUMENTS. IN PHILOSOPHY WE SPOT DESCARTES AND	KANT	, SWIFT AND SCHOPENHAUER, BUTLER AND BERGSON, RICHARD
		KANTIAN	
LION PREFACE(11)	AND FLATTERIES, CALLED PRAISES. THEN THE	KANTIAN	MORAL LAW WITHIN YOU MAKES YOU CONCEIVE YOUR GOD AS
LION PREFACE(90)	SO, WHAT I AM ENGAGED IN IS A CRITICISM (IN THE	KANTIAN	SENSE) OF AN ESTABLISHED BODY OF BELIEF WHICH HAS
SUPR III SD(72)	WHO CAN AND DOES REASON, AND WHO, APPLYING THE	KANTIAN	TEST TO HIS CONDUCT, CAN TRULY SAY TO US, IF
BARB PREFACE(216)	AND COWARDLY INFAMY. HIS CONDUCT STANDS THE	KANTIAN	TEST, WHICH PETER SHIRLEY'S DOES NOT. PETER SHIRLEY
		KANT'S	
LION PREFACE(11)	AND SUNSET, GROWTHS AND HARVESTS AND DECAY, AND	KANT'S	TWO WONDERS OF THE STARRY HEAVENS ABOVE US AND THE
		KAPITAL	
METH PREFACE(R62)	SOCIALISM IN THE WIDELY READ FIRST VOLUME OF DAS	KAPITAL	: EVERY REFERENCE IT MADE TO WORKERS AND CAPITALISTS
FABL PREFACE(77)	AT ITS CONVENTICLES AND IN ITS CHAPELS, WITH DAS	KAPITAL	AS ITS BIBLE AND GOSPEL, JUST AS COBDENIST
METH PREFACE(R61)	AND HE PUBLISHED THE FIRST VOLUME OF HIS DAS	KAPITAL	IN 1867. THE REVOLT AGAINST ANTHROPOMORPHIC
METH PREFACE(R62)	EPOCH-MAKING IN THE MINDS OF ITS READERS AS DAS	KAPITAL	. THERE WAS NOTHING ABOUT SOCIALISM IN THE WIDELY
METH PREFACE(R62)	POWER OF OBSERVATION: THERE WAS NOT A FACT IN DAS	KAPITAL	THAT HAD NOT BEEN TAKEN OUT OF A BOOK, NOR A
		KARL	
ROCK I (233)	JEW NAMED HARRY MARKS-- /HILDA/ DONT YOU MEAN	KARL	MARX? /SIR ARTHUR/ THATS THE MAN. KARL MARX. GET ME
ANNA (302)	LEARN TO READ THE BIBLE WITHOUT LEARNING TO READ	KARL	MARX? WHY DO YOU NOT STAND TO YOUR GUNS AND JUSTIFY
MILL PREFACE(128)	INTERESTS THE COUNTRY IS MISGOVERNED. SINCE	KARL	MARX AND FRIEDRICH ENGELS EXPOSED THE HORRIBLE
FABL PREFACE(66)	AND IBSEN, NEWTON AND EINSTEIN, ADAM SMITH AND	KARL	MARX ARRIVE ONLY ONCE AT INTERVALS OF HUNDREDS OF
FABL PREFACE(88)	IS SUCCESSFUL, ESPECIALLY IF HE RANKS THOSE OF	KARL	MARX AS BLASPHEMOUS, AND HISTORY AS ENDING WITH
BUOY 1 (13)	THEY WOULD DIE OF HORROR AT THEIR OWN WICKEDNESS.	KARL	MARX CHANGED THE MIND OF THE WORLD BY SIMPLY TELLING
FABL PREFACE(97)	MACAULAY, AUSTIN, COBDEN, AND BRIGHT, UNTIL	KARL	MARX DEALT IT A MORTAL BLOW BY SHEWING FROM OFFICIAL
METH PREFACE(R61)	AS DARWIN DISCREDITED THE GARDEN OF EDEN.	KARL	MARX HAD PROCLAIMED IN HIS COMMUNIST MANIFESTO OF 1848
ROCK PREFACE(189)	ROOM OF THE BRITISH MUSEUM WAS SACRED; BUT IF	KARL	MARX HAD SENT THE RENT OF HIS VILLA IN MAITLAND PARK TO
ROCK I (233)	BEAT THEM AT THEIR OWN SILLY GAME. I'LL JUST TURN	KARL	MARX INSIDE-OUT FOR THEM. (THE HOUSEHOLD GONG SOUNDS).
FABL PREFACE(77)	WITH THE COLLEGE OF CARDINALS, COMINFORM MAKES	KARL	MARX ITS DEITY AND THE KREMLIN HIS VATICAN. IT WORSHIPS
FABL PREFACE(98)	EQUALITY, AND FRATERNITY, WAS CONVICTED BY	KARL	MARX OF BEING THE WORST AND WICKEDEST ON RECORD; AND
ROCK I (220)	UP HALF THE NIGHT AFTER A HARD DAY'S WORK TO READ	KARL	MARX OR ANYONE ELSE? NO FEAR. YOUR HEARTS ARE NOT IN
3PLA PREFACE(R39)	THE FIELDS OF PHILOSOPHY, POLITICS, AND ART.	KARL	MARX SAID OF STUART MILL THAT HIS EMINENCE WAS DUE TO
METH PREFACE(R15)	ROUSSEAU WAS HUNTED FROM FRONTIER TO FRONTIER;	KARL	MARX STARVED IN EXILE IN A SOHO LODGING; RUSKIN'S
ROCK I (233)	THE MAN. KARL MARX. GET ME EVERY BLESSED BOOK BY	KARL	MARX THAT YOU CAN FIND TRANSLATED INTO ENGLISH; AND
ROCK I (218)	ANYTHING THEY DONT WANT TO KNOW. OLD DR MARX--	KARL	MARX THEY CALL HIM NOW-- MY FATHER KNEW HIM WELL--
ROCK II (267)	THE DUSTBIN. YET THEY GOT THEIR IDEAS FROM US.	KARL	MARX THOUGHT IT ALL OUT IN BLOOMSBURY. LENIN LEARNT HIS
GENV III (73)	AND DANGEROUS TROUBLE? /THE NEWCOMER/	KARL	MARX WAS TOLERATED IN ENGLAND: HE WOULDNT HAVE BEEN
BUOY II (21)	OR WHY, UNLESS YOU READ KARL MARX. /SHE/ I READ	KARL	MARX WHEN I WAS FIFTEEN. THAT IS WHY I AM HERE INSTEAD
GENV III (73)	TRAFFIC; AND ALL THE TIME THEY WERE PROVIDING	KARL	MARX WITH THE FINEST READING ROOM IN THE WORLD WHILST
GENV III (72)	RUSSIA GET HER IDEAS? FROM ENGLAND. IN RUSSIA	KARL	MARX WOULD HAVE BEEN SENT TO SIBERIA AND FLOGGED TO
ROCK PREFACE(189)	THAT PERSON TO WALK ALONG PICCADILLY STARK NAKED.	KARL	MARX WRITING THE DEATH WARRANT OF PRIVATE PROPERTY IN
MTH2 (63)	TOSH. I HAVE NO OBJECTION WHATEVER TO DENOUNCE	KARL	MARX. ANYTHING I CAN SAY AGAINST DARWIN WILL PLEASE A
METH PREFACE(R61)	RECEIVED DARWIN WITH OPEN ARMS. DARWIN AND	KARL	MARX. BESIDES, THE SOCIALISTS HAD AN EVOLUTIONARY
ROCK I (233)	YOU MEAN KARL MARX? /SIR ARTHUR/ THATS THE MAN.	KARL	MARX. GET ME EVERY BLESSED BOOK BY KARL MARX THAT YOU
BULL PREFACE(71)	POLITICAL EDUCATION, AS I BEGAN MINE, BY READING	KARL	MARX. IT IS TRUE THAT I HAD OCCASION TO POINT OUT THAT
BARB PREFACE(212)	ITS COLLISION WITH THE CLASS-CONFLICT THEORY OF	KARL	MARX. NIETZSCHE, AS I GATHER, REGARDED THE
APPL II (267)	IS BUILT ON ENGLISH HISTORY, WRITTEN IN LONDON BY	KARL	MARX. /PROTEUS/ YES; AND THE ENGLISH KING HAS
MTH2 (62)	(TO SAVVY) I UNDERSTAND. YOU ARE A DISCIPLE OF	KARL	MARX. /SAVVY/ NO, NO. KARL MARX'S ECONOMICS ARE ALL
BUOY II (21)	YOU HAVNT A NOTION OF HOW OR WHY, UNLESS YOU READ	KARL	MARX. /SHE/ I READ KARL MARX WHEN I WAS FIFTEEN. THAT
GENV III (66)	BOURGEOIS TRADITION, CONTRARY TO THE TEACHINGS OF	KARL	MARX. /SIR O./ WELL, SO MUCH THE BETTER. I CAN HARDLY
ANNA (302)	TO READ. /STRAMMFEST/ TO READ SEDITION. TO READ	KARL	MARX. /THE GRAND DUCHESS/ PSHAW! HOW COULD THEY LEARN
GENV I (47)	I STILL HAVE LIFE ENOUGH LEFT IN ME TO DENY IT.	KARL	MARX-- ANTICHRIST-- SAID THAT THE SWEET AND ENNOBLING
MTH2 (62)	YOU ARE A DISCIPLE OF KARL MARX. /SAVVY/ NO, NO.	KARL	MARX'S ECONOMICS ARE ALL ROT. /LUBIN/ (AT LAST A
ROCK II (254)	THEY HAD ACQUIRED FROM READING THE WORKS OF	KARL	MARX'S REVOLUTIONARY PREDECESSOR ROUSSEAU. THAT BIT OF
GENV III (82)	IT WAS, AND JOHN RUSKIN'S GOSPEL COMPARED WITH	KARL	MARX'S WAS LIKE BOILING BRANDY COMPARED WITH MILK AND
GENV PREFACE(24)	EVEN WHEN THEY HAVE READ PLATO, THE GOSPELS, AND	KARL	MARX, AND TO THAT EXTENT KNOW WHAT THEY HAVE TO DO,
GENV PREFACE(25)	BUTLER AND BERGSON, RICHARD WAGNER AND	KARL	MARX, BLAKE AND SHELLEY, RUSKIN AND MORRIS, WITH DOZENS
ROCK I (219)	WONT GO DOWN. /HIPNEY/ YOU SEE, YOU HAVNT READ	KARL	MARX, HAVE YOU? /SIR ARTHUR/ MR HIPNEY, WHEN THE
LION PREFACE(76)	OF COMMUNISM AND JESUISM. JUST AS IN OUR OWN TIME	KARL	MARX, NOT CONTENT TO TAKE POLITICAL ECONOMY AS HE FOUND
GENV IV (117)	UNDERSTANDS THE PAMPHLETS, THE THREE VOLUMES OF	KARL	MARX, THE THEORIES OF THE IDEALISTS, THE RANTING OF THE
GENV III (82)	TO THE NEW JERUSALEM IS THE RACE THAT PRODUCED	KARL	MARX, WHO PRODUCED SOVIET RUSSIA. /THE JUDGE/ RACE!
DOCT PREFACE(59)	THE FIELD OF BIOLOGICAL STATISTICS BY PROFESSOR	KARL	PEARSON AND HIS COLLEAGUES, I AM OUT OF MY DEPTH AT THE
DOCT PREFACE(59)	MATHEMATICIANS; AND I CANNOT RESIST PROFESSOR	KARL	PEARSON'S IMMENSE CONTEMPT FOR, AND INDIGNANT SENSE OF
FABL PREFACE(95)	THE ACQUAINTANCE OF THE EDITOR OF BIOMETRIKA,	KARL	PEARSON, WHO MAINTAINED THAT NO THEORY COULD BE VALID
		KARMA	
LION PREFACE(89)	IN ORDER TO PROVIDE AN UNLIMITED FIELD FOR	KARMA	TO BE WORKED OUT BY THE UNREDEEMED SINNER. THE BELIEF
LION PREFACE(88)	INSIST THAT THE SMALLEST OF OUR SINS BRINGS ITS	KARMA	, ALSO INSIST ON INDIVIDUAL IMMORTALITY AND
		KARTEL	
LION PREFACE(54)	STOCK, REPRESENTED BY THE TRUST, OR COMBINE, OR	KARTEL	, THE TRUST WILL PRESENTLY FREEZE YOU OUT AND ROPE
		KASPAR	
MIS. PREFACE(70)	OF THEIR CHILDREN. BETTER CLAUDE DUVAL THAN	KASPAR	HAUSER. LABORERS WHO ARE CONTEMPTUOUSLY ANTI-CLERICAL
		KASSASSIN	
PRES (155)	YOU NEVER KNEW THAT THE HERO OF THE CHARGE AT	KASSASSIN	WAS A WOMAN: YET SHE WAS: IT WAS I, ROSA CARMINA
PRES (154)	WHICH I SLEW FIVE EGYPTIANS WITH MY OWN HAND AT	KASSASSIN	, WHERE I SERVED AS A TROOPER. /MITCHENER/ LORD
		KATHARINE	
SUPR PREFACE(R20)	MATRIMONIAL ADVENTURER. ONCE HE IS ASSURED THAT	KATHARINE	HAS MONEY, HE UNDERTAKES TO MARRY HER BEFORE HE

GETT PREFACE(186)	ON WHICH HENRY VIII PROCURED HIS DIVORCE FROM	KATHARINE	OF ARAGON TO THE PLEAS ON WHICH AMERICAN WIVES
PHIL I SD(69)	KEMBLE AS HAMLET, MRS SIDDONS AS QUEEN	KATHARINE	PLEADING IN COURT, MACREADY AS WERNER (AFTER
		KATHLEEN	
BULL I (87)	IRELAND YOUVE GOT TO CALL THE UNFORTUNATE ISLAND	KATHLEEN	NI HOOLIHAN AND PRETEND SHE'S A LITTLE OLD WOMAN.
		KATINKA	
BARB PREFACE(209)	ON THE PEOPLE WHO SAW THROUGH HIM; TO FASCINATE	KATINKA	(WHO CUT POTTS SO RUTHLESSLY AT THE END OF THE
		KAWTOOM	
CAPT I (223)	KNOW. /DRINKWATER/ GAWDN, GAVNER, GAWDN. GAWDN O	KAWTOOM	-- STETCHER STENDS IN TRIFAWLGR SQUARE TO THIS DY.
		KEAN	
CATH PREFACE(157)	HAND. IN THE NINETEENTH CENTURY, THE CAREERS OF	KEAN	, MACREADY, BARRY SULLIVAN, AND IRVING, OUGHT TO HAVE
FABL PREFACE(66)	OF BRANDY, MAKE HIM A DIPSOMANIAC, LIKE EDMUND	KEAN	, ROBSON, AND DICKENS ON HIS LAST AMERICAN TOUR. OR,
		KEAN'S	
LADY PREFACE(233)	PLAYGOERS, ALL SPEAKING OF GARRICK'S RICHARD, AND	KEAN'S	OTHELLO, AND IRVING'S SHYLOCK, AND FORBES ROBERTSON'S
		KEARNEY	
CAPT III (283)	YOU MUSTNT LET SIR HOWARD MAKE A SPEECH, CAPTAIN	KEARNEY	: HIS DOCTORS HAVE POSITIVELY FORBIDDEN ANYTHING OF
CAPT III (286)	HOWARD/ (RISING TO PROTEST) CICELY! CAPTAIN	KEARNEY	: THIS MAN TOLD ME-- /LADY CICELY/ (SWIFTLY
CAPT III (281)	HAS SUCH A NICE FACE! DONT YOU THINK SO, CAPTAIN	KEARNEY	? (HE GASPS, SPEECHLESS). AND NOW WILL YOU EXCUSE
CAPT III (289)	HOUR DID YOU SAY WE WERE TO LUNCH AT, CAPTAIN	KEARNEY	? /KEARNEY/ YOU RECALL ME TO MY DOOTY, LADY
CAPT III (287)	ME. DONT YOU THINK THAT WAS NICE OF HIM, CAPTAIN	KEARNEY	? /KEARNEY/ I SHOULD HAVE DONE THE SAME MYSELF,
CAPT III (277)	YOU COULD MAKE A POOR SIMPLE SAILOR LIKE CAPTAIN	KEARNEY	BELIEVE ANYTHING. THE PROPER THING FOR YOU TO DO,
CAPT III (284)	SO MUCH BETTER, DEAR CAPTAIN KEARNEY. (SILENCE.	KEARNEY	COMPOSES HIMSELF TO SPEAK. SHE BREAKS OUT AGAIN).
CAPT III (281)	ORDERS, SIR. (HE GOES OUT, UNRUFFLED, LEAVING	KEARNEY	DUMBFOUNDED). /SIR HOWARD/ (CONTEMPLATING KEARNEY'S
CAPT III (282)	KEARNEY. THE LEDDY SENT ME ON AN ERRAND. (	KEARNEY	GRUNTS). I THOAGHT I SHOULD BE LATE. BUT THE FIRST
CAPT III SD(279)	ADMIT HIS CAPTAIN, AND GOES OUT). CAPTAIN HAMLIN	KEARNEY	IS A ROBUSTLY BUILT WESTERN AMERICAN, WITH THE KEEN,
CAPT III (285)	THAT WAS MY FIRST HASTY CONCLUSION, CAPTAIN	KEARNEY	. BUT IT APPEARS THAT THE COMPACT BETWEEN THEM WAS
CAPT III (281)	SEAT ON KEARNEY'S RIGHT) FORTUNATELY NOT, CAPTAIN	KEARNEY	. HALF A DOZEN SUCH WOMEN WOULD MAKE AN END OF LAW
CAPT III (281)	WITH DISMAY) I AM REALLY VERY SORRY, CAPTAIN	KEARNEY	. I AM QUITE AWARE THAT LADY CICELY HAS NO RIGHT
CAPT III (287)	SENSATION). I TOLD YOU THEY QUARRELLED, CAPTAIN	KEARNEY	. I SAID SO, DIDNT I? /REDBROOK/ (CRISPLY)
CAPT III (280)	HAS TAKEN SO SERIOUS A LIBERTY, CAPTAIN	KEARNEY	. IT IS A MANIA OF HERS-- SIMPLY A MANIA. WHY DID
CAPT III (283)	/LADY CICELY/ EVER SO MUCH BETTER, DEAR CAPTAIN	KEARNEY	. (SILENCE. KEARNEY COMPOSES HIMSELF TO SPEAK. SHE
CAPT III (279)	(AS HE ENTERS) SO GLAD YOUVE COME, CAPTAIN	KEARNEY	. /KEARNEY/ (COMING BETWEEN SIR HOWARD AND LADY
CAPT III SD(281)	TOUCHING THEIR CAPS, AND STAND IN A GROUP BEHIND	KEARNEY	. /KEARNEY/ (TO SIR HOWARD) YOU WILL BE GLAHD TO
CAPT III (286)	AND RESUMING HIS SEAT) I BEG YOUR PARDON, CAPTAIN	KEARNEY	. /LADY CICELY/ THEN SIDI CAME. /KEARNEY/ SIDNEY!
CAPT III (282)	HOWARD. /SIR HOWARD/ THIS IS MR RANKIN, CAPTAIN	KEARNEY	. /RANKIN/ EXCUSE MY DELAY, CAPTAIN KEARNEY. THE
CAPT III (282)	KEARNEY. /RANKIN/ EXCUSE MY DELAY, CAPTAIN	KEARNEY	. THE LEDDY SENT ME ON AN ERRAND. (KEARNEY GRUNTS).
CAPT III (286)	MAKE THEM CLEAN AND WHITEWASH THOROUGHLY, CAPTAIN	KEARNEY	. THEN CAPTAIN BRASSBOUND AND SIR HOWARD TURNED OUT
CAPT III (280)	THATS WHAT ENGLISH PEOPLE ARE LIKE, CAPTAIN	KEARNEY	. THEY WONT HEAR OF ANYTHING CONCERNING YOUR POOR
CAPT III (280)	I BEG YOU WILL NOT TALK NONSENSE TO CAPTAIN	KEARNEY	. YOUR IDEAS ON SOME SUBJECTS ARE REALLY HARDLY
CAPT III (272)	THEM BEFORE THE INQUIRY, OR THEYLL GIVE CAPTAIN	KEARNEY	QUITE A FALSE IMPRESSION OF WHAT HAPPENED. /RANKIN/
CAPT III SD(283)	ON HIS LEFT. SIR HOWARD RISES PUNCTILIOUSLY WHEN	KEARNEY	RISES AND SITS WHEN HE SITS. /KEARNEY/ IS THIS
CAPT III SD(283)	FALL BACK GALLANTLY TO ALLOW HER TO PASS.	KEARNEY	RISES TO RECEIVE HER, AND STARES WITH SOME SURPRISE
CAPT III (280)	ARE REALLY HARDLY DECOROUS. /LADY CICELY/ (TO	KEARNEY	) THATS WHAT ENGLISH PEOPLE ARE LIKE, CAPTAIN
CAPT III (283)	REST. (BRASSBOUND JOINS REDBROOK AND JOHNSON.	KEARNEY	SITS DOWN AGAIN, AFTER INVITING LADY CICELY, WITH A
CAPT III SD(279)	OUT! I BELIEVE YOU KNOW EVERY BOLT IN THAT SHIP.	KEARNEY	SOFTENS PERCEPTIBLY. /SIR HOWARD/ I AM REALLY VERY
CAPT III (287)	HURT AND DISCOURAGED) I'M SORRY YOU WISH CAPTAIN	KEARNEY	TO UNDERSTAND THAT I AM AN UNTRUTHFUL WITNESS. /SIR
CAPT III (288)	FOOL. /LADY CICELY/ OF COURSE I DID. NOW, CAPTAIN	KEARNEY	, DO YOU WANT ME-- DOES SIR HOWARD WANT ME-- DOES
CAPT II (270)	" MOGADOR HARBOR, 26 SEPT 1899. CAPTAIN HAMLIN	KEARNEY	, OF THE CRUISER SANTIAGO, PRESENTS THE COMPLIMENTS
		KEARNEY'S	
CAPT III (278)	APPEARS AT THE DOOR. /BLUEJACKET/ CAPTAIN	KEARNEY'S	CAWMPLIMENTS TO LADY WAYNFLETE; AND MAY HE COME
CAPT III (281)	DUMBFOUNDED). /SIR HOWARD/ (CONTEMPLATING	KEARNEY'S	EXPRESSION WITH DISMAY) I AM REALLY VERY SORRY,
CAPT III (272)	ME IT WILL NOT LOOK JUDEECIAL TO HAVE CAPTAIN	KEARNEY'S	OFFICERS SQUATTING ON THE FLOOR. /LADY CICELY/ OH,
CAPT III (281)	CHAIR). /SIR HOWARD/ (RESUMING HIS SEAT ON	KEARNEY'S	RIGHT) FORTUNATELY NOT, CAPTAIN KEARNEY. HALF A
		KEATS	
MILL PREFACE(133)	BY TITIAN, A BALLAD BY MACAULAY AND A STANZA BY	KEATS	. BUT AT LEAST HE IS FREE TO FIND OUT ALL THIS FOR
		KEB	
CAPT II (249)	YUSS, AN HORDER HUZ ABAHT AS IF WE WAS	KEB	TAHTS! AN THE KEPN AFRIDE TO TALK BAWCK AT ER! LADY
		KEEGAN	
BULL IV (180)	TO KEEGAN) STICK TO THE ENGLISHMAN, MR	KEEGAN	: HE HAS A BAD NAME HERE; BUT AT LEAST HE CAN FORGIVE
BULL IV (181)	MY TONE ENORMOUSLY. I FEEL SINCERELY OBLIGED TO	KEEGAN	: HE HAS MADE ME FEEL A BETTER MAN: DISTINCTLY
BULL IV (176)	HIS HAND WARMLY) YOU SHALL NEVER REGRET IT, MR	KEEGAN	: I GIVE YOU MY WORD FOR THAT. I SHALL BRING MONEY
BULL II (101)	HAT TO HER: HE DOES NOT TAKE IT OFF. /NORA/ MR	KEEGAN	: I WANT TO SPEAK TO YOU A MINUTE IF YOU DONT MIND.
BULL IV (177)	THEIR MINERALS; AND THEN WE SHALL SEE. /LARRY/ MR	KEEGAN	: IF YOU ARE GOING TO BE SENTIMENTAL ABOUT IRELAND, I
BULL II (103)	/NORA/ (BLUSHING WITH DELIGHT) YOURE JOKING, MR	KEEGAN	: I'M SURE YAR. /KEEGAN/ MY WAY OF JOKING IS TO TELL
BULL IV (155)	/BROADBENT/ YOUR IDEA IS A VERY CLEVER ONE, MR	KEEGAN	: REALLY MOST BRILLIANT: I SHOULD NEVER HAVE THOUGHT
BULL IV (173)	TO A CROSSING SWEEPER. /BROADBENT/ YES, MR	KEEGAN	: THIS PLACE MAY HAVE AN INDUSTRIAL FUTURE, OR IT MAY
BULL IV (172)	AT WHICH HE SMILES AND SHAKES HIS HEAD) YES, MR	KEEGAN	: YOURE QUITE RIGHT. THERES POETRY IN EVERYTHING,
BULL IV (154)	IRISHMAN, EH? /LARRY/ ARE YOU REALLY MAD, MR	KEEGAN	? /AUNT JUDY/ (SHOCKED) OH, LARRY, HOW COULD YOU
BULL IV (147)	/NORA/ I DONT KNOW HOW YOU CAN LAUGH. DO YOU, MR	KEEGAN	? /KEEGAN/ (GRIMLY) WHY NOT? THERE IS DANGER,
BULL II (99)	PATSY: WHAT DID I TELL YOU ABOUT CALLIN ME FATHER	KEEGAN	AN YOUR REVERENCE? WHAT DID FATHER DEMPSEY TELL YOU
BULL II (109)	DEMPSEY? /PATSY/ WELL, HWAT WAS I TO DO? FATHER	KEEGAN	BID ME TELL YOU MISS NORA WAS GONE TO THE ROUN TOWER.
BULL IV (169)	I THINK I'LL GO IN NOW. I SEE LARRY AND MR	KEEGAN	COMING UP THE HILL; AND I'M NOT FIT TO TALK TO THEM.
BULL IV (153)	HOW STUPID OF ME! I'M SO SORRY. (HE PATS	KEEGAN	CONSOLINGLY ON THE BACK). JOHN BULL'S WITS ARE STILL
BULL IV (146)	WI DHE RING IN ITS SNOUT. (ROARS OF LAUGHTER:	KEEGAN	GLARES AT THEM). BEFORE BROADBINT KNEW HWERE HE WAS,
BULL IV (172)	WAKING UP FROM HIS REVERIE AND BUSTLING	KEEGAN	GOODHUMOREDLY) AND THEN I SHALL WAKE YOU UP A BIT.
BULL III (133)	WHISHT, MAN! YOURE WORSE THAN MAD PETHER	KEEGAN	HIMSELF. /BROADBENT/ (WHO HAS LISTENED IN THE
BULL II (109)	HOW OFTEN HAVE YOU HEARD ME BID YOU CALL MISTER	KEEGAN	IN HIS PROPER NAME, THE SAME AS I DO? FATHER KEEGAN
BULL II (109)	IN HIS PROPER NAME, THE SAME AS I DO? FATHER	KEEGAN	INDEED! CANT YOU TELL THE DIFFERENCE BETWEEN YOUR
BULL II (100)	SINNER OR CURSE AT A BEGGAR, REMEMBER THAT PETHER	KEEGAN	IS A WORSE SINNER AND A WORSE BEGGAR, AND KEEP THE
BULL IV SD(145)	ATMOSPHERE BETWEEN THE TWO SIDES OF THE ROOM.	KEEGAN	IS EXTRAORDINARILY STERN: NO GAME OF BACKGAMMON COULD
BULL IV (169)	DEMPSEY HIMSELF. /NORA/ YOU LITTLE KNOW PETER	KEEGAN	. HE'D SEE THROUGH ME AS IF I WAS A PANE O GLASS.
BULL IV (152)	HANDS EFFUSIVELY) MOST HAPPY TO MEET YOU, MR	KEEGAN	. I HAVE HEARD OF YOU, THOUGH I HAVE NOT HAD THE
BULL II (101)	ADORATION) SURE IT'S YOUR BLESSIN I WANT, FADHER	KEEGAN	. I'LL HAVE NO LUCK WIDHOUT IT. /KEEGAN/ (SHOCKED)
BULL IV (152)	/AUNT JUDY/ OH, I FORGOT. YOUVE NOT MET MR	KEEGAN	. LET ME INTROJOOSHA. /BROADBENT/ (SHAKING HANDS
BULL IV (153)	AH! IT WAS ONLY YOUR DELIGHTFUL IRISH HUMOR, MR	KEEGAN	. OF COURSE, OF COURSE. HOW STUPID OF ME! I'M SO
BULL IV (154)	THAT I AM MAD. /NORA/ AH, DONT TALK LIKE THAT, MR	KEEGAN	. /BROADBENT/ (ENCOURAGINGLY) NOT AT ALL, NOT AT
BULL IV (153)	I'M SURE YOU DONT THINK ANYTHING OF THE SORT, MR	KEEGAN	. /BROADBENT/ (EMPHATICALLY) THANK YOU, MISS REILLY:
BULL IV SD(171)	BROADBENT ARRIVES, CONVERSING ENERGETICALLY WITH	KEEGAN	. /BROADBENT/ NOTHING PAYS LIKE A GOLFING HOTEL, IF
BULL IV (174)	OF THAT, I HAVE FAITH IN IRELAND. GREAT FAITH, MR	KEEGAN	. /KEEGAN/ AND WE HAVE NONE: ONLY EMPTY ENTHUSIASMS
BULL IV (176)	RATHER A STRONG EXPRESSION IN THAT CONNEXION, MR	KEEGAN	. /KEEGAN/ NOT FROM A MAN WHO KNOWS THAT THIS WORLD
BULL IV (169)	/BROADBENT/ JUST WAIT AND SAY SOMETHING NICE TO	KEEGAN	. THEY TELL ME HE CONTROLS NEARLY AS MANY VOTES AS
BULL IV (154)	ASK HIM SUCH A THING? /LARRY/ I DONT THINK MR	KEEGAN	MINDS. (TO KEEGAN) WHATS THE TRUE VERSION OF THE
BULL II (109)	WHATS THAT YOU SAY? /PATSY/ (FRIGHTENED) FADHER	KEEGAN	-- /FATHER DEMPSEY/ HOW OFTEN HAVE YOU HEARD ME BID
BULL IV (180)	KEEGAN'S RIGHT, BROADBENT ADDS, CONFIDENTIALLY TO	KEEGAN	) STICK TO THE ENGLISHMAN, MR KEEGAN: HE HAS A BAD
BULL IV (154)	/LARRY/ I DONT THINK MR KEEGAN MINDS. (TO	KEEGAN	) WHATS THE TRUE VERSION OF THE STORY OF THAT BLACK
BULL IV (147)	BEDAD I'M SORRY FOR YOUR POOR BRUDDHER, MISTHER	KEEGAN	; BUT I RECOMMEND YOU TO THRY HIM WID A COUPLE OF
BULL IV (177)	THING. I DONT IN THE LEAST MIND YOUR CHAFF, MR	KEEGAN	; BUT LARRY'S RIGHT ON THE MAIN POINT. THE WORLD
BULL II (109)	GOOD LAD (GOING). /PATSY/ (TO AUNT JUDY) FADHER	KEEGAN	SEZ-- /FATHER DEMPSEY/ (TURNING SHARPLY ON HIM)

BULL IV SD(145) AS A BED FOR BROADBENT. AGAINST THE WALL BEHIND KEEGAN STANDS A MAHOGANY SIDEBOARD. A DOOR LEADING TO THE
BULL II SD(101) ON WHICH HER FATE HANGS JUST AT PRESENT. KEEGAN TOUCHES HIS HAT TO HER: HE DOES NOT TAKE IT OFF.
BULL II (102) O WATER TO LOOK AT. (THE GRASSHOPPER CHIRPS: KEEGAN TURNS HIS HEAD AND ADDRESSES IT IN THE VERNACULAR).
BULL IV (172) OF IT, AS YOU MAY IMAGINE, POOR NORA! WELL, MR KEEGAN , AS I SAID, I BEGIN TO SEE MY WAY HERE. I BEGIN TO
BULL IV (180) IN EITHER CASE IT WOULD BE AN IMPERTINENCE, MR KEEGAN , AS YOUR APPROVAL IS NOT OF THE SLIGHTEST
BULL IV (175) SOUND LIBERAL PRINCIPLES. YOU AGREE WITH ME, MR KEEGAN , DONT YOU? /KEEGAN/ SIR: I MAY EVEN VOTE FOR YOU.
BULL IV (180) THE CHURCH OF ENGLAND CONTAINED A FEW MEN LIKE MR KEEGAN , I SHOULD CERTAINLY JOIN IT. /KEEGAN/ YOU DO ME TOO
BULL IV SD(151) TO PARLIAMENTARY CANDIDATES. NORA, AUNT JUDY, KEEGAN , LARRY, AND CORNELIUS ARE LEFT IN THE PARLOR. LARRY
BULL IV (173) THE INTEREST. /BROADBENT/ AH, YOU ARE A POET, MR KEEGAN , NOT A MAN OF BUSINESS. /LARRY/ WE WILL LEND
BULL IV (178) WILL COME. /BROADBENT/ (SERIOUSLY) TOO TRUE, MR KEEGAN , ONLY TOO TRUE. AND MOST ELOQUENTLY PUT. IT REMINDS
BULL II (100) TALK TO ME AND PRAY FOR ME BY THE NAME OF PETHER KEEGAN , SO YOU WILL. AND WHEN YOURE ANGRY AND TEMPTED TO
BULL IV SD(145) FROM THE GARDEN, IS IN THE MIDDLE; AND AT IT SETS KEEGAN , THE CENTRAL FIGURE IN A RATHER CROWDED APARTMENT.
BULL II (98) MURDHER! (BESIDE HIMSELF, CALLING) FADHER KEEGAN ! FADHER KEEGAN! /THE MAN/ (TURNING) WHO'S THERE?
BULL II (98) (BESIDE HIMSELF, CALLING) FADHER KEEGAN! FADHER KEEGAN ! /THE MAN/ (TURNING) WHO'S THERE? WHATS THAT? (

KEEGAN'S

BULL II (100) GRASSHOPPER, REMEMBER THAT THE DONKEY'S PETHER KEEGAN'S BROTHER, AND THE GRASSHOPPER PETER KEEGAN'S FRIEND.
BULL IV SD(168) BUT THIS TIME HE ENJOYS NEITHER THE STIMULUS OF KEEGAN'S CONVERSATION NOR THE PLEASURE OF TERRIFYING PATSY
BULL II (100) KEEGAN'S BROTHER, AND THE GRASSHOPPER PETER KEEGAN'S FRIEND. AND WHEN YOURE TEMPTED TO THROW A STONE AT
BULL II (101) GRASSHOPPER CHIRPS. PATSY, TERRIFIED, CLUTCHES AT KEEGAN'S HANDS) DONT SET IT ON ME, FADHER: I'LL DO ANYTHIN
BULL IV SD(145) THE WALL, ONE AT EACH END OF THE SIDEBOARD. KEEGAN'S HAT IS ON THE ONE NEAREST THE INNER DOOR; AND HIS
BULL IV (148) SAVIN YOUR PRESENCE, MISS REILLY, AND MISTHER KEEGAN'S . DHERE! I WONT SAY ANUDDHER WORD. /NORA/ I'M
BULL IV (153) MAKING AN ASS OF YOURSELF. YOU DONT UNDERSTAND MR KEEGAN'S PECULIAR VEIN OF HUMOR. /BROADBENT/ (INSTANTLY
BULL IV (179) /BROADBENT/ (COMING DOWN THE HILL AGAIN TO KEEGAN'S RIGHT HAND) BUT YOU KNOW, SOMETHING MUST BE DONE.
BULL IV (180) AWAY UP THE HILL, BUT PRESENTLY STROLLS BACK ON KEEGAN'S RIGHT. BROADBENT ADDS, CONFIDENTIALLY TO KEEGAN)
BULL IV SD(145) WITH HER FEET ON THE FENDER. A LITTLE TO KEEGAN'S RIGHT, IN FRONT OF THE TABLE, AND ALMOST SITTING ON
BULL IV (157) AND SHUTS UP THE BACKGAMMON BOARD. /AUNT JUDY/ KEEGAN'S VERY QUEER TODAY. HE HAS HIS MAD FIT ON HIM.

KEEL

HART I (81) DEAR; BUT THAT WAS FOR THE SHIP WITH THE MAGNETIC KEEL THAT SUCKED UP SUBMARINES. LIVING AT THE RATE WE DO,

KEELING

HART PREFACE(18) A CLASS, OUR MOST EFFICIENT SOLDIERS (FREDERICK KEELING , FOR EXAMPLE), WERE NOT DUPED FOR A MOMENT BY THE

KEEN

NEVR II (238) OF IT GOES THROUGH THE FATHER WITH SO KEEN A PANG THAT HE TREMBLES ALL OVER; HIS BROW BECOMES WET;
BULL IV (166) HE LIKES EM SOLID AND BOUNCING AND RATHER KEEN ABOUT HIM. IT'S A VERY CONVENIENT DIFFERENCE; FOR WEVE
POSN PREFACE(369) MEMBER, SON OF AN IRISH CHANCELLOR, PRESENTING A KEEN AND JOYOUS FRONT TO ENGLISH INTELLECTUAL SLOTH. ABOVE
CLEO IV SD(166) TWISTED AND HORNED AT THE ENDS, AND A CONSCIOUSLY KEEN AND PRETENTIOUS EXPRESSION, IS SQUATTING ON THE FLOOR
LION I (118) AND A THICK NECK: A MAN WHOSE SENSIBILITIES ARE KEEN AND VIOLENT TO THE VERGE OF MADNESS. SPINTHO IS A
CATH PREFACE(158) WHO HAS ANY FEELING OF HIS BUSINESS THERE IS A KEEN AND WHIMSICAL JOY IN DIVINING AND REVEALING A SIDE OF
SUPR I SD(46) MAKES A FRANTIC DEMONSTRATION; BUT VIOLET'S COOL KEEN ANGER EXTINGUISHES IT. /VIOLET/ YOU! OH, HOW
PLES PREFACE(R12) A PUBLIC-SPIRITED MANAGER, OR AN AUTHOR WITH A KEEN ARTISTIC CONSCIENCE, MAY CHOOSE TO PURSUE HIS BUSINESS
DEST SD(149) THEM ALL IN HIS BOYHOOD, AND NOW, HAVING A KEEN DRAMATIC FACULTY, IS EXTREMELY CLEVER AT PLAYING UPON
3PLA PREFACE(R32) TO NATURE, OF THE FAITHLESS WILL AND THE KEEN EYES THAT THE FAITHLESS WILL IS TOO WEAK TO BLIND: ALL
2TRU III (110) WHICH MAY BE A BREATH OF LIFE, BUT OF A LIFE TOO KEEN FOR ME TO BEAR, AND THEREFORE FOR ME A BLAST OF DEATH.
BUOY IV (50) BILLIONS WILL STOP WHEN I DIE. WOULD YOU BE AS KEEN IF THERE WERE NO BILLIONS? /JUNIUS/ JUST AS KEEN. HOW
ARMS II SD(23) MAN OF COOL TEMPERAMENT AND LOW BUT CLEAR AND KEEN INTELLIGENCE, WITH THE COMPLACENCY OF THE SERVANT WHO
LADY PREFACE(209) UP THE PESSIMISM OF SHAKESPEAR AND SWIFT WITH KEEN INTEREST. HE DELIGHTED IN A HIDEOUS CONCEPTION WHICH HE
BUOY IV (50) KEEN IF THERE WERE NO BILLIONS? /JUNIUS/ JUST AS KEEN . HOW OFTEN MUST I TELL YOU THAT I AM MAD ABOUT HER?
SIM II (58) HAVE LOST FAITH IN US; BUT YOUR WITS ARE STILL KEEN . /MAYA/ PRAI WE BESEECH THEE. ABOLISH THE INCUBUS.
METH PREFACE(R13) BE DONE IN A LIFETIME BY EXTRAORDINARY ABILITY, KEEN NATURAL APTITUDE, EXCEPTIONAL OPPORTUNITIES, AND
MIS. (136) MADE AN ENORMOUS PILE IN BUSINESS WITHOUT BEING KEEN ON MONEY, YOULL FIND THAT THEY ALL HAVE A SLATE OFF.
HART II (87) IS THE SOUL OF GOODNESS-- AND SHE IS NOT AT ALL KEEN ON MY DOING THE SAME. /MANGAN/ ANYHOW, YOU DONT WANT TO
ARMS II (31) SERBIAN ARMY? /PETKOFF/ A VOLUNTEER, OF COURSE: KEEN ON PICKING UP HIS PROFESSION. (CHUCKLING) WE SHOULDNT
DOCT I (100) BUT, MY DEAR BLENKINSOP, YOU USED TO BE RATHER KEEN ON SCIENCE. /BLENKINSOP/ AH, I USED TO BE A LOT OF
METH PREFACE(R21) IN THE EIGHTEENTH CENTURY NATURALISTS WERE VERY KEEN ON THE INFUSORIAN AMOEBAS, AND WERE MUCH STRUCK BY THE
LADY PREFACE(210) OR OTHER, NO DOUBT FINDING THAT PEOPLE WHO WERE KEEN ON THIS SORT OF CONVERSATION WERE RATHER SCARCE. HE
BULL IV (163) AT ALL (SHE TURNS HER FACE AWAY WITH A KEEN PANG OF SHAME AND ADDS) NO MORE THAN MYSELF.
CAPT NOTES (300) AS A LEGISLATOR MAY BE TAKEN AS PROVED BY THE KEEN PHILOSOPHY OF THE TRAVELS AND TALES HE HAS SINCE TOSSED
MTH4 I (169) INDEED? PRAY, MAY I ASK WHAT IT IS? I AM A KEEN POLITICIAN, AND MAY PERHAPS BE OF SOME USE. (HE PUTS
GETT (269) HOUSE, AND TO HAVE IT TO MYSELF. I HAVE A VERY KEEN SENSE OF BEAUTY AND FITNESS AND CLEANLINESS AND ORDER.
DOCT PREFACE(7) MUST ACQUIT THE PRISONER. THUS A JUDGE WITH A KEEN SENSE OF LAW (A VERY RARE PHENOMENON ON THE BENCH, BY
BULL PREFACE(16) THE IRISH MASSES. OUR DELICACY IS PART OF A KEEN SENSE OF REALITY WHICH MAKES US A VERY PRACTICAL, AND
LADY PREFACE(223) OF A DOZEN PASSAGES IN WHICH HE (POSSIBLY WITH A KEEN SENSE OF THE FUN OF SCANDALIZING THE MODEST COUGHERS)
PHIL III SD(147) AWE, FEELING FOR THE FIRST TIME THE PRESENCE OF A KEEN SORROW.
ARMS II SD(20) HIS JEALOUSLY OBSERVANT EYE; HIS NOSE, THIN, KEEN , AND APPREHENSIVE IN SPITE OF THE PUGNACIOUS HIGH
DEVL I SD(7) MAN TOO, WITH A THICK SANGUINE NECK; AND HIS KEEN , CHEERFUL MOUTH CUTS INTO SOMEWHAT FLESHY CORNERS. NO
DEST SD(161) IN THE NOSTRILS, CHARACTER IN THE CHIN: ALL KEEN , REFINED, AND ORIGINAL. SHE IS VERY FEMININE, BUT BY
CAPT III SD(279) IS A ROBUSTLY BUILT WESTERN AMERICAN, WITH THE KEEN , SQUEEZED, WIND BEATEN EYES AND OBSTINATELY ENDURING

KEENER

AUGS (274) SO STRONG AN ANTI-GERMAN FEELING. LIFE AFFORDS NO KEENER PLEASURE THAN FINDING A BROTHER-IN-LAW'S NAME IN THE

KEENEST

LION PREFACE(40) HAVE HAD TO CONFESS TO THE JEWS, WHO WERE THE KEENEST CRITICS OF THE CHRISTIANS, THAT JESUS WAS EITHER AN
SUPR HANDBOK(224) INTOLERABLE PAIN IS PRODUCED BY PROLONGING THE KEENEST PLEASURE. THE MAN WITH TOOTHACHE THINKS EVERYONE

KEENLY

CLEO I (112) HIM. THEY COME DOWN THE CORRIDOR, CAESAR PEERING KEENLY ABOUT AT THE STRANGE ARCHITECTURE, AND AT THE PILLAR
FANY III (321) SUSPICIOUSLY. MRS KNOX BOWS GRAVELY, LOOKING KEENLY AT DORA AND TAKING HER MEASURE WITHOUT PREJUDICE).
BARB II SD(290) UNDERSHAFT, SEATED ON A FORM, AND STILL KEENLY ATTENTIVE, LOOKS HARD AT ADOLPHUS. ADOLPHUS LOOKS
GETT PREFACE(230) AND THRUST HIM INTO PRISON, HE SUDDENLY BECOMES KEENLY CRITICAL OF THEM, AND OF THE ARGUMENTS BY WHICH THEY
GETT PREFACE(223) BUT TO TAKE A VITAL PROCESS IN WHICH WE ARE KEENLY INTERESTED PERSONAL INSTRUMENTS AND ASK US TO REGARD
BULL I (93) I'D RATHER. NORA HAS A FORTUNE. /BROADBENT/ (KEENLY INTERESTED) EH? HOW MUCH? /DOYLE/ FORTY PER ANNUM.
CAND II (107) TABLE AND SITS ON THE SOFA. HER FEELINGS ARE KEENLY STIRRED). IT'S NO BUSINESS OF YOURS WHETHER MY HEART
SUPR III (117) MY MISTRESS NEVER SAW EVERY BLEMISH IN HER MORE KEENLY THAN I. I WAS NOT DUPED: I TOOK HER WITHOUT
ROCK PREFACE(180) CRITIC TO BOOT, I FELT THE DISAPPOINTMENT SO KEENLY THAT I HAVE BEEN EVER SINCE IN THE CONDITION OF THE
PYGM EPILOG (297) WAY OUT DAWNS ON THEM) SHE FELT THEIR EFFECTS TOO KEENLY TO BE SATISFIED WITH HER POSITION. CLARA HAD A
CLEO IV (171) (EXULTANT) AHA! /POTHINUS/ (RAISING HIS EYES KEENLY TO HERS) IS CLEOPATRA THEN INDEED A QUEEN, AND NO
DEVL III (58) PUBLIC) NO, SIR: I FEEL MY OWN DEFICIENCIES TOO KEENLY TO PRESUME SO FAR. IF YOU WILL KINDLY ALLOW ME, I
CAPT III (280) /KEARNEY/ WE OFTEN FEEL THAT DEPRIVATION VERRY KEENLY , LADY WAYNFLETE. /LADY CICELY/ MY UNCLE IS FIRST
DEVL III (64) /RICHARD/ (INDIGNANTLY) SHAME! /BURGOYNE/ (KEENLY , WITH A HALF SMILE) IF YOU ARE NOT HER HUSBAND, SIR,

KEENNESS

CLEO II SD(118) REST OF HIS FACE. HE MAINTAINS AN AIR OF MAGPIE KEENNESS AND PROFUNDITY, LISTENING TO WHAT THE OTHERS SAY
BULL PREFACE(19) GENIUS, INSTEAD OF PRODUCING INTELLECTUAL KEENNESS AND SCRUPULOUSNESS, PRODUCED MERE DELIRIUM. HE WAS
BULL PREFACE(22) PEG-AWAY INDUSTRY, PERSONAL AMBITION, AND PARTY KEENNESS . ENGLISH STUPIDITY EXCUSED. I DO NOT CLAIM IT AS A

KEEP

HART II (116) KNOW BETTER. A SOUL IS A VERY EXPENSIVE THING TO KEEP : MUCH MORE SO THAN A MOTOR CAR. /CAPTAIN SHOTOVER/ IS
CAND II (113) YES? /MORELL/ HOW MANY SERVANTS DOES YOUR FATHER KEEP ? /MARCHBANKS/ (PETTISHLY) OH, I DONT KNOW. (HE
O'FL (219) TELL ME THEY KNOCKED TEN SHILLINGS OFF YOU FOR MY KEEP ? /MRS O'FLAHERTY/ (SOOTHING HIM) NO, DARLINT: THEY
FABL IV (114) WHAT I AM GOING TO DICTATE IS FOR THE PRINTER; SO KEEP A CARBON COPY. IT IS FOR THE NEW EDITION OF MY BOOK ON
MIS. PREFACE(95) NATURAL SELECTION; AND IT WOULD BE AS ABSURD TO KEEP A CHILD IN DELUSIVE IGNORANCE OF SO POTENT A FACTOR IN
ARMS III (72) BUT WHO WANTS TWENTY HORSES? WE'RE NOT GOING TO KEEP A CIRCUS. /CATHERINE/ (SEVERELY) MY DAUGHTER, SIR, IS
MIS. (113) /JOHNNY/ (STUNG INTO SUDDEN VIOLENCE) NOW YOU KEEP A CIVIL TONGUE IN YOUR HEAD. I'LL STAND NONE OF YOUR

2TRU II (73)	TALK, TALK-- /THE COUNTESS/ (HALF RISING) YOU	KEEP	A CIVIL TONGUE IN YOUR HEAD: DO YOU HEAR? /THE
2TRU II (68)	SWEETIE. SWEETIE IS BALAAM'S ASS. /THE COUNTESS/	KEEP	A CIVIL TONGUE IN YOUR HEAD, POPSY. I-- /AUBREY/ (
DEVL I (13)	HER. /MRS DUDGEON/ (THREATENINGLY) YOUD BETTER	KEEP	A CIVIL TONGUE IN YOUR HEAD. (HE GOES SULKILY TOWARDS
MTH5 (239)	MALE FIGURE/ (GLARING) HA! /THE FEMALE FIGURE/	KEEP	A CIVIL TONGUE IN YOUR HEAD, YOU. /THE NEWLY BORN/ OH,
MILL II (171)	NOT YOUR DOCTOR: I AM NOT IN GENERAL PRACTICE. I	KEEP	A CLINIC FOR PENNILESS MAHOMETAN REFUGEES; AND I WORK
2TRU I (28)	DOSE OF THE LATEST FASHIONABLE OPIATE THAT WOULD	KEEP	A COCK ASLEEP TIL HALF PAST ELEVEN ON A MAY MORNING.
GENV III (68)	BE INTERNATIONAL STATESMEN; BUT NONE OF YOU COULD	KEEP	A COFFEE STALL AT LIMEHOUSE BECAUSE YOU WOULD HAVE TO
JITT III (55)	HOUSE WHERE HIS WIFE AND DAUGHTER ARE. HE HAS TO	KEEP	A CONSULTING ROOM SOMEWHERE WHERE THEY CAN COME. THE
SIM PREFACE(17)	HAVING MY HEAD SHOT OFF." THE REPLY " YOU MUST	KEEP	A CREDIT BALANCE ALWAYS AT THE NATIONAL BANK" IS
POSN PREFACE(410)	BUT ON THE LEAST ATTEMPT ON HIS PART TO	KEEP	A DISORDERLY HOUSE UNDER COVER OF OPENING A THEATRE HE
DOCT PREFACE(18)	ON MAKING THEMSELVES LOVELY THAN WOULD SUFFICE TO	KEEP	A DOZEN UGLY WOMEN HONEST; AND THIS ENABLES THEM TO
WIDO I (16)	SYMPATHETICALLY) QUITE SO. MAY I DEPEND ON YOU TO	KEEP	A FAIR DISTANCE, AND SO SPARE ME THE NECESSITY OF
GENV I (42)	I AM THE ONLY BISHOP IN ENGLAND WHO CAN AFFORD TO	KEEP	A FOOTMAN NOW-- THAT MY FOOTMAN IS A CELL. /HE/ A
APPL INTRLUD(249)	I THOUGHT SO. /ORINTHIA/ OH, STUPID! STUPID! GO	KEEP	A GROCER'S SHOP: THAT IS WHAT YOU ARE FIT FOR. DO YOU
MTH1 II (28)	YOUR TONGUE BE ACCURST FOR SUCH BLASPHEMY! /EVE/	KEEP	A GUARD ON YOUR OWN TONGUE; AND DO NOT CURSE MY SON. IT
WIDO II (32)	LIKE TO KNOW? ME THAT WRINGS THE MONEY OUT TO	KEEP	A HOME OVER MY CHILDREN, OR YOU THAT SPEND IT AND TRY
BUOY III (46)	WHAT ALL INDEPENDENT WOMEN DO WITH THEIR MEANS.	KEEP	A HUSBAND ON THEM. /MRS SECONDBORN/ IS A HUSBAND A DOG
MIS. (160)	(PROMPTLY) FIFTY-EIGHT. /LINA/ THANK YOU. I	KEEP	A LIST OF ALL MY OFFERS. I LIKE TO KNOW WHAT I'M
NEVR I (212)	AS YOURS. /DOLLY/ BESIDES, IT CANT BE GOOD TO	KEEP	A LOT OF QUESTIONS BOTTLED UP INSIDE YOU. YOU DID IT,
APPL I (219)	HIS MIND TO POLITICS AS LONG AS HE CAN AFFORD TO	KEEP	A MOTOR CAR? /NICOBAR/ HOW MANY VOTED AT THE LAST
ROCK PREFACE(190)	THAT A SOCIALIST COULD NOT CONSISTENTLY	KEEP	A MOTOR CAR, ALMOST SUCCEEDED IN MAKING A PUBLIC
BULL PREFACE(17)	BEING GENERALLY STRAITENED BY AN ATTEMPT TO	KEEP	A PARK AND A STABLE ON AN INCOME WHICH WOULD NOT
MILL I (140)	HAVE SO MANY CLIENTS DRIVEN TO DESPAIR THAT YOU	KEEP	A PRESCRIPTION FOR THEM? /SAGAMORE/ I DO. IT'S
NEVR II (235)	IS IT? /PHILIP/ I DONT KNOW. FINCH: DOES HE	KEEP	A PUBLIC HOUSE? /M'COMAS/ (RISING, SCANDALIZED) NO,
MRS III (230)	LET OUT THE WORD HOTEL AND EVERYBODY SAYS YOU	KEEP	A PUBLIC-HOUSE. YOU WOULDNT LIKE PEOPLE TO SAY THAT OF
HART I (56)	HAD SOME CAPITAL. HE FOUGHT HIS WAY ALONG, TO	KEEP	A ROOF OVER OUR HEADS AND BRING US UP WELL; BUT IT WAS
CAND III (142)	AND SUSPICIONS. I WILL NOT LIVE WITH YOU AND	KEEP	A SECRET FROM YOU. I WILL NOT SUFFER THE INTOLERABLE
CAND II (113)	/BURGESS/ (WITH GRAVE DISAPPROVAL) DONT YOU	KEEP	A SERVANT NOW, JAMES? /MORELL/ YES; BUT SHE ISNT A
MIS. (134)	ALL THAT THE CIRCUMSTANCES THAT CONDEMNED ME TO	KEEP	A SHOP ARE THE BIGGEST TRAGEDY IN MODERN LIFE. I OUGHT
CLEO III (145)	OF FOLLOWING ARMS! /APOLLODORUS/ I DO NOT	KEEP	A SHOP. MINE IS A TEMPLE OF THE ARTS. I AM A WORSHIPPER
PPP (202)	I HAVE ALWAYS PRETENDED NOT TO NOTICE IT; BUT YOU	KEEP	A SIPHON FOR YOUR PRIVATE USE IN MY HAT-BOX. /MAGNESIA/
PYGM EPILOG (301)	COLONEL, WHO HAD BEEN COMPELLED FOR SOME YEARS TO	KEEP	A SUFFICIENT SUM ON CURRENT ACCOUNT AT HIS BANKERS TO
HART III (133)	PEOPLE LIKE MISS DUNN'S FATHER TO WORK THEM, AND	KEEP	A TIGHT HAND SO AS TO MAKE THEM PAY. OF COURSE I MAKE
MRS PREFACE(178)	LARGE, WHICH WILL FINALLY DECIDE THE MATTER, TO	KEEP	A VIGILANT EYE ON GENTLEMEN WHO WILL STAND ANYTHING AT
NEVR II (248)	ACRID CONTEMPT) RUBBISH, MAN! WHAT HAVE YOU TO	KEEP	A WIFE ON? YOU CANT MARRY HER. /VALENTINE/ WHO WANTS
VWOO 3 (136)	POINT? /Z/ WELL, THAT IT'S REALLY CHEAPER TO	KEEP	A WIFE THAN TO PAY AN ASSISTANT, LET ALONE THAT YOU
MTH4 II (185)	RACE OF ARMAMENTS IN PRINCIPLE; STILL, WE MUST	KEEP	AHEAD OR BE WIPED OUT. /ZOO/ YOU CAN MAKE THE GASES FOR
DOCT V (176)	NOT KILL, BUT NEEDST NOT STRIVE OFFICIOUSLY TO	KEEP	ALIVE. I SUPPOSE-- YES: I KILLED HIM. /JENNIFER/ AND
MIS. PREFACE(4)	OF INDUCING HIM TO MAKE A SERIOUS EFFORT TO	KEEP	ALIVE. THE MOMENT HE SEES DEATH APPROACH, HE GETS INTO
APPL II (263)	THE OLD ENGLISH NOTIONS WHICH OUR TOURISTS TRY TO	KEEP	ALIVE. WHEN YOU FIND SOME COUNTRY GENTLEMAN KEEPING UP
PYGM PREFACE(202)	RELATIONS WITH THE MEN WHO UNDERRATE IT, AND WHO	KEEP	ALL THE BEST PLACES FOR LESS IMPORTANT SUBJECTS WHICH
ROCK II (238)	LUMP IT. /SIR DEXTER/ YOU REALLY BELIEVE HE CAN	KEEP	ALL THE MONSTROUS PROMISES HE HAS MADE? /BASHAM/ NO:
SUPR IV (148)	IN ENGLAND. ONE HISTORIC OWNER CANT AFFORD TO	KEEP	ALL THE ROOMS DUSTED: THE OTHER CANT AFFORD THE DEATH
POSN (465)	AS A BAD MAN. SO LET BROTHER DANIELS MARRY US TO	KEEP	ALL THE ROTTENNESS IN THE FAMILY. WHAT DO YOU SAY,
BARB II (303)	/MRS BAINES/ I HOPE WE SHALL HAVE ENOUGH TO	KEEP	ALL THE SHELTERS OPEN. LORD SAXMUNDHAM HAS PROMISED US
GETT PREFACE(222)	MEN CAN BE LED TO COMPROMIZE THEMSELVES; AND TO	KEEP	ALL THE SKELETONS CAREFULLY LOCKED UP IN THE FAMILY
ROCK II (247)	THEIR OWN TIME AND YOUR LABOR. /BLEE/ WE KNOW.	KEEP	ALL THE SOFT JOBS FOR YOUR LOT AND THE HARD ONES FOR
SUPR I (34)	JUST THEN THAT I GOT SOMETHING THAT I WANTED TO	KEEP	ALL TO MYSELF INSTEAD OF SHARING IT WITH YOU. /ANN/ I
GENV III (66)	IT FOR YOU. I HAD NO IDEA IT WAS HEAVY. DO YOU	KEEP	ALL YOUR MONEY IN IT? /THE WIDOW/ MONEY! NO: IT IS
DOCT III (131)	BUT IT'S SO SORDID, DEAREST. I HATE MONEY. I CANT	KEEP	ALWAYS BOTHERING YOU FOR MONEY, MONEY, MONEY. THATS
FABL PREFACE(93)	ALL EVENTS THAT DO NOT MATTER. WERE I TO	KEEP	ALWAYS IN MIND EVERY EXPERIENCE OF MY 93 YEARS LIVING
LION EPILOG (147)	AND THEREFORE HATED BY THE HAVE-AND-HOLDERS, WHO	KEEP	ALWAYS IN RESERVE TWO SURE WEAPONS AGAINST THEM. THE
DOCT IV (165)	DEAR. ONLY ONE OF THOSE LITTLE SECRETS THAT MEN	KEEP	AMONG THEMSELVES. WELL, ALL YOU CHAPS HAVE THOUGHT
HART PREFACE(6)	OF THE MEDIEVAL ROBBER BARON, IT QUALIFIES MEN TO	KEEP	AN ESTATE OR A BUSINESS GOING IN ITS OLD ROUTINE
GENV IV (91)	OF THAT LEAGUE, SIGNOR. /BBDE/ MY COUNTRY HAS TO	KEEP	AN EYE ON FOOLS. THE SCRIPTURE TELLS US THAT IT IS
GETT (314)	WHAT ABOUT HIS HOME? /LEO/ THE WIFE OUGHT TO	KEEP	AN EYE ON HIM, AND SEE THAT HE IS COMFORTABLE AND TAKES
BUOY III (35)	YOU KNOWS ANYTHING ABOUT MONEY; SO I HAD BETTER	KEEP	AN EYE ON YOU AND HIM. WHERE IS DADDY? /SIR F./ MR
APPL INTRLUD(253)	IN RUIN. WE TWO ALSO HAVE OUR ORBITS, AND MUST	KEEP	AN INFINITE DISTANCE BETWEEN US TO AVOID A DISASTROUS
MIS. (136)	IT TO YOURSELF IS ONLY ANOTHER METHOD. I SHOULD	KEEP	AN OPEN MIND ABOUT IT. /JOHNNY/ HAS IT EVER OCCURRED TO
JITT II SD(33)	FULLY HER LOT AS A GOOD BOURGEOISE WITH A HOME TO	KEEP	AND A FAMILY TO MANAGE ON A SLENDER INCOME THAT SHE IS
MIS. PREFACE(12)	TOO. TWO ADULT PARENTS, IN SPITE OF A HOUSE TO	KEEP	AND AN INCOME TO EARN, CAN STILL INTERFERE TO A
FABL VI (128)	PHYSICISTS AND CHEMISTS ADORE THEIR CHILDREN AND	KEEP	ANIMALS AS PETS. /YOUTH 2/ LOOK HERE, TEACHER. TALK
PHIL II (108)	/SYLVIA/ OH, THE USUAL THING. ENOUGH TO	KEEP	ANY OTHER WOMAN FROM GETTING HIM. /CHARTERIS/ JUST SO.
MILL IV (202)	KEEP MY HUSBAND, CANNOT KEEP EVEN A LOVER, CANNOT	KEEP	ANYTHING BUT MY MONEY? THERE YOU SIT BEFORE MY VERY
CURE (226)	SAID IT. /REGINALD/ (WILDLY) THEN WHY DO YOU	KEEP	ASKING ME THE SAME QUESTIONS OVER AND OVER AGAIN? IT'S
GETT (264)	TAKE HOLIDAYS FROM ONE ANOTHER IF THEY ARE TO	KEEP	AT ALL FRESH. NOT THAT I EVER GOT TIRED OF HER, MAAM;
HART II (119)	I TELL YOU IT'S DANGEROUS TO KEEP ME. I CANT	KEEP	AWAKE AND ALERT. /ELLIE/ WHAT DO YOU RUN AWAY FOR? TO
METH PREFACE(R13)	AT WORK ALL DAY EARNING A LIVING THAT HE CANNOT	KEEP	AWAKE FOR FIVE MINUTES OVER A BOOK? IS THERE ANY HOPE
ARMS I (21)	I? THATS WHAT I WANT TO KNOW: WHERE AM I? MUST	KEEP	AWAKE. NOTHING KEEPS ME AWAKE EXCEPT DANGER: REMEMBER
PLES PREFACE(R17)	MARCHING TUNE ON THE GERMAN CONCERTINA. THEY MUST	KEEP	AWAY FROM MY PLAYS: THAT IS ALL. THERE IS NO REASON,
DOCT I (106)	EXPEDIENTS, OF COURSE; BUT AS TREATMENT, NO, NO.	KEEP	AWAY FROM THE CHEMIST'S SHOP, MY DEAR RIDGEON, WHATEVER
ARMS I (18)	(DECISIVELY) NOW DO WHAT I TELL SHUTTERS. AND	KEEP	AWAY FROM THE WINDOW, WHATEVER YOU DO. IF THEY SEE ME
KING PREFACE(154)	FOUNDATION OF THE GREAT CULT OF FRIENDSHIP SHOULD	KEEP	AWAY FROM THEATRES AND FREQUENT WORSE PLACES. STILL,
MTH5 (239)	ART, ARJILLAX? /STREPHON/ THEY LOOK DANGEROUS.	KEEP	AWAY FROM THEM. /ECRASIA/ NO NEED TO TELL US THAT,
SUPR IV (159)	BE WHAT I AM IN THAT RESPECT. /ANN/ THEN YOU MUST	KEEP	AWAY FROM THEM, AND ONLY DREAM ABOUT THEM. I WOULDNT
GENV IV (105)	IS EVER SATISFIED. ENOUGH. YOU HAVE YOUR WARNING.	KEEP	AWAY; AND YOU WILL BE NEITHER BEATEN NOR ROBBED. KEEP
GENV IV (105)	AWAY; AND YOU WILL BE NEITHER BEATEN NOR ROBBED.	KEEP	AWAY, I TELL YOU. THE WORLD IS WIDE ENOUGH FOR BOTH OF
GETT (268)	(SHE RISES AND GOES TO THE CHAIR ON THE HEARTH)	KEEP	AWAY, YOU WRETCH. /THE GENERAL/ BUT FOR THAT PIPE, I
CAND I (103)	ME, AND KNOW THAT I UNDERSTAND HER. IF YOU	KEEP	BACK ONE WORD OF IT FROM HER-- IF YOU ARE NOT READY TO
BASH III (121)	BASHVILLE, CONSTABLES, AND OTHERS. /POLICEMAN/	KEEP	BACK YOUR BRUISED PRISONER LEST HE SHOCK THIS WELLBRED
CLEO PRO2 (102)	FROM THE SPEARS, SCREAMING TO THOSE BEHIND TO	KEEP	BACK. BELZANOR'S VOICE DOMINATES THE DISTURBANCE AS HE
POSN (456)	CHUCK HIM OUT. SILENCE. YOU CANT COME IN HERE.	KEEP	BACK. STRAPPER RUSHES TO THE DOOR AND FORCES HIS WAY
CLEO PRO2 (102)	COME, COME. SPEAK TO BELZANOR. /A WOMAN/ OH,	KEEP	BACK. YOU ARE THRUSTING ME ON THE SPEARHEADS. A HUGE
CLEO III (161)	/RUFIO/ (DRAWING HIS SWORD) HA, TREACHERY!	KEEP	BACK, CAESAR: I SAW THE SHAWL MOVE: THERE IS SOMETHING
GENV IV (120)	IN IT ON CONDITION THAT THEY WORK LIKE BEES AND	KEEP	BARELY ENOUGH OF THE HONEY TO KEEP THEMSELVES MISERABLY
DOCT PREFACE(41)	THEIR DUTIES WITH RELIEF TO HUNT, TO GARDEN, TO	KEEP	BEES, TO GO INTO SOCIETY, AND THE LIKE. IN THE SAME WAY
LION II (144)	GROWLING. THE EMPEROR CLUTCHES ANDROCLES).	KEEP	BETWEEN US. /ANDROCLES/ NEVER BE AFRAID OF ANIMALS,
CAND I (87)	WAGES WOULD HAVE DRIVEN THEM TO THE STREETS TO	KEEP	BODY AND SOUL TOGETHER. (GETTING ANGRIER AND ANGRIER)
WIDO II (40)	UNFORTUNATE CREATURES THAT HAVE HARDLY ENOUGH TO	KEEP	BODY AND SOUL TOGETHER-- MADE BY SCREWING, AND
MRS PREFACE(151)	OF THEM ARE FORCED TO RESORT TO PROSTITUTION TO	KEEP	BODY AND SOUL TOGETHER. INDEED ALL ATTRACTIVE
BULL IV (180)	AND FINE WORDS ARE CHEAP IN IRELAND: YOU CAN	KEEP	BOTH FOR MY FRIEND HERE, WHO IS STILL IMPOSED ON BY
2TRU II (65)	AND THE ONLY WAY TO MAKE SURE OF THAT IS TO	KEEP	CHANGING THE MAN; FOR THE SAME MAN CAN NEVER KEEP IT
MIS. PREFACE(24)	ALL ABOUT THESE WONDERFUL SCHOOLS THAT YOU CANNOT	KEEP	CHILDREN OR EVEN ADULTS OUT OF, AND THESE TEACHERS WHOM
MIS. PREFACE(26)	PERSON THAT THE OBJECT OF THE LESSONS IS TO	KEEP	CHILDREN OUT OF MISCHIEF, AND NOT TO QUALIFY THEM FOR
BULL I (90)	/DOYLE/ (INTERRUPTING HIM) YOU MEAN THAT YOU	KEEP	CLEAR OF YOUR FATHER BECAUSE HE DIFFERS FROM YOU ABOUT
BASH III (120)	THAT PLUGGED ME IN THE EYE WHICH I PERFORCE	KEEP	CLOSING. PITY ME, MY TRAINING WASTED AND MY BLOWS
2TRU III (103)	UNDISTURBED IF VISIONS AND WANDERING THOUGHTS	KEEP	COMING BETWEEN YOU AND IT. AND A PIOUS MAN SHOULD NOT
BARB II (288)	WHY DO YOU KEEP THINKING ABOUT IT? WHY DOES IT	KEEP	COMING UP AGAINST YOU IN YOUR MIND? YOURE NOT GETTING
HART II (112)	WONT HAVE HIM THERE. DO YOU EXPECT SERVANTS TO	KEEP	COMPANY WITH THIEVES AND ALL SORTS? /CAPTAIN SHOTOVER/
BUOY PREFACE(6)	THAN ANY SOLVER OF PHYSICAL PROBLEMS, MY READERS	KEEP	COMPLAINING IN PRIVATE LETTERS AND PUBLIC CRITICISMS
SUPR HANDBOK(205)	AND CRUELTY, GLUTTONY, AND CREDULITY	KEEP	COWARDICE IN COUNTENANCE. WE CUT THE THROAT OF A CALF
MRS IV (250)	YOU KNOW ABOUT IT? I'LL NEVER MENTION IT. I'LL	KEEP	CROFTS AWAY. I'LL NOT TROUBLE YOU MUCH: YOU SEE I HAVE
MILL PREFACE(125)	THE DOMINANTS AND RECESSIVES, HAVE EXISTED AND	KEEP	CROPPING UP AS INDIVIDUALS, AND EXCITING ANTIPATHIES OR
ARMS III (50)	TREES; AND THE OFFICERS SEND FOR THEIR WIVES TO	KEEP	DISCIPLINE! (HE BEGINS TO FOLD AND DOCKET THE
GENV IV (126)	COME, OLD MAN, DONT TAKE IT SO HARD. I USED TO	KEEP	DOGS MYSELF; BUT I HAD TO GIVE IT UP: I COULDNT BEAR
GENV IV (102)	AND WHAT I SAY IS THAT WAR IS NECESSARY TO	KEEP	DOWN THE POPULATION. /BBDE/ THIS MAN IS A FOOL. WAR
ROCK II (278)	WHEREVER I WENT I ROSE BECAUSE I COULDNT	KEEP	DOWN. BUT I AM PROLETARIAN, BONE AND BLOOD, IF THATS

ROCK II (261)	AGAINST HIM, THEN TWENTY THOUSAND CONSTABLES CAN	KEEP	EIGHT MILLION CITIZENS IN ORDER. BUT IF THE CITIZENS
DEVL III (71)	NOISILY AWAY, SHOUTING) NOW THEN, DRESS UP AND	KEEP	EM BACK, WILL YOU. CRIES OF HUSH AND SILENCE ARE HEARD
GETT PREFACE(252)	OR OURSELVES FROM THEM. AND ALL THE TIME WE SHALL	KEEP	ENTHUSIASTICALLY INVESTING HER TRADE WITH EVERY
MILL IV (202)	A MILLIONAIRESS, CANNOT KEEP MY HUSBAND, CANNOT	KEEP	EVEN A LOVER, CANNOT KEEP ANYTHING BUT MY MONEY? THERE
MILL IV (199)	I AM CANNOT AFFORD ANYTHING. I HAVE TO FIGHT TO	KEEP	EVERY PENNY I POSSESS, EVERY BEGGAR, EVERY BLACKMAILER,
DEVL III (55)	YOU BE SILENT? /JUDITH/ YES. /RICHARD/ YOU WILL	KEEP	FAITH? /JUDITH/ I WILL KEEP-- (SHE BREAKS DOWN,
FANY II (286)	OFF IT. /KNOX/ (RISING RESTLESSLY) I CANT. I	KEEP	FANCYING EVERYBODY KNOWS IT AND IS SNIGGERING ABOUT IT.
HART PREFACE(6)	AS BOND STREET TRADESMEN AND DOMESTIC SERVANTS	KEEP	FASHIONABLE SOCIETY GOING WITHOUT ANY INSTRUCTION IN
METH PREFACE(R15)	IDLENESS AND LUXURY, LEARNS TO SHOOT AND RIDE AND	KEEP	FIT WITH ALL THE ASSISTANCE AND GUIDANCE THAT CAN BE
FOUN (215)	THAT REFERS TO MY PRIVATE HOUSE, MADAM. I DONT	KEEP	FOOD HERE. /MERCER/ I HAVE A SANDWICH FOR MY LUNCH,
BARB I (252)	AS LONG AS WE ARE IN THE SAME HOUSE; BUT I CANT	KEEP	FOUR FAMILIES IN FOUR SEPARATE HOUSES. YOU KNOW HOW
MTH4 I (172)	APPETITIES AND SUPERSTITIONS, OR IS UNABLE TO	KEEP	FREE FROM PAIN AND DEPRESSION, HE NATURALLY BECOMES
JOAN 6 (145)	HILLS; TO MAKE ME BREATHE FOUL DAMP DARKNESS, AND	KEEP	FROM ME EVERYTHING THAT BRINGS ME BACK TO THE LOVE OF
DEVL I (9)	SHALL BE PUNISHED. WHY SHOULD WE DO OUR DUTY AND	KEEP	GOD'S LAW IF THERE IS TO BE NO DIFFERENCE MADE BETWEEN
JOAN 2 (86)	THAT THE LAND IS THINE TO RULE RIGHTEOUSLY AND	KEEP	GOD'S PEACE IN, AND NOT TO PLEDGE AT THE PAWNSHOP AS A
HART PREFACE(34)	AS THE MORE POPULAR PASTIMES, COULD NEVERTHELESS	KEEP	GOING IN THE HANDS OF YOUNG ADVENTURERS WHO WERE DOING
CLEO III (153)	MEN PASS THE ALARM TO THE SOUTH POSTS. ONE MAN	KEEP	GUARD HERE. THE REST WITH ME-- QUICK. THE TWO AUXILIARY
JOAN 5 (120)	NOW CAST ME OUT WOULD BE LIKE STRONG TOWERS TO	KEEP	HARM FROM ME. BUT I AM WISER NOW; AND NOBODY IS ANY THE
BARB II (297)	IF I COULD BELIEVE THAT IT WOULD ELP TO	KEEP	HATHERS STRIGHT. /BARBARA/ SO IT WILL, SNOBBY. HOW
FANY I SD(276)	AND CONFIDENTIAL THAT IT IS VERY DIFFICULT TO	KEEP	HER AT A DISTANCE BY ANY PROCESS SHORT OF FLINGING HER
DEVL III (74)	GUILTILY) I DUNNO, SIR. SHE'S THAT ARTFUL-- CANT	KEEP	HER AWAY. /BURGOYNE/ YOU WERE BRIBED. /SERGEANT/ (
FANY III (308)	I WONT STAY HERE IF SHE HAS TO HIDE. I'LL	KEEP	HER COMPANY IN THE PANTRY. (SHE FOLLOWS DORA). /BOBBY/
O'FL (222)	A FORTUNE OF TEN POUNDS? /O'FLAHERTY/ LET HER	KEEP	HER FORTUNE. I WOULDNT TOUCH HER WITH THE TONGS IF SHE
MTH2 (86)	/LUBIN/ BY THE WAY, BARNABAS, IS YOUR DAUGHTER TO	KEEP	HER GOOD LOOKS ALL THE TIME? /FRANKLYN/ WILL IT
LION PROLOG (107)	BEING ADDICTED TO ANIMALS. HOW IS ANY WOMAN TO	KEEP	HER HOUSE CLEAN WHEN YOU BRING IN EVERY STRAY CAT AND
HART II (92)	INTO SUCH A BEAST'S CLAWS JUST BECAUSE HE WILL	KEEP	HER IN AN EXPENSIVE HOUSE AND MAKE HER WEAR DIAMONDS TO
HART II (122)	HE IS ONLY TOO THANKFUL TO ANYONE WHO WILL	KEEP	HER IN GOOD HUMOUR FOR HIM. /HECTOR/ AND AS SHE HAS ALL
BUOY III (37)	AND BECAME ONLY HER MATTER-OF-FACT HUSBAND. TO	KEEP	HER IN GOOD HUMOR AND HEALTH I HAD TO INVITE AND
KING I (197)	HE WAS, I THREW CHURCHILL IN HER WAY PURPOSELY TO	KEEP	HER IN GOOD HUMOR, WHAT STRUCK ME MOST IN THE AFFAIR
PRES (160)	PLAY THE VERY DEVIL IF THE OTHER WOMEN DIDNT	KEEP	HER IN PRETTY STRICT ORDER. I DONT APPROVE OF
PYGM I (214)	WITH HER KERBSTONE ENGLISH: THE ENGLISH THAT WILL	KEEP	HER IN THE GUTTER TO THE END OF HER DAYS. WELL, SIR, IN
CLEO III SD(149)	TAXED, AS HE HAS OCCASIONALLY TO STRIKE AT HER TO	KEEP	HER OFF BETWEEN A BLOW AND A GUARD WITH APOLLODORUS.
CLEO III (149)	ENOUGH BY MYSELF IF IT WERENT FOR THE OLD WOMAN.	KEEP	HER OFF ME: THAT IS ALL THE HELP I NEED. /CENTURION/
PYGM V (276)	AS YOU WISH, LADY. ANYTHING TO HELP HENRY TO	KEEP	HER OFF MY HANDS. (HE DISAPPEARS THROUGH THE WINDOW).
MRS II (202)	AND WITHOUT EITHER A PROFESSION OR TWOPENCE TO	KEEP	HER ON. ASK SAM, IF YOU DONT BELIEVE ME. (TO THE
JOAN 1 (70)	DID SHE GET INTO MY PRESENCE? IF THE DAUPHIN CAN	KEEP	HER OUT HE IS A BETTER MAN THAN I TAKE HIM FOR. (
MTH4 III (197)	ASK YOU TO TELL THE ORACLE WHAT YOU WANT, AND NOT	KEEP	HER SITTING THERE ALL DAY. /THE ELDERLY GENTLEMAN/ (
BUOY III (37)	A SUCCESSION OF INTERESTING YOUNG MEN TO	KEEP	HER SUPPLIED WITH WHAT I CALL SUNDAY HUSBANDS. /MRS
HART PREFACE(14)	RETURN OF THE FLOOD, COULD HARDLY BE EXPECTED TO	KEEP	HER TEMPER SWEET WHEN SHE KNEW AT LAST WHAT IT WAS TO
NEVR II (258)	FIND THAT SHE MUST SPEAK SHORTLY AND POINTEDLY TO	KEEP	HER VOICE STEADY) WHY SHOULD YOU, PRAY? /VALENTINE/ OF
BULL PREFACE(27)	IT IS THE AIM OF HIS PRIEST TO MAKE HIM AND	KEEP	HIM A SUBMISSIVE CONSERVATIVE; AND NOTHING BUT GROSS
PHIL II (125)	THEN? /GRACE/ DO YOU EXPECT ME TO HELP YOU TO	KEEP	HIM AFTER THE WAY YOU HAVE BEHAVED? /JULIA/ (TRYING
MTH2 (74)	A DAY UNTIL METCHNIKOFF DIED. HE THOUGHT IT WOULD	KEEP	HIM ALIVE FOR EVER; AND HE DIED OF IT. /CONRAD/ YOU
LION PREFACE(57)	DO YOU GIVE A MAN AN INCOME FOR? OBVIOUSLY TO	KEEP	HIM ALIVE. SINCE IT IS EVIDENT THAT THE FIRST CONDITION
LION PREFACE(57)	SHALL PRODUCE AN EQUIVALENT FOR WHAT IT COSTS TO	KEEP	HIM ALIVE, WE MAY QUITE RATIONALLY COMPEL HIM TO
BUOY IV (49)	PAYING. /SHE/ IF I MARRY HIM I SHALL HAVE TO	KEEP	HIM AND MANAGE FOR HIM. BUT THAT IS NOT ALTOGETHER A
MIS. PREFACE(92)	KNOWING HOW TROUBLESOME THEY MAY BE, THAT YOU	KEEP	HIM AWAY FROM THE VENUS OF MILO ONLY TO FIND HIM IN THE
DEST (163)	HER AS A FORTIFICATION) OH, THANK YOU, GENERAL.	KEEP	HIM AWAY. /NAPOLEON/ NONSENSE, SIR. THIS IS CERTAINLY A
PHIL III (136)	(STILL CONTEMPLATING REMBRANDT) I DID MY BEST TO	KEEP	HIM FROM DISTURBING YOU, PARAMORE. /PARAMORE/ (
BULL PREFACE(45)	CALLED TOMMY LIKE A CHILD. HE HAS NO REAL WORK TO	KEEP	HIM FROM GOING MAD EXCEPT HOUSEMAID'S WORK: ALL THE
DEVL II (36)	JUDITH: WILL YOU GIVE MR DUDGEON HIS TEA, AND	KEEP	HIM HERE UNTIL I RETURN. /JUDITH/ (WHITE AND
GETT (300)	FROM THAT HORRIBLE MURDERER. THEY WOULD NOT EVEN	KEEP	HIM IMPRISONED FOR LIFE. FOR TWENTY YEARS SHE HAD TO
MRS II (208)	/MRS WARREN/ (LAUGHING HEARTILY) YOU SHOULD	KEEP	HIM IN BETTER ORDER, SAM. GOODNIGHT. HERE: TAKE GEORGE
FANY III (306)	/MARGARET/ AND NOW HE WANTS ME TO CUT YOU DEAD TO	KEEP	HIM IN COUNTENANCE. WELL, I SHANT: NOT IF MY WHOLE
CAND I (86)	WHEN I PAY A MAN, AN' 'IS LIVIN DEPENS ON ME, I	KEEP	HIM IN 'IS PLACE. /MORELL/ (RATHER SHORTLY) I ALWAYS
FABL PREFACE(82)	SEPARATELY, NOR PROVIDE A SPECIAL POLICEMAN TO	KEEP	HIM (OR HER) IN ORDER, ALL CIVILIZED PERSONS EXCEPT
NEVR I (216)	AWAY FROM HIM. I HAVE KEPT HIM OUT OF YOUR LIFE:	KEEP	HIM NOW OUT OF MINE BY NEVER MENTIONING HIM TO ME
METH PREFACE(R53)	AND MISTRUSTED THE PRIEST, WE COULD AT LEAST	KEEP	HIM OUT OF THE HOUSE; BUT WHAT OF THE MODERN DARWINIST
PYGM II SD(218)	LOUDLY, AND REQUIRING ALMOST AS MUCH WATCHING TO	KEEP	HIM OUT OF UNINTENDED MISCHIEF. HIS MANNER VARIES FROM
KING I (194)	IT WAS EXHAUSTED; BUT IT STILL CAN HURT. HEAVEN	KEEP	HIM OUT OF YOUR HAND! THAT IS ALL I CAN SAY. ABSALOM!
UNPL PREFACE(R9)	EVERY DESPOT MUST HAVE ONE DISLOYAL SUBJECT TO	KEEP	HIM SANE. EVEN LOUIS THE ELEVENTH HAD TO TOLERATE HIS
BULL PREFACE(45)	HIS OFFICER HAS NOT EVEN HOUSEKEEPER'S WORK TO	KEEP	HIM SANE. THE WORK OF ORGANIZING AND COMMANDING BODIES
FANY III (315)	OF THE HILL. HE HAS NO POWERS INSIDE HIMSELF TO	KEEP	HIM STEADY; SO LET HIM CLING TO THE POWERS OUTSIDE HIM.
FANY I (281)	TALKED TO HIM LIKE A MOTHER, AND TRIED MY BEST TO	KEEP	HIM STRAIGHT; BUT I DONT DENY I LIKE A BIT OF FUN
MTH4 I (166)	ABOUT AND TALKING TO SECONDARIES AND I MUST	KEEP	HIM STRICTLY TO HEEL, THE ELDERLY GENTLEMAN RETURNS,
CAPT NOTES (300)	IT PUT HIM IN PRISON, BUT HAD NOT SENSE ENOUGH TO	KEEP	HIM THERE, YET HIS GETTING OUT OF PRISON WAS AS NOTHING
BULL IV (171)	A TREASURE TO HIM, HE THINKS SO NOW; AND YOU CAN	KEEP	HIM THINKING SO IF YOU LIKE. /NORA/ I WASNT THINKING O
PRES (146)	SHE SAYS, HE'S GOT SOMEBODY THATLL BE ABLE TO	KEEP	HIM WHEN THE SUPERTAX IS PUT UP TO TWENTY SHILLINGS IN
O'FL (219)	WAS THAT" SAYS I: " TEN SHILLINGS A WEEK WOULDNT	KEEP	HIM," SURE I THOUGHT THE MORE I SAID THE MORE THEYD
MIS. (133)	FORGET. AS HE HAS A MUCH SOFTER JOB, AND WANTS TO	KEEP	HIMSELF BEFORE THE PUBLIC, HIS CRY IS, " DONT YOU
GETT PREFACE(237)	SHORT SPAN IN THIS VALE OF TEARS RATHER THAN TO	KEEP	HIMSELF CONSTANTLY READY TO MEET HIS GOD. THE ONLY
BULL II (100)	WAS JEALOUS OF YOU? /KEEGAN/ (SCOLDING HIM TO	KEEP	HIMSELF FROM SMILING) HOW DAR YOU, PATSY FARRELL, PUT
MILL I (160)	FOR HALF THE MONEY; BUT THE AMERICAN COULD ONLY	KEEP	HIMSELF UP TO THE EXCITEMENT OF IT BY PAYING TWICE AS
MTH1 II (29)	IS HIS BROTHER'S KEEPER, BECAUSE HIS BROTHER CAN	KEEP	HIMSELF. BUT AM I IDLE? IN REJECTING YOUR DRUDGERY,
CATH 4 (194)	I WILL NEVER SPEAK TO HIM AGAIN. YOUR MAJESTY CAN	KEEP	HIM, AS FAR AS I AM CONCERNED. /CATHERINE/ I WOULD NOT
DOCT PREFACE(17)	WHOSE MANAGERS, CLERKS, WAREHOUSEMEN AND LABORERS	KEEP	HIS BUSINESS GOING WHILST HE IS IN BED OR IN HIS CLUB,
2TRU PREFACE(12)	HAVE TO ASK YOU FOR A SUBSCRIPTION TOMORROW TO	KEEP	HIS CHURCH GOING. AND THAT IS " LIBERTY: THOU CHOICEST
APPL I SD(225)	LOOKS REPROACHFULLY AT HER, STRUGGLING HARD TO	KEEP	HIS COUNTENANCE. THE OTHERS ARE BEGINNING TO JOIN IN
ROCK PREFACE(176)	THAT THE POPE TOLD GALILEO THAT HE REALLY MUST	KEEP	HIS DISCOVERIES TO HIMSELF, AND THAT GALILEO CONSENTED
LION PREFACE(86)	THEIR MORAL FORCE FROM HIS CREDIT, AND SO HAD TO	KEEP	HIS GOSPEL ALIVE. WHEN THE PROTESTANTS TRANSLATED THE
BULL IV (171)	COME BACK HERE AN LIVE ON IT, AN IF I HAVE TO	KEEP	HIS HOUSE FOR HIM, AT ALL EVENTS I CAN KEEP YOU OUT OF
FANY III (312)	IT. SIMMONS TOLD ME. /GILBEY/ YES: HE NEVER COULD	KEEP	HIS MOUTH QUIET: HE TOLD ME YOUR AUNT WAS A
ARMS III (73)	(PRETENDING TO SULK) THE LADY SAYS THAT HE CAN	KEEP	HIS TABLECLOTHS AND HIS OMNIBUSES. I AM NOT HERE TO BE
GETT PREFACE(242)	UNDER EXISTING CIRCUMSTANCES, ADVISE A WOMAN TO	KEEP	HOUSE WITH A MAN WITHOUT INSISTING ON HIS MARRYING HER,
FANY PREFACE(255)	AND COWARDICE, OR INDEED ANYTHING BUT HOW TO	KEEP	HUNGER AND CONCUPISCENCE AND FASHIONABLE DRESSING
DOCT PREFACE(65)	THE NUMBER OF PEOPLE WHO ARE ILL, AND WHOM HE CAN	KEEP	ILL, BUT ON THE NUMBER OF PEOPLE WHO ARE WELL. HE IS
DEVL III (74)	AND TAKING HER HAND) HERE, MADAM: YOU HAD BETTER	KEEP	INSIDE THE LINES; BUT STAND HERE BEHIND US; AND DONT
FANY I (278)	LONGED TO GIVE IT TO ME. /GILBEY/ MARIA: IF YOU	KEEP	INTERRUPTING WITH SILLY QUESTIONS, I SHALL GO OUT OF MY
SUPR IV (148)	DROVE ME AND MINE OUT OF IRELAND. WELL, YOU CAN	KEEP	IRELAND. ME AND ME LIKE ARE COMING BACK TO BUY ENGLAND;
BARB II (305)	SHELTER ANOTHER TIED HOUSE FOR HIM, AND ASK ME TO	KEEP	IT? /BILL/ ROTTEN DRANKEN WHISKY IT IS TOO. /MRS
2TRU I (43)	FACT IS, I AM A CLERGYMAN. BUT I MUST ASK YOU TO	KEEP	IT A DEAD SECRET; FOR MY FATHER, WHO IS AN ATHEIST,
DOCT II (123)	BUT IF A JEW MAKES AN AGREEMENT, HE MEANS TO	KEEP	IT AND EXPECTS YOU TO KEEP IT. IF HE WANTS MONEY FOR A
PYGM II (230)	COMES FORWARD). DONT BURN THAT, MRS PEARCE. I'LL	KEEP	IT AS A CURIOSITY. (HE TAKES THE HAT). /MRS PEARCE/
HART PREFACE(11)	KEPT HIS HEAD COMPLETELY EXCEPT THOSE WHO HAD TO	KEEP	IT BECAUSE THEY HAD TO CONDUCT THE WAR AT FIRST HAND. I
LADY (250)	PLEASE YOUR MAJESTY. /ELIZABETH/ SEE THAT YOU	KEEP	IT BETTER IN FUTURE. YOU HAVE LET PASS A MOST DANGEROUS
2TRU III (97)	I WANT TO CLEAN UP THIS FILTHY WORLD AND	KEEP	IT CLEAN. THERE MUST BE OTHER WOMEN WHO WANT IT TOO.
FANY II (296)	WHAT WE HAVE TO CONSIDER NOW, IF ONLY WE CAN	KEEP	IT DARK, I DONT CARE FOR ANYTHING ELSE. /MARGARET/ DONT
ROCK II (246)	CANT AFFORD TO LIVE IN IT. I CANT AFFORD EVEN TO	KEEP	IT DUSTED. YOU CAN HAVE IT FOR A HUNDRED A YEAR. /SIR
WIDO II (32)	TWO THERE-- YOURE WELCOME TO MY PLACE IF I CANT	KEEP	IT FOR MYSELF-- AND YOULL HEAR A LITTLE PLAIN SPEAKING,
MIS. (177)	UNSEXED-- /TARLETON/ DONT BEGIN AGAIN, OLD CHAP.	KEEP	IT FOR TRAFALGAR SQUARE. /HYPATIA'S VOICE OUTSIDE/ NO,
CAPT III (295)	WERE YOUR PICTURE, WOULD YOU LIKE YOUR SON TO	KEEP	IT FOR YOUNGER AND BETTER WOMEN TO SEE? /LADY CICELY/
GETT SD(260)	BISHOP HAS LONG SINCE ABANDONED THE ATTEMPT TO	KEEP	IT GOING. IT HANGS ABOVE THE OAK CHEST. THE KITCHEN IS
MIS. PREFACE(60)	IS YOUNG ENOUGH TO BE INSTINCTIVELY DOCILE, AND	KEEP	IT IN A CONDITION OF UNREMITTED TUTELAGE UNDER THE
GENV IV (95)	A FAILING THAT MAY RUIN YOU UNLESS YOU LEARN TO	KEEP	IT IN CHECK. /BBDE/ AND WHAT IS THAT, PRAY? /BATTLER/
MILL I (142)	HAVE YOU A SENSE OF HUMOR? /SAGAMORE/ I TRY TO	KEEP	IT IN CHECK; BUT I AM AFRAID I HAVE A LITTLE. YOU
DOCT PREFACE(60)	PATIENT HAS A PREJUDICE THE DOCTOR MUST EITHER	KEEP	IT IN COUNTENANCE OR LOSE HIS PATIENT. IF PEOPLE ARE
MIS. PREFACE(95)	OF SO POTENT A FACTOR IN EVOLUTION AS TO	KEEP	IT IN IGNORANCE OF RADIATION OR CAPILLARY ATTRACTION.

2TRU II (58)	IN CAMP YOU MUST NEVER FORGET DISCIPLINE. WE	KEEP	IT IN THE BACKGROUND; BUT IT IS ALWAYS THERE AND ALWAYS
FABL III (111)	IN YOUR POCKET. /THE GENTLEMAN/ YOU NEED NOT	KEEP	IT IN YOUR POCKET. YOU CAN BUY A DECENT SUIT OF CLOTHES
DOCT III (143)	WISH YOU WOULD. YOUD PAY ME SOMETHING HANDSOME TO	KEEP	IT OUT OF COURT AFTERWARDS (B.B., BAFFLED, FLINGS AWAY
PLES PREFACE(R8)	POWER THAT NOT THE CHURCH OF ENGLAND ITSELF COULD	KEEP	IT OUT. HERE MY ACTIVITY AS A SOCIALIST HAD PLACED ME
HART I (73)	CAN ALWAYS GET SOME WHEN YOU WANT: THE SERVANTS	KEEP	IT STEWING ALL DAY. THE KITCHEN VERANDA IS THE BEST
VWOO 2 (131)	IN A VILLAGE SHOP IN A QUIET PLACE, WITH ME TO	KEEP	IT STRAIGHT AND LOOK AFTER YOU. /A/ MAY I ASK HOW MUCH
CLEO II (128)	RUFIO'S SCABBARD, POTHINUS. I MAY NOT BE ABLE TO	KEEP	IT THERE IF YOU WAIT TOO LONG. SENSATION. /POTHINUS/ (
DOCT II (121)	/BLENKINSOP/ (ALMOST BREAKING DOWN) I OUGHT TO	KEEP	IT TO MYSELF, I KNOW. I CANT TELL YOU, RIDGEON, HOW
MRS III (230)	WHY WE'RE SO RESERVED ABOUT IT. BY THE WAY, YOULL	KEEP	IT TO YOURSELF, WONT YOU? SINCE IT'S BEEN A SECRET SO
BULL III (130)	OWNED HIS OWN PROPERTY OR COULD HAVE AFFORDED TO	KEEP	IT UP DECENTLY IF HE'D WANTED TO. BUT I TELL YOU PLUMP
PYGM III (252)	HIM NO HARM WHAT I COULD SEE. BUT THEN HE DID NOT	KEEP	IT UP REGULAR. (CHEERFULLY) ON THE BURST, AS YOU MIGHT
HART III (136)	HOW ARE WE TO HAVE ANY SELF-RESPECT IF WE DONT	KEEP	IT UP THAT WE'RE BETTER THAN WE REALLY ARE? /LADY
JITT II (30)	/LENKHEIM/ I'M GLAD OF THAT. OF COURSE YOU MUST	KEEP	IT UP TO EDITH THAT THERE WAS NOTHING WRONG. /FESSLER/
MTH4 II (187)	SENSE. /ZOZIM/ QUITE, I SHOULD SAY. YOU NEED NOT	KEEP	IT UP WITH ME. /THE ENVOY/ (SUDDENLY MAKING HIMSELF
MRS IV (249)	YOU UP TO BE RESPECTABLE? AND HOW CAN YOU	KEEP	IT UP WITHOUT MY MONEY AND MY INFLUENCE AND LIZZIE'S
2TRU II (65)	KEEP CHANGING THE MAN; FOR THE SAME MAN CAN NEVER	KEEP	IT UP. IN ALL MY LIFE I HAVE KNOWN ONLY ONE MAN THAT
MRS IV (240)	WORLD. /FRANK/ THIS IS MOST ELOQUENT, PRADDY.	KEEP	IT UP. /PRAED/ OH, I ASSURE YOU I HAVE CRIED-- I SHALL
LADY PREFACE(217)	POSITION AS SOON AS HE GAINED THE MEANS TO	KEEP	IT UP. THIS SIDE IDOLATRY. THERE IS ANOTHER MATTER
JOAN 2 (86)	I'LL RISK IT. I WARN YOU I SHANT BE ABLE TO	KEEP	IT UP; BUT I'LL RISK IT. YOU SHALL SEE. (RUNNING TO
SUPR III (140)	YOU IDIOTS: NOTHING SOUNDS MORE RESPECTABLE.	KEEP	IT UP, I TELL YOU. THE SOLDIERS LINE THE ROAD,
HART II (122)	ABSURD IN EVENING DRESS. /RANDALL/ STILL, YOU DO	KEEP	IT UP, OLD CHAP. NOW, I ASSURE YOU I HAVE NOT AN ATOM
DOCT PREFACE(79)	YOUR MIND HOW MANY DOCTORS THE COMMUNITY NEEDS TO	KEEP	IT WELL. DO NOT REGISTER MORE OR LESS THAN THIS NUMBER;
MTH5 (212)	IT IS A BEAUTIFUL AND HOLY COMPACT; AND I WILL	KEEP	IT WHILST I LIVE. ARE YOU GOING TO BREAK IT? /THE
SUPR II (56)	IS THAT YOU LOSE MONEY BY A MOTOR CAR UNLESS YOU	KEEP	IT WORKIN. MIGHT AS WELL AVE A PRAM AND A NUSSMAID TO
GENV I (32)	ON THE CONTRARY, IT IS ESSENTIAL THAT YOU SHOULD	KEEP	IT. BUT I THINK I CAN MAKE IT MORE INTERESTING FOR YOU.
MIS. (169)	SHOP FOR IT: YOULL GET NO JUSTICE HERE: WE DONT	KEEP	IT. HUMAN NATURE IS WHAT WE STOCK. /THE MAN/ HUMAN
DOCT II (123)	AGREEMENT, HE MEANS TO KEEP IT AND EXPECTS YOU TO	KEEP	IT. IF HE WANTS MONEY FOR A TIME, HE BORROWS IT AND
FABL I (102)	/M. A. M./ HERE IT IS IN BLACK AND WHITE. YOU MAY	KEEP	IT. I'LL BUY ANOTHER, HURRAH! HURRAH! ! HURRAH! !
APPL I (240)	THE INFIRMITIES OF HIS NATURE WOULD ALLOW HIM TO	KEEP	IT. MY NATURE IS ALSO SUBJECT TO INFIRMITY. ARE YOU
SUPR HANDBOK(195)	DESIRED IT ENOUGH TO NERVE THEM TO GET IT AND	KEEP	IT. THE ECONOMISTS WHO DISCOVERED THAT DEMAND CREATED
PYGM EPILOG (299)	BECAUSE ELIZA AND HER FREDDY DID NOT KNOW HOW TO	KEEP	IT. TRUE, ELIZA HAD NOT TO BEGIN AT THE VERY BEGINNING:
HART PREFACE(11)	I SHOULD NOT HAVE KEPT MY OWN (AS FAR AS I DID	KEEP	IT) IF I HAD NOT AT ONCE UNDERSTOOD THAT AS A SCRIBE
OVER PREFACE(158)	SOLELY BECAUSE SOCIETY CONSPIRED TO DRIVE HIM TO	KEEP	ITS OWN LOWER MORALITY IN COUNTENANCE IN THIS MISERABLE
JITT III (79)	NOBODY CAN KEEP THEM. THIS SECRET WOULDNT	KEEP	ITSELF. COME! STOP CRYING. IF ONLY YOU WOULD BE
DOCT V (178)	BUT IT IS LIKE ALL SECRETS: IT WILL NOT	KEEP	ITSELF. THE BURIED TRUTH GERMINATES AND BREAKS THROUGH
POSN PREFACE(376)	HEAD. THE OTHERS, FOR THE MOMENT, HAD NO HEADS TO	KEEP	. AND THE FASHION IN WHICH THEY PROPOSED TO WREAK THEIR
APPL I (218)	AT THAT IF YOU KNOW HOW MUCH TEMPER I HAVE TO	KEEP	. (HE STRAIGHTENS UP AND BECOMES IMPRESSIVELY
GENV IV (123)	YOU WILL SETTLE WITH ME HOW MUCH OF IT YOU MAY	KEEP	. /BATTLER/ WHAT! YOU TOO! SO THE ENCIRCLEMENT IS
JITT I (23)	THAT WAS NOTHING: ONLY A SECRET THAT THREE CAN	KEEP	. WHAT ABOUT THE RISK OF BEING FOUND WITH A DEAD ONE..
MIS. (131)	NO, THANK YOU. I SHALL TAKE JOLLY GOOD CARE TO	KEEP	JOEY OUT OF THIS UNTIL HYPATIA IS PAST PRAYING FOR.
KING I (206)	/NELL/ ROWLEY DARLING: YOU MUST LEARN TO	KEEP	KING CHARLES'S HEAD OUT OF YOUR CONVERSATION. YOU TALK
KING I (204)	BETRAYED-- ROWLEY DARLING: I CANNOT GO ON IF YOU	KEEP	LAUGHING AT ME. IF ONLY MR DRYDEN HAD GIVEN ME SOME
OVER (183)	OH, YES. GREGORY HAS AN IDEA THAT MARRIED WOMEN	KEEP	LISTS OF THE MEN THEYLL MARRY IF THEY BECOME WIDOWS.
CAND III (145)	AND LOVE FOR HIM, AND STAND SENTINEL ALWAYS TO	KEEP	LITTLE VULGAR CARES OUT. I MAKE HIM MASTER HERE, THOUGH
AUGS (269)	A RISE! /THE CLERK/ WHAT ARE THEY DYING FOR? TO	KEEP	ME ALIVE, AINT IT? WELL, WHATS THE GOOD OF THAT IF I'M
6CAL (102)	OLD ONE IS BECOMING TOO STRAIT FOR ME. WILL YOU	KEEP	ME BEGGING SO? /THE KING/ I SEE VERY WELL THAT I SHALL
CLEO I (108)	LONELINESS) IT WOULD NOT TAKE ANY NOTICE OF ME OR	KEEP	ME COMPANY. I AM GLAD YOU HAVE COME: I WAS VERY LONELY.
POSN (446)	IN ME-- WHEN I HAVE PEOPLE TO SHEW OFF BEFORE AND	KEEP	ME GAME, I'M ALL RIGHT; BUT IVE LOST MY NERVE FOR BEING
DOCT IV (161)	ONLY USE IT UP. RIDGEON: GIVE ME SOMETHING TO	KEEP	ME GOING FOR A FEW MINUTES-- NOT ONE OF YOUR CONFOUNDED
HART III (133)	SO AS TO MAKE THEM PAY. OF COURSE I MAKE THEM	KEEP	ME GOING PRETTY WELL; BUT IT'S A DOG'S LIFE; AND I DONT
WIDO II (47)	AWAY: PROMISE ME THAT YOU WILL SEND HIM AWAY AND	KEEP	ME HERE WITH YOU AS WE HAVE ALWAYS-- (SEEING TRENCH)
VWOO 1 (122)	I OFTEN WISH I HAD A DIRTY ONE TO EXERCISE ME AND	KEEP	ME IN HEALTH. WOMEN ARE SO SET ON CLEAN COLLARS THAT
JOAN 6 (138)	AM NOT, MAY GOD BRING ME TO IT: IF I AM, MAY GOD	KEEP	ME IN IT! /LADVENU/ THAT IS A VERY GOOD REPLY, MY
JOAN 5 (116)	THE ENGLISH AT ORLEANS! YOU LOCKED THE GATES TO	KEEP	ME IN; AND IT WAS THE TOWNSFOLK AND THE COMMON PEOPLE
2TRU II (70)	IVE TRIED CROSSWORD PUZZLES TO OCCUPY MY MIND AND	KEEP	ME OFF PLANNING ROBBERIES; BUT WHAT CROSSWORD PUZZLE IS
GENV II (53)	ROUND THE EMPIRE, AND GOT ME THIS JOB HERE-- TO	KEEP	ME OUT OF HIS WAY, I SUPPOSE. ANYHOW HERE I AM, YOU
2TRU II (70)	LIVE BY IT? YOU WANTED ME TO TAKE TO DRINK TO	KEEP	ME QUIET. BUT I DONT LIKE BEING DRUNK; AND WHAT WOULD
WIDO II (34)	INDEED: I ASSURE YOU IT IS. /BLANCHE/ IT WOULD	KEEP	ME RATHER SHORT IN MY HOUSEKEEPING, DEAREST BOY, IF I
MIS. (172)	YOURSELF. /THE MAN/ DAMN YOU! YOURE TRYING TO	KEEP	ME TALKING UNTIL SOMEBODY COMES. (HE RAISES THE PISTOL
MTH2 (58)	I NEVER HEARD OF HIM. TELL ME ALL ABOUT HIM.	KEEP	ME UP TO DATE. /SAVVY/ IT'S NOT A POET. I AM SAVVY, NOT
BULL IV (170)	YEARS WAS NOT LONG ENOUGH, AND THAT YOU MIGHT	KEEP	ME WAITING A DAY LONGER. WELL, YOU WERE MISTAKEN. I'M
KING I (172)	ROWLEY DARLING: HOW LONG MORE ARE YOU GOING TO	KEEP	ME WAITING IN THE STREET? /CHARLES/ YOU ARE KNOWN TO
FOUN (220)	MY EMOTIONS CARRIES ME AWAY. I IMPLORE YOU NOT TO	KEEP	ME WAITING. MY SOUL, MY SOUL IS THRILLING AS IT NEVER
FANY II (295)	SUSPENSE. /KNOX/ HOW LONG MORE ARE YOU GOING TO	KEEP	ME WAITING, AMELIA? DO YOU THINK I'M MADE OF IRON?
POSN (449)	TO US: MAKE NO MISTAKE ABOUT THAT. /BLANCO/ LORD	KEEP	ME WICKED TILL I DIE! NOW IVE SAID MY LITTLE PRAYER.
POSN (456)	NOT GOOD ENOUGH TO KISS THE BOOK. /BLANCO/ LORD	KEEP	ME WICKED TILL I DIE! I'M GAME FOR ANYTHING WHILE
HART II (119)	/CAPTAIN SHOTOVER/ I TELL YOU IT'S DANGEROUS TO	KEEP	ME. I CANT KEEP AWAKE AND ALERT. /ELLIE/ WHAT DO YOU
FANY PROL,SD(266)	HIDES FROM HIM ALL THE DANGERS AND DISGRACES THAT	KEEP	MEN OF FINER PERCEPTION IN CHECK. THE COUNT APPROACHES
BARB II (279)	THEY WANT YOUNG MEN THERE: THEY CANT AFFORD TO	KEEP	MEN OVER FORTY-FIVE. THEYRE VERY SORRY-- GIVE YOU A
KING I (177)	IN MY PRESENCE? /NELL/ IT IS NOT FAIR OF HER TO	KEEP	MENTIONING MY PROFESSION WHEN I CANNOT DECENTLY MENTION
FANY III (310)	SUCH THINGS? /JUGGINS/ MY BROTHER CAN AFFORD TO	KEEP	ME, SIR. THE TRUTH IS, HE OBJECTS TO MY BEING IN
BARB II SD(273)	THAN OF THE MOON, AND BEING COMPELLED TO	KEEP	MORE OF THEIR CLOTHES IN THE PAWNSHOP, AND LESS ON
GETT PREFACE(211)	AND BY THE UNWRITTEN LAW OF NECESSITY NO MAN CAN	KEEP	MORE WIVES THAN HE CAN AFFORD; SO THAT A MAN WITH FOUR
MTH2 (63)	BEHAVE HIMSELF, THAT I HAVE NOT BEEN ABLE TO	KEEP	MY ACADEMIC READING UP TO DATE. I HAVE KEPT MY CLASSICS
MTH3 (100)	LIVE ON THE EAST COAST: IT IS HARD ENOUGH TO	KEEP	MY BLOOD WARM HERE. BESIDES, MY FRIEND, IT WOULD NOT BE
DEVL III (77)	AFRAID SHE WAS RIGHT; SO, BY YOUR LEAVE, YOU MAY	KEEP	MY COAT AND I'LL KEEP YOURS. /RICHARD/ MINISTER-- I
CYMB FORWORD(135)	NO LONGER SURPRISE ANYBODY. I REALLY COULD NOT	KEEP	MY COUNTENANCE OVER THE IDENTIFICATION OF GUIDERIUS BY
KING II (232)	I AM NO REAL KING: THAT THE UTMOST I CAN DO IS TO	KEEP	MY CROWN ON MY HEAD AND MY HEAD ON MY SHOULDERS. HOW
CAND I (86)	IN 'IS PLACE. /MORELL/ (RATHER SHORTLY) I ALWAYS	KEEP	MY CURATES IN THEIR PLACES AS MY HELPERS AND COMRADES.
DEVL I (23)	SHALL LIVE IN CLOVER. GO ON. /HAWKINS/-- " AND	KEEP	MY DEAF FARM LABOURER PRODGER FESTON IN HIS SERVICE."
BARB III (321)	NEED. WHEN OTHER PEOPLE WANT SOMETHING TO	KEEP	MY DIVIDENDS DOWN, YOU WILL CALL OUT THE POLICE AND
BARB III (321)	ON THOSE MEASURES. WHEN I WANT ANYTHING TO	KEEP	MY DIVIDENDS UP, YOU WILL DISCOVER THAT MY WANT IS A
KING I (193)	YOUR EYE ON THE ORANGEMAN, JAMIE. /JAMES/ I SHALL	KEEP	MY EYE ON YOUR PROTESTANT BASTARD MONMOUTH. WHY DO YOU
MTH5 (258)	THE MATTER WITH ME. I WANT TO LIE DOWN. I CANNOT	KEEP	MY EYES OPEN. /ECRASIA/ YOU ARE FALLING ASLEEP. YOU
DEVL III (67)	HANDCUFF ME, WILL YOU; OR I'LL NOT UNDERTAKE TO	KEEP	MY FINGERS OFF HIM. THE SERGEANT TAKES OUT A PAIR OF
HART PREFACE(11)	WAS UNDER THE MOST SERIOUS PUBLIC OBLIGATION TO	KEEP	MY GRIP ON REALITIES; BUT THIS DID NOT SAVE ME FROM A
GENV III (69)	AND WHEN I MEET A GOD MURDERER I CAN HARDLY	KEEP	MY HANDS OFF MY GUN. /THE JEW/ AFTER ALL, MADAM, YOUR
GETT (337)	IF YOU ASK ME ANOTHER QUESTION I SHANT BE ABLE TO	KEEP	MY HANDS OFF YOU (SHE DASHES DISTRACTEDLY PAST HIM TO
MILL IV (203)	YOU ARE TWO STONE HEAVIER THAN I; AND I CANNOT	KEEP	MY HEAD AT INFIGHTING AS YOU CAN. YOU DO NOT SUIT. I
KING I (197)	SEE WHAT I GET BY IT! NOT MUCH, PERHAPS; BUT I	KEEP	MY HEAD ON MY SHOULDERS. IT TAKES A MAN OF BRAINS TO DO
KING II (224)	THESE WOMEN DO NOT KEEP THEIR HOLD ON ME: I	KEEP	MY HOLD ON THEM. I HAVE A BIT OF NEWS FOR YOU ABOUT
MILL IV (202)	JUST THAT I, BECAUSE I AM A MILLIONAIRESS, CANNOT	KEEP	MY HUSBAND, CANNOT KEEP EVEN A LOVER, CANNOT KEEP
PYGM V (273)	IN MY OLD AGE? I HAVE TO DYE MY HAIR ALREADY TO	KEEP	MY JOB AS A DUSTMAN. IF I WAS ONE OF THE DESERVING
ROCK I (229)	FOR DIGESTION NOR FOR ENOUGH SLEEP, AND HAVING TO	KEEP	MY MIND AT FULL STRETCH ALL THE TIME STRUGGLING WITH
MTH2 (57)	TO PLAY AS MANY AS SIXTY-SIX GAMES OF BRIDGE TO	KEEP	MY MIND OFF THE NEWS FROM THE FRONT. /BURGE/ (
FANY II (285)	BEEN VERY QUEER EVER SINCE IT HAPPENED. I CANT	KEEP	MY MIND ON BUSINESS AS I OUGHT; AND I WAS DEPENDING ON
VWOO 3 (137)	THIS VERY DAY, I'LL GO THIS VERY MINUTE. YOU CAN	KEEP	MY MONTH. YOU DONT KNOW WHEN YOURE WELL OFF. YOURE
JOAN EPILOG (157)	AND SAY THAT TOP-SIDE-UP IS RIGHT-SIDE-UP; AND I	KEEP	MY NOSE PRETTY CLOSE TO THE GROUND. AND I ASK YOU, WHAT
FANY III (297)	ME TO CALL YOU SIR; AND AS I TAKE THE MONEY, I	KEEP	MY PART OF THE BARGAIN. /BOBBY/ WOULD YOU CALL ME SIR
SUPR II (66)	NO, HECTOR: YOU PROMISED ME NOT TO. /HECTOR/ I'LL	KEEP	MY PRAWMIS UNTIL YOU RELEASE ME FROM IT. BUT I FEEL
DEVL II (46)	HIM SAFELY OUT OF HARM'S WAY." I PROMISED: I CANT	KEEP	MY PROMISE. HE SAID, " DONT FOR YOUR LIFE LET HIM KNOW
JITT I (23)	TO BE GOOD TO ME HE WILL NEVER LET ME LIVE TO	KEEP	MY PROMISE. /BRUNO/ I COULD NOT HAVE PAINED YOU LIKE
DEVL II (45)	/JUDITH/ NO: THIS IS HOW I BREAK IT. I CANNOT	KEEP	MY PROMISES TO HIM: WHY SHOULD I KEEP MY PROMISES TO
DEVL II (46)	I CANNOT KEEP MY PROMISES TO HIM: WHY SHOULD I	KEEP	MY PROMISES TO YOU? /ANDERSON/ DONT SPEAK SO
SUPR II (69)	EMPLOYER AND ENGINEER; I SHALL ALWAYS KNOW HOW TO	KEEP	MY PROPER DISTANCE, AND NOT INTRUDE MY PRIVATE AFFAIRS
JITT III (60)	HOW TIDY YOU KEPT HIS HOUSE FOR HIM, JUST AS I	KEEP	MY ROOM. YOU DID YOUR DUTY: NOBODY CAN BLAME YOU. BUT
GLIM (175)	YOUR TEMPER, SIGNOR COUNT. /FERRUCCIO/ I'LL NOT	KEEP	MY TEMPER. IVE AN UNCONTROLLABLE TEMPER. I GET BLINDING

ROCK II (235)	THE UNPOPULAR DIE HARD WHO COULDNT BE TRUSTED TO	KEEP	MY TEMPER. SO I STOOD DOWN. I SACRIFICED MYSELF. I TOOK
APPL I (218)	A FOOL AS SOME FOOLS THINK ME. I MAY NOT ALWAYS	KEEP	MY TEMPER. YOU WOULD NOT BE SURPRISED AT THAT IF YOU
NEVR IV (282)	IT BEST TO SPELL MYSELF B. DOUBLE-O.N., AND TO	KEEP	MY WITS PRETTY SHARP ABOUT ME. BUT I'M TAKING UP YOUR
PHIL II (130)	OH WELL, JO, IF THAT IS YOUR DECISION, I MUST	KEEP	MY WORD AND ABIDE BY IT. BETTER SIT DOWN AND MAKE
FANY EPILOG (329)	I PROMISED MY DAUGHTER YOUR OPINION; AND I MUST	KEEP	MY WORD. GENTLEMEN: YOU ARE THE CHOICE AND MASTER
MRS II (214)	NIGHT, WHEN I WAS SO TIRED I COULD HARDLY	KEEP	MYSELF AWAKE, WHO SHOULD COME UP FOR A HALF OF SCOTCH
MIS. (169)	A WEEK TO SPEND ON BOOKS WHEN I CAN HARDLY	KEEP	MYSELF DECENT? I GET BOOKS AT THE FREE LIBRARY.
MTH2 (56)	TO BE REMINDED OF THAT. IN PEACE TIME I USED TO	KEEP	MYSELF FRESH FOR MY WORK BY BANISHING ALL WORLDLY
2TRU III (97)	THINGS FOR ME THAT I OUGHT TO DO FOR MYSELF TO	KEEP	MYSELF IN HEALTH. THEY PREYED ON ME TO KEEP THEMSELVES
MILL IV (204)	BREATHE. I WILL LIVE IN UTTER LONELINESS AND	KEEP	MYSELF SACRED UNTIL I FIND THE RIGHT MAN-- THE MAN WHO
JITT III (59)	TO KEEP THE HOUSE SPICK AND SPAN I CANT ALWAYS	KEEP	MYSELF SPICK AND SPAN; AND I KNOW HE WAS PARTICULAR
PHIL II (122)	DISCOVERIES, AND WHAT I OUGHT TO READ TO	KEEP	MYSELF UP TO DATE. BUT PERHAPS YOURE BUSY. /PARAMORE/
POSN PREFACE(424)	CHURCH. IF MOB CENSORSHIP CANNOT BE TRUSTED TO	KEEP	NAUGHTY PLAYWRIGHTS IN ORDER, STILL LESS CAN IT BE
ROCK PREFACE(151)	TO GOVERN AS AGAINST THE PARLIAMENT AND WOULD	KEEP	NO BARGAIN WITH IT. PARLIAMENT DENIED HIS RIGHT, AND
PYGM I (208)	THE GENTLEMAN. IVE A RIGHT TO SELL FLOWERS IF I	KEEP	OFF THE KERB. (HYSTERICALLY) I'M A RESPECTABLE GIRL:
MTH5 (231)	BOTH PERISHED TOGETHER MISERABLY? /MARTELLUS/	KEEP	OFF THE PRIMITIVE TRIBES, PYGMALION. THEY INTEREST YOU;
SIM II (83)	ENOUGH TO UNDERSTAND ME, NOR CLEVER ENOUGH TO	KEEP	OFF THE ROCKS OF SOCIAL RUIN. IVE GROWN FOND ENOUGH OF
DEST (189)	NOT AFRAID OF THEM. /LIEUTENANT/ (RETREATING)	KEEP	OFF. (SEIZING THE HILT OF THE SABRE) KEEP OFF, I TELL
DEST (189)	KEEP OFF. (SEIZING THE HILT OF THE SABRE)	KEEP	OFF, I TELL YOU. /LADY/ (TO NAPOLEON) THEY BELONG TO
PHIL III (140)	HAS NO MORAL QUALITIES. /CHARTERIS/ (RETREATING)	KEEP	OFF, JULIA. REMEMBER YOUR NEW OBLIGATIONS TO PARAMORE.
CLEO III (148)	AT FTATATEETA, AND BRANDISHING HIS PILUM)	KEEP	OFF, THERE. /CLEOPATRA/ (RUNNING TO APOLLODORUS)
APPL II (276)	AT YOUR NOT COMING INTO THE HOUSE WITH US TO	KEEP	OLD ENGLAND IN FRONT AND LEAD A NEW PARTY AGAINST
MRS II (210)	/MRS WARREN/ (PUZZLED, THEN ANGRY) DONT YOU	KEEP	ON ASKING ME QUESTIONS LIKE THAT. (VIOLENTLY) HOLD
MTH4 I (146)	I DONT KNOW: I-- I-- I-- I SHALL GO MAD IF YOU	KEEP	ON ASKING ME TO TELL YOU THINGS THAT EVERYBODY KNOWS.
DOCT PREFACE(21)	DO CURE TO THE SATISFACTION OF THE PEOPLE WHO	KEEP	ON BUYING THEM. I HAVE NEVER BEEN ABLE TO PERCEIVE ANY
ROCK I (217)	AND BREAKS YOUR HEART AND DOES NO GOOD; BUT YOU	KEEP	ON DOING IT. THEYVE OFTEN WANTED ME TO GO INTO
ROCK I (216)	AT YOUR DEBATES! THEY DONT DO NO GOOD. BUT YOU	KEEP	ON HOLDING THEM. IT'S A SORT OF SATISFACTION TO YOU
PYGM II (218)	YOU HEAR NO DIFFERENCE AT FIRST; BUT YOU	KEEP	ON LISTENING, AND PRESENTLY YOU FIND THEYRE ALL AS
GETT (280)	/LEO/ IT'S NOT THAT IVE EXHAUSTED IT; BUT HE WILL	KEEP	ON REPEATING IT WHEN I WANT TO READ OR GO TO SLEEP. AND
OVER (182)	ME; BUT (IF YOU DONT MIND) I'D RATHER YOU DIDNT	KEEP	ON SAYING SO. /JUNO/ IS THERE THEN NO HOPE FOR ME?
2TRU I (36)	OR DEAD. /THE ELDERLY LADY/ OH, DARLING, DONT	KEEP	ON SAYING THAT. YOU KNOW IT'S NOT TRUE; AND IT DOES
BUOY IV (56)	A MINUTE AGO I DID NOT KNOW WHY I WANTED TO	KEEP	ON TERMS WITH YOU ALL. YOU HAVE SHOVED IT DOWN MY
GENV IV (113)	I WAS ACCUSED OF HAVING A TECHNIQUE. CAN WE NOT	KEEP	ON THE PLAIN TRACK OF COMMONSENSE? /DEACONESS/ BUT
BASH I (96)	HIGHT HELLISH. AS FOR THY DOG, WHY DOST THOU	KEEP	ONE AND BARK THYSELF? BEGONE. /MELLISH/ I'LL NOT
DEST (166)	WITH PRETTY PITEOUSNESS) GENERAL: I ONLY WANT TO	KEEP	ONE LITTLE PRIVATE LETTER. ONLY ONE. LET ME HAVE IT.
ROCK PREFACE(152)	THEM. I THEN EXTERMINATE MY SHEPHERDS AND	KEEP	ONLY A FEW GAMEKEEPERS, BUT I MAY DO MUCH BETTER BY
GETT (336)	IS STRONG ENOUGH TO CLOSE A DOOR THAT I MEAN TO	KEEP	OPEN. YOU CANT ESCAPE ME. IF YOU PERSIST, I'LL GO INTO
POSN PREFACE(391)	OF THE REVELS, APPOINTED IN 1544 BY HENRY VIII TO	KEEP	ORDER AMONG THE PLAYERS AND MUSICIANS OF THAT DAY WHEN
ROCK PREFACE(186)	A GREAT DEAL TO THE HIGH PRIEST; AND I CANNOT	KEEP	ORDER IN JEWRY EXCEPT BY DEALING WITH JEWISH FOOLS
DOCT PREFACE(5)	THE SORT OF CONSCIENCE THAT MAKES IT POSSIBLE TO	KEEP	ORDER ON A PIRATE SHIP, OR IN A TROOP OF BRIGANDS. IT
MTH4 I (165)	TO DO IT. YOU KNOW VERY WELL THAT THEY COULD ONLY	KEEP	ORDER-- SUCH AS IT WAS-- BY THE VERY COERCION AND
GENV IV (97)	TRIFLED WITH? /JUDGE/ YOU MAY DEPEND ON ME TO	KEEP	ORDER, MR BATTLER. DAME BEGONIA IS MAKING A MOST
ROCK II (261)	MILLIONS. /SIR DEXTER/ MY UNION JACK MEN WOULD	KEEP	ORDER, OR THEYD KNOW THE REASON WHY. /BASHAM/ AND WHO
GETT (339)	NOT TO MENTION ME? /MRS GEORGE/ SO THAT WE MIGHT	KEEP	OUR ASSIGNATION IN HEAVEN. /THE BISHOP/ (RISING AND
MRS II (213)	THEM IF MOTHER HADNT HALF-MURDERED US TO	KEEP	OUR HANDS OFF THEM. THEY WERE THE RESPECTABLE ONES.
FABL VI (126)	THEY MAY BE KEEPING US FOR THEIR AMUSEMENT, AS WE	KEEP	OUR PETS. I TOLD YOU THE UNIVERSE IS A JOKE. THAT IS MY
HART II (117)	BECAUSE THEY WANT TO PERSUADE US THAT WE CAN	KEEP	OUR SOULS IF WE LET THEM MAKE SLAVES OF OUR BODIES. I
SUPR HANDBOK(209)	OF EVERY PROFESSION AND EVERY PUBLIC OFFICE TO	KEEP	OUT EVERY ABLE MAN WHO IS NOT A SOPHIST OR A LIAR. A
MIS. PREFACE(92)	WHEN THEY PASS THROUGH THE STREETS THEY HAVE TO	KEEP	OUT IN THE WHEELED TRAFFIC TO AVOID THE TEMPTATIONS OF
FANY PROLOG (259)	MY EARS ARE OFFENDED BY THE COCKNEY TWANG; I	KEEP	OUT OF HEARING OF IT AND SPEAK AND LISTEN TO ITALIAN. I
LIED (192)	FIFTEEN SECONDS. BUT I AM ACTIVE ENOUGH TO	KEEP	OUT OF HIS REACH FOR FIFTEEN SECONDS; AND AFTER THAT I
KING I (218)	WELL TO BE PLEASANT COMPANY; SO I TAKE CARE TO	KEEP	OUT OF HIS WAY. BESIDES, LOUISE, WHEN I MAKE YOU ALL
BUOY IV (58)	BETTERER IS ENOUGH IN ONE FAMILY. /OLD BILL/	KEEP	OUT OF IT THEN, YOU. YOU WERE BORN TO TALK AND SAY
CAPT II (248)	IF SHE HAD ANY SENSE OF DANGER, PERHAPS SHE WOULD	KEEP	OUT OF IT. /BRASSBOUND/ WELL, SIR, IF SHE WERE TEN LADY
2TRU II (53)	INTERPRETER TO ME. AND DONT COME BACK WITH HIM.	KEEP	OUT OF MY SIGHT. /MEEK/ (HESITATES) ER-- /TALLBOYS/ (
NEVR I (223)	WHERE THEY ARE, AND DONT CARE, SO LONG AS THEY	KEEP	OUT OF MY WAY. (VALENTINE, WITH A HITCH OF HIS
ROCK PREFACE(162)	MAY DO AND WHAT THEY MAY NOT DO IF THEY ARE TO	KEEP	OUT OF THE HANDS OF THE POLICE. OUR FINANCIERS KNOW
ARMS I (10)	MAN/ (GRIMLY) THE FIRST MAN IN WILL FIND OUT.	KEEP	OUT OF THE WAY; AND DONT LOOK. IT WONT LAST LONG; BUT
MIS. PREFACE(8)	PLACES SEEMS TO HAVE BEEN SIMPLY TO MAKE THEM	KEEP	OUT OF THEIR FATHER'S WAY, WHICH WAS NO DOUBT WHAT HE
HART III (142)	/MAZZINI/ I SHALL TAKE PARTICULAR CARE TO	KEEP	OUT OF YOUR HOUSE, LADY UTTERWORD. /LADY UTTERWORD/ YOU
JOAN 5 (116)	ARMOR ON THEMSELVES AND ON THEIR POOR HORSES TO	KEEP	OUT THE ARROWS; AND WHEN THEY FALL THEY CANT GET UP,
SIM PRO,2, (29)	QUITE. THERE ARE NETS BELOW, AND A PALISADE TO	KEEP	OUT THE SHARKS. THE SHOCK WILL DO HIM GOOD. /THE Y.W./
DOCT I (83)	ANSWER THE DOOR, I KNOW WHO TO LET IN AND WHO TO	KEEP	OUT, AND THAT REMINDS ME OF THE POOR LADY. I THINK HE
ROCK II (268)	BUSINESS, THEN LET HIM COME OUT OF PARLIAMENT AND	KEEP	OUT, IT WILL TAKE THE LIFE OUT OF HIM AND LEAVE HIM A
CAPT I (230)	HOWARD/ PROBABLY, UNLESS YOU HAD TAKEN CARE TO	KEEP	OUTSIDE THE LAW AGAINST CONSPIRACY. WHENEVER YOU WISH
LADY PREFACE(223)	OUT THAT THE DARK LADY'S BRAINS COULD NO MORE	KEEP	PACE WITH HIS THAN ANNE HATHAWAY'S, IF THERE WERE ANY
JOAN PREFACE(36)	THE FACE OF FACT AND HISTORY PRETEND TO BE), CAN	KEEP	PACE WITH THE PRIVATE JUDGMENT OF PERSONS OF GENIUS
APPL PREFACE(184)	AND COMMUNISM OR NOT, BUT WHETHER DEMOCRACY CAN	KEEP	PACE WITH THE DEVELOPMENTS OF BOTH THAT ARE BEING
APPL PREFACE(184)	OF IT CAN REPAIR THE RAVAGES OF THE WAR AND	KEEP	PACE WITH THE GROWING REQUIREMENTS OF CIVILIZATION.
PLES PREFACE(R12)	THE FEW ACCREDITED AUTHORS ARE SO LITTLE ABLE TO	KEEP	PACE WITH THEIR COMMISSIONS, THAT HE IS ALWAYS APT TO
2TRU PREFACE(20)	FREEDOM OF THOUGHT AND FACILITY OF CHANGE TO	KEEP	PACE WITH THOUGHT. NOW THIS DOES NOT MEAN IN THE LEAST
POSN PREFACE(425)	CHAMBERLAIN, OR ANYONE ELSE, WERE TO ATTEMPT TO	KEEP	PARSIFAL FROM US TO SPARE THE FEELINGS OF THESE PEOPLE,
APPL PREFACE(188)	SIT ONE OR TWO POOR MEN WHO HAVE WORKED HARD TO	KEEP	PARTY POLITICS ALIVE IN THE CONSTITUENCY. THEY OUGHT TO
BARB III (321)	PAYS US. YOU WILL MAKE WAR WHEN IT SUITS US, AND	KEEP	PEACE WHEN IT DOESNT. YOU WILL FIND OUT THAT TRADE
MIS. PREFACE(27)	WE COME UP AGAINST THE ABUSE OF SCHOOLS TO	KEEP	PEOPLE IN IGNORANCE AND ERROR, SO THAT THEY MAY BE
ARMS I (20)	NECESSARY. /RAINA/ IF YOU WILL BE SO GOOD AS TO	KEEP	PERFECTLY STILL WHILST I AM AWAY. /THE MAN/ CERTAINLY.
BULL PREFACE(50)	THESE TOWERS ARE PIGEON-HOUSES; FOR THE VILLAGERS	KEEP	PIGEONS JUST AS AN ENGLISH FARMER KEEPS POULTRY. TRY TO
ARMS II (34)	ME NOW? WHAT WOULD THE HALF DOZEN SERGIUSES WHO	KEEP	POPPING IN AND OUT OF THIS HANDSOME FIGURE OF MINE SAY
POSN (456)	/SHERIFF/ (SAVAGELY) WHATS THIS NOISE? CANT YOU	KEEP	QUIET THERE? IS THIS A SHERIFF'S COURT OR IS IT A
CATH 4 (193)	WHAT SHE LIKES; BUT GET THE STRAPS OFF. /CLAIRE/	KEEP	QUIET, DEAR: I CANNOT GET THEM OFF IF YOU MOVE.
MIS. (185)	(SILENCE). LEAVE IT AT THAT. ENOUGH SAID. YOU	KEEP	QUIET, JOHNNY. MR PERCIVAL: YOURE WHITEWASHED. SO ARE
JOAN 5 (121)	TURN HER FROM IT. /CHARLES/ IF ONLY SHE WOULD	KEEP	QUIET, OR GO HOME! THEY FOLLOW HER DISPIRITEDLY.
CATH 4 (193)	GET THEM OFF IF YOU MOVE. /CATHERINE/ (CALMLY)	KEEP	QUITE STILL, CAPTAIN (SHE TICKLES HIM). /EDSTASTON/
PYGM III (256)	THERE IS SOME NEW CHANGE. (CLOSER AGAIN) WE	KEEP	RECORDS OF EVERY STAGE-- DOZENS OF GRAMOPHONE DISKS AND
GETT (354)	YOU MERELY RIDICULOUS AS A PREACHER, BECAUSE YOU	KEEP	REFERRING ME TO PLACES AND DOCUMENTS AND ALLEGED
BUOY III (38)	AND WHAT ABOUT SOLOMON? /SIR F./ DO PRAY LET US	KEEP	RELIGION OUT OF THIS DISCUSSION. SURELY RELIGION IS ONE
MIS. PREFACE(39)	THAT YOU KNOW YOURSELF, THERE IS A TENDENCY TO	KEEP	REPEATING THE ALREADY LEARNT LESSON RATHER THAN BREAK
MIS. PREFACE(77)	IS NOT TO FIX PEOPLE, BUT TO ROOT THEM UP. WE	KEEP	REPEATING THE SILLY PROVERB THAT A ROLLING STONE
GENV I (31)	NO HANKY PANKY. I AM RESPECTABLE; AND I MEAN TO	KEEP	RESPECTABLE. /HE/ I PLEDGE YOU MY WORD THAT MY
JITT I (12)	SIR, I WISH ALL THE OTHER GENTLEMEN THAT	KEEP	ROOMS HERE ON THE QUIET TO ENJOY THEMSELVES WERE LIKE
DEVL III (55)	/RICHARD/ YOU WILL KEEP FAITH? /JUDITH/ I WILL	KEEP	-- (SHE BREAKS DOWN, SOBBING). /RICHARD/ (TAKING HER
PYGM II (237)	HANDSOME GIRL. AS A DAUGHTER SHE'S NOT WORTH HER	KEEP	; AND SO I TELL YOU STRAIGHT. ALL I ASK IS MY RIGHTS AS
KING I (165)	A VERY SIMILAR WEAKNESS FOR WOMEN; SO YOU MUST	KEEP	SALLY OUT OF HIS WAY. /MRS BASHAM/ INDEED! IF HE TRIES
MTH3 (108)	BUT (RECOVERING) IT ISNT TRUE, YOU KNOW. LET US	KEEP	SANE. /CONFUCIUS/ (TO THE ARCHBISHOP) YOU WISH US TO
KING I (185)	THAT-- YOU MUST CONTINUALLY COME DOWN TO EARTH TO	KEEP	SANE. YOU MUST SEE: YOU MUST FEEL: YOU MUST MEASURE.
SIM I (50)	SUCH THINGS INTO MY HEAD. I AM TRYING SO HARD TO	KEEP	SANE; BUT YOU ARE TERRIFYING ME. IF ONLY I COULD BRING
MTH5 (256)	TOO MUCH ABOUT IT IF I WERE YOU. YOU HAVE TO	KEEP	SANE, YOU KNOW. THE TWO ANCIENTS LOOK AT ONE ANOTHER;
ROCK I (202)	THAT: I HAVE NOT YET BECOME A COMPLETE IDIOT. YOU	KEEP	SAYING THE FAMILY, THE FAMILY, THE FAMILY. /HILDA/
SUPR HANDBOK(204)	EGGS AND KEEP THEM AS THE RED INDIAN USED TO	KEEP	SCALPS. COERCION WITH THE LASH IS AS NATURAL TO AN
FABL PREFACE(94)	AND ONE WHICH NEVER FORGETS. ANYHOW, WE MUST	KEEP	SCHOOLMASTERS AWAY FROM THE PANEL TESTS. MY OWN SCHOOL
BASH II,1, (104)	HIM AWAY. I WILL NOT SEE THE WRETCH. HOW DARE HE	KEEP	SECRETS FROM ME? I'LL PUNISH HIM. PRAY SAY I'M NOT AT
PRES (134)	ARE REALLY THE MOST MERCIFUL IN THE END. YOU	KEEP	SENDING THESE MISGUIDED WOMEN TO HOLLOWAY AND KILLING
FANY EPILOG (334)	ONLY BE TRUE TO YOURSELF, MISS O'DOWDA.	KEEP	SERIOUS. GIVE UP MAKING SILLY JOKES. SUSTAIN THE NOTE
DEST (186)	MYSELF TO COOK AND BECAME AN INNKEEPER; AND NOW I	KEEP	SERVANTS TO DO THE WORK, AND HAVE NOTHING TO DO MYSELF
FABL PREFACE(84)	ENDURE FOR A WEEK, OUR POLITICIANS AND PARTISANS	KEEP	SHOUTING THEIR ABHORRENCE OF COMMUNISM AS IF THEIR
LION I (112)	/CENTURION/ (HORRIFIED) SILENCE, I TELL YOU!	KEEP	SILENCE THERE. DID ANYONE EVER HEAR THE LIKE OF THIS..
CLEO PRO1 (93)	MORE LIGHT. SETTLE YE THEREFORE IN YOUR SEATS AND	KEEP	SILENT; FOR YE ARE ABOUT TO HEAR A MAN SPEAK, AND A

MTH5 (223)	/ACIS/ FAIR PLAY, ARJILLAX! IF SHE IS TO	KEEP	SILENT, LET HER ALONE. /ECRASIA/ I SHALL NOT INTERRUPT,
MIS. (158)	UNDERSTAND THEM, QUITE QUIETLY AND HAPPILY, AND	KEEP	SIX BALLS IN THE AIR ALL THE TIME, YOU ARE IN PERFECT
HART II (120)	YOU CAN AWAKEN YOURSELF WITH RUM. I DRINK NOW TO	KEEP	SOBER; BUT THE DREAMS ARE CONQUERING: RUM IS NOT WHAT
DOCT III (142)	TIME BUT CONSPIRING WITH THE FAMILY SOLICITOR TO	KEEP	SOME RASCAL OUT OF JAIL AND SOME FAMILY OUT OF
JOAN 2 (74)	MY LORD CHAMBERLAIN: PLEASE! PLEASE! WE MUST	KEEP	SOME SORT OF ORDER. (TO THE DAUPHIN) AND YOU, SIR: IF
JOAN 2 (71)	IS A SORT OF IDOL. AT ANY RATE HE HAS TO LEARN TO	KEEP	STILL AND SUFFER FOOLS PATIENTLY. BESIDES, MY DEAR LORD
O'FL (207)	NOW, MAYBE, SIR PEARCE? /SIR PEARCE/ (UNABLE TO	KEEP	STILL, WALKING AWAY FROM O'FLAHERTY) SURPRISED! I'M
SUPR IV (147)	OF ITS TRADITIONS? CANNOT ANY WELL BRED WOMAN	KEEP	SUCH A HOUSE FOR HIM? /MALONE/ NO: SHE MUST BE BORN TO
MIS. PREFACE(27)	THAT VERY REASON THE GREATEST CARE IS TAKEN TO	KEEP	SUCH BENEFICIALLY SUBVERSIVE KNOWLEDGE FROM US, WITH
FANY II (289)	ANOTHER POLICEMAN AND GO BACK TO HOLLOWAY THAN	KEEP	TALKING ROUND AND ROUND IT LIKE THIS. IF YOURE GOING TO
NEVR I (221)	ARE THEY FOR? (DOGMATICALLY) THE PROPER WAY TO	KEEP	TEETH GOOD IS TO GIVE THEM PLENTY OF USE ON BONES AND
DOCT III (153)	SURELY-- /MRS DUBEDAT/ OH, IT IS SO CRUEL TO	KEEP	TELLING ME THAT. IT SEEMS ALL RIGHT; AND IT PUTS ME IN
ROCK I (222)	OFF BEFORE IT BECOMES IMPOSSIBLE. /HILDA/ BUT I	KEEP	TELLING YOU, SIR ARTHUR, THAT IF YOU WILL TALK TO
PRES (156)	GONE. AND NOW, MY DEAR LADY, IS IT NECESSARY TO	KEEP	THAT LOADED PISTOL TO MY NOSE ALL THROUGH OUR
NEVR I (214)	OFFICER DID PROPOSE TO ME; AND I TOLD HIM TO	KEEP	THAT SORT OF THING FOR WOMEN WHO WERE YOUNG ENOUGH TO
2TRU II (61)	AWAY THE WHOLE SHOW. /THE COUNTESS/ WELL, YOU	KEEP	THAT UMBRELLA TO YOURSELF NEXT TIME. WHAT DO YOU
DEVL II (48)	THE BLASPHEMY. HE THROWS THE PURSE ON THE TABLE).	KEEP	THAT. IVE TAKEN 25 DOLLARS. /JUDITH/ HAVE YOU FORGOTTEN
MTH2 (83)	BE BLUE MURDER. IT'S OUT OF THE QUESTION. WE MUST	KEEP	THE ACTUAL SECRET TO OURSELVES. /CONRAD/ (STARING AT
BULL III (142)	CAT THE CAIBLE. MIKE IT A PRESENT TO GERMANY TO	KEEP	THE AOWL KYZER BUSY FOR A WAWL; AND GIVE POOR AOWLD
DEVL EPILOG (83)	PROPOSITION 2. THE OFFICERS AND SOLDIERS MAY	KEEP	THE BAGGAGE BELONGING TO THEM. THE GENERALS OF THE
FABL II (105)	TO DUST THE HOUSES WITH VACUUM CLEANERS AND	KEEP	THE BANKS AND THE TELEPHONE SERVICES AND THE WIRELESS
LION PREFACE(88)	FANCY OF INTELLECTUALLY UNTRAINED PEOPLE WHO	KEEP	THE BIBLE ON THE SAME SHELF WITH NAPOLEON'S BOOK OF
NEVR III (267)	MAKER OF CANNONS AND THE MAKER OF ARMOR PLATES TO	KEEP	THE CANNON BALLS OUT, YOU BUILD A SHIP PROOF AGAINST
SUPR II (49)	WITH A VIEW TO LUNCHING HERE. IF NOT, I'LL	KEEP	THE CAR ON THE GO ABOUT HERE TIL YOU COME. /TANNER/
PYGM I (207)	HOLD YOUR TONGUE, CLARA. (TO THE GIRL) YOU CAN	KEEP	THE CHANGE. /THE FLOWER GIRL/ OH, THANK YOU, LADY. /THE
MRS I (192)	HER, OFTEN ENOUGH. BUT SHE'S SO DETERMINED TO	KEEP	THE CHILD ALL TO HERSELF THAT SHE WOULD DENY THAT IT
MIS. PREFACE(31)	WHAT IT WAS. AND THAT OBJECT, I REPEAT, IS TO	KEEP	THE CHILDREN OUT OF MISCHIEF: MISCHIEF MEANING FOR THE
DEVL III (66)	OUT: THEYVE DONE WITH YOU. /CHRISTY/ AND I MAY	KEEP	THE CHINA PEACOCKS? /RICHARD/ (JUMPING UP) GET OUT.
ARMS I (9)	AND SNATCHING THE CLOAK) A GOOD IDEA! I'LL	KEEP	THE CLOAK; AND YOU'LL TAKE CARE THAT NOBODY COMES IN AND
LION I (118)	PULL YOURSELF TOGETHER, MAN. HOLD YOUR HEAD UP.	KEEP	THE CORNERS OF YOUR MOUTH FIRM; AND TREAT ME
DOCT PREFACE(68)	A BODY OF MEN TRAINED AND PAID BY THE COUNTRY TO	KEEP	THE COUNTRY IN HEALTH IT WILL REMAIN WHAT IT IS AT
GETT PREFACE(236)	THAT EVERY POSSIBLE EFFORT HAS BEEN MADE TO	KEEP	THE COUPLE UNITED AGAINST THEIR WILLS, SUCH PRIVACY
MRS IV (249)	ARE. BUT IT'S NOT: IT'S ALL ONLY A PRETENCE, TO	KEEP	THE COWARDLY SLAVISH COMMON RUN OF PEOPLE QUIET. DO YOU
ROCK I (196)	TO DO. NO, P.M.: THE RIGHT ALTERNATIVE IS MINE:	KEEP	THE CROWD AMUSED. YOU OUGHT TO KNOW THAT, I THINK,
ROCK I (198)	COULDNT. ONLY, IT WOULD DO SUCH A LOT OF GOOD--	KEEP	THE CROWD QUIET TALKING ABOUT IT FOR A FORTNIGHT.
KING I (218)	WHY DONT YOU CHOOSE? /CHARLES/ I PREFER TO	KEEP	THE CROWN AND THE GRAND MANNER UP MY SLEEVE UNTIL I
KING I (190)	TO SEE THAT THE MONARCHY IS GONE AND THAT I	KEEP	THE CROWN BY MY WITS, ARE FOOLISH ENOUGH TO BELIEVE
POSN (446)	SOMEONE ELSE-- SOMEONE ROTTENER THAN YOURSELF TO	KEEP	THE DEVIL IN ME. STRAPPER KEMP WILL DO. OR A FEW OF
ROCK PREFACE(170)	GLADLY, AND THE EASYGOING ONES FIND OUT HOW TO	KEEP	THE ENERGETIC ONES BUSY, THERE MAY BE AS GOOD
MTH1 II (21)	DOWN BY A DEWDROP. HE INVENTED THE ALTAR TO	KEEP	THE FIRE ALIVE. HE CHANGED THE BEASTS HE KILLED INTO
GETT (351)	YOU AND BOXER MUST GO THERE AND BE READY TO	KEEP	THE FIRST ARRIVALS TALKING TIL WE COME. WE HAVE TO
BARB III (317)	IS FIT FOR NOTHING BUT TEACHING. IF YOU WANT TO	KEEP	THE FOUNDRY IN THE FAMILY, YOU HAD BETTER FIND AN
MTH1 I (13)	TOO! I AM TIRED OF PULLING THESE THINGS UP TO	KEEP	THE GARDEN PLEASANT FOR US FOR EVER. /THE SERPENT/ THEY
SIM PREFACE(8)	ACTIVITIES CALLED SPORT, WHICH ARE NEEDED TO	KEEP	THE GENTRY IN HEALTH, MUST BE UNPAID AND UNPRODUCTIVE:
O'FL (222)	COMES FROM THE PORCH) OH, IT'S A SHAME FOR YOU TO	KEEP	THE GIRL FROM HER JUTIES, DINNY. YOU MIGHT GET HER INTO
DOCT PREFACE(73)	CAPACITY OF AN EXPERT ADVISING THE AUTHORITIES,	KEEP	THE GOVERNMENT ITSELF FREE OF SUPERSTITION. IF ITALIAN
HART III (147)	FIRES BURNING. /NURSE GUINNESS/ (GRIMLY) THEYLL	KEEP	THE HOME FIRES BURNING FOR US: THEM UP THERE. /RANDALL/
HART III (147)	THAT YOU ARE NOT AFRAID; AND BE GOOD. PLAY US	KEEP	THE HOME FIRES BURNING. /NURSE GUINNESS/ (GRIMLY)
GENV IV (100)	COALMINER IS TO HEW THE COAL OUT OF THE EARTH TO	KEEP	THE HOME FIRES BURNING, BUT THE SOLDIER'S BUSINESS IS
JITT III (59)	IT. /AGNES/ I DONT SAY I WASNT, BUT SHE HADNT TO	KEEP	THE HOUSE FOR HIM. SHE HAD NOTHING TO DO BUT PLEASE
JITT III (59)	SCIENCE NOR CARE ABOUT IT. IF I HAVE TO	KEEP	THE HOUSE SPICK AND SPAN I CANT ALWAYS KEEP MYSELF
MTH1 II (24)	I MAKE A MERE CONVENIENCE OF ADAM: I WHO SPIN AND	KEEP	THE HOUSE, AND BEAR AND REAR CHILDREN, AND AM A WOMAN
GETT (317)	THIS CONTRACT. I'LL NOT HAVE IT SO. IF I'M TO	KEEP	THE HOUSE, I SHALL EXPECT CECIL TO PAY ME AT LEAST AS
OVER (190)	HARM OF IT? WE'RE NOT PERFECT; BUT AS LONG AS WE	KEEP	THE IDEAL BEFORE US-- /GREGORY/ HOW? /JUNO/ BY
DEST (154)	SEE HOW YOU ENJOY LOOKING ON AT ME WHILST I	KEEP	THE INN FOR YOU AND WAIT ON YOU! WELL, I SHALL ENJOY
MILL III (180)	IT'S YOURS, AND ANOTHER EVERY WEDNESDAY IF YOU	KEEP	THE INSPECTOR OFF ME. /EPIFANIA/ IT'S NO USE RINGING
MTH2 (51)	LAND VALUES; AND TO DOING SOMETHING OR OTHER TO	KEEP	THE IRISH QUIET. DOES THAT SATISFY YOU? /FRANKLYN/ IT
FOUN (212)	OF STRIKING MELODRAMATIC ATTITUDES? HOW DARE YOU	KEEP	THE LADY WAITING? I'M VERY MUCH ANNOYED. /MERCER/ I'M
CAPT II (268)	MY HEAD FOR HIS. /SIDI/ IT IS WELL. YOU SHALL	KEEP	THE MAN, AND GIVE ME THE WOMAN IN PAYMENT. /SIR HOWARD
2TRU II (56)	AND REPORT GRACIOUS MESSAGES FROM YOU, BETTER	KEEP	THE MEAT AND THE BIRDS, SIR: THEY WILL BE WELCOME AFTER
CAPT II (252)	OUT THROUGH THE ARCH). /BRASSBOUND/ (TO JOHNSON)	KEEP	THE MEN OUT OF THIS UNTIL THE SHEIKH COMES. I HAVE
SIM PRO,1, (23)	RIGHT IF YOU EAT PROPERLY AND STOP DRINKING AND	KEEP	THE OFFICE DUSTED AND YOUR NICE WHITE CLOTHES CLEAN AND
KING I (167)	HE WAS EXECUTED FOR PRACTISING IT. BUT WE	KEEP	THE OLD SIGNBOARD UP OVER THE DOOR OF THE OLD SHOP. AND
2TRU III (104)	BUT IF I SETTLE DOWN WITH THIS GIRL SHE WILL	KEEP	THE OTHERS OFF. I'M A BIT TIRED OF ADVENTURES.
DOCT III (151)	EAT REGULARLY; SLEEP WELL; KEEP YOUR SPIRITS UP;	KEEP	THE PATIENT CHEERFUL; HOPE FOR THE BEST; NO TONIC LIKE
SIM II (54)	PARTIES, ABOUT NOTHING. WE SHALL NEVER BE ABLE TO	KEEP	THE PEACE BETWEEN THEM. THE QUEBEC HAS GOT ALONGSIDE
GENV PREFACE(5)	FOR WAR, WE TRIED TO APPEASE GERMANY AND YET	KEEP	THE PEACE WITH SOVIET RUSSIA. ENGLAND FRIGHTENED AND
ANNA (300)	GRAND DUCHESS/ YOU REALLY MEAN THAT? YOU WOULD	KEEP	THE PEOPLE IN THEIR HOPELESS SQUALID MISERY? YOU WOULD
KING I (195)	SORT-- AND THE MONEYED MEN OF THE CITY. THEY WILL	KEEP	THE PEOPLE'S NOSES TO THE GRINDSTONE NO MATTER WHAT
POSN PREFACE(424)	IN ORDER, STILL LESS CAN IT BE TRUSTED TO	KEEP	THE PIONEERS OF THOUGHT IN COUNTENANCE; AND I SUBMIT
FANY PROLOG (260)	OF US MUST LIVE IN ENGLAND, YOU KNOW, JUST TO	KEEP	THE PLACE GOING. BESIDES-- THOUGH, MIND YOU, I DONT SAY
POSN PREFACE(416)	THE REAL EXPERTS ARE ALL IN THE CONSPIRACY TO	KEEP	THE POLICE OUT OF THE THEATRE. AND THEY ARE SO
OVER PREFACE(162)	INTEREST IN PSYCHOLOGY. BUT THE FINE ARTIST MUST	KEEP	THE POLICEMAN OUT OF HIS STUDIES OF SEX AND STUDIES OF
POSN (437)	THE WHARF. /ELDER DANIELS/ YES; BUT WE HAVE TO	KEEP	THE PRISONER HERE TIL HE COMES. /BABSY/ WHAT DO YOU
DOCT PREFACE(79)	TO CURE DISEASE AS YOU TREAT FORTUNE TELLERS. 9.	KEEP	THE PUBLIC CAREFULLY INFORMED, BY SPECIAL STATISTICS
HART II (105)	CHAINS WITH HIM? /MANGAN/ THATS RIGHT, HUSHABYE.	KEEP	THE PYJAMAS, MY LADY; AND MUCH GOOD MAY THEY DO YOU.
MTH3 (129)	(HE SITS DOWN). /BARNABAS/ AND IF I REFUSE TO	KEEP	THE SECRET? /CONFUCIUS/ I SHALL HAVE YOU SAFE IN A
MTH3 (130)	/BURGE-LUBIN/ (LAUGHING INDULGENTLY) HE WILL	KEEP	THE SECRET ALL RIGHT, I KNOW BARNABAS. YOU NEEDNT
DEST SD(162)	LIEUTENANT. ONLY, HER ELEGANCE AND RADIANT CHARM	KEEP	THE SECRET OF HER SIZE AND STRENGTH. SHE IS NOT,
SUPR II (64)	OH, TELL HIM, TELL HIM. WE SHALL NEVER BE ABLE TO	KEEP	THE SECRET UNLESS EVERYBODY KNOWS WHAT IT IS. MR
BARB II (303)	NEARER TO THE DRUM) HAVE WE GOT MONEY ENOUGH TO	KEEP	THE SHELTER OPEN? /MRS BAINES/ I HOPE WE SHALL HAVE
POSN PREFACE(426)	INTO A MERE COMMITTEE TO AVOID UNPLEASANTNESS AND	KEEP	THE STAGE " IN GOOD TASTE"? IT IS NO MORE POSSIBLE FOR
BULL II (100)	KEEGAN IS A WORSE SINNER AND A WORSE BEGGAR, AND	KEEP	THE STONE AND THE CURSE FOR HIM THE NEXT TIME YOU MEET
APPL INTRLUD(248)	GREAT. WHAT ARE THEY FOR? THESE DULL SLAVES? TO	KEEP	THE STREETS SWEPT FOR ME. TO ENABLE ME TO REIGN OVER
NEVR II (246)	BUT YOU ARE THE MOST THOUGHTFUL OF MEN. NO:	KEEP	THE SUNSHADES AND GIVE ME THE CAMP STOOLS (TAKING
SIM II (65)	TO SAY, PRA? MY BRAIN IS NOT STRONG ENOUGH TO	KEEP	THE THREAD OF MY REMARKS. I OUGHT TO HAVE WRITTEN IT
BARB III (335)	(DETERMINEDLY) NO: NONE OF THAT. YOU MUST	KEEP	THE TRUE FAITH OF AN ARMORER, OR YOU DONT COME IN HERE.
HART III (137)	THIS GARDEN IN WHICH YOU ARE NOT A DOG BARKING TO	KEEP	THE TRUTH OUT! /HECTOR/ THINK OF LADY UTTERWORD'S
HART PREFACE(28)	THAT APE THEM WILL BE QUITE SUFFICIENT TO	KEEP	THE TWO GOING UNTIL THE NEXT WAR. FOR THE INSTRUCTION
CLEO II (135)	YES: I FORGOT. GO QUICKLY AND WORK, CAESAR; AND	KEEP	THE WAY OVER THE SEA OPEN FOR MY MARK ANTONY. (SHE
2TRU I (45)	TRUST YOU WITH IT HOW DO I KNOW THAT YOU WILL NOT	KEEP	THE WHOLE PRICE FOR YOURSELF? /THE BURGLAR/ SWEETIE:
MRS III (229)	AND THE EXPLANATIONS IT WOULD SAVE IF WE WERE TO	KEEP	THE WHOLE THING IN THE FAMILY, SO TO SPEAK. ASK YOUR
SHAK (142)	DEAD AND TURNED TO CLAY MAY STOP A HOLE TO	KEEP	THE WIND AWAY. OH THAT THAT EARTH WHICH KEPT THE WORLD
2TRU I (29)	ME. /THE ELDERLY LADY/ BUT HOW DID IT GET IN! I	KEEP	THE WINDOWS CLOSED SO CAREFULLY. AND THERE IS A SHEET
BUOY II (22)	KEEPS THE WOMAN AND RESTS THERE. /SHE/ YOU DO NOT	KEEP	THE WOMAN IN THIS CASE. SHE HAS HAD ENOUGH OF YOU. GET
METH PREFACE(R36)	DECIDED THAT THE MOUNTAINS ARE GREAT WEIGHTS TO	KEEP	THE WORLD FROM BEING BLOWN AWAY INTO SPACE. BUT WE
MIS. PREFACE(39)	FOR SOMETHING ELSE TO TEACH; AND YOU THEREFORE	KEEP	THE WRETCHED CHILD REPEATING ITS CATECHISM AGAIN AND
CYMB V (141)	HANDKERCHIEF. /POSTHUMUS/ YEA, BLOODY CLOTH, I'LL	KEEP	THEE; FOR I WISH'D THOU SHOULDST BE COLOUR'D THUS. YOU
APPL PREFACE(183)	HAD TO BE TAUGHT TO DO IT ECONOMICALLY, AND TO	KEEP	THEIR ACCOUNTS PROPERLY, BY GOVERNMENT OFFICIALS. OUR
MIS. PREFACE(7)	OF SERVANTS IT IS IMPOSSIBLE TO INDUCE PARENTS TO	KEEP	THEIR CHILDREN AT HOME INSTEAD OF PAYING SCHOOLMASTERS
JOAN PREFACE(29)	OR THE PECULIAR PEOPLE, OR THE PARENTS WHO	KEEP	THEIR CHILDREN FROM THE ELEMENTARY SCHOOL, OR ANY OF
2TRU I (48)	CHRISTIAN NAME BY DISTANT COUSINS WHO WILL NOT	KEEP	THEIR DISTANCE, THE INVASION OF HER PRIVACY AND
GENV III SD(68)	NEWCOMER. THE REST BECOME DISCREETLY SILENT, BUT	KEEP	THEIR EARS OPEN. /THE JEW/ MY GOOD SIR, WHAT IS YOUR
CLEO III SD(152)	QUAY AND LOOKS OUT OVER THE HARBOR. THE SENTINELS	KEEP	THEIR EYES ON HIM MALIGNANTLY. /APOLLODORUS/ (
SUPR III SD(74)	NONE OF THEM ARE ARMED; AND THE UNGLOVED ONES	KEEP	THEIR HANDS IN THEIR POCKETS BECAUSE IT IS THEIR
KING II (224)	YOU DO NOT UNDERSTAND. THESE WOMEN DO NOT	KEEP	THEIR HOLD ON ME: I KEEP MY HOLD ON THEM. I HAVE A BIT
OVER PREFACE(156)	IT; AND THE PRACTITIONERS WHO KNOW MOST ABOUT IT	KEEP	THEIR KNOWLEDGE VERY JEALOUSLY TO THEMSELVES. WHICH IS

BARB I (268)	NOT ASHAMED OF IT. I AM NOT ONE OF THOSE MEN WHO	KEEP	THEIR MORALS AND THEIR BUSINESS IN WATER-TIGHT
GENV PREFACE(13)	FAR DEMOCRATIC THAT THEY MUST FOR THEIR OWN SAKES	KEEP	THEIR SLAVES ALIVE AND EFFICIENT, USE THEIR POWERS TO
VWOO 2 (130)	TABLE INSTEAD OF KEEPING THEM WHERE A LADY SHOULD	KEEP	THEM: UP YOUR SLEEVE. /Z/ WELL, WHERES THE HARM? /A/
ROCK I (196)	NOTHING TO LISTEN TO OR LOOK AT. THE MEETINGS	KEEP	THEM AMUSED. THEY SAVE US TROUBLE. /SIR ARTHUR/ THATS
SUPR HANDBOK(204)	IN ALCOHOL, AND TO STEAL BIRDS' EGGS AND	KEEP	THEM AS THE RED INDIAN USED TO KEEP SCALPS. COERCION
GENV III (86)	ALL THE SOLDIERS AND POLICE IN THE WORLD WILL NOT	KEEP	THEM AWAY FROM IT. /THE SECRETARY/ (MUSING) HM!
CLEO II (142)	HAVE COME TO PUT OUT THE FIRE. THE LIBRARY WILL	KEEP	THEM BUSY WHILST WE SEIZE THE LIGHTHOUSE. EH? (HE
ARMS I (6)	ON HER WAY TO THE DOOR) OH NO, DEAR: YOU MUST	KEEP	THEM FASTENED. YOU WOULD BE SURE TO DROP OFF TO SLEEP
CAND II (105)	OF THING-- ALWAYS HAD TO HAVE LOVE AFFAIRS TO	KEEP	THEM FROM GOING MAD. /PROSERPINE/ (RISING, OUTRAGED)
LION PREFACE(17)	TO THE PROSPECT OF HEAVEN TO CONSOLE THE POOR AND	KEEP	THEM FROM INSURRECTION ALSO CURBS THE VICIOUS BY
DEST (187)	FROM CROSSING, AND YOU BLAZING AWAY AT THEM TO	KEEP	THEM FROM SETTING THE BRIDGE ON FIRE? DID YOU NOTICE
DOCT I (107)	NOW, SIR PATRICK. HOW LONG MORE ARE YOU GOING TO	KEEP	THEM HORSES STANDING IN THE DRAUGHT? /SIR PATRICK/
GETT (332)	THEIR HUSBANDS INTO ALL SORTS OF WICKEDNESS TO	KEEP	THEM IN GOOD HUMOR. SINJON: BE OFF WITH YOU: THIS
FABL PREFACE(79)	SENSUAL PARADISE AND A VERY DISGUSTING HELL TO	KEEP	THEM IN ORDER. WHETHER HE INVENTED HIS CONVERSATIONS
ROCK II (261)	THEYD KNOW THE REASON WHY. /BASHAM/ AND WHO WOULD	KEEP	THEM IN ORDER, I SHOULD LIKE TO KNOW: SILLY AMATEURS.
GETT PREFACE(218)	HUSBAND OR WIFE YET BORN KEEPS THEM OR EVER CAN	KEEP	THEM IN THE IDEAL SENSE. MARRIAGE AS A MAGIC SPELL. THE
FABL PREFACE(68)	TO EXPERIMENT WITH; FOR THE BASIC INCOME WILL	KEEP	THEM IN THE NORMAL GROOVES. SO MUCH FOR THE ECONOMICS
MTH4 I (157)	MY CELLAR. I DO NOT DENY THEIR EXISTENCE; BUT I	KEEP	THEM IN THEIR PROPER PLACE, WHICH IS NOT, IF I MAY BE
BUOY III (35)	WHEN THEY ARE ALL RUINED THEY WILL EXPECT ME TO	KEEP	THEM ON MY ANNUITY. I CANT AND WONT. SO NOW GIVE ME A
2TRU PREFACE(10)	AND SENSE OF SOCIAL IMPORTANCE AND UTILITY TO	KEEP	THEM ON VERY GOOD TERMS WITH THEMSELVES AND THEIR
2TRU III (108)	ARE AT THEIR WITS' END FOR SOME OCCUPATION TO	KEEP	THEM OUT OF MISCHIEF. THEY WANT TO INTRODUCE THE ONLY
MTH3 (131)	NON-ADULT RACES AND GUIDE THEM AND TRAIN THEM AND	KEEP	THEM OUT OF MISCHIEF UNTIL THEY GROW UP TO BE CAPABLE
SIM II (54)	TO SINK THEM IF THEY DONT STOP. HOW AM I TO	KEEP	THEM QUIET? /PRA/ DONT KEEP THEM QUIET. THEIR
SIM II (54)	STOP. HOW AM I TO KEEP THEM QUIET? /PRA/ DONT	KEEP	THEM QUIET. THEIR SQUABBLES WILL MAKE THEM FORGET WHAT
GENV PREFACE(5)	NEVER DO MAKE THEIR WILLS, AND THE REST SELDOM	KEEP	THEM REVISED AND UP TO DATE, STATES, HOWEVER
PYGM IV (267)	HER JEWELS). WILL YOU TAKE THESE TO YOUR ROOM AND	KEEP	THEM SAFE. I DONT WANT TO RUN THE RISK OF THEIR BEING
2TRU PREFACE(4)	LADIES TAKING UP OCCUPATIONS AND INTERESTS WHICH	KEEP	THEM SO BUSY DOING PROFESSIONAL OR PUBLIC WORK THAT
CAND II SD(121)	HIS FACE, AND INTERLACING HIS FINGERS RIGIDLY TO	KEEP	THEM STEADY. /CANDIDA/ (TO MORELL, RELIEVED AND
6CAL (96)	I WILL DEAL WITH THEM. /THE QUEEN/ DO NOT	KEEP	THEM TOO LONG IN THE COLD, DEAREST SIR. /THE KING/ (
GENV III (85)	HER BRAINS ON HER SLEEVE AS MEN DO. SHE SHOULD	KEEP	THEM UP IT. MEN LIKE TO BE LISTENED TO. /BEGONIA/ I
FANY PROLOG (269)	THE YOUNG CAN DO FOR THE OLD, TO SHOCK THEM AND	KEEP	THEM UP TO DATE. BUT I KNOW THAT THIS PLAY WILL SHOCK
DEVL I (18)	THEM. KEEP THEM UP TO THE MARK, MINISTER.	KEEP	THEM UP TO THE MARK. COME! (WITH A SPRING HE SEATS
DEVL I (18)	STILL AT THE GOOD WORK, STILL SHEPHERDING THEM.	KEEP	THEM UP TO THE MARK, MINISTER. KEEP THEM UP TO THE
JITT II (50)	BUT IF I AM TO KEEP UP APPEARANCES, YOU MUST	KEEP	THEM UP TOO. IF I AM TO PRETEND TO BE A GOOD WOMAN, YOU
CAPT I (239)	AND IT WILL BE TROUBLE ENOUGH, I ASSURE YOU, TO	KEEP	THEM WASHED AND FED WITHOUT THAT. /BRASSBOUND/ (
MIS. (165)	THEM. I DIDNT MAKE THEM: I DONT LIKE THEM: I WONT	KEEP	THEM. NOW WHAT WILL YOU DO? /PERCIVAL/ BOLT. (HE RUNS
SUPR HANDBOK(222)	TREATED AS HUMAN BEINGS IT IS NOT WORTH WHILE TO	KEEP	THEM. THE RELATION OF MASTER AND SERVANT IS
JITT III (79)	THAT IF SECRETS DONT KEEP THEMSELVES, NOBODY CAN	KEEP	THEM. THIS SECRET WOULDNT KEEP ITSELF. COME! STOP
DOCT PREFACE(79)	THAT INVALIDS, MEANING PERSONS WHO CANNOT	KEEP	THEMSELVES ALIVE BY THEIR OWN ACTIVITIES, CANNOT,
2TRU III (97)	TO KEEP MYSELF IN HEALTH. THEY PREYED ON ME TO	KEEP	THEMSELVES ALIVE: THEY PRETENDED THEY WERE MAKING ME
GENV IV (120)	LIKE BEES AND KEEP BARELY ENOUGH OF THE HONEY TO	KEEP	THEMSELVES MISERABLY ALIVE. RUSSIA BELONGS TO THE
MTH3 (130)	THERE ARE NO SECRETS EXCEPT THE SECRETS THAT	KEEP	THEMSELVES. CONSIDER, THERE ARE THOSE FILMS AT THE
JITT III (74)	IT IS NO USE KEEPING SECRETS WHEN THEY WILL NOT	KEEP	THEMSELVES. I HAVE MADE HER HAPPY: THAT IS ALL I CARE
JITT III (79)	YOU HAVE JUST SAID YOURSELF THAT IF SECRETS DONT	KEEP	THEMSELVES, NOBODY CAN KEEP THEM. THIS SECRET WOULDNT
PRES (145)	MARCH. (THE ORDERLY OBEYS). THATS THE WAY TO	KEEP	THESE CHAPS UP TO THE MARK. (THE ORDERLY RETURNS).
SUPR III (134)	HIS GOING IS A POLITICAL DEFEAT. I CANNOT	KEEP	THESE LIFE WORSHIPPERS: THEY ALL GO. THIS IS THE
NEVR I (219)	BECOMES UNBEARABLE. /DOLLY/ (SUDDENLY, TO	KEEP	THINGS GOING) HOW OLD ARE YOU, MR CRAMPTON? /GLORIA/ (
FANY II (287)	ROUND THE HOUSE LOOKING UP AT US. YOU SHOULDNT	KEEP	THINKING ABOUT IT. /KNOX/ I KNOW I SHOULDNT. YOU HAVE
BARB II (288)	ER SILLY LITTLE FACE. /BARBARA/ THEN WHY DO YOU	KEEP	THINKING ABOUT IT? WHY DOES IT KEEP COMING UP AGAINST
LION II (135)	MY MASTER IS CRUCIFIED AFRESH. /ANDROCLES/ JUST	KEEP	THINKING HOW CRUELLY YOU MIGHT HURT THE POOR
DEVL II (42)	DANGER; BUT IT IS YOUR DANGER; AND I CANT	KEEP	THINKING OF IT: I CANT, I CANT: MY MIND GOES BACK TO
APPL I (213)	MY HEALTH, AND ALMOST LOST MY REASON, TRYING TO	KEEP	THIS CABINET TOGETHER IN THE FACE OF THE CUNNINGEST
FANY II (296)	ONLY ONE THING I CARE ABOUT IN THE WORLD: TO	KEEP	THIS DARK. I'M YOUR FATHER. I ASK YOU HERE ON MY
MIS. PREFACE(64)	RELIGION, LAW, AND CONVENTION IS AN ATTEMPT TO	KEEP	THIS FORCE WITHIN BENEFICENT BOUNDS. WHAT CORRUPTS
MTH1 I (11)	THAT ONE IS HIS OWN KIND. /EVE/ WHY DID LILITH	KEEP	THIS FROM HIM? /THE SERPENT/ BECAUSE IF HE COULD DO
HART I (46)	THEM IS HESIONE HUSHABYE, WHO INVITED YOU HERE. I	KEEP	THIS HOUSE: SHE UPSETS IT. I DESIRE TO ATTAIN THE
MTH4 II (176)	IN LESS THAN THREE HOURS. /NAPOLEON/ YOU CAN	KEEP	THIS IDLE FABLE OF DISCOURAGEMENT FOR PEOPLE CREDULOUS
ROCK II (238)	MADE? /BASHAM/ NO: OF COURSE HE CANT. BUT HE CAN	KEEP	THIS ONE. HE CAN RAISE THE PAY OF THE RANKS AND DOUBLE
GETT PREFACE(221)	TO GET THEIR DAUGHTERS " OFF THEIR HANDS" AND TO	KEEP	THOSE WHO ARE ALREADY MARRIED EFFECTUALLY ENSLAVED BY
MILL PREFACE(116)	THAN EITHER DECLARE MODERN WAR IMPOSSIBLE OR ELSE	KEEP	THROWING MASSES OF INFANTRY IN THE OLD FASHION AGAINST
JITT II (36)	ACROSS THE ROOM) OH, THESE COMMONPLACES! HOW YOU	KEEP	THROWING THEM AT ME! NONE OF US KNOW WHAT MY FATHER
SIM I (42)	THEE. /MAYA/ STRIVE NOT, BELOVED: I WILL	KEEP	THY SOUL FOR THEE. /THE 2 YOUTHS/ (TOGETHER,
KING I (221)	A SECRET, MR BEAUTYMONGER? THE CLOCK DOES NOT	KEEP	TIME. IF IT DID THERE WOULD BE NO FURTHER NEED FOR THE
2TRU III (82)	AND I DONT HOLD WITH IT. KEEP TO YOUR CLASS: I'LL	KEEP	TO MINE. /SWEETIE/ MY CLASS! GARN! I'M NO COUNTESS;
CAPT II (263)	/BRASSBOUND/ YES. DANGER FOR ALL OF US UNLESS I	KEEP	TO MY BARGAIN WITH THIS FANATIC. /LADY CICELY/ WHAT
BARB III (313)	GET NO DEEPER HOLD, STRONG AS HE IS. /BARBARA/	KEEP	TO THAT; AND THE END WILL BE RIGHT. NOW TELL ME WHAT
GENV IV (120)	PRAY, GENTLEMEN, NO MORE RECRIMINATIONS. LET US	KEEP	TO THE POINT OF THE SUPERIOR RACE AND THE DIVINE
APPL I (224)	BECAUSE I AM GOOD FOR NOTHING ELSE. BUT I CAN	KEEP	TO THE POINT -- WHEN IT SUITS ME. AND I CAN KEEP YOU TO
BARB II (294)	FANCY IN THE SAME BREATH WITH IT. /UNDERSHAFT/	KEEP	TO THE POINT. WE HAVE TO WIN HER; AND WE ARE NEITHER OF
PYGM II (226)	TO TALK LIKE A LADY. /MRS PEARCE/ WILL YOU PLEASE	KEEP	TO THE POINT, MR HIGGINS? I WANT TO KNOW ON WHAT TERMS
JOAN 1 (67)	OUR COUNTRIES AND OUR LANGUAGES, AND MEANT US TO	KEEP	TO THEM. IF IT WERE NOT SO IT WOULD BE MURDER TO KILL
GETT PREFACE(197)	BOTH PARENTS AND CHILDREN BECOME MORBID IF THEY	KEEP	TO THEMSELVES. WHAT IS MORE, WHEN LARGE FAMILIES WERE
PYGM III (246)	HAS STRICT ORDERS AS TO HER BEHAVIOR. SHE'S TO	KEEP	TO TWO SUBJECTS: THE WEATHER AND EVERYBODY'S HEALTH--
2TRU III (82)	ALONE UPSETTING THE MEN; AND I DONT HOLD WITH IT.	KEEP	TO YOUR CLASS: I'LL KEEP TO MINE. /SWEETIE/ MY CLASS!
CAPT II (252)	BUSINESS TO TALK OVER. WHEN HE DOES COME, WE MUST	KEEP	TOGETHER ALL: SIDI EL ASSIF'S NATURAL INSTINCT WILL BE
CAPT II SD(266)	BY OSMAN AND A TROOP OF ARABS. BRASSBOUND'S MEN	KEEP	TOGETHER ON THE ARCHWAY SIDE, BACKING THEIR CAPTAIN.
ROCK I (197)	JUST WHAT THEY ARE SURE TO RISE AT. I MUST	KEEP	TRAFALGAR SQUARE GOING NIGHT AND DAY. A FEW LABOR M.P.S
METH PREFACE(R25)	GET THEM BECAUSE YOU WANT THEM BADLY ENOUGH TO	KEEP	TRYING FOR THEM UNTIL THEY COME. NOBODY KNOWS HOW:
METH PREFACE(R22)	DISUSE. IF YOU HAVE NO EYES, AND WANT TO SEE, AND	KEEP	TRYING TO SEE, YOU WILL FINALLY GET EYES. IF, LIKE A
LADY (237)	NOT SO AMAZEDLY AT ME; BUT MARK WHAT I SAY. I	KEEP	TRYST HERE TONIGHT WITH A DARK LADY. SHE PROMISED TO
SUPR II (54)	GET MARRIED AS SOON AS POSSIBLE, AND A MAN'S TO	KEEP	UNMARRIED AS LONG AS HE CAN. YOU HAVE YOUR POEMS AND
GETT (262)	WE ARE NO LONGER BOYS AND GIRLS. YOU CANT	KEEP	UP A BROKEN HEART ALL YOUR LIFE. IT MUST BE NEARLY
DOCT IV SD(159)	HE HAS PERFORCE BECOME A JOURNALIST, AND HAS TO	KEEP	UP AN AIR OF HIGH SPIRITS THROUGH A DAILY STRUGGLE WITH
MTH5 (217)	AND YOUR COMPANIONS HERE WILL TEACH YOU HOW TO	KEEP	UP AN IMITATION OF HAPPINESS DURING YOUR FOUR YEARS BY
3PLA PREFACE(R15)	OF THEIR VICES, WITH ALL THEIR LABORED EFFORTS TO	KEEP	UP AN UNDERSTANDING OF FURTIVE NAUGHTINESS BETWEEN THE
JITT II (50)	YOU DEFY ME. I WILL NOT BE UNKIND; BUT IF I AM TO	KEEP	UP APPEARANCES, YOU MUST KEEP THEM UP TOO. IF I AM TO
MILL II SD(166)	WITH RICKETY SILVER CRUETS AND SALT CELLARS TO	KEEP	UP APPEARANCES. THE TABLE CLOTHS ARE COARSE, AND ARE
ANNA (293)	WITHOUT EVEN RISING, WITHOUT KISSING HER HAND, TO	KEEP	UP APPEARANCES BEFORE THE ESCORT. IT WILL BREAK MY
GETT PREFACE(226)	OF WHOLLY UNNATURAL FEELINGS CAN IT BE MADE TO	KEEP	UP APPEARANCES. IF THE SENTIMENTAL THEORY OF FAMILY
DOCT PREFACE(28)	FOR THE MOST PART OF VERY POOR MEN STRUGGLING TO	KEEP	UP APPEARANCES BEYOND THEIR MEANS, FIND THEMSELVES
BULL PREFACE(64)	CONSTITUTIONALLY TIMID; BUT I FIND IT POSSIBLE TO	KEEP	UP APPEARANCES, AND CAN EVEN FACE THE RISK OF BEING RUN
ARMS II (34)	NO, SIR. /SERGIUS/ VERY FATIGUING THING TO	KEEP	UP FOR ANY LENGTH OF TIME, LOUKA. ONE FEELS THE NEED OF
APPL INTRLUD(249)	DIFFICULTY. JEMIMA WOULD NOT THINK IT RIGHT TO	KEEP	UP HER PRESENT INTIMACY WITH ME IF I WERE MARRIED TO
2TRU III (103)	IS NOW SO ENORMOUSLY RICH THAT I CANNOT AFFORD TO	KEEP	UP HIS ACQUAINTANCE. NEITHER NEED YOU KEEP UP THAT OF
SUPR IV (146)	NONSENSE, MR MALONE: YOU MUST ENABLE YOUR SON TO	KEEP	UP HIS POSITION. IT IS HIS RIGHT. /MALONE/ (GRIMLY) I
FANY III (321)	(A LITTLE NERVOUS ABOUT IT; BUT TRYING TO	KEEP	UP HIS SPIRITS) MISS DELANEY: MR AND MRS KNOX. (KNOX,
CAPT II (257)	AS THE PROPERTY NOW COSTS 150 POUNDS A YEAR TO	KEEP	UP INSTEAD OF BRINGING IN ANYTHING, I AM AFRAID IT
POSN PREFACE(375)	WITH MYSELF, IT WAS NONE THE LESS NECESSARY TO	KEEP	UP ITS PRESTIGE IN EVERY POSSIBLE WAY, NOT ONLY FOR THE
MILL PREFACE(118)	TO PRIVATE ENTERPRISE, PARLIAMENT WAS ABLE TO	KEEP	UP ITS REPUTATION BY SIMPLY MAINTAINING AN EFFECTIVE
ARMS II (27)	BULGARIA. I DONT MIND A GOOD WASH ONCE A WEEK TO	KEEP	UP MY POSITION; BUT ONCE A DAY IS CARRYING THE THING TO
PHIL I (86)	AFFECTATION) IT'S VERY KIND OF YOU TO TRY TO	KEEP	UP MY SPIRITS BY MAKING LIGHT OF IT, CHARTERIS. BUT I
BUOY IV (55)	ACCEPT NO FEES FOR IT; BUT I SHALL BE GLAD TO	KEEP	UP OUR ACQUAINTANCE, IF THAT WILL BE AGREEABLE TO YOU.
2TRU III (103)	TO KEEP UP HIS ACQUAINTANCE. NEITHER NEED YOU	KEEP	UP THAT OF YOUR SON. BY THE WAY, HE PASSES HERE AS THE
MIS. (154)	OR HER LIFE. IT'S A POINT OF HONOR WITH US TO	KEEP	UP THAT TRADITION. USUALLY SEVERAL OF US DO IT; BUT IT
POSN (437)	WHILE I AM ELDER HERE, I SHALL UMBLY ENDEAVOR TO	KEEP	UP THE DIGNITY OF HIM I SERVE TO THE BEST OF MY SMALL
MIS. (146)	HAVE THOUGHT YOUR CASE WAS QUITE DIFFERENT. YOU	KEEP	UP THE MIDDLE-CLASS TRADITION: THE DAY SCHOOL AND THE
BULL IV (180)	THINK THESE THINGS CANNOT BE SAID TOO OFTEN: THEY	KEEP	UP THE MORAL TONE OF THE COMMUNITY. AS YOU KNOW, I

MRS III	(222)	AND WIFE OR BROTHER AND SISTER-- THEY CANT	KEEP	UP THE POLITE HUMBUG THATS SO EASY FOR TEN MINUTES ON
PYGM V	(275)	ESPECIALLY NOW THAT MR DOOLITTLE IS ABLE TO	KEEP	UP THE POSITION YOU HAVE THRUST ON HER; BUT SHE SAYS
SUPR PREFACE	(R18)	ORDINARY MAN'S MAIN BUSINESS IS TO GET MEANS TO	KEEP	UP THE POSITION AND HABITS OF A GENTLEMAN, AND THE
MRS PREFACE	(176)	SHAMED THE NEWSPAPERS WHICH SUPPORT A TARIFF TO	KEEP	UP THE PRICE OF EVERY AMERICAN COMMODITY EXCEPT
GENV IV	(96)	THE WORSE OF AT HOME FOR THAT. HOW ARE WE TO	KEEP	UP THE SELFRESPECT OF OUR PEOPLE UNLESS WE CONFRONT THE
BARB III	(324)	AND THE CLERKS HAVE TALL HATS AND HYMNBOOKS AND	KEEP	UP THE SOCIAL TONE BY REFUSING TO ASSOCIATE ON EQUAL
GETT	(287)	FAMILIES STUCK TO THE MARRIAGE TRADITION SO AS TO	KEEP	UP THE SUPPLY OF VESTAL VIRGINS, WHO HAD TO BE
GETT PREFACE	(208)	PROCESS AS FAR AS NUMBERS GO. IT IS HARDER TO	KEEP	UP THE SUPPLY OF ELEPHANTS THAN OF SPARROWS AND
GETT PREFACE	(208)	AND FOR THE SAME REASON IT WILL BE HARDER TO	KEEP	UP THE SUPPLY OF HIGHLY CULTIVATED MEN AND WOMEN THAN
BARB I	(255)	WAY; AND HE PRETENDS TO CONSIDER HIMSELF BOUND TO	KEEP	UP THE TRADITION AND ADOPT SOMEBODY TO LEAVE THE
CATH 2	(174)	/CATHERINE/ (SITTING UP) THEY MAKE ME DO IT TO	KEEP	UP THEIR OWN LITTLE DIGNITIES? SO? /NARYSHKIN/
FANY III	(306)	MEN HAVE TO DO SOME AWFULLY MEAN THINGS TO	KEEP	UP THEIR RESPECTABILITY. BUT YOU CANT BLAME THEM FOR
WIDO II	(41)	THEM JUST LIKE OTHER PEOPLE. DO YOU SUPPOSE I CAN	KEEP	UP THOSE ROOFS FOR NOTHING? /TRENCH/ YES: THATS ALL
OVER	(182)	OF THEM! I ASK YOU, HOW DO YOU EXPECT A WOMAN TO	KEEP	UP WHAT YOU CALL HER SENSIBILITY WHEN THIS SORT OF
KING II	(226)	STRONGER IN YOUR MIND THAN EVER; AND NOBODY CAN	KEEP	UP WITH YOU WALKING. /CHARLES/ NEVERTHELESS, BELOVED, I
KING II	(230)	MUCH EXERCISE: YOU WALK AND WALK AND NOBODY CAN	KEEP	UP WITH YOU; YOU ARE ALWAYS GARDENING OR SAILING OR
LION II	(138)	AT HIS TELLING YOU TO THINK OF YOURSELF TO	KEEP	UP YOUR HEART. I SAY, THINK OF YOURSELF AND BURN THE
DOCT I	(88)	VERY INTERESTING TO ME NOW, COLLY. /RIDGEON/ YOU	KEEP	UP YOUR INTEREST IN SCIENCE, DO YOU? /SIR PATRICK/
MTH5	(256)	HE-ANCIENT/ I FIND IT MORE AND MORE DIFFICULT TO	KEEP	UP YOUR LANGUAGE. ANOTHER CENTURY OR TWO AND IT WILL BE
BARB II	(276)	HIM AT THE CORNER OF THE TABLE). /RUMMY/ (GAILY)	KEEP	UP YOUR OLD ART! NEVER SAY DIE! /SHIRLEY/ I'M NOT AN
SIM PRO,3,	(30)	ANY. WE DONT EAT IT. /THE Y.W./ THEN HOW DO YOU	KEEP	UP YOUR STRENGTH? /THE PRIEST/ IT KEEPS ITSELF UP.
KING I	(200)	THEY THINK OF US? MR NEWTON HAS HIS POSITION TO	KEEP	UP. /CHARLES/ IT IS THE JUDGMENT OF HEAVEN ON YOU FOR
MRS I	(188)	FOR HONORIA. BESIDES, I HAVE NO MYSTERIES TO	KEEP	UP; AND IT SEEMS SHE HAS. I SHALL USE THAT ADVANTAGE
MTH1 II	(21)	LEAVE US IN PEACE. THE WORLD IS WIDE ENOUGH TO	KEEP	US APART. /EVE/ WHY DO YOU WANT TO DRIVE HIM AWAY? HE
MTH4 I	(170)	YOU ONLY ENCOURAGE THE SIN OF PRIDE IN US, AND	KEEP	US LOOKING DOWN AT YOU INSTEAD OF UP TO SOMETHING
MIS. PREFACE	(79)	WITH OUR PARENTS BY WHICH THE SCHOOL WAS BOUND TO	KEEP	US OUT OF THEIR WAY FOR HALF THE DAY AT ALL HAZARDS.
JITT III	(59)	FATHER? WHY SHOULD OUR BEING MOTHER AND DAUGHTER	KEEP	US SO FAR APART? /AGNES/ WHAT A THING TO SAY, CHILD.
MTH4 II	(186)	FROM HER. I HOPE THIS ZOZIM CHAP IS NOT GOING TO	KEEP	US WAITING MUCH LONGER; FOR I FEEL FAR FROM COMFORTABLE
MTH5	(246)	CHILDREN HAVE PLAYED WITH DOLLS. /ECRASIA/ YOU	KEEP	USING THAT WORD. WHAT ARE DOLLS, PRAY? /THE
GENV IV	(114)	DESCRIBES HIM AS YOUR VALET. /BBDE/ I DO NOT	KEEP	VALETS. BUT IN SO FAR AS FLANCO IS STRIVING TO SAVE HIS
DOCT I	(102)	THE MOON. AND THE WORST OF IT IS, I'M TOO POOR TO	KEEP	WELL MYSELF ON THE COOKING I HAVE TO PUT UP WITH. IVE
KING I	(166)	ME, I HAVE COME HERE UNINVITED. MY BUSINESS WILL	KEEP	WHILE YOU DISCHARGE YOURS WITH THIS NOBLEMAN-- SO
KING PREFACE	(157)	FOR THE WOMEN IMMEDIATELY USED THEIR VOTE TO	KEEP	WOMEN OUT OF PARLIAMENT. AFTER SEVENTEEN YEARS OF IT
SIM II	(70)	IS ALL. YOU WILL NO LONGER EXIST. DONT LET ME	KEEP	YOU ALL STANDING. SIT DOWN IF YOU LIKE. NEVER MIND ME:
FANY III	(310)	HIM UNTIL HE GETS OVER IT. /GILBEY/ AND IS HE TO	KEEP	YOU ALL THAT TIME? OR ARE YOU TO SPEND YOUR SAVINGS IN
APPL II	(265)	I SUPPOSE I SHALL END AS AMERICAN EMPEROR JUST TO	KEEP	YOU AMUSED. /THE QUEEN/ I NEVER DESIRE ANYTHING THAT IS
BUOY II	(23)	LET ME SLEEP INDOORS? /SHE/ THE SAXOPHONE WOULD	KEEP	YOU AWAKE. /HE/ ON THE CONTRARY, MUSIC ALWAYS SENDS ME
DEVL I	(5)	AND LIE DOWN, SINCE YOU HAVNT FEELING ENOUGH TO	KEEP	YOU AWAKE. YOUR HISTORY ISNT FIT FOR YOUR OWN EARS TO
BULL PREFACE	(34)	ARE BOTH EQUALLY OPPOSED TO MINE, WHICH IS TO	KEEP	YOU BOTH EQUALLY POWERLESS AGAINST ME IN ORDER THAT I
CAND II	(109)	LEAVE YOU TO YORESELF, MR MORCHBANKS. IVE COME TO	KEEP	YOU COMPANY. (MARCHBANKS LOOKS UP AT HIM IN
DEST	(187)	THE RIVER: THE AUSTRIANS BLAZING AWAY AT YOU TO	KEEP	YOU FROM CROSSING, AND YOU BLAZING AWAY AT THEM TO KEEP
MIS.	(163)	BUT A KISS; AND I'LL FIGHT LIKE THE DEVIL TO	KEEP	YOU FROM GETTING THAT. BUT WE MUST PLAY ON THE HILL AND
BULL IV	(161)	I'M FOND OF TOM. /NORA/ OH, WELL, DONT LET ME	KEEP	YOU FROM HIM. /LARRY/ I KNOW QUITE WELL THAT MY
DEVL I	(14)	YOU AND KNOW YOURE THERE: THEYRE AS MUCH BOUND TO	KEEP	YOU FROM STARVATION AS I AM. AT ANY RATE THEY MIGHT
BUOY 1	(16)	WILL YOU PAY MY FARE? /FATHER/ YES: ANYTHING TO	KEEP	YOU FROM TOMFOOLING IN THE PARKS. AND IT WILL KEEP YOUR
BARB II	(283)	I DONT WANT TO GET SHUT OF YOU. I WANT TO	KEEP	YOU HERE AND SAVE YOUR SOUL. YOUD BETTER STAY: YOURE
MIS.	(171)	AND WEARING MY LIFE OUT FOR A SALARY THAT WOULDNT	KEEP	YOU IN CIGARS. YOULL NEVER BELIEVE THAT A CLERK'S A MAN
DOCT PREFACE	(5)	GOOD OR BAD, PROVIDED YOU GET ENOUGH PEOPLE TO	KEEP	YOU IN COUNTENANCE BY DOING IT ALSO. IT IS THE SORT OF
SUPR IV	(167)	WIFE CAN PUT ON A CAP AND MAKE HERSELF UGLY TO	KEEP	YOU IN COUNTENANCE, LIKE MY GRANDMOTHER. /TANNER/ SO
6CAL	(99)	AGAINST YOUR BETTERS, WHOM GOD HAS APPOINTED TO	KEEP	YOU IN OBEDIENCE AND LOYALTY. YOU ARE TRAITORS; AND AS
MIS.	(113)	OF A LOT OF SAVAGE TRIBES. AND YET HE COULDNT	KEEP	YOU IN ORDER. I DONT SET UP TO BE HALF THE MAN YOUR
CLEO IV	(177)	THE MASTER. OUR GODS SENT THE NORTH WEST WINDS TO	KEEP	YOU IN OUR HANDS; BUT YOU HAVE BEEN TOO STRONG FOR
MTH2	(52)	AGREEMENT WITH THE LEADERS OF THE OPPOSITION TO	KEEP	YOU IN POWER ON CONDITION THAT YOU DROPPED ALL
DOCT III	(153)	SHE SITS ON THE EASEL CHAIR). THANK YOU. I WONT	KEEP	YOU LONG; BUT I MUST TELL YOU THE WHOLE TRUTH. LISTEN.
DEVL I	(20)	DUDGEON MEANS NO OFFENCE, I FEEL SURE. I WILL NOT	KEEP	YOU ONE SECOND, MR DUDGEON. JUST WHILE I GET MY
GENV I	(35)	OUT). /SHE/ YOU CAN SIT DOWN. /NEWCOMER/ I WILL	KEEP	YOU ONLY A MINUTE, MISS. (HE SITS AND TAKES OUT SOME
POSN	(440)	ELDER DANIELS HERE TO GIVE HIM A CHANCE TO	KEEP	YOU OUT OF HELL, I'D TAKE THE JOB OF TWISTING YOUR NECK
BULL IV	(171)	TO KEEP HIS HOUSE FOR HIM, AT ALL EVENTS I CAN	KEEP	YOU OUT OF IT; FOR IVE DONE WITH YOU; AND I WISH I'D
GETT	(336)	YOU HAVE A MISCHIEVOUS TONGUE. THATS ENOUGH TO	KEEP	YOU OUT OF MY HOUSE. /HOTCHKISS/ IT MUST BE RATHER A
2TRU II	(73)	SWEETIE; AND I'LL GIVE YOU A HIDING THAT WILL	KEEP	YOU SCREAMING FOR HALF AN HOUR. (SWEETIE SUBSIDES). I
DOCT IV	(162)	/LOUIS/ SIT DOWN, WONT YOU? IT'S A SHAME TO	KEEP	YOU STANDING ABOUT. /SIR PATRICK/ YES, YES. THANK YOU.
FANY III	(314)	ARE MARKED OUT FOR YOU; FOR YOUVE NOTHING ELSE TO	KEEP	YOU STRAIGHT. /KNOX/ (ANGRILY) AND IS A MAN NEVER TO
VWOO 2	(128)	THINK I HAVE THE SORT OF COMMON SENSE YOU NEED TO	KEEP	YOU STRAIGHT. AND YOU BEING A WIDOWER KNOW WHAT TO
APPL I	(224)	KEEP TO THE POINT -- WHEN IT SUITS ME. AND I CAN	KEEP	YOU TO THE POINT, SIR, WHETHER IT SUITS YOU OR NOT.
ROCK I	(207)	IN THE WELSH MOUNTAINS, WHERE SHE WANTS TO	KEEP	YOU UNDER OBSERVATION FOR SIX WEEKS. THAT WOULD REALLY
DEST	(155)	CAPTURED BY THE ACCURSED AUSTRIANS. HE DARE NOT	KEEP	YOU WAITING IF HE WERE AT LIBERTY. /NAPOLEON/ (TURNING
JITT II	(41)	GO, YOU MUST, AND YOU MAY DEPEND ON ME NOT TO	KEEP	YOU WAITING TOO LONG BEFORE I GO TO WORK ON THE
JOAN 2	(71)	IT IS THE DAUPHIN'S ROYAL PRIVILEGE TO	KEEP	YOU WAITING, IS IT NOT? /LA TREMOUILLE/ DAUPHIN BE
O'FL	(212)	WITH SPITE AND ENVY. BUT SURE, SHE SHOULDNT	KEEP	YOU WAITING, SIR. /SIR PEARCE/ OH, THATS ALL RIGHT: SHE
MIS.	(120)	MOTHER. /MRS TARLETON/ ALL RIGHT: DONT LET US	KEEP	YOU. NEVER MIND ABOUT THAT CROCK: I'LL GET THE GIRL TO
2TRU II	(55)	A LETTER I HOPE THE BRIGANDS WILL CATCH YOU AND	KEEP	YOU. /MEEK/ THERE ARE NO BRIGANDS, SIR. /TALLBOYS/ NO
MIS.	(126)	THERES YOUR FATHER, AND BUNNY WITH HIM. /BENTLEY/	KEEP	YOUNG. KEEP YOUR EYE ON ME. THATS THE TIP FOR YOU.
BULL III	(141)	YOU CALL ME PADDY? /HODSON/ (UNMOVED) YOU JAST	KEEP	YOUR AIR ON AND LISTEN TO ME. YOU AWRISH PEOPLE ARE TOO
VWOO 3	(134)	FORGET MYSELF. /Z/ (RISING) VERY WELL: YOU CAN	KEEP	YOUR BALANCE SHEET TO YOURSELF. I WILL GO ON WITH THE
APPL I	(236)	THE PRIME MINISTER WOULD HAVE BEEN UNABLE TO	KEEP	YOUR BROTHER-IN-LAW OUT OF THE CABINET. /BALBUS/ (
HART III	(136)	PHYSICAL COLDS AS WELL AS MORAL ONES; SO PLEASE	KEEP	YOUR CLOTHES ON. /MANGAN/ I'LL DO AS I LIKE: NOT WHAT
APPL I	(222)	INDUSTRIES TO BIG BUSINESS MEN AS LONG AS THEY	KEEP	YOUR CONSTITUENTS QUIET WITH HIGH WAGES, THE MORE I
BARB I	(271)	MAY GO. YOU ARE NOT FIT FOR PRAYERS: YOU CANNOT	KEEP	YOUR COUNTENANCE. /LOMAX/ OH I SAY! (HE GOES OUT).
PYGM II	(234)	TAKE HER AWAY. DO YOU SUPPOSE I'M GOING TO	KEEP	YOUR DAUGHTER FOR YOU? /DOOLITTLE/ (REMONSTRATING)
O'FL	(219)	PHARISEE I'M THINKING YOU MEAN, SIR; BUT YOU CAN	KEEP	YOUR DIRTY MONEY THAT YOUR KING GRUDGES A POOR OLD
APPL I	(219)	I MEAN THAT WHEN YOU DISAGREE WITH US YOU ARE TO	KEEP	YOUR DISAGREEMENT TO YOURSELF. /MAGNUS/ THAT WOULD BE A
CLEO III	(147)	HIS PILUM TOWARDS THE PALACE) PASS IN THERE; AND	KEEP	YOUR DISTANCE. (TURNING TO FTATATEETA) COME WITHIN A
CURE	(232)	/STREGA/ (STOPPING) I REALLY CANNOT PLAY IF YOU	KEEP	YOUR EARS STOPPED. IT IS AN INSULT. LEAVE THE ROOM.
JOAN 1	(62)	YOU DITHERING IMBECILE. STAY WITHIN CALL; AND	KEEP	YOUR EYE ON HER. I SHALL HAVE HER UP HERE AGAIN.
MIS.	(126)	FATHER, AND BUNNY WITH HIM. /BENTLEY/ KEEP YOUNG.	KEEP	YOUR EYE ON ME. THATS THE TIP FOR YOU. BENTLEY AND MR
GENV II	(54)	WANT TO KNOW WHAT REAL ENGLISH PUBLIC OPINION IS,	KEEP	YOUR EYE ON ME. I'M NOT A BIT AFRAID OF WAR: REMEMBER
HART II	(107)	HIS SHOULDERS. /RANDALL/ (ENTERING WITH A POKER)	KEEP	YOUR EYE ON THIS DOOR, MANGAN. I'LL LOOK AFTER THE
KING I	(193)	ON THE SANDS, BUT IN THE MUD OF THE NORTH SEA.	KEEP	YOUR EYE ON THE ORANGEMAN, JAMIE. /JAMES/ I SHALL KEEP
MTH5	(220)	ASK QUESTIONS. FOR THE FIRST DAY OR TWO YOU MUST	KEEP	YOUR EYES AND EARS OPEN AND YOUR MOUTH SHUT. CHILDREN
MTH5	(206)	NOW, THEN, ANCIENT SLEEPWALKER, WHY DONT YOU	KEEP	YOUR EYES OPEN AND MIND WHERE YOU ARE GOING? /THE
FANY I	(283)	MIRTH) OH MY! ISNT SHE AN OLD LOVE? HOW DO YOU	KEEP	YOUR FACE STRAIGHT? /JUGGINS/ IT IS WHAT I AM PAID
DEVL I	(12)	THERE WHEN I COME BACK AFTER DRESSING MYSELF. AND	KEEP	YOUR FINGERS OFF THE RAISINS IN THAT CAKE. AND TELL
SUPR III	(77)	(REBUKING HIS EXCITEMENT) DU CALME, DUVAL:	KEEP	YOUR HAIR ON. THEY TAKE IT QUIETLY. LET US DESCEND AND
ARMS III	(56)	I DID. WHO TAUGHT YOU TO TRIM YOUR NAILS, AND	KEEP	YOUR HANDS CLEAN, AND BE DAINTY ABOUT YOURSELF, LIKE A
WIDO II	(27)	I WILL PROSECUTE YOU MYSELF. THE WAY TO	KEEP	YOUR HANDS CLEAN IS TO GAIN THE CONFIDENCE OF YOUR
MTH4 I	(165)	/THE ELDERLY GENTLEMAN/ TCHA! /ZOO/ BUT YOU CAN	KEEP	YOUR HANDS IN THE WRONG PLACE. IN YOUR NEIGHBORS'
CLEO III	(146)	MISTRESS OF THE QUEEN'S HOUSEHOLD. /CENTURION/	KEEP	YOUR HANDS OFF OUR MEN, MISTRESS; OR I WILL HAVE YOU
ARMS I	(10)	TO HER) THERES JUST HALF A CHANCE, IF YOU	KEEP	YOUR HEAD. /RAINA/ (DRAWING THE CURTAIN BEFORE HIM)
MTH4 I	(165)	IN THE RIGHT PLACE. /ZOO/ OF COURSE. YOU CANNOT	KEEP	YOUR HEART IN ANY PLACE BUT THE RIGHT PLACE. /THE
LION II	(138)	THINK OF ME, SISTER. THINK OF YOURSELF. THAT WILL	KEEP	YOUR HEART UP. THE CAPTAIN LAUGHS SARDONICALLY.
CAND II	(111)	(ASIDE TO MARCHBANKS) YORR HE IS. JUST YOU	KEEP	YOUR HEYE ON IM AND SEE. (RISING MOMENTOUSLY) I'M
GETT	(317)	OF COURSE I SHALL WORK WHEN I'M MARRIED. I SHALL	KEEP	YOUR HOUSE. /SYKES/ OH, THAT! /REGINALD/ YOU CALL THAT
AUGS	(278)	IF HE'D MADE A COPY OF THAT PAPER. /AUGUSTUS/	KEEP	YOUR IMPERTINENT SURMISES TO YOURSELF, SIR. REMEMBER
PYGM I	(212)	/THE DAUGHTER/ (VIOLENTLY) WILL YOU PLEASE	KEEP	YOUR IMPERTINENT REMARKS TO YOURSELF. /THE NOTE TAKER/
DEST	(177)	BRIGHT FLUSH IN HER CHEEKS) OH, YOU ARE TOO BAD.	KEEP	YOUR LETTERS. READ THE STORY OF YOUR OWN DISHONOR IN
BARB II	(289)	BILL. /BILL/ AW DIDNT AWST YOU. CAWNT YOU NEVER	KEEP	YOUR MAHTH SHAT? OY AWST THE GENLMN. /CUSINS/ (
FANY II	(286)	YOUD BETTER GO BACK TO THE SHOP AND TRY TO	KEEP	YOUR MIND OFF IT. /KNOX/ (RISING RESTLESSLY) I CANT. I

KING I	(186)	FOR YOUR PILLS. HOW MUCH SHALL IT BE? /NEWTON/	KEEP	YOUR MONEY FOR THE APOTHECARY, MADAM: HE WILL BE AMPLY
ARMS III	(56)	LEVAS, AND BUY ME FOR 10! (RISING SCORNFULLY)	KEEP	YOUR MONEY. YOU WERE BORN TO BE A SERVANT. I WAS NOT.
BUOY 1	(16)	YOU FROM TOMFOOLING IN THE PARKS. AND IT WILL	KEEP	YOUR MOTHER QUIET FOR A WHILE. /SON/ BETTER SAY NOTHING
DOCT III	(145)	ANYTHING LIKE THIS! (TO LOUIS) WELL, YOU CAN	KEEP	YOUR NUCIFORM SAC, AND YOUR TUBERCULAR LUNG, AND YOUR
CAND III	(130)	A MONTH AGO IN YOUR PRESENCE. /MORELL/ DID YOU	KEEP	YOUR OATH? /MARCHBANKS/ (SUDDENLY PERCHING HIMSELF ON
NEVR IV	(302)	THE GLORIA OF MY IMAGINATION. /GLORIA/ (PROUDLY)	KEEP	YOUR OWN GLORIA: THE GLORIA OF YOUR IMAGINATION. (HER
MILL IV	(200)	PLEASE! PLEASE! DO KEEP YOUR TEMPER. /ADRIAN/	KEEP	YOUR OWN TEMPER. HAS SHE LAMED YOU FOR LIFE? HAS SHE
DEVL III	(62)	SHE CANNOT FIND WORDS). /RICHARD/ IS THIS HOW YOU	KEEP	YOUR PROMISE? /JUDITH/ IF I AM NOT TO SPEAK, YOU MUST.
DEVL II	(45)	(HE SITS DOWN BESIDE HER). IS THIS HOW YOU	KEEP	YOUR PROMISE THAT I SHANT BE ASHAMED OF MY BRAVE WIFE?
FOUN	(216)	CHANCELLOR/ SILENCE, MERCER. HAVE THE GOODNESS TO	KEEP	YOUR RADICALISM TO YOURSELF IN THE PRESENCE OF THIS
CLEO II	(129)	FOR IT WAS DONE BY MY COUNSEL. THANKS TO US, YOU	KEEP	YOUR REPUTATION FOR CLEMENCY, AND HAVE YOUR VENGEANCE
MTH3	(110)	CAN GUESS THE EXPLANATION OF THAT. /CONFUCIUS/ TO	KEEP	YOUR SECRET, YOU HAD TO DIE. /BURGE-LUBIN/ BUT DASH IT
MRS II	(217)	SORT OF MOTHER DO YOU TAKE ME FOR! HOW COULD YOU	KEEP	YOUR SELF-RESPECT IN SUCH STARVATION AND SLAVERY? AND
DOCT III	(151)	ON ME; DONT FRET; EAT REGULARLY; SLEEP WELL;	KEEP	YOUR SPIRITS UP; KEEP THE PATIENT CHEERFUL; HOPE FOR
OVER	(185)	THE GOODNESS, SIR, IN ADDRESSING THIS LADY, TO	KEEP	YOUR TEMPER AND REFRAIN FROM USING PROFANE LANGUAGE?
MILL IV	(200)	DO YOU HEAR? /SAGAMORE/ PLEASE! PLEASE! DO	KEEP	YOUR TEMPER. /ADRIAN/ KEEP YOUR OWN TEMPER. HAS SHE
JOAN 4	(102)	JOHN, I HAD RATHER YOU DID NOT, UNLESS YOU CAN	KEEP	YOUR TEMPER. /THE CHAPLAIN/ IT IS ONLY THIS. I SPEAK
MIS.	(198)	PRISONER? /TARLETON/ HOLD YOUR TONGUE. /HYPATIA/	KEEP	YOUR TEMPER. /PERCIVAL/ (COMING BETWEEN THEM) LORD
NEVR IV	(296)	/CRAMPTON/ (ANXIOUSLY, RISING TO RESTRAIN HIM)	KEEP	YOUR TEMPER, M'COMAS. DONT LET US QUARREL. BE PATIENT.
GLIM	(175)	PIECES AND THROW YOU INTO THE LAKE. /SQUARCIO/	KEEP	YOUR TEMPER, SIGNOR COUNT. /FERRUCCIO/ I'LL NOT KEEP MY
POSN	(465)	FOR FEEMY. OH MY! FEEMY! /FEEMY/ (SHORTLY)	KEEP	YOUR TONGUE OFF ME, WILL YOU? /BLANCO/ FEEMY WAS A
O'FL	(226)	IN CONVERSATION WITH YOU AT THE FAIR. YOU CAN	KEEP	YOUR UGLY STINGY LUMP OF A SON; FOR WHAT HE IS BUT A
MTH4 III	(194)	AS YOU FEEL. IT DOESNT MATTER HOW YOU BEHAVE. BUT	KEEP	YOUR WITS ABOUT YOU WHEN THE PYTHONESS ASCENDS, OR YOU
NEVR II	(236)	FOR A MOMENT ON THE STEPS AS SHE FOLLOWS THEM)	KEEP	YOUR WITS ABOUT YOU, WILLIAM. THERE WILL BE FIREWORKS.
PHIL I	(82)	COME. /JULIA/ BUT ARE YOU IN EARNEST? WILL YOU	KEEP	YOUR WORD? /CHARTERIS/ (SMILING SUBTLY) NOW YOU ARE
ARMS III	(60)	BRIDE. /LOUKA/ WE SHALL SEE WHETHER YOU DARE	KEEP	YOUR WORD. AND TAKE CARE. I WILL NOT WAIT LONG.
DEVL I	(15)	PRESENCE, IF YOU CAN HELP IT, ESSIE; AND TRY TO	KEEP	YOURSELF AND ALL WOMANHOOD UNSPOTTED BY CONTACT WITH
SUPR HANDBOOK	(221)	IN HONOR UNTIL YOU HAVE ACHIEVED IT. BETTER	KEEP	YOURSELF CLEAN AND BRIGHT: YOU ARE THE WINDOW THROUGH
MRS II	(215)	COULD YOU SAVE OUT OF FOUR SHILLINGS A WEEK AND	KEEP	YOURSELF DRESSED AS WELL? NOT YOU. OF COURSE, IF YOURE
2TRU II	(73)	FROM NOW. YOU WILL ALWAYS FEEL SPLENDID IF YOU	KEEP	YOURSELF FIT. /THE PATIENT/ FIT FOR WHAT? A LOST DOG
MIS.	(126)	/BENTLEY'S VOICE/ (IN THE GARDEN) YOUVE GOT TO	KEEP	YOURSELF FRESH: TO LOOK AT THESE THINGS WITH AN OPEN
DOCT I	(84)	YES. /EMMY/ THATS MY DUCKY DIAMOND! NOW	KEEP	YOURSELF TIDY AND DONT GO MESSING ABOUT AND DIRTYING
MRS IV	(251)	HARD, SELFISH WOMAN WHEN I MEET HER. WELL,	KEEP	YOURSELF TO YOURSELF: I DONT WANT YOU. BUT LISTEN TO
MTH4 II	(190)	TRADITION OF SOCIAL PROMISCUITY, COULD YOU	KEEP	YOURSELVES SO ENTIRELY TO YOURSELVES. /ZOZIM/ (
DEVL III	(77)	SO, BY YOUR LEAVE, YOU MAY KEEP MY COAT AND I'LL	KEEP	YOURS. /RICHARD/ MINISTER-- I SHOULD SAY CAPTAIN. I
POSN	(453)	I ONLY ARGUE THAT IF THE HORSE HAD BEEN WORTH ITS	KEEP	, YOU WOULDNT HAVE LENT IT TO STRAPPER, AND STRAPPER
INCA	(239)	LESS. BUT SHE HAD SUCH A NUMBER OF RELATIVES TO	KEEP	! IT WAS QUITE HEARTBREAKING: I HAD TO RAISE HER WAGES

KEEPER

MTH1 II	(26)	HIMSELF ALSO, AND LOOK TO HIMSELF. HE WAS NOT MY	KEEPER	ANY MORE THAN I WAS HIS: WHY DID HE NOT KILL ME?
LION II	(131)	FEET) SH! ATTENTION THERE! THE EMPEROR. (THE	KEEPER	BOLTS PRECIPITATELY INTO THE PASSAGE. THE GLADIATORS
LION II	(146)	THE FUGITIVES STEAL CAUTIOUSLY IN. THE MENAGERIE	KEEPER	COMES FROM THE PASSAGE WITH OTHER KEEPERS ARMED WITH
MTH1 II	(26)	THE VOICE THOUGHT I WAS NOTHING BUT MY BROTHER'S	KEEPER	. IT FOUND THAT I WAS MYSELF, AND THAT IT WAS FOR
LION I	(114)	AND TAKE HIS RECEIPT, COUNTERSIGNED BY THE	KEEPER	OF THE BEASTS AND THE ACTING MANAGER. YOU UNDERSTAND
JOAN 4	(96)	YOUR SERVICE, MY LORD: BACHELOR OF THEOLOGY, AND	KEEPER	OF THE PRIVATE SEAL TO HIS EMINENCE THE CARDINAL OF
ARMS II	(31)	US. HIS FATHER WAS A HOTEL AND LIVERY STABLE	KEEPER	; AND HE OWED HIS FIRST STEP TO HIS KNOWLEDGE OF
FABL IV	(114)	LOOSE, AND EVERY ELEPHANT HAD TO HAVE AN ARMED	KEEPER	TO RESTRAIN IT. IT HAD ALSO BEEN NOTICED THAT HUMAN
BARB PREFACE	(224)	BY PROSTITUTION AS UNSCRUPULOUSLY AS A HOTEL	KEEPER	TRADES IN WAITERS' LABOR CHEAPENED BY TIPS, OR
DEVL I	(18)	THAT MAKES HIM JUMP LIKE A NEGLIGENT WICKET	KEEPER	, AND COMES INTO THE MIDDLE OF THE ROOM, WHERE HE
MTH1 II	(29)	YES: A LIFE IN WHICH NO MAN IS HIS BROTHER'S	KEEPER	, BECAUSE HIS BROTHER CAN KEEP HIMSELF. BUT AM I
LION II SD	(141)	BY HIS CO-RELIGIONISTS, AND BY THE MENAGERIE	KEEPER	, WHO GOES TO THE GLADIATORS. THE GLADIATORS DRAW
LION II SD	(130)	I COULD -- THEY ARE SEPARATED BY THE MENAGERIE	KEEPER	, WHO RUSHES IN FROM THE PASSAGE, FURIOUS. /THE

KEEPERS

LION II	(147)	FIRST MAN WHO LAYS HANDS ON HIM. (THE MENAGERIE	KEEPERS	AND THE GLADIATORS RUSH FOR ANDROCLES. THE LION
MIS. PREFACE	(40)	REMARK THAT IF BOARDING SCHOOLS ARE PLACES WHOSE	KEEPERS	ARE DRIVEN TO SUCH MONSTROUS MEASURES LEST MORE
LION II	(146)	KEEPER COMES FROM THE PASSAGE WITH OTHER	KEEPERS	ARMED WITH IRON BARS AND TRIDENTS). TAKE THOSE
MTH1 II	(26)	THE MEN WHO ARE CONTENT TO BE THEIR BROTHERS'	KEEPERS	INSTEAD OF THEIR MASTERS, ARE DESPISED AND REJECTED,
2TRU III	(96)	COMPANIES, RAILWAYS, MOTOR CAR PEOPLE, HOTEL	KEEPERS	, DRESSMAKERS, SERVANTS, ALL TRYING TO GET MY MONEY
ROCK II	(263)	EMPTIED AGAIN BY WEST END TRADESMEN AND HOTEL	KEEPERS	, FASHIONABLE DOCTORS AND LAWYERS AND PARSONS AND
MRS PREFACE	(178)	OF WOMEN AT STARVATION WAGES, OR RESTAURANT	KEEPERS	; OR NEWSPAPER PROPRIETORS, OR IN SOME OTHER MORE OR

KEEPIN

WIDO III	(53)	'A BIN URT BY SEEIN THEIR NAMES IN A BLUEBOOK AS	KEEPIN	A FEVER DEN. THEIR AGENT GOT SO FRIENDLY WITH ME OVER
SUPR III	(83)	ON THE TURF) HEAR HIM TALK, ONE UD THINK SHE WAS	KEEPIN	COMPANY WITH HIM. (HE TURNS HIS BACK ON THEM AND
BARB II	(286)	FOR YOU? ME AND MY LIKE. WHATS KEP US POOR?	KEEPIN	YOU RICH. I WOULDNT HAVE YOUR CONSCIENCE, NOT FOR ALL

KEEPING

APPL I	(240)	GULP IT DOWN, SIR. IT WONT GET ANY SWEETER BY	KEEPING	: WHAT? /LYSISTRATA/ OH, FOR GOD'S SAKE, SIGN, SIR.
SUPR I	(14)	AN OMNIBUS, ASHAMED TO HIRE A HANSOM INSTEAD OF	KEEPING	A CARRIAGE, ASHAMED OF KEEPING ONE HORSE INSTEAD OF
GETT SD	(259)	ON A HOUSE BUILT FOR THE GLORY OF GOD, INSTEAD OF	KEEPING	A COMPETITIVE EYE ON THE ADVANTAGE OF SENDING IN THE
GETT PREFACE	(251)	OTHELLO'S WORST AGONY IS THE THOUGHT OF "	KEEPING	A CORNER IN THE THING HE LOVES FOR OTHERS' USES."
PYGM EPILOG	(296)	WHETHER SHE HAD QUITE GIVEN UP HER NOTION OF	KEEPING	A FLOWER SHOP. SHE REPLIED THAT SHE HAD THOUGHT OF
GETT PREFACE	(195)	OF AS A VERY TYPICAL ENGLISH PATERFAMILIAS	KEEPING	A ROOF OVER THE HEAD OF HIMSELF AND HIS DAUGHTERS BY
GETT SD	(260)	PERFECT MANNERS WHICH CAN BE ACQUIRED ONLY IN	KEEPING	A SHOP FOR THE SALE OF NECESSARIES OF LIFE TO LADIES
CLEO III	(145)	A PATRICIAN. /SENTINEL/ A PATRICIAN! A PATRICIAN	KEEPING	A SHOP INSTEAD OF FOLLOWING ARMS! /APOLLODORUS/ I
MRS II	(202)	CHEAP COMMODITY, MY LAD. IF YOU HAVE NO MEANS OF	KEEPING	A WIFE, THAT SETTLES IT: YOU CANT HAVE VIVIE.
ROCK PREFACE	(191)	MISGIVINGS AS TO WHETHER THEY ARE REALLY WORTH	KEEPING	ALIVE IN A HIGHLY CIVILIZED COMMUNITY; BUT THAT WILL
BUOY 1	(14)	FOR LACK OF IT. /FATHER/ WELL, MY BOY, YOU ARE	KEEPING	ALIVE PRETTY COMFORTABLY. WHY SHOULD YOU SAW THROUGH
LION II	(146)	ATTACHMENT TO THE OLD NOR RASH AND UNPRACTICAL IN	KEEPING	AN OPEN MIND FOR THE NEW, BUT TO MAKE THE BEST OF
DOCT PREFACE	(27)	PROBABLY WILL NOT EXIST (EXCEPT AS A PRETEXT FOR	KEEPING	AN ORDINARY HOTEL) TWO YEARS HENCE. IN A POOR
MTH4 I	(166)	THERE. IT IS A VERY OLD AND VERY CRUDE METHOD OF	KEEPING	ANIMALS FROM STRAYING. /THE ELDERLY GENTLEMAN/ WE
PLES PREFACE	(R12)	OF PROFIT AND THE MAXIMUM OF SOCIAL USEFULNESS BY	KEEPING	AS CLOSE AS HE CAN TO THE HIGHEST MARKETABLE LIMIT
FABL PREFACE	(70)	PETER ACTUALLY STRUCK A MAN AND HIS WIFE DEAD FOR	KEEPING	BACK MONEY FROM THE COMMON STOCK. THE TRANSLATORS
LION PROLOG	(108)	OH! (SHE FAINTS). /ANDROCLES/ (QUAKING, BUT	KEEPING	BETWEEN THE LION AND MEGAERA) DONT YOU COME NEAR MY
ARMS II	(42)	HIS CARD-CASE, AND STOPS TO WRITE HIS ADDRESS,	KEEPING	CATHERINE IN AN AGONY OF IMPATIENCE. AS HE HANDS HER
MIS. PREFACE	(75)	AND DISEASE AND VICE; BUT STILL THE PRACTICE OF	KEEPING	CHILDREN BARELY ALIVE AT THE CHARGE OF THE COMMUNITY
MIS.	(122)	I NEVER QUITE AGREED WITH YOUR FATHER'S NOTION OF	KEEPING	CLEAR OF THEM, AND SENDING YOU TO A SCHOOL THAT WAS
2TRU III	(104)	DO YOU SAY? /THE SERGEANT/ WELL, I DONT MIND	KEEPING	COMPANY FOR A WHILE, SUSAN, JUST TO SEE HOW WE GET
FANY III	(327)	I PROPOSE, WITH YOUR PERMISSION, TO BEGIN	KEEPING	COMPANY THIS AFTERNOON, IF MRS GILBEY CAN SPARE ME.
O'FL	(225)	AN O'FLAHERTY YET THAT WOULD DEMEAN HIMSELF BY	KEEPING	COMPANY WITH A DIRTY DRISCOLL; AND IF I SEE YOU NEXT
GETT PREFACE	(243)	PROTECT THE WIVES AND DAUGHTERS OF THE MARRIED BY	KEEPING	COMPANY WITH THE BACHELORS FOR HIRE FOR AS LONG OR
FANY I	(283)	CANT UNDERSTAND THEM. BOBBY NEVER TOLD ME HE WAS	KEEPING	COMPANY WITH YOU. HIS OWN MOTHER! /DORA/ (
BULL PREFACE	(5)	NOW CONFIDENT THAT THEIR BATTLE IS WON, ARE	KEEPING	COMPARATIVELY QUIET, WHILST IN THE EAST THE QUESTION
LIED	(202)	HIS COAT TAIL, AND PULLING HIM DOWN AGAIN, WHILST	KEEPING	FAST HOLD OF TEDDY WITH THE OTHER HAND) NOT UNTIL
SUPR HANDBOOK	(186)	AS A TROUBLESOME PACK OF HOUNDS ONLY WORTH	KEEPING	FOR THE SPORT OF HUNTING WITH THEM. CAESAR'S
BUOY 1	(13)	AMERICAN BANKS, THOUGH WHOLE NATIONS ARE BARELY	KEEPING	HALF ALIVE FOR LACK OF IT. /FATHER/ WELL, MY BOY,
DEVL III	(52)	/RICHARD/ (HOLDING HER HAND AND SMILING, BUT	KEEPING	HER ALMOST AT ARMS LENGTH) I AM VERY SURE I SHOULDNT
JITT II SD	(27)	JITTA HAS TAKEN REFUGE IN AN ILLNESS, AND IS	KEEPING	HER BED. HER HUSBAND, PROFESSOR ALFRED LENKHEIM, IS
CAND II	(109)	HURRIES PAST HIM AT THE UTMOST POSSIBLE DISTANCE,	KEEPING	HER EYES ON HIS FACE UNTIL HE TURNS FROM HER AND
DEVL II	(29)	(SHE ATTEMPTS TO EMBRACE HIM). /ANDERSON/ (	KEEPING	HER OFF) TAKE CARE, MY LOVE: I'M WET. WAIT TILL I
MRS II	(201)	GIRL WANTS TO GET MARRIED, NO GOOD CAN COME OF	KEEPING	HER UNMARRIED. /REV. S./ (ASTOUNDED) BUT MARRIED TO
CAND II	(107)	FACE IN HIS HANDS). /PROSERPINE/ (AMAZED, BUT	KEEPING	HER WITS ABOUT HER: HER POINT OF HONOR IN ENCOUNTERS
FOUN	(212)	I DIDNT LET HIM IN, MY LORD. HE CAME IN. I WAS	KEEPING	HIM FROM YOU AT THE RISK OF MY LIFE WHEN YOU CAME IN
NEVR II	(252)	DOWN. SIT DOWN, WONT YOU? (SHE LOOKS AT HIM,	KEEPING	HIM IN SUSPENSE. HE FORCES HIMSELF TO UTTER THE
CAPT III	(284)	(REMONSTRATING) CICELY! /KEARNEY/ (GRIMLY	KEEPING	HIS COUNTENANCE) YOUR LADYSHIP'S CAWMPLIMENTS WILL

GENV III (70)	MESSAGES, WITHDRAWING FROM THE CONVERSATION, BUT	KEEPING	HIS EARS OPEN). /THE COMMISSAR/ (TAKING THE VACATED
MTH5 (214)	TO STREPHON) LOOK AT ME. /STREPHON/ (SULKILY	KEEPING	HIS FACE AVERTED) THANK YOU; BUT I DONT WANT TO BE
ROCK II (236)	THE PAPERS (HE OFFERS HIS PAPER). /SIR ARTHUR/ (	KEEPING	HIS HANDS BEHIND HIS BACK TO WARM THEM) I REMEMBER
SUPR HANDBOK(224)	WOMAN DESIRES TO ENJOY THE TASTE OF WINE BY	KEEPING	HIS MOUTH ALWAYS FULL OF IT. THE MOST INTOLERABLE
DEVL II (42)	EXCLAIMING) OH, HEAVEN HELP ME! /ANDERSON/ (	KEEPING	HIS SEAT AND HOLDING HER HANDS WITH RESOLUTE
BARB III (320)	MASTERS, A GOD! AT TWENTYFOUR, TOO! /STEPHEN/ (	KEEPING	HIS TEMPER WITH DIFFICULTY) YOU ARE PLEASED TO BE
JOAN 6 (128)	STOLE THE BISHOP OF SENLIS'S HORSE. /CAUCHON/ (	KEEPING	HIS TEMPER WITH DIFFICULTY) THIS IS NOT A POLICE
DEVL III (58)	COURT CANNOT WAIT ANY LONGER FOR HIM. /SWINDON/ (	KEEPING	HIS TEMPER WITH DIFFICULTY) THE STAFF IS PERFECTLY
SUPR II (53)	MAETERLINCK'S BOOK ABOUT THE BEE? /OCTAVIUS/ (	KEEPING	HIS TEMPER WITH DIFFICULTY) I AM NOT DISCUSSING
MIS. PREFACE(21)	IMPOSITIONS, OR SUFFER EXTRA IMPRISONMENTS -- "	KEEPING	IN" WAS THE PHRASE IN MY TIME -- OR LET A MASTER
GETT PREFACE(249)	MEET THIS OR THAT PRACTICAL EMERGENCY INSTEAD OF	KEEPING	IT ADJUSTED TO THE WHOLE SCHEME OF LIFE, IS THAT YOU
MIS. PREFACE(15)	ON MORE OR LESS HYPOCRITICAL PRETENCES) AND	KEEPING	IT CONTINUALLY AT HOME. MOST WORKING FOLK TODAY
MIS. (136)	THE SHOW AWAY IS A METHOD LIKE ANY OTHER METHOD.	KEEPING	IT TO YOURSELF IS ONLY ANOTHER METHOD. I SHOULD KEEP
SUPR IV (147)	I BUY IT FOR HIM, AND GIVE HIM THE MEANS OF	KEEPING	IT UP. /VIOLET/ WHAT DO YOU MEAN BY A WIFE WORTHY OF
HART II (122)	THE DAYS OF MY VANITY; AND HESIONE INSISTS ON MY	KEEPING	IT UP. SHE MAKES ME WEAR THESE RIDICULOUS THINGS (
DEST (179)	IN THAT CASE THERE CAN BE NO OBJECTION TO YOUR	KEEPING	IT. ALL I WANTED WAS TO PREVENT YOUR READING IT. (
MIS. PREFACE(87)	OF SOCIAL INTERCOURSE, AND THE FAMILY, INSTEAD OF	KEEPING	ITSELF TO ITSELF, AS THE EVIL OLD SAYING IS, AND
SIM PREFACE(14)	FORTY." IN THEIR CASE THERE WAS NO PROPER ACCOUNT	KEEPING	. IN THE NATURE OF THINGS A HUMAN CREATURE MUST
GENV PREFACE(3)	BREAK IN MY DOOR, AND WRECK MY GRANDFATHER CLOCK,	KEEPING	ME FOR NINE YEARS OF MY LIFE SUBJECT TO A CONTINUAL
MIS. PREFACE(21)	ME INSTEAD OF PAINFULLY EARNING THEIR BREAD BY	KEEPING	ME FROM ANNOYING MY ELDERS THEY WOULD HAVE TURNED ME
LION PREFACE(62)	OF THE THEOLOGIANS WHO CONCEIVED GOD AS A MAGNATE	KEEPING	MEN AND ANGELS AS LORD ROTHSCHILD KEEPS BUFFALOES
WIDO III (54)	FROM KEEPING MY MOUTH SHUT? NO: IT CAME FROM	KEEPING	MY EARS AND EYES OPEN. BLANCHE COMES IN, FOLLOWED BY
O'FL PREFACE(203)	OF WITS; AND I AM AFRAID I GAVE GREAT OFFENCE BY	KEEPING	MY HEAD IN THIS MATTER OF IRISH RECRUITING. WHAT CAN
ROCK I (207)	I KNOW THAT YOU HAVE SACRIFICED YOURSELF TO	KEEPING	MY HOUSE AND SEWING ON MY BUTTONS; AND I AM NOT
SUPR I (45)	RAMSDEN, AND NOT YOURS. I HAVE MY REASONS FOR	KEEPING	MY MARRIAGE A SECRET FOR THE PRESENT. /RAMSDEN/ ALL
NEVR II (242)	OF CHOOSING A PROFESSION YET? /PHILIP/ I AM	KEEPING	MY MIND OPEN ON THAT SUBJECT, WILLIAM? /WAITER/
WIDO III (54)	IVE GOT ON ME! DO YOU THINK ALL THAT CAME FROM	KEEPING	MY MOUTH SHUT? NO: IT CAME FROM KEEPING MY EARS AND
METH PREFACE(R16)	IS OBTAINED BY HEREDITY, BY SIMPLE PURCHASE, BY	KEEPING	NEWSPAPERS AND PRETENDING THAT THEY ARE ORGANS OF
FANY PROLOG (264)	THE PRINCIPLE OF DIVISION OF LABOR TOO FAR. THIS	KEEPING	OF THE HONESTY AND THE OTHER QUALITIES IN SEPARATE
OVER (191)	ADMITTED-- TOGETHER /GREGORY/ WHATS THE GOOD OF	KEEPING	ON AT THAT? /MRS JUNO/ OH, NOT THAT AGAIN, PLEASE.
BARB II SD(285)	YOU MUST COME. JENNY COMES TO BARBARA, PURPOSELY	KEEPING	ON THE SIDE NEXT BILL, LEST HE SHOULD SUPPOSE THAT
SUPR I (14)	HANSOM INSTEAD OF KEEPING A CARRIAGE, ASHAMED OF	KEEPING	ONE HORSE INSTEAD OF TWO AND A GROOM-GARDENER
HART I (81)	FOR SEVEN YEARS ON 500 POUNDS. /MRS HUSHABYE/ NOT	KEEPING	OPEN HOUSE AS WE DO HERE, DADDIEST. /CAPTAIN
MILL PREFACE(136)	WHEN THEY ARE AT A LOSS FOR ANY BETTER EXCUSE FOR	KEEPING	OTHER PEOPLE IN THE KITCHEN AND THEMSELVES IN THE
APPL INTRLUD(253)	BETWEEN US TO AVOID A DISASTROUS COLLISION.	KEEPING	OUR DISTANCE IS THE WHOLE SECRET OF GOOD MANNERS;
ROCK PREFACE(172)	SHORT OF MONEY. IT IS THE IMPORTANCE OF	KEEPING	OUR INCULCATED ILLUSIONS UP TO DATE THAT THROWS OUR
ARMS II (30)	OF ATTACKING MERCILESSLY WHEN YOU ARE STRONG, AND	KEEPING	OUT OF HARM'S WAY WHEN YOU ARE WEAK. THAT IS THE
DOCT PREFACE(20)	THEIR BREAD. DOCTORING IS NOT EVEN THE ART OF	KEEPING	PEOPLE IN HEALTH (NO DOCTOR SEEMS ABLE TO ADVISE
GETT PREFACE(193)	IMPRISONMENT WHICH THEY CALLED EDUCATION; AND OF	KEEPING	PIANOS IN THEIR HOUSES, NOT FOR MUSICAL PURPOSES,
SUPR HANDBOK(227)	FOR GAMING IS COMMON, THOUGH A PASSION FOR	KEEPING	ROULETTE TABLES IS UNKNOWN. GAMBLING PROMISES THE
FABL PREFACE(93)	STAR, HOW LONG WILL IT TAKE A LONDON MOTOR BUS	KEEPING	SCHEDULE TIME TO TRAVEL FROM MILLBANK TO WESTMINSTER
JITT III (74)	IN EDITH) SHE GUESSED. SHE KNEW. IT IS NO USE	KEEPING	SECRETS WHEN THEY WILL NOT KEEP THEMSELVES. I HAVE
ARMS III (54)	I GOT THROUGH TO PIROT I HAD TO PUT IT IN SAFE	KEEPING	SOMEHOW. I THOUGHT OF THE RAILWAY CLOAK ROOM; BUT
MTH2 (52)	SOCIETY AND DESTINY; AND THE IMPOSSIBILITY OF	KEEPING	SUCH A TEAM TOGETHER WILL FORCE YOU TO SELL THE PASS
DOCT V (179)	/RIDGEON/ EVERYBODY EXCEPT HIMSELF. BY	KEEPING	THAT BACK HE LOST THE RIGHT TO SACRIFICE YOU, AND
AUGS (280)	ALL THIS TALK ABOUT WAR SAVING, AND SECRECY, AND	KEEPING	THE BLINDS DOWN AT NIGHT, AND SO FORTH, IS ALL VERY
MIS. PREFACE(40)	NOT A RIGHT TO DO IS TO MAKE THIS AN EXCUSE FOR	KEEPING	THE CHILD SLAVING FOR TEN HOURS AT PHYSICAL
GETT PREFACE(235)	OUR SEX INSTITUTIONS EXCEPT A POLICE DES MOEURS	KEEPING	THE FIELD FOR A COMPETITION AS TO WHICH SEX SHALL
HART III SD(149)	OH, I HOPE SO. RANDALL AT LAST SUCCEEDS IN	KEEPING	THE HOME FIRES BURNING ON HIS FLUTE.
LION PREFACE(60)	TO A FARCE: LAW BECOMES MERELY AN INSTRUMENT FOR	KEEPING	THE POOR IN SUBJECTION; AND ACCUSED WORKMEN ARE
LION PREFACE(10)	IS GOOD FOR CHILDREN AND SERVES MORALITY,	KEEPING	THE POOR IN GOODHUMOR OR IN AWE BY PROMISING REWARDS
PLES PREFACE(R13)	SHOULD BE ATTAINABLE IN THEATRICAL MANAGEMENT BY	KEEPING	THE PUBLIC IN CONSTANT TOUCH WITH THE HIGHEST
MTH3 (116)	OTHERS LIKE YOU, HAD THEY NOT THE SAME REASON FOR	KEEPING	THE SECRET? /THE ARCHBISHOP/ THAT IS TRUE. BUT I
DEST (179)	AGO, NOTHING ELSE WOULD SATISFY YOU. /LADY/ (	KEEPING	THE TABLE CAREFULLY BETWEEN THEM) TEN MINUTES AGO
ROCK II (282)	LIVES OF THE MILLIONS OF PEOPLE WHOSE LABOR WAS	KEEPING	THE WHOLE SHOW GOING WERE NOT WORTH LIVING. I KNEW
GETT (313)	DUTY AND SEE. DOING YOUR DUTY IS YOUR BUSINESS:	KEEPING	THE WORLD GOING IS IN HIGHER HANDS. /LESBIA/
DOCT III (147)	ME IN WASTING MY TALENTS-- SUCH AS THEY ARE-- IN	KEEPING	THEM ALIVE. AFTER ALL, IF MY FEES ARE HIGH, I HAVE
GENV II (61)	MEN WANT TO FIGHT HOW DO YOU PREVENT THEM? BY	KEEPING	THEM APART, NOT BY BRINGING THEM TOGETHER. WHEN THE
CLEO II SD(130)	WHO CLOSE UP IN THEIR REAR AND GO OUT AFTER THEM,	KEEPING	THEM MOVING WITHOUT MUCH CEREMONY. THE KING IS LEFT
JOAN PREFACE(4)	TO BE OBLIGED TO HER FOR SETTING THEM RIGHT AND	KEEPING	THEM OUT OF MISCHIEF. NOW IT IS ALWAYS HARD FOR
LION PREFACE(7)	LET THEM EXECUTE HIM AS THE CHEAPEST WAY OF	KEEPING	THEM QUIET, ON THE FORMAL PLEA THAT HE HAD COMMITTED
SUPR II SD(48)	IN THE LEAST DEFERENTIAL, BUT COOL AND RETICENT,	KEEPING	THEM QUITE EFFECTUALLY AT A DISTANCE WHILST GIVING
VWOO 2 (130)	YOU PLAY WITH YOUR CARDS ON THE TABLE INSTEAD OF	KEEPING	THEM WHERE A LADY SHOULD KEEP THEM: UP YOUR SLEEVE.
JOAN PREFACE(13)	FOR PURPOSES FAR TRANSCENDING THE PURPOSE OF	KEEPING	THESE INDIVIDUALS ALIVE AND PROSPEROUS AND
NEVR IV (285)	EVERYBODY HAS GONE TO THIS FANCY BALL INSTEAD OF	KEEPING	TO OUR APPOINTMENT HERE. /VALENTINE/ OH, HE'LL COME
ARMS I (8)	SNOW, HIS BELT AND THE STRAP OF HIS REVOLVER-CASE	KEEPING	TOGETHER THE TORN RUINS OF THE BLUE TUNIC OF A
BULL IV (170)	WORLD. YOU WILL FIND YOUR WORK CUT OUT FOR YOU	KEEPING	TOM'S HOUSE AND ENTERTAINING TOM'S FRIENDS AND
6CAL PREFACE(89)	OF LIKE A MODERN CONSTITUTIONAL MONARCH ON PARADE	KEEPING	UP AN ELABORATE FICTION OF LIVING IN A POLITICAL
DEVL I (18)	HER LOOK OF UNDISGUISED HATRED). WELL, MOTHER:	KEEPING	UP APPEARANCES AS USUAL? THATS RIGHT, THATS RIGHT.
SUPR IV (148)	ME TO UNDERTAKE THIS WITH ABSOLUTELY NO MEANS OF	KEEPING	UP HIS POSITION. /MALONE/ (ALARMED) STOP A BIT,
BUOY IV (57)	FERDINAND/ I SEE. BUT AT LEAST YOULL NOT MIND MY	KEEPING	UP MY ACQUAINTANCE WITH THE FAMILY. /DARKIE/ NOT A
GETT PREFACE(184)	ON VARIOUS OTHER GROUNDS TO BE HOODWINKED BY THE	KEEPING	UP OF THE VERY THINNEST APPEARANCES, MOST OF THEM
SUPR HANDBOK(180)	JUST AS WE ARE NOT NORMALLY CONSCIOUS OF	KEEPING	UP OUR CIRCULATION BY OUR HEART-PUMP, THOUGH IF WE
APPL II (263)	KEEP ALIVE. WHEN YOU FIND SOME COUNTRY GENTLEMAN	KEEPING	UP THE OLD ENGLISH CUSTOMS AT CHRISTMAS AND SO
AUGS (268)	AND THE FATE OF THE BRITISH EMPIRE, DEPEND ON OUR	KEEPING	UP THE SUPPLY OF SHELLS, YOU ARE WASTING MONEY ON
FABL VI (126)	US WITH PHOSPHORUS. /YOUTH 1/ THEY MAY BE	KEEPING	US FOR THEIR AMUSEMENT, AS WE KEEP OUR PETS. I TOLD
MIS. PREFACE(98)	CHOICE, NO ONE HAS A RIGHT TO DEPRIVE US OF IT BY	KEEPING	US FROM ANY WORK OF ART OR ANY WORK OF ART FROM US.
JOAN 2 (71)	WHAT THE DEVIL DOES THE DAUPHIN MEAN BY	KEEPING	US WAITING LIKE THIS? I DONT KNOW HOW YOU HAVE THE
LION PREFACE(34)	MANGER, AND OF THE SHEPHERDS ABIDING IN THE FIELD	KEEPING	WATCH OVER THEIR FLOCKS BY NIGHT, AND HOW THE ANGEL
PYGM EPILOG (298)	STRUGGLED WITH AND STIFLED FOR THE SAKE OF	KEEPING	WELL WITH SOCIETY, WERE PRECISELY THOSE BY WHICH
ARMS III SD(46)	THERE IS ONE OBJECT, HOWEVER, HOPELESSLY OUT OF	KEEPING	WITH ITS SURROUNDINGS. THIS IS A SMALL KITCHEN
ROCK II (255)	YOU THE TROUBLE OF THINKING FOR YOURSELF AND	KEEPING	YOU OFF THE ROCKS. /BLEE/ YOU HAVNT KEPT US OFF THE
FOUN (211)	I-- OH, BY THE WAY, WONT YOU SIT DOWN? EXCUSE ME	KEEPING	YOU STANDING ALL THIS TIME. MACDUFF: A CHAIR. /THE
DEVL II (32)	(REMORSEFULLY) OH YES, I FORGOT. IVE BEEN	KEEPING	YOU WAITING ALL THIS TIME. (SHE GOES TO THE FIRE
DOCT III (139)	BUT YOU WERE SMELLING OUT A SCANDAL INSTEAD OF	KEEPING	YOUR MIND CLEAN AND WHOLESOME. I CAN JUST PLAY WITH
O'FL (212)	LOOKS AT HIS WATCH). IT'S TEATIME. I WONDER WHATS	KEEPING	YOUR MOTHER. /O'FLAHERTY/ IT'S NICELY COCKED UP THE
POSN (455)	AT A RAINBOW LIKE A DAMNED SILLY FOOL INSTEAD OF	KEEPING	YOUR WITS ABOUT YOU; AND WE STOLE UP ON YOU AND HAD
VWOO 3 (139)	OUT OF THE CORNER OF YOUR EYE IN SPITE OF YOUR	KEEPING	YOURSELF SO MUCH TO YOURSELF-- DID YOU NEVER SAY " I

KEEPINGS-IN

MIS. PREFACE(72)	DOES AT PRESENT, IN SPITE OF ALL THE CANINGS AND	KEEPINGS-IN	. THE PURSUIT OF LEARNING. WHEN THE PURSUIT OF

KEEPS

KING I (165)	DRESSED LIKE A NOBLEMAN. VERY TALL. VERY DARK.	KEEPS	A LACKEY. HAS A PACK OF DOGS WITH HIM. /NEWTON/ OHO!
DOCT PREFACE(16)	IN A COUPLE OF HOURS; AND IF THE SURGEON ALSO	KEEPS	A NURSING HOME, HE MAKE CONSIDERABLE PROFITS AT THE
MIS. PREFACE(25)	LOVE INTO LOATHING. ANOTHER FRIEND OF MINE WHO	KEEPS	A SCHOOL IN THE SUBURBS, AND WHO DEEPLY DEPLORES MY "
DOCT PREFACE(21)	USED TO FASCINATE THE ALCHEMISTS. ON WEEK DAYS HE	KEEPS	A SHOP IN WHICH HE SELLS PACKETS OF PENNYROYAL,
POSN (443)	BUT I KNOW BETTER. I TELL YOU, BLANCO, WHAT	KEEPS	AMERICA TODAY THE PUREST OF THE NATIONS IS THAT WHEN
LION PREFACE(62)	MAGNATE KEEPING MEN AND ANGELS AS LORD ROTHSCHILD	KEEPS	BUFFALOES AND EMUS AT TRING, MONEY THE MIDWIFE OF
BUOY III (38)	DO WITH LEGAL INSTITUTIONS. /MRS THIRDBORN/ GOD	KEEPS	BUTTING IN SOMEHOW. /SIR F./ SURELY THAT IS NOT THE
CAPT II (263)	SIR HOWARD, STILL VERY CRUSTY AND DETERMINED. HE	KEEPS	CLOSE TO JOHNSON, WHO COMES TO BRASSBOUND'S RIGHT,
HART I (73)	AND THE GRAVEL PIT WITH A CAVE WHERE HE	KEEPS	DYNAMITE AND THINGS OF THAT SORT. HOWEVER, ITS
LADY PREFACE(209)	TO WHICH THE HISTORY OF MANKIND AND THE UNIVERSE	KEEPS	ETERNALLY REPEATING ITSELF WITHOUT THE SLIGHTEST
CAND I (100)	GIVEN US A WORLD THAT NOTHING BUT OUR OWN FOLLY	KEEPS	FROM BEING A PARADISE. I WILL HELP YOU TO BELIEVE THAT

PHIL III (144) TO THE FIRE, WATCHING THEM, WHILST THE COLONEL KEEPS GUARD ON THE OTHER SIDE), /GRACE/ (SPEAKING IN A LOW
HART II (122) MORE: SHE DOESNT REALLY CARE FOR THE MEN SHE KEEPS HANGING ABOUT HER; BUT HOW IS THE WORLD TO KNOW THAT?
DEST SD(172) THAT IN ACTING, TOO, SHE HAS MET HER MATCH. HE KEEPS HER A MOMENT IN SUSPENSE; THEN SUDDENLY CLEARS UP HIS
DEVL II (33) AT THE MEZZOTINTED DIVINE ON THE WALL. JUDITH KEEPS HER EYES ON THE TEA CADDY). IS IT STILL RAINING? (HE
KING II (224) YOU ARE FINISHED WITH ALL WOMEN! YET PORTSMOUTH KEEPS HER HOLD ON YOU, AND NELLIE THE PLAYER. AND NOW
MILL I (152) KNOWS HOW TO ORDER A DINNER BETTER. THATS WHAT KEEPS HIM AT THE TOP IN THE CITY. /SAGAMORE/ THANK YOU: I
BULL PREFACE(40) ROOTED IN DISHONOR STANDS; AND FAITH UNFAITHFUL KEEPS HIM FALSELY TRUE. THE CURSE OF NATIONALISM. IT IS
MIS. PREFACE(42) OF THE SLAVE WITH THE HELPLESSNESS THAT KEEPS HIM IN SERVITUDE; AND THIS PROBLEM IS FORTUNATELY NOT
BULL III (117) IN TO THE ROOM IN WHICH HE RECEIVES RENTS AND KEEPS HIS BOOKS AND CASH, KNOWN IN THE HOUSEHOLD AS " THE
NEVR II SD(225) WAS DETERMINED NOT TO LET THEM HAVE THEIR WAY. HE KEEPS HIS BROW RESOLUTELY WIDE OPEN, AS IF, AGAIN, HE HAD
CATH 1 (166) EDSTASTON, STILL SUSPICIOUS, SHAKES HIS HEAD AND KEEPS HIS PISTOLS READY). REACH IT MYSELF. (HE REACHES
MTH1 I (18) THAT TIME AND NO OTHER WOMAN. /EVE/ AND IF ADAM KEEPS HIS VOW I WILL LOVE NO OTHER MAN UNTIL HE DIES. /THE
OVER (180) PART OF THE ROMANCE OF A JOURNEY IS THAT A MAN KEEPS IMAGINING THAT SOMETHING MIGHT HAPPEN; AND HE CANT DO
FABL PREFACE(93) DOES NOT TEACH. HE CANES OR IMPOSITIONS OR " KEEPS IN" THE PUPILS WHO CANNOT ANSWER POINTLESS QUESTIONS
PHIL I (88) CRAVEN: SO IT IS. /CHARTERIS/ EXACTLY. THATS WHAT KEEPS IT SO SELECT: NOBODY BUT PEOPLE WHOSE REPUTATIONS ARE
GETT PREFACE(249) MIGHTY, PUT THE CHURCH IN HIS POCKET, WHERE HE KEEPS IT TO THIS DAY, IN SPITE OF THE OCCASIONAL SAINTS AND
SUPR HANDBOK(227) THE ROULETTE TABLE PAYS NOBODY EXCEPT HIM THAT KEEPS IT. NEVERTHELESS A PASSION FOR GAMING IS COMMON,
GETT PREFACE(218) THAN THE CHERUBIM. POSSIBLY THE GREAT MAJORITY KEEPS ITS MARRIAGE VOWS IN THE TECHNICAL DIVORCE COURT
PYGM EPILOG (289) REACH-ME-DOWNS OF THE RAGSHOP IN WHICH ROMANCE KEEPS ITS STOCK OF " HAPPY ENDINGS" TO MISFIT ALL STORIES.
BULL PREFACE(47) TO SEE THAT IN THE FIELD, DISCIPLINE EITHER KEEPS ITSELF UP OR GOES TO PIECES; FOR HUMANITY UNDER FIRE IS A
SIM PRO,3, (30) DO YOU KEEP UP YOUR STRENGTH? /THE PRIEST/ IT KEEPS ITSELF UP. /THE Y.W./ OH, HOW COULD THAT BE? (TO THE
2TRU PREFACE(13) TOGETHER-- OR TWO OR THREE BILLIONS-- FOR KEEPS . 2. GOVERNMENT IS NEITHER AUTOMATIC NOR ABSTRACT: IT
DEST (176) I NOT FORBIDDEN YOU TO SPEAK OF MY WIFE? (SHE KEEPS LOOKING CURIOUSLY AT HIM, TAKING NO ACCOUNT OF THE
ARMS I (21) TO KNOW: WHERE AM I? MUST KEEP AWAKE. NOTHING KEEPS ME AWAKE EXCEPT DANGER: REMEMBER THAT: (INTENTLY)
MRS IV (241) (MERCILESS TO HERSELF) NO: IT'S GOOD FOR ME. IT KEEPS ME FROM BEING SENTIMENTAL. /FRANK/ (BANTERING HER)
KING II (224) HER BECAUSE SHE IS INTELLIGENT AND LADYLIKE AND KEEPS ME IN TOUCH WITH FRANCE AND THE FRENCH COURT, TO SAY
ROCK I (206) WRONG WITH THAT, IS THERE? OF COURSE I KNOW IT KEEPS ME TOO MUCH AWAY FROM HOME. THAT GIVES YOU A SORT OF
BARB III (344) MY BRAVEST ENEMY. THAT IS THE MAN WHO KEEPS ME UP TO THE MARK. /CUSINS/ YOU KNOW, THE CREATURE IS
BARB II (278) WANTS ER. SHE'LL KNAOW WOT THET MEANS; AND IF SHE KEEPS ME WITIN ITLL BE WORSE. YOU STOP TO JAWR BECK AT ME;
ROCK PREFACE(183) PREFER IT AS A PLAIN UNDERSTANDABLE THING WHICH KEEPS MEN'S KNIVES OFF ONEANOTHER'S THROATS TO YOUR PEACE
PLES PREFACE(R9) OF THE RAY: IT IS BY A BLIND INSTINCT THAT HE KEEPS ON BUILDING UP HIS MASTERPIECES UNTIL THEIR PINNACLES
ROCK I (217) DOES GOING TO CHURCH DO HIM? NOT A SCRAP. BUT HE KEEPS ON DOING THEM ALL THE SAME. /SIR ARTHUR/ BUT SURELY
SUPR I (11) BEEN REFUSING ALL THE WAY FROM RICHMOND; BUT ANN KEEPS ON SAYING THAT OF COURSE SHE'S ONLY AN ORPHAN; AND
MTH2 (40) BIRD? /HASLAM/ OH: YES. THERES A BIRD THERE THAT KEEPS ON SINGING " STICK IT OR CHUCK IT: STICK IT OR CHUCK
APPL I SD(201) IN A RUSSIAN BLOUSE AND PEAKED CAP, WHICH HE KEEPS ON. HE IS FIFTY, HEAVILY BUILT AND AGGRESSIVELY
MILL I (162) CONVENIENT TO BE MARRIED. IT IS RESPECTABLE. IT KEEPS OTHER MEN OFF. IT GIVES ME A FREEDOM THAT I COULD NOT
FANY II (285) THAN ME. HE'S NOT LOOKING AFTER ANYTHING; AND HE KEEPS OUT OF MY WAY. HIS MANNER'S NOT NATURAL. HE HASNT
INCA (250) ON THE MOUTH ORGAN REALLY SCREAMINGLY. CHIPS KEEPS OWLS AND RABBITS, SPOTS MOTOR BICYCLES. THE CORSAIR
MIS. PREFACE(6) THOUGH IN THE RELATIVELY SMALL CLASS WHICH KEEPS PLENTY OF SERVANTS IT IS IMPOSSIBLE TO INDUCE PARENTS
BULL PREFACE(50) VILLAGERS KEEP PIGEONS JUST AS AN ENGLISH FARMER KEEPS POULTRY. TRY TO IMAGINE THE FEELINGS OF AN ENGLISH
MILL IV (191) IF HE OVERDREW BY FIVE POUNDS; BUT THE MANAGER KEEPS PRESSING OVERDRAFTS ON HER: IT MAKES HIM MISERABLE
PYGM III (256) GOT SOME SILLY BEE IN HER BONNET ABOUT ELIZA. SHE KEEPS SAYING " YOU DONT THINK, SIR": DOESNT SHE, PICK?
ARMS I (20) MISTAKE. MY FATHER IS A VERY HOSPITABLE MAN: HE KEEPS SIX HOTELS; BUT I COULDNT TRUST HIM AS FAR AS THAT.
MTH4 I (146) GENTLEMAN/ WHAT IS A TERTIARY? EVERYBODY HERE KEEPS TALKING TO ME ABOUT PRIMARIES AND SECONDARIES AND
HART III (129) INTO THE LIGHT, WITH MANGAN) I THINK I SHALL. HE KEEPS TELLING ME HE HAS A PRESENTIMENT THAT HE IS GOING TO
GETT (284) NOTHING IS MORE DREADFUL THAN A HUSBAND WHO KEEPS TELLING YOU EVERYTHING HE THINKS, AND ALWAYS WANTS TO
METH PREFACE(R82) IS ALWAYS WITH US, AND, LIKE PORTRAIT PAINTING, KEEPS THE ARTIST SUPPLIED WITH SUBJECT MATTER IN THE
KING I (192) COLLECT THE TAXES. HOW DOES KING LOUIS DO IT? HE KEEPS THE BIGGEST ARMY IN EUROPE; AND HE KEEPS YOU INTO THE
BUOY II (22) THAT IS NOT NATURAL. IN NATIVE LIFE THE WOMAN KEEPS THE HOUSE AND WORKS THERE: THE MAN KEEPS THE WOMAN AND
BUOY III (39) WHICH OF US TWO IS THE REASONABLE ONE? WHO KEEPS THE HOUSE FOR YOU? WHO LOOKS AFTER YOUR CLOTHES? WHO
SHAK PREFACE(135) FACIAL EXPRESSION, IMPOSSIBLE FOR LIVING ACTORS, KEEPS THE IMAGINATION OF THE SPECTATORS CONTINUOUSLY
BARB III (324) ME, THEORETICALLY. PRACTICALLY, EVERY MAN OF THEM KEEPS THE MAN JUST BELOW HIM IN HIS PLACE. I NEVER MEDDLE
O'FL (221) SHE HADNT HALF THE JEWELRY OF MRS SULLIVAN THAT KEEPS THE POPSHOP IN DRUMPOGUE. AND SHE DRESSES HER HAIR
SUPR HANDBOK(179) CAPITALISTIC, OR COLLECTIVIST, PROVIDED IT KEEPS THE RACE AFOOT (THE HIVE AND THE ANTHILL BEING AS
MRS I SD(181) A BIG CANVAS UMBRELLA, STUCK IN THE GROUND, KEEPS THE SUN OFF THE HAMMOCK, IN WHICH A YOUNG LADY LIES
DOCT PREFACE(5) THE PATIENT, OR EXTIRPATES AN INTERNAL ORGAN AND KEEPS THE WHOLE NATION PALPITATING FOR DAYS WHILST THE
BUOY II (22) WOMAN KEEPS THE HOUSE AND WORKS THERE: THE MAN KEEPS THE WOMAN AND RESTS THERE. /SHE/ YOU DO NOT KEEP THE
BUOY III (34) SHE HAS NO MANNERS AT HOME, AND NO EDUCATION. SHE KEEPS THEM FOR VISITORS. NO CLASS. /SIR F./ MY DEAR GOOD
GETT PREFACE(218) DIVORCE COURT SENSE. NO HUSBAND OR WIFE YET BORN KEEPS THEM OR EVER CAN KEEP THEM IN THE IDEAL SENSE.
GETT (342) FLY INTO IT BY MERE ATMOSPHERIC PRESSURE. ALICE KEEPS THEM OUT NOW. MRS COLLINS KNOWS. /MRS GEORGE/ (A
GETT PREFACE(253) THEY GIVE PARENTS A COMMON INTEREST WHICH KEEPS TOGETHER MANY A COUPLE WHO, IF CHILDLESS, WOULD
ARMS III (72) TO A VERY COMFORTABLE ESTABLISHMENT. SERGIUS KEEPS TWENTY HORSES. /BLUNTSCHLI/ BUT WHO WANTS TWENTY
BULL PREFACE(44) FROM A FORMAL CONCESSION OF NATURAL RIGHTS, AND KEEPS UP AN ILLUSION OF SAFEGUARDING THEM BY AN ELABORATE
BULL IV (161) LESS. /NORA/ I-- (HER TEARS CHOKE HER; BUT SHE KEEPS UP APPEARANCES DESPERATELY). /LARRY/ (QUITE
2TRU I SD(28) FOR THE INVALID. THE DOCTOR IS INDIFFERENT, BUT KEEPS UP HIS BEDSIDE MANNER CAREFULLY, THOUGH HE EVIDENTLY
JITT II (27) OH, MRS HALDENSTEDT IS OLD-FASHIONED. SHE KEEPS UP THE CONVENTION THAT BECAUSE EDITH IS A YOUNG
HART II (94) THE HARD CASES AMONG THE WORKPEOPLE. BUT MANGAN KEEPS US IN ORDER. HE IS DOWN ON US ABOUT EVERY EXTRA
LADY (250) THE NAUGHTIEST OF HER SUBJECTS. HO THERE! WHO KEEPS WARD ON THE QUEEN'S LODGINGS TONIGHT? /THE WARDER/ I
MIS. (132) IN IT BUT SOME IDEAS THAT THE CHAP THAT WRITES IT KEEPS WORRYING, LIKE A CAT CHASING ITS OWN TAIL. I CAN STAND
GETT (277) I COULDNT STAND HER TOUCHING ME; AND NOW SHE KEEPS WRITING TO ME. AND THEN I'M HELD UP IN THE PUBLIC
KING I (192) IT? HE KEEPS THE BIGGEST ARMY IN EUROPE; AND HE KEEPS YOU INTO THE BARGAIN. HE HARDLY KNOWS WHAT A
JOAN EPILOG (159) THAT DONT MEAN ANYTHING, YOU KNOW; BUT IT KEEPS YOU MARCHING. YOUR SERVANT, LADIES AND GENTLEMEN. WHO
KING I (172) DOOR, MR NEWTON. (LOOKING ROUND HER) AND WHO KEEPS YOUR HOUSE SO BEAUTIFULLY? I THOUGHT PHILOSOPHERS

KEEPSAKE

JITT II (42) HE WISHED TO LEAVE YOU SOMETHING VALUABLE AS A KEEPSAKE . YOU WERE HIS FRIEND. /LENKHEIM/ (SCORNFULLY) A
JITT II (42) YOU WERE HIS FRIEND. /LENKHEIM/ (SCORNFULLY) A KEEPSAKE ! DONT TALK NONSENSE, JITTA: A MAN DOES NOT GIVE

KEIR

LION PREFACE(31) ROYAL DESCENT. JOHN THE BAPTIST MAY HAVE BEEN A KEIR HARDIE; BUT THE JESUS OF MATTHEW IS OF THE
HART PREFACE(13) BEGUN WITH A SUCCESSFUL ATTEMPT TO ASSASSINATE KEIR HARDIE, AND ENDED WITH AN UNSUCCESSFUL ONE TO

KELLNER

WIDO I (5) THE HOTEL. THE WAITER COMES OUT WITH THE BEER). KELLNER : CECI-LA EST NOTRE TABLE. EST CE QUE VOUS COMPRENEZ

KELLY

BULL III (143) /HODSON/ WOT ELSE? /MATTHEW/ YOUR SOWL TO MORRIS KELLY ! WHY DIDNT YOU TELL ME THAT BEFORE? THE DIVIL AN

KELMSCOTT

BARB PREFACE(219) NUMBER OF THE ILLUSTRATED LONDON NEWS AND THE KELMSCOTT CHAUCER IS SILLY: THEY PREFER THE NEWS. THE

KELTIC

BULL I (85) ENOUGH. OF COURSE YOU HAVE THE MELANCHOLY OF THE KELTIC RACE-- /DOYLE/ (BOUNDING OUT OF HIS CHAIR) GOOD

KEMAL

ROCK II (268) /THE DUKE/ THERES NOTHING TO PREVENT YOU. LOOK AT KEMAL PASHA! LOOK AT MUSSOLINI! LOOK AT HITLER! LOOK AT

KEMBLE

PHIL I SD(69) HUNG WITH THEATRICAL ENGRAVINGS AND PHOTOGRAPHS: KEMBLE AS HAMLET, MRS SIDDONS AS QUEEN KATHARINE PLEADING IN

KEMP

POSN (463) HIMSELF BE TOOK LIKE A HARE IN A TRAP BY STRAPPER KEMP : A LAD WHOSE BACK I OR ANY GROWN MAN HERE COULD BREAK
POSN (453) HAVNT PROVED YET THAT I TOOK THE HORSE. STRAPPER KEMP : HAD I THE HORSE WHEN YOU TOOK ME OR HAD I NOT?
POSN (448) TOWN LIKE THIS THAN TEN HORSE-THIEVES. /FEEMY/ MR KEMP : WILL YOU STAND BY AND HEAR ME INSULTED IN THAT LOW
POSN (437) IN. /JESSIE/ BUT THEY CANT TRY HIM TIL SHERIFF KEMP COMES BACK FROM THE WHARF. /ELDER DANIELS/ YES; BUT WE
POSN SD(447) FEW OF THOSE SCRATCHING DEVILS OF WOMEN. STRAPPER KEMP COMES BACK. /ELDER DANIELS/ (TO STRAPPER) HE'S GONE
POSN SD(448) DOWN ON THE STEP OF THE SHERIFF'S DAIS). SHERIFF KEMP COMES IN: A STOUT MAN, WITH LARGE FLAT EARS, AND A NECK

POSN (446) HE WONT BE TOO CLEVER FOR THE BOYS AND SHERIFF KEMP IF YOU PUT THEM ON HIS TRAIL. /BLANCO/ YES, HE WILL. IT
POSN (436) WELL, I MUST SAY IT DOES SICKEN ME TO SEE SHERIFF KEMP PUTTING DOWN HIS FOOT, AS HE CALLS IT. WHY DONT HE PUT
POSN (440) MINISTERING ANGEL THOU. GO OUT TO THEM, STRAPPER KEMP ; AND TELL THEM ABOUT YOUR BIG BROTHER'S LITTLE HORSE
POSN (445) ROAST ME ALIVE OR CUT ME TO RIBBONS; BUT STRAPPER KEMP SHALL NEVER HAVE THE LAUGH ON ME OVER THAT JOB. LET
POSN (446) THAN YOURSELF TO KEEP THE DEVIL IN ME. STRAPPER KEMP WILL DO, OR A FEW OF THOSE SCRATCHING DEVILS OF WOMEN.
POSN SD(439) ELDER DANIELS, THE SHERIFF'S BROTHER STRAPPER KEMP , AND A FEW OTHERS WITH BLANCO. STRAPPER IS A LAD JUST
POSN SD(438) PRISONER. BLANCO POSNET IS BROUGHT IN BY STRAPPER KEMP , THE SHERIFF'S BROTHER, AND A CROSS-EYED MAN CALLED

KEN

BARB II (300) PINES. WELL, IF AW CAWNT SETTISFAW YOU ONE WY, AW KEN ANATHER. LISTEN EAH! AW ED TWO QUID SIVED AGEN THE
BARB II (280) /BILL/ (SULLENLY) AW'M NAO MUSIC AWL WRASTLER. KEN HE BOX? /SHIRLEY/ YES: AN YOU CANT. /BILL/ WOT! AW
BARB II (289) I CANT TEAR MYSELF AWAY FROM HER. /BILL/ WELL, AW KEN . (TO BARBARA) EAH! DO YOU KNAOW WHERE AW'M GOWIN TO,
CAPT I (220) MAWNDS KENNOT RAWSE TO CHRISTIENNITY LAWK HAHRS KEN , GAVNER: THETS AH IT IS. WEOLL, EZ HAW WAS SYIN, IF A

KENDAL

PHIL I SD(69) AS RICHARD III (AFTER LONG), ELLEN TERRY, MRS KENDAL , ADA REHAN, SARAH BERNHARDT, HENRY ARTHUR JONES, SIR

KENNEL

JOAN 4 (103) LEARNED, VENERABLE PIOUS MEN, ARE THRUST INTO THE KENNEL BY EVERY IGNORANT LABORER OR DAIRYMAID WHOM THE DEVIL
HART III (140) SHOTOVER/ IT IS NOT MY HOUSE: IT IS ONLY MY KENNEL . /HECTOR/ WE HAVE BEEN TOO LONG HERE. WE DO NOT LIVE
6CAL (104) THROUGH THE STREETS ON A CHAIN AND LODGED IN A KENNEL . /THE KING/ BE MERCIFUL, LADY. I HAVE ASKED YOU FOR
ROCK PREFACE(167) THE RUSSIAN PEASANTRY THE FATHER LIVES IN A LOUSY KENNEL , AT NO MAN'S CALL BUT HIS OWN, AND EXTRACTS A
SUPR HANDBOK(222) GENTLEMEN ARE PERMITTED TO HAVE FRIENDS IN THE KENNEL , BUT NOT IN THE KITCHEN. DOMESTIC SERVANTS, BY
6CAL (97) HOUND. /PETER/ I AM A GOOD DOG, BUT NOT OF YOUR KENNEL , NEDDY. /THE KING/ NEDDY! ! ! ! /PETER/ ORDER
GLIM (176) /FERRUCCIO/ TO THE DEVIL WITH YOUR MANGY KENNEL ! YOU WANT TO TELL EVERY TRAVELLER THAT COUNT

KENNELLED

CLEO NOTES (205) RUNNING WILD IN THE WOODS IS DIFFERENT FROM MAN KENNELLED IN A CITY SLUM; THAT A DOG SEEMS TO UNDERSTAND A

KENNELS

6CAL (94) THAT THESE DOGS WOULD HAVE COME OUT OF THEIR KENNELS AND GROVELLED FOR MERCY AT MY SUMMONS. AM I NOT

KENNINGTON

3PLA PREFACE(R28) PERFORMED FOR A FEW WEEKS AT A SUBURBAN THEATRE (KENNINGTON) IN OCTOBER 1899 BY MR MURRAY CARSON. THEY TOOK

KENNINTAHN

BARB II (283) IS SHE? (VINDICTIVELY) THEN AW'M GOWIN TO KENNINTAHN ARTER HER. (HE CROSSES TO THE GATE; HESITATES;
BARB II (299) IT CAM FROM ORF THE GRAHND IN PAWKINSES CORNER IN KENNINTAHN . IT GOT RABBED ORF BE MAW SHAOULDERS: SEE?
BARB II (283) AFTERWARDS. /BILL/ (SLINKING OFF) AW'LL GOW TO KENNINTAHN TO BE AHT O REACH O YOUR TANGUE. (SUDDENLY
BARB II (289) OUT TO TELL ME SO. /BILL/ YOU LOY. AW'M GOWIN TO KENNINTAHN , TO SPIT IN TODGER FAIRMAWL'S EYE. AW BESHED

KENNOT

CAPT I (220) THAT IS SOMETHING. /DRINKWATER/ THEIR MAWNDS KENNOT RAWSE TO CHRISTIENNITY LAWK HAHRS KEN, GAVNER: THETS

KENSINGTON

LIED SD(187) THE ROOM IS FURNISHED IN THE MOST APPROVED SOUTH KENSINGTON FASHION: THAT IS, IT IS AS LIKE A SHOP WINDOW AS
LIED SD(188) AND PRETENSIONS APART, A VERY ORDINARY SOUTH KENSINGTON FEMALE OF ABOUT 37, HOPELESSLY INFERIOR IN
HART PREFACE(7) OF A COLONY OF COBRAS AND RATTLESNAKES IN KENSINGTON GARDENS. IN THE PROPHETIC WORKS OF CHARLES
FANY II (286) WITHOUT HIS TUTOR; AND I SAW THE TUTOR IN KENSINGTON HIGH STREET THE VERY DAY SHE TOLD ME. /KNOX/ IF
PYGM EPILOG (297) TO SOME EXTENT RIDICULED AND MIMICKED IN WEST KENSINGTON LIKE EVERYBODY ELSE THERE, SHE WAS ACCEPTED AS A
PYGM PREFACE(199) DAYS WHEN THE IMPERIAL INSTITUTE ROSE IN SOUTH KENSINGTON , AND JOSEPH CHAMBERLAIN WAS BOOMING THE EMPIRE,
LIED (201) THE SMARTEST WOMAN IN THE SMARTEST SET IN SOUTH KENSINGTON , AND THE HANDSOMEST, AND THE CLEVEREST, AND THE

KENSINGTONIAN

METH PREFACE(R34) CLASS IN THE HOUSE OF A DOCTOR IN THE KENSINGTONIAN QUARTER OF LONDON. THEY FELL TO TALKING ABOUT

KENT

DEVL EPILOG (81) AT HOME BY THE FACT THAT LORD GEORGE'S TRIP TO KENT HAD NOT BEEN INTERFERED WITH, AND THAT NOBODY KNEW
ROCK II (266) BEMROSE/ (VERY SOLEMNLY) OF KENT, ARTHUR: OF KENT . NOT OF CEYLON. (HE GOES OUT). /GLENMORISON/ I THINK
ROCK II (266) ARE A NATIVE. /SIR BEMROSE/ (VERY SOLEMNLY) OF KENT , ARTHUR: OF KENT, NOT OF CEYLON. (HE GOES OUT).
BULL PREFACE(18) MAKING A MANKIND AND A WOMANKIND THAT KENT , MIDDLESEX, AND EAST ANGLIA CANNOT PRODUCE AND DO NOT
GENV III (83) YOU ARE NOT A SCOT, NOR AN IRISHMAN, NOR A MAN OF KENT , NOR A MAN OF DEVON, NOR A WELSHMAN-- /SIR O./ ONE OF
DEVL EPILOG (81) DISPOSED TO BE BALKED OF HIS PROJECTED VISIT TO KENT , THEY WERE NOT SIGNED THEN AND WERE FORGOTTEN ON HIS

KENTIN

BARB II (282) IN HEAVEN. /BILL/ (SULLENLY) I WANT NAN O YOUR KENTIN JAWR. I SPOWSE YOU THINK AW CAM EAH TO BEG FROM YOU,

KENTISH

DEVL EPILOG (83) GERMAIN OVERESTIMATED THE IMPORTANCE OF HIS KENTISH HOLIDAY, AND UNDERESTIMATED THE DIFFICULTY OF
BULL PREFACE(50) AS UNACCOUNTABLE TO AN ENGLISH VILLAGER AS A KENTISH OAST-HOUSE TO AN EGYPTIAN. THESE TOWERS ARE
MIS. (181) SICK MAN) I JOHN BROWN OF 4 CHESTERFIELD PARADE KENTISH TOWN DO HEREBY VOLUNTARILY CONFESS THAT ON THE 31ST
PYGM I (213) FAT ONE. THIS IS AN AGE OF UPSTARTS. MEN BEGIN IN KENTISH TOWN WITH 80 POUNDS A YEAR, AND END IN PARK LANE
PYGM I (213) LANE WITH A HUNDRED THOUSAND. THEY WANT TO DROP KENTISH TOWN; BUT THEY GIVE THEMSELVES AWAY EVERY TIME THEY
MIS. (179) I, JOHN BROWN, OF 4 CHESTERFIELD PARADE, KENTISH TOWN, DO HEREBY VOLUNTARILY CONFESS THAT ON THE 31ST
MIS. (179) DO YOU LIVE? /GUNNER/ 4 CHESTERFIELD PARADE, KENTISH TOWN, N.W. /PERCIVAL/ (DICTATING) I, JOHN BROWN, OF

KENTON

SIM PREFACE(19) ORDER OF THEIR APPEARANCE) WERE PLAYED BY GODFREY KENTON , ARTHUR RIDLEY, EILEEN BELDON, DEREK PRENTICE, CECIL

KENWORTHY

ROCK I (226) DO YOU THINK BATTLESHIPS ARE ANY REAL USE NOW? KENWORTHY SAYS THEYRE NOT: AND HE WAS IN THE NAVY. IT WOULD

KEP

BULL I (80) THE FIVE POUNDS OFF; FOR YOUR EXPINSES MUST BE KEP DOWN WID A STHRONG HAND; AN-- (HE IS INTERRUPTED BY THE
BULL III (127) VERY WELL WHEN SOLID MEN LIKE DORAN AN MATT WERE KEP FROM OWNIN LAND. BUT HWAT MAN IN HIS SENSES EVER WANTED
DEVL III (50) TO WAIT. /SERGEANT/ NO, MUM, NOT A MINUTE. WE KEP HIM IN THE BRIDEWELL FOR THE NIGHT; AND HE'S JUST BEEN
CAND I (91) AT ALL. WHY, I KNOW A CLORGYMAN WHAT 'AS BIN KEP HOUT OF HIS JOB FOR YORRS BY THE BISHOP O LONDON.
WIDO III (53) GEV NO EVIDENCE. BUT I'LL TELL YOU WHAT I DID. I KEP IT BACK, JAST TO OBLIGE ONE OR TWO PEOPLE WHOSE FEELINS
CAND III (136) YOURSELF. /BURGESS/ SO YOU DID, JAMES. IT FAIR KEP ME AWAKE TO THE LARS' WORD. DIDNT IT, MISS GORNETT?
BARB II (286) YOUR MILLIONS FOR YOU? ME AND MY LIKE. WHATS KEP US POOR? KEEPIN YOU RICH. I WOULDNT HAVE YOUR

KEPHALUS

CLEO NOTES (207) AND POLEMARCHUS ON HIS WAY TO THE HOUSE OF KEPHALUS ? " AND SO ON. CLEOPATRA. CLEOPATRA WAS ONLY

KEPLER

KING I (212) IN HAND: ONE WHICH SHOULD PLACE ME IN LINE WITH KEPLER , COPERNICUS, AND GALILEO AS A MASTER ASTRONOMER, AND

KEPN

CAPT I (237) (INDIGNANTLY) EAH, AW SY! NAH LOOK EAH, KEPN : MAW NIME IS DRINKWORTER. YOU AWSK EM ET SIN JORN'S IN
CAPT III (291) BY THEIR PRUDERY). /DRINKWATER/ NAOW, LOOK EAH, KEPN : THAT YNT RAWT. DROR A LAWN SOMEWHERE. /JOHNSON/ I SAY
CAPT II (248) SAY? /DRINKWATER/ WEOLL, WOT DID YER SY YRSEOLF, KEPN ? FUST TAWM AW YEVER SEE Y' AFRIDE OF ENNYBODY. (THE
CAPT II (249) HORDER HUZ ABAHT AS IF WE WAS KEB TAHTS! AN THE KEPN AFRIDE TO TALK BAWCK AT ER! LADY CICELY RETURNS WITH
CAPT II (249) ARCH, FOLLOWED BY REDBROOK). /DRINKWATER/ NAH, KEPN BRARSBAHND: YOU GOT SATHINK TO SY TO THE LIDY, YNT YR?
CAPT I (221) ME, YR HONOR. NAH SAMMUN ES BIN A TEOLLN YOU THET KEPN BRARSBAHND AN BLECK PAKEETOW IS HAW-DENTICALLY THE SIME
CAPT I (220) IS WORNTED, THERE'S MAW FRIEND AND COMMAWNDER KEPN BRARSBAHND OF THE SCHOONER THENKSGIVIN, AN IS CREW,
CAPT I (223) OO WOULD YOU SPOWSE WAS THE MARSTER TO WICH KEPN BRARSBAHND SERVED APPRENTICE, AS YR MAWT SY? /RANKIN/

CAPT I	(235)	HIS VOICE AND NARROWLY ESCAPING A SQUEAK OF PAIN)	KEPN	BRARSBAHND. (HE GETS AS FAR FROM THE HOUSE AS
CAPT I	(234)	STREET PIANNER HAHTELLIAN, LIDY: THETS WOT E IS.	KEPN	BRARSBAHND'S RESPECTS TO YR HONORS; AN E AWITES YR
CAPT III	(283)	NAME IS BRASSBOUND. /DRINKWATER/ (OFFICIOUSLY)	KEPN	BRARSBAHND, OF THE SCHOONER THENKSGIV-- /REDBROOK/ (
CAPT I	(221)	CAPTAIN BRASSBOUND? /DRINKWATER/ (GUILTILY)	KEPN	BRARSBAHND! E'S-- WEOLL, E'S MAW KEPN, GAVNER.
CAPT III	(292)	WE BE? /DRINKWATER/ BRARSBAHND YNT THE OWNLY	KEPN	IN THE WORLD. WOT MIKES A KEPN IS BRINES AN KNOLLIDGE O
CAPT III	(292)	YNT THE OWNLY KEPN IN THE WORLD. WOT MIKES A	KEPN	IS BRINES AN KNOLLIDGE O LAWF. IT YNT THET THERS NAOW
CAPT II	(244)	NAOW! NAOW, LIDY: DOWNT YOU GOW DISTURBIN THE	KEPN	. AWLL SEE TO IT. /LADY CICELY/ (GRAVELY) I WAS SURE
CAPT II	(265)	THAT CHOICE. /DRINKWATER/ (RUNNING IN) LOOK EAH,	KEPN	. EAHS ANATHER LOT CAMMIN FROM THE SAHTH HEAST.
CAPT I	(236)	(UNABLE TO CONTAIN HIMSELF) NAH, NAH, LOOK EAH,	KEPN	. IF YOU WANT TO BE MODDIST, BE MODDIST ON YOUR AOWN
CAPT II	(262)	COLOR, IS NOW LIVELY RED. /DRINKWATER/ LOOK EAH,	KEPN	. (BRASSBOUND SPRINGS UP AND RECOVERS HIMSELF
CAPT II	(263)	AND BRING THE PRISONER. /DRINKWATER/ RAWT,	KEPN	. (HE RUNS OUT). /LADY CICELY/ IS THERE REALLY ANY
CAPT II	(248)	ME WHILE SHE IS HERE. /DRINKWATER/ THETS RAWT,	KEPN	. LETS EAH YOU STEBLISH YR HAWTHORITY. (BRASSBOUND
CAPT I	(236)	HOLD YOUR TONGUE. /DRINKWATER/ (ABJECTLY) YUSS,	KEPN	. /RANKIN/ I UNDERSTOOD IT WAS YOUR BUSINESS TO PROVIDE
CAPT II	(265)	(APPALLED, ALMOST IN TEARS) NAOW, NAOW. LISSEN,	KEPN	(POINTING TO SIR HOWARD): E'LL GIVE HUZ FAWV UNNERD
CAPT I	(221)	/RANKIN/ YES. WELL? /DRINKWATER/ (FEEBLY)	KEPN	OF THE SCHOONER THENKSGIVIN, GAVNER. /RANKIN/ (
CAPT III	(285)	RAWT, GAVNER. THETS JEST AH IT WORS. THE	KEPN	-- /REDBROOK/ (AGAIN SUPPRESSING HIM) SHUT UP, YOU
CAPT I	(223)	GAVNER; AN THEY SY: YOU SMAGGLES WANNE THING,	KEPN	; WAH NOT HANATHER? /RANKIN/ WEVE COME TO IT AT LAST.
CAPT I	(238)	HUZ TO RAN AHRSEOLVS INTO DINEGER WITHAHT NAOW	KEPN	TO TEOLL US WOT TO DO. NAOW, LIDY: HOONAWTED WE STEND:
CAPT I	(221)	GUILTILY) KEPN BRARSBAHND! E'S-- WEOLL, E'S MAW	KEPN	, GAVNER. /RANKIN/ YES. WELL? /DRINKWATER/ (FEEBLY)
CAPT I	(237)	(CHUCKLING: THE ITALIAN IS ALSO GRINNING) NAH,	KEPN	, NAH! OWP YR PRAHD O Y'SEOLF NAH. /BRASSBOUND/ I
CAPT I	(236)	REMONSTRANCE) NAH, NAH, NAH! NAH LOOK EAH,	KEPN	, Y' KNAOW-- /BRASSBOUND/ (BETWEEN HIS TEETH) HOLD
			KEPN'S	
CAPT II	(249)	AND DISILLUSION) DOWNT AWSK ME, MISTE JORNSN. THE	KEPN'S	NAOW CLAWSS ARTER ALL. /BRASSBOUND/ (A LITTLE
			KEPT	
KING I	(172)	TO MARRY. /NEWTON/ IS MY HOUSE BEAUTIFULLY	KEPT	? I HAVE NEVER NOTICED IT. THIS IS MRS BASHAM, MY
MTH4 I	(142)	DO YOU NOT KNOW THAT RULES ARE MEANT TO BE	KEPT	? /THE ELDERLY GENTLEMAN/ BY THE LOWER CLASSES, NO
GETT	(276)	ABOUT THOSE-- /LEO/ (INSISTING) HAVE? YOU?	KEPT	? YOUR? PROMISES? HAVE YOU RUBBED YOUR HEAD WITH THE
FANY I	(280)	FOURTEEN DAYS OF IT: I'M ALL THE BETTER FOR BEING	KEPT	A BIT QUIET. YOU MUSTNT LET IT PREY ON YOUR MIND.
FANY PROLOG	(263)	WAS BY HER, I HOPE? /SAVOYARD/ NO: THATS BEEN	KEPT	A DEAD SECRET. I JUST SAID YOUR DAUGHTER HAS ASKED FOR
MTH3	(129)	AND WRECK HUMAN SOCIETY. THIS DISCOVERY MUST BE	KEPT	A DEAD SECRET. (HE SITS DOWN). /BARNABAS/ AND IF I
BASH III	(120)	FATHER'S LIFE, WHENAS IN TOWN THOU MIGHTST HAVE	KEPT	A GUARDIAN EYE ON HIM-- WHATS THAT? A FLYING
FANY III	(326)	I APPRENTICED MYSELF TO AN OLD BUTLER OF OURS WHO	KEPT	A HOTEL. HE TAUGHT ME MY PRESENT BUSINESS, AND GOT ME A
HART II	(85)	OF ILL-NATURE, YOU KNOW. AND YOULL ADMIT THAT I	KEPT	A JOB FOR HIM WHEN I HAD FINISHED WITH HIM. BUT
MIS.	(113)	YOU WHEN YOU WERE A KID. FOR TWENTY-FIVE YEARS HE	KEPT	A PLACE TWICE AS BIG AS ENGLAND IN ORDER: A PLACE FULL
O'FL	(220)	ONE; AND THANKFUL HE WAS TO ME TO BE ALIVE AND	KEPT	A PRISONER IN EASE AND COMFORT, AND ME LEFT FIGHTING IN
MIS. PREFACE	(85)	PEOPLE HOLD THAT BLOOD RELATIONSHIP SHOULD BE	KEPT	A SECRET FROM THE PERSONS RELATED, AND THAT THE
MIS.	(135)	ON JOHN, BECAUSE HE WAS A RATE COLLECTOR AND JOHN	KEPT	A SHOP. IT HURT HIS PRIDE TO HAVE TO BORROW MONEY SO
JOAN 6	(141)	/LADVENU/ (PRESSING THE POINT HARD) HAVE THEY	KEPT	A SINGLE PROMISE TO YOU SINCE YOU WERE TAKEN AT
MTH5	(211)	SOMEHOW MY FEELINGS BEGAN TO CHANGE BIT BY BIT, I	KEPT	A SORT OF INTEREST IN YOUR HEAD AND ARMS LONG AFTER I
MIS.	(129)	THE FIRST ONE: THE REGULATION NATURAL CHAP. HE	KEPT	A TAME PHILOSOPHER IN THE HOUSE: A SORT OF COLERIDGE OR
LADY PREFACE	(207)	THE DARK LADY, FAR FROM BEING A MAID OF HONOR,	KEPT	A TAVERN IN OXFORD AND WAS THE MOTHER OF DAVENANT THE
3PLA PREFACE	(R12)	MOST LONDON THEATRES SEEM TO EXIST, WOULD HAVE	KEPT	A THEATRE DEVOTED EXCLUSIVELY TO THE HIGHEST DRAMA OPEN
DOCT PREFACE	(79)	ACTIVITIES, CANNOT, BEYOND REASON, EXPECT TO BE	KEPT	ALIVE BY THE ACTIVITY OF OTHERS. THERE IS A POINT AT
6CAL PREFACE	(90)	PLAY WITH GOOD PARTS WILL HOLD THE STAGE AND BE	KEPT	ALIVE BY THE ACTORS FOR CENTURIES AFTER THE
CAPT NOTES	(306)	LEARNING TO SPEAK. HOWEVER THAT MAY BE, IT IS	KEPT	ALIVE ONLY BY THE LITERATE CLASSES WHO ARE REMINDED
LION PREFACE	(57)	THAT THE FIRST CONDITION ON WHICH HE CAN BE	KEPT	ALIVE WITHOUT ENSLAVING SOMEBODY ELSE IS THAT HE SHALL
CLEO NOTES	(206)	STEADY RECRUITING FROM THE COUNTRY THAT LONDON IS	KEPT	ALIVE. THIS DOES NOT SEEM AS IF THE CHANGE SINCE JOB'S
GETT	(276)	THEY CAN HARDLY BELIEVE THEIR EYES), HAVE YOU	KEPT	ALL YOUR PROMISES? /REGINALD/ OH, DONT BEGIN BOTHERING
MIS.	(129)	WITH SOMEONE OR ANOTHER. AND THE NATURAL FATHER	KEPT	AN OPEN MIND AND BELIEVED WHATEVER PAID HIM BEST.
JOAN 2,SD	(80)	SIDE OF THE ROOM; AND A CLEAR PATH ACROSS IS	KEPT	AND LINED BY THE COURTIERS. CHARLES IS IN THIS PATH IN
MIS. PREFACE	(16)	THEORY OF THE FAMILY; YET THE DOGS ARE	KEPT	AND THE CHILDREN ARE BANISHED. CHILD FANCIERS. THERE
GENV II	(61)	NOT BY BRINGING THEM TOGETHER. WHEN THE NATIONS	KEPT	APART WAR WAS AN OCCASIONAL AND EXCEPTIONAL THING: NOW
BUOY III	(46)	SECONDBORN/ IS A HUSBAND A DOG OR A CAT TO BE	KEPT	AS A PET? I NEVER HEARD SUCH NONSENSE. /HE/ DOGS ARE
3PLA PREFACE	(R33)	FROM BEN JOHNSON TO MR FRANK HARRIS, HAVE ALWAYS	KEPT	AS FAR ON THIS SIDE IDOLATRY AS I. AS TO OUR ORDINARY
2TRU III	(90)	AND GOING ELSEWHERE. TO EXPIATE THIS BLASPHEMY I	KEPT	AS MUCH UNDER FIRE AS POSSIBLE; BUT MY NERVE FAILED
2TRU I	(36)	THATS VERY TRUE. THE DOCTOR SAID SHE WAS TO BE	KEPT	AS QUIET AS POSSIBLE. /THE NURSE/ (LEADING HER TO THE
CURE	(227)	PRETENDED NOT TO SEE IT. THEY WORRIED ME, AND	KEPT	ASKING ME THE SAME THING OVER AND OVER AGAIN, AND WROTE
DOCT PREFACE	(52)	WE DO NOT DRINK ITS MILK AND EAT ITS FLESH, IS	KEPT	AT A GREATER DISTANCE IN OUR IMAGINATION THAN OUR
MILL PREFACE	(120)	HAD RETURNED TO FIND THAT THE MEN WHO HAD BEEN	KEPT	AT HOME IN THE FACTORIES COMFORTABLY EARNING GOOD
NEVR IV	(289)	TO VALENTINE'S. MRS CLANDON, WHO HAS ALL ALONG	KEPT	AT THE OPPOSITE SIDE OF THE ROOM IN ORDER TO AVOID
MIS. PREFACE	(39)	BEING ABLE TO REPEAT ALL THE PARADIGMS; AND I WAS	KEPT	AT THIS, OR RATHER KEPT IN A CLASS WHERE THE MASTER
BASH PREFACE	(88)	SIT DOWN WITH AN OPEN BOOK IN THEIR HANDS, CAN BE	KEPT	AWAKE AND ALERT VERY EFFECTUALLY IN THE THEATRE BY A
PPP	(204)	NOT A MOMENT MUST BE LOST. THE PATIENT MUST BE	KEPT	AWAKE AT ALL COSTS. CONSTANT AND VIOLENT MOTION IS
SUPR I	(38)	VANITY, AS YOU CALL IT. /ANN/ YOU NEED NOT HAVE	KEPT	AWAY FROM ME ON THAT ACCOUNT. /TANNER/ FROM YOU ABOVE
MIS.	(127)	TO READ THE BIBLE WHEN YOU KNOW THEY WONT. I WAS	KEPT	AWAY FROM THE BIBLE FOR FORTY YEARS BY BEING TOLD TO
DOCT PREFACE	(7)	OF THE MEDICAL PROFESSION. THIS MENACE IS	KEPT	BEFORE THE PUBLIC BY THE PECULIAR PEOPLE. THE
FABL PREFACE	(70)	THE VATICAN, AND THE SECRET COULD NO LONGER BE	KEPT	BY FORBIDDING CATHOLICS TO READ THE BIBLE. THE PEOPLE
BULL PREFACE	(68)	ADMINISTRATION OF IRISH JUSTICE; IRISH ORDER WAS	KEPT	BY IRISH POLICE; IRISH TAXES WERE COLLECTED BY IRISH
GLIM	(171)	IS AN INN, FATHER, NOT TWENTY YARDS AWAY. IT'S	KEPT	BY MY FATHER, SQUARCIO. /THE FRIAR/ AND IS THERE A BARN
BULL IV	(170)	RIGHTLY KNOW WHAT I WANTED TO SAY; AND MY TONGUE	KEPT	CLACKING TO COVER THE LOSS I WAS AT. WELL, IVE BEEN
MTH2	(56)	TO ME AT A MEETING WHERE THE SUFFRAGETTES	KEPT	DISTURBING ME. THEY HAD TO BE CARRIED OUT KICKING AND
GETT PREFACE	(241)	FORGETTING MY OWN DEMONSTRATION THAT THE RATE IS	KEPT	DOWN IN WASHINGTON BY THE ECONOMIC SLAVERY OF WOMEN;
ROCK PREFACE	(147)	AND DEER AND RATS AND FOXES ARE KILLED, OR "	KEPT	DOWN" AS WE PUT IT, MANKIND MUST PERISH; AND THAT
HART PREFACE	(33)	AIDED THEATRES THERE, COURT AND MUNICIPAL,	KEPT	DRAMA OF THE KIND I DEALT IN ALIVE; SO THAT I WAS
HART I	(78)	SHOTOVER/ WHAT THEN IS TO BE DONE? ARE WE TO BE	KEPT	FOR EVER IN THE MUD BY THESE HOGS TO WHOM THE UNIVERSE
KING I	(174)	A PRETTY HOUSE. A PRETTY PHILOSOPHER. A HOUSE	KEPT	FOR YOU TO MEET YOUR WOMEN IN. /MRS BASHAM/ (COMING
SUPR PREFACE	(R11)	QUESTIONS SHALL BE HELD OPEN AND THEIR DISCUSSION	KEPT	FREE, CANNOT PRETEND TO RELISH THESE JOYLESS ATTEMPTS
GETT PREFACE	(245)	THE INNOCENT, WHO HAVE BEEN EITHER CAREFULLY	KEPT	FROM ANY KNOWLEDGE OF THEIR DANGER, OR ERRONEOUSLY LED
METH PREFACE	(R14)	DID NOT ACT AS PRISONS IN WHICH THE IMMATURE ARE	KEPT	FROM WORRYING THE MATURE) THAT SAVE US FROM BEING
2TRU III	(98)	OF SOLDIERING, I TAKE IT, IS THAT THE WORLD IS	KEPT	GOING BY THE PEOPLE WHO WANT THE RIGHT THING KILLING
CATH PREFACE	(157)	WHO REALLY KEPT THE THEATRE GOING, AND WERE	KEPT	GOING BY THE THEATRE, DID NOT CATER FOR THE GREAT
HART PREFACE	(6)	THOSE WHO LIVED WITHIN THEIR INCOMES WERE REALLY	KEPT	GOING BY THEIR SOLICITORS AND AGENTS, BEING UNABLE TO
FABL V	(117)	FOOLS: IT IS IMPOSSIBLE TO UNDERSTAND HOW THEY	KEPT	GOING FOR A WEEK, MUCH LESS FOR YEARS. THEY HAD NOT
GENV PREFACE	(21)	YEAR, WAS EMPEROR FOR FOURTEEN YEARS. MUSSOLINI	KEPT	GOING FOR MORE THAN TWENTY, SO DID LOUIS NAPOLEON.
JOAN PREFACE	(17)	WITH A MIND SO EXCEPTIONALLY POWERFUL THAT IT	KEPT	HER IN CONTINUAL TROUBLE WITH THE MEDICAL AND MILITARY
JOAN PREFACE	(19)	DROWNED BY A TERRIBLE FATHER AND HER BIG BROTHERS	KEPT	HER QUIET UNTIL THE FATHER HAD LOST HIS TERRORS AND THE
JITT II SD	(33)	DISTINGUISHED SOCIALLY. HER SENSE OF DUTY HAS	KEPT	HER UPRIGHT; AND HER UPRIGHTNESS HAS GIVEN HER A
MRS II	(213)	AND HAD A FRIED-FISH SHOP DOWN BY THE MINT, AND	KEPT	HERSELF AND FOUR DAUGHTERS OUT OF IT. TWO OF US WERE
PHIL III	(136)	YOU, PARAMORE. /PARAMORE/ (GRATEFULLY) YOU	KEPT	HIM EXACTLY THE RIGHT TIME, TO A SECOND. (FORMALLY)
FANY PROLOG	(272)	BE IN THE DRAWING ROOM. YOU SHOULD NOT HAVE	KEPT	HIM HERE. /FANNY/ I KNOW. DONT SCOLD ME: I HAD
NEVR I	(216)	IF I HAD NOT TAKEN YOU AWAY FROM HIM. I HAVE	KEPT	HIM OUT OF YOUR LIFE: KEEP HIM NOW OUT OF MINE BY NEVER
FANY I	(281)	DESERVED THIS. IVE DONE MY DUTY AS A FATHER. IVE	KEPT	HIM SHELTERED. (ANGRY WITH HER) CREATURES LIKE YOU
KING PREFACE	(156)	DE KEROUALLE, WHO, AS AN AGENT OF LOUIS XIV,	KEPT	HIM UNDER THE THUMB OF THAT SUN OF MONARCHS AS HIS
APPL II	(258)	HAVE TOLD HIM TO WRITE FOR AN AUDIENCE, AND THEN	KEPT	HIM WAITING A WEEK FOR IT. /MAGNUS/ WHAT! WHEN WE
MTH1 II	(21)	HE KILLED INTO MEAT BY THE FIRE ON THE ALTAR. HE	KEPT	HIMSELF ALIVE BY EATING MEAT. HIS MEAL COST HIM A DAY'S
HART PREFACE	(11)	COMPARISON. I DO NOT KNOW WHETHER ANYONE REALLY	KEPT	HIS HEAD COMPLETELY EXCEPT THOSE WHO HAD TO KEEP IT
MIS.	(150)	LIGHTED BESIDE YOU LIKE A BIRD. /PERCIVAL/ HOW HE	KEPT	HIS HEAD I CANT IMAGINE. FRANKLY, I DIDNT. THE
POSN PREFACE	(376)	OF PUBLIC LIFE, AND OF THE SINGLE PEER WHO	KEPT	HIS HEAD. THE OTHERS, FOR THE MOMENT, HAD NO HEADS TO
JITT III	(60)	IMPETUOUSLY) OH, I KNOW VERY WELL HOW TIDY YOU	KEPT	HIS HOUSE FOR HIM, JUST AS I KEEP MY ROOM. YOU DID YOUR
PPP	(199)	OF A LIFETIME. FORMERLY IT WAS GEORGE'S. I	KEPT	HIS HOUSE, OR RATHER, HIS LODGINGS. I MENDED HIS
MRS II	(214)	LABORER IN THE DEPTFORD VICTUALLING YARD, AND	KEPT	HIS ROOM AND THE THREE CHILDREN NEAT AND TIDY ON
BUOY PREFACE	(6)	GENERATION CLAMORS FOR A MIRACLE." BUT AS MAHOMET	KEPT	HIS TEMPER UNDER THE SAME THOUGHTLESS PRESSURE, SO, I
BULL PREFACE	(59)	HIM THE GREATNESS OF THE EMPIRE, AS IT WAS, HE	KEPT	HIS VIEWS TO HIMSELF UNTIL IT WAS TOO LATE TO DO
SIM PRO,1,	(25)	HAD RHODES'S LUCK. MOTHER, FAREWELL: YOUR SON HAS	KEPT	HIS WORD." (HE TIES THE LABEL TO THE LAPEL OF HIS
MIS.	(200)	IS DISGUSTING. IT IS NOT HEALTHY. YOUR WOMEN ARE	KEPT	IDLE AND DRESSED UP FOR NO OTHER PURPOSE THAN TO BE

MIS. PREFACE(39)	THE PARADIGMS; AND I WAS KEPT AT THIS, OR RATHER	KEPT	IN A CLASS WHERE THE MASTER NEVER ASKED ME TO DO IT
MILL PREFACE(122)	THE VERSAILLES TREATY BY WHICH GERMANY WAS TO BE	KEPT	IN A CONDITION OF PERMANENT, DECISIVE, AND HUMILIATING
LION PREFACE(65)	FOR SOCIAL PURPOSES MAY BE KILLED, OR MAY BE	KEPT	IN ASYLUMS WITH A VIEW TO STUDYING THEIR CONDITION AND
LION II (147)	NOT IF THEY ARE IN CAGES. THEY SHOULD NOT BE	KEPT	IN CAGES. THEY MUST BE ALL LET OUT. /THE EMPEROR/ I
GETT PREFACE(199)	FANATICISM. WHAT PEOPLE CALL GOODNESS HAS TO BE	KEPT	IN CHECK JUST AS CAREFULLY AS WHAT THEY CALL BADNESS;
METH PREFACE(R68)	FOR AN UNPOPULAR STEP WILL SERVE IF IT CAN BE	KEPT	IN COUNTENANCE FOR A FORTNIGHT: THAT IS, UNTIL THE
HART PREFACE(16)	BE TAUGHT THE LANGUAGE OF LUTHER AND GOETHE, WERE	KEPT	IN COUNTENANCE BY THE MOST IMPUDENT REPUDIATIONS OF
OVER PREFACE(168)	THE CONTRARY IS AN ABSURD MORALITY, AND CAN BE	KEPT	IN COUNTENANCE ONLY BY HYPOCRISY. WHEN PEOPLE WERE
METH PREFACE(R74)	OPPORTUNIST CARDINALS AND BISHOPS, HAVE BEEN	KEPT	IN CREDIT BY CANONIZED SAINTS WHOSE SECRET WAS THEIR
BULL PREFACE(56)	FEW SPARE SENTENCES OF FLOGGING SHOULD HAVE BEEN	KEPT	IN HAND TO PROVIDE AGAINST ACCIDENTS. IN ANY CASE THERE
BULL IV (179)	YOUR PITY WILL DO IT! /KEEGAN/ IN THE ACCOUNTS	KEPT	IN HEAVEN, MR DOYLE, A HEART PURIFIED OF HATRED MAY BE
O'FL (224)	TO LIVE IN IRELAND WHERE IVE BEEN IMPOSED ON AND	KEPT	IN IGNORANCE, AND TO DIE WHERE THE DIVIL HIMSELF
APPL PREFACE(184)	AND CONTROL BY SEPARATE PRIVATE INDIVIDUALS	KEPT	IN ORDER BY THEIR COMPETITION FOR OUR CUSTOM, BUT
MRS PREFACE(159)	THAT IS, A LICENTIOUSLY IRREGULAR GROUP TO BE	KEPT	IN ORDER IN A ROUGH AND READY WAY BY A MAGISTRATE WHO
BARB III (323)	SIR." AND THATS ALL. /CUSINS/ BUT JONES HAS TO BE	KEPT	IN ORDER. HOW DO YOU MAINTAIN DISCIPLINE AMONG YOUR
POSN PREFACE(411)	THAT SUCH INFAMOUS POWERS OF OPPRESSION SHOULD BE	KEPT	IN RESPONSIBLE HANDS AND NOT LEFT AT THE DISPOSAL OF
MIS. PREFACE(41)	SISTERS IN THE EAST AND NURSES IN THE WEST ARE	KEPT	IN SERVITUDE. BUT IN A SOCIETY OF EQUALS (THE ONLY
GENV III (72)	SIBERIA AND FLOGGED TO DEATH. IN ENGLAND HE WAS	KEPT	IN THE BRITISH MUSEUM AT THE PUBLIC EXPENSE AND LET
O'FL (210)	SHE THOUGHT IT OUGHT TO FILL UP MINE TOO. IT'S	KEPT	IRELAND POOR, BECAUSE INSTEAD OF TRYING TO BETTER
MTH5 (246)	OH! HAVE YOU GOT IT STILL? /THE SHE-ANCIENT/ I	KEPT	IT A FULL WEEK. /ECRASIA/ EVEN IN YOUR CHILDHOOD, THEN,
CLEO PRO1 (93)	HAND AND WITH THE OTHER SMOTE OFF HIS HEAD, AND	KEPT	IT AS IT WERE A PICKLED CABBAGE TO MAKE A PRESENT TO
GENV IV (129)	AND RISING) I KILLED MY BEST FRIEND WITH THIS. I	KEPT	IT TO KILL MYSELF. IT IS USELESS NOW: GOD WILL EXECUTE
BARB III (330)	THE TOWN) BEING YOURS! AND THAT YOU HAVE	KEPT	IT TO YOURSELF ALL THESE YEARS! /UNDERSHAFT/ IT DOES
JITT II (28)	CERTAINLY WE WERE FRIENDS AT COLLEGE; AND WE	KEPT	IT UP AFTERWARDS. BUT HE NEVER TOLD ME MUCH ABOUT
MRS III (221)	HAIR: HE'S IN MUCH BETTER PRACTICE THAN YOU. HAS	KEPT	IT UP EVER SINCE, PROBABLY. HE'S TAKEN HIMSELF OFF
2TRU II (65)	UP. IN ALL MY LIFE I HAVE KNOWN ONLY ONE MAN THAT	KEPT	IT UP TIL HE DIED. /THE PATIENT/ (INTERESTED) AH!
CAPT I (229)	HE QUITE SIMPLY TOOK THE ESTATE FOR HIMSELF AND	KEPT	IT. /RANKIN/ BUT HOW ABOUT THE LAW? /SIR HOWARD/ THE
GLIM (186)	I SHOULD HAVE DIED OF IT IF IT COULD HAVE	KEPT	ITS GRIP OF ME. BUT YOU HELPED ME OUT OF IT. /GIULIA/
CAND III (130)	HIMSELF ON THE BACK OF THE EASY CHAIR) IT	KEPT	ITSELF SOMEHOW UNTIL ABOUT TEN MINUTES AGO. UP TO THAT
POSN PREFACE(390)	CERTAIN SPECIFIED POISONS OF WHICH A SCHEDULE IS	KEPT	. NOBODY IS FORBIDDEN TO SELL MINERALS WITHOUT A
WIDO III (54)	BEFOREHAND, YOU KNOW, NO MATTER HOW DARK THEYRE	KEPT	. /SARTORIUS/ (INTERESTED, BUT CAUTIOUS) WELL?
2TRU I (46)	POPSY AND I ARE AS GOOD COMPANY AS EVER YOU	KEPT	. /THE PATIENT/ NO, SWEETIE: YOU ARE A COMMON LITTLE
PYGM III (251)	THEY ALL THOUGHT SHE WAS DEAD; BUT MY FATHER HE	KEPT	LADLING GIN DOWN HER THROAT TIL SHE CAME TO SO SUDDEN
APPL PREFACE(179)	GAS OR HOT AIR, AND SENT UP SO THAT YOU SHALL BE	KEPT	LOOKING UP AT THE SKY WHILST OTHER PEOPLE ARE PICKING
KING I (196)	THAT HE GOT HIS START IN LIFE AS YOUR BARBARA'S	KEPT	MAN? /CHARLES/ I KNOW THAT THE POOR LAD RISKED
BUOY IV (49)	WHAT ABOUT YOU? DO YOU WANT TO BE ANY WOMAN'S	KEPT	MAN? /JUNIUS/ I DONT WANT ANYTHING BUT YOUR DAUGHTER.
O'FL (210)	WHAT GOOD HAS IT EVER DONE HERE IN IRELAND? IT'S	KEPT	ME IGNORANT BECAUSE IT FILLED UP MY MOTHER'S MIND, AND
CAND I (92)	IMPETUOUSLY) OH BOTHER YOUR UNDERSTANDING! YOUVE	KEPT	ME LATE FOR CANDIDA. (WITH COMPASSIONATE FERVOR) MY
2TRU III (102)	SIR, THE COLORS, THE FEAR OF DISGRACING THEM HAS	KEPT	ME OFF THE DRINK MANY A TIME. /TALLBOYS/ MAN: I DO NOT
LADY PREFACE(208)	ACQUAINTANCE WITH HIM, IN THE COURSE OF WHICH HE	KEPT	ME PRETTY CLOSELY ON THE TRACK OF HIS WORK AT THE
MRS PREFACE(151)	CRITIC OF OUR MOST RESPECTED SOCIAL INSTITUTIONS	KEPT	ME SO CONTINUALLY IN HOT WATER THAT THE ADDITION OF
POSN (443)	UNSPOTTED; AND WHEN I WENT BACK TO WORK, THE WORK	KEPT	ME STEADY. CAN YOU SAY AS MUCH, BLANCO? DID YOUR
ARMS II (26)	WHOLE AUSTRIAN EMPIRE FIRST; AND THAT WOULD HAVE	KEPT	ME TOO LONG AWAY FROM YOU. I MISSED YOU GREATLY.
MTH2 (63)	TO KEEP MY ACADEMIC READING UP TO DATE. I HAVE	KEPT	MY CLASSICS BRUSHED UP OUT OF SHEER LOVE FOR THEM; BUT
2TRU I (38)	AND THE NURSES HAD TO TREAT THEM ACCORDINGLY. I	KEPT	MY EYES OPEN THERE, AND LEARNT A LITTLE OF THE GAME. (
SUPR I (45)	ONE OF THE WRETCHES OF WHOM HE APPROVES. I HAVE	KEPT	MY MARRIAGE A SECRET FOR MY HUSBAND'S SAKE. BUT NOW I
HART PREFACE(11)	CONDUCT THE WAR AT FIRST HAND. I SHOULD NOT HAVE	KEPT	MY OWN (AS FAR AS I DID KEEP IT) IF I HAD NOT AT ONCE
MILL I (155)	GREAT AN IDIOT TO COMPREHEND HIS OWN AUDACITY-- I	KEPT	MY PROMISE TO MY FATHER. I HANDED HIM A CHEQUE FOR A
MIS. (202)	IT WASNT LOST ON ME. I'M A THINKING MAN. I	KEPT	MY TEMPER. YOULL ADMIT THAT. /LINA/ (FRANKLY) OH YES.
JOAN EPILOG (158)	HIS ARMOUR AND SURCOAT CHEERFULLY) I HAVE	KEPT	MY WORD: THE ENGLISH ARE GONE. /JOAN/ PRAISED BE GOD!
MILL I (155)	GAVE HIM A SORT OF GREATNESS. I AM IMPULSIVE: I	KEPT	MY WORD AND MARRIED HIM INSTANTLY. THEN, TOO LATE, I
MRS IV (251)	ALL GO BECAUSE I HAD YOU TO LOOK FORWARD TO. I	KEPT	MYSELF LONELY FOR YOU. YOUVE NO RIGHT TO TURN ON ME NOW
BASH II,1, (108)	MANY A TWO DAYS BRUISE HATH RUTHLESS GIVEN, HATH	KEPT	NO DUNGEON LOCKED FOR TWENTY YEARS, HATH SLAIN NO
MIS. PREFACE(32)	BOY AND GIRL ON CONDITION THAT A RECORD SHOULD BE	KEPT	OF THEIR SUBSEQUENT CAREERS AND COMPARED WITH THE
DOCT PREFACE(61)	DEMAND FOR IT; NOR CAN THE GROSSEST QUACKERY BE	KEPT	OFF THE MARKET IF THERE IS A DEMAND FOR IT. FASHIONS
3PLA PREFACE(R19)	THAT IS, THE PLAY IN WHICH LOVE IS CAREFULLY	KEPT	OFF THE STAGE, WHILST IT IS ALLEGED AS THE MOTIVE OF
ANNA (290)	FOR SEVEN CENTURIES. THE PANJANDRUMS HAVE	KEPT	OUR PLACE FOR US AT THEIR COURTS, HONORED US, PROMOTED
GETT PREFACE(197)	OF LOVE." FRANCIS PLACE TELLS US THAT HE	KEPT	OUT OF HIS FATHER'S WAY BECAUSE HIS FATHER NEVER PASSED
6CAL (105)	HIS WORDS ARE DISGUSTING. SUCH OBJECTS SHOULD BE	KEPT	OUT OF MY SIGHT: WOULD YOU HAVE ME BEAR YOU A MONSTER?
GENV III (80)	THE PLACE! AND ME, AN ELECTED REPRESENTATIVE,	KEPT	OUT OF PARLIAMENT BY THE POLICE! /THE JUDGE/ I COME TO
MIS. PREFACE(95)	MORE, THE THEORY OF NATURAL SELECTION CANNOT BE	KEPT	OUT OF SCHOOLS, BECAUSE MANY OF THE NATURAL FACTS THAT
MIS. PREFACE(70)	ARE SO LARGE THAT THE CHILDREN'S QUARTERS CAN BE	KEPT	OUT OF THE PARENTS' WAY LIKE THE SERVANTS' QUARTERS.
UNPL PREFACE(R18)	PIANOFORTE MUSIC. THE BOOKS AND MUSIC CANNOT BE	KEPT	OUT, BECAUSE THEY ALONE CAN MAKE THE HIDEOUS BOREDOM OF
MRS PREFACE(176)	THE JOURNALISTS WHO HAD DONE ALL THE MISCHIEF	KEPT	PAYING VICE THE HOMAGE OF ASSUMING THAT IT IS
SUPR III (102)	ONE; AND WITH SUCH A MAJORITY AS MINE I CANNOT BE	KEPT	PERMANENTLY OUT OF OFFICE. /DON JUAN/ I THINK, ANA, YOU
CLEO IV (176)	FUR-- THE LITTLE KING'S BEAR LEADER, WHOM YOU	KEPT	PRISONER. /CAESAR/ (ANNOYED) AND HAS HE NOT ESCAPED..
METH PREFACE(R80)	BUT IN MATHEMATICS AND PHYSICS THE FAITH IS STILL	KEPT	PURE, AND YOU MAY TAKE THE LAW AND LEAVE THE LEGENDS
METH PREFACE(R75)	THAN EVER IN THE PROCESS. THUS THE WORLD IS	KEPT	SANE LESS BY THE SAINTS THAN BY THE VAST MASS OF THE
MTH4 I (171)	FORGET THAT THE ANSWERS OF THE ORACLE CANNOT BE	KEPT	SECRET OR MISREPRESENTED. THEY ARE WRITTEN AND
ARMS I (4)	AUSTRIAN OFFICERS LIKE CHAFF, AND YOU! YOU	KEPT	SERGIUS WAITING A YEAR BEFORE YOU WOULD BE BETROTHED TO
SUPR III (115)	FOR WITH A WONDERFUL INSTINCTIVE CUNNING, SHE	KEPT	SILENT AND ALLOWED ME TO GLORIFY HER: TO MISTAKE MY OWN
GETT PREFACE(256)	OF MARRIAGE. IF OUR DOMESTIC LAWS ARE	KEPT	SO INHUMAN THAT THEY AT LAST PROVOKE A FURIOUS GENERAL
METH PREFACE(R74)	FOR THEIR INSTINCTIVE RIGHTEOUSNESS, WHO HAVE	KEPT	SWEET THE TRADITION THAT GOOD PEOPLE FOLLOW A LIGHT
MRS III (232)	OF THE CADS WHO DO. THERE ARE NO SECRETS BETTER	KEPT	THAN THE SECRETS EVERYBODY GUESSES. IN THE CLASS OF
MIS. (134)	/JOHNNY/ (SARCASTIC) OH! YOU THINK YOUVE ALWAYS	KEPT	THAT TO YOURSELF, DO YOU, GOVERNOR? I KNOW YOUR
MIS. PREFACE(31)	I DID NOT KNOW WHAT TO REPLY. AS THE SCHOOL	KEPT	THE CHILDREN QUIET DURING MY WORKING HOURS, I DID NOT
BULL PREFACE(55)	TWO HOURS TO KILL AS WELL AS FOUR MEN, THEY	KEPT	THE ENTERTAINMENT GOING BY FLOGGING EIGHT MEN WITH
HART PREFACE(16)	FRONTIERS IN THE GREAT REALM OF THE HUMAN MIND,	KEPT	THE EUROPEAN COMITY OF THAT REALM LOFTILY AND EVEN
METH PREFACE(R32)	EARLIER PHILOSOPHERS, FROM PLATO TO LEIBNITZ, HAD	KEPT	THE HUMAN MIND OPEN FOR THE THOUGHT OF THE UNIVERSE AS
GENV PREFACE(22)	TO THE LEFT" FOLLOWED BY " SWINGS TO THE RIGHT"	KEPT	THE NEWSPAPERS AND THE POLITICAL WINDBAGS AMUSED AND
INCA (248)	THE LION, THE LION WILL SPRING. THE INCA HAD	KEPT	THE PEACE FOR YEARS. THOSE WHO ATTACKED HIM WERE
INCA (249)	ONE DAY DO JUSTICE TO THE INCA AS THE MAN WHO	KEPT	THE PEACE WITH NOTHING BUT HIS TONGUE AND HIS
MILL IV (189)	IT WAS SO UNTIL QUITE LATELY, SIR. MY FATHER	KEPT	THE PIG AND WHISTLE. SO DID HIS FOREFATHERS RIGHT BACK
JOAN PREFACE(46)	WHICH JOAN HAD UNCONSCIOUSLY ANTICIPATED,	KEPT	THE QUESTIONS WHICH AROSE IN HER CASE BURNING UP TO OUR
MIS. PREFACE(106)	OF MEN, MONSTROUSLY OUTNUMBERED, REPEATEDLY	KEPT	THE RUSSIAN TROOPS PARALYSED WITH TERROR BY PURE
HART PREFACE(5)	FREETHINKING, AND HARDLY EVER WENT TO CHURCH OR	KEPT	THE SABBATH EXCEPT BY A LITTLE EXTRA FUN AT WEEK-ENDS.
DOCT V (178)	MONSTROUS, TOO GROTESQUE. WE CRUEL DOCTORS HAVE	KEPT	THE SECRET FROM YOU FAITHFULLY; BUT IT IS LIKE ALL
DOCT II (122)	YES I DID. I SHOULD HAVE LIKED VERY MUCH TO HAVE	KEPT	THE SKETCH AND GOT IT AUTOGRAPHED. /B.B./ BUT WHY DIDNT
CATH PREFACE(157)	TIME; BUT THE PLAYWRIGHTS PROPER, WHO REALLY	KEPT	THE THEATRE GOING, AND WERE KEPT GOING BY THE THEATRE,
METH PREFACE(R84)	A DESTRUCTIVE, DERISORY, CRITICAL, NEGATIVE ART,	KEPT	THE THEATRE OPEN WHEN SUBLIME TRAGEDY PERISHED. FROM
SHAK (142)	TO KEEP THE WIND AWAY. OH THAT THAT EARTH WHICH	KEPT	THE WORLD IN AWE SHOULD PATCH A WALL T' EXPEL THE
MIS. (136)	MRS TARLETON. THEY PRETENDED TO LIKE ME BECAUSE I	KEPT	THEIR BROTHERS FROM MURDERING THEM; BUT I DIDNT LIKE
MRS PREFACE(175)	NEW YORK JOURNALISTS THAT THE FEW AMONG THEM WHO	KEPT	THEIR FEET MORALLY AND INTELLECTUALLY COULD DO NOTHING
GENV PREFACE(22)	MUCH MORE PROMPTLY THAN PARLIAMENTS. THEY HAVE	KEPT	THEIR HEADS AND KNOWN THEIR LIMITATIONS. ORDINARY
HART PREFACE(20)	THROUGH THE COUNTRY. MEN WHO UP TO THAT TIME HAD	KEPT	THEIR HEADS NOW LOST THEM UTTERLY. " KILLING SALOON
HART PREFACE(11)	WAR, NOT IN THE FIELD, BUT AT HOME, AND	KEPT	THEIR HEADS, CAN POSSIBLY UNDERSTAND THE BITTERNESS OF
APPL INTRLUD(247)	AGAINST ME: I WAS PERFECTLY FAITHFUL TO THEM. I	KEPT	THEIR HOUSES BEAUTIFULLY: I FED THEM BETTER THAN THEY
MIS. PREFACE(98)	BIBLE HAS DRIVEN MANY PEOPLE MAD WHO MIGHT HAVE	KEPT	THEIR SANITY HAD THEY BEEN ALLOWED TO READ MUCH LOWER
INCA (240)	THEIR LUXURIES, THEY GAVE UP THEIR DOCTORS, BUT	KEPT	THEIR WEEK-END HOTELS, CLOSING EVERY CAREER TO ME
FABL PREFACE(67)	LABORERS GOT IN THE NINETEENTH CENTURY,	KEPT	THEM ALIVE FOR THIRTY YEARS OR SO, BUT LEFT NO SURPLUS
MIS. PREFACE(22)	A YEAR TO THE INSTITUTION. THAT WAS WHY HE WAS	KEPT	THERE AGAINST HIS WILL. THAT WAS WHY HE WAS KEPT THERE
MIS. PREFACE(22)	KEPT THERE AGAINST HIS WILL. THAT WAS WHY HE WAS	KEPT	THERE WHEN HIS EXPULSION WOULD HAVE BEEN AN UNSPEAKABLE
CATH PREFACE(154)	ENORMOUS AND UTTERLY INDECOROUS SCALE. CATHERINE	KEPT	THIS VAST GUIGNOL THEATRE OPEN FOR NEARLY HALF A
CAND II (113)	BUT SHE ISNT A SLAVE; AND THE HOUSE LOOKS AS IF I	KEPT	THREE. THAT MEANS THAT EVERYONE HAS TO LEND A HAND.
MILL I (151)	ARE VERY USEFUL THINGS IF YOU WANT THE HOUSE	KEPT	TIDY, DEAR. THE TELEPHONE RINGS. SAGAMORE ATTENDS TO
MIS. PREFACE(84)	MAIN POINT TO GRASP HERE IS THAT FAMILIES ARE NOT	KEPT	TOGETHER AT PRESENT BY FAMILY FEELING BUT BY HUMAN
GENV PREFACE(22)	IN OBSCURITY HARDLY MATTERS; FOR THEY WERE	KEPT	TOO BUSY TO BOTHER THEMSELVES ABOUT HAPPINESS; AND THE

MRS PREFACE(157)	ALL EVENTS, AS LONG AS THE TEMPTING SIDE OF IT IS	KEPT	TOWARDS THE PUBLIC, AND SOFTENED BY PLENTY OF SENTIMENT
3PLA PREFACE(R12)	LOATHING? AND YET THAT IS JUST WHAT THE THEATRES	KEPT	TRYING TO DO ALMOST ALL THE TIME I WAS DOOMED TO ATTEND
METH PREFACE(R23)	HABIT, SOLELY BECAUSE HE WANTED TO, AND	KEPT	TRYING UNTIL IT WAS ADDED UNTO HIM. HOW ACQUIREMENTS
FABL III (112)	THAT YOULL BE ENLISTED IN THE MILITARY POLICE OR	KEPT	UNDER TUTELAGE IN A LABOR BRIGADE. OR YOU MAY BE
PRES (140)	/BALSQUITH/ I DO. HOW DO YOU THINK PARTIES ARE	KEPT	UP? NOT BY THE SUBSCRIPTIONS OF THE LOCAL
FANY EPILOG (331)	AND A FEEBLE AIR OF INTELLECTUAL PRETENTIOUSNESS	KEPT	UP ALL THROUGH TO PERSUADE YOU THAT IF THE AUTHOR HASNT
PYGM EPILOG (294)	HIS PROSPECTS CONSISTED OF A HOPE THAT IF HE	KEPT	UP APPEARANCES SOMEBODY WOULD DO SOMETHING FOR HIM. THE
MTH3 (132)	THAT OVERAWED ME. I CONFESS THAT, THOUGH I HAVE	KEPT	UP APPEARANCES, I HAVE ALWAYS BEEN AFRAID OF THE
MIS. (154)	IT HAPPENS THAT JUST AT THIS MOMENT IT IS BEING	KEPT	UP BY ONE OF MY BROTHERS ONLY. EARLY THIS MORNING I GOT
BARB III (315)	SUPPOSE THIS WICKED AND IMMORAL TRADITION CAN BE	KEPT	UP FOR EVER? DO YOU PRETEND THAT STEPHEN COULD NOT
SUPR III (93)	A RELATIVE. AT ALL EVENTS, FAMILY TIES ARE RARELY	KEPT	UP HERE. YOUR FATHER IS QUITE ACCUSTOMED TO THIS: HE
DOCT PREFACE(72)	TO PLACE HER IMAGE IN A COTTAGE THAT IS NOT	KEPT	UP TO THAT HIGH STANDARD OF SUNDAY CLEANLINESS TO WHICH
MTH4 II (185)	YOU EXPECT IT FROM US; SO I SUPPOSE IT MUST BE	KEPT	UP. WILL YOU WAIT HERE UNTIL ZOZIM COMES, PLEASE (SHE
JITT III (75)	WE ARE ALONE AND THERE ARE NO APPEARANCES TO BE	KEPT	UP. YOU SWORE NOT TO, AND YOU HAVE BEEN TALKING TO ME
ROCK II (255)	AND KEEPING YOU OFF THE ROCKS. /BLEE/ YOU HAVNT	KEPT	US OFF THE ROCKS. WE'RE ON THE ROCKS, THE WHOLE LOT OF
GENV I (43)	MY HOTEL. HIS INTEREST IN THE CHURCH OF ENGLAND	KEPT	US UP TALKING LONG AFTER MY USUAL HOUR FOR RETIREMENT.
HART II (96)	WANTED ME: YOU AND PAPA. /MRS HUSHABYE/ YOU HAVE	KEPT	US WAITING SO LONG THAT IT ALMOST CAME TO-- WELL, NEVER
CAPT NOTES (304)	AS FAR AS MY SOCIAL EXPERIENCE GOES (AND I HAVE	KEPT	VERY MIXED COMPANY) THERE IS NO CLASS IN ENGLISH
PRES (152)	MUCH LONGER IS THE ANTI-SUFFRAGET LEAGUE TO BE	KEPT	WAITING? (SHE PASSES HIM CONTEMPTUOUSLY AND SITS DOWN
APPL I (201)	AT A QUARTER TO TWELVE. HOW LONG MORE AM I TO BE	KEPT	WAITING? /SEMPRONIUS/ (WITH CHEERFUL POLITENESS) GOOD
KING I (172)	MADAM. I AM ASHAMED THAT YOU SHOULD HAVE BEEN	KEPT	WAITING AT THE WRONG SIDE OF MY DOOR. /NELLY/ IT IS AN
DEVL III (73)	YOU THINK THIS IS A PLEASANT SORT OF THING TO BE	KEPT	WAITING FOR? YOUVE MADE UP YOUR MIND TO COMMIT MURDER:
GETT (302)	NO RIGHT TO CONDEMN HIM. I'M SORRY YOU HAVE BEEN	KEPT	WAITING TWENTY MINUTES; BUT I MYSELF HAVE WAITED TWENTY
APPL INTRLUD(254)	IMPOSSIBLE, BELOVED. JEMIMA DOES NOT LIKE TO BE	KEPT	WAITING. /ORINTHIA/ OH, BOTHER JEMIMA! YOU SHALL NOT
WIDO II (27)	BY NO MEANS. SIT DOWN, PRAY. I FEAR YOU HAVE BEEN	KEPT	WAITING. /TRENCH/ (TAKING BLANCHE'S CHAIR) NOT AT ALL.
BULL PREFACE(6)	ONE WAY IN WHICH THE POWER OF THE PRIEST CAN BE	KEPT	WITHIN ITS PROPER LIMITS IN IRELAND IS BY SETTING THE
LION PREFACE(64)	ITSELF TO ABSURDITY IF ITS APPLICATION WERE NOT	KEPT	WITHIN THE LIMITS WHICH NATURE SETS TO THE SELF-CONTROL
POSN (454)	LET IT BE DRAGGED IN THE MUD BY YOUR BROTHER'S	KEPT	WOMAN. GREAT EXCITEMENT AMONG THE WOMEN. THE MEN MUCH
NEVR IV (286)	AND M'COMAS. /MRS CLANDON/ I AM SO SORRY TO HAVE	KEPT	YOU ALL WAITING. A GROTESQUELY MAJESTIC STRANGER, IN A
INCA (238)	A TREASURE. THE ARCHDEACON SAYS HE WOULD HAVE	KEPT	YOU IF HE COULD POSSIBLY HAVE AFFORDED IT. MOST
BARB III (321)	THAT YOU HAVE MADE SO MUCH OF IT. BUT IT HAS	KEPT	YOU IN CIRCLES WHERE YOU ARE VALUED FOR YOUR MONEY AND
BARB I (250)	RISES; AND COMES TO THE SETTEE). I HAVE NOT	KEPT	YOU WAITING VERY LONG, I THINK. /STEPHEN/ NOT AT ALL.
DOCT IV (170)	EMBROIDERED, OVER HER ARM) I'M SO SORRY TO HAVE	KEPT	YOU WAITING. /SIR PATRICK/ DONT MENTION IT, MADAM.
NEVR I (216)	VALENTINE RETURNS. /VALENTINE/ I HOPE IVE NOT	KEPT	YOU WAITING. THAT LANDLORD OF MINE IS REALLY AN
ROCK II (236)	BED THIS MORNING, EH? FRIGHTFULLY SORRY TO HAVE	KEPT	YOU WAITING, BASHAM. WHATS WRONG WITH THE FOREIGN
CLEO IV (191)	IS IT ANY MAGIC OF MINE, THINK YOU, THAT HAS	KEPT	YOUR ARMY AND THIS WHOLE CITY AT BAY FOR SO LONG?
JITT III (76)	ROMANTICALLY: YOU BEHAVED VERY SENSIBLY. YOU	KEPT	YOUR HEAD, AND DID JUST THE RIGHT THING. YOU SAVED YOUR
ROCK PREFACE(177)	THAT THE SECRET OF THE EARTH'S MOTION COULD BE	KEPT	, AND FEARING THAT RELIGION COULD NOT STAND THE SHOCK
LADY PREFACE(230)	THE REAL NATURE OF THE MYSTERIOUS RESTRAINT THAT	KEPT	" ELIZA AND OUR JAMES" FROM TEACHING SHAKESPEAR TO BE
		KEPTIN	
PYGM I (210)	HER PRONUNCIATION EXACTLY) " CHEER AP,	KEPTIN	; N' BAW YA FLAHR ORF A PORE GEL." /THE FLOWER GIRL/
		KERAMIC	
MIS. SD(110)	HIGHLY ORNATE PUNCHBOWL IN THE SAME STYLE AS THE	KERAMIC	DISPLAY IN THE PAVILION. WICKER CHAIRS AND LITTLE
		KERB	
PYGM I (208)	IVE A RIGHT TO SELL FLOWERS IF I KEEP OFF THE	KERB	. (HYSTERICALLY) I'M A RESPECTABLE GIRL: SO HELP ME, I
		KERBSTONE	
GETT PREFACE(244)	AS POSSIBLE OF THE PATHOLOGY OF MARRIAGE AND ITS	KERBSTONE	BREAKWATER. ONLY, AS THERE SEEMS TO BE NO BOTTOM
PYGM I (214)	/THE NOTE TAKER/ YOU SEE THIS CREATURE WITH HER	KERBSTONE	ENGLISH: THE ENGLISH THAT WILL KEEP HER IN THE
PYGM III (246)	SHE'S A COMMON FLOWER GIRL. I PICKED HER OFF THE	KERBSTONE	. /MRS HIGGINS/ AND INVITED HER TO MY AT-HOME!
CAPT I SD(218)	NATURE, A BOARD SCHOOL EDUCATION, AND SOME	KERBSTONE	PRACTICE HAVING MADE HIM A BIT OF AN ORATOR. HIS
		KERENSKY	
ROCK PREFACE(168)	HAVE NO SOONER READ IN THE TIMES A LETTER FROM MR	KERENSKY	ASSURING ME THAT IN THE UKRAINE THE STARVING PEOPLE
		KERISCHIN	
CAND I (87)	AGIN ME. WELL, IVE COME TO HACT THE PART OF A	KERISCHIN	. (OFFERING HIS HAND) I FORGIVE YOU, JAMES.
CAND I (89)	WITH MY HOWN DAUGHRTER'S USBAN. COME, JAMES: BE A	KERISCHIN	, AND SHAKE ANDS. (HE PUTS HIS HAND SENTIMENTALLY
		KERNDEWCE	
CAPT NOTES (303)	THE SAME WORD, WHEN UTTERED BY LADY CICELY, AS	KERNDEWCE	, TO SUGGEST THE ENGLISH PRONUNCIATION TO AMERICAN
		KEROSINE	
SUPR HANDBOK(207)	AND GOODNESS GO. AND WHEN A NEGRO IS DIPPED IN	KEROSINE	AND SET ON FIRE IN AMERICA AT THE PRESENT TIME, HE
		KEROUALLE	
KING I SD(179)	HER GRACE THE DUCHESS OF PORTSMOUTH. LOUISE DE	KEROUALLE	, A FRENCHWOMAN WHO AT 30 RETAINS HER FAMOUS
KING PREFACE(154)	NELLY, CASTLEMAINE, AND THE FRENCHWOMAN LOUISE DE	KEROUALLE	, WHOM WE CALLED MADAME CARWELL. SO I BRING THE
KING PREFACE(156)	INFLUENCED BY WOMEN, ESPECIALLY BY LOUISE DE	KEROUALLE	, WHO, AS AN AGENT OF LOUIS XIV, KEPT HIM UNDER
		KERRICKTER	
CAPT I (237)	GOW ORN, GOW ORN. SR AHRD EZ ERD WITNESSES TO MAW	KERRICKTER	AFOAH. E KNAOWS AH MECH TO BLIEVE OF EM. /LADY
CAPT I (220)	THET WORS. LEF THE COURT WITHAHT A STINE ON MAW	KERRICKTER	, AW DID. /RANKIN/ (WITH SOME INDIGNATION) I
		KERRY	
SUPR IV SD(142)	MATERIAL OF HIS SPEECH WAS PERHAPS THE SURLY	KERRY	BROGUE; BUT THE DEGRADATION OF SPEECH THAT OCCURS IN
CAPT I (219)	EM. SOR EM AWR (HIRE) A HARAB AN TWO KROOBOYS TO	KERRY	THEIR LAGGIGE. THORT AWD CAM AN TEOLL YER. /RANKIN/
		KET	
CAPT I (219)	ENGINEST JADGE IN HINGLAND! -- AWLUS GIVES THE	KET	WEN ITS ROBBRY WITH VOYLENCE, BLESS IS AWT. AW SY
		KETCH	
FABL II (105)	THE SECOND, FOR A HUNDRED AND FIFTY THOUSAND.	KETCH	COULD AFFORD IT: HIS BACKYARD IS CHOCK FULL OF
O'FL (208)	HE COULD FEEL TO THE TIME SHE WAS TOO SLOW TO	KETCH	HIM; BUT I'M FOND OF HER; AND I'M NOT ASHAMED OF IT.
FABL II (106)	YOUR JOB, DIDNT IT? /C.-IN-C./ NOT A BIT OF IT.	KETCH	IS FAR TOO CUNNING TO GO TO WAR WITH US. HE DID NOT GO
BULL II (99)	DIVIL, WHAT CALL HAVE YOU TO FEAR IT? IF I COULD	KETCH	IT, I'D MAKE YOU TAKE IT HOME WIDJA IN YOUR HAT FOR A
		KETCHEWAYO	
FABL II (107)	HAVE WE THAT AFTER SELLING HIS INVENTION TO	KETCHEWAYO	IN AFRICA HE DID NOT SELL IT OVER AGAIN IN
FABL II (105)	HE SOLD IT TO THE SOUTH AFRICAN NEGRO HITLER,	KETCHEWAYO	THE SECOND, FOR A HUNDRED AND FIFTY THOUSAND.
		KETLEP	
BARB II (282)	NOT ME. AW DOWNT WANT YOUR BREAD AND SCRIPE AND	KETLEP	. AW DONT BLIEVE IN YOUR GAWD, NO MORE THAN YOU DO
		KETTLE	
DEVL II SD(28)	FOR ROASTING, AND BROAD FENDER, ON WHICH STAND A	KETTLE	AND A PLATE OF BUTTERED TOAST. THE DOOR, BETWEEN THE
DOCT III SD(131)	COLOR, BRUSHES, CHARCOAL, A SMALL LAY FIGURE, A	KETTLE	AND SPIRIT-LAMP, AND OTHER ODDS AND ENDS. BY THE
OVER (188)	DARLING, THERES NO USE IN THE POT CALLING THE	KETTLE	BLACK. /GREGORY/ WHEN YOU SAY DARLING, MAY I ASK
SUPR PREFACE(R26)	AND IT CERTAINLY WAS NOT FOR THE POT TO CALL THE	KETTLE	BLACK. THE ARISTOCRACY HE DEFENDED, IN SPITE OF THE
SUPR III (106)	LEGISLATURE, AND HEARD THE POT LECTURING THE	KETTLE	FOR ITS BLACKNESS, AND MINISTERS ANSWERING QUESTIONS.
SUPR III (104)	ALL THE INTELLIGENCE. /THE DEVIL/ AND A PRETTY	KETTLE	OF FISH THEY MAKE OF IT BETWEEN THEM. DID I NOT SAY,
CAPT II (263)	HE WAS HERE. /LADY CICELY/ WELL, THATS A PRETTY	KETTLE	OF FISH, ISNT IT? /BRASSBOUND/ I WILL DO WHAT I CAN
DEVL II (32)	THIS TIME. (SHE GOES TO THE FIRE AND PUTS ON THE	KETTLE	). /ANDERSON/ (GOING TO THE PRESS AND TAKING HIS

KETTLE-HOLDER

GETT (348) STATE. YOUR LIVER-PAD HAS BEEN MADE INTO A KETTLE-HOLDER . YOURE NO MORE FIT TO BE LEFT TO YOURSELF

KEW

PYGM EPILOG (301) THAT THEY SHOULD COMBINE THE LONDON SCHOOL WITH KEW GARDENS. ELIZA, TO WHOM THE PROCEDURE OF THE DICKENSIAN
GENV II (49) /THE SECRETARY/ SIT DOWN. /BEGONIA/ (COMPLYING) KEW (SHORT FOR THANK YOU). /THE SECRETARY/ (GRAVELY) YOU
FABL I SD(101) APPROACHES HER; TAKES TWO-PENCE FROM HER; SAYS " KEW ," SHORT FOR " THANK-YOU"; AND GIVES HER A TICKET. A

KEY

PRES (131) A KEY IN IT. (HE OPENS THE LETTER; TAKES OUT A KEY AND A NOTE; AND READS) " DEAR MITCH"-- WELL, I'M
JOAN 1 (61) YOUR FATHER WITH ORDERS TO PUT YOU UNDER LOCK AND KEY AND THRASH THE MADNESS OUT OF YOU. WHAT HAVE YOU TO SAY
DEVL I (12) IN THE CUPBOARD, WHICH SHE LOCKS, POCKETING THE KEY CAREFULLY), /CHRISTY/ (LINGERING AT THE FIRE) YOUD
PRES (132) MINISTER ASKING ME TO RELEASE THE WOMAN WITH THIS KEY IF SHE PADLOCKS HERSELF, AND TO HAVE HER SHEWN UP AND
PRES (131) (HE PICKS THE LETTER UP.) IT DOES SEEM TO HAVE A KEY IN IT. (HE OPENS THE LETTER; TAKES OUT A KEY AND A
JITT PREFACE(7) WHICH AFFECT, NOT THE STORY ITSELF, BUT ONLY THE KEY IN WHICH IT ENDS. THOUGH THE ASSUMPTIONS OF THE AUDIENCE
CURE (229) WAY. I MADE MY MOTHER LOCK IT AND TAKE AWAY THE KEY . I FELT SURE THEYD LET SOMEBODY IN THAT WAY IF SHE
MRS IV SD(235) DOWN THE OFFICE. SOMEBODY TRIES THE DOOR WITH A KEY . /FRANK/ (CALLING) COME IN. IT'S NOT LOCKED. VIVIE
FANY I (277) IN THE WORLD, AS ONE MAY SAY: SAFE UNDER LOCK AND KEY . /GILBEY/ (HORRIFIED, PITIABLE) OH MY-- (HIS BREATH
CURE (231) BECAUSE SHE GAVE ME THE KEY; AND IT WAS THE RIGHT KEY . /REGINALD/ BUT WHAT DID SHE DO THAT FOR? WHO ARE YOU,
OVER PREFACE(167) IT CAN, I HAVE ALWAYS CONTENDED, BE DONE IN THE KEY OF FARCICAL COMEDY; AND OVERRULED IS A TRIFLING
SIM II (85) LIFE IS WITHIN ME. /PRA/ BUT YOU HAVE GIVEN THE KEY OF IT TO ME, THE MAN. /PROLA/ YES: I NEED YOU AND YOU
MILL I (162) ASK? I HAVE NOT CARRIED A WATCH SINCE I LOST THE KEY OF MY FATHER'S OLD REPEATER. /PATRICIA/ IT IS TEN
PRES (131) NOW; AND SHE DOWNFACES US THAT YOUVE GOT THE KEY OF THE PADLOCK IN A LETTER IN A BUFF ENVELOPE, AND THAT
DEVL III (50) NODS TO THE TWO SOLDIERS, AND SHEWS THEM THE KEY OF THE ROOM IN HIS HAND. THEY WITHDRAW). YOUR GOOD LADY,
HART I (70) UTTERWORD/ (DASHING IN) HESIONE: WHERE IS THE KEY OF THE WARDROBE IN MY ROOM? MY DIAMONDS ARE IN MY
OVER PREFACE(166) ITS SUBJECT. NOW IF ALL THIS CAN BE DONE IN THE KEY OF TRAGEDY AND PHILOSOPHIC COMEDY, IT CAN, I HAVE ALWAYS
BASH II,1, (111) /LYDIA/ O HEAVEN! YOU BLEED. /CASHEL/ LEND ME A KEY OR OTHER FRIGID OBJECT, THAT I MAY PUT IT DOWN MY BACK,
MRS II (206) OF A THEATRICALLY DEVOTED MOTHER, ADDS IN A LOWER KEY) MAKE YOUR MIND EASY: THE YOUNG PUP HAS NO MORE CHANCE
CURE (231) KNOW IT'S THE RIGHT ONE, BECAUSE SHE GAVE ME THE KEY ; AND IT WAS THE RIGHT KEY. /REGINALD/ BUT WHAT DID SHE
6CAL PREFACE(90) SO HAPHAZARD THAT IT IS ONLY BY PICKING OUT ITS KEY SITUATIONS AND ARRANGING THEM IN THEIR SIGNIFICANT ORDER
DOCT PREFACE(37) IT IS USELESS TO ASSURE US THAT THERE IS NO OTHER KEY TO KNOWLEDGE EXCEPT CRUELTY. WHEN THE VIVISECTOR OFFERS
UNPL PREFACE(R23) IMPLICIT IN THE BEST PLAYS, AND ARE OFTEN THE KEY TO THEIR APPROPRIATE RENDERING; BUT MOST ACTORS ARE SO
LION PREFACE(78) FROM WHICH HE ESCAPES BY THE USE OF A SKELETON KEY , IS MORE TERRIBLE THAN ANY HE MET WHILST THE BUNDLE WAS

KEYBOARD

CURE SD(230) RINGS IN THE SAME WAY; SITTING DOWN TO THE KEYBOARD AND FINDING IT TOO NEAR TO THE PIANO, THEN TOO FAR,
CURE (233) BE REALLY KIND OF YOU. (SHE GOES BACK TO THE KEYBOARD AND SITS DOWN TO PLAY). /REGINALD/ (CROSSING TO
PHIL I SD(69) GRAND, IS ON THE SHAKESPEAR SIDE, OPEN, WITH THE KEYBOARD AT RIGHT ANGLES TO THE WALL. THE PIECE OF MUSIC ON
PYGM II SD(217) SIDE WALL, IS OCCUPIED BY A GRAND PIANO, WITH THE KEYBOARD AT THE END FURTHEST FROM THE DOOR, AND A BENCH FOR
CURE SD(225) HE WOULD FIND ON HIS LEFT A GRAND PIANO WITH THE KEYBOARD END TOWARDS HIM, AND A SMALLER DOOR BEYOND THE
PHIL I (72) LIKE THIS. (HE SITS DOWN ON THE BASS END OF THE KEYBOARD . GRACE PUTS HER FINGERS IN HER EARS. HE RISES AND
PYGM II SD(217) FOR THE PLAYER EXTENDING THE FULL LENGTH OF THE KEYBOARD . ON THE PIANO IS A DESSERT DISH HEAPED WITH FRUIT
CURE (231) PLEASE! (HE STOPS HER BY SHUTTING THE KEYBOARD LID). WHO LET YOU IN? /THE LADY/ (RISING
METH PREFACE(R29) BUT WITH SUCH AN APTITUDE FOR SHORTHAND AND KEYBOARD MANIPULATION THAT HE IS A STENOGRAPHER OR PIANIST
METH PREFACE(R28) IN EATING A SANDWICH, DRAW HIM TO THE LIFE. THE KEYBOARD OF A PIANO IS A DEVICE I HAVE NEVER BEEN ABLE TO
CURE (233) LET ME PLAY IT FOR YOU. (HE SITS DOWN AT THE KEYBOARD) I DONT THINK YOU BELIEVE I CAN PLAY. /STREGA/
PHIL I (71) DOWN ON THE PIANO STOOL, WITH HER BACK TO THE KEYBOARD). AH, YOU DONT WANT TO HEAR ANY MORE OF THE STORY.
PHIL I (85) AND LAYS IT ASIDE; THEN CLOSES THE LID OVER THE KEYBOARD). /JULIA/ (PASSING BETWEEN THE SOFA AND PIANO TO
CURE (231) SEND FOR A DOCTOR. (SHE SITS DOWN AGAIN TO THE KEYBOARD). /REGINALD/ (FALLING ON HIS KNEES) YOU MUSTNT
PYGM II (230) THE EAST WIND. (HE SITS DOWN ON THE BENCH AT THE KEYBOARD). SO HERE I AM, A CONFIRMED OLD BACHELOR, AND
CURE (234) TAKE THAT (SHE KNOCKS HIM SPRAWLING OVER THE KEYBOARD)! BEAUTIFUL DOLL INDEED! /REGINALD/ OH, I SAY!
MIS. PREFACE(51) CLASS HAVE BEEN FORCED TO SPEND OVER THE KEYBOARD , FINGERING SCALES, HOW MANY OF THEM COULD BE
CURE (234) /STREGA/ (PAUSING WITH HER HANDS RAISED OVER THE KEYBOARD , READY TO POUNCE ON THE CHORDS) WILL YOU EVER SAY

KEYBOARDS

METH PREFACE(R29) WE ARE FORCED TO SUSPECT EITHER THAT KEYBOARDS AND SHORTHAND ARE OLDER INVENTIONS THAN WE
FABL V (118) THEIR MONTHS TALLY WITH THE MOON. IN MUSIC THEIR KEYBOARDS HAD ONLY TWELVE NOTES IN THE OCTAVE INSTEAD OF OUR
MTH5 (237) EARS AND RECORD A DISPARAGING REMARK ON THEIR KEYBOARDS , THEIR BRAINS BECOME CONSCIOUS OF THE

KEYHOLE

CATH 1 (172) INTO A ROOM WITHOUT FIRST LOOKING THROUGH THE KEYHOLE ? (TAKING HIS SWORD FROM THE TABLE AND PUTTING IT
GETT (293) AT THE DOOR. I TOLD HIM I SHOULD LOOK THROUGH THE KEYHOLE IF HE DIDNT ANSWER. I LOOKED THROUGH THE KEYHOLE. HE
GETT (286) GOT ALL THAT IVE TOLD YOU OUT OF HER THROUGH THE KEYHOLE . COME, ALICE (SHE VANISHES. MRS BRIDGENORTH
GETT (293) KEYHOLE IF HE DIDNT ANSWER. I LOOKED THROUGH THE KEYHOLE . HE WAS SITTING ON HIS BED, READING A BOOK. (
APPL INTRLUD(256) THE BEAST! HE MUST HAVE LOOKED THROUGH THE KEYHOLE . (SHE THROWS HER HAND UP WITH A GESTURE OF
MRS PREFACE(160) ENTERS; DISMISSES THE DUENNA; AND LISTENS AT THE KEYHOLE OF HIS DAUGHTER'S NUPTIAL CHAMBER, UTTERING VARIOUS
CATH 1 (172) YES? /PATIOMKIN/ GO AND LOOK THROUGH THE KEYHOLE OF THE IMPERIAL BED-CHAMBER; AND BRING ME WORD

KEYHOLES

CATH 1 (172) AND THE PERFECTLY SIMPLE THING IS TO LOOK THROUGH KEYHOLES . ANOTHER EPIGRAM: THE FIFTH THIS MORNING! WHERE
CATH 1 (172) YET. /VARINKA/ FI DONC! I DO NOT LOOK THROUGH KEYHOLES . /PATIOMKIN/ (EMERGING, HAVING ARRANGED HIS SHIRT

KEYS

HART II (109) ACETYLENE WELDING PLANT AND A BUNCH OF SKELETON KEYS ? I SHALL WANT A FORGE, AND A SMITHY, AND A SHOP, AND
PYGM II (221) (WALKING UP AND DOWN THE ROOM, RATTLING HIS KEYS AND HIS CASH IN HIS POCKETS) YOU KNOW, PICKERING, IF
CURE SD(230) PIANIST BEFORE SHE AT LAST STRIKES THE KEYS AND PRELUDES BRILLIANTLY. AT THE SOUND, REGINALD, WITH
FANY I (278) A SHOP IN GREEN STREET, IVORY INLAID, WITH GOLD KEYS AND RUSSIA LEATHER BELLOWS; AND BOBBY KNEW I HANKERED
PYGM III (245) AND WALKING ABOUT, JINGLING HIS MONEY AND HIS KEYS IN HIS TROUSER POCKETS) BESIDES, THEYRE ALL IDIOTS.
FANY I (278) A SQUIFFER IS. /DORA/ WELL, REMEMBER IT HAS GOLD KEYS . THE MAN WOULDNT TAKE A PENNY LESS THAN 15 POUNDS FOR
6CAL SD(97) HALTERS, EACH CARRYING A BUNCH OF MASSIVE IRON KEYS . THEIR LEADER, EUSTACHE DE ST PIERRE, KNEELS AT THE
FANY I (278) YARDS, I'LL STAND YOU THAT SQUIFFER WITH THE GOLD KEYS ." /MRS GILBEY/ DOES HE CALL HIS TUTOR HOLY JOE TO HIS
DOCT V (177) QUIET CONVICTION) NO. DOCTORS THINK THEY HOLD THE KEYS OF LIFE AND DEATH; BUT IT IS NOT THEIR WILL THAT IS
2TRU I (35) MOST OF THEM, YOU FOOL. THEY THINK I HAVE THE KEYS OF LIFE AND DEATH IN MY POCKET; BUT I HAVE NOTHING BUT
METH PREFACE(R28) UP A FLUTE WITH A NEWLY INVENTED ARRANGEMENT OF KEYS ON IT, AND PLAY IT AT ONCE WITH HARDLY A MISTAKE. WE
6CAL SD(97) BEHIND HIM, AND, FOLLOWING HIS EXAMPLE, LAY THEIR KEYS ON THE GROUND. THEY ARE DEEPLY CAST DOWN, BEARING
BASH II,1, (111) THE WELLING LIFE STREAM. /LYDIA/ (GIVING HIM HER KEYS) OH, WHAT HAVE YOU DONE? /CASHEL/ FLUSH ON THE BOKO
JOAN PREFACE(37) BEEN SAFER FOR AN ASPIRANT TO THE CHAIR AND THE KEYS TO PASS AS A MORIBUND DOTARD THAN AS AN ENERGETIC
FABL PREFACE(86) AND AMATEUR, ARE POPULAR, AND ARE THE KEYS TO SUCCESS IN ELECTIONS. THE MARXIST CLASS WAR. THE
6CAL SD(97) DOES NOT NOTICE THIS UNTIL PETER FLINGS DOWN HIS KEYS WITH A VIOLENCE WHICH SUGGESTS THAT HE WOULD VERY

KEYSTONE

SUPR HANDBOK(218) THE PRIVATE IS AS CONFUSED AS THE NOTION THAT THE KEYSTONE NEED BE STRONGER THAN THE COPING STONE. WHERE
GETT PREFACE(205) FOR THEM TO BE SUPERIOR TO THE REST THAN FOR THE KEYSTONE OF AN ARCH TO BE OF HARDER STONE THAN THE COPING.
CAND I (89) OF THIS OBSERVATION ON BURGESS IS TO REMOVE THE KEYSTONE OF HIS MORAL ARCH. HE BECOMES BODILY WEAK, AND,
SUPR III (110) HIS IDEALS, HIS HEROISMS, PROVIDED THAT THE KEYSTONE OF THEM ALL IS THE WORSHIP OF WOMAN, OF MOTHERHOOD,
FABL PREFACE(70) GOD. SUCH A HERESY, IF PUBLISHED, WOULD KNOCK THE KEYSTONE OUT OF THE ARCH OF BRITISH CIVILIZATION. THERE WAS
JOAN 4 (105) DIGNITIES FROM THE KING, BECAUSE THERE MUST BE A KEYSTONE TO THE ARCH OF HUMAN SOCIETY; BUT WE HOLD OUR LANDS

KHAKI

O'FL (216) YOU ALWAYS WERE. THERE! IT WONT BE SEEN ON THE KHAKI : IT'S NOT LIKE THE OLD RED COAT THAT WOULD SHEW UP
HART PREFACE(30) FRONT. IN 1915 I SAW IN THE THEATRES MEN IN KHAKI IN JUST THE SAME PREDICAMENT. TO EVERYONE WHO HAD MY
ANNA (297) I KNOW ABOUT THEM? /STRAMMFEST/ THEY TRAVEL IN KHAKI . THEY DO NOT TRAVEL IN FULL DRESS COURT UNIFORM AS
HART PREFACE(22) THAT IN 1914, THEY WOULD NEVER HAVE GOT ME INTO KHAKI ." AND THAT, OF COURSE, WAS PRECISELY WHY IT HAD BEEN
HART PREFACE(22) IMPOSSIBLE TO ESTIMATE WHAT PROPORTION OF US, IN KHAKI OR OUT OF IT, GRASPED THE WAR AND ITS POLITICAL
HART PREFACE(37) TO CONFIRM THE PEACE, ENGLAND IS NO LONGER IN KHAKI ; AND A VIOLENT REACTION IS SETTING IN AGAINST THE
O'FL SD(205) GENERAL SIR PEARCE MADIGAN, AN ELDERLY BARONET IN KHAKI , BEAMING WITH ENTHUSIASM, ARRIVES. O'FLAHERTY RISES

AUGS (277) COME IN. (THE CLERK ENTERS, CLEAN SHAVEN AND IN KHAKI , WITH AN OFFICIAL PAPER AND AN ENVELOPE IN HIS HAND).

KHAKI-CLAD

BULL PREFACE(51) 13TH OF JUNE LAST THERE DROVE TO THE VILLAGE FOUR KHAKI-CLAD BRITISH OFFICERS WITH GUNS, ONE OF THEM BEING A

KHAN

BUOY 1 (13) SLAUGHTER AND DESTRUCTION THAN ATTILA AND GENGHIS KHAN AND ALL THE OTHER SCOURGES OF GOD EVER VENTURED ON. I
MILL PREFACE(117) TO SUPPOSE POSSIBLE. MUSSOLINI, HITLER AND RIZA KHAN BEGAN IN THE RANKS, AND HAVE NO MARENGOS TO THEIR
GENV PREFACE(22) NERO, PAUL OF RUSSIA, OUR JAMES THE SECOND, RIZA KHAN IN IRAN, AND SOME OF THE SMALL FRY OF DEGENERATE

KHARTOUM

LION PREFACE(97) OF OFFERING BIBLES FOR SALE IN THE STREETS OF KHARTOUM . TURN TO FRANCE, A COUNTRY TEN TIMES MORE INSULAR

KHAYYAM

GETT PREFACE(196) AS TO THE RESPECTABLE VOLUPTUARY, WHO JOINS OMAR KHAYYAM CLUBS AND VIBRATES TO SWINBURNE'S INVOCATION OF

KHEDIVE

BULL PREFACE(32) EGYPT TO PUT AN END TO THE MISGOVERNMENT OF THE KHEDIVE AND REPLACE HIM BY LORD CROMER FOR THE SAKE OF THE
BULL PREFACE(65) AND CLEMENCY AS THE OCCUPATION MAY ALLOW THE KHEDIVE TO PERFORM, AND THAT IN THE MEANTIME THEIR DETENTION

KHEIRALLAH'S

BULL PREFACE(55) OF THE ARRANGEMENT THROUGH SAID SULEIMAN KHEIRALLAH'S INCONSIDERATE INDISPOSITION MADE THE EXECUTION

KICE

CAPT I (227) FORELOCK) AWLL ENG ABAHT WITHIN ILE, GAVNER, HIN KICE AW SHOULD BE WORNTED. (HE GOES INTO THE HOUSE WITH
CAPT I (227) AW SPERRITS O YOUTH, Y' LAWDSHIP. WORTERLEOO ROWD KICE . WOT THEY CALLS OOLIGANISM. /SIR HOWARD/ OH! YOU WERE

KICK

APPL I (224) EVER THE BEST OF FRIENDS. I AM THE LAST TO KICK A MAN WHEN HE'S DOWN. /CRASSUS/ I MAY BE A JOBBER; BUT
CATH 1 (165) MADAM, THAT YOUR UNCLE HAD BETTER NOT ATTEMPT TO KICK AN ENGLISH OFFICER DOWNSTAIRS. /PATIOMKIN/ YOU WANT ME
2TRU PREFACE(20) TO ANYONE BOLD ENOUGH TO ASSUME DICTATORSHIP AND KICK ASIDE THE IMPOTENT OFFICIAL GOVERNMENT UNTIL HE HAD
CATH 1 (167) OF DIAMONDS. AND RUBIES. GET OUT. (HE AIMS A KICK AT THE SERGEANT, WHO FLEES). PUT UP YOUR PISTOLS,
MIS. (197) FATHER HAD KICKED HIM UNTIL HE WAS BIG ENOUGH TO KICK BACK. PATSY BEGGED HIM OFF. I ASKED THAT MAN WHAT IT
LADY PREFACE(212) FIXED PRACTICE AND UNGOVERNABLE IMPULSE IT IS TO KICK CONVENTIONAL DIGNITY WHENEVER HE SEES IT. HARRIS "
BARB II (278) YOU AND TELL ER TO CAM AHT AFORE AW CAM IN AND KICK ER AHT. TELL ER BILL WALKER WANTS ER. SHE'LL KNAOW WOT
GETT (304) MR HOTCHKISS. /REGINALD/ (RISING) HOW COULD I KICK HIM OUT OF THE HOUSE? HE'S STRONGER THAN ME: HE COULD
GENV IV (127) GENERAL A PERFECT GENTLEMAN. I NEVER WANTED TO KICK HIM WHILE HE WAS SPEAKING. I WANTED TO KICK YOU TWO ALL
CAPT II (265) A YELL) NAOW! (BRASSBOUND TURNS ON HIM AS IF TO KICK HIM. HE SCRAMBLES AWAY AND TAKES REFUGE BEHIND SIR
PHIL I (89) AN UNWOMANLY WOMAN! IF I WERENT AN INVALID, I'D KICK HIM. /CHARTERIS/ OH DONT SAY THAT. IT WAS I. /CRAVEN/ (
MIS. (187) OH YOU LITTLE WRETCH! STOP HIM, MR PERCIVAL. KICK HIM. /TARLETON/ STEADY ON, STEADY ON. EASY, BUNNY,
METH PREFACE(R12) HAVING KNOCKED THE OTHER HALF DOWN, IS TRYING TO KICK IT TO DEATH, AND MAY SUCCEED: A PROCEDURE WHICH IS,
6CAL (94) HIS FEET. BY GOD, I WILL HAVE THAT HEAD: I WILL KICK IT TO MY DOGS TO EAT. I WILL CHOP HIS INSOLENT HERALD
MIS. PREFACE(41) TO LIE: TEACH IT TO WALK AND YOU TEACH IT HOW TO KICK ITS MOTHER TO DEATH. THE GREAT PROBLEM OF SLAVERY FOR
CATH 2 (182) IT WILL BE AN EXCUSE FOR NOT GOING BACK TO HER. KICK ME HARD. /PATIOMKIN/ YAH! (HE FLINGS HER ON THE BED
GETT (304) HAVE KICKED ME OUT IF IT CAME TO THAT. HE DID KICK ME OUT: WHAT ELSE WAS IT BUT KICKING OUT, TO TAKE MY
2TRU PREFACE(21) BOOTS IN WHICH HE WALKS OVER IT; FOR HE MAY NOT KICK ME OUT OF MY HOUSE INTO THE STREET WITH HIS BOOTS; BUT
POSN PREFACE(376) MY WRETCHED LITTLE PAMPHLET AT MY HEAD AND TO KICK ME OUT OF THE ROOM WAS THE PASSIONATE IMPULSE WHICH
MIS. (119) JOHNNY, OLD CHAP: I BEG YOUR PARDON. WHY DONT YOU KICK ME WHEN I GO ON LIKE THAT? /LORD SUMMERHAYS/ AS WE
CATH 1 (163) I PICKED HIM UP; AND HE KICKED ME. THEY ALL KICK ME WHEN YOU KICK THEM. GOD KNOWS THAT IS NOT JUST,
LION I (119) ARE. /SPINTHO/ (GASPING) THATS IT: STRANGLE ME. KICK ME. BEAT ME. REVILE ME. OUR LORD WAS BEATEN AND
CATH 2 (182) AS HE STARTS IN PURSUIT OF THE CHAMBERLAIN) KICK ME. DISABLE ME. IT WILL BE AN EXCUSE FOR NOT GOING BACK
LION I (124) YOU BEASTLY GOAT, OR -- /SPINTHO/ YES: BEAT ME: KICK ME. I FORGIVE YOU: MIND THAT. /FERROVIUS/ (SPURNING
OVER (192) KICK OTHER MEN DOWNSTAIRS. /JUNO/ WELL, I CANT KICK MR LUNN DOWNSTAIRS. WE'RE ON THE GROUND FLOOR. /MRS
PYGM V (288) UP MY FINGER TO BE AS GOOD AS YOU, I COULD JUST KICK MYSELF. /HIGGINS/ (WONDERING AT HER) YOU DAMNED
FANY II (291) WINDMILL AND KNOCK A POLICEMAN DOWN BY A GLORIOUS KICK ON THE HELMET. OH, IF THEYD ALL FOUGHT AS WE TWO FOUGHT
OVER (192) SPOKE WITH THE GREATEST CONTEMPT OF MEN WHO DIDNT KICK OTHER MEN DOWNSTAIRS. /JUNO/ WELL, I CANT KICK MR LUNN
CATH 1 (163) YOU REFUSE TO SEE THE MOST EXALTED PERSONS, YOU KICK PRINCES AND GENERALS DOWNSTAIRS, AND THEN YOU SEE AN
MILL II (170) (SENDING HIM THROUGH THE DOOR WITH A MULE KICK) ROTTER! BOUNDER! STINKER! (SHE SNATCHES HIS HAT
CAPT III (284) YOU? (AGAIN HE PUSHES HIM BACK WITH A FURTIVE KICK). /SIR HOWARD/ (REMONSTRATING) CICELY! /KEARNEY/ (
MIS. PREFACE(7) IT, SEND IT FLYING FROM THE ROOM WITH A CUFF OR A KICK ; AND THE EXPERIENCE WILL BE AS INSTRUCTIVE TO THE
2TRU I (42) GOOD LOOKS. AND IF HER PUNCH IS ANYTHING LIKE HER KICK SHE WILL BE AN INVALUABLE BODYGUARD FOR US TWO
CATH 2 (181) PUFF, TURNING INTO A GROWL)! (HE SPITS). I MUST KICK SOMEBODY. /NARYSHKIN/ (FLYING PRECIPITATELY THROUGH
CAPT III (298) LEFT TO MYSELF, IVE BECOME HALF A BRIGAND. I CAN KICK THAT LITTLE GUTTERSCRUB DRINKWATER; BUT I FIND MYSELF
FABL II (106) YOU, WHAT COULD YOU HAVE DONE EXCEPT WHAT I DID? KICK THE FELLOW OUT. /OLDHAND/ LISTEN TO ME. I AM, AS YOU
CATH 1 (163) UP; AND HE KICKED ME. THEY ALL KICK ME WHEN YOU KICK THEM. GOD KNOWS THAT IS NOT JUST, LITTLE FATHER!
2TRU II (74) MISERABLE; AND I'M MISERABLE; AND I SHALL JUST KICK YOU AND BEAT YOU TO A JELLY. SHE RUSHES AT HIM. HE
JOAN 1 (58) NO EGGS! WHO STOLE THEM? TELL ME THAT, BEFORE I KICK YOU OUT THROUGH THE CASTLE GATE FOR A LIAR AND A SELLER
PRES (152) OUT OF THE ROOM THIS INSTANT, YOU FOOL; OR I'LL KICK YOU OUT. /THE ORDERLY/ (CIVILLY) I DONT MIND THAT,
APPL INTRLUD(244) RATHER YOU KICKED ME. /MAGNUS/ I SHOULD LIKE TO KICK YOU SOMETIMES, WHEN YOU ARE SPECIALLY AGGRAVATING. BUT
GENV IV (127) TO KICK HIM WHILE HE WAS SPEAKING. I WANTED TO KICK YOU TWO ALL THE TIME. /THE BETROTHED/ STEADY, GONNY,
CATH 1 (165) OFFICER DOWNSTAIRS. /PATIOMKIN/ YOU WANT ME TO KICK YOU UPSTAIRS: EH? YOU WANT AN AUDIENCE OF THE EMPRESS.
CATH 1 (173) AS HE IS CARRIED OUT) YOU MUST COME. IF YOU KICK YOU WILL BLACKEN MY EYES. /PATIOMKIN/ COME, BABY, COME.
PYGM V (287) TO KISS YOU WITH AND A THICK PAIR OF BOOTS TO KICK YOU WITH. IF YOU CANT APPRECIATE WHAT YOUVE GOT, YOUD
NEVR I (207) HE HAS HAD FOR MONTHS. (HE GIVES THE CHAIR A KICK , AS IF IT WERE VALENTINE). /DOLLY/ IT'S TOO BEASTLY. I
BARB II (297) IF YOU HAD GIVEN YOUR POOR MOTHER JUST ONE MORE KICK , WE SHOULD HAVE GOT THE WHOLE FIVE SHILLINGS! /PRICE/

KICKED

CATH 1 (165) YOU WITH UNUSUAL CIVILITY, CAPTAIN. HE HAS JUST KICKED A GENERAL DOWNSTAIRS. /EDSTASTON/ A RUSSIAN GENERAL,
SUPR HANDBOK(221) SAME SOCIAL PRODUCT AS THE GAROTTER WHO HAS BEEN KICKED BY HIS FATHER AND CUFFED BY HIS MOTHER UNTIL HE HAS
BULL PREFACE(61) NATIVES KNOCKED A SOLDIER OFF HIS DONKEY AND KICKED HIM IN THE STOMACH: HIS INJURIES ARE SERIOUS. IN THE
GENV IV (127) DEAD; BUT HE DOES NOT KNOW IT. HISTORY WOULD HAVE KICKED HIM OUT WERE NOT HISTORY NOW ON ITS DEATHBED.
MIS. (197) FOR KICKING HIS FATHER. HE SAID HIS FATHER HAD KICKED HIM UNTIL HE WAS BIG ENOUGH TO KICK BACK. PATSY
MIS. (197) THAT MAN WHAT IT FELT LIKE THE FIRST TIME HE KICKED HIS FATHER, AND FOUND THAT IT WAS JUST LIKE KICKING
CATH 1 (163) /THE SERGEANT/ (ON HIS KNEES) LITTLE FATHER: YOU KICKED HIS HIGHNESS DOWNSTAIRS. /PATIOMKIN/ (FLINGING HIM
APPL PREFACE(176) AND PROCEDURE. WHEN WE SEE PARLIAMENTS LIKE OURS KICKED INTO THE GUTTER BY DICTATORS, BOTH IN KINGDOMS AND
JOAN PREFACE(6) CROWNED AND THE ENGLISH KING WHOSE CROWN SHE HAD KICKED INTO THE LOIRE, WERE EQUALLY GLAD TO BE RID OF HER.
CAPT I SD(234) WITH EVERY APPEARANCE OF HAVING BEEN VIOLENTLY KICKED . MARZO IMMEDIATELY HURRIES DOWN THE GARDEN ON SIR
MIS. (197) YOUVE KICKED ME HARDER THAN BILL BURT EVER KICKED . /LORD SUMMERHAYS/ IT'S NO USE, TARLETON. SPARE
JOAN PREFACE(39) US TO REMIND THEM THAT THEY HAVE BODIES TO BE KICKED . THE VATICAN WAS NEVER SOULLESS: AT WORST IT WAS A
MRS PREFACE(153) FURIOUSLY THAT SIR GEORGE CROFTS OUGHT TO BE KICKED . WHAT A TRIUMPH FOR THE ACTOR, THUS TO REDUCE A
BULL PREFACE(53) TO HAVE THEIR THROATS CUT FOR MURDERING HER; AND KICKED (WITH NAKED FEET, FORTUNATELY); BUT AT THIS POINT
MIS. (197) I HAVNT KICKED YOU, PAPA. /TARLETON/ YOUVE KICKED ME HARDER THAN BILL BURT EVER KICKED. /LORD
SIM II (56) SUCCESSES: YOU AND LADY FARWATERS. /HYERING/ YOU KICKED ME INTO THE SEA. /SIR CHARLES/ YOU MADE LOVE TO LADY
SIM PRO,3, (31) THE SEA) WELL, IF YOU WANT TO KNOW, THIS BLIGHTER KICKED ME INTO THE SEA; AND WHEN I'D SWALLOWED A TON OR TWO
GETT (304) THE HOUSE? HE'S STRONGER THAN ME: HE COULD HAVE KICKED ME OUT IF IT CAME TO THAT. HE DID KICK ME OUT: WHAT
FANY II (293) THROUGH THE STREETS TO THE POLICE STATION. THEY KICKED ME WITH THEIR KNEES; THEY TWISTED MY ARMS; THEY
APPL INTRLUD(244) ME WHEN MY HEART DEMANDS LOVE. I HAD RATHER YOU KICKED ME. /MAGNUS/ I SHOULD LIKE TO KICK YOU SOMETIMES,
CATH 1 (163) LIE. HE FELL DOWNSTAIRS. I PICKED HIM UP; AND HE KICKED ME. THEY ALL KICK ME WHEN YOU KICK THEM. GOD KNOWS
BUOY IV (54) NOT DEMUR. IN ANY OTHER FAMILY HE WOULD HAVE BEEN KICKED OUT OF THE HOUSE. /OLD BILL/ I LIKE THE FELLOW. /SIR
KING I (194) OATES. /JAMES/ TITUS OATES! A NAVY CHAPLAIN KICKED OUT OF THE SERVICE FOR THE SINS OF SODOM AND
2TRU III (90) AS CURED ON THE THIRD OF THE MONTH: SHE HAD BEEN KICKED OUT ON THE FIRST, THE TRAINED STAFF COULD STAND A
GENV II (51) ANXIOUS ABOUT THAT: THE REPUBLICANS WILL SOON BE KICKED OUT, THE PEOPLE MAY BE MISLED FOR A WHILE; BUT THEY
CAPT II SD(242) AND OPENS HIS EYES SLEEPILY. A DOOR IS VIOLENTLY KICKED OUTSIDE; AND THE VOICE OF DRINKWATER IS HEARD RAISING
SIM PRO,3, (30) I SAY, REVEREND. WHAT ABOUT THE POOR LAD YOU KICKED OVER THE CLIFF? IS HE REALLY SAFE? I DONT FEEL EASY
DEST SD(157) ARE YOU ALL ASLEEP HERE? THE OTHER DOOR IS KICKED RUDELY OPEN. A DUSTY SUB-LIEUTENANT BURSTS INTO THE
HART II (117) THEY WOULDNT OBEY ME UNLESS I SWORE AT THEM AND KICKED THEM AND BEAT THEM WITH MY FISTS. FOOLISH PEOPLE TOOK
FANY EPILOG (331) OF BEING DUKES AND MILLIONAIRES. THE HEROINE GETS KICKED THROUGH THE MUD: REAL MUD. THERES NO PLOT. ALL THE

BULL PREFACE(53) MAN-- NOT A FOREIGNER AND NOT AN UNBELIEVER-- WAS KICKED TO DEATH IN THE STREETS OF LONDON BECAUSE THE ACTION
MIS. (193) WAS BEHAVING LIKE A VERY FINE GENTLEMAN; BUT HE KICKED VOLNEY FOR SAYING THAT WHAT FRANCE WANTED WAS THE
GETT (303) GENERAL/ I DONT DEFEND REGINALD. HE SHOULD HAVE KICKED YOU OUT OF THE HOUSE, MR HOTCHKISS. /REGINALD/ (
MIS. (197) SUMMERHAYS! THINK OF THAT! /HYPATIA/ I HAVNT KICKED YOU, PAPA. /TARLETON/ YOUVE KICKED ME HARDER THAN
JOAN 2,SD(73) THE EXPRESSION OF A YOUNG DOG ACCUSTOMED TO BE KICKED , YET INCORRIGIBLE AND IRREPRESSIBLE. BUT HE IS

KICKING
MTH5 (214) /ACIS/ MORE THAN READY, ANCIENT. SHOUTING AND KICKING AND CURSING. WE HAVE CALLED TO HER TO BE QUIET AND
MTH2 (56) KEPT DISTURBING ME. THEY HAD TO BE CARRIED OUT KICKING AND MAKING A HORRID DISTURBANCE. /CONRAD/ NO: IT WAS
MIS. (189) THE TENTH POSSESSOR OF A FOOLISH FACE CARRIED OUT KICKING AND SCREAMING BY A WOMAN. (TO PERCIVAL) YOU CROWED
HART II (117) MYSELF TO THE DEVIL. IT SAVED MY SOUL FROM THE KICKING AND SWEARING THAT WAS DAMNING ME BY INCHES. /ELLIE/
MIS. (197) HIS FATHER, AND FOUND THAT IT WAS JUST LIKE KICKING ANY OTHER MAN. HE LAUGHED AND SAID THAT IT WAS THE
SIM II (61) SOMETHING ABOUT HER DARK BEAUTY THAT-- /PROLA/ (KICKING HIM) SILENCE, SIMPLETON. LET THE UNSPEAKABLE REMAIN
CATH 1 (163) DOWNSTAIRS. /PATIOMKIN/ (FLINGING HIM DOWN AND KICKING HIM) YOU LIE, YOU DOG. YOU LIE. /THE SERGEANT/
MIS. (197) WAS A LABORER HERE. I WAS GOING TO SACK HIM FOR KICKING HIS FATHER. HE SAID HIS FATHER HAD KICKED HIM UNTIL
METH PREFACE(R12) BY THE NEWSPAPERS OF THEIR EXPLOITERS THAT THE KICKING IS NOT ONLY A SOUND COMMERCIAL INVESTMENT, BUT AN
LIED (200) PROUD OF IT, ARNT YOU? YAH! YOURE NOT WORTH KICKING . HENRY SUDDENLY EXECUTES THE FEAT KNOWN TO
MTH5 (213) YET? THE HOUR OF BIRTH IS OVERDUE. THE BABY IS KICKING LIKE MAD. SHE WILL BREAK HER SHELL PREMATURELY. /THE
SIM II (61) REMAIN UNSPOKEN. /IDDY/ I DONT MIND YOUR KICKING ME, PROLA: YOU UNDERSTAND; AND THAT IS ENOUGH FOR
GENV I (41) BUT I SHALL HAVE SOME DOUGH TO SPEND. I HAVE BEEN KICKING MY HEELS HERE FOR MONTHS FAKING NEWS FOR MY PEOPLE
GETT (304) TO THAT. HE DID KICK ME OUT: WHAT ELSE WAS IT BUT KICKING OUT, TO TAKE MY WIFE'S AFFECTIONS FROM ME AND
GLIM (175) /THE FRIAR/ ANOTHER MIRACLE OF SAINT BARBARA. (KICKING THE DOOR) COME OUT, WHELP! COME OUT, RAT. COME OUT
BARB III (327) /UNDERSHAFT/ (STRIDING ACROSS TO STEPHEN AND KICKING THE PROSTRATE DUMMY BRUTALLY OUT OF HIS WAY) NO: THE
CAPT II (242) HORSESHOE ARCH, HOT AND EXCITED, AND RUNS ROUND, KICKING THE SLEEPERS). NAH THEN. GIT AP. GIT AP, WILL YR,
FANY III (316) DO WHAT WE LIKE, AND OUR OWN SONS AND DAUGHTERS KICKING THEIR HEELS ALL OVER THE PLACE? (TO KNOX) I WAS
MILL IV (188) QUIET. YOU ARE SO QUIET: I'M NEVER AFRAID OF YOUR KICKING UP A ROW ABOUT NOTHING. THE RIVER IS SO SMOOTH. I
MTH5 (215) I WANT TO BE BORN: I WANT TO BE BORN. (VIOLENT KICKING WITHIN THE EGG, WHICH ROCKS SO HARD THAT IT HAS TO
CATH 1 (165) EMPRESS. /EDSTASTON/ I HAVE SAID NOTHING ABOUT KICKING , SIR. IF IT COMES TO THAT, MY BOOTS SHALL SPEAK FOR

KICKINGS
APPL PREFACE(173) TANTRUMS, BULLYINGS, SNEERINGS, SWEARINGS, KICKINGS : IN SHORT, THE COMMONER VIOLENCES AND

KICKS
ROCK II (270) THEM INTO THE WAY THEY SHOULD GO WITH AS MANY KICKS AS MAY BE NEEDFUL TO MAKE A THOROUGH JOB OF IT.
CAPT II (250) YOU HAVE MY AUTHORITY TO ORDER HIM AS MANY KICKS AS YOU THINK GOOD FOR HIM; AND I WILL SEE THAT HE GETS
MTH3 (97) REFUSAL TO BE GOVERNED AT ALL. A HORSE THAT KICKS EVERYONE WHO TRIES TO HARNESS AND GUIDE HIM MAY BE A
CATH 2 (178) SHE HAS AN IMPULSE OF DISGUST). HOG. (SHE KICKS HIM AS HARD AS SHE CAN). OH! YOU HAVE BROKEN MY TOE.
SUPR I (13) DO THAN LISTEN TO YOUR FOOLERIES (HE POSITIVELY KICKS HIS WAY TO HIS TABLE AND RESUMES HIS SEAT). /TANNER/
MTH4 II (181) HIS EYES) QUARTER! KAMERAD! TAKE IT, MADAM (HE KICKS IT TOWARDS HER): I SURRENDER. /THE ORACLE/ GIVE ME
MTH1 I (3) EYES? /ADAM/ IT IS NOT ONLY ITS EYES. LOOK. (HE KICKS IT). /EVE/ OH DONT! WHY DOESNT IT WAKE? /ADAM/ I
SUPR II (50) IN SEVENTEEN MINUTES. (THE CHAUFFEUR, FURIOUS, KICKS THE CAR WITH A GROAN OF VEXATION). HOW LONG WERE YOU?
HART II (101) UP! SO YOU THINK IVE BEEN ASLEEP, DO YOU? (HE KICKS THE CHAIR VIOLENTLY BACK OUT OF HIS WAY, AND GETS
MTH1 II SD(20) GOES ON DIGGING WITHOUT RAISING HIS HEAD). CAIN KICKS THE HURDLE OUT OF HIS WAY, AND STRIDES INTO THE
CATH 1 (168) /PATIOMKIN/ GET OUT. (HE SNATCHES THE GOBLET AND KICKS THE SERGEANT OUT, NOT MALICIOUSLY BUT FROM HABIT,
GETT (335) SAY? WHAT DARE HE SAY? /MRS GEORGE/ SUPPOSE HE KICKS YOU OUT OF THE HOUSE? /HOTCHKISS/ HOW CAN HE? IVE
BULL PREFACE(11) IT ARE SITTING ON BENGAL; AND THE MORE BENGAL KICKS , THE MORE BERMONDSEY IS NEGLECTED, EXCEPT BY THE TAX

KID
CAPT II (247) WASNT IT? WERE YOU EVER CALLED-- /REDBROOK/ THE KID ? YES. /LADY CICELY/ BUT WHY-- /REDBROOK/ (
BARB II (299) E CALLED ME BRADDHER, AN DAHNED ME AS IF AW WAS A KID AND E WAS ME MATHER WORSHIN ME A SETTERDA NAWT. AW EDNT
POSN (464) HIMSELF? WHY SHOULD HE GO HARD ON THE INNOCENT KID AND GO SOFT ON A ROTTEN THING LIKE ME? WHY DID I GO
CAPT II (249) SHEIKH'S AUDIENCE CHAMBER, AND TO PUT ME AND THE KID HANDY IN HIS BEDROOM IN CASE MARZO GETS ERYSIPELAS AND
MIS. (114) THEY DID TRY THAT ON ME ONCE, WHEN I WAS A SMALL KID . A SILLY GOVERNESS DID IT. I YELLED FIT TO BRING DOWN
MIS. (113) WHY HE DIDNT LICK IT OUT OF YOU WHEN YOU WERE A KID . FOR TWENTY-FIVE YEARS HE KEPT A PLACE TWICE AS BIG AS
FABL VI (126) RACES. I PICKED IT UP FROM HIM WHEN I WAS A KID . OF COURSE THE OLD MAN IS NOW OUT-OF-DATE: I DONT TAKE
BARB I (262) HE HASNT SEEN SARAH SINCE SHE WAS A LITTLE KID . /LADY BRITOMART/ NOT SINCE SHE WAS A LITTLE KID,
POSN (458) AND WENT TO BITS WHEN YOU PLAYED OFF THE SICK KID ON HIM. WELL, I GUESS THAT CLEARS ME. I'M NOT THAT SORT.
MIS. (144) DID YOU EVER MAKE MUD PIES WHEN YOU WERE A KID -- BEG PARDON: A CHILD. /LORD SUMMERHAYS/ I HOPE NOT.
POSN (462) A COLLECTION FOR THE BEREAVED MOTHER OF THE LATE KID THAT SHEWED UP BLANCO POSNET. /THE BOYS/ A COLLECTION.
POSN (466) IT'S COME OVER ME AGAIN, SAME AS WHEN THE KID TOUCHED ME, SAME AS WHEN YOU SWORE A LIE TO SAVE MY
2TRU II (71) ANXIOUS WORRYING MOTHER AS COMPLETELY AS A WEANED KID , AND I NO LONGER HATE HER. MY SLAVERY TO COOKS STUFFING
POSN (459) WITH THE FEVER. HE SAID IT WAS A LITTLE JUDAS KID , AND THAT IT WAS BETRAYING HIM WITH A KISS, AND THAT
BARB I (262) KID. /LADY BRITOMART/ NOT SINCE SHE WAS A LITTLE KID , CHARLES, AS YOU EXPRESS IT WITH THAT ELEGANCE OF
BULL IV (181) (REFLECTIVELY) ONCE, WHEN I WAS A SMALL KID , I DREAMT I WAS IN HEAVEN. (THEY BOTH STARE AT HIM).
POSN (458) CATCH ME PUTTING MY NECK IN A NOOSE FOR ANYBODY'S KID ! /THE FOREMAN/ DONT YOU GO PUTTING HER UP TO WHAT TO
POSN (458) THE THROAT-- FRANTICALLY) DEAD! THE LITTLE JUDAS KID ! THE CHILD I GAVE MY LIFE FOR! (HE BREAKS INTO

KIDBROOK
CAPT II (249) WORK THE BUCKET. /LADY CICELY/ SO GOOD OF YOU, MR KIDBROOK . (SHE MAKES FOR THE HORSESHOE ARCH, FOLLOWED BY

KIDD
BARB PREFACE(232) OF THE BUCCANEERS OF THE SPANISH MAIN. CAPTAIN KIDD WOULD HAVE MAROONED A MODERN TRUST MAGNATE FOR CONDUCT

KIDDIN
SUPR II (70) ARE PROTECTED FROM WOMEN. /STRAKER/ GARN! YOURE KIDDIN . /TANNER/ (RESOLUTELY) STAY BEHIND THEN. IF YOU
SUPR II (69) COURSE IT'S NOT MY BUSINESS; BUT YOU NEEDNT START KIDDIN ME ABOUT IT. /TANNER/ I AM NOT KIDDING. I DONT KNOW

KIDDING
SUPR II (69) START KIDDIN ME ABOUT IT. /TANNER/ I AM NOT KIDDING . I DONT KNOW WHY. /STRAKER/ (CHEERFULLY SULKY) OH,
MTH3 (131) NOT A DOUBT OF IT. THEY MUST HAVE BEEN KIDDING US, THEY WERE, WERENT THEY? /CONFUCIUS/ YOU LOOKED

KIDDY
CAND II (115) TELL ER FAIRY STORIES WHEN SHE WAS ONY A LITTLE KIDDY NOT THAT IGH (INDICATING A STATURE OF TWO FEET OR
CAPT II (242) THE SLEEPERS). NAH THEN. GIT AP. GIT AP, WILL YR, KIDDY REDBROOK. (HE GIVES THE YOUNG GENTLEMAN A RUDE
SIM I (48) /THE CLERGYMAN/ NOT AT ALL. MY SISTER WAS THE KIDDY ; SO I BECAME THE IDDY. DO PLEASE CALL ME THAT. AND BE

KIDNAP
2TRU I (47) A KIDNAP. /THE NURSE/ WHAT DO YOU MEAN? STAGE A KIDNAP . /THE BURGLAR/ IT'S QUITE SIMPLE. WE KIDNAP MOPS:
2TRU I (47) ANOTHER IDEA. A REGULAR DAZZLER. LETS STAGE A KIDNAP . /THE NURSE/ WHAT DO YOU MEAN? STAGE A KIDNAP. /THE
CATH 4 (188) NOT INTIMIDATED. I AM AN ENGLISHMAN; AND YOU CAN KIDNAP ME; BUT YOU CANT BULLY ME. /NARYSHKIN/ REMEMBER TO
2TRU I (47) A KIDNAP. /THE BURGLAR/ IT'S QUITE SIMPLE. WE KIDNAP MOPS: THAT IS, WE SHALL HIDE HER IN THE MOUNTAINS OF
ROCK PREFACE(160) WILFUL MURDER, OR LEVY WAR AGAINST THE CROWN, OR KIDNAP , OR THROW VITRIOL, IS NOT ONLY TO LIMIT SOCIAL

KIDNAPPED
GENV II (58) YOU SET FOOT IN THEIR COUNTRY. YOU MAY EVEN BE KIDNAPPED AND CARRIED THERE: REMEMBER NAPOLEON AND THE DUC
SIM I (39) IN DESPERATE PROTEST) BUT I HAVE. I HAVE. THEY KIDNAPPED ME AT WESTON SUPER MARE WHERE I WAS DOING LOCUM
MRS PREFACE(180) MOTOR CAR IN WHICH THE HEROINE OF THE FILM WAS KIDNAPPED , AND THE FASHIONABLE CLOTHES OF THE TWO VERY
2TRU I (47) /THE PATIENT/ (EXCITED) GREECE! DALMATIA! KIDNAPPED ! BRIGANDS! RANSOMED! (COLLAPSING A LITTLE)

KIDNAPPING
2TRU I (49) UNEXPECTEDLY POWERFUL MIND. PRAY HEAVEN THAT IN KIDNAPPING YOU I AM NOT BITING OFF MORE THAN I CAN CHEW.

KIDNAPS
SUPR PREFACE(R39) OF THE HUMAN SPIRIT, AND, WORST OF ALL, KIDNAPS YOUNG PEOPLE AS PUPILS AND PERSUADES THEM THAT HIS

KIDNEY
BARB PREFACE(239) THAT ALL OVER THE WORLD PROLETARIANS OF THE DUCAL KIDNEY ARE NOW REVELLING IN " THE WHIFF OF DYNAMITE" (THE

LADY	(248)	A WRESTLER; WHILST, IN THE OTHER, ONE OF THE SAME	KIDNEY	SHEWETH HER WIT BY SAYING ENDLESS NAUGHTINESSES TO A
			KIDS	
CAPT II	(269)	CHURCH NEXT SUNDER! LAWK A BLOOMIN LOT O CHERRITY	KIDS	: YOU SEE IF SHE DOWNT. /LADY CICELY/ (BUSILY)
BUOY III	(39)	RID OF YOUR CRAZY NOTIONS ABOUT YOUR HUSBAND. THE	KIDS	FILL HIS PLACE. /MRS THIRDBORN/ NOT AFTER THEY ARE SIX,
MTH2	(79)	CLAUSE, INTO THE MUSEUM. YOU SHEW THE	KIDS	THE PILTDOWN SKULL; AND YOU SAY, " THATS ADAM. THATS
MTH2	(40)	WOODMAN AND LIVE IN A HOVEL WITH HIM AND A LOT OF	KIDS	TUMBLING OVER ONE ANOTHER, JUST BECAUSE THE FELLOW HAS
MTH1 II	(30)	IT WOULD COME TO, JUST AS IT CAME TO LAMBS AND	KIDS	WHEN ABEL BEGAN WITH SHEEP AND GOATS. YOU ARE A POOR
MTH1 II	(25)	AND EAT PARTRIDGES AND DOVES, AND THE FLESH OF	KIDS	WHOSE MILK YOU WILL STEAL FOR ME? /ADAM/ YOU ARE HARD
SUPR III	(80)	BIT BETTER THAN THAT IF YOU LIKE. /MENDOZA/ WINE,	KIDS	, MILK, CHEESE, AND BREAD CAN BE PROCURED FOR READY
			KIDY	
CAPT II	(265)	BLOOMIN AWD PAWK DEMONSTRATION. AW BLIEVE ITS THE	KIDY	FROM KINTORFY. (GENERAL ALARM. ALL LOOK TO
			KIKKERONIAN	
GENV IV	(99)	FROM THESE ABOMINABLE MODERN MISPRONUNCIATIONS.	KIKKERONIAN	IS AN INSULT TO MY OLD SCHOOL. I INSIST ON
GENV IV	(99)	ACTION. OUT OF THE RAGBAG OF STALE JOURNALISM AND	KIKKERONIAN	LATIN-- /SIR O./ I PROTEST. I BEG. I ASK THE
			KILKENNY	
SIM II	(54)	ON RECORD. THEY ARE QUARRELLING ALREADY LIKE	KILKENNY	CATS. /SIR CHARLES/ WHAT ABOUT? /HYERING/ OH,
			KILL	
DOCT I	(90)	WHEN THE PATIENT IS IN THE NEGATIVE PHASE AND YOU	KILL	: INOCULATE WHEN THE PATIENT IS IN THE POSITIVE PHASE
LION II	(136)	/ANDROCLES/ BROTHER, BROTHER: LET THEM RAGE AND	KILL	: LET US BE BRAVE AND SUFFER. YOU MUST GO AS A LAMB TO
KING I	(195)	BUT JUST NOW IT IS NOT OATES THAT WE HAVE TO	KILL	: THE PEOPLE WOULD SAY THAT HE WAS MURDERED BY THE
MTH5	(243)	IN THE SAME MANNER) WHICH OF YOU SHALL WE	KILL	? /THE FEMALE FIGURE/ KILL US BOTH. HOW COULD EITHER
LADY PREFACE	(219)	ASKS " HATES ANY MAN THE THING HE WOULD NOT	KILL	? " HE IS EXPRESSING THE NATURAL AND PROPER SENTIMENTS
ROCK PREFACE	(150)	" HATES ANY MAN THE THING HE WOULD NOT	KILL	? " SAID SHYLOCK NAIVELY. BUT WE WHITE MEN, AS WE
METH PREFACE	(R59)	THAT CONCEIT OUT OF US; AND NOW, THOUGH WE MAY	KILL	A FLEA WITHOUT THE SMALLEST REMORSE, WE AT ALL EVENTS
SIM PREFACE	(4)	SIGHT AND IS CONTINUALLY SEEKING FOR AN EXCUSE TO	KILL	A FRIEND TO ACQUIRE TROPHIES ENOUGH TO ATTRACT A WIFE.
DOCT V	(177)	REMEMBER YOU ALWAYS AS A LITTLE MAN WHO TRIED TO	KILL	A GREAT ONE. /RIDGEON/ PARDON ME. I SUCCEEDED.
METH PREFACE	(R71)	END WE DO NOT YET KNOW. WHEN WOLVES COMBINE TO	KILL	A HORSE, THE DEATH OF THE HORSE ONLY SETS THEM FIGHTING
GLIM	(188)	MAD; AND THIS MAKES US THINK IT VERY UNLUCKY TO	KILL	A MADMAN. AND SINCE FROM WHAT FATHER SQUARCIO AND I
DOCT I	(91)	RESPECTABLE PRACTITIONER CAN GET. IF I WANTED TO	KILL	A MAN I SHOULD KILL HIM THAT WAY. /EMMY/ (LOOKING IN)
GLIM	(180)	WHAT DOES GIULIETTA SAY? /GIULIA/ I SHOULD NOT	KILL	A MAN IF I HATED HIM. YOU CANNOT TORMENT A MAN WHEN HE
CLEO PR01	(92)	SAID, " THY COUNSEL IS EXPEDIENT; BUT IF WE	KILL	A MAN OUTSIDE THE LAW WE SET OURSELVES IN THE PLACE OF
GLIM	(183)	AND DOING SOMETHING. I SHOULD NOT LIKE TO	KILL	A MAN WITH A GOOD SOUL. IVE HAD A DOG THAT HAD, I'M
GLIM	(183)	MONEY HONESTLY. WHEN I SAID I SHOULD NOT LIKE TO	KILL	A MAN WITH A GOOD SOUL, I MEANT KILLING ON MY OWN
LION II	(127)	IT. THE PEOPLE INDEED! DO YOU SUPPOSE WE WOULD	KILL	A MAN WORTH PERHAPS FIFTY TALENTS TO PLEASE THE
POSN	(435)	(ELDERLY AND WISE) I DONT SAY IT'S RIGHT TO	KILL	A MAN, IN A PLACE LIKE THIS, WHERE EVERY MAN HAS TO
ROCK PREFACE	(188)	THEIR FRUITS YE SHALL KNOW THEM. BEWARE HOW YOU	KILL	A THOUGHT THAT IS NEW TO YOU. FOR THAT THOUGHT MAY BE
JOAN 5	(112)	AS I LOVE PITOU, MY OLD SHEEP DOG. PITOU COULD	KILL	A WOLF. YOU WILL KILL THE ENGLISH WOLVES UNTIL THEY GO
HART I	(77)	HER IF SHE PERSISTS. /MRS HUSHABYE/ NOTHING WILL	KILL	ADDY: SHE IS AS STRONG AS A HORSE. (RELEASING HIM) NOW
2TRU III	(95)	TO STAND BY THEMSELVES, NOT CLINGERS. I WOULD	KILL	ALL THE CLINGERS. MOTHERS CLING: DAUGHTERS CLING: WE
GETT PREFACE	(208)	WHEN THE QUEEN KILLS HIM AND THE QUONDAM FEMALES	KILL	ALL THE REST (SUCH AT LEAST ARE THE ACCOUNTS GIVEN BY
CLEO II	(134)	BE THE FIRST, BUT IF HE LOVES ME, I WILL MAKE HIM	KILL	ALL THE REST. TELL ME: IS HE STILL BEAUTIFUL? DO HIS
ROCK II	(261)	IT MARKS HIM OUT AS AN ENEMY IN UNIFORM; AND TO	KILL	AN ENEMY IN UNIFORM AT SIGHT IS NOT MURDER: IT'S
JOAN 1	(67)	TO THEM. IF IT WERE NOT SO IT WOULD BE MURDER TO	KILL	AN ENGLISHMAN IN BATTLE; AND YOU, SQUIRE, WOULD BE IN
FABL I	(102)	I SHALL NOT BRING THEM INTO THIS WICKED WORLD TO	KILL	AND BE KILLED. AN EXCITED MIDDLE-AGED MAN COMES ALONG
MTH1 II	(34)	OF THE VOICE THAT THEY SHOULD DIG AND FIGHT AND	KILL	AND DIE FOR EVER. /ADAM/ IF THEY ARE LAZY AND HAVE A
MTH1 II	(34)	SHORTEN THEIR LIVES, THEY WILL DIG AND FIGHT AND	KILL	AND DIE; AND THEIR BABY ENOCHS WILL TELL THEM THAT IT
3PLA PREFACE	(R22)	BE CHEERED AS A PATRIOT BECAUSE HE IS WILLING TO	KILL	AND GET KILLED FOR THE SAKE OF CONFERRING HIMSELF AS AN
GENV IV	(107)	THE BLOOD FEUD; AND I SHALL DREAM AND DREAM AND	KILL	AND KILL. I CALL ON YOU TO CONDEMN HIM. /BBDE/ AND
HART PREFACE	(18)	IN THE PUBLIC EYE, SO THAT THEY MIGHT GO OUT TO	KILL	AND MAIM MEN AS GENTLE AS THEMSELVES. THESE MEN, WHO
BARB PREFACE	(246)	UNLIKE OUR RAILWAY SHAREHOLDERS (I AM ONE) WHO	KILL	AND MAIM SHUNTERS BY HUNDREDS TO SAVE THE COST OF
MTH5	(241)	THOUGHTLESS: I DID NOT FORESEE THAT THEY WOULD	KILL	AND PRETEND TO BE PERSONS THEY WERE NOT, AND DECLARE
BUOY II	(22)	/SHE/ WHAT IS THE WOMAN TO EAT IF YOU DO NOT	KILL	ANIMALS FOR HER? /HE/ SHE CAN BE A VEGETARIAN. I AM.
BUOY II	(22)	I HAVE LEARNT HERE THAT IF WE VEGETARIANS DO NOT	KILL	ANIMALS THE ANIMALS WILL KILL US. IT IS THE FLESH
DOCT I	(113)	OF A GREAT MAN. /RIDGEON/ YOU ARE ASKING ME TO	KILL	ANOTHER MAN FOR HIS SAKE; FOR AS SURELY AS I UNDERTAKE
SUPR III	(124)	HAVE SERVED HIS COUNTRY IF HE HAD REFUSED TO	KILL	ANY ENEMY OF SPAIN UNLESS HE PERSONALLY HATED HIM? CAN
HART II	(90)	IT ON PURPOSE? /GUINNESS/ NOW IS IT LIKELY I'D	KILL	ANY MAN ON PURPOSE. I FELL OVER HIM IN THE DARK; AND
CLEO II	(137)	GET OUT IF YOU CAN, AND TELL YOUR FRIENDS NOT TO	KILL	ANY MORE ROMANS IN THE MARKET PLACE. OTHERWISE MY
SIM II	(60)	YOU SO INTENSELY THAT IF IT WERE IN MY NATURE TO	KILL	ANYTHING I SHOULD KILL YOU. /IDDY/ THERE NOW! I OUGHT
MILL PREFACE	(113)	TO END WAR, AND THAT THE PEOPLE HE WANTS THEM TO	KILL	ARE DIABOLICAL SCOUNDRELS; AND IF HE IS FORCED TO
DEVL I SD	(3)	MOST HIGHMINDED COURSE FOR THEM TO PURSUE IS TO	KILL	AS MANY OF ONE ANOTHER AS POSSIBLE, AND THAT MILITARY
BULL PREFACE	(55)	PAPERS DESCRIBED IT), THUS HAVING TWO HOURS TO	KILL	AS WELL AS FOUR MEN, THEY KEPT THE ENTERTAINMENT GOING
BARB PREFACE	(217)	ME A POINT OF HONOR FOR WHICH I AM PREPARED TO	KILL	AT THE RISK OF MY OWN LIFE. THIS PREPAREDNESS IS, AS HE
GLIM	(180)	YOU CANNOT TORMENT A MAN WHEN HE IS DEAD. MEN	KILL	BECAUSE THEY THINK IT IS WHAT THEY CALL A SATISFACTION.
MTH1 II	(27)	HAVE YOU OF YOUR THOUSAND YEARS? I COULD	KILL	BOTH OF YOU; AND YOU COULD NO MORE DEFEND YOURSELVES
MIS. PREFACE	(74)	IS REGARDED WITH HORROR; BUT YOU MAY AND DO	KILL	CHILDREN IN A HUNDRED AND FIFTY WAYS PROVIDED YOU DO
OVER PREFACE	(163)	PRESENT MURDER. MACBETH MUST NO MORE REALLY	KILL	DUNCAN THAN HE MUST HIMSELF BE REALLY SLAIN BY MACDUFF.
MTH4 II	(178)	I HAVE NEVER SHED BLOOD WITH MY OWN HAND. THEY	KILL	EACH OTHER: THEY DIE WITH SHOUTS OF TRIUMPH ON THEIR
INCA	(256)	ARE MILLIONS. DO YOU SUPPOSE THEY WOULD REALLY	KILL	EACH OTHER IF THEY DIDNT WANT TO, MERELY FOR THE SAKE
SUPR III	(112)	PLACE, INSTEAD OF MERELY KILLING TIME WE HAVE TO	KILL	ETERNITY, GO AHEAD BY ALL MEANS. /DON JUAN/ (SOMEWHAT
MTH2	(46)	THE WAR; BUT NOW THAT THEY HAVE MANAGED TO HALF	KILL	EUROPE BETWEEN THEM, I CANT BE CIVIL TO THEM, AND I
MTH4 II	(180)	WILLING NOT ONLY TO RISK THEIR OWN LIVES BUT TO	KILL	EVERYONE WHO REFUSES TO TAKE THAT RISK. BUT IF WAR
MTH4 I	(168)	OLD! YOU ARE A CHILD: AN EVIL CHILD. WE	KILL	EVIL CHILDREN HERE. WE DO IT EVEN AGAINST OUR OWN WILLS
BUOY III	(47)	MUST CHANGE ITS AIR AND RESTORE ITS PEACE LEST IT	KILL	FATHER BUOYANT INSTEAD OF GIVING HIM A FORETASTE OF
HART I	(78)	WHAT IS THE DYNAMITE FOR? /CAPTAIN SHOTOVER/ TO	KILL	FELLOWS LIKE MANGAN. /HECTOR/ NO USE. THEY WILL ALWAYS
GENV IV	(107)	TO ME AND BEGS ME TO FORGIVE HER; AND I HAVE TO	KILL	HER AGAIN. I LONG TO GO MAD; BUT I CANNOT: EACH TIME I
CLEO PRO2	(102)	HER PICTURE IN OUR MOUTHS. HE WILL CONQUER AND	KILL	HER BROTHER, AND REIGN IN EGYPT WITH CLEOPATRA FOR HIS
JITT II	(31)	HE IS AFRAID THAT HER GRIEF FOR HER FATHER WILL	KILL	HER FEELING FOR HIM; SO YOUD BETTER TAKE EDITH IN HAND:
HART I	(77)	ME; BUT I HATE HER; SO IT IS HELL. I SHALL	KILL	HER IF SHE PERSISTS. /MRS HUSHABYE/ NOTHING WILL KILL
2TRU III	(96)	IT GIVES WAY, IT'S A BIT OF HIGH EXPLOSIVE. HE'LL	KILL	HER IF SHE PUSHES HIM TOO FAR. /THE PATIENT/ LET HIM
MTH5	(242)	MALE FIGURE/ NO! I HAVE DONE NO HARM: SHE HAS.	KILL	HER IF YOU LIKE: YOU HAVE NO RIGHT TO KILL ME. /THE
2TRU III	(96)	IF SHE PUSHES HIM TOO FAR. /THE PATIENT/ LET HIM	KILL	HER. I AM YOUNG AND STRONG: I WANT A WORLD WITHOUT
GENV IV	(107)	MY DEAREST FRIEND; AND ETIQUETTE OBLIGED ME TO	KILL	HER. IN MY DREAMS NIGHT AFTER NIGHT SHE COMES TO ME AND
KING II	(226)	THAT IS A LIE: IF ANYONE ELSE SAID IT I WOULD	KILL	HER. YOU ARE THE VERY BEST HUSBAND THAT EVER LIVED.
GENV IV	(108)	NO: I TELL YOU I CANNOT BEAR IT. FORBID HER TO	KILL	HERSELF OR I WILL LEAVE THE COURT. /JUDGE/ SENORA: I
GENV IV	(107)	I CANNOT BEAR THIS. ORDER THAT WOMAN NOT TO	KILL	HERSELF. /BBDE/ NO. IF SHE HAS A ROMAN SOUL, WHO DARES
MTH5	(241)	WAS I TO KNOW THAT A LITTLE THING LIKE THAT WOULD	KILL	HIM? I SHOULDNT DIE IF HE CUT OFF MY ARM OR LEG.
PRES	(137)	THEIR HUSBANDS DO. (TO THE ORDERLY) DID SHE	KILL	HIM? /THE ORDERLY/ NO, SIR. HE GOT A STINGER ON HIS
MTH5	(241)	FEMALE FIGURE/ HE MADE ME. I HAD AS MUCH RIGHT TO	KILL	HIM AS HE HAD TO MAKE ME. AND HOW WAS I TO KNOW THAT A
MTH1 II	(21)	AT ME; AND THEN CAME MY GREAT IDEA: WHY NOT	KILL	HIM AS HE KILLED THE BEASTS? I STRUCK; AND HE DIED.
LION PREFACE	(66)	DOES IT? IT WOULD HAVE BEEN FAR EASIER TO	KILL	HIM AS KINDLY AS POSSIBLE, OR TO LABEL HIM AND LEAVE
LION II	(140)	STRIKE FERROVIUS: I'LL GO INTO THE ARENA AND	KILL	HIM FIRST. (HE MAKES A WILD DASH INTO THE PASSAGE. AS
GLIM	(183)	NEVER DONE ANYTHING OR BEEN ANYTHING; AND I WILL	KILL	HIM FOR TEN CROWNS WITH AS LITTLE REMORSE AS I WOULD
ROCK PREFACE	(148)	OR UNSCRUPULOUS THAT IF HIS NEIGHBORS DO NOT	KILL	HIM HE WILL KILL OR RUIN HIS NEIGHBORS; SO THAT THERE
LION II	(133)	THAT HE WOULD VANQUISH ME. IF I HAD HAD TO	KILL	HIM I SHOULD NOT HAVE HAD THE MONEY. /CAESAR/ (
GLIM	(180)	EVERY DAY IS A LONG DREAD OF LOSING HIM. BETTER	KILL	HIM IF THERE BE NO OTHER ESCAPE. /FERRUCCIO/ HOW WELL
GETT PREFACE	(236)	DESIRES TO LIVE, AND WHY THE PERSON WHO WISHES TO	KILL	HIM SHOULD NOT BE GRATIFIED. ALSO WHETHER HE CAN PROVE
DOCT I	(91)	CAN GET. IF I WANTED TO KILL A MAN I SHOULD	KILL	HIM THAT WAY. /EMMY/ (LOOKING IN) WILL YOU SEE A LADY
GLIM	(180)	/FERRUCCIO/ AND IF YOU LOVED HIM? WOULD YOU	KILL	HIM THEN? /GIULIA/ PERHAPS. IF YOU LOVE A MAN YOU ARE
LION II	(140)	(RISING) OH, THAT IS UNWORTHY. CAN THEY NOT	KILL	HIM WITHOUT DISHONORING HIM? /ANDROCLES/ (SCRAMBLING
LION II	(133)	WILL SHEW THEIR DISPLEASURE BY NOT LETTING YOU	KILL	HIM, AND WHEN YOUR TURN COMES, THEY WILL REMEMBER IT
DOCT II	(129)	/SIR PATRICK/ DONT TALK WICKED NONSENSE. YOU CANT	KILL	HIM. BUT YOU CAN LEAVE HIM IN OTHER HANDS. /RIDGEON/ IN
KING II	(226)	NO. HE WILL TRY, POOR BOY; BUT JAMIE WILL	KILL	HIM. HE IS HIS MOTHER'S SON; AND HIS MOTHER WAS

GLIM	(175)	ARE VERY POOR, MY FATHER AND I. AND I AM NOT TO	KILL	HIM. I AM ONLY TO DECOY HIM HERE; FOR HE IS A DEVIL FOR
CLEO IV	(180)	THE WALL. BREAK HIM ON THE STONES. KILL, KILL,	KILL	HIM. /FTATATEETA/ (SHEWING ALL HER TEETH) THE DOG
LION II	(135)	GLADIATORS. /FERROVIUS/ IT DOES NOT HURT A MAN TO	KILL	HIM. /LAVINIA/ NOTHING BUT FAITH CAN SAVE YOU.
MTH5	(238)	UP IN CONSTERNATION. /ARJILLAX/ SHE MEANT TO	KILL	HIM. /STREPHON/ THIS IS HORRIBLE. /THE FEMALE FIGURE/ (
2TRU III	(103)	OTHER MAN WOULD, BUT NOT IN MY PRESENCE. I SHOULD	KILL	HIM. /THE ELDER/ WE ARE ALL SLAVES, BUT AT LEAST YOUR
DEST SD	(149)	THAT A CANNON BALL, IF IT STRIKES A MAN, WILL	KILL	HIM. TO A THOROUGH GRASP OF THIS REMARKABLE DISCOVERY
CLEO III	(150)	IF HE DRAWS HIS SWORD AGAIN INSIDE THE LINES,	KILL	HIM. TO YOUR POSTS. MARCH. HE GOES OUT, LEAVING TWO
KING II	(226)	CHANCE. THEY MAY CALL IN ORANGE BILLY BEFORE THEY	KILL	HIM; AND THEN IT WILL HARDLY BE DECENT FOR BILLY TO
MTH5	(242)	GOOD. IS IT MY FAULT IF I WAS NOT MADE PROPERLY?	KILL	HIM; BUT SPARE ME. /THE MALE FIGURE/ NO! I HAVE DONE
CATH 4	(194)	DONT EVER DO THIS TO A MAN AGAIN. KNOUT HIM;	KILL	HIM; ROAST HIM; BASTE HIM; HEAD, HANG, AND QUARTER HIM;
GETT PREFACE	(237)	IS SO PAINFUL TO HIM THAT HE OFTEN THREATENS TO	KILL	HIMSELF AND SOMETIMES EVEN DOES IT, YET WE EXPECT HIM
MIS.	(118)	PUBLIC BUSINESS IS THAT IT NEVER ENDS. A MAN MAY	KILL	HIMSELF AT IT. /JOHNNY/ OR HE CAN SPEND MORE ON IT THAN
GENV PREFACE	(21)	TWELVE YEARS OF KILLING OTHER PEOPLE HE HAD TO	KILL	HIMSELF, AND LEAVE HIS ACCOMPLICES TO BE HANGED. THE
GETT PREFACE	(236)	FOR PROTECTION FROM SOMEONE WHO THREATENS TO	KILL	HIM, ON THE SIMPLE GROUND THAT HE DESIRES TO LIVE, THE
DOCT PREFACE	(75)	CERTAINLY MAKE HIM A GOOD DEAL WORSE AND PERHAPS	KILL	HIM, WHEREAS IF YOU MADE PRECISELY THE SAME INOCULATION
HART I	(79)	OF COLOR). /HECTOR/ PRECISELY. WELL, DARE YOU	KILL	HIS INNOCENT GRANDCHILDREN? /CAPTAIN SHOTOVER/ THEY
KING II	(226)	AND THEN IT WILL HARDLY BE DECENT FOR BILLY TO	KILL	HIS WIFE'S FATHER. BUT THEY WILL GET RID OF JAMIE
BARB III	(322)	YOU KNOW, TO THINK OF THE LOT OF BEGGARS WE COULD	KILL	IF IT CAME TO FIGHTING. (TO UNDERSHAFT, WITH SUDDEN
OVER PREFACE	(163)	PUGILISTS AND GLADIATORS WILL ACTUALLY FIGHT AND	KILL	IN PUBLIC WITHOUT SHAME, EVEN AS A SPECTACLE FOR MONEY.
ARMS III	(58)	LIKE HEROES. PSHA! THE COURAGE TO RAGE AND	KILL	IS CHEAP. I HAVE AN ENGLISH BULL TERRIER WHO HAS AS
CYMB FORWORD	(136)	IT IS SO EASY THAT IF IT WERE POSSIBLE TO	KILL	IT IT WOULD HAVE BEEN BURLESQUED TO DEATH BY TOM THUMB,
DOCT PREFACE	(22)	BE SUMMED UP IN THE FORMULA: FIND THE MICROBE AND	KILL	IT. AND EVEN THAT THEY DID NOT KNOW HOW TO DO. THE
DOCT I	(98)	THE REMEDY? A VERY SIMPLE ONE. FIND THE GERM AND	KILL	IT. /SIR PATRICK/ SUPPOSE THERES NO GERM? /B.B./
FABL VI	(124)	ANSWER ITS RIDDLES? /YOUTH 1/ WHY SHOULD IT	KILL	ITSELF IF ANYONE DID ANSWER THEM? TELL ME THAT.
LION PREFACE	(16)	THAT NOTHING THAT YOU COULD DO TO IT COULD	KILL	IT, AND THAT WHEN YOU BURIED IT, IT WOULD RISE AGAIN IN
CLEO V	(200)	TO SAVE YOUR LIFE FROM IT? /CAESAR/ (PROMPTLY)	KILL	IT, MAN, WITHOUT MALICE, JUST AS IT WOULD KILL ME. WHAT
DOCT PREFACE	(25)	GERM BEING IN THE SCRAPINGS, AND, LEST YOU SHOULD	KILL	IT, YOU TAKE NO PRECAUTIONS AGAINST OTHER GERMS BEING
GENV IV	(107)	FEUD; AND I SHALL DREAM AND DREAM AND KILL AND	KILL	. I CALL ON YOU TO CONDEMN HIM. /BBDE/ AND CONDEMN YOU.
SIM II	(66)	AND IF THEY ARE INCAPABLE OF FEELING IT? /JANGA/	KILL	. /KANCHIN/ KILL. /VASHTI/ KILL. /MAYA/ KILL. /PROLA/
SIM II	(66)	IT? /JANGA/ KILL. /KANCHIN/ KILL. /VASHTI/	KILL	. /MAYA/ KILL. /PROLA/ THEY CAN DO THAT AS EASILY AS I.
SIM II	(66)	KILL. /KANCHIN/ KILL. /VASHTI/ KILL. /MAYA/	KILL	. /PROLA/ THEY CAN DO THAT AS EASILY AS I. ANY FOOL
SIM II	(66)	INCAPABLE OF FEELING IT? /JANGA/ KILL. /KANCHIN/	KILL	. /VASHTI/ KILL. /MAYA/ KILL. /PROLA/ THEY CAN DO THAT
MTH1 I	(16)	THOUGHT! /THE SERPENT/ KILL, KILL, KILL,	KILL	. THAT IS THE WORD. /EVE/ THE NEW ADAMS AND EVES MIGHT
DOCT I	(91)	CURE: IF IT'S UNDER POINT EIGHT, INOCULATE AND	KILL	. THATS MY DISCOVERY: THE MOST IMPORTANT THAT HAS BEEN
BUOY II	(22)	/HE/ MY WHAT? /SHE/ YOUR TROPHIES THAT YOU DARE	KILL	. THE SCALPS OF OUR ENEMIES. /HE/ I HAVE NEVER KILLED
GLIM	(177)	IT MUST BE AS HE SAYS. IT IS HIS PROFESSION TO	KILL	. WHAT COULD YOU DO AGAINST HIM? IF YOU WANT TO BEAT
MTH1 II	(26)	VOICE WOULD TELL OUR CHILDREN THAT THEY MUST NOT	KILL	. WHY DID IT NOT TELL CAIN THAT? /CAIN/ IT DID; BUT I
DEVL III	(73)	(FIXING HIS EYES ON HIM) " THOU SHALT NOT	KILL	." THE BOOK DROPS IN BRUDENELL'S HANDS. /CHAPLAIN/ (
KING II	(226)	HIS MOTHER WAS NOTHING. THEN THE PROTESTANTS WILL	KILL	JAMIE; AND THE DUTCH LAD WILL SEE HIS CHANCE AND TAKE
DOCT III	(141)	PLEASE. PUT MINNIE IN PRISON. PUT ME IN PRISON.	KILL	JENNIFER WITH THE DISGRACE OF IT ALL. AND THEN, WHEN
SHAK PREFACE	(135)	PALLS, AND THEY CAN SURVIVE TREATMENT THAT WOULD	KILL	LIVE ACTORS. WHEN I FIRST SAW THEM IN MY BOYHOOD
DEVL II	(44)	POOH! /JUDITH/ (PASSIONATELY) DO YOU WANT TO	KILL	ME? DO YOU THINK I CAN BEAR TO LIVE FOR DAYS AND DAYS
SUPR III	(127)	WHAT DO YOU MEAN? DID I KILL YOU OR DID YOU	KILL	ME? /DON JUAN/ WHICH OF US WAS THE BETTER FENCER?
CYMB V	(145)	WERE I TEN TIMES FAITHLESS, HAVE SENT A SLAVE TO	KILL	ME? /GUIDERIUS/ (SHUDDERING) ALL THE WORLD SHOULD DIE
LION I	(113)	YOUR DEATH WILL PROVE NOTHING. /LAVINIA/ THEN WHY	KILL	ME? /THE CAPTAIN/ I MEAN THAT TRUTH, IF THERE BE ANY
2TRU I	(37)	AND CLOSE THOSE CURTAINS AT ONCE. DO YOU WANT TO	KILL	ME? THE NURSE TURNS ALL THE LIGHTS FULL ON. /THE
MTH1 II	(26)	MY KEEPER ANY MORE THAN I WAS HIS: WHY DID HE NOT	KILL	ME? THERE WAS NO MORE TO PREVENT HIM THAN THERE WAS TO
MTH4 I	(168)	HAVE HAD A VERY NARROW ESCAPE. DO NOT ATTEMPT TO	KILL	ME AGAIN; FOR AT THE FIRST SIGN IN YOUR VOICE OR FACE I
GENV IV	(100)	I MUST CUT HIS IF I CAN. AM I TO ALLOW HIM TO	KILL	ME AND RAVISH MY WIFE AND DAUGHTERS? /JUDGE/ I THINK
MTH3	(125)	(DISREGARDING THIS OUTBURST) IF YOU WERE TO	KILL	ME AS I STAND HERE, YOU WOULD HAVE TO APPOINT AN INDIAN
MTH4 I	(169)	OF THIS. (OFFERING HIS CHEST FOR THE SACRIFICE)	KILL	ME AT ONCE; AND MUCH GOOD MAY MY DEATH DO YOU! /ZOO/
POSN	(453)	YOURSELF, SHERIFF. I SAY THIS IS A CONSPIRACY TO	KILL	ME BETWEEN FEEMY AND STRAPPER BECAUSE I WOULDNT TOUCH
MTH5	(233)	BEAST. HE WAS AFRAID OF ME, AND ACTUALLY TRIED TO	KILL	ME BY SNATCHING UP THINGS AND STRIKING AT ME WITH THEM.
JOAN 1	(59)	NO EGGS. THERE WILL BE NONE -- NOT IF YOU WERE TO	KILL	ME FOR IT -- AS LONG AS THE MAID IS AT THE DOOR.
PHIL I	(81)	KNEES AND WRITHING). OH, I'M MAD: I'M MAD: YOULL	KILL	ME IF YOU DESERT ME. /CHARTERIS/ (PETTING HER) MY DEAR
CLEO PRO1	(91)	SHALT DIE," THEN SAID CAESAR, " I WILL BREAK IT:	KILL	ME WHO CAN." AND HE BROKE IT. AND POMPEY WENT FOR HIM,
FANY I	(280)	ON YOUR MIND. /GILBEY/ THE DISGRACE OF IT WILL	KILL	ME. AND IT WILL LEAVE A MARK ON HIM TO THE END OF HIS
CAPT I	(232)	CANNIBALS AND ALL SORTS. EVERYBODY SAID THEYD	KILL	ME. BUT WHEN I MET THEM, I SAID HOWDYEDO? AND THEY
MILL III	(186)	CHANGE OUR WAYS I CANT GO ON: I CANT GO ON: ITLL	KILL	ME. GO UP AND STOP HER, JOE. DONT LET HER TALK: JUST
MTH1 II	(22)	TO KILL YOU, IN SPITE OF MY FEAR THAT YOU WOULD	KILL	ME. I HAVE STRIVEN WITH A BOAR AND WITH A LION AS TO
JITT I	(12)	(SHAKING HIS HEAD DECISIVELY) IT WOULD PROBABLY	KILL	ME. I KNOW. I AM A DOCTOR. (HE TAKES THE GLASS FROM
MILL IV	(198)	STRONGER THAN I AM: HE CAN BATTER ME, TORTURE ME,	KILL	ME. IT IS THE LAST ARGUMENT OF THE LOWER NATURE AGAINST
JITT III	(61)	THRESHOLD. /AGNES/ OH, HOW DREADFUL! THIS WILL	KILL	ME. (TO EDITH, RISING) OH, NOW I KNOW WHAT YOU ARE.
2TRU III	(89)	OVERWHELMED) MY SON A CLERGYMAN! THIS WILL	KILL	ME. /AUBREY/ (COOLLY TAKING ANOTHER STONE, ON HIS
CLEO IV	(189)	I AM ONLY A DREAMER. /CLEOPATRA/ BUT THEY WILL	KILL	ME. /CAESAR/ AND WHY NOT? /CLEOPATRA/ IN PITY--
FANY II	(295)	I DONT KNOW WHAT I SHALL DO: I DONT INDEED: ITLL	KILL	ME. /MARGARET/ YOU SHOULDNT HAVE PRAYED FOR ME TO BE
DEST	(153)	BUT UNHAPPILY I AM NOT STRONG ENOUGH. SHE WOULD	KILL	ME. /NAPOLEON/ THAT WILL DO EQUALLY WELL. /GIUSEPPE/
CYMB V	(145)	/IMOGEN/ AND THEREUPON YOU BADE YOUR SERVANT	KILL	ME. /POSTHUMUS/ IT SEEMED NATURAL. /IMOGEN/ STRIKE ME
O'FL	(210)	THEM BECAUSE I WAS AFEARD THAT, IF I DIDNT, THEYD	KILL	ME. /SIR PEARCE/ (GIVING IT UP, AND SITTING DOWN
MTH5	(243)	EYES ARE FIXED ON THE HE-ANCIENT) SPARE HER; AND	KILL	ME. /STREPHON/ THATS BETTER. /THE NEWLY BORN/ MUCH
2TRU I	(36)	TAKE THIS HATEFUL WOMAN AWAY. SHE WANTS TO	KILL	ME. /THE ELDERLY LADY/ OH NO, DEAR: SHE HAS BEEN SO
MTH5	(242)	HAS. KILL HER IF YOU LIKE: YOU HAVE NO RIGHT TO	KILL	ME. /THE NEWLY BORN/ DO YOU HEAR THAT? THEY WANT TO
NEVR II	(253)	GO. /CRAMPTON/ I-- I'M CHOKING. YOU WANT TO	KILL	ME. SOME-- I-- (HIS VOICE STIFLES: HE IS ALMOST IN A
CLEO V	(200)	KILL IT, MAN, WITHOUT MALICE, JUST AS IT WOULD	KILL	ME. WHAT DOES THIS PARABLE OF THE LION MEAN? /RUFIO/
MTH1 II	(27)	OFFER MYSELF TO EVERY MAN TO BE KILLED IF HE CAN	KILL	ME. WITHOUT DANGER I CANNOT BE GREAT. THAT IS HOW I PAY
METH PREFACE	(R58)	OF A MAN IS MURDER. IT IS SOMETIMES NECESSARY TO	KILL	MEN AS IT IS ALWAYS NECESSARY TO KILL TIGERS; BUT THE
KING I	(175)	WORD, I WILL THROW YOU DOWNSTAIRS. /BARBARA/ DO.	KILL	ME; AND BE HAPPY WITH THAT LOW STAGE PLAYER. YOU HAVE
MTH1 I	(13)	CAN BE. /EVE/ IT SHALL BE. /THE SERPENT/ IT IS.	KILL	ME; AND YOU WILL FIND ANOTHER SNAKE IN THE GARDEN
O'FL	(208)	SHE MUSTNT FIND OUT. IT'S NOT THAT SHE'D HALF	KILL	ME, AS BIG AS I AM AND AS BRAVE AS I AM. IT'S THAT I'M
GLIM	(176)	ENOUGH TO MAKE HIM BREAK YOU ON THE WHEEL IF YOU	KILL	ME, BUT NOT ENOUGH TO PAY FOR ALL THE MASSES THAT WOULD
MTH4 II	(181)	ARE PLENTY MORE WHERE THEY CAME FROM. IF YOU	KILL	ME, OR PUT A STOP TO MY ACTIVITY (IT IS THE SAME
DOCT PREFACE	(22)	THEY DID NOT KNOW HOW TO DO. THE SIMPLEST WAY TO	KILL	MOST MICROBES IS TO THROW THEM INTO AN OPEN STREET OR
BUOY 1	(12)	ALL THE COUNTER-REVOLUTIONISTS; AND THEN HAD TO	KILL	MOST OF THE REVOLUTIONISTS. REVOLUTION IS DIRTY WORK
MTH1 II	(22)	BY THE MAN I FEAR MOST AND DESIRE TO FIGHT AND	KILL	MOST, AND EACH HOST SHALL TRY TO KILL THE OTHER HOST.
CLEO II	(131)	I, FOR ONE, WILL TAKE NO PRISONERS. I WILL	KILL	MY ENEMIES IN THE FIELD; AND THEN YOU CAN PREACH AS
MTH1 II	(22)	I DO NOT WANT TO KILL WOMEN. I DO NOT WANT TO	KILL	MY MOTHER. AND FOR HER SAKE I WILL NOT KILL YOU, THOUGH
DOCT II	(129)	A MEMBER OF A HIGH AND GREAT PROFESSION, I'M TO	KILL	MY PATIENT. /SIR PATRICK/ DONT TALK WICKED NONSENSE.
CAND I	(101)	STOP, MORELL: IF YOU STRIKE ME, I'LL	KILL	MYSELF: I WONT BEAR IT. (ALMOST IN HYSTERICS) LET ME
HART I	(79)	SHARPLY) FELLOW FEELING? /HECTOR/ NO. I SHOULD	KILL	MYSELF IF I BELIEVED THAT. I MUST BELIEVE THAT MY
ARMS III	(60)	ON THE BREAST). COWARD! LIAR! FOOL! SHALL I	KILL	MYSELF LIKE A MAN, OR LIVE AND PRETEND TO LAUGH AT
MTH5	(244)	/STREPHON/ IF YOU MAKE ME BELIEVE THAT, I SHALL	KILL	MYSELF NOW. /THE NEWLY BORN/ OH NO. I WANT YOU. I LOVE
MILL I	(141)	YOUR AFFAIRS. /EPIFANIA/ AND YOU EXPECT ME TO	KILL	MYSELF TO MAKE MONEY FOR YOU? /SAGAMORE/ WELL, IT IS
MTH5	(244)	YOU ARE A GHASTLY LOT, YOU ANCIENTS. I SHALL	KILL	MYSELF WHEN I AM FOUR YEARS OLD. WHAT DO YOU LIVE FOR?
GENV IV	(107)	YOU CAN DO. THEN MY DREAMS WILL CEASE AND I SHALL	KILL	MYSELF. AS FOR HIM, LET HIM BEAR THE BRAND AS BEST HE
WIDO III	(50)	AS SHE RISES) IF YOU SAY IT, PAPA, I WILL	KILL	MYSELF. IT IS NOT TRUE. IF HE WERE HERE ON HIS KNEES
GENV IV	(129)	I KILLED MY BEST FRIEND WITH THIS. I KEPT IT TO	KILL	MYSELF. IT IS USELESS NOW: GOD WILL EXECUTE HIS OWN
MTH3	(111)	MAN'S EXPECTATION OF LIFE. /THE ARCHBISHOP/ I DID	KILL	MYSELF. IT WAS QUITE EASY. I LEFT A SUIT OF CLOTHES BY
SUPR IV	(157)	FOR MY SAKE. /OCTAVIUS/ (DESPERATELY) ANN! I'LL	KILL	MYSELF. /ANN/ OH NO, YOU WONT: THAT WOULDNT BE KIND.
DOCT III	(154)	HIMSELF BY A REALLY BAD ACTION, I SHOULD	KILL	MYSELF. /RIDGEON/ COME! DONT EXAGGERATE. /MRS DUBEDAT/
MIS.	(170)	ARGUE WITH YOU. I CAME HERE TO KILL YOU AND THEN	KILL	MYSELF. /TARLETON/ BEGIN WITH YOURSELF. IF YOU DONT
GETT	(339)	THIS DAY, IF I FIND YOU OUT TO BE A FRAUD, I'LL	KILL	MYSELF. /THE BISHOP/ WHAT! KILL YOURSELF FOR FINDING
MTH1 II	(27)	SOONER THAN FACE A THOUSAND YEARS OF IT I SHOULD	KILL	MYSELF, AS THE VOICE SOMETIMES TEMPTS ME TO DO ALREADY.
MILL I	(140)	YOUR EXECUTORS. /EPIFANIA/ FOR ADVISING ME HOW TO	KILL	MYSELF! /SAGAMORE/ NOT TODAY. TOMORROW. /EPIFANIA/ WHY
CLEO II	(139)	THE GATE, POTHINUS. BID HIM URGE YOUR PEOPLE TO	KILL	NO MORE OF MY SOLDIERS, FOR YOUR SAKE. /POTHINUS/ MY
METH PREFACE	(R46)	TOO: THAT, FOR INSTANCE, A HARD WINTER WILL	KILL	OFF A WEAKLY CHILD AS THE BUCKET KILLS OFF A WEAKLY
MIS. PREFACE	(3)	YOU WENT ON BREEDING, YOU WOULD FINALLY HAVE TO	KILL	OLD PEOPLE TO MAKE ROOM FOR YOUNG ONES. NOW DEATH IS
ROCK PREFACE	(164)	BECAUSE THERE IS ONE SORT OF BIRD YOU MUST NOT	KILL	ON ANY PRETEXT WHATEVER: NAMELY, THE GOOSE THAT LAYS

LION II	(128)	BUT DONT THEY EVER JUST ONLY PRETEND TO	KILL	ONE ANOTHER? WHY SHOULDNT YOU PRETEND TO DIE, AND GET
LION II	(127)	ENTER THE PASSAGE. /LAVINIA/ WILL THEY REALLY	KILL	ONE ANOTHER? /SPINTHO/ YES, IF THE PEOPLE TURN DOWN
BARB III	(320)	TRUTH AND JUSTICE AND THE WHOLE DUTY OF MAN, AND	KILL	ONE ANOTHER AT THAT GAME. WHAT A COUNTRY! WHAT A
MTH2	(77)	IT WAS SO EXCITING THAT ALL THE OTHERS BEGAN TO	KILL	ONE ANOTHER FOR SPORT, AND THUS INVENTED WAR, THE
SUPR III	(109)	AGAINST SON AND BROTHER AGAINST BROTHER, AND	KILL	ONE ANOTHER FOR THE GREAT CATHOLIC IDEA OF ABOLISHING
MTH4 I	(165)	DENOUNCING AND DEPLORING. THEY HAD ACTUALLY TO	KILL	ONE ANOTHER FOR PREACHING THEIR OWN GOSPEL, OR BE
BARB III	(335)	EVER DONE IN THIS WORLD UNTIL MEN ARE PREPARED TO	KILL	ONE ANOTHER IF IT IS NOT DONE. AFTER THAT, THERE WAS
SIM II	(66)	AND THERE ARE MORE OF THEM. /JANGA/ SET THEM TO	KILL	ONE ANOTHER; AND RULE. /KANCHIN/ DIVIDE AND GOVERN.
BUOY 1	(11)	NO COMPROMISE IS POSSIBLE. WHAT ARE WE TO DO?	KILL	ONEANOTHER? /FATHER/ NONSENSE! THERE ARE
JOAN 1	(69)	OF THE MONEY THEY WILL MAKE IN RANSOMS: IT IS NOT	KILL	OR BE KILLED WITH THEM, BUT PAY OR BE PAID. BUT I WILL
MTH4 I	(169)	IT WAKENED AND SPRUNG OUT AT ME, WARNING ME TO	KILL	OR BE KILLED. I MUST NOW RECONSIDER MY WHOLE POLITICAL
BUOY II	(23)	THE KILLER AND WOMAN THE LIFE GIVER. CAN YOU	KILL	OR NOT? /HE/ I CAN SHOOT A LITTLE, THOUGH FEW
ROCK PREFACE	(148)	THAT IF HIS NEIGHBORS DO NOT KILL HIM HE WILL	KILL	OR RUIN HIS NEIGHBORS; SO THAT THERE IS NOTHING FOR IT
MTH4 I	(164)	YOU DISOBEY THEM WITHOUT BEING STRONG ENOUGH TO	KILL	OR TORTURE THEM. /THE ELDERLY GENTLEMAN/ THAT MAY BE AN
MTH3	(120)	TIMES DID NOT KILL THEMSELVES. THEY DID NOT EVEN	KILL	OTHER PEOPLE. /MRS LUTESTRING/ YOU NEVER KILL YOURSELF,
MRS IV	(241)	THOSE TWO GOSPELS IN THE WORLD, WE HAD BETTER ALL	KILL	OURSELVES; FOR THE SAME TAINT IS IN BOTH, THROUGH AND
JOAN 2	(83)	BUT I AM QUIET AND SENSIBLE; AND I DONT WANT TO	KILL	PEOPLE: I ONLY WANT TO BE LEFT ALONE TO ENJOY MYSELF IN
BARB III	(340)	NAMES UNTIL AT LAST THEY GET THE COURAGE TO	KILL	; AND YOUR SIX HUNDRED AND SEVENTY FOOLS BECOME A
MILL PREFACE	(123)	FAR STRONGER THAN MUSSOLINI'S THAT HE WAS ABLE TO	KILL	SEVENTY-SEVEN OF HIS MOST DANGEROUS OPPONENTS AT A BLOW
GETT PREFACE	(210)	BORN IN ABOUT EQUAL NUMBERS. UNFORTUNATELY, WE	KILL	SO MANY OF OUR MALE CHILDREN IN INFANCY THAT WE ARE
POSN	(441)	LOST YOUR BIG BROTHER'S HORSE, AND YOULL WANT TO	KILL	SOMEBODY TO RELIEVE YOUR ROTTEN FEELINGS WHEN HE LICKS
2TRU II	(73)	SUBSIDES). I WANT TO BEAT SOMEBODY: I WANT TO	KILL	SOMEBODY. I SHALL END BY KILLING THE TWO OF YOU. WHAT
DEST	(153)	NONE. /NAPOLEON/ (WITH CORSICAN FACETIOUSNESS)	KILL	SOMETHING AND BRING ME ITS BLOOD. /GIUSEPPE/ (
CLEO IV	(183)	IS NOT HOCUS-POCUS. TO DO IT PROPERLY, WE SHOULD	KILL	SOMETHING TO PLEASE HIM; BUT PERHAPS HE WILL ANSWER
MTH5	(239)	HAND NEARLY AS LARGE AS A FINGER NAIL: ENOUGH TO	KILL	TEN MEN. THERE IS NO PULSE, NO BREATH. /ECRASIA/ BUT
MTH4 I	(168)	MEANING TO HURT ME. IT WAS THE INSTINCT TO	KILL	THAT YOU ROUSED IN ME. I DID NOT KNOW IT WAS IN MY
HART I	(79)	SOFA) DO NOT DECEIVE YOURSELF: THEY DO USE IT. WE	KILL	THE BETTER HALF OF OURSELVES EVERY DAY TO PROPITIATE
2TRU III	(86)	GOES OUT SKETCHING: THE LOOTNANTS GO OUT AND	KILL	THE BIRDS AND ANIMALS, OR PLAY POLO. THEY WONT FLEE
CAPT I	(232)	ENGLAND IF YOU WERE KILLED; AND THE SULTAN WOULD	KILL	THE CHIEF TO PACIFY THE ENGLISH GOVERNMENT. /LADY
MIS.	(204)	SHALL NOT ALLOW IT. /MRS TARLETON/ DO YOU WANT TO	KILL	THE CHILD? HE SHANT GO. /BENTLEY/ I WILL. I'LL LIE
JOAN PREFACE	(40)	OR REMINDED THAT A'S NEGLECT OF SANITATION MAY	KILL	THE CHILD OF B TWO MILES OFF, OR START AN EPIDEMIC IN
POSN	(464)	TELL ME THAT IF YOU CAN. HE CANT HAVE WANTED TO	KILL	THE CHILD. WHY DID HE MAKE ME GO SOFT ON THE CHILD IF
FABL VI	(128)	THOUGHT. THE MONGOOSE MUST BE INSPIRED TO	KILL	THE COBRA, THE CHEMIST TO DISTIL POISONS, THE PHYSICIST
SUPR II	(55)	US AS THE SPIDER KILLS HER MATE OR AS THE BEES	KILL	THE DRONE. AND THEY WOULD BE RIGHT IF WE WERE GOOD FOR
JOAN 5	(112)	OLD SHEEP DOG. PITOU COULD KILL A WOLF. YOU WILL	KILL	THE ENGLISH WOLVES UNTIL THEY GO BACK TO THEIR COUNTRY
BARB III	(339)	THEY POISON US MORALLY AND PHYSICALLY: THEY	KILL	THE HAPPINESS OF SOCIETY: THEY FORCE US TO DO AWAY WITH
FABL I	(103)	CAN REPLACE THEM; BUT KILL THE WOMEN AND YOU	KILL	THE HUMAN RACE. /YOUNG WOMAN/ THAT WONT STOP WAR.
FABL I	(103)	DISCOVER A POISON GAS LIGHTER THAN AIR! IT MAY	KILL	THE INHABITANTS OF A CITY; BUT IT WILL LEAVE THE CITY
CLEO PRO1	(92)	THOU HAST IMPERIAL INSTINCTS. WILT THOU THEREFORE	KILL	THE LESSER DOG FOR US? " AND HE SAID, " I WILL; FOR I
JOAN EPILOG	(162)	THAN THE MASTER OF TOULOUSE; BUT I COULD NOT	KILL	THE MAID. SHE IS UP AND ALIVE EVERYWHERE. /THE EARL OF
LION II	(133)	IF IT WERE MY MASTER'S WILL, AND THAT I COULD	KILL	THE MAN WHO KILLS ME IF I CHOSE. /THE EDITOR/ PUT ON
MTH4 I	(161)	UNTIL HE HAD DIPT IT IN SOME POISONOUS ACID TO	KILL	THE MICROBES, WAS NO LONGER GIVEN TITLES, PENSIONS, AND
PRES	(135)	FROM MATTER. SHOOT DOWN THE MATTER AND YOU	KILL	THE MIND. /BALSQUITH/ BUT HANG IT ALL-- /MITCHENER/ (
DEST	(192)	THE NATIVES THE GOSPEL OF PEACE. THE NATIVES	KILL	THE MISSIONARY: HE FLIES TO ARMS IN DEFENCE OF
CLEO PRO1	(92)	WHICH IS THE BIGGER DOG OF THE TWO; AND YE SHALL	KILL	THE OTHER DOG FOR HIS SAKE AND THEREBY EARN HIS FAVOR."
MTH1 II	(22)	FIGHT AND KILL MOST. AND EACH HOST SHALL TRY TO	KILL	THE OTHER HOST. THINK OF THAT! ALL THOSE MULTITUDES OF
MTH1 II	(22)	A BOAR AND WITH A LION AS TO WHICH OF US SHOULD	KILL	THE OTHER. I HAVE STRIVEN WITH A MAN: SPEAR TO SPEAR
MTH3	(120)	AND YOU HAVE NOT ENERGY OR CONVICTION ENOUGH TO	KILL	THE OTHERS. BESIDES, HOW CAN YOU BLAME THEM WHEN YOU
BULL III	(122)	INEVITABLE RESULTS, GET VIRTUOUSLY INDIGNANT AND	KILL	THE PEOPLE THAT CARRY OUT YOUR LAWS. /AUNT JUDY/ SURE
KING I	(195)	THE GREAT FIRE OF LONDON AND THE PLAGUE. WE MUST	KILL	THE POPISH PLOT FIRST. WHEN WE HAVE DONE THAT, GOD HELP
POSN PREFACE	(425)	WOULD BE A FAR WORSE TYRANNY, BECAUSE IT WOULD	KILL	THE RELIGIOUS AND POLITICAL LIFE OF THE COUNTRY
ARMS III	(60)	HER AND CATCHING HER FIERCELY IN HIS ARMS) I WILL	KILL	THE SWISS; AND AFTERWARDS I WILL DO AS I PLEASE WITH
KING I	(205)	AND IMMORALITY OF THE STAGE AS WILL EITHER	KILL	THE THEATRE OR SHAME IT INTO DECENCY; BUT THESE LINES
APPL I	(229)	THAT THE PRIME MINISTER DOES NOT REALLY WISH TO	KILL	THE VETO. HE ONLY WISHES TO MOVE IT TO NEXT DOOR.
GENV I	(40)	ABSOLUTELY. HE NEVER SPOKE TO ME AFTER I HAD TO	KILL	THE WOMAN WE BOTH LOVED MORE THAN WE LOVED ONEANOTHER.
GENV IV	(103)	A FOOL. IF THE OBJECT OF WAR IS EXTERMINATION,	KILL	THE WOMEN: THE MEN DO NOT MATTER. /BBDE/ THE OBJECT OF
FABL I	(103)	DOES NOT MATTER: THE WOMEN CAN REPLACE THEM; BUT	KILL	THE WOMEN AND YOU KILL THE HUMAN RACE. /YOUNG WOMAN/
GENV IV	(102)	IS BEING BLOWN TO SMITHEREENS BY HER BABY'S COT.	KILL	THE WOMEN; AND WHERE WILL YOUR POPULATION BE? EGAD, YOU
GENV I	(40)	YOUR CLASS? MY BROTHERS HAD TO FIGHT DUELS AND	KILL	THEIR BEST FRIENDS BECAUSE IT WAS ETIQUETTE. /SHE/ BUT
SUPR HANDBOK	(186)	DEFEATED BY THE DETERMINATION OF HIS SOLDIERS TO	KILL	THEIR ENEMIES IN THE FIELD INSTEAD OF TAKING THEM
GENV IV	(100)	THE SOLDIER'S BUSINESS IS TO BURN THE HOMES AND	KILL	THEIR INHABITANTS. THAT IS NOT A PART OF CIVILIZATION:
MTH2	(87)	THEIR POLITICAL INCOMPETENCE WAS THAT THEY HAD TO	KILL	THEIR OWN SONS. IT WAS THE WAR CASUALTY LISTS AND THE
BULL PREFACE	(67)	FREEDOM, THE VICTORIOUS ARTILLERISTS PROCEEDED TO	KILL	THEIR PRISONERS OF WAR IN A DRAWN-OUT STRING OF
BARB III	(346)	/BARBARA/ POWER TO BURN WOMEN'S HOUSES DOWN AND	KILL	THEIR SONS AND TEAR THEIR HUSBANDS TO PIECES. /CUSINS/
CLEO PRO2	(100)	MONEY FOR SOME OF THEM. BETTER LET THE ROMANS	KILL	THEM: IT IS CHEAPER. /BELZANOR/ (AWESTRUCK AT HIS
CLEO PRO2	(100)	THE WOMEN FROM THE ROMANS? /BELZANOR/ WHY NOT	KILL	THEM? /PERSIAN/ BECAUSE WE SHOULD HAVE TO PAY BLOOD
GENV PREFACE	(17)	DO NOTHING WITH THEIR UNWALLED PRISONERS BUT	KILL	THEM AND BURN THE CORPSES THEY COULD NOT BURY, AND EVEN
O'FL	(209)	HE SAYS: " QUITE RIGHT. BUT" SAYS HE " YOU CAN	KILL	THEM AND DO THEM A GOOD TURN AFTERWARDS TO SHEW YOUR
MTH5	(242)	HAVE ONE ANOTHER KILLED. /ARJILLAX/ MONSTROUS!	KILL	THEM BOTH. /THE HE-ANCIENT/ SILENCE. THESE THINGS ARE
ROCK PREFACE	(148)	AND KNOCKING A CLERGYMAN ON THE HEAD. BUT TO	KILL	THEM IS QUITE REASONABLE AND VERY NECESSARY. PRESENT
MTH5	(240)	ENOUGH: I COULD SMASH THEM. AS IT IS, HOW AM I TO	KILL	THEM WITHOUT MAKING A HORRIBLE MESS? /THE MALE FIGURE/
HART I	(79)	YOU CANT SPARE THEM UNTIL YOU HAVE THE POWER TO	KILL	THEM. AT THE PRESENT THEY HAVE THE POWER TO KILL YOU.
FABL VI	(128)	FORM, AND GROW UP TO BE IDIOTS OR SAVAGES. WE	KILL	THEM. BUT WE ARE OURSELVES A THROW-BACK TO THE
MTH4 I	(173)	WHAT WILL YOU DO WITH YOUR UNDESIRABLES? /ZOO/	KILL	THEM. OUR TERTIARIES ARE NOT AT ALL SQUEAMISH ABOUT
BARB III	(340)	GUNS. DONT PREACH AT THEM: DONT REASON WITH THEM.	KILL	THEM. /BARBARA/ KILLING. IS THAT YOUR REMEDY FOR
MTH3	(128)	BUT WHAT CAN WE DO TO THEM? /BARNABAS/	KILL	THEM. /BURGE-LUBIN/ NONSENSE! /BARNABAS/ LOCK THEM UP.
HART I	(79)	WHEN WE BELIEVE IN OURSELVES, WE SHALL	KILL	THEM. /HECTOR/ IT IS THE SAME SEED. YOU FORGET THAT
PYGM III	(251)	THE NEW SMALL TALK. TO DO A PERSON IN MEANS TO	KILL	THEM. /MRS EYNSFORD HILL/ (TO ELIZA, HORRIFIED) YOU
HART I	(79)	ARE OUR TERRORS TO THEIRS? GIVE ME THE POWER TO	KILL	THEM; AND I'LL SPARE THEM IN SHEER-- /CAPTAIN SHOTOVER/
ROCK PREFACE	(155)	NEIGHBORS, HAVE NOT BEEN TORTURED, BUT ORDERED TO	KILL	THEMSELVES IN THE MOST PAINLESS MANNER KNOWN TO THEIR
MTH3	(120)	WHY THE POOR IN THOSE EVIL OLD TIMES DID NOT	KILL	THEMSELVES. THEY DID NOT EVEN KILL OTHER PEOPLE. /MRS
SUPR III SD	(73)	THEM. BUT AS SOCIETY HAS NOT THE COURAGE TO	KILL	THEM, AND, WHEN IT CATCHES THEM, SIMPLY WREAKS ON THEM
O'FL	(209)	HE SAYS. " I KNOW IT'S MY JUTY AS A SOLDIER TO	KILL	THEM" I SAYS. " THATS RIGHT, DINNY," HE SAYS: " QUITE
GENV III	(69)	ME? IF YOU WERE CHRISTIANS YOU WOULD HELP ME TO	KILL	THIS DIRTY JEW. DID YOU HEAR WHAT HE SAID? /SIR O./
MTH1 II	(25)	YOU PAMPER ME AS HE PAMPERS HIS WOMAN? WILL YOU	KILL	TIGERS AND BEARS UNTIL I HAVE A HEAP OF THEIR SKINS TO
METH PREFACE	(R58)	TO KILL MEN AS IT IS ALWAYS NECESSARY TO	KILL	TIGERS; BUT THE OLD THEORETIC DISTINCTION BETWEEN THE
MTH1 I	(16)	THERE WILL BE AN END. /ADAM/ NO: THEY WILL NOT	KILL	US: THEY WILL FEEL AS I DO. THERE IS SOMETHING AGAINST
SUPR II	(55)	CHILDREN'S BREAD INSTEAD OF MAKING IT, THEY WOULD	KILL	US AS THE SPIDER KILLS HER MATE OR AS THE BEES KILL THE
MTH5	(243)	WHICH OF YOU SHALL WE KILL? /THE FEMALE FIGURE/	KILL	US BOTH. HOW COULD EITHER OF US LIVE WITHOUT THE
METH PREFACE	(R85)	AS FLIES TO WANTON BOYS ARE WE TO THE GODS: THEY	KILL	US FOR THEIR SPORT." EVER SINCE SHAKESPEAR, PLAYWRIGHTS
MTH4 II	(190)	WE UNDERSTAND YOU ONLY TOO WELL, SIR. WELL,	KILL	US. END THE LIVES YOU HAVE MADE MISERABLY UNHAPPY BY
MTH1 I	(16)	IS THE WORD. /EVE/ THE NEW ADAMS AND EVES MIGHT	KILL	US. I SHALL NOT MAKE THEM. (SHE SITS ON THE ROCK AND
BUOY II	(22)	VEGETARIANS DO NOT KILL ANIMALS THE ANIMALS WILL	KILL	US. IT IS THE FLESH EATERS WHO LET THE ANIMALS LIVE.
SUPR IV	(169)	LET ME GO: I CANT BEAR IT. /TANNER/ NOR I. LET IT	KILL	US. /ANN/ YES: I DONT CARE. I AM AT THE END OF MY
DOCT V	(174)	AND MRS WALPOLE HAS TO TELL THE GARDENER NOT TO	KILL	WASPS WHEN MR WALPOLE IS LOOKING. BUT THERE ARE DOCTORS
JOAN PREFACE	(24)	BUT ITS PURPOSE WAS NOT TO DEPICT JOAN, BUT TO	KILL	WITH RIDICULE EVERYTHING THAT VOLTAIRE RIGHTEOUSLY
SUPR III SD	(73)	ONE OR TWO OF THEM, PERHAPS, IT WOULD BE WISER TO	KILL	WITHOUT MALICE IN A FRIENDLY AND FRANK MANNER; FOR
MTH1 II	(22)	BUT HE KILLED HIM. /CAIN/ I DO NOT WANT TO	KILL	WOMEN. I DO NOT WANT TO KILL MY MOTHER. AND FOR HER
FABL I	(103)	OFF TO BE BURNT DIE OF RADIATION. BESIDES, BOMBS	KILL	WOMEN. KILLING MEN DOES NOT MATTER: THE WOMEN CAN
MIS.	(170)	LISTEN TO YOU AND ARGUE WITH YOU. I CAME HERE TO	KILL	YOU AND THEN KILL MYSELF. /TARLETON/ BEGIN WITH
ARMS III	(61)	FOOT. HORSEBACK'S TOO DANGEROUS: I DONT WANT TO	KILL	YOU IF I CAN HELP IT. /RAINA/ (HURRYING FORWARD
KING II	(226)	GRANDMOTHER. THEY KILLED MY FATHER. THEY WOULD	KILL	YOU IF I WERE NOT A LITTLE TOO CLEVER FOR THEM: THEY
ARMS III	(50)	IF SERGIUS KNEW, HE WOULD CHALLENGE YOU AND	KILL	YOU IN A DUEL. /BLUNTSCHLI/ BLESS ME! THEN DONT TELL
GLIM	(184)	IT MAKES NO DIFFERENCE. IF THEY TWO IN THERE	KILL	YOU IT WILL BE NO MORE TO ME-- EXCEPT FOR THE MONEY--
MILL I	(140)	BE PURE HYDROCYANIC ACID, ONE SIP OF WHICH WILL	KILL	YOU LIKE A THUNDERBOLT. /EPIFANIA/ (FINGERING THE
SUPR III	(127)	/THE STATUE/ MURDERING! WHAT DO YOU MEAN? DID I	KILL	YOU OR DID YOU KILL ME? /DON JUAN/ WHICH OF US WAS THE
CLEO V	(200)	MEN AT HER BIDDING. I THOUGHT SHE MIGHT BID IT	KILL	YOU SOME DAY. WELL, HAD I NOT BEEN CAESAR'S PUPIL, WHAT

ARMS I	(19)	IN THE HOUSE OF IGNORANT COUNTRYFOLK WHO WOULD	KILL	YOU THE MOMENT THEY SAW YOUR SERBIAN UNIFORM, BUT AMONG
KING I	(195)	THE PROTECTOR OF YOUR LIFE, BECAUSE NOBODY WILL	KILL	YOU TO MAKE ME KING; BUT I TAKE THAT AS THE HIGHEST
MTH1 I	(17)	HE RISES THREATENINGLY). GIVE IT TO ME; OR I WILL	KILL	YOU WHEN NEXT I CATCH YOU ASLEEP. /EVE/ (THROWING HER
DEVL III	(53)	NOT TOO LATE. CALL ME AS WITNESS: THEY WILL NEVER	KILL	YOU WHEN THEY KNOW HOW HEROICALLY YOU HAVE ACTED.
CLEO II	(137)	NOT SHARE MY CELEBRATED CLEMENCY, WILL PROBABLY	KILL	YOU. BRITANNUS: PASS THE WORD TO THE GUARD; AND FETCH
BARB III	(343)	I WILL HAVE YOUR DUE HEED AND RESPECT, OR I WILL	KILL	YOU. BUT YOUR LOVE! DAMN YOUR IMPERTINENCE! /CUSINS/
CURE	(229)	FAITH IN PILLS. BUT I SHANT LEAVE YOU ENOUGH TO	KILL	YOU. (HE PUTS ON HIS HAT). /REGINALD/ YOULL TELL THEM,
GLIM	(186)	/GIULIA/ NO, SIGNOR: I'LL HELP THEM TO	KILL	YOU. /FERRUCCIO/ MY BACK IS TO THE WALL, THEN?
PHIL III	(147)	WHY? /JULIA/ BECAUSE I AM NOT BRAVE ENOUGH TO	KILL	YOU. /GRACE/ (TAKING HER IN HER ARMS AS SHE SINKS,
LIED	(192)	YOU THINK FOR A MOMENT HE'D STAND IT? HE'D JUST	KILL	YOU. /HE/ (COMING TO A SUDDEN STOP AND SPEAKING WITH
SIM II	(60)	IF IT WERE IN MY NATURE TO KILL ANYTHING I SHOULD	KILL	YOU. /IDDY/ THERE NOW! I OUGHT TO BE WOUNDED AND
FABL VI	(130)	MY MAGNETIC FIELD. IF I TURNED IT ON IT WOULD	KILL	YOU. /MAIDEN 5/ DONT PROVOKE HIM, NUMBER THREE. I FEEL
MTH4 I	(168)	SO UTTERLY EVIL THAT IF YOU DO NOT STOP I WILL	KILL	YOU. /THE ELDERLY GENTLEMAN/ (APPREHENDING HIS DANGER)
ARMS I	(18)	RECKLESSLY, AND PULLS HIM QUITE ROUND). THEYLL	KILL	YOU. /THE MAN/ (COOLLY, BUT ATTENTIVELY) NEVER MIND:
WIDO II	(46)	THAT NOISE, I TELL YOU, UNLESS YOU WANT ME TO	KILL	YOU. /THE PARLORMAID/ (PROTESTING AND IMPLORING, BUT
HART I	(79)	KILL THEM. AT THE PRESENT THEY HAVE THE POWER TO	KILL	YOU. THERE ARE MILLIONS OF BLACKS OVER THE WATER FOR
MTH1 II	(27)	A COUPLE OF SHEEP. I SPARE YOU; BUT OTHERS MAY	KILL	YOU. WHY NOT LIVE BRAVELY, AND DIE EARLY AND MAKE ROOM
MTH1 I	(16)	OF IT. /EVE/ THE VOICE DOES NOT TELL ME NOT TO	KILL	YOU. YET I DO NOT WANT YOU TO DIE BEFORE ME. NO VOICE
GLIM	(176)	AND WHY, PRAY? /SQUARCIO/ SOMEONE ELSE MIGHT	KILL	YOUR EXCELLENCY; AND, AS YOU SAY, MY ILLUSTRIOUS BARON
DEST	(153)	THE LADY UPSTAIRS, AND MY WIFE. /NAPOLEON/	KILL	YOUR WIFE. /GIUSEPPE/ WILLINGLY, YOUR EXCELLENCY; BUT
JOAN 6	(137)	KNOW WHAT YOU ARE SAYING, CHILD. DO YOU WANT TO	KILL	YOURSELF? DO YOU NOT BELIEVE THAT YOU ARE
DEVL III	(52)	VEHEMENTLY) DO YOU REALIZE THAT YOU ARE GOING TO	KILL	YOURSELF? /RICHARD/ THE ONLY MAN I HAVE ANY RIGHT TO
SIM PRO,3,	(32)	BORN AGAIN. /THE PRIEST/ DO YOU STILL WISH TO	KILL	YOURSELF? /THE E.O./ WHEN YOU HAVE BEEN THROUGH WHAT I
GETT	(339)	BE A FRAUD, I'LL KILL MYSELF. /THE BISHOP/ WHAT!	KILL	YOURSELF FOR FINDING OUT SOMETHING! FOR BECOMING A
JITT III	(58)	YOUR EYES ARE OPENED WITH A BANG; AND YOU COULD	KILL	YOURSELF FOR HAVING BEEN SO BLIND. IF I COULD ONLY FIND
ROCK I	(200)	YOU SHOULD HAVE COME HOME TO BED. YOU WILL	KILL	YOURSELF IF YOU TRY TO GET THROUGH YOUR WORK AND ATTEND
GENV IV	(108)	LEAVE THE COURT. /JUDGE/ SENORA: I FORBID YOU TO	KILL	YOURSELF. BUT I WILL SENTENCE THE SLAYER OF YOUR
MTH3	(120)	OF A POUND. /THE ARCHBISHOP/ I WONDER YOU DID NOT	KILL	YOURSELF. I OFTEN WONDER WHY THE POOR IN THOSE EVIL OLD
MTH5	(244)	YOU WILL FIND OUT WHEN YOU GROW UP. YOU WILL NOT	KILL	YOURSELF. /STREPHON/ IF YOU MAKE ME BELIEVE THAT, I
GETT	(339)	MYSELF. /THE BISHOP/ WHY ON EARTH SHOULD YOU	KILL	YOURSELF-- NOT TO MENTION ME? /MRS GEORGE/ SO THAT WE
MTH3	(119)	OTHER PEOPLE. /MRS LUTESTRING/ YOU CAN ALWAYS	KILL	YOURSELF, AS COOK DID; BUT THAT WAS INFLUENZA. LONG
MTH3	(120)	KILL OTHER PEOPLE. /MRS LUTESTRING/ YOU NEVER	KILL	YOURSELF, BECAUSE YOU ALWAYS MAY AS WELL WAIT UNTIL
ARMS I	(6)	CRUEL! DO YOU SUPPOSE THEY WOULD HESITATE TO	KILL	YOU-- OR WORSE? /RAINA/ (TO LOUKA) LEAVE THE SHUTTERS
GLIM	(175)	BE BROUGHT TO JUSTICE. /SQUARCIO/ SO THAT IF I	KILL	YOU-- /FERRUCCIO/ YOUR BARON WILL LOSE TEN CROWNS
GLIM	(178)	THEM. /GIULIA/ IT WOULD HAVE BEEN A GOOD DEED TO	KILL	YOU, I THINK. /FERRUCCIO/ KILLING IS ALWAYS SPORT, MY
HART II	(127)	DREAD WARRIOR? /HECTOR/ SOME DAY I SHALL	KILL	YOU, IF YOU GO TOO FAR. I THOUGHT YOU WERE A FOOL.
MTH1 II	(22)	HER, I COULD NOT RESIST THE SPORT OF TRYING TO	KILL	YOU, IN SPITE OF MY FEAR THAT YOU WOULD KILL ME. I HAVE
ARMS III	(60)	HIS ARMS, PASSIVE AND STEADFAST) THE SWISS WILL	KILL	YOU, PERHAPS. HE HAS BEATEN YOU IN LOVE. HE MAY BEAT
MTH1 II	(22)	TO KILL MY MOTHER. AND FOR HER SAKE I WILL NOT	KILL	YOU, THOUGH I COULD SEND THIS SPEAR THROUGH YOU WITHOUT
GLIM	(179)	THAT IF YOU HAVE TEN CROWNS IN YOUR PURSE, AND WE	KILL	YOU, WE CAN GIVE THEM TO THE BARON. IT WOULD BE THE
CYMB V	(145)	AN IF YOU DO, BY THOR'S GREAT HAMMER STROKE I'LL	KILL	YOU, WERE YOU FIFTY SONS-IN-LAW. /BELARIUS/ PEACE, BOY:
MTH1 II	(23)	TO MAKE MEN FOR YOU TO KILL! /ADAM/ OR TO	KILL	YOU, YOU FOOL. /CAIN/ MOTHER: THE MAKING OF MEN IS YOUR
PYGM IV	(263)	BECAUSE I WANTED TO SMASH YOUR FACE. I'D LIKE TO	KILL	YOU, YOU SELFISH BRUTE. WHY DIDNT YOU LEAVE ME WHERE
PHIL II	(126)	HE WILL COME! /JULIA/ HOW I SHOULD LIKE TO	KILL	YOU! I DONT KNOW WHY I DONT. /GRACE/ YES: YOU LIKE TO
MTH4 I	(168)	YOU DEAD. /THE ELDERLY GENTLEMAN/ I ATTEMPT TO	KILL	YOU! WHAT A MONSTROUS ACCUSATION! /ZOO/ (FROWNS)!
MTH1 I	(16)	IN THE GARDEN WILL TELL THEM THAT THEY MUST NOT	KILL	, AS IT TELLS ME. /THE SERPENT/ THE VOICE IN THE GARDEN
BULL PREFACE	(68)	AS THE BLACK AND TANS) WITH CARTE BLANCHE TO	KILL	, BURN, AND DESTROY, SAVE ONLY THAT THEY MUST STOP
SUPR HANDBOK	(202)	DONE; AND OUR MILITARY AND NAVAL EXPEDITIONS TO	KILL	, BURN, AND DESTROY TRIBES AND VILLAGES FOR KNOCKING AN
DOCT V	(176)	I DID. IT REALLY COMES TO THAT. THOU SHALT NOT	KILL	, BUT NEEDST NOT STRIVE OFFICIOUSLY TO KEEP ALIVE. I
MTH4 II	(186)	MERELY US FOUR POOR WEAK CREATURES THEY WANT TO	KILL	, BUT THE ENTIRE RACE OF MAN, EXCEPT THEMSELVES. /THE
CLEO IV	(180)	FROM THE WALL. BREAK HIM ON THE STONES. KILL,	KILL	, KILL HIM. /FTATATEETA/ (SHEWING ALL HER TEETH) THE
MTH1 I	(16)	A FRIGHTFUL THOUGHT! /THE SERPENT/ KILL, KILL,	KILL	, KILL. THAT IS THE WORD. /EVE/ THE NEW ADAMS AND EVES
CLEO IV	(180)	HIM DOWN FROM THE WALL. BREAK HIM ON THE STONES.	KILL	, KILL, KILL HIM. /FTATATEETA/ (SHEWING ALL HER TEETH)
MTH1 I	(16)	! WHAT A FRIGHTFUL THOUGHT! /THE SERPENT/ KILL,	KILL	, KILL, KILL. THAT IS THE WORD. /EVE/ THE NEW ADAMS AND
MTH1 I	(16)	! ! WHAT A FRIGHTFUL THOUGHT! /THE SERPENT/	KILL	, KILL, KILL, KILL. THAT IS THE WORD. /EVE/ THE NEW
DEVL III	(52)	/RICHARD/ THE ONLY MAN I HAVE ANY RIGHT TO	KILL	, MRS ANDERSON. DONT BE CONCERNED: NO WOMAN WILL LOSE
SUPR III	(106)	THE WORSHIP OF A DESPOT BECAUSE A DESPOT CAN	KILL	, OR PARLIAMENTARY COCK-FIGHTING. I SPENT AN EVENING
PHIL II	(118)	SPEARMEN. /CRAVEN/ (HOTLY) NAKED SPEARMEN CAN	KILL	, PARAMORE. I RISKED MY LIFE! DONT FORGET THAT.
GLIM	(175)	AM FERRUCCIO, COUNT FERRUCCIO, THE MAN YOU ARE TO	KILL	, THE MAN YOUR DEVIL OF A DAUGHTER IS TO DECOY, THE MAN
MTH1 II	(23)	TO BE A MERE CONVENIENCE TO MAKE MEN FOR YOU TO	KILL	! /ADAM/ OR TO KILL YOU, YOU FOOL. /CAIN/ MOTHER: THE

KILLED

LIED	(202)	/SHE/ YOU SHANT, TEDDY: YOU SHANT. YOU WILL BE	KILLED	: HE IS A PRIZEFIGHTER. /HER HUSBAND/ (VENGEFULLY)
MIS.	(149)	EVERYBODY SHRIEKS. /MRS TARLETON/ OH, ARE THEY	KILLED	? JOHN: ARE THEY KILLED? /LORD SUMMERHAYS/ ARE YOU
MTH3	(130)	YOUR OBJECT IN REVEALING HIS AGE IS TO GET HIM	KILLED	? /BARNABAS/ (DESPERATE) BURGE: ARE YOU GOING TO
CLEO II	(142)	OH, YOU ARE NOT REALLY GOING INTO BATTLE TO BE	KILLED	? /CAESAR/ NO, CLEOPATRA. NO MAN GOES TO BATTLE TO
GLIM	(185)	YOU GIVE ST CECILIA A PICTURE IF SHE LETS ME BE	KILLED	? /GIULIA/ NO; BUT I CAN GIVE HER MANY PRAYERS.
HART III	(147)	/RANDALL/ BUT WHAT SHALL I DO IF YOU ARE	KILLED	? /LADY UTTERWORD/ YOU WILL PROBABLY BE KILLED, TOO,
MIS.	(153)	THING TO SAY! DIDNT YOU KNOW YOU MIGHT HAVE BEEN	KILLED	? /LINA/ THAT WAS WHY I WENT UP. /HYPATIA/ OF
PYGM III	(251)	YOU SURELY DONT BELIEVE THAT YOUR AUNT WAS	KILLED	? /LIZA/ DO I NOT! THEM SHE LIVED WITH WOULD HAVE
MIS.	(149)	TARLETON/ OH, ARE THEY KILLED? JOHN: ARE THEY	KILLED	? /LORD SUMMERHAYS/ ARE YOU HURT? IS ANYTHING
GLIM	(177)	WHO WANTED ME TO ABSOLVE HER FOR GETTING ME	KILLED	? /SQUARCIO/ THE POOR MUST LIVE AS WELL AS THE RICH,
SUPR II	(55)	NOT COUNTIN THE MEDITERRANEAN. /TANNER/ HOW MANY	KILLED	? /STRAKER/ TWO SILLY SHEEP. WHAT DOES IT MATTER?
ARMS I	(15)	WANTS TO GET THERE BEFORE THE OTHERS AND BE	KILLED	? THEN THEY ALL COME. YOU CAN TELL THE YOUNG ONES BY
BASH PREFACE	(90)	BARABBAS AS THAT HE WAS A ROBBER, OR THAT HE HAD	KILLED	A CERTAIN MAN IN A SEDITION, QUITE FAILED TO INTEREST
MIS. PREFACE	(31)	A SCOUNDREL WHO HAS RIFLED A BIRD'S NEST OR	KILLED	A HARMLESS SNAKE ENCOURAGES THE CHILDREN TO GO AND DO
BULL PREFACE	(53)	SELFISH AGGRESSION. ONE OF THEM HAD APPARENTLY	KILLED	A WOMAN AND WOUNDED THREE MEN WITH HIS GUN: IN FACT
MTH1 II	(21)	HIM AFTER THAT? /CAIN/ WHOSE FAULT WAS IT THAT I	KILLED	ABEL? WHO INVENTED KILLING? DID I? NO: HE INVENTED
MTH1 II	(21)	MY WORK SOMETIMES. /ADAM/ YOU MADE ABEL ALSO. HE	KILLED	ABEL. CAN YOU BEAR TO LOOK AT HIM AFTER THAT? /CAIN/
BARB PREFACE	(246)	TO PAY OFF HIS SCORE, HE MIGHT POSSIBLY HAVE	KILLED	ADAM AND EVE FOR THE MERE SAKE OF A SECOND LUXURIOUS
LION II	(128)	YOU THOUGHT! WHO CARES WHAT YOU THINK? YOULL BE	KILLED	ALL RIGHT ENOUGH. /SPINTHO/ (GROANS AND AGAIN HIDES
MTH5	(266)	WELL ENOUGH IN THE GARDEN. AND NOW THE FOOLS HAVE	KILLED	ALL THE ANIMALS; AND THEY ARE DISSATISFIED BECAUSE
BUOY 1	(12)	OF THE WORLD BUT A CIVIL WAR AS WELL. THEY FIRST	KILLED	ALL THE COUNTER-REVOLUTIONISTS; AND THEN HAD TO KILL
BULL PREFACE	(52)	WITH IN THEIR SLAUGHTER OF TURKEYS, HAD	KILLED	AN ENGLISH FARMER'S WIFE. ABD-EL-NEBI, HER HUSBAND,
BUOY II	(22)	THE SCALPS OF OUR ENEMIES. /HE/ I HAVE NEVER	KILLED	ANYBODY. I DONT WANT TO. I WANT A DECENT LIFE FOR
FABL VI	(128)	A THROW-BACK TO THE TWENTIETH CENTURY, AND MAY BE	KILLED	AS IDIOTS AND SAVAGES IF WE MEET A LATER AND HIGHER
DOCT IV	(157)	/SIR PATRICK/ COME COME! WHEN YOUVE BOTH	KILLED	AS MANY PEOPLE AS I HAVE IN MY TIME YOULL FEEL HUMBLE
LION PREFACE	(102)	THEIR SENSE OF HIS HOSTILITY BY GETTING HIM	KILLED	AS SOON AS POSSIBLE. HE WAS, IN SHORT, A
GENV PREFACE	(12)	FOREIGN EXPLORERS, VISITORS, AND PASSENGERS ARE	KILLED	AS STRANGERS. THE VENEER OF CIVILIZATION WHICH
METH PREFACE	(R52)	IMAGINATION AND PHILOSOPHY IN HIM WHICH DARWINISM	KILLED	AS WEEDS. HOW WAS IT THAT HE DID NOT SEE THAT HE WAS
DEST	(156)	/NAPOLEON/ HER HUSBAND'S CHARGER, NO DOUBT.	KILLED	AT LODI, POOR FELLOW. /THE LADY'S VOICE/ (THE TWO
DEVL EPILOG	(83)	MANNER OF A BORN HIGH COMEDIAN, IF HE HAD BEEN	KILLED	AT SARATOGA, WITH ALL HIS COMEDIES UNWRITTEN, AND HIS
HART PREFACE	(22)	WORLD SAFE FOR DEMOCRACY." HIS BROTHER WOULD BE	KILLED	AT THE FRONT. IMMEDIATELY HE WOULD THROW UP HIS WORK
MTH4 I	(169)	BE USELESS UNLESS ALL THE OTHER SHORTLIVERS WERE	KILLED	AT THE SAME TIME. BESIDES, IT IS A MEASURE WHICH
ROCK PREFACE	(155)	AT WHICH HERETICS LIKE SOCRATES, WHO WAS	KILLED	BECAUSE HE WAS WISER THAN HIS NEIGHBORS, HAVE NOT
DOCT IV	(156)	(DRILY) IT'S A LITTLE HARD ON A LAD TO BE	KILLED	BECAUSE HIS WIFE HAS TOO HIGH AN OPINION OF HIM.
POSN PREFACE	(386)	PRINCIPLE THAT ALL KINGS, GOOD OR BAD, SHOULD BE	KILLED	BECAUSE KINGSHIP AND FREEDOM CANNOT LIVE TOGETHER.
BARB PREFACE	(237)	SO EXHAUSTED AS TO BE NO LONGER DANGEROUS, HE IS	KILLED	BY A CAUTIOUS MATADOR. BUT THE IRONIC CONTRAST
HART PREFACE	(13)	STATESMAN IN EUROPE, JAURES, WAS SHOT AND	KILLED	BY A GENTLEMAN WHO RESENTED HIS EFFORTS TO AVERT THE
GENV PREFACE	(3)	TEN TO FIFTEEN INHABITANTS OF THESE ISLANDS WERE	KILLED	BY AIR RAIDS EVERY DAY; AND A DOZEN OR SO OUT OF
GETT PREFACE	(196)	BUT YOUNG CHILDREN MAY BE, AND QUITE OFTEN ARE,	KILLED	BY HER CUDDLING AND CODDLING AND DOCTORING AND
FABL II	(106)	PLACE IN THE WORLD, AND IS NOW LYING DEAD THERE,	KILLED	BY HIS OWN POISON GAS? /OLDHAND/ SERVE THE SCOUNDREL
BULL PREFACE	(20)	WENT LIKE A LAMB TO THE SLAUGHTER), GOT HIMSELF	KILLED	BY HIS PASSION FOR EXPOSING HIMSELF TO DEATH IN THAT
CATH 4	(190)	YOU ! HOW SURE ONE FEELS THAT THE PROPOSAL IS	KILLED	BY HIS WIT AND ECONOMIC PENETRATION: KILLED NEVER TO
HART PREFACE	(13)	IN CASES WHERE THE EVIDENCE AS TO THEIR BEING	KILLED	BY ILL TREATMENT WAS SO UNEQUIVOCAL THAT THE VERDICT
CYMB FORWORD	(135)	BY THE MOLE ON HIS NECK. THAT DEVICE WAS	KILLED	BY MADDISON MORTON, ONCE A FAMOUS FARCE WRITER, NOW
CAPT I	(232)	I'M ONLY TALKING COMMONSENSE. WHY DO PEOPLE GET	KILLED	BY SAVAGES? BECAUSE INSTEAD OF BEING POLITE TO THEM,

MTH4 II (180)	WANTS TO LIVE FOR EVER. TO MAKE HIM RISK BEING	KILLED	BY THE ENEMY I HAVE TO CONVINCE HIM THAT IF HE
GENV PREFACE(21)	FOR A STRANGER TO TRAVEL THERE WITHOUT BEING	KILLED	BY THE NATIVE DANAKILS HE WAS RENDERING THE SAME
ROCK PREFACE(156)	HIS ACCOMPLICES BY THE PROMISE THAT HE SHOULD BE	KILLED	BY THE SIXTH BLOW OF THE BAR. THE WHEEL AND THE STAVE
LADY PREFACE(231)	A DRUNKEN AND SENSUAL ASSASSIN, AND IS PRESENTLY	KILLED	CONTEMPTUOUSLY BEFORE OUR EYES IN SPITE OF HIS HEDGE
MTH2 (77)	BUT WHEN HE INVENTED BIRTH, AND ANYONE WHO WAS	KILLED	COULD BE REPLACED, HE COULD AFFORD TO LET HIMSELF GO.
MTH2 (77)	HE DARED NOT HAVE LOST HIS TEMPER; FOR IF HE HAD	KILLED	EVE HE WOULD HAVE BEEN LONELY AND BARREN TO ALL
GENV IV (100)	KNOW THAT SO MANY CHILDREN WILL BE RUN OVER AND	KILLED	EVERY WEEK. BUT WE CANNOT STOP THE TRAFFIC BECAUSE OF
LION II (128)	HIS FACE) ! ! ! /LAVINIA/ THEN IS NOBODY EVER	KILLED	EXCEPT US POOR CHRISTIANS? /THE EDITOR/ IF THE
ROCK PREFACE(148)	MURDERER PLEADING THAT THOUGH A RABBIT SHOULD BE	KILLED	FOR BEING MISCHIEVOUS HE HIMSELF SHOULD BE SPARED
6CAL PREFACE(89)	PRETTY HARD, HIS FATHER HAVING BEEN MISERABLY	KILLED	FOR TAKING HIS JOB TOO LIGHTLY. BUT THE JOURNALIST
3PLA PREFACE(R22)	A PATRIOT BECAUSE HE IS WILLING TO KILL AND GET	KILLED	FOR THE SAKE OF CONFERRING HIMSELF AS AN INSTITUTION
O'FL (210)	SIT THERE WEARING THE VICTORIA CROSS FOR HAVING	KILLED	GOD KNOWS HOW MANY GERMANS; AND YOU TELL ME YOU DONT
PYGM III (251)	/LIZA/ DO I NOT! THEM SHE LIVED WITH WOULD HAVE	KILLED	HER FOR A HAT-PIN, LET ALONE A HAT. /MRS EYNSFORD
CAPT III (295)	SIGHT). /BRASSBOUND/ (TEARING IT QUIETLY) YOU	KILLED	HER FOR ME THAT DAY IN THE CASTLE; AND I AM BETTER
PHIL II (112)	ANOTHER MOMENT. I SHOULD HAVE TAKEN A KNIFE AND	KILLED	HER. I SHOULD HAVE-- CUTHBERTSON APPEARS, STUFFING
PYGM III (252)	SPIRITS DOWN HER THROAT LIKE THAT. IT MIGHT HAVE	KILLED	HER. /LIZA/ NOT HER. GIN WAS MOTHER'S MILK TO HER.
DEVL II SD(40)	FROM HIS ARMS TO THE GROUND AS IF THE KISS HAD	KILLED	HER. /RICHARD/ (GOING QUICKLY TO THE SERGEANT) NOW,
MTH3 (118)	ONE OTHER. SHE WAS A COOK. SHE GREW TIRED, AND	KILLED	HERSELF. /THE ARCHBISHOP/ DEAR ME! HOWEVER, HER
ROCK I (205)	TREAT ME BADLY! YOU! ! I COULD HAVE	KILLED	HER, POOR LITTLE DEVIL. HE SITS DOWN; AND SHE PASSES
FABL V (119)	MEN AND WOMEN. /HERM./ THAT WAS NOT WHY THEY	KILLED	HIM: THEY BELIEVED ANYONE WHO PROMISED THAT MUCH.
MTH1 II (28)	REPLACE HIM WHEN HE WAS GONE, YOU WOULD NOT HAVE	KILLED	HIM: YOU WOULD HAVE RISKED YOUR OWN LIFE TO SAVE HIS.
DOCT V (175)	BEEN A LONGER ONE. /RIDGEON/ YOU KNOW THEN THAT I	KILLED	HIM? /JENNIFER/ (SUDDENLY MOVED AND SOFTENED) OH,
ANNA (291)	IS CONVULSED WITH SOBS). /SCHNEIDEKIND/ THEY HAVE	KILLED	HIM? /STRAMMFEST/ A DAGGER HAS BEEN STRUCK THROUGH
FABL V (119)	THEY BELIEVED ANYONE WHO PROMISED THAT MUCH. THEY	KILLED	HIM BECAUSE HE MADE A RIOT IN THEIR TEMPLE AND DROVE
FABL V (119)	WAS IN THEMSELVES, AND PROMISING THAT IF THEY	KILLED	HIM HE WOULD RISE FROM THE DEAD AND ESTABLISH A
HART II (106)	/MAZZINI/ OH, MY DEAR MRS HUSHABYE, I MIGHT HAVE	KILLED	HIM (HE THROWS THE PISTOL ON THE TABLE AND STAGGERS
POSN (435)	NOTHING, OR ONLY JUST TO SHEW THAT THE MAN THAT	KILLED	HIM WASNT AFRAID OF HIM. BUT MEN ARE LIKE CHILDREN
JITT III (61)	AS IF I WERE BLEEDING TO DEATH OF THE WOUND THAT	KILLED	HIM. AS I SEE HIM NOW HE IS QUITE DIFFERENT FROM WHAT
HART II (90)	BY MAZZINI DUNN). OH, MISS HESSY, IVE BEEN AND	KILLED	HIM. MAZZINI RUNS ROUND THE BACK OF THE CHAIR TO
MTH1 II (22)	HE LOVES ME. /ADAM/ HE LOVED HIS BROTHER. BUT HE	KILLED	HIM. /CAIN/ I DO NOT WANT TO KILL WOMEN. I DO NOT
DOCT V (176)	OFFICIOUSLY TO KEEP ALIVE, I SUPPOSE-- YES: I	KILLED	HIM. /JENNIFER/ AND YOU TELL ME THAT! TO MY FACE!
HART II (90)	INSENSIBLE) OH, MY GOOD LORD, I HOPE I HAVNT	KILLED	HIM, SIR! MR MANGAN! SIR! (SHE SHAKES HIM; AND HE
DOCT IV (157)	IT THIS TIME. /B.B./ WHAT DO YOU MEAN? /WALPOLE/	KILLED	HIM. THE WORST CASE OF NEGLECTED BLOOD-POISONING I
JITT II (29)	A VERY STRONG EMOTION OR EXCITEMENT MIGHT HAVE	KILLED	HIM; BUT A SETTLED MARRIED MAN WITH A WIFE AND A
DEVL EPILOG (85)	OTHERS HAVE NARRATED HOW LADY HARRIET'S HUSBAND	KILLED	HIMSELF IN A DUEL, BY FALLING WITH HIS HEAD AGAINST A
LION PREFACE(30)	AN ADVOCATE OF PHYSICAL FORCE; AND THAT HE HAD	KILLED	HIS MAN. THE CHOICE OF BARABBAS THUS APPEARS AS A
MTH5 (262)	MANY TIMES. BUT MIGHTIER CREATURES THAN THEY HAVE	KILLED	HOPE AND FAITH, AND PERISHED FROM THE EARTH; AND I
PRES (148)	OF THE OTHER QUARTER. IF THREE-QUARTERS OF US WAS	KILLED	HOW MANY PEOPLE WOULD THERE BE IN ENGLAND IN ANOTHER
CAPT II (260)	/LADY CICELY/ DO YOU THINK SHE WOULD REALLY HAVE	KILLED	HOWARD, AS SHE THREATENED, IF HE HADNT SENT HER TO
MTH1 II (27)	ME THAT I MUST OFFER MYSELF TO EVERY MAN TO BE	KILLED	IF HE CAN KILL ME. WITHOUT DANGER I CANNOT BE GREAT.
ARMS I (8)	/RAINA/ YES. /THE MAN/ WELL, I DONT INTEND TO GET	KILLED	IF I CAN HELP IT. (STILL MORE FORMIDABLY) DO YOU
CLEO III (148)	PASS. /CLEOPATRA/ I WILL MAKE CAESAR HAVE YOU	KILLED	IF YOU DO NOT OBEY ME. /SENTINEL/ HE WILL DO WORSE TO
CYMB V (143)	YOUR HELP, MY LORD POSTHUMUS: YOU NEVER	KILLED	IMOGEN TILL NOW. HELP! HELP! /IMOGEN/ OH, LET ME
OVER PREFACE(167)	AND HOW HE IS HANGED. I SHOULD HAVE HAD YOU	KILLED	IN A MUCH LESS DISGUSTING, HYPOCRITICAL, AND
CLEO II (142)	BUT THEY DO GET KILLED. MY SISTER'S HUSBAND WAS	KILLED	IN BATTLE. YOU MUST NOT GO. LET HIM GO (POINTING TO
MTH1 II (27)	A THOUSAND YEARS. WHEN YOU FIGHTERS DO NOT GET	KILLED	IN FIGHTING ONE ANOTHER OR FIGHTING THE BEASTS, YOU
MTH2 (87)	HAVE BOTH SURVIVED THE WAR. BUT THEIR SONS WERE	KILLED	IN IT. /SAVVY/ (SOBERED) YES. JIM'S DEATH KILLED
FABL I (102)	SEEMS SUCH A LITTLE ONE. MY ELDEST BROTHER WAS	KILLED	IN NORMANDY WHEN WE WERE LIBERATING FRANCE THERE. HIS
BULL PREFACE(69)	THEIR STATIONS BURNT; OR THEY WERE AMBUSHED AND	KILLED	IN PETTY BATTLES. THOSE WHO GAVE WARNINGS OR
METH PREFACE(R51)	INSTANCE, A FAMILY COULD ACQUIRE A HABIT OF BEING	KILLED	IN RAILWAY ACCIDENTS, AND YET WEISMANN BEGAN TO
METH PREFACE(R84)	WAS ASSUMED BY PLAYS IN WHICH EVERYONE WAS	KILLED	IN THE LAST ACT, JUST AS, IN SPITE OF MOLIERE, PLAYS
CLEO II (136)	HEAD) THIS, CAESAR; AND TWO OF MY COMRADES	KILLED	IN THE MARKET PLACE. /CAESAR/ (QUIET, BUT ATTENDING)
O'FL (212)	WHEN THE DAY COMES TO YOU THAT YOUR COMRADE IS	KILLED	IN THE TRENCH BESIDE YOU, AND YOU DONT AS MUCH AS
MTH1 II (21)	TO KEEP THE FIRE ALIVE. HE CHANGED THE BEASTS HE	KILLED	INTO MEAT BY THE FIRE ON THE ALTAR. HE KEPT HIMSELF
APPL I (205)	BUSINESS: AT LEAST THE PERSON WHO IS TO BE	KILLED	IS USUALLY CONCEITED ENOUGH TO THINK SO. I THINK THAT
ROCK PREFACE(155)	IN SCOTLAND) VITRIOL THROWERS, WHO CAN BE LEGALLY	KILLED	. A RUNAWAY CONVICT CAN ALSO BE SUMMARILY SHOT BY A
FABL I (102)	BRING THEM INTO THIS WICKED WORLD TO KILL AND BE	KILLED	. AN EXCITED MIDDLE-AGED MAN COMES ALONG WAVING A
LION PREFACE(84)	OF THEIR BEING INSULTED, TORTURED, AND	KILLED	. AND THE SAME IS TRUE OF JESUS. BUT IT REQUIRES THE
ROCK PREFACE(147)	HAS NO SENTIMENTAL DOUBTS THAT THEY MUST BE	KILLED	. AS TO TIGERS AND POISONOUS SNAKES, THEIR
MILL PREFACE(112)	COURTIERS. BUT OUR PETTY FIRESIDE TYRANTS ARE NOT	KILLED	. CHRISTINA OF SWEDEN WOULD NOT HAVE HAD TO ABDICATE
LION PROLOG (108)	TOTTERS AFTER HIM). /MEGAERA/ NO, ANDY: YOULL BE	KILLED	. COME BACK. THE LION UTTERS A LONG SNORING SIGH.
GLIM (175)	COME OUT, WHELP: COME OUT, RAT. COME OUT AND BE	KILLED	. COME OUT AND BE BEATEN TO A JELLY. COME OUT, DOG,
CLEO V (198)	DISLIKED THE IDEA OF DYING: I HAD RATHER BE	KILLED	. FAREWELL. /RUFIO/ (WITH A SIGH, RAISING HIS HANDS
CLEO IV (187)	INTO STONE BECAUSE YOU THINK SOME ONE HAS BEEN	KILLED	. I CANNOT BEAR IT. (SHE PURPOSELY BREAKS DOWN AND
MTH4 I (169)	AND SPRUNG OUT AT ME, WARNING ME TO KILL OR BE	KILLED	. I MUST NOW RECONSIDER MY WHOLE POLITICAL POSITION.
GENV PREFACE(20)	WORTH KILLING AS CADE, TYLER, AND ESSEX WERE	KILLED	. IN PRISON, HE AND HIS COMPANION-SECRETARY HESS,
2TRU III (89)	RIGHT) NOT A BIT OF IT: FATHERS ARE NOT SO EASILY	KILLED	. IT WAS AT THE UNIVERSITY THAT I BECAME WHAT WAS
ARMS I (8)	MY UNIFORM? SERB! IF I'M CAUGHT I SHALL BE	KILLED	. (MENACINGLY) DO YOU UNDERSTAND THAT? /RAINA/ YES.
CLEO II (142)	BATTLE TO BE KILLED. /CLEOPATRA/ BUT THEY DO GET	KILLED	. MY SISTER'S HUSBAND WAS KILLED IN BATTLE. YOU MUST
GENV III (77)	IS A FACT; AND A SPIRIT IS A FACT THAT CANNOT BE	KILLED	. /ALL THE REST/ BUT-- /THE SECRETARY/ (SHOUTING
LION II (128)	VIRGINS WANT TO HAVE ONE OF HIS PET FIGHTING MEN	KILLED	. /ANDROCLES/ BUT DONT THEY EVER JUST ONLY PRETEND TO
MTH5 (242)	DO YOU HEAR THAT? THEY WANT TO HAVE ONE ANOTHER	KILLED	. /ARJILLAX/ MONSTROUS! KILL THEM BOTH. /THE
APPL I (205)	A GREAT MANY PEOPLE WHO IN MY OPINION OUGHT TO BE	KILLED	. /BOANERGES/ (SARCASTIC) YOUD LIKE TO BE ABLE TO
CLEO III (163)	CLEOPATRA--- /CLEOPATRA/ YOU WANT ME TO BE	KILLED	. /CAESAR/ (STILL MORE GRAVELY) MY POOR CHILD: YOUR
CLEO II (142)	NO, CLEOPATRA. NO MAN GOES TO BATTLE TO BE	KILLED	. /CLEOPATRA/ BUT THEY DO GET KILLED. MY SISTER'S
BULL IV (146)	RABELAISIANISM). /NORA/ IT'S WELL MR DOYLE WASNT	KILLED	. /DORAN/ FAITH IT WASNT O LARRY WE WERE THINKIN JUS
BULL IV (149)	WE HAVE, MR BROADBENT. IT'S A MERCY YOU WERENT	KILLED	. /DORAN/ KILT! IT'S A MERCY DHERES TWO BONES OF YOU
GLIM (179)	MORE BY BREAKING ME ON THE WHEEL IF THE COUNT IS	KILLED	. /GIULIA/ THAT IS TRUE. SANDRO DID NOT THINK OF
PYGM V (284)	ARE ALWAYS SHRIEKING TO HAVE TROUBLESOME PEOPLE	KILLED	. /LIZA/ I'M NO PREACHER: I DONT NOTICE THINGS LIKE
HART II (91)	MAY LAUGH, MRS HUSHABYE; BUT I MIGHT HAVE BEEN	KILLED	. /MRS HUSHABYE/ I COULDNT HAVE HELPED LAUGHING EVEN
MIS. (179)	/MRS TARLETON/ OH, JOHN! YOU MIGHT HAVE BEEN	KILLED	. /TARLETON/ -- AND WAS PREVENTED FROM DOING SO ONLY
MTH4 II (186)	TO A PARTY HERE WHICH WANTS TO HAVE US ALL	KILLED	. /THE WIFE/ (TERRIFIED) US! BUT WE HAVE DONE
DOCT PREFACE(21)	PATIENT WAS A HARDY OLD LADY WHO WAS NOT EASILY	KILLED	. SHE RECOVERED WITH NO WORSE RESULT THAN HER
BARB III (328)	LITTLE; AND ONLY THE PEOPLE QUITE CLOSE TO IT ARE	KILLED	. STEPHEN, WHO IS QUITE CLOSE TO IT, LOOKS AT IT
GENV IV (99)	YOUNG HEROES ARE THE KILLERS, THEY ARE ALSO THE	KILLED	. THEY RISK THEIR OWN LIVES. /JUDGE/ LET US THEN ADD
MIS. PREFACE(43)	IF A MAN IS UNBEARABLY MISCHIEVOUS, HE MUST BE	KILLED	. THIS IS A MERE MATTER OF NECESSITY, LIKE THE
KING I (202)	TUT, GEORGE! THE MAN IN THE PLAY IS GOING TO BE	KILLED	. TO CONSOLE HIMSELF HE CRIES SOUR GRAPES: THAT IS
GETT (267)	I WON ALL THE EARLY ONES BY TRYING TO GET	KILLED	. YOU KNOW WHY. /LESBIA/ BUT YOU HAD A CHARMED LIFE?
DOCT PREFACE(34)	TO DESPATCH HIM QUICKLY AND MERCIFULLY. TO GET	KILLED	LAWFULLY HE MUST VIOLATE SOMEBODY ELSE'S RIGHT TO
MILL PREFACE(112)	COULD NOT BE MADE TO UNDERSTAND THIS, THEY WERE	KILLED	LIKE MAD DOGS BY THEIR OWN COURTIERS. BUT OUR PETTY
APPL PREFACE(182)	AND DID SUCH APPALLING THINGS THAT THEY HAD TO BE	KILLED	LIKE MAD DOGS. ONLY, IT WAS NOT THE PEOPLE THAT ROSE
FABL PREFACE(65)	I WAS ONCE SHEWN THE DAGGER WITH WHICH MAJOR SIRR	KILLED	LORD EDWARD FITZGERALD; BUT THE WORD DAGGER GOT
DOCT V (176)	IS A DANGEROUS MEDICINE: IT CURED BLENKINSOP: IT	KILLED	LOUIS DUBEDAT. WHEN I HANDLE IT, IT CURES. WHEN
JITT II (37)	DEAREST: DONT CRY LIKE THAT. /EDITH/ IT NEARLY	KILLED	ME TO SEE HIM SITTING THERE, AS HE OFTEN DID, STARING
3PLA PREFACE(R9)	A CRITIC OF THE LONDON THEATRES. THEY VERY NEARLY	KILLED	ME. I HAD SURVIVED SEVEN YEARS OF LONDON'S MUSIC,
MILL II (170)	HELP! HELP! /EPIFANIA/ YOU BRUTE! YOU HAVE	KILLED	ME. (SHE TOTTERS TO THE NEAREST CHAIR AND SINKS INTO
SUPR III (93)	THAT IF HIS FOOT HAD NOT SLIPPED HE WOULD HAVE	KILLED	ME. NO DOUBT HE IS RIGHT: I WAS NOT A GOOD FENCER. I
3PLA PREFACE(R17)	WRITING ABOUT THEM; AND THAT IS HOW THEY NEARLY	KILLED	ME. YET THE MANAGERS MEAN WELL. THEIR SELF-RESPECT IS
MTH4 II (186)	WITH HER. YOU WOULD NOT BELIEVE: SHE VERY NEARLY	KILLED	ME. YOU HEARD WHAT SHE SAID JUST NOW. SHE BELONGS TO
CLEO V (200)	MEAN? /RUFIO/ WHY, CLEOPATRA HAD A TIGRESS THAT	KILLED	MEN AT HER BIDDING. I THOUGHT SHE MIGHT BID IT KILL
MILL IV (197)	HE BEEN RUN OVER? /ADRIAN/ THIS WOMAN HAS HALF	KILLED	ME; AND SHE ASKS HAVE I HURT MYSELF! I FELL DOWN THE
SUPR IV (171)	I FEEL STRONG ENOUGH NOW. BUT YOU VERY NEARLY	KILLED	ME, JACK, FOR ALL THAT. /MALONE/ A ROUGH WOOER, EH..
MTH2 (87)	KILLED IN IT. /SAVVY/ (SOBERED) YES. JIM'S DEATH	KILLED	MOTHER. /HASLAM/ AND THEY NEVER SAID A WORD ABOUT
GENV IV (129)	TAKING HER PISTOL FROM HER HANDBAG AND RISING) I	KILLED	MY BEST FRIEND WITH THIS. I KEPT IT TO KILL MYSELF.
CLEO I (108)	LIVE IN THE PALACE AT ALEXANDRIA WHEN I HAVE	KILLED	MY BROTHER, WHO DROVE ME OUT OF IT. WHEN I AM OLD
JITT I (16)	SELF-CONCEIT IS IMPENETRABLE. HIS CHEERFUL GRIN	KILLED	MY CONSCIENCE. I HOLD UP MY HEAD NOW EVERYWHERE: I AM
KING II (226)	/CHARLES/ THEY KILLED MY GREAT GRANDMOTHER. THEY	KILLED	MY FATHER. THEY WOULD KILL YOU IF I WERE NOT A LITTLE

KING II (226)	SO AFRAID OF THE PROTESTANTS? /CHARLES/ THEY	KILLED	MY GREAT GRANDMOTHER. THEY KILLED MY FATHER. THEY
CAPT II (256)	ENGLAND IS? /BRASSBOUND/ HE KNOWS THAT THE MAHDI	KILLED	MY MASTER GORDON, AND THAT THE MAHDI DIED IN HIS BED
MIS. (123)	COULDNT HELP IT. IT WAS AS GOOD AS TELLING ME I'D	KILLED	MY OWN CHILD. I HAD TO GO AWAY; BUT BEFORE I WAS OUT
MTH3 (110)	MIMIC THE VOICE OF A CENTENARIAN? BETTER HAVE	KILLED	MYSELF. /BARNABAS/ YOU OUGHT TO HAVE KILLED YOURSELF.
CATH 4 (190)	IS KILLED BY HIS WIT AND ECONOMIC PENETRATION:	KILLED	NEVER TO BE MENTIONED AGAIN AMONG EDUCATED PEOPLE!
DOCT PREFACE(34)	WE LEGISLATE ON THE ASSUMPTION THAT NO MAN MAY BE	KILLED	ON THE STRENGTH OF A DEMONSTRATION THAT HE WOULD BE
GETT PREFACE(209)	FOR IF A LARGE PROPORTION OF WOMEN WERE	KILLED	OR DISABLED, NO POSSIBLE READJUSTMENT OF OUR MARRIAGE
MTH4 II (180)	IN TERRIBLE TRIALS. THEIR FEAR OF BEING	KILLED	OR ENSLAVED BY THE ENEMY, THEIR BELIEF THAT THEY ARE
CLEO IV (187)	RIGHT: IT IS DREADFUL TO THINK OF ANYONE BEING	KILLED	OR EVEN HURT; AND I HOPE NOTHING REALLY SERIOUS HAS--
GENV PREFACE(4)	THE IMPRESSION LEFT BEING THAT THE ALLIES HAD	KILLED	OR TAKEN PRISONER TENS OF THOUSANDS OF AXIS TROOPS
JOAN 2 (84)	BED, AND NOT LIVE IN CONTINUAL TERROR OF BEING	KILLED	OR WOUNDED. PUT COURAGE INTO THE OTHERS, AND LET THEM
HART PREFACE(19)	YEARS. NOT ONLY WERE SHAKESPEARS AND PLATOS BEING	KILLED	OUTRIGHT; BUT MANY OF THE BEST HARVESTS OF THE
DOCT I (89)	TRIED THESE MODERN INOCULATIONS A BIT MYSELF. IVE	KILLED	PEOPLE WITH THEM; AND IVE CURED PEOPLE WITH THEM; BUT
CLEO IV (193)	EXECUTIONER THAT IF POTHINUS HAD BEEN PROPERLY	KILLED	-- IN THE THROAT-- HE WOULD NOT HAVE CALLED OUT. YOUR
LION PREFACE(8)	WHO COULD BE PERSECUTED, STONED, SCOURGED, AND	KILLED	; AND HE WAS A GOD, IMMORTAL AND ALL-POWERFUL, ABLE
CAPT I (232)	WOULD GET INTO TROUBLE WITH ENGLAND IF YOU WERE	KILLED	; AND THE SULTAN WOULD KILL THE CHIEF TO PACIFY THE
2TRU III (92)	WERE STUFFED WITH, AND DIDNT WANT TO GO. HE WAS	KILLED	; AND WHEN IT CAME OUT AFTERWARDS THAT HE WAS RIGHT,
FABL PREFACE(76)	LIQUIDATION. CALVIN AGREED THAT SERVETUS MUST BE	KILLED	; BUT HE OBJECTED HUMANELY TO HIS BEING BURNED.
APPL I (205)	OF PERSONS WHO IN MY OPINION OUGHT NOT TO BE	KILLED	; BUT I MAY NOT EVEN ISSUE DEATH WARRANTS FOR A GREAT
MTH4 II (184)	ABOUT TEN YEARS LATER, HARDLY ANY SOLDIERS WERE	KILLED	; BUT SEVEN OF THE CAPITAL CITIES OF EUROPE WERE
MILL II (173)	I REMEMBER WHEN I BEGAN AS A YOUNG SURGEON I	KILLED	SEVERAL PATIENTS BY MY OPERATIONS BECAUSE I HAD BEEN
MTH3 (96)	SO! /CONFUCIUS/ THE KING AND HIS LOYAL SUBJECTS	KILLED	SIMON FOR FORCING HIS FRENCH PARLIAMENT ON THEM. THE
CLEO IV (185)	RUFIO ASCENDED. /CLEOPATRA/ YOUR SOLDIERS HAVE	KILLED	SOMEBODY, PERHAPS. WHAT DOES IT MATTER? THE MURMUR
ROCK PREFACE(187)	BARABBAS, WHO HAS GONE FURTHER THAN YOU AND	KILLED	SOMEBODY, WHEREAS I UNDERSTAND THAT YOU HAVE ONLY
ARMS II (29)	OF SCIENTIFIC WARFARE. TWO MAJOR-GENERALS GOT	KILLED	STRICTLY ACCORDING TO MILITARY ETIQUETTE. THE TWO
GENV PREFACE(8)	IN SOME OF THE AIR RAIDS, MORE WOMEN WERE	KILLED	THAN MEN. THE TURNING POINT OF THE WAR WAS THE SIEGE
MTH5 (241)	INDEED HE DID. /THE HE-ANCIENT/ THE CREATURE HAS	KILLED	THAT POOR YOUTH. /THE SHE-ANCIENT/ (SEEING THE BODY
MTH5 (221)	BORN; AND A FLASH OF LIGHTNING BURNT IT OFF AND	KILLED	THE ANCIENT WHO WAS DELIVERING ME. WITHOUT A HAIR ON
MTH1 II (21)	THEN CAME MY GREAT IDEA: WHY NOT KILL HIM AS HE	KILLED	THE BEASTS? I STRUCK; AND HE DIED, JUST AS THEY DID.
METH PREFACE(R44)	RELIEF WITH A GREAT " OUF! " WELL, WHEN DARWIN	KILLED	THE GOD WHO OBJECTED TO CHLOROFORM, EVERYBODY WHO HAD
MTH5 (231)	WAS CALLED CANCER, UNTIL THE LOWER FORM OF LIFE	KILLED	THE HIGHER, AND BOTH PERISHED TOGETHER MISERABLY?
ROCK PREFACE(150)	THE CATEGORY OF MALIGNANT OR MAN OF BLOOD, AND	KILLED	THE KING AS AN AFFIRMATION THAT EVEN KINGS MUST NOT
LION II SD(141)	GLADIATORS AND EXCLAIMS, EXHAUSTED) BOYS: HE'S	KILLED	THE LOT. /THE EMPEROR/ (AGAIN BURSTING FROM HIS BOX,
2TRU III (90)	OH, WHAT A LIE! IT WAS THE OTHER NURSES THAT	KILLED	THE MEN; WAKING THEM UP AT SIX IN THE MORNING AND
2TRU III (106)	ANYTHING AGAIN AS LONG AS I LIVE. I'D HAVE	KILLED	THE ONLY ONE I HAD LEFT IF SHE HADNT RUN AWAY FROM
MTH5 (233)	AS THEIR BODIES WERE CONCERNED. THAT WAS HOW I	KILLED	THE POOR BEAST OF A MAN. I HADNT PROVIDED FOR HIS
MILL PREFACE(133)	THE TSAR. BUT THE BULLET WAS A NUMBER SEVEN: IT	KILLED	THE TSAR VERY EFFICIENTLY; BUT IT CAME BACK LIKE A
O'FL PREFACE(201)	OF DUBLIN TO RUINS, AND THE BRITISH COMMANDERS	KILLED	THEIR LEADING PRISONERS OF WAR IN COLD BLOOD MORNING
APPL PREFACE(182)	ONLY, IT WAS NOT THE PEOPLE THAT ROSE UP AND	KILLED	THEM. THEY WERE DISPATCHED QUITE PRIVATELY BY A VERY
MTH4 I (165)	ONE ANOTHER FOR PREACHING THEIR OWN GOSPEL, OR BE	KILLED	THEMSELVES. /THE ELDERLY GENTLEMAN/ THE BLOOD OF THE
BARB PREFACE(217)	AND ENDOWED BY PEOPLE WHO WOULD OTHERWISE BE	KILLED	THEMSELVES, OR OF THE MOUTH-HONOR PAID TO POVERTY AND
LADY PREFACE(212)	AND SHEWN THAT, COMPARED WITH THE CAPITALISM THAT	KILLED	THEM, THEY WERE HEROES AND MARTYRS. HE HAS DONE THIS
POSN PREFACE(427)	ARE CERTAINTIES. IT IS NOT CERTAIN THAT I WILL BE	KILLED	THIS YEAR IN A RAILWAY ACCIDENT; BUT IT IS CERTAIN
SIM PREFACE(5)	OF OVERWHELMING EVIDENCE THAT VACCINATION HAS	KILLED	THOUSANDS OF CHILDREN IN A QUITE HORRIBLE WAY WHEREAS
MTH2 (87)	HADNT BEEN A PARSON I'D HAVE HAD TO GO OUT AND BE	KILLED	TOO, TO ME THE AWFUL THING ABOUT THEIR POLITICAL
POSN (436)	COMMITTEE EVER GETS HOLD OF YOU, YOUD BETTER HAVE	KILLED	TWENTY MEN THAN AS MUCH AS STOLE A SADDLE OR BRIDLE,
LION I (119)	WITH A BILLY GOAT (ANDROCLES BRIGHTENS UP) THAT	KILLED	TWO LEOPARDS AND ATE A TURKEY-COCK. YOU CAN HAVE HIM
2TRU III (106)	THREE MEAT MEALS A DAY? DO YOU KNOW THAT I HAVE	KILLED	TWO OF MY CHILDREN BECAUSE THEY TOLD ME THAT? MY OWN
FABL VI (126)	THE SUPERMEN WOULD HAVE TRAMPED ON US AND	KILLED	US, OR POISONED US WITH PHOSPHORUS. /YOUTH 1/ THEY
PRES (148)	HELP YOURSELVES. IF THREE-QUARTERS OF YOU WAS	KILLED	WE COULD REPLACE YOU WITH THE HELP OF THE OTHER
LION PREFACE(28)	DESTINY AS A GOD BY ANNOUNCING THAT HE WILL BE	KILLED	WHEN HE GOES TO JERUSALEM; FOR IF HE IS REALLY THE
JOAN 1 (69)	THEY WILL MAKE IN RANSOMS: IT IS NOT KILL OR BE	KILLED	WITH THEM, BUT PAY OR BE PAID. BUT I WILL TEACH THEM
DEST (157)	THATS NOT THE VOICE OF A WOMAN WHOSE HUSBAND WAS	KILLED	YESTERDAY. /GIUSEPPE/ HUSBANDS ARE NOT ALWAYS
2TRU I (40)	ARE YOU GOING TO LIE THERE FOR EVER? HAS SHE	KILLED	YOU? /THE BURGLAR/ (RISING SLOWLY TO HIS KNEES) AS
GLIM (176)	OF BACCHUS! I FORGOT THAT TRICK. I SHOULD HAVE	KILLED	YOU WHEN MY BLOOD WAS HOT. /SQUARCIO/ WILL YOUR
ARMS III (51)	IT. BUT I DID IT TO SAVE YOUR LIFE. HE WOULD HAVE	KILLED	YOU. THAT WAS THE SECOND TIME I EVER UTTERED A
DOCT PREFACE(6)	HUSBAND, WIFE, BROTHER, OR SISTER, " YOU HAVE	KILLED	YOUR LOST DARLING BY YOUR CREDULITY." THE PECULIAR
MTH3 (110)	HAVE KILLED MYSELF. /BARNABAS/ YOU OUGHT TO HAVE	KILLED	YOURSELF. AS AN HONEST MAN YOU WERE ENTITLED TO NO
SUPR III (95)	TRUE. REMAIN OBDURATE, MY BOY. I WISH I HAD	KILLED	YOU, AS I SHOULD HAVE DONE BUT FOR AN ACCIDENT. THEN
BARB PREFACE(216)	POUNDS A YEAR, SHALL BE PAINLESSLY BUT INEXORABLY	KILLED	, AND EVERY HUNGRY HALF NAKED CHILD FORCIBLY FATTENED
SIM PREFACE(17)	WHO THINK THAT MURDERERS SHOULD BE JUDICIALLY	KILLED	, BUT THAT THE LIVES OF THE MOST MISCHIEVOUS
BULL PREFACE(56)	EVERYTHING THEY WERE ACCUSED OF. THEY WERE THEN	KILLED	, FLOGGED, OR SENT TO PENAL SERVITUDE. THIS WAS THE
GETT PREFACE(209)	THREE-QUARTERS OF THE MEN IN THIS COUNTRY WERE	KILLED	, IT WOULD BE ABSOLUTELY NECESSARY TO ADOPT THE
LION PREFACE(65)	SELF-CONTROL ENOUGH FOR SOCIAL PURPOSES MAY BE	KILLED	, OR MAY BE KEPT IN ASYLUMS WITH A VIEW TO STUDYING
ROCK PREFACE(147)	UNLESS RABBITS AND DEER AND RATS AND FOXES ARE	KILLED	, OR " KEPT DOWN" AS WE PUT IT, MANKIND MUST PERISH;
LION II (133)	FERROVIUS. I SHALL GO INTO MY BOX AND SEE YOU	KILLED	, SINCE YOU SCORN THE PRETORIAN GUARD. (HE GOES INTO
HART III (147)	KILLED? /LADY UTTERWORD/ YOU WILL PROBABLY BE	KILLED	, TOO, RANDALL. NOW PLAY YOUR FLUTE TO SHEW THAT YOU
O'FL (209)	THE SOULS OF THE HUNDREDS OF GERMANS YOU SAY YOU	KILLED	" SAYS HE; " FOR MANY AND MANY OF THEM WERE BAVARIANS
DOCT IV (157)	DIE UNDER THE ANAESTHETIC. /B.B./ (OFFENDED)	KILLED	! REALLY, WALPOLE, IF YOUR MONOMANIA WERE NOT WELL
		KILLER	
BUOY II (23)	OF THEM. NO MATTER WHAT WE EAT, MAN IS STILL THE	KILLER	AND WOMAN THE LIFE GIVER. CAN YOU KILL OR NOT? /HE/
SUPR I (21)	AT TANNER OVER HER SHOULDER), AND JACK THE GIANT	KILLER	. (SHE GOES PAST HER MOTHER TO OCTAVIUS) AND JACK'S
SIM PRO;2, (26)	NOT US. NOT LIKELY. THERES SHARKS THERE. AND	KILLER	WHALES, WORSE THAN ANY SHARKS. /THE Y.W./ IT LOOKS
ROCK PREFACE(178)	JOSHUA WAS ANY MORE REAL THAN JACK THE GIANT	KILLER	, AND THAT GALILEO MIGHT PLAY SKITTLES WITH THE WHOLE
		KILLERS	
MTH1 II (31)	MOTHER EVE. THE DIGGERS COME: THE FIGHTERS AND	KILLERS	COME: THEY ARE BOTH VERY DULL; FOR THEY EITHER
BUOY II (22)	/SHE/ COWARDS ARE NO USE TO WOMEN. THEY NEED	KILLERS	. WHERE ARE YOUR SCALPS? /HE/ MY WHAT? /SHE/ YOUR
FABL VI (128)	TO BE BIG GAME HUNTERS, JUDGES, EXECUTIONERS, AND	KILLERS	OF ALL SORTS, OFTEN THE MOST AMIABLE OF MORTALS
KING II (226)	TRYING HARD ENOUGH, DAMN THEM! THEY ARE GREAT	KILLERS	, THESE PROTESTANTS, JAMIE HAS JUST ONE CHANCE. THEY
GENV IV (99)	REMEMBER, SIR, THAT IF OUR YOUNG HEROES ARE THE	KILLERS	, THEY ARE ALSO THE KILLED. THEY RISK THEIR OWN
		KILLINEY	
O'FL (215)	THE FOAM OF THE SEA, CAME UP OUT OF THE WATER IN	KILLINEY	BAY OFF BRAY HEAD. SHE SAYS THAT MOSES BUILT THE
		KILLING	
CLEO IV (190)	WE ARE A PARCEL OF FOOLS? I MEAN NO HARM BY	KILLING	: I DO IT AS A DOG KILLS A CAT, BY INSTINCT. WE ARE
MTH1 II (21)	FAULT WAS IT THAT I KILLED ABEL? WHO INVENTED	KILLING	? DID I? NO: HE INVENTED IT HIMSELF. I FOLLOWED
ROCK PREFACE(148)	PLEADING HIS CLERGY. WHEN THE NECESSITY FOR	KILLING	A DANGEROUS HUMAN BEING ARISES, AS IT STILL DOES
CLEO NOTES (210)	CIVIL LIFE MERE CAPACITY FOR WORK-- THE POWER OF	KILLING	A DOZEN SECRETARIES UNDER YOU, SO TO SPEAK, AS A
2TRU III (98)	UP TO DO. BUT THATS A VERY DIFFERENT THING FROM	KILLING	A MAN BECAUSE HE'S A GERMAN AND HE KILLING YOU
POSN (435)	I NEVER SHOULD LOOK AT IT IN THAT WAY. I DO THINK	KILLING	A MAN IS WORSE ANY DAY THAN STEALING A HORSE.
POSN (436)	I SAY STEALING A HORSE IS TEN TIMES WORSE THAN	KILLING	A MAN. AND IF THE VIGILANCE COMMITTEE EVER GETS HOLD
MTH3 (128)	WE GIVE? /BARNABAS/ WHAT REASON CAN YOU GIVE FOR	KILLING	A SNAKE? NATURE TELLS YOU TO DO IT. /BURGE-LUBIN/
GENV PREFACE(26)	BEFORE IT EVAPORATES THROUGH THE STRATOSPHERE OF	KILLING	ALL THE INHABITANTS OF A CITY WITHOUT DAMAGING ITS
MTH4 I (173)	TO WANT TO DIE, AND TO SETTLE THE DIFFICULTY BY	KILLING	ALL THE REST OF YOU? /ZOO/ OH, HE IS ONE OF THE
METH PREFACE(R16)	AND SPORTSMEN TO WHOM FIGHTING IS A RELIGION AND	KILLING	AN ACCOMPLISHMENT; WHILST POLITICAL POWER, USELESS
MTH5 (260)	OF IT, CAIN, MY FIRST-BORN? /CAIN/ I INVENTED	KILLING	AND CONQUEST AND MASTERY AND THE WINNOWING OUT OF
SUPR III (109)	THAT MATTERS, BUT THE FEAR OF DEATH. IT IS NOT	KILLING	AND DYING THAT DEGRADES US, BUT BASE LIVING, AND
MTH2 (77)	WAR, THE STEEPEST STEP OF ALL. THEY EVEN TOOK TO	KILLING	ANIMALS AS A MEANS OF KILLING TIME, AND THEN, OF
DOCT PREFACE(38)	BY PAY DAYS AND QUARTER DAYS, BUT BY SEASONS FOR	KILLING	ANIMALS FOR SPORT; THE FOX, THE HARE, THE OTTER, THE
MILL PREFACE(124)	BETWEEN THEM ANY GENTILE HAS THE SAME REASON FOR	KILLING	ANY JEW AT SIGHT AS THE ROMAN SOLDIER HAD FOR
BUOY 1 (12)	ALL THE CHANGES COULD HAVE BEEN EFFECTED WITHOUT	KILLING	ANYBODY. YOU MUST LISTEN TO REASON? /SON/ YES; BUT
MILL PREFACE(124)	ANY JEW AT SIGHT AS THE ROMAN SOLDIER HAD FOR	KILLING	ARCHIMEDES. NOW NO DOUBT JEWS ARE MOST OBNOXIOUS
ROCK PREFACE(147)	AND APOLOGETICALLY AS WELL AS THOROUGHLY.	KILLING	AS A POLITICAL FUNCTION, THAT KILLING IS A NECESSITY
GENV PREFACE(20)	THE GOVERNMENT ENOUGH TO BE CONSIDERED WORTH	KILLING	AS CADE, TYLER, AND ESSEX WERE KILLED. IN PRISON, HE

LION EPILOG (148)	OF COMMON PEOPLE'S LIVES, AND AMUSES HIMSELF WITH	KILLING	AS CARELESSLY AS WITH SPARING, IS THE SORT OF
MTH1 II (26)	FOOL THAN YOU? /EVE/ YOU SAID THERE WOULD BE NO	KILLING	BECAUSE THE VOICE WOULD TELL OUR CHILDREN THAT THEY
ROCK PREFACE(147)	OR PACKS OF HOUNDS AS METHODS OF EXTERMINATION.	KILLING	CAN BE CRUELLY OR KINDLY DONE; AND THE DELIBERATE
CATH 3 (184)	OWWWGH! /CLAIRE/ HELP! HELP! THEY ARE	KILLING	CHARLES. HELP! /NARYSHKIN/ (SEIZING HER AND
FANY I SD(276)	DISPOSITION, VERY TOLERABLE GOOD LOOKS, AND	KILLING	CLOTHES. SHE IS SO AFFABLE AND CONFIDENTIAL THAT IT
CAPT I (231)	THINK, HOWARD, THAT NOTHING PREVENTS PEOPLE	KILLING	EACH OTHER BUT THE FEAR OF YOUR HANGING THEM FOR IT.
ROCK PREFACE(164)	TO SECURE THIS CONDITION OF SOCIAL STABILITY BY	KILLING	EVERYONE WHO FELL INTO HIS POWER AND REFUSED TO BE
GENV PREFACE(11)	TO B.C., WHICH HAVE DEVELOPED THE TECHNIQUE OF	KILLING	FROM THE SINGLE COMBATS OF THE TROJAN WAR, FOUGHT
2TRU III (98)	GODLESS RULERS OF THIS WORLD. THOSE THAT DID THE	KILLING	HADNT EVEN THE DEVILMENT TO COMFORT THEM: WHAT
DEVL EPILOG (85)	CLAIMED HER. THE WYANDOTTE SETTLED THE DISPUTE BY	KILLING	HER AND BRINGING HER SCALP TO BURGOYNE. BURGOYNE LET
ROCK PREFACE(148)	OF RELIGION TO EXPLAIN TO HIM THAT WE ARE NOT	KILLING	HIM AT ALL, BUT ONLY EXPEDITING HIS TRANSFER TO AN
ROCK PREFACE(148)	AN ETERNITY OF BLISS. THE POLITICAL NECESSITY FOR	KILLING	HIM IS PRECISELY LIKE THAT FOR KILLING THE COBRA OR
HART PREFACE(10)	HUMAN BEING COULD BE CUT OUT WITHOUT NECESSARILY	KILLING	HIM THEY CUT OUT; AND HE OFTEN DIED (UNNECESSARILY
GETT PREFACE(237)	RIGHT IN OTHERS CAN RECONCILE THE COMMUNITY TO	KILLING	HIM. FROM THIS FUNDAMENTAL RIGHT MANY OTHERS ARE
CYMB V (149)	YOU ARRIVED JUST NOW I, AS YOU SAW, WAS HOT ON	KILLING	HIM. LET HIM BEAR WITNESS THAT I DREW ON HIM TO
O'FL (223)	AND HE KILLING THE GERMANS AND THE GERMANS	KILLING	HIM, BAD CESS TO THEM! MY BOY IS TAKEN FROM ME AND
ROCK PREFACE(147)	THOROUGHLY. KILLING AS A POLITICAL FUNCTION. THAT	KILLING	IS A NECESSITY IS BEYOND QUESTION BY ANY THOUGHTFUL
APPL I (205)	THEIR HEADS, THERE IS SO LITTLE IN THEM. STILL,	KILLING	IS A SERIOUS BUSINESS: AT LEAST THE PERSON WHO IS TO
GLIM (178)	A GOOD DEED TO KILL YOU, I THINK. /FERRUCCIO/	KILLING	IS ALWAYS SPORT, MY GIULIACCIA. /SANDRO'S VOICE/ (
MIS. PREFACE(98)	TO BE A GOOD ANGEL AS FAST AS IT CAN WITHOUT	KILLING	ITSELF IN THE PROCESS, WHICH IS A DANGEROUS ONE.
MTH1 II (21)	THE DISCOVERER OF BLOOD. HE WAS THE INVENTOR OF	KILLING	. HE FOUND OUT THAT THE FIRE OF THE SUN COULD BE
MTH1 II (30)	YOU WITH YOUR DIRTY DIGGING, OR HE WITH HIS DIRTY	KILLING	. I CANNOT THINK IT WAS FOR EITHER OF THESE CHEAP
BARB PREFACE(242)	MORAL DIFFERENCE BETWEEN OFFICIAL AND UNOFFICIAL	KILLING	. IN SHORT, ALL MEN ARE ANARCHISTS WITH REGARD TO
BARB III (340)	THEM: DONT REASON WITH THEM. KILL THEM. /BARBARA/	KILLING	. IS THAT YOUR REMEDY FOR EVERYTHING? /UNDERSHAFT/
BUOY II (22)	YOU HUNTED OR FISHED FOR ME? /HE/ NO. I HATE	KILLING	. /SHE/ HAVE YOU FOUGHT FOR ME? /HE/ NO. I AM A
MTH4 I (173)	OUR TERTIARIES ARE NOT AT ALL SQUEAMISH ABOUT	KILLING	. /THE ELDERLY GENTLEMAN/ GRACIOUS POWERS! /ZOO/ (
MTH1 II (34)	BE NO MORE DIGGING NOR SPINNING, NOR FIGHTING NOR	KILLING	. SHE SPINS RESIGNEDLY; HE DIGS IMPATIENTLY.
ROCK PREFACE(147)	THE CRUELTY AND THE ENJOYMENT OF IT, NOT IN THE	KILLING	. THE SACREDNESS OF HUMAN LIFE. IN LAW WE DRAW A
MTH1 II (27)	FIGHTING AND OF HUNTING: IN A WORD, THE CRAFT OF	KILLING	. WHAT CERTAINTY HAVE YOU OF YOUR THOUSAND YEARS? I
MILL PREFACE(132)	NOBODY GAVE HIM THE LEAST CREDIT FOR ANYTHING BUT	KILLING	. WHEN THE GLORY TURNED TO SHAME ON THE ROAD BACK
WIDO III SD(66)	TO TRENCH. COKANE CROSSES TO BLANCHE IN HIS MOST	KILLING	MANNER. /COKANE/ HOW DO YOU DO, MISS SARTORIUS?
FABL V (118)	TWICE A YEAR; AND IT TOOK ONE OF THE WORST OF THE	KILLING	MATCHES THEY CALLED WARS TO MAKE THEM GO EVEN THAT
GLIM (176)	IF THE SUM WERE LARGER YOUR BARON WOULD WIN IT BY	KILLING	ME HIMSELF AND BREAKING SOMEBODY ELSE ON THE WHEEL
APPL I (205)	SO. I THINK THAT IF THERE WERE A QUESTION OF	KILLING	ME -- /BOANERGES/ (GRIMLY) THERE MAY BE, SOMEDAY. I
FABL I (103)	DIE OF RADIATION. BESIDES, BOMBS KILL WOMEN.	KILLING	MEN DOES NOT MATTER: THE WOMEN CAN REPLACE THEM; BUT
GLIM (183)	/FERRUCCIO/ THERE IS NOTHING TO BE GAINED BY	KILLING	ME, GIULIACCIA. /GIULIA/ PERHAPS; BUT I DO NOT KNOW.
ROCK I (225)	WAS OVERWORKING: BURNING THE CANDLE AT BOTH ENDS:	KILLING	MYSELF. IT DOESNT MATTER. I HAVE MADE MY WILL.
GETT (339)	I HAVE SOMETIMES THOUGHT OF KILLING YOU, AND THEN	KILLING	MYSELF. /THE BISHOP/ WHY ON EARTH SHOULD YOU KILL
MIS. PREFACE(74)	THE OTHER TWO WOULD RAISE IT. AT PRESENT THE	KILLING	OF A FOX EXCEPT BY A PACK OF FOXHOUNDS IS REGARDED
METH PREFACE(R58)	AN ANIMAL MURDER IN EXACTLY THE SAME SENSE AS THE	KILLING	OF A MAN IS MURDER. IT IS SOMETIMES NECESSARY TO
MIS. PREFACE(43)	THIS IS A MERE MATTER OF NECESSITY, LIKE THE	KILLING	OF A MAN-EATING TIGER IN A NURSERY, A VENOMOUS SNAKE
METH PREFACE(R58)	EQUALITY OF ALL LIVING THINGS. IT MAKES THE	KILLING	OF AN ANIMAL MURDER IN EXACTLY THE SAME SENSE AS THE
ROCK PREFACE(147)	OF HUMAN LIFE. IN LAW WE DRAW A LINE BETWEEN THE	KILLING	OF HUMAN ANIMALS AND NON-HUMAN ONES, SETTING THE
HART I (79)	SOFA). I TELL YOU I HAVE OFTEN THOUGHT OF THIS	KILLING	OF HUMAN VERMIN. MANY MEN HAVE THOUGHT OF IT. DECENT
KING II (230)	YOU A SON TO INHERIT THE CROWN AND SAVE ALL THIS	KILLING	OF MONMOUTH AND JAMES AND THE HANDING OVER OF YOUR
2TRU PREFACE(10)	CALLS, AND HAVING EVERY MONTH SET APART FOR THE	KILLING	OF SOME PARTICULAR BIRD OR ANIMAL. IT MEANS BEING A
GLIM (183)	NOT LIKE TO KILL A MAN WITH A GOOD SOUL, I MEANT	KILLING	ON MY OWN ACCOUNT: NOT PROFESSIONALLY. /FERRUCCIO/
2TRU III (98)	KILLING THE WRONG PEOPLE. IT WAS INNOCENT MEN	KILLING	ONE ANOTHER. /THE PATIENT/ JUST FOR THE FUN OF IT.
2TRU III (92)	WAS RIGHT, AND THAT WE WERE ALL A PARCEL OF FOOLS	KILLING	ONE ANOTHER FOR NOTHING. SHE LOST THE COURAGE TO
SUPR III (109)	THEY WILL NEVER BE AT A LOSS FOR AN EXCUSE FOR	KILLING	ONE ANOTHER. /DON JUAN/ WHAT OF THAT? IT IS NOT
GENV PREFACE(21)	MIGHTY FAR WEST OF AMERICA. AFTER TWELVE YEARS OF	KILLING	OTHER PEOPLE HE HAD TO KILL HIMSELF, AND LEAVE HIS
METH PREFACE(R59)	REMORSE, WE AT ALL EVENTS KNOW THAT WE ARE	KILLING	OUR COUSIN. NO DOUBT IT SHOCKS THE FLEA WHEN THE
ROCK PREFACE(147)	A CHIEF OF POLICE TO THE POLITICAL NECESSITY FOR	KILLING	PEOPLE: A NECESSITY SO DISTRESSING TO THE STATESMEN
GLIM (183)	FOOL THEN AS TO SPOIL YOUR OWN TRADE BY SOMETIMES	KILLING	PEOPLE FOR NOTHING? /SQUARCIO/ ONE KILLS A SNAKE
ARMS III (55)	GRIEF! A MAN WHO HAS BEEN DOING NOTHING BUT	KILLING	PEOPLE FOR YEARS! WHAT DOES HE CARE? WHAT DOES ANY
CLEO IV (187)	HE IS AS DEAD AS POMPEY. WE ARE QUITS NOW, AS TO	KILLING	-- YOU AND I. /CAESAR/ (SHOCKED) ASSASSINATED! --
CLEO PRO1 (92)	BEING A ROMAN, ART ACCUSTOMED TO THIS KIND OF	KILLING	; FOR THOU HAST IMPERIAL INSTINCTS. WILT THOU
HART PREFACE(20)	HAD KEPT THEIR HEADS NOW LOST THEM UTTERLY. "	KILLING	SALOON PASSENGERS! WHAT NEXT? " WAS THE ESSENCE OF
3PLA PREFACE(R32)	AND THACKERAYS HUDDLE UP THE MATTER AT THE END BY	KILLING	SOMEBODY AND COVERING YOUR EYES WITH THE
ROCK PREFACE(155)	A TRAITOR, THE MOST CRUEL AND OBSCENE METHOD OF	KILLING	THAT THE HUMAN IMAGINATION COULD CONCEIVE AT ITS
ROCK PREFACE(148)	FOR KILLING HIM IS PRECISELY LIKE THAT FOR	KILLING	THE COBRA OR THE TIGER: HE IS SO FEROCIOUS OR
O'FL (223)	MAD HE IS WITH THE ROARING OF THE CANNONS AND HE	KILLING	THE GERMANS AND THE GERMANS KILLING HIM, BAD CESS TO
2TRU III (98)	KEPT GOING BY THE PEOPLE WHO WANT THE RIGHT THING	KILLING	THE PEOPLE WHO WANT THE WRONG THING. WHEN THE
2TRU III (98)	YOU BECAUSE YOURE AN ENGLISHMAN. WE WERE NOT	KILLING	THE RIGHT PEOPLE IN 1915. WE WERENT EVEN KILLING THE
2TRU II (73)	SOMEBODY: I WANT TO KILL SOMEBODY. I SHALL END BY	KILLING	THE TWO OF YOU. WHAT ARE WE, WE THREE GLORIOUS
2TRU III (98)	KILLING THE RIGHT PEOPLE IN 1915. WE WERENT EVEN	KILLING	THE WRONG PEOPLE. IT WAS INNOCENT MEN KILLING ONE
PRES (134)	SENDING THESE MISGUIDED WOMEN TO HOLLOWAY AND	KILLING	THEM SLOWLY AND INHUMANLY BY RUINING THEIR HEALTH;
LION II (140)	THINK? /THE CAPTAIN/ WHAT CAN HAPPEN? THEY ARE	KILLING	THEM, I SUPPOSE. /ANDROCLES/ (RUNNING IN THROUGH
PYGM V (284)	ONLY ONE WAY OF ESCAPING TROUBLE; AND THATS	KILLING	THINGS. COWARDS, YOU NOTICE, ARE ALWAYS SHRIEKING TO
METH PREFACE(R78)	OR MATERIAL SUBSTANTIALITY OF SOME LEGEND, AND	KILLING	THOSE WHO REFUSE TO ACCEPT IT AS HISTORICAL OR
LION PREFACE(86)	CHARLEMAGNE MADE CHRISTIANITY COMPULSORY BY	KILLING	THOSE WHO REFUSED TO EMBRACE IT; AND THOUGH THIS
SUPR III (112)	STILL, SINCE IN THIS PLACE, INSTEAD OF MERELY	KILLING	TIME WE HAVE TO KILL ETERNITY, GO AHEAD BY ALL
MTH2 (77)	THEY EVEN TOOK TO KILLING ANIMALS AS A MEANS OF	KILLING	TIME, AND THEN, OF COURSE, ATE THEM TO SAVE THE LONG
BARB PREFACE(217)	IS NOT THE DUPE OF THAT PUBLIC SENTIMENT AGAINST	KILLING	WHICH IS PROPAGATED AND ENDOWED BY PEOPLE WHO WOULD
SIM PREFACE(17)	WITH THE INSTINCTIVE SHRINKING FROM OUTRIGHT	KILLING	WHICH MAKES SO MANY PEOPLE SIGN PETITIONS FOR THE
ARMS I (6)	PEOPLE WERE NOT SO CRUEL. WHAT GLORY IS THERE IN	KILLING	WRETCHED FUGITIVES? /CATHERINE/ CRUEL! DO YOU
2TRU III (98)	FROM KILLING A MAN BECAUSE HE'S A GERMAN AND HE	KILLING	YOU BECAUSE YOURE AN ENGLISHMAN. WE WERE NOT KILLING
MTH4 I (164)	BY BEATING YOU, IMPRISONING YOU, TORTURING YOU,	KILLING	YOU IF YOU DISOBEY THEM WITHOUT BEING STRONG ENOUGH
LION II (137)	LET MY DEATH ATONE FOR BOTH. I FEEL AS IF I WERE	KILLING	YOU. /ANDROCLES/ DONT THINK OF ME, SISTER. THINK OF
DOCT V (177)	OF MY TAKING THE LAW INTO MY OWN HANDS, AND	KILLING	YOU. /RIDGEON/ I AM SO HOPELESSLY IDIOTIC ABOUT YOU
CLEO III (150)	DO NOT WANT TO GO BEYOND THE LINES, LET ME FINISH	KILLING	YOUR SENTINEL AND DEPART WITH THE QUEEN. /CENTURION/
GETT (339)	REASON! /MRS GEORGE/ I HAVE SOMETIMES THOUGHT OF	KILLING	YOU, AND THEN KILLING MYSELF. /THE BISHOP/ WHY ON
MTH1 II (21)	AND LIVED AS HE HAD LIVED, BY THE CHASE, BY THE	KILLING	, AND BY THE FIRE. AM I NOT BETTER THAN YOU?
SUPR HANDBOK(196)	HAVE BEEN MADE, BY THE PEOPLE WHO WANT IT	KILLING	, COERCING, AND INTIMIDATING THE PEOPLE WHO DONT
MTH1 II (22)	ALL THOSE MULTITUDES OF MEN FIGHTING, FIGHTING,	KILLING	, KILLING! THE FOUR RIVERS RUNNING WITH BLOOD! THE
DOCT PREFACE(22)	AUTHORITIES. IN THE FIRST FRENZY OF MICROBE	KILLING	, SURGICAL INSTRUMENTS WERE DIPPED IN CARBOLIC OIL,
MTH4 II (186)	GOING TO TAKE IN ALL THE POWERS. IF IT COMES TO	KILLING	, TWO CAN PLAY AT THAT GAME, LONGLIVED OR
PYGM III (251)	THAT, YOUNG MAN? I BET I GOT IT RIGHT. /FREDDY/	KILLING	! /MRS EYNSFORD HILL/ I'M SURE I HOPE IT WONT TURN
MTH1 II (22)	MULTITUDES OF MEN FIGHTING, FIGHTING, KILLING,	KILLING	! THE FOUR RIVERS RUNNING WITH BLOOD! THE SHOUTS

KILL'D

CYMB V (141)	LADY'S KINGDOM: 'TIS ENOUGH THAT, BRITAIN, I HAVE	KILL'D	THY MISTRESS. PEACE! I'LL GIVE NO WOUND TO THEE. I

KILLS

CLEO IV (190)	I MEAN NO HARM BY KILLING: I DO IT AS A DOG	KILLS	A CAT, BY INSTINCT. WE ARE ALL DOGS AT YOUR HEELS; BUT
GLIM (183)	ONE KILLS A SNAKE FOR NOTHING, EXCELLENCY. ONE	KILLS	A DOG FOR NOTHING SOMETIMES. /SANDRO/ (
GENV I (38)	KILLS ANYONE IT'S AN EXECUTION; BUT IF ANYONE	KILLS	A PRESIDENT IT'S AN ASSASSINATION. /THE WIDOW/ AND IS
GLIM (183)	KILLING PEOPLE FOR NOTHING? /SQUARCIO/ ONE	KILLS	A SNAKE FOR NOTHING, EXCELLENCY. ONE KILLS A DOG FOR
SIM PREFACE(4)	THERE ARE MANY DEGREES. THE ABYSSINIAN DANAKIL	KILLS	A STRANGER AT SIGHT AND IS CONTINUALLY SEEKING FOR AN
HART II (98)	SEE ME GETTING A SMASHER RIGHT IN THE FACE THAT	KILLS	A WHOLE PART OF MY LIFE: THE BEST PART THAT CAN NEVER
CAPT I (231)	MAN OF THEM BELIEVES HE WILL GO TO HEAVEN IF HE	KILLS	AN UNBELIEVER. /LADY CICELY/ BLESS YOU, DEAR MR
GENV PREFACE(10)	OF MOLECULES, ESCAPES BY SLOW RADIATION AND BOTH	KILLS	AND CURES LIVING ORGANISMS, LEAVING BEHIND IT NOT
GENV I (38)	THE EARTHLY PARADISE. /SHE/ SURELY IF A PRESIDENT	KILLS	ANYONE IT'S AN EXECUTION; BUT IF ANYONE KILLS A
MTH1 II (30)	DIVINE SUSTENANCE FROM THE SKIES? HE STEALS AND	KILLS	FOR HIS FOOD; AND MAKES UP IDLE POEMS OF LIFE AFTER
SUPR II (55)	OF MAKING IT, THEY WOULD KILL US AS THE SPIDER	KILLS	HER MATE OR AS THE BEES KILL THE DRONE. AND THEY WOULD
JITT I (14)	OF A UNIVERSITY PROFESSOR, HIS RESPECTABILITY	KILLS	HER SOUL. THEY BOTH BECOME MERE SHELLS OF THEIR FORMER
GETT PREFACE(208)	THE QUEEN HAS FOUND HER MATE, WHEN THE QUEEN	KILLS	HIM AND THE QUONDAM FEMALES KILL ALL THE REST (SUCH

SUPR PREFACE(R13)	SEEKS PRIVATE REDRESS WITH THE SWORD, DON JUAN	KILLS	HIM WITHOUT AN EFFORT. NOT UNTIL THE SLAIN FATHER
JOAN 2 (83)	AND WHENEVER I FIND A FRIEND I CAN CARE FOR, HE	KILLS	HIM. /JOAN/ WHY DOST LET HIM? /CHARLES/ (PETULANTLY
CLEO NOTES (210)	YOU, SO TO SPEAK, AS A LIFE-OR-DEATH COURIER	KILLS	HORSES-- ENABLES MEN WITH COMMON IDEAS AND
BARB PREFACE(231)	TO FLOG HIM IF HE STRIKES, TO MURDER HIM IF HE	KILLS	. BY EXAMPLE AND PRECEPT THE LAW AND PUBLIC OPINION
DOCT I (89)	THAT THE INOCULATION THAT OUGHT TO CURE SOMETIMES	KILLS	. /SIR PATRICK/ I COULD HAVE TOLD YOU THAT. IVE TRIED
FABL PREFACE(90)	THAT THE PROPHYLACTIC NOT ONLY FAILS TO CURE BUT	KILLS	. WHEN VACCINATION WAS MADE COMPULSORY AS A PREVENTIVE
DOCT I (107)	ROUND. AND FOR ALL YOU KNOW, BLOOMFIELD BONINGTON	KILLS	LESS PEOPLE THAN YOU DO. /RIDGEON/ OH, VERY LIKELY.
LION II (133)	MASTER'S WILL, AND THAT I COULD KILL THE MAN WHO	KILLS	ME IF I CHOSE. /THE EDITOR/ PUT ON THAT ARMOR.
DOCT PREFACE(22)	NOURISHES THE TUBERCLE BACILLUS HANDSOMELY AND	KILLS	MEN. THE POPULAR THEORY OF DISEASE IS THE COMMON
DOCT PREFACE(15)	PATIENTS, VISIBLY MAKES MUCH MORE THAN YOU DO AND	KILLS	NO MORE PEOPLE. A DOCTOR'S CHARACTER CAN NO MORE STAND
METH PREFACE(R46)	WINTER WILL KILL OFF A WEAKLY CHILD AS THE BUCKET	KILLS	OFF A WEAKLY PUPPY. THEN THERE IS THE FARM LABORER.
DOCT V (176)	IT, IT CURES. WHEN ANOTHER MAN HANDLES IT, IT	KILLS	-- SOMETIMES. /JENNIFER/ (NAIVELY: NOT YET TAKING IT
ROCK II (282)	THAN SEE YOU UNHAPPY. THAT SORT OF UNHAPPINESS	KILLS	; AND IF YOU DIE I'LL DIE TOO. (SHE THROWS HERSELF
JITT III (72)	OF YOUR FATHER'S LOVE. BUT THE REAL PERSON ALWAYS	KILLS	THE IMAGINED PERSON. /EDITH/ HE SAID THAT ONCE.
DOCT PREFACE(6)	THE DOCTOR DOES SOMETHING. SOMETIMES WHAT HE DOES	KILLS	THE PATIENT; BUT YOU DO NOT KNOW THAT; AND THE DOCTOR
DOCT PREFACE(5)	OF HIM. BUT IF HE OPERATES ON THE THROAT AND	KILLS	THE PATIENT, OR EXTIRPATES AN INTERNAL ORGAN AND KEEPS
LION II (128)	TO DIANA: SHE'S A HUNTRESS, YOU KNOW, AND	KILLS	THINGS. /THE EDITOR/ THAT DONT MATTER. YOU CAN CHOOSE
SUPR HANDBOK(219)	CANNOT, TEACHES. A LEARNED MAN IS AN IDLER WHO	KILLS	TIME WITH STUDY. BEWARE OF HIS FALSE KNOWLEDGE: IT IS
HART I (81)	HARPOON CANNON? /CAPTAIN SHOTOVER/ NO USE. IT	KILLS	WHALES, NOT MEN. /MRS HUSHABYE/ WHY NOT? YOU FIRE THE
GLIM (185)	IF YOURS IS DIFFERENT. I SHALL SEE WHEN MY FATHER	KILLS	YOU. /FERRUCCIO/ DO YOU KNOW WHAT I AM THINKING,
PRES (132)	SIR; AND DONT PRESUME TO ARGUE. EVEN IF SHE	KILLS	YOU, IT IS YOUR DUTY TO DIE FOR YOUR COUNTRY. RIGHT
		KILT	
PRES (148)	OTHER DHRUDGERY. WHAT WOULD YOU DO IF WE WAS ALL	KILT	? WOULD YOU GO TO BED AND HAVE TWINS? /MITCHENER/
MTH5 SD(205)	SLOWLY DESCENDS THEM. EXCEPT FOR A SORT OF LINEN	KILT	CONSISTING MAINLY OF A GIRDLE CARRYING A SPORRAN AND A
BULL III (132)	YOU TELL HIM DHAT ME MOTHER'S ANT WAS SHOT AND	KILT	DEAD IN THE STHREET O ROSSCULLEN BE A SOLJER IN THE
BULL IV (149)	SURE IT'S ONLY NATURAL. SURE YOU MIGHT HAVE BEEN	KILT	. A YOUNG MAN, FEELING THAT HE MUST LAUGH OR BURST,
MTH3 SD(103)	THROAT, SET IN A BLACK STOCK. HE WEARS A SORT OF	KILT	OF BLACK RIBBONS, AND SOFT BLACK BOOTS THAT BUTTON HIGH
O'FL (211)	MEN THAN ME: AND WHAT BETTER AM I NOW THAT IVE	KILT	THEM? WHAT BETTER IS ANYBODY? /SIR PEARCE/ (HUFFED,
O'FL (210)	SUCH THING. I KNOW QUITE WELL WHY I KILT THEM. I	KILT	THEM BECAUSE I WAS AFEARD THAT, IF I DIDNT, THEYD KILL
O'FL (210)	I TELL YOU NO SUCH THING. I KNOW QUITE WELL WHY I	KILT	THEM. I KILT THEM BECAUSE I WAS AFEARD THAT, IF I
O'FL (211)	AND MAYBE AS GOOD AS OURSELVES. THE BOSHES I	KILT	WAS MORE KNOWLEDGABLE MEN THAN ME: AND WHAT BETTER AM I
SHAK SD(140)	AND MACBETH APPEAR, ROB IN HIGHLAND TARTAN AND	KILT	WITH CLAYMORE, MACBETH IN KINGLY COSTUME. /MACBETH/
BULL IV (149)	IT'S A MERCY YOU WERENT KILLED. /DORAN/	KILT	! IT'S A MERCY DHERES TWO BONES OF YOU LEFT HOULDIN
		KIMONO	
PYGM II (240)	CLEAN YOUNG JAPANESE LADY IN A SIMPLE BLUE COTTON	KIMONO	PRINTED CUNNINGLY WITH SMALL WHITE JASMINE BLOSSOMS.
		KIN	
PPP (203)	EAH! EAH! WOTS THIS? WOTS ALL THIS NOISE? AH	KIN	ENNYBODY SLEEP THROUGH IT? (LOOKING AT THE FLOOR AND
METH PREFACE(R58)	HOW ONE TOUCH OF DARWIN MAKES THE WHOLE WORLD	KIN	. ANOTHER HUMANITARIAN INTEREST IN DARWINISM WAS THAT
PPP (203)	E KIN SLEEP THROUGH THE NOISE YOU THREE MIKES E	KIN	SLEEP THROUGH ENNYTHINK. /MAGNESIA/ DETESTABLE
PPP (203)	IF YOU WAKE THAT MAN HE DIES. /THE LANDLORD/ IF E	KIN	SLEEP THROUGH THE NOISE YOU THREE MIKES E KIN SLEEP
MIS. PREFACE(16)	THAT WOULD PRODUCE IT EQUALLY IF THEY WERE OF NO	KIN	TO ONE ANOTHER, OR IT IS A MORE OR LESS MORBID SURVIVAL
CYMB V (143)	(INTERPOSING) HANDS OFF MY MASTER! HE IS	KIN	TO THE KING. /POSTHUMUS/ (TO CYMBELINE) CALL OFF YOUR
BARB II (289)	ROT! THERE AINT NAO SACH A THING AS A SAOUL. AH	KIN	YOU TELL WEVVER AWVE A SAOUL OR NOT? YOU NEVER SEEN IT.
		KIND	
METH PREFACE(R83)	MEANT IRRESISTIBLE IMPULSE OF THE LOFTIEST	KIND	: FOR EXAMPLE A PASSION FOR ASTRONOMY OR FOR TRUTH. FOR
GENV I (32)	AM AN ARYAN; BUT I TELL THEM I AM NOTHING OF THE	KIND	: I'M AN ENGLISHWOMAN. NOT A COMMON ENGLISHWOMAN, OF
MRS PREFACE(156)	OUT ON INQUIRY TO BE SIMPLY THE PRETTY, DAINTY	KIND	: THAT IS, THE ONLY KIND THAT GETS THE CHANCE OF ACTING
GENV IV (98)	CERTAINLY. I SHALL VALUE IT. /BBDE/ YOU ARE VERY	KIND	: YOU ALMOST DISARM ME. BUT MAY I SAY THAT YOUR
MIS. (155)	EM. /MRS TARLETON/ INDEED YOULL DO NOTHING OF THE	KIND	: YOULL STAY HERE QUIETLY WITH LORD SUMMERHAYS. YOUD
NEVR II (255)	WITHOUT BEING SUPPOSED TO HAVE DESIGNS OF THAT	KIND	? AS IF THERE WERE NO OTHER INTERESTS! NO OTHER
APPL INTRLUD(248)	DO YOU DENY THAT THERE WAS SOME SUGGESTION OF THE	KIND	? /ORINTHIA/ HOW DARE YOU CHALLENGE ME TO DENY IT? I
GETT PREFACE(198)	YOUNG PEOPLE TO MAKE IT A RULE TO DO AT LEAST ONE	KIND	ACTION EVERY DAY, FEEL VERY MUCH AS I SHOULD IF I HEARD
GETT PREFACE(198)	TO SUPPLY OCCASION FOR SEVERAL THOUSAND MILLION	KIND	ACTIONS PER ANNUM, THE EFFECT ON THE CHARACTER OF THE
MTH5 (228)	IS FULL OF FORCES AND POWERS AND ENERGIES OF ONE	KIND	AND ANOTHER, THE SAP RISING IN A TREE, THE STONE
CAPT II (261)	YOUR MOTHER'S LIFETIME, WHEN YOU COULD HAVE BEEN	KIND	AND FORBEARING WITH HER. HURTING YOUR UNCLE WONT DO HER
3PLA PREFACE(R20)	THAT A MAN OR WOMAN CANNOT BE COURAGEOUS AND	KIND	AND FRIENDLY UNLESS INFATUATEDLY IN LOVE WITH SOMEBODY
SUPR HANDBOK(207)	WERE LIGHTED BY EARNESTLY PIOUS PEOPLE, WHO WERE	KIND	AND GOOD AS KINDNESS AND GOODNESS GO, AND WHEN A NEGRO
SIM I (41)	IT MEANS EVERYTHING THAT IS GOOD AND LOVELY AND	KIND	AND HOLY. I DONT PROFESS TO GO ANY FURTHER THAN THAT.
DEVL II (36)	WHEREAS, OF COURSE, YOU HAVE REALLY BEEN SO	KIND	AND HOSPITABLE AND CHARMING TO ME THAT I ONLY WANT TO
FANY I (280)	ONE; AND THATLL DO IT. IF YOUD LIKE TO BE VERY	KIND	AND NICE YOU COULD PAY THE LOT; BUT I CANT DENY THAT IT
DOCT V (178)	WILL KNOW WHAT YOU ARE CARING FOR. /JENNIFER/ (	KIND	AND QUIET) I AM NOT ANGRY WITH YOU ANY MORE, SIR
JITT II (47)	FOR YOU. /LENKHEIM/ HA! AND WERE YOU EQUALLY	KIND	AND THOUGHTFUL FOR HIS WIFE, EH? /JITTA/ (EARNESTLY)
MTH2 (67)	MR LUBIN; OR SHALL I THANK YOU FOR YOUR VERY	KIND	AND WELCOME VISIT, AND SAY GOOD EVENING? /LUBIN/ (
JOAN PREFACE(55)	SAKE, AND LIKE IT SO MUCH WHEN IT IS GOOD OF ITS	KIND	AND WELL DONE THAT THEY TEAR THEMSELVES AWAY FROM IT
MIS. PREFACE(18)	IN CERTAIN PHASES OF CIVILIZATION PEOPLE OF THIS	KIND	ARE APT TO GET THE UPPER HAND OF MORE AMIABLE AND
GETT (344)	IN FROM THE STUDY. /HOTCHKISS/ WILL YOU BE SO	KIND	AS TO TELL ME WHETHER I AM DREAMING? IN THERE I HAVE
GETT (326)	COALS WERE ALIKE, AND TRIED THE THIRTEEN SHILLING	KIND	BECAUSE IT SEEMED CHEAP. IT PROVED UNEXPECTEDLY
FANY EPILOG (328)	BUT TO ME, WHO HAVE NEVER SEEN ANYTHING OF THIS	KIND	BEFORE, THE EFFECT OF THIS PLAY IS TERRIBLY
MTH4 III SD(194)	CONTEMPLATE THE VOID WITH AWE. ORGAN MUSIC OF THE	KIND	CALLED SACRED IN THE NINETEENTH CENTURY BEGINS. THEIR
KING I (212)	THE SIDE OF THE PAINTER. BUT IN A MATTER OF THIS	KIND	CAN I, AS FOUNDER OF THE ROYAL SOCIETY, RANK THE
MILL PREFACE(110)	CAPITALIST, A JUSTICE OF THE PEACE MAY BE A GOOD	KIND	CHRISTIAN SOUL, OWING HIS POSITION, AS MOST OF US DO,
PYGM PREFACE(199)	OF A POPULAR PLAY. THERE HAVE BEEN HEROES OF THAT	KIND	CRYING IN THE WILDERNESS FOR MANY YEARS PAST. WHEN I
LION PROLOG (109)	TERRIFYING CLASH). OH, MUSTNT FRIGHTEN UM'S GOOD	KIND	DOCTOR, UM'S AFFECTIONATE NURSEY. THAT DIDNT HURT AT
GETT (325)	IMPERTINENCE WITH SHAME AND CONFUSION. YOU WERE	KIND	ENOUGH TO ANSWER THAT MR COLLINS WAS LOOKING OUT FOR A
GENV IV (114)	AND NOW I AM HAPPY: I AM WHAT THE GENTLEMAN IS	KIND	ENOUGH TO DESCRIBE AS AMIABLE. OH, WHY WILL YOU NOT DO
WIDO II (25)	YES, SIR. DR TRENCH ASKED HIS WAY OF ME, AND WAS	KIND	ENOUGH TO DRIVE ME FROM THE STATION. /SARTORIUS/ WHERE
LIED (194)	READY TO BEHAVE LIKE A GENTLEMAN IF YOU WILL BE	KIND	ENOUGH TO EXPLAIN EXACTLY HOW. /SHE/ (A LITTLE
CAND III (137)	YOU ALL HAD SUPPER? /LEXY/ MR BURGESS HAS BEEN	KIND	ENOUGH TO GIVE US A REALLY SPLENDID SUPPER AT THE
PRES (154)	NOT A WEAPON: IT IS A CURIOSITY. IF YOU WOULD BE	KIND	ENOUGH TO PLACE IT IN SOME MUSEUM INSTEAD OF POINTING
AUGS (272)	QUALITY; BUT HE WOULD NOT HEAR OF IT. HE WAS	KIND	ENOUGH TO SAY HE COULD NOT BELIEVE THAT A GERMAN
DOCT II (124)	IF I WERE SEEN SPEAKING TO YOU, UNLESS YOU WERE	KIND	ENOUGH TO SAY YOU CALLED ME TO ASK WHETHER THE MOTOR
MTH3 (126)	GROWN UP ENOUGH EVEN FOR THAT, THOUGH YOU WERE	KIND	ENOUGH TO SAY THAT I FRIGHTEN YOU. /BURGE-LUBIN/
KING I (166)	BY CHANCE AT YOUR DOOR; AND HIS FAVORITE DOG WAS	KIND	ENOUGH TO TAKE A FANCY TO ME. /CHARLES/ SHE IS NEVER
MIS. (181)	MUCH OR NOT ENOUGH. LORD SUMMERHAYS: WILL YOU BE	KIND	ENOUGH TO WITNESS THE DECLARATION THIS MAN HAS JUST
DOCT PREFACE(13)	OPERATION IS AS CERTAIN AS ANYTHING OF THE	KIND	EVER CAN BE. THUS THE CONSERVATIVE SURGEON AND THE
CAPT II (244)	SURE YOU WOULD, MR DRINKWATER. YOU HAVE SUCH A	KIND	FACE. (SHE TURNS BACK AND GOES OUT THROUGH THE SMALL
NEVR III (277)	ARE MEN WHO HAVE A GOOD DEAL OF FEELING, AND	KIND	FEELING TOO, WHICH THEY ARE NOT ABLE TO EXPRESS. WHAT
O'FL (213)	SURE, I KNOW SHE WOULD, SIR. SHE WAS ALWAYS A	KIND	FRIEND TO THE POOR. LITTLE HER LADYSHIP KNEW, GOD HELP
PYGM I (215)	(TO PICKERING, AS HE PASSES HER) BUY A FLOWER,	KIND	GENTLEMAN. I'M SHORT FOR MY LODGING. /PICKERING/ I
JOAN 1 (62)	SQUIRE. JACK WILL COME WILLINGLY: HE IS A VERY	KIND	GENTLEMAN, AND GIVES ME MONEY TO GIVE TO THE POOR. I
MIS. (140)	DO YOU MEAN TO TELL ME THAT NOTHING OF THAT	KIND	HAD EVER HAPPENED BEFORE? THAT NO MAN HAD EVER--
CATH PREFACE(157)	SOPHOCLES, AND EURIPIDES; BUT NOTHING OF THE	KIND	HAPPENED: THESE ACTORS PLAYED THE WORKS OF DEAD
JOAN PREFACE(11)	IMAGINATION HAD BEEN OF THE SAME VIVIDLY DRAMATIC	KIND	HE MIGHT HAVE SEEN THE GHOST OF PYTHAGORAS WALK INTO
SUPR IV SD(142)	IN HIS FINERY, THOUGH IN A WORKING DRESS OF ANY	KIND	HE WOULD LOOK DIGNIFIED ENOUGH. HE IS A BULLET CHEEKED
HART II (87)	LEMONS. YOUVE BEEN WASTING YOUR GRATITUDE: MY	KIND	HEART IS ALL ROT. I'M SICK OF IT. WHEN I SEE YOUR
CAPT III (274)	RADIANT) OH, HOW GOOD OF YOU! YOU HAVE A REAL	KIND	HEART OF GOLD, MR RANKIN. NOW, BEFORE YOU GO, SHALL WE
CAPT I (239)	YOU, CAPTAIN BRASSBOUND. I FEEL SURE YOU HAVE A	KIND	HEART. YOU HAVE SUCH NICE EYES. /SIR HOWARD/ (
CATH 4 (193)	(TO CATHERINE) DARLING LITTLE MOTHER! YOU HAVE A	KIND	HEART, THE KINDEST IN EUROPE. HAVE PITY. HAVE MERCY. I
HART PREFACE(34)	THERE, COURT AND MUNICIPAL, KEPT DRAMA OF THE	KIND	I DEALT IN ALIVE; SO THAT I WAS INDEBTED TO THE EMPEROR
CAPT I (227)	/SIR HOWARD/ INDEED! THATS THE FIRST CASE OF THE	KIND	I HAVE EVER MET. /DRINKWATER/ LAWD, SR AHRD, WOT
GENV IV (121)	TO EFFECT THIS DESTRUCTION, AND TO RETALIATE IN	KIND	IF THEY ARE USED AGAINST YOU? /SIR O./ WHAT ELSE CAN
GENV PREFACE(9)	AND MUNITION FACTORIES MADE RETALIATION IN	KIND	IMPOSSIBLE. OUR FLAME THROWING FROM TANKS FINISHED THE
JOAN PREFACE(32)	IS BY FAR THE MOST MODEST PRETENSION OF THE	KIND	IN EXISTENCE. COMPARED WITH OUR INFALLIBLE DEMOCRACIES,

SUPR I (23)	RECKLESSLY, BECAUSE THEY ARE UNSELFISH, THEY ARE	KIND	IN LITTLE THINGS. BECAUSE THEY HAVE A PURPOSE WHICH IS
NEVR II (250)	COMPLIMENT AND AN HONOR TO US, MR CRAMPTON, VERY	KIND	INDEED. THE MORE YOU ARE AT HOME HERE, SIR, THE BETTER
NEVR I (206)	TIME, IT WILL BE IMPOSSIBLE FOR ME TO ACCEPT YOUR	KIND	INVITATION TO LUNCH. (HE RISES WITH AN AIR OF
MIS. PREFACE(38)	SHOULD BE RELEASED FROM ANY OBLIGATION OF THE	KIND	. A LIFE'S WORK IS LIKE A DAY'S WORK: IT CAN BEGIN
GENV IV SD(87)	SUGGESTS A SITTING OR HEARING OR MEETING OF SOME	KIND	. A WASTE PAPER BASKET IS AVAILABLE. THE SECRETARY OF
MILL I (145)	WOULD BE AN ARDENT LOVER. HE WAS NOTHING OF THE	KIND	. ALL HIS ARDOR WAS IN HIS FISTS. NEVER SHALL I FORGET
JOAN PREFACE(50)	THE AIR, WITHOUT PUBLIC RESPONSIBILITIES OF ANY	KIND	. ALL SHAKESPEAR'S CHARACTERS ARE SO: THAT IS WHY THEY
MTH3 (105)	WHAT A BRAIN! /THE ARCHBISHOP/ NOTHING OF THAT	KIND	. ASSUME IN THE ORDINARY SENSE THAT I WAS BORN IN THE
JITT II (29)	BE FORGIVEN FOR DYING IN AN ADVENTURE OF THAT	KIND	. BUT A MAN OF SCIENCE! UNFORTUNATE, TO SAY THE LEAST:
SUPR HANDBOK(221)	CANCEL ONE ANOTHER, BUT SIMILARS THAT BREED THEIR	KIND	. CRIME IS ONLY THE RETAIL DEPARTMENT OF WHAT, IN
WIDO I (7)	THANK YOU. (TO SARTORIUS) THIS IS REALLY TOO	KIND	. HARRY: BRING YOUR CHAIR ROUND. /SARTORIUS/ YOU ARE
GENV IV (107)	MY HUSBAND WANTED SATISFACTION OF ANOTHER	KIND	. HE GOT IT FROM MY DEAREST FRIEND; AND ETIQUETTE
LADY PREFACE(209)	BY PROFESSION A MAN OF LETTERS OF AN UNCOMMERCIAL	KIND	. HE WAS A SPECIALIST IN PESSIMISM; HAD MADE A
DOCT PREFACE(44)	TO BE CAPABLE OF PASSIONATE WICKEDNESS OF ANY	KIND	. HERE, THEN, WE HAVE IN VIVISECTION, AS IN ALL THE
GETT PREFACE(222)	AS TO ORDER AND COMFORT, BUT NOT A DIFFERENCE IN	KIND	. HOWEVER, IT IS NOT BY ANY REFORM OF THE MARRIAGE LAWS
CATH 4 (192)	/EDSTASTON/ (INDIGNANTLY) I AM NOTHING OF THE	KIND	. I HAVE BEEN MENTIONED IN DISPATCHES AS A HIGHLY
BARB I (255)	ANOTHER SON! I NEVER SAID ANYTHING OF THE	KIND	. I NEVER DREAMT OF SUCH A THING. THIS IS WHAT COMES OF
OVER (182)	YOU ARE? /MRS LUNN/ I NEVER SAID ANYTHING OF THE	KIND	. I'M NOT AT ALL INSENSIBLE BY NATURE; BUT (I DONT
CYMB FORWORD(135)	DRAMA, AND INDEED OF SERIOUS LITERATURE OF ANY	KIND	. IT IS SO OUT-OF-PLACE THERE THAT SHAKESPEAR NEVER
CATH 4 (191)	I DONT KNOW A WORD OF GERMAN; BUT THAT SOUNDED	KIND	. (BECOMING HYSTERICAL) LITTLE MOTHER, BEAUTIFUL
CLEO IV (182)	ARE TO BE LIKE OTHER PEOPLE: IDLE, LUXURIOUS, AND	KIND	. (SHE STRETCHES HER HAND TO HIM ALONG THE TABLE).
PHIL III (141)	HIM. /CRAVEN/ DONT RUB IT IN, JULIA: IT'S NOT	KIND	. NO MAN IS QUITE HIMSELF WHEN HE'S CROSSED IN LOVE. (
POSN PREFACE(391)	UNDER A CENSORSHIP OF A GROTESQUELY UNSUITABLE	KIND	. NO PLAY CAN BE PERFORMED IF THE LORD CHAMBERLAIN
SUPR I SD(16)	MODERATELY AS POSSIBLE, NOTHING WHATEVER OF THE	KIND	. NOT THAT OCTAVIUS'S ADMIRATION IS IN ANY WAY
NEVR I (217)	/PHILIP/ OH, THERE ARE LOTS OF PEOPLE OF THAT	KIND	. OLD CHAMICO USED TO THRASH HIS WIFE AND DAUGHTERS
MIS. (150)	(TAKING OFF HIS GOGGLES) YOURE REALLY MORE THAN	KIND	. /BENTLEY/ WHY, IT'S JOEY PERCIVAL. /PERCIVAL/ HALLO,
PYGM V (271)	VISIT I REMEMBER MAKING SOME SILLY JOKE OF THE	KIND	. /DOOLITTLE/ AH! YOU MAY WELL CALL IT A SILLY JOKE.
MTH1 I (11)	ALL THINGS EXCEPT ONE; AND THAT ONE IS HIS OWN	KIND	. /EVE/ WHY DID LILITH KEEP THIS FROM HIM? /THE
PHIL II (122)	MORE CARE OF YOU, DOCTOR. /PARAMORE/ YOU ARE TOO	KIND	. /GRACE/ IT IS YOU WHO ARE TOO KIND-- TO YOUR
APPL INTRLUD(248)	DENY. OF COURSE THERE WAS A SUGGESTION OF THE	KIND	. /MAGNUS/ I THOUGHT SO. /ORINTHIA/ OH, STUPID!
NEVR II (231)	/GLORIA/ (GRAVELY ATTENTIVE) MR M'COMAS IS VERY	KIND	. /M'COMAS/ (NERVOUSLY) NOT AT ALL, MY DEAR YOUNG
CATH 1 (168)	FOR ENGLISH GENTLEMEN TO TAKE PRESENTS OF THAT	KIND	. /PATIOMKIN/ ARE YOU REALLY AN ENGLISHMAN?
SUPR I (6)	ASHAMED OF ME FOR NOT BEING A BIG SUCCESS OF SOME	KIND	. /RAMSDEN/ (GETTING UP AND PLANTING HIMSELF WITH HIS
SUPR III (135)	SERVICE. /THE STATUE/ WITH PLEASURE: YOURE MOST	KIND	. /THE DEVIL/ THIS WAY, COMMANDER. WE GO DOWN THE OLD
SIM PREFACE(15)	AND THAT THERE NEVER WILL BE ANYTHING OF THE	KIND	. THE ONLY CONCLUSION THE PIOUS WILL DRAW IS THAT I, AT
BARB II SD(273)	HONESTY OR ALTRUISTIC CONSIDERATIONS OF ANY	KIND	. THE WOMAN IS A COMMONPLACE OLD BUNDLE OF POVERTY AND
GENV I (46)	WITH TRIBAL SUPERSTITIONS OF THE MOST BARBAROUS	KIND	. THEY BELIEVE IN HUMAN SACRIFICES, IN WHAT THEY CALL
FABL IV (115)	BECAME LESS CAPABLE OF ORGANIZED ACTION OF ANY	KIND	. THEY COULD NOT OR WOULD NOT MAKE POLITICAL ALLIANCES,
GENV I (45)	ITS DOCTRINES ARE OF THE MOST SUBVERSIVE	KIND	. THEY HAVE PENETRATED TO MY OWN HOUSEHOLD. MY WIFE IS
MTH3 (109)	YEARS. /THE ARCHBISHOP/ NO. NOTHING OF THE	KIND	. THEY SIMPLY BELIEVED THAT MANKIND COULD LIVE ANY
SUPR I (8)	TANNER, IT'S NOT FAIR: IT'S NOT RIGHT: IT'S NOT	KIND	. WHAT ARE YOU GOING TO DO ABOUT IT? /OCTAVIUS/ BUT
SUPR III (126)	AS HARD TO ESCAPE WHEN I WAS CRUEL AS WHEN I WAS	KIND	. WHEN THE LADY'S INSTINCT WAS SET ON ME, THERE WAS
SUPR IV (157)	MYSELF. /ANN/ OH! NO, YOU WONT: THAT WOULDNT BE	KIND	. YOU WONT HAVE A BAD TIME. YOU WILL BE VERY NICE TO
LION PREFACE(76)	WHICH IS STILL THE MOST AMAZING THING OF THE	KIND	KNOWN TO US, BEING INTELLECTUALLY AN INVETERATE ROMAN
PYGM I (207)	(HOPEFULLY) I CAN GIVE YOU CHANGE FOR A TANNER,	KIND	LADY. /THE MOTHER/ (TO CLARA) GIVE IT TO ME. (CLARA
SUPR II (65)	EXPERIENCE TO KNOW WHAT MYSTIFICATIONS OF THIS	KIND	LEAD TO. /HECTOR/ (WITH STRONG SYMPTOMS OF MORAL
MIS. PREFACE(73)	WHILST THERE IS SO LITTLE PROVISION OF THIS	KIND	MADE FOR CHILDREN, I HAVE MORE THAN ONCE THOUGHT OF
JOAN EPILOG (161)	THEY ALL SAY " YES, PARSON: WE ALL KNOW YOU ARE A	KIND	MAN, AND WOULD NOT HARM A FLY." THAT IS A GREAT COMFORT
CATH PREFACE(155)	OF LIFE, CHARACTER, OR HISTORY, FEATS OF THIS	KIND	MAY TICKLE AN AUTHOR'S TECHNICAL VANITY; BUT HE IS
MIS. PREFACE(18)	THE CHILDREN IN AFTER LIFE. THE TRUE CRY OF THE	KIND	MOTHER AFTER HER LITTLE ROSARY OF KISSES IS " RUN AWAY,
CATH PREFACE(156)	CRUDE NATURE; AND I PREFER TO ADMIT THAT IN THIS	KIND	MY DRAMATIS PERSONAE ARE, AS THEY SHOULD BE, OF THE
CAPT II (245)	(TURNING TO SIR HOWARD) THATS THE CURSE O THIS	KIND	O LIFE, SIR: YOU GOT TO ASSOCIATE WITH ALL SORTS. MY
WIDO I (21)	HAS BEEN OF THE MOST EXPENSIVE AND COMPLETE	KIND	OBTAINABLE; AND HER SURROUNDINGS HAVE BEEN
LION PREFACE(36)	SUPPRESS FOR THE SAKE OF PRODUCING THIS	KIND	OF AMENITY IS THE REPROACH ADDRESSED TO JESUS FOR
JOAN PREFACE(8)	OF THE HUMAN SPECIES, AND NOT AS A DIFFERENT	KIND	OF ANIMAL WITH SPECIFIC CHARMS AND SPECIFIC
GETT PREFACE(196)	VERY WELL IN A BOOK (FOR PEOPLE WHO LIKE THAT	KIND	OF BOOK); BUT IN ACTUAL LIFE SHE IS A NUISANCE.
MIS. (129)	THE HOUSE: A SORT OF COLERIDGE OR HERBERT SPENCER	KIND	OF CARD, YOU KNOW. THAT WAS THE SECOND FATHER. THEN HIS
GENV I (35)	AND THE LABOR PARTY; BUT IT WAS WON BY AN UPSTART	KIND	OF CHAP WHO CALLED HIMSELF A BUSINESS DEMOCRAT. HE GOT
JOAN PREFACE(54)	BUT I LIKE POLICE NEWS AND DIVORCE NEWS AND ANY	KIND	OF DANCING OR DECORATION THAT HAS AN APHRODISIAC EFFECT
GENV III (83)	WHAT IS A MONGREL? I THOUGHT IT WAS A CHEAP	KIND	OF DOG. /THE JUDGE/ SO IT IS, MADAM. I APPLIED THE WORD
METH PREFACE(R48)	THAT IF WE ONCE ADMIT THE EXISTENCE OF ANY	KIND	OF FORCE, HOWEVER UNINTELLIGENT, AND STRETCH OUT THE
PHIL I (92)	SO SHE WENT STRAIGHT OFF. /CUTHBERTSON/ VERY	KIND	OF HER INDEED. I'M REALLY ASHAMED-- /CRAVEN/ DONT
FANY PROLOG (263)	HUMAN. I WAS SURPRISED. /THE COUNT/ EXTREMELY	KIND	OF HIM. /SAVOYARD/ THEN I WENT TO VAUGHAN, BECAUSE HE
DOCT PREFACE(16)	SAME TIME BY RUNNING WHAT IS THE MOST EXPENSIVE	KIND	OF HOTEL. THESE GAINS ARE SO GREAT THAT THEY UNDO MUCH
LION PREFACE(72)	AND FAMILY TIES AS THE CLAIM OF A PARTICULAR	KIND	OF INDIVIDUAL TO BE FREE FROM THEM BECAUSE THEY HAMPER
JITT III (74)	DISMAY), THATS VERY KIND OF YOU, EDITH, AND VERY	KIND	OF JITTA TO INCLUDE ME IN THE NUMBER OF HUSBANDS SHE
CLEO PRO1 (92)	BUT THOU, BEING A ROMAN, ART ACCUSTOMED TO THIS	KIND	OF KILLING; FOR THOU HAST IMPERIAL INSTINCTS. WILT THOU
BULL PREFACE(57)	AND BULLY THE UNIONISTS NEARER HOME. THAT	KIND	OF LOYALTY, NOT BEING A NATURAL PRODUCT, HAS TO BE
GENV III (83)	MADAM. I APPLIED THE WORD FIGURATIVELY TO A CHEAP	KIND	OF MAN: THAT IS, TO AN ENORMOUS MAJORITY OF THE HUMAN
GENV III (74)	BEEN MORE CONSIDERATE. BUT I HAD NEVER MET THAT	KIND	OF MAN BEFORE. THE ONLY OTHER BRITISH BISHOP I HAD MET
DEST (160)	YOU OUGHT TO BE ABLE TO TELL FROM HIS CONDUCT THE	KIND	OF MAN HE WAS. /NAPOLEON/ PSHA! WHAT WAS HE LIKE?
DEST (160)	/NAPOLEON/ YES, YES, SIR: NO DOUBT YOU WILL. WHAT	KIND	OF MAN WAS HE? /LIEUTENANT/ WELL, I SHOULD THINK YOU
CLEO NOTES (205)	AND LUXURIOUS FOOD AND SHELTER WILL PRODUCE A	KIND	OF MAN WITH WHOM THE COMMON LABORER IS SOCIALLY
GETT (307)	THAT. IT AINT SO EASY TO STOP IT AS THE EARNEST	KIND	OF PEOPLE THINK. /EDITH/ I KNEW YOU WOULD AGREE WITH
SUPR HANDBOK(178)	ALWAYS BEEN SILENCED BY THE SAME QUESTION: WHAT	KIND	OF PERSON IS THIS SUPERMAN TO BE? YOU ASK, NOT FOR A
PYGM II (232)	THAT I'M AN ARBITRARY OVERBEARING BOSSING	KIND	OF PERSON. I CANT ACCOUNT FOR IT. MRS PEARCE RETURNS.
POSN PREFACE(371)	THE VERY WORST PRACTICABLE EXAMPLES OF THE	KIND	OF PLAY IT PROFESSED TO EXTIRPATE. FOR IT MUST BE
FANY PROLOG (269)	THEATRES OF THE MOST SUPERIOR KIND-- YOU KNOW THE	KIND	OF PLAYS I MEAN? /TROTTER/ (EMPHATICALLY) I THINK I
CATH PREFACE(153)	STATESMEN WITH WHOM SHE PLAYED THIS MISCHIEVOUS	KIND	OF POLITICAL CHESS HAD ANY NOTION OF THE REAL HISTORY
MIS. PREFACE(71)	FOR THEM FREEDOM WILL NOT MEAN THE EXPENSIVE	KIND	OF SAVAGERY NOW CALLED " THE SIMPLE LIFE." THIS
LADY PREFACE(228)	AS HE FEELS ON ALL OCCASIONS; AND THIS RARE	KIND	OF SINCERITY IS ALL OVER THE SONNETS. SHAKESPEAR, WE
BARB II (274)	IT? YOU SAID YOU WAS A PAINTER. /PRICE/ NOT THAT	KIND	OF SNOB, BUT THE GENTEEL SORT. I'M TOO UPPISH, OWING TO
BARB III (312)	DRINKING, MAY I ASK? /CUSINS/ A MOST DEVILISH	KIND	OF SPANISH BURGUNDY, WARRANTED FREE FROM ADDED ALCOHOL:
DOCT III (133)	ARE COMING THIS MORNING. ISNT IT EXTRAORDINARILY	KIND	OF THEM, LOUIS, TO INSIST ON COMING? ALL OF THEM, TO
FANY EPILOG (329)	A BIT. ANY CLEVER MODERN GIRL COULD TURN OUT THAT	KIND	OF THING BY THE YARD. /THE COUNT/ THEN, SIR, TOMORROW I
BULL PREFACE(19)	AND INEVITABLE. WELLINGTON'S FORMULA FOR THAT	KIND	OF THING WAS A WELL-KNOWN IRISH ONE: " SIR: DONT BE A
MTH5 (209)	THAT IS RATHER SILLY? WE CANNOT GO ON AS IF THIS	KIND	OF THING, THIS DANCING AND SWEETHEARTING, WERE
GETT (280)	TO A REAL GROWN-UP MAN. /REGINALD/ THIS IS THE	KIND	OF THING, YOU KNOW-- (HELPLESSLY) WELL, THERE IT IS!
MTH4 II (176)	FRIEND THE ENVOY. AS YOU ARE SUPERIOR TO THAT	KIND	OF THING, YOU MAY CONSULT ME NOW. (SHE LEADS THE WAY
KING I (209)	LET IT PASS, MR ROWLEY. THIS PAINTER HAS ONE	KIND	OF UNDERSTANDING: I HAVE ANOTHER. THERE IS ONLY ONE
PYGM II (235)	HAVE TRUSTED ME WITH IT, GOVERNOR. SHE'S THAT	KIND	OF WOMAN: YOU KNOW. I HAD TO GIVE THE BOY A PENNY AFORE
TRFL (83)	WISDOM, OR THEIR FIGURES CHARACTERLESS; FOR THIS	KIND	OF WORK WOULD BE UNBEARABLE IF IT ADDED DEFICIENCY TO
NEVR IV (287)	(SHAKING HIS HEAD) OH NO, MAAM. IT'S VERY	KIND	OF YOU: VERY LADYLIKE AND AFFABLE INDEED, MAAM; BUT I
MRS I (182)	A PAPER KNIFE AMONG ITS PENDANTS). /PRAED/ VERY	KIND	OF YOU INDEED, MISS WARREN. (SHE SHUTS THE GATE WITH A
MTH2 (47)	DAUGHTER. /SAVVY/ (NOT DARING TO APPROACH) VERY	KIND	OF YOU TO COME. JOYCE BURGE STANDS FAST AND SAYS
AUGS (280)	HAND) GOODBYE. GOODBYE. SO SORRY TO LOSE YOU.	KIND	OF YOU TO COME; BUT THERE WAS NO REAL DANGER. YOU SEE,
FANY PROLOG (266)	/SAVOYARD/ MR FLAWNER BANNAL. /THE COUNT/ VERY	KIND	OF YOU TO COME, MR BANNAL. /BANNAL/ DONT MENTION IT.
MTH5 (256)	AFRAID WE DO NOT QUITE SUCCEED. /STREPHON/ VERY	KIND	OF YOU TO COME AT ALL AND TALK TO US, I'M SURE.
JOAN EPILOG (162)	BEAR NO MALICE, MY LORD. /WARWICK/ JUST SO. VERY	KIND	OF YOU TO MEET ME IN THAT WAY: A TOUCH OF TRUE
FANY I (283)	STANDING UP) DONT MENTION IT. I'M SURE IT'S MOST	KIND	OF YOU TO RECEIVE ME AT ALL. /MRS GILBEY/ I MUST GO OFF
FANY PROLOG (267)	AFRAID. EVERY NUANCE IS PERFECT. /FANNY/ IT'S SO	KIND	OF YOU TO SAY SO, MR TROTTER, BUT THAT ISNT WHATS THE
PYGM V (277)	UNHAPPY IF YOU FORGOT ME. /PICKERING/ IT'S VERY	KIND	OF YOU TO SAY SO, MISS DOOLITTLE. /LIZA/ IT'S NOT
GETT (291)	MY DEAR BOXER! /HOTCHKISS/ (DELIGHTED) HOW	KIND	OF YOU TO SAY SO, GENERAL! YOURE QUITE RIGHT: I AM A
MTH2 (55)	LEADER OF THE LIBERAL PARTY. HOWEVER, IT IS VERY	KIND	OF YOU TO TAKE IT OFF MY HANDS, IF THE PARTY WILL LET
MRS III (228)	FROM THE MONEY POINT OF VIEW. /VIVIE/ IT'S VERY	KIND	OF YOU TO TELL ME ALL THIS. /CROFTS/ OH WELL, COME,
PHIL I (86)	/CRAVEN/ (WITH MILITARY AFFECTATION) IT'S VERY	KIND	OF YOU TO TRY TO KEEP UP MY SPIRITS BY MAKING LIGHT OF
DEVL III (51)	/RICHARD/ MRS ANDERSON: THIS VISIT IS VERY	KIND	OF YOU. AND HOW ARE YOU AFTER LAST NIGHT? I HAD TO

SIM PRO,3, (32)	IT IS A CHRISTIAN FACE. /THE PRIEST/ IT IS VERY	KIND	OF YOU. I WILL READ THE TRACT WITH THE GREATEST
CURE (233)	DO. WHAT AN ADVERTISEMENT! IT WILL BE REALLY	KIND	OF YOU. (SHE GOES BACK TO THE KEYBOARD AND SITS DOWN
SUPR IV (150)	ROBINSON. /HECTOR/ I THANK YOU, TOO. IT'S VERY	KIND	OF YOU. MY FATHER KNOWS NO BETTER. /MALONE/ (FURIOUSLY
JITT II (34)	HER HANDKERCHIEF) THANK YOU. I'M SURE IT'S VERY	KIND	OF YOU. /LENKHEIM/ (CLEARING HIS THROAT AND SNIFFING)
MILL IV (194)	DAMAGED LIMBS ALONG THE COUCH) WELL, IT'S MOST	KIND	OF YOU; AND I REALLY CANT STAND ANY LONGER. BUT I DONT
LION II (128)	WHEN HE GOES OFF DUTY. /ANDROCLES/ NO: IT'S VERY	KIND	OF YOU; BUT I FEEL I CANT SAVE MYSELF THAT WAY. /THE
JITT III (74)	(THE TWO WOMEN SPRING UP IN DISMAY). THATS VERY	KIND	OF YOU, EDITH, AND VERY KIND OF JITTA TO INCLUDE ME IN
SUPR II (61)	(GRATEFULLY) IT'S VERY THOUGHTFUL AND VERY	KIND	OF YOU, JACK, TO OFFER ME THIS LOVELY HOLIDAY,
MTH2 (55)	NOBODY DOUBTED THAT YOU MEANT WELL. /BURGE/ VERY	KIND	OF YOU, LUBIN. LET ME REMARK THAT YOU CANNOT LEAD A
CAPT I (219)	CAM AN TEOLL YER. /RANKIN/ THANK YOU. ITS VERRA	KIND	OF YOU, MR DRINKWOTTER. /DRINKWATER/ DOWNT MENTION IT,
JITT I (12)	CARE NEVER TO SEE HER. /THE GENTLEMAN/ THATS VERY	KIND	OF YOU, MRS BILLITER. (HE RISES TO GO TO THE TABLE).
NEVR II (250)	ON THE BEACH HERE. /WAITER/ (WITH EMOTION) VERY	KIND	OF YOU, SIR, TO PUT IT AS IF IT WAS NOT A COMPLIMENT
2TRU I (37)	ELDERLY LADY/ (WHISPERING) I WILL INDEED. HOW	KIND	OF YOU! YOU WILL LET ME KNOW IF ANYTHING-- /THE NURSE/
MILL IV (199)	CHURCH AND CHAPEL, EVERY INSTITUTION OF EVERY	KIND	ON EARTH IS BUSY FROM MORNING TO NIGHT TRYING TO BLEED
WIDO III (54)	AN OLD FRIEND OF OURS. /LICKCHEESE/ AND A	KIND	ONE TO ME. I HOPE I SEE YOU WELL, MISS BLANCHE.
CAPT NOTES (301)	SOFT CRUEL HEARTS AND STRIKE FIRE FROM THE HARD	KIND	ONES. HE HANDLES THE OTHER LETHAL WEAPONS AS FAMILIARLY
MIS. PREFACE(71)	BEGUN IN BOY SCOUTING AND EXCURSIONS OF ONE	KIND	OR ANOTHER. THE DISCOVERY THAT ANYTHING, EVEN SCHOOL
MIS. (195)	TO MARRY ONE ANOTHER BY CIRCUMSTANCES OF ONE	KIND	OR ANOTHER; AND HE ASSURES ME THAT IF MARRIAGES WERE
GETT SD(260)	HIS TONE ALWAYS IMPLIES THAT HE DOES IT WITH YOUR	KIND	PERMISSION. WITHAL BY NO MEANS SERVILE: RATHER GALLANT
PYGM EPILOG (296)	TWO MONTHS. THE RESULT WAS A CONVERSION OF A	KIND	QUITE COMMON TODAY. A MODERN ACTS OF THE APOSTLES WOULD
SIM I (43)	AND PROFFERS HER HAND)! /THE CLERGYMAN/ MOST	KIND	-- ER. (HE SHAKES). LADY FARWATERS SITS DOWN IN THE
HART III (138)	/MANGAN/ (SNIFFING AND WIPING HIS EYES) IT ISNT	KIND	-- (HIS EMOTION CHOKES HIM). /LADY UTTERWORD/ YOU ARE
NEVR I (210)	ER-- IF YOU DONT MIND-- I MEAN IF YOU WILL BE SO	KIND	-- (TO THE PARLORMAID, TESTILY) WHAT IS IT? /THE
WIDO II (36)	BEEN DISAGREEABLE? /TRENCH/ NO: HE HAS BEEN VERY	KIND	-- TO ME, AT LEAST. IT'S NOT THAT. IT'S NOTHING YOU CAN
PHIL II (122)	YOU ARE TOO KIND. /GRACE/ IT IS YOU WHO ARE TOO	KIND	-- TO YOUR PATIENTS. YOU SACRIFICE YOURSELF. HAVE A
FANY PROLOG (269)	WAY FOR REPERTORY THEATRES OF THE MOST SUPERIOR	KIND	-- YOU KNOW THE KIND OF PLAYS I MEAN? /TROTTER/ (
MILL IV (194)	DOES. /ADRIAN/ BUT I DO. YOU ARE MOST	KIND	; BUT I CANNOT CLAIM THE PRIVILEGE OF A FRIEND AND AT
BULL IV (149)	THE SHOCK OFF? /BROADBENT/ YOURE ALL REALLY TOO	KIND	; BUT THE SHOCK HAS QUITE PASSED OFF. /DORAN/ (
SUPR I (45)	SAKE, FORGIVE US. /VIOLET/ YES: ANN HAS BEEN	KIND	; BUT THEN ANN KNEW. /TANNER/ (WITH A DESPERATE
PHIL I (72)	FROM THE PIANO, SAYING) NO, MY DEAR: IVE BEEN	KIND	; IVE BEEN FRANK; IVE BEEN EVERYTHING THAT A
MIS. PREFACE(80)	ABSOLUTELY WITHOUT THE SMALLEST FRICTION OF ANY	KIND	; YET WHEN HER DEATH SET ME THINKING CURIOUSLY ABOUT
FANY PROLOG (269)	US: HE WOULD FORGIVE ME FOR ANYTHING OF THAT	KIND	SOONER OR LATER; BUT HE NEVER GIVES WAY ON A POINT OF
MRS PREFACE(156)	SIMPLY THE PRETTY, DAINTY KIND: THAT IS, THE ONLY	KIND	THAT GETS THE CHANCE OF ACTING ON SUCH REASONING. READ
2TRU PREFACE(8)	ME MORE UNHAPPY THAN ANYTHING ELSE OF AN ACCEPTED	KIND	THAT I CAN IMAGINE. FOR, JUST AS THE BEAN-FEASTER CAN
DOCT I (83)	LADY. I THINK HE OUGHT TO SEE HER. SHE'S JUST THE	KIND	THAT PUTS HIM IN A GOOD TEMPER. (SHE DUSTS REDPENNY'S
ROCK PREFACE(162)	PROVIDED THEY OBSERVE A FEW CONDITIONS OF THIS	KIND	THEY ARE FREE TO ENTER UPON A SERIES OF QUITE
CAPT II (262)	SHOULDER) OH NO. I AM SURE YOU HAVE DONE LOTS OF	KIND	THINGS AND BRAVE THINGS, IF YOU COULD ONLY RECOLLECT
NEVR III (278)	THE OTHER SIDE OF IT! THINK OF THE PEOPLE WHO DO	KIND	THINGS IN AN UNKIND WAY! PEOPLE WHOSE TOUCH HURTS,
METH PREFACE(R34)	OF A QUITE SIMPLE, STRAIGHTFORWARD, AND PROPER	KIND	TO ASCERTAIN WHETHER THE EXPRESSION OF ATHEISTIC
ARMS III (61)	CUSTOM IN BULGARIA TO ALLOW INVITATIONS OF THAT	KIND	TO BE TRIFLED WITH. /BLUNTSCHLI/ (WARMLY) POOH! DONT
KING II (233)	BARBARA THAT THE PROTESTANT WIFE WOULD NOT BE SO	KIND	TO HER AS YOU ARE, AND WOULD HAVE HER OUT OF THE
SUPR III (134)	AND COURTEOUS TO MEN AS YOUR DAUGHTER HERE WAS	KIND	TO HER PET CATS AND DOGS; BUT SUCH KINDNESS IS A DENIAL
SUPR I (29)	YOU TO GO TO VIOLET AT ONCE AND BE PARTICULARLY	KIND	TO HER. /ANN/ I HAVE SEEN HER, JACK. AND I AM SORRY TO
6CAL (105)	KING/ HEAR THAT, DEAREST: HE CALLS THEE LASS. BE	KIND	TO HIM. HE IS ONLY A POOR OLD CUR WHO HAS LOST HALF HIS
SUPR II SD(61)	HIS FAULT, AND MAKE A POINT OF BEING SPECIALLY	KIND	TO HIM. HIS CHIVALROUS MANNERS TO WOMEN, AND HIS
NEVR IV (283)	HEARD BY CRAMPTON). THERE HE IS, MISS CLANDON. BE	KIND	TO HIM. I'LL LEAVE YOU WITH HIM FOR A MOMENT. (HE GOES
JOAN 6 (122)	PIOUS PETER. /THE PAGE/ NO, MY LORD. I SHALL BE	KIND	TO HIM, BECAUSE, WHEN THE MAID IS BROUGHT IN, PIOUS
MIS. (168)	JUST AT THIS MOMENT; BUT IVE NO DOUBT SHE WAS	KIND	TO ME AND WE WERE HAPPY TOGETHER. IF YOU HAVE A WORD TO
SUPR I (20)	WHO HAS MADE ALL THE DIFFICULTY. COME, JACK! BE	KIND	TO ME IN MY SORROW. YOU DONT REFUSE TO ACCEPT ME AS
GENV II (63)	EXCITED ABOUT IT. (TO THE SECRETARY) YOU WERE SO	KIND	TO ME JUST NOW THAT I THOUGHT YOU HAD A RIGHT TO KNOW
SIM I (48)	I BECAME THE IDDY. DO PLEASE CALL ME THAT, AND BE	KIND	TO ME. I AM WEAKMINDED AND LOSE MY HEAD VERY EASILY;
SIM I (48)	KNOW I AM NO CATCH FOR MAYA. STILL, SHE WAS VERY	KIND	TO ME. IN FACT-- BUT PERHAPS I OUGHTNT TO TELL YOU
FANY II (287)	THIS IS MONSIEUR DUVALLET, WHO HAS BEEN EXTREMELY	KIND	TO ME. MONSIEUR DUVALLET: MY MOTHER. (DUVALLET BOWS).
BULL IV (165)	WHEN YOU FOUND ME HERE THAT TIME, I LET YOU BE	KIND	TO ME, AND CRIED IN YOUR ARMS, BECAUSE I WAS TOO
SUPR I (12)	YOUR NECK. /OCTAVIUS/ THIS SORT OF TALK IS NOT	KIND	TO ME, JACK. /TANNER/ (RISING AND GOING TO OCTAVIUS TO
PYGM V (288)	HAD A FINER EAR THAN YOU. AND I CAN BE CIVIL AND	KIND	TO PEOPLE, WHICH IS MORE THAN YOU CAN. AHA! THATS DONE
DOCT IV (165)	THAT, RIDGEON. THAT WAS GOOD. JENNIFER, DEAR: BE	KIND	TO RIDGEON ALWAYS; BECAUSE HE WAS THE LAST MAN WHO
BULL IV (160)	I'M AFRAID I'M BORING YOU, NORA, THOUGH YOURE TOO	KIND	TO SAY SO. /NORA/ ARE YOU WANTING TO GET BACK TO
PRES (147)	NOT COMPARE A RISK OF THAT HARMLESS DOMESTIC	KIND	TO THE FEARFUL RISKS OF THE BATTLEFIELD. /MRS FARRELL/
CAND I (98)	EITHER OF US WILL BE ANYTHING BUT PATIENT AND	KIND	TO THE OTHER, WHATEVER WE MAY HAVE TO SAY. /MARCHBANKS/
BULL PREFACE(69)	WHO GAVE WARNINGS OR INFORMATION OF ANY HELPFUL	KIND	TO THEM WERE MERCILESSLY EXECUTED WITHOUT PRIVILEGE OF
PYGM V (280)	/PICKERING/ (SQUEEZING ELIZA'S ELBOW GENTLY) BE	KIND	TO THEM, ELIZA. MAKE THE BEST OF IT. /LIZA/ (FORCING A
BULL PREFACE(28)	ARE OFTEN TRADITIONALLY FOND OF NEGROES AND	KIND	TO THEM, WITH SUBSTANTIAL RETURNS IN HUMBLE AFFECTION;
PYGM II (224)	OVER ANYONE. ALL I PROPOSE IS THAT WE SHOULD BE	KIND	TO THIS POOR GIRL. WE MUST HELP HER TO PREPARE AND FIT
MIS. PREFACE(63)	THEMSELVES AND FEND FOR THEMSELVES, BUT ARE TOO	KIND	TO THROW THEM ON THEIR OWN RESOURCES WITH THE FEROCITY
SIM PRO,3, (31)	THESE HEATHEN IDOLATERS VERY TRYING. IS IT REALLY	KIND	TO TREAT THEM ACCORDING TO THEIR FOLLY INSTEAD OF TO
LIED (191)	GUESTS HERE: HE IS AN HONORABLE MAN: HE HAS BEEN	KIND	TO US; HE HAS PERHAPS LOVED YOU AS WELL AS HIS PROSAIC
PHIL II (118)	DR PARAMORE. CHEER UP. YOUVE BEEN MOST	KIND	TO US; AND YOUVE DONE PAPA A LOT OF GOOD. /PARAMORE/ (
KING I (177)	I CAN NEVER BE UNFAITHFUL. /NELL/ YES: YOU ARE	KIND	TO US; BUT WE ARE NOTHING TO YOU. (SIGHING) I WOULD
SUPR III (134)	ALSO OUTSIDE THE MORAL WORLD. THIS DON JUAN WAS	KIND	TO WOMEN AND COURTEOUS TO MEN AS YOUR DAUGHTER HERE WAS
DEVL I (17)	WE KNOW WHO YOU ARE; BUT WE ARE WILLING TO BE	KIND	TO YOU IF YOU ARE A GOOD GIRL AND DESERVE IT. WE ARE
MRS PREFACE(156)	WILL REASON IN THIS WAY. BUT ALAS! THAT CERTAIN	KIND	TURNS OUT ON INQUIRY TO BE SIMPLY THE PRETTY, DAINTY
PYGM EPILOG (297)	(FOR NOBODY EVER FACES UNPLEASANT TRUTHS OF THIS	KIND	UNTIL THE POSSIBILITY OF A WAY OUT DAWNS ON THEM) SHE
GETT PREFACE(255)	IT IS IMPOSSIBLE TO PUSH RATIONAL MEASURES OF ANY	KIND	VERY FAR: THE WOLF AT THE DOOR WILL COMPEL US TO LIVE
NEVR III (277)	YOUR EYES OPENED. THERE WE DO UNKIND THINGS IN A	KIND	WAY: WE SAY BITTER THINGS IN A SWEET VOICE: WE ALWAYS
GETT (357)	/HOTCHKISS/ SINCE YOU PUT IT IN THAT MORE THAN	KIND	WAY, POLLY, ABSOLUTELY NOTHING. /MRS GEORGE/ HM! LIKE
OVER PREFACE(161)	CONSIDERED A HERESIARCH OF THE MOST EXTRAVAGANT	KIND	WHEN I EXPRESSED MY OPINION, AT THE OUTSET OF MY CAREER
DOCT PREFACE(25)	INOCULATION. YET THIS IS THE ONLY STUFF OF THE	KIND	WHICH IS PREPARED AND SUPPLIED EVEN IN STATE
PPP SD(193)	SIDE IS A CHEST OF DRAWERS OF THAT DISASTROUS	KIND	WHICH, RECALCITRANT TO THE OPENER UNTIL SHE IS PROVOKED
HART I (53)	IS MAZZINI DUNN. MAZZINI WAS A CELEBRITY OF SOME	KIND	WHO KNEW ELLIE'S GRANDPARENTS. THEY WERE BOTH POETS,
DOCT III (151)	DOWN A TUBE OF SOME REALLY STIFF ANTI-TOXIN. ANY	KIND	WILL DO. DONT FORGET. GOODBYE, COLLY. (HE GOES OUT).
MRS PREFACE(156)	WILL TELL YOU THAT ONLY GIRLS OF A CERTAIN	KIND	WILL REASON IN THIS WAY. BUT ALAS! THAT CERTAIN KIND
MILL PREFACE(130)	AND UNIVERSITY EDUCATION EQUIPS ARMIES OF THIS	KIND	WITH APPROPRIATE STAFFS OF OFFICERS. WHEN BOTH ARE
OVER (172)	YOU CALL BEING HORRID. WITH A BEAUTIFUL, WITTY,	KIND	WOMAN, THERES NO TIME FOR SUCH FOLLIES. IT'S SO
APPL PREFACE(187)	A SHILLING TO OUR LITTLE FLOWER SHOW, HAS A	KIND	WORD FOR THE CHILDREN WHEN HE PASSES, AND IS A VICTIM
SUPR II (58)	KINDEST WAY, TOO. /ANN/ (GOING TO OCTAVIUS) HOW	KIND	YOU ARE, TAVY! HOW HELPFUL! HOW WELL YOU UNDERSTAND!
CLEO V SD(199)	IN BLACK, WITHOUT ORNAMENTS OR DECORATION OF ANY	KIND	, AND THUS MAKING A STRIKING FIGURE AMONG THE
BARB PREFACE(230)	HIS DEED, FIRST BY GETTING PUNISHED FOR IT IN	KIND	, AND, WHEN THAT RELIEF IS DENIED HIM, BY FINING
SUPR IV (157)	HIS SELF-CONTROL) I KNOW YOU MEAN TO BE	KIND	, ANN. JACK HAS PERSUADED YOU THAT CYNICISM IS A GOOD
ROCK PREFACE(161)	FOR INSTANT EXEMPLARY EXTERMINATIONS OF THIS	KIND	, ANY MORE THAN FOR THE GROWING URGENCY OF HOW TO
CATH 1 (166)	ME. TOO DRUNK TO SPEAK PROPLY. IF YOU WOULD BE SO	KIND	, DARLING. GREEN BORLE. (EDSTASTON, STILL SUSPICIOUS,
POSN PREFACE(368)	AS CASUAL SERVANTS OF A SPECIALLY DISORDERLY	KIND	, DEMANDED, NOT THE ABOLITION OF THE INSTITUTION, BUT
POSN PREFACE(412)	CENSORSHIP OF A MORE ENLIGHTENED AND INDEPENDENT	KIND	, EXERCISED BY THE MOST EMINENT AVAILABLE AUTHORITIES,
BULL PREFACE(29)	TO ANY IRISHMAN OF HIS ACQUAINTANCE, AND BE	KIND	, HOSPITABLE, AND SERVICEABLE IN HIS INTERCOURSE WITH
SUPR III (80)	MISCONCEPTION) OH NO, NO, NO: NOTHING OF THE	KIND	, I ASSURE YOU. WE NATURALLY HAVE MODERN VIEWS AS TO
LION PROL,SD(105)	HIS ARMS AND LEGS AND BACK, THOUGH WIRY OF THEIR	KIND	, LOOK SHRIVELLED AND STARVED. HE CARRIES A BIG BUNDLE,
AUGS (282)	IN MY WALLET, . . . /AUGUSTUS/ NOTHING OF THE	KIND	, MADAM. I HAVE IT HERE IN MY POCKET. (HE TAKES THE
6CAL (95)	/THE KING/ DO I NOT KNOW IT? HAVE I NOT BEEN	KIND	, MAGNANIMOUS? HAVE I NOT DONE ALL THAT CHRISTIAN
BULL II (108)	ON THE SOFA IN THE PARLOR. /BROADBENT/ YOURE VERY	KIND	, MISS DOYLE; BUT REALLY I'M ASHAMED TO GIVE YOU SO
GENV I (43)	HELP: YOU WILL SYMPATHIZE. /RUSSIAN/ YOU ARE VERY	KIND	, MY LORD: I AM QUITE AT YOUR SERVICE. /BISHOP/ (
OVER PREFACE(155)	TO ENGAGE IN UNCONVENTIONAL ADVENTURES OF ANY	KIND	, NOT ONLY BECAUSE THEY HAVE NEITHER TIME NOR
SUPR III (129)	ONLY OBTUSE; NOT SELF-RESPECTING, ONLY VAIN; NOT	KIND	, ONLY SENTIMENTAL; NOT SOCIAL, ONLY GREGARIOUS; NOT
MIS. PREFACE(44)	WORDS IT MUST NOT PERSECUTE DOCTRINES OF ANY	KIND	, OR WHAT IS CALLED BAD TASTE, AND MUST INSIST ON ALL
DOCT IV (158)	/MRS DUBEDAT/ (COMFORTED AND TOUCHED) YOU ARE SO	KIND	, SIR RALPH, BUT DONT GIVE ME MUCH HOPE OR I SHALL CRY;
BULL III (139)	THE BETTER FOR IT. /HODSON/ I'M SURE YOURE VERY	KIND	, SIR; BUT IT DONT SEEM TO MATTER TO ME WHETHER THEY
PRES (149)	AND IT GEV ME THE UMP. I SHOULD TAKE IT VERY	KIND	, SIR, IF YOUD LET ME OFF THE DRILL AND LET ME SHAVE
GETT SD(293)	A YOUNG GENTLEMAN WITH GOOD LOOKS OF THE SERIOUS	KIND	, SOMEWHAT CAREWORN BY AN EXACTING CONSCIENCE, AND JUST

2TRU II (63) THERES A DEAR. /THE PATIENT/ DO NOTHING OF THE KIND , SWEETIE. LET HIM WAIT ON HIMSELF. /THE COUNTESS/ (
METH PREFACE(R20) HAVE SINCE SURVIVED SIMPLY BY REPRODUCING THEIR KIND , THEN YOU WERE NOT AN EVOLUTIONIST. IF YOU BELIEVED,
MIS. PREFACE(61) SCHOOLROOM OR NURSERY. THE CHILD IS TAUGHT TO BE KIND , TO BE RESPECTFUL, TO BE QUIET; NOT TO ANSWER BACK, TO
NEVR IV (283) YOURE GOING TO MAKE IMPOSSIBLE CONDITIONS OF THIS KIND , WE MAY AS WELL GO BACK HOME AT ONCE. /CRAMPTON/ BUT
CLEO I (114) DEATH; BUT YOU SHALL ALWAYS BE MY KING: MY NICE, KIND , WISE, GOOD OLD KING. /CAESAR/ OH, MY WRINKLES, MY
SUPR IV (155) CALL ON HIM ON THE WAY. /MALONE/ IF YOULL BE SO KIND , YES. AND MAY I ASK WHO-- /TANNER/ MR ROEBUCK RAMSDEN,

KINDER

CATH 4 (193) ME. /CATHERINE/ WELL, JUST TO SHEW YOU HOW MUCH KINDER A RUSSIAN SAVAGE CAN BE THAN AN ENGLISH ONE (THOUGH
2TRU I (30) I KNOW YOU HAVE, DOCTOR: NOBODY COULD HAVE BEEN KINDER . BUT IT REALLY DID NOT DO HER ANY GOOD. SHE GOT
KING I (190) SOMETIMES ASK MYSELF WHETHER IT WOULD NOT BE FAR KINDER OF ME TO PUSH THE EXCLUSION BILL THROUGH AND SAVE YOU
DOCT PREFACE(15) AND A BETTER DRAINED AND VENTILATED HOUSE. IT IS KINDER TO GIVE HIM A BOTTLE OF SOMETHING ALMOST AS CHEAP AS
JITT II (38) MOTHER AS YOU LOVED YOUR FATHER, YOU WOULD BE KINDER TO HER. YOU THINK OF HIM AS A MAN WHOSE WIFE HAS
PYGM EPILOG (302) COLONEL HAS TO ASK HER FROM TIME TO TIME TO BE KINDER TO HIGGINS; AND IT IS THE ONLY REQUEST OF HIS THAT
POSN PREFACE(428) IF RESORT TO HIM IS TO BE OPTIONAL. LET ME BE KINDER TO HIM THAN HE HAS BEEN TO ME, AND UNCOVER FOR HIM
ROCK I (231) SET OF TEETH I THINK IT IS BETTER FOR HIM, AND KINDER TO HIM, TO PULL THEM ALL OUT AND REPLACE THEM WITH A
MILL PREFACE(118) TWIST) AND COULD NOT BE ADMINISTERED IN ANY KINDER WAY WITHOUT WEAKENING THE WILLINGNESS OF ITS

KINDERGARTEN

FABL PREFACE(72) THIS FORMULA TO ALL PARENTS, NURSES, AND KINDERGARTEN TEACHERS, AS IT EFFECTS ITS PURPOSE AND THEN
MIS. PREFACE(24) CURE. OR YOU CAN BUY A CHEAPER PLATE INSCRIBED KINDERGARTEN , AND IMAGINE, OR LEAVE OTHERS TO IMAGINE, THAT

KINDEST

SUPR II (57) MISUNDERSTAND, JACK. ANN IS SHEWING YOU THE KINDEST CONSIDERATION, EVEN AT THE COST OF DECEIVING YOU.
CATH 4 (193) DARLING LITTLE MOTHER: YOU HAVE A KIND HEART, THE KINDEST IN EUROPE. HAVE PITY, HAVE MERCY. I LOVE YOU. (
KING I (215) STUPIDEST. NELLY IS THE WITTIEST: SHE IS ALSO THE KINDEST . LOUISE IS THE LOVELIEST AND CLEVEREST. SHE IS ALSO
KING I (173) YOU ARE THE WISEST MAN IN ENGLAND, AND THE KINDEST . /CHARLES/ AND THE BUSIEST, NELLY. COME. HE HAS
JITT PREFACE(4) MY PLAYS WERE NOT PLAYS, AND URGING ME, IN THE KINDEST SPIRIT, TO CEASE MY VAIN EFFORTS TO ENTER A
SUPR II (58) HER DUTY, JACK; AND YOU KNOW IT. DOING IT IN THE KINDEST WAY, TOO. /ANN/ (GOING TO OCTAVIUS) HOW KIND YOU

KINDLE

CAND I (100) FEELING AND EUGENE'S OBDURACY) THEN HELP TO KINDLE IT IN THEM-- IN ME-- NOT TO EXTINGUISH IT. IN THE

KINDLED

CAPT NOTES (302) WITH MY MOTHER. HER INTEREST WAS INSTANTLY KINDLED ; AND THE FOLLOWING CONVERSATION ENSUED. " WHO IS

KINDLES

MTH4 I (157) I APPROACH THIS SUBJECT THE DIVINE SPARK IN ME KINDLES AND GLOWS, THE CORRUPTIBLE BECOMES INCORRUPTIBLE,

KINDLIER

BARB II (283) SELP ME GAWD IF AW DOWNT! /BARBARA/ (A SHADE KINDLIER , IF POSSIBLE) IT'S NO USE, BILL. SHE'S GOT ANOTHER

KINDLINESS

SUPR HANDBOK(207) THE FEAR OF REVOLT; AND THERE ARE THE EFFECTS OF KINDLINESS AND AFFECTION. LET IT BE REPEATED THEREFORE THAT
BULL PREFACE(55) WALRUS PLEDGES HIMSELF IN EVERY CASE FOR THE KINDLINESS OF THE OFFICIAL CARPENTER. ONE MAN WAS ACTUALLY
BULL PREFACE(28) OF AUTHENTIC EXAMPLES OF THE CONCURRENCE OF HUMAN KINDLINESS WITH POLITICAL RANCOR. SLAVES AND SCHOOLBOYS
ANNA (299) IN YOUR ILLUSIONS ABOUT US? (SHE SHAKES OFF HER KINDLINESS , AND SITS DOWN IN HIS CHAIR) NOW TELL ME, WHAT
MIS. PREFACE(16) AFFECTION, AS DISTINGUISHED FROM SIMPLE KINDLINESS , MAY OR MAY NOT EXIST: WHEN IT DOES IT EITHER
DOCT I SD(85) HIS COMBINATION OF SOFT MANNERS AND RESPONSIVE KINDLINESS , WITH A CERTAIN UNSEIZABLE RESERVE AND A

KINDLING

MTH4 I (162) TO THE HAND OF THE NEXT, EACH GENERATION KINDLING IT TO A BRIGHTER, PROUDER FLAME. THUS EACH
DOCT PREFACE(16) MAKESHIFTS OF HOMES WHERE EVEN BUNDLES OF KINDLING WOOD ARE LUXURIES TO BE ANXIOUSLY ECONOMIZED. THE

KINDLY

JOAN 6 (133) PALE TODAY. ARE YOU NOT WELL? /JOAN/ THANK YOU KINDLY : I AM WELL ENOUGH. BUT THE BISHOP SENT ME SOME CARP;
BULL II (109) TO TEA? /FATHER DEMPSEY/ NOT TO-NIGHT, THANK YOU KINDLY : I HAVE BUSINESS TO DO AT HOME. (HE TURNS TO GO,
BARB PREFACE(237) THE SPLENDOR, THE HAPPINESS, THE ATMOSPHERE OF KINDLY ADMIRATION SURROUNDING THE YOUNG COUPLE, AND THE
DEVL III (58) TOO KEENLY TO PRESUME SO FAR. IF YOU WILL KINDLY ALLOW ME, I WILL SIT AT THE FEET OF GAMALIEL. (HE
CAPT III (282) YOUR COMPLIMENTS TO LEDDY CEECILY, AND WOULD SHE KINDLY ALLOW THE PRISONERS TO COME IN, AS YOU WERE ANXIOUS
HART III (141) TO ME. /MAZZINI/ BUT WHAT A VERY NATURAL AND KINDLY AND CHARMING HUMAN FEELING, LADY UTTERWORD! /LADY
NEVR I SD(208) AFFECTIONS. HER VOICE AND WAYS ARE ENTIRELY KINDLY AND HUMANE; AND SHE LENDS HERSELF CONSCIENTIOUSLY TO
MTH4 I (161) MAY SAY, IMAGINATION WITHOUT MICROSCOPES WAS KINDLY AND OFTEN COURAGEOUS, BECAUSE IT WORKED ON THINGS OF
PHIL II (129) IF YOULL ONLY GIVE HIM TIME. YOU KNOW YOURE A KINDLY AND SENSIBLE MAN AS WELL AS A DEUCEDLY CLEVER ONE,
LION PREFACE(66) IT? IT WOULD HAVE BEEN FAR EASIER TO KILL HIM AS KINDLY AS POSSIBLE, OR TO LABEL HIM AND LEAVE HIM TO HIS
BULL IV (149) NOT A MAN IN THE TOWN WOULD SAY LESS (MURMURS OF KINDLY ASSENT). WONT YOU COME DOWN TO DOOLAN'S AND HAVE A
MIS. PREFACE(84) MUTUAL HELP AND CONSOLATION AS ANY OTHER FORM OF KINDLY ASSOCIATION CULTIVATES THEM; BUT THE ADDITION OF A
CATH 4 (196) /EDSTASTON/ (FOLLOWING THE EMPRESS AND RESUMING KINDLY BUT JUDICIALLY) AFTER ALL, THOUGH YOUR MAJESTY IS OF
JOAN 5 (111) THEN, OH THEN -- /DUNOIS/ (INTERRUPTING HER KINDLY BUT NOT SYMPATHETICALLY) THEN, JOAN, WE SHALL HEAR
LION II (129) DONT SAY THAT. THIS IS DREADFUL. YOU MEAN SO KINDLY BY ME THAT IT SEEMS QUITE HORRIBLE TO DISOBLIGE YOU.
NEVR III (277) ATTENTIONS AND PAYING INSINCERE COMPLIMENTS IN A KINDLY CHARMING WAY. IF YOU LIVED IN LONDON, WHERE THE WHOLE
NEVR IV (294) CLANDON/ THIS IS MR BOHUN, DOLLY, WHO HAS VERY KINDLY COME TO HELP US THIS EVENING. /DOLLY/ OH, THEN HE
DEVL I (14) TO BE CONSOLED AND EDIFIED, AND TO APPRECIATE THE KINDLY CONDESCENSION OF THE REMARK) YOU ARE NOT GOING TO BE
GETT SD(289) PEOPLE WITH A SWEET FORBEARANCE (IMPLYING A KINDLY CONSIDERATION FOR THEIR STUPIDITY) WHICH INFURIATES
ROCK PREFACE(147) OF EXTERMINATION. KILLING CAN BE CRUELLY OR KINDLY DONE; AND THE DELIBERATE CHOICE OF CRUEL WAYS, AND
GENV IV (124) /JUDGE/ IT IS NOT INTELLIGIBLE TO ME. WILL YOU KINDLY EXPLAIN? /SECRETARY/ THE ORBIT OF THE EARTH IS THE
DEVL II (39) WELL, I'M NOT ASHAMED OF THEM: THANK YOU KINDLY FOR THE APOLOGY. (HE HOLDS OUT HIS HANDS).
CATH 1 (166) EVERYTHING. READ LERRER INCE-INCE-ISTASTANEOUSLY. KINDLY GIVE ME VINEGAR BORLE. GREEN BORLE. ONLY TO SOBER ME.
BARB PREFACE(240) UNNATURAL ABOMINATION UNDER RATIONAL AND KINDLY HUMAN CIRCUMSTANCES. THEN COMES THE CLIMAX OF IRONY
GETT PREFACE(226) WHO, THROUGH TOTAL DISUSE, HAVE LOST THE POWER OF KINDLY HUMAN SPEECH AND CAN ONLY SCOLD AND COMPLAIN: THERE
JITT I SD(11) GOING GREY, VERY DISTINGUISHED IN APPEARANCE AND KINDLY IN MANNER. /MRS BILLITER/ (RETURNING) WHY WILL YOU
FANY PROLOG (266) VERY GREATLY INDEBTED TO YOU, GENTLEMEN, FOR SO KINDLY INDULGING HER WHIM. (THE DRESSING BELL SOUNDS. THE
ARMS III (68) MY LIFE. /PETKOFF/ (EXASPERATED) RAINA: WILL YOU KINDLY INFORM ME, IF I AM NOT ASKING TOO MUCH, WHICH OF
CLEO II SD(120) THE BUSINESS IN HAND IS IN MARKED CONTRAST TO THE KINDLY INTEREST OF CAESAR, WHO LOOKS AT THE SCENE, WHICH IS
HART II (110) GOOD EVENING, LADIES AND GENTLEMEN; AND THANK YOU KINDLY . HE IS HURRYING OUT WHEN HE IS CONFRONTED IN THE
ARMS III (57) A SMOOTH, ELDERLY MANNER) OH NO, SIR: THANK YOU KINDLY . I WAS ONLY SPEAKING TO THIS FOOLISH GIRL ABOUT HER
APPL I (199) OH WELL, COME! THAT WAS FRIENDLY AND KINDLY . IT SHEWS HE HAD SOMETHING INSIDE HIM AFTER ALL.
PYGM II (238) /DOOLITTLE/ NOT ME, GOVERNOR, THANK YOU KINDLY . IVE HEARD ALL THE PREACHERS AND ALL THE PRIME
FANY PROLOG (271) TO BE SINCERE AND SIMPLE, TO BE UNASSUMING AND KINDLY . IVE LIVED A BLAMELESS LIFE. IVE SUPPORTED THE
JITT I (13) PROMISE. /MRS BILLITER/ THANK YOU, SIR. THANK YOU KINDLY . (SHE GOES OUT, CLOSING THE DOOR VERY SOFTLY BEHIND
DOCT PREFACE(19) CASES SCIENTIFICALLY; AND SHOULD FEEL ABOUT THEM KINDLY . LET US SEE WHAT GUARANTEES WE HAVE: FIRST FOR THE
NEVR IV (301) AGAIN TO HER, OFFERING HIS HAND). LET US PART KINDLY . /GLORIA/ (ENORMOUSLY RELIEVED, AND IMMEDIATELY
WIDO II (38) HE OPENS THE DOOR, AND CALLS) MR COKANE: WILL YOU KINDLY JOIN US HERE. /COKANE/ (IN THE CONSERVATORY) COMING,
HART II (108) NO. I'M SORRY TO BE INHOSPITABLE; BUT WILL YOU KINDLY LEAVE THE HOUSE? /THE BURGLAR/ RIGHT. I'LL GO TO THE
LION I (115) THE SAME TIME. WHY WILL YOU NOT CHOOSE RATHER A KINDLY LOVE AND AN HONORABLE ALLIANCE? /LAVINIA/ THEY
MIS. PREFACE(19) CONFUSE YOUR AFFECTIONS; BUT A CONSCIENTIOUS AND KINDLY MEDDLER MAY LITERALLY WORRY YOU OUT OF YOUR SENSES.
BUOY II (20) LEARN NOTHING. /HE/ AND HERE YOU WAIT UNTIL THAT KINDLY NATIVE COMES AND FEEDS YOU, LIKE ELIJAH'S RAVENS.
LION PREFACE(7) FOR DISCUSSION: GROWN MEN AND WOMEN MAY SPEAK KINDLY OF A HARMLESS CREATURE WHO UTTERS AMIABLE SENTIMENTS
DOCT III (147) PATRICK/ WELL, MR DUBEDAT, AS SIR RALPH HAS VERY KINDLY OFFERED TO TAKE CHARGE OF YOUR CASE, AND AS THE TWO
WIDO I (7) THANK YOU, BLANCHE: THIS GENTLEMAN VERY KINDLY OFFERS US HIS TABLE, IF YOU WOULD PREFER IT.
CAPT II (262) (QUITE UNDERSTANDING, AND PUTTING HER HAND KINDLY ON HIS SHOULDER) OH NO. I AM SURE YOU HAVE DONE LOTS
PYGM IV (264) PARTY. BUT THATS ALL OVER NOW. (HE PATS HER KINDLY ON THE SHOULDER. SHE WRITHES). THERES NOTHING MORE TO
CLEO II (121) OF MY LORD THE KING. /CAESAR/ (PATTING PTOLEMY KINDLY ON THE SHOULDER) SO YOU ARE THE KING. DULL WORK AT
BARB I SD(263) SURFACE, A STOUTISH, EASYGOING ELDERLY MAN, WITH KINDLY PATIENT MANNERS, AND AN ENGAGING SIMPLICITY OF
BARB III (339) I HAD MY WILL: NOW I AM A USEFUL, BENEFICENT, KINDLY PERSON. THAT IS THE HISTORY OF MOST SELF-MADE
BARB PREFACE(221) TO RECOGNIZE A MAN OF GENIUS IF SOMEBODY WILL KINDLY POINT HIM OUT TO THEM. HAVING POINTED MYSELF OUT IN
WIDO III (58) LITERY STYLE, AND THATS THE TRUTH; SO MR COKANE KINDLY PUTS IT INTO MY LETTERS AND DRAFT PROSPECTUSES AND

PYGM PREFACE(202)	UNDERRATED SUBJECT TO MAINTAIN SERENE AND	KINDLY	RELATIONS WITH THE MEN WHO UNDERRATE IT, AND WHO KEEP
SIM II (64)	QUARTET, IF IT WANTS TO GIVE ANOTHER CONCERT,	KINDLY	REMOVE ITSELF OUT OF HEARING. /KANCHIN/ SILENCE FOR
BUOY III (30)	DONE I HAVE TO SEE TO IT. /MRS THIRDBORN/ (VERY	KINDLY	) DONT MIND HER, SIR FERDINAND. SHE ALWAYS TALKS THE
CLEO II (131)	YOU ARE WELCOME TO STAY IF YOU WISH. /CAESAR/ (	KINDLY	) GO, MY BOY. I WILL NOT HARM YOU; BUT YOU WILL BE
HART II (95)	MISTAKEN. /MRS HUSHABYE/ (LEANING TOWARDS HIM	KINDLY	) HAVE I BEEN A BEAST? /MAZZINI/ (PULLING HIMSELF
DEVL III (62)	IN A PERFECTLY WORKMANLIKE AND AGREEABLE WAY. (	KINDLY	) LET ME PERSUADE YOU TO BE HANGED, MR ANDERSON?
ARMS I (10)	TO INTIMIDATE RAINA. /THE MAN/ (SINCERELY AND	KINDLY	) NO USE, DEAR: I'M DONE FOR. (FLINGING THE CLOAK TO
ROCK I (225)	NOR ANY OF THE CHILDREN? /THE LADY/ (SMILING	KINDLY	) NO. YOUR DEATH. /SIR ARTHUR/ (RELIEVED) WELL,
CLEO II (121)	SHYLY TO OFFER HIS CHAIR) CAESAR-- /CAESAR/ (	KINDLY	) NO, NO, MY BOY: THAT IS YOUR CHAIR OF STATE. SIT
MRS IV (252)	NOT WANTED. (SHE TURNS TO THE DOOR). /VIVIE/ (	KINDLY	) WONT YOU SHAKE HANDS? /MRS WARREN/ (AFTER LOOKING
2TRU II (58)	MOST CERTAINLY NOT. YOUR INTENTION IS NATURAL AND	KINDLY	; BUT IF YOU TREAT A PRIVATE SOLDIER AS A HUMAN BEING
MIS. PREFACE(23)	" BRINGING UP" CHILDREN. I SHALL BE ASKED WITH	KINDLY	SCORN WHETHER I HAVE HEARD OF FROEBEL AND PESTALOZZI,
CAPT III (284)	COME TO THAT PRESENTLY. MR RAHNKIN: WILL YOU	KINDLY	TAKE UP THE PARABLE? /RANKIN/ ON THE VERY DAY THAT
BARB I (262)	ME TO BE SARCASTIC, CHARLES. ADOLPHUS: WILL YOU	KINDLY	TELL ME WHERE I WAS. /CUSINS/ (SWEETLY) YOU WERE
MRS PREFACE(174)	ONE IS OCCUPIED BY THE DECLARATION OF THE PAPER'S	KINDLY	THEATRE CRITIC, THAT THE PERFORMANCE LEFT HIM "
DEVL III (76)	(TO THE EXECUTIONER IN THE CART-- VERY POLITELY)	KINDLY	UNDO MR DUDGEON. THE EXECUTIONER TAKES THE ROPE FROM
FOUN (214)	TIMID WARD OF THE COURT FEELS AT THE SOUND OF HIS	KINDLY	VOICE AND THE ENCOURAGING BEAM, TWINKLING WITH HUMOR,
BULL II SD(107)	ENERGY OR GRIP, PLACID WITHOUT TRANQUILLITY,	KINDLY	WITHOUT CONCERN FOR OTHERS: INDEED WITHOUT MUCH
JITT I (12)	ALL: I KNOW HOW ANXIOUS YOU ARE ABOUT ME, AND HOW	KINDLY	YOU MEAN IT. BUT I AM ALL RIGHT NOW; AND I-- I-- (HE
GETT PREFACE(227)	AS ON A VISIT IN A STRANGE HOUSE, AND AS FRANKLY,	KINDLY	, AND EASILY IN A STRANGE HOUSE AS AT HOME. IN THE
JOAN PREFACE(7)	IS THE DRINKING WATER OF FRANCE ASCETIC), VERY	KINDLY	, AND, THOUGH A BRAVE AND HARDY SOLDIER, UNABLE TO
CAND I (98)	AND PUTS HIS HAND ON HIS SHOULDER STRONGLY AND	KINDLY	, DISREGARDING HIS ATTEMPT TO SHAKE IT OFF). COME:
PYGM II (239)	POUNDS I THINK YOU SAID. /DOOLITTLE/ THANK YOU	KINDLY	, GOVERNOR. /HIGGINS/ YOURE SURE YOU WONT TAKE TEN..
PYGM I (207)	IS FOR YOUR FLOWERS. /THE FLOWER GIRL/ THANK YOU	KINDLY	, LADY. /THE DAUGHTER/ MAKE HER GIVE YOU THE CHANGE.
MIS. (191)	/GUNNER/ (FOLLOWING HER OBEDIENTLY) THANK YOU	KINDLY	, MADAM. (SHE GOES OUT. BEFORE PASSING OUT AFTER
LION PREFACE(70)	MOUNTAINS. IT IS PRECISELY AS PEOPLE BECOME MORE	KINDLY	, MORE CONSCIENTIOUS, MORE READY TO SHOULDER THE
MTH2 (54)	MR BARNABAS? (HE SPEAKS VERY COMFORTABLY AND	KINDLY	, MUCH AS IF HE WERE THE HOST, AND FRANKLYN AN
BULL III (140)	/MATTHEW/ WELL, I'LL BE GOIN. GOOD MORNIN TO YOU	KINDLY	, SIR. /BROADBENT/ YOU HAVE SOME DISTANCE TO GO, MR

KINDNESS

6CAL (95)	CHIVALRY COULD REQUIRE OF ME? AND THEY ABUSE MY	KINDNESS	: IT ONLY ENCOURAGES THEM: THEY DESPISE ME FOR IT.
PHIL I (72)	A LOVERS' QUARREL. (GRACE WINCES). FRANKNESS AND	KINDNESS	: ONE IS AS BAD AS THE OTHER. ESPECIALLY FRANKNESS.
DEVL II (46)	POOR FELLOW! YOU SAID GOODBYE TO HIM IN ALL	KINDNESS	AND CHARITY, JUDITH, I HOPE. /JUDITH/ I KISSED HIM.
MIS. PREFACE(14)	THE CHILD HAS NO DEFENCE IN ANY CASE EXCEPT THE	KINDNESS	AND CONSCIENCE OF THE ADULT; AND THE ADULT HAD
SUPR HANDBOK(207)	EARNESTLY PIOUS PEOPLE, WHO WERE KIND AND GOOD AS	KINDNESS	AND GOODNESS GO. AND WHEN A NEGRO IS DIPPED IN
BARB PREFACE(239)	OF MALICE, THE ONE MAN WHO STILL HAS FAITH IN THE	KINDNESS	AND INTELLIGENCE OF HUMAN NATURE IS THE FULMINATOR,
BULL IV (149)	GLAD IT HAPPENED, BECAUSE IT HAS BROUGHT OUT THE	KINDNESS	AND SYMPATHY OF THE IRISH CHARACTER TO AN EXTENT I
MIS. PREFACE(74)	CLOTHING, LODGING, INSTRUCTION, AND PARENTAL	KINDNESS	FOR THE ASKING. FOR THE MATTER OF THAT, SO SHOULD
MIS. (182)	AND TO DO WHAT IN ME LIES TO PROVE WORTHY OF HIS	KINDNESS	IN GIVING ME ANOTHER CHANCE AND REFRAINING FROM
MIS. (180)	AND TO DO WHAT IN ME LIES TO PROVE WORTHY OF HIS	KINDNESS	IN GIVING ME ANOTHER CHANCE-- /BENTLEY/ " ANOTHER
SUPR III (134)	HERE WAS KIND TO HER PET CATS AND DOGS; BUT SUCH	KINDNESS	IS A DENIAL OF THE EXCLUSIVELY HUMAN CHARACTER OF
CLEO IV (171)	AS GOOD TO HIM. NAY, ASK HIS VERY HORSE! HIS	KINDNESS	IS NOT FOR ANYTHING IN ME: IT IS IN HIS OWN NATURE.
DOCT PREFACE(50)	INTERESTING EXPERIMENT) TO THE SIMPLEST ACT OF	KINDNESS	. AND IN THE LIGHT OF THAT TRUTH IT IS CLEAR THAT
DOCT PREFACE(19)	WE HAVE: FIRST FOR THE SCIENCE, AND THEN FOR THE	KINDNESS	. ARE DOCTORS MEN OF SCIENCE? I PRESUME NOBODY
DOCT PREFACE(30)	NOW DEAL WITH THE MORE PAINFUL SUBJECT OF MEDICAL	KINDNESS	. DOCTORS AND VIVISECTION. THE IMPORTANCE TO OUR
PYGM V (286)	ABOUT? /LIZA/ (MUCH TROUBLED) I WANT A LITTLE	KINDNESS	. I KNOW I'M A COMMON IGNORANT GIRL, AND YOU A
DOCT II (121)	MISERABLE POVERTY TO YOUR DINNER AFTER ALL YOUR	KINDNESS	. IT'S NOT THAT YOU WONT ASK ME AGAIN; BUT IT'S SO
CAND I (98)	SHALL SEE WHETHER THIS IS A TIME FOR PATIENCE AND	KINDNESS	. (MORELL, FIRM AS A ROCK, LOOKS INDULGENTLY AT
LION PREFACE(74)	HIS MIRACLES ON SENTIENT SUBJECTS WAS AN ACT OF	KINDNESS	. JOHN DECLARES THAT HE HEALED THE WOUND OF THE MAN
BARB PREFACE(236)	GENEROSITY, TENDERNESS, DELICACY, PITY AND	KINDNESS	. THE CONFIRMATION OF THAT DOUBT, AT WHICH OUR
NEVR II (247)	ACQUAINTANCES, IVE HAD RESPECT FROM THEM: AYE,	KINDNESS	. WOULD ONE OF THEM HAVE SPOKEN TO ME AS THAT GIRL
HART II (85)	IF WE CHOOSE TO MAKE THE BEST OF IT. YOUR	KINDNESS	OF HEART WILL MAKE IT EASY FOR ME. /MANGAN/ (
HART II (85)	LIKE DELIBERATE UNPLEASANTNESS IN HIS VOICE)	KINDNESS	OF HEART, EH? I RUINED YOUR FATHER, DIDNT I?
GETT (338)	/THE BISHOP/ (TURNING TO MRS GEORGE WITH GREAT	KINDNESS	OF MANNER) I'M SORRY YOU HAVE BEEN WORRIED (HE
DOCT PREFACE(42)	EARS AND TAILS OF DOGS AND HORSES. LET CRUELTY OR	KINDNESS	OR ANYTHING ELSE ONCE BECOME CUSTOMARY AND IT WILL
PYGM IV (264)	IF CONDESCENDING TO A TRIVIAL SUBJECT OUT OF PURE	KINDNESS	). I SHOULDNT BOTHER ABOUT IT IF I WERE YOU. I
SUPR III (125)	THEIR CHASTITY, THEIR THRIFT, AND THEIR LOVING	KINDNESS	; AND TO BASE YOUR INSTITUTIONS ON THESE
CATH 4 (196)	PATRONIZINGLY IN HIS OWN) I FEEL YOUR MAJESTY'S	KINDNESS	SO MUCH THAT I REALLY CANNOT LEAVE YOU WITHOUT A
GETT PREFACE(199)	BEYOND THE STRICT LETTER OF THE LAW IN THE WAY OF	KINDNESS	THAN WE HAVE NOW AGAINST EXCESS IN THE OPPOSITE
SIM PRO,1, (23)	BY HIS OUTBURST). /WILKS/ WOULD YOU HAVE THE	KINDNESS	TO CLEAR OUT, MISS. WE'RE BUSY. YOURE PASSED ALL
HART I (59)	TO STARBOARD)-- GRATEFUL TO HIM FOR HIS	KINDNESS	TO DEAR FATHER. I KNOW. ANYBODY ELSE? /ELLIE/ WHAT
BUOY III (46)	SWINGING A CENSER. /THE PRIEST/ WILL YOU HAVE THE	KINDNESS	TO FOLLOW YOUR FRIENDS AND LEAVE ME TO PURIFY THIS
FABL PREFACE(77)	HUMANE (INDEED, AS SOME THINK, TOO HUMANE IN HIS	KINDNESS	TO HIS DOZEN DOGS AND HALF DOZEN MISTRESSES), COULD
BARB I (264)	SOME THINGS. (HE OFFERS HIS HAND WITH PATERNAL	KINDNESS	TO LOMAX). /LOMAX/ (JERKILY SHAKING HIS HAND)
MILL IV (202)	NOTES AND NEVER ASKED ME TO REPAY THEM. WHY?	KINDNESS	TO ME? LOVE OF ME? NO: THE SWANK OF A POOR MAN
CLEO IV (171)	EVERYONE AS HE DOES WITH DOGS AND CHILDREN. HIS	KINDNESS	TO ME IS A WONDER: NEITHER MOTHER, FATHER, NOR
INCA (237)	AND SELF-DENIAL BOTH AT ONCE; AND AN ACT OF	KINDNESS	TO ME, AS I AM OUT OF PLACE. /THE PRINCESS/ I'M SO
HART I (54)	HIS). I MUST THANK YOU, MRS HUSHABYE, FOR YOUR	KINDNESS	TO MY DAUGHTER. I'M AFRAID SHE WOULD HAVE HAD NO
POSN PREFACE(417)	MURRAY AND MR LAURENCE HOUSMAN, WHO, IN PURE	KINDNESS	TO THE MANAGERS, ASKED WHETHER IT WOULD NOT BE
LIED (203)	I HARDLY LIKE TO ASK; BUT IT WOULD BE A REAL	KINDNESS	TO US BOTH. /HE/ WHAT CAN I DO? /HER HUSBAND/ (
BULL II (116)	MISS REILLY, OR EXPRESS MY SENSE OF YOUR	KINDNESS	WHEN I AM IN SUCH A DISGUSTING STATE. HOW COULD I
DEVL III (54)	THEY COULD ALL RISE TO SOME SORT OF GOODNESS AND	KINDNESS	WHEN THEY WERE IN LOVE (THE WORD LOVE COMES FROM
BULL IV (149)	/BROADBENT/ MAY I SAY HOW DEEPLY I FEEL THE	KINDNESS	WITH WHICH I HAVE BEEN OVERWHELMED SINCE MY
GETT PREFACE(196)	ON THEIR THESIS THEY ARE SOMETIMES TALKING ABOUT	KINDNESS	, AND SOMETIMES ABOUT MERE APPETITE. IN EITHER
PYGM V (287)	AS IF I WAS A BABY OR A PUPPY. IF I CANT HAVE	KINDNESS	, I'LL HAVE INDEPENDENCE. /HIGGINS/ INDEPENDENCE..
2TRU III (99)	RAISE HIS HAND TO A WOMAN, SAVE IN THE WAY OF	KINDNESS	, IS UNWORTHY THE NAME OF BRITON. /TALLBOYS/ I AM
GETT (276)	RAISE HIS HAND TO A WOMAN, SAVE IN THE WAY OF	KINDNESS	, IS UNWORTHY THE NAME OF BRIDGENORTH. (HE SITS
GETT PREFACE(227)	AND CONSCIOUS AND STUDIED ACTS OF ARTIFICIAL	KINDNESS	, MAY BE DEFEATED IN A LARGE FAMILY BY THE HEALTHY
MRS IV (246)	TENDERNESS) YOU KNOW THAT PRADDY IS THE SOUL OF	KINDNESS	, MRS WARREN. PRADDY: WHAT DO YOU SAY? GO OR
MILL I (149)	YOU KNOW. I WENT WHERE I COULD FIND PEACE AND	KINDNESS	, TO MY GOOD SWEET DARLING POLLY. SO THERE!
POSN (465)	A CHILD WITH A NEW TOY: YOU AND YOUR BIT OF HUMAN	KINDNESS	! /THE WOMAN/ HOW MANY WOULD HAVE DONE IT WITH

KINDRED

CLEO I (106)	BUT NO OTHER CAESAR, NO AIR NATIVE TO ME, NO MAN	KINDRED	TO ME, NONE WHO CAN DO MY DAY'S DEED, AND THINK MY

KIND-HEARTED

BULL IV (163)	/NORA/ (WONDERING AT HIM) I THINK YOURE A VERY	KIND-HEARTED	MAN, MR BROADBENT; BUT YOU SEEM TO ME TO HAVE

KINDS

LION PREFACE(72)	THE EXPLORERS, THE RESTLESSLY ENERGETIC OF ALL	KINDS	: IN SHORT, BY THE ADVENTUROUS. THE GREATEST SACRIFICE
POSN PREFACE(368)	OF THE COMMUNITY STILL BELIEVES THAT ART OF ALL	KINDS	IS INHERENTLY SINFUL. WHY THE GOVERNMENT INTERFERED.
JOAN PREFACE(48)	AND MAGICIANS AND MONSTERS AND FAIRY TALES OF ALL	KINDS	. THE PROPORTION OF MARVEL TO IMMEDIATELY CREDIBLE
KING I (200)	A FAST DAY. ALL I NEED IS THREE OR FOUR DIFFERENT	KINDS	OF FISH. /MRS BASHAM/ NO, SIR: IN THIS HOUSE YOU WILL
DOCT PREFACE(59)	AS TO CIRCUMCISION AND THE DECLARING CERTAIN	KINDS	OF FLESH UNCLEAN BY THE JEWS. TO ADVERTIZE ANY REMEDY
BULL IV (177)	WITHOUT BECOMING BETTER OR WORSE. IT PRODUCES TWO	KINDS	OF MEN IN STRANGE PERFECTION: SAINTS AND TRAITORS. IT
2TRU PREFACE(7)	RARELY) ARTISTIC AND POLITICAL " CAUSES" OF ALL	KINDS	, MOSTLY WITHOUT STOPPING TO EXAMINE WHETHER THE
UNPL PREFACE(R24)	OF THE ABOVE ARGUMENTS, OF WORKS OF A MIXTURE OF	KINDS	, PART NARRATIVE, PART HOMILY, PART DESCRIPTION, PART
DOCT PREFACE(61)	BY LAYMEN, INCLUDING QUACKS AND FADDISTS OF ALL	KINDS	, THAT THE PUBLIC WAS SUFFICIENTLY IMPRESSED TO MAKE
METH PREFACE(R46)	SEXUAL SELECTION, AND VARIATION LEADING TO NEW	KINDS	, THERE IS NOTHING TO PUZZLE YOU IN DARWINISM. THAT
GETT PREFACE(215)	BY SETTLEMENTS AND PRIVATE CONTRACTS OF VARIOUS	KINDS	, WOULD BECOME THE PRACTICE OF THE RICH: THAT IS,

KING

KING II (226)	LAD WILL SEE HIS CHANCE AND TAKE IT. HE WILL BE	KING	: A PROTESTANT KING. SO YOU MUST MAKE FOR PORTUGAL.
JOAN 2 (83)	ENJOY MYSELF IN MY OWN WAY. I NEVER ASKED TO BE A	KING	: IT WAS PUSHED ON ME. SO IF YOU ARE GOING TO SAY " SON
CLEO I (114)	WHIP THEM TO DEATH; BUT YOU SHALL ALWAYS BE MY	KING	: MY NICE, KIND, WISE, GOOD OLD KING. /CAESAR/ OH, MY
JOAN 5 (112)	AND FALLING ON HER KNEE) SIRE: I HAVE MADE YOU	KING	: MY WORK IS DONE. I AM GOING BACK TO MY FATHER'S FARM.
KING I (191)	THEM DO IT. CHARLES: YOU HAVNT THE SPIRIT OF A	KING	: THAT IS WHAT IS THE MATTER WITH YOU. AS LONG AS THEY

APPL INTRLUD(253)	TIME? AFTER ALL, WHAT ARE YOU PAID FOR? TO BE A	KING	: THAT IS, TO WIPE YOUR BOOTS ON COMMON PEOPLE.
KING II (232)	HOW OFTEN HAVE I TOLD YOU THAT I AM NO REAL	KING	: THAT THE UTMOST I CAN DO IS TO KEEP MY CROWN ON MY
APPL I (230)	WHY SHOULD I? /BALBUS/ BECAUSE YOURE THE	KING	: THATS WHY. /MAGNUS/ DOES IT FOLLOW? /PROTEUS/ IF TWO
APPL I (225)	ARE AT PRESENT ENGAGED IN A TUG OF WAR WITH THE	KING	: THE TUG OF YOUR LIVES. YOU THINK YOU HAVE WON. YOU
KING II (232)	CHOPPED HER HEAD OFF. MY FATHER WAS A PROTESTANT	KING	: THEY CHOPPED HIS HEAD OFF FOR TRYING TO GOVERN THEM
CYMB V (146)	TAKE HIM FROM OUR PRESENCE. /BELARIUS/ STAY, SIR	KING	: THIS MAN IS BETTER THAN THE MAN HE SLEW, AS WELL
6CAL (102)	QUEEN/ A VERY VERY LITTLE THING, SIR. YOU ARE THE	KING	: YOU HAVE AT YOUR DISPOSAL THOUSANDS OF LIVES: ALL OUR
APPL I (207)	THAT BE? YOURE KING. /MAGNUS/ AND WHAT IS THE	KING	? AN IDOL SET UP BY A GROUP OF PLUTOCRATS SO THAT THEY
6CAL (98)	WAY FOR ONE OF THY DEGREE TO SPEAK TO AN ANOINTED	KING	? BEAR THYSELF AS BEFITS ONE OF THY DEGREE IN THE
KING II (229)	OLD NOLL FOUND THAT OUT. WHY AM I A POPULAR	KING	? BECAUSE I AM A LAZY FELLOW. I ENJOY MYSELF AND LET
APPL I (211)	OF IT THEMSELVES. HOW DID YOU GET ON WITH THE	KING	? /BOANERGES/ RIGHT AS RAIN, JOE. YOU LEAVE THE KING
KING II (226)	HIM FROM SUCCEEDING YOU AND BECOME A PROTESTANT	KING	? /CHARLES/ NO. HE WILL TRY, POOR BOY; BUT JAMIE WILL
6CAL (99)	AM I NOT YOUR OVERLORD? AM I NOT YOUR ANOINTED	KING	? /EUSTACHE/ THAT IS YOUR CLAIM, SIR; AND YOU HAVE
6CAL (98)	RESISTANCE FOR ALL THESE MONTHS TO ME, YOUR	KING	? /EUSTACHE/ SIR, WE ARE NOT FELLOWS. WE ARE FREE
ROCK PREFACE(181)	NOT HAPPEN IN MY KINGDOM. /PILATE/ THEN YOU ARE A	KING	? /JESUS/ YOU SAY SO. I CAME INTO THIS WORLD AND WAS
APPL INTRLUD(246)	LISTEN TO ME, MAGNUS. WHY CAN YOU NOT BE A REAL	KING	? /MAGNUS/ IN WHAT WAY, BELOVEDEST? /ORINTHIA/ SEND
KING I (187)	/JAMES/ (IMPERIOUSLY) WHERE IS HIS MAJESTY THE	KING	? /NEWTON/ (RISING IN UNGOVERNABLE WRATH) SIR: I
APPL I (212)	COUNTRY HAS BEEN GOVERNED DURING THAT TIME BY THE	KING	? /NICOBAR/ I DONT SEE THAT. WE -- /PROTEUS/ (
APPL I (227)	THAT. SO, IN FUTURE, NO SPEECHES. /MAGNUS/ A DUMB	KING	? /PROTEUS/ OF COURSE WE CANNOT OBJECT TO SUCH
CLEO II (120)	(LOOKING AT POTHINUS AND PTOLEMY) WHICH IS THE	KING	? THE MAN OR THE BOY? /POTHINUS/ I AM POTHINUS, THE
6CAL (99)	WHY DID THEY TAKE ARMS AGAINST THEIR ANOINTED	KING	? WHY SHOULD I HAVE MERCY ON THEM OR ON YOU?
METH PREFACE(R32)	COULD THEY EXPECT WITH SUCH A MINISTRY AND SUCH A	KING	? " STUFF! " SAID GOETHE: " I AM NOT THINKING OF THESE
KING I (200)	" ISNT THAT A DAINTY DISH TO SET BEFORE A	KING	? " YOUR FAST WILL BE A REAL FAST, JAMIE, FOR THE FIRST
APPL I (201)	AND THAT HE IS COMING HERE TODAY TO GIVE THE	KING	A PIECE OF HIS MIND, OR WHAT HE CALLS HIS MIND, ABOUT
APPL PREFACE(173)	THAT I HAVE PACKED THE CARDS BY MAKING THE	KING	A WISE MAN AND THE MINISTER A FOOL. BUT THAT IS NOT AT
DEVL EPILOG (81)	NOT DAWN ON HIM UNTIL MANY MONTHS AFTERWARDS) THE	KING	ACTUALLY TOOK ADVANTAGE OF HIS BEING A PRISONER OF WAR
JOAN 5 (113)	FRANCE! /THE ARCHBISHOP/ (STERNLY) MAID: THE	KING	ADDRESSED HIMSELF TO ME, NOT TO YOU. YOU FORGET
APPL II (275)	SAY WHAT I THINK. (HE IS TAKING HIS HAT WHEN THE	KING	ADDRESSES HIM). /MAGNUS/ SO I HAVE NOT UPSET THE APPLE
KING I (219)	IS IN THE WORST POSSIBLE TASTE. CHARLES: BE A	KING	AGAIN; AND FORBID IT. /CHARLES/ NOBODY BUT BARBARA
KING I (190)	IN FRANCE. /JAMES/ AND LEAVE THEMSELVES WITHOUT A	KING	AGAIN! NOT THEY! THEY HAD ENOUGH OF THAT UNDER OLD
KING I (217)	SILENCE. /FOX/ IN THE PRESENCE OF THIS EARTHLY	KING	ALL YOU GREAT NOBLES BECOME DUMB FLUNKEYS. WHAT WILL
KING I (218)	THE NEW ROYAL SOCIETY. HERE IS GODFREY KNELLER! A	KING	AMONG PAINTERS. I CAN MAKE YOU DUCHESSES AND YOUR SONS
METH PREFACE(R66)	GOD; AND ROYALISTS ARE CONTENT TO WORSHIP THE	KING	AND ASK THE POLICEMAN. BUT GOD'S TRUSTIEST LIEUTENANTS
GETT (350)	MIGHT AS WELL GO TOO. SO HE PLAYED GOD SAVE THE	KING	AND CLEARED OUT THE CHURCH. HE'S COMING TO THE
CLEO II (124)	OWN ROYAL BLOOD. PTOLEMY AND CLEOPATRA ARE BORN	KING	AND CONSORT JUST AS THEY ARE BORN BROTHER AND SISTER.
ROCK PREFACE(147)	IT JUSTICE OR CAPITAL PUNISHMENT OR OUR DUTY TO	KING	AND COUNTRY OR ANY OTHER CONVENIENT VERBAL WHITEWASH
O'FL (227)	HOW I WAS LONGING TO BE BACK TAKING MY PART FOR	KING	AND COUNTRY WITH THE OTHERS, I WAS LYING, AS YOU WELL
O'FL (208)	IT A BIT OCCASIONALLY MYSELF. AFTER ALL, IT'S FOR	KING	AND COUNTRY, BUT IF YOU WONT MIND MY SAYING IT,
BUOY II (23)	BEATERS, NO GROOMS, NO STABLES, NO SOLDIERS, NO	KING	AND COUNTRY, I SHOULD HAVE TO LEARN TO MAKE BOWS AND
GENV II (51)	MISLED FOR A WHILE; BUT THEY ALWAYS COME BACK TO	KING	AND COUNTRY. /THE SECRETARY/ AND NOW, MISS BROWN, I
ROCK I (227)	ABOUT PROGRESS AND LIBERTY INSTEAD OF ABOUT	KING	AND COUNTRY. /SIR ARTHUR/ OF COURSE I MAKE SPEECHES:
O'FL (206)	LISTENING TO THEM, AND THE CALLING FOR CHEERS FOR	KING	AND COUNTRY, AND THE SALUTING THE FLAG TIL I'M STIFF
LADY PREFACE(230)	" POOR, BARE, FORKED ANIMAL" THAT CALLS ITSELF A	KING	AND FANCIES ITSELF A GOD, THAT ONE WONDERS WHAT WAS THE
SUPR HANDBOK(217)	MAN, HE CUTS ITS HEAD OFF. HE WHO SLAYS A	KING	AND HE WHO DIES FOR HIM ARE ALIKE IDOLATERS. ROYALTY,
JOAN 4 (106)	MENTIONED THE PEERAGE, AND THINKS ONLY OF THE	KING	AND HERSELF. /WARWICK/ QUITE SO. THESE TWO IDEAS OF
MTH3 (96)	(SURPRISED) YOU DONT SAY SO! /CONFUCIUS/ THE	KING	AND HIS LOYAL SUBJECTS KILLED SIMON FOR FORCING HIS
ROCK II (267)	/BASHAM/ I HAVE A JOLLY GOOD MIND TO GO TO THE	KING	AND MAKE HIM TAKE THE BIT BETWEEN HIS TEETH AND ARREST
MTH5 (237)	THE SACRED LIFE FORCE. THERE IS ONE PERSON OF THE	KING	AND ONE OF THE QUEEN; BUT THE LIFE FORCE OF THE KING
MTH5 (238)	REMEMBER THAT THOUGH THERE IS ONE PERSON OF THE	KING	AND ONE OF THE QUEEN, YET THESE TWO PERSONS ARE NOT
APPL II SD(257)	FROM THE LAWN BY A CENTRAL FLIGHT OF STEPS. THE	KING	AND QUEEN ARE SITTING APART NEAR THE CORNERS OF THE
MTH5 (237)	AND ONE OF THE QUEEN; BUT THE LIFE FORCE OF THE	KING	AND QUEEN IS ALL ONE: THE GLORY EQUAL, THE MAJESTY
POSN PREFACE(398)	DISALLOW THE INCESTUOUS RELATIONSHIP BETWEEN THE	KING	AND QUEEN. HE WOULD PROBABLY INSIST ON THE SUBSTITUTION
APPL I SD(210)	OH, THATS ALL RIGHT, THATS QUITE ALL RIGHT. THE	KING	AND THE PRINCESS GO OUT, APPARENTLY MUCH PLEASED.
JOAN PREFACE(45)	THE FACT THAT SHE INSISTED ON THIS WHILST THE	KING	AND THE REST TIMIDLY AND FOOLISHLY THOUGHT THEY COULD
APPL I SD(216)	HAND AND PLANTS THEM SIDE BY SIDE BETWEEN THE	KING	AND THE TABLE OF PAMPHILIUS. /AMANDA/ THERE YOU ARE,
O'FL (206)	AND THE LISTENING TO THEM PLAYING GOD SAVE THE	KING	AND TIPPERARY, AND THE TRYING TO MAKE MY EYES LOOK
MTH5 (238)	THOUGHT-OUT AND HAND-MADE. THE ACTIONS OF THE	KING	ARE CAUSED, AND THEREFORE DETERMINED, FROM THE
O'FL SD(205)	END OF IT. THE LAST FOUR BARS OF GOD SAVE THE	KING	ARE HEARD IN THE DISTANCE, FOLLOWED BY THREE CHEERS.
SUPR PREFACE(R22)	OR SENTIMENTAL UXORIOUSNESS; AND THE TENNYSONIAN	KING	ARTHUR POSING AT GUINEVERE BECOMES DON QUIXOTE
JOAN PREFACE(27)	OF EMOTION, AUTHOR OF A YANKEE AT THE COURT OF	KING	ARTHUR, IN WHICH THE HEROES AND HEROINES OF MEDIEVAL
ROCK PREFACE(150)	OF MALIGNANT OR MAN OF BLOOD, AND KILLED THE	KING	AS AN AFFIRMATION THAT EVEN KINGS MUST NOT SURVIVE IF
APPL I (207)	SO THAT THEY CAN RULE THE COUNTRY WITH THE	KING	AS THEIR SCAPEGOAT AND PUPPET. PRESIDENTS, NOW, ARE
KING I (192)	I MUST. AND I KNOW THAT I MUST. TO PLAY THE	KING	AS YOU WOULD HAVE ME I SHOULD NEED OLD NOLL'S ARMY; AND
O'FL (217)	ALL FULL OF YOU SHAKING HANDS WITH THE ENGLISH	KING	AT BUCKINGHAM PALACE? /O'FLAHERTY/ I DIDNT SHAKE HANDS
JOAN 5 (111)	HIRE. /DUNOIS/ WELL, YOUR MAJESTY IS AN ANOINTED	KING	AT LAST. HOW DO YOU LIKE IT? /CHARLES/ I WOULD NOT GO
APPL II (258)	/THE QUEEN/ MUST! ! AN AMERICAN MUST SEE THE	KING	AT ONCE, WITHOUT AN AUDIENCE! WELL! /MAGNUS/ (
APPL I (206)	HAVE RISEN AS YOU HAVE DONE. AS FOR ME, I AM A	KING	BECAUSE I WAS THE NEPHEW OF MY UNCLE, AND BECAUSE MY
APPL I (213)	THAT A REPUBLICAN PRESIDENT HAS MORE POWER THAN A	KING	BECAUSE THE PEOPLE KNOW THAT THEY NEED A STRONG MAN TO
KING II (229)	FATHERS. WHAT GOOD IS THAT? /CATHERINE/ YOU ARE	KING	BECAUSE YOU ARE THE SON OF YOUR FATHER. AND YOU ARE THE
APPL I (203)	SAY THINGS TO YOU THAT HAVE NEVER BEEN SAID TO A	KING	BEFORE? /MAGNUS/ I AM VERY GLAD INDEED TO HEAR IT, MR
APPL I (232)	HE IS SETTLING THE WHOLE BUSINESS WITH THE	KING	BEHIND OUR BACKS. THAT IS WHAT JOE ALWAYS CONTRIVES TO
JOAN 4 (105)	KING SOLE AND ABSOLUTE AUTOCRAT. INSTEAD OF THE	KING	BEING MERELY THE FIRST AMONG HIS PEERS, HE BECOMES
BULL PREFACE(7)	HIS OWN. SHUT HIM UP IN DERRY WITH AN ENGLISH	KING	BESIEGING HIM, AND HE DOES NOT SHRIEK FOR THE GERMANS
APPL INTRLUD(253)	BOOTS ON COMMON PEOPLE. /MAGNUS/ YES; BUT THIS	KING	BUSINESS, AS THE AMERICANS CALL IT, HAS GOT ITSELF SO
POSN PREFACE(364)	THE COMMITTEE FROM THE FEAR OF DISPLEASING THE	KING	BY ANY PROPOSAL TO ABOLISH THE CENSORSHIP OF THE LORD
JOAN PREFACE(8)	WHEN THEY WERE STRAINING THEMSELVES TO PLEASE THE	KING	BY PRAISING HER, EVER CLAIMED THAT SHE WAS PRETTY. ALL
APPL PREFACE(173)	BE CAREFUL NOT TO CHOOSE THE WEAPONS AT WHICH THE	KING	CAN BEAT HIM. RATHER WILL HE IN COLD BLOOD OPPOSE TO
KING I (210)	A CANNON BALL FROM THE MIGHTIEST CANNON THE	KING	CAN LEND YOU, AND THOUGH YOU HAD THE STRENGTH OF
ROCK II (259)	DEXTER/ YOU CANNOT PROROGUE PARLIAMENT. ONLY THE	KING	CAN PROROGUE PARLIAMENT. /SIR ARTHUR/ PRECISELY. KINGS
APPL II (268)	RESIGNS! WHAT ARE YOU DRIVING AT? /CRASSUS/ A	KING	CANNOT RESIGN. /NICOBAR/ YOU MIGHT AS WELL TALK OF
APPL I (212)	YOURE PRIME MINISTER YOURE NOT GOD ALMIGHTY. THE	KING	CANT DO ANYTHING EXCEPT WHAT WE ADVISE HIM TO DO. HOW
APPL II (272)	PLANS. /NICOBAR/ WHAT PLANS? /BALBUS/ A RETIRED	KING	CANT HAVE PLANS AND A FUTURE. /MAGNUS/ WHY NOT? I AM
APPL I (201)	ABOUT THE CRISIS. /SEMPRONIUS/ WHAT DOES THE	KING	CARE ABOUT THE CRISIS? THERE HAS BEEN A CRISIS EVERY
JOAN 5 (115)	VICTORIES OF OURS WERE WON WITHOUT GENERALSHIP.	KING	CHARLES: YOU HAVE SAID NO WORD IN YOUR PROCLAMATIONS OF
JOAN EPIL,SD(152)	FULL OF SUMMER LIGHTNING AFTER MANY DAYS OF HEAT.	KING	CHARLES THE SEVENTH OF FRANCE, FORMERLY JOAN'S DAUPHIN,
JOAN 2,SD(73)	AT COURT ATTENTION. THE DAUPHIN, AGED 26, REALLY	KING	CHARLES THE SEVENTH SINCE THE DEATH OF HIS FATHER, BUT
KING I SD(166)	ANNOUNCES VISITORS. /SALLY/ MR ROWLEY AND MR FOX.	KING	CHARLES THE SECOND, AGED 50, APPEARS AT THE DOOR, BUT
KING II (234)	CHAMBER LIKE THAT! NOBODY WOULD TAKE YOU FOR	KING	CHARLES THE SECOND WITHOUT THAT WIG. NOW. (SHE PUTS
KING I (161)	" IN GOOD	KING	CHARLES'S GOLDEN DAYS", ACT I. THE LIBRARY IN THE HOUSE
KING (151)	" IN GOOD	KING	CHARLES'S GOLDEN DAYS": A TRUE HISTORY THAT NEVER
APPL I (205)	/MAGNUS/ OH, QUITE. I HAVE NOT FORGOTTEN	KING	CHARLES'S HEAD. WELL, I HOPE IT WILL BE SETTLED BY A
KING I (206)	/NELL/ ROWLEY DARLING: YOU MUST LEARN TO KEEP	KING	CHARLES'S HEAD OUT OF YOUR CONVERSATION. YOU TALK TOO
ROCK II (259)	ON. /SIR DEXTER/ THAT WAS HOW CROMWELL CUT OFF	KING	CHARLES'S HEAD. HIS COMMISSIONERS FOUND OUT AFTERWARDS
ROCK PREFACE(150)	OF SOCIAL CRITICISM AND NO TIME TO INVENT IT.	KING	CHARLES'S HEAD. IT WAS, BY THE WAY, THE ENGLISH
JOAN 5,SD(111)	A CHANCE. /DUNOIS/ THAT IS TRUE. (HE LAUGHS).	KING	CHARLES, WITH BLUEBEARD ON HIS LEFT AND LA HIRE ON HIS
MRS PREFACE(173)	SIR JOHN FALSTAFF AN ATTACK ON KNIGHTHOOD, AND	KING	CLAUDIUS AN ATTACK ON ROYALTY. HERE AGAIN THE CLAMOR
FANY III (313)	SPIRITS; AND I MAKE A MERIT OF IT, AND I'M THE	KING	COCKATOO OF THE CONVIVIAL COCKATOOS. NEVER PUT YOURSELF
KING I (202)	HIS OWN FAVORITE RECITATION PRESENTLY; BUT THE	KING	COMES FIRST. NOW LISTEN. (HE RISES. THEY ALL RISE,
KING I (217)	/CHARLES/ NO, NO, NO. NOT A WORD MORE. THE	KING	COMMANDS IT. DEAD SILENCE. THEY SIT AS IF IN CHURCH,
SUPR HANDBOK(214)	THE KINGS IN EUROPE WERE MADE AS FREE TOMORROW AS	KING	COPHETUA, NOBODY BUT THEIR AUNTS AND CHAMBERLAINS WOULD
JOAN 4 (106)	ONLY THE KING'S SERVANTS IN THEIR EYES. THE	KING	COULD BREAK US ACROSS HIS KNEE ONE BY ONE; AND THEN
APPL I (233)	YOU SINGLEHANDED. THERE WAS A TIME WHEN THE	KING	COULD DEPEND ON THE SUPPORT OF THE ARISTOCRACY AND THE
APPL I (200)	WERE GULLS; AND GULLS ARE NOT DECORATIVE. OUR	KING	COULD HAVE LIVED THERE FOR THIRTY YEARS WITH NOTHING
APPL I (230)	A DEMAGOGUE MAY STEAL A HORSE WHERE A	KING	DARE NOT LOOK OVER A HEDGE. /LYSISTRATA/ I DOUBT IF
JOAN EPILOG (154)	NOW, CAN THEY? /LADVENU/ NOT CHARLEMAGNE NOR	KING	DAVID HIMSELF WAS MORE SACREDLY CROWNED. /CHARLES/ (
GENV III (69)	/THE WIDOW/ YOU WILL BE TELLING ME NEXT THAT	KING	DAVID WAS A JEW, I SUPPOSE. /SIR O./ WELL,
MILL PREFACE(125)	GOT FORTIFIED SOMEWHERE IN THE PAST BY THAT OF	KING	DAVID. HE CANNOT GET OVER THE FACT THAT THE LOST TRIBES

GENV III (69)	WILL REMEMBER THAT OUR SAVIOR WAS OF THE HOUSE OF	KING	DAVID. /THE WIDOW/ YOU WILL BE TELLING ME NEXT THAT
CAND I (101)	OLD STORY: YOULL FIND IT IN THE BIBLE. I IMAGINE	KING	DAVID, IN HIS FITS OF ENTHUSIASM, WAS VERY LIKE YOU. (
METH PREFACE(R78)	BIRDS: THEY WILL NOT READ EVEN THE CHRONICLES OF	KING	DAVID, WHICH MAY VERY WELL BE TRUE, AND ARE CERTAINLY
APPL PREFACE(171)	POTHER ABOUT? I HAD WRITTEN A COMEDY IN WHICH A	KING	DEFEATS AN ATTEMPT BY HIS POPULARLY ELECTED PRIME
SUPR HANDBOK(214)	AND DESIRES A PEDIGREE. AND IN THAT HE IS RIGHT.	KING	DEMOS MUST BE BRED LIKE ALL OTHER KINGS; AND WITH MUST
APPL I (230)	UNDERSTOOD IT IF THEY HAD; WHEREAS, FOR WHAT A	KING	DOES, HE, AND HE ALONE, IS HELD RESPONSIBLE. A
6CAL PREFACE(89)	A KING EDWARD WHO DID NOT BEHAVE LIKE THE SON OF	KING	EDWARD THE SEVENTH SEEMED UNNATURAL AND INDECENT TO
6CAL PREFACE(89)	THE JOURNALIST CRITICS KNEW NOTHING OF THIS. A	KING	EDWARD WHO DID NOT BEHAVE LIKE THE SON OF KING EDWARD
HART I (62)	LIFE OF THE TIGER FROM A HUNTING PARTY: ONE OF	KING	EDWARD'S HUNTING PARTIES IN INDIA. THE KING WAS
GENV PREFACE(21)	MUSSO, AND CHILDISHLY REFUSE TO CALL HIS PUPPET	KING	EMPEROR. BUT WE DID THROW STONES, AND MADE NO PROTEST
APPL INTR,SD(243)	IS A LARGE SETTEE IN THE MIDDLE OF THE ROOM. THE	KING	ENTERS AND WAITS ON THE THRESHOLD. /ORINTHIA/ (
APPL I SD(214)	MEMORANDUM OF UNDERSTANDING ARRIVED AT -- THE	KING	ENTERS, WITH AMANDA, POSTMISTRESS GENERAL, A MERRY LADY
KING PREFACE(156)	ENOUGH OF THAT UNDER CROMWELL, AND GRUDGED THEIR	KING	EVEN THE LIFEGUARDS WHICH WERE THE NUCLEUS OF SUCH AN
KING I (220)	KNELLER. THERE IS A COVER LAID FOR YOU; AND THE	KING	EXPECTS YOU. /NEWTON/ THE LINES ARE NOT STRAIGHT, MR
O'FL (219)	THEY SAYS, " BECAUSE YOU SAVE THAT BY THE	KING	FEEDING HIM." " INDEED! " SAYS I: " I SUPPOSE IF I'D
JOAN 4 (106)	THE TWO ARE SELDOM THE SAME. WHERE WOULD THE	KING	FIND COUNSELLORS TO PLAN AND CARRY OUT SUCH A POLICY
PYGM II (228)	PALACE IN A CARRIAGE, BEAUTIFULLY DRESSED. IF THE	KING	FINDS OUT YOURE NOT A LADY, YOU WILL BE TAKEN BY THE
SUPR HANDBOK(217)	SERVANT'S HALL OF THE SOVEREIGN. VULGARITY IN A	KING	FLATTERS THE MAJORITY OF THE NATION. THE FLUNKEYISM
MTH3 (96)	ALWAYS DID WAS TO GRANT SUPPLIES TO THE	KING	FOR LIFE WITH ENTHUSIASTIC EXPRESSIONS OF LOYALTY, LEST
KING II (234)	ON. /CATHERINE/ NO: YOU ARE NOT THAT SORT OF	KING	FOR ME. BUT WILL IT BE A REAL CONVERSION? I THINK YOU
APPL II (270)	AS YOU DONT INTERFERE WITH HIM. JUST THE RIGHT	KING	FOR US. NOT PIG-HEADED. NOT MEDDLESOME. THINKS THAT
CLEO II (125)	LEFT BY AULUS GABINIUS WHEN HE SET UP YOUR TOY	KING	FOR YOU? /ACHILLAS/ (SUDDENLY ASSERTING HIMSELF) AND
KING I (207)	/JAMES/ (TO FOX) YOU WOULD LIKE TO HAVE A	KING	FOR YOUR FOLLOWER, EH? /FOX/ I DESIRE FRIENDS, NOT
JOAN 2 (84)	HE SITS ENTHRONED, A PITEOUS FIGURE) HERE IS THE	KING	FOR YOU! LOOK YOUR FILL AT THE POOR DEVIL. /JOAN/
APPL INTRLUD(255)	(PANTING BUT GREATLY PLEASED WITH HERSELF) THE	KING	FORGETS EVERYTHING WHEN HE IS HERE. SO DO I, I AM
DEVL III SD(70)	IS THE DEVIL'S DISCIPLE AND NOT THE MINISTER THAT	KING	GEORGE AND HIS TERRIBLE GENERAL ARE ABOUT TO HANG:
DEVL EPILOG (83)	REMOTE AND INFERIOR CREATURES, THE COLONISTS. AND	KING	GEORGE AND THE REST OF THE NATION AGREED, ON THE WHOLE,
DEVL I (27)	AND WOBBLES WITH FEAR) EH? WOULD THAT SHEW THAT	KING	GEORGE MEANT BUSINESS-- HA? /ANDERSON/ (PERFECTLY
O'FL (208)	HALL AT BUCKINGHAM PALACE THIS DAY, AND	KING	GEORGE POLISHING HIS JACKBOOTS FOR HIM IN THE SCULLERY.
CATH 4 (187)	(SURPRISED) WHY? /EDSTASTON/ HIS MAJESTY	KING	GEORGE THE THIRD WILL SEND FOR SIX OF THEM WHEN THE
DEVL III (61)	OF YOUR OBLIGATIONS AS A SUBJECT OF HIS MAJESTY	KING	GEORGE THE THIRD. /RICHARD/ I AM AWARE, SIR, THAT HIS
DEVL III (61)	/RICHARD/ I AM AWARE, SIR, THAT HIS MAJESTY	KING	GEORGE THE THIRD IS ABOUT TO HANG ME BECAUSE I OBJECT
DEVL III (62)	AVERAGE MARKSMANSHIP OF THE ARMY OF HIS MAJESTY	KING	GEORGE THE THIRD? IF WE MAKE YOU UP A FIRING PARTY,
DEVL I (26)	NO, NO! /RICHARD/ YES, YOU ARE. YOU HAVNT DAMNED	KING	GEORGE UP HILL AND DOWN DALE AS I HAVE; BUT YOUVE
DEVL III (61)	BUT TO BE SWINDLED BY A PIG-HEADED LUNATIC LIKE	KING	GEORGE-- /SWINDON/ (SCANDALIZED) CHUT, SIR-- SILENCE!
DEVL II (39)	MUM. DUTY! ANTHONY ANDERSON: I ARREST YOU IN	KING	GEORGE'S NAME AS A REBEL. /JUDITH/ (POINTING AT
GENV II (51)	SMALLEST CHILD THERE, I PRESENTED THE BOUQUET TO	KING	GEORGE'S SISTER, WHO CAME TO OUR PRIZE GIVING. SAY A
DEVL II (30)	THE SEAT AND MAKING HER SIT DOWN WITH HIM) ONLY	KING	GEORGE, MY DEAR. HE'S RETURNING TO BARRACKS, OR HAVING
DEVL EPILOG (81)	AND WHEN HE AT LAST OBTAINED A COMMITTEE, THE	KING	GOT RID OF IT BY A PROROGATION. WHEN BURGOYNE REALIZED
O'FL (219)	SIR; BUT YOU CAN KEEP YOUR DIRTY MONEY THAT YOUR	KING	GRUDGES A POOR OLD WIDOW; AND PLEASE GOD THE ENGLISH
LADY (244)	(CUTTING THEM SHORT) HOW KNOW YOU THAT	KING	HARRY WAS INDEED YOUR FATHER? /ELIZABETH/ ZOUNDS! NOW
APPL II (260)	THE PRODIGAL SON AT THIS MOMENT. /THE QUEEN/ THE	KING	HAS A CABINET MEETING IN TEN MINUTES, MR VANHATTAN.
APPL I (201)	SELF-ASSERTIVE. /BOANERGES/ LOOK HERE. THE	KING	HAS AN APPOINTMENT WITH ME AT A QUARTER TO TWELVE. HOW
6CAL (100)	WRATH) HOT W--! /EUSTACHE/ ALAS, MADAM, WHEN THE	KING	HAS ENDED HIS BUSINESS WITH US WE SHALL NEED NOTHING
KING I (168)	TO THE NEW SO-CALLED ROYAL SOCIETY WHICH THE	KING	HAS ESTABLISHED, TO ENQUIRE, IT SEEMS, INTO THE NATURE
APPL I (225)	WON. YOU HAVNT. ALL THAT HAS HAPPENED IS THAT THE	KING	HAS LET GO THE ROPE. YOU ARE SPRAWLING ON YOUR BACKS;
APPL I (218)	ITS EXISTENCE? /NICOBAR/ WHAT WE SAY IS THAT THE	KING	HAS NO RIGHT TO REMIND HIS SUBJECTS OF ANYTHING
APPL II (267)	BY KARL MARX. /PROTEUS/ YES; AND THE ENGLISH	KING	HAS SIDETRACKED YOU AGAIN. (TO MAGNUS) WHAT ABOUT THE
JOAN 5 (119)	YOU, AND WILL NOT RESCUE YOU. AND HIS MAJESTY THE	KING	HAS TOLD YOU THAT THE THRONE HAS NOT THE MEANS OF
JOAN 5 (109)	THEY WANT TO SEE YOU AGAIN. /JOAN/ NO: LET THE	KING	HAVE ALL THE GLORY. /DUNOIS/ HE ONLY SPOILS THE SHOW,
KING I (169)	TEN DEGREES BACKWARD AS A SIGN FROM GOD TO GOOD	KING	HEZEKIAH WHO WAS DYING OF A BOIL UNTIL THE PROPHET
JOAN 1 (58)	SIR, YOU KNOW YOU ARE A GREATER MAN HERE THAN THE	KING	HIMSELF. /ROBERT/ PRECISELY. AND NOW, DO YOU KNOW WHAT
APPL PREFACE(173)	MOMENT FOR A DEMEANOR AS URBANE AS THAT OF THE	KING	HIMSELF, THUS EMPLOYING TWO SETS OF WEAPONS TO THE
APPL INTRLUD(243)	/ORINTHIA/ I DIDNT SAY I WAS ENGAGED. TELL THE	KING	I DONT WANT TO SEE HIM. /MAGNUS/ HE AWAITS YOUR
KING I (197)	I AM, AS YOU SAY, NO KING. TO BE WHAT YOU CALL A	KING	I LACK MILITARY AMBITION; I LACK CRUELTY. I HAVE TO
KING I (190)	A DAMNED COWARD, CHARLES. I AM NOT. WHEN I AM	KING	I SHALL REIGN: THESE FELLOWS SHALL FIND WHAT A KING'S
APPL I (202)	/BOANERGES/ WELL, I TOLD ONE OF THEM TO TELL THE	KING	I WAS HERE, AND TO LOOK SHARP ABOUT IT. HE LOOKED AT ME
KING PREFACE(155)	OF CURIOUSLY MIXED BLOOD, AND ENDED AS THE FIRST	KING	IN ENGLAND WHOSE KINGSHIP WAS PURELY SYMBOLIC, AND WHO
APPL I (224)	AND A SULTAN. /MAGNUS/ BUT WHAT INTEREST HAS A	KING	IN FLATTERING A SUBJECT? /AMANDA/ SUPPOSE SHE'S A
OVER PREFACE(165)	AS ENJOYING INTENSELY THE PERFORMANCE OF THE	KING	IN HAMLET BECAUSE ANYBODY COULD SEE THAT THE KING WAS
KING I (193)	THOUGHT! I GRANT YOU HE HAS NOT THE MAKINGS OF A	KING	IN HIM: I AM NOT BLIND TO HIS WEAKNESSES. BUT SURELY HE
KING I (218)	AND THEIR LITTLE COURTS. HERE IS PASTOR FOX, A	KING	IN HIS MEETING HOUSE, THOUGH HIS MEETINGS ARE AGAINST
6CAL (101)	BY GOD, I WILL BE MASTER IN MY OWN HOUSE AND	KING	IN MY OWN CAMP. TAKE THESE FELLOWS OUT AND HANG THEM IN
JOAN 2 (81)	FROM ORLEANS AND FROM FRANCE, AND TO CROWN YOU	KING	IN THE CATHEDRAL AT RHEIMS, WHERE ALL TRUE KINGS OF
SUPR HANDBOK(198)	JUST AS THE SAME QUALITIES WHICH MAKE THE LION	KING	IN THE FOREST ENSURE HIS DESTRUCTION WHEN HE ENTERS A
KING I (218)	ARE AGAINST THE LAW. HERE IS MR NEWTON, A	KING	IN THE NEW ROYAL SOCIETY. HERE IS GODFREY KNELLER: A
MRS PREFACE(156)	AN OFFICER OF THE ROYAL HOUSEHOLD, PLACES THE	KING	IN THE POSITION OF SAYING TO THE DRAMATIST " THUS, AND
JOAN 2 (86)	TO HIM FOR EVER AND EVER, AND BECOME THE GREATEST	KING	IN THE WORLD AS HIS STEWARD AND HIS BAILIFF, HIS
APPL I (202)	WHO I AM AS WELL AS I DO MYSELF. GO AND TELL THE	KING	I'M WAITING FOR HIM. D'YE SEE? " SO HE TOOK HIMSELF OFF
APPL INTRLUD(246)	LIFE -- WITH ME. WHAT YOU NEED TO MAKE YOU A REAL	KING	IS A REAL QUEEN. /MAGNUS/ BUT I HAVE GOT ONE.
ANNA (290)	AND STINK. (HE RISES, EXALTED BY HIS THEME). A	KING	IS A SPLENDID REALITY, A MAN RAISED ABOVE US LIKE A
BASH II,2, (118)	/LYDIA/ HERCULES CANNOT WITHSTAND HIM. SEE: THE	KING	IS DOWN; THE TALLEST CHIEF IS UP, HEELS OVER HEAD,
6CAL (101)	AND READY. /THE QUEEN/ OH, YOU MISTAKE, SIR: THE	KING	IS INCAPABLE OF REVENGE: MY HUSBAND IS THE FLOWER OF
CLEO II SD(130)	KEEPING THEM MOVING WITHOUT MUCH CEREMONY. THE	KING	IS LEFT IN HIS CHAIR, PITEOUS, OBSTINATE, WITH
O'FL (210)	MAN! THERES NO LORD LIEUTENANT IN ENGLAND: THE	KING	IS LORD LIEUTENANT. IT'S A SIMPLE QUESTION OF
APPL I (213)	THE KING IS WORKING THE PRESS AGAINST US. THE	KING	IS MAKING SPEECHES. THINGS HAVE COME TO A HEAD. HE SAID
APPL I (210)	COMPREHENSIVELY) WELL, SAY WHAT YOU WILL, THE	KING	IS NO FOOL, NOT WHEN YOU KNOW HOW TO HANDLE HIM.
APPL II (270)	BE SAID FOR IT, I HAVE NO OBJECTION. /PLINY/ ONE	KING	IS NO WORSE THAN ANOTHER, IS HE? /BOANERGES/ IS HE ANY
APPL INTRLUD(243)	MOMENT BECAUSE THEY ARE IN THE PALACE, AND THE	KING	IS NOT A GENTLEMAN, I MUST TAKE A HOUSE OUTSIDE. I AM
APPL I (225)	YOU, MY OWN CHARACTER IS FAR TOO VULNERABLE. A	KING	IS NOT ALLOWED THE LUXURY OF A GOOD CHARACTER. OUR
APPL I (226)	A SENSE OF HUMOR IS NOT A CRIME. AND WHEN THE	KING	IS NOT SETTING ME OFF, YOU ARE. /BOANERGES/ WHERE IS
6CAL SD(103)	CARRY PETER TO THE KING, AND FLING HIM DOWN. THE	KING	IS NOW GRINNING. HIS PAROXYSM OF TEARS HAS COMPLETELY
APPL II (274)	YOU REALLY THINK OF ME: NO REAL CRITICISM OF THE	KING	IS POSSIBLE. I HAVE NEVER BEEN ABLE TO SPEAK MY MIND AS
KING II (225)	GOOD CHRISTIANS. BUT BARBARA MAY BE RIGHT. WHEN A	KING	IS SHUNNED, AND HIS HEIR IS COURTED, HIS DEATH IS NOT
MTH5 (237)	GLORY EQUAL. THE MAJESTY CO-ETERNAL. SUCH AS THE	KING	IS SO IS THE QUEEN, THE KING THOUGHT-OUT AND HAND-MADE,
APPL I (226)	HAVE IN FACT NEVER BEEN MADE TO THEM. THUS EVERY	KING	IS SUPPOSED TO BE A LIBERTINE; AND AS, ODDLY ENOUGH, HE
SUPR HANDBOK(188)	GENERAL IS SET UP AS AN ALEXANDER; HIS	KING	IS THE FIRST GENTLEMAN IN THE WORLD; HIS POPE IS A
LION PREFACE(17)	MUST BE NOTED. THE CONSUMMATION OF PRAISE FOR A	KING	IS TO DECLARE THAT HE IS THE SON OF NO EARTHLY FATHER,
APPL I (213)	(THUNDEROUSLY) ORDER ORDER! /PROTEUS/ THE	KING	IS WORKING THE PRESS AGAINST US. THE KING IS MAKING
KING I (187)	WRATH) SIR: I NEITHER KNOW NOR CARE WHERE THE	KING	IS. THIS IS MY HOUSE; AND I DEMAND TO BE LEFT IN PEACE
APPL PREFACE(180)	EVERY BOY CAN BE AN ENGINE DRIVER OR A PIRATE	KING	. A NATION OF PRIME MINISTERS OR DICTATORS IS AS ABSURD
CATH PREFACE(159)	SPEECH RIDICULOUSLY LONG; AND WANTED TO PLAY THE	KING	. ANYHOW, WHETHER HE HAD THE WIT TO UTTER IT OR NOT,
O'FL PREFACE(202)	THE FORM OF DEVOTION TO ENGLAND AND ENGLAND'S	KING	. APPEAL TO HIS DISCONTENT, HIS DEADLY BOREDOM, HIS
APPL I (207)	/MAGNUS/ YES, YES: EVERYBODY FLATTERS THE	KING	. BUT EVERYBODY HAS NOT YOUR TACT. AND, MAY I SAY?
KING I (195)	ENGLAND IS GOVERNED BY ITS MOB INSTEAD OF BY ITS	KING	. BUT I TELL YOU, CHARLES, WHEN I AM KING THERE SHALL
APPL II (271)	AND IT WILL BRING US FACE TO FACE WITH A NEW	KING	. BUT THE NEW PROBLEMS AND THE NEW KING WILL NOT MAKE
BUOY IV (58)	MANAGE A FISH AND CHIPS BUSINESS. /FIFFY/ TRUE, O	KING	. BUT WE ARE NEEDED IN THE WORLD BETTERING BUSINESS,
JOAN 1 (64)	WELL, SHE MARRIED HER DAUGHTER TO THE ENGLISH	KING	. CAN YOU BLAME THE WOMAN? /POULENGEY/ I BLAME NOBODY.
KING I (200)	WILL CALL THEMSELVES PURVEYORS TO HIS MAJESTY THE	KING	. CREDIT WILL BE UNLIMITED. /JAMES/ REMEMBER THAT THIS
CLEO II (121)	PTOLEMY KINDLY ON THE SHOULDER) SO YOU ARE THE	KING	. DULL WORK AT YOUR AGE, EH? (TO POTHINUS) YOUR
CLEO II (132)	THAT VERY CLEVER, /CAESAR/ BRITANNUS: ATTEND THE	KING	. GIVE HIM IN CHARGE TO THAT POTHINUS FELLOW. (
KING II (230)	CONTENTED. IT IS THE WORST OF LUCK TO BE BORN A	KING	. GIVE ME A SKILLED TRADE AND EIGHT OR TEN SHILLINGS A
KING II (229)	A MODEL POPE. /CATHERINE/ MY FATHER WAS A GREAT	KING	. HE FOUGHT THE SPANIARDS AND SET PORTUGAL FREE FROM
APPL INTRLUD(251)	ACROSS THE SKY THAT YOU AND I ARE QUEEN AND	KING	. HOW CAN YOU HESITATE? WHAT ATTRACTION IS THERE FOR
KING I (199)	ELSE. AND THEY ALONE ARE FAITHFUL TO THE ELDERLY	KING	. I AM FIFTY, JAMIE, FIFTY: DONT FORGET THAT. AND WOMEN
APPL INTRLUD(254)	A JELLY. /MAGNUS/ A REAL MAN WOULD NEVER DO AS A	KING	. I AM ONLY AN IDOL, MY LOVE; AND ALL I CAN DO IS TO
CYMB V (145)	PSHAW! THAT WAS CLOTEN: SON, HE SAID, TO THE	KING	. I CUT HIS HEAD OFF. /CYMBELINE/ MARRY, THE GODS

APPL I (207)	MAN IN THE COUNTRY I SHOULD STILL BE ITS	KING	. I HAVE NOT WON MY POSITION BY MY MERITS. IF I HAD
KING II (227)	HAD LEARNT THAT MUCH THERE WAS AN END OF ME AS A	KING	. I KNEW TOO MUCH. /CATHERINE/ WITH WHAT YOU HAVE
APPL I (204)	HEARD EVERYTHING THAT COULD POSSIBLY BE SAID TO A	KING	. I SHALL BE GRATEFUL FOR THE SMALLEST NOVELTY.
CLEO I (114)	MAKE ALL THE MEN I LOVE KINGS. I WILL MAKE YOU A	KING	. I WILL HAVE MANY YOUNG KINGS, WITH ROUND, STRONG
APPL I (240)	HAVE HEARD WHY THE TWO LADIES CANNOT SUPPORT THE	KING	. IS THERE ANYBODY WHO CAN? SILENCE. /MAGNUS/ I SEE
APPL I (202)	ON YOUR ACCESSION? /SEMPRONIUS/ (RETURNING) THE	KING	. (HE GOES TO HIS TABLE AND TAKES THE VISITOR'S CHAIR
KING II (234)	COMPLETE HIS TOILET). NOW YOU LOOK EVERY INCH A	KING	. (MAKING HIM A FORMAL CURTSEY) YOUR MAJESTY'S VISIT
MIS. (135)	IS REALLY GREAT. I'M SURE HE WAS MEANT TO BE A	KING	. MY FATHER LOOKED DOWN ON JOHN, BECAUSE HE WAS A RATE
CLEO II (119)	SON OF AULETES THE FLUTE BLOWER WHO WAS YOUR	KING	. MY SISTER BERENICE DROVE HIM FROM HIS THRONE AND
6CAL PREFACE(90)	IS AS INCONCEIVABLE BY THEM AS A MEDIEVAL	KING	. NOW A PLAYWRIGHT'S DIRECT BUSINESS IS SIMPLY TO
KING I (190)	/CHARLES/ YOU COULD NOT LEAVE THEM WITHOUT A	KING	. PROTESTANT KINGS-- STUART KINGS-- ARE SIX A PENNY IN
CLEO II (126)	LIFE BEFORE CATO AND JUBA OF NUMIDIA, THE AFRICAN	KING	. /ACHILLAS/ (FOLLOWING UP POTHINUS'S SPEECH
MTH3 (96)	WAS THE POWER OF WITHHOLDING SUPPLIES FROM THE	KING	. /BURGE-LUBIN/ PRECISELY. THAT GREAT ENGLISHMAN SIMON
CLEO II (120)	I AM POTHINUS, THE GUARDIAN OF MY LORD THE	KING	. /CAESAR/ (PATTING PTOLEMY KINDLY ON THE SHOULDER) SO
CLEO I (114)	ALWAYS BE MY KING: MY NICE, KIND, WISE, GOOD OLD	KING	. /CAESAR/ OH, MY WRINKLES, MY WRINKLES! AND MY
JOAN 4 (105)	TO GOD; AND GOD WILL THEN VEST THEM WHOLLY IN THE	KING	. /CAUCHON/ NEED YOU FEAR THAT? YOU ARE THE MAKERS OF
KING I (196)	IN THE FACE. BUT IN FRANCE THERE IS A REAL	KING	. /CHARLES/ HE HAS A REAL ARMY AND REAL GENERALS. AND
KING I (220)	DUCHESS: IT IS MY RIGHT TO BE TAKEN IN BY THE	KING	. /CHARLES/ (RISING AND RESIGNEDLY GIVING HER HIS ARM)
KING II (229)	WHETHER THE PEOPLE SHOULD NOT CHOOSE THEIR	KING	. /CHARLES/ NOT THE ENGLISH PEOPLE. THEY WOULD CHOOSE
CYMB V (145)	PEACE, BOY: WE'RE IN THE PRESENCE OF THE	KING	. /IMOGEN/ OH, CADWAL, CADWAL, YOU AND POLYDORE, MY
JOAN 1 (60)	BAUDRICOURT; AND I TAKE NO ORDERS EXCEPT FROM THE	KING	. /JOAN/ (REASSURINGLY) YES, SQUIRE: THAT IS ALL
KING I (209)	QUIET, BARBARA. DO NOT PRESUME TO CONTRADICT YOUR	KING	. /KNELLER/ IF THERE IS A SCIENCE OF LINES, DO I NOT
MIS. (135)	GAVE HIM A HUNDRED IN HIS BIG WAY. JUST LIKE A	KING	. /LORD SUMMERHAYS/ NOT AT ALL. I HAD FIVE KINGS TO
APPL I (207)	(NOT QUITE CONVINCED) HOW CAN THAT BE? YOURE	KING	. /MAGNUS/ AND WHAT IS THE KING? AN IDOL SET UP BY A
APPL I (227)	KING. /PROTEUS/ (IMPLACABLY) A DUMB	KING	. /MAGNUS/ HM! WHAT NEXT? /PROTEUS/ THE WORKING OF
APPL INTRLUD(243)	ROUND) WHO IS THAT? /MAGNUS/ HIS MAJESTY THE	KING	. /ORINTHIA/ I DONT WANT TO SEE HIM. /MAGNUS/ HOW SOON
6CAL (97)	AND CHILDREN, ARE AT THE MERCY OF THIS GREAT	KING	. /PETER/ YOU MISTAKE HIM FOR HIS GRANDFATHER. GREAT!
APPL I (227)	LAID" AND SO FORTH. BUT POLITICALLY, YES: A DUMB	KING	. /PLINY/ (TO SOFTEN IT) A CONSTITUTIONAL KING.
CYMB V (143)	HANDS OFF MY MASTER! HE IS KIN TO THE	KING	. /POSTHUMUS/ (TO CYMBELINE) CALL OFF YOUR BULLDOGS,
CLEO II (119)	LET POTHINUS, THE KING'S GUARDIAN, SPEAK FOR THE	KING	. /POTHINUS/ (SUPPRESSING HIS IMPATIENCE WITH
APPL I (227)	KING. /PLINY/ (TO SOFTEN IT) A CONSTITUTIONAL	KING	. /PROTEUS/ (IMPLACABLY) A DUMB KING. /MAGNUS/ HM!
APPL I SD(238)	BREAKS IT IMPRESSIVELY AS HE ADDRESSES THE	KING	. /PROTEUS/ YOU HEAR THAT, SIR. YOUR ONE SUPPORTER IN
6CAL (93)	TELL ME ANYTHING. I MIGHT BE A DOG INSTEAD OF A	KING	. /THE PRINCE/ (ABOUT TO KNEEL) MAJESTY-- /THE KING/
APPL II SD(265)	AND PUTS THE QUEEN'S CHAIR IN THE CENTRE FOR THE	KING	. /THE QUEEN/ (SHAKING HANDS) HOW DO YOU DO, MR
KING II (226)	CHANCE AND TAKE IT. HE WILL BE KING: A PROTESTANT	KING	. SO YOU MUST MAKE FOR PORTUGAL. /CATHERINE/ BUT SUCH
KING I (190)	TO GO ON MY TRAVELS AND LEAVE THEM WITHOUT A	KING	. THAT IS THE WAY TO BRING THEM DOWN ON THEIR
POSN PREFACE(364)	EXCEPTIONAL CROSS FIRE. FIRST, THERE WAS THE	KING	. THE CENSOR IS A MEMBER OF HIS HOUSEHOLD RETINUE; AND
KING II (232)	THE PORTUGUESE CAN BELIEVE IN A CHURCH AND OBEY A	KING	. THE ENGLISH ROBBED THE CHURCH AND DESTROYED IT: IF A
JOAN 2 (87)	WITH IT REPEATEDLY) SILENCE FOR HIS MAJESTY THE	KING	. THE KING SPEAKS. (PEREMPTORILY) WILL YOU BE SILENT
JOAN 1 (64)	SHOULD JOIN THE DUKE OF BURGUNDY AND THE ENGLISH	KING	. THEY HOLD HALF THE COUNTRY, RIGHT DOWN TO THE LOIRE.
KING I (193)	ENGLISH LOUIS, THE BRITISH ROI SOLEIL, THE SUN	KING	. THIS IS A DEUCED FOGGY CLIMATE FOR SUN KINGS, JAMIE.
CLEO II (120)	SPEAK! /ACHILLAS/ BUT TWO ROMAN LEGIONS, O	KING	. THREE THOUSAND SOLDIERS AND SCARCE A THOUSAND
KING I (197)	DREAMS OF GLORY ABOUT THEM. I AM, AS YOU SAY, NO	KING	. TO BE WHAT YOU CALL A KING I LACK MILITARY AMBITION;
6CAL (102)	DO ANYTHING I WANT. I MIGHT AS WELL BE A DOG AS A	KING	. YOU TREAT ME LIKE A BABY. /THE QUEEN/ AH NO: YOU ARE
KING I (191)	LOSE MY PLACE IN WESTMINSTER ABBEY WHEN YOU ARE	KING	. YOUR PRINCIPLES MIGHT OBLIGE YOU TO THROW MY CARCASE
MIS. (135)	BUT AT LAST ONE DAY HE SAID TO ME, " JOHN IS A	KING	." /BENTLEY/ HOW MUCH DID HE BORROW ON THAT OCCASION..
BULL PREFACE(43)	WOULD STILL BE AS GOOD AS ENGLAND'S.	KING	JAMES THE FIRST PROVED SO CLEVERLY AND CONCLUSIVELY
KING I (195)	THE PEOPLE OF ENGLAND WILL HAVE TO CHOOSE BETWEEN	KING	JAMES THE SECOND AND KING TITUS OATES. AND JAMES AND
KING I (168)	WARRANT FOR SUPPOSING THAT REVELATION CEASED WHEN	KING	JAMES'S PRINTERS FINISHED WITH THE BIBLE? /FOX/ I DO
CYMB FORWORD(134)	LIKE THE CERES SCENE IN THE TEMPEST, TO PLEASE	KING	JAMIE, OR ELSE BECAUSE AN IRRESISTIBLE FASHION HAD SET
POSN PREFACE(420)	POLITICAL COMPREHENSION NOR POLITICAL VIRTUE THAN	KING	JOHN. WHEN HENRY VII CALMLY PROCEEDED TO TEAR UP MAGNA
SHAK (141)	/SHAKES/ WHERE IS THY HAMLET? COULDST THOU WRITE	KING	LEAR? /SHAV/ AYE, WITH HIS DAUGHTERS ALL COMPLETE.
3PLA PREFACE(R34)	FORGIVE HENRY IRVING FOR PRODUCING A VERSION OF	KING	LEAR SO MUTILATED THAT THE NUMEROUS CRITICS WHO HAD
POSN PREFACE(418)	JOURNEY, OR A MANAGER WHETHER HE MAY PRODUCE	KING	LEAR WITHOUT RISK OF PROSECUTION, THE SOLICITOR WILL
METH PREFACE(R85)	CONDITION WAS ONE OF DESPAIR. HIS TOWERING	KING	LEAR WOULD BE ONLY A MELODRAMA WERE IT NOT FOR ITS
MIS. (199)	ADVICE. READ SOMETHING. /TARLETON/ I'LL READ	KING	LEAR. /HYPATIA/ DONT. I'M VERY SORRY, DEAR. /TARLETON/
CYMB FORWORD(133)	THE STAGE, WHICH HAD PRODUCED A HAPPY ENDING TO	KING	LEAR, CIBBER'S RICHARD III, A LOVE SCENE IN THE TOMB OF
POSN PREFACE(418)	CLIENT THAT BOTH OF THEM ARE OBSCENE LIBELS; THAT	KING	LEAR, CONTAINING AS IT DOES PERHAPS THE MOST APPALLING
APPL I (224)	BY FLATTERING THEM; AND NOW THAT YOU ARE THE ONLY	KING	LEFT IN THE CIVILIZED HALF OF EUROPE NATURE SEEMS TO
MTH5 (238)	AND THE ACTIONS OF THE QUEEN ARE LIKEWISE. THE	KING	LOGICAL AND PREDETERMINED AND INEVITABLE, AND THE QUEEN
APPL I SD(225)	AMANDA BURSTS INTO UNCONTROLLABLE LAUGHTER. THE	KING	LOOKS REPROACHFULLY AT HER, STRUGGLING HARD TO KEEP HIS
APPL I SD(226)	THERE IS A RATHER GRIM SILENCE, DURING WHICH THE	KING	LOOKS ROUND IN VAIN FOR SOME ENCOURAGING RESPONSE.
APPL I (200)	THEY SAY THAT WHERE THERE IS NOTHING THE	KING	LOSES HIS RIGHTS. MY FATHER FOUND THAT WHERE THERE IS
MILL IV (203)	MRS FITZFASSENDEN. WHEN THERE IS NOTHING, THE	KING	LOSES HIS RIGHTS. /EPIFANIA/ OH, I CAN BEAR NO MORE OF
KING I (192)	/JAMES/ THE ARMY WILL COLLECT THE TAXES. HOW DOES	KING	LOUIS DO IT? HE KEEPS THE BIGGEST ARMY IN EUROPE; AND
KING I (192)	AS I DO. FRENCH MONEY IS AS GOOD AS ENGLISH.	KING	LOUIS GETS LITTLE ENOUGH FOR IT: I TAKE CARE OF THAT.
KING I (196)	THRONE AT VERSAILLES: NOT ONE OF THEM DARE LOOK	KING	LOUIS STRAIGHT IN THE FACE. BUT IN FRANCE THERE IS A
KING I (202)	IT BEAUTIFULLY. HE IS ALMOST AS GOOD AN ACTOR AS	KING	LOUIS; AND HE HAS REALLY MORE OF THE GRAND AIR.
APPL II (259)	WHAT THE DEVIL IS THE MATTER? /VANHATTAN/	KING	MAGNUS: BETWEEN YOUR COUNTRY AND MINE THERE IS A DEBT.
APPL II (259)	A YEAR TO BALANCE THE ACCOUNT. /VANHATTAN/	KING	MAGNUS: FOR THE MOMENT, FORGET FIGURES. BETWEEN YOUR
APPL II (272)	WHERE'S YOUR MANNERS? WHERE'S YOUR EDUCATION?	KING	MAGNUS: WE PART; BUT WE PART AS STRONG MEN PART: AS
APPL PREFACE(174)	ADOPTED BY THE ANTAGONISTS IN THE SCRAP BETWEEN	KING	MAGNUS AND MR JOSEPH PROTEUS IS SEEN TO BE A PLAIN
APPL I (202)	PUNCTUALITY IS THE POLITENESS OF KINGS; AND	KING	MAGNUS IS A MODEL IN THAT RESPECT. YOUR ARRIVAL CANNOT
APPL I (204)	STAMP, I THINK. AM I RIGHT? /BOANERGES/ YOU ARE,	KING	MAGNUS. AN INDIARUBBER STAMP. THATS WHAT YOU HAVE GOT
APPL I (203)	AND CREDULOUS) I SHOULD JUST THINK YOU HAVE,	KING	MAGNUS. I HAVE MADE YOU SIT UP ONCE OR TWICE, EH?
APPL II (260)	YESTERDAY. /VANHATTAN/ IT HAS. IT HAS INDEED,	KING	MAGNUS. /MAGNUS/ THEN WHAT IS IT? I HAVE NOT TIME TO
APPL PREFACE(174)	BE MADE TO YIELD A FARTHING FOR IT BY SUBSIDIES.	KING	MAGNUS'S LITTLE TACTICAL VICTORY, WHICH BULKS SO
APPL I SD(203)	TURNS TO THE DOOR IN HIS CHAIR WITHOUT RISING.	KING	MAGNUS, A TALLISH STUDIOUS LOOKING GENTLEMAN OF 45 OR
APPL (170)	MATTHEW BOULTON AS BOANERGES, CEDRIC HARDWICKE AS	KING	MAGNUS, EVE TURNER AS THE PRINCESS ROYAL, CHARLES
APPL II (258)	SHE LEARNS THE NATURE OF MY ERRAND HERE. THIS,	KING	MAGNUS, IS A GREAT HISTORIC SCENE: ONE OF THE GREATEST,
APPL II (260)	LIKE TO SEE THE FACES OF YOUR CABINET MINISTERS,	KING	MAGNUS, WHEN THEY HEAR WHAT I HAVE TO TELL YOU.
APPL I (223)	THEIR BREATHS) AHA-A-A-A-H! ! ! /PROTEUS/ NOW,	KING	MAGNUS! OUR CARDS ARE ON THE TABLE. WHAT HAVE YOU TO
JOAN PREFACE(50)	HAD NO MORE FEUDAL QUALITY THAN HIS SUCCESSOR THE	KING	MAKER HAS IN THE PLAY OF HENRY VI. WE SHOULD HAVE SEEN
SUPR HANDBOK(213)	MARRIED, WHEREAS IT MATTERED VERY MUCH WHOM THE	KING	MARRIED. THE WAY IN WHICH ALL CONSIDERATIONS OF THE
APPL II (261)	OUR CONDITIONS WILL BE THAT YOU SHALL BE EMPEROR.	KING	MAY BE GOOD ENOUGH FOR THIS LITTLE ISLAND; BUT IF WE
APPL I (229)	OUR CONSTITUENTS ARE REMINDED EVERY DAY THAT THE	KING	MAY VETO ANYTHING THAT PARLIAMENT DOES? DO YOU EXPECT
APPL II (270)	SHOULD HAVE HAD NOTICE OF THIS. BUT I SUPPOSE THE	KING	MUST DO AS HE THINKS RIGHT. /PROTEUS/ THEN THE GOAT
CLEO II (133)	WHAT NONSENSE! YOU MUST REMEMBER THAT YOU ARE A	KING	NOW: I HAVE MADE YOU ONE. KINGS DONT WORK. /CAESAR/
LION PREFACE(90)	THE STARS WOULD FALL FROM HEAVEN AND HE BECOME	KING	OF AN EARTHLY PARADISE. BUT IT IS EASY AND REASONABLE
MILL PREFACE(114)	THE PHYSICAL STRENGTH AND FEROCITY OF A	KING	OF BEASTS, THE POLITICAL GENIUS OF A KING OF MEN, THE
3PLA PREFACE(R31)	OF THAT SYSTEM ON US THROUGH THE MOUTH OF THE	KING	OF BROBDINGNAG, AND DESCRIBED MAN AS THE YAHOO,
SUPR PREFACE(R23)	GENIUS BEING A WOMAN, THEN THE GAME IS ONE FOR A	KING	OF CRITICS: YOUR GEORGE SAND BECOMES A MOTHER TO GAIN
CLEO II (119)	PLACES HIMSELF AT HIS LEFT HAND. /POTHINUS/ THE	KING	OF EGYPT HAS A WORD TO SPEAK. /THEODOTUS/ (IN A SQUEAK
CLEO II (133)	LITTLE KITTEN? EH? /CLEOPATRA/ MY FATHER WAS	KING	OF EGYPT; AND HE NEVER WORKED. BUT HE WAS A GREAT KING,
INCA (255)	KINGS NOWADAYS BELONG TO THE POORER CLASSES. THE	KING	OF ENGLAND DOES NOT EVEN ALLOW HIMSELF WINE AT DINNER.
JOAN 4 (102)	SHE, NOT THE CHURCH! SHE SENDS LETTERS TO THE	KING	OF ENGLAND GIVING HIM GOD'S COMMAND THROUGH HER TO
KING I (207)	SHALL NOT HAVE ME. I SHALL DIE IN MY BED, AND DIE	KING	OF ENGLAND IN SPITE OF THEM. /FOX/ THIS IS NOT
LION PREFACE(97)	HUNDRED AND SIXTEEN AND A HALF MILLIONS. THE	KING	OF ENGLAND IS THE DEFENDER OF THE FAITH; BUT WHAT FAITH
JOAN 1 (67)	TO YOU WHETHER HE IS THE DUKE OF BURGUNDY OR THE	KING	OF ENGLAND OR THE KING OF FRANCE? WHAT HAS THEIR
O'FL (209)	FOR THE SOULS OF THE BOSHES? " I SAYS. " LET THE	KING	OF ENGLAND PAY FOR THEM" I SAYS; " FOR IT WAS HIS
BULL PREFACE(30)	AS A BUREAUCRACY DERIVING AUTHORITY FROM THE	KING	OF ENGLAND. IT CANNOT CAST HIM OFF WITHOUT CASTING OFF
KING II (229)	AND ONE OF MY NIECES SUCCEEDS HIM JACK WILL BE	KING	OF ENGLAND. /CATHERINE/ PERHAPS THE CHURCH SHOULD
KING I (206)	YOU HAVE NOT SEEN ME PRACTISE IT. BUT I AM	KING	OF ENGLAND; AND MY HEAD IS STILL ON MY SHOULDERS.
DOCT PREFACE(31)	ESCAPADES. HAD HE BEEN A NINETEENTH-CENTURY	KING	OF ENGLAND, HE WOULD HAVE HAD TO WAIT FOR SOME HUGE
6CAL SD(93)	DAY OF THE SIEGE. THE PAVILION OF EDWARD III,	KING	OF ENGLAND, IS ON YOUR LEFT AS YOU FACE THE WALLS. THE
JOAN 6 (127)	COURTEOUS TO YOU, MASTER DE STOGUMBER, OR TO THE	KING	OF ENGLAND, TO ASSUME THAT ENGLISH IS THE DEVIL'S
JOAN 1 (67)	DUKE OF BURGUNDY OR THE KING OF ENGLAND OR THE	KING	OF FRANCE? WHAT HAS THEIR LANGUAGE TO DO WITH IT?

DOCT PREFACE(18)	BUT (IF VASARI IS TO BE BELIEVED) WHEN THE	KING	OF FRANCE ENTRUSTED HIM WITH MONEY TO BUY PICTURES FOR
JOAN EPILOG (157)	PRETTY CLOSE TO THE GROUND. AND I ASK YOU, WHAT	KING	OF FRANCE HAS DONE BETTER, OR BEEN A BETTER FELLOW IN
JOAN 2 (84)	BREAD FOR THEE; AND I TELL THEE THEY COUNT NO MAN	KING	OF FRANCE UNTIL THE HOLY OIL HAS BEEN POURED ON HIS
KING I (219)	HOW MUCH HE HAS: SHE GETS IT FOR HIM FROM THE	KING	OF FRANCE. /LOUISE/ THIS SUBJECT OF CONVERSATION IS IN
JOAN 5 (120)	FRANCE WOULD HAVE FRIENDS AT THE COURT OF THE	KING	OF FRANCE; AND I FIND ONLY WOLVES FIGHTING FOR PIECES
KING PREFACE(156)	HE WAS CLEVER ENOUGH TO GET IT FROM THE CATHOLIC	KING	OF FRANCE; FOR, THOUGH HEAD OF THE CHURCH OF ENGLAND,
JOAN EPILOG (158)	FELLOW IN HIS LITTLE WAY? /JOAN/ ART REALLY	KING	OF FRANCE, CHARLIE? BE THE ENGLISH GONE? /DUNOIS/ (
KING I (192)	YOU ARE. DO YOU THINK I WILL BE IN THE PAY OF THE	KING	OF FRANCE, WHOSE BITTER BREAD WE HAD TO EAT IN OUR
JOAN 1 (60)	YES, SQUIRE! THAT IS ALL RIGHT. MY LORD IS THE	KING	OF HEAVEN. /ROBERT/ WHY, THE GIRL'S MAD. (TO THE
JOAN 3 (90)	YOUR OWN? /JOAN/ NO: THE HELP AND COUNSEL OF THE	KING	OF HEAVEN. WHICH IS THE WAY TO THE BRIDGE? /DUNOIS/
JOAN 1 (67)	UNDERSTAND THAT A BIT. WE ARE ALL SUBJECT TO THE	KING	OF HEAVEN; AND HE GAVE US OUR COUNTRIES AND OUR
SIM II (61)	ORACLES OF THE WISE ARE UNHEEDED. SILENCE FOR THE	KING	OF IDIOTS. /MAYA/ (ALSO ENSHRINING HERSELF) SPEAK.
MTH5 (237)	THE INEVITABLE. MY NAME IS OZYMANDIAS,	KING	OF KINGS: LOOK ON MY WORKS, YE MIGHTY, AND DESPAIR.
KING I (217)	BECOME DUMB FLUNKEYS. WHAT WILL YOU BE WHEN THE	KING	OF KINGS CALLS YOU FROM YOUR GRAVES TO ANSWER FOR YOUR
MTH5 (243)	UNTIL HE REACHES HER HAND) I KNEW I WAS REALLY A	KING	OF KINGS. (TO THE OTHERS) ILLUSIONS, FAREWELL: WE ARE
METH PREFACE(R66)	MADE A GOOD RIDDANCE OF HIM. THE VICEROYS OF THE	KING	OF KINGS. NOW IN POLITICS IT IS MUCH EASIER TO DO
MTH5 (237)	HER) IS CLEOPATRA-SEMIRAMIS, CONSORT OF THE	KING	OF KINGS, AND THEREFORE QUEEN OF QUEENS. YE ARE THINGS
CLEO I (115)	ON HER STATE? /CAESAR/ FOR A CITIZEN OF ROME. A	KING	OF KINGS, TOTATEETA. /CLEOPATRA/ (STAMPING AT HER) HOW
APPL INTRLUD(244)	YOU ALWAYS HAVE A PRETTY EXCUSE. YOU ARE THE	KING	OF LIARS AND HUMBUGS. YOU CANNOT UNDERSTAND HOW A
DOCT V (172)	/RIDGEON/ (READING THE TITLE) THE STORY OF A	KING	OF MEN. BY HIS WIFE. (HE LOOKS AT THE PORTRAIT
JOAN PREFACE(12)	CHRONOLOGY, WHICH ESTABLISHES HIM AS THE	KING	OF MENTAL CONJURORS, BUT A BEDLAMITE KING WHOSE
MILL PREFACE(114)	OF A KING OF BEASTS, THE POLITICAL GENIUS OF A	KING	OF MEN, THE STRATEGIC CUNNING AND TACTICAL GUMPTION OF
DOCT V (178)	/RIDGEON/ WHAT TRUTH! WHY, THAT LOUIS DUBEDAT,	KING	OF MEN, WAS THE MOST ENTIRE AND PERFECT SCOUNDREL, THE
DOCT V (178)	EXCLAIMING) OH, MY KING OF MEN! /RIDGEON/	KING	OF MEN! OH, THIS IS TOO MONSTROUS, TOO GROTESQUE. WE
DOCT V (178)	IN A PAROXYSM OF REMORSE, EXCLAIMING) OH, MY	KING	OF MEN! /RIDGEON/ KING OF MEN! OH, THIS IS TOO
KING II (229)	/CHARLES/ THANK YOU. AND YOUR BROTHER ALFONSO WAS	KING	OF PORTUGAL BECAUSE HE WAS THE SON OF HIS FATHER. WAS
BULL PREFACE(10)	WHICH IS THE MODERN IMPERIAL IDEA. TO SINGE THE	KING	OF SPAIN'S BEARD; PICK HIS POCKET; AND RUN AWAY, WAS,
BULL PREFACE(20)	SUPREME TRIBUTE OF THE EXQUISITE COWARD TO THE	KING	OF TERRORS (FOR, BELIEVE ME, YOU CANNOT BE A HERO
ROCK PREFACE(181)	IN THE SAME CIRCUMSTANCES. /PILATE/ ARE YOU THE	KING	OF THE JEWS? /JESUS/ DO YOU REALLY WANT TO KNOW? OR
LION PREFACE(7)	TREASON AGAINST ROME BY SAYING THAT HE WAS THE	KING	OF THE JEWS. HE WAS NOT FALSELY ACCUSED, NOR DENIED
KING I (187)	DAUGHTER OF THE SOUTH: WHO WAS SHE? AND THE	KING	OF THE SOUTH? AND HE THAT COMETH AGAINST HIM? AND THE
CYMB V (147)	MARK WELL, LUCIUS, MARK. THERE SPAKE THE FUTURE	KING	OF THIS RUDE ISLAND. /GUIDERIUS/ WITH YOU, SIR THIEF,
LADY (242)	ANGELS, AS INDEED YOU DO, YET KNOW THAT I AM THE	KING	OF WORDS-- /THE LADY/ A KING, HA! /THE MAN/ NO LESS.
MTH5 (241)	WITH HIS KNEES KNOCKING) MY NAME IS OZYMANDIAS,	KING	OF-- /THE HE-ANCIENT/ (WITH A CONTEMPTUOUS GESTURE)
APPL I (208)	HIS EYEBROWS)! /BOANERGES/ (CONTINUING) NO	KING	ON EARTH IS AS SAFE IN HIS JOB AS A TRADE UNION
DEST (193)	BULLIES YOU ON MANLY PRINCIPLES; HE SUPPORTS HIS	KING	ON LOYAL PRINCIPLES AND CUTS OFF HIS KING'S HEAD ON
JOAN 4 (106)	PEOPLE FOLLOW THEIR FEUDAL LORDS, AND KNOW THE	KING	ONLY AS A TRAVELLING SHOW, OWNING NOTHING BUT THE
BULL PREFACE(11)	BE KINGS AND CHIEFS BECAUSE THEY IMAGINE THAT A	KING	OR A CHIEF IS AN IDLE VOLUPTUARY WITH LOTS OF MONEY,
APPL I (212)	DOESNT WORK. WHAT MAN HAS EVER APPROACHED A	KING	OR A MINISTER AND BEEN ABLE TO PICK HIM UP FROM THE
APPL I (205)	NOT DEAD. WHAT MAN HAS EVER APPROACHED EITHER A	KING	OR A MINISTER AND BEEN ABLE TO PICK HIM UP FROM THE
LADY PREFACE(232)	THROUGH AND THROUGH. NOBODY IN HIS PLAYS, WHETHER	KING	OR CITIZEN, HAS ANY CIVIL PUBLIC BUSINESS OR CONCEPTION
LION PREFACE(98)	SUCH LUDICROUSLY PAROCHIAL DELUSIONS. NO ENGLISH	KING	OR FRENCH PRESIDENT CAN POSSIBLY GOVERN ON THE
APPL I (206)	BREAKS DOWN IN EVERY REAL EMERGENCY, BECAUSE NO	KING	OR MINISTER IS THE VERY LEAST LITTLE BIT LIKE A STAMP:
GENV IV (93)	AND ROB THE PEOPLE WITHOUT INTERFERENCE FROM	KING	OR PRIEST; BUT THE PEOPLE ALWAYS FOLLOW THEIR BORN
DOCT PREFACE(5)	TO THE PATIENT. THE WONDER IS THAT THERE IS A	KING	OR QUEEN LEFT ALIVE IN EUROPE. DOCTORS' CONSCIENCES.
APPL PREFACE(171)	THE ENTIRELY PERSONAL TRIUMPH OF THE HEREDITARY	KING	OVER THE ELECTED MINISTER TO BE A TRIUMPH OF AUTOCRACY
CLEO II (120)	/THEODOTUS/ (WITH MUCH PRESENCE OF MIND) THE	KING	PERMITS THE ROMAN COMMANDER TO ENTER! CAESAR, PLAINLY
APPL II SD(277)	HANDS IMPULSIVELY; AND GOES WITH AMANDA. THE	KING	PLUNGES INTO DEEP THOUGHT. PRESENTLY THE QUEEN COMES
CLEO II SD(118)	IS TO TOTTENHAM COURT ROAD. THE YOUNG	KING	PTOLEMY DIONYSUS (AGED TEN) IS AT THE TOP OF THE
CLEO V (196)	THE WAR, APOLLODORUS? /APOLLODORUS/ THE LITTLE	KING	PTOLEMY WAS DROWNED. /BELZANOR/ DROWNED! HOW?
CLEO II (137)	DO YOU KNOW THAT YOU ARE IN ALEXANDRIA, AND THAT	KING	PTOLEMY, WITH AN ARMY OUTNUMBERING YOUR LITTLE TROOP A
APPL I (236)	WHAT SORT OF ANIMALS ARE YOU -- YOU MEN? THE	KING	PUTS BEFORE US THE MOST SERIOUS QUESTION OF PRINCIPLE
POSN PREFACE(393)	BY THE WAY IN WHICH THE CENSORSHIP MAKES THE	KING	RESPONSIBLE FOR THE CONTENTS OF EVERY PLAY. ONE
APPL I SD(232)	OBLIGE WITH A SONG. (HE RESUMES HIS SEAT). THE	KING	RETURNS WITH PROTEUS, WHO LOOKS GLUM. ALL RISE. THE TWO
APPL II SD(264)	IT IS NOT THE CLIMATE. IT IS THE HORSE SHOW. THE	KING	RISES VERY THOUGHTFULLY; AND VANHATTAN FOLLOWS HIS
APPL II (274)	SHALL NATURALLY ENDEAVOR TO FORM A PARTY. MY SON	KING	ROBERT WILL HAVE TO CALL ON SOME PARTY LEADER WHO CAN
KING I (190)	HOWEVER UNPOPULAR IT MAY MAKE ME. WHEN I AM	KING	-- AS I SHALL BE, IN MY OWN RIGHT, AND NOT BY THE LEAVE
KING II (229)	/CATHERINE/ PERHAPS THE CHURCH SHOULD SELECT THE	KING	-- OR THE QUEEN. /CHARLES/ THE CHURCH HAS FAILED OVER
APPL I (205)	IDEALIZE THEIR RULERS? IN THE OLD DAYS THE	KING	-- POOR MAN! -- WAS A GOD, AND WAS ACTUALLY CALLED GOD
APPL I (220)	THAT IS WHY THE PEOPLE TRUST US. (TO THE	KING	) AND THAT IS WHY YOU WILL HAVE TO GIVE WAY TO US. WE
APPL II (261)	HIS SEAT). /THE QUEEN/ (LOOKING ANXIOUSLY AT THE	KING	) DONT YOU THINK SO, MAGNUS? /MAGNUS/ (PULLING
6CAL (96)	SOLDIER, THE GREATEST BABY OF THEM ALL. (TO THE	KING	) HAVE YOU PUT ON YOUR FLANNEL BELLY BAND, DEAREST?
APPL I (236)	/BOANERGES/ ORDER! ORDER! /LYSISTRATA/ (TO THE	KING	) I BEG YOUR PARDON, SIR; BUT REALLY -- AT A MOMENT
APPL II (273)	SHAME! /PROTEUS/ SHUT UP, YOU BABY. (TO THE	KING	) I SAY, WHATS THE GAME? /MAGNUS/ THERE IS NO IMPOSING
JOAN PREFACE(19)	THE DESPERATE SITUATION OF THE UNCROWNED	KING	) SHOULD NOT HAVE SIMPLY GONE TO THE COURT AS A MAID,
6CAL (104)	YOU SHALL SUFFER FOR THIS INSOLENCE. (TO THE	KING	) WILL YOU, MY LORD, STAND BY AND HEAR ME SPOKEN TO IN
APPL II (271)	THERE, CHILDREN! STEADY! STEADY! (TO THE	KING	) YOU HAVE BROUGHT US ALL ROUND, SIR, AS USUAL.
APPL I (216)	ME: I SHOULD HAVE SAID AMANDA. (HE SITS NEXT THE	KING	). /AMANDA/ DONT MENTION IT, DARLING. /BOANERGES/
KING I (172)	NOT COME UP TO US. (HE RISES IN DISMISSAL OF THE	KING	). /CHARLES/ (RISING) I SEE I MUST TAKE MY LEAVE.
APPL I (211)	TO BUSINESS. (HE TAKES THE CHAIR VACATED BY THE	KING	). SEMPRONIUS AND PAMPHILIUS AT ONCE RISE AND GO OUT
JOAN 5 (110)	I HAVE CROWNED CHARLES AND MADE HIM A REAL	KING	; AND ALL THE HONORS HE IS HANDING OUT HAVE GONE TO
SUPR III (83)	DOWN AGAIN AND BE FRIENDLY. A CAT MAY LOOK AT A	KING	; AND EVEN A PRESIDENT OF BRIGANDS MAY LOOK AT YOUR
JOAN 2 (75)	CRAZY WENCH. /CHARLES/ (TURNING) BUT I AM THE	KING	; AND I WILL. /LA TREMOUILLE/ (BRUTALLY) THEN SHE
O'FL (206)	GRATIFYING SIDE TO IT, TOO. AFTER ALL, HE IS OUR	KING	; AND IT'S OUR OWN COUNTRY, ISNT IT? /O'FLAHERTY/
APPL I (213)	HAVE LEADING ARTICLES THIS MORNING SUPPORTING THE	KING	; AND THE LATEST ADDITION TO THE CABINET HERE IS A
GENV IV (126)	HEAVEN I SHALL LOSE MY JESUS. THERE HE WILL BE A	KING	; AND THERE WILL BE NO MORE TROUBLES AND SORROWS AND
KING I (195)	LIFE, BECAUSE NOBODY WILL KILL YOU TO MAKE ME	KING	; BUT I TAKE THAT AS THE HIGHEST COMPLIMENT YOU COULD
JOAN PREFACE(43)	AND MAINTAINED. A BISHOP WILL DEFER TO AND OBEY A	KING	; BUT LET A CURATE VENTURE TO GIVE HIM AN ORDER,
JOAN EPILOG (152)	I BRING YOU GLAD TIDINGS OF GREAT JOY. REJOICE, O	KING	; FOR THE TAINT IS REMOVED FROM YOUR BLOOD, AND THE
O'FL (206)	SAYS THEYRE PROUD TO KNOW ME, JUST THE WAY THE	KING	SAID WHEN HE PINNED THE CROSS ON ME. AND IT'S AS TRUE
ROCK II (264)	BASHAM: YOU WILL GET THE SACK THE DAY AFTER THE	KING	SENDS FOR ME. DOMESDAY! YOU HAVE GONE GAGA: GO HOME TO
APPL II (272)	HEARTS WHEN I CONCLUDE BY SAYING THAT WHATSOEVER	KING	SHALL REIGN -- /AMANDA/ YOULL BE THE VICAR OF BRAY,
JOAN PREFACE(6)	SHE HAD DISGRACED AND DEFEATED, THE FRENCH	KING	SHE HAD CROWNED AND THE ENGLISH KING WHOSE CROWN SHE
LION PREFACE(55)	BRITISH CONSERVATIVE HESITATES TO SAY THAT HIS	KING	SHOULD BE MUCH POORER THAN MR ROCKEFELLER, OR TO
KING II (231)	INTO YOUR MOUTH AT LAST; AND YOU HAVE BEEN A	KING	SINCE YOU WERE OLD ENOUGH TO USE YOUR POWER. BUT I! MY
APPL I SD(216)	BOANERGES HASTILY RISES AND SITS DOWN AGAIN. THE	KING	SITS IN PLINY'S CHAIR. LYSISTRATA AND THE REST OF THE
APPL I SD(203)	WITH ME. /MAGNUS/ (GRATEFULLY) THANK YOU. THE	KING	SITS. PAMPHILIUS SITS. SEMPRONIUS RETURNS TO HIS TABLE
6CAL SD(106)	FOR SHAME! FOR SHAME! HAVE MEN NO DECENCY? THE	KING	SNATCHES HER INTO HIS ARMS, LAUGHING BOISTEROUSLY. THE
FANY PREFACE(255)	AND ASSISTED THE MAKE-UP BY WHICH MR CLAUDE	KING	SO SUCCESSFULLY SIMULATED HIS PERSONAL APPEARANCE. THE
JOAN 4 (105)	DEVICE TO SUPERSEDE THE ARISTOCRACY, AND MAKE THE	KING	SOLE AND ABSOLUTE AUTOCRAT. INSTEAD OF THE KING BEING
JOAN 2 (87)	REPEATEDLY) SILENCE FOR HIS MAJESTY THE KING. THE	KING	SPEAKS. (PEREMPTORILY) WILL YOU BE SILENT THERE? (
BASH II,2, (116)	MAUL HIM. /WORTHINGTON/ HAVE NO FEAR. HARK! THE	KING	SPEAKS. /CETEWAYO/ YE SONS OF THE WHITE QUEEN: TELL ME
APPL I (235)	IGNORANCE AND POPULAR POVERTY. TODAY ONLY THE	KING	STANDS ABOVE THAT TYRANNY. YOU ARE DANGEROUSLY SUBJECT
6CAL SD(106)	/THE QUEEN/ NO NO: FOR SHAME! FOR SHAME! THE	KING	STOPS HER MOUTH WITH A KISS. PETER BRAYS MELODIOUSLY IN
6CAL SD(101)	OUT AND HANG THEM IN THEIR WHITE BEARDS. THE	KING	TAKES HIS PLACE ON HIS CHAIR OF STATE WITH HIS ARMS
SUPR PREFACE(R14)	THAN WORDSWORTH JUST AS IT MADE PETER A BOLDER	KING	THAN GEORGE III; BUT AS IT WAS, AFTER ALL, ONLY A
O'FL (207)	OFF MY BACK IF I'D EVER LET ON TO HAVE ANY OTHER	KING	THAN PARNELL. /SIR PEARCE/ (RISING, PAINFULLY SHOCKED)
KING I (196)	FROM HER FATHER'S HEAD? ROCHESTER CALLED YOU THE	KING	THAT NEVER SAID A FOOLISH THING AND NEVER DID A WISE
SUPR HANDBOK(213)	MILITARY EFFICIENCY. WELL, NOWADAYS IT IS NOT THE	KING	THAT RULES, BUT THE TINKER. DYNASTIC WARS ARE NO LONGER
JOAN 1 (69)	ON THE SOIL OF FRANCE; AND THERE WILL BE BUT ONE	KING	THERE: NOT THE FEUDAL ENGLISH KING, BUT GOD'S FRENCH
KING I (195)	BY ITS KING. BUT I TELL YOU, CHARLES, WHEN I AM	KING	THERE SHALL BE NO SUCH NONSENSE. YOU JEER AT ME AND SAY
MTH5 (238)	SUCH AS THE KING IS SO IS THE QUEEN, THE	KING	THOUGHT-OUT AND HAND-MADE, THE QUEEN THOUGHT-OUT AND
KING II (228)	BE THE MAKINGS OF A CAPABLE COUNCIL AND A CAPABLE	KING	THREE OR FOUR TIMES OVER, IF ONLY WE KNEW HOW TO PICK
KING I (195)	HAVE TO CHOOSE BETWEEN KING JAMES THE SECOND AND	KING	TITUS OATES, AND JAMES AND THE CHURCH-- AND THERE IS
POSN PREFACE(394)	LORD CHAMBERLAIN IT WOULD BE IMPOSSIBLE FOR THE	KING	TO ALLOW THE LICENCE TO BE ISSUED, AS HE WOULD THEREBY
APPL II SD(266)	AND BALBUS. A PAUSE, PROTEUS WAITING FOR THE	KING	TO BEGIN. HE, DEEP IN THOUGHT, SAYS NOTHING. THE
APPL I (211)	/BOANERGES/ RIGHT AS RAIN, JOE. YOU LEAVE THE	KING	TO ME. I KNOW HOW TO HANDLE HIM. IF I'D BEEN IN THE

JOAN PREFACE(3)	PATRONIZED HER OWN KING, AND SUMMONED THE ENGLISH	KING	TO REPENTANCE AND OBEDIENCE TO HER COMMANDS. SHE
APPL I (215)	TABLE, WHERE SHE STANDS WAITING FOR THE	KING	TO SIT DOWN.) /PROTEUS/ THIS IS WHAT I HAVE TO PUT UP
KING II (231)	AND THEIR RELIGION WHEN THEY MADE ME THEIR BOY	KING	TO SPITE OLD NOLL. I SOMETIMES THINK RELIGION AND
O'FL (210)	WOULD TO YOU, SIR. IT MEANS ENGLAND AND ENGLAND'S	KING	TO YOU. TO ME AND THE LIKE OF ME, IT MEANS TALKING
KING I (215)	AND TURNING IT OVER TO IDENTIFY IT) HAS THE	KING	TORN UP A WORK OF MINE? I LEAVE THE COUNTRY THIS
6CAL PREFACE(89)	MODERN LONDON JOURNALISTS. THEIR ONLY NOTION OF A	KING	WAS A PLEASANT AND HIGHLY RESPECTABLE GENTLEMAN IN A
OVER PREFACE(165)	KING IN HAMLET BECAUSE ANYBODY COULD SEE THAT THE	KING	WAS AN ACTOR, AND RESENTING GARRICK'S HAMLET BECAUSE IT
HART I (62)	OF KING EDWARD'S HUNTING PARTIES IN INDIA. THE	KING	WAS FURIOUS: THAT WAS WHY HE NEVER HAD HIS MILITARY
SUPR PREFACE(R28)	FOR A MOMENT. COULD IT BE THAT THE DIAMOND	KING	WAS NO GENTLEMAN AFTER ALL? HOWEVER, IT WAS EASY TO
KING I (183)	MUST NOT DO HIM ANY HARM; FOR IF WE POISON THE	KING	WE SHALL BE EXECUTED IN THE MOST HORRIBLE MANNER. IT
KING II (231)	IN OUR FORTUNES! ALL YOUR HOPES OF BEING A	KING	WERE CUT OFF! YOU WERE AN EXILE, AN OUTCAST, A
KING II (226)	YOU ARE GONE. BUT JAMES IS A CATHOLIC. WHEN HE IS	KING	WHAT HAVE I TO FEAR? OR DO YOU BELIEVE YOUR SON
APPL I (212)	STOP SQUABBLING. WHAT ARE WE GOING TO SAY TO THE	KING	WHEN HE COMES IN? IF YOU WILL ONLY HOLD TOGETHER AND
MTH3 (97)	YOU CALLED IT, AND CUTTING OFF THE HEAD OF YOUR	KING	WHENEVER HE HAPPENED TO BE A LOGICAL SCOT AND TRIED TO
ROCK PREFACE(151)	CROWN WITH HIS SON, AND, AFTER EJECTING THE NEXT	KING	WHO BROKE IT, A STILL HARDER ONE WITH HIS DUTCH
APPL PREFACE(174)	UNDER DOG IN THE CONFLICT. BUT TO ME IT IS THE	KING	WHO IS DOOMED TO BE TRAGICALLY IN THAT POSITION IN THE
LION PREFACE(3)	AND YET CLAIMS TO BE A PATRIOTIC SUBJECT OF THE	KING	WHO MAKES THEM. WE HAVE ALWAYS HAD A CURIOUS FEELING
APPL PREFACE(172)	WITH A DOCILITY WHICH CANNOT BE IMPOSED ON A	KING	WHO WORKS AT HIS JOB; FOR THE KING WORKS CONTINUOUSLY
JOAN PREFACE(12)	AS THE KING OF MENTAL CONJURORS, BUT A BEDLAMITE	KING	WHOSE AUTHORITY NO ONE NOW ACCEPTS. ON THE SUBJECT OF
JOAN PREFACE(6)	THE FRENCH KING SHE HAD CROWNED AND THE ENGLISH	KING	WHOSE CROWN SHE HAD KICKED INTO THE LOIRE, WERE EQUALLY
KING II (234)	I COULD BELIEVE IT. /CHARLES/ YOU MEAN I AM THE	KING	WHOSE WORD NO MAN RELIES ON. /CATHERINE/ NO: YOU ARE
CLEO II (123)	THIS IS HOW SHE TREATS ME ALWAYS. IF I AM A	KING	WHY IS SHE ALLOWED TO TAKE EVERYTHING FROM ME?
JOAN 4 (105)	QUITE SOUND THEOLOGICALLY, MY LORD. BUT THE	KING	WILL HARDLY CARE, PROVIDED HE REIGN. IT IS AN ABSTRACT
6CAL (101)	OUR HEARTHS AND HOMES TO THE LAST EXTREMITY. THE	KING	WILL NOT BE BAULKED OF HIS REVENGE; AND WE ARE SHRIVEN
APPL II (271)	WITH A NEW KING. BUT THE NEW PROBLEMS AND THE NEW	KING	WILL NOT MAKE US FORGET OUR OLD COUNSELLOR, MONARCH,
CLEO II (120)	THE FORCE AND EMPHASIS OF POLITICAL PASSION) THE	KING	WILL NOT SUFFER A FOREIGNER TO TAKE FROM HIM THE THRONE
KING II (226)	MUST GO BACK TO PORTUGAL, WHERE YOUR BROTHER THE	KING	WILL TAKE CARE OF YOU. YOU WILL NEVER BE SAFE HERE,
JOAN 4 (105)	OUR OWN TENANTS. NOW BY THE MAID'S DOCTRINE THE	KING	WILL TAKE OUR LANDS -- OUR LANDS! -- AND MAKE THEM A
BULL PREFACE(36)	THE TRADITIONAL COUNTER LEGEND, " TO HELL WITH	KING	WILLIAM! " (OF GLORIOUS, PIOUS, AND IMMORTAL MEMORY);
APPL PREFACE(171)	THE COMEDIC PARADOX OF THE SITUATION IS THAT THE	KING	WINS, NOT BY EXERCISING HIS ROYAL AUTHORITY, BUT BY
APPL PREFACE(173)	THE TWO, BOTH PLAY WITH EQUAL SKILL; AND THE	KING	WINS, NOT BY GREATER ASTUTENESS, BUT BECAUSE HE HAS THE
CLEO II (119)	(SUPPRESSING HIS IMPATIENCE WITH DIFFICULTY) THE	KING	WISHED TO SAY THAT THE GODS WOULD NOT SUFFER THE
APPL I (235)	DO! THE PERSONS YOU DARE NOT OFFEND! WELL, A	KING	WITH A LITTLE COURAGE MAY TACKLE THEM FOR YOU.
KING I SD(189)	UNWORTHY TO UNLOOSE. HE RISES AND CONFRONTS THE	KING	WITH DIGNITY. /CHARLES/ WILL YOU GET UP, JAMIE, AND NOT
CLEO II SD(119)	COURT-BRED PRINCES OF ALL AGES. ALL RECEIVE THE	KING	WITH REVERENCES. HE COMES DOWN THE STEPS TO A CHAIR OF
DOCT PREFACE(11)	TO SOCIAL REFORM, THE STRANGLING OF THE LAST	KING	WITH THE ENTRAILS OF THE LAST PRIEST, SUBSTITUTED
APPL PREFACE(172)	IMPOSED ON A KING WHO WORKS AT HIS JOB; FOR THE	KING	WORKS CONTINUOUSLY WHILST HIS MINISTERS ARE IN OFFICE
BULL PREFACE(11)	THE NEGLECT OF HIS OWN PROPER AFFAIRS, THAN THE	KING	WOULD HAVE DIED OF CAPTIVITY. BERMONDSEY GOES TO THE
POSN PREFACE(364)	OF THE WORD) BY THE SLIGHTEST INTIMATION THAT THE	KING	WOULD PREFER NOT TO MEET THEM; AND THIS WAS A HEAVY
JOAN 2 (84)	YOUR FILL AT THE POOR DEVIL. /JOAN/ THOURT NOT	KING	YET, LAD: THOURT BUT DAUPHIN. BE NOT LED AWAY BY THEM
MILL PREFACE(110)	HELPLESSLY INTO THE HANDS OF THE BORN BOSSES. A	KING	, A PRELATE, A SQUIRE, A CAPITALIST, A JUSTICE OF THE
CLEO II (120)	OF OUR EGYPT. (A SHOUT OF APPLAUSE). TELL THE	KING	, ACHILLAS, HOW MANY SOLDIERS AND HORSEMEN FOLLOW THE
LION PREFACE(8)	TO RECEIVE THE VICTORIA CROSS AT THE HANDS OF THE	KING	, ALTHOUGH HE WAS IN FACT A MECHANIC, NOBODY THINKS OF
CLEO II (133)	OF EGYPT; AND HE NEVER WORKED. BUT HE WAS A GREAT	KING	, AND CUT OFF MY SISTER'S HEAD BECAUSE SHE REBELLED
6CAL SD(103)	HERE. THE THREE MEN-AT-ARMS CARRY PETER TO THE	KING	, AND FLING HIM DOWN. THE KING IS NOW GRINNING. HIS
JOAN 2 (75)	AN ANGEL. AND SHE IS COMING TO ME: TO ME, THE	KING	, AND NOT TO YOU, ARCHBISHOP, HOLY AS YOU ARE. SHE
PRES (139)	THE ONLY SON OF WHAT THEY CALL A SODA	KING	, AND ORDERS A CURATE TO LICK HIS BOOTS. AND WHEN THE
BULL PREFACE(11)	HAVE SUFFERED AS MUCH BY SUCH A FOLLY AS THE	KING	, AND PROBABLY DIED SOONER OF WORRY, ANXIETY, EXPENSE,
JOAN PREFACE(3)	IN THE FLESH ON EARTH. SHE PATRONIZED HER OWN	KING	, AND SUMMONED THE ENGLISH KING TO REPENTANCE AND
JOAN 4 (106)	PEOPLE'S THOUGHTS AND HEARTS WERE TURNED TO THE	KING	, AND THEIR LORDS BECAME ONLY THE KING'S SERVANTS IN
JOAN 2,SD(80)	IS STANDING THEATRICALLY ON THE DAIS, PLAYING THE	KING	, AND, LIKE THE COURTIERS, ENJOYING THE JOKE RATHER
JOAN PREFACE(44)	SOON COLLAPSED AND OBEYED. AND SO ON UP TO THE	KING	, AS WE HAVE SEEN. THIS WOULD HAVE BEEN UNBEARABLY
APPL PREFACE(173)	IF HE FINDS HIMSELF INVOLVED IN A DUEL WITH HIS	KING	, BE CAREFUL NOT TO CHOOSE THE WEAPONS AT WHICH THE
JOAN 4 (105)	WE HOLD OUR LANDS AND DIGNITIES FROM THE	KING	, BECAUSE THERE MUST BE A KEYSTONE TO THE ARCH OF HUMAN
JOAN 1 (69)	BE BUT ONE KING THERE: NOT THE FEUDAL ENGLISH	KING	, BUT GOD'S FRENCH ONE. /ROBERT/ (TO POULENGEY) THIS
MRS PREFACE(160)	PARENTS TO MARRY THE DAUGHTER OF A NEIGHBORING	KING	, BUT LOVES ANOTHER MAIDEN. THE SCENE REPRESENTS A HALL
KING I (194)	WHAT! ! ! /CHARLES/ AND I, WHO AM CALLED A	KING	, CANNOT GET RID OF HIM. THIS HOUSE IS ISAAC NEWTON'S;
KING I (190)	THERE HAS BEEN NO REAL RESTORATION: YOU ARE NO	KING	, CLEVERLY AS YOU PLAY WITH THESE WHIGS AND TORIES.
DOCT PREFACE(26)	PRINCE-- NO, NOT EVEN THE SON OF A CHICAGO MEAT	KING	, COULD AFFORD THE TREATMENT. YET IT IS DOUBTFUL
O'FL (207)	DIVIL A PERCH OF IT EVER I OWNED. AND AS TO THE	KING	, GOD HELP HIM, MY MOTHER WOULD HAVE TAKEN THE SKIN OFF
6CAL (94)	FOR MERCY AT MY SUMMONS. AM I NOT THEIR LAWFUL	KING	, HA? /THE PRINCE/ UNDOUBTEDLY, SIR. THEY-- /THE KING/
LADY (242)	KNOW THAT I AM THE KING OF WORDS-- /THE LADY/ A	KING	, HA! /THE MAN/ NO LESS. WE ARE POOR THINGS, WE MEN
APPL II (269)	REPUBLICAN I HAVE NO RESPECT FOR HIS MAJESTY AS A	KING	, I HAVE A GREAT RESPECT FOR HIM AS A STRONG MAN. BUT
JOAN 2 (85)	OF THAT SORT? /JOAN/ I CAN TURN THEE INTO A	KING	, IN RHEIMS CATHEDRAL; AND THAT IS A MIRACLE THAT WILL
6CAL SD(96)	AND A GROUP OF NOBLEMEN ATTENDANT ON THE	KING	, INCLUDING SIR WALTER MANNY AND THE LORDS DERBY,
LADY PREFACE(231)	REBEL BY APPEALING TO THE DIVINITY THAT HEDGES A	KING	, IS A DRUNKEN AND SENSUAL ASSASSIN, AND IS PRESENTLY
SUPR HANDBOK(191)	WHERE THE ARTIZAN IS BETTER EDUCATED THAN THE	KING	, IT TAKES A MUCH BIGGER MAN TO BE A SUCCESSFUL
CLEO II SD(118)	HE HAS FINE TAWNY HAIR, LIKE FUR. PTOLEMY, THE	KING	, LOOKS MUCH OLDER THAN AN ENGLISH BOY OF TEN; BUT HE
KING I (217)	I LOVE YOU WHEN YOU PUT ON YOUR ROYALTY. MY	KING	, LOUIS QUATORZE, LE GRAND MONARQUE, LE ROI SOLEIL,
GENV IV (93)	THEIR BORN LEADER. WHEN THERE IS NO LEADER, NO	KING	, NO PRIEST, NOR ANY BODY OF LAW ESTABLISHED BY DEAD
APPL I (235)	BE BORNE ON A KING'S SHOULDERS. BUT HE MUST BE	KING	, NOT A PUPPET. YOU WOULD BE RESPONSIBLE FOR A PUPPET:
PYGM II (229)	WELL, WHAT I SAY IS RIGHT. I WONT GO NEAR THE	KING	, NOT IF I'M GOING TO HAVE MY HEAD CUT OFF. IF I'D
JOAN 5 (114)	VOICES. WHY DONT THE VOICES COME TO ME? I AM	KING	, NOT YOU. /JOAN/ THEY DO COME TO YOU; BUT YOU DO NOT
GENV IV (93)	HAS DELIVERED YOU FROM THE LAW OF PRIEST AND	KING	, OF LANDLORD AND CAPITALIST, ONLY TO BRING YOU UNDER
POSN PREFACE(428)	WORKS AS SWEET LAVENDER, PETER PAN, THE SILVER	KING	, OR ANY OF THE 99 PER CENT OF PLAYS THAT ARE EQUALLY
HART PREFACE(10)	THE BODIES OF THEIR FELLOW-CITIZENS AS NEITHER	KING	, POPE, NOR PARLIAMENT DARE EVER HAVE CLAIMED. THE
GENV IV (99)	EXERCISE A PERSONAL AUTHORITY UNATTAINABLE BY ANY	KING	, PRESIDENT, OR MINISTER. THAT IS SIMPLE, NATURAL,
APPL II SD(266)	LEFT IS NICOBAR, CRASSUS, BOANERGES, AMANDA, THE	KING	, PROTEUS, LYSISTRATA, PLINY, AND BALBUS. A PAUSE,
6CAL SD(97)	IN AN ATTITUDE OF INTENSE RECALCITRANCE. THE	KING	, SCOWLING FIERCELY AT ST PIERRE AND THE REST, DOES NOT
JOAN PREFACE(17)	FOR A MEDIEVAL CAPTAIN, OR EVEN A MEDIEVAL	KING	, THAN ITS MERE PHYSICAL DIFFICULTY AS A MILITARY
BARB PREFACE(224)	OR A LIBRARY IS THE SON-IN-LAW OF A CHICAGO MEAT	KING	, THAT YOUNG CLERGYMAN HAS, LIKE BARBARA, A VERY BAD
JOAN PREFACE(45)	TO FORGE SUCH A CHAIN SHE NEEDED TO BE THE	KING	, THE ARCHBISHOP OF RHEIMS, THE BASTARD OF ORLEANS, AND
JOAN PREFACE(44)	ORDERED EVERYBODY ABOUT, FROM HER UNCLE TO THE	KING	, THE ARCHBISHOP, AND THE MILITARY GENERAL STAFF. HER
KING I (196)	CALL HIM, DARED TO INTERFERE WITH ME, A CATHOLIC	KING	, THE POPE COULD TAKE HIS PART AGAINST ME IN THE FACE
2TRU PREFACE(15)	THESE RIVAL VIEWS OF THE SITUATION. THE PIRATE	KING	, THE ROBBER BARON, AND THE MANCHESTER MAN PRODUCED
JOAN 2 (84)	GOD PUTS ON THEE. IF THOU FAIL TO MAKE THYSELF	KING	, THOULT BE A BEGGAR: WHAT ELSE ART FIT FOR? COME!
ROCK PREFACE(151)	THE VICTORIOUS ELECTION WINNERS EXTERMINATED THE	KING	, VERY LOGICALLY. FINDING THAT THEIR AUTHORITY STILL
KING I (202)	LOUIS. /JAMES/ PRAY SILENCE FOR HIS MAJESTY THE	KING	, WHO IS GOING TO MAKE A FOOL OF HIMSELF TO PLEASE THE
APPL II SD(277)	FOR DINNER. COME ON, LIKE A GOOD LITTLE BOY. THE	KING	, WITH A GRIMACE OF HOPELESS TENDERNESS, ALLOWS HIMSELF
APPL II (275)	ON AS BEFORE. THE CRISIS IS A WASHOUT. (TO THE	KING	, WITH DEADLY CONCENTRATION) I WILL NEVER FORGIVE YOU
APPL II SD(258)	FIRST AT HIM, AND THEN APPEALINGLY AT THE	KING	, WITH HER HANDS BEING VIGOROUSLY WRUNG AND WAVED UP
ROCK PREFACE(151)	DUTCH GRANDSON BEFORE THEY ALLOWED THE TITLE OF	KING	, WITH NINE TENTHS OF THE MEANING KNOCKED OUT OF IT, TO
CLEO II (124)	FROM ME? /CLEOPATRA/ YOU ARE NOT TO BE	KING	, YOU LITTLE CRY-BABY. YOU ARE TO BE EATEN BY THE
CLEO IV (172)	THIS. YOU THINK THAT BY MAKING MY BROTHER	KING	, YOU WILL RULE IN EGYPT, BECAUSE YOU ARE HIS GUARDIAN
APPL I (240)	KISS)! /MAGNUS/ SHOULD NOT THE QUEEN SUPPORT THE	KING	, YOUR MAJESTY? /AMANDA/ SORRY, SIR; BUT THERE ISNT
APPL I (229)	WHEN I AM ASKED FOR A PLEDGE, " YOU MUST ASK THE	KING	"? /MAGNUS/ I HAVE TO SAY " YOU MUST ASK THE PRIME
FOUN (210)	THE INFANT. I'M BRABAZON. I'LL CALL THEE HAMLET!	KING	! FATHER! ROYAL DANE: WILT THOU NOT ANSWER ME? (
APPL I (207)	/MAGNUS/ YOU FLATTER ME. /BOANERGES/ FLATTER A	KING	! NEVER. NOT BILL BOANERGES. /MAGNUS/ YES, YES:
KING II (234)	VISIT HAS MADE ME VERY HAPPY. LONG LIVE THE	KING	! /CHARLES/ MAY THE QUEEN LIVE FOR EVER! HE THROWS UP
BASH II,1, (110)	SDEATH! IS IT HALF-PAST TWO? THE KING! THE	KING	! /LYDIA/ THE KING! WHAT MEAN YOU? /CASHEL/ I MUST
ARMS II (33)	AT HIM WITH ADMIRATION AND WORSHIP) MY HERO! MY	KING	! /SERGIUS/ MY QUEEN! (HE KISSES HER ON THE
BASH II,1, (110)	/CASHEL/ SDEATH! IS IT HALF-PAST TWO? THE	KING	! THE KING! /LYDIA/ THE KING! WHAT MEAN YOU?
6CAL (94)	IN THE EYES WITH HIS HEAD UP AS IF I-- I, HIS	KING	! WERE DIRT BENEATH HIS FEET. BY GOD, I WILL HAVE THAT
BASH II,1, (110)	HALF-PAST TWO? THE KING! THE KING! /LYDIA/ THE	KING	! WHAT MEAN YOU? /CASHEL/ I MUST MEET A MONARCH THIS

KINGCRAFT

KING I (207)	OF ENGLAND IN SPITE OF THEM. /FOX/ THIS IS NOT	KINGCRAFT	: IT IS CHICANERY. PROTESTANTISM GIVES THE LIE TO

KING I (198)	I OUGHT NOT TO TALK TO YOU ABOUT GOVERNMENT AND	KINGCRAFT	: YOU DONT UNDERSTAND THESE MATTERS AND NEVER
FABL PREFACE(69)	AS FANCIES AND FICTIONS. MENDACITY COMPULSORY IN	KINGCRAFT	AND PRIESTCRAFT. THIS LANDS THEM IN THE QUAINTEST
KING I (206)	YOU PRACTISE IT, CHARLES. WHAT IS IT? /CHARLES/	KINGCRAFT	. /JAMES/ OF WHICH YOU HAVE NOT THE FAINTEST
BARB PREFACE(220)	IS NOT SIN, SUFFERING, GREED, PRIESTCRAFT,	KINGCRAFT	, DEMAGOGY, MONOPOLY, IGNORANCE, DRINK, WAR,
		KINGDOM	
CYMB V (141)	ITALIAN GENTRY, AND TO FIGHT AGAINST MY LADY'S	KINGDOM	: 'TIS ENOUGH THAT, BRITAIN, I HAVE KILL'D THY
MILL PREFACE(114)	PERSON WHO HAS A CAPACITY FOR KINGSHIP BUT HAS NO	KINGDOM	AND MUST THEREFORE ACQUIRE A READYMADE ONE WHICH IS
APPL I (208)	THAT THEY HAVE THE VOTE, AND THAT THEIRS IS THE	KINGDOM	AND THE POWER AND THE GLORY. I SAY TO THEM " YOU ARE
APPL II (276)	AS IF ANOTHER PLANET WERE CRASHING INTO US. THE	KINGDOM	AND THE POWER AND THE GLORY WILL PASS FROM US AND
2TRU III (112)	OUT UNTO ALL LANDS AND REALIZE FOR US AT LAST THE	KINGDOM	AND THE POWER AND THE GLORY FOR EVER AND EVER. AMEN.
LION PREFACE(38)	AND RETAINS UNDISTURBED HIS VIEW OF THE	KINGDOM	AS A LOCALITY AS DEFINITE AS JERUSALEM OR
KING II (233)	TO HER AS YOU ARE, AND WOULD HAVE HER OUT OF THE	KINGDOM	BEFORE SHE COULD SAY JACK ROBINSON. SO NOW SHE HAS
KING I (187)	AGAINST HIM? AND THE VILE PERSON WHO OBTAINS THE	KINGDOM	BY FLATTERIES? AND MICHAEL? WHO WAS MICHAEL? (HE
KING II (231)	WERE AN EXILE, AN OUTCAST, A FUGITIVE. YET YOUR	KINGDOM	DROPPED INTO YOUR MOUTH AT LAST; AND YOU HAVE BEEN A
LADY PREFACE(229)	LUDICROUS EXTRAVAGANCE, MAKING RICHARD OFFER HIS	KINGDOM	FOR A HORSE AND OTHELLO DECLARE OF CASSIO THAT " HAD
CLEO II (119)	DAUGHTERS MY SISTER CLEOPATRA WOULD SNATCH THE	KINGDOM	FROM ME AND REIGN IN MY PLACE. BUT THE GODS WOULD
ROCK PREFACE(186)	YOU UNDERTOOK TO SUPERSEDE THE ROMAN EMPIRE BY A	KINGDOM	IN WHICH YOU AND NOT CAESAR ARE TO OCCUPY THE
JOAN 4 (107)	IS THE REALM OF CHRIST'S KINGDOM. DIVIDE THAT	KINGDOM	INTO NATIONS, AND YOU DETHRONE CHRIST. DETHRONE
LION PREFACE(28)	THE POSITION THEY SHALL OCCUPY IN HEAVEN WHEN HIS	KINGDOM	IS ESTABLISHED. HE REBUKES THEM STRENUOUSLY FOR
ROCK II (264)	A CIVILIZATION COMPARED TO WHICH YOUR LITTLE	KINGDOM	IS NO BETTER THAN A CONCENTRATION CAMP. WHAT YOU
ROCK PREFACE(181)	ME FOR JUDGMENT. WHAT HAVE YOU DONE? /JESUS/ MY	KINGDOM	IS NOT OF THIS WORLD: IF IT WERE, MY FOLLOWERS WOULD
BUOY II (26)	ARE THROWING THE HATCHET AFTER THE HANDLE. HIS	KINGDOM	IS WITHIN US; BUT IT IS FOR US TO ADMINISTER IT.
KING I (168)	NATURE MAKES YOU THE BEST MANNERED MAN IN THE	KINGDOM	. AND NOW, WHAT ABOUT THE REVELATIONS? /FOX/ I AM
JOAN 4 (107)	ONLY ONE REALM, AND THAT IS THE REALM OF CHRIST'S	KINGDOM	. DIVIDE THAT KINGDOM INTO NATIONS, AND YOU DETHRONE
6CAL (102)	BANQUET THEM: FEAST THEM: GIVE THEM MY CROWN, MY	KINGDOM	. GIVE THEM THE CLOTHES OFF MY BACK, THE BREAD OUT
KING I (194)	YES, AT PRESENT HE IS THE MOST POPULAR MAN IN THE	KINGDOM	. HE IS LODGED IN MY PALACE AT WHITEHALL WITH A
MTH2 (79)	THE MOST INSPIRED PARTY LEADER, IN THE	KINGDOM	. I TAKE OFF MY HAT TO HIM. I, JOYCE BURGE, GIVE HIM
UNPL PREFACE(R9)	SAY AS IF I WERE THE MOST IMPORTANT PERSON IN THE	KINGDOM	. MY PLEASING TOIL WAS TO REPORT UPON ALL THE WORKS
SIM II (63)	OF REPUBLICS AND THEIR JOBBERIES. PROCLAIM A	KINGDOM	. /MAYA/ OR A QUEENDOM. /IDDY/ OH YES: LET US MAKE
ROCK PREFACE(181)	ME. BUT THAT SORT OF THING DOES NOT HAPPEN IN MY	KINGDOM	. /PILATE/ THEN YOU ARE A KING? /JESUS/ YOU SAY SO.
POSN PREFACE(431)	PROVOCATION. THE MOST TURBULENT AUDIENCE IN THE	KINGDOM	. THE DIRECTORS OF THE IRISH NATIONAL THEATRE, LADY
LADY (249)	TO LOOK TO AND NOT THE GREATNESS OF THIS YOUR	KINGDOM	. THEREFORE NOW MUST YOUR MAJESTY TAKE UP THAT GOOD
LION PREFACE(35)	BEGS JESUS TO REMEMBER HIM WHEN HE COMES INTO HIS	KINGDOM	, TO WHICH JESUS REPLIES, " THIS DAY SHALT THOU BE
GENV PREFACE(20)	ESTABLISH THE KINGDOM OF GOD ON EARTH-- A GERMAN	KINGDOM	OF A GERMAN GOD-- BY MILITARY CONQUEST OF THE REST
SIM II (63)	AND THE UNITY OF ALL LIVING SOULS IN THE CATHOLIC	KINGDOM	OF GOD AND HIS CHURCH. /LADY FARWATERS/ THAT SOUNDS
LION PREFACE(3)	ATTEMPTS AT IT BY INADEQUATE PEOPLE, SUCH AS THE	KINGDOM	OF GOD IN MUNSTER, WHICH WAS ENDED BY A CRUCIFIXION
ROCK PREFACE(188)	THE BEAST OF PREY IS NOT STRIVING TO RETURN: THE	KINGDOM	OF GOD IS STRIVING TO COME. THE EMPIRE THAT LOOKS
ROCK PREFACE(187)	AND BLASPHEMY THE WORLD WOULD STAND STILL AND THE	KINGDOM	OF GOD NEVER BE A STAGE NEARER. THE ROMAN EMPIRE
GENV PREFACE(20)	OF A CHOSEN RACE, WAS DESTINED TO ESTABLISH THE	KINGDOM	OF GOD ON EARTH-- A GERMAN KINGDOM OF A GERMAN GOD--
ROCK PREFACE(188)	FOR THAT THOUGHT MAY BE THE FOUNDATION OF THE	KINGDOM	OF GOD ON EARTH. /PILATE/ IT MAY ALSO BE THE RUIN OF
SUPR HANDBOK(185)	OURSELVES EXCLUSIVELY TO THE ESTABLISHMENT OF THE	KINGDOM	OF GOD," THOUGH THE AMERICAN NATION DECLARED THAT
JOAN PREFACE(37)	BRING PEACE AND THE REIGN OF THE SAINTS IN THE	KINGDOM	OF GOD, BUT THEIR FRUITFUL INTERACTION IN A COSTLY
ROCK PREFACE(188)	ARE THE UNIVERSAL COWARD: I, STANDING FOR THE	KINGDOM	OF GOD, HAVE BRAVED EVERYTHING, LOST EVERYTHING, AND
SUPR HANDBOK(185)	" DEVOTED EXCLUSIVELY TO THE ESTABLISHMENT OF THE	KINGDOM	OF GOD," AND CARING NO MORE FOR PROPERTY AND
LION PREFACE(33)	AS " ONE WHO ALSO HIMSELF WAS LOOKING FOR THE	KINGDOM	OF GOD," WHICH SUGGESTS THAT HE WAS AN INDEPENDENT
LION PREFACE(17)	IT WILL PRESENTLY PASS AWAY AND BE REPLACED BY A	KINGDOM	OF HAPPINESS, JUSTICE, AND BLISS IN WHICH THE RICH
BUOY III (33)	OF A NEEDLE THAN FOR A RICH WOMAN TO ENTER THE	KINGDOM	OF HEAVEN? /MRS SECONDBORN/ OH, YOU ARE RELIGIOUS.
LION PREFACE(38)	" LO, HERE! " AND " LO, THERE! " BECAUSE THE	KINGDOM	OF HEAVEN IS WITHIN THEM. BUT LUKE HAS NO SENSE THAT
LION PREFACE(38)	THAT PEOPLE MUST NOT GO ABOUT ASKING WHERE THE	KINGDOM	OF HEAVEN IS, AND SAYING " LO, HERE! " AND " LO,
LION PREFACE(50)	CONFIRMED ARE, ROUGHLY, THE FOLLOWING: 1. THE	KINGDOM	OF HEAVEN IS WITHIN YOU. YOU ARE THE SON OF GOD; AND
LION PREFACE(62)	US THAT WE AND OUR FATHER ARE ONE; THAT AS THE	KINGDOM	OF HEAVEN IS WITHIN US WE NEED NOT GO ABOUT LOOKING
LION PREFACE(31)	BOOKS WOULD BE ONE OF THE PLEASURES OF THE	KINGDOM	OF HEAVEN ON EARTH. CLASS TYPE OF MATTHEW'S JESUS.
ANNA (299)	INDEMNITIES, AND MERELY WISHES TO ESTABLISH THE	KINGDOM	OF HEAVEN ON EARTH THROUGHOUT THE UNIVERSE. (HE
CAND I (100)	OWN HOME. YOU WILL BE ONE OF THE MAKERS OF THE	KINGDOM	OF HEAVEN ON EARTH; AND-- WHO KNOWS? -- YOU MAY BE A
CAND II (118)	AND YOU THINK IT'S ALL ENTHUSIASM FOR THE	KINGDOM	OF HEAVEN ON EARTH; AND SO DO THEY. YOU DEAR SILLY!
LION PREFACE(21)	TO THE PEOPLE TO REPENT OF THEIR SINS, AS THE	KINGDOM	OF HEAVEN WAS AT HAND. LUKE ADDS THAT HE ALSO
LION PREFACE(102)	ADMITTING THAT CAESAR, WHO PRESUMABLY HAD THE	KINGDOM	OF HEAVEN WITHIN HIM AS MUCH AS ANY DISCIPLE, HAD
CAND I (82)	THATS A FORETASTE OF WHAT WILL BE BEST IN THE	KINGDOM	OF HEAVEN WE ARE TRYING TO ESTABLISH ON EARTH. THAT
ROCK PREFACE(157)	IT WAS IMPOSSIBLE FOR A RICH MAN TO ENTER THE	KINGDOM	OF HEAVEN), AGAINST ALL THE INTERESTS, CLASSES,
LION PREFACE(51)	SEA AS EVER CAME OUT OF IT, AND BETTER, IN THE	KINGDOM	OF HEAVEN, WHICH, AS AFORESAID, IS WITHIN YOU. THERE
SIM I (53)	/MAYA/ (SITTING DOWN BESIDE HIM) AND THIS IS THE	KINGDOM	OF LOVE. THE THREE EMBRACE WITH INTERLACED ARMS AND
FABL V (119)	HIM HE WOULD RISE FROM THE DEAD AND ESTABLISH A	KINGDOM	OF RIGHTEOUSNESS NOT AMONG ANGELS IN THE CLOUDS BUT
HART PREFACE(28)	ATTAIN IT? AT ALL EVENTS IT IS CLEAR THAT THE	KINGDOM	OF THE PRINCE OF PEACE HAS NOT YET BECOME THE
HART PREFACE(28)	OF THE PRINCE OF PEACE HAS NOT YET BECOME THE	KINGDOM	OF THIS WORLD. HIS ATTEMPTS AT INVASION HAVE BEEN
ROCK PREFACE(179)	ORDEAL AS A PRELUDE TO THE ESTABLISHMENT OF HIS	KINGDOM	ON EARTH? A MODERN PASSION PLAY IMPOSSIBLE. THE
ROCK PREFACE(175)	THE DEAD AND COME AGAIN IN GLORY TO ESTABLISH HIS	KINGDOM	ON EARTH FOR EVER, IT DOES NOT MATTER TO OUR PRESENT
LION PREFACE(44)	HIS PROMISE TO RETURN IN GLORY AND ESTABLISH HIS	KINGDOM	ON EARTH WITHIN THE LIFETIME OF MEN THEN LIVING, WAS
LION PREFACE(28)	WORLD A SECOND TIME IN GLORY AND ESTABLISH HIS	KINGDOM	ON EARTH. HE FEARS THAT THIS MAY LEAD TO THE
CAPT II (252)	OFFICE; BUT IT WILL NOT BE ENOUGH TO SAVE HIS	KINGDOM	-- ANY MORE THAN IT WOULD SAVE YOUR LIFE, IF YOUR
ROCK PREFACE(188)	THAT LOOKS BACK IN TERROR SHALL GIVE WAY TO THE	KINGDOM	THAT LOOKS FORWARD WITH HOPE. TERROR DRIVES MEN MAD:
JOAN 2 (86)	TO KNEEL IN THE CATHEDRAL AND SOLEMNLY GIVE THY	KINGDOM	TO HIM FOR EVER AND EVER, AND BECOME THE GREATEST
KING I (193)	/JAMES/ PSHA! THERE IS NOT A PLOT IN THE	KINGDOM	TO MURDER EITHER OF US THAT HE IS NOT AT THE BOTTOM
KING II (230)	MONMOUTH AND JAMES AND THE HANDING OVER OF YOUR	KINGDOM	TO THE HOLLANDER. I AM TEMPTED TO DO IT BECAUSE THEN
DOCT PREFACE(30)	OF THE VIVISECTORS, EVERY DOCTOR IN THE	KINGDOM	WOULD GAIN SUBSTANTIALLY BY THE IMMENSE RELIEF AND
POSN PREFACE(391)	THROUGH EVERY PLAY THAT IS PRODUCED IN THE	KINGDOM	YEAR IN, YEAR OUT, WHY THE LORD CHAMBERLAIN? WHAT
CLEO IV (182)	OF MEN WHO ARE NOT GREAT! SHALL I MAKE YOU A NEW	KINGDOM	, AND BUILD YOU A HOLY CITY THERE IN THE GREAT
SUPR III (97)	OF FATE WAS THIS COLD SELFISH EGOTIST SENT TO MY	KINGDOM	, AND YOU TAKEN TO THE ICY MANSIONS OF THE SKY!
JOAN 2 (74)	DAUPHIN) AND YOU, SIR: IF YOU CANNOT RULE YOUR	KINGDOM	, AT LEAST TRY TO RULE YOURSELF. /CHARLES/ ANOTHER
LION PREFACE(37)	PRESENTLY COME BACK TO EARTH AND ESTABLISH HIS	KINGDOM	, HAVING DULY DIED AND RISEN AGAIN AFTER THREE DAYS.
LION PREFACE(30)	DEATH TIL THEY SEE THE SON OF MAN COMING IN HIS	KINGDOM	" DESTROYED THE LAST POSSIBILITY OF THE PROMISED
		KINGDOMS	
DEST (186)	FAR WORSE THAN THAT. HE OFFERS ME NO CROWNS AND	KINGDOMS	: HE EXPECTS TO GET EVERYTHING FOR NOTHING:
APPL PREFACE(176)	OURS KICKED INTO THE GUTTER BY DICTATORS, BOTH IN	KINGDOMS	AND REPUBLICS, IT IS FOOLISH TO WAIT UNTIL THE
ROCK PREFACE(179)	SUCH IMPORTANCE AT THE PRESENT CRISIS, WHEN THE	KINGDOMS	ARE BREAKING UP, AND UPSTART RULERS ARE SOWING
LION EPILOG (150)	THE BRITISH EMPIRE, THE FRENCH REPUBLIC, AND THE	KINGDOMS	OF ITALY, JAPAN, AND SERBIA) ACTUALLY SUCCEEDED IN
DEST (186)	GALLEY SLAVE IN THE OTHER: WHO SHEWS YOU ALL THE	KINGDOMS	OF THE EARTH AND OFFERS TO MAKE YOU THEIR MASTER ON
JOAN PREFACE(6)	DIE NATURAL DEATHS IN ALL THE GLORY OF THE	KINGDOMS	OF THIS WORLD, PROVING THAT IT IS FAR MORE
ROCK PREFACE(188)	ON EARTH. /PILATE/ IT MAY ALSO BE THE RUIN OF ALL	KINGDOMS	, ALL LAW, AND ALL HUMAN SOCIETY. IT MAY BE THE
		KINGFISHER	
JOAN 3 (92)	/DUNOIS/ (RUNNING BACK) WHAT IS IT? THE	KINGFISHER	? (HE LOOKS EAGERLY FOR IT UP THE RIVER).
JOAN 3 (89)	(HE TURNS AWAY FROM HIM) MARY IN THE BLUE SNOOD,	KINGFISHER	COLOR: WILL YOU GRUDGE ME A WEST WIND? /A
JOAN 3 (88)	WHERE? WHO? THE MAID? /THE PAGE/ NO: THE	KINGFISHER	. LIKE BLUE LIGHTNING. SHE WENT INTO THAT BUSH.
JOAN 3 (92)	IT UP THE RIVER). /JOAN/ (JOINING THEM) OH, A	KINGFISHER	! WHERE? /THE PAGE/ NO: THE WIND, THE WIND, THE
		KINGLINESS	
SUPR HANDBOK(217)	BECOMES SANE AND NEVER COMPLETELY RECOVERS HIS	KINGLINESS	. THE COURT IS THE SERVANT'S HALL OF THE
		KINGLY	
CYMB V (147)	WITH YOU, SIR THIEF, TO TUTOR ME? NO, NO: THIS	KINGLY	BUSINESS HAS NO CHARM FOR ME. WHEN I LIVED IN A CAVE
SHAK SD(140)	TARTAN AND KILT WITH CLAYMORE, MACBETH IN	KINGLY	COSTUME, /MACBETH/ THUS FAR INTO THE BOWELS OF THE
APPL INTRLUD(246)	LIVE A REALLY NOBLE AND BEAUTIFUL LIFE -- A	KINGLY	LIFE -- WITH ME. WHAT YOU NEED TO MAKE YOU A REAL
		KINGPOSTS	
METH PREFACE(R38)	CONTRIVED, CORDS AND LEVERS, GIRDERS AND	KINGPOSTS	, CIRCULATING SYSTEMS OF PIPES AND VALVES,

KING'S

APPL I (212)	YOUD USE A BIT OF WOOD AND BRASS AND RUBBER? THE	KING'S	A LIVE MAN; AND WHAT MORE ARE YOU, WITH YOUR BLESSED
KING I (220)	/CHARLES/ (HOLDING HER FAST) YOU ARE ON THE	KING'S	ARM. BEHAVE YOURSELF. (HE TAKES HER OUT FORCIBLY).
JOAN 3 (93)	AND HANDING HIS BATON TO JOAN) YOU COMMAND THE	KING'S	ARMY. I AM YOUR SOLDIER. /THE PAGE/ (LOOKING DOWN
CLEO IV (176)	FELLOW WITH HAIR LIKE SQUIRREL'S FUR-- THE LITTLE	KING'S	BEAR LEADER, WHOM YOU KEPT PRISONER. /CAESAR/ (
JOAN 4 (101)	VILLAGE GIRL IS OF EQUAL VALUE WITH YOURS OR YOUR	KING'S	BEFORE THE THRONE OF GOD; AND MY FIRST DUTY IS TO
APPL I (231)	ABOUT ARE FOOTBALL AND REFRESHMENTS. LICK THE	KING'S	BOOTS: THAT IS ALL YOU ARE FIT FOR. (HE DASHES OUT
KING I (187)	/JAMES/ SIR: I AM THE DUKE OF YORK, THE	KING'S	BROTHER. /NEWTON/ I AM ISAAC NEWTON, THE PHILOSOPHER.
CLEO II SD(120)	FRANK CURIOSITY OF A CHILD, AND THEN TURNS TO THE	KING'S	CHAIR: BRITANNUS AND RUFIO POSTING THEMSELVES NEAR
KING I (187)	THIRTYFIVE DAYS. FIVE MONTHS DIFFERENCE! AND THE	KING'S	DAUGHTER OF THE SOUTH: WHO WAS SHE? AND THE KING OF
CLEO II (122)	DEBT DUE TO ROME BY EGYPT, CONTRACTED BY THE	KING'S	DECEASED FATHER TO THE TRIUMVIRATE; AND THAT IT IS
APPL I (235)	DAUGHTERS WILL SOON MAKE HIM UNDERSTAND THAT THE	KING'S	DISPLEASURE IS STILL A SENTENCE OF SOCIAL DEATH
JOAN 1 (68)	BLACKER THAN THE DEVIL HIMSELF, OR OF THE ENGLISH	KING'S	FATHER? /JOAN/ YOU MUST NOT BE AFRAID, ROBERT --
6CAL SD(97)	LEADER, EUSTACHE DE ST PIERRE, KNEELS AT THE	KING'S	FEET. FOUR OF HIS FELLOW VICTIMS, PIERS DE WISSANT,
ROCK II (247)	THE VOICE OF THE PEERAGE, OF THE CITY, OF THE	KING'S	FORCES. YOU WILL NOW HEAR THE VOICE OF THE
CLEO II (120)	HORSEMEN FOLLOW THE ROMAN? /THEODOTUS/ LET THE	KING'S	GENERAL SPEAK! /ACHILLAS/ BUT TWO ROMAN LEGIONS, O
CLEO II (121)	AND THIS GENTLEMAN? /THEODOTUS/ ACHILLAS, THE	KING'S	GENERAL. /CAESAR/ (TO ACHILLAS, VERY FRIENDLY) A
JOAN 2 (84)	SOME GOOD IN THEE, CHARLIE; BUT IT IS NOT YET A	KING'S	GOOD. /CHARLES/ WE SHALL SEE. I AM NOT SUCH A FOOL AS
APPL I (229)	THE CORPSE? /PROTEUS/ NO. I CANNOT CARRY ON THE	KING'S	GOVERNMENT UNLESS I CAN GIVE PLEDGES AND CARRY THEM
APPL I (214)	AND TELL THE COUNTRY THAT WE CANT CARRY ON THE	KING'S	GOVERNMENT UNDER CONDITIONS WHICH DESTROY OUR
CLEO II (128)	SAFER THERE. /POTHINUS/ THIS IS A TRICK. I AM THE	KING'S	GUARDIAN! I REFUSE TO STIR. I STAND ON MY RIGHT HERE.
CLEO II (119)	WOULD NOT SUFFER. /THEODOTUS/ LET POTHINUS, THE	KING'S	GUARDIAN, SPEAK FOR THE KING. /POTHINUS/ (
6CAL (104)	DO YOU NOT KNOW THAT YOUR LIFE IS IN THE	KING'S	HAND? DO YOU EXPECT ME TO RECOMMEND YOU TO HIS MERCY
APPL II SD(277)	LYSISTRATA POCKETS HER HANDKERCHIEF; SHAKES THE	KING'S	HANDS IMPULSIVELY; AND GOES WITH AMANDA. THE KING
APPL I (224)	/NICOBAR/ SUPPOSE HE HAS A LOT OF MONEY, AND THE	KING'S	HARD UP! /PROTEUS/ SUPPOSE HE IS A PRIME MINISTER,
DEST (193)	HIS KING ON LOYAL PRINCIPLES AND CUTS OFF HIS	KING'S	HEAD ON REPUBLICAN PRINCIPLES. HIS WATCHWORD IS
BUOY 1 (12)	HAND OF THE MONARCHY CROMWELL HAD TO CUT OFF THE	KING'S	HEAD. THE FRENCH REVOLUTION TRIED HARD TO BE LIBERAL
BULL PREFACE(30)	IRELAND IT IS NOT " LOYALTY" TO DRINK THE ENGLISH	KING'S	HEALTH AND STAND UNCOVERED TO THE ENGLISH NATIONAL
BULL PREFACE(17)	SOLDIER TAKES THE KING'S SHILLING AND DRINKS THE	KING'S	HEALTH; AND THE IRISH SQUIRE TAKES THE TITLE DEEDS OF
ANNA (299)	ALL GREAT TRUTHS BEGIN AS BLASPHEMIES. ALL THE	KING'S	HORSES AND ALL THE KING'S MEN CANNOT SET UP MY
BUOY III (32)	ELECTION. /SIR F./ DO NOT DEPEND ON THAT. ALL THE	KING'S	HORSES AND ALL THE KING'S MEN CANNOT BRING BACK THE
MILL IV (210)	IDOLS ARE SWEPT AWAY SOONER OR LATER; AND ALL THE	KING'S	HORSES AND ALL THE KING'S MEN CANNOT SET THEM UP
POSN PREFACE(403)	CHAMBERLAIN, WHO IS AT LEAST AN OFFICIAL OF THE	KING'S	HOUSEHOLD AND A NOMINEE OF THE GOVERNMENT. THE LORD
POSN PREFACE(392)	WHICH MAKES IT UNDESIRABLE THAT A MEMBER OF THE	KING'S	HOUSEHOLD SHOULD BE RESPONSIBLE FOR THE CHARACTER AND
POSN PREFACE(367)	A CERTIFICATE FROM THE CHIEF OFFICER OF THE	KING'S	HOUSEHOLD THAT THE PLAY WAS A PROPER ONE. A TWO
HART PREFACE(17)	DUKES FROM THE ROLL OF OUR PEERAGE, CHANGING THE	KING'S	ILLUSTRIOUS AND HISTORICALLY APPROPRIATE SURNAME FOR
APPL I (202)	THE VISITOR'S CHAIR IN HIS HAND, READY FOR THE	KING'S	INSTRUCTIONS AS TO WHERE TO PLACE IT). PAMPHILIUS
KING I (184)	THINGS TO DO THAN TO PEDDLE LOVE CHARMS TO THE	KING'S	LADIES. /LOUISE/ (IRONICALLY) YES: TO ENTERTAIN THE
APPL I (200)	LET ME ADD THAT IN THIS PALACE, WHEN THE	KING'S	LETTERS ARE NOT READY FOR HIM AT 12 O'CLOCK, A
APPL I SD(197)	AS HE SITS AT ONE OF THE TABLES OPENING THE	KING'S	LETTERS, PAMPHILIUS, MIDDLE AGED, SHEWS HIS LEFT AS
APPL I (213)	AND THE LATEST ADDITION TO THE CABINET HERE IS A	KING'S	MAN, I RESIGN. GENERAL CONSTERNATION EXCEPT ON THE
POSN PREFACE(391)	OF THE THEATRE, IS A DIRECT DESCENDANT OF THE	KING'S	MASTER OF THE REVELS, APPOINTED IN 1544 BY HENRY VIII
BUOY III (32)	DEPEND ON THAT. ALL THE KING'S HORSES AND ALL THE	KING'S	MEN CANNOT BRING BACK THE UNEARNED INCOMES OF THE
ANNA (299)	AS BLASPHEMIES. ALL THE KING'S HORSES AND ALL THE	KING'S	MEN CANNOT SET UP MY FATHER'S THRONE AGAIN. IF THEY
MILL IV (210)	OR LATER; AND ALL THE KING'S HORSES AND ALL THE	KING'S	MEN CANNOT SET THEM UP AGAIN; BUT THE SAINTS SHALL
6CAL (99)	THAT SHAKES US. WE KNEEL TO IMPLORE YOUR	KING'S	MERCY FOR OUR WRETCHED AND STARVING TOWNSFOLK, NOT
APPL I (226)	FEMALES. TO GAIN THE REPUTATION OF BEING THE	KING'S	MISTRESS THEY WOULD DO ALMOST ANYTHING EXCEPT GIVE
KING I (219)	LIKE A DAIRYMAID: YOU THINK THERE IS NO END TO A	KING'S	MONEY. HERE IS MY NELLY, WHO IS MORE CAREFUL OF MY
POSN PREFACE(416)	FROM THE PURLIEUS OF OUR THEATRICAL WORLD AS THE	KING'S	NAVAL CAREER FROM THE ISLE OF DOGS? THE MOMENT WE
BULL PREFACE(10)	ONE; BUT IF DRAKE HAD PUT A CHAIN ROUND THE	KING'S	NECK AND LED HIM ROUND A PRISONER FOR THE REST OF HIS
DEVL III (71)	YOU WHAT I'LL DO, TO TEACH YOU TO CORRUPT THE	KING'S	OFFICER. I'LL PUT YOU UNDER ARREST UNTIL THE
APPL PREFACE(173)	THUS EMPLOYING TWO SETS OF WEAPONS TO THE	KING'S	ONE. THIS GIVES HIM THE ADVANTAGES OF HIS OWN
6CAL SD(100)	THAT THE QUEEN'S ARRIVAL WASHES OUT ALL THE	KING'S	ORDERS. /THE QUEEN/ SIR, WHAT IS THIS THEY TELL ME..
MRS PREFACE(160)	MAIDEN. THE SCENE REPRESENTS A HALL IN THE	KING'S	PALACE AT NIGHT. THE WEDDING HAS TAKEN PLACE THAT
DOCT PREFACE(9)	SAVE": THEIR REPUTATION STANDS, LIKE AN AFRICAN	KING'S	PALACE, ON A FOUNDATION OF DEAD BODIES; AND THE
6CAL (93)	GROOM RUNNING AFTER HIM. /THE PRINCE/ HERE IS THE	KING'S	PAVILION WITHOUT A SINGLE ATTENDANT TO ANNOUNCE ME.
6CAL SD(93)	HAINAULT IS ON YOUR RIGHT. BETWEEN THEM, NEAR THE	KING'S	PAVILION, IS A TWO-SEATED CHAIR OF STATE FOR PUBLIC
APPL PREFACE(173)	HIM. RATHER WILL HE IN COLD BLOOD OPPOSE TO THE	KING'S	PERFECT BEHAVIOR AN INTENTIONAL MISBEHAVIOR AND
KING I (217)	APOLOGIZES FOR HIS LAPSE INTO ROYALTY. ONLY, THE	KING'S	PERSON IS NOT TO BE DISCUSSED. /LOUISE/ BUT, CHARLES,
GETT (273)	I CAN NEVER FORGET WHAT I FELT: IT WAS ONLY THE	KING'S	PERSONAL REQUEST-- VIRTUALLY A COMMAND-- THAT STOPPED
SUPR HANDBOK(213)	THE WAY IN WHICH ALL CONSIDERATIONS OF THE	KING'S	PERSONAL RIGHTS, OF THE CLAIMS OF THE HEART, OF THE
CYMB V (142)	SHEATH YOUR SWORD, YOU LOUT. /IACHIMO/ IN THE	KING'S	PRESENCE I MUST YIELD PERFORCE; BUT AS A PERSON OF
CYMB V (142)	PULLS POSTHUMUS BACK. /ARVIRAGUS/ IN THE	KING'S	PRESENCE SHEATH YOUR SWORD, YOU LOUT. /IACHIMO/ IN
APPL I (202)	OH YES: IVE HEARD OF YOU. YOURE ONE OF THE	KING'S	PRIVATE SECRETARIES. /PAMPHILIUS/ I AM. AND WHAT HAVE
APPL I (241)	/SEMPRONIUS/ ONCE FOR ALL, MR PROTEUS, THE	KING'S	PRIVATE SECRETARIES MUST HEAR EVERYTHING, SEE
POSN PREFACE(418)	FITCH'S THE WOMAN IN THE CASE? PUT THE PROPOSED	KING'S	PROCTOR IN OPERATION TOMORROW; AND WHAT WILL BE THE
GETT PREFACE(257)	TO THE STATE ACTING ON THE PETITION OF THE	KING'S	PROCTOR OR OTHER SUITABLE FUNCTIONARY, WHO MAY,
GETT (276)	HER AND THE GENERAL) OH, REJJY! WHAT WILL THE	KING'S	PROCTOR SAY? /REGINALD/ DAMN THE KING'S PROCTOR!
POSN PREFACE(417)	TO ESTABLISH FOR THEIR ASSISTANCE A SORT OF	KING'S	PROCTOR TO WHOM PLAYS MIGHT BE REFERRED FOR AN
POSN PREFACE(419)	ANY SERVICE TO HIM. THE VERDICT OF THE PROPOSED	KING'S	PROCTOR WOULD BE NOTHING BUT COUNSEL'S OPINION
POSN PREFACE(417)	TO AN EXTENT NEVER DREAMT OF BY ANY NOVELIST, A	KING'S	PROCTOR. ANOTHER HARE WAS STARTED BY PROFESSOR
GETT PREFACE(254)	BRINGING UP THEIR CHILDREN TO THEIR TRADE, THE	KING'S	PROCTOR, INSTEAD OF PURSUING HIS PRESENT PURELY
GETT (276)	WILL THE KING'S PROCTOR SAY? /REGINALD/ DAMN THE	KING'S	PROCTOR! /LEO/ NAUGHTY. WELL, I SUPPOSE I MUST KISS
JOAN 4 (96)	LORD. /THE NOBLEMAN/ OR BUY HER. I WILL OFFER A	KING'S	RANSOM. /THE CHAPLAIN/ A KING'S RANSOM! FOR THAT
JOAN 4 (96)	I WILL OFFER A KING'S RANSOM. /THE CHAPLAIN/ A	KING'S	RANSOM! FOR THAT SLUT! /THE NOBLEMAN/ ONE HAS TO
POSN PREFACE(429)	NO DOUBT SUCCEED AS THEY DO TODAY. BUT COULD THE	KING'S	READER OF PLAYS LIVE ON HIS FEES FROM THESE PLAYS
APPL PREFACE(171)	IN SHORT, TO REDUCE HIM TO A CIPHER. THE	KING'S	REPLY IS THAT RATHER THAN BE A CIPHER HE WILL ABANDON
POSN PREFACE(364)	IS A MEMBER OF HIS HOUSEHOLD RETINUE; AND AS A	KING'S	RETINUE HAS TO BE JEALOUSLY GUARDED TO AVOID
6CAL SD(97)	THE REST BY PASSING BEHIND THE ROYAL CHAIR TO THE	KING'S	RIGHT AND PLANTING HIMSELF STIFFLY ERECT IN AN
6CAL SD(96)	ARE JOINED BY THE BLACK PRINCE, WHO STANDS AT THE	KING'S	RIGHT HAND AND TAKES CHARGE OF JOHN OF GAUNT. /THE
APPL II SD(266)	WHEN THEY ARE SEATED, THEIR ORDER FROM THE	KING'S	RIGHT TO HIS LEFT IS NICOBAR, CRASSUS, BOANERGES,
APPL II SD(257)	NEAR THE CORNERS OF THE STEPS, THE QUEEN TO THE	KING'S	RIGHT. HE IS READING THE EVENING PAPER: SHE IS
KING I (194)	/CHARLES/ LET ME TELL YOU A SECRET, JAMIE! A	KING'S	SECRET. PETER THE FISHERMAN DID NOT KNOW EVERYTHING.
JOAN 4 (106)	TO THE KING, AND THEIR LORDS BECAME ONLY THE	KING'S	SERVANTS IN THEIR EYES, THE KING COULD BREAK US
BULL PREFACE(17)	A VERY COARSE PEOPLE. THE IRISH SOLDIER TAKES THE	KING'S	SHILLING AND DRINKS THE KING'S HEALTH; AND THE IRISH
APPL I (235)	WOULD BREAK YOUR BACKS MAY STILL BE BORNE ON A	KING'S	SHOULDERS, BUT HE MUST BE KING, NOT A PUPPET. YOU
CLEO II (122)	WE HAVE BEEN AT STRIFE HERE, BECAUSE THE	KING'S	SISTER CLEOPATRA FALSELY CLAIMS HIS THRONE. THE
CLEO II (122)	SISTER CLEOPATRA FALSELY CLAIMS HIS THRONE. THE	KING'S	TAXES HAVE NOT BEEN COLLECTED FOR A WHOLE YEAR.
CLEO II (121)	REMINDS ME. I WANT SOME MONEY. /POTHINUS/ THE	KING'S	TREASURY IS POOR, CAESAR. /CAESAR/ YES: I NOTICE THAT
CLEO II (122)	THE TREASURES OF THE TEMPLE AND THE GOLD OF THE	KING'S	TREASURY SHALL BE SENT TO THE MINT TO BE MELTED DOWN
CLEO II (122)	IMPOSSIBLE. THERE IS NOT SO MUCH MONEY IN THE	KING'S	TREASURY. /CAESAR/ (ENCOURAGINGLY) ONLY SIXTEEN
CLEO II (121)	THE COUNCIL CHAMBER OF THE CHANCELLORS OF THE	KING'S	TREASURY, CAESAR. /CAESAR/ AH! THAT REMINDS ME. I
CLEO II (121)	AND YOU, SIR, ARE--? /THEODOTUS/ THEODOTUS, THE	KING'S	TUTOR. /CAESAR/ YOU TEACH MEN HOW TO BE KINGS,
JOAN 4 (97)	CALL HIM THE CARDINAL OF ENGLAND, I BELIEVE. OUR	KING'S	UNCLE. /CAUCHON/ MESSIRE JOHN DE STOGUMBER: I AM
APPL I (213)	OF THE NEW CHAMBER OF COMMERCE BUILDING THAT THE	KING'S	VETO IS THE ONLY REMAINING DEFENCE OF THE PEOPLE
BARB I (253)	AT CAMBRIDGE IT WAS THE SAME. A LITTLE BRUTE AT	KING'S	WHO WAS ALWAYS TRYING TO GET UP REVIVALS, SPOILT MY
KING I (190)	I SHALL REIGN: THESE FELLOWS SHALL FIND WHAT A	KING'S	WILL IS WHEN HE REIGNS BY DIVINE RIGHT. THEY WILL GET
CLEO II (119)	BY SHEER SELF-OPINIONATIVENESS) PEACE FOR THE	KING'S	WORD! /PTOLEMY/ (WITHOUT ANY VOCAL INFLEXIONS: HE
POSN PREFACE(416)	NOTION THAT A THEATRE IS AN ALSATIA WHERE THE	KING'S	WRIT DOES NOT RUN, AND WHERE ANY WICKEDNESS IS
CLEO II (125)	REIGN JOINTLY IN EGYPT. /ACHILLAS/ WHAT OF THE	KING'S	YOUNGER BROTHER AND CLEOPATRA'S YOUNGER SISTER?

KINGS

BULL I (96)	NEVER FEAR. YOURE ALL DESCENDED FROM THE ANCIENT	KINGS	: I KNOW THAT. (COMPLACENTLY) I'M NOT SO TACTLESS AS
MTH5 (237)	THE INEVITABLE. MY NAME IS OZYMANDIAS, KING OF	KINGS	: LOOK ON MY WORKS, YE MIGHTY, AND DESPAIR. THERE IS A
CLEO II (139)	HIS FISTS). BUT HARKEN, THEODOTUS, TEACHER OF	KINGS	: YOU WHO VALUED POMPEY'S HEAD NO MORE THAN A SHEPHERD
KING II (229)	THE SON OF HIS FATHER. WAS HE ALSO THE BEST OF	KINGS	? /CATHERINE/ OH, HE WAS DREADFUL. HE WAS BARELY FIT

JOAN 4 (106)	NEED YOU FEAR THAT? YOU ARE THE MAKERS OF	KINGS	AFTER ALL. YORK OR LANCASTER IN ENGLAND, LANCASTER OR
ROCK II (259)	CAN PROROGUE PARLIAMENT. /SIR ARTHUR/ PRECISELY.	KINGS	ALWAYS HAVE PROROGUED PARLIAMENT AND GOVERNED WITHOUT
CAPT I (232)	I SAID HOWDYEDO? AND THEY WERE QUITE NICE. THE	KINGS	ALWAYS WANTED TO MARRY ME. /SIR HOWARD/ THAT DOES NOT
JOAN EPILOG (160)	TIP TOP COMPANY TOO: EMPERORS AND POPES AND	KINGS	AND ALL SORTS. THEY CHIP ME ABOUT GIVING THAT YOUNG
GENV IV (93)	/BBDE/ NEVER. PLUTOCRACY HAS CUT OFF THE HEADS OF	KINGS	AND ARCHBISHOPS TO MAKE ITSELF SUPREME AND ROB THE
MILL PREFACE(110)	WHAT IS THE UNITED STATES TO DO WITH ITS MONEY	KINGS	AND BOSSES? WHAT ARE WE TO DO WITH OURS? HOW IS THE
JOAN EPILOG (167)	SOLDIER/ WELL, WHAT DO THEY ALL AMOUNT TO, THESE	KINGS	AND CAPTAINS AND BISHOPS AND LAWYERS AND SUCH LIKE?
BULL PREFACE(11)	FOLLY OF THE IGNORANT SIMPLETONS WHO LONG TO BE	KINGS	AND CHIEFS BECAUSE THEY IMAGINE THAT A KING OR A CHIEF
KING II (229)	OTHER COUNTRY, THE MAKINGS OF HALF A DOZEN DECENT	KINGS	AND COUNCILS; BUT THEY ARE MOSTLY IN PRISON. IF WE
GENV IV (112)	BORN A NOBODY, AND NOW IN COMMAND ABOVE ALL	KINGS	AND KAISERS. FOR MY SUPPORT IS NO DEAD JEW, BUT A
APPL PREFACE(174)	MONEY PRINTS: MONEY BROADCASTS: MONEY REIGNS; AND	KINGS	AND LABOR LEADERS ALIKE HAVE TO REGISTER ITS DECREES,
CLEO PRO1 (92)	" LO: THESE ROMANS WHICH HAVE LENT MONEY TO OUR	KINGS	AND LEVIED A DISTRAINT UPON US WITH THEIR ARMS, CALL
LADY PREFACE(231)	OF SOCIAL PATHOLOGY. THEN CONSIDER SHAKESPEAR'S	KINGS	AND LORDS AND GENTLEMEN! WOULD EVEN JOHN BALL OR
BUOY 1 (15)	IS THE SPORT OF LABOR PARTIES. /SON/ WHAT COULD	KINGS	AND PARTIES DO WITHOUT ARMIES OF PROLETARIANS? WAR IS
JOAN PREFACE(22)	DOGGEDNESS, AND HER ACCEPTANCE OF GREAT LORDS AND	KINGS	AND PRELATES AS SUCH WITHOUT IDOLATRY OR SNOBBERY,
METH PREFACE(R64)	SLAVERY. PEOPLE WERE TIRED OF GOVERNMENTS AND	KINGS	AND PRIESTS AND PROVIDENCES, AND WANTED TO FIND OUT
GENV IV (93)	PRIEST, NOR ANY BODY OF LAW ESTABLISHED BY DEAD	KINGS	AND PRIESTS, YOU HAVE MOB LAW, LYNCHING LAW, GANGSTER
MTH5 (237)	SUN AND THE BLIND FIRE; BUT THE KINGS OF	KINGS	AND QUEEN OF QUEENS ARE NOT ACCIDENTS OF THE EGG: THEY
KING I (218)	WOULD BE MERE DUKES OR DUCHESSES IF THEY COULD BE	KINGS	AND QUEENS? /NELL/ DUKES WILL BE SIX A PENNY IF YOU
MIS. PREFACE(103)	GUILLOTINE THE SEIGNEURS; CHOP OFF THE HEADS OF	KINGS	AND QUEENS AND SET UP DEMOCRACY ON THE RUINS OF
KING I (218)	YOU ARE A QUEEN. I TELL YOU THE WORLD IS FULL OF	KINGS	AND QUEENS AND THEIR LITTLE COURTS. HERE IS PASTOR
KING I (219)	CHARLES. WHAT YOU WERE SAYING ABOUT LITTLE	KINGS	AND QUEENS BEING EVERYWHERE WAS VERY TRUE. YOU ARE
CLEO II (124)	HERE, AND NOT CONVERSANT WITH OUR LAWS. THE	KINGS	AND QUEENS OF EGYPT MAY NOT MARRY EXCEPT WITH THEIR
O'FL (217)	A NICE THING FOR A POOR BOY TO BE MADE MUCH OF BY	KINGS	AND QUEENS, AND SHOOK HANDS WITH BY THE HEIGHTH OF HIS
SUPR HANDBOK(217)	HE WHO DIES FOR HIM ARE ALIKE IDOLATERS. ROYALTY.	KINGS	ARE NOT BORN: THEY ARE MADE BY ARTIFICIAL
JOAN PREFACE(49)	COMPLETELY PERSONAL AND SELFISH EVEN IN THEM. HIS	KINGS	ARE NOT STATESMEN: HIS CARDINALS HAVE NO RELIGION: A
APPL I (226)	ME. /CRASSUS/ I HOPE YOUR MAJESTY RECOGNIZES THAT	KINGS	ARE NOT THE ONLY PEOPLE TO WHOM CERTAIN SORTS OF MUD
LADY PREFACE(216)	MADE BY A VERY ELABORATE PROCESS OF CULTURE. EVEN	KINGS	ARE TAUGHT AND COACHED AND DRILLED FROM THEIR EARLIEST
LION PREFACE(45)	WHO WILL NOT BELIEVE MATTHEW'S STORY OF THREE	KINGS	BRINGING COSTLY GIFTS TO THE CRADLE OF JESUS, BELIEVE
JOAN PREFACE(23)	ANY WORLD BUT THE TRIBAL WORLD, WROTE LETTERS TO	KINGS	CALLING ON THEM TO MAKE MILLENNIAL REARRANGEMENTS.
KING I (217)	DUMB FLUNKEYS. WHAT WILL YOU BE WHEN THE KING OF	KINGS	CALLS YOU FROM YOUR GRAVES TO ANSWER FOR YOUR LIVES..
KING I (177)	IT STRIKES UPON MY LIFE. I AM CALLED. EARTHLY	KINGS	CANNOT STAY ME. LET ME PASS. /CHARLES/ STAND BACK, MR
6CAL (102)	HIMSELF. YOU SAID ONCE THAT YOU WOULD LEAD TEN	KINGS	CAPTIVE TO MY FEET. MUCH AS I HAVE BEGGED FROM YOU I
LION PREFACE(20)	ENOUGH TO LIVE IN A HOUSE IN BETHLEHEM TO WHICH	KINGS	COULD BRING GIFTS OF GOLD WITHOUT PROVOKING ANY
CLEO II (133)	THAT YOU ARE A KING NOW: I HAVE MADE YOU ONE.	KINGS	DONT WORK. /CAESAR/ OH! WHO TOLD YOU THAT, LITTLE
APPL I (207)	OF THE REPUBLICAN STATES HAVE? AMBITIOUS	KINGS	ENVY THEM. /BOANERGES/ WHAT'S THAT? I DONT FOLLOW
SUPR HANDBOK(190)	POLITICIAN WHO ONCE HAD TO LEARN HOW TO FLATTER	KINGS	HAS NOW TO LEARN HOW TO FASCINATE, AMUSE, COAX,
O'FL (218)	FOR WHO I LIKE; AND I'LL SHAKE HANDS WITH WHAT	KINGS	I LIKE; AND IF YOUR OWN SON IS NOT GOOD ENOUGH FOR
MILL PREFACE(116)	CIRCUMSTANCES COULD AND INDEED MUST HAVE BECOME	KINGS	IF THEY HAD BEEN UNGOVERNABLE ENOUGH TO DESIRE IT.
KING I (192)	NO DOUBT; BUT THE BRITISH PEOPLE DO NOT MAKE	KINGS	IN ENGLAND. THE CROWN IS IN THE HANDS OF THE DAMNED
SUPR HANDBOK(214)	MORE POPULAR, DOMESTIC, AND ROMANTIC. IF ALL THE	KINGS	IN EUROPE WERE MADE AS FREE TOMORROW AS KING COPHETUA,
SUPR III (107)	CONSCIOUSNESS OF HAVING THE BLOOD OF THE OLD SEA	KINGS	IN HIS VEINS. CALL HIM LIAR AND THIEF; AND HE WILL
LION PREFACE(34)	GO TO THE STABLE AND TAKE THE PLACE OF THE	KINGS	IN MATTHEW'S CHRONICLE. SO COMPLETELY HAS THIS STORY
PYGM EPILOG (289)	THE EXAMPLE BY PLAYING QUEENS AND FASCINATING	KINGS	IN THE THEATRE IN WHICH SHE BEGAN BY SELLING ORANGES.
LION PREFACE(18)	THE TITLE OF GOD. ILLOGICALLY, SUCH DIVINE	KINGS	INSIST A GOOD DEAL ON THEIR ROYAL HUMAN ANCESTORS.
MRS PREFACE(157)	TO STREET" IS LOUDER THAN THE VOICES OF ALL THE	KINGS	. I AM NOT DEPENDENT ON THE THEATRE, AND CANNOT BE
6CAL (102)	BEGGED FROM YOU I HAVE NEVER ASKED FOR MY TEN	KINGS	. I ASK ONLY FOR SIX OLD MERCHANTS, MEN BENEATH YOUR
CLEO I (114)	KINGS. /CLEOPATRA/ I WILL MAKE ALL THE MEN I LOVE	KINGS	. I WILL MAKE YOU A KING. I WILL HAVE MANY YOUNG
MTH5 (243)	REACHES HER HAND) I KNEW I WAS REALLY A KING OF	KINGS	. (TO THE OTHERS) ILLUSIONS, FAREWELL: WE ARE GOING
6CAL (104)	YOU LIE IN YOUR TEETH, THOUGH YOU WERE FIFTY	KINGS	. NO MAN ALIVE SHALL PITY PETER HARDMOUTH, A DOG OF
METH PREFACE(R66)	GOOD RIDDANCE OF HIM. THE VICEROYS OF THE KING OF	KINGS	. NOW IN POLITICS IT IS MUCH EASIER TO DO WITHOUT GOD
BUOY 1 (15)	WAR IS A SPORT. IT USED TO BE THE SPORT OF	KINGS	. NOW IT IS THE SPORT OF LABOR PARTIES. /SON/ WHAT
APPL I (224)	OR NOT. /MAGNUS/ AT ALL EVENTS YOU DO NOT FLATTER	KINGS	. ONE OF THEM, AT LEAST, IS GRATEFUL TO YOU FOR THAT.
CLEO PRO2 (97)	MYSELF. I AM PERSIAN, AND DESCENDED FROM MANY	KINGS	. /BEL AFFRIS/ (TO THE GUARDSMEN) HAIL, COUSINS! (
KING II (230)	LIKE. IT IS WHAT THEY WOULD DO IF THEY WERE	KINGS	. /CATHERINE/ YOU ARE NOT LAZY: I WISH YOU WERE: I
JOAN EPILOG (154)	LIE THROUGH PALACES, NOR MY CONVERSATION BE WITH	KINGS	. /CHARLES/ (FOLLOWING HIM TOWARDS THE DOOR, AND
KING II (229)	THE SON OF YOUR FATHER. AND YOU ARE THE BEST OF	KINGS	. /CHARLES/ THANK YOU. AND YOUR BROTHER ALFONSO WAS
CLEO I (114)	MAKING ME A QUEEN. /CAESAR/ BUT QUEENS LOVE ONLY	KINGS	. /CLEOPATRA/ I WILL MAKE ALL THE MEN I LOVE KINGS. I
APPL INTRLUD(249)	IT. IF YOU DO NOT, YOU ARE NOT ONE OF NATURE'S	KINGS	. /MAGNUS/ SUBLIME! NOTHING BUT GENUINE INSPIRATION
JOAN 4 (106)	POLITICAL CARDINALS, BETWEEN THE BARONS AND THE	KINGS	. THE DEVIL DIVIDES US AND GOVERNS. I SEE YOU ARE NO
FANY PROLOG (258)	ALWAYS BE GOD SAVE THE QUEEN, NO MATTER HOW MANY	KINGS	MAY SUCCEED. I FOUND ENGLAND BEFOULED WITH
ROCK PREFACE(150)	AND KILLED THE KING AS AN AFFIRMATION THAT EVEN	KINGS	MUST NOT SURVIVE IF THEY ARE MALIGNANT. THIS WAS MUCH
APPL I (230)	RESPONSIBILITY AND THE VETO NOW BELONG NEITHER TO	KINGS	NOR DEMAGOGUES AS SUCH, BUT TO WHOEVER IS CLEVER
INCA (255)	YOU ARE TOO POOR. YOU HAVE TO EAT WAR BREAD.	KINGS	NOWADAYS BELONG TO THE POORER CLASSES. THE KING OF
JOAN 4 (105)	IN THESE LETTERS OF HERS, SHE PROPOSES TO ALL THE	KINGS	OF EUROPE, AS SHE HAS ALREADY PRESSED ON CHARLES, A
JOAN 2 (81)	KING IN THE CATHEDRAL AT RHEIMS, WHERE ALL TRUE	KINGS	OF FRANCE ARE CROWNED. /CHARLES/ (TRIUMPHANT, TO THE
MTH5 (237)	BY THE BRAINLESS SUN AND THE BLIND FIRE; BUT THE	KINGS	OF KINGS AND QUEEN OF QUEENS ARE NOT ACCIDENTS OF THE
ROCK PREFACE(156)	STUDIED AND ARRANGED THAT CARTOUCHE, ONE OF THE	KINGS	OF SCOUNDRELISM, WAS BRIBED TO BETRAY HIS ACCOMPLICES
JOAN 4 (103)	MESSENGER OF GOD, AND WROTE IN GOD'S NAME TO THE	KINGS	OF THE EARTH. HER LETTERS TO THEM ARE GOING FORTH
KING I (190)	THEM WITHOUT A KING. PROTESTANT KINGS-- STUART	KINGS	-- ARE SIX A PENNY IN EUROPE TODAY. THE DUTCH LAD'S
APPL I (202)	THEY SAY THAT POLITENESS IS THE PUNCTUALITY OF	KINGS	-- /SEMPRONIUS/ THE OTHER WAY ABOUT, MR BOANERGES.
KING I (190)	COULD NOT LEAVE THEM WITHOUT A KING. PROTESTANT	KINGS	-- STUART KINGS-- ARE SIX A PENNY IN EUROPE TODAY. THE
APPL I (202)	MR BOANERGES. PUNCTUALITY IS THE POLITENESS OF	KINGS	; AND KING MAGNUS IS A MODEL IN THAT RESPECT. YOUR
CAPT II (267)	SHEIKHS OF FRANGUESTAN. SHE GOES UNVEILED AMONG	KINGS	; AND ONLY PRINCES MAY TOUCH HER HAND. /LADY CICELY/
JOAN 4 (106)	YOU NEED NOT FEAR, MY LORD. SOME MEN ARE BORN	KINGS	; AND SOME ARE BORN STATESMEN. THE TWO ARE SELDOM THE
SUPR HANDBOK(214)	IS RIGHT. KING DEMOS MUST BE BRED LIKE ALL OTHER	KINGS	; AND WITH MUST THERE IS NO ARGUING. IT IS IDLE FOR AN
LION PREFACE(102)	DIVINE RIGHT OF KINGS, AND PROVOKED MEN TO CUT	KINGS	' HEADS OFF TO RESTORE SOME SENSE OF PROPORTION IN THE
JOAN 4 (105)	THE CHURCH? /WARWICK/ HER IDEA IS THAT THE	KINGS	SHOULD GIVE THEIR REALMS TO GOD, AND THEN REIGN AS
APPL I (206)	HE IS A LIVING SOUL. /BOANERGES/ A SOUL, EH? YOU	KINGS	STILL BELIEVE IN THAT, I SUPPOSE. / MAGNUS/ I FIND THE
ROCK PREFACE(151)	PROPERTY. HAVING DISPOSED OF THE DIVINE RIGHT OF	KINGS	THE POLITICAL LIQUIDATORS TURNED THEIR ATTENTION
MIS. (135)	A KING. /LORD SUMMERHAYS/ NOT AT ALL. I HAD FIVE	KINGS	TO MANAGE IN JINGHISKAHN; AND I THINK YOU DO YOUR
6CAL (102)	BABY. /THE QUEEN/ AH NO: YOU ARE THE GREATEST OF	KINGS	TO ME, THE NOBLEST OF MEN, MY DEAREST LORD AND MY
BUOY 1 (14)	COMMIT SUICIDE? A HUNDRED YEARS AGO THERE WERE	KINGS	TO SPUNGE ON. NOWADAYS THERE ARE REPUBLICS EVERYWHERE;
SIM PREFACE(6)	SINS. THE CHRISTIAN CHURCHES AND THE CHRISTIAN	KINGS	WERE DRIVEN TO THE SAME DEVICE; AND WHEN I EVOLVED
CLEO PRO2 (103)	TO BE PAINTED ON THE WALL IN THE PYRAMIDS OF THE	KINGS	WHOM MY FATHERS SERVED. THE WOMEN LAUGH TRIUMPHANTLY.
JITT II (50)	WHY SHOULD YOU NOT SHAKE HANDS WITH ALL THE	KINGS	, AND DINE WITH ALL THE PRESIDENTS, AND HAVE GALA
LION PREFACE(102)	THAT ENDED IN THE THEORY OF THE DIVINE RIGHT OF	KINGS	, AND PROVOKED MEN TO CUT KINGS' HEADS OFF TO RESTORE
JOAN PREFACE(37)	GREAT POPES ARE AS RARE AND ACCIDENTAL AS GREAT	KINGS	, AND THAT IT HAS SOMETIMES BEEN SAFER FOR AN ASPIRANT
MTH5 (237)	IS CLEOPATRA-SEMIRAMIS, CONSORT OF THE KING OF	KINGS	, AND THEREFORE QUEEN OF QUEENS. YE ARE THINGS HATCHED
APPL I (224)	AT LEAST, IS GRATEFUL TO YOU FOR THAT. /PROTEUS/	KINGS	, AS YOU AND I VERY WELL KNOW, RULE THEIR MINISTERS BY
MILL IV (210)	THEY ARE THE ONE SPECIES YOU CANNOT LIQUIDATE.	KINGS	, EMPERORS, CONQUERORS, PONTIFFS AND ALL THE OTHER
POSN PREFACE(386)	THE EXTREME REPUBLICAN PRINCIPLE THAT ALL	KINGS	, GOOD OR BAD, SHOULD BE KILLED BECAUSE KINGSHIP AND
KING I (193)	SUN KING. THIS IS A DEUCED FOGGY CLIMATE FOR SUN	KINGS	, JAMIE. /JAMES/ SO YOU THINK, CHARLES. BUT THE
GENV II SD(49)	WITH ENGRAVED PRINTS OR ENLARGED PHOTOGRAPHS OF	KINGS	, PRESIDENTS, AND DICTATORS, MOSTLY IN MILITARY
2TRU PREFACE(19)	ITSELF TO BE REFORMED BY A PLUTOCRACY OF PIRATE	KINGS	, ROBBER BARONS, COMMERCIAL ADVENTURERS, MONEYLENDERS,
MILL PREFACE(110)	THE PAPAL CHAIR? HOW DO COMMON SOLDIERS BECOME	KINGS	, SHAHS, AND DICTATORS? WHY DOES A HEREDITARY PEER
CLEO II (121)	KING'S TUTOR. /CAESAR/ YOU TEACH MEN HOW TO BE	KINGS	, THEODOTUS. THAT IS VERY CLEVER OF YOU. (LOOKING AT
APPL PREFACE(184)	TOO, SOME OF THEM. IF THEY HAVE NOT LAWS AND	KINGS	, THEY HAVE BY-LAWS AND CHAIRMEN. AND YOU AND I, THE
APPL I (224)	SHE USED TO HAVE TO DIVIDE BETWEEN HALF A DOZEN	KINGS	, THREE EMPERORS, AND A SULTAN. /MAGNUS/ BUT WHAT
CLEO I (115)	STATE? /CAESAR/ FOR A CITIZEN OF ROME. A KING OF	KINGS	, TOTATEETA. /CLEOPATRA/ (STAMPING AT HER) HOW DARE
KING PREFACE(156)	THE TRUTH IS THAT CHARLES, LIKE MOST ENGLISH	KINGS	, WAS CONTINUALLY IN MONEY DIFFICULTIES BECAUSE THE
CLEO I (114)	I WILL MAKE YOU A KING. I WILL HAVE MANY YOUNG	KINGS	, WITH ROUND, STRONG ARMS; AND WHEN I AM TIRED OF THEM
SUPR PREFACE(R30)	HIM. NAPOLEON PROVIDED TALMA WITH A PIT OF	KINGS	, WITH WHAT EFFECT ON TALMA'S ACTING IS NOT RECORDED.
JOAN PREFACE(22)	WITH PEOPLE OF ALL CLASSES, FROM LABORERS TO	KINGS	, WITHOUT EMBARRASSMENT OR AFFECTATION, AND GOT THEM
GENV PREFACE(11)	A GASEOUS NEBULA. IT SEEMS THAT IF " THE SPORT OF	KINGS	" IS TO CONTINUE IT MUST BE FOUGHT UNDER QUEENSBERRY

		KINGSHIP	
POSN PREFACE(386)	ALL KINGS, GOOD OR BAD, SHOULD BE KILLED BECAUSE	KINGSHIP	AND FREEDOM CANNOT LIVE TOGETHER. UNDER CERTAIN
MILL PREFACE(114)	USURPER? THE PERSON WHO HAS A CAPACITY FOR	KINGSHIP	BUT HAS NO KINGDOM AND MUST THEREFORE ACQUIRE A
KING PREFACE(155)	AND ENDED AS THE FIRST KING IN ENGLAND WHOSE	KINGSHIP	WAS PURELY SYMBOLIC, AND WHO WAS CLEVER ENOUGH TO
METH PREFACE(R59)	CONCEPTION OF GODHEAD AS BEING, LIKE EARTHLY	KINGSHIP	, A SUPREME CLASS DISTINCTION INSTEAD OF THE ROCK
		KINGSLAND	
CAND I SD(77)	VERMIN PRESERVE FOR ALL THE PETTY FAUNA OF	KINGSLAND	, HACKNEY, AND HOXTON. A BANDSTAND, AN UNFURNISHED
		KINGSTON	
INCA (232)	LONDON, ON 16TH DECEMBER 1917, WITH GERTRUDE	KINGSTON	AS ERMYNTRUDE, HELEN MORRIS AS THE PRINCESS, NIGEL
HART PREFACE(36)	OF THE ADAM-ADELPHIAN DECORATION ON WHICH MISS	KINGSTON	HAD LAVISHED SO MUCH TASTE AND CARE, THE LITTLE
CATH PREFACE(155)	ITS EXPONENTS. THOSE WHO HAVE SEEN MISS GERTRUDE	KINGSTON	PLAY THE PART OF CATHERINE WILL HAVE NO DIFFICULTY
CATH PREFACE(155)	THE PLAY INTO EXISTENCE. I ONCE RECOMMENDED MISS	KINGSTON	PROFESSIONALLY TO PLAY QUEENS. NOW IN THE MODERN
CATH PREFACE(158)	IMPERTINENCES, I AM QUITE SURE THAT MISS GERTRUDE	KINGSTON	, WHO FIRST MADE HER REPUTATION AS AN IMPERSONATOR
		KINGSTON'S	
CATH PREFACE(155)	QUEENS ARE NOT WORTH A TINKER'S OATH? MISS	KINGSTON'S	COMMENT ON MY SUGGESTION, THOUGH MORE ELEGANTLY
		KINK	
DOCT I (105)	THERES NO SUCH ORGAN. IT'S A MERE ACCIDENTAL	KINK	IN THE MEMBRANE, OCCURRING IN PERHAPS TWO-AND-A-HALF
		KINSHIP	
MIS. PREFACE(84)	COMPULSORY AFFECTION AS AN ATTRIBUTE OF NEAR	KINSHIP	IS NOT ONLY UNNECESSARY, BUT POSITIVELY DETRIMENTAL;
NEVR II (250)	TO BE COLD, BUT SUPREMELY INDIFFERENT TO THEIR	KINSHIP	. HE GREETS HER WITH A GROWL). WELL? /GLORIA/ I
SUPR PREFACE(R26)	TAILORING, BY THE GLAMOR OF ARISTOCRATIC	KINSHIP	. WELL, WE TWO KNOW THESE TRANSFIGURED PERSONS,
MIS. PREFACE(84)	ALARM NOBODY. WE CANNOT BREAK UP THE FACTS OF	KINSHIP	NOR ERADICATE ITS NATURAL EMOTIONAL CONSEQUENCES.
METH PREFACE(R59)	WAS NOT JUSTIFIED; FOR THIS SENSE OF THE	KINSHIP	OF ALL FORMS OF LIFE IS ALL THAT IS NEEDED TO MAKE
DOCT PREFACE(78)	VITAL DOGMAS OF HONOR, LIBERTY, COURAGE, THE	KINSHIP	OF ALL LIFE, FAITH THAT THE UNKNOWN IS GREATER THAN
		KINSMAN	
CAPT II (267)	/OSMAN/ (SCANDALIZED) WOMAN: TOUCH NOT THE	KINSMAN	OF THE PROPHET. /LADY CICELY/ OH, I SEE. I'M BEING
CAPT II (266)	ONE IS NOT HERE. /BRASSBOUND/ SIDI EL ASSIF,	KINSMAN	OF THE PROPHET: YOU ARE WELCOME. /REDBROOK/ (WITH
CAPT II (252)	THE SHEIKH SIDI EL ASSIF-- /OSMAN/ (PROUDLY)	KINSMAN	TO THE PROPHET. /BRASSBOUND/ TELL HIM WHAT YOU HAVE
CAPT II (269)	UPON THEE, THOU MOON AT THE FULL! WHERE IS THY	KINSMAN	, THE CADI OF FRANGUESTAN? I AM HIS FRIEND, HIS
		KINSMEN	
CLEO PRO2 (101)	CANNOT LIVE ON ITS PAY. BUT HEAR ME FURTHER, O YE	KINSMEN	OF OSIRIS. /THE GUARDSMEN/ SPEAK, O SUBTLE ONE. HEAR
MIS. PREFACE(30)	AS MAY EXIST BETWEEN HER AND HER NEAREST	KINSMEN	, AND HAS NO KNOWLEDGE OF THE CONDITION WHICH, IF
		KINTAFI	
CAPT II (265)	HALLAM: YOU HAVE ONE CHANCE LEFT. THE CADI OF	KINTAFI	STANDS SUPERIOR TO THE SHEIKH AS THE RESPONSIBLE
CAPT II (270)	OF THE UNITED STATES TO THE CADI MULEY OTHMAN EL	KINTAFI	, AND ANNOUNCES THAT HE IS COMING TO LOOK FOR THE
CAPT NOTES (302)	AND HOW HE FELL INTO THE HANDS OF THE CADI OF	KINTAFI	, WHO RIGHTLY HELD THAT THERE WAS MORE DANGER TO
		KINTORFY	
CAPT II (265)	PAWK DEMONSTRATION. AW BLIEVE ITS THE KIDY FROM	KINTORFY	. (GENERAL ALARM. ALL LOOK TO BRASSBOUND).
		KIOSK	
CAND I SD(77)	PITCHES, A GYMNASIUM, AND AN OLD FASHIONED STONE	KIOSK	ARE AMONG ITS ATTRACTIONS. WHEREVER THE PROSPECT IS
		KIPLING	
MTH4 I (167)	A THOUSAND YEARS AGO THERE WERE TWO AUTHORS NAMED	KIPLING	. ONE WAS AN EASTERN AND A WRITER OF MERIT: THE
GENV I (36)	KIPLING PUTS IT. /NEWCOMER/ NO: I DONT HOLD WITH	KIPLING	. TOO IMPERIALIST FOR ME. I'M A DEMOCRAT. /SHE/ BUT
MIS. (132)	NO. WRONG PRINCIPLE. YOU WANT TO REMEMBER. READ	KIPLING	. " LEST WE FORGET." /JOHNNY/ IF KIPLING WANTS TO
GENV I (36)	(BRIGHTLY) " AND NEVER THE TWAIN SHALL MEET," AS	KIPLING	PUTS IT. /NEWCOMER/ NO: I DONT HOLD WITH KIPLING.
MIS. (132)	READ KIPLING. " LEST WE FORGET." /JOHNNY/ IF	KIPLING	WANTS TO REMEMBER, LET HIM REMEMBER. IF HE HAD TO
BULL PREFACE(19)	BETWEEN ENGLISH AND IRISH BY MOORE AND MR	KIPLING	, OR EVEN BY PARNELL AND GLADSTONE. SIR BOYLE ROCHE
BULL PREFACE(18)	THE CONTEMPORARY BRITISH PRIVATE; WHILST AS TO MR	KIPLING	, YOU WILL SEE THAT HE HAS NOT, AND UNLESS HE
MIS. PREFACE(37)	AT PRESENT. YOU MAY SAY OF THEM, PARAPHRASING MR	KIPLING	, " WHAT DO THEY KNOW OF PLATO THAT ONLY PLATO
		KIPLINGIZED	
MTH4 I (167)	APPLIED TO MYSELF. YOU HAVE ACTUALLY	KIPLINGIZED	ME. /ZOO/ KIPLINGIZED! WHAT IS THAT? /THE
MTH4 I (167)	MYSELF. YOU HAVE ACTUALLY KIPLINGIZED ME. /ZOO/	KIPLINGIZED	! WHAT IS THAT? /THE ELDERLY GENTLEMAN/ ABOUT
		KIPLING'S	
MIS. PREFACE(57)	THAN LIBERAL EDUCATION. THE SAILOR IN MR RUDYARD	KIPLING'S	CAPTAINS COURAGEOUS, TEACHING THE BOY THE NAMES OF
BULL PREFACE(18)	MOORE'S VISIONARY MINSTREL BOY WITH MR RUDYARD	KIPLING'S	QUASI-REALISTIC SOLDIERS THREE, YOU MAY YAWN OVER
GETT PREFACE(225)	COUNSELLOR SHE PROBABLY LEAVES THEM NOWHERE. MR	KIPLING'S	QUESTION WHAT CAN THEY KNOW OF ENGLAND THAT ONLY
BULL PREFACE(12)	SPECIALLY AN ENGLISHMAN'S BURDEN, AS MOST OF MR	KIPLING'S	READERS SEEM TO INTERPRET IT. TRIBES MUST MAKE
FABL PREFACE(93)	EVER SEEN. BUT THIS DOES NOT DISCONCERT ME.	KIPLING'S	" LEST WE FORGET" IS OFTEN LESS URGENT THAN " LEST
		KIRBY	
GETT (292)	THE NAVY BOASTS TWO SUCH MARTYRS IN CAPTAINS	KIRBY	AND WADE, WHO WERE SHOT FOR REFUSING TO FIGHT UNDER
		KISS	
PHIL I (83)	YOU COME WITHOUT ANOTHER WORD IF I GIVE YOU A	KISS	? /JULIA/ I WILL DO ANYTHING YOU WISH, DARLING.
2TRU III (87)	THAT THOUGH THERE IS A POINT AT WHICH I'D RATHER	KISS	A WOMAN THAN DO ANYTHING ELSE IN THE WORLD, YET I'D
HART I (76)	TAKE CARE, DEAR CHILD. I DONT BELIEVE ANY MAN CAN	KISS	ADDY WITHOUT FALLING IN LOVE WITH HER. (SHE GOES INTO
2TRU III (110)	SWEAR; USE DIRTY WORDS; DRINK COCKTAILS;	KISS	AND CARESS AND CUDDLE UNTIL GIRLS WHO ARE LIKE ROSES AT
2TRU III (87)	OH, WELL, KISS ME AND HAVE DONE WITH IT. YOU CANT	KISS	AND TALK ABOUT RELIGION AT THE SAME TIME. /THE ELDER/ (
MIS. (193)	SAY TO THAT? /PERCIVAL/ AS A GENTLEMAN, I DO NOT	KISS	AND TELL. AS A MERE MAN: A MERE CAD, IF YOU LIKE, I SAY
O'FL SD(220)	WITHOUT LOSING HER IRISH DIGNITY, TAKES THE	KISS	AS APPRECIATIVELY AS A CONNOISSEUR MIGHT TAKE A GLASS
DEVL II (40)	THAT YOU LOVE ME LIKE A WIFE UNLESS YOU GIVE ONE	KISS	BEFORE I GO. HE APPROACHES HER AND HOLDS OUT HIS ARMS.
OVER PREFACE(164)	IMPOSSIBLE FOR ANY SPECTATOR TO MISTAKE A STAGE	KISS	FOR A REAL ONE. IN ENGLAND, ON THE CONTRARY, REALISM IS
BARB PREFACE(223)	THE REGULAR SALVATION ARMY JOKES, AND SNATCHES A	KISS	FROM HER LOVER ACROSS HIS DRUM, THE DEVOTEES OF THE
DEVL II SD(40)	DROPPING FROM HIS ARMS TO THE GROUND AS IF THE	KISS	HAD KILLED HER. /RICHARD/ (GOING QUICKLY TO THE
HART I (70)	SHOTOVER/ STUFF! EVERYONE KISSES MY DAUGHTER.	KISS	HER AS MUCH AS YOU LIKE (HE MAKES FOR THE PANTRY).
LADY (247)	I-- /ELIZABETH/ GO (THE DARK LADY TRIES TO	KISS	HER HAND). NO MORE. GO (THE DARK LADY GOES,
LADY (242)	THE VIRGINALS. LET HER PLAY SO TO ME; AND I'LL	KISS	HER HANDS, BUT UNTIL THEN, YOU ARE MY QUEEN; AND I'LL
NEVR II (248)	HER. /VALENTINE/ WHO WANTS TO MARRY HER? I'LL	KISS	HER HANDS; I'LL KNEEL AT HER FEET; I'LL LIVE FOR HER;
HART I (72)	STILL SMILES). /MRS HUSHABYE/ CALL HER ADDY; AND	KISS	HER LIKE A GOOD BROTHER-IN-LAW; AND HAVE DONE WITH IT.
JITT II SD(33)	SENTENCES. JITTA HAS TO DRAW THE GIRL TO HER, AND	KISS	HER ON THE BROW. ALFRED LEADS MRS HALDENSTEDT TO THE
CATH 4 (195)	HIS ARMS) EMBRACE HER, VICTOR OF BUNKER'S HILL.	KISS	HER TILL SHE SWOONS. /THE SERGEANT/ RECEIVE HER IN THE
VWOO 2,SD(132)	YOU. /Z/ THANKS VERY MUCH. SHE TEMPTS HIM TO	KISS	HER. /A/ NO! ! ! (HE STRIDES OUT).
WIDO I (13)	YOU ACTUALLY KISSED-- /TRENCH/ YOU DIDNT SEE ME	KISS	HER. /COKANE/ WE NOT ONLY SAW BUT HEARD IT: THE REPORT
SIM I (48)	KNOW I SHOULD HAVE EXPLAINED THAT. BUT SHE LET ME	KISS	HER. /MRS HYERING/ THAT MUST HAVE BEEN A THRILL, MR
DEST (183)	SISTER'S A VERY PRETTY WOMAN. (HE ATTEMPTS TO	KISS	HER). /LADY/ (SLIPPING AWAY FROM HIM) OH, LIEUTENANT!
ARMS II (35)	(CHARMED) WITTY AS WELL AS PRETTY. (HE TRIES TO	KISS	HER). /LOUKA/ (AVOIDING HIM) NO: I DONT WANT YOUR
PYGM III (245)	DAY: YOU PROMISED NOT TO COME. (AS HE BENDS TO	KISS	HER, SHE TAKES HIS HAT OFF, AND PRESENTS IT TO HIM).
PYGM V (289)	DEAR. /HIGGINS/ GOODBYE, MOTHER. (HE IS ABOUT TO	KISS	HER, WHEN HE RECOLLECTS SOMETHING). OH, BY THE WAY,
SUPR IV (160)	DEAR. (SHE PATS HIS CHEEK; HAS AN IMPULSE TO	KISS	HIM AND THEN ANOTHER IMPULSE OF DISTASTE WHICH PREVENTS
BASH II,2, (116)	BEHOLD! THE CHAMPION COMES. /LYDIA/ OH, I COULD	KISS	HIM NOW HERE, BEFORE ALL THE WORLD. HIS BOXING THINGS
WIDO II (25)	MY DEAR CHILD. (SHE RESPONDS BY GOING OVER TO	KISS	HIM. A TAP AT THE DOOR). COME IN. LICKCHEESE ENTERS,

JITT III (80)	FOLLOWED BY MRS HALDENSTEDT. /EDITH/ HERE HE IS.	KISS	HIM. /FESSLER/ (HASTILY) TCHUT! (TAKING JITTA'S
ARMS II (26)	US! (SHE STOOPS OVER THE BACK OF HIS CHAIR TO	KISS	HIM). HAVE THEY BROUGHT YOU FRESH COFFEE? /PETKOFF/
JITT I SD(26)	HER. SHE GOES TO HIM, AND CANNOT TOUCH HIM OR	KISS	HIM; BUT SHE MAKES THE SIGN OF THE CROSS OVER HIM;
POSN (459)	DOWN HIS NECK AND CALLED HIM DADDY AND TRIED TO	KISS	HIM; FOR IT WAS NOT RIGHT IN ITS HEAD WITH THE FEVER.
ANNA (290)	ABOVE US LIKE A GOD. YOU CAN SEE HIM; YOU CAN	KISS	HIS HAND; YOU CAN BE CHEERED BY HIS SMILE AND TERRIFIED
OVER PREFACE(164)	PHYSICAL INCIDENTS OF SEX. ON THE FRENCH STAGE A	KISS	IS AS OBVIOUS A CONVENTION AS THE THRUST UNDER THE ARM
PHIL III (139)	(WITH GENUINE EMOTION, HE TAKES HER HAND TO	KISS	IT AGAIN). /JULIA/ (SNATCHING HER HAND AWAY IN
ARMS I SD(7)	THAT ARE BEYOND ALL EXPRESSION. SHE DOES NOT	KISS	IT OR PRESS IT TO HER BREAST, OR SHEW IT ANY MARK OF
WIDO III SD(64)	THE PORTRAIT FROM THE EASEL, AND IS ABOUT TO	KISS	IT WHEN, TAKING A SECOND LOOK ROUND TO REASSURE HIMSELF
CATH 4 (192)	AN EMPRESS ALLOWS YOU TO SEE HER FOOT YOU SHOULD	KISS	IT. CAPTAIN EDSTASTON: YOU ARE A BOOBY. /EDSTASTON/ (
DEST (164)	HER HAND). /LIEUTENANT/ (BENDING GALLANTLY TO	KISS	IT) OH, MADAM, NOT THE LEA-- (CHECKING HIMSELF AND
MRS III (227)	ARE MY FIRST PLAYMATE. (HE CATCHES HER HAND TO	KISS	IT, BUT CHECKS HIMSELF TO LOOK ROUND FIRST. VERY
PHIL II (116)	(SHE CATCHES CRAVEN'S LEFT HAND AND STOOPS TO	KISS	IT, HIS RIGHT HAND BEING STILL ON CUTHBERTSON'S
MRS II (199)	NEVER YOU MIND, MY DEAR: IT'S ONLY A MOTHERLY	KISS	. GO AND MAKE LOVE TO VIVIE. /FRANK/ SO I HAVE. /MRS
GENV II (53)	GENTLEMAN I MUST SAY: NEVER ASKED SO MUCH AS A	KISS	. I WAS DISAPPOINTED. /THE SECRETARY/ DISAPPOINTED AT
ARMS III (67)	WELL, ONLY A JOKE, LITTLE ONE. COME: GIVE ME A	KISS	. (SHE KISSES HIM). NOW GIVE ME THE COAT. /RAINA/ NO:
PYGM V SD(289)	SHE'LL BUY EM ALL RIGHT ENOUGH. GOODBYE. THEY	KISS	. MRS HIGGINS RUNS OUT. HIGGINS, LEFT ALONE, RATTLES
6CAL SD(106)	FOR SHAME! THE KING STOPS HER MOUTH WITH A	KISS	. PETER BRAYS MELODIOUSLY IN THE DISTANCE.
CAND II (121)	A GRAPPLING IRON INTO MY HEART THAN GIVEN ME THAT	KISS	. /CANDIDA/ (AMAZED) MY DEAR: WHATS THE MATTER?
PHIL I (83)	I'LL COME, DEAR, IF YOU WISH IT. GIVE ME ONE	KISS	. /CHARTERIS/ (EXASPERATED) THIS IS TOO MUCH. NO: I'M
DEST (183)	DESTINY OF HUMANITY! (MAKING FOR HER) ONLY A	KISS	. /LADY/ (RETREATING ROUND THE TABLE) NOT UNTIL YOU
BUOY IV (48)	/PRIEST/ TRULY NO. THE TEMPLE WILL SANCTIFY YOUR	KISS	. /OLD BILL/ GOOD. IT IS CURIOUS HOW HAPPY I ALWAYS
SUPR I (41)	ALWAYS ONE WHO KISSES AND ONE WHO ONLY ALLOWS THE	KISS	. TAVY WILL KISS; AND YOU WILL ONLY TURN THE CHEEK. AND
PHIL II (131)	(HE SLIPS HIS ARM ROUND HER WAIST) JUST ONE	KISS	. TO SOOTHE ME. /GRACE/ (COMPLACENTLY OFFERING HER
DEVL II (40)	I OUGHT TO-- IT'S MURDER-- /RICHARD/ NO: ONLY A	KISS	(SOFTLY TO HER) FOR HIS SAKE. /JUDITH/ I CANT. YOU
6CAL (103)	FOR THE QUEEN'S MERCY? /PETER/ YAH! HENPECKED!	KISS	MAMMY! /THE KING/ (CHUCKLES) ! ! /THE QUEEN/ (
HART I (50)	I AM ARIADNE. I'M LITTLE PADDY PATKINS. WONT YOU	KISS	ME? (SHE GOES TO HIM AND THROWS HER ARMS ROUND HIS
ROCK II (281)	THAT. /LADY CHAVENDER/ THE BRUTE! HOW DARE HE	KISS	ME? (SHE RUBS THE PLACE WITH HER HANDKERCHIEF). /SIR
HART I (70)	NOT. /MRS HUSHABYE/ THEN WHAT BUSINESS HAD YOU TO	KISS	ME? /THE GENTLEMAN/ I THOUGHT I WOULD LIKE TO. THE
2TRU III (87)	HAS TO MAKE ROOM FOR. /SWEETIE/ OH, WELL,	KISS	ME AND HAVE DONE WITH IT. YOU CANT KISS AND TALK ABOUT
HART II (98)	I WAS TO QUARREL WITH YOU AND CALL YOU NAMES! DO	KISS	ME AND SAY YOURE NOT ANGRY WITH ME. /ELLIE/ (FIERCELY)
HART I (76)	DARLING, HE HAS ACTUALLY CONDESCENDED TO	KISS	ME AT LAST. I SHALL GO INTO THE GARDEN: IT'S COOLER NOW
MIS. (163)	HILL AND CHASE ME THROUGH THE BRACKEN. YOU MAY	KISS	ME IF YOU CATCH ME. /PERCIVAL/ I SHALL DO NOTHING OF
MIS. (126)	ANYBODY BE IN LOVE WITH BUNNY? I LIKE HIM TO	KISS	ME JUST AS I LIKE A BABY TO KISS ME. I'M FOND OF HIM;
HART I (53)	AND EXPLOSIVELY) HESIONE: ARE YOU GOING TO	KISS	ME OR ARE YOU NOT? /MRS HUSHABYE/ WHAT DO YOU WANT TO
ARMS II (35)	CONSIDERS RIGHT. I THOUGHT FROM YOUR TRYING TO	KISS	ME THAT YOU HAD GIVEN UP BEING SO PARTICULAR. /SERGIUS/
MIS. (126)	I LIKE HIM TO KISS ME JUST AS I LIKE A BABY TO	KISS	ME. I'M FOND OF HIM; AND HE NEVER BORES ME; AND I SEE
HART I (76)	YOU ARE MY BROTHER-IN-LAW. HESIONE ASKED YOU TO	KISS	ME. (HE SEIZES HER IN HIS ARMS, AND KISSES HER
BASH III (123)	/ADELAIDE/ MY SON! /CASHEL/ MY MOTHER! DO NOT	KISS	ME. MY VISAGE IS TOO SORE. /POLICEMAN/ THE LADY HID
HART I (53)	SEPARATED FOR TWENTY-THREE YEARS. YOU OUGHT TO	KISS	ME. /MRS HUSHABYE/ TOMORROW MORNING, DEAR, BEFORE YOU
FANY III (304)	FEELING MEAN ABOUT THIS AFTERWARDS. YOUD BETTER	KISS	ME. YOU NEEDNT EVER DO IT AGAIN. /BOBBY/ IF I'M NO
FANY III (304)	WHAT YOU CALL FUN, I SHOULD ASK THE FRENCHMAN TO	KISS	ME-- OR JUGGINS. /BOBBY/ (RISING AND RETREATING TO THE
MIS. PREFACE(22)	A HANDSOME YOUTH, BEEN KISSED BY HER. SHE DID NOT	KISS	ME; AND NOBODY EVER DREAMT OF EXPELLING ME. THE TRUTH
BULL PREFACE(19)	HE HAD TO COMMAND, WITHOUT ONE GUSH OF THE "	KISS	ME, HARDY" EMOTION WHICH ENABLED NELSON TO IDOLIZE HIS
FANY III (304)	PREPARING TO USE FORCE) NOW, I'LL MAKE YOU	KISS	ME, JUST TO PUNISH YOU. (SHE SEIZES HIS WRIST; PULLS
BUOY IV (48)	OUT). /OLD BILL/ SHALL I PROFANE THE TEMPLE IF I	KISS	MY DAUGHTER HERE? I AM FOND OF HER. /PRIEST/ TRULY NO.
MIS. (141)	OTHER OLD MEN, SO (OFFERING HER HAND) YOU MAY	KISS	MY HAND IF THAT WILL BE ANY FUN FOR YOU. /LORD'
PRES (168)	HAND). /LADY CORINTHIA/ (TO BALSQUITH) YOU MAY	KISS	MY HAND, IF YOU WISH. /BALSQUITH/ (CAUTIOUSLY) I THINK
CURE (237)	VOICE TO WELCOME ME HOME, OF A SILKY MOUSTACHE TO	KISS	MY WEARY FINGERS WHEN I RETURN FROM A TITANIC STRUGGLE
3PLA PREFACE(R30)	BY SURREPTITIOUSLY IMPRINTING A HEARTBROKEN	KISS	ON A STRAY LOCK OF HER HAIR WHILST HE UTTERED THE
ARMS I (4)	PULLS HER MOTHER DOWN ON THE OTTOMAN; AND THEY	KISS	ONE ANOTHER FRANTICALLY). /CATHERINE/ (WITH SURGING
BARB II (290)	NOT FOR THE FIRST TIME, AS PEOPLE CANNOT	KISS	OVER A BIG DRUM WITHOUT PRACTICE. UNDERSHAFT COUGHS).
6CAL (96)	DEAREST SIR. /THE KING/ (UXORIOUSLY WAVING HER A	KISS	) MY LOVE! THE QUEEN GOES INTO HER PAVILION; AND A
PHIL I (83)	HER IN HIS ARMS AND GIVES HER AN UNCEREMONIOUS	KISS	). NOW REMEMBER YOUR PROMISE. COME ALONG. /JULIA/ THAT
GETT (266)	GOOD MORNING, DEAR LITTLE SISTER. (THEY	KISS	): /LESBIA/ GOOD MORNING, COLLINS. HOW WELL YOU ARE
2TRU I (43)	MORE LIKE AN ENGLISH GENTLEMAN. (SHE WAVES HIM A	KISS	). /THE NURSE/ WELL I'LL BE DA-- /THE BURGLAR/
ARMS I (6)	COMES BACK FOR A MOMENT). WISH ME JOY. (THEY	KISS	). THIS IS THE HAPPIEST NIGHT OF MY LIFE-- IF ONLY
APPL I (240)	OF YOU: THATS WHAT I SAY. /AMANDA/ (WAFTS HIM A	KISS	)! /MAGNUS/ SHOULD NOT THE QUEEN SUPPORT THE KING,
APPL I (216)	/BOANERGES/ ORDER, ORDER! /AMANDA/ (WAVES HIM A	KISS	)! ! /MAGNUS/ PRIME MINISTER: THE WORD IS WITH YOU.
MIS. (163)	BE AFRAID, LITTLE BOY: YOULL GET NOTHING BUT A	KISS	; AND I'LL FIGHT LIKE THE DEVIL TO KEEP YOU FROM
BUOY 1 SD(17)	GOOD FATHER; AND I SHALL NOT FORGET IT. THEY	KISS	; AND THE SON GOES.
2TRU I (49)	ON HIS LEFT. /THE PATIENT/ HERE I AM, POPS. ONE	KISS	; AND THEN-- LEAD ON. /THE BURGLAR/ GOOD. YOUR
SUPR I (41)	AND ONE WHO ONLY ALLOWS THE KISS. TAVY WILL	KISS	; AND YOU WILL ONLY TURN THE CHEEK. AND YOU WILL THROW
DOCT III (140)	A GOOD TIME THAT CAN NEVER BE TAKEN FROM US; SO	KISS	; PART GOOD FRIENDS; AND SHE BACK TO SERVICE, AND I
NEVR IV (303)	(TUMULTUOUSLY) OH, MY FEELINGS! I WANT TO	KISS	SOMEBODY; AND WE BAR IT IN THE FAMILY. WHERES FINCH?
SIM II (77)	CHILDREN: GO AWAY. NOW THAT MAYA HAS GONE TO	KISS	SOMEBODY, THERE IS NOTHING LEFT FOR YOU TO GLORIFY BUT
INCA SD(242)	BOW TO THE PRINCESS; GOES TO THE DOOR; WAFTS A	KISS	SURREPTITIOUSLY TO ERMYNTRUDE; AND GOES OUT. /THE
POSN (456)	TO ME NEXT TIME, FOR ALL I'M NOT GOOD ENOUGH TO	KISS	THE BOOK. /BLANCO/ LORD KEEP ME WICKED TILL I DIE! I'M
POSN (454)	/JESSIE/ THATS RIGHT. SHE DIDNT OUGHT TO BE LET	KISS	THE BOOK. /EMMA/ HOW COULD THE LIKE OF HER TELL THE
PPP (197)	TUMBLER TO ADOLPHUS) PLEDGE ME, ADOLPHUS. /FITZ/	KISS	THE CUP, MAGNESIA. PLEDGE HER, MAN. DRINK DEEP.
GETT (327)	PLACE WHERE SHE HAD BEEN. A HIDEOUS TEMPTATION TO	KISS	THE DOORSTEP BECAUSE HER FOOT HAD PRESSED IT MADE ME
LADY (243)	HANDS. BUT UNTIL THEN, YOU ARE MY QUEEN; AND I'LL	KISS	THOSE LIPS THAT HAVE DROPT MUSIC ON MY HEART. (HE PUTS
ARMS II (34)	THERE TO EXCHANGE LOOKS WITH HIM AND WAVE HIM A	KISS	WITH BOTH HANDS. HE LOOKS AFTER HER WITH EMOTION FOR A
LION I (117)	OF HIM). DO YOU TURN THE OTHER CHEEK WHEN THEY	KISS	YOU? /LAVINIA/ (STARTING) WHAT? /LENTULUS/ DO YOU
2TRU III (87)	I DONT WANT YOU NOW. /THE SERGEANT/ YOU WILL IF I	KISS	YOU HALF A DOZEN TIMES, MORE THAN YOU EVER WANTED
PRES (168)	CORRECT THING IN EVERY WAY, I AM QUITE WILLING TO	KISS	YOU IF YOU WISH IT. /MRS FARRELL/ YOUD ONLY FEEL LIKE A
PYGM V (287)	WITH LOTS OF MONEY, AND A THICK PAIR OF LIPS TO	KISS	YOU WITH AND A THICK PAIR OF BOOTS TO KICK YOU WITH. IF
SIM I (41)	MAKE ME FEEL AS I HAVE NEVER FELT BEFORE. I MUST	KISS	YOU. (HE DOES SO AND FINDS THAT SHE IS ALIVE. SHE
HART I (48)	APPROACHING HER WITH OUTSTRETCHED ARMS) COME AND	KISS	YOUR AUNT, DARLING. /ELLIE/ I'M ONLY A VISITOR. IT IS
JOAN 5 (119)	CHILDREN AND THEIR INVALIDS TO HEAL: THEY WILL	KISS	YOUR HANDS AND FEET, AND DO WHAT THEY CAN, POOR SIMPLE
SIM I (41)	YOU ARE! HOW I WISH YOU WERE ALIVE AND I COULD	KISS	YOUR LIVING LIPS INSTEAD OF THE PAINT ON A HARD WOODEN
O'FL (216)	OF THE FINEST SOLDIER IN IRELAND. COME AND	KISS	YOUR OLD MOTHER, DINNY DARLINT. (O'FLAHERTY DOES SO
GETT (276)	PROCTOR! /LEO/ NAUGHTY. WELL, I SUPPOSE I MUST	KISS	YOU; BUT DONT ANY OF YOU TELL. (SHE KISSES HIM. THEY
LION I (118)	/LENTULUS/ DO YOU TURN THE OTHER CHEEK WHEN THEY	KISS	YOU, FASCINATING CHRISTIAN? /LAVINIA/ DONT BE FOOLISH.
DEST (184)	SMILE, SHE CHANGES THE GESTURE INTO WAFTING HIM A	KISS	, AND RUNS OUT THROUGH THE INNER DOOR, ELECTRIFIED. HE
POSN (459)	JUDAS KID, AND THAT IT WAS BETRAYING HIM WITH A	KISS	, AND THAT HE'D SWING FOR IT. AND THEN HE GAVE ME THE
WIDO I (12)	HE KISSES HER AGAIN). /BLANCHE/ (OVERCOME BY THE	KISS	, BUT HOLDING ON TO HER POINT) BUT HARRY-- /TRENCH/ (
PHIL I (83)	PROMISE. COME ALONG. /JULIA/ THAT WAS NOT A NICE	KISS	, DEAREST. I WANT ONE OF OUR OLD REAL KISSES.
PHIL I (70)	QUAINTLY AT HER). THAT MUST POSITIVELY BE MY LAST	KISS	, GRACE; OR I SHALL BECOME DOWNRIGHT SILLY. LET US
CATH 4 (196)	ONE KISS! AND ON THE FOREHEAD! FISH. SEE HOW I	KISS	, THOUGH IT IS ONLY MY HORRIBLY UGLY OLD UNCLE (SHE
OVER PREFACE(164)	OFFENSIVE, NO MATTER WHETHER IT BE A PRAYER OR A	KISS	, UNLESS IT IS PRESENTED WITH A CONVINCING APPEARANCE
CLEO IV (180)	WELCOME, APOLLODORUS. (SHE GIVES HIM HER HAND TO	KISS	, WITH HER OTHER ARM ABOUT CAESAR). /APOLLODORUS/
ARMS III (73)	MAN. YOU ACCEPTED ME. YOU GAVE ME YOUR HAND TO	KISS	, YOUR BED TO SLEEP IN, AND YOUR ROOF TO SHELTER ME.
CATH 4 (196)	NO OBJECTION. /VARINKA/ (DISGUSTED) ONLY ONE	KISS	! AND ON THE FOREHEAD! FISH. SEE HOW I KISS, THOUGH

KISSED

MIS. PREFACE(22)	AND IN THAT CASE THE CULPRIT, A BOARDER, HAD	KISSED	A HOUSEMAID, OR POSSIBLY, BEING A HANDSOME YOUTH,
SUPR I (34)	WITH OUR ARMS ROUND ONE ANOTHER, AND	KISSED	AT PARTING, AND HERE MOST CONSCIENTIOUSLY ROMANTIC.
INCA (244)	WITH SOFT HAIR AND A BEARD. I COULDNT BEAR BEING	KISSED	BY A BRISTLY PERSON. (SHE RUNS OUT, THE MANAGER
MIS. PREFACE(22)	OR POSSIBLY, BEING A HANDSOME YOUTH, BEEN	KISSED	BY HER. SHE DID NOT KISS ME; AND NOBODY EVER DREAMT
HART I (53)	YOU NOT? /MRS HUSHABYE/ WHAT DO YOU WANT TO BE	KISSED	FOR? /LADY UTTERWORD/ I DONT WANT TO BE KISSED; BUT
PHIL II (110)	SCENE LAST NIGHT. IMAGINE HER SAYING I HAD	KISSED	HER WITHIN THE LAST TWO DAYS! /GRACE/ (RISING
SIM I (48)	THEN ON WHAT GROUND? OH, I SHOULDNT HAVE	KISSED	HER. /MRS HYERING/ OHO! YOU SAID IT WAS SHE WHO
DEVL II (46)	KINDNESS AND CHARITY, JUDITH, I HOPE. /JUDITH/ I	KISSED	HIM. /ANDERSON/ WHAT! JUDITH! /JUDITH/ ARE YOU
DEVL II (47)	THAT IS WHY HE WENT IN YOUR COAT. THAT IS WHY I	KISSED	HIM. /ANDERSON/ (EXPLODING) BLOOD AN' OWNS! (HIS
ARMS II SD(37)	WITH A SUPERB GESTURE, SHE PRESENTS HER ARM TO BE	KISSED	. AMAZED, HE LOOKS AT HER; AT THE ARM; AT HER AGAIN;
SUPR I (33)	THE TRUTH ABOUT; I STOLE THINGS I DIDNT WANT; I	KISSED	LITTLE GIRLS I DIDNT CARE FOR. IT WAS ALL BRAVADO:

PHIL I	(76)	IN LOVE WITH ME: HOW IT IS NOT TWO DAYS SINCE YOU	KISSED	ME AND TOLD ME THAT THE FUTURE WOULD BE AS HAPPY AS
O'FL	(207)	THAT WAS HOW IT WAS, SIR. AND SURE THE POOR WOMAN	KISSED	ME AND WENT ABOUT THE HOUSE SINGING IN HER OLD CRACKY
MIS.	(193)	MR PERCIVAL CHASED ME THROUGH THE HEATHER AND	KISSED	ME. /LORD SUMMERHAYS/ AS A GENTLEMAN, MR PERCIVAL,
SIM I	(48)	BUT PERHAPS I OUGHTNT TO TELL YOU THIS-- SHE	KISSED	ME. /SIR CHARLES/ INDEED? THAT SHEWS THAT SHE
MIS.	(185)	DISTRESS) YOU CHASED ME THROUGH THE HEATHER AND	KISSED	ME. YOU SHOULDNT HAVE DONE THAT IF YOU WERE NOT IN
GETT	(345)	/MRS GEORGE/ (WAKING) WHAT WAS THAT? WHO	KISSED	MY HAND? (TO THE BISHOP, EAGERLY) WAS IT YOU? (HE
DOCT V	(177)	HAVE EXPECTED TO CARE FOR YOU! /RIDGEON/ WHO	KISSED	MY HANDS. WHO BELIEVED IN ME. WHO TOLD ME HER
JITT III	(77)	THAT I AM A DON JUAN. TO BE PRECISE, I HAVE	KISSED	OTHER WOMEN TWICE. I WAS DRUNK BOTH TIMES. AND I HAD
WIDO I	(13)	WITH THE USAGES OF SOCIETY? YOU ACTUALLY	KISSED	-- /TRENCH/ YOU DIDNT SEE ME KISS HER. /COKANE/ WE
CATH 2	(180)	SMILING AND EXTENDING HER HAND TO HIM TO BE	KISSED	) COURTIER! /EDSTASTON/ (KISSING IT) NOT AT ALL.
CATH 4	(198)	THAT JUST ONCE. (VARINKA PUTS HER FACE UP TO BE	KISSED	). EH? NO, NO, NO, NO: YOU DONT MEAN THAT, YOU KNOW.
HART I	(53)	KISSED FOR? /LADY UTTERWORD/ I DONT WANT TO BE	KISSED	; BUT I DO WANT YOU TO BEHAVE PROPERLY AND DECENTLY.
POSN	(456)	SAY THE WORDS. /FEEMY/ WORSE PEOPLE THAN ME HAS	KISSED	THAT BOOK. WHAT WRONG IVE DONE, MOST OF YOU WENT
MTH4 I	(155)	AND WOMEN FLUNG THEMSELVES DOWN AND PASSIONATELY	KISSED	THE SOIL OF IRELAND, CALLING ON THE YOUNG TO EMBRACE
KING II	(226)	SO YOU MUST MAKE FOR HOME THE MOMENT I HAVE	KISSED	YOU GOODBYE FOR THE LAST TIME. /CATHERINE/ (ALMOST
SIM II	(60)	WAS EITHER SO FUNNY OR SO PITEOUS THAT I HAVE	KISSED	YOU INSTEAD. /IDDY/ YOU MAKE ME HAPPIER THAN I HAVE
SIM I	(48)	HER. /MRS HYERING/ OHO! YOU SAID IT WAS SHE WHO	KISSED	YOU. /THE CLERGYMAN/ YES: I KNOW I SHOULD HAVE
HART I	(72)	GRAVE COURTESY). /MRS HUSHABYE/ SHE WANTS TO BE	KISSED	, HECTOR. /LADY UTTERWORD/ HESIONE! (BUT SHE STILL
			KISSES	
CATH 4	(195)	/VARINKA/ SHE BEGS YOU FOR A THOUSAND DEAR LITTLE	KISSES	ALL OVER HER BODY. /CLAIRE/ (VEHEMENTLY) I DO NOT. (
SUPR I	(41)	VERY MUCH ABOUT TAVY. BUT THERE IS ALWAYS ONE WHO	KISSES	AND ONE WHO ONLY ALLOWS THE KISS. TAVY WILL KISS; AND
JITT III	(80)	(OVERJOYED) OH, THINK OF THAT! EDITH (SHE	KISSES	EDITH)! DOCTOR (SHE KISSES THE DOCTOR)! PROFESSOR
PYGM EPILOG	(296)	FIRST MEETING: A SENTIMENT WHICH EARNED HIM MANY	KISSES	FROM HIS WIFE. HE ADDED THAT HE HAD ALWAYS BEEN
GENV II	(53)	YOU? /BEGONIA/ OH NO! THERE WERE PLENTY OF	KISSES	GOING FROM BETTER LOOKING CHAPS. BUT HE WAS A BIT OF
JITT I	(24)	NOTHING MATTERS BUT JITTA, JITTA, JITTA (HE	KISSES	HER AGAIN AND AGAIN). I AM NEITHER WEAK NOR AFRAID
WIDO I	(12)	/TRENCH/ WHAT MORE CAN I SAY THAN THIS? (HE	KISSES	HER AGAIN). /BLANCHE/ (OVERCOME BY THE KISS, BUT
CATH 3,SD	(184)	KNOUTED IF WE STAY? /EDSTASTON/ DO, DEAREST. HE	KISSES	HER AND LETS HER GO, EXPECTING HER TO RUN INTO THE
JITT I	(24)	AWAY) LIFE: YES: THIS IS LIFE, AND THIS (HE	KISSES	HER EYES), AND THIS (HE KISSES HER LIPS). WHAT A
BULL IV	(165)	NORA: THATS REALLY MOST DELICATELY WOMANLY (HE	KISSES	HER HAND CHIVALROUSLY). /NORA/ (LOOKING EARNESTLY
JITT I	(18)	THIEF AM I. I FEEL THAT THROUGH AND THROUGH. (HE	KISSES	HER HAND PASSIONATELY). I HAVE TAKEN A PRICELESS
ARMS II	SD(38)	I AM SO HAPPY TODAY. HE GOES QUICKLY TO HER, AND	KISSES	HER HAND REMORSEFULLY. CATHERINE COMES OUT AND CALLS
PHIL II	(117)	BY THE STAIRCASE DOOR, FOLLOWED BY SYLVIA, WHO	KISSES	HER HAND TO THE BUST AS SHE PASSES. CRAVEN STARES
FANY I	(284)	WELL, I'M OFF. TOOTLE LOO, CHARLIE DARLING. (SHE	KISSES	HER HAND TO HIM AND GOES).
CAPT II	SD(262)	THAT. HE LOOKS UP AT HER FOR A MOMENT; THEN	KISSES	HER HAND. SHE PRESSES HIS AND TURNS AWAY WITH HER
MRS II	(209)	TAKES HER HAND) GOOD-NIGHT, DEAR MRS WARREN. (HE	KISSES	HER HAND. SHE SNATCHES IT AWAY, HER LIPS TIGHTENING,
DEST	(164)	TWINS. /LIEUTENANT/ THAT ACCOUNTS FOR IT. (HE	KISSES	HER HAND). A THOUSAND PARDONS. I DIDNT MIND ABOUT THE
CAND I	(103)	AN HOUR. (SHE PUTS A FINAL TOUCH TO THE BOW. HE	KISSES	HER HAND). DONT BE SILLY. /MARCHBANKS/ I WANT TO
OVER	(183)	YOU WILL. /MRS LUNN/ WELL, PERHAPS I WILL. (HE	KISSES	HER HAND). NOW DONT BEGIN ABUSING THE PRIVILEGE.
SUPR II	(58)	HOUSEKEEPING. /OCTAVIUS/ I FLY, DEAREST ANN (HE	KISSES	HER HAND). /ANN/ (TENDERLY) RICKY TICKY TAVY! HE
PRES	(168)	WOMAN. IVE MADE AN EXTREMELY WISE CHOICE. (HE	KISSES	HER HAND). /LADY CORINTHIA/ (TO BALSQUITH) YOU MAY
6CAL	(95)	/THE PRINCE/ HOW DO YOU, LADY MOTHER? (HE	KISSES	HER HAND). /THE KING/ (SOLICITOUSLY) MADAM: ARE YOU
LION II	(146)	/LAVINIA/ YES, HANDSOME CAPTAIN: YOU MAY. (HE	KISSES	HER HAND). /THE EMPEROR/ AND NOW, MY FRIENDS, THOUGH
ANNA	(298)	TO ME OF THE ONLY POWER I RECOGNIZE ON EARTH (HE	KISSES	HER HAND). /THE GRAND DUCHESS/ (INDULGENTLY)
GETT	(345)	I'M NOT REPUDIATING THAT HONOR. ALLOW ME (HE	KISSES	HER HAND). /MRS GEORGE/ THANK YOU FOR THAT. IT WAS
GETT	(334)	YOU HAVE THAWED THE LONG-FROZEN SPRINGS (HE	KISSES	HER HAND), FORGIVE ME; AND THANK YOU: BLESS YOU-- (
JITT I	SD(26)	BUT SHE MAKES THE SIGN OF THE CROSS OVER HIM;	KISSES	HER HAND; CROSSES HERSELF; AND HURRIES OUT, CLOSING
CAPT III	(299)	SOMEHOW ON THE SECRET OF COMMAND AT LAST (HE	KISSES	HER HANDS): THANKS FOR THAT, AND FOR A MAN'S POWER
NEVR II	(260)	/VALENTINE/ GOODBYE. FORGIVE ME. (HE RAPIDLY	KISSES	HER HANDS, AND RUNS AWAY TO THE STEPS, WHERE HE MEETS
JITT II	SD(31)	I HOPE TO FIND YOU QUITE WELL THEN, DEAR LADY. HE	KISSES	HER HAND, AND GOES OUT. WHEN HE HAS GONE, LENKHEIM
ARMS III	(70)	LADY: THE BEST WISHES OF A GOOD REPUBLICAN! (HE	KISSES	HER HAND, TO RAINA'S GREAT DISGUST, AND RETURNS TO
JITT I	(24)	AND THIS (HE KISSES HER EYES), AND THIS (HE	KISSES	HER LIPS). WHAT A FOOL I WAS WITH MY IRON
NEVR III	SD(276)	IS TRUE. GLORIA, BEHIND THE CHAIR, STOOPS AND	KISSES	HER MOTHER'S HAIR, A DEMONSTRATION WHICH DISCONCERTS
ARMS II	(33)	MY HERO! MY KING! /SERGIUS/ MY QUEEN! (HE	KISSES	HER ON THE FOREHEAD). /RAINA/ HOW I HAVE ENVIED YOU,
CLEO V	(202)	DO NOT THINK WE SHALL MEET AGAIN. FAREWELL. (HE	KISSES	HER ON THE FOREHEAD. SHE IS MUCH AFFECTED AND BEGINS
BARB II	(290)	NOT AT ALL. (HE IS SUDDENLY SOFTENED, AND	KISSES	HER OVER THE DRUM, EVIDENTLY NOT FOR THE FIRST TIME,
CLEO IV	SD(185)	EXPRESSION. THEN SHE FLINGS HER ARMS ROUND HER;	KISSES	HER REPEATEDLY AND SAVAGELY; AND TEARS OFF HER JEWELS
HART I	(76)	YOU TO KISS ME. (HE SEIZES HER IN HIS ARMS, AND	KISSES	HER STRENUOUSLY). OH! THAT WAS A LITTLE MORE THAN
NEVR II	(259)	OUR MOMENT OF COURAGE! (HE DRAWS HER TO HIM;	KISSES	HER WITH IMPETUOUS STRENGTH; AND LAUGHS BOYISHLY).
HART I	(69)	HESIONE. (INSTEAD OF TAKING HER HAND HE	KISSES	HER. AT THE SAME MOMENT THE CAPTAIN APPEARS IN THE
ARMS II	(30)	(PATTING HER CHEEK) MY LITTLE PET GIRL. (HE	KISSES	HER. SHE GOES TO THE CHAIR LEFT BY NICOLA FOR
2TRU III	(86)	IN A VERY HEARTY EMBRACE) NOT A MAN, EH? (HE	KISSES	HER) HOW DOES THAT FEEL, JUDY? /SWEETIE/ (
PHIL II	(131)	OFFERING HER CHEEK) FOOLISH BOY! (HE	KISSES	HER). NOW COME ALONG. (THEY GO OUT TOGETHER).
GETT	(334)	(HE SUDDENLY SNATCHES HER INTO HIS ARMS AND	KISSES	HER). OH! YOU DARE DO THAT AGAIN, YOU YOUNG
KING II	(223)	HUSBAND; AND I COUNT IT A GREAT PRIVILEGE. (HE	KISSES	HER). /CATHERINE/ YES YES; BUT WHY CHOOSE YOU MY
BARB II	(277)	AND SAVED MY SOUL, HAVNT YOU? (JENNY, TOUCHED,	KISSES	HER). SIT DOWN AND REST A BIT: YOU MUST BE READY TO
GENV I	(41)	A SCOOP FOR ME, HONEY! YOU ARE A PEACH. (HE	KISSES	HER). SOMEONE KNOCKS AT THE DOOR. /SHE/ SHSH!
O'FL	(220)	OF THE BRASS OUT OF MY MOUTH. (HE SEIZES HER AND	KISSES	HER). TERESA, WITHOUT LOSING HER IRISH DIGNITY, TAKES
BARB II	(285)	I DONT, MAJOR, BLESS HIS POOR HEART! (BARBARA	KISSES	HER; AND SHE RUNS AWAY MERRILY INTO THE SHELTER. BILL
PYGM III	(258)	NOW. THE THING'S DONE. GOODBYE, MOTHER. (HE	KISSES	HER, AND FOLLOWS PICKERING). /PICKERING/ (TURNING
PYGM V	(268)	GOOD MORNING. (HE CHECKS HIS IMPATIENCE AND	KISSES	HER, WHILST THE PARLOR-MAID GOES OUT). WHAT IS IT?
MTH5	(225)	NEWLY BORN/ (FLINGS HER ARMS ROUND HIS NECK AND	KISSES	HIM ENTHUSIASTICALLY). /MARTELLUS/ (RISES; CARRIES
MTH5	(234)	TRUE! HOW GREAT OF YOU, DARLING STREPHON! (SHE	KISSES	HIM IMPULSIVELY). /STREPHON/ (PASSIONATELY) LET ME
SUPR III	(78)	MON FRERE! (HE EMBRACES HIM RAPTUROUSLY AND	KISSES	HIM ON BOTH CHEEKS). /STRAKER/ (DISGUSTED) ERE, GIT
CAND II	(121)	YOU UNDERSTAND NOTHING. (SHE LAUGHS, AND	KISSES	HIM TO CONSOLE HIM. HE RECOILS AS IF STABBED, AND
SUPR II	SD(66)	/VIOLET/ ARE THEY LOOKING? /HECTOR/ NO. SHE	KISSES	HIM. /VIOLET/ HAVE YOU BEEN TELLING LIES FOR MY
GETT	(276)	I MUST KISS YOU; BUT DONT ANY OF YOU TELL. (SHE	KISSES	HIM. THEY CAN HARDLY BELIEVE THEIR EYES). HAVE YOU
DOCT III	(132)	HIM AND DRAG HIM DOWN FROM THE CLOUDS. (SHE	KISSES	HIM). AND NOW, DEAR, WONT YOU FINISH THOSE DRAWINGS
2TRU III	(106)	I MEANT IT: I AM GREATLY OBLIGED TO YOU. (SHE	KISSES	HIM). BUT NOW WHAT AM I TO DO? HOW AM I TO BEHAVE IN
MIS.	(126)	KNOW ABOUT IT, MY LAD. HOW DO, PATSY! (HYPATIA	KISSES	HIM). HOW IS MY CHICKABIDDY? (HE KISSES MRS
ROCK I	(208)	/LADY CHAVENDER/ THANK YOU, DARLING. (SHE	KISSES	HIM). MAY I TELL FLAVIA SHE IS FORGIVEN? /SIR
ARMS III	(67)	A JOKE, LITTLE ONE. COME: GIVE ME A KISS. (SHE	KISSES	HIM). NOW GIVE ME THE COAT. /RAINA/ NO: I AM GOING TO
NEVR IV	(303)	TO CRAMPTON) OH, YOURE JUST IN TIME. (SHE	KISSES	HIM). NOW (LEADING HIM FORWARD) BLESS THEM. /GLORIA/
NEVR IV	(302)	IF-- (HER GRIP OF HIS ARMS TIGHTENS; AND SHE	KISSES	HIM). OH LORD! (BREATHLESS) OH, I-- (HE GASPS) I
BARB III	(349)	ME MY PLACE AND MY WORK. GLORY HALLELUJAH! (SHE	KISSES	HIM). /CUSINS/ MY DEAREST: CONSIDER MY DELICATE
HART II	(114)	YOU ARE RIGHT. /ELLIE/ GOODNIGHT, DEAREST. (SHE	KISSES	HIM). /MAZZINI/ GOODNIGHT, LOVE. (HE MAKES FOR THE
GETT	(301)	WHIMPERING) OH REJJY (SHE RUNS TO HIM AND	KISSES	HIM). /REGINALD/ (WRATHFULLY) BE OFF. (SHE RETURNS
DEVL II	SD(40)	WITH A SUDDEN EFFORT, THROWS HER ARMS ROUND HIM;	KISSES	HIM; AND SWOONS AWAY, DROPPING FROM HIS ARMS TO THE
MRS II	SD(199)	UPTURNED FACE FOR A MOMENT, TEMPTED. AT LAST SHE	KISSES	HIM, AND IMMEDIATELY TURNS AWAY, OUT OF PATIENCE WITH
JITT I	(14)	IT HERE, AND HERE, AND STRAIGHT DOWN HERE. (SHE	KISSES	HIS BROW). NO: THEY ARE NOT GONE YET. /BRUNO/ IT IS
ROCK I	(208)	HER. /LADY CHAVENDER/ (SMILING) DEAREST. (SHE	KISSES	HIS FINGERS AND GOES OUT, GIVING HIM A PARTING SMILE
CAND III	(146)	DIVINES HER INTENTION AND FALLS ON HIS KNEES, SHE	KISSES	HIS FOREHEAD. THEN HE FLIES OUT INTO THE NIGHT. SHE
DOCT III	(155)	HIM TO ME. /RIDGEON/ AT ALL HAZARDS. (SHE	KISSES	HIS HAND. HE RISES HASTILY). NO: YOU HAVE NOT HEARD
DEST	(171)	HIM) IS WHY WE ALL BEGIN TO WORSHIP YOU. (SHE	KISSES	HIS HANDS). /NAPOLEON/ (EMBARRASSED) TUT! TUT!
JOAN 4	(97)	(HE EXTENDS HIS HAND TO THE CHAPLAIN, WHO	KISSES	HIS RING.) /WARWICK/ DO ME THE HONOR TO BE SEATED. (
MIS. PREFACE	(18)	CRY OF THE KIND MOTHER AFTER HER LITTLE ROSARY OF	KISSES	IS " RUN AWAY, DARLING." IT IS NICER THAN " HOLD YOUR
ARMS I	(16)	(HE HANDS HER THE PICTURE. SHE DELIBERATELY	KISSES	IT AND LOOKS HIM STRAIGHT IN THE FACE BEFORE
GLIM	(172)	SEE. (HE TAKES HER HAND IN HIS. SHE KNEELS AND	KISSES	IT FERVENTLY) OH, IT'S TRUE. YOU ARE A SAINT. HEAVEN
GETT	(345)	BEHIND HER, HE PICKS UP HER HAND FROM HER LAP AND	KISSES	IT OVER HER SHOULDER). /MRS GEORGE/ (WAKING) WHAT
CLEO V	(198)	BUT A TRIFLE SHAMEFACED, TAKES HIS HAND AND	KISSES	IT SHEEPISHLY). /BELZANOR/ (TO THE PERSIAN) THIS
DEVL III	(50)	MY WIFE. MY ADORED ONE. (HE TAKES HER HAND AND	KISSES	IT WITH A PERVERSE, RAFFISH GALLANTRY). HOW LONG DO
HART II	(115)	SHOTOVER/ WELL, ONE TURNS THE CHEEK: THE OTHER	KISSES	IT. ONE PROVIDES THE CASH: THE OTHER SPENDS IT.
ARMS II	SD(30)	HER HAND: HE DROPS CHIVALROUSLY ON ONE KNEE AND	KISSES	IT. /PETKOFF/ (ASIDE TO CATHERINE, BEAMING WITH
LIED	(189)	AURORA. (HE TAKES HER HAND FROM HIS SHOULDER AND	KISSES	IT. SHE SITS DOWN ON THE STOOL. HE REMAINS NEAR THE
DEVL I	(27)	ALSO CLENCHED, HANGS DOWN. ESSIE SEIZES IT AND	KISSES	IT, HER TEARS FALLING ON IT. HE STARTS AND LOOKS AT
ARMS II	(35)	/LOUKA/ (AVOIDING HIM) NO: I DONT WANT YOUR	KISSES	. GENTLEFOLK ARE ALL ALIKE: YOU MAKING LOVE TO ME
SIM II	(74)	IDDY! I'LL GO AND SOOTHE HIM WITH A THOUSAND	KISSES	. (SHE RUNS AFTER HIM). /HYERING/ (TO SIR CHARLES)

PHIL I (83)	A NICE KISS, DEAREST. I WANT ONE OF OUR OLD REAL	KISSES	. /CHARTERIS/ (FURIOUS) OH, GO TO THE DEUCE. (HE
CLEO IV (173)	ROMAN, THAT SHE MAY BUY IT BACK FROM HIM WITH HER	KISSES	. /FTATATEETA/ FOOL! DID SHE NOT TELL YOU THAT SHE
CURE (237)	QUIVERING FRAME AND SMOTHER IT WITH PASSIONATE	KISSES	. /REGINALD/ (TRANSPORTED) LET IT BE ME, LET IT BE
SUPR I SD(17)	HER ENTRY AND HER RECEPTION BY RAMSDEN, WHOM SHE	KISSES	. THE LATE MR WHITEFIELD WOULD BE GRATIFIED ALMOST TO
FANY III SD(324)	TO MARGARET'S HANDSHAKE WITH ENTHUSIASM,	KISSES	JUGGINS ON BOTH CHEEKS, AND SINKS INTO HIS CHAIR,
ROCK II (281)	BE PERFECTLY HAPPY. GOOD OLD MOTHER-IN-LAW. (HE	KISSES	LADY CHAVENDER, WHO IS TOO ASTOUNDED TO RESIST OR
JITT III (80)	DOCTOR (SHE KISSES THE DOCTOR)! PROFESSOR (SHE	KISSES	LENKHEIM)! DIDNT I SAY SHE WAS OUR GOOD ANGEL?
MIS. (126)	HYPATIA KISSES HIM). HOW IS MY CHICKABIDDY? (HE	KISSES	MRS TARLETON'S HAND AND POSES EXPANSIVELY IN THE
HART I (70)	YOU THAT-- /CAPTAIN SHOTOVER/ STUFF! EVERYONE	KISSES	MY DAUGHTER. KISS HER AS MUCH AS YOU LIKE (HE MAKES
SIM I (41)	IMAGE; BUT HIS FEET HAVE BEEN WORN AWAY BY THE	KISSES	OF CHRISTIAN PILGRIMS. YOU MAKE ME FEEL AS I HAVE
MILL IV (203)	BOISTEROUSLY) HA HA! ONE FOR YOU, EPPY. (HE	KISSES	PATRICIA). /SAGAMORE/ (SMILING) I AM AFRAID THE
SIM II (73)	A NOISE LIKE A VACUUM CLEANER. /MAYA/ (WAFTING	KISSES	) GOODBYE, SILLY OLD EXCELSIOR. THE NOISE STOPS.
CAND I (92)	IN MORELL'S ARMS, OFFERS HIM HER CHEEK, WHICH HE	KISSES	). JAMES AND ME IS COME TO A NUNNERSTANNIN. A
CATH 4 (196)	ROUND PATIOMKIN'S NECK AND COVERS HIS FACE WITH	KISSES	). /THE SERGEANT/ (MOVED TO TEARS) SAINTED NICHOLAS!
ARMS III (69)	YOU. (SHE TIMIDLY GIVES HIM HER HAND, WHICH HE	KISSES	). THAT TOUCH MAKES ME YOUR AFFIANCED WIFE. /SERGIUS/
JITT III (80)	THAT! EDITH (SHE KISSES EDITH)! DOCTOR (SHE	KISSES	THE DOCTOR)! PROFESSOR (SHE KISSES LENKHEIM)!
LIED SD(187)	KISSING IT; KISSES THE GLOVES ONE AFTER ANOTHER;	KISSES	THE FAN; GASPS A LONG SHUDDERING SIGH OF ECSTASY;
LIED SD(187)	HIS NOSE INTO ITS SOFTNESS AND KISSING IT;	KISSES	THE GLOVES ONE AFTER ANOTHER; KISSES THE FAN; GASPS A
NEVR II (248)	BE ENOUGH FOR ME. LOOK AT HER BOOK! SEE! (HE	KISSES	THE HANDKERCHIEF). IF YOU OFFERED ME ALL YOUR MONEY
JOAN 2,SD(83)	PASSES JOAN, SHE FALLS ON HER KNEES, AND	KISSES	THE HEM OF HIS ROBE FERVENTLY. HE SHAKES HIS HEAD IN
WIDO II (34)	SOB BREAKS FROM HIM; AND HE CATCHES HER HANDS AND	KISSES	THEM PASSIONATELY. THEN, LOOKING INTO HER EYES WITH
JITT I (22)	ME. /JITTA/ SO BE IT. (HE SNATCHES HER HANDS AND	KISSES	THEM). I PROMISE YOU THAT IF I SURVIVE THE DAY THAT
BARB III (325)	YOU SOMETIMES. (SHE TAKES HER FATHER'S HANDS AND	KISSES	THEM). YOU HAVE GIVEN ME BACK MY HAPPINESS: I FEEL IT
WIDO III (66)	TO SEE YOU. (SHE GIVES HIM HER HAND, WHICH HE	KISSES	WITH GALLANTRY). /LICKCHEESE/ (ON TRENCH'S LEFT, IN
GETT (335)	TELL HIM IF YOU DARE. IF I CHOOSE TO TAKE TEN	KISSES	, HOW WILL YOU PREVENT ME? /MRS GEORGE/ YOU COME
GETT (335)	HIM TO THAT, YOU WOULD SUFFER A THOUSAND STOLEN	KISSES	, WOULDNT YOU? /MRS GEORGE/ (IN UTTER

KISSING

CLEO V (197)	BY NAME, RUFIO. (THEY SHOUT AGAIN). /RUFIO/ (	KISSING	CAESAR'S HAND) AY: I AM CAESAR'S SHIELD; BUT OF WHAT
CATH 4 (196)	/EDSTASTON/ (PLUCKING UP SOME GENIALITY, AND	KISSING	CLAIRE CEREMONIOUSLY ON THE BROW) I HAVE NO
HART I (52)	NO ONE, AND BEING NEGLECTED AND ABANDONED. (	KISSING	HER AGAIN). MY POOR LOVE! (SHE DEPOSITS ELLIE ON
ARMS II (30)	BEHIND HER FATHER'S CHAIR. /RAINA/ (STOOPING AND	KISSING	HER FATHER) DEAR FATHER! WELCOME HOME! /PETKOFF/ (
CLEO II (135)	MARK ANTONY. (SHE RUNS OUT THROUGH THE LOGGIA,	KISSING	HER HAND TO MARK ANTONY ACROSS THE SEA). /CAESAR/ (
LIED (188)	PUTS DOWN THE MIRROR AS SHE ENTERS. /HE/ (	KISSING	HER HAND) AT LAST! /SHE/ HENRY: SOMETHING DREADFUL
CATH 4 (198)	DEVON, WILL ALWAYS FIND ME. (TO VARINKA,	KISSING	HER HAND) GOODBYE, MADEMOISELLE: GOODBYE, LITTLE
LADY (250)	THE PALACE GATES ARE BETWEEN US. /SHAKESPEAR/ (	KISSING	HER HAND) MY BODY GOES THROUGH THE GATE INTO THE
6CAL (102)	KNEEL GRATEFULLY TO THE QUEEN. /EUSTACHE/ (	KISSING	HER HAND) MADAM: OUR RANSOM SHALL BUY YOU A
GENV IV (88)	AND I'M NOT EXACTLY A NOBODY. /THE BETROTHED/ (	KISSING	HER HAND) MY OWNEST AND BESTEST, YOU ARE A DAME OF
PHIL III (138)	AND REJOICE DISINTERESTEDLY IN THE HAPPINESS OF (	KISSING	HER HAND) MY DEAR JULIA, (KISSING THE OTHER) MY
CLEO IV (182)	WELL, FOR ONCE I WILL SACRIFICE MY COMFORT-- (	KISSING	HER HAND) THERE! (HE TAKES A DRAUGHT OF WINE). NOW
ANNA (293)	HAVE TO RECEIVE HER WITHOUT EVEN RISING, WITHOUT	KISSING	HER HAND, TO KEEP UP APPEARANCES BEFORE THE ESCORT.
CATH 4 (196)	BUT YOU DID NOT THINK SO. FAREWELL. /EDSTASTON/ (	KISSING	HER HAND, WHICH, INSTEAD OF RELEASING, HE HOLDS
CAND II (126)	/MORELL/ (TAKING HER TENDERLY IN HIS ARMS AND	KISSING	HER ON THE FOREHEAD) AH, I THOUGHT IT WAS I WHO
NEVR III (264)	HAS TURNED TO GLORIA TO THE EXTENT OF-- /DOLLY/--	KISSING	HER-- /PHILIP/-- ON THE TERRACE-- /DOLLY/ (
HART I (52)	/MRS HUSHABYE/ ELLIE, MY DARLING, MY PETTIKINS (	KISSING	HER): HOW LONG HAVE YOU BEEN HERE? IVE BEEN AT HOME
GETT (276)	AMONG THE PHILISTINES. /LEO/ (TO LESBIA,	KISSING	HER) GOOD MORNING, (COMING TO MRS BRIDGENORTH) HOW
MRS II (219)	MOTHER FOR IT, WONT YOU? /VIVIE/ I WILL, DEAR. (	KISSING	HER) GOODNIGHT. /MRS WARREN/ (WITH UNCTION)
PYGM III (245)	/MRS HIGGINS/ GO HOME AT ONCE. /HIGGINS/ (	KISSING	HER) I KNOW, MOTHER. I CAME ON PURPOSE. /MRS
BARB II (307)	MONEY? /BARBARA/ (IMPULSIVELY GOING TO HER AND	KISSING	HER) NO, NO: GOD HELP YOU, DEAR, YOU MUST: YOU ARE
2TRU I (49)	STILL LEAVES SOMETHING TO BE DESIRED; BUT (	KISSING	HER) YOUR BREATH IS SWEET: YOU BREATHE THE AIR OF
HART I (53)	(SHE PUSHES HER BACK INTO THE CHAIR INSTEAD OF	KISSING	HER, AND POSTS HERSELF BEHIND IT). YOU DO LOOK A
JOAN 3 (93)	INTO TEARS AND FLINGING HER ARMS ROUND DUNOIS,	KISSING	HIM ON BOTH CHEEKS) DUNOIS, DEAR COMRADE IN ARMS,
BUOY IV (49)	(HE GOES). /SHE/ (RUSHING TO OLD BILL AND	KISSING	HIM) DADDYEST! /OLD BILL/ (RETURNING HER EMBRACE)
BUOY IV (53)	(THROWING HER ARMS ROUND OLD BILL'S NECK AND	KISSING	HIM) DADDY! DADDY! DADDY! THE NATIVE COMES IN AND
MTH2 (41)	/THE SIMPLE-LIFER/ (SWOOPING ON CONRAD AND	KISSING	HIM) HALLO, NUNK. YOURE BEFORE YOUR TIME. /CONRAD/
PHIL III (143)	LOVE. /JULIA/ (LOOKING UP AT HIM TEARFULLY, AND	KISSING	HIS HAND) DONT MIND THEM. YOU DIDNT MEAN IT, DADDY.
FANY III (327)	FRANCE IT WOULD BE IMPOSSIBLE. BUT HERE-- AH! (	KISSING	HIS HAND) LA BELLE ANGLETERRE!
DEST (171)	THE FIRST SUBJECT TO SWEAR ALLEGIANCE. (AGAIN	KISSING	HIS HAND) MY EMPEROR! /NAPOLEON/ (OVERCOME,
DEST (190)	AND TRULY WITHOUT SHAMMING, I DO YOU HOMAGE (	KISSING	HIS HAND). /NAPOLEON/ (QUICKLY WITHDRAWING IT)
GETT SD(285)	TO HIS WIFE AND SITS DOWN, TAKING HER HAND AND	KISSING	IT BY WAY OF BEGINNING A CONVERSATION WITH HER. /THE
ARMS I (20)	TAKE MY HAND. (SHE OFFERS IT AGAIN). /THE MAN/ (	KISSING	IT WITH HIS HANDS BEHIND HIS BACK) THANKS, GRACIOUS
JITT III (80)	(HASTILY) TCHUT! (TAKING JITTA'S HAND, AND	KISSING	IT) I OWE YOU MY LIFE'S HAPPINESS, MRS LENKHEIM.
CATH 2 (180)	TO HIM TO BE KISSED) COURTIER! /EDSTASTON/ (	KISSING	IT) NOT AT ALL. YOUR MAJESTY IS VERY GOOD. I HAVE
LIED SD(187)	HANDS, NESTLING HIS NOSE INTO ITS SOFTNESS AND	KISSING	IT; KISSES THE GLOVES ONE AFTER ANOTHER; KISSES THE
HART II (98)	YOU CAN HELP ME OVER IT BY A LITTLE COAXING AND	KISSING	, WHEN I WANT ALL THE STRENGTH I CAN GET TO LEAN ON:
JITT III (74)	POLITENESS). /EDITH/ (TO LENKHEIM, AFTER	KISSING	JITTA RATHER DEFIANTLY) MRS LENKHEIM DID NOT SAY A
HART II (99)	BUT I WARN YOU THAT WHEN I AM NEITHER COAXING AND	KISSING	NOR LAUGHING, I AM JUST WONDERING HOW MUCH LONGER I
HART I (50)	(DISENGAGING HIMSELF) YOU SHOULD GROW OUT OF	KISSING	STRANGE MEN: THEY MAY BE STRIVING TO ATTAIN THE
MTH4 I (156)	REALLY. THAT SCENE OF THE IRISH LANDING HERE AND	KISSING	THE GROUND MIGHT HAVE HAPPENED TO A HUNDRED PEOPLE.
PHIL III (138)	HAPPINESS OF (KISSING HER HAND) MY DEAR JULIA, (	KISSING	THE OTHER) MY BEAUTIFUL JULIA. (SHE TEARS HER HANDS
ARMS II (29)	(SHE HOLDS OUT BOTH HER HANDS). /SERGIUS/ (	KISSING	THEM WITH SCRUPULOUS GALLANTRY) MY DEAR MOTHER, IF I
2TRU III (87)	SILENT; AND LET MEN RISE TO SOMETHING NOBLER THAN	KISSING	THEM. THE SERGEANT, INTERESTED AND OVERAWED, SITS
GENV II (53)	/THE SECRETARY/ DISAPPOINTED AT HIS NOT	KISSING	YOU? /BEGONIA/ OH NO: THERE WERE PLENTY OF KISSES
MIS. (119)	/LORD SUMMERHAYS/ AND ALL THE WOMEN HAVE BEEN	KISSING	YOU AND PITYING YOU EVER SINCE TO STOP YOUR CRYING.
HART I (70)	APPEARS IN THE DOORWAY). YOU WILL EXCUSE MY	KISSING	YOUR DAUGHTER, CAPTAIN, WHEN I TELL YOU THAT--
MRS PREFACE(160)	AND DECLARING, WITH A SHIVER, THAT A SOUND OF	KISSING	, WHICH HE SUPPOSES TO PROCEED FROM WITHIN, MAKES

KISSUMS

MRS II (209)	HIM TO THE GARDEN GATE. /FRANK/ (TO VIVIE)	KISSUMS	? /VIVIE/ (FIERCELY) NO. I HATE YOU. (SHE TAKES A
LION PROLOG (109)	ANDY WANDY. (THE LION LICKS HIS FACE). YES,	KISSUMS	ANDY WANDY. (THE LION, WAGGING HIS TAIL VIOLENTLY,

KIT

PRES (137)	AFTER LUNCH. PARADE THEM FOR THAT PURPOSE! FULL	KIT	. DONT GRIN AT ME, SIR. RIGHT ABOUT FACE. MARCH. THE
SUPR II (64)	THE ARRANGEMENTS. I MUST SEE TO MY TRAVELLING	KIT	. MRS WHITEFIELD LOOKS BEWILDERED; BUT ANN DRAWS HER
HART II (109)	/LADY UTTERWORD/ NONSENSE: YOU HAVE YOUR BURGLING	KIT	. /THE BURGLAR/ WHATS A JEMMY AND A CENTREBIT AND AN
SUPR II (70)	MY ROOMS FOR MY KIT; THEN TO YOUR ROOMS FOR YOUR	KIT	; THEN BREAK THE RECORD FROM LONDON TO DOVER OR
SUPR II (70)	TO THE BANK FOR MONEY; THEN TO MY ROOMS FOR MY	KIT	; THEN TO YOUR ROOMS FOR YOUR KIT; THEN BREAK THE RECORD

KITCHEN

PYGM II (223)	OFF ANY OTHER WAY. IS THERE A GOOD FIRE IN THE	KITCHEN	? /MRS PEARCE/ (PROTESTING) YES; BUT-- /HIGGINS/ (
DEVL I SD(5)	THE DOOR AND OPENS IT, LETTING INTO THE STUFFY	KITCHEN	A LITTLE OF THE FRESHNESS AND A GREAT DEAL OF THE
O'FL (220)	YOU HAVE A SUP OF GOOD BLACK TEA FOR ME IN THE	KITCHEN	AFTERWARDS, ACUSHLA. THAT WASHY DRAWING ROOM TEA
PYGM II (228)	YOURE NAUGHTY AND IDLE YOU WILL SLEEP IN THE BACK	KITCHEN	AMONG THE BLACK BEETLES, AND BE WALLOPED BY MRS
GETT (324)	WHAT! THAT! (SHE MAKES A HALF TOUR OF THE	KITCHEN	AND ENDS RIGHT IN FRONT OF HIM). YOUNG MAN: DO YOU
DEVL I SD(3)	DUDGEON, OF NEW HAMPSHIRE, IS SITTING UP IN THE	KITCHEN	AND GENERAL DWELLING ROOM OF HER FARM HOUSE ON THE
MRS II (203)	ON TOO! /VIVIE/ (GOING TO THE DOOR OF THE	KITCHEN	AND OPENING IT, IGNORING HER MOTHER) NOW, ABOUT
SUPR PREFACE(R21)	WITH CONDESCENSION, EVEN WITH CHIVALRY, AS IF THE	KITCHEN	AND THE NURSERY WERE LESS IMPORTANT THAN THE OFFICE
MILL PREFACE(136)	ANY BETTER EXCUSE FOR KEEPING OTHER PEOPLE IN THE	KITCHEN	AND THEMSELVES IN THE DRAWING ROOM. I SAY CHEERFULLY
CAND I SD(78)	ROOM, USED FOR ALL MEALS, IN FRONT, AND THE	KITCHEN	AT THE BACK. UPSTAIRS, ON THE LEVEL OF THE HALL
MRS I SD(181)	AND WITHIN REACH OF HER HAND, IS A COMMON	KITCHEN	CHAIR, WITH A PILE OF SERIOUS-LOOKING BOOKS AND A
KING I (181)	DARES TO MEASURE THE DAYS OF THE ALMIGHTY BY HIS	KITCHEN	CLOCK, YOU TAKE HIS WORD BEFORE THE WORD OF GOD!
HART I SD(43)	THAT IT IS A SHELVED PANTRY WITH BOTTLES AND	KITCHEN	CROCKERY, ON THE STARBOARD SIDE, BUT CLOSE TO THE
MRS II SD(207)	OUT OF THE COTTAGE. THE CLERGYMAN APPEARS AT THE	KITCHEN	DOOR. /REV. S./ (LOOKING ROUND) WHERE IS SIR
NEVR II SD(245)	ASSISTANT ALONG WITH HIM INTO THE HOTEL BY THE	KITCHEN	ENTRANCE, LEAVING THE LUNCHEON PARTY TO THEMSELVES.
NEVR II SD(240)	GOES TO THE SERVICE TABLE AND BECKONS TO THE	KITCHEN	ENTRANCE, WHENCE ISSUE A YOUNG WAITER WITH SOUP
DEVL I SD(4)	AT THE RISK OF NODDING THEMSELVES INTO THE	KITCHEN	FIRE. MRS DUDGEON SLEEPS WITH A SHAWL OVER HER HEAD,
DEVL II SD(28)	THE CHIEF DWELLING ROOM HAS THE SAME SORT OF	KITCHEN	FIREPLACE, WITH BOILER, TOASTER HANGING ON THE BARS,

GENV PREFACE(12)	AT THEIR WORK AS MOTHERS, NURSES, COOKS, AND	KITCHEN	GARDENERS. THERE ARE STILL PLACES IN THE WORLD WHERE
MTH1 II SD(20)	CLOSE AT HAND THE END OF A LOG HOUSE ABUTS ON A	KITCHEN	GARDEN. ADAM IS DIGGING IN THE MIDDLE OF THE GARDEN.
O'FL (226)	MINUTE AND TEAR ONE ANOTHER'S EYES OUT IN THE	KITCHEN	IF YOU LIKE. IN WITH YOU. THE TWO MEN SEIZE THE TWO
GETT SD(259)	A FINE MORNING IN THE SPRING OF 1908 THE NORMAN	KITCHEN	IN THE PALACE OF THE BISHOP OF CHELSEA LOOKS VERY
DOCT PREFACE(15)	STEAM HEATING, AND MACHINERY THAT TURNS THE	KITCHEN	INTO A LABORATORY AND ENGINE HOUSE COMBINED, MANAGE,
GETT SD(260)	STANDS AGAINST THE WALL. ACROSS THE MIDDLE OF THE	KITCHEN	IS A BIG TIMBER TABLE SURROUNDED BY ELEVEN STOUT
GETT SD(260)	KEEP IT GOING. IT HANGS ABOVE THE OAK CHEST. THE	KITCHEN	IS OCCUPIED AT PRESENT BY THE BISHOP'S LADY, MRS
GETT SD(259)	HE IS A MAN OF HUMBLE MIND; BUT BECAUSE THE	KITCHEN	IS ONE OF THE FINEST ROOMS IN THE HOUSE. THE BISHOP
MRS II SD(207)	DAMN YOU! BEFORE SHE CAN RETORT THE DOOR OF THE	KITCHEN	IS OPENED; AND THE VOICES OF THE OTHERS ARE HEARD
GETT SD(259)	AFFAIR FROM TUMBLING DOWN BY ITS OWN WEIGHT. THE	KITCHEN	IS THE BISHOP'S FAVORITE ROOM. THIS IS NOT AT ALL
GETT SD(275)	TOGETHER). IT IS TOO LATE: LEO IS ALREADY IN THE	KITCHEN	. COLLINS GOES OUT, MUTELY ABANDONING A SITUATION
SUPR HANDBOK(222)	TO HAVE FRIENDS IN THE KENNEL, BUT NOT IN THE	KITCHEN	, DOMESTIC SERVANTS, BY MAKING SPOILED CHILDREN OF
MRS II SD(198)	LEFT-HAND SIDE WALL IS THE DOOR LEADING TO THE	KITCHEN	. FARTHER BACK AGAINST THE SAME WALL IS A DRESSER
WIDO III SD(51)	GOES OUT BEAMING, FULL OF THE NEWS FOR THE	KITCHEN	. LICKCHEESE CLINCHES THE SITUATION BY A TRIUMPHANT
MRS II (204)	PARSON TAKES MRS WARREN; AND THEY PASS INTO THE	KITCHEN	. PRAED AND CROFTS FOLLOW. ALL EXCEPT PRAED CLEARLY
GETT SD(326)	RESOLUTION, GOES SWIFTLY TO THE MIDDLE OF THE	KITCHEN	. /HOTCHKISS/ CECIL. REJJY. (STARTLED BY HIS
KING I (162)	THE FISH HAWKER. HE'S PAUNCHING THE RABBIT IN THE	KITCHEN	. /SALLY/ YES, MAAM. (SHE GOES). /MRS BASHAM/ THREE
O'FL (212)	AT THE SAME TABLE AS YOU, SIR, INSTEAD OF IN THE	KITCHEN	. SHE'LL BE AFTER DRESSING IN THE HEIGHTH OF
HART II (112)	HIS YEARS). /GUINNESS/ I SUPPOSE YOU MEAN THE	KITCHEN	. THEY WONT HAVE HIM THERE. DO YOU EXPECT SERVANTS
PYGM II (236)	COME YOU CAN TAKE HER AWAY. YOU CAN WAIT IN THE	KITCHEN	. THIS WAY, PLEASE. DOOLITTLE, MUCH TROUBLED,
HART II (121)	GONE TO BED; BUT THE FATHER YOU GAVE ME IS IN THE	KITCHEN	. YOU KNEW QUITE WELL ALL ALONG. COME. (SHE DRAWS
CAPT II (249)	WELL: MARZO'S IN YOUR BED. LADY WANTS TO MAKE A	KITCHEN	OF THE SHEIKH'S AUDIENCE CHAMBER, AND TO PUT ME AND
MIS. PREFACE(87)	OF A SEPARATE HOME, OR A PRIVATE NURSERY OR	KITCHEN	OR MOTHER-IN-LAW, OR ANYTHING THAT CONSTITUTES THE
BARB III (348)	IT GO; ONLY SHE THOUGHT IT WAS THE HOUSES AND THE	KITCHEN	RANGES AND THE LINEN AND CHINA, WHEN IT WAS REALLY
BASH II,2, (113)	OF OUR FACTORIES, AND BY THE MILLION PATENT	KITCHEN	RANGES OF HAPPY ENGLISH HOMES. /CETEWAYO/ WHEN FIRST
GETT (296)	BRIDGENORTH/ (TRANSFIXED IN THE MIDDLE OF THE	KITCHEN	) AND CECIL! ! /LESBIA/ AND SINJON! /THE BISHOP/
CAND III (130)	GO TO BED. I'LL TELL HER. (SHE GOES OUT TO THE	KITCHEN	). /MORELL/ (LOOKING STERNLY DOWN AT MARCHBANKS)
MRS II (205)	WITH HIS VIVVUMS FOR THIS. (HE PASSES INTO THE	KITCHEN	). /MRS WARREN/ (WITHIN) HERE, VIVIE: COME ON YOU
HART I (46)	(QUITE UNCONCERNED, SHE GOES ON HER WAY TO THE	KITCHEN	). /THE CAPTAIN/ MADAM: WILL YOU FAVOR ME WITH YOUR
GETT (270)	AND WALKS ACROSS TO THE OTHER SIDE OF THE	KITCHEN	). /THE GENERAL/ (MOODILY) HA! THATS WHATS THE
MRS II (204)	ONLY TWO ARE WANTED. (SHE OPENS THE DOOR OF THE	KITCHEN	). WILL YOU TAKE MY MOTHER IN, MR GARDNER. (THE
ARMS II (27)	YOU TOUCH A BUTTON; SOMETHING TINKLES IN THE	KITCHEN	; AND THEN NICOLA COMES UP. /PETKOFF/ WHY NOT SHOUT
2TRU I (38)	JUST SHOVES A HANDFUL OF THIS INTO IT. COMMON	KITCHEN	SALT. NO MORE SCREAMING. UNDERSTAND? /THE PATIENT/
2TRU I (38)	BEDSIDE TABLE. IT CONTAINS ABOUT HALF A POUND OF	KITCHEN	SALT). DO YOU KNOW WHAT THAT IS AND WHAT IT'S FOR..
3PLA PREFACE(R31)	LIFE IN DESPAIR AND DISCARDING THE TRUMPERY MORAL	KITCHEN	SCALES IN WHICH THEY TRY TO WEIGH THE UNIVERSE,
NEVR I (222)	MY PATIENTS HAVNT ALL FORMED THEIR CHARACTERS ON	KITCHEN	SOAP. /CRAMPTON/ (SUDDENLY GRIPPING HIM BY THE ARM
DEVL I SD(4)	THE SMOKY MANTELSHELF FOR ROASTING. THE PLAIN	KITCHEN	TABLE IS OPPOSITE THE FIRE, AT HER ELBOW, WITH A
ARMS III SD(46)	OF KEEPING WITH ITS SURROUNDINGS. THIS IS A SMALL	KITCHEN	TABLE, MUCH THE WORSE FOR WEAR, FITTED AS A WRITING
DEVL II SD(28)	BOARDS, AND FASTENS WITH A LATCH. THE TABLE IS A	KITCHEN	TABLE, WITH A TREACLE COLORED COVER OF AMERICAN
GETT SD(259)	WINDOW IS THE LARGEST; AND IF WE LOOK INTO THE	KITCHEN	THROUGH IT WE SEE FACING US THE SOUTH WALL WITH
GETT (354)	QUESTION FOR ME FOR EVER. (HE PROWLS ACROSS THE	KITCHEN	TO THE GARDEN DOOR, DEEP IN THOUGHT). /SOAMES/
GETT SD(279)	LET HIM COME. LET THEM ALL COME. HE CROSSES THE	KITCHEN	TO THE OAK CHEST AND SITS SULKILY ON IT. MRS
NEVR II SD(241)	WITH HOT PLATES, BRINGS IN THE FISH FROM THE	KITCHEN	TO THE SERVICE TABLE, AND BEGINS SLICING IT.
GETT (304)	OUR BUSINESS IS ABOUT EDITH? (HE FUMES UP THE	KITCHEN	TO THE TOWER AND BACK TO HIS CHAIR). /MRS
GETT (296)	WITH AN EXCLAMATION OF DISGUST, CROSSES THE	KITCHEN	TOWARDS THE STUDY DOOR). BUT, MY DEAR REJJY, ARE YOU
GETT (288)	OF TRUMPERY. /REGINALD/ (LURCHING ACROSS THE	KITCHEN	TOWARDS THE HEARTH WITH HIS HANDS IN HIS POCKETS)
HART I (73)	WANT: THE SERVANTS KEEP IT STEWING ALL DAY. THE	KITCHEN	VERANDA IS THE BEST PLACE TO ASK. MAY I SHEW YOU? (
MILL II SD(166)	HARD AND UNCOMFORTABLE. THE CUTLERY IS CHEAP	KITCHEN	WARE, WITH RICKETY SILVER CRUETS AND SALT CELLARS TO
BARB II (291)	A MAN OF HIM: IT FINDS A WORM WRIGGLING IN A BACK	KITCHEN	, AND LO! A WOMAN! MEN AND WOMEN OF RANK TOO, SONS
DEVL II SD(28)	IN FACT, THE EVOLUTION OF THE MINISTER'S	KITCHEN	, DINING ROOM AND DRAWING ROOM INTO THREE SEPARATE
DEVL I (18)	FROM HIS NEIGHBORHOOD TO THE OTHER SIDE OF THE	KITCHEN	, HOLDING HER SKIRT INSTINCTIVELY AS IF TO SAVE IT
INCA (239)	IT HAS NOT BEEN WAITING. STRAIGHT FROM THE	KITCHEN	, MADAM, BELIEVE ME. /ERMYNTRUDE/ SEND THE MANAGER
NEVR II SD(225)	NEARER THE PARAPET THERE LURKS A WAY TO THE	KITCHEN	, MASKED BY A LITTLE TRELLIS PORCH. THE TABLE AT
CAND II (115)	SITTING DOWN) MARIA IS READY FOR YOU NOW IN THE	KITCHEN	, MRS MORELL. (CANDIDA RISES). THE ONIONS HAVE
GETT PREFACE(192)	AND THEIR WIVES WENT THROUGH THE ROUTINE OF THE	KITCHEN	, NURSERY, AND DRAWING-ROOM JUST AS THEY WENT
MRS II SD(208)	TO ORDER THE BUTTER. PRAED COMES IN FROM THE	KITCHEN	, PUTTING UP HIS HANDKERCHIEF, WHICH HE HAS BEEN
MIS. PREFACE(16)	BUILDING WITH THEM? THE HOME MAY BE A THIEVES'	KITCHEN	, THE MOTHER A PROCURESS, THE FATHER A VIOLENT
KING PREFACE(158)	BY THE FEMALE MAJORITY WHOSE WORLD IS THE	KITCHEN	, THE NURSERY, AND THE DRAWINGROOM IF SUCH A LUXURY
MTH4 I (157)	AND TELL THEM THAT THERE ARE BLACKBEETLES IN MY	KITCHEN	, WASHING SODA IN MY LAUNDRY, AND COAL IN MY CELLAR.
		KITCHENER	
PRES PREFACE(130)	MITCHENER, BY THE WAY, IS NOT THE LATE LORD	KITCHENER	, BUT AN EARLIER AND MORE HIGHLY CONNECTED
		KITED	
MILL I (159)	BEEN DISHONORED. /ALASTAIR/ NOT ONE OF THEM. WE	KITED	THEM ALL. BUT IT WAS A HEARTBREAKING JOB. /ADRIAN/ I
		KITES	
BARB III (313)	CHARITABLE INSTITUTIONS WOULD BE DOWN ON HIM LIKE	KITES	ON A BATTLE FIELD IF HE GAVE HIS NAME. /LADY
LADY PREFACE(219)	ERE THIS, I SHOULD HAVE FATTED ALL THE REGION	KITES	WITH THIS SLAVE'S OFFAL." REALLY ONE IS TEMPTED TO
		KITING	
MILL I (159)	TWO HUNDRED POUNDS. AND SO YOU GO SPENDING AND	KITING	FROM HUNDREDS TO THOUSANDS AND FROM RISKS OF EIGHTEEN
MILL I (159)	JOB. /ADRIAN/ I DONT UNDERSTAND. WHAT DOES	KITING	MEAN? /SAGAMORE/ IT IS QUITE SIMPLE. YOU PAY FOR
MILL I (159)	THE FIRST NIGHT: WE WERE SIGNING CHEQUES AND	KITING	THEM ALL THE TIME. OF COURSE IT WAS EASIER AFTER A
		KITTEN	
CLEO II (133)	WORK. /CAESAR/ OH! WHO TOLD YOU THAT, LITTLE	KITTEN	? EH? /CLEOPATRA/ MY FATHER WAS KING OF EGYPT; AND
AUGS (282)	AND THAT I WAS A HUN. HE LAPPED IT UP LIKE A	KITTEN	. . . . /AUGUSTUS/ YOU DONT MEAN TO SAY THAT -- /THE
CLEO IV (171)	THAT DEPENDED ON CLEOPATRA BEING A LITTLE NURSERY	KITTEN	. NOW THAT CLEOPATRA IS A QUEEN, THE PLAN IS UPSET.
CLEO I (111)	LITTLE GIRL; AND YOU ARE DESCENDED FROM THE BLACK	KITTEN	. YOU ARE BOTH A GIRL AND A CAT. /CLEOPATRA/ (
CLEO I (109)	WHAT! /CLEOPATRA/ THIS IS ONLY A DEAR LITTLE	KITTEN	OF A SPHINX. WHY, THE GREAT SPHINX IS SO BIG THAT IT
CLEO I (108)	GREAT-GRANDMOTHER'S GREAT-GRANDMOTHER WAS A BLACK	KITTEN	OF THE SACRED WHITE CAT; AND THE RIVER NILE MADE HER
CLEO PRO2 (102)	SHE IS DESCENDED FROM THE RIVER NILE AND A BLACK	KITTEN	OF THE SACRED WHITE CAT. WHAT THEN? /PERSIAN/ WHY,
CLEO II (134)	OLDER; SO THAT HE MIGHT NOT THINK ME A MERE	KITTEN	, AS YOU DO! BUT PERHAPS THAT IS BECAUSE YOU ARE
CLEO I (114)	WHILE FTATATEETA ESCAPES). /CAESAR/ YOU SCRATCH,	KITTEN	, DO YOU? /CLEOPATRA/ (BREAKING FROM HIM) I WILL
FANY I (278)	BUT HOLY JOE LIKES IT: FAIRLY LAPS IT UP LIKE A	KITTEN	, POOR OLD DEAR. WELL, BOBBY SAYS TO ME, " DARLING--"
		KITTENISHNESS	
GETT SD(275)	LEO'S RESTLESSNESS IS MUCH LESS LOVABLE THAN THE	KITTENISHNESS	WHICH COMES FROM A RICH AND FRESH VITALITY.
		KITTENS	
FANY PROLOG (268)	I SHOULD SAY DAMN CAMBRIDGE. AS IT IS, I BLAME MY	KITTENS	. AND NOW LET ME WARN YOU. IF YOURE GOING TO BE A
FANY PROLOG (268)	FABIAN SOCIETY, KITTENS. IMPERTINENT LITTLE	KITTENS	. BLAME THEM. SMACK THEM. I GUESS WHAT IS ON YOUR
FANY PROLOG (268)	" BLAME MY KITTENS! " OBSERVE, MISS O'DOWDA:	KITTENS	. I SAY AGAIN IN THE TEETH OF THE WHOLE CAMBRIDGE
FANY PROLOG (268)	THE TEETH OF THE WHOLE CAMBRIDGE FABIAN SOCIETY,	KITTENS	. IMPERTINENT LITTLE KITTENS. BLAME THEM. SMACK
METH PREFACE(R46)	COUNTRY HOUSE WHO HAS NOT TAKEN A LITTER OF	KITTENS	OR PUPPIES TO THE BUCKET, AND DROWNED ALL OF THEM
FANY PROLOG (268)	" BLAME MY CATS! " NO: I SUBSTITUTE " BLAME MY	KITTENS	! " OBSERVE, MISS O'DOWDA: KITTENS. I SAY AGAIN IN
		KITTY	
MRS IV (245)	IN VIVIE'S CHAIR TO SCRIBBLE A NOTE). MY DEAR	KITTY	: COME IN! COME IN. MRS WARREN COMES IN, LOOKING
MRS IV (245)	WONT SHE SEE ME, DONT YOU THINK? /PRAED/ MY DEAR	KITTY	: DONT DISTRESS YOURSELF. WHY SHOULD SHE NOT? /MRS
MRS I (190)	YOURE AFRAID I'LL BULLY HER. /PRAED/ MY DEAR	KITTY	: YOU THINK I'M OFFENDED. DONT IMAGINE THAT: PRAY
MRS II (207)	AS HE SEES NO SIGN OF SYMPATHY IN HER) LOOK HERE,	KITTY	: YOURE A SENSIBLE WOMAN: YOU NEEDNT PUT ON ANY MORAL
MRS I (191)	MIGHT HEAR US FROM THE WINDOW. LOOK HERE: DID	KITTY	EVER TELL YOU WHO THAT GIRL'S FATHER IS? /PRAED/
MRS II (201)	OF COURSE IT'S IMPOSSIBLE. DONT BE A FOOL,	KITTY	. /MRS WARREN/ (NETTLED) WHY NOT? ISNT MY DAUGHTER
MRS IV (246)	HANDS WITH HER). /PRAED/ (SADLY) GOODBYE,	KITTY	. /MRS WARREN/ (SNIVELLING)-- GOOBYE! PRAED GOES.
MRS II (208)	/MRS WARREN/ BYEBYE, PRADDY. /PRAED/ BYEBYE,	KITTY	. THEY SHAKE HANDS AFFECTIONATELY AND GO OUT TOGETHER.

MRS I (192) ARE PROBABLY ON MUCH MORE CONFIDENTIAL TERMS WITH KITTY THAN I AM. SURELY YOU CAN ASK HER THE QUESTION
MRS I (190) /PRAED/ ONLY THAT VIVIE IS A GROWN WOMAN. PRAY, KITTY , TREAT HER WITH EVERY RESPECT. /MRS WARREN/ (WITH

K.C.B
MIS. (113) AS YOU ARE OF YOUR FATHER'S TITLE AND HIS K.C.B ., AND ALL THE REST OF IT. MY FATHER BEGAN IN A LITTLE
MIS. (111) TO YOU. IF YOU THINK THAT BECAUSE YOUR FATHER'S A K.C.B ., AND YOU WANT TO MARRY MY SISTER, YOU CAN MAKE

K.C.M.G
ROCK II (253) NEED NOT WARN US, SIR BROADFOOT BASHAM, D.S.O., K.C.M.G ., O.B.E. IN THE CLASS WAR YOUR MYRMIDONS WILL BE

KLAXON
2TRU II SD(51) VISIBLE. AN ARMY HUT ON THE HITHER SIDE, WITH A KLAXON ELECTRIC HORN PROJECTING FROM A BOARD ON THE WALL.
2TRU II SD(78) AS A PRIVATE THAN AS A COLONEL, EH? THE KLAXON SOUNDS STRIDENTLY. THE COLONEL DRAWS HIS REVOLVER AND

KLEPTOMANIAC
FANY III (312) KEEP HIS MOUTH QUIET: HE TOLD ME YOUR AUNT WAS A KLEPTOMANIAC . /MRS KNOX/ IT WASNT TRUE, MR GILBEY. SHE USED

KLINGSOR
HART PREFACE(5) WERE BORN, HORRIBLY MISPLACED, INTO THE GARDEN OF KLINGSOR ; BUT SOMETIMES ONE CAME UPON HORSEBREAKERS AND

KLISSOURA
ARMS III (61) O'CLOCK I SHALL BE IN THE DRILLING-GROUND ON THE KLISSOURA ROAD, ALONE, ON HORSEBACK, WITH MY SABRE. DO YOU

KLOOTZ
LADY PREFACE(212) IMPERIALIST AN ANACHARSIS KLOOTZ, TO ANACHARSIS KLOOTZ A WASHINGTON, TO MRS PROUDIE A DON JUAN, TO ASPASIA A
LADY PREFACE(212) TO THE BISMARCKIAN IMPERIALIST AN ANACHARSIS KLOOTZ , TO ANACHARSIS KLOOTZ A WASHINGTON, TO MRS PROUDIE A

KNACK
BULL IV (152) ORATOR, MR BROADBENT. /BROADBENT/ OH, IT'S ONLY A KNACK . ONE PICKS IT UP ON THE PLATFORM. IT STOKES UP THEIR
CAND I (101) GAB, NOTHING MORE AND NOTHING LESS. WHAT HAS YOUR KNACK OF FINE TALKING TO DO WITH THE TRUTH, ANY MORE THAN
SUPR PREFACE(R10) PURSUITS OF A VESTRYMAN. NO DOUBT THAT LITERARY KNACK OF MINE WHICH HAPPENS TO AMUSE THE BRITISH PUBLIC

KNACKERS
BARB II (281) OUT OF A JOB BEFORE. GOOD WORKER. AND SENT TO THE KNACKERS LIKE AN OLD HORSE! /BARBARA/ NO MATTER: IF YOU DID

KNAGG
FANY I (282) AND I CANT GET IT AT PERRY AND JOHN'S. /DORA/ KNAGG AND PANTLE'S: ONE AND FOURPENCE. IT'S MACHINE

KNAOW
BULL III (142) IT. YOU DANNO WOT AWDSHIP IS OWVER EAH: ALL YOU KNAOW IS AH TO AHL ABAHT IT. YOU TIKE THE BISCUIT AT THET,
BARB II (278) SEE? BAT AW'LL LET ER KNAOW; AND AW'LL LET YOU KNAOW . AW'M GOWING TO GIVE HER A DOIN THATLL TEACH ER TO
BARB II (301) WE'LL TAKE NOTHING LESS. /BILL/ (BITTERLY) AW KNAOW . ME AN MAW FEW SHILLINS IS NOT GOOD ENAFF FOR YOU.
BARB II (310) HAS A TWINGE OF REMORSE). BUT THETS AW RAWT, YOU KNAOW . NATHINK PASNL. NAOW MELLICE. SAO LONG, JUDY. (HE
BARB II (289) FAIR OR IS IT NOT? YOURE A GENLMN: YOU OUGHTER KNAOW . /BARBARA/ TWO BLACK EYES WONT MAKE ONE WHITE ONE,
CAPT I (236) NAH, NAH, NAH! NAH LOOK EAH, KEPN, Y' KNAOW -- /BRASSBOUND/ (BETWEEN HIS TEETH) HOLD YOUR TONGUE.
CAPT I (222) NETRAL STITE BEIN GREEN, AN E EVIN BLECK AIR, Y' KNAOW -- /RANKIN/ (CUTTING HIM SHORT) I SEE. AND NOW I WILL
BARB II (278) A CARSE FOR ER OR YOU: SEE? BAT AW'LL LET ER KNAOW ; AND AW'LL LET YOU KNAOW, AW'M GOWING TO GIVE HER A
CAPT I (225) YOU OUGHTER BIN BAWN A CHRISTIAN, YOU OUGHT. YOU KNAOW TOO MACH. /RANKIN/ YOU HAVE BROAT ONNLY TROUBLE AND
BARB II (289) /BILL/ WELL, AW KEN. (TO BARBARA) EAH! DO YOU KNAOW WHERE AW'M GOWIN TO, AND WOT AW'M GOWIN TO DO?
BARB II (299) A BIT SNOWY. /BILL/ SAO IT IS SNAOWY. YOU WANT TO KNAOW WHERE THE SNAOW CAM FROM, DOWNT YOU? /BARBARA/ YES.
BARB II (278) KICK ER AHT. TELL ER BILL WALKER WANTS ER. SHE'LL KNAOW WOT THET MEANS; AND IF SHE KEEPS ME WITIN ITLL BE
BULL III (142) AT THET, YOU DO. OI'M A OWM RULER, OI EM. DO YOU KNAOW WOY? /MATTHEW/ (EQUALLY CONTEMPTUOUS) D'YE KNOW,
BARB II (277) TRUCULENTLY, DRIVING HER DOWN THE YARD. /BILL/ AW KNAOW YOU. YOURE THE ONE THAT TOOK AWY MAW GIRL. YOURE THE
CAPT I (219) INTER THE MAHNTNS OR SECH LAWK. WEOLL, AS YOU KNAOW , GAVNER, THET CAHNT BE DONE EAH WITHAHT A HESCORT.
CAPT II (244) ATHER LITTLE SUVVICE? MIKE YRSEOLF AT OWM, Y' KNAOW , LIDY. /LADY CICELY/ (CONSIDERATELY) DONT GO IF YOUD
BULL III (141) WOT PRAWCE MAW GRENFAWTHER, OI SHOULD LAWK TO KNAOW , THAT FITTED AP A FUST CLAWSS SHOP AND BUILT AP A

KNAOWED
CAPT I (227) AHRD, WOT JAGGINSES THEM JURYMEN WAS! YOU AN ME KNAOWED IT TOO, DIDNT WE? /SIR HOWARD/ I DARESAY WE DID. I
CAPT I (223) THET THERE STRITEFORARD MAN Y' MIDE MENTION ON KNAOWED WOT E WAS ATORKIN ABAHT: OO WOULD YOU SPOWSE WAS THE

KNAOWS
CAPT I (237) AHRD EZ ERD WITNESSES TO MAW KERRICKTER AFOAH. E KNAOWS AH MECH TO BLIEVE OF EM. /LADY CICELY/ CAPTAIN

KNAPSACK
DEST SD(151) SOLDIER CARRIES A FIELD MARSHAL'S BATON IN HIS KNAPSACK , BUT BECAUSE HE HOPES TO CARRY AT LEAST HALF A

KNAVE
LADY (241) MY LIFE! ARE YOU BY CHANCE MAKING LOVE TO ME, KNAVE ? /THE MAN/ NAY: TIS YOU WHO HAVE MADE THE LOVE: I
MIS. PREFACE(67) THE ENGLISHMAN OBEYS LIKE A SHEEP, EVADES LIKE A KNAVE , OR TRIES TO MURDER HIS OPPRESSOR. MERELY CRITICIZED

KNAVISH
MRS PREFACE(178) IS EQUALLY LIKELY THAT THEY MAY BE COLLECTED AND KNAVISH . AT ALL EVENTS, TO PROHIBIT THE PLAY IS TO PROTECT

KNEE
MTH5 (225) A DEAD STATUE. (HE TAKES THE NEWLY BORN ON HIS KNEE : SHE IS FLATTERED AND VOLUPTUOUSLY RESPONSIVE).
POSN (463) I OR ANY GROWN MAN HERE COULD BREAK AGAINST HIS KNEE ? I'M A ROTTENER FRAUD AND FAILURE THAN THE ELDER
ARMS II SD(30) PRESENTS HER HAND: HE DROPS CHIVALROUSLY ON ONE KNEE AND KISSES IT. /PETKOFF/ (ASIDE TO CATHERINE, BEAMING
BULL I (95) /BROADBENT/ (WHO HAS BEEN NURSING HIS KNEE AND REFLECTING, APPARENTLY RATHER AGREEABLY) YOU KNOW,
BULL III SD(120) HAVE PERHAPS WORN A LONG TAILED FRIEZE COAT AND KNEE BREECHES IN HIS TIME; BUT NOW HE IS DRESSED RESPECTABLY
CATH 1,SD(161) HIS HUGE HAIRY CHEST, NOR HIS HALF-BUTTONED KNEE BREECHES, NOR HIS LEGS. THESE ARE PARTLY CLAD IN SILK
BARB III (339) DOWN FROM TIME TO TIME TO THANK HEAVEN FOR IT: KNEE DRILL, I THINK YOU CALL IT. IT IS CHEAP WORK CONVERTING
MRS IV SD(235) UP IN HEAPS OF PAPERS AND BOOKS. THIS TABLE HAS KNEE HOLES AND CHAIRS RIGHT AND LEFT AND IS VERY UNTIDY. THE
ARMS III (69) (APPROVINGLY) YOU ARE RIGHT. (HE BENDS HIS KNEE IN HIS GRANDEST MANNER) FORGIVE ME. /LOUKA/ I FORGIVE
CATH 3 (184) AH, WOULD YOU, DAMN YOU! (HE DRIVES HIS KNEE INTO THE SERGEANT'S EPIGASTRIUM, AND STRUGGLES
ARMS III SD(51) BEFORE HER WITH HER HANDS CLASPED ROUND HER KNEE . BLUNTSCHLI, QUITE TOUCHED, GOES TO THE OTTOMAN WITH A
PYGM II (231) KNOWS NO BETTER: SHE LEARNT IT AT HER MOTHER'S KNEE . BUT SHE MUST NOT HEAR IT FROM YOUR LIPS. /HIGGINS/ (
ANNA (297) YOU HAVE BEEN DANDLED ON MY GRANDMOTHER'S KNEE . BY THAT GRACIOUS ACTION THE DOWAGER PANJANDRINA MADE
CYMB V (147) /BELARIUS/ I AM TOO BLUNT AND SAUCY: HERE'S MY KNEE . ERE I ARISE I WILL PREFER MY SONS. THEN SPARE NOT THE
BARB II (278) DOOR OF THE SHELTER. SHE FALLS ON HER HAND AND KNEE . RUMMY HELPS HER UP AGAIN). /PRICE/ (RISING, AND
ANNA (294) STRAMMFEST. MY GRANDMOTHER DANDLED YOU ON HER KNEE . /STRAMMFEST/ (BURSTING INTO TEARS) O GOD, YES.
CATH 2 (180) CAPTAIN: WE ARE PLEASED. (HE FALLS ON HIS KNEE . SHE TAKES HIS CHEEKS IN HER HANDS; TURNS UP HIS FACE;
CLEO III (148) PILUM AT APOLLODORUS, WHO DROPS EXPERTLY ON ONE KNEE . THE PILUM PASSES WHIZZING OVER HIS HEAD AND FALLS
NEVR IV (289) (GETTING UP AND SPEAKING ACROSS TO HIM WITH ONE KNEE ON THE OTTOMAN) BUT IT'S PERFECTLY SIMPLE-- /BOHUN/ (
JOAN 4 (106) IN THEIR EYES. THE KING COULD BREAK US ACROSS HIS KNEE ONE BY ONE; AND THEN WHAT SHOULD WE BE BUT LIVERIED
MILL IV (197) ABOUT DISLOCATED KNEES: THEY WANTED TO CUT MY KNEE OPEN TO SEE WHAT WAS THE MATTER WITH IT. I HAD TO TAKE
CLEO PRO2 (96) FOR THE NEW COMER. /PERSIAN/ (RISING FROM HIS KNEE) ARE EVIL TIDINGS, THEN, SO HONORABLE? /BELZANOR/ O
CAND II (119) LEANING OVER TO HIM WITH HER ARMS ON HIS KNEE) EUGENE'S ALWAYS RIGHT. HE'S A WONDERFUL BOY: I HAVE
PHIL I (71) HIS CHIN ON HIS RIGHT HAND AND HIS ELBOW ON HIS KNEE) I HAVE SAT ALONE WITH HER JUST AS I AM SITTING WITH
MTH4 II (177) A MOMENT'S HESITATION, SINKS RESPECTFULLY ON ONE KNEE) I-- /THE ORACLE/ OH, RISE, RISE, ARE YOU SO FOOLISH
JOAN 5 (112) BETWEEN CHARLES AND BLUEBEARD, AND FALLING ON HER KNEE) SIRE: I HAVE MADE YOU KING: MY WORK IS DONE. I AM
ANNA (298) MORE TO YOU? /STRAMMFEST/ (FALLING ON HIS KNEE) YOU ARE, GOD HELP ME, ALL THAT IS LEFT TO ME OF THE
LIED (190) DO? (SUDDENLY THROWING HIS HEAD AWAY FROM HER KNEE) YOU DONT SEEM TO THINK A BIT ABOUT TEDDY. (SHE JUMPS
MTH1 I (4) ON THE GROUND BESIDE HIM, AND GRASPING HIS KNEE) YOU MUST BE CAREFUL. PROMISE ME YOU WILL BE CAREFUL.
DEVL III (55) NEVER ASK YOU ANYTHING AGAIN. (SHE CLASPS HIS KNEE). I BEG AND PRAY IT OF YOU. /RICHARD/ IF I DO, WILL
CAND II (117) DOWN, AND SEATS HERSELF ON THE CARPET BESIDE HIS KNEE). NOW (PATTING HIS HAND) YOURE BEGINNING TO LOOK
CYMB V (143) (HE STRIKES POSTHUMUS AND BRINGS HIM DOWN ON ONE KNEE). /ARVIRAGUS/ YOU DOG, HOW DARE YOU (THREATENING

CATH 2 (180)	HIS CHEEK COQUETTISHLY: HE BOWS ALMOST TO HIS	KNEE	). THE PETIT LEVER IS OVER. (SHE TURNS TO GO INTO THE
ANNA (301)	YOURSELF, SIR. /STRAMMFEST/ (DROPPING ON HIS	KNEE	SUBMISSIVELY) NOW AT LAST YOU SPEAK LIKE YOUR ROYAL
INCA PROLOG (234)	MAMMON, MAMMON! I AM PUNISHED NOW FOR BOWING THE	KNEE	TO HIM. IS THERE NOTHING LEFT OF YOUR SETTLEMENT?
NEVR II (228)	OUT OF EVERYTHING, BECAUSE IVE REFUSED TO BOW THE	KNEE	TO SOCIALISM. /MRS CLANDON/ (SHOCKED) SOCIALISM!
MTH4 II (179)	NAY, YOU ARE MY SUPERIOR: HAVE I NOT BOWED MY	KNEE	TO YOU BY INSTINCT? YET I CHALLENGE YOU TO A TEST OF
CAPT I (221)	SOW? /RANKIN/ THAT IS SO. (DRINKWATER SLAPS HIS	KNEE	TRIUMPHANTLY. THE MISSIONARY PROCEEDS DETERMINEDLY) AND
6CAL (96)	RUNS IN EXCITEDLY. /JOHN OF GAUNT/ (BENDING HIS	KNEE	VERY PERFUNCTORILY) SIRE: THEY HAVE SURRENDERED: THE
MILL IV (197)	WHOLE FLIGHT OF STAIRS. MY ANKLE WAS SPRAINED. MY	KNEE	WAS TWISTED. THE SMALL BONE OF MY LEG WAS BROKEN. I
LADY PREFACE(230)	OF THEM THAT " CROOK THE PREGNANT HINGES OF THE	KNEE	WHERE THRIFT MAY FOLLOW FAWNING." THINK OF ROSENCRANTZ,
CAND II (111)	HIS OPINIONS-- /BURGESS/ (TOUCHING HIM ON THE	KNEE	WITH HIS FOREFINGER, AND PRESSING IT TO HOLD HIS
BARB II (275)	WAS A PIOUS WOMAN THAT TAUGHT ME ME PRAYERS AT ER	KNEE	, AN HOW I USED TO COME HOME DRUNK AND DRAG HER OUT O
MILL IV (196)	ON THE STRENGTH OF A SPRAINED ANKLE, A DISLOCATED	KNEE	, AND A LUMP ON MY HEAD THE SIZE OF AN OSTRICH'S EGG..
NEVR IV SD(293)	OF THE COMPANY, THE HARLEQUIN DOWN ON HIS LEFT	KNEE	, AND THE COLUMBINE STANDING ON HIS RIGHT KNEE, WITH
MTH5 (234)	OF LIE THEY WILL TELL. GIVE THEM A CLIP BELOW THE	KNEE	, AND THEY WILL JERK THEIR FOOT FORWARD. GIVE THEM A
CAND II (120)	NOT A BIT. (SHE TAKES HER ARMS FROM HIS	KNEE	, AND TURNS THOUGHTFULLY, SINKING INTO A MORE RESTFUL
BULL III (136)	DHATS THE STYLE, BEGOB! (HE SMITES HIS	KNEE	, AND WINKS AT MATT). /MATTHEW/ MORE POWER TO YOU,
CATH 4 (197)	ME MORE WHEN YOU SEE YOUR LITTLE ONES ROUND YOUR	KNEE	, AND YOUR MAN THERE BY THE FIRESIDE IN THE WINTER
CAPT I (222)	WAW, ITS THE NIME IS BLESSED MATHER GIVE IM AT ER	KNEE	, BLESS IS LITTLE AWT! THER YNT NAOW AWM IN IT. SHE
CLEO PRO2,SD(95)	WHO, WITH HIS SPEAR ON THE GROUND BESIDE HIS	KNEE	, IS STOOPING TO THROW DICE WITH A SLY-LOOKING YOUNG
NEVR IV SD(293)	KNEE, AND THE COLUMBINE STANDING ON HIS RIGHT	KNEE	, WITH HER ARMS CURVED OVER HER HEAD. UNLIKE THEIR
KING PREFACE(153)	GWYNN'S WAIST, OR WITH MOLL DAVIS SEATED ON HIS	KNEE	, WITH THE VOLUPTUOUS TERMAGANT CASTLEMAINE RAGING IN
PRES (137)	TO SANDSTONE. HE IS ONLY BRINGING YOU " ON THE	KNEE	," AS WE SAY IN THE ARMY. COULD ANY OTHER LIVING MAN
LION PREFACE(16)	" RIGHT BARBAROUSLEE," CUTTING HIM " OFF AT	KNEE	" WITH YOUR SCYTHES, SCOURGING HIM WITH YOUR FLAILS,

KNEEL

MTH4 III (194)	WIFE/ (TO ZOO, IN A REVERENT WHISPER) SHALL WE	KNEEL	? /ZOO/ (LOUDLY) YES, IF YOU WANT TO. YOU CAN STAND
JOAN EPILOG (164)	SHALL BE LAWFUL AND LAUDABLE FOR THE FAITHFUL TO	KNEEL	AND ADDRESS THEIR PRAYERS THROUGH HER TO THE MERCY
2TRU III (111)	IS THE MARK OF THE MAN: LET LESSER CREATURES	KNEEL	AND CRAWL: WE WILL NOT KNEEL AND WE DO NOT BELIEVE."
2TRU III (111)	LET LESSER CREATURES KNEEL AND CRAWL: WE WILL NOT	KNEEL	AND WE DO NOT BELIEVE." BUT WHAT NEXT? IS NO ENOUGH?
NEVR II (248)	WANTS TO MARRY HER? I'LL KISS HER HANDS; I'LL	KNEEL	AT HER FEET; I'LL LIVE FOR HER; I'LL DIE FOR HER; AND
FABL PREFACE(74)	SKY AND ASKED " WHO MADE ALL THAT? " DID NOT	KNEEL	BESIDE THOSE WHO REPLIED THAT IT MADE ITSELF, OR
NEVR II (244)	INQUIRED. /DOLLY/ THE SERVANTS COME IN LENT AND	KNEEL	DOWN BEFORE YOU AND CONFESS ALL THE THINGS THEYVE
BARB III (339)	EATING BREAD AND TREACLE, AND BEING FORCED TO	KNEEL	DOWN FROM TIME TO TIME TO THANK HEAVEN FOR IT; KNEE
CATH 2,SD(177)	PATIOMKIN WITH SO TERRIBLE AN EXPRESSION THAT ALL	KNEEL	DOWN HASTILY EXCEPT EDSTASTON, WHO IS SPRAWLING ON THE
LION EPILOG (152)	AT THE LABORATORIES, OR INFIDELS WHO REFUSE TO	KNEEL	DOWN WHEN A PROCESSION OF DOCTORS GOES BY. BUT THE
6CAL SD(102)	WILL YOU GO, CURSES ON YOU. THE FIVE BURGESSES	KNEEL	GRATEFULLY TO THE QUEEN. /EUSTACHE/ (KISSING HER
6CAL SD(97)	DE WISSANT, JEAN D'AIRE, AND GILLES D'OUDEBOLLE,	KNEEL	IN PAIRS BEHIND HIM, AND, FOLLOWING HIS EXAMPLE, LAY
JOAN 2 (86)	CLOTHES, AND I COME FROM GOD TO TELL THEE TO	KNEEL	IN THE CATHEDRAL AND SOLEMNLY GIVE THY KINGDOM TO HIM
6CAL (99)	IS IT FOR ME TO ACCUSE YOU OF ANYTHING? HERE WE	KNEEL	IN THE DUST BEFORE YOU, NAKED AND WITH THE ROPES ON
JOAN EPILOG (164)	MERCY SEAT. /JOAN/ OH NO. IT IS FOR THE SAINT TO	KNEEL	. (SHE FALLS ON HER KNEES, STILL RAPT). /THE
MTH4 III SD(195)	PERHAPS IT WOULD BE IN BETTER TASTE. THE TWO MEN	KNEEL	. THE VAPOR OF THE ABYSS THICKENS; AND A DISTANT ROLL
CLEO PRO1 (89)	RA, WHO WAS ONCE IN EGYPT A MIGHTY GOD. YE CANNOT	KNEEL	NOR PROSTRATE YOURSELVES; FOR YE ARE PACKED IN ROWS
BARB III (348)	IF WE TURN FROM THE CHURCHES THEY BUILD, WE MUST	KNEEL	ON THE STONES OF THE STREETS THEY PAVE. AS LONG AS
6CAL (93)	A DOG INSTEAD OF A KING. /THE PRINCE/ (ABOUT TO	KNEEL	) MAJESTY-- /THE KING/ NO NO: ENOUGH OF THAT. YOUR
MTH4 III (195)	MORE THAN I BARGAINED FOR. ARE YOU GOING TO	KNEEL	; OR HOW? /THE ELDERLY GENTLEMAN/ PERHAPS IT WOULD BE
LION I (115)	TO YOU WHAT CHRIST MEANS TO ME? NO: WE SHOULD	KNEEL	SIDE BY SIDE BEFORE HER ALTAR LIKE TWO CHILDREN. BUT
DEST (167)	HER EYES FULL OF TENDER PLEADING, AND IS ABOUT TO	KNEEL	TO HIM AGAIN). /NAPOLEON/ (BRUSQUELY) GET UP, GET UP.
BULL PREFACE(45)	AND PERVERTS A MUSKETRY DRILL ORDER TO MAKE THEM	KNEEL	TO HIM AS AN ACT OF PERSONAL HUMILIATION, AND THEREBY
6CAL (99)	AND OUR NAKED CONDITION THAT SHAKES US. WE	KNEEL	TO IMPLORE YOUR KING'S MERCY FOR OUR WRETCHED AND
BULL II (101)	/KEEGAN/ (SHOCKED) GET UP OUT O THAT, MAN. DONT	KNEEL	TO ME: I'M NOT A SAINT. /PATSY/ (WITH INTENSE
CLEO II (139)	MORE THAN A SHEPHERD VALUES AN ONION, AND WHO NOW	KNEEL	TO ME, WITH TEARS IN YOUR OLD EYES, TO PLEAD FOR A FEW

KNEELIN

BARB II (299)	WAS SIVIN ANATHER MENN'S KNEES AT THE TAWM. E WAS	KNEELIN	ON MOY ED, E WAS. /JENNY/ WHO WAS KNEELING ON YOUR
BARB II (299)	DEAR ART"! AN ER BLOWK-- THIRTEEN STUN FOUR! --	KNEELIN	WIV ALL IS WIGHT ON ME. FANNY, AINT IT? /JENNY/ OH

KNEELING

JOAN 3 (93)	CHANGED. (HE CROSSES HIMSELF) GOD HAS SPOKEN. (	KNEELING	AND HANDING HIS BATON TO JOAN) YOU COMMAND THE
PPP (206)	FEET. /FITZ/ THATS DONE IT! WHEW! /MAGNESIA/ (	KNEELING	AT THE LEFT HAND OF THE STATUE) FOR EVER AND FOR
PPP (206)	STATUE) FOR EVER AND FOR EVER, ADOLPHUS. /FITZ/ (	KNEELING	AT THE RIGHT HAND OF THE STATUE) THE REST IS
CAND III (145)	FONDLY AGAINST HIS). /MORELL/ (QUITE OVERCOME,	KNEELING	BESIDE HER CHAIR AND EMBRACING HER WITH BOYISH
NEVR III (262)	YOU KNOW I NEVER ASK QUESTIONS. /GLORIA/ (	KNEELING	BESIDE HER CHAIR) I KNOW, I KNOW. (SHE SUDDENLY
LIED (195)	ME TO FIND THE WAY BACK TO THE HEIGHTS. /SHE/ (	KNEELING	BESIDE HIM AND PLEADING) IF YOU WOULD ONLY BE
CLEO II (133)	THINK I MUST EAT YOU, AFTER ALL. /CLEOPATRA/ (	KNEELING	BESIDE HIM AND LOOKING AT HIM WITH EAGER INTEREST,
PPP (205)	LISTENING AT THE DOCTOR'S CHEST) DEAD! /FITZ/ (	KNEELING	BY THE LANDLORD, AND RAISING HIS HAND, WHICH DROPS
CATH 2 (174)	UP ABRUPTLY) POTZTAUSEND! (CONTEMPLATING THE	KNEELING	COURTIERS) OH, GET UP, GET UP. (ALL RISE). YOUR
JOAN 2,SD(83)	THE ROBE FROM HER; AND GOES OUT. SHE IS LEFT	KNEELING	DIRECTLY IN THE DUCHESS'S WAY. /THE DUCHESS/ (
2TRU III SD(107)	A HEAP OF PASSPORTS FROM HIS SATCHEL ON THE SAND,	KNEELING	DOWN TO SORT OUT THE PATIENT'S. /TALLBOYS/ WHAT IS
LION I (119)	YOU. /LENTULUS/ HAW! GOOD! (INDICATING THE	KNEELING	FERROVIUS). IS THIS ONE OF THE TURN-THE-OTHER-CHEEK
JOAN 5,SD(109)	OUT OF THE NAVE AFTER THE CORONATION. JOAN IS	KNEELING	IN PRAYER BEFORE THE STATION. SHE IS BEAUTIFULLY
BARB II (299)	E WAS KNEELIN ON MOY ED, E WAS. /JENNY/ WHO WAS	KNEELING	ON YOUR HEAD? /BILL/ TODGER WAS. E WAS PRYIN FOR
CLEO PRO2,SD(96)	THE GROUP ROUND THE STORYTELLER DIES AWAY. THE	KNEELING	PERSIAN, WINNING THE THROW, SNATCHES UP THE STAKE
GENV II SD(49)	WITH TINY FIGURES, ALSO IN MILITARY UNIFORMS,	KNEELING	ROUND HER FEET AND BOWING THEIR HEADS PIOUSLY
LADY (246)	NO WOMAN CAN RESIST. /SHAKESPEAR/ FLATTERIES! (	KNEELING	) OH, MADAM, I PUT MY CASE AT YOUR ROYAL FEET. I
CATH 3,SD(184)	AT THEM, CLAIRE, AS HE IS TAKING THE PISTOLS THE	KNEELING	SERGEANT SUDDENLY DROPS THEM; FLINGS HIMSELF
CATH 4 (195)	IF YOULL ONLY LET ME ALONE. /THE SERGEANT/ (	KNEELING	TO HER) PARDON HIM, PARDON HIM, LEST THE MIGHTY MAN
CATH 4 (195)	THIS IS PERFECTLY RIDICULOUS. /VARINKA/ (	KNEELING	TO HER) PARDON HIM, PARDON HIM, LITTLE DELIGHT,
JOAN EPILOG (165)	HAVE DRAGGED THROUGH THE MIRE. /WARWICK/ (	KNEELING	TO HER) THE CUNNING COUNSELLORS PRAISE THEE,
JOAN EPILOG (165)	THE FREEDOM OF THE LIVING SOUL. /THE SOLDIER/ (	KNEELING	TO HER) THE WICKED OUT OF HELL PRAISE THEE, BECAUSE
JOAN EPILOG (165)	ARE TURNED INTO BLESSINGS. /THE INQUISITOR/ (	KNEELING	TO HER) THE JUDGES IN THE BLINDNESS AND BONDAGE OF
JOAN EPILOG (165)	IS NOTHING BETWEEN THEM AND HEAVEN. /DUNOIS/ (	KNEELING	TO HER) THE DYING SOLDIERS PRAISE THEE, BECAUSE
JOAN EPILOG (165)	NOT QUENCHED IS A HOLY FIRE. /THE EXECUTIONER/ (	KNEELING	TO HER) THE TORMENTORS AND EXECUTIONERS PRAISE
JOAN EPILOG (165)	GUILTLESS OF THE DEATH OF THE SOUL. /CHARLES/ (	KNEELING	TO HER) THE UNPRETENDING PRAISE THEE, BECAUSE THOU
JOAN EPILOG (165)	BETWEEN THEM AND THE JUDGMENT. /THE ARCHBISHOP/ (	KNEELING	TO HER) THE PRINCES OF THE CHURCH PRAISE THEE,
JOAN EPILOG (165)	BODY, YET IN MY SOUL I HAVE SEEN GOD. /CAUCHON/ (	KNEELING	TO HER) THE GIRLS IN THE FIELD PRAISE THEE; FOR
JOAN EPILOG (165)	THEY HAVE TIED THEIR OWN SOULS. /DE STOGUMBER/ (	KNEELING	TO HER) THE FOOLISH OLD MEN ON THEIR DEATHBEDS
CLEO II (139)	THEM AWAY WITH THE HELP OF BOOKS. /THEODOTUS/ (	KNEELING	, WITH GENUINE LITERARY EMOTION: THE PASSION OF THE

KNEELS

GLIM (172)	LET ME SEE. (HE TAKES HER HAND IN HIS. SHE	KNEELS	AND KISSES IT FERVENTLY) OH, IT'S TRUE. YOU ARE A
CAPT III (299)	BETTER THAN THE WIFE OF BLACK PAQUITO. (HE	KNEELS	AND TAKES HER HANDS) YOU CAN DO NO MORE FOR ME NOW: I
NEVR III (273)	WOMAN. /VALENTINE/ OH DONT, GLORIA, DONT. (HE	KNEELS	AT HER FEET) /GLORIA/ GET UP! GET UP! HOW DARE
GETT (338)	IF YOU RESPECT NOTHING ELSE. I FORBID YOU. (HE	KNEELS	AT HER FEET). WHAT ARE YOU DOING? GET UP: DONT BE A
SUPR III (84)	OF HOTEL BILLS SCRAWLED WITH MANUSCRIPT, AND	KNEELS	AT THE FIRE TO DECIPHER THEM, POKING IT WITH A STICK
6CAL SD(97)	IRON KEYS. THEIR LEADER, EUSTACHE DE ST PIERRE,	KNEELS	AT THE KING'S FEET, FOUR OF HIS FELLOW VICTIMS, PIERS
ARMS III (56)	I PROMISE YOU. (HE THROWS THE LOGS DOWN AND	KNEELS	AT THE STOVE). /LOUKA/ YOU SHALL NEVER BE MASTER IN
CLEO I SD(114)	YOURSELF, MISTRESS? FTATATEETA, CRUSHED,	KNEELS	BEFORE CLEOPATRA, WHO CAN HARDLY BELIEVE HER EYES.
CLEO IV SD(185)	FTATATEETA DRAGS HERSELF SLEEPILY TO THE ALTAR;	KNEELS	BEFORE RA; AND REMAINS THERE IN PRAYER. CAESAR GOES
SUPR IV (170)	HAVE PROMISED TO MARRY JACK. (SHE SWOONS. VIOLET	KNEELS	BY HER AND CHAFES HER HAND. TANNER RUNS ROUND TO HER
JITT I (25)	ON THE LIGHT) BRUNO. (SHE RUSHES TO HIM AND	KNEELS	BY HIM), BRUNO: SPEAK TO ME IF YOU CAN: IS IT YOUR
MTH5 SD(239)	TO HIM? THEY LOOK ON ANXIOUSLY AS MARTELLUS	KNEELS	DOWN AND EXAMINES THE BODY OF PYGMALION. /MARTELLUS/
WIDO III (66)	(HE SHUTS HIS EYES TIGHT AND GRINS. SHE SUDDENLY	KNEELS	DOWN BESIDE HIM WITH HER BREAST AGAINST HIS
DEVL III (74)	SQUARE). /BURGOYNE/ (NODDING APPROVINGLY AS SHE	KNEELS	) AH, QUITE SO. DO NOT DISTURB HER, MR BRUDENELL:
CLEO II (141)	AGAIN, AND SETTING OUT HIS LEG FOR BRITANNUS, WHO	KNEELS	TO PUT ON HIS GREAVES) NEITHER DO I LIKE TO BE
GLIM (172)	QUITE CLOSE TO MY EAR IF YOU SPEAK LOW. (SHE	KNEELS	WITH HER BREAST AGAINST HIS ARM AND HER CHIN ON HIS

		KNEES	
CATH 2 (177)	AT EDSTASTON) WHAT IS THIS? /PATIOMKIN/ (ON HIS	KNEES	: TEARFULLY) I DONT KNOW. I AM DRUNK. WHAT IS THIS.
MILL IV (197)	AND NONE OF THEM KNEW ANYTHING ABOUT DISLOCATED	KNEES	: THEY WANTED TO CUT MY KNEE OPEN TO SEE WHAT WAS THE
JOAN 2 (86)	AGAINST GOD: THE ENGLISH WILL FALL ON THEIR	KNEES	AND BEG THEE LET THEM RETURN TO THEIR LAWFUL HOMES IN
FOUN (219)	PRISON ANOTHER MINUTE-- NOT IF I WENT DOWN ON MY	KNEES	AND BEGGED HIM TO LET ME STAY. OF COURSE I REFUSED TO
LION I (121)	SUFFERING AND DEATH. /LENTULUS/ (FALLING ON HIS	KNEES	AND BURSTING INTO TEARS) OH, HELP ME, MOTHER!
CLEO III (163)	COME, RUFIO. /CLEOPATRA/ (SCRAMBLING TO HER	KNEES	AND CLINGING TO HIM) NO NO. DO NOT LEAVE ME, CAESAR. (
KING I (177)	/FOX/ GOD HAS STOPPED IT. (HE FALLS ON HIS	KNEES	AND COLLAPSES, SHIVERING LIKE A MAN RECOVERING FROM A
2TRU II SD(58)	ON THE RUG, AND LISTENS TO THEM, HUGGING HER	KNEES	AND HER UMBRELLA, AND TRYING TO LOOK AS INDIGENOUS AS
LION PROLOG (106)	DOWN SADLY ON THE GROUND WITH HIS ELBOWS ON HIS	KNEES	AND HIS HEAD IN HIS HANDS) WE ALL HAVE TO THINK OF
CAND III (134)	DISTRACTEDLY ON THE SOFA, WITH HIS ELBOWS ON HIS	KNEES	AND HIS HEAD PROPPED ON HIS CLENCHED FISTS).
CAND I (95)	(HE SITS DOWN ON THE SOFA, HIS ELBOWS ON HIS	KNEES	AND HIS TEMPLES BETWEEN HIS FISTS, WITH AN EXPRESSION
ROCK II SD(273)	AND LOOKS RATHER SICK, WITH HIS ELBOWS ON HIS	KNEES	AND HIS TEMPLES ON HIS FISTS. BARKING AND MISS
PYGM I (206)	A SHODDY BLACK COAT THAT REACHES NEARLY TO HER	KNEES	AND IS SHAPED TO HER WAIST. SHE HAS A BROWN SKIRT WITH
MTH5 (243)	OZYMANDIAS: DO YOU HEAR THAT? (SHE RISES ON HER	KNEES	AND LOOKS RAPTLY INTO SPACE). QUEEN OF QUEENS! (SHE
LION II SD(143)	ANDROCLES SHIVERS AT THE SOUND; THEN FALLS ON HIS	KNEES	AND PRAYS. THE GRATING RISES WITH A CLASH. THE LION
NEVR IV (284)	(QUICKLY) YES, MOTHER. (SHE TURNS TO HIM ON HER	KNEES	AND SEIZES HIS HANDS). NOW LISTEN. NO TREASON TO HER:
CURE (232)	START AT ONCE. /REGINALD/ (RUNNING TO HER ON HIS	KNEES	AND SNATCHING AT HER HANDS) NO, YOU SHANT. (SHE RISES
2TRU III (111)	KNELT MURMURING " I BELIEVE" WE STAND WITH STIFF	KNEES	AND STIFFER NECKS SHOUTING " UP, ALL! THE ERECT
CLEO III (155)	IN WITH YOU. /FTATATEETA/ (FALLING ON HER	KNEES	AND STRETCHING HER HANDS OVER THE WATERS) GODS OF THE
NEVR III (268)	PLAN OF ATTACK: YOU KNOW: GOING DOWN ON HIS	KNEES	AND SWEARING TO LOVE, HONOR, AND OBEY AND SO ON. /MRS
MTH2 SD(47)	BY SIDE, HUNCHED UP WITH THEIR ELBOWS ON THEIR	KNEES	AND THEIR CHINS ON THEIR HANDS, PROVIDING BURGE WITH A
LADY (244)	TEACH YOU-- /THE DARK LADY/ (RISING FROM HER	KNEES	AND THROWING HERSELF BETWEEN THEM) WILL: IN GOD'S NAME
HART II (114)	BREAK. /LADY UTTERWORD/ (FLINGING HERSELF ON HER	KNEES	AND THROWING HER ARMS ROUND HIM) PAPA: DONT SAY YOU
2TRU I (42)	SPRINGS HALF UP, THREATENINGLY. HE FALLS ON HIS	KNEES	AND THROWS UP HIS HANDS). KAMERAD, MISS MOPPLY:
PHIL I (81)	BREAKS DOWN, ROCKING HER HEAD DESPERATELY ON HIS	KNEES	AND WRITHING). OH, I'M MAD: I'M MAD: YOULL KILL ME IF
MIS. SD(115)	ON HER KNEES BY BENTLEY. MRS TARLETON, WHOSE	KNEES	ARE STIFFER, BENDS OVER HIM AND TRIES TO LIFT HIM. MRS
MTH4 I (152)	YOU? /ZOO/ FIFTY-SIX. /THE ELDERLY GENTLEMAN/ MY	KNEES	ARE TREMBLING. I FEAR I AM REALLY ILL. NOT SO YOUNG AS
PHIL II (124)	(SUDDENLY THROWING HERSELF TRAGICALLY ON HER	KNEES	AT GRACE'S FEET) DONT TAKE HIM FROM ME. OH DONT-- DONT
KING II SD(234)	STALKS OUT. SHE RISES AND THROWS HERSELF ON HER	KNEES	AT HER PRIE-DIEU.
CATH 4 (192)	/CLAIRE/ (SEEING HIM AND THROWING HERSELF ON HER	KNEES	AT HIS SIDE). OH, HOW DARE THEY TIE YOU UP LIKE THAT!
BARB II (299)	SOUR MIRTHLESS HUMOR) AW WAS SIVIN ANATHER MENN'S	KNEES	AT THE TAWM. E WAS KNEELIN ON MOY ED, E WAS. /JENNY/
SIM II (67)	DOWN TO THE LAWN AND THROWING THEMSELVES ON THEIR	KNEES	BEFORE HER) HAIL! /PROLA/ WILL YOU PROVOKE ME TO BOX
DEST (171)	AND COURAGE; AND THAT (SUDDENLY SINKING ON HER	KNEES	BEFORE HIM) IS WHY WE ALL BEGIN TO WORSHIP YOU. (SHE
JOAN 2 (81)	WITH EMOTION) OH, MY LORD! (SHE FALLS ON BOTH	KNEES	BEFORE HIM, WITH BOWED HEAD, NOT DARING TO LOOK UP) MY
HART II (110)	THERE TWO OF YOU? /THE BURGLAR/ (FALLING ON HIS	KNEES	BEFORE THE CAPTAIN IN ABJECT TERROR) OH MY GOOD LORD,
MIS. SD(115)	BY MRS TARLETON, AND THROWS HERSELF ON HER	KNEES	BY BENTLEY. MRS TARLETON, WHOSE KNEES ARE STIFFER,
PPP (194)	/PHYLLIS/ (IMPULSIVELY THROWING HERSELF ON HER	KNEES	BY HER MISTRESS'S SIDE, AND CLASPING HER ROUND THE
JOAN EPIL,SD(152)	AT THE PICTURES IN FOUQUET'S BOCCACCIO WITH HIS	KNEES	DOUBLED UP TO MAKE A READING DESK. BESIDE THE BED ON
LADY (243)	DARK LADY/ (RECOGNIZING HER AND FALLING ON HER	KNEES	IN ABJECT TERROR) WILL: I AM LOST: I HAVE STRUCK THE
BULL II (101)	HIT ME WITH IT. /PATSY/ (THROWING HIMSELF ON HIS	KNEES	IN AN ECSTASY OF ADORATION) SURE IT'S YOUR BLESSIN I
MTH2 (44)	TO LIVE, EH? /THE PARLOR MAID/ (DROPPING ON HER	KNEES	IN CONSTERNATION) I MEANT NO OFFENCE, SIR. /CONRAD/
CLEO I (110)	SCRAMBLES DOWN TO THE SAND; AND FALLS ON HER	KNEES	IN FRANTIC SUPPLICATION, SHRIEKING) BITE HIM IN TWO,
DEVL III (74)	AWAY WITH A FRIGHTFUL SHUDDER, AND FALLS ON HER	KNEES	IN PRAYER. BRUDENELL COMES TOWARDS HER FROM THE BACK
CATH 4 (189)	YOU GRINNING AT? /NARYSHKIN/ (FALLING ON HIS	KNEES	IN TERROR) BE MERCIFUL, LITTLE MOTHER. MY HEART IS IN
JOAN PREFACE(33)	OUR INFALLIBLE PARLIAMENTS, THE POPE IS ON HIS	KNEES	IN THE DUST CONFESSING HIS IGNORANCE BEFORE THE THRONE
MTH5 (253)	AND FOUR OF MY ELBOWS RESTING ON FOUR OF MY	KNEES	. AND SUDDENLY IT CAME INTO MY MIND THAT THIS
CATH 3 (185)	BEAR. HE HAS BROKEN MY SWEETBREAD WITH HIS STRONG	KNEES	. GOD KNOWS POOR FOLK SHOULD NOT BE SET UPON SUCH
6CAL (98)	BETTER DOG OF THE TWO. /THE KING/ DRAG HIM TO HIS	KNEES	. HAMSTRING HIM IF HE RESISTS. THREE MEN-AT-ARMS DASH
SUPR II SD(48)	WITH BENT BACK AND HANDS SUPPORTED ON HIS	KNEES	. HIS LEATHERN OVERCOAT AND PEAKED CAP PROCLAIM HIM
CATH 3,SD(185)	BACK AND FASTEN HIS WRISTS TOGETHER BEHIND HIS	KNEES	. NEXT THEY PUT A BROAD STRAP ROUND HIS RIBS, FINALLY
BULL IV (147)	THING LIKE A WHEEL ON TOP OF A STICK BETWEEN HIS	KNEES	. /AUNT JUDY/ LORD HAVE MERCY ON US! /NORA/ I DONT
CATH 4,SD(188)	WHERE SHE HAS ENTERED. THE SOLDIERS FALL ON THEIR	KNEES	. /CATHERINE/ OBEY YOUR ORDERS. THE SOLDIERS SEIZE
MTH4 III SD(196)	UP WITH YOU, ETH. THE TWO WOMEN RISE TO THEIR	KNEES	. /THE ENVOY/ WHAT I WANT TO ASK IS THIS. (HE REFERS
2TRU I (44)	AT FULL LENGTH WITH MY HEAD PILLOWED ON SWEETIE'S	KNEES	. /THE PATIENT/ YOU CAN LEAVE SWEETIE OUT, POPS. HER
MTH4 III SD(195)	ELDERLY GENTLEMAN MANAGES TO GET ON HIS HANDS AND	KNEES	. /ZOO/ COME ON, DADDY: YOU ARE NOT AFRAID. SPEAK TO
BULL PREFACE(70)	CRAWL PAST OFFICIAL BUILDINGS ON THEIR HANDS AND	KNEES	. THE EFFECT WAS TO MAKE BRITISH IMPERIAL RULE
6CAL SD(98)	MEN-AT-ARMS DASH AT PETER AND DRAG HIM TO HIS	KNEES	. THEY TAKE HIS HALTER AND TIE HIS ANKLES AND WRISTS
BULL PREFACE(7)	SHOULD BE ABLE TO FACE HOME RULE WITHOUT HIS	KNEES	KNOCKING SHAMEFULLY IN THE FACE OF A CONTEMPTUOUS
MTH5 (241)	MALE FIGURE/ (TRYING TO ASSERT HIMSELF WITH HIS	KNEES	KNOCKING) MY NAME IS OZYMANDIAS, KING OF-- /THE
6CAL (103)	HARM YOU MAY HAVE DONE YOURSELF FLOPPING ON YOUR	KNEES	LIKE THAT? /THE QUEEN/ I HAVE DONE MYSELF NO HARM,
SUPR III (83)	STRAKER! /STRAKER/ (SCRAMBLING UP ON HIS	KNEES	MOST INDIGNANTLY) LOOK HERE: LOUISA STRAKER IS MY
PPP (200)	AND FITZ/ (THROWING THEMSELVES ON THEIR	KNEES	ON EITHER SIDE OF HIM) FOR OUR SAKES, ADOLPHUS,
JOAN 1 (59)	(ROBERT HAS TO LET HIM DROP. HE SQUATS ON HIS	KNEES	ON THE FLOOR, CONTEMPLATING HIS MASTER RESIGNEDLY).
PYGM IV SD(267)	HER OWN TRIUMPH; AND FINALLY GOES DOWN ON HER	KNEES	ON THE HEARTHRUG TO LOOK FOR THE RING.
PYGM V (285)	TO COME BACK FOR? /HIGGINS/ (BOUNCING UP ON HIS	KNEES	ON THE OTTOMAN AND LEANING OVER IT TO HER) FOR THE FUN
PHIL II (106)	(HE FOLLOWS HER). /SYLVIA/ (JUMPING UP ON HER	KNEES	ON THE SETTEE, AND SPEAKING OVER THE BACK OF IT) WHATS
FANY II (296)	THIS DARK. I'M YOUR FATHER. I ASK YOU HERE ON MY	KNEES	-- IN THE DUST, SO TO SPEAK-- NOT TO LET IT OUT.
2TRU I (40)	KILLED YOU? /THE BURGLAR/ (RISING SLOWLY TO HIS	KNEES	) AS NEARLY AS DOESNT MATTER. OH, SWEETIEST, WHY DID
2TRU II (60)	FORGETTING HERSELF AND SCRAMBLING FORWARD TO HER	KNEES	) BUT YOU-- /THE COUNTESS/ (STOPPING HER WITH A
WIDO III (50)	(CATCHING HER ARM AND ARRESTING HER ON HER	KNEES	) COME, MY CHILD! YOU MUST NOT TRIFLE WITH ME AS IF I
MTH4 III (196)	TO YOUR QUESTIONS. /THE ENVOY/ (RISING TO HIS	KNEES	) I SHALL BE ONLY TOO GLAD TO GET BACK ALIVE ON ANY
6CAL (102)	DEAREST DEAREST LOVE. (THROWING HERSELF ON HER	KNEES	) LISTEN: DO AS YOU WILL: I WILL NOT SAY ANOTHER WORD:
CATH 1 (163)	IS GENERAL VOLKONSKY? /THE SERGEANT/ (ON HIS	KNEES	) LITTLE FATHER: YOU KICKED HIS HIGHNESS DOWNSTAIRS.
JOAN 6 (149)	YOUR HEART, THEN -- THEN -- (FALLING ON HIS	KNEES	) O GOD, TAKE AWAY THIS SIGHT FROM ME! O CHRIST,
MTH5 (241)	POOH! /THE MALE FIGURE/ (FALLING ON HIS	KNEES	) OH DONT, SIR. DONT. SHE DID IT, SIR: INDEED SHE DID.
WIDO II (45)	GO. /THE PARLORMAID/ (PITEOUSLY, FALLING ON HER	KNEES	) OH NO, MISS BLANCHE. DONT SEND ME AWAY FROM YOU:
MRS II (211)	WARREN/ (DISTRACTED, THROWING HERSELF ON HER	KNEES	) OH NO, NO. STOP, STOP. I AM YOUR MOTHER: I SWEAR IT.
MILL IV (192)	/ALASTAIR/ (SITTING UP AND TAKING IT ON HIS	KNEES	) OH, I AM SORRY: I FORGOT. (HE SIGNS). THERE YOU
BULL II (98)	COMES BACK AND FINDS THE LABORER, WHO CLASPS HIS	KNEES	) PATSY FARRELL! WHAT ARE YOU DOING HERE? /PATSY/ OH
FABL I (103)	(THOUGHTFULLY, LETTING THE NEWSPAPER DROP ON HIS	KNEES	) THAT IS AN IDEA. /YOUNG WOMAN/ WHAT IDEA? /YOUNG
DEST (167)	/NAPOLEON/ (LAUGHING GRIMLY AND SLAPPING HIS	KNEES	) THAT IS THE ONE QUESTION YOU MUST NEVER ASK A
CURE (231)	TO THE KEYBOARD). /REGINALD/ (FALLING ON HIS	KNEES	) YOU MUSTNT PLAY. YOU REALLY MUSTNT. I CANT STAND IT.
CLEO IV (189)	(TERRIFIED, RUNNING TO HIM AND FALLING ON HER	KNEES	) YOU WILL NOT DESERT ME, CAESAR. YOU WILL DEFEND THE
DEST (166)	NO-- (SHE BREAKS OFF, AND THROWS HERSELF ON HER	KNEES	). AH, GENERAL, LET ME GO: LET ME GO WITHOUT ASKING
DEVL III (54)	OH, ONE MOMENT MORE. (SHE THROWS HERSELF ON HER	KNEES	). I PRAY TO YOU-- /RICHARD/ HUSH! (CALLING) COME
CATH 2 (174)	MAJESTY IS AWAKE. (THE COURT FALLS ON ITS	KNEES	). /ALL/ GOOD MORNING TO YOUR MAJESTY. /NARYSHKIN/
PHIL II (115)	WITH HIS HEAD ON HIS HANDS AND HIS ELBOWS ON HIS	KNEES	). /CUTHBERTSON/ (WHO HAS BEEN REJOICING WITH JULIA
MIS. (126)	AND SITS DOWN ON IT WITH HIS BACK AGAINST HER	KNEES	). /TARLETON/ OLD! THATS ALL YOU KNOW ABOUT IT, MY
MTH4 III (195)	DAUGHTER/ (PITEOUSLY) OH! (SHE FALLS ON HER	KNEES	). /THE ENVOY/ WHEW! STAND BY ME, POPPA. THIS IS A
LION I (118)	HANDS IN SILENT PRAYER; AND THROWS HIMSELF ON HIS	KNEES	). THATS THE WAY TO MANAGE THEM, EH! THIS FINE FELLOW
CLEO III SD(155)	LEFT. HIS HELMET, FULL OF DATES, IS BETWEEN HIS	KNEES	; AND A LEATHERN BOTTLE OF WINE IS BY HIS SIDE. BEHIND
NEVR I (211)	BACK; PLACES HIS KNUCKLES SYMMETRICALLY ON HIS	KNEES	; AND OPENS HIS CASE). DOLLY AND I HAVE BEEN TALKING
CATH 3,SD(184)	SERGEANT GOES TO EDSTASTON; PLUMPS DOWN ON HIS	KNEES	; AND TAKES OUT A MAGNIFICENT PAIR OF PISTOLS WITH
2TRU II SD(77)	WITH AN AIR OF DISARMING INNOCENCE; FALLS ON HER	KNEES	; LIFTS HER PALMS; AND SMITES THE GROUND WITH HER
2TRU I SD(40)	TACKLES THE PATIENT. THE PATIENT SWOOPS AT HER	KNEES	; LIFTS HER; AND SENDS HER FLYING. SHE COMES DOWN WITH
FANY II (293)	TO THE POLICE STATION. THEY KICKED ME WITH THEIR	KNEES	; THEY TWISTED MY ARMS; THEY TAUNTED AND INSULTED ME;
BASH II,2, (118)	SHOOTS TO ITS MARK; AND THE LAST AFRICAN UPON HIS	KNEES	SUES PITEOUSLY FOR QUARTER. (RUSHING INTO CASHEL'S
BASH I (98)	GODS THAT WILL NOT SPARE THIS MAN, UPON YOUR	KNEES	TAKE THE DISPARITY TWIXT HIS AGE AND MINE. NOW FROM
GETT (338)	HIS HOME THIS AFTERNOON; AND I SHALL REMAIN ON MY	KNEES	TIL THE BISHOP COMES IN AND SEES US. WHAT WILL HE
CATH 4 (195)	THE EMPRESS'S SIDE TO CLAIRE AND FALLING ON HIS	KNEES	TO HER) PARDON HIM, PARDON HIM, LITTLE CHERUB! LITTLE
CAPT I (223)	(DRILY) AND DO YE GO DOWN ON YOUR BENDED	KNEES	TO HIM TO DO IT? /DRINKWATER/ (SOMEWHAT ABASHED)
CAPT I (223)	GAVNER, NOT IF WE GOWS DAHN ON AHR BLOOMIN BENDED	KNEES	TO IM TO DO IT. /RANKIN/ (DRILY) AND DO YE GO DOWN ON
GETT (338)	BE A FOOL. /HOTCHKISS/ POLLY: I ASK YOU ON MY	KNEES	TO LET ME MAKE GEORGE'S ACQUAINTANCE IN HIS HOME THIS
MILL I (155)	YOU WON MY HAND, FOR WHICH ALL EUROPE WAS ON ITS	KNEES	TO ME. WHAT YOU DESERVED WAS FIVE YEARS PENAL
PHIL II (126)	PITIFUL THING. DO YOU THINK I NEED GO DOWN ON MY	KNEES	TO MEN TO MAKE THEM COME TO ME? THAT MAY BE YOUR

MRS III SD(229)	HE GRINS; LEANS FORWARD WITH HIS ELBOWS ON HIS	KNEES	TO PROD WITH HIS STICK AT SOME UNFORTUNATE INSECT IN
JOAN 6 (143)	NOTHING BUT BEGGING THIS DAMNABLE WITCH ON YOUR	KNEES	TO RECANT ALL THROUGH THIS TRIAL. /THE INQUISITOR/ (
SIM PRO,2, (29)	I WAS AFRAID TO MAKE AN END OF IT. (HE BENDS HIS	KNEES	TO SPRING, BUT CANNOT). I WILL. (HE MAKES ANOTHER
CYMB V (140)	THAT; BUT WHEN THE TRUMPET SOUNDS THEYRE ON THEIR	KNEES	TO US. /PHILARIO/ WELL, CAPTAIN, I MUST HASTEN BACK TO
MILL III (181)	SO CRUEL AS TO REPORT THEM THEYD GO DOWN ON THEIR	KNEES	TO YOU TO SPARE THEM. /THE MAN/ YOU THAT KNOW SUCH A
WIDO III (50)	MYSELF. IT IS NOT TRUE. IF HE WERE HERE ON HIS	KNEES	TONIGHT, I WOULD WALK OUT OF THE HOUSE SOONER THAN
CAPT II SD(242)	WITH THEIR REEFER COATS UNDER THEIR HEADS, THEIR	KNEES	UPLIFTED, AND THEIR CALVES LAID COMFORTABLY ON THE
NEVR III (277)	YOU HAD HIM AT YOUR MERCY; YOU BROUGHT HIM TO HIS	KNEES	WHEN YOU THREATENED TO MAKE THE MATTER PUBLIC BY
CAPT II (265)	DID YOU, YOU DOG. /DRINKWATER/ (FALLING ON HIS	KNEES	WITH A YELL) NAOW! (BRASSBOUND TURNS ON HIM AS IF TO
SUPR III (83)	/STRAKER/ (SECRETLY DAUNTED, BUT RISING FROM HIS	KNEES	WITH AN AIR OF RECKLESS PUGNACITY) I AINT AFRAID OF
BARB II (306)	YOU EVER SEEN A THOUSAND PEOPLE FALL ON THEIR	KNEES	WITH ONE IMPULSE AND PRAY? COME WITH US TO THE
WIDO II SD(43)	BEGGARED, WITH HIS CLASPED KNUCKLES BETWEEN HIS	KNEES	, A LIVING PICTURE OF DISILLUSION. COKANE COMES
JOAN 2,SD(83)	AS THE ARCHBISHOP PASSES JOAN, SHE FALLS ON HER	KNEES	, AND KISSES THE HEM OF HIS ROBE FERVENTLY. HE SHAKES
WIDO II (43)	SLOWLY UNLACES HIS FINGERS; PUTS HIS HANDS ON HIS	KNEES	, AND LIFTS HIMSELF UPRIGHT; PULLS HIS WAISTCOAT
CATH 1,SD(161)	WHICH HE OCCASIONALLY HITCHES UP TO HIS	KNEES	, AND PRESENTLY SHAKES DOWN TO HIS SHINS, BY HIS
ARMS III (56)	MASTER IN MINE. /NICOLA/ (TURNING, STILL ON HIS	KNEES	, AND SQUATTING DOWN RATHER FORLORNLY ON HIS CALVES,
MTH4 III (201)	PERPLEXED AND WRETCHED MAN. (HE FALLS ON HIS	KNEES	, AND STRETCHES HIS HANDS IN ENTREATY OVER THE ABYSS).
MTH4 III SD(195)	SEE THE PYTHONESS. THE ENVOY'S WIFE FALLS ON HER	KNEES	, AND TAKES REFUGE IN PRAYER. /THE DAUGHTER/ (
BARB II (299)	/BARBARA/ PITY YOU DIDNT RUB SOME OFF WITH YOUR	KNEES	, BILL! THAT WOULD HAVE DONE YOU A LOT OF GOOD.
ARMS I (15)	USE TRYING TO FIGHT. THE WOUNDS ARE MOSTLY BROKEN	KNEES	, FROM THE HORSES CANNONING TOGETHER. /RAINA/ UGH!
SUPR IV (161)	AND SITS CLOSE TO HER WITH HIS ELBOWS ON HIS	KNEES	, GIVING HER HIS WHOLE ATTENTION). I DONT KNOW WHY IT
CLEO PRO2 (103)	OF THE COURTYARD, WHERE, AS THEY FLING HER ON HER	KNEES	, HE DRAWS A MURDEROUS LOOKING KNIFE). WHERE IS SHE..
DEVL II SD(49)	DIE. ESSIE SCREAMS WITH TERROR AND FALLS ON HER	KNEES	, HIDING HER FACE. JUDITH, WITHOUT HEEDING HER, LOOKS
6CAL (97)	HAVE BRAINED EDWARD WITH THEM. /THE KING/ ON YOUR	KNEES	, HOUND. /PETER/ I AM A GOOD DOG, BUT NOT OF YOUR
CAND III SD(128)	FACE UPWARDS, AND THROWS BACK HIS HEAD ACROSS HER	KNEES	, LOOKING UP AT HER. /MARCHBANKS/ OH, IVE BEEN SO
BULL IV (146)	FARRLL IN THE BACK SATE WI DHE PIG BETWEEN HIS	KNEES	, N ME BOULD ENGLISH BOYOH IN FRONT AT THE MACHINERY,
SIM II (76)	POLL-IT-TICKS. PART OF THE AUDIENCE FELL TO THEIR	KNEES	, REPEATING THE CONFESSION. OTHERS RUSHED FRANTICALLY
CAND III (146)	AND AS HE DIVINES HER INTENTION AND FALLS ON HIS	KNEES	, SHE KISSES HIS FOREHEAD. THEN HE FLIES OUT INTO THE
DEVL I (27)	TEARS! THE DEVIL'S BAPTISM! (SHE FALLS ON HER	KNEES	, SOBBING. HE STOOPS GOODNATUREDLY TO RAISE HER,
JOAN EPILOG (164)	IT IS FOR THE SAINT TO KNEEL. (SHE FALLS ON HER	KNEES	, STILL RAPT). /THE GENTLEMAN/ (PUTTING UP HIS PAPER,
6CAL SD(103)	RETIRE, BOWING TO THE QUEEN, WHO, STILL ON HER	KNEES	, WAVES HER HAND GRACIOUSLY TO THEM. /THE QUEEN/ WILL
CAND III (128)	IF YOU ONLY KNEW. (HE TURNS QUITE OVER ON HIS	KNEES	, WITH HIS HANDS CLASPED AND HIS ARMS ON HER LAP, AND
CLEO I (113)	HERE. (MENACINGLY) CLEOPATRA-- /CAESAR/ ON YOUR	KNEES	, WOMAN: AM I ALSO A CHILD THAT YOU DARE TRIFLE WITH

KNELL

SUPR HANDBOK(179)	MAKE ANY SERIOUS IMPRESSION ON PROPERTY. THE	KNELL	OF THAT OVERRATED INSTITUTION WILL NOT SOUND UNTIL IT

KNELLER

KING I (218)	A KING IN THE NEW ROYAL SOCIETY. HERE IS GODFREY	KNELLER	: A KING AMONG PAINTERS. I CAN MAKE YOU DUCHESSES
KING I (208)	ARE BOTH ALMOST AS ANGRY AS BARBARA. /NEWTON/ MR	KNELLER	: I WILL DISPUTE WITH YOU NO MORE. YOU DO NOT
KING I (220)	YOUR VICTUALS WILL BE COLD. /NEWTON/ (RISING) MR	KNELLER	: WILL YOU TAKE HER GRACE OF CLEVELAND, AS YOU ARE
KING I (221)	YOUR CHOICE OF A HUNDRED HEAVENS. /MRS BASHAM/ MR	KNELLER	: YOUR DINNER WILL BE COLD; AND YOU WILL BE LATE FOR
KING I (209)	HE LIES. /CHARLES/ AND WHAT DO YOU SAY, MR	KNELLER	? /KNELLER/ SIR: I DO NOT SAY: I KNOW. THE RIGHT
KING I (220)	/MRS BASHAM/ WILL YOU TAKE THE PLAYER WOMAN, MR	KNELLER	? /NELL/ NO NO. THE PLAYER WOMAN GOES WITH HER DEAR
KING I (216)	CALLED A BLUESTOCKING. ALL I MEANT WAS THAT MR	KNELLER	AND MR NEWTON SEEM TO MEAN EXACTLY THE SAME THING;
KING I (208)	(SCRUTINIZING IT ADMIRINGLY) SPLENDID! HAS MR	KNELLER	DONE THIS? NOBODY CAN CATCH A LIKENESS AS HE CAN.
KING PREFACE(154)	DATE; SO I HAD TO FALL BACK ON GODFREY KNELLER.	KNELLER	HAD NOT HOGARTH'S BRAINS; BUT I HAVE HAD TO ENDOW
KING I (212)	IT. /CHARLES/ DO NOT BE AN IDIOT, BARBARA: MR	KNELLER	IS PAYING YOU THE GREATEST COMPLIMENT IN TAKING YOU
KING I (220)	YOU. /NEWTON/ THE LINES ARE NOT STRAIGHT, MR	KNELLER	, GRAVITATION BENDS THEM. AND AT BOTTOM I KNOW NO
KING PREFACE(154)	MY CHOSEN DATE; SO I HAD TO FALL BACK ON GODFREY	KNELLER	. KNELLER HAD NOT HOGARTH'S BRAINS; BUT I HAVE HAD
KING I (220)	THERE IS NO ONE LEFT FOR YOU TO TAKE IN, MR	KNELLER	. MR NEWTON MUST TAKE ME IN AND COME LAST. /KNELLER/
KING I (209)	YOU ARE CERTAINLY A VERY SKILFUL DRAUGHTSMAN, MR	KNELLER	. /KNELLER/ CAN ANYONE HERE DRAW A LINE BETTER THAN
KING I (220)	/MRS BASHAM/ YOU WILL DO NOTHING OF THE SORT, MR	KNELLER	. THERE IS A COVER LAID FOR YOU; AND THE KING
KING I (209)	IT BETTER THAN ANYONE? /CHARLES/ GRANTED, MR	KNELLER	. WHAT THEN? /KNELLER/ THIS MAN HERE, THIS CRAZY
KING PREFACE(154)	WITH A VICTORIOUS ANTAGONIST. IN POINT OF DATE	KNELLER	JUST FITTED IN. BUT I MUST MAKE AN EXCEPTION TO THIS
KING I (209)	DUKE'S LEFT). /CHARLES/ MR NEWTON IS OUR HOST, MR	KNELLER	; AND HE IS A VERY EMINENT PHILOSOPHER. WILL YOU NOT
KING I SD(208)	COMES IN FROM THE GARDEN, FOLLOWED BY GODFREY	KNELLER	, A DUTCHMAN OF 34, WELL DRESSED AND ARROGANT. THEY
KING I (199)	WITH YOU THIS MORNING TO COME ON HERE. MR GODFREY	KNELLER	, THE NEW DUTCH PAINTER, WITH A LOAD OF IMPLEMENTS
KING I (214)	FULFIL BEFORE WE GO. I MUST RECONCILE HIM WITH MR	KNELLER	, WHO MUST PAINT HIS PORTRAIT TO HANG IN THE ROOMS
KING I (213)	/CHARLES/ SO YOU, TOO, ARE A PHILOSOPHER, MR	KNELLER	! /KNELLER/ SIR: WHEN A MAN HAS THE GIFT OF A

KNELT

LION I (120)	I NEVER HAD A HAPPY MOMENT AFTER THAT UNTIL I HAD	KNELT	AND ASKED HIS FORGIVENESS BY HIS BEDSIDE IN THE
MTH4 II (177)	WHICH EVEN YOU DESPISE? /NAPOLEON/ (RISING) I	KNELT	IN SPITE OF MYSELF. I COMPLIMENT YOU ON YOUR
2TRU III (111)	OUR CREEDS: IN THE DESECRATED TEMPLES WHERE WE	KNELT	MURMURING " I BELIEVE" WE STAND WITH STIFF KNEES AND
CLEO IV (171)	THAT IS ALL. /CLEOPATRA/ FOR THAT YOU WOULD HAVE	KNELT	TO CAESAR. NO, POTHINUS: YOU CAME WITH SOME PLAN THAT

KNEW

BARB PREFACE(225)	THE CROSS, HE WAS PERHAPS BETTER INSPIRED THAN HE	KNEW	: SUCH KNOWLEDGE, FOR THE DAUGHTER OF ANDREW
MIS. (128)	YOU? /BENTLEY/ YES. THATS AN IDEA OF MINE. I	KNEW	A CHAP NAMED JOEY PERCIVAL AT OXFORD (YOU KNOW I WAS
MIS. PREFACE(23)	GREEK. WHEN I WENT THERE AS A VERY SMALL BOY I	KNEW	A GOOD DEAL OF LATIN GRAMMAR WHICH I HAD BEEN TAUGHT IN
GETT (278)	SHE KNEW NO MORE ABOUT LIFE THAN A CHILD. /LEO/ I	KNEW	A GREAT DEAL MORE ABOUT IT THAN A GREAT BABY LIKE YOU.
DOCT III (142)	ARGUMENT THEY FALL BACK ON INTIMIDATION. I NEVER	KNEW	A LAWYER YET WHO DIDNT THREATEN TO PUT ME IN PRISON
PYGM EPILOG (299)	PRETENTIOUS, AND THOROUGHLY INEFFICIENT SCHOOLS,	KNEW	A LITTLE LATIN. IT WAS VERY LITTLE, BUT ENOUGH TO MAKE
JITT III (63)	WRETCHED NIGHT; BUT SHE NEVER CAN RESIST THEM. I	KNEW	A MAN WHO WAS MARRIED THREE TIMES; AND EVERY ONE OF HIS
FABL PREFACE(72)	THEY MAY BE WORSE THAN NO SCHEME AT ALL. I	KNEW	A MAN WHOSE YOUTH WAS MADE MISERABLE BY A DREAD OF HELL
LIED (203)	RORY? THEY CANT RESIST YOU: NONE OF EM. NEVER	KNEW	A MAN YET THAT COULD HOLD OUT THREE DAYS. /SHE/ DONT BE
DOCT III (142)	TO PUT ME IN PRISON SOONER OR LATER. I NEVER	KNEW	A PARSON WHO DIDNT THREATEN ME WITH DAMNATION. AND NOW
GENV III (74)	HAVE BOLSHEVIKS NO DECENCY? /THE NEWCOMER/ I	KNEW	A PRIEST ONCE WHO-- /THE SECRETARY/ NO, PLEASE. THE
WIDO III (60)	THE VESTRIES USED TO BE US OURSELVES. NOBODY EVER	KNEW	A WORD ABOUT THE ELECTION; AND WE USED TO GET TEN OF US
JOAN PREFACE(49)	ABOUT THESE MEN AND THEIR CIRCLE THAN SHAKESPEAR	KNEW	ABOUT FALCONBRIDGE AND THE DUKE OF AUSTRIA, OR ABOUT
JITT II (29)	DIDNT YOU KNOW THAT HE WAS ILL? /LENKHEIM/ OH, I	KNEW	ABOUT HIS HEART AND SO FORTH. BUT MANY A PATIENT WITH
MRS II (214)	OFF WATERLOO BRIDGE. POOR FOOL: THAT WAS ALL HE	KNEW	ABOUT IT! BUT I WAS MORE AFRAID OF THE WHITELEAD
DEVL EPILOG (81)	HAD NOT BEEN INTERFERED WITH, AND THAT NOBODY	KNEW	ABOUT THE OVERSIGHT OF THE DISPATCH. THE POLICY OF THE
BARB PREFACE(208)	STRANGE AND SIGNIFICANT, THOUGH I ALREADY	KNEW	ALL ABOUT ALNASCHAR AND DON QUIXOTE AND SIMON TAPPERTIT
PYGM V (275)	SHE'D BEEN. /HIGGINS/ (IMPATIENTLY) BUT SHE	KNEW	ALL ABOUT THAT. WE DIDNT MAKE SPEECHES TO HER, IF THATS
INCA (254)	DINNER. I NEVER FORGET A FACE. /ERMYNTRUDE/ YOU	KNEW	ALL ALONG! /THE INCA/ (BITTERLY, THROWING HIMSELF
JOAN PREFACE(26)	NOT KNOW WHAT EVERYBODY KNOWS. I WISH EVERYBODY	KNEW	ALL THAT HE KNOWS. ONE FEELS ANTIPATHIES AT WORK IN HIS
O'FL (213)	OR ANY OTHER CHRISTIANS. OH, HER LADYSHIP NEVER	KNEW	ALL THAT WAS GOING ON BEHIND HER BACK: HOW WOULD SHE..
MTH3 (92)	WHATS WRONG NOW? /BARNABAS/ IF YOU ONLY	KNEW	ALL THE PROTESTS I HAVNT MADE, YOU WOULD BE SURPRISED
O'FL (206)	" BEDAD, MAM," I SAYS TO HER, " IF THE GENERAL	KNEW	ALL THE RABBITS I SNARED ON HIM, AND ALL THE SALMON I
SIM II (83)	GOOD. THAT IS EXACTLY WHAT I AM. /PROLA/ BUT I	KNEW	ALSO THAT NOBODY BUT A FOOL WOULD BE FRIVOLOUS ENOUGH
FANY II (287)	HAD HAPPENED. IT SEEMS UNNATURAL, AS IF THEY ALL	KNEW	AND DIDNT CARE. /MRS KNOX/ IF THEY KNEW, JO, THERED BE
DEST (191)	YOU HADNT. THATS THE MEANEST THING I EVER	KNEW	ANY MAN DO; BUT IT EXACTLY FULFILLED YOUR PURPOSE; AND
DOCT II (122)	HE SAID THAT THE JEWS WERE THE ONLY PEOPLE WHO	KNEW	ANYTHING ABOUT ART, AND THAT THOUGH HE HAD TO PUT UP
MILL IV (197)	IN THREE HARLEY STREET SURGEONS; AND NONE OF THEM	KNEW	ANYTHING ABOUT DISLOCATED KNEES: THEY WANTED TO CUT MY
LION I (117)	LETS CHAFF THEM. /METELLUS/ AWFUL BRUTES. IF YOU	KNEW	AS MUCH ABOUT THEM AS I DO YOU WOULDNT WANT TO CHAFF
JOAN PREFACE(10)	WAS NOT ILLITERATE. HE HAD BEEN TO SCHOOL, AND	KNEW	AS MUCH LATIN AND GREEK AS MOST UNIVERSITY PASSMEN
METH PREFACE(R30)	BEGAN TO CULTIVATE THEM. MY PRE-DARWINIAN UNCLE	KNEW	AS WELL AS DARWIN THAT THE RACE-HORSE AND THE
JITT II (44)	COLLABORATOR! WHAT ARE YOU TALKING ABOUT? HE	KNEW	AS WELL AS I DID THAT I WAS ONLY WAITING FOR THE
GLIM (187)	I WAS FORCED AT LAST TO BELIEVE IN GRIM DEATH I	KNEW	AT LAST WHAT BELIEF WAS, AND THAT I HAD NEVER BELIEVED
HART PREFACE(14)	BE EXPECTED TO KEEP HER TEMPER SWEET WHEN SHE	KNEW	AT LAST WHAT IT WAS TO HIDE IN CELLARS AND UNDERGROUND
BASH II,1, (106)	MY HEAPED-UP STAKES, MY UNDEFEATED RECORD; BUT I	KNEW	BEHIND THEIR BLAZE A HATEFUL SECRET LURKED. /LYDIA/
SUPR I (19)	DISAPPROVE. I ACCEPT IT. MY FATHER LOVED ME AND	KNEW	BEST WHAT WAS GOOD FOR ME. /RAMSDEN/ OF COURSE I
AUGS PREFACE(261)	PRESTIGE. BUT OUR GOVERNMENT DEPARTMENTS	KNEW	BETTER: THEIR PROBLEM WAS HOW TO WIN THE WAR WITH
METH PREFACE(R21)	THEN LIVING WHO KNEW BETTER. LINNAEUS HIMSELF	KNEW	BETTER BEFORE HE DIED. IN THE LAST EDITION OF HIS
JITT II (51)	HE WISHED IT: THAT IS ENOUGH FOR ME. HE	KNEW	BETTER THAN EITHER OF US WHAT IS BEST FOR US.

FABL PREFACE(73)	ON THE OTHER HAND IF GALILEO, THE MAN OF SCIENCE,	KNEW	BETTER THAN JOSHUA, AND LINNEUS AND DARWIN BETTER THAN
JITT III (66)	HIM. I COULDNT. /JITTA/ OH NO, MRS HALDENSTEDT: I	KNEW	BETTER THAN THAT. NOTHING ANNOYS A MAN MORE THAN A
BULL PREFACE(59)	TO TELL THE TRUTH IN THIS FASHION. THE PRISONERS	KNEW	BETTER THAN TO ATTEMPT IT. ON THE SCAFFOLD, DARWEESH
BULL PREFACE(51)	COULD GET FROM THE OMDEH'S DEPUTY, WHO	KNEW	BETTER THAN TO DARE AN ABSOLUTE REFUSAL, WAS THE PRETTY
JITT PREFACE(3)	OUTSIDE RECOGNIZED THEATRICAL COMMERCE. TREBITSCH	KNEW	BETTER. HE ALSO KNEW ENGLISH. HE WAS QUITE UNKNOWN TO
METH PREFACE(R21)	FANCIERS, AND STOCK BREEDERS THEN LIVING WHO	KNEW	BETTER. LINNAEUS HIMSELF KNEW BETTER BEFORE HE DIED. IN
INCA PREFACE(231)	TO BE TRIFLING HEARTLESSLY WITH A DEADLY PERIL. I	KNEW	BETTER; AND I HAVE REPRESENTED CAESAR AS KNOWING BETTER
METH PREFACE(R9)	BUFFON. EVERY LITERATE CHILD AT THAT TIME	KNEW	BUFFON'S NATURAL HISTORY AS WELL AS ESOP'S FABLES. AND
O'FL PREFACE(202)	SIMPLY TO THE BUSINESS OF OBTAINING RECRUITS. I	KNEW	BY PERSONAL EXPERIENCE AND OBSERVATION WHAT ANYONE
CLEO PRO1 (90)	UNTIL THEY BECAME GREAT MASTERS OF THAT ART, AND	KNEW	BY WHAT LAWS IT COULD BE MADE TO APPEAR SEEMLY AND
METH PREFACE(R11)	OFF BY THIS SPECIALIZATION FROM THE MAJORITY WHO	KNEW	DARWIN ONLY BY HIS SPURIOUS REPUTATION, THAT THEY WERE
PHIL I (86)	THEY NEVER SAID A WORD OF IT TO US. WE TWO, WHO	KNEW	EACH OTHER BEFORE THEY WERE BORN, MIGHT NEVER HAVE MET
HART I (53)	DUNN. MAZZINI WAS A CELEBRITY OF SOME KIND WHO	KNEW	ELLIE'S GRANDPARENTS. THEY WERE BOTH POETS, LIKE THE
JITT PREFACE(3)	COMMERCE. TREBITSCH KNEW BETTER. HE ALSO	KNEW	ENGLISH. HE WAS QUITE UNKNOWN TO ME WHEN HE APPEARED
SUPR II (52)	WANT TO SPEAK TO YOU ABOUT ANN. /TANNER/ STRAKER	KNEW	EVEN THAT. HE LEARNT IT AT THE POLYTECHNIC, PROBABLY.
JITT III (57)	/AGNES/ I CANT SEE ANYTHING CLEARLY. I THOUGHT I	KNEW	EVERYBODY THAT IT COULD POSSIBLY BE; BUT THERE'S
MIS. PREFACE(47)	BECAUSE THEIR PARENTS AND GUARDIANS AND TEACHERS	KNEW	EVERYTHING SO MUCH BETTER THAN SOCRATES OR SOLON? IT
KING I (213)	A BOATSWAIN ONCE IN MY FLAGSHIP WHO THOUGHT HE	KNEW	EVERYTHING. /FOX/ PERHAPS HE DID. DIVINE GRACE TAKES
MILL I (160)	TOURING RIGHTS, ALL SORTS OF RIGHTS THAT I NEVER	KNEW	EXISTED, AND BEGAN SELLING THEM TO ONE ANOTHER UNTIL
DEVL I (25)	I WAS BROUGHT UP IN THE OTHER SERVICE; BUT I	KNEW	FROM THE FIRST THAT THE DEVIL WAS MY NATURAL MASTER AND
SIM II (83)	A HELP OR A HINDRANCE? /PROLA/ PRA: I ALWAYS	KNEW	FROM THE VERY BEGINNING THAT YOU WERE AN
SUPR PREFACE(R33)	PROJECTIONS OF THE DEEPEST HUMANITY HE	KNEW	HAVE THE SAME DEFECT: THEIR CHARACTERS AND MANNERS ARE
JITT II (34)	TO UPHOLD, MY DEAR EDITH, BELIEVE ME. /AGNES/ HE	KNEW	HE COULD DEPEND ON YOU. I HAVE A PACKET OF PAPERS
FANY I (278)	IT; BUT HE COULDNT AFFORD IT, POOR LAD, THOUGH I	KNEW	HE JUST LONGED TO GIVE IT TO ME. /GILBEY/ MARIA: IF YOU
NEVR II (232)	WHATEVER IT IS. HE SAID I WAS LIKE HIS MOTHER. I	KNEW	HE MUST MEAN HIS DAUGHTER. /PHILIP/ (VERY SERIOUSLY)
CAPT III (284)	NEVER SEE SIR HOWRRD AGAIN, BECAUSE HIS MASTER	KNEW	HE WAS A CHRISTIAN AND WOULD TAKE HIM OUT OF THE HANDS
MIS. (166)	STAND THERE BY HER OPEN GRAVE AND DENY THAT YOU	KNEW	HER? /TARLETON/ (TRYING TO RECOLLECT) WHAT DID YOU
SUPR I (8)	ARE, HE WILL ALWAYS BE WELCOME BECAUSE HE	KNEW	HER DEAR FATHER. /RAMSDEN/ (OUT OF PATIENCE) THAT
MTH2 (70)	WAS GOVERNED ALL THAT TIME BY A LITTLE WOMAN WHO	KNEW	HER OWN MIND? /SAVVY/ HEAR, HEAR! /LUBIN/ THAT OFTEN
CLEO PRO1 (92)	FATHERS IN THE DAYS WHEN ENGLAND WAS LITTLE, AND	KNEW	HER OWN MIND, AND HAD A MIND TO KNOW INSTEAD OF A
FANY PROLOG (261)	TOLD ME I GOT THE IDEA THAT YOUR DAUGHTER	KNEW	HER WAY ABOUT HERE, AND HAD SEEN A LOT OF PLAYS. HE HAD
JOAN EPILOG (154)	ALL RIGHT IN THE END: SHE WAS NOT THAT SORT: I	KNEW	HER. IS HER REHABILITATION COMPLETE? I MADE IT PRETTY
PHIL III (141)	IVE PERSECUTED HER WITH MY ADDRESSES EVER SINCE I	KNEW	HER. IT'S BEEN NO USE: SHE UTTERLY DESPISES ME. A
MIS. (167)	PICTURES. GOOD BOY! /THE MAN/ ONE OF THEM AS YOU	KNEW	HER. THE OTHER AS SHE BECAME WHEN YOU FLUNG HER ASIDE.
ROCK I (213)	WE BROUGHT TOFFY HERE, SIR ARTHUR, BECAUSE WE	KNEW	HE'D SPEAK TO YOU AS A DOCK LABORER WOULD SPEAK TO YOU
APPL PREFACE(191)	GATTIE, WITH WHOM I WAS PERSONALLY ACQUAINTED. I	KNEW	HIM FIRST AS THE AUTHOR OF A PLAY. HE WAS A DISTURBING
DOCT V (172)	THE PORTRAIT FRONTISPIECE). AY: THERE HE IS. YOU	KNEW	HIM HERE, I SUPPOSE. /THE SECRETARY/ OH, WE KNEW HIM.
APPL I (197)	MY JOB HERE IN THE PALACE. ALL OUR ROYAL PEOPLE	KNEW	HIM QUITE WELL: HE WAS BEHIND THE SCENES WITH THEM.
ROCK I (218)	DR MARX-- KARL MARX THEY CALL HIM NOW-- MY FATHER	KNEW	HIM WELL-- THOUGHT THAT WHEN HE'D EXPLAINED THE
PYGM PREFACE(200)	BUT HE WOULD NOT SUFFER FOOLS GLADLY. THOSE WHO	KNEW	HIM WILL RECOGNIZE IN MY THIRD ACT THE ALLUSION TO THE
DOCT V (172)	KNEW HIM HERE, I SUPPOSE. /THE SECRETARY/ OH, WE	KNEW	HIM. BETTER THAN SHE DID. SIR COLENSO, IN SOME WAYS,
JITT III (73)	YES. YOU HAVE BEEN A DAUGHTER TO ME EVER SINCE I	KNEW	HIM. BUT WE MUST BE VERY CAREFUL, VERY DISCREET. YOU
MTH3 (112)	WHEN HE WAS BETWEEN SIXTY AND SEVENTY. I	KNEW	HIM. /BURGE-LUBIN/ (DEPRESSED) AH! BUT HE DIED. /THE
SIM II (59)	PEACE. /VASHTI/ LET HIM BE AS HE WAS BEFORE WE	KNEW	HIM. /MAYA/ WHEN WE WERE HAPPY. /VASHTI/ WHEN HE WAS
LION PREFACE(24)	POLITICALLY. THE JEW AS JESUS, HIMSELF A JEW,	KNEW	HIM, NEVER DREAMT OF SUCH THINGS, AND COULD FOLLOW
3PLA PREFACE(R33)	WHO NEVER COULD BE PERSUADED THAT SHAKESPEAR	KNEW	HIS BUSINESS BETTER THAN THEY, HAVE EVER BEEN THE MOST
JITT II (37)	DID NOT SEE YOU. JUST THINK. HE WAS A DOCTOR: HE	KNEW	HIS DANGER BETTER THAN ANYONE. WHEN A MAN FINDS HIMSELF
CYMB V (140)	A TRAITOR, MUST HAVE BEEN RECALLED. THAT FELLOW	KNEW	HIS JOB. THESE FAT CIVILIANS WHEN WE'RE AT PEACE, ROB
MTH4 III (200)	FRAUD. /THE ENVOY/ HE WAS CAPABLE OF ANYTHING: I	KNEW	HIS PRIVATE SECRETARY. AND NOW WHAT ARE WE GOING TO
BULL I (84)	HIS FATHER, WHO CAME FROM MY PART OF IRELAND. I	KNEW	HIS UNCLES, MATT AND ANDY HAFFIGAN OF ROSSCULLEN.
BULL III (124)	UNDER A MORAL OBLIGATION OR I AM NOT. I WISH I	KNEW	HOW DRUNK I WAS. /LARRY/ WELL, YOU WERE EVIDENTLY IN A
NEVR I (212)	BY A GIBE FROM HER) MY DEAR DOLLY: IF YOU ONLY	KNEW	HOW GLAD I AM THAT IT IS NOTHING BUT A JOKE TO YOU,
WIDO II (26)	NOT THAT I MAKE MUCH ACCOUNT OF HIM; BUT IF YOU	KNEW	HOW HE HAS WORRIED ME OVER THAT STAIRCASE-- /SARTORIUS/
DEST (160)	IT NEAR THE TABLE AND SITS DOWN). IF YOU ONLY	KNEW	HOW HUNGRY AND TIRED I AM, YOUD HAVE MORE
FANY PROLOG (267)	NERVOUS THAN I AM ALREADY, MR TROTTER. IF YOU	KNEW	HOW I FEEL! /TROTTER/ NATURALLY: YOUR FIRST PARTY:
JITT II (38)	(RESTLESS AGAIN, PACING UP AND DOWN). OH, IF YOU	KNEW	HOW INFAMOUSLY ALL THOSE PEOPLE WHO CALL ON US
MRS PREFACE(153)	BE MORE NEEDED THAN I KNEW; AND YET I THOUGHT I	KNEW	HOW LITTLE THE OTHERS KNOW. DO NOT SUPPOSE, HOWEVER,
MTH3 (98)	BIG DOG; AND HE IS THE BEST FELLOW I KNOW. IF YOU	KNEW	HOW MUCH UGLIER YOU ARE THAN A CHOW, YOU WOULDNT START
LIED (194)	AFTER BREAKING MY PET FAN, I THINK. /HE/ IF YOU	KNEW	HOW NEAR I WAS TO BREAKING TEDDY'S PET WIFE AND
VWOO 3 (138)	TEMPER AGAIN. /Z/ I WILL IF I LIKE. AND IF YOU	KNEW	HOW NEAR I WAS TO PUTTING A COUPLE OF EXTRA WORDS IN,
CLEO III (156)	A MAD EXPEDITION. WE SHALL BE BEATEN. I WISH I	KNEW	HOW OUR MEN ARE GETTING ON WITH THAT BARRICADE ACROSS
BUOY IV (53)	OF YOU. /JUNIUS/ YOU THINK SO. BUT IF YOU ONLY	KNEW	HOW QUICKLY I CAN LOSE MONEY. HE CAN ONLY MAKE IT. /OLD
HART PREFACE(11)	WAS LEFT TO IT WAS THE BOAST THAT AT LEAST IT	KNEW	HOW TO DIE: A MELANCHOLY ACCOMPLISHMENT WHICH THE
CLEO IV (175)	AND FENCE A BIT: HE MIGHT BE WORSE, IF HE ONLY	KNEW	HOW TO HOLD HIS TONGUE. /CAESAR/ THE GODS FORBID HE
KING II (228)	CAPABLE KING THREE OR FOUR TIMES OVER, IF ONLY WE	KNEW	HOW TO PICK THEM. NOBODY HAS FOUND OUT HOW TO DO IT:
KING II (229)	BUT THEY ARE MOSTLY IN PRISON. IF WE ONLY	KNEW	HOW TO PICK THEM OUT AND LABEL THEM, THEN THE PEOPLE
PRES (165)	THE SIDE OF THE HEAD FOR TELLIN ME THAT IF I ONLY	KNEW	HOW TO PLAY ME CARDS I COULD MARRY ANY GENERAL ON THE
O'FL (215)	GREAT MEN WAS IRISH. SHE SAYS THE ENGLISH NEVER	KNEW	HOW TO READ THEIR OWN BOOKS UNTIL WE TAUGHT THEM. SHE
MRS II (217)	ARE IN THE GUTTER? BECAUSE I ALWAYS	KNEW	HOW TO RESPECT MYSELF AND CONTROL MYSELF. WHY IS LIZ
KING I (190)	OF THAT UNDER OLD NOLL'S MAJOR-GENERALS. NOLL	KNEW	HOW TO RULE: I WILL SAY THAT FOR HIM; AND I THANK HIM
FANY PROLOG (262)	THE NOTION OF HAVING CRITICS WAS NEW. I HARDLY	KNEW	HOW TO SET ABOUT IT. THEY DONT EXPECT PRIVATE
HART III (134)	OWN POCKET. THE SYNDICATE FOUND THE MONEY: THEY	KNEW	HOW USEFUL I SHOULD BE TO THEM IN THE GOVERNMENT. /LADY
MIS. PREFACE(77)	ALDGATE PUMP. TO OTHERS, WHO WOULD MOVE IF THEY	KNEW	HOW, TRAVELLING IS SURROUNDED WITH IMAGINARY
3PLA PREFACE(R32)	WHO KNEW HUMAN WEAKNESS SO WELL, NEVER	KNEW	HUMAN STRENGTH OF THE CAESARIAN TYPE. HIS CAESAR IS AN
3PLA PREFACE(R32)	HAS BEEN BEFOREHAND. BUT SHAKESPEAR, WHO	KNEW	HUMAN WEAKNESS SO WELL, NEVER KNEW HUMAN STRENGTH OF
BULL IV (146)	KEEGAN GLARES AT THEM). BEFORE BROADBINT	KNEW	WHERE HE WAS, THE PIG WAS UP HIS BACK AND OVER INTO HIS
MIS. PREFACE(39)	THE MASTER NEVER ASKED ME TO DO IT BECAUSE HE	KNEW	I COULD, AND THEREFORE DEVOTED HIMSELF TO TRAPPING THE
MIS. (139)	WANTED OR NOT, BECAUSE WHEN I READ YOUR LETTER I	KNEW	I HAD TO COME. /HYPATIA/ WHY? /LORD SUMMERHAYS/ OH
ROCK I (220)	1917. /SIR ARTHUR/ I MUST READ MARX, MR HIPNEY. I	KNEW	I HAD TO DEAL WITH A SENTIMENTAL REVOLT AGAINST
MTH4 I (162)	WILL LAST YOUR TIME: IT WILL NOT LAST MINE. IF I	KNEW	I HAD TO DIE IN TWENTY YEARS IT WOULD NOT BE WORTH MY
FANY I (278)	GOLD KEYS AND RUSSIA LEATHER BELLOWS; AND BOBBY	KNEW	I HANKERED AFTER IT; BUT HE COULDNT AFFORD IT, POOR
OVER (173)	YOU BEGAN MAKING LOVE TO ME. /GREGORY/ BUT YOU	KNEW	I LOVED YOU ALL ALONG. /MRS JUNO/ YES, OF COURSE; BUT I
DOCT II (122)	POWER TO SAY NO, MR SCHUTZMACHER. OF COURSE, I	KNEW	I OUGHTNT TO LEND MONEY TO A YOUNG FELLOW IN THAT WAY;
PHIL I (72)	MY BETTER SELF THAT WAS SPEAKING, AND THAT SHE	KNEW	I STILL REALLY LOVED HER. WHEN I WROTE IT TO HER WITH
MTH5 (221)	IS THAT TRUE, OR IS IT NOT? /ARJILLAX/ EVERYBODY	KNEW	I WAS AN EXTRAORDINARY PERSON. WHEN I WAS BORN MY BEARD
CAPT III (282)	IN, AS YOU WERE ANXIOUS TO SEE HER AGAIN. THEN I	KNEW	I WAS IN TIME. /KEARNEY/ OH, THAT WAS IT, WAS IT? MAY
ROCK I (225)	HAVE BEEN DYING A LONG TIME. /SIR ARTHUR/ WELL, I	KNEW	I WAS OVERWORKING: BURNING THE CANDLE AT BOTH ENDS:
MTH5 (243)	FEEBLY TOWARDS HER UNTIL HE REACHES HER HAND) I	KNEW	I WAS REALLY A KING OF KINGS. (TO THE OTHERS)
JITT III (73)	WHO BETTER COULD IT BE? OF COURSE IT WAS YOU. I	KNEW	IT ALL ALONG, ONLY I COULDNT RECOLLECT. OH, DARLING!
JITT II (36)	WE WERE LEFT IN THE DARK. /JITTA/ NO, NO. NO ONE	KNEW	IT EXCEPT HIMSELF. /EDITH/ (PASSIONATELY) MY MOTHER
MTH2 (56)	FOR THE FIRST TIME) YOURE RIGHT: IT WAS. I	KNEW	IT HAD SOMETHING TO DO WITH WOMEN. MY MEMORY NEVER
SUPR I (46)	HAVE ALL BEEN TALKING ABOUT ME! IF MY HUSBAND	KNEW	IT HE WOULD NEVER LET ME SPEAK TO ANY OF YOU AGAIN. (
ROCK II (282)	THE WHOLE SHOW GOING WERE NOT WORTH LIVING. I	KNEW	IT QUITE WELL; BUT I WAS ABLE TO PUT IT OUT OF MY MIND
2TRU I (30)	WHO KNOWS HER CONSTITUTION. DEAR OLD DR NEWLAND	KNEW	IT SO WELL FROM HER VERY BIRTH. /THE DOCTOR/
ARMS I (5)	SO SELDOM LIKE THAT! INDEED NEVER, AS FAR AS I	KNEW	IT THEN. (REMORSEFULLY) ONLY THINK, MOTHER: I DOUBTED
SUPR I (15)	AN ADVANCED MAN BEFORE YOU WERE BORN. /TANNER/ I	KNEW	IT WAS A LONG TIME AGO. /RAMSDEN/ I AM AS ADVANCED AS
ARMS I (16)	GOT WIND OF THE CARTRIDGE BUSINESS SOMEHOW, AND	KNEW	IT WAS A SAFE JOB. /RAINA/ THAT IS TO SAY, HE WAS A
LION I (116)	THANK YOU FOR TRYING TO SAVE ME. /THE CAPTAIN/ I	KNEW	IT WAS NO USE; BUT ONE TRIES IN SPITE OF ONE'S
PHIL II (116)	DAD, YOU MAY BET. (COMING TO CRAVEN) BESIDES, I	KNEW	IT WAS NONSENSE ALL ALONG. (PETTING HIM) POOR DEAR OLD
MTH2 (54)	(NOT AT ALL PUT OUT) YES: YOU ARE QUITE RIGHT. I	KNEW	IT WAS SOMETHING ABOUT AMERICA. (HE PATS FRANKLYN'S
CAPT II (258)	/LADY CICELY/ NO: I DONT SUPPOSE YOU EVEN	KNEW	IT WAS TORN. SOME MEN ARE BORN UNTIDY. YOU CANNOT VERY
DEVL I SD(17)	SOMETHING THAT WOULD CHANGE THEIR TUNE IF THEY	KNEW	IT. ANDERSON IS UNEASY: THE LOVE OF SOLEMN FAMILY
DEVL II (32)	FONDER OF RICHARD THAN YOU ARE OF ME, IF YOU ONLY	KNEW	IT. EH! /JUDITH/ OH, DONT SAY THAT: DONT SAY THAT,
PHIL II (98)	MAY AS WELL MAKE A CLEAN BREAST OF IT: EVERYBODY	KNEW	IT. I MARRIED FOR MONEY. /CUTHBERTSON/ (ENCOURAGINGLY)
SUPR III (92)	! ! /DON JUAN/ NO: HE IS IN HEAVEN. /ANA/ I	KNEW	IT. MY NOBLE FATHER! HE IS LOOKING DOWN ON US NOW.
PHIL II (116)	SHOULDER). /SYLVIA/ (CONTEMPTUOUSLY) I	KNEW	IT. OF COURSE IT WAS NOTHING BUT EATING TOO MUCH. I
NEVR II (232)	HER PERPLEXEDLY. /DOLLY/ (WITH CONVICTION) I	KNEW	IT. PHIL: CHALKSTONES IS OUR FATHER! /M'COMAS/

JITT III (59)	AN EXCELLENT WIFE TO HIM, MRS HALDENSTEDT; AND HE	KNEW	IT. /AGNES/ I DONT SAY I WASNT. BUT SHE HADNT TO KEEP
PHIL III (139)	ME. I WAS LIKE A CHILD IN YOUR HANDS; AND YOU	KNEW	IT. /CHARTERIS/ YES, MY DEAR. THAT MEANS THAT WHENEVER
KING I (169)	THAT IS BECAUSE IT IS IN THE HOLY BIBLE! I NEVER	KNEW	IT. /NEWTON/ ON REFLECTION, THE SUN HAS STOPPED THREE
FANY III (312)	EVER TELL YOU MY FATHER DRANK? /KNOX/ NO. BUT I	KNEW	IT. SIMMONS TOLD ME. /GILBEY/ YES: HE NEVER COULD KEEP
GENV III (77)	THE TRUEST FRIEND OF ALL THE POWERS IF THEY ONLY	KNEW	IT. THAT IS THE STRENGTH OF MY POSITION HERE. EACH OF
DEVL I (10)	HAVE DONE IT IF I HAD BEEN WITH HIM; AND WELL HE	KNEW	IT. THAT WAS WHY HE STOLE AWAY LIKE A THIEF TO TAKE
CATH 2 (179)	REVIEW, MADAM. /VARINKA/ (TRIUMPHANTLY) AHA! I	KNEW	IT. YOUR MAJESTY WORE THE HUSSAR UNIFORM. HE SAW HOW
CLEO PRO1 (90)	ITS MIND WAS LITTLE AND ITS WORK WAS SIMPLE. IT	KNEW	ITS OWN MIND AND DID ITS OWN WORK; AND THE GODS PITIED
GENV II (62)	MADE THE MOST AWFUL EXHIBITION OF HIMSELF. AND HE	KNEW	IT, POOR LAMB, AND WOULD NEVER HAVE GONE IN FOR IT IF
METH PREFACE(R20)	I KNEW PERFECTLY WELL, WITHOUT KNOWING THAT I	KNEW	IT, THAT THE VALIDITY OF A STORY IS NOT THE SAME AS THE
DEVL II (32)	POOH! HAVENT YOU OFTEN THOUGHT THAT IF THEY ONLY	KNEW	IT, THEY WERE BETTER FRIENDS TO THEIR ENEMIES THAN TO
FANY I (276)	A MONSIGNOR! AND YOURE CATHOLICS! AND I NEVER	KNEW	IT, THOUGH IVE KNOWN BOBBY EVER SO LONG! BUT OF COURSE
OVER PREFACE(165)	SIMULATIVE ILLUSION. THE THEATRE, AS I FIRST	KNEW	IT, WAS A PLACE OF WINGS AND FLATS WHICH DESTROYED BOTH
MRS I (185)	WHAT A MONSTROUS, WICKED, RASCALLY SYSTEM! I	KNEW	IT! I FELT AT ONCE THAT IT MEANT DESTROYING ALL THAT
ARMS I (15)	(BREATHLESS, FORGIVING HIM EVERYTHING) AH, I	KNEW	IT! TELL ME. TELL ME ABOUT HIM. /THE MAN/ HE DID IT
KING I (194)	WHAT I KNOW, AND NOT WITH WHAT PETER AND MARTIN	KNEW	. ANYHOW, THE LONG AND THE SHORT OF IT IS THAT YOU MUST
SIM I (41)	IT IS THE CHRISTIAN RELIGION. I THOUGHT EVERYBODY	KNEW	. BUT THEN OF COURSE YOU ARE A HEATHEN. /PROLA/ WHAT
JITT III (61)	WHAT HAVE YOU DONE? /EDITH/ (COOLLY) TOLD HER I	KNEW	. I HAD TO. /FESSLER/ (CLOSING THE DOOR, AND COMING
2TRU I (43)	WHO IS AN ATHEIST, WOULD DISINHERIT ME IF HE	KNEW	. I WAS SECRETLY ORDAINED WHEN I WAS UP AT OXFORD. /THE
JITT III (74)	WITH HER WARM INTEREST IN EDITH) SHE GUESSED. SHE	KNEW	. IT IS NO USE KEEPING SECRETS WHEN THEY WILL NOT KEEP
CURE (227)	MUSTNT GAMBLE. /REGINALD/ BUT I WASNT GAMBLING. I	KNEW	. IT ISNT GAMBLING IF YOU KNOW THAT THE SHARES WILL GO
CAND III (128)	I'M EVER SO MUCH OLDER THAN YOU, IF YOU ONLY	KNEW	. (HE TURNS QUITE OVER ON HIS KNEES, WITH HIS HANDS
JITT III (60)	HEAD. I WONDER WHAT YOU WOULD SAY IF YOU REALLY	KNEW	. /EDITH/ (SCORNFULLY) IF I REALLY KNEW! DO YOU
JITT III (73)	THAT THEY WOULD NEVER SPEAK TO ME AGAIN IF THEY	KNEW	. /EDITH/ MORE SHAME FOR THEM! DO SUCH PEOPLE MATTER?
OVER (175)	AGAIN. /MRS JUNO/ I'M SORRY. I THOUGHT YOU	KNEW	. /GREGORY/ YOU THOUGHT I WAS A LIBERTINE? /MRS JUNO/
CAPT III (274)	SIR HOWARD'S NEPHEW, THE SON OF THE BROTHER YOU	KNEW	. /RANKIN/ (OVERWHELMED) I SAW THE LIKENESS THE NIGHT
BARB I (254)	KNOW THE UNDERSHAFT MOTTO: UNASHAMED. EVERYBODY	KNEW	. /STEPHEN/ BUT YOU SAID THAT WAS WHY YOU SEPARATED.
SUPR I (45)	US. /VIOLET/ YES: ANN HAS BEEN KIND; BUT THEN ANN	KNEW	. /TANNER/ (WITH A DESPERATE GESTURE) OH! ! !
VWOO 1 (118)	HOW DID YOU FIND OUT? /A/ I DIDNT FIND OUT. I	KNEW	. /Z/ WHO TOLD YOU? /A/ NOBODY TOLD ME. /Z/ THEN HOW
JITT I (24)	WHEN I CLIMBED THOSE TERRIBLE STAIRS JUST NOW, I	KNEW	. YOU WOULD HAVE TO GIVE YOUR NAME TO THE POLICE. OUR
PHIL I (78)	WAS SUCH SUFFERING IN MY HAPPINESS THAT I HARDLY	KNEW	JOY FROM PAIN. (SHE SINKS ON THE PIANO STOOL, AND
POSN PREFACE(415)	PERVERSE PARADOX WHEN I SAID THAT THE WITNESS WHO	KNEW	LEAST ABOUT THE THEATRE WAS HENRY IRVING. YET A
MIS. PREFACE(80)	OF OBSERVATION, DIVINATION, AND STORY-TELLING, HE	KNEW	LESS ABOUT HIS FATHER AND MOTHER THAN ABOUT MOST OF THE
HART PREFACE(5)	AS A RULE, HOWEVER, THE TWO WERE APART AND	KNEW	LITTLE OF ONE ANOTHER; SO THE PRIME MINISTER FOLK HAD
ARMS II (30)	A THING? /SERGIUS/ (WITH FIRE) EVERYONE THAT	KNEW	ME. BUT ENOUGH OF MYSELF AND MY AFFAIRS. HOW IS RAINA;
BULL II (100)	THE PEOPLE. /PATSY/ BUT WASNT IT ONLY BECAUSE YOU	KNEW	MORE LATN THAN FATHER DEMPSEY THAT HE WAS JEALOUS OF
HART III (144)	THOUGH THE PEOPLE IN THE SOCIETIES THOUGHT THEY	KNEW	MORE THAN MANGAN, MOST OF THEM WOULDNT HAVE JOINED IF
JOAN PREFACE(53)	WILL DOUBT THAT THIS IS WHAT WOULD HAPPEN IF I	KNEW	MY BUSINESS SO LITTLE AS TO LISTEN TO THESE WELL
PHIL III (142)	I WAS TAKEN ABACK; I WONT DENY IT. BUT I	KNEW	MY DUTY; AND I DID IT. I GAVE HER UP, AND WISHED
HART I (64)	AWAY FOR NEARLY A MONTH; AND I HAD NO IDEA YOU	KNEW	MY WIFE, OR THAT YOU WERE COMING HERE. I AM NONE THE
JOAN EPILOG (156)	NOW TELL ME WHAT HAS HAPPENED SINCE YOU WISE MEN	KNEW	NO BETTER THAN TO MAKE A HEAP OF CINDERS OF ME?
HART PREFACE(21)	DROPPING INTO HIS EGG-CUP, THEIR WRATH AND HORROR	KNEW	NO BOUNDS. THEY DECLARED THAT THIS WOULD PUT A NEW
MIS. PREFACE(98)	OUR CHILDREN LEFT THEM MORE LITERATE THAN IF THEY	KNEW	NO LITERATURE AT ALL, WHICH WAS THE PRACTICAL
GETT (278)	WOMAN. I HAD NO RIGHT AT MY AGE TO MARRY LEO: SHE	KNEW	NO MORE ABOUT LIFE THAN A CHILD. /LEO/ I KNEW A GREAT
MIS. PREFACE(57)	BY THE SAME MEANS. THESE CHILDREN, GROWN UP,	KNEW	NO OTHER METHODS OF TRAINING. FINALLY THE EVIL THAT WAS
BUOY III (36)	COMMAND OF MY SOUL. AND ALL FOR A MAN OF WHOM I	KNEW	NOTHING: A PASSING VAGABOND WHO HAD BEGGED A MEAL FROM
BUOY III (29)	I KNOW ALL ABOUT HOUSEKEEPING BECAUSE OUR MOTHER	KNEW	NOTHING ABOUT IT AND CARED LESS. SHE PREFERRED
ARMS II (31)	THESE FOREIGNERS HADNT SHEWN US HOW TO DO IT: WE	KNEW	NOTHING ABOUT IT; AND NEITHER DID THE SERBS. EGAD,
GENV PREFACE(4)	EMERGENCY. AS A MATTER OF FACT THE NATION	KNEW	NOTHING ABOUT IT. HAD WE BEEN TOLD, THE GERMANS WOULD
MIS. (141)	THINK OF IT! I WAS ENGAGED TO YOUR SON; AND YOU	KNEW	NOTHING ABOUT IT. HE WAS AFRAID TO TELL YOU: HE BROUGHT
MIS. (123)	ASKED ME WHAT SYSTEM I HAD. I SAID I WAS SURE I	KNEW	NOTHING ABOUT SUCH THINGS, AND HADNT WE BETTER CHANGE
FANY III (314)	GUIDED HER, AND WHAT HARM THERE WAS IN IT SHE	KNEW	NOTHING ABOUT. /GILBEY/ OH, COME, MRS KNOX! GIRLS ARE
MRS II (214)	OURSELVES TO BE SUPERIOR TO THE CHILDREN THAT	KNEW	NOTHING AND WENT NOWHERE-- AND WE STAYED THERE UNTIL
HART II (87)	HER HANDS) HOW STRANGE! THAT MY MOTHER, WHO	KNEW	NOTHING AT ALL ABOUT BUSINESS, SHOULD HAVE BEEN QUITE
PYGM EPILOG (300)	WITH BOTANICAL NOMENCLATURE. UNFORTUNATELY HE	KNEW	NOTHING ELSE; AND ELIZA, THOUGH SHE COULD COUNT MONEY
JOAN PREFACE(22)	THE WEIGHT AND PROPORTION OF SOCIAL FORCES. SHE	KNEW	NOTHING OF IRON HANDS IN VELVET GLOVES: SHE JUST USED
METH PREFACE(R52)	MUST HAVE KNOWN ABOUT THE BOUND FEET EVEN IF HE	KNEW	NOTHING OF THE MUTILATIONS, THE CLIPPED EARS AND DOCKED
LION PREFACE(18)	FOR SUSPECTING INTERPOLATION IS THAT ST PAUL	KNEW	NOTHING OF THE DIVINE BIRTH, AND TAUGHT THAT JESUS CAME
6CAL PREFACE(89)	HIS JOB TOO LIGHTLY. BUT THE JOURNALIST CRITICS	KNEW	NOTHING OF THIS. A KING EDWARD WHO DID NOT BEHAVE LIKE
GENV PREFACE(4)	FORTITUDE IN THE FACE OF THE DEADLY PERIL WE	KNEW	NOTHING OF. ALL THIS WAS NECESSARY AND INEVITABLE. IT
BARB PREFACE(208)	LANGUAGE I DO NOT KNOW THREE WORDS, AND OF WHOM I	KNEW	NOTHING UNTIL YEARS AFTER THE SHAVIAN ANSCHAUUNG WAS
MIS. PREFACE(80)	DAYS (I HAD ALMOST SAID OF FORTY MINUTES) THAN I	KNEW	OF MY MOTHER AT THE END OF FORTY YEARS. A CONTEMPORARY
MIS. (170)	DO WITH YOU? /TARLETON/ WELL, YOU SAY SHE AND I	KNEW	ONE ANOTHER AND PARTED. SHE MUST HAVE HAD SOMETHING OFF
SUPR III (139)	/OCTAVIUS/ WHY, VIOLET, I THOUGHT YOU HARDLY	KNEW	ONE ANOTHER BEFORE THIS TRIP, YOU AND MALONE! /VIOLET/
JITT I (17)	I MEAN THAT MY DAUGHTER-- BORN BEFORE WE	KNEW	ONE ANOTHER-- IS YOUR DAUGHTER. /JITTA/ EDITH! WHAT DO
MTHS (118)	THERE WERE OTHERS. DID YOU? /MRS LUTESTRING/ I	KNEW	ONE OTHER. SHE WAS A COOK. SHE GREW TIRED, AND KILLED
KING I (181)	OF ALL THREE OF US IS THAT IF THE COMMON PEOPLE	KNEW	OUR REAL MINDS THEY WOULD HANG US AND BURY US IN
ARMS III (62)	AFFIANCED HUSBAND BEHIND HIS. BLUNTSCHLI: YOU	KNEW	OUR RELATIONS; AND YOU DECEIVED ME. IT IS FOR THAT THAT
METH PREFACE(R20)	DID NOT PERPLEX MY INFANT MIND IN THE LEAST: I	KNEW	PERFECTLY WELL, WITHOUT KNOWING THAT I KNEW IT, THAT
MIS. PREFACE(106)	KNOW WHEN THEY WERE BEATEN, WHEREAS WELLINGTON	KNEW	PRECISELY WHEN HE WAS NOT BEATEN. THE UNBLUFFABLE WOULD
HART II (121)	BUT THE FATHER YOU GAVE ME IS IN THE KITCHEN. YOU	KNEW	QUITE WELL ALL ALONG. COME. (SHE DRAWS HIM OUT INTO
ARMS II (43)	HE SHEWS CAPTAIN BLUNTSCHLI OUT HERE WHEN HE	KNEW	QUITE WELL I WAS IN THE LIBRARY; AND THEN HE GOES
DOCT V (178)	I AM NOT ANGRY WITH YOU ANY MORE, SIR COLENSO. I	KNEW	QUITE WELL THAT YOU DID NOT LIKE LOUIS; BUT IT IS NOT
METH PREFACE(R9)	A COPY OF MAN AND SUPERMAN. AS IT WAS, SHE	KNEW	QUITE WELL WHAT HE WANTED; FOR THIS WAS BEFORE THE
MTH4 I (163)	NOW LISTEN TO ME, YOU LITTLE EPHEMERAL THING. I	KNEW	QUITE WELL WHAT YOU MEANT BY YOUR TORCH HANDED ON FROM
GETT (302)	WHAT MAN EVER HAS? I NEVER SUSPECTED-- I NEVER	KNEW	-- ARE YOU JOKING? OR HAVE WE ALL GONE MAD? /THE
CAPT II (255)	EXISTENCE. I AFFIRM THAT MOST SOLEMNLY. I NEVER	KNEW	-- NEVER DREAMT-- THAT MY BROTHER MILES LEFT A SON. AS
HART III (143)	ALL VERY WELL TO MAKE FUN OF ME; BUT IF YOU ONLY	KNEW	-- /HECTOR/ (IMPATIENTLY) HOW IS ALL THIS GOING TO
MTH2 (53)	BUT LUBIN! OH MY STARS, LUBIN! ! IF YOU ONLY	KNEW	-- THE PARLOR MAID OPENS THE DOOR AND ANNOUNCES A
MRS PREFACE(153)	IN IT". TRULY MY PLAY MUST BE MORE NEEDED THAN I	KNEW	; AND YET I THOUGHT I KNEW HOW LITTLE THE OTHERS KNOW.
CATH PREFACE(153)	DYNASTIC DIPLOMACY WHICH WAS THE ONLY WORLD SHE	KNEW	SHE WAS MORE THAN A MATCH FOR HIM AND FOR ALL THE REST
PYGM IV (261)	A BIT NERVOUS. /HIGGINS/ OH, SHE WASNT NERVOUS. I	KNEW	SHE'D BE ALL RIGHT. NO; IT'S THE STRAIN OF PUTTING THE
PRES (134)	BUT GEORGINA? /MITCHENER/ GEORGINA WOULD IF SHE	KNEW	SHE'D BE SHOT IF SHE DIDNT. THATS HOW THE THING WOULD
GENV II (53)	A COUNTY COUNCIL SCHOLARSHIP AND WAS EDUCATED AND	KNEW	SHORTHAND AND A BIT OF FRENCH AND ALL THAT, AND THAT I
METH PREFACE(R81)	BEAR IT, THE DULL DAUBS OF HILTON AND HAYDON, WHO	KNEW	SO MUCH MORE ABOUT DRAWING AND SCUMBLING AND GLAZING
MIS. (168)	RISES IN YOU AT THE SIGHT OF THE FACE YOU ONCE	KNEW	SO WELL? /TARLETON/ (TOO MUCH ABSORBED IN THE
DEVL I SD(16)	LOOKING OUT. HAWKINS SMILES SECRETIVELY AS IF HE	KNEW	SOMETHING THAT WOULD CHANGE THEIR TUNE IF THEY KNEW IT.
MIS. (111)	DIFFERENT. BY THE TIME I WAS BORN, THE OLD COUPLE	KNEW	SOMETHING. SO I CAME OUT ALL BRAINS AND NO MORE BODY
SUPR I (15)	DESIRE FOR THAT SORT OF NOTORIETY. BLESS YOU, I	KNEW	THAT ANSWER WOULD COME AS WELL AS I KNOW THAT A BOX OF
FABL PREFACE(71)	HOUSES IN WHICH CASES OF FEVER HAD OCCURRED, I	KNEW	THAT EXPERIMENTS HAD PROVED THAT THE FUMES OF BURNING
PYGM EPILOG (291)	OF THE MARRIED WOMAN). TO PUT IT SHORTLY, SHE	KNEW	THAT FOR SOME MYSTERIOUS REASON HE HAD NOT THE MAKINGS
CATH 2 (179)	THINGS. I SPEAK AS A PRACTICAL MAN. AND I NEVER	KNEW	THAT FOREIGNERS HAD ANY POLICY; I ALWAYS THOUGHT THAT
METH PREFACE(R30)	KNEW THAT THE SAME THING IS TRUE OF PIGEONS. HE	KNEW	THAT GARDENERS HAD SPENT THEIR LIVES TRYING TO BREED
PYGM EPILOG (302)	THERE WAS ANY SWANK ABOUT HIM: NOBODY BUT ELIZA	KNEW	THAT HE HAD BEEN CHRISTENED FREDERICK CHALLONER. ELIZA
MILL PREFACE(122)	DEFIANCE BY ANY WORD OF ARGUMENT OR DIPLOMACY. HE	KNEW	THAT HIS ATTITUDE WAS SAFE AND SURE OF SUCCESS; AND HE
POSN PREFACE(378)	INNOCENT LADY TOLD ME AFTERWARDS THAT SHE NEVER	KNEW	THAT I COULD SMILE SO BEAUTIFULLY, AND THAT SHE THOUGHT
JITT III (68)	AND CONTINUING) WELL, THAT VERY MOMENT I	KNEW	THAT I HAD BEEN BELIEVING ALL ALONG-- BUT I DONT THINK
AUGS (276)	AM GOING TO SAY TO YOU; FOR IF THE BRITISH PUBLIC	KNEW	THAT I HAD SAID IT, I SHOULD BE AT ONCE HOUNDED DOWN AS
SUPR III (101)	IT IS TRUE. FROM THE BEGINNING OF MY CAREER I	KNEW	THAT I SHOULD WIN IN THE LONG RUN BY SHEER WEIGHT OF
SUPR III (122)	GAVE IN AND ALLOWED ANA'S MOTHER TO MARRY ME-- I	KNEW	THAT I WAS PLANTING THORNS IN MY PILLOW, AND THAT
POSN PREFACE(370)	BEGINNING, THIS WAS A BAD BEGINNING. EVERYBODY	KNEW	THAT IN ENGLAND THE CENSORSHIP WOULD NOT BE CRUSHED BY
ROCK II (265)	CONNECTION BETWEEN INDIA AND ENGLAND BECAUSE I	KNEW	THAT IN THE COURSE OF NATURE AND BY THE JUSTICE OF
DOCT III (154)	BEAUTY: DONT THINK ME VAIN FOR KNOWING IT. I	KNEW	THAT MEN OF GENIUS ALWAYS HAD A TERRIBLE STRUGGLE WITH
WIDO II (43)	RIGHT TO THROW STONES. BUT, ON MY HONOR, I NEVER	KNEW	THAT MY HOUSE WAS A GLASS ONE UNTIL YOU POINTED IT OUT.
SIM PRO,1, (25)	" I AM INDISPENSABLE" I SAYS. AND ALL THE TIME I	KNEW	THAT NOBODY NEEDNT BE IN THE OFFICE, AND THAT ANY JEW
HART PREFACE(3)	IN WHICH EUROPE WAS STIFLING ITS SOUL; AND HE	KNEW	THAT OUR UTTER ENERVATION AND FUTILIZATION IN THAT
BULL PREFACE(7)	CABINET. HE WAS NOT AFRAID OF HIS COUNTRYMEN: HE	KNEW	THAT PROTESTANTISM COULD HOLD ITS OWN ONLY TOO WELL IN

BULL PREFACE(69)	RECONQUEST, MASSACRE, AND REPLANTATION WHICH IT	KNEW	THAT PUBLIC OPINION IN ENGLAND AND AMERICA WOULD NOT
JITT II (39)	WAS NOT THAT. THE WORLD WOULD FORGIVE HIM IF IT	KNEW	THAT SHE IS WHAT I KNOW SHE MUST BE IF HE LOVED HER.
SUPR I (33)	DIDNT LIKE THE TRUE STORIES. /ANN/ OF COURSE I	KNEW	THAT SOME OF THE THINGS COULDNT HAVE HAPPENED. BUT--
CURE (226)	YOU ARE AN UNDER-SECRETARY IN THE WAR OFFICE. YOU	KNEW	THAT THE ARMY WAS GOING TO BE PUT ON VEGETARIAN DIET,
HART PREFACE(3)	FEW AMATEURS WHOSE HOBBY IS FOREIGN POLICY EVEN	KNEW	THAT THE GUNS WERE LOADED. A RUSSIAN PLAYWRIGHT,
PRES (155)	LADY! /MRS BANGER/ HOW CAN YOU TELL? YOU NEVER	KNEW	THAT THE HERO OF THE CHARGE AT KASSASSIN WAS A WOMAN:
METH PREFACE(R30)	OF PRODUCING CROSS VARIETIES UNKNOWN TO ADAM. HE	KNEW	THAT THE SAME THING IS TRUE OF PIGEONS. HE KNEW THAT
HART II (86)	BE IN TOO GREAT A HURRY TO WAIT FOR HIS MARKET. I	KNEW	THAT THE SUREST WAY TO RUIN A MAN WHO DOESNT KNOW HOW
HART PREFACE(18)	GRIEF; BUT THEY ONLY EMBITTERED THOSE WHO	KNEW	THAT THE YOUNG MEN WERE HAVING THEIR TEETH SET ON EDGE
METH PREFACE(R30)	TO MODERN RACING AND INDUSTRIAL HAULAGE. HE	KNEW	THAT THERE ARE NEARLY TWO HUNDRED DIFFERENT SORTS OF
2TRU III (97)	BELONG TO THE POOR, AND DONT WANT TO. I ALWAYS	KNEW	THAT THERE WERE THOUSANDS OF POOR PEOPLE; AND I WAS
FANY PROLOG (262)	BESIDES, I DIDNT KNOW WHAT TO OFFER THEM. I	KNEW	THAT THEY WERE CHEAPER THAN ACTORS, BECAUSE THEY GET
MTH4 I (160)	HE HAD HUNG HIS HAT ON IT. /ZOO/ (LAUGHING) HE	KNEW	THAT TRAVELLERS ARE AMUSING ONLY WHEN THEY ARE TELLING
BULL I (96)	DISGRACEFULLY. /DOYLE/ BY GEORGE, IF SHE ONLY	KNEW	THAT TWO MEN WERE TALKING ABOUT HER LIKE THIS--!
GETT (294)	DOESNT CARE WHAT SHE SAYS. /REGINALD/ WELL: YOU	KNEW	THAT WHEN YOU PROPOSED TO HER. /SYKES/ YES; BUT I DIDNT
BARB I (257)	COMES FROM ANDREW. /STEPHEN/ (SHOCKED) I NEVER	KNEW	THAT. /LADY BRITOMART/ WELL, YOU SURELY DIDNT SUPPOSE
HART III (139)	ABSOLUTELY NOTHING. /MAZZINI/ WELL OF COURSE I	KNEW	THAT, LADY UTTERWORD. BUT IF PEOPLE BELIEVE IN HIM AND
JOAN 2 (81)	TO THE COURT) YOU SEE, ALL OF YOU: SHE	KNEW	THE BLOOD ROYAL. WHO DARE SAY NOW THAT I AM NOT MY
MRS III (225)	YOU ARE WRONG: YOU KNOW NOTHING ABOUT HER. IF YOU	KNEW	THE CIRCUMSTANCES AGAINST WHICH MY MOTHER HAD TO
3PLA PREFACE(R33)	ANTONYS AND OCTAVIUSES OF ITS TIME, WHO AT LEAST	KNEW	THE DIFFERENCE BETWEEN LIFE AND RHETORIC. IT WILL BE
MTH2 (70)	THE PEOPLE WOULDNT LISTEN TO REASON. BESIDES, I	KNEW	THE DUTCH WOULDNT GIVE HIM UP. /SAVVY/ OH, DONT START
DOCT PREFACE(6)	THIS HOLDS GOOD IN POLITICAL PRACTICE. IF MANKIND	KNEW	THE FACTS, AND AGREED WITH THE DOCTORS, THEN THE
PYGM III (252)	HE'D POURED SO MUCH DOWN HIS OWN THROAT THAT HE	KNEW	THE GOOD OF IT. /MRS EYNSFORD HILL/ DO YOU MEAN HE
BUOY 1 (13)	GOD EVER VENTURED ON. I TELL YOU, IF PEOPLE ONLY	KNEW	THE HISTORY OF THEIR OWN TIMES THEY WOULD DIE OF HORROR
HART PREFACE(19)	AND HAD NO CHILDREN OF THEIR OWN TO LOSE, YET	KNEW	THE INESTIMABLE LOSS TO THE WORLD OF FOUR YEARS OF THE
LIED (189)	BUT I DONT MIND HIS BROTHERS. NOW IF YOU ONLY	KNEW	THE LEAST LITTLE THING ABOUT THE WORLD, HENRY, YOUD
JITT II (28)	IT. SHE WAS VERY FOND OF HER FATHER. /LENKHEIM/ I	KNEW	THE MOTHER AND DAUGHTER NEVER GOT ON VERY WELL
PYGM EPILOG (299)	ELIZA HAD NOT TO BEGIN AT THE VERY BEGINNING: SHE	KNEW	THE NAMES AND PRICES OF THE CHEAPER FLOWERS; AND HER
SUPR I (37)	FOOTING. I HAD BECOME A NEW PERSON; AND THOSE WHO	KNEW	THE OLD PERSON LAUGHED AT ME. THE ONLY MAN WHO BEHAVED
DOCT III (154)	YES: I UNDERSTAND. /MRS DUBEDAT/ OH, IF YOU ONLY	KNEW	THE OTHER SIDE OF HIM AS I DO! DO YOU KNOW, DOCTOR,
SUPR I (33)	I DONT WANT TO REMIND YOU OF ANYTHING. BUT I	KNEW	THE PEOPLE THEY HAPPENED TO, AND HEARD ABOUT THEM.
METH PREFACE(R33)	AND EDWARD VII TOO, FOR THAT MATTER). NOBODY WHO	KNEW	THE THEORY WAS ADDING ANYTHING TO IT. THIS SLUMP NOT
BARB II (307)	I WILL DO MY BEST. I COULD VAMP A BASS IF I	KNEW	THE TUNE. /CUSINS/ IT IS A WEDDING CHORUS FROM ONE OF
SUPR PREFACE(R19)	THE DAY I FIRST SET FOOT ON THIS FOREIGN SOIL I	KNEW	THE VALUE OF THE PROSAIC QUALITIES OF WHICH IRISHMEN
SUPR PREFACE(R19)	TEACH ENGLISHMEN TO BE ASHAMED AS WELL AS I	KNEW	THE VANITY OF THE POETIC QUALITIES OF WHICH ENGLISHMEN
DOCT I (93)	FOR THE ILLNESS AND THE GUINEAS IT COSTS HIM. I	KNEW	THE WALPOLES WELL FIFTEEN YEARS AGO. THE FATHER USED TO
CLEO PRO1 (92)	A SOLDIER THAT HAD ONCE SERVED POMPEY, AND THAT	KNEW	THE WAYS OF ROME AND WAS FULL OF HER LUSTS. AND THEY
CAPT III (287)	/LADY CICELY/ WHAT NONSENSE! AS IF ANYBODY EVER	KNEW	THE WHOLE TRUTH ABOUT ANYTHING! (SITTING DOWN, MUCH
BULL PREFACE(14)	STRONG AFFECTION AND LOYALTY IN AN IRISHMAN WHO	KNEW	THE WORLD AND WAS MOVED ONLY TO DISLIKE, MISTRUST,
ARMS I (19)	SAW THAT, DEAR YOUNG LADY. I SAW AT ONCE THAT YOU	KNEW	THE WORLD. /RAINA/ HAVE YOU EVER SEEN THE OPERA OF
SIM II (56)	THE DREAM WHICH UNITED PROLA AND PRA AS YOU FIRST	KNEW	THEM, AND THEN UNITED US ALL SIX, HAS ENDED IN A SINGLE
MTH1 I (9)	DEATH AS YOU SAW IT WHEN THE FAWN FELL; AND SHE	KNEW	THEN THAT SHE MUST FIND OUT HOW TO RENEW HERSELF AND
HART II (112)	SO BILLY DUNN WAS POOR NURSE'S LITTLE ROMANCE. I	KNEW	THERE HAD BEEN SOMEBODY. /RANDALL/ THEY WILL FIGHT
FANY III (321)	RUDOLPH SAY I'M A REGULAR PIG. I'M SURE I NEVER	KNEW	THERE WAS ANYTHING WRONG WITH ME. BUT LIVE AND LEARN.
CLEO V (199)	THIS LEAVETAKING? /CAESAR/ (ENLIGHTENED) AH, I	KNEW	THERE WAS SOMETHING. (TO RUFIO) HOW COULD YOU LET ME
GETT (264)	WITHIN SIGHT OF HER. WOULDNT GO TO BED UNLESS SHE	KNEW	THEY WAS ALL SAFE AT HOME AND THE DOOR LOCKED, AND THE
LION PREFACE(93)	SHOULD BE LESS CAREFUL HOW I COMMITTED THEM IF I	KNEW	THEY WOULD COST ME NOTHING." THEN, TOO, THERE IS THE
KING I (211)	CALCULATION, WITHOUT EVEN A SCHOOLBOY'S ALGEBRA,	KNEW	THIS WHEN I, WHO WAS BORN ONE OF THE GREATEST
PHIL I (89)	ALWAYS A WOMAN AT THE BOTTOM OF IT. WELL, WE	KNEW	THIS WHEN WE FOUNDED THE CLUB; BUT WE NOTICED THAT THE
2TRU PREFACE(22)	BY A CONTRIVED SINGULARITY. ST VINCENT DE PAUL	KNEW	THOROUGHLY WELL WHAT HE WAS ABOUT WHEN HE CONSTITUTED
FABL PREFACE(76)	POSTULANT TO TELL A FLAT LIE WHICH BOTH OF THEM	KNEW	TO BE A LIE, AND HE TOLD IT WITHOUT A BLUSH. THE
MTH3 (109)	THAT MANKIND COULD LIVE ANY LENGTH OF TIME IT	KNEW	TO BE ABSOLUTELY NECESSARY TO SAVE CIVILIZATION FROM
HART PREFACE(32)	FROM THE FIELD, WERE AS MUCH PLEASED BY WHAT THEY	KNEW	TO BE STALE AND FOOLISH AS THE NOVICES BY WHAT THEY
JITT II (43)	THIS. WHAT DID HE TELL YOU? /JITTA/ OF COURSE I	KNEW	TOO LITTLE OF THE WORK YOU AND HE WERE DOING TOGETHER
KING II (227)	THAT MUCH THERE WAS AN END OF ME AS A KING. I	KNEW	TOO MUCH. /CATHERINE/ WITH WHAT YOU HAVE TAUGHT ME I
DOCT II (116)	YOU DONT KNOW WHAT YOUVE DONE FOR ME. I NEVER	KNEW	UNTIL NOW HOW DEADLY AFRAID I WAS-- HOW I HAD COME TO
MIS. PREFACE(80)	CURIOUSLY ABOUT OUR RELATIONS, I REALIZED THAT I	KNEW	VERY LITTLE ABOUT HER, INTRODUCE ME TO A STRANGE WOMAN
JITT III (56)	ME. WHATEVER I MAY HAVE SAID WHEN I WAS UPSET, I	KNEW	VERY WELL ALL ALONG THAT BRUNO NEVER WENT WITH COMMON
FANY III (312)	THAT NEVER ASKED HER BEFORE. /GILBEY/ I NEVER	KNEW	WE COULD LIVE WITHOUT BEING RESPECTABLE. /MRS GILBEY/
CLEO PRO1 (92)	AND INFLUENCE AMONG YOU." AND THEY SAID, " WE	KNEW	WELL THOU WOULDST NOT DO IT FOR NOTHING: THOU SHALT
HART PREFACE(35)	SOLDIERS WHO DID NOT KNOW WHAT A THEATRE WAS,	KNEW	WHAT A CHURCH WAS. AND THEY HAD BEEN TAUGHT TO RESPECT
ARMS III (56)	MIND THE MAJOR BEING A LITTLE IMPATIENT; FOR THEY	KNEW	WHAT A GOOD SERVANT I WAS-- AFTER MAKING A FOOL AND A
JOAN EPILOG (154)	TO HER! /CHARLES/ YOU CANNOT. NONE OF US EVER	KNEW	WHAT ANYTHING MEANT TO HER. SHE WAS LIKE NOBODY ELSE;
GENV IV (94)	YOU MEAN THAT YOU WOULD KNOW WHAT TO DO WHEN YOU	KNEW	WHAT ENGLAND WAS GOING TO DO? /BATTLER/ I KNOW ALREADY
MIS. (174)	SAY IT'S A SCANDAL AND AN INFAMY. IF PEOPLE ONLY	KNEW	WHAT GOES ON IN THIS SO-CALLED RESPECTABLE HOUSE IT
O'FL (206)	FOR THE SAKE OF A LITTLE REST AND QUIET. I NEVER	KNEW	WHAT HARD WORK WAS TIL I TOOK TO RECRUITING. WHAT WITH
DEVL II (46)	FURTHER EFFORT TO CONCEAL HIS ANXIETY). I WISH I	KNEW	WHAT HAS FRIGHTENED YOU SO. WAS THERE A STRUGGLE? DID
BARB II (282)	FULFILS HIMSELF IN MANY WAYS; AND I DARESAY HE	KNEW	WHAT HE WAS ABOUT WHEN HE MADE A SECULARIST OF YOU, SO
LION PREFACE(7)	THE CHARGE, JESUS REPEATED THE OFFENCE. HE	KNEW	WHAT HE WAS DOING: HE HAD ALIENATED NUMBERS OF HIS OWN
SUPR III (84)	COMMIT SUCH A CRIME AGAINST HIMSELF IF HE REALLY	KNEW	WHAT HE WAS DOING. HOW CAN YOU LOOK ROUND AT THESE
GENV IV (109)	THERE ARE OTHERS, ERNEST. /DEACONESS/ IF YOU	KNEW	WHAT I WAS, WHAT I AM, ALL THAT YOU ARE DOING HERE
JOAN 2 (78)	OR OUR SOLDIERS SACRIFICE THEIR LIVES. IF THEY	KNEW	WHAT IS REALLY HAPPENING INSTEAD OF WHAT SEEMS TO THEM
2TRU PREFACE(18)	AND SAPPHIRA FOR VIOLATING IT. IF OUR NEWSPAPERS	KNEW	WHAT IS REALLY HAPPENING IN THE WORLD, OR COULD
MIS. (197)	HE LAUGHED AND SAID THAT IT WAS THE OLD MAN THAT	KNEW	WHAT IT FELT LIKE. THINK OF THAT, SUMMERHAYS! THINK OF
GETT (333)	THEY SPOILT ME FOR ALL THEY WERE WORTH. I NEVER	KNEW	WHAT IT WAS TO WANT MONEY OR ANYTHING THAT MONEY COULD
PRES (133)	IT UNCONDITIONALLY. /BALSQUITH/ YES, BEFORE WE	KNEW	WHAT IT WAS. IT WAS UNWORKABLE, YOU KNOW. /MITCHENER/ I
DEVL III (73)	THAT YOU SHOULD THINK THAT, MR DUDGEON. IF YOU	KNEW	WHAT MY COMMISSION COST ME, AND WHAT MY PAY IS, YOU
SUPR III (117)	RESEMBLANCES TO HER FATHER AND MOTHER BY WHICH I	KNEW	WHAT SHE WOULD BE LIKE IN THIRTY YEARS' TIME. I NOTED
MILL PREFACE(122)	BUT HE HAD ONE QUALITY IN COMMON WITH IL DUCE: HE	KNEW	WHAT THE VICTORIOUS ALLIES WOULD FIGHT FOR AND WHAT
POSN PREFACE(421)	CATASTROPHES. AT ALL EVENTS, WHETHER THEY	KNEW	WHAT THEY WERE DOING OR NOT, THERE CAN BE NO QUESTION
BARB III (336)	OWN POWER; AND THE CONSEQUENCE WAS THAT I NEVER	KNEW	WHAT TO DO WITH MYSELF. WHEN I JOINED IT, I HAD NOT
BUOY III (45)	TO RUN AWAY. MY SECOND MARRIAGE WAS A SUCCESS: I	KNEW	WHAT TO EXPECT. SECOND MARRIAGES ARE THE QUIETEST AND
PHIL II (107)	A LOT IN THOSE DAYS, DID DAD. THE DOCTOR NEVER	KNEW	WHAT WAS WRONG WITH HIM UNTIL PARAMORE DISCOVERED A
KING I (203)	THESE POOR FELLOWS THEIR FIFTEEN SHILLINGS IF YOU	KNEW	WHAT WOMEN COST. /FOX/ WHAT MANNER OF WORLD IS THIS
DOCT II (120)	REALLY HARDLY BORROWING; FOR HE SAID HEAVEN ONLY	KNEW	WHEN HE COULD PAY ME. I COULDNT REFUSE. IT APPEARS THAT
BUOY III (36)	HE WOULD FOLLOW ME TO THE ENDS OF THE EARTH IF HE	KNEW	WHERE I WAS; AND WE SHOULD BOTH MAKE FOOLS OF OURSELVES
2TRU PREFACE(18)	PROPERTY IN THE PHYSICAL EARTH, BEFORE THE CHURCH	KNEW	WHERE IT WAS (IT HAS NOT QUITE LOCATED ITSELF YET) IT
HART PREFACE(23)	INTO THE WAY BY THE BLESSED FACT THAT THEY NEVER	KNEW	WHERE THE WAY WAS. THUS WHILST ALL THE EFFICIENCY OF
BARB PREFACE(210)	I EVER READ A WORD BY SCHOPENHAUER, OR EVEN	KNEW	WHETHER HE WAS A PHILOSOPHER OR A CHEMIST. THE
BUOY III (39)	NOR BOTHERED ABOUT BEETHOVEN; BUT I ALWAYS	KNEW	WHETHER IT WAS A FINE DAY OR A WET ONE WITHOUT ANY
FANY EPILOG (330)	THEN HOW COULD YOU WRITE ABOUT THEM UNTIL YOU	KNEW	WHICH WAS PINERO AND WHICH WAS JONES? BESIDES, WHAT
AUGS (265)	DID YOU TELL THEM WHO YOU WERE? /THE CLERK/ THEY	KNEW	WHO I WAS. THATS WHY THEY WOULDNT LET ME UP. /AUGUSTUS/
CAPT I (229)	I AM NO LAWYER, SIR HOWRRD. /LADY CICELY/ I NEVER	KNEW	YOU HAD A BROTHER, HOWARD? /SIR HOWARD/ (NOT PLEASED
NEVR II (236)	I WAS TO BE HIS FATHER. TODAY, AS SOON AS HE	KNEW	YOU WERE COMING, SIR, HE TRIED TO PUT IT UP ON ME THAT
ROCK I (203)	MINISTER AND HIS ASSAILANT. /LADY CHAVENDER/ I	KNEW	YOU WERE COMING HERE TO MAKE A SCENE AND DISTURB YOUR
GENV IV (95)	YOUR COUNTRYMEN THOUGHT YOU A HERO. BUT AS YOU	KNEW	YOU WERE QUITE SAFE, WE WERE NOT IMPRESSED. /BBDE/ YOU
GETT (307)	IT AS THE EARNEST KIND OF PEOPLE THINK. /EDITH/ I	KNEW	YOU WOULD AGREE WITH ME, COLLINS. THANK YOU.
SUPR I (45)	RAMSDEN: I HAVE BORNE YOUR HARD WORDS BECAUSE I	KNEW	YOU WOULD BE SORRY FOR THEM WHEN YOU FOUND OUT THE
BARB I (258)	HIS MONEY. /LADY BRITOMART/ THANK YOU, STEPHEN: I	KNEW	YOU WOULD GIVE ME THE RIGHT ADVICE WHEN IT WAS PROPERLY
SUPR I (33)	GET YOU INTO TROUBLE. AND YOU WERE ONLY A BOY. I	KNEW	YOU WOULD GROW OUT OF THEM. PERHAPS I WAS WRONG.
BASH III (124)	TREAT THY WIFE? /CASHEL/ THERE SPAKE MY FATE: I	KNEW	YOU WOULD SAY THAT. OH, MOTHERS, MOTHERS, WOULD YOU BUT
BULL IV (165)	THATS RIGHT, THATS RIGHT: THATS MAGNIFICENT. I	KNEW	YOU WOULD SEE WHAT A FIRST-RATE THING THIS WILL BE FOR
MIS. (183)	PUT THE LID ON THIS JOB IN A MASTERLY MANNER. I	KNEW	YOU WOULD. I TOLD YOU ALL TO LET WELL ALONE. YOU
LIED (197)	IN THE HONOR OF A GENTLEMAN. /SHE/ DEAREST BOY, I	KNEW	YOU WOULD, I-- SH! (SHE RUSHES TO THE DOOR, AND HOLDS
BULL IV (159)	TO ANSWER IT, BUT I HAVNT HAD A MOMENT; AND I	KNEW	YOU WOULDNT MIND. YOU SEE, I AM SO AFRAID OF BORING YOU
PHIL II (127)	AM GOING TO COMPLAIN TO THE COMMITTEE. /SYLVIA/ I	KNEW	YOUD OVERDO IT SOME DAY, JULIA. /CRAVEN/ DO YOU KNOW
DOCT I (94)	HANDY INSTRUMENT. /WALPOLE/ (CONFIDENTLY) I	KNEW	YOUD SEE ITS POINTS. /SIR PATRICK/ YES: I REMEMBER THAT

PYGM V (288)	NON-RESISTANT) WRING AWAY. WHAT DO I CARE? I	KNEW	YOUD STRIKE ME SOME DAY. (HE LETS HER GO, STAMPING
JITT I (11)	LIFT, SIR? IT ISNT AS IF ANYONE IN THIS HOUSE	KNEW	YOU. AND FOR THAT MATTER YOU MEET PEOPLE ON THE STAIRS
WIDO III (54)	/BLANCHE/ WHY, IT'S MR LICKCHEESE! I HARDLY	KNEW	YOU. /LICKCHEESE/ I FIND YOU A LITTLE CHANGED YOURSELF,
DOCT IV (162)	THE BLESSING OF MY LIFE. I NEVER LIVED UNTIL I	KNEW	YOU. /LOUIS/ (HIS EYES GLISTENING) THEN YOU MUST
CAPT II (247)	CICELY/ (SHAKING HANDS) HOWDYEDO? OF COURSE I	KNEW	YOUR FATHER-- DUNHAM WASNT IT? WERE YOU EVER CALLED--
JOAN 4 (99)	(REASSURED) AH! YOU HEAR, MESSIRE JOHN? I	KNEW	YOUR LORDSHIP WOULD NOT FAIL US. PARDON MY
SUPR PREFACE(R9)	MATURE AGE WHEN YOU MADE THE SUGGESTION; AND YOU	KNEW	YOUR MAN. IT IS HARDLY FIFTEEN YEARS SINCE, AS TWIN
PYGM EPILOG (295)	NOT LAST TWO YOUNG PEOPLE FOR EVER; AND THEY BOTH	KNEW	, AND ELIZA FELT AS WELL, THAT THEY MUST SHIFT FOR
BULL PREFACE(50)	THAT THEY WERE WILD BIRDS, AS EVERYBODY IN CHINA	KNEW	, AND THAT THE PRETENDED INDIGNATION OF THE FARMERS WAS
OVER (175)	THAT. I THOUGHT YOU LIKED ME, BUT THAT YOU	KNEW	, AND WOULD BE GOOD. /GREGORY/ (STRETCHING HIS HANDS
LION PREFACE(41)	MORE A MAN OF THE WORLD THAN THE OTHERS, AND	KNEW	, AS MERE CHRONICLERS AND ROMANCERS NEVER KNOW, WHAT
SUPR III (125)	THAT HER CONSTANT COMPANIONSHIP MIGHT, FOR ALL I	KNEW	, BECOME INTOLERABLY TEDIOUS TO ME; THAT I COULD NOT
FANY II (290)	I HEARD WORDS THAT I DIDNT EVEN KNOW THAT I	KNEW	, COMING OUT OF MY MOUTH JUST AS IF SOMEBODY ELSE HAD
SUPR III (93)	WE NEVER CONFESSED IT-- THE DEATH OF ANYONE WE	KNEW	, EVEN THOSE WE LIKED BEST, WAS ALWAYS MINGLED WITH A
O'FL (213)	A KIND FRIEND TO THE POOR. LITTLE HER LADYSHIP	KNEW	, GOD HELP HER, THE DEPTH OF DIVILMENT THAT WAS IN US:
ARMS III (50)	IT WAS IN THIS HOUSE YOU TOOK REFUGE. IF SERGIUS	KNEW	, HE WOULD CHALLENGE YOU AND KILL YOU IN A DUEL.
FANY II (287)	THEY ALL KNEW AND DIDNT CARE. /MRS KNOX/ IF THEY	KNEW	, JO, THERED BE A CROWD ROUND THE HOUSE LOOKING UP AT
MILL IV (191)	TO PAY THE MORTGAGE INTEREST. THE NEXT THING WE	KNEW	, THE GIRL HAD PAID OFF THE MORTGAGE AND GOT THE WHIP
LION PROLOG (106)	A LIFE HIS WIFE LEADS HIM! " OH, IF THEY ONLY	KNEW	! AND YOU THINK I DONT KNOW. BUT I DO, I DO, (
JITT III (60)	REALLY KNEW. /EDITH/ (SCORNFULLY) IF I REALLY	KNEW	! DO YOU SUPPOSE ANY GIRL OF MY AGE NOWADAYS DOES NOT
MIS. (183)	TARLETON/ (SHOCKED) IS LUCY DEAD? AND I NEVER	KNEW	! (WITH AN EFFUSION OF TENDERNESS) AND YOU HERE BEING
ARMS III (55)	/BLUNTSCHLI/ HOTELS! NONSENSE. IF YOU ONLY	KNEW	! OH, IT'S TOO RIDICULOUS! EXCUSE ME: I MUST GIVE MY
DEST (170)	/NAPOLEON/ (WITH ANGRY DERISION) IF THEY ONLY	KNEW	! PRAY DO YOU KNOW? /LADY/ YES. I HAD THE MISFORTUNE
DEST (170)	THEY HAVE NO EXPERIENCE OF THEM. OH, IF THEY ONLY	KNEW	! /NAPOLEON/ (WITH ANGRY DERISION) IF THEY ONLY

KNICKERBOCKERS

CAPT NOTES (306)	OF A STREET BOY TO A BLACK MAN OR TO A LADY IN	KNICKERBOCKERS	. I HAVE MADE ONLY THE MOST PERFUNCTORY
NEVR I (205)	I ASSURE YOU. LORD DE CRESCI'S SISTER BICYCLES IN	KNICKERBOCKERS	; AND THE RECTOR'S WIFE ADVOCATES DRESS
ARMS II SD(23)	JACKET WITH EMBROIDERED BORDER, SASH, WIDE	KNICKERBOCKERS	, AND DECORATED GAITERS. HIS HEAD IS SHAVED

KNICKERS

2TRU I (48)	AND WOOL. REAL SILK STOCKINGS WITHOUT LADDERS.	KNICKERS	: HOW DARINGLY MODERN! SHOES: HEELS ONLY TWO
MTH3 SD(99)	HER SHOULDERS TO HER CHAIR. SHE IS IN CORSET,	KNICKERS	, AND SILK STOCKINGS. /BURGE-LUBIN/ (HORRIFIED) I

KNIFE

MRS I (182)	AT HER BELT, WITH A FOUNTAIN PEN AND A PAPER	KNIFE	AMONG ITS PENDANTS). /PRAED/ VERY KIND OF YOU INDEED,
BULL IV (147)	FOR ME OR ANYWAN ELSE TO GO OVER EXCEPT WID A	KNIFE	AN FORK. /AUNT JUDY/ WHY DIDNT MR BROADBENT STOP THE
KING I (213)	NOT DRAW, BUT WHICH ANY FOOL CAN MAKE WITH A	KNIFE	AND A LUMP OF SUGAR, I BELIEVE IN NONE OF THESE
BUOY II (20)	/SHE/ YOU NEED NOT LOOK ROUND FOR A TUMBLER AND A	KNIFE	AND FORK. DRINK FROM THE CALABASH; EAT FROM YOUR
MIS. PREFACE(40)	ONES: THE CHILD MUST LEARN TO WALK, TO USE A	KNIFE	AND FORK, TO SWIM, TO RIDE A BICYCLE, TO ACQUIRE
PHIL II (112)	OUT IN ANOTHER MOMENT. I SHOULD HAVE TAKEN A	KNIFE	AND KILLED HER. I SHOULD HAVE-- CUTHBERTSON APPEARS,
ROCK PREFACE(154)	OF CLERGY, AND OF HANNIBAL CHOLLOP WITH HIS BOWIE	KNIFE	AND PISTOL. LET US THEN ASSUME THAT PRIVATE PROPERTY,
DEVL I (12)	ON ONE OF WHICH SHE PUTS A BARNBRACK WITH A	KNIFE	BESIDE IT. ON THE OTHER SHE SHAKES SOME BISCUITS OUT
CLEO IV (184)	SLAVE. /CAESAR/ NOTHING. /RUFIO/ A MAN WITH A	KNIFE	IN HIM, I'LL SWEAR. /CAESAR/ (RISING) A MURDER!
GLIM (182)	THE SCRUFF OF YOUR NECK, OR HIS DAUGHTER THRUST A	KNIFE	IN YOUR THROAT, SIGNOR? /FERRUCCIO/ IT WOULD BE MANY
CLEO III (145)	THE SENTINEL'S ARMS FROM BEHIND) THRUST YOUR	KNIFE	INTO THE DOG'S THROAT, APOLLODORUS. (THE CHIVALROUS
DOCT IV (160)	/THE NEWSPAPER MAN/ OH, I SAY: YOU HAVE GOT YOUR	KNIFE	INTO US, HAVNT YOU? /WALPOLE/ (VINDICTIVELY) I WISH
DOCT I (105)	ROT: THE CASES ARE ALL BLOOD-POISONING; AND THE	KNIFE	IS THE REAL REMEDY. BYE-BYE, SIR PADDY. HAPPY TO HAVE
CAPT II (258)	HIS BLACK BLOOD, I WOULD DRAIN THEM EMPTY WITH MY	KNIFE	. I HAVE NO RELATIONS. I HAD A MOTHER: THAT WAS ALL.
DEVL II (37)	THE SECOND PLATE, AND HANDS IT TO HER, WITH THE	KNIFE	. THE ACTION SHEWS QUICKLY HOW WELL HE KNOWS THAT SHE
DEVL II (37)	THE TABLE NEAREST THE PRESS. THERE IS A PLATE AND	KNIFE	LAID THERE. THE OTHER PLATE IS LAID NEAR IT: BUT
MRS II (209)	(CUTTING A PAGE OF HER BOOK WITH THE PAPER	KNIFE	ON HER CHATELAINE) HAS IT REALLY NEVER OCCURRED TO
SUPR III (136)	HIM; THROWING HIM ON HIS BACK; AND DRAWING A	KNIFE	) I STAB THE MAN WHO STIRS. (HE BLOCKS THE WAY. THE
CLEO PRO2 (104)	SLAY HER. /PERSIAN/ (THREATENING HER WITH HIS	KNIFE	) PERSIA HAS BUT ONE GOD; YET HE LOVES THE BLOOD OF
CLEO PRO2 (105)	PERISH ON THE SPEARS OF THE ROMANS. (LIFTING HIS	KNIFE	) TASTE DEATH. /FTATATEETA/ NOT FROM THEE, BABY. (SHE
CLEO PRO2 (103)	HER ON HER KNEES, HE DRAWS A MURDEROUS LOOKING	KNIFE	). WHERE IS SHE? WHERE IS SHE? OR-- (HE THREATENS
CLEO V (201)	ROMAN OF THE NOBLEST; NOT OLD AND RIPE FOR THE	KNIFE	; NOT LEAN IN THE ARMS AND COLD IN THE HEART; NOT
PHIL II (96)	(SYLVIA RISES, HORRIFIED). I SHALL REQUIRE A	KNIFE	SPECIALLY MADE TO GET AT IT. THE MAN WHO IS WAITING
CLEO PRO1 (93)	BUT THE GODS LAUGHED; FOR SEPTIMIUS WAS BUT A	KNIFE	THAT POMPEY HAD SHARPENED; AND WHEN IT TURNED AGAINST
CLEO PRO2 (104)	(HER VOICE DIES AWAY AS THE PERSIAN PUTS HIS	KNIFE	TO HER THROAT). /BEL AFFRIS/ (LAYING A HAND ON
DOCT PREFACE(14)	ON KNOW BETTER. THE PATIENT DOES NOT FEEL THE	KNIFE	, AND THE OPERATION IS THEREFORE ENORMOUSLY
DOCT PREFACE(36)	INSIDE A MAN'S BODY EXCEPT BY EXPLORING IT WITH A	KNIFE	, OR TO FIND OUT WHAT THE SUN IS MADE OF WITHOUT

KNIGHT

MRS (150)	1902, WITH MADGE MCINTOSH AS VIVIE, JULIUS	KNIGHT	AS PRAED, FANNY BROUGH AS MRS WARREN, CHARLES
JOAN 3 (90)	IF YOU DELIVERED ME FROM FEAR I SHOULD BE A GOOD	KNIGHT	FOR A STORY BOOK, BUT A VERY BAD COMMANDER OF THE
ARMS II (33)	INSPIRED ME. I HAVE GONE THROUGH THE WAR LIKE A	KNIGHT	IN A TOURNAMENT WITH HIS LADY LOOKING DOWN AT HIM!
PPP (199)	MY HUSBAND SHALL BE MY HERO, MY LOVER, MY PERFECT	KNIGHT	. HE SHALL SHIELD ME FROM ALL CARE AND TROUBLE. HE
6CAL (95)	KING/ I HAVE NOT THREATENED THE LIFE OF A SINGLE	KNIGHT	. I HAVE SAID THAT NO MAN OF GENTLE CONDITION AND
DOCT I (83)	AND FOLLOWING HER) WHAT? /EMMY/ HE'S BEEN MADE A	KNIGHT	. MIND YOU DONT GO DR RIDGEONING HIM IN THEM LETTERS.
CLEO III (148)	/CLEOPATRA/ APOLLODORUS: YOU ARE MY PERFECT	KNIGHT	; AND I WILL ALWAYS BUY MY CARPETS THROUGH YOU. (
CLEO IV (188)	BEAUTIFUL. YOU SHOULD HAVE CALLED UPON ME, YOUR	KNIGHT	; AND IN FAIR DUEL I SHOULD HAVE SLAIN THE SLANDERER.
AUGS (264)	DOGS! /THE CLERK/ WHY DID THEY GIVE YOUNG BILL	KNIGHT	TWO AND SEVENPENCE, AND NOT GIVE ME EVEN MY TRAM
3PLA PREFACE(R37)	IMMENSE DIFFERENCE IN SCOPE BETWEEN THE PERFECT	KNIGHT	VERCINGETORIX AND HIS GREAT CONQUEROR JULIUS CAESAR.
JOAN 4 (100)	BARONY. BUT AS I AM AN EARL, AND TALBOT IS ONLY A	KNIGHT	, I MAY MAKE BOLD TO ACCEPT THE COMPARISON. (TO THE
BARB PREFACE(217)	AND COMMAND THEM WITHOUT SUPERIORITY. FROISSART'S	KNIGHT	, IN PLACING THE ACHIEVEMENT OF A GOOD LIFE BEFORE
AUGS (263)	IN HIM, BURSTS INTO FLAME). YOUNG BILL	KNIGHT	, THAT I TOOK WITH ME, GOT TWO AND SEVENPENCE. I GOT
DOCT I (106)	TO SIR PATRICK) SO THATS WHY THEY MADE ME A	KNIGHT	! AND THATS THE MEDICAL PROFESSION! /SIR PATRICK/

KNIGHTED

3PLA PREFACE(R17)	TIME IN THE SIXTIES UNTIL THE FIRST ACTOR WAS	KNIGHTED	IN THE NINETIES. THE MANAGER MAY NOT WANT GOOD

KNIGHTHOOD

POSN PREFACE(388)	OF FINE ART. TODAY WE HAVE ON THE ROLL OF	KNIGHTHOOD	ACTORS, AUTHORS, AND MANAGERS. THE ROGUE AND
AUGS (266)	ECONOMY. I CAME DOWN HERE TO PROMISE THE MAYOR A	KNIGHTHOOD	FOR HIS EXERTIONS. /THE CLERK/ THE MAYOR! WHERE
DOCT I SD(84)	OF AGE. JUST AT PRESENT THE ANNOUNCEMENT OF HIS	KNIGHTHOOD	IN THE MORNING PAPERS MAKES HIM SPECIALLY
DOCT I (98)	TO YOU, RIDGEON; AND I AM GLAD TO THINK THAT YOUR	KNIGHTHOOD	IS THE RESULT. /RIDGEON/ I AM DEEPLY OBLIGED TO
DOCT I (106)	THE DOOR WITH HIM) I WILL. AND THANK YOU FOR THE	KNIGHTHOOD	. GOODBYE. /B.B./ (STOPPING AT THE DOOR, WITH
DOCT I (97)	SIR COLENSO, EH? WELCOME TO THE ORDER OF	KNIGHTHOOD	. /RIDGEON/ (SHAKING HANDS) THANK YOU, B.B.
DOCT I (113)	ALL MY OLD FRIENDS TO A DINNER TO CELEBRATE MY	KNIGHTHOOD	-- YOUVE SEEN ABOUT IT IN THE PAPERS, HAVNT YOU?
PLES PREFACE(R14)	MOST OF IT THERE. SUCH MANAGERSHIP WOULD CARRY A	KNIGHTHOOD	WITH IT; AND SUCH A THEATRE WOULD BE THE NEEDED
MRS PREFACE(173)	ON THE ARMY, SIR JOHN FALSTAFF AN ATTACK ON	KNIGHTHOOD	, AND KING CLAUDIUS AN ATTACK ON ROYALTY. HERE

KNIGHTHOODS

GETT PREFACE(223)	WITHOUT ANY HOPE OF SEATS IN PARLIAMENT,	KNIGHTHOODS	, OR POSTS IN THE GOVERNMENT, BECAUSE PARTY

KNIGHTLY

3PLA PREFACE(R38)	THE MAN, WITH ITS COMEDIC CONFLICT BETWEEN THE	KNIGHTLY	BULGARIAN AND THE MOMMSENITE SWISS CAPTAIN.
3PLA PREFACE(R37)	HE DID SO ACCORDING TO HIS OWN ESSENTIALLY	KNIGHTLY	CONCEPTION OF A GREAT STATESMAN-COMMANDER. BUT IN
6CAL (95)	SHALL BE DENIED QUARTER AND RANSOM. IT WAS THEIR	KNIGHTLY	DUTY TO MAKE A SHOW OF ARMS AGAINST ME. BUT (
SUPR HANDBOK(204)	ARTICLES, AND THE VIVISECTOR WHO PLEDGES HIS	KNIGHTLY	HONOR THAT NO ANIMAL OPERATED ON IN THE
3PLA PREFACE(R38)	AND CARLYLE, RAISE A SHRIEK OF CONCERN FOR THEIR	KNIGHTLY	IDEAL AS IF NOBODY HAD EVER QUESTIONED ITS

KNIGHT'S

BARB PREFACE(217)	COULD BE ACHIEVED BY ROBBING AND PILLING. IF THE	KNIGHT'S	CONTEMPORARIES HAD BEEN ALL AS RESOLUTE AS HE,

KNIGHTS

JOAN 5 (116) COCK HIS NOSE AT ME; BUT REMEMBER THE DAY YOUR KNIGHTS AND CAPTAINS REFUSED TO FOLLOW ME TO ATTACK THE
JOAN 5 (109) AT COURT. /JOAN/ WHY DO ALL THESE COURTIERS AND KNIGHTS AND CHURCHMEN HATE ME? WHAT HAVE I DONE TO THEM? I
JOAN 6 (145) I COULD LET THE BANNERS AND THE TRUMPETS AND THE KNIGHTS AND SOLDIERS PASS ME AND LEAVE ME BEHIND AS THEY
JOAN 5 (116) BASTARD, YOUR ART OF WAR IS NO USE, BECAUSE YOUR KNIGHTS ARE NO GOOD FOR REAL FIGHTING. WAR IS ONLY A GAME TO
JOAN 1 (69) WAY TO SAVE YOUR SKIN IS TO RUN AWAY. OUR KNIGHTS ARE THINKING ONLY OF THE MONEY THEY WILL MAKE IN
SUPR PREFACE(R28) DIVIDENDS, AND EAT GRATUITOUSLY, LIKE THE KNIGHTS IN DON QUIXOTE'S BOOKS OF CHIVALRY. THE CITY PAPERS
JOAN 5 (116) WILL STOP TO BARGAIN ABOUT RANSOMS, AS HALF YOUR KNIGHTS LIVE BY DOING? NO: THEY WILL FIGHT TO WIN; AND THEY
JOAN PREFACE(52) I THINK THEY ARE MISTAKEN. THE EXPERIENCED KNIGHTS OF THE BLUE PENCIL, HAVING SAVED AN HOUR AND A HALF
6CAL (99) GENEROSITY AS NOBLEMEN, ON YOUR CHIVALRY AS GOOD KNIGHTS , TO BEAR WITNESS FOR US THAT IT IS THE COLD OF THE

KNIGHTSBRIDGE

AUGS (275) NOT SITTING ON ROYAL COMMISSIONS OR ON DUTY AT KNIGHTSBRIDGE BARRACKS. BY GAD, MADAM, IF THE SIREN COMES
PRES (157) POCKET. WHEN I SANG TOSTI'S GOODBYE FOR EVER AT KNIGHTSBRIDGE IN 1880 THE WHOLE REGIMENT WEPT. YOU ARE TOO

KNIPPERDOLLINGS

LION PREFACE(10) AND CONQUERORS AS WELL AS BY SAVONAROLAS AND KNIPPERDOLLINGS . AND AS THEY KNOW, VERY SENSIBLY, THAT A

KNITS

GETT (312) BASKET) HERE HE IS. (SHE RESUMES HER SEAT, AND KNITS). SOAMES COMES IN IN CASSOCK AND BIRETTA. HE SALUTES

KNITTED

DEVL III SD(58) SITS DOWN AND BEGINS TO READ THE REPORT WITH KNITTED BROWS AND CAREWORN LOOKS, REFLECTING ON HIS
APPL II (275) RISING AND SPEAKING SLOWLY, WITH HIS BROWS DEEPLY KNITTED) HAS YOUR MAJESTY GOT THAT ULTIMATUM ON YOU?
BULL IV (150) FOR ROSSCULLEN! /AUNT JUDY/ (WAVING A HALF KNITTED SOCK) HIP HIP HURRAY! THE CHEERS ARE GIVEN WITH

KNITTING

BULL IV (160) BY THE TENDERNESS OF HIS SINGING, PUTS DOWN HER KNITTING AT THIS VERY UNEXPECTED SENTIMENT, AND STARES AT
GETT (312) BRIDGENORTH/ (COMING BACK FROM THE STUDY WITH A KNITTING BASKET) HERE HE IS. (SHE RESUMES HER SEAT, AND
GETT (319) HAD COST ME. /MRS BRIDGENORTH/ (PUTTING DOWN HER KNITTING IN AMAZEMENT) EDITH! WHO EVER HEARD OF SUCH A
MILL IV SD(188) PATRICIA, IN HER GLADDEST SUMMER RAGS, IS KNITTING IN THE MIDDLE CHAIR OPPOSITE, FULL OF QUIET
APPL II SD(266) ALONG THE TERRACE. SEMPRONIUS FOLLOWS WITH HER KNITTING . /MAGNUS/ (SITTING DOWN) BE SEATED, LADIES AND
MILL IV SD(194) PATRICIA RETURNS TO HER CHAIR, AND RESUMES HER KNITTING . /SAGAMORE/ (TAKING A CHAIR NEXT PATRICIA ON HER
WIDO III SD(49) LOBBY. BLANCHE HAS HER WORKBASKET AT HAND, AND IS KNITTING . SARTORIUS, CLOSER TO THE FIRE, HAS A NEWSPAPER,
APPL II SD(257) RIGHT. HE IS READING THE EVENING PAPER: SHE IS KNITTING . SHE HAS A LITTLE WORK TABLE ON HER RIGHT, WITH A
MIS. PREFACE(102) A BROKEN DOWN LOCOMOTIVE BY PRODDING IT WITH A KNITTING NEEDLE. AND THIS IS NOT AT ALL BECAUSE THEY ARE
BULL IV (158) RISES). I'LL BORRY HIM, SO I WILL. (SHE PUTS HER KNITTING ON THE TABLE AND FOLLOWS HIM OUT, WITH A RESOLUTE
SIM II (82) (RISING) PROLA: SHALL I BRING YOU SOME KNITTING TO OCCUPY YOU? /PROLA/ NO, THANK YOU. I HAVE SOME
OVER (184) HEART IS A POTATO? OR A TURNIP? OR A BALL OF KNITTING WOOL? THAT YOU CAN THROW IT AWAY LIKE THIS? /MRS
OVER (184) LIKE THIS? /MRS LUNN/ I DONT THROW AWAY BALLS OF KNITTING WOOL. A MAN'S HEART SEEMS TO ME MUCH LIKE A SPONGE:
BULL IV SD(158) A CATCH IN HER THROAT SHE TAKES UP AUNT JUDY'S KNITTING , AND MAKES A PRETENCE OF GOING ON WITH IT. /NORA/
BULL IV SD(145) JUDY, A LITTLE FURTHER BACK, SITS FACING THE FIRE KNITTING , WITH HER FEET ON THE FENDER. A LITTLE TO KEEGAN'S

KNIVES

METH PREFACE(R53) EFFORT TO USE THEIR MINDS INSTEAD OF THEIR KNIVES AND EYES, AND ESTABLISHED AN ABOMINABLE TRADITION
ARMS III (73) HUNDRED EIDER-DOWN QUILTS. I HAVE TEN THOUSAND KNIVES AND FORKS, AND THE SAME QUANTITY OF DESSERT SPOONS. I
MRS II (205) WARREN/ (WITHIN) OF COURSE THERE IS (CLATTER OF KNIVES AND GLASSES AS SHE MOVES THE THINGS ON THE TABLE).
LION PREFACE(65) IS SUDDENLY AND PAINFULLY PINCHED. PEOPLE FLING KNIVES AND LIGHTED PARAFFIN LAMPS AT ONE ANOTHER IN A
MIS. PREFACE(29) DOES AS A MATTER OF FACT LEAD TO THE DRAWING OF KNIVES AND PISTOLS, AND SEX DISCUSSION LEADS TO OBSCENITY,
MRS II (203) THE REST ARE DONE: MRS ALISON HAS ONLY PLATES AND KNIVES FOR FOUR. /PRAED/ OH, IT DOESNT MATTER ABOUT ME. I--
DEVL III (57) GERMAN DRAGOONS, AND INDIANS WITH SCALPING KNIVES . THESE ARE THE COUNTRYMEN ON WHOSE DEVOTION YOU
KING I (199) RECEIVE ANY MORE OF YOUR GUESTS. I HAVE NOT KNIVES NOR PLATES NOR GLASSES ENOUGH. I HAVE HAD TO BORROW
ROCK PREFACE(183) AS A PLAIN UNDERSTANDABLE THING WHICH KEEPS MEN'S KNIVES OFF ONEANOTHER'S THROATS TO YOUR PEACE WHICH IS
MIS. (157) SO. /TARLETON/ BILLIARD BALLS AND CUES? PLATES, KNIVES , AND FORKS? TWO PARAFFIN LAMPS AND A HATSTAND?
BASH II,1, (113) HER BOOTS; BECAUSE I LOVE HER I HAVE CLEANED HER KNIVES , DOING IN THIS THE OFFICE OF A BOY, WHILST, LIKE THE
DEVL EPILOG (85) WITH THE REFERENCE TO INDIANS WITH SCALPING KNIVES , WHO, WITH THE TROOPS HIRED FROM GERMANY, MADE UP

KNOALEDGE

CAND I (85) HALF PAST NINE IN THE MORNING. WHY DO YOU SAY " KNOALEDGE " IN CHURCH, THOUGH YOU ALWAYS SAY " KNOLLEDGE" IN

KNOB

CAND I (82) I FORGOT. (MORELL HALTS AND TURNS WITH THE DOOR KNOB IN HIS HAND). YOUR FATHER-IN-LAW IS COMING ROUND TO SEE
DEVL III (69) THAT SAFE-CONDUCT. (HE PUTS HIS HAND TO THE DOOR KNOB TO OPEN IT). /SWINDON/ (WHO HAS NOT BUDGED) GENERAL

KNOBS

CAPT II SD(242) WITH GILDED EDGES, AND ORNAMENTED WITH GILT KNOBS . ON THE CEMENT FLOOR ARE MATTINGS, SHEEPSKINS, AND

KNOCK

FANY II (291) HE COULDNT WHIRL HIS LEG LIKE A WINDMILL AND KNOCK A POLICEMAN DOWN BY A GLORIOUS KICK ON THE HELMET. OH,
FANY III (303) SWING HIS LEG ROUND LIKE THE HAND OF A CLOCK AND KNOCK A POLICEMAN DOWN WITH IT. HE WAS IN WORMWOOD SCRUBBS
BULL PREFACE(62) LAW RESPECTED. THE RESULT IS THAT THREE NATIVES KNOCK A SOLDIER OFF HIS DONKEY AND ROB HIM. THEREUPON MR
CAPT I (238) LOOKS FOR SICH. IT TIKES A HAWBITRAIRY WANNE TO KNOCK AHT THEM EATHEN SHIKES, AW TEOLL YER. /BRASSBOUND/
GENV III (83) NOTES OF THE DISCUSSION). YOU SEE, JUDGE. IF YOU KNOCK ALL THIS NONSENSE OF BELONGING TO SUPERIOR RACES OUT
AUGS (278) HE COULD GET. /AUGUSTUS/ AND DID YOU DARE TO KNOCK AT MY DOOR AND INTERRUPT MY BUSINESS WITH THIS LADY TO
DOCT III SD(136) AS A PHYSICIAN, NOT AS A COMMERCIAL TRAVELLER. A KNOCK AT THE DOOR. LOUIS GOES UNCONCERNEDLY TO OPEN IT,
DEVL II (44) I CAN BEAR TO LIVE FOR DAYS AND DAYS WITH EVERY KNOCK AT THE DOOR-- EVERY FOOTSTEP-- GIVING ME A SPASM OF
MRS IV (244) EXPECT FROM THE MOST ORDINARY TRANSACTIONS. (A KNOCK AT THE DOOR). I WONDER WHO THIS IS. WOULD YOU MIND
AUGS (277) A FORGETFUL OLD" -- (SHE IS INTERRUPTED BY A KNOCK AT THE DOOR). /AUGUSTUS/ (IMPATIENTLY) COME IN. (THE
DOCT I (82) CANT TAKE ANY NEW PATIENTS, WHEN THE MOMENT A KNOCK COMES TO THE DOOR, IN YOU BOUNCE TO ASK WHETHER HE CAN
MTH3 (111) THREE TIMES. WHEN I PERSUADED THE AUTHORITIES TO KNOCK DOWN ALL OUR TOWNS AND REBUILD THEM FROM THE
WIDO III (54) SUPPOSE I'D GOT WIND OF A NEW STREET THAT WOULD KNOCK DOWN ROBBINS'S ROW AND TURN BURKE'S WALK INTO A
GETT (347) MY SOLEMN WORD THAT IF I EVER COMMIT A CRIME I'LL KNOCK HER DOWN BEFORE A WITNESS AND GO OFF TO BRIGHTON WITH
HART II (101) CAN GIVE TO A MAN WHO BREAKS ALL THE RULES IS TO KNOCK HIM DOWN. WHAT WOULD YOU SAY IF I WERE TO BOX YOUR
METH PREFACE(R45) AND PREDESTINATION. NOTHING WILL KNOCK INTO HIS HEAD THE FATEFUL DISTINCTION BETWEEN
DOCT IV SD(156) IN, IS HANGING UP HIS BESIDE THEM. THERE IS A KNOCK . HE OPENS THE DOOR AND FINDS RIDGEON THERE. /WALPOLE/
PPP (195) (SOMEONE KNOCKS AT THE DOOR). THAT IS ADOLPHUS'S KNOCK . (FITZ'S FACE TURNS A DAZZLING GREEN). WHAT HAS
BASH II,1, (103) /LYDIA/ (TURNING PALE) BASHVILLE, DIDST HEAR? A KNOCK . /BASHVILLE/ MADAM: TIS BYRON'S KNOCK. SHALL I ADMIT
BASH II,1, (103) HEAR? A KNOCK. /BASHVILLE/ MADAM: TIS BYRON'S KNOCK . SHALL I ADMIT HIM? /LUCIAN/ REEKING FROM THE RING!
BASH II,2, (117) WITH A CERTAIN DELICATE SCREW I WITHOUT VIOLENCE KNOCK MY FOEMAN OUT. MARK HOW HE FALLS UPON HIS FACE! THE
DOCT PREFACE(3) GUINEAS IF HE DECIDES IN OUR FAVOR, I CANNOT KNOCK MY SHINS SEVERELY WITHOUT FORCING ON SOME SURGEON THE
APPL I (206) MUCH MATTER ABOUT ME: THE DOCTOR SAYS I OUGHT TO KNOCK OFF A STONE OR TWO; BUT THERE'S SOMETHING MORE TO ME
O'FL (212) OVER THESE RECRUITING MEETINGS. HOWEVER, WE CAN KNOCK OFF FOR THE REST OF THE DAY; AND TOMORROW'S SUNDAY.
2TRU I (47) /THE NURSE/ IF YOU COULD JUMP OUT OF BED TO KNOCK OUT POPSY AND ME YOU CAN JUMP OUT TO DRESS YOURSELF
FANY III (322) AND WHERE ELSE ARE WOMEN TRAINED TO BOX AND KNOCK OUT THE TEETH OF POLICEMEN AS A PROTEST AGAINST
BASH II,1, (103) CROWD THE PERFECT PINK OF HIS CONDITION"-- (A KNOCK). /LYDIA/ (TURNING PALE) BASHVILLE, DIDST HEAR? A
GENV II (61) EXPERIENCE HERE TAUGHT ME HOW HOPELESS IT IS TO KNOCK SUPERNATIONALISM-- /SIR O./ SUPER WHAT? DID YOU SAY
METH PREFACE(R40) GENIUS, WHILST ADMITTING PALEY'S FACTS, COULD KNOCK THE BRAINS OUT OF PALEY BY THE DISCOVERY OF A METHOD
JOAN PREFACE(47) CENTURY, AND STILL MORE THE TWENTIETH, CAN KNOCK THE FIFTEENTH INTO A COCKED HAT IN POINT OF
FABL PREFACE(70) NOT SEE GOD. SUCH A HERESY, IF PUBLISHED, WOULD KNOCK THE KEYSTONE OUT OF THE ARCH OF BRITISH CIVILIZATION.
KING I (198) WHAT YOU NEED IS A BIT OF MY SEA TRAINING TO KNOCK THE NONSENSE OUT OF YOU. /CHARLES/ SO YOU WILL TRY
O'FL (216) BETTER. YOULL NEVER HAVE A QUIET WORLD TIL YOU KNOCK THE PATRIOTISM OUT OF THE HUMAN RACE. /SIR PEARCE/
GENV IV (123) LANGUAGE OF DIPLOMACY-- WE SHOULD BE OBLIGED TO KNOCK THE STUFFING OUT OF YOU. THAT IS OUR BRITISH METHOD OF
SUPR III SD(72) GO STRAIGHT TO THE GUARDIANS FOR RELIEF, AND KNOCK THE WHOLE SOCIAL SYSTEM TO PIECES WITH MOST BENEFICIAL
GETT PREFACE(245) MISCONDUCT ONLY, RUN INTO DANGER BLINDFOLD. ONCE KNOCK THIS FACT INTO PEOPLE'S MINDS, AND THEIR
BARB PREFACE(210) POLITE NOR PROFOUND, WAS PROBABLY INTENDED TO KNOCK THIS NONSENSE VIOLENTLY ON THE HEAD. A SENTENCE
PHIL I (74) DAY FOR YOUR COLDNESS, YOUR-- (A VIOLENT DOUBLE KNOCK WITHOUT. THEY START AND LISTEN, STILL IN ONE ANOTHER'S

BARB II (278)	YOU GOWIN TO FETCH AHT MOG EBBIJEM; OR EM AW TO	KNOCK	YOUR FICE OFF YOU AND FETCH HER MESELF? /JENNY/ (
		KNOCKABOUT	
LIED PREFACE(185)	OF HUSBAND, WIFE, AND LOVER, OR THE FUN OF	KNOCKABOUT	FARCE. I HAVE TAKEN BOTH, AND GOT AN ORIGINAL
		KNOCKED	
BULL I (95)	DONT KNOW WHAT IRISH PRIDE IS. ENGLAND MAY HAVE	KNOCKED	A GOOD DEAL OF IT OUT OF ME; BUT SHE'S NEVER BEEN IN
BULL PREFACE(61)	IRRIGATION INSPECTOR. TWO DAYS AGO THREE NATIVES	KNOCKED	A SOLDIER OFF HIS DONKEY AND KICKED HIM IN THE
ROCK I (223)	DAVY COULDNT STAND THE WAY THE PEOPLE WERE	KNOCKED	ABOUT. HE SCREAMED TO THEM TO STAND. THE INSPECTOR
BULL PREFACE(53)	INJURY, BUT NOT BEFORE THEY HAD BEEN SEVERELY	KNOCKED	ABOUT, ONE OF THEM HAVING ONE OF THE BONES OF HIS
WIDO III (60)	THE NORTH THAMES ICED MUTTON COMPANY. THEYLL BE	KNOCKED	DOWN INSIDE OF TWO YEAR TO MAKE ROOM FOR THE NEW
VWOO 2 (127)	THEY WERE ALL RIGHT; BUT THE OLD PARTS WERE HALF	KNOCKED	DOWN; AND I COULDNT SEE ANY GLORY OR GRANDEUR
GETT (274)	AT SCHOOL YOU HAD A THEORY THAT WOMEN LIKED BEING	KNOCKED	DOWN, I REMEMBER. /REGINALD/ YOURE A NICE,
MTH4 III SD(198)	LIGHTNING AND THUNDER. THE ELDERLY GENTLEMAN IS	KNOCKED	FLAT; BUT AS HE IMMEDIATELY SITS UP AGAIN DAZEDLY IT
GETT (273)	BUT TO HIT HER! ABSOLUTELY TO HIT HER! HE	KNOCKED	HER DOWN-- KNOCKED HER FLAT DOWN ON A FLOWERBED IN
GETT (273)	ABSOLUTELY TO HIT HER! HE KNOCKED HER DOWN--	KNOCKED	HER FLAT DOWN ON A FLOWERBED IN THE PRESENCE OF HIS
FANY I (279)	BE! "; AND I GAVE HIS HELMET A CHUCK BEHIND THAT	KNOCKED	IT OVER HIS EYES, AND DID A BUNK. /MRS GILBEY/ DID A
MILL I (145)	A DEGREE THAT I WENT FOR HIM WITH MY FISTS. HE	KNOCKED	ME OUT WITH THAT ABOMINABLE PUNCH IN THE FIRST
2TRU I (44)	DELICATE! IT'S NOT FIVE MINUTES SINCE YOU	KNOCKED	ME OUT, AND THREW SWEETIE ALL OVER THE ROOM. IF YOU
CATH 1 (170)	MURDERED HIM. (SUBSIDING A LITTLE) HE ALSO	KNOCKED	MY EYE OUT; BUT (SITTING DOWN PLACIDLY) I SUCCEEDED
O'FL (219)	(SOOTHING HIM) NO, DARLINT: THEY ONLY	KNOCKED	OFF HALF A CROWN. I PUT UP WITH IT BECAUSE IVE GOT
SUPR HANDBOK(196)	THOSE WHO RESISTED IT WOULD BE FINED, SOLD UP,	KNOCKED	ON THE HEAD BY POLICEMEN, THROWN INTO PRISON, AND IN
MTH3 (118)	APRON, WHO OPENED THE HOUSE DOOR WHEN PEOPLE	KNOCKED	OR RANG, AND WAS EITHER YOUR TYRANT OR YOUR SLAVE. I
MILL I (145)	PUNCH IN THE FIRST EXCHANGE. HAVE YOU EVER BEEN	KNOCKED	OUT BY A PUNCH IN THE SOLAR PLEXUS? /SAGAMORE/ NO,
ROCK PREFACE(151)	TITLE OF KING, WITH NINE TENTHS OF THE MEANING	KNOCKED	OUT OF IT, TO BE USED AS A MATTER OF CONVENIENCE
FANY II (295)	PRETENDING, PRETENDING. THANK HEAVEN IVE HAD IT	KNOCKED	OUT OF ME ONCE FOR ALL! /MRS KNOX/ (GREATLY
FABL PREFACE(89)	STANLEY JEVONS WOULD PASS IT, THOUGH AFTER HE HAD	KNOCKED	OUT RICARDO AND THE REST WITH HIS CORRECT
FANY III (302)	JUMPING UP, TRIUMPHANT) IVE BEATEN YOU HOLLOW. I	KNOCKED	OUT TWO OF HIS TEETH. IVE GOT ONE OF THEM. HE SOLD
FANY II (291)	HELD OUT HIS HAND WITH HIS TWO TEETH IN IT THAT I	KNOCKED	OUT. I SAID IT WAS ALL RIGHT; THAT I HAD HEARD
FANY I (280)	I COULDNT ALLOW THAT: HE MIGHT HAVE HAD HIS EYE	KNOCKED	OUT. /GILBEY/ (TO DORA, ANGRILY) LISTEN HERE, YOU.
HART II (111)	GET CAUGHT WHEN YOURE ACTUALLY TRYING TO. I HAVE	KNOCKED	OVER ALL THE CHAIRS IN A ROOM WITHOUT A SOUL PAYING
LION PREFACE(79)	OF THE CROSS. IN FACT, NO SOONER HAD JESUS	KNOCKED	OVER THE DRAGON OF SUPERSTITION THAN PAUL BOLDLY SET
MIS. (120)	I'M NOT ALLOWED TEA. AND I'M ASHAMED TO SAY IVE	KNOCKED	OVER YOUR BEAUTIFUL PUNCH-BOWL. YOU MUST LET ME
BULL PREFACE(52)	OUT OF THEM AGAIN, ONE OF THE COACHMEN BEING	KNOCKED	SENSELESS. THEY THEN " AGREED TO RUN," THE
O'FL (219)	FACE. /O'FLAHERTY/ (FURIOUS) DO YOU TELL ME THEY	KNOCKED	TEN SHILLINGS OFF YOU FOR MY KEEP? /MRS O'FLAHERTY/
KING I (191)	I AM AN AGREEABLE SORT OF FELLOW: OLD NEWCASTLE	KNOCKED	THAT INTO ME WHEN I WAS A BOY. LIVING AT THE HAGUE
BULL PREFACE(59)	WOUNDED; THE VILLAGERS HAD LOST THEIR TEMPERS AND	KNOCKED	THE INVADERS ABOUT; AND THE OLDER MEN AND WATCHMEN
METH PREFACE(R12)	AT THE PRESENT MOMENT ONE HALF OF EUROPE, HAVING	KNOCKED	THE OTHER HALF DOWN, IS TRYING TO KICK IT TO DEATH,
FANY II (293)	THAT DUVALLET SWUNG HIS LEG LIKE A WINDMILL AND	KNOCKED	THE POLICEMAN DOWN. AND THEN THREE POLICEMEN RUSHED
ROCK II (267)	HAVE A SPECIAL CABINET FOR IT; AND IT HAS	KNOCKED	THE WHOLE PLACE TO PIECES. WHERE SHOULD YOU AND I BE
METH PREFACE(R65)	FETICHISM. BETWEEN THE TWO OF THEM RELIGION WAS	KNOCKED	TO PIECES; AND WHERE THERE HAD BEEN A GOD, A CAUSE,
MTH2 (70)	THE RELATION OF NAUGHTY CHILDREN WHOSE HEADS SHE	KNOCKED	TOGETHER WHEN THEIR TEMPERS AND QUARRELS BECAME
FANY II (288)	I DID. I HAD THAT SATISFACTION AT ALL EVENTS. I	KNOCKED	TWO OF HIS TEETH OUT. /KNOX/ AND YOU SIT THERE
MIS. (150)	AVIATOR/ I'M REALLY VERY SORRY. I'M AFRAID IVE	KNOCKED	YOUR VINERY INTO A COCKED HAT. (EFFUSIVELY) YOU
		KNOCKER	
HART I (69)	TO RING. /CAPTAIN SHOTOVER/ WHY SHOULD THERE BE A	KNOCKER	? WHY SHOULD THE BELL RING? THE DOOR IS OPEN. /THE
HART I (69)	MY INTRUDING IN THIS FASHION; BUT THERE IS NO	KNOCKER	ON THE DOOR; AND THE BELL DOES NOT SEEM TO RING.
DOCT I (83)	BACK, HE SAID. ALL THE REST WILL BE HERE TOO: THE	KNOCKER	WILL BE GOING ALL DAY. WHAT I'M AFRAID OF IS THAT
		KNOCKERS	
CLEO IV (189)	STREETS AGAIN REACHES THEM). DO YOU HEAR? THESE	KNOCKERS	AT YOUR GATE ARE ALSO BELIEVERS IN VENGEANCE AND IN
		KNOCKING	
ARMS II (28)	ARE YOU DEAF? DONT YOU HEAR MAJOR SARANOFF	KNOCKING	? BRING HIM ROUND THIS WAY. (HE PRONOUNCES THE
ROCK PREFACE(148)	A TILE FOR FLYING OFF A ROOF IN A STORM AND	KNOCKING	A CLERGYMAN ON THE HEAD. BUT TO KILL THEM IS QUITE
MIS. (204)	WITH YOU. /LINA/ (SLAPPING HIM ON THE BACK AND	KNOCKING	A GHASTLY WHITE SMILE INTO HIS FACE) YOU SHALL. I
BULL PREFACE(61)	OF SUNSTROKE HAD BEEN PREDISPOSED TO IT BY THE	KNOCKING	ABOUT HE HAD SUFFERED AND BY HIS FLIGHT UNDER THE
SUPR HANDBOK(202)	KILL, BURN, AND DESTROY TRIBES AND VILLAGES FOR	KNOCKING	AN ENGLISHMAN ON THE HEAD ARE SO COMMON A PART OF
ARMS I (10)	THE NOISE SUBSIDES SUDDENLY. /LOUKA/ (OUTSIDE,	KNOCKING	AT THE BEDROOM DOOR) MY LADY! MY LADY! GET UP
JOAN EPILOG (160)	OLD CHANTY: RUM TUM TRUMPLE -- HULLO! WHO'S THAT	KNOCKING	AT THE DOOR? THEY LISTEN. A LONG GENTLE KNOCKING
UNPL PREFACE(R10)	AN ENLIGHTENMENT UNKNOWN TO MY SCHOOLDAYS, CAME	KNOCKING	AT THE DOOR TOO: I GLANCED BACK AT MY OLD COLUMNS
ARMS II (27)	REFINED PEOPLE NOTICE SUCH THINGS. /SERGIUS/ (	KNOCKING	AT THE STABLE GATES) GATE, NICOLA! /PETKOFF/
PHIL II (104)	TO THE OPPOSITE RECESS BY WAY OF THE FENDER,	KNOCKING	DOWN THE FIREIRONS WITH A CRASH AS HE DOES SO).
PYGM I (206)	A FLOWER GIRL, WHO IS HURRYING IN FOR SHELTER,	KNOCKING	HER BASKET OUT OF HER HANDS. A BLINDING FLASH OF
LION II SD(143)	CAR; FINALLY RUBS HIMSELF AGAINST ANDROCLES,	KNOCKING	HIM OVER. ANDROCLES, SUPPORTING HIMSELF ON HIS
JOAN EPIL,SD(160)	KNOCKING AT THE DOOR? THEY LISTEN. A LONG GENTLE	KNOCKING	IS HEARD. /CHARLES/ COME IN. THE DOOR OPENS; AND AN
GENV I (41)	SOMEONE KNOCKS AT THE DOOR. /SHE/ SHSH! SOMEONE	KNOCKING	. THEY SEPARATE HASTILY, HE GOING TO THE STOVE AND
GETT (278)	CHEEK TO PRETEND TO BELIEVE ALL THAT ROT ABOUT MY	KNOCKING	LEO ABOUT AND LEAVING HER FOR-- FOR A-- A-- UGH!
KING I (188)	PRIVILEGE WITH ME DOES NOT RUN TO THE LENGTH OF	KNOCKING	MY BROTHER DOWN. IT IS A SERIOUS MATTER TO LAY
DEVL I (5)	I DARESAY. DROPPED OFF! (FIERCELY, AS THE	KNOCKING	RECOMMENCES) WHY DONT YOU GET UP AND LET YOUR UNCLE
MTH5 (241)	FIGURE/ (TRYING TO ASSERT HIMSELF WITH HIS KNEES	KNOCKING	) MY NAME IS OZYMANDIAS, KING OF-- /THE HE-ANCIENT/
BULL PREFACE(7)	BE ABLE TO FACE HOME RULE WITHOUT HIS KNEES	KNOCKING	SHAMEFULLY IN THE FACE OF A CONTEMPTUOUS ENGLAND
2TRU III SD(81)	A GOTHIC SUGGESTION WHICH HAS BEEN ASSISTED BY	KNOCKING	THE TOP OF THE OPENING INTO SOMETHING LIKE A
2TRU III SD(112)	FAVORITE IS THE WOMAN OF ACTION, WHO BEGINS BY	KNOCKING	THE WIND OUT OF THE RASCAL, AND ENDS WITH A
ARMS II SD(25)	THATS THE SECRET OF SUCCESS IN SERVICE. A LOUD	KNOCKING	WITH A WHIP HANDLE ON A WOODEN DOOR IS HEARD FROM
KING I (188)	PERSONAGE. /NEWTON/ SIR: I HAD NO INTENTION OF	KNOCKING	YOUR ROYAL BROTHER DOWN. HE FELL AND DRAGGED ME
DEVL I SD(4)	DOOR, NOT LOUD ENOUGH TO WAKE THE SLEEPERS. THEN	KNOCKING	, WHICH DISTURBS MRS DUDGEON A LITTLE. FINALLY THE
		KNOCK-OUT	
MTH2 (56)	OVER THAT BUSINESS, BURGE! DO YOU REMEMBER THE	KNOCK-OUT	BLOW? /BURGE/ IT CAME OFF: DONT FORGET THAT. DO
MILL I (148)	POSE OF A MARTYR) YES: STRIKE ME. SHEW HER YOUR	KNOCK-OUT	PUNCH. LET HER SEE HOW YOU TREAT WOMEN. /ALASTAIR/
		KNOCKS	
GETT (276)	THAT SHOULD NOT BE FORGIVEN TO A MAN. WHEN A MAN	KNOCKS	A WOMAN DOWN (LEO GIVES A LITTLE SHRIEK OF LAUGHTER
JOAN 3 (92)	TO PRAYERS: THEY UNDERSTAND NOTHING BUT HARD	KNOCKS	AND SLASHES. I WILL NOT GO TO CHURCH UNTIL WE HAVE
LION II (133)	THEY FIGHT FAIRLY. (HE GOES UP TO HIS BOX, AND	KNOCKS	AT IT. IT IS OPENED FROM WITHIN BY THE CAPTAIN, WHO
DEVL II (32)	WHEN I WAS OUT? /JUDITH/ NO, ONLY-- (SOMEONE	KNOCKS	AT THE DOOR. WITH A START WHICH BETRAYS HER INTENSE
MRS IV SD(239)	THAT YOU KNOW OF, FORTUNATELY FOR YOU. SOMEONE	KNOCKS	AT THE DOOR. /FRANK/ MY CURSE UPON YOUR CALLER,
GENV I SD(41)	YOU ARE A PEACH. (HE KISSES HER). SOMEONE	KNOCKS	AT THE DOOR. /SHE/ SHSH! SOMEONE KNOCKING. THEY
GENV I SD(29)	SPEECH AND MANNERS ARE LONDON SUBURBAN. SOMEBODY	KNOCKS	AT THE DOOR. SHE HASTILY TAKES HER HEELS OFF THE
DOCT III (133)	COME IF IT DIDNT AMUSE THEM, ANYHOW. (SOMEONE	KNOCKS	AT THE DOOR). I SAY! IT'S NOT TIME YET, IS IT? /MRS
PPP (195)	MAGNESIA/ MY SWEET MOTHER-IN-LAW! (SOMEONE	KNOCKS	AT THE DOOR). THAT IS ADOLPHUS'S KNOCK. (FITZ'S FACE
DEVL I (13)	DOOR IN HER FACE). NICE MANNERS, THAT! (SOMEONE	KNOCKS	AT THE HOUSE DOOR: SHE TURNS AND CRIES INHOSPITABLY)
CYMB V (143)	HAVE A PLAY WITH THIS? THERE LIES THY PART (HE	KNOCKS	HER DOWN WITH A BLOW OF HIS FIST). /GUIDERIUS/
CURE (234)	OH, YOU BEAUTIFUL DOLL. /STREGA/ TAKE THAT (SHE	KNOCKS	HIM SPRAWLING OVER THE KEYBOARD)! BEAUTIFUL DOLL
CAND I (99)	A PIECE OF WHOLESOME PLAIN SPEAKING FOR YOU. (HE	KNOCKS	IN THE LESSON WITH A NOD IN HIS OLD WAY, AND POSTS
DEVL I SD(7)	AND VILLAINS, THE SCUM OF THE EARTH! SOMEONE	KNOCKS	. /CHRISTY/ (WITHOUT MOVING) THATS THE MINISTER.
DEVL III (54)	WHAT WORSE-- CAN IT MEAN TO ME? (THE SERGEANT	KNOCKS	. THE BLOW ON THE DOOR JARS ON HER HEART). OH, ONE
APPL INTR,SD(255)	CLEARS HIS THROAT AND BLOWS HIS NOSE NOISILY; AND	KNOCKS	LOUDLY AND REPEATEDLY. THE TWO COMBATANTS CEASE
2TRU II (68)	I SHALL GET USED TO IT IN TIME. BUT AT PRESENT IT	KNOCKS	ME TO PIECES. I SHALL SIMPLY HAVE TO GO AWAY IF YOU
DEVL I (15)	ONLY-- MY FATHER WAS A SMUGGLER; AND-- (SOMEONE	KNOCKS	). /JUDITH/ THEY ARE BEGINNING TO COME. NOW REMEMBER
PRES (136)	(SOMEONE OUTSIDE TRIES TO OPEN THE DOOR AND THEN	KNOCKS	). WHATS THAT? /MITCHENER/ WHO'S THERE? /THE
SHAK SD(140)	NINE-- AT THE COUNT OF NINE SHAV SPRINGS UP AND	KNOCKS	SHAKES DOWN WITH A RIGHT TO THE CHIN. /SHAV/ (
SHAK SD(139)	UP YOUR HANDS. /SHAV/ COME ON. THEY SPAR. SHAKES	KNOCKS	SHAV DOWN WITH A STRAIGHT LEFT AND BEGINS COUNTING
CAND II (121)	ROOM TO THE FIREPLACE; PROTESTING AS HE GOES, AND	KNOCKS	THE ASHES OUT OF HIS PIPE ON THE BARS). MORELL SITS

MIS. (147) THING THE EMPIRE. EDUCATES US. OPENS OUR MINDS. KNOCKS THE BIBLE OUT OF US. AND CIVILIZES THE OTHER CHAPS.
MTH5 SD(241) OO! OOH! /THE HE-ANCIENT/ SILENCE, I SAY. HE KNOCKS THE MALE AUTOMATON UPRIGHT BY A VERY LIGHT FLIP UNDER
LADY (243) YOUR FILTHY TRULL. (WITH TWO VIGOROUS CUFFS, SHE KNOCKS THE PAIR ASUNDER, SENDING THE MAN, WHO IS UNLUCKY
BASH II,1, (105) TOUCHED. OPEN THE DOOR. /BASHVILLE/ DESTRUCTION KNOCKS THEREAT. I SMILE, AND OPEN. (BASHVILLE OPENS THE
UNPL PREFACE(R10) IN THEIR CRADLES. I LISTENED TO THEIR VIGOROUS KNOCKS WITH EXULTATION FOR THE RACE, WITH PENURIOUS ALARM
GETT (347) DO MAKE HIM SEE THAT THERE ARE NO WORMS BEFORE HE KNOCKS YOU DOWN, EDITH. WHERES REJJY? /REGINALD/ (COMING

KNOLL
BULL II SD(111) CAR BY CARRYING THE ROAD PARTLY ROUND THE KNOLL AND PARTLY THROUGH A CUTTING; SO THAT THE WAY FROM THE
BULL II SD(111) GREENSWARD ON IT. THE ROAD ONCE RAN OVER THIS KNOLL ; BUT MODERN ENGINEERING HAS TEMPERED THE LEVEL TO THE
BULL II SD(111) SOME FIFTY YARDS SOUTH OF THE ROAD ON A KNOLL WITH A CIRCLE OF WILD GREENSWARD ON IT. THE ROAD ONCE

KNOLLEDGE
CAND I (85) " KNOALEDGE" IN CHURCH, THOUGH YOU ALWAYS SAY " KNOLLEDGE " IN PRIVATE CONVERSATION! BAH! DO YOU THINK I

KNOLLIDGE
CAPT III (292) KEPN IN THE WORLD. WOT MIKES A KEPN IS BRINES AN KNOLLIDGE O LAWF. IT YNT THET THERS NAOW SITCH PUSSON: ITS

KNOT
PPP (201) IT? /FITZ/ TRY THE BUN. /ADOLPHUS/ (GNAWING THE KNOT OF HAIR AT THE BACK OF THE BUST'S HEAD: IT MAKES HIM
GETT PREFACE(216) STITCH IS RIPPED, IS VERY APPLICABLE TO THE KNOT OF MARRIAGE. REMOTENESS OF THE FACTS FROM THE IDEAL.
CAPT I SD(217) FLANNEL SHIRT WITH WHITE COLLAR, A GREEN SAILOR KNOT TIE WITH A CHEAP PIN IN IT, HE WEARS A SUIT OF CLEAN

KNOTS
CAPT III (284) THE CADI STIMULATED HIMSELF TO SOME TEN KNOTS AN HOUR, AND LODGED YOU AND YOUR MEN IN MOGADOR JAIL
JOAN EPILOG (165) PRAISE THEE, BECAUSE THOU HAST CUT THE KNOTS IN WHICH THEY HAVE TIED THEIR OWN SOULS. /DE
CAPT III (284) OF THAT INFORMATION THE SANTIAGO MADE THE TWENTY KNOTS TO MOGADOR HARBOR INSIDE OF FIFTY-SEVEN MINUTES.

KNOTTED
DEVL II (42) KNOW-- (DISTRACTED, SHE BURIES HER FACE IN HER KNOTTED HANDS). /ANDERSON/ (BREAKING DOWN AND COMING TO

KNOUT
CATH 4 (194) ANGEL MOTHER, DONT EVER DO THIS TO A MAN AGAIN. KNOUT HIM; KILL HIM; ROAST HIM; BASTE HIM; HEAD, HANG, AND
CATH 3 (186) HE WILL RECEIVE A HUNDRED AND ONE BLOWS OF THE KNOUT . (HE LAUGHS AND GOES OUT, NURSING HIS BITTEN
MIS. (175) GALLOWS; LET THEMSELVES BE CUT IN PIECES WITH THE KNOUT , OR DRIVEN THROUGH THE FROZEN SNOWS OF SIBERIA,

KNOUTED
CATH 4 (190) RUSH OUT) NARYSHKIN: ARE YOU WAITING TO BE KNOUTED ? (NARYSHKIN BACKS OUT HASTILY). CATHERINE AND
ANNA (297) AND YOU WERE THERE WITH YOUR OWN PASSPORT, THEY KNOUTED HIM. /THE GRAND DUCHESS/ OH! STRAMMFEST: SEND THESE
CATH 3 (184) TO LOSE. /CLAIRE/ MAY I TELL HER SHE WILL BE KNOUTED IF WE STAY? /EDSTASTON/ DO, DEAREST. HE KISSES HER
CATH 2 (181) (TURNING FROM THE DOOR) SHE WILL HAVE HIM KNOUTED . HE IS A DEAD MAN. /THE PRINCESS DASHKOFF/ BUT WHAT
CATH 4 (192) THERE, ON YOUR LIFE. DRAG HER BACK. YOU WILL BE KNOUTED . IT IS HOPELESS, MADEMOISELLE: YOU MUST OBEY
CATH 3 (183) BECAUSE I DIDNT PARTICULARLY WANT TO HAVE YOU KNOUTED , AND TO BE HANGED OR SENT TO SIBERIA MYSELF.

KNOW
PHIL II (128) IN HIS AGITATION) WELL, TO GET A LITTLE REST, YOU KNOW : A BUSY PROFESSIONAL MAN LIKE THAT! HE'S NOT HAD A
DOCT I (105) BROMIDE. IF THAT DOESNT ANSWER A STIMULANT, YOU KNOW : A LITTLE PHOSPHORUS AND STRYCHNINE. IF YOU CANT
KING II (228) ANY OF THEM WHAT HIS SECT BELIEVES HE DOES NOT KNOW : ALL HE CAN SAY IS THAT THE MEN OF THE OTHER SECTS
FABL PREFACE(74) THAT IT MADE ITSELF, OR RETORTED " WE DONT KNOW : AND NEITHER DO YOU," I, AS A CREATIVE EVOLUTIONIST,
FANY I (279) THE NOD; SO WE STARTED TO WALK, VERY JOLLY, YOU KNOW : ARM IN ARM, AND DANCING ALONG, SINGING AND ALL THAT.
ROCK I (221) WE PRIME MINISTERS HAVE TO BE, MR HIPNEY! YOU KNOW : DONT YOU? (HE OFFERS HIS HAND TO SIGNIFY THAT THE
NEVR III (268) TO GIVE UP HIS OLD FASHIONED PLAN OF ATTACK: YOU KNOW : GOING DOWN ON HIS KNEES AND SWEARING TO LOVE, HONOR,
MTH2 (47) LEAVE NOT A RACK BEHIND." THATS BIOLOGY, YOU KNOW : GOOD SOUND BIOLOGY. (HE SITS DOWN. SO DO THE OTHERS,
HART I (58) CONCERT. I WAS SINGING THERE. AS AN AMATEUR, YOU KNOW : HALF A GUINEA FOR EXPENSES AND THREE SONGS WITH THREE
ARMS III (61) TO BLUNTSCHLI) WHAT ABOUT? /BLUNTSCHLI/ I DONT KNOW : HE HASNT TOLD ME. BETTER NOT INTERFERE, DEAR YOUNG
2TRU II (70) A LOT IN THE WAR, JUST FOR THE ROMANCE OF IT, YOU KNOW : HE MEANT NO HARM. BUT HE'D NEVER SHOT ANYONE WITH
JITT I (19) KNOW. YES: HE NOT ONLY DOES NOT KNOW: HE WILL NOT KNOW : HE REFUSES TO KNOW. AND THAT REFUSAL, BECAUSE IT IS
JITT I (19) NOT LET HIMSELF KNOW. YES: HE NOT ONLY DOES NOT KNOW : HE WILL NOT KNOW: HE REFUSES TO KNOW. AND THAT
PHIL I (91) POOR CHILD. I'LL HAVE TO APOLOGIZE FOR HER, YOU KNOW : HER GOING AWAY IS A DOWNRIGHT SLAP IN THE FACE FOR
JOAN 1 (69) UP FOR HIS HALO RATHER APPREHENSIVELY) I DONT KNOW : HOW DID SHE GET INTO MY PRESENCE? IF THE DAUPHIN CAN
PYGM V (281) WAY. BUT DONT SAY NOTHING TO ELIZA. SHE DONT KNOW : I ALWAYS HAD A DELICACY ABOUT TELLING HER.
JITT III (73) ABOUT ME AS YOU DO. HE IS RIGHT ABOUT ME, YOU KNOW : I AM NOT A GOOD WOMAN. HAVE YOU QUITE FORGOTTEN THAT
MIS. (115) BUNNY! THAT WAS A NAUGHTY WORD. /BENTLEY/ YES, I KNOW : I BEG YOUR PARDON. (HE RISES, AND EXTRICATES HIMSELF
WIDO I (18) IS SARTORIUS? /TRENCH/ (TAKEN ABACK) I DONT KNOW : I DIDNT ASK. IT'S A SORT OF QUESTION YOU CANT VERY
VWOO 3 (138) OF MARRIAGE. /Z/ (REMORSEFULLY) OH, I DIDNT KNOW : I DIDNT INDEED. I WAS ONLY JOKING. (SHE SITS AGAIN)
FANY II (285) WHAT MAKES YOU THINK THAT? /KNOX/ WELL, I DONT KNOW : I DIDNT LIKE TO TELL YOU: YOU HAVE ENOUGH TO WORRY
GETT (346) THE DEVIL DID HE DO THAT FOR? /SYKES/ OH, I DONT KNOW : I DIDNT MAKE ANY BARGAIN WITH HIM. (TO MRS GEORGE)
FANY PROLOG (261) TO SAY IT IS A MODERN PLAY? /SAVOYARD/ I DONT KNOW : I DIDNT READ IT. I HANDED IT TO BILLY BURJOYCE-- THE
MRS I (186) NOT FROM ANY SHORTCOMING ON YOUR PART, YOU KNOW : I DONT MEAN THAT. BUT YOU ARE SO DIFFERENT FROM HER
VWOO 1 (116) LIKE IT IN THE SEASON, IS THERE? /A/ I DONT KNOW : I HAVE NEVER BEEN THERE. /Z/ (DISAPPOINTED) OH, YOU
FANY III (314) BUT I DO SAY THAT SHE DIDNT KNOW WHAT WE KNOW : I MEAN THE WAY CERTAIN TEMPTATIONS GET A SUDDEN HOLD
CAND II (109) (PASSIONATELY) NO: ANSWER ME. I WANT TO KNOW : I MUST KNOW. I CANT UNDERSTAND IT. I CAN SEE NOTHING
CURE (234) LIKE IT? /REGINALD/ AWFULLY. OH, I SAY, YOU KNOW : I REALLY DO WISH YOU BELONGED TO ME. (STREGA
LION I (118) FOR? /LENTULUS/ (IRRESOLUTELY) LOOK HERE, YOU KNOW : I -- YOU-- I -- /LAVINIA/ STUFF! GO ABOUT YOUR
FOUN (211) SITS DOWN). /BRABAZON/ DONT MENTION IT. WELL, YOU KNOW : I WANT SOME GOOD HOME INFLUENCE TO STEADY ME. YOU SEE
GENV I (31) I'D SEE ALL THE GREAT MEN. I AM AMBITIOUS, YOU KNOW : I WON A LONDON COUNTY COUNCIL SCHOLARSHIP. I WANTED A
MTH4 I (146) IT IS A CIVILIZED COUNTRY. (DESPERATELY) I DONT KNOW : I-- I-- I-- I SHALL GO MAD IF YOU KEEP ON ASKING ME
FOUN (214) THOSE OF HIS OWN HEAD." THATS A NASTY ONE, YOU KNOW : ISNT IT? IT MEANS THAT YOUR BRAINS ARE WOOLLY,
SUPR I (35) AND WOMANHOOD MEAN IN MOST PEOPLE'S MOUTHS? YOU KNOW : IT MEANS THE BEGINNING OF LOVE. BUT LOVE BEGAN LONG
KING II (227) AND MARRIED RICHMOND. /CATHERINE/ OH, I KNOW, I KNOW : IT WAS THE ONLY TIME I EVER WAS JEALOUS. WELL, I
CAND I (87) IS PRIVILEGED TO BE A BIT OF A FOOL, YOU KNOW : IT'S ONY BECOMIN IN 'IS PROFESSION THAT HE SHOULD.
MTH4 II (179) CANNOT SEE THEM. YOU FEEL YOURSELF MY SUPERIOR, I KNOW : NAY, YOU ARE MY SUPERIOR: HAVE I NOT BOWED MY KNEE TO
ARMS I (16) HER, APOLOGIZING). PERHAPS I'M QUITE WRONG, YOU KNOW : NO DOUBT I AM. MOST LIKELY HE HAD GOT WIND OF THE
DEST (189) OH, I SAY, GENERAL! NO, LOOK HERE, YOU KNOW : NOBODY CAN SAY I'M A COWARD AFTER LODI. BUT TO ASK ME
MRS IV (246) WILL STAY HERE. /MRS WARREN/ (SCARED) I DONT KNOW : PERHAPS I'D BETTER GO. WE'RE DISTURBING YOU AT YOUR
ROCK II (261) WHO WOULD KEEP THEM IN ORDER, I SHOULD LIKE TO KNOW : SILLY AMATEURS. AND LET ME REMIND YOU OF ONE THING.
DOCT V (179) ERROR) HE WAS ONE OF THE MEN WHO KNOW WHAT WOMEN KNOW : THAT SELF-SACRIFICE IS VAIN AND COWARDLY. /RIDGEON/
GETT (289) HERE UNTIL AFTER THE CEREMONY. /HOTCHKISS/ YES, I KNOW : THATS JUST IT. MAY I HAVE A WORD WITH YOU IN
MRS III (224) IT'S A REGULAR OLD THIRTEENTH CENTURY CHURCH, YOU KNOW : THE GOV'NOR'S EVER SO FOND OF IT, BECAUSE HE GOT UP A
LIED (198) OFF A SET OF SONGS TO THE SUNRISE. AURORA, YOU KNOW : THE ROSY FINGERED AURORA. THEYRE ALL ABOUT AURORA.
FANY II (294) THEM IN A REVERENT TONE OF VOICE. /MARGARET/ I KNOW : THE TONE THAT SHEWS THEY DONT MEAN ANYTHING REAL TO
JITT I (17) THINK OF THE MOST HARDENED MATERIALIST YOU KNOW : THE VERY LAST MAN YOU COULD IMAGINE LENDING HIMSELF
MTH1 I (18) THAT IS TRUE. WHAT IS A FOOL? /EVE/ I DO NOT KNOW : THE WORD CAME TO ME. IT IS WHAT YOU ARE WHEN YOU
DOCT III (133) THIS PLACE, WONT YOU? IT'S ONLY A STUDIO, YOU KNOW : THERES NO REAL CONVENIENCE FOR LIVING HERE. BUT WE
AUGS (283) AT RUMPELMEISTER'S? . . . RUM-PEL-MEISTER'S. YOU KNOW : THEY CALL IT ROBINSON'S NOW. . . . RIGHT. TA TA. (
CAND I (103) JUSTIFIABLE-- /MARCHBANKS/ (CUTTING HIM SHORT) I KNOW : TO LIE. IT WILL BE USELESS. GOODBYE, MR CLERGYMAN. AS
CAND II (120) WITH HER HANDS IN HER LAP). SOME DAY HE WILL KNOW : WHEN HE IS GROWN UP AND EXPERIENCED, LIKE YOU. AND HE
ARMS I (21) OF FALLING). WHERE AM I? THATS WHAT I WANT TO KNOW : WHERE AM I? MUST KEEP AWAKE. NOTHING KEEPS ME AWAKE
BULL IV (174) THE UNION, POOR OLD CHAP! HE'S WORKED OUT, YOU KNOW : YOU CAN SEE IT. /KEEGAN/ POOR LOST SOUL, SO CUNNINGLY
JOAN 6 (149) I WOULD HAVE TORN HER FROM THEIR HANDS. YOU DONT KNOW : YOU HAVNT SEEN: IT IS SO EASY TO TALK WHEN YOU DONT
MIS. (202) WITH INCREASED RESPECT) HAVE YOU INDEED? I DIDNT KNOW : YOULL EXCUSE MY MISTAKE, I HOPE. BUT THE PRINCIPLE IS
BARB II (282) REMEMBER HOW) BILL WALKER? (RECOLLECTING) OH, I KNOW : YOURE THE MAN THAT JENNY HILL WAS PRAYING FOR INSIDE
FANY III (316) DO TOMORROW MORNING? /GILBEY/ WHY SHOULDNT I KNOW ? ARE WE CHILDREN NOT TO BE LET DO WHAT WE LIKE, AND
PHIL I (70) TRANFIELD FOR MONEY? /CHARTERIS/ HOW DO I KNOW ? BESIDES, YOU MIGHT HAVE MARRIED HIM NOT BECAUSE YOU
GETT PREFACE(225) WHAT CAN THEY KNOW OF ENGLAND THAT ONLY ENGLAND KNOW ? DISPOSES NOT ONLY OF THE PATRIOTS WHO ARE SO
DOCT III (152) YOU MEAN? /MRS DUBEDAT/ OH, DO YOU THINK I DONT KNOW ? DO YOU THINK IT HAS NEVER HAPPENED BEFORE? WHY DOES
JITT III (72) RECOLLECT. I-- I SOMETIMES WONDER DOES EVERYBODY KNOW ? DOES MY MOTHER KNOW? /JITTA/ (QUICKLY) YOUR MOTHER

GENV I	(42)	COMMERCIAL PROSPERITY. ARE PEOPLE MAD? DONT THEY	KNOW ?	DONT THEY CARE? /HE/ MY! MY! MY! (HE TAKES A
MIS.	(193)	YOU THAT I OUGHT TO KNOW OR THAT BENTLEY OUGHT TO	KNOW ?	HAVE YOU SAID ANYTHING TO MR PERCIVAL? /HYPATIA/ MR
VWOO 1	(118)	FOR A MOMENT THAT YOU WERE. /Z/ BUT HOW COULD YOU	KNOW ?	HOW DID YOU FIND OUT? /A/ I DIDNT FIND OUT. I KNEW.
ROCK II	(243)	/GLENMORISON/ FIFTY. /SIR JAFNA/ HOW DO YOU	KNOW ?	HOW DO YOU KNOW? THE WAY I AM PLUNDERED AT EVERY
MTH3	(112)	HOW DO I KNOW! /THE ARCHBISHOP/ YES: HOW DO YOU	KNOW ?	I DID NOT BEGIN EVEN TO SUSPECT UNTIL I WAS NEARLY
MTH5	(207)	SEE. YOU ARE GROWING UP. /THE MAIDEN/ HOW DO YOU	KNOW ?	I DO NOT LOOK SO MUCH OLDER, DO I? /THE ANCIENT/
ARMS II	(24)	IF-- /LOUKA/ (TURNING ON HIM QUICKLY) HOW DO YOU	KNOW ?	I NEVER TOLD YOU! /NICOLA/ (OPENING HIS EYES
MILL I	(143)	THE REST OF IT. HOW CAN I LAUGH AT THINGS I DONT	KNOW ?	IF I AM LAUGHING-- AND AM I REALLY LAUGHING? -- I
FABL VI	(122)	TO ASK QUESTIONS. IS THERE NOTHING YOU WANT TO	KNOW ?	IF NOT, THE SIXTH FORM IS NOT FOR YOU: IT IS OUT OF
GETT	(352)	IT IF YOURE NOT REMAINING. /HOTCHKISS/ HOW DO I	KNOW ?	IS MY DESTINY ANY LONGER IN MY OWN HANDS? GO: ASK
PRES	(140)	THE STANDING OF HIS MAN BETTER! WHY DIDNT HE	KNOW ?	IT WAS HIS BUSINESS TO KNOW. HE OUGHT TO BE FLOGGED.
MILL II	(172)	WHATEVER THE MATTER. /EPIFANIA/ HOW DO YOU	KNOW ?	IT'S MY HAND, NOT YOURS. /THE DOCTOR/ YOU WOULD
GETT	(300)	NOT GOING TO COMMIT MURDER. /EDITH/ HOW DO YOU	KNOW ?	IVE SOMETIMES WANTED TO MURDER SLATTOX. HAVE YOU
CAND I	(85)	PRIVATE CONVERSATION! BAH! DO YOU THINK I DONT	KNOW ?	(SHE GOES BACK TO THE TYPEWRITER). HERE! COME AND
DEVL III	(53)	HEART. /JUDITH/ (ALMOST IN A WHISPER) HOW DO YOU	KNOW ?	(SHE PUTS HER HANDS ON HIS SHOULDERS AND LOOKS
FANY I	(275)	GILBEY/ DONT JUMP TO CONCLUSIONS, ROB. HOW DO YOU	KNOW ?	(TO JUGGINS) IS SHE A LADY, JUGGINS? YOU KNOW WHAT
BARB I	(267)	YES; BUT WHAT ABOUT THE CANNON BUSINESS, DONT YOU	KNOW ?	(TO UNDERSHAFT) GETTING INTO HEAVEN IS NOT EXACTLY
WIDO II	(32)	WHICH OF US IS THE WORSE, I SHOULD LIKE TO	KNOW ?	ME THAT WRINGS THE MONEY OUT TO KEEP A HOME OVER MY
ROCK I	(201)	AT HER) DONT REMIND ME OF IT: DO YOU THINK I DONT	KNOW ?	MY BRAIN IS OVERWORKED: MY MENTAL GRASP IS STRETCHED
BARB II	(279)	EM TRY YOU. THEYLL FIND THE DIFFER. WHAT DO YOU	KNOW ?	NOT AS MUCH AS HOW TO BEEYAVE YOURSELF-- LAYIN YOUR
SUPR II	(69)	ME! ! ! /STRAKER/ MEAN TO TELL ME YOU DIDNT	KNOW ?	OH, COME, MR TANNER! /TANNER/ (IN FIERCE EARNEST)
JITT III	(73)	HAS SUFFERED EVER SINCE. /EDITH/ BUT HOW DO YOU	KNOW ?	OH, TELL ME. YOU MUST TELL ME NOW. /JITTA/ WHEN YOU
HART I	(63)	HER) HESIONE: YOU ARE A WITCH. HOW DO YOU	KNOW ?	OH, YOU ARE THE MOST SYMPATHETIC WOMAN IN THE WORLD.
FABL VI	(125)	HAVE A CREATOR. /TEACHER/ MUST IT? HOW DO YOU	KNOW ?	ONE OF THE ANCIENT GODS, NAMED NAPOLEON, POINTED TO
ROCK PREFACE	(181)	KING OF THE JEWS? /JESUS/ DO YOU REALLY WANT TO	KNOW ?	OR HAVE THOSE PEOPLE OUTSIDE PUT IT INTO YOUR HEAD
FOUN	(217)	I THINK I AM. /THE LORD CHANCELLOR/ DONT YOU	KNOW ?	/ANASTASIA/ NO. I WAS BROUGHT UP IN WHAT YOU MIGHT
VWOO 1	(118)	YOU? /A/ NOBODY TOLD ME. /Z/ THEN HOW DID YOU	KNOW ?	/A/ (EXASPERATED) HOW DO I KNOW THAT A PARROT ISNT
PRES	(163)	WHAT ARE ITS CONVENIENCES, I SHOULD LIKE TO	KNOW ?	/BALSQUITH/ WELL, WHEN YOU TELL PEOPLE THAT THEY ARE
MTH3	(111)	FOR ME. /THE ARCHBISHOP/ (COOLLY) HOW DO YOU	KNOW ?	/BARNABAS/ (TAKEN ABACK) HOW DO I KNOW! /THE
ARMS III	(73)	HAVE YOU? /SERGIUS/ HOW THE DEUCE DO I	KNOW ?	/BLUNTSCHLI/ HAVE YOU FOUR THOUSAND? /SERGIUS/ NO.
MTH2	(53)	NOT I. /FRANKLYN/ DO YOU MEAN TO SAY YOU DID NOT	KNOW ?	/BURGE/ (SITTING DOWN AGAIN WITH A SHRUG) OH, I HAD
HART II	(120)	AGAIN. /CAPTAIN SHOTOVER/ WHY? /ELLIE/ DONT YOU	KNOW ?	/CAPTAIN SHOTOVER/ NO. /ELLIE/ HEARTBREAK. I FELL IN
FABL II	(105)	WHAT THE DEVIL ARE WE TO DO? HOW MUCH DO YOU	KNOW ?	/C.-IN-C./ ONLY THAT THERE IS NOT ONE OF GOD'S
BULL III	(127)	HIS LEFT? WHAT DID HE EVER SUFFER, I'D LIKE TO	KNOW ?	/CORNELIUS/ THATS JUST WHAT I SAY. I WASNT COMPARIN
NEVR I	(213)	/GLORIA/ DO YOU INTEND THAT WE SHALL NEVER	KNOW ?	/DOLLY/ OH GLORIA, DONT. IT'S BARBAROUS. /GLORIA/ (
BULL I	(94)	BUT SHE IS WAITING FOR ME. /BROADBENT/ HOW DO YOU	KNOW ?	/DOYLE/ SHE WRITES TO ME-- ON HER BIRTHDAY. SHE USED
HART I	(59)	WAS NOT TELLING LIES. /MRS HUSHABYE/ HOW DO YOU	KNOW ?	/ELLIE/ SHAKESPEAR WOULD HAVE SAID IF HE WAS.
MILL I	(161)	WHAT WOULD SHE BE WITHOUT HER MONEY, I'D LIKE TO	KNOW ?	/EPIFANIA/ NOBODY IS ANYBODY WITHOUT MONEY.
FANY PROLOG	(272)	THE STAGIRITE! DO YOU MEAN TO SAY YOU DONT	KNOW ?	/FANNY/ HAVNT THE LEAST NOTION. /THE COUNT/ THE
JITT II	(43)	ON HER, A SUSPICION FLASHING ON HIM) HOW DO YOU	KNOW ?	/JITTA/ (CHECKING HERSELF, FEELING THAT HER TEMPER
JITT III	(72)	WONDER DOES EVERYBODY KNOW? DOES MY MOTHER	KNOW ?	/JITTA/ (QUICKLY) YOUR MOTHER DOES NOT KNOW. YOUR
JITT III	(72)	COULD NEVER UNDERSTAND. /EDITH/ JITTA: DO YOU	KNOW ?	/JITTA/ YES. /EDITH/ JITTA! ! ! /JITTA/ YES. I
DEST	(175)	WHEN HE CAN AVOID IT ALL BY TAKING CARE NOT TO	KNOW ?	/LADY/ (REVOLTED) SUPPOSE THAT PACKET CONTAINED A
DEST	(170)	ANGRY DERISION) IF THEY ONLY KNEW! PRAY DO YOU	KNOW ?	/LADY/ YES. I HAD THE MISFORTUNE TO BE BORN GOOD. (
MIS.	(196)	SUCH NONSENSE! DO YOU THINK YOUNG PEOPLE DONT	KNOW ?	/LORD SUMMERHAYS/ I'M SURE THEY DONT FEEL. TARLETON:
MTH2	(65)	WOULD KNOW-- /BURGE/ WHAT DO YOU KNOW THAT I DONT	KNOW ?	/LUBIN/ I KNOW THAT WE ARE TAKING UP TOO MUCH OF MR
HART I	(67)	HER ALL THE SAME. /CAPTAIN SHOTOVER/ HOW DO YOU	KNOW ?	/MANGAN/ (PLAYING THE STRONG MAN) I INTEND TO. I
MTH4 II	(176)	THE MIDDLE OF THE COURTYARD). WHAT DO YOU WANT TO	KNOW ?	/NAPOLEON/ (FOLLOWING HER) MADAM: I HAVE NOT COME
NEVR I	(203)	OF COURSE. PERHAPS I AM. /VALENTINE/ DONT YOU	KNOW ?	/PHILIP/ NOT IN THE LEAST. /DOLLY/ IT'S A WISE
MRS IV	(242)	HEAR! /VIVIE/ (STARING AT HIM) IS THAT ALL YOU	KNOW ?	/PRAED/ CERTAINLY THAT IS ALL. /VIVIE/ THEN YOU
DOCT II	(119)	TO FIND A WORSE MAN. /SIR PATRICK/ HOW DO YOU	KNOW ?	/RIDGEON/ COME NOW, SIR PADDY, NO GROWLING. HAVE
MILL IV	(202)	IS THERE FOR A MILLIONAIRESS, I SHOULD LIKE TO	KNOW ?	/SAGAMORE/ IN THE COURTS-- /EPIFANIA/ I AM NOT
MTH2	(84)	IT MIGHT HAPPEN TO THE PARLORMAID. HOW DO WE	KNOW ?	/SAVVY/ THE PARLORMAID! OH, THATS NONSENSE, NUNK.
LIED	(188)	KNOW WHAT WOMAN IT WAS? /HE/ BUT HOW WILL THEY	KNOW ?	/SHE/ HOW WILL THEY KNOW! WHY, MY NAME IS ALL OVER
JOAN 2	(78)	SHE WILL. /LA TREMOUILLE/ WHY? HOW IS SHE TO	KNOW ?	/THE ARCHBISHOP/ SHE WILL KNOW WHAT EVERYBODY IN
MTH3	(112)	MAY BE IN THE SAME BOAT WITH YOU, FOR ALL WE	KNOW ?	/THE ARCHBISHOP/ YOU MAY. THEREFORE I ADVISE YOU TO
MTH3	(115)	MET ANY CASE BUT MY OWN. /CONFUCIUS/ HOW DO YOU	KNOW ?	/THE ARCHBISHOP/ WELL, NO ONE HAS EVER TOLD ME THAT
GETT	(281)	AT ALL. /LEO/ YES: THATS JUST IT. HOW DID YOU	KNOW ?	/THE BISHOP/ OH, I SHOULD SAY MOST IMAGINATIVE AND
GETT	(339)	YOUR DUTY TO REBUKE ME. BUT DO YOU THINK I DONT	KNOW ?	/THE BISHOP/ I DONT REBUKE YOU. WHO AM I THAT I
MTH4 III	(197)	YOU HAVE THE CHANCE? WHAT IS IT YOU WANT TO	KNOW ?	/THE ENVOY/ (PATRONIZING HER IN THE MANNER OF A
SUPR III	(89)	I KNOW I AM NOT IN HELL. /DON JUAN/ HOW DO YOU	KNOW ?	/THE OLD WOMAN/ BECAUSE I FEEL NO PAIN. /DON JUAN/
2TRU III	(96)	BETWEEN YOU AND MY SON, WHOM YOU SEEM TO	KNOW ?	/THE PATIENT/ POPSY STOLE MY NECKLACE, AND GOT ME TO
NEVR I	(201)	WEEKS. IS THERE ANYTHING ELSE YOU WOULD LIKE TO	KNOW ?	/THE YOUNG LADY/ (THE HINT QUITE LOST ON HER) ANY
FABL VI	(125)	YOU DONT KNOW. I DONT KNOW. /TEACHER/ WHY DONT WE	KNOW ?	/YOUTH 2/ BECAUSE WE DONT, THATS WHY. /TEACHER/ NO.
FABL VI	(123)	AND YOU, NUMBER THREE, DO YOU REALLY WANT TO	KNOW ?	/YOUTH 3/ NO. I DIDNT KNOW THAT CONES BURY
BULL III	(109)	AT ALL. HWERES NORA? /AUNT JUDY/ OH, HOW DO I	KNOW ?	SHE SLIPPED OUT A LITTLE WHILE AGO: I THOUGHT SHE
FANY II	(296)	WOMAN: IS THIS A TIME FOR PRAYING? DOES ANYBODY	KNOW ?	THATS WHAT WE HAVE TO CONSIDER NOW. IF ONLY WE CAN
ROCK II	(243)	FIFTY. /SIR JAFNA/ HOW DO YOU KNOW? HOW DO YOU	KNOW ?	THE WAY I AM PLUNDERED AT EVERY TURN! (TO SIR
PHIL I	(88)	THAN ANY OF THE REST OF THEM, I SHOULD LIKE TO	KNOW ?	THEY ARE ALWAYS SAYING THINGS LIKE THAT BEHIND MY
VWOO 2	(130)	MEN DO RUN AFTER ME. /A/ WHY? /Z/ OH, HOW DO I	KNOW ?	THEY DONT KNOW, THEMSELVES. BUT THE LOT OF MONEY
DOCT III	(142)	GOING TO DIE IN SIX MONTHS. /LOUIS/ HOW DO YOU	KNOW ?	THIS FOR B.B. IS THE LAST STRAW. HE COMPLETELY LOSES
MTH2	(88)	WONT BE ONE OF US, ANYHOW. /FRANKLYN/ HOW DO YOU	KNOW ?	THIS IS UNANSWERABLE. NONE OF THEM HAVE ANYTHING
CAND II	(105)	BEING OUTSIDE HER CODE OF MANNERS) HOW DO I	KNOW ?	WHY DO YOU ASK ME? /MARCHBANKS/ I BEG YOUR PARDON.
FABL VI	(125)	TO LIVE? /YOUTH 3/ HOW THE DEVIL DOES ANYBODY	KNOW ?	YOU DONT KNOW. I DONT KNOW. /TEACHER/ WHY DONT WE
GETT	(307)	AFTER ALL, WHAT CAN THEY SAY THAT YOU DONT	KNOW ?	YOU PICK IT UP AS THEY GO ON TALKING. (HE GOES TO
MIS. PREFACE	(37)	" WHAT DO THEY KNOW OF PLATO THAT ONLY PLATO	KNOW ?	" IF OUR UNIVERSITIES WOULD EXCLUDE EVERYBODY WHO HAD
CAND I	(91)	HUSED TO WONDER YOU WAS LET PREACH AT ALL. WHY, I	KNOW A	CLORGYMAN WHAT 'AS BIN KEP HOUT OF HIS JOB FOR YORRS
SUPR IV	(163)	ANOTHER WOMAN MAKES EYES AT ME, SHE'LL REFUSE TO	KNOW A	COQUETTE. SHE WILL DO JUST WHAT SHE LIKES HERSELF
GETT	(356)	TENS THAT DO. /MRS GEORGE/ WE'RE NOT ANGELS. I	KNOW A	FEW SCANDALS; BUT MOST OF US ARE TOO DULL TO BE
JOAN 5	(118)	I AM A POOR GIRL, AND SO IGNORANT THAT I DO NOT	KNOW A	FROM B. HOW COULD I BE PROUD? AND HOW CAN YOU SAY
JOAN PREFACE	(10)	ALL. JOAN WAS ABSOLUTELY ILLITERATE. " I DO NOT	KNOW A	FROM B" SHE SAID. BUT MANY PRINCESSES AT THAT TIME
BULL III	(139)	(TO BROADBENT, DEFERENTIALLY) OF COURSE I	KNOW A	GENTLEMAN LIKE YOU WOULD NOT COMPARE ME TO THE
JITT I	(12)	THERE ARE PEOPLE AND PEOPLE IN THIS WORLD; AND I	KNOW A	GENTLEMAN WHEN I SEE HIM. AND I FEEL SURE YOUR LADY
SUPR I	(32)	IMPOSED ON THEM. BUT TELL ME THIS: DID YOU EVER	KNOW A	GOOD BOY? /ANN/ OF COURSE. ALL BOYS ARE FOOLISH
MIS. PREFACE	(27)	CONSTITUTION, UNLESS ITS PUBLICLY ACTIVE CITIZENS	KNOW A	GOOD DEAL OF CONSTITUTIONAL HISTORY, LAW, AND
LIED	(201)	AND THE MOST FETCHING TO EXPERIENCED MEN WHO	KNOW A	GOOD THING WHEN THEY SEE IT, WHATEVER SHE MAY BE TO
LION PREFACE	(4)	THINKER AS YOU WILL FIND ANYWHERE. I GRANT YOU I	KNOW A	GREAT DEAL MORE ABOUT ECONOMICS AND POLITICS THAN
DOCT III	(139)	STRAIGHT AWAY THAT SHE HADNT GOT ANY. YOU DONT	KNOW A	LADY WHEN YOU SEE ONE. /B.B./ (MAJESTICALLY) WHAT DO
WIDO III	(53)	THREATENING MOVEMENT). NOW DONT FLY OUT AT ME. I	KNOW A	LANDLORD THAT OWNED AS BEASTLY A SLUM AS YOU COULD
CAPT I	(233)	THAT SOUNDS PROMISING. BUT I SHOULD LIKE TO	KNOW A	LITTLE MORE ABOUT HIM BEFORE I TRUST MYSELF IN HIS
MILL I	(164)	I AM ONE OF THOSE UNFORTUNATE PEOPLE-- YOU MUST	KNOW A	LOT OF THEM-- I DARESAY MANY OF THEM HAVE SAT IN THIS
BARB I	(250)	YOUVE BEEN TO INDIA AND JAPAN. YOU MUST	KNOW A	LOT OF THINGS, NOW; UNLESS YOU HAVE WASTED YOUR TIME
FABL III	(112)	PENCE TABLE. I CANT ADD TWO AND TWO TOGETHER. I	KNOW A	LOT, AND CAN DO NOTHING. WHEN I TELL THE CLEVER CHAPS
NEVR III	(277)	IS ONE OF FALSE GOOD-FELLOWSHIP, AND YOU MAY	KNOW A	MAN FOR TWENTY YEARS WITHOUT FINDING OUT THAT HE
JITT PREFACE	(5)	ATROCI SPASIMI, AND THE HERO HIMSELF MAY NOT	KNOW A	MOMENT OF HAPPINESS OR SECURITY UNTIL MISFORTUNE DOGS
ROCK II	(272)	LIKE OF YOU AND ME. YOU COME AND LUNCH WITH ME: I	KNOW A	NICE LITTLE PLACE WHERE THE COOKING'S GOOD AND THE
SUPR I	(38)	TAKE A STEP WITHOUT RUNNING TO YOU FOR LEAVE. I	KNOW A	POOR WRETCH WHOSE ONE DESIRE IN LIFE IS TO RUN AWAY
DOCT PREFACE	(4)	CHARACTER: IT HAS AN INFAMOUS CHARACTER. I DO NOT	KNOW A	SINGLE THOUGHTFUL AND WELL-INFORMED PERSON WHO DOES
MILL IV	(191)	SO THAN YOU THINK, OLD BOY, BECAUSE I HAPPEN TO	KNOW A	WOMAN OF THAT STAMP. BY THE WAY, I TELEGRAPHED FOR A
CATH 4	(191)	(TENDERLY) GELIEBTER! /EDSTASTON/ I DONT	KNOW A	WORD OF GERMAN; BUT THAT SOUNDED KIND. (BECOMING
DOCT III	(138)	PATRICK/ NOT QUITE, MR DUBEDAT. DO YOU HAPPEN TO	KNOW A	YOUNG WOMAN NAMED MINNIE TINWELL? /LOUIS/ MINNIE! I
FANY III	(301)	HER) WHAT DO YOU KNOW ABOUT HER? WHAT DO YOU	KNOW	ABOUT ALL THIS SORT OF THING? /MARGARET/ WHAT SORT OF
POSN PREFACE	(415)	AN ACTOR-MANAGER IS THE LESS HE IS LIKELY TO	KNOW	ABOUT ANY THEATRE EXCEPT HIS OWN. WHEN THE COMMITTEE OF
O'FL	(218)	THE MIGHTY FINE POLITICIAN, ARNT YOU? MUCH YOU	KNOW	ABOUT BELGIANS OR FOREIGN PARTS OR THE WORLD YOURE
BULL I	(84)	HIS BROGUE? /DOYLE/ HIS BROGUE! A FAT LOT YOU	KNOW	ABOUT BROGUES! IVE HEARD YOU CALL A DUBLIN ACCENT THAT
HART II	(86)	OF COURSE YOU DONT UNDERSTAND: WHAT DO YOU	KNOW	ABOUT BUSINESS? YOU JUST LISTEN AND LEARN. YOUR
DEVL III	(65)	PROPERLY, YOU JUMPING JACKASS. WHAT DO THEY	KNOW	ABOUT DICK? /CHRISTY/ WELL, YOU ARE DICK, AINT YOU?

LADY PREFACE(225)	HANDS, WE KNOW MUCH MORE ABOUT SHAKESPEAR THAN WE	KNOW	ABOUT DICKENS OR THACKERAY: THE ONLY DIFFICULTY IS THAT
GETT (332)	ALL THE SAME. BESIDES, WHAT DOES MISS GRANTHAM	KNOW	ABOUT EITHER MEN OR WOMEN? SHE'S GOT TOO MUCH
APPL II (273)	/BOANERGES/ PAID BY THE STATE! IS THAT ALL YOU	KNOW	ABOUT ELECTIONEERING IN ENGLAND? /PROTEUS/ YOU WILL
ROCK I (206)	/LADY CHAVENDER/ OH, YOUR VOTERS! WHAT DO THEY	KNOW	ABOUT GOVERNMENT? FOOTBALL, PRIZEFIGHTING, WAR: THAT
KING II (228)	THAT TOM, DICK AND HARRY MATTER. WHAT DO THEY	KNOW	ABOUT GOVERNMENT? /CHARLES/ NOTHING; BUT THEY HATE IT.
FANY III (301)	HIS SEAT ON THE TABLE BESIDE HER) WHAT DO YOU	KNOW	ABOUT HER? WHAT DO YOU KNOW ABOUT ALL THIS SORT OF
MTH5 (227)	OF BIOLOGICAL SCIENCE. /ARJILLAX/ IS THAT ALL WE	KNOW	ABOUT HIM? IT DOESNT AMOUNT TO VERY MUCH, DOES IT?
MTH2 (81)	DO WE KNOW ABOUT HIM, BARNABAS? WHAT DOES ANYONE	KNOW	ABOUT HIM? /CONRAD/ WE KNOW THIS ABOUT HIM WITH
POSN (464)	THERE IS ONE ABOVE, BLANCO. /BLANCO/ WHAT DO YOU	KNOW	ABOUT HIM? YOU THAT ALWAYS TALK AS IF HE NEVER DID
BUOY IV (58)	GENTLEMAN WOULD DREAM OF SAYING. THAT IS ALL WE	KNOW	ABOUT HIM. DONT MARRY HIM, CLEMMY. /SECONDBORN/ MY
MTH2 (81)	CAN. /BURGE/ (WITH ZEALOUS REVERENCE) WHAT DO WE	KNOW	ABOUT HIM, BARNABAS? WHAT DOES ANYONE KNOW ABOUT HIM?
MIS. (113)	GOT THAT OUT OF YOUR HALFPENNY PAPER. A LOT YOU	KNOW	ABOUT HIM! /JOHNNY/ I DONT SET UP TO BE ABLE TO DO
OVER PREFACE(167)	THE MATTER HAD BEEN IN MY HANDS. WHAT I WANT TO	KNOW	ABOUT IS THE MURDER. HOW DID YOU FEEL WHEN YOU
PRES (149)	TO MY ORDERS AND NOT TO IZ, E SAYS: WHAT DOES E	KNOW	ABOUT IT? E SAYS. YOU DIDNT GIVE ME ANY ORDERS, I
AUGS (269)	FOR IT -- WHAT? . . . BUT HOW COULD SHE POSSIBLY	KNOW	ABOUT IT? I HAVNT MENTIONED IT TO A SOUL, EXCEPT, OF
MRS IV (250)	GIVE IT UP-- NOT FOR ANYBODY. BUT WHAT NEED YOU	KNOW	ABOUT IT? I'LL NEVER MENTION IT. I'LL KEEP CROFTS
NEVR I (223)	BE MISERABLE. /VALENTINE/ OH COME! WHAT DO YOU	KNOW	ABOUT IT? /CRAMPTON/ I'M NOT A BACHELOR. /VALENTINE/
MTH5 (221)	SILLY TONGUE, YOU CONCEITED HUMBUG. WHAT DO YOU	KNOW	ABOUT IT? /ECRASIA/ I KNOW WHAT EVERY PERSON OF
GETT (277)	AND A PRECIOUS GREEN ONE AT THAT. WHAT DO YOU	KNOW	ABOUT IT? /THE GENERAL/ AM I TO UNDERSTAND THAT THE
MTH5 (229)	(TO ECRASIA, QUARRELSOMELY) WHAT DO YOU	KNOW	ABOUT IT? YOU ARE NOT AN ARTIST. /ACIS/ SHUT YOUR
DOCT PREFACE(76)	HAD EVER HEARD OF IT. TO THE PATIENT WHO DOES NOT	KNOW	ABOUT IT HE WILL SAY NOTHING. TO THE PATIENT WHO DOES,
FANY PROLOG (264)	LONDON THATLL LIKE IT IF THEY CAN ONLY BE GOT TO	KNOW	ABOUT IT. BESIDES, BANNAL'S KNOWLEDGE OF THE THEATRE IS
2TRU II (65)	THAT MARRIED MY SISTER: THAT WAS HOW I CAME TO	KNOW	ABOUT IT. /AUBREY/ AND HIS ARDOR NEVER PALLED? DAY IN
MIS. (123)	INDECENT. WE JUST DONT MENTION IT OR PRETEND TO	KNOW	ABOUT IT; AND THERES AN END OF IT. BUT ALL THE
O'FL (211)	/O'FLAHERTY/ (PRESERVING HIS DIGNITY) I DONT	KNOW	ABOUT IT'S BEING A GREAT WAR, SIR. IT'S A BIG WAR; BUT
MIS. (126)	HER KNEES). /TARLETON/ OLD! THATS ALL YOU	KNOW	ABOUT IT, MY LAD. HOW DO, PATSY! (HYPATIA KISSES
MRS IV (249)	ABOUT ME. WHAT DO THE PEOPLE THAT TAUGHT YOU	KNOW	ABOUT LIFE OR ABOUT PEOPLE LIKE ME? WHEN DID THEY EVER
VWOO 1 (117)	LIKE YOU TO GET ME RIGHT. AFTER ALL, WHAT DO YOU	KNOW	ABOUT ME? I WILL TELL YOU THE WHOLE OF MY LIFE IF YOU
2TRU I (44)	PATIENT/ JUST LIKE HER IMPUDENCE! HOW DID SHE	KNOW	ABOUT ME? /THE BURGLAR/ SIMPLY ENOUGH. IN HER LILY
GLIM (177)	IF THAT IS WHAT YOU MEAN. /GIULIA/ HOW DID YOU	KNOW	ABOUT MY SANDRO AND HIS MOTHER? HOW WERE YOU SO WISE
2TRU III (105)	LIKE HERSELF. /MRS MOPPLY/ ISNT SHE? WHAT DO YOU	KNOW	ABOUT MYSELF? MY REAL SELF? THEY TOLD ME LIES; AND I
MIS. PREFACE(30)	THAT THE RIGHT TO KNOW ALL THERE IS TO	KNOW	ABOUT ONESELF IS A NATURAL HUMAN RIGHT THAT SWEEPS AWAY
JOAN PREFACE(11)	SHEW HOW LITTLE OUR MATTER-OF-FACT HISTORIANS	KNOW	ABOUT OTHER PEOPLE'S MINDS, OR EVEN ABOUT THEIR OWN.
MIS. PREFACE(80)	YOU MUST POSE FOR BETTER FOR WORSE. HOW LITTLE WE	KNOW	ABOUT OUR PARENTS. THE RELATION BETWEEN PARENT AND
PYGM I (211)	THE NOTE TAKER) SEE HERE: WHAT CALL HAVE YOU TO	KNOW	ABOUT PEOPLE WHAT NEVER OFFERED TO MEDDLE WITH YOU?
JITT II (43)	HAD BUILT ON IT. /LENKHEIM/ TO YOU! WHAT DO YOU	KNOW	ABOUT PSYCHIATRY? WHY SHOULD HE SACRIFICE HIS
LADY PREFACE(216)	ADVENTURE SCHOOL. THEY PROVE, AS EVERYTHING WE	KNOW	ABOUT SHAKESPEAR SUGGESTS, THAT HE THOUGHT OF THE
MRS II (198)	DOWN). /MRS WARREN/ NEVER YOU MIND. WHAT DO YOU	KNOW	ABOUT SUCH THINGS? YOURE ONLY A BOY. (SHE GOES TO THE
CAPT II (259)	A SET OF CHAINS ON HIM? /LADY CICELY/ OH, I DONT	KNOW	ABOUT THAT, MR H-- I MEAN CAPTAIN BRASSBOUND. MEN ARE
GENV I (39)	TO PUT A STOP TO? /SHE/ OH, DONT ASK ME. ALL I	KNOW	ABOUT THE LEAGUE IS THAT IT PAYS MY SALARY. JUST GIVE
SUPR III (137)	TIKE TO THE MAHNTNS. /MENDOZA/ IDIOT, WHAT DO YOU	KNOW	ABOUT THE MOUNTAINS? ARE YOU A SPANIARD? YOU WOULD BE
MILL IV (189)	QUITE COMFORTABLE. /PATRICIA/ I SHOULD LIKE TO	KNOW	ABOUT THE OLD PIG IF IT'S ROMANTIC. IF YOU CAN SPARE
SUPR I (6)	BOY, NONSENSE! YOURE TOO MODEST. WHAT DOES SHE	KNOW	ABOUT THE REAL VALUE OF MEN AT HER AGE? (MORE
ANNA (296)	EVERY DAY FROM HAKONSBURG TO POTTERDAM. WHAT DO I	KNOW	ABOUT THEM? /STRAMMFEST/ THEY TRAVEL IN KHAKI. THEY DO
WIDO III (57)	I HATE THE IDEA OF SUCH THINGS. I DONT WANT TO	KNOW	ABOUT THEM. I LOVE YOU BECAUSE YOU BROUGHT ME UP TO
MTH4 I (157)	BY TEN THOUSAND YEARS. /ZOO/ YES; BUT WHAT DO WE	KNOW	ABOUT THIS BREATH OF LIFE THAT PUFFS YOU UP SO
KING I (176)	FOX FOR THE FIRST TIME) WHAT DOES THIS PERSON	KNOW	ABOUT WOMEN? /FOX/ ONLY WHAT THE WOMAN IN MYSELF
HART I (59)	YES. AT LEAST-- /MRS HUSHABYE/ I DONT WANT TO	KNOW	ABOUT " AT LEAST": I WANT TO KNOW THE WORST. GIRLS OF
FANY III (319)	THAT THE FOOTMAN IS OFFERING HIM CAKE) SHE DOESNT	KNOW	ABOUT-- ABOUT HIS GRACE, YOU KNOW. /MRS GILBEY/ PERHAPS
POSN PREFACE(427)	A NICE AMIABLE COMMITTEE OF ELDERLY GENTLEMEN (I	KNOW	ALL ABOUT ELDERLY GENTLEMEN, BEING ONE MYSELF) WHOSE
JITT II (45)	/LENKHEIM/ OH, STUFF! WHO WAS THE WOMAN? YOU	KNOW	ALL ABOUT HER: I CAN SEE IT IN YOUR EYES. (HE TAKES
BULL I (83)	IN GLASGOW. NEVER WAS IN IRELAND IN HIS LIFE. I	KNOW	ALL ABOUT HIM. /BROADBENT/ BUT HE SPOKE-- HE BEHAVED
BUOY III (29)	OUR FATHER KNOWS EVERYTHING ABOUT IT. BUT I	KNOW	ALL ABOUT HOUSEKEEPING BECAUSE OUR MOTHER KNEW NOTHING
ROCK II (262)	I HAVE SEEN THESE THINGS. I HAVE DONE THEM. I	KNOW	ALL ABOUT IT: YOU KNOW NOTHING ABOUT IT. IT MEANS
JITT III (78)	PRICE OF MY WIFE. WELL, WHOSE FAULT IS IT THAT I	KNOW	ALL ABOUT IT? WHO LET THE SECRET OUT? YOU DID.
DOCT I (97)	TO BE TAUGHT MY BUSINESS BY YOUR YOUNG CHAPS, I	KNOW	ALL ABOUT IT. IVE HANDLED THESE ANTI-TOXINS EVER SINCE
JITT II (45)	FACE TO FACE), AHA! YOU KNOW WHO SHE WAS. YOU	KNOW	ALL ABOUT IT. /JITTA/ (RISING INDIGNANTLY AND LETTING
MRS IV (241)	AWAY. /VIVIE/ OH, DO YOU THINK MR PRAED DOES NOT	KNOW	ALL ABOUT MY MOTHER? (TURNING ON PRAED) YOU HAD
PYGM III (249)	WE'RE SUPPOSED TO BE CIVILIZED AND CULTURED-- TO	KNOW	ALL ABOUT POETRY AND PHILOSOPHY AND ART AND SCIENCE,
ROCK I (220)	AND WOMAN THAT DOES READ HIM A CONCEIT THAT THEY	KNOW	ALL ABOUT POLITICAL ECONOMY AND CAN LOOK DOWN ON THE
ROCK II (275)	HEADS FILLED WITH NONSENSE. /ALOYSIA/ OF COURSE I	KNOW	ALL ABOUT PSYCHO-ANALYSIS. I EXPLAINED TO HIM THAT HE
SIM II (79)	YES? . . . WHAT? . . . YES: AMAZING NEWS: WE	KNOW	ALL ABOUT THAT. WHAT IS THE LATEST? . . . YES: " PLOT
WIDO II (39)	YOU I PROMISED HER TO DO SO? /TRENCH/ YES, I	KNOW	ALL ABOUT THAT, MR SARTORIUS; AND I'M GREATLY OBLIGED
PYGM III (255)	IT MORE CONVENIENT-- /MRS HIGGINS/ QUITE SO. I	KNOW	ALL ABOUT THAT: IT'S AN EXCELLENT ARRANGEMENT. BUT
FANY PROLOG (267)	NOT FIT FOR ELDERLY PEOPLE TO SEE. /FANNY/ OH, I	KNOW	ALL ABOUT THAT; BUT YOU CANT UNDERSTAND WHAT IT MEANS
OVER (175)	/GREGORY/ (INTERRUPTING HER) YES, YES: I	KNOW	ALL ABOUT THAT. IT'S NOT ROMANTIC: IT'S NOT DON JUAN:
MTH3 (124)	AS SHAREHOLDERS? /BARNABAS/ NOTHING LIKE IT. I	KNOW	ALL ABOUT THE OLD JOINT STOCK COMPANIES. THE
POSN (464)	TO YOUR SOUL, BLANCO. /BLANCO/ OH YES: YOU	KNOW	ALL ABOUT THE LORD, DONT YOU? YOURE IN THE LORD'S
MIS. PREFACE(24)	MONSIEUR DELCROZE CALLS OUT " HOP! " OH YES: I	KNOW	ALL ABOUT THESE WONDERFUL SCHOOLS THAT YOU CANNOT KEEP
NEVR I (203)	OH, WE ARE, WE ARE. IT'S ALL OVER, PHIL: THEY	KNOW	ALL ABOUT US IN ENGLAND. (TO VALENTINE) OH, YOU CANT
WIDO III (53)	NO: THAT AINT LICKCHEESE'S WAY. BESIDES, THEY	KNOW	ALL ABOUT YOU ALREADY. THEM STAIRS THAT YOU AND ME
BARB II (281)	SINCE YOUVE MADE FRIENDS WITH US, WE WANT TO	KNOW	ALL ABOUT YOU. NAMES AND ADDRESSES AND TRADES.
GETT (356)	WELL, I SUPPOSE, YOUR PETTY TRADESMEN'S SET. YOU	KNOW	ALL ITS SCANDALS AND HYPOCRISIES, ITS JEALOUSIES AND
CAND I (99)	WARM THEM). /MARCHBANKS/ OH, DO YOU THINK I DONT	KNOW	ALL THAT? DO YOU THINK THAT THE THINGS PEOPLE MAKE
PRES (133)	/BALSQUITH/ YES, YES, MY DEAR MITCHENER: I	KNOW	ALL THAT AS WELL AS YOU DO: I ARGUED WITH HIM UNTIL I
BULL I (84)	(INTERRUPTING HIM VERY IMPATIENTLY) YES, YES: I	KNOW	ALL THAT AS WELL AS YOU DO. /BROADBENT/ OH WELL, OF
MRS IV (248)	YOU ARE VERY RICH. /MRS WARREN/ BUT YOU DONT	KNOW	ALL THAT THAT MEANS: YOURE TOO YOUNG. IT MEANS A NEW
JOAN 5 (117)	IT OFTEN MAKE THE BEST JOB OF IT. /DUNOIS/ I	KNOW	ALL THAT. I DO NOT FIGHT IN THE OLD WAY: I HAVE LEARNT
JITT I (21)	AS BRUNO'S, /JITTA/ (IMPATIENTLY) OH YES, YES: I	KNOW	ALL THAT. IT SOUNDS LIKE A SENTENCE FROM YOUR ANNUAL
FABL III (112)	IN WHICH CASE YOULL BE LIQUIDATED. /THE TRAMP/ I	KNOW	ALL THAT. WHAT GOOD WILL IT DO YOU? WHY ARE YOU
APPL I (210)	HIGHNESS. I'M PROUD OF IT. /ALICE/ OH YES, I	KNOW	ALL THAT, MR BOANERGES. BUT YOU DONT LOOK THE PART. YOU
HART II (123)	IT IS A POSE LIKE ANY OTHER. IN THIS HOUSE WE	KNOW	ALL THE POSES: OUR GAME IS TO FIND OUT THE MAN UNDER
MTH3 (100)	SO TANTALIZING TO SEE YOU AND TALK TO YOU, AND TO	KNOW	ALL THE TIME THAT YOU ARE TWO HUNDRED MILES AWAY, AND
GLIM (177)	THEY ARE INURED TO TOIL AND ENDURANCE. BESIDES, I	KNOW	ALL THE TRICKS. /THE GIRL/ DO NOT ATTEMPT TO QUARREL
MIS. PREFACE(30)	INCAPABLE OF UNDERSTANDING THAT THE RIGHT TO	KNOW	ALL THERE IS TO KNOW ABOUT ONESELF IS A NATURAL HUMAN
MTH1 II (27)	OF YEARS? I HAVE NOT LIVED AS LONG AS YOU; BUT I	KNOW	ALL THERE IS TO BE KNOWN OF THE CRAFT OF DIGGING. BY
CATH 1 (166)	THE QUEEN. ALL RIGHT, EH? /EDSTASTON/ HOW DO YOU	KNOW	ALL THIS? /PATIOMKIN/ (CROWING FANTASTICALLY) IN ER
BUOY IV (48)	WORLD TO PUT MY NOSE INTO A TEMPLE. HOWEVER, YOU	KNOW	ALL THIS. I AM REPEATING MYSELF, AND BORING YOU. LEAVE
LIED (196)	AT PRESENT. NOW JUST LISTEN TO ME. I SUPPOSE YOU	KNOW	ALL THOSE POEMS BY HEART. /HE/ YES, BY HEART. (RAISING
BUOY III (29)	AM NATURALLY SOMEWHAT AT A LOSS. HOW MUCH DO YOU	KNOW	ALREADY OF THE BUSINESS I AM TO PUT BEFORE YOU?
CAND II (107)	YOU, FOR ALL THAT. /MARCHBANKS/ YOU NEEDNT. I	KNOW	ALREADY THAT IT MUST. /PROSERPINE/ BUT MIND! IF YOU
GENV IV (94)	KNEW WHAT ENGLAND WAS GOING TO DO? /BATTLER/ I	KNOW	ALREADY WHAT YOU COULD DO. NOTHING. I TORE UP YOUR
GETT PREFACE(245)	AND MORE SINCERE ONE. WE WHO DO NOT WANT TO	KNOW	ALSO DO NOT WANT TO GO BLIND, TO GO MAD, TO BE
2TRU II (55)	IT, EH? /MEEK/ SO THEY SAY, SIR. /TALLBOYS/ YOU	KNOW	ALSO THAT UNDER THE ARTICLES OF WAR ANY SOLDIER WHO
BULL PREFACE(12)	IN OUR EXPLORATIONS AND COLONIZATIONS. I	KNOW	ALSO THAT WHAT COMPELS US TO PUSH OUR FRONTIERS FARTHER
GETT (271)	SO, GENERAL. /THE GENERAL/ (EMPHATICALLY) YOU	KNOW	ALSO, DONT YOU, THAT ANY MAN WHO CAN SEE ANYTHING
CAPT II (252)	OUT WHEN SIR HOWARD SPEAKS). /SIR HOWARD/ YOU	KNOW	ALSO, MR JOHNSON, I HOPE, THAT YOU CAN DEPEND ON ME.
DEVL III (66)	(IMPATIENTLY) YAH! (TO CHRISTY) HE WANTS TO	KNOW	AM I MINISTER ANDERSON. TELL HIM, AND STOP GRINNING
MTH3 (115)	WHAT WAS HAPPENING TO ME, I WAS OLD ENOUGH TO	KNOW	AND FEAR THE FEROCIOUS HATRED WITH WHICH HUMAN ANIMALS,
JITT III (60)	FEEL ANYTHING THAT LITTLE CHILDREN OUGHT NOT TO	KNOW	AND FEEL, JUST WHEN I, AS A WOMAN, MOST WANT THE
GENV PREFACE(25)	HOW THEIR LITTLE HEADS CAN CARRY ALL THEY	KNOW	AND RANKING THEM AS PASSING RICH ON FOUR HUNDRED POUNDS
3PLA PREFACE(R26)	MR ROBERT BUCHANAN, A DRAMATIST WHO KNOWS WHAT I	KNOW	AND REMEMBERS WHAT I REMEMBER OF THE HISTORY OF THE
SUPR I (10)	RAMSDEN: GET ME OUT OF IT SOMEHOW. YOU DONT	KNOW	ANN AS WELL AS I DO. SHE'LL COMMIT EVERY CRIME A
DEVL III (65)	EXCHANGING LOOKS. /SWINDON/ (TO CHRISTY) DO YOU	KNOW	ANTHONY ANDERSON, THE PRESBYTERIAN MINISTER? /CHRISTY/
GETT PREFACE(205)	WHO GOVERNS THE STREET TRAFFIC TO BE OR TO	KNOW	ANY BETTER THAN THE PEOPLE WHO OBEY THE WAVE OF HIS
MTH4 II (184)	ENVOY/ (COMING BETWEEN HIS WIFE AND ZOO) I DONT	KNOW	ANY HISTORY: A MODERN PRIME MINISTER HAS SOMETHING
PHIL II (105)	SHE'S TO BE FOUND. /CHARTERIS/ I SHALL NEVER	KNOW	ANY MORE, SYLVIA. SHE'S QUARRELLED WITH ME. /SYLVIA/

PYGM V	(270)	IN THE CHIPPENDALE CHAIR). /MRS HIGGINS/ DO YOU	KNOW	ANY OF HER PEOPLE? /PICKERING/ ONLY HER FATHER: THE
DEVL I	(15)	THOUGHTFUL HOUSEKEEPER THAN MRS DUDGEON). DO YOU	KNOW	ANY OF YOUR FATHER'S RELATIVES? /ESSIE/ NO. THEY
MTH1 II	(25)	WHY NOT BRING THEM UP FROM CHILDHOOD NEVER TO	KNOW	ANY OTHER LOT, SO THAT THEY MAY BELIEVE THAT WE ARE
FANY II	(294)	YOU SHOULD MIX A LITTLE WITH PEOPLE WHO DONT	KNOW	ANY OTHER WORDS. BUT WHEN I SAID THAT ABOUT A DESCENT
LIED	(195)	SERVICE. WHAT DO YOU WISH ME TO DO? /SHE/ DO YOU	KNOW	ANYBODY ELSE NAMED AURORA? /HE/ NO. /SHE/ THERES NO
KING I	(203)	ABOUT. KYNASTON PLAYED WOMEN IN HIS PLAYS. I DONT	KNOW	ANY. WE CANNOT AFFORD THEM NOWADAYS. THEY REQUIRE
HART I	(71)	WITH MY HUSBAND ONLY TEN MINUTES AGO; AND I DIDNT	KNOW	ANYONE ELSE HAD COME. IT MUST BE A VISITOR. (SHE GOES
POSN PREFACE	(371)	KNOW NOTHING ABOUT THAT AND DO NOT WANT TO	KNOW	ANYTHING: ALL THAT THEY DO KNOW IS THAT INCEST,
NEVR IV	(302)	LORD! (BREATHLESS) OH, I-- (HE GASPS) I DONT	KNOW	ANYTHING ABOUT WOMEN: TWELVE YEARS EXPERIENCE IS NOT
MILL I	(143)	TO YOU. /SAGAMORE/ BUT, MY DEAR LADY, I DONT	KNOW	ANYTHING ABOUT YOUR DISTRESS, YOUR DISGRACE, THE MESS
BUOY III	(33)	WILL LIVE ON COMPANY DIRECTORSHIPS. YOU NEED NOT	KNOW	ANYTHING ABOUT THE BUSINESSES; YOUR NAME ON THE
MRS I	(187)	MONEY TO MAKE THINGS SMOOTH. BUT DONT IMAGINE I	KNOW	ANYTHING ABOUT MY MOTHER. I KNOW FAR LESS THAN YOU DO.
MRS III	(223)	GONE BACK TO TOWN. /PRAED/ BUT YOUR MOTHER DOESNT	KNOW	ANYTHING ABOUT MRS WARREN, DOES SHE? (HE PICKS UP THE
MTH1 II	(25)	I WILL STAY AS I AM. /CAIN/ YOU NEITHER OF YOU	KNOW	ANYTHING ABOUT LIFE. YOU ARE SIMPLE COUNTRY FOLK. YOU
GETT PREFACE	(245)	A RIGHTEOUS AIR, AND BECOMES " I DONT WANT TO	KNOW	ANYTHING ABOUT THE DISEASES WHICH ARE THE JUST
HART II	(93)	POOR DEAR MANGAN INDEED! /MAZZINI/ BUT HE DOESNT	KNOW	ANYTHING ABOUT MACHINERY. HE NEVER GOES NEAR THE MEN:
HART III	(134)	THEY SHOULDNT DO IT THEMSELVES EITHER. I MAY NOT	KNOW	ANYTHING ABOUT MY OWN MACHINERY; BUT I KNOW HOW TO
PYGM II	(224)	WHY NOT? /MRS PEARCE/ WHY NOT! BUT YOU DONT	KNOW	ANYTHING ABOUT HER. WHAT ABOUT HER PARENTS? SHE MAY BE
BULL IV	(159)	OF HARD WORK. /NORA/ YES: IT'S HARD FOR ME TO	KNOW	ANYTHING ABOUT YOU IF YOU NEVER TELL ME ANYTHING.
GENV II	(63)	LOBBY UNTIL SHE KNOWS THE WAY. SHE NEED NOT	KNOW	ANYTHING ELSE. /THE SECRETARY/ BUT SHE IS A COMPLETE
BARB I	(266)	MEN. FEW OF THEM KNOW GREEK; AND NONE OF THEM	KNOW	ANYTHING ELSE; BUT THEIR POSITION IS UNCHALLENGEABLE.
MTH2	(66)	GOING TO LET THEM OFF LIKE THIS? HOW ARE THEY TO	KNOW	ANYTHING IF NOBODY EVER TELLS THEM? IF YOU DONT, I
JITT III	(60)	I AM TO BE A GOOD LITTLE CHILD, AND NOT	KNOW	ANYTHING NOR FEEL ANYTHING THAT LITTLE CHILDREN OUGHT
MILL I	(152)	UNDERSTAND, OF COURSE, THAT I AM NOT SUPPOSED TO	KNOW	ANYTHING OF HIS RELATIONS WITH MY WIFE, WHATEVER THEY
GETT PREFACE	(258)	ARE TOO POORLY PAID IN THIS COUNTRY TO	KNOW	ANYTHING THAT IS FIT FOR PUBLICATION. CONCLUSIONS, TO
GENV IV	(97)	HE DOESNT KNOW WHAT PECKHAM IS. THESE PEOPLE DONT	KNOW	ANYTHING. /THE SECRETARY/ PECKHAM IS ANOTHER PART OF
JITT II	(28)	MOST DOMESTICATED OF MEN. THAT IS, UNLESS YOU	KNOW	ANYTHING. YOU WERE SO INTIMATE WITH HIM, YOU KNOW.
MRS IV	(242)	THAT IS ALL. /VIVIE/ THEN YOU NEITHER OF YOU	KNOW	ANYTHING. YOUR GUESSES ARE INNOCENCE ITSELF COMPARED TO
MRS II	(201)	WARREN/ (DEFIANTLY) I KNOW NO REASONS. IF YOU	KNOW	ANY, YOU CAN TELL THEM TO THE LAD, OR TO THE GIRL, OR
OVER	(182)	I DONT KNOW WHY; FOR ALL THE VOLCANIC WOMEN I	KNOW	ARE PLAIN LITTLE CREATURES WITH SANDY HAIR. I DONT
KING I	(170)	THERES A LADY IN A COACH AT THE DOOR WANTS TO	KNOW	ARE YOU READY TO TAKE A DRIVE WITH HER. /CHARLES/ ANY
MRS I	(185)	OR ELECTRICITY OR INSURANCE. I DONT EVEN	KNOW	ARITHMETIC WELL. OUTSIDE MATHEMATICS, LAWN-TENNIS,
JOAN 4	(108)	AND SUBTLE FOR A POOR CLERK LIKE MYSELF. BUT I	KNOW	AS A MATTER OF PLAIN COMMONSENSE THAT THE WOMAN IS A
DOCT IV	(157)	CASE. YOU KNOW, COLLY, BY JUPITER, IF I DIDNT	KNOW	AS A MATTER OF SCIENTIFIC FACT THAT I'D BEEN
DOCT I	(107)	AND A VERY GOOD PROFESSION, TOO, MY LAD. WHEN YOU	KNOW	AS MUCH AS I KNOW OF THE IGNORANCE AND SUPERSTITION OF
POSN PREFACE	(416)	ARE SO SUCCESSFUL THAT EVEN THE POLICE DO NOT	KNOW	AS MUCH AS THEY SHOULD. THE POLICE SHOULD HAVE BEEN
MIS. PREFACE	(50)	FAMOUS NAME IN LITERATURE. I SHOULD PROBABLY	KNOW	AS MUCH LATIN AS FRENCH, IF LATIN HAD NOT BEEN MADE THE
BARB II	(292)	ARE DEAD OR ARE PINED FOR STILL; BUT WHOE'ER CAN	KNOW	AS THE LONG DAYS GO THAT TO LIVE IS HAPPY, HAS FOUND
BULL PREFACE	(11)	THE RED MAN, TO CIVILIZE THESE PLACES; THOUGH I	KNOW	AS WELL AS ANYONE THAT THERE ARE MANY DETESTABLE
2TRU III	(96)	TO LOOK AT WHAT THEY CALL NEW SKIES, THOUGH THEY	KNOW	AS WELL AS I DO THAT IT IS ONLY THE SAME OLD SKY
PHIL II	(103)	THAT? /CUTHBERTSON/ I DECLINE TO EXPLAIN. YOU	KNOW	AS WELL AS I DO. I'M GOING DOWNSTAIRS NOW TO ORDER
MTH4 II	(188)	WITH US ON THIS EXPEDITION, THOUGH OF COURSE YOU	KNOW	AS WELL AS I DO THAT HE HAS IMPOSED HIMSELF ON MY PARTY
MTH4 I	(167)	I SHALL NOT EXPLAIN, MADAM. I BELIEVE YOU	KNOW	AS WELL AS I DO. (HE SITS DOWN ON THE BOLLARD IN
BUOY IV	(55)	HERE. /OLD BILL/ COME, COME, FLOPPER! YOU	KNOW	AS WELL AS I DO THAT PEOPLE WHO MARRY FOR MONEY ARE
LION PREFACE	(58)	ALL STRIVE TOWARDS AN INDEPENDENT INCOME. WE ALL	KNOW	AS WELL AS JESUS DID THAT IF WE HAVE TO TAKE THOUGHT
BARB III	(349)	INDEPENDENT AND TO ACT AND THINK FOR YOURSELF? I	KNOW	AS WELL AS POSSIBLE WHAT THAT CRY OF " MAMMA, MAMMA,"
DOCT III	(153)	WE HAVE SEEN SO MANY DOCTORS: I HAVE COME TO	KNOW	AT LAST WHEN THEY ARE ONLY TALKING AND CAN DO NOTHING.
MIS. PREFACE	(37)	STREET DOES. AND THIS IS JUST WHAT THEY DO NOT	KNOW	AT PRESENT. YOU MAY SAY OF THEM, PARAPHRASING MR
BARB II	(295)	TO HER AS YOU HAVE BEEN TALKING TO ME, YOU DONT	KNOW	BARBARA. /UNDERSHAFT/ MY FRIEND: I NEVER ASK FOR WHAT I
MTH3	(130)	INDULGENTLY) HE WILL KEEP THE SECRET ALL RIGHT. I	KNOW	BARNABAS. YOU NEEDNT WORRY. /CONFUCIUS/ (TROUBLED AND
MIS. PREFACE	(45)	NOT ONLY BECAUSE ANY OF THEM MAY FOR ALL WE	KNOW	BE ON THE RIGHT TRACK BUT BECAUSE IT IS IN THE CONFLICT
GENV II	(63)	TO ME JUST NOW THAT I THOUGHT YOU HAD A RIGHT TO	KNOW	BEFORE ANYONE ELSE. (TO SIR O.) AND IT'S SPLENDID NEWS
WIDO II	(40)	WHY DID YOU NOT SAY SO BEFORE? /TRENCH/ I DIDNT	KNOW	BEFORE. /SARTORIUS/ (PROVOKED) THEN YOU OUGHT TO HAVE
CAND III	(129)	OH, NOW I CANT SAY ANYTHING: ALL THE WORDS I	KNOW	BELONG TO SOME ATTITUDE OR OTHER-- ALL EXCEPT ONE.
SUPR III	(98)	SURE HE WOULD BE UNCOMFORTABLE? OF COURSE YOU	KNOW	BEST: YOU BROUGHT HIM HERE ORIGINALLY; AND WE HAD THE
BULL IV	(169)	DISCONSOLATE AND UNCONVINCED) WELL, PRAPS YOU	KNOW	BEST WHAT THEY DO IN ENGLAND. THEY MUST HAVE VERY
ARMS III	(70)	YOU WERE FONDER OF HIM THAN OF SERGIUS. YOU	KNOW	BEST WHETHER I WAS RIGHT. /BLUNTSCHLI/ WHAT NONSENSE!
SUPR I	(6)	I OUGHT TO TELL YOU OR NOT! /OCTAVIUS/ YOU	KNOW	BEST. /RAMSDEN/ IT WAS SOMETHING ABOUT HIS DAUGHTER.
ROCK I	(199)	NICE OLD BRIC-A-BRAC THERE. /HILDA/ OH WELL! YOU	KNOW	BEST. /SIR ARTHUR/ (ENERGETICALLY) AND NOW TO WORK.
2TRU I	(29)	OH, DONT YOU THINK, DEAR DOCTOR-- OF COURSE YOU	KNOW	BEST; BUT I AM SO TERRIBLY ANXIOUS-- DONT YOU THINK YOU
CAND II	(124)	ALL THE GOOD WE HAVE BEEN DOING. OF COURSE YOU	KNOW	BEST; BUT-- (HE SHRUGS HIS SHOULDERS AND WANDERS TO
CLEO II	(137)	REST, EGYPT FOR THE EGYPTIANS! /RUFIO/ WELL, YOU	KNOW	BEST, I SUPPOSE. IS THAT ALL? /CAESAR/ THAT IS ALL.
CAPT III	(275)	DREADFULLY. I'M AFRAID, MR RANKIN-- THOUGH YOU	KNOW	BEST, OF COURSE-- THAT WE ARE BOUND NOT TO REPEAT
GETT	(341)	IN THAT STATE. WOULD YOU MARRY NOW THAT YOU	KNOW	BETTER IF YOU WERE A WIDOWER? /THE BISHOP/ I'M OLD
SUPR I	(45)	(BOWING TO THE STORM) I HAVE NO DEFENCE: I SHALL	KNOW	BETTER IN FUTURE THAN TO TAKE ANY WOMAN'S PART. WE HAVE
ROCK II	(282)	AND I WAS DOING THE BEST THAT COULD BE DONE. I	KNOW	BETTER NOW: I KNOW THAT IT CAN BE HELPED, AND HOW IT
MILL II	(177)	NOR TO YOUR MOTHER EITHER, IT SEEMS. WELL, YOU	KNOW	BETTER NOW. I AM TO GIVE YOU A HUNDRED AND FIFTY
JITT III	(58)	OF COURSE NEITHER OF US WAS GROWING YOUNGER. I	KNOW	BETTER NOW. OH, WHAT A FOOL I WAS! BUT THAT IS HOW
JOAN 5	(114)	OF SEEING THE EFFECT SHE IS PRODUCING) BUT I DO	KNOW	BETTER THAN ANY OF YOU SEEM TO. AND I AM NOT PROUD: I
APPL INTRLUD	(246)	THEY DONT NOTICE THE CHANGE. BESIDES, YOU SHOULD	KNOW	BETTER THAN ANYONE ELSE THAT WHEN A MAN GETS TIRED OF
SUPR III	(119)	ERROR. COME, ANA! DO NOT LOOK SHOCKED: YOU	KNOW	BETTER THAN ANY OF US THAT MARRIAGE IS A MANTRAP BAITED
MIS. PREFACE	(46)	IF ADULTS WILL FRANKLY GIVE UP THEIR CLAIM TO	KNOW	BETTER THAN CHILDREN WHAT THE PURPOSES OF THE LIFE
GETT	(355)	RELIGIONS. WHO ARE YOU, ANYHOW, THAT YOU SHOULD	KNOW	BETTER THAN MAHOMET OR CONFUCIUS OR ANY OF THE OTHER
BULL II	(114)	SPRING OF BITTERNESS) I SHOULD THINK YOU OUGHT TO	KNOW	BETTER THAN ME WHETHER YOURE INTERFERING WITH HIM.
ROCK I	(198)	I WONDER WHAT HE MEANT BY SAYING THAT I OUGHT TO	KNOW	BETTER THAN MOST MEN. WHAT OUGHT I TO KNOW BETTER THAN
ROCK I	(198)	TO KNOW BETTER THAN MOST MEN. WHAT OUGHT I TO	KNOW	BETTER THAN MOST MEN? /HILDA/ I THINK HE MEANT THAT
MIS. PREFACE	(11)	FOR HIM. HANDEL'S PARENTS NO DOUBT THOUGHT THEY	KNOW	BETTER THAN THEIR CHILD WHEN THEY TRIED TO PREVENT HIS
BARB II	(295)	OF HIS COWARDICE BY PREACHING HUMILITY: WE	KNOW	BETTER THAN THAT. WE THREE MUST STAND TOGETHER ABOVE
SUPR IV	(162)	MY MIND. IT ONLY SETS TAVY AGAINST ME. BUT YOU	KNOW	BETTER THAN THAT. SO IF YOU MARRY HER, DONT PUT THE
6CAL	(101)	HIS CONSORT) HA! DO YOU, MASTER MERCHANT? YOU	KNOW	BETTER THAN THE QUEEN! YOU AND YOUR LIKE KNOW WHAT TO
FABL PREFACE	(88)	CANDIDATES WHO ARE PLOUGHED BECAUSE THEY	KNOW	BETTER THAN THEIR EXAMINERS, YET ARE AS UNCONSCIOUS OF
NEVR II	(257)	/VALENTINE/ NO, NO, NO, NO, NO. NOT LOVE: WE	KNOW	BETTER THAN THAT. LET'S CALL IT CHEMISTRY. YOU CANT
BARB III	(341)	WICKEDNESS. AND YOU, ADOLPHUS, OUGHT TO	KNOW	BETTER THAN TO GO ABOUT SAYING THAT WRONG THINGS ARE
O'FL	(207)	IF YOUD BEEN BROUGHT UP BY MY MOTHER, SIR, YOUD	KNOW	BETTER THAN TO JOKE ABOUT HER. WHAT I'M TELLING YOU IS
SIM II	(69)	CLOTHES. /THE ANGEL/ REALLY, YOUR PEOPLE OUGHT TO	KNOW	BETTER THAN TO SHOOT AT AN ANGEL. /MAYA/ ARE YOU AN
PHIL II	(105)	OF THE ELDER SISTER! /JULIA/ YOU OUGHT TO	KNOW	BETTER THAN TO ENCOURAGE A CHILD TO MAKE HERSELF
FOUN	(211)	/BRABAZON/ NOTHING TODAY, THANK YOU. AND NOW, I	KNOW	BETTER THAN TO TAKE UP THE TIME OF A BUSY MAN. HAPPY TO
O'FL	(218)	IN, GOD HELP YOU! /MRS O'FLAHERTY/ WHY WOULDNT I	KNOW	BETTER THAN YOU? AMMENT I YOUR MOTHER? /O'FLAHERTY/
NEVR IV	(295)	TERMS) NO YOU WOULDNT: YOU THINK YOU WOULD; BUT I	KNOW	BETTER THAN YOU. YOUD WANT THIS YOUNG LADY HERE TO GIVE
6CAL	(101)	YOU LITTLE KNOW YOUR HUSBAND, MADAM. WE	KNOW	BETTER WHAT TO EXPECT FROM EDWARD PLANTAGENET. /THE
HART II	(116)	THE MORE SOUL YOU HAVE. YOUNG PEOPLE NOWADAYS	KNOW	BETTER. A SOUL IS A VERY EXPENSIVE THING TO KEEP: MUCH
SUPR IV	(171)	A SPECTATOR, I AM ONE OF THE PRINCIPALS; AND I	KNOW	BETTER. ANN: STOP TEMPTING TAVY, AND COME BACK TO ME.
FANY I	(280)	/DORA/ SO YOU ALWAYS SAY, YOU OLD DEARS. BUT YOU	KNOW	BETTER. BOBBY CAME TO ME: I DIDNT COME TO HIM. /GILBEY/
CLEO III	(151)	BUSINESS. /FIRST AUXILIARY/ YES: YOU OUGHT TO	KNOW	BETTER. GET OFF WITH YOU. /SECOND AUXILIARY/ (LOOKING
POSN	(436)	ARE. WAIT TIL YOUR OWN HORSE IS STOLEN, AND YOULL	KNOW	BETTER. I HAD AN UNCLE THAT DIED OF THIRST IN THE SAGE
POSN	(443)	NOT IF I WAS TO STARVE FOR IT TOMORROW. BUT I	KNOW	BETTER. I TELL YOU, BLANCO, WHAT KEEPS AMERICA TODAY
CLEO PRO2	(101)	NOT WE. AT MEMPHIS YE DEEM HER A QUEEN: HERE WE	KNOW	BETTER. I WILL TAKE HER ON THE CRUPPER OF MY HORSE.
FANY III	(315)	COME, MRS KNOX, DONT TELL ME KNOX IS A SINNER. I	KNOW	BETTER. I'M SURE YOUD BE THE FIRST TO BE SORRY IF
GETT	(298)	TO HOTCHKISS) SORRY; BUT YOU ARE OLD ENOUGH TO	KNOW	BETTER. (TO THE OTHERS) AND NOW SINCE THERE IS TO BE
2TRU II	(61)	SAY A THING LIKE THAT; BUT YOURE EXPECTED TO	KNOW	BETTER. /AUBREY/ MOPS: YOUVE SHOCKED SWEETIE. /THE
BARB III	(321)	GOVERNS ENGLAND; BUT YOU MUST ALLOW ME TO THINK I	KNOW	BETTER. /UNDERSHAFT/ AND WHAT DOES GOVERN ENGLAND,
POSN PREFACE	(371)	SUFFICIENT TO DROWN THE PROTESTS OF THE FEW WHO	KNOW	BETTER. THE ACHILLES HEEL OF THE CENSORSHIP IS
MTH4 I	(164)	IT, BUT OUR MINDS ARE GREATER THAN THE FACTS. WE	KNOW	BETTER. THE GREATEST ANCIENT TEACHERS, FOLLOWED BY THE
DOCT PREFACE	(14)	PAINLESS, PEOPLE WHO HAVE BEEN OPERATED ON	KNOW	BETTER. THE PATIENT DOES NOT FEEL THE KNIFE, AND THE
CAPT II	(255)	EVERYTHING I DID WHEN I WAS ATTORNEY GENERAL. YOU	KNOW	BETTER. THERE IS SOME EXCUSE FOR HIS MOTHER. SHE WAS AN
FABL PREFACE	(79)	OTHER COUNTRIES " POLICE STATES." I, BEING IRISH,	KNOW	BETTER, TO RETURN TO THE INVETERACY OF IDOLATRY. TEN
FABL II	(107)	PUBLIC THINKS IT IS THE OTHER WAY ABOUT; BUT WE	KNOW	BETTER. WE MUST BE PREPARED FOR WAR BEFORE EVERYTHING.

O'FL	(216)	THE GERMANS, THOUGH THEYRE EDUCATED AND OUGHT TO	KNOW	BETTER. YOULL NEVER HAVE A QUIET WORLD TIL YOU KNOCK
FABL PREFACE	(63)	OR BRIDGE, CAN TAKE IN THE TENSOR CALCULUS. I	KNOW	BETTER, AND CAN ONLY HOPE THAT A BATCH OF CHILDISH
ROCK II	(257)	TO BE GOVERNED AT ALL. EVEN YOU, WHO OUGHT TO	KNOW	BETTER, ARE ALWAYS COMPLAINING OF THE INCOME TAX. /THE
JITT II	(30)	NOT EXIST FOR HER. WHAT AN EYE-OPENER FOR US WHO	KNOW	BETTER! (SENTENTIOUSLY) AND YET, WHATEVER VIEW WE MAY
MTH3	(98)	YOU THINK I'M AFRAID OF YOU, YOU JOLLY WELL DONT	KNOW	BURGE-LUBIN: THATS ALL. /CONFUCIUS/ YOU ARE BRAVE: YES.
HART III	(136)	YOU, MR MANGAN, I HAVE BEEN THROUGH IT ALL; AND I	KNOW	BY EXPERIENCE THAT MEN AND WOMEN ARE DELICATE PLANTS
CATH 2,SD	(177)	SEE THAT SHE IS TRYING NOT TO LAUGH, AND	KNOW	BY EXPERIENCE THAT SHE WILL NOT SUCCEED. THEY RISE,
BASH I	(94)	/CASHEL/ WHO KNOWS? WE SHALL. THAT MUCH I	KNOW	BY INSTINCT. WHATS YOUR NAME? /LYDIA/ LYDIA CAREW.
GENV IV	(113)	THERE IS ETERNAL PEACE. I KNOW SO MANY CASES. I	KNOW	BY MY OWN EXPERIENCE. /SECRETARY/ YOU ARE AN AMIABLE
CATH 2	(175)	(SHE TURNS AGAIN TO NARYSHKIN) YOU SHOULD	KNOW	BY THIS TIME THAT I AM FRANK AND ORIGINAL IN CHARACTER,
BULL I	(85)	TEMPER: IT'S NOT MEANT FOR YOU, AS YOU OUGHT TO	KNOW	BY THIS TIME. (HE SITS DOWN AGAIN, A LITTLE ASHAMED OF
ROCK PREFACE	(182)	YOU AGAIN, WHAT IS TRUTH? /JESUS/ IT IS WHAT YOU	KNOW	BY YOUR EXPERIENCE TO BE TRUE OR FEEL IN YOUR SOUL MUST
NEVR IV	(296)	YES YOU ARE: YOU THINK YOURE NOT; BUT YOU ARE. I	KNOW	BY YOUR EYEBROWS. /BOHUN/ (CAPITULATING) MRS CLANDON:
MRS III	(230)	MYSTERY ABOUT IT: DONT THINK THAT. OF COURSE YOU	KNOW	BY YOUR MOTHER'S BEING IN IT THAT IT'S PERFECTLY
KING I	(170)	CONFRONTED WITH THE ENORMITY OF WHAT HE DOES NOT	KNOW	CAN THINK MUCH OF WHAT HE DOES KNOW. BUT WHAT IS THE
AUGS	(270)	WHAT YOU MIGHT CALL A LADY. SHE WANTS TO	KNOW	CAN YOU SEE HER IF I LET HER UP. /AUGUSTUS/ OH, YOU
KING PREFACE	(157)	WITH HIS APPETITE FOR BARBARA VILLIERS DO NOT	KNOW	CHALK FROM CHEESE BIOLOGICALLY. THE FUTURE OF WOMEN IN
CLEO I	(115)	TELL HIM. /CAESAR/ HE WILL NOT ASK ME. HE WILL	KNOW	CLEOPATRA BY HER PRIDE, HER COURAGE, HER MAJESTY, AND
PYGM I	(214)	/THE NOTE TAKER/ (EAGERLY) ARE YOU? DO YOU	KNOW	COLONEL PICKERING, THE AUTHOR OF SPOKEN SANSCRIT? /THE
ROCK II	(279)	SELDOM FULFILS ALL OUR EXPECTATIONS. YOU DONT	KNOW	DAVID YET. /ALOYSIA/ I WILL FIND HIM A JOB AND SEE THAT
PRES	(166)	BE A FOOL, CHILD. (TO MITCHENER) SHE WANTS TO	KNOW	DO I REALLY LOVE YOU. (INTO THE TELEPHONE) IT'S LIKELY
PYGM V	(286)	HAVE TO GIVE UP FEELING NEGLECTED IF THE MEN YOU	KNOW	DONT SPEND HALF THEIR TIME SNIVELLING OVER YOU AND THE
BULL IV	(158)	/LARRY/ WELL, WHAT IS THERE TO SAY? YOU SEE, WE	KNOW	EACH OTHER SO WELL. /NORA/ (A LITTLE CONSOLED) YES: OF
KING I	(218)	LOUIS AND I PLAYED TOGETHER WHEN WE WERE BOYS. WE	KNOW	EACH OTHER TOO WELL TO BE PLEASANT COMPANY; SO I TAKE
FANY EPILOG	(330)	IT IS. IF HE DOESNT, HE CANT COMPLAIN IF I DONT	KNOW	EITHER. I'M NOT THE AUTHOR. /THE COUNT/ BUT IS IT A
MTH2	(65)	OR A PARK. I AM A YORKSHIREMAN, MY FRIEND. I	KNOW	ENGLAND; AND YOU DONT. IF YOU DID YOU WOULD KNOW--
JITT II	(47)	TOLD ME EVERYTHING. /JITTA/ (BITTERLY) DONT YOU	KNOW	ENOUGH ALREADY? /LENKHEIM/ (POINTING TO THE
BUOY IV	(58)	OF YOU WANT TO BETTER THE WORLD WHEN YOU DONT	KNOW	ENOUGH OF IT TO MANAGE A FISH AND CHIPS BUSINESS.
CAND II	(122)	YOU BACK AGAIN. /CANDIDA/ THANK YOU, LEXY. YOU	KNOW	EUGENE, DONT YOU? /LEXY/ OH YES. HOW DO YOU DO,
SUPR IV	(143)	IS IT? THANK YOU. /STRAKER/ WHY, YOU DONT	KNOW	EVEN HER NAME? /THE IRISHMAN/ YES I DO, NOW THAT YOUVE
JITT III	(61)	BUT THAT POOR WOMAN, AS YOU CALL HER, DID NOT	KNOW	EVEN HOW TO BEGIN. /FESSLER/ YOUR GRIEF IS CARRYING YOU
MILL I	(156)	PREFERENCE AND A DEFERRED ORDINARY. HE WOULD NOT	KNOW	EVEN HOW TO BEGIN. /ADRIAN/ BUT HOW DID HE BEGIN? MY
FABL V	(121)	FROM? CAN YOU TELL ME? /ROSE/ NO; BUT WHEN WE	KNOW	EVEN THAT, IT WILL BE ONLY ANOTHER GRAIN OF SAND ON THE
PYGM III	(249)	ART AND SCIENCE, AND SO ON; BUT HOW MANY OF US	KNOW	EVEN THE MEANINGS OF THESE NAMES? (TO MISS HILL) WHAT
HART II	(93)	WHEN HE GETS IT. HE IS SUCH A BABY THAT HE DOESNT	KNOW	EVEN WHAT TO EAT AND DRINK: HE HAS RUINED HIS LIVER
CAPT III	(279)	HOW CLEVER OF YOU TO FIND OUT! I BELIEVE YOU	KNOW	EVERY BOLT IN THAT SHIP. KEARNEY SOFTENS PERCEPTIBLY.
BULL I	(77)	BUT I SHOULD LIKE TO EXPLAIN-- /TIM/ SURE I	KNOW	EVERY WORD YOURE GOIN TO SAY BEFORE YEV SAID IT. I KNOW
GETT	(325)	I MIND NOTHING BUT MY DUTIES. /THE BISHOP/ YOU	KNOW	EVERYBODY NOW, I THINK. /MRS GEORGE/ (TURNING TO THE
GETT	(357)	/MRS GEORGE/ HM! LIKE MOST MEN, YOU THINK YOU	KNOW	EVERYTHING A WOMAN WANTS, DONT YOU? BUT THE THING ONE
KING I	(221)	HAS TO CORRECT IT FROM TIME TO TIME. CAN YOU, WHO	KNOW	EVERYTHING BECAUSE YOU AND GOD ARE BOTH ARTISTS, TELL
KING I	(194)	A KING'S SECRET. PETER THE FISHERMAN DID NOT	KNOW	EVERYTHING. NEITHER DID MARTIN LUTHER. /JAMES/ NEITHER
APPL I	(242)	MUST HEAR EVERYTHING, SEE EVERYTHING, AND	KNOW	EVERYTHING. /PROTEUS/ SINGULARLY ENOUGH, MR SEMPRONIUS,
GLIM	(174)	OF THE WINDOW AND BROKE HIS ARM. /THE GIRL/ YOU	KNOW	EVERYTHING. /THE FRIAR/ SAINT BARBARA, MY DAUGHTER,
APPL I	(205)	WILL HAVE TO LET THEM DO IT, BECAUSE YOU CANNOT	KNOW	EVERYTHING; AND EVEN IF YOU COULD YOU CANNOT DO
JOAN 5	(116)	LET HER HAVE HER WAY, DUNOIS: SHE DOES NOT	KNOW	EVERYTHING; BUT SHE HAS GOT HOLD OF THE RIGHT END OF
FABL VI	(124)	ONLY FIRST FORM CHILDREN, WHO THINK THEIR PARENTS	KNOW	EVERYTHING, ASK WHY. IN THE SIXTH FORM YOU ARE SUPPOSED
PYGM I	(211)	(AMAZED) WELL, WHO SAID I DIDNT? BLY ME! YOU	KNOW	EVERYTHING, YOU DO. /THE FLOWER GIRL/ (STILL NURSING
JITT III	(57)	GET IT BY LIFTING UP HIS LITTLE FINGER. OH, I	KNOW	EXACTLY HOW HE DECEIVED US. /LENKHEIM/ (RISING,
JOAN 5	(115)	FINDING TROOPS FOR HER AND FEEDING THEM. BUT I	KNOW	EXACTLY HOW MUCH GOD DID FOR US THROUGH THE MAID, AND
FABL VI	(129)	BY GOD. ANYHOW THEY ARE WHISPERED; AND I WANT TO	KNOW	EXACTLY HOW. /TEACHER/ LIKE ALL YOUNG THINGS YOU WANT
MIS. PREFACE	(105)	DEFENSIBLE AND DELIGHTFUL AMUSEMENT WHEN YOU	KNOW	EXACTLY WHAT YOU ARE DOING AND WHERE FANCY ENDS AND
DOCT PREFACE	(61)	BUT THEY NO LONGER DARE SAY AS MUCH UNTIL THEY	KNOW	EXACTLY WHERE THEY ARE; FOR MANY VERY DESIRABLE
MTH4 II	(177)	WOMAN: ONE HUNDRED AND SEVENTY IF YOU WISH TO	KNOW	EXACTLY. /NAPOLEON/ (FOLDING HIS ARMS) I AM NOT
DEST	(171)	AN IMPERTINENCE IN ME TO TELL YOU WHAT YOU MUST	KNOW	FAR BETTER THAN I DO. BUT YOU ARE NOT ANGRY WITH ME,
MRS I	(187)	DONT IMAGINE I KNOW ANYTHING ABOUT MY MOTHER. I	KNOW	FAR LESS THAN YOU DO. /PRAED/ (VERY ILL AT EASE) IN
DEST	(168)	RUN AWAY: FEAR IS THE MAINSPRING OF WAR. FEAR! I	KNOW	FEAR WELL, BETTER THAN YOU, BETTER THAN ANY WOMAN. I
ARMS II	(24)	THE MISTRESS THAT SHE WOULDNT HAVE THE MASTER	KNOW	FOR A THOUSAND LEVAS. I KNOW THINGS ABOUT HIM THAT SHE
JITT III	(72)	LET HIM TOUCH ME. /JITTA/ MY DEAR! HOW CAN HE	KNOW	FOR CERTAIN? YOU DO NOT KNOW FOR CERTAIN YOURSELF.
JITT III	(58)	THEY SAY. BUT IT WILL NEVER COMFORT ME UNTIL I	KNOW	FOR CERTAIN THAT THE HAPPINESS HE HAD WITH ME WAS THE
FABL I	(103)	BUT THE WHOLE NEUTRAL WORLD. WE DO NOT AS YET	KNOW	FOR CERTAIN THAT THE BOMB THAT DISINTEGRATED HIROSHIMA
FABL PREFACE	(82)	QUOTED A CERTAIN EX-COLONEL WHO SAID TO ME " I	KNOW	FOR CERTAIN THAT THE RECTOR IS THE FATHER OF HIS
MRS I	(192)	/CROFTS/ (CATCHING HIM UP CUNNINGLY) YOU	KNOW	FOR CERTAIN THAT I'M NOT? /PRAED/ I KNOW NOTHING ABOUT
2TRU III	(103)	MIND WHAT FOR. A FORTNIGHT MIGHT DO; BUT I DONT	KNOW	FOR CERTAIN YET. THERES SOMETHING STEADYING ABOUT HIM;
JITT III	(72)	MY DEAR: HOW CAN HE KNOW FOR CERTAIN? YOU DO NOT	KNOW	FOR CERTAIN YOURSELF. /EDITH/ I KNOW I CANT PROVE IT.
JITT III	(71)	MY FATHER COULD GO WITH LOW WOMEN-- IF HE DID NOT	KNOW	FOR CERTAIN, AS I KNOW, THAT THE WOMAN MY FATHER LOVED
PHIL II	(108)	CERTAINLY NOT. PRINCIPLE'S THE POOREST REASON I	KNOW	FOR MAKING YOURSELF NASTY. /SYLVIA/ BOSH! IBSEN!
ROCK I	(210)	THIS WHAT? ? /OXFORD YOUTH/ OH, CHUCK IT. YOU	KNOW	FRENCH AS WELL AS I DO. /SIR ARTHUR/ OH. FAUX BONHOMME,
ROCK II	(243)	MONEY! NOT AT ALL. I AM A POOR MAN. I NEVER	KNOW	FROM ONE MOMENT TO ANOTHER WHETHER I AM WORTH THIRTEEN
MIS. PREFACE	(44)	TO SCHOOLMASTER THE FUTURE BY PRETENDING TO	KNOW	GOOD FROM EVIL IN TENDENCY, OR PROTECT CITIZENS AGAINST
3PLA PREFACE	(R25)	ITS MERITS TO THE HUGE MAJORITY WHO DONT	KNOW	GOOD WORK FROM BAD. IT DOES THEM GOOD; AND IT DOES ME
BARB I	(266)	GREEK SCHOLARS ARE PRIVILEGED MEN. FEW OF THEM	KNOW	GREEK; AND NONE OF THEM KNOW ANYTHING ELSE; BUT THEIR
JITT III	(54)	HE TELLS? /FESSLER/ I AM QUITE SURE HE DID NOT	KNOW	HALF HIS OWN GREATNESS. /AGNES/ THEN WILL YOU TELL ME
SUPR II	(51)	REGENT STREET! CHELSEA! THE BOROUGH! -- I DONT	KNOW	HALF THEIR CONFOUNDED NAMES: THESE ARE HIS
CAPT III	(286)	REMONSTRATING) CICELY! /LADY CICELY/ HE DID: YOU	KNOW	HE DID. YOU TOLD ME TO TELL THE EXACT TRUTH. /KEARNEY/
JOAN 1	(61)	/JOAN/ HIS FRIENDS CALL HIM SO, SQUIRE: I DID NOT	KNOW	HE HAD ANY OTHER NAME. JACK -- /ROBERT/ THAT IS
BARB II	(305)	AGAINST THE ANSWER TO OUR PRAYERS? /BARBARA/ I	KNOW	HE HAS A SOUL TO BE SAVED. LET HIM COME DOWN HERE; AND
DOCT III	(153)	KNOWS HIM OR EVER CAN KNOW HIM. I AM HIS WIFE. I	KNOW	HE HAS LITTLE FAULTS: IMPATIENCE, SENSITIVENESS, EVEN
GETT PREFACE	(222)	TO ASK A YOUNG MAN HIS INTENTIONS WHEN YOU	KNOW	HE HAS NO INTENTIONS, BUT IS UNABLE TO DENY THAT HE HAS
ARMS I	(15)	BUT I DONT BELIEVE THE FIRST MAN IS A COWARD. I	KNOW	HE IS A HERO! /THE MAN/ (GOODHUMOREDLY) THATS WHAT
BASH II,1,	(102)	OF THE PANLEY BOY, THE DUTCHMAN, GLUTTON AS WE	KNOW	HE IS, SEEMED THIS TIME LIKELY TO GO HUNGRY. CASHEL WAS
JITT III	(54)	SCIENCE. /AGNES/ SO I HAVE ALWAYS UNDERSTOOD. I	KNOW	HE THOUGHT SO HIMSELF. /FESSLER/ (INDIGNANT) OH NO: HE
O'FL	(215)	IN GLASNEVIN. /SIR PEARCE/ BOSH! HOW DOES SHE	KNOW	HE WAS? DID YOU EVER ASK HER? /O'FLAHERTY/ I DID,
INCA PROLOG	(233)	WAS A MILLIONAIRE. /ERMYNTRUDE/ HOW DID YOU	KNOW	HE WAS A MILLIONAIRE? /THE ARCHDEACON/ HE CAME FROM
KING I	(180)	IT IS WITH HIM, NOT WITH YOU, CHERI. I DID NOT	KNOW	HE WAS HOLDING A RECEPTION. /CHARLES/ MR NEWTON IS NOT
HART II	(120)	HEARTBREAK. I FELL IN LOVE WITH HECTOR, AND DIDNT	KNOW	HE WAS MARRIED. /CAPTAIN SHOTOVER/ HEARTBREAK? ARE YOU
JITT III	(59)	I CANT ALWAYS KEEP MYSELF SPICK AND SPAN; AND I	KNOW	HE WAS PARTICULAR ABOUT SUCH THINGS. THATS WHERE SHE
O'FL	(215)	DID SHE SAY? /O'FLAHERTY/ SHE ASKED ME HOW DID I	KNOW	HE WASNT, AND FETCHED ME A CLOUT ON THE SIDE OF MY
DEVL II	(31)	I DO HATE HIM. I CANT GET HIM OUT OF MY MIND: I	KNOW	HE WILL BRING HARM WITH HIM. HE INSULTED YOU: HE
BARB III	(339)	WILL HE BE THE BETTER FOR THAT? /UNDERSHAFT/ YOU	KNOW	HE WILL. DONT BE A HYPOCRITE, BARBARA. HE WILL BE
HART II	(87)	HIM THE TRUTH OR BURST. WHAT STOPS ME IS THAT I	KNOW	HE WOULDNT BELIEVE ME. HE'D THINK IT WAS MY MODESTY, AS
SUPR IV	(148)	I DO. I MEAN ALL I SAY. /VIOLET/ THEN YOU DONT	KNOW	HECTOR AS I DO. HE IS ROMANTIC AND FADDY-- HE GETS IT
ROCK II	(284)	/SIR ARTHUR/ NEVER MIND, DEAR: THE POLICE ALL	KNOW	HER: SHE'LL COME TO NO HARM. SHE'LL BE BACK FOR TEA.
MRS III	(225)	THE BOND BETWEEN YOUR MOTHER AND ME: THATS WHY I	KNOW	HER BETTER THAN YOULL EVER KNOW HER. /VIVIE/ YOU ARE
JOAN 1	(63)	SHE'S A BOURGEOISE. THAT MATTERS A GOOD DEAL. I	KNOW	HER CLASS EXACTLY. HER FATHER CAME HERE LAST YEAR TO
PHIL II	(130)	SO NERVOUS THAT I CANT ANSWER FOR MYSELF UNTIL I	KNOW	HER DECISION. MRS TRANFIELD WILL TELL YOU WHAT A TIME
JOAN EPILOG	(159)	WHO TOLD YOU THAT? /JOAN/ NEVER MIND. WOULD YOU	KNOW	HER IF YOU SAW HER AGAIN? /THE SOLDIER/ NOT I. THERE
JITT III	(72)	REAL TO ME. BESIDES, I HAVE A QUEER SENSE THAT I	KNOW	HER QUITE AS WELL AS A REAL PERSON; THAT SHE IS HERE
SUPR I	(22)	SHE IS THE SAME TO EVERYBODY, JACK: YOU	KNOW	HER WAYS. /TANNER/ YES: SHE BREAKS EVERYBODY'S BACK
PHIL III	(146)	TO ADVANCE) TAKE CARE. SHE'S GOING TO HIT YOU. I	KNOW	HER. CHARTERIS STOPS AND LOOKS CAUTIOUSLY AT JULIA,
NEVR II	(252)	NO RIGHT TO GIVE ME YOUR SISTER'S NAME. I DONT	KNOW	HER. /CRAMPTON/ YOURE TALKING NONSENSE. THERE ARE
MRS III	(225)	ME: THATS WHY I KNOW HER BETTER THAN YOULL EVER	KNOW	HER. /VIVIE/ YOU ARE WRONG: YOU KNOW NOTHING ABOUT HER.
MTH1 II	(23)	PAINS! HA! POOR WRETCH: DO YOU THINK I DO NOT	KNOW	HER, AND KNOW YOU, BETTER THAN THAT? DO YOU RISK YOUR
LION II	(132)	HER. /CAESAR/ IS THAT ALL? /ANDROCLES/ YOU DONT	KNOW	HER, CAESAR, OR YOU WOULDNT SAY THAT. /CAESAR/ AH,
GETT	(286)	BRIDGENORTH/ -- SOME GREAT MAN WHO WILL NEVER	KNOW	HER, NEVER TOUCH HER, AS SHE IS ON EARTH, BUT WHOM SHE
MIS.	(166)	DOUBT SHE WAS AN EXCELLENT WOMAN. /THE MAN/ NOT	KNOW	HER! DO YOU DARE TO STAND THERE BY HER OPEN GRAVE AND
FANY I	(274)	AS IF THE BOY WAS IN PRISON. /GILBEY/ HOW DO YOU	KNOW	HE'S NOT IN PRISON? IT'S GOT ON MY NERVES SO, THAT I'D
SUPR IV	(155)	OR A PATENT ARTICLE-- /TANNER/ HE'S A MAN. I	KNOW	HIM: HIS PRINCIPLES ARE THOROUGHLY COMMERCIAL. LET US

MILL I (138)	AND HEAVY WEIGHT BOXER? /THE LADY/ DO YOU	KNOW	HIM? /SAGAMORE/ EVERY MORNING WE SWIM TOGETHER AT THE
MTH2 (41)	FROM THAT COMMANDING POSITION). /FRANKLYN/ YOU	KNOW	HIM? /SAVVY/ RATHER. SIT DOWN, BILL. /FRANKLYN/ MR
ARMS I (16)	LOYAL TO HER IDEALS) INDEED! WOULD YOU	KNOW	HIM AGAIN IF YOU SAW HIM? /THE MAN/ SHALL I EVER
HART I (61)	/MRS HUSHABYE/ YOU DONT KNOW HIM; AND YOU	KNOW	HIM ALMOST INTIMATELY. HOW LUCID! /ELLIE/ I MEAN THAT
HART II (93)	YOU WILL BE SURPRISED WHEN YOU COME TO	KNOW	HIM BETTER: HE IS REALLY THE MOST HELPLESS OF MORTALS.
BULL II (114)	WITH HIM. YOUVE SEEN HIM OFTENER THAN I HAVE. YOU	KNOW	HIM BETTER THAN I DO, BY THIS TIME. YOUVE COME TO ME
ARMS III (52)	STARTLED) OH! DO YOU THINK SO? /BLUNTSCHLI/ YOU	KNOW	HIM BETTER THAN I DO. /RAINA/ I WONDER-- I WONDER IS
SUPR III (139)	TONE-- /ANN/ DONT MIND HIM, GRANNY: YOU OUGHT TO	KNOW	HIM BY THIS TIME (SHE TAKES HIS ARM AND COAXES HIM
HART I (61)	HIM TO SPEAK TO. /MRS HUSHABYE/ BUT YOU WANT TO	KNOW	HIM EVER SO MUCH MORE INTIMATELY, EH? /ELLIE/ NO NO: I
WIDO I (10)	THAT HE'S PLEASANT ENOUGH; BUT THEN YOUVE GOT TO	KNOW	HIM FIRST, HAVNT YOU? /BLANCHE/ (IMPATIENTLY)
DOCT PREFACE(69)	BE ITS OWN SALVATION. FOR THE M.O.H. AS WE	KNOW	HIM IS ONLY THE BEGINNING OF THAT ARMY OF PUBLIC
MTH4 I (160)	ME, AND MAKE ME MORE DETERMINED THAN EVER NOT TO	KNOW	HIM ON ANY TERMS. /ZOO/ YET YOU WOULD BE MUCH MORE
LION PREFACE(84)	WITH THE WORD RELIGION; WHILST OTHERS, WHO	KNOW	HIM ONLY BY MISREPRESENTATION AS A SENTIMENTAL PACIFIST
WIDO I (22)	POSITION AND AFFAIRS; AND I HAVE LONG DESIRED TO	KNOW	HIM PERSONALLY. /COKANE/ (AGAIN OBSEQUIOUS, BUT STILL
MTH5 (226)	BESIDE ECRASIA, ON HER LEFT). /MARTELLUS/ YOU	KNOW	HIM QUITE WELL. PYGMALION. /ECRASIA/ (INDIGNANTLY)
HART I (61)	SO MUCH MORE INTIMATELY, EH? /ELLIE/ NO NO: I	KNOW	HIM QUITE-- ALMOST INTIMATELY. /MRS HUSHABYE/ YOU DONT
MTH4 I (159)	HIS ORGANS AND ANALYZE THEM CHEMICALLY, WOULD YOU	KNOW	HIM THEN? /THE ELDERLY GENTLEMAN/ CERTAINLY NOT. ANY
HART I (61)	WHAT DOES THAT MEAN? /ELLIE/ WELL, OF COURSE I	KNOW	HIM TO SPEAK TO. /MRS HUSHABYE/ BUT YOU WANT TO KNOW
CAND I (95)	THINK OF MY FATHER? /MARCHBANKS/ I-- I HARDLY	KNOW	HIM YET. HE SEEMS TO BE A VERY NICE OLD GENTLEMAN.
DOCT III (153)	AS NOBODY ELSE IN THE WORLD KNOWS HIM OR EVER CAN	KNOW	HIM. I AM HIS WIFE. I KNOW HE HAS LITTLE FAULTS:
SUPR HANDBOK(194)	THE HILL WILL NEVER BE CLIMBED BY MAN AS WE	KNOW	HIM. IT NEED NOT BE DENIED THAT IF WE ALL STRUGGLED
CAPT III (281)	/SIR HOWARD/ (DRILY) YES, I THINK I	KNOW	HIM. /KEARNEY/ BRING IN THE PRISONERS. /BLUEJACKET/ (
HART I (59)	OF COURSE I DONT TELL EVERYBODY. BESIDES, I DONT	KNOW	HIM. /MRS HUSHABYE/ DONT KNOW HIM! WHAT DOES THAT
WIDO III (51)	YES, SIR. BUT INDEED, SIR, YOUD SCARCELY	KNOW	HIM. /SARTORIUS/ (FROWNING) HM! STARVING, I SUPPOSE.
APPL I (198)	BY THE WAY, IS HE ALIVE? I SHOULD LIKE TO	KNOW	HIM. /SEMPRONIUS/ NO. HE DIED IN 1962, OF SOLITUDE.
MIS. (150)	WAY! BEFORE HE COMES IN: LET ME EXPLAIN. I DONT	KNOW	HIM. /TARLETON/ EH? /PERCIVAL/ HAVNT EVEN LOOKED AT
MTH4 I (159)	EVERY DAY WHEN I AM AT HOME. BUT I REFUSE TO	KNOW	HIM. /ZOO/ IF YOU COULD SEE HIM MUCH MORE DISTINCTLY
KING I (161)	HOME TO RECEIVE HIM. /MRS BASHAM/ ROWLEY? I DONT	KNOW	HIM. THIS IS NO HOUR TO CALL ON MR NEWTON. /THE MAID/
FANY PROLOG (264)	OF THE THEATRE IS AN INSIDE KNOWLEDGE. WE	KNOW	HIM; AND HE KNOWS US. HE KNOWS THE ROPES: HE KNOWS HIS
HART I (61)	ALMOST INTIMATELY. /MRS HUSHABYE/ YOU DONT	KNOW	HIM; AND YOU KNOW HIM ALMOST INTIMATELY. HOW LUCID!
SUPR II (51)	YOU MIND HIM, MR ROBINSON. HE LIKES TO TALK. WE	KNOW	HIM, DONT WE? /OCTAVIUS/ (EARNESTLY) BUT THERES A
WIDO I (10)	ISNT AN EASY MAN TO TACKLE. OF COURSE, NOW THAT I	KNOW	HIM, I SEE THAT HE'S PLEASANT ENOUGH; BUT THEN YOUVE
DEVL III (51)	FAULT WITH EVERYTHING THIS SIDE OF HALF PAST, I	KNOW	HIM, SIR: I SERVED WITH HIM IN PORTUGAL. YOU MAY COUNT
GLIM (173)	TO ALL THE OTHER YOUNG MEN. /THE GIRL/ YOU	KNOW	HIM, THEN! /THE FRIAR/ NO NO NO NO. I'M TOO OLD TO
CLEO II (134)	HELP YOUR FATHER. /CLEOPATRA/ (ENRAPTURED) YOU	KNOW	HIM! /CAESAR/ (NODDING) I DO. /CLEOPATRA/ HAS HE COME
HART I (59)	BESIDES, I DONT KNOW HIM. /MRS HUSHABYE/ DONT	KNOW	HIM! WHAT DOES THAT MEAN? /ELLIE/ WELL, OF COURSE I
DEVL III (57)	I SUPPOSE, SIR, THE BRITISH OFFICER NEED NOT	KNOW	HIS BUSINESS: THE BRITISH SOLDIER WILL GET HIM OUT OF
SUPR III (105)	IF IT HAD WANTED MONEY INSTEAD OF FOOD. I	KNOW	HIS CLUMSY TYPEWRITERS AND BUNGLING LOCOMOTIVES AND
DEVL II (31)	DONT YOU WANT HIM TO BE WARNED? /JUDITH/ HE MUST	KNOW	HIS DANGER. OH, TONY, IS IT WRONG TO HATE A BLASPHEMER
CAPT II (247)	LET ME INTRODOOCE MR REDBROOK. YOUR LADYSHIP MAY	KNOW	HIS FATHER, THE VERY REV. DEAN REDBROOK. (HE GOES TO
ROCK II (269)	OF DOMESDAY, MR HIPNEY. /HIPNEY/ BLESS YOU, I	KNOW	HIS GRACE. ABOUT TOWN, AS YOU MIGHT SAY, THOUGH WEVE
WIDO II (26)	TELL YOU WHAT HE SAID. /SARTORIUS/ HM! DO YOU	KNOW	HIS NAME? /LICKCHEESE/ YES, SIR. SPEAKMAN. /SARTORIUS/
MIS. (199)	ME RIGHT! PARENTS AND CHILDREN! NO MAN SHOULD	KNOW	HIS OWN CHILD. NO CHILD SHOULD KNOW ITS OWN FATHER. LET
SUPR II (56)	WHO WILL TOUCH HIS HAT AND	KNOW	HIS PLACE. I AM ENRY'S SLAVE, JUST AS UNCLE JAMES WAS
CLEO II (135)	IS THE MOST BEAUTIFUL OF OUR GODS. BUT I WANT TO	KNOW	HIS REAL NAME. /CAESAR/ HIS NAME IS MARK ANTONY.
BULL III (127)	TO BE COMPARED TO PATSY FARRLL, THAT DOESNT HARLY	KNOW	HIS RIGHT HAND FROM HIS LEFT? WHAT DID HE EVER SUFFER,
2TRU II (60)	LIT UP AT ONCE AND SAID " DEAR AUBREY BAGOT! I	KNOW	HIS SISTER INTIMATELY. WE WERE ALL THREE CHILDREN
BULL IV (147)	MINE. /NORA/ HE MEANS THE PIG, MR DORAN. YOU	KNOW	HIS WAY. /DORAN/ (RISING GALLANTLY TO THE OCCASION)
FANY I (276)	TO COME HERE; BUT THEN WHAT WAS I TO DO? YOU	KNOW	HOLY JOE, BOBBY'S TUTOR, DONT YOU? BUT OF COURSE YOU
CURE (231)	APPROACHING HER) WELL, YOU KNOW, IT'S SO HARD TO	KNOW	HOW A CROCODILE WOULD PLAY. /THE LADY/ STUFF! (SHE
OVER PREFACE(167)	CEREMONIES DO NOT INTEREST ME IN THE LEAST, I	KNOW	HOW A MAN IS TRIED, AND HOW HE IS HANGED. I SHOULD HAVE
MILL I (156)	YOU FEELS LIKE A NEEDY ADVENTURER. YOU DONT	KNOW	HOW A MAN TO WHOM A HUNDRED POUNDS IS A CONSIDERABLE
BARB III (321)	IT IS IMPOSSIBLE TO BE ANGRY WITH YOU. YOU DONT	KNOW	HOW ABSURD ALL THIS SOUNDS TO ME. YOU ARE VERY PROPERLY
JITT I (22)	COULD NEVER HAVE WRITTEN IT WITHOUT HIM. AND YOU	KNOW	HOW AMBITIOUS HE IS. I CAN DEPEND ON ALFRED ABSOLUTELY.
JITT I (12)	TABLE, SNUBBED). /THE GENTLEMAN/ NOT AT ALL: I	KNOW	HOW ANXIOUS YOU ARE ABOUT ME, AND HOW KINDLY YOU MEAN
DOCT IV (160)	PRESENTLY. HE WANTS TO SEE YOU BECAUSE HE DOESNT	KNOW	HOW BAD HE IS. WE'LL ALLOW YOU TO WAIT A FEW MINUTES TO
BARB I (259)	ARMCHAIR, INTO WHICH HE THROWS HIMSELF). I DONT	KNOW	HOW BARBARA WILL TAKE IT. EVER SINCE THEY MADE HER A
BUOY PREFACE(5)	THAN ONCE EVERY FIFTEEN YEARS OR SO. I DO NOT	KNOW	HOW COMMON THEY ARE; FOR I NEVER HEARD ANYONE BUT MR
CAND III (133)	HANDS TOUCH ME. /MORELL/ YOU YOUNG IMP, DO YOU	KNOW	HOW DANGEROUS IT IS TO SAY THAT TO ME? OR (WITH A
MIS. (194)	MY DEAR MISS TARLETON: DONT BE SO NAUGHTY. I	KNOW	HOW DELIGHTFUL IT IS TO SHOCK AN OLD MAN; BUT THERE IS
FANY PREFACE(255)	GIVEN UNDER THE CIRCUMSTANCES, OR THAT I DO NOT	KNOW	HOW DIFFICULT IT IS TO FIND OUT A WAY OF GETTING INTO
HART I (49)	VERY STRANGE: HE HAS BEEN JUST LIKE THAT TO ME. I	KNOW	HOW DREADFUL IT MUST BE: MY OWN FATHER IS ALL THE WORLD
CAND I (96)	CABMAN. I KNOW IT'S UTTERLY SILLY; BUT YOU DONT	KNOW	HOW DREADFUL SUCH THINGS ARE TO ME-- HOW I SHRINK FROM
MIS. (115)	THEM). THATS ALL RIGHT. JOHNNY FRIGHTENED ME. YOU	KNOW	HOW EASY IT IS TO HURT ME; AND I'M TOO SMALL TO DEFEND
MIS. PREFACE(87)	AFFECTED OR MORBID. FAMILY MOURNING. I DO NOT	KNOW	HOW FAR THIS DETESTABLE CUSTOM OF MOURNING IS CARRIED
CAPT II (252)	NOTE THE HOUR OF HIS GOING, THAT HIS MASTER MAY	KNOW	HOW FAST HE RIDES. /OSMAN/ THE BELIEVER'S WORD SHALL
GETT (275)	ASKED TO COME; AND I HAVE ASKED YOU TO GO. YOU	KNOW	HOW FOND I AM OF LEO; AND YOU KNOW WHAT SHE WOULD FEEL
DEST (158)	LIKE TO KNOW, GENERAL. (WITH EMOTION) YOU DONT	KNOW	HOW FOND I WAS OF THAT HORSE. /NAPOLEON/ (ANGRILY
ARMS I (17)	AH, TRUE, DEAR YOUNG LADY: YOURE ALWAYS RIGHT. I	KNOW	HOW GOOD YOUVE BEEN TO ME: TO MY LAST HOUR I SHALL
PYGM PREFACE(202)	IN ITS REQUIREMENTS!); FOR ALTHOUGH I WELL	KNOW	HOW HARD IT IS FOR A MAN OF GENIUS WITH A SERIOUSLY
JITT I (21)	NO, I CANNOT, NEVER. /BRUNO/ (SOOTHING HER) I	KNOW	HOW HARD IT IS FOR YOU, DARLING. THAT IS WHY I HAVE NOT
2TRU I (46)	YOU LIKE. IF YOU WERE LADIES AND GENTLEMEN, YOUD	KNOW	HOW HARD IT IS NOT TO DO WHAT EVERYBODY ELSE DOES. /THE
DEVL III (53)	ME AS WITNESS: THEY WILL NEVER KILL YOU WHEN THEY	KNOW	HOW HEROICALLY YOU HAVE ACTED. /RICHARD/ (WITH SOME
SUPR II (66)	MIDDLE CLASS. /VIOLET/ IT'S TOO RIDICULOUS. YOU	KNOW	HOW I DISLIKE SAYING SUCH THINGS TO YOU, HECTOR; BUT IF
HART I (75)	I DO NOT LIKE BEING ATTRACTED. BUT YOU HAD BETTER	KNOW	HOW I FEEL IF YOU ARE GOING TO STAY HERE. /LADY
ROCK II (255)	MISS BROLLIKINS, ISNT IT? /ALOYSIA/ YOU DONT	KNOW	HOW I FEEL; AND YOU NEVER WILL. WE ARE GOING TO SAVE
GENV III (78)	WAS MADE BY MY GRANDFATHER. UPON MY HONOR I DONT	KNOW	HOW I GOT LANDED WHERE I AM. I AM QUITE AN ORDINARY
PHIL II (98)	DAN. (SENTIMENTALLY) SOME DAY THE WORLD WILL	KNOW	HOW I LOVED THAT WOMAN. BUT SHE WAS INCAPABLE OF
JITT I (20)	BRUNO: CANT THAT WAIT A LITTLE? YOU	KNOW	HOW I VALUE YOUR WORK; BUT WE HAVE SO LITTLE TIME LEFT
JITT II (36)	CARE? /JITTA/ HE WAS TOO CONSIDERATE TO LET YOU	KNOW	HOW ILL HE WAS. /EDITH/ HE TOLD EVERYONE ELSE. WE WERE
GETT (350)	THE TRUTH IS, THEYRE WILD WITH CURIOSITY TO	KNOW	HOW IT ALL HAPPENED. THE ORGANIST HELD ON UNTIL THE
MILL I (153)	ADRIAN: I HAVE NO SENSE OF HUMOR; AND YOU	KNOW	HOW IT ANNOYS ME WHEN YOU TALK THE SORT OF NONSENSE
CAPT II (258)	HALF OUT. /BRASSBOUND/ (DISCONCERTED) I-- I DONT	KNOW	HOW IT GOT TORN. /LADY CICELY/ YOU SHOULD NOT GET
JOAN 2 (79)	IT WILL NOT BE A MIRACLE FOR ME, BECAUSE I SHALL	KNOW	HOW IT HAS BEEN DONE, AND MY FAITH WILL NOT BE
OVER (193)	I'M VERY SORRY I LET YOU IN FOR ALL THIS. I DONT	KNOW	HOW IT IS THAT WE CONTRIVE TO MAKE FEELINGS LIKE OURS,
MRS I (184)	/VIVIE/ YES, FIFTY POUNDS. PERHAPS YOU DONT	KNOW	HOW IT WAS. MRS LATHAM, MY TUTOR AT NEWNHAM, TOLD MY
ROCK I (221)	THROUGH THE MASKED DOOR. /SIR ARTHUR/ DO YOU	KNOW	HOW LATE IT IS? TO WORK! WORK! WORK! WORK! COME
DOCT PREFACE(34)	HIS MOTHER INTO THE STOVE BECAUSE HE DESIRES TO	KNOW	HOW LONG AN ADULT WOMAN WILL SURVIVE AT A TEMPERATURE
JITT III (63)	YES I DO. /FESSLER/ THEN I WONT. YOU SEE, I DONT	KNOW	HOW LONG THIS MOOD OF YOURS WILL LAST. /EDITH/ LIFE IS
INCA (240)	OF IMPORTANCE; AND I VENTURE TO ASK YOU TO LET ME	KNOW	HOW LONG YOU INTEND TO HONOR US WITH YOUR PRESENCE.
MIS. PREFACE(33)	MONEY AND GIVE AND TAKE CHANGE, AND, GENERALLY,	KNOW	HOW MANY BEANS MAKE FIVE. IT MUST KNOW SOME LAW, WERE
METH PREFACE(R28)	TO BE A FENCER, OR THE ASTRONOMER ROYAL TO	KNOW	HOW MANY BEANS MAKE FIVE ANY BETTER THAN HIS
JOAN 5 (117)	THE LESSON OF AGINCOURT, OF POITIERS AND CRECY. I	KNOW	HOW MANY LIVES ANY MOVE OF MINE WILL COST; AND IF THE
O'FL PREFACE(202)	IT IS NOT COMMON AT PRESENT. NO ONE WILL EVER	KNOW	HOW MANY MEN JOINED THE ARMY IN 1914 AND 1915 TO ESCAPE
ROCK I (230)	TO HEALTH THAN AN UNDEREXERCISED BODY. YOU	KNOW	HOW MEN BECOME BONE LAZY FOR WANT OF BODILY EXERCISE.
VWOO 2 (129)	TO BUY HER AN ANNUITY SHE'D SELL IT. /A/ I DONT	KNOW	HOW MUCH ANNUITIES COST. /Z/ YOU WILL FIND IT IN
JITT II (36)	BECAUSE WE HAVE MORE EXPERIENCE OF MEN, AND	KNOW	HOW MUCH BETTER WHAT HE WAS THAN YOU ARE YET OLD ENOUGH
JITT III (68)	THE MOST WONDERFUL DIFFERENCE TO ME. YOU DONT	KNOW	HOW MUCH GOOD YOU HAVE DONE ME. IT ONLY SHEWS HOW
DEVL III (54)	YOUR SAKE, I LIED AS MEN ALWAYS LIE TO WOMEN. YOU	KNOW	HOW MUCH I HAVE LIVED WITH WORTHLESS MEN-- AYE, AND
SUPR IV (159)	I ACCEPT MY ILL LUCK. BUT I DONT THINK YOU QUITE	KNOW	HOW MUCH IT HURTS. /ANN/ YOU ARE SO SOFTHEARTED! IT'S
POSN PREFACE(416)	OF THEATRES FROM THE POINT OF VIEW OF THOSE WHO	KNOW	HOW MUCH MONEY CAN BE MADE OUT OF THEM BY MANAGERS WHO
JOAN 2 (71)	DAUPHIN BE DAMNED! SAVING YOUR REVERENCE. DO YOU	KNOW	HOW MUCH MONEY HE OWES ME? /THE ARCHBISHOP/ MUCH MORE
JOAN 6 (131)	I HAVE TO DO MAY SEEM CRUEL TO THOSE WHO DO NOT	KNOW	HOW MUCH MORE CRUEL IT WOULD BE TO LEAVE IT UNDONE, I
CLEO IV (167)	PLEASE, AND NOT WHOM I PLEASE. I SHOULD LIKE TO	KNOW	HOW MUCH OF HER GOLD PIECE THAT HARP GIRL WILL HAVE TO
JOAN 2 (79)	TREMOUILLE/ WELL, I WISH I WERE CLEVER ENOUGH TO	KNOW	HOW MUCH OF YOU IS GOD'S ARCHBISHOP AND HOW MUCH IS THE
BULL III (138)	WE HAVE GOOD WARRANT FOR IT; SO I'D LIKE TO	KNOW	HOW MUCH SPOIL THERE IS BEFORE I COMMIT MESELF. (HE
APPL I (218)	TEMPER. YOU WOULD NOT BE SURPRISED AT THAT IF YOU	KNOW	HOW MUCH TEMPER I HAVE TO KEEP. (HE STRAIGHTENS UP AND

MTH5	(222)	US! OUTRAGED US! PROFANED HIS ART! YOU	KNOW	HOW MUCH WE HOPED FROM THE TWELVE BUSTS HE PLACED IN
MRS IV	(247)	IT: I WAS INTENDING TO DOUBLE IT. ONLY LET ME	KNOW	HOW MUCH YOU WANT. /VIVIE/ YOU KNOW VERY WELL THAT THAT
CAPT III	(298)	DO IT? /LADY CICELY/ I'M AFRAID YOU DONT QUITE	KNOW	HOW ODD A MATCH IT WOULD BE FOR ME ACCORDING TO THE
MTH4 I	(163)	EVER EXISTED OUTSIDE YOUR IMAGINATION. I DO NOT	KNOW	HOW OLD YOU ARE: YOU LOOK ABOUT FIVE HUNDRED-- /THE
ARMS III	(47)	YOU HAVNT BEEN CAMPAIGNING, CATHERINE: YOU DONT	KNOW	HOW PLEASANT IT IS FOR US TO SIT HERE, AFTER A GOOD
BARB I	(253)	KEEP FOUR FAMILIES IN FOUR SEPARATE HOUSES. YOU	KNOW	HOW POOR MY FATHER IS: HE HAS BARELY SEVEN THOUSAND A
POSN PREFACE	(368)	IT COULD INFLUENCE BRITISH GOVERNMENTS LITTLE	KNOW	HOW REMOTE FROM PUBLIC OPINION AND HOW FULL OF THEIR
MRS IV	(248)	HALF WHISPERING. /MRS WARREN/ VIVIE: DO YOU	KNOW	HOW RICH I AM? /VIVIE/ I HAVE NO DOUBT YOU ARE VERY
INCA	(236)	DO I DO? I AM NOT USED TO THE TELEPHONE: I DONT	KNOW	HOW -- WHAT! OH, I CAN HEAR YOU SPEAKING QUITE
JITT II	(31)	FOR HIM; SO YOUD BETTER TAKE EDITH IN HAND: YOU	KNOW	HOW SHE CLINGS TO YOU. SHE IS LIKE HER FATHER IN THAT:
JITT III	(68)	COULD NEVER HAVE CARED FOR HER. /JITTA/ YOU DONT	KNOW	HOW SHE GOT HIM THERE. BUT I KNOW THAT IF HE REALLY
DOCT I	(101)	USED TO READ THE MEDICAL PAPERS AT FIRST; BUT YOU	KNOW	HOW SOON A MAN DROPS THAT; BESIDES, I CANT AFFORD THEM;
CAND III	(144)	UNDER ALL SORTS OF GLORIOUS CIRCUMSTANCES! YOU	KNOW	HOW STRONG HE IS (I HOPE HE DIDNT HURT YOU): HOW
GENV III	(67)	REALLY NEED NOT SHOOT HIM. /THE WIDOW/ YOU DONT	KNOW	HOW STRONG PUBLIC OPINION IS IN THE EARTHLY PARADISE.
SUPR HANDBOK	(209)	SOCIAL SYSTEM, CAN BE IMAGINED ONLY BY THOSE WHO	KNOW	HOW SUDDENLY A CIVILIZATION WHICH HAS LONG CEASED TO
HART II	(119)	LIKE ME, THE DREAMS COME BY THEMSELVES. YOU DONT	KNOW	HOW TERRIBLE THAT IS: YOU ARE YOUNG: YOU SLEEP AT NIGHT
WIDO I	(18)	WITH YOUR WIFE, DOESNT IT CONCERN YOUR FAMILY TO	KNOW	HOW THAT MONEY WAS MADE? DOESNT IT CONCERN YOU-- YOU,
KING II	(228)	SCOTTISH, HARDLY AT ALL ENGLISH. WHEN I WANT TO	KNOW	HOW THE GREAT LUMP OF MY SUBJECTS WILL TAKE ANYTHING I
CLEO PRO2	(99)	A MOVING WALL OF SHIELDS COMING TOWARDS US. YOU	KNOW	HOW THE HEART BURNS WHEN YOU CHARGE A FORTIFIED WALL;
OVER PREFACE	(156)	OF THE FACT THAT MOST SECTIONS OF SOCIETY DO NOT	KNOW	HOW THE OTHER SECTIONS LIVE. INDUSTRY IS THE MOST
2TRU PREFACE	(7)	ARE EXCEPTIONAL. THE RICH, IT IS SAID, DO NOT	KNOW	HOW THE POOR LIVE; BUT NOBODY INSISTS ON THE MORE
2TRU PREFACE	(7)	ON THE MORE MISCHIEVOUS FACT THAT THE POOR DO NOT	KNOW	HOW THE RICH LIVE. THE RICH ARE A MINORITY; AND THEY
CYMB FORWORD	(136)	EVEN IN THE TWO LONG LOST PRINCES, I WANTED TO	KNOW	HOW THEIR CHARACTERS WOULD REACT TO THE ECLAIRCISSEMENT
JOAN PREFACE	(23)	ENGLISH READERS WOULD PROBABLY LIKE TO	KNOW	HOW THESE IDOLIZATIONS AND REACTIONS HAVE AFFECTED THE
CAPT III	(278)	HOWARD, NOT A BIT. OF COURSE YOURE RIGHT: YOU	KNOW	HOW THESE THINGS OUGHT TO BE DONE. I'LL DO EXACTLY WHAT
BULL III	(119)	PORTER IS WHAT THEY LIKE, SIR. I'M SURE I DONT	KNOW	HOW THEY CAN STAND IT. GIVE ME BEER, I SAY. /BROADBENT/
MTH5	(219)	I CAN SEE. THEY NEVER ENJOY THEMSELVES. I DONT	KNOW	HOW THEY CAN STAND IT. THEY DONT EVEN COME TO OUR
SUPR II	(59)	/ANN/ IT WAS THAT DREADFUL BOOK OF YOURS. YOU	KNOW	HOW TIMID MOTHER IS. ALL TIMID WOMEN ARE CONVENTIONAL:
APPL II	(270)	BY BREAKAGES, LIMITED. AND REALLY I HARDLY	KNOW	HOW TO ANSWER HIM. /CRASSUS/ THINGS ARE LIKE THAT
ROCK II	(267)	WITH THE UTMOST DEFERENCE THAT I SIMPLY DONT	KNOW	HOW TO ASSERT MYSELF AND BULLY PEOPLE. THIRD, I'M SO
GETT PREFACE	(206)	NOTHING BUT THEIR DUE IN THE ASSURANCE " I	KNOW	HOW TO ATTAIN OUR ENDS BETTER THAN YOU," AND STAKING
PYGM II	(239)	YOURE A MAN, AND SHE'S ONLY A WOMAN AND DONT	KNOW	HOW TO BE HAPPY ANYHOW. /HIGGINS/ PICKERING: IF WE
JOAN 5	(115)	LONG ENOUGH THE ENEMY WILL STOP FIRST. YOU DONT	KNOW	HOW TO BEGIN A BATTLE; AND YOU DONT KNOW HOW TO USE
OVER	(173)	JUNO/ I DONT UNDERSTAND. /GREGORY/ WELL, I HARDLY	KNOW	HOW TO BEGIN TO EXPLAIN. BUT THE ROOT OF THE MATTER IS
MIS.	(190)	HAVE NEITHER SENSE ENOUGH NOR STRENGTH ENOUGH TO	KNOW	HOW TO BEHAVE YOURSELF IN A DIFFICULTY OF ANY SORT. I
NEVR II	(234)	BY INDIGNATION) CERTAINLY NOT. MY CHILDREN	KNOW	HOW TO BEHAVE THEMSELVES. /PHILIP/ NO, WILLIAM: THIS
FANY III	(318)	HAPPENING WITH A SERVANT; AND WE NONE OF US	KNOW	HOW TO BEHAVE. /JUGGINS/ IT'S QUITE SIMPLE, MADAM. I'M
MILL II	(176)	THIS IS VERY INTERESTING. /EPIFANIA/ NONSENSE! I	KNOW	HOW TO BUY AND SELL, IF THAT IS WHAT YOU MEAN. /THE
SUPR III	(105)	TO LIVE; BUT FOR LACK OF BRAINS THEY DID NOT	KNOW	HOW TO CARRY OUT THEIR PURPOSE, AND SO DESTROYED
HART II	(127)	YOU I AM GOING TO PUNISH HER. YOU SHALL SEE: I	KNOW	HOW TO DEAL WITH WOMEN. I'M REALLY VERY SLEEPY. SAY
PYGM V	(288)	BACK INTO HIS SEAT ON THE OTTOMAN). AHA! NOW I	KNOW	HOW TO DEAL WITH YOU. WHAT A FOOL I WAS NOT TO THINK OF
2TRU I	(38)	TAKE FIVE THOUSAND A YEAR TO BE A NURSE. BUT I	KNOW	HOW TO DEAL WITH YOU AND YOUR LIKE, BECAUSE I WAS ONCE
KING I	(188)	/JAMES/ A CLUB OF DAMNABLE HERETICS. I SHALL	KNOW	HOW TO DEAL WITH THEM. /NEWTON/ (RISING IN A FURY AND
BUOY PREFACE	(3)	MIRACLES. AS TRUEBLUE BRITONS THE MEDIUMS DO NOT	KNOW	HOW TO DEFEND THEMSELVES. THEY ONLY ARGUE-BARGUE. THEY
HART I	(56)	DIFFICULTY OF NOT HAVING CAPITAL ENOUGH. I DONT	KNOW	HOW TO DESCRIBE IT TO YOU. /MRS HUSHABYE/ POOR ELLIE!
GENV I	(37)	(RISING AND GOING TO THE DOOR) WELL, YOU	KNOW	HOW TO DO BUSINESS HERE: THERES NO MISTAKE ABOUT THAT.
ARMS II	(42)	TO PHILIPPOPOLIS; AND WE DONT IN THE LEAST	KNOW	HOW TO DO IT. /BLUNTSCHLI/ (SUDDENLY ATTENTIVE AND
MTH2	(59)	AND ASK HIM TO HOLD MY HAND. /LUBIN/ HE WOULDNT	KNOW	HOW TO DO IT, MY DEAR. BURGE HAS A REPUTATION AS A
GENV PREFACE	(24)	EXTENT KNOW WHAT THEY HAVE TO DO, THEY DO NOT	KNOW	HOW TO DO IT, AND STICK IN THE OLD GROOVES FOR WANT OF
KING II	(233)	AND WHEN I HAVE THROWN HIM OVER, AS I SHALL	KNOW	HOW TO DO PRESENTLY, THERE WILL BE AN END OF HIM. BUT
INCA	(237)	A SOLDIER AND IS EXPECTING A WAR BABY, BUT I DONT	KNOW	HOW TO DO WITHOUT HER. IVE TRIED MY VERY BEST; BUT
DOCT PREFACE	(22)	MICROBE AND KILL IT. AND EVEN THAT THEY DID NOT	KNOW	HOW TO DO. THE SIMPLEST WAY TO KILL MOST MICROBES IS TO
BULL I	(76)	/BROADBENT/ (LAUGHING) YOU IRISHMEN CERTAINLY DO	KNOW	HOW TO DRINK. (POURING SOME WHISKY FOR HIMSELF) NOW
MILL II	(168)	ANY MONEY, AND THE PEOPLE WHO HAVE MONEY NEVER	KNOW	HOW TO ENJOY THEMSELVES? /EPIFANIA/ YOU ARE NOT MAKING
MILL II	(168)	DAY UP THE RIVER. WHY IS IT THAT THE PEOPLE WHO	KNOW	HOW TO ENJOY THEMSELVES NEVER HAVE ANY MONEY, AND THE
FANY III	(307)	MR BOBBY GILBEY. (DUVALLET BOWS). I REALLY DONT	KNOW	HOW TO EXPLAIN OUR RELATIONSHIPS. BOBBY AND I ARE LIKE
MILL III	(185)	AND THE BANK LENDS IT TO YOU IF IT THINKS YOU	KNOW	HOW TO EXTEND YOUR BUSINESS. /THE WOMAN/ (TERRIFIED)
BULL IV	(172)	CASE) IN THE MOST MODERN PROSAIC THINGS, IF YOU	KNOW	HOW TO EXTRACT IT (HE EXTRACTS A CIGAR FOR HIMSELF AND
MTH4 II	(179)	GLORY. /THE ORACLE/ NO DOUBT THEN YOU WISH TO	KNOW	HOW TO EXTRICATE YOURSELF FROM THIS UNFORTUNATE
OVER	(192)	OF US COULD BEAT THE OTHER, AS WE NEITHER OF US	KNOW	HOW TO FIGHT. WE SHOULD ONLY BLACKEN EACH OTHER'S EYES
CAPT III	(291)	COAT AND WAISTCOAT TOGETHER). DOES ANY MAN HERE	KNOW	HOW TO FOLD UP THIS SORT OF THING PROPERLY? /REDBROOK/
MIS. PREFACE	(107)	OF LUCK, CUNNING, AND FOLLY, BE EXPECTED TO	KNOW	HOW TO GOVERN? THE MERELY LUCKY ONES AND THE
MIS. PREFACE	(107)	DISASTROUS THAN A GOVERNING CLASS THAT DOES NOT	KNOW	HOW TO GOVERN. AND HOW CAN THIS RABBLE OF THE CASUAL
MIS.	(118)	TO HIM STILL: I HAVE NO INFLUENCE. BESIDES, YOU	KNOW	HOW TO HANDLE MEN. SEE HOW YOU HANDLED ME WHEN I WAS
APPL I	(210)	WHAT YOU WILL. THE KING IS NO FOOL. NOT WHEN YOU	KNOW	HOW TO HANDLE HIM. /PAMPHILIUS/ OF COURSE, THAT MAKES
APPL I	(211)	RIGHT AS RAIN, JOE. YOU LEAVE THE KING TO ME. I	KNOW	HOW TO HANDLE HIM. IF I'D BEEN IN THE CABINET THESE
HART II	(86)	KNEW THAT THE SUREST WAY TO RUIN A MAN WHO DOESNT	KNOW	HOW TO HANDLE MONEY IS TO GIVE HIM SOME. I EXPLAINED MY
ARMS II	(37)	UP HER SLEEVES, FEELING HER BRUISED ARMS) YOU	KNOW	HOW TO HURT WITH YOUR TONGUE AS WELL AS WITH YOUR
PYGM EPILOG	(299)	TIME, SIMPLY BECAUSE ELIZA AND HER FREDDY DID NOT	KNOW	HOW TO KEEP IT. TRUE, ELIZA HAD NOT TO BEGIN AT THE
SUPR II	(69)	AS BETWEEN EMPLOYER AND ENGINEER, I SHALL ALWAYS	KNOW	HOW TO KEEP MY PROPER DISTANCE, AND NOT INTRUDE MY
WIDO II	(41)	MY YOUNG FRIEND: THESE POOR PEOPLE DO NOT	KNOW	HOW TO LIVE IN PROPER DWELLINGS: THEY WOULD WRECK THEM
HART PREFACE	(10)	TO THE GENERAL MEDICAL COUNCIL. THOSE WHO DO NOT	KNOW	HOW TO LIVE MUST MAKE A MERIT OF DYING. HEARTBREAK
MIS.	(194)	CONSTANT MONEY DIFFICULTIES BECAUSE I SIMPLY DONT	KNOW	HOW TO LIVE ON THE THOUSAND A YEAR SCALE. AS TO ASK A
2TRU III	(88)	MADNESS. MY WIFE HAS DIED CURSING ME. I DO NOT	KNOW	HOW TO LIVE WITHOUT HER: WE WERE UNHAPPY TOGETHER FOR
MTH1 II	(34)	DIE BEFORE THEY HAVE SENSE ENOUGH TO	KNOW	HOW TO LIVE. /ADAM/ NO MATTER. (HE SPITS ON HIS HANDS,
HART PREFACE	(11)	ABOUT IT. HEARTBREAK HOUSE, IN SHORT, DID NOT	KNOW	HOW TO LIVE, AT WHICH POINT ALL THAT WAS LEFT TO IT WAS
BUOY II	(23)	CARE TO BE NEXT TO ME AT A SHOOT. BUT I DO NOT	KNOW	HOW TO LOAD THE GUN: I MUST HAVE A LOADER. I CANNOT
ROCK II	(275)	I AM A READING THINKING MODERN WOMAN; AND I	KNOW	HOW TO LOOK AT THESE THINGS OBJECTIVELY AND
LION I	(114)	TONE, HUMANE AND URGENT) LAVINIA: DO CHRISTIANS	KNOW	HOW TO LOVE? /LAVINIA/ (COMPOSEDLY) YES, CAPTAIN:
FABL VI	(131)	/YOUTH 3/ ROT! YOU WANT TO KNOW TOO MUCH. WE	KNOW	HOW TO MAKE CYCLOTRONS AND HUNDRED INCH TELESCOPES. WE
MILL I	(156)	A HUNDRED AND FIFTY. I SHOULD VERY MUCH LIKE TO	KNOW	HOW TO MAKE IT UP TO FIFTY THOUSAND. YOU ARE SO RICH,
CAND III	(143)	(IMPRESSED) THATS A GOOD BID, EUGENE. NOW I	KNOW	HOW TO MAKE MY CHOICE. SHE PAUSES AND LOOKS CURIOUSLY
HART II	(124)	PERSON. WHATS THE MATTER? /HECTOR/ I DO NOT	KNOW	HOW TO MANAGE YOUR FRIEND RANDALL. NO DOUBT YOU DO.
HART PREFACE	(30)	PART OF IT UTTERLY INCOMPREHENSIBLE. HE DID NOT	KNOW	HOW TO PLAY HIS PART OF THE GAME. HE COULD UNDERSTAND
MTH1 I	(5)	HAVE IT. IT MUST NOT BE, I TELL YOU. YET I DO NOT	KNOW	HOW TO PREVENT IT. /EVE/ THAT IS JUST WHAT I FEEL; BUT
INCA	(254)	SUCH PERFECT SYMPATHY. WILL YOU -- I HARDLY	KNOW	HOW TO PUT THIS -- WILL YOU BE MINE? /ERMYNTRUDE/ OH,
METH PREFACE	(R9)	ACT OF 1870 HAD PRODUCED SHOP ASSISTANTS WHO	KNOW	HOW TO READ AND KNOW NOTHING ELSE. THE CELEBRATED
2TRU PREFACE	(24)	ADVANTAGE OF AT LEAST KNOWING THAT THEIR RULERS	KNOW	HOW TO READ AND WRITE, WHICH THEY DO NOT ENJOY AT
MIS.	(158)	SORRY TO SAY. /LINA/ THAT IS BECAUSE YOU DO NOT	KNOW	HOW TO READ IT. PUT IT UP BEFORE YOU ON A STAND; AND
MRS II	(204)	CLEARLY DISAPPROVE OF THE ARRANGEMENT, BUT DO NOT	KNOW	HOW TO RESIST IT. VIVIE STANDS AT THE DOOR LOOKING IN
BULL I	(78)	PREPARED TO FACE THAT. /TIM/ NEVER FEAR, SIR. WE	KNOW	HOW TO RESPICT A BRAVE INNIMY. /BROADBENT/ WHAT I
2TRU I	(45)	YOURE A CLERGYMAN ALL RIGHT, POPS. BUT I DONT	KNOW	HOW TO SELL THE NECKLACE. /THE BURGLAR/ I DO. LET ME
ARMS II	(38)	DISTRACTED OVER THOSE THREE REGIMENTS. HE DOESNT	KNOW	HOW TO SEND THEM TO PHILIPPOPOLIS; AND HE OBJECTS TO
MIS.	(173)	GO AND HAVE A GOOD SPREE WITH, I WONDER WOULD YOU	KNOW	HOW TO SET ABOUT IT. DO YOU EVER TAKE A HOLIDAY? /THE
DOCT PREFACE	(80)	ABLE TO PAY FOR IT DIRECTLY YOURSELF, EVEN IF YOU	KNOW	HOW TO SET ABOUT IT. OTHERWISE YOU WILL BE WHAT MOST
KING I	(184)	LOVE WITH ME-- WHICH GOD FORBID! -- I SHOULD NOT	KNOW	HOW TO SET ABOUT IT. I SHOULD LEARN TO PLAY SOME
WIDO II	(35)	BE ABSURD, HARRY: BE GOOD; AND LISTEN TO ME: I	KNOW	HOW TO SETTLE IT. YOU ARE TOO PROUD TO OWE ANYTHING TO
PYGM EPILOG	(294)	IT LASTED A LONG TIME BECAUSE FREDDY DID NOT	KNOW	HOW TO SPEND MONEY, NEVER HAVING HAD ANY TO SPEND, AND
HART III	(134)	NOT KNOW ANYTHING ABOUT MY OWN MACHINERY; BUT I	KNOW	HOW TO STICK A RAMROD INTO THE OTHER FELLOW'S, AND NOW
SUPR III	(79)	CARRIED THREE BRAVE COMRADES OF OURS, WHO DID NOT	KNOW	HOW TO STOP IT, INTO GRANADA, AND CAPSIZED THEM
MTH4 III	(198)	GESTURE OF STILLING THE TEMPEST) THATS ENOUGH. WE	KNOW	HOW TO TAKE A HINT. I'LL PUT THE CASE IN THREE WORDS. I
MTH5	(218)	NEVER HEARD SUCH NONSENSE IN ALL MY LIFE. I SHALL	KNOW	HOW TO TAKE CARE OF MYSELF. /THE SHE-ANCIENT/ SO YOU
PHIL I	(89)	UNWOMANLY WOMEN WHO WORK FOR THEIR LIVING, AND	KNOW	HOW TO TAKE CARE OF THEMSELVES, NEVER GIVE ANY TROUBLE.
HART I	(61)	ANY AT ALL. /MRS HUSHABYE/ WELL, NO HARM IF YOU	KNOW	HOW TO TAKE CARE OF YOURSELF. MAY I ASK HIS NAME?
FANY EPILOG	(330)	I CAN SEE IT ALL RIGHT ENOUGH; BUT HOW AM I TO	KNOW	HOW TO TAKE IT? IS IT SERIOUS, OR IS IT SPOOF? IF THE
MRS I	(190)	DEAL MORE BESIDES. DONT YOU INTERFERE, PRADDY: I	KNOW	HOW TO TREAT MY OWN CHILD AS WELL AS YOU DO. (PRAED,
FOUN	(212)	WE HAVE NO AEROPLANE; AND IF WE HAD WE SHOULDNT	KNOW	HOW TO USE IT. HARK! A VISITOR AT THE DOOR. (THEY

JOAN 3	(91)	AND OF PLACING THE BIG GUNS. YOU SOLDIERS DO NOT	KNOW	HOW TO USE THE BIG GUNS: YOU THINK YOU CAN WIN BATTLES
JOAN 5	(115)	YOU DONT KNOW HOW TO BEGIN A BATTLE; AND YOU DONT	KNOW	HOW TO USE YOUR CANNONS. AND I DO. SHE SQUATS DOWN ON
DEST	(156)	CAN SEE THAT YOU ARE A GREAT MAN, GENERAL: YOU	KNOW	HOW TO WAIT. IF IT WERE A CORPORAL NOW, OR A
WIDO II	(31)	HALF ROOM: AYE, OR QUARTER ROOM. IT PAYS WHEN YOU	KNOW	HOW TO WORK IT, SIR. NOTHING LIKE IT. IT'S BEEN
GENV I	(34)	THE CORRECT COURSE. /SHE/ BUT I'M NOT SURE THAT I	KNOW	HOW TO WRITE A LETTER WITH ALL THOSE POLICE COURT
KING II	(228)	THE RESPONSES OF BARBARA, CHIFFINCH, AND JAMIE, I	KNOW	HOW TOM, DICK AND HARRY WILL TAKE IT, AND IT IS NEVER
APPL II	(267)	TO FORCE THIS ISSUE TO ITS LOGICAL END? YOU	KNOW	HOW UNENGLISH IT IS TO DO THAT? /PROTEUS/ MY PEOPLE
SUPR IV	(156)	GUIDE THAN MY OWN SELFISHNESS. /OCTAVIUS/ OH, I	KNOW	HOW UNSELFISH YOU ARE, ANN. BUT BELIEVE ME-- THOUGH I
ARMS II	(34)	SH! LET ME BE THE WORSHIPPER, DEAR. YOU LITTLE	KNOW	HOW UNWORTHY EVEN THE BEST MAN IS OF A GIRL'S PURE
FABL V	(119)	BEING TOO YOUNG AND NOT ENOUGH OF A FINANCIER TO	KNOW	HOW USEFUL AND NECESSARY THEY WERE TO PILGRIMS. HIS
DOCT III	(140)	SCIENTIFICALLY TRAINED, MR DUBEDAT, YOU WOULD	KNOW	HOW VERY SELDOM AN ACTUAL CASE BEARS OUT A PRINCIPLE.
MTH4 II	(186)	GOT TO SEE THIS ORACLE. THE FOLKS AT HOME WONT	KNOW	HOW WE HAVE BEEN TREATED: ALL THEYLL KNOW IS THAT IVE
6CAL	(98)	THE ROYAL PRESENCE, OR BY HOLY PAUL-- /PETER/ YOU	KNOW	HOW WE HAVE BORNE OURSELVES IN HIS ROYAL PRESENCE THESE
MRS I	(191)	BE MEETING THE GIRL EVERY DAY. WE DONT EXACTLY	KNOW	HOW WE OUGHT TO FEEL TOWARDS HER. /PRAED/ WHAT
CLEO II	(123)	/CAESAR/ DO NOT FEAR, POTHINUS: THE PEOPLE	KNOW	HOW WELL WINE TASTES IN WOODEN CUPS. IN RETURN FOR YOUR
HART I	(53)	IT? /ELLIE/ HE IS NOT A HOG, HESIONE. YOU DONT	KNOW	HOW WONDERFULLY GOOD HE WAS TO MY FATHER, AND HOW
SIM II	(61)	TO DRIVE ANYBODY MAD, AND SHE IS WISE ENOUGH TO	KNOW	HOW WORTHLESS I AM. I LOVE PROLA BECAUSE SHE IS FAR
BULL IV	(147)	/AUNT JUDY/ LORD HAVE MERCY ON US! /NORA/ I DONT	KNOW	HOW YOU CAN LAUGH. DO YOU, MR KEEGAN? /KEEGAN/ (
PYGM II	(219)	OH, SOMETHING DREADFUL, SIR, REALLY. I DONT	KNOW	HOW YOU CAN TAKE AN INTEREST IN IT. /HIGGINS/ (TO
SUPR I	(14)	TO PITY YOU. /RAMSDEN/ (HOTLY) I DONT WANT TO	KNOW	HOW YOU FEEL TOWARDS ME, MR TANNER. /TANNER/ ANN WILL
MTH3	(113)	YOU? SHE WILL BRING US BACK TO REAL LIFE. I DONT	KNOW	HOW YOU FELLOWS FEEL; BUT I'M JUST GOING DOTTY.
JOAN 2	(71)	MEAN BY KEEPING US WAITING LIKE THIS? I DONT	KNOW	HOW YOU HAVE THE PATIENCE TO STAND THERE LIKE A STONE
DEST	(193)	/LADY/ W-W-W-W-W-WH! DO STOP A MOMENT. I WANT TO	KNOW	HOW YOU MAKE ME OUT TO BE ENGLISH AT THIS RATE.
MTH3	(98)	SO HAVE YOU, YOU OLD HUMBUG. ALL THE SAME, I DONT	KNOW	HOW YOU STAND THE WORK YOU DO. YOU SEEM TO ME
GETT	(278)	IT THAN A GREAT BABY LIKE YOU. I'M SURE I DONT	KNOW	HOW YOULL GET ON WITH NO ONE TO TAKE CARE OF YOU: I
ROCK I	(197)	DO ANYTHING ELSE. IN THE FIRST PLACE, THEY DONT	KNOW	HOW. IN THE SECOND, THEY ARE AFRAID. I AM INSTRUCTING
CAND I	(82)	I AM GOING TO DAWDLE TODAY. /LEXY/ YOU! YOU DONT	KNOW	HOW. /MORELL/ (RISING) HA! HA! DONT I? I'M GOING TO
MIS. PREFACE	(102)	LET THEM. ALWAYS THE MACHINE. IN SHORT, THEY DONT	KNOW	HOW. THEY TRY TO REFORM SOCIETY AS AN OLD LADY MIGHT
BULL III	(127)	LIFE? /CORNELIUS/ WE'RE TIRED OF HIM. HE DOESNT	KNOW	HWERE TO STOP. EVERY MAN CANT OWN LAND; AND SOME MEN
FANY III	(315)	/KNOX/ NOW, DONT TAKE ON LIKE THAT, AMELIA. YOU	KNOW	I ALWAYS GAVE IN TO YOU THAT YOU WERE RIGHT ABOUT
2TRU I	(36)	ARM COAXINGLY BUT FIRMLY). /THE ELDERLY LADY/ I	KNOW	I AM: I AM READY TO DROP. HOW SYMPATHETIC OF YOU TO
DEST	(167)	LIKE A MAN ENJOYING SOME SECRET JOKE). HOW DO YOU	KNOW	I AM A BRAVE MAN? /LADY/ (AMAZED) YOU! GENERAL
APPL I	(231)	(IN HIS GRANDEST MANNER) WELL, MADAM, I	KNOW	I AM A NEWCOMER: EVERYTHING MUST HAVE A BEGINNING. I AM
SIM I	(48)	/THE CLERGYMAN/ (MUCH DEJECTED) I SUPPOSE SO. I	KNOW	I AM NO CATCH FOR MAYA. STILL, SHE WAS VERY KIND TO ME.
SUPR III	(89)	SOCIETY. /THE OLD WOMAN/ I TELL YOU, WRETCH, I	KNOW	I AM NOT IN HELL. /DON JUAN/ HOW DO YOU KNOW? /THE OLD
DEVL II	(34)	FIREPLACE AND SETS IT ON THE HOB). /RICHARD/ I	KNOW	I AM NOT WELCOME FOR MY OWN, MADAM. (HE RISES). BUT I
JITT I	(22)	INHUMAN: A MOCKERY, AN IMPOSSIBILITY. /BRUNO/ I	KNOW	I AM PUTTING YOUR LOVE TO THE CRUELLEST TEST; BUT OH,
PHIL II	(111)	BUT THE PHILOSOPHER SAYS YOU ARE RIGHT. /GRACE/ I	KNOW	I AM RIGHT. AND SO WE MUST PART. /CHARTERIS/ NOT AT
JOAN 5	(114)	TO. AND I AM NOT PROUD: I NEVER SPEAK UNLESS I	KNOW	I AM RIGHT. /BLUEBEARD/ HA HA! /CHARLES/ JUST SO. (
SUPR IV	(156)	UNSELFISH YOU ARE, ANN. BUT BELIEVE ME-- THOUGH I	KNOW	I AM SPEAKING IN MY OWN INTEREST-- THERE IS ANOTHER
SIM II	(83)	LEFT. DID YOU EVER REALLY CARE FOR ME? I	KNOW	I BEGAN AS A PASSION AND HAVE ENDED AS A HABIT, LIKE
PYGM V	(278)	ME AS A FLOWER GIRL, AND ALWAYS WILL; BUT I	KNOW	I CAN BE A LADY TO YOU, BECAUSE YOU ALWAYS TREAT ME AS
SUPR III	(97)	JUAN/ (NAUSEATED) EXCUSE ME: I AM GOING. YOU	KNOW	I CANNOT STAND THIS. /THE DEVIL/ (ANGRILY) YES: I KNOW
CAND III	(137)	TOO FAST, PROSS? /PROSERPINE/ MUCH TOO FAST. YOU	KNOW	I CANT DO MORE THAN NINETY WORDS A MINUTE. (SHE
PYGM V	(287)	ALL THE TIME THAT YOURE NOTHING BUT A BULLY. YOU	KNOW	I CANT GO BACK TO THE GUTTER, AS YOU CALL IT, AND THAT
PHIL I	(81)	DEAR LOVE, DONT CRY: DONT GO ON IN THIS WAY. YOU	KNOW	I CANT HELP IT. /JULIA/ (SOBBING AS HE RISES AND
JITT III	(72)	YOU DO NOT KNOW FOR CERTAIN YOURSELF. /EDITH/ I	KNOW	I CANT PROVE IT. BUT I AM CERTAIN, AND I WILL DEVOTE MY
DOCT V	(174)	BRUTE. /RIDGEON/ (QUIVERING) OH, DONT. YOU	KNOW	I DID NOT KNOW YOU WERE HERE. /JENNIFER/ (RAISING HER
ARMS II	(34)	LOUKA. /LOUKA/ (PRETENDING TO PULL) OH, SIR, YOU	KNOW	I DIDNT MEAN THAT. I'M SURPRISED AT YOU! /SERGIUS/ (
MIS.	(189)	IVE MADE A SILLY EXHIBITION OF MYSELF HERE. I	KNOW	I DIDNT RISE TO THE OCCASION. I KNOW THAT IF YOUD BEEN
MIS.	(186)	BAD. /MRS TARLETON/ NOW DONT BE RUDE, JOHNNY: YOU	KNOW	I DONT LIKE IT. (TO GUNNER) A CUP OF TEA WILL PICK YOU
VWOO 2	(130)	SORT AND DONT RUN AFTER WOMEN. /A/ HOW DO YOU	KNOW	I DONT RUN AFTER WOMEN? /Z/ WELL, IF YOU WANT TO KNOW,
CAPT I	(228)	HE HAS BEEN SO FRANK AND TRUTHFUL WITH US. YOU	KNOW	I DONT THINK ANYBODY CAN PAY ME A GREATER COMPLIMENT
GETT	(269)	THE SAME TIME. /THE GENERAL/ MY DEAR LESBIA: YOU	KNOW	I DONT WISH TO BE IMPERTINENT; BUT THESE ARE NOT
PHIL I	(79)	(POLITELY) I BEG YOUR PARDON, MY DEAR. I	KNOW	I HAVE A HABIT OF REPEATING MYSELF. THE POINT IS THAT
BULL IV	(164)	YOU SAY SUCH FUNNY THINGS. /BROADBENT/ YES: I	KNOW	I HAVE A STRONG SENSE OF HUMOR WHICH SOMETIMES MAKES
NEVR III	(276)	REAL ADVICE: YOUR SINCERE, FRIENDLY ADVICE. YOU	KNOW	I HAVE ALWAYS TRUSTED YOUR JUDGMENT. I PROMISE YOU THE
BUOY III	(28)	HERE IS MOST UNSUITABLE. DOES THE FAMILY	KNOW	I HAVE ARRIVED? /THE PRIEST/ HERE THEY ARE. THE
PHIL I	(80)	YOU HAVE SAID IT SEVERAL TIMES THIS EVENING. I	KNOW	I HAVE BEEN WICKED, ODIOUS, BAD: I SAY NOTHING IN
NEVR III	(269)	ONE HAS ANY RIGHT TO TRY: NOT EVEN HER MOTHER. I	KNOW	I HAVE LOST YOUR CONFIDENCE, JUST AS I HAVE LOST THIS
BARB I	(251)	WELL, ADVISE ME. /STEPHEN/ (MUCH PERPLEXED) YOU	KNOW	I HAVE NEVER INTERFERED IN THE HOUSEHOLD-- /LADY
BARB I	(254)	AND UNGRATEFUL OF YOU TO SAY SUCH A THING. YOU	KNOW	I HAVE NEVER TREATED ANY OF YOU AS CHILDREN. I HAVE
PYGM III	(245)	WHENEVER THEY MEET YOU. /HIGGINS/ NONSENSE! I	KNOW	I HAVE NO SMALL TALK; BUT PEOPLE DONT MIND. (HE SITS
APPL I	(206)	YOU KNOW, IF YOU MUST CALL ME ANYTHING AT ALL. I	KNOW	I HAVE TOO MUCH MATTER ABOUT ME: THE DOCTOR SAYS I
BARB III	(311)	OVER BARBARA) I'M AWFULLY SORRY, BARBARA. YOU	KNOW	I HELPED YOU ALL I COULD WITH THE CONCERTINA AND SO
SUPR I	(12)	TO HER ABOUT IT; AND SHE SAID I WAS RIGHT. YOU	KNOW	I LOVE HER, MR RAMSDEN; AND JACK KNOWS IT TOO. IF JACK
FANY II	(291)	SOMEHOW. IT WAS THE SINGING, I SUPPOSE: YOU	KNOW	I LOVE SINGING A GOOD SWINGING HYMN; AND I FELT IT WAS
SUPR IV	(156)	FORGIVE ME: I MUST SPEAK OF IT. I LOVE YOU. YOU	KNOW	I LOVE YOU. /ANN/ WHATS THE GOOD, TAVY? YOU KNOW THAT
PHIL I	(80)	I'M TOO MISERABLE TO ARGUE-- TO THINK. I ONLY	KNOW	I LOVE YOU. YOU REPROACH ME WITH NOT WANTING TO MARRY
APPL INTRLUD	(255)	/MAGNUS/ LISTEN, ORINTHIA. DONT BE ABSURD. YOU	KNOW	I MUST GO. DO BE GOOD. /ORINTHIA/ ONLY TEN MINUTES
NEVR III	(262)	/GLORIA/ (RETURNING) YES. /MRS CLANDON/ YOU	KNOW	I NEVER ASK QUESTIONS. /GLORIA/ (KNEELING BESIDE HER
MRS I	(190)	OFFENDED. DONT IMAGINE THAT: PRAY DONT. BUT YOU	KNOW	I OFTEN NOTICE THINGS THAT ESCAPE YOU; AND THOUGH YOU
OVER	(189)	IS A PROMISE. I CANT TELL A DELIBERATE LIE. I	KNOW	I OUGHT TO BE SORRY; BUT THE FLAT FACT IS THAT I'M NOT
DOCT III	(151)	MATTER? ARE YOU DISAPPOINTED? /MRS DUBEDAT/ I	KNOW	I OUGHT TO BE VERY GRATEFUL. BELIEVE ME, I AM VERY
FANY I	(276)	GENTEELLY) I DONT KNOW WHAT YOULL SAY TO ME: YOU	KNOW	I REALLY HAVE NO RIGHT TO COME HERE; BUT THEN WHAT WAS
CURE	(230)	THE PILL) IT WAS AWFULLY SILLY OF ME. BUT YOU	KNOW	I REALLY SAW THE THING. /THE DOCTOR/ YOU NEEDNT TROUBLE
INCA	(238)	IMPORTANCE TO THAT. /ERMYNTRUDE/ (GUSHING) OH, I	KNOW	I SHALL. /THE PRINCESS/ YOU MUST NOT EXPECT TOO MUCH.
APPL II	(268)	SO I SHOULD BE MAKING PERSONAL PROMISES WHICH I	KNOW	I SHOULD BREAK -- WHICH IN FACT I MUST BREAK BECAUSE I
SIM I	(48)	IT WAS SHE WHO KISSED YOU. /THE CLERGYMAN/ YES: I	KNOW	I SHOULD HAVE EXPLAINED THAT. BUT SHE LET ME KISS HER.
GETT	(357)	TO DO SO; BUT I THINK I SHOULD NOT DO SO. I	KNOW	I SHOULD NOT DO SO. /HOTCHKISS/ NEITHER SHALL I BE ABLE
FANY II	(287)	US. YOU SHOULDNT KEEP THINKING ABOUT IT. /KNOX/ I	KNOW	I SHOULDNT. YOU HAVE YOUR RELIGION, AMELIA; AND I'M
DOCT I	(110)	YOU? /MRS DUBEDAT/ YES, I BEG YOUR PARDON. I	KNOW	I SHOULDNT-- (GIVING WAY AGAIN) OH, PLEASE, SAY THAT
MRS I	(189)	FAULT: I THOUGHT YOUD HAVE HAD THE GUMPTION TO	KNOW	I WAS COMING BY THE 3.10 TRAIN. VIVIE: PUT YOUR HAT ON,
JOAN 3	(89)	NOT IN TIME TO SEE THEM YESTERDAY. /DUNOIS/ YOU	KNOW	I WAS EXPECTING THE MAID WHEN YOU SET UP YOUR YELPING.
MILL I	(151)	SAY BLENDERBLAND? /EPIFANIA/ ADRIAN! HOW DID HE	KNOW	I WAS HERE? /SAGAMORE/ ASK THE GENTLEMAN TO WAIT. (HE
CAPT I	(236)	FATHERLESS! /SIR HOWARD/ (STARTLED) I DID NOT	KNOW	I WAS SO FAVORABLY SPOKEN OF IN THESE PARTS, CAPTAIN
HART II	(95)	CLEVER WHEN YOU TALK ABOUT HER. /MAZZINI/ I DIDNT	KNOW	I WAS SO VERY STUPID ON OTHER SUBJECTS. /MRS HUSHABYE/
MIS.	(128)	I KNEW A CHAP NAMED JOEY PERCIVAL AT OXFORD (YOU	KNOW	I WAS TWO MONTHS AT BALLIOL BEFORE I WAS SENT DOWN FOR
PHIL II	(125)	AND IMPULSIVELY GOODNATURED INSTEAD OF TRAGIC) I	KNOW	I WAS WRONG TO ACT AS I DID LAST NIGHT. I BEG YOUR
HART I	(55)	THAT OF MY FATHER! /MRS HUSHABYE/ I WAS. YOU	KNOW	I WAS. /ELLIE/ (WITH DIGNITY) I WILL LEAVE YOUR HOUSE
MIS.	(118)	SUMMERHAYS/ NOT AT ALL. /JOHNNY/ OH YES I WAS: I	KNOW	I WAS. WELL, IF MY BLESSED FATHER HAD COME IN HE'D HAVE
DOCT IV	(161)	PROMISE ME SOMETHING. /MRS DUBEDAT/ YES, YES: YOU	KNOW	I WILL. (IMPLORINGLY) ONLY, MY LOVE, MY LOVE, DONT
6CAL	(102)	(THROWING HER ARMS ROUND HIM) OH, DEAR SIR, YOU	KNOW	I WOULD DIE TO SPARE YOU A MOMENT'S DISTRESS. THERE,
2TRU I	(37)	I WILL INDEED. HOW KIND OF YOU! YOU WILL LET ME	KNOW	IF ANYTHING-- /THE NURSE/ YES, YES. I PROMISE TO COME
MILL IV	(189)	BUT I MUSTNT DISTURB YOU TALKING. YOU WILL LET ME	KNOW	IF THERES ANYTHING I CAN DO TO MAKE YOU QUITE
GLIM	(185)	OF THE CHRIST IN THE PICTURE IN CHURCH. I DO NOT	KNOW	IF YOURS IS DIFFERENT. I SHALL SEE WHEN MY FATHER KILLS
MRS III	(229)	I'M IN NO HURRY. IT WAS ONLY JUST TO LET YOU	KNOW	IN CASE YOUNG GARDNER SHOULD TRY TO TRAP YOU. LEAVE THE
BULL IV	(176)	ORDERLY AS THE CLEANEST AND MOST ORDERLY PLACE I	KNOW	IN IRELAND, WHICH IS OUR POETICALLY NAMED MOUNTJOY
3PLA PREFACE	(R24)	PHILOSOPHY, I TAUGHT MY CRITICS THE LITTLE THEY	KNOW	IN MY QUINTESSENCE OF IBSENISM; AND NOW THEY TURN THEIR
JITT II	(39)	HAVING DIED IN THE ARMS OF SOME VILE CREATURE. I	KNOW	IN MY SOUL THAT SHE WAS NOT THAT. THE WORLD WOULD
GENV IV	(117)	BY STREET LIFE AND TRADE UNIONISM, WILL	KNOW	IN THEIR SOULS THAT I AM THE SALVATION OF THE WORLD.
ARMS I	(18)	YOU MUST TRUST TO OUR HOSPITALITY. YOU DO NOT YET	KNOW	IN WHOSE HOUSE YOU ARE. I AM A PETKOFF. /THE MAN/ A PET
CLEO PRO1	(92)	LITTLE, AND KNEW HER OWN MIND, AND HAD A MIND TO	KNOW	INSTEAD OF A CIRCULATION OF NEWSPAPERS. WHEREFORE LOOK
BULL III	(128)	HAD A THOUGHT AGEN YOU OR THE HOLY CHURCH. I	KNOW	I'M A BIT HASTY WHEN I THINK ABOUT THE LAN. I AX YOUR
PYGM V	(286)	(MUCH TROUBLED) I WANT A LITTLE KINDNESS. I	KNOW	I'M A COMMON IGNORANT GIRL, AND YOU A BOOK-LEARNED
SUPR I	(21)	WITH HER FINGER; THEN COMES BACK TO RAMSDEN). YOU	KNOW	I'M BEGINNING TO THINK THAT GRANNY IS RATHER A PIECE OF
CAPT III	(275)	/LADY CICELY/ OH, IVE THOUGHT OF THAT. YOU	KNOW	I'M GOING BACK TO ENGLAND BY WAY OF ROME, MR RANKIN;

MIS.	(178)	IN BOXING, AND I'LL FIGHT YOU FAST ENOUGH. YOU	KNOW	I'M NO GOOD OR YOU DARENT BULLY ME LIKE THIS.
BULL IV	(166)	RIGHT TO BE PARTICULAR. /BROADBENT/ (HUMBLY) I	KNOW	I'M NOT GOOD ENOUGH FOR YOU, NORA. BUT NO MAN IS, YOU
MRS III	(228)	NO MAN IS MORE SENSIBLE OF THAT THAN I AM, I	KNOW	I'M NOT PERFECT: THATS ONE OF THE ADVANTAGES OF BEING A
FANY III	(317)	GOOD ENOUGH FOR YOU? /MRS KNOX/ NO, JO: YOU	KNOW	I'M NOT. WHAT BETTER WERE MY PEOPLE THAN YOURS, FOR ALL
MIS.	(141)	NORTH POLE TO FALL IN LOVE WITH ME AS YOU. YOU	KNOW	I'M ONLY A LINENDRAPER'S DAUGHTER WHEN ALL'S SAID. I
NEVR I	(211)	FAR, TO ONE OF THEM. (RHETORICALLY) THE SORT YOU	KNOW	IS BASED ON MUTUAL RESPECT, ON RECOGNITION OF THE RIGHT
BUOY PREFACE	(6)	OF REMINDING THEM CALMLY THAT, LIKE NEWTON, ALL I	KNOW	IS BUT A GRAIN OF SAND PICKED UP ON THE VERGE OF THE
HART II	(104)	THE MATTER? /ELLIE/ THIS GENTLEMAN WANTS TO	KNOW	IS HE NEVER TO HAVE THE LAST WORD? /LADY UTTERWORD/ (
JITT III	(70)	LOOKING STRAIGHT AT HER) AND NOW WHAT I WANT TO	KNOW	IS HOW I AM TO MAKE YOU LAUGH. FOR YOU WILL GO MAD IF
APPL PREFACE	(182)	DUTIES AS INTOLERABLE BURDENS. WHAT WE WANT TO	KNOW	IS HOW LITTLE GOVERNMENT WE CAN GET ALONG WITH WITHOUT
BUOY IV	(60)	MUST TAKE MY CHANCE. YES. /DARKIE/ WHAT I WANT TO	KNOW	IS HOW MANY OF YOU ARE STAYING FOR LUNCH. THE CURTAIN
CAND III	(132)	INTENTLY TO QUESTION MORELL). WHAT I WANT TO	KNOW	IS HOW YOU GOT PAST THE FLAMING SWORD THAT STOPPED ME.
DOCT PREFACE	(33)	PAUSE HERE TO EXPLAIN THEIR ERROR. THE RIGHT TO	KNOW	IS LIKE THE RIGHT TO LIVE. IT IS FUNDAMENTAL AND
JITT I	(17)	OH, A MAN! THE MOST HOPELESS MATERIALIST I	KNOW	IS MY HUSBAND; AND I DO NOT WANT TO BE REMINDED OF HIM
ROCK I	(208)	YOU FOR THAT BURST OF APPLAUSE: WHICH I WELL	KNOW	IS NO MERE TRIBUTE TO MY POOR ELOQUENCE, BUT THE
PRES	(147)	DID SHE? /MRS FARRELL/ FAITH, I DUNNA. ALL I	KNOW	IS SHE WALKED UP TO HIM AS BOLD AS BRASS N SAID, "
BARB I	(251)	I KNOW SO LITTLE ABOUT THEM; AND WHAT I DO	KNOW	IS SO PAINFUL! IT IS SO IMPOSSIBLE TO MENTION SOME
FABL V	(120)	WERE ETHICALLY RIGHT; BUT THE UTMOST THAT WE	KNOW	IS STILL NO MORE THAN HIS GRAIN OF SAND. I WOULD LIKE
BUOY III	(46)	MATHEMATICAL THEORY EXPRESSING HIM. ALL WE	KNOW	IS THAT HE LEAVES MUCH OF IT TO US; AND WE MAKE A
2TRU III	(111)	I HAVE LOST MY NERVE AND AM INTIMIDATED: ALL I	KNOW	IS THAT I MUST FIND THE WAY OF LIFE, FOR MYSELF AND ALL
POSN PREFACE	(371)	DO NOT WANT TO KNOW ANYTHING: ALL THAT THEY DO	KNOW	IS THAT INCEST, PROSTITUTION, ABORTION, CONTAGIOUS
MTH4 II	(186)	WONT KNOW HOW WE HAVE BEEN TREATED: ALL THEYLL	KNOW	IS THAT IVE STOOD FACE TO FACE WITH THE ORACLE AND HAD
METH PREFACE	(R25)	COME. NOBODY KNOWS HOW: NOBODY KNOWS WHY: ALL WE	KNOW	IS THAT THE THING ACTUALLY TAKES PLACE. WE RELAPSE
APPL I	(228)	DO WITH POLITICS. THE NEXT THING THEY	KNOW	IS THAT THEIR PET SHARES HAVE DROPPED FIFTEEN POINTS;
BUOY III	(32)	HAVE ANY INCOMES. HAVE YOU? /THE WIDOWER/ ALL I	KNOW	IS THAT WHAT MONEY I NEED APPEARS TO MY CREDIT IN MY
GENV IV	(105)	HIM! IS HE A BLOND BEAST? THE BLONDEST BEAST I	KNOW	IS THE CALABRIAN BULL. I HAVE NO DESIRE TO FIGURE AS A
DOCT IV	(166)	BENDS DOWN AND LISTENS). /WALPOLE/ HE WANTS TO	KNOW	IS THE NEWSPAPER MAN HERE. /THE NEWSPAPER MAN/ (
MTH4 III	(198)	JUST SO. THE ELECTION. NOW WHAT WE WANT TO	KNOW	IS THIS: OUGHT WE TO DISSOLVE IN AUGUST, OR PUT IT OFF
GETT	(299)	OF IT I SHALL SET YOU A BETTER EXAMPLE. I WANT TO	KNOW	IS THIS TRUE. (SHE PRODUCES A PAMPHLET AND TAKES IT TO
MIS.	(113)	YOU PLEASE: IT WONT STICK TO ME. WHAT I WANT TO	KNOW	IS THIS. HOW IS IT THAT YOUR FATHER, WHO I SUPPOSE IS
FANY I	(278)	AND ME DISGRACED FOR EVER; AND ALL YOU CARE TO	KNOW	IS WHAT A SQUIFFER IS. /DORA/ WELL, REMEMBER IT HAS
JITT III	(57)	IT COULD POSSIBLY BE; BUT THERE'S NOBODY. ALL I	KNOW	IS WHAT HE LIKED AND WHAT HE WANTED, AND HOW EASILY HE
KING I	(189)	YOU WOULD BURN THE LOT. /CHARLES/ WHAT I WANT TO	KNOW	IS WHAT YOU ARE DOING HERE WHEN YOU SHOULD BE IN
PYGM IV	(266)	TO HEAR ANYTHING MORE ABOUT THAT. ALL I WANT TO	KNOW	IS WHETHER ANYTHING BELONGS TO ME. MY OWN CLOTHES WERE
FOUN	(211)	WITH ME WHEN YOU CAME IN. NOW WHAT I WANT TO	KNOW	IS, CAN YOU GET ME AN ENGAGEMENT? AS YOUR WARD, I HAVE
MTH4 II	(184)	OF HISTORY, AS YOU MIGHT SAY. BUT WHAT I WANT TO	KNOW	IS, HOW DID WAR COME BACK AGAIN? AND HOW DID THEY MAKE
FANY III	(321)	DONT MIND ME, MRS GILBEY. /KNOX/ WHAT I WANT TO	KNOW	IS, WHATS TO BE THE END OF THIS? IT'S NOT FOR ME TO
JOAN 6	(136)	VANITY, JOAN. YOU STAND IN GREAT PERIL. /JOAN/ I	KNOW	IT: HAVE I NOT BEEN PUNISHED FOR MY VANITY? IF I HAD
DEVL I	(10)	ROPE ROUND HIS NECK-- AYE, TO PETER DUDGEON. YOU	KNOW	IT: OLD ELI HAWKINS, THE MAN TO WHOSE PULPIT YOU
SUPR I	(5)	/RAMSDEN/ HOW DO WE KNOW THAT, OCTAVIUS? HE MAY	KNOW	IT: WE CANNOT TELL. COME! DONT GRIEVE. (OCTAVIUS
6CAL	(95)	OF SILVER FOR A FLYING FOE. /THE KING/ DO I NOT	KNOW	IT? HAVE I NOT BEEN KIND, MAGNANIMOUS? HAVE I NOT
MTH1 I	(4)	IT MUST NOT BE. /EVE/ WE BOTH KNOW IT. HOW DO WE	KNOW	IT? /ADAM/ THERE IS A VOICE IN THE GARDEN THAT TELLS
ROCK I	(229)	ARTHUR. A FORTNIGHT'S GOLF: THATS THE CURE. I	KNOW	IT ALL BY HEART. SO SUPPOSE WE DROP IT, AND PART
HART I	(78)	IS ENMITY BETWEEN OUR SEED AND THEIR SEED. THEY	KNOW	IT AND ACT ON IT, STRANGLING OUR SOULS. THEY BELIEVE IN
MIS.	(124)	OF HER BOY) NOW DONT BEGIN ABOUT MY JOHNNY. YOU	KNOW	IT ANNOYS ME. JOHNNY'S AS CLEVER AS ANYBODY ELSE IN HIS
LIED	(201)	IT'S ADMITTED BY THE BEST PEOPLE; AND NOT TO	KNOW	IT ARGUES YOURSELF UNKNOWN. THREE OF OUR FIRST
GETT	(357)	EIGHTH? /SOAMES/ I DO NOT MERELY BELIEVE THAT: I	KNOW	IT AS A LAWYER. /HOTCHKISS/ WOULD YOU STEAL A TURNIP
METH PREFACE	(R38)	MUCKRAKERS COULD FAIL TO SEE THIS, AND EVEN TO	KNOW	IT AS PART OF THEIR OWN CONSCIOUSNESS. YET TO ADMIT IT
APPL I	(207)	OH! I DONT SAY THAT. /MAGNUS/ COME COME! YOU	KNOW	IT AS WELL AS I DO. WELL, IF IT HAPPENS YOU WILL HAVE
APPL INTRLUD	(246)	AND UGLIER THAN THE OLD. /ORINTHIA/ WHY SHOULD I	KNOW	IT BETTER THAN ANYONE ELSE? /MAGNUS/ WHY, BECAUSE YOU
ROCK II	(264)	ROSY: YOU ARE A DAMNED FOOL; AND YOU OUGHT TO	KNOW	IT BY THIS TIME. PANDRANATH: YOU ARE ONLY A SILLY
MIS. PREFACE	(82)	FAMILY AFFECTION. UNTIL THE FAMILY AS WE	KNOW	IT CEASES TO EXIST, NOBODY WILL DARE TO ANALYZE
ARMS III	(54)	IT. /RAINA/ PAWNED IT! ! ! /BLUNTSCHLI/ I	KNOW	IT DOESNT SOUND NICE; BUT IT WAS MUCH THE SAFEST PLAN.
PHIL II	(113)	GO TO ITALY MYSELF. I'LL REDISCOVER MY DISEASE: I	KNOW	IT EXISTS; I FEEL IT; AND I'LL PROVE IT IF I HAVE TO
MILL PREFACE	(133)	AMUSEMENT; SO THAT THE COUNTRYSIDE MAY COME TO	KNOW	IT FROM BEHIND THE SCENES, WHEN, THOUGH IT WILL STILL
SUPR I	(44)	THAT I AM IN THE RIGHT, I MEAN. /TANNER/ OH, THEY	KNOW	IT IN THEIR HEARTS, THOUGH THEY THINK THEMSELVES BOUND
ROCK I	(220)	DEVELOP INTO COMMUNISM, AND THAT WHOEVER DOESNT	KNOW	IT IS AN IGNORANT NOBODY OR A HALF-EDUCATED COLLEGE
DEST	(171)	/LADY/ (STRUGGLING WITH HAPPY TEARS) YES, I	KNOW	IT IS AN IMPERTINENCE IN ME TO TELL YOU WHAT YOU MUST
SUPR III	(124)	MARRY ANY MAN SHE DOES NOT PERSONALLY LOVE? YOU	KNOW	IT IS NOT SO: THE WOMAN OF NOBLE BIRTH MARRIES AS THE
CLEO IV	(186)	IS TRUE. (HE DOES NOT RESPOND TO THE CARESS) YOU	KNOW	IT IS TRUE, RUFIO. THE MURMUR WITHOUT SUDDENLY SWELLS
SIM I	(38)	WHAT I SAY, THOUGH IT IS THE SIMPLE TRUTH. I	KNOW	IT IS VERY HARD TO BELIEVE. /PROLA/ IN THE UNEXPECTED
ROCK I	(206)	NOT MUCH WRONG WITH THAT, IS THERE? OF COURSE I	KNOW	IT KEEPS ME TOO MUCH AWAY FROM HOME. THAT GIVES YOU A
DOCT II	(124)	YOU HAVE NO RIGHT TO ASK. /THE MAID/ YES, SIR, I	KNOW	IT LOOKS LIKE THAT. BUT WHAT AM I TO DO? /SIR PATRICK/
GETT	(262)	HELP TELLING HER; SO WHENEVER WE MEET, THOUGH I	KNOW	IT MAKES HER AVOID ME. (HE ALL BUT WEEPS). /MRS
HART III	(139)	A WORD OF THAT. /ELLIE/ NEITHER DO I. BUT I	KNOW	IT MEANS SOMETHING. /MANGAN/ DONT SAY THERE WAS ANY
ARMS I	(18)	OR NOT TIRED, YOU CAN ALWAYS DO A THING WHEN YOU	KNOW	IT MUST BE DONE. WELL, THAT PIPE MUST BE GOT DOWN: (HE
BUOY III	(40)	THE WORLD EVER STAYS PUT FOR TEN SECONDS. WE CAN	KNOW	IT ONLY RELATIVELY AT ANY MOMENT. YET MOST PEOPLE CAN
FABL III	(112)	TELL ME I'M IGNORANT AND CRAZY. AND SO I AM: I	KNOW	IT ONLY TOO WELL. YOUD BETTER GIVE ME A MEAL OR THE
JOAN 5	(112)	THE BEGINNING. /ALL THE OTHERS/ WHAT! /JOAN/ I	KNOW	IT SOMEHOW. /DUNOIS/ NONSENSE! /JOAN/ JACK: DO YOU
SUPR PREFACE	(R26)	ARE MEASURED BY THE BRITISH THEATRE AS YOU	KNOW	IT TODAY, CAN EITHER HANDLE THIS COLOSSAL TASK
PHIL I	(85)	AND CRAVEN WERE ACQUAINTED. /CRAVEN/ WHY, I DIDNT	KNOW	IT UNTIL TONIGHT. IT'S A MOST EXTRAORDINARY THING. WE
CLEO IV	(193)	HIS WORK. /CLEOPATRA/ (ENIGMATICALLY) HOW DO YOU	KNOW	IT WAS A MAN? /RUFIO/ (STARTLED, AND PUZZLED) IT WAS
POSN	(452)	YOU EVER TRIED TO SELL. /THE SHERIFF/ HOW DO YOU	KNOW	IT WAS A ROTTEN HORSE IF YOU DIDNT STEAL IT? /BLANCO/
2TRU I	(29)	I HAD SUCH HOPES OF THAT LAST BOTTLE; BUT YOU	KNOW	IT WAS AFTER THAT THAT SHE DEVELOPED MEASLES. /THE
MIS. PREFACE	(98)	VERSION IS A GREAT WORK OF ART AS WELL, TO	KNOW	IT WAS BETTER THAN KNOWING NO ART, WHICH ALSO WAS THE
2TRU II	(65)	DONT GET THAT MUCH TO LOOK BACK ON. BESIDES, YOU	KNOW	IT WAS FOR YOUR OWN GOOD, POPSY. WE WERENT REALLY
MTH4 I	(169)	INSTINCT TO KILL THAT YOU ROUSED IN ME. I DID NOT	KNOW	IT WAS IN MY NATURE: NEVER BEFORE HAS IT WAKENED AND
LIED	(188)	DEAR, OF COURSE IT WAS VERY NICE OF YOU; AND I	KNOW	IT WAS MY OWN FAULT AS MUCH AS YOURS. I OUGHT TO HAVE
MRS I	(190)	HERSELF FACE TO FACE WITH PRAED). COME, PRADDY, I	KNOW	IT WAS ONLY YOUR TENDER-HEARTEDNESS. YOURE AFRAID I'LL
2TRU II	(59)	SIMPLE AND DIRECT. I LIKE IT. /TALLBOYS/ I DIDNT	KNOW	IT WAS VULGAR. IT IS CONCISE. /THE COUNTESS/ OF COURSE
VWOO 3	(143)	ABOVE ME AND BEYOND ME DROVE ME ON. THATS WHY I	KNOW	IT WILL BE ALL RIGHT. DONT BE AFRAID. I CANT MAKE A
MIS.	(134)	I KNOW YOUR OPINION OF ME AS WELL AS YOU	KNOW	IT YOURSELF. IT TAKES ONE MAN OF BUSINESS TO APPRECIATE
INCA	(255)	THE WORST OF IT IS, I AM INTELLIGENT ENOUGH TO	KNOW	IT. AND I SHALL BE BEATEN IN CONSEQUENCE, BECAUSE MY
DEVL II	(40)	TRYING TO SPARE YOU THE TRUTH; BUT YOU HAD BETTER	KNOW	IT. ARE YOU LISTENING TO ME? (SHE SIGNIFIES ASSENT).
APPL INTRLUD	(245)	KNOW IT. /MAGNUS/ IT IS, AS YOU SAY, A LIE; AND I	KNOW	IT. BUT I DID NOT SAY IT. /ORINTHIA/ YOU IMPLIED IT.
ARMS III	(51)	DONT TALK OF IT IN THAT FLIPPANT WAY. I LIED: I	KNOW	IT. BUT I DID IT TO SAVE YOUR LIFE. HE WOULD HAVE
MRS III	(228)	A MIDDLE-AGED MAN; FOR I'M NOT A YOUNG MAN, AND I	KNOW	IT. BUT MY CODE IS A SIMPLE ONE, AND, I THINK, A GOOD
APPL PREFACE	(184)	DEATH POWERS. I NEED NOT LABOR THIS POINT: WE ALL	KNOW	IT. BUT WHAT WE DO NOT ALL REALIZE IS THAT WE ARE
DEVL II	(30)	SAY; AND YOURE QUITE RIGHT. OH, QUITE RIGHT: I	KNOW	IT. BUT-- I SUPPOSE I'M NOT BRAVE: THATS ALL. MY HEART
SUPR II	(58)	RIGHT. ANN WAS ONLY DOING HER DUTY, JACK; AND YOU	KNOW	IT. DOING IT IN THE KINDEST WAY, TOO. /ANN/ (GOING TO
JITT III	(75)	BUT SHE WILL NEVER KNOW IT. SHE DOESNT WANT TO	KNOW	IT. EDITH DID. THAT MAKES ALL THE DIFFERENCE. I HAVE
MIS. PREFACE	(87)	OR ANYTHING THAT CONSTITUTES THE FAMILY AS WE	KNOW	IT. EVEN BLOOD RELATIONSHIP IS MIRACULOUSLY ABSTRACTED
CAPT I	(225)	TROUBLE AND EXPENSE TO MY DOOR, HASSAN; AND YOU	KNOW	IT. HAVE I EVER CHARGED YOUR WIFE AND CHILDREN FOR MY
GENV IV	(127)	UNDELUDED. /BBDE/ FLANCO IS DEAD; BUT HE DOES NOT	KNOW	IT. HISTORY WOULD HAVE KICKED HIM OUT WERE NOT HISTORY
MTH1 I	(4)	NOT BE. I KNOW THAT IT MUST NOT BE. /EVE/ WE BOTH	KNOW	IT. HOW DO WE KNOW IT? /ADAM/ THERE IS A VOICE IN THE
JITT II	(49)	/JITTA/ YOU ARE IN MY HANDS, ALFRED; AND YOU	KNOW	IT. I CAN GIVE THE WHOLE SCANDAL AWAY IF YOU DEFY ME. I
MILL I	(149)	YOU KNOW THAT, PRAY? /PATRICIA/ NEVER MIND HOW I	KNOW	IT. I DO. /ALASTAIR/ IT WAS QUITE INNOCENT; BUT WHERE
BARB III	(313)	YOU? /CUSINS/ YES: THAT IS OUR UNDERSTANDING. I	KNOW	IT. I HOLD TO IT. UNLESS HE CAN WIN ME ON THAT HOLIER
BARB II	(302)	/UNDERSHAFT/ YOU REALLY THINK SO? /MRS BAINES/ I	KNOW	IT. I REMEMBER 1886, WHEN YOU RICH GENTLEMEN HARDENED
APPL INTRLUD	(249)	PLACE OUT. I AM ONE OF NATURE'S QUEENS; AND THEY	KNOW	IT. IF YOU DO NOT, YOU ARE NOT ONE OF NATURE'S KINGS.
2TRU III	(85)	DO YOU KNOW THAT? /SWEETIE/ NEVER YOU MIND HOW I	KNOW	IT. IT'S NOTHING TO DO WITH YOU. /THE SERGEANT/ NOTHING
CAPT II	(252)	IT, I THINK. /JOHNSON/ (PHLEGMATICALLY) YES: WE	KNOW	IT. (HE IS GOING OUT WHEN SIR HOWARD SPEAKS). /SIR
DEST	(167)	HIS SHOULDER) YOURE TALKING NONSENSE; AND YOU	KNOW	IT. (SHE SITS DOWN SUBMISSIVELY ON THE COUCH. WHEN HE
SIM II	(84)	REST OF THE JIGSAW PUZZLES: I AM A WOMAN AND I	KNOW	IT. LET MEN DESPAIR AND BECOME CYNICS AND PESSIMISTS
MTH2	(49)	HAS NEVER REPRESENTED THE PEOPLE; AND YOU	KNOW	IT. LORD DUNREEN IS THE BITTEREST OLD TORY LEFT ALIVE.
BUOY IV	(55)	LOVE GUARANTEES NOTHING. I KNOW THIS. YOU	KNOW	IT. MY DAUGHTER KNOWS IT. THE YOUNG MAN KNOWS IT. ARE
CLEO NOTES	(207)	IN THE PLAY. I CAN ONLY IMITATE HUMANITY AS I	KNOW	IT. NOBODY KNOWS WHETHER SHAKESPEAR THOUGHT THAT

JITT II	(38)	(ANGRY) I DO NOT THINK IT: I KNOW IT. YOU	KNOW	IT. PLEASE LET US HAVE NO MORE OF THE POOR CHILD
DEVL I	(26)	REBELLIOUS WORD. WELL, WE'RE ALL REBELS; AND YOU	KNOW	IT. /ALL THE MEN/ (EXCEPT ANDERSON) NO, NO, NO!
2TRU III	(91)	SWEETIE. /SWEETIE/ THEY WERE JEALOUS; AND YOU	KNOW	IT. /AUBREY/ I DARESAY THEY WERE. ANYHOW, SWEETIE AND I
KING I	(218)	SO YOU CAN TELL IT TO HER, ROWLEY DARLING, IF YOU	KNOW	IT. /CHARLES/ IT IS BECAUSE IN THE THEATRE YOU ARE A
MTH3	(99)	/CONFUCIUS/ HER NUMBER IS-- /BURGE-LUBIN/ I	KNOW	IT. /CONFUCIUS/ (RISING) I CANNOT UNDERSTAND HER
OVER	(179)	WOMAN'S VOICE/ THIS IS THE WAY TO THE LOUNGE. I	KNOW	IT. /GREGORY/ GREAT HEAVEN! WE'RE BOTH MAD. THATS MY
JITT I	(17)	THAN SHE LOVES HER OWN MOTHER, THOUGH SHE MAY NOT	KNOW	IT. /JITTA/ (THOUGHTFULLY) STRANGE. AND I LOVE YOUR
CAPT II	(261)	ME. I AM GOING TO DO MY DUTY AS A SON; AND YOU	KNOW	IT. /LADY CICELY/ BUT I SHOULD HAVE THOUGHT THAT THE
DOCT III	(144)	YOURE A SOUND METHODIST, MY LAD; ONLY YOU DONT	KNOW	IT. /LOUIS/ (SERIOUSLY ANNOYED FOR THE FIRST TIME)
APPL INTRLUD	(245)	TO TALK ABOUT BUT MEN: FOR THAT IS A LIE; AND YOU	KNOW	IT. /MAGNUS/ IT IS, AS YOU SAY, A LIE; AND I KNOW IT.
BULL III	(130)	THAN LET HIM COME UP THAT STEP; AND WELL YOU	KNOW	IT. /MATTHEW/ (BLACK WITH RAGE, IN A LOW GROWL) LEMMY
FANY III	(324)	ANY SATISFACTION. /GILBEY/ NO YOU DONT, NOT IF I	KNOW	IT. /MRS KNOX/ HE OUGHT TO, MR GILBEY. /GILBEY/ WELL,
APPL I	(222)	HIS MAJESTY'S SUGGESTIONS IN THE MARGIN; AND YOU	KNOW	IT. /PROTEUS/ HAVE YOU ALL DONE PLAYING STRAIGHT INTO
ARMS I	(19)	(STIFLING A HEAVY SIGH OF WEARINESS) THEN I DONT	KNOW	IT. /RAINA/ I THOUGHT YOU MIGHT HAVE REMEMBERED THE
DOCT II	(128)	BLENKINSOP ISNT THAT SORT OF GOOD MAN; AND YOU	KNOW	IT. /RIDGEON/ IT WOULD BE SIMPLER IF BLENKINSOP COULD
POSN	(441)	SAW ME WITH THAT HORSE YOU CANT TOUCH ME; AND YOU	KNOW	IT. /STRAPPER/ IS THAT THE LAW, ELDER? /ELDER DANIELS/
SUPR III	(84)	YOUR CAREER TO A MONOMANIA. /MENDOZA/ I	KNOW	IT. /TANNER/ NO YOU DONT. NO MAN WOULD COMMIT SUCH A
MTH5	(207)	WHEN ANYTHING NO LONGER INTERESTS US WE NO LONGER	KNOW	IT. /THE MAIDEN/ YOU HAVNT TOLD ME HOW I SHEW MY AGE.
JITT III	(75)	IS THAT SHE GUESSES IT TOO; BUT SHE WILL NEVER	KNOW	IT. SHE DOESNT WANT TO KNOW IT. EDITH DID. THAT MAKES
ROCK II	(253)	IT. WHAT WE WANT WE SHALL HAVE TO TAKE; AND WE	KNOW	IT. THE GOOD OF THE COMMUNITY IS NOTHING TO YOU: YOU
CAPT I	(231)	CICELY: YOU ARE TALKING GREAT NONSENSE; AND YOU	KNOW	IT. THESE PEOPLE HAVE NO LAWS TO RESTRAIN THEM, WHICH
MRS IV	(249)	THE CLEVER PEOPLE, THE MANAGING PEOPLE, ALL	KNOW	IT. THEY DO AS I DO, AND THINK WHAT I THINK. I KNOW
SUPR II	(59)	YOUTH TO AGE! LOOK AT FASHIONABLE SOCIETY AS YOU	KNOW	IT. WHAT DOES IT PRETEND TO BE? AN EXQUISITE DANCE OF
GENV III	(74)	GROOVES. YOU ARE A BOLSHEVIK; BUT NOBODY WOULD	KNOW	IT. YOU HAVE THE APPEARANCE, THE DRESS, THE CULTURE OF
JITT II	(38)	CHILD! /EDITH/ (ANGRY) I DO NOT THINK IT: I	KNOW	IT. YOU KNOW IT. PLEASE LET US HAVE NO MORE OF THE POOR
SUPR II	(61)	YOU ARE TALKING THE GREATEST NONSENSE; AND YOU	KNOW	IT. YOU WOULD NEVER DO ANYTHING TO HURT ME. /TANNER/
MIS.	(130)	FRIEND MR PERCIVAL DOWN HERE? /BENTLEY/ NOT IF I	KNOW	IT. YOUD THROW ME OVER THE MOMENT YOU SET EYES ON HIM.
DEVL II	(44)	DANGER? /JUDITH/ (BITTERLY) OH, YOU WONT GO. I	KNOW	IT. YOULL STAY; AND I SHALL GO MAD. /ANDERSON/ MY DEAR,
DEVL III	(65)	DO (IMPLYING THAT SWINDON MUST BE AN ASS NOT TO	KNOW	IT). /SWINDON/ IS HE HERE? /CHRISTY/ (STARING ROUND)
MIS.	(121)	A HUMBUG, YOU KNOW, LORD SUMMERHAYS. JOHN DOESNT	KNOW	IT; AND JOHNNY DOESNT KNOW IT; BUT YOU AND I KNOW IT,
SUPR I	(41)	A SUBTLE INTEREST (SHE LAUGHS)-- JUST SO: YOU	KNOW	IT; AND YOU TRIUMPH IN IT. OPENLY AND SHAMELESSLY
LION PREFACE	(15)	IN THE SCIENTIFIC SOCIOLOGICAL WAY IN WHICH WE	KNOW	IT; BUT HIS INSTINCT SERVED HIM BETTER THAN KNOWLEDGE
CATH 1	(167)	ARE BARBARIANS, DRUNKEN PIGS. CATHERINE DOES NOT	KNOW	IT; BUT WE ARE. CATHERINE'S A GERMAN. BUT I HAVE GIVEN
MIS.	(121)	JOHN DOESNT KNOW IT; AND JOHNNY DOESNT	KNOW	IT; BUT YOU AND I KNOW IT, DONT WE? NOW THATS
NEVR IV	(297)	MR BOHUN! /BOHUN/ OH YES YOU DO: YOU DONT	KNOW	IT; BUT YOU DO. /GLORIA/ (RISING) STOP. I WARN YOU, MR
MILL IV	(196)	NOT SWEAR TO SUCH A LIE. /SAGAMORE/ HOW DO YOU	KNOW	IT'S A LIE? YOU DONT KNOW WHAT HAPPENED AT THE END.
PHIL II	(119)	HIM) WHY DONT YOU GET MARRIED, PARAMORE? YOU	KNOW	IT'S A SCANDALOUS THING FOR A MAN IN YOUR PROFESSION TO
VWOO 1	(122)	/Z/ OH, I HAVE HAD PLENTY OF OFFERS. BUT YOU	KNOW	IT'S A TERRIBLE THING TO BE A POOR MAN'S WIFE WHEN YOU
PHIL II	(104)	MAY I TAKE YOU DOWN? /JULIA/ NO, REALLY: YOU	KNOW	IT'S AGAINST THE RULES OF THE CLUB TO CODDLE WOMEN IN
ROCK I	(198)	THE DOOR; THEN HESITATES AND ADDS) BY THE WAY, I	KNOW	IT'S ASKING A LOT; BUT IF YOU COULD GIVE US A TURN IN
2TRU II	(69)	ME! WE'RE ALWAYS PLANNING ROBBERIES, OF COURSE I	KNOW	IT'S MOSTLY IMAGINATION; BUT THE FUN IS IN THE PLANNING
O'FL	(209)	HOLY CHURCH, TO LOVE YOUR ENEMIES? " HE SAYS. " I	KNOW	IT'S MY JUTY AS A SOLDIER TO KILL THEM" I SAYS. " THATS
ROCK I	(232)	THAT SORT OF THING MYSELF OCCASIONALLY; AND YOU	KNOW	IT'S NO USE GIVING TRACTS TO A MISSIONARY. BUT I FEEL
2TRU I	(36)	LADY/ OH, DARLING, DONT KEEP ON SAYING THAT. YOU	KNOW	IT'S NOT TRUE; AND IT DOES HURT ME SO. /THE NURSE/ YOU
BULL IV	(163)	NOT. I DONT MEAN IT. AT LEAST I DO MEAN IT; BUT I	KNOW	IT'S PREMATURE. I HAD NO RIGHT TO TAKE ADVANTAGE OF
ROCK I	(198)	SORRY TO HAVE TAKEN UP SO MUCH OF YOUR TIME: I	KNOW	IT'S PRICELESS. (HE HURRIES TO THE DOOR; THEN
CURE	(231)	OF THE SORT. IT'S THE DUCHESS OF DUNMOW'S ROOM. I	KNOW	IT'S THE RIGHT ONE, BECAUSE SHE GAVE ME THE KEY; AND IT
WIDO III	(65)	AS SHE SEES IT). AHA! YOU REMEMBER THAT. YOU	KNOW	IT'S TRUE: YOU CANT DENY IT. (SHE SITS DOWN, AND
FANY II	(290)	KNOX/ (REPROACHFULLY) MARGARET! /MARGARET/ YOU	KNOW	IT'S TRUE. /MRS KNOX/ MARGARET: IF YOURE GOING TO BE
DOCT III	(152)	TO HAVE HIM. BUT OH, I WISH IT HAD BEEN YOU. I	KNOW	IT'S UNREASONABLE; I CANT EXPLAIN; BUT I HAD SUCH A
CAND I	(95)	WONDERING HOW MUCH I OUGHT TO GIVE THE CABMAN. I	KNOW	IT'S UTTERLY SILLY; BUT YOU DONT KNOW HOW DREADFUL SUCH
DEVL II	(32)	HIM; AND THEN IT WONT MATTER. /JUDITH/ OH, I	KNOW	IT'S WRONG TO HATE ANYBODY; BUT-- /ANDERSON/ (GOING
DEVL I	(20)	OF THIS. LEAVE MY HOUSE. /RICHARD/ HOW DO YOU	KNOW	IT'S YOUR HOUSE UNTIL THE WILL IS READ? (THEY LOOK AT
BULL PREFACE	(52)	WITH AN IRRITATED MOB, ESPECIALLY IF YOU DO NOT	KNOW	ITS LANGUAGE. HAD THE SHOOTING PARTY BEEN IN THE CHARGE
MIS. PREFACE	(11)	FORCE. YOU ARE ASSUMING THAT THE CHILD DOES NOT	KNOW	ITS OWN BUSINESS, AND THAT YOU DO. IN THIS YOU ARE SURE
MIS.	(199)	NO MAN SHOULD KNOW HIS OWN CHILD. NO CHILD SHOULD	KNOW	ITS OWN FATHER. LET THE FAMILY BE ROOTED OUT OF
JOAN 6	(131)	THE STAKE MYSELF SOONER THAN DO IT IF I DID NOT	KNOW	ITS RIGHTEOUSNESS, ITS NECESSITY, ITS ESSENTIAL MERCY.
CAND III	(145)	OUT. I MAKE HIM MASTER HERE, THOUGH HE DOES NOT	KNOW	IT, AND COULD NOT TELL YOU A MOMENT AGO HOW IT CAME TO
PHIL III	(145)	ME-- UNLESS YOU, SYLVIA: EH? /SYLVIA/ NOT IF I	KNOW	IT, CHARTERIS. /CHARTERIS/ (TO THEM ALL) YOU SEE!
MIS.	(121)	KNOW IT; AND JOHNNY DOESNT KNOW IT; BUT YOU AND I	KNOW	IT, DONT WE? NOW THATS SOMETHING THAT EVEN YOU CANT
2TRU II	(55)	FOR RANSOM. YOU KNOW THAT. YOU DONT THINK IT: YOU	KNOW	IT, EH? /MEEK/ SO THEY SAY, SIR. /TALLBOYS/ YOU KNOW
KING I	(189)	CHARLES: I AM A PRINCE. /CHARLES/ OH, DO I NOT	KNOW	IT, GOD HELP YOU! /JAMES/ OUR FATHER LOST HIS HEAD BY
BARB I	(266)	NEVER EDUCATED. /LOMAX/ (ENCOURAGINGLY) NOBODY'D	KNOW	IT, I ASSURE YOU. YOU LOOK ALL RIGHT, YOU KNOW.
CAPT II	(252)	OVER. /BRASSBOUND/ YOU CAN DEPEND ON ME; AND YOU	KNOW	IT, I THINK. /JOHNSON/ (PHLEGMATICALLY) YES: WE KNOW
APPL PREFACE	(178)	AGAINST ARE WORTH TAKING. DEMOCRACY, AS YOU	KNOW	IT, IS SELDOM MORE THAN A LONG WORD BEGINNING WITH A
CAND I	(97)	THAT! YOU BELIEVE THAT! /MORELL/ (BUOYANTLY) I	KNOW	IT, MY LAD. LAROCHEFOUCAULD SAID THAT THERE ARE
BARB II	(301)	/MRS BAINES/ NO, SIR: THE WHOLE NATION DOES NOT	KNOW	IT, OR WE SHOULD NOT BE CRIPPLED AS WE ARE FOR WANT OF
SUPR I	(40)	WILL BE VERY UNHAPPY. /TANNER/ YES; BUT HE WONT	KNOW	IT, POOR DEVIL. HE IS A THOUSAND TIMES TOO GOOD FOR
MIS.	(145)	/TARLETON/ SHE HAD ME THERE, THOUGH SHE DOESNT	KNOW	IT, POOR INNOCENT LAMB! PUBLIC SCANDAL EXAGGERATES
SUPR I	(14)	PERSON I HAVE EVER MET. /TANNER/ (SERIOUSLY) I	KNOW	IT, RAMSDEN. YET EVEN I CANNOT WHOLLY CONQUER SHAME. WE
KING I	(218)	AT ALL. TELL HER THE REASON, NELL. /NELL/ I DONT	KNOW	IT, ROWLEY DARLING. I NEVER WAS AN ORANGE GIRL; BUT I
ROCK II	(271)	IF I DIDNT. YOU COULD DO IT IF YOU LIKED; AND YOU	KNOW	IT, SIR BROADFOOT. BUT PERHAPS YOUR CONSCIENCE WOULDNT
MIS. PREFACE	(107)	AS LONG AS YOU HAVE THE COMPULSORY SCHOOL AS WE	KNOW	IT, WE SHALL HAVE SUBMISSIVENESS INCULCATED. WHAT IS
POSN	(461)	HERE, HOLD HARD. /THE FOREMAN/ NOT IF WE	KNOW	IT, YOU DONT. /THE BOYS/ (BARRING THE WAY TO THE DOOR)
2TRU I	(40)	TABLE AS A BULWARK FOR THE JEWEL CASE) NOT IF I	KNOW	IT, YOU SHANT. /THE BURGLAR/ (APPROACHING HER) YOU
ANNA	(297)	/STRAMMFEST/ IT IS QUITE SIMPLE, AS YOU VERY WELL	KNOW	. A DOZEN TRAVELLERS ARRIVE AT THE BOUNDARY. THE
CURE	(236)	WOMAN. /REGINALD/ YOU ARE A WONDERFUL WOMAN, YOU	KNOW	. ADORED ONE-- WOULD YOU MIND MY TAKING A LITTLE
MILL I	(164)	YOU CAME TO CONSULT ME ABOUT? /ALASTAIR/ I DONT	KNOW	. AFTER TEN MINUTES OF EPPY I NEVER DO KNOW WHETHER I
GETT	(311)	BISHOP/ I'M SORRY TO SAY I DONT. BUT SOAMES WILL	KNOW	. ALICE: WHERE IS SOAMES? /HOTCHKISS/ HE'S IN THERE (
ARMS I	(21)	(HE STUMBLES AGAINST THE BED). AH YES: NOW I	KNOW	. ALL RIGHT NOW. I'M TO GO TO BED, BUT NOT TO SLEEP. BE
SUPR IV	(167)	OF BLUE EYES HE MEETS IN THE STREET. /ANN/ YES, I	KNOW	. ALL THE SAME, JACK, MEN LIKE THAT ALWAYS LIVE IN
GENV IV	(126)	HER). /NEWCOMER/ OH COME COME! THIS WONT DO, YOU	KNOW	. ALL YOU PEOPLE SEEM TO THINK YOU WERE GOING TO LIVE
CATH 1	(170)	YOU? /EDSTASTON/ AS YOU DID NOT GIVE IT, I DONT	KNOW	. ALLOW ME TO ADD THAT I HAVE NOT ASKED FOR YOUR
BUOY PREFACE	(3)	HAVE WRITTEN THIS PLAY I MUST REPLY THAT I DO NOT	KNOW	. AMONG THE MANY SECTS OF PECULIAR PEOPLE WHICH ENGLAND
MIS.	(203)	AND SHOULDNT BE ALLOWED, FOR THEIR OWN GOOD, YOU	KNOW	. AND FOR THE GOOD OF MORALITY IN GENERAL. YOU AGREE
JITT II	(38)	POLITE TO SPEAK AS HORRIBLY AS THEY THINK; BUT I	KNOW	. AND MY MOTHER ENCOURAGES THEM. SHE ACTUALLY LIKES TO
2TRU III	(95)	MY CHILD IS DYING. SHE MAY BE DEAD FOR ALL I	KNOW	. AND NOBODY IS DOING ANYTHING: NOBODY CARES. OH DEAR,
CAND II	(108)	DENY IT. /MARCHBANKS/ (COMPASSIONATELY) YES, I	KNOW	. AND SO YOU HAVNT THE COURAGE TO TELL HIM?
JITT I	(19)	DOES NOT KNOW: HE WILL NOT KNOW: HE REFUSES TO	KNOW	. AND THAT REFUSAL, BECAUSE IT IS UNCONSCIOUS, BINDS MY
DOCT III	(139)	WELL, YOU SET UP TO APPRECIATE JENNIFER, YOU	KNOW	. AND YOU DESPISE ME, DONT YOU? /RIDGEON/ (CURTLY) I
HART II	(85)	ON PURPOSE! /MANGAN/ NOT OUT OF ILL-NATURE, YOU	KNOW	. AND YOULL ADMIT THAT I KEPT A JOB FOR HIM WHEN I HAD
HART I	(59)	TO HIM FOR HIS KINDNESS TO DEAR FATHER. I	KNOW	. ANYBODY ELSE? /ELLIE/ WHAT DO YOU MEAN? /MRS
APPL I	(210)	MR BOANERGES, BUT YOU DONT LOOK THE PART, YOU	KNOW	. ANYONE CAN SEE THAT YOU BELONG NATURALLY TO THE
MTH5	(207)	TOLD ME HOW I SHEW MY AGE. THAT IS WHAT I WANT TO	KNOW	. AS A MATTER OF FACT I AM OLDER THAN THIS BOY HERE:
MTH5	(235)	/PYGMALION/ OH YES. A QUESTION IS A STIMULUS, YOU	KNOW	. ASK HIM ONE. /ACIS/ (TO THE MALE FIGURE) WHAT DO YOU
BULL II	(113)	THE VOICE IS JUST AS BEAUTIFUL IN THE DARK, YOU	KNOW	. BESIDES, IVE HEARD A GREAT DEAL ABOUT YOU FROM LARRY.
ROCK I	(232)	WHAT FOR? /SIR ARTHUR/ WELL, BRACING, YOU	KNOW	. BRACING. /THE LADY/ CURIOUS, HOW IDLE PEOPLE ARE
MTH5	(211)	MAIDEN/ WHY SHOULD THEY? /STREPHON/ OH, I DONT	KNOW	. BUT DONT YOU WANT TO TOUCH ME? YOU USED TO. /THE
APPL I	(209)	GRATIFICATION) WELL, I DONT CALL MYSELF THAT, YOU	KNOW	. BUT I BELIEVE THE EXPRESSION IS IN USE, AS YOU MIGHT
LION PROLOG	(106)	OH, IF THEY ONLY KNEW! AND YOU THINK I DONT	KNOW	. BUT I DO, I DO, (SCREAMING) I DO. /ANDROCLES/ YES,
ROCK I	(206)	AND YET I AM VERY VERY FOND OF YOU, AS YOU	KNOW	. BUT I HAVE A GRUDGE AGAINST YOUR CAREER. /SIR ARTHUR/
JITT III	(73)	THAT. I DONT WANT THAT SORT OF MOTHER. /JITTA/ I	KNOW	. BUT I MUSTNT TAKE YOUR DEVOTION-- IT IS DEVOTION,
DOCT II	(123)	JUST LIKE THE MERCHANT OF VENICE, YOU	KNOW	. BUT IF A JEW MAKES AN AGREEMENT, HE MEANS TO KEEP IT
GETT	(330)	I DONT KNOW THAT I LOVE HIM. HE'S MY HUSBAND, YOU	KNOW	. BUT IF I GOT ANXIOUS ABOUT GEORGE'S HEALTH, AND I
PYGM II	(237)	WAS AS POOR AS ME. NOT THAT I MEAN ANY HARM, YOU	KNOW	. BUT IF LIZA IS GOING TO HAVE A BIT OUT OF THIS, WHY
BUOY III	(34)	THIRDBORN/ INCLUDING SOME THINGS NOBODY OUGHT TO	KNOW	. BUT IT IS NOT HER FAULT. /MRS SECONDBORN/ SHE HAS NO
MTH5	(243)	MUSIC. /ARJILLAX/ WHY? /THE NEWLY BORN/ I DONT	KNOW	. BUT IT WOULD. THE MUSICIANS PLAY. /THE FEMALE FIGURE/

DOCT II	(117)	COME TO DREAD THE WORST. I NEVER DARED LET MYSELF	KNOW	. BUT NOW THE RELIEF HAS COME: NOW I KNOW. LOUIS
CAPT II	(261)	/LADY CICELY/ HE SAYS HE COULDNT, YOU	KNOW	. BUT PERHAPS THE REAL REASON WAS THAT HE DIDNT LIKE
JITT III	(67)	CONSULTING A DOCTOR. THERE ARE SUCH PEOPLE, YOU	KNOW	. BUT SUPPOSE SHE WAS WHAT YOU THINK! WOULD A WOMAN
APPL I	(219)	PUT HIS FOOT DOWN AND STOP IT. /CRASSUS/ YES: I	KNOW	. BUT THAT IS NOT DEMOCRACY. /BOANERGES/ DEMOCRACY BE
BUOY 1	(10)	DOING WELL; AND YOU ARE DOING NOTHING. /SON/ I	KNOW	. BUT THE ONLY PROFESSION THAT APPEALS TO ME IS ONE
3PLA PREFACE	(R18)	LIVE ON PRETENCES, AS THE MASTERFUL MINORITY WELL	KNOW	. BUT THE TIMID MAJORITY, IF IT RULES NOWHERE ELSE, AT
SUPR I	(6)	WAS HIS PARTIALITY: WE WERE VERY OLD FRIENDS, YOU	KNOW	. BUT THERE WAS SOMETHING ELSE HE USED TO SAY ABOUT
MTH3	(106)	WHEN THEY ARE THREE. JUST TO BREAK THEM IN, YOU	KNOW	. BUT THEY BECOME SELF-SUPPORTING, OR NEARLY SO, AT
GENV IV	(96)	I DONT KNOW. WHERE DO THEY STAND WITH US? I DONT	KNOW	. BUT THEY KNOW WHAT ENGLAND INTENDS. THEY KNOW WHAT TO
MILL I	(140)	DONT TAKE IT. /EPIFANIA/ WHY? /SAGAMORE/ I DONT	KNOW	. BUT THEY NEVER DO. /EPIFANIA/ I WILL. AND I HOPE YOU
KING I	(170)	HE DOES NOT KNOW CAN THINK MUCH OF WHAT HE DOES	KNOW	. BUT WHAT IS THE PRECESSION OF THE EQUINOXES? IF I
HART I	(65)	HOW CAN YOU LOVE A LIAR? /MRS HUSHABYE/ I DONT	KNOW	. BUT YOU CAN, FORTUNATELY. OTHERWISE THERE WOULDNT BE
GENV I	(34)	SCATTERED OVER EUROPE, VERY EMINENT PERSONS, YOU	KNOW	. CAN I DO ANYTHING? /NEWCOMER/ (LOOKING AT THE
MTH3	(101)	MET THEIR DEATH BY DROWNING. /BURGE-LUBIN/ YES: I	KNOW	. CAN YOU EXPLAIN IT? /CONFUCIUS/ IT CANNOT BE
MTH1 I	(7)	I WHO WHISPERED THE WORD TO YOU THAT YOU DID NOT	KNOW	. DEAD. DEATH. DIE. /EVE/ (SHUDDERING) WHY DO YOU
DOCT IV	(161)	TO THE DOCTORS-- LAUGHING TO MYSELF. THEY	KNOW	. DEAREST: DONT CRY. IT MAKES YOU UGLY; AND I CANT BEAR
DOCT III	(151)	ON-- PROBABLY ON TUESDAY NEXT; BUT I WILL LET YOU	KNOW	. DEPEND ON ME; DONT FRET; EAT REGULARLY; SLEEP WELL;
MRS PREFACE	(153)	AND YET I THOUGHT I KNEW HOW LITTLE THE OTHERS	KNOW	. DO NOT SUPPOSE, HOWEVER, THAT THE CONSTERNATION OF
LION II	(139)	THE INCENSE? SONS TAKE AFTER THEIR MOTHERS, YOU	KNOW	. DO YOU WANT YOUR SON TO BE A COWARD? /THE CAPTAIN/ (
MTH4 III	(198)	AS I WAS SAYING-- WHERE WAS I? /ZOO/ I DONT	KNOW	. DOES ANYBODY? /THE ELDERLY GENTLEMAN/ (TACTFULLY)
WIDO III	(52)	I SEE. /LICKCHEESE/ I OWE IT PARTLY TO YOU, YOU	KNOW	. DOES THAT SURPRISE YOU? /SARTORIUS/ IT DOESNT
MIS.	(110)	OH! AND WHOS TO FETCH IT? /BENTLEY/ DONT	KNOW	. DONT CARE. PROVIDENCE, PROBABLY. IF NOT, YOUR MOTHER
DOCT IV	(165)	BEG YOUR PARDON. /LOUIS/ THAT WAS OLD WALPOLE, I	KNOW	. DONT GRIEVE, WALPOLE. I'M PERFECTLY HAPPY. I'M NOT IN
FANY PROLOG	(272)	YOU SHOULD NOT HAVE KEPT HIM HERE. /FANNY/ I	KNOW	. DONT SCOLD ME: I HAD SOMETHING IMPORTANT TO SAY TO
SUPR III	(79)	NO PRICKLY PEARS AND BROILED RABBITS, YOU	KNOW	. DONT TELL ME YOU CANT DO US A BIT BETTER THAN THAT IF
GETT	(296)	MORNING: I DONT KNOW WHY. I'M HIS BEST MAN, YOU	KNOW	. DONT YOU THINK IT GIVES ME A CERTAIN RIGHT TO BE
DEST	(182)	(IMPORTANTLY) YOU MUSNT DELAY ME, YOU	KNOW	. DUTY, MADAM, DUTY. /LADY/ (IMPLORINGLY) OH, SIR,
BARB II	(274)	YUS, I DESSAY. /THE MAN/ YUS, YOU DESSAY! I	KNOW	. EVERY LOAFER THAT CANT DO NOTHINK CALLS ISSELF A
BULL IV	(152)	A SPEECH, MISS DOYLE; BUT THEY LIKE IT, YOU	KNOW	. EVERYTHING HELPS IN ELECTIONEERING. LARRY TAKES THE
HART I	(55)	ELLIE: MANGAN HAS COME: I THOUGHT YOUD LIKE TO	KNOW	. EXCUSE ME, MRS HUSHABYE: THE STRANGE OLD GENTLEMAN--
NEVR II	(235)	OF THE CROOKED BILLET, IS IT? /PHILIP/ I DONT	KNOW	. FINCH: DOES HE KEEP A PUBLIC HOUSE? /M'COMAS/ (
SUPR II	(53)	IS SO DEVOUT, SO PERFECT, SO-- /TANNER/ YES: I	KNOW	. GO ON. /OCTAVIUS/ YOU SEE, UNDER THIS NEW
VWOO 1	(120)	HA! /Z/ WHAT IS THERE FUNNY IN THAT? /A/ I DONT	KNOW	. HA HA! THE POSTMAN'S DAUGHTER HATH RIPE RED LIPS:
WIDO II	(36)	HARRY; BUT I'M SURE THERES SOMETHING I OUGHT TO	KNOW	. HAS PAPA BEEN DISAGREEABLE? /TRENCH/ NO: HE HAS BEEN
DEVL II	(41)	HAS HAPPENED? /JUDITH/ (STILL ASTRAY) I DONT	KNOW	. HAVE I BEEN ASLEEP? I SUPPOSE-- (SHE STOPS
FOUN	(222)	MY OWN BOY. /BRABAZON/ YES, BUT LOOK HERE, YOU	KNOW	. HAVE YOU ANY MONEY? /ANASTASIA/ NOT A RAP.
MTH4 I	(167)	/ZOO/ NO: EVEN YOU CAN TELL ME THINGS I DO NOT	KNOW	. HAVNT YOU NOTICED THAT ALL THE TIME YOU HAVE BEEN
PYGM V	(277)	WELL! ! /PICKERING/ OH, THATS ONLY HIS WAY, YOU	KNOW	. HE DOESNT MEAN IT. /LIZA/ OH, I DIDNT MEAN IT EITHER,
ROCK I	(217)	HE SELL IT IF IT WAS LEFT ON HIS HANDS? HE DONT	KNOW	. HE DONT KNOW NOTHING OF THE BUSINESS THAT HIS LIFE
APPL I	(198)	KNOW WHAT THOUGHT MEANT. VERY FEW PEOPLE DO, YOU	KNOW	. HE HAD VISION: ACTUAL BODILY VISION, I MEAN; AND HE
ROCK PREFACE	(167)	HE KNOWS THINGS THAT UNIVERSITY PROFESSORS DO NOT	KNOW	. HE IS BRUTALIZED BY EXCESSIVE MUSCULAR LABOR; HE IS
HART II	(124)	THAT HE IS YOUR HUSBAND. /LADY UTTERWORD/ I	KNOW	. HE IS JEALOUS. AS IF HE HAD ANY RIGHT TO BE! HE
HART II	(96)	(CONTEMPLATING MANGAN WITHOUT INTEREST) I	KNOW	. HE IS ONLY ASLEEP. WE HAD A TALK AFTER DINNER; AND HE
PRES	(140)	WHY DIDNT HE KNOW? IT WAS HIS BUSINESS TO	KNOW	. HE OUGHT TO BE FLOGGED. /BALSQUITH/ PROBABLY HE WILL
BUOY IV	(49)	EMBRACE) MY BABZY! WHO IS THE MAN? /SHE/ I DONT	KNOW	. HE WANTS TO MARRY ME. /OLD BILL/ DOES HE INDEED? DO
DOCT V	(173)	OF THE PRIVATE DOCTOR. WELL, BLENKINSOP OUGHT TO	KNOW	. HE WAS A PRIVATE DOCTOR LONG ENOUGH HIMSELF. COME!
MRS III	(223)	PAPER AND SITS DOWN TO READ IT). /FRANK/ I DONT	KNOW	. HER JOURNEY TO TOWN LOOKS AS IF SHE DID. NOT THAT MY
SUPR III	(130)	LOVE AND BEAUTY; BUT HERE-- /DON JUAN/ OH YES: I	KNOW	. HERE THERE IS NOTHING BUT LOVE AND BEAUTY. UGH! IT
FANY I	(282)	OF A LADY? /GILBEY/ (BITTERLY) OH YES: I	KNOW	. HERE! I MUST BUY THE LAD'S SALVATION, I SUPPOSE. HOW
ROCK I	(213)	GOOD MANNERS WOULD LET HIM. AND HE'S RIGHT, YOU	KNOW	. HE'S RUDE; BUT HE'S RIGHT. /OXFORD YOUTH/ YOURS
MRS II	(203)	YOU SHOULDNT GO OFF LIKE THAT WITHOUT LETTING ME	KNOW	. HOW COULD I TELL WHAT HAD BECOME OF YOU? AND NIGHT
FANY II	(293)	MARGARET? I'M NOT BLAMING YOU: I ONLY WANT TO	KNOW	. HOW COULD YOU BRING YOURSELF TO DO IT? /MARGARET/ I
FABL VI	(128)	CENTURIES. /MAIDEN 5/ YES: THAT IS WHAT I WANT TO	KNOW	. HOW OLD IS THE WORLD? /TEACHER/ WE DO NOT KNOW. WE
AUGS	(272)	SUBJECT, UNHAPPILY. /THE LADY/ OH, I KNOW, I	KNOW	. HOW SHAMEFULLY YOU HAVE BEEN TREATED! WHAT
WIDO I	(10)	(HE SITS NEAR HER). /BLANCHE/ (SHARPLY) I DONT	KNOW	. HOW SHOULD I? YOU HAD NO RIGHT TO SPEAK TO ME THAT
FANY I	(277)	GET ON. GET ON. /DORA/ OH, OF COURSE YOU WOULDNT	KNOW	. HOW SILLY OF ME! IT'S A RATHER GO-AHEAD SORT OF
PHIL I	(86)	OH, THATS MY DAUGHTER'S NAME. SHE'S A WIDOW, YOU	KNOW	. HOW UNCOMMONLY WELL YOU LOOK, DAN! THE YEARS HAVNT
JITT I	(12)	HIS HEAD DECISIVELY) IT WOULD PROBABLY KILL ME. I	KNOW	. I AM A DOCTOR. (HE TAKES THE GLASS FROM HER). THANK
KING I	(174)	AS WE HAVE ANY RIGHT TO ASK FOR. /NELLY/ YES, I	KNOW	. I AM COMING. (SHE RISES AND GOES TO CHARLES, WHOSE
CATH 2	(177)	/PATIOMKIN/ (ON HIS KNEES: TEARFULLY) I DONT	KNOW	. I AM DRUNK. WHAT IS THIS, VARINKA? /EDSTASTON/ (
SIM I	(37)	WISH TO GO, BY THE WAY? /THE CLERGYMAN/ I DONT	KNOW	. I AM LOST. /PRA/ LOST? /THE CLERGYMAN/ YES. QUITE
PYGM V	(278)	TAKES OFF HIS BOOTS ALL OVER THE PLACE. /LIZA/ I	KNOW	. I AM NOT BLAMING HIM. IT IS HIS WAY, ISNT IT? BUT IT
SIM II	(82)	THINK OF YOU AS A SEPARATE POSSIBILITY. /PRA/ I	KNOW	. I AM PART OF THE FURNITURE OF YOUR HOUSE. I AM A
FABL PREFACE	(91)	THEY CAN BE INVITED TO INDICATE THE BOOKS THEY	KNOW	. I AM QUITE AWARE OF THE POSSIBILITY OF MISLEADING
ROCK II	(280)	SAY OR DO NEXT. IF SHE WERE A LADY I'D ALWAYS	KNOW	. I AM SO TIRED OF WELLBRED PEOPLE, AND PARTY POLITICS,
MTH2	(55)	WELL, JUST WHAT YOU ARE DOING, IF YOU WANT TO	KNOW	. I AM TRYING TO ENLIST MR BARNABAS'S VALUABLE SUPPORT
CAND II	(123)	GOT IT. /LEXY/ IT WAS REPLY PAID. /MORELL/ YES, I	KNOW	. I ANSWERED IT. I CANT GO. /CANDIDA/ BUT WHY, JAMES..
MRS IV	(248)	THINK OVER IT. (SOOTHINGLY) YOURE SHOCKED, I	KNOW	. I CAN ENTER INTO YOUR FEELINGS; AND I THINK THEY DO
FABL VI	(124)	/YOUTH 3/ YES. /TEACHER/ HOW? /YOUTH 3/ I DONT	KNOW	. I CANT FIND WORDS FOR IT: I'M NO TALKER. BUT I CAN DO
JITT II	(30)	DOES SHE SUSPECT ANYBODY? /FESSLER/ I DONT	KNOW	. I CANT SEE THROUGH HER; AND THE WORST OF IT IS, SHE
DOCT II	(121)	BREAKING DOWN) I OUGHT TO KEEP IT TO MYSELF, I	KNOW	. I CANT TELL YOU, RIDGEON, HOW ASHAMED I AM OF
CAND II	(109)	NO: ANSWER ME. I WANT TO KNOW: I MUST	KNOW	. I CANT UNDERSTAND IT. I CAN SEE NOTHING IN HIM BUT
CLEO PRO2	(104)	/FTATATEETA/ PERSIAN: AS OSIRIS LIVES, I DO NOT	KNOW	. I CHID HER FOR BRINGING EVIL DAYS UPON US BY TALKING
NEVR II	(257)	TO A TONE OF UTTER RECKLESSNESS) I DONT	KNOW	. I DONT CARE. (BURSTING OUT REPROACHFULLY) OH, MISS
FABL VI	(125)	3/ HOW THE DEVIL DOES ANYBODY KNOW? YOU DONT	KNOW	. I DONT KNOW. /TEACHER/ WHY DONT WE KNOW? /YOUTH 2/
MIS.	(144)	ARE YOU? /LORD SUMMERHAYS/ DONT ASK ME. I DONT	KNOW	. I DONT KNOW. TARLETON RETURNS FROM THE VESTIBULE.
PYGM II	(235)	WITH IT, GOVERNOR. SHE'S THAT KIND OF WOMAN: YOU	KNOW	. I HAD TO GIVE THE BOY A PENNY AFORE HE TRUSTED ME
ROCK PREFACE	(185)	WHY DO YOU THINK SO? /JESUS/ I DO NOT THINK: I	KNOW	. I HAVE IT FROM GOD. /PILATE/ I HAVE THE SAME SORT OF
FABL PREFACE	(79)	HE LISTENED FOR THE VOICE OF GOD, WE SHALL NEVER	KNOW	. I HAVE JUST HAD A LETTER FROM A MAN WHO, HAVING MADE
MILL III	(181)	ABOMINABLE. THERE IS NOTHING MORE FOR ME TO	KNOW	. I HAVE YOU IN THE HOLLOW OF MY HAND. GIVE ME SOME
VWOO 3	(135)	MANNERS HAVE IMPROVED, HAVNT THEY? /A/ I DONT	KNOW	. I KNOW THAT THEY ARE NO LONGER DISINTERESTED AND
JITT II	(35)	DEAR. BUT THERE ARE THINGS IT IS BETTER NOT TO	KNOW	. I KNOW THEM; AND I ONLY WISH I COULD CHANGE PLACES
DOCT III	(133)	YOU, DEAR, DONT YOU? /LOUIS/ (FONDLY) I	KNOW	. I KNOW. I'M A WRETCH; AND YOURE AN ANGEL. OH, IF ONLY
NEVR III	(262)	/GLORIA/ (KNEELING BESIDE HER CHAIR) I	KNOW	. I KNOW. (SHE SUDDENLY THROWS HER ARM ABOUT HER
O'FL	(206)	ME. /SIR PEARCE/ (SOOTHINGLY) YES, YES: I	KNOW	. I KNOW. ONE DOES GET FED UP WITH IT: I'VE BEEN DOG
KING I	(172)	FRIEND ROWLEY. /NELLY/ (RUNNING TO FOX) I	KNOW	. I KNOW. THE MAN IN THE LEATHER BREECHES. /FOX/ (
NEVR I	(215)	MY DEARS: I DO NOT MEAN THAT YOU ARE TOO YOUNG TO	KNOW	. I MEAN THAT YOU ARE TOO YOUNG TO BE TAKEN INTO MY
AUGS	(280)	BUSY. /AUGUSTUS/ YES; BUT NOT BEFORE LUNCH, YOU	KNOW	. I NEVER CAN DO MUCH BEFORE LUNCH. AND I'M NO GOOD AT
CAND II	(111)	MY SON-IN-LAW JAMES ERE? /MARCHBANKS/ I DONT	KNOW	. I NEVER CAN REMEMBER DATES. A FEW MONTHS, PERHAPS.
HART I	(57)	RUINED. /MRS HUSHABYE/ HOW? /ELLIE/ I DONT	KNOW	. I NEVER COULD UNDERSTAND. BUT IT WAS DREADFUL. WHEN
ARMS II	(36)	THE LAST FIVE MINUTES. WHO IS HE? /LOUKA/ I DONT	KNOW	. I NEVER SAW HIM. I ONLY HEARD HIS VOICE THROUGH THE
DOCT III	(137)	FROM THE OTHER-- /WALPOLE/ I WALKED INTO IT, YOU	KNOW	. I OFFERED IT. /RIDGEON/ -- THEY COULD AFFORD IT. BUT
MTH5	(254)	YOU DID NOT ALWAYS THINK SO, ACIS. /ACIS/ OH, I	KNOW	. I OFFERED YOU MY LOVE ONCE, AND ASKED FOR YOURS.
GLIM	(184)	ME, GIULIACCIA. /GIULIA/ PERHAPS; BUT I DO NOT	KNOW	. I SAW SANDRO MAKE A SIGN TO MY FATHER: THAT IS WHY
DOCT III	(137)	IT'S QUITE SAFE: HE CANT SELL IT FOR A YEAR, YOU	KNOW	. I SAY, MY DEAR WALPOLE, I AM SORRY. (HE PLACES HIS
INCA	(237)	TO WANT ANYTHING NOW, ON ACCOUNT OF THE WAR, YOU	KNOW	. I SENT MY MAID AWAY AS A PUBLIC DUTY; AND NOW SHE HAS
MTH5	(218)	SO YOU THINK. /THE NEWLY BORN/ I DONT THINK: I	KNOW	. I SHALL ENJOY LIFE FOR EVER AND EVER. /THE
MRS II	(200)	YOURSELF! BUT WHAT ABOUT PRADDY? /CROFTS/ DONT	KNOW	. I SUPPOSE HE CAN SLEEP AT THE INN. /MRS WARREN/ HAVNT
GETT	(270)	WOMAN YOU DONT UNDERSTAND? /THE GENERAL/ I DONT	KNOW	. I SUPPOSE I LOVE YOU. /LESBIA/ WELL, BOXER, YOU CAN
BULL IV	(178)	IT REMINDS ME OF POOR RUSKIN: A GREAT MAN, YOU	KNOW	. I SYMPATHIZE. BELIEVE ME, I'M ON YOUR SIDE. DONT
OVER	(174)	JUNO/ NO: PLEASE DONT EXPLAIN. I DONT WANT TO	KNOW	. I TAKE YOUR WORD FOR IT. BESIDES, IT DOESNT MATTER
SIM I	(38)	WHO IS THIS GENTLEMAN? /PRA/ HE DOES NOT SEEM TO	KNOW	. I THINK HE HAS ESCAPED FROM THE ASYLUM. /THE
MTH2	(88)	TO SAVVY) NOR YOU, I SUPPOSE? /SAVVY/ OH, I DONT	KNOW	. I THOUGHT I WAS FOR A MOMENT. I CAN BELIEVE, IN A
HART III	(143)	UP CHILD TO PLAY AT EARTHQUAKES WITH. /MAZZINI/ I	KNOW	. I USED OFTEN TO THINK ABOUT THAT WHEN I WAS YOUNG.
FANY III	(298)	/BOBBY/ BUT YOUD HAVE TO MAKE SOME EXCUSE, YOU	KNOW	. I WANT TO GIVE IT A GENTLEMANLY TURN: TO SAY I'M NOT
MILL I	(149)	I WENT TO MISS SMITH: SHE'S NOT A PRONOUN, YOU	KNOW	. I WENT WHERE I COULD FIND PEACE AND KINDNESS. TO MY
MILL I	(142)	THE LAW, OR IS IT NOT? /SAGAMORE/ I REALLY DONT	KNOW	. I WILL LOOK IT UP IN MY LAW BOOKS. /EPIFANIA/ YOU

PRES	(136)	IT; AND I KNOW. /BALSQUITH/ I HAVNT; AND I DONT	KNOW	. I WISH THOSE GUNS DIDNT MAKE SUCH A DEVIL OF A NOISE.
HART I	(59)	WOULD HAVE FOUND HIM OUT IF SHE HAD LIVED, YOU	KNOW	. I WONDER WAS THAT WHY HE STRANGLED HER! /ELLIE/
GETT	(292)	THE BAPTISM SERVICE. THATS NOT A BIT REAL, YOU	KNOW	. IF I MAY SAY SO, YOU WOULD BOTH FEEL SO MUCH MORE AT
LION II	(139)	/THE CAPTAIN/ BUT FOR WHAT? /LAVINIA/ I DONT	KNOW	. IF IT WERE FOR ANYTHING SMALL ENOUGH TO KNOW, IT
FANY EPILOG	(330)	SIMPLE QUESTION. /BANNAL/ SIMPLE ENOUGH WHEN YOU	KNOW	. IF IT'S BY A GOOD AUTHOR, IT'S A GOOD PLAY.
MRS II	(201)	/MRS WARREN/ (REFLECTIVELY) WELL, SAM, I DONT	KNOW	. IF THE GIRL WANTS TO GET MARRIED, NO GOOD CAN COME OF
FABL PREFACE	(87)	THAT PRACTICAL PEOPLE ARE CONSTRUCTIVE AND DO	KNOW	. IF THEY ARE AND DO, WHY ARE WE IN OUR PRESENT
MTH3	(98)	I HAVE A BIG DOG; AND HE IS THE BEST FELLOW I	KNOW	. IF YOU KNEW HOW MUCH UGLIER YOU ARE THAN A CHOW, YOU
INCA	(238)	/THE PRINCESS/ (ALARMED) OH, I'M SURE I DONT	KNOW	. IF YOU LIKE, OF COURSE; BUT DO YOU THINK I OUGHT TO?
MIS.	(136)	WONDERFUL MAN; BUT HE'S NOT QUITE ALL THERE, YOU	KNOW	. IF YOU NOTICE, HE'S DIFFERENT FROM ME; AND WHATEVER
SUPR II	(67)	IF I WERE TO-- OH, WELL, NO MATTER. /HECTOR/ I	KNOW	. IF YOU WERE TO MARRY THE SON OF AN ENGLISH
GENV II	(51)	SEAPORT OF THE EARTHLY PARADISE. /BEGONIA/ I	KNOW	. IN CENTRAL AMERICA, ISNT IT? /THE SECRETARY/ YES.
BUOY PREFACE	(4)	HIMSELF BE BURNT RATHER THAN RECANT HIS " I DONT	KNOW	. INSTRUCT ME"? WHEN I WAS A SMALL BOY I SAW A
FANY EPILOG	(332)	INCAPABLE OF THE NOTE OF PASSION. /BANNAL/ YES, I	KNOW	. INTELLECT WITHOUT EMOTION. THATS RIGHT. I ALWAYS SAY
JITT II	(47)	STOP: WHERE ARE YOU GOING? /JITTA/ I DONT	KNOW	. INTO THE STREETS, I SUPPOSE. /LENKHEIM/ OH, DAMN YOUR
LIED	(201)	HUSBAND/ WHAT IS MRS BOMPAS TO YOU, I'D LIKE TO	KNOW	. I'LL TELL YOU WHAT MRS BOMPAS IS. SHE'S THE SMARTEST
DOCT III	(133)	YOU, DEAR, DONT YOU? /LOUIS/ (FONDLY) I KNOW, I	KNOW	. I'M A WRETCH; AND YOURE AN ANGEL. OH, IF ONLY I WERE
MIS.	(161)	YELLOW PATCHES THAT WONT COME OFF. SHORT WIND. I	KNOW	. I'M ASHAMED OF MYSELF. I COULD DO NOTHING ON THE HIGH
CAND I	(100)	DOING. TAKE CARE. /MARCHBANKS/ (RUTHLESSLY) I	KNOW	. I'M DOING IT ON PURPOSE. I TOLD YOU I SHOULD STAGGER
OVER	(188)	US YOU ARE ADDRESSING? /MRS LUNN/ I REALLY DONT	KNOW	. I'M GETTING HOPELESSLY CONFUSED. /JUNO/ WHY DONT YOU
MTH2	(42)	IS GOING, SAVVY. HE HAS AN ENGAGEMENT. /SAVVY/ I	KNOW	. I'M THE ENGAGEMENT. /CONRAD/ IN THAT CASE, WOULD YOU
FANY III	(318)	GILBEY? ANYBODY MAY BE THE SON OF A DUKE, YOU	KNOW	. IS HE LEGITIMATE? /GILBEY/ GOOD LORD! I NEVER
FANY EPILOG	(330)	WHAT SORT OF PLAY IS THIS? THATS WHAT I WANT TO	KNOW	. IS IT A COMEDY OR A TRAGEDY? IS IT A FARCE OR A
CAND II	(112)	ABOVE IT. BUT IS IT RIGHT? THATS WHAT I WANT TO	KNOW	. IS IT RIGHT? /MORELL/ THATS A QUESTION FOR THE
DOCT III	(152)	BONINGTON-- /MRS DUBEDAT/ YES, I KNOW, I	KNOW	. IT IS A GREAT PRIVILEGE TO HAVE HIM. BUT OH, I WISH
MTH4 III	(200)	HAVE ASKED. SHE WOULD HAVE ANSWERED THEM, YOU	KNOW	. IT IS ALWAYS LIKE THAT. I WILL GO AND ARRANGE TO HAVE
MTH1 I	(3)	OH DONT! WHY DOESNT IT WAKE? /ADAM/ I DONT	KNOW	. IT IS NOT ASLEEP. /EVE/ NOT ASLEEP? /ADAM/ TRY.
BARB III	(346)	HAVE NO POWER, AND THAT HE HAS NONE. /CUSINS/ I	KNOW	. IT IS NOT FOR MYSELF ALONE. I WANT TO MAKE POWER FOR
JOAN 4	(94)	BEEN DEFEATED. /THE NOBLEMAN/ THAT HAPPENS, YOU	KNOW	. IT IS ONLY IN HISTORY BOOKS AND BALLADS THAT THE
HART I	(58)	WHY ARNT YOU ROLLING IN MONEY? /ELLIE/ I DONT	KNOW	. IT SEEMS VERY UNFAIR TO ME. YOU SEE, MY FATHER WAS
DOCT I	(98)	THE PROOF OF THE PUDDING IS IN THE EATING, YOU	KNOW	. IT WAS AN IMMENSE SUCCESS. IT ACTED LIKE MAGIC ON THE
FANY II	(291)	BUT HOW DID IT ALL BEGIN? /MARGARET/ OH, I DONT	KNOW	. IT WAS BOAT-RACE NIGHT, THEY SAID. /MRS KNOX/
DEST	(187)	FOUND IT? I WAS THE FIRST MAN TO CROSS; AND I	KNOW	. IT WAS MY HORSE THAT FOUND IT. (WITH CONVICTION, AS
BASH I	(95)	IS A PART OF WHAT I AM. WHAT THAT IS YOU MUST NOT	KNOW	. IT WOULD END ALL BETWEEN US. AND YET THERE'S NO
BULL I	(77)	AT ALL COSTS (HE DRINKS). /TIM/ SURE I	KNOW	. IT'S AWFUL (HE DRINKS). I SEE YOURE A GOOD LIBERAL
SUPR II	(49)	IF YOU LIKE EASY GOING, YOU CAN TAKE A BUS, YOU	KNOW	. IT'S CHEAPER. YOU PAY ME TO SAVE YOUR TIME AND GIVE
MTH2	(76)	YOU. /BURGE/ (TO FRANKLYN) I WISH YOU WOULD, YOU	KNOW	. IT'S IMPORTANT. VERY IMPORTANT. /FRANKLYN/ WELL,
GETT	(268)	LESBIA. I'M FIFTY: YOU ARE-- /LESBIA/ YES, I	KNOW	. IT'S NO USE, BOXER. WHEN WILL YOU BE OLD ENOUGH TO
MIS.	(168)	OF THAT SORT BY THE BUSHEL: THE DOOM SORT, YOU	KNOW	. IT'S ODD, ISNT IT, THAT YOU AND I SHOULD BE LIKE ONE
MIS.	(111)	/BENTLEY/ I -- /JOHNNY/ NO, STOP! I DONT WANT TO	KNOW	. IT'S ONLY A DODGE TO START AN ARGUMENT. /BENTLEY/
PHIL II	(99)	HERE TOO. /CUTHBERTSON/ (SYMPATHETICALLY) I	KNOW	. IT'S THE SAME WITH GRACE. SHE'S ALWAYS HERE. /CRAVEN/
DEVL III	(51)	(GAILY) UPON MY LIFE, MRS ANDERSON, I DONT	KNOW	. IVE BEEN ASKING MYSELF THAT QUESTION EVER SINCE; AND
DOCT IV	(161)	ME THE HORRIBLE STRAIN OF PRETENDING THAT I DONT	KNOW	. IVE BEEN LYING THERE LISTENING TO THE DOCTORS--
MIS.	(114)	DOWN THE PASSAGE THERE. HE -- /BENTLEY/ OH YES: I	KNOW	. IVE READ IT. " THE ROMANCE OF BUSINESS, OR THE STORY
CAPT II	(247)	ASK ONE OF YOUR MEN TO TURN OUT. YOU WONT MIND, I	KNOW	. (ALL THE MEN STARE AT HER. EVEN DRINKWATER FORGETS
DOCT II	(126)	/WALPOLE/ HULLO! YOU MUSTNT NEGLECT THIS, YOU	KNOW	. (ALL TOGETHER) /BLENKINSOP/ (PUTTING HIS FINGERS IN
MIS.	(113)	TO RECOVER HIMSELF) I'M SORRY I INTRUDED: I DIDNT	KNOW	. (BREAKING DOWN AGAIN) OH YOU BEAST! YOU PIG!
CAND II	(109)	OH! /MARCHBANKS/ YOU DO UNDERSTAND; AND YOU	KNOW	. (DETERMINED TO HAVE AN ANSWER) IS IT POSSIBLE FOR A
PYGM IV	(265)	THAT HE WILL EAT AN APPLE), YOU MIGHT MARRY, YOU	KNOW	. (HE BITES A LARGE PIECE OUT OF THE APPLE AND MUNCHES
CAND II	(113)	KEEP? /MARCHBANKS/ (PETTISHLY) OH, I DONT	KNOW	. (HE MOVES TO THE SOFA, AS IF TO GET AS FAR AS
SUPR II	(52)	AND YOU TWO WANT TO TALK ABOUT YOUR LADIES, I	KNOW	. (HE PRETENDS TO BUSY HIMSELF ABOUT THE CAR, BUT
BULL II	(109)	ANYTHING I CAN DO FOR YOU IN THIS PARISH, LET ME	KNOW	. (HE SHAKES HANDS WITH BROADBENT). /BROADBENT/ (
APPL II	(269)	(HE SITS DOWN). /PLINY/ YOURE NOT SERIOUS, YOU	KNOW	. (HE SITS DOWN). /NICOBAR/ YOU CANT UPSET THE APPLE
MTH5	(235)	A LITTLE SOMETHING. YOU DANCE SO BEAUTIFULLY, YOU	KNOW	. (HE SITS DOWN NEXT MARTELLUS, AND WHISPERS TO HIM)
MRS I	(193)	YOU: YOURE JUST THE SORT OF FELLOW SHE OUGHT TO	KNOW	. (HE SMILES, AND RAISES THE CHARMING VOICE ALMOST TO
ARMS I	(21)	WHAT AM I LOOKING FOR? SLEEP-- DANGER-- DONT	KNOW	. (HE STUMBLES AGAINST THE BED). AH YES: NOW I KNOW.
PYGM III	(254)	SO FEW PARTIES, POOR CHILD! SHE DOESNT QUITE	KNOW	. (MRS HIGGINS, SEEING THAT HER EYES ARE MOIST, TAKES
DOCT I	(88)	TEMPTATIONS OF LOVE. THE OLD WOMAN SAID SHE DIDNT	KNOW	. (RIDGEON LAUGHS). WELL, I MAKE YOU THE SAME ANSWER.
CAND I	(81)	WATCH AND PRAY, LEXY: WATCH AND PRAY. /LEXY/ I	KNOW	. (RISING WITTILY TO THE OCCASION) BUT HOW CAN I WATCH
FANY PROLOG	(260)	HER NOT TO HAVE AN ENGLISH HERO. THAT IS ALL I	KNOW	. (RUEFULLY) I HAVNT BEEN CONSULTED EVEN ABOUT THE
CLEO II	(136)	CAESAR-- /CAESAR/ (ANTICIPATING HIM) YES: I	KNOW	. (RUFIO AND BRITANNUS COME DOWN THE HALL FROM THE
WIDO I	(18)	SARTORIUS MAY BE A RETIRED BURGLAR FOR ALL I	KNOW	. (SARTORIUS AND BLANCHE, READY FOR DINNER, COME FROM
DEST	(175)	OH! (SINKING BACK INTO THE CHAIR) I-- I DONT	KNOW	. (SHE BREAKS DOWN). /NAPOLEON/ AHA! I THOUGHT SO: A
NEVR III	(262)	/GLORIA/ (KNEELING BESIDE HER CHAIR) I KNOW, I	KNOW	. (SHE SUDDENLY THROWS HER ARM ABOUT HER MOTHER AND
FANY II	(293)	EXCEPT WHEN THEYRE TREATED LIKE LADIES, I DONT	KNOW	. (SHE THROWS HERSELF INTO A CORNER OF THE SOFA). /MRS
DOCT IV	(170)	YOU KNOW. /MRS DUBEDAT/ OH, THANK YOU: I DIDNT	KNOW	. (SIR PATRICK GOES). /WALPOLE/ GOODBYE. I BLAME
WIDO II	(24)	SAY, PAPA? /SARTORIUS/ HIS PEOPLE? I DONT	KNOW	. (STILL BUSY). ANOTHER PAUSE. /BLANCHE/ WHAT DOES HE
PHIL II	(126)	OF THIS CLUB ARE SO EXTRAORDINARY THAT I DONT	KNOW	. (TO GRACE) MAY I ASK, MADAM, WHETHER YOU HAVE ANY
BARB III	(342)	IS, THERE WILL THE EAGLES BE GATHERED, DONT YOU	KNOW	. (TO UNDERSHAFT) EH? WHAT? /UNDERSHAFT/ PRECISELY.
PYGM III	(249)	SORRY. (BEAMING SUDDENLY) I SUPPOSE I AM, YOU	KNOW	. (UPROARIOUSLY) HA, HA! /MISS EYNSFORD HILL/ (WHO
DOCT II	(127)	WIFE. WE MUST NOT JUDGE HIM TOO HASTILY, YOU	KNOW	. (WITH UNCTION) GOOOOOOOODNIGHT, PADDY. BLESS YOU,
ROCK II	(247)	WASTE THEIR OWN TIME AND YOUR LABOR. /BLEE/ WE	KNOW	. KEEP ALL THE SOFT JOBS FOR YOUR LOT AND THE HARD ONES
NEVR IV	(299)	/GLORIA/ (PETULANTLY) I DONT KNOW. YES, I DO	KNOW	. LET US GO AND SEE THE DANCING. THEY GO TOWARDS THE
MTH3	(108)	HOME TO ONE-- BUT (RECOVERING) IT ISNT TRUE, YOU	KNOW	. LET US KEEP SANE. /CONFUCIUS/ (TO THE ARCHBISHOP)
GETT	(326)	WHAT ARE YOU AFRAID OF? /HOTCHKISS/ I DONT	KNOW	. LISTEN TO ME. I WAS A YOUNG FOOL LIVING BY MYSELF IN
MTH3	(102)	BUT FOUR, DROWNED OR NOT? /BURGE-LUBIN/ I DONT	KNOW	. LOOK HIM UP IN THE ENCYCLOPEDIA BRITANNICA.
DOCT II	(117)	MYSELF KNOW. BUT NOW THE RELIEF HAS COME: NOW I	KNOW	. LOUIS DUBEDAT COMES FROM THE HOTEL, IN HIS OVERCOAT,
FOUN	(217)	INSTITUTION. THEY FOUND ME ON THE DOORSTEP, YOU	KNOW	. MIGHT HAVE HAPPENED TO ANYBODY, MIGHTNT IT? /MERCER/
BARB III	(313)	/LOMAX/ THAT WAS RATHER FINE OF THE OLD MAN, YOU	KNOW	. MOST CHAPS WOULD HAVE WANTED THE ADVERTISEMENT.
PYGM II	(241)	TO SEE YOUR DAUGHTER. IT'S YOUR DUTY, YOU	KNOW	. MY BROTHER IS A CLERGYMAN; AND HE COULD HELP YOU IN
MRS IV	(251)	YOU ARE: NO MERCY FOR YOURSELF OR ANYONE ELSE. I	KNOW	. MY EXPERIENCE HAS DONE THAT FOR ME ANYHOW: I CAN TELL
MTH5	(257)	TO FIND YOU ALL RATHER SILLY. /STREPHON/ I	KNOW	. MY GIRL WENT OFF THIS MORNING. SHE HADNT SLEPT FOR
JOAN 2	(75)	WAS PRAYING, AND TOLD HIM EVERYTHING HE WANTED TO	KNOW	. MY POOR FATHER HAD TWO SAINTS, MARIE DE MAILLE AND
JOAN 5	(114)	HOW DO YOU KNOW YOU ARE RIGHT? /JOAN/ I ALWAYS	KNOW	. MY VOICES-- /CHARLES/ OH, YOUR VOICES, YOUR VOICES.
CATH 4	(198)	EH? NO, NO, NO: YOU DONT MEAN THAT, YOU	KNOW	. NAUGHTY! (TO THE SERGEANT) GOODBYE, MY FRIEND. YOU
ROCK I	(197)	ARTHUR/ WHAT OPPORTUNITY? /BASHAM/ THEY DONT	KNOW	. NEITHER DO I. IT'S ONLY A PHRASE THAT MEANS NOTHING:
GENV I	(31)	RIGHT. /HE/ HOW ALL RIGHT? /SHE/ MORALLY, YOU	KNOW	. NO HANKY PANKY. I AM RESPECTABLE; AND I MEAN TO KEEP
GENV IV	(94)	/BBDE/ YOU DONT KNOW! ! /SIR O./ I DONT	KNOW	. NOR DO YOU, MR BATTLER. NOR YOU, SIGNOR. /BBDE/ DO
OVER	(179)	/MRS JUNO/ OH, DONT MAKE ME SAY IT. OF COURSE I	KNOW	. NOTHING-- NOT LIFE NOR DEATH NOR SHAME NOR ANYTHING
POSN	(451)	HANGING HORSE-THIEVES IS JUSTICE; SO NOW YOU	KNOW	. NOW THEN: WEVE WASTED ENOUGH TIME. HUSTLE WITH YOUR
DEST	(188)	/LIEUTENANT/ YES, DROP IT. YOURE MY PRISONER, YOU	KNOW	. OF COURSE I DONT BELIEVE IN ANY SUCH RUBBISH; BUT
ROCK I	(218)	YOU CANT TEACH PEOPLE ANYTHING THEY DONT WANT TO	KNOW	. OLD DR MARX-- KARL MARX THEY CALL HIM NOW-- MY FATHER
BARB I	(268)	GET ON WITHOUT CANNONS; BUT IT ISNT RIGHT, YOU	KNOW	. ON THE OTHER HAND, THERE MAY BE A CERTAIN AMOUNT OF
MTH4 I	(151)	GENTLEMAN/ MARRIAGE MAKES A DIFFERENCE, YOU	KNOW	. ONE CAN SAY THINGS TO A MARRIED LADY THAT WOULD
O'FL	(206)	/SIR PEARCE/ (SOOTHINGLY) YES, YES: I KNOW, I	KNOW	. ONE DOES GET FED UP WITH IT: I'VE BEEN DOG TIRED
MIS.	(170)	SHE MUST HAVE HAD SOMETHING OFF ME THEN, YOU	KNOW	. ONE DOESNT GET OUT OF THESE THINGS FOR NOTHING. HANG
VWOO 3	(136)	THE MANY DAYS WITH NOTHING TO EAT? /A/ I DONT	KNOW	. ONE DOES, SOMEHOW. STOP ASKING QUESTIONS; AND LET US
FANY I	(283)	WHY DID YOU CHANGE HATS WITH HIM? /DORA/ I DONT	KNOW	. ONE DOES, YOU KNOW. /MRS GILBEY/ I NEVER DID. THE
DOCT I	(86)	GOOD. PARRISH'S CHEMICAL FOOD: PHOSPHATES, YOU	KNOW	. ONE TABLESPOONFUL TO A TWELVE-OUNCE BOTTLE OF WATER:
BULL III	(122)	THE STONES. /BROADBENT/ THAT WAS MAGNIFICENT, YOU	KNOW	. ONLY A GREAT RACE IS CAPABLE OF PRODUCING SUCH MEN.
SIM I	(46)	I-- /PRA/ PRECISELY. YOU DONT KNOW. WELL, WE DO	KNOW	. OUR FOUR WONDERFUL CHILDREN HAVE ALL SORTS OF
APPL INTRLUD	(245)	GO AS FAR AS YOURS, I SUPPOSE. /MAGNUS/ I DONT	KNOW	. OUR MINDS GO TOGETHER HALF WAY. WHETHER IT IS THAT
PHIL II	(107)	YES: THATS WHAT MADE PARAMORE'S REPUTATION, YOU	KNOW	. PAPA USED TO GET BAD OCCASIONALLY; BUT WE ALWAYS
BARB II	(282)	WOT CALL AS SHE TO PRY FOR ME? /BARBARA/ I DONT	KNOW	. PERHAPS IT WAS YOU THAT CUT HER LIP. /BILL/ (
HART I	(56)	DESCRIBE IT TO YOU. /MRS HUSHABYE/ POOR ELLIE! I	KNOW	. PULLING THE DEVIL BY THE TAIL. /ELLIE/ (HURT) OH NO.
MIS.	(131)	VERY TRUE. STILL, DEMOCRACY'S ALL RIGHT, YOU	KNOW	; READ MILL. READ JEFFERSON. /LORD SUMMERHAYS/ YES.
OVER	(176)	I THOUGHT IT THE MOST DELICATE WAY OF LETTING YOU	KNOW	. / MRS JUNO/ WELL, YOU ARE A DAISY, I MUST SAY. I

MILL IV	(194)	DEAR! DEAR! /ALASTAIR/ EPPY IS LIKE THAT, YOU	KNOW	. /ADRIAN/ YES: I KNOW NOW. BUT I OUGHT NOT TO BE HERE:
APPL I	(231)	WHAT ARE WE TO DO NOW? THATS WHAT I WANT TO	KNOW	. /AMANDA/ (INCORRIGIBLE) I SUGGEST A LITTLE COMMUNITY
DEVL II	(41)	ASLEEP? I SUPPOSE-- (SHE STOPS BLANKLY). I DONT	KNOW	. /ANDERSON/ (GROANING) HEAVEN FORGIVE ME, I LEFT YOU
VWOO 1	(118)	THE WOMEN, ISNT IT? IF YOU WERE A WOMAN YOUD	KNOW	. /A/ I AM A WOMAN; AND YOU ARE A MAN, WITH A SLIGHT
VWOO 3	(136)	REMEDY IS SIMPLE. I SHALL NOT MARRY. /Z/ YOU DONT	KNOW	. /A/ NEITHER DO YOU. /Z/ YES I DO. YOU HAVE MARRIED
2TRU II	(66)	WELL, THE TRAVELLERS WERE JUST AS BAD, YOU	KNOW	. /AUBREY/ JUST AS BAD! SAY JUST AS GOOD. FICKLENESS
2TRU III	(91)	PART OF IT? THE COUNTESS VALBRIONI WOULD LIKE TO	KNOW	. /AUBREY/ WE MAY AS WELL BE FRANK UP TO THE POINT AT
APPL I	(224)	YOU ARE A GENTLEMAN, SIR. WE SHANT RUB IT IN, YOU	KNOW	. /BALBUS/ EVER THE BEST OF FRIENDS. I AM THE LAST TO
PRES	(136)	RUN, BELIEVE ME! IVE SEEN PLENTY OF IT; AND I	KNOW	. /BALSQUITH/ I HAVNT; AND I DONT KNOW. I WISH THOSE
FANY EPILOG	(334)	A LITTLE LIKE BERNARD SHAW. THE FABIAN TOUCH, YOU	KNOW	. /BANNAL/ (COMING TO HER ENCOURAGINGLY) A JOLLY GOOD
GENV IV	(94)	COULD YOU DO, FACTS OR NO FACTS? /SIR O./ I DONT	KNOW	. /BATTLER/ /BBDE/ YOU DONT KNOW! ! ! /SIR O./ I
GENV IV	(127)	STEADY, GONNY, STEADY! MUSTNT BE RUDE, YOU	KNOW	. /BEGONIA/ OH, WHAT DOES IT MATTER NOW? AS WE SHALL
CLEO PRO2	(98)	NO RELIGION. I HAVE FOUGHT AGAINST THEM; AND I	KNOW	. /BELZANOR/ (DERISIVELY) WERE YOU FRIGHTENED,
WIDO I	(23)	IT AS SETTLED. YOU HAVNT MADE ANY PROMISE, YOU	KNOW	. /BLANCHE/ (EARNESTLY) YES, I HAVE: I PROMISED PAPA
CAPT II	(261)	HER. HURTING YOUR UNCLE WONT DO HER ANY GOOD, YOU	KNOW	. /BRASSBOUND/ IT WILL TEACH OTHER SCOUNDRELS TO
MTH2	(65)	UNANSWERED? /CONRAD/ WE HAVNT ASKED YOU ANY, YOU	KNOW	. /BURGE/ MAY I TAKE THAT AS A MARK OF CONFIDENCE?
CAND II	(115)	/MORELL/ (SHORTLY, WRITING A TELEGRAM) I DONT	KNOW	. /BURGESS/ (SENTIMENTALLY) HE TALKS VERY PRETTY. I
CLEO III	(157)	THE RUBICON MAY BE IN THESE PAPERS, FOR ALL WE	KNOW	. /CAESAR/ PUT THEM IN THE FIRE. /BRITANNUS/ PUT THEM--
MTH1 II	(29)	OR FATIGUE-- /EVE/ SELFISH AND IDLE, CAIN. I	KNOW	. /CAIN/ SELFISH, YES: A LIFE IN WHICH NO MAN IS HIS
HART II	(111)	THE FACE OF PROVIDENCE, IF THATS WHAT YOU WANT TO	KNOW	. /CAPTAIN SHOTOVER/ GUINNESS: YOU REMEMBER THIS MAN..
KING I	(170)	ANY NAME? /SALLY/ NO, SIR. SHE SAID YOUD	KNOW	. /CHARLES/ A DUCHESS, WOULD YOU SAY? /SALLY/ OH NO,
PHIL I	(91)	CUTHBERTSON MAY BE OFFENDED ALREADY FOR ALL I	KNOW	. /CHARTERIS/ OH, NEVER MIND ABOUT HIM. MRS TRANFIELD
WIDO I	(17)	MARIA, ABOUT BLANCHE AND ME. TO TELL HER, YOU	KNOW	. /COKANE/ TELL HER ABOUT BLANCHE AND YOU! TELL HER
GENV I	(47)	IS LIVING IN. /SHE/ HE'S AN ENGLISH BISHOP, YOU	KNOW	. /COMMISSAR/ WELL? IS HE NOT A RATIONAL HUMAN BEING?
MTH3	(96)	WHO COULD DO NOTHING COULDNT HAVE DONE THAT, YOU	KNOW	. /CONFUCIUS/ I DID NOT SAY YOU COULD DO NOTHING. YOU
MTH3	(133)	WE TO DO? SOMETHING MUST BE DONE ABOUT IT, YOU	KNOW	. /CONFUCIUS/ LET US SIT STILL, AND MEDITATE IN SILENCE
PHIL II	(130)	JULIA'S REALLY A MOST DETERMINED WOMAN, YOU	KNOW	. /CRAVEN/ (STARTING UP) WELL, UPON MY LIFE! UPON MY
PHIL II	(98)	DAN? WHY NOT? WE CANT GET ON WITHOUT IT, YOU	KNOW	. /CRAVEN/ (WITH SINCERE FEELING) I GOT TO BE VERY
BARB III	(334)	IN THE EYE! WHY, I GET ONLY EIGHT HUNDRED, YOU	KNOW	. /CUSINS/ BY THE WAY, MAC, I AM A CLASSICAL SCHOLAR,
BARB I	(266)	KNOW IT, I ASSURE YOU. YOU LOOK ALL RIGHT, YOU	KNOW	. /CUSINS/ LET ME ADVISE YOU TO STUDY GREEK, MR
NEVR I	(213)	DROP IT. WE DIDNT THINK YOUD MIND. I DONT WANT TO	KNOW	. /DOLLY/ (COMING OFF THE TABLE) I'M SURE I DONT. OH,
NEVR I	(213)	LIES WE TELL, WE REPLIED TRUTHFULLY THAT WE DIDNT	KNOW	. /DOLLY/ NEITHER DID WE. /PHILIP/ SH! THE RESULT WAS
CAPT I	(223)	APPRENTICE, AS YR MAWT SY? /RANKIN/ I DONT	KNOW	. /DRINKWATER/ GAWDN, GAVNER, GAWDN. GAWDN O KAWTOOM--
JOAN 5	(112)	(CONTINUING HEEDLESSLY) A HEALTHY LIFE, YOU	KNOW	. /DUNOIS/ BUT A DULL ONE. /BLUEBEARD/ YOU WILL FIND
JITT III	(63)	SAY THAT TO YOUR FATHER. YOU TAKE AFTER HIM, YOU	KNOW	. /EDITH/ IF I DO I MUST TAKE CARE NOT TO MAKE THE
JITT II	(36)	BETTER WHAT HE WAS THAN YOU ARE YET OLD ENOUGH TO	KNOW	. /EDITH/ (RISING AND PACING RESTLESSLY ACROSS THE
HART II	(84)	HAS BEEN TALKING TO ME ABOUT YOU. YOU AND ME, YOU	KNOW	. /ELLIE/ (INTERESTED) THE CAPTAIN! WHAT DID HE SAY?
HART I	(64)	I WAS YOUR AGE. HE IS REALLY RATHER SPLENDID, YOU	KNOW	. /ELLIE/ (TURNING ON HER) SPLENDID! YES: SPLENDID
MILL III	(180)	IF YOU LOOK ROUND A BIT. THERE ARE OTHERS, YOU	KNOW	. /EPIFANIA/ GIVE ME THE ADDRESS OF THE OTHERS. IF I AM
MILL IV	(210)	A MAD DOG. YOU ARE A BLOATED CAPITALIST, YOU	KNOW	. /EPIFANIA/ I AM A CAPITALIST HERE; BUT IN RUSSIA I
MILL III	(184)	/THE MAN/ HERE! I'M NOT YOUR CLERK, YOU	KNOW	. /EPIFANIA/ YOU WILL BE, SOON. DO AS I TELL YOU. /THE
BUOY 1	(11)	TO LIVE ON AN OLD AGE PENSION! THAT HAPPENS, YOU	KNOW	. /FATHER/ IN OUR CASE IT HAPPENS THE OTHER WAY. THERE
MTH2	(70)	DIVINE PURPOSE, HE WILL COME OUT ALL RIGHT, YOU	KNOW	. /FRANKLYN/ THE KAISER FELT LIKE THAT. DID HE COME OUT
FANY I	(282)	WOULD THAT DO, OLD DEAR? THERE ARE OTHERS, YOU	KNOW	. /GILBEY/ THATS TRUE. I MUST SEND THE BOY HIMSELF
MIS.	(186)	THIS ISNT ALCOHOL. SLOE GIN. VEGETARIAN, YOU	KNOW	. /GUNNER/ (HESITATING) IS IT A FRUIT BEVERAGE?
MTH2	(38)	(IN GHOSTLY TONES) WE'RE NOT CHURCH PEOPLE, YOU	KNOW	. /HASLAM/ OH, I DONT MIND THAT, IF YOU DONT. THE
GENV I	(30)	CONDUCT IT ALL RIGHT. IT'S NEVER IN A HURRY, YOU	KNOW	. /HE/ BUT REALLY-- PARDON ME IF I AM TAKING TOO MUCH
LIED	(196)	KNOWS! HOWEVER, YOURE A POET, AND YOU OUGHT TO	KNOW	. /HE/ WHAT DOES IT MATTER-- NOW? /SHE/ IT MATTERS A
GENV I	(32)	/SHE/ THEY ARE. BUT I MUSTNT TAKE BRIBES, YOU	KNOW	. /HE/ YOU NEED NOT. ANY FRIENDLY SERVICE I MAY BE ABLE
PYGM II	(218)	REALLY AMAZING. I HAVNT TAKEN HALF OF IT IN, YOU	KNOW	. /HIGGINS/ WOULD YOU LIKE TO GO OVER ANY OF IT AGAIN?
MIS.	(144)	MIGHT BE-- /LORD SUMMERHAYS/ HIS DAUGHTER: YES, I	KNOW	. /HYPATIA/ I WAS GOING TO SAY HIS GRANDDAUGHTER. /LORD
SIM II	(71)	WELL, IT'S HARDLY WHAT WE WERE LED TO EXPECT, YOU	KNOW	. /JANGA/ " THE HEAVENS SHALL PASS AWAY WITH A GREAT
FANY III	(299)	THINGS A BIT. DENMARK HILL ISNT CAMBERWELL, YOU	KNOW	. /JUGGINS/ I HAVE NOTICED, SIR, THAT DENMARK HILL
FANY III	(310)	SUIT YOU IF YOURE DISSATISFIED-- IN REASON, YOU	KNOW	. /JUGGINS/ I REALIZE MY ADVANTAGES, SIR; BUT IVE
FANY III	(311)	TO PART WITH YOU. YOUR BROTHER ISNT A DUKE, YOU	KNOW	. /JUGGINS/ UNFORTUNATELY, HE IS, SIR. TOGETHER
BULL IV	(176)	(GOODHUMOREDLY) WELL, YES, I'M AFRAID I DO, YOU	KNOW	. /KEEGAN/ THEN PERHAPS YOU WILL CONFESS TO THE ASS'S
BULL IV	(154)	WAS TOO BIG A JOKE TO SWALLOW ALL AT ONCE, YOU	KNOW	. /KEEGAN/ YOU MUST ALSO ALLOW FOR THE FACT THAT I AM
JOAN 2	(75)	WILL READ IT FOR YOU IF YOU LIKE. I CAN READ, YOU	KNOW	. /LA TREMOUILLE/ (WITH INTENSE CONTEMPT, NOT AT ALL
BARB I	(263)	IT MUST BE A REGULAR CORKER FOR HIM, DONT YOU	KNOW	. /LADY BRITOMART/ IS THIS A MOMENT TO GET ON MY
BARB I	(263)	THERES NOTHING TO BE EXACTLY PROUD OF, DONT YOU	KNOW	. /LADY BRITOMART/ WELL, TRY AND LOOK AS IF THERE WAS.
JITT II	(28)	KNOW ANYTHING. YOU WERE SO INTIMATE WITH HIM, YOU	KNOW	. /LENKHEIM/ WAS I REALLY INTIMATE WITH HIM? CERTAINLY
GETT	(317)	THEYLL BE HIS CHILDREN AS WELL AS YOURS, YOU	KNOW	. /LEO/ DONT BE INDELICATE, REJJY. /EDITH/ YOU ARE
MIS.	(173)	I WAS GLAD TO GET BACK TO THE OFFICE. NOW YOU	KNOW	. /LINA/ COME TO THE GYMNASIUM: I'LL TEACH YOU HOW TO
PYGM V	(278)	YOU TO SPEAK; AND I COULDNT HAVE DONE THAT, YOU	KNOW	. /LIZA/ (TRIVIALLY) OF COURSE: THAT IS HIS
MIS.	(143)	WELL, ISNT IT? BEING A MAN, YOU OUGHT TO	KNOW	. /LORD SUMMERHAYS/ IT REQUIRES SOME NATURAL TALENT,
PPP	(198)	PLEASE NOT POOR ADOLPHUS YET. I STILL LIVE, YOU	KNOW	. /MAGNESIA/ THE VITAL SPARK BUT FLASHES BEFORE IT
APPL I	(229)	(CONSOLING HIM) THATS THE CONSTITUTION, YOU	KNOW	. /MAGNUS/ QUITE. I ONLY MENTION IT TO SHEW THAT THE
APPL I	(207)	PERHAPS NOT. STILL, I AM A REPUBLICAN, YOU	KNOW	. /MAGNUS/ THAT IS WHAT HAS ALWAYS SURPRISED ME. DO YOU
SUPR IV	(148)	TAKE CARE OF HIM. NOT A FADDY SORT OF PERSON, YOU	KNOW	. /MALONE/ SOMEBODY LIKE YOU, PERHAPS? /VIOLET/ (
FANY III	(303)	LIGHT OF IT, MEG; BUT THIS IS A BIT THICK, YOU	KNOW	. /MARGARET/ DO YOU FEEL YOU COULDNT MARRY A WOMAN WHOS
FANY III	(305)	DOES HIM CREDIT: HE ALWAYS WAS A GENTLEMAN, YOU	KNOW	. /MARGARET/ DOES HIM CREDIT! TO INSULT YOU LIKE
SUPR III	(78)	OR SHOW-FOOR? IT MAKES ALL THE DIFFERENCE, YOU	KNOW	. /MENDOZA/ (EXPLAINING) WE SHOULD EXPECT RANSOM FOR A
PRES	(133)	WE KNEW WHAT IT WAS. IT WAS UNWORKABLE, YOU	KNOW	. /MITCHENER/ I DONT KNOW. WHY IS IT UNWORKABLE?
CAND II	(125)	THAT, JAMES. IT'S ONY THAT IT AINT SUNDAY, YOU	KNOW	. /MORELL/ I'M SORRY. I THOUGHT YOU MIGHT LIKE TO BE
JITT I	(10)	GIRL/ (GRINNING) OH, IT'S NOTHING TO ME. BUT I	KNOW	. /MRS BILLITER/ YOU KNOW TOO MUCH, YOU DO. ARE THEY
GETT	(301)	THINK IT QUITE LIKELY. BUT OF COURSE I DONT	KNOW	. /MRS BRIDGENORTH/ BUT BLESS ME! MARRIAGE IS NOT A
NEVR I	(213)	/GLORIA/ (ADVANCING) MOTHER: WE HAVE A RIGHT TO	KNOW	. /MRS CLANDON/ (RISING AND FACING HER) GLORIA! "
DOCT IV	(170)	AND SETTLE EVERYTHING. THATS THE LAW, YOU	KNOW	. /MRS DUBEDAT/ OH, THANK YOU: I DIDNT KNOW. (SIR
FANY I	(283)	HATS WITH HIM? /DORA/ I DONT KNOW. ONE DOES, YOU	KNOW	. /MRS GILBEY/ I NEVER DID. THE THINGS PEOPLE DO! I
FANY III	(319)	SHE DOESNT KNOW ABOUT-- ABOUT HIS GRACE, YOU	KNOW	. /MRS GILBEY/ PERHAPS SHE DOES. DOES SHE, MR JUGGINS?
HART II	(108)	/THE BURGLAR/ IT'S COMPOUNDING A FELONY, YOU	KNOW	. /MRS HUSHABYE/ THIS IS UTTERLY RIDICULOUS. ARE WE TO
OVER	(176)	ASKING THEM TO THROW ME OUT? YOU OUGHT TO, YOU	KNOW	. /MRS JUNO/ WHAT! MAKE A SCANDAL IN THE FACE OF THE
BUOY III	(34)	GET OVER. SHE KNOWS THINGS A LADY OUGHT NOT TO	KNOW	. /MRS THIRDBORN/ INCLUDING SOME THINGS NOBODY OUGHT TO
MRS II	(199)	SO MUCH AS HER MOTHER. SHE AINT SO HANDSOME, YOU	KNOW	. /MRS WARREN/ (TAKEN ABACK BY HIS ASSURANCE) WELL,
DEST	(158)	OTHERWISE AT HAVING SOME REMARKABLE NEWS) I DONT	KNOW	. /NAPOLEON/ (UNABLE TO BELIEVE HIS EARS) YOU DONT
KING I	(184)	WIG. /LOUISE/ BUT YOU ARE AN ALCHEMIST: YOU MUST	KNOW	. /NEWTON/ THEN I AM NOT AN ALCHEMIST. BUT THE CHANGING
APPL I	(215)	JOE! DONT MAKE A SCENE. YOU ASKED FOR IT, YOU	KNOW	. /NICOBAR/ WHAT DO YOU GO PROVOKING LIZZIE FOR LIKE
BULL II	(112)	REILLY. MY NAME IS BROADBENT. LARRY'S FRIEND, YOU	KNOW	. /NORA/ (CHILLED) AND HAS MR DOYLE NOT COME WITH
BUOY IV	(49)	IT. /OLD BILL/ WHATS HIS NAME? /SHE/ I DONT	KNOW	. /OLD BILL/ THE DEVIL YOU DONT! /SHE/ (TO HIM) WHATS
BUOY IV	(48)	IS EMPTY THE GODS TAKE POSSESSION. AND THE GODS	KNOW	. /OLD BILL/ YES: I SUPPOSE THATS IT. BUT IT'S A QUEER
MILL I	(165)	/ALASTAIR/ NO: THAT SOUNDS SILLY. LITERARY, YOU	KNOW	. /PATRICIA/ MORE OF A MIND MATE, I SHOULD CALL IT.
MIS.	(195)	MIGHT HAVE SOME SORT OF PREFERENCE FOR PATSY, YOU	KNOW	. /PERCIVAL/ WELL, BUT DOES THAT MATTER, DO YOU THINK?
NEVR II	(241)	ISNT IT? IT'S JUST AS BAD FOR US, YOU	KNOW	. /PHILIP/ SH! DOLLY: WE ARE BOTH WANTING IN TACT. (
PYGM II	(242)	THEIR PLACE A BIT. I WOULDNT SPEAK TO THEM, YOU	KNOW	. /PICKERING/ BETTER WAIT TIL WE GET YOU SOMETHING
MRS I	(186)	WHAT YOU HOPE AS WHAT YOU BELIEVE, THAT I WANT TO	KNOW	. /PRAED/ WELL, FRANKLY, I AM AFRAID YOUR MOTHER WILL
SIM II	(57)	IT. /HYERING/ THEY DARENT USE THEIR BOMBS, YOU	KNOW	. /PRA/ TRUE; BUT WHAT IS TO PREVENT THEM FROM TAKING
SIM II	(72)	/MRS HYERING/ BUT WHICH? THATS WHAT I WANT TO	KNOW	. /PROLA/ THERE IS NOTHING NEW IN THIS TAKING OF THE
ARMS III	(51)	STORY ABOUT THE ICE PUDDING WAS A-- A-- A-- YOU	KNOW	. /RAINA/ (WINCING) AH, DONT TALK OF IT IN THAT
CURE	(228)	LOATHE IT. /THE DOCTOR/ THATS VERY SERIOUS, YOU	KNOW	. /REGINALD/ WHY IS IT SERIOUS? /THE DOCTOR/ WELL,
DOCT III	(139)	ESPECIALLY YOU, RIDGEON. I HAD YOU THAT TIME, YOU	KNOW	. /RIDGEON/ HOW, PRAY? /LOUIS/ WELL, YOU SET UP TO
DOCT II	(129)	/SIR PATRICK/ PERHAPS SHE WONT HAVE YOU, YOU	KNOW	. /RIDGEON/ (WITH A SELF-ASSURED SHAKE OF THE HEAD)
DOCT I	(85)	AND BELSIZE AVENUE. LOONY SCHUTZMACHER, YOU	KNOW	. /RIDGEON/ WHAT! LOONY! (HE SHAKES HANDS
MTH2	(69)	/HASLAM/ GOD COUNTS FOREIGNERS, YOU	KNOW	. /SAVVY/ (WITH INTENSE SATISFACTION) WELL SAID, BILL.
ROCK II	(275)	AND WAS JEALOUS OF YOU. THE EDIPUS COMPLEX, YOU	KNOW	. /SIR ARTHUR/ AND WHAT DID HE SAY TO THAT? /ALOYSIA/
ROCK II	(275)	HE TOLD ME TO GO TO HELL. HE'S LIKE THAT, YOU	KNOW	. /SIR ARTHUR/ YES, A HASTY BOY. /ALOYSIA/ HE IS, JUST
ROCK I	(212)	WELL, THE UNEMPLOYED ARE-- WELL, UNEMPLOYED, YOU	KNOW	. /SIR ARTHUR/ WE HAVE PROVIDED FOR THE UNEMPLOYED.
CAPT III	(276)	IT WILL LOOK SO DREADFUL. YOUR OWN NEPHEW, YOU	KNOW	. /SIR HOWARD/ CICELY: AN ENGLISH JUDGE HAS NO NEPHEWS,

GENV IV	(95)	OF INTEREST, YOU SAID FRANKLY YOU DID NOT	KNOW	. /SIR O./ WELL, I DONT. /BATTLER/ AND YOU CALL
GENV II	(63)	MY SHIP COMES HOME: THE SIX HUNDRED A YEAR, YOU	KNOW	. /SIR O./ WILL A FIVE POUND NOTE BE ANY USE (HE
CURE	(233)	/REGINALD/ (RAVISHED) OH! I CAN STAND THAT, YOU	KNOW	. /STREGA/ (IRONICALLY, STILL PRELUDING) THANK YOU.
2TRU III	(86)	IF IT ISNT, WHERE ARE WE? THATS WHAT I WANT TO	KNOW	. /SWEETIE/ AND IS THIS ALL YOU CARE ABOUT? SITTING
DEVL III	(65)	IS HE HERE? /CHRISTY/ (STARING ROUND) I DONT	KNOW	. /SWINDON/ DO YOU SEE HIM? /CHRISTY/ NO. /SWINDON/
SUPR I	(44)	WHY SHOULD THEY NOT? /VIOLET/ BUT THEY DONT	KNOW	. /TANNER/ DONT KNOW WHAT? /VIOLET/ THEY DONT KNOW
FABL VI	(125)	DEVIL DOES ANYBODY KNOW? YOU DONT KNOW. I DONT	KNOW	. /TEACHER/ WHY DONT WE KNOW? /YOUTH 2/ BECAUSE WE
MTH3	(108)	DROWNED FOUR TIMES OVER. YOU ARE NOT A CAT, YOU	KNOW	. /THE ARCHBISHOP/ THAT IS VERY EASY TO UNDERSTAND.
GETT	(285)	TO LET THEM? THEY MAY BE MARRIED WOMEN, YOU	KNOW	. /THE BISHOP/ THEY ALWAYS ARE. THIS ONE IS. (TO MRS
GETT	(281)	DISTINCTION, LEO. /LEO/ JUST OCCASIONALLY, YOU	KNOW	. /THE BISHOP/ (SITTING DOWN COSILY BESIDE HER) QUITE
GETT	(340)	/MRS GEORGE/ ONE THING I SHOULD LIKE YOU TO	KNOW	. /THE BISHOP/ YES? /MRS GEORGE/ WE DIDNT CHEAT YOUR
SIM I	(48)	THE IDIOT. /MRS HYERING/ OH! I AM SORRY: I DIDNT	KNOW	. /THE CLERGYMAN/ NOT AT ALL. MY SISTER WAS THE KIDDY;
LION II	(129)	GO INTO THE ARENA WITH THE REST, MY HONOR, YOU	KNOW	. /THE EDITOR/ HONOR! THE HONOR OF A TAILOR?
MTH4 III	(195)	TO HER. SHE WONT WAIT HERE ALL DAY FOR YOU, YOU	KNOW	. /THE ELDERLY GENTLEMAN/ (RISING VERY DEFERENTIALLY
GETT	(282)	EMPIRE, BOXER. YOURE A BRITISH GENERAL, YOU	KNOW	. /THE GENERAL/ WHAT HAS THAT TO DO WITH POLYGAMY?
GETT	(287)	OF MARRIAGE. I'M JUST AT THE ROMAN BUSINESS, YOU	KNOW	. /THE GENERAL/ (COMING FROM THE GARDEN DOOR TO THE
INCA	(246)	WILL GET HIS MONEY BACK. NOBODY WOULD BUY IT, YOU	KNOW	. /THE INCA/ MAY I ASK WHY? /ERMYNTRUDE/ WELL, LOOK AT
INCA	(248)	HIM. /ERMYNTRUDE/ WELL, HE STARTED IT, YOU	KNOW	. /THE INCA/ MADAM, BE JUST. WHEN THE HUNTERS SURROUND
GENV III	(79)	NEWCOMER/ I'M A RETIRED BUILDER, IF YOU WANT TO	KNOW	. /THE JUDGE/ HE HAS HAD ABILITY ENOUGH TO CONDUCT A
CURE	(231)	(RETREATING TIMIDLY) IT'S MY ROOM, YOU	KNOW	. /THE LADY/ IT'S NOTHING OF THE SORT. IT'S THE DUCHESS
INCA	(242)	THE HOUSE WHENEVER ANYONE WASHES HIS HANDS, I	KNOW	. /THE MANAGER/ (GALLANT) YOU ARE HARD TO PLEASE,
MTH2	(45)	TO DO WITH IT? HE MAY LIVE AS LONG AS YOU, YOU	KNOW	. /THE PARLOR MAID/ THATS JUST IT, SIR. YOU SEE, HE
SIM PRO,3,	(33)	DEVOTION IN WOMEN. HE ONCE DID IN ME; SO I	KNOW	. /THE PRIEST/ DONT BE VINDICTIVE, PROLA. I DONT DO IT
SIM PRO,3,	(31)	GOD HAS MANY NAMES. /THE L.T./ NOT WITH US, YOU	KNOW	. /THE PRIEST/ YES: EVEN WITH YOU. THE FATHER, THE SON,
2TRU III	(82)	HERSELF NO AIRS) YOU NEEDNT STAND UP FOR ME, YOU	KNOW	. /THE SERGEANT/ (STIFFLY) BEG PARDON, YOUR LADYSHIP.
MTH5	(256)	WE COULD MANAGE PRETTY WELL BY OURSELVES, YOU	KNOW	. /THE SHE-ANCIENT/ TELL ME, ACIS: DO YOU EVER THINK OF
JOAN EPILOG	(161)	COMFORT TO ME. FOR I AM NOT CRUEL BY NATURE, YOU	KNOW	. /THE SOLDIER/ WHO SAID YOU WERE? /DE STOGUMBER/
GENV I	(37)	ATTEND TO. IT'S ONLY INTELLECTUAL BUSINESS, YOU	KNOW	. /THE WIDOW/ BUT DO THEY NOT TAKE PART IN THE ASSEMBLY
POSN	(459)	GOT TO TELL US THE TRUTH. THATS THE LAW, YOU	KNOW	. /THE WOMAN/ THE MAN LOOKED A BAD MAN. HE CURSED ME;
SIM PRO,1,	(24)	LOOK HERE: YOU CANT GO ON LIKE THIS, YOU	KNOW	. /THE Y.W./ WHAT WERE YOU GOING TO DO WITH YOURSELF
MTH5	(208)	/THE MAIDEN/ (TRAGICALLY PENSIVE) I DONT	KNOW	. /THE YOUTH/ THEN THERE IS SOMETHING THE MATTER. IS
WIDO III	(63)	DO YOU KNOW THAT YOU AINT? THATS WHAT WE WANT TO	KNOW	. /TRENCH/ (SULKILY) I WONT HAVE THE RELATIONS BETWEEN
BARB I	(268)	AT LEAST UNLESS YOURE DOWNRIGHT IMMORAL, DONT YOU	KNOW	. /UNDERSHAFT/ YOU HARDLY APPRECIATE MY POSITION, MR
BARB I	(267)	SHOCKED) BUT NOT YOUR SORT OF BLOOD AND FIRE, YOU	KNOW	. /UNDERSHAFT/ MY SORT OF BLOOD CLEANSES: MY SORT OF
BARB III	(316)	YOU MAY HAVE GOOD BLOOD IN YOUR VEINS FOR ALL YOU	KNOW	. /UNDERSHAFT/ TRUE. PROBABLY I HAVE. THAT IS ANOTHER
NEVR III	(266)	AT, MRS CLANDON? /MRS CLANDON/ I THINK YOU	KNOW	. /VALENTINE/ GLORIA? /MRS CLANDON/ YES, GLORIA.
NEVR II	(255)	STRENGTH'S INFECTIOUS. /GLORIA/ WEAKNESS IS, I	KNOW	. /VALENTINE/ (WITH CONVICTION) YOURE STRONG. DO YOU
SIM II	(58)	HIM, NOT I. /MAYA/ WE WERE YOUNG: WE DID NOT	KNOW	. /VASHTI/ HELP US, PRA. YOU HAVE LOST FAITH IN US; BUT
FABL VI	(124)	WHY DOES SHE TELL LIES? THAT IS WHAT I WANT TO	KNOW	. /YOUTH 3/ THE SPHINX STORY IS ROT. WHY SHOULD THE
VWOO 2	(126)	TWO: THATS TWO AND TENPENCE, ISNT IT? /A/ I DONT	KNOW	. /Z/ HOVIS, TUPPENCE HALFPENNY. THREE SHILLINGS AND A
BARB II	(281)	OF ANYBODY BUT MYSELF. /BARBARA/ (GUESSING) I	KNOW	. SECULARIST? /SHIRLEY/ (HOTLY) DID I OFFER TO DENY
GETT	(304)	US GOOD ADVICE-- TOLD US WHAT TO DO WHEN WE DIDNT	KNOW	. SHE FOUND OUT THAT I WASNT ANY USE TO HER AND HE WAS;
GETT	(351)	I SHOULD LIKE YOU TO DROP IN AFTER A WHILE, YOU	KNOW	. SHE GETS SO CROSS AND UPSET WHEN THERES NOBODY TO
AUGS	(274)	THAT FOR? /THE LADY/ I CANT IMAGINE. BUT THIS I	KNOW	. SHE MADE A BET WITH HIM THAT SHE WOULD COME DOWN HERE
HART I	(71)	THE GARDEN WITH MISS DUNN? /MRS HUSHABYE/ I DONT	KNOW	. SHE QUARRELLED MORTALLY WITH MY HUSBAND ONLY TEN
GETT	(329)	WHEN YOU ARE THE HUSBAND? SHE ISNT CLEVER, YOU	KNOW	. SHE'S ONLY SILLY-CLEVER. /HOTCHKISS/ (UNEASILY
SHAK	(142)	TO MEND THEM. /SHAKES/ TAUGHT WHAT YOU COULD NOT	KNOW	. SING IF YOU CAN MY CLOUD CAPPED TOWERS, MY GORGEOUS
FOUN	(211)	NO: WHAT I WANT IS A WIFE. NOT A YOUNG WOMAN, YOU	KNOW	. SOMEONE OLD ENOUGH TO BE MY MOTHER: SAY THIRTY OR SO.
BARB I	(270)	RATHER A STRONG ORDER TO BEGIN WITH, DONT YOU	KNOW	. SUPPOSE I SING THOURT PASSING HENCE, MY BROTHER. IT'S
MIS.	(144)	SUMMERHAYS/ DONT ASK ME. I DONT KNOW. I DONT	KNOW	. TARLETON RETURNS FROM THE VESTIBULE. HYPATIA SITS
GENV II	(60)	O./ I MEAN WHAT EVERYBODY MEANS. SANCTIONS, YOU	KNOW	. THAT IS PLAIN ENGLISH. OIL, FOR INSTANCE. /JUDGE/
JOAN EPILOG	(161)	WHAT CRUELTY WAS LIKE. I HAD NOT SEEN IT, YOU	KNOW	. THAT IS THE GREAT THING: YOU MUST SEE IT. AND THEN
PRES	(142)	YOU KNOW-- /BALSQUITH/ STOP. STOP, I SAY. I DONT	KNOW	. THAT IS THE DIFFERENCE BETWEEN YOUR JOB AND MINE.
MIS.	(129)	OF COLERIDGE OR HERBERT SPENCER KIND OF CARD, YOU	KNOW	. THAT WAS THE SECOND FATHER. THEN HIS MOTHER WAS AN
JOAN EPILOG	(159)	NOBLE CAPTAIN: I HAVE A DAY OFF. EVERY YEAR, YOU	KNOW	. THATS MY ALLOWANCE FOR MY ONE GOOD ACTION. /CAUCHON/
POSN	(445)	WHAT MADE ME SUCH A FOOL? THATS WHAT I WANT TO	KNOW	. THATS THE GREAT SECRET. /ELDER DANIELS/ (AT THE
BULL III	(123)	YOU LAUGHING AT? /LARRY/ (STOPPING DEAD) I DONT	KNOW	. THATS THE SORT OF THING AN IRISHMAN LAUGHS AT. HAS
MRS I	(184)	THE THIRD WRANGLER. JUST THE RIGHT PLACE, YOU	KNOW	. THE FIRST WRANGLER IS ALWAYS A DREAMY, MORBID FELLOW,
FABL II	(107)	OURSELVES MAY HAVE IT UP ITS SLEEVE FOR ALL WE	KNOW	. THE GAS MAY COME IN AT THAT WINDOW WHILE WE ARE
MIS.	(155)	THE DEVIL ARE THEY? /LORD SUMMERHAYS/ I THINK I	KNOW	. THE LAST TIME I SAW THAT LADY, SHE DID SOMETHING I
KING I	(172)	ROWLEY. /NELLY/ (RUNNING TO FOX) I KNOW. I	KNOW	. THE MAN IN THE LEATHER BREECHES. /FOX/ (STUBBORNLY
FANY II	(291)	MADE YOU GET OUT OF THE BUS? /MARGARET/ I DONT	KNOW	. THE MEETING GOT ON MY NERVES, SOMEHOW. IT WAS THE
O'FL	(220)	YOUR TEMPER ABOUT IT. I ONLY THOUGHT I'D LIKE TO	KNOW	. THE NICE FOOL I'D LOOK IF I WENT ABOUT SHEWING OFF A
MRS II	(213)	MOTHER PRETENDED HE WAS A GENTLEMAN; BUT I DONT	KNOW	. THE OTHER TWO WERE ONLY HALF SISTERS: UNDERSIZED,
GENV II	(54)	ALWAYS DO: THE REAL LADIES AND GENTLEMEN, YOU	KNOW	. THE OTHERS ARE ODDITIES AND OUTSIDERS. IF YOU WANT TO
KING I	(210)	SAY, MR KNELLER? /KNELLER/ SIR: I DO NOT SAY: I	KNOW	. THE RIGHT LINE, THE LINE OF BEAUTY, IS A CURVE. MY
SIM I	(40)	THE NAME OF THE MORNING STAR. PHOSPHORUS, YOU	KNOW	. THE STUFF THEY MAKE MATCHES WITH. SUCH A NAME TO
MTH5	(256)	IT IF I WERE YOU. YOU HAVE TO KEEP SANE, YOU	KNOW	. THE TWO ANCIENTS LOOK AT ONE ANOTHER; SHRUG THEIR
SUPR I	(21)	(INNOCENTLY) OH, IS THERE HARM IN IT? I DIDNT	KNOW	. THEN I CERTAINLY WONT CALL YOU THAT. MAY I CALL YOU
JITT III	(72)	YOU CANT PUT ME OFF THAT WAY. I TELL YOU I	KNOW	. THERE IS SOME WOMAN WHO WAS REAL TO MY FATHER; AND HE
GETT	(350)	HAPPENED TO THE WEDDING PARTY? /SYKES/ I DONT	KNOW	. THERE WASNT A SOUL IN THE CHURCH WHEN WE WERE MARRIED
POSN	(452)	/THE FOREMAN/ BESIDES, YOU NEEDNT HANG HIM, YOU	KNOW	. THERES PLENTY OF WILLING HANDS TO TAKE THAT JOB OFF
SUPR III	(128)	HURT YOU. YOUR FRIENDS ARE ALL THE DULLEST DOGS I	KNOW	. THEY ARE NOT BEAUTIFUL: THEY ARE ONLY DECORATED. THEY
INCA	(243)	INDEED? WHICH SON? /THE PRINCESS/ I DONT	KNOW	. THEY HAVNT SETTLED WHICH. IT'S A DREADFUL THING TO BE
JOAN 1	(64)	HIS MOTHER SAYS HE ISNT; AND SHE OUGHT TO	KNOW	. THINK OF THAT! THE QUEEN DENYING THE LEGITIMACY OF
2TRU II	(76)	POSSIBLY WANT WITH MAROONS? /TALLBOYS/ I DONT	KNOW	. THIS EXPEDITION HAS BEEN SENT OUT WITHOUT THE
JITT III	(71)	TABLE, AND HALF SITTING AGAINST ITS EDGE) YES: I	KNOW	. THIS HOUSE HAS BEEN A SORT OF MADHOUSE SINCE MY
FANY III	(310)	AND RETIRING TO THE HEARTHRUG IN DUDGEON) OH, I	KNOW	. VERY WELL: GO. THE SOONER THE BETTER. /MRS GILBEY/
MTH3	(106)	YEAR 1910. AM I A THIEF? /CONFUCIUS/ I DO NOT	KNOW	. WAS THAT ONE OF YOUR PROFESSIONS? /THE ARCHBISHOP/
BUOY II	(21)	DO WE GO ON TALKING TO ONEANOTHER? /SHE/ I DONT	KNOW	. WE ARE DANGEROUS TO ONEANOTHER. FINISH YOUR FOOD; AND
BUOY PREFACE	(5)	ESSENTIALLY THE SAME AS A PLAYWRIGHT? I DO NOT	KNOW	. WE BOTH GOT SOME SATISFACTION FROM IT OR WE WOULD NOT
SUPR III	(99)	NOT THAT WE DONT ADMIRE YOUR INTELLECT, YOU	KNOW	. WE DO. BUT I LOOK AT THE MATTER FROM YOUR OWN POINT
FABL VI	(128)	KNOW. HOW OLD IS THE WORLD? /TEACHER/ WE DO NOT	KNOW	. WE LOST COUNT IN THE DARK AGES THAT FOLLOWED THE
BULL IV	(169)	WELL, WE MUSNT BE STIFF AND STAND-OFF, YOU	KNOW	. WE MUST BE THOROUGHLY DEMOCRATIC, AND PATRONIZE
HART II	(94)	RUIN THE BUSINESS IN A YEAR. I'VE TRIED; AND I	KNOW	. WE SHOULD SPEND TOO MUCH ON EVERYTHING. WE SHOULD
PHIL I	(86)	SUBJECT. BUT IT'S BETTER THAT CUTHBERTSON SHOULD	KNOW	. WE USED TO BE VERY CLOSE FRIENDS, AND ARE SO STILL, I
AUGS	(274)	HE BECAME BLUELOO. /THE LADY/ OH, INDEED: I DIDNT	KNOW	. WELL, BLUELOO IS SIMPLY INFATUATED WITH MY
FANY I	(278)	IT'S A SORT OF NAME IVE GOT. DARLING DORA, YOU	KNOW	. WELL, HE SAYS, " DARLING, IF YOU CAN GET HOLY JOE TO
SIM I	(46)	I DONT KNOW-- I-- /PRA/ PRECISELY. YOU DONT	KNOW	. WELL, WE DO KNOW. OUR FOUR WONDERFUL CHILDREN HAVE
BARB II	(309)	AND HE PINCHED YOUR POUND AT A QUARTER TO TWO. I	KNOW	. WELL, YOU CANT AFFORD TO LOSE IT. I'LL SEND IT TO
JITT III	(61)	MAKE YOU REALLY ILL. /EDITH/ (SCORNFULLY) YES, I	KNOW	. WHAT CANT BE CURED MUST BE ENDURED; SO LET US GET
MIS.	(176)	/TARLETON/ YOU CANT LEAVE IT AT THAT, YOU	KNOW	. WHAT DID YOU SEE MY DAUGHTER DOING? /GUNNER/ AFTER
BARB III	(342)	AND WE HAVE TO FIT THEM IN SOMEHOW, DONT YOU	KNOW	. WHAT I MEAN IS THAT YOU CANT GO CUTTING EVERYBODY;
BULL IV	(181)	THE OTHER SIDE OF THE HALL. I DIDNT ENJOY IT, YOU	KNOW	. WHAT IS IT LIKE IN YOUR DREAMS? /KEEGAN/ IN MY
GENV I	(31)	WELL, WE HAVE THEIR NAMES ON OUR NOTEPAPER, YOU	KNOW	. WHAT MORE CAN THEY DO? YOU CANT EXPECT THEM TO SIT
ROCK I	(217)	HIS LITTLE BIT OF A JOB ON COME FROM? HE DONT	KNOW	. WHAT WILL HAPPEN TO IT WHEN IT GOES OUT OF THE
O'FL	(223)	HAPPENED TO EVERYBODY? THATS WHAT I WANT TO	KNOW	. WHATS HAPPENED TO YOU THAT I THOUGHT ALL THE WORLD OF
MIS.	(170)	BROUGHT HIM A LITTLE CAPITAL. /THE MAN/ I DONT	KNOW	. WHATS THAT GOT TO DO WITH YOU? /TARLETON/ WELL, YOU
BULL III	(124)	IRISH VOICE! /LARRY/ (SYMPATHETICALLY) YES, I	KNOW	. WHEN I FIRST WENT TO LONDON I VERY NEARLY PROPOSED TO
2TRU II	(68)	IVE LIVED AT THAT ADDRESS MYSELF; AND I	KNOW	. WHEN I LOVE A MAN NOW IT'S ALL LOVE AND NOTHING ELSE.
METH PREFACE	(R71)	IN FINANCE. HOW IT WILL ALL END WE DO NOT YET	KNOW	. WHEN WOLVES COMBINE TO KILL A HORSE, THE DEATH OF THE
CAPT I	(239)	DO YOU PROPOSE TO GO? /SIR HOWARD/ I HARDLY	KNOW	. WHERE CAN WE GO, MR RANKIN? /RANKIN/ TAKE MY ADVICE,
ROCK I	(217)	HE BUY IT IF IT STOPPED COMING TO HIM? HE DONT	KNOW	. WHERE COULD HE SELL IT IF IT WAS LEFT ON HIS HANDS.
ROCK I	(217)	DONE THEIR LITTLE BITS OF JOBS ON IT? HE DONT	KNOW	. WHERE COULD HE BUY IT IF IT STOPPED COMING TO HIM?
GENV IV	(96)	INTENTIONS ARE I MUST FRANKLY SAY THAT I DONT	KNOW	. WHERE DO THEY STAND WITH US? I DONT KNOW. BUT THEY
BARB III	(327)	JAPANESE VICTORY? /UNDERSHAFT/ OH, I DONT	KNOW	. WHICH SIDE WINS DOES NOT CONCERN US HERE. NO: THE
BUOY II	(21)	ME NOW THAT YOU HAVE YOUR MEAL? /HE/ I DONT	KNOW	. WHY DO WE GO ON TALKING TO ONEANOTHER? /SHE/ I DONT

PRES	(134)	IT WAS UNWORKABLE, YOU KNOW. /MITCHENER/ I DONT	KNOW	. WHY IS IT UNWORKABLE? /BALSQUITH/ I MEAN THE PART
KING II	(223)	HOW LONG HAVE I BEEN ASLEEP? /CATHERINE/ I NOT	KNOW	. WHY LEAVE YOU YOUR THINGS ABOUT ALL OVER MY ROOM? I
JITT I	(19)	KNOWLEDGE THAT HE MUST NOT LET HIMSELF	KNOW	. YES: HE NOT ONLY DOES NOT KNOW: HE WILL NOT KNOW: HE
NEVR IV	(299)	I WONDER? /GLORIA/ (PETULANTLY) I DONT	KNOW	. YES, I DO KNOW. LET US GO AND SEE THE DANCING. THEY
INCA	(236)	WHAT! A LADY? OH, A PERSON. OH YES: I	KNOW	. YES, PLEASE, SEND HER UP. HAVE MY SERVANTS FINISHED
BARB III	(314)	(CUNNINGLY) NOT AS A DRUMMER, THOUGH, YOU	KNOW	. YOU ARE A VERY CLEARHEADED BRAINY CHAP, DOLLY; AND IT
VWOO 3	(141)	YOU AND ME? /A/ YOU ARE INEXPERIENCED. YOU DONT	KNOW	. YOU ARE THE DUPE OF THOUGHTLESS WORDS LIKE
SUPR II	(50)	TANNER IS GITTIN AT YOU WITH IS ENRY STRAKER, YOU	KNOW	. YOU CALL IT HENERY, BUT I DONT MIND, BLESS YOU!
MIS.	(137)	NO USE PRETENDING THEYRE ROCKS. /JOHNNY/ I DONT	KNOW	. YOU CAN DRAW A LINE AND MAKE OTHER CHAPS TOE IT.
JITT III	(58)	OF THE SCANDAL. BELIEVE ME, IT'S BETTER NOT TO	KNOW	. YOU COULD NOT HURT HER WITHOUT HURTING YOURSELF AND
CAND II	(108)	NOT ANY ONE PARTICULAR PERSON. /MARCHBANKS/ I	KNOW	. YOU FEEL THAT YOU COULD LOVE ANYBODY THAT OFFERED--
JITT II	(47)	WHAT DOES THAT TITLE-PAGE MEAN? /JITTA/ YOU	KNOW	. YOU HAVE SAID WHAT IT MEANS. /LENKHEIM/ I WANT TO
BARB III	(343)	OF MISERY. /CUSINS/ WELL, LOVE. /UNDERSHAFT/ I	KNOW	. YOU LOVE THE NEEDY AND THE OUTCAST: YOU LOVE THE
JOAN 6	(149)	HAVNT SEEN: IT IS SO EASY TO TALK WHEN YOU DONT	KNOW	. YOU MADDEN YOURSELF WITH WORDS: YOU DAMN YOURSELF
BUOY PREFACE	(4)	OR TURF BOOKMAKING OR PEDDLING, I DO NOT	KNOW	. YOU MAY SAY IT WAS BECAUSE I HAD A TALENT THAT WAY.
DOCT III	(153)	IT IS DIFFERENT WITH YOU. I FEEL THAT YOU	KNOW	. YOU MUST LISTEN TO ME, DOCTOR. (WITH SUDDEN
JITT III	(62)	MUST BE CAREFUL NOT TO IDEALIZE A PERSON YOU DONT	KNOW	. YOU SEE, EVERYBODY IS AN IDEAL PERSON TO US UNTIL WE
MTH3	(116)	/THE ARCHBISHOP/ THAT IS TRUE. BUT I SHOULD	KNOW	. YOU SHORT-LIVED PEOPLE ARE SO CHILDISH. IF I MET A
CAND II	(118)	/MORELL/ (SHOCKED) CANDIDA! /CANDIDA/ OH, I	KNOW	. YOU SILLY BOY: YOU THINK IT'S YOUR SOCIALISM AND YOUR
CATH 1	(165)	AND AGREEABLE MANNER. /PATIOMKIN/ PSHA! I	KNOW	. YOU THINK IF SHE ONCE SETS EYES ON YOUR FACE AND YOUR
CURE	(226)	HARM IN-- /THE DOCTOR/ YES, YES, YES: I KNOW, I	KNOW	. YOU THINK YOU MADE A FOOL OF YOURSELF BEFORE THAT
BULL I	(88)	TO THE ENGLISH LEVEL OF SELF-GOVERNMENT, YOU	KNOW	. YOU UNDERSTAND ME? /DOYLE/ PERFECTLY. AND ROSSCULLEN
BARB II	(280)	BUT YOULL COME TO IT YOURSELF; AND THEN YOULL	KNOW	. YOULL COME TO IT SOONER THAN A TEETOTALLER LIKE ME,
PYGM III	(254)	WORD. /PICKERING/ DONT. IT'S NOT COMPULSORY, YOU	KNOW	. YOULL GET ON QUITE WELL WITHOUT IT. /MRS EYNSFORD
JITT III	(72)	KNOW? /JITTA/ (QUICKLY) YOUR MOTHER DOES NOT	KNOW	. YOUR MOTHER COULD NEVER UNDERSTAND. /EDITH/ JITTA: DO
MRS I	(182)	MISTAKEN THE DAY. THAT WOULD BE JUST LIKE ME, YOU	KNOW	. YOUR MOTHER ARRANGED THAT SHE WAS TO COME DOWN FROM
MRS I	(191)	PRAED. I ASK YOU AS A PARTICULAR FAVOR. IF YOU DO	KNOW	(MOVEMENT OF PROTEST FROM PRAED)-- I ONLY SAY, IF YOU
JOAN 5	(117)	THE NUMBERS ON HER SIDE; AND SHE HAS WON. BUT I	KNOW	JOAN; AND I SEE THAT SOME DAY SHE WILL GO AHEAD WHEN
MIS.	(145)	WAS SO SURPRISED IN MY LIFE AS WHEN I CAME TO	KNOW	JOHNNY AS A MAN OF BUSINESS AND FOUND OUT WHAT HE WAS
MIS.	(124)	OH, I SAY NOTHING AGAINST YOUR DARLING: WE ALL	KNOW	JOHNNY'S PERFECTION. /MRS TARLETON/ DONT BE CROSS,
OVER	(190)	SELF-SACRIFICE. /GREGORY/ OH YES: IF, IF, IF. YOU	KNOW	JOLLY WELL THAT SELF-SACRIFICE DOESNT WORK EITHER WHEN
2TRU II	(68)	THE LEAST CURIOSITY ABOUT MY LOVELY SERGEANT: I	KNOW	JUST WHAT HE'LL SAY AND WHAT HE'LL DO. I JUST WANT HIM
SIM PRO,3,	(34)	OFFICER. /SIR CHARLES/ AH, OF COURSE: YES. YOU	KNOW	LADY FARWATERS BY SIGHT. WHICH WAY DID SHE GO? /THE
BULL IV	(167)	WOULDNT HAVE DONE AT ALL, NOT AT ALL. YOU DONT	KNOW	LARRY AS I DO, MY DEAR. HE HAS ABSOLUTELY NO CAPACITY
JOAN 5	(117)	STICK. FIGHTING IS NOT WHAT IT WAS; AND THOSE WHO	KNOW	LEAST ABOUT IT OFTEN MAKE THE BEST JOB OF IT. /DUNOIS/
OVER PREFACE	(155)	WRITE MOST SINCERELY AND FAVORABLY ABOUT POLYGAMY	KNOW	LEAST ABOUT IT; AND THE PRACTITIONERS WHO KNOW MOST
MIS. PREFACE	(52)	IS SHAM. THOSE WHO HAVE BEEN TAUGHT MOST	KNOW	LEAST. ANTICHRIST, AMONG THE WORST EFFECTS OF THE
MTH4 I	(159)	MADAM. THE DULLEST FISH COULD NOT POSSIBLY	KNOW	LESS OF THE MAJESTY OF THE OCEAN THAN MANY GEOGRAPHERS
PYGM PREFACE	(202)	HIM, OF THE LATER GENERATIONS OF PHONETICIANS I	KNOW	LITTLE. AMONG THEM TOWERS THE POET LAUREATE, TO WHOM
OVER	(173)	IVE BEEN ABLE TO ALLOW MYSELF TO FALL IN LOVE. I	KNOW	LOTS OF CHARMING WOMEN; BUT THE WORST OF IT IS, THEYRE
FOUN	(211)	I HAVE A RIGHT TO EXPECT THAT OF YOU. YOU MUST	KNOW	LOTS OF PEOPLE WHO COULD GIVE ME A START. AND THERES
DOCT III	(153)	BUT I MUST TELL YOU THE WHOLE TRUTH. LISTEN. I	KNOW	LOUIS AS NOBODY ELSE IN THE WORLD KNOWS HIM OR EVER CAN
MTH1 II	(27)	AND MAKE ROOM FOR OTHERS? WHY, I-- I! THAT	KNOW	MANY MORE CRAFTS THAN EITHER OF YOU, AM TIRED OF MYSELF
VWOO 1	(116)	AT MARGATE. /Z/ (EAGERLY) OH, I AM SO GLAD YOU	KNOW	MARGATE. THERES NO PLACE LIKE IT IN THE SEASON, IS
HART I	(49)	THE SOFA, SUFFUSED WITH EMOTION) PAPA! DONT YOU	KNOW	ME? I'M YOUR DAUGHTER. /THE CAPTAIN/ NONSENSE! MY
FANY III	(305)	PANTRY TIL YOURE DISENGAGED. /MARGARET/ DONT YOU	KNOW	ME? /DORA/ (COMING TO THE MIDDLE OF THE ROOM AND
CYMB V	(142)	LOST AND WON. PASS ON. /POSTHUMUS/ DO YOU NOT	KNOW	ME? /IACHIMO/ NO. /POSTHUMUS/ LOOK CLOSER. YOU HAVE
NEVR II	(227)	AT HER QUAINTLY FROM UNDER THE UMBRELLA) DONT YOU	KNOW	ME? /MRS CLANDON/ (INCREDULOUSLY, LOOKING HARD AT
HART I	(52)	UTTERWORD/ HESIONE: IS IT POSSIBLE THAT YOU DONT	KNOW	ME? /MRS HUSHABYE/ (CONVENTIONALLY) OH COURSE I
APPL I	(202)	CAN HE HAVE MY NAME! " MY LAD" I SAID: " NOT TO	KNOW	ME ARGUES YOURSELF UNKNOWN. YOU KNOW WHO I AM AS WELL
DOCT V	(178)	BE AS ANGRY WITH ME AS YOU LIKE: AT LEAST YOU	KNOW	ME AS I REALLY AM. IF YOU EVER COME TO CARE FOR AN
APPL INTRLUD	(251)	SO BECAUSE YOU HAVE NO IMAGINATION. AND YOU DONT	KNOW	ME BECAUSE I HAVE NEVER LET YOU REALLY POSSESS ME. I
GENV IV	(122)	TO MAKE YOU EMPEROR OF THE UNIVERSE? YOU SHOULD	KNOW	ME BETTER (HE RESUMES HIS SEAT MAJESTICALLY).
HART I	(54)	HOME. /LADY UTTERWORD/ YOU ARE PRETENDING NOT TO	KNOW	ME ON PURPOSE. I WILL LEAVE THE HOUSE. MAZZINI DUNN
MRS PREFACE	(154)	THE THING THAT MOST NEEDS SAYING, THAT THOSE WHO	KNOW	ME PERSONALLY REPROACH ME, NOT FOR WRITING THIS PLAY,
VWOO 2	(128)	/Z/ HOW MUCH BETTER DO YOU THINK YOU WILL	KNOW	ME WHEN WE HAVE TALKED FOR TWENTY YEARS? /A/ THAT IS
NEVR III	(272)	AWAY FROM HIM. HE CONTINUES, TO MRS CLANDON) I	KNOW	MEN WHOSE WIVES LOVE THEM; AND THEY GO ON EXACTLY LIKE
O'FL	(206)	SHAKES HANDS WITH ME AND SAYS THEYRE PROUD TO	KNOW	ME, JUST THE WAY THE KING SAID WHEN HE PINNED THE CROSS
DEST	(165)	TO WIPE AWAY A TEAR). /NAPOLEON/ I SEE YOU DONT	KNOW	ME, MADAM, OR YOU WOULD SAVE YOURSELF THE TROUBLE OF
2TRU III	(85)	/THE SERGEANT/ NOTHING TO DO WITH ME! YOU DONT	KNOW	ME, MY LASS. SOME MEN WOULD JUST ORDER YOU OFF; BUT TO
SUPR III	(92)	/DON JUAN/ DONA ANA DE ULLOA! /ANA/ WHAT? YOU	KNOW	ME! /DON JUAN/ AND YOU FORGET ME! /ANA/ I CANNOT SEE
SUPR PREFACE	(R34)	AND DAVID COPPERFIELD. AT THE END OF THE BOOK YOU	KNOW	MICAWBER, WHEREAS YOU ONLY KNOW WHAT HAS HAPPENED TO
GETT	(329)	BUT AT LEAST LET ME KNOW YOUR SOUL AS YOU SEEM TO	KNOW	MINE. DO YOU LOVE THIS ABSURD COAL MERCHANT. /MRS
WIDO III	(63)	OF THE UNT AS FAR AS YOUNG LADIES IS CONCERNED. I	KNOW	MISS BLANCHE: SHE HAS HER FATHER'S EYE FOR BUSINESS.
MRS IV	(241)	THE GOSPEL OF ART IS THE ONLY ONE I CAN PREACH. I	KNOW	MISS WARREN IS A GREAT DEVOTEE OF THE GOSPEL OF GETTING
BULL PREFACE	(14)	I AM PERSUADED FURTHER-- WITHOUT PRETENDING TO	KNOW	MORE ABOUT IT THAN ANYONE ELSE-- THAT BROADBENT'S
HART II	(109)	ACCOUNT. WHY NOT SET UP AS A LOCKSMITH? YOU MUST	KNOW	MORE ABOUT LOCKS THAN MOST HONEST MEN? /THE BURGLAR/
INCA	(243)	DONT THINK YOULL SUIT. I FEEL SURE NOW THAT YOU	KNOW	MORE ABOUT MEN THAN YOU SHOULD. /ERMYNTRUDE/ I AM A
JITT III	(62)	HIM SO? /FESSLER/ MY DEAR, I AM A MAN; AND I	KNOW	MORE ABOUT MEN'S WAYS THAN YOU DO. A MAN IS A VERY
MILL I	(144)	/EPIFANIA/ LIKE ALL SOLICITORS YOU THINK YOU	KNOW	MORE ABOUT MY HUSBAND THAN I DO. WELL, I TELL YOU THAT
MTH4 I	(161)	ANATOMICAL OR CHEMICAL FACTS WERE NOT SUPPOSED TO	KNOW	MORE ABOUT SCIENCE THAN THE COLLECTOR OF USED POSTAGE
POSN PREFACE	(415)	HARDLY A FIRST-NIGHTER IN HIS GALLERY WHO DID NOT	KNOW	MORE ABOUT THE LONDON THEATRES AND THE PROGRESS OF
MTH3	(96)	/BURGE-LUBIN/ LOOK HERE, CONFUCIUS: YOU	KNOW	MORE HISTORY THAN I DO, OF COURSE; BUT DEMOCRACY--
MIS. PREFACE	(80)	AND IF WE TAKE NATURALLY TO ONE ANOTHER I WILL	KNOW	MORE OF HER AND SHE OF ME AT THE END OF FORTY DAYS (I
SUPR PREFACE	(R17)	THE STATUE. I FEEL SURE YOU WOULD LIKE TO	KNOW	MORE OF THAT STATUE-- TO DRAW HIM OUT WHEN HE IS OFF
MTH4 I	(159)	NOT KNOWLEDGE OF IT: IF IT WERE, THE FISH WOULD	KNOW	MORE OF THE SEA THAN THE GEOGRAPHERS AND THE
GETT	(333)	WHAT YOU REALLY FEEL ABOUT THEM. AND THATS HOW I	KNOW	MORE OF THE WORLD THAN YOU. /LESBIA/ THE CHINESE KNOW
BUOY III	(31)	SUCH AN EXTRAORDINARY MAN, THAT I SHOULD LIKE TO	KNOW	MORE OF YOU. YOU BELONG TO A NEW GENERATION, QUITE
GETT	(342)	FAINT CONVULSION PASSING LIKE A WAVE OVER HER) I	KNOW	MORE THAN EITHER OF YOU. ONE OF YOU HAS NOT YET
ROCK II	(270)	WITH WHEN THEYRE HURT, AND NOT TO PRETEND THEY	KNOW	MORE THAN GOD ALMIGHTY DOES. GIVE EM A CHOICE BETWEEN
CLEO II	(133)	INTRODUCED US THE OTHER NIGHT; AND YOU THINK YOU	KNOW	MORE THAN I DO ALREADY. /CLEOPATRA/ (TAKEN DOWN, AND
JITT III	(60)	YOU SUPPOSE ANY GIRL OF MY AGE NOWADAYS DOES NOT	KNOW	MORE THAN YOU WERE EVER TAUGHT? /AGNES/ (SHRIEKING)
CYMB V	(141)	OF PERIL MYSELF I'LL DEDICATE. LET ME MAKE MEN	KNOW	MORE VALOUR IN ME THAN MY HABITS SHEW. GODS, PUT THE
BUOY 1	(14)	TO ME, MY BOY, YOU ARE CLEVERER THAN I AM. YOU	KNOW	MORE. YOU KNOW TOO MUCH. YOU TALK TOO WELL. I HAVE
OVER PREFACE	(156)	KNOW LEAST ABOUT IT; AND THE PRACTITIONERS WHO	KNOW	MOST ABOUT IT KEEP THEIR KNOWLEDGE VERY JEALOUSLY TO
FANY I	(276)	BUT OF COURSE YOU DO. /GILBEY/ (WITH DIGNITY) I	KNOW	MR JOSEPH GRENFELL, THE BROTHER OF MONSIGNOR GRENFELL,
SUPR IV	(144)	IS NOT MY PRINCIPAL: I TOOK IT TO OBLIGE HER. I	KNOW	MR MALONE; AND HE AINT YOU, NOT BY A LONG CHALK. AT THE
PYGM EPILOG	(299)	AND THAT LADY ALSO DESIRED ABOVE ALL THINGS TO	KNOW	MR WELLS AND SELL PRETTY THINGS TO HIM, SHE OFFERED
PYGM III	(248)	/MRS HIGGINS/ SO GLAD YOUVE COME. DO YOU	KNOW	MRS EYNSFORD HILL-- MISS EYNSFORD HILL? (EXCHANGE OF
DOCT I	(95)	THE FIVE PER CENT. I'LL GIVE YOU AN INSTANCE. YOU	KNOW	MRS JACK FOLJAMBE: THE SMART MRS FOLJAMBE? I OPERATED
SUPR II	(70)	ON YOUR FACE. IF YOU AINT SPOTTED THAT, YOU DONT	KNOW	MUCH ABOUT THESE SORT OF THINGS. (SERENE AGAIN)
CYMB FORWORD	(133)	THAT EVERYONE BEHIND THE SCENES IN A THEATRE MUST	KNOW	MUCH BETTER THAN SHAKESPEAR HOW PLAYS SHOULD BE
ROCK PREFACE	(175)	TO BE ALTERED TO PLEASE CATHOLIC AUTHORITIES WHO	KNOW	MUCH LESS ABOUT CATHOLICISM THAN I DO. IN AMERICA BOOKS
LADY PREFACE	(225)	FACT, WITH THE PLAYS AND SONNETS IN OUR HANDS, WE	KNOW	MUCH MORE ABOUT SHAKESPEAR THAN WE KNOW ABOUT DICKENS
SUPR I	(31)	DO PLEASE DROP IT. WHY DO YOU SAY THINGS THAT YOU	KNOW	MUST PAIN ME? I DO MY BEST TO PLEASE YOU, JACK: I
NEVR I	(219)	(LOOKING MORE EARNESTLY AT HER) SO YOU WANT TO	KNOW	MY AGE, DO YOU? I'M FIFTY SEVEN. /DOLLY/ (WITH
MTH2	(47)	ENSUING SITTING. /FRANKLYN/ I FORGET WHETHER YOU	KNOW	MY BROTHER CONRAD. HE IS A BIOLOGIST. /BURGE/ (
MTH4 II	(177)	NOT GRUDGE ME THE NECESSARY TIME, MADAM, WHEN YOU	KNOW	MY CASE. I AM A MAN GIFTED WITH A CERTAIN SPECIFIC
LADY	(250)	IT MAY PROVE SO. BUT OF THIS I AM CERTAIN (FOR I	KNOW	MY COUNTRYMEN) THAT UNTIL EVERY OTHER COUNTRY IN THE
PYGM III	(254)	I SHOULD, MOST AWFULLY. /MRS HIGGINS/ WELL, YOU	KNOW	MY DAYS. /FREDDY/ YES. THANKS AWFULLY. GOODBYE. (HE
GLIM	(179)	THAT I DID NOT MEAN MY GIULIETTA TO TELL YOU. I	KNOW	MY DUTY TO YOUR EXCELLENCY BETTER THAN THAT.
LADY	(242)	LADY/ GRAMERCY FOR YOUR SERMON, SIR, I HOPE I	KNOW	MY DUTY. /THE MAN/ THIS IS NO SERMON, BUT THE LIVING
JITT III	(62)	DISAPPOINTMENT TO YOU. /EDITH/ NEVER FEAR. I	KNOW	MY FATHER TOO WELL. (TURNING FIERCELY ON HIM) BUT THAT
PYGM III	(241)	SHALL TAKE YOU HOME. /LIZA/ NOT HIM. YOU DONT	KNOW	MY FATHER. ALL HE COME HERE FOR WAS TO TOUCH YOU FOR
SIM I	(40)	I ASSURE YOU. NOT MY FATHER'S CHILDREN. YOU DONT	KNOW	MY FATHER. EVEN MY CHRISTIAN NAME IS PHOSPHOR. /PRA/ IS
2TRU III	(105)	THINK YOU MEAN; BUT YOU HAVE JUST HIT IT: I DONT	KNOW	MY HEAD FROM MY HEELS. WHY DID THEY TELL ME THAT
HART I	(66)	REALLY! /MRS HUSHABYE/ (TO MANGAN) DO YOU	KNOW	MY HUSBAND, MR MANGAN (SHE INDICATES HECTOR). /MANGAN/

MILL IV	(198)	YOU. /EPIFANIA/ AN ACTION! VERY WELL: YOU	KNOW	MY INVARIABLE RULE. FIGHT HIM TO THE LAST DITCH, NO
FABL II	(107)	A DIPLOMATIST; AND I THINK YOULL ADMIT THAT I	KNOW	MY JOB AFTER MY FIFTEEN YEARS IN THE FOREIGN OFFICE.
WIDO II	(31)	BELIEVE THAT KNOWS WHAT SUCH PROPERTIES ARE. I	KNOW	MY MERITS, DR TRENCH, AND WILL SPEAK FOR MYSELF IF NO
MRS III	(225)	(WINCING; THEN LOOKING AT HIM STEADILY) TODAY I	KNOW	MY MOTHER BETTER THAN YOU DO. /FRANK/ HEAVEN FORBID!
MRS I	(187)	/VIVIE/ DONT SUPPOSE ANYTHING, MR PRAED. I HARDLY	KNOW	MY MOTHER. SINCE I WAS A CHILD I HAVE LIVED IN ENGLAND,
MTH3	(111)	PRETENDING THAT I HAD LOST MY MEMORY, AND DID NOT	KNOW	MY NAME OR MY AGE OR ANYTHING ABOUT MYSELF. UNDER
BUOY III	(36)	MARRIED. SO I FLED; AND HERE I AM. HE DOES NOT	KNOW	MY NAME, NOR I HIS. BUT WHEN I THINK OF HIM EVERYTHING
FANY EPILOG	(333)	SHAW, SHAW, SHAW! DO CHUCK IT. IF YOU WANT TO	KNOW	MY OPINION ABOUT SHAW-- /TROTTER/ NO, PLEASE, WE DONT.
DOCT III	(150)	RIDGEON AND SIR RALPH BLOOMFIELD BONINGTON. THEY	KNOW	MY OPINION. GOOD AFTERNOON TO YOU, MAAM. (HE BOWS AND
BARB III	(342)	ANDREW: YOU ARE A VULGAR TRADESMAN. NOW YOU ALL	KNOW	MY OPINION; AND MY CONSCIENCE IS CLEAR, AT ALL EVENTS (
JITT III	(64)	YOUR WAITING. EVERYBODY SEEMS TO THINK THEY	KNOW	MY OWN MIND BETTER THAN I DO MYSELF. I CAN ONLY TELL
ARMS III	(57)	THE SECRET OF IT. AND YOU MAY DEPEND ON ME TO	KNOW	MY PLACE IF YOU GET PROMOTED. THINK OVER IT, MY GIRL.
BASH II,1,	(105)	ENTERS, IN TEARS. A SOLEMN PAUSE.) /CASHEL/ YOU	KNOW	MY SECRET? /LYDIA/ YES. /CASHEL/ AND THEREUPON YOU
FOUN	(218)	/ANASTASIA/ SAY NO MORE. OF COURSE YOU COULD NOT	KNOW	MY SOCIAL POSITION. /MERCER/ DONT SAY THAT, MISS. YOU
PYGM III	(248)	(BOWING) AHDEDO? /MRS HIGGINS/ I DONT THINK YOU	KNOW	MY SON, PROFESSOR HIGGINS. /FREDDY/ (GOING TO HIGGINS)
HART III	(138)	ISNT CONCEITED. ARE YOU, PETTIKINS? /ELLIE/ I	KNOW	MY STRENGTH NOW, HESIONE. /MANGAN/ BRAZEN, I CALL YOU.
MTH4 I	(152)	UNINTERESTING, EXCEPT TO THEMSELVES. I SHOULDNT	KNOW	MY TWO ELDEST IF I MET THEM. /THE ELDERLY GENTLEMAN/ (
BULL IV	(174)	ARE IRISHMEN, BUT BECAUSE THEYRE DUFFERS, AND I	KNOW	MY WAY ABOUT. /KEEGAN/ HAVE YOU CONSIDERED WHAT IS TO
KING I	(177)	UNFAITHFUL. /CHARLES/ WRONG, PASTOR. YOU DO NOT	KNOW	MY WIFE. TO HER ONLY I CAN NEVER BE UNFAITHFUL. /NELL/
APPL II	(272)	ME TO SAY -- COMRADE. (HEAR HEARS AD LIBITUM). I	KNOW	MY WORDS WILL FIND AN ECHO IN ALL YOUR HEARTS WHEN I
SUPR III	(132)	THE LINE OF LEAST RESISTANCE: NOW I WANT TO	KNOW	MYSELF AND MY DESTINATION, AND CHOOSE MY PATH; SO I
PYGM II	(241)	AINT SUCH A MUG AS TO PUT UP MY CHILDREN TO ALL I	KNOW	MYSELF. HARD ENOUGH TO HOLD THEM IN WITHOUT THAT. IF
GENV III	(84)	YOU CAN POSSESS ME FOR THE PRICE OF A DINNER, YOU	KNOW	NEITHER YOUR OWN PLACE NOR MINE. /THE JEW/ I ASK
MRS I	(185)	INSURANCE COMPANIES, AND SO ON; BUT I	KNOW	NEXT TO NOTHING ABOUT ENGINEERING OR ELECTRICITY OR
PYGM II	(239)	GOVERNOR: MARRY ELIZA WHILE SHE'S YOUNG AND DONT	KNOW	NO BETTER. IF YOU DONT YOULL BE SORRY FOR IT AFTER. IF
BULL III	(119)	CALL IT STIRABOUT, SIR: THATS HOW IT WAS. THEY	KNOW	NO BETTER, SIR. /BROADBENT/ ALL RIGHT: I'LL HAVE SOME
INCA	(242)	/ERMYNTRUDE/ IN YOUR HIGHNESS'S SERVICE I	KNOW	NO FEAR. YOUR HIGHNESS CAN LEAVE ALL UNPLEASANT PEOPLE
KING I	(220)	KNELLER. GRAVITATION BENDS THEM. AND AT BOTTOM I	KNOW	NO MORE ABOUT GRAVITATION THAN YOU DO ABOUT BEAUTY.
GENV II	(55)	/THE SECRETARY/ THEY ARE QUITE INNOCENT: THEY	KNOW	NO MORE ABOUT IT THAN I DID. THE WHOLE THING WAS DONE
METH PREFACE	(R49)	EFFECTS OF CIRCUMSTANTIAL SELECTION; THAT I NEED	KNOW	NO MORE ABOUT DARWINISM THAN A BUTTERFLY KNOWS OF A
JOAN PREFACE	(49)	AT CHATEAUDUN, IS A SUGGESTIVE HELP. BUT I REALLY	KNOW	NO MORE ABOUT THESE MEN AND THEIR CIRCLE THAN
FANY I	(274)	OF REPROBATION." " AS YOU MAY IMAGINE! " AND WE	KNOW	NO MORE ABOUT IT THAN THE BABE UNBORN. /MRS GILBEY/
LION PREFACE	(91)	AND DOES NOT ALTER IT AT ALL FOR THOSE WHO	KNOW	NO MORE ABOUT MODERN PALEOGRAPHY THAN ARCHBISHOP USSHER
POSN	(455)	COMPANY AND NO TALENT FOR PLAYING THE HARP-- I	KNOW	NO MORE OF THAT HORSE'S WHEREABOUTS THAN YOU DO
GENV PREFACE	(7)	TO THINK INTENSELY AND THINK WRONG. STATESMEN WHO	KNOW	NO PAST HISTORY ARE DANGEROUS BECAUSE CONTEMPORARY
SUPR IV	(163)	THAT MAKES HER ALMOST SOMETHING FOR WHICH I	KNOW	NO POLITE NAME. /MRS WHITEFIELD/ (IN MILD
MRS II	(201)	KNOW THE REASONS-- /MRS WARREN/ (DEFIANTLY) I	KNOW	NO REASONS. IF YOU KNOW ANY, YOU CAN TELL THEM TO THE
ARMS II	(24)	AT ME, TEN YEARS IN THEIR SERVICE. DO YOU THINK I	KNOW	NO SECRETS? I KNOW THINGS ABOUT THE MISTRESS THAT SHE
DOCT I	(100)	THERE ARE NO CHANCES OF MEETING YOU GREAT MEN. I	KNOW	NOBODY BUT THE ST ANNE'S MEN OF MY OWN DAY. (TO
ARMS III	(60)	THERE AGAIN. WHETHER THAT IS AN INSULT I NEITHER	KNOW	NOR CARE: TAKE IT AS YOU PLEASE. BUT (VEHEMENTLY) I
LION PREFACE	(69)	INSTINCT; AND THE MASS OF MANKIND NEITHER	KNOW	NOR CARE MUCH ABOUT FREEDOM OF CONSCIENCE, WHICH IS
2TRU I	(39)	WE ARE HERE FOR, POPSY. /THE PATIENT/ I NEITHER	KNOW	NOR CARE WHAT YOU ARE HERE FOR. ALL I CAN TELL YOU IS
KING I	(187)	(RISING IN UNGOVERNABLE WRATH) SIR: I NEITHER	KNOW	NOR CARE WHERE THE KING IS. THIS IS MY HOUSE; AND I
CAND I	(95)	NOT A BAD ONE. WELL, I NEVER MET A MAN AS DIDNT	KNOW	NORTN FOLGIT AFORE. (ABASHED AT HIS OWN NOISINESS)
CLEO IV	(177)	TO YOUR OFFER. /POTHINUS/ I WILL DEAL PLAINLY. I	KNOW	NOT BY WHAT STRANGE GODS YOU HAVE BEEN ENABLED TO
LADY	(246)	WOULD PUT HIS HAND TO. I AM ALL DISORDERED: I	KNOW	NOT WHAT I AM SAYING TO YOUR MAJESTY: I AM OF ALL
LION PREFACE	(34)	OF HIS PERSECUTORS ON THE GROUND THAT " THEY	KNOW	NOT WHAT THEY DO." ACCORDING TO MATTHEW, IT IS PART OF
CYMB V	(147)	THE TRUTH AND FACE IT. /BELARIUS/ ROYAL SIR: I	KNOW	NOT WHAT TO SAY: NOT YOU NOR I CAN TELL OUR CHILDREN'S
BASH III	(126)	OF LADY WORTHINGTON. /CASHEL/ UNHAPPY MAN, YOU	KNOW	NOT WHAT YOU DO. /LYDIA/ NAY, TIS A MATCH OF MOST
PPP	(194)	HER ROUND THE WAIST) OH, MY BELOVED MISTRESS, I	KNOW	NOT WHY OR HOW; BUT I FEEL THAT I SHALL NEVER SEE YOU
MTH1 II	(29)	I NOT EMBRACED EVILS AND AGONIES OF WHICH YOU	KNOW	NOTHING? THE ARROW IS LIGHTER IN THE HAND THAN THE
FANY III	(303)	THE FRENCHMAN? /MARGARET/ (FACING HIM AGAIN) I	KNOW	NOTHING ABOUT THE FRENCHMAN EXCEPT THAT HE'S A VERY
HART II	(112)	(IRRITABLY) YOU ARE NOT MARRIED; AND YOU	KNOW	NOTHING ABOUT IT, RANDALL. HOLD YOUR TONGUE. /RANDALL/
LION II	(127)	PEOPLE TURN DOWN THEIR THUMBS. /THE EDITOR/ YOU	KNOW	NOTHING ABOUT IT. THE PEOPLE INDEED! DO YOU SUPPOSE WE
JOAN 1	(66)	MY FATHER SOMETIMES CALLS HIMSELF D'ARC; BUT I	KNOW	NOTHING ABOUT IT. YOU MET MY FATHER. HE -- /ROBERT/
DOCT I	(88)	YOUVE BROUGHT US BACK TO INOCULATION. /RIDGEON/ I	KNOW	NOTHING ABOUT SMALLPOX. MY LINE IS TUBERCULOSIS AND
CATH 2	(179)	FEATS IN THE IMPERIAL BED. /EDSTASTON/ I	KNOW	NOTHING ABOUT HER MAJESTY'S EMINENCE IN POLICY OR
DOCT II	(120)	KNOW THAT A MAN'S SOUND ON THESE TWO POINTS, YOU	KNOW	NOTHING ABOUT HIM. /B.B./ AH, CYNIC, CYNIC! /WALPOLE/
GETT	(339)	THAT HUMOR IS A DIVINE ATTRIBUTE. /MRS GEORGE/ I	KNOW	NOTHING ABOUT DIVINE ATTRIBUTES OR WHATEVER YOU CALL
POSN PREFACE	(371)	OR CHARMING ROMANCES: OUR TRIBAL CITIZENS	KNOW	NOTHING ABOUT THAT AND DO NOT WANT TO KNOW ANYTHING:
MTH2	(66)	YOU CANT. YOU DIDNT READ MY BOOK; AND YOU	KNOW	NOTHING ABOUT IT. YOU JUST HOLD YOUR TONGUE. /SAVVY/ I
MIS. PREFACE	(48)	SIMPLY A PIECE OF IMPUDENCE ON YOUR PART, AS YOU	KNOW	NOTHING ABOUT IT EXCEPT THAT AS GOOD MEN AS YOU HAVE
2TRU II	(52)	SIR. THAT IS HIS ANSWER, SIR. /TALLBOYS/ I	KNOW	NOTHING ABOUT IT. WHO SENT YOU? /THE RIDER/ COLONEL
NEVR I	(212)	DESCRIBE IT TO YOU: FORTUNATELY FOR YOU, YOU	KNOW	NOTHING ABOUT IT. (SHE SITS DOWN, PANTING). /DOLLY/ (
CLEO III	(145)	IT IS A UNIVERSAL PASSWORD. /SENTINEL/ I	KNOW	NOTHING ABOUT UNIVERSAL PASSWORDS. EITHER GIVE ME THE
SUPR II	(51)	HIM AS AN OLD SCHOOL FELLOW. /STRAKER/ YOU DONT	KNOW	NOTHING ABOUT IT, MR TANNER. IT'S NOT THE BOARD SCHOOL
MTH3	(104)	IF THEY LIVE TWO OR THREE CENTURIES. /BARNABAS/ I	KNOW	NOTHING ABOUT THEIR WORKING AND PRODUCING. THAT IS NOT
KING I	(184)	ANY PRICE YOU LIKE. /NEWTON/ I TELL YOU, MADAM, I	KNOW	NOTHING ABOUT SUCH THINGS. IF I WISHED TO MAKE YOU FALL
MRS II	(210)	AND THE PROFESSION I INTEND TO PURSUE. I	KNOW	NOTHING ABOUT YOU. WHAT IS THAT WAY OF LIFE WHICH YOU
MRS III	(225)	YOULL EVER KNOW HER. /VIVIE/ YOU ARE WRONG: YOU	KNOW	NOTHING ABOUT HER. IF YOU KNEW THE CIRCUMSTANCES
MRS I	(192)	YOU KNOW FOR CERTAIN THAT I'M NOT? /PRAED/ I	KNOW	NOTHING ABOUT IT, I TELL YOU, ANY MORE THAN YOU. BUT
BUOY IV	(49)	ANYTHING BUT YOUR DAUGHTER. I DONT KNOW WHY. I	KNOW	NOTHING ABOUT HER; AND SHE KNOWS NOTHING ABOUT ME. I AM
SIM II	(70)	ABOUT IT; BERLIN, ROME, MADRID, AND GENEVA	KNOW	NOTHING ABOUT IT; AND MOSCOW SAYS THE BRITISH
ROCK II	(255)	AND SERVE ME JOLLY WELL RIGHT! YOU JUST	KNOW	NOTHING ABOUT IT, BECAUSE YOUVE NEVER HAD TO COMMAND;
ROCK II	(258)	WELL. THAT THEY DONT GOVERN AND CANT GOVERN AND	KNOW	NOTHING ABOUT GOVERNMENT EXCEPT THAT IT ALWAYS SUPPORTS
ROCK II	(262)	I HAVE DONE THEM. I KNOW ALL ABOUT IT: YOU	KNOW	NOTHING ABOUT IT. IT MEANS EXTERMINATION; AND WHEN IT
PYGM V	(269)	RELATIVE OF HERS THAT SHE'S GONE TO. SOMEBODY WE	KNOW	NOTHING ABOUT. (TO THE PARLOR-MAID) SEND HIM UP,
GENV IV	(124)	NO MORE TIME TO SPEND TRIFLING HERE WITH MEN WHO	KNOW	NOTHING AND BELIEVE NOTHING. (HE MOVES TOWARDS THE
MTH4 I	(157)	SHIRK MY RESPONSIBILITIES BY PRETENDING THAT I	KNOW	NOTHING AND THEREFORE CAN BELIEVE NOTHING. WE CANNOT
BARB PREFACE	(208)	SUCH AS CHARLES O'MALLEY AND HARRY LORREQUER, I	KNOW	NOTHING BUT THE NAMES AND SOME OF THE ILLUSTRATIONS.
METH PREFACE	(R9)	PRODUCED SHOP ASSISTANTS WHO KNOW HOW TO READ AND	KNOW	NOTHING ELSE. THE CELEBRATED BUFFOON WAS NOT A
JOAN PREFACE	(27)	COURT THAT TRIED HER; AND UNTIL YOU FEEL THAT YOU	KNOW	NOTHING ESSENTIAL ABOUT HER. THAT THE MISSISSIPPI PILOT
MRS I	(185)	SUPPOSED TO KNOW SOMETHING ABOUT SCIENCE; BUT I	KNOW	NOTHING EXCEPT THE MATHEMATICS IT INVOLVES. I CAN MAKE
HART I	(68)	SHOTOVER/ (STOPPING AND TURNING ON HIM) I	KNOW	NOTHING MORE THAN I HAVE SEEN IN HER EYE. SHE WILL
BUOY III	(42)	I FOUND OUT WHO SHE WAS BUT NOT WHAT SHE IS. I	KNOW	NOTHING OF HER TASTES, HER INTELLIGENCE, HER MANNERS,
MTH5	(226)	/ARJILLAX/ ASK MARTELLUS: DO NOT ASK ME. I	KNOW	NOTHING OF HIM. (HE LEAVES MARTELLUS, AND SITS DOWN
JITT III	(78)	HIS, HE DID SO ON THE UNDERSTANDING THAT I WAS TO	KNOW	NOTHING OF HIS RELATIONS WITH YOU. HE HADNT QUITE SUCH
MILL I	(142)	WHAT EVERYBODY WAS DOING EVERY DAY, SOLICITORS	KNOW	NOTHING OF LAW: THEY ARE ONLY GOOD AT PRACTICE, AS THEY
MIS. PREFACE	(31)	TO WHOM I MENTIONED MY INTENTION SAID, " YOU	KNOW	NOTHING OF MODERN EDUCATION: SCHOOLS ARE NOT NOW WHAT
POSN PREFACE	(416)	AND SUCCESSFUL MANAGERS LIKE MR ALEXANDER, WHO	KNOW	NOTHING OF SUCH ABUSES, AND DENY, WITH PERFECT
2TRU PREFACE	(6)	NOW BE DISMISSED AS AN ILLUSION OF THE POOR WHO	KNOW	NOTHING OF THE LIVES OF THE RICH. POVERTY, WHEN IT
GENV PREFACE	(15)	HIS CHRISTLIKE SON. JUST SO TODAY CONSERVATIVES	KNOW	NOTHING OF THE TORY CREED, BUT ARE CONVINCED THAT THE
ROCK I	(217)	IT WAS LEFT ON HIS HANDS? HE DONT KNOW. HE DONT	KNOW	NOTHING OF THE BUSINESS THAT HIS LIFE DEPENDS ON. TURN
SIM PREFACE	(16)	THE FAIR; BUT TIME ENOUGH FOR OUR PEOPLE, WHO	KNOW	NOTHING OF THE BUTTON MOULDER AND HAVE BEEN ASSURED BY
GENV I	(44)	ENGLISHMAN INTO A CELL. /COMMISSAR/ HAVE WE? I	KNOW	NOTHING OF YOUR FOOTMAN. IF HE IS INTELLIGENT ENOUGH TO
MTH5	(250)	ART. THERE IS A MAGIC AND MYSTERY IN ART THAT YOU	KNOW	NOTHING OF. /THE SHE-ANCIENT/ YES, CHILD: ART IS THE
MRS III	(225)	AMONG THOROUGHLY IMMORAL PEOPLE THAT YOU	KNOW	NOTHING OF. YOUVE TOO MUCH CHARACTER. THATS THE BOND
APPL PREFACE	(188)	APPROACHES, TWO OR THREE PERSONS OF WHOM I	KNOW	NOTHING WRITE TO ME SOLICITING MY VOTE AND ENCLOSING A
GLIM	(174)	SAINT BARBARA, MY DAUGHTER, SAINT BARBARA. I	KNOW	NOTHING. BUT WHERE HAVE YOU SEEN FERRUCCIO? SAINT
KING I	(182)	SHAME FOR QUARRELLING OVER A MATTER OF WHICH WE	KNOW	NOTHING. BY THE WAY, WHERE WERE WE WHEN WE BEGAN TO
MTH1 II	(27)	MYSELF FREE TO LEARN NOBLER CRAFTS OF WHICH YOU	KNOW	NOTHING. I KNOW THE CRAFT OF FIGHTING AND OF HUNTING:
ARMS II	(41)	JUST RETURNED WITH MY FUTURE SON-IN-LAW; AND THEY	KNOW	NOTHING. IF THEY DID, THE CONSEQUENCES WOULD BE
DEST	(174)	ONLY MY PRIVATE LETTERS FROM PARIS, OF WHICH YOU	KNOW	NOTHING. /LADY/ (PROMPT AND BUSINESSLIKE) GENERAL: LET
FABL VI	(131)	SAMPLING US. /YOUTH 1/ HE TOLD US NOTHING. WE	KNOW	NOTHING. /YOUTH 3/ ROT! YOU WANT TO KNOW TOO MUCH. WE
CLEO PRO2	(100)	THE PRIDE AND HONOR OF WAR, OF WHICH THESE ROMANS	KNOW	NOTHING. SO WE ESCAPED WITH OUR LIVES; AND I AM COME TO
NEVR II	(229)	YOU TO EXPLAIN EVERYTHING TO THE CHILDREN. THEY	KNOW	NOTHING; AND NOW THAT WE HAVE COME BACK TO ENGLAND IT
CYMB V	(140)	YOU. WHERE, THINK YOU, IS IACHIMO? /CAPTAIN/ I	KNOW	NOT. AND YET I THINK HE CANNOT BE FAR OFF. /PHILARIO/

CAPT NOTES	(300)	INTO THE HOUSE OF COMMONS. HOW HE DID IT I	KNOW	NOT; BUT THE THING CERTAINLY HAPPENED, SOMEHOW. THAT HE
LION II	(141)	NO. WHAT HAVE YOU DONE, FERROVIUS? /FERROVIUS/ I	KNOW	NOT; BUT THERE WAS BLOOD BEHIND MY EYES; AND THERES
INCA	(254)	INCA/ TRUE: I HAD FORGOTTEN MY MAGNETISM. BUT YOU	KNOW	NOW THAT BENEATH THE TRAPPINGS OF IMPERIAL MAJESTY
LION II	(138)	MERE DREAMS BESIDE THAT INEXORABLE REALITY. I	KNOW	NOW THAT I AM NOT DYING FOR STORIES OR DREAMS. DID YOU
FANY II	(295)	LITTLE HOLE OF A HOUSE AND ALL ITS PRETENCES. I	KNOW	NOW THAT I AM STRONGER THAN YOU AND PAPA. I HAVNT FOUND
PHIL III	(138)	YOU. HOW I HAVE LOOKED FORWARD TO THIS DAY! YOU	KNOW	NOW THAT I DONT WANT YOU TO MARRY ME OR TO LOVE ME;
GETT	(263)	SHE WONDERS WHEN I AM GOING TO GROW OUT OF IT. I	KNOW	NOW THAT I SHALL NEVER GROW OUT OF IT. /MRS
FANY II	(293)	IT'S ALL OVER I'M RATHER PROUD OF IT; THOUGH I	KNOW	NOW THAT I'M NOT A LADY; BUT WHETHER THATS BECAUSE
BULL IV	(179)	HAVE TOLD ME THIS MORNING WHERE HELL IS? YET YOU	KNOW	NOW THAT IT IS HERE. DO NOT DESPAIR OF FINDING HEAVEN:
MTH3	(126)	ARE THE MOST HELPLESS DURING THEIR IMMATURITY. I	KNOW	NOW THAT IT TOOK ME A WHOLE CENTURY TO GROW UP. I BEGAN
HART III	(141)	/LADY UTTERWORD/ SO I THOUGHT, MR DUNN. BUT I	KNOW	NOW THAT IT WAS ONLY THE LAST OF MY INFLUENZA. I FOUND
SUPR HANDBOK	(206)	WE BELIEVE, THE EGYPTIANS BUILT THE PYRAMIDS. WE	KNOW	NOW THAT THE CRUSADE AGAINST CHATTEL SLAVERY IN THE XIX
BARB II	(302)	MAAM. THE WINDOWS OF EAVEN AV BIN OPENED TO ME. I	KNOW	NOW THAT THE RICH MAN IS A SINNER LIKE MYSELF. /RUMMY/
HART II	(117)	EVEN YOUR BODY. /ELLIE/ OLD-FASHIONED AGAIN. WE	KNOW	NOW THAT THE SOUL IS THE BODY, AND THE BODY THE SOUL.
SUPR PREFACE	(R27)	AS THE TERRORS OF THE DEGENERACY MONGERS; AND WE	KNOW	NOW THAT THERE IS NO HEREDITARY " GOVERNING CLASS" ANY
INCA	(249)	WILL ALL BE SORRY FOR THIS.' AND THEY ARE. THEY	KNOW	NOW THAT THEY HAD BETTER HAVE RELIED ON THE SWORD OF
ARMS III	(63)	AND I SAW SOMETHING I DID NOT UNDERSTAND THEN. I	KNOW	NOW THAT YOU WERE MAKING LOVE TO HER. /SERGIUS/ (WITH
METH PREFACE	(R71)	SICK AND TIRED OF THE WHOLE BUSINESS, AND	KNOW	NOW VERY WELL THAT IT SHOULD NEVER HAVE BEEN ALLOWED TO
GENV IV	(114)	/SECRETARY/ NO: I HAVE SAID ENOUGH. YOU	KNOW	NOW WHAT AN IMPOSSIBLE JOB I HAVE HERE AS SECRETARY TO
CAPT III	(293)	CAPTAIN TO PUT OUT TO SEA. AND HER CAPTAIN DOESNT	KNOW	NOW WHETHER TO TURN HER HEAD NORTH OR SOUTH. /LADY
MILL IV	(194)	EPPY IS LIKE THAT, YOU KNOW. /ADRIAN/ YES: I	KNOW	NOW. BUT I OUGHT NOT TO BE HERE: SAGAMORE SHOULD NOT
2TRU III	(98)	AND THAT MY SOUL WAS STARVING ON THEM. I	KNOW	NOW. I HAVE FOUND MYSELF OUT THOROUGHLY-- IN MY DREAM.
MIS.	(137)	CROSS AND WHEN HE WAS PLEASED; AND THATS ALL WE	KNOW	NOW, WITH ALL HIS TALK. IT NEVER STOPS: TALK, TALK,
GETT PREFACE	(224)	PROBABLY SOME OF THE TRUTH LIES BOTH WAYS. I ALSO	KNOW	OF A HOUSEHOLD CONSISTING OF THREE FAMILIES, A HAVING
GLIM	(185)	THEM BEFORE HIM). /FERRUCCIO/ THAT REMINDS ME. I	KNOW	OF A PAINTER IN THE NORTH THAT CAN PAINT SUCH BEAUTIFUL
CAND III	(140)	JAMES. /MORELL/ (TAKEN ABACK) MY DEAR: I DONT	KNOW	OF ANY RIGHT THAT MAKES ME MASTER. I ASSERT NO SUCH
PYGM III	(249)	OF SCIENCE? (INDICATING FREDDY) WHAT DOES HE	KNOW	OF ART OR SCIENCE OR ANYTHING ELSE? WHAT THE DEVIL DO
SIM II	(81)	CIVILIZATION PERISHES AS ALL THE ANCIENT ONES WE	KNOW	OF DID. WE ARE NOT BEING PUNISHED TODAY: WE ARE BEING
GETT PREFACE	(225)	THEM NOWHERE. MR KIPLING'S QUESTION WHAT CAN THEY	KNOW	OF ENGLAND THAT ONLY ENGLAND KNOW? DISPOSES NOT ONLY
FANY II	(296)	BUT IS SHE GOING TO RUIN US? TO LET EVERYBODY	KNOW	OF HER DISGRACE AND SHAME? TO TEAR ME DOWN FROM THE
SUPR III	(124)	PEASANTS? AND HOW MUCH DOES EVEN THE PEASANT	KNOW	OF HIS BRIDE OR SHE OF HIM BEFORE HE ENGAGES HIMSELF..
MTH1 II	(23)	TO YOU THAN LOVE BETWEEN US? /CAIN/ WHAT DOES HE	KNOW	OF LOVE? ONLY WHEN HE HAS FOUGHT, WHEN HE HAS FACED
MRS II	(209)	(GALLED BY VIVIE'S INDIFFERENCE) WHAT DO YOU	KNOW	OF MEN, CHILD, TO TALK THAT WAY ABOUT THEM? YOULL HAVE
DEVL II	(46)	MY PROMISE. HE SAID, " DONT FOR YOUR LIFE LET HIM	KNOW	OF MY DANGER," IVE TOLD YOU OF IT. HE SAID THAT IF YOU
DEVL II	(40)	OUT OF HARM'S WAY. DONT FOR YOUR LIFE LET HIM	KNOW	OF MY DANGER; BUT IF HE FINDS IT OUT, TELL HIM THAT HE
POSN	(452)	HORSE IF YOU DIDNT STEAL IT? /BLANCO/ I DONT	KNOW	OF MY OWN KNOWLEDGE. I ONLY ARGUE THAT IF THE HORSE HAD
PYGM III	(249)	ANYTHING ELSE? WHAT THE DEVIL DO YOU IMAGINE I	KNOW	OF PHILOSOPHY? /MRS HIGGINS/ (WARNINGLY) OR OF
MIS. PREFACE	(37)	OF THEM, PARAPHRASING MR KIPLING, " WHAT DO THEY	KNOW	OF PLATO THAT ONLY PLATO KNOW? " IF OUR UNIVERSITIES
PYGM III	(249)	OF THESE NAMES? (TO MISS HILL) WHAT DO YOU	KNOW	OF POETRY? (TO MRS HILL) WHAT DO YOU KNOW OF
PYGM III	(249)	YOU KNOW OF POETRY? (TO MRS HILL) WHAT DO YOU	KNOW	OF SCIENCE? (INDICATING FREDDY) WHAT DOES HE KNOW OF
JOAN 6	(147)	INQUISITOR/ OH, QUITE INNOCENT. WHAT DOES SHE	KNOW	OF THE CHURCH AND THE LAW? SHE DID NOT UNDERSTAND A
FANY PROLOG	(261)	A HUNDRED YEARS AGO? MY DAUGHTER DOES NOT	KNOW	OF THE EXISTENCE OF SUCH A THING. I REFER TO THE
PRES	(150)	O STEPNEY. (ALMOST IN TEARS) WHAT DO YOU	KNOW	OF THE FEELINGS OF A RESPECTABLE FAMILY IN THE MIDDLE
DOCT I	(107)	TOO, MY LAD. WHEN YOU KNOW AS MUCH AS I	KNOW	OF THE IGNORANCE AND SUPERSTITION OF THE PATIENTS,
FABL V	(118)	IS UNCONCEIVABLE, AND START FROM WHAT WE REALLY	KNOW	OF THE PRESENT. HE SHUTS HIS BOOK AND THROWS IT AWAY.
MTH4 I	(173)	TELL ME ACCOUNTS FOR A GREAT DEAL OF THE LITTLE I	KNOW	OF THE PRIVATE LIFE OF OUR GREAT MEN. WE MUST BE VERY
MIS. PREFACE	(64)	IS HUMAN WILL. IT IS THE HIGHEST ORGANIZATION WE	KNOW	OF THE WILL THAT HAS CREATED THE WHOLE UNIVERSE. NOW
SIM PREFACE	(7)	THE MOST DAMNABLE CRIMES. BUT THOUGH WE	KNOW	OF THESE FAILURES OF INFERNAL TERRORISM WE HAVE NO
MILL IV	(209)	ALL THESE MEN IN ONE. WHAT DO THE UNMARRIED	KNOW	OF THIS INFINITELY DANGEROUS HEART TEARING EVERCHANGING
JITT III	(64)	/JITTA/ I HOPE NOT. TELL ME: DOES MY HUSBAND	KNOW	OF THIS NEW TURN? /FESSLER/ NOT YET. PERHAPS YOU HAD
CAPT II	(255)	FORWARD TO CLAIM IT. THREE MINUTES AGO I DID NOT	KNOW	OF YOUR EXISTENCE. I AFFIRM THAT MOST SOLEMNLY. I NEVER
GENV PREFACE	(15)	HAVE WRECKED ALL THE EARLIER CIVILIZATIONS WE	KNOW	OF. THE ANCIENT EMPIRES WERE NOT DESTROYED BY FOREIGN
MRS IV	(239)	WAY. NO OTHER WAY, IN FACT. /VIVIE/ NONE THAT YOU	KNOW	OF, FORTUNATELY FOR YOU. SOMEONE KNOCKS AT THE DOOR.
SUPR IV	(145)	COMPOSURE. HE CONTINUES SLOWLY) NOW I DONT	KNOW	ON HWAT TERMS YOUNG PEOPLE ASSOCIATE IN ENGLISH
JITT III	(70)	THE GRAVE; BUT THEM PLAY THE MERRIEST TUNES THEY	KNOW	ON THEIR WAY BACK. /EDITH/ HOW UNFEELING! /JITTA/ YES;
PYGM II	(226)	PLEASE KEEP TO THE POINT, MR HIGGINS? I WANT TO	KNOW	ON WHAT TERMS THE GIRL IS TO BE HERE. IS SHE TO HAVE
PHIL I	(85)	THE FAMOUS IBSENIST PHILOSOPHER. /CRAVEN/ OH, WE	KNOW	ONE ANOTHER ALREADY. CHARTERIS IS QUITE AT HOME IN OUR
GETT PREFACE	(201)	THE MAJORITY OF MARRIED COUPLES NEVER GET TO	KNOW	ONE ANOTHER AT ALL: THEY ONLY GET ACCUSTOMED TO HAVING
SUPR II	(61)	WE OUGHT TO SEE MORE OF ONE ANOTHER AND COME TO	KNOW	ONE ANOTHER BETTER. (GRATEFULLY) IT'S VERY THOUGHTFUL
NEVR II	(255)	HORRIBLE THING THAT A MAN AND A WOMAN CAN HARDLY	KNOW	ONE ANOTHER WITHOUT BEING SUPPOSED TO HAVE DESIGNS OF
PHIL I	(83)	(SITTING ON THE FLOOR) IMPOSSIBLE. THEY DONT	KNOW	ONE ANOTHER. /CHARTERIS/ (DESPERATELY) I TELL YOU
6CAL	(104)	PROVINCE; SO I ALSO AM A DOG OF CHAMPAGNE. WE	KNOW	ONE ANOTHER'S BARK. (TURNING ON HIM WITH BRISTLING
NEVR II	(234)	CONSEQUENTLY, HE IS ONLY OUR SOLICITOR. DO YOU	KNOW	ONE CRAMPTON, OF THIS TOWN? /WAITER/ COCK-EYED.
GETT PREFACE	(224)	PHENOMENON AMONG ENTIRELY LAW-ABIDING PEOPLE. I	KNOW	ONE LADY WHO HAS BEEN MARRIED FIVE TIMES. SHE IS, AS
JOAN 2	(72)	THEY NEVER MET A SOUL EXCEPT THE COUNTRY FOLK. I	KNOW	ONE OF THEM: DE POULENGEY. HE SAYS SHE'S AN ANGEL. IF
KING I	(205)	DARLING? I DONT KNOW WHAT IT IS ALL ABOUT: I	KNOW	ONLY MY PART AND MY CUE. ALL I CAN SAY IS THAT WHEN
MIS.	(116)	HIS BROW). FEEL BETTER NOW? (JOHNNY NODS). I	KNOW	ONLY ONE PERSON ALIVE WHO COULD DRIVE ME TO THE POINT
PRES	(165)	OF THIS COMMUNICATION, MRS FARRELL; BUT I	KNOW	ONLY ONE WOMAN IN THE COUNTRY WHOSE PRACTICAL ABILITY
2TRU PREFACE	(9)	I HAVE HAD MY AFTERNOONS AS AN IDLE RICH MAN, AND	KNOW	ONLY TOO WELL WHAT IT IS LIKE. IT MAKES ME FEEL
FABL PREFACE	(78)	IN ENGLAND I, AN OLD JOURNALIST AND AGITATOR,	KNOW	ONLY TOO WELL THAT BOTH PLATFORM AND PRESS ARE GAGGED
SUPR I	(40)	HOW I FEEL FOR TAVY, DONT YOU? /TANNER/ I	KNOW	ONLY TOO WELL WHAT IS GOING TO HAPPEN TO POOR TAVY.
JOAN 1	(58)	THAT. /STEWARD/ (DESPERATE) I KNOW, SIR. I	KNOW	ONLY TOO WELL. THERE IS NO MILK: THERE ARE NO EGGS:
GLIM	(178)	TO MYSELF-- THE LIFE OF THOUGHT AND POETRY-- I	KNOW	ONLY TWO PLEASURES: CRUELTY AND LUST. I DESIRE REVENGE:
KING I	(222)	IS A HABIT THAT IS GROWING ON YOU. WHAT DO THEY	KNOW	OR CARE ABOUT THE PERRY HEALING OF MERCURY THAT
BARB III	(319)	MOVEMENT). WELL, COME! IS THERE ANYTHING YOU	KNOW	OR CARE FOR? /STEPHEN/ (RISING AND LOOKING AT HIM
ARMS II	(24)	MAKE THE MISTRESS FEEL THAT NO MATTER WHAT YOU	KNOW	OR DONT KNOW, SHE CAN DEPEND ON YOU TO HOLD YOUR TONGUE
MIS.	(193)	MR PERCIVAL SAID ANYTHING TO YOU THAT I OUGHT TO	KNOW	OR THAT BENTLEY OUGHT TO KNOW? HAVE YOU SAID ANYTHING
PHIL III	(134)	(JULIA, INTERESTED, LOOKS UP AT HIM QUICKLY): I	KNOW	OTHER BEAUTIFUL WOMEN. IT IS YOUR HEART, YOUR
CLEO III	(152)	ME, OR TO WATCH THE EGYPTIANS? /SENTINEL/ WE	KNOW	OUR DUTY. /APOLLODORUS/ THEN WHY DONT YOU DO IT? THERE
GETT	(271)	I ONLY FEEL UTTERLY AT A LOSS. /LESBIA/ WELL, YOU	KNOW	OUR FAMILY RULE. WHEN AT A LOSS CONSULT THE
DOCT III	(143)	ARE A THOROUGHGOING SPECIMEN. /SIR PATRICK/ YOU	KNOW	OUR OPINION OF YOU NOW, AT ALL EVENTS. /LOUIS/ (
MILL III	(186)	/THE WOMAN/ CAUSE YOU DONT UNDERSTAND IT, JOE. WE	KNOW	OUR OWN WAYS; AND THOUGH WE'RE POOR OUR WAYS HAVE NEVER
CAND III	(137)	TRAY. /CANDIDA/ WHO WILL HAVE SOME LEMONADE? YOU	KNOW	OUR RULES; TOTAL ABSTINENCE. (SHE PUTS THE TRAY ON THE
HART I	(45)	HOUSE IS FULL OF SURPRISES FOR THEM THAT DONT	KNOW	OUR WAYS. /CAPTAIN SHOTOVER/ (LOOKING IN FROM THE HALL
WIDO III	(65)	SOME WAY OF MAKING IT PROFITABLE. OH, I	KNOW	PAPA; AND I KNOW YOU, AND FOR THE SAKE OF THAT, YOU
PRES	(141)	DO FOR ME. DONT BE WEAK-KNEED, BALSQUITH. YOU	KNOW	PERFECTLY WELL THAT THE REAL GOVERNMENT OF THIS COUNTRY
2TRU I	(45)	HAVE TO SELL IT AS A BURGLAR TO A MAN WHO WILL	KNOW	PERFECTLY WELL THAT I HAVE STOLEN IT. I SHALL BE LUCKY
ROCK I	(207)	MALE OR FEMALE, THREE GUINEAS TO TELL ME WHAT I	KNOW	PERFECTLY WELL ALREADY: THAT MY BRAIN'S OVERWORKED AND
ROCK I	(228)	WILL MAKE YOU TAKE IT SERIOUSLY. /SIR ARTHUR/ I	KNOW	PERFECTLY WELL HOW TO CURE MYSELF. THE CURE IS AS
SUPR I	(28)	COULD NOT STAMMER MORE CONFUSEDLY. AND YET YOU	KNOW	PERFECTLY WELL HE'S INNOCENT, TAVY. /RAMSDEN/ (
SUPR I	(15)	VIRTUES. YOU DONT MEAN THAT I HAVNT GOT THEM: YOU	KNOW	PERFECTLY WELL THAT I AM AS SOBER AND HONEST A CITIZEN
SUPR IV	(163)	I DONT. BUT WHAT ANNOYS ME IS THAT ANN DOES. I	KNOW	PERFECTLY WELL THAT ALL THIS ABOUT HER BEING A LIAR AND
BULL IV	(169)	AS FATHER DEMPSEY HIMSELF. /NORA/ YOU LITTLE	KNOW	PETER KEEGAN. HE'D SEE THROUGH ME AS IF I WAS A PANE O
MRS IV	(249)	IT. THEY DO AS I DO, AND THINK WHAT I THINK. I	KNOW	PLENTY OF THEM. I KNOW THEM TO SPEAK TO, TO INTRODUCE
MILL I	(139)	SHEET OF PAPER AND WRITING) I SHOULD LIKE TO	KNOW	POLLY, /EPIFANIA/ PRAY WHY? /SAGAMORE/ (TALKING AS HE
CLEO IV	(186)	SWELLS TO A ROAR AND SUBSIDES. /RUFIO/ I SHALL	KNOW	PRESENTLY. (HE MAKES FOR THE ALTAR IN THE BURLY TROT
PYGM V	(274)	WHAT DID WE DO TO HER? /MRS HIGGINS/ I THINK I	KNOW	PRETTY WELL WHAT YOU DID. THE GIRL IS NATURALLY RATHER
GETT	(283)	I STILL WANT TO HAVE A LOT OF INTERESTING MEN TO	KNOW	QUITE INTIMATELY-- TO SAY EVERYTHING I THINK OF TO
DEVL II	(38)	AT REST IN MY LIFE THAN AT THIS MOMENT; AND YET I	KNOW	QUITE WELL I COULD NEVER LIVE HERE. IT'S NOT IN MY
HART II	(84)	YOU DONT MIND, THEN? /ELLIE/ OF COURSE I	KNOW	QUITE WELL THAT OUR ENGAGEMENT-- /MANGAN/ OH! YOU CALL
LION PREFACE	(6)	GREATER THAN HIS JUDGES. WAS JESUS A COWARD? I	KNOW	QUITE WELL THAT THIS IMPRESSION OF SUPERIORITY IS NOT
BULL IV	(161)	WELL, DONT LET ME KEEP YOU FROM HIM. /LARRY/ I	KNOW	QUITE WELL THAT MY DEPARTURE WILL BE A RELIEF. RATHER A
MTH4 I	(170)	GUIDED BY THE ORACLE; BUT WE ARE NOT DECEIVED: WE	KNOW	QUITE WELL THAT HE HAS COME HERE SO THAT WHEN HE GOES
SIM I	(44)	/MRS HYERING/ DONT APOLOGIZE, MR HAMMINGTAP. WE	KNOW	QUITE WELL WHAT OUR DAUGHTERS ARE CAPABLE OF WHEN THEY
APPL I	(228)	/NICOBAR/ WHAT DO YOU MEAN? /LYSISTRATA/ YOU	KNOW	QUITE WELL WHAT I MEAN. WHEN WILL YOU LEARN, NICOBAR,
DOCT V	(178)	THINK THAT YOU HAVE SHOCKED ME SO DREADFULLY. I	KNOW	QUITE WELL WHAT YOU MEAN BY HIS SELFISHNESS. HE
O'FL	(210)	PARDON, SIR PEARCE, I TELL YOU NO SUCH THING. I	KNOW	QUITE WELL WHY I KILT THEM. I KILT THEM BECAUSE I WAS

HART II	(124)	YOU ARE THE MOST PETTISH CREATURE. /RANDALL/ YOU	KNOW	QUITE WELL, ARIADNE, THAT I HAVE NOT AN OUNCE OF
FANY II	(296)	YOURS. I CANT EVEN PRAY FOR HER NOW; FOR I DONT	KNOW	RIGHTLY WHAT TO PRAY FOR. /KNOX/ DONT TALK NONSENSE,
CURE	(234)	SEEM QUITE IGNORANT OF THE BEST MUSIC. DONT YOU	KNOW	RUM TUM TIDDLE, AND ALEXANDER'S RAG TIME BAND, AND TAKE
FANY PROLOG	(261)	I HANDED IT TO BILLY BURJOYCE-- THE PRODUCER, YOU	KNOW	-- AND LEFT IT TO HIM TO SELECT THE COMPANY AND SO ON.
PYGM III	(246)	HEALTH-- FINE DAY AND HOW DO YOU DO, YOU	KNOW	-- AND NOT TO LET HERSELF GO ON THINGS IN GENERAL. THAT
DOCT I	(90)	AND DOWNS-- NATURE BEING ALWAYS RHYTHMICAL, YOU	KNOW	-- AND THAT WHAT THE INOCULATION DOES IS TO STIMULATE
FANY EPILOG	(334)	SHAKESPEAR'S-- HAMLET OR THE LADY OF LYONS, YOU	KNOW	-- BUT STILL, A FIRSTRATE LITTLE BIT OF WORK. (HE
FOUN	(219)	WAS A PLUMP, CHUBBY, TEMPTING SORT OF MAN, YOU	KNOW	-- CAME INTO MY CELL AND REMONSTRATED WITH ME, I
MRS I	(190)	(CROFTS SULKILY OBEYS). /PRAED/ I THINK, YOU	KNOW	-- IF YOU DONT MIND MY SAYING SO-- THAT WE HAD BETTER
SIM I	(46)	(BEWILDERED) HER CONSCIENCE? I SUPPOSE-- I DONT	KNOW	-- I-- /PRA/ PRECISELY. YOU DONT KNOW. WELL, WE DO
DEVL II	(42)	YOURE ABOUT IT. /JUDITH/ OH STOP, STOP. YOU DONT	KNOW	-- (DISTRACTED, SHE BURIES HER FACE IN HER KNOTTED
FANY III	(318)	BEFORE MY TIME. /GILBEY/ WELL BUT LOOK HERE YOU	KNOW	-- (HE HESITATES). /JUGGINS/ YES, SIR? /KNOX/ I KNOW
HART II	(87)	WELL TOGETHER. /MANGAN/ WELL, BUT LOOK HERE, YOU	KNOW	-- (HE STOPS, QUITE AT A LOSS). /ELLIE/ (PATIENTLY)
GETT	(280)	MAN. /REGINALD/ THIS IS THE KIND OF THING, YOU	KNOW	-- (HELPLESSLY) WELL, THERE IT IS! /THE GENERAL/ (
BARB I	(264)	(REMONSTRATING) NO BUT LOOK HERE DONT YOU	KNOW	-- (OVERCOME) OH I SAY! /LADY BRITOMART/ (RECOVERING
MRS III	(230)	BUSINESS IN MY SET-- THE COUNTY SET, YOU	KNOW	-- OUR SET IT WILL BE IF YOU THINK BETTER OF MY OFFER.
PRES	(142)	WHO WILL SELL THEIR SOULS FOR FIVE SHILLINGS. YOU	KNOW	-- /BALSQUITH/ STOP. STOP, I SAY. I DONT KNOW. THAT IS
MTH2	(65)	KNOW ENGLAND; AND YOU DONT. IF YOU DID YOU WOULD	KNOW	-- /BURGE/ WHAT DO YOU KNOW THAT I DONT KNOW? /LUBIN/
NEVR II	(232)	INTIMATE RELATIONSHIP WITH US A MAN WHOM WE DONT	KNOW	-- /DOLLY/ (VEHEMENTLY) AN AWFUL OLD MAN! (
PHIL II	(124)	WHAT OUR PAST HAS BEEN-- HOW I LOVE HIM. YOU DONT	KNOW	-- /GRACE/ GET UP; AND DONT BE A FOOL. SUPPOSE ANY ONE
MIS.	(183)	HALLO, MOTHER: THIS IS ALL VERY WELL, YOU	KNOW	-- /PERCIVAL/ BUT MAY I POINT OUT, MRS TARLETON, THAT--
MRS I	(187)	YOUR MOTHER'S LIFE HAS BEEN-- ER-- I SUPPOSE YOU	KNOW	-- /VIVIE/ DONT SUPPOSE ANYTHING, MR PRAED. I HARDLY
HART I	(55)	HESIONE! MY FATHER SELFISH! HOW LITTLE YOU	KNOW	-- SHE IS INTERRUPTED BY MAZZINI, WHO RETURNS, EXCITED
CAPT II	(255)	WE MET YOU. AS TO HER DEATH, YOU KNOW-- YOU MUST	KNOW	-- THAT SHE DIED IN HER NATIVE COUNTRY, YEARS AFTER OUR
WIDO I	(18)	IS DELIGHTED, AND ASKING US-- BLANCHE AND ME, YOU	KNOW	-- TO STAY WITH HER, AND SO FORTH. YOU KNOW WHAT I
CAPT II	(255)	THE EVENING WE MET YOU. AS TO HER DEATH, YOU	KNOW	-- YOU MUST KNOW-- THAT SHE DIED IN HER NATIVE COUNTRY,
ROCK PREFACE	(147)	CITIZEN THAT NOBODY EXCEPT MYSELF (AS FAR AS I	KNOW	) HAS VENTURED TO EXAMINE IT DIRECTLY ON ITS OWN
HART I	(49)	SISTER, MY NEPHEWS AND NIECES (ONE OUGHT TO, YOU	KNOW	), AND I WAS LOOKING FORWARD TO IT. AND NOW THE STATE
MTH4 III	(196)	BEEN TOLD NOT TO DO IT. ASK HER WHAT YOU WANT TO	KNOW	; AND BE QUICK ABOUT IT. /THE ELDERLY GENTLEMAN/ (
DEVL II	(35)	PARTICULARS. /RICHARD/ PSHA! NOT I: HE DOESNT	KNOW	; AND I DONT CARE. (VIOLENTLY) BE OFF, YOU OAF. (
FANY PROLOG	(270)	I'M DELIGHTED TO FIND THERES SOMETHING YOU DONT	KNOW	; AND I SHANT SPOIL YOU BY DISPELLING AN IGNORANCE
WIDO III	(60)	ENOUGH TO MAKE IT LOOK LIKE A MODEL DWELLING, YOU	KNOW	; AND LET THE OTHER BLOCK TO ME ON FAIR TERMS FOR A
SIM II	(73)	BEGINNING OF ITS RESPONSIBLE MATURITY. SO NOW YOU	KNOW	; AND MY BUSINESS WITH YOU IS ENDED. (HE RISES). IS
FABL VI	(123)	INTO THE CLAY. /TEACHER/ GOOD, NUMBER TWO. I DONT	KNOW	; AND NEITHER DOES ANYONE ELSE. AND YOU, NUMBER THREE,
FABL PREFACE	(89)	IS " GRANTED; BUT HOW? " UNFORTUNATELY I DONT	KNOW	; AND NEITHER DOES ANYONE ELSE; BUT AS SOMEBODY MUST
SUPR II	(49)	HENRY: THERE ARE THINGS IT IS NOT GOOD FOR YOU TO	KNOW	; AND THIS WAS ONE OF THEM. HOWEVER, CHEER UP: WE ARE
MRS II	(211)	OH YES YOU CAN, IF YOU LIKE. I HAVE A RIGHT TO	KNOW	; AND YOU KNOW VERY WELL THAT I HAVE THAT RIGHT. YOU
JITT I	(15)	(SHE LAUGHS, SMOOTHING HIS GREY HAIR). YES: I	KNOW	; BUT GREY AS I AM, I AM STILL A HOBBLEDEHOY; JUST A
MRS PREFACE	(166)	GO TO THE THEATRE AS OFTEN AS THE CRITICS, I WELL	KNOW	; BUT I AM TOO WELL EQUIPPED FOR THE STRIFE TO BE
BUOY III	(35)	YOU DO IT TO GET AWAY FROM ME. YOU THINK I DONT	KNOW	; BUT I DO. AM I WICKED AND IGNORANT AND UNREASONABLE?
JITT III	(55)	IT WAS OVER AND WE SETTLED DOWN, TROUBLES CAME I	KNOW	; BUT I HAD MY MEMORIES, AND COULD SIT AND THINK OF
JITT I	(11)	STAIRS AS WELL AS IN THE LIFT. /THE GENTLEMAN/ I	KNOW	; BUT I MUSTNT LET THE LIFTMEN SEE ME COMING HERE TOO
JOAN 6	(133)	WAS FRESH. /JOAN/ YOU MEANT TO BE GOOD TO ME, I	KNOW	; BUT IT IS A FISH THAT DOES NOT AGREE WITH ME. THE
JOAN EPILOG	(159)	TAIL AND STUMPLEDUM: THAT DONT MEAN ANYTHING, YOU	KNOW	; BUT IT KEEPS YOU MARCHING. YOUR SERVANT, LADIES AND
WIDO II	(28)	IT'S THE SORT OF HOUSE NOBODY CAN LIVE IN, YOU	KNOW	; BUT IT'S A NICE THING FOR HIM TO OFFER. DONT YOU
FANY PROLOG	(264)	HIM ABOUT ARISTOTLE? /SAVOYARD/ WELL, I DONT	KNOW	; BUT IT'S ONE OF THE RECOGNIZED WAYS OF CHAFFING HIM.
CAND II	(124)	/LEXY/ (CONFIDENTIALLY) WELL, I DONT EXACTLY	KNOW	; BUT SHE SPOKE VERY STRANGELY TO ME THIS MORNING. I'M
FANY PROLOG	(264)	ENGLISHMAN WOULD! THEY DONT COUNT REALLY, YOU	KNOW	; BUT STILL IT'S RATHER THE THING TO HAVE THEM. GUNN IS
DEST	(185)	PRESENCE OF MY REGIMENT? NOT THAT I MIND, YOU	KNOW	; BUT STILL NO REGIMENT LIKES TO HAVE ALL THE OTHER
FABL PREFACE	(92)	GENIUS AND THE IDIOT? AGAIN, I DO NOT	KNOW	; BUT WE CAN AT LEAST CALL IN THE PROFESSIONAL
SUPR III	(106)	STORY IS IN THE BIBLE. WHAT ELSE HE SAYS I DO NOT	KNOW	; FOR IT IS ALL IN A LONG POEM WHICH NEITHER I NOR
O'FL	(209)	TONING DOWN. I DONT ASK YOU TO DROP IT, YOU	KNOW	; FOR IT'S POPULAR, UNDOUBTEDLY; BUT STILL, THE TRUTH
MTH4 II	(184)	GASES YOU SPEAK OF? WE SHOULD BE GLAD TO	KNOW	; FOR THEY MIGHT COME IN VERY HANDY IF WE HAVE TO FIGHT
POSN PREFACE	(361)	" THE STAGE PLAYS" MEANS IN THIS TITLE I DO NOT	KNOW	; NOR DOES ANYONE ELSE. THE NUMBER OF THE BLUEBOOK IS
MTH5	(232)	MY OWN BODY. SCULPTORS DO THAT SOMETIMES, YOU	KNOW	; THOUGH THEY PRETEND THEY DONT. /MARTELLUS/ HM!
ARMS II	(39)	YOU. /RAINA/ (WITH COOL IMPERTINENCE) OH, I	KNOW	SERGIUS IS YOUR PET. I SOMETIMES WISH YOU COULD MARRY
PHIL III	(143)	/CRAVEN/ DONT WORRY YOUR SISTER, SYLVIA. YOU	KNOW	SHE CANT BEAR IT. /SYLVIA/ I SPEAK FOR HER GOOD, DAD.
APPL I	(215)	DO YOU GO PROVOKING LIZZIE FOR LIKE THAT? YOU	KNOW	SHE HAS A TEMPER. /LYSISTRATA/ THERE IS NOTHING
JITT II	(39)	WOULD FORGIVE HIM IF IT KNEW THAT SHE IS WHAT I	KNOW	SHE MUST BE IF HE LOVED HER. OH, WHY DOES SHE NOT DEFY
PYGM III	(234)	THESE TWO MONTHS PAST. /HIGGINS/ THEN HOW DID YOU	KNOW	SHE WAS HERE? /DOOLITTLE/ (" MOST MUSICAL, MOST
DOCT III	(141)	/LOUIS/ DOES IT! WHY CANT YOU THINK? HOW DO YOU	KNOW	SHE WASNT MARRIED ALREADY TOO? /B.B./ WALPOLE!
JITT III	(72)	DESOLATION MUST BE AS GREAT AS MINE: GREATER, I	KNOW	SHE WILL LOVE ME BECAUSE I AM HIS DAUGHTER. AND I KNOW
INCA	(238)	I AM SURE SHE HAD NEVER DONE IT BEFORE; AND I	KNOW	SHE WOULD NEVER HAVE DONE IT AGAIN, SHE WAS SO TRULY
O'FL	(213)	GLAD TO WELCOME YOUR MOTHER. /O'FLAHERTY/ SURE, I	KNOW	SHE WOULD, SIR. SHE WAS ALWAYS A KIND FRIEND TO THE
DOCT III	(149)	YOU GO, SIR PATRICK, LET ME FETCH JENNIFER. I	KNOW	SHE'D LIKE TO SEE YOU, IF YOU DONT MIND. (HE GOES TO
BARB I	(251)	THAT PERHAPS I OUGHT; BUT REALLY, MOTHER, I	KNOW	SO LITTLE ABOUT THEM; AND WHAT I DO KNOW IS SO
BUOY IV	(53)	OH, WHY, WHY AM I INFATUATED WITH YOU? I	KNOW	SO MANY APPARENTLY SUPERIOR WOMEN. /SHE/ SAME HERE.
GENV IV	(113)	AND IN THAT LOVE THERE IS ETERNAL PEACE. I	KNOW	SO MANY CASES, I KNOW BY MY OWN EXPERIENCE. /SECRETARY/
MTH4 I	(167)	HAVE NEVER ASKED US ANY QUESTIONS, ALTHOUGH WE	KNOW	SO MUCH MORE THAN YOU DO? /THE ELDERLY GENTLEMAN/ I AM
2TRU II	(75)	YOU THINK SO, SIR? /TALLBOYS/ I DONT THINK SO: I	KNOW	SO. DONT BE A FOOL, MAN. PULL YOURSELF TOGETHER, AND
LIED	(195)	SAYING NO IN THAT FROZEN PIGHEADED WAY. YOU MUST	KNOW	SOME AURORA OR OTHER SOMEWHERE. /HE/ YOU SAID YOU WERE
ARMS II	(24)	YOU LIKE ME THE BETTER FOR IT, DONT YOU? BUT I	KNOW	SOME FAMILY SECRETS THEY WOULDNT CARE TO HAVE TOLD,
MIS. PREFACE	(33)	GENERALLY, KNOW HOW MANY BEANS MAKE FIVE. IT MUST	KNOW	SOME LAW, WERE IT ONLY A SIMPLE SET OF COMMANDMENTS,
BARB II	(304)	LORD SAXMUNDHAM, OTHERS WOULD FOLLOW. DONT YOU	KNOW	SOMEBODY? COULDNT YOU? WOULDNT YOU? (HER EYES FILL
MRS I	(185)	AND NOTHING BUT MATHEMATICS. I'M SUPPOSED TO	KNOW	SOMETHING ABOUT SCIENCE; BUT I KNOW NOTHING EXCEPT THE
LION PREFACE	(9)	TASK OF GOING STEADILY THROUGH THEM, UNLESS YOU	KNOW	SOMETHING OF THE HISTORY OF THE HUMAN IMAGINATION AS
DEVL II	(36)	RICHARD ADDS, A LITTLE SHAMEFACEDLY) WE SHALL	KNOW	SOON ENOUGH. /ANDERSON/ WELL, PERHAPS YOU WILL LET ME
MILL III	(181)	KNEES TO YOU TO SPARE THEM. /THE MAN/ YOU THAT	KNOW	SUCH A LOT OUGHT TO KNOW THAT A BUSINESS LIKE THIS CANT
DOCT III	(136)	YOU MUST HAVE GREAT INFLUENCE WITH THEM. YOU MUST	KNOW	SUCH LOTS OF THINGS ABOUT THEM-- PRIVATE THINGS THAT
ROCK I	(201)	IT WAS ABOUT THE FAMILY. /SIR ARTHUR/ WELL, I	KNOW	THAT: I HAVE NOT YET BECOME A COMPLETE IDIOT. YOU KEEP
HART II	(122)	KEEPS HANGING ABOUT HER; BUT HOW IS THE WORLD TO	KNOW	THAT? IT'S NOT FAIR TO HASTINGS. IT'S NOT FAIR TO ME.
CAPT I	(223)	BEFORE, MR DRINKWOTTER. IT MEANS PIRATE. DO YE	KNOW	THAT? /DRINKWATER/ BLESS YE AWT, Y' CAWNT BE A PAWRIT
MIS.	(183)	WHEN SHE CAME TO ME IN HER TROUBLE. DIDNT YOU	KNOW	THAT? /GUNNER/ NO. SHE NEVER TALKED TO ME ABOUT
SUPR IV	(149)	YOUR POSITION HAS BEEN GOT BY MY MONEY: DO YOU	KNOW	THAT? /HECTOR/ WELL, YOUVE JUST SPOILED IT ALL BY
CAND III	(140)	YOU TO STAY? JAMES IS MASTER HERE. DONT YOU	KNOW	THAT? /MARCHBANKS/ (FLUSHING WITH A YOUNG POET'S RAGE
FANY II	(289)	BUT THEY SHOULDNT HAVE HAPPENED TO YOU. DONT YOU	KNOW	THAT? /MARGARET/ THEY SHOULDNT HAPPEN TO ANYBODY, I
2TRU III	(85)	GIVE YOU IN SOME GAOLS. /THE SERGEANT/ HOW DO YOU	KNOW	THAT? /SWEETIE/ NEVER YOU MIND HOW I KNOW IT. IT'S
MTH4 I	(153)	BRITON WHO WAS ALIVE IN THEIR TIME. DONT YOU	KNOW	THAT? /THE ELDERLY GENTLEMAN/ DO NOT QUIBBLE, MADAM. I
INCA	(254)	IN DISGUISE. /THE INCA/ GOOD HEAVENS: HOW DO YOU	KNOW	THAT? WHO HAS BETRAYED ME? /ERMYNTRUDE/ HOW COULD I
SUPR I	(15)	YOU, I KNEW THAT ANSWER WOULD COME AS WELL AS I	KNOW	THAT A BOX OF MATCHES WILL COME OUT OF AN AUTOMATIC
MILL III	(181)	THEM. /THE MAN/ YOU THAT KNOW SUCH A LOT OUGHT TO	KNOW	THAT A BUSINESS LIKE THIS CANT AFFORD ANY LUXURIES.
BULL I	(92)	WHAT ON EARTH-- /DOYLE/ IT'S QUITE SIMPLE. YOU	KNOW	THAT A CATERPILLAR-- /BROADBENT/ A CATERPILLAR! ! !
MTH5	(241)	KILL HIM AS HE HAD TO MAKE ME. AND HOW WAS I TO	KNOW	THAT A LITTLE THING LIKE THAT WOULD KILL HIM? I
NEVR III	(266)	MATTERS, THAT I HAVE NOT COMMON SENSE ENOUGH TO	KNOW	THAT A MAN WHO COULD MAKE AS MUCH WAY IN ONE INTERVIEW
DOCT II	(120)	THEM IS A CHEQUE. THE OTHER IS A WOMAN. UNTIL YOU	KNOW	THAT A MAN'S SOUND ON THESE TWO POINTS, YOU KNOW
VWOO 1	(118)	HOW DID YOU KNOW? /A/ (EXASPERATED) HOW DO I	KNOW	THAT A PARROT ISNT A BIRD OF PARADISE? /Z/ THEYRE
METH PREFACE	(R69)	AND HISTORY TO APPRECIATE THE RISK, AND TO	KNOW	THAT A REVOLUTION ALWAYS SEEMS HOPELESS AND IMPOSSIBLE
PYGM II	(224)	PROPERLY SAYS, GARN! MARRIED INDEED! DONT YOU	KNOW	THAT A WOMAN OF THAT CLASS LOOKS A WORN OUT DRUDGE OF
2TRU PREFACE	(8)	ITS DAILY PRACTICE AND ITS REMOTER RESULTS; AND I	KNOW	THAT A YEAR OF IT WOULD MAKE ME MORE UNHAPPY THAN
MIS.	(155)	OF WOMAN IS THAT TO HAVE IN OUR HOUSE WHEN YOU	KNOW	THAT ALL HINDHEAD WILL BE CALLING ON US TO SEE THAT
MRS II	(205)	GOOD. LET US TALK LEARNEDLY. MISS WARREN: DO YOU	KNOW	THAT ALL THE MOST ADVANCED THINKERS ARE AGREED THAT
BULL I	(83)	/DOYLE/ LIKE AN IRISHMAN! ! MAN ALIVE, DONT YOU	KNOW	THAT ALL THIS TOP-O-THE-MORNING AND BROTH-OF-A-BOY AND
NEVR III	(276)	TIME MIDWAY BETWEEN DOLLY AND MRS CLANDON). YOU	KNOW	THAT ALL THIS IS A MADE UP CASE-- THAT FERGUS DOES NOT
ROCK II	(266)	POLITICS WONT BEAR THINKING ABOUT? DIDNT YOU	KNOW	THAT AS A NATION WE HAVE LOST THE TRICK OF THINKING?
MRS PREFACE	(153)	WILL ARISE: EVERY MAN AND WOMAN PRESENT WILL	KNOW	THAT AS LONG AS POVERTY MAKES VIRTUE HIDEOUS AND THE
BARB I	(252)	I DONT MEAN THAT YOU ARE NOT TO BE CONSULTED: YOU	KNOW	THAT AS WELL AS I DO. (STEPHEN CLOSES HIS LIPS AND IS
MTH4 I	(156)	COULDNT HAVE HAPPENED TO A HUNDRED THOUSAND: YOU	KNOW	THAT AS WELL AS I DO. AND WHAT A RIDICULOUS THING TO

SUPR III	(132)	NOT THE TOOL OF ANY BLUNDERING UNIVERSAL FORCE. I	KNOW	THAT BEAUTY IS GOOD TO LOOK AT; THAT MUSIC IS GOOD TO
MTH2	(67)	A YAWN) WITH PLEASURE, MR BARNABAS. OF COURSE YOU	KNOW	THAT BEFORE I CAN ADOPT ANY NEW PLANK IN THE PARTY
FABL III	(112)	YOU MAY BE ONE OF THE ARTFUL DODGERS WHO	KNOW	THAT BEGGING IS EASIER AND HAPPIER THAN BOSSING. /THE
SUPR III	(99)	TRUTH IS, YOU HAVE-- I WONT SAY NO HEART; FOR WE	KNOW	THAT BENEATH ALL YOUR AFFECTED CYNICISM YOU HAVE A WARM
WIDO II	(39)	DR TRENCH: I WILL BE PLAIN WITH YOU. I	KNOW	THAT BLANCHE HAS A QUICK TEMPER. IT IS PART OF HER
ARMS III	(68)	WHEN I WROTE THAT ON THE PHOTOGRAPH, I DID NOT	KNOW	THAT CAPTAIN BLUNTSCHLI WAS MARRIED. /BLUNTSCHLI (
CAPT III	(275)	WORD, MR RANKIN. (HE COMES BACK). THE CADI DIDNT	KNOW	THAT CAPTAIN BRASSBOUND WAS SIR HOWARD'S NEPHEW, DID
BASH I	(95)	YELLS, AND SCREAMST MY NAME FOR ALL THE WORLD TO	KNOW	THAT CASHEL BYRON IS TRAINING HERE FOR COMBAT.
CURE	(226)	BUT YOU CANT PERSUADE ME THAT IF YOU HAPPEN TO	KNOW	THAT CERTAIN SHARES ARE GOING TO RISE YOU SHOULDNT BUY
MIS. PREFACE	(63)	CAN, OFTEN BAFFLING THOSE SENSITIVE PARENTS WHO	KNOW	THAT CHILDREN SHOULD THINK FOR THEMSELVES AND FEND FOR
FABL VI	(123)	YOU REALLY WANT TO KNOW? /YOUTH 3/ NO. I DIDNT	KNOW	THAT CONES BURY THEMSELVES; AND I DONT CARE A DUMP
PRES	(141)	THE GOVERNMENT OF THE MASSES BY THE CLASSES. YOU	KNOW	THAT DEMOCRACY IS DAMNED NONSENSE, AND THAT NO CLASS
GENV IV	(93)	WHO ARE YOU CALLING LOWER ORDERS? DONT YOU	KNOW	THAT DEMOCRACY HAS PUT AN END TO ALL THAT? /BBDE/ ON
ROCK II	(266)	ON YOUR HOLIDAY INSTEAD OF THINKING? DIDNT YOU	KNOW	THAT ENGLISH POLITICS WONT BEAR THINKING ABOUT? DIDNT
CLEO PRO1	(89)	TO ME THEN, OH YE COMPULSORILY EDUCATED ONES.	KNOW	THAT EVEN AS THERE IS AN OLD ENGLAND AND A NEW, AND YE
GETT	(290)	BECAUSE IVE SEEN TOO MUCH ACTIVE SERVICE NOT TO	KNOW	THAT EVERY MAN'S NERVE PLAYS HIM FALSE AT ONE TIME OR
MTH4 II	(176)	NOT SPEAKING OF AN AGRICULTURAL FIELD. DO YOU NOT	KNOW	THAT EVERY MASS OF MATTER IN MOTION CARRIES WITH IT AN
O'FL	(208)	HER AFTER FUNKING A FIGHT. THAT WAS HOW I GOT TO	KNOW	THAT FIGHTING WAS EASIER THAN IT LOOKED, AND THAT THE
METH PREFACE	(R68)	SUFFER THIS OR THAT: THEY ALLOWED THEMSELVES TO	KNOW	THAT FOR THEIR OWN PERSONAL PURPOSES, WHICH ARE LIMITED
FABL PREFACE	(71)	NOT HAVE THOUGHT OF THAT. ALL PLAYWRIGHTS SHOULD	KNOW	THAT HAD I NOT SUSPENDED MY ARTISTIC ACTIVITY TO WRITE
ROCK II	(263)	IN THE CLASS WAR ANY MORE THAN YOU DO, DEXY. I	KNOW	THAT HALF THE WORKING CLASS IS SLAVING AWAY TO PILE UP
KING I	(196)	WHAT! THAT HENPECKED BOOBY! I SUPPOSE YOU	KNOW	THAT HE GOT HIS START IN LIFE AS YOUR BARBARA'S KEPT
CAPT I	(228)	SIR HOWARD? /SIR HOWARD/ (ABRUPTLY) DONT YOU	KNOW	THAT HE IS DEAD? /RANKIN/ (MUCH SHOCKED) NEVER HAIRD
NEVR II	(233)	FATHER FOR US! /M'COMAS/ (ANGRILY) HOW DO YOU	KNOW	THAT HE IS NOT NICE? AND WHAT RIGHT HAVE YOU TO CHOOSE
JOAN 1	(64)	A CORNER, EXCEPT THAT HE WONT FIGHT. WE DONT EVEN	KNOW	THAT HE IS THE DAUPHIN: HIS MOTHER SAYS HE ISNT; AND
BULL III	(126)	IS HE GOING TO RETIRE? /CORNELIUS/ NO: I DONT	KNOW	THAT HE IS. /LARRY/ (INTERROGATIVELY) WELL? THEN?
MILL II	(169)	ON SO MUCH OF WHAT OTHER PEOPLE MADE; BUT I DO	KNOW	THAT HE LOST FOUR FIFTHS OF IT BY BEING FAR ENOUGH
GENV IV	(111)	IF YOU HAD EVER HAD GOD'S WORK TO DO YOU WOULD	KNOW	THAT HE NEVER DOES IT HIMSELF. WE ARE HERE TO DO IT FOR
ROCK I	(220)	OR WRONG, BECAUSE I DONT KNOW WHAT HE SAID. BUT I	KNOW	THAT HE PUTS INTO EVERY MAN AND WOMAN THAT DOES READ
DOCT III	(153)	THAT ARE TOO TRIVIAL FOR HIM TO NOTICE. I	KNOW	THAT HE SOMETIMES SHOCKS PEOPLE ABOUT MONEY BECAUSE HE
CAND I	(83)	ARGUING WITH SOMEBODY. HE ASKED ME TO LET YOU	KNOW	THAT HE WAS COMING. /MORELL/ (HALF INCREDULOUS) BUT HE
JITT II	(29)	HE WOULD PEG OUT FIRST? /FESSLER/ BUT DIDNT YOU	KNOW	THAT HE WAS ILL? /LENKHEIM/ OH, I KNEW ABOUT HIS HEART
FABL II	(106)	TO THE ENEMY. /C.-IN-C./ WHAT! DONT YOU	KNOW	THAT HE WENT TO LIVE IN THE ISLE OF WIGHT AS THE SAFEST
JITT III	(72)	IT. I KNOW THAT SHE CANNOT BE VERY FAR OFF. I	KNOW	THAT HER GRIEF AND DESOLATION MUST BE AS GREAT AS MINE:
INCA	(241)	BUT HER HIGHNESS WAS SO GRACIOUS. I DID NOT	KNOW	THAT HER HIGHNESS WAS AT ALL PARTICULAR. /ERMYNTRUDE/
LION II	(135)	HOUR OF TRIAL. /FERROVIUS/ THAT IS WHAT I FEAR. I	KNOW	THAT I AM A FIGHTER. HOW CAN I FEEL SURE THAT I AM A
ROCK II	(249)	/SIR JAFNA/ YOU HAVE HEARD OF ME, MR MAYOR. YOU	KNOW	THAT I AM A MAN WHO KNOWS WHAT HE IS TALKING ABOUT.
BUOY II	(24)	/HE/ STAY, PRESUMPTUOUS ONE. I WOULD HAVE YOU TO	KNOW	THAT I AM A MASTER OF ARTS OF THE UNIVERSITY OF OXFORD,
CLEO I	(115)	CLEOPATRA GOES ON EAGERLY, TO CAESAR) CAESAR WILL	KNOW	THAT I AM A QUEEN WHEN HE SEES MY CROWN AND ROBES, WILL
VWOO 2	(128)	MAN EXPECTS THE EARTH. /A/ HOW DO YOU	KNOW	THAT I AM A WIDOWER? /Z/ YOU TOLD ME. /A/ DID I? WHEN
SIM II	(61)	IN THEM. I CANNOT BEAR BEING LOVED, BECAUSE I	KNOW	THAT I AM A WORM, AND THAT NOBODY COULD LOVE ME UNLESS
ARMS I	(9)	CUTTING HIM SHORT) YOU WILL SHOOT ME. HOW DO YOU	KNOW	THAT I AM AFRAID TO DIE? /THE MAN/ (CUNNINGLY) AH;
MTH4 I	(153)	AS IT IS, I HAVE TO BE CONTENT AND PROUD TO	KNOW	THAT I AM DESCENDED FROM BOTH THOSE HEROES. /ZOO/ YOU
SIM II	(61)	FOR BEING OUT OF ALL PATIENCE WITH ME, BECAUSE I	KNOW	THAT I AM ENOUGH TO DRIVE ANYBODY MAD, AND SHE IS WISE
SUPR I	(44)	/TANNER/ DONT KNOW WHAT? /VIOLET/ THEY DONT	KNOW	THAT I AM IN THE RIGHT, I MEAN. /TANNER/ OH, THEY KNOW
SUPR I	(8)	BUT THERE ARE LIMITS TO SOCIAL TOLERATION. YOU	KNOW	THAT I AM NOT A BIGOTED OR PREJUDICED MAN. YOU KNOW
CLEO V	(197)	GOVERNOR! WHAT ARE YOU DREAMING OF? DO YOU NOT	KNOW	THAT I AM ONLY THE SON OF A FREEDMAN? /CAESAR/ (
SUPR I	(8)	THAT I AM NOT A BIGOTED OR PREJUDICED MAN. YOU	KNOW	THAT I AM PLAIN ROEBUCK RAMSDEN WHEN OTHER MEN WHO HAVE
CLEO PRO1	(89)	WITHOUT JUDGMENT. LOOK UPON MY HAWK'S HEAD; AND	KNOW	THAT I AM RA, WHO WAS ONCE IN EGYPT A MIGHTY GOD. YE
CLEO III	(148)	(FLUSHING ANGRILY) HOW DARE YOU? DO YOU	KNOW	THAT I AM THE QUEEN? /SENTINEL/ I HAVE MY ORDERS. YOU
LADY	(242)	WITH THE TONGUES OF ANGELS, AS INDEED YOU DO, YET	KNOW	THAT I AM THE KING OF WORDS-- /THE LADY/ A KING, HA!
WIDO III	(63)	IF SHE'S AGREEABLE? /TRENCH/ (SHORTLY) I DONT	KNOW	THAT I AM. (SARTORIUS RISES INDIGNANTLY). /LICKCHEESE/
JOAN 3	(90)	ME TO THE WRONG SIDE OF THE RIVER. DO YOU NOT	KNOW	THAT I BRING YOU BETTER HELP THAN EVER CAME TO ANY
SUPR I	(18)	BY THE LACK OF ANY RESPONSE, CONTINUES) I DONT	KNOW	THAT I CAN CONSENT TO ACT UNDER SUCH CONDITIONS. MR
JITT III	(64)	NOT YET. PERHAPS YOU HAD BETTER TELL HIM. I DONT	KNOW	THAT I CAN GO ON WORKING HERE EVERY DAY IF EDITH STICKS
PYGM II	(228)	ME SPEAK TO THE GIRL PROPERLY IN PRIVATE. I DONT	KNOW	THAT I CAN TAKE CHARGE OF HER OR CONSENT TO THE
APPL II	(268)	IS PAST. YOU THINK YOU CAN DO WITHOUT ME; AND I	KNOW	THAT I CANNOT DO WITHOUT YOU. I DECIDE, OF COURSE, IN
MIS.	(142)	YOU KNOW THE BODILY INFIRMITIES OF THE OLD. YOU	KNOW	THAT I DARENT EAT ALL THE RICH THINGS YOU GOBBLE UP AT
GLIM	(179)	NOT CLEVER, EXCELLENCY. AT THE SAME TIME YOU MUST	KNOW	THAT I DID NOT MEAN MY GIULIETTA TO TELL YOU. I KNOW MY
MTH2	(65)	IF YOU DID YOU WOULD KNOW-- /BURGE/ WHAT DO YOU	KNOW	THAT I DONT KNOW? /LUBIN/ I KNOW THAT WE ARE TAKING UP
APPL I	(230)	I DOUBT IF THAT IS ANY LONGER TRUE, SIR. I	KNOW	THAT I GET BLAMED FOR EVERYTHING THAT GOES WRONG IM MY
SUPR I	(5)	I ALWAYS INTENDED TO THANK HIM-- TO LET HIM	KNOW	THAT I HAD NOT TAKEN ALL HIS CARE OF ME AS A MATTER OF
DEVL II	(44)	/ANDERSON/ DO YOU THINK IT WOULD BE BETTER TO	KNOW	THAT I HAD RUN AWAY FROM MY POST AT THE FIRST SIGN OF
DOCT III	(133)	DUBEDAT/ (PUTTING HER ARMS ROUND HIS NECK) YOU	KNOW	THAT I HATE LECTURING, AND THAT I DONT FOR A MOMENT
JITT I	(18)	THAT SHE HAS TAKEN SOMETHING FROM YOU. /JITTA/ I	KNOW	THAT I HAVE A DIVINE RIGHT TO YOU. AND I KNOW THAT SHE
WIDO II	(34)	MY DEAR: IT'S NO LAUGHING MATTER. DO YOU	KNOW	THAT I HAVE A BARE SEVEN HUNDRED A YEAR TO LIVE ON?
2TRU III	(106)	MEDICINE AND THREE MEAT MEALS A DAY? DO YOU	KNOW	THAT I HAVE KILLED TWO OF MY CHILDREN BECAUSE THEY TOLD
PHIL III	(133)	OH, I HATE THAT LOOK IN THEIR FACES. DO YOU	KNOW	THAT I HAVE NEVER HAD ONE HUMAN BEING CARE FOR ME SINCE
APPL I	(227)	THE PALACE BACK STAIRS MUST CEASE. /MAGNUS/ YOU	KNOW	THAT I HAVE NO CONTROL OF THE PRESS. THE PRESS IS IN
APPL II	(270)	YOU ANYTHING ELSE TO PROPOSE? /BOANERGES/ I DONT	KNOW	THAT I HAVE ON THE SPUR OF THE MOMENT. WE SHOULD HAVE
CAND II	(119)	(LOOKING AT HER WITH TROUBLED INTENSITY) YOU	KNOW	THAT I HAVE PERFECT CONFIDENCE IN YOU, CANDIDA.
WIDO I	(15)	MENTION? /TRENCH/ ONLY THAT-- THAT-- NO: I DONT	KNOW	THAT I HAVE, EXCEPT THAT I LOVE-- /SARTORIUS/ (
JOAN 6	(133)	DID YOU JUMP FROM THE TOWER? /JOAN/ HOW DO YOU	KNOW	THAT I JUMPED? /D'ESTIVET/ YOU WERE FOUND LYING IN THE
FANY II	(290)	I CALLED NAMES. I HEARD WORDS THAT I DIDNT EVEN	KNOW	THAT I KNEW, COMING OUT OF MY MOUTH JUST AS IF SOMEBODY
ARMS III	(63)	HIM, AND SAYS, IN A LOWER, INTENSER TONE) DO YOU	KNOW	THAT I LOOKED OUT OF THE WINDOW AS I WENT UPSTAIRS, TO
ARMS III	(59)	I WOULD SET YOU ON THE THRONE BY MY SIDE. YOU	KNOW	THAT I LOVE ANOTHER WOMAN, A WOMAN AS HIGH ABOVE YOU AS
FANY PROLOG	(269)	GIVES WAY ON A POINT OF ART. I DARENT LET HIM	KNOW	THAT I LOVE BEETHOVEN AND WAGNER; AND AS TO STRAUSS, IF
GETT	(330)	LOVE YOUR JORJY PORJY? /MRS GEORGE/ OH, I DONT	KNOW	THAT I LOVE HIM. HE'S MY HUSBAND, YOU KNOW. BUT IF I
JITT I	(22)	HIM) NO, NO, BRUNO: YOU ARE ASKING TOO MUCH. YOU	KNOW	THAT I LOVE YOU AS MY MAN, WITHOUT A THOUGHT OF YOUR
MTH1 I	(16)	BUT I WAS NOT CONFUSED IN MY MIND. IF I DID NOT	KNOW	THAT I LOVED EVE, AT LEAST I DID NOT KNOW THAT SHE
CAPT I	(221)	ASSURE YER, GAVNER. /RANKIN/ I WOULD HAVE YOU TO	KNOW	THAT I MET HIM PRIVATELY, MR DRINKWOTTER. HIS BROTHER
CAND II	(120)	GROWN UP AND EXPERIENCED, LIKE YOU. AND HE WILL	KNOW	THAT I MUST HAVE KNOWN. I WONDER WHAT HE WILL THINK OF
KING I	(192)	HIM. HOW CAN YOU STOOP? /CHARLES/ I MUST. AND I	KNOW	THAT I MUST, TO PLAY THE KING AS YOU WOULD HAVE ME I
PHIL II	(106)	OH, I KNOW YOU, MY LAD. /CHARTERIS/ THEN YOU	KNOW	THAT I NEVER PAY ANY SPECIAL ATTENTION TO ANY WOMAN.
SUPR III	(100)	TEMPERAMENT: I DONT UNDERSTAND IT: I DONT	KNOW	THAT I PARTICULARLY WANT TO UNDERSTAND IT; BUT IT TAKES
DOCT IV	(163)	DUBEDAT/ I'M LISTENING. I SHALL NOT FORGET. YOU	KNOW	THAT I PROMISE. /LOUIS/ WELL, THATS ABOUT ALL; EXCEPT
KING II	(230)	WITH. /CATHERINE/ I AM TORN TEN DIFFERENT WAYS. I	KNOW	THAT I SHOULD MAKE YOU DIVORCE ME AND MARRY A YOUNG
CAND I	(103)	RAPTURE) BECAUSE SHE WILL UNDERSTAND ME, AND	KNOW	THAT I UNDERSTAND HER. IF YOU KEEP BACK ONE WORD OF IT
HART I	(77)	TURN. BUT IT HAS NEVER COME OFF. /HECTOR/ I DONT	KNOW	THAT I WANT IT TO COME OFF. IT WAS DAMNED DANGEROUS.
PHIL II	(122)	INDIFFERENCE, AND RISING CARELESSLY) I DONT	KNOW	THAT I WAS GOING TO SAY ANYTHING MORE. IF I WERE YOU I
2TRU III	(97)	DIDNT KNOW THAT THE RICH WERE MISERABLE. I DIDNT	KNOW	THAT I WAS MISERABLE. I DIDNT KNOW THAT OUR
KING I	(168)	IF YOU SO DESIRE. BUT I OWED IT TO YOU TO LET YOU	KNOW	THAT I WAS NOT DECEIVED BY YOUR NEW NAME. /CHARLES/ I
BULL II	(100)	WORK. WHEN IT TOOK AWAY MY PAPERS IT MEANT YOU TO	KNOW	THAT I WAS ONLY A POOR MADMAN, UNFIT AND UNWORTHY TO
AUGS	(267)	IN YOUR SPEECH LAST NIGHT. /AUGUSTUS/ I DID NOT	KNOW	THAT I WAS TALKING TO AN IMBECILE. YOU OUGHT TO BE
JOAN 3	(91)	DISPLAYS OF PERSONAL COURAGE. BESIDES, YOU MUST	KNOW	THAT I WELCOME YOU AS A SAINT, NOT AS A SOLDIER. I HAVE
JITT III	(68)	YOU DONT KNOW HOW SHE GOT HIM THERE. BUT I	KNOW	THAT IF HE REALLY OPENED HIS HEART TO HER, HE TALKED TO
SUPR IV	(155)	THE PRICE: THEY WERE YOUNG AND GREEDY, AND DIDNT	KNOW	THAT IF THE SHARES WERE WORTH WHAT WAS BID FOR THEM
MRS PREFACE	(164)	IF THEIR HOUSES ARE CONDUCTED VICIOUSLY. THEY	KNOW	THAT IF THEY LOSE THEIR CHARACTER, THE COUNTY COUNCIL
PRES	(141)	AND IF THEY MADE A FUSS, SHOOT THEM DOWN. YOU	KNOW	THAT IF WE NEED PUBLIC OPINION TO SUPPORT US, WE CAN
JITT III	(72)	MUST LEARN TO EXPECT DISAPPOINTMENTS. HOW DO YOU	KNOW	THAT IF YOU FOUND THIS WOMAN SHE WOULD NOT DISAPPOINT
SIM PRO,2,	(27)	PLACE. THE CLIMATE IS SOMETHING TERRIBLE. DO YOU	KNOW	THAT IF YOU HADNT COME IN THIS MORNING I'D HAVE DONE
MIS.	(189)	HERE. I KNOW I DIDNT RISE TO THE OCCASION. I	KNOW	THAT IF YOUD BEEN MY MOTHER, YOUD HAVE BEEN ASHAMED OF
LIED	(189)	LEAST LITTLE THING ABOUT THE WORLD, HENRY, YOUD	KNOW	THAT IN A LARGE FAMILY, THOUGH THE SISTERS QUARREL WITH
DOCT IV	(165)	PUZZLING IT OUT FOR HIMSELF WEAKLY) I	KNOW	THAT IN AN ACCIDENTAL SORT OF WAY, STRUGGLING THROUGH
MILL IV	(203)	YOU WILL; BUT I SHOULD RATHER LIKE THE WORLD TO	KNOW	THAT IN MY LITTLE WAY I WAS ABLE TO TAKE THE BEST AND
PRES	(141)	OF A LABOR MAJORITY IN PARLIAMENT. YOU	KNOW	THAT IN THAT CASE WE SHOULD DISFRANCHISE THE MOB, AND
APPL I	(221)	FOUR SQUARE MILES OF CONFECTIONERY WORKS! DO YOU	KNOW	THAT IN THE CHRISTMAS CRACKER TRADE BIRMINGHAM IS THE

SUPR III (113)	TRUE. BUT I AM QUITE CONTENT WITH BRAIN ENOUGH TO	KNOW	THAT I'M ENJOYING MYSELF. I DONT WANT TO UNDERSTAND
GETT (262)	DO YOU ALWAYS CALL LESBIA MY SISTER? DONT YOU	KNOW	THAT IT ANNOYS HER MORE THAN ANY OF THE REST OF YOUR
MILL III (180)	CAN AFFORD AND NOT A PENNY MORE. YOU SEEM TO	KNOW	THAT IT CAN AFFORD FIVE SHILLINGS. WELL, IF YOU KNOW
ROCK II (282)	THE BEST THAT COULD BE DONE. I KNOW BETTER NOW: I	KNOW	THAT IT CAN BE HELPED, AND HOW IT CAN BE HELPED. AND
MILL III (180)	FIVE SHILLINGS. WELL, IF YOU KNOW THAT, YOU	KNOW	THAT IT CANT AFFORD ANY MORE. TAKE YOUR FIVE SHILLINGS
SUPR PREFACE(R30)	FOR THAT PUBLIC IN THIS ENTERPRISE; BUT I	KNOW	THAT IT HAS THE FRIENDLIEST DISPOSITION TOWARDS YOU AND
CAND I (100)	HIGHER POWERS THAN I CAN EVER PRETEND TO. I WELL	KNOW	THAT IT IS IN THE POET THAT THE HOLY SPIRIT OF MAN--
GETT (326)	FROM THAT WOMAN'S HUSBAND. AT THAT TIME I DID NOT	KNOW	THAT IT IS NOT TRUE ECONOMY TO BUY THE LOWEST PRICED
CAND II (122)	FRIGHTFULLY. I FEEL HIS PAIN IN MY OWN HEART. I	KNOW	THAT IT IS NOT YOUR FAULT: IT IS SOMETHING THAT MUST
SUPR III (124)	OF ALL HUMAN RELATIONS. /DON JUAN/ HOW DO YOU	KNOW	THAT IT IS NOT THE GREATEST OF ALL HUMAN RELATIONS?
METH PREFACE(R83)	UNTIL IT IS AS FAMILIAR AS POP GOES THE WEASEL,	KNOW	THAT IT IS SANE AND METHODICAL. AS SUCH, IT MUST
FANY EPILOG (329)	DISMAY. PRAY DELIVER YOUR VERDICT. MR BANNAL: YOU	KNOW	THAT IT IS THE CUSTOM AT A COURT MARTIAL FOR THE
KING I (203)	NO EXCEPTION TO THIS. I HAVE TOO GOOD REASON TO	KNOW	THAT IT IS TRUE. BUT BEWARE HOW YOU LET THESE BOLD
SUPR III (132)	THEY MAY SAY OF ME IN CHURCHES ON EARTH, I	KNOW	THAT IT IS UNIVERSALLY ADMITTED IN GOOD SOCIETY THAT
DOCT IV (168)	/SIR PATRICK/ WHEN YOURE AS OLD AS I AM, YOULL	KNOW	THAT IT MATTERS VERY LITTLE HOW A MAN DIES. WHAT
MTH1 I (4)	MIGHT BE. /ADAM/ NO, I TELL YOU IT MUST NOT BE. I	KNOW	THAT IT MUST NOT BE. /EVE/ WE BOTH KNOW IT. HOW DO WE
ARMS III (50)	SUDDEN EARNESTNESS) I DO INDEED. BUT THEY DONT	KNOW	THAT IT WAS IN THIS HOUSE YOU TOOK REFUGE. IF SERGIUS
GETT (340)	YOU EVER FORGIVE ME? /MRS GEORGE/ YOU COULDNT	KNOW	THAT IT WAS ONLY THE COAL MERCHANT'S WIFE, COULD YOU..
LION PREFACE(47)	IN WHICH NEWTON PROVED IT, AND DOES NOT EVEN	KNOW	THAT IT WAS WRITTEN IN LATIN. IF YOU PRESS AN ULSTER
MTH1 I (17)	AS LONG AS YOU DO NOT KNOW THE FUTURE YOU DO NOT	KNOW	THAT IT WILL NOT BE HAPPIER THAN THE PAST. THAT IS
GETT (262)	TWENTY YEARS SINCE SHE REFUSED YOU. AND YOU	KNOW	THAT IT'S NOT BECAUSE SHE DISLIKES YOU, BUT ONLY THAT
OVER (178)	OF THE SORT: I SEE THAT IT'S NOT WORTH IT: I	KNOW	THAT IT'S WRONG: I HAVE NEVER IN MY LIFE BEEN COOLER,
MIS. (189)	MY DAY, MIND YOU--- I'M GOOD FOR SOMETHING TOO. I	KNOW	THAT IVE MADE A SILLY EXHIBITION OF MYSELF HERE. I KNOW
GETT PREFACE(246)	HAD FIVE MINUTES' EXPERIENCE OF LOVE THEY WOULD	KNOW	THAT LOVE IS ITSELF A TYRANNY REQUIRING SPECIAL
PLES PREFACE(R16)	THEM I MUST FRANKLY TAKE THE SUPERIOR POSITION. I	KNOW	THAT MANY MANAGERS ARE WHOLLY DEPENDENT ON THEM, AND
JOAN 6 (124)	CASE TODAY AND HASTEN TO HER DEFENCE IF I DID NOT	KNOW	THAT MEN FAR MY SUPERIORS IN LEARNING AND PIETY, IN
APPL I (236)	WELL, PERHAPS IT WOULD SURPRISE YOU ALL TO	KNOW	THAT MIKE DOESNT DRINK AS MUCH AS I DO. /AMANDA/ YOU
SUPR III SD(79)	THE ROAD; FOR IT IS NOW STARLIGHT; AND THEY	KNOW	THAT MOTOR CARS HAVE LAMPS WHICH CAN BE TURNED TO
LADY PREFACE(221)	REEKS. I LOVE TO HEAR HER SPEAK; YET WELL I	KNOW	THAT MUSIC HATH A FAR MORE PLEASING SOUND. I GRANT I
SUPR I (7)	WITH IMPRESSIVE GRAVITY). NOW, OCTAVIUS, I	KNOW	THAT MY DEAD FRIEND WAS RIGHT WHEN HE SAID YOU WERE A
GETT (357)	MY HAND FOR THAT FORBIDDEN FRUIT BEFORE; AND I	KNOW	THAT MY HAND WILL ALWAYS COME BACK EMPTY, TO DISBELIEVE
SUPR IV (156)	KNOW I LOVE YOU. /ANN/ WHATS THE GOOD, TAVY? YOU	KNOW	THAT MY MOTHER IS DETERMINED THAT I SHALL MARRY JACK.
MIS. (156)	TAKE HER CHANCE. /LORD SUMMERHAYS/ STILL, YOU	KNOW	THAT MY NAME MUST NOT BE ASSOCIATED WITH ANY SCANDAL.
6CAL (102)	HARDLY BUY ME A NEW GIRDLE; AND OH, DEAR SIR, YOU	KNOW	THAT MY OLD ONE IS BECOMING TOO STRAIT FOR ME. WILL YOU
MIS. (201)	GIVE ME A HOME, A POSITION. HE TELLS ME I MUST	KNOW	THAT MY PRESENT POSITION IS NOT ONE FOR A NICE WOMAN.
PYGM I (207)	SERVICES OF A DENTIST). /THE MOTHER/ HOW DO YOU	KNOW	THAT MY SON'S NAME IS FREDDY, PRAY? /THE FLOWER GIRL/
SIM PREFACE(7)	TERRORISM WE HAVE NO RECORD OF ITS SUCCESSES. WE	KNOW	THAT NAIVE ATTEMPTS TO BRIBE DIVINE JUSTICE LED TO A
JITT I (19)	NOT SUCH A CONFOUNDEDLY BAD PSYCHOLOGIST HE WOULD	KNOW	THAT NATURE MEANT YOU TO BE MY WIFE. IT IS A STROKE OF
AUGS (274)	YOU HAD A GERMAN BROTHER-IN-LAW, MADAM, YOU WOULD	KNOW	THAT NOTHING ELSE IN THE WORLD PRODUCES SO STRONG AN
BUOY III (43)	CANNOT DO EQUATIONS, I AM MATHEMATICIAN ENOUGH TO	KNOW	THAT NOTHING IS STATIONARY: EVERYTHING IS MOVING AND
ANNA (297)	IS SATISFIED. /THE GRAND DUCHESS/ THEN HOW DO YOU	KNOW	THAT ONE OF THE PASSPORTS WAS MINE? /STRAMMFEST/ A
INCA (252)	AFTER ALL, ANY FOOL CAN BE A SOLDIER: WE	KNOW	THAT ONLY TOO WELL IN PERUSALEM, WHERE EVERY FOOL IS A
2TRU III (97)	I DIDNT KNOW THAT I WAS MISERABLE. I DIDNT	KNOW	THAT OUR RESPECTABILITY WAS UPPISH SNOBBERY AND OUR
CATH 1 (170)	YOU THINK SHE MURDERED HIM? /EDSTASTON/ I	KNOW	THAT PEOPLE HAVE SAID SO. /PATIOMKIN/ (THUNDEROUSLY:
LION PREFACE(62)	NATURE IMPOSES ON ALL HUMAN BEINGS ALIKE. WE	KNOW	THAT PEOPLE NEED BREAD AND BOOTS WITHOUT WAITING FOR
VWOO 3 (138)	MORE IN LIFE THAN A JOB AND A SALARY. /A/ I	KNOW	THAT PERFECTLY WELL. THERE IS ONE THING WE ARE ALL OUT
ROCK II (278)	AND A COME-DOWN FOR HIM. /LADY CHAVENDER/ WE BOTH	KNOW	THAT POINT OF VIEW, MISS BROLLIKINS; BUT IT IS YOU, NOT
FABL PREFACE(84)	MATHEMATICAL. NONE OF OUR POLITICIANS SEEMS TO	KNOW	THAT POLITICAL ACTION, LIKE ALL EARTHLY ACTION, MUST
POSN PREFACE(421)	OR OF ARCHBISHOP LAUD. ONE OF THEM DID NOT	KNOW	THAT POLITICS MEANT ANYTHING MORE THAN PARTY
JITT III (73)	/JITTA/ YES. /EDITH/ JITTA! ! ! /JITTA/ YES, I	KNOW	THAT POOR CRIMINAL. I KNOW WHAT HAS BECOME OF HER. I
BARB PREFACE(209)	AT THE END OF THE STORY); BUT FOR ALL THAT, WE	KNOW	THAT POTTS PLAYS AN ENORMOUS PART IN OURSELVES AND IN
MRS IV (246)	OF REAL COMPASSION IN HIS AIRY TENDERNESS) YOU	KNOW	THAT PRADDY IS THE SOUL OF KINDNESS, MRS WARREN.
FANY II (294)	HORRIFIED) OH, DONT SAY SUCH A THING AS THAT. I	KNOW	THAT PRAYER CAN SET US FREE; THOUGH YOU COULD NEVER
2TRU PREFACE(21)	SELF-ELECTED AS GENTLEMEN AND LADIES. WE	KNOW	THAT PRIVATE PROPERTY DISTRIBUTES WEALTH, WORK, AND
MTH4 I (164)	YES, YES, YES, DADDY: WE LONGLIVED PEOPLE	KNOW	THAT QUITE WELL. BUT DID ANY OF THEIR DISCIPLES EVER
MILL IV (196)	VERY WELL, SAGAMORE. YOU SEE MY CONDITION: YOU	KNOW	THAT RIGHT AND JUSTICE ARE ON MY SIDE. I SHALL NOT
MTH4 I (142)	TO GO ABOUT HERE WITHOUT NURSES. DO YOU NOT	KNOW	THAT RULES ARE MEANT TO BE KEPT? /THE ELDERLY
JITT III (72)	IS HOW. I HAVE THOUGHT AND THOUGHT ABOUT IT. I	KNOW	THAT SHE CANNOT BE VERY FAR OFF. I KNOW THAT HER GRIEF
CAPT II (255)	OUR LAST MEETING. PERHAPS YOU WERE TOO YOUNG TO	KNOW	THAT SHE COULD HARDLY HAVE EXPECTED TO LIVE LONG.
JITT I (18)	I KNOW THAT I HAVE A DIVINE RIGHT TO YOU. AND I	KNOW	THAT SHE HAS NOT. /BRUNO/ THERE ARE OTHER RIGHTS BESIDE
DEST (188)	/LADY/ (MYSTERIOUSLY) WELL, DO YOU	KNOW	THAT SHE IS A WITCH? /GIUSEPPE/ (IN TERROR, CROSSING
PYGM II (234)	YOU MUST HAVE. HOW ELSE COULD YOU POSSIBLY	KNOW	THAT SHE IS HERE? /DOOLITTLE/ DONT TAKE A MAN UP LIKE
APPL I (210)	I WAS GLAD TO SEE THAT. SHE DOESNT SEEM TO	KNOW	THAT SHE IS THE PRINCESS ROYAL, EH? /SEMPRONIUS/ WELL,
BASH II,1, (106)	HECUBA THOU POINTEST DARKLY AT MY LOVELY COUSIN.	KNOW	THAT SHE IS TO ME, AND I TO HER, WHAT NEVER CANST THOU
MTH1 I (16)	DID NOT KNOW THAT I LOVED EVE, AT LEAST I DID NOT	KNOW	THAT SHE MIGHT CEASE TO LOVE ME, AND COME TO LOVE SOME
JOAN 5 (118)	TRUTH. /THE ARCHBISHOP/ THEY DID. /JOAN/ BUT YOU	KNOW	THAT SHE WAS SPEAKING THE TRUTH. YOU WOULD NOT LET THEM
JITT III (59)	HAD WITH THE OTHER WOMAN THE WRONG SORT. HOW DO I	KNOW	THAT SHE WASNT A CLEVERER WOMAN THAN I AM? I DONT CARE
JITT III (72)	SHE WILL LOVE ME BECAUSE I AM HIS DAUGHTER. AND I	KNOW	THAT SHE WILL BE SOMEBODY WORTHY OF HIM. /JITTA/ EDITH,
PHIL III (143)	HER GOOD, DAD. ALL THE WORLD CANT BE EXPECTED TO	KNOW	THAT SHE'S THE FAMILY BABY. /JULIA/ YOU WILL GET YOUR
SUPR I (6)	HER FATHER'S WISH WOULD BE SACRED TO HER. DO YOU	KNOW	THAT SINCE SHE GREW UP TO YEARS OF DISCRETION, I DONT
DOCT PREFACE(23)	SHE WAS SNUBBED AS AN IGNORANT FEMALE WHO DID NOT	KNOW	THAT SMALLPOX CAN BE PRODUCED ONLY BY THE IMPORTATION
GENV IV (100)	PRACTICAL VIEW. IT IS LIKE THE LONDON TRAFFIC. WE	KNOW	THAT SO MANY CHILDREN WILL BE RUN OVER AND KILLED EVERY
JOAN 1 (67)	PUTTING SUCH NONSENSE INTO YOUR HEAD? DONT YOU	KNOW	THAT SOLDIERS ARE SUBJECT TO THEIR FEUDAL LORD, AND
PHIL III (139)	OF BEING ANGELICALLY GOOD AND FORGIVING. OH, I	KNOW	THAT SORT OF GOODNESS! YOU MAY HAVE THOUGHT ON THESE
ARMS III (57)	MY HUSBAND. YOU WOULD MAKE MORE OUT OF ME. OH, I	KNOW	THAT SOUL OF YOURS. /NICOLA/ (GOING CLOSER TO HER FOR
BUOY II (19)	AS A GRADUATE OF OXFORD UNIVERSITY? /SHE/ I	KNOW	THAT STUNT, MY LAD. THE WANDERING SCHOLAR TURNS UP HERE
GENV IV (96)	AND FIFTY. /JUDGE/ STILL, SIR MIDLANDER, YOU	KNOW	THAT SUCH AN ACTIVITY AS THOUGHT EXISTS. /SIR O./ YOU
JITT III (79)	HIS GREATNESS-- FOR WHATEVER YOU MAY SAY I	KNOW	THAT THAT BOOK IS THE GREATEST THAT EVER WAS WRITTEN--
APPL I (201)	YOUNG CHAP. I WAS GOING TO SAY THAT I SUPPOSE YOU	KNOW	THAT THAT BULL-ROARER BOANERGES HAS JUST BEEN TAKEN
3PLA PREFACE(R17)	YOU FROM BEING AS EXQUISITE A CREATURE, IF YOU	KNOW	THAT THE ACCIDENT OF MATRIMONY (SAY WITH AN OFFICER OF
SUPR PREFACE(R34)	FEET ON SOLID GROUND, VIVID AND AMUSING, YOU	KNOW	THAT THE AUTHOR HAS MUCH TO SHEW AND NOTHING TO TEACH.
FANY I (274)	TALK NONSENSE, ROB. YOU OUGHT TO BE THANKFUL TO	KNOW	THAT THE BOY IS ALIVE AFTER HIS DISAPPEARING LIKE THAT
GENV I (30)	NOBODY EVER COMES IN HERE: PEOPLE DONT SEEM TO	KNOW	THAT THE COMMITTEE EXISTS. /HE/ DO YOU MEAN THAT YOU
BULL IV (149)	PERIL THROUGH WHICH WE HAVE ALL PASSED-- FOR I	KNOW	THAT THE DANGER TO THE BYSTANDERS WAS AS GREAT AS TO
FANY PROLOG (270)	IF YOU HAD BEEN EDUCATED AT OXFORD, YOU WOULD	KNOW	THAT THE DEFINITION OF A PLAY HAS BEEN SETTLED EXACTLY
GENV I (38)	WHAT A COINCIDENCE! /THE WIDOW/ THEN YOU	KNOW	THAT THE EARTHLY PARADISE IS ONE OF THE LEADING STATES
DEST (194)	LEANING A LITTLE ON HIS SHOULDER. /LADY/ DO YOU	KNOW	THAT THE ENGLISH SAY THAT A MAN'S STAR IS NOT COMPLETE
MILL PREFACE(125)	SMATTERING OF MENDELISM IS ALL THAT ONE NEEDS TO	KNOW	THAT THE ETERNAL FUSION OF RACES DOES NOT ALWAYS BLEND
POSN PREFACE(408)	AS A BAR TO ANY SUCH PROCEEDINGS. ABOVE ALL, THEY	KNOW	THAT THE EXAMINER OF PLAYS IS FREE FROM THE PRESSURE OF
UNPL PREFACE(R15)	OF DOING AWAY WITH THEM. NAY, I MYSELF, THOUGH I	KNOW	THAT THE EXAMINER IS NECESSARILY AN ODIOUS AND
JOAN 4 (104)	OR A BLOCKHEAD BECAUSE, AS A TRAVELLED MAN, I	KNOW	THAT THE FOLLOWERS OF MAHOMET PROFESS GREAT RESPECT FOR
DEST SD(152)	BY AN IRRUPTION OF FRENCH TROOPS AT SIX O' CLOCK,	KNOW	THAT THE FRENCH COMMANDER HAS QUARTERED HIMSELF IN THIS
FABL II (106)	IT WILL BE YOUR DOING. /C.-IN-C./ HOW WAS I TO	KNOW	THAT THE GAS WAS ANY GOOD? I GET DOZENS OF SUCH
MILL IV (196)	/THE MANAGER/ I AM SORRY, MADAM: I DID NOT	KNOW	THAT THE GENTLEMAN WAS YOUR HUSBAND. HOWEVER, YOU ARE
SUPR IV (148)	OF COURSE IT IS VERY SCANDALOUS; BUT SURELY YOU	KNOW	THAT THE GOVERNMENT WILL SOONER OR LATER PUT A STOP TO
ROCK I (224)	UNDER THE BANNER OF THE PRINCE OF PEACE, WE	KNOW	THAT THE HEART OF ENGLAND IS THE ENGLISH HOME. NOT THE
BULL PREFACE(31)	OF EXPENSES WITH THE BRITISH TAXPAYER, THEY	KNOW	THAT THE IRISH COAST IS FOR THE ENGLISH
POSN (451)	SWEAR THE JURY, A ROTTEN SHERIFF YOU ARE NOT TO	KNOW	THAT THE JURY'S GOT TO BE SWORN. /THE FOREMAN/ (
BARB PREFACE(236)	AND ALLIES OF THEIR SWEATERS AND OPPRESSORS, THEY	KNOW	THAT THE LARGE SUBSCRIPTIONS WHICH HELP TO SUPPORT THE
SUPR PREFACE(R38)	OF WHAT OTHERS HAVE SAID OR WRITTEN AFORETIME. I	KNOW	THAT THE LEISURELY TRICKS WHICH THEIR WANT OF
JOAN 2 (76)	HIRE/ I DO NOT KNOW WHAT A COINCIDENCE IS. I DO	KNOW	THAT THE MAN IS DEAD, AND THAT SHE TOLD HIM HE WAS
JOAN PREFACE(19)	AND BY THAT TIME SHE HAD SENSE ENOUGH TO	KNOW	THAT THE MASCULINE AND MILITARY LIFE WAS NOT A MERE
DOCT PREFACE(58)	THE RISK. THAT HAS ALWAYS BEEN THE CASE. WE NOW	KNOW	THAT THE MEDIEVAL HORROR OF LEPROSY WAS OUT OF ALL
JITT III (68)	OF COURSE YOU DONT: IT'S TOO SILLY. BUT DO YOU	KNOW	THAT THE MOMENT YOU TOOK THAT WEIGHT OFF MY MIND, AND
APPL I (208)	TRUE. YOU ARE QUITE RIGHT TO REMIND ME OF IT. I	KNOW	THAT THE MONARCHY MAY COME TO AN END AT ANY MOMENT, BUT
BULL I (94)	WHAT D'YE MEAN BY HM! /BROADBENT/ OF COURSE I	KNOW	THAT THE MORAL CODE IS DIFFERENT IN IRELAND. BUT IN
2TRU III SD(112)	NO PARSNIPS. A FEW OF THE CHOICER SPIRITS WILL	KNOW	THAT THE PENTECOSTAL FLAME IS ALWAYS ALIGHT AT THE

PRES	(137)	RED HAS THROWN UP? /MITCHENER/ HOW CAN I? YOU	KNOW	THAT THE PEOPLE ARE DEVOTED HEART AND SOUL TO
KING I	(196)	IN LIFE AS YOUR BARBARA'S KEPT MAN? /CHARLES/ I	KNOW	THAT THE POOR LAD RISKED BREAKING HIS BONES BY JUMPING
APPL I	(210)	NEW MINISTER. WE SHALL MEET AGAIN PRESENTLY: YOU	KNOW	THAT THE PRIME MINISTER IS CALLING ON ME TODAY WITH
GETT PREFACE	(243)	ALL THESE GENTLEMEN ARE CELIBATES, EVEN THOUGH WE	KNOW	THAT THE QUESTION MUST BE ANSWERED VERY EMPHATICALLY IN
GENV IV	(112)	AS PIONEER, NOT AS CAMP FOLLOWER. AS PIONEER I	KNOW	THAT THE REAL OBSTACLE TO HUMAN PROGRESS IS THE SORT OF
BULL III	(139)	YOUR SUPPORT THIS MORNING. I VALUE IT BECAUSE I	KNOW	THAT THE REAL HEART OF A NATION IS THE CLASS YOU
CAND I	(84)	INSTEAD OF MERE EMOTIONS LIKE US, AND TO	KNOW	THAT THE REASON WE DONT SHARE YOUR AMOROUS DELUSIONS IS
2TRU III	(97)	NOT KNOWING HOW TO READ AND WRITE. BUT I DIDNT	KNOW	THAT THE RICH WERE MISERABLE. I DIDNT KNOW THAT I WAS
CURE	(227)	I WASNT GAMBLING. I KNEW. IT ISNT GAMBLING IF YOU	KNOW	THAT THE SHARES WILL GO UP. IT'S A CERT. /THE DOCTOR/
GETT	(321)	ON HIM) WHAT RIGHT HAVE YOU TO SAY SO? YOU	KNOW	THAT THE SINS THAT ARE WASTING AND MADDENING THIS
JOAN 6	(139)	MICHAEL THE ARCHANGEL? /COURCELLES/ HOW DO YOU	KNOW	THAT THE SPIRIT WHICH APPEARS TO YOU IS AN ARCHANGEL..
2TRU PREFACE	(21)	BE SEEN CARRYING A PARCEL DOWN BOND STREET. WE	KNOW	THAT THE STRAINS SET UP BY SUCH A DIVISION OF INTERESTS
MILL PREFACE	(122)	HITLER WAS POLITICAL PSYCHOLOGIST ENOUGH TO	KNOW	THAT THE TIME HAD ARRIVED WHEN IT WOULD BE QUITE
MTH5	(210)	HERE WITH GREATER AND GREATER RELUCTANCE; AND I	KNOW	THAT THE TIME WILL SOON COME-- PERHAPS IT HAS COME
2TRU III	(87)	OF YOU. YOU, SIR, ARE NOT AN IGNORANT MAN: YOU	KNOW	THAT THE UNIVERSE IS WRECKED. /SWEETIE/ (CLINGING TO
DOCT PREFACE	(47)	ANIMALS ARE COMPLETELY PAINLESS; ALTHOUGH HE MUST	KNOW	THAT THE VERY EXPERIMENTS WHICH FIRST PROVOKED THE
KING PREFACE	(155)	WAS PURELY SYMBOLIC, AND WHO WAS CLEVER ENOUGH TO	KNOW	THAT THE WORK OF THE REGICIDES COULD NOT BE UNDONE, AND
BARB II	(304)	DEADLY THIRST BY THAT WICKED SKY SIGN? DO YOU	KNOW	THAT THE WORST THING I HAVE HAD TO FIGHT HERE IS NOT
SUPR PREFACE	(R38)	NOT FACE THE TOIL OF WRITING A SINGLE SENTENCE. I	KNOW	THAT THERE ARE MEN WHO, HAVING NOTHING TO SAY AND
MIS. PREFACE	(93)	NO MATTER WHAT ITS RACE AND COLOR MAY BE, SHOULD	KNOW	THAT THERE ARE BLACK MEN AND BROWN MEN AND YELLOW MEN,
MIS. PREFACE	(93)	SOCIALISTS AND UNSOCIALISTS, SO IT SHOULD	KNOW	THAT THERE ARE CHRISTIANS AND MAHOMETANS AND BUDDHISTS
DOCT PREFACE	(62)	AND KNOWLEDGE ATTRIBUTED TO THEM); AND THOUGH I	KNOW	THAT THERE ARE MEDICAL BLACKGUARDS AS WELL AS MILITARY,
GETT	(321)	THERE ARE MILLIONS OF YEARS BEHIND US; AND WE	KNOW	THAT THERE ARE MILLIONS BEFORE US. MRS BRIDGENORTH'S
BULL PREFACE	(12)	AS TO THE FREEDOM OF NATIONALISM FROM ABUSE. I	KNOW	THAT THERE ARE ABUSES IN ENGLAND WHICH WOULD NOT EXIST
APPL I	(221)	TAKE GATESHEAD AND MIDDLESBOROUGH ALONE! DO YOU	KNOW	THAT THERE HAS NOT BEEN A DAY'S UNEMPLOYMENT THERE FOR
GENV II	(52)	WAS I INTERESTED IN THE LEAGUE? LET ME SEE. YOU	KNOW	THAT THERE IS A SOCIETY CALLED THE LEAGUE OF NATIONS
METH PREFACE	(R16)	RULED UNDERSTAND HIGH POLITICS. THEY DO NOT EVEN	KNOW	THAT THERE IS SUCH A BRANCH OF KNOWLEDGE AS POLITICAL
JOAN 6	(142)	LAW. /THE CHAPLAIN/ (RISING, PURPLE WITH FURY) I	KNOW	THAT THERE IS NO FAITH IN A FRENCHMAN. (TUMULT, WHICH
FANY PREFACE	(255)	OR MOTOR CAR. NOWADAYS WE DO NOT SEEM TO	KNOW	THAT THERE IS ANY OTHER TEST OF CONDUCT EXCEPT
O'FL	(211)	LITTLE PENSION IT CARRIES? DO YOU THINK I DONT	KNOW	THAT THERES HUNDREDS OF MEN AS BRAVE AS ME THAT NEVER
DEVL I	(19)	FROM HIS RELATIVES, ANDERSON, SENSIBLE ENOUGH TO	KNOW	THAT THESE DEMONSTRATIONS CAN ONLY GRATIFY AND
LIED	(191)	ME. /HE/ I NEVER THOUGHT OF DOING SO, DEAREST: I	KNOW	THAT THESE TRIVIALITIES ARE NOTHING TO YOU. WHAT WAS I
LADY PREFACE	(229)	EVERYBODY, INCLUDING THE WORKERS THEMSELVES,	KNOW	THAT THEY ARE DIRTY, DRUNKEN, FOUL-MOUTHED, IGNORANT,
VWOO 3	(135)	HAVE IMPROVED, HAVNT THEY? /A/ I DONT KNOW. I	KNOW	THAT THEY ARE NO LONGER DISINTERESTED AND SINCERE. /Z/
GENV II	(56)	DENIES ANY KNOWLEDGE OF IT. MOST OF THEM DID NOT	KNOW	THAT THEY ARE MEMBERS. /SIR O./ DO YOU MEAN TO SAY THAT
CAND I	(80)	I THINK. /MORELL/ JUST LIKE ANARCHISTS NOT TO	KNOW	THAT THEY CANT HAVE A PARSON ON SUNDAY! TELL THEM TO
FANY I	(283)	MAN A MONTH FOR WEARING HERS? /JUGGINS/ I DIDNT	KNOW	THAT THEY DID, MADAM. /MRS GILBEY/ IT DOESNT SEEM
MRS PREFACE	(154)	HELL; AND THE GIRLS AMONG WHOM THEY ARE WORKING	KNOW	THAT THEY DO NOT BELIEVE IN IT, AND WOULD LAUGH AT THEM
MTH2	(84)	TO, BUT BECAUSE THE SOUL DEEP DOWN IN THEM WILL	KNOW	THAT THEY MUST, IF THE WORLD IS TO BE SAVED. /LUBIN/ (
ROCK PREFACE	(162)	OUT OF THE HANDS OF THE POLICE. OUR FINANCIERS	KNOW	THAT THEY MUST NOT FORGE SHARE CERTIFICATES NOR
APPL I	(213)	HAS MORE POWER THAN A KING BECAUSE THE PEOPLE	KNOW	THAT THEY NEED A STRONG MAN TO PROTECT THEM AGAINST THE
JITT III	(56)	HE SAW THERE WERE COMMON WOMEN; BUT HOW DO YOU	KNOW	THAT THEY WERE NOT HIS PATIENTS? /AGNES/ DONT DECEIVE
GENV PREFACE	(7)	ON BOSWORTH FIELD AND THE IRONSIDES AT NASEBY	KNOW	THAT THEY WERE EXCHANGING IT FOR WHIG PLUTOCRACY.
GENV PREFACE	(7)	COMBATANTS IN THE BATTLE OF HASTINGS DID NOT	KNOW	THAT THEY WERE INAUGURATING FEUDALISM FOR FOUR
GENV III	(74)	ENGLISH CLERGY ARE NOT LIKE THAT. YOU WOULD NOT	KNOW	THAT THEY WERE CLERGY AT ALL IF IT WERE NOT FOR THEIR
ARMS III	(64)	BOUNDING HALF ACROSS THE ROOM). /RAINA/ DONT YOU	KNOW	THAT THEYRE ENGAGED? /SERGIUS/ NICOLA! ARE FRESH
ARMS I	(15)	COME BUNCHED UP UNDER THE NUMBER ONE GUARD: THEY	KNOW	THAT THEYRE MERE PROJECTILES, AND THAT IT'S NO USE
CAPT III	(273)	POOR CAPTAIN BRASSBOUND! DOES NOT YOUR LEDDYSHIP	KNOW	THAT THIS BRASSBOUND IS-- HEAVEN FORGIVE ME FOR JUDGING
JOAN PREFACE	(55)	WHICH HAVE NOTHING TO DO WITH ART. I	KNOW	THAT THIS IS HARD ON THE PSEUDO-CRITICS AND ON THE
ANNA	(304)	(SHE MARCHES AS IF IN FRONT OF A REGIMENT). I	KNOW	THAT THIS MAN ALONE CAN ROUSE THE ARMY TO ENTHUSIASM.
SUPR I	(7)	WAS RIGHT WHEN HE SAID YOU WERE A GENEROUS LAD. I	KNOW	THAT THIS MAN WAS YOUR SCHOOLFELLOW, AND THAT YOU FEEL
FANY PROLOG	(269)	TO SHOCK THEM AND KEEP THEM UP TO DATE. BUT I	KNOW	THAT THIS PLAY WILL SHOCK HIM ARTISTICALLY; AND THAT
MTH4 I	(161)	TO YOUR INORDINATELY LONG LIVES. DO YOU NOT	KNOW	THAT THIS QUESTION WAS FAMILIAR TO MEN WHO DIED BEFORE
VWOO 3	(141)	I AM NOT A MATERIALIST; I AM A POET; AND I	KNOW	THAT TO BE IN YOUR ARMS WILL NOT GRATIFY MY SENSES AT
SUPR III	(132)	ARE ALL GOOD TO THINK ABOUT AND TALK ABOUT. I	KNOW	THAT TO BE WELL EXERCISED IN THESE SENSATIONS,
CAPT II	(264)	THAT CANT BE DONE WITHOUT DISCIPLINE: YOU	KNOW	THAT TOO. I'LL TAKE MY PART WITH THE REST UNDER
LADY	(242)	I SPEAK OF IS THE POWER OF IMMORTAL POESY. FOR	KNOW	THAT VILE AS THIS WORLD IS, AND WORMS AS WE ARE, YOU
2TRU II	(77)	AFRAID OF US. /TALLBOYS/ YES, BECAUSE THEY DONT	KNOW	THAT WE ARE A MERE HANDFUL OF MEN. BUT IF THIS WOMAN IS
PRES	(141)	STANDS LESS OF IT THAN THE WORKING CLASS. YOU	KNOW	THAT WE ARE ALREADY DISCUSSING THE STEPS THAT WILL HAVE
AUGS	(269)	HORROR) A RISE! HORATIO FLOYD BEAMISH! DO YOU	KNOW	THAT WE ARE AT WAR? /THE CLERK/ (FEEBLY IRONICAL) I
DEVL III	(69)	LAST NIGHT AND DROVE US OUT; SO THAT WE MAY	KNOW	THAT WE ARE DEALING WITH AN OFFICER OF IMPORTANCE.
NEVR II	(235)	/PHILIP/ (IMPRESSIVELY) WILLIAM: HE DOES NOT	KNOW	THAT WE ARE HIS FAMILY. HE HAS NOT SEEN US FOR EIGHTEEN
GETT PREFACE	(249)	DIFFERENCE IN VALUE BETWEEN HUMAN BEINGS, WE MAY	KNOW	THAT WE ARE IN THE SLAVE-MARKET, WHERE THE CONCEPTION
METH PREFACE	(R59)	WITHOUT THE SMALLEST REMORSE, WE AT ALL EVENTS	KNOW	THAT WE ARE KILLING OUR COUSIN. NO DOUBT IT SHOCKS THE
MTH2	(65)	WHAT DO YOU KNOW THAT I DONT KNOW? /LUBIN/ I	KNOW	THAT WE ARE TAKING UP TOO MUCH OF MR BARNABAS'S TIME. (
APPL II	(265)	A RESERVATION. /THE QUEEN/ NONSENSE, DEAR! THEY	KNOW	THAT WE ARE THEIR NATURAL SUPERIORS. YOU CAN SEE IT BY
ARMS II	(27)	/PETKOFF/ I DID MY BEST. I TOOK CARE TO LET THEM	KNOW	THAT WE HAVE A LIBRARY. /CATHERINE/ AH; BUT YOU DIDNT
SUPR II	(49)	A LITTLE. (LOOKING AT HIS WATCH) I SUPPOSE YOU	KNOW	THAT WE HAVE COME FROM HYDE PARK CORNER TO RICHMOND IN
FABL II	(107)	AND MAKE THE GAS OURSELVES. WHEN THE OTHER STATES	KNOW	THAT WE HAVE PLENTY OF IT NONE OF THEM WILL DARE TO
ROCK II	(257)	OF WHAT HAPPENS AS A SPECIAL INTERVIEW: YOU	KNOW	THAT WE LABOR INTELLIGENTSIA HAVE TO LIVE BY OUR
BUOY 1	(11)	THEM? THE STREETS ARE FULL OF THEM. AND HOW DO I	KNOW	THAT WE SHALL NOT LOSE ALL OUR MONEY AND FALL INTO
GETT	(321)	THAT THE WORLD ITSELF WAS GOING TO LAST. NOW WE	KNOW	THAT WE SHALL HAVE TO GO THROUGH WITH IT. WE HAVE FOUND
WIDO I	(11)	PERHAPS-- /BLANCHE/ WHAT OTHER TIME? HOW DO YOU	KNOW	THAT WE SHALL EVER MEET AGAIN? (DESPERATELY) TELL ME
WIDO II	(34)	DONT MAKE A JOKE OF IT: I'M SERIOUS. DO YOU	KNOW	THAT WE SHALL BE VERY POOR? /BLANCHE/ IS THAT WHAT
SUPR I	(33)	BUT WHAT A DEVIL OF A CHILD YOU MUST HAVE BEEN TO	KNOW	THAT WEAKNESS AND TO PLAY ON IT FOR THE SATISFACTION OF
DOCT II	(116)	NO: DONT CRY. YOUR HUSBAND HAD BETTER NOT	KNOW	THAT WEVE BEEN TALKING ABOUT HIM. /MRS DUBEDAT/ (
HART II	(99)	ALL THE SAME. WHAT I MEAN BY THAT IS THAT I	KNOW	THAT WHAT HAS HAPPENED TO ME WITH MARCUS WILL NOT
MTH4 II	(175)	ON SIMPLETONS. I BELIEVE THAT WHAT IS, IS. I	KNOW	THAT WHAT IS NOT, IS NOT. THE ANTICS OF A WOMAN SITTING
MTH4 I	(167)	THAT BEFORE. AND I AM AN EXPERIENCED TRAVELLER. I	KNOW	THAT WHAT THE TRAVELLER OBSERVES MUST REALLY EXIST, OR
GETT	(294)	YOU PROPOSED TO HER. /SYKES/ YES; BUT I DIDNT	KNOW	THAT WHEN WE WERE MARRIED I SHOULD BE LEGALLY
SUPR III	(120)	WHEN THIS SHALL CEASE TO BE TRUE? DO YOU NOT	KNOW	THAT WHERE THERE IS A WILL THERE IS A WAY? THAT
JOAN 4	(106)	THAT THERE IS A WILL TO POWER IN THE WORLD. I	KNOW	THAT WHILE IT LASTS THERE WILL BE A STRUGGLE BETWEEN
FABL VI	(125)	ASK WHY. IN THE SIXTH FORM YOU ARE SUPPOSED TO	KNOW	THAT WHY IS UNANSWERABLE. /YOUTH 3/ NONSENSE. WHY IS
WIDO III	(63)	YOU SAY YOU DONT KNOW THAT YOU ARE, BUT DO YOU	KNOW	THAT YOU AINT? THATS WHAT WE WANT TO KNOW. /TRENCH/ (
PHIL I	(85)	/CHARTERIS/ I WAS ONLY GOING TO SAY THAT I DIDNT	KNOW	THAT YOU AND CRAVEN WERE ACQUAINTED. /CRAVEN/ WHY, I
CLEO II	(137)	/POTHINUS/ (SCORNFULLY) I YOUR PRISONER! DO YOU	KNOW	THAT YOU ARE IN ALEXANDRIA, AND THAT KING PTOLEMY, WITH
BARB II	(294)	INTERESTING, MR UNDERSHAFT. OF COURSE YOU	KNOW	THAT YOU ARE MAD. /UNDERSHAFT/ (WITH REDOUBLED FORCE)
CLEO I	(115)	ROBES, WILL HE NOT? /CAESAR/ NO. HOW SHALL HE	KNOW	THAT YOU ARE NOT A SLAVE DRESSED UP IN THE QUEEN'S
SUPR III	(97)	CANNOT STAND THIS. /THE DEVIL/ (ANGRILY) YES: I	KNOW	THAT YOU ARE NO FRIEND OF MINE. /THE STATUE/ WHAT HARM
MTH4 I	(143)	NOTICEABLY STIFF? /THE WOMAN/ PERHAPS YOU DO NOT	KNOW	THAT YOU ARE ON THE WEST COAST OF IRELAND, AND THAT IT
BULL IV	(153)	INSINCERE. /KEEGAN/ DO NOT BE OFFENDED, SIR: I	KNOW	THAT YOU ARE QUITE SINCERE. THERE IS A SAYING IN THE
WIDO I	(4)	NOTHING BUT THAT NORFOLK JACKET. HOW ARE THEY TO	KNOW	THAT YOU ARE WELL CONNECTED IF YOU DO NOT SHEW IT BY
WIDO III	(63)	TRENCH) COME, NOW, DR TRENCH! YOU SAY YOU DONT	KNOW	THAT YOU ARE, BUT DO YOU KNOW THAT YOU AINT? THATS
JITT I	(16)	IS RUTHLESS AND SHAMELESS. /BRUNO/ JITTA: DO YOU	KNOW	THAT YOU BELONGED TO ME BEFORE WE EVER SAW ONE
DOCT III	(155)	HIM; YOU MUST MAKE HIM QUITE WELL AGAIN FOR ME. I	KNOW	THAT YOU CAN DO IT AND THAT NOBODY ELSE CAN. I IMPLORE
BUOY 1	(10)	IS ONE THAT I CANNOT AFFORD. /FATHER/ HOW DO YOU	KNOW	THAT YOU CANNOT AFFORD IT? HAVE I EVER STINTED YOU IN
LION PREFACE	(52)	NOT MAKE MEN GOOD BY ACT OF PARLIAMENT, WE NOW	KNOW	THAT YOU CANNOT MAKE THEM GOOD IN ANY OTHER WAY, AND
NEVR II	(256)	(WITH CONVICTION) YOURE STRONG. DO YOU	KNOW	THAT YOU CHANGED THE WORLD FOR ME THIS MORNING? I WAS
HART III	(137)	OF MY SOUL. I ONLY WANTED TO FEEL MY STRENGTH: TO	KNOW	THAT YOU COULD NOT ESCAPE IF I CHOSE TO TAKE YOU.
MILL I	(156)	WHAT IT FEELS LIKE TO BE IN THE ARMS OF A MAN AND	KNOW	THAT YOU COULD BUY HIM UP TWENTY TIMES OVER AND NEVER
CLEO IV	(188)	IN ALL THE WORLD CAN BE FOUND, NOW OR FOREVER, TO	KNOW	THAT YOU DID WRONG, THAT MAN WILL HAVE EITHER TO
KING I	(171)	IN MY PRESENCE. /CHARLES/ I APOLOGIZE. I DID NOT	KNOW	THAT YOU DISAPPROVED OF THE PLAYHOUSE, MRS BASHAM. /MRS
SIM I	(42)	YOU ARE GODS AND GODDESSES OR REAL PEOPLE. I ONLY	KNOW	THAT YOU FILL MY HEART WITH INEXPRESSIBLE LONGINGS.
DOCT I	(111)	IN YOUR EYES (SHE HASTILY WIPES HER EYES): I	KNOW	THAT YOU HAVE A TORRENT OF ENTREATIES READY FOR ME THE
BULL IV	(164)	UNFEELING! NONSENSICAL! /NORA/ DONT YOU	KNOW	THAT YOU HAVE SAID THINGS TO ME THAT NO MAN OUGHT TO
ROCK I	(207)	END OF ME. /SIR ARTHUR/ YES, YES, MY PETTUMS. I	KNOW	THAT YOU HAVE SACRIFICED YOURSELF TO KEEPING MY HOUSE
MIS.	(163)	/HYPATIA/ DROPPED DOWN FROM THE SKY. DONT YOU	KNOW	THAT YOU MUST ALWAYS GO ON LIKE THIS WHEN YOU GET THE

SUPR I	(34)	TELLING YOU ABOUT MY ADVENTURES; BUT HOW DO YOU	KNOW	THAT YOU STOPPED THE ADVENTURES? /ANN/ DO YOU MEAN TO
BARB III	(333)	DETAILS AND LEAVE YOUR FINAL DECISION OPEN. YOU	KNOW	THAT YOU WILL HAVE TO CHANGE YOUR NAME. DO YOU OBJECT
BARB III	(346)	BUT FOR REALITY AND FOR POWER. /BARBARA/ YOU	KNOW	THAT YOU WILL HAVE NO POWER, AND THAT HE HAS NONE.
MTH1 II	(33)	LIVE FOR EVER? YOU THINK YOU COULD, BECAUSE YOU	KNOW	THAT YOU WILL NEVER HAVE TO MAKE YOUR THOUGHT GOOD. BUT
2TRU I	(45)	CATCH IN THIS. IF I TRUST YOU WITH IT HOW DO I	KNOW	THAT YOU WILL NOT KEEP THE WHOLE PRICE FOR YOURSELF?
FANY PROLOG	(263)	ME SEE. AS YOU DONT LIKE ENGLISH PEOPLE, I DONT	KNOW	THAT YOULL GET ON WITH TROTTER, BECAUSE HE'S THOROUGHLY
PYGM I	(207)	THANK YOU, LADY. /THE MOTHER/ NOW TELL ME HOW YOU	KNOW	THAT YOUNG GENTLEMAN'S NAME. /THE FLOWER GIRL/ I DIDNT.
ANNA	(299)	DUCHESS/ M'YES; BUT -- (RISING) STRAMMFEST: YOU	KNOW	THAT YOUR CAUSE -- THE CAUSE OF THE DYNASTY -- IS LOST.
JOAN 6	(145)	THEM AWAY FROM ME, OR FROM ANY HUMAN CREATURE, I	KNOW	THAT YOUR COUNSEL IS OF THE DEVIL, AND THAT MINE IS OF
GLIM	(176)	(FERRUCCIO MAKES A DEMONSTRATION). OH, I	KNOW	THAT YOUR EXCELLENCY HAS BEEN TAUGHT BY FENCERS AND
BULL III	(129)	DOES IT MATTER TO US WHAT YOUR OPINIONS ARE? YOU	KNOW	THAT YOUR FATHER'S BOUGHT HIS PLACE HERE, JUST THE SAME
BARB I	(258)	IT SHALL BE AS YOU WISH. YOU WILL BE GLAD TO	KNOW	THAT YOUR GRANDFATHER CONCURS. BUT HE THINKS I OUGHT TO
6CAL	(104)	ARE YOU MAD, MASTER BURGESS? DO YOU NOT	KNOW	THAT YOUR LIFE IS IN THE KING'S HAND? DO YOU EXPECT ME
SIM I	(48)	WAY. I CANT MAKE SENSE OF WHAT YOU ARE SAYING. I	KNOW	THAT YOUR MEANING MUST BE PERFECTLY RIGHT AND
MRS IV	(242)	AND ABOVE THE SCOPE OF THE LAW, THAT THOUGH I	KNOW	THAT YOUR MOTHER IS AN UNMARRIED WOMAN, I DO NOT
DOCT III	(142)	BUT THERE ARE OTHER LAWS TO RECKON WITH. DO YOU	KNOW	THAT YOURE GOING TO DIE? /LOUIS/ WE'RE ALL GOING TO
MIS.	(118)	COURSE IF NOBODY AGREES WITH YOU, HOW ARE YOU TO	KNOW	THAT YOURE NOT A FOOL? /LORD SUMMERHAYS/ QUITE SO.
WIDO III	(57)	NOT; BUT THE PEOPLE WE WANT TO MIX WITH NOW DONT	KNOW	THAT, AND IT WAS NOT MY FAULT; SO I DONT SEE WHY I
BULL II	(98)	/THE MAN/ SURE IT'S THE WISE GRASSHOPPER YAR TO	KNOW	THAT. BUT TELL ME THIS, MISTHER UNWORLDLY WISEMAN: WHY
GENV IV	(124)	IT TAKES US A YEAR TO GET ROUND. /JUDGE/ WE ALL	KNOW	THAT. BUT THE MESSAGE SAYS THAT THE ORBIT IS JUMPING TO
APPL I	(227)	SENT TO THEM WITH A ROYAL COMMAND. /PROTEUS/ WE	KNOW	THAT, BUT THOUGH THESE MEN ARE RICHER THAN YOU, THEY
CLEO II	(133)	NO: THAT WOULD BE VERY SILLY OF ME: OF COURSE I	KNOW	THAT. BUT-- (SUDDENLY) ARE YOU ANGRY WITH ME?
BULL III	(126)	WOULD NOT BE POPULAR ENOUGH. /CORNELIUS/ I DONT	KNOW	THAT, DO YOU, BARNEY? /DORAN/ THERES TOO MUCH
PYGM II	(228)	NO USE EXPLAINING. AS A MILITARY MAN YOU OUGHT TO	KNOW	THAT. GIVE HER HER ORDERS: THATS WHAT SHE WANTS. ELIZA:
JITT III	(71)	YOUR FATHER'S DAUGHTER! /EDITH/ OH, OF COURSE I	KNOW	THAT. I DONT EXPECT HIM TO FEEL THE SAME AFFECTION. BUT
CLEO IV	(187)	NOT BETRAYED YOU, CAESAR: I SWEAR IT. /CAESAR/ I	KNOW	THAT. I HAVE NOT TRUSTED YOU. (HE TURNS FROM HER, AND
MTH2	(49)	VIOLENCE ON THE LAND OF OUR FATHERS. /FRANKLYN/ I	KNOW	THAT. I KNOW WHO YOU ARE, AND THE EARTH-SHAKING PART OF
BULL I	(96)	YOURE ALL DESCENDED FROM THE ANCIENT KINGS: I	KNOW	THAT. (COMPLACENTLY) I'M NOT SO TACTLESS AS YOU THINK,
GLIM	(180)	THE WATER, FATHER SQUARCIO. TRUST A FISHERMAN TO	KNOW	THAT. NOBODY CAN TELL THAT DROWNING WAS NOT AN
GENV I	(38)	ARE PROPERLY ATTENDED TO. /SHE/ CAN IT? I DIDNT	KNOW	THAT. OF COURSE I SHALL BE ONLY TOO PLEASED TO APPLY
JITT II	(31)	ON THEM. I HAVE BEEN REALLY TOO ILL. I HOPE THEY	KNOW	THAT. /FESSLER/ (WITH AFFECTIONATE DEFERENCE) THEY
JITT III	(77)	IT MIGHT RESTORE YOUR HAPPINESS A LITTLE TO	KNOW	THAT. /JITTA/ ALFRED: I WILL NEVER SPEAK TO YOU NOR
JITT II	(46)	WHAT I ENJOYED I SHALL HAVE TO PAY FOR. I	KNOW	THAT. /LENKHEIM/ YOU AND HE WERE LOVERS? /JITTA/ (
CAPT II	(248)	YOU BE GOOD ENOUGH TO LET LADY CICELY WAYNFLETE	KNOW	THAT. /SIR HOWARD/ (SITTING UP ON THE DIVAN AND
ROCK II	(249)	BUT THE LAND QUESTION. /THE MAYOR/ YES: WE ALL	KNOW	THAT. /SIR JAFNA/ THEN YOU WILL VOTE FOR SIR ARTHUR
MTH4 II	(186)	SAFE WITH ME: YOU OUGHT TO HAVE SENSE ENOUGH TO	KNOW	THAT. /THE ELDERLY GENTLEMAN/ I AM SORRY TO SAY, MOLLY,
DOCT III	(155)	I DO NOT GIVE MY TRUST BY HALVES. /RIDGEON/ I	KNOW	THAT. WELL, I AM GOING TO TEST YOU-- HARD. WILL YOU
MTH2	(48)	TO BE? YOU ARE A MAN OF ENORMOUS INFLUENCE. WE	KNOW	THAT. WEVE ALWAYS KNOWN IT. WE HAVE TO CONSULT YOU
MIS.	(140)	CALL IT. /LORD SUMMERHAYS/ PLEASE BELIEVE THAT I	KNOW	THAT. WHEN MEN OF MY AGE-- /HYPATIA/ (IMPATIENTLY) OH,
2TRU II	(55)	A BRITISH LADY WHO IS BEING HELD FOR RANSOM. YOU	KNOW	THAT. YOU DONT THINK IT: YOU KNOW IT, EH? /MEEK/ SO
DOCT PREFACE	(6)	WHAT HE DOES KILLS THE PATIENT; BUT YOU DO NOT	KNOW	THAT; AND THE DOCTOR ASSURES YOU THAT ALL THAT HUMAN
LION II	(138)	HE IS NOT A HUMORIST: HE WAS RIGHT. YOU OUGHT TO	KNOW	THAT, CAPTAIN: YOU HAVE BEEN FACE TO FACE WITH DEATH.
LION II	(139)	/THE CAPTAIN/ WHAT IS GOD? /LAVINIA/ WHEN WE	KNOW	THAT, CAPTAIN, WE SHALL BE GODS OURSELVES. /THE
BARB III	(313)	AND DIVINER DREAMS THAN THE FIRESIDE ONES. YOU	KNOW	THAT, DONT YOU? /CUSINS/ YES: THAT IS OUR
HART I	(74)	AND CARRIES THEM BEYOND HONOR AND DISHONOR. YOU	KNOW	THAT, DONT YOU? /LADY UTTERWORD/ PERHAPS I DO, HECTOR.
OVER	(179)	ON EARTH OR IN HEAVEN CAN PART US NOW. YOU	KNOW	THAT, DONT YOU? /MRS JUNO/ OH, DONT MAKE ME SAY IT. OF
GENV I	(36)	OF COURSE THEYRE NOT. JUST THE OPPOSITE. YOU	KNOW	THAT, DONT YOU? /SHE/ OH, QUITE, QUITE. /NEWCOMER/
MTH3	(109)	DOUBT OF YOUR ABSOLUTE VERACITY, ARCHBISHOP. YOU	KNOW	THAT, DONT YOU? /THE ARCHBISHOP/ QUITE, MR PRESIDENT.
GLIM	(174)	IS ONE OF THE SEVEN DEADLY SINS. /THE GIRL/ I	KNOW	THAT, FATHER; AND BELIEVE ME, I'M HUMBLE AND GOOD. I
ROCK I	(196)	IS MINE: KEEP THE CROWD AMUSED. YOU OUGHT TO	KNOW	THAT, I THINK, BETTER THAN MOST MEN. /SIR ARTHUR/ I!
JOAN 6	(141)	IN THE WISDOM OF SCHOLARS. /LADVENU/ WE	KNOW	THAT, JOAN: WE ARE NOT SO FOOLISH AS YOU THINK US. TRY
SUPR I	(5)	AND CRIES UNAFFECTEDLY). /RAMSDEN/ HOW DO WE	KNOW	THAT, OCTAVIUS? HE MAY KNOW IT: WE CANNOT TELL. COME!
MILL I	(149)	HARDLY SLEPT ALL NIGHT. /EPIFANIA/ HOW DO YOU	KNOW	THAT, PRAY? /PATRICIA/ NEVER MIND HOW I KNOW IT. I DO.
BULL II	(100)	YOUR CHURCH IS RIGHT OR WRONG. /PATSY/ SURE I	KNOW	THAT, SIR. /KEEGAN/ THE CHURCH LET ME BE ITS PRIEST AS
BARB III	(329)	THE SCIENTIFIC INTEREST OF THE SUBJECT) DID YOU	KNOW	THAT, UNDERSHAFT? HAVE YOU EVER TRIED? /UNDERSHAFT/
ANNA	(292)	SPEAK LOUDER, WILL YOU: I AM A GENERAL . . . I	KNOW	THAT, YOU DOLT. HAVE YOU CAPTURED THE OFFICER THAT WAS
ARMS III	(67)	HEARD MISS RAINA SAY THAT I DID, SIR. /PETKOFF/ I	KNOW	THAT, YOU IDIOT. WAS IT TRUE? /NICOLA/ I AM SURE MISS
MILL III	(180)	THAT IT CAN AFFORD FIVE SHILLINGS. WELL, IF YOU	KNOW	THAT, YOU KNOW THAT IT CANT AFFORD ANY MORE. TAKE YOUR
MIS.	(142)	CANT UNDERSTAND MY HOLIER FEELINGS, AT LEAST YOU	KNOW	THE BODILY INFIRMITIES OF THE OLD. YOU KNOW THAT I
JOAN 4	(103)	BED. WE HAVE SUCH PEOPLE HERE IN FRANCE TOO: I	KNOW	THE BREED. IT IS CANCEROUS: IF IT BE NOT CUT OUT,
ROCK II	(258)	/SIR DEXTER/ (IMPATIENTLY) YES, YES: WE	KNOW	THE CANT OF ALL THE TUPPENY-HAPENY DICTATORS WHO THINK
2TRU III	(96)	ALL THE MORNING, EVER SINCE SHE ARRIVED; AND I	KNOW	THE COLONEL. HE HAS A TEMPER; AND WHEN IT GIVES WAY,
CAND I	(97)	MARRIAGES BUT NO DELIGHTFUL ONES. YOU DONT	KNOW	THE COMFORT OF SEEING THROUGH AND THROUGH A THUNDERING
2TRU II	(53)	OF THE BRITISH EMPIRE, DO YOU? /MEEK/ NO, SIR. I	KNOW	THE COUNTRY. I CAN SPEAK THE DIALECTS A LITTLE.
MTH1 II	(27)	LEARN NOBLER CRAFTS OF WHICH YOU KNOW NOTHING. I	KNOW	THE CRAFT OF FIGHTING AND OF HUNTING: IN A WORD, THE
3PLA PREFACE	(R31)	ABOUT IT ROMANTICALLY IS DESPAIR. HOW WELL WE	KNOW	THE CRIES OF THAT DESPAIR! VANITY OF VANITIES, ALL IS
GETT PREFACE	(245)	INNOCENT AND MISSES THE GUILTY BECAUSE THE GUILTY	KNOW	THE DANGER AND TAKE ELABORATE PRECAUTIONS AGAINST IT,
CAPT II	(259)	MY TRAP WAS LAID FOR HIM, NOT FOR YOU. DO YOU	KNOW	THE DANGER YOU ARE IN? /LADY CICELY/ THERES ALWAYS A
DOCT I	(114)	REALLY GOOD ONES? /RIDGEON/ YES. I WILL LET YOU	KNOW	THE DATE IN THE COURSE OF TOMORROW. LEAVE ME YOUR
MILL I	(145)	IF I LIKE. IT IS YOUR BUSINESS AS A SOLICITOR TO	KNOW	THE DETAILS. I MADE A VERY COMMON MISTAKE. I THOUGHT
BARB III	(319)	/STEPHEN/ (RISING AND LOOKING AT HIM STEADILY) I	KNOW	THE DIFFERENCE BETWEEN RIGHT AND WRONG. /UNDERSHAFT/ (
DOCT I	(107)	/RIDGEON/ OH, VERY LIKELY. BUT HE REALLY OUGHT TO	KNOW	THE DIFFERENCE BETWEEN A VACCINE AND AN ANTI-TOXIN.
BULL I	(84)	YOUR HAT ON, A BROGUE. HEAVEN HELP YOU! YOU DONT	KNOW	THE DIFFERENCE BETWEEN CONNEMARA AND RATHMINES. (WITH
CYMB FORWORD	(138)	RECOMMEND MY VERSION. THE AUDIENCE WILL NOT	KNOW	THE DIFFERENCE; AND THE FEW CRITICS WHO HAVE READ
VWOO 1	(121)	THAT YOU ARE NOT A LADY? /Z/ THE AMERICANS DONT	KNOW	THE DIFFERENCE: THEY THINK MY TELEPHONE TALK IS
2TRU I	(47)	A COUNTESS. WE SHALL GO ABROAD, WHERE NOBODY WILL	KNOW	THE DIFFERENCE. YOU SHALL HAVE A SPLENDID FOREIGN
ARMS III	(71)	TAKEN ABACK). NEXT TIME, I HOPE YOU WILL	KNOW	THE DIFFERENCE BETWEEN A SCHOOLGIRL OF SEVENTEEN AND A
ARMS II	(36)	WILL MARRY HIM, WHETHER HE LIKES IT OR NOT. I	KNOW	THE DIFFERENCE BETWEEN THE SORT OF MANNER YOU AND SHE
MTH5	(207)	/THE YOUTH/ YOU OLD FISH! I BELIEVE YOU DONT	KNOW	THE DIFFERENCE BETWEEN A MAN AND A WOMAN. /THE ANCIENT/
MILL I	(156)	/EPIFANIA/ NONSENSE! THE CREATURE DOES NOT	KNOW	THE DIFFERENCE BETWEEN A CUMULATIVE PREFERENCE AND A
BULL I	(93)	HAVE IT, I CAN GET IT INTO ENGINEERING FOR YOU: I	KNOW	THE EDITOR. /DOYLE/ LETS GET BACK TO BUSINESS. I'D
JOAN PREFACE	(4)	MOST ATTRACTIVE. IF SHE HAD BEEN OLD ENOUGH TO	KNOW	THE EFFECT SHE WAS PRODUCING ON THE MEN WHOM SHE
NEVR III	(262)	ONE. PERHAPS I SHALL WRITE IT FOR YOU-- WHEN I	KNOW	THE END OF IT. (SHE GOES BACK TO THE WINDOW). /MRS
CLEO PRO1	(92)	AND YOUR LUSTS AND STUPIDITIES, AND NOW, WOULD YE	KNOW	THE END OF POMPEY, OR WILL YE SLEEP WHILE A GOD
BULL I	(78)	PROPERLY, AS ESTATES ARE HANDLED IN ENGLAND. YOU	KNOW	THE ENGLISH PLAN, MR HAFFIGAN, DONT YOU? /TIM/ BEDAD I
SUPR I	(8)	WOMAN. AND HER FATHER IS GONE. WE DONT AS YET	KNOW	THE EXACT TERMS OF HIS WILL; BUT HE OFTEN TALKED IT
LADY	(247)	/SHAKESPEAR/ I AM NOT CRUEL, MADAM; BUT YOU	KNOW	THE FABLE OF JUPITER AND SEMELE. I COULD NOT HELP MY
SUPR HANDBOK	(207)	OF OUR MOST REPUTABLE CIRCLES; AND, IF YOU	KNOW	THE FACTS AND ARE STRONG ENOUGH TO LOOK THEM IN THE
DOCT PREFACE	(6)	LUNATIC. BUT MANKIND DOES NOT AGREE, AND DOES NOT	KNOW	THE FACTS. ALL THAT CAN BE SAID FOR MEDICAL POPULARITY
GENV IV	(96)	YOU SEE, THINKING IS VERY LITTLE USE UNLESS YOU	KNOW	THE FACTS, AND WE NEVER DO KNOW THE POLITICAL FACTS
PYGM II	(237)	A FATHER'S HEART, AS IT WERE. /PICKERING/ WELL, I	KNOW	THE FEELING; BUT REALLY IT SEEMS HARDLY RIGHT--
MTH1 I	(17)	IS HOPE? /THE SERPENT/ AS LONG AS YOU DO NOT	KNOW	THE FUTURE YOU DO NOT KNOW THAT IT WILL NOT BE HAPPIER
CAPT II	(252)	(STRUCK) IS THAT SO, CAPTAIN? /BRASSBOUND/ I	KNOW	THE GENTLEMAN'S VALUE-- BETTER PERHAPS THAN HE KNOWS IT
PYGM II	(235)	WEST COUNTRY MYSELF. (TO DOOLITTLE) HOW DID YOU	KNOW	THE GIRL WAS HERE IF YOU DIDNT SEND HER? /DOOLITTLE/
BULL III	(135)	DEAL OF TRUTH IN IT. NOW I AM A LIBERAL. YOU	KNOW	THE GREAT PRINCIPLES OF THE LIBERAL PARTY. PEACE--
DOCT V	(178)	YOU ARE CRUEL, CRUEL. WHEN HE WAS ALIVE I DID NOT	KNOW	THE GREATNESS OF MY BLESSING. I WORRIED MEANLY ABOUT
POSN PREFACE	(402)	WOULD HAVE BECOME A POLICE DES MOEURS. THOSE WHO	KNOW	THE HISTORY OF SUCH POLICE FORCES ON THE CONTINENT WILL
MTH3	(96)	WAS HER PECULIAR AND SUPREME GLORY. /CONFUCIUS/ I	KNOW	THE HISTORY OF YOUR COUNTRY PERFECTLY WELL. IT PROVES
MTH3	(95)	HONEST AND COMPETENT? /BURGE-LUBIN/ YOU DO NOT	KNOW	THE HISTORY OF THIS COUNTRY. WHAT WOULD MY ANCESTORS
CAND III	(145)	MAN'S VOICE-- NO LONGER A BOY'S-- IN THE WORDS) I	KNOW	THE HOUR WHEN IT STRIKES. I AM IMPATIENT TO DO WHAT
WIDO III	(58)	OF YOU, DOCTOR. YOU NEVER BIN HERE BEFORE; BUT I	KNOW	THE HOUSE BETTER THAN MY OWN. /BLANCHE/ HERE THEY ARE.
WIDO I	(6)	/COKANE/ AH, YOU ARE YOUNG, DEAR BOY: YOU DONT	KNOW	THE IMPORTANCE OF THESE THINGS: APPARENTLY IDLE
GETT PREFACE	(217)	CONFIDENCE. SPEAKING FOR MYSELF, I CAN SAY THAT I	KNOW	THE INSIDE HISTORY OF PERHAPS HALF A DOZEN MARRIAGES.
GENV III	(70)	SIR ORPHEUS: YOU REMEMBER ME, SENORA. YOU	KNOW	THE JUDGE, BOSS. /THE SECRETARY/ DO ME THE HONOR TO
FANY PROLOG	(269)	THEATRES OF THE MOST SUPERIOR KIND-- YOU	KNOW	THE KIND OF PLAYS I MEAN? /TROTTER/ (EMPHATICALLY) I
JOAN 4	(106)	LONG AS THE PEOPLE FOLLOW THEIR FEUDAL LORDS, AND	KNOW	THE KING ONLY AS A TRAVELLING SHOW, OWNING NOTHING BUT
INCA	(241)	YOU CAN TRIFLE WITH ME. I AM A LADY'S MAID; AND I	KNOW	THE LADIES' MAIDS AND VALETS OF ALL THE ARISTOCRACIES

GETT	(310)	THE MISSION. /HOTCHKISS/ BUT HOW AM I TO	KNOW	THE LADY? /COLLINS/ SHE HAS GONE TO THE CHURCH IN
OVER	(185)	TRY TO LOOK LIKE AN UNMARRIED MAN. I HAPPEN TO	KNOW	THE LADY YOU DISAPPOINTED. I TRAVELLED IN THE SAME SHIP
JITT PREFACE	(5)	BE A WONDERFUL FEAT FOR A TRANSLATOR WHO DOES NOT	KNOW	THE LANGUAGE. HOWEVER, WHEN IT COMES TO TRANSLATING A
CLEO IV	(169)	INSCRUTABLY AT HIM. /CHARMIAN/ I SEE YOU DO NOT	KNOW	THE LATEST NEWS, POTHINUS. /POTHINUS/ WHAT IS THAT?
GETT	(297)	ON MY HONOR, NO. ALL I SAID WAS THAT I DIDNT	KNOW	THE LAW WHEN I ASKED YOU TO BE MY WIFE. /EDITH/ AND YOU
JOAN 6	(142)	TAKE ITS COURSE. MASTER DE STOGUMBER. AND YOU	KNOW	THE LAW. /THE CHAPLAIN/ (RISING, PURPLE WITH FURY) I
DEVL I	(22)	BORN ANNIE PRIMROSE"-- YOU SEE HE DID NOT	KNOW	THE LAW, MR DUDGEON: YOUR MOTHER WAS NOT BORN ANNIE:
SUPR III	(124)	IN LOVE WITH AND MARRY HIM! /ANA/ YES, JUAN: WE	KNOW	THE LIBERTINE'S PHILOSOPHY. ALWAYS IGNORE THE
LADY PREFACE	(211)	ON SHAKESPEAR GAVE ME GREAT DELIGHT. TO THOSE WHO	KNOW	THE LITERARY WORLD OF LONDON THERE WAS A SHARP STROKE
DEVL II	(49)	HIS OLD QUIET AND IMPRESSIVE CONVICTION) YOU DONT	KNOW	THE MAN YOURE MARRIED TO. (ESSIE RETURNS. HE SWOOPS AT
ROCK I	(221)	OF IT; AND I DONT PRETEND TO. /HIPNEY/ DID YOU	KNOW	THE MAYOR WELL, SRARTHUR? YOU CALLED HIM YOUR OLD
LION I	(115)	IN MY GOD NOR IN THEIR OWN -- MEN WHO DO NOT	KNOW	THE MEANING OF THE WORD RELIGION -- WHEN THESE MEN DRAG
DOCT III	(143)	A BIT. IT'S ONLY A WORD: A WORD THAT YOU DONT	KNOW	THE MEANING OF. WHAT IS A SCOUNDREL? /B.B./ YOU ARE A
KING I	(182)	ALWAYS DEFIED GOD AND BETRAYED WOMEN. HE DOES NOT	KNOW	THE MEANING OF THE WORD RELIGION. HE LAUGHED AT IT IN
ARMS II	(23)	BE WARNED IN TIME, LOUKA: MEND YOUR MANNERS. I	KNOW	THE MISTRESS. SHE IS SO GRAND THAT SHE NEVER DREAMS
BUOY III	(43)	THAT IS TRUE. ARE YOU A MATHEMATICIAN? /HE/ I	KNOW	THE MULTIPLICATION TABLE, AND CAN DO VERY SIMPLE SUMS:
VWOO 3	(135)	OF COURSE, WHEN PEOPLE ARE TOO IGNORANT TO	KNOW	THE NAMES OF WHAT THEY EAT, THAT IS ANOTHER MATTER. /Z/
SUPR I SD	(5)	AS WELL AS IN HIS BLACK CLOTHES. RAMSDEN SEEMS TO	KNOW	THE NATURE OF THE BEREAVEMENT. AS THE VISITOR ADVANCES
2TRU I	(39)	MY ROOM AT NIGHT? /THE NURSE/ YOU SEE, YOU DONT	KNOW	THE NATURE OF THE BUSINESS YET. IT'S GOT TO BE DONE
2TRU III	(100)	I AM SURE. (TOGETHER) /THE ELDER/ MAY I CRAVE TO	KNOW	THE NATURE OF THE DISTINGUISHED SERVICE WHICH HAS WON
BULL III	(121)	IT'S MADE A GREAT CHANGE, LARRY. YOUD HARLY	KNOW	THE OLD TENANTS NOW. YOUD THINK IT WAS A LIBERTY TO
GETT	(324)	BROUGHT IT UP TO THE PRESENT DAY. BUT ENOUGH TO	KNOW	THE PART PLAYED IN IT BY MISS GRANTHAM. /MRS
DEVL II	(35)	WAIT A MOMENT. YOUR BROTHER MUST BE ANXIOUS TO	KNOW	THE PARTICULARS. /RICHARD/ PSHA! NOT I: HE DOESNT
MTH2	(85)	FAMILIES. HE HAS TO THINK OF THE FUTURE AND	KNOW	THE PAST. HIS OFFICE IS THE REAL MODERN CONFESSIONAL.
JOAN 2	(84)	THEE. DRESSING UP DONT FILL EMPTY NODDLE. I	KNOW	THE PEOPLE: THE REAL PEOPLE THAT MAKE THY BREAD FOR
MRS I	(193)	AM I. WHAT ARE YOU UP TO IN THESE PARTS? DO YOU	KNOW	THE PEOPLE HERE? /PRAED/ YES: I'M SPENDING THE DAY
CAPT I	(232)	/LADY CICELY/ BUT I ALWAYS GO EVERYWHERE. I	KNOW	THE PEOPLE HERE WONT TOUCH ME. THEY HAVE SUCH NICE
GENV IV	(96)	USE UNLESS YOU KNOW THE FACTS. AND WE NEVER DO	KNOW	THE POLITICAL FACTS UNTIL TWENTY YEARS AFTER. SOMETIMES
SIM II	(65)	A WORLD OF POLITICAL FACTS, BECAUSE WE SHALL NOT	KNOW	THE POLITICAL FACTS FOR YEARS TO COME. WE MUST
ARMS II	(24)	HER CIGARET, AND STAMPS ON IT). CHILD: YOU DONT	KNOW	THE POWER SUCH HIGH PEOPLE HAVE OVER THE LIKE OF YOU
ROCK II	(237)	OF PARASITISM. /SIR DEXTER/ YOU DONT EVEN	KNOW	THE PRESENT LAW. YOU HAVE THE VERMINOUS PERSONS ACT.
DEVL III	(65)	YOU SEE HIM? /CHRISTY/ NO. /SWINDON/ YOU SEEM TO	KNOW	THE PRISONER? /CHRISTY/ DO YOU MEAN DICK? /SWINDON/
MILL I	(163)	OUT INTO THE COUNTRY SOMEWHERE AND LUNCH THERE. I	KNOW	THE QUAINTEST LITTLE PLACE UP THE RIVER. GOODBYE, MR
HART III	(139)	LIFE WITH A BLESSING! THAT IS WHAT I WANT. NOW I	KNOW	THE REAL REASON WHY I COULDNT MARRY MR MANGAN: THERE
ROCK II	(261)	MY UNION JACK MEN WOULD KEEP ORDER, OR THEYD	KNOW	THE REASON WHY. /BASHAM/ AND WHO WOULD KEEP THEM IN
KING I	(218)	ORANGE GIRL OR QUEEN. OR EVEN A MAN. BUT I DONT	KNOW	THE REASON WHY. SO YOU CAN TELL IT TO HER, ROWLEY
MRS II	(201)	/REV. S./ BUT SURELY, MY DEAR MRS WARREN, YOU	KNOW	THE REASONS-- /MRS WARREN/ (DEFIANTLY) I KNOW NO
NEVR III	(267)	PROTECT HER AGAINST THE WILES OF MAN. WELL, YOU	KNOW	THE RESULT: THE OLD FASHIONED MAN GOT ROUND HER. THE
GETT	(340)	AT IT. /THE BISHOP/ POOR PEOPLE! IT'S SO HARD TO	KNOW	THE RIGHT PLACE TO LAUGH, ISNT IT? /MRS GEORGE/ I
JITT I	(19)	ME. SOMETHING YOU CAN UNDERSTAND ONLY WHEN YOU	KNOW	THE RIGHTS OF IT. /JITTA/ (REPELLED AND ANXIOUS) BUT
POSN	(441)	/STRAPPER/ I'LL GET A WITNESS ALL RIGHT ENOUGH. I	KNOW	THE ROAD HE TOOK; AND I'LL ASK AT EVERY HOUSE WITHIN
MIS. PREFACE	(33)	WASTING OTHER PEOPLE'S TIME: THAT IS, IT MUST	KNOW	THE RULES OF THE ROAD, BE ABLE TO READ PLACARDS AND
MRS II	(214)	LIZ WENT OUT ONE NIGHT AND NEVER CAME BACK. I	KNOW	THE SCHOOLMISTRESS THOUGHT I'D SOON FOLLOW HER EXAMPLE;
CAND III SD	(146)	HIM). AH, JAMES! THEY EMBRACE. BUT THEY DO NOT	KNOW	THE SECRET IN THE POET'S HEART.
BULL I	(77)	WORD YOURE GOIN TO SAY BEFORE YEV SAID IT. I	KNOW	THE SORT O MAN YAR. AN SO YOURE THINKIN O COMIN TO
FANY PROLOG	(269)	I MEAN? /TROTTER/ (EMPHATICALLY) I THINK I	KNOW	THE SORT OF ENTERTAINMENTS YOU MEAN. BUT PLEASE DO NOT
DEST	(160)	USE TRYING TO PUT THE BLAME ON ME. HOW WAS I TO	KNOW	THE SORT OF FELLOW HE WAS? (HE TAKES A CHAIR FROM
JOAN 1	(60)	HA! YOU BELIEVE SHE PRAYS, YOU IDIOT. I	KNOW	THE SORT OF GIRL THAT IS ALWAYS TALKING TO SOLDIERS.
HART II	(110)	/THE BURGLAR/ WELL, HOW DO I KNOW, CAPTAIN? YOU	KNOW	THE SORT OF LIFE YOU AND ME HAS LED. ANY YOUNG LADY OF
MIS.	(159)	YOU MUST HAVE DRIVEN LOTS OF MEN CRAZY. YOU	KNOW	THE SORT OF MAN I AM, DONT YOU? SEE THROUGH ME AT A
BULL IV	(165)	NO POWERS OF EXPRESSION. /NORA/ I DONT THINK YOU	KNOW	THE SORT OF MAN YOU ARE AT ALL. WHATEVER MAY BE THE
HART II	(101)	THE FLOOR. BUT IVE FOUND YOU ALL OUT, ANYHOW. I	KNOW	THE SORT OF PEOPLE I'M AMONG NOW. IVE HEARD EVERY WORD
FANY PROLOG	(260)	AND HER PERAMBULATOR WAS A GONDOLA. NOW YOU	KNOW	THE SORT OF PEOPLE WE ARE, MR SAVOYARD. YOU CAN IMAGINE
MRS I	(186)	OF IT, AND WENT OFF TO CHANCERY LANE. NOW YOU	KNOW	THE SORT OF PERFECTLY SPLENDID MODERN YOUNG LADY I AM.
MRS IV	(249)	ABOUT IT, GOES ON CALMLY) MOTHER: YOU DONT AT ALL	KNOW	THE SORT OF PERSON I AM. I DONT OBJECT TO CROFTS MORE
VWOO 2	(125)	BEEN BROADCASTED ON THE WIRELESS AS LOST. YOU	KNOW	THE SORT OF THING. MISSING FROM HIS HOME SINCE JANUARY
PHIL II	(102)	YOUR HEART IS STILL MINE"-- AND SO ON: YOU	KNOW	THE SORT OF THING-- " EVER AND ALWAYS YOUR LOVING
MRS IV	(251)	WILL SPARE YOU? /MRS WARREN/ (VIOLENTLY) OH, I	KNOW	THE SORT YOU ARE: NO MERCY FOR YOURSELF OR ANYONE ELSE.
PRES	(139)	INFERNAL YOUNG FOOL CHUBBS-JENKINSON IS, NOT TO	KNOW	THE STANDING OF HIS MAN BETTER! WHY DIDNT HE KNOW? IT
CAND I	(96)	PRESENT, I SUPPOSE: YOU ARE TOO MUCH OF A POET TO	KNOW	THE STATE A WOMAN FINDS HER HOUSE IN WHEN SHE'S BEEN
BULL II	(102)	OH DONT SAY THAT. /KEEGAN/ WHY NOT? DONT YOU	KNOW	THE STORY? HOW I CONFESSED A BLACK MAN AND GAVE HIM
GETT	(324)	STORY OF THE GENERAL'S LIFE? /THE BISHOP/ YOU	KNOW	THE STORY OF HIS LIFE, THEN? /MRS GEORGE/ NOT ALL. WE
MILL III	(180)	OH, MAAM, HAVE SOME FEELING FOR US. YOU DONT	KNOW	THE STRUGGLE WE HAVE TO LIVE. /THE MAN/ (ROUGHLY)
SUPR HANDBOK	(178)	TO SATISFY THE DEMAND OF HOUSEWIVES WHO DO NOT	KNOW	THE TECHNICAL DIFFERENCES BETWEEN A TUBER AND A
SIM II	(65)	WHAT REALLY HAPPENED WAS QUITE DIFFERENT. WE DONT	KNOW	THE TRUTH ABOUT ANY OF OUR STATESMEN UNTIL THEY ARE
LION PREFACE	(51)	THE WORLD IS SO BADLY GOVERNED THAT THOSE WHO	KNOW	THE TRUTH CAN HARDLY BEAR TO LIVE IN IT, AN OBJECTION
ROCK PREFACE	(185)	FROM SEVERAL GODS. /JESUS/ IN SO FAR AS YOU	KNOW	THE TRUTH YOU HAVE IT FROM MY GOD, WHO IS YOUR HEAVENLY
ROCK II	(284)	THE RED FLAG? /LADY CHAVENDER/ NO. I DONT	KNOW	THE TUNE. I CAUGHT THE FIRST TWO WORDS. " ENGLAND,
BARB I	(254)	WAS NOT THE SORT OF THING HE DID. BESIDES, YOU	KNOW	THE UNDERSHAFT MOTTO: UNASHAMED. EVERYBODY KNEW.
CLEO II	(138)	POSTERITY AS A BARBAROUS SOLDIER TOO IGNORANT TO	KNOW	THE VALUE OF BOOKS? /CAESAR/ THEODOTUS: I AM AN AUTHOR
JITT I	(20)	LEFT THAT I DARE NOT PUT THIS OFF ANY LONGER. YOU	KNOW	THE VALUE OF MY BOOK. WELL, YOU MUST TAKE CHARGE OF IT.
BULL PREFACE	(31)	UNION JACK WITHOUT THE SMALLEST SCRUPLE; BUT THEY	KNOW	THE VALUE OF THE CHANNEL FLEET, AND WILL CLING CLOSER
JITT III	(58)	LECTURE ON VARIETIES OF SLEEP-- /AGNES/ STUFF! I	KNOW	THE VARIETY OF SLEEP HE LEARNT FROM HER. (LOOKING AT
BULL I	(85)	YOU IN THE FACE. WHY, MAN ALIVE, LOOK AT ME! YOU	KNOW	THE WAY I NAG, AND WORRY, AND CARP, AND CAVIL, AND
SUPR III	(133)	STAND A SENTIMENTAL ONE, SENOR COMMANDER: YOU	KNOW	THE WAY TO THE FRONTIER OF HELL AND HEAVEN. BE GOOD
ROCK II	(275)	THESE THINGS OBJECTIVELY AND SCIENTIFICALLY. YOU	KNOW	THE WAY YOU MEET THOUSANDS OF PEOPLE AND THEY MEAN
DEST	(189)	/LIEUTENANT/ YOUD BETTER GO FIRST: I DONT	KNOW	THE WAY. /GIUSEPPE/ YOU CANT MISS IT. BESIDES (
CAND I	(84)	HUMAN HEART YOU HAVE, MR LEXY MILL! HOW WELL YOU	KNOW	THE WEAKNESSES OF WOMAN, DONT YOU? IT MUST BE SO NICE
FABL PREFACE	(75)	BEFORE MICAH, AND REPUDIATED EVERY PRETENCE TO	KNOW	THE WILL OF GOD, FORBIDDING EVEN THE MENTION OF HIS
DEVL I	(22)	INWARDLY) YOU KNOW WHAT I THINK, MR ANDERSON: YOU	KNOW	THE WORD I GAVE TO IT. /ANDERSON/ IT CANNOT BE HELPED,
MIS. PREFACE	(23)	I HAVE HEARD OF FROEBEL AND PESTALOZZI, WHETHER I	KNOW	THE WORK THAT IS BEING DONE BY MISS MASON AND THE
BARB II	(301)	BEEN SHEWN OVER THE SHELTER, MR UNDERSHAFT? YOU	KNOW	THE WORK WE'RE DOING, OF COURSE. /UNDERSHAFT/ (VERY
APPL I	(208)	(CONFIDENTLY) THEY WONT THROW ME OVER. YOU DONT	KNOW	THE WORKERS, MAGNUS: YOU HAVE NEVER BEEN A WORKER.
MIS. PREFACE	(37)	AND TALK AND CRITICIZE TO ANY PURPOSE, THEY MUST	KNOW	THE WORLD OUTSIDE THE UNIVERSITY AT LEAST AS WELL AS
ROCK II	(247)	LABOR AND PUTTING DOWN STRIKES YOU DONT	KNOW	THE WORLD YOURE LIVING IN; AND THATS ALL ABOUT IT. /SIR
PHIL II	(103)	TO HER. /CHARTERIS/ (MOURNFULLY) HOW LITTLE YOU	KNOW	THE WORLD, COLONEL! THE NEW WOMAN IS NOT LIKE THAT.
KING I	(186)	SHE WOULD NOT TAKE IT. /LOUISE/ HOW LITTLE YOU	KNOW	THE WORLD, MONSIEUR! NOBODY REFUSES A GOLDEN GUINEA.
MRS II	(217)	DONT YOU BE LED ASTRAY BY PEOPLE WHO DONT	KNOW	THE WORLD, MY GIRL. THE ONLY WAY FOR A WOMAN TO PROVIDE
GETT	(328)	IS SWEEPING ME AWAY WILL NOT SPARE YOU. I MUST	KNOW	THE WORST AT ONCE. WHAT WAS YOUR FATHER? /MRS GEORGE/
HART I	(59)	I DONT WANT TO KNOW ABOUT " AT LEAST": I WANT TO	KNOW	THE WORST. GIRLS OF YOUR AGE FALL IN LOVE WITH ALL
KING I	(212)	ARCHBISHOPS IMPOSTORS. /NEWTON/ YOU DO NOT	KNOW	THE WORST, SIR. I HAVE ANOTHER BOOK IN HAND: ONE WHICH
APPL PREFACE	(191)	ABOUT BREAKAGES, LIMITED. LIKE ALL SOCIALISTS WHO	KNOW	THEIR BUSINESS I HAVE AN EXASPERATED SENSE OF THE
METH PREFACE	(R16)	DESTRUCTIVELY, IS QUITE GENUINE: THE INSTRUCTORS	KNOW	THEIR BUSINESS, AND REALLY MEAN THE LEARNERS TO
JOAN 6	(135)	THE INQUIRIES ARE CARRIED ON BY PEOPLE WHO DO NOT	KNOW	THEIR LEGAL BUSINESS. /COURCELLES/ BUT THE WOMAN IS A
INCA	(252)	FOOLS TALK OF CRUSHING THE INCA; BUT THEY LITTLE	KNOW	THEIR MAN. TELL ME THIS. WHY DID ST HELENA EXTINGUISH
MIS.	(184)	ENJOYING PERCIVAL'S SUDDEN REVERSE. THEY	KNOW	THEIR MOTHER). /PERCIVAL/ (GASPING) MRS TARLETON: I
MIS. PREFACE	(27)	FROM BAD BLOOD ALL THEIR LIVES; WHEREAS MEN WHO	KNOW	THEIR OPPONENTS AND UNDERSTAND THEIR CASE, QUITE
PYGM IV	(262)	THATS WHAT DRIVES ME MAD: THE SILLY PEOPLE DONT	KNOW	THEIR OWN SILLY BUSINESS. (RISING) HOWEVER, IT'S OVER
CLEO I	(113)	SILENT. (TO CLEOPATRA) IS THIS HOW YOUR SERVANTS	KNOW	THEIR PLACES? SEND HER AWAY; AND DO YOU (TO THE
BULL IV	(180)	I KNOW THEIR VALUE. /KEEGAN/ YOU MEAN YOU DONT	KNOW	THEIR VALUE. /LARRY/ (ANGRILY) I MEAN WHAT I SAY.
BULL IV	(180)	FRIEND HERE, WHO IS STILL IMPOSED ON BY THEM. I	KNOW	THEIR VALUE. /KEEGAN/ YOU MEAN YOU DONT KNOW THEIR
MIS. PREFACE	(52)	LONG AS THE FAMILY AND THE SCHOOL PERSIST AS WE	KNOW	THEM: THAT IS, AS LONG AS THE RIGHTS OF CHILDREN ARE SO
3PLA PREFACE	(R11)	WHO HAVE THEIR OWN DRESSES AND DRAWING ROOMS, AND	KNOW	THEM TO BE A MERE MASQUERADE BEHIND WHICH THERE IS
MRS IV	(249)	AND THINK WHAT I THINK. I KNOW PLENTY OF THEM. I	KNOW	THEM TO SPEAK TO, TO INTRODUCE YOU TO, TO MAKE FRIENDS
FANY PROLOG	(258)	MR SAVOYARD: THE DIFFICULTY IS THAT SO FEW OF US	KNOW	THEM WHEN WE SEE THEM. WE HAVE INHERITED FROM THE PAST
ROCK PREFACE	(187)	EMPIRE ON IT? /JESUS/ BY THEIR FRUITS YE SHALL	KNOW	THEM. BEWARE HOW YOU KILL A THOUGHT THAT IS NEW TO YOU.
APPL INTRLUD	(251)	MEN ARE FOOLS AND MORAL COWARDS WHEN YOU COME TO	KNOW	THEM. BUT YOU ARE LESS OF A FOOL AND LESS OF A MORAL

BARB I	(269)	NAMES THE BETTER. YOU NEEDNT TALK TO ME: I	KNOW	THEM. IVE HAD SCORES OF THEM THROUGH MY HANDS:
KING I	(213)	DO NOT PROVE THINGS. THEY DO NOT NEED TO. THEY	KNOW	THEM. /NEWTON/ THIS IS FALSE. YOUR NOTION OF A
MTH4 I	(171)	THE OPPOSITION CAN OBTAIN COPIES. ALL THE NATIONS	KNOW	THEM. SECRET DIPLOMACY HAS BEEN TOTALLY ABOLISHED.
BUOY 1	(11)	/FATHER/ YOU NEED NOT SPEAK TO THEM. YOU NEED NOT	KNOW	THEM. YOU DO NOT MIX WITH THEM. AND THEY ARE NOT
JITT II	(35)	BUT THERE ARE THINGS IT IS BETTER NOT TO KNOW. I	KNOW	THEM; AND I ONLY WISH I COULD CHANGE PLACES WITH YOU.
CLEO PRO2,SD	(95)	NINETEEN AND A HALF CENTURIES YOUNGER THAN WE	KNOW	THEM; BUT YOU WOULD NOT GUESS THAT FROM THEIR
3PLA PREFACE	(R11)	THEY IMAGINE THEMSELVES CHRISTIANS THAN WHEN THEY	KNOW	THEMSELVES JEWS. ALL THAT CAN FAIRLY BE SAID OF THE
KING I	(179)	SYMBOLIZED, BECAUSE THOUGH WE FEEL THEM WE DO NOT	KNOW	THEM, MR NEWTON HAVING NOT YET DISCOVERED THEIR NATURE,
MILL PREFACE	(130)	ASSUME THAT THE SOLDIER AND HIS OFFICER AS WE	KNOW	THEM, THE ORANGE AND PAPIST RIOTERS OF BELFAST, THE
DOCT V	(175)	IT WOULD HAVE BEEN A LONGER ONE. /RIDGEON/ YOU	KNOW	THEN THAT I KILLED HIM? /JENNIFER/ (SUDDENLY MOVED
MTH1 I	(10)	HAPPENED TO A LILITH THAT NEVER WAS. SHE DID NOT	KNOW	THEN THAT IMAGINATION IS THE BEGINNING OF CREATION. YOU
CLEO PRO2	(98)	AFFRIS) AY: THE TALE OF THE BATTLE. /BEL AFFRIS/	KNOW	THEN, THAT I AM A NOVICE IN THE GUARD OF THE TEMPLE OF
GETT	(339)	WHO AM I THAT I SHOULD REBUKE YOU? BESIDES, I	KNOW	THERE ARE DISCUSSIONS IN WHICH THE POKER IS THE ONLY
HART I	(59)	NOW WE'RE COMING TO IT. TELL ME ALL ABOUT HIM. I	KNOW	THERE MUST BE SOMEBODY, OR YOUD NEVER HAVE BEEN SO
MTH5	(206)	ANCIENT/ (MILD, BLAND, AND INDULGENT) I DID NOT	KNOW	THERE WAS A NURSERY HERE, OR I SHOULD NOT HAVE TURNED
HART II	(121)	DOOR. /HECTOR/ I BEG YOUR PARDON. WE DID NOT	KNOW	THERE WAS ANYONE HERE. /ELLIE/ (RISING) THAT MEANS
ROCK I	(224)	! (HE SINKS BACK INTO HIS CHAIR). I DIDNT	KNOW	THERE WAS ANYONE IN THE ROOM. THE LADY NEITHER MOVES
MTH3	(124)	WHETHER WE WORK OR NOT. WE WORK PARTLY BECAUSE WE	KNOW	THERE WOULD BE NO DIVIDENDS IF WE DID NOT, AND PARTLY
BASH II,1,	(103)	THE POLICE. THIS BRUTAL SAILOR SHALL BE MADE TO	KNOW	THERE'S LAW IN ENGLAND. /LUCIAN/ DO NOT INTERRUPT HIM:
WIDO III	(52)	OF THE HOUSING OF THE WORKING CLASSES. YOU	KNOW	THERES A ROYAL COMMISSION ON IT, DONT YOU? /SARTORIUS/
ARMS III	(67)	HER CHOCOLATE CREAM SOLDIER: A SOUVENIR." NOW YOU	KNOW	THERES SOMETHING MORE IN THIS THAN MEETS THE EYE; AND
GENV IV	(115)	TO IT. /JUDGE/ (BEFORE FLANCO SITS DOWN) YOU	KNOW	THESE GENTLEMEN, I THINK. /FLANCO/ (SITTING DOWN
WIDO III	(54)	THE BUILDINGS COMPENSATED FOR. SOMEBODY HAS TO	KNOW	THESE THINGS BEFOREHAND, YOU KNOW, NO MATTER HOW DARK
JOAN 1	(68)	OF THEM WERE LEFT BEHIND, WOUNDED. I CAME TO	KNOW	THESE THREE POOR GODDAMS QUITE WELL. THEY HAD NOT HALF
SUPR PREFACE	(R26)	THE GLAMOR OF ARISTOCRATIC KINSHIP. WELL, WE TWO	KNOW	THESE TRANSFIGURED PERSONS, THESE COLLEGE PASSMEN,
MTH2	(84)	LIKING IS NOT WILLING. SEE WHAT THEY DO WHEN THEY	KNOW	THEY MUST. /FRANKLYN/ DO NOT MISTAKE MERE IDLE FANCIES
JOAN 6	(150)	AT CHRIST. THEY WERE FRENCH PEOPLE, MY LORD: I	KNOW	THEY WERE FRENCH. /WARWICK/ HUSH? SOMEONE IS COMING.
MIS.	(127)	OF TELLING CHILDREN TO READ THE BIBLE WHEN YOU	KNOW	THEY WONT. I WAS KEPT AWAY FROM THE BIBLE FOR FORTY
BULL IV	(151)	OH NO HE WONT: HE'S NOT AN IRISHMAN. HE'LL NEVER	KNOW	THEYRE LAUGHING AT HIM; AND WHILE THEYRE LAUGHING HE'LL
MIS.	(122)	WE ALL DO THAT: THATS ONLY HUMAN NATURE. BUT YOU	KNOW	THEYVE NO NOTION OF DECENCY. I SHALL NEVER FORGET THE
ARMS II	(24)	HAVE THE MASTER KNOW FOR A THOUSAND LEVAS. I	KNOW	THINGS ABOUT HIM THAT SHE WOULDNT LET HIM HEAR THE LAST
ARMS II	(24)	OF FOR SIX MONTHS IF I BLABBED THEM TO HER. I	KNOW	THINGS ABOUT RAINA THAT WOULD BREAK OFF HER MATCH WITH
ARMS II	(24)	THEIR SERVICE. DO YOU THINK I KNOW NO SECRETS? I	KNOW	THINGS ABOUT THE MISTRESS THAT SHE WOULDNT HAVE THE
CLEO IV	(172)	AND WHO WOULD HURT ME. /POTHINUS/ DOES CAESAR	KNOW	THIS? /CLEOPATRA/ YES. /POTHINUS/ AND HE IS NOT
CAND I	(103)	HER. /MORELL/ (PUZZLED) WHY DO YOU WANT HER TO	KNOW	THIS? /MARCHBANKS/ (WITH LYRIC RAPTURE) BECAUSE SHE
KING I	(207)	NEVER HAVE BEEN PUT THERE. BUT HOW DO YOU COME TO	KNOW	THIS? THINGS COME TO MY KNOWLEDGE BY THE GRACE OF GOD;
MTH2	(82)	WHAT DOES ANYONE KNOW ABOUT HIM? /CONRAD/ WE	KNOW	THIS ABOUT HIM WITH ABSOLUTE CERTAINTY. THE POWER MY
BARB PREFACE	(233)	AND CIRCUMSTANTIAL NECESSITIES. STRONG PEOPLE	KNOW	THIS AND COUNT UPON IT. IN NOTHING HAVE THE
MTH4 I	(140)	ITS HEADQUARTERS A THOUSAND YEARS AGO. FEW PEOPLE	KNOW	THIS INTERESTING CIRCUMSTANCE NOW; BUT I ASSURE YOU IT
BULL I	(91)	I DONT WANT TO INTERRUPT YOU, LARRY; BUT YOU	KNOW	THIS IS ALL GAMMON. THESE DIFFERENCES EXIST IN ALL
PHIL II	(127)	YOUD OVERDO IT SOME DAY, JULIA. /CRAVEN/ DO YOU	KNOW	THIS LADY, JO? /CUTHBERTSON/ THIS IS MY DAUGHTER, MRS
FANY II	(289)	A MONTH, BUT WITH THE OPTION OF A FINE. I DID NOT	KNOW	THIS UNTIL I WAS RELEASED, WHEN MY FIRST ACT WAS TO PAY
CLEO IV	(171)	WE WILL OR NO. AND SHE WHO IS WISE ENOUGH TO	KNOW	THIS WILL REIGN WHEN CAESAR DEPARTS. /POTHINUS/ YOU
BARB PREFACE	(235)	TO BILL. IN REAL LIFE BILL WOULD PERHAPS NEVER	KNOW	THIS. BUT I, THE DRAMATIST WHOSE BUSINESS IT IS TO SHEW
BUOY IV	(55)	WHAT YOU CALL CULTURE. LOVE GUARANTEES NOTHING. I	KNOW	THIS. YOU KNOW IT. MY DAUGHTER KNOWS IT. THE YOUNG MAN
MIS.	(191)	HEARTILY AS I DO. IT IS AS WELL THAT YOU SHOULD	KNOW	THIS, MY YOUNG FRIEND; SO THAT YOU MAY RECOGNIZE IN
BARB I	(254)	/STEPHEN/ HE MARRIED WITHOUT LETTING YOU	KNOW	THIS! /LADY BRITOMART/ (RATHER TAKEN ABACK BY THIS
BARB PREFACE	(208)	A NORWEGIAN AUTHOR OF WHOSE LANGUAGE I DO NOT	KNOW	THREE WORDS, AND OF WHOM I KNEW NOTHING UNTIL YEARS
JOAN PREFACE	(16)	TO HAVE THE MOST VILLAINOUS RACIAL POISON WE	KNOW	THRUST INTO THEIR VEINS? THE ONE WHO TOLD THEM THE
MILL III	(184)	WHO ARE YOU CALLING SWEATERS? /EPIFANIA/ MAN,	KNOW	THYSELF. YOU SWEAT YOURSELF: YOU SWEAT YOUR WIFE: YOU
MTH4 II	(179)	ACROSS A FRONTIER AND A CHAIN OF MOUNTAINS AND	KNOW	TO A MILE EXACTLY WHERE THEY WILL BE AT THE END OF
SUPR HANDBOK	(204)	INCANTATIONS WITH BURNING SULPHUR (WHICH THEY	KNOW	TO BE USELESS) BECAUSE THE PEOPLE BELIEVE IN IT AS
MTH3	(132)	DOMINATED AND INTIMIDATED BY PEOPLE WHOM I NOW	KNOW	TO HAVE BEEN WEAKER AND SILLIER THAN I, BECAUSE THERE
SUPR HANDBOK	(219)	WHEN A MAN TEACHES SOMETHING HE DOES NOT	KNOW	TO SOMEBODY ELSE WHO HAS NO APTITUDE FOR IT, AND GIVES
CAND I	(103)	LAY THE TRUTH AT HER FEET AS I AM-- THEN YOU WILL	KNOW	TO THE END OF YOUR DAYS THAT SHE REALLY BELONGS TO ME
DOCT PREFACE	(19)	AND DRUNKEN, AS THEIR WIVES AND CHILDREN	KNOW	TO THEIR COST. NOT ONLY DO THESE TALENTED ENERGETIC
APPL PREFACE	(193)	OF THE TRAIN, AS THOSE WHO LIVE WITHIN EARSHOT	KNOW	TO THEIR COST), AND THE RAILWAY PORTERS WHO DUMP THE
CLEO IV	(173)	LISTEN TO HIM. BEGONE! /POTHINUS/ (DARKLY) I	KNOW	TO WHOM I MUST GO NOW. /FTATATEETA/ (SUSPICIOUSLY) TO
SUPR III	(88)	WHY NOT, SENORA? /THE OLD WOMAN/ YOU DO NOT	KNOW	TO WHOM YOU ARE SPEAKING. I AM A LADY, AND A FAITHFUL
WIDO II	(32)	YOU WILL. /COKANE/ (WITH DIGNITY) DO YOU	KNOW	TO WHOM YOU ARE SPEAKING, MY GOOD MAN? /LICKCHEESE/ (
CURE	(231)	IT'S NO BUSINESS OF YOURS, HOWEVER, YOUD BETTER	KNOW	TO WHOM YOU ARE SPEAKING. I AM STREGA THUNDRIDGE. (SHE
SUPR IV	(161)	I DONT KNOW WHICH IS BEST FOR A YOUNG MAN: TO	KNOW	TOO LITTLE, LIKE YOU, OR TOO MUCH, LIKE JACK. TANNER
BUOY 1	(16)	I TELL YOU AGAIN YOU ARE TOO CLEVER: YOU	KNOW	TOO MUCH: I CAN DO NOTHING WITH YOU. I WONDER HOW MANY
ROCK I	(199)	LAST YEAR. /SIR ARTHUR/ NO: THESE PARSONS	KNOW	TOO MUCH ABOUT THAT. BESIDES, THIS IS NOT THE TIME TO
MILL II	(173)	NOR ATTRACTIVE TO ME EXCEPT WHEN THEY ARE ILL. I	KNOW	TOO MUCH ABOUT THEM, INSIDE AND OUT. YOU ARE PERFECTLY
ROCK I	(213)	TIME HE OPENS HIS MOUTH. /BLEE/ WE WORKING FOLKS	KNOW	TOO MUCH OF BAD LANGUAGE AND BAD MANNERS TO SEE ANY FUN
FABL VI	(131)	LIFE. /THE TEACHER/ ENOUGH. WE CAN NEVER WANT TO	KNOW	TOO MUCH. ATTENTION! (ALL RISE). YOU WILL GET AT THE
ROCK I	(217)	WOULDNT HAVE A CHANCE AGAINST HIM. BUT NOT ME: I	KNOW	TOO MUCH. IT WOULD BE THE END OF ME, AS IT'S BEEN THE
MILL III	(181)	/THE MAN/ I DONT LIKE THE PEOPLE I EMPLOY TO	KNOW	TOO MUCH. /EPIFANIA/ I SEE. THEY MIGHT CALL IN THE
LION II	(128)	AN ACTOR? /THE EDITOR/ SEE HERE: YOU WANT TO	KNOW	TOO MUCH. THERE WILL BE NO PRETENDING ABOUT THE NEW
FABL VI	(131)	WE KNOW NOTHING. /YOUTH 3/ ROT! YOU WANT TO	KNOW	TOO MUCH. WE KNOW HOW TO MAKE CYCLOTRONS AND HUNDRED
BUOY 1	(14)	YOU ARE CLEVERER THAN I AM. YOU KNOW MORE. YOU	KNOW	TOO MUCH. YOU TALK TOO WELL. I HAVE THOUGHT A GOOD DEAL
JITT I	(10)	NOTHING TO ME. BUT I KNOW. /MRS BILLITER/ YOU	KNOW	TOO MUCH, YOU DO. ARE THEY PAID FOR? /THE FLOWER GIRL/
HART I	(63)	DRESS) YOU SHANT GO. I COULDNT BE SO MISTAKEN: I	KNOW	TOO WELL WHAT LIARS ARE LIKE. SOMEBODY HAS REALLY TOLD
ROCK II	(253)	BE WELL PAID. /THE DUKE/ MYRMIDONS! /ALOYSIA/ WE	KNOW	TOO WELL WHAT WE HAVE TO EXPECT FROM YOUR JANISSARIES.
MIS.	(187)	YOU AGAIN, LEAVE IT AT THAT. /BENTLEY/ I WANT TO	KNOW	TOO. HYPATIA'S ENGAGED TO ME. /HYPATIA/ BENTLEY: IF YOU
OVER	(188)	MY PROMISE. I SOLEMNLY DECLARE THAT I DID NOT	KNOW	UNTIL THIS EVENING THAT MRS JUNO WAS MARRIED. SHE WILL
DEVL I	(6)	TO NEVINSTOWN WE FOUND HIM ILL IN BED. HE DIDNT	KNOW	US AT FIRST. THE MINISTER SAT UP WITH HIM AND SENT ME
MILL III	(186)	TO THEM. AND WHO WOULD SPEAK TO US? WHO WOULD	KNOW	US OR GIVE US A HELPING HAND IN HARD TIMES IF WE BEGAN
HART II	(104)	FEEL LONELY WITHOUT US ALL NOW, AFTER COMING TO	KNOW	US SO WELL. /MANGAN/ (WITH SOMETHING LIKE A YELL OF
NEVR II	(235)	HE HAS NOT SEEN US FOR EIGHTEEN YEARS. HE WONT	KNOW	US. (TO EMPHASIZE THE COMMUNICATION, PHIL SEATS
MRS I	(197)	GONE INTO THE CHURCH! WELL, I NEVER! DONT YOU	KNOW	US, SAM? THIS IS GEORGE CROFTS, AS LARGE AS LIFE AND
NEVR III	(265)	I AM GOING TO SPEAK OF A SUBJECT OF WHICH I	KNOW	VERY LITTLE: PERHAPS NOTHING. I MEAN LOVE. /VALENTINE/
OVER PREFACE	(166)	UP TO THE POINT AT WHICH THEY LEARN THAT THEY	KNOW	VERY LITTLE ABOUT THEMSELVES, AND THAT THEY DO NOT SEEM
LADY PREFACE	(225)	THAT THEY ARE FORCED TO BEGIN BY SAYING THAT WE	KNOW	VERY LITTLE ABOUT SHAKESPEAR. AS A MATTER OF FACT, WITH
PYGM V	(287)	AGAINST ME: I'M ALWAYS IN THE WRONG. BUT YOU	KNOW	VERY WELL ALL THE TIME THAT YOURE NOTHING BUT A BULLY.
GETT	(273)	THEIR OWN WAY AND GETTING WELL TRAINED. YOU	KNOW	VERY WELL HE COULDNT AFFORD TO MARRY UNTIL THE
JITT II	(32)	CLUNG TO YOU. /JITTA/ TO ME! /LENKHEIM/ YES: YOU	KNOW	VERY WELL HE DID. IF I HAD DIED YOU WOULD HAVE BEEN UP
MIS.	(124)	TO CLEVERNESS. JERRY WOULD DRIVE ME MAD: YOU	KNOW	VERY WELL HES A FOOL: EVEN JOHNNY THINKS HIM A FOOL.
JITT III	(60)	DARE-- /EDITH/ (CONTINUING IMPETUOUSLY) OH, I	KNOW	VERY WELL HOW TIDY YOU KEPT HIS HOUSE FOR HIM, JUST AS
GETT	(317)	FARE, AS SO MANY WOMEN HAVE TO DO. /SYKES/ YOU	KNOW	VERY WELL I WOULD GRUDGE YOU NOTHING, EDIE. /EDITH/
O'FL	(219)	IT BECAUSE IVE GOT THE OLD AGE PENSION; AND THEY	KNOW	VERY WELL I'M ONLY SIXTY-TWO; SO IVE THE BETTER OF THEM
MIS. PREFACE	(81)	PARENT AS A FELLOW-CREATURE, WHILST THE PARENTS	KNOW	VERY WELL THAT THE CHILDREN ARE ONLY THEMSELVES OVER
MTH1 I	(5)	OF THE HORROR OF HAVING TO BE HERE FOREVER. BUT I	KNOW	VERY WELL THAT WHAT YOU MEAN IS THE HORROR OF HAVING TO
MTH2	(51)	A MUD BATH FOR EVERY SOUL CONCERNED IN IT. YOU	KNOW	VERY WELL THAT IT WILL NOT BE FOUGHT ON PRINCIPLE.
JOAN 1	(64)	THEY HAVE PARIS. THEY HAVE THIS CASTLE: YOU	KNOW	VERY WELL THAT WE HAD TO SURRENDER IT TO THE DUKE OF
BULL I	(89)	YOURE PARTLY RIGHT IN THAT: AT ALL EVENTS I	KNOW	VERY WELL THAT IF I HAD BEEN THE SON OF A LABORER
BULL III	(122)	THAT TOOK IT AFTER THEM? /LARRY/ (ANGRILY) YOU	KNOW	VERY WELL THAT BILLY BYRNE NEVER PAID IT. HE ONLY
JITT III	(62)	YES: BUT YOU WANT THE TRUTH, DONT YOU? YOU	KNOW	VERY WELL THAT GOETHE WAS A GREAT MAN; BUT THE FINE
JITT II	(35)	YOU NEED NOT SPEAK TO ME LIKE THAT. YOU	KNOW	VERY WELL THAT WHAT IS THE MATTER IS NOT MERELY THE
SUPR II	(53)	TO YOU, IT IS TO ME, AND TO HER. /TANNER/ YOU	KNOW	VERY WELL THAT SHE IS AS FREE TO CHOOSE AS YOU ARE.
MTH4 I	(165)	PREVENTED THEM FROM REALLY WANTING TO DO IT. YOU	KNOW	VERY WELL THAT THEY COULD ONLY KEEP ORDER-- SUCH AS IT
MTH5	(257)	OF YEARS? /ACIS/ OH, DONT TALK ABOUT IT. WHY, I	KNOW	VERY WELL THAT I HAVE ONLY FOUR YEARS OF WHAT ANY
MRS II	(201)	S./ (COLLAPSING HELPLESSLY INTO HIS CHAIR) YOU	KNOW	VERY WELL THAT I COULDNT TELL ANYONE THE REASONS. BUT
MRS II	(211)	CAN, IF YOU LIKE. I HAVE A RIGHT TO KNOW; AND YOU	KNOW	VERY WELL THAT I HAVE THAT RIGHT. YOU CAN REFUSE TO
PHIL I	(87)	NOT ALWAYS. DONT EXAGGERATE, CHARTERIS. YOU	KNOW	VERY WELL THAT THOUGH I JOINED THE CLUB ON GRACE'S
WIDO II	(38)	/TRENCH/ I AM DOING NOTHING OF THE SORT. YOU	KNOW	VERY WELL THAT WHAT YOU ARE SAYING IS DISGRACEFULLY

MRS IV	(250)	I'M LESS. I'M CERTAIN I'M LESS SENTIMENTAL. I	KNOW	VERY WELL THAT FASHIONABLE MORALITY IS ALL A PRETENCE,
MRS IV	(247)	ONLY LET ME KNOW HOW MUCH YOU WANT. /VIVIE/ YOU	KNOW	VERY WELL THAT THAT HAS NOTHING TO DO WITH IT. FROM
GENV III	(67)	HE HAS MADE THAT SPEECH OVER AND OVER AGAIN. YOU	KNOW	VERY WELL THAT AFTER A CERTAIN AGE A MAN HAS ONLY ONE
MILL I	(162)	TOO MUCH THE GENTLEMAN TO MENTION IT; BUT YOU	KNOW	VERY WELL THAT YOUR OWN BEHAVIOR HASNT BEEN SO VERY
ROCK II	(258)	THEY ARE THE REAL GOVERNMENT OF THE COUNTRY. THEY	KNOW	VERY WELL THAT THEY DONT GOVERN AND CANT GOVERN AND
ROCK II	(265)	POINT LIKE THIS IS IN VERY BAD TASTE. AND YOU	KNOW	VERY WELL THAT THE COUNTRY CANNOT DO WITHOUT DEXY. DEXY
FANY III	(300)	OFF DUTY? WHAT DO YOU MEAN? /MARGARET/ YOU	KNOW	VERY WELL WHAT I MEAN, BOBBY! DID YOU EVER CARE ONE
HART II	(113)	NOT, LADY UTTERWORD. REALLY! /LADY UTTERWORD/ I	KNOW	VERY WELL WHAT YOU MEANT. THE IMPUDENCE! /ELLIE/ WHAT
JITT II	(37)	MY MOTHER WONT SPEAK TO ME ABOUT IT; BUT I	KNOW	VERY WELL WHAT SHE IS THINKING. THEY WHISPER ALL DAY AT
ROCK II	(250)	TO LIVE THERE. /ALOYSIA/ DONT PREVARICATE. YOU	KNOW	VERY WELL WHAT I MEAN. IT IS WRITTEN IN BLOOD AND TEARS
ROCK II	(242)	IN SHORT, YOU WILL MAKE UTOPIAN PROMISES THAT YOU	KNOW	VERY WELL WILL NEVER BE CARRIED OUT. /GLENMORISON/ YOU
CAND I	(83)	PHOTOGRAPH AND STARES AUSTERELY AT HER). AND YOU	KNOW	VERY WELL YOU THINK ME DOWDY AND SECOND RATE ENOUGH.
ARMS II	(44)	LETS HAVE NO MORE NONSENSE ABOUT GOING AWAY. YOU	KNOW	VERY WELL YOURE NOT GOING BACK TO SWITZERLAND YET.
CAND II	(118)	THEM. /MORELL/ (WITH ENERGETIC SERIOUSNESS) YOU	KNOW	VERY WELL, CANDIDA, THAT I OFTEN BLOW THEM UP SOUNDLY
HART II	(123)	AGAIN. /HECTOR/ WHAT CONSPIRACY? /RANDALL/ YOU	KNOW	VERY WELL, SIR. A CONSPIRACY TO MAKE ME OUT TO BE
SUPR IV	(165)	MOTHER! COME, NOW: YOU MUSTNT CRY ANY MORE: YOU	KNOW	VIOLET DOESNT LIKE IT (MRS WHITEFIELD DRIES HER EYES,
MRS I	(193)	WARREN. /FRANK/ (ENTHUSIASTICALLY) WHAT! DO YOU	KNOW	VIVIE? ISNT SHE A JOLLY GIRL? I'M TEACHING HER TO
MTH2	(50)	HAVE EITHER BELIEFS OR PRINCIPLES. WHAT WE DID	KNOW	WAS THAT YOUR GOVERNMENT WAS FORMED LARGELY OF MEN WHO
FANY III	(316)	YOU I WAS A SINNER? /MRS GILBEY/ NOW, ROB, YOU	KNOW	WE ARE ALL SINNERS. WHAT ELSE IS RELIGION? /GILBEY/ I
WIDO I	(15)	PEOPLE WONT EXPECT US TO ENTERTAIN THEM: THEYLL	KNOW	WE CANT AFFORD IT. BUT THEYLL ENTERTAIN US: THEY ALWAYS
BUOY II	(24)	DO YOU MEAN BY OUR NOT BELIEVING? HOW DO YOU	KNOW	WE DO NOT BELIEVE? /THE NATIVE/ HE WHO BELIEVES IN HIS
ROCK I	(213)	TO USE ANY OF YOUR WEST END LANGUAGE HERE. YOU	KNOW	WE DONT LIKE IT. /SIR ARTHUR/ THATS RIGHT, MISS
SUPR I	(39)	DONT MIND YOUR QUEER OPINIONS ONE LITTLE BIT. YOU	KNOW	WE HAVE ALL BEEN BROUGHT UP TO HAVE ADVANCED OPINIONS.
OVER PREFACE	(169)	NOT ONLY THE COMPARATIVELY HARMLESS LIES THAT WE	KNOW	WE OUGHT NOT TO TELL, BUT THE RUINOUS LIES THAT WE
WIDO II	(32)	MY GOOD MAN? /LICKCHEESE/ (RECKLESSLY) I	KNOW	WELL ENOUGH WHO I'M SPEAKING TO. WHAT DO I CARE FOR
PYGM V	(287)	FRIENDS IN THE WORLD BUT YOU AND THE COLONEL. YOU	KNOW	WELL I COULDNT BEAR TO LIVE WITH A LOW COMMON MAN AFTER
CAND III	(133)	WIFE: I WANT NO MORE OF YOUR POETIC FRIPPERIES. I	KNOW	WELL THAT IF I HAVE LOST HER LOVE AND YOU HAVE GAINED
JOAN 5	(112)	WOULD REALLY RATHER GO HOME. /JOAN/ (BITTERLY) I	KNOW	WELL THAT NONE OF YOU WILL BE SORRY TO SEE ME GO. (SHE
JOAN 4	(106)	THE MAID IF WE STRIVE AGAINST ONE ANOTHER. I	KNOW	WELL THAT THERE IS A WILL TO POWER IN THE WORLD. I KNOW
MTH5	(262)	I WILL HAVE PATIENCE WITH THEM STILL; THOUGH I	KNOW	WELL THAT WHEN THEY ATTAIN IT THEY SHALL BECOME ONE
DEVL I	(21)	BY ME AND DECLARE THAT I AM OF SOUND MIND AND	KNOW	WELL WHAT I AM DOING AND THAT THIS IS MY REAL WILL
CLEO PRO1	(91)	AND HIDING OUR HANDIWORK AS A SHAMEFUL THING. YE	KNOW	WELL WHAT I MEAN; FOR THIS IS ONE OF YOUR OWN SINS. AND
GETT	(356)	I'M NOT A MAN OF SENTIMENT, BUT A MAN OF HONOR. I	KNOW	WELL WHAT WILL HAPPEN TO ME WHEN ONCE I CROSS THE
FANY III	(311)	BEGIN TO TAKE LIBERTIES, JUGGINS, NOW THAT YOU	KNOW	WE'RE LOTH TO PART WITH YOU. YOUR BROTHER ISNT A DUKE,
SUPR I	(44)	NOT? /VIOLET/ BUT THEY DONT KNOW. /TANNER/ DONT	KNOW	WHAT? /VIOLET/ THEY DONT KNOW THAT I AM IN THE RIGHT,
MIS.	(139)	I DO IT OF MY OWN FREE WILL. /HYPATIA/ I DONT	KNOW	WHAT A BLACKMAILER IS. I HAVNT EVEN THAT MUCH
SIM PREFACE	(5)	COCK WOULD COME DOWN THE CHIMNEY, THEY DID NOT	KNOW	WHAT A CHIMNEY WAS, BUT HE THREATENED THEM WITH THE
MTH4 II	(189)	/ZOZIM/ WHAT IS A CHURCH? /THE ENVOY/ NOT	KNOW	WHAT A CHURCH IS! WELL! /THE ELDERLY GENTLEMAN/ YOU
JOAN 2	(76)	DROWNED. A MERE COINCIDENCE. /LA HIRE/ I DO NOT	KNOW	WHAT A COINCIDENCE IS. I DO KNOW THAT THE MAN IS DEAD,
GETT	(277)	WHAT THAT FEELS LIKE TO A DECENT MAN? DO YOU	KNOW	WHAT A DECENT MAN FEELS ABOUT HIS WIFE'S NAME? HOW
FABL III	(113)	THEM TO DO WHAT WAS DONE LAST TIME. BUT I NEVER	KNOW	WHAT A GENIUS WILL BE UP TO NEXT, EXCEPT THAT IT WILL
ARMS II	(35)	ENGAGED TO WITH HER MAID. /LOUKA/ IT'S SO HARD TO	KNOW	WHAT A GENTLEMAN CONSIDERS RIGHT. I THOUGHT FROM YOUR
GENV III	(84)	WITH A JEW IN MY LIFE. /THE JEW/ THEN YOU DO NOT	KNOW	WHAT A GOOD DINNER IS. COME! TRY DINING WITH A JEW FOR
DEVL II	(32)	THAT: DONT SAY THAT, TONY, EVEN IN JEST. YOU DONT	KNOW	WHAT A HORRIBLE FEELING IT GIVES ME. /ANDERSON/ (
MIS. PREFACE	(12)	IGNORANT AND SILLY ENOUGH TO SUPPOSE THAT THEY	KNOW	WHAT A HUMAN BEING OUGHT TO BE, AND WHO STICK AT
SUPR I	(20)	DEAR FATHER'S WILL IS TO BE CARRIED OUT. YOU DONT	KNOW	WHAT A JOY THAT IS TO ME AND TO MY MOTHER! (SHE GOES
GETT PREFACE	(257)	JUDGE OR BISHOP. DO NOT ASK SOMEBODY WHO DOES NOT	KNOW	WHAT A JUDGE IS, OR WHAT A BISHOP IS, OR WHAT THE LAW
ARMS I	(19)	LUXURY INDEED, DEAR YOUNG LADY. /RAINA/ DO YOU	KNOW	WHAT A LIBRARY IS? /THE MAN/ A LIBRARY? A ROOMFUL OF
ROCK I	(198)	YOU ARE SUCH A WONDERFUL SPEAKER YOU OUGHT TO	KNOW	WHAT A MAGICAL EFFECT A FINE SPEECH HAS ON A CROWD.
MIS.	(112)	TRIAL HERE BECAUSE MY MOTHER THINKS A GIRL SHOULD	KNOW	WHAT A MAN IS LIKE IN THE HOUSE BEFORE SHE MARRIES HIM.
GETT	(333)	WHAT A WOMAN IS LIKE WHEN HER HAIR'S PULLED. I	KNOW	WHAT A MAN IS LIKE WHEN HE'S BIT. I KNOW WHAT THEYRE
GETT	(333)	MORE OF THE WORLD THAN YOU. /LESBIA/ THE CHINESE	KNOW	WHAT A MAN IS LIKE WHEN HE IS CUT INTO A THOUSAND
ROCK II	(255)	IS NEVER IN FAVOR OF ANY MEASURE. THEY DONT	KNOW	WHAT A MEASURE IS. WHAT THEY WANT IS THEIR ORDERS, AND
FABL II	(106)	BLOKE. DO YOU KNOW WHAT AN ISOTOPE IS? DO YOU	KNOW	WHAT A MESON IS? I DONT: NEITHER DO YOU. WHAT COULD
HART II	(97)	ALONE. /MAZZINI/ (AFFECTIONATELY) OH, WELL, I	KNOW	WHAT A NUISANCE PARENTS ARE, DEAR. I WILL BE GOOD AND
MTH4 I	(142)	YOU TAKE ME FOR A PAUPER? /THE WOMAN/ I DO NOT	KNOW	WHAT A PAUPER IS. YOU MUST TELL ME WHO YOU ARE, IF IT
KING I	(172)	/NELLY/ (GOING PAST CHARLES TO NEWTON) I DONT	KNOW	WHAT A PHILOSOPHER IS, MR NEWTON; BUT YOU LOOK ONE,
O'FL	(212)	THINK, SIR; FOR HOW WOULD A GENTLEMAN LIKE YOU	KNOW	WHAT A POOR IGNORANT CONCEITED CREATURE I WAS WHEN I
ROCK I	(196)	DAY AT THESE MEETINGS, SIR DEXTER RIGHTSIDE-- YOU	KNOW	WHAT A REGULAR OLD DIEHARD HE IS-- HEARD A SPEAKER SAY
MTH3	(93)	UNLESS OUR FIGURES ARE UNCHALLENGEABLE. YOU	KNOW	WHAT A ROW THERE WAS OVER THOSE LAST THREE YEARS, AND
O'FL	(208)	GO ON DECEIVING HER, CANT I? IT'S LITTLE YOU	KNOW	WHAT A SON'S LOVE CAN DO, SIR. DID YOU EVER NOTICE WHAT
HART PREFACE	(35)	PLEASE NOTE THAT ALL THESE SOLDIERS WHO DID NOT	KNOW	WHAT A THEATRE WAS, KNEW WHAT A CHURCH WAS. AND THEY
HART PREFACE	(35)	SOLDIERS AT THE BEGINNING OF THE WAR, DOES NOT	KNOW	WHAT A THEATRE IS, BUT PLEASE NOTE THAT ALL THESE
BULL II	(102)	A WAY. BUT NEVER MIND THE BLACK MAN. NOW THAT YOU	KNOW	WHAT A TRAVELLED MAN I AM, WHAT CAN I DO FOR YOU? (
LION PROLOG	(108)	AND WHEN I'M EATEN BY THE WILD BEASTS YOULL	KNOW	WHAT A WIFE YOUVE LOST. (SHE DASHES INTO THE JUNGLE
GETT	(333)	WITH DISGUST) NO. /MRS GEORGE/ WELL, I DID. I	KNOW	WHAT A WOMAN IS LIKE WHEN HER HAIR'S PULLED. I KNOW
NEVR II	(251)	NOT WITHIN MY CONTROL. I AM NOT SURE THAT I QUITE	KNOW	WHAT AFFECTION MEANS. (SHE TURNS AWAY WITH AN EVIDENT
FABL II	(106)	A DIPLOMATIST, NOT A LABORATORY BLOKE. DO YOU	KNOW	WHAT AN ISOTOPE IS? DO YOU KNOW WHAT A MESON IS? I
HART PREFACE	(30)	BOY I WAS TAKEN TO THE OPERA. I DID NOT THEN	KNOW	WHAT AN OPERA WAS, THOUGH I COULD WHISTLE A GOOD DEAL
SUPR III	(74)	ABLY REPRESENTED BY OUR ONE ANARCHIST, WHO DOESNT	KNOW	WHAT ANARCHISM MEANS (LAUGHTER)-- /THE ANARCHIST/ (
PYGM V	(269)	ACROSS THE ROOM) BUT I CANT FIND ANYTHING. I DONT	KNOW	WHAT APPOINTMENTS IVE GOT. I'M-- (PICKERING COMES IN.
PYGM V	(278)	WAS NOTHING MORE THAN THAT IN IT. BUT DO YOU	KNOW	WHAT BEGAN MY REAL EDUCATION? /PICKERING/ WHAT?
MRS IV	(237)	HAD A BROTHER? /VIVIE/ NO. /FRANK/ THEN YOU DONT	KNOW	WHAT BEING BROTHER AND SISTER FEELS LIKE? NOW I HAVE
MTH4 I	(168)	TRIUMPHANT) AHA! I HAVE MADE YOU BLUSH. NOW YOU	KNOW	WHAT BLUSHING MEANS. BLUSHING WITH SHAME! /ZOO/
PHIL I	(89)	THE CONTRARY, AFTER ALL, WHAT CAN WE DO? YOU	KNOW	WHAT BREAKS UP MOST CLUBS FOR MEN AND WOMEN. THERES A
JITT III	(66)	BUSINESS AND PRETENDS TO UNDERSTAND IT. DO YOU	KNOW	WHAT BRUNO ALWAYS TALKED TO ME ABOUT? WHAT IT ALWAYS
GENV IV	(97)	WHAT IS CAMBERWELL? /BEGONIA/ OH! HE DOESNT	KNOW	WHAT CAMBERWELL IS! /THE SECRETARY/ CAMBERWELL, MR
BUOY III	(44)	SHOULD BE ONE IN EVERY CHURCH. PEOPLE WOULD THEN	KNOW	WHAT CHANCES THEY ARE TAKING. SHOULD FIRST COUSINS
VWOO 1	(116)	WHAT DID YOU EXPECT IT TO BE? /Z/ WELL, I DIDNT	KNOW	WHAT COLOR THE SEA MIGHT BE IN THESE PARTS. I ALWAYS
SIM I	(37)	LOST. I DONT KNOW WHERE I AM. I MEAN I DONT EVEN	KNOW	WHAT COUNTRY I AM IN. /PRA/ YOU ARE IN THE UNEXPECTED
JOAN EPILOG	(161)	I DID A VERY CRUEL THING ONCE BECAUSE I DID NOT	KNOW	WHAT CRUELTY WAS LIKE. I HAD NOT SEEN IT, YOU KNOW.
APPL I	(213)	OTHER DEFENCE IS THERE? DEMOCRACY? YAH! WE	KNOW	WHAT DEMOCRACY IS WORTH. WHAT WE NEED IS A STRONG MAN.
GENV IV	(111)	YES, THE EXECUTIONS COME ALONG ALL RIGHT. WE	KNOW	WHAT DICTATORS ARE. /BBDE/ YES: THE TRIFLERS AND
DOCT I	(107)	TO BEHAVE MYSELF BEFORE I LEARNT YOU TO DO IT. I	KNOW	WHAT DOCTORS ARE: SITTING TALKING TOGETHER ABOUT
JITT III	(79)	TRY TO CONSOLE ME WITHOUT SNEERING AT ME. DO YOU	KNOW	WHAT EDITH CALLED YOU? /LENKHEIM/ NO. YOU CAN TELL ME
GENV IV	(96)	DO THEY STAND WITH US? I DONT KNOW. BUT THEY	KNOW	WHAT ENGLAND INTENDS. THEY KNOW WHAT TO EXPECT FROM US.
MTH5	(221)	HUMBUG. WHAT DO YOU KNOW ABOUT IT? /ECRASIA/ I	KNOW	WHAT EVERY PERSON OF CULTURE KNOWS: THAT THE BUSINESS
JOAN 2	(78)	HOW IS SHE TO KNOW? /THE ARCHBISHOP/ SHE WILL	KNOW	WHAT EVERYBODY IN CHINON KNOWS: THAT THE DAUPHIN IS THE
JOAN PREFACE	(26)	ME. I CANNOT BELIEVE THAT ANATOLE FRANCE DOES NOT	KNOW	WHAT EVERYBODY KNOWS. I WISH EVERYBODY KNEW ALL THAT HE
O'FL	(209)	TALK TO FATHER QUINLAN, IS IT! DO YOU	KNOW	WHAT FATHER QUINLAN SAYS TO ME THIS VERY MORNING? /SIR
DEST	(167)	MATTER) AH, YOU CAN LAUGH AT FEAR. THEN YOU DONT	KNOW	WHAT FEAR IS. /NAPOLEON/ TELL ME THIS. SUPPOSE YOU
GETT	(290)	/HOTCHKISS/ (SUNNILY) MY DEAR GENERAL, I DONT	KNOW	WHAT FEAR MEANS IN THE MILITARY SENSE OF THE WORD. IVE
ARMS III	(61)	POOH! DONT TALK TO ME ABOUT BULGARIA. YOU DONT	KNOW	WHAT FIGHTING IS. BUT HAVE IT YOUR OWN WAY. BRING YOUR
FANY I	(273)	(FLINGING AWAY TOWARDS HIS CHAIR) HOW DO I	KNOW	WHAT FOR? /MRS GILBEY/ WHAT DOES HE SAY? /GILBEY/ (
GETT	(264)	ANXIOUS SOUL; AND SHE WAS NEVER BROUGHT UP TO	KNOW	WHAT FREEDOM IS TO SOME PEOPLE. YOU SEE, FAMILY LIFE IS
FANY III	(320)	LAUGHS AT A FRENCHMAN'S JOKES? /GILBEY/ WE ALL	KNOW	WHAT FRENCH JOKES ARE. /JUGGINS/ BELIEVE ME: YOU DO
GENV III	(75)	FUTILE DONT KNOW WHAT GOES ON HERE. THEY DONT	KNOW	WHAT GENEVA MEANS TO US. THE POWERS THINK WE ARE
BUOY III	(46)	COMES TO THAT: LEAVE IT TO GOD, THOUGH WE DO NOT	KNOW	WHAT GOD IS, AND ARE STILL SEEKING A GENERAL
GENV III	(75)	TRUE. THOSE WHO THINK THE LEAGUE FUTILE DONT	KNOW	WHAT GOES ON HERE. THEY DONT KNOW WHAT GENEVA MEANS TO
MIS. PREFACE	(47)	THE BEST-BEHAVED CHILD, BECAUSE I REALLY DO NOT	KNOW	WHAT GOOD CONDUCT IS; BUT I WILL GLADLY TAKE THE
JITT III	(55)	AS MUCH AS THE BUTTER AND EGGS, YOU WOULD WANT TO	KNOW	WHAT HAD BECOME OF IT ALL. /FESSLER/ (SITTING DOWN
HART II	(96)	HE ASKED ME TO. /MAZZINI/ BUT IT'S DANGEROUS. YOU	KNOW	WHAT HAPPENED TO ME. /ELLIE/ (UTTERLY INDIFFERENT) OH,
CATH 1	(170)	IT IS NOT LUCKY TO BE CATHERINE'S HUSBAND. YOU	KNOW	WHAT HAPPENED TO PETER? /EDSTASTON/ (SHORTLY: SITTING
MILL IV	(196)	/SAGAMORE/ HOW DO YOU KNOW IT'S A LIE? YOU DONT	KNOW	WHAT HAPPENED AT THE END. YOU HAD CONCUSSION OF THE
FANY III	(317)	WE NEVER THOUGHT WE'D WANT TO DO. AND THEN YOU	KNOW	WHAT HAPPENS: COMPLAINTS AND QUARRELS AND HUFF AND
PYGM V	(273)	FOR ALL THE HAPPINESS THEY EVER HAS. THEY DONT	KNOW	WHAT HAPPINESS IS. BUT I, AS ONE OF THE UNDESERVING
JITT III	(73)	! ! /JITTA/ YES. I KNOW THAT POOR CRIMINAL. I	KNOW	WHAT HAS BECOME OF HER. I KNOW WHAT SHE DID. I KNOW

JOAN 2 (72)	LAMB, ARCHBISHOP. GOOD DAY, MY LORD. DO YOU	KNOW	WHAT HAS HAPPENED TO LA HIRE? /LA TREMOUILLE/ HE HAS
FANY I (277)	WAS ALL YOUR FAULT? I'M HALF DISTRACTED. I DONT	KNOW	WHAT HAS HAPPENED TO THE BOY! HE'S BEEN LOST THESE
SUPR PREFACE(R34)	OF THE BOOK YOU KNOW MICAWBER, WHEREAS YOU ONLY	KNOW	WHAT HAS HAPPENED TO DAVID, AND ARE NOT INTERESTED
CLEO IV (186)	I HAVE BEEN HERE WITH YOU ALL THE TIME. HOW CAN I	KNOW	WHAT HAS HAPPENED? /CAESAR/ (REFLECTIVELY) THAT IS
MILL I (152)	I HAVE HIM UP? /EPIFANIA/ CERTAINLY. I WANT TO	KNOW	WHAT HE IS DOING HERE. /ALASTAIR/ I DONT MIND. YOU
KING I (210)	/NEWTON/ (TERRIBLY PERTURBED) THIS MAN DOES NOT	KNOW	WHAT HE IS SAYING. TAKE HIM AWAY; AND LEAVE ME IN
JITT III (71)	IT THAT. /EDITH/ BUT YOU CANT THINK THAT. DO YOU	KNOW	WHAT HE SAID? /JITTA/ NO. ANYTHING VERY DREADFUL?
JITT II (47)	YOU HAVE SAID WHAT IT MEANS. /LENKHEIM/ I WANT TO	KNOW	WHAT HE SAID. /JITTA/ THAT YOU ARE TO BE THE FATHER TO
ROCK I (220)	WHAT MARX SAID WAS RIGHT OR WRONG, BECAUSE I DONT	KNOW	WHAT HE SAID. BUT I KNOW THAT HE PUTS INTO EVERY MAN
MTH2 (49)	KNOW WHERE THEY ARE WITH LORD DUNREEN. THEY	KNOW	WHAT HE THINKS RIGHT AND WHAT HE THINKS WRONG. WITH
LION PREFACE(15)	ASKED YOU FOR NOTHING BUT FAITH. LUTHER DID NOT	KNOW	WHAT HE WAS DOING IN THE SCIENTIFIC SOCIOLOGICAL WAY IN
POSN (460)	A GOOD ACTION IT WAS BECAUSE HE WAS TOO DRUNK TO	KNOW	WHAT HE WAS DOING. SO IT'S NO HARM TO HANG HIM. SHE
DEVL II (45)	COAT). I'D BETTER TAKE HIM HIS OWN COAT. I	KNOW	WHAT HE'LL SAY-- (IMITATING RICHARD'S SARDONIC MANNER)
ROCK II (278)	HE WANTS TO MARRY A FACTORY GIRL. BUT I DO NOT	KNOW	WHAT HIS ATTITUDE WILL BE WHEN A FACTORY GIRL WANTS TO
GENV III (79)	I COME TO OUR DEMOCRATIC FRIEND HERE. I DO NOT	KNOW	WHAT HIS BUSINESS IS-- /THE NEWCOMER/ I'M A RETIRED
NEVR II (249)	AND MAKING HIS FORTUNE IN A HURRY, NO DOUBT. I	KNOW	WHAT HIS SIX WEEKS' EARNINGS COME TO. (HE CROSSES THE
MILL II (177)	BEATEN TOO. /THE DOCTOR/ HOPELESSLY. YOU DO NOT	KNOW	WHAT HOMELESS POVERTY IS; AND ALLAH THE COMPASSIONATE
DOCT I (107)	THEY OUGHT TO BE WITH THEIR POOR PATIENTS. AND I	KNOW	WHAT HORSES ARE, SIR PATRICK. I WAS BROUGHT UP IN THE
GETT (286)	BRIDGENORTH/ (RISING) NOT DRESSED! DOES SHE	KNOW	WHAT HOUR IT IS? /LESBIA/ SHE HAS LOCKED HERSELF INTO
ROCK I (221)	BLESS YOUR INNOCENCE, SRARTHUR, YOU DONT	KNOW	WHAT HUMBUG IS YET. WAIT TIL YOURE A LABOR LEADER. (HE
CATH 1 (164)	/PATIOMKIN/ DARLING BELOVED, I AM DRUNK; BUT I	KNOW	WHAT I AM DOING. I WISH TO STAND WELL WITH THE ENGLISH.
GLIM (185)	SEE WHEN MY FATHER KILLS YOU. /FERRUCCIO/ DO YOU	KNOW	WHAT I AM THINKING, GIULIETTA? /GIULIA/ NO, SIGNOR.
DOCT V (178)	IS MY JUSTIFICATION AND MY REWARD. NOW YOU	KNOW	WHAT I DID AND WHAT I THOUGHT OF HIM. BE AS ANGRY WITH
SUPR III (104)	AS I. NOT MERELY THE NEED TO DO, BUT THE NEED TO	KNOW	WHAT I DO, LEST IN MY BLIND EFFORTS TO LIVE I SHOULD BE
VWOO 3 (143)	YOU ARE SURE YOU FEEL HAPPY ABOUT IT? /A/ I DONT	KNOW	WHAT I FEEL ABOUT IT. GO AND DO AS YOU ARE TOLD; AND
DOCT II (116)	NIGHT I CAN BEGIN TO BE HAPPY AT LAST. YOU DONT	KNOW	WHAT I FEEL. SHE SITS DOWN IN TEARS. THEY CROWD ABOUT
MILL IV (199)	AS MAY BE). /ADRIAN/ (TO EPIFANIA) NOW YOU	KNOW	WHAT I FELT. IT SERVES YOU RIGHT. /EPIFANIA/ YES: GO
SUPR I (5)	DROPPED WITHOUT A MOMENT'S WARNING. HE WILL NEVER	KNOW	WHAT I FELT. (HE TAKES OUT HIS HANDKERCHIEF AND CRIES
MTH1 I (5)	ON ME. I CAN NEVER BE ALONE. YOU ALWAYS WANT TO	KNOW	WHAT I HAVE BEEN DOING. IT IS A BURDEN. YOU SHOULD TRY
PRES (152)	I'M EXTREMELY SORRY. YOU REALLY DO NOT	KNOW	WHAT I HAVE TO PUT UP WITH. THIS IMBECILE, INCOMPETENT,
ROCK I (204)	RISES TO GO). /FLAVIA/ YOU NEEDNT GO, HILDA. YOU	KNOW	WHAT I HAVE TO ENDURE. /DAVID/ DAMN ALL THIS PARALYZING
SIM PREFACE(17)	THE CITIZEN WILL SAY " I REALLY MUST	KNOW	WHAT I MAY DO AND WHAT I MAY NOT DO WITHOUT HAVING MY
PYGM IV (266)	IN THE MIDDLE OF THE NIGHT? /LIZA/ I WANT TO	KNOW	WHAT I MAY TAKE AWAY WITH ME. I DONT WANT TO BE ACCUSED
PHIL II (97)	A SCIENTIFIC MAN, PERHAPS, LIKE YOURSELF. BUT YOU	KNOW	WHAT I MEAN: A MAN. (HE STRIKES HIMSELF A SOUNDING
AUGS (279)	REPORT YOURSELF FOR DISOBEYING ORDERS. NOW DO YOU	KNOW	WHAT I MEAN? /THE CLERK/ NOW LOOK HERE. I AINT GOING
APPL INTRLUD(249)	WOULD THINK IT ILLNATURED. /ORINTHIA/ OH, YOU	KNOW	WHAT I MEAN. DIVORCE HER. MAKE HER DIVORCE YOU. IT IS
PYGM II (230)	STANDING OVER HIM GRAVELY) COME, HIGGINS! YOU	KNOW	WHAT I MEAN. IF I'M TO BE IN THIS BUSINESS I SHALL FEEL
GETT (349)	UNFORTUNATE IN MY CHOICE OF EXPRESSIONS; BUT YOU	KNOW	WHAT I MEAN. I FEEL SURE YOU WOULD BE HAPPIER AS MY
WIDO I (18)	YOU KNOW-- TO STAY WITH HER, AND SO FORTH. YOU	KNOW	WHAT I MEAN. JUST TELL HER ALL ABOUT IT IN A CHATTY
FANY I (275)	KNOW? (TO JUGGINS) IS SHE A LADY, JUGGINS? YOU	KNOW	WHAT I MEAN. /JUGGINS/ IN THE SENSE IN WHICH YOU ARE
APPL I (227)	AND WINKING -- /MAGNUS/ WINKING! /PROTEUS/ YOU	KNOW	WHAT I MEAN. THE BEST SPEECH IN THE WORLD CAN BE READ
MTH1 II (33)	ENOUGH FOR YOU. /CAIN/ MURDER IS NOT DEATH. YOU	KNOW	WHAT I MEAN. THOSE WHOM I SLAY WOULD DIE IF I SPARED
BULL IV (170)	AT. WELL, IVE BEEN THINKING EVER SINCE; AND NOW I	KNOW	WHAT I OUGHT TO HAVE SAID. IVE COME BACK TO SAY IT.
MIS. (177)	IN MY PRESENCE? /GUNNER/ (TURNING WHITE) YOU	KNOW	WHAT I SAW AND HEARD, HYPATIA, WITH A GLEAM OF TRIUMPH
BARB II (293)	I FEEL INTENSELY AFRAID OF IT; AND I DONT	KNOW	WHAT I SHALL DO WITH BARBARA OR WHAT SHE WILL DO WITH
FANY II (295)	WITH THE PROMPTINGS OF THE DEVIL, THEN I DONT	KNOW	WHAT I SHALL DO; I DONT INDEED; ITLL KILL ME.
SUPR IV (165)	(AS THEY GO UP THROUGH THE GARDEN) I DONT	KNOW	WHAT I SHALL DO WHEN YOU ARE GONE, WITH NO ONE BUT ANN
GENV IV (94)	I DO NOT KNOW WHAT YOU COULD DO, OR THAT I DO NOT	KNOW	WHAT I SHOULD DO. /SIR O./ BOTH, SIGNOR. /BBDE/ WHAT
BULL III (127)	SUFFERED. /MATTHEW/ NEVER MIND HWAT I SUFFERED. I	KNOW	WHAT I SUFFERED ADHOUT YOU TELLIN ME. BUT DID I EVER
CATH 4 (194)	SEEMS TO THINK THAT YOU ENJOYED IT. /CLAIRE/ I	KNOW	WHAT I THINK. I WILL NEVER SPEAK TO HIM AGAIN. YOUR
CLEO IV (176)	TO YOU. /CAESAR/ (GRAVELY) MY FRIEND: I ALREADY	KNOW	WHAT I THINK. COME TO YOUR OFFER. /POTHINUS/ I WILL
DEVL I (22)	AND THIS IS MY REWARD! (RAGING INWARDLY) YOU	KNOW	WHAT I THINK, MR ANDERSON: YOU KNOW THE WORD I GAVE TO
BULL IV (170)	I WAS JUST AS WRETCHED AS YOU. I DIDNT RIGHTLY	KNOW	WHAT I WANTED TO SAY; AND MY TONGUE KEPT CLACKING TO
MILL I (146)	HAVE PUT ME OFF IT WITH YOUR FOOLING; AND I DONT	KNOW	WHAT I WANT. THAT IS A HORRIBLE STATE OF MIND. I AM A
MTH1 II (30)	A BEAR. I DO NOT WANT TO EAT CHILDREN. I DO NOT	KNOW	WHAT I WANT, EXCEPT THAT I WANT TO BE SOMETHING HIGHER
JOAN 6 (149)	OH! YOU SAW IT, THEN? /THE CHAPLAIN/ I DID NOT	KNOW	WHAT I WAS DOING. I AM A HOTHEADED FOOL; AND I SHALL BE
NEVR III (265)	VALENTINE. I MARRIED BEFORE I WAS OLD ENOUGH TO	KNOW	WHAT I WAS DOING. AS YOU HAVE SEEN FOR YOURSELF, THE
ROCK II (260)	TO TRY YOUR TWENTY THOUSAND POLICE ON ME. DO YOU	KNOW	WHAT I WILL DO? /SIR ARTHUR/ WHAT? /SIR DEXTER/ I
GENV III (69)	OF PRINCIPLE. /THE WIDOW/ (TO THE JEW) DO YOU	KNOW	WHAT I WOULD DO IF I WERE A PRESIDENT? /THE JEW/ NO.
MRS IV (251)	I DONT WANT YOU. BUT LISTEN TO THIS. DO YOU	KNOW	WHAT I WOULD DO WITH YOU IF YOU WERE A BABY AGAIN?
BULL I (95)	AT THE POSSIBILITY OF MY HAVING ANY. YOU DONT	KNOW	WHAT IRISH PRIDE IS. ENGLAND MAY HAVE KNOCKED A GOOD
BULL II (115)	STRUGGLING WITH A SURGE OF EMOTION) YOU DONT	KNOW	WHAT I-- (HE CHOKES FOR A MOMENT AND THEN BLURTS OUT
MIS. (160)	YOU. I KEEP A LIST OF ALL MY OFFERS. I LIKE TO	KNOW	WHAT I'M CONSIDERED WORTH. /TARLETON/ LET ME LOOK.
OVER (178)	HIMSELF DESPERATELY) NO. I'M NOT RECKLESS. I	KNOW	WHAT I'M DOING: MY CONSCIENCE IS AWAKE. OH, WHERE IS
PHIL II (124)	IN THAT RIDICULOUS ATTITUDE! /JULIA/ I HARDLY	KNOW	WHAT I'M DOING. I DONT CARE WHAT I'M DOING: I'M TOO
ARMS I (5)	HIM. /CATHERINE/ DONT ASK ME FOR PROMISES UNTIL I	KNOW	WHAT I'M PROMISING. /RAINA/ WELL, IT CAME INTO MY HEAD
SUPR IV (147)	IN MONEY. I DARESAY YOU THINK THAT SORDID; BUT I	KNOW	WHAT I'M TALKING ABOUT. ME FATHER DIED OF STARVATION IN
MIS. (147)	AND TEN MILES HIGH BETWEEN PARENT AND CHILD. I	KNOW	WHAT I'M TALKING ABOUT. IVE GIRLS IN MY EMPLOYMENT:
MIS. (175)	ARE YOU TALKING ABOUT, YOUNG MAN? /GUNNER/ I	KNOW	WHAT I'M TALKING ABOUT. I WENT INTO THAT TURKISH BATH A
O'FL (218)	SHELLS BURSTING ON THE TOP OF ME? I TELL YOU I	KNOW	WHAT I'M TALKING ABOUT. I'D BE ASHAMED TO STAY AT HOME
DOCT I (101)	THAT YOU CAN ONLY GET AT THE OPERATING TABLE. I	KNOW	WHAT I'M TALKING ABOUT: IVE BEEN A SURGEON AND A
KING I (221)	NOT KNOW WHAT IT IS. /NEWTON/ I DO. BUT I DO NOT	KNOW	WHAT IS AMISS WITH IT. NOT UNTIL THE WORLD FINDS THIS
NEVR II (251)	FATHER? /GLORIA/ PERFECTLY. /CRAMPTON/ DO YOU	KNOW	WHAT IS DUE TO ME AS YOUR FATHER? /GLORIA/ FOR
MIS. (189)	HER GRAVELY) DONT YOU BE ALARMED, MAAM. I	KNOW	WHAT IS DUE TO YOU AS A LADY AND TO MYSELF AS A
SUPR PREFACE(R25)	OF WISDOM" SAID WILLIAM BLAKE; FOR " YOU NEVER	KNOW	WHAT IS ENOUGH UNLESS YOU KNOW WHAT IS MORE THAN
MTH4 I (164)	THEIR CHRISTLIKE PRINCIPLES? IT IS NOT ENOUGH TO	KNOW	WHAT IS GOOD: YOU MUST BE ABLE TO DO IT. THEY COULDNT
APPL II (265)	IS NOT GOOD FOR YOU, MAGNUS. YOU DO NOT ALWAYS	KNOW	WHAT IS GOOD FOR YOU. /MAGNUS/ WELL, WELL, WELL, WELL!
SIM II (65)	IT. BUT HOW IS SHE TO BE AN EMPRESS IF SHE DOESNT	KNOW	WHAT IS HAPPENING EVERYWHERE? /MRS HYERING/ SHE CAN
SUPR PREFACE(R25)	FOR " YOU NEVER KNOW WHAT IS ENOUGH UNLESS YOU	KNOW	WHAT IS MORE THAN ENOUGH"). THERE IS A POLITICAL ASPECT
JOAN 2 (73)	TO YOU? /LA TREMOUILLE/ IT IS MY BUSINESS TO	KNOW	WHAT IS PASSING BETWEEN YOU AND THE GARRISON AT
MIS. PREFACE(47)	BUT EXCEPT IN THAT VERY SHALLOW SENSE I DONT	KNOW	WHAT IS THE MATTER WITH YOU; AND I CANT UNDERTAKE TO
MIS. (199)	RIGHT THING. I CANT DO THE RIGHT THING. I DONT	KNOW	WHAT IS THE RIGHT THING. I'M BEATEN; AND SHE KNOWS IT.
HART III (130)	HESIONE HAD ANY NOTION OF HOW TO LIVE? DONT YOU	KNOW	WHAT IS WRONG WITH IT? /HECTOR/ WE ARE WRONG WITH IT.
MILL I (156)	MILLION IS MERE PIN MONEY. /EPIFANIA/ NOR DO YOU	KNOW	WHAT IT FEELS LIKE TO BE IN THE ARMS OF A MAN AND KNOW
KING I (205)	/NELL/ BUT HOW CAN I, ROWLEY DARLING? I DONT	KNOW	WHAT IT IS ALL ABOUT: I KNOW ONLY MY PART AND MY CUE.
APPL PREFACE(181)	MOVEMENT VERY FEW PEOPLE WHO TAKE PART IN IT	KNOW	WHAT IT IS ALL ABOUT. I ONCE SAW A REAL POPULAR
SUPR IV SD(141)	GARDEN OF A VILLA IN GRANADA. WHOEVER WISHES TO	KNOW	WHAT IT IS LIKE MUST GO TO GRANADA TO SEE. ONE MAY
FABL VI (130)	ARE YOU SUCH A BODY? /RAPHAEL/ I AM CURIOUS TO	KNOW	WHAT IT IS LIKE TO BE A BODY. CURIOSITY NEVER DIES.
DEVL I (15)	QUESTIONS ABOUT HIM, ESSIE. YOU ARE TOO YOUNG TO	KNOW	WHAT IT IS TO BE A BAD MAN. BUT HE IS A SMUGGLER; AND
GENV I (32)	I DARENT GIVE IT UP FOR ANYTHING CHANCY. YOU DONT	KNOW	WHAT IT IS TO BE OUT OF A JOB. /HE/ I SHALL NOT ASK YOU
MTH1 II (23)	OF THE LAST RALLY OF HIS STRENGTH, CAN HE	KNOW	WHAT IT IS TO REST IN LOVE IN THE ARMS OF A WOMAN. ASK
OVER (172)	NO OTHER WAY OF ENTERTAINING EACH OTHER. YOU DONT	KNOW	WHAT IT IS TO BE ALONE WITH A WOMAN WHO HAS LITTLE
GETT (269)	HAD THE STRANGEST ADVENTURES WITH THEM? DO YOU	KNOW	WHAT IT IS TO LOOK AT A MERE REAL MAN AFTER THAT? A
SUPR IV (152)	POVERTY IS. /HECTOR/ (FERVIDLY) WELL, I WAWNT TO	KNOW	WHAT IT IS. I WAWNT'BE A MAHN. VIOLET: YOU COME ALONG
BUOY III (30)	SO IF YOUR POSITION IS EXCEPTIONAL, I HAD BETTER	KNOW	WHAT IT IS. /DARKIE/ WELL, AS I AM THE ONLY FEMALE, I
KING I (221)	THE PERIHELION OF MERCURY. /KNELLER/ I DO NOT	KNOW	WHAT IT IS. /NEWTON/ I DO. BUT I DO NOT KNOW WHAT IS
DOCT I (91)	YES. THERES SOMETHING THE MATTER WITH ME. I DONT	KNOW	WHAT IT IS. /SIR PATRICK/ NEITHER DO I. I SUPPOSE YOUVE
APPL II (260)	IN A POSITION TO TELL IT TO THEM, BECAUSE I DONT	KNOW	WHAT IT IS. /VANHATTAN/ THE PRODIGAL, SIR, HAS RETURNED
MTH1 II (34)	ALONE. THERE IS SOMETHING ELSE. WE DO NOT YET	KNOW	WHAT IT IS; BUT SOME DAY WE SHALL FIND OUT; AND THEN WE
HART III (143)	FOR EVER. I'M ALWAYS EXPECTING SOMETHING. I DONT	KNOW	WHAT IT IS; BUT LIFE MUST COME TO A POINT SOMETIME.
SUPR HANDBOK(206)	THE WORLD WILL NOT BEAR THINKING OF TO THOSE WHO	KNOW	WHAT IT IS, EVEN WITH THE LARGEST DISCOUNT FOR THE
MIS. PREFACE(78)	A MOTHER OF MY ACQUAINTANCE THAT SHE WOULD NEVER	KNOW	WHAT IT MEANT TO BE HURT UNTIL SHE WAS HURT THROUGH HER
CLEO NOTES (203)	MEAN THE OUTSIDE MEMBRANE OF A REED: I DO NOT	KNOW	WHAT IT OUGHT TO BE CALLED. IN THE BURNT MICE RECEIPT I
BARB PREFACE(245)	EVIL IN THE FACE WITHOUT ILLUSION, HE WILL NEVER	KNOW	WHAT IT REALLY IS, OR COMBAT IT EFFECTUALLY. THE FEW
POSN (453)	SAID A WORD ABOUT THE HORSE AT ALL. HOW WAS I TO	KNOW	WHAT IT WAS IN YOUR MIND TO DO? /BLANCO/ BEAR WITNESS
METH PREFACE(R44)	HE LIKES ABOUT DARWIN; BUT ANYONE WHO WANTS TO	KNOW	WHAT IT WAS TO BE A LAMARCKIAN DURING THE LAST QUARTER
HART PREFACE(30)	HAD NEVER BEEN IN A THEATRE BEFORE AND DID NOT	KNOW	WHAT IT WAS, AT ONE OF OUR GREAT VARIETY THEATRES I SAT

JOAN 6	(149)	AT ALL. /THE CHAPLAIN/ I MEANT NO HARM. I DID NOT	KNOW	WHAT IT WOULD BE LIKE. /WARWICK/ (HARDENING) OH! YOU
SUPR IV	(152)	HAVE YOU GOT TO SAY-- ANY OF YOU? /MALONE/ I	KNOW	WHAT IVE GOT TO SAY. SHE'S MARRIED A BEGGAR. /HECTOR/
BARB II	(275)	TO LET ON WE'RE NO WORSE THAN OTHER PEOPLE? YOU	KNOW	WHAT LADIES AND GENTLEMEN ARE. /PRICE/ THIEVIN SWINE!
PYGM II	(220)	MR HIGGINS? /THE FLOWER GIRL/ WHY SHOULDNT I? I	KNOW	WHAT LESSONS COST AS WELL AS YOU DO; AND I'M READY TO
WIDO II	(29)	OH, GENTLEMEN, YOURE YOUNG; AND YOU DONT	KNOW	WHAT LOSS OF EMPLOYMENT MEANS TO THE LIKE OF ME. WHAT
SIM I	(52)	IN YOUR THOUGHTS INSTEAD OF ONE, THEN YOU DO NOT	KNOW	WHAT LOVE CAN BE. /IDDY/ BUT IT'S JUST THE CONTRARY.
MTH5	(254)	I DENY IT TO YOU, ACIS? /ACIS/ YOU DIDNT EVEN	KNOW	WHAT LOVE WAS. /ECRASIA/ OH! I ADORED YOU, YOU STUPID
LIED	(188)	EVER MAN LOVED WOMAN BEFORE. BUT THEY WILL NOT	KNOW	WHAT MAN IT WAS. /SHE/ WHAT GOOD IS THAT TO ME IF
JITT II	(39)	DAY IN HER SHAME AND MISERY. OH, EDITH, WE DONT	KNOW	WHAT MEANNESSES WE ARE CAPABLE OF UNTIL WE ARE TRIED.
POSN	(436)	QUIET ONES, TOO. /JESSIE/ OH, DONT TALK TO ME. I	KNOW	WHAT MEN ARE. OF COURSE HE AINT AFRAID TO SHOOT AND HE
PYGM II	(227)	ELIZA. /LIZA/ (HALTING, TEMPTED) HOW DO I	KNOW	WHAT MIGHT BE IN THEM? IVE HEARD OF GIRLS BEING
LADY	(245)	BREAK WITH HIM FOR EVER. OH, MADAM, IF YOU WOULD	KNOW	WHAT MISERY IS, LISTEN TO THIS MAN THAT IS MORE THAN
NEVR II	(241)	(STRIKING IN MELLIFLUOUSLY) ALL RIGHT, SIR. WE	KNOW	WHAT MR CRAMPTON LIKES HERE, SIR. (HE GOES INTO THE
MRS II	(207)	DEARIE: HAVE YOU HAD A GOOD SUPPER? /VIVIE/ YOU	KNOW	WHAT MRS ALISON'S SUPPERS ARE. (SHE TURNS TO FRANK AND
MRS II	(213)	VERY EASY, ISNT IT? HERE! WOULD YOU LIKE TO	KNOW	WHAT MY CIRCUMSTANCES WERE? /VIVIE/ YES: YOU HAD
JITT II	(36)	HOW YOU KEEP THROWING THEM AT ME! NONE OF US	KNOW	WHAT MY FATHER WAS: HE WAS THROWN AWAY AMONG US. (
BARB II	(304)	WHY NOT, DEAR? /BARBARA/ WHY NOT! DO YOU	KNOW	WHAT MY FATHER IS? HAVE YOU FORGOTTEN THAT LORD
MIS.	(171)	NO. THATS JUST IT: IVE NO BUSINESS TO DO. DO YOU	KNOW	WHAT MY LIFE IS? I SPEND MY DAYS FROM NINE TO SIX--
JOAN 6	(142)	A FRENCHMAN. (TUMULT, WHICH HE SHOUTS DOWN). I	KNOW	WHAT MY LORD THE CARDINAL OF WINCHESTER WILL SAY WHEN
BULL II	(103)	MY EYES HAD NEVER BEEN OPENED TO THEM. I DID NOT	KNOW	WHAT MY OWN HOUSE WAS LIKE, BECAUSE I HAD NEVER BEEN
BARB III	(333)	(TAKEN ABACK) TEN PER CENT! WHY, MAN, DO YOU	KNOW	WHAT MY PROFITS ARE? /CUSINS/ ENORMOUS, I HOPE:
SUPR II	(65)	SOME YOUNG FOOL WHO HAS NOT ENOUGH EXPERIENCE TO	KNOW	WHAT MYSTIFICATIONS OF THIS KIND LEAD TO. /HECTOR/ (
BULL III	(124)	/LARRY/ ARISTOCRACY BE BLOWED! DO YOU	KNOW	WHAT NORA EATS? /BROADBENT/ EATS! WHAT DO YOU MEAN..
MTH5	(213)	STREPHON. I AM GETTING ON FOR THREE MYSELF; AND I	KNOW	WHAT OLD AGE IS. I HATE TO SAY " I TOLD YOU SO"; BUT
CAPT III	(298)	WELL, I HAVNT GOT IT. I CAN GIVE AN ORDER WHEN I	KNOW	WHAT ORDER TO GIVE. I CAN MAKE MEN OBEY IT, WILLING OR
O'FL	(212)	COULDNT MAKE ONE RIGHT, THERE, SIR! NOW YOU	KNOW	WHAT O'FLAHERTY V.C. THINKS; AND YOURE WISER SO THAN
FABL III	(112)	PROSPERO: IT'S AUTOLYCUS. /THE GENTLEMAN/ IF YOU	KNOW	WHAT OTHER PEOPLE OUGHT TO DO, YOULL BE TOO BUSY
METH PREFACE	(R83)	ONE OF PHYSICAL MOVEMENT, I SHOULD MUCH LIKE TO	KNOW	WHAT OTHER STORM THAN THE ATOMIC STORM COULD HAVE
GENV IV	(97)	BUT WHAT IS PECKHAM? /BEGONIA/ OH! HE DOESNT	KNOW	WHAT PECKHAM IS. THESE PEOPLE DONT KNOW ANYTHING. /THE
SUPR IV	(165)	TELL ME: POLITENESS IS ALL VERY WELL; BUT I	KNOW	WHAT PEOPLE THINK-- (SHE TALKS HERSELF AND VIOLET OUT
SUPR IV	(152)	WOUNDED AND FULL OF CONCERN) HECTOR: YOU DONT	KNOW	WHAT POVERTY IS. /HECTOR/ (FERVIDLY) WELL, I WAWNT TO
GENV II	(54)	OTHERS ARE ODDITIES AND OUTSIDERS. IF YOU WANT TO	KNOW	WHAT REAL ENGLISH PUBLIC OPINION IS, KEEP YOUR EYE ON
JOAN 2	(73)	THE CURTAINS. /CHARLES/ OH, ARCHBISHOP, DO YOU	KNOW	WHAT ROBERT DE BAUDRICOURT IS SENDING ME FROM
BUOY III	(43)	IT IS THE TRADE OF SHAM SCIENTISTS WHO DO NOT	KNOW	WHAT SCIENCE MEANS. /SECONDBORN/ THAT IS TRUE. ARE YOU
JITT III	(73)	POOR CRIMINAL. I KNOW WHAT HAS BECOME OF HER. I	KNOW	WHAT SHE DID. I KNOW WHAT SHE HAS SUFFERED EVER SINCE.
JITT III	(73)	WHAT HAS BECOME OF HER. I KNOW WHAT SHE DID. I	KNOW	WHAT SHE HAS SUFFERED EVER SINCE. /EDITH/ BUT HOW DO
SUPR IV	(162)	(PEACEFULLY) OH, VERY LIKELY YOU WILL: YOU	KNOW	WHAT SHE IS WHEN SHE HAS SET HER MIND ON ANYTHING. BUT
MILL III	(186)	YOURSELF. OH, DONT SIT THERE DITHERING: YOU DONT	KNOW	WHAT SHE MAY BE DOING. OH! OH! OH! (SHE CAN SAY NO
MTH5	(212)	WANT THE GIRL WHO IS TO BE BORN TODAY. HOW DO I	KNOW	WHAT SHE WILL BE LIKE? I WANT YOU. /THE MAIDEN/ YOU
GETT	(275)	YOU TO GO. YOU KNOW HOW FOND I AM OF LEO; AND YOU	KNOW	WHAT SHE WOULD FEEL IF SHE CAME IN AND FOUND YOU HERE.
PYGM II	(218)	SIR, SHE SAYS YOULL BE GLAD TO SEE HER WHEN YOU	KNOW	WHAT SHE'S COME ABOUT. SHE'S QUITE A COMMON GIRL, SIR.
MIS.	(156)	THAT YOUNG WOMAN'S RIGHT IN HER HEAD. DO YOU	KNOW	WHAT SHE'S JUST ASKED FOR? /TARLETON/ CHAMPAGNE? /MRS
DEST	(186)	FOR CIVILIANS; BUT IT WONT WORK IN THE ARMY. YOU	KNOW	WHAT SOLDIERS ARE, GENERAL: THEY WILL HAVE MEN OF
SUPR HANDBOK	(178)	SORT OF MAN YOU WANT. UNFORTUNATELY YOU DO NOT	KNOW	WHAT SORT OF MAN YOU WANT. SOME SORT OF GOODLOOKING
FANY II	(291)	BIT THE SORT OF GIRL I THOUGHT MYSELF. AND I DONT	KNOW	WHAT SORT OF PERSON YOU REALLY ARE, OR WHAT SORT OF
GENV I	(47)	REASONABLE PERSON; BUT THIS MAN DOES NOT SEEM TO	KNOW	WHAT SORT OF WORLD HE IS LIVING IN. /SHE/ HE'S AN
FANY EPILOG	(331)	/BANNAL/ NO. /VAUGHAN/ (CONTEMPTUOUSLY) DO YOU	KNOW	WHAT STYLE IS? /BANNAL/ WELL, I SUPPOSE YOUD CALL
GETT	(277)	AS MRS REGINALD BRIDGENORTH: LEO'S NAME: DO YOU	KNOW	WHAT THAT FEELS LIKE TO A DECENT MAN? DO YOU KNOW WHAT
SUPR I	(10)	RAMSDEN AS HE EXCLAIMS /TANNER/ RAMSDEN: DO YOU	KNOW	WHAT THAT IS? /RAMSDEN/ (LOFTILY) NO, SIR. /TANNER/
2TRU I	(38)	ABOUT HALF A POUND OF KITCHEN SALT). DO YOU	KNOW	WHAT THAT IS AND WHAT IT'S FOR? /THE PATIENT/ IS IT
ROCK I	(219)	WITHOUT EVER HAVING READ A WORD OF HIM. BUT I	KNOW	WHAT THAT MAN DID FOR THEM AS DID READ HIM. /SIR
HART II	(94)	IS THE MATTER WITH ME IS THAT I AM POOR. YOU DONT	KNOW	WHAT THAT MEANS AT HOME. MIND: I DONT SAY THEY HAVE
GETT	(276)	YES, YES. NEARLY EVERY NIGHT. /LEO/ NEARLY! I	KNOW	WHAT THAT MEANS. HAVE YOU WORN YOUR LIVER PAD? /THE
MILL I	(139)	HAVE BARELY SEVEN HUNDRED THOUSAND A YEAR. DO YOU	KNOW	WHAT THAT MEANS TO A WOMAN BROUGHT UP ON AN INCOME OF
BARB II	(295)	FOR BUYING IT. /CUSINS/ I DONT THINK YOU QUITE	KNOW	WHAT THE ARMY DOES FOR THE POOR. /UNDERSHAFT/ OH YES I
GENV III	(75)	OR IMPOSSIBLE THAT USED TO BE EASY. YOU DONT	KNOW	WHAT THE ATMOSPHERE OF GENEVA IS. WHEN I CAME HERE I
POSN PREFACE	(366)	MAY NOT UNDERSTAND IT, MAY NOT LIKE IT, MAY NOT	KNOW	WHAT THE AUTHOR IS DRIVING AT, MAY HAVE NO KNOWLEDGE OF
JOAN 6	(142)	OF WINCHESTER WILL SAY WHEN HE HEARS OF THIS. I	KNOW	WHAT THE EARL OF WARWICK WILL DO WHEN HE LEARNS THAT
O'FL	(225)	YOURE SPEAKING TO. THAT I MAYTNT SIN! BUT I DONT	KNOW	WHAT THE GOOD GOD WAS THINKING ABOUT WHEN HE MADE THE
ARMS II	(34)	THE TABLE, OPPOSITE HER, AND SAYS) LOUKA: DO YOU	KNOW	WHAT THE HIGHER LOVE IS? /LOUKA/ (ASTONISHED) NO,
BULL IV	(153)	THE WORDS-- LET NOT THE RIGHT SIDE OF YOUR BRAIN	KNOW	WHAT THE LEFT SIDE DOETH. I LEARNT AT OXFORD THAT THIS
PYGM II	(223)	TALK OF SUCH THINGS. I'M A GOOD GIRL, I AM; AND I	KNOW	WHAT THE LIKE OF YOU ARE, I DO. /HIGGINS/ WE WANT NONE
MRS I	(185)	BRING. /VIVIE/ CULTURE! MY DEAR MR PRAED: DO YOU	KNOW	WHAT THE MATHEMATICAL TRIPOS MEANS? IT MEANS GRIND,
NEVR IV	(299)	NOT TO YOU. NOT TO HER, PERHAPS. BUT I	KNOW	WHAT THE MEN FELT. (WITH LUDICROUSLY GENUINE
ROCK PREFACE	(176)	MUST HAVE BEEN WRITTEN BY SOMEBODY WHO DID NOT	KNOW	WHAT THE PHYSICAL UNIVERSE WAS REALLY LIKE. I AM QUITE
CAPT II	(256)	THE LAW AND THE PROPHETS. /SIR HOWARD/ DOES HE	KNOW	WHAT THE POWER OF ENGLAND IS? /BRASSBOUND/ HE KNOWS
SIM I SD	(37)	THOUGH NOT WARMLY SO. HE EVIDENTLY WANTS TO	KNOW	WHAT THE STRANGER IS DOING IN HIS GARDEN. /THE
O'FL	(219)	IT! /MRS O'FLAHERTY/ ALLOWANCE, IS IT! DO YOU	KNOW	WHAT THE THIEVING BLACKGUARDS DID ON ME? THEY CAME TO
O'FL	(210)	/O'FLAHERTY/ ARRA, SIR, HOW THE DIVIL DO I	KNOW	WHAT THE WAR IS ABOUT? /SIR PEARCE/ (RISING AGAIN AND
SUPR IV	(153)	THE MONEY THAN MADE FRIENDS AND STARVED. YOU DONT	KNOW	WHAT THE WORLD IS: I DO. /HECTOR/ NO, NO, NO. THATS
MRS IV	(248)	YOUVE BEEN TAUGHT WRONG ON PURPOSE: YOU DONT	KNOW	WHAT THE WORLD IS REALLY LIKE. /VIVIE/ (ARRESTED)
DEST	(174)	YOU AT YOUR TRICKS AGAIN? DO YOU THINK I DONT	KNOW	WHAT THESE PAPERS CONTAIN? I'LL TELL YOU. FIRST, MY
2TRU PREFACE	(22)	AND PASTORS WHO MEDDLE WITH FAMILY AFFAIRS SHOULD	KNOW	WHAT THEY ARE TALKING ABOUT. ANOTHER IMPORTANT MODERN
MTH4 I	(160)	DANGEROUS TO SHEW TOO MUCH TO PEOPLE WHO DO NOT	KNOW	WHAT THEY ARE LOOKING AT. I THINK THAT A MAN WHO IS
6CAL	(103)	/JOHN OF GAUNT/ SIR: THE MEN-AT-ARMS WANT TO	KNOW	WHAT THEY ARE TO DO WITH THIS FELLOW? /THE KING/ AYE,
KING I	(192)	THE NAVY IF WE CALLED IT SHIP MONEY, AND LET THEM	KNOW	WHAT THEY ARE PAYING FOR. /JAMES/ I SHALL MAKE THEM
MIS. PREFACE	(30)	OF THEIR WHOLE LIVES DEPENDS WITHOUT LETTING THEM	KNOW	WHAT THEY ARE UNDERTAKING. ALLEGED NOVELTIES IN MODERN
MTH2	(84)	DOING FROM THEMSELVES: THEY WILL TAKE CARE NOT TO	KNOW	WHAT THEY ARE DOING. THEY WILL LIVE THREE HUNDRED
ARMS I	(9)	ME INTO THE STREET TO AMUSE THEMSELVES WITH: I	KNOW	WHAT THEY ARE. ARE YOU PREPARED TO RECEIVE THAT SORT OF
KING II	(230)	THEY ARE WILL NOT BEAR THINKING OF BY THOSE WHO	KNOW	WHAT THEY ARE. THAT IS WHAT THE PEOPLE LIKE. IT IS WHAT
SUPR I	(32)	BOYS' SECRETS ARE JUST LIKE MEN'S; AND YOU	KNOW	WHAT THEY ARE! /TANNER/ (OBSTINATELY) NO I DONT WHAT
HART II	(125)	HAVE OFFENDED YOU. (TURNING TO HECTOR) DO YOU	KNOW	WHAT THEY CALL HIM, HECTOR? /HECTOR/ PLEASE DONT TELL
APPL I	(204)	YOU ARE ONLY A CONSTITUTIONAL MONARCH. DO YOU	KNOW	WHAT THEY CALL THAT IN BELGIUM? /MAGNUS/ AN
DEVL I	(25)	DO NOT YOU INTERRUPT MINE. (TO ESSIE) DO YOU	KNOW	WHAT THEY CALL ME, ESSIE? /ESSIE/ DICK. /RICHARD/ (
CURE	(236)	ON DEPUTATIONS, AND FIGHTING THE POLICE. DO YOU	KNOW	WHAT THEY CALL ME? /STREGA/ (PLAYING SOFTLY) WHAT DO
GENV PREFACE	(24)	THE GOSPELS, AND KARL MARX, AND TO THAT EXTENT	KNOW	WHAT THEY HAVE TO DO, THEY DO NOT KNOW HOW TO DO IT,
ARMS II	(24)	/NICOLA/ (WITH COMPASSIONATE SUPERIORITY) DO YOU	KNOW	WHAT THEY WOULD DO IF THEY HEARD YOU TALK LIKE THAT?
LIED	(201)	THEY START A REPERTORY THEATRE; AND I THINK THEY	KNOW	WHAT THEYRE ABOUT AS WELL AS YOU. THE ONLY MEMBER OF
GETT	(333)	I KNOW WHAT A MAN IS LIKE WHEN HE'S BIT. I	KNOW	WHAT THEYRE BOTH LIKE WHEN YOU TELL THEM WHAT YOU
GETT	(307)	IS TO GET THE YOUNG PEOPLE TIED UP BEFORE THEY	KNOW	WHAT THEYRE LETTING THEMSELVES IN FOR. THERES MISS
SUPR III	(94)	EXCUSE ME; BUT IT DOES SO BORE ME. THEY DONT	KNOW	WHAT THEYRE TALKING ABOUT: I DO. THEY THINK THEY HAVE
PRES	(149)	ORDERS IS ALL RIGHT; BUT THE OFFICERS DONT	KNOW	WHAT THEYRE TALKIN ABOUT. WHY, THE ORSES KNOWS BETTER
MIS.	(131)	NATIVE PRINCES, IN FACT) AND VOTERS WHO DONT	KNOW	WHAT THEYRE VOTING ABOUT. I DONT UNDERSTAND THESE
FANY III	(321)	SHE SITS). BOBBY'S GIVEN ME THE SQUIFFER. DO YOU	KNOW	WHAT THEYVE BEEN DOING DOWNSTAIRS? YOUD NEVER GUESS.
MRS III	(230)	(RISING, ALMOST BESIDE HERSELF) TAKE CARE. I	KNOW	WHAT THIS BUSINESS IS. /CROFTS/ (STARTING, WITH A
DEVL III	(68)	FIRST TIME WITHOUT HIS TITLE). SWINDON: DO YOU	KNOW	WHAT THIS IS (SHEWING HIM THE LETTER)? /SWINDON/
MTH5	(211)	THE COMFORT IN THE WORLD. /STREPHON/ BUT YOU DONT	KNOW	WHAT THIS MEANS TO ME. IT MEANS THAT YOU ARE DYING TO
PRES	(140)	NO NOTICE. /MITCHENER/ (BREAKING DOWN) YOU DONT	KNOW	WHAT THIS MEANS TO ME, BALSQUITH. I LOVE THE ARMY. I
APPL I	(198)	MY DEAR PAM: MY FATHER NEVER THOUGHT. HE DIDNT	KNOW	WHAT THOUGHT MEANT. VERY FEW PEOPLE DO, YOU KNOW. HE
GETT	(293)	HE HAD FINISHED THE BOOK. I ASKED HIM DID HE	KNOW	WHAT TIME IT WAS, AND WHETHER HE HAPPENED TO RECOLLECT
POSN PREFACE	(433)	NOR SANCTIONED BY CUSTOM, IT IS DIFFICULT TO	KNOW	WHAT TO CALL IT UNTIL IT ADVISES THE LORD CHAMBERLAIN
BULL I	(79)	PLEASE, YOU MUST COME AS MY-- MY-- WELL, I HARDLY	KNOW	WHAT TO CALL IT. IF WE CALL YOU MY AGENT, THEYLL SHOOT
GENV IV	(94)	YOU TO SAY TO THAT, ERNEST? /BATTLER/ I SHOULD	KNOW	WHAT TO DO: HAVE NO DOUBT ABOUT THAT. /SIR O./ YOU MEAN
DOCT I	(105)	RIDGEON. DONT FRET ABOUT YOUR HEALTH: YOU	KNOW	WHAT TO DO: IF YOUR LIVER IS SLUGGISH, A LITTLE MERCURY
DOCT IV	(170)	/B.B./ I WILL SEND THE PROPER PEOPLE: THEY WILL	KNOW	WHAT TO DO: YOU SHALL HAVE NO TROUBLE. GOODBYE, MY DEAR
GENV I	(42)	WOULD BE INVALUABLE TO ME; FOR I REALLY DONT	KNOW	WHAT TO DO OR WHERE TO GO HERE. I AM MET WITH
SUPR I	(30)	I NEVER MEANT TO BE SELFISH. IT'S SO HARD TO	KNOW	WHAT TO DO WHEN ONE WISHES EARNESTLY TO DO RIGHT.

GENV IV	(94)	ABOUT THAT. /SIR O./ YOU MEAN THAT YOU WOULD	KNOW	WHAT TO DO WHEN YOU KNEW WHAT ENGLAND WAS GOING TO DO?
HART II	(93)	COST. AND THE WORST OF IT IS, POOR MANGAN DOESNT	KNOW	WHAT TO DO WITH HIS MONEY WHEN HE GETS IT. HE IS SUCH A
MTH4 I	(171)	LEAVING COMMON MEN MORE LEISURE THAN THEY WILL	KNOW	WHAT TO DO WITH. /ZOO/ DADDY! THE MAN WHOSE LIFE IS
GENV PREFACE	(17)	WERE NOT FIENDS IN HUMAN FORM; BUT THEY DID NOT	KNOW	WHAT TO DO WITH THE THOUSANDS THROWN ON THEIR CARE.
MRS III	(223)	THE HOUSE). /REV. S./ HE'S SO IMPETUOUS. I DONT	KNOW	WHAT TO DO WITH HIM, MR PRAED. /FRANK/ (RETURNING WITH
WIDO III	(65)	LOOK-- YOU DONT KNOW WHAT TO SAY; AND YOU DONT	KNOW	WHAT TO DO. BUT AFTER ALL, I REALLY DONT SEE WHAT ANY
DEVL II	(43)	QUITE DISTRACTED. /JUDITH/ I MAY WELL BE. I DONT	KNOW	WHAT TO DO. I DONT KNOW WHAT TO DO. (TEARING HER HANDS
GETT	(298)	LEAST-- IF IT WERE NOT FOR MY MOTHER-- OH, I DONT	KNOW	WHAT TO DO. IVE BEEN SO FOND OF YOU; AND WHEN THE WORRY
DEVL II	(43)	I MAY WELL BE. I DONT KNOW WHAT TO DO. I DONT	KNOW	WHAT TO DO. (TEARING HER HANDS AWAY). I MUST SAVE HIM.
SUPR IV	(170)	GOES TO VIOLET'S ASSISTANCE, BUT DOES NOT	KNOW	WHAT TO DO. MRS WHITEFIELD HURRIES BACK INTO THE VILLA.
HART I	(64)	LITTLE HOUSE. /ELLIE/ (IN GREAT DISTRESS) I DONT	KNOW	WHAT TO DO. PLEASE, MAY I SPEAK TO PAPA? DO LEAVE ME.
DOCT II	(116)	/WALPOLE/ THERES NO REAL DIFFICULTY, IF ONLY YOU	KNOW	WHAT TO DO. /MRS DUBEDAT/ OH, HOW CAN I EVER THANK
HART I	(51)	PLEASE-- (HE GOES OUT). LADY UTTERWORD: I DONT	KNOW	WHAT TO DO. YOUR FATHER PERSISTS IN BELIEVING THAT MY
FANY III	(299)	CLOSER TO YOU. /BOBBY/ WHAT A NUISANCE! I DONT	KNOW	WHAT TO DO. YOU KNOW, JUGGINS, YOUR COOL SIMPLE-MINDED
PHIL III	(134)	AND LOOKS UNEASILY ABOUT HER). OH, I DONT	KNOW	WHAT TO DO. YOU WILL EXPECT TOO MUCH FROM ME. (SHE
MILL PREFACE	(127)	SAID ST PAUL. " HE HAS GONE MAD; AND WE DONT	KNOW	WHAT TO DO." " DONT TELL ANYBODY" ADDED ST PETER. AND
GENV IV	(124)	AND WE SHALL HAVE MANY CONVERTS. WE CATHOLICS	KNOW	WHAT TO DO; AND I HAVE NO MORE TIME TO SPEND TRIFLING
PYGM II	(237)	WHY NOT ME TOO? /HIGGINS/ (TROUBLED) I DONT	KNOW	WHAT TO DO, PICKERING. THERE CAN BE NO QUESTION THAT AS
GENV IV	(96)	KNOW. BUT THEY KNOW WHAT ENGLAND INTENDS. THEY	KNOW	WHAT TO EXPECT FROM US. WE HAVE NO SPECULATIVE PLANS.
VWOO 2	(128)	TO KEEP YOU STRAIGHT. AND YOU BEING A WIDOWER	KNOW	WHAT TO EXPECT FROM A WOMAN. AN INEXPERIENCED MAN
MTH2	(43)	MAY BE FALSE; BUT AT LEAST THEY EXIST. THE WOMEN	KNOW	WHAT TO EXPECT AND WHAT IS EXPECTED OF THEM. SAVVY
6CAL	(101)	KNOW BETTER THAN THE QUEEN! YOU AND YOUR LIKE	KNOW	WHAT TO EXPECT FROM YOUR LORDS AND RULERS! WELL, THIS
DEVL I	(11)	DUDGEON/ (WITHOUT LOOKING AT HIM) THE LORD WILL	KNOW	WHAT TO FORBID AND WHAT TO ALLOW WITHOUT YOUR HELP.
FANY PROLOG	(262)	AND SO THEY HAVE NO AGENTS. BESIDES, I DIDNT	KNOW	WHAT TO OFFER THEM. I KNEW THAT THEY WERE CHEAPER THAN
FABL V	(120)	CREATIVE POWER; BUT TO PRAY EFFECTIVELY YOU MUST	KNOW	WHAT TO PRAY FOR. IN THE SIXTEENTH CENTURY THERE WAS A
MIS. PREFACE	(31)	WAS GOING TO DO FOR THE VILLAGE SCHOOL. I DID NOT	KNOW	WHAT TO REPLY. AS THE SCHOOL KEPT THE CHILDREN QUIET
FANY EPILOG	(329)	FOR THE PRESENT. /BANNAL/ YOU DONT EXPECT ME TO	KNOW	WHAT TO SAY ABOUT A PLAY WHEN I DONT KNOW WHO THE
ROCK II	(277)	WHEN THIS UNDERSTANDING IS VIOLATED. WE DONT	KNOW	WHAT TO SAY OR WHAT TO DO. WELL. YOU HAVE VIOLATED IT
O'FL	(221)	KNOW WHAT TO SAY TO ME, POOR WOMAN! AND I DIDNT	KNOW	WHAT TO SAY TO HER, GOD HELP ME! /TERESA/ YOULL HAVE A
O'FL	(221)	AN IRISH LOOK ABOUT HER EYEBROWS. AND SHE DIDNT	KNOW	WHAT TO SAY TO ME, POOR WOMAN! AND I DIDNT KNOW WHAT
OVER	(189)	ME, DEAR. /MRS JUNO/ (THOUGHTFULLY) I DONT	KNOW	WHAT TO SAY. I MUST THINK OVER IT. I HAVE ALWAYS BEEN
BUOY III	(31)	BUT IT WORKS PRAGMATICALLY. /SIR F./ I HARDLY	KNOW	WHAT TO SAY. YOU ARE SUCH AN UNUSUALLY OUTSPOKEN
WIDO III	(65)	AS FOOLISH AS A MAN COULD LOOK-- YOU DONT	KNOW	WHAT TO SAY; AND YOU DONT KNOW WHAT TO DO. BUT AFTER
LION PREFACE	(95)	SHE HAD CONCEIVED OF THE HOLY GHOST, WE SHOULD	KNOW	WHAT TO THINK: A REMARK WHICH WOULD NEVER HAVE OCCURRED
FANY II	(286)	WHEN A GIRL RUNS AWAY FROM HOME LIKE THAT, PEOPLE	KNOW	WHAT TO THINK OF HER AND HER PARENTS. /KNOX/ SHE HAD A
MTH5	(237)	FEMALE FIGURE/ HOW CAN YOU EXPECT MY HUSBAND TO	KNOW	WHAT TO THINK OF YOU IF YOU GIVE HIM HIS BREAKFAST
JOAN 4	(104)	CALL THE ZEAL OF THE CHRISTIAN CHURCH BIGOTRY I	KNOW	WHAT TO THINK. /WARWICK/ THEY ARE ONLY EAST AND WEST
KING I	(167)	IS A VERY UNUSUAL ONE, REQUIRES THAT I SHOULD	KNOW	WHAT TOM, DICK AND HARRY HAVE TO SAY TO ONEANOTHER. I
ARMS III	(59)	UP; THEY ALL HAVE SCHOOLBOY'S IDEAS. YOU DONT	KNOW	WHAT TRUE COURAGE IS. /SERGIUS/ (IRONICALLY) INDEED!
BULL II	(99)	N WE ALL KNOW YOURE NOT A MAN; N HOW DO WE	KNOW	WHAT UD HAPPEN TO US IF WE SHEWED ANY DISRESPECT TO
CLEO NOTES	(203)	PRICK IT, OR RUB IT TILL IT BLEEDS. I DO NOT	KNOW	WHAT VINE RAG IS. I TRANSLATE LITERALLY." APPARENT
FOUN	(211)	HAVE BEEN INDULGED. I WAS TOO YOUNG. HOW DID I	KNOW	WHAT WAS GOOD FOR ME? I PUT IT TO YOU AS ONE MAN TO
2TRU III	(101)	ALL THE HONORS GO TO A BRIGADIER WHO DID NOT EVEN	KNOW	WHAT WAS HAPPENING? IN THE ARMY THESE THINGS AVERAGE
2TRU II	(54)	I HAD TO DO IT FOR HIM. /TALLBOYS/ HOW DID YOU	KNOW	WHAT WAS IN COLONEL SAXBY'S LETTER? /MEEK/ I READ IT
JITT III	(60)	YOU HAVE TO COMPLAIN OF. YOU USED TO TRUST ME TO	KNOW	WHAT WAS RIGHT FOR YOU, AND NOW YOU HAVE SUDDENLY
KING II	(227)	GOOD. IN PORTUGAL THERE IS THE HOLY CHURCH: WE	KNOW	WHAT WE BELIEVE; AND WE ALL BELIEVE THE SAME THINGS.
KING I	(211)	ONE MORNING. /CHARLES/ BUT, MR NEWTON, MAY WE NOT	KNOW	WHAT WE HAVE DONE TO MOVE YOU THUS? WHAT DIABOLICAL
FANY III	(314)	SAY SHE WAS IGNORANT. BUT I DO SAY THAT SHE DIDNT	KNOW	WHAT WE KNOW: I MEAN THE WAY CERTAIN TEMPTATIONS GET A
HART I	(58)	ALL LOST THEIR MONEY. IT WAS DREADFUL. I DONT	KNOW	WHAT WE SHOULD HAVE DONE BUT FOR MR MANGAN. /MRS
LIED	(191)	TIME. I HAVE THOUGHT DEEPLY OVER THIS; AND I	KNOW	WHAT WE TWO MUST DO, SOONER OR LATER. /SHE/ NO, HENRY.
GETT	(308)	WITH IT IN BLACK AND WHITE; AND THEN WE SHALL	KNOW	WHAT WE'RE ABOUT. /HOTCHKISS/ QUITE RIGHT, MR ALDERMAN.
ANNA	(295)	ME. /STRAMMFEST/ COME, COME, PRISONER! DO YOU	KNOW	WHAT WILL HAPPEN TO YOU IF YOU COMPEL ME TO TAKE A
ANNA	(295)	TONE WITH YOU? /THE GRAND DUCHESS/ NO. BUT I	KNOW	WHAT WILL HAPPEN TO YOU. /STRAMMFEST/ PRAY WHAT,
2TRU I	(38)	WHOM YOU CAN ILLTREAT AS YOU PLEASE? DO YOU	KNOW	WHAT WILL HAPPEN TO YOU WHEN MY MOTHER COMES IN THE
LIED	(188)	/SHE/ WHAT GOOD IS THAT TO ME IF EVERYBODY WILL	KNOW	WHAT WOMAN IT WAS? /HE/ BUT HOW WILL THEY KNOW? /SHE/
DOCT V	(179)	PITYING HIS ERROR) HE WAS ONE OF THE MEN WHO	KNOW	WHAT WOMEN KNOW: THAT SELF-SACRIFICE IS VAIN AND
BARB III	(348)	SHED, OR BE ONE OF BODGER'S BARMAIDS. DO YOU	KNOW	WHAT WOULD HAVE HAPPENED IF YOU HAD REFUSED PAPA'S
ROCK I	(213)	SOMETHING SILLY TO TALK ABOUT, YOURE HAPPY. BUT I	KNOW	WHAT WOULD MAKE YOU SIT UP AND DO SOMETHING. /SIR
DOCT IV	(165)	NO, DUBEDAT. NOT AT ALL. /LOUIS/ YES, YOU HAVE. I	KNOW	WHAT YOU ALL THINK OF ME. DONT IMAGINE I'M SORE ABOUT
DEVL II	(30)	ANY THE LESS SOUNDLY FOR THAT. /JUDITH/ YES, I	KNOW	WHAT YOU ALWAYS SAY; AND YOURE QUITE RIGHT. OH, QUITE
JOAN 1	(58)	KING HIMSELF. /ROBERT/ PRECISELY. AND NOW, DO YOU	KNOW	WHAT YOU ARE? /STEWARD/ I AM NOBODY, SIR, EXCEPT THAT
DOCT V	(178)	EVER COME TO CARE FOR AN ELDERLY MAN, YOU WILL	KNOW	WHAT YOU ARE CARING FOR. /JENNIFER/ (KIND AND QUIET) I
SUPR II	(49)	CAR IS CAPABLE OF 84 MILES AN HOUR; AND I ALREADY	KNOW	WHAT YOU ARE CAPABLE OF WHEN THERE IS A RIVAL CAR ON
APPL I	(220)	THEY KNOW WHEN THEY ARE WELL OFF; AND THEY DONT	KNOW	WHAT YOU ARE GRUMBLING ABOUT; AND THATS WHAT WILL BEAT
JOAN 4	(98)	LET ME REMIND -- /WARWICK/ (INTERPOSING) I	KNOW	WHAT YOU ARE GOING TO SAY, MY LORD. DUNOIS DEFEATED ME
JOAN 4	(94)	(POOHPOOHING) OH, ORLEANS! /THE CHAPLAIN/ I	KNOW	WHAT YOU ARE GOING TO SAY, MY LORD: THAT WAS A CLEAR
GETT	(300)	MOTHER). /THE BISHOP/ (READING THE TITLE) DO YOU	KNOW	WHAT YOU ARE GOING TO DO? BY A WOMAN WHO HAS DONE IT.
GETT	(269)	BUT YOUR SENTIMENTS ARE SO CORRECT THAT I ALWAYS	KNOW	WHAT YOU ARE GOING TO SAY BEFORE YOU FINISH. YOU SEE,
BARB I	(260)	AND SARAH ON THE SETTEE). I DONT IN THE LEAST	KNOW	WHAT YOU ARE LAUGHING AT, ADOLPHUS. I AM SURPRISED AT
JOAN 6	(143)	I WILL SIGN IT. /THE INQUISITOR/ WOMAN: YOU MUST	KNOW	WHAT YOU ARE PUTTING YOUR HAND TO. READ IT TO HER,
MTH2	(82)	OF IT. UNTIL YOU HAVE YOUR BILL DRAFTED YOU DONT	KNOW	WHAT YOU ARE REALLY DOING: THAT IS MY EXPERIENCE.
BARB III	(336)	AM A PART. /BARBARA/ (STARTLED) FATHER! DO YOU	KNOW	WHAT YOU ARE SAYING; OR ARE YOU LAYING A SNARE FOR MY
JOAN 6	(139)	/CAUCHON/ WRETCHED WOMAN: AGAIN I ASK YOU, DO YOU	KNOW	WHAT YOU ARE SAYING? /THE INQUISITOR/ YOU WRESTLE IN
JOAN 6	(137)	(PLEADING WITH HER URGENTLY) YOU DO NOT	KNOW	WHAT YOU ARE SAYING, CHILD. DO YOU WANT TO KILL
ANNA	(303)	STAND FOR THE REVOLUTION. /STRAMMFEST/ YOU DO NOT	KNOW	WHAT YOU ARE SAYING. THIS IS PURE BOLSHEVISM. ARE YOU,
O'FL	(210)	AND STANDING OVER HIM) WHAT! O'FLAHERTY: DO YOU	KNOW	WHAT YOU ARE SAYING? YOU SIT THERE WEARING THE
FABL PREFACE	(92)	WOULD BE CAPABLE, BUT WITH A BLANK " I DONT	KNOW	WHAT YOU ARE TALKING ABOUT." THIS WILL NOT PROVE THAT
SIM II	(71)	TO SAY NOTHING OF THE DAY OF JUDGMENT, THEY DONT	KNOW	WHAT YOU ARE TALKING ABOUT. THE OTHERS-- THE PIOUS
JITT III	(61)	THIS WILL KILL ME. (TO EDITH, RISING) OH, NOW I	KNOW	WHAT YOU ARE. JUST AS BAD AS YOUR FATHER! JUST AS BAD
PHIL I	(76)	SHE SHALL NOT. SHE SHALL STAY HERE. SHE SHALL	KNOW	WHAT YOU ARE, AND HOW YOU HAVE BEEN IN LOVE WITH ME:
OVER	(194)	ON FOOTLING ABOUT IT? /JUNO/ (HUFFILY) I DONT	KNOW	WHAT YOU CALL FOOTLING-- /MRS JUNO/ (CUTTING HIM
HART III	(134)	SO FAR? /MANGAN/ ACHIEVEMENTS? WELL, I DONT	KNOW	WHAT YOU CALL ACHIEVEMENTS; BUT IVE JOLLY WELL PUT A
GENV IV	(94)	NOR YOU, SIGNOR. /BBDE/ DO YOU MEAN THAT I DO NOT	KNOW	WHAT YOU COULD DO, OR THAT I DO NOT KNOW WHAT I SHOULD
CAPT III	(284)	DO YOU FOLLOW ME SO FAR? /BRASSBOUND/ YES, I	KNOW	WHAT YOU DID AND WHAT THE CADI DID. THE POINT IS, WHY
MILL IV	(196)	OF WHAT HAPPENED BEFORE THE ASSAULT. HOW DO YOU	KNOW	WHAT YOU DID IN THESE MOMENTS? /ADRIAN/ LOOK HERE. ARE
CAND III	(135)	(DESPERATELY) BUT WHAT HAVE I DONE? /CANDIDA/ I	KNOW	WHAT YOU HAVE DONE: AS WELL AS IF I HAD BEEN HERE ALL
JITT III	(60)	THINGS ARE SO SERIOUS WITH US? /AGNES/ I DONT	KNOW	WHAT YOU HAVE TO COMPLAIN OF. YOU USED TO TRUST ME TO
BUOY IV	(57)	WITH THE FAMILY. /DARKIE/ NOT A BIT. LET ME	KNOW	WHAT YOU LIKE TO EAT AND DRINK: THAT IS ALL. I MUST GO
HART I	(59)	ABOUT IT? YOU ARE SUCH A SPHINX: I NEVER	KNOW	WHAT YOU MEAN. /MRS HUSHABYE/ DESDEMONA WOULD HAVE
JITT III	(71)	FOR YOURSELF? /EDITH/ (STRAIGHTENING UP) I DONT	KNOW	WHAT YOU MEAN. /JITTA/ DOCTOR FESSLER SAYS YOU HAVE
CAND II	(120)	HIM. /MORELL/ (QUITE AT A LOSS) YES. NO. I DONT	KNOW	WHAT YOU MEAN. /CANDIDA/ (EXPLAINING) IF HE LEARNS IT
DEVL III	(63)	THAT YOU ARE NOT HIS WIFE? /JUDITH/ I DONT	KNOW	WHAT YOU MEAN. I SAY THAT HE IS NOT MY HUSBAND-- THAT
SIM I	(44)	CLERGYMAN/ I COULDNT HELP IT. I MEAN-- /PROLA/ WE	KNOW	WHAT YOU MEAN. YOU NEED NOT EXPLAIN. /THE CLERGYMAN/
WIDO III	(50)	OUT-- /BLANCHE/ I AM NOT STANDING OUT. I DONT	KNOW	WHAT YOU MEAN. (SHE TRIES TO RISE AND GO AWAY).
PYGM III	(255)	WHAT IS SHE? /PICKERING/ (SLOWLY) I THINK I	KNOW	WHAT YOU MEAN, MRS HIGGINS. /HIGGINS/ WELL, DASH ME IF
HART I	(48)	(SITTING DOWN WITH A FLOUNCE ON THE SOFA) I	KNOW	WHAT YOU MUST FEEL. OH, THIS HOUSE, THIS HOUSE! I COME
O'FL	(218)	/O'FLAHERTY/ AND IF YOU ARE ITSELF, HOW CAN YOU	KNOW	WHAT YOU NEVER SEEN AS WELL AS ME THAT WAS DUG INTO THE
PRES	(157)	I SOLEMNLY PROTEST-- /LADY CORINTHIA/ OH, I	KNOW	WHAT YOU OFFICERS ARE. TO YOU A WOMAN'S HONOR IS
ARMS III	(52)	DO YOU MEAN WHAT YOU SAID JUST NOW? DO YOU	KNOW	WHAT YOU SAID JUST NOW? /BLUNTSCHLI/ I DO. /RAINA/ (
MTH5	(246)	ARE STILL CAPABLE OF THANKING, THOUGH YOU DO NOT	KNOW	WHAT YOU THANK. YOU ARE A THANKING LITTLE ANIMAL, A
JOAN 5	(115)	FLAGS WITH CROSSED ANKLES, POUTING. /DUNOIS/ I	KNOW	WHAT YOU THINK OF US, GENERAL JOAN. /JOAN/ NEVER MIND
GETT	(284)	YOU EVERYTHING HE THINKS, AND ALWAYS WANTS TO	KNOW	WHAT YOU THINK. /LEO/ (STRUCK BY THIS) WELL, THATS
2TRU I	(34)	LOTS OF PEOPLE BELIEVE IN THE BOTTLES AND WOULDNT	KNOW	WHAT YOU WERE TALKING ABOUT IF YOU SUGGESTED THE REAL
ROCK II	(236)	YOU WERE TOO DRUNK LAST NIGHT AT THE GUILDHALL TO	KNOW	WHAT YOU WERE SAYING, YOUD BETTER READ THE PAPERS (HE
GENV II	(52)	YES, FANCY THAT! /THE SECRETARY/ BUT DID YOU NOT	KNOW	WHAT YOU WERE DOING? YOU CONDUCTED THE CORRESPONDENCE
PYGM III	(245)	BESIDES, THEYRE ALL IDIOTS. /MRS HIGGINS/ DO YOU	KNOW	WHAT YOU WOULD DO IF YOU REALLY LOVED ME, HENRY?
LION I	(126)	(TO SPINTHO, WHO IS QUAKING AND LOITERING) I	KNOW	WHAT YOULL BE AT THAT DINNER. YOULL BE THE EMETIC. (HE

FANY I	(276)	/DORA/ (SITTING DOWN GENTEELLY) I DONT	KNOW	WHAT YOULL SAY TO ME! YOU KNOW I REALLY HAVE NO RIGHT
MRS IV	(248)	WILL BLAME YOU: YOU MAY TAKE MY WORD FOR THAT. I	KNOW	WHAT YOUNG GIRLS ARE; AND I KNOW YOULL THINK BETTER OF
MRS II	(213)	VIVIE IS IMPRESSED IN SPITE OF HERSELF). D'YOU	KNOW	WHAT YOUR GRAN'MOTHER WAS? /VIVIE/ NO. /MRS WARREN/ NO
MRS II	(211)	/VIVIE/ WHO WAS MY FATHER? /MRS WARREN/ YOU DONT	KNOW	WHAT YOURE ASKING. I CANT TELL YOU. /VIVIE/ (
CAPT II	(268)	/SIR HOWARD/ IMPOSSIBLE. /BRASSBOUND/ YOU DONT	KNOW	WHAT YOURE DOING. /LADY CICELY/ OH, DONT I? IVE NOT
NEVR II	(252)	STOP! DONT SAY ANYTHING MORE YET: YOU DONT	KNOW	WHAT YOURE DOING. DO YOU WANT TO DRIVE ME MAD? (SHE
PHIL II	(124)	DONT BE SO CRUEL. GIVE HIM BACK TO ME. YOU DONT	KNOW	WHAT YOURE DOING-- WHAT OUR PAST HAS BEEN-- HOW I LOVE
FANY EPILOG	(331)	/THE COUNT/ BUT-- /GUNN/ (INTERRUPTING HIM) I	KNOW	WHAT YOURE GOING TO SAY, COUNT. YOURE GOING TO SAY THAT
DOCT II	(121)	/BLENKINSOP/ (STOPPING HIM RESOLUTELY) NO: I	KNOW	WHAT YOURE GOING TO SAY; BUT I WONT TAKE IT. IVE NEVER
DOCT II	(126)	HIS FINGERS IN HIS EARS) NO, NO: IT'S NO USE. I	KNOW	WHAT YOURE GOING TO SAY: IVE SAID IT OFTEN TO OTHERS. I
NEVR III	(266)	GLORIA. (INTERPOSING AS SHE IS ABOUT TO SPEAK) I	KNOW	WHAT YOURE GOING TO SAY: IVE NO MONEY. /MRS CLANDON/ I
NEVR IV	(301)	NOT MAKING ADVANCES TO YOU? /VALENTINE/ POOH! I	KNOW	WHAT YOURE GOING TO SAY. YOU THINK YOURE NOT ORDINARY:
MIS.	(158)	TABLE). /MRS TARLETON/ WELL, I'M SURE I DONT	KNOW	WHAT YOURE TALKING ABOUT; AND I ONLY HOPE YOU KNOW
CAND II	(109)	HIM BY AN AIR OF COOL PROPRIETY) I SIMPLY DONT	KNOW	WHAT YOURE TALKING ABOUT. I DONT UNDERSTAND YOU.
SIM PRO 2,	(27)	NOT MARRY A COLORED WOMAN? /THE E.O./ YOU DONT	KNOW	WHAT YOURE TALKING ABOUT. IVE TRIED. BUT NOW THEYRE ALL
VWOO 3	(141)	WELL AS FINE THINGS TO SAY. /A/ SENSES! YOU DONT	KNOW	WHAT YOURE TALKING ABOUT. LOOK AROUND YOU. HERE IN THIS
MTH4 II	(189)	AT THE GUILDHALL! /ZOZIM/ DISCOURAGE ME IF I	KNOW	WHAT YOURE TALKING ABOUT! I WISH ZOO WOULD COME: SHE
DOCT II	(116)	BE A DOCTOR! (THEY LAUGH). DONT LAUGH. YOU DONT	KNOW	WHAT YOUVE DONE FOR ME. I NEVER KNEW UNTIL NOW HOW
MRS IV	(236)	SMOKING). GO AHEAD. /FRANK/ WELL, I WANT TO	KNOW	WHAT YOUVE DONE-- WHAT ARRANGEMENTS YOUVE MADE. /VIVIE/
VWOO 2	(131)	NO: YOU WILL NOT SEE. /Z/ WELL, WHAT? /A/ I DONT	KNOW	WHAT. I WILL NOT COMMIT MYSELF. WE'LL SEE. /Z/ JUST SO:
MTH5	(208)	MAIDEN/ YES. SOMETHING IS HAPPENING TO ME. I DONT	KNOW	WHAT. /THE YOUTH/ YOU NO LONGER LOVE ME. I HAVE SEEN IT
FANY III	(318)	(HE HESITATES). /JUGGINS/ YES, SIR? /KNOX/ I	KNOW	WHATLL CLINCH IT, GILBEY. YOU LEAVE IT TO ME. (TO
VWOO 2	(130)	BUT THERE WAS SOMETHING ABOUT YOU: I DONT EXACTLY	KNOW	WHAT; BUT IT MADE ME FEEL THAT I COULD DO WITH YOU IN
NEVR II	(248)	AND TALKING FASTER AND FASTER) CRAMPTON: DO YOU	KNOW	WHATS BEEN THE MATTER WITH ME TODAY? YOU DONT SUPPOSE,
NEVR III	(273)	(HE COMES BETWEEN THEM). NOW LOOK HERE, YOU BOTH	KNOW	WHATS GOING ON: DONT YOU? GLORIA TURNS QUICKLY, AS IF
DEST	(190)	ON THAT POOR LIEUTENANT'S HORSE. SO YOU SEE I	KNOW	WHATS IN THEM; AND YOU DONT. /NAPOLEON/ EXCUSE ME: I
CAPT III	(291)	BRANDYFACED JACK: YOURE LOOKING AT THESE STUDS. I	KNOW	WHATS IN YOUR MIND. /DRINKWATER/ (INDIGNANTLY) NAOW
FANY III	(317)	IT ALL MY LIFE: WE'RE IGNORANT. WE DONT REALLY	KNOW	WHATS RIGHT AND WHATS WRONG. WE'RE ALL RIGHT AS LONG AS
NEVR IV	(284)	AFRAID I'M SOMETIMES A LITTLE IRRITABLE; BUT I	KNOW	WHATS RIGHT AND REASONABLE ALL THE TIME, EVEN WHEN I
NEVR IV	(284)	IT! WHY, THATS MYSELF: MYSELF ALL OVER. I	KNOW	WHATS RIGHT AND DIGNIFIED AND STRONG AND NOBLE, JUST AS
PYGM II	(221)	PROPOSE TO PAY ME FOR THE LESSONS? /LIZA/ OH, I	KNOW	WHATS RIGHT. A LADY FRIEND OF MINE GETS FRENCH LESSONS
DOCT I	(94)	OVERWORK, I SUPPOSE. /WALPOLE/ (SWIFTLY) I	KNOW	WHATS THE MATTER WITH YOU. I CAN SEE IT IN YOUR
PYGM IV	(263)	TO BECOME OF ME? /HIGGINS/ HOW THE DEVIL DO I	KNOW	WHATS TO BECOME OF YOU? WHAT DOES IT MATTER WHAT
DOCT II	(129)	A PRETTY GOOD FLAIR FOR THAT SORT OF THING. I	KNOW	WHEN A WOMAN IS INTERESTED IN ME. SHE IS. /SIR PATRICK/
MILL PREFACE	(115)	HAD LEARNT AT THE MILITARY ACADEMY, AND DID NOT	KNOW	WHEN HE WAS BEATEN UNTIL IT WAS TOO LATE TO DO ANYTHING
MIS.	(137)	THE LAW, HOW MUCH BETTER IT WOULD BE! WE SHOULD	KNOW	WHEN HE WAS CROSS AND WHEN HE WAS PLEASED; AND THATS
KING II	(227)	NOTHING EXCEPT WHAT YOU HAVE MADE ME. WHAT DID I	KNOW	WHEN I CAME HERE? ONLY WHAT THE NUNS TEACH A
KING I	(161)	MAID/ PLEASE, MRS BASHAM, A MR ROWLEY WANTS TO	KNOW	WHEN THE MASTER WILL BE AT HOME TO RECEIVE HIM. /MRS
SUPR III	(101)	HAVE DONE. BUT THE ENGLISH REALLY DO NOT SEEM TO	KNOW	WHEN THEY ARE THOROUGHLY MISERABLE. AN ENGLISHMAN
APPL I	(220)	PAY THEM. WELL, THE VOTERS LIKE HIGH WAGES. THEY	KNOW	WHEN THEY ARE WELL OFF; AND THEY DONT KNOW WHAT YOU ARE
MIS. PREFACE	(106)	TO NEY AND D'ERLON, WHO, ON THAT FIELD, DID NOT	KNOW	WHEN THEY WERE BEATEN, WHEREAS WELLINGTON KNEW
FANY I	(282)	MY BOY IN PRISON, ISNT IT? /DORA/ I'D LIKE TO	KNOW	WHEN THEYLL LET HIM OUT. /GILBEY/ YOU WOULD, WOULD
DEST	(193)	PEOPLE. /NAPOLEON/ YES, TOO STUPID SOMETIMES TO	KNOW	WHEN THEYRE BEATEN. BUT I GRANT THAT YOUR BRAINS ARE
APPL I	(228)	MINE. /MAGNUS/ FRANK, MR PROTEUS. /PROTEUS/ I	KNOW	WHEN TO BE FRANK. I LEARNT THE TRICK FROM YOUR MAJESTY.
ROCK II	(256)	TO THAT OLD BIRD BUTTERING YOU UP. YOU JUST DONT	KNOW	WHEN TO GO. /ALOYSIA/ (MOVING TO THE HEARTHRUG, BEHIND
FANY III	(323)	IT IS BECAUSE WE HAVE NOT SENSE ENOUGH TO	KNOW	WHEN WE ARE BEATEN. AT WATERLOO, HAD WE KNOWN WHEN WE
JOAN 5	(114)	EVERY TIME WE HAVE TRUSTED TO THEM. WE NEVER	KNOW	WHEN WE ARE BEATEN: THAT IS OUR GREAT FAULT. /JOAN/ YOU
JOAN 5	(114)	BEATEN: THAT IS OUR GREAT FAULT. /JOAN/ YOU NEVER	KNOW	WHEN YOU ARE VICTORIOUS: THAT IS A WORSE FAULT. I SHALL
PRES	(162)	YOU AND YOUR HIGH F IN ALT! HOW ARE YOU TO	KNOW	WHEN YOU HAVNT MADE HER COMFORTABLE UNLESS SHE HAS A
VWOO 3	(137)	THIS VERY MINUTE. YOU CAN KEEP MY MONTH. YOU DONT	KNOW	WHEN YOURE WELL OFF. YOURE SELFISH. I DONT WONDER YOUR
DOCT I	(92)	ANYHOW. BUT I HAVE A CURIOUS ACHING: I DONT	KNOW	WHERE: I CANT LOCALIZE IT. SOMETIMES I THINK IT'S MY
PYGM V	(273)	HIGGINS/ HENRY: DONT BE ABSURD. IF YOU WANT TO	KNOW	WHERE ELIZA IS, SHE IS UPSTAIRS. /HIGGINS/ (AMAZED)
SIM I	(37)	LOST? /THE CLERGYMAN/ YES, QUITE LOST. I DONT	KNOW	WHERE I AM. I MEAN I DONT EVEN KNOW WHAT COUNTRY I AM
MIS.	(187)	A VULGAR BUSINESS HABIT; BUT I CONFESS I LIKE TO	KNOW	WHERE I AM. /TARLETON/ I DONT. WHEREVER YOU ARE, YOURE
MILL I	(154)	ALL CRAZY. /SAGAMORE/ STEADY! STEADY! I HARDLY	KNOW	WHERE I AM. YOU ARE ALL CONSULTING ME; BUT NONE OF YOU
PYGM I	(211)	BYSTANDER/ (NOT ATTENDING TO HER) DO YOU	KNOW	WHERE I COME FROM? /THE NOTE TAKER/ (PROMPTLY)
JITT III	(55)	TELL ME: THERE IS A BOOK SOMEWHERE; AND I WANT TO	KNOW	WHERE IT IS. DID HE GO MAD AND DESTROY IT? IF NOT, WHO
FANY II	(288)	ANY MISTAKE I'M READY TO APOLOGIZE. BUT I WANT TO	KNOW	WHERE MY DAUGHTER HAS BEEN FOR THE LAST FORTNIGHT.
MTH2	(83)	THE THING WILL HAPPEN. /FRANKLYN/ WE DONT	KNOW	WHERE OR WHEN OR TO WHOM IT WILL HAPPEN. IT MAY HAPPEN
BARB I	(259)	ME SOMETIMES. IT'S NOT LADYLIKE: I'M SURE I DONT	KNOW	WHERE SHE PICKED IT UP. ANYHOW, BARBARA SHANT BULLY ME;
PHIL II	(105)	AND COMES A STEP NEARER TO LISTEN). YOU GENERALLY	KNOW	WHERE SHE'S TO BE FOUND. /CHARTERIS/ I SHALL NEVER KNOW
MIS.	(134)	YOU NEVER HAVE BEEN, A REAL MAN OF BUSINESS. I	KNOW	WHERE TARLETON'S WOULD HAVE BEEN THREE OR FOUR TIMES IF
PRES	(162)	FOR ME BY WAGNER. I'M NOT WAGNER. HOW DOES HE	KNOW	WHERE THE SHOE PINCHES ME? HOW DO YOU KNOW WHERE THE
PRES	(162)	HE KNOW WHERE THE SHOE PINCHES ME? HOW DO YOU	KNOW	WHERE THE SHOE PINCHES YOUR WASHERWOMAN? YOU AND YOUR
MTH2	(49)	NEVER KNOW WHERE THEY ARE. WITH YOU THEY NEVER	KNOW	WHERE THEY ARE. /BURGE/ (AMAZED) WITH ME! /FRANKLYN/
MTH2	(49)	BELIEFS AND PRINCIPLES TO OFFER. THE PEOPLE	KNOW	WHERE THEY ARE WITH LORD DUNREEN. THEY KNOW WHAT HE
MTH2	(49)	HE THINKS WRONG. WITH YOUR FOLLOWERS THEY NEVER	KNOW	WHERE THEY ARE. WITH YOU THEY NEVER KNOW WHERE THEY
NEVR I	(223)	INTRODUCE YOU, SIR. I'M HAPPY TO SAY THAT I DONT	KNOW	WHERE THEY ARE, AND DONT CARE, SO LONG AS THEY KEEP OUT
DOCT III	(150)	AM NEEDED-- AND NEEDED I SHALL BE FINALLY-- THEY	KNOW	WHERE TO FIND ME; AND I AM ALWAYS AT YOUR SERVICE. SO
METH PREFACE	(R70)	ALL POLITICAL STABILITY: NAMELY, THAT YOU NEVER	KNOW	WHERE TO HAVE THE POLITICIANS. IF THE FEAR OF GOD WAS
MIS.	(136)	WRONG AND THEN STICKS TO IT. AT ALL EVENTS YOU	KNOW	WHERE TO HAVE HIM. /LORD SUMMERHAYS/ THAT MAY NOT BE
MIS. PREFACE	(19)	LIFE FOR THEMSELVES. A SELFISH TYRANT YOU	KNOW	WHERE TO HAVE, AND HE (OR SHE) AT LEAST DOES NOT
CAND I SD	(93)	FULL STRENGTH. MISERABLY IRRESOLUTE, HE DOES NOT	KNOW	WHERE TO STAND OR WHAT TO DO. HE IS AFRAID OF BURGESS,
MIS. PREFACE	(59)	CHILDREN WILL NOT SURVIVE. THE DIFFICULTY IS TO	KNOW	WHERE TO STOP. TO ILLUSTRATE THIS, LET US CONSIDER THE
GENV III	(73)	AND EVERY COPY OF HIS BOOKS. BUT THEY DID NOT	KNOW	WHERE TO STRIKE. THEY PERSECUTED POOR MEN FOR MAKING
MIS.	(187)	GENTLEMAN HAS BEEN ATTENDED TO, I SHOULD LIKE TO	KNOW	WHERE WE ARE. IT MAY BE A VULGAR BUSINESS HABIT; BUT I
MIS.	(191)	IT'S NO USE SHIRKING IT, PAT. WE'D BETTER	KNOW	WHERE WE ARE. /LORD SUMMERHAYS/ COME, MISS TARLETON.
HART II	(84)	FIRST TIME YOUVE USED THE WORD; AND I DIDNT QUITE	KNOW	WHERE WE STOOD: THATS ALL. (HE SITS DOWN IN THE WICKER
ARMS I SD	(10)	AN OFFICER WITH WHAT DOES THIS MEAN, SIR? DO YOU	KNOW	WHERE YOU ARE? THE NOISE SUBSIDES SUDDENLY. /LOUKA/ (
MRS II	(199)	TWO INCHES THICK OF CHEEK ALL OVER YOU. I DONT	KNOW	WHERE YOU GOT IT. NOT FROM YOUR FATHER, ANYHOW.
ROCK II	(274)	YOU WEST END PEOPLE USE! I'M SURE I DONT	KNOW	WHERE YOU PICK IT UP. /SIR ARTHUR/ IT DOESNT MEAN
WIDO II	(40)	I SAID NOTHING OF THE SORT. I SAY THAT I DID NOT	KNOW	WHERE YOUR MONEY CAME FROM BEFORE. /SARTORIUS/ THAT IS
GETT	(299)	PROMISE IS A PROMISE. /REGINALD/ WE DONT WANT TO	KNOW	WHETHER A PROMISE IS A PROMISE OR NOT. CANT YOU ANSWER
HART PREFACE	(11)	THEIR EMPEROR, WAS TAME IN COMPARISON. I DO NOT	KNOW	WHETHER ANYONE REALLY KEPT HIS HEAD COMPLETELY EXCEPT
FANY III	(322)	A STRANGER, AS YOU ARE TO US, WITHOUT WANTING TO	KNOW	WHETHER HE INTENDED TO BEHAVE HONORABLY? /DUVALLET/
MILL I	(164)	I DONT KNOW. AFTER TEN MINUTES OF EPPY I NEVER DO	KNOW	WHETHER I AM STANDING ON MY HEAD OR MY HEELS.
MTH3	(119)	COMPLICATIONS MUST BE FRIGHTFUL. REALLY I HARDLY	KNOW	WHETHER I DO WANT TO LIVE MUCH LONGER THAN OTHER
NEVR II	(259)	NOW THAT I THINK DOWN INTO IT SERIOUSLY, I DONT	KNOW	WHETHER I LIKE YOU OR NOT. /GLORIA/ (LOOKING DOWN AT
PYGM III	(253)	HAVE CHANGED SO MUCH THAT I SOMETIMES DONT	KNOW	WHETHER I'M AT A RESPECTABLE DINNERTABLE OR IN A SHIP'S
ARMS III	(62)	NO FAVORS. WHY, THE YOUNG LADY DOESNT EVEN	KNOW	WHETHER I'M MARRIED OR NOT. /RAINA/ (FORGETTING
HART III	(137)	HAVE IT YOUR OWN WAY. ONLY LET ME ALONE. I DONT	KNOW	WHETHER I'M ON MY HEAD OR MY HEELS WHEN YOU ALL START
GETT	(352)	STUDY. /HOTCHKISS/ YOUR BROTHER-IN-LAW WISHES TO	KNOW	WHETHER I'M TO STAY FOR THE WEDDING BREAKFAST. TELL
OVER	(186)	NO OPINION AT ALL ABOUT ME. SHE DOESNT SEEM TO	KNOW	WHETHER I'M WICKED OR COMIC. SHE DOESNT SEEM TO CARE.
PRES	(148)	/MRS FARRELL/ THEYVE COME ABOUT THE VOTE. I DONT	KNOW	WHETHER IT'S DHEM DHAT WANT IT OR DHEM DHAT DOESNT WANT
SUPR III	(89)	CAN I HAVE IT SET RIGHT? /DON JUAN/ I DO NOT	KNOW	WHETHER MISTAKES CAN BE CORRECTED HERE. PROBABLY THEY
SIM II	(60)	THAT DOES NOT SETTLE MY DIFFICULTIES. I DONT	KNOW	WHETHER OTHER PEOPLE ARE LIKE ME OR NOT-- /LADY
JITT III	(67)	YOU MAKE SUCH A FUSS ABOUT HER? YOU DONT EVEN	KNOW	WHETHER SHE WAS NOT A PATIENT WHO HAD TO CONCEAL THE
GETT	(286)	SHE WONT OPEN THE DOOR. AND SHE SAYS SHE DOESNT	KNOW	WHETHER SHE'S GOING TO BE MARRIED OR NOT TIL SHE'S
DEST	(179)	OUT OF ITS REACH AND SAYS) BUT DONT YOU WANT TO	KNOW	WHETHER THE AUSTRIANS ARE AT MANTUA OR PESCHIERA?
DOCT I	(90)	YOU CURE. /SIR PATRICK/ AND PRAY HOW ARE YOU TO	KNOW	WHETHER THE PATIENT IS IN THE POSITIVE OR THE NEGATIVE
GETT PREFACE	(183)	THE CONTRARY, IN FACT; CONSEQUENTLY, I DO NOT	KNOW	WHETHER THEY MAKE LESS FUSS THAN ORDINARY PEOPLE WHEN
ROCK I	(228)	EYES. /SIR ARTHUR/ (BRIGHTENING) WELL, I DONT	KNOW	WHETHER THIS IS REAL OR NOT; BUT IT'S ELECTRIC, AND
SUPR PREFACE	(R26)	SARSPAN BUSINESS AS HE GOT HIS MONEY BY." DO YOU	KNOW	WHETHER TO LAUGH OR CRY AT THE NOTION THAT THEY, POOR
ROCK I	(220)	THEM RIGHT ROUND THE OTHER WAY TO YOURS. I DONT	KNOW	WHETHER WHAT MARX SAID WAS RIGHT OR WRONG, BECAUSE I
SIM I	(42)	THEM, YOUNG SWIMMER? /THE CLERGYMAN/ OH, I DONT	KNOW	WHETHER YOU ARE GODS AND GODDESSES OR REAL PEOPLE. I
BULL II	(103)	EMBARRASSED) OH, ONLY IDLE CURIOSITY. I WANTED TO	KNOW	WHETHER YOU FOUND IRELAND-- I MEAN THE COUNTRY PART OF
MTH2	(54)	WHY HAS SHE NEVER COME TO SEE US? /BURGE/ I DONT	KNOW	WHETHER YOU HAVE NOTICED, LUBIN, THAT I AM PRESENT.

2TRU III (98)	IS FROM THREE TO FORTY MILES OFF, AND YOU DONT	KNOW	WHETHER YOU HAVE ONLY MADE A HARMLESS HOLE IN THE
SUPR PREFACE(R27)	MISSIONARY INTO CRUDE AFRICAN IDOLATRY. I DO NOT	KNOW	WHETHER YOU HAVE ANY ILLUSIONS LEFT ON THE SUBJECT OF
PYGM I (209)	WHAT DID YOU TAKE DOWN MY WORDS FOR? HOW DO I	KNOW	WHETHER YOU TOOK ME DOWN RIGHT? YOU JUST SHEW ME WHAT
PYGM I (212)	SAME TO ME AS ANY LADY'S. /THE NOTE TAKER/ I DONT	KNOW	WHETHER YOUVE NOTICED IT; BUT THE RAIN STOPPED ABOUT
OVER (182)	I'M NOT AT ALL INSENSIBLE BY NATURE; BUT (I DONT	KNOW	WHETHER YOUVE NOTICED IT) I AM WHAT PEOPLE CALL RATHER
MRS III (230)	I'LL TELL YOU ALL ABOUT IT IF YOU LIKE. I DONT	KNOW	WHETHER YOUVE FOUND IN TRAVELLING HOW HARD IT IS TO
SUPR IV (161)	/MRS WHITEFIELD/ WELL, NEVER MIND, TAVY. I DONT	KNOW	WHICH IS BEST FOR A YOUNG MAN: TO KNOW TOO LITTLE, LIKE
MILL IV (188)	ROW ABOUT NOTHING. THE RIVER IS SO SMOOTH. I DONT	KNOW	WHICH IS MORE COMFORTING, YOU OR THE RIVER, WHEN I
MRS II (198)	IT ON THE TABLE. /MRS WARREN/ O LORD! I DONT	KNOW	WHICH IS THE WORST OF THE COUNTRY, THE WALKING OR THE
SIM PRO,3, (30)	ALL THESE DIFFERENT GODS. IT IS SO DIFFICULT TO	KNOW	WHICH IS WHICH. /THE PRIEST/ THEY ARE NOT DIFFERENT
MTH1 II (30)	AND SPEAR. BOTH SIT ON THE GROUND). I HARDLY	KNOW	WHICH OF YOU SATISFIES ME LEAST, YOU WITH YOUR DIRTY
MIS. (122)	TO DO AWAY WITH THEM ALL AND TRY ANOTHER. I DIDNT	KNOW	WHICH WAY TO LOOK WHEN SHE BEGAN TALKING ABOUT IT: I
PYGM II (241)	/LIZA/ I HAD A GOOD MIND TO BREAK IT. I DIDNT	KNOW	WHICH WAY TO LOOK. BUT I HUNG A TOWEL OVER IT, I DID.
PRES (150)	ME IN THE STREET WITH THIS UNIFORM ON, I ARDLY	KNOW	WHICH WAY TO LOOK. THERE NEVER WAS A SOLDIER IN MY
CAPT I (233)	/RANKIN/ HIS AGENT, OR MATE! I DONT RIGHTLY	KNOW	WHICH. /LADY CICELY/ OH, IF HE HAS A MATE NAMED FELIX
CATH 3 (186)	I WILL GO TO THE EMPRESS MYSELF: SHE CANNOT	KNOW	WHO CAPTAIN EDSTASTON IS -- WHO WE ARE. /THE SERGEANT/
MIS. (139)	CLEVER, GROWN-UP, HIGH-CLASS, EXPERIENCED MAN I	KNOW	WHO HAS GIVEN HIMSELF AWAY TO ME BY MAKING AN UTTER
SUPR I (27)	OF COURSE YOU ARE QUITE RIGHT, TAVY; BUT WE DONT	KNOW	WHO HE IS: VIOLET WONT TELL US. /TANNER/ WHAT ON EARTH
SUPR II (64)	HIM ABOUT THIS TRIP? /TANNER/ WE DONT	KNOW	WHO HE IS. /HECTOR/ (RETIRING INTO HIS SHELL IN A VERY
MRS I (191)	FATHER WAS? /CROFTS/ (SUSPICIOUSLY) THEN YOU	KNOW	WHO HE WAS? /PRAED/ (WITH A TOUCH OF TEMPER) I SAID
MTH2 (45)	AND NOT EVEN	KNOW	WHO HE WAS. /CONRAD/ WELL, WHY NOT? FOR ALL YOU KNOW,
NEVR I (213)	THAT WE HAD A FATHER, AND THAT YOU PROBABLY	KNOW	WHO HE WAS. /MRS CLANDON/ (HER AGITATION RETURNING)
NEVR I (214)	ANSWER IS PRETTY OBVIOUS. A WOMAN WHO DOES NOT	KNOW	WHO HER FATHER WAS CANNOT ACCEPT SUCH AN OFFER. /MRS
APPL I (202)	" NOT TO KNOW ME ARGUES YOURSELF UNKNOWN. YOU	KNOW	WHO I AM AS WELL AS I DO MYSELF. GO AND TELL THE KING
CAND II (110)	DONE IT NOW. NO HUSE A-TALKIN TO ME. I'LL LET YOU	KNOW	WHO I AM. (PROSERPINE SHIFTS HER PAPER CARRIAGE WITH A
HART I (69)	(STOPPING HIM) BUT I'M AFRAID YOU DONT	KNOW	WHO I AM. /CAPTAIN SHOTOVER/ DO YOU SUPPOSE THAT AT MY
JOAN 2 (78)	AND LET US ARRANGE SO THAT SHE WILL NOT	KNOW	WHO I AM. YOU WILL PRETEND TO BE ME. (HE GOES OUT
MIS. (197)	JOY OF YOUR BARGAIN. /PERCIVAL/ IF YOU WISH TO	KNOW	WHO I AM-- /TARLETON/ I DONT CARE A TINKER'S CURSE WHO
GLIM (175)	(SQUARCIO COMES OUT, SWORD IN HAND). DO YOU	KNOW	WHO I AM, DOG? /SQUARCIO/ (IMPRESSED) NO, YOUR
APPL I (202)	CHAP COMES OVER TO ME AND PRETENDS HE DOESNT	KNOW	WHO I AM! ASKS ME CAN HE HAVE MY NAME! " MY LAD" I
WIDO II (46)	DID I ASK YOU ABOUT LICKCHEESE? YOU BEAST: YOU	KNOW	WHO I MEAN: YOURE DOING IT ON PURPOSE. /THE PARLORMAID/
SUPR I (10)	/TANNER/ MEAN! (HE HOLDS UP THE WILL). DO YOU	KNOW	WHO IS APPOINTED ANN'S GUARDIAN BY THIS WILL?
KING I (194)	TALKING JUST NOW ABOUT YOUR POPULARITY. DO YOU	KNOW	WHO IS THE MOST POPULAR MAN IN ENGLAND AT PRESENT?
BARB I (263)	YES, MY LADY. (HE GOES). /LOMAX/ DOES MORRISON	KNOW	WHO IT IS? /LADY BRITOMART/ OF COURSE. MORRISON HAS
DEVL I (14)	FROM THE DOOR). NEVER MIND HER, MRS ANDERSON: YOU	KNOW	WHO SHE IS AND WHAT SHE IS. IF SHE GIVES YOU ANY
JITT II (45)	SHOULDERS AND TURNS HER FACE TO FACE). AHA! YOU	KNOW	WHO SHE WAS. YOU KNOW ALL ABOUT IT. /JITTA/ (RISING
FANY EPILOG (329)	ME TO KNOW WHAT TO SAY ABOUT A PLAY WHEN I DONT	KNOW	WHO THE AUTHOR IS, DO YOU? /THE COUNT/ WHY NOT?
FANY PROLOG (270)	IS THE STAGIRITE? /TROTTER/ (SHOCKED) YOU DONT	KNOW	WHO THE STAGIRITE WAS! /FANNY/ SORRY. NEVER HEARD OF
MILL III (184)	/THE WOMAN/ OH NO: THAT WOULDNT BE RIGHT. WE DONT	KNOW	WHO THEY ARE; AND MR SUPERFLEW DOES. BESIDES, WE
DOCT I (83)	COMFORT WITH ANYBODY BUT ME TO ANSWER THE DOOR. I	KNOW	WHO TO LET IN AND WHO TO KEEP OUT. AND THAT REMINDS ME
2TRU III (105)	THROUGH THE BOTTOMLESS ABYSS. /MRS MOPPLY/ I DONT	KNOW	WHO YOU ARE OR WHAT YOU THINK YOU MEAN; BUT YOU HAVE
MTH2 (49)	LAND OF OUR FATHERS. /FRANKLYN/ I KNOW THAT. I	KNOW	WHO YOU ARE. AND THE EARTH-SHAKING PART OF IT TO ME IS
CATH 1 (164)	HIGHNESS WHO I AM. /PATIOMKIN/ I DONT WANT TO	KNOW	WHO YOU ARE. WHAT DO YOU WANT? /EDSTASTON/ AN AUDIENCE
DEVL I (17)	(ENCOURAGINGLY) THATS RIGHT. THATS RIGHT. WE	KNOW	WHO YOU ARE; BUT WE ARE WILLING TO BE KIND TO YOU IF
KING I (216)	OF THAT DIVINE NATURE? /KNELLER/ SIR: I DO NOT	KNOW	WHO YOU ARE; BUT I WILL PAINT YOUR PORTRAIT. /CHARLES/
MIS. (147)	A THOUSAND YEARS ITLL BE CONSIDERED BAD FORM TO	KNOW	WHO YOUR FATHER AND MOTHER ARE. EMBARRASSING. BETTER
MIS. (169)	WHAT ARE YOU DRIVING AT? /TARLETON/ WELL, DO YOU	KNOW	WHO YOUR FATHER WAS? /THE MAN/ I SEE WHAT YOU MEAN
CLEO III (157)	TO GRASP THE SITUATION) WELL, WE SHALL NOW	KNOW	WHO YOUR FOES ARE. THE NAME OF EVERY MAN WHO HAS
MILL I (138)	I DRAW UP THE WILL IT WILL BE NECESSARY FOR ME TO	KNOW	WHO YOUR HUSBAND IS. /THE LADY/ MY HUSBAND IS A FOOL
O'FL (225)	MANNERS. BE ASHAMED OF YOURSELF, DO; AND LEARN TO	KNOW	WHO YOURE SPEAKING TO. THAT I MAYTNT SIN! BUT I DONT
MRS II (210)	(AGAIN RAISING HER VOICE ANGRILY) DO YOU	KNOW	WHO YOURE SPEAKING TO, MISS? /VIVIE/ (LOOKING ACROSS
MRS I (195)	GOV'NOR! COME IN. /REV. S./ NO, SIR; NOT UNTIL I	KNOW	WHOSE GARDEN I AM ENTERING. /FRANK/ IT'S ALL RIGHT.
KING I (218)	NOTHING CAN MAKE A COURTIER OF HER. DO YOU	KNOW	WHY? /BARBARA/ BECAUSE THE ORANGE GIRL HAS THE GUTTER
ARMS III (63)	A COWARD AS WELL. I REFUSE TO FIGHT YOU. DO YOU	KNOW	WHY? /BLUNTSCHLI/ NO; BUT IT DOESNT MATTER. I DIDNT
OVER (172)	UNCOMPLIMENTARY; BUT IT ISNT REALLY. DO YOU	KNOW	WHY HALF THE COUPLES WHO FIND THEMSELVES SITUATED AS WE
FANY I (280)	BEEN THERE FOR HIM TO GO TO? TELL ME THAT. YOU	KNOW	WHY HE WENT TO YOU, I SUPPOSE. /DORA/ (CHARITABLY) IT
CLEO IV (167)	NOT YOU BE A SILLY LITTLE EGYPTIAN FOOL. DO YOU	KNOW	WHY I ALLOW YOU ALL TO CHATTER IMPERTINENTLY JUST AS
BUOY III (36)	YOUR VERY INTERESTING RELATIVES, I REALLY DO NOT	KNOW	WHY I AM STAYING, ESPECIALLY AS YOU APPEAR TO BE TAKING
PHIL II (126)	/JULIA/ HOW I SHOULD LIKE TO KILL YOU! I DONT	KNOW	WHY I DONT. /GRACE/ YES: YOU LIKE TO GET OUT OF YOUR
CATH 1 (168)	WELL, IN A SORT OF WAY I DO; THOUGH I DONT	KNOW	WHY I SHOULD. BUT MY INSTRUCTIONS ARE THAT I AM TO SEE
MILL II (173)	YOU EVEN COMMON CURIOSITY? DONT YOU WANT TO	KNOW	WHY I THREW THAT BEAST DOWNSTAIRS? DONT YOU WANT TO
BUOY IV (56)	AWAY. THIS IS TOO SUDDEN. A MINUTE AGO I DID NOT	KNOW	WHY I WANTED TO KEEP ON TERMS WITH YOU ALL. YOU HAVE
HART I (65)	THIS HOUSE, HESIONE, AND EVEN ABOUT YOU. I DONT	KNOW	WHY I'M TALKING TO YOU SO CALMLY. I HAVE A HORRIBLE
SUPR IV (161)	KNEES, GIVING HER HIS WHOLE ATTENTION). I DONT	KNOW	WHY IT IS THAT OTHER PEOPLE'S CHILDREN ARE SO NICE TO
DOCT IV (169)	B.B. DEATH MAKES PEOPLE GO ON LIKE THAT. I DONT	KNOW	WHY IT SHOULD; BUT IT DOES. BY THE WAY, WHAT ARE WE
PYGM II (240)	BOWL OF SOAP SMELLING LIKE PRIMROSES. NOW I	KNOW	WHY LADIES IS SO CLEAN. WASHING'S A TREAT FOR THEM.
DEVL III (54)	ANOTHER MAN'S INTO IT, I COULD NOT DO IT. I DONT	KNOW	WHY NOT: I SEE MYSELF AS A FOOL FOR MY PAINS; BUT I
CLEO III (160)	WHY NOT? /RUFIO/ THE EGYPTIANS WILL LET YOU	KNOW	WHY NOT IF THEY HAVE THE SENSE TO MAKE A RUSH FROM THE
MRS III (225)	ADROITLY FINISHING THE SENTENCE FOR HER) I SHOULD	KNOW	WHY SHE IS WHAT SHE IS, SHOULDNT I? WHAT DIFFERENCE
CLEO PRO2 (103)	WILL. /FTATATEETA/ (WITH A DERISIVE LAUGH) NOW I	KNOW	WHY THE GODS HAVE TAKEN HER OUT OF OUR HANDS. (THE
JOAN 1 (68)	THEY HAD NOT HALF MY STRENGTH. /ROBERT/ DO YOU	KNOW	WHY THEY ARE CALLED GODDAMS? /JOAN/ NO. EVERYONE CALLS
GLIM (173)	BARBARA TELLS ME EVERYTHING. /THE GIRL/ THEN YOU	KNOW	WHY WE CANT MARRY YET. /THE FRIAR/ HE IS TOO POOR. HIS
SUPR IV (158)	IT SEEMS QUITE SIMPLE. BUT I DOUBT IF WE EVER	KNOW	WHY WE DO THINGS. THE ONLY REALLY SIMPLE THING IS TO GO
O'FL (210)	KNOWS HOW MANY GERMANS; AND YOU TELL ME YOU DONT	KNOW	WHY YOU DID IT! /O'FLAHERTY/ ASKING YOUR PARDON, SIR
CAND I (102)	AFRAID. WHEN MY WIFE COMES BACK SHE WILL WANT TO	KNOW	WHY YOU HAVE GONE. AND WHEN SHE FINDS THAT YOU ARE
SUPR II (69)	AS LAST. /TANNER/ WHY? /STRAKER/ GARN! YOU	KNOW	WHY. COURSE IT'S NOT MY BUSINESS; BUT YOU NEEDNT START
BUOY IV (49)	I DONT WANT ANYTHING BUT YOUR DAUGHTER. I DONT	KNOW	WHY. I KNOW NOTHING ABOUT HER; AND SHE KNOWS NOTHING
GETT (296)	CALLS A MAN THAT ON HIS WEDDING MORNING: I DONT	KNOW	WHY. I'M HIS BEST MAN, YOU KNOW. DONT YOU THINK IT
WIDO I (10)	EVERYBODY IS AFRAID OF PAPA: I'M SURE I DONT	KNOW	WHY. (SHE SITS DOWN AGAIN, POUTING A LITTLE). /TRENCH/
AUGS (274)	HIGHCASTLE: BLUELOO AS YOU CALL HIM: I DONT	KNOW	WHY. /AUGUSTUS/ (EXPLAINING) HE WAS ORIGINALLY CALLED
GETT (267)	ALL THE EARLY ONES BY TRYING TO GET KILLED. YOU	KNOW	WHY. /LESBIA/ BUT YOU HAD A CHARMED LIFE? /THE
SUPR II (69)	ME ABOUT IT. /TANNER/ I AM NOT KIDDING. I DONT	KNOW	WHY. /STRAKER/ (CHEERFULLY SULKY) OH, VERY WELL. ALL
OVER (182)	CREATURE WITH VOLCANIC PASSIONS: I'M SURE I DONT	KNOW	WHY; FOR ALL THE VOLCANIC WOMEN I KNOW ARE PLAIN LITTLE
MTH3 (113)	CERTAINLY IS A BIT OF A TERROR. I DONT EXACTLY	KNOW	WHY; FOR SHE IS NOT AT ALL BAD-LOOKING. /BARNABAS/ (
GENV IV (129)	IT'S NO USE GOING ON MAKING MOTOR CARS THAT YOU	KNOW	WILL NEVER RUN. /BATTLER/ YES: WHEN THE ALTERNATIVE IS
FANY III (322)	INTENTIONS? HOW? /MARGARET/ HE WANTS TO	KNOW	WILL YOU MARRY ME. /MRS GILBEY/ WHAT A THING TO SAY!
BARB II (275)	BRONTERRE O'BRIEN PRICE, THE CONVERTED PAINTER. I	KNOW	WOT THEY LIKE. I'LL TELL EM HOW I BLASPHEMED AND
BARB II (274)	FOR ME FELLOW WORKERS. FOURTH, I'M FLY ENOUGH TO	KNOW	WOTS INSIDE THE LAW AND WOTS OUTSIDE IT; AND INSIDE IT
BASH II,1, (106)	/LUCIAN/ IS THERE WORSE TO COME? /CASHEL/	KNOW	YE NOT THEN MY MOTHER IS AN ACTRESS? /LUCIAN/ HOW
MRS II (208)	US TO BE THINKING OF HOME. YOUR MOTHER DOES NOT	KNOW	YET THAT WE HAVE VISITORS. /PRAED/ I'M AFRAID WE'RE
MTH4 III (199)	PUBLIC? /THE ENVOY/ THAT DOESNT MATTER. I DONT	KNOW	YET. WE WILL FIND A QUESTION ALL RIGHT ENOUGH. THE
MTH1 II (28)	WOMAN THE CREATOR AND MAN THE DESTROYER. I	KNOW	YOU: I AM YOUR MOTHER. YOU ARE IDLE: YOU ARE SELFISH.
SUPR IV (155)	IS ALSO ONE OF OUR CIRCLE. /MALONE/ GLAD TO	KNOW	YOU ALSO, MR TANNER. /TANNER/ THANKS. (MALONE AND
KING I (198)	/JAMES/ CHARLES! WE MUST NOT PART LIKE THIS. YOU	KNOW	YOU ALWAYS STAND BY ME AS FAR AS YOU DARE. I OUGHT NOT
MRS II (206)	WATCHING YOUR WAY OF LOOKING AT HER. REMEMBER: I	KNOW	YOU AND WHAT YOUR LOOKS MEAN. /CROFTS/ THERES NO HARM
JOAN 1 (57)	OR AM I A COWBOY? /STEWARD/ OH, SIR, YOU	KNOW	YOU ARE A GREATER MAN HERE THAN THE KING HIMSELF.
JOAN EPILOG (161)	SHOCK." AND THEY ALL SAY " YES, PARSON: WE ALL	KNOW	YOU ARE A KIND MAN, AND WOULD NOT HARM A FLY." THAT IS
MTH4 I (168)	YOU CANNOT BELIEVE THAT I AM A MURDERER. /ZOO/ I	KNOW	YOU ARE A MURDERER. IT IS NOT MERELY THAT YOU THREW
HART II (118)	PERSON IN THE HOUSE I CAN SAY WHAT I LIKE TO. I	KNOW	YOU ARE FOND OF ME. SIT DOWN. (SHE DRAWS HIM TO THE
PYGM V (277)	IT'S NOT BECAUSE YOU PAID FOR MY DRESSES. I	KNOW	YOU ARE GENEROUS TO EVERYBODY WITH MONEY. BUT IT WAS
FABL III (111)	GOOD FOR NOTHING ELSE. /THE GENTLEMAN/ HOW DO YOU	KNOW	YOU ARE GOOD FOR NOTHING ELSE? /THE TRAMP/ WELL, WHAT
MTH4 I (170)	DONE YOU? YOU COME TO US FOR ADVICE WHEN YOU	KNOW	YOU ARE IN DIFFICULTIES. BUT YOU NEVER KNOW YOU ARE IN
MTH4 I (170)	YOU KNOW YOU ARE IN DIFFICULTIES. BUT YOU NEVER	KNOW	YOU ARE IN DIFFICULTIES UNTIL TWENTY YEARS AFTER YOU
SUPR II (59)	HER MIND IN THAT ABOMINABLE WAY? /ANN/ I	KNOW	YOU ARE INCAPABLE OF BEHAVING BADLY-- /TANNER/ THEN WHY
ROCK I (223)	BOTH OF YOU, AND ENTERTAIN YOUR NEW FRIENDS. YOU	KNOW	YOU ARE NOT ALLOWED TO COME IN HERE WHEN I AM AT WORK.
CLEO IV (187)	TEARS: YOU SHALL NOT BE TROUBLED WITH THEM. I	KNOW	YOU ARE NOT ANGRY, BUT ONLY SAD; ONLY I AM SO SILLY, I
SUPR IV (158)	NAUGHTILY). I'M SHOCKING YOU, I SUPPOSE. BUT YOU	KNOW	YOU ARE REALLY GETTING A SORT OF SATISFACTION ALREADY

JOAN 5	(114)	EXCLAIMING TOGETHER) /THE ARCHBISHOP/ HOW DO YOU	KNOW	YOU ARE RIGHT? /JOAN/ I ALWAYS KNOW. MY VOICES--
BULL II	(113)	AH, NOW YOURE CHAFFING ME, MISS REILLY: YOU	KNOW	YOU ARE. YOU MUSTNT CHAFF ME. I'M VERY MUCH IN EARNEST
PHIL III	(140)	IF THE PEOPLE YOU TALK SO CLEVERLY TO COULD ONLY	KNOW	YOU AS I KNOW YOU! SOMETIMES I WONDER AT MYSELF FOR
MRS III	(222)	YOU WOULD BE MORE RESPECTFUL TO YOUR FATHER. YOU	KNOW	YOU CAN BE SO NICE WHEN YOU LIKE. /FRANK/ MY DEAR
BULL IV	(156)	WILL YOU EXCUSE ME? /AUNT JUDY/ TO BE SURE: YOU	KNOW	YOU CAN COME IN N NOUT AS YOU LIKE. /KEEGAN/ WE CAN
PYGM V	(283)	DO WITHOUT YOU: DONT THINK I CANT. /HIGGINS/ I	KNOW	YOU CAN. I TOLD YOU YOU COULD. /LIZA/ (WOUNDED,
MTH2	(48)	ON WASTING YOUR PARTY FUNDS ON THE STRAND? YOU	KNOW	YOU CANNOT WIN IT. /BURGE/ WE CANNOT WIN IT; BUT YOU--
MTH2	(44)	SIR. /CONRAD/ YOU DIDNT GIVE ANY. BUT YOU	KNOW	YOU COULD LIVE A DEVIL OF A LONG LIFE IF YOU REALLY
LION PROLOG	(107)	TOOK THE BREAD OUT OF MY MOUTH TO FEED THEM: YOU	KNOW	YOU DID: DONT ATTEMPT TO DENY IT. /ANDROCLES/ ONLY WHEN
GETT	(304)	MAN COULD TO PREVENT THE SMASH. /REGINALD/ OH, I	KNOW	YOU DID: I DONT BLAME YOU: PEOPLE DONT DO THESE THINGS
DEVL III	(51)	OF REASON FOR ACTING AS I DID. /JUDITH/ YOU	KNOW	YOU DID IT FOR HIS SAKE, BELIEVING HE WAS A MORE WORTHY
DEST	(187)	AND TURNED OLD BEAULIEU'S FLANK FOR YOU. YOU	KNOW	YOU DIDNT DARE GIVE THE ORDER TO CHARGE THE BRIDGE
VWOO 3	(138)	IT FOR THE WORLD IF I'D KNOWN. /A/ NEVER MIND: I	KNOW	YOU DIDNT MEAN IT. BY THE WAY, I MADE AN INCONSIDERATE
CURE	(225)	COUCH, NOT VERY GENTLY) OF COURSE YOU DIDNT. I	KNOW	YOU DIDNT. /REGINALD/ I NEVER-- /THE DOCTOR/ (
PYGM V	(283)	OF THE OTTOMAN WITH HER FACE TO THE HEARTH) I	KNOW	YOU DID, YOU BRUTE. YOU WANTED TO GET RID OF ME.
LION PROLOG	(106)	(SCREAMING) I DO. /ANDROCLES/ YES, MY DEAR: I	KNOW	YOU DO. /MEGAERA/ THEN WHY DONT YOU TREAT ME PROPERLY
2TRU I	(32)	OUT WHEN SHE HESITATES AND COMES BACK). DOCTOR: I	KNOW	YOU DONT BELIEVE IN INOCULATIONS; BUT I CANT HELP
SUPR I	(41)	CARRIAGE OF HER SHOULDERS). /TANNER/ OH, I	KNOW	YOU DONT CARE VERY MUCH ABOUT TAVY. BUT THERE IS ALWAYS
PYGM IV	(263)	WHAT BECOMES OF YOU? /LIZA/ YOU DONT CARE. I	KNOW	YOU DONT CARE. YOU WOULDNT CARE IF I WAS DEAD. I'M
MRS II	(212)	HER FACE IN HER HANDS). DONT DO THAT, MOTHER: YOU	KNOW	YOU DONT FEEL IT A BIT. (MRS WARREN TAKES DOWN HER
BARB II	(297)	ME TO THE PAPERS. (HE MAKES A WRY FACE). YES: I	KNOW	YOU DONT LIKE IT; BUT IT MUST BE DONE. THE STARVATION
PYGM II	(228)	OR CONSENT TO THE ARRANGEMENT AT ALL. OF COURSE I	KNOW	YOU DONT MEAN HER ANY HARM; BUT WHEN YOU GET WHAT YOU
SUPR I	(39)	MINDED? /TANNER/ THATS THE DANGER OF IT. I	KNOW	YOU DONT MIND, BECAUSE YOUVE FOUND OUT THAT IT DOESNT
GETT	(292)	AND CONFESS YOUR REAL CONVICTIONS. YOU	KNOW	YOU DONT REALLY THINK A BISHOP THE EQUAL OF A CURATE,
BULL I	(75)	TO WAIT IF I WASNT IN. /HODSON/ WELL SIR, I DIDNT	KNOW	YOU EXPECTED HIM; SO I THOUGHT IT BEST TO-- TO-- NOT TO
HART II	(103)	CANT BEAR IT. HAVE I BROKEN YOUR HEART? I DIDNT	KNOW	YOU HAD ONE. HOW COULD I? /MANGAN/ I'M A MAN, AINT I?
MIS. PREFACE	(97)	WHO HAS NOT STOLEN YOUR WATCH BECAUSE HE DID NOT	KNOW	YOU HAD ONE. VIRTUE CHOOSES GOOD FROM EVIL; AND WITHOUT
CLEO IV	(187)	EMOTION AND TO PUT IT BRAVELY AWAY). BUT THERE: I	KNOW	YOU HATE TEARS: YOU SHALL NOT BE TROUBLED WITH THEM. I
PPP	(201)	AT HIS DEATHBED IN CURL PAPERS. /MAGNESIA/ WE	KNOW	YOU HAVE A GOOD HEART, PHYLLIS. TAKE THIS (GIVING HER
DEST	(195)	WHICH HE HAS JUST PLACED). /LADY/ YES; BUT YOU	KNOW	YOU HAVE THE LETTER IN YOUR POCKET. (HE SMILES; TAKES
MILL I	(148)	TO ENDURE THIS? /PATRICIA/ (SOOTHINGLY) YES: WE	KNOW	YOU HAVE TO PUT UP WITH A LOT, DEARY;-- /EPIFANIA/ (
SUPR I	(40)	DO YOU THINK I HAVE DESIGNS ON TAVY? /TANNER/ I	KNOW	YOU HAVE. /ANN/ (EARNESTLY) TAKE CARE, JACK. YOU MAY
2TRU I	(30)	MONSTER: THREE TIMES! /THE ELDERLY LADY/ OH, I	KNOW	YOU HAVE, DOCTOR: NOBODY COULD HAVE BEEN KINDER. BUT IT
MIS.	(124)	REALLY COULDNT STICK IT OUT WITH JERRY, MOTHER. I	KNOW	YOU LIKED HIM; AND NOBODY CAN DENY THAT HES A SPLENDID
PHIL I	(80)	BUT WHY? WE COULD BE SO HAPPY. YOU LOVE ME: I	KNOW	YOU LOVE ME. I FEEL IT. YOU SAY " MY DEAR" TO ME: YOU
ROCK I	(218)	NOT A MAN WOULD STOP TO LISTEN TO ME. MIND YOU, I	KNOW	YOU MEAN IT AS A COMPLIMENT THAT I'D MAKE A GOOD
SUPR IV	(157)	THAT HE IS ONLY RECOVERING HIS SELF-CONTROL) I	KNOW	YOU MEAN TO BE KIND, ANN. JACK HAS PERSUADED YOU THAT
CAPT III	(277)	WOULD MISUNDERSTAND ME. /LADY CICELY/ NO: SHE'D	KNOW	YOU MEAN WELL. AND WHEN YOU CAME HOME AND SAID, " MARY:
BULL III	(135)	IS ABOUT TO REPLY) DHERE NOW! DHATS ENOUGH! WE	KNOW	YOU MEAN WELL; AN I'M NOT ANGRY WITH YOU. /BROADBENT/
MIS.	(153)	TARLETON/ OH, WHAT A THING TO SAY! DIDNT YOU	KNOW	YOU MIGHT HAVE BEEN KILLED? /LINA/ THAT WAS WHY I WENT
BULL IV	(174)	OF THIS UNBUSINESSLIKE VIEW) YES, YES; BUT YOU	KNOW	YOU MIGHT SAY THAT OF ANY COUNTRY. THE FACT IS, THERE
MIS.	(116)	/MRS TARLETON/ NO DEAR, NOT A SAVAGE; BUT YOU	KNOW	YOU MUSNT CALL OUR VISITOR NAUGHTY NAMES. /BENTLEY/ OH,
NEVR II	(259)	ABOUT TO SPEAK: HE STOPS HER DEPRECATINGLY) OH, I	KNOW	YOU MUSNT TELL ME WHETHER YOU LIKE ME OR NOT; BUT--
POSN	(439)	OUT. AH, WOULD YOU? NOW, THEN: GET ALONG. YOU	KNOW	YOU MUST GO, WHATS THE USE OF SCRATCHING LIKE THAT?
FANY III	(301)	DID YOU LEARN IT FROM A FRENCHWOMAN? YOU	KNOW	YOU MUST HAVE LEARNT IT FROM SOMEBODY. /BOBBY/ NOT A
APPL I	(240)	THAT YOU CAN SAY WILL MAKE ANY DIFFERENCE. YOU	KNOW	YOU MUST SIGN. WHY NOT SIGN AND HAVE DONE WITH IT?
MIS.	(163)	QUICKLY FROM HER TOUCH) NO, NO: DONT YOU	KNOW	YOU MUSTNT GO ON LIKE THIS WITH A PERFECT STRANGER?
FANY III	(316)	THAT-- /MRS GILBEY/ NOW DONT BE NAUGHTY, ROB. YOU	KNOW	YOU MUSTNT SET YOURSELF UP AGAINST RELIGION? /GILBEY/
PYGM II	(232)	IT WOULD BE A BETTER EXAMPLE TO THE GIRL. YOU	KNOW	YOU NEARLY CHOKED YOURSELF WITH A FISHBONE IN THE JAM
GETT	(284)	SO YOU SHALL, MY DEAR, IF YOU ARE LUCKY. BUT YOU	KNOW	YOU NEEDNT MARRY THEM ALL. THINK OF ALL THE BUTTONS YOU
ARMS I	(19)	TO BE SURE. HOW STUPID OF ME! /RAINA/ YOU	KNOW	YOU NEVER HEARD OF THEM UNTIL THIS MOMENT. HOW CAN YOU
MTH3	(92)	YOU MAY, MY DEAR BARNABAS, AT ANY TIME. YOU	KNOW	YOU NEVER LOOK WHERE YOU ARE GOING WHEN YOU ARE
KING I	(193)	WHY DO YOU MAKE A PET OF THAT WORTHLESS FELLOW?	KNOW	YOU NOT HE IS LONGING FOR YOUR DEATH SO THAT HE MAY
PHIL III	(137)	HE MAKES HIS CHAIR FLY BACK TO THE TABLE). I	KNOW	YOU NOW, LEONARD CHARTERIS, THROUGH AND THROUGH, IN ALL
SUPR I	(21)	YOU SAY ON PURPOSE TO SHOCK PEOPLE: THOSE WHO	KNOW	YOU PAY NO ATTENTION TO THEM. BUT, IF YOU LIKE, I'LL
SUPR III	(138)	AND RAMSDEN). /HECTOR/ WHY, SO DO I. /OCTAVIUS/ I	KNOW	YOU PERFECTLY WELL, SIR; BUT I CANT THINK WHERE I HAVE
CATH 4	(188)	MAJESTY: TELL THESE FELLOWS TO UNSTRAP ME. YOU	KNOW	YOU REALLY OWE ME AN APOLOGY. /CATHERINE/ YOU THINK YOU
SIM PRO,1,	(22)	AT THIS HOUR OF THE MORNING TOO! DONT YOU	KNOW	YOU SHOULDNT? /THE E.O./ (TO WILKS) TAKE HER AWAY,
MIS.	(114)	IT UP YET. /JOHNNY/ DONT TALK ROT, CHILD. YOU	KNOW	YOU SIMPLY MAKE ME PITY YOU. /BENTLEY/ " ROMANCE OF
LADY	(244)	DOG-- /SHAKESPEAR/ (CUTTING THEM SHORT) HOW	KNOW	YOU THAT KING HARRY WAS INDEED YOUR FATHER?
AUGS	(270)	. . . POOH! DONT YOU BE NERVOUS, OLD CHAP, I	KNOW	YOU THINK ME A FOOL; BUT I'M NOT SUCH A FOOL AS ALL
MRS II	(199)	FACE IN HER HANDS AND TURNING IT UP TO HER): I	KNOW	YOU THROUGH AND THROUGH BY YOUR LIKENESS TO YOUR
MTH3	(115)	WOMAN SO SUPERIOR TO ALL COMMON WEAKNESSES AS WE	KNOW	YOU TO BE. /MRS LUTESTRING/ I MAY HAVE REASONS WHICH
LADY	(241)	DROP LIKE HONEY. /THE LADY/ (WITH COLD MAJESTY)	KNOW	YOU TO WHOM YOU SPEAK, SIR, THAT YOU DARE EXPRESS
2TRU II	(60)	WAY, COUNTESS, I MET THREE PEOPLE YESTERDAY WHO	KNOW	YOU VERY WELL. /THE PATIENT/ (FORGETTING HERSELF AND
NEVR II	(254)	TO MARRYING ME PERSONALLY? /GLORIA/ I DO NOT	KNOW	YOU WELL ENOUGH, MR VALENTINE, TO HAVE ANY OPINION ON
BUOY IV	(56)	/DARKIE/ OH! I BEG YOUR PARDON. I DID NOT	KNOW	YOU WERE ENGAGED. IT IS ONLY TO ASK WHETHER YOU WILL
MILL I	(152)	DO, ALASTAIR? MR SAGAMORE, I PRESUME. I DID NOT	KNOW	YOU WERE ENGAGED. /SAGAMORE/ YOUR ARRIVAL IS QUITE
GENV II	(62)	SIR ORPHEUS) OH, I BEG YOUR PARDON: I DIDNT	KNOW	YOU WERE ENGAGED. /THE SECRETARY/ THIS IS SIR ORPHEUS
PRES	(150)	FOR HIM BY HIS RELATIONS. THE COUNTRY DIDNT	KNOW	YOU WERE GOING TO DO THAT OR IT'D NEVER AVE STOOD IT.
MIS.	(120)	HIM. /MRS TARLETON/ OH, LORD SUMMERHAYS, I DIDNT	KNOW	YOU WERE HERE. WONT YOU HAVE SOME TEA? /LORD
DOCT V	(174)	(QUIVERING) OH, DONT. YOU KNOW I DID NOT	KNOW	YOU WERE HERE. /JENNIFER/ (RAISING HER HEAD A LITTLE
MILL IV	(193)	TWO FRIENDS, ALASTAIR: I ASSURE YOU I DID NOT	KNOW	YOU WERE HERE. SAGAMORE SAID SOME FRIENDS WHO WOULD BE
DOCT I	(114)	YOU AGAIN AND AGAIN. YOU HAVE MADE ME SO HAPPY: I	KNOW	YOU WILL ADMIRE HIM AND LIKE HIM. THIS IS MY ADDRESS. (
DOCT I	(114)	/MRS DUBEDAT/ YOU ARE VERY GENEROUS. THANK YOU. I	KNOW	YOU WILL CURE HIM. GOODBYE. /RIDGEON/ I WILL. GOODBYE.
6CAL	(102)	/THE KING/ NO: YOU ASK NOTHING BECAUSE YOU	KNOW	YOU WILL GET EVERYTHING. (HE RISES, SHOUTING). TAKE
JITT I	(21)	TO BRING MYSELF TO TELL YOU UNTIL TODAY. BUT I	KNOW	YOU WILL NOT FAIL ME. /JITTA/ DONT SAY THAT, BRUNO, AS
APPL II	(277)	DID ANYONE EVER HEAR OF SUCH A THING! YOU	KNOW	YOU WILL NOT SLEEP IF YOU THINK AFTER SEVEN O'CLOCK.
DEVL II	(44)	BETTER FOR HIM TO DIE! SO MUCH GREATER! BUT I	KNOW	YOU WILL TAKE YOUR OWN WAY AS HE TOOK IT. I HAVE NO
CAPT III	(275)	HALF BEWILDERED) I'LL DO MY BEST. /LADY CICELY/ I	KNOW	YOU WILL. (AS HE IS GOING OUT) OH! ONE WORD, MR
CAPT III	(275)	WAITING TO CARRY THE PORTMANTEAU. YOU WILL: I	KNOW	YOU WILL. (SHE EDGES HIM TO THE DOOR). AND DO YOU.
SUPR IV	(154)	YOULL TRY TO BRING HIM TO HIS SENSES, VIOLET: I	KNOW	YOU WILL. /VIOLET/ I HAD NO IDEA HE COULD BE SO
SUPR I	(42)	THE WHOLE AFFAIR. /OCTAVIUS/ (VERY WRETCHED) I	KNOW	YOU WISH ME TO TAKE VIOLET AWAY, MISS RAMSDEN. I WILL.
PYGM V	(278)	BETTER THAN A SCULLERY-MAID; THOUGH OF COURSE I	KNOW	YOU WOULD HAVE BEEN JUST THE SAME TO A SCULLERY-MAID IF
DOCT V	(174)	THE COURSE OF MY ANATOMICAL WORK. /JENNIFER/ YOU	KNOW	YOU WOULD NOT DARE TO SAY SUCH A SILLY THING AS THAT TO
MIS.	(120)	WHAT? /JOHNNY/ GOING TO MEET THE GOVERNOR. YOU	KNOW	YOU WOULDNT THINK IT; BUT THE GOVERNOR LIKES BUNNY
WIDO III	(64)	YOU WISH, YES. /LICKCHEESE/ (CHEERILY) DIDNT I	KNOW	YOU WOULD! /SARTORIUS/ (AT THE STUDY DOOR, TO COKANE)
FANY III	(315)	STARVED, WE AND THE CHILD. /MRS KNOX/ HOW DO YOU	KNOW	YOUD HAVE STARVED? ALL THE OTHER THINGS MIGHT HAVE
WIDO III	(65)	OF MAKING IT PROFITABLE. OH, I KNOW PAPA; AND I	KNOW	YOU, AND FOR THE SAKE OF THAT, YOU COME BACK HERE--
KING I	(188)	AND THE COURT TO RESORT TO? GO AWAY. /JAMES/ I	KNOW	YOU. YOU ARE A FOLLOWER OF THE ARCH INFIDEL GALILEO!
DEST	(165)	AN EFFECT OF SMILING THROUGH HER TEARS) YES, I DO	KNOW	YOU. YOU ARE THE FAMOUS GENERAL BUONAPARTE. (SHE GIVES
MTH3	(129)	SINGLE SOUL WITH YOU. /BARNABAS/ I UNDERSTAND. I	KNOW	YOU. YOU THINK YOU ARE ONE OF THEM. /CONFUCIUS/ MR
WIDO II	(46)	SUBDUED VOICE) LET ME GO, MISS BLANCHE: YOU	KNOW	YOULL BE SORRY: YOU ALWAYS ARE. REMEMBER HOW DREADFULLY
MRS IV	(248)	WORD FOR THAT. I KNOW WHAT YOUNG GIRLS ARE; AND I	KNOW	YOULL THINK BETTER OF IT WHEN YOUVE TURNED IT OVER IN
KING I	(182)	OR ON THE EARTH BENEATH. I AM AFRAID YOU DO NOT	KNOW	YOUR CATECHISM, MR FOX. /CHARLES/ (LAUGHING)
ROCK II	(277)	I SHOULD WANT TO MARRY DAVID. /ALOYSIA/ I	KNOW	YOUR CLASS POINT OF VIEW, LADY CHAVENDER. YOU THINK IT
PRES	(154)	REVOLVER AND POINTING IT AT HIS NOSE) YOU LITTLE	KNOW	YOUR COUNTRYWOMEN, GENERAL MITCHENER. /MITCHENER/ (
DOCT I	(93)	LEANING RESIGNEDLY AGAINST IT. /SIR PATRICK/ I	KNOW	YOUR CUTLER WALPOLES AND THEIR LIKE. THEYVE FOUND OUT
ANNA	(292)	SPEAKING? . . . WHY DIDNT YOU SAY SO? DONT YOU	KNOW	YOUR DUTY? NEXT TIME YOU WILL LOSE YOUR STRIPE. . . .
NEVR I	(223)	IN THE SAME IDLE STRAIN) I REALLY SHOULD LIKE TO	KNOW	YOUR FAMILY, MR CRAMPTON. (HE POURS SOME HOT WATER
6CAL	(101)	IS THE FLOWER OF CHIVALRY. /EUSTACHE/ YOU LITTLE	KNOW	YOUR HUSBAND, MADAM. WE KNOW BETTER WHAT TO EXPECT FROM
FABL II	(107)	AFTER MY FIFTEEN YEARS IN THE FOREIGN OFFICE. YOU	KNOW	YOUR JOB TOO AS A SOLDIER: I DONT QUESTION IT. THAT
APPL I	(218)	WHO IS TO BE ITS SPOKESMAN TODAY? /PROTEUS/ I	KNOW	YOUR MAJESTY'S OPINION OF ME; BUT LET -- /MAGNUS/ (
CAPT I	(238)	STAY AT HOME AND LET ME TAKE CHARGE OF IT. I	KNOW	YOUR MEN WILL GET ON PERFECTLY WELL IF THEYRE PROPERLY
MIS.	(166)	CUT UP ROUGH. FACE IT LIKE A MAN. YOU SEE I DIDNT	KNOW	YOUR MOTHER; BUT IVE NO DOUBT SHE WAS AN EXCELLENT
MTH4 I	(147)	NOT CALL ME DADDY AT ONCE? /THE MAN/ I DID NOT	KNOW	YOUR NAME WAS DADDY. /THE ELDERLY GENTLEMAN/ MY NAME IS
BUOY IV	(50)	/SHE/ I CANT LEAVE YOU OUT, DADDY. BUT YOU WILL	KNOW	YOUR NATURAL PLACE IN MY HOUSE: YOU HAVE ALWAYS KNOWN

GENV II	(62)	OH, MOST PLEASED TO MEET YOU, SIR ORPHEUS. I	KNOW	YOUR NEPHEW. WE ARE QUITE DEAR FRIENDS (SHE SHAKES SIR
GENV III	(85)	PRETTY HEAD. /BEGONIA/ GO ON: I AM USED TO IT. I	KNOW	YOUR OPINION OF ME: I AM THE ONLY PERFECT IDIOT IN
MIS.	(134)	KEPT THAT TO YOURSELF, DO YOU, GOVERNOR? I	KNOW	YOUR OPINION OF ME AS WELL AS YOU KNOW IT YOURSELF. IT
CATH 4	(187)	ISNT MY FAULT. (TO THE SOLDIERS, INSOLENTLY) YOU	KNOW	YOUR ORDERS? YOU REMEMBER WHAT YOU HAVE TO DO WHEN THE
FANY III	(310)	POLICE COURT. (TO JUGGINS) WELL, I SUPPOSE YOU	KNOW	YOUR OWN BUSINESS BEST. I TAKE YOUR NOTICE: YOU CAN GO
MIS.	(146)	IN THE DAY SCHOOL PART OF IT. AT ALL EVENTS, YOU	KNOW	YOUR OWN CHILDREN. /TARLETON/ DO WE? I'M NOT SO SURE
PYGM II	(240)	PARDON, MISS. /THE JAPANESE LADY/ GARN! DONT YOU	KNOW	YOUR OWN DAUGHTER? EXCLAIMING SIMULTANEOUSLY
NEVR I	(207)	IT FAIR TO ASK ME TO LUNCH WITH YOU WHEN YOU DONT	KNOW	YOUR OWN FATHER? /DOLLY/ AFTER ALL, OUR GRANDFATHER IS
WIDO II	(40)	TRIFLING WITH ME, SIR. YOU SAID THAT YOU DID NOT	KNOW	YOUR OWN MIND BEFORE. /TRENCH/ I SAID NOTHING OF THE
FABL VI	(124)	WHATEVER YOU SAY. /TEACHER/ SO YOU SHALL. YOU	KNOW	YOUR OWN MIND, THOUGH YOU CANNOT SPEAK IT. /YOUTH 3/ I
DEVL III	(72)	ASKED ME TO CHOOSE THE ROPE BECAUSE YOU DONT	KNOW	YOUR OWN TRADE WELL ENOUGH TO SHOOT ME PROPERLY. WELL,
ARMS III	(57)	AS THE WAY TO GET ON AS A SERVANT: YOUVE GOT TO	KNOW	YOUR PLACE: THATS THE SECRET OF IT. AND YOU MAY DEPEND
BARB I	(252)	BRITOMART/ DONT BE TOO SURE OF THAT, STEPHEN. I	KNOW	YOUR QUIET, SIMPLE, REFINED, POETIC PEOPLE LIKE
GETT	(356)	GEORGE/ NO. /HOTCHKISS/ YES. THINK AGAIN. YOU	KNOW	YOUR SET PRETTY WELL, I SUPPOSE, YOUR PETTY TRADESMEN'S
SUPR IV	(145)	INTIMACY BETWEEN THE PARTIES. /VIOLET/ YES: I	KNOW	YOUR SON VERY WELL, MR MALONE. HAVE YOU ANY OBJECTION?
FABL III	(111)	YOU ARE ON THAT TACK YOU WONT GIVE ME ANYTHING: I	KNOW	YOUR SORT. GOOD MORNING. (HE STARTS TO GO). /THE GIRL/
GETT	(329)	AND MAKE ME DO WHAT YOU LIKE. BUT AT LEAST LET ME	KNOW	YOUR SOUL AS YOU SEEM TO KNOW MINE. DO YOU LOVE THIS
SUPR I	(18)	WE ARE AGREED THAT WE CAN DECIDE NOTHING UNTIL WE	KNOW	YOUR VIEWS. I AM AFRAID I SHALL HAVE TO ASK YOU TO
FANY PROLOG	(260)	BECAUSE IT EXPLAINS WHY IT IS YOU DONT SEEM TO	KNOW	YOUR WAY ABOUT MUCH IN ENGLAND. I HOPE, BY THE WAY,
PHIL II	(129)	TO PROPOSE IF YOULL ONLY GIVE HIM TIME. YOU	KNOW	YOURE A KINDLY AND SENSIBLE MAN AS WELL AS A DEUCEDLY
POSN	(447)	YOURE ONE OF THE ROTTENEST. /STRAPPER/ YOU	KNOW	YOURE DONE, AND THAT YOU MAY AS WELL BE HANGED FOR A
NEVR I	(203)	NO. /PHILIP/ WELL, COME, DOLLY: HOW DO YOU	KNOW	YOURE NOT? /DOLLY/ (CHEERED) OH, I FORGOT. OF COURSE.
BULL II	(99)	FADHER DEMPSEY SEZ YOURE NOT A PRIEST; N WE ALL	KNOW	YOURE NOT A MAN; N HOW DO WE KNOW WHAT UD HAPPEN TO US
PRES	(165)	MITCHENER. (TO MITCHENER) DONT YOU BE AFEARD: I	KNOW	YOURE SANE ENOUGH WHEN YOURE NOT TALKIN ABOUT THE
SUPR I	(35)	MY SOUL. /ANN/ OH, DO BE SENSIBLE, JACK. YOU	KNOW	YOURE TALKING NONSENSE. /TANNER/ THE MOST SOLEMN
DEVL I	(14)	YOUR FATHER'S PEOPLE HAD BETTER SEE YOU AND	KNOW	YOURE THERE: THEYRE AS MUCH BOUND TO KEEP YOU FROM
CAND I	(95)	AT HIS OWN NOISINESS) GOODBYE, MR MORCHBANKS: I	KNOW	YOURE TOO IGHBRED TO TAKE MY PLEASANTRY IN BAD PART.
LADY	(244)	STREETS. OH GOD! OH GOD! /SHAKESPEAR/ LEARN TO	KNOW	YOURSELF BETTER, MADAM. I AM AN HONEST GENTLEMAN OF
CYMB V	(145)	TO WOMEN. /IMOGEN/ YOU AT LEAST HAVE GRACE TO	KNOW	YOURSELF FOR WHAT YOU ARE. MY HUSBAND THINKS THAT ALL
MRS II	(199)	BY YOUR LIKENESS TO YOUR FATHER, BETTER THAN YOU	KNOW	YOURSELF. DONT YOU GO TAKING ANY SILLY IDEAS INTO YOUR
PYGM III	(255)	HIM) COME, HIGGINS: YOU MUST LEARN TO	KNOW	YOURSELF. I HAVNT HEARD SUCH LANGUAGE AS YOURS SINCE WE
MIS. PREFACE	(39)	AS IT IS LESS TROUBLE TO SET A LESSON THAT YOU	KNOW	YOURSELF, THERE IS A TENDENCY TO KEEP REPEATING THE
MIS.	(158)	WHAT YOURE TALKING ABOUT; AND I ONLY HOPE YOU	KNOW	YOURSELVES. HOWEVER, YOU SHALL HAVE WHAT YOU WANT, OF
WIDO II	(35)	AND THEN WE SHALL BE QUITS. NOW, NOW, HARRY, YOU	KNOW	YOUVE NOT A WORD TO SAY AGAINST THAT. /TRENCH/ IT'S
MTH1 II	(23)	POOR WRETCH: DO YOU THINK I DO NOT KNOW HER, AND	KNOW	YOU, BETTER THAN THAT? DO YOU RISK YOUR LIFE WHEN YOU
PHIL II	(106)	BE YOUR FATHER? /SYLVIA/ (KNOWINGLY) OH, I	KNOW	YOU, MY LAD. /CHARTERIS/ THEN YOU KNOW THAT I NEVER PAY
PHIL III	(140)	YOU TALK SO CLEVERLY TO COULD ONLY KNOW YOU AS I	KNOW	YOU! SOMETIMES I WONDER AT MYSELF FOR EVER CARING FOR
BULL IV	(172)	OH NO! IT WONT DO THAT: NOT THE LEAST DANGER. YOU	KNOW	, A CHURCH BELL CAN MAKE A DEVIL OF A NOISE WHEN IT
CAPT NOTES	(301)	(VELASQUEZ BEING NO LONGER AVAILABLE). HE IS, I	KNOW	, A SCOTCH LAIRD. HOW HE CONTRIVES TO BE AUTHENTICALLY
LION PREFACE	(75)	WAS NEVER CONCERNED FOR A MOMENT, AS FAR AS WE	KNOW	, ABOUT WHETHER HIS CONDUCT WAS SINFUL OR NOT; SO THAT
BUOY III	(37)	EXIST AT ALL EXCEPT IN MY IMAGINATION. SO NOW YOU	KNOW	, ALL OF YOU. LET US CHANGE THE SUBJECT. /SIR F./ NOT,
BULL I	(95)	AND REFLECTING, APPARENTLY RATHER AGREEABLY) YOU	KNOW	, ALL THIS SOUNDS RATHER INTERESTING. THERES THE IRISH
GENV II	(53)	PROUD; AND I'M QUITE USED TO BEING A SUCCESS. YOU	KNOW	, ALTHOUGH I WAS ALWAYS AT THE TOP OF MY CLASS AT
BARB III	(322)	POINT OF VIEW AS IT WERE. YOURE GETTING ON, YOU	KNOW	, AND ALL THAT. /SARAH/ YOU DONT MIND CHOLLY'S
CAPT III	(275)	FOR MY BROTHER THERE: HE'S AMBASSADOR, YOU	KNOW	, AND HAS TO BE VERY PARTICULAR AS TO WHAT HE WEARS. I
FABL PREFACE	(86)	RIDDLE OF THE UNIVERSE? WHEN I REPLY THAT I DONT	KNOW	, AND HAVE NO PANACEA, I AM TOLD THAT I AM NOT
LION II	(128)	COULDNT SACRIFICE TO DIANA: SHE'S A HUNTRESS, YOU	KNOW	, AND KILLS THINGS. /THE EDITOR/ THAT DONT MATTER. YOU
SIM PREFACE	(7)	BY FIRM BELIEVERS IN THE BRIMSTONE; BUT WE DO NOT	KNOW	, AND NEVER SHALL KNOW, HOW MANY CRIMES WERE REFRAINED
KING I	(194)	NO; BUT I MUST DO THE BEST I CAN WITH WHAT I	KNOW	, AND NOT WITH WHAT PETER AND MARTIN KNEW. ANYHOW, THE
GENV I	(31)	SAY ALL. THERES THE HEAD OFFICE IN PARIS, YOU	KNOW	, AND SOME OFFICES IN OTHER COUNTRIES. I SUPPOSE THEY
SUPR I	(44)	ABOUT MORALITY AND PROPRIETY AND SO FORTH. BUT I	KNOW	, AND THE WHOLE WORLD REALLY KNOWS, THOUGH IT DARE NOT
ARMS I	(9)	ADDING, WITH CUTTING EMPHASIS) SOME SOLDIERS, I	KNOW	, ARE AFRAID TO DIE. /THE MAN/ (WITH GRIM GOODHUMOR)
METH PREFACE	(R12)	STUDENTS OF THIS SCIENCE IN ENGLAND, AS FAR AS I	KNOW	, ARE MY FRIENDS SIDNEY AND BEATRICE WEBB. IT HAS TAKEN
MTH4 II	(185)	AFTER THIS? /ZOO/ I DONT EXPECT ANYTHING. I	KNOW	, AS A MATTER OF EXPERIENCE, THAT YOU WILL BE
HART PREFACE	(38)	PROSTRATE FOE, CAN ONLY BE GUESSED BY THOSE WHO	KNOW	, AS HE DOES, HOW HOPELESS IS REMONSTRANCE, AND HOW
DOCT I	(99)	TAKE ANY COLORING MATTER. CONSEQUENTLY, THOUGH WE	KNOW	, AS SCIENTIFIC MEN, THAT THEY EXIST, WE CANNOT SEE
BARB II	(292)	I THINK, MY FRIEND, THAT IF YOU WISH TO	KNOW	, AS THE LONG DAYS GO, THAT TO LIVE IS HAPPY, YOU MUST
JITT III	(60)	TAUGHT? /AGNES/ (SHRIEKING) WHAT? /EDITH/ I	KNOW	, AS WELL AS YOU DO, WHERE MY FATHER DIED, AND HOW HE
MTH2	(61)	GONE INTO POLITICAL ECONOMY AT THE TIME. AS YOU	KNOW	, AT THE UNIVERSITY I WAS A CLASSICAL SCHOLAR; AND MY
DOCT PREFACE	(9)	AND HE GETS LITTLE SYMPATHY, EVEN FROM LAYMEN WHO	KNOW	, BECAUSE HE HAS BROUGHT THE INCREDULITY ON HIMSELF. IF
CATH 4	(197)	I CANNOT MAKE ALLOWANCES. YOUR MAJESTY HAS, I	KNOW	, BEEN UNFORTUNATE IN YOUR EXPERIENCE AS A MARRIED
KING II	(224)	NELLY IS A GOOD CREATURE; AND SHE AMUSES ME. YOU	KNOW	, BELOVED, ONE GETS TIRED OF COURT LADIES AND THEIR
MTH2	(46)	BURGE, PERHAPS. /SAVVY/ (DISAPPOINTED) OH, THEY	KNOW	, BILL. WHY DIDNT YOU TELL US HE WAS COMING? I HAVE
GETT	(283)	ONLY ENGLISH FAMILY LIFE. GOOD MORNING. /LEO/ YOU	KNOW	, BISHOP, IT'S VERY DEAR OF YOU TO TAKE MY PART; BUT
WIDO III	(57)	NO, MY DEAR: OF COURSE NOT. BUT DO YOU	KNOW	, BLANCHE, THAT MY MOTHER WAS A VERY POOR WOMAN, AND
DOCT I	(107)	NOT ENOUGH GOOD ONES TO GO ROUND. AND FOR ALL YOU	KNOW	, BLOOMFIELD BONINGTON KILLS LESS PEOPLE THAN YOU DO.
NEVR III	(276)	AN UNSUITABLE MARRIAGE (NOBODY'S FAULT, YOU	KNOW	, BUT PURELY ACCIDENTAL INCOMPATIBILITY OF TASTES);
HART I	(54)	MIND PAPA, DO YOU? HE IS AS MAD AS A HATTER, YOU	KNOW	, BUT QUITE HARMLESS, AND EXTREMELY CLEVER. YOU WILL
BULL PREFACE	(32)	ALERTNESS-- IS TEMPERED, AS WE IRISH WELL	KNOW	, BY AN ABSURD SUSCEPTIBILITY TO INTIMIDATION. FOR LET
AUGS PREFACE	(261)	AT AUGUSTUS IN THE THEATRE, NOTHING, AS FAR AS I	KNOW	, CAME OF MY DRAMATIC REDUCTION OF HIM TO ABSURDITY.
CAND III	(141)	DID YOU-- (SHE STOPS)? /MORELL/ (ASHAMED) YOU	KNOW	, CANDIDA, THAT I HAVE A TEMPER TO STRUGGLE WITH. AND
HART II	(110)	(HE RELEASES HIM). /THE BURGLAR/ WELL, HOW DO I	KNOW	, CAPTAIN? YOU KNOW THE SORT OF LIFE YOU AND ME HAS
CAPT III	(297)	MARRY ANYBODY BUT YOURSELF. /LADY CICELY/ DO YOU	KNOW	, CAPTAIN PAQUITO, THAT IVE MARRIED NO LESS THAN
HART II	(111)	MY FELLOW-CREATURES, AND NEVER DID, AS YOU WELL	KNOW	, CAPTAIN. BUT WHAT I DO IS INNOCENT AND PIOUS. I
CAPT III	(280)	NEXT TIME? /LADY CICELY/ I'M SO SORRY. BUT YOU	KNOW	, CAPTAIN, THE ONE THING THAT ONE MISSES ON BOARD OF A
KING II	(225)	TO. /CATHERINE/ I FORGIVE MY ENEMIES, AS YOU WELL	KNOW	, CHARLES. IT IS MY DUTY AS A CATHOLIC AND A CHRISTIAN.
PHIL I	(90)	HE TURNS TO CHARTERIS, GRUMBLING). NOW REALLY YOU	KNOW	, CHARTERIS, THIS IS DEVILISH AWKWARD: UPON MY LIFE IT
GETT	(318)	IT. AND HE DOES OTHER THINGS, AS YOU EVIDENTLY	KNOW	, COLLINS. THEREFORE I GIVE YOU NOTICE THAT I SHALL
DOCT IV	(157)	/B.B./ IT'S AN ENORMOUSLY INTERESTING CASE. YOU	KNOW	, COLLY, BY JUPITER, IF I DIDNT KNOW AS A MATTER OF
MILL I	(152)	FATHER'S REPUTATION, AND HAS NEVER, AS FAR AS I	KNOW	, CONTRIBUTED AN IDEA TO ANY OF THEM. /ALASTAIR/ BE
DOCT II	(122)	THE NERVE TO REFUSE. I COULDNT VERY WELL, YOU	KNOW	, COULD I? /SCHUTZMACHER/ I DONT UNDERSTAND THAT. I
MTH5	(234)	THEY ARE AUTOMATA. /PYGMALION/ (UNCONVINCED) I	KNOW	, DEAR OLD CHAP; BUT THERE REALLY IS SOME EVIDENCE THAT
MIS.	(122)	EXACTLY; BUT YOUVE GOT TO PICK UP THEIR WAYS. YOU	KNOW	, DEAR, I NEVER QUITE AGREED WITH YOUR FATHER'S NOTION
JITT II	(36)	HIM: NONE OF US WERE ANYTHING TO HIM. /JITTA/ YOU	KNOW	, DEAR, THAT YOU ARE UNJUST TO HIM WHEN YOU SAY SO.
JITT III	(61)	OH, THAT! HOW YOU FRIGHTENED ME! BUT YOU	KNOW	, DEAR, YOU MUSTNT WORRY TOO MUCH ABOUT YOUR FATHER.
JITT III	(62)	NOT DEATH. /FESSLER/ (PROSAICALLY) WELL, YOU	KNOW	, DEATH IS A SORT OF DESTINY AS WELL. IF YOU ARE RIGHT,
MILL IV	(204)	OF THE WILL OF ALLAH. /ALASTAIR/ LOOK HERE, YOU	KNOW	, DOC: THAT WONT GO DOWN IN THIS COUNTRY. WE DONT
DOCT III	(154)	ONLY KNEW THE OTHER SIDE OF HIM AS I DO! DO YOU	KNOW	, DOCTOR, THAT IF LOUIS DISHONORED HIMSELF BY A REALLY
DOCT V	(174)	WHO HAD NONE. /JENNIFER/ CLEVER BRUTES? DO YOU	KNOW	, DOCTOR, THAT SOME OF THE DEAREST AND MOST FAITHFUL
PYGM II	(220)	/THE FLOWER GIRL/ GOOD ENOUGH FOR YE-OO. NOW YOU	KNOW	, DONT YOU? I'M COME TO HAVE LESSONS, I AM. AND TO PAY
SUPR IV	(143)	ON THE STEPS WITH SUDDEN SUSPICION) WELL, YOU	KNOW	, DONT YOU? /THE IRISHMAN/ DO I? /STRAKER/ (HIS
DOCT I	(114)	GOODBYE. (THEY SHAKE HANDS). BY THE WAY, YOU	KNOW	, DONT YOU, THAT TUBERCULOSIS IS CATCHING. YOU TAKE
GETT	(271)	GENERAL/ THEY ARE MEANT TO. VERY WELL. NOW YOU	KNOW	, DONT YOU, THAT YOUR SERVICES TO THE COMMUNITY AS A
CAPT II	(261)	THE REAL REASON WAS THAT HE DIDNT LIKE HER. YOU	KNOW	, DONT YOU, THAT IF YOU DONT LIKE PEOPLE YOU THINK OF
CURE	(229)	YOU WITH A VIEW TO A CORONER'S INQUEST. YOU	KNOW	, DONT YOU, THAT OPIUM IS A POISON? /REGINALD/ YES,
O'FL	(209)	WHAT DID HE SAY? /O'FLAHERTY/ HE SAYS " YOU	KNOW	, DONT YOU" HE SAYS " THAT IT'S YOUR DUTY, AS A
PYGM II	(237)	JUDICIALLY). /PICKERING/ I THINK YOU OUGHT TO	KNOW	, DOOLITTLE, THAT MR HIGGINS'S INTENTIONS ARE ENTIRELY
HART II	(93)	HE WONT HAVE A DOG'S CHANCE AGAINST ELLIE. YOU	KNOW	, ELLIE HAS REMARKABLE STRENGTH OF CHARACTER. I THINK
GENV II	(61)	NOW. /SIR O./ POOH! THEY CANT DO ANYTHING, YOU	KNOW	, EXCEPT MAKE SPEECHES AND WRITE ARTICLES. THEY ARE
GETT PREFACE	(243)	HIRING IS ENDED. AND SUCH AN INSTITUTION, AS WE	KNOW	, EXISTS AMONG US. IT IS COMMONLY SPOKEN OF AND THOUGHT
BASH II,2,	(114)	A MILLION MILES BY SEA TO LEARN HOW MEN CAN LIE!	KNOW	, FATHER WEBBER, MEN BECOME CIVILIZED THROUGH TWIN
LION I	(123)	CONTAMINATED HIM). /LAVINIA/ (LAUGHING) YOU	KNOW	, FERROVIUS, I AM NOT ALWAYS A CHRISTIAN. I DONT THINK
DEST	(158)	WHERE INDEED? THATS JUST WHAT I SHOULD LIKE TO	KNOW	, GENERAL. (WITH EMOTION) YOU DONT KNOW HOW FOND I WAS
BASH II,2,	(116)	HEARD OF ANY DAY BY SUCH AS LIKES THE JOB. I DONT	KNOW	, GOVERNOR, AS ENNYTHINK REMAINS FOR ME TO SAY.
MRS III	(221)	A THING. /FRANK/ (COMPASSIONATELY) HOW DO YOU	KNOW	, GOV'NOR, WHAT YOU SAID AND THOUGHT LAST NIGHT?
METH PREFACE	(R63)	MORAL ATMOSPHERE. NEVER IN HISTORY, AS FAR AS WE	KNOW	, HAD THERE BEEN SUCH A DETERMINED, RICHLY SUBSIDIZED,
GENV III	(69)	HE DID NOT MEAN TO BLASPHEME. ETHNOLOGICALLY, YOU	KNOW	, HE WAS RIGHT. ONLY ETHNOLOGICALLY, OF COURSE. /THE

BULL III (139) OH WELL, DONT BE TOO STAND-OFFISH, YOU KNOW , HODSON. I SHOULD LIKE YOU TO BE POPULAR. IF IT COSTS
SIM PREFACE(7) BRIMSTONE; BUT WE DO NOT KNOW, AND NEVER SHALL KNOW , HOW MANY CRIMES WERE REFRAINED FROM THAT WOULD HAVE
CAPT I (227) THEY MUST WANT IT MORE THAN WE DO; AND YOU KNOW , HOWARD, THAT MAHOMETANS NEVER SPEND MONEY IN DRINK.
JOAN EPILOG (155) EVER SINCE? /CHARLES/ OH, NOT SO BAD. DO YOU KNOW , I ACTUALLY LEAD MY ARMY OUT AND WIN BATTLES? DOWN
GENV III (85) I HAVE DINED WITH YOU THREE TIMES ALREADY. YOU KNOW , I AM A LITTLE AFRAID OF YOU, YOU ARE SO DEEP AND
CURE (231) OR ELSE LEAVE THE ROOM. /REGINALD/ BUT, YOU KNOW , I AM ILL. /STREGA/ THEN GO TO BED, AND SEND FOR A
BARB I (266) GIRL. /UNDERSHAFT/ NEVER MIND ME, MY DEAR. AS YOU KNOW , I AM NOT A GENTLEMAN; AND I WAS NEVER EDUCATED.
ROCK I (198) HAS ON A CROWD. /SIR ARTHUR/ (MUSING) DO YOU KNOW , I AM NOT AT ALL SURE THAT THERE IS NOT SOMETHING IN
BULL IV (180) KEEP UP THE MORAL TONE OF THE COMMUNITY. AS YOU KNOW , I CLAIM THE RIGHT TO THINK FOR MYSELF IN RELIGIOUS
LION II (129) HONOR IS TOO STRONG AN EXPRESSION. STILL, YOU KNOW , I COULDNT ALLOW THE TAILORS TO GET A BAD NAME THROUGH
MTH5 (235) ANYTHING ORIGINAL? /PYGMALION/ NO. BUT THEN, YOU KNOW , I DO NOT ADMIT THAT ANY OF US CAN DO ANYTHING REALLY
BARB II (290) BUT SUPPOSE BARBARA FINDS YOU OUT! /CUSINS/ YOU KNOW , I DO NOT ADMIT THAT I AM IMPOSING ON BARBARA. I AM
BULL I (96) MORE AND MORE CARRIED AWAY BY HIS NEW FANCY). YOU KNOW , I HAVE A SORT OF PRESENTIMENT THAT MISS REILLY IS A
MRS I (184) OF EVERYTHING. BUT THINGS ARE IMPROVING. DO YOU KNOW , I HAVE BEEN IN A POSITIVE STATE OF EXCITEMENT ABOUT
HART III (132) BAITED OUT OF ALL PRUDENCE) WELL, IF YOU WANT TO KNOW , I HAVE NO MONEY AND NEVER HAD ANY. /MRS HUSHABYE/
KING II (227) FROM ME AND MARRIED RICHMOND. /CATHERINE/ OH, I KNOW , I KNOW: IT WAS THE ONLY TIME I EVER WAS JEALOUS.
AUGS (272) A PLEASANT SUBJECT, UNHAPPILY. /THE LADY/ OH, I KNOW , I KNOW. HOW SHAMEFULLY YOU HAVE BEEN TREATED! WHAT
DOCT III (152) RALPH BLOOMFIELD BONINGTON-- /MRS DUBEDAT/ YES, I KNOW , I KNOW. IT IS A GREAT PRIVILEGE TO HAVE HIM. BUT OH,
CURE (226) MEANT ANY HARM IN-- /THE DOCTOR/ YES, YES, YES: I KNOW , I KNOW. YOU THINK YOU MADE A FOOL OF YOURSELF BEFORE
MRS I (191) THATS WHAT PUZZLES ME ABOUT IT. WHY, FOR ALL I KNOW , I MIGHT BE HER FATHER. /PRAED/ YOU! IMPOSSIBLE!
BUOY III (31) SIR FERDINAND, WHATS THE LATEST? /SIR F./ YOU KNOW , I PRESUME, THAT YOUR FATHER'S MONEY, NOW PRACTICALLY
HART II (95) ATTITUDE, QUITE INTERESTED IN MAZZINI NOW) YOU KNOW , I REALLY THINK YOU MUST LOVE ELLIE VERY MUCH; FOR YOU
LION I (120) FOOLISHLY, AND STRIKES HIM AGAIN FEEBLY). YOU KNOW , I SHOULD FEEL ASHAMED IF I LET MYSELF BE STRUCK LIKE ,
SIM I (47) OH YES: I WISH I HADNT. IT TORTURES ME. YOU KNOW , I SHOULD HAVE ENJOYED BEING A PIRATE'S CHAPLAIN
JITT III (66) ME! /JITTA/ YES, YOU, YOU, YOU. DO YOU KNOW , I SOMETIMES WANTED TO SHAKE HIM FOR NOT TAKING A
POSN (449) SO. MORNING, SHERIFF. /THE SHERIFF/ MORNING. YOU KNOW , I SUPPOSE, THAT IF YOUVE STOLE A HORSE AND THE JURY
CAPT II (264) (UNEXPECTEDLY ACQUIESCING) VERY GOOD. YOU KNOW , I SUPPOSE, THAT IF YOU BREAK MY BARGAIN WITH SIDI,
WIDO III (51) I WAS NOT ASKING AFTER YOUR HEALTH, SIR, AS YOU KNOW , I THINK, AS WELL AS I DO. WHAT IS YOUR BUSINESS?
DEVL I (19) PASTOR, FOR THE SAKE OF OLD TIMES. /ANDERSON/ YOU KNOW , I THINK, MR DUDGEON, THAT I DO NOT DRINK BEFORE
KING I (162) WELL, NEVER MIND. I WILL ASK MR NEWTON. HE'LL KNOW , IF ANYBODY WILL, OR STOP, ASK JACK THE FISH HAWKER.
VWOO 2 (130) /A/ LOVE AT FIRST SIGHT! WHAT? /Z/ OH NO. YOU KNOW , IF I FELL IN LOVE WITH A MAN I'D NEVER MARRY HIM: HE
INCA (248) DOWN, MILLIONS OF MEN PERISH. /ERMYNTRUDE/ YOU KNOW , IF I HAD A MOUSTACHE LIKE THAT, IT WOULD TURN MY
BARB I (261) THICK. /LOMAX/ (HANDSOMELY) NOT THAT I MIND, YOU KNOW , IF SARAH DONT. (HE SITS). /LADY BRITOMART/ (
MTH2 (41) HIS FORMER LOW GHOSTLY TONE) YOU NEEDNT GO, YOU KNOW , IF YOU ARE REALLY INTERESTED. /HASLAM/ (FED UP)
FOUN (216) MUST BE SOMETHING AWFULLY WRONG ABOUT YOU, YOU KNOW , IF YOU GET ONLY THE THIRTY-THIRD OF WHAT HE GETS.
APPL I (206) I THINK I'D RATHER YOU CALLED ME A SOUL, YOU KNOW , IF YOU MUST CALL ME ANYTHING AT ALL. I KNOW I HAVE
BULL III (121) WAS HE INDUSTRIOUS? THATS REMARKABLE, YOU KNOW , IN AN IRISHMAN. /LARRY/ INDUSTRIOUS! THAT MAN'S
FANY III (299) A DEVILISH COOL WAY OF LAYING DOWN THE LAW. YOU KNOW , IN MY CLASS YOU HAVE TO WRAP UP THINGS A BIT. DENMARK
ROCK II (282) AND THE END OF HYPOCRISY. DO YOU THINK I DIDNT KNOW , IN THE DAYS OF MY GREAT SPEECHES AND MY ROARING
DOCT PREFACE(53) JENNER, NOR ANY OTHER DOCTOR EVER, AS FAR AS I KNOW , INCULCATED THE POPULAR NOTION THAT EVERYBODY GOT
FANY III (299) OF WHICH YOU WILL GET THE WORSE. /BOBBY/ BUT, YOU KNOW , I'M NOT REALLY WORTHY OF HER. /JUGGINS/ PROBABLY SHE
SUPR IV (163) OF IT UNTIL TAVY TOLD ME SHE SAID I DID. BUT, YOU KNOW , I'M VERY FOND OF TAVY: HE'S A SORT OF SON TO ME; AND
JOAN 4 (98) OF LORRAINE! /CAUCHON/ SIR JOHN TALBOT, WE ALL KNOW , IS A FIERCE AND FORMIDABLE SOLDIER, MESSIRE; BUT I
FABL V (120) AGREE ON WHAT SORT OF MIND WE NEEDED. PRAYER, WE KNOW , IS A GREAT CREATIVE POWER; BUT TO PRAY EFFECTIVELY
MIS. PREFACE(100) PROTESTANT MANIFESTO EVER WRITTEN, AS FAR AS I KNOW , IS HOUSTON CHAMBERLAIN'S FOUNDATIONS OF THE
SUPR HANDBOK(180) TO GOOD BREEDING; AND EQUALITY, AS ALL ECONOMISTS KNOW , IS INCOMPATIBLE WITH PROPERTY. BESIDES, EQUALITY IS
GENV IV (119) LET US RIDE CAREFULLY. LEADERSHIP, WE TWO KNOW , IS MYSTICAL. THEN LET US NOT PRETEND TO UNDERSTAND
BARB PREFACE(220) NEW, EVEN ON THE STAGE. WHAT IS NEW, AS FAR AS I KNOW , IS THAT ARTICLE IN UNDERSHAFT'S RELIGION WHICH
LION II (139) KNOW. IF IT WERE FOR ANYTHING SMALL ENOUGH TO KNOW , IT WOULD BE TOO SMALL TO DIE FOR. I THINK I'M GOING
VWOO 2 (130) I DONT RUN AFTER WOMEN? /Z/ WELL, IF YOU WANT TO KNOW , IT'S BECAUSE YOU DIDNT RUN AFTER ME. YOU MIGHTNT
PHIL II (117) ROT ABOUT MODERN SCIENCE? BETWEEN OURSELVES, YOU KNOW , IT'S HORRIBLY CRUEL: YOU MUST ADMIT THAT IT'S A
GENV IV (129) MEN WHO WILL FOLLOW US. /SIR O./ STILL, YOU KNOW , IT'S NO USE GOING ON MAKING MOTOR CARS THAT YOU KNOW
FANY III (303) IT A RELIEF? /BOBBY/ (RISING STIFFLY) BUT YOU KNOW , IT'S NOT THE SAME FOR A GIRL. A MAN MAY DO THINGS A
CURE (231) CAUTIOUSLY RISING AND APPROACHING HER) WELL, YOU KNOW , IT'S SO HARD TO KNOW HOW A CROCODILE WOULD PLAY. /THE
JITT III (68) /AGNES/ (HOLDING HER) OH, DONT GO YET. YOU KNOW , IT'S VERY FUNNY HOW ONE'S MIND WORKS. /JITTA/ (
INCA (238) I SUPPOSE HE MUST HAVE BEEN. I WONDER! YOU KNOW , IT'S VERY SHARP OF YOU TO FIND THAT OUT. I HOPE YOU
PHIL II (99) LOOKING ROUND FOR THEM. /CRAVEN/ (RISING) DO YOU KNOW , IVE A GREAT MIND TO JOIN, JUST TO SEE WHAT IT'S LIKE.
ARMS III (52) STRANGE IT IS TO BE TALKED TO IN SUCH A WAY! YOU KNOW , IVE ALWAYS GONE ON LIKE THAT. /BLUNTSCHLI/ YOU MEAN
GETT (288) ALICE TO LET ANYTHING STAND IN THE WAY. BUT, YOU KNOW , IVE SEEN ONE OF OUR DAUGHTERS AFTER ANOTHER-- ETHEL,
SUPR I (25) IT WERE A NICELY UNDERDONE CHOP. /OCTAVIUS/ YOU KNOW , JACK, I SHOULD HAVE TO RUN AWAY FROM YOU IF I DID NOT
CAND II (119) AND FONDER OF HIM ALL THE TIME I WAS AWAY. DO YOU KNOW , JAMES, THAT THOUGH HE HAS NOT THE LEAST SUSPICION OF
JITT II (44) DO IT? WHERE IS THE SENSE IN IT? I BELIEVE YOU KNOW , JITTA. /JITTA/ REALLY, ALFRED--! I MUST GO BACK TO
FANY III (299) WHAT A NUISANCE! I DONT KNOW WHAT TO DO. YOU KNOW , JUGGINS, YOUR COOL SIMPLE-MINDED WAY OF DOING IT
FANY PROLOG (260) /SAVOYARD/ SOME OF US MUST LIVE IN ENGLAND, YOU KNOW , JUST TO KEEP THE PLACE GOING. BESIDES-- THOUGH, MIND
GENV III (75) MENTION. /THE NEWCOMER/ HULLO, MAAM! YOU KNOW , LADIES DONT SAY THINGS LIKE THAT IN MY COUNTRY. /THE
BULL I (92) LIKE AWE). I DONT WISH TO BE IMPERTINENT, AS YOU KNOW , LARRY; BUT ARE YOU SURE SHE HAS NOTHING TO DO WITH
BULL I (93) /BROADBENT/ (WITH HEARTY ADMIRATION) NOW YOU KNOW , LARRY, THAT WOULD NEVER HAVE OCCURRED TO ME. YOU
PHIL II (106) TO ANY WOMAN. /SYLVIA/ (THOUGHTFULLY) DO YOU KNOW , LEONARD, I REALLY BELIEVE YOU. I DONT THINK YOU CARE
MIS. (121) A THING A PRETTY TURN! YOURE A HUMBUG, YOU KNOW , LORD SUMMERHAYS. JOHN DOESNT KNOW IT; AND JOHNNY
MIS. (121) WHAT? /MRS TARLETON/ CALLED HER THE GIRL. YOU KNOW , LORD SUMMERHAYS, IT'S A FUNNY THING; BUT NOW I'M
DOCT III (150) NO USE HERE; AND I MUST BE GETTING BACK. AS YOU KNOW , MAAM, I'M NOT IN PRACTICE NOW; AND I SHALL NOT BE IN
BULL PREFACE(7) SEEMS TO SERVE HER OWN TURN. THERE ARE, I KNOW , MEN AND WOMEN WHO ARE POLITICAL PERVERTS BY NATURE.
GETT (296) THE STUDY WITH THE BISHOP). /HOTCHKISS/ DO YOU KNOW , MISS BRIDGENORTH, I SHOULD MOST AWFULLY LIKE TO HEAR
WIDO I (9) VERY GOOD INDEED. (SERIOUSLY) BUT DO YOU KNOW , MISS SARTORIUS, THERE ACTUALLY ARE JOHANNIS CHURCHES
OVER (194) MOTHER; AND I'M SORRY SHE'S DEAD; BUT REALLY, YOU KNOW , MOST WOMEN ARE MOTHERS; AND THEY ALL DIE SOME TIME OR
PYGM III (245) GO HOME AT ONCE. /HIGGINS/ (KISSING HER) I KNOW , MOTHER. I CAME ON PURPOSE. /MRS HIGGINS/ BUT YOU
NEVR I (213) AGAIN). /GLORIA/ (INEXORABLY) WE HAVE A RIGHT TO KNOW , MOTHER. /MRS CLANDON/ (INDIGNANTLY) AH! YOU INSIST.
GETT (311) THE FIRST CLAUSE IN AN AGREEMENT, USUALLY? YOU KNOW , MR ALDERMAN. /COLLINS/ (AT A LOSS) WELL, SIR, THE
BULL III (135) HIMSELF FOR A POLITICAL DELIVERANCE) WELL, YOU KNOW , MR DOYLE, THERES A STRONG DASH OF TORYISM IN THE
FANY III (316) THERE! /MRS KNOX/ (WITH GENTLE PITY) HOW DO YOU KNOW , MR GILBEY, WHAT YOULL DO TOMORROW MORNING? /GILBEY/
MTH2 (59) RESTLESS) DONT LET HIM SHUT YOU UP, MR BURGE. YOU KNOW , MR LUBIN, I AM FRIGHTFULLY INTERESTED IN THE LABOR
SUPR I (6) OH, IF ONLY I THOUGHT I HAD A CHANCE! YOU KNOW , MR RAMSDEN, I DONT CARE ABOUT MONEY OR ABOUT WHAT
SUPR II (70) SORT OF THINGS. (SERENE AGAIN) EX-CUSE ME, YOU KNOW , MR TANNER; BUT YOU ASKED ME AS MAN TO MAN; AND I TOLD
JITT III (69) HELP IT. /JITTA/ (LOOKING HARD AT HER) YOU KNOW , MRS HALDENSTEDT, I WAS VERY VERY FOND OF HIM. /AGNES/
PYGM V (269) /PICKERING/ WE CANT LET HER GO LIKE THIS. YOU KNOW , MRS HIGGINS. WHAT WERE WE TO DO? /MRS HIGGINS/ YOU
HART II (91) FORMERLY, AND HAS TO DRINK TOO LITTLE NOW. YOU KNOW , MRS HUSHABYE, I REALLY THINK HE HAS BEEN HYPNOTIZED.
MTH3 (116) HE SAYS. THAT IS HIS LITTLE JOKE. DO YOU KNOW , MRS LUTESTRING, HE HAD ALMOST TALKED US INTO
O'FL (224) BELGIANS. SIR PEARCE/ YES: HE'S QUITE RIGHT, YOU KNOW , MRS O'FLAHERTY: QUITE RIGHT THERE. /MRS O'FLAHERTY/
MTH3 (130) BURGE: I SPOKE TO YOU. /BURGE-LUBIN/ WELL, YOU KNOW , MY DEAR BARNABAS, CONFUCIUS IS A VERY LONG-HEADED
GETT (349) GENERAL/ (RISING, HORRIFIED) NO, NO, YOU MUST KNOW , MY DEAR LESBIA, THAT I WAS NOT USING THE WORD IN ITS
MRS I (183) /PRAED/ WELL, IN MAKING YOU CONVENTIONAL. YOU KNOW , MY DEAR MISS WARREN, I AM A BORN ANARCHIST. I HATE
MRS III (222) OVER HERE! HE MUST HAVE BEEN EVER SO DRUNK. YOU KNOW , MY DEAR PRADDY, MY MOTHER WOULDNT STAND MRS WARREN
BARB I (256) RIGHT AND WRONG, IF HE HAD BEEN IN THE HOUSE. YOU KNOW , MY DEAR, YOUR FATHER WAS A VERY ATTRACTIVE MAN IN
JOAN 6 (150) MARTIN. /LADVENU/ (ENIGMATICALLY) WE DO NOT KNOW , MY LORD. IT MAY HAVE ONLY JUST BEGUN. /WARWICK/ WHAT
ROCK I (205) SUCH A HORRID WICKED THING TO SAY. DONT YOU KNOW , MY LOVE, THAT YOU ARE THE BEST OF WIVES? THE VERY
HART II (103) BOSS, IS IT? /MANGAN/ (SHORTLY) IF YOU WANT TO KNOW , MY NAME'S ALFRED. /MRS HUSHABYE/ (SPRINGING UP)
KING I (173) MR NEWTON WILL TELL YOU. I SHOULD BE GLAD TO KNOW , MYSELF. /NEWTON/ FLUXIONS, MADAM, ARE THE RATES OF
WIDO III (54) SOMEBODY HAS TO KNOW THESE THINGS BEFOREHAND, YOU KNOW , NO MATTER HOW DARK THEYRE KEPT. /SARTORIUS/ (
OVER (185) /JUNO/ AHA! YOU CONFESS IT. WELL, IF YOU WANT TO KNOW , NOBODY TOLD ME. EVERYBODY FALLS IN LOVE WITH MY WIFE.
CAND II (123) TOMORROW. /LEXY/ (INTIMIDATED, BUT URGENT) I KNOW , OF COURSE, THAT THEY MAKE THE MOST UNREASONABLE
VWOO 1 (118) I NEVER COULD BRING MYSELF TO BELIEVE THAT. I KNOW , OF COURSE, THAT MEN HAVE THEIR WEAKNESSES AND THEIR
MTH4 I (163) REALLY, MADAM-- /ZOO/ (CONTINUING); BUT I KNOW , OF COURSE, THAT YOU ARE AN ORDINARY SHORTLIVER. WELL,
BUOY IV (52) DADDY. WE SHALL LIVE IN PARK LANE. /JUNIUS/ YOU KNOW , OF COURSE, THAT THERE ARE PLENTY OF RATTLERS AND
MRS I (191) /PRAED/ NONE. /CROFTS/ (NOT BELIEVING HIM) I KNOW , OF COURSE, THAT YOU PERHAPS MIGHT FEEL BOUND NOT TO
BARB PREFACE(217) AS AN INSTITUTION, WHAT ELSE CAN THEY DO? THEY KNOW , OF COURSE, THAT THEY ARE RICH BECAUSE OTHERS ARE
HART I (59) (BEHIND THE SOFA, SCOLDING DOWN AT HER) YOU KNOW , OF COURSE, THAT IT'S NOT HONORABLE OR GRATEFUL TO
POSN PREFACE(374) ATTENTION TO THE BUSINESS THAT THEY DID NOT KNOW , OR HAD FORGOTTEN, THAT THEY HAD ALREADY BEEN SUPPLIED

LION PREFACE(47)	EITHER HE WILL HAVE TO CONFESS THAT HE DOESNT	KNOW	, OR HE WILL SAY THAT NEWTON PROVED IT. BUT HE HAS NOT
OVER (180)	NO REASON! AT LEAST I SUPPOSE NOT. BUT, YOU	KNOW	, PART OF THE ROMANCE OF A JOURNEY IS THAT A MAN KEEPS
BARB PREFACE(226)	AT THE HEIGHT OF THEIR VOGUE. EVENTUALLY, AS WE	KNOW	, PERFECTLY RESPECTABLE CITIZENS AND EARNEST
PYGM II (221)	HIS KEYS AND HIS CASH IN HIS POCKETS) YOU	KNOW	, PICKERING, IF YOU CONSIDER A SHILLING, NOT AS A
PYGM II (232)	SIR. THATS ALL. (SHE GOES OUT). /HIGGINS/ YOU	KNOW	, PICKERING, THAT WOMAN HAS THE MOST EXTRAORDINARY
HART II (100)	RICH YOUNG MEN CAN GET RID OF THEIR WIVES, YOU	KNOW	, PRETTY CHEAPLY. BUT THIS OBJECT, AS YOU CALL HIM, CAN
MIS. PREFACE(44)	IS THE NATURE OF CREATION, WHICH, AS WE NOW	KNOW	, PROCEEDS BY EVOLUTION. EVOLUTION FINDS ITS WAY BY
ARMS III (72)	A QUESTION OF YOUR POSITION; BUT HANG IT, YOU	KNOW	, RAINA IS ACCUSTOMED TO A VERY COMFORTABLE
BASH III (126)	THE FACE OF MAN? /CASHEL/ TIS FATE'S DECREE. FOR	KNOW	, RASH YOUTH, THAT IN THIS STAR CROST WORLD FATE DRIVES
VWOO 3 (143)	/A/ SO DO I. /Z/ I'M NOT A BIT LIKE THAT, YOU	KNOW	, REALLY. SOMETHING ABOVE ME AND BEYOND ME DROVE ME ON.
CAPT I (233)	HE IS. HIS TELLING YOU SO FRANKLY PROVES IT. YOU	KNOW	, REALLY, HOWARD, ALL THOSE POOR PEOPLE WHOM YOU TRY
APPL I (224)	FOR THAT. /PROTEUS/ KINGS, AS YOU AND I VERY WELL	KNOW	, RULE THEIR MINISTERS BY FLATTERING THEM; AND NOW THAT
GENV III (72)	AT THE SHOOTING CONVERSATION) BUT DONT YOU	KNOW	, SENORA, THAT YOU MUSTNT GO ABOUT SHOOTING PEOPLE
ARMS II (24)	FEEL THAT NO MATTER WHAT YOU KNOW OR DONT	KNOW	, SHE CAN DEPEND ON YOU TO HOLD YOUR TONGUE AND SERVE
PYGM III (257)	NEW ELIZAS, SPEAKING TOGETHER /HIGGINS/ YOU	KNOW	, SHE HAS THE MOST EXTRAORDINARY QUICKNESS OF EAR:
PHIL II (98)	OF VALUING A TRUE MAN'S AFFECTION. DO YOU	KNOW	, SHE OFTEN SAID SHE WISHED SHE'D MARRIED YOU INSTEAD.
CLEO PRO2 (105)	THE WAY TO THE SEA. WHAT SHE WOULD HAVE IT	KNOW	, SHE TELLS INTO THE EARS OF THE SACRED CATS; AND ON
ROCK II (243)	THEY ALL SIT DOWN). /SIR BEMROSE/ I HAPPEN TO	KNOW	, SIR JAFNA, THAT YOUR ENTERPRISES STAND AT TWENTY
DOCT II (126)	ON. WE CANT ALL GO TO ST MORITZ OR TO EGYPT, YOU	KNOW	, SIR RALPH. DONT TALK ABOUT IT. EMBARRASSED SILENCE.
JOAN 1 (58)	TOO: DO NOT FORGET THAT. /STEWARD/ (DESPERATE) I	KNOW	, SIR. I KNOW ONLY TOO WELL. THERE IS NO MILK: THERE
O'FL (227)	COUNTRY WITH THE OTHERS, I WAS LYING, AS YOU WELL	KNOW	, SIR. NOW I CAN GO AND SAY IT WITH A CLEAR CONSCIENCE.
O'FL (205)	YOU FOR MY GUEST HERE TODAY. /O'FLAHERTY/ SURE I	KNOW	, SIR. YOU HAVE TO PUT UP WITH A LOT FROM THE LIKE OF
2TRU III (104)	ITS VANITIES-- AND WEVE GOT TO LIVE IN IT, YOU	KNOW	, SIR-- SHE APPEALS TO ME. /AUBREY/ TAKE CARE,
APPL II (275)	HIS HAT) WELL, I AM GLAD NOTHING'S HAPPENED. YOU	KNOW	, SIR, NOTHING EVER REALLY DOES HAPPEN IN THE CABINET.
APPL II (264)	OLD ENGLAND -- CAN LAST FOR EVER. PROGRESS, YOU	KNOW	, SIR, PROGRESS, PROGRESS! /MAGNUS/ JUST SO, JUST SO.
ARMS I (14)	JUST NOW. /RAINA/ (LOFTILY) FRIGHTEN ME! DO YOU	KNOW	, SIR, THAT THOUGH I AM ONLY A WOMAN, I THINK I AM AT
ARMS III (52)	/RAINA/ (STARING HAUGHTILY AT HIM) DO YOU	KNOW	, SIR, THAT YOU ARE INSULTING ME? /BLUNTSCHLI/ I CANT
ARMS III (69)	THAN HER CONFIDENTIAL SERVANT. I INTEND, AS YOU	KNOW	, SIR, TO SET UP A SHOP LATER ON IN SOFIA; AND I LOOK
BULL IV (179)	THE HILL AGAIN TO KEEGAN'S RIGHT HAND) BUT YOU	KNOW	, SOMETHING MUST BE DONE. /KEEGAN/ YES: WHEN WE CEASE
MTH2 (39)	IT FOR NINE HUNDRED YEARS. I SHOULD CHUCK IT. YOU	KNOW	, SOMETIMES, WHEN THE BISHOP, WHO IS THE MOST PRICELESS
SUPR I (25)	THE DOOR). /ANN/ STOP, JACK. GRANNY: HE MUST	KNOW	, SOONER OR LATER. /RAMSDEN/ OCTAVIUS: I HAVE A VERY
BARB I (253)	UNDER COVER OF GIVING CREDIT FOR THE CANNONS. YOU	KNOW	, STEPHEN, IT'S PERFECTLY SCANDALOUS, THOSE TWO MEN,
CURE (236)	MONEY FOR MYSELF. I AM A POOR LITTLE THING, I	KNOW	, STREGA; BUT I COULD MAKE A HOME FOR YOU. I HAVE GREAT
2TRU II (67)	SAKE DONT START CRYING. /THE PATIENT/ FOR ALL YOU	KNOW	, SWEETIE, THE SERGEANT MAY BE A HAPPILY MARRIED MAN.
SIM II (60)	ME HAPPIER THAN I HAVE BEEN FOR MONTHS. BUT, YOU	KNOW	, THAT DOES NOT SETTLE MY DIFFICULTIES. I DONT KNOW
JITT III (72)	LOW WOMEN-- IF HE DID NOT KNOW FOR CERTAIN, AS I	KNOW	, THAT THE WOMAN MY FATHER LOVED MUST HAVE BEEN ONE OF
PYGM V (279)	WAY WITH HER; BUT IT WAS NO USE. YOU TOLD ME, YOU	KNOW	, THAT WHEN A CHILD IS BROUGHT TO A FOREIGN COUNTRY, IT
LADY (249)	WHICH IS BUT A LARGER STAGE. OF LATE, AS YOU	KNOW	, THE CHURCH TAUGHT THE PEOPLE BY MEANS OF PLAYS; BUT
BARB III (344)	THE MAN WHO KEEPS ME UP TO THE MARK. /CUSINS/ YOU	KNOW	, THE CREATURE IS REALLY A SORT OF POET IN HIS WAY.
MTH2 (45)	WHO HE WAS. /CONRAD/ WELL, WHY NOT? FOR ALL YOU	KNOW	, THE MAN YOU ARE GOING TO MARRY MAY BE YOUR
PHIL I (90)	IS, CUTHBERTSON, MRS TRANFIELD, WHO IS, AS YOU	KNOW	, THE MOST THOUGHTFUL OF WOMEN, TOOK IT INTO HER HEAD
MRS II (204)	A PARTICULARLY ABLE PERSON. /FRANK/ WELL, YOU	KNOW	, THE OLD MAN IS NOT ALTOGETHER SUCH A FOOL AS HE
SUPR PREFACE(R18)	OF MODERN LONDON LIFE, A LIFE IN WHICH, AS YOU	KNOW	, THE ORDINARY MAN'S MAIN BUSINESS IS TO GET MEANS TO
BULL IV (172)	BE THE ROAR OF THY WATERS." /BROADBENT/ YOU	KNOW	, THE ROAR OF A MOTOR BOAT IS QUITE PRETTY. /KEEGAN/
GENV I (44)	IT. MY BUSINESS WILL TAKE ONLY A MOMENT. AS YOU	KNOW	, THE SOVIET GOVERNMENT HAS GONE AS FAR AS POSSIBLE IN
MIS. (132)	AND THERES AN END OF IT. /TARLETON/ STILL, YOU	KNOW	, THE SUPERMAN MAY COME. THE SUPERMAN'S AN IDEA. I
JOAN 5 (120)	GILLES DE RAIS TWIRLS HIS BEARD. /BLUEBEARD/ YOU	KNOW	, THE WOMAN IS QUITE IMPOSSIBLE. I DONT DISLIKE HER,
VWOO 2 (130)	ME. /A/ WHY? /Z/ OH, HOW DO I KNOW? THEY DONT	KNOW	, THEMSELVES. BUT THE LOT OF MONEY THEY SPEND ON THINGS
BASH III (123)	FOR NOW I DO APPROACH MY TRAGEDY'S CATASTROPHE.	KNOW	, THEN, THAT HEAVEN DID BLESS ME WITH AN ONLY SON, A
GENV II (57)	I AGREE WITH THAT-- IN PRINCIPLE. STILL, YOU	KNOW	, THERE ARE PEOPLE YOU CAN TAKE INTO COURT AND PEOPLE
BARB III (341)	OIL ON THE TROUBLED WATERS) THE FACT IS, YOU	KNOW	, THERE IS A CERTAIN AMOUNT OF TOSH ABOUT THIS NOTION
O'FL (206)	MYSELF ON PARADE MANY A TIME. BUT STILL, YOU	KNOW	, THERES A GRATIFYING SIDE TO IT, TOO. AFTER ALL, HE IS
BULL III (138)	IT WAS A PRETTY OBVIOUS MOVE, I SHOULD THINK. YOU	KNOW	, THESE FELLOWS HAVE PLENTY OF SHREWDNESS IN SPITE OF
BARB III (329)	/LOMAX/ (LECTURING TO THE COMPANY GENERALLY) YOU	KNOW	, THESE HIGH EXPLOSIVES DONT GO OFF LIKE GUNPOWDER,
MIS. (114)	YOU HAVNT GOT MORE THAN ONE IDEA! IF YOU WANT TO	KNOW	, THEY DID TRY THAT ON ME ONCE, WHEN I WAS A SMALL KID.
CURE (227)	CATS? THERES A QUESTION TO REFLECT ON! YOU	KNOW	, THEY OUGHT TO HAVE MADE ME A PHILOSOPHER. /THE
SIM PRO,3, (31)	WITH HIS BACK TO THE SEA) WELL, IF YOU WANT TO	KNOW	, THIS BLIGHTER KICKED ME INTO THE SEA; AND WHEN I'D
PHIL I (87)	HARPING ON CUTHBERTSON'S INCONSISTENCY) WELL, YOU	KNOW	, THIS IS UNEXPECTED! NOW IT'S REALLY VERY UNEXPECTED.
MTH3 (131)	ENGLISH BE HANGED! IT'S COMMON SENSE. YOU	KNOW	, THOSE TWO PEOPLE GOT US HYPNOTIZED: NOT A DOUBT OF
CLEO PRO2 (103)	(THE GUARDSMEN START AND LOOK AT ONE ANOTHER).	KNOW	, THOU FOOLISH SOLDIER, THAT THE QUEEN HAS BEEN MISSING
HART III (144)	PAMPHLETS. THAT WAS ALL I COULD DO. BUT, YOU	KNOW	, THOUGH THE PEOPLE IN THE SOCIETIES THOUGHT THEY KNEW
MTH2 (72)	YOU, WHO HAVNT LIFTED A FINGER, AS FAR AS I	KNOW	, TO HELP US THROUGH THIS AWFUL CRISIS WHICH HAS LEFT
SIM PRO,3, (29)	ON HER LEFT NEAREST THE IMAGES. /THE Y.W./ YOU	KNOW	, TO ME THIS IS A FUNNY SORT OF LUNCH. YOU BEGIN WITH
JITT II (30)	OF HOURS TODAY. JUST IN A DRESSING-GOWN, YOU	KNOW	, TO SIT ABOUT A BIT. /FESSLER/ OH, GOOD. WELL, I MUST
BARB III (322)	IT GIVES YOU A RIPPING FEELING OF SECURITY, YOU	KNOW	, TO THINK OF THE LOT OF BEGGARS WE COULD KILL IF IT
MRS PREFACE(173)	BY THEIR FATHER'S PROFESSION. THESE CRITICS MUST	KNOW	, TOO, FROM HISTORY IF NOT FROM EXPERIENCE, THAT WOMEN
GENV IV (127)	NATURALLY. /THE BETROTHED/ MINE HAVNT. YOU	KNOW	, UNCLE, I THINK THERES SOMETHING IN YOUR NOTION OF
BARB I (266)	I'M AWFULLY SORRY, LADY BRIT; BUT REALLY YOU	KNOW	, UPON MY SOUL! (HE SITS ON THE SETTEE BETWEEN LADY
LION PREFACE(10)	BY SAVONAROLAS AND KNIPPERDOLLINGS. AND AS THEY	KNOW	, VERY SENSIBLY, THAT A LITTLE RELIGION IS GOOD FOR
FABL PREFACE(87)	AND WON THE ELECTION FOR THEM. THIS, AS FAR AS I	KNOW	, WAS THE FIRST NON-PARTY TEST EVER APPLIED TO
MTH5 (228)	I PROMISE YOU I WILL NOT DETAIN YOU LONG. WE	KNOW	, WE CHILDREN OF SCIENCE, THAT THE UNIVERSE IS FULL OF
LION PREFACE(41)	AND KNEW, AS MERE CHRONICLERS AND ROMANCERS NEVER	KNOW	, WHAT ACTUALLY HAPPENS AWAY FROM BOOKS AND DESKS. BUT
HART II (101)	/MRS HUSHABYE/ PETTIKINS: DONT MAKE ME CRY. YOU	KNOW	, WHAT YOU SAID ABOUT MY MAKING A HOUSEHOLD PET OF HIM
BARB III (314)	OF COUNTENANCE) WELL, DRIVEL IS DRIVEL, DONT YOU	KNOW	, WHATEVER A MAN'S AGE. /LADY BRITOMART/ IN GOOD
DOCT I (86)	FOOD. /SCHUTZMACHER/ I TAKE IT MYSELF, YOU	KNOW	, WHEN I FEEL RUN DOWN. GOODBYE. YOU DONT MIND MY
GENV II (50)	/BEGONIA/ OH, THEN THATS QUITE ALL RIGHT. YOU	KNOW	, WHEN I WAS AT SCHOOL I WAS CHOSEN FIVE TIMES TO
BULL IV (167)	NOT GOOD ENOUGH FOR YOU, NORA, BUT NO MAN IS, YOU	KNOW	, WHEN THE WOMAN IS A REALLY NICE WOMAN. /NORA/ OH, I'M
DOCT I (86)	NO BRASS PLATE. IT WAS A SHOP WINDOW: RED, YOU	KNOW	, WITH BLACK LETTERING, DOCTOR LEO SCHUTZMACHER,
LION II (131)	/METELLUS/ AN INCONCEIVABLE LIBERTY! DO YOU NOT	KNOW	, WOMAN, THAT THE EMPEROR CAN DO NO WRONG AND THEREFORE
KING I (174)	THE HOUSE THIS INSTANT OR I DO. /BARBARA/ DO YOU	KNOW	, WOMAN, THAT YOU ARE SPEAKING OF THE DUCHESS OF
CAND I (95)	IT WILL PLEASE YOU. /CANDIDA/ (TOUCHED) DO YOU	KNOW	, YOU ARE A VERY NICE BOY, EUGENE, WITH ALL YOUR
MRS I (183)	SUPPOSE SHE DOES (HE SITS DOWN). /VIVIE/ DO YOU	KNOW	, YOU ARE JUST LIKE WHAT I EXPECTED. I HOPE YOU ARE
ARMS III (52)	OF THE WORLD. /RAINA/ (WONDERINGLY) DO YOU	KNOW	, YOU ARE THE FIRST MAN I EVER MET WHO DID NOT TAKE ME
CAPT II (258)	AND REFLECTIVELY UPWARD MEANWHILE). DO YOU	KNOW	, YOU ARE WONDERFULLY LIKE YOUR UNCLE. /BRASSBOUND/
BUOY IV (56)	BUOYANT WAY! IT SAVES A LOT OF TIME. NOW THAT YOU	KNOW	, YOU HAD BETTER STAY TO LUNCH. /SIR FERDINAND/ NO. I
MRS I (191)	OF PROTEST FROM PRAED)-- I ONLY SAY, IF YOU	KNOW	, YOU MIGHT AT LEAST SET MY MIND AT REST ABOUT HER. THE
CAPT III (275)	AT THE INQUIRY THAT THE CADI SAID. HE DIDNT	KNOW	, YOU SEE. /RANKIN/ (CANNILY) I TAKE YOUR POINT, LEDDY
BULL III (142)	WOY? /MATTHEW/ (EQUALLY CONTEMPTUOUS) D'YE	KNOW	, YOURSELF? /HODSON/ YUS OI DO. IT'S BECAUSE OI WANT A
GETT PREFACE(245)	CRY OF THE SOUL IS " DONT TELL ME: I DONT WANT TO	KNOW	," AND WHERE FRANTIC DENIALS AND FURIOUS SUPPRESSIONS
DOCT PREFACE(69)	NEVER ONCE DARING TO SAY EITHER " I DONT	KNOW	," OR " I DONT AGREE," FOR THE STRENGTH OF THE
FABL VI (124)	THINGS ALWAYS ASK IT, AND WILL NOT TAKE " I DONT	KNOW	" FOR AN ANSWER. CAN ANY OF YOU TELL ME THE STORY OF
DOCT PREFACE(78)	SAINTS, THEY ARE NOTHING BUT EMPIRICS WHO SAY " I	KNOW	" INSTEAD OF " I AM LEARNING," AND PRAY FOR CREDULITY
GETT PREFACE(245)	FACED. IN THIS PARTICULAR CASE " I DONT WANT TO	KNOW	" TAKES A RIGHTEOUS AIR, AND BECOMES " I DONT WANT TO
BULL IV (159)	AFFAIRS YOU DONT UNDERSTAND AND PEOPLE YOU DONT	KNOW	! AND YET WHAT ELSE HAVE I TO WRITE ABOUT? I BEGIN A
MRS II (201)	(SITTING UP IN SOME CONSTERNATION) I SAY, YOU	KNOW	! COME! /REV. S./ (RISING, STARTLED OUT OF HIS
MTH2 (48)	IT TO A RIGHT HONORABLE. BUT THE STRAND, YOU	KNOW	! DO COME OFF IT. /FRANKLYN/ YOU MUST EXCUSE MY
BULL I (93)	IT'S ALL TOMMY ROT; BUT IT'S SO BRILLIANT, YOU	KNOW	! HOW THE DICKENS DO YOU THINK OF SUCH THINGS! YOU
DEST (165)	TABLE BY THE LIEUTENANT) I BRAVE! HOW LITTLE YOU	KNOW	! I HAVE SPENT THE DAY IN AN AGONY OF FEAR. I HAVE A
CAND II (113)	/MORELL/ (VERY GRAVELY) SO MANY THAT YOU DONT	KNOW	! (MORE AGGRESSIVELY) WHEN THERES ANYTHING
BARB I (261)	/LOMAX/ (STILL REMONSTRANT) BUT REALLY, DONT YOU	KNOW	! OH I SAY! /LADY BRITOMART/ (FRIGIDLY) WHAT DO YOU
CAND III (140)	/CANDIDA/ (WITH INFINITE REPROACH) YOU DONT	KNOW	! OH, JAMES! JAMES! (TO EUGENE, MUSINGLY) I WONDER
DEST (158)	/NAPOLEON/ (UNABLE TO BELIEVE HIS EARS) YOU DONT	KNOW	! /LIEUTENANT/ NO MORE THAN YOU DO, GENERAL. NOW I
PRES (134)	BUT YOU CANT SHOOT THEM DOWN! WOMEN, YOU	KNOW	! /MITCHENER/ (STRADDLING CONFIDENTLY) YES YOU CAN.
MTH3 (112)	DO YOU KNOW? /BARNABAS/ (TAKEN ABACK) HOW DO I	KNOW	! /THE ARCHBISHOP/ YES: HOW DO YOU KNOW? I DID NOT
BARB III (344)	STRONGLY REMONSTRANT) YOUR OWN DAUGHTER, YOU	KNOW	! /UNDERSHAFT/ SO I SEE. (TO CUSINS) WELL, MY FRIEND,
LIED (188)	/HE/ BUT HOW WILL THEY KNOW? /SHE/ HOW WILL THEY	KNOW	! WHY, MY NAME IS ALL OVER THEM: MY SILLY, UNHAPPY
GENV IV (94)	/SIR O./ I DONT KNOW. /BATTLER/ /BBDE/ YOU DONT	KNOW	! ! ! /SIR O./ I DONT KNOW. NOR DO YOU, MR BATTLER.

			KNOWED	
PYGM I	(212)	BLAST. /THE SARCASTIC BYSTANDER/ THERE! I	KNOWED	HE WAS A PLAIN-CLOTHES COPPER. /THE BYSTANDER/ THAT
			KNOWEST	
SHAK	(139)	RIVALLING MINE? /SHAV/ NAY, WHO ART THOU, THAT	KNOWEST	NOT THESE FEATURES PICTURED THROUGHOUT THE GLOBE?
			KNOWETH	
LION PREFACE	(39)	OF LUKE. INDEED, THE JEWS SAY OF HIM " HOW	KNOWETH	THIS MAN LETTERS, HAVING NEVER LEARNT? " JOHN THE
			KNOWING	
SUPR III	(132)	ON THE WORK." /THE DEVIL/ WHAT IS THE USE OF	KNOWING	? /DON JUAN/ WHY, TO BE ABLE TO CHOOSE THE LINE OF
DEST	SD(150)	EMIGRATION AS AFORESAID; PARTLY BY HIS FACULTY OF	KNOWING	A COUNTRY, WITH ALL ITS ROADS, RIVERS, HILLS AND
O'FL	(224)	AMONG HEATHENS AND PAGANS AND SAVAGES, AND ME NOT	KNOWING	A WORD OF THEIR LANGUAGE NOR THEM OF MINE?
GENV IV	(114)	IT IS AGONY TO HAVE TO LISTEN TO ALL THIS TALK,	KNOWING	AS I DO THAT NOTHING CAN COME OF IT. HAVE PITY ON
GETT	(333)	HAUGHTILY) AND PRAY HOW DOES THAT PREVENT ME FROM	KNOWING	AS MUCH ABOUT MEN AND WOMEN AS PEOPLE WHO HAVE NO
GETT PREFACE	(231)	QUITE AS TOUCHINGLY AS WE) ARE MUCH MORE LIBERAL,	KNOWING	AS THEY DO THAT MONOGAMY WILL TAKE CARE OF ITSELF
ROCK II	(282)	REMIND ME THAT IT WAS ALL HOT AIR, I COULDNT HELP	KNOWING	AS WELL AS ANY OF THOSE DAMNED SOCIALISTS THAT
GETT PREFACE	(217)	IF YOU GET INTO THE PAPERS, THE PRETENCE OF NOT	KNOWING	BECOMES IMPOSSIBLE. BUT IT IS HARDLY TOO MUCH TO SAY
INCA PREFACE	(231)	I KNEW BETTER; AND I HAVE REPRESENTED CAESAR AS	KNOWING	BETTER HIMSELF. BUT IT WAS ONE OF THE QUAINTNESSES
MIS. PREFACE	(61)	THAT THE PROGRESS OF THE WORLD DEPENDS ON YOUR	KNOWING	BETTER THAN YOUR ELDERS, ARE JUST AS IMPORTANT AS
FABL VI	(129)	LIKE ALL YOUNG THINGS YOU WANT TO BEGIN BY	KNOWING	EVERYTHING. I CAN GIVE YOU ONLY THE ADVICE OF THE
LION II	(135)	FOOL! (HE BITES HIS LIPS IRRESOLUTELY, NOT	KNOWING	EXACTLY WHAT TO DO). /ANDROCLES/ (TO FERROVIUS)
CAPT II	(260)	HE HAD A FELLOW FEELING FOR THE THIEF,	KNOWING	HE WAS A THIEF HIMSELF. DO YOU FORGET THAT HE SENT
FANY III	(305)	BUT I DO THINK IT'S NOT QUITE THE SAME THING MY	KNOWING	HER AND YOU KNOWING HER. /DORA/ OF COURSE IT ISNT,
FANY III	(306)	NOT QUITE THE SAME THING MY KNOWING HER AND YOU	KNOWING	HER. /DORA/ OF COURSE IT ISNT, OLD MAN. (TO
MIS.	(178)	TARLETON'S CONDUCT, SINCE I HAVE HAD THE HONOR OF	KNOWING	HER, HAS BEEN, I NEED HARDLY SAY, IN EVERY RESPECT
MTH4 I	(159)	KNOWING IT. /ZOO/ WELL, YOU CAN SEE A MAN WITHOUT	KNOWING	HIM, CAN YOU NOT? /THE ELDERLY GENTLEMAN/ (
JOAN 3	(88)	YOU INTO THE RIVER. /THE PAGE/ (NOT AFRAID,	KNOWING	HIS MAN) IT LOOKED FRIGHTFULLY JOLLY, THAT FLASH OF
PYGM EPILOG	(298)	LIFE SUDDENLY BEGAN TO MOVE WITH HER. WITHOUT	KNOWING	HOW OR WHY, SHE BEGAN TO MAKE FRIENDS AND ENEMIES.
ROCK II	(267)	I'M SO HORRIBLY HARD UP FOR POCKET MONEY WITHOUT	KNOWING	HOW TO DO WITHOUT IT THAT IVE LOST ALL MY
2TRU III	(97)	BEING DIRTY AND DRUNKEN AND DISHONEST, AND NOT	KNOWING	HOW TO READ AND WRITE. BUT I DIDNT KNOW THAT THE
MIS. PREFACE	(92)	YOU ARE SO CAREFUL OF YOUR BOY'S MORALS,	KNOWING	HOW TROUBLESOME THEY MAY BE, THAT YOU KEEP HIM AWAY
MIS. PREFACE	(20)	BREAD. YOU HAVE NOT EVEN THE SATISFACTION OF	KNOWING	HOW YOU ARE TORTURING HIM AND HOW HE LOATHES YOU;
ARMS III	(55)	WITH THE DOCUMENTS IN HIS HAND). /LOUKA/ (	KNOWING	INSTINCTIVELY THAT SHE CAN ANNOY RAINA BY
MIS. PREFACE	(16)	AND CRUEL AS CHILDREN NECESSARILY ARE WITHOUT	KNOWING	IT OR MEANING IT, CANNOT BE CALLED NATURAL: IN FACT
SUPR HANDBOK	(188)	HE ACTUALLY DOES IT HIMSELF EVERY DAY WITHOUT	KNOWING	IT. HE WILL THEREFORE MAKE NO OBJECTION TO THE
DOCT III	(154)	HAD EVEN A LITTLE BEAUTY: DONT THINK ME VAIN FOR	KNOWING	IT. I KNEW THAT MEN OF GENIUS ALWAYS HAD A TERRIBLE
MTH4 I	(159)	CAN BE AWARE OF THE EXISTENCE OF A THING WITHOUT	KNOWING	IT. /ZOO/ WELL, YOU CAN SEE A MAN WITHOUT KNOWING
DOCT PREFACE	(61)	CANNOT MAKE HIM CHANGE HIS DAILY HABITS WITHOUT	KNOWING	IT. THE REFORMS ALSO COME FROM THE LAITY. IN THE
SUPR IV	(158)	HIS BROKEN HEART AND DELICATE ATTITUDE WITHOUT	KNOWING	IT) I DONT DOUBT THAT. YOU WILL ENRAPTURE HIM
MRS PREFACE	(166)	HAVE BEEN DRIVING AT FOR A LONG TIME PAST WITHOUT	KNOWING	IT) IS FAR LESS HOPEFUL THAN MY OWN DETERMINATION TO
SUPR III	(113)	COMMANDER, YOU WOULD ENJOY YOURSELF WITHOUT	KNOWING	IT, AND SO LOSE ALL THE FUN. /THE STATUE/ TRUE, MOST
LIED	(189)	HIM. THEY CAN DO IT TO HER VERY FACE WITHOUT HER	KNOWING	IT, BECAUSE THEY ALWAYS HAVE A LOT OF STUPID LOW
DEVL I	SD(3)	OF ANY SORT, AND IS CONSEQUENTLY, WITHOUT	KNOWING	IT, THE MOST LICENTIOUS WOMAN IN THE PARISH ON THE
PHIL I	(92)	WHAT HAS BEEN GOING ON HERE? I INSIST ON	KNOWING	. GRACE HAS NOT GONE TO BED: I HAVE SEEN AND SPOKEN
MILL I	(139)	PREFERS HER TO YOU SHE MUST BE INDEED WORTH	KNOWING	. I SHALL CERTAINLY MAKE HIM INTRODUCE ME.
HART I	(75)	ALLOWED WITHIN ARMS LENGTH OF ANY WOMAN WORTH	KNOWING	. /HECTOR/ I SEE. YOU ARE NEITHER A BOHEMIAN WOMAN
GENV III	(78)	LADY, WHOSE NAME I HAVE NOT THE PLEASURE OF	KNOWING	. /THE JEW/ TRY DOLORES. /THE WIDOW/ I SUPPOSE YOU
LION PREFACE	(46)	MILES WAS THE PROPER DISTANCE. THE KAISER,	KNOWING	JUST AS LITTLE ABOUT IT AS THE CONQUEROR, WOULD SEND
MIS. PREFACE	(98)	WORK OF ART AS WELL; TO KNOW IT WAS BETTER THAN	KNOWING	NO ART, WHICH ALSO WAS THE PRACTICAL ALTERNATIVE. IT
SUPR III	(91)	WE WERE ALIVE; AND WE STILL THINK IN THAT WAY,	KNOWING	NO OTHER, BUT WE CAN APPEAR TO ONE ANOTHER AT WHAT
FANY III	(319)	DOWNSTAIRS, AND WE HAVING A PARTY UP HERE AND	KNOWING	NOTHING ABOUT IT? /JUGGINS/ YES, SIR. I HAVE TO DO
CAPT II	(256)	FOR HIS MOTHER. SHE WAS AN UNEDUCATED BRAZILIAN,	KNOWING	NOTHING OF ENGLISH SOCIETY, AND DRIVEN MAD BY
ROCK PREFACE	(180)	GO ON FROM HORROR TO HORROR BREATHLESSLY,	KNOWING	NOTHING OF THE CONSTITUTIONAL QUESTIONS AT ISSUE.
FANY PREFACE	(255)	NO OTHER REASON THAN THAT OTHER PEOPLE DO IT, AND	KNOWING	NOTHING OF GOOD AND EVIL, OF COURAGE AND COWARDICE,
JITT II	(42)	OH, YOURE THERE. /JITTA/ WHAT IS THE MATTER? (	KNOWING	ONLY TOO WELL, AND VERY ANGRY AT HIS CONTEMPTUOUS
CATH PREFACE	(153)	TAKE THE NAME OF LIBERALISM IN VAIN WITHOUT	KNOWING	OR CARING ENOUGH ABOUT ITS MEANING EVEN TO TALK AND
LADY PREFACE	(234)	SHYLOCK, AND FORBES ROBERTSON'S HAMLET WITHOUT	KNOWING	OR CARING HOW MUCH THESE HAD TO DO WITH CRIED" WAS
PLES PREFACE	(R15)	THAT I HAVE NO GRIEVANCE AGAINST OUR THEATRES.	KNOWING	QUITE WELL WHAT I WAS DOING, I HAVE HEAPED
SUPR II	SD(62)	EXTREMELY DIFFICULT TO DECIDE WHETHER HE IS WORTH	KNOWING	; FOR WHILST HIS COMPANY IS UNDENIABLY PLEASANT AND
LADY	(238)	MASTER WARDER: IS IT NOT A STRANGE THING THAT WE,	KNOWING	THAT ALL WOMEN ARE FALSE, SHOULD BE AMAZED TO FIND
SUPR PREFACE	(R37)	AND THOUGHTFUL WRITER." AND THE ORDINARY CITIZEN,	KNOWING	THAT AN AUTHOR WHO IS WELL SPOKEN OF BY A
DOCT PREFACE	(64)	IF HE HAS NO ASSISTANT, OFTEN DOES NOT UNDRESS,	KNOWING	THAT HE WILL BE CALLED UP BEFORE HE HAS SNATCHED AN
POSN PREFACE	(403)	THINKS TWICE BEFORE HE REFUSES A LICENCE,	KNOWING	THAT HIS REFUSAL IS FINAL AND MAY PROMPTLY BE MADE
HART I	(44)	LADY/ WAITING FOR SOMEBODY TO SHEW SOME SIGNS OF	KNOWING	THAT I HAVE BEEN INVITED HERE. /THE WOMANSERVANT/
METH PREFACE	(R20)	MIND IN THE LEAST: I KNEW PERFECTLY WELL, WITHOUT	KNOWING	THAT I KNEW IT, THAT THE VALIDITY OF A STORY IS NOT
SUPR PREFACE	(R39)	AND OBLIGED. BUT I NEVER DREAM OF REFORMING,	KNOWING	THAT I MUST TAKE MYSELF AS I AM AND GET WHAT WORK I
CLEO II	(134)	COULD YOU NOT PERSUADE HIM TO ASK ME-- WITHOUT	KNOWING	THAT I WANTED HIM TO? /CAESAR/ (TOUCHED BY HER
ANNA	(300)	OF ME, OF ME! STANDING THERE FOR YOU TO GAPE AT,	KNOWING	THAT I WAS NO GODDESS, BUT ONLY A GIRL LIKE ANY
MIS. PREFACE	(65)	US MRS HEEP TEACHING HER SON TO " BE UMBLE,"	KNOWING	THAT IF HE CARRIED OUT THAT PRECEPT HE MIGHT BE
GENV IV	(125)	TO SELL GILT-EDGED IN ANY QUANTITY, AT ANY PRICE,	KNOWING	THAT IF THIS STORY GETS ABOUT BEFORE SETTLING DAY HE
MIS. PREFACE	(42)	RUMBUSTIOUS PONY WITH LITTLE SPURS ON MY HEELS (	KNOWING	THAT IN MY AGITATION I WOULD USE THEM
MIS. PREFACE	(3)	EONS AND FOR EVER AFTER, WE DIE VOLUNTARILY,	KNOWING	THAT IT IS TIME FOR US TO BE SCRAPPED, TO BE
GETT	(300)	BRINGING UP HER CHILDREN BY HER OWN WORK, AND	KNOWING	THAT JUST WHEN THEY WERE GROWN UP AND BEGINNING
JOAN 6	(131)	AND BECAUSE THE PEOPLE HAVE YIELDED THEM UP,	KNOWING	THAT THE HOLY OFFICE WOULD DEAL WITH THEM. BEFORE
O'FL PREFACE	(202)	AND EVEN, IF NO BETTER MAY BE, FOR ENGLAND.	KNOWING	THAT THE IGNORANCE AND INSULARITY OF THE IRISHMAN IS
BULL IV	(177)	DESTRUCTION. BUT HE COMES TO BROWSE HERE WITHOUT	KNOWING	THAT THE SOIL HIS HOOF TOUCHES IS HOLY GROUND.
2TRU PREFACE	(24)	BUT THEY WOULD GAIN THE ADVANTAGE OF AT LEAST	KNOWING	THAT THEIR RULERS KNOW HOW TO READ AND WRITE, WHICH
OVER	(173)	OF MEETING IT ON EVERY BEAUTIFUL WOMAN, AND	KNOWING	THAT THERE IS A HUSBAND ROUND THE CORNER? I HAVE
MTH5	(206)	NOT AT ALL. YOU REPEAT THAT OLD PHRASE WITHOUT	KNOWING	THAT THERE WAS ONCE A CREATURE ON EARTH CALLED A
KING PREFACE	(158)	OF THEM ARE FOR GIVING ALL POWER TO THE MEN,	KNOWING	THAT THEY CAN GET ROUND THEM WITHOUT BEING HAMPERED
SUPR I	(24)	FROM THEM, TO SURPRISE THEIR INMOST SECRETS,	KNOWING	THAT THEY HAVE THE POWER TO ROUSE HIS DEEPEST
POSN PREFACE	(428)	OPPOSITION FROM THE MANAGER. FOR THE MANAGER,	KNOWING	THAT THREE OF MY PLAYS HAVE BEEN REFUSED A LICENCE,
DEST	(168)	COME SAFELY OUT WITH THAT LETTER IN YOUR HAND,	KNOWING	THAT WHEN THE HOUR CAME, YOUR FEAR HAD TIGHTENED,
MILL PREFACE	(133)	WITH THE HIGHEST ACADEMIC HONORS WITHOUT	KNOWING	THE DIFFERENCE BETWEEN A CHANTY AND A SYMPHONY, A
BULL PREFACE	(37)	OF THE ORDINARY ENGLISHMAN, WHO, INSTEAD OF	KNOWING	THE DISTINCTIVE TENETS OF HIS CHURCH OR SECT,
MIS. PREFACE	(85)	OR BROTHERS OR SISTERS, PASSES THEM BY WITHOUT	KNOWING	THEM. AND FOR SUCH A VIEW THERE IS THIS TO BE SAID:
CLEO PRO2,SD	(95)	THAT JULIUS CAESAR IS INVADING HIS COUNTRY. NOT	KNOWING	THIS, IS INTENT ON HIS GAME WITH THE PERSIAN, WHOM,
MIS. PREFACE	(66)	OF A CLEVER WIFE WHO REPUDIATES VOTES FOR WOMEN,	KNOWING	WELL THAT WHILST THE MAN IS MASTER, THE MAN'S
JITT III	(74)	OF DIVORCING HER AT PRESENT. /EDITH/ (NOT	KNOWING	WHAT ELSE TO SAY) IT WASNT THAT. MRS LENKHEIM NEVER
MRS III	(232)	AND I ADMITTED YOU JUST NOW TO THE FAMILIARITY OF	KNOWING	WHAT I THINK OF YOU. /CROFTS/ (WITH SERIOUS
MIS. PREFACE	(24)	GREAT TEACHERS, IS THE COMPLETEST OF TYRANTS,	KNOWING	WHAT IS RIGHT AND THAT HE MUST AND WILL HAVE THE
PYGM I	(209)	WHAT IS WRONG WITH HER. A REMOTER GROUP, NOT	KNOWING	WHAT THE MATTER IS, CROWD IN AND INCREASE THE NOISE
MILL PREFACE	(121)	THE FACT STARING THEM IN THE FACE THAT IL DUCE,	KNOWING	WHAT THE PEOPLE WANTED AND GIVING IT TO THEM, WAS
GETT	(314)	THERES THE YOUNG THINGS THAT MARRY FOR LOVE, NOT	KNOWING	WHAT THEYRE DOING, AND THE OLD THINGS THAT MARRY FOR
BULL I	(88)	YOULL FIND ALL THAT CHAFFING AND DRINKING AND NOT	KNOWING	WHAT TO BE AT IN PECKHAM JUST THE SAME AS IN
FANY II	(286)	AWAY HER HANDKERCHIEF) IT ONLY ENDS IN OUR NOT	KNOWING	WHAT TO BELIEVE. MRS GILBEY TOLD ME BOBBY WAS IN
ROCK PREFACE	(169)	AND COMFORTABLE TUTELAGE AND ROUTINE, NOT	KNOWING	WHAT TO DO WITH THEMSELVES WHEN AT LIBERTY. A LIFE
JITT II	(28)	BY ALL SORTS OF SURMISES AND SUSPICIONS, NOT	KNOWING	WHAT TO THINK, ASKING HERSELF EVERY MINUTE WHETHER
DEVL III	(59)	MEAN TO SAY THAT YOUVE BROUGHT ME HERE WITHOUT	KNOWING	WHO I AM? /SWINDON/ AS A MATTER OF FORM, SIR, GIVE
NEVR IV	(295)	THIS IS SOMETHING REALLY SERIOUS. I INSIST ON	KNOWING	WHO MISS CLANDON SAID THAT TO. /DOLLY/ PERHAPS PHIL
BULL PREFACE	(66)	POSSIBLY TURN ON HIM AND REND HIM, ALSO WITHOUT	KNOWING	WHY. THE ONE THING THEY WILL NOT DO IS TO BLAME
BULL PREFACE	(66)	IDOLIZED LORD CROMER AND LORD MILNER WITHOUT	KNOWING	WHY. THEY WILL NOW VERY POSSIBLY TURN ON HIM AND
BULL PREFACE	(66)	THEN, MEN OF BOTH PARTIES IDOLIZED HIM WITHOUT	KNOWING	WHY, JUST AS THEY HAD FORMERLY IDOLIZED LORD CROMER
MIS.	(152)	MAY I NOW ASK TO BE ALLOWED THE PLEASURE OF	KNOWING	YOUR NAME? /THE PASSENGER/ MY NAME IS LINA
GETT PREFACE	(193)	QUITE COMPLICATED SYSTEMS OF PAYING VISITS AND "	KNOWING	" ONE ANOTHER. THEY FELT A LITTLE VULGAR WHEN THEY

KNOWINGLY

2TRU II	(55)	THAT UNDER THE ARTICLES OF WAR ANY SOLDIER WHO	KNOWINGLY	DOES WHEN ON ACTIVE SERVICE ANY ACT CALCULATED TO
JITT I	(19)	BINDS MY SENSE OF HONOR AS IF HE SPARED US	KNOWINGLY	. /JITTA/ (CHANGING HER TONE, AND TRYING TO
PHIL II	(106)	MAN WHO MIGHT NEARLY BE YOUR FATHER? /SYLVIA/ (	KNOWINGLY	) OH, I KNOW YOU, MY LAD. /CHARTERIS/ THEN YOU

KNOWLEDGABLE

O'FL	(211)	AS GOOD AS OURSELVES. THE BOSHES I KILT WAS MORE	KNOWLEDGABLE	MEN THAN ME: AND WHAT BETTER AM I NOW THAT IVE

KNOWLEDGE

SUPR HANDBOK	(219)	WHO KILLS TIME WITH STUDY. BEWARE OF HIS FALSE	KNOWLEDGE	: IT IS MORE DANGEROUS THAN IGNORANCE. ACTIVITY IS
WIDO III	(52)	IT TO YOU, SARTORIUS. IT WASNT MONEY: IT WAS	KNOWLEDGE	: KNOWLEDGE OF THE GREAT PUBLIC QUESTION OF THE
MTH2	(76)	AND OMNISCIENCE. GREATER POWER AND GREATER	KNOWLEDGE	: THESE ARE WHAT WE ARE ALL PURSUING EVEN AT THE
DOCT PREFACE	(37)	ON VIVISECTION IS NOT AN ATTACK ON THE RIGHT TO	KNOWLEDGE	: WHY, INDEED, THOSE WHO HAVE THE DEEPEST
DOCT PREFACE	(37)	REMAINS: DO WE ALL REALLY WISH TO BE SPARED THAT	KNOWLEDGE	? ARE HUMANE METHODS REALLY TO BE PREFERRED TO
MTH1 I	(16)	AND DESIRE MY DEATH. CAN YOU FIND A NAME FOR THAT	KNOWLEDGE	? /THE SERPENT/ JEALOUSY. JEALOUSY.
ARMS I	(11)	MANNER). COULD ANYONE HAVE GOT IN WITHOUT YOUR	KNOWLEDGE	? WERE YOU ASLEEP? /RAINA/ NO: I HAVE NOT BEEN
2TRU III	(89)	YOU OBJECTED. HOW COULD I HAVE DONE IT WITH YOUR	KNOWLEDGE	? YOU WOULD HAVE STOPPED MY ALLOWANCE. /THE
DOCT PREFACE	(35)	SOCIETY, " MAY I TORTURE MY MOTHER IN PURSUIT OF	KNOWLEDGE	? " SOCIETY REPLIES, " NO." IF HE PLEADS, "WHAT!
DOCT PREFACE	(50)	DESTROY THE WHOLE RACE IN TORMENT, ACQUIRING	KNOWLEDGE	ALL THE TIME FROM HIS HIGHLY INTERESTING
DOCT PREFACE	(50)	BY HIS OWN METHODS. THERE ARE MANY PATHS TO	KNOWLEDGE	ALREADY DISCOVERED; AND NO ENLIGHTENED MAN DOUBTS
SIM II	(85)	FOR MORE KNOWLEDGE AND MORE POWER, THOUGH THE NEW	KNOWLEDGE	ALWAYS CONTRADICTS THE OLD, AND THE NEW POWER IS
3PLA PREFACE	(R36)	FOUNDED ON A GENUINE SUPERIORITY OF TECHNICAL	KNOWLEDGE	AND APTITUDE: HE IS SOMETIMES A BETTER ANATOMICAL
BUOY PREFACE	(4)	BY SOMEBODY ELSE, BEING UNACCOUNTABLY BEYOND HIS	KNOWLEDGE	AND CAPACITY. WHO THAT SOMEBODY ELSE WAS IS THE
MIS. PREFACE	(25)	IT TOOK FOUR YEARS OF HARROW TO OBLITERATE THAT	KNOWLEDGE	AND CHANGE THE LOVE INTO LOATHING. ANOTHER FRIEND
SIM PREFACE	(3)	AND THE AUTHOR IS ASSUMING A HIGH DEGREE OF	KNOWLEDGE	AND CULTURE IN HIS AUDIENCE. THIS OCCURS OFTENER
JOAN 4	(103)	BE LIKE WHEN THE CHURCH'S ACCUMULATED WISDOM AND	KNOWLEDGE	AND EXPERIENCE, ITS COUNCILS OF LEARNED, VENERABLE
METH PREFACE	(R38)	SEE, IF NOT TO EXTEND HIS CONSCIOUSNESS AND HIS	KNOWLEDGE	AND HIS POWER? THAT PURPOSE WAS AT WORK
SIM II	(85)	THEN I, PRA, MUST CONTINUE TO STRIVE FOR MORE	KNOWLEDGE	AND MORE POWER, THOUGH THE NEW KNOWLEDGE ALWAYS
JOAN PREFACE	(14)	BY THE FACT THAT MEN WILL, IN THE PURSUIT OF	KNOWLEDGE	AND OF SOCIAL READJUSTMENTS FOR WHICH THEY WILL
JOAN PREFACE	(14)	THERE IS NO MORE MYSTERY ABOUT THIS APPETITE FOR	KNOWLEDGE	AND POWER THAN ABOUT THE APPETITE FOR FOOD: BOTH
FABL VI	(127)	AND POWER. /TEACHER/ YES; FOR THE PURSUIT OF	KNOWLEDGE	AND POWER INVOLVES THE SLAUGHTER AND DESTRUCTION
FABL VI	(127)	OUR THICK SKULLS IN THEIR CONTINUAL PURSUIT OF	KNOWLEDGE	AND POWER, SINCE THEY NEED OUR HANDS AND BRAINS AS
FABL VI	(127)	PUTS THAT INTO OUR HEADS? NOT THE PURSUIT OF	KNOWLEDGE	AND POWER. /TEACHER/ YES; FOR THE PURSUIT OF
FABL V	(121)	THEM ALL UP. WHAT THEN? /ROSE/ THE PURSUIT OF	KNOWLEDGE	AND POWER WILL NEVER END.
FABL V	(119)	WHICH ARE NORMAL WITH US IN OUR PURSUIT OF	KNOWLEDGE	AND POWER, AND CULMINATE IN OUR EXPLORATIONS AND
DEST	(192)	MIDDLE PEOPLE WHO ARE DANGEROUS: THEY HAVE BOTH	KNOWLEDGE	AND PURPOSE. BUT THEY, TOO, HAVE THEIR WEAK POINT.
MTH4 I	(157)	THEREFORE CAN BELIEVE NOTHING. WE CANNOT DISCLAIM	KNOWLEDGE	AND SHIRK RESPONSIBILITY. WE MUST PROCEED ON
DOCT III	(155)	SLOWLY) MRS DUBEDAT: DO YOU REALLY BELIEVE IN MY	KNOWLEDGE	AND SKILL AS YOU SAY YOU DO? /MRS DUBEDAT/
PHIL III	(132)	MATTER WITH YOU; SO THAT YOU MIGHT CALL OUT MY	KNOWLEDGE	AND SYMPATHY. AS IT IS, I CAN ONLY ADMIRE YOU, AND
MTH2	(83)	THERE IS FOR THEM TO DO. /CONRAD/ SPREAD THAT	KNOWLEDGE	AND THAT CONVICTION; AND AS SURELY AS THE SUN WILL
CLEO NOTES	(208)	ONLY SHEWS THE WIDE DIFFERENCE BETWEEN COMMON	KNOWLEDGE	AND THE INTELLECTUAL GAME CALLED SCIENCE. WE HAVE
PYGM IV	(267)	DAMN MY OWN FOLLY IN HAVING LAVISHED HARD-EARNED	KNOWLEDGE	AND THE TREASURE OF MY REGARD AND INTIMACY ON A
GENV II	(53)	SEE. /THE SECRETARY/ WERE YOU EXAMINED AS TO YOUR	KNOWLEDGE	AND UNDERSTANDING OF THE COVENANT OF THE LEAGUE,
DOCT PREFACE	(8)	RESULT OF HIS FORMER PRETENCES TO INFINITE	KNOWLEDGE	AND UNERRING SKILL. HE HAS TAUGHT THE JURY AND THE
O'FL	(222)	OVER YOU, CHILD, AT ALL AT ALL? /O'FLAHERTY/	KNOWLEDGE	AND WISDOM HAS COME OVER ME WITH PAIN AND FEAR AND
MIS. PREFACE	(45)	IT IS IN THE CONFLICT OF OPINION THAT WE WIN	KNOWLEDGE	AND WISDOM. HOWEVER TERRIBLE THE WOUNDS SUFFERED
FABL PREFACE	(78)	WHO BELIEVE THAT MY INCOME IS UNLIMITED, MY	KNOWLEDGE	AND WISDOM INFINITE, MY NAME A GUARANTEE OF
BUOY II	(25)	POUNDS FOR IT. /THE NATIVE/ IT IS IMPOSSIBLE.	KNOWLEDGE	AND WISDOM CANNOT BE PURCHASED LIKE FASHIONABLE
NEVR II	(258)	EXCUSE MY REMINDING YOU THAT YOUR REASON AND YOUR	KNOWLEDGE	AND YOUR EXPERIENCE ARE NOT INFALLIBLE. AT LEAST I
DOCT PREFACE	(51)	CONCEPTION OF WHAT SCIENCE MEANS. THE PATHS TO	KNOWLEDGE	ARE COUNTLESS. ONE OF THESE PATHS IS A PATH
FOUN	(215)	YET YOUR MATURE WISDOM AND UNPARALLELED LEGAL	KNOWLEDGE	ARE FREELY AT THE SERVICE OF ALL DESERVING
MRS PREFACE	(173)	AND POLITICALLY. BUT BOTH OBSERVATION AND	KNOWLEDGE	ARE LEFT BEHIND WHEN JOURNALISTS GO TO THE
METH PREFACE	(R16)	DO NOT EVEN KNOW THAT THERE IS SUCH A BRANCH OF	KNOWLEDGE	AS POLITICAL SCIENCE; BUT BETWEEN THEM THEY CAN
BULL PREFACE	(27)	DOCILE; HE IS REVERENT; HE IS CONTENT TO REGARD	KNOWLEDGE	AS SOMETHING NOT HIS BUSINESS; HE IS A CHILD
DOCT PREFACE	(37)	ONLY KNOWLEDGE WE LOSE BY FORBIDDING CRUELTY IS	KNOWLEDGE	AT FIRST HAND OF CRUELTY ITSELF, WHICH IS
DOCT PREFACE	(62)	USUAL CREDULITY AS TO THE MIRACULOUS POWERS AND	KNOWLEDGE	ATTRIBUTED TO THEM); AND THOUGH I KNOW THAT THERE
GETT PREFACE	(231)	A RELATION IS CREATED WHICH HAS NEVER TO MY	KNOWLEDGE	BEEN SHARED BY THREE PERSONS EXCEPT WHEN ALL THREE
KING I	(207)	HOW DO YOU COME TO KNOW THIS? THINGS COME TO MY	KNOWLEDGE	BY THE GRACE OF GOD; YET THE SAME THINGS HAVE COME
LION PREFACE	(15)	KNOW IT; BUT HIS INSTINCT SERVED HIM BETTER THAN	KNOWLEDGE	COULD HAVE DONE; FOR IT WAS INSTINCT RATHER THAN
SUPR I	(24)	OF OURSELVES; AND HE WHO ADDS A JOT TO SUCH	KNOWLEDGE	CREATES NEW MIND AS SURELY AS ANY WOMAN CREATES
METH PREFACE	(R88)	MY READERS. BUT I NEVER FORGOT THAT WITHOUT	KNOWLEDGE	EVEN WISDOM IS MORE DANGEROUS THAN MERE
DOCT PREFACE	(37)	TO ASSURE US THAT THERE IS NO OTHER KEY TO	KNOWLEDGE	EXCEPT CRUELTY. WHEN THE VIVISECTOR OFFERS US THAT
SUPR III	(132)	BRAIN-- A PHILOSOPHER'S BRAIN-- TO GRASP THIS	KNOWLEDGE	FOR ME AS THE HUSBANDMAN'S HAND GRASPS THE PLOUGH
ROCK PREFACE	(185)	IT FROM GOD. /PILATE/ I HAVE THE SAME SORT OF	KNOWLEDGE	FROM SEVERAL GODS. /JESUS/ IN SO FAR AS YOU KNOW
DOCT PREFACE	(50)	IT IS CLEAR THAT THE EXEMPTION OF THE PURSUIT OF	KNOWLEDGE	FROM THE LAWS OF HONOR IS THE MOST HIDEOUS
MIS. PREFACE	(27)	IS TAKEN TO KEEP SUCH BENEFICIALLY SUBVERSIVE	KNOWLEDGE	FROM US, WITH THE RESULT THAT IN PUBLIC LIFE WE
FANY III	(299)	REPEATEDLY, BUT NEVER WITH SUCCESS, AS FAR AS MY	KNOWLEDGE	GOES. /BOBBY/ YOU HAVE A DEVILISH COOL WAY OF
PYGM EPILOG	(295)	RIGHT, WITHOUT HIGGINS'S CONSENT, TO EXPLOIT THE	KNOWLEDGE	HE HAD GIVEN HER; FOR HIS KNOWLEDGE SEEMED TO HER
APPL PREFACE	(172)	SHARE OF DOMINATING ABILITY AND RELEVANT	KNOWLEDGE	HE IS HELPLESS IN THE HANDS OF HIS OFFICIALS. HE
DOCT PREFACE	(37)	HAND OF CRUELTY ITSELF, WHICH IS PRECISELY THE	KNOWLEDGE	HUMANE PEOPLE WISH TO BE SPARED. BUT THE QUESTION
SUPR HANDBOK	(228)	HYPOCRISY BECOMES GOOD TASTE. WHERE THERE IS NO	KNOWLEDGE	IGNORANCE CALLS ITSELF SCIENCE. IF THE WICKED
DOCT PREFACE	(78)	WITH US. BUT WE SHALL STILL PICK UP ALL OUR	KNOWLEDGE	IN PURSUIT OF SOME WILL O' THE WISP OR OTHER. WHAT
DOCT PREFACE	(33)	THAT IGNORANCE IS BLISS, AND THAT " A LITTLE	KNOWLEDGE	IS A DANGEROUS THING" (A LITTLE BEING THE MOST
GENV PREFACE	(16)	BUT I CAN INCREASE THEIR KNOWLEDGE. A LITTLE	KNOWLEDGE	IS A DANGEROUS THING; BUT WE MUST TAKE THAT RISK
DOCT PREFACE	(33)	IN THIS WAY FOR THE UNCONDITIONED PURSUIT OF	KNOWLEDGE	IS AS IDLE AS ALL DREAMS OF UNCONDITIONED
DOCT PREFACE	(37)	OF THAT RIGHT ARE THE LEADERS OF THE ATTACK. NO	KNOWLEDGE	IS FINALLY IMPOSSIBLE OF HUMAN ATTAINMENT; FOR
DOCT PREFACE	(34)	SUBJECTS TO PURSUE KNOWLEDGE ON THE GROUND THAT	KNOWLEDGE	IS IN ITSELF A BAD THING, OR THAT IT IS POSSIBLE
GETT PREFACE	(217)	SAY: TO WIT, THAT NO MARRIAGE OF WHICH I HAVE ANY	KNOWLEDGE	IS IN THE LEAST LIKE THE IDEAL MARRIAGE. I DO NOT
MILL IV	(206)	HE NEVER TOOK OUT A PATENT. HE BELIEVED THAT	KNOWLEDGE	IS NO MAN'S PROPERTY. AND HE HAD NEITHER TIME NOR
MILL II	(176)	CARE FOR MONEY: I CARE FOR KNOWLEDGE. /EPIFANIA/	KNOWLEDGE	IS NO USE WITHOUT MONEY. ARE YOU MARRIED? /THE
DOCT PREFACE	(34)	HIS OTHER RIGHTS AT THE SAME TIME. THE RIGHT TO	KNOWLEDGE	IS NOT THE ONLY RIGHT; AND ITS EXERCISE MUST BE
GETT	(333)	A THOUSAND PIECES, OR BOILED IN OIL. THAT SORT OF	KNOWLEDGE	IS OF NO USE TO ME. I'M AFRAID WE SHALL NEVER GET
MRS I	(196)	WITH THESE WORDS, WHICH I SHALL NEVER FORGET, "	KNOWLEDGE	IS POWER" SHE SAID; " AND I NEVER SELL POWER."
GENV PREFACE	(16)	CHANGE THEIR MINDS; BUT I CAN INCREASE THEIR	KNOWLEDGE	. A LITTLE KNOWLEDGE IS A DANGEROUS THING; BUT WE
FABL VI	(125)	WE DONT. THATS WHY. /TEACHER/ NO. WHY IS BEYOND	KNOWLEDGE	. ALL THE WHYS LEAD TO THE GREAT INTERROGATION
MTH4 I	(156)	PASSED AWAY THE IRISH RACE VANISHED FROM HUMAN	KNOWLEDGE	. AND THE DISPERSED JEWS DID THE SAME LEST THEY
DOCT PREFACE	(71)	VIVISECTOR, OR THE BEST WE CAN MAKE OF OUR REAL	KNOWLEDGE	. BUT I MAY REMIND THOSE WHO CONFUSEDLY IMAGINE
MTH4 I	(161)	IT WORKED ON THINGS OF WHICH IT HAD SOME REAL	KNOWLEDGE	. BUT IMAGINATION WITH MICROSCOPES, WORKING ON A
DOCT PREFACE	(34)	HAVE TOO MUCH OF IT. LIMITATIONS OF THE RIGHT TO	KNOWLEDGE	. BUT NEITHER DOES ANY GOVERNMENT EXEMPT THE
DOCT PREFACE	(32)	WOULD BE GONE. THE HIGHER MOTIVE. THE TREE OF	KNOWLEDGE	. BUT THE GREATEST FORCE OF ALL ON THE SIDE OF
SUPR HANDBOK	(219)	THAN IGNORANCE. ACTIVITY IS THE ONLY ROAD TO	KNOWLEDGE	. EVERY FOOL BELIEVES WHAT HIS TEACHERS TELL HIM,
POSN	(452)	DIDNT STEAL IT? /BLANCO/ I DONT KNOW OF MY OWN	KNOWLEDGE	. I ONLY ARGUE THAT IF THE HORSE HAD BEEN WORTH
DOCT PREFACE	(33)	BE INDUCED TO PLUCK THE APPLE FROM THE TREE OF	KNOWLEDGE	. I SHOULD HAVE SWALLOWED EVERY APPLE ON THE TREE
MTH1 I	(5)	MOVING ABOUT IN HIS AGITATION) I CANNOT BEAR THIS	KNOWLEDGE	. I WILL NOT HAVE IT. IT MUST NOT BE, I TELL YOU.
SUPR HANDBOK	(219)	ITS AUTHOR ATTAINS IMPARTIAL JUDGMENT AND PERFECT	KNOWLEDGE	. IF A HORSE COULD WAIT AS LONG FOR ITS SHOES AND
MIS. PREFACE	(40)	AND AS STRONG AS SANDOW. THE REWARDS AND RISKS OF	KNOWLEDGE	. IN A WORD, WE CANNOT COMPLETELY EDUCATE A CHILD;
DOCT PREFACE	(34)	IT IS JUST SO IN THE CASE OF THE RIGHT TO	KNOWLEDGE	. IT IS A RIGHT THAT IS AS YET VERY IMPERFECTLY
FANY III	(318)	I BELIEVE SO, SIR. I CANT SAY FROM PERSONAL	KNOWLEDGE	. IT WAS BEFORE MY TIME. /GILBEY/ WELL BUT LOOK
CAND I	(83)	LOOK AT CANDIDA BEFORE SHE GROWS OUT OF HIS	KNOWLEDGE	. (HE RESIGNS HIMSELF TO THE INEVITABLE, AND GOES
MILL II	(176)	DOCTOR/ NO. I DO NOT CARE FOR MONEY: I CARE FOR	KNOWLEDGE	. /EPIFANIA/ KNOWLEDGE IS NO USE WITHOUT MONEY.
BUOY II	(25)	TRUTHFULLY ONLY OUT OF ONE'S OWN WISDOM AND	KNOWLEDGE	. /HE/ NOT AT OXFORD. UNLESS YOU ARE A HUNDRED
LION I	(116)	IT WAS NO USE; BUT ONE TRIES IN SPITE OF ONE'S	KNOWLEDGE	. /LAVINIA/ SOMETHING STIRS, EVEN IN THE IRON
SIM II	(64)	THE BURDEN OF THOUGHT. /VASHTI/ THE BURDEN OF	KNOWLEDGE	. /MAYA/ THE BURDEN OF RIGHTEOUSNESS. /VASHTI/ THE
GENV III	(80)	SPIRIT OF GENEVA. WHAT YOU LACK IS NOT MIND BUT	KNOWLEDGE	. /THE NEWCOMER/ MY WIFE SAYS I'M PIGHEADED. HOW
MTH4 I	(159)	ALL I CAN GRANT YOU IS THAT THEY INCREASED OUR	KNOWLEDGE	. /ZOO/ NONSENSE! CONSCIOUSNESS OF A FACT IS NOT
LIED	(199)	THATS NOT A FACT. I CAME BY THEM WITHOUT HER	KNOWLEDGE	. SHE DIDNT SHEW THEM TO ME. /HE/ DOES NOT THAT

DOCT PREFACE(51)	ALL THE OTHER PROFESSIONS ARE DOING: NAMELY, MORE	KNOWLEDGE	. THE JURIES WHICH SEND THE POOR PECULIARS TO
DOCT PREFACE(51)	BECAUSE IT IS INDISPENSABLE TO THE FULNESS OF HIS	KNOWLEDGE	. THOU ART THE MAN. I SHALL NOT BE AT ALL
LION PREFACE(90)	APPERTAINING TO DIVINITY THAT IS WITHIN THEIR	KNOWLEDGE	. THUS THE GOSPELS AS MEMOIRS AND SUGGESTIVE
FANY PROLOG (264)	BANNAL'S KNOWLEDGE OF THE THEATRE IS AN INSIDE	KNOWLEDGE	. WE KNOW HIM; AND HE KNOWS US. HE KNOWS THE
MTH2 (71)	THAT IS MERE ENERGY WITHOUT INTELLECT AND WITHOUT	KNOWLEDGE	. YOUR MIND IS NOT A TRAINED MIND: IT HAS NOT BEEN
DOCT PREFACE(35)	WITHOUT TORTURING A DOG, YOU MUST DO WITHOUT	KNOWLEDGE	," A FALSE ALTERNATIVE. BUT IN PRACTICE YOU CANNOT
DOCT PREFACE(50)	DISCOVERED. THE TRUTH IS, IF THE ACQUISITION OF	KNOWLEDGE	JUSTIFIES EVERY SORT OF CONDUCT, IT JUSTIFIES ANY
BARB PREFACE(242)	TO ADMINISTER ANY LAW THAT IS BASED ON IDEAS OR	KNOWLEDGE	LESS THAN HALF A CENTURY OLD, THEY DISAGREE WITH
METH PREFACE(R88)	TO MAKE A VERBAL DISTINCTION BETWEEN SCIENCE AND	KNOWLEDGE	LEST I SHOULD MISLEAD MY READERS. BUT I NEVER
DOCT PREFACE(34)	THAT PARTICULAR ADDITION TO THE STORE OF HUMAN	KNOWLEDGE	MAY BE. A MAN WHO DID SO WOULD HAVE SHORT WORK
DOCT PREFACE(33)	ACTIVITY; BUT NONE THE LESS THE RIGHT TO	KNOWLEDGE	MUST BE REGARDED AS A FUNDAMENTAL HUMAN RIGHT. THE
DOCT PREFACE(34)	IT IS ADMITTED THAT AN ADULT PERSON IN PURSUIT OF	KNOWLEDGE	MUST NOT BE REFUSED IT ON THE GROUND THAT HE WOULD
MTH2 (69)	BEGINNING TO HAVE A GLIMMER OF THE WISDOM AND	KNOWLEDGE	NEEDED FOR THEIR OWN GOVERNMENT. /LUBIN/ QUITE AN
PYGM EPILOG (300)	THREE PARTS DID NOT CARRY WITH IT THE SLIGHTEST	KNOWLEDGE	OF ACCOUNTS OR BUSINESS: COLONEL PICKERING HAD TO
MIS. PREFACE(93)	AN IMPARTIALLY COMMUNICATED HISTORICAL OBJECTIVE	KNOWLEDGE	OF ALL THE CREEDS AND CHURCHES. JUST AS A CHILD,
JOAN PREFACE(10)	SHE MUST HAVE HAD A DIVINE REVELATION. THIS	KNOWLEDGE	OF AND INTEREST IN PUBLIC AFFAIRS WAS NOTHING
PYGM EPILOG (300)	SAVE MONEY BY ENGAGING A BOOKKEEPER WITH SOME	KNOWLEDGE	OF BUSINESS. HOW, THEY ARGUED, COULD YOU POSSIBLY
MIS. PREFACE(25)	FRIENDS WAS LED TO GENUINE LOVE AND CONSIDERABLE	KNOWLEDGE	OF CLASSICAL LITERATURE BY AN IRISH SCHOOLMASTER
METH PREFACE(R87)	THERE IS NO TRACE IN HIS PLAYS OF ANY FAITH IN OR	KNOWLEDGE	OF CREATIVE EVOLUTION AS A MODERN SCIENTIFIC FACT.
GETT PREFACE(192)	ARTICLES INFORMED BY AT LEAST SOME PRETENCE OF	KNOWLEDGE	OF ECONOMICS, HISTORY, AND CONSTITUTIONAL LAW,
BULL PREFACE(65)	PERSONAL AND SOCIAL CREDENTIALS, AND AN INTIMATE	KNOWLEDGE	OF EGYPT AND THE EGYPTIANS, CAN FIND IT IN MR
FANY III (322)	OH FATHER: HOW CAN YOU? /DUVALLET/ I'M AFRAID MY	KNOWLEDGE	OF ENGLISH IS NOT ENOUGH TO UNDERSTAND.
METH PREFACE(R57)	BROUGHT INTENSE RELIEF AS WELL AS AN ENLARGED	KNOWLEDGE	OF FACTS TO THE HUMANITARIANS. HE DESTROYED THE
MTH5 (260)	I AM JUSTIFIED. FOR I CHOSE WISDOM AND THE	KNOWLEDGE	OF GOOD AND EVIL; AND NOW THERE IS NO EVIL; AND
LION PREFACE(4)	CORRUPT THAT ORDER MIGHT BE, BY PEOPLE WITH NO	KNOWLEDGE	OF GOVERNMENT AND NO POWER TO CONSTRUCT POLITICAL
LADY PREFACE(210)	HIM REVEREND. IT MAY VERY WELL BE THAT HE GOT HIS	KNOWLEDGE	OF HEBREW IN READING FOR THE CHURCH; AND THERE WAS
MIS. PREFACE(80)	HEAVENS, IT DOES NOT MATTER WHICH AS FAR AS ONE'S	KNOWLEDGE	OF HER IS CONCERNED: THE BROOMSTICK IS THERE AND
CLEO NOTES (209)	ASK DOES ANYONE WHO, IN THE LIGHT OF A COMPETENT	KNOWLEDGE	OF HIS OWN AGE, HAS STUDIED HISTORY FROM
ARMS II (31)	STABLE KEEPER; AND HE OWED HIS FIRST STEP TO HIS	KNOWLEDGE	OF HORSE-DEALING. (WITH MOCK ENTHUSIASM) AH, HE
MILL IV (195)	UNFORTUNATELY I HAVE NEITHER YOUR MUSCLE NOR YOUR	KNOWLEDGE	OF HOW TO PUNCH. BUT I WILL TAKE LESSONS WHEN I
DEST SD(149)	PRODIGIOUS POWERS OF WORK, AND A CLEAR REALISTIC	KNOWLEDGE	OF HUMAN NATURE IN PUBLIC AFFAIRS, HAVING SEEN IT
NEVR I (217)	AND THE ENGLISH VARIETY, DOLL. TRUST MY	KNOWLEDGE	OF HUMAN NATURE. (HE RESUMES HIS POSITION ON THE
NEVR I (207)	A LOT OF MONEY, THOUGH. /PHILIP/ I DOUBT IT. MY	KNOWLEDGE	OF HUMAN NATURE LEADS ME TO BELIEVE THAT IF HE HAD
NEVR I (203)	MAKE TO YOU? /PHILIP/ (MATURELY) NO, DOLLY: MY	KNOWLEDGE	OF HUMAN NATURE CONFIRMS MR VALENTINE'S JUDGMENT.
NEVR I (211)	DEAL LATELY; AND I DONT THINK, JUDGING FROM MY	KNOWLEDGE	OF HUMAN NATURE-- WE DONT THINK THAT YOU (
NEVR I (213)	AND BREAD AND BUTTER FOR A FORTNIGHT PAST. NOW MY	KNOWLEDGE	OF HUMAN NATURE LEADS ME TO BELIEVE THAT WE HAD A
NEVR II (230)	WELL, SO HE IS: IT'S NOT OUR FAULT. /PHILIP/ MY	KNOWLEDGE	OF HUMAN NATURE IS FAIRLY EXTENSIVE, MR M'COMAS;
NEVR II (231)	I HOPE IT WILL DESERVE IT, MR M'COMAS. MY	KNOWLEDGE	OF HUMAN NATURE TEACHES ME NOT TO EXPECT TOO MUCH.
KING I (198)	FAULT THAT YOU HAVE NO HEAD FOR POLITICS AND NO	KNOWLEDGE	OF HUMAN NATURE. YOU NEED NOT BE ANXIOUS ABOUT ME.
MTH4 I (159)	/ZOO/ NONSENSE! CONSCIOUSNESS OF A FACT IS NOT	KNOWLEDGE	OF IT: IF IT WERE, THE FISH WOULD KNOW MORE OF THE
GENV II (56)	COMMITTEE; AND EVERY ONE OF THEM DENIES ANY	KNOWLEDGE	OF IT. MOST OF THEM DID NOT KNOW THAT THEY ARE
LION PREFACE(20)	TO JESUS, NOR ANY INDICATION OF HIS HAVING ANY	KNOWLEDGE	OF IT. THE NARRATIVE, IN FACT, PROCEEDS IN ALL
FABL PREFACE(88)	THE TESTS TEND TO EXCLUDE BORN RULERS.	KNOWLEDGE	OF LANGUAGES, DEAD AND FOREIGN, PUTS A MEZZOFANTI,
MIS. PREFACE(39)	GROUND. AT SCHOOL I BEGAN WITH A FAIRLY COMPLETE	KNOWLEDGE	OF LATIN GRAMMAR IN THE CHILDISH SENSE OF BEING
BARB III (319)	DONT SAY SO! WHAT! NO CAPACITY FOR BUSINESS, NO	KNOWLEDGE	OF LAW, NO SYMPATHY WITH ART, NO PRETENSION TO
SIM PREFACE(15)	SO SURE ABOUT BRUTUS AND CROMWELL. OUR GENERAL	KNOWLEDGE	OF MANKIND, IF WE DARE BRING IT INTO PLAY, WOULD
SUPR PREFACE(R29)	OR INDEED ANYTHING ELSE THAT TURNS UPON A	KNOWLEDGE	OF MANKIND. HENCE IT HAS BEEN POINTED OUT THAT
CAPT III (274)	AGAINST HIM IN MY OPINION, BECAUSE YOU HAVE MORE	KNOWLEDGE	OF MEN THAN ANYONE ELSE HERE. PERHAPS I'M
JOAN PREFACE(22)	BEING ONLY A LASS WHEN ALL IS SAID, LACKED THEIR	KNOWLEDGE	OF MEN'S VANITIES AND OF THE WEIGHT AND PROPORTION
CAPT NOTES (300)	HOLY) BY CUNNINGHAME GRAHAM. MY OWN FIRST HAND	KNOWLEDGE	OF MOROCCO IS BASED ON A MORNING'S WALK THROUGH
FABL IV (116)	AND BEER, BEEF AND MUTTON, BECAME A SEARCH FOR	KNOWLEDGE	OF NATURE AND POWER OVER IT, AND A DESIRE FOR
ROCK PREFACE(177)	PHYSICAL MATTERS WITH EVERY ADVANCE MADE IN OUR	KNOWLEDGE	OF NATURE. IN TREATING THE LEGEND OF JOSHUA'S
SUPR I (24)	AS WE REALLY ARE. OUR MINDS ARE NOTHING BUT THIS	KNOWLEDGE	OF OURSELVES; AND HE WHO ADDS A JOT TO SUCH
SUPR IV (170)	/TANNER/ (RISING) I YIELD TO YOUR SUPERIOR	KNOWLEDGE	OF PHYSIOLOGY, HENRY. (HE WITHDRAWS TO THE CORNER
MIS. PREFACE(27)	EXIST IN SCHOOLS; BUT EVERY ADULT WHO DERIVES HIS	KNOWLEDGE	OF PUBLIC AFFAIRS FROM THE NEWSPAPERS CAN TAKE IN,
LION PREFACE(41)	THIS VERISIMILITUDE MAY BE DRAMATIC ART BACKED BY	KNOWLEDGE	OF PUBLIC LIFE; BUT EVEN AT THAT WE MUST NOT
BARB I (256)	ALL HAVE GROWN UP WITHOUT PRINCIPLES, WITHOUT ANY	KNOWLEDGE	OF RIGHT AND WRONG, IF HE HAD BEEN IN THE HOUSE.
SUPR HANDBOK(212)	ENOUGH NOURISHMENT, NO CAPITAL, NO CREDIT, AND NO	KNOWLEDGE	OF SCIENCE OR BUSINESS, THEY WOULD, IF THE STATE
LION PREFACE(84)	WITNESSED ONE OF HIS PLAYS; BUT NOBODY WITH ANY	KNOWLEDGE	OF SHAKESPEAR OR MOLIERE COULD POSSIBLY DETEST
BARB PREFACE(222)	OUR THEATRE CRITICS, BUT ACTUALLY OUTSIDE THEIR	KNOWLEDGE	OF SOCIETY. INDEED NOTHING COULD BE MORE
FABL PREFACE(91)	TEST THEIR EXECUTIVE SKILL BUT TO ASCERTAIN THEIR	KNOWLEDGE	OF THE BEST MUSIC AND THEIR INTEREST IN AND
O'FL (210)	DOWN AGAIN) YES, YES, OF COURSE; BUT HAVE YOU NO	KNOWLEDGE	OF THE CAUSES OF THE WAR? OF THE INTERESTS AT
MIS. PREFACE(30)	BETWEEN HER AND HER NEAREST KINSMEN, AND HAS NO	KNOWLEDGE	OF THE CONDITION WHICH, IF NOT FORESEEN, MUST COME
2TRU II (53)	IT, SIR. /TALLBOYS/ WHERE DID YOU PICK UP YOUR	KNOWLEDGE	OF THE COUNTRY? /MEEK/ I WAS MOSTLY A SORT OF
CAPT NOTES (300)	SURROUNDINGS, ITS ATMOSPHERE, ITS GEOGRAPHY, ITS	KNOWLEDGE	OF THE EAST, ITS FASCINATING CADIS AND KROOBOYS
POSN PREFACE(366)	KNOW WHAT THE AUTHOR IS DRIVING AT, MAY HAVE NO	KNOWLEDGE	OF THE ETHICAL, POLITICAL, AND SECTARIAN
SUPR HANDBOK(175)	PERSON UNDER THE AGE OF THIRTY, WHO, HAVING ANY	KNOWLEDGE	OF THE EXISTING SOCIAL ORDER, IS NOT A
MIS. PREFACE(78)	OF THE OBLIGATIONS IT IS INCURRING AND A	KNOWLEDGE	OF THE FACT THAT THESE OBLIGATIONS ARE BEING
JITT PREFACE(4)	WITH A QUITE MINOR MATTER. I CAN NEITHER CLAIM	KNOWLEDGE	OF THE GERMAN LANGUAGE NOR PLEAD IGNORANCE OF IT.
WIDO III (52)	YOU, SARTORIUS. IT WASNT MONEY: IT WAS KNOWLEDGE:	KNOWLEDGE	OF THE GREAT PUBLIC QUESTION OF THE OUSING OF THE
CAND I (84)	BELIEVE ME? YOU THINK I'M JEALOUS? OH, WHAT A	KNOWLEDGE	OF THE HUMAN HEART YOU HAVE, MR LEXY MILL! HOW
POSN PREFACE(417)	FIRST PLACE, NO LAWYER WITH THE MOST ELEMENTARY	KNOWLEDGE	OF THE LAW OF LIBEL IN ITS VARIOUS APPLICATIONS TO
MTH5 (219)	THE ONES THAT ATTEND TO US HAVE TO BRUSH UP THEIR	KNOWLEDGE	OF THE LANGUAGE ONCE A YEAR OR SO. NOTHING MAKES
APPL PREFACE(172)	TO THEM IN EXPERIENCE, IN CUNNING, IN EXACT	KNOWLEDGE	OF THE LIMITS OF THEIR RESPONSIBILITY AND
JOAN 4 (107)	PRESUMPTIONS. BUT AS A PRIEST I HAVE GAINED A	KNOWLEDGE	OF THE MINDS OF THE COMMON PEOPLE; AND THERE YOU
MIS. PREFACE(72)	THAT IT CAN NO MORE GO TO THE SEASIDE WITHOUT A	KNOWLEDGE	OF THE MULTIPLICATION AND PENCE TABLES THAN IT CAN
DOCT PREFACE(32)	ONLY), IS AS NOTHING COMPARED TO THE THIRST FOR	KNOWLEDGE	OF THE PHILOSOPHER, THE POET, THE BIOLOGIST, AND
UNPL PREFACE(R17)	OF THE CENSORSHIP, WITHOUT ANY ACTION OR	KNOWLEDGE	OF THE PLAY ON ITS PART, WAS SUFFICIENT TO
OVER PREFACE(159)	-- ON THE PARTIES CONCERNED. FEW PEOPLE HAVE ANY	KNOWLEDGE	OF THE SAVAGE PUNISHMENTS THAT ARE LEGALLY
BARB III (319)	ART, NO PRETENSION TO PHILOSOPHY; ONLY A SIMPLE	KNOWLEDGE	OF THE SECRET THAT HAS PUZZLED ALL THE
FANY PROLOG (264)	ONLY BE GOT TO KNOW ABOUT IT. BESIDES, BANNAL'S	KNOWLEDGE	OF THE THEATRE IS AN INSIDE KNOWLEDGE. WE KNOW
SUPR III (82)	DIRTY! /MENDOZA/ IT SHEWED HER EXTRAORDINARY	KNOWLEDGE	OF THE WORLD; FOR IT IS UNDOUBTEDLY TRUE, OUR
WIDO I (23)	NOT AT ALL. A LITTLE TACT, MR SARTORIUS, A LITTLE	KNOWLEDGE	OF THE WORLD, A LITTLE EXPERIENCE OF WOMEN-- (
GENV PREFACE(16)	ENDING AS A SAGE WITH A VERY SCRAPPY AND PARTIAL	KNOWLEDGE	OF THE WORLD. I DO NOT SEE WHY I SHOULD NOT HAVE
MRS III (228)	WHEN I FIRST CAME INTO THE PROPERTY. IVE USED MY	KNOWLEDGE	OF THE WORLD TO INVEST MY MONEY IN WAYS THAT OTHER
GETT PREFACE(245)	WHO HAVE BEEN EITHER CAREFULLY KEPT FROM ANY	KNOWLEDGE	OF THEIR DANGER, OR ERRONEOUSLY LED TO BELIEVE
ARMS II (32)	IF SUCH WOMEN EXIST, WE SHOULD BE SPARED THE	KNOWLEDGE	OF THEM. /PETKOFF/ POOH! NONSENSE! WHAT DOES IT
KING I (214)	LIKE FINE LADIES WHO HAVE ONLY A DISHONEST	KNOWLEDGE	OF THEM. /CHARLES/ BE QUIET, NELLY: YOU ARE MAKING
KING I (214)	SOMETIMES TO MAKE THEM; SO THEY HAVE AN HONEST	KNOWLEDGE	OF THEM, AND ARE NOT ASHAMED LIKE FINE LADIES WHO
LION PREFACE(19)	MOTHER. WITH NO MORE SCHOLARLY EQUIPMENT THAN A	KNOWLEDGE	OF THESE HABITS OF THE HUMAN IMAGINATION, ANYONE
CAPT NOTES (302)	ABETS ME IN MY CAREER AS A DRAMATIST, I OWE MY	KNOWLEDGE	OF THOSE MAIN FACTS OF THE CASE WHICH BECAME
DOCT PREFACE(52)	IS CAN ONLY BE REALIZED BY THOSE WHO HAVE SOME	KNOWLEDGE	OF VITAL STATISTICS, AND OF THE ILLUSIONS WHICH
DOCT PREFACE(55)	BATH, THE OWNING OF THIRTY PAIRS OF TROUSERS, A	KNOWLEDGE	OF WAGNER'S MUSIC, A PEW IN CHURCH, ANYTHING, IN
JOAN PREFACE(21)	NAPOLEON: SHE HAD HIS EYE FOR ARTILLERY AND HIS	KNOWLEDGE	OF WHAT IT COULD DO. SHE DID NOT EXPECT BESIEGED
BULL II (106)	/FATHER DEMPSEY/ (WITH GENTLE EMPHASIS) I HAVE A	KNOWLEDGE	OF WHAT THE ROUN TOWERS WERE, IF THATS WHAT YOU
HART PREFACE(22)	IN THE LIGHT OF ANY PHILOSOPHY OF HISTORY OR	KNOWLEDGE	OF WHAT WAR IS. I DOUBT WHETHER IT WAS AS HIGH AS
BULL PREFACE(29)	ADJUSTED TO YOUR TAXABLE CAPACITY BY AN INTIMATE	KNOWLEDGE	OF YOUR AFFAIRS VERIFIED IN THE CONFESSIONAL!
DOCT PREFACE(34)	NOW OPENLY FORBIDS ITS SUBJECTS TO PURSUE	KNOWLEDGE	ON THE GROUND THAT KNOWLEDGE IS IN ITSELF A BAD
MIS. PREFACE(43)	ADULTS ARE OFTEN EXPOSED TO RISKS OUTSIDE THEIR	KNOWLEDGE	OR BEYOND THEIR COMPREHENSION OR POWERS OF
MIS. PREFACE(62)	WHO VENTURES TO GIVE HIMSELF AIRS OF SUPERIOR	KNOWLEDGE	OR TASTE, AND GENERALLY TO TAKE LUCIFER FOR ONE'S
GETT (265)	BLESS YOU, MAAM, SHE DONE IT FIVE TIMES TO MY OWN	KNOWLEDGE	; AND THEN GEORGE GAVE UP TELLING US ABOUT IT, HE
DOCT PREFACE(50)	TO BE DISCOVERED. INDEED, ALL PATHS LEAD TO	KNOWLEDGE	; BECAUSE EVEN THE VILEST AND STUPIDEST ACTION
MTH2 (61)	OF GRAVITATION. I SPEAK, IF I MAY SAY SO, WITH	KNOWLEDGE	; FOR I HAVE MADE A SPECIAL STUDY OF THE LABOR
PYGM EPILOG (295)	EXPLOIT THE KNOWLEDGE HE HAD GIVEN HER; FOR HIS	KNOWLEDGE	SEEMED TO HER AS MUCH HIS PRIVATE PROPERTY AS HIS
NEVR II (258)	OH YES, YOU ARE. MY REASON TELLS ME SO: MY	KNOWLEDGE	TELLS ME SO: MY EXPERIENCE TELLS ME SO. /GLORIA/
BARB PREFACE(225)	FUTURE, TO GO BACK TO THE SALVATION ARMY WITH THE	KNOWLEDGE	THAT EVEN THE SALVATIONISTS THEMSELVES ARE NOT
JITT I (19)	INDEED IT IS ONLY LUCK, AND NOT HIS SUBCONSCIOUS	KNOWLEDGE	THAT HE MUST NOT LET HIMSELF KNOW. YES: HE NOT

MILL PREFACE(111)	THE MAGNITUDE AND DIFFICULTY OF HIS JOB, AND THE	KNOWLEDGE	THAT IF HE MAKES A MESS OF IT HE WILL FALL AS
2TRU PREFACE(11)	ARE SIMPLY ADDITIONAL COCKTAILS, AND HIS SURE	KNOWLEDGE	THAT IF HE TELLS YOU THE TRUTH ABOUT YOURSELF AND
SUPR III (108)	TO MAKE YOU FIGHT IS A LITTLE HOT BLOOD AND THE	KNOWLEDGE	THAT IT'S MORE DANGEROUS TO LOSE THAN TO WIN. /DON
BUOY IV (59)	AWAY BY THE PASSION FOR MEASURING TRUTH AND	KNOWLEDGE	THAT POSSESSED AND DROVE THEM? WILL YOU SET ABOVE
LADY PREFACE(213)	THE COUNTRY. IT WAS THE FIRST TIME WITHIN MY	KNOWLEDGE	THAT SUCH A FORECAST PROVED TRUE. WILDE, THOUGH
HART I (80)	OF OURSELVES EVERY DAY TO PROPITIATE THEM. THE	KNOWLEDGE	THAT THESE PEOPLE ARE THERE TO RENDER ALL OUR
GENV IV (90)	SCANDALOUS. /THE JUDGE/ NOT AT ALL, SENORA. THE	KNOWLEDGE	THAT WE ALL LIVE IN PUBLIC, AND THAT THERE ARE NO
ROCK II (243)	A BIG PUBLICLY USEFUL THING WELL DONE, AND THE	KNOWLEDGE	THAT WITHOUT ME IT COULD NOT BE DONE? SHALL I NOT
MIS. PREFACE(97)	ONE. VIRTUE CHOOSES GOOD FROM EVIL; AND WITHOUT	KNOWLEDGE	THERE CAN BE NO CHOICE. AND EVEN THIS IS A
MTH2 (76)	THANK GOD! AS THERE IS NO LIMIT TO POWER AND	KNOWLEDGE	THERE CAN BE NO END. " THE POWER AND THE GLORY,
DOCT PREFACE(30)	THAT IN THE PURSUIT OF THEIR PROFESSIONAL	KNOWLEDGE	THEY SHOULD BE FREE FROM THE RESTRAINTS OF LAW, OF
BARB PREFACE(209)	ENOUGH LUCK, ENOUGH TACT OR SKILL OR ADDRESS OR	KNOWLEDGE	TO CARRY THINGS OFF BETTER THAN HE DID; TO IMPOSE
DOCT PREFACE(26)	WHICH THEY HAVE NEITHER THE MEANS NOR THE	KNOWLEDGE	TO PERFORM, THERE IS STILL NO GRASP OF THE
DOCT PREFACE(34)	WITHOUT IT. PARENTS AND PRIESTS MAY FORBID	KNOWLEDGE	TO THOSE WHO ACCEPT THEIR AUTHORITY; AND SOCIAL
OVER PREFACE(156)	PRACTITIONERS WHO KNOW MOST ABOUT IT KEEP THEIR	KNOWLEDGE	VERY JEALOUSLY TO THEMSELVES. WHICH IS HARDLY FAIR
FABL V (120)	FAMOUS MATHEMATICIAN WHO DECLARED THAT OUR UTMOST	KNOWLEDGE	WAS NO MORE THAN A GRAIN OF SAND PICKED UP ON THE
MIS. PREFACE(47)	YOUR CONDITION; AND I WILL BRING THE VERY LITTLE	KNOWLEDGE	WE HAVE TO YOUR TREATMENT; BUT EXCEPT IN THAT VERY
DOCT PREFACE(37)	ANY PARTICULAR METHOD CAN CUT US OFF FROM THE	KNOWLEDGE	WE HOPE TO GAIN BY IT. THE ONLY KNOWLEDGE WE LOSE
DOCT PREFACE(37)	THE KNOWLEDGE WE HOPE TO GAIN BY IT. THE ONLY	KNOWLEDGE	WE LOSE BY FORBIDDING CRUELTY IS KNOWLEDGE AT
SUPR PREFACE(R23)	SPECIAL PLEADING FOR PLEASURE, EXCITEMENT, AND	KNOWLEDGE	WHEN HE IS YOUNG, AND FOR CONTEMPLATIVE
GENV IV (87)	NOT. I AM HERE TO BE ABLE TO REPORT FROM PERSONAL	KNOWLEDGE	WHETHER ANY NOTICE HAS BEEN TAKEN OF THE SUMMONSES
SUPR III (131)	MY DOG'S PURPOSES; BUT MY OWN BRAIN LABORS AT A	KNOWLEDGE	WHICH DOES NOTHING FOR ME PERSONALLY BUT MAKE MY
HART PREFACE(22)	AND THAT THIS COULD NOT BE DONE BY APPEALS TO A	KNOWLEDGE	WHICH THEY DID NOT POSSESS, AND A COMPREHENSION OF
MIS. PREFACE(94)	AND REPUDIATIONS AS THEIR LIFE DEEPENS AND THEIR	KNOWLEDGE	WIDENS. BUT WHAT IS TO GUIDE THE CHILD BEFORE ITS
DOCT PREFACE(33)	AND DESPAIRING, TO HOPE THAT THE THIRST FOR	KNOWLEDGE	WILL EITHER DIMINISH OR CONSENT TO BE SUBORDINATED
DOCT PREFACE(35)	PEOPLE SAY IN EFFECT " IF YOU CANNOT ATTAIN TO	KNOWLEDGE	WITHOUT BURNING YOUR MOTHER YOU MUST DO WITHOUT
DOCT PREFACE(35)	THE WISEST PEOPLE SAY, " IF YOU CANNOT ATTAIN TO	KNOWLEDGE	WITHOUT TORTURING A DOG, YOU MUST DO WITHOUT
JOAN PREFACE(16)	STUPIDITY, CRUELTY, MUCKRAKING CURIOSITY,	KNOWLEDGE	WITHOUT WISDOM, AND EVERYTHING THAT THE ETERNAL
PYGM V (288)	TO THINK OF IT BEFORE! YOU CANT TAKE AWAY THE	KNOWLEDGE	YOU GAVE ME. YOU SAID I HAD A FINER EAR THAN YOU.
DOCT PREFACE(35)	AND NOBODY SAYS, " YES, BECAUSE IN THE PURSUIT OF	KNOWLEDGE	YOU MAY DO AS YOU PLEASE." JUST AS EVEN THE
MIS. PREFACE(14)	LITTLE ANIMAL, WITH AN INSATIABLE APPETITE FOR	KNOWLEDGE	, AND CONSEQUENTLY A MADDENING PERSISTENCE IN
SUPR III (104)	IGNORANCE: WHEREAS, ALAS! STUPIDITY HAS ALL THE	KNOWLEDGE	, AND IMAGINATION ALL THE INTELLIGENCE. /THE
MIS. PREFACE(38)	BY INVENTING NEW IDEAS OR EXTENDING THE DOMAIN OF	KNOWLEDGE	, AND INSISTS ON A READY-MADE ROUTINE. IT MAY COME
DOCT PREFACE(4)	THE MOST REVOLTING CRUELTIES IN THE PURSUIT OF	KNOWLEDGE	, AND JUSTIFIES THEM ON GROUNDS WHICH WOULD
DOCT II (122)	SAID THAT HIS WIFE WAS GREATLY STRUCK WITH MY	KNOWLEDGE	, AND THAT SHE ALWAYS ADMIRED JEWS. THEN HE ASKED
MIS. PREFACE(72)	LIBERTIES ARE ATTACHED TO THE ACQUISITION OF	KNOWLEDGE	, AND THE CHILD FINDS THAT IT CAN NO MORE GO TO
LION PREFACE(83)	ALL SORTS OF MARTYRDOMS FOR THE ENLARGEMENT OF	KNOWLEDGE	, AND THE ENRICHMENT AND INTENSIFICATION OF LIFE (
DOCT PREFACE(34)	NEITHER DOES ANY GOVERNMENT EXEMPT THE PURSUIT OF	KNOWLEDGE	, ANY MORE THAN THE PURSUIT OF LIFE, LIBERTY, AND
MTH4 I (161)	OF GROTESQUE CREATURES OF WHOSE NATURE IT HAD NO	KNOWLEDGE	, BECAME A CRUEL, TERROR-STRICKEN, PERSECUTING
DOCT PREFACE(34)	HAVE SHORT WORK MADE NOT ONLY OF HIS RIGHT TO	KNOWLEDGE	, BUT OF HIS RIGHT TO LIVE AND ALL HIS OTHER
BULL PREFACE(40)	INSUFFERABLE OF ALL WINDBAGS. IT REQUIRES NEITHER	KNOWLEDGE	, CHARACTER, CONSCIENCE, DILIGENCE IN PUBLIC
MIS. PREFACE(28)	TABOO IN SCHOOLS. THE SUPPRESSION OF ECONOMIC	KNOWLEDGE	, DISASTROUS AS IT IS, IS QUITE INTELLIGIBLE. ITS
BUOY IV (60)	IS NOT ENOUGH: THE APPETITE FOR MORE TRUTH, MORE	KNOWLEDGE	, FOR MEASUREMENT AND PRECISION, IS FAR MORE
BARB PREFACE(225)	HE WAS PERHAPS BETTER INSPIRED THAN HE KNEW: SUCH	KNOWLEDGE	, FOR THE DAUGHTER OF ANDREW UNDERSHAFT, WILL
BUOY PREFACE(6)	UP ON THE VERGE OF THE OCEAN OF UNDISCOVERED	KNOWLEDGE	, I HAVE SOME DIFFICULTY IN REFRAINING FROM SOME
APPL I (205)	EMPEROR-GOD HAD NOT INFINITE WISDOM, INFINITE	KNOWLEDGE	, INFINITE POWER; BUT HE HAD SOME: PERHAPS EVEN AS
DOCT PREFACE(33)	AND UNCONDITIONAL IN ITS ASSUMPTION THAT	KNOWLEDGE	, LIKE LIFE, IS A DESIRABLE THING, THOUGH ANY FOOL
SIM PREFACE(8)	THY MIGHT; FOR THERE IS NO WORK, NOR DEVICE, NOR	KNOWLEDGE	, NOR WISDOM, IN THE GRAVE WHITHER THOU GOEST." WE
BULL IV (173)	YOU FORGET, SIR, THAT WE, WITH OUR CAPITAL, OUR	KNOWLEDGE	, OUR ORGANIZATION, AND MAY I SAY OUR ENGLISH
MIS. (125)	AS THE OTHER INSTINCT. ONE OF THEM, TO MY CERTAIN	KNOWLEDGE	, REFUSED A MAN SHE WAS IN LOVE WITH, AND MARRIED
DOCT PREFACE(51)	SCIENTIFIC TO INFER THAT WHAT ATTRACTS HIM IS NOT	KNOWLEDGE	, SINCE THERE ARE OTHER PATHS TO THAT, BUT
DEST (192)	OF THEM; FOR THE LOW ARE UNSCRUPULOUS WITHOUT	KNOWLEDGE	, SO THAT THEY MAKE AN IDOL OF ME; WHILST THE HIGH
APPL PREFACE(186)	INTERESTS ARE CONSTANTLY IN CONFLICT WITH THE	KNOWLEDGE	, THE WISDOM, AND THE PUBLIC SPIRIT AND REGARD FOR
HART PREFACE(10)	OF AN ADDITION TO THE BODY OF SCIENTIFIC	KNOWLEDGE	, THEY OPERATED AND VIVISECTED AND INOCULATED AND
PYGM V (271)	AT PRESENT IN ENGLAND, TO THE BEST OF YOUR	KNOWLEDGE	, WAS ALFRED DOOLITTLE, A COMMON DUSTMAN.
BARB PREFACE(207)	WITHOUT COURAGE, WITHOUT MEANS, WITHOUT	KNOWLEDGE	, WITHOUT SKILL, WITHOUT ANYTHING REAL EXCEPT HIS
DOCT PREFACE(35)	WITHOUT BURNING YOUR MOTHER YOU MUST DO WITHOUT	KNOWLEDGE	," SO THE WISEST PEOPLE SAY, " IF YOU CANNOT
2TRU III (89)	ORDAINED! YOU DARED TO GET ORDAINED WITHOUT MY	KNOWLEDGE	! /AUBREY/ OF COURSE. YOU OBJECTED. HOW COULD I

KNOWLES

CATH PREFACE(157)	HARDLY REGULAR PROFESSIONAL PLAYWRIGHTS. SHERIDAN	KNOWLES	, BULWER LYTTON, WILLS, AND TENNYSON PRODUCED A FEW

KNOWN

SUPR II (64)	A MISALLIANCE) HER MARRIAGE HAS NOT YET BEEN MADE	KNOWN	: SHE DESIRES THAT IT SHALL NOT BE MENTIONED FOR THE
NEVR III (267)	OUT. YOU BUILD A SHIP PROOF AGAINST THE BEST GUN	KNOWN	: SOMEBODY MAKES A BETTER GUN AND SINKS YOUR SHIP. YOU
MIS. (168)	AS YOU PASSED IN THE STREET IF I WERE TO MAKE IT	KNOWN	? /TARLETON/ YOU READ A GOOD DEAL, DONT YOU? /THE
WIDO II (40)	OF RESPECT). HOW THE DEUCE COULD I HAVE	KNOWN	? YOU DIDNT TELL ME. /SARTORIUS/ YOU ARE TRIFLING
LION PREFACE(64)	WITHIN THE REACH OF MEN OF AVERAGE HEIGHT. I HAVE	KNOWN	A CASE OF AN UNFORTUNATE CHILD BEING BEATEN FOR NOT
2TRU I (30)	THANK YOU: I FELT SURE YOU WOULD. I HAVE SO OFTEN	KNOWN	A CHANGE OF MEDICINE WORK WONDERS. /THE DOCTOR/ WHEN
POSN (436)	HIM; AND SERVE HIM RIGHT, TOO. /EMMA/ I HAVE	KNOWN	A CHILD THAT WAS BORN CROOKED BECAUSE ITS MOTHER HAD
NEVR II (232)	WE HAVE NEVER SEEN THE FACE OF A RELATIVE: NEVER	KNOWN	A CLAIM EXCEPT THE CLAIM OF FREELY CHOSEN FRIENDSHIP.
DOCT I (101)	AND A CONSULTANT FOR TWENTY YEARS; AND IVE NEVER	KNOWN	A GENERAL PRACTITIONER RIGHT IN HIS DIAGNOSIS YET.
DOCT III (140)	SPEAKING, HE OUGHT TO HAVE LIVED. I HAVE ACTUALLY	KNOWN	A MAN DIE OF A DISEASE FROM WHICH HE WAS,
DOCT III (149)	SINCE I HAVE KNOWN YOU. SINCE RICHMOND I HAVE NOT	KNOWN	A MOMENT'S FEAR. AND IT USED TO BE NOTHING BUT FEAR.
BULL PREFACE(30)	OF VIEW IT IS COWARDICE AND DISHONOR. I HAVE	KNOWN	A PROTESTANT GO TO DUBLIN CASTLE TO BE SWORN IN AS A
MTH3 (130)	/CONFUCIUS/ (UNMOVED) HAVE YOU EVER	KNOWN	A PUBLIC MAN WHO WAS NOT WHAT VITUPERATIVE PEOPLE
JOAN PREFACE(48)	PLAY WHICH FOLLOWS. IT CONTAINS ALL THAT NEED BE	KNOWN	ABOUT HER; BUT AS IT IS FOR STAGE USE I HAVE HAD TO
METH PREFACE(R52)	BE BORN WITH ABNORMALLY SMALL FEET? HE MUST HAVE	KNOWN	ABOUT THE BOUND FEET EVEN IF HE KNEW NOTHING OF THE
METH PREFACE(R9)	IF MY UNCLE HAD BEEN ALIVE, HE WOULD HAVE	KNOWN	ALL ABOUT DARWIN, AND KNOWN IT ALL WRONG. IN SPITE OF
JITT I (24)	YOU? I COULD HAVE RELIEVED YOUR MIND. I HAVE	KNOWN	ALL ALONG THAT YOU WERE ILL; AND MY ONLY FEAR WAS THAT
HART PREFACE(22)	TO A CANDIDATE WHOM I WAS SUPPORTING " IF I HAD	KNOWN	ALL THAT IN 1914, THEY WOULD NEVER HAVE GOT ME INTO
SIM II (60)	A DISCOVERY AS REGARDS MYSELF. /VASHTI/ ENOUGH IS	KNOWN	ALREADY. /MAYA/ SEEK NO FURTHER: THERE IS NOTHING
SUPR HANDBOK(188)	PLEASURE WITH STERILITY, NOW UNIVERSALLY	KNOWN	AND ACCESSIBLE, ENABLE THESE PERSONS TO WEED
DOCT PREFACE(78)	LIFE, FAITH THAT THE UNKNOWN IS GREATER THAN THE	KNOWN	AND IS ONLY THE AS YET UNKNOWN, AND RESOLUTION TO FIND
SUPR IV (159)	THINK I COULD MARRY SUCH A WOMAN-- I, WHO HAVE	KNOWN	AND LOVED YOU? /ANN/ HM! WELL, AT ALL EVENTS, SHE
JOAN PREFACE(37)	VALUE AND VIRTUE CANNOT BE APPARENT UNTIL IT IS	KNOWN	AND UNDERSTOOD AS SUCH. IF ANY SIMPLE PRIEST FOR WHOM
GENV III (73)	NOT A VIRTUE. IF THE BRITISH GOVERNMENT HAD	KNOWN	AND UNDERSTOOD WHAT MARX WAS DOING, AND WHAT ITS
METH PREFACE(R36)	WAS ALSO SEMPITERNAL: HE ASSUMED THAT ALL THINGS,	KNOWN	AND UNKNOWN, WERE CAUSED. HENCE IT WAS THAT I FOUND
PLES PREFACE(R12)	OF A PLAY, THE EASE WITH WHICH DRAMATIC AUTHORS,	KNOWN	AND UNKNOWN, GET THEIR WORKS PERFORMED MUST NEEDS SEEM
BULL IV (167)	I DONT. /NORA/ IT WAS ONLY THAT I'D NEVER	KNOWN	ANYBODY ELSE THAT I COULD CARE FOR; AND I WAS FOOLISH
JITT III (67)	I WORRIED HIM ABOUT THINGS THAT HE NEEDNT HAVE	KNOWN	ANYTHING ABOUT. IT'S IN MY NATURE: I CANT HELP IT.
HART I (48)	WHEN I WAS A CHILD I WAS USED TO IT: I HAD NEVER	KNOWN	ANYTHING BETTER, THOUGH I WAS UNHAPPY, AND LONGED ALL
APPL I (198)	TO FEEL ABOUT WHEN HE GREW UP. HE'D NEVER HAVE	KNOWN	ANYTHING IF HE HADNT BEEN TAUGHT AT SCHOOL. HE COULDNT
SUPR I (24)	SINCE MARRIAGE BEGAN, THE GREAT ARTIST HAS BEEN	KNOWN	AS A BAD HUSBAND. BUT HE IS WORSE: HE IS A
MILL PREFACE(120)	ON IT. SUCH A MAN WAS MUSSOLINI. HE HAD BECOME	KNOWN	AS A JOURNALIST BY CHAMPIONING THE DEMOBILIZED
LION PREFACE(25)	ARE TWO OBVIOUS REASONS FOR HIS DISLIKE OF BEING	KNOWN	AS A WORKER OF MIRACLES. ONE IS THE NATURAL OBJECTION
BUOY PREFACE(3)	ANY FAMOUS SCRIPTURE. FOR INSTANCE, THE PECULIARS	KNOWN	AS BACONIANS BELIEVE, WITH ALL THE EVIDENCE AGAINST
JOAN PREFACE(14)	POWER THAN ABOUT THE APPETITE FOR FOOD: BOTH ARE	KNOWN	AS FACTS AND AS FACTS ONLY, THE DIFFERENCE BETWEEN
KING I (172)	BREECHES. /FOX/ (STUBBORNLY SEATED) I AM ALSO	KNOWN	AS GEORGE FOX. /NELLY/ (CLAPPING HIM ON THE SHOULDER)
HART III (144)	MOST OF THEM WOULDNT HAVE JOINED IF THEY HAD	KNOWN	AS MUCH . YOU SEE THEY HAD NEVER HAD ANY MONEY TO
BUOY III (28)	FAMILY OF YOUR CLIENT MR BASTABLE BUOYANT, BETTER	KNOWN	AS OLD BILL BUOYANT THE BILLIONAIRE. I AM A WIDOWER.
SIM II (57)	OF THE ABOMINABLE LIBERTINE AND DAMNABLE APOSTATE	KNOWN	AS PHOSFOR HAMMINGTAP. THE PATIENCE OF THE HOLY ISLAND
SIM I (44)	YOU MAY ADDRESS AS PROLA, AND THIS GENTLEMAN,	KNOWN	AS PRA, ARE BOTH ENTIRELY ORIENTAL, AND VERY DOMINANT
MTH4 I (140)	OF THE BRITISH COMMONWEALTH, DURING A PERIOD NOW	KNOWN	AS THE EXILE. THEY WERE ITS HEADQUARTERS A THOUSAND
SIM I (48)	FOR? /THE CLERGYMAN/ WELL, IN OUR HOME I WAS	KNOWN	AS THE IDIOT. /MRS HYERING/ OH! I AM SORRY: I DIDNT
2TRU PREFACE(17)	PARTY; AND THE HOLY OFFICE AND ITS FAMILIARS ARE	KNOWN	AS THE KOMINTERN AND THE GAY PAY OO. THERE IS THE
JOAN EPILOG (163)	TO ANNOUNCE TO YOU THAT JOAN OF ARC, FORMERLY	KNOWN	AS THE MAID, HAVING BEEN THE SUBJECT OF AN INQUIRY

BULL PREFACE(4)	AND FOUGHT ON A PROGRAM OF ENGLISH SOCIAL REFORM,	KNOWN	AS THE NEWCASTLE PROGRAM, DRAWN UP BY MY FRIEND AND
ARMS III (72)	TO TAKE. THE PETKOFFS AND THE SARANOFFS ARE	KNOWN	AS THE RICHEST AND MOST IMPORTANT FAMILIES IN THE
MRS II (201)	WILL STAY OUT AS LONG AS POSSIBLE. HE HAS NEVER	KNOWN	BEFORE WHAT IT IS TO STRAY OVER THE HEATH ON A SUMMER
JOAN 4 (99)	/CAUCHON/ IF SHE HAD, MY LORD, I SHOULD HAVE	KNOWN	BETTER THAN TO HAVE TRUSTED MYSELF HERE WITHIN YOUR
FOUN (211)	COULD HAVE BEEN MORE IDIOTIC. YOU OUGHT TO HAVE	KNOWN	BETTER. NO: THE CHURCH IS NOT IN MY LINE. NATURE
GETT (261)	AFFABLE LADY, MAAM, FOR A BISHOP'S LADY. I HAVE	KNOWN	BISHOPS' LADIES THAT WOULD FAIRLY PROVOKE YOU TO UP
FANY I (276)	YOURE CATHOLICS! AND I NEVER KNEW IT, THOUGH IVE	KNOWN	BOBBY EVER SO LONG! BUT OF COURSE THE LAST THING YOU
ROCK PREFACE(191)	OFF AS STANDARDS OF WORTH GET ESTABLISHED AND	KNOWN	BY PRACTICE. IN THE MEANTIME THE TERROR WILL ACT AS A
MRS I (189)	MAY I SHAKE HANDS WITH A YOUNG LADY WHOM I HAVE	KNOWN	BY REPUTATION VERY LONG AS THE DAUGHTER OF ONE OF MY
DOCT PREFACE(58)	THE CROPPING OF DOGS' EARS. SO IS THE LESS WIDELY	KNOWN	CONTROVERSY AS TO CIRCUMCISION AND THE DECLARING
MILL II (172)	A DISEASE FOR WHICH I DO NOT PRESCRIBE. THE ONLY	KNOWN	CURE IS A REVOLUTION; BUT THE MORTALITY RATE IS HIGH;
GENV IV (93)	DEMOCRACY. THANK YOUR STARS YOU HAVE NEVER	KNOWN	DEMOCRACY IN ENGLAND. I HAVE RESCUED MY COUNTRY FROM
DOCT PREFACE(11)	WHEN THE PATIENT IS THE SAME. ANYONE WHO HAS EVER	KNOWN	DOCTORS WELL ENOUGH TO HEAR MEDICAL SHOP TALKED
NEVR IV (282)	SIR. MY OWN NAME IS BOON, SIR, THOUGH I AM BEST	KNOWN	DOWN HERE AS BALMY WALTERS, SIR. BY RIGHTS I SHOULD
VWOO 2 (128)	YOU ANY INTENTIONS? /A/ DONT BE IN A HURRY. WEVE	KNOWN	EACH OTHER LESS THAN TEN MINUTES. /Z/ HOW MUCH BETTER
SUPR I (31)	HIM) BUT ISNT THAT ONLY NATURAL, JACK? WE HAVE	KNOWN	EACH OTHER SINCE WE WERE CHILDREN. DO YOU REMEMBER--
ROCK II (258)	NO ENGLISHMAN WOULD SUBMIT TO, THOUGH WEVE	KNOWN	EVER SINCE WE GAVE THEM THE VOTE THAT THEYD SUBMIT TO
UNPL PREFACE(R24)	THE COUNTLESS HEROES AS TO WHOM NOTHING IS EVER	KNOWN	EXCEPT THAT THEY WEAR NICE CLOTHES, LOVE THE HEROINE,
LION PROLOG (109)	DANCING WITH A GREAT BRUTE BEAST THAT YOU HAVNT	KNOWN	FOR TEN MINUTES AND THAT WANTS TO EAT YOUR OWN WIFE.
GETT PREFACE(218)	AND THE DAY AFTER MEETS A WOMAN HE HAS	KNOWN	FOR TWENTY YEARS, HE FINDS, SOMETIMES TO HIS OWN
APPL II (264)	EXAMPLE. /MAGNUS/ I MUST THINK OVER THIS. I HAVE	KNOWN	FOR YEARS PAST THAT IT WAS ON THE CARDS. WHEN I WAS
DOCT I (88)	OLD CARDINAL SAYS IN BROWNING'S PLAY? " I HAVE	KNOWN	FOUR AND TWENTY LEADERS OF REVOLT." WELL, IVE KNOWN
SUPR III (128)	MY OWN HEALTH, MY OWN FORTUNE, I HAVE NEVER	KNOWN	HAPPINESS. IT WAS NOT LOVE FOR WOMAN THAT DELIVERED ME
2TRU II (64)	SWEETIE WANTS A NEW FACE EVERY FORTNIGHT. I HAVE	KNOWN	HER FALL IN LOVE WITH A NEW FACE TWICE IN THE SAME
MRS III (230)	IT THAT IT'S PERFECTLY STRAIGHT AND HONEST. IVE	KNOWN	HER FOR MANY YEARS; AND I CAN SAY OF HER THAT SHE'D
BULL III (123)	YOU TO COME TO BUSINESS? YOU CAN HARDLY HAVE	KNOWN	HER FOR MORE THAN A COUPLE OF HOURS. /BROADBENT/ I AM
HART II (121)	YES; BUT I AM ON INTIMATE TERMS WITH HER. I HAVE	KNOWN	HER FOR YEARS. /HECTOR/ IT TOOK HER YEARS TO GET TO
ROCK I (205)	WAS QUITE RIGHT. IT IS THE FIRST TIME I HAVE EVER	KNOWN	HER TO BE RIGHT ABOUT ANYTHING. I AM A BAD WIFE AND A
PYGM III (246)	HER. /HIGGINS/ YOU DIDNT. I ASKED HER. IF YOUD	KNOWN	HER YOU WOULDNT HAVE ASKED HER. /MRS HIGGINS/ INDEED!
MTH4 I (141)	WOMAN/ YOU SPOKE OF A LADY DOCTOR. THE WORD IS	KNOWN	HERE ONLY AS THE NAME OF A BUTTERFLY. /THE ELDERLY
CLEO II (122)	AH, I FORGOT. I HAVE NOT MADE MY COMPANIONS	KNOWN	HERE. POTHINUS: THIS IS BRITANNUS, MY SECRETARY. HE IS
BASH III (122)	/LYDIA/ I THOUGHT HIS MOTHER HARDLY WOULD HAVE	KNOWN	HIM, SO CRUSHED HIS COUNTENANCE. /ADELAIDE/ A RIBALD
PRES (152)	CORINTHIA FANSHAWE, THE PRESIDENT OF THE LEAGUE,	KNOWN	IN MUSICAL CIRCLES-- I AM NOT MUSICAL-- AS THE
ARMS I (19)	THE FAMILY OF THE PETKOFFS, THE RICHEST AND BEST	KNOWN	IN OUR COUNTRY. /THE MAN/ OH YES, OF COURSE. BEG YOUR
ARMS III (73)	SWITZERLAND? /BLUNTSCHLI/ MY RANK IS THE HIGHEST	KNOWN	IN SWITZERLAND: I AM A FREE CITIZEN. /CATHERINE/ THEN,
BULL III (117)	HE RECEIVES RENTS AND KEEPS HIS BOOKS AND CASH,	KNOWN	IN THE HOUSEHOLD AS " THE OFFICE." THIS CHAIR, LIKE
DOCT I SD(96)	CREDULITY ON ALL BUT THE STRONGEST MINDS. HE IS	KNOWN	IN THE MEDICAL WORLD AS B.B.; AND THE ENVY ROUSED BY
GENV I (39)	HE WAS RE-ELECTED THREE TIMES, AND IS NOW	KNOWN	IN THE PARADISE AS THE FATHER OF HIS COUNTRY. /SHE/
SIM PREFACE(9)	TO BE A CROSS AND A DISGRACE; AND THE LOWEST RANK	KNOWN	IS THAT OF LABORER. THE OBJECT OF EVERYONE'S AMBITION
METH PREFACE(R9)	ALIVE, HE WOULD HAVE KNOWN ALL ABOUT DARWIN, AND	KNOWN	IT ALL WRONG. IN SPITE OF THE EFFORTS OF GRANT ALLEN
MTH4 I (169)	I AM AT THE MERCY OF A MADWOMAN: I MIGHT HAVE	KNOWN	IT FROM THE BEGINNING. I CAN BEAR NO MORE OF THIS. (
MILL II (173)	HIPPOPOTAMUS, YOU ARE A BASHIBAZOUK. I MIGHT HAVE	KNOWN	IT FROM YOUR RIDICULOUS TARBOOSH. YOU SHOULD TAKE IT
BULL PREFACE(7)	WELL IN A FREE IRELAND; AND EVEN IF HE HAD NOT	KNOWN	IT HE WOULD HAVE TAKEN HIS CHANCE RATHER THAN SELL HIS
BUOY IV (50)	YOUR NATURAL PLACE IN MY HOUSE: YOU HAVE ALWAYS	KNOWN	IT IN YOUR OWN. I CAN TRUST YOU. /JUNIUS/ I HAVE NO
JITT II (49)	THIS MISERABLE BREAK-UP OF OUR MARRIAGE BECOMES	KNOWN	IT WILL BREAK UP THAT POOR WOMAN'S WIDOWHOOD AS WELL?
SUPR II (59)	/TANNER/ (HIS EYE FLASHING) HA! I MIGHT HAVE	KNOWN	IT. THE MOTHER! ALWAYS THE MOTHER! /ANN/ IT WAS THAT
MTH2 (48)	OF ENORMOUS INFLUENCE. WE KNOW THAT. WEVE ALWAYS	KNOWN	IT. WE HAVE TO CONSULT YOU WHETHER WE LIKE IT OR NOT.
SUPR II (49)	THEYRE HERE ALREADY. /THE CHAUFFEUR/ IF I'D	KNOWN	IT! (WITH DEEP REPROACH) WHY DIDNT YOU TELL ME, MR
FABL IV (114)	STRONGEST, MOST FERTILE, MOST PASSIONATE ANIMALS	KNOWN	. BUT THEY WERE ALSO THE MOST FEROCIOUS, BEING SO
CAND II (120)	LIKE YOU. AND HE WILL KNOW THAT I MUST HAVE	KNOWN	. I WONDER WHAT HE WILL THINK OF ME THEN. /MORELL/ NO
NEVR II (253)	TO TURN YOU FROM ME! WHEN YOU NEED NEVER HAVE	KNOWN	. (UNDER A GRINDING, AGONIZED BREATH) CURSE HER!
POSN (435)	A ROPE ROUND THEIR OWN NECKS IF ALL THEY DID WAS	KNOWN	. LET ALONE THE MESS IT MAKES. /LOTTIE/ I WISH WE
VWOO 3 (138)	I WOULDNT HAVE SAID IT FOR THE WORLD IF I'D	KNOWN	. /A/ NEVER MIND: I KNOW YOU DIDNT MEAN IT. BY THE
POSN (436)	DONT BELIEVE ANY OF US LIKE IT, IF THE TRUTH WERE	KNOWN	. /BABSY/ OUR SHERIFF IS A REAL STRONG MAN. YOU WANT A
HART I (46)	I THINK MY FATHER IS THE BEST MAN I HAVE EVER	KNOWN	. /THE CAPTAIN/ HE MUST BE GREATLY CHANGED. HAS HE
DOCT III (136)	PRIVATE THINGS THAT THEY WOULDNT LIKE TO HAVE	KNOWN	. THEY WOULDNT DARE TO REFUSE YOU. /RIDGEON/ (
APPL INTRLUD(251)	LESS OF A MORAL COWARD THAN ANY MAN I HAVE EVER	KNOWN	. YOU HAVE ALMOST THE MAKINGS OF A FIRST RATE WOMAN IN
GETT PREFACE(190)	FOR PLEASURE, SEEING AS HE DOES THAT THE	KNOWN	LIBERTINES OF HIS PARISH ARE VISIBLY SUFFERING MUCH
BULL III (118)	ALL RIGHT ANYWHERE BUT IN THEIR OWN COUNTRY. IVE	KNOWN	LOTS OF EM IN ENGLAND, AND GENERALLY LIKED EM. BUT
GENV I (33)	MOST OF THEM MYSELF. /SHE/ OH, DONT SAY THAT. IVE	KNOWN	LOTS OF QUITE NICE JEWS. WHAT I SAY IS WHY PICK ON THE
MIS. PREFACE(50)	OPEN A BOOK IF THEY WERE NOT FORCED TO. I HAVE	KNOWN	MANY SUCH PERSONS WHO HAVE BEEN FORCED TO THE POINT OF
BULL IV (163)	GOING TO PRESS YOU FOR AN ANSWER BEFORE YOU HAVE	KNOWN	ME FOR 24 HOURS. I AM A REASONABLE MAN, I HOPE; AND I
FANY II (292)	(CONTINUING) HE DID, JUST AS IF HE HAD	KNOWN	ME FOR YEARS. WE GOT ON TOGETHER LIKE OLD FRIENDS. HE
GETT (306)	AND CECIL WILL ALLOW HIM-- /EDITH/ COLLINS HAS	KNOWN	ME FROM MY CHILDHOOD: I'M SURE HE WILL AGREE WITH ME.
MIS. (121)	WE HAD BARELY A HUNDRED A YEAR. YOU SHOULD HAVE	KNOWN	ME WHEN I WAS FORTY! I TALKED LIKE A DUCHESS; AND IF
GENV III (80)	THE MORE BRILLIANT. /SIR O./ TRUE. TRUE. I HAVE	KNOWN	MEN WHO COULD HOLD THE HOUSE OF COMMONS SPELLBOUND FOR
SUPR HANDBOK(184)	IT IS EASY TO UNDERSTAND WHY THE ONLY GENERALLY	KNOWN	MODERN EXPERIMENT IN BREEDING THE HUMAN RACE TOOK
MILL II (169)	THINK MONEY UNINTERESTING! OH, YOU SHOULD HAVE	KNOWN	MY FATHER! /ADRIAN/ I AM VERY GLAD I DID NOT.
NEVR IV (300)	THAT I SHOULD NOT HAVE KNOWN WHAT WAS COMING, AND	KNOWN	MY OWN MISERABLE WEAKNESS? /VALENTINE/ (SCOLDING AT
CAND II (111)	I WOULDNT GIVE TO HEVERYBODY. OW LONG AVE YOU	KNOWN	MY SON-IN-LAW JAMES ERE? /MARCHBANKS/ I DONT KNOW. I
MIS. PREFACE(3)	GET 50 POUNDS: ALL THE 50 POUND NOTES I HAVE EVER	KNOWN	OF HAVE BEEN MORE EASILY EARNED THAN A LABORIOUS
METH PREFACE(R29)	CASTES AND TRADES AND CLASSES WERE THE BEST	KNOWN	OF SOCIAL INSTITUTIONS, AND IN SOME CASES OF PUBLIC
MTH1 II (27)	AS LONG AS YOU; BUT I KNOW ALL THERE IS TO BE	KNOWN	OF THE CRAFT OF DIGGING. BY QUITTING IT I HAVE SET
GENV PREFACE(12)	TO BE GOVERNED AT ALL. LAW HAS BEEN POPULARLY	KNOWN	ONLY AS OPPRESSION AND TAXATION, AND POLITICS AS A
2TRU II (65)	MAN CAN NEVER KEEP IT UP. IN ALL MY LIFE I HAVE	KNOWN	ONLY ONE MAN THAT KEPT IT UP TIL HE DIED. /THE
DOCT I (88)	FOUR AND TWENTY LEADERS OF REVOLT." WELL, IVE	KNOWN	OVER THIRTY MEN THAT FOUND OUT HOW TO CURE
KING PREFACE(157)	AS EXISTING, OR EVER HAVING EXISTED, AT ANY	KNOWN	PERIOD OF ENGLISH HISTORY. IT IS TO BE NOTED THAT THE
BULL PREFACE(43)	THEY CANNOT BE DEDUCED FROM THE PRINCIPLES OF ANY	KNOWN	POLITICAL SYSTEM. IF THEY COULD, THEY WOULD NOT BE
2TRU II (57)	OF THE FOREIGN ACCENTS OF ALL THE WAITERS SHE HAS	KNOWN	). /TALLBOYS/ TAKE MY CHAIR. (HE GOES BEHIND IT AND
DOCT PREFACE(24)	OF THE MOST DISCREDITABLE AND DREADED DISEASE	KNOWN	; AND DOCTORS, TO SAVE THE CREDIT OF THE INOCULATION,
FANY II (289)	FIST. I SHOULD HAVE DONE SO WITH PLEASURE HAD I	KNOWN	; BUT AS IT WAS, I STRUCK HIM ON THE EAR WITH MY
FABL IV (114)	THIS WAS NOT SURPRISING, AS IT HAD LONG BEEN	KNOWN	THAT BULLS AND ELEPHANTS, FED ON GRASS AND LEAVES,
METH PREFACE(R87)	I WAS QUITE CONSCIOUS OF THIS; FOR I HAD ALWAYS	KNOWN	THAT CIVILIZATION NEEDS A RELIGION AS A MATTER OF LIFE
JITT III (67)	WHAT SORT OF WOMEN MUST THEY BE? SHE MUST HAVE	KNOWN	THAT HE COULD NEVER HAVE CARED FOR HER. /JITTA/ YOU
APPL PREFACE(192)	OF HAVING UNDER-RATED HIM) THAT I HAD NEVER	KNOWN	THAT HE WAS AN ENGINEER, AND HAD TAKEN HIM TO BE THE
MRS PREFACE(168)	OF THAT DREARY MIMANTHROPOMETRY ARE SO WELL	KNOWN	THAT IT IS ALMOST IMPOSSIBLE FOR ITS SLAVES TO WRITE
MTH2 (50)	HUN WOULD EVER HAVE COME TO THE GATE IF HE HAD	KNOWN	THAT IT WOULD BE SHUT IN HIS FACE ON PRINCIPLE? DID
LION PREFACE(50)	MULTIPLICATION OF OUR OWN NUMBERS, HAVE ALWAYS	KNOWN	THAT JESUS HAD A REAL MESSAGE, AND HAVE FELT THE
PYGM V (277)	SLIGHTEST PROVOCATION. AND I SHOULD NEVER HAVE	KNOWN	THAT LADIES AND GENTLEMEN DIDNT BEHAVE LIKE THAT IF
MRS PREFACE(165)	FOUR YEARS; AND I HAVE SPARED NO PAINS TO MAKE	KNOWN	THAT MY PLAYS ARE BUILT TO INDUCE, NOT VOLUPTUOUS
MIS. (112)	I HOPE, THAT I SHOULD HAVE COME DOWN IF I HAD	KNOWN	THAT THAT WAS HOW YOU ALL FEEL ABOUT ME. (HE MAKES
GENV PREFACE(10)	TO SAY NOTHING OF MY OWN. IT IS ALREADY	KNOWN	THAT THE ENERGY THAT MAKES URANIUM OUT OF MOLECULES,
FABL IV (116)	HARDEST PHYSICAL EXERCISE DAILY. IT WAS ALREADY	KNOWN	THAT THE VIGILS AND FASTS OF SAINTS DID NOT WEAKEN
KING I (169)	SOLDIER, HAD HE BEEN A PHILOSOPHER HE WOULD HAVE	KNOWN	THAT TO STOP THE NEAREST SPECK OF DUST WOULD HAVE
KING I (178)	THEIR PULPITS AND THEIR ALTARS; AND LET IT BE	KNOWN	THAT WHAT THE WORLD NEEDS TO BRING IT BACK TO GOD IS
GETT (349)	CHANGED MY MIND. (TO HOTCHKISS) I MIGHT HAVE	KNOWN	THAT YOU WERE TOO CLEVER TO BE REALLY A GENTLEMAN. (
CLEO IV (177)	UP BUCKETS OF FRESH WATER FROM THEM. WE HAVE	KNOWN	THAT YOUR GODS ARE IRRESISTIBLE, AND THAT YOU ARE A
2TRU II (77)	ADVANCING ON US. /THE COUNTESS/ (ALARMED) IF I'D	KNOWN	THAT, YOU WOULDNT HAVE GOT ME HERE. IS THAT SO,
DOCT I SD(81)	ENTRANCE OF AN OLD SERVING-WOMAN WHO HAS NEVER	KNOWN	THE CARES, THE PREOCCUPATIONS, THE RESPONSIBILITIES,
VWOO 3 (142)	IF THE FEMALE NOBODIES WHO SNAPPED THEM UP HAD	KNOWN	THE ENORMITY OF THEIR OWN PRESUMPTION? I BELIEVE THEY
MRS PREFACE(152)	OF THEIR PROFESSION, NO AUTHOR WHO HAS EVER	KNOWN	THE EXULTATION OF SENDING THE PRESS INTO AN HYSTERICAL
GETT (300)	TO ME THAN MR BALFOUR'S OR MR ASQUITH'S. IF I HAD	KNOWN	THE LAW I WOULD NEVER HAVE CONSENTED. I DONT BELIEVE
ROCK II (276)	DOESNT CARE A RAP FOR DOMESTIC HAPPINESS. I HAVE	KNOWN	THE MOST REMARKABLE CHILDREN COME OF THE MOST
DOCT I (105)	THE OPERATION WILL DO THEM NO HARM: INDEED, IVE	KNOWN	THE NERVOUS SHAKE-UP AND THE FORTNIGHT IN BED DO
GENV PREFACE(22)	THAN PARLIAMENTS. THEY HAVE KEPT THEIR HEADS AND	KNOWN	THEIR LIMITATIONS. ORDINARY MORTALS LIKE NERO, PAUL OF
CLEO II (140)	TO GUARD HIM, EH? /RUFIO/ AGH! I MIGHT HAVE	KNOWN	THERE WAS SOME FOX'S TRICK BEHIND YOUR FINE TALKING. (
DOCT I (104)	TEN TIMES THE MAN HE WAS. /BLENKINSOP/ IVE	KNOWN	THINGS LIKE THAT HAPPEN. THEY CANT BE EXPLAINED.

LION PREFACE(26)	ACCORDING TO MATTHEW HIMSELF, JESUS MUST HAVE	KNOWN	THIS ONLY TOO WELL; FOR WHEREVER HE WENT HE WAS
MTH2 (49)	I AM, IF I MISTAKE NOT, JOYCE BURGE, PRETTY WELL	KNOWN	THROUGHOUT EUROPE, AND INDEED THROUGHOUT THE WORLD, AS
DOCT I SD(81)	NAME, SHE HAS NO DISCOVERED SURNAME, AND IS	KNOWN	THROUGHOUT THE DOCTOR'S QUARTER BETWEEN CAVENDISH
LION PREFACE(94)	ALLOWS YOU. THE HONEST TEACHER WHO HAS TO MAKE	KNOWN	TO A NOVICE THE FACTS ABOUT CHRISTIANITY CANNOT IN ANY
KING I (174)	FIT INTO MY WAY OF LIFE. MR ROWLEY: YOU ARE WELL	KNOWN	TO BE AS INTERESTED IN LADIES AS I AM INTERESTED IN
ROCK PREFACE(171)	OF A HELL THE DETAILS OF WHICH HE MUST HAVE	KNOWN	TO BE HIS OWN INVENTION EVEN IF HE DID BELIEVE
BARB PREFACE(235)	OF EVENTS IN REAL LIFE, HAVE CONTRIVED TO MAKE IT	KNOWN	TO BILL, WITH THE RESULT THAT THE SALVATION ARMY LOSES
BULL II SD(104)	ONE OF THE LAST SURVIVORS OF THE PUBLIC VEHICLES	KNOWN	TO EARLIER GENERATIONS AS BEEYANKINY CARS, THE IRISH
DOCT PREFACE(6)	THE ASSENT OF THE MAJORITY IS THE ONLY SANCTION	KNOWN	TO ETHICS. NO DOUBT THIS HOLDS GOOD IN POLITICAL
KING I (172)	KEEP ME WAITING IN THE STREET? /CHARLES/ YOU ARE	KNOWN	TO EVERYONE PRESENT, MISTRESS GWYNN, I THINK. MAY I
BUOY III (41)	WE ARE UNIVERSITY MEN NONE THE LESS. IF A MAN IS	KNOWN	TO HAVE BEEN AT OXFORD OR CAMBRIDGE NOBODY EVER ASKS
APPL II (261)	TYPIST IN OUR BUREAU WHO CAN SPELL IT; BUT HE IS	KNOWN	TO HIS FRIENDS AS MICK O'RAFFERTY. /MAGNUS/ THE
BULL PREFACE(68)	LET LOOSE A SPECIALLY RECRUITED FORCE (	KNOWN	TO HISTORY AS THE BLACK AND TANS) WITH CARTE BLANCHE
JOAN PREFACE(4)	WOULD HAVE BEEN ONE OF THE MOST ODIOUS PERSONS	KNOWN	TO HISTORY INSTEAD OF ONE OF THE MOST ATTRACTIVE. IF
AUGS (263)	IN MY PRESENCE. OUR STATESMEN ARE THE GREATEST	KNOWN	TO HISTORY. OUR GENERALS ARE INVINCIBLE. OUR ARMY IS
WIDO I (7)	NAME IS SARTORIUS; AND I HAVE THE HONOR OF BEING	KNOWN	TO LADY ROXDALE, WHO IS, I BELIEVE, A NEAR RELATIVE OF
MTH5 (246)	INSULT IT. /THE HE-ANCIENT/ CHILDREN HAVE BEEN	KNOWN	TO MAKE DOLLS OUT OF RAGS, AND TO CARESS THEM WITH THE
ROCK PREFACE(177)	NO MODEL DEFENCE, AND THERE IS NO MODERN TREATISE	KNOWN	TO ME WHICH QUITE SUPPLIES THIS NEED. STUART MILL'S
JOAN 4 (96)	SERVICE. /CAUCHON/ YOUR LORDSHIP'S FAME IS WELL	KNOWN	TO ME. /WARWICK/ THIS REVEREND CLERIC IS MASTER JOHN
JITT PREFACE(5)	ARE IN THE DICTIONARY. IT WAS NOT BY ANY PROCESS	KNOWN	TO MEN OF LEARNING, BUT RATHER BY SOME TELEPATHIC
GETT PREFACE(232)	HAPPILY WITHOUT EACH OTHER. IN EVERY OTHER CASE	KNOWN	TO ME, EITHER FROM OBSERVATION OR RECORD, THE
DOCT III (146)	ELSE. WELL, IF YOU APPLY ANY SCIENTIFIC TEST	KNOWN	TO ME, YOU WILL ACHIEVE A REDUCTIO AD ABSURDUM. YOU
DOCT III (150)	IN FACT I HAVE THEM; AND THEY ARE PERFECTLY WELL	KNOWN	TO MY COLLEAGUES. IF I AM NEEDED-- AND NEEDED I SHALL
BULL IV (155)	THERE IS ONLY ONE PLACE OF HORROR AND TORMENT	KNOWN	TO MY RELIGION; AND THAT PLACE IS HELL. THEREFORE IT
FABL PREFACE(99)	AS ATOMIC BOMB MANUFACTURE REMAINS A TRADE SECRET	KNOWN	TO ONLY ONE STATE, IT WILL BE THE MAINSTAY OF PEACE
BULL IV SD(151)	HEARD OUTSIDE SAYING GOODNIGHT IN EVERY INFLEXION	KNOWN	TO PARLIAMENTARY CANDIDATES. NORA, AUNT JUDY, KEEGAN,
LIED SD(200)	WORTH KICKING. HENRY SUDDENLY EXECUTES THE FEAT	KNOWN	TO PUGILISTS AS SLIPPING, AND CHANGES SIDES WITH
GENV IV (121)	STARVATION AND RUIN, EXTERMINATION BY EVERY MEANS	KNOWN	TO SCIENCE. YOU HAVE REDUCED ONE ANOTHER TO SUCH A
LION PREFACE(95)	THE TEACHER OF CHRISTIANITY HAS THEN TO MAKE	KNOWN	TO THE CHILD, FIRST THE SONG OF JOHN BARLEYCORN, WITH
POSN PREFACE(362)	MYSELF AND A NUMBER OF GENTLEMEN LESS WELL	KNOWN	TO THE GENERAL PUBLIC, BUT IMPORTANT IN THE WORLD OF
3PLA PREFACE(R29)	LOVED, OR WAS THAT WOMAN HERSELF, OR WAS EVEN	KNOWN	TO THE SAVER AS MUCH AS BY SIGHT? NEVER. WHEN WE WANT
MRS PREFACE(179)	BEST INSTRUMENT FOR WARNING THE MEN, AND MAKING	KNOWN	TO THE WOMEN THE ADDRESSES OF THE ORGANIZATION FOR
ROCK PREFACE(155)	TO KILL THEMSELVES IN THE MOST PAINLESS MANNER	KNOWN	TO THEIR JUDGES, BUT FROM THAT SUMMIT THERE WAS A
AUGS (273)	HER SOMEWHAT LOFTILY) ALL THAT IS PERFECTLY WELL	KNOWN	TO THIS DEPARTMENT, MADAM. /THE LADY/ (SURPRISED AND
MIS. PREFACE(94)	THAT ALLAH IS SIMPLY THE NAME BY WHICH GOD IS	KNOWN	TO TURKS AND ARABS, WHO ARE JUST AS ELIGIBLE FOR
DOCT I SD(96)	EVEN BROKEN BONES, IT IS SAID, HAVE BEEN	KNOWN	TO UNITE AT THE SOUND OF HIS VOICE; HE IS A BORN
GENV PREFACE(9)	A CLOUD OF FLAMING GAS IN WHICH NO FORM OF LIFE	KNOWN	TO US COULD SURVIVE FOR A MOMENT. THAT SUCH EXPLOSIONS
GENV IV (124)	BE FROZEN STIFF. NOT A TRACE OF ANY SORT OF LIFE	KNOWN	TO US WILL BE POSSIBLE ON THIS EARTH. /THE JEW/ (
LION PREFACE(76)	WHICH IS STILL THE MOST AMAZING THING OF THE KIND	KNOWN	TO US. BEING INTELLECTUALLY AN INVETERATE ROMAN
DEVL III (66)	LAST, HAVE YOU? /SWINDON/ DUDGEON IS A NAME WELL	KNOWN	TO US, EH? /RICHARD/ YES: PETER DUDGEON, WHOM YOU
CAPT I (235)	THIS IS SIR HOWARD HALLAM, WHO WILL BE WELL	KNOWN	TO YE AS ONE OF HER MAJESTY'S JUDGES. /BRASSBOUND/ (
KING I (172)	MISTRESS GWYNN, I THINK. MAY I MAKE OUR HOST	KNOWN	TO YOU? THE EMINENT PHILOSOPHER, MR NEWTON. /NELLY/ (
POSN (452)	IN A FORENSIC MANNER) SHERIFF: THE ELDER, THOUGH	KNOWN	TO YOU AND TO ALL HERE AS NO BROTHER OF MINE AND THE
GENV I (46)	SOCIETY. I WARNED OUR SECRET POLICE, FORMERLY	KNOWN	TO YOU AS THE GAY PAY OOH. THEY FOLLOWED UP THE CLUE
KING I (167)	/NEWTON/ I HAD FORGOTTEN TO MAKE THIS LADY	KNOWN	TO YOU, GENTLEMEN. MRS BASHAM: MY HOUSEKEEPER, AND THE
METH PREFACE(R49)	ANY PURPOSE, IMMEDIATE OR ULTERIOR, HE MUST HAVE	KNOWN	VERY LITTLE ABOUT CATS. BUT A THOROUGHGOING
METH PREFACE(R51)	BEEN ACQUIRED BY A SIMILAR PROCESS, HE WOULD HAVE	KNOWN	WHAT A HABIT IS: THAT IS, AN ACTION VOLUNTARILY
2TRU II (54)	A LETTER TO A PRIVATE SOLDIER. HE CANNOT HAVE	KNOWN	WHAT HE WAS DOING. YOU MUST HAVE REPRESENTED YOURSELF
PYGM II (229)	NOT IF I'M GOING TO HAVE MY HEAD CUT OFF. IF I'D	KNOWN	WHAT I WAS LETTING MYSELF IN FOR, I WOULDNT HAVE COME
MTH1 II (33)	NEVER HAVE TO MAKE YOUR THOUGHT GOOD. BUT I HAVE	KNOWN	WHAT IT IS TO SIT AND BROOD UNDER THE TERROR OF
HART II (98)	IT'S EASY FOR YOU TO TALK: YOU HAVE NEVER	KNOWN	WHAT IT IS TO WANT MONEY; AND YOU CAN PICK UP MEN AS
HART PREFACE(40)	ON GENERAL B'S SOLDIERS? AND HAD THE STAGE MADE	KNOWN	WHAT THE PRIME MINISTER AND THE SECRETARY OF STATE FOR
JOAN PREFACE(52)	THINGS THEY ACTUALLY WOULD HAVE SAID IF THEY HAD	KNOWN	WHAT THEY WERE REALLY DOING. AND BEYOND THIS NEITHER
GETT (289)	WONDERED WHETHER THEYD HAVE GONE QUIETLY IF THEYD	KNOWN	WHAT THEY WERE DOING. IVE A HORRIBLE MISGIVING ABOUT
NEVR IV (300)	HAVE BEEN ON MY GUARD? THAT I SHOULD NOT HAVE	KNOWN	WHAT WAS COMING, AND KNOWN MY OWN MISERABLE WEAKNESS?
FANY III (323)	TO KNOW WHEN WE ARE BEATEN. AT WATERLOO, HAD WE	KNOWN	WHEN WE WERE BEATEN, WE SHOULD HAVE RETREATED; TRIED
MIS. (151)	I HOPE, SATISFIED AT LAST, LORD SUMMERHAYS: A MAN	KNOWN	WHEREVER THE BRITISH FLAG WAVES. HIS SON BENTLEY,
HART II (112)	/GUINNESS/ WHY DIDNT YOU SHOOT HIM, SIR? IF I'D	KNOWN	WHO HE WAS, I'D HAVE SHOT HIM MYSELF. (SHE GOES OUT).
NEVR II (235)	NO, NO, NO. YOUR FATHER, SIR, IS A WELL	KNOWN	YACHT BUILDER, AN EMINENT MAN HERE. /WAITER/ (
GENV II (57)	THEY WILL AFFIRM OUR EXISTENCE, WHICH IS HARDLY	KNOWN	YET. THEY WILL EXERCISE OUR POWER, WHICH IS HARDLY
SUPR I (38)	YOU WILL TRY TO GET INTO A CIRCLE WHICH HAS NEVER	KNOWN	YOU EXCEPT AS AN ANGEL. /ANN/ SO IT WAS ONLY YOUR
FANY III (305)	YES IT IS. /DORA/ WELL, I SHOULD NEVER HAVE	KNOWN	YOU OUT OF THE UNIFORM. HOW DID YOU GET OUT? YOU WERE
LIED (195)	THINK I WOULD EVER HAVE ENCOURAGED YOU IF I HAD	KNOWN	YOU WERE SUCH A LITTLE DEVIL? /HE/ DONT DRAG ME
INCA (243)	OH, I BEG YOUR PARDON. OF COURSE I OUGHT TO HAVE	KNOWN	YOU WOULD NOT HAVE SPOKEN LIKE THAT IF YOU WERE NOT
DOCT III (149)	OH, LIFE HAS BEEN WORTH LIVING SINCE I HAVE	KNOWN	YOU. SINCE RICHMOND I HAVE NOT KNOWN A MOMENT'S FEAR.
WIDO II (40)	/SARTORIUS/ (PROVOKED) THEN YOU OUGHT TO HAVE	KNOWN	YOUR OWN MIND ON A POINT OF SUCH VITAL IMPORTANCE.
BASH III (124)	WHERE IS THY STING? /POLICEMAN/ SIR: HAD I	KNOWN	YOUR QUALITY, THIS COP I HAD AVERTED; BUT IT IS TOO
CLEO NOTES (205)	IN FACT, ARE NOT TO THE POINT. IT HAS BEEN	KNOWN	, AS FAR BACK AS OUR RECORDS GO, THAT MAN RUNNING WILD
FABL PREFACE(88)	BE ACCEPTED BY THE ELDERLY EXAMINERS, SOON BECOME	KNOWN	, ENABLING PROFESSIONAL CRAMMERS TO COACH ANY SIXTH
MIS. (190)	MORE THAN ANY MAN IN THIS ROOM, IF THE TRUTH WERE	KNOWN	, I EXPECT, THATS WHATS GOING TO SMASH UP YOUR
DOCT IV (157)	REALLY, WALPOLE, IF YOUR MONOMANIA WERE NOT WELL	KNOWN	, I SHOULD TAKE SUCH AN EXPRESSION VERY SERIOUSLY.
FANY II (295)	WANT ME TO BE ENLIGHTENED. IF THE TRUTH WERE	KNOWN	, I SUSPECT WE ALL WANT OUR PRAYERS TO BE ANSWERED
JOAN 6 (149)	(LAMENTABLY) I LET THEM DO IT. IF I HAD	KNOWN	, I WOULD HAVE TORN HER FROM THEIR HANDS. YOU DONT
FOUN (218)	RESUME YOUR SEAT, I BEG. /MERCER/ IF I HAD ONLY	KNOWN	, MISS! PARK LANE! I COULD BITE MY TONGUE OUT FOR MY
DOCT III (141)	OF COURSE NOT. DONT YOU SEE THAT IF SHE HAD	KNOWN	, SHE WOULDNT HAVE CONSIDERED HERSELF MY WIFE? YOU
GENV I (44)	YOU RECOGNIZE ME? /BISHOP/ A BOLSHIE! IF I HAD	KNOWN	, SIR, I SHOULD HAVE REPUDIATED YOUR ADVANCES WITH
ARMS I (16)	THINKING HE'D DONE THE CLEVEREST THING EVER	KNOWN	, WHEREAS HE OUGHT TO BE COURTMARTIALLED FOR IT. OF
LION I (124)	FEEL CONSOLED) YES: I DARESAY IF THE TRUTH WERE	KNOWN	, YOURE ALL AS BAD AS I AM. /LAVINIA/ (
WIDO II (40)	/TRENCH/ (MUCH INJURED) I OUGHT TO HAVE	KNOWN	! COKANE! IS THIS REASONABLE? (COKANE'S FEATURES

KNOWS

SUPR IV (162)	THOUGH WHAT HE SEES IN HER SO WONDERFUL, GOODNESS	KNOWS	: I DONT. IT'S NO USE TELLING TAVY THAT ANN PUTS
MRS III (228)	MEAN TO PRAISE MYSELF. I HAVE MY FAULTS, HEAVEN	KNOWS	: NO MAN IS MORE SENSIBLE OF THAT THAN I AM. I KNOW
GETT (264)	PEOPLE. YOU SEE, FAMILY LIFE IS ALL THE LIFE SHE	KNOWS	: SHE'S LIKE A BIRD BORN IN A CAGE, THAT WOULD DIE IF
MTH5 (221)	/ECRASIA/ I KNOW WHAT EVERY PERSON OF CULTURE	KNOWS	: THAT THE BUSINESS OF THE ARTIST IS TO CREATE BEAUTY.
JOAN 2 (78)	SHE WILL KNOW WHAT EVERYBODY IN CHINON	KNOWS	: THAT THE DAUPHIN IS THE MEANEST-LOOKING AND
JITT I (22)	CAN I DEPEND ON YOU? /JITTA/ (HALF BEATEN) WHO	KNOWS	? I CANNOT DEPEND ON MYSELF. THIS SACRIFICE IS NO
2TRU I (29)	A BREATH OF FRESH AIR FOR ME! /THE DOCTOR/ WHO	KNOWS	? IT MAY HAVE LURKED HERE SINCE THE HOUSE WAS BUILT.
DEST (156)	SHE COME FROM? /GIUSEPPE/ (WITH A SHRUG) WHO	KNOWS	? SHE ARRIVED HERE JUST BEFORE YOUR EXCELLENCY IN A
BASH I (94)	/LYDIA/ WHY SHOULD WE MEET AGAIN? /CASHEL/ WHO	KNOWS	? WE SHALL. THAT MUCH I KNOW BY INSTINCT. WHATS YOUR
CAND I (100)	OF THE KINGDOM OF HEAVEN ON EARTH; AND-- WHO	KNOWS	? -- YOU MAY BE A MASTER BUILDER WHERE I AM ONLY A
MIS. (139)	BLACKMAILER, MY DEAR YOUNG LADY, IS A PERSON WHO	KNOWS	A DISGRACEFUL SECRET IN THE LIFE OF ANOTHER PERSON,
MTH2 (39)	THERES A LIVING IN THE FAMILY, OR ONE'S GOVERNOR	KNOWS	A PATRON, ONE GETS SHOVED INTO THE CHURCH BY ONE'S
PYGM I (211)	IN THE NOTE TAKER'S FAVOR, EXCLAMATIONS OF HE	KNOWS	ALL ABOUT IT. TOLD HIM PROPER. HEAR HIM TELL THE TOFF
ARMS II (36)	RIGHT TO TAKE UP MY WORDS LIKE THAT. THE MISTRESS	KNOWS	ALL ABOUT IT. AND I TELL YOU THAT IF THAT GENTLEMAN
BUOY III (32)	ANYTHING ABOUT MAKING MONEY BECAUSE OUR FATHER	KNOWS	ALL ABOUT IT. /SIR F./ HAS HE NEVER TAUGHT YOU
SUPR II (51)	TAVY, DONT START HIM ON POLITICAL ECONOMY. HE	KNOWS	ALL ABOUT IT; AND WE DONT. YOURE ONLY A POETIC
MTH4 III (198)	NEVER MIND THE BRIBERY AND LIES. THE ORACLE	KNOWS	ALL ABOUT THAT. THE POINT IS THAT THOUGH OUR FIVE
BARB III (317)	AFTERNOON. /UNDERSHAFT/ (TO LADY BRITOMART) HE	KNOWS	ALL ABOUT THE TRADITION, I SUPPOSE? /LADY BRITOMART/
CAPT II (256)	BED AND WENT TO PARADISE. /SIR HOWARD/ THEN HE	KNOWS	ALSO THAT ENGLAND'S VENGEANCE WAS ON THE MAHDI'S
GETT PREFACE(189)	TO THIS QUESTION IS AN ANSWER WHICH EVERYBODY	KNOWS	AND NOBODY LIKES TO GIVE. WHAT IS DRIVING OUR
LADY PREFACE(222)	ENDURE A MAN WHO DOTES WITHOUT DOUBTING; WHO	KNOWS	AND WHO IS HUGELY AMUSED AT THE ABSURDITY OF HIS
BULL III (139)	BE YOU, LARRY DOYLE. SOME PEOPLE THINK NO ONE	KNOWS	ANYTHIN BUT DHEMSELVES. (TO BROADBENT, DEFERENTIALLY)
2TRU I (34)	POWER THAT GIVES US OUR LIFE AND THAT NONE OF US	KNOWS	ANYTHING ABOUT. LOTS OF PEOPLE BELIEVE IN THE BOTTLES
BUOY III (29)	WHATEVER. BUSINESS MEANS MONEY; AND NONE OF US	KNOWS	ANYTHING ABOUT MONEY BECAUSE OUR FATHER KNOWS
BUOY III (32)	/DARKIE/ I TOLD YOU SO, SIR FERDINAND. NONE OF US	KNOWS	ANYTHING ABOUT MAKING MONEY BECAUSE OUR FATHER KNOWS
BUOY III (35)	DO FOOLISH THINGS WITH THEIR MONEY. NONE OF YOU	KNOWS	ANYTHING ABOUT MONEY; SO I HAD BETTER KEEP AN EYE ON

JITT II (28)	TO PRETEND TO BE IN THE DARK. BUT OF COURSE SHE	KNOWS	AS WELL AS YOU OR I; AND IT MADDENS HER TO HAVE TO
ROCK I (210)	/THE OXFORD YOUTH/ (DISCORDANTLY) OH, HE	KNOWS	AS WELL AS YOU DO, ALOYSIA. (HE ADVANCES OFFENSIVELY
DOCT II (129)	ME. SHE IS. /SIR PATRICK/ WELL, SOMETIMES A MAN	KNOWS	BEST; AND SOMETIMES HE KNOWS WORST. YOUD MUCH BETTER
MTH3 (133)	WHOM THE MIRACLE HAS HAPPENED, BUT THE ARCHBISHOP	KNOWS	BETTER NOW. HE WILL ADVERTIZE IN TERMS WHICH ONLY THE
PRES (149)	KNOW WHAT THEYRE TALKIN ABOUT. WHY, THE ORSES	KNOWS	BETTER SOMETIMES. " FOURS," SAYS LIEUTENANT TREVOR AT
CYMB FORWORD(133)	STUDIOS TODAY THAT EVERYONE IN A FILM STUDIO	KNOWS	BETTER THAN ANY PROFESSIONAL PLAYWRIGHT HOW A PLAY
POSN PREFACE(389)	MAY DO AND WHAT HE MAY NOT DO; AND, THOUGH NO ONE	KNOWS	BETTER THAN A MAGISTRATE THAT A SINGLE ILL-CONDUCTED
JOAN 5 (114)	OF HUBRIS. /CHARLES/ YES: SHE THINKS SHE	KNOWS	BETTER THAN EVERYONE ELSE. /JOAN/ (DISTRESSED, BUT
2TRU PREFACE(21)	OF ALL THE REST" AS SAINTS OR RULERS. PROVIDENCE	KNOWS	BETTER THAN TO PROVIDE ARMIES CONSISTING EXCLUSIVELY
APPL I (218)	QUITE FRANKLY, MY OPINION OF YOU IS THAT NO MAN	KNOWS	BETTER THAN YOU WHEN TO SPEAK AND WHEN TO LET OTHERS
LION II (131)	BE FORGIVEN? /LAVINIA/ I EXPECT THE EMPEROR	KNOWS	BETTER. ANYHOW, WE FORGIVE HIM. /THE CHRISTIANS/
MILL IV (201)	NOT HAVE BEEN COMPROMISED, BUT MRS FITZFASSENDEN	KNOWS	BETTER. SHE KNOWS THE PRIVILEGES OF HER SEX TO A
APPL PREFACE(171)	MUST AT ONCE ACCEPT IT JOYFULLY AS SUCH. HE	KNOWS	BETTER. THE CHANGE WOULD RALLY THE ANTI-DEMOCRATIC
POSN PREFACE(416)	THEATRES. THE OTHER IS THE SILENT SECTION WHICH	KNOWS	BETTER, BUT IS VERY WELL CONTENT TO BE PUBLICLY
MTH5 (230)	OF ITS BIRTH. WHY, THE NEWLY BORN THERE ALREADY	KNOWS	BY INSTINCT MANY THINGS THAT THEIR GREATEST PHYSICISTS
SUPR III (110)	NATURE'S BEHEST IN THE MOST ECONOMICAL WAY. SHE	KNOWS	BY INSTINCT THAT FAR BACK IN THE EVOLUTIONAL PROCESS
BULL III (128)	WE WANT A NEW CLASS O MAN IN PARLIAMENT: ONE DHAT	KNOWS	DHAT THE FARMER'S THE REAL BACKBONE O THE COUNTRY, N
BUOY III (29)	AMATEUR BOXER. ANOTHER IS A HISTORIAN AND	KNOWS	ELEVEN LANGUAGES. HE IS ALSO A PEDESTRIAN AND WALKS
JITT I (18)	QUITE HANDY CURVE DIAGRAMS FOR MY LECTURES. HE	KNOWS	EVERYTHING: WHAT HE LACKS IS A SENSE OF THE
BUOY III (29)	US KNOWS ANYTHING ABOUT MONEY BECAUSE OUR FATHER	KNOWS	EVERYTHING ABOUT IT, BUT I KNOW ALL ABOUT HOUSEKEEPING
PRES (142)	AFTER TWENTY YEARS IN THE ARMY A MAN THINKS HE	KNOWS	EVERYTHING. AFTER TWENTY MONTHS IN THE CABINET HE
BARB III (320)	WANTS TO DO. HE KNOWS NOTHING; AND HE THINKS HE	KNOWS	EVERYTHING. THAT POINTS CLEARLY TO A POLITICAL CAREER.
KING I (219)	VERY THOUGHTFUL ABOUT MONEY. /BARBARA/ YES: SHE	KNOWS	EXACTLY HOW MUCH HE HAS: SHE GETS IT FOR HIM FROM THE
MTH4 II (180)	FOR EVER: HE HOPES TO ESCAPE FOR SIX MONTHS, BUT	KNOWS	HE CANNOT ESCAPE FOR SIX YEARS. THE RISK OF BANKRUPTCY
DOCT II (123)	HE MUST PAY IT AT THE END OF THE TIME. IF HE	KNOWS	HE CANT PAY, HE BEGS IT AS A GIFT. /RIDGEON/ COME,
SUPR II (57)	AWAY DOWN THE AVENUE WITH THE AIR OF A MAN WHO	KNOWS	HE IS NO LONGER WANTED). /ANN/ (COMING BETWEEN
DOCT II (123)	IF HE WANTS MONEY FOR A TIME, HE BORROWS IT AND	KNOWS	HE MUST PAY IT AT THE END OF THE TIME. IF HE KNOWS HE
MILL II (176)	ANY OF THEM, AND THE OWNER DARE NOT REFUSE: HE	KNOWS	HE WILL NEVER GET SUCH AN OFFER AGAIN. /THE DOCTOR/
2TRU I (38)	THING SHE DOES IS TO OPEN HER MOUTH. A NURSE WHO	KNOWS	HER BUSINESS JUST SHOVES A HANDFUL OF THIS INTO IT.
2TRU I (30)	NO: DONT SAY THAT. SHE MUST BE NEAR A DOCTOR WHO	KNOWS	HER CONSTITUTION. DEAR OLD DR NEWLAND KNEW IT SO WELL
DEST (176)	WITH A VERY ABLE AND AMBITIOUS HUSBAND WHO	KNOWS	HER THROUGH AND THROUGH: KNOWS THAT SHE HAS LIED TO
ROCK I (212)	WHY DONT YOU CALL HIM BY THE NAME THE EAST END	KNOWS	HIM BY? OLD HIPNEY, GOOD OLD HIPNEY. /OLD HIPNEY/ (
DOCT III (153)	LISTEN. I KNOW LOUIS AS NOBODY ELSE IN THE WORLD	KNOWS	HIM OR EVER CAN KNOW HIM. I AM HIS WIFE. I KNOW HE HAS
DOCT V (171)	COMMISSIONAIRE WONT LET ANYONE THROUGH UNLESS HE	KNOWS	HIM. WE HAVE A FEW PEOPLE WHO LIKE TO COME BEFORE THE
JOAN 5 (118)	I A WITCH! /THE ARCHBISHOP/ PETER CAUCHON	KNOWS	HIS BUSINESS. THE UNIVERSITY OF PARIS HAS BURNT A
KING I (200)	NO, SIR: MR NEWTON WOULD NOT LIKE THAT: HE	KNOWS	HIS DUTIES AS YOUR HOST. AND IF YOU WILL EXCUSE ME
MIS. PREFACE(87)	THE BLINDS OF THE LONG STREET IN WHICH NOBODY	KNOWS	HIS NEIGHBOR AND EVERYONE WISHES TO DECEIVE HIM AS TO
FANY III (321)	TO INTERFERE BETWEEN YOU AND YOUR SON, GILBEY: HE	KNOWS	HIS OWN INTENTIONS BEST, NO DOUBT, AND PERHAPS HAS
BULL IV (176)	I HAD BETTER VOTE FOR AN EFFICIENT DEVIL THAT	KNOWS	HIS OWN MIND AND HIS OWN BUSINESS THAN FOR A FOOLISH
SUPR IV (156)	I SAID THAT. I DONT FOR A MOMENT THINK THAT JACK	KNOWS	HIS OWN MIND. BUT IT'S CLEAR FROM MY FATHER'S WILL
CAND II (110)	SEVERITY) MR MORCHBANKS IS A GENTLEMAN, AND	KNOWS	HIS PLACE, WHICH IS MORE THAN SOME PEOPLE DO.
FANY PROLOG (265)	KNOW HIM; AND HE KNOWS US. HE KNOWS THE ROPES: HE	KNOWS	HIS WAY ABOUT: HE KNOWS WHAT HE'S TALKING ABOUT. /THE
METH PREFACE(R25)	TO KEEP TRYING FOR THEM UNTIL THEY COME. NOBODY	KNOWS	HOW: NOBODY KNOWS WHY: ALL WE KNOW IS THAT THE THING
O'FL (210)	WEARING THE VICTORIA CROSS FOR HAVING KILLED GOD	KNOWS	HOW MANY GERMANS; AND YOU TELL ME YOU DONT KNOW WHY
DEVL I (13)	PATHETIC CREATURE TO ANY SYMPATHETIC OBSERVER WHO	KNOWS	HOW ROUGH A PLACE THE WORLD IS. ONE FEELS, ON THE
JITT III (65)	THIS IS A MARKED HOUSE: EVERYBODY DESERTS IT. WHO	KNOWS	HOW SOON I SHALL BE LEFT ALONE HERE TO HAUNT THE PLACE
APPL I (218)	PROTEUS. I OWN I LIKE A PRIME MINISTER THAT	KNOWS	HOW TO BE A PRIME MINISTER. WHY DO YOU LET THEM TAKE
ROCK II (277)	A LOSS. APPARENTLY MY SON WAS NOT AT A LOSS. HE	KNOWS	HOW TO DEAL WITH YOU: I DO NOT. I MUST REALLY REFER
BUOY III (32)	WILL SEE TO THAT. /DARKIE/ NONE OF US WOMEN	KNOWS	HOW TO DO HOUSEWORK. /SIR F./ I AM AFRAID YOU WILL
MIS. (182)	/GUNNER/ (OPPRESSED AND DISCONCERTED, HARDLY	KNOWS	HOW TO GET OUT OF THE ROOM) YES, SIR. I-- (HE TURNS
CLEO V (198)	/BELZANOR/ (TO THE PERSIAN) THIS ROMAN	KNOWS	HOW TO MAKE MEN SERVE HIM. /PERSIAN/ AY: MEN TOO
GETT SD(323)	MRS GEORGE: SHE IS NOT AFRAID OF COLORS, AND	KNOWS	HOW TO MAKE THE MOST OF THEM. NOT AT ALL A LADY IN
MILL I (152)	/ALASTAIR/ BE FAIR TO HIM, EPPY. NO MAN IN LONDON	KNOWS	HOW TO ORDER A DINNER BETTER. THATS WHAT KEEPS HIM AT
HART II (87)	IS THAT HE'S A BLAMED FOOL, AND I AM A MAN THAT	KNOWS	HOW TO TAKE CARE OF HIMSELF. (HE THROWS HIMSELF BACK
SUPR I (37)	ONE. (CONFUSED) OH! YOU ARE SO SILLY: ONE NEVER	KNOWS	HOW TO TAKE YOU. /TANNER/ YOU MUST TAKE ME QUITE
DEVL II (35)	HER HAND) YOU HEAR THAT, JUDITH? MR DUDGEON	KNOWS	HOW TO TURN A COMPLIMENT. THE LATCH IS LIFTED FROM
PHIL I (75)	WILL FACE IT. I HAVE NOTHING TO LOSE. EVERYBODY	KNOWS	HOW YOU HAVE TREATED ME: YOU HAVE BOASTED OF YOUR
DEST (192)	PATIENTLY UNTIL THERE COMES INTO HIS MIND, NO ONE	KNOWS	HOW, A BURNING CONVICTION THAT IT IS HIS MORAL AND
CAND II (125)	IS SO CRITICAL OF SERMONS. (LOOKING AT HIM) HE	KNOWS	I AM AFRAID OF HIM: HE TOLD ME AS MUCH THIS MORNING.
HART II (123)	AND CHILDISH AND EVERYTHING I AM NOT. EVERYONE	KNOWS	I AM JUST THE OPPOSITE. /HECTOR/ (RISING) SOMETHING
PHIL II (112)	HE SHOULD SHUT UP THE SHOP SOMETIMES. HEAVEN	KNOWS	I AM ONLY TOO ANXIOUS TO FORGET HIS SCIENCE, SINCE IT
POSN (452)	UP, BLANCO, AS FAR AS MY EVIDENCE GOES. EVERYBODY	KNOWS	I BORROWED ONE OF THE SHERIFF'S HORSES FROM STRAPPER
GENV I (40)	DO IT AS A SELF-RESPECTING WIFE AND MOTHER. GOD	KNOWS	I DID NOT WANT TO DO IT: I LOVED HER: I WOULD HAVE LET
SUPR II (58)	YOU LOVE HER, TAVY, DONT YOU? /OCTAVIUS/ SHE	KNOWS	I DO. /ANN/ HUSH. FOR SHAME, TAVY! /TANNER/ OH, I
BULL IV (169)	INTO THE CABINET, PERHAPS, EH? /NORA/ GOD	KNOWS	I DONT GRUDGE YOU ME MONEY! BUT TO LOWER MESELF TO
POSN (460)	BACK ON HER THERE, WILL YOU? /THE WOMAN/ GOD	KNOWS	I DONT WANT TO SEE HER COMMIT MURDER. (SHE FOLDS HER
GETT (279)	IN THE WORLD HAS BEEN EXHAUSTED LONG AGO. HEAVEN	KNOWS	I HAVE EXHAUSTED THE CONVERSATION OF THE BRITISH ARMY
MTH2 (69)	MY HUMAN LIMITATIONS VERY ACUTELY. /BURGE/ GOD	KNOWS	I HAVE OFTEN FELT THAT I COULD NOT GO ON IF IT HAD NOT
HART II (125)	THAT I HAVE LOVED THIS DEMON ALL MY LIFE; BUT GOD	KNOWS	I HAVE PAID FOR IT (HE SITS DOWN IN THE DRAUGHTSMAN'S
ROCK I (202)	HE IS MAKING TROUBLE FOR HIMSELF; AND GOODNESS	KNOWS	I HAVE TROUBLE ENOUGH WITHOUT MAKING ANY MORE. PUT
MRS II (218)	BUT I CANT STAND SAYING ONE THING WHEN EVERYONE	KNOWS	I MEAN ANOTHER. WHATS THE USE IN SUCH HYPOCRISY? IF
O'FL (211)	THEM HOW I FOUGHT THE KAISER, THAT ALL THE WORLD	KNOWS	I NEVER SAW IN MY LIFE, THAN TELL THEM THE TRUTH. BUT
CATH 4 (195)	FOUGHT WITH THE STRENGTH OF LIONS AND BEARS. GOD	KNOWS	I SHALL CARRY A BROKEN SWEETBREAD TO MY GRAVE.
ANNA (300)	HAVE DONE IT, WOULD YOU NOT? /STRAMMFEST/ GOD	KNOWS	I WOULD! /THE GRAND DUCHESS/ YOU REALLY MEAN THAT?
WIDO II (32)	I THINK YOUR FRIEND WILL SAY A WORD FOR ME NOW HE	KNOWS	I'M NOT IN FAULT. /TRENCH/ (RISING ANGRILY) I WILL
2TRU II (62)	JUST TELL A THUNDERING SILLY LIE THAT EVERYONE	KNOWS	IS A LIE, AND A MURMUR OF PLEASED ASSENT WILL HUM UP
BULL PREFACE(24)	THAT THE MEMBER OF THE IRISH PROTESTANT CHURCH	KNOWS	IS THAT HE IS NOT A ROMAN CATHOLIC. THE DECORATIONS OF
DOCT PREFACE(59)	IN THE STREET KNOWS NOTHING OF BIOMETRIKA: ALL HE	KNOWS	IS THAT " YOU CAN PROVE ANYTHING BY FIGURES," THOUGH
FANY II (286)	RESTLESSLY) I CANT. I KEEP FANCYING EVERYBODY	KNOWS	IT AND IS SNIGGERING ABOUT IT. I'M AT PEACE NOWHERE
APPL I (212)	WAY AS USUAL, BECAUSE ONE MAN THAT HAS A MIND AND	KNOWS	IT CAN ALWAYS BEAT TEN MEN WHO HAVNT AND DONT. /PLINY/
CAPT II (252)	THE GENTLEMAN'S VALUE-- BETTER PERHAPS THAN HE	KNOWS	IT HIMSELF. I SHALL NOT LOSE SIGHT OF IT. JOHNSON NODS
PYGM PREFACE(202)	SOCIAL AMENITY FROM ITS NURSLINGS: (HEAVEN	KNOWS	IT IS NOT EXORBITANT IN ITS REQUIREMENTS!); FOR
CATH 2 (174)	WHY DO THEY DO IT, NARYSHKIN? /NARYSHKIN/ GOD	KNOWS	IT IS NOT FOR YOUR SAKE, LITTLE MOTHER. BUT YOU SEE IF
JITT I (19)	THAT I MAY NEVER HAVE TO SPEAK OF IT AGAIN. GOD	KNOWS	IT IS NOT TO INVOLVE YOU IN MY STRUGGLES WITH MYSELF,
CATH 1 (172)	ARM) YES, YES, YES, LITTLE ENGLISH FATHER: GOD	KNOWS	IT IS YOUR DUTY TO BE BRAVE AND WAIT ON THE EMPRESS.
CATH 1 (163)	/THE SERGEANT/ BE MERCIFUL, LITTLE FATHER. GOD	KNOWS	IT IS YOUR DUTY TO SEE HIM! (TO VARINKA) INTERCEDE
JITT I (17)	/BRUNO/ NOT AT ALL: IT IS NOT NEW: EVERYBODY	KNOWS	IT NOWADAYS IN THE ROUGH. BUT IT HAS NEVER BEEN WORKED
PYGM II (239)	JUST BECAUSE I'M NOT HER LAWFUL HUSBAND. AND SHE	KNOWS	IT TOO. CATCH HER MARRYING ME! TAKE MY ADVICE,
SUPR I (12)	RIGHT. YOU KNOW I LOVE HER, MR RAMSDEN; AND JACK	KNOWS	IT TOO. IF JACK LOVED A WOMAN, I WOULD NOT COMPARE HER
BUOY IV (55)	YOU KNOW IT. MY DAUGHTER KNOWS IT. THE YOUNG MAN	KNOWS	IT. ARE WE MAD BECAUSE WE ACT AND SPEAK ACCORDINGLY..
ROCK II (256)	OH! PRIVATE BUSINESS? /ALOYSIA/ I DONT CARE WHO	KNOWS	IT, BUT PERHAPS YOU WOULD. /BARKING/ SHE MEANS TO
FANY EPILOG (332)	/BANNAL/ THERE CAN BE NO DOUBT OF THAT: EVERYBODY	KNOWS	IT. BUT SHAW DOESNT WRITE HIS PLAYS AS PLAYS. ALL HE
LIED (188)	I'M THE ONLY AURORA IN LONDON; AND EVERYBODY	KNOWS	IT. I BELIEVE I'M THE ONLY AURORA IN THE WORLD. AND
DEVL II (36)	ABOUT THAT. I HATE AND DREAD YOU; AND MY HUSBAND	KNOWS	IT. IF YOU ARE NOT HERE WHEN HE COMES BACK, HE WILL
VWOO 1 (117)	HEAVENS, NO. PLEASE DONT. /Z/ OH, I DONT CARE WHO	KNOWS	IT. /A/ EVIDENTLY. YOU WOULD HARDLY OFFER TO TELL IT
PHIL I (75)	TO ME: YOU HAVE NO RIGHT TO BE HERE; AND SHE	KNOWS	IT. /CHARTERIS/ I THINK YOU HAD BETTER LET ME TAKE YOU
HART II (89)	THAT YOURE IN LOVE WITH HER HUSBAND. /ELLIE/ SHE	KNOWS	IT. /MANGAN/ YOU TOLD HER! ! ! /ELLIE/ SHE TOLD ME.
MIS. (199)	KNOW WHAT IS THE RIGHT THING. I'M BEATEN; AND SHE	KNOWS	IT. SUMMERHAYS: TELL ME WHAT TO DO. /LORD SUMMERHAYS/
KING I (183)	I MAKE NO SECRET OF WHO HE IS: ALL THE WORLD	KNOWS	IT. THE LOVE CHARM MUST NOT DO HIM ANY HARM; FOR IF HE
BUOY IV (55)	NOTHING. I KNOW THIS. YOU KNOW IT. MY DAUGHTER	KNOWS	IT. THE YOUNG MAN KNOWS IT. ARE WE MAD BECAUSE WE ACT
BULL IV (180)	MYSELF A BIT OF A-- OF A-- WELL, I DONT CARE WHO	KNOWS	IT-- A BIT OF A UNITARIAN; BUT IF THE CHURCH OF
SUPR IV (151)	MY DEAR SIR, THE LADY IS MARRIED ALREADY. HECTOR	KNOWS	IT; AND YET HE PERSISTS IN HIS INFATUATION. TAKE HIM
POSN (435)	FREE WITH ONE ANOTHER IN THE WAY OF SHOOTING. GOD	KNOWS	IT'S HARD ENOUGH TO HAVE TO BRING A BOY INTO THE WORLD
SIM II (79)	BUT, IDDY,-- /PROLA/ LET HIM GO, THE PIGEON	KNOWS	ITS WAY HOME. LADY FARWATERS SINKS BACK INTO HER SEAT.
GENV IV (127)	CANNOT BE INFLUENCED. IT KNOWS THE TRUTH AS GOD	KNOWS	IT, AND WILL INSTRUCT US ACCORDINGLY. ANYONE WHO
BARB II (301)	/UNDERSHAFT/ (VERY CIVILLY) THE WHOLE NATION	KNOWS	IT, MRS BAINES. /MRS BAINES/ NO, SIR: THE WHOLE NATION
JOAN 6 (147)	THE PROCEDURE MAY BE USEFUL LATER ON: ONE NEVER	KNOWS	. AND THE SOONER IT IS OVER, THE BETTER FOR THAT POOR

CYMB V (147)	INTO THEM; MY BREEDING WAS, SIR, AS YOUR HIGHNESS	KNOWS	. COME HITHER, BOYS, AND PAY YOUR LOVES AND DUTIES TO
MTH4 I (146)	ON ASKING ME TO TELL YOU THINGS THAT EVERYBODY	KNOWS	. COUNTRIES WHERE YOU CAN TRAVEL COMFORTABLY. WHERE
JITT I (18)	LACKS: IS A SENSE OF THE SIGNIFICANCE OF WHAT HE	KNOWS	. I AM REALLY SORRY FOR HIM, AND SHOULD LIKE TO HELP
JOAN PREFACE(26)	THAT ANATOLE FRANCE DOES NOT KNOW WHAT EVERYBODY	KNOWS	. I WISH EVERYBODY KNEW ALL THAT HE KNOWS. ONE FEELS
HART I (62)	HE ONE OF THE ABERDEEN DARNLEYS? /ELLIE/ NOBODY	KNOWS	. JUST FANCY! HE WAS FOUND IN AN ANTIQUE CHEST-- /MRS
JOAN PREFACE(26)	KNOWS. I WISH EVERYBODY KNEW ALL THAT HE	KNOWS	. ONE FEELS ANTIPATHIES AT WORK IN HIS BOOK. HE IS NOT
GENV IV (102)	MY UNDERSTUDY HERE. HE TOO HAS BEEN A SOLDIER. HE	KNOWS	. /BATTLER/ WE ALL BEGIN AS UNDERSTUDIES, AND END,
MTH2 (40)	WHAT LIFE REALLY MEANS. SHE HAS TO DIE BEFORE SHE	KNOWS	. /HASLAM/ (AGREEABLY) THATS IT. /FRANKLYN/ SHE HASNT
PYGM II (240)	AND I DONT CARE WHO HEARS ME SAY IT. MRS PEARCE	KNOWS	. /HIGGINS/ WHAT WAS WRONG, MRS PEARCE? /MRS PEARCE/
SIM II (64)	IS SHE WHO UNITES. /VASHTI/ PROLA IS SHE WHO	KNOWS	. /MAYA/ NO ONE CAN WITHSTAND PROLA. /PROLA/ BE QUIET,
GETT (342)	PRESSURE. ALICE KEEPS THEM OUT NOW. MRS COLLINS	KNOWS	. /MRS GEORGE/ (A FAINT CONVULSION PASSING LIKE A
GETT (319)	OF IT BETTER THAN THE REAL THING, AS EVERY NURSE	KNOWS	. /SOAMES/ ARE YOU SURE THAT ANY OF US, YOUNG OR OLD,
GETT (311)	IN THESE LITTLE MATTERS. PERHAPS HIS LORDSHIP	KNOWS	. /THE BISHOP/ I'M SORRY TO SAY I DONT. BUT SOAMES
LADY (238)	WHAT STRAIN OF MUSIC, SIR? I'M NO MUSICIAN, GOD	KNOWS	. /THE MAN/ THERE IS MUSIC IN YOUR SOUL: MANY OF YOUR
MILL IV (198)	/SAGAMORE/ TOKO! WHAT IS TOKO? /ALASTAIR/ SHE	KNOWS	. TOKO IS AN INFALLIBLE MEDICINE FOR CALMING THE
BULL III (127)	HANS? TELL ME THAT, CORNY DOYLE, AND YOU THAT	KNOWS	. WAS I FIT FOR THE RESPONSIBILITY OR WAS I NOT?
JOAN 1 (57)	HA! YOU JEST ABOUT IT. /STEWARD/ NO, SIR, GOD	KNOWS	. WE ALL HAVE TO GO WITHOUT EGGS JUST AS YOU HAVE,
MTH3 (98)	THE ASSURED CERTAINTY OF THE MAN WHO SEES AND	KNOWS	. YOUR GENIAL BLUSTER, YOUR CHEERY SELF-CONFIDENCE,
DOCT I SD(96)	A COLOSSAL HUMBUG: THE FACT BEING THAT, THOUGH HE	KNOWS	JUST AS MUCH (AND JUST AS LITTLE) AS HIS
MIS. PREFACE(27)	WHO KNOWS ONLY THE OFFICIAL SIDE OF A CONTROVERSY	KNOWS	LESS THAN NOTHING OF ITS NATURE. THE ABLER A
MIS. PREFACE(51)	THAT ITS SCHOLASTIC CULTURE IS A SHAM; THAT IT	KNOWS	LITTLE ABOUT LITERATURE OR ART AND A GREAT DEAL ABOUT
HART I (61)	NO. ON PURPOSE. HE LIKED TALKING TO ME. HE	KNOWS	LOTS OF THE MOST SPLENDID PEOPLE. FASHIONABLE WOMEN
JITT I (19)	TOGETHER: WE ARE PROFESSIONAL COLLEAGUES. HE	KNOWS	ME INTIMATELY; AND IF HE WERE NOT SUCH A CONFOUNDEDLY
DOCT III (138)	/LOUIS/ MINNIE! I SHOULD THINK I DO; AND MINNIE	KNOWS	ME TOO. SHE'S A REALLY NICE GOOD GIRL, CONSIDERING HER
DOCT PREFACE(20)	FOLLOW THE LITERATURE OF THE SCIENTIFIC MOVEMENT,	KNOWS	MORE ABOUT IT THAN THOSE DOCTORS (PROBABLY A LARGE
HART II (93)	TAKE THE LEAST INTEREST IN THE WORKS: HE HARDLY	KNOWS	MORE ABOUT THEM THAN YOU DO. PEOPLE ARE CRUELLY UNJUST
SUPR PREFACE(R31)	MY PROOFS, DELIGHTED LONDON WITH A SERVANT WHO	KNOWS	MORE THAN HIS MASTERS. THE CONCEPTION OF MENDOZA
DOCT PREFACE(10)	THE SAKE OF MAKING THE PATIENT BELIEVE THAT SHE	KNOWS	MORE THAN THE DOCTOR, BUT SHE DARE NOT, FOR HER
GETT PREFACE(217)	HALF A DOZEN MARRIAGES. ANY FAMILY SOLICITOR	KNOWS	MORE THAN THIS; BUT EVEN A FAMILY SOLICITOR, HOWEVER
GETT PREFACE(204)	BUT ON THE CONTRARY TO CONVINCE THEM THAT HE	KNOWS	MUCH BETTER THAN THEY DO, AND THEREFORE DIFFERS FROM
MRS II (210)	BREATHLESS) YOU YOUNG IMP! /VIVIE/ EVERYBODY	KNOWS	MY REPUTATION, MY SOCIAL STANDING, AND THE PROFESSION
ARMS II (44)	CAPTAIN BLUNTSCHLI REALLY WISHES TO STAY. HE	KNOWS	MY WISHES. /BLUNTSCHLI/ (IN HIS DRIEST MILITARY
PYGM II (231)	HOT. IT BEGINS WITH THE SAME LETTER AS BATH. SHE	KNOWS	NO BETTER: SHE LEARNT IT AT HER MOTHER'S KNEE. BUT SHE
GETT PREFACE(204)	US SEEM TO THINK, TO CONVINCE THE VOTERS THAT HE	KNOWS	NO BETTER THAN THEY AS TO THE METHODS OF ATTAINING
MTH1 II (29)	BEAR THAN A MAN; FOR THE BEAR IS NOT ASHAMED: HE	KNOWS	NO BETTER. IF YOU ARE CONTENT, LIKE THE BEAR, I AM
FOUN (218)	CHANCELLOR/ FORGET THE RUDENESS OF MY CLERK: HE	KNOWS	NO BETTER. RESUME YOUR SEAT, I BEG. /MERCER/ IF I HAD
SUPR IV (150)	THANK YOU, TOO. IT'S VERY KIND OF YOU. MY FATHER	KNOWS	NO BETTER. /MALONE/ (FURIOUSLY CLENCHING HIS FISTS)
CYMB V (144)	ARE A GENTLEMAN, GIVE HIM THE LIE. /IACHIMO/ HE	KNOWS	NO BETTER, MADAM. WE MADE A WAGER, HE AND I, IN ITALY
BULL PREFACE(47)	AND THEIR HONEST AND GENEROUS INDIGNATION	KNOWS	NO BOUNDS: THEY FEEL ABOUT THEM LIKE MEN, NOT LIKE
FABL PREFACE(88)	A LEGISLATOR OR ADMINISTRATOR, ABOVE A SOLON WHO	KNOWS	NO LANGUAGE BUT HIS OWN. IT PUTS FACILITY IN DOING SET
MIS. PREFACE(52)	MAY HAVE BECOME THROUGH DISUSE; BUT THE CHILD	KNOWS	NO OTHER WAY OF LIFE THAN THE SLAVE'S WAY. BORN FREE,
HART PREFACE(40)	LOYALLY SILENT; FOR THE ART OF THE DRAMATIC POET	KNOWS	NO PATRIOTISM; RECOGNIZES NO OBLIGATION BUT TRUTH TO
METH PREFACE(R49)	OF THE LIZARD, " DOES NOT WISH TO AVOID DEATH;	KNOWS	NOTHING ABOUT DEATH," WHAT HAS HAPPENED BEING SIMPLY
HART II (97)	YOUR EARS TIGHT; AND SHUT YOUR EYES TOO. HESIONE	KNOWS	NOTHING ABOUT ME: SHE HASNT THE LEAST NOTION OF THE
JITT III (54)	NEVER SAID SO. /AGNES/ DO YOU THINK A MAN'S WIFE	KNOWS	NOTHING ABOUT HIS THOUGHTS EXCEPT WHAT HE TELLS?
BUOY IV (49)	DONT KNOW WHY. I KNOW NOTHING ABOUT HER; AND SHE	KNOWS	NOTHING ABOUT ME. I AM SIMPLE MAD ON THE SUBJECT. /OLD
SIM II (70)	REPORTS THE JUDGMENT DAY IN FULL SWING; BUT PARIS	KNOWS	NOTHING ABOUT IT; HILVERSUM KNOWS NOTHING ABOUT IT;
SIM II (70)	BUT PARIS KNOWS NOTHING ABOUT IT; HILVERSUM	KNOWS	NOTHING ABOUT IT; BERLIN, ROME, MADRID, AND GENEVA
DOCT PREFACE(59)	ORDINARY SOCIOLOGIST. NOW THE MAN IN THE STREET	KNOWS	NOTHING OF BIOMETRIKA: ALL HE KNOWS IS THAT " YOU CAN
MTH2 (77)	THIS FAIRY TALE, DOCTOR BARNABAS? SURELY SCIENCE	KNOWS	NOTHING OF GENESIS, OR OF ADAM AND EVE. /CONRAD/ THEN
GETT PREFACE(201)	KNOWS NOTHING OF THE MAN'S WORKING LIFE AND HE	KNOWS	NOTHING OF HER WORKING LIFE (HE CALLS IT HER HOME
MTH2 (78)	IS BOUND TO EXPLAIN IT. YOU TELL ME THAT SCIENCE	KNOWS	NOTHING OF IT. THEN SCIENCE IS MORE IGNORANT THAN THE
CAPT I (218)	BAW THE LAWK O ME, GAVNER. /RANKIN/ A MISSIONARY	KNOWS	NOTHING OF LEKS OF THAT SOART, OR OF DISLEKS EITHER.
GETT PREFACE(201)	SLEEP IN THE SAME ROOM. IN MOST CASES THE WOMAN	KNOWS	NOTHING OF THE MAN'S WORKING LIFE AND HE KNOWS NOTHING
GETT PREFACE(217)	A FAMILY SOLICITOR, HOWEVER LARGE HIS PRACTICE,	KNOWS	NOTHING OF THE MILLION HOUSEHOLDS WHICH HAVE NO
DOCT PREFACE(28)	FOLLY: ALL THIS, SO PUZZLING TO THE OBSERVER WHO	KNOWS	NOTHING OF THE ECONOMIC SIDE OF THE QUESTION, AND ONLY
GENV III (75)	BUT IN LITTLE WAYS OF WHICH THE PUBLIC	KNOWS	NOTHING WE SIDETRACK THEM. WE SABOTAGE THEM. WE SHAME
PRES (142)	TWENTY MONTHS IN THE CABINET HE KNOWS THAT HE	KNOWS	NOTHING. /MITCHENER/ WE LEARN FROM HISTORY--
JITT I (19)	BE MY WIFE. IT IS A STROKE OF LUCK FOR US THAT HE	KNOWS	NOTHING-- IF INDEED IT IS ONLY LUCK, AND NOT HIS
BARB III (320)	/UNDERSHAFT/ OH, JUST WHAT HE WANTS TO DO. HE	KNOWS	NOTHING; AND HE THINKS HE KNOWS EVERYTHING. THAT
METH PREFACE(R49)	KNOW NO MORE ABOUT DARWINISM THAN A BUTTERFLY	KNOWS	OF A LIZARD'S APPETITE; AND THAT THE PROOF THAT I
SUPR PREFACE(R33)	BY THOSE CHARACTERS INTO WHICH HE PUTS WHAT HE	KNOWS	OF HIMSELF, HIS HAMLETS AND MACBETHS AND LEARS AND
JOAN 4 (107)	AND ANTI-CHRISTIAN; FOR THE CATHOLIC CHURCH	KNOWS	ONLY ONE REALM, AND THAT IS THE REALM OF CHRIST'S
MIS. PREFACE(27)	SUBJECT CAN BE TAUGHT DOGMATICALLY. HE WHO	KNOWS	ONLY THE OFFICIAL SIDE OF A CONTROVERSY KNOWS LESS
DOCT II (123)	YOU SEE, WHEN AN ENGLISHMAN BORROWS, ALL HE	KNOWS	OR CARES IS THAT HE WANTS MONEY; AND HE'LL SIGN
BULL I (86)	WHICH IT TALKS OLD-FASHIONED NONSENSE WHICH IT	KNOWS	PERFECTLY WELL TO BE A CENTURY BEHIND THE TIMES. THATS
CATH 3 (185)	BROKEN MY SWEETBREAD WITH HIS STRONG KNEES . GOD	KNOWS	POOR FOLK SHOULD NOT BE SET UPON SUCH DANGEROUS
FABL PREFACE(94)	OR THEIR SYMBOLS FROM THE MATERIAL OBJECTS IT	KNOWS	QUITE WELL HOW TO COUNT, TO ME A AND B, WHEN THEY
METH PREFACE(R46)	ACTS IN MORE WAYS THAN HE HAS YET NOTICED; FOR HE	KNOWS	QUITE WELL, AS YOU WILL FIND IF YOU ARE NOT TOO PROUD
BARB I (259)	MAKE DIFFICULTIES. I AM NERVOUS ENOUGH, GOODNESS	KNOWS	; BUT I DONT SHEW IT. SARAH AND BARBARA COME IN WITH
PYGM III (249)	THINK THEY OUGHT TO THINK IS BAD ENOUGH, LORD	KNOWS	; BUT WHAT THEY REALLY THINK WOULD BREAK UP THE WHOLE
GETT PREFACE(184)	TO MARRIAGE. HOW COMMON THEY ARE NOBODY	KNOWS	; FOR IN SPITE OF THE POWERFUL PROTECTION AFFORDED TO
MRS II (216)	THAT ANY WOMAN WOULD DO FOR PLEASURE, GOODNESS	KNOWS	; THOUGH TO HEAR THE PIOUS PEOPLE TALK YOU WOULD
ARMS I (11)	I HAVE FOUND A RUSSIAN OFFICER, THANK HEAVEN: HE	KNOWS	SERGIUS. (SPEAKING THROUGH THE DOOR TO SOMEONE
MILL IV (193)	TIRED OF PAYING US UNEXPECTED VISITS NOW THAT SHE	KNOWS	SHE CAN DEPEND ON ME. (HE GOES OUT, BUT IMMEDIATELY
MILL III (181)	LOOKING AT HER SHOES. SHE'S GOT US; AND SHE	KNOWS	SHE'S GOT US. /EPIFANIA/ I DO NOT LIKE THIS
MRS PREFACE(155)	THE SAFEST ADVISER ON THE SUBJECT OF WHICH HE	KNOWS	SO LITTLE. IF I DO NOT DRAW THE SAME CONCLUSION, IT IS
AUGS (274)	IN THE GERMAN CASUALTY LIST. /THE LADY/ NOBODY	KNOWS	THAT BETTER THAN I. WAIT UNTIL YOU HEAR WHAT I HAVE
ROCK II (283)	I'M NOT THE MAN FOR THE JOB, DARLING; AND NOBODY	KNOWS	THAT BETTER THAN YOU. AND I SHALL HATE THE MAN WHO
GETT PREFACE(233)	MUST GIVE WAY, LEGAL TIE OR NO LEGAL TIE; BUT HE	KNOWS	THAT EITHER ONE OR THE OTHER MUST GO. AND A SENSIBLE
SUPR PREFACE(R20)	SAVE THE WOMAN THE TROUBLE OF SCHEMING: PROSPERO	KNOWS	THAT HE HAS ONLY TO THROW FERDINAND AND MIRANDA
LION PREFACE(93)	HE HAS NO SUCH HAPPINESS. HE IS A THIEF AND	KNOWS	THAT HE IS A THIEF. NOTHING CAN RUB THAT OFF HIM. HE
MTH1 II SD(20)	NOT-QUITE-AT-EASE MANNER OF A REVOLTED SON WHO	KNOWS	THAT HE IS NOT FORGIVEN NOR APPROVED OF. /CAIN/ (TO
DEVL I (9)	HE IS SEATED HE ADDS, IN THE TONE OF A MAN WHO	KNOWS	THAT HE IS OPENING A DIFFICULT SUBJECT) HAS CHRISTY
PRES (142)	EVERYTHING. AFTER TWENTY MONTHS IN THE CABINET HE	KNOWS	THAT HE KNOWS NOTHING. /MITCHENER/ WE LEARN FROM
GENV PREFACE(3)	IS NOT VERY TERRIFYING EVEN WHEN EACH OF US	KNOWS	THAT HE OR SHE IS AS LIKELY AS NOT TO BE ONE OF THE
GETT (262)	BEAR WITH ME IN A LITTLE THING LIKE THAT. SHE	KNOWS	THAT HER NAME STICKS IN MY THROAT. BETTER CALL HER
PYGM EPILOG (302)	ANY SUCH TRIAL! -- WILL EVER ALTER THIS. SHE	KNOWS	THAT HIGGINS DOES NOT NEED HER, JUST AS HER FATHER DID
MRS III SD(231)	SWEARING AND RAGING FOULLY TO HIMSELF. BUT HE	KNOWS	THAT HIS CUE IS TO BE SYMPATHETIC. HE TAKES REFUGE IN
MIS. PREFACE(4)	A POOR JOB AND HAD BETTER BE REMANUFACTURED. HE	KNOWS	THAT HIS DEATH WILL MAKE ROOM FOR A BIRTH; AND HE
BARB PREFACE(245)	HAVE REAL MORAL RESPONSIBILITY UNTIL EVERYONE	KNOWS	THAT HIS DEEDS ARE IRREVOCABLE, AND THAT HIS LIFE
POSN PREFACE(396)	(REPORT, PAGE 330), FEELS WITH THE PUBLIC, AND	KNOWS	THAT HIS OFFICE COULD NOT SURVIVE A WIDESPREAD
MIS. PREFACE(69)	PRIG IF HE DOES NOT GO TO SCHOOL, AND THE COSTER	KNOWS	THAT HIS SON WILL BECOME AN ILLITERATE HOOLIGAN IF HE
LIED (192)	BELIEVE ME, NOTHING WILL HAPPEN. YOUR HUSBAND	KNOWS	THAT I AM CAPABLE OF DEFENDING MYSELF. UNDER SUCH
APPL INTRLUD(249)	THE SUN IN THE HEAVENS? (RISING AGAIN) EVERYONE	KNOWS	THAT I AM THE REAL QUEEN. EVERYONE TREATS ME AS THE
MTH2 (46)	THERE TO CONTEST THE PARLIAMENTARY SEAT. BURGE	KNOWS	THAT I HAVE A FOLLOWING, AND THINKS I COULD GET INTO
2TRU II (76)	ME TO SEARCH HER LUGGAGE AT ONCE, BEFORE SHE	KNOWS	THAT I HAVE FOUND HER OUT. /THE COUNTESS/ BUT I HAVE
SUPR I (42)	WHAT IS THE USE OF SAYING NO, ROEBUCK? OCTAVIUS	KNOWS	THAT I WOULD NOT TURN ANY TRULY CONTRITE AND REPENTANT
JITT III (63)	LOT OF THAT AS A DOCTOR. LOOK AT YOUR MOTHER: SHE	KNOWS	THAT IF SHE EATS PRAWNS AND CUCUMBERS SHE WILL HAVE A
SUPR I (6)	CHARACTER INCOMPLETE IF HE IS NOT AMBITIOUS. SHE	KNOWS	THAT IF SHE MARRIED ME SHE WOULD HAVE TO REASON
MIS. PREFACE(3)	MACHINE ANSWERING THE SAME PURPOSE. HE ALSO	KNOWS	THAT IF SOME DEVIL WERE TO CONVINCE US THAT OUR DREAM
DOCT PREFACE(11)	OF HIS OWN OPINION TO RUIN ANOTHER MAN BY IT. HE	KNOWS	THAT IF SUCH CONDUCT WERE TOLERATED IN HIS PROFESSION
MIS. PREFACE(105)	ATTEMPT TO BETTER A HOPELESS WORLD. THE WISE MAN	KNOWS	THAT IMAGINATION IS NOT ONLY A MEANS OF PLEASING
POSN (452)	TOWN YESTERDAY AND PUT UP IN MY HOUSE. EVERYBODY	KNOWS	THAT IN THE MORNING THE HORSE WAS GONE AND YOU WERE
GETT (280)	WHY DO THEY WANT TO MARRY US? BESIDES, REJJY	KNOWS	THAT I'M QUITE FOND OF HIM. I LIKE HIM BECAUSE HE
CATH 1 (163)	ME. THEY ALL KICK ME WHEN YOU KICK THEM. GOD	KNOWS	THAT IS NOT JUST, LITTLE FATHER! /PATIOMKIN/ (LAUGHS
MIS. PREFACE(4)	THAT HE ASPIRED TO BE AND FELL SHORT OF. HE	KNOWS	THAT IT IS THROUGH DEATH AND REBIRTH THAT THIS

MIS. PREFACE(51)	TO THE FINAL EXTREMITY OF THE UNIVERSITY DEGREE	KNOWS	THAT ITS SCHOLASTIC CULTURE IS A SHAM; THAT IT KNOWS
DEST (176)	HUSBAND WHO KNOWS HER THROUGH AND THROUGH:	KNOWS	THAT SHE HAS LIED TO HIM ABOUT HER AGE, HER INCOME,
DEVL II (37)	THE KNIFE. THE ACTION SHEWS QUICKLY HOW WELL HE	KNOWS	THAT SHE HAS AVOIDED HER USUAL PLACE SO AS TO BE AS
DEST (176)	ABOUT EVERYTHING THAT SILLY WOMEN LIE ABOUT:	KNOWS	THAT SHE IS INCAPABLE OF FIDELITY TO ANY PRINCIPLE OR
SUPR I (18)	VOICE, IGNORING HER MOTHER'S BAD TASTE) MAMMA	KNOWS	THAT SHE IS NOT STRONG ENOUGH TO BEAR THE WHOLE
MIS. (128)	NATURE TO PUT A FALSE MASK OF AGE ON HER WHEN SHE	KNOWS	THAT SHE'S AS YOUNG AS EVER? WHY SHOULD SHE LOOK IN
3PLA PREFACE(R29)	THE CHARM AND THE PEACE AND THE SANCTITY, BUT	KNOWS	THAT SUCH MATERIAL COMFORTS ARE NOT FOR HIM. WHEN THE
LION PROLOG (107)	THE SAME THING, ONLY TEN TIMES WORSE? EVERYBODY	KNOWS	THAT THE CHRISTIANS ARE THE VERY LOWEST OF THE LOW.
GENV PREFACE(16)	AS OUR BIGGEST HEADS CAN HOLD; AND A CITIZEN WHO	KNOWS	THAT THE EARTH IS ROUND AND OLDER THAN SIX THOUSAND
ROCK I (199)	AT THE CHURCH HOUSE. BESIDES, EVERYBODY	KNOWS	THAT THE FAMILY MEANS THE BRITISH FAMILY. BY THE WAY,
JOAN PREFACE(26)	ENTER; WHEREAS LANG WAS A SCOT, AND EVERY SCOT	KNOWS	THAT THE GREY MARE IS AS LIKELY AS NOT TO BE THE
LION PREFACE(55)	THE HORSE-SHOE IS HIS. BUT THE BLACKSMITH	KNOWS	THAT THE HORSE-SHOE DOES NOT BELONG SOLELY TO HIM, BUT
MTH5 (238)	EAR AND JAR TOO REPUGNANTLY ON MY SENSORIUM, WHO	KNOWS	THAT THE INEVITABLE RESPONSE TO THAT STIMULUS MAY NOT
CAPT II (256)	WHAT THE POWER OF ENGLAND IS? /BRASSBOUND/ HE	KNOWS	THAT THE MAHDI KILLED MY MASTER GORDON, AND THAT THE
CLEO NOTES (211)	WHEN A COMMON MAN TRIES HARDEST TO GET IT. HE	KNOWS	THAT THE REAL MOMENT OF SUCCESS IS NOT THE MOMENT
GETT PREFACE(219)	NOW THIS IS VIOLENTLY UNTRUE. EVERY ADULT	KNOWS	THAT THE RELATION IN QUESTION CAN AND DOES EXIST
MTH1 I (14)	MAN IS DEEPER IN HIS THOUGHT THAN I AM. THE WOMAN	KNOWS	THAT THERE IS NO SUCH THING AS NOTHING: THE MAN KNOWS
MTH1 I (14)	THAT THERE IS NO SUCH THING AS NOTHING: THE MAN	KNOWS	THAT THERE IS NO SUCH DAY AS TOMORROW. I DO WELL TO
DOCT PREFACE(11)	TO HEAR MEDICAL SHOP TALKED WITHOUT RESERVE	KNOWS	THAT THEY ARE FULL OF STORIES ABOUT EACH OTHER'S
JOAN 6 (130)	STRIVEN WITH THESE DIABOLICAL MADNESSES; AND IT	KNOWS	THAT THEY BEGIN ALWAYS BY VAIN AND IGNORANT PERSONS
SUPR HANDBOK(210)	ADVANCE DIES IN HIS BOSOM AS HE WATCHES THEM: HE	KNOWS	THAT THEY WILL DO JUST WHAT THEIR FATHERS DID, AND
MTH5 (219)	OFF TO MOODLE ABOUT DOING NOTHING; THOUGH SHE	KNOWS	THAT THIS IS FESTIVAL DAY. /THE NEWLY BORN/ WHAT IS
BULL IV (176)	CONNEXION, MR KEEGAN. /KEEGAN/ NOT FROM A MAN WHO	KNOWS	THAT THIS WORLD IS HELL. BUT SINCE THE WORD OFFENDS
SUPR II (50)	BUT THIS CHAP HAS BEEN EDUCATED. WHATS MORE, HE	KNOWS	THAT WE HAVNT. WHAT WAS THAT BOARD SCHOOL OF YOURS,
BARB PREFACE(216)	HAVING GRASPED THE FACT THAT POVERTY IS A CRIME,	KNOWS	THAT WHEN SOCIETY OFFERED HIM THE ALTERNATIVE OF
LION II (144)	SECRET. HE'LL BE AS GENTLE AS A LAMB WHEN HE	KNOWS	THAT YOU ARE HIS FRIEND. STAND QUITE STILL; AND SMILE;
FANY III (309)	EXPECTING MR AND MRS KNOX TO TEA. /GILBEY/ HE	KNOWS	THAT. (HE SITS DOWN. THEN, TO JUGGINS) WHAT IS IT?
HART III (131)	UNIVERSITY; HE HAS BEEN IN THE FOREIGN OFFICE; HE	KNOWS	THE BEST PEOPLE AND HAS LIVED ALL HIS LIFE AMONG THEM.
JOAN 2 (75)	AND NOT TO YOU, ARCHBISHOP, HOLY AS YOU ARE. SHE	KNOWS	THE BLOOD ROYAL IF YOU DONT. (HE STRUTS UP TO THE
MRS II (200)	COURSE WE SHALL ONLY BE TOO HAPPY. I SUPPOSE HE	KNOWS	THE DUKE PERSONALLY. /FRANK/ OH, EVER SO INTIMATELY!
LION PREFACE(55)	CAN GO NO FURTHER. BY THIS TIME NOBODY WHO	KNOWS	THE FIGURES OF THE DISTRIBUTION DEFENDS THEM. THE MOST
POSN (441)	THAT THE LAW, ELDER? /ELDER DANIELS/ THE SHERIFF	KNOWS	THE LAW. I WOULDNT SAY FOR SURE; BUT I THINK IT WOULD
DEST SD(150)	ALL ITS ROADS, RIVERS, HILLS AND VALLEYS, AS HE	KNOWS	THE PALM OF HIS HAND; AND LARGELY BY THAT NEW FAITH OF
MILL IV (201)	BUT MRS FITZFASSENDEN KNOWS BETTER. SHE	KNOWS	THE PRIVILEGES OF HER SEX TO A HAIR'S BREADTH AND
FANY PROLOG (264)	KNOWLEDGE. WE KNOW HIM; AND HE KNOWS US. HE	KNOWS	THE ROPES: HE KNOWS HIS WAY ABOUT: HE KNOWS WHAT HE'S
SIM II (65)	THEY ARE DEAD AND CANT TAKE LIBEL ACTIONS. NOBODY	KNOWS	THE SORT OF PEOPLE WE REALLY ARE. THE PAPERS HAVE BEEN
MRS PREFACE(172)	MUST BE A CACODEMON. WELL, DOES ANYBODY WHO	KNOWS	THE SPORTING WORLD REALLY BELIEVE THAT BOOKMAKERS ARE
JOAN PREFACE(53)	OF THE PRESS WOULD BE UNANIMOUS. NOBODY WHO	KNOWS	THE STAGE HISTORY OF SHAKESPEAR WILL DOUBT THAT THIS
LADY PREFACE(213)	BY CHAPTERS FROM THE HAND OF ARTEMUS WARD. YET HE	KNOWS	THE TASTE AND THE VALUE OF HUMOR. HE WAS ONE OF THE
GENV IV (127)	YOU SHOCK ME. THE CHURCH CANNOT BE INFLUENCED. IT	KNOWS	THE TRUTH AS GOD KNOWS IT, AND WILL INSTRUCT US
MIS. PREFACE(9)	UP A CHILD IN THE WAY IT SHOULD GO. NOW NOBODY	KNOWS	THE WAY A CHILD SHOULD GO. ALL THE WAYS DISCOVERED SO
MRS I (183)	TO MEET YOUR MOTHER? /VIVIE/ (COOLLY) WHY? SHE	KNOWS	THE WAY. /PRAED/ (DISCONCERTED) ER-- I SUPPOSE SHE
GENV II (63)	PILOT HER THROUGH THE DIVISION LOBBY UNTIL SHE	KNOWS	THE WAY. SHE NEED NOT KNOW ANYTHING ELSE. /THE
MILL III (184)	IT JUST THE SAME OLD ROUND TO THE SAME PLACES. HE	KNOWS	THE WHOLESALERS. MR SUPERFLEW IS SUPERFLUOUS. WE SHALL
SUPR II SD(48)	AND THAT, TOO, RATHER CYNICALLY, LIKE A MAN WHO	KNOWS	THE WORLD WELL FROM ITS SEAMY SIDE. HE SPEAKS SLOWLY
BARB III (332)	AND THE AGENT GENERAL FOR SOUTH WESTERN AUSTRALIA	KNOWS	THEM PERSONALLY AND HAS ASSURED ME THAT THEY ARE MOST
BUOY III (34)	MAKES A DIFFERENCE WE CANNOT GET OVER. SHE	KNOWS	THINGS A LADY OUGHT NOT TO KNOW. /MRS THIRDBORN/
ROCK PREFACE(167)	PURPOSES HAS TO BE CLASSED AS IGNORANT, THOUGH HE	KNOWS	THINGS THAT UNIVERSITY PROFESSORS DO NOT KNOW. HE IS
CLEO NOTES (211)	BENCH FASHION, TELL A LIE WHICH EVERYBODY	KNOWS	TO BE A LIE (AND CONSEQUENTLY EXPECTS HIM AS A MATTER
GETT (355)	IS ONLY ONE RELIGION FOR ME: THAT WHICH MY SOUL	KNOWS	TO BE TRUE; BUT EVEN IRRELIGION HAS ONE TENET; AND
FANY PROLOG (264)	IS AN INSIDE KNOWLEDGE. WE KNOW HIM; AND HE	KNOWS	US. HE KNOWS THE ROPES: HE KNOWS HIS WAY ABOUT: HE
MIS. PREFACE(4)	HE GETS INTO BED AND SENDS FOR A DOCTOR. HE	KNOWS	VERY WELL AT THE BACK OF HIS CONSCIENCE THAT HE IS
MIS. PREFACE(3)	THEMSELVES. BUT THE INTELLIGENTLY IMAGINATIVE MAN	KNOWS	VERY WELL THAT IT IS WASTE OF LABOR TO MAKE A MACHINE
JOAN 4 (95)	YOU TO BE SO WITH IMPUNITY. BUT YOUR LORDSHIP	KNOWS	VERY WELL THAT I AM NOT ATTACHED TO THE SOIL IN A
CATH 4 (195)	LEST THE MIGHTY MAN BRING HIS WHIP TO YOU. GOD	KNOWS	WE ALL NEED PARDON! /CLAIRE/ (AT THE TOP OF HER
CATH 3 (184)	SOLDIERS WHO HAVE BROUGHT THEM TO YOU; FOR GOD	KNOWS	WE GET BUT LITTLE TO DRINK. /EDSTASTON/ (
CATH 3 (185)	PETERSBURG, LITTLE SPITFIRE. /THE SERGEANT/ GOD	KNOWS	WE HAVE NO ORDERS TO HARM YOU, LITTLE MOTHER. OUR DUTY
MTH2 (56)	/BURGE/ I WISH YOUD BE SERIOUS, LUBIN. GOD	KNOWS	WE HAVE PASSED THROUGH TIMES TERRIBLE ENOUGH TO MAKE
HART PREFACE(38)	HIS INSPIRED MESSAGES BECAME SCRAPS OF PAPER. HE	KNOWS	WELL THAT FROM THE PEACE CONFERENCE WILL COME, IN
DOCT PREFACE(70)	FOR LIFE IN AN OVERCROWDED PROFESSION, AND	KNOWS	WELL THAT " A GOOD BEDSIDE MANNER" WILL CARRY HIM TO
CLEO IV (185)	THAT SHE IS DRUNK WITH WINE. NOT SO RUFIO: HE	KNOWS	WELL THE RED VINTAGE THAT HAS INEBRIATED HER). /RUFIO/
DEST SD(152)	OF RED WINE. THE LANDLORD, GIUSEPPE GRANDI, SHE	KNOWS	WELL. HE IS A SWARTHY VIVACIOUS SHREWDLY CHEERFUL
ARMS III (70)	AND I, A COMMONPLACE SWISS SOLDIER WHO HARDLY	KNOWS	WHAT A DECENT LIFE IS AFTER FIFTEEN YEARS OF BARRACKS
KING I (193)	AND HE KEEPS YOU INTO THE BARGAIN. HE HARDLY	KNOWS	WHAT A PARLIAMENT IS. HE DRAGOONS THE PROTESTANTS OUT
BULL PREFACE(63)	DILLON, REPRESENTING THE IRISH PARTY, WHICH WELL	KNOWS	WHAT BRITISH OCCUPATIONS AND FINDLAY " LOYALISM" MEAN,
PHIL I (88)	RENDERED BY WOMANLY WOMEN AND MANLY MEN AND DEUCE	KNOWS	WHAT ELSE. IS IT AT THE IBSEN CLUB THAT YOU SEE ALL
6CAL (103)	(RAISING HER) : YOU SHOULD BE MORE CAREFUL: WHO	KNOWS	WHAT HARM YOU MAY HAVE DONE YOURSELF FLOPPING ON YOUR
O'FL (212)	AND YOURE WISER SO THAN THE OTHERS THAT ONLY	KNOWS	WHAT HE DONE. /SIR PEARCE/ (MAKING THE BEST OF IT,
APPL I (231)	(THOUGHTFUL) TAKE IT EASY, FRIENDS. JOE	KNOWS	WHAT HE IS ABOUT. /LYSISTRATA/ OF COURSE HE DOES. I
ROCK II (249)	OF ME, MR MAYOR. YOU KNOW THAT I AM A MAN WHO	KNOWS	WHAT HE IS TALKING ABOUT. WELL, I TELL YOU THAT THE
POSN PREFACE(430)	WOULD SETTLE THE WHOLE DIFFICULTY, BUT NO MAN	KNOWS	WHAT HE MEANS BY COMMON SENSE, THOUGH EVERY MAN CAN
GENV PREFACE(16)	POLITICAL PARTIES AND CLUBS IN WHICH NONE OF THEM	KNOWS	WHAT HE OR SHE IS TALKING ABOUT. SOME OF THEM HAVE
FANY PROLOG (265)	HE KNOWS THE ROPES: HE KNOWS HIS WAY ABOUT: HE	KNOWS	WHAT HE'S TALKING ABOUT. /THE COUNT/ (WITH A LITTLE
FANY EPILOG (330)	IS IT SERIOUS, OR IS IT SPOOF? IF THE AUTHOR	KNOWS	WHAT HIS PLAY IS, LET HIM TELL US WHAT IT IS. IF HE
3PLA PREFACE(R26)	OF PLAYS, MR ROBERT BUCHANAN, A DRAMATIST WHO	KNOWS	WHAT I KNOW AND REMEMBERS WHAT I REMEMBER OF THE
MILL I (154)	NOT THINK IT? WHAT DO YOU MEAN? /ALASTAIR/ HE	KNOWS	WHAT I MEAN. /EPIFANIA/ SOME SILLY JOKE, I SUPPOSE.
NEVR I (217)	I MUST GET THAT NAME RIGHT, OR HEAVEN	KNOWS	WHAT I SHALL CALL HIM. /GLORIA/ PHIL: CAN YOU BELIEVE
SIM II (65)	/IDDY/ PROLA CAN RULE THIS HOUSE BECAUSE SHE	KNOWS	WHAT IS HAPPENING IN IT. BUT HOW IS SHE TO BE AN
SUPR II (64)	NEVER BE ABLE TO KEEP THE SECRET UNLESS EVERYBODY	KNOWS	WHAT IT IS. MR MALONE: IF YOU GO TO NICE WITH VIOLET,
SUPR IV (154)	TAKE ONE OF THEM UNTIL IVE SEEN IT. ONE NEVER	KNOWS	WHAT MAY BE WRONG WITH THESE PLACES. /MALONE/ I WONT.
GENV III (76)	GUNWOMAN HERE: I HATE HER BECAUSE SHE IS HEAVEN	KNOWS	WHAT MIXTURE OF SPANIARD AND INDIAN AND SAVAGE. /THE
WIDO I (17)	AND INVITATIONS AND CONGRATULATIONS AND THE DEUCE	KNOWS	WHAT NOT. SO JUST PUT IT IN SUCH A WAY THAT AUNT MARIA
MIS. PREFACE(30)	MAN AND THE WOMAN. HE IS LED TO BELIEVE THAT SHE	KNOWS	WHAT SHE IS PROMISING, AND THAT HE IS IN NO DANGER OF
PRES (132)	UP. /THE ORDERLY/ ME UNLOCK HER! I DURSENT. LORD	KNOWS	WHAT SHE'D DO TO ME. /MITCHENER/ (PEPPERILY, RISING)
PHIL II (96)	PLUMP MYSELF DOWN ON A SEAT BESIDE HER: GOODNESS	KNOWS	WHAT SHE'D THINK I WANTED! THATS ONE OF THE DELIGHTS
ROCK II (269)	BY PROMISING THEM TO HANG THE KAISER, OR LORD	KNOWS	WHAT SILLINESS THAT SHOULDNT HAVE IMPOSED ON A CHILD
WIDO II (31)	ON HIS PROPERTIES THAN ANYONE WOULD BELIEVE THAT	KNOWS	WHAT SUCH PROPERTIES ARE. I KNOW MY MERITS, DR TRENCH,
INCA (252)	GREAT A MAN AS THE INCA. AND -- WELL, EVERYBODY	KNOWS	WHAT THE INCA'S UNCLE WAS. /ERMYNTRUDE/ MY EXPERIENCE
ROCK PREFACE(182)	OF THE GODS IS NOW AND ALWAYS; AND ALL THE WORLD	KNOWS	WHAT THE PEACE OF YOUR JEWISH GOD MEANS. HAVE I NOT
JITT I (16)	I HAVE TO ENDURE BETWEEN TIMES. AND WHO	KNOWS	WHAT WOULD HAPPEN IF I WERE TO BREAK UP YOUR HOME AND
MTH2 (50)	RESPONSIBLE POSITION. NEITHER I NOR ANYONE ELSE	KNOWS	WHAT YOUR BELIEFS ARE, OR EVEN WHETHER YOU HAVE EITHER
ARMS III (70)	NOBLE NATURES AND CAVALRY CHARGES AND GOODNESS	KNOWS	WHAT! AND I, A COMMONPLACE SWISS SOLDIER WHO HARDLY
SUPR III (94)	BEAUTY, ITS HOLINESS, ITS SPIRITUALITY, ITS DEVIL	KNOWS	WHAT! -- EXCUSE ME; BUT IT DOES SO BORE ME. THEY DONT
APPL PREFACE(173)	BECAUSE HE HAS THE ACE OF TRUMPS IN HIS HAND AND	KNOWS	WHEN TO PLAY IT, AS THE PRETTIER PLAYER OF THE TWO HE
APPL I (236)	YOU CARRY IT BETTER, BERT. /PLINY/ MIKE NEVER	KNOWS	WHEN TO STOP. /CRASSUS/ THE TIME FOR MIKE TO STOP IS
HART II (120)	BE SO MUCH WATER. GO GET ME ANOTHER: GUINNESS	KNOWS	WHERE IT IS. YOU HAD BETTER SEE FOR YOURSELF THE
PYGM III (256)	TO HER PRESENT PITCH. BESIDES, SHE'S USEFUL. SHE	KNOWS	WHERE MY THINGS ARE, AND REMEMBERS MY APPOINTMENTS AND
MIS. (136)	MEMBER OF MY CLUB WANTS TO STEAL MY UMBRELLA, HE	KNOWS	WHERE TO FIND IT. IF A MAN PUT UP FOR THE CLUB WHO HAD
DEST (181)	ABOUT PUTTING A MAN UNDER ARREST: ONE NEVER	KNOWS	WHERE TO FIND-- (HE TALKS HIMSELF OUT OF THE ROOM).
JITT III (65)	DOWN WOEFULLY BESIDE HER). HE'S GONE; AND HEAVEN	KNOWS	WHETHER HE WILL EVER COME BACK. THIS IS A MARKED
CLEO IV (182)	ANYTHING. MY BRAINS ARE ASLEEP. BESIDES, WHO	KNOWS	WHETHER I SHALL RETURN TO ROME? /RUFIO/ (ALARMED)
O'FL (212)	DID WAS BRAVE AND MANLY, ANYHOW. /O'FLAHERTY/ GOD	KNOWS	WHETHER IT WAS OR NOT, BETTER THAN YOU NOR ME.
CLEO NOTES (207)	I CAN ONLY IMITATE HUMANITY AS I KNOW IT. NOBODY	KNOWS	WHETHER SHAKESPEAR THOUGHT THAT ANCIENT ATHENIAN
ARMS III (54)	REDEEMED IT THE DAY BEFORE YESTERDAY. HEAVEN ONLY	KNOWS	WHETHER THE PAWNBROKER CLEARED OUT THE POCKETS OR NOT.
SUPR PREFACE(R14)	HAD YOU AND I BEEN IN HIS PLACE AT HIS AGE, WHO	KNOWS	WHETHER WE MIGHT NOT HAVE DONE AS HE DID, UNLESS
METH PREFACE(R37)	EDUCATED CHILD OVER THE AGE OF SIX, ONE HARDLY	KNOWS	WHICH IS THE MORE APPALLING: THE ABJECTNESS OF THE
BARB PREFACE(242)	GOES FREE ALTHOUGH EVERYBODY IN THE DISTRICT	KNOWS	WHO HE IS AND WHAT HE HAS DONE. THEY DO NOT BETRAY

ROCK II (263)	AND LADIES' MAIDS AND SCULLERY MAIDS AND DEUCE	KNOWS	WHO NOT. /THE DUKE/ HOW TRUE, ARTHUR! HOW PROFOUNDLY
ARMS II (40)	BUT HE ASKS FOR YOU, MADAM. AND I DONT THINK HE	KNOWS	WHO YOU ARE: HE SAID THE LADY OF THE HOUSE. HE GAVE ME
JOAN 2 (72)	GODDAMS, DESERTERS, ROBBERS, AND LORD	KNOWS	WHO; AND THEY NEVER MET A SOUL EXCEPT THE COUNTRY
METH PREFACE(R25)	THEM UNTIL THEY COME. NOBODY KNOWS HOW: NOBODY	KNOWS	WHY: ALL WE KNOW IS THAT THE THING ACTUALLY TAKES
GENV IV (124)	BY DISTANCES CALLED QUANTUMS OR QUANTA. NOBODY	KNOWS	WHY. IF THE EARTH IS JUMPING TO A WIDER ORBIT IT IS
JITT II (28)	HERSELF AWAY? /FESSLER/ WOMEN DO, SOMETIMES. GOD	KNOWS	WHY! BUT MEANWHILE, POOR MRS HALDENSTEDT IS MOST
DOCT PREFACE(21)	VIRGINIA SNAKE ROOT WILL BE AN INGREDIENT. HEAVEN	KNOWS	WHY! VIRGINIA SNAKE ROOT FASCINATES THE IMAGINATION
GETT PREFACE(183)	AND ASTONISHED WHEN I, WHO AM SUPPOSED (HEAVEN	KNOWS	WHY!) TO HAVE THE MOST ADVANCED VIEWS ATTAINABLE ON
DOCT II (129)	SOMETIMES A MAN KNOWS BEST; AND SOMETIMES HE	KNOWS	WORST. YOUD MUCH BETTER CURE THEM BOTH. /RIDGEON/ I
MRS I (193)	THIS (PUTTING DOWN THE RIFLE). I'M SO GLAD SHE	KNOWS	YOU: YOURE JUST THE SORT OF FELLOW SHE OUGHT TO KNOW.
CATH 1 (166)	TELL US WHAT TO DO. OUR LIVES ARE YOURS; BUT GOD	KNOWS	YOU ARE NOT FIT TO DIE. /PATIOMKIN/ (ABSURDLY
POSN (452)	STRAPPER BECAUSE MY OWN'S GONE LAME. EVERYBODY	KNOWS	YOU ARRIVED IN THE TOWN YESTERDAY AND PUT UP IN MY
LION I (122)	(HASTILY) DONT SLAP ME ON THE BACK, BROTHER. SHE	KNOWS	YOU MEAN ME. /FERROVIUS/ HOW I WISH I WERE WEAK LIKE
FANY PROLOG (267)	INNOCENT: EVERYBODY WHO READS YOUR ARTICLES	KNOWS	YOURE AS INNOCENT AS A LAMB. /TROTTER/ WHAT! /FANNY/
BULL II (103)	WOMEN; BUT I'LL TELL YOU THIS. THE MORE A MAN	KNOWS	, AND THE FARTHER HE TRAVELS, THE MORE LIKELY HE IS TO
FOUN (211)	LEG YOURSELF OCCASIONALLY FOR ALL THE PUBLIC	KNOWS	, EH? EVEN IF YOU ARE VIRTUOUS, I SHOULD PROBABLY
CATH 1 (164)	TO HER SACRED MAJESTY THE EMPRESS. GOD	KNOWS	, HE NEEDS YOUR COUNTENANCE AND PROTEC-- (HE VANISHES
BARB PREFACE(243)	BROUGHT TO REPUDIATE THE LAWS AND INSTITUTIONS HE	KNOWS	, HE WILL REPUDIATE THE VERY CONCEPTION OF LAW AND THE
LADY (248)	WHAT THEY BEST LIKE; AND WHAT THEY BEST LIKE, GOD	KNOWS	, IS NOT THEIR OWN BETTERMENT AND INSTRUCTION, AS WE
CATH 2 (175)	MY SUFFERINGS. /THE PRINCESS DASHKOFF/ GOD	KNOWS	, LITTLE MOTHER, WE ALL IMPLORE YOU TO GIVE YOUR
APPL I (230)	DO IS DONE BY THE WILL OF THE PEOPLE, WHO, GOD	KNOWS	, NEVER DREAMT OF IT, AND WOULD NOT HAVE UNDERSTOOD IT
SUPR I (44)	SO FORTH. BUT I KNOW, AND THE WHOLE WORLD REALLY	KNOWS	, THOUGH IT DARE NOT SAY SO, THAT YOU WERE RIGHT TO
JOAN 6 (140)	/LADVENU/ MY LORD: WHAT SHE SAYS IS, GOD	KNOWS	, VERY WRONG AND SHOCKING; BUT THERE IS A GRAIN OF
2TRU II (72)	TO BE A GENTLEMAN? SWEETIE IS BAD ENOUGH, HEAVEN	KNOWS	, WITH HER VULGARITY AND HER LOW CUNNING: ALWAYS
PRES (156)	IT'S NOT LOADED. IT'S HEAVY ENOUGH, GOODNESS	KNOWS	, WITHOUT PUTTING BULLETS IN IT. /MITCHENER/ (
SUPR III (83)	FAMILY OF FIGHTERS; AND AS YOUR SISTER WELL	KNOWS	, YOU WOULD HAVE AS MUCH CHANCE AGAINST ME AS A
LIED (196)	SEEMS APPROPRIATE ENOUGH AT PRESENT, GOODNESS	KNOWS	! HOWEVER, YOURE A POET, AND YOU OUGHT TO KNOW. /HE/
PYGM II (229)	(COMING OFF THE PIANO RESTLESSLY) OH, LORD	KNOWS	! I SUPPOSE THE WOMAN WANTS TO LIVE HER OWN LIFE; AND
MTH3 (118)	/MRS LUTESTRING/ WHAT! WHEN THE PRESIDENT	KNOWS	! IT WILL BE ALL OVER THE PLACE BEFORE THE END OF THE
BULL II (110)	DOIN AT THE ROUN TOWER? /AUNT JUDY/ OH, THE LORD	KNOWS	! ROMANCIN, I SUPPOSE. PRAPS SHE THINKS LARRY WOULD
LIED (203)	AT HIM) WHAT SHE CAN SEE IN YOU, GOODNESS ONLY	KNOWS	! /HER HUSBAND/ (BEAMING WITH REMORSE) MY DEAR CHAP,
VWOO 3 (137)	COULD GET ANOTHER ASSISTANT FOR? /A/ HEAVEN ONLY	KNOWS	! /Z/ (IN A FURY) I'LL GO THIS VERY DAY. I'LL GO
		KNOX	
LADY PREFACE(212)	TO MRS PROUDIE A DON JUAN, TO ASPASIA A JOHN	KNOX	: IN SHORT, TO EVERYONE HIS COMPLEMENT RATHER THAN HIS
FANY III (312)	AS IT WERE, AN ACCIDENT. /GILBEY/ IT'S NO USE,	KNOX	: LOOK IT IN THE FACE. DID I EVER TELL YOU MY FATHER
FANY III (320)	/GILBEY/ DONT BE A FOOL, MARIA. LOOK HERE,	KNOX	: WE CANT LET THIS GO ON. PEOPLE CANT BE ALLOWED TO
FANY III (324)	IS ABOVE ME. CAN YOU MAKE ANYTHING OUT OF IT,	KNOX	? /KNOX/ THE LONG AND SHORT OF IT SEEMS TO BE THAT HE
FANY I (281)	HAVE THE KNOXES TO DINNER EVERY FRIDAY. MARGARET	KNOX	AND BOBBY ARE AS GOOD AS ENGAGED. MR KNOX IS MY
FANY III (317)	YOUR PEOPLE WERE IN THE WHOLESALE AND THOUGHT	KNOX	AND GILBEY WASNT GOOD ENOUGH FOR YOU? /MRS KNOX/ NO,
FANY I (281)	WITH THE EXAMPLE OF A RELIGIOUS WOMAN LIKE MRS	KNOX	BEFORE HIS EYES? I CANT UNDERSTAND HOW HE COULD BRING
FANY III (321)	ACKNOWLEDGES THE INTRODUCTION SUSPICIOUSLY. MRS	KNOX	BOWS GRAVELY, LOOKING KEENLY AT DORA AND TAKING HER
FANY II SD(296)	TO LET IT OUT. /MARGARET/ I'LL TELL EVERYBODY.	KNOX	COLLAPSES IN DESPAIR. MRS KNOX TRIES TO PRAY AND
FANY II SD(295)	THE THINGS THAT USED TO HOLD ME CAN HOLD ME NOW.	KNOX	COMES BACK, UNABLE TO BEAR HIS SUSPENSE. /KNOX/ HOW
FANY II SD(285)	BOOKS AND ALBUMS ON IT, AND CHAIRS NEAR IT. MR	KNOX	COMES IN ALMOST FURTIVELY, A TROUBLED MAN OF FIFTY,
FANY II SD(287)	SHE THROWS UP THE SASH AND LEANS OUT. MARGARET	KNOX	COMES IN, FLUSTERED AND ANNOYED. SHE IS A STRONG,
FANY II SD(287)	SHE IS ANNOYED. /MARGARET/ MOTHER. MOTHER. MRS	KNOX	DRAWS IN HER HEAD AND CONFRONTS HER DAUGHTER. /MRS
FANY III (318)	WITH HIS DUTIES, HANDING ROUND CUPS OF TEA AS MRS	KNOX	FILLS THEM). SHRIEKS OF LAUGHTER FROM BELOW STAIRS
FANY III SD(320)	DUVALLET COMES IN BEHAVING HIMSELF PERFECTLY.	KNOX	FOLLOWS. /MARGARET/ OH-- LET ME INTRODUCE. MY FRIEND
FANY II (290)	/DUVALLET/ OH PLEASE! IT DOES NOT MATTER. (	KNOX	HANDS HIM TWO SOVEREIGNS). IF YOU INSIST-- (HE POCKETS
FANY II SD(285)	MAN WITH WHITE HAIR AND THIN SMOOTH SKIN, WHILST	KNOX	HAS COARSE BLACK HAIR, AND BLUE JAWS WHICH NO DILIGENCE
FANY II SD(290)	DONT RING, JO. SEE THE GENTLEMAN OUT YOURSELF.	KNOX	HASTILY SEES DUVALLET OUT. MOTHER AND DAUGHTER SIT
FANY PREFACE(255)	ALL AS DEAD AS MUTTON. OUT OF THE MOUTH OF MRS	KNOX	I HAVE DELIVERED ON THEM THE JUDGMENT OF HER GOD. THE
FANY III (308)	HIM TO THE DOOR). YOU UNDERSTAND, SIR, THAT MISS	KNOX	IS A LADY ABSOLUTELY COMME IL FAUT? /DUVALLET/
FANY II SD(285)	WHICH NO DILIGENCE IN SHAVING CAN WHITEN. MRS	KNOX	IS A PLAIN WOMAN, DRESSED WITHOUT REGARD TO FASHION,
FANY III (315)	UNTO YOU. /GILBEY/ COME, MRS KNOX, DONT TELL ME	KNOX	IS A SINNER. I KNOW BETTER. I'M SURE YOUD BE THE FIRST
FANY I (281)	KNOX AND BOBBY ARE AS GOOD AS ENGAGED. MR	KNOX	IS MY HUSBAND'S PARTNER. MRS KNOX IS VERY RELIGIOUS;
FANY III (316)	AS IF I'D REALLY DONE ANYTHING. /MRS GILBEY/ MRS	KNOX	IS SPEAKING FOR YOUR GOOD, ROB. /GILBEY/ WELL, I DONT
FANY I (281)	AS ENGAGED. MR KNOX IS MY HUSBAND'S PARTNER. MRS	KNOX	IS VERY RELIGIOUS; BUT SHE'S QUITE CHEERFUL. WE DINE
FANY II SD(285)	ACT II. ON THE AFTERNOON OF THE SAME DAY, MRS	KNOX	IS WRITING NOTES IN HER DRAWING ROOM, AT A
FANY III (321)	TO KEEP UP HIS SPIRITS) MISS DELANEY: MR AND MRS	KNOX	. (KNOX, AS HE RESUMES HIS SEAT, ACKNOWLEDGES THE
FANY III (300)	JUGGINS RETURNS. /JUGGINS/ (ANNOUNCING) MISS	KNOX	. MARGARET COMES IN. JUGGINS WITHDRAWS. /MARGARET/
BULL PREFACE(38)	LEGITIMATE SUCCESSOR OF MARTIN LUTHER AND JOHN	KNOX	. NOWADAYS, HOWEVER, VOLTAIRE'S JOKES ARE EITHER
FANY III (325)	HER WHETHER OR NO. /BOBBY/ I FEEL I OUGHT TO, MRS	KNOX	. /GILBEY/ HOLD YOUR TONGUE. MIND YOUR OWN BUSINESS.
FANY III (304)	TO ME, ANYHOW. /BOBBY/ (HUFFED) I'M SORRY, MISS	KNOX	. /MARGARET/ GOODBYE, MR GILBEY. (SHE TURNS ON HER
FANY III (326)	TO PROPOSE THAT SOLUTION OF YOUR PROBLEM, MR	KNOX	. /MRS GILBEY/ WELL, I NEVER! /KNOX/ D'YE MEAN IT?
FANY III (314)	I'M OBLIGED TO YOU FOR YOUR GOOD OPINION, MRS	KNOX	. /MRS KNOX/ WELL, I WILL SAY FOR YOU, MR GILBEY, THAT
FANY III (307)	OR THE NEW ICELAND WRESTLING. ADMIRABLE, MISS	KNOX	. THE ATHLETIC YOUNG ENGLISHWOMAN IS AN EXAMPLE TO ALL
FANY III (311)	/JUGGINS/ (ENTERING AND ANNOUNCING) MR AND MRS	KNOX	. THE KNOXES COME IN. JUGGINS TAKES TWO CHAIRS FROM THE
FANY II SD(287)	HE'S OUT OF SIGHT. KNOX RUSHES FROM THE ROOM. MRS	KNOX	LOOKS ANXIOUSLY AND EXCITEDLY FROM THE WINDOW, THEN SHE
FANY II (288)	OVERWHELMED, SITS AT THE OTHER SIDE OF THE TABLE.	KNOX	REMAINS STANDING IN THE MIDDLE OF THE ROOM). /DUVALLET/
FANY II SD(287)	ROUND THE HOUSE. DO DO SOMETHING TO STOP HIM.	KNOX	RETURNS WITH A GOOD-LOOKING YOUNG MARINE OFFICER.
FANY II SD(290)	HER EXAMPLE. THEY LOOK AT ONE ANOTHER AGAIN. MR	KNOX	RETURNS. /KNOX/ (SHORTLY AND STERNLY) AMELIA: THIS IS
FANY II SD(287)	TELL YOU. CATCH THE MAN BEFORE HE'S OUT OF SIGHT.	KNOX	RUSHES FROM THE ROOM. MRS KNOX LOOKS ANXIOUSLY AND
FANY III (317)	I NEVER DENIED THAT YOUVE A GREAT INTELLECT, MRS	KNOX	-- /MRS KNOX/ OH, GET ALONG WITH YOU, GILBEY, IF YOU
FANY III (313)	BEEN GOING IT QUITE FAR ENOUGH, ROB. (TO MRS	KNOX	) HE WONT GET UP IN THE MORNINGS NOW: HE THAT WAS
FANY III (311)	HOSTESS. THEN HE WITHDRAWS. /MRS GILBEY/ (TO MRS	KNOX	) HOW ARE YOU, DEAR? /MRS KNOX/ NICELY, THANK YOU.
FANY III (314)	GILBEY) THATS A NEW NAME HE'S GOT FOR ME. (TO	KNOX	) I TELL YOU, JO, THIS DOESNT SIT WELL ON YOU. YOU MAY
FANY III (316)	KICKING THEIR HEELS ALL OVER THE PLACE? (TO	KNOX	) I WAS NEVER ONE TO INTERFERE BETWEEN MAN AND WIFE,
FANY III (318)	HIM WITH SUSPICION. /GILBEY/ (WHISPERING TO	KNOX	) YOU ASK HIM. /KNOX/ (TO JUGGINS/ JUST A WORD WITH
FANY III (316)	WAS NEVER ONE TO INTERFERE BETWEEN MAN AND WIFE,	KNOX	; BUT IF MARIA STARTED ORDERING ME ABOUT LIKE THAT--
FANY II SD(290)	AT ONE ANOTHER WITHOUT SAYING A WORD. MRS	KNOX	SLOWLY SITS DOWN. MARGARET FOLLOWS HER EXAMPLE. THEY
FANY III (311)	AND SHE TAKES THE CHAIR NEAREST MRS GILBEY. MR	KNOX	TAKES THE OTHER CHAIR). /GILBEY/ (SITTING DOWN) I WAS
FANY III (326)	FEEL I AM A MAN WITH A CHARACTER. IT IS FOR MISS	KNOX	TO DECIDE. /MARGARET/ I GOT INTO A FRIGHTFUL ROW ONCE
FANY III (309)	GILBEY/ OH, JUGGINS, WE'RE EXPECTING MR AND MRS	KNOX	TO TEA. /GILBEY/ HE KNOWS THAT. (HE SITS DOWN. THEN,
FANY II SD(296)	TELL EVERYBODY. KNOX COLLAPSES IN DESPAIR. MRS	KNOX	TRIES TO PRAY AND CANNOT. MARGARET STANDS INFLEXIBLE.
FANY III (326)	TO HEAR. /JUGGINS/ I WILL EXPLAIN; BUT ONLY MRS	KNOX	WILL UNDERSTAND. I ONCE INSULTED A SERVANT. RASHLY; FOR
FANY III (321)	UP HIS SPIRITS) MISS DELANEY: MR AND MRS KNOX. (	KNOX	, AS HE RESUMES HIS SEAT, ACKNOWLEDGES THE INTRODUCTION
FANY III (315)	HAVE BEEN ADDED UNTO YOU. /GILBEY/ COME, MRS	KNOX	, DONT TELL ME KNOX IS A SINNER. I KNOW BETTER. I'M
FANY II (288)	PERFECTLY. (HE SPEAKS ENGLISH BETTER THAN	KNOX	, HAVING LEARNT IT ON BOTH SIDES OF THE ATLANTIC).
FANY III (325)	/GILBEY/ WELL, IF THATS YOUR RELIGION, AMELIA	KNOX	, I WANT NO MORE OF IT. WOULD YOU INVITE THEM TO YOUR
FANY III (323)	ONE IS A HUMAN BEING-- AN END IN HIMSELF. OH, MRS	KNOX	, IF ONLY YOUR MILITARY GENIUS WERE EQUAL TO YOUR MORAL
FANY III (313)	ALL THOSE LESSONS WE PAID FOR. /GILBEY/ LORD,	KNOX	, IT WAS LUCKY YOU AND ME GOT LET IN TOGETHER. I TELL
FANY II (288)	(SHE SITS BETWEEN THE TABLE AND THE SOFA. MRS	KNOX	, OVERWHELMED, SITS AT THE OTHER SIDE OF THE TABLE.
FANY III (319)	MADAM. /GILBEY/ WHOS WITH HIM? /JUGGINS/ MISS	KNOX	, SIR. /GILBEY/ MISS KNOX! ARE YOU SURE? IS THERE
FANY III (311)	/GILBEY/ (SITTING DOWN) I WAS JUST SAYING,	KNOX	, WHAT IS THE WORLD COMING TO? /KNOX/ (APPEALING TO
FANY II (289)	I SHOULD BE DEALT WITH LENIENTLY. YET MISS	KNOX	, WHO USED HER FIST, GOT A MONTH, BUT WITH THE OPTION
FANY II SD(285)	WINDOW ON THE LEFT, BOTH FURTHER AWAY THAN MRS	KNOX	, WHOSE BACK IS PRESENTED TO AN OBSOLETE UPRIGHT PIANO
FANY III (319)	HIM? /JUGGINS/ MISS KNOX, SIR. /GILBEY/ MISS	KNOX	! ARE YOU SURE? IS THERE ANYONE ELSE? /JUGGINS/ ONLY
FANY III (314)	IT SHE KNEW NOTHING ABOUT. /GILBEY/ OH, COME, MRS	KNOX	! GIRLS ARE NOT SO INNOCENT AS ALL THAT. /MRS KNOX/ I
		KNOXES	
FANY III SD(311)	(ENTERING AND ANNOUNCING) MR AND MRS KNOX. THE	KNOXES	COME IN. JUGGINS TAKES TWO CHAIRS FROM THE WALL AND
FANY III (321)	FOR HER ON GILBEY'S RIGHT, OPPOSITE THE	KNOXES	). THANK YOU. (SHE SITS). BOBBY'S GIVEN ME THE
FANY I (281)	I'M AT HOME ON FIRST THURSDAYS, AND WE HAVE THE	KNOXES	TO DINNER EVERY FRIDAY. MARGARET KNOX AND BOBBY ARE

		KNOX'S	
FANY III (319)	DID EVER ANYBODY HEAR OF SUCH A THING? /GILBEY/	KNOX'S	DAUGHTER SHEWN INTO MY PANTRY! /KNOX/ MARGARET
FANY II (288)	DEBONAIR) BUT IT'S VERY NATURAL. I UNDERSTAND MR	KNOX'S	FEELINGS PERFECTLY. (HE SPEAKS ENGLISH BETTER THAN
FANY III (326)	MILLIONAIRES, I COULD NOT HAVE ASPIRED TO MISS	KNOX'S	HAND. BUT AS A SOBER, HONEST, AND INDUSTRIOUS
FANY II SD(285)	AGAINST THE WALL. ANYONE PLACED SO AS TO SEE MRS	KNOX'S	LEFT PROFILE, WILL HAVE THE DOOR ON THE RIGHT AND THE
FANY III SD(321)	MR GILBEY, DUVALLET BOWS AND SITS DOWN ON MR	KNOX'S	LEFT, JUGGINS PLACING A CHAIR FOR HIM. /DORA/ NOW,
LION PREFACE(83)	SUCCESSORS GET THE UPPER HAND, AS IN GENEVA (	KNOX'S	" PERFECT CITY OF CHRIST") AND IN SCOTLAND AND
		KNUCKLE	
SUPR III (105)	MUSEUMS, AND SO FEW AND IMPERFECT AT THAT, THAT A	KNUCKLE	BONE OR A TOOTH OF ONE OF THEM IS PRIZED BEYOND THE
MIS. (191)	MIND: I'M NOT KNUCKLING DOWN TO ANY MAN HERE. I	KNUCKLE	DOWN TO MRS TARLETON BECAUSE SHE'S A WOMAN IN A
		KNUCKLES	
DOCT I (95)	HIS HANDS OUT OF HIS CUFFS AS HE SETS HIS	KNUCKLES	AKIMBO). /EMMY/ (LOOKING IN) SIR RALPH BLOOMFIELD
MILL II (171)	IF YOU DIDNT BELIEVE ME. I MUST HAVE SPRAINED MY	KNUCKLES	AND MY WRIST ON THAT BEAST'S CHIN. /THE DOCTOR/
WIDO II SD(43)	AT THE FLOOR, MORALLY BEGGARED, WITH HIS CLASPED	KNUCKLES	BETWEEN HIS KNEES, A LIVING PICTURE OF DISILLUSION.
JITT I (15)	TAP AT THE DOOR IN THE MORNING. THE TAP WITH BONY	KNUCKLES	. THE CALLER. /JITTA/ DEATH! OH, WHY WILL YOU
BASH II,2, (117)	OFF HIS GLOVES AND ATTACKS CASHEL WITH HIS BARE	KNUCKLES	.) /THE CROWD/ UNFAIR! THE RULES! /CETEWAYO/ THE
ROCK II (251)	HEAR HEAR! (THEY HAMMER ON THE TABLE WITH THEIR	KNUCKLES	), /THE DUKE/ (VERY APPRECIATIVE) WHAT A
NEVR I (211)	ATTENTIVE. PHIL STRAIGHTENS HIS BACK; PLACES HIS	KNUCKLES	SYMMETRICALLY ON HIS KNEES; AND OPENS HIS CASE).
KING I SD(163)	IN CALCULATION, HIS FISTS CLENCHED, TAPPING HIS	KNUCKLES	TOGETHER TO TICK OFF THE STAGES OF THE EQUATION. HE
BASH II,1, (107)	A PRIZEFIGHTER, AND MAUL POOR MARINERS WITH NAKED	KNUCKLES	, IS NO WORK FOR YOU. /CASHEL/ THOU DOST ARRAIGN
		KNUCKLING	
MIS. (191)	LINGERS FOR A MOMENT TO WHISPER) MIND: I'M NOT	KNUCKLING	DOWN TO ANY MAN HERE. I KNUCKLE DOWN TO MRS
		KOCH'S	
DOCT PREFACE(26)	WHICH LED TO THE HASTY DROPPING IN 1894 OF	KOCH'S	TUBERCULIN WERE NOT ACCIDENTS, BUT PERFECTLY ORDERLY
DOCT I (89)	ALSO THAT YOU UNDERTOOK TO CURE HER WITH	KOCH'S	TUBERCULIN. /RIDGEON/ AND INSTEAD OF CURING HER, IT
		KODAKS	
CAPT NOTES (301)	AND MODERN MAUSER ARE TO HIM AS UMBRELLAS AND	KODAKS	ARE TO ME. HIS TALES OF ADVENTURE HAVE THE TRUE
		KOENIG	
CURE (232)	PLAYING LISZT'S TRANSCRIPTION OF SCHUBERT'S ERL	KOENIG	). /REGINALD/ (PUTS HIS FINGERS IN HIS EARS, BUT
		KOEPENIK	
METH PREFACE(R66)	ONLY AN IMPOSTOR, AND THAT THE EXPOSURE OF THIS	KOEPENIK	CAPTAIN OF THE HEAVENS, FAR FROM PROVING THAT THERE
		KOHELETH	
LION PREFACE(86)	IN OPEN COMPETITION WITH THE SAYINGS OF PAUL AND	KOHELETH	AND DAVID AND SOLOMON AND THE AUTHORS OF JOB AND
FABL PREFACE(63)	THE SERMONS OF BUNYAN, AND THE WISECRACKS OF	KOHELETH	AND ECCLESIASTICUS. HARD WORKERS WHO DEVOUR MY
3PLA PREFACE(R40)	LASTED 300 YEARS, THOUGH HE GOT NO FURTHER THAN	KOHELETH	THE PREACHER, WHO DIED MANY CENTURIES BEFORE HIM;
LADY PREFACE(210)	SHAKESPEAR, AND THE DARK LADY, AND SWIFT, AND	KOHELETH	, AND THE CYCLES, AND THE MYSTERIOUS MOMENTS WHEN A
SUPR III (131)	THE PROFOUND TRUTH OF THE SAYING OF MY FRIEND	KOHELETH	, THAT THERE IS NOTHING NEW UNDER THE SUN. VANITAS
		KOMINTERN	
2TRU PREFACE(17)	HOLY OFFICE AND ITS FAMILIARS ARE KNOWN AS THE	KOMINTERN	AND THE GAY PAY OO. THERE IS THE POPULAR SAFEGUARD
GENV I (47)	AND YOU HAVE JUST BEEN TOLD THAT THE RUSSIAN	KOMINTERN	IS ANALOGOUS TO THE CHURCH OF ENGLAND. /BISHOP/ (
GENV I (47)	OF ENGLAND! ! /COMMISSAR/ COMRADE BISHOP: THE	KOMINTERN	IS THE STATE CHURCH IN RUSSIA EXACTLY AS THE
GENV I (47)	WHICH IT HAS PLEASED GOD TO CALL THEM. DOES YOUR	KOMINTERN	TEACH THAT BLASPHEMY OR DOES IT NOT? /COMMISSAR/
GENV I (47)	BUT SURELY, SURELY, YOU WOULD NOT COMPARE THE	KOMINTERN	TO THE CHURCH OF ENGLAND! ! /COMMISSAR/ COMRADE
GENV I (47)	INSTITUTION, ENDOWED BY OUR GOVERNMENT, THE	KOMINTERN	, WERE TO SEND ITS AGENTS INTO ENGLAND TO TEACH
		KOMISCH	
CATH 4 (190)	SILENCE. CATHERINE READS ON. /CATHERINE/ WIE	KOMISCH	! /EDSTASTON/ AHEM! AHEM! SILENCE. /CATHERINE/ (
		KONG	
BUOY III (27)	NOT HOLY. WE ARE IN BELGRAVE SQUARE, NOT IN HONG	KONG	. /THE PRIEST/ SIR: IN MANY OLD ENGLISH HOUSES THERE IS
		KOOSH	
MTH4 I (154)	GULF, THE TOBOGGANS AND FUNICULARS OF THE HINDOO	KOOSH	. CAN YOU WONDER THAT I TURN, WITH A HUNGRY HEART, TO
		KOPEK	
CATH 2 (175)	; BUT NOW THAT I AM EMPRESS HE NEVER GIVES ME A	KOPEK	. WHEN I HAVE HEADACHES AND COLICS I ENVY THE
		KORAN	
POSN PREFACE(393)	PROPHET, OR OF THE ENGLISH TRANSLATIONS OF THE	KORAN	IN THE PREFACES TO WHICH MAHOMET IS CRITICIZED AS AN
LION PREFACE(17)	THE VICIOUS BY THREATENING THEM WITH HELL. IN THE	KORAN	WE FIND MAHOMET DRIVEN MORE AND MORE TO THIS EXPEDIENT
		KORATES	
CAND I (86)	BRIGHTENS UP AND GOES OUT. /BURGESS/ SPOILIN YOUR	KORATES	AS USUAL, JAMES. GOOD MORNIN. WHEN I PAY A MAN, AN'
		KOWTOWED	
BARB I (253)	JUDEA." BUT THAT WAS NOT SO BAD AS THE WAY I WAS	KOWTOWED	TO EVERYWHERE BECAUSE MY FATHER WAS MAKING MILLIONS
		KREMLIN	
FABL PREFACE(77)	COMINFORM MAKES KARL MARX ITS DEITY AND THE	KREMLIN	HIS VATICAN. IT WORSHIPS HIS APOSTLES AT ITS
FABL PREFACE(84)	WITH A VIEW TO EQUALITY OF INCOME THAN THE	KREMLIN	, STALIN'S RUSSO-FABIAN SLOGAN, SOCIALISM IN A
		KREUTZER	
MIS. PREFACE(82)	FROM ITS ACTUAL PARENTS. NOT EVEN TOLSTOY, IN THE	KREUTZER	SONATA, HAS SAID ALL THAT WE SUSPECT ABOUT IT. WHEN
		KRISHNA	
JOAN PREFACE(15)	THE MIND'S EYE TO THE BODY'S, THE VISIONARY SEES	KRISHNA	OR THE BUDDHA OR THE BLESSED VIRGIN OR ST CATHERINE
LION PREFACE(98)	IS MORE THAN THE BUDDHA, OR JEHOVAH MORE THAN	KRISHNA	, OR JESUS MORE OR LESS HUMAN THAN MAHOMET OR
		KRONSTADT	
ROCK II (239)	LOT HAVE BEEN WITHOUT THE BALTIC FLEET AND THE	KRONSTADT	SAILORS? DO YOU SUPPOSE THE BRITISH NAVY, WITH
		KROOBOYS	
CAPT NOTES (300)	KNOWLEDGE OF THE EAST, ITS FASCINATING CADIS AND	KROOBOYS	AND SHEIKHS AND MUD CASTLES FROM AN EXCELLENT BOOK
CAPT I SD(224)	A MOORISH PORTER COMES FROM THE HOUSE WITH TWO	KROOBOYS	. /THE PORTER/ (AT THE DOOR, ADDRESSING RANKIN)
CAPT I (225)	(HE GOES CHEERFULLY INTO THE HOUSE WITH THE	KROOBOYS	). /DRINKWATER/ JIST THORT EED TRAH IT ORN, E DID.
CAPT I (219)	TO PUT EM. SOR! EM AWR (HIRE) A HARAB AN TWO	KROOBOYS	TO KERRY THEIR LAGGIGE. THORT AWD CAM AN TEOLL YER.
CAPT III (275)	AND HE WILL. IT WILL BE QUITE EASY: THERE ARE TWO	KROOBOYS	WAITING TO CARRY THE PORTMANTEAU. YOU WILL: I KNOW
CAPT I (226)	VILLAINOUS A TRIO AS THAT MOOR AND THE TWO	KROOBOYS	, TO WHOM YOU GAVE FIVE DOLLARS WHEN THEY WOULD
CAPT I (226)	TO CARRY OUR LUGGAGE UP! AND TWO PERFECT PETS OF	KROOBOYS	! DID YOU NOTICE THEIR FACES, HOWARD? /SIR
		KROPOTKIN	
BARB PREFACE(218)	OF LIFE-- MEN LIKE RUSKIN AND WILLIAM MORRIS AND	KROPOTKIN	-- HAVE ENORMOUS SOCIAL APPETITES AND VERY
		KRUGER	
LION PREFACE(102)	PROPHESIED THE DOWNFALL OF THE LATE PRESIDENT	KRUGER	IF HE HAD SURVIVED TO HIS TIME, BUT, WHEN CHALLENGED,

KULAK
ROCK PREFACE(154) A CORPORATE STATE, A SOVIET COMMISSAR EJECTING A KULAK AND ADDING HIS ACRES TO A COLLECTIVE FARM, ARE ALL
ROCK PREFACE(164) ABILITY PARALYZED. FOOD RAN SHORT. VERY SOON THE KULAK HAD TO BE THROWN BACK INTO HIS FARM AND TOLD TO CARRY
ROCK PREFACE(149) THE OLD CONSERVATIVE PROFESSIONAL CLASS AND THE KULAK OR PROSPEROUS FARMER CLASS HAS BEEN CHECKED ONLY BY
ROCK PREFACE(164) NUMBERS WAS CRUSHINGLY DISAPPOINTED. WHEN THE KULAK WAS THROWN OUT OF HIS FARM, AND HIS FARMING ABILITY
ROCK PREFACE(164) EDUCATIONAL LIST. THEY ALSO PROSCRIBED THE KULAK , THE ABLE, HARDHEADED, HARDFISTED FARMER WHO WAS

KULAKS
ROCK PREFACE(168) WHEN THE EXTINCTION OF THE BOURGEOISIE AND THE KULAKS AND THE OLD ARISTOCRACY IS COMPLETE, AND THE RUSSIAN
ROCK PREFACE(164) FOR THE MORAL OUTLOOK OF THE BOURGEOISIE AND THE KULAKS WAS DANGEROUSLY ANTI-SOCIAL. BUT THE RESULTS WERE

KULIN
GETT PREFACE(185) LOVE. IN THE BRITISH EMPIRE WE HAVE UNLIMITED KULIN POLYGAMY, MUSLIM POLYGAMY LIMITED TO FOUR WIVES, CHILD
GETT PREFACE(211) CARRIAGES AND MOTORS AS WE CAN AFFORD TO PAY FOR. KULIN POLYGYNY, THOUGH UNLIMITED, IS NOT REALLY A POPULAR

KULTUR
INCA (248) RISES WITH IT. NOT WHAT YOU CALL CULTURE; BUT KULTUR , A WORD SO MUCH MORE SIGNIFICANT THAT I HARDLY

KURT
GENV PREFACE(19) HIS GRASP. HE HAD THE IMMEDIATE PRECEDENT OF KURT EISNER'S SUCCESSFUL PUTSCH TO ENCOURAGE HIM. BUT EISNER

KU-KLUX
ROCK PREFACE(150) NIGGER IS A DEAD NIGGER" SAY THE AMERICANS OF THE KU-KLUX TEMPERAMENT. " HATES ANY MAN THE THING HE WOULD NOT

KU-KLUX-KLANS
MILL PREFACE(130) AND HINDU IRRECONCILABLES OF THE EAST AND THE KU-KLUX-KLANS AND LYNCHING MOBS OF THE WEST, HAVE PASSED

KVASS
CATH 1 (163) MUCH FRENCH BRANDY AND TOO LITTLE GOOD RUSSIAN KVASS . /PATIOMKIN/ (WITH SUDDEN FURY) WHY ARE VISITORS OF

KYBOSH
GENV IV (123) BUT ENCIRCLED, NO. /NEWCOMER/ IT PUTS THE KYBOSH ON BATTLERISM ANYHOW. THE TELEPHONE RINGS AGAIN. /ALL

KYD
BASH PREFACE(87) IN AN EIGHTEENTH CENTURY SYMPHONY, IN PEELE, KYD , GREENE, AND THE HISTORIES OF SHAKESPEAR. ACCORDINGLY,

KYNASTON
KING I (203) THAT AUTHOR THE OLD ACTORS USED TO TALK ABOUT. KYNASTON PLAYED WOMEN IN HIS PLAYS. I DONT KNOW ANY. WE

KYZER
BULL III (142) MIKE IT A PRESENT TO GERMANY TO KEEP THE AOWL KYZER BUSY FOR A WAWL; AND GIVE POOR AOWLD ENGLAND A

L
GENV I (42) /BISHOP/ NO: NOT THAT SORT OF CELL. C.E. DOUBLE L . A COMMUNIST CELL. LIKE A BEE IN A HIVE. PLANTED ON ME BY
GENV II (53) LOTS OF PRIZES AND CERTIFICATES; AND THERE WAS MY L . C. C. SCHOLARSHIP. YOU SEE, I HAVE SUCH A GOOD MEMORY:
CAPT I SD(218) OF PRONOUNCING IT PROPERLY. AS TO HIS YOL FOR L (A COMPENDIOUS DELIVERY OF THE PROVINCIAL EH-AL), AND
GETT (262) BETTER CALL HER YOUR SISTER THAN TRY TO CALL HER L -- (HE ALMOST BREAKS DOWN) L-- WELL, CALL HER BY HER NAME
GETT (262) THAN TRY TO CALL HER L-- (HE ALMOST BREAKS DOWN) L -- WELL, CALL HER BY HER NAME AND MAKE A FOOL OF MYSELF BY
UNPL PREFACE(R22) THE EXTREME INSTANCE IS A PURE PANTOMIME, LIKE L ' ENFANT PRODIGUE, IN WHICH THE DIALOGUE, THOUGH IT
PYGM PREFACE(201) CURRENT ONES WITH WHICH YOU WRITE M, N, AND U, L , P, AND Q, SCRIBBLING THEM AT WHATEVER ANGLE COMES

LA
FANY III (327) IMPOSSIBLE. BUT HERE-- AH! (KISSING HIS HAND) LA BELLE ANGLETERRE!
MTH2 (58) SHORT FOR SAVAGE. /LUBIN/ (PATTING HER HAND) LA BELLE SAUVAGE. /HASLAM/ (RISING AND SURRENDERING SAVVY
BUOY III (42) /SHE/ MY MISTAKE. THEY RHYME. /HE/ BON SOIR LA COMPAGNIE. THIS ROOM IS LIKE A TEMPLE. ARE YOU ENGAGED IN
MRS PREFACE(159) CONFORM TO THE STRICTEST RULES OF THE PERIOD WHEN LA DAME AUX CAMELLIAS WAS STILL A FORBIDDEN PLAY, AND WHEN
MRS PREFACE(161) HENRY IV, MEASURE FOR MEASURE, TIMON OF ATHENS, LA DAME AUX CAMELLIAS, THE PROFLIGATE, THE SECOND MRS
PYGM IV (260) BEGINS HALF SINGING HALF YAWNING AN AIR FROM LA FANCIULLA DEL GOLDEN WEST. SUDDENLY HE STOPS AND
PHIL I (89) WOMEN. THERES A QUARREL-- A SCANDAL-- CHERCHEZ LA FEMME-- ALWAYS A WOMAN AT THE BOTTOM OF IT. WELL, WE KNEW
MILL PREFACE(116) AND PAGEANTRY AND PATRIOTIC BRAGGADOCIO TO MAKE LA GLOIRE GLORIOUS. AND ALL THIS BECAUSE, LIKE WILLIAM THE
HART PREFACE(14) BY SHRUGGING THEIR SHOULDERS AND SAYING " C'EST LA GUERRE." ENGLAND, INVIOLATE FOR SO MANY CENTURIES THAT
JOAN 5 (112) I WANT TO. BUT I SHALL MISS YOU AT TIMES. /JOAN/ LA HIRE: IN SPITE OF ALL YOUR SINS AND SWEARS WE SHALL MEET
JOAN 2 (72) DAY, MY LORD. DO YOU KNOW WHAT HAS HAPPENED TO LA HIRE? /LA TREMOUILLE/ HE HAS SWORN HIMSELF INTO A FIT,
JOAN PREFACE(19) TO THE TRANSVAAL, TO SEND D'ALENCON, DE RAIS, LA HIRE AND THE REST TO THE RELIEF OF DUNOIS AT ORLEANS,
JOAN 2,SD(72) LA HIRE IS FRIGHTENED OUT OF HIS WITS. CAPTAIN LA HIRE COMES IN: A WAR DOG WITH NO COURT MANNERS AND
JOAN PREFACE(22) SHE ALLOWED TO THE INCORRIGIBLY BLASPHEMOUS LA HIRE EQUALLY WITH HERSELF. THE VALUE OF THIS PRUDERY WAS
JOAN 2 (72) HE HAS JUST FALLEN INTO A WELL AND BEEN DROWNED. LA HIRE IS FRIGHTENED OUT OF HIS WITS. CAPTAIN LA HIRE COMES
JOAN 2,SD(80) IS IN THIS PATH IN THE MIDDLE OF THE ROOM. LA HIRE IS ON HIS RIGHT. THE ARCHBISHOP, ON HIS LEFT, HAS
JOAN 2 (71) BLUEBEARD! WHY ANNOUNCE HIM? /THE PAGE/ CAPTAIN LA HIRE IS WITH HIM. SOMETHING HAS HAPPENED, I THINK. GILLES
JOAN 5,SD(111) KING CHARLES, WITH BLUEBEARD ON HIS LEFT AND LA HIRE ON HIS RIGHT, COMES FROM THE VESTRY, WHERE HE HAS
JOAN 2,SD(73) TO THE ARCHBISHOP'S LEFT HAND. BLUEBEARD AND LA HIRE RETIRE TOWARDS THE CURTAINS. /CHARLES/ OH,
JOAN PREFACE(17) WERE NOT UNREASONABLE: HER MILITARY COLLEAGUE LA HIRE WAS IN COMMAND OF A CONSIDERABLE FORCE NOT SO VERY
JOAN PREFACE(18) MISCALCULATED: WHEN SHE WAS LED TO THE STAKE, AND LA HIRE WAS NOT THUNDERING AT THE GATES OF ROUEN NOR
JOAN 5,SD(111) THE PILLAR. DUNOIS IS LEFT BETWEEN CHARLES AND LA HIRE. /DUNOIS/ WELL, YOUR MAJESTY IS AN ANOINTED KING AT
JOAN 5 (112) TO THE MORE CONGENIAL NEIGHBORHOOD OF DUNOIS AND LA HIRE). /LA HIRE/ WELL, I SHALL BE ABLE TO SWEAR WHEN I
JOAN 2 (75) STRUTS UP TO THE CURTAINS BETWEEN BLUEBEARD AND LA HIRE). /THE ARCHBISHOP/ YOU CANNOT BE ALLOWED TO SEE THIS
JOAN 2,SD(87) (HE DESCENDS FROM THE DAIS). GENERAL AMAZEMENT. LA HIRE, DELIGHTED, SLAPS HIS STEEL THIGH-PIECE WITH HIS
MIS. (162) THE WORKTABLE AND SOBS). /LINA/ (GOING TO HIM) O LA LA! (SHE SLAPS HIM VIGOROUSLY, BUT NOT UNKINDLY, ON THE
SUPR HANDBOK(177) TO TWEEDLEDEE: PLUS CA CHANGE, PLUS C'EST LA MEME CHOSE. BUT THE CHANGES FROM THE CRAB APPLE TO THE
JITT PREFACE(5) COUNT IN IL TROVATORE, LIVE ONLY TO CENTUPLICAR LA MORTE DE THE HERO IN MILLE ATROCI SPASIMI, AND THE HERO
WIDO III (61) A MAN MUST LIVE. /COKANE/ JE N'EN VOIS PAS LA NECESSITE. /TRENCH/ SHUT UP, BILLY; OR ELSE SPEAK SOME
SIM PREFACE(8) A JUG OF MILK DOWN BOND STREET OR THE RUE DE LA PAIX. A WHITE PERSON DOING SUCH A THING IN CAPETOWN WOULD
SUPR III (75) I NEVER SAID SO. BE FAIR, MENDOZA. 3. JE DEMANDE LA PAROLE. C'EST ABSOLUMENT FAUX. C'EST FAUX! FAUX! !
JOAN PREFACE(25) RELIGION, WRITTEN BY A HOSTAGE OR A SLAVE; AND LA PUCELLE MAKES BUTLER'S THEORY ALMOST CONVINCING. VOLTAIRE
JOAN PREFACE(24) WHO BURLESQUED HOMER IN A MOCK EPIC CALLED LA PUCELLE. IT IS THE FASHION TO DISMISS THIS WITH VIRTUOUS
BUOY IV (59) AS SURELY AS OUR APPETITES FOR BEEF AND BRANDY. LA ROCHEFOUCAULD TOLD YOU TWO CENTURIES AGO THAT THOUGH THE
MIS. PREFACE(45) ON THE MOUNT, AND MACHIAVELLI'S PRINCE, AND LA ROCHEFOUCAULD'S MAXIMS, AND HYMNS ANCIENT AND MODERN, AND
OVER PREFACE(159) OF THE OPPOSITE SEX, AND WHO EVEN COUNTENANCE LA ROCHEFOUCAULD'S REMARK THAT VERY FEW PEOPLE WOULD EVER
HART PREFACE(15) MACHINERY DESTROYED BY SIMPLE POLICE RAIDS A LA RUSSE, AND PERSONS ARRESTED AND SHOT WITHOUT ANY PRETENCE
JOAN 2,SD(80) ON HIS LEFT, HAS TAKEN HIS PLACE BY THE DAIS: LA TREMOUILLE AT THE OTHER SIDE OF IT. THE DUCHESS DE LA
JOAN 2,SD(73) A VERY PIOUS BEGINNING, CAPTAIN. BLUEBEARD AND LA TREMOUILLE LAUGH AT HIM. THE PAGE RETURNS. /THE PAGE/ HIS
JOAN 2,SD(83) ACROSS TO THE DOOR, FOLLOWED BY THE DUCHESS AND LA TREMOUILLE. AS THE ARCHBISHOP PASSES JOAN, SHE FALLS ON
JOAN 2,SD(81) IN THE LAUGH, AND JUMPS DOWN FROM THE DAIS BESIDE LA TREMOUILLE. JOAN, ALSO ON THE BROAD GRIN, TURNS BACK,
JOAN 2 (83) OLD GRUFF-AND-GRUMP? /CHARLES/ HE IS THE DUKE DE LA TREMOUILLE. /JOAN/ WHAT BE HIS JOB? /CHARLES/ HE
JOAN 2 (81) BLESSING, WONT YOU? /BLUEBEARD/ (WHISPERING TO LA TREMOUILLE) THE OLD FOX BLUSHES. /LA TREMOUILLE/ ANOTHER
JOAN 2 (72) AND PLANTING HIMSELF BETWEEN THE ARCHBISHOP AND LA TREMOUILLE). THIS IS NOTHING TO JOKE ABOUT. IT IS WORSE
JOAN 2 (74) AHA! ASK THAT BULLY THERE (POINTING TO LA TREMOUILLE). /LA TREMOUILLE/ (FURIOUS) HOLD YOUR TONGUE.
JOAN 2 (74) /CHARLES/ (COMING BACK AND PEERING ROUND LA TREMOUILLE'S LEFT SHOULDER) I WILL READ IT FOR YOU IF YOU
JOAN 2,SD(71) BEARING, AND THE LORD CHAMBERLAIN, MONSEIGNEUR DE LA TREMOUILLE, A MONSTROUS ARROGANT WINESKIN OF A MAN, ARE
JOAN 2,SD(80) AT THE OTHER SIDE OF IT. THE DUCHESS DE LA TREMOUILLE, PRETENDING TO BE THE QUEEN, SITS IN THE
SUPR III (78) HE SAY BOURGEOIS, HE SAY COMPROMISE. JAMAIS DE LA VIE! MISERABLE MENTEUR-- /STRAKER/ SEE HERE, CAPTAIN
MIS. (162) WORKTABLE AND SOBS). /LINA/ (GOING TO HIM) O LA LA ! (SHE SLAPS HIM VIGOROUSLY, BUT NOT UNKINDLY, ON THE

LABAN'S

BULL PREFACE(59)	HOUSE, WHERE HIS MOTHER SAT ON IT, LIKE RACHEL ON	LABAN'S	STOLEN TERAPHIM, UNTIL SHE WAS DRAGGED OFF. A

LABEL

GETT (312)	PARENTS, YOUNG GENTLEMEN, BE VERY CAREFUL NOT TO	LABEL	A HELPLESS CHILD WITH VIEWS WHICH IT MAY COME TO HOLD
KING PREFACE(158)	SPECIFIC ORGAN OR HORMONE THAT A BIOLOGIST CAN	LABEL	AS THE SOUL, SO WE CHRISTEN IT THE HOLY GHOST OR THE
LION PREFACE(66)	EASIER TO KILL HIM AS KINDLY AS POSSIBLE, OR TO	LABEL	HIM AND LEAVE HIM TO HIS CONSCIENCE, OR TO TREAT HIM
3PLA PREFACE(R23)	COMPARISON IS THAT THE PAINTER INVARIABLY DOES SO	LABEL	HIS PICTURE. WHAT IS A ROYAL ACADEMY CATALOGUE BUT A
LION PREFACE(50)	RATHER THAN A DECLARATION OF SENTIMENT OR A	LABEL	OF IDOLATRY. THE DOCTRINES IN WHICH JESUS IS THUS
FABL PREFACE(87)	AND CREATIVE EVOLUTIONIST IF I MUST HAVE A	LABEL	OF SOME SORT. AT PRESENT I AM STUCK ALL OVER WITH
SIM PRO,1, (25)	(HE SITS AT THE TABLE AND WRITES ON A LUGGAGE	LABEL	; THEN READS WHAT HE HAS WRITTEN) " HERE LIES A MAN
FABL PREFACE(87)	OR TWO TO OFFER; BUT THAT IS THE HEROIC	LABEL	THAT ALL WORLDBETTERERS ASPIRE TO, AND SOME HAVE EVEN
HART PREFACE(12)	ENEMY. SWINDLERS WERE EMBOLDENED TO TAKE OFFICES;	LABEL	THEMSELVES ANTI-ENEMY LEAGUES; AND SIMPLY POCKET THE
KING II (229)	PRISON. IF WE ONLY KNEW HOW TO PICK THEM OUT AND	LABEL	THEM, THEN THE PEOPLE COULD HAVE THEIR CHOICE OUT OF
SIM PRO,1, (25)	YOUR SON HAS KEPT HIS WORD." (HE TIES THE	LABEL	TO THE LAPEL OF HIS COAT) WHERES THAT FOOL'S GUN? (
GETT SD(323)	ALL A LADY IN LESBIA'S USE OF THE TERM AS A CLASS	LABEL	, SHE PROCLAIMS HERSELF TO THE FIRST GLANCE AS THE

LABELLED

DOCT PREFACE(21)	WAS A LITTLE DEPRESSED. DIGITALIS BEING A DRUG	LABELLED	AS A HEART SPECIFIC BY THE PROFESSION, HE PROMPTLY
FABL PREFACE(69)	SAINT JANUARIUS, AND SAYING MASS OVER A JAWBONE	LABELLED	AS THAT OF SAINT ANTHONY OF PADUA. WHEN THE PEOPLE
APPL PREFACE(192)	AND THERE, SURE ENOUGH, I FOUND A WORKSHOP, DULY	LABELLED	AS THE PREMISES OF THE NEW TRANSPORT COMPANY,
FABL V SD(117)	THE SCENE IS UNCHANGED; BUT THE BUILDING IS NOW	LABELLED	GENETIC INSTITUTE. ON THE TERRACE, SEATED ROUND A
BARB PREFACE(208)	WHAT CAME, TEN YEARS LATER, TO BE PERFUNCTORILY	LABELLED	IBSENISM? I WAS NOT IBSENIST EVEN AT SECOND HAND;
FABL VI SD(122)	FABLE. AS BEFORE, EXCEPT THAT THE BUILDING IS NOW	LABELLED	SIXTH FORM SCHOOL: SCHEDULED HISTORIC MONUMENT. ON
UNPL PREFACE(R24)	AS I DO MYSELF. FINALLY, A WORD AS TO WHY I HAVE	LABELLED	THE THREE PLAYS IN THIS FIRST VOLUME UNPLEASANT.
DOCT PREFACE(21)	HE SELLS PACKETS OF PENNYROYAL, DANDELION, ETC.,	LABELLED	WITH LITTLE LISTS OF THE DISEASES THEY ARE SUPPOSED
SIM PRO,3, (31)	/THE PRIESTESS/ (SHARPLY) ARE YOUR TEMPLES THEN	LABELLED	" FOR MEN ONLY"? /THE L.T./ (SHOCKED) OH,
PRES (133)	PUT ON OUR GLOVES WITH FRENCH CHALK. EVERYTHING'S	LABELLED	" MADE IN CAMBERWELL." /MITCHENER/ AS A TARIFF

LABELS

GENV PREFACE(15)	ABHORRENCE WHEN THEY ARE PRESENTED WITHOUT THEIR	LABELS	. I WAS BAPTIZED AS A MEMBER OF THE THEN ESTABLISHED
FABL PREFACE(87)	OF SOME SORT. AT PRESENT I AM STUCK ALL OVER WITH	LABELS	LIKE A TOURIST'S TRUNK. I CANNOT CALL MYSELF THE WAY
GENV PREFACE(15)	FRIENDS (QUAKERS), RITUALISTS, ALL BEARING	LABELS	WHICH NONE OF THEM CAN DEFINE, AND WHICH INDICATE

LABOR

GETT PREFACE(222)	BETWEEN TRADE UNIONISM AND UNORGANIZED CASUAL	LABOR	: A HUGE DIFFERENCE, NO DOUBT, AS TO ORDER AND
ROCK II (244)	MY ORIENTAL BLOOD. NATIONALIZED LAND: COMPULSORY	LABOR	: ABOLITION OF RATES: STRIKES MADE CRIMINAL: I
ROCK II (253)	USUAL. /BLEE/ THE POLICE COME FROM THE RANKS OF	LABOR	: DONT FORGET THAT. /BASHAM/ THATS NOT HOW THEY LOOK
MILL IV (205)	/EPIFANIA/ YOU CANNOT CHANGE THE MARKET PRICE OF	LABOR	: NOT ALLAH HIMSELF CAN DO THAT. BUT I CAME TO THIS
SUPR HANDBOK(206)	WITHOUT APOLOGY DEMANDED A RETURN TO COMPULSORY	LABOR	: THAT IS, TO THE METHODS BY WHICH, AS WE BELIEVE, THE
MTH5 (261)	WITHOUT UNDERSTANDING. IS THIS ENOUGH? OR SHALL I	LABOR	AGAIN? SHALL I BRING FORTH SOMETHING THAT WILL SWEEP
SUPR PREFACE(R35)	MR BLACKMAILER, MR CAD, MR DRUNKARD, MR	LABOR	AGITATOR AND SO FORTH, CAN READ THE PILGRIM'S PROGRESS
ROCK II (247)	AND TELL THEM THEY SHOULD VOTE FOR COMPULSORY	LABOR	AND DOING AWAY WITH STRIKES? /BLEE/ ARNT THE WORKERS
ROCK II (255)	DOWN OUR ANSWER. EITHER YOU DROP COMPULSORY	LABOR	AND DROP COMPENSATION OR NEVER SHEW YOUR FACE IN THE
BULL PREFACE(56)	THREE TO IMPRISONMENT FOR A YEAR WITH HARD	LABOR	AND FIFTY LASHES, AND FIVE TO FIFTY LASHES. LORD
BULL III (131)	ABILITY, NOR CAPITAL, NOR ANYTHING BUT MERE BRUTE	LABOR	AND GREED IN HIM, HEAVEN HELP HIM! /DORAN/ WELL,
2TRU PREFACE(14)	FROM DAY TO DAY AND THE JUST SHARING OF THE	LABOR	AND LEISURE INVOLVED. THUS THE INDIVIDUAL CITIZEN HAS
ROCK II (247)	THE BRITISH WORKINGMAN WILL LISTEN TO COMPULSORY	LABOR	AND PUTTING DOWN STRIKES YOU DONT KNOW THE WORLD YOURE
APPL PREFACE(193)	THE MEANS OF EFFECTING AN ENORMOUS SAVING OF	LABOR	AND SMASH. BUT INSTEAD OF BEING RECEIVED WITH OPEN
BULL PREFACE(56)	FLOGGEES ENOUGH; SO THESE THREE HAD A YEAR'S HARD	LABOR	APIECE IN ADDITION TO THEIR FLOGGINGS. SIX OTHERS WERE
CLEO NOTES (204)	OUT THAT HE GETS TWICE AS MUCH MONEY FOR HIS	LABOR	AS HIS FATHER DID IN THE SAME TRADE, AND THAT HIS
ROCK I (216)	CAN LIVE ON A PENNY A DAY. WHAT CAN WE DO AGAINST	LABOR	AT A PENNY A DAY AND POWER FOR NEXT TO NOTHING OUT OF
SIM PREFACE(17)	FOR THE LIFE OF HIM SEE WHY HE SHOULD NOT EMPLOY	LABOR	AT A PROFIT, OR BUY THINGS SOLELY TO SELL THEM AGAIN
SUPR III (113)	WERE HER OBJECT, START OFF ON ANOTHER LINE AND	LABOR	AT THE CLUMSY ELEPHANT AND THE HIDEOUS APE, WHOSE
FABL III (112)	THE MILITARY POLICE OR KEPT UNDER TUTELAGE IN A	LABOR	BRIGADE. OR YOU MAY BE CLASSED AS DANGEROUS AND
SUPR HANDBOK(179)	THAT IT DISTRIBUTES SOCIAL WEALTH AND THE SOCIAL	LABOR	BURDEN IN A GROTESQUELY INEQUITABLE MANNER) DID NOT
MILL III (181)	LIKE THIS CANT AFFORD ANY LUXURIES. IT'S A CHEAP	LABOR	BUSINESS, AS LONG AS I GET WOMEN TO WORK FOR THEIR
APPL I (234)	WERE CALLED IN THE DAYS OF THAT RASH STATESMAN	LABOR	CABINETS, DO NOT MISUNDERSTAND ME: I DO NOT WANT THE
ROCK II (240)	OF CONSERVATISM. THATS THE WAY TO DISH THESE	LABOR	CHAPS AND RED FLAGGERS AND ALL THE REST OF THE SCUM
BARB PREFACE(224)	CHARITY SERMON WAS AN EMPLOYER TRADING IN FEMALE	LABOR	CHEAPENED BY PROSTITUTION AS UNSCRUPULOUSLY AS A HOTEL
BARB PREFACE(224)	AS A HOTEL KEEPER TRADES IN WAITERS'	LABOR	CHEAPENED BY TIPS, OR COMMISSIONAIRES' LABOR CHEAPENED
BARB PREFACE(224)	LABOR CHEAPENED BY TIPS, OR COMMISSIONAIRES'	LABOR	CHEAPENED BY PENSIONS; OR THAT THE ONLY PATRON WHO CAN
FABL PREFACE(72)	BEEN MANY YEARS TO ADDRESS YOU, I ETC. ETC." THE	LABOR	CHURCH DID NOT LAST; BUT THE REACTION DID; AND THE
FABL PREFACE(72)	HIM INTO SOCIALISM, WHEREUPON HE FOUNDED A	LABOR	CHURCH IN WHICH ALL THE MEETINGS BEGAN BY CALLING ON
BARB III (330)	MEN PRESENTED THEM TO ME IN YOUR WILLIAM MORRIS	LABOR	CHURCH. /CUSINS/ OH! IT NEEDED ONLY THAT. A LABOR
BARB III (330)	CHURCH. /CUSINS/ OH! IT NEEDED ONLY THAT. A	LABOR	CHURCH! (HE MOUNTS THE FIRESTEP DISTRACTEDLY, AND
ROCK II (247)	COLLEAGUES. /SIR ARTHUR/ (BEAMING) GENTLEMEN: A	LABOR	DEPUTATION FROM THE ISLE OF CATS. THE ONE ELEMENT THAT
GETT PREFACE(238)	OF WOMEN IN ALL CIVILIZED CITIES. WILL THE	LABOR	EXCHANGE FIND EMPLOYERS FOR HER? IF NOT, WHAT WILL IT
GETT PREFACE(238)	MAKING MARRIAGE A CONDITION OF THE HIRING.	LABOR	EXCHANGES AND THE WHITE SLAVERY. SUPPOSE, AGAIN, A
GETT PREFACE(239)	AS ELIGIBLE AS THAT OF THE WOMEN FOR WHOM THE	LABOR	EXCHANGES ARE FINDING INDEPENDENT WORK? WILL NOT MANY
GETT PREFACE(238)	OF THE DAY (1910) A QUESTION WITH REGARD TO THE	LABOR	EXCHANGES IT HAS VERY WISELY ESTABLISHED THROUGHOUT
GETT PREFACE(238)	SUPPOSE, AGAIN, A WOMAN PRESENTS HERSELF AT THE	LABOR	EXCHANGE, AND STATES HER TRADE AS THAT OF A WHITE
SUPR HANDBOK(206)	THE MOST EFFECTIVE NOR THE LEAST HUMANE METHOD OF	LABOR	EXPLOITATION; AND THE WORLD IS NOW FEELING ITS WAY
SUPR III (111)	WITHOUT CONSULTING HER, TAKING HER DOMESTIC	LABOR	FOR GRANTED AS THE FOUNDATION OF IT. /ANA/ THAT IS
BUOY IV (55)	GUINEA PIGS. NO USE: THAT GAME IS UP. THE NEW	LABOR	GOVERNMENT GIVES SUCH JOBS TO SUPERANNUATED TRADE
BUOY III (32)	SURELY THIS SHORTAGE WILL NOT LAST FOR EVER. THE	LABOR	GOVERNMENT, WHICH IS RESPONSIBLE FOR THESE ROBBERIES
MILL PREFACE(119)	IN VAIN DID THE VOTERS USE THEIR VOTES TO PLACE A	LABOR	GOVERNMENT, WITH A CABINET OF SOCIALISTS, ON THE
SUPR HANDBOK(206)	AND ITS MITIGATION. NOW THAT THE FREEDOM OF WAGE	LABOR	HAS PRODUCED A SCARCITY OF IT, AS IN SOUTH AFRICA, THE
SUPR HANDBOK(194)	DISTRIBUTION OF WEALTH AND ALLOTMENT OF	LABOR	HAVE ARISEN THROUGH AN UNSCIENTIFIC ECONOMIC SYSTEM,
ROCK II (244)	FIND IT WHERE THEY FIND IT, IN THE PRODUCT OF THE	LABOR	I EMPLOY. AT PRESENT I HAVE TO PAY EXORBITANT AND
KING I (181)	CALCULATION. DO YOU MEAN TO TELL ME THAT ALL THE	LABOR	I HAVE BESTOWED ON THAT BOOK HAS BEEN WASTED? /FOX/
CLEO NOTES (206)	I ASK THIS QUESTION BECAUSE THE SCARCITY OF	LABOR	IN AMERICA RELATIVELY TO THE DEMAND FOR IT HAS LED TO
GENV PREFACE(16)	RUTHLESS DESPOTS OUT FOR NOTHING BUT EXPLOITING	LABOR	IN PURSUIT OF SURPLUS VALUE, AS MARX CALLED RENT,
GETT (288)	IT ALL THE SAME: ON CORDITE, ON DRINK, ON CHINESE	LABOR	IN SOUTH AFRICA, ON ALL SORTS OF TRUMPERY. /REGINALD/
BULL PREFACE(4)	IMPASSIONED DEFENCE OF THE EMPLOYMENT OF CHINESE	LABOR	IN SOUTH AFRICA WITHOUT CONSIDERING THE FACT THAT
ROCK II (257)	HAPPENS AS A SPECIAL INTERVIEW: YOU KNOW THAT WE	LABOR	INTELLIGENTSIA HAVE TO LIVE BY OUR BRAINS. AU REVOIR.
SUPR HANDBOK(182)	IN HIS MILL AND THE COTTON SPINNER IN HIS	LABOR	INTO A MERE PERMISSION TO TRADE OR WORK ON STRINGENT
BULL PREFACE(4)	WAS EQUALLY VALID FOR THE INTRODUCTION OF CHINESE	LABOR	INTO LANCASHIRE. AND AS THE PEOPLE OF LANCASHIRE WERE
GENV III (68)	GOVERNMENT IN 1906 WHEN IT WANTED TO LET CHINESE	LABOR	INTO LANCASHIRE! /THE JEW/ YOUR OWN COUNTRY! WHO
APPL I (220)	AND HARDSHIP STILL EXIST: IN OTHER WORDS, WHERE	LABOR	IS CHEAP. WE LIVE IN COMFORT ON THE IMPORTED PROFITS
CAND I SD(85)	MAN, OFFENSIVE AND CONTEMPTUOUS TO PEOPLE WHOSE	LABOR	IS CHEAP, RESPECTFUL TO WEALTH AND RANK, AND QUITE
ROCK II (251)	CRIED TO GOD FOR IN VAIN IS UPON YOU NOW THAT	LABOR	IS COMING TO ITS OWN; AND IT IS YOUR TURN NOW TO GET
SIM PREFACE(9)	PAYEE LOSES CASTE AND IS NO LONGER CALLED MISTER.	LABOR	IS HELD TO BE A CROSS AND A DISGRACE; AND THE LOWEST
2TRU PREFACE(21)	INORDINATELY RICH AND PASSIONATELY CONVINCED THAT	LABOR	IS SO DISGRACEFUL TO THEM THAT THEY DARE NOT BE SEEN
2TRU PREFACE(14)	8. LEISURE IS THE SPHERE OF INDIVIDUAL LIBERTY:	LABOR	IS THE SPHERE OF SLAVERY. 9. PEOPLE WHO THINK THEY CAN
MTH1 I (9)	MAKE US DIFFERENT? /THE SERPENT/ I TELL YOU THE	LABOR	IS TOO MUCH FOR ONE. TWO MUST SHARE IT. /EVE/ DO YOU
LION PREFACE(100)	LIVES OF THE UNFORTUNATE INHABITANTS OUT OF WHOSE	LABOR	IT COULD BE MADE. AT THIS MOMENT ULSTER IS REFUSING TO
ROCK I (209)	AND GENTLEMEN, I NEED NOT LABOR THE POINT." THEN	LABOR	IT FOR THE NEXT TEN MINUTES. THAT WILL DO. THAT WILL
BARB PREFACE(233)	BAILEY DOCK OR IN THE RANKS OF CASUAL UNSKILLED	LABOR	. AND THE MORALITY OF BILL'S CHARACTERISTICS VARIES
MTH1 II (32)	MADE THIS WHEEL FOR ME WHICH HAS SAVED ME SO MUCH	LABOR	. AND THERE IS ENOCH, WHO WALKS ON THE HILLS, AND
DOCT I (105)	BUT, AFTER ALL, WHAT IS OPERATING? ONLY MANUAL	LABOR	. BRAIN-- BRAIN REMAINS MASTER OF THE SITUATION. THE
SUPR HANDBOK(226)	HE HAS NOT EARNED IS GENEROUS WITH OTHER PEOPLE'S	LABOR	. EVERY GENUINELY BENEVOLENT PERSON LOATHES ALMSGIVING
ROCK II (247)	ARE GOING TO HEAR, SIR ARTHUR, IS THE VOICE OF	LABOR	. (SHE REMAINS STANDING). /BLEE/ THE VERDICT OF
FABL PREFACE(97)	OF THE PREVALENT RUTHLESS EXPLOITATION OF	LABOR	. ROBERT OWEN HAD CALLED FOR A NEW MORAL WORLD AS
ROCK II (247)	WHO DO NOTHING BUT WASTE THEIR OWN TIME AND YOUR	LABOR	. /BLEE/ WE KNOW. KEEP ALL THE SOFT JOBS FOR YOUR LOT
KING I (211)	ANY OTHER MAN THAN ISAAC NEWTON TWENTY YEARS HARD	LABOR	. /CHARLES/ I HAVE SEEN THAT BOOK, AND BEEN ASTOUNDED

GENV IV (91)	IS IN THE RANKS OF SILENT AND BLINDLY OBEDIENT	LABOR	. /NEWCOMER/ OH, THATS YOUR GAME, IS IT? WHO ARE YOU
SUPR II (51)	SAYS. I BELIEVE MOST INTENSELY IN THE DIGNITY OF	LABOR	. /STRAKER/ (UNIMPRESSED) THATS BECAUSE YOU NEVER
ROCK II (244)	HE NOW STEALS. IN ADDITION I SHALL HAVE CHEAP	LABOR	. THAT IS NOT ORIENTAL EMOTION: IT IS BRITISH
MRS PREFACE(170)	WEST END OF IT ON MONEY EARNED BY SOMEBODY ELSE'S	LABOR	. THE NOTION THAT PROSTITUTION IS CREATED BY THE
MIS. PREFACE(6)	BOYS AND GIRLS DO A SUBSTANTIAL SHARE OF FARM	LABOR	. THIS IS WHY IT IS NECESSARY TO COERCE POOR PARENTS
DOCT PREFACE(67)	RECOGNIZED THE ADVANTAGES OF DIVISION OF	LABOR	. UNDER SUCH CONDITIONS NO STATISTICS AS TO THE
SUPR II (51)	ANY, MR ROBINSON. MY BUSINESS IS TO DO AWAY WITH	LABOR	. YOULL GET MORE OUT OF ME AND A MACHINE THAN YOU WILL
MTH2 (57)	/BURGE/ BUT I AM IN THE TRUEST SENSE MYSELF A	LABOR	LEADER. I-- (HE STOPS, AS LUBIN HAS RISEN WITH A
ROCK I (221)	DONT KNOW WHAT HUMBUG IS YET. WAIT TIL YOURE A	LABOR	LEADER. (HE WINKS AT HIS HOST AND MAKES FOR THE
APPL PREFACE(174)	MONEY BROADCASTS: MONEY REIGNS; AND KINGS AND	LABOR	LEADERS ALIKE HAVE TO REGISTER ITS DECREES, AND EVEN,
GLIM (182)	HIS SCREWS FOR WHAT THEY WILL FETCH: THEY GO TO	LABOR	LIKE ANY PEASANT'S BEAST, BUT OUR NOBILITY DOES NOT
PRES (141)	EVER BE FACE TO FACE WITH THE POSSIBILITY OF A	LABOR	MAJORITY IN PARLIAMENT. YOU KNOW THAT IN THAT CASE WE
GENV II (62)	COMMUNISTS ARE PUTTING UP A CANDIDATE AGAINST THE	LABOR	MAN; AND THE LIBERALS ARE CONTESTING THE SEAT AS WELL.
DOCT PREFACE(18)	SUCCESSFUL ONES. IN THE RANKS OF ORDINARY SKILLED	LABOR	MANY MEN ARE TO BE FOUND WHO EARN GOOD WAGES AND ARE
ROCK II (255)	FROM ME. I AM NO COMMUNIST: I AM A RESPECTABLE	LABOR	MAN, AS LAW ABIDING AS ANY MAN HERE. I AM WHAT NONE OF
SUPR HANDBOK(212)	ENTERPRISE THROWING ITS HUMAN REFUSE ON THE CHEAP	LABOR	MARKET AND THE WORKHOUSE; AND THE REFUSE OF THE NEW
FABL PREFACE(95)	WHILST " UNIVERSITY ENGINEERS" ARE DRUGS IN THE	LABOR	MARKET COMPARED TO THOSE WHO GO STRAIGHT FROM THEIR
DOCT PREFACE(70)	ARE IN ALL CLASSES WHEN A DEARTH IN THEIR	LABOR	MARKET MAKES THEM INDISPENSABLE; BUT THE AVERAGE
SUPR III (109)	HAVE MADE FREE WHITE CHRISTIANS CHEAPER IN THE	LABOR	MARKET THAN BLACK HEATHEN SLAVES SOLD BY AUCTION AT
SUPR HANDBOK(212)	SUCCESSFUL OR NOT, WOULD HAVE TO BE THROWN ON THE	LABOR	MARKET; BUT THE UNSUCCESSFUL ONES WOULD NOT ENTITLE
ROCK II (263)	WOULD FIGHT FOR THEIR OWN SKINS. CAN YOU GET A	LABOR	MEMBER INTO PARLIAMENT IN THE PLACES WHERE THEY ARE IN
MTH2 (61)	IMAGINARY NEW PRINCIPLES AND NEW POLITICS, THE	LABOR	MEMBERS WILL FIND THAT THE IMMUTABLE LAWS OF POLITICAL
ROCK II (235)	GUARD OF LIBERALS AND HIS RAGTAG AND BOBTAIL OF	LABOR	MEN AND SOCIALISTS AND LAWYERS AND
ROCK I (218)	BE THE END OF ME, AS IT'S BEEN THE END OF ALL THE	LABOR	MEN THAT HAVE DONE IT. THE CABINET IS FULL OF LABOR
ROCK I (218)	MEN THAT HAVE DONE IT. THE CABINET IS FULL OF	LABOR	MEN THAT STARTED AS RED-HOT SOCIALISTS; AND WHAT
ROCK I (197)	KEEP TRAFALGAR SQUARE GOING NIGHT AND DAY. A FEW	LABOR	M.P.S WOULD HELP. YOU HAVE A RARE LOT OF GASBAGS UNDER
ROCK I (220)	/HIPNEY/ LORD BLESS YOU, SRARTHUR, THE	LABOR	MOVEMENT IS ROTTEN WITH BOOK LEARNING; AND YOUR PEOPLE
MTH2 (59)	MR LUBIN, I AM FRIGHTFULLY INTERESTED IN THE	LABOR	MOVEMENT, AND IN THEOSOPHY, AND IN RECONSTRUCTION
3PLA PREFACE(R9)	BETWEEN THE LEISURE OF A PERSIAN CAT AND THE	LABOR	OF A COCKNEY CAB HORSE IS NOT GREATER THAN THE
MTH2 (77)	COURSE, ATE THEM TO SAVE THE LONG AND DIFFICULT	LABOR	OF AGRICULTURE. I ASK YOU TO CONTEMPLATE OUR FATHERS
FABL IV (114)	NEW PARAGRAPH, AHEM! AS THIS CHANGE SAVED THE	LABOR	OF BREEDING ANIMALS FOR FOOD, AND SUPPORTED HUMAN
KING I (213)	THINKING. THEY ARE TRIFLES BESIDE OUR GREAT	LABOR	OF CREATION AND INTERPRETATION. /JAMES/ I HAD A
MTH1 II (28)	IT WAS LILITH WHO DID WRONG WHEN SHE SHARED THE	LABOR	OF CREATION SO UNEQUALLY BETWEEN MAN AND WIFE. IF YOU,
SUPR III (111)	LEFT AT HIS DISPOSAL BY SAVING HIM THE EXHAUSTING	LABOR	OF GESTATION. THIS SUPERFLUOUS ENERGY HAS GONE TO HIS
SUPR PREFACE(R34)	BRINK OF THE RIVER OF DEATH OVER THE STRIFE AND	LABOR	OF HIS PILGRIMAGE, AND SAY " YET DO I NOT REPENT ME";
2TRU PREFACE(14)	THE PROBLEM IS HOW TO EVADE HIS SHARE IN THE	LABOR	OF PRODUCTION, TO INCREASE HIS SHARE IN THE
MTH1 II (30)	I NEVER HAVE THESE THOUGHTS: I! WHO HAVE THE	LABOR	OF THE CHILD-BEARING: I! WHO HAVE THE DRUDGERY OF
MTH3 (125)	YOU WE LEAVE THE MOST TROUBLESOME PART OF THE	LABOR	OF THE NATION TO THEM. AND A GOOD JOB TOO: WHY SHOULD
MILL PREFACE(119)	OF ESCAPE WAS FOR THE GOVERNMENT TO ORGANIZE THE	LABOR	OF THE UNEMPLOYED FOR THE SUPPLY OF THEIR OWN NEEDS.
CAND III (145)	EVERY WORD. WHAT I AM YOU HAVE MADE ME WITH THE	LABOR	OF YOUR HANDS AND THE LOVE OF YOUR HEART. YOU ARE MY
SUPR III SD(72)	TO IMAGINATIVE DECORATION. THE RANKS OF UNSKILLED	LABOR	OFFER NO SUCH POSITIONS. WE MISUSE OUR LABORERS
GENV I (30)	THE MAGNIFICENT PALACE OF THE INTERNATIONAL	LABOR	OFFICE AND THE NEW QUARTERS OF THE SECRETARIAT, I
APPL I (213)	CHAIR IN DESPERATION) THIS IS A NICE THING. TWO	LABOR	PAPERS HAVE LEADING ARTICLES THIS MORNING SUPPORTING
BUOY 1 (15)	TO BE THE SPORT OF KINGS. NOW IT IS THE SPORT OF	LABOR	PARTIES. /SON/ WHAT COULD KINGS AND PARTIES DO WITHOUT
BULL PREFACE(71)	INDUSTRIAL PROLETARIAT ORGANIZED IN TRADE UNIONS,	LABOR	PARTIES, AND THE UBIQUITOUS SODALITIES OF THAT NEW
ROCK PREFACE(152)	IN TRADE UNIONS, MUNICIPAL AND PARLIAMENTARY	LABOR	PARTIES, AND THE LIKE, AND MAINTAINING A SORT OF
PRES (138)	ARE UNPOPULAR. /BALSQUITH/ WHEN THE LEADER OF THE	LABOR	PARTY APPEALED TO ME AND TO THE HOUSE LAST YEAR NOT TO
PRES (163)	/MITCHENER/ NO. FOR YOU NOW TELL ME THAT THE	LABOR	PARTY DEMANDS VOTES FOR WOMEN. THAT MAKES IT
FABL PREFACE(83)	ENTERPRISES NOT YET RIPE FOR NATIONALIZATION. THE	LABOR	PARTY IN ENGLAND NATIONALIZED AS MANY INDUSTRIES AS IT
MIS. PREFACE(36)	ON CHILDREN. IF WE DID, THEY WOULD SOON OUTDO THE	LABOR	PARTY IN THEIR CLAIM FOR A RIGHT TO WORK BILL. IN ANY
PRES (162)	/MITCHENER/ INFERNAL IMPUDENCE! /BALSQUITH/ THE	LABOR	PARTY IS TAKING THE SAME LINE. THEY SAY THE MEN GOT
ROCK II (252)	LIKE. I'M NOT ARGUING. I'M TELLING YOU THAT THE	LABOR	PARTY OF THE ISLE OF CATS PUTS DOWN ITS FOOT AND SAYS
PRES (138)	/BALSQUITH/ -- AND THE FEELING WAS THAT THE	LABOR	PARTY WERE SOULLESS CADS. /MITCHENER/ SO THEY ARE.
APPL PREFACE(188)	HAD IT WRITTEN FOR HIM AT THE HEADQUARTERS OF THE	LABOR	PARTY. A FOURTH, THE MOST HOPELESSLY OUT OF DATE OF
MTH2 (57)	THAT YOU MAY BOTH BE COMPLETELY SUPERSEDED BY THE	LABOR	PARTY. /BURGE/ BUT I AM IN THE TRUEST SENSE MYSELF A
ROCK II (252)	WHO ARE YOU CALLING A LIBERAL? I REPRESENT THE	LABOR	PARTY. /SIR BEMROSE/ YOURE A NO COMPENSATION MAN, ARNT
GENV I (35)	OUR USUAL PEOPLE: THE NATIONAL PARTY AND THE	LABOR	PARTY; BUT IT WAS WON BY AN UPSTART KIND OF CHAP WHO
GENV I (35)	GOT A CLEAR MAJORITY OVER THE NATIONALS AND THE	LABOR	PARTY; SO IT WAS UP TO HIM TO FORM A GOVERNMENT. AND
CAND I (80)	GUILD OF ST MATTHEW ON MONDAY. INDEPENDENT	LABOR	PARTY, GREENWICH BRANCH, ON THURSDAY. MONDAY,
ROCK I (197)	THE ANARCHISTS, THE SYNDICALISTS, THE OFFICIAL	LABOR	PARTY, THE INDEPENDENT LABOR PARTY, THE SALVATION
ROCK I (197)	THE OFFICIAL LABOR PARTY, THE INDEPENDENT	LABOR	PARTY, THE SALVATION ARMY, THE CHURCH ARMY AND THE
MTH2 (61)	DO NOT REALIZE. TAKE ALL THIS FUSS ABOUT THE	LABOR	PARTY, WITH ITS IMAGINARY NEW PRINCIPLES AND NEW
MTH2 (57)	BUT WITHOUT A PRETENCE OF INTEREST). /LUBIN/ THE	LABOR	PARTY! OH NO, MR BARNABAS. NO, NO, NO, NO. (HE
ROCK II (249)	TELL YOU THAT THE FUNDAMENTAL QUESTION IS NOT THE	LABOR	QUESTION BUT THE LAND QUESTION. /THE MAYOR/ YES: WE
MTH2 (61)	KNOWLEDGE; FOR I HAVE MADE A SPECIAL STUDY OF THE	LABOR	QUESTION. /FRANKLYN/ (WITH INTEREST AND SOME
MTH2 (57)	THEM; TAKES HER HAND; AND DROPS THE SUBJECT OF	LABOR	). WELL, MY DEAR YOUNG LADY? WHAT IS THE LATEST
PRES (139)	FLOGGING HIM; SO NOW HE WILL GET TWO YEARS' HARD	LABOR	; AND SERVE HIM RIGHT! /BALSQUITH/ I BET YOU A GUINEA
BULL III (131)	LIFT OUR HEADS FROM THE DUST IF WE TRADE IN CHEAP	LABOR	; AND SERVE US RIGHT TOO! IF I GET INTO PARLIAMENT,
ROCK II (253)	THEY FEEL THAT THEYVE ESCAPED FROM THE RANKS OF	LABOR	; AND THEYRE PROUD OF IT. THEY HAVE A STATUS WHICH
APPL PREFACE(195)	SAVING MUCH DANGEROUS AND DEMORALIZINGLY CASUAL	LABOR	; AND TRANSFIGURING THE UNDERPAID STEVEDORE INTO A
ROCK PREFACE(167)	NOT KNOW. HE IS BRUTALIZED BY EXCESSIVE MUSCULAR	LABOR	; HE IS DIRTY; HIS FREEDOM FROM CIVILIZED CONTROL
MIS. PREFACE(57)	MONSTROUS EVEN IF IT WERE TRUE; FOR THERE IS NO	LABOR	THAT MIGHT NOT BE IMPOSED ON A CHILD OR AN ADULT ON
ROCK I (209)	OF ONE MIND, MY LORDS AND GENTLEMEN. I NEED NOT	LABOR	THE POINT." THEN LABOR IT FOR THE NEXT TEN MINUTES.
APPL PREFACE(184)	POWERS ARE LIFE AND DEATH POWERS. I NEED NOT	LABOR	THIS POINT: WE ALL KNOW IT. BUT WHAT WE DO NOT ALL
LION PREFACE(56)	POSSIBLE IN THAT DIRECTION BUT TO PAY A WORKER BY	LABOR	TIME: SO MUCH AN HOUR OR DAY OR WEEK OR YEAR. BUT HOW
LION PREFACE(56)	TO DO WITH THE PRODUCT IS TO FEED HIS LAMBS.	LABOR	TIME, SO MAKER'S RIGHT AS AN ALTERNATIVE TO TAKING THE
GENV IV (103)	SEVERAL FEET OF SOLID PAVEMENT, COSTING YEARS OF	LABOR	TO CONSTRUCT. /SIR O./ DO YOU SERIOUSLY PROPOSE THAT
MIS. PREFACE(3)	MAN KNOWS VERY WELL THAT IT IS WASTE OF	LABOR	TO MAKE A MACHINE THAT WILL LAST TEN YEARS, BECAUSE IT
SUPR HANDBOK(196)	MISLEADER OF THE PEOPLE, AND IMPRISONED WITH HARD	LABOR	TO SHEW HIM HOW MUCH SINCERITY THERE IS IN THE
FANY PROLOG (264)	SEEMS TO ME TO CARRY THE PRINCIPLE OF DIVISION OF	LABOR	TOO FAR, THIS KEEPING OF THE HONESTY AND THE OTHER
MIS. PREFACE(34)	AGITATE FOR THE UNCOMPROMISING ABOLITION OF CHILD	LABOR	UNDER OUR CAPITALIST SYSTEM. IT IS NOT THE LEAST OF
GENV II (62)	IN. I SHALL BE THE PATRIOTIC CANDIDATE; AND THE	LABOR	VOTE WILL BE A SPLIT VOTE; FOR THE COMMUNISTS ARE
ROCK II (282)	NAMES, THE LIVES OF THE MILLIONS OF PEOPLE WHOSE	LABOR	WAS KEEPING THE WHOLE SHOW GOING WERE NOT WORTH
MTH4 I (171)	SERVICE, SO SCIENTIFICALLY THAT THE BURDEN OF	LABOR	WILL CEASE TO BE PERCEPTIBLE, LEAVING COMMON MEN MORE
GETT PREFACE(257)	FOOTING AS OTHER WORK: THAT IS, ON THE FOOTING OF	LABOR	WORTHY OF ITS HIRE; AND PROVIDE FOR UNEMPLOYMENT IN IT
ROCK PREFACE(162)	BALANCE SHEETS YOU WILL BE SHOT; IF YOU EXPLOIT	LABOR	YOU WILL BE SHOT; AND IT WILL BE USELESS TO PLEAD THAT
SUPR III (76)	/MENDOZA/ (URBANELY) UNDOUBTEDLY. ALL MADE BY	LABOR	, AND ON ITS WAY TO BE SQUANDERED BY WEALTHY VAGABONDS
MTH4 I (171)	OF MILES APART. WE HOPE SHORTLY TO ORGANIZE THEIR	LABOR	, AND PRESS NATURAL FORCES INTO THEIR SERVICE, SO
GETT (301)	TO TEN YEARS PENAL SERVITUDE, TWO YEARS HARD	LABOR	, AND THE LOSS OF ALL CIVIL RIGHTS, NOT COUNTING THAT
MRS PREFACE(177)	TO THESE THE EMPLOYERS WHO PROFIT BY CHEAP FEMALE	LABOR	, AND THE SHAREHOLDERS WHOSE DIVIDENDS DEPEND ON IT (
MTH5 (260)	SON? /ADAM/ I MADE THE EARTH BRING FORTH BY MY	LABOR	, AND THE WOMAN BRING FORTH BY MY LOVE. AND THIS IS
HART PREFACE(15)	THE MOST SCIENTIFIC ORGANIZATION AND ECONOMY OF	LABOR	, AND THOUGH NO FACT WAS BETTER ESTABLISHED THAN THAT
SUPR PREFACE(R9)	PER ALIUM FACIT PER SE. ITS PROFITS, LIKE ITS	LABOR	, BELONG TO ME: ITS MORALS, ITS MANNERS, ITS
SUPR HANDBOK(206)	WITHIN OUR OWN TIME IN THE FORM OF FREE WAGE	LABOR	, HAS ENCOUNTERED THE SAME PERSONAL AND COMMERCIAL
SUPR III (76)	WEALTH. /THE SULKY SOCIAL-DEMOCRAT/ ALL MADE BY	LABOR	, MIND YOU. /MENDOZA/ (URBANELY) UNDOUBTEDLY. ALL
BARB II (303)	AND GRATIFYING TO ALL LARGE EMPLOYERS OF	LABOR	, MRS BAINES. /MRS BAINES/ BARBARA: JENNY: I HAVE GOOD
DOCT PREFACE(18)	ATTRACTIVENESS: THEY EXPEND MORE THOUGHT,	LABOR	, SKILL, INVENTIVENESS, TASTE AND ENDURANCE ON MAKING
FANY PREFACE(255)	CAPTURE BY THE POLICE, AND A MONTH'S HARD	LABOR	, THAN DRIFT ALONG FROM THEIR CRADLES TO THEIR GRAVES
MIS. PREFACE(35)	A PUNISHMENT AND A CURSE. IN AVOWED PRISONS, HARD	LABOR	, THE ONLY ALLEVIATION OF A PRISONER'S LOT, IS TREATED
MILL I (159)	IT OBLIGES YOU, ON PAIN OF EIGHTEEN MONTHS HARD	LABOR	, TO INDUCE ANOTHER FRIEND OR HOTEL MANAGER TO CASH
BULL IV (174)	NOW TO TAKE ON MEN OVER FORTY EVEN FOR UNSKILLED	LABOR	, WHICH I SUPPOSE IS ALL HAFFIGAN WOULD BE GOOD FOR.
APPL I (209)	TO HIS BLOUSE). /BOANERGES/ THE UNIFORM OF	LABOR	, YOUR ROYAL HIGHNESS. I'M PROUD OF IT. /ALICE/ OH
ARMS III (47)	DRAWS UP THE ORDERS; AND I SIGN EM. DIVISION OF	LABOR	! (BLUNTSCHLI PASSES HIM A PAPER). ANOTHER ONE?

LABORATORIES

HART PREFACE(9)	BLINDED BY THE DOLTISH MATERIALISM OF THE	LABORATORIES	AS THE UNCULTURED WORLD OUTSIDE. BUT BEING AN
FABL V (120)	BODY AND NOT THE BODY THE MIND. DEMOLISH ALL THE	LABORATORIES	. BUILD TEMPLES IN WHICH WE CAN PRAY AND PRAY

METH PREFACE(R53)	IS WRONG WITH ALL THE BARREN CRUELTIES OF THE	LABORATORIES	. DARWIN'S FOLLOWERS DID NOT THINK OF THIS.
FABL V (120)	OUT OF MATERIAL SUBSTANCES IN BIOCHEMICAL	LABORATORIES	. I WAS MANUFACTURED THAT WAY MYSELF; AND SO
MTH5 (227)	WERE MADE OVER AND OVER AGAIN IN THE CRUDE	LABORATORIES	OF THE SILLY-CLEVER AGES; BUT NOTHING CAME OF
MTH4 I (161)	OF THE PSEUDO-CHRISTIAN ERA, WHEN ALL THEIR	LABORATORIES	WERE DEMOLISHED, AND ALL THEIR APPARATUS
DOCT PREFACE(29)	OF TREATMENTS THAT INVOLVE HIGHLY ORGANIZED	LABORATORIES	, HOSPITALS, AND PUBLIC INSTITUTIONS GENERALLY,
LION EPILOG (152)	FLAT-EARTH MEN, SCOFFERS AT THE	LABORATORIES	, OR INFIDELS WHO REFUSE TO KNEEL DOWN WHEN A
		LABORATORY	
DOCT PREFACE(26)	RESISTANCE TO IT, TO ASCERTAIN THE RIGHT MOMENT A	LABORATORY	AND A STAFF OF EXPERTS ARE NEEDED. THE GENERAL
FABL III (112)	WELL. I'LL HAVE YOU ARRESTED AND PUT THROUGH THE	LABORATORY	AND CLASSIFIED. THAT IS THE LAW, COMPULSORY FOR
DOCT PREFACE(15)	AND MACHINERY THAT TURNS THE KITCHEN INTO A	LABORATORY	AND ENGINE HOUSE COMBINED, MANAGE, WHEN THEY ARE
DOCT PREFACE(26)	NEEDED. THE GENERAL PRACTITIONER, HAVING NO SUCH	LABORATORY	AND NO SUCH EXPERIENCE, HAS ALWAYS CHANCED IT,
KING I (200)	TO LOOK AFTER IT. I MUST TURN THEM ALL OUT OF THE	LABORATORY	AND SEND THEM UP HERE WHILE I LAY THE TABLE
FABL III (111)	ELSE AM I GOOD FOR? YOU CAN TAKE ME INTO YOUR	LABORATORY	AND TRY IF YOU LIKE. THERE IS A CANTEEN THERE,
DOCT I SD(81)	BY ANSWERING HIS LETTERS, ACTING AS HIS DOMESTIC	LABORATORY	ASSISTANT, AND MAKING HIMSELF INDISPENSABLE
DOCT I (90)	SEND A DROP OF THE PATIENT'S BLOOD TO THE	LABORATORY	AT ST ANNE'S; AND IN FIFTEEN MINUTES I'LL GIVE
KING I (180)	I UNDERSTAND THAT YOU, MR ROWLEY, HAVE A PRIVATE	LABORATORY	AT WHITEHALL, IN WHICH YOU ARE ATTEMPTING THE
FABL II (106)	AUTHORITIES TELL ME. YOURE A DIPLOMATIST, NOT A	LABORATORY	BLOKE. DO YOU KNOW WHAT AN ISOTOPE IS? DO YOU
METH PREFACE(R53)	COMMITTED BY CRUEL MEN WHO WERE ATTRACTED TO THE	LABORATORY	BY THE FACT THAT IT WAS A SECRET REFUGE LEFT BY
DOCT PREFACE(50)	BEEN CARRIED OUT BY SKILLED PHYSIOLOGISTS UNDER	LABORATORY	CONDITIONS. THE EARTHQUAKE IN SAN FRANCISCO
LION PREFACE(88)	LIKE SIR WILLIAM CROOKES DEMONSTRATE BY	LABORATORY	EXPERIMENTS THAT " MEDIUMS" LIKE DUNGLAS HOME CAN
MIS. PREFACE(33)	PLEASURES, THAT ITS SACRIFICE IN A HOSPITAL OR	LABORATORY	EXPERIMENT MIGHT SAVE MILLIONS OF LIVES, ETC.
DOCT PREFACE(40)	AN UNDOUBTED TRUTH, BUT ASCERTAINABLE WITHOUT	LABORATORY	EXPERIMENTS BY A SIMPLE INQUIRY ADDRESSED TO THE
DOCT PREFACE(76)	ALMROTH AS A DANGEROUS MAN IF HIS PRACTICE IN THE	LABORATORY	HAD NOT LED HIM TO THE CONCLUSION THAT THE
MTH2 (79)	YOU TAKE THE SPECTACLED SCIENCE STUDENT FROM THE	LABORATORY	IN OWENS COLLEGE; AND WHEN HE ASKS YOU FOR A
DOCT PREFACE(75)	WHATEVER MAY BE THE CASE IN SIR ALMROTH'S FAMOUS	LABORATORY	IN ST MARY'S HOSPITAL. IT WOULD HAVE BECOME
MIS. PREFACE(49)	THE SCHOOLMASTER IS ANOTHER EXPERIMENT; AND A	LABORATORY	IN WHICH ALL THE EXPERIMENTS BEGAN EXPERIMENTING
PYGM II SD(217)	NEXT DAY AT 11 A.M. HIGGINS'S	LABORATORY	IN WIMPOLE STREET. IT IS A ROOM ON THE FIRST
PHIL II (96)	TO TRY BEFORE FITTING IT AND SENDING IT TO THE	LABORATORY	. I AM AFRAID IT WOULD NOT DO TO BRING SUCH
MTH5 (241)	TWO THINGS? /MARTELLUS/ HE MADE THEM IN HIS	LABORATORY	. I MOULDED THEIR LIMBS. I AM SORRY. I WAS
DOCT III (150)	BE IN HIS PROPER PLACE, IN THE BACTERIOLOGICAL	LABORATORY	. I SHALL BE IN MY PROPER PLACE, AT THE BEDSIDE.
MTH5 (232)	AND SWALLOWED THEM. HE DRANK EVERY FLUID IN THE	LABORATORY	. I TRIED TO EXPLAIN TO HIM THAT HE MUST TAKE
METH PREFACE(R53)	AS WE SHUDDER NOW WHEN WE PASS A PHYSIOLOGICAL	LABORATORY	. IF WE DREADED AND MISTRUSTED THE PRIEST, WE
PYGM IV SD(260)	THE WIMPOLE STREET	LABORATORY	. MIDNIGHT. NOBODY IN THE ROOM. THE CLOCK ON THE
DOCT PREFACE(44)	HAD NOT FELT SICK AT HIS FIRST EXPERIENCE IN THE	LABORATORY	. NOT THAT THIS CAN EXONERATE ANY VIVISECTOR FROM
FABL III SD(109)	OF STEEL AND GLASS IS INSCRIBED ANTHROPOMETRIC	LABORATORY	. ON THE TERRACE BEFORE IT A BENCH AND CHAIRS.
FABL III SD(110)	THANK YOU. HE TAKES THE TICKET AND GOES INTO THE	LABORATORY	. /THE GENTLEMAN/ HE WILL BE A HEAVEN-SENT
FABL III (111)	IF YOULL SUBMIT TO A TEST OF YOUR CAPACITY IN OUR	LABORATORY	. /THE TRAMP/ IT WOULD BE ROBBING YOU. I TELL YOU
METH PREFACE(R73)	CANNOT BE ISOLATED AND EXPERIMENTED WITH IN THE	LABORATORY	. SECOND, THAT FORCE, BEING BY DEFINITION
MTH5 (235)	LIVING ORGANISM THAT CAN BE PRODUCED IN THE	LABORATORY	. THE BEST TISSUES WE CAN MANUFACTURE WILL NOT
MTH4 I (158)	ITS LIFE THAN ROGER BACON EVER DISCOVERED IN HIS	LABORATORY	. WHEN I WAS SEVEN YEARS OLD I DISCOVERED THE
MTH5 (229)	ATTEMPTS WERE MADE TO PRODUCE PROTOPLASM IN THE	LABORATORY	. WHY WERE THESE SYNTHETIC PLASMS, AS THEY CALLED
MTH5 (226)	THAT SOULLESS CREATURE! A SCIENTIST! A	LABORATORY	PERSON! /ARJILLAX/ PYGMALION PRODUCE A WORK OF
MTH5 (243)	LABORATORY, AND DESTROY THEM WITH THE REST OF THE	LABORATORY	REFUSE. (SOME OF THEM MOVE TO OBEY). TAKE CARE:
METH PREFACE(R73)	A LIVING SOUL. THE NEW VITALISTS, FILLED BY THEIR	LABORATORY	RESEARCHES WITH A SENSE OF THE MIRACULOUSNESS OF
FABL III (113)	HA! HA! HA! HA! HA! HA! (HE GOES INTO THE	LABORATORY	ROARING WITH LAUGHTER). /THE GENTLEMAN/ TWO BIG
FABL III (111)	I'LL GET YOU SOME BREAD. (SHE GOES INTO THE	LABORATORY	). /THE TRAMP/ LOOK AT THAT, NOW! ASK; AND IT
MTH5 (229)	THAT THE SO-CALLED SCIENTIST GRUBS UP IN HIS	LABORATORY	SLOWLY AND STUPIDLY LONG AFTERWARDS. /ARJILLAX/ (
SUPR HANDBOK(204)	THAT NO ANIMAL OPERATED ON IN THE PHYSIOLOGICAL	LABORATORY	SUFFERS THE SLIGHTEST PAIN. HYPOCRISY IS AT ITS
DOCT PREFACE(40)	HIS OWN FAVORITE METHOD OF EXPERIMENT, SUGGESTED	LABORATORY	TESTS OF THE VIVISECTOR'S EMOTIONS. TAKE THE
FABL PREFACE(90)	BARBARISM WHEN THEY ARE IN FACT EXALTING EVERY	LABORATORY	VIVISECTOR AND QUACK IMMUNIZER ABOVE JESUS AND ST
MTH5 (245)	HAND. THERE ARE TWO OF PYGMALION'S PUPILS AT THE	LABORATORY	WHO HELPED HIM TO MANUFACTURE THE BONES AND
METH PREFACE(R31)	AND THE SCALPEL FORCED IT ON THE VISION OF MERE	LABORATORY	WORKERS WHO COULD NOT THINK AND HAD NO RELIGION.
LION PREFACE(63)	DEMAND MAY BE LIMITED TO THE MEREST HANDFUL OF	LABORATORY	WORKERS, AND IN WHICH NEVERTHELESS THE WHOLE
FABL III (110)	SECRETIONS AND REACTIONS AND SO ON. QUITE EASY	LABORATORY	WORK. /THE TOURIST/ THAT WILL SUIT ME DOWN TO THE
MTH5 (243)	TAKE THESE TWO ABOMINATIONS AWAY TO PYGMALION'S	LABORATORY	, AND DESTROY THEM WITH THE REST OF THE
MTH5 (250)	THIS MAKESHIFT, CAN BE MADE BY A BOY IN A	LABORATORY	, AND IS HELD BACK FROM DISSOLUTION ONLY BY MY
METH PREFACE(R55)	WALLOWING IN THE INFAMIES OF THE VIVISECTOR'S	LABORATORY	, AND SOLEMNLY OFFERING US AS EPOCH-MAKING
HART PREFACE(10)	THAT MEDICINE WAS THE BUSINESS OF THE CHEMIST'S	LABORATORY	, AND SURGERY OF THE CARPENTER'S SHOP, AND ALSO
FABL V (118)	THE SEMINAL FLUIDS WHICH OUR CHEMISTS MAKE IN THE	LABORATORY	, AND WHICH IT IS OUR BUSINESS TO EXPERIMENT
MTH5 (230)	IF IT WERE POSSIBLE TO MAKE PROTOPLASM IN THE	LABORATORY	, IT MUST BE EQUALLY POSSIBLE TO BEGIN HIGHER UP
DOCT I (110)	YOU MUST TAKE MY WORD FOR IT THAT IT IS SO. MY	LABORATORY	, MY STAFF, AND MYSELF ARE WORKING AT FULL
MILL IV (207)	THE NURSE, THE FUNERAL, THE DISPOSAL OF THE	LABORATORY	, THE CHANGE TO A CHEAPER LODGING, HAD LEFT HER
DOCT PREFACE(44)	THIS ACQUIRED INDIFFERENCE WITH THEM INTO THE	LABORATORY	, WHERE ANY ATROCITY IS POSSIBLE, BECAUSE ALL
KING I (191)	YOUR PICTURES, AND YOUR MUSIC, AND YOUR CHEMICAL	LABORATORY	, YOU LET THEM DO AS THEY LIKE. THE MERRY
		LABORED	
3PLA PREFACE(R15)	HAD THE COURAGE OF THEIR VICES. WITH ALL THEIR	LABORED	EFFORTS TO KEEP UP AN UNDERSTANDING OF FURTIVE
JOAN PREFACE(29)	INDICTMENT. THE POINT NEED BE NO FURTHER	LABORED	, JOAN WAS PERSECUTED ESSENTIALLY AS SHE WOULD BE
		LABORER	
MTH4 II (178)	TASTES AND HABITS. I HAVE THE VIRTUES OF A	LABORER	: INDUSTRY AND INDIFFERENCE TO PERSONAL COMFORT. BUT
SUPR III SD(72)	GENTLEMAN AN ARTIST MAY MAKE AN UNEDUCATED MANUAL	LABORER	AN ABLEBODIED PAUPER. THERE ARE MEN WHO FALL
METH PREFACE(R46)	DOING ON A VERY SMALL SCALE. THERE IS HARDLY A	LABORER	ATTACHED TO AN ENGLISH COUNTRY HOUSE WHO HAS NOT
MIS. PREFACE(42)	THOUGH THEY ARE ALL EQUALLY HIS SLAVES: THE	LABORER	BEING IN FACT LESS DEPENDENT ON HIS FAVOR THAN THE
MIS. PREFACE(103)	OF A SLAVE CAN BE FREE. IT IS LIKE SAYING TO A	LABORER	BROUGHT UP ON A FAMILY INCOME OF THIRTEEN SHILLINGS
DOCT PREFACE(21)	WAS JUDICIOUS OR NOT: THE POINT IS, THAT A FARM	LABORER	CONSULTING A HERBALIST WOULD HAVE BEEN TREATED IN
ROCK II (244)	WAGES. WHY? BECAUSE OUT OF THOSE WAGES THE	LABORER	HAS TO PAY HALF OR QUARTER AS RENT TO THE LANDLORD.
MIS. (197)	WHY? /TARLETON/ (TO THE OTHERS) BILL BURT WAS A	LABORER	HERE. I WAS GOING TO SACK HIM FOR KICKING HIS
MTH2 (65)	AND YOUNGER SON CLASS. I DEFY YOU TO FIND A FARM	LABORER	IN ENGLAND WITH BROKEN BOOTS. CALL A MECHANIC ONE OF
MRS II (214)	TO US AS A MODEL BECAUSE SHE MARRIED A GOVERNMENT	LABORER	IN THE DEPTFORD VICTUALLING YARD, AND KEPT HIS ROOM
MTH2 (65)	AS A MARK OF CONFIDENCE? /CONRAD/ IF I WERE A	LABORER	IN YOUR CONSTITUENCY, I SHOULD ASK YOU A BIOLOGICAL
BULL I (89)	I KNOW VERY WELL THAT IF I HAD BEEN THE SON OF A	LABORER	INSTEAD OF THE SON OF A COUNTRY LANDAGENT, I SHOULD
SUPR HANDBOK(194)	ACROBAT AND THE BENT BACK OF THE RHEUMATIC FIELD	LABORER	IS A DIFFERENCE PRODUCED BY CONDITIONS, NOT BY
ROCK II (244)	PAY HALF OR QUARTER AS RENT TO THE LANDLORD. THE	LABORER	IS IGNORANT: HE THINKS HE IS ROBBED BY THE LANDLORD;
SUPR III (121)	UGLINESS AND IMPOTENCE AND DEATH. THE CHILDLESS	LABORER	IS MORE TORMENTED BY HIS WIFE'S IDLENESS AND HER
CLEO NOTES (205)	WILL PRODUCE A KIND OF MAN WITH WHOM THE COMMON	LABORER	IS SOCIALLY INCOMPATIBLE. THE SAME THING IS TRUE OF
SUPR HANDBOK(206)	PICK UP ANOTHER ONE FOR NOTHING, AS YOU CAN A	LABORER	, BUT THIS NATURAL CHECK ON INCONSIDERATE
MTH2 (66)	THE MAN OF HER CHOICE, WHETHER HE BE LORD OR	LABORER	. MAY I COUNT ON YOUR SUPPORT? /BURGE/ (HURLING
JOAN 1 (63)	MAKES MONEY BY IT, AND LIVES BY IT. STILL, NOT A	LABORER	. NOT A MECHANIC. HE MIGHT HAVE A COUSIN A LAWYER,
BULL III (131)	O THE LAND FOR DHEMSELVES, MUCH LESS GIVE IT TO A	LABORER	. /LARRY/ (NOW THOROUGHLY ROUSED) THEN LET THEM
MTH4 I (142)	STANDING. I AM NOT A CHILD, NOR AN AGRICULTURAL	LABORER	. /THE WOMAN/ (SEVERELY) THEY APPLY TO YOU VERY
METH PREFACE(R46)	KILLS OFF A WEAKLY PUPPY. THEN THERE IS THE FARM	LABORER	. SHAKESPEAR'S TOUCHSTONE, A COURT-BRED FOOL, WAS
SIM PREFACE(9)	A DISGRACE; AND THE LOWEST RANK KNOWN IS THAT OF	LABORER	. THE OBJECT OF EVERYONE'S AMBITION IS AN UNEARNED
2TRU PREFACE(6)	HAVE BEEN FOURTEEN THOUSAND TIMES AS HAPPY AS THE	LABORER	LUCKY ENOUGH TO BE EARNING TWO POUNDS A WEEK. THOSE
MIS. PREFACE(65)	SLIGHTEST CHALLENGE TO THEIR AUTHORITY. THUS A	LABORER	MAY BE DIRTY, DRUNKEN, UNTRUTHFUL, SLOTHFUL,
2TRU PREFACE(6)	THAT IF HE DRANK A BOTTLE OF WINE A DAY THE	LABORER	MUST HAVE DRUNK FOURTEEN THOUSAND. THE UNLOADING
LION PREFACE(56)	TIMES AS MUCH MONEY AS AN ENGLISH AGRICULTURAL	LABORER	OF GOOD GENERAL CHARACTER. NAME THE PRINCIPAL
MILL IV (205)	AND THE WAGES YOU PAY WOULD BE A FORTUNE TO A	LABORER	ON THE NILE. BUT WHAT OF THE OLD PEOPLE WHOSE
JOAN 4 (103)	MEN, ARE THRUST INTO THE KENNEL BY EVERY IGNORANT	LABORER	OR DAIRYMAID WHOM THE DEVIL CAN PUFF UP WITH THE
LION PREFACE(18)	FAMILY, IN RESISTING IT, WERE TRYING TO DO A	LABORER	OUT OF HIS RIGHTS, IT IS QUITE POSSIBLE THAT MATTHEW
PRES (140)	NEPHEW HAS BEEN TREATED LIKE ANY COMMON	LABORER	; AND WHILE ENGLAND IS REELING UNDER THE SHOCK, A
UNPL PREFACE(R11)	DEGRADATION LOOMING BEFORE ME AS AN AGRICULTURAL	LABORER	SEES THE WORKHOUSE. SO I SAID " I WILL BEGIN WITH
SUPR III (109)	AT THE BLOCK. /DON JUAN/ NEVER FEAR! THE WHITE	LABORER	SHALL HAVE HIS TURN TOO. BUT I AM NOT NOW DEFENDING
CLEO NOTES (206)	COCKNEY PROLETARIAN IS SO INFERIOR TO THE VILLAGE	LABORER	THAT IT IS ONLY BY STEADY RECRUITING FROM THE
LION PREFACE(57)	VIRTUES IN WHICH MR BARNATO EXCEEDED THE	LABORER	THREE THOUSANDFOLD; AND GIVE IN FIGURES THE LOSS
GENV PREFACE(23)	WITH LESS, AND THAT THE MOST LIMITED CRAFTSMAN OR	LABORER	WHO CAN DO NOTHING WITHOUT DIRECTION FROM A THINKER,

MTH2 (66)	I AM ASKING THE QUESTION IN THE CHARACTER OF A	LABORER	WHO EARNED THIRTEEN SHILLINGS A WEEK BEFORE THE WAR
SUPR III (106)	I SAW A MAN DIE: HE WAS A LONDON BRICKLAYER'S	LABORER	WITH SEVEN CHILDREN. HE LEFT SEVENTEEN POUNDS CLUB
ROCK I (213)	BECAUSE WE KNEW HE'D SPEAK TO YOU AS A DOCK	LABORER	WOULD SPEAK TO YOU IF HIS GOOD MANNERS WOULD LET
MIS. (165)	OF ALL SLAVERIES. HOW WOULD YOU LIKE IT IF EVERY	LABORER	YOU MET IN THE ROAD WERE TO MAKE LOVE TO YOU? NO.
HART PREFACE(27)	THAN THUNDER IN THE HAND OF EVERY VILLAGE	LABORER	, AND FOUND ON THE MESSINES RIDGE THE CRATERS OF THE
BULL II (98)	TOWARDS THE BROW OF THE HILL. IMMEDIATELY A YOUNG	LABORER	, HIS FACE DISTORTED WITH TERROR, SLIPS ROUND FROM
JOAN PREFACE(9)	BASED ON THE ASSUMPTION THAT HE WAS AN ILLITERATE	LABORER	, IN THE FACE OF THE PLAINEST EVIDENCE THAT HIS
MRS II (217)	ADVISE ME TO TRY THE WATERLOO BAR, OR MARRY A	LABORER	, OR EVEN GO INTO THE FACTORY? /MRS WARREN/ (
LADY PREFACE(216)	SAID, WITH THE OBJECT OF PROVING SHAKESPEAR A	LABORER	, THAT HE COULD HARDLY WRITE HIS NAME. WHY? BECAUSE
APPL I (210)	BUT I HAVE EARNED MY BREAD BY MY HANDS, NOT AS A	LABORER	, THOUGH, I AM A SKILLED MECHANIC, OR WAS UNTIL MY
BULL II (98)	WHATS THAT? (HE COMES BACK AND FINDS THE	LABORER	, WHO CLASPS HIS KNEES) PATSY FARRELL! WHAT ARE YOU
		LABORER'S	
SUPR HANDBOK(180)	EVEN PROPERTY AND MARRIAGE, WHICH LAUGH AT THE	LABORER'S	PETTY COMPLAINT THAT HE IS DEFRAUDED OF " SURPLUS
LION PREFACE(61)	OF THE OTHER. TO HANG ME FOR CUTTING A DOCK	LABORER'S	THROAT AFTER MAKING MUCH OF ME FOR LEAVING HIM TO
MRS PREFACE(175)	THAT MYSELF. I HAVE SEEN AN OXFORD AGRICULTURAL	LABORER'S	WIFE LOOKING CHEERFUL ON EIGHT SHILLINGS A WEEK;
		LABORERS	
ANNA (290)	EMPTY WORDS USED BY VULGAR TRADESMEN AND COMMON	LABORERS	: MERE WIND AND STINK. (HE RISES, EXALTED BY HIS
BARB III (324)	LABORERS; THE FOREMEN DRIVE AND BULLY BOTH THE	LABORERS	AND ARTISANS; THE ASSISTANT ENGINEERS FIND FAULT
GETT PREFACE(191)	PROFESSIONAL MEN, ARTISTS, AND EVEN WITH	LABORERS	AND ARTISANS AS FAR AS MUSCULAR EXERTION GOES, THEY
BULL PREFACE(47)	NORMAL CIRCUMSTANCES, MUCH LIKE ANY OTHER BODY OF	LABORERS	AND GENTLEMEN. MANY OF US COUNT AMONG OUR PERSONAL
ROCK PREFACE(170)	SUCH ARTIFICIAL PRODUCTS AS OUR AGRICULTURAL	LABORERS	AND URBAN MECHANICS, OUR COUNTRY GENTLEMEN AND CITY
CLEO NOTES (206)	BE MORE ADVANCED THAN THE COUNTRY; AND THE FIELD	LABORERS	AND VILLAGE ARTISANS OF TODAY MUST BE MUCH LESS
MIS. PREFACE(63)	HAVE QUITE A MAJORITY. AT PRESENT THE CHILDREN OF	LABORERS	ARE SOON MOBILE AND ABLE TO SHIFT FOR THEMSELVES,
SIM PREFACE(9)	LAVISHED ANNUALLY ON LADIES AND GENTLEMEN WHILST	LABORERS	ARE UNDERFED, ILL CLOTHED, AND SLEEPING TWO OR
DOCT PREFACE(55)	MORE MEANS AND BETTER NURTURE THAN THE MASS OF	LABORERS	ENJOY, CAN BE STATISTICALLY PALMED OFF AS A
SIM PREFACE(10)	THE NECESSARY PERSECUTION, SUCH AS TRANSPORTING	LABORERS	FOR READING THE WORKS OF THOMAS PAINE, OR
FABL PREFACE(67)	WEEK PER FAMILY, WHICH WAS THE SHARE AGRICULTURAL	LABORERS	GOT IN THE NINETEENTH CENTURY, KEPT THEM ALIVE FOR
SUPR III SD(72)	LABOR OFFER NO SUCH POSITIONS. WE MISUSE OUR	LABORERS	HORRIBLY; AND WHEN A MAN REFUSES TO BE MISUSED, WE
LION PREFACE(58)	BEING AS MISCHIEVOUS AS THE EXCESSIVE TOIL OF THE	LABORERS	. ANYHOW, THE MORAL IS CLEAR. THE TWO MAIN PROBLEMS
GETT PREFACE(208)	MEN AND WOMEN THAN IT NOW IS OF AGRICULTURAL	LABORERS	. BEES GET OUT OF THIS DIFFICULTY BY A SPECIAL
BULL III (128)	IN THE TOWNS, OR FOR THE FOOLISHNESS OF THE	LABORERS	. /DORAN/ AYE; AN DHAT CAN AFFORD TO LIVE IN LONDON
DOCT PREFACE(17)	WHOSE MANAGERS, CLERKS, WAREHOUSEMEN AND	LABORERS	KEEP HIS BUSINESS GOING WHILST HE IS IN BED OR IN
MTH2 (65)	/LUBIN/ ND YOU WOULDNT, MY DEAR DOCTOR.	LABORERS	NEVER ASK QUESTIONS. /BURGE/ ASK IT NOW. I HAVE
LION PREFACE(18)	AS A BARONET WAS SUPPORTED BY AN ASSOCIATION OF	LABORERS	ON THE GROUND THAT THE TICHBORNE FAMILY, IN
ROCK PREFACE(152)	I NO LONGER NEED TOLERATE THE EXISTENCE OF THE	LABORERS	; SO I DRIVE THEM OFF MY LAND, WHICH IS MY LEGAL
BARB III (324)	THE SWEEPERS; THE ARTISANS SNUB THE UNSKILLED	LABORERS	; THE FOREMEN DRIVE AND BULLY BOTH THE LABORERS AND
DOCT PREFACE(29)	OR THE PUBLIC TECHNICAL EDUCATION OF UNSKILLED	LABORERS	' SONS TO COMPETE WITH HIM, SO THE DOCTOR WILL
MRS PREFACE(175)	BOOTH AS HAVING TESTIFIED THAT THERE ARE MANY	LABORERS	' WIVES WHO ARE HAPPY AND CONTENTED ON EIGHTEEN
MTH3 (120)	THEN: MISERABLE PITTANCES FOR WORN-OUT OLD	LABORERS	TO DIE ON. I THOUGHT I SHOULD BE FOUND OUT IF I
ROCK PREFACE(152)	TO GROW WHEAT ON IT, I NEED MANY AGRICULTURAL	LABORERS	TO ENABLE ME TO DO IT; AND I TOLERATE THEIR
JOAN PREFACE(22)	TO AND DEALT WITH PEOPLE OF ALL CLASSES, FROM	LABORERS	TO KINGS, WITHOUT EMBARRASSMENT OR AFFECTATION, AND
BULL IV (178)	TEMPER BY EMPLOYING HIM TO SLAVE-DRIVE YOUR	LABORERS	VERY EFFICIENTLY; AND (LOW AND BITTER) WHEN AT
MIS. (200)	WE CAN BUY PETROL AT THE BEACON. WITH A FEW	LABORERS	WE CAN GET HER OUT ON TO THE PORTSMOUTH ROAD AND
JOAN PREFACE(43)	AND TO SOME EXTENT OVER HER FATHER'S HIRED	LABORERS	WHEN HE HIRED ANY, BUT OVER NO ONE ELSE ON EARTH.
MIS. PREFACE(70)	CHILDREN. BETTER CLAUDE DUVAL THAN KASPAR HAUSER.	LABORERS	WHO ARE CONTEMPTUOUSLY ANTI-CLERICAL IN THEIR
MILL PREFACE(130)	WERE NEVER-DO-WELLS, MENTAL DEFECTIVES, AND	LABORERS	WITH THE MINDS AND HABITS OF SERFS. MILITARY
ROCK PREFACE(150)	SPECIES. LADIES AND GENTLEMEN CLASS REBELLIOUS	LABORERS	WITH VERMIN. THE DOMINICANS, THE WATCHDOGS OF GOD,
FABL PREFACE(67)	WROTE ASKING ME DID I REALIZE THAT HIS ARMY OF	LABORERS	WOULD BE DESTITUTE AND HELPLESS WITHOUT HIM. I
SUPR II (51)	OF ME AND A MACHINE THAN YOU WILL OUT OF TWENTY	LABORERS	, AND NOT SO MUCH TO DRINK EITHER. /TANNER/ FOR
MIS. PREFACE(42)	HIS SOLICITOR OR HIS DOCTOR AS HE TREATS HIS	LABORERS	, THOUGH THEY ARE ALL EQUALLY HIS SLAVES: THE
BARB PREFACE(234)	PEASANTS, GROCERS AND ARISTOCRATS, ARTISANS AND	LABORERS	, WASHERWOMEN AND DUCHESSES, IN WHICH ALL THE
		LABORING	
OVER PREFACE(158)	CONTEMPTIBLE, AND COWARDLY CUCKOLD. AND THE	LABORING	CLASS IS DIVIDED INTO THE RESPECTABLE SECTION WHICH
		LABORIOUS	
MTH5 (230)	MOST FAMOUS MATHEMATICIANS YEARS OF PROLONGED AND	LABORIOUS	CALCULATIONS REQUIRING SUCH INTENSE MENTAL
SUPR PREFACE(R10)	A REASONABLE, PATIENT, CONSISTENT, APOLOGETIC,	LABORIOUS	PERSON, WITH THE TEMPERAMENT OF A SCHOOLMASTER AND
ROCK PREFACE(168)	BY THE BANK OF ENGLAND (ONLY ENORMOUSLY MORE	LABORIOUS	), STRAINS ALL THE WIT AND INDUSTRY OF THE RUSSIAN
MIS. PREFACE(3)	EVER KNOWN OF HAVE BEEN MORE EASILY EARNED THAN A	LABORIOUS	SIXPENCE; BUT THE DIFFICULTY OF INDUCING A MAN TO
MTH4 II (191)	UNNECESSARILY PAINFUL, MY BOYHOOD UNNECESSARILY	LABORIOUS	, BY RIDICULOUS PREPARATIONS FOR A LENGTH OF DAYS
METH PREFACE(R28)	BY MILLIONS, ARE CASES IN WHICH A LONG,	LABORIOUS	, CONSCIOUS, DETAILED PROCESS OF ACQUIREMENT HAS
		LABORIOUSLY	
GENV IV (98)	IT CANNOT BE PRACTISED EFFECTIVELY WITHOUT A	LABORIOUSLY	ACQUIRED TECHNIQUE. /SIR O./ BUT I AM AN
BULL II SD(105)	AT HIS HEELS. THE PRIEST FOLLOWS. PATSY LAGS	LABORIOUSLY	BEHIND. /CORNELIUS/ THIS IS A BIT OF A CLIMB, MR
PHIL I (79)	DARE TREAT ME AS YOU ARE DOING NOW. /CHARTERIS/ (	LABORIOUSLY	GOING BACK TO HIS ARGUMENT) IT WAS UNDERSTOOD
MIS. PREFACE(49)	AND HIS HISTORY OF SCOTLAND FROM END TO END MOST	LABORIOUSLY	. ONCE, STUNG BY THE AIRS OF A SCHOOLFELLOW WHO
JITT PREFACE(4)	WHILST THE ENGLISH CRITICS WERE STILL EXPLAINING	LABORIOUSLY	THAT MY PLAYS WERE NOT PLAYS, AND URGING ME, IN
3PLA PREFACE(R35)	MERE GLEANERS, OR, WORSE THAN THAT, FOOLS WHO GO	LABORIOUSLY	THROUGH ALL THE MOTIONS OF THE REAPER AND BINDER
AUGS (282)	WHAT! /THE CLERK/ (LAUGHING SLOWLY AND	LABORIOUSLY	, WITH INTENSE ENJOYMENT) HA HA! HA HA HA!
		LABORS	
CLEO PRO2 (101)	GROWS OLD NOW: HE IS PAST FIFTY AND FULL OF	LABORS	AND BATTLES. HE IS TOO OLD FOR THE YOUNG WOMEN; AND
SUPR III (131)	SERVES ONLY MY DOG'S PURPOSES; BUT MY OWN BRAIN	LABORS	AT A KNOWLEDGE WHICH DOES NOTHING FOR ME PERSONALLY
APPL II (266)	WELL IN ANYTHING. AND NOW I LEAVE YOU ALL TO YOUR	LABORS	. SHE GOES OUT ALONG THE TERRACE. SEMPRONIUS FOLLOWS
		LABOURER	
DEVL I (23)	GO ON. /HAWKINS/-- " AND KEEP MY DEAF FARM	LABOURER	PRODGER FESTON IN HIS SERVICE." /RICHARD/ PRODGER
		LABOUR'S	
SHAK PREFACE(136)	NOT HAVE WRITTEN VENUS AND ADONIS NOR LOVE'S	LABOUR'S	LOST. ONE DOES NOT FORGET BUNYAN'S " THE LATIN I
SHAK PREFACE(136)	WORKS AS VENUS AND ADONIS, LUCRECE, AND LOVE'S	LABOUR'S	LOST, COULD NOT POSSIBLY HAVE BEEN WRITTEN BY AN
		LABYRINTHS	
SUPR HANDBOK(193)	CIVILIZED PEOPLE (THAT IS, PEOPLE MASSED IN THE	LABYRINTHS	OF SLUMS WE CALL CITIES), HALF THEIR BODILY LIFE
		LACE	
FANY I (282)	GILBEY/ (UNRUFFLED) WHERE DID YOU BUY THAT WHITE	LACE	? I WANT SOME TO MATCH A COLLARET OF MY OWN; AND I
PPP (202)	MY HAT-BOX. /MAGNESIA/ I USE IT FOR WASHING OLD	LACE	; BUT NO MATTER: HE SHALL HAVE IT (SHE PRODUCES A
		LACED	
CAPT I SD(234)	BLUE SERGE, A DILAPIDATED ALPINE HAT, AND BOOTS	LACED	WITH SCRAPS OF TWINE. HE REMAINS NEAR THE DOOR, WHILST
		LACERATE	
CLEO NOTES (203)	IT BECAUSE IN MOST OF THE OTHERS YOU HAVE TO	LACERATE	THE SKIN, PRICK IT, OR RUB IT TILL IT BLEEDS. I DO
		LACERATED	
DOCT PREFACE(54)	AS TETANUS WAS THEN SUPPOSED TO BE INDUCED) BY A	LACERATED	WOUND. THERE WERE NO STATISTICS AVAILABLE AS TO
		LACERATION	
DOCT PREFACE(39)	ESPECIALLY THOSE INVOLVING BLOODSHED, BLOWS, AND	LACERATION	. A CRAZE FOR CRUELTY CAN BE DEVELOPED JUST AS A
		LACHEND	
HART PREFACE(40)	TO CRY WITH BRYNHILD, " LASS' UNS VERDERBEN,	LACHEND	ZU GRUNDE GEH'N" SOONER THAN DECEIVE OR BE DECEIVED;

LACHRYMOSE

CAND I (87) IMPUDENCE! /BURGESS/ (RETREATING, WITH ALMOST LACHRYMOSE DEPRECATION OF THIS TREATMENT) IS THAT BECOMIN
MILL IV (201) AND TAKING HIS HEAD IN HIS HANDS, SHAKEN, ALMOST LACHRYMOSE) IS THERE ANY JUSTICE FOR A MAN AGAINST A

LACHRYMOSELY

CAPT II (250) SURE IT WOULD HURT MR DRINKWATER. /DRINKWATER/ (LACHRYMOSELY) LIDY'S HINKYP'BLE O SICH BAWBROUS USAGE.
MIS. (188) MAAM: I REGARD YOU WITH RESPECT AND AFFECTION. (LACHRYMOSELY) YOU WERE VERY GOOD TO MY MOTHER: MY POOR

LACING

MIS. (114) FATHER DIDNT GIVE YOUR THIN SKIN A JOLLY GOOD LACING WITH A CANE! /BENTLEY/ PITY YOU HAVNT GOT MORE THAN

LACK

LADY (247) BECOMING A COURTIER LIKE THE REST OF THEM. YOU LACK ADVANCEMENT. /SHAKESPEAR/ " LACK ADVANCEMENT." BY YOUR
LADY (247) OF THEM. YOU LACK ADVANCEMENT. /SHAKESPEAR/ " LACK ADVANCEMENT." BY YOUR MAJESTY'S LEAVE: A QUEENLY
MILL PREFACE(130) WHICH CERTAIN PEOPLE GET PUSHED EVEN WHEN THEY LACK AMBITION AND ARE FAR TOO INTELLIGENT TO BELIEVE THAT
BULL PREFACE(23) PROTESTANT PARNELL, ALTHOUGH THERE WAS NO LACK AMONG US OF FLUENT IMBECILES, WITH MAJESTIC PRESENCES
KING I (197) WHAT YOU CALL A KING I LACK MILITARY AMBITION; I LACK CRUELTY. I HAVE TO MANAGE PROTESTANTS WHO ARE SO
KING I (178) AND TAKE ON THEMSELVES DIVINE POWERS WHEN THEY LACK DIVINE ATTRIBUTES. AM I TO HOLD MY PEACE IN THE FACE OF
LADY PREFACE(219) BE," HE SAYS, " BUT I AM PIGEON-LIVERED, AND LACK GALL TO MAKE OPPRESSION BITTER; ELSE, ERE THIS, I
SIM PREFACE(4) BUT I BELIEVE THEY ARE CAPABLE ENOUGH AND ONLY LACK INSTRUCTION. I WONDER HOW MANY OF THEM HAVE GIVEN
MIS. PREFACE(107) CONSTRUCTIVE, UTOPIAN IMAGINATION, WHICH LACK IS A GHASTLY DEFECT. FREEDOM FROM IMAGINATIVE ILLUSION
MIS. PREFACE(107) NOT ONLY IN A LACK OF ROMANTIC IMAGINATION, WHICH LACK IS A MERIT, BUT OF THE REALISTIC, CONSTRUCTIVE, UTOPIAN
GENV III (80) PRECISELY. THAT IS THE SPIRIT OF GENEVA. WHAT YOU LACK IS NOT MIND BUT KNOWLEDGE. /THE NEWCOMER/ MY WIFE SAYS
GETT PREFACE(244) LACKED WHAT NO WOMAN WITH PLENTY OF MONEY NEED LACK . THE FACT THAT, ACCORDING TO THE TESTIMONY OF MEN WHO
METH PREFACE(R12) THE EXPLOITERS, THEY FALL INTO POVERTY WHEN THEY LACK LUCRATIVE SPECIFIC TALENTS. AT THE PRESENT MOMENT ONE
KING I (197) AS YOU SAY, NO KING, TO BE WHAT YOU CALL A KING I LACK MILITARY AMBITION; I LACK CRUELTY. I HAVE TO MANAGE
LADY PREFACE(231) CONTEND THAT ONE OF SHAKESPEAR'S DEFECTS IS HIS LACK OF AN INTELLIGENT COMPREHENSION OF FEUDALISM. HE HAD OF
HART PREFACE(29) TO INTRODUCE A PLAY IN THE FORM OF A BOOK FOR LACK OF AN OPPORTUNITY OF PRESENTING IT IN ITS PROPER MODE
SUPR I (18) NOTHING TO SAY. RAMSDEN, A LITTLE RUFFLED BY THE LACK OF ANY RESPONSE, CONTINUES) I DONT KNOW THAT I CAN
SUPR III (105) THESE THINGS LIVED AND WANTED TO LIVE; BUT FOR LACK OF BRAINS THEY DID NOT KNOW HOW TO CARRY OUT THEIR
FABL PREFACE(86) IN SPAIN THEY WERE UTTERLY DEFEATED THROUGH LACK OF COMPETENT MINISTERS AND COMMANDERS. THE STRUGGLE IS
SUPR II SD(62) ENGLISH LIFE SEEMS TO HIM TO SUFFER FROM A LACK OF EDIFYING RHETORIC (WHICH HE CALLS MORAL TONE);
APPL I (234) PRACTICAL ABILITY, THEIR COMPARATIVE POVERTY AND LACK OF EDUCATION, OR, LET ME HASTEN TO ADD, THEIR HATRED OF
CLEO NOTES (207) AS FAR AS IT IS CHILDISHNESS OF CHARACTER AND NOT LACK OF EXPERIENCE, IS NOT A MATTER OF YEARS. IT MAY BE
BULL PREFACE(17) MORE IN IT THAN THAT. IF THERE IS AN ENTIRE LACK OF GALL IN THE FEELING OF THE IRISH GENTRY TOWARDS THE
FANY PROL,SD(266) AND NEGATIVELY BY A COMFORTABLE IGNORANCE AND LACK OF INTUITION WHICH HIDES FROM HIM ALL THE DANGERS AND
BUOY 1 (13) WHOLE NATIONS ARE BARELY KEEPING HALF ALIVE FOR LACK OF IT. /FATHER/ WELL, MY BOY, YOU ARE KEEPING ALIVE
LADY PREFACE(215) WAS AT A SOCIAL DISADVANTAGE THROUGH HIS LACK OF MIDDLE-CLASS TRAINING. THEY ARE ROWDY, ILL-MANNERED,
3PLA PREFACE(R36) ARTISTIC, MATHEMATICAL AND LINGUISTIC, WHO FOR LACK OF NEW IDEAS, OR INDEED OF ANY IDEAS WORTH MENTIONING,
METH PREFACE(R55) WANT OF MASTERY OF THEIR OWN SUBJECT, THE DULLEST LACK OF OBSERVATION OF THE FORCES UPON WHICH NATURAL
LIED (201) SWINE! D'YE HEAR? /HE/ (WITH A DEPLORABLE LACK OF POLISH) YOU CALL ME A SWINE AGAIN AND I'LL LAND YOU
APPL I (234) TO DISTINCTION CLOSED TO THEM EITHER BY THEIR LACK OF PRACTICAL ABILITY, THEIR COMPARATIVE POVERTY AND
METH PREFACE(R85) PLAYWRIGHTS HAVE BEEN STRUGGLING WITH THE SAME LACK OF RELIGION; AND MANY OF THEM WERE FORCED TO BECOME
MIS. PREFACE(107) QUALIFICATION OFTEN CONSISTS NOT ONLY IN A LACK OF ROMANTIC IMAGINATION, WHICH LACK IS A MERIT, BUT OF
SUPR PREFACE(R27) CRITICS WHO, IF THEY CANNOT GOVERN IN PERSON FOR LACK OF SPARE ENERGY OR SPECIFIC TALENT FOR ADMINISTRATION,
ROCK PREFACE(168) SHORT OF BOOTS AND TIGHTENING ITS BELT FOR LACK OF SUFFICIENT FOOD. I MUST NOT SUGGEST THAT THIS HAS
KING PREFACE(159) WILL FALL SHORT AND PERHAPS BREAK DOWN FOR LACK OF SUFFICIENT DIRECTION. COMPETENT WOMEN, OF WHOM
BUOY PREFACE(4) ANY OTHER SON OF A DOWNSTART GENTLEMAN DRIVEN BY LACK OF UNEARNED INCOME TO BECOME AN INCOMPETENT MERCHANT
GETT PREFACE(243) THAT POVERTY MEANS HUNGER, AN INTOLERABLE LACK OF VARIETY AND PLEASURE, AND, IN SHORT, ALL SORTS OF
APPL PREFACE(195) UNDER HIS INSULTS AND SHOCKED BY HIS UTTER LACK OF VENERATION FOR BIGWIGS, BESIDES BEING HAMPERED AS
GETT PREFACE(192) HEROINE'S PERSON ON THE STRENGTH OF A STAGGERING LACK OF VIRTUE. INDEED THEIR ONLY CONCEPTION OF THE MEANING
METH PREFACE(R66) POLICEMAN. BUT GOD'S TRUSTIEST LIEUTENANTS OFTEN LACK OFFICIAL CREDENTIALS. THEY MAY BE PROFESSED ATHEISTS
CURE PREFACE(224) THE SCENES CAN BE EMPLOYED; BUT THE RESULT WILL LACK SPONTANEITY. THERE IS, HOWEVER, NO PRESSING REASON WHY

LACKED

GENV IV (102) ECSTASY OF LOVE. WHEN HAS A WARLIKE RACE EVER LACKED CHILDREN? /THE BETROTHED/ VERY ROMANTIC AND ALL
CLEO NOTES (212) HUMOR, THERE IS NO MORE REASON TO ASSUME THAT HE LACKED IT THAN TO ASSUME THAT HE WAS DEAF OR BLIND. IT IS
BARB PREFACE(207) OF LIFE, A POIGNANT QUALITY THAT ROMANTIC FICTION LACKED . THE BOOK, IN SPITE OF ITS FIRST FAILURE, IS NOT
BARB PREFACE(218) SO FAR, HOWEVER, THEIR ATTACK ON SOCIETY HAS LACKED SIMPLICITY. THE POOR DO NOT SHARE THEIR TASTES NOR
UNPL PREFACE(R7) THIS PROVISION AS MIGHT BE SUPPOSED, NOT THAT I LACKED THE DRAMATIST'S GIFT, AS FAR AS THAT IS CONCERNED, I
JOAN PREFACE(22) BUT SHE, BEING ONLY A LASS WHEN ALL IS SAID, LACKED THEIR KNOWLEDGE OF MEN'S VANITIES AND OF THE WEIGHT
PYGM PREFACE(199) TO DISLIKE. HENRY SWEET, THEN A YOUNG MAN, LACKED THEIR SWEETNESS OF CHARACTER: HE WAS ABOUT AS
GENV PREFACE(17) DEAL WITH SUCH A SITUATION. WELL, THEY SIMPLY LACKED THESE QUALITIES. THEY WERE NOT FIENDS IN HUMAN FORM;
INCA (252) WHICH I SHOULD BE THE LAST TO DENY. NAPOLEON LACKED VERSATILITY. AFTER ALL, ANY FOOL CAN BE A SOLDIER: WE
GETT PREFACE(244) FUN, OR THE LIKE, SHE IS REALLY SAYING THAT SHE LACKED WHAT NO WOMAN WITH PLENTY OF MONEY NEED LACK. THE

LACKEY

KING I (165) LIKE A NOBLEMAN. VERY TALL. VERY DARK. KEEPS A LACKEY . HAS A PACK OF DOGS WITH HIM. /NEWTON/ OHO! SO THAT
KING I (161) AND VERY DARK, AND A LOT OF DOGS WITH HIM, AND A LACKEY . NOT A PERSON YOU COULD SHUT THE DOOR IN THE FACE

LACKEYS

HART PREFACE(39) A PEASANT; THE LORD OF HELLAS IS LEVEL WITH HIS LACKEYS IN REPUBLICAN SWITZERLAND; PRIME MINISTERS AND
KING I (196) WITH THE SQUIREARCHY. WHAT ARE THEY IN FRANCE? LACKEYS ROUND THE THRONE AT VERSAILLES: NOT ONE OF THEM DARE

LACKING

ROCK PREFACE(191) A SORT OF SOCIAL CONSCIENCE WHICH IS DANGEROUSLY LACKING AT PRESENT, AND WHICH NONE OF OUR MODEL EDUCATIONAL
OVER PREFACE(168) SOME SPECIFIC QUALITY PRESENT IN A MURDERER AND LACKING IN ME. AND, IF SO, WHAT THAT QUALITY IS. IN JUST THE
ROCK II (247) FROM THE ISLE OF CATS. THE ONE ELEMENT THAT WAS LACKING IN OUR COUNCILS. YOU HAVE HEARD THE VOICE OF THE
MRS PREFACE(165) ARE EQUALLY INDIGNANT WITH ME. THEY REVILE ME AS LACKING IN PASSION, IN FEELING, IN MANHOOD. SOME OF THEM
SUPR I (28) AMONG US-- /TANNER/ OR ANY MAN NOTORIOUSLY LACKING IN SELF-CONTROL. /RAMSDEN/ (AGHAST) DO YOU DARE TO
SIM I (46) WITH ME. I AM CONVINCED THAT THERE IS SOMETHING LACKING IN THE CONSTITUTION OF THE CHILDREN. IT MAY BE A
BULL PREFACE(55) PAPERS, NOS. 3 AND 4, EGYPT, 1906, ARE NOT LACKING IN UNCONSCIOUS HUMOR. THE OFFICIAL WALRUS PLEDGES
KING PREFACE(158) WHO BELIEVE THAT THE SOUL IS A MASCULINE ORGAN LACKING IN WOMEN, AS CERTAIN PHYSICAL ORGANS ARE, AND IS THE
DOCT PREFACE(68) OF HEALTH) ARE IN THE NEW POSITION: WHAT IS LACKING IS APPRECIATION OF THE CHANGE, NOT ONLY BY THE
BULL I SD(73) PURCHASED IS CHEAP; NOR IS ANYTHING THEY WANT LACKING . ON THE WALLS HANG A LARGE MAP OF SOUTH AMERICA, A
MRS IV (241) ABOUT YOU TODAY, VIV, WHICH HAS HITHERTO BEEN LACKING . /PRAED/ (REMONSTRATING) MY DEAR FRANK: ARNT YOU A
BULL PREFACE(61) THE LEVER WHICH HAS, UP TO THE PRESENT, BEEN LACKING TO THE VENAL AGITATORS WHO ARE AT THE HEAD OF THE

LACKS

PLES PREFACE(R17) IS THAT MY TALENT, THOUGH NOT UNENTERTAINING, LACKS ELEVATION OF SENTIMENT AND SERIOUSNESS OF PURPOSE.
JITT I (18) FOR MY LECTURES. HE KNOWS EVERYTHING: WHAT HE LACKS IS A SENSE OF THE SIGNIFICANCE OF WHAT HE KNOWS. I AM
JOAN 2,SD(72) HE IS DETERMINED TO MAKE HIMSELF AGREEABLE, BUT LACKS NATURAL JOYOUSNESS, AND IS NOT REALLY PLEASANT. IN
JITT II SD(27) WHO IS ENGAGED TO BRUNO'S DAUGHTER EDITH. ALFRED LACKS THE DISTINCTION AND HEROIC TOUCH OF BRUNO; BUT PROSAIC
BULL PREFACE(55) LEAST SENSATIONAL FORM OF PUBLIC EXECUTION: IT LACKS THOSE ELEMENTS OF BLOOD AND TORTURE FOR WHICH THE

LACQUER

HART I SD(49) EMERGES FROM THE PANTRY WITH A TRAY OF CHINESE LACQUER AND A VERY FINE TEA-SET ON IT. HE RESTS IT
NEVR III SD(261) OF LINCRUSTA WALTON IN PLUM COLOR AND BRONZE LACQUER , WITH DADO AND CORNICE; THE ORMOLU CONSOLES IN THE

LAD

BULL III (134) HE AT ALL AT ALL? /FATHER DEMPSEY/ HE'S A CLEVER LAD : DHERES THE MAKING OF A MAN IN HIM YET. /MATTHEW/ (IN
CAND I (97) TO EUGENE WITH AFFECTIONATE SERIOUSNESS), MY DEAR LAD : IN A HAPPY MARRIAGE LIKE OURS, THERE IS SOMETHING VERY
JOAN 2 (84) AT THE POOR DEVIL. /JOAN/ THOURT NOT KING YET, LAD : THOURT BUT DAUPHIN. BE NOT LED AWAY BY THEM AROUND
DOCT II (128) WORLD ISNT GOING TO BE MADE SIMPLE FOR YOU, MY LAD : YOU MUST TAKE IT AS IT IS. YOUVE TO HOLD THE SCALES
SUPR I (5) VERY ROOM-- HE SAID TO ME: " TAVY IS A GENEROUS LAD AND THE SOUL OF HONOR; AND WHEN I SEE HOW LITTLE
O'FL (227) ALL FOR WAR'S ALARUMS NOW. I ALWAYS WAS A QUIET LAD BY NATURAL DISPOSITION. /SIR PEARCE/ STRICTLY BETWEEN

MIS. (134)	OF HURTING HIS FEELINGS, BECAUSE, AFTER ALL, THE	LAD	CANT HELP IT; BUT IVE NEVER THOUGHT JOHNNY WORTH
FANY III (306)	AND A RESPECTABLE MARRIAGE, OR TO STOP A DECENT	LAD	FROM SETTLING HIMSELF. I HAVE A CONSCIENCE; THOUGH I
KING I (193)	SUSPICION TO PUT INTO MY MIND. I THOUGHT THE	LAD	HAD ABUSED MY AFFECTION UNTIL IT WAS EXHAUSTED; BUT IT
FANY I (278)	NO HOLDING HIM. HE DOES ENJOY LIFE MORE THAN ANY	LAD	I EVER MET. /GILBEY/ NEVER YOU MIND HOW HE'S BEEN
SUPR PREFACE(R36)	MEN OF GOOD FAMILY AND HIGH FEEDING); THAT BRISK	LAD	IGNORANCE, TALKATIVE, BY-ENDS OF FAIRSPEECH AND HIS
MIS. (184)	YOU THINK I'M A FOOL? I WONDER YOU CAN LOOK THE	LAD	IN THE FACE AFTER BULLYING HIM AND MAKING HIM SIGN THOSE
PYGM V (285)	/LIZA/ HE HAS A RIGHT TO IF HE LIKES, POOR	LAD	. AND HE DOES LOVE ME. /HIGGINS/ (GETTING OFF THE
2TRU II (66)	NOT ME. NOT MUCH. I'M THROUGH WITH YOU, MY	LAD	. AND I CANT QUITE FANCY THE COLONEL: HE'S TOO OLD, AND
JOAN EPILOG (155)	ARE YOU A GHOST, JOAN? /JOAN/ HARDLY EVEN THAT,	LAD	. CAN A POOR BURNT-UP LASS HAVE A GHOST? I AM BUT A
LION I (122)	HIM AWAY. THE SPIRIT HAS OVERWROUGHT HIM, POOR	LAD	. CARRY HIM GENTLY TO HIS HOUSE; AND LEAVE THE REST TO
O'FL (206)	PEARCE/ (LAUGHING) YOURE WELCOME TO THEM ALL, MY	LAD	. COME (HE MAKES HIM SIT DOWN AGAIN ON THE GARDEN
POSN (452)	ELDER DANIEL IS COME TO JUDGMENT ALL RIGHT, MY	LAD	. ELDER: THE FLOOR IS YOURS. (THE ELDER RISES). GIVE
CAPT III (274)	CECILY: I MUST GO TO THE PRISON AND SEE THE	LAD	. HE MAY HAVE BEEN A BIT WILD; BUT I CANT LEAVE POOR
MIS. (126)	/TARLETON/ OLD! THATS ALL YOU KNOW ABOUT IT, MY	LAD	. HOW DO, PATSY! (HYPATIA KISSES HIM). HOW IS MY
SUPR I (7)	FRIEND WAS RIGHT WHEN HE SAID YOU WERE A GENEROUS	LAD	. I KNOW THAT THIS MAN WAS YOUR SCHOOLFELLOW, AND THAT
GETT (330)	LOVE IS NOT QUITE SO CHEAP AN ARTICLE AS THAT, MY	LAD	. I WOULDNT CROSS THE STREET TO HAVE ANOTHER LOOK AT
MRS II (202)	YOU. YOUR LOVE'S A PRETTY CHEAP COMMODITY, MY	LAD	. IF YOU HAVE NO MEANS OF KEEPING A WIFE, THAT SETTLES
FANY I (277)	NO FEELING. YOU DONT CARE WHAT BECOMES OF THE	LAD	. (HE SITS DOWN SAVAGELY). /DORA/ (SOOTHINGLY) YOUVE
DOCT I (87)	THE DOOR). /SIR PATRICK/ THANK YOU. THATS A GOOD	LAD	. (REDPENNY VANISHES). THEY ALL PUT UP WITH ME, THESE
CAND I (97)	THAT! /MORELL/ (BUOYANTLY) I KNOW IT, MY	LAD	. LAROCHEFOUCAULD SAID THAT THERE ARE CONVENIENT
DOCT IV (168)	NO, PLEASE, PADDY: DONT BE HARD ON THE POOR	LAD	. NOT NOW, NOT NOW. AFTER ALL, WAS HE SO BAD? HE HAD
JOAN EPILOG (155)	PLAINLY VISIBLE AS HE SITS UP) THOU LOOKS OLDER,	LAD	. /CHARLES/ I AM OLDER. AM I REALLY ASLEEP? /JOAN/
PHIL II (106)	FATHER? /SYLVIA/ (KNOWINGLY) OH, I KNOW YOU, MY	LAD	. /CHARTERIS/ THEN YOU KNOW THAT I NEVER PAY ANY SPECIAL
DEST (162)	TRIUMPH. /LIEUTENANT/ SO IVE GOT YOU, MY	LAD	. SO YOUVE DISGUISED YOURSELF, HAVE YOU? (IN A VOICE
BUOY II (19)	OXFORD UNIVERSITY? /SHE/ I KNOW THAT STUNT, MY	LAD	. THE WANDERING SCHOLAR TURNS UP HERE ABOUT TWICE A
MIS. (167)	WOMAN. /TARLETON/ SHE'D HAVE DONE THAT ANYHOW, MY	LAD	. WE ALL GROW OLD. LOOK AT ME! (SEEING THAT THE MAN IS
DOCT I (107)	/SIR PATRICK/ AND A VERY GOOD PROFESSION, TOO, MY	LAD	. WHEN YOU KNOW AS MUCH AS I KNOW OF THE IGNORANCE AND
BULL II (109)	YOUR REVERENCE. /FATHER DEMPSEY/ THATS A GOOD	LAD	(GOING). /PATSY/ (TO AUNT JUDY) FADHER KEEGAN SEZ--
POSN SD(439)	KEMP, AND A FEW OTHERS WITH BLANCO. STRAPPER IS A	LAD	JUST TURNING INTO A MAN: STRONG, SELFISH, SULKY, AND
O'FL (207)	ALWAYS HAS BEEN, THAT EVER TAUGHT A POOR INNOCENT	LAD	LIKE MYSELF TO PRAY NIGHT AND MORNING TO ST PATRICK TO
CAPT I SD(217)	HIS FRAME AND FLESH ARE THOSE OF AN ILL-NOURISHED	LAD	OF SEVENTEEN; BUT HIS AGE IS INSCRUTABLE: ONLY THE
METH PREFACE(R32)	1830, WHEN DARWIN WAS AN APPARENTLY UNPROMISING	LAD	OF TWENTY-ONE, UNTIL 1859, WHEN HE TURNED THE WORLD
BASH III (121)	AND NEVER SEE ME MORE. /CASHEL/ I GO. THE MEANEST	LAD	ON THY ESTATE WOULD NOT BETRAY ME THUS. BUT TIS NO
KING I (196)	KEPT MAN? /CHARLES/ I KNOW THAT THE POOR	LAD	RISKED BREAKING HIS BONES BY JUMPING OUT OF BARBARA'S
GENV II (53)	BY THE CONSERVATIVE CANDIDATE: AN INNOCENT YOUNG	LAD	ROLLING IN MONEY. HE SAW THAT I WAS A CUT ABOVE THE
FANY III (310)	DO IT, JUGGINS: PAY YOUR OWN WAY LIKE AN HONEST	LAD	; AND DONT EAT YOUR BROTHER'S BREAD WHILE YOURE ABLE TO
ANNA (291)	ACCUSE YOU OF TREASON TO THE REVOLUTION, MY	LAD	; AND THEY WOULD IMMEDIATELY SHOOT YOU, UNLESS YOU CRIED
FANY I (274)	ROB, BOBBY MIGHT GET INTO A SCRAPE LIKE ANY OTHER	LAD	; BUT HE'D NEVER DO ANYTHING LOW. JUGGINS, THE FOOTMAN,
JOAN 3 (91)	IS MORE TROUBLE THAN IT IS WORTH. /JOAN/ AYE,	LAD	; BUT YOU CANNOT FIGHT STONE WALLS WITH HORSES: YOU MUST
DOCT III (144)	AND WATER IN MILK. YOURE A SOUND METHODIST, MY	LAD	; ONLY YOU DONT KNOW IT. /LOUIS/ (SERIOUSLY ANNOYED FOR
DOCT IV (156)	/SIR PATRICK/ (DRILY) IT'S A LITTLE HARD ON A	LAD	TO BE KILLED BECAUSE HIS WIFE HAS TOO HIGH AN OPINION OF
MIS. (183)	I DONT BELIEVE A WORD OF IT. IF THE POOR	LAD	WAS THERE IN THE TURKISH BATH, WHO HAS A BETTER RIGHT TO
BULL II (107)	A SIGHT OF HIM FOR EIGHTEEN YEARS, N HE ONY A	LAD	WHEN HE LEFT US. /BROADBENT/ IT'S NOT LARRY'S FAULT: HE
POSN (463)	BE TOOK LIKE A HARE IN A TRAP BY STRAPPER KEMP: A	LAD	WHOSE BACK I OR ANY GROWN MAN HERE COULD BREAK AGAINST
KING II (226)	THE PROTESTANTS WILL KILL JAMIE; AND THE DUTCH	LAD	WILL SEE HIS CHANCE AND TAKE IT. HE WILL BE KING: A
SIM PRO;3, (30)	THE PRIEST) I SAY, REVEREND. WHAT ABOUT THE POOR	LAD	YOU KICKED OVER THE CLIFF? IS HE REALLY SAFE? I DONT
MIS. (113)	SWINE, SWINE! NOW! /JOHNNY/ ALL RIGHT, MY	LAD	, ALL RIGHT. SLING YOUR MUD AS HARD AS YOU PLEASE: IT
METH PREFACE(R74)	CLARIFIED BY IT. IF YOU TAKE AN ENGLISH VILLAGE	LAD	, AND TEACH HIM THAT RELIGION MEANS BELIEVING THAT THE
ROCK I (211)	TIME FOR PERSIFLAGE? /SIR ARTHUR/ CAMOUFLAGE, MY	LAD	, CAMOUFLAGE. DO YOU EXPECT ME TO TAKE YOU SERIOUSLY IN
GLIM (179)	GIULIA RETURNS WITH SANDRO. /GIULIA/ THIS IS THE	LAD	, EXCELLENCY. SANDRO: THIS IS HIS LORDSHIP COUNT
BULL II (99)	CALLOW, FLAXEN POLLED, SMOOTHFACED, DOWNY CHINNED	LAD	, FULLY GROWN BUT NOT YET FULLY FILLED OUT, WITH BLUE
APPL I (213)	I SHOULD STAND A BETTER CHANCE THAN YOU, MY	LAD	, IF WE WERE A REPUBLIC, AND THE PEOPLE COULD CHOOSE.
FANY I (275)	IT WASNT THAT SHE MAY TELL US SOMETHING ABOUT THE	LAD	, [illegible]
2TRU III (83)	AFTER MY OWN AFFAIRS. WHAT I LOOK TO YOU FOR, MY	LAD	, IS A BIT OF FUN. /THE SERGEANT/ QUITE. BUT WHEN MEN
MIS. (186)	HE-- /MRS TARLETON/ NOW STOP JOKING THE POOR	LAD	, JOHN: I WONT HAVE IT. HE'S BEEN WORRIED TO DEATH
MTH3 (93)	WHO DARES DISPUTE IT? /BURGE-LUBIN/ NOBODY, DEAR	LAD	, NOBODY. DONT FLY OUT AT ME. IT IS EVIDENT THAT YOU
FANY PROLOG (259)	YOU ARE TOO YOUNG. /SAVOYARD/ I WAS QUITE A	LAD	, OF COURSE. BUT I HAD A JOB IN THE ORIGINAL PRODUCTION
MRS II (201)	IF YOU KNOW ANY, YOU CAN TELL THEM TO THE	LAD	, OR TO THE GIRL, OR TO YOUR CONGREGATION, IF YOU LIKE.
APPL II (269)	MONARCH. /PLINY/ OH, COME! DONT BE HARD ON THE	LAD	, SIR. HE HAS PLENTY OF BRAINS. /MAGNUS/ OH YES, YES,
MIS. (127)	SELECTION. YOU GET IT OUT OF YOUR HEAD, MY	LAD	, THAT I'M GOING TO DIE BECAUSE I'M WEARING OUT OR
FANY I (278)	HANKERED AFTER IT; BUT HE COULDNT AFFORD IT, POOR	LAD	, THOUGH I KNEW HE JUST LONGED TO GIVE IT TO ME.
FANY I (281)	(CHARITABLY) IT WAS DULL FOR HIM AT HOME, POOR	LAD	, WASNT IT? /MRS GILBEY/ OH NO. I'M AT HOME ON FIRST
BUOY II (19)	TURNS UP HERE ABOUT TWICE A WEEK. /HE/ " MY	LAD	" EH? THAT IS AN ENDEARMENT. WE ARE GETTING ON. WHAT
APPL I (202)	WHO I AM! ASKS ME CAN HE HAVE MY NAME! " MY	LAD	" I SAID: " NOT TO KNOW ME ARGUES YOURSELF UNKNOWN. YOU
SIM PRO;1, (25)	CECIL RHODES: YOU SEE IF I'M NOT." " NOT YOU, MY	LAD	" SHE SAYS, " EVERYTHING WHAT COMES TO YOU YOU THROW IT
DOCT IV (167)	(RISING, SHOCKED) MY DEAR COLLY! THE POOR	LAD	! HE DIED SPLENDIDLY. /SIR PATRICK/ AYE! THAT IS HOW
MIS. (191)	IVE OVER-EXCITED MYSELF. /MRS TARLETON/ POOR	LAD	! NO WONDER, AFTER ALL YOUVE GONE THROUGH! YOU WANT TO
DOCT II (118)	DEE-LIGHTFUL COUPLE! CHARMING WOMAN! GIFTED	LAD	! REMARKABLE TALENT! GRACEFUL OUTLINES! PERFECT
MIS. (169)	/TARLETON/ NO: THATS WHAT YOU CALL IT. COME, MY	LAD	! WHATS THE MATTER WITH YOU? YOU DONT LOOK STARVED;

LADDER

JOAN 5 (116)	FOLLOW ME HALF NAKED INTO THE MOAT AND UP THE	LADDER	AND OVER THE WALL. WITH THEM IT IS MY LIFE OR THINE,
PHIL II (123)	DOES NOT LOOK HIS WAY. HE TAKES HIS FEET FROM THE	LADDER	AND SITS UP). WHEW! (JULIA WANDERS ALONG HIS SIDE
CLEO III (159)	NOT FOR MY HEAD HAVE IT CARRIED UP THAT NARROW	LADDER	FROM THE CAUSEWAY. /RUFIO/ SWING IT UP BY THE CRANE,
BUOY II SD(18)	WHERE THERE IS A WOODEN HOUSE ON POSTS, WITH A	LADDER	FROM THE STOEP OR VERANDAH TO THE GROUND. THE ROOF IS
CLEO III (163)	OURSELVES HERE. /APOLLODORUS/ I HAVE THROWN THE	LADDER	INTO THE SEA. THEY CANNOT GET IN WITHOUT IT. /RUFIO/
BARB III SD(326)	LEFT THE END OF A SHED RAISED ON PILES, WITH A	LADDER	OF THREE OR FOUR STEPS UP TO THE DOOR, WHICH OPENS
PYGM EPILOG (296)	FOR SO MANY YEARS TO THAT STEP OF THE SOCIAL	LADDER	ON WHICH RETAIL TRADE IS IMPOSSIBLE. THIS DIFFICULTY
DEVL III SD(70)	APPROACHES AND THE ARRIVAL OF THE BEADLE WITH THE	LADDER	REMAINS THE ONLY SIGN OF PREPARATION. BUT AT LAST
PHIL II (106)	AND PERCHES HIMSELF REFLECTIVELY ON THE STEP	LADDER	). /SYLVIA/ SHE CANT TAKE THINGS EASY: CAN SHE, OLD
MTH2 (77)	CAME CRASHING DOWN ALL THE STEPS OF THIS JACOB'S	LADDER	THAT REACHED FROM PARADISE TO A HELL ON EARTH IN
JOAN 3 (91)	THE STONIEST WALL. /JOAN/ I WILL BE FIRST UP THE	LADDER	WHEN WE REACH THE FORT, BASTARD. I DARE YOU TO FOLLOW
DEVL III SD(72)	THE PRISONER TO MOUNT. THEN HE CLIMBS THE TALL	LADDER	WHICH STANDS AGAINST THE GALLOWS, AND CUTS THE STRING
JOAN 3 (91)	IT) AYE, LASS; BUT A GOOD HEART AND A STOUT	LADDER	WILL GET OVER THE STONIEST WALL. /JOAN/ I WILL BE
JOAN 3 (93)	EYES ARE BLINDED WITH TEARS. SET MY FOOT ON THE	LADDER	, AND SAY " UP, JOAN." /DUNOIS/ (DRAGGING HER OUT)
LADY (242)	WHO THINKS THAT THE SKY IS AT THE TOP OF HIS	LADDER	, AND SO TAKES IT ON HIM TO REBUKE ME FOR FLYING. I
BARB II SD(273)	IN THE LOFT ABOVE IT WITHOUT ANY BALCONY OR	LADDER	, BUT WITH A PULLEY RIGGED OVER IT FOR HOISTING
DEVL III SD(70)	OF THE UPRIGHTS, OUT OF REACH OF THE BOYS. ITS	LADDER	, TOO, HAS BEEN BROUGHT OUT AND PLACED IN POSITION BY

LADDERS

2TRU I (48)	SILK AND WOOL. REAL SILK STOCKINGS WITHOUT	LADDERS	. KNICKERS: HOW DARINGLY MODERN! SHOES: HEELS ONLY
JOAN EPILOG (155)	THE MOAT UP TO MY WAIST IN MUD AND BLOOD. UP THE	LADDERS	WITH THE STONES AND HOT PITCH RAINING DOWN. LIKE

LADDIE

METH PREFACE(R79)	PARTS OF THE WORLD, AND BE VERY GLAD TO FIND HIS	LADDIE	AS INTERESTED IN SUCH THINGS AS IN MARBLES OR POLICE
JOAN EPILOG (155)	REALLY DEAD? /JOAN/ AS DEAD AS ANYBODY EVER IS,	LADDIE	. I AM OUT OF THE BODY. /CHARLES/ JUST FANCY! DID IT
JOAN 5 (117)	/JOAN/ (FLATTERED) SIXTEEN THOUSAND POUNDS! EH,	LADDIE	, HAVE THEY OFFERED THAT FOR ME? THERE CANNOT BE SO

LADDIES

KING I (203)	AND-- WOULD YOU BELIEVE IT, GEORGE? -- THOSE	LADDIES	WILL NOT PLAY NOW FOR LESS THAN FIFTEEN SHILLINGS A

LADEN

BULL I SD(73)	THE OUTER DOOR IS OPENED, AND A VALET COMES IN	LADEN	WITH A LARGE GLADSTONE BAG AND A STRAP OF RUGS. HE
NEVR II SD(246)	NOTICE THE RETURN OF THE WAITER FROM THE HOTEL,	LADEN	WITH CRAMPTON'S COAT, VALENTINE'S STICK, A COUPLE OF
CLEO II (137)	/RUFIO/ YES. FIVE GOOD SHIPS, AND A BARGE	LADEN	WITH OIL GRAPPLED TO EACH. BUT IT IS NOT MY DOING: THE

		LADIES	
GENV IV (129)	OUT). /JUDGE/ (TO THE DEACONESS AND THE WIDOW)	LADIES	: I AM AFRAID THERE IS NOTHING MORE TO BE DONE HERE.
KING I (179)	WILL WAIT UPON YOU AT SOME HAPPIER MOMENT. COME,	LADIES	: WE MUST LEAVE MR NEWTON TO HIS MATHEMATICS. (HE IS
O'FL (216)	SELF? AND HOW IS HER LADYSHIP AND ALL THE YOUNG	LADIES	? OH, IT'S RIGHT GLAD WE ARE TO SEE YOUR HONOR BACK
PRES (145)	WHAT A LIFE! (TO THE ORDERLY) WHERE ARE THE	LADIES	? /THE ORDERLY/ IN NO. 17, SIR. /MITCHENER/ SHEW MR
DOCT PREFACE(38)	HAVING EACH ITS APPOINTED DATE FOR SLAUGHTER. THE	LADIES	AMONG US WORE HATS AND CLOAKS AND HEAD-DRESSES
LADY PREFACE(232)	ONE. HE MIGHT HAVE BEEN JILTED BY TEN DARK	LADIES	AND BEEN NONE THE WORSE FOR IT; BUT HIS TREATMENT BY
PPP (206)	OUT FOR THE NEXT PERFORMANCE. PASS ALONG, PLEASE,	LADIES	AND GENTLEMEN: PASS ALONG.
BUOY II (21)	AND FULL OF THEIR SNOBBERY. BUT FAILURES AS	LADIES	AND GENTLEMEN. /HE/ NOTHING LEFT BUT TO LIVE ON
ROCK I (205)	POST-WAR FASHION INSTEAD OF TEACHING THEM TO BE	LADIES	AND GENTLEMEN. BESIDES, FLAVIA WAS RIGHT. I DO TREAT
ROCK I (214)	THAT THEY ARE RANSOMING THEIR RICHES. YOU,	LADIES	AND GENTLEMEN, WILL HAVE TO PUT YOUR HANDS IN YOUR
ROCK II (247)	NOW HEAR THE VOICE OF THE PROLETARIAT. SIT DOWN,	LADIES	AND GENTLEMEN. /THE MAYOR/ (RUDELY) WHO ARE YOU
MILL IV (199)	WITH GREAT DIGNITY). /ALASTAIR/ QUITE SAFE NOW,	LADIES	AND GENTLEMEN. (HE PICKS UP HIS ILLUSTRATED PAPER,
BARB II (275)	WE'RE NO WORSE THAN OTHER PEOPLE? YOU KNOW WHAT	LADIES	AND GENTLEMEN ARE. /PRICE/ THIEVIN SWINE! WISH I AD
MIS. (165)	CONVENTIONALITY AMONG THOROUGHLY WELL-BROUGHT UP	LADIES	AND GENTLEMEN. /HYPATIA/ ANOTHER TALKER! MEN LIKE
APPL I (216)	HIS CHAIR). /MAGNUS/ (SWEETLY) SHALL WE SIT,	LADIES	AND GENTLEMEN? BOANERGES HASTILY RISES AND SITS DOWN
APPL I (220)	THE IMPORTED PROFITS OF THAT CAPITAL. WE ARE ALL	LADIES	AND GENTLEMEN NOW. /NICOBAR/ WELL, WHAT MORE DO YOU
APPL PREFACE(177)	YOUR GRACES AND REVERENCES, MY LORDS,	LADIES	AND GENTLEMEN, FELLOW-CITIZENS OF ALL DEGREES: I AM
APPL II (266)	HER KNITTING. /MAGNUS/ (SITTING DOWN) BE SEATED,	LADIES	AND GENTLEMEN. THEY TAKE CHAIRS OF ONE SORT OR
APPL I (232)	EXCUSE FOR FLYING OUT. /CRASSUS/ IN MY OPINION,	LADIES	AND GENTLEMEN, WE HAVE DONE OUR BIT, AND MAY LEAVE
APPL I (231)	SUPPOSE I MUST DO IT MYSELF, AS USUAL. EXCUSE ME,	LADIES	AND GENTLEMEN. HE RISES. THE REST RISE. HE GOES OUT.
APPL I (240)	APPEAL HAS BEEN IN VAIN. I DO NOT REPROACH YOU,	LADIES	AND GENTLEMEN, BECAUSE I PERCEIVE THAT YOUR SITUATION
APPL I (241)	OUT, I WILL SIGN WITHOUT ANOTHER WORD. MEANWHILE,	LADIES	AND GENTLEMEN, AU REVOIR! HE RISES. ALL RISE. HE
MIS. PREFACE(17)	WITH CHILDREN EXACTLY AS SOME ECCENTRIC OLD	LADIES	AND GENTLEMEN FILL THEIRS WITH CATS. IN SUCH PLACES
MIS. PREFACE(37)	TO LEARN MANNERS AND BECOME UNCHALLENGEABLE	LADIES	AND GENTLEMEN. THE SOCIAL PRESSURE WHICH EFFECTS
OVER PREFACE(167)	HIS TRIAL, WITH THE NAMES OF THE DISTINGUISHED	LADIES	AND GENTLEMEN WHO HONORED HIM WITH THEIR PRESENCE ON
HART PREFACE(4)	OF A PRISON FOR HORSES WITH AN ANNEX FOR THE	LADIES	AND GENTLEMEN WHO RODE THEM, HUNTED THEM, TALKED
HART II (110)	WISH TO BE ANYTHING BUT AGREEABLE. GOOD EVENING,	LADIES	AND GENTLEMEN; AND THANK YOU KINDLY. HE IS HURRYING
JOAN EPILOG (159)	KNOW; BUT IT KEEPS YOU MARCHING. YOUR SERVANT,	LADIES	AND GENTLEMEN. WHO ASKED FOR A SAINT? /JOAN/ BE YOU
PYGM V (277)	PROVOCATION. AND I SHOULD NEVER HAVE KNOWN THAT	LADIES	AND GENTLEMEN DIDNT BEHAVE LIKE THAT IF YOU HADNT
LION II (147)	I THANK YOUR WORSHIP. I THANK YOU ALL,	LADIES	AND GENTLEMEN. COME, TOMMY. WHILST WE STAND TOGETHER,
LION II (142)	NEVER BEEN THE SLIGHTEST IDEA OF HARMING THEM.	LADIES	AND GENTLEMEN: YOU ARE ALL FREE. PRAY GO INTO THE
GETT PREFACE(233)	I HAD ALMOST SAID NOT AT ALL UNUSUAL. YOUNG	LADIES	AND GENTLEMEN IN THE GREENSICKLY CONDITION WHICH IS
GETT (308)	/COLLINS/ I TELL YOU THE TRUTH, MY LORD AND	LADIES	AND GENTLEMEN: I DONT TRUST MY JUDGMENT ON THIS
GETT (358)	PLEASE, MY LORDS AND GENTLEMEN. BY YOUR LEAVE,	LADIES	AND GENTLEMEN: WAY FOR THE MAYORESS. MRS GEORGE TAKES
BULL PREFACE(3)	INTO THE WASTE PAPER BASKET BECAUSE A HANDFUL OF	LADIES	AND GENTLEMEN OBJECTED TO IT, AND THE ARMY OFFICERS'
BULL PREFACE(28)	OF ENGLISH RULE. IF YOU WOULD BE GOOD ENOUGH,	LADIES	AND GENTLEMEN OF ENGLAND, TO TAKE YOUR THUMB AWAY AND
BULL PREFACE(40)	HE VOTES LIBERAL INSTEAD OF CONSERVATIVE. ENGLISH	LADIES	AND GENTLEMEN WHO WOULD PERISH SOONER THAN SHOOT A
ROCK PREFACE(149)	RUSSIA, WHERE THE EXTERMINATION OF THE CLASS OF	LADIES	AND GENTLEMEN OF SO-CALLED INDEPENDENT MEANS HAS
ROCK PREFACE(150)	ALL DIFFERENTLY COLORED FOLK AS INFERIOR SPECIES,	LADIES	AND GENTLEMEN CLASS REBELLIOUS LABORERS WITH VERMIN,
ROCK PREFACE(153)	THOUGH IT IS NEVER MENTIONED AS SUCH, AND	LADIES	AND GENTLEMEN ARE CAREFULLY EDUCATED TO BE
MILL PREFACE(129)	WOULD REMAIN; AND IF THEY WERE STILL EDUCATED AS	LADIES	AND GENTLEMEN ARE EDUCATED TODAY, AND CONSEQUENTLY
SIM PREFACE(14)	NO USE TO ITSELF AND IS THERE SOLELY TO SUPPORT	LADIES	AND GENTLEMEN, YOU NEED NOT BOTHER ABOUT THIS: YOU
SIM PREFACE(12)	OF THE VERY POOR TO BECOME SINECURISTS LIKE	LADIES	AND GENTLEMEN. MY OWN ACQUAINTANCE WITH SUCH A
SIM PREFACE(9)	OF THE COUNTRY'S INCOME ARE LAVISHED ANNUALLY ON	LADIES	AND GENTLEMEN WHILST LABORERS ARE UNDERFED, ILL
2TRU I (46)	CRIMINALS: YOU CAN DO WHAT YOU LIKE. IF YOU WERE	LADIES	AND GENTLEMEN, YOUD KNOW HOW HARD IT IS NOT TO DO
2TRU I (46)	MORE AT EASE WITH US IF I INFORM YOU THAT WE ARE	LADIES	AND GENTLEMEN. MY OWN RANK-- NOT THAT I WOULD PRESUME
CAND II (110)	(FRETFULLY) IT'S WELL YOU AND I ARE NOT	LADIES	AND GENTLEMEN: I'D TALK TO YOU PRETTY STRAIGHT IF MR
CAPT NOTES (304)	UP, GUN, ETC., MR SWEET'S EVIDENCE IS CONCLUSIVE.	LADIES	AND GENTLEMEN IN SOUTHERN ENGLAND PRONOUNCE THEM AS
3PLA PREFACE(R17)	THE FACT THAT HIS CHARACTERS DO NOT BEHAVE AS	LADIES	AND GENTLEMEN ARE POPULARLY SUPPOSED TO BEHAVE. IF
SUPR HANDBOK(198)	WORTH THE GUILLOTINING OF ALL THOSE UNLUCKY	LADIES	AND GENTLEMEN, USELESS AND MISCHIEVOUS AS MANY OF
SUPR HANDBOK(222)	TO THE NUMBER AND VORACITY OF ITS PARASITES.	LADIES	AND GENTLEMEN ARE PERMITTED TO HAVE FRIENDS IN THE
DEVL I (18)	/RICHARD/ (ON THE THRESHOLD, TAKING OFF HIS HAT)	LADIES	AND GENTLEMEN: YOUR SERVANT, YOUR VERY HUMBLE
DEVL I (20)	WHERE HE TAKES THE RAILED CHAIR IN HIS HAND).	LADIES	AND GENTLEMEN: AS THE ELDEST SON OF MY LATE FATHER,
SUPR IV (170)	UPRIGHT AND SELF-POSSESSED). /STRAKER/ NOW THEN,	LADIES	AND GENTLEMEN: SHE DONT WANT A CROWD ROUND HER: SHE
FABL PREFACE(79)	OF HISTORY IS WHETHER JESUS, DENOUNCED BY THE	LADIES	AND GENTLEMEN OF HIS TIME AS A SABBATH BREAKER, A
KING I (202)	TO PLEASE THE QUAKER. /CHARLES/ FORGIVE JAMIE,	LADIES	AND GENTLEMEN. HE WILL GIVE YOU HIS OWN FAVORITE
GENV II (54)	I DO. THE BEST SORT OF PEOPLE ALWAYS DO: THE REAL	LADIES	AND GENTLEMEN, YOU KNOW, THE OTHERS ARE ODDITIES AND
GENV PREFACE(12)	AND THEIR WIVES IS DANGEROUSLY THIN. EVEN ENGLISH	LADIES	AND GENTLEMEN " GO FANTEE" OCCASIONALLY. CHRISTMAS
GENV IV (89)	CHAIR, GREETING THEM AS HE GOES) GOOD MORNING,	LADIES	AND GENTLEMEN. GOOD MORNING, MADEMOISELLE. GOOD
GENV IV (105)	ERNEST! YOU THINK YOURSELF A BLOND BEAST.	LADIES	AND GENTLEMEN, LOOK AT HIM! IS HE A BLOND BEAST?
CLEO IV SD(167)	FOLLOWING WITH HER HARP, AMID THE LAUGHTER OF THE	LADIES	AND SLAVES. /CLEOPATRA/ NOW, CAN ANY OF YOU AMUSE
KING I (199)	NOISE YOUR PEOPLE WERE MAKING. THERE ARE THE TWO	LADIES	AND THE PLAYER WOMAN, AND YOURSELF AND YOUR ROYAL
KING II (224)	ME. YOU KNOW, BELOVED, ONE GETS TIRED OF COURT	LADIES	AND THEIR CONVERSATION, ALWAYS THE SAME. /CATHERINE/
WIDO I (12)	GATE). /WAITER/ TABLE D'HOTE IN DWENDY MINUTES,	LADIES	AND ZHENTELLMENN. (HE GOES INTO THE HOTEL).
CLEO IV SD(166)	OF THE ROOM; THE REST ON THE GROUND. CLEOPATRA'S	LADIES	ARE ALL YOUNG, THE MOST CONSPICUOUS BEING CHARMIAN
SUPR III (90)	JUAN/ NOT AT ALL: YOU ARE A LADY; AND WHEREVER	LADIES	ARE IS HELL. DO NOT BE SURPRISED OR TERRIFIED: YOU
BUOY III (28)	BILL BUOYANT THE BILLIONAIRE. I AM A WIDOWER. THE	LADIES	ARE MY BROTHERS' WIVES. ONE BROTHER IS ABSENT: HE
MRS I (183)	DISPOSED TO BE FRIENDS WITH ME! YOU MODERN YOUNG	LADIES	ARE SPLENDID: PERFECTLY SPLENDID! /VIVIE/ (
SIM II SD(58)	PROLA IS SITTING ON THE EASTERN SEAT. ALL FIVE	LADIES	ARE TAKING TEA. PRA COMES FROM THE HOUSE WITH SIR
KING I (174)	ROWLEY: YOU ARE WELL KNOWN TO BE AS INTERESTED IN	LADIES	AS I AM INTERESTED IN THE SCRIPTURES; AND I THANK YOU
CLEO V SD(199)	FIGURE AMONG THE BRILLIANTLY DRESSED BEVY OF	LADIES	AS SHE PASSES THROUGH IT, COMES FROM THE PALACE AND
ROCK II (273)	/BARKING/ (BARRING HER WAY WITH AN ARM OF IRON)	LADIES	BE DAMNED! YOURE NO LADY. (HE COMES PAST THE TABLE
2TRU III (82)	I DONT. I SAW A LOT OF THAT IN THE WAR: PRETTY	LADIES	BRIGHTENING UP THE HOSPITALS AND LOSING THEIR SILLY
APPL I (240)	NOW, ANYBODY ELSE? WE HAVE HEARD WHY THE TWO	LADIES	CANNOT SUPPORT THE KING. IS THERE ANYBODY WHO CAN?
MTH4 III SD(198)	THAT HE IS NONE THE WORSE FOR THE SHOCK. THE	LADIES	COWER IN TERROR. THE ENVOY'S HAT IS BLOWN OFF; BUT HE
LION I (114)	SHE CHOOSES TO SACRIFICE AS ALL WELLBRED ROMAN	LADIES	DO. I HAVE NO MORE TO SAY TO THE PRISONERS.
GENV III (75)	MENTION. /THE NEWCOMER/ HULLO, MAAM! YOU KNOW,	LADIES	DONT SAY THINGS LIKE THAT IN MY COUNTRY. /THE WIDOW/
JOAN 2,SD(80)	LADY IN WAITING: MY DEAR! HER HAIR! ALL THE	LADIES	EXPLODE IN UNCONTROLLABLE LAUGHTER. /BLUEBEARD/ (
ROCK II (273)	YOU GET OUT AND WAIT FOR YOUR TURN. /ALOYSIA/	LADIES	FIRST, IF YOU PLEASE, SIR ARTHUR-- /BARKING/ (
SUPR III (139)	ME: IT WAS YOU WHO CLAIMED MY ACQUAINTANCE. THE	LADIES	FOLLOWED YOUR EXAMPLE. HOWEVER, THIS DISPLAY OF THE
NEVR I (207)	THE PARLORMAID APPEARS. /THE PARLORMAID/ TWO	LADIES	FOR YOU, MISS. YOUR MOTHER AND SISTER, MISS, I THINK.
MIS. SD(116)	DEAR: HE'LL BE HIMSELF PRESENTLY. COME. THE TWO	LADIES	GO OUT THROUGH THE INNER DOOR WITH BENTLEY, WHO TURNS
O'FL (221)	WHERE IT USED TO BE, AND NOT WHERE THE OTHER	LADIES	HAD IT. AND SHE HAD LITTLE BROOCHES IN HER EARS,
NEVR III (280)	DOWNSTAIRS AT THE OFFICE, SIR, FIVE SHILLINGS:	LADIES	HALF PRICE IF ACCOMPANIED BY A GENTLEMAN. /PHILIP/ (
NEVR IV (282)	WEARILY AND TIMIDLY ON THE OTTOMAN. /WAITER/ THE	LADIES	HAVE GONE FOR A TURN THROUGH THE GROUNDS TO SEE THE
KING I (179)	TO PROCEED WITH IT IN THE NECESSARY SOLITUDE. THE	LADIES	HAVE NOT WASTED MY TIME: I HAVE TO THANK HER GRACE OF
KING I (174)	! /NEWTON/ -- AND I BEG YOU WILL BRING NO MORE	LADIES	HERE UNTIL I HAVE TIME TO SET ASIDE A DAY OF
SIM I (50)	YOU THAT NOT ONLY VASHTI AND MAYA, BUT ALL THE	LADIES	HERE, ARE INCLUDED IN THE SUPERFAMILY COMPACT. /IDDY/
LADY PREFACE(218)	PEOPLE ABOUT WHO IDOLIZED SHAKESPEAR AS AMERICAN	LADIES	IDOLIZE PADEREWSKI, AND WHO CARRIED BARDOLATRY, EVEN
6CAL SD(100)	TOO GOOD FOR HIM. THE QUEEN HURRIES IN WITH HER	LADIES	IN GREAT CONCERN. THE MEN-AT-ARMS RELEASE THE
FANY PROLOG (267)	UNUSUAL IN THAT, I'M SORRY TO SAY. HALF THE YOUNG	LADIES	IN LONDON SPEND THEIR EVENINGS MAKING THEIR FATHERS
BULL IV (181)	OF PALE BLUE SATIN PLACE, WITH ALL THE PIOUS OLD	LADIES	IN OUR CONGREGATION SITTING AS IF THEY WERE AT A
OVER PREFACE(166)	OBVIOUS FANCY BALL MASQUERADING OF SUBURBAN YOUNG	LADIES	IN THE SAME CHARACTER. HOLDING THE MIRROR UP TO
JOAN 2,SD(80)	SITS IN THE CONSORT'S CHAIR, WITH A GROUP OF	LADIES	IN WAITING CLOSE BY, BEHIND THE ARCHBISHOP. THE
MTH4 II SD(182)	DISGUISED BY A GOOD TAILOR. THE DRESS OF THE	LADIES	IS COEVAL WITH THAT OF THE ELDERLY GENTLEMAN, AND
WIDO III (63)	AS MARRIED MEN, IS OUT OF THE UNT AS FAR AS YOUNG	LADIES	IS CONCERNED. I KNOW MISS BLANCHE: SHE HAS HER
PYGM II (240)	OF SOAP SMELLING LIKE PRIMROSES. NOW I KNOW WHY	LADIES	IS SO CLEAN. WASHING'S A TREAT FOR THEM. WISH THEY
3PLA PREFACE(R15)	THEM THAT MOST OF IBSEN'S HEROINES WERE NAUGHTY	LADIES	. AND THEY TRIED TO PRODUCE IBSEN PLAYS BY MAKING
JOAN EPILOG (161)	JOAN. /THE NEWCOMER/ EXCUSE ME, GENTLE LORDS AND	LADIES	. DO NOT LET ME DISTURB YOU. ONLY A POOR OLD HARMLESS
POSN (439)	OF SCRATCHING LIKE THAT? NOW, LADIES, LADIES,	LADIES	. HOW WOULD YOU LIKE IT IF YOU WERE GOING TO BE
SUPR II (52)	THE CAR; AND YOU TWO WANT TO TALK ABOUT YOUR	LADIES	. I KNOW. (HE PRETENDS TO BUSY HIMSELF ABOUT THE
SUPR PREFACE(R22)	BEFORE THE PRIMNESSES OF OUR BEHAVIOR FOR YOUNG	LADIES	. IT IS ASSUMED THAT THE WOMAN MUST WAIT, MOTIONLESS,
MIS. (143)	SHEW ME WHAT? /HYPATIA/ GIRLS WITHERING INTO	LADIES	. LADIES WITHERING INTO OLD MAIDS. NURSING OLD WOMEN.
6CAL (104)	I AM NOT SKILLED IN DEALING WITH FINE HANDSOME	LADIES	. LEAVE ME TO SETTLE MY BUSINESS WITH YOUR HENPECKED
ROCK I (230)	SANITARY. NO NEWSPAPERS, NO LETTERS, NO IDLE	LADIES	. NO BOOKS EXCEPT IN THE AFTERNOON AS A REST FROM

GETT	(311)	GENTLEMEN CAN BE PUT IN. /LEO/ NOT ANY NUMBER OF	LADIES	. ONLY ONE LADY. BESIDES, THAT CREATURE WASNT A LADY.
JOAN EPILOG	(160)	A SAINT, AT YOUR SERVICE, NOBLE LORDS AND LOVELY	LADIES	. /CHARLES/ AND AFTER TWELVE? /THE SOLDIER/ AFTER
KING I	(184)	TO DO THAN TO PEDDLE LOVE CHARMS TO THE KING'S	LADIES	. /LOUISE/ (IRONICALLY) YES: TO ENTERTAIN THE
MIS.	(176)	SEE? /GUNNER/ I CANT TELL YOU IN THE PRESENCE OF	LADIES	. /MRS TARLETON/ OH, YOU ARE TIRESOME. AS IT IF
SUPR III	(139)	BUT PERFECTLY AUDIBLE WHISPER) SEVERAL DIFFERENT	LADIES	. /RAMSDEN/ (ANGRILY) WELL, WHAT IS THAT TO YOU,
MTH4 II	(190)	ARRANGE ALL THAT, NEVER MIND HOW. LET US JOIN THE	LADIES	. /THE ELDERLY GENTLEMAN/ (THROWING OFF HIS
SUPR III	(125)	FIRST TELL ME WHAT YOU USED TO SAY TO THE	LADIES	. /THE STATUE/ I! OH, I SWORE THAT I WOULD BE
VWOO 2	(130)	A GENTLEMAN. I AM ACCUSTOMED TO ASSOCIATE WITH	LADIES	. THAT MEANS THAT I AM ACCUSTOMED TO SPEAK UNDER
GETT	(308)	/COLLINS/ WE ARE AT PRESENT SIX MEN TO FOUR	LADIES	. THATS NOT FAIR. /REGINALD/ NOT FAIR TO THE MEN, YOU
MIS.	SD(150)	IN THROUGH THE PAVILION WITH JOHNNY AND THE TWO	LADIES	. THE PASSENGER COMES BETWEEN PERCIVAL AND TARLETON,
KING I	(174)	RISING) NO NO NO NO NO, MADAM. I CANNOT ENTERTAIN	LADIES	. THEY DO NOT FIT INTO MY WAY OF LIFE. MR ROWLEY: YOU
MTH4 II	(192)	IF I TRIED. IT SOUNDED FINE. AH! HERE COME THE	LADIES	. TO HIS RELIEF, THEY HAVE JUST APPEARED ON THE
2TRU PREFACE	(21)	AND THE RACKETEERS, SELF-ELECTED AS GENTLEMEN AND	LADIES	. WE KNOW THAT PRIVATE PROPERTY DISTRIBUTES WEALTH,
ARMS III	(74)	IN THE EVENING ON TUESDAY FORTNIGHT. GRACIOUS	LADIES	(HIS HEELS CLICK) GOOD EVENING. (HE MAKES THEM A
CLEO IV	(169)	SHORE WITH MUCH CONCEIT WASHED OUT OF YOU. (THE	LADIES	LAUGH. CLEOPATRA RISES IMPATIENTLY). BEGONE, ALL OF
CLEO IV	SD(169)	AND DO NOT UNDERSTAND THESE MATTERS. THE	LADIES	LAUGH. CLEOPATRA LOOKS INSCRUTABLY AT HIM. /CHARMIAN/
CLEO IV	SD(167)	/IRAS/ WE CAN EASILY FIND OUT THAT FOR YOU. THE	LADIES	LAUGH. /CLEOPATRA/ (FROWNING) YOU LAUGH; BUT TAKE
CLEO IV	(167)	THIS TIME FTATATEETA HAS BEEN VIRTUOUS. (ALL THE	LADIES	LAUGH-- NOT THE SLAVES). POTHINUS HAS BEEN TRYING TO
CLEO IV	(168)	IS WORSE THAN BEING RELIGIOUS, AT OUR AGES. (THE	LADIES	LAUGH). /CLEOPATRA/ CEASE THAT ENDLESS CACKLING, WILL
CLEO IV	(169)	YOU BY THE HAIR AND THROW YOU INTO THE SEA. (THE	LADIES	LAUGH). /CLEOPATRA/ SHE IS RIGHT, POTHINUS: YOU WILL
PRES	(148)	TO TAKE THESE CLOTHES TO MR BALSQUITH WHEN THE	LADIES	LEAVE. THE ORDERLY COMES IN. /THE ORDERLY/ LADY
LADY	(246)	HATH STRUCK A NOTE OF MUSIC OUT OF THEE. " OF ALL	LADIES	MOST DEJECT AND WRETCHED." (HE MAKES A NOTE OF IT).
LADY	(246)	NOT WHAT I AM SAYING TO YOUR MAJESTY: I AM OF ALL	LADIES	MOST DEJECT AND WRETCHED-- /SHAKESPEAR/ HA! AT LAST
GETT	(307)	FIND IS THE FULL HORROR OF THE SITUATION. THESE	LADIES	NOT ONLY REFUSE OUR HONORABLE OFFERS, BUT AS I
LION PREFACE	(11)	POINT: FOR INSTANCE, IF SAVONAROLA ONLY TELLS THE	LADIES	OF FLORENCE THAT THEY OUGHT TO TEAR OFF THEIR JEWELS
3PLA PREFACE	(R18)	THIS POINT OF VIEW IS NOT CAUGHT BY THE CLEVER	LADIES	OF HEDDA'S OWN CLASS, WHO RECOGNIZE THE PORTRAIT,
BARB PREFACE	(239)	WAY ON THE UNFAILING TACT AND GOOD TASTE OF THE	LADIES	OF OUR ROYAL HOUSES, WHO, THOUGH PRESUMABLY OF FULL
LION II	(128)	DOWN THEIR THUMBS, THATS ANOTHER MATTER. THEYRE	LADIES	OF RANK. /LAVINIA/ DOES THE EMPEROR EVER INTERFERE..
SIM I	(48)	MR HAMMINGTAP; UNLESS IT INCLUDES ALL THE	LADIES	OF THE FAMILY. YOU WILL NOT BE ALLOWED TO PICK AND
JITT III	(62)	WELL THAT GOETHE WAS A GREAT MAN; BUT THE FINE	LADIES	OF WEIMAR WERE SHOCKED BY HIS MARRIAGE. ROUSSEAU WAS
CLEO III	(162)	I A DOLPHIN, CAESAR, TO CROSS THE SEAS WITH YOUNG	LADIES	ON MY BACK? MY BOAT IS SUNK: ALL YOURS ARE EITHER AT
ROCK PREFACE	(165)	WHEREBY ALL EDUCATED PERSONS, HOWEVER OBVIOUSLY	LADIES	OR GENTLEMEN, WHO WERE WILLING TO ASSURE THE
GETT	(311)	THATS A MERE MATTER OF FORM, MAAM. ANY NUMBER OF	LADIES	OR GENTLEMEN CAN BE PUT IN. /LEO/ NOT ANY NUMBER OF
MRS PREFACE	(169)	PLAY TEACHES. THOSE WHO WERE " SURPRISED TO SEE	LADIES	PRESENT" WERE MEN; AND WHEN THEY PROCEEDED TO EXPLAIN
PHIL II	(124)	HIS ARM AS IF TO GO WITH HIM). /GRACE/ WHEN TWO	LADIES	QUARREL IN THIS CLUB, IT IS AGAINST THE RULES TO
APPL II	SD(273)	ELECTION. ALL THE REST EXCEPT BOANERGES AND	LADIES	RISE IN CONSTERNATION. /PROTEUS/ THIS IS TREACHERY.
CATH 2,	SD(176)	AND SITS DOWN, THRUSTING HER FEET OUT). THE TWO	LADIES	RUSH TO HER FEET, EACH CARRYING A SLIPPER. CATHERINE,
SIM II	(58)	/PRA/ (SITTING DOWN BETWEEN THE TWO BRITISH	LADIES	) THEY MAY COME BACK. /HYERING/ (SITTING BESIDE
GETT PREFACE	(225)	BE MUCH MORE EXPERT AT IT THAN MOST MONOGAMIC	LADIES	; AND AS A COMPANION AND COUNSELLOR SHE PROBABLY
SUPR I	SD(17)	CHAIRS FROM THE WALL, AND PLACE THEM FOR THE TWO	LADIES	; BUT ANN COMES TO TANNER AND TAKES HIS CHAIR, WHICH
POSN	(436)	COMES IN. /ELDER DANIELS/ SORRY TO DISTURB YOU,	LADIES	; BUT THE VIGILANCE COMMITTEE HAS TAKEN A PRISONER;
LION PREFACE	(36)	POSSIBLE THOSE PICTURES WHICH NOW HANG IN MANY	LADIES	' CHAMBERS, IN WHICH JESUS IS REPRESENTED EXACTLY AS
INCA	(250)	AND PAINTS MOST ABOMINABLY. JACK JOHNSON TRIMS	LADIES	' HATS, AND BOXES WITH PROFESSIONALS HIRED FOR THAT
SIM II	(80)	PROTEST BY LADY GUSHING, PRESIDENT OF THE TITLED	LADIES	' LEAGUE OF SOCIAL SERVICE, ON THE INEQUALITY OF
INCA	(241)	WITH ME. I AM A LADY'S MAID; AND I KNOW THE	LADIES	' MAIDS AND VALETS OF ALL THE ARISTOCRACIES OF EUROPE
ROCK II	(263)	AND JOCKEYS, BUTLERS AND HOUSEKEEPERS AND	LADIES	' MAIDS AND SCULLERY MAIDS AND DEUCE KNOWS WHO NOT.
BUOY III	(34)	IT ALL BEFORE SHE WAS TEN, AND WAS SENT TO A	LADIES	' SCHOOL. /MRS SECONDBORN/ NOTHING COULD MAKE A REAL
KING I	(179)	ABSOLUTELY FREE FROM THE PLEASANT DISTURBANCE OF	LADIES	' SOCIETY-- IS NOW NECESSARY TO ME; AND I MUST BEG
NEVR II	(246)	ARTICLES AND OFFERS THE PARASOLS TO PHIL). THE	LADIES	' SUNSHADES, SIR. NASTY GLARE OFF THE SEA TODAY, SIR:
GETT	(261)	THEM AND ASKING THEM ABOUT THE FAMILY-- ACTUALLY	LADIES	SAYING " WHERE HAVE WE MET BEFORE? " AND ALL SORTS OF
PYGM I	(206)	AS SHE CAN AFFORD TO BE; BUT COMPARED TO THE	LADIES	SHE IS VERY DIRTY. HER FEATURES ARE NO WORSE THAN
APPL I	(226)	ROYAL ADVANTAGE THAT YOU ENJOY, THAT THE MORE THE	LADIES	TAKE AWAY YOUR CHARACTER THE BETTER THE PEOPLE LIKE
2TRU PREFACE	(4)	HAD ANY SELF AT ALL. HERE AND THERE YOU FIND RICH	LADIES	TAKING UP OCCUPATIONS AND INTERESTS WHICH KEEP THEM
3PLA PREFACE	(R18)	OF POPULAR PLAYS WOULD SOON CONVINCE THESE CLEVER	LADIES	THAT A HEROINE WHO ATONES IN THE LAST ACT BY
PYGM I	(215)	AT LAST, HALLO! (TO THE GIRL) WHERE ARE THE TWO	LADIES	THAT WERE HERE? /THE FLOWER GIRL/ THEY WALKED TO THE
GETT	(261)	MAAM, FOR A BISHOP'S LADY. I HAVE KNOWN BISHOPS'	LADIES	THAT WOULD FAIRLY PROVOKE YOU TO UP AND CHEEK THEM;
MRS II	(214)	TO THE CATHEDRAL, ONE OF THE MOST RESPECTABLE	LADIES	THERE. CHAPERONES GIRLS AT THE COUNTY BALL, IF YOU
MIS.	(122)	WITH A MARCHIONESS, TWO DUCHESSES, AND NO END OF	LADIES	THIS AND THAT. OF COURSE IT WAS ONLY A COMMITTEE:
BARB PREFACE	(224)	HE HAS ONLY TO FOLLOW UP THE INCOME OF THE SWEET	LADIES	TO ITS INDUSTRIAL SOURCE, AND THERE HE WILL FIND MRS
SUPR III	(125)	DO NOT WORK SMOOTHLY? /THE STATUE/ WHAT USED THE	LADIES	TO SAY, JUAN? /DON JUAN/ OH, COME! CONFIDENCE FOR
SUPR III	(139)	THAT WILL DO, MY FRIEND. YOU DO NOT EXPECT THESE	LADIES	TO TREAT YOU AS AN ACQUAINTANCE, I SUPPOSE, BECAUSE
ROCK II	(277)	HAS HE PICKED YOU OUT FROM AMONG THE THOUSAND	LADIES	TO WHOM HE IS INDIFFERENT? TO USE YOUR OWN
MIS. PREFACE	(73)	PERSUADING CHILDREN THAT HE IS NOT HUMAN, JUST AS	LADIES	USED TO PERSUADE THEM THAT THEY HAVE NO LEGS.
DOCT PREFACE	(42)	CLUBS THEM TO DEATH IN WHOLESALE MASSACRE BECAUSE	LADIES	WANT SEALSKIN JACKETS; OR AS FANCIERS BLIND SINGING
SUPR III	(124)	WHEN I WAS ON EARTH, AND MADE THOSE PROPOSALS TO	LADIES	WHICH, THOUGH UNIVERSALLY CONDEMNED, HAVE MADE ME SO
APPL I	(226)	THEIR CLAIM. SIDE BY SIDE WITH THEM ARE THE	LADIES	WHO ARE REALLY UNSCRUPULOUS. THEY ARE SO CAREFUL OF
GETT PREFACE	(215)	WOULD NOT STOP THERE. THE STRONG-MINDED	LADIES	WHO ARE RESOLVED TO BE MISTRESSES IN THEIR OWN HOUSES
GETT	SD(306)	IN THROUGH THE TOWER, IN ALDERMAN'S ROBES. THE	LADIES	WHO ARE STANDING SIT DOWN HASTILY, AND LOOK AS
ROCK PREFACE	(152)	WILD DEER, AND COLLECT MONEY FROM GENTLEMEN AND	LADIES	WHO ENJOY SHOOTING THEM. I THEN EXTERMINATE MY
KING I	(214)	KNOWLEDGE OF THEM, AND ARE NOT ASHAMED LIKE FINE	LADIES	WHO HAVE ONLY A DISHONEST KNOWLEDGE OF THEM.
DOCT PREFACE	(17)	HUMBUG WHO EVER PRESCRIBED ETHER TONICS TO	LADIES	WHOSE NEED FOR TONICS IS OF PRECISELY THE SAME
GETT	SD(260)	A SHOP FOR THE SALE OF NECESSARIES OF LIFE TO	LADIES	WHOSE SOCIAL POSITION IS SO UNQUESTIONABLE THAT THEY
BUOY III	(32)	LIVE IN GATE LODGES AND GARDENERS' COTTAGES. YOUR	LADIES	WILL HAVE TO DO THE HOUSEWORK. YOUR CLOTHES WILL HAVE
GETT	(316)	HUSBANDS WILL ALSO BE OUTCASTS; AND THE POOR	LADIES	WILL OCCASIONALLY PINE FOR MALE SOCIETY. /LESBIA/
BARB PREFACE	(224)	TO ACCEPT MONEY FROM ANYBODY EXCEPT SWEET OLD	LADIES	WITH INDEPENDENT INCOMES AND GENTLE AND LOVELY WAYS
MIS. PREFACE	(90)	AND THAT MUSIC IS MADE BY A FEW WELL-INTENTIONED	LADIES	WITH THE HELP OF A HARMONIUM, CAN HEAR MASSES BY
DOCT PREFACE	(66)	DRESSINGS, PRESCRIBING ETHER DRAMS FOR	LADIES	WITH TIMID LEANINGS TOWARDS DIPSOMANIA, AND GENERALLY
MIS.	(143)	ME WHAT? /HYPATIA/ GIRLS WITHERING INTO LADIES.	LADIES	WITHERING INTO OLD MAIDS. NURSING OLD WOMEN. RUNNING
SUPR I	(46)	LIKE A NAUGHTY CHILD BY YOUNG GIRLS AND OLD	LADIES	WITHOUT ANY SERIOUS DUTIES AND RESPONSIBILITIES.
LADY	(243)	FOR I HAD HOPED THAT EVEN THE VILEST OF MY	LADIES	WOULD NOT HAVE DISHONORED MY COURT BY WANTONING WITH
GETT	(330)	FOR LOVE LIKE THE ROBINS IN WINTER, AS THE GOOD	LADIES	YOURE ACCUSTOMED TO ARE. YOULL HAVE TO BE VERY
NEVR IV	SD(282)	FAULT FOR BEING SO AFFABLE, SIR. I'LL TELL THE	LADIES	YOURE HERE, SIR. (HE GOES OUT INTO THE GARDEN
CLEO V	SD(195)	BROAD STEPS OF THE GATE, CROWDED WITH CLEOPATRA'S	LADIES	, ALL IN THEIR GAYEST ATTIRE, ARE LIKE A FLOWER
BUOY III	SD(28)	A MIDDLE-AGED WIDOWER, A YOUNGER MAN, TWO MARRIED	LADIES	, AN UNMARRIED GIRL OF 20, AND AN IRREVERENT YOUTH OF
INCA	(240)	BY A CIVIL WAITER WHO IS ACCUSTOMED TO WAIT ON	LADIES	, AND NOT, LIKE YOU, ON COMMERCIAL TRAVELLERS. /THE
SUPR III	(120)	WELL, YOU HAVE DONE YOUR BEST, YOU VIRTUOUS	LADIES	, AND OTHERS OF YOUR WAY OF THINKING, TO BEND MAN'S
FANY II	(293)	REALLY A LADY EXCEPT WHEN THEYRE TREATED LIKE	LADIES	, I DONT KNOW. (SHE THROWS HERSELF INTO A CORNER OF
SUPR II	(49)	PUT IN THE WHOLE MORNING IN THERE TALKIN TO THE	LADIES	, I'LL PUT THE CAR IN THE GARAGE AND MAKE MYSELF
POSN	(439)	THE USE OF SCRATCHING LIKE THAT? NOW, LADIES,	LADIES	, LADIES. HOW WOULD YOU LIKE IT IF YOU WERE GOING TO
POSN	(439)	GO. WHATS THE USE OF SCRATCHING LIKE THAT? NOW,	LADIES	, LADIES, LADIES. HOW WOULD YOU LIKE IT IF YOU WERE
CLEO IV	SD(166)	IN HER BOUDOIR IN THE PALACE, AMONG A BEVY OF HER	LADIES	, LISTENING TO A SLAVE GIRL WHO IS PLAYING THE HARP
PRES	(145)	MUTINY? /THE ORDERLY/ WHAT AM I TO SAY TO THE	LADIES	, SIR? /BALSQUITH/ YOU DONT MIND MY SEEING THEM
CATH 2,	SD(174)	TO AWAKEN. THE PRINCESS DASHKOFF, WITH TWO	LADIES	, STANDS A LITTLE IN FRONT OF THE LINE OF COURTIERS,
JOAN 2	(77)	INVINCIBLE DUNOIS, THE DARLING OF ALL THE	LADIES	, THE BEAUTIFUL BASTARD. IS IT LIKELY THAT THE
PRES	(152)	WITH A SLIGHT CHUCKLE OF SATISFACTION) AND NOW,	LADIES	, TO WHAT AM I INDEBTED-- /MRS BANGER/ LET ME
PRES	(153)	/MITCHENER/ ARMING YOURSELVES! BUT, MY DEAR	LADIES	, UNDER THE LATEST PROCLAMATION WOMEN ARE STRICTLY
OVER	(181)	I SANG " FAREWELL AND ADIEU TO YOU DEAR SPANISH	LADIES	," THAT YOU WERE BY BIRTH A LADY OF SPAIN? YOUR
JOAN 2	(80)	IN DEPRECATION OF THEIR MERRIMENT) SSH -- SSH!	LADIES	! LADIES! ! /JOAN/ (NOT AT ALL EMBARRASSED) I
POSN	(438)	(DISTURBANCE). THEY ARE BRINGING HIM IN. NOW	LADIES	! PLEASE, PLEASE. THEY RISE RELUCTANTLY. HANNAH,
DEVL I	(18)	AS JUDITH SITS DOWN). AS USUAL, LOOKING AFTER THE	LADIES	! /UNCLE TITUS/ (INDIGNANTLY) BE ASHAMED OF
BASH IIT1,	(108)	SPOIL DOES WHAT ITS TRADESMEN TELL IT. OH, YOUR	LADIES	! SEALSKINNED AND EGRET-FEATHERED; ALL DEFIANCE TO
JOAN 2	(80)	OF THEIR MERRIMENT) SSH -- SSH! LADIES!	LADIES	! ! /JOAN/ (NOT AT ALL EMBARRASSED) I WEAR IT LIKE

LADIES-IN-WAITING

GLIM	(181)	NOT GIVE FIFTY CROWNS FOR ONE OF MY MOTHER'S	LADIES-IN-WAITING	. FIFTY PENCE, YOU MUST MEAN. /SQUARCIO/

LADLING

PYGM III	(251)	ALL THOUGHT SHE WAS DEAD; BUT MY FATHER HE KEPT	LADLING	GIN DOWN HER THROAT TIL SHE CAME TO SO SUDDEN THAT

LAD'S

MIS.	(203)	/MRS TARLETON/ DONT MAKE TOO MUCH NOISE. THE	LAD'S	ASLEEP. /TARLETON/ CHICKABIDDY: WE HAVE SOME NEWS FOR
DOCT IV	(156)	PHASE. /SIR PATRICK/ NEGATIVE OR POSITIVE, THE	LAD'S	DONE FOR. HE WONT LAST OUT THE AFTERNOON. HE'LL GO
KING I	(190)	ARE SIX A PENNY IN EUROPE TODAY. THE DUTCH	LAD'S	GRANDFATHER-IN-LAW WAS OUR GRANDFATHER. YOUR DAUGHTER
CYMB V	(142)	TO BE YOUR ROYAL HIGHNESS'S PRISONER, NOT THIS	LAD'S	. /LUCIUS/ HIS CLAIM IS VALID, SIR. HIS BLOOD IS
FANY I	(282)	(BITTERLY) OH YES: I KNOW. HERE! I MUST BUY THE	LAD'S	SALVATION, I SUPPOSE. HOW MUCH WILL YOU TAKE TO CLEAR

LADS

APPL I	(217)	GENTLY, AMANDA, GENTLY. THREE VERY PROMISING	LADS	: THEY DO YOU CREDIT. /AMANDA/ I NEVER WANTED THEM TO
MIS.	(128)	TO DISGUST YOUNG WOMEN WITH ME, AND GIVE THE	LADS	A TURN. /MRS TARLETON/ JOHN: I WONT HAVE IT. THATS A
MIS. PREFACE	(38)	SIX UNDER GAS LAMPS IN UNDERGROUND CITY OFFICES.	LADS	AND LASSES IN THEIR TEENS WILL PROBABLY BE ABLE TO
BULL PREFACE	(52)	STICK; HASSAN MAHFOUZ USED A STICK ALSO; AND THE	LADS	AND LOAFERS BEGAN TO THROW STONES AND BRICKS. FIVE
BULL PREFACE	(52)	REVOLT TO THE ENTIRE MOSLEM WORLD); AND ALL THE	LADS	AND LOAFERS IN THE PLACE WERE PRESENTLY ON THE SPOT.
BULL PREFACE	(53)	OFFICERS HAD BEEN TAKEN OUT OF THE HANDS OF THE	LADS	AND THE LOAFERS, OF ABD-EL-NEBI AND HASSAN MAHFOUZ, BY
MIS. PREFACE	(6)	AS NURSEMAIDS AND GENERAL SERVANTS, AND THE	LADS	AS ERRAND BOYS. IN THE COUNTRY BOTH BOYS AND GIRLS DO A
MIS.	(117)	ARRESTED WHEN THEY ARE LITTLE MORE THAN COLLEGE	LADS	. BENTLEY DOESNT REALLY MEAN TO BE OFFENSIVE. YOU CAN
BARB II	(305)	THINK OF THE WIDOWS AND ORPHANS! THE MEN AND	LADS	TORN TO PIECES WITH SHRAPNEL AND POISONED WITH
INCA	(249)	THEN, WITH INDULGENT PATERNAL CONTEMPT) EXCELLENT	LADS	, MADAM. VERY HONEST AFFECTIONATE CREATURES. I HAVE
APPL I	(211)	THEIR BIT OF FUN WITH YOU AS A NEW COMER. COME,	LADS	! ENOUGH OF FOOLING: LETS GET TO BUSINESS. (HE TAKES

LADVENU

JOAN	6,SD(150)	HUSH? SOMEONE IS COMING. CONTROL YOURSELF.	LADVENU	COMES BACK THROUGH THE COURTYARD TO WARWICK'S RIGHT
JOAN EPIL	,SD(152)	IT ENERGETICALLY, MAKING A DEAFENING CLATTER.	LADVENU	ENTERS, 25 YEARS OLDER, STRANGE AND STARK IN
JOAN	6,SD(151)	WILL DO HIMSELF SOME MISCHIEF. AFTER HIM, QUICK.	LADVENU	HURRIES OUT, WARWICK URGING HIM. THE EXECUTIONER
JOAN	6 (151)	/WARWICK/ (WITH A WRY SMILE, THINKING OF WHAT	LADVENU	SAID) THE LAST OF HER? HM! I WONDER!
JOAN	6,SD(136)	SIGH. THE INQUISITOR PURSES HIS LIPS AND FROWNS.	LADVENU	SHAKES HIS HEAD PITIFULLY. /D'ESTIVET/ SHE IMPUTES
JOAN	6,SD(147)	RISE IN DISORDER, AND FOLLOW THE SOLDIERS, EXCEPT	LADVENU	, WHO HAS HIDDEN HIS FACE IN HIS HANDS. /CAUCHON/ (

LADY

SUPR III	(100)	THERE IS A GREAT GULF FIXED. /THE DEVIL/ DEAR	LADY	: A PARABLE MUST NOT BE TAKEN LITERALLY. THE GULF IS
ARMS I	(12)	THEY SEE THEM EVERYWHERE. (POLITELY) GRACIOUS	LADY	: A THOUSAND PARDONS. GOODNIGHT. (MILITARY BOW, WHICH
CYMB V	(149)	EVEN SORRY. /POSTHUMUS/ I'M TOO HAPPY. /IACHIMO/	LADY	: A WORD. WHEN YOU ARRIVED JUST NOW I, AS YOU SAW, WAS
DEST	(191)	EMPHASIS) CONSCIENCE OF YOURS? I TOOK YOU FOR A	LADY	: AN ARISTOCRAT. WAS YOUR GRANDFATHER A SHOPKEEPER,
DOCT II	(116)	CROWD ABOUT HER TO CONSOLE HER. /B.B./ MY DEAR	LADY	: COME COME! COME COME! (VERY PERSUASIVELY) COME
DEST	(161)	WHAT ARE YOU THINKING OF, LIEUTENANT? IT'S A	LADY	: DONT YOU HEAR? IT'S A WOMAN'S VOICE. /LIEUTENANT/
HART II	(107)	/THE BURGLAR/ WELL, YOUVE GOT THEM BACK,	LADY	: HAVNT YOU? CAN YOU GIVE ME BACK THE YEARS OF MY LIFE
BASH III	(122)	PEACE, THERE! EXCUSE HIS DAMAGED FEATURES,	LADY	: HE'S PARADISE; AND THIS ONE'S BYRON'S TRAINER,
2TRU II	(73)	HER FELLOW CREATURES-- /THE PATIENT/ I AM NOT A	LADY	: I AM FREE NOW TO SAY WHAT I PLEASE. HOW DO YOU LIKE
ARMS I	(16)	A COMIC GESTURE OF DESPAIR) IT'S NO USE, DEAR	LADY	: I CANT MAKE YOU SEE IT FROM THE PROFESSIONAL POINT OF
ARMS I	(20)	HIS HANDS BEHIND HIS BACK) THANKS, GRACIOUS YOUNG	LADY	: I FEEL SAFE AT LAST. AND NOW WOULD YOU MIND BREAKING
FABL PREFACE	(69)	HOLY TRINITY, THE SCARLET WOMAN AS WELL AS OUR	LADY	: IN SHORT AS MANY DEMONS AS SAINTS. AT FIRST, HOWEVER,
ARMS III	(52)	TOLD ONLY TWO LIES IN YOUR WHOLE LIFE. DEAR YOUNG	LADY	: ISNT THAT RATHER A SHORT ALLOWANCE? I'M QUITE A
JITT III	(57)	/LENKHEIM/ (DRAWING A LITTLE CLOSER TO HER) DEAR	LADY	: MAY I ASK YOU A VERY INDISCREET QUESTION? I SHALL
NEVR II	(231)	/M'COMAS/ (NERVOUSLY) NOT AT ALL, MY DEAR YOUNG	LADY	: NOT AT ALL. AT THE SAME TIME, THIS IS RATHER SUDDEN.
MTH3	(123)	AND PUT YOU ON YOUR TRIAL. /BURGE-LUBIN/ MY DEAR	LADY	: OUR CHINESE AND COLORED FRIENDS ARE PERFECTLY HAPPY.
NEVR IV	(305)	IN MY OWN HOUSE, SIR: MY WIFE WAS LIKE YOUR YOUNG	LADY	: SHE WAS OF A COMMANDING AND MASTERFUL DISPOSITION,
WIDO I	(16)	YOU MY PEOPLE ARNT A BIT SNOBBISH. BLANCHE IS A	LADY	: THATLL BE GOOD ENOUGH FOR THEM. /SARTORIUS/ (MOVED)
ARMS III	(70)	SIDE AFTER ALL. (TO LOUKA) GRACIOUS YOUNG	LADY	: THE BEST WISHES OF A GOOD REPUBLICAN! (HE KISSES
BUOY III	(41)	HASTILY AND COMES STRAIGHT TO HER. /NATIVE/ PINK	LADY	: THE MAN HAS COME. /SHE/ HERE! ! ! /NATIVE/ IN THIS
NEVR II	(228)	FOR THAT. /M'COMAS/ HOWLED AT! MY DEAR GOOD	LADY	: THERE IS NOTHING IN ANY OF THOSE VIEWS NOWADAYS TO
ARMS I	(13)	AS HE TAKES THE PISTOL) NO USE, DEAR YOUNG	LADY	: THERES NOTHING IN IT. IT'S NOT LOADED. (HE MAKES A
VWOO 2	(130)	PROTECTION TO BOTH PARTIES. YOU ARE NOT A	LADY	: YOU ARE A VILLAGER; BUT SOMEBODY HAS EDUCATED YOU--
SUPR III	(90)	VIRTUE AND PROPRIETY! /DON JUAN/ PATIENCE,	LADY	: YOU WILL BE PERFECTLY HAPPY AND AT HOME HERE. AS
PRES	(166)	TELEPHONE) WAIT LE YOURE MARRIED YOURSELF, ME FINE	LADY	: YOULL FIND OUT THAT EVERY WOMAN'S A CHARWOMAN FROM
ARMS I	(12)	BUT A MISS IS AS GOOD AS A MILE. DEAR YOUNG	LADY	: YOUR SERVANT TO THE DEATH. I WISH FOR YOUR SAKE I HAD
ARMS I	(17)	SOLDIER? /THE MAN/ AH, TRUE, DEAR YOUNG	LADY	: YOURE ALWAYS RIGHT. I KNOW HOW GOOD YOUVE BEEN TO ME:
2TRU II	(67)	FOR ME. /THE COUNTESS/ NO IT ISNT. YOURE A REAL	LADY	: YOURE BROKEN IN TO BE DULL. BESIDES, YOU HAVE POPSY.
NEVR IV	(295)	DONT YOU TRY TO PUT ME OUT OF COUNTENANCE, YOUNG	LADY	: YOURE TOO YOUNG TO DO IT. (HE TAKES M'COMAS'S CHAIR
OVER	(186)	YOU, SIR, ASPERSE THE CHARACTER OF THAT SWEET	LADY	? A LADY WHOM I HAVE TAKEN UNDER MY PROTECTION. /JUNO/
ARMS III	(65)	/BLUNTSCHLI/ WHAT ELSE CAN HE DO, DEAR	LADY	? HE MUST DEFEND HIMSELF SOMEHOW. COME (VERY
WIDO I	(21)	MUCH IN THE STYLE OF A PROSPECTUS OF THE YOUNG	LADY	? I THROW OUT THE SUGGESTION AS A MATTER OF TASTE.
2TRU III	(101)	/TALLBOYS/ NONE. /THE ELDER/ BUT--? THE BRITISH	LADY	? IN THEIR CLUTCHES? /TALLBOYS/ SHE HAS BEEN IN MY
AUGS	(271)	SHE IS. (TO THE LADY) MAY I OFFER YOU A CHAIR,	LADY	? (HE PLACES A CHAIR AT THE WRITING-TABLE OPPOSITE
ARMS III	(56)	AND BE DAINTY ABOUT YOURSELF, LIKE A FINE RUSSIAN	LADY	? ME! DO YOU HEAR THAT? ME! (SHE TOSSES HER HEAD
SUPR III	(97)	DON JUAN, YOUR SERVANT. (POLITELY) AND A STRANGE	LADY	? MY RESPECTS, SENORA. /ANA/ ARE YOU-- /THE DEVIL/ (
WIDO I	(17)	YOU, MY FRIEND; AND FORGET THAT I AM WRITING TO A	LADY	? NEVER! /TRENCH/ BOSH, BILLY: DONT PRETEND YOU DONT
INCA	(236)	FOR A CONVERSATION). HOW WONDERFUL! WHAT! A	LADY	? OH, A PERSON. OH YES: I KNOW. YES, PLEASE, SEND HER
PPP	(206)	YOUR WAY IF I LEAVE THEM THERE UNTIL MORNING, MY	LADY	? OR SHALL I BRING UP THE ASHPAN AND TAKE THEM AWAY..
GETT	(310)	THE MISSION. /HOTCHKISS/ BUT HOW AM I TO KNOW THE	LADY	? /COLLINS/ SHE HAS GONE TO THE CHURCH IN STATE, SIR,
GETT	(309)	DENIED TO US. WHAT IS THE SOCIAL POSITION OF THIS	LADY	? /COLLINS/ THE HIGHEST IN THE BOROUGH, SIR. SHE IS MY
KING I	(204)	ORANGES IN DRURY LANE THAN YOU ARE NOW AS A COURT	LADY	? /FOX/ DID YOU SELL ORANGES IN DRURY LANE? /NELL/
FANY I	(282)	THINK ANY WOMAN WOULD THAT HAD THE FEELINGS OF A	LADY	? /GILBEY/ (BITTERLY) OH YES! I KNOW. HERE! I MUST
BULL III	(118)	ABOUT ME LAST NIGHT WHEN I CAME IN WITH THAT	LADY	? /HODSON/ (SURPRISED) NO, SIR. /BROADBENT/ NOT ANY--
BARB III	(314)	MY LADY; OR IS HE AT HOME HERE, SO TO SPEAK, MY	LADY	? /LADY BRITOMART/ ANNOUNCE HIM. /MORRISON/ THANK YOU,
BARB I	(263)	/MORRISON/ MIGHT I SPEAK A WORD TO YOU, MY	LADY	? /LADY BRITOMART/ NONSENSE! SHEW HIM UP. /MORRISON/
HART I	(45)	WHO IS THIS MISGUIDED AND UNFORTUNATE YOUNG	LADY	? /NURSE GUINNESS/ SHE SAYS MISS HESSY INVITED HER,
ARMS III	(73)	HUNDRED HORSES! WHEW! /SERGIUS/ WHAT SAYS THE	LADY	? /RAINA/ (PRETENDING TO SULK) THE LADY SAYS THAT HE
ARMS III	(65)	OVER IN A FRIENDLY WAY. WHERE IS THIS OTHER YOUNG	LADY	? /RAINA/ LISTENING AT THE DOOR, PROBABLY. /SERGIUS/ (
CAPT I	(236)	(IGNORING THIS ANNOUNCEMENT) WHO IS THE	LADY	? /RANKIN/ LADY CEECILY WAYNFLETE, HIS LORDSHIP'S
VWOO 1	(121)	/A/ HAVE THEY FOUND OUT HERE THAT YOU ARE NOT A	LADY	? /Z/ THE AMERICANS DONT KNOW THE DIFFERENCE: THEY
SUPR IV	(143)	ROUND HIM WITH LIVELY CURIOSITY) THE YOUNG	LADY	? THATS MISS VIOLET, EH? /STRAKER/ (STOPPING ON THE
MTH2	(57)	DROPS THE SUBJECT OF LABOR). WELL, MY DEAR YOUNG	LADY	? WHAT IS THE LATEST NEWS? WHATS GOING ON? HAVE YOU
FOUN	(213)	CLASS OF GENTLEMAN IS IT, PRAY, THAT GIVES A	LADY	A CHAIR? /MERCER/ OH, I'M SURE I BEG YOUR PARDON,
DEVL III	(59)	FOR HER. QUITE SO, QUITE SO. (BLANDLY) GIVE THE	LADY	A CHAIR; AND MAKE HER THOROUGHLY COMFORTABLE. THE
MIS.	(154)	OH WELL, NEVER MIND: HYPATIA WILL LEND THE	LADY	A GOWN. /LINA/ THANK YOU: I'M QUITE COMFORTABLE AS I
DEVL III	(64)	DOWN). SIT DOWN, MADAM, WHILST WE WAIT. GIVE THE	LADY	A NEWSPAPER. /RICHARD/ (INDIGNANTLY) SHAME!
FANY III	(308)	DOOR). YOU UNDERSTAND, SIR, THAT MISS KNOX IS A	LADY	ABSOLUTELY COMME IL FAUT? /DUVALLET/ PERFECTLY. BUT
LADY PREFACE	(221)	IF SHAKESPEAR DID ALL THE SUFFERING AND THE DARK	LADY	ALL THE CRUELTY. BUT WHY DOES HE NOT PUT HIMSELF IN THE
SUPR II	(66)	OPPORTUNITY TO LET ME HAVE A FEW WORDS WITH THE	LADY	ALONE. I SHALL HAVE TO CRY OFF THIS TRIP; AND IT'S
PYGM EPILOG	(299)	TALK TO THE LADY OF THE FURNITURE SHOP, AND THAT	LADY	ALSO DESIRED ABOVE ALL THINGS TO KNOW MR WELLS AND SELL
2TRU I	SD(27)	SHEWS THAT THE BED IS A SICK BED AND THE YOUNG	LADY	AN INVALID. THE FURNITURE INCLUDES A VERY HANDSOME
PYGM V	(278)	OF SPEAKING, AND SO ON), THE DIFFERENCE BETWEEN A	LADY	AND A FLOWER GIRL IS NOT HOW SHE BEHAVES, BUT HOW SHE'S
2TRU I	SD(28)	(IT COLLAPSES). THE DOOR OPENS; AND AN ELDERLY	LADY	AND A YOUNG DOCTOR COME IN. THE LADY STEALS ALONG ON
JOAN 2	(75)	OH, GOD FORGIVE ME, WHAT AM I SAYING? -- BY OUR	LADY	AND ALL THE SAINTS, THIS MUST BE THE ANGEL THAT STRUCK
SIM PREFACE	(14)	WORK OF A CONSTITUTION WHICH HAD ABOLISHED THE	LADY	AND GENTLEMAN EXACTLY AS THE INQUISITION CARRIED OUT
OVER	SD(171)	OVERRULED. A	LADY	AND GENTLEMAN ARE SITTING TOGETHER ON A CHESTERFIELD IN
NEVR II	(236)	CLANDON WILL BE DOWN PRESENTLY, SIR. THE YOUNG	LADY	AND GENTLEMAN WERE JUST TALKING ABOUT YOUR FRIEND, SIR.
NEVR III	(262)	OF MRS CLANDON, CONVERSING MEANWHILE). THE YOUNG	LADY	AND GENTLEMAN HAVE JUST COME BACK, MAAM: THEY HAVE BEEN
PHIL I	SD(69)	THE PHILANDERER. ACT I. A	LADY	AND GENTLEMAN ARE MAKING LOVE TO ONE ANOTHER IN THE
PHIL I	SD(69)	NEAR THE PIANO IS A SOFA, ON WHICH THE	LADY	AND GENTLEMAN ARE SEATED AFFECTIONATELY SIDE BY SIDE,
NEVR II	(226)	SIR, VERY TAKING INDEED; ESPECIALLY THE YOUNG	LADY	AND GENTLEMAN. /THE GENTLEMAN/ MISS DOROTHEA AND MR
CAPT I	SD(225)	THEM EATHENS IS JAST LAWK YOU AN' ME, GAVNER. A	LADY	AND GENTLEMAN, BOTH ENGLISH, COME INTO THE GARDEN. THE
WIDO I	SD(5)	THE RIVERSIDE GATE). OH, I SAY! HERE THEY ARE. A	LADY	AND GENTLEMAN, FOLLOWED BY A PORTER WITH SOME LIGHT

PYGM I SD(205)	THERE ARE ALREADY SEVERAL PEOPLE, AMONG THEM A	LADY	AND HER DAUGHTER IN EVENING DRESS. THEY ARE ALL PEERING
MIS. (182)	OF FOUNDATION I APOLOGIZE MOST HUMBLY TO THE	LADY	AND HER FAMILY FOR MY CONDUCT AND I PROMISE MR TARLETON
MIS. (180)	/PERCIVAL/ I APOLOGIZE MOST HUMBLY TO THE	LADY	AND HER FAMILY FOR MY CONDUCT-- (HE WAITS FOR BENTLEY
DEVL I SD(16)	SOFA, WHERE HE SITS DOWN WARMLY BETWEEN HIS OWN	LADY	AND HIS BROTHER'S. ANDERSON HANGS UP HIS HAT AND WAITS
MIS. (164)	MR PERCIVAL! YOU SIT DOWN IN THE PRESENCE OF A	LADY	AND LEAVE HER STANDING. (HE RISES HASTILY). HA, HA!
ARMS III (70)	WHY, BLESS MY HEART AND SOUL, LOOK AT THE YOUNG	LADY	AND LOOK AT ME. SHE, RICH, YOUNG, BEAUTIFUL, WITH HER
ARMS II (33)	DEED, OR THINK AN IGNOBLE THOUGHT. /SERGIUS/ MY	LADY	AND MY SAINT! (HE CLASPS HER REVERENTLY). /RAINA/ (
FOUN (215)	MADAM: I MUST REQUEST YOU TO SPEAK LIKE A	LADY	AND NOT LIKE A PROCESSION OF THE UNEMPLOYED. THE HOUSE
GETT (311)	THE DRAFT). /LEO/ AND YOU HAVE GOT ONLY ONE	LADY	AND ONE GENTLEMAN. THERE OUGHT TO BE TWO GENTLEMEN.
2TRU I SD(35)	AND PRESSES THE BUTTON REPEATEDLY). THE ELDERLY	LADY	AND THE NIGHT NURSE COME RUNNING IN. THE NURSE IS
MIS. (189)	BE ALARMED, MAAM. I KNOW WHAT IS DUE TO YOU AS A	LADY	AND TO MYSELF AS A GENTLEMAN. I REGARD YOU WITH RESPECT
MRS PREFACE(180)	THE GIRLS AND SHEWED THEM THE RISKS THEY RAN. THE	LADY	APPEALED TO ME TO HELP HER TO PROTEST. AFTER CONVINCING
2TRU II (78)	ENOUGH. WHY HAVE YOU PASSED YOURSELF OFF ON THIS	LADY	AS A NATIVE SERVANT? BEING A SERVANT IS NO LARK.
HART PREFACE(30)	THE OPERA SINGERS. I PICKED OUT ONE MASSIVE DARK	LADY	AS ALBONI, AND WONDERED HOW SOON SHE WOULD STAND UP AND
O'FL (217)	AND TIMES I HAVE SAID THAT MISS AGNES WOULD BE MY	LADY	AS HER MOTHER WAS BEFORE HER! DIDNT I, DINNY? /SIR
CAND I (86)	DISAPPOINTEDLY AT HER) YOURE NOT THE SAME YOUNG	LADY	AS HUSED TO TYPEWRITE FOR HIM? /PROSERPINE/ NO.
LADY PREFACE(207)	UP TO DATE. WHY, THEN, DID I INTRODUCE THE DARK	LADY	AS MISTRESS FITTON? WELL, I HAD TWO REASONS. THE PLAY
SUPR I SD(43)	SHE IS AS IMPENITENT AND SELF-POSSESSED A YOUNG	LADY	AS ONE WOULD DESIRE TO SEE AMONG THE BEST BEHAVED OF
WIDO II (36)	IS NO LONGER EVEN AN IMITATION OF THE VOICE OF A	LADY	AS SHE EXCLAIMS) I HATE SECRETS; AND I DONT LIKE TO BE
SUPR HANDBOK(226)	I DEMURRED TO THE DESCRIPTION OF A CERTAIN YOUNG	LADY	AS " THE PRETTY MISS SO AND SO." MY AUNT REBUKED ME BY
FANY III (324)	THINK OF HIS INSPIRING WORDS, WHEN THE	LADY	ASKED HIM WHETHER BRITISH SOLDIERS EVER RAN AWAY. " ALL
BARB II (275)	WE AZ TO MAKE AZ TO BE WISPERED TO ONE	LADY	AT A TIME. IT AINT RIGHT, SPITE OF ALL THEIR PIETY.
MRS III (226)	/FRANK/ (GRACEFULLY) THAT WOULD PUT THE OLD	LADY	AT EVER SUCH A DISADVANTAGE. NO, VIV: YOUR INFATUATED
MIS. PREFACE(5)	ME TO A HEAVIER ARTICLE. I MUST HAVE SEEN THAT	LADY	AT LEAST FOUR TIMES IN THE TWENTY YEARS FOLLOWING. SHE
LADY PREFACE(207)	OF JEALOUSY BETWEEN QUEEN ELIZABETH AND THE DARK	LADY	AT THE EXPENSE OF THE UNFORTUNATE BARD. NOW THIS, IF
SUPR PREFACE(R11)	EMOTIONS. SOMETIMES WE GRUMBLE UNGALLANTLY AT THE	LADY	BECAUSE SHE DOES NOT ACT AS WELL AS SHE LOOKS. BUT IN A
MIS. (177)	THE MONSTROUS AND BLACKGUARDLY LIE THAT THIS	LADY	BEHAVED IMPROPERLY IN MY PRESENCE? /GUNNER/ (TURNING
PRES (166)	HER DAUGHTER-IN-LAW'S MOTHER TO BE A GENERAL'S	LADY	BETTHER THAN TO BE A CHARWOMAN. (INTO THE TELEPHONE)
SIM PRO,3, (33)	/THE PRIEST/ NO MATTER: I SHALL SOON GET THE POOR	LADY	BEYOND THE DOGLIKE STAGE. /THE E.O./ (WHO HAS BEEN
DOCT I (82)	HE CAN SEE SOMEBODY? /EMMY/ I SAID THERES A	LADY	BOTHERING ME TO SEE THE DOCTOR. THAT ISNT ASKING. ITS
DOCT I (82)	IMMEDIATELY BEGINNING TO DUST THE COUCH) THERES A	LADY	BOTHERING ME TO SEE THE DOCTOR. /REDPENNY/ (DISTRACTED
DOCT I (82)	ISNT ASKING. ITS TELLING. /REDPENNY/ WELL, IS THE	LADY	BOTHERING YOU ANY REASON FOR YOU TO COME BOTHERING ME
BARB I (271)	TO. I INSIST ON YOUR STAYING. /CUSINS/ MY DEAR	LADY	BRIT: THERE ARE THINGS IN THE FAMILY PRAYER BOOK THAT I
BARB I (262)	APPROVAL) PRECISELY. /LOMAX/ LOOK HERE, DOLLY:	LADY	BRIT DIDNT SAY THAT. /LADY BRITOMART/ (VEHEMENTLY) I
BARB III (313)	STREETS. /CUSINS/ YOUR ORDERS ARE ALREADY OBEYED,	LADY	BRIT. /BARBARA/ DOLLY: WERE YOU EVER REALLY IN EARNEST
BARB I (266)	UPON MY SOUL! (HE SITS ON THE SETTEE BETWEEN	LADY	BRITOMART AND UNDERSHAFT, QUITE OVERCOME). /BARBARA/
BARB III SD(330)	IS NO DANGER. (HE SITS BESIDE HER ON THE SHELL).	LADY	BRITOMART ARRIVES FROM THE TOWN WITH A BOUQUET. /LADY
BARB I (259)	OF SUPPORTING THEIR WIVES. (THE BUTLER ENTERS:	LADY	BRITOMART GOES BEHIND THE SETTEE TO SPEAK TO HIM).
BARB I SD(249)	ON HIS LEFT. NEAR THE WINDOW IS AN ARMCHAIR.	LADY	BRITOMART IS A WOMAN OF FIFTY OR THEREABOUTS, WELL
BARB III SD(311)	ACT III. NEXT DAY AFTER LUNCH	LADY	BRITOMART IS WRITING IN THE LIBRARY IN WILTON CRESCENT.
BARB III (322)	AND GET READY, MAMMA: THE CARRIAGE IS WAITING. (	LADY	BRITOMART LEAVES THE ROOM). /UNDERSHAFT/ (TO SARAH)
BARB I SD(263)	CONFUSION). ANDREW UNDERSHAFT COMES IN. ALL RISE.	LADY	BRITOMART MEETS HIM IN THE MIDDLE OF THE ROOM BEHIND
BARB III (318)	END OF TREATING ME AS A CHILD, IF YOU PLEASE. (	LADY	BRITOMART RECOILS, DEEPLY WOUNDED BY HIS TONE). UNTIL
BARB I (259)	TO COME DOWN HERE AT ONCE. (MORRISON WITHDRAWS.	LADY	BRITOMART TURNS TO STEPHEN). NOW REMEMBER, STEPHEN: I
BARB I SD(249)	AFTER DINNER IN JANUARY 1906, IN THE LIBRARY IN	LADY	BRITOMART UNDERSHAFT'S HOUSE IN WILTON CRESCENT. A
BARB III (342)	CHOLLY IS THE USUAL TICKET. /UNDERSHAFT/ (TO	LADY	BRITOMART) BIDDY-- /LADY BRITOMART/ (VIOLENTLY) DONT
BARB I (264)	HANDS IN HIS) HOW ARE YOU, MY YOUNG FRIEND? (TO	LADY	BRITOMART) HE IS VERY LIKE YOU, MY LOVE. /CUSINS/ YOU
BARB III (317)	(COLDLY) GOOD AFTERNOON. /UNDERSHAFT/ (TO	LADY	BRITOMART) HE KNOWS ALL ABOUT THE TRADITION, I
BARB I SD(260)	HER. CONSEQUENTLY HE HAS NOT ATTEMPTED TO RESIST	LADY	BRITOMART'S ARRANGEMENTS TO THAT END. ALL FOUR LOOK AS
BARB III (349)	MEANS, ALWAYS RUNNING TO ME! /SARAH/ (TOUCHING	LADY	BRITOMART'S RIBS WITH HER FINGER TIPS AND IMITATING A
BARB I SD(249)	BEHIND HIM ON HIS LEFT; THE DOOR BEHIND HIM ON	LADY	BRITOMART'S SIDE; AND A WINDOW WITH A WINDOW SEAT
BARB I SD(249)	IS VACANT AT PRESENT) WOULD HAVE, ON HIS RIGHT,	LADY	BRITOMART'S WRITING TABLE, WITH THE LADY HERSELF BUSY
BARB III (323)	HIM). /CUSINS/ (MOODILY WALKING ACROSS TO	LADY	BRITOMART'S WRITING TABLE) WHY ARE WE TWO COMING TO
BARB III SD(325)	RESPONSIBLY; AND CROSSES THE ROOM TO THE DOOR.	LADY	BRITOMART, DRESSED FOR OUT-OF-DOORS, OPENS IT BEFORE HE
BARB III (344)	OF YOUR HEALTH. (CALLING) BILTON! (HE TURNS TO	LADY	BRITOMART, WHO RISES). MY DEAR: LET US LEAVE THESE TWO
BARB I SD(271)	(LANGUIDLY) VERY WELL, MAMMA. (SHE GOES).	LADY	BRITOMART, WITH A SUDDEN FLOUNCE, GIVES WAY TO A LITTLE
BARB III (314)	(OVERWHELMED) YOU ARE SO AWFULLY STRONG-MINDED,	LADY	BRIT-- /LADY BRITOMART/ RUBBISH! (MORRISON COMES IN).
BARB III (312)	I HAVE NEVER BEFORE VENTURED TO REPROACH YOU,	LADY	BRIT; BUT HOW COULD YOU MARRY THE PRINCE OF DARKNESS..
BARB I (266)	NOT, LEAVE THE ROOM. /LOMAX/ I'M AWFULLY SORRY,	LADY	BRIT; BUT REALLY YOU KNOW, UPON MY SOUL! (HE SITS ON
BARB I (261)	FOR US? /CUSINS/ (CAUTIOUSLY) IF I MAY SAY SO,	LADY	BRIT, I THINK CHARLES HAS RATHER HAPPILY EXPRESSED WHAT
BARB III (331)	/CUSINS/ IT IS TRUE. YOU ACCUSED ME YOURSELF,	LADY	BRIT, OF JOINING THE ARMY TO WORSHIP BARBARA; AND SO I
LADY PREFACE(223)	GENERALLY PUTS AN END TO SONNETS. THAT THE DARK	LADY	BROKE SHAKESPEAR'S HEART, AS MR HARRIS WILL HAVE IT SHE
LADY PREFACE(209)	AND THE NEWS THAT HE WAS CONVINCED SHE WAS A DARK	LADY	BY TRACES OF PAINT STILL DISCERNIBLE. IN DUE COURSE HE
2TRU II (59)	GLANCES). I HAVE SENT A MESSAGE TO THE OLD	LADY	BY WIRELESS TO SAY THAT PAYMENT OF A RANSOM IS OUT OF
GETT PREFACE(233)	WOULD ACT IN THE SAME WAY. IF A ROMANTIC YOUNG	LADY	CAME INTO HER HOUSE AND PROPOSED TO ADORE HER HUSBAND
SUPR III (90)	TERRIFIED: YOU WILL FIND EVERYTHING HERE THAT A	LADY	CAN DESIRE, INCLUDING DEVILS WHO WILL SERVE YOU FROM
OVER PREFACE(156)	AND THE DIVORCE COURTS -- THAT A GENTLEMAN AND A	LADY	CANNOT BE ALONE TOGETHER INNOCENTLY. AND THAT IS
POSN (459)	IN A DIFFICULTY HERE. IF BLANCO WAS THE MAN, THE	LADY	CANT, AS A WHITE WOMAN, GIVE HIM AWAY. SHE OUGHTNT TO
KING PREFACE(154)	FOR SUCH. AND ANYONE WHO IS MORE INTERESTED IN	LADY	CASTLEMAINE'S HIPS THAN IN FOX'S FOUNDATION OF THE
KING I SD(174)	TO GO OUT, THE DUCHESS OF CLEVELAND, 39, FORMERLY	LADY	CASTLEMAINE, AND BORN BARBARA VILLIERS, BURSTS INTO THE
CAPT I (236)	THIS ANNOUNCEMENT) WHO IS THE LADY? /RANKIN/	LADY	CEECILY WAYNFLETE, HIS LORDSHIP'S SISTER-IN-LAW. /LADY
ROCK II SD(277)	AND REPORT. THEY ARE ABOUT TO SHAKE HANDS WHEN	LADY	CHAVENDER COMES IN THROUGH THE MASKED DOOR. /LADY
ROCK I SD(203)	TO LIVE IN THIS HOUSE WITH HER A MOMENT LONGER.	LADY	CHAVENDER FOLLOWS HER IN, SPEAKING AS SHE ENTERS, AND
ROCK II (276)	HAVNT YOU? /SIR ARTHUR/ QUITE. THE MOMENT I SAW	LADY	CHAVENDER I SAID " THATS THE WOMAN FOR ME." /ALOYSIA/
ROCK I (204)	MISS HANWAYS: WOULD YOU MIND-- /HILDA/ YES,	LADY	CHAVENDER (SHE RISES TO GO). /FLAVIA/ YOU NEEDNT GO,
ROCK II (234)	/SIR DEXTER/ NONSENSE! HE MUST SEE ME. DOES	LADY	CHAVENDER SUPPOSE THAT A PRIME MINISTER CAN STAND THE
ROCK II (234)	HIS GETTING A MOVE ON? /HILDA/ (MUCH WORRIED)	LADY	CHAVENDER WONT ALLOW HIM TO BE DISTURBED. SHE SAYS HIS
ROCK I (195)	COME OVER FROM SCOTLAND YARD. HE IS TALKING TO	LADY	CHAVENDER. /SIR ARTHUR/ (RISING AND MAKING FOR THE
ROCK II (277)	DAVID. /ALOYSIA/ I KNOW YOUR CLASS POINT OF VIEW,	LADY	CHAVENDER. YOU THINK IT WOULD BE A BIG CATCH FOR ME AND
ROCK I (201)	GRASPING HIS TEMPLES DISTRACTEDLY) OH DEAR! HAS	LADY	CHAVENDER'S SISTER-IN-LAW BEEN MAKING A FUSS AGAIN?
ROCK II (281)	HAPPY. GOOD OLD MOTHER-IN-LAW. (HE KISSES	LADY	CHAVENDER, WHO IS TOO ASTOUNDED TO RESIST OR SPEAK).
CAPT I SD(234)	GAVNER. (HE GOES OFFICIOUSLY INTO THE HOUSE).	LADY	CICELY AND RANKIN SIT DOWN AS BEFORE TO RECEIVE THE
CAPT III SD(279)	CENTURY OR TWO. MEANWHILE HE PRESENTS HIMSELF TO	LADY	CICELY AS A BLUNT SAILOR WHO HAS SOMETHING TO SAY TO
CAPT III (288)	WITH WHICH YOU HAVE GIVEN YOUR EVIDENCE. (	LADY	CICELY BEAMS ON HIM GRATEFULLY AND SITS DOWN
CAPT II SD(267)	TAKING HIM INTO THE GROUP BEHIND BRASSBOUND.	LADY	CICELY COMES FORWARD BETWEEN BRASSBOUND AND THE SHEIKH,
CAPT II SD(244)	TABLE AND SITS ON THE SADDLE, RATHER EXHAUSTED.	LADY	CICELY COMES TO DRINKWATER. /LADY CICELY/ WHERE IS
CAPT III SD(293)	AND IS LOOKING AT IT WITH GRIM DISTASTE WHEN	LADY	CICELY ENTERS. HIS BACK IS TOWARDS HER; AND HE DOES NOT
CAPT II (247)	LADY SIS. (HE FOLLOWS JOHNSON TO THE PATIENT.	LADY	CICELY GOES TOO). NOW, COUNT MARZO. (MARZO GROANS AS
CAPT II SD(258)	ON BRASSBOUND'S WRATH-BLURRED PERCEPTION THAT	LADY	CICELY HAS AT SOME UNNOTICED STAGE IN THE PROCEEDINGS
CAPT III (281)	SORRY, CAPTAIN KEARNEY. I AM QUITE AWARE THAT	LADY	CICELY HAS NO RIGHT WHATEVER TO GIVE ORDERS TO YOUR
CAPT II SD(253)	/BRASSBOUND/ JUSTICE ON A THIEF AND A MURDERER.	LADY	CICELY LAYS DOWN HER WORK AND LOOKS UP ANXIOUSLY. /SIR
CAPT II (256)	BRASSBOUND WITH HIS FISTS CLENCHED; SO THAT	LADY	CICELY LIFTS ONE EYE FROM HER WORK TO ASSURE HERSELF
CAPT III (286)	TO ME. /KEARNEY/ (SOMEWHAT STERNLY, SUSPECTING	LADY	CICELY OF ARISTOCRATIC ATHEISM) BUT YOU ARE A CHRISTIAN
CAPT II SD(267)	HAS HIS OTHER ARM. REDBROOK HASTENS TO RELIEVE	LADY	CICELY OF MARZO, TAKING HIM INTO THE GROUP BEHIND
CAPT III SD(282)	AND SIR HOWARD. FINALLY BRASSBOUND APPEARS WITH	LADY	CICELY ON HIS ARM. HE IS IN FASHIONABLE FROCK COAT AND
CAPT III (285)	MAY I ASK HAVE YOU HAD ANY CONVERSATION WITH	LADY	CICELY ON THIS SUBJECT? /RANKIN/ (NAIVELY) YES. (SIR
CAPT II SD(268)	AFTER A MOMENT OF STUPEFACTION, HURRIES OUT.	LADY	CICELY PUTS ON HER HAT AND PINS IT TO HER HAIR, THE
CAPT II (254)	BUT I AM NOT GOING TO STRIKE HIM. (	LADY	CICELY RELEASES HIM, AND SITS DOWN, MUCH PERPLEXED.
CAPT II SD(252)	IT. JOHNSON NODS GRAVELY, AND IS GOING OUT WHEN	LADY	CICELY RETURNS SOFTLY BY THE LITTLE DOOR AND CALLS TO
CAPT II SD(249)	TAHTS! AN THE KEPN AFRIDE TO TALK BAWCK AT ER!	LADY	CICELY RETURNS WITH REDBROOK. SHE CARRIES THE JAR FULL
CAPT II SD(246)	IS ABOUT TO ASK JOHNSON FOR AN EXPLANATION, WHEN	LADY	CICELY RETURNS THROUGH THE LITTLE DOOR, AND COMES
CAPT II SD(248)	BUT INCREDULOUS NOD). /DRINKWATER/ EAH, EAH!	LADY	CICELY RETURNS WITH JOHNSON AND REDBROOK. SHE CARRIES A
CAPT II SD(253)	COURTYARD. /JOHNSON/ RIGHT, MAAM. (HE GOES OUT).	LADY	CICELY SITS DOWN AT THE TINY TABLE, AND BEGINS
CAPT I SD(228)	(HE GOES INTO THE HOUSE WITH SOFT STEPS).	LADY	CICELY SITS DOWN ON THE BENCH UNDER THE TAMARISK.
CAPT III (284)	/RANKIN/ ON THE VERY DAY THAT SIR HOWRRD AND	LADY	CICELY STARTED ON THEIR EXCURSION I WAS APPLIED TO FOR
CAPT II (243)	NAMED-- AS IT AFTERWARDS APPEARS-- JOHNSON.	LADY	CICELY WALKS BESIDE MARZO. REDBROOK, A LITTLE
CAPT II (248)	AND NO ONE ELSE. WILL YOU BE GOOD ENOUGH TO LET	LADY	CICELY WAYNFLETE KNOW THAT. /SIR HOWARD/ (SITTING UP

CAPT II (270)	THE TWO BRITISH TRAVELLERS SIR HOWARD HALLAM AND	LADY	CICELY WAYNFLETE, IN THE CADI'S JURISDICTION. AS THE
CAPT I (226)	/SIR HOWARD/ (INTRODUCING HER) MY SISTER-IN-LAW,	LADY	CICELY WAYNFLETE, MR RANKIN. /RANKIN/ I AM GLAD TO BE
3PLA PREFACE(R30)	SINCE NEITHER JULIUS CAESAR, CLEOPATRA, NOR	LADY	CICELY WAYNFLETE HAVE ANY EXTERNAL POLITICAL CONNEXION
CAPT II (248)	YOU WILL HAVE AMPLE OPPORTUNITY FOR SPEAKING TO	LADY	CICELY YOURSELF WHEN SHE RETURNS. (DRINKWATER
CAPT I SD(235)	HOWARD; THEN WITH SOME SURPRISE AND UNEASINESS AT	LADY	CICELY. FINALLY HE COMES DOWN INTO THE MIDDLE OF THE
CAPT II (264)	EXCUSE MY MENTIONING IT. /SIR HOWARD/ MYSELF AND	LADY	CICELY. /BRASSBOUND/ WHAT! A JUDGE COMPOUND A FELONY!
CAPT I SD(234)	DRINKWATER COMES FORWARD BETWEEN SIR HOWARD AND	LADY	CICELY. /DRINKWATER/ YR HONOR'S SERVANT. (TO THE
CAPT II (247)	GOES TO MARZO). /REDBROOK/ HAPPY TO OBLIGE YOU,	LADY	CICELY. /LADY CICELY/ (SHAKING HANDS) HOWDYEDO? OF
CAPT II SD(269)	CADI COMES IMPETUOUSLY FORWARD BETWEEN HIM AND	LADY	CICELY. /THE CADI/ NOW WOE UPON THEE, SIDI EL ASSIF,
CAPT III (290)	AND THE PETTY OFFICER). /SIR HOWARD/ (TO	LADY	CICELY) CICELY: IN THE COURSE OF MY PROFESSIONAL CAREER
CAPT I (237)	ANSWER, YOU DOG, WHEN THE LADY ORDERS YOU. (TO	LADY	CICELY) DO NOT ADDRESS HIM AS MR DRINKWATER, MADAM! HE
CAPT III (288)	/DRINKWATER/ (IN INTENSE DISTRESS, APPEALING TO	LADY	CICELY) DOWNT LET EM BURN EM, LIDY. THEY DASSENT IF YOU
CAPT I (238)	YOU A SYIN ORN? WE CAWNT GOW WITHAHT YER. (TO	LADY	CICELY) NAOW, LIDY: IT WOULDNT BE FOR YR HOWN GOOD. YER
CAPT III (280)	THE BLUEJACKET REAPPEARS. /BLUEJACKET/ (TO	LADY	CICELY) PRISONERS COMING UP THE HILL, MARM. /KEARNEY/ (
CAPT III (279)	/KEARNEY/ (COMING BETWEEN SIR HOWARD AND	LADY	CICELY) WHEN WE PARTED YESTERDAY AHFTERNOON, LADY
CAPT II (263)	/BRASSBOUND/ SIDI EL ASSIF AND FIFTY MEN! (TO	LADY	CICELY) YOU WERE TOO LATE: I GAVE YOU UP MY VENGEANCE
CAPT III (276)	VERY GOOD. (HE COMES TO THE TABLE AND TAKES	LADY	CICELY'S CHAIR). /RANKIN/ OO REVOIR, LEDDY CEECILY.
CAPT NOTES (304)	INCREDIBILITIES? AND SO I AM COMPELLED TO HIDE	LADY	CICELY'S SPEECH UNDER THE VEIL OF CONVENTIONAL
CAPT I (229)	(WITH MOISTENING EYES, WHICH AT ONCE TOUCH	LADY	CICELY'S SYMPATHY) I'M RIGHT SORRY-- RIGHT SORRY. /SIR
CAPT III SD(272)	A JUG AND SOME GLASSES NEAR THE INKSTAND WHEN	LADY	CICELY'S VOICE IS HEARD AT THE DOOR, WHICH IS BEHIND
CAPT II (248)	OF IT. /BRASSBOUND/ WELL, SIR, IF SHE WERE TEN	LADY	CICELYS, SHE MUST CONSULT ME WHILE SHE IS HERE.
CAPT I (241)	SEEMS SO. /BRASSBOUND/ ON YOUR HEAD BE IT! (TO	LADY	CICELY, ACCEPTING HER HAND AT LAST) GOODNIGHT. HE GOES.
CAPT II SD(253)	YOU ARE MY PRISONER. /SIR HOWARD/ PRISONER!	LADY	CICELY, AFTER A SINGLE GLANCE UP, CONTINUES STITCHING,
CAPT II (254)	TERMS TO ME? /BRASSBOUND/ I DO. (HE TURNS TO	LADY	CICELY, AND ADDS, POINTING CONTEMPTUOUSLY TO SIR
CAPT NOTES (303)	THEN WHY NOT SPELL THE SAME WORD, WHEN UTTERED BY	LADY	CICELY, AS KERNDEWCE, TO SUGGEST THE ENGLISH
CAPT II (255)	THAT YOU ARE. DID HE TELL THE MISSIONARY THAT,	LADY	CICELY, EH? /LADY CICELY/ (SYMPATHETICALLY) POOR
CAPT II SD(257)	WRATHFULLY. THE REST, EXCEPT BRASSBOUND AND	LADY	CICELY, FOLLOW. BRASSBOUND WALKS UP AND DOWN THE ROOM,
CAPT I (226)	I AM SORRY TO HAVE TO WARN YOU, MR RANKIN, THAT	LADY	CICELY, FROM TRAVELLING IN AFRICA, HAS ACQUIRED A HABIT
CAPT III SD(283)	HE IS QUITE OUT OF COUNTENANCE-- A SHAVEN SAMSON.	LADY	CICELY, HOWEVER, IS GREATLY PLEASED WITH IT; AND THE
CAPT II SD(267)	WE HIDE HER FACE BEFORE SHE ENTERS? /SIDI/ NO.	LADY	CICELY, WHO HAS RESUMED HER TRAVELLING EQUIPMENT, AND
CAPT II SD(257)	UNCONSCIOUSLY ENTERS UPON AN UNEQUAL CONTEST WITH	LADY	CICELY, WHO SITS QUIETLY STITCHING. IT SOON BECOMES
CAPT III (283)	JOHNSON. KEARNEY SITS DOWN AGAIN, AFTER INVITING	LADY	CICELY, WITH A SOLEMN GESTURE, TO TAKE THE VACANT
CAPT II (248)	HOWARD/ CAPTAIN BRASSBOUND: IF YOU CAN FRIGHTEN	LADY	CICELY, YOU WILL CONFER A GREAT OBLIGATION ON HER
MILL I SD(137)	A ROOM WHICH SUGGESTS OPULENCE, AND IN WHICH	LADY	CLIENTS WILL LOOK THEIR BEST, EVERYTHING IS WELL DUSTED
GETT (310)	YOU MIGHT REMEMBER YOUR MANNERS, SINJON. THE	LADY	COMES FIRST. (SHE GOES BEHIND HIM AND STOOPS TO LOOK
DOCT I SD(108)	THE GLASS AND GOES TO THE WRITING-TABLE). THE	LADY	COMES IN. EMMY GOES OUT AND SHUTS THE DOOR. RIDGEON,
6CAL SD(95)	DOG'S DEATH THEY DESERVE. THEY SHALL-- A COURT	LADY	COMES IN. /THE COURT LADY/ SIR: THE QUEEN. SSSH! /THE
LADY SD(243)	ON YOUR LIFE, TAKE YOUR HANDS FROM ME. THE DARK	LADY	COMES STOOPING ALONG THE TERRACE BEHIND THEM LIKE A
INCA PROLOG (233)	ON THE TOP STEP. A FASHIONABLY DRESSED	LADY	COMES THROUGH THE CURTAINS AND CONTEMPLATES HIM WITH
LADY PREFACE(218)	FOOLS AND SCOUNDRELS, DOES NOT DATE FROM THE DARK	LADY	COMPLICATION: HE SEEMS TO HAVE BEEN BORN WITH IT. IF IN
FANY EPILOG (334)	IS THIS TRUE? /FANNY/ IT IS. I DID A MONTH WITH	LADY	CONSTANCE LYTTON; AND I'M PROUDER OF IT THAN I EVER WAS
PRES (159)	YOU ARE EXTREMELY VULGAR, GENERAL. /MITCHENER/	LADY	CORINTHIA: YOU HAVE MY PISTOL. WILL YOU HAVE THE
PRES (166)	DOOR, USHERING IN LADY CORINTHIA. /THE ORDERLY/	LADY	CORINTHIA FANSHAWE TO SPEAK TO YOU, SIR. /LADY
PRES SD(152)	OF PROTEST) NO-- MRS BANGER COMES IN FOLLOWED BY	LADY	CORINTHIA FANSHAWE. MRS BANGER IS A MASCULINE WOMAN OF
PRES (152)	SECRETARY OF THE ANTI-SUFFRAGET LEAGUE. THIS IS	LADY	CORINTHIA FANSHAWE, THE PRESIDENT OF THE LEAGUE, KNOWN
PRES (148)	LADIES LEAVE. THE ORDERLY COMES IN. /THE ORDERLY/	LADY	CORINTHIA FANSHAWE AND MRS BANGER WANT TO SEE YOU, SIR.
PRES (145)	NAMES? /THE ORDERLY/ YES, SIR. THE PRESIDENT IS	LADY	CORINTHIA FANSHAWE; AND THE SECRETARY IS MRS BANGER.
PRES (145)	ME WHEN YOUVE DONE WITH THEM. I UNDERSTAND THAT	LADY	CORINTHIA IS A VERY FASCINATING WOMAN. WHO IS SHE, BY
PRES (152)	CONFIDENCE IN THE CHAIR NEXT THE FIREPLACE.	LADY	CORINTHIA TAKES THE CHAIR ON THE OPPOSITE SIDE OF THE
PRES (167)	/MITCHENER/ AND EXTREMELY PROUD OF IT,	LADY	CORINTHIA. /LADY CORINTHIA/ (CONTEMPTUOUSLY) SHE SUITS
PRES SD(166)	SHE SAYS. THE ORDERLY OPENS THE DOOR, USHERING IN	LADY	CORINTHIA. /THE ORDERLY/ LADY CORINTHIA FANSHAWE TO
PRES (158)	DISGRACEFUL TO YOU AS THEY ARE UNDESERVED BY ME,	LADY	CORINTHIA. SUCH SUSPICIONS INVITE THE CONDUCT THEY
PRES (168)	(SHE SHUTS IT AND COMES BETWEEN MITCHENER AND	LADY	CORINTHIA). /MITCHENER/ POOR WRETCH! THE DAY AFTER
PRES (167)	AT LEAST, ARE NOT A PHILISTINE. /BALSQUITH/ NO,	LADY	CORINTHIA; BUT I'M A CONFIRMED BACHELOR. I DONT WANT A
PRES (160)	INFERNAL NONSENSE IT IS. BUT I TELL YOU PLAINLY,	LADY	CORINTHIA, THAT THERE IS ONE GAME THAT I DISLIKE MORE
PRES SD(152)	A POWERFUL VOICE AND GREAT PHYSICAL STRENGTH.	LADY	CORINTHIA, WHO IS ALSO OVER THIRTY, IS BEAUTIFUL AND
DEST (155)	EXCEPT THE LADY. I CANNOT ANSWER FOR HER; BUT NO	LADY	COULD RESIST YOU, GENERAL. /NAPOLEON/ (SOURLY,
SUPR HANDBOK(202)	FORTH AS MUCH PITY AS CAN BE COUNTED ON BY ANY	LADY	CRIMINAL. THE JUDICIAL USE OF TORTURE TO EXTORT
MRS III (228)	WHAT I'M DRIVING AT. I WANT TO SETTLE DOWN WITH A	LADY	CROFTS. I SUPPOSE YOU THINK ME VERY BLUNT, EH? /VIVIE/
MRS III (228)	APPRECIATE THE OFFER: THE MONEY, THE POSITION,	LADY	CROFTS, AND SO ON. BUT I THINK I WILL SAY NO, IF YOU
GETT PREFACE(224)	OF PICTURE POST-CARDS, AND, WHEN AN ENAMOURED	LADY	CUSTOMER DEMANDS A PORTRAIT OF HER FAVORITE ACTOR OR A
ROCK II (280)	FLESH OCCASIONALLY; BUT SHE WONT BORE ME AS A	LADY	DAUGHTER-IN-LAW WOULD. I SHALL BE ALWAYS WONDERING WHAT
LADY PREFACE(209)	WHETHER HE WAS RIGHT OR WRONG ABOUT THE DARK	LADY	DID NOT MATTER URGENTLY TO ME: SHE MIGHT HAVE BEEN
MIS. PREFACE(80)	SYMPATHY WAS IMPOSSIBLE; AND IF THE UNFORTUNATE	LADY	DID NOT PERISH, IT WAS BECAUSE, AS I NOW COMFORT MYSELF
MIS. PREFACE(42)	AMUSED AT MY TERRORS. YET WHEN THAT SAME	LADY	DISCOVERED THAT I HAD FOUND A COPY OF THE ARABIAN
2TRU III SD(94)	TALLBOYS DOWN THE PATH THROUGH THE GAP, THE	LADY	DISTRACTED AND INSISTENT, THE COLONEL ALMOST EQUALLY
MIS. (199)	I WANTED TO MARRY JOEY. WHAT DID THE POLISH	LADY	DO TO YOU? /BENTLEY/ (TURNING HIS HEAD AWAY) I'D
SUPR PREFACE(R20)	IS NO NEED FOR PERDITA TO CAPTURE FLORIZEL AS THE	LADY	DOCTOR IN ALL'S WELL THAT ENDS WELL (AN EARLY IBSENITE
ROCK I (228)	/THE LADY/ (RELEASING HIM) ONLY YOUR WIFE'S	LADY	DOCTOR. DID SHE NOT TELL YOU TO EXPECT ME? /SIR
MTH4 I (141)	ABOUT A BUTTERFLY. /THE WOMAN/ YOU SPOKE OF A	LADY	DOCTOR. THE WORD IS KNOWN HERE ONLY AS THE NAME OF A
MTH4 I (141)	YOU? /THE ELDERLY GENTLEMAN/ I HAVE NO NEED OF A	LADY	DOCTOR, THANK YOU, MADAM. /THE WOMAN/ (SHAKING HER
PYGM II (227)	ANY FUTURE TO THINK OF. NO, ELIZA: DO AS THIS	LADY	DOES: THINK OF OTHER PEOPLE'S FUTURES; BUT NEVER THINK
2TRU I SD(28)	DOES NOT THINK THE CASE SO SERIOUS AS THE	LADY	DOES. SHE COMES TO THE BEDSIDE ON THE INVALID'S LEFT.
ARMS III (62)	I HAVE RECEIVED NO FAVORS. WHY, THE YOUNG	LADY	DOESNT EVEN KNOW WHETHER I'M MARRIED OR NOT. /RAINA/ (
POSN PREFACE(408)	WEAR TWICE AS MANY PETTICOATS AS AN ORDINARY	LADY	DOES, AND SELDOM EXHIBIT MORE THAN THEIR ANKLES.
2TRU III (95)	/THE SERGEANT/ YOU WILL BE, MISS, IF THE OLD	LADY	DRIVES THE COLONEL TOO HARD. SHE HAS BEEN AT HIM ALL
CURE SD(230)	SOMEBODY UNLOCKS THE CENTRAL DOORS. A LOVELY	LADY	ENTERS WITH A BOUQUET IN HER HAND. SHE LOOKS ABOUT HER;
GENV IV SD(108)	AN ATTRACTIVE AND VERY VOLUBLE MIDDLEAGED ENGLISH	LADY	ENTERS. SHE IS DRESSED AS A DEACONESS AND CARRIES A
FANY II (293)	ONLY SHOPKEEPERS, OR BECAUSE NOBODY'S REALLY A	LADY	EXCEPT WHEN THEYRE TREATED LIKE LADIES, I DONT KNOW. (
CAPT II (243)	LAWD ELLAM AN LIDY WINEFLETE? /REDBROOK/	LADY	FAINT, EH? /DRINKWATER/ FYNT! NOT LAWKLY. WORNTED TO
SIM I (47)	/THE CLERGYMAN/ HOW CAN ONE HELP BEING ATTRACTED,	LADY	FARWATERS? THEYRE QUITE BEAUTIFUL. /LADY FARWATERS/
SIM I (49)	DO I. PRA AND PROLA THINK THEY UNDERSTAND IT; BUT	LADY	FARWATERS AND I DONT; AND WE DONT PRETEND TO. WE ARE
SIM PRO,3, (34)	/SIR CHARLES/ AH, OF COURSE: YES. YOU KNOW	LADY	FARWATERS BY SIGHT. WHICH WAY DID SHE GO? /THE E.O./ I
SIM I SD(42)	IT GLOWS. (SHE ALSO THROWS HER ARM ROUND HIM).	LADY	FARWATERS COMES FROM THE HOUSE, AND PAUSES AT THE TOP
SIM II SD(58)	THERE. VASHTI AND MAYA ARE IN THEIR SHRINES.	LADY	FARWATERS IS SITTING ON THE WESTERN STONE SEAT, WITH
SIM II SD(79)	LET HIM GO. THE PIGEON KNOWS ITS WAY HOME.	LADY	FARWATERS SINKS BACK INTO HER SEAT. THERE IS A MOMENT
SIM I SD(43)	/THE CLERGYMAN/ MOST KIND-- ER. (HE SHAKES).	LADY	FARWATERS SITS DOWN IN THE MIDDLE OF THE OTHER STONE
SIM I (48)	MAY I TRY TO EXPLAIN? /THE CLERGYMAN/ PLEASE DO,	LADY	FARWATERS. BUT I WISH YOU WOULDNT CALL ME MR
SIM I (49)	SORT OF WAY AND CALL ME IDDY. NOW GO ON,	LADY	FARWATERS. EXCUSE ME FOR INTERRUPTING YOU SO LONG.
SIM I (50)	/IDDY/ (IMPLORINGLY) TWO YOUNG HUSBANDS,	LADY	FARWATERS. OH PLEASE, TWO. /LADY FARWATERS/ I THINK
SIM II (56)	THEM; AND I HAD ONLY TWO SUCCESSES: YOU AND	LADY	FARWATERS. /HYERING/ YOU KICKED ME INTO THE SEA. /SIR
SIM I (43)	MIDDLE OF THE STONE SEAT NEAREST THE STEPS. /PRA/	LADY	FARWATERS. /LADY FARWATERS/ (SMILES AND PROFFERS HER
SIM II (56)	ME INTO THE SEA. /SIR CHARLES/ YOU MADE LOVE TO	LADY	FARWATERS. /PRA/ I HAD TO USE THAT METHOD WITH VERY
SIM I (48)	MEANING MUST BE PERFECTLY RIGHT AND RESPECTABLE,	LADY	FARWATERS; BUT IT SOUNDS LIKE A DREADFUL SORT OF
SIM I SD(44)	PROLA SITS DOWN ON SIR CHARLES'S LEFT, AND PRA ON	LADY	FARWATERS' LEFT. /LADY FARWATERS/ YOU HAVE MADE THE
SIM I (43)	I AM SO SORRY. /HYERING/ NOT AT ALL. (HE SITS ON	LADY	FARWATERS' RIGHT). /PRA/ (INDICATING THE PARAPET OF
SIM PRO,3, (34)	OH BOY, WHAT DO YOU THINK OF THIS ABODE OF LOVE?	LADY	FARWATERS, AS WHITE AS CANTERBURY VEAL, HAS FALLEN FOR
SIM I SD(43)	SOCIALLY, BUT STILL VERY MUCH HER OLD SELF.	LADY	FARWATERS, ONCE A GAUNT AND AFFECTED TOURIST VISITING
SIM II (56)	TO USE THAT METHOD WITH VERY CRUDE NOVICES; AND	LADY	FARWATERS, WITH HER ENGLISH LADYLIKE BRINGING-UP, WAS
SUPR PREFACE(R36)	BY-ENDS OF FAIRSPEECH AND HIS MOTHER-IN-LAW	LADY	FEIGNING, AND OTHER REPUTABLE GENTLEMEN AND CITIZENS,
VWOO 2 (127)	ONE SORT OR ANOTHER IN THE BIG DRAWING ROOM; BUT	LADY	FLOPPING CANT FLOP ON MORE THAN ONE, CAN SHE? /A/ (
BUOY III (42)	DO I UNDERSTAND THAT YOU PROPOSE TO MARRY THIS	LADY	FOR HER MONEY, AND ARE APOLOGIZING FOR WANTING TO MARRY
PYGM II (221)	THE LESSONS? /LIZA/ OH, I KNOW WHATS RIGHT. A	LADY	FRIEND OF MINE GETS FRENCH LESSONS FOR EIGHTEENPENCE AN
SUPR PREFACE(R37)	THE FACT THAT THE WRITER HAS OPINIONS. THE OLD	LADY	FROM COLCHESTER WAS RIGHT TO SUN HER SIMPLE SOUL IN THE
PYGM III (258)	THE MANNERS AND HABITS THAT DISQUALIFY A FINE	LADY	FROM EARNING HER OWN LIVING WITHOUT GIVING HER A FINE
2TRU III (100)	BRIGANDAGE HERE. I HAVE RESCUED A BRITISH	LADY	FROM THE CLUTCHES OF THE BRIGANDS. THE GOVERNMENT IS
MIS. (193)	REALLY A GENTLEMAN OR WAS HE NOT? HE MADE THE	LADY	GET OUT OF THE WAY OF THE PORTER AND SAID, " RESPECT

SUPR III (81)	SORT O WOMAN, ALL BUT THE COOKIN. ER NAME WAS	LADY	GLADYS PLANTAGENET, WASNT IT? /MENDOZA/ NO, SIR: SHE
DEST (180)	DOOR TO, AND COMES TO THE MIDDLE OF THE ROOM. THE	LADY	GOES A LITTLE WAY INTO THE VINEYARD TO AVOID HIM).
LADY (247)	TRIES TO KISS HER HAND). NO MORE. GO (THE DARK	LADY	GOES, CONVULSED). YOU HAVE BEEN CRUEL TO THAT POOR FOND
MIS. (153)	I'M IN A DIFFICULTY. I CANT UNDERSTAND A	LADY	GOING UP IN AN AEROPLANE FOR FAMILY REASONS. IT'S RUDE
DOCT I (95)	I OPERATED AT EASTER ON HER SISTER-IN-LAW,	LADY	GORRAN, AND FOUND SHE HAD THE BIGGEST SAC I EVER SAW:
POSN PREFACE(432)	IT INSPIRED SEVERAL APPROVING SERMONS. LATER ON,	LADY	GREGORY AND MR YEATS BROUGHT THE PLAY TO LONDON AND
POSN PREFACE(431)	THE DIRECTORS OF THE IRISH NATIONAL THEATRE,	LADY	GREGORY AND MR WILLIAM BUTLER YEATS, ROSE TO THE
POSN PREFACE(432)	CONCESSION IN RETURN FOR HAVING MY OWN WAY. BUT	LADY	GREGORY AND MR YEATS NOT ONLY WOULD NOT YIELD AN INCH,
LADY SD(239)	O-O-O-H! (HE MAKES A NOTE OF THEM). A CLOAKED	LADY	GROPES HER WAY FROM THE PALACE AND WANDERS ALONG THE
SIM II (80)	WHERE CASUALTIES HAVE BEEN COMPARATIVELY FEW.	LADY	GUSHING HAS SINCE DISAPPEARED. THERE IS GENERAL
SIM II (80)	THE MORNING POST CONTAINS AN ELOQUENT PROTEST BY	LADY	GUSHING, PRESIDENT OF THE TITLED LADIES' LEAGUE OF
MRS PREFACE(180)	PAPERS THAT HE HAD GIVEN AS HIS REASON THAT THE	LADY	HAD PARADED THE ALLUREMENTS OF VICE, AND THAT SUCH
GETT PREFACE(231)	THE FAMOUS CASE OF NELSON AND SIR WILLIAM AND	LADY	HAMILTON. THE SECRET OF THIS HOUSEHOLD OF THREE WAS NOT
GETT PREFACE(232)	THAT BOTH THE HUSBAND AND NELSON WERE DEVOTED TO	LADY	HAMILTON, BUT THAT THEY WERE ALSO APPARENTLY DEVOTED TO
GETT PREFACE(188)	AND FORMED A MENAGE A TROIS WITH SIR WILLIAM AND	LADY	HAMILTON, WAS IDOLIZED. SHELLEY MIGHT HAVE HAD AN
DEVL EPILOG (85)	WITH EXAGGERATIONS, BY BURGOYNE, CONCERNING	LADY	HARRIET ACLAND. OTHERS HAVE NARRATED HOW LADY HARRIET'S
DEVL EPILOG (86)	A COLD SHORTLY AFTER HIS RETURN TO ENGLAND; AND	LADY	HARRIET REMAINED A WIDOW UNTIL HER DEATH IN 1815. THE
DEVL EPILOG (85)	FALLING WITH HIS HEAD AGAINST A PEBBLE; AND HOW	LADY	HARRIET THEN MARRIED THE WARRIOR CHAPLAIN. ALL THIS,
DEVL EPILOG (85)	LADY HARRIET ACLAND. OTHERS HAVE NARRATED HOW	LADY	HARRIET'S HUSBAND KILLED HIMSELF IN A DUEL, BY FALLING
2TRU III (105)	APOLOGY IN THE LEAST. MY APOLOGY IS COMPLETE. THE	LADY	HAS A RIGHT TO IT. MY ACTION WAS INEXCUSABLE. BUT NO
HART I (46)	DO YOU SUPPOSE, WOMAN, THAT BECAUSE THIS YOUNG	LADY	HAS BEEN INSULTED AND NEGLECTED, YOU HAVE THE RIGHT TO
MILL IV (205)	AND HAPPINESS. BUT ALL THIS TALK IS IDLE. THIS	LADY	HAS EASILY FULFILLED THE CONDITION IMPOSED BY MY
GENV IV (113)	AND AS A COMMON BASIS OF AGREEMENT, THIS	LADY	HAS PROPOSED THE POLICY OF THE SERMON ON THE MOUNT.
NEVR II (249)	NATURAL, SIR, I'M SURE, SIR, AT YOUR AGE. THE	LADY	HAS SENT ME FOR HER BOOK, SIR. MIGHT I TAKE THE LIBERTY
NEVR IV (304)	AN ENGAGEMENT BETWEEN THESE TWO YOUNG PEOPLE. THE	LADY	HAS SOME PROPERTY, AND (LOOKING AT CRAMPTON) WILL
BULL IV (150)	BUILDING HAS BEEN WRECKED: AN AGED AND INFIRM	LADY	HAS SUFFERED AN IMPACT FOR WHICH I FEEL PERSONALLY
LADY (238)	EEN CHEAPEN THAT WHICH WE BUY EVERY DAY. THIS	LADY	HAS TO MAKE A PRESENT TO A WARDER NIGH EVERY NIGHT OF
CATH 2 (180)	BUT I NEVER SAID I ADMIRED YOUR MAJESTY. THE	LADY	HAS TWISTED MY WORDS. /VARINKA/ YOU DONT ADMIRE HER,
LADY (238)	/THE MAN/ VILLAIN: WOULDST TELL ME THAT MY DARK	LADY	HATH EVER DONE THUS BEFORE? THAT SHE MAKETH OCCASIONS
SUPR II (64)	ALL CONVINCED) TOO AMERICAN, EH? MUST THE YOUNG	LADY	HAVE A CHAPERONE? /OCTAVIUS/ IT'S NOT THAT, MALONE--
LADY PREFACE(221)	JOY THAT DERIDED SORROW? THINK OF THE POOR DARK	LADY	HAVING TO STAND UP TO THIS UNBEARABLE POWER OF
ARMS II (35)	A GENTLEMAN DOES NOT DISCUSS THE CONDUCT OF THE	LADY	HE IS ENGAGED TO WITH HER MAID. /LOUKA/ IT'S SO HARD TO
LADY PREFACE(222)	YORICK'S FAVOR SHE MUST COME AT LAST. TO THE DARK	LADY	HE MUST SOMETIMES HAVE SEEMED CRUEL BEYOND DESCRIPTION:
AUGS (282)	I'M HIS BROTHER, IDIOT. . . . THAT YOU, BLUELOO?	LADY	HERE AT LITTLE PIFFLINGTON WANTS TO SPEAK TO YOU. HOLD
MIS. (160)	HIM GREAT-- IT FRIGHTENS A WOMAN. /LINA/ THE	LADY	HERE IS YOUR WIFE, ISNT SHE? DONT YOU CARE FOR HER?
NEVR IV (295)	BUT I KNOW BETTER THAN YOU. YOUD WANT THIS YOUNG	LADY	HERE TO GIVE UP DRESSING LIKE A STAGE COLUMBINE IN THE
MTH3 (113)	TUT TUT! I AM NOT FRIVOLLING. I DID NOT ASK THE	LADY	HERE. WHICH OF YOU DID? /CONFUCIUS/ IT IS HER OFFICIAL
BARB I SD(249)	RIGHT, LADY BRITOMART'S WRITING TABLE, WITH THE	LADY	HERSELF BUSY AT IT; A SMALLER WRITING TABLE BEHIND HIM
BASH III (123)	KISS ME. MY VISAGE IS TOO SORE. /POLICEMAN/ THE	LADY	HID HIM. THIS IS A REGULAR PLANT. YOU CANNOT BE UP TO
JITT I SD(13)	OF THE ROOM OPEN. IMMEDIATELY AFTERWARDS A VEILED	LADY	HURRIES IN LIKE A HUNTED CREATURE. HE FOLLOWS HER;
MRS I (186)	KNOW THE SORT OF PERFECTLY SPLENDID MODERN YOUNG	LADY	I AM. HOW DO YOU THINK I SHALL GET ON WITH MY MOTHER..
MIS. (181)	DOING SO ONLY BY THE TIMELY ARRIVAL OF THE POLISH	LADY	I FURTHER CONFESS THAT I WAS GUILTY OF UTTERING AN
AUGS (270)	/AUGUSTUS/ OH, YOU MEAN AM I DISENGAGED. TELL THE	LADY	I HAVE JUST RECEIVED NEWS OF THE GREATEST IMPORTANCE
KING I (186)	SHALL I GIVE ONE OF THE NEW GOLDEN GUINEAS TO THE	LADY	I SHOCKED IF I MEET HER ON THE STAIRS? /NEWTON/ NO.
MIS. (151)	HAD THE FAINTEST NOTION THAT MY PASSENGER WAS A	LADY	I SHOULDNT HAVE LEFT YOU TO SHIFT FOR YOURSELF IN THAT
ROCK I (207)	GO ON LIKE THIS. PROMISE ME THAT YOU WILL SEE THE	LADY	I SPOKE TO YOU ABOUT-- IF YOU WONT SEE A PROPER DOCTOR.
MILL IV (192)	WERE NOT THAT THE PROPRIETRESS OF THIS HOTEL, THE	LADY	I TOLD YOU OF, IS A MRS FITZFASSENDEN. /ALASTAIR/ (
MRS II (213)	OR WOULDNT RATHER HAVE GONE TO COLLEGE AND BEEN A	LADY	IF I'D HAD THE CHANCE? /VIVIE/ EVERYBODY HAS SOME
KING I (170)	/SALLY/ (BURSTING IN) MR ROWLEY: THERES A	LADY	IN A COACH AT THE DOOR WANTS TO KNOW ARE YOU READY TO
PYGM II (228)	MONTHS, LEARNING HOW TO SPEAK BEAUTIFULLY, LIKE A	LADY	IN A FLORIST'S SHOP. IF YOURE GOOD AND DO WHATEVER
PYGM II (220)	WANT, MY GIRL? /THE FLOWER GIRL/ I WANT TO BE A	LADY	IN A FLOWER SHOP STEAD OF SELLING AT THE CORNER OF
SUPR I SD(41)	BACK WITH MISS RAMSDEN, A HARDHEADED OLD MAIDEN	LADY	IN A PLAIN BROWN SILK GOWN, WITH ENOUGH RINGS, CHAINS,
PYGM II (228)	OF SEVEN-AND-SIXPENCE TO START LIFE WITH AS A	LADY	IN A SHOP. IF YOU REFUSE THIS OFFER YOU WILL BE A MOST
PYGM II (222)	THE ONE FOR THE OTHER IF YOU WISH TO BECOME A	LADY	IN A SHOP. LIZA, UTTERLY BEWILDERED, STARES HELPLESSLY
PYGM II (240)	A DAINTY AND EXQUISITELY CLEAN YOUNG JAPANESE	LADY	IN A SIMPLE BLUE COTTON KIMONO PRINTED CUNNINGLY WITH
APPL I SD(215)	AND LYSISTRATA, POWERMISTRESS GENERAL, A GRAVE	LADY	IN ACADEMIC ROBES, ON HIS RIGHT. ALL RISE. THE PRIME
SUPR II (67)	SHEW ME THE DOOR FOR MARRYING THE MOST PERFECT	LADY	IN ENGLAND MERELY BECAUSE SHE HAS NO HANDLE TO HER
GETT SD(266)	THE TOWER. SHE IS A TALL, HANDSOME, SLENDER	LADY	IN HER PRIME; THAT IS, BETWEEN 36 AND 55. SHE HAS WHAT
CAPT NOTES (306)	OBJECTION OF A STREET BOY TO A BLACK MAN OR TO A	LADY	IN KNICKERBOCKERS. I HAVE MADE ONLY THE MOST
GETT SD(323)	KNOWS HOW TO MAKE THE MOST OF THEM. NOT AT ALL A	LADY	IN LESBIA'S USE OF THE TERM AS A CLASS LABEL. SHE
MRS II (217)	IT WOULDNT BE FOR HER OWN HAPPINESS. ASK ANY	LADY	IN LONDON SOCIETY THAT HAS DAUGHTERS; AND SHE'LL TELL
PPP SD(193)	THE DOOR A PEDESTAL BEARS A PORTRAIT BUST OF THE	LADY	IN PLASTER. THERE IS A FAN ON THE DRESSING-TABLE, A
DEST (163)	WITH HIM! WITH WHOM, SIR? WHY DO YOU TREAT THIS	LADY	IN SUCH A FASHION? /LIEUTENANT/ LADY! HE'S A MAN!
POSN (456)	OR IS IT A SALOON? /BLANCO/ DONT INTERRUPT A	LADY	IN THE ACT OF HANGING A GENTLEMAN. WHERES YOUR
BARB II (285)	IF SHE'D LET ME. YOURE NO GENTLEMAN, TO HIT A	LADY	IN THE FACE. (BILL, WITH GREATER THINGS MOVING IN HIM,
BASH II,1, (109)	TURN FOOTMAN, AND HIS EAGER DAME SINK THE GREAT	LADY	IN THE OBSEQUIOUS HOUSEMAID! OH, AT SUCH MOMENTS I
POSN (447)	/STRAPPER/ (CALLING TO THOSE WITHOUT) SHEW THE	LADY	IN THERE. FEEMY EVANS COMES IN. SHE IS A YOUNG WOMAN OF
APPL I SD(214)	WITH AMANDA, POSTMISTRESS GENERAL, A MERRY	LADY	IN UNIFORM LIKE THE MEN, ON HIS LEFT, AND LYSISTRATA,
JOAN 2 (80)	FOR THE DAUPHIN. /THE DUCHESS/ (TO THE NEAREST	LADY	IN WAITING) MY DEAR! HER HAIR! ALL THE LADIES EXPLODE
MIS. (164)	SURELY THERE IS NOTHING THAT CAN WOUND ANY	LADY	IN-- (HE HESITATES, NOT QUITE CONVINCED). AT LEAST--
BUOY II (19)	THEM ON THE STOEP. /THE NATIVE/ (CALLING TO THE	LADY	INSIDE) AHAIYA! MISSY'S RATIONS. PINK PERSON LOAFING
NEVR IV (297)	TO HER NOT BEARING HER FATHER'S NAME. THE OTHER	LADY	INTENDS TO GET MARRIED. /GLORIA/ (FLUSHING) MR BOHUN!
ROCK II (280)	WHAT SHE WILL SAY OR DO NEXT. IF SHE WERE A	LADY	I'D ALWAYS KNOW. I AM SO TIRED OF WELLBRED PEOPLE, AND
GENV III (81)	HIS OPINIONS. /THE COMMISSAR/ I MUST PROTEST. THE	LADY	IS A BOURGEOISE: I AM A COMMUNIST. HOW CAN THERE BE THE
FANY I SD(273)	ROCKING-CHAIR ON THE LADY'S SIDE OF THE ROOM. THE	LADY	IS A PLACID PERSON. HER HUSBAND, MR ROBIN GILBEY, NOT
JITT I (12)	A GENTLEMAN WHEN I SEE HIM, AND I FEEL SURE YOUR	LADY	IS A REAL LADY, AND ALWAYS THE SAME LADY; THOUGH OF
CAPT I SD(225)	HIS WHITE HAT AND SUMMERY RACECOURSE ATTIRE. THE	LADY	IS BETWEEN THIRTY AND FORTY, TALL, VERY GOODLOOKING,
DEST (157)	THE INNER DOOR) GO. ATTEND TO YOUR BUSINESS: THE	LADY	IS CALLING YOU. (HE GOES TO THE FIREPLACE AND STANDS
2TRU III (99)	AWARE OF THAT, SIR. I NEED NO REMINDER. THE	LADY	IS ENTITLED TO AN APOLOGY. SHE SHALL HAVE IT. /THE
HART I (51)	CAPTAIN/ WHAT DOES IT MATTER WHETHER THE YOUNG	LADY	IS EXPECTED OR NOT? SHE IS WELCOME. THERE ARE BEDS:
2TRU III (99)	FIND THEIR WAY HOME. (THE VOICE OF THE ELDERLY	LADY	IS HEARD RETURNING). OH! HERE SHE COMES AGAIN! MRS
PYGM III (249)	MOTHER'S HEAD TO ELIZA TO INDICATE TO HER WHICH	LADY	IS HER HOSTESS). ELIZA, WHO IS EXQUISITELY DRESSED,
HART I (45)	OF HOUSE, BY HEAVENS! A YOUNG AND ATTRACTIVE	LADY	IS INVITED HERE. HER LUGGAGE IS LEFT ON THE STEPS FOR
AUGS SD(279)	AND RUSHES HIM THROUGH THE DOOR. THE MOMENT THE	LADY	IS LEFT ALONE, SHE SNATCHES A SHEET OF OFFICIAL PAPER
SUPR IV (151)	FOR THIS LADY, PRAY? /TANNER/ MY DEAR SIR, THE	LADY	IS MARRIED ALREADY. HECTOR KNOWS IT; AND YET HE
PPP SD(193)	BESIDE THE CHEST OF DRAWERS PROCLAIMS THAT THE	LADY	IS MARRIED. HER OWN BOOTS ARE BESIDE THE CUPBOARD. THE
ARMS III (71)	AGES! I'M THIRTY-FOUR: I DONT SUPPOSE THE YOUNG	LADY	IS MUCH OVER SEVENTEEN. (THIS ESTIMATE PRODUCES A
CLEO III (146)	NO! (CORRECTING HIMSELF POLITELY) NOT THAT THE	LADY	IS NOT A STRIKING FIGURE IN HER OWN WAY. BUT (
KING I (175)	PATIENCE, PATIENCE, PATIENCE. MRS BASHAM: THE	LADY	IS NOT IN A STATE OF REASON: I WILL PROVE TO YOU THAT
GETT (270)	APPETITES-- /LESBIA/ AS I SAID BEFORE, AN ENGLISH	LADY	IS NOT THE SLAVE OF HER APPETITES. THAT IS WHAT AN
JOAN 2 (83)	AT THE FIGURE CUT BY THE MAGNIFICENTLY DRESSED	LADY	IS NOT WHOLLY COMPLIMENTARY). /LA TREMOUILLE/ (VERY
MIS. (154)	THE LADY. /MRS TARLETON/ DONT BE SILLY, JOHN. THE	LADY	IS ONLY JOKING, I'M SURE. (TO LINA) I SUPPOSE YOUR
GENV IV (110)	THIS COURT, SIR, IS THAT THERE ARE NO POLICE. THE	LADY	IS RAISING A POINT OF GENERAL IMPORTANCE: ONE WE MUST
NEVR II (247)	THE LEAVES TO MARK THE PAGE), THE ELDER YOUNG	LADY	IS READING IT AT PRESENT. (VALENTINE TAKES IT
LADY PREFACE(228)	BUT THE LANGUAGE OF THE SONNETS TO THE DARK	LADY	IS THE LANGUAGE OF PASSION: THEIR CRUELTY SHEWS IT.
ARMS III (57)	TO BE ORDERED ABOUT. THE WAY TO GET ON AS A	LADY	IS THE SAME AS THE WAY TO GET ON AS A SERVANT: YOUVE
APPL PREFACE(175)	THE SPLENDIDLY HONEST AND DEVOTED DIE-HARD	LADY	IS TOO SCORNFULLY TACTLESS TO HELP MUCH; BUT WITH A
OVER SD(171)	A DOOR. THE GENTLEMAN IS ON THE LADY'S RIGHT. THE	LADY	IS VERY ATTRACTIVE, WITH A MUSICAL VOICE AND SOFT
GENV III (81)	AM DEALING WITH THE FACTS. IT IS EVIDENT THAT THE	LADY	IS WRONG AS TO THE FACTS, BECAUSE THE INHABITANTS OF A
MTH2 (54)	SO. JUST SO. (LOOKING ROUND AT SAVVY) THE YOUNG	LADY	IS--? /FRANKLYN/ MY DAUGHTER, SAVVY. SAVVY COMES FROM
GETT (305)	OF NATURE. /LESBIA/ BUT IF SHE IS AN ENGLISH	LADY	IT IS HER RIGHT AND HER DUTY TO STAND OUT FOR HONORABLE
GENV III (79)	POINT OUT THAT WHATEVER IS THE MATTER WITH THIS	LADY	IT IS NOT STUPIDITY. SHE SPEAKS SEVERAL LANGUAGES. HER
CYMB V (149)	THAT CHEST HAD SMOTHERED YOU. /IACHIMO/ DEAR	LADY	IT VERY NEARLY DID. /IMOGEN/ I WILL NOT LAUGH. I MUST
DOCT IV (158)	YOU ARE HIS BEST PHYSICIAN AFTER ALL, DEAR	LADY	. AN INSPIRATION! CORNWALL: OF COURSE, YES, YES, YES.
LADY PREFACE(207)	HELD FATAL TO THE STRONGEST CLAIM TO BE THE DARK	LADY	. AND SO, UNLESS IT CAN BE SHEWN THAT SHAKESPEAR'S

SUPR HANDBOK	(178)	DEMAND FOR A PERFECT GENTLEMAN AND A PERFECT	LADY	. AND, AFTER ALL, NO MARKET DEMAND IN THE WORLD TAKES
PYGM V	(276)	WOULD YOU MIND? /DOOLITTLE/ AS YOU WISH,	LADY	. ANYTHING TO HELP HENRY TO KEEP HER OFF MY HANDS. (HE
FOUN	(217)	TO COME HERE AND TALK UP TO US AS IF YOU WAS A	LADY	. BE OFF WITH YOU; AND BE ASHAMED OF YOURSELF, YOU
GETT	(311)	PUT IN. /LEO/ NOT ANY NUMBER OF LADIES. ONLY ONE	LADY	. BESIDES, THAT CREATURE WASNT A LADY. /REGINALD/ YOU
2TRU II	(59)	CERTAINLY DO IF THEY DARE LAY A HAND ON A BRITISH	LADY	. BUT I CANNOT COUNTENANCE SUCH A CONCESSION TO
SUPR IV	(146)	I DARESAY YOU ARE AN AMIABLE AND EXCELLENT YOUNG	LADY	. BUT I HAVE OTHER VIEWS FOR HECTOR. /VIOLET/ HECTOR
VWOO 1	(118)	DE LUCKS AND ALL THAT, THAT I AM AN EDUCATED	LADY	. BUT I'M NOT. /A/ I NEVER SUPPOSED FOR A MOMENT THAT
KING I	(199)	HAS FRENCH BRAINS AND MANNERS, AND IS ALWAYS A	LADY	. BUT THEY ARE NOW MY FRIENDS ONLY: AFFECTIONATE
MIS.	(173)	WITH PAIN-- THEN GO TO THE GYMNASIUM WITH THAT	LADY	. BUT YOULL BE MORE COMFORTABLE IN JAIL. /LINA/ (
MILL III	(180)	POSTCARD TO THE HOME OFFICE. /THE MAN/ LOOK HERE,	LADY	. CANT WE ARRANGE THIS? WHAT GOOD WILL IT DO YOU TO
KING I	(212)	MEN. I AM NOT A HEATHEN GODDESS: I AM A CHRISTIAN	LADY	. CHARLES ALWAYS ENCOURAGES INFIDELS AND LIBERTINES TO
BUOY IV	(58)	/SIR FERDINAND/ YES, IF YOU CAN FIND THE	LADY	. DRESS BETTER; AND OIL YOUR HAIR. BABZY COMES BACK
PPP	(206)	US. GOODNIGHT, PHYLLIS. /PHYLLIS/ GOODNIGHT, MY	LADY	. GOODNIGHT, SIR. SHE RETIRES. /MAGNESIA/ AND NOW,
LADY	(240)	SPEECH WITH YOU HERE? /THE MAN/ WHY, YES, FAIR	LADY	. HAVE YOU FORGOT IT? /THE LADY/ I HAVE WALKED IN MY
JITT II	(31)	I HOPE TO FIND YOU QUITE WELL THEN, DEAR	LADY	. HE KISSES HER HAND, AND GOES OUT. WHEN HE HAS GONE,
HART I	(47)	GUINNESS/ THATS NO TALK TO OFFER TO A YOUNG	LADY	. HERE, DUCKY, HAVE SOME TEA; AND DONT LISTEN TO HIM (
BUOY II	(18)	THAT TO YOU? /HE/ IF YOU HAVE, HE IS ONLY A MAN.	LADY	. I ALSO AM A MAN. BUT YOU DO NOT LOOK MARRIED. HAVE
ARMS I	(12)	MAN/ AUSTRIAN! NOT I. DONT HATE ME, DEAR YOUNG	LADY	. I AM A SWISS, FIGHTING MERELY AS A PROFESSIONAL
ARMS I	(11)	STIFF MILITARY CARRIAGE) GOOD EVENING, GRACIOUS	LADY	. I AM SORRY TO INTRUDE; BUT THERE IS A SERB HIDING ON
MIS. PREFACE	(32)	GUIDANCE. " YOU OUGHT TO GIVE A PRIZE" SAID THE	LADY	. I ASKED IF THERE WAS A PRIZE FOR GOOD CONDUCT. AS I
DEST	(155)	AT YOUR EXCELLENCY'S DISPOSAL, EXCEPT THE	LADY	. I CANNOT ANSWER FOR HER; BUT NO LADY COULD RESIST
2TRU II	(60)	AT THE SMITER. /TALLBOYS/ ONE OF THEM WAS A	LADY	. I HAPPENED TO MENTION YOUR BROTHER'S NAME; AND SHE
6CAL	(104)	AND LODGED IN A KENNEL. /THE KING/ BE MERCIFUL,	LADY	. I HAVE ASKED YOU FOR MANY FAVORS, AND HAD THEM
GETT	(261)	YOU ARE A VERY AFFABLE LADY, MAAM, FOR A BISHOP'S	LADY	. I HAVE KNOWN BISHOPS' LADIES THAT WOULD FAIRLY
CAPT NOTES	(303)	FOR EXAMPLE MY AMERICAN CAPTAIN AND MY ENGLISH	LADY	. I HAVE SPELT THE WORD CONDUCE, AS UTTERED BY THE
2TRU III	(97)	PATIENT/ YOU FOOL, THERE IS NO SUCH THING AS A	LADY	. I HAVE THE INSTINCTS OF A GOOD HOUSEKEEPER: I WANT TO
ARMS I	(20)	OWN HAND) BETTER NOT TOUCH MY HAND, DEAR YOUNG	LADY	. I MUST HAVE A WASH FIRST. /RAINA/ (TOUCHED) THAT IS
ARMS II	(41)	BUT PHILOSOPHICAL) AT ONCE, GRACIOUS	LADY	. I ONLY CAME TO THANK YOU AND RETURN THE COAT YOU LENT
ARMS I	(19)	MONTH IN VIENNA. /THE MAN/ I SAW THAT, DEAR YOUNG	LADY	. I SAW AT ONCE THAT YOU KNEW THE WORLD. /RAINA/ HAVE
KING I	(215)	IS THE LOVELIEST AND CLEVEREST. SHE IS ALSO A	LADY	. I SHOULD LIKE TO HAVE PORTRAITS OF ALL THREE AS THEY
DOCT I	(83)	WHO TO KEEP OUT, AND THAT REMINDS ME OF THE POOR	LADY	. I THINK HE OUGHT TO SEE HER. SHE'S JUST THE KIND THAT
GENV IV	(114)	CASES-- /DEACONESS/ OH, I WAS NOT AN AMIABLE	LADY	. I WAS A PERFECT FIEND, JEALOUS, QUARRELSOME, FULL OF
GETT	(340)	TO MAKE YOU THINK THE LETTERS WERE FROM A FINE	LADY	. I WROTE ON CHEAP PAPER; AND I NEVER COULD SPELL. /THE
MRS II	(216)	OF IT. BUT OF COURSE IT'S NOT WORTH WHILE FOR A	LADY	. IF YOU TOOK TO IT YOUD BE A FOOL; BUT I SHOULD HAVE
MRS IV	(250)	LIKES GOOD SOCIETY, AND HAS THE AIR OF BEING A	LADY	. IMAGINE ME IN A CATHEDRAL TOWN! WHY, THE VERY ROOKS
PPP	(193)	DOES IT NOT? /PHYLLIS/ ELEVEN AT NIGHT, MY	LADY	. IN THE MORNING IT MEANS HALF-PAST TWO; SO IF YOU HEAR
ARMS III	(52)	/BLUNTSCHLI/ (PROMPTLY) INSTINCT, DEAR YOUNG	LADY	. INSTINCT, AND EXPERIENCE OF THE WORLD. /RAINA/ (
ARMS I	(14)	HIM). UGH! DONT DO THINGS SO SUDDENLY, GRACIOUS	LADY	. IT'S MEAN TO REVENGE YOURSELF BECAUSE I FRIGHTENED
ROCK II	(273)	WITH AN ARM OF IRON) LADIES BE DAMNED! YOURE NO	LADY	. (HE COMES PAST THE TABLE TO SIR ARTHUR'S RIGHT). SIR
CLEO III	(148)	US. /APOLLODORUS/ I SHALL NOT NEED THEIR HELP,	LADY	. (HE DRAWS HIS SWORD). NOW, SOLDIER: CHOOSE WHICH
DOCT IV	(170)	DO: YOU SHALL HAVE NO TROUBLE. GOODBYE, MY DEAR	LADY	. (HE GOES). /RIDGEON/ GOODBYE. (HE OFFERS HIS HAND).
BARB I	(263)	NONSENSE! SHEW HIM UP. /MORRISON/ YES, MY	LADY	. (HE GOES). /LOMAX/ DOES MORRISON KNOW WHO IT IS?
ARMS III	(54)	THATS THE SWISS NATIONAL CHARACTER, DEAR	LADY	. (HE RETURNS TO THE TABLE). /RAINA/ OH, I WISH I HAD
2TRU III	(97)	SAY IT, MOPS; BUT YOU HAVE NOT THE INSTINCTS OF A	LADY	. (HE SITS DOWN MOODILY ON A STONE A LITTLE WAY UP THE
MIS.	(173)	TO NINE AS WELL. /TARLETON/ DONT SWEAR. THATS A	LADY	. (HE THROWS THE PISTOL ON THE WRITING TABLE). /THE
BARB III	(314)	GO AND LET HIM IN. /MORRISON/ THANK YOU, MY	LADY	. (HE WITHDRAWS). /LADY BRITOMART/ CHILDREN: GO AND
NEVR IV	(297)	YOURSELF IN THE DIRECTION INDICATED BY THIS YOUNG	LADY	. (M'COMAS IS ABOUT TO PROTEST). NO: DONT INTERRUPT
DOCT I	(91)	HE'LL WAIT ALL RIGHT. HE'S TALKING TO THE POOR	LADY	. (SHE GOES OUT). /SIR PATRICK/ WELL? WHAT IS IT?
HART I	(51)	RIGHT. I'LL TELL THEM ALL THEY MUST CALL YOU MY	LADY	. (SHE TAKES HER TRAY OUT WITH UNDISTURBED PLACIDITY).
DEST	(155)	IN MY OPINION, EXCELLENCY, A FINE FIGURE OF A	LADY	. (SLYLY) SHALL I LAY THE TABLE FOR HER COLLATION
2TRU III	(101)	/AUBREY/ I INVENTED THE BRIGANDS AND THE BRITISH	LADY	. (TO TALLBOYS) BY THE WAY, COLONEL, THE IMPRESSIVE
MILL IV	(201)	FEMININE-- WHEN IT IS HER CUE TO PLAY THE PERFECT	LADY	. LONG BEFORE WE CAN GET THE CASE INTO THE LISTS THE
PYGM II	(220)	CALLED A BAGGAGE WHEN IVE OFFERED TO PAY LIKE ANY	LADY	. MOTIONLESS, THE TWO MEN STARE AT HER FROM THE OTHER
LADY	(240)	HOW DO YOU DARE? /THE MAN/ BE NOT WROTH WITH ME,	LADY	. MY MISTRESS IS A MARVELLOUS PROPER WOMAN. BUT SHE
ARMS III	(61)	HASNT TOLD ME. BETTER NOT INTERFERE, DEAR YOUNG	LADY	. NO HARM WILL BE DONE: IVE OFTEN ACTED AS SWORD
SUPR III	(91)	JUAN/ NO MORE REAL DEVILS THAN YOU WILL BE A REAL	LADY	. NOTHING IS REAL HERE. THAT IS THE HORROR OF
ARMS II	(37)	/LOUKA/ THAT SORT OF APOLOGY MAY SATISFY A	LADY	. OF WHAT USE IS IT TO A SERVANT? /SERGIUS/ (RUDELY
BARB I	(266)	BARBARA: YOU HAVE HAD THE EDUCATION OF A	LADY	. PLEASE LET YOUR FATHER SEE THAT; AND DONT TALK LIKE A
BASH II,1,	(104)	A CONSUMMATION DEVOUTLY TO BE WISHED BY ANY	LADY	. PRAY, DO YOU WISH THIS MAN TO COME AGAIN? /LYDIA/
PPP SD	(195)	IN HIS RIGHT HAND BODE ILL FOR THE SLEEPING	LADY	. PROVIDENTIALLY SHE SNEEZES ON THE VERY BRINK OF
DOCT I SD	(109)	A GOOD DEAL OF THE ELEGANCE AND DIGNITY OF A FINE	LADY	. RIDGEON, WHO IS EXTREMELY SUSCEPTIBLE TO THE BEAUTY
MILL I	(164)	(TO ALASTAIR) YOUR WIFE IS A MOST EXTRAORDINARY	LADY	. /ALASTAIR/ (UTTERS A STIFLED HOWL)! /PATRICIA/ HE
FOUN	(216)	RADICALISM TO YOURSELF IN THE PRESENCE OF THIS	LADY	. /ANASTASIA/ WHY DO YOU ALLOW YOUR CLERK TO BE A
MIS.	(180)	I THINK IT'S S, Z, C, Z-- BETTER SAY THE POLISH	LADY	. /BENTLEY/ (WRITING) " THE POLISH LADY"? /TARLETON/
CAPT III	(289)	/KEARNEY/ THE BOOKS WILL BE HANDED OVER TO THE	LADY	. /DRINKWATER/ (IN A SMALL VOICE) THENKYER, LIDY. (HE
PYGM III	(258)	I SEE. THE PROBLEM OF HOW TO PASS HER OFF AS A	LADY	. /HIGGINS/ I'LL SOLVE THAT PROBLEM. IVE HALF SOLVED IT
HART II	(109)	UP QUICKLY) I SHALL HAVE TO BUY A LOT OF TOOLS,	LADY	. /LADY UTTERWORD/ NONSENSE: YOU HAVE YOUR BURGLING
HART I	(71)	ADDY. /HECTOR/ (APPARENTLY SURPRISED) NOT THIS	LADY	. /LADY UTTERWORD/ (SMILING) WHY NOT? /HECTOR/ (
GETT	(347)	A WITNESS AND GO OFF TO BRIGHTON WITH ANOTHER	LADY	. /LESBIA/ THATS WHAT YOU CALL PROVIDING FOR
BASH II,1,	(101)	WHOSE, DID YOU SAY? /BASHVILLE/ CASHEL'S, MY	LADY	. /LYDIA/ LUCIAN: YOUR HAND-- A CHAIR-- /BASHVILLE/
PYGM II	(226)	DONT WANT TO TALK GRAMMAR. I WANT TO TALK LIKE A	LADY	. /MRS PEARCE/ WILL YOU PLEASE KEEP TO THE POINT, MR
MIS.	(178)	/GUNNER/ I NEVER SAID ANYTHING AGAINST THE	LADY	. /MRS TARLETON/ OH, LISTEN TO THAT! /BENTLEY/ WHAT A
MIS.	(154)	DUFFER; BUT THEN I'M DREAMING YOU AS WELL AS THE	LADY	. /MRS TARLETON/ DONT BE SILLY, JOHN. THE LADY IS ONLY
DEST	(156)	/GIUSEPPE/ YES, EXCELLENCY. THE STRANGE	LADY	. /NAPOLEON/ STRANGE? WHERE DOES SHE COME FROM?
MILL I	(153)	THANK YOU. I HOPE I AM NOT INTERRUPTING THIS	LADY	. /PATRICIA/ NOT AT ALL. DONT MIND ME. /SAGAMORE/ (
ARMS I	(19)	YOU LIVE IN GREAT LUXURY INDEED, DEAR YOUNG	LADY	. /RAINA/ DO YOU KNOW WHAT A LIBRARY IS? /THE MAN/ A
ARMS III	(71)	HAVE PUT EVERYTHING RIGHT, I HOPE, GRACIOUS YOUNG	LADY	. /RAINA/ (GOING TO THE TABLE TO FACE HIM) I QUITE
SUPR IV	(170)	TAKE CARE. SOMETHING'S THE MATTER WITH THE	LADY	. /RAMSDEN/ WHAT DOES THIS MEAN? /VIOLET/ (RUNNING
GETT	(311)	ONLY ONE LADY. BESIDES, THAT CREATURE WASNT A	LADY	. /REGINALD/ YOU SHUT YOUR HEAD, LEO. THIS IS A GENERAL
DOCT I	(93)	SHEW MR WALPOLE UP. /EMMY/ HE'S TALKING TO THE	LADY	. /RIDGEON/ (EXASPERATED) DID I NOT TELL YOU-- EMMY
DOCT I	(95)	FOLLOWING ME. HE'S STAYED DOWN TO TALK TO THAT	LADY	. /RIDGEON/ (EXPLODING) I TOLD YOU TO TELL THAT LADY--
CAPT II	(248)	ROUGH, SIR HOWARD. I HAVE NO WISH TO FRIGHTEN THE	LADY	. /SIR HOWARD/ CAPTAIN BRASSBOUND: IF YOU CAN FRIGHTEN
PYGM I	(207)	YOUR FLOWERS. /THE FLOWER GIRL/ THANK YOU KINDLY,	LADY	. /THE DAUGHTER/ MAKE HER GIVE YOU THE CHANGE. THESE
PPP	(204)	MAGNESIA TENDERLY) IT LOOKS LIKE IT. HOLD UP, MY	LADY	. /THE DOCTOR/ NOT A MOMENT MUST BE LOST. THE PATIENT
LION II	(135)	ENOUGH. I'M TO BE THROWN TO THE LIONS WITH THE	LADY	. /THE EDITOR/ THEN GET OUT OF THE WAY AND HOLD YOUR
MRS I SD	(181)	TAKES STOCK OF THE PLACE; AND SEES THE YOUNG	LADY	. /THE GENTLEMAN/ (TAKING OFF HIS HAT) I BEG YOUR
PPP	(194)	HAS HAPPENED TO HIM. YOUR BED IS READY, MY	LADY	. /THE LADY/ THANK YOU, PHYLLIS. (SHE RISES AND
PPP	(193)	THE CLOCK STRIKE, PHYLLIS? /PHYLLIS/ SIXTEEN, MY	LADY	. /THE LADY/ THAT MEANS ELEVEN O'CLOCK, DOES IT NOT?
LADY	(237)	SIR, YOU ARE A BETTER PAYMASTER THAN YOUR DARK	LADY	. /THE MAN/ WOMEN ARE THRIFTY, MY FRIEND. /THE
PYGM I	(207)	I CAN GIVE YOU CHANGE FOR A TANNER, KIND	LADY	. /THE MOTHER/ (TO CLARA) GIVE IT TO ME. (CLARA PARTS
SUPR III	(90)	ALL, ALL! /DON JUAN/ AND YET WE MEET HERE, DEAR	LADY	. /THE OLD WOMAN/ LISTEN TO ME. MY FATHER WAS SLAIN BY
PPP	(204)	BACK WITH A DOCTOR. /PHYLLIS/ THE MEDICAL MAN, MY	LADY	. /THE POLICEMAN/ A POISON CASE, SIR. /THE DOCTOR/ DO
SIM PRO,1,	(22)	E.O./ VERY WELL. BACK YOU GO BY THE NEXT BOAT, MY	LADY	. /THE Y.W./ (UNMOVED) AT THIS HOUR OF THE MORNING
MILL II	(176)	I WANT TO MARRY YOU. /THE DOCTOR/ NOTHING DOING,	LADY	. SCIENCE IS MY BRIDE. /EPIFANIA/ YOU CAN HAVE SCIENCE
HART II	(108)	/THE BURGLAR/ I'M TOO OLD TO BE GIV A HIDING,	LADY	. SEND FOR THE POLICE AND HAVE DONE WITH IT. IT'S ONLY
SIM PRO,3,	(31)	HIS SEAT) YOU SHOULD NOT BE RUDE TO THE POOR	LADY	. SHE IS ENGLISH, AND DOESNT UNDERSTAND. /THE
HART I SD	(44)	IN THE PANTRY WITHOUT NOTICING THE YOUNG	LADY	. SHE PLACES THE BOTTLES ON THE SHELF AND FILLS HER
LADY	(237)	WHAT I SAY. I KEEP TRYST HERE TONIGHT WITH A DARK	LADY	. SHE PROMISED TO BRIBE THE WARDER. I GAVE HER THE
SUPR IV	(143)	TAKEN SERIOUSLY. /STRAKER/ I'LL GO TELL THE YOUNG	LADY	. SHE SAID YOUD PREFER TO STAY HERE (HE TURNS TO GO UP
AUGS	(270)	THERES A FEMALE DOWNSTAIRS: WHAT YOU MIGHT CALL A	LADY	. SHE WANTS TO KNOW CAN YOU SEE HER IF I LET HER UP.
JOAN PREFACE	(22)	AND PLAYWRIGHTS HAVE PRETENDED: A ROMANTIC YOUNG	LADY	. SHE WAS A THOROUGH DAUGHTER OF THE SOIL IN HER
2TRU III	(82)	WHITE WOMAN WITHIN FIFTY MILES; AND SHE'S A REAL	LADY	. SHE WOULDNT LOOK AT YOU. /THE SERGEANT/ WELL, THATS A
FOUN	(221)	/BRABAZON/ QUITE OUT OF THE QUESTION, MY DEAR	LADY	. SIR CARDONIUS WILL TELL YOU THAT YOU ARE TOO YOUNG,
BUOY II	(21)	/HE/ AND I CAN STAND ANYTHING EXCEPT AN ENGLISH	LADY	. THAT GAME IS UP, DANCING AND GAMBLING, DRINKING
SUPR IV	(149)	YOUVE IMPERSONATED ME AND STOLEN A MARCH ON THIS	LADY	. THATS DISAWNERABLE. /MALONE/ (THREATENINGLY) NOW YOU
GETT PREFACE	(232)	THE CLERGYMAN, IS THE MORE SUITABLE MATE FOR THE	LADY	. THE CLERGYMAN, WHO HAS A TEMPER, IS FIRST TEMPTED TO
ANNA	(294)	TELL HIM TO LET GO. /STRAMMFEST/ RELEASE THE	LADY	. THE SOLDIERS TAKE THEIR HANDS OFF HER. ONE OF THEM

ARMS II (32) HIS WAY INTO THE BEDROOM OF A YOUNG BULGARIAN LADY . THE YOUNG LADY WAS ENCHANTED BY HIS PERSUASIVE
LADY PREFACE(220) OF THE DESPAIR OF A HEART BROKEN BY THE DARK LADY . THERE IS AN IRREPRESSIBLE GAIETY OF GENIUS WHICH
BUOY II (18) WHATS YOUR BUSINESS? /HE/ NO BUSINESS, DEAR LADY . TREAT ME AS A PASSING TRAMP. /SHE/ WELL, PASS DOUBLE
2TRU II (61) /AUBREY/ OH NO, NO, NO, MOPS. DAMN IT, BE A LADY . WHATS THE MATTER, SWEETIE? /THE COUNTESS/ YOU
HART I (49) OUT A CUP GREEDILY. /THE CAPTAIN/ YOUR TEA, YOUNG LADY . WHAT! ANOTHER LADY! I MUST FETCH ANOTHER CUP (HE
JITT III (56) IT WAS ALWAYS THE SAME WOMAN, AND THAT SHE WAS A LADY . WHEN SHE RAN AWAY SHE TOOK THAT BOOK WITH HER: YOU
LADY PREFACE(209) OF MISTRESS MARY FITTON WITH THE DARK LADY . WHETHER HE WAS RIGHT OR WRONG ABOUT THE DARK LADY DID
PRES (157) DEAR LADY! /LADY CORINTHIA/ I AM NOT YOUR DEAR LADY . YOU ARE NOT THE FIRST MAN WHO HAS CONCLUDED THAT
SIM PRO,1, (22) I-- ER-- (COLLECTING HIMSELF) LOOK HERE, YOUNG LADY . YOU HAVE TO ANSWER QUESTIONS HERE, NOT TO ASK THEM.
JOAN EPILOG (160) /THE SOLDIER/ (CHEERFULLY) NO GREAT TORMENT, LADY . YOU SEE I WAS USED TO WORSE. /CHARLES/ WHAT! WORSE
BARB III (314) BRITOMART/ ANNOUNCE HIM. /MORRISON/ THANK YOU, MY LADY . YOU WONT MIND MY ASKING, I HOPE. THE OCCASION IS IN A
CAPT III (280) WAYNFLETE, HE IS NOT FORBIDDEN TO TAKE ANY OTHER LADY . YOURS IS AN EXTRAORDINAIRY COUNTRY-- TO AN AMERRICAN.
2TRU II (58) HIS OWN INITIATIVE, OR CALL YOU ANYTHING BUT " MY LADY ." IF THERE IS ANYTHING WE CAN DO FOR YOU WE SHALL BE
SUPR III (139) (TO OCTAVIUS) YOU, SIR, OFTEN BROUGHT THIS LADY (ANN) AND HER MOTHER TO DINNER ON YOUR WAY TO THE
CLEO III (152) /APOLLODORUS/ (TO THE PORTERS) FOLLOW THIS LADY (INDICATING FTATATEETA); AND OBEY HER. THE PORTERS
ARMS III (68) TO? /RAINA/ TO NEITHER OF THEM. THIS YOUNG LADY (INTRODUCING LOUKA, WHO FACES THEM ALL PROUDLY) IS THE
GENV III (70) ONLY A JEW COULD MENTION SUCH A THING TO A LADY (SHE GIVES UP THE STRUGGLE AND RESUMES HER SEAT). THE
DEST (163) /NAPOLEON/ NONSENSE, SIR. THIS IS CERTAINLY A LADY (SHE SUDDENLY DROPS HIS ARM AND BLUSHES AGAIN); AND
SUPR III (138) (TO HECTOR) YOU, SIR, USED TO COME WITH THIS LADY (VIOLET) TO LUNCH. (TO OCTAVIUS) YOU, SIR, OFTEN
KING I (167) /NEWTON/ I HAD FORGOTTEN TO MAKE THIS LADY KNOWN TO YOU, GENTLEMEN. MRS BASHAM: MY HOUSEKEEPER,
KING I (199) THE JEALOUS LADY WOULDNT LEAVE UNTIL THE FRENCH LADY LEFT; AND THE PLAYER WOMAN IS AS CURIOUS AS A MAGPIE
HART I SD(44) BOTTLES. AS SHE RETURNS WITH THESE, THE YOUNG LADY LETS HER BOOK DROP, AWAKENING HERSELF, AND STARTLING
MRS I SD(181) KEEPS THE SUN OFF THE HAMMOCK, IN WHICH A YOUNG LADY LIES READING AND MAKING NOTES, HER HEAD TOWARDS THE
MILL III (180) /THE WOMAN/ HUSH, HUSH, JOE: DONT SPEAK TO THE LADY LIKE THAT. YOU SEE, MAAM: THERES NOT A SOUL. /EPIFANIA/
ARMS II (33) THE WAR LIKE A KNIGHT IN A TOURNAMENT WITH HIS LADY LOOKING DOWN AT HIM! /RAINA/ AND YOU HAVE NEVER BEEN
DEST (173) HAND UNFOLDING THE PAPER INVOLUNTARILY STOPS. THE LADY LOOKS AT HIM ENIGMATICALLY, IN TRANQUIL SILENCE. HE
BASH I (97) WILTSTOKEN'S HOLY BELL HEARKENING, WILTSTOKEN'S LADY LOVING BREATHLESSLY. /MELLISH/ THE LADY OF THE CASTLE!
PPP (194) /PHYLLIS/ (EMPHASIZING THE TITLE) LADY MAGNESIA FITZTOLLEMACHE. /LADY MAGNESIA/ IN CASE WE
PPP SD(194) I WILL. PHYLLIS WITHDRAWS, OVERCOME BY EMOTION. LADY MAGNESIA SWITCHES OFF THE ELECTRIC LIGHT, AND
3PLA PREFACE(R20) TO PRETEND THAT THE HERO IS IN LOVE WITH A YOUNG LADY MANUFACTURED FOR THE PURPOSE, AND TO IMPLY THAT IT IS
BASH I (95) LIVES IN THIS CASTLE! OWNS THIS PARK! A LADY MARRY A PRIZEFIGHTER! IMPOSSIBLE. AND YET THE
DOCT PREFACE(53) INOCULATION, BY WHICH VOLTAIRE, CATHERINE II AND LADY MARY WORTLEY MONTAGU SO CONFIDENTLY EXPECTED TO SEE THE
SUPR III (119) NOR CONDEMNED BY PUBLIC OPINION. THAT SUCH A LADY MAY BE MORE LAW ABIDING THAN THE POOR GIRL WHOM WE USED
LADY PREFACE(222) THOUGH SHE PAINT AN INCH THICK (WHICH THE DARK LADY MAY HAVE DONE), TO YORICK'S FAVOR SHE MUST COME AT
LADY PREFACE(222) DREAM AGAIN." WHICH IS VERY LOVELY; BUT THE DARK LADY MAY HAVE HAD THAT VICE IN HER EARS WHICH CLOTEN
GENV III (72) IS AS GOOD AS ANOTHER. I AM NOT A JEW; BUT THE LADY MAY SHOOT ME BECAUSE I AM A COMMUNIST. /THE WIDOW/ HOW
APPL I (215) IN REGARD TO THE PREROGATIVE; AND I FIND THE TWO LADY MEMBERS, THE POSTMISTRESS GENERAL AND THE POWERMISTRESS
SUPR I (32) /ANN/ TEMPTED! JACK! /TANNER/ YES, MY DEAR LADY MEPHISTOPHELES, TEMPTED. YOU WERE INSATIABLY CURIOUS AS
MIS. PREFACE(102) KNOW HOW. THEY TRY TO REFORM SOCIETY AS AN OLD LADY MIGHT TRY TO RESTORE A BROKEN DOWN LOCOMOTIVE BY
APPL II SD(265) THE PROCESSION, FOLLOWED IMMEDIATELY BY THE TWO LADY MINISTERS, THE QUEEN RISES AS PROTEUS TURNS TO HER.
LADY PREFACE(223) WIDE WORLD DREAMING OF THINGS TO COME." THE DARK LADY MOST LIKELY THOUGHT THIS SIDE OF HIM INSUFFERABLY
6CAL (95) DEAR CHILD: WELCOME. /THE PRINCE/ HOW DO YOU, LADY MOTHER? (HE KISSES HER HAND). /THE KING/ (
ROCK I SD(224) I DIDNT KNOW THERE WAS ANYONE IN THE ROOM. THE LADY NEITHER MOVES NOR SPEAKS. SHE LOOKS AT HIM WITH
CAPT III (289) ITALIAN) WHAT? WHATS THAT YOU SAY? /MARZO/ NO LADY NURSE DAM RASCAL. ONLY SAINT. SHE SAINT. SHE GET ME TO
SUPR III (91) ENTIRELY DAMNED. WE CULTIVATE OUR HEARTS. AS A LADY OF 77, YOU WOULD NOT HAVE A SINGLE ACQUAINTANCE IN
GENV I SD(37) OPENS IN HIS FACE; AND A WIDOW COMES IN: A CREOLE LADY OF ABOUT FORTY, WITH THE REMAINS OF A GORGEOUS AND
METH PREFACE(R39) SPIRIT" AS POINTEDLY AS HE PLEASED; OUR SOVEREIGN LADY OF ELIZABETH MIGHT RATIFY THE ARTICLE AGAIN AND AGAIN;
MIS. (151) VANISHES. I'M PROUD TO RECEIVE IN MY HOUSE A LADY OF EVIDENT REFINEMENT AND DISTINCTION. ALLOW ME TO
2TRU PREFACE(4) TO BE A HOUSEMAID AND CAN BE HERSELF; BUT THE LADY OF FASHION NEVER HAS A MOMENT OFF: SHE HAS TO BE
CLEO NOTES (208) NOT THE TYPICAL GREEK-CULTURED, EDUCATED EGYPTIAN LADY OF HER TIME. TO REPRESENT HER BY ANY SUCH TYPE WOULD BE
BUOY III (34) /MRS SECONDBORN/ NOTHING COULD MAKE A REAL LADY OF HER. SHE DRESSES LIKE A LADY, AND CAN TALK LIKE A
FANY I SD(275) VISITOR). MISS DELANEY COMES IN. SHE IS A YOUNG LADY OF HILARIOUS DISPOSITION, VERY TOLERABLE GOOD LOOKS,
FANY EPILOG (334) SAY IT'S LIKE ONE OF SHAKESPEAR'S-- HAMLET OR THE LADY OF LYONS, YOU KNOW-- BUT STILL, A FIRSTRATE LITTLE BIT
PYGM IV (265) FLOWERS. I DIDNT SELL MYSELF. NOW YOUVE MADE A LADY OF ME I'M NOT FIT TO SELL ANYTHING ELSE. I WISH YOUD
PYGM EPILOG (294) MOTHER IT PERHAPS APPEARED AS A MARRIAGE TO SOME LADY OF MEANS WHO COULD NOT RESIST HER BOY'S NICENESS. FANCY
GENV III (78) WE ARE FAIN. O SANGUINE AND SUBTLE DOLORES OUR LADY OF PAIN." /THE JOURNALIST/ SWINBURNE, SIR ORPHEUS. /SIR
FANY III (322) I HAVE MET AT A VARIETY THEATRE A CHARMING YOUNG LADY OF PERFECT RESPECTABILITY, AND ENJOYED A DANCE WITH HER
OVER (181) DEAR SPANISH LADIES," THAT YOU WERE BY BIRTH A LADY OF SPAIN? YOUR SPLENDID ANDALUSIAN BEAUTY SPEAKS FOR
LIED (199) I NEED NOT TELL YOU THAT MRS BOMPAS IS A LADY OF STAINLESS HONOR, WHO HAS NEVER CAST AN UNWORTHY
HART II (110) THE SORT OF LIFE YOU AND ME HAS LED. ANY YOUNG LADY OF THAT AGE MIGHT BE MY DAUGHTER ANYWHERE IN THE WIDE
APPL I (217) HAS NEVER FORGIVEN ME FOR NOT MAKING HER FIRST LADY OF THE ADMIRALTY. SHE HAS THREE NEPHEWS IN THE NAVY.
PLES PREFACE(R18) EUROPE, BETWEEN STAMBOULOFF AND AN EMINENT LADY OF THE BULGARIAN COURT WHO TOOK EXCEPTION TO HIS
BASH I (94) ME NOT WHENCE I COME, NOR WHAT I AM. YOU ARE THE LADY OF THE CASTLE. I HAVE BUT THIS HARD AND BLACKENED HAND
BASH I (97) LADY LOVING BREATHLESSLY. /MELLISH/ THE LADY OF THE CASTLE! THOU ART MAD. /CASHEL/ TIS THOU ART MAD
LADY (241) UNABASHED) NOT I, NOT CARE NEITHER. YOU ARE SOME LADY OF THE COURT, BELIKE. TO ME THERE ARE BUT TWO SORTS OF
JOAN PREFACE(10) DOMREMY WOULD HAVE DEFERRED TO HER AS THE YOUNG LADY OF THE FARM. THE DIFFERENCE BETWEEN JOAN'S CASE AND
PYGM EPILOG (299) AFTERWARDS. AND AS SHE HAPPENED TO TALK TO THE LADY OF THE FURNITURE SHOP, AND THAT LADY ALSO DESIRED ABOVE
SIM I (38) AWE AND ADMIRATION) OH DEAR! IS THIS THE LADY OF THE HOUSE? /PROLA/ (COMING PAST PRA TO THE
ARMS II (40) I DONT THINK HE KNOWS WHO YOU ARE: HE SAID THE LADY OF THE HOUSE. HE GAVE ME THIS LITTLE TICKET FOR YOU. (
MIS. PREFACE(31) EVEN A BEGINNING WAS BROUGHT HOME TO ME BY THE LADY OF THE MANOR IN THE LITTLE VILLAGE IN HERTFORDSHIRE
GENV I SD(37) IMPOSING STYLE AND DRESS AT ONCE REDUCE THE YOUNG LADY OF THE OFFICE TO NERVOUS ABJECTION. /THE WIDOW/ ARE YOU
LADY (237) THE DARK LADY OF THE SONNETS. FIN DE SIECLE 15-1600. MIDSUMMER NIGHT
LADY PREFACE(207) PREFACE TO THE DARK LADY OF THE SONNETS. HOW THE PLAY CAME TO BE WRITTEN. I HAD
LADY (206) THE DARK LADY OF THE SONNETS. 1910. THE DARK LADY OF THE SONNETS WAS FIRST PERFORMED AT THE HAYMARKET
LADY (205) THE DARK LADY OF THE SONNETS. 1910. THE DARK LADY OF THE SONNETS WAS
HART PREFACE(33) APPEAL TO OUR NATIONAL CULTURE. MY PLAY, THE DARK LADY OF THE SONNETS, WAS ONE OF THE INCIDENTS OF THAT
JOAN PREFACE(9) PLEASE HERSELF AT TIMES WITH BEING THE YOUNG LADY OF THIS CASTLE. HER MOTHER AND BROTHERS WERE ABLE TO
BASH I (94) /CASHEL/ (THUNDERSTRUCK) DO NOT SAY YOU ARE THE LADY OF THIS GREAT DOMAIN. /LYDIA/ I AM. /CASHEL/ ACCURSED
FANY III (325) THE MAN SHE MAKES UP HER MIND TO MARRY. SHE IS A LADY OF VERY DETERMINED CHARACTER. /KNOX/ YES: IF HE'D HAVE
PYGM II (225) THE GUTTER AND DRESS YOU BEAUTIFULLY AND MAKE A LADY OF YOU. /MRS PEARCE/ STOP, MR HIGGINS. I WONT ALLOW IT.
MTH3 (121) THAT HAS BEEN YOUR OWN FAULT. IF I MAY SAY SO, A LADY OF YOUR ATTRACTIONS NEED NEVER HAVE BEEN LONELY. /MRS
WIDO III (57) AND A LITTLE WISTFULLY) I SEE I HAVE MADE A REAL LADY OF YOU, BLANCHE. /BLANCHE/ (DEFIANTLY) WELL? ARE YOU
ROCK PREFACE(165) AGAINST IT IF YOU ACCUSE ANY RUSSIAN OF BEING A LADY OR A GENTLEMAN. INCOMPATIBILITY OF PEASANTRY WITH
SIM PREFACE(8) FASHIONABLE THOROUGHFARE. NOBODY HAS EVER SEEN A LADY OR GENTLEMAN CARRYING A JUG OF MILK DOWN BOND STREET OR
3PLA PREFACE(R14) SCENERY WITHIN REACH OF THE LONDONER. THE LEADING LADY OR GENTLEMAN MAY BE AS TEMPTING TO THE ADMIRER IN THE
CATH 1 (172) BEEN BADLY BROUGHT UP, LITTLE DARLING. WOULD ANY LADY OR GENTLEMAN WALK UNANNOUNCED INTO A ROOM WITHOUT FIRST
DOCT PREFACE(16) NOR PRACTICABLE. AND EVERY HYPOCHONDRIACAL RICH LADY OR GENTLEMAN WHO CAN BE PERSUADED THAT HE OR SHE IS A
MRS III (232) IN THE CLASS OF PEOPLE I CAN INTRODUCE YOU TO. NO LADY OR GENTLEMAN WOULD SO FAR FORGET THEMSELVES AS TO
CAPT I (237) CAPTAIN. /BRASSBOUND/ ANSWER, YOU DOG, WHEN THE LADY ORDERS YOU. (TO LADY CICELY) DO NOT ADDRESS HIM AS MR
BUOY III (34) DIFFERENCE WE CANNOT GET OVER. SHE KNOWS THINGS A LADY OUGHT NOT TO KNOW. /MRS THIRDBORN/ INCLUDING SOME
AUGS (281) THICK POKER. I RANG FOR YOU TO SHEW THE LADY OUT. /THE CLERK/ SHE'S GONE. SHE RUN OUT LIKE A RABBIT.
LADY (248) FROM THE STAGE, WHERE INDEED I CANNOT HAVE MY LADY PHYSICIAN PRESENTED AT ALL, SHE BEING TOO HONEST A
HART I (44) /THE WOMANSERVANT/ GOD BLESS US! (THE YOUNG LADY PICKS UP THE BOOK AND PLACES IT ON THE TABLE). SORRY TO
2TRU II (59) SUCH THINGS HAVE BEEN DONE; AND THE POOR LADY POINTS OUT VERY JUSTLY THAT I CANNOT REPLACE HER
AUGS (270) EXCEPT, OF COURSE, DEAR LUCY. . . . OH, TOTO AND LADY POPHAM AND THAT LOT: THEY DONT COUNT: THEYRE ALL RIGHT.
3PLA PREFACE(R14) I DID NOT FIND THAT MATTERS WERE IMPROVED BY THE LADY PRETENDING TO BE " A WOMAN WITH A PAST," VIOLENTLY
SIM I (51) NATURE ALWAYS HELPS. /IDDY/ (RISING) THANK YOU, LADY PROLA. YES: THAT WILL BE A GREAT HELP. /PROLA/ COME. (
DEST SD(195) LOOKING AT THE LETTER) I WONDER! THE STRANGE LADY PUTS THE LETTER DOWN ALIGHT ON THE SNUFFERS TRAY, AND
AUGS (282) WITH A SHRUG, GOES UP THE MIDDLE OF THE ROOM. THE LADY RESUMES HER CONVERSATION WITH THE TELEPHONE) WHAT? . .
AUGS SD(281) /AUGUSTUS/ WHAT ON EARTH DOES SHE MEAN? THE LADY RETURNS. /THE LADY/ MAY I USE YOUR TELEPHONE?
PRES (141) THEN YOUR PROMISE TO TAKE COMMAND IF LADY RICHMOND CONSENTS? /MITCHENER/ ON CONDITION THAT I
PRES (141) /MITCHENER/ THE OLD GIRL? /BALSQUITH/ WELL, LADY RICHMOND. APOLOGIZE TO HER. ASK HER LEAVE TO ACCEPT THE
PRES (140) NOT BE SERIOUS? HERE ARE WE, FACE TO FACE WITH LADY RICHMOND'S GRAVE DISPLEASURE; AND YOU TALK TO ME ABOUT
PRES (140) TO ATTEND TO THAN EXPLOSIONS, GREAT HEAVENS! LADY RICHMOND'S NEPHEW HAS BEEN TREATED LIKE ANY COMMON
PRES (139) THE BLOTTER). HE HAS THREE AUNTS IN THE PEERAGE; LADY RICHMOND'S ONE OF THEM (MITCHENER PUNCTUATES THESE
MRS PREFACE(179) BY THE AGENTS OF THE WHITE SLAVE TRAFFIC. THE LADY RIGHTLY CONCLUDED THAT MUCH THE BEST INSTRUMENT FOR
WIDO I (22) RENTAL OF A VERY EXTENSIVE REAL ESTATE IN LONDON. LADY ROXDALE IS ONE OF THE HEAD LANDLORDS; AND DR TRENCH

WIDO I	(20)	WITH." /SARTORIUS/ (QUICKLY) BY NO MEANS:	LADY	ROXDALE MUST JUDGE OF THAT FOR HERSELF. LET IT STAND AS
WIDO I	(18)	IF YOU WISH, NOTHING EASIER. BUT IF YOU THINK	LADY	ROXDALE WILL PASS IT OVER, I DIFFER FROM YOU. I MAY BE
WIDO I	(18)	A CHATTY WAY, I DARESAY I CAN COMMUNICATE IT TO	LADY	ROXDALE WITH BECOMING DELICACY. WHAT IS SARTORIUS?
WIDO I	(6)	THE WAY, HARRY, I HAVE OFTEN MEANT TO ASK YOU: IS	LADY	ROXDALE YOUR MOTHER'S SISTER OR YOUR FATHER'S? THIS
WIDO I	(19)	DEPENDS ON THE WAY THE MATTER IS PUT TO	LADY	ROXDALE. BUT AS TO THAT, YOU MAY RELY ON ME. I
WIDO II	(28)	/COKANE/ LADY ROXDALE, MY DEAR SIR: HE MEANS	LADY	ROXDALE. DO EXPRESS YOURSELF WITH A LITTLE MORE TACT,
WIDO III	(57)	WAITING FOR THE CONSENT OF THE GROUND LANDLORD,	LADY	ROXDALE. /BLANCHE/ LADY ROXDALE! /SARTORIUS/ YES. BUT
WIDO I	(20)	THAT IS, TRENCH'S DEAR AUNT MARIA, MY FRIEND	LADY	ROXDALE. YOU UNDERSTAND THAT I AM ONLY DRAFTING A
WIDO I	(15)	TO SEIZE AN ADVANTAGE, AND YET DEFERRING TO	LADY	ROXDALE'S RELATIVE) SO FAR, NO. I MAY SAY THAT YOUR
WIDO II	(28)	A LETTER). /SARTORIUS/ AUNT MARIA? /COKANE/	LADY	ROXDALE, MY DEAR SIR: HE MEANS LADY ROXDALE. DO EXPRESS
WIDO II	(28)	WITH A LITTLE MORE TACT, MY DEAR FELLOW. /TRENCH/	LADY	ROXDALE, OF COURSE. UNCLE HARRY-- /COKANE/ SIR HARRY
WIDO I	(7)	SARTORIUS; AND I HAVE THE HONOR OF BEING KNOWN TO	LADY	ROXDALE, WHO IS, I BELIEVE, A NEAR RELATIVE OF YOURS.
WIDO III	(57)	OF THE GROUND LANDLORD, LADY ROXDALE. /BLANCHE/	LADY	ROXDALE! /SARTORIUS/ YES, BUT I SHALL EXPECT THE
DOCT I	(96)	/RIDGEON/ (EXPLODING) I TOLD YOU TO TELL THAT	LADY	-- (EMMY VANISHES). /WALPOLE/ (JUMPING UP AGAIN) OH,
NEVR I	(218)	/CRAMPTON/ THANK YOU; BUT WONT THIS YOUNG	LADY	-- (INDICATING GLORIA, WHO IS CLOSE TO THE CHAIR)?
2TRU III	(105)	A RIGHT TO IT. MY ACTION WAS INEXCUSABLE, BUT NO	LADY	-- NO HUMAN BEING-- HAS A RIGHT TO IMPOSE A FALSEHOOD
FANY PROLOG	(267)	HE IS. /TROTTER/ (REMONSTRATING) MY DEAR YOUNG	LADY	-- /FANNY/ I DONT MEAN MORALLY INNOCENT: EVERYBODY WHO
JITT I	(10)	/A GIRL'S VOICE/ (THE ACCENT IS NOT THAT OF A	LADY	) GENTLEMAN ORDERED THESE, SUPPOSE IT'S ALL RIGHT, ISNT
DEST	(188)	THE SABRE) NO SUCH MAN! EH, GENERAL? (TO THE	LADY	) I SAY: WHERES MY HORSE? /LADY/ SAFE AT BORGHETTO,
DEST	(188)	IN THE UNMISTAKEABLE VOICE OF THE STRANGE	LADY	) LIEUTENANT: I AM YOUR PRISONER. (SHE OFFERS HIM HER
DEST	(164)	AGAINST THE BETTER SIDE OF YOUR NATURE. (TO THE	LADY	) MADAM: MY APOLOGIES. I THOUGHT YOU WERE THE SAME
AUGS	(271)	/THE CLERK/ (TO AUGUSTUS) HERE SHE IS. (TO THE	LADY	) MAY I OFFER YOU A CHAIR, LADY? (HE PLACES A CHAIR
AUGS	(282)	WANTS TO SPEAK TO YOU. HOLD THE LINE. (TO THE	LADY	) NOW, MADAM (HE HANDS HER THE RECEIVER). /THE LADY/
CURE	(231)	OH! OH! (HE LOOKS AT THE PIANO AND SEES THE	LADY	) OH I SAY! /THE LADY/ WHAT ON EARTH DO YOU MEAN BY
HART I	(46)	READY BEFORE SHE HAS FINISHED IT. (TO THE YOUNG	LADY	) TAKE OFF YOUR HAT, DUCKY; AND MAKE YOURSELF AT HOME
LADY	(243)	JEALOUSLY. /THE MAN/ (UNAWARE OF THE DARK	LADY	) THEN CEASE TO MAKE MY HANDS TREMBLE WITH THE STREAMS
AUGS	(281)	YOU? (INTO THE TELEPHONE) WHAT? . . . (TO THE	LADY	) WHOM DO YOU WANT TO GET ON TO? /THE LADY/ BLUELOO.
LADY	(240)	IN A SINGLE WORD. CAN THIS BE MY MARY? (TO THE	LADY	) WHY DO YOU SPEAK IN A STRANGE VOICE, AND UTTER POETRY
AUGS	(279)	SOLDIER NOW. (HE SHUTS THE DOOR AND COMES TO THE	LADY	). THANK HEAVEN, THE WAR HAS GIVEN US THE UPPER HAND OF
BULL I	(96)	AGAIN) I EXPECT TO FIND MISS REILLY A PERFECT	LADY	; AND I STRONGLY ADVISE YOU TO COME AND HAVE ANOTHER
HART II	(105)	THATS RIGHT, HUSHABYE. KEEP THE PYJAMAS, MY	LADY	; AND MUCH GOOD MAY THEY DO YOU. /HECTOR/ (ADVANCING
GENV IV	(113)	MY OWN EXPERIENCE. /SECRETARY/ YOU ARE AN AMIABLE	LADY	; AND NO DOUBT THERE ARE, AS YOU SAY, OTHER CASES--
CAPT I	(237)	WILL ORDER MY MEN TO BEHAVE THEMSELVES BEFORE THE	LADY	; AND THEY SHALL OBEY THEIR ORDERS. BUT THE LADY WILL
BULL I	(95)	ME FAVORABLY. SHE SEEMS TO HAVE THE FEELINGS OF A	LADY	; AND THOUGH WE MUST FACE THE FACT THAT IN ENGLAND HER
SUPR III	(90)	I AM NOBODY! /DON JUAN/ NOT AT ALL: YOU ARE A	LADY	; AND WHEREVER LADIES ARE IS HELL. DO NOT BE SURPRISED
VWOO 1	(116)	YOU CALL IT? /A/ OH, CALL IT WHAT YOU LIKE, DEAR	LADY	; BUT I HAVE FIVE HUNDRED WORDS TO WRITE BEFORE LUNCH;
GENV IV	(97)	/BATTLER/ I APPLAUD YOUR LOCAL PATRIOTISM, YOUNG	LADY	; BUT I PRESS FOR AN ANSWER TO MY QUESTION. WHAT DOES "
GLIM	(171)	AND THIRTEEN YEARS OLD, BY THE GRACE OF OUR	LADY	; BUT I STILL REMEMBER ALL MY LATIN; AND I CAN BIND AND
KING II	(224)	/CATHERINE/ AND NELLY? SHE CAN PLAY THE FINE	LADY	; BUT IS SHE ONE? /CHARLES/ NELLY IS A GOOD CREATURE;
MIS.	(201)	THIS YOUNG GENTLEMAN. HE IS ENGAGED TO THIS YOUNG	LADY	; BUT NO MATTER FOR THAT: HE MAKES LOVE TO ME BECAUSE I
DOCT II	(115)	RIGHT, QUITE RIGHT. SORRY TO LOSE YOU, MY DEAR	LADY	; BUT SIR PATRICK'S ORDERS ARE THE LAWS OF-- ER-- OF
CYMB V	(149)	SUFFER YOURS. YOU ARE, I SWEAR, A VERY WORTHY	LADY	; BUT STILL, NOT QUITE AN ANGEL. /IMOGEN/ NO, NOT
BUOY II	(20)	THAN I SHOULD BE IN PICCADILLY. /HE/ YES, HOLY	LADY	; BUT WHAT ABOUT YOUR CONSCIENCE? A HUNGRY MAN ASKS
GETT	(320)	DELIGHT IN PICTURES OF THE SAINTS AND OF OUR	LADY	; BUT WHEN I FALL UNDER THAT MOST TERRIBLE CURSE OF THE
FANY II	(293)	PROUD OF IT; THOUGH I KNOW NOW THAT I'M NOT A	LADY	; BUT WHETHER THATS BECAUSE WE'RE ONLY SHOPKEEPERS, OR
BARB III	(314)	WITH YOU? /MORRISON/ SHALL I ANNOUNCE HIM, MY	LADY	; OR IS HE AT HOME HERE, SO TO SPEAK, MY LADY? /LADY
FANY PROLOG	(271)	YOU. I SHALL SAY THAT YOURE A VERY FOOLISH YOUNG	LADY	; THAT YOUVE GOT INTO A VERY QUESTIONABLE SET; AND THAT
JITT I	(12)	YOUR LADY IS A REAL LADY, AND ALWAYS THE SAME	LADY	; THOUGH OF COURSE I TAKE CARE NEVER TO SEE HER. /THE
ARMS III	(68)	ARE EQUALLY ASTONISHED). THE GRACIOUS YOUNG	LADY	SAVED MY LIFE BY GIVING ME CHOCOLATE CREAMS WHEN I WAS
ARMS III	(73)	SAYS THE LADY? /RAINA/ (PRETENDING TO SULK) THE	LADY	SAYS THAT HE CAN KEEP HIS TABLECLOTHS AND HIS
ARMS I	(11)	ROOM TO GET AS FAR FROM THE DOOR AS POSSIBLE). MY	LADY	SAYS YOU ARE TO DRESS AT ONCE, AND TO-- (SHE SEES THE
MTH5	(255)	IS JUST WHAT THIS OLD GENTLEMAN AND THIS OLD	LADY	SEEM TO THINK TOO. /THE SHE-ANCIENT/ QUITE SO. /THE
MIS.	(151)	IN THAT SELFISH WAY. /LORD SUMMERHAYS/ THE	LADY	SEEMS TO HAVE SHIFTED FOR BOTH VERY EFFECTUALLY, SIR.
BARB PREFACE	(231)	ON EQUAL TERMS WITH A BLACKGUARD TO WHOM NO	LADY	SHOULD BE SEEN SPEAKING IN THE PUBLIC STREET: IN SHORT,
VWOO 2	(130)	ON THE TABLE INSTEAD OF KEEPING THEM WHERE A	LADY	SHOULD KEEP THEM: UP YOUR SLEEVE. /Z/ WELL, WHERES THE
2TRU PREFACE	(10)	THE WHOLE, THERE IS NO REASON WHY A TERRITORIAL	LADY	SHOULD NOT BE AS HAPPY AS HER DAIRYMAID, OR HER HUSBAND
ARMS III	(70)	MY DEAR MAJOR, MY DEAR MADAME, THE GRACIOUS YOUNG	LADY	SIMPLY SAVED MY LIFE, NOTHING ELSE. SHE NEVER CARED TWO
CAPT III	(292)	FROM THE WAIST DOWN, AND THE REST PIRATE.	LADY	SIS WONT SPEAK TO YOU IN IT. /BRASSBOUND/ I'LL CHANGE
CAPT III	(291)	TO YOU, BRASSBOUND, THAT THE CLOBBER BELONGS TO	LADY	SIS. AINT YOU GOING TO GIVE IT BACK TO HER?
CAPT II	SD(247)	THE REST OF THE QUESTION) CARDS AND DRINK.	LADY	SIS. (HE FOLLOWS JOHNSON TO THE PATIENT. LADY CICELY
FANY I	SD(273)	ROOM OF A HOUSE IN DENMARK HILL. AN ELDERLY	LADY	SITS AT BREAKFAST READING THE NEWSPAPER. HER CHAIR IS
PPP	SD(193)	ROOM IN A FASHIONABLE QUARTER OF LONDON A	LADY	SITS AT HER DRESSING-TABLE, WITH HER MAID COMBING HER
DEST	SD(164)	WITH CONCENTRATED IRRITATION) IDIOT! THE STRANGE	LADY	SMILES SYMPATHETICALLY. HE COMES FROWNING DOWN THE ROOM
HART I	(46)	NOW IT'S ALL RIGHT, CAPTAIN: I'LL GET THE	LADY	SOME TEA; AND HER ROOM SHALL BE READY BEFORE SHE HAS
CLEO III	(153)	BEWARE WHAT YOU DO, SIR. THOSE EGGS OF WHICH THE	LADY	SPEAKS MUST WEIGH MORE THAN A POUND APIECE. THIS BOAT
DEST	(182)	I THINK, TO PROVE THAT WILD STATEMENT. (THE	LADY	STARTS. HE ADDS, WITH CLINCHING EMPHASIS) THOSE PAPERS
2TRU I	SD(28)	AN ELDERLY LADY AND A YOUNG DOCTOR COME IN. THE	LADY	STEALS ALONG ON TIPTOE, FULL OF THE DEEPEST CONCERN FOR
DEST	SD(161)	WATCHING A MOUSEHOLE). IT OPENS; AND THE STRANGE	LADY	STEPS IN. SHE IS TALL AND EXTRAORDINARILY GRACEFUL,
CATH 4	(194)	LIKE THAT AND TICKLE HIM. /CATHERINE/ YOUR YOUNG	LADY	STILL SEEMS TO THINK THAT YOU ENJOYED IT. /CLAIRE/ I
FANY III	(319)	DOES. DOES SHE, MR JUGGINS? /JUGGINS/ THE OTHER	LADY	SUSPECTS ME, MADAM. THEY CALL ME RUDOLPH, OR THE LONG
2TRU III	(100)	CONGRATULATE ME, MY FRIENDS. MY DEAR SARAH IS	LADY	TALLBOYS AT LAST. (HE RESUMES HIS SEAT AND PORES OVER
FANY III	(319)	PLACES GILBEY'S TEA ON THE TABLE BEFORE HIM). THE	LADY	THAT CALLED ABOUT MASTER BOBBY, SIR. /KNOX/ DO YOU MEAN
GETT	(308)	MY JUDGMENT ON THIS SUBJECT. THERES A CERTAIN	LADY	THAT I ALWAYS CONSULT ON DELICATE POINTS LIKE THIS. SHE
FANY III	(298)	IN MY PLACE? /JUGGINS/ I SHOULD TELL THE YOUNG	LADY	THAT I FOUND I COULDNT FULFIL MY ENGAGEMENT. /BOBBY/
GLIM	(174)	ME, I'M HUMBLE AND GOOD, I SWEAR TO YOU BY OUR	LADY	THAT IT IS NOT FERRUCCIO'S LOVE THAT I MUST TAKE, BUT
DOCT I	(91)	HIM THAT WAY. /EMMY/ (LOOKING IN) WILL YOU SEE A	LADY	THAT WANTS HER HUSBAND'S LUNGS CURED? /RIDGEON/ NO.
MTH4 I	(151)	YOU KNOW, ONE CAN SAY THINGS TO A MARRIED	LADY	THAT WOULD PERHAPS BE IN QUESTIONABLE TASTE TO ANYONE
FANY III	(299)	THEIR CARDS ON THE TABLE. IF YOU TELL THE YOUNG	LADY	THAT YOU WANT TO JILT HER, AND SHE CALLS YOU A PIG, THE
GENV IV	(114)	AND I AM NOW GOVERNED BY JESUS. /JUDGE/ ALLOW THE	LADY	THE LAST WORD, MR LEADER. PROCEED, MR SECRETARY.
BASH II,1,	(106)	IT WAS MY GLORY. I HAD HOPED TO OFFER TO MY	LADY	THERE MY BELTS, MY CHAMPIONSHIPS, MY HEAPED-UP STAKES,
MTH3	(99)	NEGRESS/ STUPID OF ME. I WAS TALKING TO ANOTHER	LADY	THIS MORNING; AND I LEFT THE PEG IN. /BURGE-LUBIN/ BUT
CAPT III	(282)	PIERCING TONES) BRING IN THE PRISONERS. TELL THE	LADY	THOSE ARE MY ORDERS. DO YOU HEAR? TELL HER SO. (THE
DEST	SD(190)	GO OUT, ARM IN ARM). IT IS NOW STARRY NIGHT. THE	LADY	THROWS THE PACKET ON THE TABLE AND SEATS HERSELF AT HER
FANY PROLOG	(267)	THE DINNER I'M TAKEN ASIDE BY A CHARMING YOUNG	LADY	TO BE TALKED TO ABOUT THE PLAY. HOW CAN YOU EXPECT ME
GENV IV	(111)	GOD'S EFFECTIVES. THEN COMES THIS PIOUS	LADY	TO BID ME TURN TO GOD. THERE IS NO NEED: GOD HAS TURNED
CATH 2	(179)	AGAINST IT WITH ALL MY MIGHT. I APPEAL TO THIS	LADY	TO CONFIRM ME. /VARINKA/ (PRETENDING TO BE INDIGNANT)
DEVL II	(40)	OH, OF COURSE, OF COURSE. NO CALL FOR THE	LADY	TO DISTRESS HERSELF. STILL-- (IN A LOWER VOICE,
GETT	(269)	BUT THESE ARE NOT CORRECT VIEWS FOR AN ENGLISH	LADY	TO EXPRESS. /LESBIA/ THAT IS WHY I DONT EXPRESS THEM,
DEST	(180)	GENERAL. /NAPOLEON/ I CANNOT PERSUADE THIS	LADY	TO GIVE ME MUCH INFORMATION; BUT THERE CAN BE NO DOUBT
MIS.	(141)	TO MISBEHAVE HIMSELF; AND I'M TOO MUCH OF A	LADY	TO LET HIM; AND HE'S SHY AND SHEEPISH; AND I'M CORRECT
FANY I	(281)	/DORA/ WELL, WHATEVER I MAY BE, I'M TOO MUCH THE	LADY	TO LOSE MY TEMPER; AND I DONT THINK BOBBY WOULD LIKE ME
CAPT III	(286)	WITH INDIGNATION). /KEARNEY/ (CALMLY) ALLOW THE	LADY	TO PRO-CEED, SIR HOWARD HALLAM. /SIR HOWARD/ (
AUGS	(278)	AT MY DOOR AND INTERRUPT MY BUSINESS WITH THIS	LADY	TO REPEAT THIS MAN'S INEPTITUDES? /THE CLERK/ NO. I
MTH3	(127)	LADY'S WAY. /BARNABAS/ THERE IS TIME TO SEND THE	LADY	TO THE LETHAL CHAMBER BEFORE ANYTHING COMES OF YOUR
SUPR III	(119)	LAWFUL CHILDREN BORNE BY ONE HIGHLY RESPECTABLE	LADY	TO THREE DIFFERENT FATHERS IS NOT IMPOSSIBLE NOR
HART PREFACE	(36)	REVILED. WHETHER OR NO, THE FACT REMAINS THAT THE	LADY	TO WHOSE PUBLIC SPIRIT AND SENSE OF THE NATIONAL VALUE
PYGM V	(278)	GIRL, AND ALWAYS WILL; BUT I KNOW I CAN BE A	LADY	TO YOU, BECAUSE YOU ALWAYS TREAT ME AS A LADY, AND
POSN PREFACE	(378)	MY MOST VALUED LITERARY TROPHIES. AN INNOCENT	LADY	TOLD ME AFTERWARDS THAT SHE NEVER KNEW THAT I COULD
LADY	(239)	MAKING SONNETS BY MOONLIGHT. AND TO THE SAME	LADY	TOO. /THE MAN/ NO! /THE BEEFEATER/ LAST NIGHT HE STOOD
2TRU III	(91)	SIR. YOU HAVE JUST SAID THAT YOU AND THIS	LADY	TOOK THE SAME LODGING. AM I TO UNDERSTAND THAT YOU ARE
SIM PRO,3,SD	(33)	FLABBERGASTED). /THE PRIESTESS/ HUSH. LOOK. THE	LADY	TOURIST RETURNS AND AGAIN GOES TO THE PRIEST. /THE
SIM PRO,3,SD	(30)	AS HE HAS RECOVERED FROM HIS DUCKING. AN ENGLISH	LADY	TOURIST, BAEDEKER IN HAND, HAS WANDERED IN, TRYING TO
LADY	(247)	GRIEF AND SHAME. I-- /ELIZABETH/ GO (THE DARK	LADY	TRIES TO KISS HER HAND). NO MORE. GO (THE DARK LADY
HART I	SD(44)	HAS BEEN READING. A CLOCK STRIKES SIX. THE YOUNG	LADY	TURNS AND LOOKS AT HER WATCH. SHE RISES WITH AN AIR OF
MILL I	(146)	INTO THE TELEPHONE) SEND MR FITZFASSENDEN AND THE	LADY	UP. /EPIFANIA/ WE SHALL SEE NOW THE SORT OF WOMAN FOR
DEST	(156)	/GIUSEPPE/ THE LADY, EXCELLENCY. /NAPOLEON/ THE	LADY	UPSTAIRS? /GIUSEPPE/ YES, EXCELLENCY. THE STRANGE
DEST	(155)	EXCELLENCY BY ANY CHANCE CAUGHT A GLIMPSE OF THE	LADY	UPSTAIRS? /NAPOLEON/ (SITTING UP PROMPTLY) HOW OLD IS

DEST (153)	BUT YOUR EXCELLENCY'S HORSE, THE SENTINEL, THE	LADY	UPSTAIRS, AND MY WIFE. /NAPOLEON/ KILL YOUR WIFE.
DEST (161)	(PETRIFIED) WHAT WAS THAT? /GIUSEPPE/ ONLY A	LADY	UPSTAIRS, LIEUTENANT, CALLING ME. /LIEUTENANT/ LADY!
DEST (155)	YOU AND YOUR WHOLE HOUSEHOLD, INCLUDING THE	LADY	UPSTAIRS, WILL SATISFY ME. /GIUSEPPE/ WE ARE ALL
HART I (72)	/MRS HUSHABYE/ (INTRODUCING) MR MAZZINI DUNN,	LADY	UT-- OH, I FORGOT: YOUVE MET. (INDICATING ELLIE) MISS
HART I (51)	COMING TO THE TABLE TO PUT DOWN HER EMPTY CUP)	LADY	UTTERWORD: DO YOU THINK MRS HUSHABYE REALLY EXPECTS
HART I (51)	HIM TO STOP HIM) OH PLEASE-- (HE GOES OUT).	LADY	UTTERWORD: I DONT KNOW WHAT TO DO. YOUR FATHER PERSISTS
HART II (114)	BROKEN, CHILD? /HECTOR/ (RISING WITH A BOUND)	LADY	UTTERWORD: YOU ARE NOT TO BE TRUSTED. YOU HAVE MADE A
HART I (72)	TO THE BIG CHAIR, AND ADDS) WONT YOU SIT DOWN,	LADY	UTTERWORD? (SHE DOES SO VERY GRACIOUSLY). /MRS
HART I (49)	I THOUGHT I OUGHT TO GO AWAY TOO. BUT HOW CAN I,	LADY	UTTERWORD? MY LUGGAGE IS ON THE STEPS; AND THE STATION
HART III (142)	YOUR HOUSE IS NOT HEARTBREAK HOUSE: IS IT,	LADY	UTTERWORD? /HECTOR/ YET SHE BREAKS HEARTS, EASY AS HER
HART I (74)	OF A BOOK) DO YOU LIKE STORIES OF ADVENTURE,	LADY	UTTERWORD? /LADY UTTERWORD/ (PATRONIZINGLY) OF
HART II (123)	IS IT YOUR NOTION OF GOOD FORM TO GIVE AWAY	LADY	UTTERWORD? /RANDALL/ (A CHILDISHLY PLAINTIVE NOTE
HART III (132)	/ELLIE/ NOT IN THE LEAST. WHAT IS YOUR OPINION,	LADY	UTTERWORD? YOU HAVE SO MUCH GOOD SENSE. /MANGAN/ BUT
HART I SD(74)	RANDALL AND MRS HUSHABYE). ELLIE, HECTOR, AND	LADY	UTTERWORD ARE LEFT. HECTOR IS CLOSE TO LADY UTTERWORD.
HART II SD(107)	TO THE STARBOARD DOOR AND STANDS ON GUARD THERE).	LADY	UTTERWORD COMES IN AFTER RANDALL, AND GOES BETWEEN MRS
HART II SD(112)	IN DEEP ABSTRACTION; THEY ALL LOOK AFTER HIM; AND	LADY	UTTERWORD COUGHS CONSCIOUSLY. /MRS HUSHABYE/ SO BILLY
HART I (72)	THEMSELVES). /HECTOR/ BEHAVE YOURSELF, HESIONE.	LADY	UTTERWORD IS ENTITLED NOT ONLY TO HOSPITALITY BUT TO
HART III SD(129)	OUT THROUGH THE GLASS DOOR OF THE POOP, FINDS	LADY	UTTERWORD LYING VOLUPTUOUSLY IN THE HAMMOCK ON THE EAST
HART I SD(49)	ASLEEP. (HE VANISHES THROUGH THE HALF DOOR).	LADY	UTTERWORD RETIRES TO THE WINDOW TO CONCEAL HER TEARS.
HART I SD(71)	CORNER NEAR THE PANTRY. HECTOR COMES FORWARD; AND	LADY	UTTERWORD RISES LOOKING HER VERY BEST. /MRS HUSHABYE/
HART II SD(112)	MANGAN, FORGOTTEN, SITS IN THE PORT CORNER.	LADY	UTTERWORD TAKES THE BIG CHAIR. CAPTAIN SHOTOVER GOES
HART II (123)	THAT THERE IS NOT AN ATOM OF-- /HECTOR/ YES. AND	LADY	UTTERWORD TOLD ME SHE NEVER MADE SCENES. WELL, DONT
HART II (124)	EFFECT. (HE GOES TO THE GARDEN DOOR AND CALLS	LADY	UTTERWORD WITH COMMANDING EMPHASIS) ARIADNE! /LADY
HART II (113)	HAUGHTY) I WAS NOT ADDRESSING YOU PARTICULARLY,	LADY	UTTERWORD. AND I AM NOT ACCUSTOMED TO BE ASKED HOW DARE
HART III (139)	NOTHING. /MAZZINI/ WELL, OF COURSE I KNEW THAT,	LADY	UTTERWORD. BUT IF PEOPLE BELIEVE IN HIM AND ARE ALWAYS
HART I (72)	(PULLING HIMSELF TOGETHER) I BEG YOUR PARDON,	LADY	UTTERWORD. I AM EXTREMELY GLAD TO WELCOME YOU AT LAST
HART III (137)	IMMENSE WEALTH. /ELLIE/ I CANNOT COMMIT BIGAMY,	LADY	UTTERWORD. (EXCLAIMING ALL TOGETHER) /MRS HUSHABYE/
HART I (71)	I MADE A PERFECT FOOL OF MYSELF. / MRS HUSHABYE/	LADY	UTTERWORD. MY SISTER. MY YOUNGER SISTER. /MANGAN/ (
HART II (113)	HAVE BEEN BROUGHT UP. /MAZZINI/ OH, I HOPE NOT,	LADY	UTTERWORD. REALLY! /LADY UTTERWORD/ I KNOW VERY WELL
HART III (144)	MEANT HASTINGS. /MAZZINI/ OH, I BEG YOUR PARDON,	LADY	UTTERWORD. /CAPTAIN SHOTOVER/ EVERY DRUNKEN SKIPPER
HART II (121)	TAKE IT THAT WE MAY BE QUITE FRANK. I MEAN ABOUT	LADY	UTTERWORD. /HECTOR/ YOU MAY. I HAVE NOTHING TO BE FRANK
HART III (142)	TAKE PARTICULAR CARE TO KEEP OUT OF YOUR HOUSE,	LADY	UTTERWORD. /LADY UTTERWORD/ YOU WILL BE QUITE WRONG, MR
HART III (141)	SETS DOWN AS A NINCOMPOOP: DONT FORGET HIM,	LADY	UTTERWORD. /LADY UTTERWORD/ AND A VERY FASCINATING
HART I (71)	SISTER. /MANGAN/ (BOWING) PLEASED TO MEET YOU,	LADY	UTTERWORD. /LADY UTTERWORD/ (WITH MARKED INTEREST) WHO
HART I SD(74)	AND LADY UTTERWORD ARE LEFT. HECTOR IS CLOSE TO	LADY	UTTERWORD. THEY LOOK AT ELLIE, WAITING FOR HER TO GO.
HART II (123)	INTO HIS HUFF) I HAVE NOT SAID A WORD AGAINST	LADY	UTTERWORD. THIS IS JUST THE CONSPIRACY OVER AGAIN.
HART I (53)	DEEPLY GRATEFUL I AM TO HIM. /MRS HUSHABYE/ (TO	LADY	UTTERWORD) HER FATHER IS A VERY REMARKABLE MAN, ADDY.
HART III (137)	BARKING TO KEEP THE TRUTH OUT! /HECTOR/ THINK OF	LADY	UTTERWORD'S BEAUTY! HER GOOD SENSE! HER STYLE! /LADY
HART III (135)	ABOUT HESIONE BUT HER BEAUTIFUL BLACK HAIR; AND	LADY	UTTERWORD'S IS TOO PRETTY TO BE REAL. THE ONE THING
HART II (105)	GOOD MAY THEY DO YOU. /HECTOR/ (ADVANCING TO	LADY	UTTERWORD'S LEFT HAND) LET US ALL GO OUT INTO THE NIGHT
HART II SD(106)	BACK OF THE SOFA; AND THROWS HER RIGHT ARM ROUND	LADY	UTTERWORD'S NECK. /MRS HUSHABYE/ THEY WOULDNT BELIEVE
HART III SD(139)	SILK DRESSING-GOWN, COMES FROM THE HOUSE, ON	LADY	UTTERWORD'S SIDE. /MRS HUSHABYE/ OH! HERE COMES THE
HART I SD(48)	BY LADY UTTERWORD, WHO BURSTS IN MUCH FLUSTERED.	LADY	UTTERWORD, A BLONDE, IS VERY HANDSOME, VERY WELL
HART I (51)	NURSE: WILL YOU PLEASE REMEMBER THAT I AM	LADY	UTTERWORD, AND NOT MISS ADDY, NOR LOVEY, NOR DARLING,
HART I SD(52)	ELLIE. SHE IS A COUPLE OF YEARS OLDER THAN	LADY	UTTERWORD, AND EVEN BETTER LOOKING. SHE HAS MAGNIFICENT
HART I (47)	/NURSE GUINNESS/ MY GRACIOUS! IT'S MISS ADDIE,	LADY	UTTERWORD, MRS HUSHABYE'S SISTER: THE ONE I TOLD THE
HART I (71)	ONE'S HUSBAND NEVER IS, ARIADNE (HE SITS BY	LADY	UTTERWORD, ON HER RIGHT). /MRS HUSHABYE/ ONE'S SISTER'S
HART III (133)	I NEVER HEARD OF YOU. /MANGAN/ LET ME TELL YOU,	LADY	UTTERWORD, THAT THE PRIME MINISTER OF THIS COUNTRY
HART I SD(48)	AND IS HURRYING OUT WHEN SHE IS INTERCEPTED BY	LADY	UTTERWORD, WHO BURSTS IN MUCH FLUSTERED. LADY
HART III (141)	NATURAL AND KINDLY AND CHARMING HUMAN FEELING,	LADY	UTTERWORD! /LADY UTTERWORD/ SO I THOUGHT, MR DUNN, BUT
FOUN (212)	MELODRAMATIC ATTITUDES? HOW DARE YOU KEEP THE	LADY	WAITING? I'M VERY MUCH ANNOYED. /MERCER/ I'M SORRY, MY
LADY SD(240)	(SHAKING HER ARM) MARY, I SAY: ART ASLEEP? THE	LADY	WAKES; STARTS; AND NEARLY FAINTS. HE CATCHES HER ON HIS
KING I (199)	AWAY WHEN THEY CAME DOWNSTAIRS; BUT THE FRENCH	LADY	WANTED TO LOOK THROUGH MR NEWTON'S TELESCOPE; AND THE
SUPR II SD(63)	INDIFFERENCE AS THEIR COMMON LOT; AND THE POOR	LADY	WANTS TO BE EITHER LET ALONE OR LET PRATTLE ABOUT THE
CAPT II (249)	JOHNSON? /JOHNSON/ WELL: MARZO'S IN YOUR BED.	LADY	WANTS TO MAKE A KITCHEN OF THE SHEIKH'S AUDIENCE
AUGS (281)	DO YOU WANT HIM? /THE LADY/ YES. /AUGUSTUS/ THE	LADY	WANTS YOU AT THE WINDOW. /THE CLERK/ (RUSHING TO THE
LADY PREFACE(207)	OF THE UNFORTUNATE BARD. NOW THIS, IF THE DARK	LADY	WAS A MAID OF HONOR, WAS QUITE EASY. IF SHE WERE A
ARMS II (32)	THE BEDROOM OF A YOUNG BULGARIAN LADY. THE YOUNG	LADY	WAS ENCHANTED BY HIS PERSUASIVE COMMERCIAL TRAVELLER'S
ARMS II (32)	HER CONDUCT SHOULD APPEAR UNMAIDENLY. THE OLD	LADY	WAS EQUALLY FASCINATED; AND THE FUGITIVE WAS SENT ON
SUPR II (65)	(HALF APOLOGETIC, HALF HUFFY) THE YOUNG	LADY	WAS MARRIED SECRETLY; AND HER HUSBAND HAS FORBIDDEN
LADY PREFACE(207)	LET ME SAY THAT I DO NOT CONTEND THAT THE DARK	LADY	WAS MARY FITTON, BECAUSE WHEN THE CASE IN MARY'S FAVOR
LADY PREFACE(207)	HER, IF YOU PLEASE TO CONSIDER THAT THE DARK	LADY	WAS NO BETTER THAN SHE OUGHT TO HAVE BEEN) WAS
3PLA PREFACE(R14)	FOR MY OWN SEX, I CAN SAY THAT THE LEADING	LADY	WAS NOT TO EVERYBODY'S TASTE: HER PRETTY FACE OFTEN
LADY PREFACE(222)	THE ONE THING SHAKESPEAR'S PASSION FOR THE DARK	LADY	WAS NOT, WAS WHAT MR HARRIS IN ONE PASSAGE CALLS IT:
GETT (351)	AS FINAL. /COLLINS/ WHAT A PITY, MAAM! A FINE	LADY	WASTED, MAAM. (THEY SHAKE THEIR HEADS SADLY; AND MRS
DEST (178)	LOOKING OUT INTO THE VINES, DEEP IN THOUGHT. THE	LADY	WATCHES HIM IN SILENCE, SOMEWHAT SLIGHTINGLY. SUDDENLY
CAPT III (288)	ANY VIOLENCE TO THE PURE INSTINCTS OF WOMANHOOD.	LADY	WAYNFLETE! I THAHNK YOU FOR THE DELICACY WITH WHICH YOU
CAPT III (283)	IS THIS ANOTHER GENTLEMAN OF YOUR PARTY,	LADY	WAYNFLETE? I PRESUME I MET YOU LAHST NIGHT, SIR, ON
CAPT III (289)	KEARNEY? /KEARNEY/ YOU RECALL ME TO MY DOOTY,	LADY	WAYNFLETE. MY BARGE WILL BE READY TO TAKE OFF YOU AND
CAPT III (287)	/KEARNEY/ I SHOULD HAVE DONE THE SAME MYSELF,	LADY	WAYNFLETE. PROCEED. /LADY CICELY/ CAPTAIN BRASSBOUND, I
CAPT III (285)	CAN PROCEED TO PROSECUTE. THE FLOOR IS YOURS,	LADY	WAYNFLETE. /LADY CICELY/ (RISING) I CAN ONLY TELL YOU
CAPT III (280)	AHDMIRALTY HAS IN ITS WHOLE CAWNSTITOOTION,	LADY	WAYNFLETE. /LADY CICELY/ OF COURSE I HAVE. SAILORS
CAPT III (280)	WE OFTEN FEEL THAT DEPRIVATION VERRY KEENLY,	LADY	WAYNFLETE. /LADY CICELY/ MY UNCLE IS FIRST LORD OF THE
CAPT III (278)	/BLUEJACKET/ CAPTAIN KEARNEY'S CAWMPLIMENTS TO	LADY	WAYNFLETE; AND MAY HE COME IN? /LADY CICELY/ YES. BY
CAPT III (282)	IT? MAY I ASK, SIR, DID YOU NOTICE ANY SIGN ON	LADY	WAYNFLETE'S PART OF CAWMPLYING WITH THAT VERRY MODERATE
CAPT III (280)	TO LOOK AFTER THE SHIP. /KEARNEY/ STRANGER STILL,	LADY	WAYNFLETE, HE IS NOT FORBIDDEN TO TAKE ANY OTHER LADY.
CAPT III (283)	WILL YOU BEGIN WITH ME? /KEARNEY/ BY YOUR LEAVE,	LADY	WAYNFLETE, I THINK I WILL JUST BEGIN WITH MYSELF.
CAPT III (279)	LADY CICELY) WHEN WE PARTED YESTERDAY AHFTERNOON,	LADY	WAYNFLETE, I WAS UNAWARE THAT IN THE COURSE OF YOUR
ARMS III (71)	BACK HERE TO HAVE ANOTHER LOOK AT THE YOUNG	LADY	WHEN ANY OTHER MAN OF MY AGE WOULD HAVE SENT THE COAT
PHIL III (144)	MIND. BUT IF YOU ARE NOT GOING TO BEHAVE LIKE A	LADY	WHEN MRS TRANFIELD COMES INTO THIS ROOM, YOUVE GOT TO
BUOY III (34)	AND CAN TALK LIKE A LADY, AND CAN BEHAVE LIKE A	LADY	WHEN SHE LIKES; BUT SHE DOES NOT BELONG TO US. HER TEN
DOCT III (139)	AWAY THAT SHE HADNT GOT ANY. YOU DONT KNOW A	LADY	WHEN YOU SEE ONE. /B.B./ (MAJESTICALLY) WHAT DO YOU
GETT PREFACE(251)	THAT I HAD NOT THE PRESENCE OF MIND TO ASK THE	LADY	WHETHER SHE INSISTED ON HAVING A DOCTOR, A NURSE, A
GETT (285)	ALICE: IVE HAD ANOTHER LETTER FROM THE MYSTERIOUS	LADY	WHO CANT SPELL. I LIKE THAT WOMAN'S LETTERS. THERES AN
DOCT II (124)	WITH HIM. /RIDGEON/ THE WOMAN! DO YOU MEAN THE	LADY	WHO DINED HERE? THE GENTLEMAN'S WIFE? /THE MAID/ DONT
DOCT PREFACE(45)	OF LETTING THEM LOOSE ON A HUMAN CHILD. THE	LADY	WHO GETS HER CLOAK BY FLAYING A SABLE DOES NOT FLAY A
GETT PREFACE(224)	AMONG ENTIRELY LAW-ABIDING PEOPLE. I KNOW ONE	LADY	WHO HAS BEEN MARRIED FIVE TIMES. SHE IS, AS MIGHT BE
MIS. SD(115)	HIM. MRS TARLETON IS A SHREWD AND MOTHERLY OLD	LADY	WHO HAS BEEN PRETTY IN HER TIME, AND IS STILL VERY
MTH3 (123)	MINISTRY I DO NOT COME TO YOU: I GO TO THE BLACK	LADY	WHO HAS BEEN THE REAL PRESIDENT DURING YOUR PRESENT
MRS PREFACE(179)	BE EXHIBITED IN PLACE OF PUBLIC ENTERTAINMENT, A	LADY	WHO HAS DEVOTED HERSELF TO THE CHARITABLE WORK OF
BUOY IV (54)	INTERRUPTED BY THE ARRIVAL FROM AMERICA OF THE	LADY	WHO HAS JUST LEFT US. I WAS INTERRUPTED AGAIN BY THE
GETT PREFACE(224)	ME THAT PEOPLE ARE THE WORSE FOR A CHANGE. THE	LADY	WHO HAS MARRIED AND MANAGED FIVE HUSBANDS MUST BE MUCH
MRS PREFACE(160)	OFFICER FINDS HIMSELF IN AN INN WITH A FRENCH	LADY	WHO HAS WOUNDED HIS NATIONAL VANITY. HE RESOLVES TO
2TRU II (55)	IN THIS DISTRICT AND TO RESCUE A BRITISH	LADY	WHO IS BEING HELD FOR RANSOM. YOU KNOW THAT. YOU DONT
GETT PREFACE(227)	CHILDREN PREMATURELY AND FAR TOO FREQUENTLY. THE	LADY	WHO SAYS THAT AS HER RELIGION IS LOVE, HER CHILDREN
SUPR I (13)	BUY IT, SIR. IT HAS BEEN SENT ME BY SOME FOOLISH	LADY	WHO SEEMS TO ADMIRE YOUR VIEWS. I WAS ABOUT TO DISPOSE
FOUN (216)	NOT MY BUSINESS TO BE A FATHER TO EVERY YOUNG	LADY	WHO WALKS INTO MY OFFICE. /ANASTASIA/ NOT YOUR
DOCT PREFACE(21)	DOSE. FORTUNATELY THE PATIENT WAS A HARDY OLD	LADY	WHO WAS NOT EASILY KILLED. SHE RECOVERED WITH NO WORSE
MRS I (189)	HANDS. /CROFTS/ MAY I SHAKE HANDS WITH A YOUNG	LADY	WHOM I HAVE KNOWN BY REPUTATION VERY LONG AS THE
OVER (186)	SIR, ASPERSE THE CHARACTER OF THAT SWEET LADY? A	LADY	WHOM I HAVE TAKEN UNDER MY PROTECTION. /JUNO/
CATH PREFACE(154)	AS A RUSSIAN, BUT AS A HIGHLY DOMESTICATED GERMAN	LADY	WHOSE HOUSEHOLD ROUTINE WAS NOT AT ALL SO UNLIKE THAT
GENV I (37)	THE LEAGUE OF NATIONS? /NEWCOMER/ NO, MAAM. THIS	LADY	WILL DO ALL YOU REQUIRE (HE GOES OUT). /THE WIDOW/ AM
WIDO I (21)	VERY CLEARLY EXPRESSED. /SARTORIUS/ " THE YOUNG	LADY	WILL INHERIT THE BULK OF HER FATHER'S FORTUNE, AND WILL
CATH 1 (171)	BEAUTIFUL DARLING. /EDSTASTON/ MY RESPECT FOR THE	LADY	WILL NOT PERMIT IT. /VARINKA/ RESPECT! HOW CAN YOU
CAPT I (237)	LADY; AND THEY SHALL OBEY THEIR ORDERS. BUT THE	LADY	WILL PLEASE UNDERSTAND THAT I TAKE MY OWN WAY WITH THEM
FANY III (298)	WITHOUT BEING SUED FOR BREACH OF PROMISE IF THE	LADY	WISHES TO BE PAID FOR HER DISAPPOINTMENT. /BOBBY/ BUT
FANY I (275)	/JUGGINS/ (PRESENTING THE SALVER TO MR GILBEY)	LADY	WISHES TO SEE MR BOBBY'S PARENTS, SIR, /GILBEY/ (

2TRU PREFACE(10)	LUMP. BUT THEN THEY ARE NEITHER IDLE NOR FREE. A	LADY	WITH A BIG HOUSE TO MANAGE, AND THE REARING OF A FAMILY
MILL IV (190)	THINGS. BUT THE VERY NEXT DAY AN AMERICAN	LADY	WITH A BOATING PARTY BOUGHT THEM RIGHT OFF THE TABLE
MIS. (178)	SHOULD HAVE THOUGHT OF THAT BEFORE YOU ATTACKED A	LADY	WITH A DASTARDLY SLANDER. I'M WAITING FOR YOUR
SIM PRO,3, (34)	M.T./ EXCUSE ME: I HAVE MISLAID MY WIFE. ENGLISH	LADY	WITH A GUIDE BOOK. WEARS GLASSES. BI-FOCALS. /THE Y.W./
2TRU I SD(27)	IN ONE OF THE RICHEST CITIES IN ENGLAND. A YOUNG	LADY	WITH AN UNHEALTHY COMPLEXION IS ASLEEP IN THE BED. A
MTH2 SD(41)	MESS OF HIS DEPARTURE, A VIGOROUS SUNBURNT YOUNG	LADY	WITH HAZEL HAIR CUT TO THE LEVEL OF HER NECK, LIKE AN
DEVL III (66)	IN THE MINISTER'S HOUSE, SITTING AT TEA WITH THE	LADY	WITH HIS COAT OFF, QUITE AT HOME. IF HE ISNT MARRIED TO
PYGM V (277)	GARDEN; AND NOW SHE PRETENDS TO PLAY THE FINE	LADY	WITH ME. /MRS HIGGINS/ (PLACIDLY) YES, DEAR; BUT YOULL
LADY PREFACE(207)	TO SHAKESPEAR, I HAVE IDENTIFIED THE DARK	LADY	WITH MISTRESS MARY FITTON. FIRST, LET ME SAY THAT I DO
3PLA PREFACE(R14)	IN THE CONTEMPLATION OF A BEAUTEOUS YOUNG LEADING	LADY	WITH VOLUPTUOUS CONTOURS AND LONGLASHED EYES, PAINTED
BASH III (126)	OH, CHANGE THAT TITLE FOR THE SWEETER ONE OF	LADY	WORTHINGTON. /CASHEL/ UNHAPPY MAN, YOU KNOW NOT WHAT
DOCT PREFACE(72)	IN TWENTY; AND THEY COULD HARDLY DOUBT THAT OUR	LADY	WOULD BE DELIGHTED. PERHAPS THEY DO NOWADAYS; FOR
NEVR II (227)	OF COURSE, SIR, IF IT WERE TRUE, THE YOUNG	LADY	WOULD HAVE SEEN THE RESEMBLANCE TOO, SIR. /THE
SUPR III (124)	INFREQUENTLY MET IN SOME SUCH WAY AS THIS. THE	LADY	WOULD SAY THAT SHE WOULD COUNTENANCE MY ADVANCES,
2TRU II (73)	THERE ARE CERTAIN DISGUSTING TRUTHS THAT NO	LADY	WOULD THROW IN THE TEETH OF HER FELLOW CREATURES-- /THE
KING I (199)	THROUGH MR NEWTON'S TELESCOPE; AND THE JEALOUS	LADY	WOULDNT LEAVE UNTIL THE FRENCH LADY LEFT; AND THE
SUPR IV (146)	I DARESAY YOU ARE PREPARED FOR THAT. WHEN A YOUNG	LADY	WRITES TO A YOUNG MAN TO COME TO HER QUICK, QUICK,
OVER (185)	LOOK LIKE AN UNMARRIED MAN. I HAPPEN TO KNOW THE	LADY	YOU DISAPPOINTED. I TRAVELLED IN THE SAME SHIP WITH
FANY III (325)	AS DISGRACEFUL. IT IS GENTLEMANLY TO MARRY THE	LADY	YOU MAKE LOVE TO. /GILBEY/ (AGHAST) MY BOY IS TO MARRY
2TRU I (46)	AND A LIAR. BUT YOU AMUSE ME. IF YOU WERE A REAL	LADY	YOU WOULDNT AMUSE ME. YOUD BE AFRAID TO BE SO
ARMS I (11)	HIDING ON THE BALCONY. WILL YOU AND THE GRACIOUS	LADY	YOUR MOTHER PLEASE TO WITHDRAW WHILST WE SEARCH?
CAPT III (280)	THEY SAID, WELL, SIR, WILL YOU TALK TO THE	LADY	YOURSELF NEXT TIME? /LADY CICELY/ I'M SO SORRY. BUT
WIDO I (13)	TO SEE. /COKANE/ NOTHING TO SEE! SHE, A PERFECT	LADY	, A PERSON OF THE HIGHEST BREEDING, ACTUALLY IN YOUR
SUPR PREFACE(R37)	IS NARRATED THAT IN THE EIGHTEENSEVENTIES AN OLD	LADY	, A VERY DEVOUT METHODIST, MOVED FROM COLCHESTER TO A
ARMS I (9)	MAN/ (WITH GRIM GOODHUMOR) ALL OF THEM, DEAR	LADY	, ALL OF THEM, BELIEVE ME. IT IS OUR DUTY TO LIVE AS
HART II (110)	IMPERTINENT. /THE BURGLAR/ (QUICKLY) ALL RIGHT,	LADY	, ALL RIGHT. IVE NO WISH TO BE ANYTHING BUT AGREEABLE.
AUGS (280)	THERE WAS NO REAL DANGER. YOU SEE, MY DEAR LITTLE	LADY	, ALL THIS TALK ABOUT WAR SAVING, AND SECRECY, AND
6CAL PREFACE(89)	FOOTBALL TEAM. TO THEM A QUEEN WAS A DIGNIFIED	LADY	, ALSO VICTORIAN AS TO HER COIFFURE, GRACIOUSLY
SUPR III (88)	YOU DO NOT KNOW TO WHOM YOU ARE SPEAKING. I AM A	LADY	, AND A FAITHFUL DAUGHTER OF THE CHURCH. /DON JUAN/ I
JITT I (12)	I SEE HIM. AND I FEEL SURE YOUR LADY IS A REAL	LADY	, AND ALWAYS THE SAME LADY; THOUGH OF COURSE I TAKE
PYGM V (278)	A LADY TO YOU, BECAUSE YOU ALWAYS TREAT ME AS A	LADY	, AND ALWAYS WILL. /MRS HIGGINS/ PLEASE DONT GRIND YOUR
GETT (270)	YOU SEE, IS THAT I REALLY AM AN ENGLISH	LADY	, AND AM PARTICULARLY PROUD OF BEING ONE. /THE GENERAL/
BUOY III (34)	HER. SHE DRESSES LIKE A LADY, AND CAN TALK LIKE A	LADY	, AND CAN BEHAVE LIKE A LADY WHEN SHE LIKES; BUT SHE
BUOY III (34)	COULD MAKE A REAL LADY OF HER. SHE DRESSES LIKE A	LADY	, AND CAN TALK LIKE A LADY, AND CAN BEHAVE LIKE A LADY
JOAN PREFACE(11)	VOICES IN THEM. IN SHORT, MUCH MORE OF A YOUNG	LADY	, AND EVEN OF AN INTELLECTUAL, THAN MOST OF THE
DOCT I SD(108)	RATHER DISTANT PROFESSIONAL MANNER, TURNS TO THE	LADY	, AND INVITES HER, BY A GESTURE, TO SIT DOWN ON THE
OVER SD(171)	HE IS OBVIOUSLY VERY MUCH IN LOVE WITH THE	LADY	, AND IS, IN FACT, YIELDING TO AN IRRESISTIBLE IMPULSE
LADY PREFACE(210)	AFFAIRS: WE TALKED ABOUT SHAKESPEAR, AND THE DARK	LADY	, AND SWIFT, AND KOHELETH, AND THE CYCLES, AND THE
DOCT III (149)	JENNIFER COMES IN. PLEASE REMEMBER THAT SHE'S A	LADY	, AND THAT YOU ARE SUPPOSED TO BE GENTLEMEN. (HE GOES
LADY PREFACE(214)	TYLER IN IDENTIFYING MARY FITTON AS THE DARK	LADY	, AND THE EARL OF PEMBROKE AS THE ADDRESSEE OF THE
ARMS I SD(4)	FARMER, BUT IS DETERMINED TO BE A VIENNESE	LADY	, AND TO THAT END WEARS A FASHIONABLE TEA GOWN ON ALL
2TRU PREFACE(9)	THE CRIMEAN HOSPITALS RATHER THAN BEHAVE LIKE A	LADY	, AND WHY MY NEIGHBOR MR APSLEY CHERRY-GARRARD, THE
GLIM (180)	THIN, WHICH WAS EXACTLY WHAT SHE DESIRED, POOR	LADY	, AS SHE WAS LOSING HER FIGURE TERRIBLY. /SQUARCIO/
SUPR III SD(72)	SOONER THAN WORK AGAINST HIS GRAIN; OR WHEN A	LADY	, BECAUSE SHE IS A LADY, WILL FACE ANY EXTREMITY OF
AUGS SD(271)	RETURNS, DEVOTEDLY USHERING A VERY ATTRACTIVE	LADY	, BRILLIANTLY DRESSED. SHE HAS A DAINTY WALLET HANGING
CAPT III SD(279)	PUT POLITELY, AS BECOMES AN OFFICER ADDRESSING A	LADY	, BUT ALSO WITH AN EMPHATICALLY IMPLIED REBUKE, AS AN
GETT (270)	MATTER IS VERY SIMPLE. AS I SAY, I AM AN ENGLISH	LADY	, BY WHICH I MEAN THAT I HAVE BEEN TRAINED TO DO
3PLA PREFACE(R21)	TO WHOM MINOR POETS ADDRESS VERSES ENTITLED TO MY	LADY	, COME TO LIFE AS THE PARLORMAIDS AND WAITRESSES OF THE
DEST (157)	ALWAYS REGRETTED, EXCELLENCY. (CALLING) COMING,	LADY	, COMING. (HE MAKES FOR THE INNER DOOR). /NAPOLEON/ (
GENV IV (89)	BRIEF FOR THE BRITISH FOREIGN OFFICE. THE	LADY	, DAME BEGONIA BROWN, REPRESENTS THE COMMITTEE FOR
2TRU II (77)	US? /TALLBOYS/ (TAPPING HIS REVOLVER) MY DEAR	LADY	, DO YOU SUPPOSE I AM CARRYING THIS FOR FUN? DONT YOU
MTH3 (121)	IF I TELL YOU. /BURGE-LUBIN/ OFFENDED! MY DEAR	LADY	, DO YOU SUPPOSE, AFTER SUCH A STUPENDOUS REVELATION,
ARMS III (51)	SITS DOWN BESIDE HER. /BLUNTSCHLI/ MY DEAR YOUNG	LADY	, DONT LET THIS WORRY YOU. REMEMBER: I'M A SOLDIER. NOW
APPL I SD(209)	AS LONG AS I AM THE NEPHEW OF MY UNCLE. A YOUNG	LADY	, DRESSED FOR WALKING, RUSHES IN IMPETUOUSLY. /THE
DEST (156)	(STARTLED) WHO'S THAT? /GIUSEPPE/ THE	LADY	, EXCELLENCY. /NAPOLEON/ THE LADY UPSTAIRS? /GIUSEPPE/
LADY PREFACE(207)	THE LATER SUGGESTION OF MR ACHESON THAT THE DARK	LADY	, FAR FROM BEING A MAID OF HONOR, KEPT A TAVERN IN
AUGS (260)	21ST JANUARY 1917, WITH LALLA VANDERVELDE AS THE	LADY	, F. B. J. SHARP AS LORD AUGUSTUS HIGHCASTLE, AND
HART I SD(44)	SIDE AND A LONG GARDEN SEAT ON THE WEST. A YOUNG	LADY	, GLOVED AND HATTED, WITH A DUST COAT ON, IS SITTING IN
JITT II (41)	UNCTUOUSLY, AS HE SHAKES HER HAND) GOODBYE, DEAR	LADY	, GOOD-BYE. /AGNES/ GOODBYE. (TO EDITH, LAUGHING A
PHIL I SD(69)	SIDE BY SIDE, IN ONE ANOTHER'S ARMS. THE	LADY	, GRACE TRANFIELD, IS ABOUT 32, SLIGHT OF BUILD,
GENV I SD(41)	BUT THE WIDOW HAS GONE AND THE YOUNG OFFICE	LADY	, GREATLY UPSET, DROPS BACK INTO HER SEAT WITH A
PYGM EPILOG (297)	WAS WHAT THE EPSOM GREENGROCER CALLED A CARRIAGE	LADY	, HAD NO EXCHANGE VALUE, APPARENTLY. IT HAD PREVENTED
SIM PRO,3,SD(32)	TRACT WITH THE GREATEST ATTENTION. THANK YOU. THE	LADY	, HAVING NO EXCUSE FOR STAYING, MOVES AWAY RELUCTANTLY
2TRU I (31)	SURE IT IS NOT HER LUNGS? /THE DOCTOR/ MY GOOD	LADY	, HER LUNGS ARE AS SOUND AS A SEAGULL'S. /THE ELDERLY
CATH 1 (162)	SERGEANT, ENTERS. /THE SERGEANT/ (SOFTLY TO THE	LADY	, HOLDING THE DOOR HANDLE) LITTLE DARLING HONEY: IS HIS
FOUN (218)	LORD CHANCELLOR/ (OVERWHELMED) MY DEAR YOUNG	LADY	, HOW CAN I APOLOGIZE-- /MERCER/ (CRUSHED) I'M SURE I
SIM I (38)	/THE CLERGYMAN/ (DISTRESSED) OH, DEAR BEAUTIFUL	LADY	, I AM NOT MAD. EVERYBODY THINKS I AM. NOBODY BELIEVES
ARMS I (18)	HER IMPATIENCE). I AM NOT INDIFFERENT, DEAR YOUNG	LADY	, I ASSURE YOU. BUT HOW IS IT TO BE DONE? /RAINA/ COME
MILL I (143)	PROVE A FORTUNE TO YOU. /SAGAMORE/ BUT, MY DEAR	LADY	, I DONT KNOW ANYTHING ABOUT YOUR DISTRESS. YOUR
2TRU III (82)	/THE SERGEANT/ (WITH STERN CONTEMPT) NO, MY	LADY	, I DONT. I SAW A LOT OF THAT IN THE WAR: PRETTY LADIES
VWOO 3 (135)	ON THEM! " AND " SPARROWGRASS VERY GOOD TODAY, MY	LADY	, IF YOU WOULD BE WANTING SOME." /A/ I POSITIVELY DENY
NEVR II (226)	PHILIP, I SUPPOSE. /WAITER/ YES, SIR. THE YOUNG	LADY	, IN GIVING AN ORDER, OR THE LIKE OF THAT, WILL SAY, "
GETT PREFACE(251)	OF OTHELLO'S OUTBURST UNTIL I ONE DAY HEARD A	LADY	, IN THE COURSE OF A PRIVATE DISCUSSION AS TO THE
ARMS I SD(3)	OUTWARDS, ALSO STAND OPEN. ON THE BALCONY A YOUNG	LADY	, INTENSELY CONSCIOUS OF THE ROMANTIC BEAUTY OF THE
FANY PROLOG (270)	THIS IS CAMBRIDGE EDUCATION! WELL, MY DEAR YOUNG	LADY	, I'M DELIGHTED TO FIND THERES SOMETHING YOU DONT KNOW;
MIS. (139)	/LORD SUMMERHAYS/ A BLACKMAILER, MY DEAR YOUNG	LADY	, IS A PERSON WHO KNOWS A DISGRACEFUL SECRET IN THE
NEVR IV (294)	/BOHUN/ (IN POWERFUL TONES) THIS IS THE YOUNGER	LADY	, IS IT? /DOLLY/ (SLIPPING DOWN OFF THE TABLE IN
PRES (156)	THANK HEAVEN SHE'S GONE. AND NOW, MY DEAR	LADY	, IS IT NECESSARY TO KEEP THAT LOADED PISTOL TO MY NOSE
MTH4 II (185)	TURNS TO ENTER THE TEMPLE). /THE ENVOY/ MY GOOD	LADY	, IS IT WORTH WHILE DRESSING-UP AND PUTTING ON FALSE
CATH 3,SD(183)	THE NEVA. CLAIRE, A ROBUST YOUNG ENGLISH	LADY	, IS LEANING ON THE RIVER WALL. SHE TURNS EXPECTANTLY
SUPR III (125)	AN IMMORAL IMPULSE. /DON JUAN/ NATURE, MY DEAR	LADY	, IS WHAT YOU CALL IMMORAL. I BLUSH FOR IT; BUT I
PYGM V (277)	REALLY NICE MANNERS; AND THAT IS WHAT MAKES ONE A	LADY	, ISNT IT? YOU SEE IT WAS SO VERY DIFFICULT FOR ME
GENV III (71)	TO SEX IN THESE WESTERN COUNTRIES. THIS HANDSOME	LADY	, IT SEEMS, HAS SOME LOVER'S QUARREL WITH THIS HANDSOME
PHIL II (127)	IT SOME DAY, JULIA. /CRAVEN/ DO YOU KNOW THIS	LADY	, JO? /CUTHBERTSON/ THIS IS MY DAUGHTER, MRS
FANY I (275)	ROB. HOW DO YOU KNOW? (TO JUGGINS) IS SHE A	LADY	, JUGGINS? YOU KNOW WHAT I MEAN. /JUGGINS/ IN THE
SUPR III (118)	I WAS IN THE ACT OF FRAMING MY EXCUSE TO THE	LADY	, LIFE SEIZED ME AND THREW ME INTO HER ARMS AS A SAILOR
GETT (261)	ALL SORTS OF PEOPLE. YOU ARE A VERY AFFABLE	LADY	, MAAM, FOR A BISHOP'S LADY. I HAVE KNOWN BISHOPS'
GETT (263)	EXCEPT YOUR SISTER, MAAM. A FINE CHARACTER OF A	LADY	, MAAM, IS MISS GRANTHAM. I HAVE AN AMBITION TO ARRANGE
DEVL III (67)	HAVE YOU ADDRESSED PROFANE LANGUAGE TO THE	LADY	, MAJOR SWINDON? /SWINDON/ (VERY ANGRY) NO, SIR,
2TRU I (46)	THE FUN WHILE I, BECAUSE I AM RESPECTABLE AND A	LADY	, MIGHT JUST AS WELL BE IN PRISON. /THE BURGLAR/ DONT
BARB III (314)	IN). WHAT IS IT? /MORRISON/ IF YOU PLEASE, MY	LADY	, MR UNDERSHAFT HAS JUST DROVE UP TO THE DOOR. /LADY
GETT SD(260)	KITCHEN IS OCCUPIED AT PRESENT BY THE BISHOP'S	LADY	, MRS BRIDGENORTH, WHO IS TALKING TO MR WILLIAM
2TRU III SD(94)	AND LAMENTATION. IT IS THAT OF THE ELDERLY	LADY	, MRS MOPPLY. SHE IS PURSUING COLONEL TALLBOYS DOWN THE
GETT (309)	(TO THE BISHOP) IVE OFTEN SPOKEN OF HER TO YOUR	LADY	, MY LORD. (TO MRS BRIDGENORTH) MRS GEORGE, MAAM. /MRS
SUPR IV (149)	BY OPENING THAT LETTER. A LETTER FROM AN ENGLISH	LADY	, NOT ADDRESSED TO YOU-- A CAWNFIDENTIAL LETTER! A
LADY PREFACE(207)	CAME TO LIGHT AND TURNED OUT TO BE THAT OF A FAIR	LADY	, NOT OF A DARK ONE. THAT SETTLES THE QUESTION, IF THE
ARMS III (53)	/BLUNTSCHLI/ (WARMLY, RISING) NO, MY DEAR YOUNG	LADY	, NO, NO, NO A THOUSAND TIMES. IT'S PART OF YOUR YOUTH:
GETT (310)	IN THE COUNTY OF BLANK, HEREINAFTER CALLED THE	LADY	, OF THE OTHER PART, WHEREBY IT IS DECLARED AND AGREED
DEVL III (63)	BUT YOU WILL NOT SAVE MINE. /BURGOYNE/ MY GOOD	LADY	, OUR ONLY DESIRE IS TO SAVE UNPLEASANTNESS. WHAT
SUPR IV (151)	THIS. IS HECTOR NOT GOOD ENOUGH FOR THIS	LADY	, PRAY? /TANNER/ MY DEAR SIR, THE LADY IS MARRIED
3PLA PREFACE(R21)	FROM A MIRACULOUS SLEEP, MEETS A BOSTON YOUNG	LADY	, PROVIDED EXPRESSLY FOR HIM TO FALL IN LOVE WITH.
GETT (322)	ALICE, PLEASE. AS I SAID BEFORE, I AM AN ENGLISH	LADY	, QUITE PREPARED TO DO WITHOUT ANYTHING I CANT HAVE ON
FANY I (279)	THATS YOURS. /MRS GILBEY/ OH, DONT BE RUDE TO THE	LADY	, ROB. /DORA/ I'M COMING TO IT, OLD DEAR: DONT YOU BE
DEST (180)	HURRIES OFF. NAPOLEON TURNS CURTLY TO THE	LADY	, SAYING) I MUST TROUBLE YOU TO REMAIN SOME MOMENTS
MIS. (155)	I THINK I KNOW. THE LAST TIME I SAW THAT	LADY	, SHE DID SOMETHING I SHOULD NOT HAVE THOUGHT POSSIBLE.
2TRU I (30)	GOOD. SHE GOT WORSE. /THE DOCTOR/ BUT, MY DEAR	LADY	, SHE WAS SICKENING FOR MEASLES. THAT WAS NOT THE FAULT
GETT PREFACE(244)	IN THIS TRADE WHO HAS THE TABLE MANNERS OF A	LADY	, SHEWS THAT PROSTITUTION IS NOT A VOCATION BUT A

LADY (238)	ARE THE ONLY PRETTY MAN IN THE WORLD? A MERRY	LADY	, SIR: A WARM BIT OF STUFF. GO TO: I'LL NOT SEE HER
NEVR II (242)	WHO IS LOOKING ABOUT FOR SOMETHING) BREAD FOR THE	LADY	, SIR? YES, SIR. (HE SERVES BREAD TO GLORIA, AND
LADY (239)	FROM WITHIN. /THE BEEFEATER/ HERE COMES YOUR	LADY	, SIR, I'LL TO T'OTHER END OF MY WARD. YOU MAY EEN TAKE
DEVL III (50)	THE ROOM IN HIS HAND. THEY WITHDRAW). YOUR GOOD	LADY	, SIR, /RICHARD/ (GOING TO HER) WHAT! MY WIFE. MY
CAPT III (281)	(AT THE DOOR) THEY ARE ENGAGED WITH THE BRITISH	LADY	, SIR. SHALL I ASK HER-- /KEARNEY/ (JUMPING UP AND
JOAN EPILOG (159)	/JOAN/ BE YOU A SAINT? /THE SOLDIER/ YES,	LADY	, STRAIGHT FROM HELL. /DUNOIS/ A SAINT, AND FROM HELL!
LADY (206)	24TH NOVEMBER 1910, BY MONA LIMERICK AS THE DARK	LADY	, SUZANNE SHELDON AS QUEEN ELIZABETH, GRANVILLE BARKER
2TRU III (103)	HE PASSES HERE AS THE HALF STEPBROTHER OF THIS	LADY	, THE COUNTESS VALBRIONI. /SWEETIE/ VALBRIONI BE
WIDO I (21)	/COKANE/ (WRITING) " ACQUAINTANCE OF A YOUNG	LADY	, THE DAUGHTER OF"-- YES? /SARTORIUS/ " OF"-- YOU HAD
WIDO I (21)	I SAID, " I HAVE MADE THE ACQUAINTANCE OF A YOUNG	LADY	, THE DAUGHTER OF--" (HE HESITATES). /COKANE/ (
SUPR PREFACE(R18)	LENGTH IN A SHAVIO-SOCRATIC DIALOGUE WITH THE	LADY	, THE STATUE, AND THE DEVIL. BUT THIS PLEASANTRY IS NOT
BULL PREFACE(51)	OF ONE ABD-EL-NEBI, A YOUNG MAN OF 25. NOW THE	LADY	, THOUGH, AS IT TURNED OUT, ONLY TEMPORARILY DISABLED
OVER (185)	YOU HAVE THE GOODNESS, SIR, IN ADDRESSING THIS	LADY	, TO KEEP YOUR TEMPER AND REFRAIN FROM USING PROFANE
HART I (48)	OH, HOW I LONGED! -- TO BE RESPECTABLE, TO BE A	LADY	, TO LIVE AS OTHERS DID, NOT TO HAVE TO THINK OF
PPP (201)	(HESITATING) IT DO SEEM A PITY, DONT IT, MY	LADY	, TO SPOIL YOUR LOVELY BUST? /ADOLPHUS/ TUSH! THIS
NEVR IV (301)	SHOCKED. YOU ARE JUST AN ORDINARY YOUNG	LADY	, TOO ORDINARY TO ALLOW TAME LIEUTENANTS TO GO AS FAR
CATH 1,SD(162)	BODILY STRENGTH, AND EXALTED RANK. A PRETTY YOUNG	LADY	, VARINKA, HIS FAVORITE NIECE, IS LOUNGING ON AN
SIM PREFACE(8)	OF HONOR AND SUCCESS IS TO BE A GENTLEMAN OR	LADY	, WHICH MEANS THAT YOUR LIVING IS EARNED FOR YOU BY
SUPR III (116)	ONE WAS VERY HARD HIT INDEED. /DON JUAN/ THEN THE	LADY	, WHO HAD BEEN HAPPY AND IDLE ENOUGH BEFORE, BECAME
CLEO III (145)	/APOLLODORUS/ MY FRIEND: THIS IS A GREAT	LADY	, WHO STANDS HIGH WITH CAESAR. /SENTINEL/ (NOT AT ALL
SIM I (44)	YOU SEE, THE FAMILY IS A MIXED ONE. THIS	LADY	, WHOM YOU MAY ADDRESS AS PROLA, AND THIS GENTLEMAN,
GENV III (78)	TAKE THE CASE OF THIS PASSIONATE AND ATTRACTIVE	LADY	, WHOSE NAME I HAVE NOT THE PLEASURE OF KNOWING. /THE
WIDO III (62)	YOU FORGET, MR LICKCHEESE, THAT THE YOUNG	LADY	, WHOSE TASTE HAS TO BE CONSIDERED, DECISIVELY OBJECTED
SUPR III SD(72)	HIS GRAIN; OR WHEN A LADY, BECAUSE SHE IS A	LADY	, WILL FACE ANY EXTREMITY OF PARASITIC DEPENDENCE
ROCK I (228)	(A DEEP SIGHING BREATH). AND NOW, MY DEAR	LADY	, WILL YOU BE GOOD ENOUGH TO TELL ME WHO THE DEVIL YOU
DEST SD(173)	WHEN IT IS NECESSARY. DO YOU UNDERSTAND? THE	LADY	, WITHOUT SPEAKING, STANDS UPRIGHT, AND TAKES A PACKET
SUPR III (116)	DONT LIKE IT YOU CAN LUMP IT. /DON JUAN/ MY DEAR	LADY	, YOU HAVE PUT MY WHOLE CASE AGAINST ROMANCE INTO A FEW
SUPR III (103)	/DON JUAN/ IN HEAVEN, AS I PICTURE IT, DEAR	LADY	, YOU LIVE AND WORK INSTEAD OF PLAYING AND PRETENDING.
NEVR III (276)	MEAN THAT, MR M'COMAS. /M'COMAS/ MY DEAR YOUNG	LADY	, YOU PICK ME UP VERY SHARPLY. BUT LET ME JUST PUT THIS
PYGM II (228)	DRESSED. IF THE KING FINDS OUT YOURE NOT A	LADY	, YOU WILL BE TAKEN BY THE POLICE TO THE TOWER OF
PYGM V (286)	STOP BEING A COMMON IDIOT. IF YOURE GOING TO BE A	LADY	, YOULL HAVE TO GIVE UP FEELING NEGLECTED IF THE MEN
DOCT III (150)	IS GIVING HER A MOST GRATIFYING SURPRISE) MY DEAR	LADY	, YOUR HUSBAND SHALL HAVE ME. /MRS DUBEDAT/ BUT--
ARMS III (57)	BUT JUST LISTEN TO MY ADVICE. IF YOU WANT TO BE A	LADY	, YOUR PRESENT BEHAVIOR TO ME WONT DO AT ALL, UNLESS
MIS. (180)	POLISH LADY. /BENTLEY/ (WRITING) " THE POLISH	LADY	"? /TARLETON/ (TO PERCIVAL) NOW IT'S YOUR TURN.
LADY PREFACE(218)	HIS THEORY THAT SHAKESPEAR'S PASSION FOR THE DARK	LADY	" CANKERED AND TOOK ON PROUD FLESH IN HIM, AND TORTURED
LADY PREFACE(222)	GRINS WITH YORICK'S SKULL, AND INVITING " MY	LADY	" TO LAUGH AT THE SEPULCHRAL HUMOR OF THE FACT THAT
ARMS I (10)	KNOCKING AT THE BEDROOM DOOR) MY LADY! MY	LADY	! GET UP QUICK AND OPEN THE DOOR. IF YOU DONT THEY
DEST (163)	TREAT THIS LADY IN SUCH A FASHION? /LIEUTENANT/	LADY	! HE'S A MAN! THE MAN I SHEWED MY CONFIDENCE IN. (
HART I (49)	CAPTAIN/ YOUR TEA, YOUNG LADY. WHAT! ANOTHER	LADY	! I MUST FETCH ANOTHER CUP (HE MAKES FOR THE PANTRY).
ARMS I (10)	(OUTSIDE, KNOCKING AT THE BEDROOM DOOR) MY	LADY	! MY LADY! GET UP QUICK AND OPEN THE DOOR. IF YOU
MIS. (151)	I SAY! /JOHNNY/ BY GEORGE! /LORD SUMMERHAYS/ A	LADY	! /HYPATIA/ A WOMAN! /TARLETON/ (TO PERCIVAL) YOU
PRES (157)	YOU ARE A DEAD MAN. /MITCHENER/ (AMAZED) MY DEAR	LADY	! /LADY CORINTHIA/ I AM NOT YOUR DEAR LADY. YOU ARE
PRES (155)	WOMEN. /MITCHENER/ (REMONSTRATING) MY DEAR	LADY	! /MRS BANGER/ HOW CAN YOU TELL? YOU NEVER KNEW THAT
DEVL I (26)	TO JUDITH) ACTUALLY DOESNT WANT TO, MOST VIRTUOUS	LADY	! /UNCLE TITUS/ HAVE A CARE, RICHARD DUDGEON. THE
DEST (161)	UPSTAIRS, LIEUTENANT, CALLING ME. /LIEUTENANT/	LADY	! /VOICE/ GIUSEPPE, GIUSEPPE: WHERE ARE YOU?
MRS II (217)	ABOUT IT TO HER, BUT THEN LIZ WAS SUCH A PERFECT	LADY	! SHE HAD THE TRUE INSTINCT OF IT; WHILE I WAS ALWAYS
ARMS I (13)	AND SAYS, WITH GRATEFUL EMOTION) BLESS YOU, DEAR	LADY	! YOU CAN ALWAYS TELL AN OLD SOLDIER BY THE INSIDE OF

LADYLIKE

BARB I (259)	ABOUT WHICH QUITE COWS ME SOMETIMES. IT'S NOT	LADYLIKE	: I'M SURE I DONT KNOW WHERE SHE PICKED IT UP.
MRS II (214)	WENT TO A CHURCH SCHOOL-- THAT WAS PART OF THE	LADYLIKE	AIRS WE GAVE OURSELVES TO BE SUPERIOR TO THE
NEVR IV (287)	HEAD) OH NO, MAAM. IT'S VERY KIND OF YOU: VERY	LADYLIKE	AND AFFABLE INDEED, MAAM; BUT I SHOULD FEEL AT A
3PLA PREFACE(R10)	IN LOVE, BUT SENTIMENTALLY, ROMANTICALLY; ALWAYS	LADYLIKE	AND GENTLEMANLIKE, JEJUNELY INSIPID. ALL THIS, TO
KING II (224)	SEEMS. I HOLD HER BECAUSE SHE IS INTELLIGENT AND	LADYLIKE	AND KEEPS ME IN TOUCH WITH FRANCE AND THE FRENCH
SIM II (56)	NOVICES; AND LADY FARWATERS, WITH HER ENGLISH	LADYLIKE	BRINGING-UP, WAS SO CRUDE THAT SHE REALLY COULD NOT
NEVR I (211)	A CURIOUS HARD EXCITEMENT, DIGNIFIED BUT DOGGED,	LADYLIKE	BUT IMPLACABLE: THE MANNER OF THE OLD GUARD) PHIL:
HART I (73)	LIFE; BUT WHAT DOES IT END IN? RESPECTABILITY. A	LADYLIKE	DAUGHTER. THE LANGUAGE AND APPEARANCE OF A CITY
BARB I (263)	COMES OFF THE TABLE, AND SITS IN HER CHAIR WITH	LADYLIKE	ELEGANCE). /LADY BRITOMART/ REMEMBER, CHARLES, THAT
MIS. (143)	HERE DOING NOTHING BUT BEING GOOD AND NICE AND	LADYLIKE	I SIMPLY WONT. STAY DOWN HERE WITH US FOR A WEEK;
2TRU II (67)	NO PICTURES. NO DANCES. NOTHING TO DO BUT BE	LADYLIKE	. AND THE ONE REALLY LOVABLE MAN GOING TO WASTE!
FANY II (290)	I HIT BACK. YES I DID. AND I DID WORSE. I WASNT	LADYLIKE	. I CURSED. I CALLED NAMES. I HEARD WORDS THAT I
CATH 4 (191)	I CAN SEE YOUR ANKLES WHEN YOU TICKLE ME: ITS NOT	LADYLIKE	. /CATHERINE/ (STICKING OUT HER TOE AND ADMIRING
2TRU I (48)	BUT WORTH FORTYFIVE GUINEAS. HAT, QUIET AND	LADYLIKE	. TAILOR MADE FROCK, COMBINATION: SILK AND WOOL.
2TRU II (67)	YOU LIKE. WHATS TO PREVENT YOU? /THE PATIENT/ MY	LADYLIKE	MORALS, I SUPPOSE. /THE COUNTESS/ MORALS YOUR
MILL IV (201)	AND LOOKING HER BEST. NO WOMAN CAN BE MORE	LADYLIKE	-- MORE FEMININE-- WHEN IT IS HER CUE TO PLAY THE
INCA (242)	PEOPLE. BUT WHEN I'M NOT PLEASED I'M NOT TOO	LADYLIKE	TO SAY SO. THATS ALL THE DIFFERENCE. THERE IS
PYGM II (227)	CHOKED BY IT) I WOULDNT HAVE ATE IT, ONLY I'M TOO	LADYLIKE	TO TAKE IT OUT OF MY MOUTH. /HIGGINS/ LISTEN,
JOAN PREFACE(26)	DETERMINED TO MAKE JOAN A BEAUTIFUL AND MOST	LADYLIKE	VICTORIAN; BUT BOTH OF THEM RECOGNIZE AND INSIST ON
WIDO III (57)	FEEL THAT WAY, AFTER YOUR BRINGING UP. IT IS THE	LADYLIKE	VIEW OF THE MATTER. SO DONT LET US QUARREL, MY
DEVL I (13)	AS HE IN VITALITY. SHE IS PRETTY AND PROPER AND	LADYLIKE	, AND HAS BEEN ADMIRED AND PETTED INTO AN OPINION
BARB II (282)	DO YOURSELF. /BARBARA/ (SUNNILY APOLOGETIC AND	LADYLIKE	, AS ON A NEW FOOTING WITH HIM) OH, I BEG YOUR
WIDO I SD(5)	STRONGMINDED YOUNG WOMAN, PRESENTABLY	LADYLIKE	, BUT STILL HER FATHER'S DAUGHTER. NEVERTHELESS
MRS II (218)	THAT YOU WERE GROWING UP LIKE LIZ: YOUVE JUST HER	LADYLIKE	, DETERMINED WAY. BUT I CANT STAND SAYING ONE THING
SUPR I SD(16)	AS FAR AS THAT GOES; AND SHE IS PERFECTLY	LADYLIKE	, GRACEFUL, AND COMELY, WITH ENSNARING EYES AND

LADY-AND-GENTLEMAN

SIM PREFACE(13)	PAY AWAY ABOUT HALF MY EARNINGS IN TRIBUTE TO THE	LADY-AND-GENTLEMAN	BUSINESS IN ORDER TO GET PERMISSION TO

LADY-IN-WAITING

CATH 1 (166)	HOME FROM AMERICA AT THE REQUEST OF AUNT FANNY,	LADY-IN-WAITING	TO THE QUEEN. ALL RIGHT, EH? /EDSTASTON/

LADY-KILLER

HART I (75)	/LADY UTTERWORD/ YOU ARE AN EXCEEDINGLY CLEVER	LADY-KILLER	, HECTOR. AND TERRIBLY HANDSOME. I AM QUITE A

LADY'S

CAPT III (289)	/KEARNEY/ I SUPPOSE YOU AND YOUR MEN ACCEPT THIS	LADY'S	ACCOUNT OF WHAT PASSED, CAPTAIN BRASSBOUND.
ARMS I SD(3)	ARMS AND THE MAN. ACT I. NIGHT. A	LADY'S	BEDCHAMBER IN BULGARIA, IN A SMALL TOWN NEAR THE
MRS I SD(181)	LEANING AGAINST THE SIDE BENCH IN THE PORCH. A	LADY'S	BICYCLE IS PROPPED AGAINST THE WALL, UNDER THE
SUPR III (105)	MUCH IN A THOUSAND CENTURIES AS THE FASHION OF A	LADY'S	BONNET IN A SCORE OF WEEKS. BUT WHEN HE GOES OUT TO
LADY PREFACE(223)	SURMISE THAT SHAKESPEAR FOUND OUT THAT THE DARK	LADY'S	BRAINS COULD NO MORE KEEP PACE WITH HIS THAN ANNE
NEVR I (201)	PARLORMAID/ (APPEARING AT THE DOOR) THE YOUNG	LADY'S	BROTHER, SIR. A HANDSOME MAN IN MINIATURE, OBVIOUSLY
SUPR III (125)	DREAMT OF ANY OF THESE THINGS; THAT UNLESS THE	LADY'S	CHARACTER AND INTELLECT WERE EQUAL OR SUPERIOR TO MY
MIS. (185)	THAT YOU COULD NOT, AS A GENTLEMAN, DISPARAGE A	LADY'S	CHARACTER. YOU AGREE WITH ME, I HOPE. /GUNNER/ YES:
NEVR IV (296)	I WILL NOT HAVE THIS, MR BOHUN: I USE THE YOUNG	LADY'S	CHRISTIAN NAME NATURALLY AS AN OLD FRIEND OF HER
LADY PREFACE(207)	IS PERHAPS LESS CERTAIN. SHAKESPEAR RUBBED IN THE	LADY'S	COMPLEXION IN HIS SONNETS MERCILESSLY; FOR IN HIS DAY
ARMS III (62)	OTTOMAN) ARE YOU? /SERGIUS/ YOU SEE THE YOUNG	LADY'S	CONCERN, CAPTAIN BLUNTSCHLI. DENIAL IS USELESS. YOU
POSN (459)	WE DONT WANT A HORSE-THIEF TO GET OFF THROUGH A	LADY'S	DELICACY. /THE FOREMAN/ NO WE DONT; AND WE DONT
AUGS (279)	BEAUTIFUL ENVELOPE FOR THE LIST, AN UNMISTAKEABLE	LADY'S	ENVELOPE. (SHE PUTS THE SHAM LIST INTO HER ENVELOPE
NEVR III (275)	SURPRISED TO FIND YOURSELF REGARDED BY THE YOUNG	LADY'S	FATHER AS A FORTUNE HUNTER. /VALENTINE/ SO I AM. DO
MILL IV (205)	I HAVE NOT FULFILLED THE CONDITION IMPOSED BY THE	LADY'S	FATHER. /EPIFANIA/ YOU NEED NOT TROUBLE ABOUT THAT.
BASH III (125)	UNSELFISHLY RENOUNCE ALL MY PRETENSIONS TO MY	LADY'S	FAVOR. /LYDIA/ WHAT, BASHVILLE! DIDST THOU LOVE ME?
GLIM (172)	POPE HIMSELF TO CARRY IT TO ROME FOR THAT BLESSED	LADY'S	FESTIVAL THERE; AND SINCE THAT MY HAND HAS NEVER
MIS. (136)	THE GOVERNOR HAS GIVEN HIMSELF AWAY, AND THE OLD	LADY'S	GONE, I'LL TELL YOU SOMETHING, LORD SUMMERHAYS. IF
GENV III (76)	YOU. /SIR O./ DEAR ME! FORTUNATELY I HAVE THE	LADY'S	GUN IN MY POCKET. BUT OF COURSE I DONT BELIEVE YOU.
PPP SD(193)	EXCEPT THE OVERTURE AND THE CRACKLING OF THE	LADY'S	HAIR AS THE MAID'S BRUSH DRAWS ELECTRIC SPARKS FROM
LADY PREFACE(207)	WHICH I SEE NO REASON TO DOUBT, AND THE	LADY'S	HAIR UNDYED, WHICH IS PERHAPS LESS CERTAIN.
NEVR II (247)	THE TAIL POCKET OF HIS DRESS COAT A BOOK WITH A	LADY'S	HANDKERCHIEF BETWEEN THE LEAVES TO MARK THE PAGE).

DEST (161) IT AND EXAMINES IT). /GIUSEPPE/ (TO NAPOLEON) A LADY'S HANDKERCHIEF, EXCELLENCY. (HE SMELLS IT). PERFUMED.
POSN PREFACE(391) SWORD OR THE ABSENCE OF A FEATHER FROM A LADY'S HEAD-DRESS WOULD BE A GRAVER MATTER THAN THE HABEAS
SUPR III (115) ALWAYS ALARMED ME; FOR THE FIRST MEANT THAT THE LADY'S IMPULSE HAD BEEN SOLELY TO THROW DOWN MY
PYGM III (258) EARNING HER OWN LIVING WITHOUT GIVING HER A FINE LADY'S INCOME! IS THAT WHAT YOU MEAN? /PICKERING/ (
SUPR III (126) PITIABLE OF FIGURES. BESIDES, I SAID " WHEN THE LADY'S INSTINCT WAS SET ON ME." IT WAS NOT ALWAYS SO; AND
SUPR III (126) WHEN I WAS CRUEL AS WHEN I WAS KIND. WHEN THE LADY'S INSTINCT WAS SET ON ME, THERE WAS NOTHING FOR IT BUT
GENV I (42) OF) MY NATIVE LANGUAGE, MY LORD. ALSO THIS LADY'S . (EXCHANGE OF BOWS). WILL YOU TAKE A PEW, MY LORD?
PYGM I (212) CHARACTER. MY CHARACTER IS THE SAME TO ME AS ANY LADY'S . /THE NOTE TAKER/ I DONT KNOW WHETHER YOUVE NOTICED
CYMB V (141) AMONG THE ITALIAN GENTRY, AND TO FIGHT AGAINST MY LADY'S KINGDOM: 'TIS ENOUGH THAT, BRITAIN, I HAVE KILL'D THY
MIS. PREFACE(16) FOR A MONTH OR TWO SPENT ELSEWHERE THAN IN A LADY'S LAP OR ROASTING ON A DRAWINGROOM HEARTHRUG. BESIDES,
OVER SD(171) IS AN UNUSED FIREPLACE. OPPOSITE IT ON THE LADY'S LEFT IS A DOOR. THE GENTLEMAN IS ON THE LADY'S RIGHT
INCA (238) OUT. I HOPE YOU ARE NOT TOO SHARP. /ERMYNTRUDE/ A LADY'S MAID HAS TO BE, YOUR HIGHNESS. (SHE PRODUCES SOME
PYGM I (214) GARDEN PARTY. I COULD EVEN GET HER A PLACE AS LADY'S MAID OR SHOP ASSISTANT, WHICH REQUIRES BETTER
INCA PROLOG (234) ARCHDEACON/ THEN, MY DEAR, YOU HAD BETTER BECOME LADY'S MAID TO A PRINCESS UNTIL YOU CAN FIND ANOTHER
INCA (237) NO, THANK YOU, YOUR HIGHNESS. I AM ONLY A LADY'S MAID. I UNDERSTOOD YOU WANTED ONE. /THE PRINCESS/ OH
INCA (241) BUT DONT THINK YOU CAN TRIFLE WITH ME. I AM A LADY'S MAID; AND I KNOW THE LADIES' MAIDS AND VALETS OF ALL
DEVL I SD(16) DERELICT NEAR THE DOOR. UNCLE TITUS, WHO IS THE LADY'S MAN OF THE FAMILY, RESCUES HER BY GIVING HER HIS
MRS III (227) MISS VIVIE. I'M QUITE AWARE THAT I'M NOT A YOUNG LADY'S MAN. /VIVIE/ INDEED, SIR GEORGE? /CROFTS/ NO; AND TO
NEVR IV (294) /BOHUN/ NO! DONT INTERRUPT, M'COMAS. THE YOUNG LADY'S METHOD IS RIGHT. (TO DOLLY, WITH TREMENDOUS
SUPR II (57) THE SORT. I ADMIT THAT THE FORMATION OF A YOUNG LADY'S MIND AND CHARACTER USUALLY CONSISTS IN TELLING HER
BASH III (121) YOUR BRUISED PRISONER LEST HE SHOCK THIS WELLBRED LADY'S NERVES. YOUR PARDON, MAAM; BUT HAVE YOU SEEN BY
CAPT III (280) THAT QUESTION TOO. I SAID, WHY DID YOU OBEY THAT LADY'S ORDERS INSTEAD OF WAITING FOR MINE? THEY SAID THEY
ARMS II (43) WHAT HAVE YOU BROUGHT THAT FOR? /NICOLA/ MY LADY'S ORDERS, MAJOR. LOUKA TOLD ME THAT-- /CATHERINE/ (
CAPT III (281) IN TO SAY THAT? /BLUEJACKET/ (CALMLY) BRITISH LADY'S ORDERS, SIR. (HE GOES OUT, UNRUFFLED, LEAVING
2TRU I (44) SIMPLY ENOUGH. IN HER LILY HAND WAS A COPY OF THE LADY'S PICTORIAL. IT CONTAINED AN ILLUSTRATED ACCOUNT OF
LADY PREFACE(221) BUT WHY DOES HE NOT PUT HIMSELF IN THE DARK LADY'S PLACE FOR A MOMENT AS HE HAS PUT HIMSELF SO
CAPT III (292) ORDERS). REDBROOK: YOU PACK THAT CLOBBER IN THE LADY'S PORTMANTEAU, AND PUT IT ABOARD THE YACHT FOR HER.
CAPT III (288) SUBJECT THAT SHOULD NEVER HAVE BEEN BROACHED IN A LADY'S PRESENCE. (HE RESUMES HIS SEAT, AND ADDS, IN A
CAPT III (292) /BRASSBOUND/ IF ONE BRASS PIN OF THAT LADY'S PROPERTY IS MISSING, I'LL HANG YOU WITH MY OWN HANDS
GETT PREFACE(221) A SEDUCER, BESIDES FACING THE UTMOST DAMAGE THE LADY'S RELATIVES CAN DO HIM, SUCH A TRANSACTION IS NOT AN
2TRU II SD(58) ON THE SAND, AND PLACES A CHAIR FOR HIM ON THE LADY'S RIGHT WITH GRINNING COURTESY. SHE THEN SEATS HERSELF
PYGM I (206) PLINTH OF THE COLUMN, SORTING HER FLOWERS, ON THE LADY'S RIGHT. SHE IS NOT AT ALL AN ATTRACTIVE PERSON. SHE
OVER SD(171) LADY'S LEFT IS A DOOR. THE GENTLEMAN IS ON THE LADY'S RIGHT. THE LADY IS VERY ATTRACTIVE, WITH A MUSICAL
PYGM I (205) HAVE GOT US A CAB BY THIS. /A BYSTANDER/ (ON THE LADY'S RIGHT) HE WONT GET NO CAB NOT UNTIL HALF-PAST ELEVEN,
MTH4 III (197) DO NOT ALLOW YOURSELF TO BE PUT DOWN BY THIS LADY'S RUDE CLAMOR, AMBROSE. TAKE NO NOTICE. PROCEED. /THE
BASH III (126) SHALL BE! /BASHVILLE/ MUST I RENOUNCE MY LOVELY LADY'S SERVICE, AND MAR THE FACE OF MAN? /CASHEL/ TIS
FANY I SD(273) WALLS, AND INCLUDING A BABY ROCKING-CHAIR ON THE LADY'S SIDE OF THE ROOM. THE LADY IS A PLACID PERSON. HER
PPP SD(193) IN AGAIN. OPPOSITE THIS CHEST OF DRAWERS, ON THE LADY'S SIDE OF THE ROOM, IS A CUPBOARD. THE PRESENCE OF A
DEST SD(180) IN TEMPER AND SPIRITS BY HIS MEAL, CHOOSES THE LADY'S SIDE OF THE ROOM, AND WAITS, MUCH AT HIS EASE, FOR
KING I (184) MUST GO. I CANNOT STAY AND LISTEN TO THIS FRENCH LADY'S TALK. (SHE GOES OUT WITH DIGNITY). /LOUISE/ I SHALL
MIS. (200) FIRST TO FALL TODAY UNDER THE LASH OF THAT YOUNG LADY'S TERRIBLE DERISION, BENTLEY. LINA, HER CAP ON, AND HER
NEVR I SD(201) A HANDSOME MAN IN MINIATURE, OBVIOUSLY THE YOUNG LADY'S TWIN, COMES IN EAGERLY. HE WEARS A SUIT OF TERRA
SUPR II (68) THE CAR AND APPROACHES TANNER). WHAT ABOUT THE LADY'S VIEWS? /TANNER/ SHE IS JUST AS WILLING TO BE LEFT TO
MTH3 (127) GENERAL. BE GOOD ENOUGH TO GET OUT OF THE LADY'S WAY. /BARNABAS/ THERE IS TIME TO SEND THE LADY TO THE
SUPR II (64) FOR THE PRESENT. /HECTOR/ I SHALL RESPECT THE LADY'S WISHES. WOULD IT BE INDISCREET TO ASK WHO HER HUSBAND
JOAN 6 (136) WITH THE SHEEP LIKE ANYONE ELSE. I WILL DO A LADY'S WORK IN THE HOUSE -- SPIN OR WEAVE -- AGAINST ANY
MIS. SD(109) OUT IN THE HALL NEAR THE SIDEBOARD, AND A LADY'S WORKTABLE, WITH TWO CHAIRS AT IT, TOWARDS THE OTHER
NEVR II (247) /WAITER/ (DISCREETLY) THATS THE YOUNGER LADY'S , SIR. (VALENTINE LETS IT GO). THANK YOU, SIR. IF

LADY'S-MAIDS

MIS. PREFACE(16) DAILY AND INTIMATE CONTACT WITH THEIR VALETS AND LADY'S-MAIDS , WHOSE INFLUENCE AND CARE ARE OFTEN DOMINANT

LADYSHIP

O'FL (216) HOW IS YOUR HONOR'S GOOD SELF? AND HOW IS HER LADYSHIP AND ALL THE YOUNG LADIES? OH, IT'S RIGHT GLAD WE
BASH III (119) MY SOLE PURPOSE HERE IS TO INQUIRE WHETHER YOUR LADYSHIP ANY BAD CHARACTERS THIS AFTERNOON HAS NOTED IN THE
BASH III (119) TO WREAK ULTION FOR THE BROKEN LAW. I WISH YOUR LADYSHIP GOOD AFTERNOON. /LYDIA/ GOOD AFTERNOON. (EXIT
O'FL (216) AND THEY TELL ME DOWN AT THE LODGE THAT HER LADYSHIP IS STAYING IN LONDON, AND THAT MISS AGNES IS TO BE
2TRU III (82) KNOW. /THE SERGEANT/ (STIFFLY) BEG PARDON, YOUR LADYSHIP . I WAS NOT AWARE OF YOUR LADYSHIP'S PRESENCE.
O'FL (213) WAS ALWAYS A KIND FRIEND TO THE POOR. LITTLE HER LADYSHIP KNEW, GOD HELP HER, THE DEPTH OF DIVILMENT THAT WAS
CAPT II (247) /JOHNSON/ LET ME INTRODOOCE MR REDBROOK. YOUR LADYSHIP MAY KNOW HIS FATHER, THE VERY REV. DEAN REDBROOK. (
O'FL (213) LIKE OURSELVES OR ANY OTHER CHRISTIANS. OH, HER LADYSHIP NEVER KNEW ALL THAT WAS GOING ON BEHIND HER BACK:
PPP (194) THE BED). GOODNIGHT. /PHYLLIS/ WILL YOUR LADYSHIP NOT UNDRESS? /THE LADY/ NOT TONIGHT, PHYLLIS. (
BASH II,1, (107) MUCH; BUT-- " NATURE'S GENTLEMAN"! I THANK YOUR LADYSHIP OF LYONS, BUT MUST BEG TO BE EXCUSED. /LYDIA/ BUT
CAPT I (238) FOLLOWED BY THE ITALIAN). /BRASSBOUND/ YOUR LADYSHIP SEES. THESE MEN SERVE ME BY THEIR OWN FREE CHOICE.
BASH III (119) TO ME. ENTER POLICEMAN. /POLICEMAN/ ASKING YOUR LADYSHIP TO PARDON ME FOR THIS INTRUSION, MIGHT I BE SO BOLD
CAPT II (250) FITS OF INSOLENCE. IF HE IS IMPERTINENT TO YOUR LADYSHIP , OR DISOBEDIENT, YOU HAVE MY AUTHORITY TO ORDER

LADYSHIP'S

CAPT III (284) /KEARNEY/ (GRIMLY KEEPING HIS COUNTENANCE) YOUR LADYSHIP'S CAWMPLIMENTS WILL BE IN ORDER AT A LATER STAGE.
2TRU III (82) PARDON, YOUR LADYSHIP. I WAS NOT AWARE OF YOUR LADYSHIP'S PRESENCE. /SWEETIE/ CAN ALL THAT STUFF, SERGEANT.

LAERTES

LADY PREFACE(218) NOT QUITE SO READY FOR TREACHERY AND MURDER AS LAERTES AND EVEN HAMLET HIMSELF (NOT TO MENTION THE
LADY PREFACE(224) HIM TO FIERCE DISGUST FOR THE SENTIMENTALITY OF LAERTES BY HER GRAVE; AND WHEN HE DISCUSSES THE SCENE WITH

LAG

GETT PREFACE(258) MARRIAGES, AND, AS IT IS OUR CAUTIOUS CUSTOM TO LAG BEHIND THE REST OF THE WORLD TO SEE HOW THEIR
FABL PREFACE(85) CIVIL WAR. IN THE SIMPLEST HOME AFFAIRS THE TIME LAG EXTENDS TO CENTURIES. FOR INSTANCE, THE PRACTICE OF
FABL PREFACE(85) TO FORESEE ITS NECESSITY OR DESIRABILITY, A TIME LAG IS CREATED DURING WHICH THE MAJORITY IS ALWAYS
FABL PREFACE(84) FACTS INTO SANE CO-OPERATION. THE POLITICAL TIME LAG . THE WORST FEATURES OF OUR SHAM-DEMOCRATIC
FABL PREFACE(98) FUTURE: HOMILIES NO USE. WHILE THE TIME LAG LASTS THE FUTURE REMAINS THREATENING. THE PROBLEM OF
FABL PREFACE(85) ACTS, IT TOOK THE BRITISH PARLIAMENT A TIME LAG OF 50 YEARS TO MAKE THEM EFFECTIVE. HOME RULE FOR

LAGER

NEVR II (239) HIM). /PHILIP/ VALENTINE--? /VALENTINE/ WOULD LAGER BE CONSIDERED VULGAR? /PHILIP/ PROBABLY. WE'LL ORDER
NEVR II (242) OUT WINE) 413, MADAM. (TO VALENTINE) LARGE LAGER FOR YOU, SIR. (TO GLORIA) 413, MISS. /DOLLY/ (
NEVR II (241) (CHEERFULLY) YES, SIR. CERTAINLY, SIR. SMALL LAGER FOR YOU, SIR. (TO CRAMPTON) SELTZER AND IRISH, SIR. (
NEVR II (242) (TO M'COMAS) APOLLINARIS, SIR. (TO DOLLY) SMALL LAGER , MISS. (TO MRS CLANDON, POURING OUT WINE) 413,

LAGERS

NEVR II (241) TO THE YOUNG WAITER) THICK. /PHILIP/ TWO SMALL LAGERS FOR THE CHILDREN AS USUAL, WILLIAM; AND ONE LARGE FOR

LAGGIGE

CAPT I (219) (HIRE) A HARAB AN TWO KROOBOYS TO KERRY THEIR LAGGIGE , THORT AWD CAM AN TEOLL YER. /RANKIN/ THANK YOU.
CAPT NOTES (305) THUS, THOUGH LUGGAGE IS PRONOUNCED BY HIM AS LAGGIGE , TURN IS NOT PRONOUNCED AS TARN, BUT AS TEUN WITH

LAGS

BARB PREFACE(242) EXAMPLE OF VIOLATING IT. IN THIS INSTANCE THE MAN LAGS BEHIND THE LAW; BUT WHEN THE LAW LAGS BEHIND THE MAN,
BARB PREFACE(242) THE MAN LAGS BEHIND THE LAW; BUT WHEN THE LAW LAGS BEHIND THE MAN, HE BECOMES EQUALLY AN ANARCHIST. WHEN
BULL II SD(105) BROADBENT AT HIS HEELS. THE PRIEST FOLLOWS. PATSY LAGS LABORIOUSLY BEHIND. /CORNELIUS/ THIS IS A BIT OF A

LAHST

CAPT III (283) YOUR PARTY, LADY WAYNFLETE? I PRESUME I MET YOU LAHST NIGHT, SIR, ON BOARD THE YACHT. /BRASSBOUND/ NO. I AM
CAPT III (284) STATES CRUISER SANTIAGO, WAS SPOKEN OFF MOGADOR LAHST THURSDAY BY THE YACHT REDGAUNTLET. THE OWNER OF THE

LAID

FANY III SD(297) GILBEY'S DINING ROOM. AFTERNOON. THE TABLE IS NOT LAID : IT IS DRAPED IN ITS ORDINARY CLOTH, WITH PEN AND INK,
GENV IV (123) SO TO SPEAK, OUR LITTLE SISTER, AND THAT IF YOU LAID A FINGER ON HER WE SHOULD-- PARDON ME IF IN MY
LION PREFACE(101) BY THE HEELS ALMOST AS PROMPTLY AS HE WOULD HAVE LAID A ROMAN CATHOLIC, THOUGH IN FIJI AT THE SAME MOMENT HE
SUPR HANDBOK(207) BE REPEATED THEREFORE THAT NO INDICTMENT IS HERE LAID AGAINST THE WORLD ON THE SCORE OF WHAT ITS CRIMINALS
BULL PREFACE(55) TO LEARN FROM THE BRITISH OFFICIAL REPORTS LAID BEFORE PARLIAMENT THAT " DUE DIGNITY WAS OBSERVED IN
INCA (246) THE RIM IS A PIECE OF THE TELEPHONE CABLE LAID BY HIS MAJESTY ACROSS THE SHIPSKEEL CANAL. THE PIN IS A
CAPT II (257) HIM WHEN HE IS WANTED. /SIR HOWARD/ YOU WILL BE LAID BY THE HEELS YET, MY FRIEND. /REDBROOK/ (WITH CHEERFUL
CAPT II (271) BRASSBOUND (LOOKING IMPLACABLY AT HIM) YOU ARE LAID BY THE HEELS, MY FRIEND, AS I SAID YOU WOULD BE. /LADY
CAPT II SD(242) HEADS, THEIR KNEES UPLIFTED, AND THEIR CALVES LAID COMFORTABLY ON THE DIVAN. THOSE WHO WEAR SHIRTS HAVE
MTH4 I (142) ALL. I FEAR YOU HAVE NOT BEEN OBSERVING THE RULES LAID DOWN FOR SHORTLIVED VISITORS. /THE ELDERLY GENTLEMAN/
PRES (142) CONFOUND IT! THAT REMINDS ME. THE GERMANS HAVE LAID DOWN FOUR MORE DREADNOUGHTS. /MITCHENER/ THEN YOU MUST
GETT PREFACE(258) OF UNEMPLOYMENT, PROBABLY ON THE PRINCIPLES LAID DOWN IN THE MINORITY REPORT OF THE ROYAL COMMISSION ON
GENV IV (110) JUDGE/ IN THE CAPACITY OF A FAMOUS PROPHET WHO LAID DOWN THE LAW IN THESE WORDS, " THIS COMMANDMENT I GIVE
CLEO V SD(195) CHARGE OF A GANGWAY, WHENCE A RED FLOORCLOTH IS LAID DOWN THE MIDDLE OF THE ESPLANADE, TURNING OFF TO THE
3PLA PREFACE(R20) OF THE PLANET MARS: A CAPITAL STORY, NOT TO BE LAID DOWN UNTIL FINISHED. LOVE INTEREST IS IMPOSSIBLE ON ITS
MTH1 I (13) WHOLE GARDEN FOR A LONG TIME! NOT UNTIL YOU HAVE LAID DOWN YOUR BURDEN AND GONE TO SLEEP FOR EVER. WHY SHOULD
GETT PREFACE(205) WORK, ONCE THE WAY IS DISCOVERED, THE METHODS LAID DOWN, AND THE MACHINERY PROVIDED, THE WORK OF THE
ROCK II (276) THE WOMAN FOR ME." /ALOYSIA/ WELL, THE MOMENT I LAID EYES ON DAVID I WENT ALL OVER LIKE THAT. YOU CANT DENY
ARMS II SD(23) SMALL TABLE, WITH TWO BENT WOOD CHAIRS AT IT, IS LAID FOR BREAKFAST WITH TURKISH COFFEE POT, CUPS, ROLLS,
CAPT II (259) IN HIS VOICE) WHY DID YOU COME HERE? MY TRAP WAS LAID FOR HIM, NOT FOR YOU. DO YOU KNOW THE DANGER YOU ARE
MILL II SD(166) LENGTH OF THE ROOM, ARE TWO SEPARATE LONG TABLES, LAID FOR LUNCH FOR ABOUT A DOZEN PEOPLE EACH. THE CHAIRS,
KING I (220) NOTHING OF THE SORT, MR KNELLER. THERE IS A COVER LAID FOR YOU; AND THE KING EXPECTS YOU. /NEWTON/ THE LINES
SUPR IV (168) /TANNER/ THE WILL IS YOURS THEN! THE TRAP WAS LAID FROM THE BEGINNING. /ANN/ (CONCENTRATING ALL HER
MIS. PREFACE(53) WAY. BORN FREE, AS ROUSSEAU SAYS, HE HAS BEEN LAID HANDS ON BY SLAVES FROM THE MOMENT OF HIS BIRTH AND
BASH III (122) PEACEMAKER, WHEN LO! THESE MINIONS OF THE LAW LAID HANDS ON ME. /BASHVILLE/ A LOVELY WOMAN, WITH
PHIL I (71) JUST EXACTLY. SHE HAS PUT HER HANDS IN MINE, AND LAID HER CHEEK AGAINST MINE, AND LISTENED TO ME SAYING ALL
LION PREFACE(101) AS TO CANNIBALISM IN ENGLAND, CROMWELL WOULD HAVE LAID HIM BY THE HEELS ALMOST AS PROMPTLY AS HE WOULD HAVE
PRES (139) SIMPLE. HE SHOULD HAVE OBEYED THE ORDER; AND THEN LAID HIS COMPLAINT AGAINST THE OFFICER IN PROPER FORM. HE
DEVL I (8) LOOKS UP AT HIM. /ANDERSON/ SISTER: THE LORD HAS LAID HIS HAND VERY HEAVILY UPON YOU. /MRS DUDGEON/ (WITH
2TRU III (97) LOOK AT MEEK! THAT MAN COULD BE AN EMPEROR IF HE LAID HIS MIND TO IT: BUT HE'D RATHER BE A PRIVATE. HE'S
GETT (345) THAT WAS JUST BURSTING TO BE SAID; AND SO IT LAID HOLD OF ME AND SAID ITSELF. THATS HOW IT IS, YOU SEE.
CLEO IV (187) AND DRIVING US INTO THE SEA STRAIGHT AWAY. WE LAID HOLD OF THIS RENEGADE IN CLEARING THEM OUT OF THE
JOAN 6 (140) /THE INQUISITOR/ THE BLESSED ST ATHANASIUS HAS LAID IT DOWN IN HIS CREED THAT THOSE WHO CANNOT UNDERSTAND
HART PREFACE(18) WISE, WITH REALLY VALUABLE WORK IN HAND, LAID IT DOWN VOLUNTARILY AND SPENT MONTHS FORMING FOURS IN
FANY I (279) HAT AND I IN HIS, THE COPS WERE VERY SPITEFUL AND LAID IT ON FOR ALL THEY WERE WORTH: DRUNK AND DISORDERLY AND
CLEO PRO2 (99) HE LAY DOWN IN A STUPOR; AND I TOOK HIS SWORD AND LAID IT ON. (DRAWING THE SWORD) LO! A ROMAN SWORD WITH
CAND III (127) A WEAPON. IF I WERE A HERO OF OLD I SHOULD HAVE LAID MY DRAWN SWORD BETWEEN US. IF MORELL HAD COME IN HE
DEVL II (37) A PLATE AND KNIFE LAID THERE. THE OTHER PLATE IS LAID NEAR IT: BUT JUDITH STAYS AT THE OPPOSITE END OF THE
HART PREFACE(20) THE SPHERE OF THE FINE ARTS, NO GREAT STRESS WAS LAID ON THAT LOSS. IMMEDIATELY AN AMAZING FRENZY SWEPT
CLEO IV SD(173) THIS TIME DRAWING ON TO DINNER TIME. THE TABLE IS LAID ON THE ROOF OF THE PALACE; AND THITHER RUFIO IS NOW
HART PREFACE(36) FROM THEM IN THE HISTORY OF THE CHURCH WERE LAID ON THE SHOULDERS OF THE THEATRE: THAT STUFFY,
LADY PREFACE(210) EXPRESSLY FOR HIS DISCOMFITURE; FOR THE STRESS I LAID ON TYLER'S CLAIMS MUST HAVE SEEMED UNACCOUNTABLE AND
MTH5 SD(226) PYGMALION, A SQUARE-FINGERED YOUTH WITH HIS FACE LAID OUT IN HORIZONTAL BLOCKS, AND A PERPETUAL SMILE OF
MTH3 (132) BY AN EXPLOSION FOR WHICH HE HAS HIMSELF LAID THE CHARGE AND LIGHTED THE FUSE. BUT I AM NOT
HART PREFACE(20) OTHERS INCLUDED SIR HUGH LANE; BUT AS HE HAD ONLY LAID THE COUNTRY UNDER GREAT OBLIGATIONS IN THE SPHERE OF
ROCK PREFACE(166) AND YET THE MOUJIK, BEING STILL THE GOOSE THAT LAID THE GOLDEN EGGS, COULD NOT BE EXTERMINATED SUMMARILY
MILL PREFACE(133) BUT IT CAME BACK LIKE A BOOMERANG AND LAID THE HOHENZOLLERNS BESIDE THE ROMANOFFS. PAGEANTRY WILL
NEVR III (271) ANGER AND AMAZEMENT); HOW MANY TIMES HE HAS LAID THE TRAP IN WHICH HE HAS CAUGHT YOU; HOW OFTEN HE HAS
3PLA PREFACE(R36) SHAKESPEAR AND MICHAEL ANGELO. BUT BOTH OF THEM LAID THEIR ARTS WASTE FOR CENTURIES BY LEADING LATER ARTISTS
CYMB V (144) MAGIC IN THEM THAT WOULD NOT LET ME REST UNTIL I LAID THEM ON MERCURY'S ALTAR. HE'S THE GOD OF THIEVES, BUT I
DEVL II (37) NEAREST THE PRESS, THERE IS A PLATE AND KNIFE LAID THERE. THE OTHER PLATE IS LAID NEAR IT: BUT JUDITH
BULL PREFACE(69) THAT WERE NOT BURNT WERE RAIDED AT NIGHT AND LAID UNDER CONTRIBUTION FOR NEEDED SUPPLIES. IF THE
MTH3 (119) PURE TERROR. I SAW THAT THE LITTLE MONEY I HAD LAID UP WOULD NOT LAST, AND THAT I MUST GO OUT AND WORK
CAND I (100) THE HEAVY BURTHEN AND GREAT GIFT OF A POET MAY BE LAID UPON YOU. /MARCHBANKS/ (UNIMPRESSED AND REMORSELESS,
BULL II SD(104) GENERATIONS AS BEEMANKINY CARS, THE IRISH HAVING LAID VIOLENT TONGUES ON THE NAME OF THEIR PROJECTOR, ONE
DOCT V (177) A TERRIBLE DISCOVERY. FROM HAVING YOUR LIFE LAID WASTE, /JENNIFER/ HOW? /RIDGEON/ NO MATTER. I HAVE
POSN (442) OWNED ANYTHING BUT OTHER PEOPLE'S PROPERTY. YOU LAID YOUR HANDS ON EVERYTHING FATHER AND MOTHER HAD WHEN
APPL I (227) " WE DECLARE THIS FOUNDATION STONE WELL AND TRULY LAID " AND SO FORTH. BUT POLITICALLY, YES! A DUMB KING.

LAIN

SUPR II (52) HER VOICE! IF YOU HAD SEEN HER TEARS! I HAVE LAIN AWAKE ALL NIGHT THINKING OF THEM. IF SHE HAD REPROACHED
MIS. PREFACE(11) THE CHILD BECOMING A GREAT RASCAL HAD ITS GENIUS LAIN IN THAT DIRECTION. HANDEL WOULD HAVE BEEN HANDEL, AND
CAND I SD(94) CANVAS SHOES. IN THESE GARMENTS HE HAS APPARENTLY LAIN IN THE HEATHER AND WADED THROUGH THE WATERS; AND THERE
DOCT PREFACE(73) HIMSELF IN A ROOM WHERE A SMALLPOX PATIENT HAS LAIN , BY PRETENDING TO EXORCISE THE DISEASE WITH BURNING

LAIRD

CAPT NOTES (301) NO LONGER AVAILABLE). HE IS, I KNOW, A SCOTCH LAIRD . HOW HE CONTRIVES TO BE AUTHENTICALLY THE TWO THINGS

LAISSER-FAIRE

METH PREFACE(R64) FREE CONTRACT, FREE COMPETITION, NATURAL LIBERTY, LAISSER-FAIRE : IN SHORT, ON " DOING THE OTHER FELLOW DOWN"
POSN PREFACE(386) EMBRACES ALL THAT IS VALUABLE IN THE DOCTRINE OF LAISSER-FAIRE AND THE METHOD OF FREE TRADE AS WELL AS ALL
DOCT PREFACE(74) OF TRIAL AND ERROR, IF YOU COME TO THAT, WHAT IS LAISSER-FAIRE BUT AN ORTHODOXY? THE MOST TYRANNOUS AND
DOCT PREFACE(73) AS OURS ANY ORTHODOXY IS BETTER THAN LAISSER-FAIRE . IF OUR POPULATION EVER COMES TO CONSIST
METH PREFACE(R75) A STATESMAN WHO IS INDIFFERENT ON PRINCIPLE, A LAISSER-FAIRE OR MUDDLE-THROUGH DOCTRINAIRE, PLAYS THE DEUCE
FABL PREFACE(83) OR CRISS-CROSSED, LENIN AND STALIN HAD TO CRY LAISSER-FAIRE TO ALL THE ENTERPRISES NOT YET RIPE FOR
FABL PREFACE(86) IS ALL FOR WELL POLICED PRIVATE PROPERTY AND LAISSER-FAIRE , THE PROLETARIAT ALL FOR STATE INDUSTRY WITH

LAITY

LION PREFACE(102) HIS DISCIPLES SHOULD SEPARATE THEMSELVES FROM THE LAITY : HE PICKED THEM UP BY THE WAYSIDE, WHERE ANY MAN OR
BULL PREFACE(37) " INFIDEL," INSTEAD OF AS THE CHAMPION OF THE LAITY AGAINST THE OFFICIAL THEOCRACY OF THE STATE CHURCH.
BULL PREFACE(39) WHO ARE TO BE FOUND AMONG THE ROMAN CATHOLIC LAITY AS PLENTIFULLY AS AMONG THE ANGLICAN CATHOLIC LAITY IN
SUPR HANDBOK(184) TOWARDS CHRISTIANITY AND ENJOIN CELIBACY ON ITS LAITY AS WELL AS ON ITS CLERGY, MARRIAGES WOULD STILL BE
BULL PREFACE(37) THE STRUGGLE BETWEEN THE PRIESTHOOD AND THE LAITY HAS PRODUCED A VAST BODY OF VOLTAIREANS. BUT THE
BULL PREFACE(39) AS PLENTIFULLY AS AMONG THE ANGLICAN CATHOLIC LAITY IN ENGLAND. SHE GETS NOTHING OUT OF IRELAND BUT
DOCT I (107) ALL PROFESSIONS ARE CONSPIRACIES AGAINST THE LAITY . AND WE CANT ALL BE GENIUSES LIKE YOU. EVERY FOOL CAN
CAND II (112) THATS A QUESTION FOR THE CHURCH, NOT FOR THE LAITY . HAS IT DONE YOU ANY HARM? THATS THE QUESTION FOR
DOCT PREFACE(61) KNOWING IT. THE REFORMS ALSO COME FROM THE LAITY . IN THE MAIN, THEN, THE DOCTOR LEARNS THAT IF HE GETS
DOCT PREFACE(61) THEM. THAT IS WHY ALL THE CHANGES COME FROM THE LAITY . IT WAS NOT UNTIL AN AGITATION HAD BEEN CONDUCTED FOR
DOCT PREFACE(47) WHAT HE DEEMS THE IGNORANT SENTIMENTALITY OF THE LAITY . WHEN THE PUBLIC CONSCIENCE STIRS UNEASILY AND
BULL PREFACE(38) TO THE IRISH DEMOCRACY-- THAT IS, TO THE CATHOLIC LAITY -- WOULD BE DELIVERED UP TO THE TYRANNY OF THE
DOCT PREFACE(11) THEY ARE ALL CONSPIRACIES AGAINST THE LAITY ; AND I DO NOT SUGGEST THAT THE MEDICAL CONSPIRACY IS
2TRU PREFACE(23) THEMSELVES ETERNALLY; THEY CAN DROP OUT INTO THE LAITY WHEN THEY PLEASE, AND IF THEY DO NOT PLEASE AND
BULL PREFACE(36) THE HERETIC. WHEN IT IS LET LOOSE, THE CATHOLIC LAITY WILL MAKE AS SHORT WORK OF SACERDOTAL TYRANNY IN
BULL PREFACE(35) A PROTESTANT NATIONAL GUARD. THE ROMAN CATHOLIC LAITY , NOW A CIPHER, WOULD ORGANIZE ITSELF; AND A REVOLT

LAKE

CLEO IV (192) RUNS OUT.) WITH THE REST, I SHALL MARCH ROUND THE LAKE AND UP THE NILE TO MEET MITHRIDATES. AWAY, LUCIUS; AND
BUOY II (26) THE SERPENTS OF THE BUSH AND THE MONSTERS OF THE LAKE ARE CHARMED, AND ASSEMBLE HERE TO LISTEN. /SHE/ (
GETT PREFACE(210) WHO OBJECTS. THUS, IT WAS NOT THE WOMEN OF SALT LAKE CITY NOR EVEN OF AMERICA WHO ATTACKED MORMON POLYGYNY.
GETT PREFACE(212) ARE SECLUDED AND MARRIAGES ARE ARRANGED. IN SALT LAKE CITY THE FREE UNSECLUDED WOMAN COULD SEE AND MEET THE
GETT PREFACE(211) TO MONOGAMY, LIKE THE LATTER-DAY SAINTS OF SALT LAKE CITY. THE ANSWER IS NOT FAR TO SEEK: THEIR POLYGYNY IS
CAND I SD(77) AND CONTAINING PLENTY OF GREENSWARD, TREES, A LAKE FOR BATHERS, FLOWER BEDS WHICH ARE TRIUMPHS OF THE
GLIM SD(171) A. D. GLOAMING. AN INN ON THE EDGE OF AN ITALIAN LAKE . A STONE CROSS WITH A PEDESTAL OF STEPS, A VERY OLD
GLIM (175) INTO FORTY THOUSAND PIECES AND THROW YOU INTO THE LAKE . /SQUARCIO/ KEEP YOUR TEMPER, SIGNOR COUNT.
FABL VI (123) A WALL ACROSS A RIVER VALLEY TO PEN IT UP AS A LAKE . /YOUTH 3/ ALL I MEANT IS WHAT THE TEACHER SAYS.

CLEO IV (192) HALF OUR FORCES MUST TAKE SHIP FOR THE WESTERN LAKE . SEE TO MY HORSE AND ARMOR. (BRITANNUS RUNS OUT.)
CLEO IV (177) A CITY AND AN ARMY. SINCE WE CUT YOU OFF FROM LAKE MAREOTIS, AND YOU DUG WELLS IN THE SALT SEA SAND AND
GENV III SD(65) OF A FASHIONABLE RESTAURANT OVERLOOKING THE LAKE OF GENEVA. THREE TEA TABLES, WITH TWO CHAIRS AT EACH,
GLIM (178) SPORT, MY GIULIACCIA. /SANDRO'S VOICE/ (ON THE LAKE) GIULIETTA! GIULIETTA! /FERRUCCIO/ (CALLING TO HIM)
BUOY II (19) THE MILK? /SHE/ YOU CAN GET A MEAL WHERE THE LAKE STEAMERS STOP, TWO MILES FARTHER ON. /HE/ TWO MILES!
GLIM (181) HER MANDOLINE. /FERRUCCIO/ I SHALL JUMP INTO THE LAKE , SQUARCIO. IF YOUR CAT BEGINS TO MIAOWL. /SANDRO/ (

LAKES
HART II (116) MUSIC AND PICTURES AND BOOKS AND MOUNTAINS AND LAKES AND BEAUTIFUL THINGS TO WEAR AND NICE PEOPLE TO BE
LION PREFACE(25) WHEN HIS DISCIPLES ARE TERRIFIED BY STORMS ON THE LAKES . HE ASKS FOR NO REWARD, BUT BEGS THE PEOPLE NOT TO
SUPR PREFACE(R15) ANTAGONIST HURLED THOSE WHO REFUSE TO REPENT INTO LAKES OF BURNING BRIMSTONE, THERE TO BE TORMENTED BY DEVILS

LALLA
AUGS (260) THE STAGE SOCIETY ON THE 21ST JANUARY 1917, WITH LALLA VANDERVELDE AS THE LADY, F. B. J. SHARP AS LORD

LAM
BARB II (275) AND DRAG HER OUT O BED BE ER SNOW WHITE AIRS, AN LAM INTO ER WITH THE POKER. /RUMMY/ THATS WHATS SO UNFAIR TO

LAMA
LION PREFACE(72) THIS DAY THE ROMAN CATHOLIC PRIEST, THE BUDDHIST LAMA , AND THE FAKIRS OF ALL THE EASTERN DENOMINATIONS

LAMARCK
METH PREFACE(R41) MUST HAVE BEEN DESIGNED TO REACH THE FOOD. BUT LAMARCK DID NOT BELIEVE THAT THE NECKS WERE SO DESIGNED IN
METH PREFACE(R47) WAS CAREFUL NOT TO CLAIM THAT HE HAD SUPERSEDED LAMARCK OR DISPROVED FUNCTIONAL ADAPTATION. IN SHORT, HE WAS
METH PREFACE(R22) WELL AS NEO-DARWINIANS. I WAS A NEO-LAMARCKIAN. LAMARCK PASSED ON FROM THE CONCEPTION OF EVOLUTION AS A
METH PREFACE(R43) RESCUER, HOPE GIVER, AND EPOCH MAKER; WHILST POOR LAMARCK WAS SWEPT ASIDE AS A CRUDE AND EXPLODED GUESSER
METH PREFACE(R41) FROM HIM NOW. HOW DID HE COME BY HIS LONG NECK? LAMARCK WOULD HAVE SAID, BY WANTING TO GET AT THE TENDER
METH PREFACE(R22) NEO-LAMARCKIANS. I CALL YOUR SPECIAL ATTENTION TO LAMARCK , BECAUSE LATER ON THERE WERE NEO-LAMARCKIANS AS
METH PREFACE(R42) THE OPEN-EYED INTELLIGENT WANTING AND TRYING OF LAMARCK , THE DARWINIAN PROCESS MAY BE DESCRIBED AS A
METH PREFACE(R22) OF IT, WHICH WAS THE METHOD OF EVOLUTION. LAMARCK , WHILST MAKING MANY INGENIOUS SUGGESTIONS AS TO THE
METH PREFACE(R22) THE BATTLE OF WATERLOO, A FRENCH SOLDIER NAMED LAMARCK , WHO HAD BEATEN HIS MUSKET INTO A MICROSCOPE AND

LAMARCKIAN
3PLA PREFACE(R21) MADMAN, OR JESTER. NAY, I BELIEVE WE SHOULD, BY LAMARCKIAN ADAPTATION, ENLARGE OUR NOSES TO THE ADMIRED
METH PREFACE(R44) BUT ANYONE WHO WANTS TO KNOW WHAT IT WAS TO BE A LAMARCKIAN DURING THE LAST QUARTER OF THE NINETEENTH CENTURY
METH PREFACE(R45) TO UNDERSTAND, MORE VISIBLE AND CONCRETE, THAN LAMARCKIAN EVOLUTION. EVOLUTION AS A PHILOSOPHY AND
METH PREFACE(R47) FUNCTIONAL ADAPTATIONS (THE CURRENT PHRASE FOR LAMARCKIAN EVOLUTION) EITHER CERTAINLY WERE OR CONCEIVABLY
METH PREFACE(R50) THE COUNTER-ASSURANCE THAT YOU ARE THE PRODUCT OF LAMARCKIAN EVOLUTION, FORMERLY CALLED FUNCTIONAL ADAPTATION
METH PREFACE(R25) RAPID AND DISASTROUS DEGENERATION. LET US FIX THE LAMARCKIAN EVOLUTIONARY PROCESS WELL IN OUR MINDS. YOU ARE
METH PREFACE(R47) REACTED AGAINST HIM FURIOUSLY; RAN UP THE LAMARCKIAN FLAG TO THE TOP-GALLANT PEAK; DECLARED WITH
METH PREFACE(R24) THE MOST ELABORATE FORMS OF ORGANIZED LIFE ON LAMARCKIAN LINES WITHOUT THE INTERVENTION OF CIRCUMSTANTIAL
METH PREFACE(R71) WESTERN POWERS HAD SELECTED THEIR ALLIES IN THE LAMARCKIAN MANNER INTELLIGENTLY, PURPOSELY, AND VITALLY, AD
METH PREFACE(R60) FACTOR IN HIS DESTINY HAD BEEN REINFORCED BY THE LAMARCKIAN VIEW OF EVOLUTION. IF THE GIRAFFE CAN DEVELOP HIS

LAMARCKIANS
METH PREFACE(R45) PRETEND THAT IT EVER CONSISTED OF DARWINIANS AND LAMARCKIANS . THE AVERAGE CITIZEN IS IRRELIGIOUS AND

LAMARCKO-SHAVIAN
METH PREFACE(R55) UPON WHICH NATURAL SELECTION WORKS. A SAMPLE OF LAMARCKO-SHAVIAN INVECTIVE. THE VITALIST PHILOSOPHERS MADE

LAMARCK'S
METH PREFACE(R32) AS WILL, WHICH IS THE METAPHYSICAL COMPLEMENT TO LAMARCK'S NATURAL HISTORY, AS IT DEMONSTRATES THAT THE
METH PREFACE(R60) WHERE THERE IS A WILL, THERE IS A WAY," CONDENSES LAMARCK'S THEORY OF FUNCTIONAL ADAPTATION INTO A PROVERB.
METH PREFACE(R43) FULL OF AMOEBAS INTO THE FRENCH ACADEMY. THOUGH LAMARCK'S WAY, THE WAY OF LIFE, WILL, ASPIRATION, AND

LAMB
JOAN 6 (144) A REVERENCE) PRAISE BE TO GOD, MY BROTHERS, THE LAMB HAS RETURNED TO THE FLOCK; AND THE SHEPHERD REJOICES IN
FANY PROLOG (267) WITTY, CHARMING BABY; BUT STILL JUST A WEE LAMB IN A WORLD OF WOLVES. CAMBRIDGE IS NOT WHAT IT WAS IN
HART I (47) GUINNESS/ OH, WHAT A THING TO DO! THE POOR LAMB IS READY TO DROP. /THE CAPTAIN/ YOU SHALL HAVE SOME OF
LION II (136) /FERROVIUS/ AYE, AYE: THAT IS RIGHT. NOT AS A LAMB IS SLAIN BY THE BUTCHER; BUT AS A BUTCHER MIGHT LET
FANY I (279) HE THOUGHT THE COPPER WOULD SEE THE JOKE. POOR LAMB . HE WAS ARGUING ABOUT IT WHEN THE TWO THAT TOOK ME
JITT III (58) VERY IRRITABLE, THOUGH HE USED TO BE A PERFECT LAMB . I THOUGHT IT WAS ONLY HIS HEALTH; FOR OF COURSE
ROCK II (240) WE MAY AS WELL BE HANGED FOR A SHEEP AS FOR A LAMB . /SIR DEXTER/ WE! WE! WE! WHO ARE WE? IF YOU MEAN
DEVL III (60) TO YOU? I MAY AS WELL BE HANGED FOR A SHEEP AS A LAMB . /SWINDON/ YOU HAVE NO RIGHT TO ASSUME THAT THE COURT
FANY PROLOG (267) READS YOUR ARTICLES KNOWS YOURE AS INNOCENT AS A LAMB . /TROTTER/ WHAT! /FANNY/ YES, MR TROTTER: IVE SEEN A
POSN (447) THAT YOU MAY AS WELL BE HANGED FOR A SHEEP AS A LAMB . SO TALK AWAY. IVE GOT MY WITNESS; AND I'LL TROUBLE
JOAN 2 (82) THAT I MAY AS WELL BE HANGED FOR A SHEEP AS A LAMB . THE COURTIERS TAKE HEART AT THIS. THERE IS MORE
DOCT I (108) /EMMY/ WELL, IT'S ALL SHE CAN AFFORD, POOR LAMB . THEM OTHERS THINK NOTHING OF HALF-A-SOVEREIGN JUST TO
SIM PRO,3, (31) THE BETTER FOR YOUR DIP. WHY, HE'S AN ANGEL, A LAMB . WHAT HAVE YOU DONE TO HIM? /THE E.O./ (SEATING
2TRU II (75) NO SIR. ALL SHE SAID WAS " MARY HAD A LITTLE LAMB ." AND WHEN YOU ASKED HER COULD SHE SPEAK FRENCH SHE
SIM II (59) WORTHY IS THE LAMB" FOR EVER YOU WOULD DRIVE THE LAMB MAD. THE NOTION IS THAT YOU CANT HAVE TOO MUCH OF A
METH PREFACE(R76) THEN WASH OURSELVES INNOCENT IN THE BLOOD OF THE LAMB ON SUNDAY AT THE COST OF A CREDO AND A PENNY IN THE
2TRU III (95) ORDINARY AFTERNOON TEA, AND A CHICKEN AND SOME LAMB OR VEAL-- /TALLBOYS/ WILL YOU BE GOOD ENOUGH-- /MRS
APPL PREFACE(183) NOW RUN TO THE GOVERNMENT FOR HELP AS A LAMB RUNS TO ITS MOTHER. THEY CANNOT EVEN MAKE AN EXTENSION
LION II (136) LET US BE BRAVE AND SUFFER. YOU MUST GO AS A LAMB TO THE SLAUGHTER. /FERROVIUS/ AYE, AYE: THAT IS RIGHT.
LION PREFACE(19) CONSISTENT PERSON. HIS REASONS FOR GOING " LIKE A LAMB TO THE SLAUGHTER" INSTEAD OF SAVING HIMSELF AS MAHOMET
POSN PREFACE(376) FOLLOWS. THE SENTENCE. I WAS TO BE ADMITTED, AS A LAMB TO THE SLAUGHTER, AND ALLOWED TO TAKE MY PLACE AS IF
BULL PREFACE(20) EVEN THE ILLUSION OF HEROISM WHEN HE WENT LIKE A LAMB TO THE SLAUGHTER), GOT HIMSELF KILLED BY HIS PASSION
BUOY III (45) DOES. I HAVE GONE TWICE TO MY WEDDINGS LIKE A LAMB TO THE SLAUGHTER HOUSE. MY TWO WIVES WERE TRIUMPHANT. I
ROCK PREFACE(179) THEIR CHAMPION PUT UP NO FIGHT: HE WENT LIKE A LAMB TO THE SLAUGHTER, DUMB. SUCH A SPECTACLE IS
2TRU II (77) WENT-- /THE PATIENT/ (ADROITLY CUTTING IN) THAT LAMB WAS SURE TO GO. GOT ME, COLONEL. HOW CLEVER OF YOU!
LION II (144) THATS THE GREAT SECRET. HE'LL BE AS GENTLE AS A LAMB WHEN HE KNOWS THAT YOU ARE HIS FRIEND. STAND QUITE
DEST (183) AND HOLDING IT) ALL RIGHT: I'LL BE AS GENTLE AS A LAMB WITH HIM. HIS SISTER'S A VERY PRETTY WOMAN. (HE
GENV II (62) AWFUL EXHIBITION OF HIMSELF, AND HE KNEW IT, POOR LAMB , AND WOULD NEVER HAVE GONE IN FOR IT IF HIS MOTHER
JOAN 2 (72) THE PAGE WITHDRAWS. /BLUEBEARD/ YOUR FAITHFUL LAMB , ARCHBISHOP. GOOD DAY, MY LORD. DO YOU KNOW WHAT HAS
CATH 4 (195) CLASPED HANDS TO CLAIRE) OH, SWEET LITTLE ANGEL LAMB , HE LOVES YOU! IT SHINES IN HIS DARLING EYES. PARDON
2TRU II (75) BUT WHAT DOES BMAL ELTTIL MEAN? /MEEK/ LITTLE LAMB , SIR. /TALLBOYS/ SHE CALLED ME A LITTLE LAMB! /MEEK/
BARB PREFACE(245) CONTENT WITH THE OLD SCAPEGOAT AND SACRIFICIAL LAMB , WE DEIFY HUMAN SAVIORS, AND PRAY TO MIRACULOUS VIRGIN
SIM II (59) HARP FOR EVER; AND IF YOU SANG " WORTHY IS THE LAMB " FOR EVER YOU WOULD DRIVE THE LAMB MAD. THE NOTION IS
MIS. (123) THAT WAS THE VERY THING HE DIED OF, POOR LITTLE LAMB ! I BURST OUT CRYING: I COULDNT HELP IT. IT WAS AS
MIS. (145) THERE, THOUGH SHE DOESNT KNOW IT, POOR INNOCENT LAMB ! PUBLIC SCANDAL EXAGGERATES ENORMOUSLY, OF COURSE;
MIS. (187) TARLETON/ NOW DONT HURT HIS FEELINGS, POOR LITTLE LAMB ! /LORD SUMMERHAYS/ (VERY STERNLY) BENTLEY: YOU ARE
2TRU II (75) LAMB, SIR. /TALLBOYS/ SHE CALLED ME A LITTLE LAMB ! /MEEK/ NO SIR. ALL SHE SAID WAS " MARY HAD A LITTLE

LAMBALLE
DEST SD(162) CHITON, NOTHING, INDEED, THAT THE PRINCESSE DE LAMBALLE MIGHT NOT HAVE WORN. HER DRESS OF FLOWERED SILK IS

LAMBETH
PRES (144) GERMAN FLEET. /MITCHENER/ YOU DARENT SAY THAT IN LAMBETH . /BALSQUITH/ I'LL SAY IT THE DAY AFTER YOU PUBLISH
SIM II (75) REMOVED TO MENTAL HOSPITAL. CHURCH ASSEMBLY AT LAMBETH PALACE DECIDES BY A LARGE MAJORITY THAT THERE HAS
PRES (144) I'M MUCH MORE INTERESTED IN THE DEATH-RATE IN LAMBETH THAN IN THE GERMAN FLEET. /MITCHENER/ YOU DARENT SAY

LAMBS
MTH1 II (30) THAT IS WHAT IT WOULD COME TO, JUST AS IT CAME TO LAMBS AND KIDS WHEN ABEL BEGAN WITH SHEEP AND GOATS. YOU ARE
JOAN 6 (145) THE TREES, THE LARKS IN THE SUNSHINE, THE YOUNG LAMBS CRYING THROUGH THE HEALTHY FROST, AND BLESSED BLESSED
METH PREFACE(R78) THEM LITERALLY MADE HIM A MADMAN WHO SLEW LAMBS INSTEAD OF FEEDING THEM. IN ENGLAND TODAY GOOD BOOKS
2TRU III (110) NUMBER OF OUR MAGAZINES, ARE NUDER THAN SHORN LAMBS . BUT THE HORROR OF THE NAKED MIND IS STILL MORE THAN

LION PREFACE(56)	A RIGHT TO DO WITH THE PRODUCT IS TO FEED HIS	LAMBS	. LABOR TIME. SO MAKER'S RIGHT AS AN ALTERNATIVE TO
ROCK II (236)	UNEMPLOYED WELL IN HAND TODAY. /BASHAM/ QUIET AS	LAMBS	. THEYRE ALL READING THE PAPERS. NEW EDITIONS EVERY
FOUN (219)	CHANCELLOR/ PARDON ME. I THOUGHT YOU SUFFRAGIST	LAMBS	PRIDED YOURSELVES ON ACTING ALWAYS ON PRINCIPLE. ON
JOAN 5 (120)	TO DEATH: FRANCE MIGHT PERISH IF ONLY OUR	LAMBS	WERE SAFE. I THOUGHT FRANCE WOULD HAVE FRIENDS AT THE
CATH 4 (196)	(MOVED TO TEARS) SAINTED NICHOLAS: BLESS YOUR	LAMBS	! /CATHERINE/ DO YOU WONDER NOW THAT I LOVE RUSSIA AS
		LAME	
LION PROLOG (107)	YOU BRING IN EVERY STRAY CAT AND LOST CUR AND	LAME	DUCK IN THE WHOLE COUNTRYSIDE? YOU TOOK THE BREAD OUT
MIS. PREFACE(21)	TO BEAT HIM SAVAGELY ENOUGH TO FORCE HIM TO	LAME	HIS MIND -- FOR JOHNSON'S GREAT MIND WAS LAMED -- BY
POSN (452)	HORSES FROM STRAPPER BECAUSE MY OWN'S GONE	LAME	. EVERYBODY KNOWS YOU ARRIVED IN THE TOWN YESTERDAY AND
LION PREFACE(25)	HE SAYS, IN EFFECT, THERE IS NOTHING IN MAKING A	LAME	MAN WALK: THOUSANDS OF LAME MEN HAVE BEEN CURED AND
LION PREFACE(23)	DISEASE AS A DEPARTMENT OF SIN, AND ON CURING A	LAME	MAN, SAYS " THY SINS ARE FORGIVEN" INSTEAD OF " ARISE
LION PREFACE(25)	NOTHING IN MAKING A LAME MAN WALK: THOUSANDS OF	LAME	MEN HAVE BEEN CURED AND HAVE WALKED WITHOUT ANY
LION PROLOG (108)	FLAPS IT PITEOUSLY BEFORE ANDROCLES). OH, HE'S	LAME	, POOR CHAP! HE'S GOT A THORN IN HIS PAW. A
		LAMED	
METH PREFACE(R14)	OR ANY OTHER SORT OF MASTERS: IT CAN ONLY BE	LAMED	AND ENSLAVED BY THEM. IT IS SAID THAT IF YOU WASH A
MIS. PREFACE(67)	CHARACTER ARE CRUELLY DISTRESSED AND MORE OR LESS	LAMED	FOR LIFE BY IT. OUR QUARRELSOMENESS, AS BETWEEN
BARB III (317)	IN DOCILITY AND WHAT THEY CALL GOOD TASTE; AND	LAMED	FOR LIFE SO THAT HE IS FIT FOR NOTHING BUT TEACHING.
MIS. PREFACE(72)	OF THE YOUNG MEN THEY COACH FOR EXAMINATIONS ARE	LAMED	FOR LIFE THEREBY; IN SPITE OF DICKENS AND HIS PICTURE
MIS. PREFACE(52)	LARGE, MAY REMEMBER HOW TO SET ABOUT IT, HOWEVER	LAMED	HIS POWER OF INITIATIVE MAY HAVE BECOME THROUGH
CAPT III (295)	YOU; BUT I'M NOT CLEVER ENOUGH TO SEIZE IT. YOUVE	LAMED	ME BY SHEWING ME THAT I TAKE LIFE THE WRONG WAY WHEN
MIS. PREFACE(21)	TO LAME HIS MIND -- FOR JOHNSON'S GREAT MIND WAS	LAMED	-- BY LEARNING HIS LESSONS, NONE OF MY SCHOOLMASTERS
MILL IV (200)	TEMPER. /ADRIAN/ KEEP YOUR OWN TEMPER. HAS SHE	LAMED	YOU FOR LIFE? HAS SHE RAISED A BUMP ON YOUR HEAD?
		LAMENT	
ROCK II (280)	OUT THROUGH THE MAIN DOOR). /DAVID/ (IN LOUD	LAMENT	TO HIS MOTHER) YOUVE RUINED MY WHOLE LIFE. (HE GOES
MTH5 SD(214)	HAS DESCENDED THE HILL PATH DURING STREPHON'S	LAMENT	, AND HAS HEARD MOST OF IT. SHE IS LIKE THE
		LAMENTABLE	
CLEO II SD(138)	IN, TEARING HIS HAIR, AND SQUEAKING THE MOST	LAMENTABLE	EXCLAMATIONS. RUFIO STEPS BACK TO STARE AT HIM,
2TRU I (40)	HER FEET. SHE'S FAINTED. /THE BURGLAR/ (UTTERS A	LAMENTABLE	GROAN AND ROLLS OVER ON HIS FACE)! ! /THE
MILL PREFACE(128)	JUDGED IN THIS LIGHT OUR PRESENT PREDICAMENT IS	LAMENTABLE	. WE NO LONGER BELIEVE IN THE OLD " SANCTIONS" (
CAPT II (246)	THETLL BRIKE MAW AWT, WOWNT IT NAH? (WITH A	LAMENTABLE	SOB, HE THROWS HIMSELF DOWN ON THE DIVAN, RAGING
		LAMENTABLY	
MTH5 (241)	INDEED SHE DID. /THE FEMALE FIGURE/ (HOWLING	LAMENTABLY	) BOOHOO! OO! OOH! /THE HE-ANCIENT/ SILENCE, I
MIS. (199)	NOW-- (HE IS BROKEN WITH EMOTION, AND CONTINUES	LAMENTABLY	) I CANT SAY THE RIGHT THING. I CANT DO THE RIGHT
JOAN 6 (149)	BUT IT WAS NOT YOUR DOING. /THE CHAPLAIN/ (	LAMENTABLY	) I LET THEM DO IT. IF I HAD KNOWN, I WOULD HAVE
MIS. (184)	IMPOSSIBLE. /BENTLEY/ (SUDDENLY BREAKING OUT	LAMENTABLY	) JOEY: HAVE YOU TAKEN HYPATIA AWAY FROM ME?
PYGM III (250)	TO ME! (THEY STARE AT HIM). COVENT GARDEN! (	LAMENTABLY	) WHAT A DAMNED THING! /MRS HIGGINS/ HENRY,
LION I (119)	AT BEING PARTED FROM IT. (ANDROCLES SNIFFS	LAMENTABLY	). AINT YOU, OLD CHAP? WELL, CHEER UP, WE MARCH
		LAMENTATION	
2TRU III SD(94)	DISTURBANCE. A VOICE IS HEARD IN COMPLAINT AND	LAMENTATION	. IT IS THAT OF THE ELDERLY LADY, MRS MOPPLY,
BASH PREFACE(90)	OF THE NAME OF GENTLEMAN, AND JAMES HEARN'S	LAMENTATION	OVER THE TRAGEDY OF CETEWAYO CAME OFF, NOT AS A
LIED (194)	FORWARD AND CATCHING AT THE FAN, WITH LOUD	LAMENTATION	) DONT BREAK MY FAN-- NO, DONT. (HE SLOWLY
		LAMENTED	
DEVL I (19)	THE WAY, DID I HEAR, OR DID I NOT, THAT OUR LATE	LAMENTED	UNCLE PETER, THOUGH UNMARRIED, WAS A FATHER?
		LAMENTING	
MRS PREFACE(165)	SPECTACLE OF A NUMBER OF RESPECTABLE GENTLEMEN	LAMENTING	BECAUSE A PLAYWRIGHT LURES THEM TO THE THEATRE BY
SUPR I (12)	AND GOING TO OCTAVIUS TO CONSOLE HIM, BUT STILL	LAMENTING	) IF HE WANTED A YOUNG GUARDIAN, WHY DIDNT HE
LION II (132)	VERY EASILY TO MY SPIRIT (BEATING HIS BREAST AND	LAMENTING	) OH, SINNER THAT I AM! (HE THROWS HIMSELF DOWN
		LAMING	
MIS. PREFACE(42)	AND PROHIBITING AND PUNISHING AND SCOLDING AND	LAMING	AND CRAMPING AND DELAYING PROGRESS AND GROWTH INSTEAD
MIS. PREFACE(52)	THE IMPRISONMENT, THE BEATING, THE TAMING AND	LAMING	, THE BREAKING OF YOUNG SPIRITS, THE ARREST OF
		LAMP	
MRS IV SD(235)	BOX, ASH PANS, AND A PORTABLE ELECTRIC READING	LAMP	ALMOST SNOWED UP IN HEAPS OF PAPERS AND BOOKS. THIS
MTH5 (212)	BECOME AS THE ANCIENTS! NEVER TO LET THE SACRED	LAMP	BE EXTINGUISHED! NEVER TO CHANGE OR FORGET! TO BE
DOCT PREFACE(61)	AND PASS HIS LANCET THROUGH THE FLAME OF A SPIRIT	LAMP	BEFORE SCRATCHING HIS ARM. BUT HE CANNOT MAKE HIM
PYGM II SD(217)	ROW OF TINY ORGAN PIPES WITH A BELLOWS, A SET OF	LAMP	CHIMNEYS FOR SINGING FLAMES WITH BURNERS ATTACHED TO A
VWOO 3 (142)	OF SENSE. WE SHALL LIGHT UP FOR ONEANOTHER A	LAMP	IN THE HOLY OF HOLIES IN THE TEMPLE OF LIFE; AND THE
2TRU I (37)	NO, NO. LEAVE ME SOMETHING TO READ BY. MY BEDSIDE	LAMP	IS NOT ENOUGH, YOU STUPID IDIOT. THE NURSE SWITCHES ON
CAND III SD(127)	MARCHBANKS ARE SITTING BY THE FIRE. THE READING	LAMP	IS ON THE MANTELSHELF ABOVE MARCHBANKS, WHO IS IN THE
HART III (146)	I MARRIED! I'LL GO ON THE ROOF FIRST. (THE	LAMP	LIGHTS UP AGAIN). THERE! MR HUSHABYE'S TURNED IT ON
MRS II SD(198)	IN THE CENTRE A TABLE STANDS WITH A LIGHTED	LAMP	ON IT. VIVIE'S BOOKS AND WRITING MATERIALS ARE ON A
CLEO I (113)	SIDE OF THE THRONE IS A SLENDER PILLAR WITH A	LAMP	ON IT.) /CAESAR/ WHAT PLACE IS THIS? /CLEOPATRA/ THIS
MRS IV (253)	PLACE AT THE WRITING-TABLE; PUSHES THE ELECTRIC	LAMP	OUT OF THE WAY; PULLS OVER A GREAT SHEAF OF PAPERS; AND
2TRU III (95)	CLING: WE ARE ALL LIKE DRUNKEN WOMEN CLINGING TO	LAMP	POSTS: NONE OF US STANDS UPRIGHT. /THE ELDER/ THERE IS
OVER SD(171)	IT IN EVENING DRESS, CATCH THE LIGHT FROM AN ARC	LAMP	SOMEWHERE; BUT THE WALLS, COVERED WITH A DARK GREEN
DOCT I SD(82)	A MICROSCOPE, SEVERAL TEST TUBES, AND A SPIRIT	LAMP	STANDING UP THROUGH ITS LITTER OF PAPERS. THERE IS A
CAND II SD(113)	CANDIDA COMES IN, WELL APRONED, WITH A READING	LAMP	TRIMMED, FILLED, AND READY FOR LIGHTING. SHE PLACES IT
VWOO 3 (142)	THE HOLY OF HOLIES IN THE TEMPLE OF LIFE; AND THE	LAMP	WILL MAKE ITS VEIL TRANSPARENT. AIMLESS LUMPS OF STONE
HART III (144)	THE WEST. THE MOON GROWS FROM A SICKLE TO AN ARC	LAMP	, AND COMES LATER AND LATER UNTIL SHE IS LOST IN THE
MRS II (218)	AND LIGHTS THE CANDLE. THEN SHE EXTINGUISHES THE	LAMP	, DARKENING THE ROOM A GOOD DEAL). BETTER LET IN SOME
MIS. PREFACE(74)	AS IF BY MAGIC, WITH NOTHING TO DO BUT RUB THE	LAMP	, LIKE ALADDIN, AND HAVE THEIR NEEDS SATISFIED. THE
		LAMPLIGHT	
LADY SD(239)	WORLD FOR THE MOST PART WILL NONE OF MY THOUGHTS.	LAMPLIGHT	STREAMS FROM THE PALACE DOOR AS IT OPENS FROM
		LAMPOONED	
FANY PREFACE(255)	THE JUDGMENT OF HER GOD. THE CRITICS WHOM I HAVE	LAMPOONED	IN THE INDUCTION TO THIS PLAY UNDER THE NAMES OF
		LAMPS	
MIS. (157)	CUES? PLATES, KNIVES, AND FORKS? TWO PARAFFIN	LAMPS	AND A HATSTAND? /LINA/ NO: THAT IS POPULAR LOW-CLASS
MIS. (158)	TOUCH NOTHING BUT CLASSICAL WORK. ANYBODY CAN DO	LAMPS	AND HATSTANDS. I CAN DO SILVER BULLETS. THAT IS REALLY
PPP SD(193)	COMBING HER HAIR. IT IS LATE; AND THE ELECTRIC	LAMPS	ARE GLOWING, APPARENTLY THE ROOM IS BEDLESS; BUT THERE
NEVR IV SD(282)	THE SAME ROOM. NINE O' CLOCK. NOBODY PRESENT. THE	LAMPS	ARE LIGHTED; BUT THE CURTAINS ARE NOT DRAWN. THE
CAND II (114)	CHARIOT! TO CARRY US UP INTO THE SKY, WHERE THE	LAMPS	ARE STARS, AND DONT NEED TO BE FILLED WITH PARAFFIN
LION PREFACE(65)	PINCHED, PEOPLE FLING KNIVES AND LIGHTED PARAFFIN	LAMPS	AT ONE ANOTHER IN A DISPUTE OVER A DINNER-TABLE. MEN
LION PREFACE(101)	IMPROVEMENT ON HINDOO SCRIPTURE, IS TO OFFER OLD	LAMPS	FOR OLDER ONES IN A MARKET WHERE THE OLDEST LAMPS,
MIS. PREFACE(38)	A DAY OR BOYS DRUDGING FROM NINE TO SIX UNDER GAS	LAMPS	IN UNDERGROUND CITY OFFICES. LADS AND LASSES IN THEIR
LION PREFACE(62)	GREATER ABUNDANCE OF LIFE; THAT WE ARE THE	LAMPS	IN WHICH THE LIGHT OF THE WORLD BURNS: THAT, IN SHORT,
CLEO I (113)	AS THE QUEEN HAS BIDDEN. (THE SLAVE LIGHTS THE	LAMPS	. MEANWHILE CLEOPATRA STANDS HESITATING, AFRAID OF
CLEO I (113)	THRONE). /CAESAR/ ORDER THE SLAVE TO LIGHT THE	LAMPS	. /CLEOPATRA/ (SHYLY) DO YOU THINK I MAY? /CAESAR/
CLEO I (113)	(TIMIDLY, TO THE SLAVE) LIGHT ALL THE	LAMPS	. /FTATATEETA/ (SUDDENLY COMING FROM BEHIND THE
CAND II (112)	SHE HAS GOT RID OF HER PUPIL, SHE IS FILLING THE	LAMPS	. /MARCHBANKS/ (STARTING UP IN THE WILDEST
CAND III (132)	IN THE SCULLERY, SLICING ONIONS AND FILLING	LAMPS	. /MARCHBANKS/ OR IN THE PULPIT, SCRUBBING CHEAP
LIED SD(187)	IN THE EVENING. THE CURTAINS ARE DRAWN AND THE	LAMPS	LIGHTED IN THE DRAWING ROOM OF HER FLAT IN CROMWELL
WIDO III SD(49)	WINTER EVENING: FIRE BURNING, CURTAINS DRAWN, AND	LAMPS	LIGHTED. SARTORIUS AND BLANCHE ARE SITTING GLUMLY NEAR
CAND III SD(127)	IN THE EVENING. THE CURTAINS ARE DRAWN, AND THE	LAMPS	LIGHTED. THE TYPEWRITER IS IN ITS CASE: THE LARGE
CLEO I (107)	MADMAN'S DREAM: THIS IS MY REALITY. THESE STARRY	LAMPS	OF YOURS I HAVE SEEN FROM AFAR IN GAUL, IN BRITAIN, IN
DEVL II SD(29)	EXCEPT FOR THE COSY FIRELIGHT AND THE DIM OIL	LAMPS	SEEN THROUGH THE WINDOW IN THE WET STREET, WHERE THERE

CLEO I (113) YOU HAVE WITH YOU: AND HOW DARE YOU ORDER THE LAMPS TO BE LIGHTED WITHOUT MY PERMISSION? (CLEOPATRA IS
CAND II (113) WITH US, EUGENE. I THINK I WILL HAND OVER THE LAMPS TO YOU. /MARCHBANKS/ I WILL STAY ON CONDITION THAT YOU
SUPR III SD(79) NOW STARLIGHT; AND THEY KNOW THAT MOTOR CARS HAVE LAMPS WHICH CAN BE TURNED TO ACCOUNT FOR LIGHTING A CARD
MILL IV SD(188) SITTERS, DIVIDED BY STATIONERY CASES AND ELECTRIC LAMPS WITH DAINTY SHADES. NEAR IT IS A TABLE WITH ALL THE
LION PREFACE(101) LAMPS FOR OLDER ONES IN A MARKET WHERE THE OLDEST LAMPS , LIKE OLD FURNITURE IN ENGLAND, ARE THE MOST HIGHLY
DOCT PREFACE(20) MORE THAN CONJURING WITH RETORTS AND SPIRIT LAMPS , MAGNETS AND MICROSCOPES, AND DISCOVERING MAGICAL

LAN
BULL III (127) THEN HWAT DID YOU MANE BE TALKIN ABOUT GIVIN HIM LAN ? /DORAN/ AISY, MATT, AISY. YOURE LIKE A BEAR WITH A
BULL III (129) YOU THINK WELL TO ASK HIM WHAT HE MANES ABOUT THE LAN ? /LARRY/ (COMING DOWN ON MATT PROMPTLY) I'LL TELL
BULL III (127) NEVER MIND HIM, /MATTHEW/ (RISING) WELL, IF ME LAN IS TO BE GIVEN TO PATSY AND HIS LIKE, I'M GOIN OURA
BULL III (128) I KNOW I'M A BIT HASTY WHEN I THINK ABOUT THE LAN . I AX YOUR PARDON FOR IT. /FATHER DEMPSEY/ (RESUMING
BULL III (127) VIOLENT IMPATIENCE) ARRA WHO'S GOIN TO GIVE YOUR LAN TO PATSY, YOWL FOOL YE? /FATHER DEMPSEY/ AISY, BARNEY,
BULL III (129) MIGHTNT HAVE A MORE INDEPINDENT MIND ABOUT THE LAN , AN BE LESS AFEERD TO SPAKE OUT ABOUT IT, DHAN AN IRISH
BULL III (127) AGEN LANLORDS. HWAT CALL HAS HE TO TALK ABOUT THE LAN , THAT NEVER WAS OUTSIDE OF A CITY OFFICE IN HIS LIFE..

LANCASHIRE
BULL PREFACE(4) AS THE PEOPLE OF LANCASHIRE WERE CONCERNED ABOUT LANCASHIRE AND NOT AT ALL ABOUT SOUTH AFRICA, THE UNIONIST
2TRU PREFACE(8) CAN LIVE LIKE A LORD FOR AN AFTERNOON, AND THE LANCASHIRE FACTORY OPERATIVE HAVE A GORGEOUS WEEK AT
BULL PREFACE(4) VALID FOR THE INTRODUCTION OF CHINESE LABOR INTO LANCASHIRE . AND AS THE PEOPLE OF LANCASHIRE WERE CONCERNED
SUPR HANDBOK(182) ANY REGARD FOR INDIVIDUAL HARD CASES, PEOPLE IN LANCASHIRE STILL SPEAK OF THEIR " PROPERTY" IN THE OLD
METH PREFACE(R64) THEY FOUND IT OUT TO THEIR COST IN THE DAYS WHEN LANCASHIRE USED UP NINE GENERATIONS OF WAGE SLAVES IN ONE
BULL PREFACE(4) LABOR INTO LANCASHIRE, AND AS THE PEOPLE OF LANCASHIRE WERE CONCERNED ABOUT LANCASHIRE AND NOT AT ALL
GENV III (68) IN 1906 WHEN IT WANTED TO LET CHINESE LABOR INTO LANCASHIRE ! /THE JEW/ YOUR OWN COUNTRY! WHO MADE YOU A

LANCASTER
ROCK I (224) ENGLISH ARE STILL WHAT WE WERE WHEN TIME-HONORED LANCASTER DESCRIBED US AS " THIS HAPPY BREED OF MEN." WE ARE
JOAN 4 (106) YOU ARE THE MAKERS OF KINGS AFTER ALL. YORK OR LANCASTER IN ENGLAND, LANCASTER OR VALOIS IN FRANCE: THEY
JOAN 4 (106) OF KINGS AFTER ALL. YORK OR LANCASTER IN ENGLAND, LANCASTER OR VALOIS IN FRANCE: THEY REIGN ACCORDING TO YOUR
ROCK II (267) AND EVEN THE CHILTERN HUNDREDS AND THE DUCHY OF LANCASTER -- WE HAVE NO DEPARTMENT FOR THINKING? THE
POSN PREFACE(369) THE SUBJECT. THE THEN CHANCELLOR OF THE DUCHY OF LANCASTER , MR HERBERT SAMUEL (NOW POSTMASTER-GENERAL), WHO

LANCE
GENV IV (88) IS NOT INTERESTED, IT SEEMS. /BEGONIA/ ONE FREE LANCE JOURNALIST LOOKED IN; BUT SHE WENT AWAY WHEN SHE FOUND
JOAN 3,SD(89) WIND DROPS; AND THE PENNON FLAPS IDLY DOWN THE LANCE ; BUT DUNOIS IS TOO MUCH OCCUPIED WITH JOAN TO NOTICE
JOAN 3 (93) HURRAY-AY-AY! (HE SNATCHES UP THE SHIELD AND LANCE , AND CAPERS OUT AFTER THEM, MAD WITH EXCITEMENT).
JOAN PREFACE(20) GIVE EXHIBITIONS OF HER DEXTERITY IN HANDLING A LANCE , AND OF HER SEAT AS A RIDER? WHY DID SHE ACCEPT

LANCED
METH PREFACE(R15) TIME TO TIME IN GIGANTIC BOILS THAT HAVE TO BE LANCED BY A MILLION BAYONETS. THIS IS THE RESULT OF

LANCELOT'S
BULL PREFACE(40) FOR THE NATIONALIST ENEMY. EVERY IRISHMAN IS IN LANCELOT'S POSITION: HIS HONOR ROOTED IN DISHONOR STANDS;

LANCET
PPP SD(205) ATTRACTED TO THE WAISTCOAT OF THE DOCTOR BY THE LANCET IN HIS POCKET. FINALLY IT LEAPS WITH FEARFUL FORCE ON
DOCT IV (160) YOU? (HE PRODUCES A CAMERA). COULD YOU HAVE A LANCET OR SOMETHING IN YOUR HAND? /WALPOLE/ PUT IT UP. IF
DOCT PREFACE(61) HE CAN CHEAT HIM WITH COLORED WATER AND PASS HIS LANCET THROUGH THE FLAME OF A SPIRIT LAMP BEFORE SCRATCHING
JOAN EPIL,SD(152) SIDE OF THE ROOM SO AS TO AVOID BLOCKING A TALL LANCET WINDOW IN THE MIDDLE. ITS CANOPY BEARS THE ROYAL ARMS
JOAN EPILOG (155) PLACE. (A FLASH OF SUMMER LIGHTNING SHEWS UP THE LANCET WINDOW. A FIGURE IS SEEN IN SILHOUETTE AGAINST IT)

LANCHESTER
SHAK PREFACE(135) MY CAREER AS A PLAYWRIGHT WAS FINISHED WHEN WALDO LANCHESTER OF THE MALVERN MARIONETTE THEATRE, OUR CHIEF

LANCHESTER'S
SHAK PREFACE(135) I ACCOMPLISHED THIS FEAT, AND WAS GRATIFIED BY MR LANCHESTER'S IMMEDIATE APPROVAL. I HAVE LEARNT PART OF MY

LAND
CLEO III (152) RECAPTURE THE PHAROS. THEY WILL ATTACK BY SEA AND LAND : BY LAND ALONG THE GREAT MOLE; BY SEA FROM THE WEST
ROCK II (244) THE LAST DROP OF MY ORIENTAL BLOOD. NATIONALIZED LAND : COMPULSORY LABOR: ABOLITION OF RATES: STRIKES MADE
KING I (196) AND SINK HIM THERE. HE IS NO GREAT GENERAL ON LAND : ON WATER HE IS NOTHING. I HAVE NEVER BEEN BEATEN AT
MTH2 (65) FROM BEING HECKLED. OUT WITH IT. IS IT ABOUT THE LAND ? /CONRAD/ NO. /BURGE/ IS IT ABOUT THE CHURCH?
FABL III (111) GET INTO THIS ISLAND? WHY WERE YOU ALLOWED TO LAND ? /HE/ I WAS A STOWAWAY, MADAM. THEY WANTED TO SEND ME
DOCT III (141) HE TO BE ALLOWED TO DEFY THE CRIMINAL LAW OF THE LAND ? /SIR PATRICK/ THE CRIMINAL LAW IS NO USE TO DECENT
FABL III (109) TO BE ON THE ISLE OF WIGHT AT ALL. WHO LET YOU LAND ? /THE TOURIST/ I CAME IN MY OWN BOAT. I LANDED ON THE
KING I (182) SHALL I ROOT OUT THE SIN OF IDOLATRY FROM THIS LAND ? WORSHIP YOUR GOD, WOMAN, NOT A DRESSED-UP PRIEST.
ANNA (300) PRISONS AGAIN WITH THE NOBLEST SPIRITS IN THE LAND ? YOU WOULD THRUST THE RISING SUN OF LIBERTY BACK INTO
SIM II (57) BY NOON TODAY" THAT CAME THIS MORNING " I SHALL LAND A SHORE PARTY EQUIPPED WITH MACHINE GUNS AND TEAR GAS
BULL III (130) THINK YOURE EVERYBODY BECAUSE YOUR FATHER WAS A LAND AGENT. /LARRY/ WHAT CALL HAVE YOU TO LOOK DOWN ON PATSY
CLEO III (152) THE PHAROS. THEY WILL ATTACK BY SEA AND LAND: BY LAND ALONG THE GREAT MOLE; BY SEA FROM THE WEST HARBOR. STIR
LION PREFACE(59) PROBLEM OF HOW TO DISTRIBUTE THE PRODUCT OF THE LAND AMONG ALL THE INDIVIDUALS IN THE COMMUNITY. EQUAL
O'FL (224) /MRS O'FLAHERTY/ IS IT TAKE ME INTO A STRANGE LAND AMONG HEATHENS AND PAGANS AND SAVAGES, AND ME NOT
LION PREFACE(59) AND DERIVATIVE. PERSONS WHO LIVE ON RENT OF LAND AND CAPITAL ARE ECONOMICALLY, THOUGH NOT LEGALLY, IN
ROCK PREFACE(152) PRIVATE PROPERTY IN LAND EXISTS. IF I POSSESS LAND AND FIND IT PROFITABLE TO GROW WHEAT ON IT, I NEED MANY
METH PREFACE(R18) ANY LEGS AT ALL; BUILDING LUNGS AND ARMS FOR THE LAND AND GILLS AND FINS FOR THE SEA; ENABLING THE MAMMAL TO
ROCK II (244) LAST NIGHT, ARTHUR: YOU MUST NATIONALIZE THE LAND AND PUT A STOP TO THIS SHAMELESS EXPLOITATION OF THE
FABL PREFACE(96) WITH ENORMOUS RENTS FOR THE PROPRIETORS OF LONDON LAND AND SEAHAM MINES, NOT EQUIVALENTLY SURTAXED. DOCTORS
ROCK II (236) NOTHING ABOUT WOMEN. MUNICIPALIZATION OF URBAN LAND AND THE BUILDING TRADE, AND CONSEQUENT EXTINCTION OF
BULL III (132) DID THE TITHES EVER COME OFF YOU? WAS YOUR LAND ANY DEARER WHEN YOU PAID THE TITHE TO THE PARSON THAN
JOAN 2 (86) BUT I SHALL NOT BE LAWFUL OWNER OF MY OWN LAND ANYHOW. WILL THE CONSECRATION PAY OFF MY MORTGAGES? I
BULL IV (173) EVERYONE OF THESE MEN HALF AS MUCH AGAIN ON THEIR LAND AS IT IS WORTH, OR EVER CAN BE WORTH, TO THEM.
ROCK II (249) DUTIES-- YOU WILL GET ALL YOUR CASH BACK AND THE LAND AS WELL. /THE MAYOR/ BLEE: I TELL YOU, DONT ARGUE.
BULL III (130) LESS GREEDY AND OPPRESSIVE TO THEM THAT HAVE NO LAND AT ALL THAN OLD NICK LESTRANGE, WHO WAS AN EDUCATED
GENV IV (104) YOU ARE OF A CERTAIN RACE OR COLOR YOU SHALL NOT LAND AT ALL. SOONER THAN LET GERMAN SOLDIERS MARCH THROUGH
BULL III (128) HOW IT IS, LARRY. ROUND ABOUT HERE, WEVE GOT THE LAND AT LAST; AND WE WANT NO MORE GOVERMENT MEDDLIN. WE WANT
BULL IV (157) AN HAFFIGAN CANT SLEEP WITH COVETN THAT CORNER O LAND AT THE FOOT OF HIS MEDDA THAT BELONGS TO DOOLAN. HE'LL
METH PREFACE(R16) OF THE WEAPONS, BATTLESHIPS, SUBMARINES, AND LAND BATTERIES BY WHICH THEY ARE APPLIED DESTRUCTIVELY, IS
ROCK PREFACE(151) AS PRIVATE PROPERTY IN LAND. FOR WHEN A TRACT OF LAND BECOMES THE PRIVATE PROPERTY OF AN INDIVIDUAL WHO HAS
DEVL I (22) AND BEQUEATH MY HOUSE AT WEBSTERBRIDGE WITH THE LAND BELONGING TO IT AND ALL THE REST OF MY PROPERTY SOEVER
CLEO III (145) /SENTINEL/ WE ARE NOT HERE TO WATCH THE LAND BUT THE SEA. CAESAR HAS JUST LANDED ON THE PHAROS. (
CLEO III SD(144) CRESSET BEACON. THE ISLAND IS JOINED TO THE MAIN LAND BY THE HEPTASTADIUM, A GREAT MOLE OR CAUSEWAY FIVE
BULL I (89) THE LANDLORDS ARE MOSTLY PROTESTANTS. WHAT WITH LAND COURTS REDUCING RENTS AND LAND PURCHASE ACTS TURNING
BULL IV (178) AND YOU WILL DEVOTE WHAT THEY SAVE TO FRESH LAND DEVELOPMENT SCHEMES. FOR FOUR WICKED CENTURIES THE
BULL IV (179) PURIFIED OF HATRED MAY BE WORTH MORE THAN EVEN A LAND DEVELOPMENT SYNDICATE OF ANGLICIZED IRISHMEN AND
BULL I (78) I'M GOING TO DEVELOP AN ESTATE THERE FOR THE LAND DEVELOPMENT SYNDICATE, IN WHICH I AM INTERESTED. I AM
ROCK PREFACE(152) HAPPENING WHEREVER PRIVATE PROPERTY IN LAND EXISTS. IF I POSSESS LAND AND FIND IT PROFITABLE TO
BULL III (131) HONEST MEN HERE CANT MAKE THAT MUCH OUT O THE LAND FOR DHEMSELVES, MUCH LESS GIVE IT TO A LABORER. /LARRY/
BARB I (255) YOUR FATHER DID; AND THEY WERE RICH ENOUGH TO BUY LAND FOR THEIR OWN CHILDREN AND LEAVE THEM WELL PROVIDED
CLEO V (196) THERE WILL BE FAMINE AND TEMPEST IN THE LAND FOR THIS. /PERSIAN/ POOH! WHY DID NOT APIS CAUSE
ROCK II (249) FOR SIR ARTHUR BECAUSE HE WILL NATIONALIZE THE LAND FOR YOU. /BLEE/ (SCORNFULLY) YES, WITH COMPENSATION!
SHAK (140) /MACBETH/ THUS FAR INTO THE BOWELS OF THE LAND HAVE WE MARCHED ON WITHOUT IMPEDIMENT. SHALL I STILL
DOCT PREFACE(70) THAT MAKE UP SO MUCH OF FAMILY LIFE) WOULD SOON LAND HIM IN THE BANKRUPTCY COURT. PRIVATE PRACTICE, THUS
ROCK I (202) GRACE, MY LORDS AND GENTLEMEN. NATIONALIZE THE LAND IF YOU WILL; NATIONALIZE OUR INDUSTRIES IF WE MUST;
KING I (190) YOU JUMP INTO THE NEAREST FISHING SMACK AND LAND IN FRANCE, /JAMES/ AND LEAVE THEMSELVES WITHOUT A KING
FABL PREFACE(96) UNDER THE SEA, MILES FROM THE PIT HEAD, OR THAT LAND IN THE CITY OF LONDON FETCHES FABULOUS PRICES PER
ROCK II (244) THINK NOTHING OF EXTORTING A MILLION AN ACRE FOR LAND IN THE CITY, A MAN CANNOT HAVE AN ADDRESS IN LONDON FOR
BULL III (130) LAZY, GOOD-FOR-NOTHING SORT OF THING TO LEAVE THE LAND IN THE HANDS OF THE OLD LANDLORDS WITHOUT CALLING THEM

2TRU PREFACE(21)	ALLOW A PERSON TO OWN A THOUSAND ACRES OF	LAND	IN THE MIDDLE OF LONDON MUCH MORE COMPLETELY THAN HE
BULL IV (171)	PAYS LIKE A GOLFING HOTEL, IF YOU HOLD THE	LAND	INSTEAD OF THE SHARES, AND IF THE FURNITURE PEOPLE
O'FL (224)	ALL THE TIME TELLING THEM HOW THEY MIGHT PUT THE	LAND	INTO DECENT TILLAGE LIKE THE FRENCH AND BELGIANS, SIR
CAPT I SD(217)	AND TAMARISKS, THE PROSPECT ENDS, AS FAR AS THE	LAND	IS CONCERNED, IN LITTLE HILLS THAT COME NEARLY TO THE
BULL III (130)	THINKS THINGS WILL BE ANY BETTER NOW THAT THE	LAND	IS HANDED OVER TO A LOT OF LITTLE MEN LIKE YOU, WITHOUT
JOAN 2 (86)	WORKING ON THE LAND; AND I TELL THEE THAT THE	LAND	IS THINE TO RULE RIGHTEOUSLY AND KEEP GOD'S PEACE IN,
BULL IV (173)	WILL NOT LEND THEM MORE ON THEIR LAND THAN THE	LAND	IS WORTH; SO THEY WILL BE ABLE TO PAY YOU THE INTEREST.
BULL IV (173)	AND HOTELS IN THE AIR. FOR THAT YOU MUST OWN OUR	LAND	. AND HOW WILL YOU DRAG OUR ACRES FROM THE FERRET'S
BULL III (127)	SOLID MEN LIKE DORAN AN MATT WERE KEP FROM OWNIN	LAND	. BUT HWAT MAN IN HIS SENSES EVER WANTED TO GIVE LAND
ROCK PREFACE(151)	GRADUALLY DISGUISED ITSELF AS PRIVATE PROPERTY IN	LAND	. FOR WHEN A TRACT OF LAND BECOMES THE PRIVATE PROPERTY
MIS. PREFACE(25)	PIPCHINS AND MRS WILFERS THROUGHOUT THIS UNHAPPY	LAND	. I WILL GO FURTHER, AND ADMIT THAT THE BRASS PLATES
BARB II (302)	OUR WORK THROUGH THE LENGTH AND BREADTH OF THE	LAND	. LET ME TELL YOU THAT THERE WOULD HAVE BEEN RIOTING
VWOO 1 (116)	OF NAPLES, ATHENS, EGYPT, AND THE HOLY	LAND	. PLEASE OCCUPY YOUR MIND WITH THEM UNTIL THE SOUP
BULL IV (179)	LAND, A NAKED LAND, AN IGNORANT AND OPPRESSED	LAND	. /BROADBENT/ BUT, HANG IT ALL, THE IDLERS WILL BRING
MTH4 I SD(148)	WOMAN WITH THE NUMBER ONE ON HER CAP ARRIVES BY	LAND	. SHE LOOKS NO OLDER THAN SAVVY BARNABAS, WHOM SHE
ROCK II (243)	WHAT ON EARTH DO YOU MEAN? /SIR JAFNA/ YOUR	LAND	MONOPOLISTS, YOUR BLACKMAILERS, YOUR ROBBER BARONS,
FABL PREFACE(96)	VOTE LIKE SHEEP FOR THE LANDLORDS, AND DENOUNCE	LAND	MUNICIPALIZATION AS ROBBERY. HAD THE LATE FAMOUS
LION PREFACE(59)	WHO POSTULATE SOME REVOLUTIONARY CHANGE LIKE	LAND	NATIONALIZATION, WHICH BY ITSELF WOULD OBVIOUSLY ONLY
ROCK II (253)	SIR ARTHUR CARRIES HIS POINT THEYLL SHED IT FOR	LAND	NATIONALIZATION. IF YOU CARRY YOURS THEYLL STAND BY
LADY PREFACE(232)	HE HAD NO NOTION OF THE FEELING WITH WHICH THE	LAND	NATIONALIZERS OF TODAY REGARD THE FACT THAT HE WAS A
LADY PREFACE(232)	BUT THE SIMPLE FACT THAT IN HIS DAY WHAT ENGLISH	LAND	NEEDED WAS INDIVIDUAL APPROPRIATION AND CULTIVATION,
SUPR III SD(73)	THEY ARE ALL COCKNEY OR AMERICAN; THEREFORE, IN A	LAND	OF CLOAKS AND SOMBREROS, THEY MOSTLY WEAR SEEDY
BULL IV (179)	WHICH SUCH IRISHMEN AS YOU HAVE TURNED INTO A	LAND	OF DERISION. /BROADBENT/ (COMING BETWEEN THEM) TAKE
MTH4 II (192)	TO DISTRESS) IT MEANS NOTHING TO HIM: IN THIS	LAND	OF DISCOURAGEMENT THE SUBLIME HAS BECOME THE
CLEO IV (172)	A CAT EATS UP MICE; AND THAT HE WILL PUT ON THIS	LAND	OF EGYPT AS A SHEPHERD PUTS ON HIS GARMENT. AND WHEN HE
CLEO IV (171)	WE ARE ALL CAESAR'S SLAVES-- ALL WE IN THIS	LAND	OF EGYPT-- WHETHER WE WILL OR NO. AND SHE WHO IS WISE
JOAN 2 (86)	SHEPHERD. THOURT NOT LAWFUL OWNER OF THY OWN	LAND	OF FRANCE TILL THOU BE CONSECRATED. /CHARLES/ BUT I
BULL PREFACE(13)	WHICH FORCED MY ARMS AND THE MAN AND MR YEATS'S	LAND	OF HEART'S DESIRE ON THE RECALCITRANT LONDON PLAYGOER,
PLES PREFACE(R7)	SUPPLIED A COMEDY OF SIGHS: MR YEATS, THE	LAND	OF HEART'S DESIRE. I, HAVING NOTHING BUT UNPLEASANT
MIS. (181)	THAT ON THE 31ST MAY 1909 I TRESPASSED ON THE	LAND	OF JOHN TARLETON AT HINDHEAD AND EFFECTED AN UNLAWFUL
MIS. (179)	/TARLETON/ (DICTATING) -- I TRESPASSED ON THE	LAND	OF JOHN TARLETON AT HINDHEAD, AND EFFECTED AN UNLAWFUL
CLEO PRO1 (93)	THAN THE DAY IN WHICH CAESAR SET FOOT IN THE	LAND	OF MY PEOPLE. AND NOW I LEAVE YOU; FOR YE ARE A DULL
MTH2 (49)	HAS EVER BURST WITH EARTH-SHAKING VIOLENCE ON THE	LAND	OF OUR FATHERS. /FRANKLYN/ I KNOW THAT. I KNOW WHO YOU
CLEO IV (181)	IT). I HAVE BEEN IN BRITAIN-- THAT WESTERN	LAND	OF ROMANCE-- THE LAST PIECE OF EARTH ON THE EDGE OF THE
2TRU I (46)	BEFORE US. YOU AND SWEETIE HAVE HAD A WEEK IN THE	LAND	OF THE MOUNTAIN AND THE FLOOD FOR SEVEN GUINEAS, TIPS
BASH II,1, (102)	THE DAY. THE DUTCHMAN LED AT ONCE, AND SEEMED TO	LAND	ON BYRON'S DICEBOX; BUT THE SEAMAN'S REACH, TOO SHORT
ROCK PREFACE(167)	SUBSISTENCE BY PRIMITIVE METHODS FROM A STRIP OF	LAND	ON WHICH A TRACTOR COULD HARDLY TURN EVEN IF HE COULD
KING II (231)	IN PORTUGAL WAS A TONGUE THAT NEVER WAS SPOKE ON	LAND	OR SEA; AND MY PORTUGUESE MADE YOU LAUGH. WE MUST
FABL I (104)	100,000 POUNDS TO THE MAN WHO FOUND OUT HOW TO	LAND	OUR ARMY IN NORMANDY IN 1945. /YOUNG WOMAN/ GOVERNMENTS
MTH4 I (143)	THE WORD. /THE ELDERLY GENTLEMAN/ IS THIS	LAND	PRIVATE PROPERTY? IF SO, I MAKE NO CLAIM. I PROFFER A
BULL I (89)	WHAT WITH LAND COURTS REDUCING RENTS AND	LAND	PURCHASE ACTS TURNING BIG ESTATES INTO LITTLE HOLDINGS,
BULL III (121)	/AUNT JUDY/ OH SURE HE'S BOUGHT HIS FARM IN THE	LAND	PURCHASE. HE'S INDEPENDENT NOW. /NORA/ IT'S MADE A
BULL PREFACE(33)	NEED FOR PAYING SERIOUS ATTENTION TO THE IRISH	LAND	QUESTION WAS SEEN IN ENGLAND. IT COST THE AMERICAN WAR
ROCK II (249)	QUESTION IS NOT THE LABOR QUESTION BUT THE	LAND	QUESTION. /THE MAYOR/ YES: WE ALL KNOW THAT. /SIR
CAND I (80)	WELL, THURSDAY THEN? /PROSERPINE/ ENGLISH	LAND	RESTORATION LEAGUE. /MORELL/ WHAT NEXT? /PROSERPINE/
ROCK PREFACE(154)	THIS (EXCEPT IN THE SPECIAL CASE OF AGRICULTURAL	LAND	) BECOMES APPARENT, AND THE QUESTION IS PROBED TO THE
JOAN 2 (86)	LAND, AND HAVE GOTTEN MY STRENGTH WORKING ON THE	LAND	; AND I TELL THEE THAT THE LAND IS THINE TO RULE
ROCK PREFACE(166)	OF GIVE US PEACE. LENIN SAID, IN EFFECT, TAKE THE	LAND	; AND IF FEUDALLY MINDED PERSONS OBSTRUCT YOU,
BULL III (127)	HE DOESNT KNOW HWERE TO STOP. EVERY MAN CANT OWN	LAND	; AND SOME MEN MUST OWN IT TO EMPLOY THEM. IT WAS ALL
JOAN 4 (95)	-- YOU SEE, I HAVE MADE MY PILGRIMAGE TO THE HOLY	LAND	; AND THE HEAVENLY POWERS, FOR THEIR OWN CREDIT, CAN
APPL PREFACE(195)	HIS SCHEME FOR TURNING THE DOCKS INTO BUILDING	LAND	; EXPEDITING THE THAMES TRAFFIC; SAVING MUCH DANGEROUS
METH PREFACE(R15)	MINDLESS FORGOTTEN NONENTITIES GOVERNED THE	LAND	; SENT MEN TO THE PRISON OR THE GALLOWS FOR BLASPHEMY
BULL IV (173)	PARDON ME, YOU WILL NOT LEND THEM MORE ON THEIR	LAND	THAN THE LAND IS WORTH; SO THEY WILL BE ABLE TO PAY YOU
ROCK II (243)	WITH IT IS THAT THE OWNERS OF ALL THE MILES OF	LAND	THAT ARE INDISPENSABLE TO MY SCHEME, AND THAT WITHOUT
SIM II (62)	TOMORROW'S THREE O'CLOCK EDITION. /KANCHIN/ THE	LAND	THAT BROUGHT FORTH IDDY BEGINS THE APOCALYPSE.
BULL IV (173)	HABITS, CAN MAKE OR LOSE TEN POUNDS OUT OF	LAND	THAT HAFFIGAN, WITH ALL HIS INDUSTRY, COULD NOT MAKE OR
ROCK II (251)	YOU GILT EDGED SECURITIES IN EXCHANGE FOR THE	LAND	THAT NO LONGER BRINGS YOU IN SHOOTING RENTS; AND YOU
MTH4 I (154)	OF TWO AND A HALF CENTURIES OF LIFE. THE	LAND	THAT ONCE EXPORTED COTTON SHIRTS AND HARDWARE NOW
GENV IV (120)	OWN THEIR COUNTRIES. THEIR PEOPLE DO NOT OWN THE	LAND	THEY STARVE IN. THEIR COUNTRIES ARE OWNED BY A HANDFUL
MILL IV (202)	OF VOLCANOES, IN THE TRACK OF AVALANCHES, ON	LAND	THROWN UP ONLY YESTERDAY BY EARTHQUAKES, BUT WITH A
ROCK PREFACE(152)	BUT I MAY DO MUCH BETTER BY LETTING MY	LAND	TO INDUSTRIALISTS FOR THE ERECTION OF FACTORIES. THEY
BULL III (127)	BUT HWAT MAN IN HIS SENSES EVER WANTED TO GIVE	LAND	TO PATSY FARRLL AN DHE LIKE O HIM? /BROADBENT/ BUT
MIS. PREFACE(71)	OF A MUCH NEEDED LAW COMPELLING PROPRIETORS OF	LAND	TO PROVIDE PLENTY OF GATES IN THEIR FENCES, AND TO
BULL IV (173)	LIGHTING. /LARRY/ WHAT IS THE USE OF GIVING	LAND	TO SUCH MEN? THEY ARE TOO SMALL, TOO POOR, TOO
OVER PREFACE(157)	POACHERS, AND DEFENDS HIS LEGAL RIGHTS OVER HIS	LAND	TO THE EXTREMEST POINT OF UNSOCIAL SAVAGERY, BUT
JOAN 4 (95)	NUT TO CRACK; AND AS HE HAS BEEN TO THE HOLY	LAND	TOO, HONORS ARE EASY BETWEEN US AS FAR AS THAT GOES.
JOAN 3 (90)	HOLD THEM AGAINST GOD. GOD DID NOT GIVE THEM THE	LAND	UNDER THOSE FORTS: THEY STOLE IT FROM HIM. HE GAVE IT
MTH2 (51)	OF LORDS; TO A REVISED SCHEME OF TAXATION OF	LAND	VALUES; AND TO DOING SOMETHING OR OTHER TO KEEP THE
WIDO III (54)	COMPENSATION FOR WHAT? /LICKCHEESE/ WHY, THE	LAND	WAS WANTED FOR AN EXTENSION OF THE MINT; AND THE
ROCK PREFACE(174)	TAKEN IN BY TENNYSON'S NOTION THAT WE LIVE IN A	LAND	WHERE A MAN CAN SAY THE THING HE WILL. THERE IS NO SUCH
MTH4 II (179)	LOSE MY POWER AND BECOME A BEGGAR IN THE	LAND	WHERE I NOW MAKE MEN DRUNK WITH GLORY. /THE ORACLE/ NO
HART II (105)	GO, BOSS MANGAN; AND WHEN YOU HAVE FOUND THE	LAND	WHERE THERE IS HAPPINESS AND WHERE THERE ARE NO WOMEN,
BULL PREFACE(7)	DISHONOR OF ACTING AS A FOREIGN GARRISON IN A	LAND	WHERE THEY ARE NOT FOREIGNERS THAT MAKES THE POSITION
BULL III (141)	TO TALK O SUFFERIN, AN YOU LIVIN ON THE FAT O THE	LAND	WID MONEY WRUNG FROM US. /HODSON/ (SUDDENLY DROPPING
MILL PREFACE(129)	ANARCHY AND HERITABLE PRIVATE PROPERTY IN	LAND	WITH ALL THEIR DISASTROUS CONSEQUENCES AND GADARENE
ROCK II (249)	(SCORNFULLY) YES, WITH COMPENSATION! TAKE THE	LAND	WITH ONE HAND AND GIVE BACK ITS CASH VALUE TO THE
ROCK PREFACE(152)	FIND THAT IT IS MORE PROFITABLE TO COVER MY	LAND	WITH SHEEP AND SELL THEIR WOOL, I HAVE TO TOLERATE THE
ROCK PREFACE(165)	THAT THEIR FATHERS HAD " WORKED ON THE	LAND	WITH THEIR HANDS" WERE ACCEPTED AS GENUINE
ROCK PREFACE(152)	ON I FIND THAT IT IS MORE PROFITABLE TO COVER MY	LAND	WITH WILD DEER, AND COLLECT MONEY FROM GENTLEMEN AND
GENV IV (104)	IS CONFRONTED BY OFFICERS WHO SAY YOU SHALL NOT	LAND	WITHOUT YOUR PASSPORT, YOUR VISA. IF YOU ARE OF A
ROCK II (251)	DROVE FROM THEIR COUNTRY TO PERISH IN A FOREIGN	LAND	WOULD TURN IN THEIR GRAVES AT THE CHINK OF A SINGLE
LIED (201)	OF POLISH) YOU CALL ME A SWINE AGAIN AND I'LL	LAND	YOU ONE ON THE CHIN THATLL MAKE YOUR HEAD SING FOR A
BULL IV (179)	HAVE LEFT IN MILLIONS BECAUSE IT IS A HUNGRY	LAND	, A NAKED LAND, AN IGNORANT AND OPPRESSED LAND.
FANY III (324)	OF YOUR ILLUSTRIOUS NELSON, ALWAYS BEATEN ON	LAND	, ALWAYS VICTORIOUS AT SEA, WHERE HIS MEN COULD NOT RUN
BULL IV (179)	IN MILLIONS BECAUSE IT IS A HUNGRY LAND, A NAKED	LAND	, AN IGNORANT AND OPPRESSED LAND. /BROADBENT/ BUT, HANG
CLEO V (197)	UTTERING THE BARBAROUS CRIES OF YOUR NATIVE	LAND	, AND AFFIRMING YOURSELF A MATCH FOR ANY FOUR OF THE
JOAN 2 (86)	/JOAN/ (EARNESTLY) CHARLIE: I COME FROM THE	LAND	, AND HAVE GOTTEN MY STRENGTH WORKING ON THE LAND; AND
MILL PREFACE(126)	BROWN AND BLACK NATIVES FOR POSSESSION OF THE	LAND	, AND OUR JAMAICAN MISCEGENATION SHOCKS PUBLIC
HART PREFACE(12)	IMPUNITY IN CIVIL LIFE, WAS NOT THE LAW OF THE	LAND	, AND THAT A VICTORIA CROSS DID NOT CARRY WITH IT A
ROCK II (260)	AND ALWAYS WILL STAND: THE STRONGEST AND GREATEST	LAND	, AND THE BIRTHPLACE OF THE NOBLEST IMPERIAL RACE, THAT
BULL III (122)	ALL OVER! MAKE BAD LAWS AND GIVE AWAY ALL THE	LAND	, AND THEN, WHEN YOUR ECONOMIC INCOMPETENCE PRODUCES
SUPR HANDBOK(182)	PROPRIETOR MAY STILL DRIVE MEN AND WOMEN OFF HIS	LAND	, DEMOLISH THEIR DWELLINGS, AND REPLACE THEM WITH SHEEP
FABL PREFACE(86)	CONDITIONS; SO THAT A PROPRIETOR SHALL HOLD HIS	LAND	, HIS SPARE MONEY (CALLED CAPITAL) ON THE SAME TERMS
BULL III (131)	OUT OF HER. IF WE CANT HAVE MEN OF HONOR OWN THE	LAND	, LETS HAVE MEN OF ABILITY. IF WE CANT HAVE MEN WITH
ROCK PREFACE(166)	ONLY ADDED TO THE PEASANTS' CRY OF GIVE US	LAND	, THE SOLDIERS' CRY OF GIVE US PEACE. LENIN SAID, IN
BULL PREFACE(19)	CAPABLE AND PROPERLY EQUIPPED ENEMY EXCEPT ON	LAND	, WHERE HE HAD NEVER BEEN SUCCESSFUL. COMPARE
ROCK PREFACE(152)	EXISTENCE OF THE LABORERS; SO I DRIVE THEM OFF MY	LAND	, WHICH IS MY LEGAL METHOD OF EXTERMINATION, RETAINING
MTH4 I SD(139)	OR HOLDFAST, AN ELDERLY GENTLEMAN SITS FACING THE	LAND	, WITH HIS HEAD BOWED AND HIS FACE IN HIS HANDS,
2TRU PREFACE(22)	ANCIENT WISDOM FROM ITS NORMAL DAY'S WORK ON THE	LAND	, WITHOUT WHICH IT WOULD BE A COUNCIL OF TRAMPS AND
LION PREFACE(61)	A WAY AS TO BE ABLE TO SAY TO EVERY PERSON IN THE	LAND	, " TAKE NO THOUGHT, SAYING WHAT SHALL WE EAT? OR WHAT
CATH 4 (190)	REVENUE OF THE COUNTRY FROM A SINGLE TAX ON	LAND	! HOW HE WITHERS IT WITH HIS IRONY! HOW HE MAKES YOU

LANDAGENT

BULL I (90)	HOW AM I TO GET ON WITH A LITTLE COUNTRY	LANDAGENT	THAT EKES OUT HIS 5 PER CENT WITH A LITTLE FARMING
BULL I (89)	THE INTERRUPTION) THERE HE IS IN ROSSCULLEN, A	LANDAGENT	WHO'S ALWAYS BEEN IN A SMALL WAY BECAUSE HE'S A
BULL I (89)	SON OF A LABORER INSTEAD OF THE SON OF A COUNTRY	LANDAGENT	, I SHOULD HAVE STRUCK MORE GRIT THAN I DID.

		LANDED	
MTH4 I (167)	YOU SEE MY WHITE HAIR? IT WAS HARDLY GREY WHEN I	LANDED	: THERE WERE PATCHES OF ITS ORIGINAL AUBURN STILL
MILL PREFACE(117)	FUMES OF T.N.T. ON THE SOMME. " THE NELSON TOUCH"	LANDED	A SECTION OF THE BRITISH FLEET AT THE BOTTOM OF THE
BULL III (118)	HATE EM. THE FEELING COME OVER ME THE MOMENT WE	LANDED	AT CORK, SIR. IT'S NO USE MY PRETENDIN, SIR: I CANT
BULL I (94)	GEORGE'S CHANNEL SINCE FOR HER SAKE-- NEVER EVEN	LANDED	AT QUEENSTOWN AND COME BACK TO LONDON THROUGH
ROCK II (246)	UTTER EXTINCTION IN THREE GENERATIONS; AND THE	LANDED	CLASSES ARE WITH YOU TO THE LAST MAN FOR IT. ACCEPT
ROCK II (244)	ENTREPRENEURS BY A USELESS, IDLE, AND PREDATORY	LANDED	CLASS. /SIR ARTHUR/ (CHUCKLING) MAGNIFICENT! I HAVE
GETT (356)	/HOTCHKISS/ AND YOU BELIEVE THAT MANY OF OUR	LANDED	ESTATES WERE STOLEN FROM THE CHURCH BY HENRY THE
CLEO III (163)	CAESAR: WE ARE CUT OFF. THE EGYPTIANS HAVE	LANDED	FROM THE WEST HARBOR BETWEEN US AND THE BARRICADE!
ROCK II (253)	WHOSE BLOOD? /BASHAM/ THE POLICE'S BLOOD. YOU	LANDED	GENTLEMEN NEVER DO A THING YOURSELVES: YOU ONLY CALL
MILL PREFACE(129)	THE UPPER MIDDLE CLASSES AND THE PRESTIGE OF THE	LANDED	GENTRY AND PEERAGE THERE HAS BEEN NO SUBSTANTIAL
2TRU PREFACE(10)	AND IMPORTANT PART OF A WELL ORDERED LIFE. THE	LANDED	GENTRY HAVE ENOUGH EXERCISE AND OCCUPATION AND SENSE
SIM PREFACE(13)	AND I CAN ASSURE THE FOREIGN OFFICE THAT THE	LANDED	GENTRY IN THE PERSON OF MY GRANDFATHER, THE TRAMWAY
ROCK II (244)	OF BUSINESS. IF YOU DESTROY THE INCOMES OF OUR	LANDED	GENTRY WHERE WILL YOU FIND THE CAPITAL THAT EXISTS
2TRU PREFACE(9)	IN THE HEIGHT OF THE SEASON. CONSOLATIONS OF THE	LANDED	GENTRY. TO SOME EXTENT THIS MISERY OF RICHES IS A NEW
MTH2 (51)	IT TO ME THAT THEY HATE THE CHURCH AND HATE THE	LANDED	GENTRY; THAT THEY ARE JEALOUS OF THE NOBILITY, AND
2TRU PREFACE(9)	WORK THAT IS ALWAYS AVAILABLE FOR THE RESIDENT	LANDED	GENTRY, WILL AT ONCE CHALLENGE THE UNQUALIFIED
MTH4 I (155)	FORBID THEM. THEY JUMPED AT THE SUGGESTION. THEY	LANDED	HERE: HERE IN GALWAY BAY, ON THIS VERY GROUND. WHEN
SIM II (70)	WELL, THEYRE NOT FOOLING: AN ANGEL HAS JUST	LANDED	HERE TO TELL US THE SAME THING. . . . AN ANGEL. A FOR
METH PREFACE(R76)	DID IN THE PILGRIM'S PROGRESS WHEN CHRISTIAN	LANDED	HIM IN THE SLOUGH OF DESPOND: THAT IS, RUN BACK IN
SUPR II SD(62)	CIVILIZATION THAN THAT IN WHICH HIS MIGRATION HAS	LANDED	HIM. ON THESE POINTS HECTOR IS NOT QUITE CONVINCED:
HART I (76)	ALWAYS FALLING IN LOVE WITH MY MOUSTACHE I GET	LANDED	IN ALL SORTS OF TEDIOUS AND TERRIFYING FLIRTATIONS IN
MTH4 I (150)	THANK YOU, THANK YOU. FOR THE FIRST TIME SINCE I	LANDED	IN THIS TERRIBLE COUNTRY I BEGIN TO FEEL AT HOME. THE
PRES (163)	AN IDEA OF THEIR OWN; AND THEN OF COURSE YOURE	LANDED	. /MITCHENER/ SH-- /BALSQUITH/ (DESPERATELY SHOUTING
BULL III (144)	HUMOR IS IN ABEYANCE: I NOTICED IT THE MOMENT WE	LANDED	. THINK OF THAT IN A COUNTRY WHERE EVERY MAN IS A
POSN (461)	/BLANCO/ (WHISPERING AT HER) SOFTY! CRY-BABY!	LANDED	LIKE ME! DOING WHAT YOU NEVER INTENDED! (TAKING UP
BARB III (316)	SERIOUSLY, MY LOVE, THE UNDERSHAFT TRADITION HAS	LANDED	ME IN A DIFFICULTY. I AM GETTING ON IN YEARS; AND MY
CLEO PRO2 (97)	HE SAYS THAT THE ROMAN JULIUS CAESAR, WHO HAS	LANDED	ON OUR SHORES WITH A HANDFUL OF FOLLOWERS, WILL MAKE
FABL III (109)	YOU LAND? /THE TOURIST/ I CAME IN MY OWN BOAT. I	LANDED	ON THE BEACH. WHAT HARM AM I DOING? /THE GIRL/ THIS
CLEO III (145)	TO WATCH THE LAND BUT THE SEA. CAESAR HAS JUST	LANDED	ON THE PHAROS. (LOOKING AT FTATATEETA) WHAT HAVE YOU
SUPR HANDBOK(182)	CLERGYMAN, OFFICER, OR CIVIL SERVANT, A	LANDED	PROPRIETOR MAY STILL DRIVE MEN AND WOMEN OFF HIS
ROCK PREFACE(166)	IN. AND IT WAS THE RESULTANT LEGIONS OF PETTY	LANDED	PROPRIETORS THAT MADE LENIN'S POSITION IMPREGNABLE.
CLEO III (149)	BEEN WITHIN THE ROMAN LINES SINCE CAESAR	LANDED	THERE? /CLEOPATRA/ YES, YES. ANSWER THAT, IF YOU
2TRU III (85)	DIDNT GET TO HEAVEN ALONG THEM. A LOT OF THEM	LANDED	UP IN THE OTHER PLACE. NO, JOHN: YOU COULD TELL A
MIS. (131)	OTHER WHERE A SINGLE FORTNIGHT OF IT WOULD HAVE	LANDED	US. /TARLETON/ VERY TRUE. STILL, DEMOCRACY'S ALL
JOAN 1 (65)	FEW MAD PEOPLE NOW. SEE WHERE THE SANE ONES HAVE	LANDED	US! /ROBERT/ (HIS IRRESOLUTENESS NOW OPENLY
GENV III (78)	GRANDFATHER. UPON MY HONOR I DONT KNOW HOW I GOT	LANDED	WHERE I AM. I AM QUITE AN ORDINARY CHAP REALLY. /THE
GENV IV (102)	WHEN YOUR WOUNDS TOOK YOU OUT OF THE TRENCHES AND	LANDED	YOU IN A HOSPITAL BED? /BBDE/ EXTREMELY GLAD. BUT
SUPR II (58)	(BLUNTLY) NOW LOOK HERE, ANN. THIS TIME YOUVE	LANDED	YOURSELF; AND IF TAVY WERE NOT IN LOVE WITH YOU PAST
SIM PRO,3, (34)	BEFORE, I THINK, HAVNT WE? /THE E.O./ WHEN YOU	LANDED	, SIR CHARLES. I AM THE EMIGRATION OFFICER. /SIR
		LANDING	
BARB III SD(329)	AND LIST SLIPPERS COMES OUT ON THE LITTLE	LANDING	AND HOLDS THE DOOR FOR LOMAX, WHO APPEARS IN THE
FANY III (320)	I'LL PUT A STOP TO THIS. (HE GOES OUT TO THE	LANDING	AND SHOUTS) MARGARET! (SUDDEN DEAD SILENCE).
LION II SD(127)	ON BOTH SIDES OF THIS PASSAGE STEPS ASCEND TO A	LANDING	AT THE BACK ENTRANCE TO THE BOX. THE LANDING FORMS A
BARB III SD(326)	WHICH OPENS OUTWARDS AND HAS A LITTLE WOODEN	LANDING	AT THE THRESHOLD, WITH A FIRE BUCKET IN THE CORNER
LION II SD(127)	TO A LANDING AT THE BACK ENTRANCE TO THE BOX. THE	LANDING	FORMS A BRIDGE ACROSS THE PASSAGE. AT THE ENTRANCE
MTH4 I (156)	DO NOT HAPPEN REALLY. THAT SCENE OF THE IRISH	LANDING	HERE AND KISSING THE GROUND MIGHT HAVE HAPPENED TO A
PYGM IV SD(260)	ELIZA OPENS THE DOOR AND IS SEEN ON THE LIGHTED	LANDING	IN OPERA CLOAK, BRILLIANT EVENING DRESS, AND
BARB III SD(326)	GASHES, HAVE BEEN SHOVED OUT OF THE WAY UNDER THE	LANDING	. A FEW OTHERS ARE NEARLY UPRIGHT AGAINST THE SHED;
HART PREFACE(20)	SOLDIERS AT NEUVE CHAPELLE AND AT THE GALLIPOLI	LANDING	. I WILL NOT GO SO FAR AS TO SAY THAT OUR CIVILIANS
KING II SD(223)	OUT THE COAT AND HANGS IT ON THE RAIL OF THE	LANDING	, RETURNING, SHE PURPOSELY CLOSES THE DOOR WITH A
BARB III SD(326)	WITH A FIRE BUCKET IN THE CORNER OF THE	LANDING	, SEVERAL DUMMY SOLDIERS, MORE OR LESS MUTILATED,
LION II (141)	MEAN? /THE EMPEROR/ (ENTHUSIASTICALLY, ON THE	LANDING	OUTSIDE HIS BOX) WHAT DOES IT MEAN? IT MEANS THAT
CLEO PRO2 (99)	UPON A CITY RABBLE FLYING FROM HIS LEGIONS, WHOSE	LANDING	THEY HAD GONE OUT TO WITHSTAND. /BELZANOR/ AND YE,
SIM PRO,1, (23)	OR LATER, OFF AND ON. HERE! I'LL GIVE YOU A	LANDING	TICKET; AND YOU JUST CLEAR OFF AND SAY NOTHING. (HE
BASH II,2, (117)	MY RIGHT AIMING BESIDE THE ANGLE OF THE JAW AND	LANDING	WITH A CERTAIN DELICATE SCREW I WITHOUT VIOLENCE
LION II SD(144)	THE EMPEROR DASHES MADLY UP THE STEPS, ACROSS THE	LANDING	, AND DOWN AGAIN ON THE OTHER SIDE, WITH THE LION IN
KING II SD(223)	WALKING STICK. THE DOOR, OPENING ON A STAIRCASE	LANDING	, IS NEAR THE HEAD OF THE COUCH, BETWEEN IT AND THE
HART PREFACE(20)	COST OF NEUVE CHAPELLE, YPRES, AND THE GALLIPOLI	LANDING	, THE FUSS ABOUT THE LUSITANIA SEEMED ALMOST A
		LANDLADIES	
SUPR IV (167)	WITH BROKEN HEARTS, AND ARE ADORED BY THEIR	LANDLADIES	, AND NEVER GET MARRIED. MEN LIKE YOU ALWAYS GET
		LANDLADY	
MILL PREFACE(112)	HAVE HAD HER OWN WAY MUCH MORE COMPLETELY AS	LANDLADY	OF THE MERMAID TAVERN THAN SHE HAD AS SOVEREIGN OF
SUPR III SD(72)	AND STARVES IN A GARRET, SPUNGING ON A POOR	LANDLADY	OR ON HIS FRIENDS AND RELATIVES SOONER THAN WORK
JITT III (55)	ROOM SOMEWHERE WHERE THEY CAN COME. THE	LANDLADY	SAID HE RENTED THE ROOM TO SEE HIS FRIENDS IN
JITT III (56)	WENT WITH COMMON WOMEN FROM THE STREETS. THE	LANDLADY	SAID IT WAS ALWAYS THE SAME WOMAN, AND THAT SHE WAS
PYGM II (235)	WHY DIDNT YOU GO FOR IT YOURSELF? /DOOLITTLE/	LANDLADY	WOULDNT HAVE TRUSTED ME WITH IT, GOVERNOR. SHE'S
PYGM II (235)	A BOY IN THE TAXI TO GIVE HIM A JAUNT. SON OF HER	LANDLADY	, HE IS. HE HUNG ABOUT ON THE CHANCE OF HER GIVING
PPP PREFACE(192)	THE LANDLORD MAY WITH EQUAL PROPRIETY BE A	LANDLADY	, IF THAT ARRANGEMENT BE BETTER SUITED TO THE
LADY PREFACE(207)	OF HONOR, WAS QUITE EASY. IF SHE WERE A TAVERN	LANDLADY	, IT WOULD HAVE STRAINED ALL PROBABILITY. SO I
		LANDLESS	
SIM PREFACE(12)	EARTH OF THE COUNTRY, MEANS THE POWER TO MAKE	LANDLESS	PEOPLE EARN THE PROPRIETORS' LIVINGS FOR THEM. SUCH
		LANDLL	
BULL IV (157)	D'YE THINK? /LARRY/ HE'LL LEND YOU MORE THAN THE	LANDLL	EVER BE WORTH TO YOU; SO FOR HEAVEN'S SAKE BE
		LANDLORD	
MTH4 I (144)	I AM SPEAKING THE PLAINEST ENGLISH. ARE YOU THE	LANDLORD	? /THE WOMAN/ (SHAKING HER HEAD) THERE IS A
GENV IV (93)	DELIVERED YOU FROM THE LAW OF PRIEST AND KING, OF	LANDLORD	AND CAPITALIST, ONLY TO BRING YOU UNDER THE LAW OF
PPP SD(205)	WIND TO THE WALL. SHE DISPOSES SIMILARLY OF THE	LANDLORD	AND DOCTOR. /PHYLLIS/ WILL THEY BE IN YOUR WAY IF I
ROCK II (244)	BUT THE ROBBED VICTIM IS ME-- ME! GET RID OF THE	LANDLORD	AND I SHALL HAVE ALL THE CAPITAL HE NOW STEALS. IN
PPP SD(205)	IM. /THE DOCTOR/ WHAT, YOU! HE POUNCES ON THE	LANDLORD	AND RUSHES HIM ROUND. /THE LANDLORD/ EAH! CHACK
GENV PREFACE(12)	THIRD OF THEIR WEEKLY EARNINGS OR MORE TO AN IDLE	LANDLORD	AS IF THAT WERE A LAW OF NATURE; BUT A COLLECTION
NEVR I (210)	YOU TO WAIT FIVE MINUTES WHILE I GET RID OF MY	LANDLORD	DOWNSTAIRS? /DOLLY/ DONT BE LONG. WE'RE HUNGRY.
WIDO II (31)	IF I SKINNED EM ALIVE. I DONT SAY HE'S THE WORST	LANDLORD	IN LONDON: HE COULDNT BE WORSE THAN SOME; BUT HE'S
WIDO III (55)	NO MOTHER! CLERGYMAN! BEAST! " THE WORST SLUM	LANDLORD	IN LONDON." " SLUM LANDLORD." OH! (SHE COVERS HER
NEVR I (206)	RENT YET. I'M EATING AND DRINKING ON CREDIT; MY	LANDLORD	IS AS RICH AS A JEW AND AS HARD AS NAILS; AND IVE
MILL II (170)	BACK. COME BACK. /THE DOCTOR/ (RETURNING) THE	LANDLORD	IS TAKING THE GENTLEMAN TO THE COTTAGE HOSPITAL IN
DOCT PREFACE(79)	A POOR DOCTOR: NOT EVEN A POOR EMPLOYER OR A POOR	LANDLORD	. 2. OF ALL THE ANTI-SOCIAL VESTED INTERESTS THE
PLES PREFACE(R9)	STAGE AT ALL, IS THE REAL ANTAGONIST OF THE SLUM	LANDLORD	. BUT THE OBVIOUS CONFLICTS OF UNMISTAKEABLE GOOD
BULL III (130)	YOUR POWER AS YOU WERE IN THE POWER OF YOUR OLD	LANDLORD	. DO YOU THINK, BECAUSE YOURE POOR AND IGNORANT AND
NEVR I (222)	YOURE QUITE HARD ENOUGH FOR ME ALREADY-- AS A	LANDLORD	. (CRAMPTON RECEIVES THIS WITH A GROWL OF GRIM
NEVR I SD(218)	HIM STRAIGHT AWAY. VALENTINE COMES BACK WITH HIS	LANDLORD	, MR FERGUS CRAMPTON IS A MAN OF ABOUT SIXTY, WITH
NEVR I (217)	OLD GENTLEMAN WITH THE TOOTHACHE. /PHILIP/ THE	LANDLORD	. /THE PARLORMAID/ MR CRAMPTON, SIR? /PHILIP/ IS
ROCK II (244)	LABORER HAS TO PAY HALF OR QUARTER AS RENT TO THE	LANDLORD	. THE LABORER IS IGNORANT: HE THINKS HE IS ROBBED
WIDO III (55)	" THE WORST SLUM LANDLORD IN LONDON." " SLUM	LANDLORD	." OH! (SHE COVERS HER FACE WITH HER HANDS, AND
BULL PREFACE(40)	VENGEANCE AND FOREIGN OPPRESSION. TRUE, HIS	LANDLORD	MAY TURN HIM OUT OF HIS COTTAGE IF HE GOES TO A
PPP PREFACE(192)	MOST USEFUL IN ENHANCING THE STAGE EFFECT. THE	LANDLORD	MAY WITH EQUAL PROPRIETY BE A LANDLADY, IF THAT
NEVR I (216)	/VALENTINE/ I HOPE IVE NOT KEPT YOU WAITING. THAT	LANDLORD	OF MINE IS REALLY AN EXTRAORDINARY OLD CHARACTER.
POSN PREFACE(363)	CONSTRUED AS IF IT CONTAINED A CLAUSE GIVING THE	LANDLORD	POWER TO BREAK IT AND EVICT THE LESSEE IF HE
BULL III (122)	WAS IT TO THEM? THE MOMENT THEYD DONE IT, THE	LANDLORD	PUT A RENT OF 5 POUNDS A YEAR ON THEM, AND TURNED
ROCK II (249)	BLEE. /THE DUKE/ ENCHANTED. I HAPPEN TO BE A	LANDLORD	-- A DUKE, IN FACT-- AND I CAN ASSURE YOU, MR

PPP (204)	TRYING ARTIFICIA_I RESPIRATION, DO IT? (TO THE	LANDLORD	) HERE! LEND A HAND, YOU. WE'D BEST TAKE HIM AND
PPP (203)	WELL, OF ALL THE ARTFUL-- (HE COLLARS THE	LANDLORD	). I ARREST YOU FOR WILFUL MURDER. /THE LANDLORD/ (
ROCK II (244)	IS IGNORANT: HE THINKS HE IS ROBBED BY THE	LANDLORD	; BUT THE ROBBED VICTIM IS ME-- ME! GET RID OF THE
WIDO III (53)	MOVEMENT). NOW DONT FLY OUT AT ME. I KNOW A	LANDLORD	THAT OWNED AS BEASTLY A SLUM AS YOU COULD FIND IN
MILL II (175)	THING IN THIS LITTLE PLACE. /EPIFANIA/ TELL THE	LANDLORD	TO STOP THE FIRST ONE THAT COMES ALONG AND BUY IT.
MRS PREFACE(170)	UP IN WRATH AGAINST THE SLUM LANDLORD, THE SLUM	LANDLORD	VERY EFFECTUALLY SHEWED HIM THAT SLUMS ARE THE
NEVR I (210)	HAD NO PATIENTS UNTIL TODAY. MY INTERVIEW WITH MY	LANDLORD	WILL BE CONSIDERABLY SMOOTHED BY THE APPARENT BOOM
ROCK PREFACE(154)	RESPONSIBLE TO THE WHOLE COMMUNITY, THE	LANDLORD	WITH HIS WRIT OF EJECTMENT AND THE EMPLOYER WITH
PPP SD(202)	THEIR CHORDS CEASE: ON THE ABRUPT ENTRANCE OF THE	LANDLORD	, A VULGAR PERSON IN PYJAMAS. /THE LANDLORD/ EAH!
PPP (205)	DOCTOR'S CHEST) DEAD! /FITZ/ (KNEELING BY THE	LANDLORD	, AND RAISING HIS HAND, WHICH DROPS WITH A THUD)
BULL III (122)	WITH FURY) I SHOULD HAVE SHOT THE CONFOUNDED	LANDLORD	, AND WRUNG THE NECK OF THE DAMNED AGENT, AND BLOWN
DEST SD(152)	OLIVES, AND A BIG WICKERED FLASK OF RED WINE. THE	LANDLORD	, GIUSEPPE GRANDI, SHE KNOWS WELL. HE IS A SWARTHY
NEVR I (223)	OF HAVING HIS FURNITURE DISTRAINED UPON BY HIS	LANDLORD	, HE MARRIES. IVE NOTICED THAT BEFORE. WELL, MARRY;
WIDO III (57)	I AM ONLY WAITING FOR THE CONSENT OF THE GROUND	LANDLORD	, LADY ROXDALE. /BLANCHE/ LADY ROXDALE!
NEVR I (209)	WITH HER FINGER TIPS. /THE PARLORMAID/ ONLY THE	LANDLORD	, MAAM. VALENTINE, IN A BLUE SERGE SUIT, WITH A
NEVR I (210)	TESTILY) WHAT IS IT? /THE PARLORMAID/ THE	LANDLORD	, SIR, WISHES TO SPEAK TO YOU BEFORE YOU GO OUT.
MRS PREFACE(170)	YOUNG GENTLEMAN ROSE UP IN WRATH AGAINST THE SLUM	LANDLORD	, THE SLUM LANDLORD VERY EFFECTUALLY SHEWED HIM
LION PREFACE(55)	DOES NOT BELONG SOLELY TO HIM, BUT TO HIS	LANDLORD	, TO THE RATE COLLECTOR AND TAXGATHERER, TO THE MEN
PPP SD(205)	FINALLY IT LEAPS WITH FEARFUL FORCE ON THE	LANDLORD	, WHO, BEING OF A GROSS AND SPONGY NATURE, ABSORBS
DEST (157)	AT THE INN DOOR, SHOUTING) HERE, SOMEONE. HOLLO!	LANDLORD	! WHERE ARE YOU? (SOMEBODY RAPS VIGOROUSLY WITH

LANDLORDISM

BULL III (127)	AN DHE LIKE O HIM? /BROADBENT/ BUT SURELY IRISH	LANDLORDISM	WAS ACCOUNTABLE FOR WHAT MR HAFFIGAN SUFFERED.
UNPL PREFACE(R12)	IT INTO A GROTESQUELY REALISTIC EXPOSURE OF SLUM	LANDLORDISM	, MUNICIPAL JOBBERY, AND THE PECUNIARY AND

LANDLORD'S

ROCK PREFACE(189)	TO THE CHANCELLOR OF THE EXCHEQUER, AND SHOT THE	LANDLORD'S	AGENTS WHEN THEY CAME TO DISTRAIN ON HIS
DEST SD(152)	ON HER RIGHT LEADING TO THE STREET ENTRY; THE	LANDLORD'S	BEST SIDEBOARD, NOW IN FULL ACTION FOR DINNER,
NEVR I (202)	THE HOUSE ISNT HIS AND THE FURNITURE IS THE	LANDLORD'S	BUT THE PROFESSIONAL PLANT IS HIRED HE GOT MY
NEVR I (200)	THE LATEST THING, IS IT? /THE DENTIST/ IT'S MY	LANDLORD'S	. /THE YOUNG LADY/ DOES HE OWN THAT TOOTHACHE

LANDLORDS

GENV IV (120)	IN. THEIR COUNTRIES ARE OWNED BY A HANDFUL OF	LANDLORDS	AND CAPITALISTS WHO ALLOW THEM TO LIVE IN IT ON
LION PREFACE(55)	FOR THESE FELLOW TRADERS OF HIS HAVE ALSO THEIR	LANDLORDS	AND MONEYLENDERS TO SATISFY. IF, THEN, SUCH SIMPLE
BULL I (89)	IN A SMALL WAY BECAUSE HE'S A CATHOLIC, AND THE	LANDLORDS	ARE MOSTLY PROTESTANTS. WHAT WITH LAND COURTS
ROCK II (246)	ARTHUR/ DEXY: YOU ARE IN A MINORITY OF ONE. THE	LANDLORDS	ARE ON MY SIDE. THE CAPITALISTS, BIG AND LITTLE,
ROCK PREFACE(166)	PRESUME TO FOLLOW IT), MEANT BRINGING THE OLD	LANDLORDS	BACK; AND THE PEASANT FOUGHT AGAINST THAT AS THE
MILL PREFACE(129)	PROPERTY CAN BE COMMUNIZED. CAPITALISTS AND	LANDLORDS	CAN BE PRESSED INTO THE SERVICE OF THE COMMUNITY,
GENV IV (120)	PEOPLE INSTEAD OF ROBBING THEM. /FLANCO/ DID YOUR	LANDLORDS	EVER ROB THE PEOPLE AS YOUR BUREAUCRACY NOW ROBS
ROCK II (249)	MY OWN POCKET AND THAT OF MY UNFORTUNATE FELLOW	LANDLORDS	IN THE FORM OF INCOME TAX, SURTAX, AND ESTATE
BARB PREFACE(242)	LODGES OF IRELAND IN THEIR LONG STRUGGLE WITH THE	LANDLORDS	. UNDER SUCH CIRCUMSTANCES, THE ASSASSIN GOES FREE
BULL III (122)	DOESNT MATTER, ANYHOW, BECAUSE THERES HARLY ANY	LANDLORDS	LEFT; AND THERLL SOON BE NONE AT ALL. /LARRY/ ON
MRS PREFACE(177)	BY MRS WARREN AND SIR GEORGE CROFTS, BUT BY THE	LANDLORDS	OF THEIR HOUSES, THE NEWSPAPERS WHICH ADVERTIZE
WIDO I (22)	ESTATE IN LONDON. LADY ROXDALE IS ONE OF THE HEAD	LANDLORDS	; AND DR TRENCH HOLDS A MORTGAGE FROM WHICH, IF I
ROCK II (240)	OF INCOME TAX AND MAKE THESE LAZY IDLE LUBBERS OF	LANDLORDS	SWEAT FOR IT. I CALL THAT THE ESSENCE OF
BULL PREFACE(28)	THE POPE IN THE VATICAN. THEY LOVE THEIR	LANDLORDS	TOO: MANY AN IRISH GENTLEMAN HAS FOUND IN HIS
ROCK II (249)	WITH ONE HAND AND GIVE BACK ITS CASH VALUE TO THE	LANDLORDS	WITH THE OTHER! NOT LIKELY. I ASK AGAIN, DO YOU
BULL III (130)	THING TO LEAVE THE LAND IN THE HANDS OF THE OLD	LANDLORDS	WITHOUT CALLING THEM TO A STRICT ACCOUNT FOR THE
3PLA PREFACE(R12)	CARPENTERS, DOORKEEPERS, ACTORS, THEATRE	LANDLORDS	, AND ALL THE OTHER PEOPLE FOR WHOSE EXCLUSIVE
FABL PREFACE(96)	POLITICALLY THAT THEY VOTE LIKE SHEEP FOR THE	LANDLORDS	, AND DENOUNCE LAND MUNICIPALIZATION AS ROBBERY.
FABL PREFACE(96)	PAST FOUR IN THE AFTERNOON EARNING RENT FOR THEIR	LANDLORDS	, AND ONLY THE REST OF THE DAY FOR THEMSELVES AND
2TRU PREFACE(20)	DO NOTHING BUT TALK, AND AN ACTUAL GOVERNMENT OF	LANDLORDS	, EMPLOYERS, AND FINANCIERS AT WAR WITH AN
MRS PREFACE(178)	MORALS OF THE THEATRE WERE EITHER MRS WARREN'S	LANDLORDS	, OR EMPLOYERS OF WOMEN AT STARVATION WAGES, OR
ROCK PREFACE(151)	SLOWLY TO ITS DERIVATORY THE DIVINE RIGHT OF	LANDLORDS	, WHICH HAD GRADUALLY DISGUISED ITSELF AS PRIVATE

LANDMARKS

CAND I SD(78)	MARX'S CAPITAL, AND HALF A DOZEN OTHER LITERARY	LANDMARKS	IN SOCIALISM. FACING HIM ON THE OTHER SIDE OF THE

LANDON

BULL III (141)	AND BUILT AP A FUST CLAWSS DRIPERY BUSINESS IN	LANDON	BY SIXTY YEARS WORK, AND THEN WAS CHACKED AHT OF IT

LANDOR

PYGM EPILOG (292)	IS A SECONDARY AFFAIR, WOULD NOT HAVE RECOMMENDED	LANDOR	TO ELIZA. PUT THAT ALONG WITH HER RESENTMENT OF

LANDOR'S

PYGM EPILOG (292)	HAVE BEEN MILTON AND THE UNIVERSAL ALPHABET.	LANDOR'S	REMARK THAT TO THOSE WHO HAVE THE GREATEST POWER OF

LANDOWNER

BULL IV (173)	DOYLE TO FORGO THE PRIDE OF BEING A SMALL	LANDOWNER	? HOW WILL BARNEY DORAN'S MILLRACE AGREE WITH
SUPR HANDBOK(203)	AND PROPHYLACTIC INOCULATIONS, IS RAMPANT; THE	LANDOWNER	WHO IS NO LONGER POWERFUL ENOUGH TO SET THE

LAND-THIEVES

HART II (112)	WITH THIEVES AND ALL SORTS? /CAPTAIN SHOTOVER/	LAND-THIEVES	AND WATER-THIEVES ARE THE SAME FLESH AND BLOOD.

LANDS

JOAN 4 (105)	WE CALL NO MAN MASTER. NOMINALLY WE HOLD OUR	LANDS	AND DIGNITIES FROM THE KING, BECAUSE THERE MUST BE A
SIM II (70)	REASONABLE TO TRY CASES IN HUNDREDS OF DIFFERENT	LANDS	AND LANGUAGES AND CREEDS AND COLORS ON THE SAME DAY IN
2TRU III (112)	A MESSAGE THE SOUND WHEREOF SHALL GO OUT UNTO ALL	LANDS	AND REALIZE FOR US AT LAST THE KINGDOM AND THE POWER
GENV PREFACE(7)	AS SHAKESPEAR DID, IN THE ENCLOSURE OF COMMON	LANDS	AS A STEP FORWARD IN CIVILIZATION. HISTORY STOPS
LADY PREFACE(232)	THAT HE WAS A PARTY TO THE ENCLOSURE OF COMMON	LANDS	AT WELLCOME. THE EXPLANATION IS, NOT A GENERAL
LION PREFACE(52)	THE SHARES WILL FALL TO ZERO AND THE	LANDS	BE UNSALEABLE. IF ONE MAN SELLS OUT AND THROWS THE
JOAN 4 (105)	TO THE ARCH OF HUMAN SOCIETY; BUT WE HOLD OUR	LANDS	IN OUR OWN HANDS, AND DEFEND THEM WITH OUR OWN SWORDS
CLEO PRO2 (104)	TO THE PERSIAN) YOU, O SUBTLE ONE: YOUR FATHER'S	LANDS	LIE FAR FROM THE NILE. SLAY HER. /PERSIAN/ (
MTH4 I (140)	HERE ON A PIOUS PILGRIMAGE TO ONE OF THE NUMEROUS	LANDS	OF MY FATHERS. WE ARE OF THE SAME STOCK, YOU AND I.
CLEO PRO2 (101)	IS DESCENDED FROM THE RIVER NILE; AND THE	LANDS	OF OUR FATHERS WILL GROW NO GRAIN IF THE NILE RISES
JOAN 4 (105)	NOW BY THE MAID'S DOCTRINE THE KING WILL TAKE OUR	LANDS	-- OUR LANDS! -- AND MAKE THEM A PRESENT TO GOD; AND
BUOY II (24)	HAVE BEEN TAUGHT THAT HE HAS OTHER NAMES IN OTHER	LANDS	; BUT HERE HIS HOLY NAME (HE BENDS HIS NECK) IS
FABL PREFACE(69)	COMPULSORY IN KINGCRAFT AND PRIESTCRAFT. THIS	LANDS	THEM IN THE QUAINTEST MORAL DILEMMAS. IT DRIVES THEM
CLEO PRO1 (90)	ROBBED THE POOR OF OTHER LANDS, AND ADDED THOSE	LANDS	TO ROME UNTIL THERE CAME A NEW ROME, RICH AND HUGE.
CLEO I (111)	TO YOU. I WILL MAKE THE RIVER NILE WATER YOUR	LANDS	TWICE A YEAR. /CAESAR/ PEACE, PEACE, MY CHILD. YOUR
BASH I (93)	SOLITUDE THAT I, LYDIA CAREW, THE OWNER OF THESE	LANDS	, ALBEIT MOST RICH, MOST LEARNED, AND MOST WISE, AM
CLEO PRO1 (90)	THEIR OWN POOR DRY, THEY ROBBED THE POOR OF OTHER	LANDS	, AND ADDED THOSE LANDS TO ROME UNTIL THERE CAME A NEW
2TRU PREFACE(18)	FRONTIERS, ENJOYING NOT ONLY THE RENT OF CHURCH	LANDS	, BUT SELLING SALVATION ON SUCH A SCALE THAT WHEN
CLEO I (106)	FROM JULIUS CAESAR! I HAVE WANDERED IN MANY	LANDS	, SEEKING THE LOST REGIONS FROM WHICH MY BIRTH INTO
LION PREFACE(52)	IS IMPOSSIBLE. IF HE SELLS HIS SHARES AND HIS	LANDS	, THEIR PURCHASER WILL CONTINUE ALL THOSE ACTIVITIES
ANNA (296)	(RISING AND SALUTING) PROLETARIANS OF ALL	LANDS	, UNITE. LIEUTENANT SCHNEIDEKIND: YOU WILL RISE AND
JOAN 4 (105)	DOCTRINE THE KING WILL TAKE OUR LANDS -- OUR	LANDS	! -- AND MAKE THEM A PRESENT TO GOD; AND GOD WILL

LANDSCAPE

APPL I (234)	DARKNESS WHILST IT LIGHTS UP EVERY CORNER OF THE	LANDSCAPE	BEHIND US. ALL THE TALENT AND GENIUS OF THE
PYGM III SD(244)	WHISTLER SIDE OF THEM) ARE ON THE WALLS. THE ONLY	LANDSCAPE	IS A CECIL LAWSON ON THE SCALE OF A RUBENS. THERE
MRS II (218)	(SHE DRAWS ASIDE THE CURTAINS OF THE WINDOW. THE	LANDSCAPE	IS SEEN BATHED IN THE RADIANCE OF THE HARVEST MOON
ARMS II SD(23)	FURTHER THE BALKAN MOUNTAINS RISE AND SHUT IN THE	LANDSCAPE	. LOOKING TOWARDS THEM FROM WITHIN THE GARDEN, THE
ARMS III (49)	LOOKS ROUND AT HER; BUT SHE IS AGAIN RAPT IN THE	LANDSCAPE	. WITH A LITTLE GUSH OF PARENTAL AFFECTION AND
SUPR III SD(71)	NATURE HERE: RATHER A MOST ARISTOCRATIC MOUNTAIN	LANDSCAPE	MADE BY A FASTIDIOUS ARTIST-CREATOR. NO VULGAR
MIS. SD(109)	THE GARDEN, AND, BEYOND IT, A BARREN BUT LOVELY	LANDSCAPE	OF HILL PROFILE WITH FIR TREES, COMMONS OF BRACKEN
GETT SD(323)	WOMAN. BUT HER BEAUTY IS WRECKED, LIKE AN AGELESS	LANDSCAPE	RAVAGED BY LONG AND FIERCE WAR. HER EYES ARE

HART I SD(44) THE GLASS DOORS LEAD DIPS TO THE SOUTH BEFORE THE LANDSCAPE RISES AGAIN TO THE HILLS. EMERGING FROM THE HOLLOW
SUPR III SD(73) IS NOT UNEXPECTED, IN SPITE OF THE SPANISH LANDSCAPE ; FOR WITH THE EXCEPTION OF ONE MAN WHO MIGHT BE
DOCT II (120) AND GOES UP TO THE BALUSTRADE, CONTEMPLATING THE LANDSCAPE VEXEDLY). /WALPOLE/ LOOK HERE, RIDGEON! THIS IS
BULL IV (160) YES. (HE GAZES THROUGH THE DOORWAY AT THE IRISH LANDSCAPE , AND SINGS, ALMOST UNCONSCIOUSLY, BUT VERY
BUOY II SD(18) STUDDED WITH HALF-SUBMERGED TREES IN A TROPICAL LANDSCAPE , COVERED WITH BUSH EXCEPT FOR A CLEARANCE BY THE
METH PREFACE(R42) CHANGES AS AN AVALANCHE MAY MAKE IN A MOUNTAIN LANDSCAPE , OR A RAILWAY ACCIDENT IN A HUMAN FIGURE. TO CALL
ARMS III SD(46) DIVAN, IS GAZING IN A DAYDREAM OUT AT THE BALKAN LANDSCAPE , WITH A NEGLECTED NOVEL IN HER LAP. THE DOOR IS

LANDSCAPES
JOAN PREFACE(18) AS SOME OTHER PEOPLE SEE IMAGINARY DIAGRAMS AND LANDSCAPES WITH NUMBERS DOTTED ABOUT THEM, AND ARE THEREBY
MTH5 (251) HAS COME UP ALIVE FROM THOSE FLAMING DEPTHS: YOUR LANDSCAPES , YOUR MOUNTAINS, ARE ONLY THE WORLD'S CAST SKINS

LANE
KING I (204) COURT LADY? /FOX/ DID YOU SELL ORANGES IN DRURY LANE ? /NELL/ THEY SAY I DID. THE PEOPLE LIKE TO BELIEVE I
BUOY IV (52) RATTLERS AND GATERS OF THE HUMAN VARIETY IN PARK LANE ? /SHE/ YES; AND YOU MAY BE ONE OF THEM. /JUNIUS/ YOU
KING I (170) BE INTRODUCED TO MISTRESS GWYNN, THE FAMOUS DRURY LANE ACTRESS? /MRS BASHAM/ (TURNING IMPERATIVELY TO
GETT (302) THE POSITIVIST CEREMONY AT NEWTON HALL IN FETTER LANE AFTER ENTERING INTO THE CIVIL CONTRACT BEFORE THE
BASH III (124) ALGERNON DE COURCY CASHEL BYRON, SIEUR OF PARK LANE AND OVERLORD OF DORSET, WHO AFTER THREE MONTHS WEDDED
MRS I (186) I WAS REALLY AT HONORIA'S CHAMBERS IN CHANCERY LANE EVERY DAY, WORKING AWAY AT ACTUARIAL CALCULATIONS FOR
MRS I (188) FRIGHTEN ME, MR PRAED. IN THAT MONTH AT CHANCERY LANE I HAD OPPORTUNITIES OF TAKING THE MEASURE OF ONE OR TWO
FOUN (218) /MERCER/ DONT SAY THAT, MISS. YOU HAVE PARK LANE IN EVERY FEATURE. /THE LORD CHANCELLOR/ (EFFUSIVELY)
MRS IV SD(235) ACT IV. HONORIA FRASER'S CHAMBERS IN CHANCERY LANE . AN OFFICE AT THE TOP OF NEW STONE BUILDINGS, WITH A
HART PREFACE(21) THAN MOST PEOPLE, THE MISFORTUNE OF THE DEATH OF LANE . I EVEN FOUND A GRIM SATISFACTION, VERY INTELLIGIBLE
BARB II (296) EXPERIENCE MEETING AT THE OTHER GATE IN CRIPPS'S LANE . IVE HARDLY EVER SEEN THEM SO MUCH MOVED AS THEY WERE
MRS I (186) STAND ANY MORE OF IT, AND WENT OFF TO CHANCERY LANE . NOW YOU KNOW THE SORT OF PERFECTLY SPLENDID MODERN
BUOY IV (52) BE OUT OF REACH OF DADDY. WE SHALL LIVE IN PARK LANE . /JUNIUS/ YOU KNOW, OF COURSE, THAT THERE ARE PLENTY
FOUN (218) DOORSTEP OF ONE OF THE VERY BEST HOUSES IN PARK LANE . /THE LORD CHANCELLOR/ (OVERWHELMED) MY DEAR YOUNG
WIDO II (31) BY THE ROOM THAN YOU CAN FOR A MANSION IN PARK LANE . /TRENCH/ I HOPE MR SARTORIUS HASNT MUCH OF THAT SORT
BARB II (302) ASKIN FOR YOU AT THE OTHER GATE IN CRIPPS'S LANE . SHE'S HEARD ABOUT YOUR CONFESSION (PRICE TURNS
ROCK PREFACE(164) BY THE SHOULDERS AND THREW DESTITUTE INTO THE LANE . THERE WERE PLAUSIBLE REASONS FOR THIS BEGINNING OF
BARB PREFACE(219) MAY OR MAY NOT PREFER MAJOR BARBARA TO THE DRURY LANE PANTOMIME; BUT HE ALWAYS PREFERS FIVE HUNDRED POUNDS TO
MRS I (187) BATTLE ROYAL WHEN MY MOTHER HEARS OF MY CHANCERY LANE PROJECT. /PRAED/ (RUEFULLY) I'M AFRAID THERE WILL.
HART PREFACE(20) AMONG OTHERS, THE OTHERS INCLUDED SIR HUGH LANE ; BUT AS HE HAD ONLY LAID THE COUNTRY UNDER GREAT
KING I (204) FREER AND HAPPIER WHEN YOU SOLD ORANGES IN DRURY LANE THAN YOU ARE NOW AS A COURT LADY? /FOX/ DID YOU SELL
APPL PREFACE(187) THE ADDRESSES. THE BOY CONCEALS HIMSELF IN THE LANE WHILST THE POSTMAN DELIVERS THE LETTERS AT THE HOUSE,
PYGM I (213) TOWN WITH 80 POUNDS A YEAR, AND END IN PARK LANE WITH A HUNDRED THOUSAND. THEY WANT TO DROP KENTISH
PYGM I (210) BETWEEN THE NOTE TAKER AND THE GENTLEMAN) PARK LANE , FOR INSTANCE. I'D LIKE TO GO INTO THE HOUSING
MRS III (234) /VIVIE/ AT HONORIA FRASER'S CHAMBERS, 67 CHANCERY LANE , FOR THE REST OF MY LIFE. (SHE GOES OFF QUICKLY IN
BULL I (77) AND I HAD A HOOKED NOSE AND A HOUSE IN PARK LANE , I SHOULD CARRY A UNION JACK HANDKERCHIEF AND A PENNY
PYGM I (215) (HE GRINS AND OPENS THE DOOR, ANGEL COURT, DRURY LANE , ROUND THE CORNER OF MICKLEJOHN'S OIL SHOP. LETS SEE
JOAN (2) 26TH MARCH 1924 IN THE NEW THEATRE IN ST MARTIN'S LANE , WITH SYBIL THORNDIKE AS THE SAINT.
FOUN (218) I BEG. /MERCER/ IF I HAD ONLY KNOWN, MISS! PARK LANE ! I COULD BITE MY TONGUE OUT FOR MY BAD MANNERS, I DO

LANERS
BULL I (86) HUMBUGS, GERMANS, JEWS, YANKEES, FOREIGNERS, PARK LANERS , COSMOPOLITAN RIFFRAFF. DONT CALL THEM ENGLISH. THEY

LANFREY
NEVR I (209) ME INTRODUCE YOU, MR VALENTINE. MY MOTHER, MRS LANFREY CLANDON. (MRS CLANDON BOWS. VALENTINE BOWS,
NEVR II (236) FORWARD BETWEEN THEM) YES, SIR. /VALENTINE/ MRS LANFREY CLANDON. /WAITER/ (WITH A SWEET SMILE OF WELCOME)
NEVR I (203) WE ARE THE CHILDREN OF THE CELEBRATED MRS LANFREY CLANDON, AN AUTHORESS OF GREAT REPUTE-- IN MADEIRA.

LANG
JOAN PREFACE(53) JOAN WOULD BE BURNT ON THE STAGE, AS MR MATHESON LANG ALWAYS IS IN THE WANDERING JEW, ON THE PRINCIPLE THAT
JOAN PREFACE(26) RATHER THAN THE VALUATION THAT IS WRONG. ANDREW LANG AND MARK TWAIN ARE EQUALLY DETERMINED TO MAKE JOAN A
JOAN PREFACE(50) AND THE CRUEL INQUISITOR OF MARK TWAIN AND ANDREW LANG ARE AS DULL AS PICKPOCKETS; AND THEY REDUCE JOAN TO THE
JOAN PREFACE(26) SHOULD BE READ AS A CORRECTIVE TO THE OTHER. LANG HAD NO DIFFICULTY IN SHEWING THAT JOAN'S ABILITY WAS
JOAN PREFACE(25) THE HISTORIES OF JOAN BY MARK TWAIN AND ANDREW LANG . MARK TWAIN WAS CONVERTED TO DOWNRIGHT WORSHIP OF JOAN
JOAN PREFACE(26) AND BUSINESS PARIS, DOES NOT ENTER; WHEREAS LANG WAS A SCOT, AND EVERY SCOT KNOWS THAT THE GREY MARE IS
JOAN PREFACE(27) CLEARLY OUT OF COURT FROM THE BEGINNING. ANDREW LANG WAS BETTER READ; BUT, LIKE WALTER SCOTT, HE ENJOYED
JOAN PREFACE(26) ABOUT IT THAN THE MISSISSIPPI PILOT. BUT THEN LANG WAS, BY LIFELONG PROFESSIONAL HABIT, A CRITIC OF

LANGUAGE
GENV I (32) THE MARKS OF A GERMAN BLOND. GERMAN IS MY NATIVE LANGUAGE : IN FACT I AM IN EVERY SENSE A GERMAN. BUT I
MIS. (174) /TARLETON/ ALL RIGHT, CHICKABIDDY: IT'S NOT BAD LANGUAGE : IT'S ONLY SOCIALISM. /MRS TARLETON/ WELL, I WONT
MTH1 I (11) STORY LILITH IMAGINED AND TOLD YOU IN YOUR SILENT LANGUAGE : THE STORY THAT WAS TOO WONDERFUL TO BE TRUE, AND
OVER (185) KEEP YOUR TEMPER AND REFRAIN FROM USING PROFANE LANGUAGE ? /MRS LUNN/ (RISING, DELIGHTED) GREGORY!
BARB III (346) THE WORLD CAN NEVER BE REALLY TOUCHED BY A DEAD LANGUAGE AND A DEAD CIVILIZATION. THE PEOPLE MUST HAVE
HART I (73) END IN? RESPECTABILITY. A LADYLIKE DAUGHTER. THE LANGUAGE AND APPEARANCE OF A CITY MISSIONARY. LET IT BE A
ROCK I (213) /BLEE/ WE WORKING FOLKS KNOW TOO MUCH OF BAD LANGUAGE AND BAD MANNERS TO SEE ANY FUN IN THEM OR THINK
FANY III (317) AND QUARRELS AND HUFF AND OFFENCE AND BAD LANGUAGE AND BAD TEMPER AND REGULAR BEWILDERMENT AS IF SATAN
SUPR HANDBOK(193) OF OUR FEELING THAT MAKES ITS DESECRATION BY VILE LANGUAGE AND COARSE HUMOR INTOLERABLE; SO THAT AT LAST WE
SIM I (39) ME ALL OVER THE WORLD, WHERE I COULDNT SPEAK THE LANGUAGE AND COULDNT EXPLAIN. /PRA/ AND THEY WANTED YOU TO
PYGM PREFACE(200) BUT A SAVAGELY DERISIVE ATTACK ON A PROFESSOR OF LANGUAGE AND LITERATURE WHOSE CHAIR SWEET REGARDED AS PROPER
JOAN PREFACE(22) OF PUBLIC DECENCY, AND WOULD NOT TOLERATE FOUL LANGUAGE AND NEGLECT OF RELIGIOUS OBSERVANCES, NOR ALLOW
3PLA PREFACE(R36) WE SEARCH FOR EXAMPLES OF A PRODIGIOUS COMMAND OF LANGUAGE AND OF GRAPHIC LINE, WE CAN THINK OF NOBODY BETTER
PYGM II (221) FACE TO ASK ME THE SAME FOR TEACHING ME MY OWN LANGUAGE AS YOU WOULD FOR FRENCH; SO I WONT GIVE MORE THAN A
PYGM III (255) MUST LEARN TO KNOW YOURSELF. I HAVNT HEARD SUCH LANGUAGE AS YOURS SINCE WE USED TO REVIEW THE VOLUNTEERS IN
FABL PREFACE(88) OR ADMINISTRATOR, ABOVE A SOLON WHO KNOWS NO LANGUAGE BUT HIS OWN. IT PUTS FACILITY IN DOING SET SUMS IN
BUOY III (41) YEARS WITHOUT LEARNING HOW TO SPEAK THEIR NATIVE LANGUAGE DECENTLY OR WRITE IT EASILY. /THE WIDOWER/ WE ARE
METH PREFACE(R28) THAN HIS BOOKKEEPER. EVEN EXCEPTIONAL COMMAND OF LANGUAGE DOES NOT IMPLY THE POSSESSION OF IDEAS TO EXPRESS:
SUPR HANDBOK(219) REVELATION. NO MAN FULLY CAPABLE OF HIS OWN LANGUAGE EVER MASTERS ANOTHER. NO MAN CAN BE A PURE
CAND I (87) /MORELL/ (HOTLY) NO, SIR: IT'S NOT BECOMING LANGUAGE FOR A CLERGYMAN. I USED THE WRONG WORD. I SHOULD
CAND I (87) DEPRECATION OF THIS TREATMENT) IS THAT BECOMIN LANGUAGE FOR A CLORGYMAN, JAMES? AND YOU SO PARTICLAR,
FANY PROLOG (271) STOP TALKING FRENCH TO ME: IT'S NOT A PROPER LANGUAGE FOR A YOUNG GIRL. GREAT HEAVENS! HOW IS IT
PYGM V (271) WORLD, AND THAT WANTED YOU TO INVENT A UNIVERSAL LANGUAGE FOR HIM? /HIGGINS/ WHAT! EZRA D. WANNAFELLER!
CAPT NOTES (304) GESPROCHENEN ENGLISCH, TRANSLATED INTO HIS NATIVE LANGUAGE FOR THE USE OF BRITISH ISLANDERS AS A PRIMER OF
SUPR HANDBOK(192) ON THESE SUBJECTS, AND CONSEQUENTLY WE HAVE NO LANGUAGE FOR THEM EXCEPT INDECENT LANGUAGE. WE THEREFORE
FABL V (118) WERE SO DISGUSTING THAT THEY HAD NO DECENT LANGUAGE FOR THEM. YOU THINK THEIR METHODS WERE LIKE OURS,
PRES (147) LANGUAGE. /MRS FARRELL/ WOULD YOU PUT UP WITH BAD LANGUAGE FROM ME BECAUSE IVE RISKED ME LIFE EIGHT TIMES IN
PYGM II (231) AND WHO THE DEVIL-- /HIGGINS/ MRS PEARCE! THIS LANGUAGE FROM YOUR LIPS! REALLY! /MRS PEARCE/ (NOT TO BE
PYGM V (272) HIGGINS. I'LL HAVE TO LEARN TO SPEAK MIDDLE CLASS LANGUAGE FROM YOU, INSTEAD OF SPEAKING PROPER ENGLISH. THATS
SUPR PREFACE(R26) " THE HOOFS OF THE SWINISH MULTITUDE," BURKE'S LANGUAGE GAVE GREAT OFFENCE BECAUSE THE IMPLIED EXCEPTIONS
ROCK I (213) YOU PROMISED NOT TO USE ANY OF YOUR WEST END LANGUAGE HERE. YOU KNOW WE DONT LIKE IT. /SIR ARTHUR/ THATS
BARB PREFACE(208) DERIVE ME FROM A NORWEGIAN AUTHOR OF WHOSE LANGUAGE I DO NOT KNOW THREE WORDS, AND OF WHOM I KNEW
PYGM V (279) IS BROUGHT TO A FOREIGN COUNTRY, IT PICKS UP THE LANGUAGE IN A FEW WEEKS, AND FORGETS ITS OWN. WELL, I AM A
MIS. (174) THIS-- /MRS TARLETON/ DONT YOU DARE USE SUCH LANGUAGE IN COMPANY. I WONT ALLOW IT. /TARLETON/ ALL RIGHT,
SUPR PREFACE(R36) IN VAIN DO I REDOUBLE THE VIOLENCE OF THE LANGUAGE IN WHICH I PROCLAIM MY HETERODOXIES. I RAIL AT THE
PYGM III (255) HANDS. /HIGGINS/ (AGGRIEVED) DO YOU MEAN THAT MY LANGUAGE IS IMPROPER? /MRS HIGGINS/ NO, DEAREST: IT WOULD
BARB III (314) AMOUNT OF TOSH ABOUT THE TIMES; BUT AT LEAST ITS LANGUAGE IS REPUTABLE. /LOMAX/ (OVERWHELMED) YOU ARE SO
BULL PREFACE(15) THAT I WAS BORN IN IRELAND, AND THAT MY NATIVE LANGUAGE IS THE ENGLISH OF SWIFT AND NOT THE UNSPEAKABLE
PYGM I (214) GIFT OF ARTICULATE SPEECH: THAT YOUR NATIVE LANGUAGE IS THE LANGUAGE OF SHAKESPEAR AND MILTON AND THE
MTH5 (256) I FIND IT MORE AND MORE DIFFICULT TO KEEP UP YOUR LANGUAGE . ANOTHER CENTURY OR TWO AND IT WILL BE IMPOSSIBLE.
MIS. PREFACE(99) LIKE SIR WALTER SCOTT AND RUSKIN, A DEAD LANGUAGE . BESIDES, MANY WHO HAVE NO EAR FOR LITERATURE OR
CLEO NOTES (203) GALEN DID NOT, AS HE QUOTES YOUR HEROINE'S OWN LANGUAGE . FOAM OF NITRE IS, I THINK, SOMETHING LIKE
BULL PREFACE(52) IRRITATED MOB, ESPECIALLY IF YOU DO NOT KNOW ITS LANGUAGE . HAD THE SHOOTING PARTY BEEN IN THE CHARGE OF A
ROCK I (213) APOLOGIZE FOR HIS DRESS, FOR HIS MANNERS, FOR HIS LANGUAGE . HE MUST SHOCK YOU EVERY TIME HE OPENS HIS MOUTH.
JOAN 1 (68) TO PERDITION. THAT IS WHAT GODDAM MEANS IN THEIR LANGUAGE . HOW DO YOU LIKE IT? /JOAN/ GOD WILL BE MERCIFUL

JITT PREFACE(5)	FEAT FOR A TRANSLATOR WHO DOES NOT KNOW THE	LANGUAGE	. HOWEVER, WHEN IT COMES TO TRANSLATING A PLAY THE
GENV III (79)	IT SOUNDS WELL; BUT ENGLISH IS NOT MY NATIVE	LANGUAGE	. I DO NOT UNDERSTAND THE FIRST LINE. " WE ARE FAIN
BASH PREFACE(89)	HYPERBOLICAL RHETORIC AND DELIBERATELY ARTIFICIAL	LANGUAGE	. MY PARODIES OF THE ELIZABETHAN MANNERISM, AND
LION EPILOG (150)	HILL IN WHICH GOD WAS WORSHIPPED IN THE GERMAN	LANGUAGE	. ONE WOULD HAVE SUPPOSED THAT THIS GROTESQUE
MTH2 (78)	IS CLASSROOM JARGON: THE OTHER IS INSPIRED HUMAN	LANGUAGE	. /LUBIN/ (CALMLY REMINISCENT) ONE OF THE FEW
PRES (147)	OF HIS SELF-CONTROL; TO BE EXCUSED A LITTLE STRONG	LANGUAGE	. /MRS FARRELL/ WOULD YOU PUT UP WITH BAD LANGUAGE
BUOY III (38)	MUST DRAG IN RELIGION, AT LEAST DO SO IN BECOMING	LANGUAGE	. /MRS THIRDBORN/ WHEN YOU REALLY BELIEVE IN GOD
PYGM V (274)	I HAD UTTERED A WORD, AND USED PERFECTLY AWFUL	LANGUAGE	. /PICKERING/ (ASTONISHED) BUT WHY? WHAT DID WE
JOAN 1 (67)	SHOULD COME INTO OUR COUNTRY AND TRY TO SPEAK OUR	LANGUAGE	. /ROBERT/ WHO HAS BEEN PUTTING SUCH NONSENSE INTO
PYGM III (246)	PUPILS BECAUSE SHE'S HAD TO LEARN A COMPLETE NEW	LANGUAGE	. SHE TALKS ENGLISH ALMOST AS YOU TALK FRENCH. /MRS
ROCK II (276)	DENY THAT HE IS A NICE BOY IN SPITE OF HIS AWFUL	LANGUAGE	. SO I SAID-- /SIR ARTHUR/ " DAVID'S THE MAN FOR
JOAN 6 (127)	TO ASSUME THAT ENGLISH IS THE DEVIL'S NATIVE	LANGUAGE	. SO LET IT PASS. THE MATTER IS NOT WHOLLY OMITTED
FABL V (118)	TO MAKE AN ALPHABET CAPABLE OF SPELLING THEIR	LANGUAGE	. THEY COUNTED THEIR GOODS IN TWELVES BUT COULD NOT
SUPR HANDBOK(192)	DINNER TABLE, A MERE DIFFICULTY OF EDUCATION AND	LANGUAGE	. WE ARE NOT TAUGHT TO THINK DECENTLY ON THESE
SUPR HANDBOK(192)	WE HAVE NO LANGUAGE FOR THEM EXCEPT INDECENT	LANGUAGE	. WE THEREFORE HAVE TO DECLARE THEM UNFIT FOR
MTH4 I (141)	/THE WOMAN/ DECENT? THERE IS NO SUCH WORD IN OUR	LANGUAGE	. WHAT DOES IT MEAN? /THE ELDERLY GENTLEMAN/ IT
MTH1 I (10)	TOLD ME WHAT SHE HAD IMAGINED IN OUR SILENT	LANGUAGE	(FOR THERE WERE NO WORDS THEN) I BADE HER DESIRE
BUOY PREFACE(6)	RESULT WAS THE MOST ABSURD BOOK IN THE ENGLISH	LANGUAGE	(HIS CHRONOLOGY) DOES NOT INVALIDATE IN THE LEAST
JITT PREFACE(4)	I CAN NEITHER CLAIM KNOWLEDGE OF THE GERMAN	LANGUAGE	NOR PLEAD IGNORANCE OF IT. I AM LIKE MOST LITERARY
O'FL (224)	AND SAVAGES, AND ME NOT KNOWING A WORD OF THEIR	LANGUAGE	NOR THEM OF MINE? /O'FLAHERTY/ A GOOD JOB THEY
BASH II,1, (100)	LEARNT YOU THAT ATROCIOUS WORD? THIS IS THE	LANGUAGE	OF A FLOWER-GIRL. /LYDIA/ TRUE. IT IS HORRIBLE.
LADY PREFACE(227)	TO PEMBROKE, EXTRAVAGANT AS IT NOW SEEMS, IS THE	LANGUAGE	OF COMPLIMENT AND FASHION, TRANSFIGURED NO DOUBT BY
GENV IV (123)	BREACH OF THE PEACE I AM UNABLE TO ADHERE TO THE	LANGUAGE	OF DIPLOMACY-- WE SHOULD BE OBLIGED TO KNOCK THE
BULL PREFACE(41)	PEOPLE, WHICH IS MOST FORTUNATELY ALSO THE NATIVE	LANGUAGE	OF HALF THE WORLD, INCLUDING ENGLAND. EVERY
BULL III (136)	YOU WHAT I FEEL ABOUT HOME RULE WITHOUT USING THE	LANGUAGE	OF HYPERBOLE. /DORAN/ SAVIN FADHER DEMPSEY'S
HART PREFACE(16)	NO ENGLISH CHILD SHOULD EVER AGAIN BE TAUGHT THE	LANGUAGE	OF LUTHER AND GOETHE, WERE KEPT IN COUNTENANCE BY
PYGM EPILOG (300)	AND HAD ACQUIRED A CERTAIN FAMILIARITY WITH THE	LANGUAGE	OF MILTON FROM HER STRUGGLES TO QUALIFY HERSELF FOR
DOCT PREFACE(78)	IT, AND ARE THEREFORE COMPELLED TO INVENT A NEW	LANGUAGE	OF NONSENSE FOR EVERY BOOK THEY WRITE, LET ME SUM
LADY PREFACE(228)	LANGUAGE OF THE SONNETS TO THE DARK LADY IS THE	LANGUAGE	OF PASSION: THEIR CRUELTY SHEWS IT. THERE IS NO
PYGM I (214)	SPEECH: THAT YOUR NATIVE LANGUAGE IS THE	LANGUAGE	OF SHAKESPEAR AND MILTON AND THE BIBLE; AND DONT
LION PREFACE(9)	TODAY THE BIBLE IS SO LITTLE READ THAT THE	LANGUAGE	OF THE AUTHORIZED VERSION IS RAPIDLY BECOMING
CAPT III (288)	SAID WHEN THE ENGLISH BENCH ADDRESSED YOU IN THE	LANGUAGE	OF THE ENGLISH FORECASTLE-- (SIR HOWARD IS ABOUT
BULL PREFACE(41)	POPULARIZING ITSELF AS AN ATTACK ON THE NATIVE	LANGUAGE	OF THE IRISH PEOPLE, WHICH IS MOST FORTUNATELY ALSO
LADY PREFACE(228)	MANLY LOYALTY DEEP ENOUGH TO BE OUTRAGED. BUT THE	LANGUAGE	OF THE SONNETS TO THE DARK LADY IS THE LANGUAGE OF
LADY PREFACE(227)	IS AN ANCHORITE COMPARED TO SHAKESPEAR. THE	LANGUAGE	OF THE SONNETS ADDRESSED TO PEMBROKE, EXTRAVAGANT
FANY II (295)	OF THIS WORLD TALKING VAINLY AND FOOLISHLY IN THE	LANGUAGE	OF THIS WORLD. BUT WHEN I HEAR YOU JUSTIFYING YOUR
CAPT III (288)	OF ANY INDIVIDUAL OF MY OWN SEX AND REPEAT THE	LANGUAGE	OF TWO ANGRY MEN? /KEARNEY/ (RISING IMPRESSIVELY)
PYGM V (277)	LIKE HIM, UNABLE TO CONTROL MYSELF, AND USING BAD	LANGUAGE	ON THE SLIGHTEST PROVOCATION. AND I SHOULD NEVER
MTH5 (219)	TO US HAVE TO BRUSH UP THEIR KNOWLEDGE OF THE	LANGUAGE	ONCE A YEAR OR SO. NOTHING MAKES ANY DIFFERENCE TO
JOAN PREFACE(7)	A BRAVE AND HARDY SOLDIER, UNABLE TO ENDURE LOOSE	LANGUAGE	OR LICENTIOUS CONDUCT. SHE WENT TO THE STAKE
PYGM PREFACE(200)	IS THAT IT CAN EXPRESS EVERY SOUND IN THE	LANGUAGE	PERFECTLY, VOWELS AS WELL AS CONSONANTS, AND THAT
SUPR IV SD(143)	A STUPID ENGLISHMAN WHO CANNOT EVEN SPEAK HIS OWN	LANGUAGE	PROPERLY. STRAKER, ON THE OTHER HAND, REGARDS THE
FANY III (305)	ALL THAT-- WELL! /MARGARET/ OH, IVE LEARNT THE	LANGUAGE	; AND I LIKE IT. IT'S ANOTHER BARRIER BROKEN DOWN.
JOAN 1 (67)	BUT HE GAVE THEM THEIR OWN COUNTRY AND THEIR OWN	LANGUAGE	; AND IT IS NOT HIS WILL THAT THEY SHOULD COME INTO
PYGM PREFACE(201)	LEGIBLE SCRIPT FOR OUR NOBLE BUT ILL-DRESSED	LANGUAGE	; BUT HE WAS LED PAST THAT BY HIS CONTEMPT FOR THE
MTH4 I (149)	DIE SOONER THAN LANGUAGES. I UNDERSTAND YOUR	LANGUAGE	; BUT I DO NOT ALWAYS UNDERSTAND YOUR THOUGHT. THE
PYGM PREFACE(200)	OF MAKING SENSE WITH THE CONTEXT, EXISTED IN ANY	LANGUAGE	SPOKEN ON EARTH. THAT LESS EXPERT MORTALS SHOULD
CLEO V (197)	/BRITANNUS/ CAESAR: I ASK YOU TO EXCUSE THE	LANGUAGE	THAT ESCAPED ME IN THE HEAT OF THE MOMENT. /CAESAR/
CYMB V (146)	NOTHING PRINCE-LIKE; FOR HE DID PROVOKE ME WITH	LANGUAGE	THAT WOULD MAKE ME SPURN THE SEA IF IT COULD SO
FANY I (281)	GIVING PEOPLE A BIT OF MY MIND I SOMETIMES USE	LANGUAGE	THATS BENEATH ME. BUT I TELL YOU ONCE FOR ALL I
FANY III (306)	LIKE A SKUNK. /BOBBY/ (MUCH RUFFLED) NICE	LANGUAGE	THAT! /DORA/ WELL, DEARIE, MEN HAVE TO DO SOME
SUPR HANDBOK(193)	OF WOMEN. ADD TO THE HORRORS OF POPULAR	LANGUAGE	THE HORRORS OF POPULAR POVERTY. IN CROWDED
JOAN 1 (67)	OF ENGLAND OR THE KING OF FRANCE? WHAT HAS THEIR	LANGUAGE	TO DO WITH IT? /JOAN/ I DO NOT UNDERSTAND THAT A
DEVL III (67)	/BURGOYNE/ HAVE YOU ADDRESSED PROFANE	LANGUAGE	TO THE LADY, MAJOR SWINDON? /SWINDON/ (VERY
BASH PREFACE(88)	ELIZABETHAN ENGLISH MAY NOT AGAIN BECOME A LIVING	LANGUAGE	TO THE ORDINARY PLAYGOER, TO PEOPLE WHO NEVER READ
JOAN 4 (101)	MEAN IN ENGLAND WHAT IT DOES IN FRANCE. IN YOUR	LANGUAGE	TRAITOR MEANS BETRAYER: ONE WHO IS PERFIDIOUS,
CAPT II (245)	BRANDYFACED JACK: I NAME YOU FOR CONDUCT AND	LANGUAGE	UNBECOMING TO A GENTLEMAN. THOSE WHO AGREE WILL
SUPR III (137)	OBJECT TO, YOU BLACKMAILIN SWINE, YOU. /MENDOZA/	LANGUAGE	UNWORTHY OF LOUISA'S BROTHER! BUT NO MATTER: YOU
AUGS (274)	TOWERING RAGE AT ITS BEING ENTRUSTED TO YOU: HIS	LANGUAGE	WAS TERRIBLE. HE ORDERED ALL THE GUNS TO BE SHIFTED
JOAN 2 (72)	WAS TOLD BY A SOLDIER THAT HE SHOULDNT USE SUCH	LANGUAGE	WHEN HE WAS AT THE POINT OF DEATH. /THE ARCHBISHOP/
BULL I (85)	(SLYLY)-- AND ALSO ITS HABIT OF USING STRONG	LANGUAGE	WHEN THERES NOTHING THE MATTER. /DOYLE/ NOTHING THE
DEVL III (56)	OPINION. I NEVER STOOP TO THAT HABIT OF PROFANE	LANGUAGE	WHICH UNFORTUNATELY COARSENS OUR PROFESSION. IF I
JITT PREFACE(4)	SUCCESSFUL AND RESPECTED PLAYWRIGHT IN THE GERMAN	LANGUAGE	WHILST THE ENGLISH CRITICS WERE STILL EXPLAINING
SUPR HANDBOK(192)	DISPOSAL, FIND NO DIFFICULTY; AND MASTERS OF	LANGUAGE	WHO THINK DECENTLY CAN WRITE POPULAR STORIES LIKE
GETT (353)	OF LOVE SHALL TELL /HOTCHKISS/ (SARDONICALLY) IN	LANGUAGE	WHOSE EXCESS IMPARTS THE POWER THEY FEEL SO WELL.
FANY I (273)	LEAVE IT AT THAT, PLEASE. WHATEVER IT IS, BAD	LANGUAGE	WONT MAKE IT BETTER. /GILBEY/ (BITTERLY) YES, PUT
CAPT NOTES (306)	AS A MEANS OF EMPHASIS, AND THAT THE LONDON	LANGUAGE	WOULD BE POORER WITHOUT IT. THE OBJECTION TO IT IS
WIDO III (61)	/TRENCH/ SHUT UP, BILLY; OR ELSE SPEAK SOME	LANGUAGE	YOU UNDERSTAND. NO, MR SARTORIUS: I SHOULD BE VERY
ROCK II (274)	YOUNG BARKING'S TITLE. /ALOYSIA/ YES HE DID. THE	LANGUAGE	YOU WEST END PEOPLE USE! I'M SURE I DONT KNOW
PYGM V (279)	A CHILD IN YOUR COUNTRY. I HAVE FORGOTTEN MY OWN	LANGUAGE	, AND CAN SPEAK NOTHING BUT YOURS. THATS THE REAL
HART PREFACE(14)	WRECKED DWELLINGS, EXCUSE A GOOD DEAL OF VIOLENT	LANGUAGE	, AND PRODUCE A WRATH ON WHICH MANY SUNS GO DOWN
PYGM PREFACE(199)	DUE PLACE. THE ENGLISH HAVE NO RESPECT FOR THEIR	LANGUAGE	, AND WILL NOT TEACH THEIR CHILDREN TO SPEAK IT.
GETT PREFACE(219)	DOES EXIST BETWEEN ENTIRE STRANGERS, DIFFERENT IN	LANGUAGE	, COLOR, TASTES, CLASS, CIVILIZATION, MORALS,
MRS PREFACE(175)	COULD DO NOTHING TO CHECK THE EPIDEMIC OF FOUL	LANGUAGE	, GROSS SUGGESTION, AND RAVING OBSCENITY OF WORD
CLEO NOTES (208)	OF EXACTLY THE SAME STOCK, AND SPEAKING THE SAME	LANGUAGE	, GROWING IN GREAT BRITAIN, IN IRELAND, AND IN
LION PREFACE(97)	MORE INSULAR IN ITS PREOCCUPATION WITH ITS OWN	LANGUAGE	, ITS OWN HISTORY, ITS OWN CHARACTER, THAN WE, WHO
FANY III (305)	BARRIER BROKEN DOWN. /BOBBY/ IT'S NOT SO MUCH THE	LANGUAGE	, MEG. BUT I THINK (HE LOOKS AT DORA AND STOPS).
GENV I (42)	ON ALL THE STYLE HE IS CAPABLE OF) MY NATIVE	LANGUAGE	, MY LORD. ALSO THIS LADY'S. (EXCHANGE OF BOWS).
BASH PREFACE(88)	PLAYGOER, TO WHOM ELIZABETHAN ENGLISH IS A DEAD	LANGUAGE	, ONLY HALF UNDERSTOOD NINE-TENTHS OF THE PLAY, AND
POSN PREFACE(362)	OF OUR CLASS GOVERNMENTS IN THE ENGLISH	LANGUAGE	, THAT WHENEVER AN ABUSE BECOMES OPPRESSIVE ENOUGH
JOAN 1 (68)	ENGLAND, AND TRIED TO LIVE THERE AND SPEAK ITS	LANGUAGE	, THE DEVIL WOULD ENTER INTO ME; AND WHEN I WAS OLD
METH PREFACE(R36)	HIM THE GREAT FIRST CAUSE, OR, IN STILL CHOICER	LANGUAGE	, THE PRIMAL CAUSE. TO THE RATIONALISTS IT WOULD
BULL PREFACE(51)	SHOOT PIGEONS; BUT AS THEY DID NOT UNDERSTAND HIS	LANGUAGE	, THE WARNING HAD NO EFFECT. THEY SENT THEIR
ROCK II (281)	THEIR VIOLENCE, THEIR BRUTALITY AND FILTHY	LANGUAGE	, THEIR SAVAGE TREATMENT OF THEIR WOMEN FOLK. THAT
LION PREFACE(20)	THE FACT THAT THE GOSPEL IS WRITTEN IN THE GREEK	LANGUAGE	, WHILST THE FIRST-HAND TRADITIONS AND THE ACTUAL
SHAK PREFACE(136)	OF BUNYAN AND COBBETT, BOTH GREAT MASTERS OF	LANGUAGE	, WHO NEVERTHELESS COULD NOT HAVE WRITTEN VENUS AND
BULL IV (162)	CUSH RHYME TO BUSH). /BROADBENT/ OH, CONFOUND THE	LANGUAGE	! NORA DARLING-- MY NORA-- THE NORA I LOVE--

LANGUAGES

SIM II (70)	TO TRY CASES IN HUNDREDS OF DIFFERENT LANDS AND	LANGUAGES	AND CREEDS AND COLORS ON THE SAME DAY IN THE SAME
BARB I (266)	BUT THEIR POSITION IS UNCHALLENGEABLE. OTHER	LANGUAGES	ARE THE QUALIFICATIONS OF WAITERS AND COMMERCIAL
BUOY III (29)	BOXER. ANOTHER IS A HISTORIAN AND KNOWS ELEVEN	LANGUAGES	, HE IS ALSO A PEDESTRIAN AND WALKS 3000 MILES
GENV III (79)	THIS LADY IT IS NOT STUPIDITY, SHE SPEAKS SEVERAL	LANGUAGES	, HER INTELLIGENCE IS REMARKABLE: SHE TAKES A
MTH4 I (149)	THOUGHT. /ZOO/ WELL, THOUGHTS DIE SOONER THAN	LANGUAGES	. I UNDERSTAND YOUR LANGUAGE; BUT I DO NOT ALWAYS
MIS. PREFACE(62)	MORAL COURAGE JUST AS HE COMES TO HATE BOOKS AND	LANGUAGES	. IN THE END, JOHN RUSKIN, TIED SO CLOSELY TO HIS
SIM II (71)	BUT EXCUSE ME: THEY DO NOT SPEAK DIFFERENT	LANGUAGES	. /THE ANGEL/ THEY SOUND DIFFERENT TO US. /SIR
ARMS III (73)	STANDING OF A GENTLEMAN; AND I HAVE THREE NATIVE	LANGUAGES	. SHEW ME ANY MAN IN BULGARIA THAT CAN OFFER AS
KING II (228)	THEM ANYTHING WE TEACH THEM GRAMMAR AND DEAD	LANGUAGES	. WHAT IS THE RESULT? PROTESTANTISM AND
SIM PRO,2, (28)	A STRANGE MAD COUNTRY WHERE THE YOUNG ARE TAUGHT	LANGUAGES	THAT ARE DEAD AND HISTORIES THAT ARE LIES, BUT ARE
SIM II (71)	THEY NEEDED IT BADLY AND HE WAS READY. THE OTHER	LANGUAGES	WILL FOLLOW. THE UNITED STATES OF AMERICA WILL BE
JOAN 1 (67)	OF HEAVEN; AND HE GAVE US OUR COUNTRIES AND OUR	LANGUAGES	, AND MEANT US TO KEEP TO THEM. IF IT WERE NOT SO
MILL PREFACE(125)	(RAPIDLY FADING, BY THE WAY), NATIONAL	LANGUAGES	, AND NATIONAL CUSTOMS. BUT THEY DETERIORATE
MTH4 I (149)	DEAD THOUGHT! I HAVE HEARD OF THE DEAD	LANGUAGES	, BUT NEVER OF THE DEAD THOUGHT. /ZOO/ WELL,
FABL PREFACE(88)	TESTS TEND TO EXCLUDE BORN RULERS. KNOWLEDGE OF	LANGUAGES	, DEAD AND FOREIGN, PUTS A MEZZOFANTI, USELESS AS
SUPR III (123)	STRANGERS TO ONE ANOTHER, SPEAKING DIFFERENT	LANGUAGES	, DIFFERING IN RACE AND COLOR, IN AGE AND
MIS. PREFACE(57)	LIKE THOSE OF THE COMMERCIAL SCHOOLMASTER).	LANGUAGES	, EVEN DEAD ONES, HAVE THEIR USES; AND, AS IT
METH PREFACE(R28)	TO EXPRESS: MEZZOFANTI, THE MASTER OF FIFTY-EIGHT	LANGUAGES	, HAD LESS TO SAY IN THEM THAN SHAKESPEAR WITH HIS

LANGUID

UNPL PREFACE(R11) WARMLY INTERESTED. BUT IT SOON APPEARED THAT THE LANGUID DEMAND OF A SMALL AND UPPISH GROUP FOR A FORM OF
JITT II (42) AIR, BUT PRETENDING TO BE LISTLESS AND LANGUID). /LENKHEIM/ (SHEWING HER THE MANUSCRIPT) LOOK AT
OVER (179) CAREFULLY. SHE IS A TALL, IMPOSING, HANDSOME, LANGUID WOMAN, WITH FLASHING DARK EYES AND LONG LASHES. THEY
JITT II SD(31) A MOMENT THROUGH THE INNER DOOR. JITTA COMES IN, LANGUID , AND DRESSED AS LENKHEIM HAS DESCRIBED. /JITTA/ OH,

LANGUIDLY

BARB I (271) WISHED YOU WERE A THOUSAND MILES AWAY. /SARAH/ (LANGUIDLY) VERY WELL, MAMMA. (SHE GOES). LADY BRITOMART,

LANGUISH

ROCK PREFACE(171) THAT ALL EVOLUTIONISTS GO TO HELL; THAT CHILDREN LANGUISH AND DIE WITHOUT BEEFSTEAKS; AND THAT WITHOUT

LANGUISHED

PYGM EPILOG (298) HER TO THINK THAT THE DUNGEON IN WHICH SHE HAD LANGUISHED FOR SO MANY UNHAPPY YEARS HAD BEEN UNLOCKED ALL

LANGUISHES

CLEO IV (184) IN ITS ARMS THAT CAESAR FOUND ME ASLEEP. (SHE LANGUISHES AT CAESAR THEN TURNS CURTLY TO THE PRIEST). GO. I
HART PREFACE(39) HAPSBURG HAS COLLAPSED; ALL HIGHEST HOHENZOLLERN LANGUISHES IN HOLLAND, THREATENED WITH TRIAL ON A CAPITAL

LANGUISHING

HART PREFACE(5) ROOM, AND THE PICTURE GALLERY WOULD BE FOUND LANGUISHING AMONG THE STABLES, MISERABLY DISCONTENTED; AND

LANGUOR

DOCT IV SD(160) MOST OF HIS CONDITION, FINDING VOLUPTUOUSNESS IN LANGUOR AND DRAMA IN DEATH. THEY ARE ALL IMPRESSED, IN SPITE
DOCT IV SD(160) HARDLY MOVE, LYING ON HIS CUSHIONS WITH COMPLETE LANGUOR ; BUT HIS MIND IS ACTIVE: IT IS MAKING THE MOST OF

LANLORDS

BULL III (127) WEVE HAD ENOUGH OF HIS FOOLISH TALK AGEN LANLORDS . HWAT CALL HAS HE TO TALK ABOUT THE LAN, THAT

LANNID

CAPT I (219) /DRINKWATER/ WOT ABAHT THEM! WAW, THEYRE EAH. LANNID AHT OF A STEAM YACHT IN MOGADOR AWBER NOT TWENTY

LANTERN

METH PREFACE(R36) A MAN WOULD CONFESS THAT HE STOOD AS WITH A DIM LANTERN IN A DENSE FOG, AND COULD SEE BUT A LITTLE WAY IN
MTH4 III (201) A FOOLISH PICTURE OF ME THROWN ON A CLOUD BY A LANTERN . HOW CAN I HELP YOU? /THE ELDERLY GENTLEMAN/ THEY
MRS PREFACE(157) TO PLACE IT IN THE LIGHT OF THE POLICEMAN'S LANTERN OR THE SALVATION ARMY SHELTER IS CHECKMATED AT ONCE
JOAN PREFACE(18) THEM THAT THE MIND'S EYE IS MORE OR LESS A MAGIC LANTERN , AND THAT THE STREET IS FULL OF NORMALLY SANE

LANTERNS

NEVR IV SD(282) WINDOW STANDS WIDE OPEN; AND STRINGS OF CHINESE LANTERNS ARE GLOWING AMONG THE TREES OUTSIDE, WITH THE
NEVR III (280) TO MRS CLANDON) WE OFTEN HAVE THEM, MAAM: CHINESE LANTERNS IN THE GARDEN, MAAM: VERY BRIGHT AND PLEASANT, VERY
NEVR IV (305) DANCES AWAY WITH GLORIA, AND DISAPPEARS AMONG THE LANTERNS , LEAVING VALENTINE GASPING). /VALENTINE/ (

LAO

LION PREFACE(95) JUST AS YOU CAN BECOME A FOLLOWER OF CONFUCIUS OR LAO TSE, AND MAY THEREFORE CALL YOURSELF A JESUIST, OR EVEN

LAODICEA

GETT PREFACE(198) IT AS THE IDEAL MARRIED STATE, THE GOSPEL OF LAODICEA . LET US TRY TO GET AT THE ROOT ERROR OF THESE
METH PREFACE(R75) THE MATTER, BUTLER'S PREACHING OF THE GOSPEL OF LAODICEA WAS A PIECE OF COMMON SENSE FOUNDED ON HIS
GETT PREFACE(198) HIS EXPERIENCE OF LIFE, PREACHED THE GOSPEL OF LAODICEA , URGING PEOPLE TO BE TEMPERATE IN WHAT THEY CALLED

LAODICEAN

FABL PREFACE(76) MASSES AND NEVER MENTION THE REFORMATION, LAODICEAN BROAD CHURCHMEN, AND LOW CHURCH PROTESTANTS. THE

LAODICEANISM

BARB PREFACE(221) THE NECESSITY AND MORALITY OF A CONSCIENTIOUS LAODICEANISM IN RELIGION AND OF AN EARNEST AND CONSTANT
GETT PREFACE(199) SALVATION WERE HEALTHY, VIRTUOUS, AND WISE, THE LAODICEANISM OF THE ORDINARY MAN MIGHT BE REGARDED AS A
JOAN PREFACE(35) THAT OF THE DOMINICANS WITH PRIESTLY LAZINESS AND LAODICEANISM , THAT OF THE JESUITS WITH PRIESTLY APATHY AND

LAP

GETT SD(261) MRS BRIDGENORTH PUTS THE TIMES DOWN IN HER LAP AND CONSIDERS COLLINS FOR A MOMENT. /MRS BRIDGENORTH/ DO
GETT (345) BEHIND HER, HE PICKS UP HER HAND FROM HER LAP AND KISSES IT OVER HER SHOULDER). /MRS GEORGE/ (WAKING)
POSN (440) SOME WICKED MAN STOLE. GO AND CRY IN YOUR MAMMY'S LAP . /STRAPPER/ (FURIOUS) YOU JOUNCE ME ANY MORE ABOUT
ARMS III SD(46) BALKAN LANDSCAPE, WITH A NEGLECTED NOVEL IN HER LAP . THE DOOR IS ON THE SAME SIDE AS THE STOVE, FARTHER
HART II (90) SIR, I HOPE I HAVNT HURT YOU PLUMPING INTO YOUR LAP LIKE THAT. (COMING TO HIM) I WAS LOOKING FOR YOU, SIR.
MIS. PREFACE(16) A MONTH OR TWO SPENT ELSEWHERE THAN IN A LADY'S LAP OR ROASTING ON A DRAWINGROOM HEARTHRUG. BESIDES, TO
6CAL PREFACE(89) NEXT MOMENT BLUBBERING LIKE A CHILD IN HIS WIFE'S LAP OR SNARLING LIKE A SAVAGE DOG AT A DAUNTLESS AND DEFIANT
CURE (234) (SATISFIED) HM! (SHE DROPS HER HANDS IN HER LAP). /REGINALD/ (WIPING HIS BROW) OH, THAT WAS FEARFULLY
CAND II (120) A MORE RESTFUL ATTITUDE WITH HER HANDS IN HER LAP). SOME DAY HE WILL KNOW: WHEN HE IS GROWN UP AND
BULL IV (146) HE WAS, THE PIG WAS UP HIS BACK AND OVER INTO HIS LAP ; AND BEDAD THE POOR BASTE DID CREDIT TO CORNY'S
HART I SD(44) READ SHAKESPEAR. PRESENTLY THE BOOK SINKS TO HER LAP ; HER EYES CLOSE; AND SHE DOZES INTO A SLUMBER. AN
CAND III (128) KNEES, WITH HIS HANDS CLASPED AND HIS ARMS ON HER LAP , AND SPEAKS WITH GROWING IMPULSE, HIS BLOOD BEGINNING
POSN (458) SETTIN ON THE GROUND WITH THE DEAD BODY ON HER LAP , STUPID-LIKE. THE HORSE WAS GRAZIN ON THE OTHER SIDE O

LAPDOG

HART I (81) /HECTOR/ (BITTERLY) I MIGHT AS WELL BE YOUR LAPDOG . /MRS HUSHABYE/ DO YOU WANT TO BE MY BREADWINNER,

LAPDOGS

JOAN 2 (85) HELPING MOTHER AT HOME. WHAT IS THINE? PETTING LAPDOGS AND SUCKING SUGARSTICKS. I CALL THAT MUCK. I TELL

LAPEL

MTH4 II SD(175) WITH MEASURED STEPS; PLACES HIS HAND IN HIS LAPEL IN THE TRADITIONAL MANNER; AND FIXES THE WOMAN WITH
SIM PRO,1, (25) HAS KEPT HIS WORD." (HE TIES THE LABEL TO THE LAPEL OF HIS COAT) WHERES THAT FOOL'S GUN? (HE OPENS A
O'FL (216) OUT HER HANDKERCHIEF; SPITS ON IT; AND SCRUBS HIS LAPEL WITH IT). OH, IT'S THE UNTIDY SLOVENLY ONE YOU ALWAYS

LAPELS

2TRU II SD(60) COSTUME AND BLACK SILKEN WRAP WITH WHITE SILK LAPELS : A CLERICAL TOUCH. /TALLBOYS/ (CONTINUING) AH,
CAPT II (262) SPOILS THE SIT OF IT. ALLOW ME. (SHE PULLS THE LAPELS OF HIS COAT VIGOROUSLY FORWARD) PUT BACK YOUR

LAPPED

AUGS (282) I WAS MY SISTER-IN-LAW AND THAT I WAS A HUN. HE LAPPED IT UP LIKE A KITTEN. . . . /AUGUSTUS/ YOU DONT MEAN

LAPPELL

CAND I (101) TOUCH ME. (MORELL GRASPS HIM POWERFULLY BY THE LAPPELL OF HIS COAT: HE COWERS DOWN ON THE SOFA AND SCREAMS

LAPPELS

NEVR I SD(218) DOUBLE BREASTED, AND WITH STOUT BUTTONS AND BROAD LAPPELS : A COAT FOR A SHIPYARD RATHER THAN A COUNTING
PHIL III (140) PARAMORE: THAT IS MY BUSINESS. (SHE GRASPS THE LAPPELS OF HIS COAT IN HER HANDS, AND LOOKS FIXEDLY AT HIM).
DEST SD(162) ALL EVENTS SHE WEARS NO JACKET WITH EXTRAVAGANT LAPPELS , NO GRECO-TALLIEN SHAM CHITON, NOTHING. INDEED,

LAPS

FANY I (278) BOBBY TAKES HIM. BUT HOLY JOE LIKES IT: FAIRLY LAPS IT UP LIKE A KITTEN, POOR OLD DEAR. WELL, BOBBY SAYS TO
LADY (240) INTO THRONES THOUGH THEY BE FIT ONLY FOR MEN'S LAPS MUST BE PUT AWAY. WHATS DONE CANNOT BE UNDONE. OUT, I
SUPR IV SD(142) COMES WITH AGE HAS ATTACKED HIS THROAT AND THE LAPS OF HIS CHEEKS; BUT HE IS STILL HARD AS AN APPLE ABOVE

ARMS II SD(37) AT HER. SHE FINISHES PACKING THE TRAY, AND LAPS THE CLOTH OVER THE EDGES, SO AS TO CARRY ALL OUT

LAPSE
BULL PREFACE(22) EDUCATED BY A PRIVATE GOVERNESS, WE SHOULD LAPSE INTO GROSS INTELLECTUAL SOTTISHNESS, AND PREFER
KING I (217) AGAIN? /CHARLES/ MR ROWLEY APOLOGIZES FOR HIS LAPSE INTO ROYALTY. ONLY, THE KING'S PERSON IS NOT TO BE
MRS PREFACE(179) 1902. P.S. (1930) ON READING THE ABOVE AFTER A LAPSE OF 28 YEARS, WITH THE BAN ON MRS WARREN WITHDRAWN AND
BASH PREFACE(88) THE SECOND ACT, ON READING OVER THE ABOVE AFTER A LAPSE OF THIRTY YEARS I AM NOT QUITE SO SURE AS I WAS THAT
3PLA PREFACE(R27) SUCH, IT WILL ASSUREDLY LOSE ITS GLOSS WITH THE LAPSE OF TIME, AND LEAVE THE DEVIL'S DISCIPLE EXPOSED AS THE
MIS. (164) DAMN YOU! (RECOVERING HIMSELF, HORRIFIED AT HIS LAPSE) I BEG YOUR PARDON; BUT SINCE WEVE BOTH FORGOTTEN

LAPSING
BUOY PREFACE(6) SO QUEER TO US TODAY, HE WAS NOT IN THE LEAST LAPSING FROM SCIENCE INTO SUPERSTITION: HE WAS LOOKING FOR
MRS IV (251) MAKE EITHER OF US HAPPY TOGETHER? /MRS WARREN/ (LAPSING RECKLESSLY INTO HER DIALECT) WE'RE MOTHER AND

LARFED
BARB II (299) AT ALL. ARF THE STREET PRYED; AN THE TATHER ARF LARFED FIT TO SPLIT THEIRSELVES. (TO BARBARA) THERE! ARE

LARFIN
PRES (148) FAIR CAUTION SHE IS. (CHUCKLING) COULDNT HELP LARFIN WHEN I SOR IM OP IT. /MITCHENER/ (HIGHLY INCENSED)

LARGE
BARB I (264) YOUR FAMILY. /UNDERSHAFT/ (SURPRISED) IS IT SO LARGE ? I AM SORRY TO SAY MY MEMORY IS FAILING VERY BADLY
MIS. (170) IN THE GUTTER? MY FATHER MAYNT HAVE BEEN IN AS LARGE A WAY AS YOU; BUT HE WAS BETTER CONNECTED; AND HIS
BULL IV (178) OUR YOUTH (HE WAFTS A WREATH OF CIGAR SMOKE AT LARGE ACROSS THE HILL). /KEEGAN/ COME, MR DOYLE! IS THIS
SUPR III SD(72) TAKE A SITUATION AS COOK OR PARLORMAID, WE MAKE LARGE ALLOWANCES FOR THEM. TO SUCH ALLOWANCES THE ABLEBODIED
BARB PREFACE(244) THEY WILL NOT MAKE ALLOWANCES. ALL MEN MAKE VERY LARGE ALLOWANCES INDEED BEFORE THEY STAKE THEIR OWN LIVES IN
BULL PREFACE(11) IN VILLAGE AND TRIBAL COMMUNITIES, AND A VERY LARGE ALLOY INDEED OF BRIGANDAGE IN OUR EXPLORATIONS AND
BARB I SD(249) UNDERSHAFT'S HOUSE IN WILTON CRESCENT. A LARGE AND COMFORTABLE SETTEE IS IN THE MIDDLE OF THE ROOM,
DOCT PREFACE(38) BUTCHERS SUPPLYING US WITH WHITE VEAL, AND WERE LARGE AND CONSTANT CONSUMERS OF PATE DE FOIE GRAS: BOTH
MRS PREFACE(177) HIGHEST PLACES IN CHURCH AND STATE) AND YOU GET A LARGE AND POWERFUL CLASS WITH A STRONG PECUNIARY INCENTIVE
GETT PREFACE(197) AS THE WORST TRICKS OF THE WORST NURSEMAIDS. LARGE AND SMALL FAMILIES. IN MOST HEALTHY FAMILIES THERE IS
CAPT I SD(235) TOWARDS ONE ANOTHER; MOUTH SET GRIMLY; NOSTRILS LARGE AND STRAINED: A FACE SET TO ONE TRAGIC PURPOSE. A MAN
DOCT PREFACE(38) ON ONE OCCASION I WAS INVITED TO SPEAK AT A LARGE ANTI-VIVISECTION MEETING IN THE QUEEN'S HALL IN
NEVR II (241) LARGE FOR THIS GENTLEMAN (INDICATING VALENTINE). LARGE APOLLINARIS FOR MR M'COMAS. /WAITER/ YES, SIR. /DOLLY/
POSN PREFACE(369) WITH A BUNCH OF CARNATIONS IN HIS BUTTONHOLE AS LARGE AS A DINNER-PLATE, WHICH WOULD HAVE MADE A BUNTHORNE
MTH5 (239) SHE HAS BITTEN A PIECE OUT OF HIS HAND NEARLY AS LARGE AS A FINGER NAIL: ENOUGH TO KILL TEN MEN. THERE IS NO
MTH3 SD(91) THE END WALL IS A SILVERY SCREEN NEARLY AS LARGE AS A PAIR OF FOLDING DOORS. THE DOOR IS ON YOUR LEFT
CLEO II SD(121) BEFORE THE IMAGE IS A BRONZE TRIPOD, ABOUT AS LARGE AS A THREE-LEGGED STOOL, WITH A STICK OF INCENSE
MRS I (197) DONT YOU KNOW US, SAM? THIS IS GEORGE CROFTS, AS LARGE AS LIFE AND TWICE AS NATURAL. DONT YOU REMEMBER ME?
DOCT PREFACE(77) STUFF TO BE TAKEN IN SPOONFULS OR IN PELLETS AS LARGE AS PEAS; AND PEOPLE WOULD NOT PAY AS MUCH FOR DROPS
2TRU III (94) THE POLITICAL PARTY FUNDS WILL BUY ME A HALO AS LARGE AS SWEETIE'S SUN HAT. THAT IS MY PROGRAM. WHAT HAVE
GETT SD(260) FURNITURE IS A CLOCK WITH A WOODEN DIAL ABOUT AS LARGE AS THE BOTTOM OF A WASHTUB. THE WEIGHTS, CHAINS, AND
MTH4 I (158) THE SKY TO BE ONLY THE CEILING OF A ROOM AS LARGE AS THE EARTH, WITH ANOTHER ROOM ON TOP OF IT. DEATH
GENV PREFACE(19) HIGHLY FLATTERING TO HANS, FRITZ, AND GRETCHEN AT LARGE AS WELL AS TO THE BEER DRINKERS IN THE CELLAR; AND
CAND I SD(78) WEDDING PRESENT), AND ON THE WALL ABOVE A LARGE AUTOTYPE OF THE CHIEF FIGURE IN TITIAN'S ASSUMPTION OF
JITT III SD(52) WIDOW FROM TIME TO TIME. THE ROOM IS LIGHTED BY A LARGE BAY WINDOW, WITH A WINDOW-SEAT UNDER IT. THE TABLE
BULL PREFACE(46) OF EXPLOSIVES FACTORIES. THEY HAVE TO HANDLE LARGE BODIES OF MEN WHOSE CARELESSNESS OR INSUBORDINATION
POSN PREFACE(408) OF PLAYS IS FREE FROM THE PRESSURE OF THAT LARGE BODY OF ENGLISH PUBLIC OPINION ALREADY ALLUDED TO,
BASH PREFACE(88) ONE EVEN IN THE THEATRE; FOR IT INCLUDES A LARGE BODY OF INTELLIGENT MANUAL AND OPEN AIR WORKERS AND
POSN PREFACE(371) AS A NEW PLAY, HE WOULD HAVE BEEN SUPPORTED BY A LARGE BODY OF PEOPLE TO WHOM INCEST IS A TABOOED SUBJECT
LION PREFACE(44) THAT THE BATTLE OF WATERLOO OCCURRED, OR THAT A LARGE BODY OF RUSSIAN TROOPS PASSED THROUGH ENGLAND IN 1914
MTH2 (63) ANYTHING I CAN SAY AGAINST DARWIN WILL PLEASE A LARGE BODY OF SINCERELY PIOUS VOTERS. IF IT WILL BE EASIER
WIDO III (56) THINK. HE LEFT A BOOK HERE FOR ME TO LOOK OVER: A LARGE BOOK IN A BLUE PAPER COVER. HAS THE GIRL PUT IT AWAY?
GETT SD(262) BRIDGENORTH IS A WELL SET UP MAN OF FIFTY, WITH LARGE BRAVE NOSTRILS, AN IRON MOUTH, FAITHFUL DOG'S EYES,
GETT (349) MAY I ASK WHY, LESBIA? /LESBIA/ (DRAWING A LARGE BREATH) TO THINK THAT AFTER ALL THE DANGERS OF THE
DOCT I SD(87) SOMETIMES RATHER ARID COMMON SENSE, HIS LARGE BUILD AND STATURE, THE ABSENCE OF THOSE ODD MOMENTS OF
INCA (250) TO RIDICULE HIS EFFORTS. /ERMYNTRUDE/ QUITE A LARGE CHOICE, EH? /THE INCA/ BUT VERY LITTLE TO CHOOSE.
DOCT PREFACE(68) EVERY SORT OF MEDICAL PRIVATE PRACTICE IN A LARGE CITY EXCEPT OBSTETRIC PRACTICE AND THE SURGERY OF
WIDO III (60) HIS. I SHOULD HARDLY FEEL JUSTIFIED IN MAKING A LARGE CLAIM FOR COMPENSATION UNDER EXISTING CIRCUMSTANCES.
BULL PREFACE(45) WHICH BUILDS UP THE CHARACTER AND RESOURCE OF THE LARGE CLASS OF CIVILIANS WHO LIVE BY IT, ONLY DEMORALIZES
GETT SD(273) MANNER AND SPEECH, BELONGING AS HE DOES TO THE LARGE CLASS OF ENGLISH GENTLEMEN OF PROPERTY (
MIS. PREFACE(22) POOR SCHOOLMASTERS, WITH THEIR SMALL SALARIES AND LARGE CLASSES, WERE AS MUCH PRISONERS AS WE WERE, AND MUCH
MIS. PREFACE(71) SOMETHING CAN BE DONE EVEN WITHIN CLASS LIMITS. LARGE COMMUNITIES OF CHILDREN OF THE SAME CLASS ARE POSSIBLE
LION PREFACE(63) SANITARY ARRANGEMENTS, ARMIES AND NAVIES. IN LARGE COMMUNITIES, WHERE EVEN THE MOST ECCENTRIC DEMANDS FOR
METH PREFACE(R39) BUT AN ANTHROPOMORPHIC IDOL: NO MATTER: PEOPLE AT LARGE COULD NOT CONCEIVE A GOD WHO WAS NOT ANTHROPOMORPHIC:
DEVL II SD(29) BASKETS IN THEIR MOUTHS, AND, AT THE CORNERS, TWO LARGE COWRIE SHELLS. A PRETTY FEATURE OF THE ROOM IS THE LOW
MIS. SD(115) IS, SHE HAS AN OPAQUE WHITE SKIN, BLACK HAIR, LARGE DARK EYES WITH BLACK BROWS AND LASHES, CURVED LIPS,
MTH1 II SD(20) FLAX. HER WHEEL, WHICH SHE TURNS BY HAND, IS A LARGE DISC OF HEAVY WOOD, PRACTICALLY A FLY-WHEEL. AT THE
HART PREFACE(14) MORE REASONABLE. BELGIUM AND FLANDERS, WHERE OVER LARGE DISTRICTS LITERALLY NOT ONE STONE WAS LEFT UPON
DOCT PREFACE(29) BY HAHNEMANN: TO WIT, THAT DRUGS WHICH IN LARGE DOSES PRODUCE CERTAIN SYMPTOMS, COUNTERACT THEM IN
BULL I SD(73) STOOL FOR ONE PERSON. IN THE MIDDLE OF THE ROOM A LARGE DOUBLE WRITING TABLE IS SET ACROSS, WITH A CHAIR AT
PYGM IV SD(261) THE CIRCULARS). ELIZA RETURNS WITH A PAIR OF LARGE DOWN-AT-HEEL SLIPPERS. SHE PLACES THEM ON THE CARPET
BULL I SD(73) CORNER IS A HATSTAND AND A TABLE CONSISTING OF LARGE DRAWING BOARDS ON TRESTLES, WITH PLANS, ROLLS OF
BARB II (303) CERTAINLY MOST CONVENIENT AND GRATIFYING TO ALL LARGE EMPLOYERS OF LABOR, MRS BAINES. /MRS BAINES/ BARBARA:
GETT PREFACE(233) CHOOSE WHICH MAN WILL OCCUPY THE PLACE THAT IS LARGE ENOUGH FOR ONE ONLY. HE IS SO FAR SHREWDLY
SIM I SD(36) THE OCEAN AND OF A BREAKWATER ENCLOSING A HARBOR, LARGE ENOUGH TO ACCOMMODATE A FLEET, BUT AT PRESENT
DEVL II SD(28) WARE, WITH MILK JUG AND BOWL TO MATCH, EACH LARGE ENOUGH TO CONTAIN NEARLY A QUART, ON A BLACK JAPANNED
GETT PREFACE(210) LARGE TO CLAIM ATTENTION, AND YET NOT LARGE ENOUGH TO ENABLE EVERY MAN TO HAVE TWO WIVES. EVEN IF
APPL PREFACE(195) HE WOULD NOT LISTEN TO YOU IF YOUR MIND WAS NOT LARGE ENOUGH TO GRASP THE IMMEDIATE NECESSITY FOR A NEW
DOCT PREFACE(54) THE PERCENTAGE DODGE. IN SOME HAMLET, BARELY LARGE ENOUGH TO HAVE A NAME, TWO PEOPLE ARE ATTACKED DURING
GETT PREFACE(242) THE NUMBER OF MEN WHO CANNOT AFFORD TO MARRY IS LARGE ENOUGH TO PRODUCE VERY SERIOUS SOCIAL RESULTS; AND THE
DOCT I (110) SHIPWRECKED MEN ON A RAFT-- A RAFT THAT IS BARELY LARGE ENOUGH TO SAVE THEM-- THAT WILL NOT SUPPORT ONE MORE.
DOCT PREFACE(58) ARE PREVENTIBLE; AND THEY ALREADY ARE TO A LARGE EXTENT PREVENTED. THE DANGERS OF INFECTION AND THE WAY
GETT PREFACE(197) SAFEGUARDS, SUCH AS THEY WERE. WE NO LONGER HAVE LARGE FAMILIES: ALL THE FAMILIES ARE TOO SMALL TO GIVE THE
MIS. PREFACE(12) SHOULD GO. THE OLD OBSERVATION THAT MEMBERS OF LARGE FAMILIES GET ON IN THE WORLD HOLDS GOOD BECAUSE IN
GETT PREFACE(197) SMALL ONES. IT USED TO BE SAID THAT MEMBERS OF LARGE FAMILIES GET ON IN THE WORLD; AND IT IS CERTAINLY TRUE
MIS. PREFACE(12) GET ON IN THE WORLD HOLDS GOOD BECAUSE IN LARGE FAMILIES IT IS IMPOSSIBLE FOR EACH CHILD TO RECEIVE
GETT PREFACE(197) SENTIMENTALITY IS MUCH MORE CHARACTERISTIC OF LARGE FAMILIES THAN SMALL ONES. IT USED TO BE SAID THAT
GETT PREFACE(197) IF THEY KEEP TO THEMSELVES. WHAT IS MORE, WHEN LARGE FAMILIES WERE THE FASHION, THEY WERE ORGANIZED AS
MIS. PREFACE(12) AS MUCH AS IF IT WERE ITS OWN FATHER. SMALL AND LARGE FAMILIES. THESE RIGHTS HAVE NOW BECOME MORE IMPORTANT
GETT PREFACE(227) ACTS OF ARTIFICIAL KINDNESS, MAY BE DEFEATED IN A LARGE FAMILY BY THE HEALTHY DERISION AND REBELLION OF
INCA (241) IS, NOT A SOUL ABOVE THE RANK OF A CURATE WITH A LARGE FAMILY WILL BE SEEN ENTERING IT. I SHAKE ITS DUST OFF
LIED (189) THING ABOUT THE WORLD, HENRY, YOUD KNOW THAT IN A LARGE FAMILY, THOUGH THE SISTERS QUARREL WITH ONE ANOTHER
ROCK PREFACE(170) TO ADD, TO HEREDITARY FIGURE HEADS). THERE IS A LARGE FIELD FOR TOLERATION HERE: THE CLEVER PEOPLE MUST
POSN SD(448) DAIS). SHERIFF KEMP COMES IN: A STOUT MAN, WITH LARGE FLAT EARS, AND A NECK THICKER THAN HIS HEAD. /ELDER
MRS I SD(188) FROM HIS STRONG FRAME, CLEAN-SHAVEN BULLDOG JAWS, LARGE FLAT EARS, AND THICK NECK: GENTLEMANLY COMBINATION OF
DOCT IV (164) BEEN REALLY SELFISH. NO ARTIST CAN: ART IS TOO LARGE FOR THAT. YOU WILL MARRY AGAIN, JENNIFER. /MRS
NEVR II (241) FOR THE CHILDREN AS USUAL, WILLIAM; AND ONE LARGE FOR THIS GENTLEMAN (INDICATING VALENTINE). LARGE
PRES (155) ISNT SHE SPLENDID! /MRS BANGER/ (RISING WITH A LARGE GESTURE) THIS VERY AFTERNOON I SHALL CAST OFF THIS
BULL I SD(73) DOOR IS OPENED, AND A VALET COMES IN LADEN WITH A LARGE GLADSTONE BAG AND A STRAP OF RUGS. HE CARRIES THEM
NEVR IV (292) WAVES HIS HAND IMPATIENTLY. THE WAITER PLACES A LARGE GLASS JUG AND THREE TUMBLERS IN THE MIDDLE). AND
CAND II (123) TO HAVE SPOKEN FOR THEM TONIGHT. THEYVE TAKEN THE LARGE HALL IN MARE STREET AND SPENT A LOT OF MONEY ON
GETT PREFACE(217) THAN THIS; BUT EVEN A FAMILY SOLICITOR, HOWEVER LARGE HIS PRACTICE, KNOWS NOTHING OF THE MILLION HOUSEHOLDS
CAPT II SD(242) IN THIS SEAT WOULD HAVE THE CHIEF ENTRANCE, A LARGE HORSESHOE ARCH, ON HIS LEFT, AND ANOTHER SADDLE SEAT
CURE SD(225) YOUNG MAN OF 22, IS PROSTRATE ON A SOFA IN A LARGE HOTEL DRAWING ROOM, CRYING CONVULSIVELY. HIS DOCTOR IS
BARB I SD(249) CONCEIVING THE UNIVERSE EXACTLY AS IF IT WERE A LARGE HOUSE IN WILTON CRESCENT, THOUGH HANDLING HER CORNER
GETT PREFACE(208) FOUR CHILDREN WOULD COST THEM MIGHT NOT BE VERY LARGE IF THE ADVANCE IN SOCIAL ORGANIZATION AND CONSCIENCE

SUPR III SD(73)	FOR MISCHIEF, IT IS JUST AS WELL THAT THEY ARE AT	LARGE	IN THE SIERRA, AND IN THE HANDS OF A CHIEF WHO LOOKS
DOCT PREFACE(20)	OCCASION. UNQUALIFIED PRACTITIONERS NOW MAKE	LARGE	INCOMES AS HYGIENISTS, AND ARE RESORTED TO AS
MIS. PREFACE(19)	BY ORGANIZED PROFESSIONAL ENTERPRISE IN	LARGE	INSTITUTIONS ESTABLISHED FOR THE PURPOSE. AND IT IS TO
BARB PREFACE(243)	OF SUCH VITAL IMPORTANCE THAT A LAWBREAKER AT	LARGE	IS HARDLY TO BE TOLERATED ON ANY PLEA. SUCH AN
MILL PREFACE(129)	THEIR COUNTRY AND AN ENRICHMENT OF THE WORLD AT	LARGE	. BUT PRIVATE PROPERTY IS NOT THE SUBJECT OF MY
INCA SD(244)	TRIM AT THE MIRROR, BEFORE THE MANAGER, WITH A	LARGE	JEWEL CASE IN HIS HAND, RETURNS, USHERING IN THE INCA.
INCA (245)	HAD SOME BUSINESS? /THE INCA/ (PRODUCING A VERY	LARGE	JEWEL CASE, AND RELAPSING INTO SOLEMNITY) I AM-
NEVR II (242)	POURING OUT WINE) 413, MADAM. (TO VALENTINE)	LARGE	LAGER FOR YOU, SIR. (TO GLORIA) 413, MISS. /DOLLY/ (
MRS I SD(181)	GARDEN, WITH ITS THATCHED ROOF AND PORCH, AND A	LARGE	LATTICED WINDOW TO THE LEFT OF THE PORCH. A PALING
FANY II (293)	REALLY. (SHE RISES AND STRETCHES HER ARMS WITH A	LARGE	LIBERATING BREATH) NOW THAT IT'S ALL OVER I'M RATHER
JOAN PREFACE(41)	SECOND, TO BEAR IN MIND THAT UNLESS THERE IS A	LARGE	LIBERTY TO SHOCK CONVENTIONAL PEOPLE, AND A WELL
SIM II (75)	CHURCH ASSEMBLY AT LAMBETH PALACE DECIDES BY A	LARGE	MAJORITY THAT THERE HAS BEEN A VISITATION. DISSENTING
DOCT PREFACE(20)	MORE ABOUT IT THAN THOSE DOCTORS (PROBABLY A	LARGE	MAJORITY) WHO ARE NOT INTERESTED IN IT, AND PRACTISE
BULL I SD(73)	ANYTHING THEY WANT LACKING. ON THE WALLS HANG A	LARGE	MAP OF SOUTH AMERICA, A PICTORIAL ADVERTISEMENT OF A
JOAN 6 (129)	SERIOUS, I MEAN NOTHING THAT MEN OF SUFFICIENTLY	LARGE	MIND TO CONDUCT AN INQUIRY LIKE THIS WOULD CONSIDER
ARMS II SD(28)	IN SPITE OF THE PUGNACIOUS HIGH BRIDGE AND	LARGE	NOSTRIL; HIS ASSERTIVE CHIN, WOULD NOT BE OUT OF PLACE
FANY II SD(287)	SHE IS A STRONG, SPRINGY GIRL OF EIGHTEEN, WITH	LARGE	NOSTRILS, AN AUDACIOUS CHIN, AND A GAILY RESOLUTE
LION I (118)	POWERFUL, CHOLERIC MAN IN THE PRIME OF LIFE, WITH	LARGE	NOSTRILS, STARING EYES, AND A THICK NECK: A MAN WHOSE
DOCT I (95)	I'D MADE SURE SHE'D HAVE AN EXCEPTIONALLY	LARGE	ONE. (HE SITS DOWN ON THE COUCH, SQUARING HIS
SUPR HANDBOK(191)	SMALL JOB WELL: HE MUDDLES RHETORICALLY THROUGH A	LARGE	ONE. WHEN A GREAT POLITICAL MOVEMENT TAKES PLACE, IT
GENV IV (91)	BE HERE. MY WILL IS PART OF THE WORLD'S WILL. A	LARGE	PART, AS IT HAPPENS. THE WORLD MOVES TOWARDS
ARMS I SD(3)	OF CHOCOLATE CREAMS, AND A MINIATURE EASEL WITH A	LARGE	PHOTOGRAPH OF AN EXTREMELY HANDSOME OFFICER, WHOSE
GENV II SD(49)	ROW OF PLASTER DOVES IN LOW RELIEF. THERE IS ONE	LARGE	PICTURE IN OILS, REPRESENTING A LIFESIZE PEACE, WITH
PYGM IV (265)	APPLE). YOU MIGHT MARRY, YOU KNOW. (HE BITES A	LARGE	PIECE OUT OF THE APPLE AND MUNCHES IT NOISILY). YOU
CAND I SD(78)	OF THE HALL DOOR, IS THE DRAWINGROOM, WITH ITS	LARGE	PLATE GLASS WINDOW LOOKING OUT ON THE PARK. IN THIS,
GETT PREFACE(209)	IT IS A SIMPLE MATTER OF NECESSITY; FOR IF A	LARGE	PROPORTION OF WOMEN WERE KILLED OR DISABLED, NO
GETT PREFACE(214)	MAY, PERHAPS, BE SUBTRACTED FOR THE PRESENT THE	LARGE	PROPORTION OF WOMEN WHO COULD NOT AFFORD THE EXTRA
GETT PREFACE(204)	THE PEOPLE ON SUCH OCCASIONS IS MOSTLY TO DRINK	LARGE	QUANTITIES OF BEER, OR, AMONG THE MORE LUXURIOUS
ROCK PREFACE(160)	UNNECESSARILY, AND TO PRIVILEGE THE	LARGE	RANGE OF INTOLERABLE MISCONDUCT THAT LIES OUTSIDE
DOCT PREFACE(12)	TO RECOMMEND OR PERFORM THE OPERATION AGAIN. THE	LARGE	RANGE OF OPERATIONS WHICH CONSIST OF AMPUTATING LIMBS
GETT (301)	(PETTING LEO, BUT SPEAKING TO THE COMPANY AT	LARGE	) BUT ISNT ALL THIS GREAT NONSENSE? WHAT LIKELIHOOD
PYGM III (254)	SILVERY LAUGHTER). /FREDDY/ (TO THE HEAVENS AT	LARGE	) WELL, I ASK YOU-- (HE GIVES IT UP, AND COMES TO MRS
HART I (57)	DEBT. BUT WHEN HE LAUNCHED OUT INTO BUSINESS ON A	LARGE	SCALE, HE HAD TO INCUR LIABILITIES. WHEN THE BUSINESS
BARB III (329)	HAVE YOU EVER TRIED? /UNDERSHAFT/ NOT ON A	LARGE	SCALE, MR LOMAX. BILTON WILL GIVE YOU A SAMPLE OF GUN
MIS. PREFACE(13)	WITH MUCH LESS DAMAGE THAN THE SINGLE CHILD. IN A	LARGE	SCHOOL THE SYSTEM MAY BE BAD; BUT THE PERSONAL
POSN PREFACE(368)	AND COMMON INFORMERS IN A COUNTRY WHERE A	LARGE	SECTION OF THE COMMUNITY STILL BELIEVES THAT ART OF
BULL IV (150)	A BILL LEGALIZING SUCH AN OPERATION. I BELIEVE A	LARGE	SECTION OF THE LIBERAL PARTY WOULD AVAIL THEMSELVES OF
MIS. PREFACE(6)	CREDIT LET HIS SON GO IN RAGS. ALSO, IN A VERY	LARGE	SECTION OF THE POPULATION, PARENTS FINALLY BECOME
HART II (87)	(HE THROWS HIMSELF BACK INTO THE BIG CHAIR WITH	LARGE	SELF-APPROVAL). NOW WHAT DO YOU THINK OF ME, MISS
APPL INTR,SD(243)	NEAR THE CORNER DIAGONALLY OPPOSITE, THERE IS A	LARGE	SETTEE IN THE MIDDLE OF THE ROOM. THE KING ENTERS AND
2TRU PREFACE(15)	JOINED THIS CATHOLIC CHURCH, LIKE A VERY	LARGE	SHIP ENTERING A VERY SMALL HARBOR, TO THE GREAT PERIL
DOCT PREFACE(68)	EVERY M.O.H. SHOULD AIM. BUT THE PROFESSION AT	LARGE	SHOULD NONE THE LESS WELCOME HIM AND SET ITS HOUSE IN
BULL IV (162)	(HOLDING HER WITH ONE ARM AND PRODUCING A	LARGE	SILK HANDKERCHIEF FROM HIS BREAST POCKET) HERES A
MRS PREFACE(151)	THAT ARE NOT MORE OR LESS VENAL. IF ON THE	LARGE	SOCIAL SCALE WE GET WHAT WE CALL VICE INSTEAD OF WHAT
BULL III SD(117)	MOST OF THE CROCKERY IS CROWDED UPON A	LARGE	SQUARE BLACK TRAY OF JAPANNED METAL. THE TEAPOT IS OF
SUPR HANDBOK(220)	OF PROMISCUOUS AMORISTIC MONOGAMY, IS FATAL TO	LARGE	STATES BECAUSE IT PUTS ITS BAN ON THE DELIBERATE
BARB PREFACE(236)	THEIR SWEATERS AND OPPRESSORS, THEY KNOW THAT THE	LARGE	SUBSCRIPTIONS WHICH HELP TO SUPPORT THE ARMY ARE
DOCT PREFACE(5)	AND THEN WEIGHT HIS DECISION WITH A BRIBE OF A	LARGE	SUM OF MONEY AND A VIRTUAL GUARANTEE THAT IF HE MAKES
BULL PREFACE(61)	DISREGARD FOR TRUTH AS TO MAKE IT EVIDENT THAT	LARGE	SUMS OF MONEY HAVE BEEN EXPENDED." MR FINDLAY IS ALSO
MRS PREFACE(172)	THE STRENGTH OF CHARACTER REQUIRED FOR HANDLING	LARGE	SUMS OF MONEY AND FOR STRICT SETTLEMENTS AND
WIDO III SD(58)	CHEERFULLY UNTIL THEY ARE ALL SEATED ROUND THE	LARGE	TABLE: TRENCH NEAREST THE FIREPLACE; COKANE NEAREST
CAND III SD(127)	LAMPS LIGHTED. THE TYPEWRITER IS IN ITS CASE: THE	LARGE	TABLE HAS BEEN CLEARED AND TIDIED: EVERYTHING
WIDO III SD(49)	IT ON A SMALL TABLE BETWEEN THEM. THERE IS A	LARGE	TABLE IN THE MIDDLE OF THE ROOM. LOOKING FROM IT
CAND I SD(78)	AT THIS MACHINE, WITH HER BACK TO THE WINDOW. THE	LARGE	TABLE IS LITTERED WITH PAMPHLETS, JOURNALS, LETTERS,
PYGM III (245)	DONT THEY? SMALL TALK INDEED! WHAT ABOUT YOUR	LARGE	TALK? REALLY, DEAR, YOU MUSTNT STAY. /HIGGINS/ I
DOCT PREFACE(30)	(A GREAT DEAL OF IT FROM SHEER GOOD NATURE) SO	LARGE	THAT AT FIRST SIGHT IT SEEMS UNACCOUNTABLE THAT THEY
MIS. PREFACE(70)	OR THE HOUSES OF THE VERY RICH, WHICH ARE SO	LARGE	THAT THE CHILDREN'S QUARTERS CAN BE KEPT OUT OF THE
GETT PREFACE(210)	A SURPLUS OF ADULT WOMEN WHICH IS SUFFICIENTLY	LARGE	TO CLAIM ATTENTION, AND YET NOT LARGE ENOUGH TO ENABLE
POSN PREFACE(386)	EMPIRES. THE LIMITS TO TOLERATION. BUT THE	LARGE	TOLERATION THESE CONSIDERATIONS DICTATE HAS LIMITS.
DOCT PREFACE(68)	ORGANIZED AT PRESENT ONLY IN HOSPITALS; THOUGH IN	LARGE	TOWNS THE PRACTICE OF CALLING IN THE CONSULTANT ACTS,
MIS. PREFACE(73)	THE COSTLY AND STRICTLY ENFORCED RESERVATION OF	LARGE	TRACTS OF COUNTRY AS DEER FORESTS AND BREEDING GROUNDS
DEST SD(152)	AT THE BACK TO THIS VINEYARD THAT IT IS ALMOST A	LARGE	VERANDA. THE BOLDER CHILDREN, MUCH EXCITED BY THE
JOAN EPIL,SD(152)	OF HIM CLOSE TO THE CORNER FARTHEST FROM HIM. A	LARGE	WATCHMAN'S RATTLE, HANDSOMELY DESIGNED AND GAILY
MTH3 (96)	MAY BE RIGHT IN THESE LITTLE DETAILS; BUT IN THE	LARGE	WE HAVE MANAGED TO HOLD OUR OWN AS A GREAT RACE. WELL,
DOCT III SD(131)	ACT III. IN DUBEDAT'S STUDIO. VIEWED FROM THE	LARGE	WINDOW THE OUTER DOOR IS IN THE WALL ON THE LEFT AT
KING I SD(161)	THE GARDEN FROM THE FIRST FLOOR THROUGH A	LARGE	WINDOW WHICH HAS AN IRON BALCONY OUTSIDE, WITH AN IRON
ARMS III SD(46)	A MOST COMFORTABLE SITTING ROOM. A ROW OF THREE	LARGE	WINDOWS SHEWS A MOUNTAIN PANORAMA, JUST NOW SEEN IN
CLEO PRO2,SD(102)	A NETWORK OF TINY WRINKLES, AND HER EYES OLD,	LARGE	, AND WISE; SINEWY HANDED, VERY TALL, VERY STRONG;
DEVL III SD(55)	OF HIGH MILITARY DISTINCTION. HIS EYES,	LARGE	, BRILLIANT, APPREHENSIVE, AND INTELLIGENT, ARE HIS
DOCT PREFACE(68)	THE HEALTH OF THE PATIENT OR OF THE COMMUNITY AT	LARGE	, BUT THE PROTECTION OF THE DOCTOR'S LIVELIHOOD AND
NEVR I (201)	WAS YOUR FIRST TOOTH, THE PRACTICE CANT BE VERY	LARGE	, CAN IT? /THE DENTIST/ NOT AS YET. (HE SHUTS THE
DEVL III SD(55)	CHAMBER IS READY FOR THE COURT MARTIAL. IT IS A	LARGE	, LOFTY ROOM, WITH A CHAIR OF STATE IN THE MIDDLE
KING I (185)	A THOUSAND MILES AWAY? /NEWTON/ IT IS VERY VERY	LARGE	, MADAM. IT IS ONE MILLION THREE HUNDRED THOUSAND
MIS. PREFACE(52)	LEARNT BEFORE HIS CONVICTION HOW TO LIVE AT	LARGE	, MAY REMEMBER HOW TO SET ABOUT IT, HOWEVER LAMED HIS
DEVL I SD(16)	HEADED BY THE SENIOR UNCLE, WILLIAM DUDGEON, A	LARGE	, SHAPELESS MAN, BOTTLE-NOSED AND EVIDENTLY NO ASCETIC
DOCT PREFACE(68)	OF THE MEDICAL PROBLEM, THEN, DEPENDS ON THE	LARGE	, SLOWLY ADVANCING, PETTISHLY RESISTED INTEGRATION OF
MIS. PREFACE(92)	AS IT SEEMS, THESE UNHAPPY LUNATICS ARE LEFT AT	LARGE	, UNREBUKED, EVEN ADMIRED AND REVERED, WHILST ARTISTS
MRS PREFACE(178)	OF THE DOUBT, I THEREFORE ADVISE THE PUBLIC AT	LARGE	, WHICH WILL FINALLY DECIDE THE MATTER, TO KEEP A

LARGELADY

PYGM EPILOG (298)	GALSWORTHY; AND GALSWORTHY EXPOSED THE VANITY OF	LARGELADY	PARK AND FINISHED HER. IT EXASPERATED HER TO THINK
PYGM EPILOG (297)	GIVE HER AN AIR OF BEING A GENUINE PRODUCT OF	LARGELADY	PARK. AND YET ITS TRADITION MADE HER REGARD A
PYGM EPILOG (293)	JOINTURE, A LAST RELIC OF THE OPULENCE OF	LARGELADY	PARK, HAD ENABLED HER TO STRUGGLE ALONG IN
PYGM I (212)	TAKER) HOW VERY CURIOUS! I WAS BROUGHT UP IN	LARGELADY	PARK, NEAR EPSOM. /THE NOTE TAKER/ (UPROARIOUSLY
PYGM EPILOG (299)	HE AND HIS ELIZA WERE THINKING OF BLACKENING THE	LARGELADY	SCUTCHEON BY OPENING A SHOP, HE FOUND THE LITTLE

LARGELY

GETT PREFACE(250)	IN SEVERAL COUNTRIES, THE REFORMATION WAS SO	LARGELY	A REBELLION AGAINST SACERDOTALISM THAT MARRIAGE WAS
GETT PREFACE(249)	TO MAKE IT HOLY, MARRIAGE WAS, AS IT STILL IS,	LARGELY	A SURVIVAL OF THE CUSTOM OF SELLING WOMEN TO MEN.
METH PREFACE(R57)	WERE DEVILS? WELL, CIRCUMSTANTIAL SELECTION IS	LARGELY	A THEORY OF COLLISIONS; THAT IS, A THEORY OF THE
LION PREFACE(95)	SATURATED WITH THIS TRADITION, JESUS HAS BEEN	LARGELY	ACCEPTED AS THE LONG EXPECTED AND OFTEN PROPHESIED
MIS. PREFACE(64)	BECAUSE BOTH SCHOOLS AND FAMILIES ARE MOSTLY VERY	LARGELY	ANARCHIC; PARENTS AND SCHOOLMASTERS ARE GOOD-NATURED
POSN PREFACE(394)	THE SUMMIT OF THEIR CATHEDRAL IN A CITY OCCUPIED	LARGELY	AND INFLUENTIALLY BY JEWS. COURT ETIQUET IS NO DOUBT
BASH PREFACE(91)	THEY WILL CONTINUE TO BE LOATHED AS THEY VERY	LARGELY	ARE AT PRESENT. BUT IF OUR CHILDREN, WHEN THEY HAVE
JOAN PREFACE(11)	FIGURE. CRIMINAL LUNATIC ASYLUMS ARE OCCUPIED	LARGELY	BY MURDERERS WHO HAVE OBEYED VOICES. THUS A WOMAN
DEST SD(150)	VALLEYS, AS HE KNOWS THE PALM OF HIS HAND; AND	LARGELY	BY THAT NEW FAITH OF HIS IN THE EFFICACY OF FIRING
BULL PREFACE(50)	TO ENTER IT. AND IN ENGLAND IT IS, IN FACT,	LARGELY	DEPENDENT FOR ITS RECRUITS ON THE REFUSE OF
JOAN PREFACE(20)	THEMSELVES WITHOUT PLENTY OF WOMEN. MEN ARE MORE	LARGELY	DISPENSABLE, AND ARE SACRIFICED ACCORDINGLY. WAS
GETT PREFACE(198)	WHICH FORMERLY TOOK EFFECT IN TYRANNY HAVE BEEN	LARGELY	DIVERTED INTO SENTIMENTALITY, AND THOUGH A LITTLE
GENV PREFACE(15)	ALTOGETHER DEFICIENT POLITICAL CAPACITY. IT IS	LARGELY	IGNORANCE OF FACTS, CREATING A VACUUM INTO WHICH ALL
PYGM PREFACE(200)	OXFORD AND ALL ITS TRADITIONS. IT MUST HAVE BEEN	LARGELY	IN HIS OWN DESPITE THAT HE WAS SQUEEZED INTO
APPL PREFACE(174)	MAGNUS'S LITTLE TACTICAL VICTORY, WHICH BULKS SO	LARGELY	IN THE PLAYHOUSE, LEAVES HIM IN A WORSE PLIGHT THAN
GENV PREFACE(9)	TERRITORY (BLOWING ITS CITIES TO SMITHEREENS	LARGELY	IN THE PROCESS) WE DISCOVERED THAT THE MANUFACTURE
POSN PREFACE(412)	AND SUPERSTITIONS WHICH NECESSARILY ENTER	LARGELY	INTO MORALITY AND PUBLIC OPINION, ARE ESSENTIAL TO
GENV IV (113)	DOES NOT AT PRESENT CONSIST EXCLUSIVELY OR EVEN	LARGELY	OF LIKEABLE PERSONS. /DEACONESS/ BUT I ASSURE YOU,
MTH2 (50)	WE DID KNOW WAS THAT YOUR GOVERNMENT WAS FORMED	LARGELY	OF MEN WHO REGARDED YOU AS A ROBBER OF HENROOSTS,
LADY PREFACE(233)	EXPRESS HIMSELF MORE FREELY IN PLAYS CONSISTING	LARGELY	OF MONOLOGUE TO BE SPOKEN BY A GREAT ACTOR FROM WHOM

DOCT PREFACE(64) TO WORK DAY AND NIGHT. IN PRACTICES WHICH CONSIST LARGELY OF WORKMEN'S CLUBS, AND IN WHICH THE PATIENTS ARE
BARB PREFACE(210) DENOUNCING THE IDOLIZED FORM AS UGLY HAS BEEN LARGELY QUOTED. THE ENGLISH CRITICS HAVE READ THAT SENTENCE;
LION PREFACE(72) THE FOLLOWING OF THE INNER LIGHT AT ALL COSTS IS LARGELY SELF-INDULGENCE, WHICH IS JUST AS SUICIDAL, JUST AS
CATH PREFACE(157) ART OF WRITING A FASHIONABLE PLAY HAD BECOME VERY LARGELY THE ART OF WRITING IT " ROUND" THE PERSONALITIES OF
MRS PREFACE(179) IN LONDON ON THE THAMES EMBANKMENT HAD TO DEAL LARGELY WITH WORKING MEN WHO HAD COME TO LONDON FROM THE
CAPT III (273) FANATICAL CHREESTIANITY OF THE AMERICANS. YE HAVE LARGELY YOURSELF TO THANK IF HE'S GONE. /LADY CICELY/ ALLAH

LARGENESS

CAND I SD(91) EYES, AND WELL SET MOUTH AND CHIN SIGNIFY LARGENESS OF MIND AND DIGNITY OF CHARACTER TO ENNOBLE HER

LARGER

MILL PREFACE(109) TO START WITH, OR POSSIBLY LESS, WHO MAKES LARGER AND LARGER PROFITS, AND INSPIRES MORE AND MORE
DOCT PREFACE(66) OF THE BEST CLASS; BUT THE RIGHT REMEDY IS A LARGER AREA AS THE SANITARY UNIT, MEDICAL ORGANIZATION.
MIS. PREFACE(79) A PET GOAT, FOUND THE ANIMAL IN THE HANDS OF A LARGER BOY THAN EITHER OF US, WHO MOCKED HIM AND REFUSED TO
GENV IV (96) TO OUR BELOVED BRITISH EMPIRE, AND UNDERTAKE ANY LARGER CARES THAT PROVIDENCE MAY IMPOSE ON US. MEANWHILE WE
PLES PREFACE(R10) BLIND, SO AS TO COMBINE AN EASIER DISGUISE WITH A LARGER CLAIM FOR SYMPATHY, SOMETHING MIGHT HAVE BEEN DONE.
POSN PREFACE(399) TENDENCY OF THE PLAY. THIS INDIFFERENCE TO THE LARGER ISSUES OF A THEATRICAL PERFORMANCE COULD NOT BE
BARB II (296) I PREFER SOBER WORKMEN. THE PROFITS ARE LARGER . /CUSINS/ -- HONEST-- /UNDERSHAFT/ HONEST WORKMEN
MIS. PREFACE(72) AS THE ART OF CANING. AND, AFTER ALL, IF LARGER LIBERTIES ARE ATTACHED TO THE ACQUISITION OF
POSN PREFACE(388) IS NO QUESTION HERE OF GIVING THE THEATRE ANY LARGER LIBERTIES THAN THE PRESS AND THE PLATFORM, OR OF
BARB PREFACE(225) LIKE HER, LEARNT IT BY TAKING THEIR PART IN THE LARGER LIFE OF THE NATION. BARBARA'S RETURN TO THE COLORS
BARB III (313) THAT HAS NOTHING TO DO WITH IT, DOLLY. THERE ARE LARGER LOVES AND DIVINER DREAMS THAN THE FIRESIDE ONES. YOU
SUPR I SD(17) AND AN ODD AIR OF CONTINUALLY ELBOWING AWAY SOME LARGER PERSON WHO IS CRUSHING HER INTO A CORNER. ONE GUESSES
DOCT V SD(172) BACK TO GET A MORE DISTANT VIEW OF ONE OF THE LARGER PICTURES. SHE HASTILY CLOSES THE BOOK AT THE SOUND;
POSN PREFACE(388) THAN THE PRESS AND THE PLATFORM, OR OF CLAIMING LARGER POWERS FOR SHAKESPEAR TO EULOGIZE BRUTUS THAN LORD
GETT PREFACE(191) GAMES WITH THEIR CHILDREN, THEIR PROSPECTS OF LARGER PROFITS OR HIGHER SALARIES, THEIR SATURDAY HALF
MILL PREFACE(109) WITH, OR POSSIBLY LESS, WHO MAKES LARGER AND LARGER PROFITS, AND INSPIRES MORE AND MORE CONFIDENCE IN HIS
MTH5 (231) EYES MORE PERFECT THAN OUR OWN, AND EARS WITH A LARGER RANGE OF SOUND; BUT THEY COULD NEITHER SEE NOR HEAR,
DOCT IV SD(160) MAN WOULD BE; AND HE IS NOT SCARED. HIS EYES LOOK LARGER ; AND HE IS SO WEAK PHYSICALLY THAT HE CAN HARDLY
BARB PREFACE(223) I CAN GATHER, THAT PEOPLE IN WHOM PASSION HAS A LARGER SCOPE ARE PASSIONLESS AND THEREFORE UNINTERESTING.
APPL PREFACE(185) ONE ANOTHER FOR OUR VOTES BY EACH PROMISING US A LARGER SHARE THAN THE OTHER OF THE PLUNDER OF THE MINORITY.
LADY (249) BE DOING IN EARNEST IN THE WORLD, WHICH IS BUT A LARGER STAGE. OF LATE, AS YOU KNOW, THE CHURCH TAUGHT THE
SUPR III SD(73) IMPOSING, PERHAPS BECAUSE THE SCENERY ADMITS OF A LARGER SWAGGER THAN PICCADILLY, PERHAPS BECAUSE OF A CERTAIN
MIS. PREFACE(5) ME WITH A BIBLE WITH A GILT CLASP AND EDGES, LARGER THAN BIBLES SIMILARLY PRESENTED TO MY SISTERS,
MTH4 III SD(195) AND AGAIN VAGUE AND SHADOWY: ABOVE ALL, SHE IS LARGER THAN LIFE-SIZE, NOT ENOUGH TO BE MEASURED BY THE
MIS. PREFACE(41) USE MONEY. THE CONSEQUENCES ARE OF COURSE MUCH LARGER THAN THE MERE ABILITY TO READ THE NAME OF A STREET OR
GETT PREFACE(253) THAT THE PROPORTION OF CHILDLESS DIVORCES IS MUCH LARGER THAN THE PROPORTION OF DIVORCES FROM ALL CAUSES. BUT
GLIM (176) DOLT. CAN YOU NOT REASON? IF THE SUM WERE LARGER YOUR BARON WOULD WIN IT BY KILLING ME HIMSELF AND

LARGE-MINDED

BULL PREFACE(14) OF THEMSELVES WITH THE MOST TOLERANT AND LARGE-MINDED GOODHUMOR, THEY WERE PERFECTLY WILLING TO ALLOW
GENV IV (113) I UNDERSTOOD THE SECRETARY TO IMPLY THAT HOWEVER LARGE-MINDED YOUR VIEW OF THE BROTHERHOOD OF MANKIND, YOU

LARGEST

SUPR HANDBOK(206) OF TO THOSE WHO KNOW WHAT IT IS, EVEN WITH THE LARGEST DISCOUNT FOR THE RESTRAINTS OF POVERTY ON THE POOR
SUPR III (100) YOU EVER BEEN IN THE COUNTRY WHERE I HAVE THE LARGEST FOLLOWING? ENGLAND. THERE THEY HAVE GREAT
PHIL II (113) BUY ANIMALS WITH, BESIDES HAVING THE RUN OF THE LARGEST HOSPITAL IN ITALY, (WITH DESPERATE RESOLUTION) BUT
PPP (200) UP A HUGE SLICE) TAKE THIS, ADOLPHUS: IT IS THE LARGEST (SHE CRAMS IT INTO HIS MOUTH). /FITZ/ HA! A LUMP
CAPT III SD(272) MOORISH WINDOWS HIGH UP IN THE ADOBE WALLS OF THE LARGEST ROOM IN LESLIE RANKIN'S HOUSE. A CLEAN COOL ROOM,
GETT SD(259) LOOK NORTH AND SOUTH. THE NORTH WINDOW IS THE LARGEST ; AND IF WE LOOK INTO THE KITCHEN THROUGH IT WE SEE
LION PREFACE(56) MENTIONED, AND THE ADDITIONAL ANOMALY THAT THE LARGEST SHARE WENT TO THE PEOPLE WHO DID NOT WORK AT ALL,
SIM PREFACE(8) IT. IT HAPPENS, HOWEVER, THAT IN ONE OF THE LARGEST STATES IN THE WORLD, RUSSIA, THE CHILDREN ARE

LARK

OVER (177) /MRS JUNO/ OR WAS IT THE USUAL AIMLESS MAN'S LARK : A MERE SHIPBOARD FLIRTATION? /GREGORY/ OH NO, NO:
OVER PREFACE(163) DOES NOT, AS IN ROMEO AND JULIET, RISE WITH THE LARK : THE WHOLE NIGHT OF LOVE IS PLAYED BEFORE THE
DOCT I (97) (ARCHLY) AHA! HA HA! AHA! (TRILLING LIKE A LARK AS HE SHAKES HIS FINGER AT WALPOLE). YOU REMOVED HER
LADY PREFACE(220) IN SHAKESPEAR'S LATEST WORKS. " HARK, HARK! THE LARK AT HEAVEN'S GATE SINGS" IS NOT THE LYRIC OF A BROKEN
2TRU II (78) LADY AS A NATIVE SERVANT? BEING A SERVANT IS NO LARK . ANSWER ME. DONT STAND THERE TRYING TO INVENT A LIE.
BARB I (270) HALF THE ARMY CAME TO THEIR FIRST MEETING FOR A LARK . (RISING) COME ALONG. (SHE THROWS HER ARM ROUND HER
APPL INTRLUD(252) AS ENCHANTING AS YOU; AND THEN WHAT A GLORIOUS LARK LIFE WILL BE! BUT AT PRESENT, WHAT I COME HERE FOR IS
FANY III (304) AS LONG AS IT IS UNDERSTOOD THAT IT IS ONLY A LARK OR A SLIP, BUT TO GO ON THE LOOSE ON PRINCIPLE; TO TALK
FANY III (304) AND I DONT PRETEND TO. I CAN UNDERSTAND A LARK ; I CAN FORGIVE A SLIP; AS LONG AS IT IS UNDERSTOOD
BARB I SD(260) LOMAX LIKES SARAH AND THINKS IT WILL BE RATHER A LARK TO MARRY HER. CONSEQUENTLY HE HAS NOT ATTEMPTED TO
HART I (59) ABOUT MANGAN: YOUD HAVE THOUGHT IT QUITE A LARK TO MARRY HIM. /ELLIE/ (BLUSHING VIVIDLY) HESIONE: YOU
FANY III (303) WALKS STRAIGHT UP TO HIM). I DIDNT DO IT FOR A LARK , BOB; I DID IT OUT OF THE VERY DEPTHS OF MY NATURE. I
2TRU II (78) YOU DONT UNDERSTAND ENGLISH? /THE PATIENT/ FOR A LARK , COLONEL. /TALLBOYS/ THATS NOT GOOD ENOUGH. WHY HAVE
OVER (182) THAT WAS WHY I MARRIED HIM. THEN IT BECAME A MILD LARK , HARDLY WORTH THE TROUBLE. AFTER THAT I FOUND IT
SIM I (45) /THE CLERGYMAN/ (TEMPTED) IT WOULD BE RATHER A LARK , WOULDNT IT? /MRS HYERING/ THATS RIGHT, MR
MRS I (194) MOTHER? /PRAED/ YES. /FRANK/ BY JOVE! WHAT A LARK ! DO YOU THINK SHE'LL LIKE ME? /PRAED/ IVE NO DOUBT
HART I (64) MARCUS DARNLEY. /MRS HUSHABYE/ (RISING) WHAT A LARK ! HE IS MY HUSBAND. /ELLIE/ BUT HOW-- (SHE STOPS
ROCK I (222) UNEMPLOYED WITH ALOYSIA AND TOFFY. /DAVID/ SUCH A LARK ! /FLAVIA/ WE SAW A POLICE CHARGE. DAVID WAS ARRESTED.
PYGM V (272) HE DOES! WHEW! (BRIGHTENING SUDDENLY) WHAT A LARK ! /PICKERING/ A SAFE THING FOR YOU, DOOLITTLE. THEY
HART I (52) ME EVEN WORTH MENTIONING! /MRS HUSHABYE/ WHAT A LARK ! SIT DOWN (SHE PUSHES HER BACK INTO THE CHAIR

LARKLIKE

SUPR II SD(57) DELIBERATION. SURPRISED BY THIS BURST OF LARKLIKE MELODY, AND JARRED BY A SARDONIC NOTE IN ITS

LARKS

JOAN 6 (145) I COULD STILL HEAR THE WIND IN THE TREES, THE LARKS IN THE SUNSHINE, THE YOUNG LAMBS CRYING THROUGH THE
MIS. PREFACE(26) ADMIT THAT IF THE SKY FELL WE SHOULD ALL CATCH LARKS . BUT I DO NOT PROPOSE TO BOTHER ABOUT A SUPPLY OF
MTH2 (73) I HOPE, THAT IF THE SKY FELL WE SHOULD ALL CATCH LARKS . /FRANKLYN/ YOUR TURN NOW, CONRAD. GO AHEAD. /CONRAD/
MRS II (199) DO COME TO VIENNA WITH ME? IT'D BE EVER SUCH LARKS . /MRS WARREN/ NO, THANK YOU. VIENNA IS NO PLACE FOR
LION I (110) AND WAIT). NOW THEN, YOU CHRISTIANS, NONE OF YOUR LARKS . THE CAPTAIN'S COMING. MIND YOU BEHAVE YOURSELVES. NO
SUPR HANDBOK(195) THAT IF THE SKY FALLS WE SHALL ALL CATCH LARKS . WE ARE NOT GOING TO TREAD THOSE PATHS: WE HAVE NOT

LARKY

FANY III (303) SEE THERE WAS NO HARM IN IT. BUT YOURE NOT THE LARKY SORT. AT LEAST YOU USENT TO BE. /MARGARET/ I'M NOT;

LARN

ROCK PREFACE(156) INVENTED TO PUNISH HIM FOR BEING A TRAITOR (OR " LARN HIM TO BE A TOAD"); AND THIS SENTENCE HAS BEEN PASSED,
GENV PREFACE(11) THIRD. VILLAGES IN INDIA ARE STILL WIPED OUT TO " LARN " THEIR MOSTLY HARMLESS INHABITANTS NOT TO SNIPE AT

LARNT

BULL II (100) OF. SURE HE HAD TO BE A FREETHINKER WHEN HE LARNT A THRADE AND WENT TO LIVE IN THE TOWN. /KEEGAN/ WELL,

LAROCHEFOUCAULD

CAND I (97) THAT! /MORELL/ (BUOYANTLY) I KNOW IT, MY LAD. LAROCHEFOUCAULD SAID THAT THERE ARE CONVENIENT MARRIAGES BUT

LAROCHEFOUCAULD'S

HART PREFACE(11) LOVE DID NOTHING BUT PROVE THE SOUNDNESS OF LAROCHEFOUCAULD'S SAYING THAT VERY FEW PEOPLE WOULD FALL IN

LAROCHEJAQUELIN

HART I (62) -- DE ROUGEMONT? /ELLIE/ (INNOCENTLY) NO: DE LAROCHEJAQUELIN , A FRENCH FAMILY. A VICOMTE. HIS LIFE HAS

LARRY

BULL III	(121)	SAME TO ME. HE USED TO BE VERY CIVIL TO MASTHER	LARRY	: A DEAL TOO CIVIL, I USED TO THINK. NOW HE'S AS SURLY
BULL I	(92)	CHARACTER. A CATERPILLAR-- /BROADBENT/ LOOK HERE,	LARRY	: DONT BE AN ASS. /DOYLE/ (INSISTING) I SAY A
BULL III	(124)	SENTIMENTALITY, ANYHOW. /BROADBENT/ THAT IS TRUE,	LARRY	: I ADMIT IT. HER VOICE HAS A MOST EXTRAORDINARY
BULL I	(91)	TO THE IRISH, BUT TO OUR ENGLISH GLADSTONE. NO,	LARRY	: I CANT HELP THINKING THAT THERES SOMETHING BEHIND
BULL III	(144)	WHATS TO GRIEVE THEM? /BROADBENT/ I DIVINED IT,	LARRY	: I SAW IT IN THEIR FACES. IRELAND HAS NEVER SMILED
BULL IV	(178)	BELIEVE ME, I'M ON YOUR SIDE. DONT SNEER,	LARRY	: I USED TO READ A LOT OF SHELLEY YEARS AGO. LET US BE
BULL III	(144)	THINK OF WHAT IT MEANS! (IMPRESSIVELY)	LARRY	: WE ARE IN THE PRESENCE OF A GREAT NATIONAL GRIEF.
BULL III	(125)	NOT WISELY BUT TOO LITTLE. /BROADBENT/ (FURIOUS)	LARRY	: YOU-- YOU-- YOU DISGUST ME. YOU ARE A DAMNED FOOL. (
BULL I	(96)	AH YES, I SUPPOSE SO. (WITH FEELING, SEVERELY)	LARRY	: YOUVE TREATED THAT POOR GIRL DISGRACEFULLY. /DOYLE/
BULL II	(112)	SHE SEES A MAN APPROACHING. /NORA/ IS THAT YOU,	LARRY	? (FRIGHTENED A LITTLE) WHO'S THAT? /BROADBENT/ (
BULL III	(126)	NODS INDEPENDENTLY. /DORAN/ HOWS YOURSELF,	LARRY	? /LARRY/ FINELY, THANK YOU. NO NEED TO ASK YOU. (
BULL III	(126)	WERE YEVER THINKIN O GOIN INTO PARLIAMENT AT ALL,	LARRY	? /LARRY/ ME! /FATHER DEMPSEY/ (ENCOURAGINGLY) YES,
BULL III	(126)	/BROADBENT/ DO YOU THINK IT WILL BEAR TWO,	LARRY	? /LARRY/ PERHAPS NOT. DONT MOVE. I'LL STAND. (HE
BULL IV	(158)	HER TEARS) IS THAT ALL YOU HAVE TO SAY TO ME,	LARRY	? /LARRY/ WELL, WHAT IS THERE TO SAY? YOU SEE, WE
BULL III	(129)	BUT SURE LARRY'S AS GOOD AS ENGLISH: ARNT YOU,	LARRY	? /LARRY/ YOU MAY PUT ME OUT OF YOUR HEAD, FATHER,
BULL II	(114)	YOU MEAN THAT IT'S AN ACT OF TREACHERY TO	LARRY	? /NORA/ DEED I DONT. WHAT HAS LARRY TO DO WITH IT..
BULL IV	(157)	D'YE THINK HE'D LEND ME 300 POUNDS ON THE FARM,	LARRY	? WHEN I'M SO HARD UP, IT SEEMS A WASTE O MONEY NOT
BULL I	(84)	ABOUT. /BROADBENT/ WHATS WRONG WITH YOU TODAY,	LARRY	? WHY ARE YOU SO BITTER? DOYLE LOOKS AT HIM
BULL III	(144)	GOING TO TAKE IT TO MR HAFFIGAN'S (HE GIVES	LARRY	A SLAP ON THE SHOULDERS THAT SENDS HIM STAGGERING OFF
BULL III	SD(123)	WATCHES HER UNTIL SHE DISAPPEARS; THEN COMES TO	LARRY	AND ADDRESSES HIM WITH SUDDEN INTENSITY. /BROADBENT/
BULL III	SD(117)	THE OFFICE." THIS CHAIR, LIKE THE TWO OCCUPIED BY	LARRY	AND BROADBENT, HAS A MAHOGANY FRAME AND IS UPHOLSTERED
BULL IV	(169)	FOR THEMSELVES. I THINK I'LL GO IN NOW. I SEE	LARRY	AND MR KEEGAN COMING UP THE HILL; AND I'M NOT FIT TO
BULL IV	SD(158)	A RESOLUTE AIR THAT BODES TROUBLE FOR CORNELIUS).	LARRY	AND NORA ARE LEFT TOGETHER FOR THE FIRST TIME SINCE
BULL III	SD(117)	ACT III. NEXT MORNING BROADBENT AND	LARRY	ARE SITTING AT THE ENDS OF A BREAKFAST TABLE IN THE
BULL IV	(167)	HAVE DONE AT ALL, NOT AT ALL. YOU DONT KNOW	LARRY	AS I DO, MY DEAR. HE HAS ABSOLUTELY NO CAPACITY FOR
BULL IV	(146)	/DORAN/ BEDAD, MAAM, SHE'S HURT BEHIND NOW; FOR	LARRY	BOWLED HER OVER LIKE A SKITTLE. (GENERAL DELIGHT AT
BULL IV	(146)	LAUGH AT, MR DORAN. /DORAN/ BEDAD, MISS REILLY,	LARRY	CLEARED SIX YARDS SIDEWAYS AT WAN JUMP IF HE CLEARED
BULL III	(143)	AND RECOMPOSES HIMSELF AS A VALET. BROADBENT AND	LARRY	COME THROUGH THE SHRUBBERY. HODSON MOVES ASIDE TO THE
BULL III	SD(126)	BROADBENT RESUMES HIS SEAT ON THE RUSTIC BENCH.	LARRY	CROSSES TO THE BENCH AND IS ABOUT TO SIT DOWN BESIDE
BULL	PREFACE(19)	ALL ENGLISHMEN TO THIS DAY. IT IS THE FORMULA OF	LARRY	DOYLE FOR TOM BROADBENT IN MY PLAY, IN SPITE OF
BULL IV	(146)	BOULD ENGLISH BOYOH IN FRONT AT THE MACHINERY, N	LARRY	DOYLE IN THE ROAD STARTIN THE INJINE WID A BED WINCH.
BULL III	(135)	SEE THE SIMPLE EXPLANATION OF ALL THIS. MY FRIEND	LARRY	DOYLE IS A MOST BRILLIANT SPEAKER; BUT HE'S A TORY: AN
BULL III	(120)	GRUDGINGLY ADMITTING IT) I SUPPOSE HE'LL BE YOUNG	LARRY	DOYLE THAT WAS. /LARRY/ YES. /MATTHEW/ (TO LARRY) I
BULL IV	(171)	I'D NEVER SEEN YOU. SO GOODBYE TO YOU, MISTER	LARRY	DOYLE. (SHE TURNS HER BACK ON HIM AND GOES HOME).
BULL III	(139)	(HUFFILY) I DONT NEED TO BE INSTHRUCTED BE YOU,	LARRY	DOYLE. SOME PEOPLE THINK NO ONE KNOWS ANYTHIN BUT
BULL II	SD(101)	WOMAN, WHOM HE WOULD EVEN CALL ETHEREAL. TO	LARRY	DOYLE, AN EVERYDAY WOMAN FIT ONLY FOR THE EIGHTEENTH
BULL III	(132)	YOUR PRIEST TO DEAL WITH THIS YOUNG MAN. NOW,	LARRY	DOYLE, WHATEVER THE BLESSED ST PETER WAS CRUCIFIED
BULL IV	SD(151)	LARRY, AND CORNELIUS ARE LEFT IN THE PARLOR.	LARRY	GOES TO THE THRESHOLD AND WATCHES THE SCENE IN THE
BULL III	SD(126)	CHAIR FROM IT, PLACING IT NEAR THE BASKET; BUT	LARRY	HAS ALREADY TAKEN THE CHAIR FROM THE OTHER END AND
BULL II	(114)	I'M BOUND TO TELL YOU, MISS REILLY, THAT	LARRY	HAS NOT ARRIVED IN ROSSCULLEN YET. HE MEANT TO GET
BULL II	(112)	ISNT IT? /BROADBENT/ LOVELY. I MUST EXPLAIN WHY	LARRY	HAS NOT COME HIMSELF. /NORA/ WHY SHOULD HE COME? HE'S
BULL II	(113)	MUCH IN EARNEST ABOUT YOU AND ABOUT LARRY. /NORA/	LARRY	HAS NOTHING TO DO WITH ME, MR BROADBENT. /BROADBENT/
BULL III	(138)	/CORNELIUS/ (RUEFULLY) I'D SET ME MIND ON	LARRY	HIMSELF FOR THE SEAT; BUT I SUPPOSE IT CANT BE HELPED.
BULL III	(135)	A STRONG DASH OF TORYISM IN THE IRISH CHARACTER.	LARRY	HIMSELF SAYS THAT THE GREAT DUKE OF WELLINGTON WAS THE
BULL IV	(146)	THE GORDN BENNETT. /NORA/ (REPROACHFULLY) AND	LARRY	IN FRONT OF IT AND ALL! IT'S NOTHIN TO LAUGH AT, MR
BULL IV	(179)	CONCEIVE AN IRISHMAN PITYING ENGLAND; BUT AS	LARRY	INTERVENES ANGRILY, HE GIVES IT UP AND TAKES TO THE
BULL I	(81)	BE THERE HALF AN HOUR BEFORE THE THRAIN STARTS. (	LARRY	IS HEARD AT THE BEDROOM DOOR, RETURNING). WHISHT: HE'S
BULL II	SD(112)	STRAINING HER EYES IN THE MOONLIGHT, WATCHING FOR	LARRY	. AT LAST SHE GIVES IT UP WITH A SOB OF IMPATIENCE,
BULL IV	(171)	(WITH CONVICTION) YOU WERE RIGHT THIS MORNING,	LARRY	. I MUST FEED UP NORA. SHE'S WEAK; AND IT MAKES HER
BULL IV	(180)	IN HAND? /BROADBENT/ I DONT AGREE WITH THAT,	LARRY	. I THINK THESE THINGS CANNOT BE SAID TOO OFTEN: THEY
BULL III	(133)	(MAKING A WRY FACE) DONT BE PARADOXICAL,	LARRY	. IT REALLY GIVES ME A PAIN IN MY STOMACH. /LARRY/
BULL I	(96)	COURSE NOT. WE OUGHT TO BE ASHAMED OF OURSELVES,	LARRY	. (MORE AND MORE CARRIED AWAY BY HIS NEW FANCY). YOU
BULL III	(122)	THEN! /AUNT JUDY/ AH, YOURE NEVER SATISFIED,	LARRY	. (TO NORA) COME ON, ALANNA, AN MAKE THE PASTE FOR
BULL I	(86)	MATTER-OF-FACTLY) THE USUAL THING IN THE COUNTRY,	LARRY	. JUST THE SAME HERE. /DOYLE/ (HASTILY) NO, NO: THE
BULL III	(126)	HANDS). /CORNELIUS/ GIVE FATHER DEMPSEY A CHAIR,	LARRY	. MATTHEW HAFFIGAN RUNS TO THE NEAREST END OF THE
BULL III	(124)	ANGEL. YOU REALLY HAVE COARSE TASTES IN THAT WAY,	LARRY	. MISS REILLY IS ONE OF THE FINER TYPES: A TYPE RARE
BULL III	(128)	GO ON. /CORNELIUS/ WELL, YOU SEE HOW IT IS,	LARRY	. ROUND ABOUT HERE, WEVE GOT THE LAND AT LAST; AND WE
BULL III	SD(131)	NOTHING LESS THAN THE SUMMARY EXCOMMUNICATION OF	LARRY	. /LARRY/ HOW IS THE MAN TO MARRY AND LIVE A DECENT
BULL III	(123)	ADDRESSES HIM WITH SUDDEN INTENSITY. /BROADBENT/	LARRY	. /LARRY/ WHAT IS IT? /BROADBENT/ I GOT DRUNK LAST
BULL II	(113)	BESIDES, IVE HEARD A GREAT DEAL ABOUT YOU FROM	LARRY	. /NORA/ (WITH BITTER INDIFFERENCE) HAVE YOU NOW?
BULL II	(113)	I'M VERY MUCH IN EARNEST ABOUT YOU AND ABOUT	LARRY	. /NORA/ LARRY HAS NOTHING TO DO WITH ME, MR
BULL IV	(165)	YOU WHO HAVE NO FEELING. YOURE AS HEARTLESS AS	LARRY	. /NORA/ WHAT DO YOU EXPECT ME TO DO? IS IT TO THROW
BULL I	(88)	EARNESTNESS BY DOYLE'S ELOQUENCE) NEVER DESPAIR,	LARRY	. THERE ARE GREAT POSSIBILITIES FOR IRELAND. HOME RULE
BULL III	(133)	IN THE GREATEST ASTONISHMENT) YOU AMAZE ME,	LARRY	. WHO WOULD HAVE THOUGHT OF YOUR COMING OUT LIKE
BULL III	(121)	INDEPENDENT NOW. /NORA/ IT'S MADE A GREAT CHANGE,	LARRY	. YOUD HARLY KNOW THE OLD TENANTS NOW. YOUD THINK IT
BULL IV	(178)	ITS SECOND BANKRUPTCY EFFICIENTLY (BROADBENT AND	LARRY	LOOK QUICKLY AT ONE ANOTHER; FOR THIS, UNLESS THE
BULL II	(99)	OATH AN SOUL I WASNT: I WAS WAITN TO MEET MASTHER	LARRY	N CARRY HIS LUGGAGE FROM THE CAR; N I FELL ASLEEP ON
BULL I	(93)	/BROADBENT/ (ATTENTIVELY, BEGINNING TO SUSPECT	LARRY	OF MISCONDUCT WITH NORA, AND RESOLVING TO GET TO THE
BULL III	SD(125)	THE WAY. THE PRIEST COMES TO THE TABLE AND SLAPS	LARRY	ON THE SHOULDER. LARRY, TURNING QUICKLY, AND
BULL III	SD(119)	AIR OF A WOMAN ACCUSTOMED TO HAVE NOTHING TO DO.	LARRY	RETURNS FROM THE SHRUBBERY. /BROADBENT/ GOOD MORNING,
BULL III	SD(117)	FRAME AND IS UPHOLSTERED IN BLACK HORSEHAIR.	LARRY	RISES AND GOES OFF THROUGH THE SHRUBBERY WITH HIS
BULL IV	(167)	FOR; AND I WAS FOOLISH ENOUGH ONCE TO THINK THAT	LARRY	-- /BROADBENT/ (DISPOSING OF THE IDEA AT ONCE)
BULL III	(120)	LARRY DOYLE THAT WAS. /LARRY/ YES. /MATTHEW/ (TO	LARRY	) I HEAR YOU DONE WELL IN AMERICA. /LARRY/ FAIRLY
BULL IV	(180)	TOO MUCH HONOR, SIR. (WITH PRIESTLY HUMILITY TO	LARRY	) MR DOYLE: I AM TO BLAME FOR HAVING UNINTENTIONALLY
BULL IV	(157)	RIGHT AFTER ALL. IT'S A CONTRAIRY WORLD. (TO	LARRY	) WHY WOULD YOU BE SUCH A FOOL AS TO LET BROADBENT
BULL III	(139)	HODSON-- /HODSON/ (COMING BETWEEN BROADBENT AND	LARRY	) YES, SIR? /BROADBENT/ I WANT YOU TO BE RATHER
BULL III	(140)	GIVE HIM A HAND WITH THE PIG IF NECESSARY. COME,	LARRY	; AND HELP ME. (HE RUSHES AWAY THROUGH THE
BULL II	(114)	SERIOUS. TELL ME THAT I'M INTERFERING WITH	LARRY	; AND I'LL GO STRAIGHT FROM THIS SPOT BACK TO LONDON
BULL III	SD(126)	THE BENCH). THEY ARE ALL NOW SEATED, EXCEPT	LARRY	; AND THE SESSION ASSUMES A PORTENTOUS AIR, AS IF
BULL I	(92)	AWE). I DONT WISH TO BE IMPERTINENT, AS YOU KNOW,	LARRY	; BUT ARE YOU SURE SHE HAS NOTHING TO DO WITH YOUR
BULL I	(91)	(SHREWDLY) I DONT WANT TO INTERRUPT YOU,	LARRY	; BUT YOU KNOW THIS IS ALL GAMMON. THESE DIFFERENCES
BULL II	SD(107)	IN HONOR OF THE OCCASION. SHE LOOKS ROUND FOR	LARRY	; IS PUZZLED; THEN STARES INCREDULOUSLY AT BROADBENT.
BULL III	(138)	IRISH ODDITY. (HODSON COMES FROM THE HOUSE.	LARRY	SITS IN DORAN'S CHAIR AND READS). OH, BY THE WAY,
BULL IV	(169)	NORA DRIES HER EYES, AND TURNS TO GO AS	LARRY	STROLLS UP THE HILL TO HER). /LARRY/ NORA. (SHE TURNS
BULL IV	SD(152)	IT, YOU KNOW. EVERYTHING HELPS IN ELECTIONEERING.	LARRY	TAKES THE CHAIR NEAR THE DOOR; DRAWS IT NEAR THE
BULL III	(129)	/DORAN/ (RALLYING HIM BLATANTLY) IS IT STILL	LARRY	THE BOULD FENIAN? /LARRY/ NO: THE BOLD FENIAN IS NOW
BULL II	(114)	TREACHERY TO LARRY? /NORA/ DEED I DONT. WHAT HAS	LARRY	TO DO WITH IT? IT'S AN ACT OF DISRESPECT AND RUDENESS
BULL III	(137)	INJA SOMEWHERE; AN HE WAS AS PLEASED AS PUNCH!	LARRY	TOLD HIM THAT IF HE'D BEEN ALIVE WHEN THE NEWS O
BULL IV	(146)	MR DOYLE WASNT KILLED. /DORAN/ FAITH IT WASNT O	LARRY	WE WERE THINKIN JUS DHEN, WI DHE PIG TAKIN THE MAIN
BULL IV	(176)	ME SOFTEN IT, AND COMPARE YOU SIMPLY TO AN ASS. (	LARRY	WHITENS WITH ANGER). /BROADBENT/ (REDDENING) AN ASS!
BULL II	(110)	KNOWS! ROMANCIN, I SUPPOSE. PRAPS SHE THINKS	LARRY	WOULD GO THERE TO LOOK FOR HER AND SEE HER SAFE HOME.
BULL I	(84)	(HE SITS DOWN AT THE WRITING TABLE OPPOSITE	LARRY	, AND ADDS, CASUALLY, BUT WITH AN ANXIOUS GLANCE AT
BULL IV	SD(151)	CANDIDATES, NORA, AUNT JUDY, KEEGAN,	LARRY	, AND CORNELIUS ARE LEFT IN THE PARLOR. LARRY GOES TO
BULL III	(137)	THOUGHT. /FATHER DEMPSEY/ YOU MIGHT FIND OUT FROM	LARRY	, CORNY, WHAT HIS MEANS ARE. GOD FORGIVE US ALL! IT'S
BULL IV	(154)	MAD, MR KEEGAN? /AUNT JUDY/ (SHOCKED) OH,	LARRY	, HOW COULD YOU ASK HIM SUCH A THING? /LARRY/ I DONT
BULL I	(90)	/BROADBENT/ (INVINCIBLE) UNMITIGATED ROT,	LARRY	, I ASSURE YOU. /DOYLE/ WELL, AT ANY RATE YOU WILL
BULL III	(123)	FROM THE ROUND TOWER WITH HER. /BROADBENT/ NO,	LARRY	, I WAS DRUNK, I AM SORRY TO SAY. I HAD TWO TUMBLERS
BULL I	(88)	HIMSELF COMFORTABLY TO LECTURE DOYLE). NOW,	LARRY	, IVE LISTENED CAREFULLY TO ALL YOUVE SAID ABOUT
BULL IV	(155)	ARE HERE. /BROADBENT/ (WITH CONVICTION) NEVER,	LARRY	, NEVER. BUT LEAVING POLITICS OUT OF THE QUESTION, I
BULL III	SD(138)	SIR. (HE FOLLOWS CORNELIUS INTO THE HOUSE).	LARRY	, NEWSPAPER STILL IN HAND, COMES BACK THROUGH THE
BULL I	(86)	THATS ENGLISH, IF YOU LIKE. /BROADBENT/ NO,	LARRY	, NO, YOU ARE THINKING OF THE MODERN HYBRIDS THAT NOW
BULL I	(95)	THE TABLE AND HIS HANDS CLENCHED) DONT DESPAIR,	LARRY	, OLD BOY: THINGS MAY LOOK BLACK; BUT THERE WILL BE A
BULL I	(90)	WITH A TWINKLE IN HIS EYE) VERY FRIENDLY OF YOU,	LARRY	, OLD MAN, BUT ALL BLARNEY. I LIKE BLARNEY; BUT IT'S
BULL I	(93)	(WITH HEARTY ADMIRATION) NOW YOU KNOW,	LARRY	, THAT WOULD NEVER HAVE OCCURRED TO ME. YOU IRISH
BULL III	(138)	CANDIDATE COMES UP. AFTER ALL, WHATEVER YOU SAY,	LARRY	, THEY LIKE AN ENGLISHMAN. THEY FEEL THEY CAN TRUST

BULL III	SD(125)	TO THE TABLE AND SLAPS LARRY ON THE SHOULDER.	LARRY	, TURNING QUICKLY, AND RECOGNIZING FATHER DEMPSEY,
BULL IV	SD(148)	END OF THE TABLE NEAREST THE GARDEN DOOR, WHILST	LARRY	, WHO ACCOMPANIES HIM, THROWS HIS MOTORING COAT ON THE
BULL IV	(172)	HE EXTRACTS A CIGAR FOR HIMSELF AND OFFERS ONE TO	LARRY	, WHO TAKES IT). IF I WAS TO BE SHOT FOR IT I COULDNT
BULL IV	(179)	YOU IRISHMEN! TOUJOURS BALLYHOOLY, EH? (	LARRY	, WITH A SHRUG, HALF COMIC, HALF IMPATIENT, TURNS AWAY
BULL IV	(175)	PATIENCE) WHY CANT YOU SAY A SIMPLE THING SIMPLY,	LARRY	, WITHOUT ALL THAT IRISH EXAGGERATION AND
BULL II	(107)	NOT YOU, LARRY! /CORNELIUS/ ARRA HOW COULD HE BE	LARRY	, WOMAN ALIVE? LARRY'S IN NO HURRY HOME, IT SEEMS. I
BULL I	(85)	OF MY BEST FRIENDS. /BROADBENT/ OH, COME,	LARRY	! DO YOURSELF JUSTICE. YOURE VERY AMUSING AND
BULL IV	(175)	DIE PRESENTLY. /BROADBENT/ (SHOCKED) OH COME,	LARRY	! DON'T BE UNFEELING. IT'S HARD ON HAFFIGAN. IT'S
BULL IV	(167)	/BROADBENT/ (DISPOSING OF THE IDEA AT ONCE)	LARRY	! OH, THAT WOULDNT HAVE DONE AT ALL, NOT AT ALL. YOU
BULL II	(107)	/AUNT JUDY/ SURELY TO GOODNESS THATS NOT YOU,	LARRY	! /CORNELIUS/ ARRA HOW COULD HE BE LARRY, WOMAN
BULL IV	(154)	BEEN TURNED EVER SINCE. /NORA/ (REPROACHFULLY)	LARRY	! /KEEGAN/ (BLANDLY) THAT IS NOT QUITE WHAT
BULL II	(107)	HEARTILY) MR BROADBENT! FANCY ME TAKIN YOU FOR	LARRY	! SURE WE HAVNT SEEN A SIGHT OF HIM FOR EIGHTEEN
BULL IV	(181)	WITH ALL THEIR TALK! /BROADBENT/ OH TUT, TUT,	LARRY	! THEY IMPROVED MY MIND: THEY RAISED MY TONE
			LARRY'S	
BULL III	(129)	IT, DHAN AN IRISH CATHOLIC. /CORNELIUS/ BUT SURE	LARRY'S	AS GOOD AS ENGLISH: ARNT YOU, LARRY? /LARRY/ YOU
BULL II	SD(104)	PARISH PRIEST, FATHER DEMPSEY; CORNELIUS DOYLE,	LARRY'S	FATHER; AND BROADBENT, ALL IN OVERCOATS AND AS STIFF
BULL II	(107)	ONY A LAD WHEN HE LEFT US. /BROADBENT/ IT'S NOT	LARRY'S	FAULT: HE WAS TO HAVE BEEN HERE BEFORE ME. HE
BULL II	(112)	ALARMED YOU, MISS REILLY. MY NAME IS BROADBENT.	LARRY'S	FRIEND, YOU KNOW. /NORA/ (CHILLED) AND HAS MR DOYLE
BULL II	(107)	ARRA HOW COULD HE BE LARRY, WOMAN ALIVE?	LARRY'S	IN NO HURRY HOME, IT SEEMS. I HAVNT SET EYES ON HIM.
BULL IV	(177)	DONT IN THE LEAST MIND YOUR CHAFF, MR KEEGAN; BUT	LARRY'S	RIGHT ON THE MAIN POINT. THE WORLD BELONGS TO THE
BULL II	(108)	HOTEL. YOULL STAY WITH US. I'D HAVE PUT YOU INTO	LARRY'S	ROOM, ONY THE BOY'S PALLYASS IS TOO SHORT FOR YOU;
BULL IV	(166)	ABOUT HER. THE IDEAL IS WHAT I LIKE. NOW	LARRY'S	TASTE IS JUST THE OPPOSITE: HE LIKES EM SOLID AND
			LARS	
CAND III	(137)	SO YOU DID, JAMES. IT FAIR KEP ME AWAKE TO THE	LARS	' WORD. DIDNT IT, MISS GORNETT? /PROSERPINE/ (
			LARYNGOSCOPE	
PYGM II	SD(217)	FLAT WRITING-TABLE, ON WHICH ARE A PHONOGRAPH, A	LARYNGOSCOPE	, A ROW OF TINY ORGAN PIPES WITH A BELLOWS, A
			LAS	
BULL III	(125)	RISES GENIALLY. /CORNELIUS/ I THINK WE ALL MET	LAS	NIGHT. /DORAN/ I HADNT THAT PLEASURE. /CORNELIUS/ TO BE
			LASCIVIOUS	
MIS.	PREFACE(88)	WE EVEN ACQUIRE THE NOTION THAT FINE ART IS	LASCIVIOUS	AND DESTRUCTIVE TO THE CHARACTER. IN CHURCH, IN
SUPR	HANDBOK(205)	IN THAT SCHOOL OF LITTLENESS CALLED THE HOME. THE	LASCIVIOUS	CLAMOR OF THE FLAGELLOMANIAC FOR MORE OF IT,
MIS.	PREFACE(17)	OF DOTING AFFECTION AND ALL THE EXCESSES OF	LASCIVIOUS	CRUELTY. YET THE PEOPLE WHO HAVE THIS MORBID
POSN	PREFACE(400)	AND ALMOST AS MUCH COARSELY VULGAR AND FURTIVELY	LASCIVIOUS	DRAMA AS WE LIKE. UNDER A COLLEGE OF CARDINALS,
SUPR III	(128)	" FRAIL." THEY ARE NOT ARTISTIC: THEY ARE ONLY	LASCIVIOUS	. THEY ARE NOT PROSPEROUS: THEY ARE ONLY RICH.
			LASH	
BULL	PREFACE(60)	YOU MUST DO AS THE EGYPTIANS DO: TERRORIZE BY THE	LASH	AND THE SCAFFOLD. THUS DOES THE EAST CONQUER ITS
POSN	(438)	THE SHERIFF'S BROTHER WANTED TO TIE HIM UP AND	LASH	HIM TIL HE CONFESSED WHAT HE'D DONE WITH IT; BUT I
LION II	(145)	CANT GET IT LOOSE. /ANDROCLES/ WE MUSTNT LET HIM	LASH	HIMSELF INTO A RAGE. YOU MUST SHEW HIM THAT YOU ARE MY
DEST	(193)	OF HIS POOR AT SIX YEARS OF AGE TO WORK UNDER THE	LASH	IN HIS FACTORIES FOR SIXTEEN HOURS A DAY. HE MAKES TWO
SUPR	HANDBOK(204)	RED INDIAN USED TO KEEP SCALPS. COERCION WITH THE	LASH	IS AS NATURAL TO AN ENGLISHMAN AS IT WAS TO SOLOMON
APPL	INTRLUD(250)	TO JEMIMA'S DIGNITY WOULD HIT ME LIKE THE	LASH	OF A WHIP ACROSS THE FACE. ABOUT YOURS, SOMEHOW, I DO
JITT II	(45)	DIRTY BUSINESS. /JITTA/ (STARTING AS FROM THE	LASH	OF A WHIP) DIRTY! OH, NEVER WAS ANYTHING PURER,
MIS.	(200)	YOU ARE NOT THE FIRST TO FALL TODAY UNDER THE	LASH	OF THAT YOUNG LADY'S TERRIBLE DERISION, BENTLEY. LINA,
LION	PREFACE(94)	P YOUR GOD IS AN OLD MAN WHOM YOU CHEAT," AND TO	LASH	THE DEADENED CONSCIENCE OF THE NINETEENTH CENTURY BACK
MIS.	PREFACE(53)	IS, CLAMORING O CLAMORING FOR WAR, FOR THE	LASH	, FOR POLICE, PRISONS, AND SCAFFOLDS IN A WILD PANIC OF
BASH	II,1, (108)	WORLD, THAT COWERS BEHIND THE GALLOWS AND THE	LASH	, THE WORLD THAT ROBS THE POOR, AND WITH THEIR SPOIL
			LASHED	
LION II	(140)	WHIP. THE ONLY TIME I EVER HIT A MAN WAS WHEN HE	LASHED	AN OLD HORSE WITH A WHIP. IT WAS TERRIBLE: I DANCED
			LASHES	
BULL	PREFACE(59)	OF THE LATTER, HE WOULD NO DOUBT HAVE HAD FIFTY	LASHES	BEFORE HIS HANGING, TO TEACH HIM THE GREATNESS OF THE
BULL	PREFACE(55)	GOING BY FLOGGING EIGHT MEN WITH FIFTY	LASHES	EACH: ELEVEN MORE THAN THE UTMOST PERMITTED BY THE
MIS.	PREFACE(56)	MADNESS: SOLDIERS WERE SENTENCED TO A THOUSAND	LASHES	FOR TRIFLING OFFENCES, WITH THE RESULT (AMONG OTHERS
LION II	(145)	THE TONE OF YOUR VOICE. (THE LION GROWLS AND	LASHES	HIS TAIL). I THINK HE'S GOING TO SPRING AT YOUR
SUPR	HANDBOK(204)	FACTS THAT THE MOSAIC LAW FORBADE MORE THAN FORTY	LASHES	IN THE NAME OF HUMANITY, AND THAT FLOGGINGS OF A
MIS.	PREFACE(56)	IN THE DAYS OF MOSES IT WAS LIMITED TO 39	LASHES	. IN THE EARLY NINETEENTH CENTURY IT HAD BECOME AN
BULL	PREFACE(56)	HARD LABOR AND FIFTY LASHES, AND FIVE TO FIFTY	LASHES	. LORD CROMER CERTIFIES THAT THESE PROCEEDINGS WERE "
OVER	(179)	LANGUID WOMAN, WITH FLASHING DARK EYES AND LONG	LASHES	. THEY MAKE FOR THE CHESTERFIELD, NOT NOTICING THE
BULL	PREFACE(58)	AWARDED HIM TWO YEARS IMPRISONMENT AND FIFTY	LASHES	. WITHOUT RUDELY CALLING THIS A USE OF TORTURE TO
SUPR	HANDBOK(204)	OF HUMANITY, AND THAT FLOGGINGS OF A THOUSAND	LASHES	WERE INFLICTED ON ENGLISH SOLDIERS IN THE XVIII AND
BULL	PREFACE(49)	WHEN FLOGGINGS OF HUNDREDS AND EVEN THOUSANDS OF	LASHES	WERE MATTERS OF ORDINARY ROUTINE, THIS DETESTABLE
BULL	PREFACE(56)	IMPRISONMENT FOR A YEAR WITH HARD LABOR AND FIFTY	LASHES	, AND FIVE TO FIFTY LASHES. LORD CROMER CERTIFIES
DEVL	EPILOG (79)	WAS THOUGHT OF ORDERING A SOLDIER A THOUSAND	LASHES	, AS IT WILL BE TO THOSE MODERN VICTIMS OF THE
MIS.	SD(115)	BLACK HAIR, LARGE DARK EYES WITH BLACK BROWS AND	LASHES	, CURVED LIPS, SWIFT GLANCES AND MOVEMENTS THAT FLASH
			LASHING	
BULL	PREFACE(63)	IT BRAVELY BY HONORABLE MEANS, INSTEAD OF WILDLY	LASHING	AND STRANGLING A HANDFUL OF POOR PEASANTS TO SCARE
			LASHINGS	
BULL	PREFACE(63)	POWER AND WOULD NOT STAND THESE BARBAROUS	LASHINGS	AND VINDICTIVE HANGINGS. YET MR DILLON,
			LASS	
BARB	PREFACE(230)	STRAIGHTWAY HE BEGINS TO TRY TO UNASSAULT THE	LASS	AND DERUFFIANIZE HIS DEED, FIRST BY GETTING PUNISHED
JOAN	2 (77)	BEAUTIFUL BASTARD. IS IT LIKELY THAT THE COUNTRY	LASS	CAN DO WHAT HE CANNOT DO? /CHARLES/ WHY DOESNT HE
JOAN	EPILOG (155)	/JOAN/ HARDLY EVEN THAT, LAD. CAN A POOR BURNT-UP	LASS	HAVE A GHOST? I AM BUT A DREAM THAT THOURT DREAMING. (
JOAN	2 (75)	BAUDRICOURT, HE IS SENDING SOME CRACKED COUNTRY	LASS	HERE -- /CHARLES/ (INTERRUPTING) NO: HE IS SENDING A
6CAL	(105)	/THE KING/ HEAR THAT, DEAREST: HE CALLS THEE	LASS	. BE KIND TO HIM, HE IS ONLY A POOR OLD CUR WHO HAS
6CAL	(105)	SAINTS IN HEAVEN AND DEVILS IN HELL. WELL SAID,	LASS	. HE NUDGES HER, TO HER EXTREME INDIGNATION. /THE KING/
MIS.	PREFACE(99)	FOR BYRON'S DON JUAN AS A PRESENT FOR A SWAIN OR	LASS	. PICKWICK IS THE SAFEST SAINT FOR US IN OUR NONAGE.
2TRU III	(85)	NOTHING TO DO WITH ME! YOU DONT KNOW ME, MY	LASS	. SOME MEN WOULD JUST ORDER YOU OFF; BUT TO ME THE MOST
BARB II	SD(276)	JENNY HILL, A PALE, OVERWROUGHT, PRETTY SALVATION	LASS	OF 18, COMES IN THROUGH THE YARD GATE, LEADING PETER
JOAN	3 (91)	GRINNING AT HER FAMILIARITY, AND ECHOING IT) AYE,	LASS	; BUT A GOOD HEART AND A STOUT LADDER WILL GET OVER THE
HART	PREFACE(40)	ENGLAND PERISH; IS READY TO CRY WITH BRYNHILD, "	LASS	' UNS VERDERBEN, LACHEND ZU GRUNDE GEH'N" SOONER THAN
LADY	(241)	BUT POUR IT OUT AT YOUR FEET. I CANNOT BUT LOVE A	LASS	THAT SETS SUCH STORE BY AN APT WORD. THEREFORE
JOAN	EPILOG (159)	TIED TWO STICKS TOGETHER, AND GAVE THEM TO A POOR	LASS	THAT WAS GOING TO BE BURNED. /THE SOLDIER/ RIGHT. WHO
JOAN	EPILOG (160)	/JOAN/ (RISING) BACK THERE! YOU! THAT GAVE THE	LASS	THE CROSS! /THE SOLDIER/ (EXCUSING HIS UNSOLDIERLY
JOAN	PREFACE(10)	TO THEM, WHEN SHE WAS CALLED A SHEPHERD	LASS	TO HER FACE SHE VERY WARMLY RESENTED IT, AND CHALLENGED
JOAN	PREFACE(22)	HAVE BECOME HAD SHE LIVED. BUT SHE, BEING ONLY A	LASS	WHEN ALL IS SAID, LACKED THEIR KNOWLEDGE OF MEN'S
BARB	PREFACE(230)	IN MY PLAY, HAVING ASSAULTED THE SALVATION	LASS	, PRESENTLY FINDS HIMSELF OVERWHELMED WITH AN
JOAN	6 (136)	LASS'S TONGUE. /JOAN/ NAY: I AM NO SHEPHERD	LASS	, THOUGH I HAVE HELPED WITH THE SHEEP LIKE ANYONE ELSE.
JOAN	2 (82)	/LA HIRE/ (WITH A HUGE CHUCKLE) WELL SAID,	LASS	! WELL SAID! /JOAN/ (IMPATIENTLY TO THE ARCHBISHOP)
			LASSALLE	
FABL	PREFACE(97)	PROSTITUTION, AND PREMATURE DEATH. FERDINAND	LASSALLE	IN GERMANY HAD ALREADY DEMONSTRATED THE INJUSTICE
SUPR	HANDBOK(198)	EVEN THE JEWS, WHO, FROM MOSES TO MARX AND	LASSALLE	, HAVE INSPIRED ALL THE REVOLUTIONS, HAVE HAD TO
FABL	PREFACE(70)	THAN THAT OF ANANIAS. " THE LIE" SAID FERDINAND	LASSALLE	" IS A EUROPEAN POWER." HE MIGHT, HOWEVER, HAVE
			LASSES	
BARB II	(286)	PETER? WILL YOU GO INTO THE SHELTER AND LEND THE	LASSES	A HAND FOR A WHILE: WE'RE WORKED OFF OUR FEET.

MIS. PREFACE(38)	GAS LAMPS IN UNDERGROUND CITY OFFICES. LADS AND	LASSES	IN THEIR TEENS WILL PROBABLY BE ABLE TO PRODUCE AS
BARB II (275)	WHAT AM I TO DO? I CANT STARVE. THEM SALVATION	LASSES	IS DEAR GOOD GIRLS; BUT THE BETTER YOU ARE, THE WORSE
SIM II (76)	RUSHED FRANTICALLY TO THE DOORS. TWO SALVATION	LASSES	STEMMED THE RUSH, AT GREAT PERSONAL DANGER TO

LASSIE

JOAN EPILOG (158)	THAT WON WAS ALWAYS YOUR WAY. I GIVE YOU BEST,	LASSIE	. I WROTE A FINE LETTER TO SET YOU RIGHT AT THE NEW
DOCT III (140)	GRUDGE HER FEW POUNDS EITHER, THE BRAVE LITTLE	LASSIE	. WHEN WE WERE CLEANED OUT, WE'D HAD ENOUGH OF IT:
SIM PRO,1, (26)	EM WHETHER I'M AN EMPIRE BUILDER OR NOT. THAT	LASSIE	SHANT SAY THAT I DIDNT LEAVE THE PLACE TIDY EITHER,
BARB III (320)	LOOK AT POOR LITTLE JENNY HILL, THE SALVATION	LASSIE	! SHE WOULD THINK YOU WERE LAUGHING AT HER IF YOU

LASSITUDE

CAPT II (243)	HIS BAW THE TAWM YOURE AWIKE. (THEY RELAPSE INTO	LASSITUDE	). WAW WASNT YOU ON THE LOOK-AHT TO GIVE US A

LASS'S

JOAN 6 (136)	US NOT BE MOVED BY THE ROUGH SIDE OF A SHEPHERD	LASS'S	TONGUE. /JOAN/ NAY; I AM NO SHEPHERD LASS, THOUGH I

LAST

CLEO NOTES (212)	HAS NOT BEEN WRONG IN ITS MORAL THEORY FOR THE	LAST	2,500 YEARS OR SO. IT MUST BE A CONSTANT PUZZLE TO MANY
NEVR II (248)	BEFORE. I'M CAPABLE OF ANYTHING: IVE GROWN UP AT	LAST	: I'M A MAN; AND IT'S YOUR DAUGHTER THATS MADE A MAN OF
NEVR II (259)	SOLID, RINGING, AND JUBILANT) AH, IT'S COME AT	LAST	: MY MOMENT OF COURAGE. (HE SEIZES HER HANDS: SHE
JOAN 6 (150)	THE CHURCH FOR HER THAT SHE MIGHT SEE IT TO THE	LAST	: SHE HAD ONLY TWO STICKS THAT SHE PUT INTO HER BOSOM.
MIS. PREFACE(65)	THE DISPOSAL OF MY WILL." IT HAS COME TO THIS AT	LAST	: THAT THAT THE PHRASE " SHE HAS A WILL OF HER OWN," OR
ROCK II (281)	ARTHUR/ DO YOU REALIZE THAT WE TWO ARE FREE AT	LAST	? FREE, DEAREST! THINK OF THAT! NO MORE CHILDREN.
MTH4 I (155)	POEM CAN DO JUSTICE TO THE END. WHEN IT CAME AT	LAST	? HARDLY TWO HUNDRED YEARS HAD ELAPSED WHEN THE CLAIMS
APPL I (220)	I WANT IT TO LAST. /NICOBAR/ WHY SHOULDNT IT	LAST	? (RISING) OWN THE TRUTH. YOU HAD RATHER HAVE THE
CAND III (131)	/MORELL/ AND YOU APPROACHED THE GATE OF HEAVEN AT	LAST	? /MARCHBANKS/ YES. /MORELL/ WELL? (FIERCELY) SPEAK,
WIDO II (28)	MAY WE REGARD THE MATTER AS SETTLED AT	LAST	? /SARTORIUS/ QUITE SETTLED. (HE RISES AND OFFERS HIS
GENV I (32)	WHAT ABOUT THE PAY? AND HOW LONG WILL THE JOB	LAST	? THE WORK HERE MAY BE DULL; AND THE PAY IS JUST SHORT
PYGM EPILOG (293)	WITH A LOUDER ROAR " THE FIRST LION THINKS THE	LAST	A BORE." THE MAN OR WOMAN WHO FEELS STRONG ENOUGH FOR
DOCT III (151)	THINGS UP. AND I MISSED SO MANY SMALL SUMS. AT	LAST	A DREADFUL THING HAPPENED. I MISSED A FIVE-POUND NOTE.
MILL III (185)	LET HER TEMPT YOU, JOE. /EPIFANIA/ WHEN HAD YOU	LAST	A HOLIDAY? /THE WOMAN/ ME! A HOLIDAY! WE CANT AFFORD
MTH2 (69)	MUCH LESS TO MORTAL MEN WHOSE WHOLE LIFE DOES NOT	LAST	A HUNDRED YEARS. /BURGE/ WE WON THE WAR: DONT FORGET
MTH2 (62)	KARL MARX'S ECONOMICS ARE ALL ROT. /LUBIN/ (AT	LAST	A LITTLE TAKEN ABACK) DEAR ME! /SAVVY/ YOU MUST EXCUSE
O'FL (224)	O'FLAHERTY/ WELL, SIR, PLEASE GOD THE WAR WILL	LAST	A LONG TIME YET; AND MAY BE I'LL DIE BEFORE IT'S OVER
GENV IV (119)	BEFORE YOU GET INTO BED, MY BOY; AND YOU MAY	LAST	A WHILE YET. LOUD APPLAUSE FROM THE BRITISH SECTION.
GETT PREFACE(205)	THE IMPULSES OF THE AVERAGE SOLDIER WOULD NOT	LAST	A YEAR. THE RESULT OF TRYING TO MAKE THE CHURCH OF
POSN PREFACE(419)	FOR DOING NOTHING? THE INSTITUTION WOULD NOT	LAST	A YEAR, EXCEPT AS A JOB FOR SOMEBODY. COUNSEL'S
MTH2 (37)	WITH HIS THOUGHT) I HAVE MADE UP MY MIND AT	LAST	ABOUT THE TIME. I MAKE IT THREE HUNDRED YEARS. /THE
BULL PREFACE(44)	TO THE MARROW. I HOPE THAT WHEN HOME RULE IS AT	LAST	ACHIEVED, ONE OF OUR FIRST LEGISLATIVE ACTS WILL BE TO
METH PREFACE(R26)	HAD NEITHER A SKULL NOR A BACKBONE. WHEN HE AT	LAST	ACQUIRED THESE ARTICLES, HE WAS FOR SOME TIME DOUBTFUL
JOAN 2 (86)	PAY OFF MY MORTGAGES? I HAVE PLEDGED MY	LAST	ACRE TO THE ARCHBISHOP AND THAT FAT BULLY. I OWE MONEY
JITT PREFACE(7)	GOES SO FAR AS TO SAY " YOU HAVE MADE MY	LAST	ACT ALMOST A COMEDY"; BUT HE IS TOO AMIABLE TO REPROACH
3PLA PREFACE(R18)	CLEVER LADIES THAT A HEROINE WHO ATONES IN THE	LAST	ACT BY COMMITTING SUICIDE MAY DO ALL THE THINGS THAT
METH PREFACE(R84)	PLAYS IN WHICH EVERYONE WAS MARRIED IN THE	LAST	ACT CALLED THEMSELVES COMEDIES. NOW NEITHER TRAGEDIES
CYMB FORWORD(134)	SURPRISE WHEN I BEGAN BY READING THE AUTHENTIC	LAST	ACT CAREFULLY THROUGH. I HAD NOT DONE SO FOR MANY
CYMB FORWORD(134)	THAT THE REVIVAL WOULD BE ALL RIGHT IF I WROTE A	LAST	ACT FOR IT. TO MY SURPRISE THIS BLASPHEMY WAS RECEIVED
HART PREFACE(41)	THE GERMANS MIGHT ON ANY NIGHT HAVE TURNED THE	LAST	ACT FROM PLAY INTO EARNEST, AND EVEN THEN MIGHT NOT
CYMB FORWORD(137)	TO MAKE FOR INDULGING IN A VARIATION ON THE	LAST	ACT OF CYMBELINE. I STAND IN THE SAME TIME RELATION TO
APPL II (273)	TO HEAR ABOUT THOSE PLANS OF YOURS. /MAGNUS/ MY	LAST	ACT OF ROYAL AUTHORITY WILL BE TO DIVEST MYSELF OF ALL
CYMB FORWORD(138)	WILL BE TOO GRATEFUL FOR MY SHORTENING OF THE	LAST	ACT TO COMPLAIN. G.B.S. AYOT ST LAWRENCE, DECEMBER
2TRU II (56)	COACHES PLY EVERY DAY ALL THE YEAR ROUND. THE	LAST	ACTIVE BRIGAND RETIRED FIFTEEN YEARS AGO, AND IS NINETY
CYMB FORWORD(133)	PLAYS NOW ON THE STAGE, GOES TO PIECES IN THE	LAST	ACT. IN FACT I MOOTED THE POINT MYSELF BY THOUGHTLESSLY
METH PREFACE(R84)	WHICH GIVES ONLY THE LAST MOMENTS OF THE	LAST	ACT. SHAKESPEAR DID NOT MAKE HAMLET OUT OF ITS FINAL
CYMB FORWORD(135)	WHICH PRECEDES IT, JUST THE THING TO SAVE THE	LAST	ACT. WITHOUT IT THE ACT IS A TEDIOUS STRING OF
CYMB FORWORD(135)	HE IS THE ONLY CHARACTER LEFT REALLY ALIVE IN THE	LAST	ACT; AND AS I CANNOT CHANGE HIM FOR THE BETTER I HAVE
MRS PREFACE(168)	IMPOSSIBLE FOR ITS SLAVES TO WRITE TOLERABLE	LAST	ACTS TO THEIR PLAYS, SO CONVENTIONALLY DO THEIR
CYMB FORWORD(137)	VORTIGERN, WHICH WAS MUCH ADMIRED AND AT	LAST	ACTUALLY PERFORMED AS A PLAY BY SHAKESPEAR, THE AFFAIR
CYMB FORWORD(136)	TROUBLE THROUGH HAVING TO UNRAVEL THEM IN THE	LAST	ACT, ESPECIALLY IN THE TWO GENTLEMEN OF VERONA AND
METH PREFACE(R84)	BY PLAYS IN WHICH EVERYONE WAS KILLED IN THE	LAST	ACT, JUST AS, IN SPITE OF MOLIERE, PLAYS IN WHICH
GETT PREFACE(236)	SUCH PRIVACY WILL ONLY BE TOLERATED WHEN WE AT	LAST	ADMIT THAT THE SOLE AND SUFFICIENT REASON WHY PEOPLE
BASH II,2, (118)	A CHAMELEON'S TONGUE SHOOTS TO ITS MARK; AND THE	LAST	AFRICAN UPON HIS KNEES SUES PITEOUSLY FOR QUARTER. (
LION PREFACE(44)	MUST FULFIL. TWO EVANGELISTS DECLARE THAT IN HIS	LAST	AGONY HE DESPAIRED, AND REPROACHED GOD FOR FORSAKING
BUOY III (45)	YOU-- IF YOU DIE-- IF WE NEVER MEET AGAIN, IT MAY	LAST	ALL MY LIFE. AND THERE ARE RIGHTS I WILL GIVE TO NO MAN
FABL PREFACE(66)	LIKE EDMUND KEAN, ROBSON, AND DICKENS ON HIS	LAST	AMERICAN TOUR. OR, NEEDING A WOMAN CAPABLE OF BEARING
METH PREFACE(R41)	HE COULD FIND, AND BRED FROM THEM UNTIL AT	LAST	AN ANIMAL WITH AN ABNORMALLY LONG NECK WAS EVOLVED BY
DOCT PREFACE(5)	A TROOP OF BRIGANDS. IT MAY BE SAID THAT IN THE	LAST	ANALYSIS THERE IS NO OTHER SORT OF HONOR OR CONSCIENCE
2TRU III (110)	A MAN WHO HAS MISSED HIS TRAIN: TOO LATE FOR THE	LAST	AND TOO EARLY FOR THE NEXT. WHAT AM I TO DO? WHAT AM
GETT (265)	BE AT HER FEET ALL DAY LONG. SHE GOT SENSIBLE AT	LAST	AND TOOK HIS ADVICE. GEORGE ALWAYS LIKED CHANGE OF
PHIL I (86)	SORT OF LIVER COMPLAINT. THE DOCTORS SAY HE CANT	LAST	ANOTHER YEAR; AND HE HAS FULLY MADE UP HIS MIND NOT TO
2TRU II (72)	THIS IS NOT ENOUGH. THE GLORIES OF NATURE DONT	LAST	ANY DECENTLY ACTIVE PERSON A WEEK, UNLESS THEYRE
NEVR III (277)	(RALLYING ALL HIS FORCES) LET ME MAKE ONE	LAST	APPEAL. MRS CLANDON: BELIEVE ME, THERE ARE MEN WHO HAVE
GETT PREFACE(218)	COUPLES WHO NEVER DISLIKE ONE ANOTHER; BUT THESE	LAST	ARE PEOPLE WHO ARE INCAPABLE OF DISLIKING ANYBODY. IF
MILL IV (198)	HE CAN BATTER ME, TORTURE ME, KILL ME. IT IS THE	LAST	ARGUMENT OF THE LOWER NATURE AGAINST THE HIGHER. MY
APPL II (275)	JOB FOR ME. (HE GOES). /PLINY/ (CHEERFUL TO THE	LAST	AS HE, TOO, GOES FOR HIS HAT) WELL, I AM GLAD NOTHING'S
JITT III (65)	REVENGE. IT'S THAT I REALLY LOVED BRUNO TO THE	LAST	AS I LOVED HIM FROM THE FIRST. HE WAS ALL I HAD THAT I
DOCT PREFACE(66)	THE FIRST DAY OF HIS PROFESSIONAL CAREER TO THE	LAST	AS THE DOCTOR IS. THE JUDGE PASSES SENTENCE OF DEATH;
JOAN 1 (64)	/ROBERT/ HE BEAT THE ENGLISH THE YEAR BEFORE	LAST	AT MONTARGIS. I WAS WITH HIM. /POULENGEY/ NO MATTER:
BARB III (347)	I ADMITTED THIS WHEN THE TURKS AND GREEKS WERE	LAST	AT WAR. MY BEST PUPIL WENT OUT TO FIGHT FOR HELLAS. MY
SUPR I (22)	TO JACK. I EMBRACE JACK. HERE ENDETH MY FIRST AND	LAST	ATTEMPT TO ASSERT MY AUTHORITY. /ANN/ YOU SEE, MAMMA,
MIS. (173)	TAKE A HOLIDAY? /THE MAN/ TAKE! I GOT FOUR DAYS	LAST	AUGUST. /TARLETON/ WHAT DID YOU DO? /THE MAN/ I DID A
GETT (326)	/THE BISHOP/ SHALL WE TRY TO GET THROUGH THE	LAST	BATCH OF LETTERS WHILST THEY ARE AWAY, SOAMES?
JITT III (53)	LETTING HERSELF DROOP) I HAVE GONE THROUGH THIS	LAST	BATCH OF LETTERS THREE TIMES OVER IN THE HOPE OF
MTH4 I (173)	ELDERLY GENTLEMAN/ (RISING) GALWAY! SHALL I AT	LAST	BE ABLE TO BOAST OF HAVING SEEN THAT MAGNIFICENT CITY?
JOAN PREFACE(38)	IT A POINT OF HONOR TO PRIVILEGE HERESY TO THE	LAST	BEARABLE DEGREE ON THE SIMPLE GROUND THAT ALL EVOLUTION
BARB I SD(249)	PEREMPTORY, ARBITRARY, AND HIGH-TEMPERED TO THE	LAST	BEARABLE DEGREE, AND WITHAL A VERY TYPICAL MANAGING
JITT II (47)	YES; AND I WILL TELL YOU SOMETHING MORE. THE	LAST	BEAT OF HIS HEART WOULD HAVE BROKEN MINE IF I HAD BEEN
MTH3 (135)	IT: I WONT RISK IT. /CONFUCIUS/ GOOD. YOU HAVE AT	LAST	BECOME PRUDENT: YOU ARE NO LONGER WHAT YOU CALL A
3PLA PREFACE(R33)	WITH THE RESULT THAT HIS PLAYS ARE AT	LAST	BEGINNING TO BE PERFORMED AS HE WROTE THEM; AND THE
ARMS III (72)	OF HIS RIVAL'S DISCOMFITURE) BLUNTSCHLI: MY ONE	LAST	BELIEF IS GONE. YOUR SAGACITY IS A FRAUD, LIKE
APPL INTRLUD(248)	WAY, ORINTHIA, WHEN YOUR DRESSMAKERS TOOK UP THAT	LAST	BILL FOR YOU, THEY WERE SPECULATING, WERE THEY NOT, IN
CAPT III (298)	THATS MY SECRET. /BRASSBOUND/ THEN THROW AWAY THE	LAST	BIT OF SELF. MARRY ME. /LADY CICELY/ (VAINLY
MTH2 (43)	YOU ARE NOT HER FATHER. /CONRAD/ I SENT HER MY	LAST	BOOK. I CAN BREAK THE ICE BY ASKING HER WHAT SHE MADE
SIM PREFACE(8)	PROPHETS WHOSE INVECTIVES AND WARNINGS FILL THE	LAST	BOOKS OF THE OLD TESTAMENT, AND THE COMMUNIST
2TRU I (29)	THE PRESCRIPTION? I HAD SUCH HOPES OF THAT	LAST	BOTTLE; BUT YOU KNOW IT WAS AFTER THAT THAT SHE
LION PREFACE(29)	AGONY OF THIRST AND PAIN ON THE CROSS AT	LAST	BREAKS HIS SPIRIT, AND HE DIES WITH A CRY OF " MY GOD:
6CAL (98)	AND AS TO THE TOWN, I WOULD HAVE BURNT IT TO THE	LAST	BRICK, AND EVERY MAN, WOMAN AND CHILD ALONG WITH IT,
APPL PREFACE(181)	FOR INSTANCE, ARE NOTHING BUT STAMPEDES. OUR	LAST	BUT ONE WAS A CONSPICUOUS EXAMPLE OF THIS. THE COW WAS
HART PREFACE(40)	OF OUR GENERALS AND ADMIRALS, UNMUZZLED AT	LAST	BY THE ARMISTICE. DURING THE WAR, GENERAL A, IN HIS
ARMS I SD(10)	AND A DIN OF TRIUMPHANT YELLS, DOMINATED AT	LAST	BY THE VOICE OF CATHERINE, INDIGNANTLY ADDRESSING AN
ARMS I (13)	CARRY CHOCOLATE INSTEAD; AND I FINISHED THE	LAST	CAKE OF THAT HOURS AGO. /RAINA/ (OUTRAGED IN HER MOST
CAND I (86)	JUST THE SAME AS HEWER, JAMES! /MORELL/ WHEN YOU	LAST	CALLED-- IT WAS ABOUT THREE YEARS AGO, I THINK-- YOU
HART PREFACE(24)	BRED IT, MUCH LESS THE SUBURBS. WHEN MATTERS AT	LAST	CAME TO THE LOOTING OF SHOPS BY CRIMINALS UNDER
CLEO PRO2,SD(95)	INFLUENTIALLY CONNECTED, BE EMPLOYED IN THE TWO	LAST	CAPACITIES BY A MODERN EUROPEAN STATE ON THE STRENGTH
APPL I (236)	CLAMOR ON ME. I ASK YOU, BEFORE YOU PLAY YOUR	LAST	CARD AND DESTROY ME, TO CONSIDER WHERE YOU WILL BE
JOAN 1 (65)	HERSELF A BIT OF A MIRACLE. ANYHOW, SHE IS THE	LAST	CARD LEFT IN OUR HAND. BETTER PLAY HER THAN THROW UP
MILL PREFACE(132)	IN THE LAST RESORT BY A WAR. IT WAS NOT ONLY THE	LAST	CARD OF NAPOLEON III BEFORE HE LOST THE GAME: IT PLAYED
GETT PREFACE(207)	SOMETIMES AGAINST ANY CHILDBEARING. THIS	LAST	CAUSE IS IMPORTANT. IT CANNOT BE REMOVED BY ANY

MILL PREFACE(111)	HAVE BEEN ABOLISHED IN ALL DIRECTIONS DURING THE	LAST	CENTURY AND A HALF, WITH THE RESULT, HOWEVER, OF
SUPR HANDBOK(182)	COTTON MANUFACTURERS DID AT THE BEGINNING OF	LAST	CENTURY, BUT THOUGH THE FACTORY CODE ON THE ONE HAND,
CYMB FORWORD(133)	HENRY IRVING AND AUGUSTIN DALY AT THE END OF THE	LAST	CENTURY, IS FOR THE MOMENT HEAVILY DISCREDITED. IT MAY
SUPR HANDBOK(181)	OF THE SCIENTIFIC IMAGINATION IN THE MIDDLE OF	LAST	CENTURY, ITS DEVOTEES ANNOUNCED THAT IT WAS A CRIME TO
GETT SD(296)	BREAKS UP. THE GENERAL FLINGS HIMSELF INTO THE	LAST	CHAIR ON THE LONG SIDE OF THE TABLE, NEAR THE GARDEN
NEVR I (206)	AND IVE DONE WITH CONSCIENCE FOR EVER. THIS IS MY	LAST	CHANCE. I SPENT MY LAST SOVEREIGN ON MOVING IN; AND I
DEVL II (40)	A LOWER VOICE, INTENDED FOR RICHARD ALONE) YOUR	LAST	CHANCE, SIR. THEY LOOK AT ONE ANOTHER SIGNIFICANTLY FOR
BASH PREFACE(90)	WAS, IT WAS BELIEVED, TO INCUR THE CURSE IN THE	LAST	CHAPTER OF REVELATIONS. EVEN IN ENGLAND THE VERY TIMID
BARB PREFACE(224)	OR THAT THE MOST GENEROUS CONTRIBUTOR AT HIS	LAST	CHARITY SERMON WAS AN EMPLOYER TRADING IN FEMALE LABOR
MTH1 II (31)	BE SURPRISED, DELIGHTED, INTERESTED; THOUGH THE	LAST	CHILD IS LIKE THE FIRST, AND HAS SAID AND DONE NOTHING
MTH4 II (184)	WAS THE END OF PSEUDO-CHRISTIAN CIVILIZATION. THE	LAST	CIVILIZED THING THAT HAPPENED WAS THAT THE STATESMEN
ROCK II (262)	THEM WILL BE RESISTED AND OBSTRUCTED TO THE VERY	LAST	CLAUSE. YOU MAY HAVE TO GO TO THE COUNTRY ON SEVERAL OF
PPP (199)	(ADOLPHUS GROANS). AND NOW, ADOLPHUS, TAKE THIS	LAST	COMFORT FROM THE UNHAPPY MAGNESIA FITZTOLLEMACHE. AS I
SIM II (77)	THE MOST SPLENDID OF ALL HER WARS! /KANCHIN/ THE	LAST	CONQUEST LEFT TO HER TO ACHIEVE! /VASHTI/ TO OVERCOME
PRES (162)	CLAMOR. I HAVE JUST TOLD THAT WOMAN THAT I AM AT	LAST	CONVINCED-- /BALSQUITH/ (JOYFULLY)-- THAT THE
LADY PREFACE(209)	RECOLLECTION OF ITS PREVIOUS OCCURRENCE IN THE	LAST	CYCLE, HE HUNTED OUT ALLUSIONS TO THIS FAVORITE THEORY
PHIL II (131)	ON HER BEHAVIOR WHICH SHE WILL REMEMBER TO THE	LAST	DAY OF HER LIFE. /CHARTERIS/ (APPROVINGLY) THAT WAS
6CAL SD(93)	AUGUST 1347, BEFORE THE WALLS OF CALAIS ON THE	LAST	DAY OF THE SIEGE. THE PAVILION OF EDWARD III, KING OF
MILL IV (209)	IT UP. /BLENDERBLAND/ YOU WILL REGRET IT TO THE	LAST	DAY OF YOUR LIFE. /EPIFANIA/ MR SAGAMORE: YOU HAVE YOUR
LION PREFACE(75)	HIM AS THE MAN WITHOUT SIN. EVEN IF WE RECKON HIS	LAST	DAYS AS THE DAYS OF HIS DELUSION, HE NONE THE LESS GAVE
PHIL II (102)	GREY IN THE HONORED SERVICE OF HIS COUNTRY, WHOSE	LAST	DAYS YOU HAVE BLIGHTED? /CHARTERIS/ (SURPRISED,
BULL IV (175)	IT MATTER WHERE AN OLD AND BROKEN MAN SPENDS HIS	LAST	DAYS, OR WHETHER HE HAS A MILLION AT THE BANK OR ONLY
JITT PREFACE(4)	FOR WHICH NATURE HAD UTTERLY UNFITTED ME. IN THE	LAST	DECADE OF THE NINETEENTH CENTURY I WAS DERIVING A
MIS. PREFACE(96)	OF THE MORAL INSTRUCTION BOOKS IT IS IN THE	LAST	DEGREE REPREHENSIBLE. IT IS OBVIOUSLY NOT TRUE AS A
2TRU II SD(52)	AIR OF HAVING RINGLETS AND A VEIL WHICH IS IN THE	LAST	DEGREE UNSOLDIERLY. HIS FIGURE IS THAT OF A BOY OF
MTH2 (83)	WHO ARE GETTING ON IN YEARS, IT WOULD BE IN THE	LAST	DEGREE UPSETTING AND EVEN DANGEROUS TO ENABLE EVERYONE
2TRU I SD(28)	WITH ITS HEAD IN ITS HANDS, AND SEEMS IN THE	LAST	DEGREE WRETCHED. /THE MONSTER/ OH! OH! ! OH! ! !
JITT (1)	LICHT, DIE FRAU OHNE DIENSTAG, DER GELIEBTE, DIE	LAST	DES BLUTES, ETC. ETC. TRANSLATED BY BERNARD SHAW.
GENV PREFACE(20)	LEARNT HIS LESSON: NAMELY, THAT PUTSCHES ARE A	LAST	DESPERATE METHOD, NOT A FIRST ONE, AND THAT ADVENTURERS
CURE PREFACE(224)	ENGLISH CONCERTINA. THAT DID JUST AS WELL. AS A	LAST	DESPERATE RESORT A PIANOLA BEHIND THE SCENES CAN BE
BULL I (78)	AN HOW CAN I HELP YOU? COMMAND ME TO THE	LAST	DHROP O ME BLOOD. /BROADBENT/ HAVE YOU EVER HEARD OF
HART PREFACE(35)	PROVINCES. BUT AT THE MOMENT WHEN THE ARMY HAS AT	LAST	DISGORGED THE SURVIVORS OF THE GALLANT BAND OF DRAMATIC
BULL PREFACE(71)	WONT HAVE IT," MEANING THAT THEY WOULD DIE IN THE	LAST	DITCH SINGING " O GOD, OUR HELP IN AGES PAST" RATHER
MILL IV (198)	YOU KNOW MY INVARIABLE RULE. FIGHT HIM TO THE	LAST	DITCH, NO MATTER WHAT IT COSTS. TAKE HIM TO THE HOUSE
MTH5 (250)	CERTAIN. /THE SHE-ANCIENT/ YES: THIS BODY IS THE	LAST	DOLL TO BE DISCARDED. WHEN I WAS A CHILD, ECRASIA, I,
SUPR HANDBOK(202)	SO COMMON A PART OF OUR IMPERIAL ROUTINE THAT THE	LAST	DOZEN OF THEM HAS NOT CALLED FORTH AS MUCH PITY AS CAN
APPL PREFACE(176)	BEST QUALIFIED RULERS, IS SO ABSURD THAT IF THE	LAST	DOZEN PARLIAMENTS HAD CONSISTED OF THE CANDIDATES WHO
PYGM II (218)	REASONABLE MOMENTS. /HIGGINS/ (AS HE SHUTS THE	LAST	DRAWER) WELL, I THINK THATS THE WHOLE SHOW. /PICKERING/
MIS. (188)	DEFIANTLY, PUGNACIOUS WITH SLOE GIN; DRAINS THE	LAST	DROP FROM HIS GLASS; THROWS IT ON THE SIDEBOARD; AND
APPL I (238)	FOR THAT, SIR; AND I WOULD BE WITH YOU TO THE	LAST	DROP OF MY BLOOD IF I DARED. BUT WHAT CAN I DO? IF I
MTH2 (56)	EXPLAINING TO ME THAT I COULDNT FIGHT TO THE	LAST	DROP OF MY BLOOD, BECAUSE I SHOULD BE DEAD LONG BEFORE
MILL II (172)	DOCTOR/ JEWESS, EH? /EPIFANIA/ CHRISTIAN, TO THE	LAST	DROP OF MY BLOOD. JEWS THROW HALF THEIR MONEY AWAY ON
ROCK II (263)	HOW PROFOUNDLY TRUE! I AM WITH YOU THERE TO THE	LAST	DROP OF MY BLOOD. /SIR ARTHUR/ WELL, THESE PARASITES
MTH3 (129)	RESIST ANY ATTEMPT TO ALTER OR UPSET IT TO THE	LAST	DROP OF MY BLOOD IF NEED BE. /BURGE-LUBIN/ OH, TUT
ROCK II (244)	COMMONSENSE. I AM WITH YOU, ARTHUR, TO THE	LAST	DROP OF MY ORIENTAL BLOOD. NATIONALIZED LAND:
APPL II (261)	SINN FEIN, AND FIGHT FOR OUR INDEPENDENCE TO THE	LAST	DROP OF OUR BLOOD? /VANHATTAN/ I SHOULD BE RIGHT SORRY
ROCK II (252)	OUR PROPERTY-- AND YOURS: YOURS, MR MAYOR, TO THE	LAST	DROP OF OUR BLOOD. /BASHAM/ (INCISIVELY RE-ENTERING
MTH2 (56)	DONT FORGET THAT. DO YOU REMEMBER FIGHTING TO THE	LAST	DROP OF YOUR BLOOD? /LUBIN/ (UNRUFFLED, TO FRANKLYN)
BULL IV (147)	DO WE NEED TO MAKE US MERRY? GO ON, BARNEY: THE	LAST	DROPS OF JOY ARE NOT SQUEEZED FROM THE STORY YET. TELL
KING I (199)	BUT HALF A DECANTER OF SHERRY THAT WAS OPENED	LAST	EASTER, AND THE REMAINS OF A MOULDY CAKE. I HAVE SENT
METH PREFACE(R21)	HIMSELF KNEW BETTER BEFORE HE DIED. IN THE	LAST	EDITION OF HIS SYSTEM OF NATURE, HE BEGAN TO WONDER
SIM PRO,1, (24)	/THE E.O./ (AT THE RAILWAY DOOR, TO WILKS, IN A	LAST	EFFORT TO ASSERT HIMSELF) CARRY ON, YOU. (HE GOES).
JITT II (51)	OWN WAY). /LENKHEIM/ (RUSHING TO THE DOOR IN A	LAST	EFFORT TO ASSERT HIMSELF, AND SHOUTING AFTER HER) IF
NEVR IV (305)	THROUGH THE WINDOW). /VALENTINE/ (MAKING A	LAST	EFFORT) MRS CLANDON: MAY I-- /PHILIP/ (FORESTALLING
APPL I (219)	A MOTOR CAR? /NICOBAR/ HOW MANY VOTED AT THE	LAST	ELECTION? NOT SEVEN PER CENT OF THE REGISTER. /BALBUS/
APPL PREFACE(183)	DEAD IN A MONTH. WHEN MR BALDWIN TRIED TO WIN THE	LAST	ELECTION BY DECLARING THAT SOCIALISM HAD BEEN A FAILURE
ROCK II (241)	BRIBED UP TO THE NECK. BUT YOUR MAJORITY AT THE	LAST	ELECTION WAS SEVENTEEN: THERE WERE THREE RECOUNTS. YOUR
APPL I (212)	THAT THOUGH WE WIPED OUT EVERY OTHER PARTY AT THE	LAST	ELECTION, AND HAVE BEEN IN POWER FOR THE LAST THREE
ROCK PREFACE(156)	ALAS! THE FIRST THING THE IRISH DID WHEN THEY AT	LAST	ENJOYED SELF-GOVERNMENT WAS TO GET RID OF THESE
LION PREFACE(29)	SACRIFICE. IN THIS NEW FRAME OF MIND HE AT	LAST	ENTERS JERUSALEM AMID GREAT POPULAR CURIOSITY; DRIVES
FANY I (274)	MY BROTHER, AS YOU MAY IMAGINE, FEELS THAT THIS	LAST	ESCAPADE HAS GONE BEYOND THE BOUNDS; AND I THINK,
MILL PREFACE(118)	THE PEOPLE VOTES THAN TO CARRY OUT REFORMS, AT	LAST	ESTABLISHED ADULT SUFFRAGE. THE RESULT WAS A COLOSSAL
POSN (453)	TO THE ELDER) DID WE OR DID WE NOT HAVE A QUARREL	LAST	EVENING ABOUT A CERTAIN ARTICLE THAT WAS LEFT BY MY
SUPR HANDBOK(202)	AS A TRIBAL CUSTOM HAS DEPRIVED US OF THE	LAST	EXCUSE FOR BELIEVING THAT OUR OFFICIAL RELIGIOUS RITES
6CAL (94)	THE MATTER STAND? THEY MUST BE SUFFERING THE	LAST	EXTREMITY OF FAMINE. THEIR WALLS MAY HOLD OUT; BUT
SIM II (68)	BY PROLA! /VASHTI/ TO FEEL HER RULE IN THE	LAST	EXTREMITY OF PAIN! /KANCHIN/ TO SUFFER FOR HER!
6CAL (101)	GUILTY FOR DEFENDING OUR HEARTHS AND HOMES TO THE	LAST	EXTREMITY. THE KING WILL NOT BE BAULKED OF HIS REVENGE;
FABL VI (122)	SIXTH AND	LAST	FABLE, AS BEFORE, EXCEPT THAT THE BUILDING IS NOW
LION PREFACE(59)	EQUAL DISTRIBUTION. WHEN THAT PROBLEM IS AT	LAST	FACED, THE QUESTION OF THE PROPORTION IN WHICH THE
PPP (194)	NEVER AGAIN MEET IN THIS WORLD, LET US TAKE A	LAST	FAREWELL. /PHYLLIS/ (EMBRACING HER WITH TEARS) MY POOR
DEVL III (74)	TO HIS HAND-- WILL NOT BE PUT OFF WITH SO COLD A	LAST	FAREWELL-- AT LAST, AS HE TRIES TO DISENGAGE HIMSELF,
JOAN 5 (117)	WHICH IS ALL YOUR FAULT, HAS COST ME THE	LAST	FARTHING I CAN BORROW. /JOAN/ THE CHURCH IS RICHER THAN
NEVR I (223)	SIR, NATURALLY, WHEN A YOUNG MAN HAS COME TO HIS	LAST	FARTHING, AND IS WITHIN TWENTY FOUR HOURS OF HAVING HIS
BULL IV (159)	/NORA/ DID JEVER GET A LETTER I WROTE YOU	LAST	FEBRUARY? /LARRY/ OH YES; AND I REALLY INTENDED TO
GETT PREFACE(191)	SPARE THE FINE EDGE OF THEIR FACULTIES AND THE	LAST	FEW INCHES OF THEIR CHESTS WITHOUT BEING ANY THE LESS
POSN PREFACE(395)	WOULD HAVE VENTURED ON IN ANY CASE. WITHIN THE	LAST	FEW MONTHS A VERY AMUSING COMEDY WITH A STRONGLY
ARMS II (32)	I HAVE HAD OF THE SEAMY SIDE OF LIFE DURING THE	LAST	FEW MONTHS HAVE MADE ME CYNICAL; BUT I SHOULD NOT HAVE
JITT I (14)	BEHIND WHEN I COME HERE INTO THE DREAMLAND. THESE	LAST	FEW MONTHS HAVE BEEN WONDERFUL, BUT THEY HAVE BEEN
MTH2 (57)	SABBATH; AND THERE HAVE BEEN SUNDAYS WITHIN THE	LAST	FEW YEARS ON WHICH I HAVE HAD TO PLAY AS MANY AS
UNPL PREFACE(R19)	DISTORTED AND FALSIFIED. IT IS ONLY WITHIN THE	LAST	FEW YEARS THAT SOME OF OUR YOUNGER ACTOR-MANAGERS HAVE
JITT III (57)	I ALWAYS THOUGHT IT WAS, AT LEAST UNTIL THE	LAST	FEW YEARS, THEN THERE WAS A SUDDEN CHANGE, UP TO THAT
LION PREFACE(100)	ALL THE PERSECUTIONS AND RELIGIOUS WARS OF THE	LAST	FIFTEEN HUNDRED YEARS. WHEN THE LATE EXPLORER SIR HENRY
DOCT I (103)	QUITE TRUE. IVE NOT PRESCRIBED A DRUG FOR THE	LAST	FIFTEEN YEARS. /B.B./ DRUGS CAN ONLY REPRESS SYMPTOMS:
LION PREFACE(96)	IT WOULD BE EASIER TO SUSTAIN THE THESIS THAT THE	LAST	FIFTY YEARS HAVE WITNESSED A DISTINCT REACTION FROM
MTH2 (74)	I AM PREPARED TO DEMONSTRATE THAT DURING THE	LAST	FIFTY YEARS, THOUGH THE CHURCH HAS OFTEN BEEN WRONG,
BASH III (121)	(HE SHUTS THE DOOR AGAIN.) NOW SHALT THOU SEE MY	LAST	FIGHT FOUGHT. EXHAUSTED AS I AM, TO CAPTURE ME WILL
MTH1 II (31)	AND ONE HARVEST IS JUST LIKE ANOTHER, AND THE	LAST	FIGHT ONLY A REPETITION OF THE FIRST. OH, I HAVE HEARD
MTH1 II (31)	TO ME OF THE LAST HARVEST, OR BOAST TO ME OF THE	LAST	FIGHT; AND ONE HARVEST IS JUST LIKE ANOTHER, AND THE
GLIM (186)	BUT THE AGONY OF MY SOUL WAS TOO DREADFUL TO	LAST	FIVE MINUTES; I SHOULD HAVE DIED OF IT IF IT COULD HAVE
ARMS II (36)	OF BEHAVING AS I HAVE BEEN BEHAVING FOR THE	LAST	FIVE MINUTES. WHO IS HE? /LOUKA/ I DONT KNOW. I NEVER
SIM II (69)	IVE BEEN LOOKING AT IT THROUGH THE WINDOW FOR THE	LAST	FIVE MINUTES. IT ISNT AN ALBATROSS. LOOK AT IT THROUGH
DEVL II SD(41)	CANDLES HAS BURNT OUT, AND THE OTHER IS AT ITS	LAST	FLICKER. /ANDERSON/ WHY, WHAT ON EARTH--? (CALLING)
PPP (201)	AWAY, MOSTLY INTO ONE ANOTHER'S FACE. ADOLPHUS AT	LAST	FLINGS FITZTOLLEMACHE TO THE FLOOR, AND PUTS THE SPOUT
DEST (154)	(FOLD): ONE BATTLE IS LIKE ANOTHER. (AT THE	LAST	FOLD, HE SLAPS THE CLOTH ON THE TABLE AND DEFTLY ROLLS
MIS. PREFACE(40)	COMPULSORY COMPLETION OF EDUCATION IS THE	LAST	FOLLY OF A ROTTEN AND DESPERATE CIVILIZATION. ALL WE
MTH5 (221)	TO TWO. YOUR GENIUS SEEMS TO HAVE BEEN IN THE	LAST	FOOT OF YOUR BEARD; FOR YOU HAVE LOST BOTH. /MARTELLUS/
MTH4 I (154)	WEST. CONSIDER THIS ISLAND ON WHICH WE STAND, THE	LAST	FOOTHOLD OF MAN ON THIS SIDE OF THE ATLANTIC: THIS
MTH1 II (27)	DOES NOT LAST FOR A THOUSAND YEARS; AND I MUST	LAST	FOR A THOUSAND YEARS. WHEN YOU FIGHTERS DO NOT GET
MTH1 II (27)	OFF THEN. THIS SPLENDID LIFE OF YOURS DOES NOT	LAST	FOR A THOUSAND YEARS; AND I MUST LAST FOR A THOUSAND
MRS II (216)	WASTER OF A WOMAN THAT THINKS HER LUCK WILL	LAST	FOR EVER. (WITH GREAT ENERGY) I DESPISE SUCH PEOPLE:
APPL II (264)	NOTHING -- NOT EVEN DEAR OLD ENGLAND -- CAN	LAST	FOR EVER. PROGRESS, YOU KNOW, SIR, PROGRESS, PROGRESS!
2TRU II (64)	FOR IT. THE MONEY WE GOT FOR THE NECKLACE WONT	LAST	FOR EVER. /AUBREY/ SWEETIE: YOU WILL HAVE TO STICK IT
MIS. (175)	IT TIL I SAW IT WITH MY OWN EYES. WELL, IT WONT	LAST	FOR EVER. THE WRITING IS ON THE WALL. ROME FELL.
BUOY III (32)	/THE WIDOWER/ BUT SURELY THIS SHORTAGE WILL NOT	LAST	FOR EVER. THE LABOR GOVERNMENT, WHICH IS RESPONSIBLE
GETT SD(259)	IN A NORMAN FORTRESS. IT IS A HOUSE BUILT TO	LAST	FOR EVER. THE WALLS AND BEAMS ARE BIG ENOUGH TO CARRY
MIS. PREFACE(3)	WITH NO IMAGINATION TRY TO MAKE THINGS WHICH WILL	LAST	FOR EVER, AND EVEN WANT TO LIVE FOR EVER THEMSELVES.
MTH1 I (14)	IS SO LIKE A MAN. THE MOMENT YOU FIND WE NEED NOT	LAST	FOR EVER, YOU TALK AS IF WE WERE GOING TO END TODAY.

ROCK II (262)	ON SEVERAL OF THEM. THE COMMITTEE STAGES WILL	LAST	FOR WEEKS AND WEEKS, NO MATTER HOW HARD YOU WORK THE
INCA (256)	JUDGMENT-SEAT AT WHICH THEY AND I SHALL ANSWER AT	LAST	FOR WHAT WE HAVE LEFT UNDONE NO LESS THAN FOR WHAT WE
FANY III (307)	PERFECTLY. /MARGARET/ BOBBY HAS SPENT THE	LAST	FORTNIGHT IN PRISON. YOU DONT MIND, DO YOU? /DUVALLET/
FANY III (307)	IT WITH AN EFFORT. /MARGARET/ DORA HAS SPENT THE	LAST	FORTNIGHT IN PRISON. /DUVALLET/ QUITE SO. I FELICITATE
FANY III (307)	YOU? /DUVALLET/ NO, NATURALLY. I HAVE SPENT THE	LAST	FORTNIGHT IN PRISON. THE CONVERSATION DROPS. MARGARET
VWOO 1 (115)	OF THE DECK. I OFTEN WONDERED WHY. /A/ WITHIN THE	LAST	FORTNIGHT YOU HAVE INSPECTED THE PRICELESS ANTIQUITIES
FANY II (288)	I WANT TO KNOW WHERE MY DAUGHTER HAS BEEN FOR THE	LAST	FORTNIGHT. /DUVALLET/ SHE HAS BEEN, I ASSURE YOU, IN A
DOCT PREFACE(12)	SKIRTS: THE TRIUMPH OF SOME SURGEON WHO HAS AT	LAST	FOUND OUT HOW TO MAKE A ONCE DESPERATE OPERATION FAIRLY
O'FL SD(205)	SEAT WITH AN IRON CHAIR AT EACH END OF IT. THE	LAST	FOUR BARS OF GOD SAVE THE KING ARE HEARD IN THE
WIDO III (50)	IS NO USE IN OUR GOING ON AS WE HAVE FOR THE	LAST	FOUR MONTHS. YOU HAVE NOT BEEN HAPPY; AND I HAVE BEEN
GETT (287)	STRAIN ITSELF UNTIL IT BREAKS. IVE TOLD OUR	LAST	FOUR PRIME MINISTERS THAT IF THEY DIDNT MAKE OUR
JOAN 6 (129)	HIS SEAT) THAT IS WHAT THE MAID SAID TO US	LAST	FRIDAY. /CAUCHON/ I WISH YOU HAD FOLLOWED HER COUNSEL,
SIM PRO,2, (28)	WEEDER OF THE GARDEN, THE SACRED SCAVENGER, THE	LAST	FRIEND ON EARTH, THE PROLONGER OF SLEEP AND THE GIVER
SUPR III (103)	GO PRESENTLY, BECAUSE THERE I HOPE TO ESCAPE AT	LAST	FROM LIES AND FROM THE TEDIOUS, VULGAR PURSUIT OF
CYMB FORWORD(134)	STUPIDITY. THE ACT IS GENUINE SHAKESPEAR TO THE	LAST	FULL STOP, AND LATE PHASE SHAKESPEAR IN POINT OF VERBAL
SUPR III (122)	STRICTLY CORRECT, I SHOULD RATHER SAY WHEN I AT	LAST	GAVE IN AND ALLOWED ANA'S MOTHER TO MARRY ME-- I KNEW
METH PREFACE(R76)	THE SUCCESS OF THE HANG THE KAISER CRY AT THE	LAST	GENERAL ELECTION SHEWS US VERY TERRIFYINGLY HOW A
PYGM EPILOG (300)	MAKING THE ENDS MEET OVER AND OVER AGAIN, AT	LAST	GENTLY INSISTED; AND ELIZA, HUMBLED TO THE DUST BY
LION PREFACE(16)	WITH THE CRAVING FOR THE REDEEMER, YOU AT	LAST	GET THE CONVICTION THAT WHEN THE REDEEMER COMES HE WILL
SUPR III SD(86)	RETRACE THEIR MELODY IN DESPAIR AND AT	LAST	GIVE IT UP, EXTINGUISHED BY WAILINGS FROM UNCANNY WIND
SIM II (74)	/KANCHIN/ HE IS OUT OF SIGHT. /MAYA/ THERE! ONE	LAST	GLINT OF THE SUN ON HIS WINGS. HE IS GONE. THE FOUR
MIS. PREFACE(46)	A POLITICIAN, BUT A GROWN-UP SCHOOLBOY WHO HAS AT	LAST	GOT A CANE IN HIS HAND, AND AS ALL THE REST OF US ARE
POSN PREFACE(429)	AS THIS MUST HAVE COME TO LORD GORELL WHEN HE AT	LAST	GRAPPLED SERIOUSLY WITH THE PROBLEM. MR HARCOURT SEIZED
MTH1 II (31)	TIME, OR TO RECEIVE A VISIT FROM THE	LAST	GREAT-GREAT-GRANDSON WHO HAS GROWN UP AND WANTS TO
LION PREFACE(96)	IN WISDOM AND LIBERALITY HAS BEEN GREATER IN THE	LAST	HALF CENTURY THAN IN THE SIXTEEN HALF CENTURIES
MIS. (137)	BORE THEIR CHILDREN! THREE OR FOUR TIMES IN THE	LAST	HALF HOUR IVE BEEN ON THE POINT OF SCREAMING. /LORD
PHIL I (82)	I HAVE BEEN ON THE POINT OF SWEARING FOR THE	LAST	HALF HOUR, /JULIA/ (DESPAIRINGLY) YOU ARE ONLY MAKING
HART II (102)	UNPLEASANT THINGS CAME INTO YOUR MIND IN THE	LAST	HALF SECOND BEFORE YOU WOKE. ELLIE RUBBED YOUR HAIR THE
DOCT III (137)	IT, BUT TO CLEAN POOR BLENKINSOP OUT OF HIS	LAST	HALF-CROWN WAS DAMNABLE. I INTEND TO GIVE HIM THAT
GETT (294)	MYSELF. IVE BEEN CONTROLLING MYSELF FOR THE	LAST	HALF-HOUR UNTIL I FEEL LIKE BURSTING. (HE SITS DOWN
DOCT IV (156)	OLD PADDY CULLEN HAS BEEN HERE WITH B.B. FOR THE	LAST	HALF-HOUR. (SIR PATRICK, WITH BAD NEWS IN HIS FACE,
VWOO 3 (142)	AND AN INTENSE LOVE WILL SEIZE US. IT WILL	LAST	HARDLY LONGER THAN THE LIGHTNING FLASH WHICH TURNS THE
MTH1 II (31)	VERY DULL; FOR THEY EITHER COMPLAIN TO ME OF THE	LAST	HARVEST, OR BOAST TO ME OF THE LAST FIGHT; AND ONE
JOAN 2 (71)	TREMOUILLE/ TWENTYSEVEN THOUSAND: THAT WAS HIS	LAST	HAUL. A COOL TWENTYSEVEN THOUSAND! /THE ARCHBISHOP/
SUPR I (38)	SO ENTIRELY AND HELPLESSLY AT HIS MERCY THAT AT	LAST	HE DARE NOT TAKE A STEP WITHOUT RUNNING TO YOU FOR
DOCT I (93)	TO FIND SOMETHING FRESH TO OPERATE ON; AND AT	LAST	HE GOT HOLD OF SOMETHING HE CALLS THE NUCIFORM SAC,
JITT II (35)	INTO HER EYES). DO YOU REMEMBER WHEN WE WERE	LAST	HERE TOGETHER? YOUR FATHER BROUGHT YOU. HE WAS RADIANT
BULL PREFACE(71)	INTEREST THAT USED TO ATTACH TO IT, HAS BECOME AT	LAST	HIGHLY INTERESTING TO THE STUDENT OF POLITICAL SCIENCE
BASH II,2, (114)	CRAFTS BY WHICH TO SLAY UNFACED FOES, UNTIL AT	LAST	HIS AGONIZED DESIRE MAKES POSSIBILITY ITS SLAVE. AND
LION PREFACE(78)	TO REACH " YONDER SHINING LIGHT"; AND WHEN AT	LAST	HIS BUNDLE FALLS OFF HIM INTO THE SEPULCHRE OF CHRIST,
MTH2 (39)	ENERGY) THERE! AGAIN! YOU SEE, CON. IT WILL	LAST	HIS TIME. LIFE IS TOO SHORT FOR MEN TO TAKE IT
BARB II (284)	WOTS IS WIGHT? /SHIRLEY/ THIRTEEN FOUR. (BILL'S	LAST	HOPE EXPIRES). /BARBARA/ GO AND TALK TO HIM, BILL.
GLIM (186)	REALLY ARE. A PRIEST SAID TO ME ONCE, " IN YOUR	LAST	HOUR EVERYTHING WILL FALL AWAY FROM YOU EXCEPT YOUR
ARMS I (17)	RIGHT. I KNOW HOW GOOD YOUVE BEEN TO ME: TO MY	LAST	HOUR I SHALL REMEMBER THOSE THREE CHOCOLATE CREAMS. IT
DEVL I (23)	HIM RATHER THAN TO OTHERS IN THE PERPLEXITY OF MY	LAST	HOUR IN THIS STRANGE PLACE." /ANDERSON/ AMEN. /THE
PPP (198)	(IN A BROKEN VOICE) FAREWELL, MAGNESIA: MY	LAST	HOUR IS AT HAND. FAREWELL, FAREWELL, FAREWELL!
HART PREFACE(24)	MOST OF THE MEN OF ACTION, OCCUPIED TO THE	LAST	HOUR OF THEIR TIME WITH URGENT PRACTICAL WORK, HAD TO
BUOY III (46)	OF PEACE. IT HAS BEEN TERRIBLY PROFANED FOR THE	LAST	HOUR. FATHER BUOYANT WILL BE HERE PRESENTLY FOR HIS
PHIL II (109)	OLD GIRL. IVE BEEN WAITING FOR YOU THIS	LAST	HOUR. I'M STARVING. /GRACE/ ALL RIGHT, DEAR. (TO
KING II (234)	SEE TO THAT WHEN THE HOUR STRIKES FOR ME: THE	LAST	HOUR. SO MY VERY BELOVEDEST WILL DIE HAPPY; AND THAT IS
GLIM (187)	YOUR RELIGION." BUT I HAVE LIVED THROUGH MY	LAST	HOUR; AND MY RELIGION WAS THE FIRST THING THAT FELL
DEVL I (9)	TO COMPLETE THE QUESTION). /ANDERSON/ YES. IN HIS	LAST	HOURS HE CHANGED HIS MIND. /MRS DUDGEON/ (WHITE WITH
MRS IV (252)	FROM THIS TIME FORTH, SO HELP ME HEAVEN IN MY	LAST	HOUR, I'LL DO WRONG AND NOTHING BUT WRONG. AND I'LL
MIS. (153)	CARE. /LINA/ I'LL TELL YOU WITH PLEASURE. FOR THE	LAST	HUNDRED AND FIFTY YEARS, NOT A SINGLE DAY HAS PASSED
GENV I (46)	MEMORIAL SERVICE SAID FOR THEM. TO THAT EXTENT AT	LAST	I CAN DEFEAT YOUR GODLESS TYRANNY. /COMMISSAR/ YOU ARE
JITT I (21)	AT WHICH I BUY HIS WIFE FROM HIM; AND NOW AT	LAST	I CAN TAKE MY HAPPINESS WITH BOTH HANDS, FREE IN MY
MTH1 I (8)	DARED! /THE SERPENT/ I DARED EVERYTHING. AND AT	LAST	I FOUND A WAY OF GATHERING TOGETHER A PART OF THE LIFE
GENV I (40)	THIS WAY. USELESS: HE WOULD NOT LISTEN TO ME. AT	LAST	I FOUND OUT THE REASON. HE WAS CARRYING ON AN INTRIGUE
GETT (343)	MYSELF. IVE NOT BEEN AFRAID OF MYSELF. AND AT	LAST	I HAVE ESCAPED FROM MYSELF, AND AM BECOME A VOICE FOR
JITT I (15)	THE MOMENTS ENDLESS UNTIL YOU COME, AND AT	LAST	I HEAR YOUR RING, I SUDDENLY BECOME LIKE A FRESHMAN
FABL PREFACE(72)	DID NOT LAST; BUT THE REACTION DID; AND THE	LAST	I HEARD OF ITS FOUNDER WAS THAT HE WAS HELPING THE
HART II (123)	AT FIRST; BUT I BECAME ACCUSTOMED TO THEM. AT	LAST	I LEARNED TO PLAY THEM. /RANDALL/ IF IT'S ALL THE SAME
CAPT I (230)	HAD MY OWN POSITION IN THE WORLD TO MAKE. BUT AT	LAST	I MADE IT. IN THE COURSE OF A HOLIDAY TRIP TO THE WEST
CAND III (144)	OF HIS LOT) I HAD MY BOOKS. I HAD NATURE. AND AT	LAST	I MET YOU. /CANDIDA/ NEVER MIND THAT JUST AT PRESENT.
FANY I (279)	AWAY LIKE A STREAK OF LIGHTNING; AND THAT WAS THE	LAST	I SAW OF HIM. I WAS COPPED IN THE DOCK ROAD MYSELF:
MTH3 (121)	RECUPERATED. I LOOKED YOUNGER AND YOUNGER. AND AT	LAST	I WAS RESTED ENOUGH TO HAVE COURAGE AND STRENGTH TO
VWOO 2 (125)	WILL BELIEVE ME WHEN I TELL YOU THAT IN JANUARY	LAST	I WAS SITTING ON THE DECK OF A SHIP NAMED THE EMPRESS
DOCT PREFACE(32)	DESCRIPTION OF THE TREATMENT OF CHARLES II IN HIS	LAST	ILLNESS TO SEE HOW STRONGLY HIS PHYSICIANS FELT THAT
MIS. PREFACE(14)	CONDITION OF NERVOUS FEEBLENESS, AND AT	LAST	IMAGINE THEMSELVES UNABLE TO WORK UNDER CONDITIONS OF
NEVR I (210)	I-- ER-- ER-- YES-- THANK YOU (HE SUCCEEDS AT	LAST	IN BLUNDERING HIMSELF OUT OF THE ROOM; BUT THE
ROCK II (261)	MASSACRE. HOW LONG DO YOU THINK A MASSACRE WOULD	LAST	IN ENGLAND TODAY? JUST AS LONG AS IT TAKES A DRUNKEN
JOAN 4 (104)	DUST BEFORE THE WORLD, AND SUBMIT HERSELF TO THE	LAST	INCH OF HER SOUL TO HER CHURCH, TO THE FIRE SHE SHALL
SUPR II (56)	YOU IN IT AS THAT CAR AND ME IF YOU DONT GIT THE	LAST	INCH OUT OF US BOTH. /TANNER/ (SOOTHINGLY) ALL RIGHT,
CLEO IV SD(173)	AN INLAID STOOL. AFTER MANY STAIRS THEY EMERGE AT	LAST	INTO A MASSIVE COLONNADE ON THE ROOF. LIGHT CURTAINS
SUPR III (115)	HIS POEMS TO FEEL MORE DEEPLY. BUT HE LED ME AT	LAST	INTO THE WORSHIP OF WOMAN. /ANA/ JUAN! /DON JUAN/ YES:
HART III (130)	YOU, ALF. THERE IS NO TRAIN AT THIS HOUR. THE	LAST	IS NINE FORTYFIVE. /MANGAN/ BUT A GOODS TRAIN. /MRS
PYGM III (253)	I DO THINK IT HORRIBLE AND UNLADYLIKE. BUT THIS	LAST	IS REALLY TOO MUCH. DONT YOU THINK SO, COLONEL
GETT PREFACE(189)	OF RELIGION AND STATESMEN TO BLURT IT OUT AT	LAST	IS THE PLAIN FACT THAT MARRIAGE IS NOW BEGINNING TO
CLEO I (107)	BELOW, WHOSE POST I NEVER COULD FIND. AND HERE AT	LAST	IS THEIR SENTINEL-- AN IMAGE OF THE CONSTANT AND
FANY II (292)	ALL. I NEVER ENJOYED ANYTHING SO MUCH. BUT AT	LAST	IT GOT SPOILT BY THE OXFORD AND CAMBRIDGE STUDENTS UP
HART I (57)	BETWEEN HER TEETH) HARD. WELL? GO ON. /ELLIE/ AT	LAST	IT SEEMED THAT ALL OUR TROUBLES WERE AT AN END. MR
METH PREFACE(R34)	SOMETHING APPROACHING TO AN ARGUMENT BEGAN. AT	LAST	IT WAS ALLEGED BY THE MOST EVANGELICAL OF THE
MTH1 I (4)	BE ALONE. I COULD NOT SIT STILL THEN. AND AT	LAST	IT WOULD HAPPEN TO ME TOO. /ADAM/ AND THEN? /EVE/ THEN
SIM II (68)	ISLANDERS WILL SEE THEIR DAY OF JUDGMENT AT	LAST	. A DISTANT FUSILLADE OF SHOTGUNS ANSWERS HER. /SIR
HART PREFACE(37)	THE NEXT PHASE. THE PRESENT SITUATION WILL NOT	LAST	. ALTHOUGH THE NEWSPAPER I READ AT BREAKFAST THIS
ARMS I (20)	BACK) THANKS, GRACIOUS YOUNG LADY: I FEEL SAFE AT	LAST	. AND NOW WOULD YOU MIND BREAKING THE NEWS TO YOUR
JOAN 4 (106)	FIRST AND LAST, AS I AM A CHURCHMAN FIRST AND	LAST	. BUT CAN WE NOT SINK OUR DIFFERENCES IN THE FACE OF A
MILL I (162)	MAN I EVER LOVED; AND I HOPE HE WILL NOT BE THE	LAST	. BUT LEGAL DIFFICULTIES DO NOT EXIST FOR PEOPLE WITH
3PLA PREFACE(R26)	RESUSCITATED FASHIONS OF THE GENERATION BEFORE	LAST	. BUT THE STAGE TRICKS OF THE DEVIL'S DISCIPLE ARE NOT,
MRS IV (244)	THE LEAST. I FEEL HE'S PERFECTLY ACCOUNTED FOR AT	LAST	. BUT WHAT A FACER FOR ME, PRADDY! I CANT MARRY HER
BULL IV (157)	TO MORTGAGE TO BUY IT. I MAY AS WELL BE FIRST AS	LAST	. D'YE THINK BROADBENT'D LEN ME A LITTLE? /LARRY/ I'M
GETT PREFACE(229)	IN ENGLAND IS TOO STRAINED AND MISCHIEVOUS TO	LAST	. EUROPE AND AMERICA HAVE LEFT US A CENTURY BEHIND IN
AUGS (279)	HAS GIVEN US THE UPPER HAND OF THESE FELLOWS AT	LAST	. EXCUSE MY VIOLENCE; BUT DISCIPLINE IS ABSOLUTELY
JOAN 5 (111)	WELL, YOUR MAJESTY IS AN ANOINTED KING AT	LAST	. HOW DO YOU LIKE IT? /CHARLES/ I WOULD NOT GO THROUGH
GLIM (187)	THAT MOMENT IN DEATH, THEN I SHALL BE A MAN AT	LAST	. I HAVE TASTED THE WATER OF LIFE FROM THE CUP OF
OVER (175)	BURDEN OF BEING GOOD HAD FALLEN FROM MY SOUL AT	LAST	. I SAW NOTHING THERE BUT A BOSOM TO REST ON: THE BOSOM
HART I (76)	HE HAS ACTUALLY CONDESCENDED TO KISS ME AT	LAST	. I SHALL GO INTO THE GARDEN: IT'S COOLER NOW (SHE
CAPT I (223)	WAW NOT HANATHER? /RANKIN/ WEVE COME TO IT AT	LAST	. I THOUGHT SO. CAPTAIN BRASSBOUND IS A SMUGGLER.
FANY III (301)	LIFE. /MARGARET/ IVE LIVED A LOT SINCE I SAW YOU	LAST	. I WASNT AT MY AUNT'S. ALL THAT TIME THAT YOU WERE IN
2TRU II (57)	MY NEW THINGS FROM PARIS HAVE ARRIVED AT	LAST	. IF YOU WOULD BE SO VERY SWEET AS TO GET THEM TO MY
BUOY 1 (13)	THE TRICK. /FATHER/ THE RUSSIAN MADNESS WILL NOT	LAST	. INDEED IT HAS COLLAPSED ALREADY. I NOW INVEST ALL MY
OVER (178)	LET THIS MOMENT SLIP? /GREGORY/ I PROTEST TO THE	LAST	. I'M AGAINST THIS. I HAVE BEEN PUSHED OVER A
DEST (194)	ME; AND WHAT BEATS A MAN FIRST WILL BEAT HIM	LAST	. (HE GOES MEDITATIVELY INTO THE MOONLIT VINEYARD AND
2TRU III (100)	ME. MY FRIENDS, MY DEAR SARAH IS LADY TALLBOYS AT	LAST	. (HE RESUMES HIS SEAT AND PORES OVER THE PAPER).
ARMS III (49)	THE DISCARDED COAT). AH, NOW I FEEL AT HOME AT	LAST	. (HE SITS DOWN AND TAKES HIS NEWSPAPER WITH A GRUNT
BARB II (296)	MUST HAVE GOT A GOOD DEAL BY IT FROM FIRST TO	LAST	. (HE SITS ON THE TABLE, WITH ONE FOOT ON THE SIDE
DEST (157)	AGAIN AND THROWING GIUSEPPE OFF) MY MAN AT	LAST	. (POINTING TO THE INNER DOOR) GO, ATTEND TO YOUR

SUPR I	(33)	HOPED THAT IT WOULD BE SOMETHING REALLY HEROIC AT	LAST	. (RECOVERING HERSELF) EXCUSE ME, JACK; BUT THE THINGS
HART II	(96)	/MRS HUSHABYE/ (RISING) OH! HERE IS ELLIE AT	LAST	. (SHE GOES BEHIND THE SOFA). /ELLIE/ (ON THE
APPL II	(264)	YOU SAY SUBMERGE? -- SOME OF US WILL SWIM TO THE	LAST	. (TO THE QUEEN) MY DEAR, THE QUEEN STRIKES HER GONG.
MIS.	(151)	OUT OF THE SKY, AND IS NOW, I HOPE, SATISFIED AT	LAST	. LORD SUMMERHAYS: A MAN KNOWN WHEREVER THE BRITISH
MIS.	(197)	MINE. /HYPATIA/ DONT ANSWER HIM, JOEY: IT WONT	LAST	. LORD SUMMERHAYS, I'M SORRY ABOUT BENTLEY; BUT JOEY'S
JITT II	(46)	(PROUDLY) YES: YOU HAVE FOUND THE RIGHT WORD AT	LAST	. LOVERS. /LENKHEIM/ (WHINING PITIABLY) AND YOU COULD
MTH4 II	(189)	I CAN ONLY PLEAD THAT WE DID REFORM OUR CHURCH AT	LAST	. NO DOUBT WE HAD TO MAKE A FEW COMPROMIZES AS A MATTER
GETT	(321)	NOT BELIEVE THAT THE WORLD ITSELF WAS GOING TO	LAST	. NOW WE KNOW THAT WE SHALL HAVE TO GO THROUGH WITH IT.
MIS.	(137)	RELIEF. /LORD SUMMERHAYS/ AT LAST! /HYPATIA/ AT	LAST	. OH, IF I MIGHT ONLY HAVE A HOLIDAY IN AN ASYLUM FOR
MIS.	(143)	ERRANDS FOR OLD MEN, GOOD FOR NOTHING ELSE AT	LAST	. OH, YOU CANT IMAGINE THE FIENDISH SELFISHNESS OF THE
MTH1 I	(13)	THEN I COULD FACE MY DAYS, HOWEVER LONG THEY MAY	LAST	. ONLY, THERE MUST BE SOME END, SOME END: I AM NOT
MTH3	SD(111)	VERY GLUM. THEIR INCREDULITY IS VANQUISHED AT	LAST	. /BURGE-LUBIN/ LOOK HERE. DO YOU CHAPS REALIZE HOW
MTH3	(134)	AFTERNOON? I AM DISPOSED TO BE APPROACHABLE AT	LAST	. /BURGE-LUBIN/ BUT FISHGUARD! TWO HUNDRED AND SEVENTY
HART II	(104)	SPEND HER LIFE WONDERING HOW LONG HER GLOVES WILL	LAST	. /CAPTAIN SHOTOVER/ (PASSING THROUGH) DONT WEAR ANY.
BASH III	(127)	HERSELF INTO HIS ARMS) YOUR BOATS ARE BURNT AT	LAST	. /CASHEL/ THIS IS THE FACE THAT BURNT A THOUSAND
JOAN EPILOG	(156)	OF THANKS TO ME FOR HAVING HAD JUSTICE DONE AT	LAST	. /CAUCHON/ (APPEARING AT THE WINDOW BETWEEN THEM)
BULL III	(129)	ONCE? IT'S A GOOD JOB YOUVE MADE UP YOUR MIND AT	LAST	. /DORAN/ (SUSPICIOUSLY) STOP A BIT: STOP A BIT.
JITT III	(64)	SEE, I DONT KNOW HOW LONG THIS MOOD OF YOURS WILL	LAST	. /EDITH/ LIFE IS SHORT: DONT WASTE ANY MORE OF YOURS
HART II	(104)	YOU WERE ONLY THINKING WHETHER YOUR GLOVES WOULD	LAST	. /ELLIE/ I SHALL NOT HAVE TO THINK ABOUT THAT WHEN WE
PHIL III	(138)	FRIEND HAS MADE A SUCCESSFUL EXPERIMENT AT	LAST	. /JULIA/ (EARNESTLY) IT IS YOU WHO ARE THE
KING I	(220)	MR KNELLER. MR NEWTON MUST TAKE ME IN AND COME	LAST	. /KNELLER/ I WILL GO HOME. I CANNOT EAT IN THIS HOUSE
JOAN 6	(141)	BURN ME NOW? /THE INQUISITOR/ YOU REALIZE IT AT	LAST	. /LADVENU/ THERE ARE EIGHT HUNDRED ENGLISH SOLDIERS
APPL II	(276)	US NAKED, FACE TO FACE WITH OUR REAL SELVES AT	LAST	. /LYSISTRATA/ SO MUCH THE BETTER, IF BY OUR REAL
NEVR II	(230)	LOOK INTO HIS EYES). WE ARE GLAD TO MEET YOU AT	LAST	. /M'COMAS/ MISS GLORIA, I PRESUME? (GLORIA SMILES
APPL I	(220)	WONDERFUL PROSPERITY, SIR. /MAGNUS/ I WANT IT TO	LAST	. /NICOBAR/ WHY SHOULDNT IT LAST? (RISING) OWN THE
CLEO III	(162)	WELL, NEVER MIND: HERE YOU ARE SAFE AND SOUND AT	LAST	. /RUFIO/ AY; AND NOW THAT SHE IS HERE, WHAT ARE WE TO
WIDO III	(52)	I' BIN GITTIN ON A LITTLE SINCE I SAW YOU	LAST	. /SARTORIUS/ SO I SEE. /LICKCHEESE/ I OWE IT PARTLY TO
ROCK II	(259)	THAT WILL BE REALLY RESPONSIBLE GOVERNMENT AT	LAST	. /SIR DEXTER/ SO THAT IS YOUR GAME, IS IT? HAS IT
SUPR II	(69)	USE. MR ROBINSON MAY AS WELL GIVE IT UP FIRST AS	LAST	. /TANNER/ WHY? /STRAKER/ GARN! YOU KNOW WHY. COURSE
INCA PROLOG	(234)	WHEN HE DIED. HE WAS A MILLIONAIRE TO THE	LAST	. /THE ARCHDEACON/ O MAMMON, MAMMON! I AM PUNISHED NOW
CLEO II	(129)	ONLY BECAUSE HE CONQUERED THEM. HIS TURN CAME AT	LAST	. /THEODOTUS/ (FLATTERINGLY) THE DEED WAS NOT YOURS,
WIDO I	(10)	GRIN. /BLANCHE/ WELL, SO YOU HAVE DONE IT AT	LAST	. /TRENCH/ YES. AT LEAST COKANE'S DONE IT. I TOLD YOU
MRS IV	(246)	CHEERFULNESS). WELL, DEARIE, SO HERE YOU ARE AT	LAST	. /VIVIE/ I AM GLAD YOU HAVE COME: I WANT TO SPEAK TO
MRS III	(229)	LESS THAN 40,000 POUNDS INTO IT, FROM FIRST TO	LAST	. /VIVIE/ (STARING AT HIM) DO YOU MEAN TO SAY YOU WERE
VWOO 1	(122)	THAT THE STEWARD IS COMING ROUND WITH THE SOUP AT	LAST	. /Z/ WELL, IT'S HALF PAST ELEVEN, ISNT IT? THE
PRES	(168)	IT'S A MERCY YOUVE FOUND ONE ANOTHER OUT AT	LAST	. THATS ENOUGH NOW.
DOCT I	(88)	FULLY A HUNDRED AND FIFTY SINCE YOURS WAS MADE	LAST	. THATS SOMETHING TO BE PROUD OF. BUT YOUR DISCOVERY'S
BULL PREFACE	(51)	WENT PIGEON-SHOOTING THERE THE YEAR BEFORE	LAST	. THE INHABITANTS COMPLAINED AND MEMORIALIZED; BUT THEY
POSN	(444)	HIM ALL THESE YEARS. BUT HE CAUGHT ME OUT AT	LAST	. THE LAUGH IS WITH HIM AS FAR AS HANGING ME GOES. (HE
KING I	(221)	COMES FIRST. BUT YOU TAKE GOOD CARE THAT HE COMES	LAST	. THE MISTRESS OF THIS AND EVERY OTHER HOUSE IS SHE WHO
LION PREFACE	(17)	SO THAT THE TWO EVENTS BECOME IDENTIFIED AT	LAST	. THERE IS THE OTHER AND MORE ARTIFICIAL SIDE OF THIS
GENV II	(58)	TROUBLE WITH ME? I AM SIMPLY A JUDGE, FIRST AND	LAST	. TO ME IT IS A CONTINUAL TROUBLE AND SCANDAL THAT
LADY PREFACE	(222)	HAVE DONE), TO YORICK'S FAVOR SHE MUST COME AT	LAST	. TO THE DARK LADY HE MUST SOMETIMES HAVE SEEMED CRUEL
FABL I	(102)	(READING THE HEADLINES) " THE WORLD AT PEACE AT	LAST	. WASHINGTON AGREES. MOSCOW AGREES. CHINA AGREES. THE
FABL V	(119)	HOW MANY AT A TIME, NOR HOW LONG THEY OUGHT TO	LAST	. WE ALL WANT THE JUST MAN MADE PERFECT; BUT WHEN OUR
HART III	(143)	WITH FOR ME: AND YET I TOO FEEL THAT THIS CANT	LAST	. WE SIT HERE TALKING, AND LEAVE EVERYTHING TO MANGAN
ROCK I	(214)	WILL BOAST THAT HE HAS MADE ME DO SOMETHING AT	LAST	. WHAT CAN I DO? DO YOU SUPPOSE THAT I CARE LESS ABOUT
MTH4 II	(180)	SEEMS TO ME THEY MIGHT AS WELL SHOOT YOU FIRST AS	LAST	. WHY DONT THEY? /NAPOLEON/ BECAUSE THEIR LOVE OF
DOCT II	(116)	YOU! FROM THIS NIGHT I CAN BEGIN TO BE HAPPY AT	LAST	. YOU DONT KNOW WHAT I FEEL. SHE SITS DOWN IN TEARS.
2TRU II	(65)	AWFULLY NICE FOR THE FIRST FEW DAYS, IT DOESNT	LAST	. YOU GET THE BEST OUT OF MEN BY HAVING THEM ALWAYS
MIS.	(122)	YOU AGAIN; AND YOU MAY AS WELL SAY NO FIRST AS	LAST	. YOU NEEDNT BE AFRAID OF THE ARISTOCRACY, DEAR: THEYRE
DEST	(158)	(WATCH IN HAND) WELL, SIR, YOU HAVE COME AT	LAST	. YOUR INSTRUCTIONS WERE THAT I SHOULD ARRIVE HERE AT
CAPT III	(299)	BLUNDERED SOMEHOW ON THE SECRET OF COMMAND AT	LAST	(HE KISSES HER HANDS): THANKS FOR THAT, AND FOR A
MRS I	(195)	TO HER. DO YOU REMEMBER THE ADVICE YOU GAVE ME	LAST	JULY, GOV'NOR? /REV. S./ (SEVERELY) YES. I ADVISED
CAND I	(92)	HE FOUND HIM SLEEPING ON THE EMBANKMENT	LAST	JUNE. HAVNT YOU NOTICED OUR NEW PICTURE (POINTING TO
BARB I	(250)	/LADY BRITOMART/ YES, YOU, OF COURSE. YOU WERE 24	LAST	JUNE. YOUVE BEEN AT HARROW AND CAMBRIDGE. YOUVE BEEN TO
DOCT PREFACE	(11)	TO SOCIAL REFORM, THE STRANGLING OF THE	LAST	KING WITH THE ENTRAILS OF THE LAST PRIEST, SUBSTITUTED
PHIL I	(70)	QUAINTLY AT HER). THAT MUST POSITIVELY BE MY	LAST	KISS, GRACE; OR I SHALL BECOME DOWNRIGHT SILLY. LET US
MTH4 I	(141)	BE AT LEAST A HUNDRED AND FIFTY YEARS SINCE I	LAST	LAUGHED. BUT IF YOU DO THAT ANY MORE I SHALL CERTAINLY
MILL I	(157)	LITTLE OPERA COMPANY WHICH WAS THEN ON ITS	LAST	LEGS IN THE SUBURBS TO ALLOW HIM TO APPEAR FOR ONE
MILL IV	(189)	RID OF THE OLD THINGS IN IT. IT WAS ON ITS	LAST	LEGS WHEN YOU SAW IT, SIR. I WAS ASHAMED OF IT.
GETT PREFACE	(235)	THAT WE ALL BELIEVE THAT OUR RELIGION IS ON ITS	LAST	LEGS, WHEREAS THE TRUTH IS THAT IT IS NOT YET BORN.
AUGS	(277)	IT IN THE -- OH, HERE IT IS! NO: THIS IS LUCY'S	LAST	LETTER. /THE LADY/ (ELEGIACALLY) LUCY'S LAST LETTER!
AUGS	(277)	LAST LETTER. /THE LADY/ (ELEGIACALLY) LUCY'S	LAST	LETTER! WHAT A TITLE FOR A PICTURE PLAY! /AUGUSTUS/ (
GENV IV	(94)	PIECES IN YOUR FACE. YOU DID NOTHING. I TOOK YOUR	LAST	LOCARNO PACT AND MARCHED 18,000 SOLDIERS THROUGH IT. I
DOCT PREFACE	(71)	SUCH ABSURD PANIC SCANDALS AS THAT OF THE	LAST	LONDON EPIDEMIC, WHERE A FEE OF HALF-A-CROWN PER
POSN PREFACE	(403)	AND MR BALFOUR MIGHT NOT IMPROBABLY COST MORE AND	LAST	LONGER THAN A CIVIL WAR. AND WHY SHOULD THE CHOSEN
SHAK PREFACE	(135)	SUPPLY ONE OF MY FAMOUS DRAMAS FOR THEM, NOT TO	LAST	LONGER THAN TEN MINUTES OR THEREABOUTS. I ACCOMPLISHED
MIS. PREFACE	(3)	HUMAN BEINGS VISIBLY WEAR OUT, THOUGH THEY	LAST	LONGER THAN THEIR FRIENDS THE DOGS. TURTLES, PARROTS,
SIM II	(70)	PLACE? OF COURSE NOT. THE WHOLE BUSINESS WILL	LAST	LONGER THAN WHAT YOU CALL A YEAR. WE GAVE THE ENGLISH
MIS.	(161)	DOESNT IT? /LINA/ IT MEANS SOMETHING THAT WILL	LAST	LONGER THAN YES. I LIKE YOU. I ADMIT YOU TO MY
SUPR III	(92)	WE HAVE A RAGE FOR 17; BUT IT DOES NOT	LAST	LONG. JUST AT PRESENT THE FASHIONABLE AGE IS 40-- OR
ARMS I	(10)	OUT. KEEP OUT OF THE WAY; AND DONT LOOK. IT WONT	LAST	LONG; BUT IT WILL NOT BE NICE. (HE DRAWS HIS SABRE AND
MILL IV	(191)	AT THEIR AGE. MY FATHER HAD A STROKE AND WONT	LAST	LONG, I'M AFRAID. AND MY MOTHER HAS GONE A BIT SILLY.
ARMS I	SD(21)	EYES CLOSE. SHE GOES TO THE DOOR, TURNING FOR A	LAST	LOOK AT HIM, SHE SEES THAT HE IS DROPPING OFF TO SLEEP.
DEVL II	(41)	SERGEANT OPENS THE DOOR). /RICHARD/ (TAKING A	LAST	LOOK ROUND HIM) GOODBYE, WIFE: GOODBYE, HOME. MUFFLE
BARB III	(316)	ON IN YEARS; AND MY PARTNER LAZARUS HAS AT	LAST	MADE A STAND AND INSISTED THAT THE SUCCESSION MUST BE
PYGM II	(237)	ALL I ASK IS MY RIGHTS AS A FATHER; AND YOURE THE	LAST	MAN ALIVE TO EXPECT ME TO LET HER GO FOR NOTHING; FOR I
MTH2	(70)	PROGRAM OF HANGING HIM? /BURGE/ STUFF! I AM THE	LAST	MAN ALIVE TO HANG ANYBODY; BUT THE PEOPLE WOULDNT
KING II	(229)	ALEXANDER BORGIA WAS A JOLLY FELLOW; AND I AM THE	LAST	MAN ALIVE TO THROW STONES AT HIM; BUT HE WAS NOT A
ROCK II	(246)	AND THE LANDED CLASSES ARE WITH YOU TO THE	LAST	MAN FOR IT, ACCEPT THE HUMBLE GRATITUDE OF A PAUPERIZED
APPL INTRLUD	(250)	ONE MAN WILL DO AS WELL AS ANOTHER, AND WHICH THE	LAST	MAN HOLDS SUBJECT TO SIX MONTHS NOTICE IN THE DIVORCE
BUOY IV	(48)	IT'S A QUEER BUSINESS: I THOUGHT I WAS THE VERY	LAST	MAN IN THE WORLD TO PUT MY NOSE INTO A TEMPLE. HOWEVER,
MRS PREFACE	(155)	AS IT DOES AT PRESENT. CONSEQUENTLY, I AM THE	LAST	MAN TO DENY THAT IF THE NET EFFECT OF PERFORMING MRS
DOCT IV	(165)	BE KIND TO RIDGEON ALWAYS; BECAUSE HE WAS THE	LAST	MAN WHO AMUSED ME. /RIDGEON/ (RELENTLESS) WAS I?
JITT I	(17)	THE MOST HARDENED MATERIALIST YOU KNOW: THE VERY	LAST	MAN YOU COULD IMAGINE LENDING HIMSELF TO SUCH A
DEVL III	(62)	IN ARMS TO HOLD THE TOWN AGAINST YOU TO THE	LAST	MAN. BUT YOU ARRIVED, UNFORTUNATELY, BEFORE WE HAD GOT
ROCK II	(254)	THE ARMY WILL BE WITH SIR ARTHUR TO THE	LAST	MAN. HE HAS THE WHOLE PROPERTIED CLASS ON HIS SIDE. BUT
DOCT PREFACE	(55)	RECOVERED WHILST THE VACCINATED SUCCUMBED TO THE	LAST	MAN, OR, TO TAKE ANOTHER COMMON INSTANCE, COMPARISONS
LION I	(121)	/ANDROCLES/ EASY, FERROVIUS, EASY: YOU BROKE THE	LAST	MAN'S JAW. LENTULUS, WITH A MOAN OF TERROR, ATTEMPTS TO
MRS I	(186)	WORLD ART CAN OPEN UP TO YOU. /VIVIE/ YES I HAVE.	LAST	MAY I SPENT SIX WEEKS IN LONDON WITH HONORIA FRASER.
ARMS III	(52)	A STRAIGHTFORWARD MAN MYSELF; BUT IT WOULDNT	LAST	ME A WHOLE MORNING. /RAINA/ (STARING HAUGHTILY AT HIM)
CAPT I	(228)	AND HOW HAVE YE BEEN, SIR HOWRRD, SINCE OUR	LAST	MEETING THAT MORNING NIGH FORTY YEAR AGO DOWN AT THE
CAPT II	(255)	SHE DIED IN HER NATIVE COUNTRY, YEARS AFTER OUR	LAST	MEETING. PERHAPS YOU WERE TOO YOUNG TO KNOW THAT SHE
2TRU III	(104)	TO YOU WHICH I MUST DISCHARGE AT ONCE. AT OUR	LAST	MEETING, I STRUCK YOU. /MRS MOPPLY/ STRUCK ME! YOU
CAPT I	(228)	GREATLY SURPRISED, PULLING HIMSELF TOGETHER) OUR	LAST	MEETING! MR RANKIN: HAVE I BEEN UNFORTUNATE ENOUGH TO
ARMS III	(50)	/RAINA/ YOU LOOK EVER SO MUCH NICER THAN WHEN WE	LAST	MET. (HE LOOKS UP, SURPRISED). WHAT HAVE YOU DONE TO
MILL IV	(197)	THAT HIS INJURIES WERE INFLICTED BY YOU WHEN YOU	LAST	MET, MRS FITZFASSENDEN. /EPIFANIA/ BY ME! AM I A
FABL V	(120)	ENZYMES AND THE REST, WE NEVER AGREE ON THE	LAST	MILLIGRAM OF EACH INGREDIENT; AND IT IS THAT MILLIGRAM
MTH4 I	(162)	CHILDHOOD. A LIE WILL LAST YOUR TIME: IT WILL NOT	LAST	MINE. IF I KNEW I HAD TO DIE IN TWENTY YEARS IT WOULD
PYGM V	(283)	TO LEAVE YOU; AND YOU ALWAYS GOT ROUND HER AT THE	LAST	MINUTE. AND YOU DONT CARE A BIT FOR HER. AND YOU DONT
BULL PREFACE	(30)	THE PEACE OF THE TOWN, YET BACK OUT AT THE	LAST	MOMENT BECAUSE HE COULD NOT BRING HIMSELF TO SWALLOW
LION I	(123)	HE'S NEVER QUITE SURE OF HIMSELF. SUPPOSE AT THE	LAST	MOMENT IN THE ARENA, WITH THE GLADIATORS THERE TO FIGHT
WIDO II	(25)	BUT DO NOT PUT OFF MY BUSINESS AGAIN TO THE	LAST	MOMENT. HAS THERE BEEN ANY FURTHER TROUBLE ABOUT THE ST
6CAL	SD(98)	AND BIND HIS MOUTH WITH IT. HE BARKS TO THE	LAST	MOMENT. JOHN OF GAUNT LAUGHS ECSTATICALLY AT THIS
HART III	(137)	CAN THROW MR MANGAN OVER AT ANY TIME UP TO THE	LAST	MOMENT. VERY FEW MEN IN HIS POSITION GO BANKRUPT. YOU
GENV IV	(129)	OR GET DRUNK. WE CANNOT WORK FOR OURSELVES TO THE	LAST	MOMENT; BUT WE CAN ALL WORK FOR HONOR. (HE GOES OUT).

METH PREFACE(R84)	ACCORDING TO A PRESCRIPTION WHICH GIVES ONLY THE	LAST	MOMENTS OF THE LAST ACT. SHAKESPEAR DID NOT MAKE HAMLET
3PLA PREFACE(R25)	COURT MARTIAL, THE SCAFFOLD, THE REPRIEVE AT THE	LAST	MOMENT, AS HE RECOGNIZES BEEFSTEAK PUDDING ON THE BILL
GENV PREFACE(8)	ENOUGH TO FRIGHTEN HER OUT OF IT? IN THE	LAST	MONTHS THE BOMBS LAUNCHED BY YOUNG BRITISH WARRIORS
HART PREFACE(29)	IS TRUE THAT THE PEOPLE WHO THOUGHT IT COULD NOT	LAST	MORE THAN SIX MONTHS WERE VERY SIGNALLY REFUTED BY THE
METH PREFACE(R27)	FROM HAND TO MOUTH, AND CAN HARDLY RECALL THE	LAST	MOVE BUT ONE, OR FORESEE THE NEXT BUT TWO. ALSO, WHEN I
METH PREFACE(R83)	ENERGY; BUT PRAY CAN ANYONE EXPLAIN THE	LAST	MOVEMENT OF HIS HAMMERKLAVIER SONATA, OPUS 106,
BUOY IV (53)	IT. /OLD BILL/ LEAVE ME OUT OF IT: I SHALL NOT	LAST	MUCH LONGER: YOU HAVE A LIFETIME TO GIVE HER. AWAY WITH
MTH2 (39)	FOR YOU; BUT IT'S GOOD ENOUGH FOR ME. IT WILL	LAST	MY TIME, ANYHOW (HE LAUGHS GOOD-HUMOREDLY). /FRANKLYN/
OVER (181)	IT'S ALWAYS THE HAPPY MARRIAGES THAT BREAK UP. AT	LAST	MY WIFE AND I AGREED THAT WE OUGHT TO TAKE A HOLIDAY.
DEVL III (51)	VISIT IS VERY KIND OF YOU. AND HOW ARE YOU AFTER	LAST	NIGHT? I HAD TO LEAVE YOU BEFORE YOU RECOVERED; BUT I
CAPT III (273)	YE NOT HEAR WHAT SIR HOWRRD TOLD ME ON THE YACHT	LAST	NIGHT? /LADY CICELY/ ALL A MISTAKE, MR RANKIN: ALL A
MRS III (221)	DO YOU KNOW, GOV'NOR, WHAT YOU SAID AND THOUGHT	LAST	NIGHT? /PRAED/ (COMING IN THROUGH THE HEDGE) GOOD
DEVL III (51)	SO SELFISH AS THAT, WHY DID YOU LET THEM TAKE YOU	LAST	NIGHT? /RICHARD/ (GAILY) UPON MY LIFE, MRS ANDERSON,
SIM II (54)	THE SAME HOUR. DO YOU SEE THAT SLOOP THAT CAME IN	LAST	NIGHT? /SIR CHARLES/ WHAT IS IT? /HYERING/ THE
GENV III (67)	MINISTER'S SPEECH IN THE DEBATE ON THE LEAGUE	LAST	NIGHT? /THE SECRETARY/ (ILLHUMOREDLY) YES. HALF ABOUT
DEVL III (69)	THEY ARE SENDING THE MAN WHO RAISED SPRINGTOWN	LAST	NIGHT AND DROVE US OUT; SO THAT WE MAY KNOW THAT WE ARE
PHIL II (125)	THIS FROM HIM. /GRACE/ I LEARNT IT FROM YOURSELF,	LAST	NIGHT AND NOW. HOW I HATE TO BE A WOMAN WHEN I SEE, BY
GENV I (43)	PLEASURE OF MAKING THIS GENTLEMAN'S ACQUAINTANCE	LAST	NIGHT AT MY HOTEL. HIS INTEREST IN THE CHURCH OF
ROCK II (236)	/BASHAM/ OH COME, P.M.! IF YOU WERE TOO DRUNK	LAST	NIGHT AT THE GUILDHALL TO KNOW WHAT YOU WERE SAYING,
ROCK II (234)	ALLOW HIM TO BE DISTURBED. SHE SAYS HIS SPEECH	LAST	NIGHT AT THE GUILDHALL BANQUET QUITE TIRED HIM OUT.
LADY (239)	THE SAME LADY TOO. /THE MAN/ NO! /THE BEEFEATER/	LAST	NIGHT HE STOOD HERE ON YOUR ERRAND, AND IN YOUR SHOES.
BARB III (318)	RECOILS, DEEPLY WOUNDED BY HIS TONE). UNTIL	LAST	NIGHT I DID NOT TAKE YOUR ATTITUDE SERIOUSLY, BECAUSE I
SIM II (70)	NAME OF INGE, I THINK. I ANNOUNCED IT TO HIM	LAST	NIGHT IN A DREAM, AND ASKED HIM WHETHER THE ENGLISH
DEVL I (5)	(ESSIE GOES OUT). SHE'D HAVE GONE TO BED	LAST	NIGHT JUST AS IF NOTHING HAD HAPPENED IF I'D LET HER.
AUGS (264)	CLERK/ YES. /AUGUSTUS/ I ADDRESSED A MEETING HERE	LAST	NIGHT -- WENT STRAIGHT TO THE PLATFORM FROM THE TRAIN.
SUPR III (137)	/STRAKER/ DO ARE YOU CALLIN COMRADE? /MENDOZA/	LAST	NIGHT THE ADVANTAGE WAS WITH ME. THE ROBBER OF THE POOR
MRS III (225)	BUT WHAT ON EARTH HAS HAPPENED TO YOU?	LAST	NIGHT WE WERE PERFECTLY AGREED AS TO YOUR MOTHER AND
BULL III (118)	SIR. /BROADBENT/ DID YOU NOTICE ANYTHING ABOUT ME	LAST	NIGHT WHEN I CAME IN WITH THAT LADY? /HODSON/ (
BULL III (118)	BEEN ENJOYING YOURSELF, YOURE A BIT HEARTY LIKE.	LAST	NIGHT YOU SEEMED RATHER LOW, IF ANYTHING. /BROADBENT/ I
ROCK II (236)	WARM THEM) I REMEMBER PERFECTLY WELL WHAT I SAID	LAST	NIGHT, AND I DRANK NOTHING BUT BARLEY WATER. /BASHAM/ (
PHIL II (109)	WELL? /CHARTERIS/ I'M AFRAID TO FACE YOU AFTER	LAST	NIGHT, CAN YOU IMAGINE A MORE HORRIBLE SCENE? DONT YOU
GENV I (44)	QUITE RECOVERED YET, I THINK. I AM YOUR FRIEND OF	LAST	NIGHT, DONT YOU RECOGNIZE ME? /BISHOP/ A BOLSHIE! IF
PHIL II (125)	OF TRAGIC) I KNOW I WAS WRONG TO ACT AS I DID	LAST	NIGHT, I BEG YOUR PARDON. I AM SORRY. I WAS MAD.
PHIL II (110)	IT IS, GRACE: YOU CANT FORGET THAT HORRIBLE SCENE	LAST	NIGHT, IMAGINE HER SAYING I HAD KISSED HER WITHIN THE
PYGM II (220)	OF GETTING BACK A BIT OF WHAT YOU CHUCKED AT ME	LAST	NIGHT, (CONFIDENTIALLY) YOUD HAD A DROP IN, HADNT
BULL IV (163)	LOWERING HIS VOICE) NORA: I WAS IN EARNEST	LAST	NIGHT, (NORA MOVES AS IF TO RISE). NO: ONE MOMENT, YOU
ROCK II (245)	/SIR ARTHUR/ NOT AT ALL. ONLY A TALK OVER	LAST	NIGHT, MAKE YOURSELF AT HOME. /SIR DEXTER/ YOU COME IN
AUGS (267)	CAPABLE OF. YOU SAID SO YOURSELF IN YOUR SPEECH	LAST	NIGHT, /AUGUSTUS/ I DID NOT KNOW THAT I WAS TALKING TO
PHIL II (100)	(TO CUTHBERTSON) ONLY WHAT WE WERE SPEAKING OF	LAST	NIGHT, /CUTHBERTSON/ WELL, CHARTERIS, I THINK THAT IS
BULL III (117)	/BROADBENT/ I HOPE THEY MADE YOU COMFORTABLE	LAST	NIGHT, /HODSON/ I WAS NO WORSE THAN YOU WERE ON THAT
DEVL III (53)	BUT I HAVE PROVIDED FOR HER: I MADE MY OWN WILL	LAST	NIGHT, /JUDITH/ (STONILY, AFTER A MOMENT'S SILENCE)
CAPT III (276)	RANKIN. I HOPE YOU GOT HOME SAFELY FROM THE YACHT	LAST	NIGHT, /RANKIN/ QUITE SAFE, THANK YE, SIR HOWRRD. /LADY
SUPR II (52)	(SELF-REPROACHFULLY) I WAS BRUTE ENOUGH TO DO SO	LAST	NIGHT, /TANNER/ BRUTE ENOUGH! WHAT DO YOU MEAN?
PYGM II (219)	OF IT) WHY, THIS IS THE GIRL I JOTTED DOWN	LAST	NIGHT, SHE'S NO USE: IVE GOT ALL THE RECORDS I WANT OF
SIM II (54)	TO THE ROADSTEAD) LOOK! FIVE MORE CRUISERS IN	LAST	NIGHT, THE PAPERS SAY IT IS THE FIRST TIME THE FLEETS
VWOO 1 (115)	PAST TEN. /A/ THE CLOCKS WERE PUT ON HALF AN HOUR	LAST	NIGHT, WE ARE GOING EAST. /Z/ I ALWAYS THINK IT ADDS TO
BUOY 1 (9)	MIND. I HAD A LONG TALK WITH YOUR MOTHER ABOUT IT	LAST	NIGHT. YOU HAVE BEEN TIED TO HER APRON STRING QUITE
BULL III (137)	WELL, LET US SAY QUOITS. I SAW TWO MEN, I THINK,	LAST	NIGHT-- BUT AFTER ALL, THESE ARE QUESTIONS OF DETAIL.
DEVL III (50)	TIP TOP, MUM. THE CHAPLAIN LOOKED IN TO SEE HIM	LAST	NIGHT; AND HE WON SEVENTEEN SHILLINGS OFF HIM AT SPOIL
BARB II (298)	IT, OF COURSE. MRS BAINES SAYS SHE PRAYED FOR IT	LAST	NIGHT; AND SHE HAS NEVER PRAYED FOR IT IN VAIN: NEVER
PHIL II (101)	IT WORTH MY WHILE TO BE EXPOSED TO SUCH SCENES AS	LAST	NIGHT'S. YOU HAD MUCH BETTER GO BACK TO JULIA, AND
PHIL II (100)	IT STRIKE YOU AS RATHER ODD, OUR BEING UP THERE	LAST	NIGHT, AND MRS TRANFIELD NOT WITH US? /CRAVEN/ WELL,
BULL III (123)	/LARRY/ WHAT IS IT? /BROADBENT/ I GOT DRUNK	LAST	NIGHT, AND PROPOSED TO MISS REILLY. /LARRY/ YOU WHAT..
ROCK II (243)	SUBSIDING) YOU WERE QUITE RIGHT AT THE GUILDHALL	LAST	NIGHT, ARTHUR: YOU MUST NATIONALIZE THE LAND AND PUT A
PYGM V (268)	FRIGHTENED HER! NONSENSE! SHE WAS LEFT	LAST	NIGHT, AS USUAL, TO TURN OUT THE LIGHTS AND ALL THAT;
CAPT III (272)	/RANKIN/ BUT YE CANNOT SEE THEM. THEY DECAMPED	LAST	NIGHT, BACK TO THEIR CASTLES IN THE ATLAS. /LADY
BARB III (322)	/UNDERSHAFT/ (TO CUSINS) QUITE WELL AFTER	LAST	NIGHT, EURIPIDES, EH? /CUSINS/ AS WELL AS CAN BE
DEVL III (54)	GOODNESS THAT ONLY COMES OUT RED HOT. WHAT I DID	LAST	NIGHT, I DID IN COLD BLOOD, CARING NOT HALF SO MUCH FOR
SIM II (76)	THE FIRST LORD OF THE ADMIRALTY, INTERVIEWED	LAST	NIGHT, SAID THAT HE COULD NOT MAKE HEAD OR TAIL OF THE
BARB III (318)	YES. (TO STEPHEN) IT IS WHAT I TOLD YOU	LAST	NIGHT, STEPHEN. /UNDERSHAFT/ (SULKILY) I UNDERSTAND
JITT II (27)	GOING ASLEEP AT YOUR AGE! YOU WERE NOT CALLED UP	LAST	NIGHT, WERE YOU? /FESSLER/ NO. BUT, BY JIMMINY,
PYGM V (279)	HAVE DONE IT ONCE; BUT NOW I CANT GO BACK TO IT.	LAST	NIGHT, WHEN I WAS WANDERING ABOUT, A GIRL SPOKE TO ME;
HART PREFACE(10)	THEY WENT ON TO OVARIES AND APPENDICES UNTIL AT	LAST	NO ONE'S INSIDE WAS SAFE. THEY EXPLAINED THAT THE HUMAN
HART PREFACE(29)	WOUNDS, IT IS NEARLY TWENTY YEARS SINCE I WAS	LAST	OBLIGED TO INTRODUCE A PLAY IN THE FORM OF A BOOK FOR
DEVL EPILOG (81)	OF COMMONS BY THE COURT PARTY; AND WHEN HE AT	LAST	OBTAINED A COMMITTEE, THE KING GOT RID OF IT BY A
METH PREFACE(R66)	NOT SEE THE SIGNIFICANCE OF THE FACT THAT ON THE	LAST	OCCASION ON WHICH GOD HAD BEEN " EXPELLED WITH A
APPL PREFACE(177)	IT AND HAVE A FANCY FOR IT OR AN INTEREST IN IT.	LAST	OCTOBER (1929) I WAS ASKED TO ADDRESS THE ENORMOUS
ARMS II (24)	ABOUT HIM THAT SHE WOULDNT LET HIM HEAR THE	LAST	OF FOR SIX MONTHS IF I BLABBED THEM TO HER. I KNOW
JOAN 6 (151)	A WRY SMILE, THINKING OF WHAT LADVENU SAID) THE	LAST	OF HER? HM! I WONDER!
JOAN 6 (151)	IS AT THE BOTTOM OF THE RIVER. YOU HAVE HEARD THE	LAST	OF HER. /WARWICK/ (WITH A WRY SMILE, THINKING OF WHAT
CAND I SD(79)	BUSILY AT HER MACHINE WHILST MORELL OPENS THE	LAST	OF HIS MORNING'S LETTERS. HE REALIZES ITS CONTENTS WITH
BULL III (121)	CORNY FOR. HE HASNT BEEN HERE SINCE HE PAID THE	LAST	OF HIS OLD RENT; AND THEN HE AS GOOD AS THREW IT IN
MRS II (202)	PENNY. HE HAS HAD HIS PATRIMONY; AND HE SPENT THE	LAST	OF IT IN JULY. (MRS WARREN'S FACE FALLS). /CROFTS/ (
DOCT IV (163)	TO DISAPPOINT THE POOR LITTLE WORMS; BUT THE	LAST	OF ME SHALL BE THE FLAME IN THE BURNING BUSH. WHENEVER
MRS II (211)	IF YOU PLEASE; BUT IF YOU DO, YOU WILL SEE THE	LAST	OF ME TOMORROW MORNING. /MRS WARREN/ OH, IT'S TOO
HART III (141)	MR DUNN. BUT I KNOW NOW THAT IT WAS ONLY THE	LAST	OF MY INFLUENZA. I FOUND THAT I WAS NOT REMEMBERED AND
2TRU PREFACE(15)	WHICH THEY CALLED THE CHURCH; AND IN DUE TIME THE	LAST	OF THE CHESTERTONS JOINED THIS CATHOLIC CHURCH, LIKE A
SUPR PREFACE(R14)	BYRON'S DON JUAN OUT OF ACCOUNT. MOZART'S IS THE	LAST	OF THE TRUE DON JUANS; FOR BY THE TIME HE WAS OF AGE,
DEVL III (68)	BURGOYNE WAITS WITH UNRUFFLED SERENITY UNTIL THE	LAST	OF THEM DISAPPEARS. THEN HE BECOMES VERY GRAVE, AND
GETT (261)	IF I WAS TO GET NERVOUS OVER MARRYING THE	LAST	OF THEM. /MRS BRIDGENORTH/ I HAVE ALWAYS SAID YOU WERE
GETT (262)	HANDS). ANOTHER NIECE TO GIVE AWAY. THIS IS THE	LAST	OF THEM. /THE GENERAL/ (VERY GLOOMY) YES, ALICE.
LION PREFACE(40)	ANY BELIEVER COMPILING A GOSPEL AFTER THE	LAST	OF THESE CONTEMPORARIES HAD PASSED AWAY, WOULD EITHER
PHIL II (127)	YOUR COMPLAINT, AND THAT JULIA MAY SOON SEE THE	LAST	OF THIS MOST OUTRAGEOUS INSTITUTION. CHARTERIS RETURNS.
MTH3 (122)	HE OUGHT TO PAINT. AND NOW THAT MY FOOT IS AT	LAST	ON THE THRESHOLD OF THE TEMPLE I FIND THAT IT IS ALSO
ROCK II (238)	GOVERNMENT, WHICH NOW, THANK HEAVEN, WONT	LAST	ONE DAY AFTER THE NEXT MEETING OF PARLIAMENT? /SIR
MIS. (135)	" AFTER ALL, HES ONLY A LINENDRAPER." BUT AT	LAST	ONE DAY HE SAID TO ME, " JOHN IS A KING," /BENTLEY/ HOW
JOAN 5 (112)	HIRE/ YOU AND I TOGETHER: YES. /JOAN/ NO: I SHALL	LAST	ONLY A YEAR FROM THE BEGINNING. /ALL THE OTHERS/ WHAT!
PYGM EPILOG (299)	AND BUY A BUTTONHOLE FROM ELIZA. NOW HERE IS A	LAST	OPPORTUNITY FOR ROMANCE. WOULD YOU NOT LIKE TO BE
BULL PREFACE(36)	IT MAY SEEM INCREDIBLE THAT LONG AFTER THE	LAST	ORANGEMAN SHALL LAY DOWN HIS CHALK FOR EVER, THE
ARMS III (49)	(TO SERGIUS, HANDING A PAPER) THATS THE	LAST	ORDER. /PETKOFF/ (JUMPING UP) WHAT! FINISHED?
SUPR III (131)	NOVEL TO US THE ACTORS, IS BUT THE HISTORY OF THE	LAST	OSCILLATION REPEATED; NAY MORE, THAT IN THE UNTHINKABLE
GETT (343)	NOT FALLEN WITHERED IN THE FIRE: I HAVE COME AT	LAST	OUT BEYOND, TO THE BACK OF GODSPEED. /THE BISHOP/ AND
MTH4 II (191)	LIVED ON THE ASSUMPTION THAT YOU WERE GOING TO	LAST	OUT FOR EVER AND EVER AND EVER. IMMORTAL, YOU THOUGHT
MTH3 (111)	IS ONLY THREE HUNDRED YEARS. /BARNABAS/ YOU WILL	LAST	OUT MY TIME ANYHOW: THATS ENOUGH FOR ME. /THE
DOCT IV (156)	NEGATIVE OR POSITIVE, THE LAD'S DONE FOR. HE WONT	LAST	OUT THE AFTERNOON. HE'LL GO SUDDENLY: IVE OFTEN SEEN
HART PREFACE(22)	BOGEY STORIES AND MELODRAMATIC NONSENSE, WHICH AT	LAST	OVERREACHED ITSELF AND MADE IT IMPOSSIBLE TO STOP THE
NEVR II (239)	CRAMPTON'S RIGHT SHOULDER) THE WHISKY'S ON THE	LAST	PAGE BUT ONE. /CRAMPTON/ LET ME ALONE, CHILD. /DOLLY/
ROCK II (241)	DOZEN MEN WHO WERE FORCED INTO BANKRUPTCY IN THE	LAST	PANIC, THOUGH THEY WERE AS SOLVENT AS YOU OR I. BUT SIR
MILL IV (205)	HEAD. YOU SOLD IT TO THE MAN SUPERFLEW FOR THE	LAST	PENNY OF HIS SAVINGS; AND THE WOMEN STILL SLAVE FOR HIM
GENV PREFACE(18)	GERMANY, DEFEATED AND SUBJECTED FAR BEYOND THE	LAST	PENNY SHE COULD SPARE, COULD BE TORN UP CLAUSE BY
SUPR I (27)	I PROTEST AGAINST IT. I AM READY TO PUT DOWN MY	LAST	PENNY TO SAVE HER FROM BEING DRIVEN TO RUN TO YOU FOR
SUPR I (13)	HAPPINESS, TAVY, I WOULD BUY IT FOR YOU WITH MY	LAST	PENNY. BUT A LIFETIME OF HAPPINESS! NO MAN ALIVE COULD
ROCK II (244)	OF THE CITY. /SIR JAFNA/ TO THE LAST VOTE, TO THE	LAST	PENNY, THESE PIRATES THINK NOTHING OF EXTORTING A
JOAN 2 (71)	ON A CHICKEN OR A SCRAP OF MUTTON. HE BORROWS MY	LAST	PENNY; AND THERE IS NOTHING TO SHEW FOR IT. (A PAGE
ROCK II (237)	ON UNEARNED INCOMES. /SIR DEXTER/ YES: TAKE OUR	LAST	PENNY! AND WHEN THE LITTLE THAT THE PRESENT RUINOUS
OVER PREFACE(155)	BE RETROGRADE, ARE OFTEN, AND INDEED MOSTLY, THE	LAST	PEOPLE IN THE WORLD TO ENGAGE IN UNCONVENTIONAL
GETT PREFACE(213)	MOTHERS FOR THE GOOD OF THE RACE ARE THE VERY	LAST	PEOPLE TO PRESS THEIR SERVICES ON THEIR COUNTRY IN THAT

MIS. (195)	YOUNG MEN; AND OLD MEN RUN AFTER YOU. AND I'M THE	LAST	PERSON IN THE WORLD TO HEAR OF IT. /HYPATIA/ HOW COULD
JITT III (63)	WHO MADE A MISTAKE LIKE THAT ONCE WOULD BE THE	LAST	PERSON IN THE WORLD TO MAKE THE SAME MISTAKE AGAIN?
LION PREFACE(30)	SECOND COMING TO BE FULFILLED. THE DEATH OF THE	LAST	PERSON WHO HAD BEEN ALIVE WHEN JESUS SAID " THERE BE
MRS PREFACE(155)	DRAMATIC METHOD THAT I HAVE NO DOUBT I SHALL AT	LAST	PERSUADE EVEN LONDON TO TAKE ITS CONSCIENCE AND ITS
HART II (96)	IT DOESNT MATTER, ANYHOW, BECAUSE I HAVE AT	LAST	PERSUADED YOUR FATHER THAT YOU DONT WANT TO MARRY HIM.
CLEO IV (181)	IN BRITAIN-- THAT WESTERN LAND OF ROMANCE-- THE	LAST	PIECE OF EARTH ON THE EDGE OF THE OCEAN THAT SURROUNDS
MIS. SD(199)	HANGING AS IF HE TOO HAD BEEN EXERCISED TO THE	LAST	PITCH OF FATIGUE. HE IS VERY SAD. THEY STARE AT HIM AS
BASH II,1, (112)	WHOSE EXPLOITS, WRIT IN MY CHARACTER FROM MY	LAST	PLACE, WOULD DAMN ME INTO OSTLERDOM. AND YET THERES AN
SHAK PREFACE(135)	PREFACE. THIS IN ALL ACTUARIAL PROBABILITY IS MY	LAST	PLAY AND THE CLIMAX OF MY EMINENCE, SUCH AS IT IS. I
SUPR III (74)	/MENDOZA/ (FORCIBLY) NO, BY THUNDER: YOUR	LAST	POINT OF ORDER TOOK HALF AN HOUR. BESIDES, ANARCHISTS
JOAN PREFACE(8)	IMBECILITIES. JOAN'S GOOD LOOKS. TO PUT THE	LAST	POINT ROUGHLY, ANY BOOK ABOUT JOAN WHICH BEGINS BY
3PLA PREFACE(R14)	TO BE MERELY TANTALIZED. THE BREAKDOWN ON THE	LAST	POINT WAS CONCLUSIVE, FOR WHEN THE MANAGERS TRIED TO
PYGM EPILOG (289)	WITH HIM. BUT AS SHE FEELS SURE OF HIM ON THAT	LAST	POINT, SHE HAS NO DOUBT AT ALL AS TO HER COURSE, AND
LION PREFACE(30)	SON OF MAN COMING IN HIS KINGDOM" DESTROYED THE	LAST	POSSIBILITY OF THE PROMISED SECOND COMING, AND BORE OUT
ROCK II (277)	WHAT YOU HAVE SAID HAS BEEN UNEXPECTED TO THE	LAST	POSSIBLE DEGREE-- /ALOYSIA/ IT HAS BEEN TRUE. /SIR
ARMS III (54)	/BLUNTSCHLI/ (TO RAINA) WILL YOU EXCUSE ME: THE	LAST	POSTAL DELIVERY THAT REACHED ME WAS THREE WEEKS AGO.
MTH3 (102)	ME? WAS OLD ARCHBISHOP HASLAM, THE PRESENT MAN'S	LAST	PREDECESSOR BUT FOUR, DROWNED OR NOT? /BURGE-LUBIN/ I
DOCT PREFACE(11)	OF THE LAST KING WITH THE ENTRAILS OF THE	LAST	PRIEST, SUBSTITUTED COMPULSORY VACCINATION FOR
GETT PREFACE(256)	DOMESTIC LAWS ARE KEPT SO INHUMAN THAT THEY AT	LAST	PROVOKE A FURIOUS GENERAL INSURRECTION AGAINST THEM AS
ROCK II (245)	SUPPORT YOU IN ANY CASE, ARTHUR. YOU HAVE AT	LAST	PUBLICLY ADMITTED THAT THE DEATH DUTIES ARE UNSOUND IN
POSN PREFACE(399)	FOR INSTANCE, HAD IT BEEN IN EXISTENCE DURING THE	LAST	QUARTER OF A CENTURY, IT WOULD HAVE PERCEIVED THAT
METH PREFACE(R44)	TO KNOW WHAT IT WAS TO BE A LAMARCKIAN DURING THE	LAST	QUARTER OF THE NINETEENTH CENTURY HAS ONLY TO READ MR
OVER (185)	WHY, HE'S MY HUSBAND. /JUNO/ THAT TAKES AWAY THE	LAST	RAG OF EXCUSE FOR SUCH CONDUCT. A NICE WORLD IT WOULD
2TRU III (110)	IS STILL MORE THAN WE CAN BEAR. THROW OFF THE	LAST	RAG OF YOUR BATHING COSTUME; AND I SHALL NOT BLENCH NOR
MTH1 II (23)	DEATH, WHEN HE HAS STRIVEN TO THE SPENDING OF THE	LAST	RALLY OF HIS STRENGTH, CAN HE KNOW WHAT IT IS TO REST
POSN PREFACE(429)	MR HARCOURT SEIZED THE OPPORTUNITY TO MAKE A	LAST	RALLY. HE SECONDED LORD GORELL'S PROPOSAL THAT THE
MIS. PREFACE(93)	EXCEEDINGLY GRAVE AT PRESENT, BECAUSE THE	LAST	RAY OF ART IS BEING CUT OFF FROM OUR SCHOOLS BY THE
MIS. PREFACE(90)	NOISE SET UP BY CHOIRS AND ORCHESTRAS) WE HAVE AT	LAST	REACHED A POINT AT WHICH, FOR EXAMPLE, A PERSON LIVING
2TRU PREFACE(19)	HAPPY, AND THE RICH HORRIBLY TORTURED. MATTERS AT	LAST	REACHED A POINT AT WHICH THERE WAS MORE LAW AND ORDER
DOCT PREFACE(70)	WHEN THE EVOLUTION OF SOCIAL ORGANIZATION AT	LAST	REACHES HIS PROFESSION, WILL BE THAT HE WILL ALWAYS
DEVL III SD(70)	REMAINS THE ONLY SIGN OF PREPARATION. BUT AT	LAST	REASSURING SHOUTS OF HERE THEY COME: HERE THEY ARE, ARE
NEVR I (216)	INDIGNANT REPULSION). THAT WOULD HAVE BEEN YOUR	LAST	RECOLLECTION OF YOUR FATHER, GLORIA, IF I HAD NOT TAKEN
FABL PREFACE(75)	AND THEN THAT IT IS HOLY AS A MEMORIAL OF THE	LAST	RECORDED SUPPER OF JESUS. NO MAN CAN BE ORDAINED A
JITT III SD(69)	IS NOT ENJOYING THE JOKE IN GOOD FAITH. JITTA AT	LAST	RECOVERS HER SELF-CONTROL WITH A DESPERATE EFFORT.
CAPT NOTES (303)	FOR EXAMPLE, CAN SPARE TIME TO LEARN THAT	LAST	REFINEMENT OF MODERN SPEECH, THE EXQUISITE DIPHTHONG, A
MILL PREFACE(132)	POINT BY AN ENEMY AT THE GATE, IS NOT ONLY THE	LAST	REFUGE OF A SCOUNDREL IN DR JOHNSON'S SENSE, IT IS FAR
SUPR PREFACE(R25)	OUR POLITICAL EXPERIMENT OF DEMOCRACY, THE	LAST	REFUGE OF CHEAP MISGOVERNMENT, WILL RUIN US IF OUR
PYGM EPILOG (293)	MONEY AND NO OCCUPATION. HIS MOTHER'S JOINTURE, A	LAST	RELIC OF THE OPULENCE OF LARGELADY PARK, HAD ENABLED
JOAN EPIL,SD(167)	PRESSING APPOINTMENT -- (HE GOES ON TIPTOE). THE	LAST	REMAINING RAYS OF LIGHT GATHER INTO A WHITE RADIANCE
FANY PROLOG (270)	I LOATHE PLAYS. /TROTTER/ (DISAPPOINTED) THAT	LAST	REMARK DESTROYS ALL THE VALUE OF YOUR ADMISSION. YOU
2TRU I (47)	A DAINTY ARIEL. /THE MONSTER/ (PICKING UP THE	LAST	REMARK OF THE PATIENT) SO HAVE YOU. NO MORE MEASLES:
CAPT II (259)	(RETURNING TO THE TAILORING QUESTION AS IF HER	LAST	REMARK WERE OF NO CONSEQUENCE WHATEVER) DID THIS SLEEVE
BULL I (81)	THE BEDROOM, SLAMMING THE DOOR AND SHATTERING THE	LAST	REMNANT OF TIM'S NERVE. THE POOR WRETCH SAVES HIMSELF
BULL I (77)	LEAGUE, AND CLAMOR FOR THE DESTRUCTION OF THE	LAST	REMNANTS OF NATIONAL LIBERTY-- /TIM/ NOT ANOTHER WORD.
CYMB V (140)	HE FOUGHT LIKE ANY LEGIONARY, SWORD IN HAND. HIS	LAST	REPORTED WORD WAS " SAVE YOURSELVES: BID ALL MAKE FOR
DEVL III (55)	IF YOU ASKED IT. YOU WILL ASK IT. IT IS MY	LAST	REQUEST: I SHALL NEVER ASK YOU ANYTHING AGAIN. (SHE
MILL PREFACE(132)	TRIES TO RALLY ITS SUBJECTS TO ITS SUPPORT IN THE	LAST	RESORT BY A WAR. IT WAS NOT ONLY THE LAST CARD OF
BULL PREFACE(68)	MOVEMENT WAS USELESS, AS ENGLAND WOULD IN THE	LAST	RESORT REPUDIATE THE CONSTITUTION AND HOLD IRELAND
APPL PREFACE(181)	MIGHT SUPPOSE THAT AT LEAST THEY WOULD ACT AS A	LAST	RESORT WHEN AN AUTOCRAT GOES MAD AND COMMITS OUTRAGEOUS
SUPR HANDBOK(196)	HEAD BY POLICEMEN, THROWN INTO PRISON, AND IN THE	LAST	RESORT " EXECUTED" JUST AS THEY ARE WHEN THEY BREAK THE
DOCT PREFACE(13)	HAVE VITALITY ENOUGH TO REGARD AN OPERATION AS A	LAST	RESORT, BUT NO SURGEON IS BOUND TO TAKE THE
DOCT PREFACE(68)	AS THE CONSULTANT IS AN EXPENSIVE LUXURY, HE IS A	LAST	RESOURCE RATHER THAN, AS HE SHOULD BE, A MATTER OF
PRES (155)	USELESS; AND YOUR TEARS AND ENTREATIES-- A MAN'S	LAST	RESOURCE-- WILL AVAIL YOU JUST AS LITTLE. I SWEEP THEM
JITT II (33)	I FELT WHEN I LAY HELPLESS, UNABLE TO PAY THE	LAST	RESPECTS TO OUR DEAR LOST FRIEND. (AS SHE SITS DOWN,
MTH4 I (154)	CENTRE SHIFTED TO BAGHDAD, AND THE ENGLISHMAN AT	LAST	RETURNED TO THE TRUE CRADLE OF HIS RACE IN MESOPOTAMIA.
ROCK I (215)	EVEN HOLD THAT TRADE IS ALREADY REVIVING. BY THE	LAST	RETURNS THE EXPORT OF SPANISH ONIONS HAS AGAIN REACHED
CYMB FORWORD(134)	NOR EXCUSE. I MUST HAVE GOT IT FROM THE	LAST	REVIVAL OF THE PLAY AT THE OLD LYCEUM THEATRE, WHEN
GENV I (38)	THAN TWO THOUSAND WHITE INHABITANTS BEFORE THE	LAST	REVOLUTION. THERE MUST BE STILL AT LEAST FIFTEEN
CLEO I (114)	HER ARMS WAVING, CRYING) I AM A REAL QUEEN AT	LAST	-- A REAL, REAL QUEEN! CLEOPATRA THE QUEEN! (CAESAR
JITT I (15)	TO SAY A THOUSAND THINGS TO YOU! AND WHEN AT	LAST	-- (SHE FINISHES THE SENTENCE BY A CARESS)! WHEN YOU
BULL II SD(112)	ENGLISH DRAWING ROOM BALLAD OF THE SEASON BEFORE	LAST	-- UNTIL SOME SLIGHT NOISE SUGGESTS A FOOTSTEP, WHEN
MTH3 (131)	TO MATURITY. /BURGE-LUBIN/ (GRASPING THE IDEA AT	LAST	) BY GEORGE, CONFUCIUS, YOURE RIGHT! I NEVER THOUGHT
CAPT I (241)	BE IT! (TO LADY CICELY, ACCEPTING HER HAND AT	LAST	) GOODNIGHT. HE GOES. IT IS BY THIS TIME STARRY NIGHT.
SIM II (59)	SIPS HIS TEA. THE SILENCE CONTINUES. /IDDY/ (AT	LAST	) I AM A FUTILE CREATURE. THEY ALL TURN AS IF STUNG AND
JOAN 2 (86)	ME AND HIM THAT SENT ME? /CHARLES/ (TEMPTED AT	LAST	) OH, IF I ONLY DARE! /JOAN/ I SHALL DARE, DARE, AND
SUPR III (140)	SULKY SOCIAL-DEMOCRAT/ (ARGUMENTATIVE TO THE	LAST	) ON THE CONTRARY, ONLY BY CAPTURING THE STATE
DEST (172)	AND MORE RIDICULOUS ALL THE TIME. /NAPOLEON/ (AT	LAST	) WELL? /LADY/ (DISCONCERTED, BUT WITH HER ARMS STILL
DOCT I (95)	DOOR; BUT THERE IS NO SIR RALPH. /RIDGEON/ (AT	LAST	) WHERE IS HE? /EMMY/ (LOOKING BACK) DRAT HIM, I
JOAN PREFACE(48)	THE UFFIZI IN FLORENCE (OR WERE WHEN I WAS THERE	LAST	). MY DUNOIS WOULD DO EQUALLY WELL FOR THE DUC
PHIL II (104)	HIS POLITEST CONSULTING-ROOM LAUGH. CRAVEN GOES	LAST	). /CRAVEN/ (AT THE DOOR, GRAVELY) COME, JULIA.
2TRU I (49)	TO SECURITY FIND IT IN THE GRAVE. FOR ME SAFETY	LAST	; AND FORWARD, FORWARD, ALWAYS FOR--" /THE NURSE/ (
MILL PREFACE(118)	THE DONKEY HAD OVERTAKEN THE CARROTS AT	LAST	; AND INSTEAD OF EATING THEM HE ALLOWED THEM TO BE
POSN (448)	BY ME TO THE END, WONT YOU? HOLD MY HAND TO THE	LAST	; AND I'LL DIE GAME. (HE PUTS OUT HIS HAND: SHE
SUPR III (94)	WITHOUT END. I HAD TO LEAVE IT TO ITS FATE AT	LAST	; AND NOW I FEAR IT IS SHOCKINGLY MUTILATED. MY POOR
JOAN 5 (113)	LET US MAKE A TREATY. OUR LUCK IS TOO GOOD TO	LAST	; AND NOW IS OUR CHANCE TO STOP BEFORE IT TURNS. /JOAN/
BULL III (128)	IS, LARRY. ROUND ABOUT HERE, WEVE GOT THE LAND AT	LAST	; AND WE WANT NO MORE GOVERMENT MEDDLIN. WE WANT A NEW
KING II (231)	YET YOUR KINGDOM DROPPED INTO YOUR MOUTH AT	LAST	; AND YOU HAVE BEEN A KING SINCE YOU WERE OLD ENOUGH TO
FABL PREFACE(72)	YOU, I ETC. ETC." THE LABOR CHURCH DID NOT	LAST	; BUT THE REACTION DID; AND THE LAST I HEARD OF ITS
GETT (350)	LORD, THAT HE HELD BACK MENDELSSOHN TIL THE VERY	LAST	; BUT WHEN THAT WAS GONE HE THOUGHT HE MIGHT AS WELL GO
DOCT IV (168)	NO GLOVES. GOOD DAY TO YOU. (HE EDGES HIM OUT AT	LAST	; SHUTS THE DOOR ON HIM; AND RETURNS TO SIR PATRICK AS
PPP (206)	/MAGNESIA/ AND NOW, HUSBAND, LET US PERFORM OUR	LAST	SAD DUTY TO OUR FRIEND. HE HAS BECOME HIS OWN MONUMENT.
SUPR PREFACE(R20)	IS SO SHALLOW THAT EVEN IN THE THEATRE, THAT	LAST	SANCTUARY OF UNREALITY, IT IMPOSES ONLY ON THE
WIDO II (29)	HAVE HAD TO DISAPPOINT HER MORE THAN ONCE SINCE I	LAST	SAW YOU. WILL YOU EXCUSE ME FOR TEN MINUTES? /COKANE/
FANY EPIL,SD(334)	GENTLEMEN. THE CURTAINS ARE DRAWN, REVEALING THE	LAST	SCENE OF THE PLAY AND THE ACTORS ON THE STAGE. THE
PHIL II (105)	YOU ARE PLEASED. WRETCH! NOW YOU HAVE LOST THE	LAST	SCRAP OF MY REGARD. (HE TURNS TO GO, BUT IS STOPPED BY
ROCK II (247)	ALREADY WITHOUT YOUR DEPRIVING THEM OF THAT	LAST	SCRAP OF THEIR LIBERTY? THE ONLY WEAPON THEY HAVE
LIED (201)	TO HER, WORTH ALL YOUR AMATEUR TRASH. AT ASCOT	LAST	SEASON THE ELDEST SON OF A DUKE EXCUSED HIMSELF FROM
2TRU PREFACE(11)	FASHIONS IN DRESS: YOU CANNOT POSSIBLY BE SEEN IN	LAST	SEASON'S GARMENTS," AND SO ON AND SO FORTH. BUT THE OLD
VWOO 2 (125)	MISSING FROM HIS HOME SINCE JANUARY THE FIRST.	LAST	SEEN IN A DECK CHAIR ON THE EMPRESS OF PATAGONIA
APPL I (228)	NO OPPORTUNITY OF DISPARAGING THE THRONE. THE	LAST	SENTENCE OF THE LEADING ARTICLE ALMOST INVARIABLY
ROCK II (237)	ACCOUNTS WITH THE LAST TRADESMAN AND TURNED THE	LAST	SERVANT INTO THE STREETS, WHERE ARE THEY TO FIND
MIS. PREFACE(53)	BROUGHT UP AS A SLAVE. HOW IS HE, WHEN HE IS AT	LAST	SET FREE, TO BE ANYTHING ELSE THAN THE SLAVE HE
HART PREFACE(22)	WHICH THEY WERE INCAPABLE. WHEN THE ARMISTICE AT	LAST	SET ME FREE TO TELL THE TRUTH ABOUT THE WAR AT THE
MILL PREFACE(116)	ARE THINGS OF THE PAST: BATTLES NOWADAYS	LAST	SEVERAL MONTHS AND THEN PETER OUT ON BARBED WIRE UNDER
BULL II SD(112)	HER EYES IN THE MOONLIGHT, WATCHING FOR LARRY. AT	LAST	SHE GIVES IT UP WITH A SOB OF IMPATIENCE, AND RETREATS
HART II (114)	LONGING ALL HER LIFE FOR SOMEONE TO BREAK IT. AT	LAST	SHE HAS BECOME AFRAID SHE HAS NONE TO BREAK. /LADY
MRS II SD(199)	LAUGHING UPTURNED FACE FOR A MOMENT, TEMPTED. AT	LAST	SHE KISSES HIM, AND IMMEDIATELY TURNS AWAY, OUT OF
HART PREFACE(8)	ABUSED IT TO THE UTMOST. BUT WHEN SHE STRUCK AT	LAST	SHE STRUCK WITH A VENGEANCE. FOR FOUR YEARS SHE SMOTE
BULL I (79)	GOODNATURE: IT'S AN IRISH WAKENESS. I'D SHARE ME	LAST	SHILLIN WITH A FRIEND. /BROADBENT/ I FEEL SURE YOU
BULL I (82)	/DOYLE/ NO DOUBT HE WOULD SHARE HIS FRIEND'S	LAST	SHILLING IF HIS FRIEND WAS FOOL ENOUGH TO LET HIM. HOW
BULL I (82)	SPIRIT ABOUT MONEY. I BELIEVE HE WOULD SHARE HIS	LAST	SHILLING WITH A FRIEND. /DOYLE/ NO DOUBT HE WOULD SHARE
GETT (263)	THE SAME SHOCK. /MRS BRIDGENORTH/ WELL, IT'S HIS	LAST	SHOCK. YOU HAVE MARRIED THE WHOLE FAMILY NOW, COLLINS.
HART III (145)	SHOTOVER/ ECHOES: NOTHING BUT ECHOES. THE	LAST	SHOT WAS FIRED YEARS AGO. /HECTOR/ AND THIS SHIP THAT
POSN PREFACE(406)	A DRINK SHOP AND A PROSTITUTION MARKET; AND THE	LAST	SHRED OF ITS DISGUISE IS STRIPPED BY THE VIRTUALLY
WIDO III (52)	ABOVE MONEY, EH? /SARTORIUS/ (HESITATES, AND AT	LAST	SHUTS THE DOOR, SAYING GUARDEDLY) HOW MUCH MONEY?
MIS. (172)	DOWN FROM HEAVEN AND RECEIVE YOUR UNHAPPY SON'S	LAST	SIGH. /THE MAN/ OH, ROT! DO YOU THINK I READ
HART I (81)	HUSHABYE/ FIVE HUNDRED POUNDS; AND I HAVE MADE IT	LAST	SINCE EASTER! /CAPTAIN SHOTOVER/ SINCE EASTER: BARELY

PPP SD(205) CANNONING THROUGH A GHASTLY QUADRILLE, AT LAST SINK INANIMATE ON THE CARPET. /MAGNESIA/ (LISTENING AT
MTH4 III (198) ROTTERJACKS-- HAVE WON EVERY BYE-ELECTION FOR THE LAST SIX MONTHS. THEY-- /THE ELDERLY GENTLEMAN/ (SCRAMBLING
MRS PREFACE(167) AND THE HABIT OF MAKE-BELIEVE BECOMES AT LAST SO ROOTED, THAT CRITICISM OF THE THEATRE INSENSIBLY
APPL II (270) OF OUR DIFFICULTY. CONSEQUENTLY IT IS THE LAST SOLUTION I COULD HAVE EXPECTED IN POLITICS, BUT I
LADY (246) MOST DEJECT AND WRETCHED-- /SHAKESPEAR/ HA! AT LAST SORROW HATH STRUCK A NOTE OF MUSIC OUT OF THEE. " OF
JITT I (15) DISTANCE-- I ALWAYS LISTEN TO THEM TO CATCH THE LAST SOUND OF YOU-- I AM STABBED WITH A FEAR THAT I HAVE
NEVR I (206) FOR EVER. THIS IS MY LAST CHANCE. I SPENT MY LAST SOVEREIGN ON MOVING IN; AND I HAVNT PAID A SHILLING OF
CATH 1 (167) THEY ALMOST UPSET EDSTASTON. WHEN THE VICTIM AT LAST STAGGERS TO HIS FEET, HE IS A PALE FRAGILE NOBLEMAN,
MILL PREFACE(127) HE FOUGHT THE GOOD FIGHT TO THE END HE WOULD AT LAST STAND IN THE PRESENCE OF HIS GOD. IN DUE COURSE HE
CLEO PR01 (91) WAS BROUGHT DOWN TO UTTER NOTHINGNESS, HE MADE A LAST STAND TO DIE HONORABLY, AND DID NOT DESPAIR; FOR HE
DEVL I (12) HAS NO DOUBT STOOD THERE UNTOUCHED SINCE THE LAST STATE OCCASION IN THE FAMILY, AND SOME GLASSES, WHICH
PYGM PREFACE(203) THE THING HAS TO BE DONE SCIENTIFICALLY, OR THE LAST STATE OF THE ASPIRANT MAY BE WORSE THAN THE FIRST. AN
FABL VI (126) THAT WE ARE THE VANGUARD OF CIVILIZATION, THE LAST STEP IN CREATIVE EVOLUTION. BUT ACCORDING TO THE THEORY
ANNA (297) /STRAMMFEST/ (RISING IN HORROR) NO: THIS IS THE LAST STRAW: I CANNOT CONSENT. IT IS IMPOSSIBLE, UTTERLY,
PYGM EPILOG (294) EXACT FIGURE. HE ABSOLUTELY REFUSED TO ADD THE LAST STRAW TO HIS BURDEN BY CONTRIBUTING TO ELIZA'S SUPPORT.
SUPR IV (152) OF ANOTHER MAN. /HECTOR/ (OUTRAGED) THIS IS THE LAST STRAW, DAD: YOU HAVE INSULTED MY WIFE. /MALONE/ YOUR
DOCT III SD(142) /LOUIS/ HOW DO YOU KNOW? THIS FOR B.B. IS THE LAST STRAW. HE COMPLETELY LOSES HIS TEMPER AND BEGINS TO
MILL I (147) SHE SETS UP A WISE FATHER! THIS IS THE LAST STRAW. /SAGAMORE/ DO SIT DOWN, MISS SMITH, WONT YOU? (
MTH5 (261) NOT SUPERSEDE THEM UNTIL THEY HAVE FORDED THIS LAST STREAM THAT LIES BETWEEN FLESH AND SPIRIT, AND
CURE SD(230) TRICKS OF THE PROFESSIONAL PIANIST BEFORE SHE AT LAST STRIKES THE KEYS AND PRELUDES BRILLIANTLY. AT THE
PHIL III (139) THEN THE REACTION WOULD COME; AND YOU WOULD AT LAST SUBSIDE INTO A SOOTHING RAPTURE OF AFFECTION WHICH GAVE
POSN PREFACE(392) IT IS ONLY OF LATE YEARS THAT ACTRESSES HAVE AT LAST SUCCEEDED IN LIVING DOWN THE ASSUMPTION THAT ACTRESS
HART III SD(149) AT THE PROSPECT) OH, I HOPE SO. RANDALL AT LAST SUCCEEDS IN KEEPING THE HOME FIRES BURNING ON HIS
GENV PREFACE(26) LONG THEY MAY BE DREAMT OF AND DESIRED, COME AT LAST SUDDENLY AND MIRACULOUSLY LIKE THE BALANCING OF THE
LION PREFACE(39) HE ACTUALLY LEANED ON THE BOSOM OF JESUS AT THE LAST SUPPER AND ASKED IN A WHISPER WHICH OF THEM IT WAS THAT
BULL II SD(104) JAUNTING CAR, BLACK AND DILAPIDATED, ONE OF THE LAST SURVIVORS OF THE PUBLIC VEHICLES KNOWN TO EARLIER
3PLA PREFACE(R31) IS VANITY! MOANS THE PREACHER, WHEN LIFE HAS AT LAST TAUGHT HIM THAT NATURE WILL NOT DANCE TO HIS
JOAN PREFACE(42) WAS TO THE GOVERNMENT OF HER DAY, HAVE WITHIN THE LAST TEN YEARS BEEN SLAUGHTERED, STARVED TO DEATH, BURNT OUT
MRS PREFACE(159) THE PLOTS OF TWO PLAYS WITNESSED WITHIN THE LAST TEN YEARS BY MYSELF AT LONDON WEST END THEATRES, ONE
PRES (142) WE DO. I HAVE THOUGHT OF NOTHING ELSE FOR THE LAST TEN YEARS. SAY WHAT YOU WILL, BALSQUITH, THE GERMANS
MIS. PREFACE(3) IT IS WASTE OF LABOR TO MAKE A MACHINE THAT WILL LAST TEN YEARS, BECAUSE IT WILL PROBABLY BE SUPERSEDED IN
2TRU I (29) IS ANY CHANCE? CAN SHE POSSIBLY SURVIVE THIS LAST TERRIBLE COMPLICATION. /THE MONSTER/ MEASLES! HE
BULL PREFACE(55) REFLECT GREAT CREDIT ON ALL CONCERNED." AS THIS LAST TESTIMONIAL APPARENTLY DOES NOT REFER TO THE VICTIMS,
METH PREFACE(R78) FEELING AGAINST THE BIBLE HAS BECOME SO STRONG AT LAST THAT EDUCATED PEOPLE NOT ONLY REFUSE TO OUTRAGE THEIR
SUPR III (109) BE A CATHOLIC IDEA. WHEN THE SPANIARD LEARNS AT LAST THAT HE IS NO BETTER THAN THE SARACEN, AND HIS PROPHET
LADY PREFACE(223) WAS TOO STUPID OR TOO MODEST NOT TO SEE AT LAST THAT IT WAS A CASE OF JUPITER AND SEMELE? SHAKESPEAR
LION PREFACE(68) WAY AT EVERY TURN, AND HAD BECOME PERSUADED AT LAST THAT NO MAN COULD FOLLOW HIS INNER LIGHT UNTIL HE WAS
DEST (163) AND LEAVE THE ROOM, SINCE YOU ARE CONVINCED AT LAST THAT THIS IS NO GENTLEMAN? /LIEUTENANT/ GENTLEMAN! I
LION PREFACE(84) FIFTY STEPHENS AND A DOZEN PETERS. ONE FEELS AT LAST THAT WHEN JESUS CALLED PETER FROM HIS BOAT, HE SPOILED
SUPR HANDBOK(193) OFFENSIVE AND NOXIOUS, WITH THE RESULT THAT AT LAST THE ASSOCIATION OF UNCLEANLINESS WITH THESE NATURAL
MILL I (158) NOT MAKE THEMSELVES HEARD ABOVE YOUR ROARING. AT LAST THE CHORUS DRAGGED YOU OFF THE STAGE; AND THE REGULAR
HART PREFACE(17) NOT THE CHILDREN HAD MADE THE SACRIFICE, UNTIL AT LAST THE COMIC PAPERS WERE DRIVEN TO SATIRIZE FAT OLD MEN,
FOUN (219) I SHALL SAY NOTHING. SUFFICE IT THAT WHEN AT LAST THE CRAVING FOR FOOD WAS STILLED, THE CRAVING FOR LOVE
SUPR PREFACE(R21) REALITY THAT DISABLES CONVENTION, DEFYING TO THE LAST THE FATE WHICH FINALLY OVERTAKES HIM, THE WOMAN'S NEED
CAPT II (256) CARE OF YOURSELF; FOR YOU ARE GOING TO SEE AT LAST THE HYPOCRISY IN THE SANCTIMONIOUS SPEECH OF THE JUDGE
HART PREFACE(12) PROVED INDICTMENTS FOR WILFUL MURDER, UNTIL AT LAST THE JUDGES AND MAGISTRATES HAD TO ANNOUNCE THAT WHAT
2TRU III (112) SHALL GO OUT UNTO ALL LANDS AND REALIZE FOR US AT LAST THE KINGDOM AND THE POWER AND THE GLORY FOR EVER AND
2TRU II (70) BUT HE'D NEVER SHOT ANYONE WITH THEM; AND AT LAST THE TEMPTATION WAS TOO GREAT AND HE WENT OUT AND SHOT
POSN SD(439) YOU LIKE IT IF YOU WERE GOING TO BE HANGED? AT LAST THE WOMEN ARE PUSHED OUT, LEAVING ELDER DANIELS. THE
GENV PREFACE(5) TO BE " LIBERATING" BECAME SO FRIGHTFUL THAT AT LAST THE WORD HAD TO BE GIVEN TO TWO OF OUR BEST
BULL PREFACE(51) FEELINGS OF DENSHAWAI WHEN ON THE 13TH OF JUNE LAST THERE DROVE TO THE VILLAGE FOUR KHAKI-CLAD BRITISH
JOAN 4 (103) RAVAGED HIS WAY WEST LIKE A WILD BEAST UNTIL AT LAST THERE STOOD ONLY THE PYRENEES AND GOD'S MERCY BETWEEN
LADY PREFACE(221) OF A SADDENED ONE. IS IT NOT CLEAR THAT TO THE LAST THERE WAS IN SHAKESPEAR AN INCORRIGIBLE DIVINE LEVITY,
DOCT III (154) /MRS DUBEDAT/ I HAD A GREAT MANY DREAMS; BUT AT LAST THEY ALL CAME TO ONE DREAM. /RIDGEON/ (WITH HALF A
CATH 2,SD(181) ANOTHER AND THEN HAS TO BOW HIS APOLOGIES. BUT AT LAST THEY ARE ALL GONE EXCEPT NARYSHKIN. /EDSTASTON/ OUF!
2TRU II (65) CHAMBERMAID GETS SO USED TO NEW FACES THAT AT LAST THEY BECOME A NECESSITY. (SHE SITS DOWN ON THE STOOL).
PYGM EPILOG (301) TO BE LEARNING NOTHING ABOUT FLOWER SHOPS. AT LAST THEY GAVE IT UP AS HOPELESS, AND SHOOK THE DUST OF THE
BARB III (340) AND CALL THEMSELVES CERTAIN NAMES UNTIL AT LAST THEY GET THE COURAGE TO KILL; AND YOUR SIX HUNDRED AND
MILL PREFACE(127) THE NEWCOMER TO FORGO HIS PROMISED PRIVILEGE. AT LAST THEY TOOK HIM BY THE ARMS AND LED HIM TO A MIGHTY
MTH1 II (29) TO THE LEVEL OF THE BEASTS. IF THAT IS TO BE THE LAST THING AS IT HAS BEEN THE FIRST, LET MANKIND PERISH. IF
MILL IV (195) WHAT HAPPENED IMMEDIATELY BEFORE THE ASSAULT: THE LAST THING I CAN RECOLLECT WAS A QUITE ORDINARY CONVERSATION
MTH3 (109) YEARS. SHE WAS SIXTY-EIGHT WHEN SHE DIED; AND THE LAST THING SHE SAID TO ME, AS I SAT BY HER BEDSIDE HOLDING
HART III (129) IS THAT REMARK YOUR OWN? /ELLIE/ NO. ONLY THE LAST THING THE CAPTAIN SAID BEFORE HE WENT TO SLEEP.
FANY I (276) IVE KNOWN BOBBY EVER SO LONG! BUT OF COURSE THE LAST THING YOU FIND OUT ABOUT A PERSON IS THEIR RELIGION.
MTH2 (84) PATERNALLY) WELL, MY DEAR BARNABAS, FOR THE LAST THIRTY YEARS THE POST HAS BROUGHT ME AT LEAST ONCE A
BUOY 1 (13) AND UNCIVILIZED. /SON/ MY DEAR FATHER: WITHIN THE LAST THIRTY YEARS WE HAVE HAD MORE HORRIBLE PERSECUTIONS AND
2TRU PREFACE(8) CONVICT ME OF CRYING SOUR GRAPES; FOR DURING THE LAST THIRTYFIVE YEARS I HAVE BEEN UNDER NO COMPULSION TO
BULL IV (178) VERY EFFICIENTLY; AND (LOW AND BITTER) WHEN AT LAST THIS POOR DESOLATE COUNTRYSIDE BECOMES A BUSY MINT IN
KING I (219) DYING, AND ALL THE REST OF YOU ARE FORGOTTEN, MY LAST THOUGHT WILL BE OF NELLY. /NELL/ ROWLEY DARLING: DONT
GETT SD(289) OR THEREABOUTS, CORRECT IN DRESS TO THE LAST THREAD OF HIS COLLAR, BUT TOO MUCH PREOCCUPIED WITH HIS
DOCT III (140) MONEY: HERS AND MINE TOO. HER THIRTY POUNDS DIDNT LAST THREE DAYS. I HAD TO BORROW FOUR TIMES AS MUCH TO SPEND
PHIL II (120) BLOW PATHOLOGICAL SCIENCE HAS RECEIVED FOR THE LAST THREE HUNDRED YEARS! /CHARTERIS/ NO, NO, NO.
APPL I (211) TO HANDLE HIM. IF I'D BEEN IN THE CABINET THESE LAST THREE MONTHS THERE'D HAVE BEEN NO CRISIS. /NICOBAR/ HE
ROCK I (221) ANOTHER I HAVNT BEEN ABLE TO DO A THING FOR THE LAST THREE WEEKS; AND IT ACCUMULATES AND ACCUMULATES. IT
MTH3 (93) YOU KNOW WHAT A ROW THERE WAS OVER THOSE LAST THREE YEARS, AND HOW NEARLY THE TOO-OLD-AT-FORTY PEOPLE
APPL I (212) THE LAST ELECTION, AND HAVE BEEN IN POWER FOR THE LAST THREE YEARS, THIS COUNTRY HAS BEEN GOVERNED DURING THAT
DOCT I (101) LOOK AT ME NOW: THIS IS MY BEST; AND IT MUST LAST TIL CHRISTMAS, WHAT CAN I DO? IVE NEVER OPENED A BOOK
MIS. (196) YES: FOR THE FIRST TIME. /PERCIVAL/ FOR THE LAST TIME? /LORD SUMMERHAYS/ (REVOLTED) SIR: YOU ARE IN
MILL PREFACE(114) DUNDERHEAD WHO ALWAYS DOES WHAT WAS DONE LAST TIME BECAUSE HE IS INCAPABLE OF CONCEIVING ANYTHING
ROCK II (242) A MUNICIPAL BANK, MY MAJORITY FELL TO SEVENTEEN LAST TIME BECAUSE I WENT TO THEM WITH EMPTY HANDS AND A
APPL PREFACE(194) OF ITS ABOLISHING ITSELF AS INFAMOUS. THE LAST TIME I SAW HIM HE CALLED ON ME TO UNFOLD A NEW SCHEME
SUPR I (5) NOW LET ME TELL YOU SOMETHING TO CONSOLE YOU. THE LAST TIME I SAW HIM-- IT WAS IN THIS VERY ROOM-- HE SAID TO
MIS. (155) ARE THEY? /LORD SUMMERHAYS/ I THINK I KNOW. THE LAST TIME I SAW THAT LADY, SHE DID SOMETHING I SHOULD NOT
JOAN 6 (135) THOU ART A RARE NOODLE, MASTER. DO WHAT WAS DONE LAST TIME IS THY RULE, EH? /COURCELLES/ (RISING) THOU
ROCK PREFACE(187) HAVE ONLY RAISED A JEW FROM THE DEAD. SO FOR THE LAST TIME SET YOUR WITS TO WORK, AND FIND ME A SOUND REASON
GENV PREFACE(14) HAD TO MARK TIME BY DOING WHAT WAS DONE LAST TIME UNTIL THE NEXT BIG BOSS CAME ALONG AND BECAME A
JITT II (32) LOVE, OR ANYTHING OF THAT SORT? /JITTA/ THE LAST TIME WE WERE AT THE THEATRE HE DISCUSSED THE PLAY WITH
FABL III (113) I CAN ALWAYS DEPEND ON THEM TO DO WHAT WAS DONE LAST TIME. BUT I NEVER KNOW WHAT A GENIUS WILL BE UP TO
JITT I (15) A FEAR THAT I HAVE HELD YOU IN MY ARMS FOR THE LAST TIME. BUT WHEN WE HAVE BEEN PARTED FOR DAYS, AND I AM
JITT I (23) (WITH DELIBERATE EMPHASIS) THIS MUST BE THE LAST TIME. (RISING, WITH A SUDDEN FANCIFUL RECKLESSNESS)
WIDO II (46) ARE. REMEMBER HOW DREADFULLY MY HEAD WAS CUT LAST TIME. /BLANCHE/ (RAGING) ANSWER ME, WILL YOU. HAVE
KING II (226) HOME THE MOMENT I HAVE KISSED YOU GOODBYE FOR THE LAST TIME. /CATHERINE/ (ALMOST IN TEARS) YOU NOT MUST TALK
SUPR IV (171) (ASIDE TO HIM) I WANT TO MAKE YOU CRY FOR THE LAST TIME. /TAVY/ (STEADFASTLY) NO MORE TEARS. I AM HAPPY
GETT (268) TWO YEARS AGO, YOU SAID " FOR THE NINTH AND LAST TIME." /THE GENERAL/ WE ARE TWO YEARS OLDER, LESBIA.
GETT (268) TO HER) LISTEN TO ME, LESBIA. FOR THE TENTH AND LAST TIME-- /LESBIA/ (INTERRUPTING) ON FLORENCE'S WEDDING
BULL IV (181) /KEEGAN/ (HALTING AND TURNING TO THEM FOR THE LAST TIME) EVERY DREAM IS A PROPHECY: EVERY JEST IS AN
WIDO II (36) THE VOICE SOFTENING AND REFINING FOR THE LAST TIME) HARRY: THERES NO USE IN OUR FENCING IN THIS WAY.
GENV PREFACE(6) POSSIBLE THINGS (EXCEPT REPEATING WHAT WAS DONE LAST TIME) IN SECURITY. THE PREFABRICATION IN ENGLAND OF
FABL II (106) THERE IS ANYTHING TO BE DONE EXCEPT WHAT WAS DONE LAST TIME. I SHALL HAVE TO DO IT. /OLDHAND/ YOU HAVE A VERY
JOAN 6 (139) NOW AS TO THIS MATTER OF THE MAN'S DRESS. FOR THE LAST TIME, WILL YOU PUT OFF THAT IMPUDENT ATTIRE, AND DRESS
MIS. (115) TO ME WHEN I ASKED YOU. " SEE WHAT WAS DONE THE LAST TIME": THAT WAS THE BEGINNING AND THE END OF YOUR
BULL I (88) STAINING AND DEGRADING, UNTIL, WHEN YOU COME AT LAST TO A COUNTRY WHERE MEN TAKE A QUESTION SERIOUSLY AND
DOCT PREFACE(73) SENSE OF HUMOR, LEST HE (OR SHE) SHOULD COME AT LAST TO BELIEVE ALL THE NONSENSE THAT MUST NEEDS BE TALKED.
GLIM (187) THAT FELL AWAY FROM ME. WHEN I WAS FORCED AT LAST TO BELIEVE IN GRIM DEATH I KNEW AT LAST WHAT BELIEF
INCA (252) REMARKABLE QUALITIES, WHICH I SHOULD BE THE LAST TO DENY, NAPOLEON LACKED VERSATILITY, AFTER ALL, ANY
JITT PREFACE(5) METHOD OF ABSORPTION, THAT I MANAGED AT LAST TO DIVINE, INFER, GUESS, AND CO-INVENT THE STORY OF
SUPR III (102) OF ROMANCE, AND OF SCIENCE ARE ALL DRIVEN AT LAST TO HAVE BUT ONE PRAYER " MAKE ME A HEALTHY ANIMAL." BUT

APPL I	(224)	KNOW. /BALBUS/ EVER THE BEST OF FRIENDS. I AM THE	LAST	TO KICK A MAN WHEN HE'S DOWN. /CRASSUS/ I MAY BE A
METH PREFACE	(R84)	IN THE THEATRE. ON THE STAGE (AND HERE I COME AT	LAST	TO MY OWN PARTICULAR FUNCTION IN THE MATTER), COMEDY,
MTH5	(212)	WOMAN TWICE YOUR AGE. I CANNOT MAKE MY CHILDHOOD	LAST	TO PLEASE YOU. THE AGE OF LOVE IS SWEET; BUT IT IS
ROCK II	(271)	ARE GROWN UP AND OFF MY HANDS. I'M FREE AT	LAST	TO PUT MY NECK IN A NOOSE IF I LIKE. /BASHAM/ I WONDER
MTH3	(97)	AND RUIN PRODUCED BY YOUR ANARCHY FORCED YOU AT	LAST	TO RECOGNIZE TWO INEXORABLE FACTS. FIRST, THAT
BULL II	SD(111)	DREAMED OF (HE CALLS IT POTTING) AND IS NOW AT	LAST	TO TASTE. HIS GOODHUMOR RISES ALMOST TO EXCITEMENT
BARB II	(298)	I WISH WE COULD DO WITHOUT IT. I AM GETTING AT	LAST	TO THINK MORE OF THE COLLECTION THAN OF THE PEOPLE'S
SUPR III	(75)	SOIL OF PALESTINE, MENDOZA WILL NOT BE THE	LAST	TO VOLUNTEER (SYMPATHETIC APPLAUSE-- HEAR, HEAR,
ANNA	(299)	WICKED IN OUR OWN DESPITE, THAT WE HAVE COME AT	LAST	TO WILL OUR OWN DESTRUCTION. /STRAMMFEST/ YOU ARE
DOCT II	(123)	/B.B./ NO, NO, MR SCHUTZMACHER. YOU INVENTED THAT	LAST	TOUCH, SERIOUSLY, NOW? /SCHUTZMACHER/ NO. YOU CANT
MTH2	SD(54)	THE END OF HIS SIXTIES, A YORKSHIREMAN WITH THE	LAST	TRACES OF SCANDINAVIAN FLAX STILL IN HIS WHITE HAIR,
ROCK II	(237)	GONE; WHEN WE HAVE CLOSED OUR ACCOUNTS WITH THE	LAST	TRADESMAN AND TURNED THE LAST SERVANT INTO THE STREETS,
JOAN PREFACE	(53)	WEARY AND DEMORALIZED AUDIENCE WOULD LOSE THEIR	LAST	TRAINS AND CURSE ME FOR WRITING SUCH INORDINATELY LONG
JOAN EPILOG	(152)	FROM YOUR CROWN. JUSTICE, LONG DELAYED, IS AT	LAST	TRIUMPHANT. /CHARLES/ WHAT ARE YOU TALKING ABOUT? WHO
BASH III	(124)	UPON THINE EAR SHALL CLANG IN THUNDER FROM THE	LAST	TRUMPET. /ADELAIDE/ A DISGRACEFUL THREAT TO LEVEL AT
PRES	(133)	OH, IMPOSSIBLE! THE PROCLAMATION OF MARTIAL LAW	LAST	TUESDAY MADE SANDSTONE VIRTUALLY DICTATOR IN THE
INCA	(240)	TO ESTABLISH A SECOND-HAND BUSINESS FAILED	LAST	TUESDAY WEEK? HAVE YOU THE HEART TO COMPLAIN TO THE
KING II	(225)	I TOLD THE SAME ONE TWICE OVER WITHIN AN HOUR	LAST	TUESDAY. THIS MORNING BARBARA CALLED ME AN OLD WRECK.
DEVL II	(29)	FROM HIS HAT AND PUTS IT ON THE FENDER; AND AT	LAST	TURNS WITH HIS HANDS OUTSTRETCHED TO JUDITH). NOW! (
GETT	(301)	GO ON? /THE GENERAL/ IVE BEEN WAITING FOR THE	LAST	TWENTY MINUTES, ALFRED. IN AMAZEMENT! IN
ANNA PREFACE	(287)	FOR ITS " TURNS" LITTLE PLAYS CALLED SKETCHES, TO	LAST	TWENTY MINUTES OR SO, AND TO ENABLE SOME FAVORITE
SIM PREFACE	(8)	TAKE IT THAT NO CIVILIZED RUSSIAN BORN WITHIN THE	LAST	TWENTY YEARS HAS ANY APPREHENSION OF HAVING TO SUFFER
3PLA PREFACE	(R18)	IT HAS HAD FROM THE WORKING CLASS DURING THE	LAST	TWENTY YEARS. LET BUT THE ATTITUDE OF THE AUTHOR BE
MTH3	(93)	YOU HAVE READ ANY BOOK EXCEPT A NOVEL FOR THE	LAST	TWENTY YEARS; FOR I WONT BELIEVE YOU. /BURGE-LUBIN/
MTH3	(93)	LIKE YOU AND ME HAVE DIED BY DROWNING DURING THE	LAST	TWO CENTURIES, AND THAT WHEN THIS INVENTION OF
KING I	SD(187)	BIBLE, WHICH, HELPED BY A MARKER, HE OPENS AT THE	LAST	TWO CHAPTERS OF THE BOOK OF DANIEL. HE PROPS HIS HEAD
APPL I	(197)	CEREMONIES AND THINGS LIKE THAT. HE ARRANGED THE	LAST	TWO CORONATIONS. THAT WAS HOW I GOT MY JOB HERE IN THE
PHIL II	(110)	IMAGINE HER SAYING I HAD KISSED HER WITHIN THE	LAST	TWO DAYS! /GRACE/ (RISING EAGERLY) WAS THAT NOT
PYGM EPILOG	(295)	MONTHS OUT OF FASHION. STILL, 500 POUNDS WILL NOT	LAST	TWO YOUNG PEOPLE FOR EVER; AND THEY BOTH KNEW, AND
SIM II	(61)	AM! MY SERMONS ARE WRETCHED STUFF, EXCEPT THESE	LAST	TWO, WHICH I THINK REALLY HAVE SOMETHING IN THEM. I
LION PREFACE	(12)	YOU WILL FIND THAT THOUGH A RELIGION MAY	LAST	UNCHANGED FOR MANY CENTURIES IN PRIMITIVE COMMUNITIES
HART I	(72)	UTTERWORD. I AM EXTREMELY GLAD TO WELCOME YOU AT	LAST	UNDER OUR ROOF (HE OFFERS HIS HAND WITH GRAVE
SIM II	(63)	CHRISTENDOM TO CELEBRATE THE PASSING AWAY OF THE	LAST	VAIN DREAM OF EARTHLY EMPIRE, AND THE UNITY OF ALL
PYGM V	(271)	A COMMON DUSTMAN. /HIGGINS/ OH, AFTER YOUR	LAST	VISIT I REMEMBER MAKING SOME SILLY JOKE OF THE KIND.
3PLA PREFACE	(R26)	BOTH HOSTILE AND FRIENDLY, WAS PROVOKED BY MY	LAST	VOLUME OF PLAYS, MR ROBERT BUCHANAN, A DRAMATIST WHO
ROCK II	(244)	HAVE THE SUPPORT OF THE CITY. /SIR JAFNA/ TO THE	LAST	VOTE, TO THE LAST PENNY. THESE PIRATES THINK NOTHING OF
FABL I	(103)	AIR AND TAKES MANY DAYS TO DISPERSE. SO IN THE	LAST	WAR GAS WAS NOT USED; AND ATOMIC BOMBS WONT BE USED IN
JOAN 5	(119)	ELSE IS WRONG. /THE ARCHBISHOP/ TAKE THIS AS YOUR	LAST	WARNING. IF YOU PERISH THROUGH SETTING YOUR PRIVATE
SUPR HANDBOK	(193)	LANGUAGE AND COARSE HUMOR INTOLERABLE; SO THAT AT	LAST	WE CANNOT BEAR TO HAVE IT SPOKEN OF AT ALL BECAUSE ONLY
MTH4 I	(154)	WHICH IT HAD OPPRESSED BUT NEVER CONQUERED, " AT	LAST	WE LEAVE YOU TO YOURSELVES; AND MUCH GOOD MAY IT DO
BARB III	(343)	WEAKENING: YOUR GRIP IS SLIPPING. COME! TRY YOUR	LAST	WEAPON. PITY AND LOVE HAVE BROKEN IN YOUR HAND:
BARB II	(300)	FROST; AN AWVE A PAHND OF IT LEFT. A MITE O MAWN	LAST	WEEK ED WORDS WITH THE JUDY E'S GOWIN TO MERRY. E GIVE
GETT	(297)	SHALL BE RESPONSIBLE FOR EVERYTHING YOU SAY. ONLY	LAST	WEEK YOU SAID ON A PUBLIC PLATFORM THAT SLATTOX AND
LIED	(197)	I'M SORRY I HAVNT BEEN ABLE TO CALL ON HER THIS	LAST	WEEK. I HOPE THERES NOTHING THE MATTER WITH HER. /HER
MIS.	(117)	MAD ON READING. HE PROMISED ANOTHER FREE LIBRARY	LAST	WEEK. IT'S RUINOUS. ITLL HIT YOU AS WELL AS ME WHEN
PYGM II	(232)	CHOKED YOURSELF WITH A FISHBONE IN THE JAM ONLY	LAST	WEEK. /HIGGINS/ (ROUTED FROM THE HEARTHRUG AND
JITT II	(27)	JIMMINY, LENKHEIM, I HAVE GONE THROUGH A LOT THIS	LAST	WEEK. /LENKHEIM/ HOW? /FESSLER/ JUST CONSIDER. IMAGINE
CLEO IV	(178)	HEARD IT BEFORE. YOU REPEATED IT TO APOLLODORUS	LAST	WEEK; AND HE THOUGHT IT WAS ALL YOUR OWN. (CAESAR'S
LION PREFACE	(90)	TO BELIEVE THAT AN OVERWROUGHT PREACHER AT	LAST	WENT MAD AS SWIFT AND RUSKIN AND NIETZSCHE WENT MAD.
GLIM	(187)	FORCED AT LAST TO BELIEVE IN GRIM DEATH I KNEW AT	LAST	WHAT BELIEF WAS, AND THAT I HAD NEVER BELIEVED IN
HART PREFACE	(14)	TO KEEP HER TEMPER SWEET WHEN SHE KNEW AT	LAST	WHAT IT WAS TO HIDE IN CELLARS AND UNDERGROUND RAILWAY
DOCT III	(153)	HAVE SEEN SO MANY DOCTORS: I HAVE COME TO KNOW AT	LAST	WHEN THEY ARE ONLY TALKING AND CAN DO NOTHING. IT IS
JITT III	(71)	SORT OF HAPPINESS TO BE ABLE TO GIVE MYSELF UP AT	LAST	WHOLLY TO MY SORROW. /JITTA/ (SITTING DOWN IN
DEVL I	(21)	GO AHEAD. /HAWKINS/ (READING) " THIS IS THE	LAST	WILL AND TESTAMENT OF ME TIMOTHY DUDGEON ON MY DEATHBED
JITT II	(43)	YOU. /LENKHEIM/ WHY MUST I? /JITTA/ IT WAS HIS	LAST	WISH: WE HAVE NO CHOICE. /LENKHEIM/ WE! ME, YOU MEAN.
BARB PREFACE	(245)	AND SOME GENEROSITY IN COMPLYING WITH THEIR	LAST	WISHES. PLACE THEM IN THE LETHAL CHAMBER AND GET RID OF
ROCK I	SD(210)	MODEST, OR PRETENDS TO BE, AND COMES IN	LAST	WITH A DISARMING SMILE RATHER AS A POOR FOLLOWER OF THE
BARB PREFACE	(240)	HE CAN TO ESCAPE, AND SENDS HIM OFF ACQUAINTED AT	LAST	WITH A FORCE THAT GOES DEEPER THAN DYNAMITE, THOUGH YOU
DEST	(166)	MEETS HER REGARD INFLEXIBLY. /LADY/ (RISING AT	LAST	WITH A QUIET LITTLE SIGH) I WILL GET THEM FOR YOU. THEY
MIS.	(141)	/HYPATIA/ THAT WAS SOMETHING HAPPENING AT	LAST	WITH A VENGEANCE. IT WAS SPLENDID. IT WAS MY FIRST PEEP
METH PREFACE	(R87)	EVOLUTION DEVELOPED I SAW THAT WE WERE AT	LAST	WITHIN REACH OF A FAITH WHICH COMPLIED WITH THE FIRST
PYGM IV	(262)	OVER AND DONE WITH; AND NOW I CAN GO TO BED AT	LAST	WITHOUT DREADING TOMORROW. ELIZA'S BEAUTY BECOMES
MTH2	(81)	SOME MORE CAPABLE AGENTS. MAN IS NOT GOD'S	LAST	WORD: GOD CAN STILL CREATE. IF YOU CANNOT DO HIS WORK
HART II	(104)	LIKE A YELL OF DESPAIR) AM I NEVER TO HAVE THE	LAST	WORD? /CAPTAIN SHOTOVER/ (APPEARING AT THE STARBOARD
NEVR II	(254)	BETTER GO. (HE PUTS ON HIS HAT). IS THAT YOUR	LAST	WORD? /GLORIA/ I HOPE SO. HE LOOKS STUBBORNLY AT HER
HART II	(104)	GENTLEMAN WANTS TO KNOW IS HE NEVER TO HAVE THE	LAST	WORD? /LADY UTTERWORD/ (COMING FORWARD TO THE SOFA) I
JITT II	(36)	JITTA) WHY DID HE NOT DIE WITH US? WHY HAD HE NO	LAST	WORD FOR US? I WAS NOTHING TO HIM: NONE OF US WERE
KING I	(186)	IN SPITE OF YOUR MILLIONS OF MILES. AND THIS	LAST	WORD HERE? /NEWTON/ ONLY SUGAR, TO SWEETEN THE
MIS. PREFACE	(90)	AND HYMNS ANCIENT AND MODERN ARE NOT PERHAPS THE	LAST	WORD OF BEAUTY AND PROPRIETY IN THE PRAISE OF GOD. IN
DOCT PREFACE	(24)	PROCEED ON THE ASSUMPTION THAT THEY COULD GET THE	LAST	WORD OF SCIENCE AS TO THE CONSTITUENTS OF THEIR
MIS. PREFACE	(57)	BABY IS DOING; AND TELL HIM HE MUSTNT" IS THE	LAST	WORD OF THE NURSERY; AND THE GRIMMEST ASPECT OF IT IS
MIS.	(135)	TO SAY SOMETHING LIKE THAT IF IT WAS TO BE HIS	LAST	WORD ON EARTH. BESIDES, HES QUITE RIGHT: MY POOR FATHER
LADY PREFACE	(232)	NOT MERELY DESPAIR OF HUMAN NATURE. HIS FIRST AND	LAST	WORD ON PARLIAMENT WAS " GET THEE GLASS EYES, AND, LIKE
ROCK PREFACE	(189)	OF PEACE. THE SACREDNESS OF CRITICISM, AND SO THE	LAST	WORD REMAINS WITH CHRIST AND HANDEL; AND THIS MUST
DEVL III	(53)	/RICHARD/ OF HEART DISEASE-- IN THE NIGHT. HER	LAST	WORD TO ME WAS HER CURSE: I DONT THINK I COULD HAVE
JOAN 6	(146)	NOT FIT THAT I SHOULD LIVE AMONG YOU. THAT IS MY	LAST	WORD TO YOU. THE SOLDIERS SEIZE HER. /CAUCHON/ (
MTH4 I	(166)	(EXHAUSTED) WELL, A WOMAN MUST HAVE THE	LAST	WORD. I WILL NOT DISPUTE IT WITH YOU. /ZOO/ GOOD. NOW
CAND III	(145)	(HE GOES TOWARDS THE DOOR). /CANDIDA/ ONE	LAST	WORD. (HE STOPS, BUT WITHOUT TURNING TO HER. SHE GOES
GENV IV	(104)	DO I CARE? I HAVE MY PRINCIPLES STILL. THATS MY	LAST	WORD. NOW GO ON AND TALK YOURSELF SILLY. /BBDE/ IT IS
VWOO 1	(116)	/A/ IT IS YOUR PRIVILEGE AS A WOMAN TO HAVE THE	LAST	WORD. PLEASE TAKE IT AND DONT END ALL YOUR REMARKS WITH
BARB III	(334)	I WILL GIVE YOU THREE FIFTHS; BUT THAT IS MY	LAST	WORD. /CUSINS/ DONE! /LOMAX/ DONE IN THE EYE! WHY, I
HART II	(104)	GET THEM, MR MANGAN. PROVIDENCE ALWAYS HAS THE	LAST	WORD. /MANGAN/ (DESPERATELY) NOW YOU ARE GOING TO COME
APPL PREFACE	(191)	THAT AT PRESENT. THE RUSSIANS ARE. THAT IS MY	LAST	WORD. THINK OVER IT. SO MUCH FOR MY BROADCAST ON
BUOY II	(23)	OF DEATH. /HE/ (RISING WEARILY) YOU HAVE THE	LAST	WORD. YOU ARE AN INHOSPITABLE WRETCH. /SHE/ AND YOU ARE
2TRU III	SD(112)	SAVED BY TALK ALONE. HE HAS GIVEN THE RASCAL THE	LAST	WORD; BUT HIS OWN FAVORITE IS THE WOMAN OF ACTION, WHO
MTH2	(38)	IS EXTRAORDINARY. MOST EXTRAORDINARY. THE VERY	LAST	WORDS I WROTE WHEN YOU INTERRUPTED ME WERE " AT LEAST
SUPR PREFACE	(R15)	GOETHE'S FAUST AND MOZART'S DON JUAN WERE THE	LAST	WORDS OF THE XVIII CENTURY ON THE SUBJECT; AND BY THE
SIM II	(76)	BE PROVIDED BY THE POET LAUREATE. THE PREMIER'S	LAST	WORDS WERE LOST THROUGH THE MISCONDUCT OF A CHERUB WHO
WIDO I	(21)	NOTE OF COLDNESS IN HIS VOICE AS HE WRITES THE	LAST	WORDS) " -- AND POSITION" /SARTORIUS/ " WHICH, HOWEVER,
CAND II	(110)	(SOMEWHAT RELIEVED BY THE TRIUMPH OF HAVING THE	LAST	WORD, AND YET HALF INCLINED TO TRY TO IMPROVE ON IT, HE
HART II	(104)	MY DEAR. THE IMPORTANT THING IS NOT TO HAVE THE	LAST	WORD, BUT TO HAVE YOUR OWN WAY. /MANGAN/ SHE WANTS
CLEO III	(165)	ON THE COPING). /BRITANNUS/ (ANXIOUSLY) ONE	LAST	WORD, CAESAR. DO NOT LET YOURSELF BE SEEN IN THE
GENV IV	(114)	NOW GOVERNED BY JESUS. /JUDGE/ ALLOW THE LADY THE	LAST	WORD, MR LEADER. PROCEED, MR SECRETARY. /SECRETARY/ NO:
APPL I	(241)	HE RISES. ALL RISE. HE MARCHES OUT. /PROTEUS/ HIS	LAST	WRIGGLE. NEVER MIND: WE HAVE HIM SAFE ENOUGH. WHAT
HART I	(80)	/MRS HUSHABYE/ WHERE IS THE SNOW THAT FELL	LAST	YEAR? /CAPTAIN SHOTOVER/ WHERE IS ALL THE MONEY YOU
PRES	(137)	UNIVERSAL COMPULSORY MILITARY SERVICE AS HE DID	LAST	YEAR? WHY, EVEN THE CHURCH REFUSED EXEMPTION. HE IS
BULL PREFACE	(61)	WHICH HAS BEEN SEDULOUSLY FOSTERED DURING THE	LAST	YEAR BY UNSCRUPULOUS AND INTERESTED AGITATORS," AGAIN,
MIS. PREFACE	(56)	TRAINED TO IT FROM CHILDHOOD IN THE SCHOOLS UNTIL	LAST	YEAR (1913), WHEN, IN WHAT MUST BE DESCRIBED AS A
PRES	(138)	THE LABOR PARTY APPEALED TO ME AND TO THE HOUSE	LAST	YEAR NOT TO THROW AWAY ALL THE LIBERTIES OF ENGLISHMEN
INCA	(251)	NOT SENSE ENOUGH TO BE AFRAID TO DIE. WITHIN THE	LAST	YEAR THE WORLD HAS PRODUCED MILLIONS OF HEROES. HAS IT
POSN PREFACE	(361)	COMMITTEE OF BOTH HOUSES OF PARLIAMENT WHICH SAT	LAST	YEAR TO INQUIRE INTO THE WORKING OF THE CENSORSHIP,
JOAN 1	(63)	I KNOW HER CLASS EXACTLY. HER FATHER CAME HERE	LAST	YEAR TO REPRESENT HIS VILLAGE IN A LAWSUIT: HE IS ONE
CLEO IV	(174)	CONCILIATED. WE HAD SEVEN OF THEM IN TEN MONTHS	LAST	YEAR. /CAESAR/ (CONTRITELY) IT IS TRUE, RUFIO! I
ROCK I	(199)	THAT YOU USED AT THE BRITISH ASSOCIATION	LAST	YEAR. /SIR ARTHUR/ NO: THESE PARSONS KNOW TOO MUCH
MIS.	(135)	IT WAS NO GOOD. FIRST IT WAS 250 POUNDS MORE THAN	LAST	YEAR. THEN IT WAS 700 POUNDS. THEN IT WAS 2000. THEN I
FANY II	(293)	IT WAS A BIT OF ENGLISH FUN. AND TALKED ABOUT	LAST	YEAR'S BOAT-RACE NIGHT WHEN IT HAD BEEN A GREAT DEAL
MTH2	(78)	HAVE GONE OUT OF FASHION AND PERISHED LIKE	LAST	YEAR'S POPULAR SONG, IS A SCIENTIFIC FACT; AND SCIENCE

MIS. (135)	PROVING THAT I'D MADE 20 POUNDS LESS THAN	LAST	YEAR, I COULD ASK HER TO LET ME CHANCE JOHNNY'S AND
POSN PREFACE(387)	JULIUS CAESAR AT HIS MAJESTY'S THEATRE IN LONDON	LAST	YEAR, MIGHT NOW ENTERTAIN VERY SERIOUSLY A PROPOSAL TO
GENV II (53)	THERES NO HARM IN IT. I'D NEVER HEARD OF IT UNTIL	LAST	YEAR, WHEN THEY OPENED A BRANCH IN CAMBERWELL WITH A
MTH1 I (10)	YOU DESIRE; YOU WILL WHAT YOU IMAGINE; AND AT	LAST	YOU CREATE WHAT YOU WILL. /EVE/ HOW CAN I CREATE OUT OF
BUOY III (32)	TO DO THE HOUSEWORK. YOUR CLOTHES WILL HAVE TO	LAST	YOU FOR YEARS. I AM HERE TO IMPRESS THESE HARD FACTS ON
BULL I (87)	WHISKY. (WITH FIERCE SHIVERING SELF-CONTEMPT) AT	LAST	YOU GET THAT YOU CAN BEAR NOTHING REAL AT ALL: YOUD
ANNA (301)	(DROPPING ON HIS KNEE SUBMISSIVELY) NOW AT	LAST	YOU SPEAK LIKE YOUR ROYAL SELF. /THE GRAND DUCHESS/ OH,
BUOY 1 (16)	THERE IS SOME SENSE IN THAT. BUT IT WOULD NOT	LAST	YOUR LIFETIME: IT WOULD ONLY GIVE YOU A START. AT
MTH4 I (162)	AND WITHER IN YOUR SECOND CHILDHOOD. A LIE WILL	LAST	YOUR TIME: IT WILL NOT LAST MINE. IF I KNEW I HAD TO
PHIL II (117)	MITRAL VALVES A LITTLE WORN PERHAPS; BUT THEYLL	LAST	YOUR TIME IF YOURE CAREFUL. DONT SMOKE TOO MUCH.
ROCK I (220)	MEDALS AND THE LIKE, SHE'S WON ENOUGH OF THEM TO	LAST	YOUR WHOLE FAMILY FOR TWO GENERATIONS. SHE CAN WIN THEM
ROCK I (224)	ON THE TABLE BETWEEN HIS ARMS. /SIR ARTHUR/ AT	LAST	, A MOMENT'S PEACE. THE WORD ROUSES THE ORATOR IN HIM.
PRES (164)	IN EARNEST. HE SAYS HE HAS MET HIS IDEAL AT	LAST	, A REALLY SOLDIERLY WOMAN. SHE WILL SIT ON HIS HEAD
MILL IV (189)	HAVE YOU DONE TO THE OLD PLACE? WHEN I WAS HERE	LAST	, A YEAR AGO, IT WAS A COMMON PUB CALLED THE PIG AND
MRS PREFACE(152)	MRS WARREN'S PROFESSION HAS BEEN PERFORMED AT	LAST	, AFTER A DELAY OF ONLY EIGHT YEARS; AND I HAVE ONCE
JOAN 1,SD(60)	AT HAVING PENETRATED TO BAUDRICOURT'S PRESENCE AT	LAST	, AND FULL OF HOPE AS TO THE RESULT. HIS SCOWL DOES NOT
GENV IV (129)	ATTITUDES IN BARDO'S MANNER: WE SHALL WORK TO THE	LAST	, AND SET AN EXAMPLE TO THE NEW RACE OF ICEPROOF MEN
MTH3 (119)	SAW THAT THE LITTLE MONEY I HAD LAID UP WOULD NOT	LAST	, AND THAT I MUST GO OUT AND WORK AGAIN. THEY HAD
HART II (100)	MOST OF MY TIME WONDERING HOW LONG MY GLOVES WILL	LAST	, ANYHOW. /MRS HUSHABYE/ (RISING SUPERBLY) ELLIE: YOU
CAND I (90)	(EXULTANT) AHA! YOURE FINDING THAT OUT AT	LAST	, ARE YOU? /BURGESS/ (PORTENTOUSLY) YES: TIMES 'AS
DEVL III (74)	NOT BE PUT OFF WITH SO COLD A LAST FAREWELL-- AT	LAST	, AS HE TRIES TO DISENGAGE HIMSELF, THROWS HERSELF ON
JOAN 4 (106)	FRIEND TO THE CHURCH: YOU ARE AN EARL FIRST AND	LAST	, AS I AM A CHURCHMAN FIRST AND LAST. BUT CAN WE NOT
DEVL II (29)	/JUDITH/ (RUNNING TO HIM) OH, HERE YOU ARE AT	LAST	, AT LAST! (SHE ATTEMPTS TO EMBRACE HIM). /ANDERSON/
GETT (321)	EARLY CHRISTIAN RULES OF LIFE WERE NOT MADE TO	LAST	, BECAUSE THE EARLY CHRISTIANS DID NOT BELIEVE THAT THE
SIM I SD(37)	ABOUT TWENTY YEARS OLDER THAN WHEN WE SAW HIM	LAST	, BUT SPLENDIDLY PRESERVED. HIS APPROACH IS DIGNIFIED
CAND I (101)	ALL-- EVEN THE HUMBLEST-- SHALL ONE DAY REAP. AND	LAST	, BUT TRUST ME, NOT LEAST, I WILL HELP YOU TO BELIEVE
PYGM III (251)	LONG AND PAINFUL PAUSE ENSUES. /MRS HIGGINS/ (AT	LAST	, CONVERSATIONALLY) WILL IT RAIN, DO YOU THINK? /LIZA/
JITT II (33)	HALDENSTEDT, HOW DEEPLY I--- /JITTA/ (GUSHING) AT	LAST	, DEAREST MRS HALDENSTEDT, I AM ABLE TO TELL YOU WHAT I
GLIM (179)	(THEY TAKE THEIR PLACES). THATS RIGHT. SERVE ME	LAST	, GIULIETTA. SANDRO IS HUNGRY. /SQUARCIO/ (TO THE
PYGM I (215)	/FREDDY/ (SPRINGING OUT OF A TAXICAB) GOT ONE AT	LAST	, HALLO! (TO THE GIRL) WHERE ARE THE TWO LADIES THAT
DEVL III (66)	RICHARD DUDGEON? /RICHARD/ YOUVE FOUND IT OUT AT	LAST	, HAVE YOU? /SWINDON/ DUDGEON IS A NAME WELL KNOWN TO
FANY PROLOG (266)	BY ALL THE MEN, EXCEPT TROTTER, WHO, GOING	LAST	, IS DETAINED BY FANNY). /FANNY/ MR TROTTER: I WANT TO
SUPR PREFACE(R36)	EVEN LITTLE FAITH, THOUGH HE GETS TO HEAVEN AT	LAST	, IS GIVEN TO UNDERSTAND THAT IT SERVED HIM RIGHT TO BE
MTH5 (248)	YOU PLAYED WITH RAG DOLLS. /THE HE-ANCIENT/ AT	LAST	, LIKE PYGMALION, YOU DEMAND FROM YOUR DOLLS THE FINAL
SUPR HANDBOK(210)	BUT THAT MAN SHOULD WILL THEM, PERCEIVE AT	LAST	, LIKE RICHARD WAGNER, THAT THE FACT TO BE FACED IS
APPL I (203)	/MAGNUS/ IT IS A GREAT PLEASURE TO MEET YOU AT	LAST	, MR BOANERGES. I HAVE FOLLOWED YOUR CAREER WITH
GETT PREFACE(234)	FOR DIVORCE, MIGHT MORE REASONABLY BE MADE THE	LAST	, OR WHOLLY EXCLUDED. THE PRESENT LAW IS PERFECTLY
GETT PREFACE(248)	ON THE ASSUMPTION THAT THE WORLD IS GOING TO	LAST	, REALLY DO BELIEVE THAT THERE WILL BE A JUDGMENT DAY,
O'FL (211)	LONG LIFE. IT'S A TRUE RESPECT I'M SHEWING YOU AT	LAST	, SIR. MAYBE YOUD RATHER HAVE ME HUMBUG YOU AND TELL
SUPR IV (160)	YOU SHALL NEVER SEE IT BLEED. /ANN/ POETIC TO THE	LAST	, TAVY. GOODBYE, DEAR. (SHE PATS HIS CHEEK; HAS AN
NEVR III (262)	AND RINGS). I HAVE FINISHED THESE PROOFS AT	LAST	, THANK GOODNESS! /GLORIA/ (STROLLING LISTLESSLY
GETT PREFACE(245)	THINGS HAPPENING TO OUR CHILDREN. WE LEARN, AT	LAST	, THAT THE MAJORITY OF THE VICTIMS ARE NOT THE PEOPLE
SUPR III (115)	LOVE IS SATISFIED": SHE ALWAYS SAID, FIRST, " AT	LAST	, THE BARRIERS ARE DOWN," AND SECOND, " WHEN WILL YOU
MTH2 (81)	UP HER MIND TO JUMP; BUT WHEN SHE MAKES IT UP AT	LAST	, THE JUMP IS BIG ENOUGH TO TAKE US INTO A NEW AGE.
JITT II (34)	THEM: WHEN THEY CAN LEAN ON US TO THE VERY	LAST	, THEN, WHEN THE PARTING COMES, THERE IS SOME
FOUN (219)	GO; BUT I HAD TO LET THE POOR MAN HAVE HIS WAY AT	LAST	, THOUGH IT TOOK TEN WARDRESSES TO PERSUADE ME TO DO
PHIL II (109)	WOMAN. /SYLVIA/ (RUNNING TO HER) HERE YOU ARE AT	LAST	, TRANFIELD, OLD GIRL. IVE BEEN WAITING FOR YOU THIS
MIS. (141)	AND I'M CORRECT AND SELF-POSSESSED; AND AT	LAST	, WHEN I CAN BEAR IT NO LONGER, I EITHER FRIGHTEN HIM
PPP SD(202)	MAGNESIA LOOSENING THE STRAPS WHEN HE MOANS. AT	LAST	, WITH A SIGH OF RELIEF, HE SINKS BACK IN THE WOMEN'S
HART I (54)	A SOFT BLACK HAT OF CLERICAL CUT. /ELLIE/ AT	LAST	! CAPTAIN SHOTOVER: HERE IS MY FATHER. /THE CAPTAIN/
SUPR III (98)	YOU. AND NOW, MY FRIEND-- I MAY CALL YOU SO AT	LAST	! COULD YOU NOT PERSUADE HIM TO TAKE THE PLACE YOU
DEVL II (29)	(RUNNING TO HIM) OH, HERE YOU ARE AT LAST, AT	LAST	! (SHE ATTEMPTS TO EMBRACE HIM). /ANDERSON/ (KEEPING
PPP (202)	DISSOLVED THE BUST. /MAGNESIA/ (SNATCHING IT) AT	LAST	! /FITZ/ YOU ARE SAVED. DRAIN IT TO THE DREGS.
MIS. (137)	AN ENORMOUS SIGH OF RELIEF. /LORD SUMMERHAYS/ AT	LAST	! /HYPATIA/ AT LAST. OH, IF I MIGHT ONLY HAVE A
LIED (188)	MIRROR AS SHE ENTERS. /HE/ (KISSING HER HAND) AT	LAST	! /SHE/ HENRY: SOMETHING DREADFUL HAS HAPPENED. /HE/
JOAN 2 (71)	SHEW FOR IT. (A PAGE APPEARS IN THE DOORWAY). AT	LAST	! /THE PAGE/ NO, MY LORD: IT IS NOT HIS MAJESTY.

LASTED

3PLA PREFACE(R40)	I HATE TO THINK THAT SHAKESPEAR HAS	LASTED	300 YEARS, THOUGH HE GOT NO FURTHER THAN KOHELETH THE
POSN (443)	IT ALL UP." DID YOU EVER SEE ME SOBER WHILE IT	LASTED	? /BLANCO/ NO; AND YOU LOOKED SO DISGUSTING THAT I
PYGM EPILOG (294)	OF 500 POUNDS FROM THE COLONEL TO ELIZA. IT	LASTED	A LONG TIME BECAUSE FREDDY DID NOT KNOW HOW TO SPEND
GLIM (186)	YOU HAVE PRETTY TEETH. /FERRUCCIO/ THE TOOTHACHE	LASTED	A WEEK; BUT THE AGONY OF MY SOUL WAS TOO DREADFUL TO
FANY III (315)	RESPECTABLE? ALL THIS FOR A PINT OF WHISKY THAT	LASTED	A WEEK! HOW LONG WOULD IT HAVE LASTED SIMMONS, I
MILL PREFACE(131)	WAS MASTER WHILST THEIR PERSONAL RELATIONS	LASTED	. AND PLEASE NOTE THAT NAPOLEON DID NOT AND COULD NOT
MTH5 (260)	DENY THAT MINE WAS A SPLENDID GAME WHILE IT	LASTED	. BUT NOW! OUT, OUT, BRIEF CANDLE! (HE VANISHES).
MTH4 I (162)	ANYTHING BUT HAVING A LITTLE PLEASURE WHILE I	LASTED	. /THE ELDERLY GENTLEMAN/ YOUNG WOMAN: YOU ARE
MTH4 I (151)	WOULD BE UNDERSTOOD AS LONG AS HUMAN NATURE	LASTED	. TO EMBARRASS IS TO BRING A BLUSH TO THE CHEEK.
BUOY II (25)	ME; FOR THE DOCTRINES OF MY TEACHERS HAVE	LASTED	MANY THOUSANDS OF CENTURIES. ONLY THE TRUTH COULD
HART PREFACE(29)	SIR DOUGLAS HAIG HAS POINTED OUT, ITS WATERLOOS	LASTED	MONTHS INSTEAD OF HOURS. BUT THERE WOULD HAVE BEEN
FANY III (315)	THAT LASTED A WEEK! HOW LONG WOULD IT HAVE	LASTED	SIMMONS, I WONDER? /MRS KNOX/ (GENTLY) OH, WELL,
SUPR II (54)	TO THE TEST OF DOMESTIC FAMILIARITY; AND IT	LASTED	THEM TO THEIR GRAVES. MARRY ANN; AND AT THE END OF A
JITT II (46)	THIS AFFAIR BEEN GOING ON? /JITTA/ OUR LOVE HAS	LASTED	THREE YEARS. /LENKHEIM/ LOVE! LOVE IN THE SORT OF
DOCT V (177)	WHO BELIEVED IN ME. WHO TOLD ME HER FRIENDSHIP	LASTED	UNTIL DEATH. /JENNIFER/ AND WHOM YOU WERE BETRAYING.
JITT III (77)	WITH YOUR DEAR FRIEND THELMA PETERSEN. THAT	LASTED	UNTIL SHE AND HER HUSBAND WENT BACK TO NORWAY.
HART PREFACE(29)	FOR WAR, OR EVEN FOR PEACE, THE WAR WOULD HAVE	LASTED	UNTIL THE BELLIGERENTS WERE SO TIRED OF IT THAT THEY
ROCK II (269)	A VISION, A HOPE AND A FAITH AND A PROMISE. IT	LASTED	UNTIL THEY DRAGGED IT DOWN TO EARTH, AS YOU MIGHT

LASTING

DOCT III (155)	(SHE TAKES HIS HAND). I HOPE THIS WILL BE A	LASTING	FRIENDSHIP. /MRS DUBEDAT/ IT WILL. MY FRIENDSHIPS
SUPR IV (169)	LET ME GO. I HAVE DARED SO FRIGHTFULLY-- IT IS	LASTING	LONGER THAN I THOUGHT. LET ME GO: I CANT BEAR IT.
ARMS II (28)	UNTIL WE'RE QUITE SURE THAT THE PEACE WILL BE A	LASTING	ONE. /NICOLA/ (AT THE GATE, ANNOUNCING) MAJOR
HART PREFACE(29)	THERE WOULD HAVE BEEN NOTHING SURPRISING IN ITS	LASTING	THIRTY YEARS, IF IT HAD NOT BEEN FOR THE FACT THAT
MIS. PREFACE(53)	SERVICE, AND FINALLY OF COMPULSORY CIVIL SERVICE	LASTING	UNTIL THE AGE OF SUPERANNUATION, ALWAYS MORE

LASTLY

DEVL I (23)	GREATLY PLEASED). GO ON. /HAWKINS/ " FOURTHLY AND	LASTLY	, THAT HE TRY TO LIVE AT PEACE WITH HIS MOTHER AS FAR

LAST-BORN

MTH1 II (31)	ALL A THOUSAND TIMES. THEY TELL ME TOO OF THEIR	LAST-BORN	: THE CLEVER THING THE DARLING CHILD SAID

LASTS

JOAN PREFACE(55)	TO SECURE A SEAT. IN COUNTRIES WHERE A PLAY	LASTS	A WEEK, THEY BRING BASKETS OF PROVISIONS AND SIT IT
BUOY IV (50)	I HAVE NO OBJECTION TO YOUR FATHER AS LONG AS HE	LASTS	. HE HAS THE BILLIONS. /OLD BILL/ THE BILLIONS WILL
2TRU II (68)	AND NOTHING ELSE. IT'S THE REAL THING WHILE IT	LASTS	. I HAVNT THE LEAST CURIOSITY ABOUT MY LOVELY
SIM I (50)	HYERING; WELL, STICK TO THE ENCHANTMENT WHILE IT	LASTS	. LET LIFE COME TO YOU. /PRA/ MAY I REMIND YOU THAT
NEVR III (264)	MAKE THE MOST OF THE NINETEENTH CENTURY WHILE IT	LASTS	. /PHILIP/ SH! HERE HE IS. /VALENTINE/ (ENTERING)
BUOY III (33)	OR NO TAXES. LETS MAKE THE MOST OF HIM WHILE HE	LASTS	. /SECONDBORN/ I FIND IT HARD TO BELIEVE THAT HE WILL
MTH1 II (31)	AS NO COUPLE CAN EVER AGAIN FEEL WHILE THE WORLD	LASTS	. WHEN I CAN BEAR NO MORE, I GO TO OUR OLD GARDEN,
VWOO 1 (121)	IS IT WORTH IT? /Z/ IT IS WHILE THE NOVELTY	LASTS	. YOU SEE, WHEN YOURE AT HOME YOU GET TIRED OF DOING
POSN PREFACE(405)	A LICENCE TO PURSUE HIS TRADE; AND THIS LICENCE	LASTS	ONLY A YEAR, AND NEED NOT BE RENEWED IF HIS HOUSE HAS
2TRU PREFACE(14)	THE PERSONAL SLAVERY OF THE COMPULSION TO WORK	LASTS	ONLY AS MANY HOURS DAILY AS SUFFICE TO DISCHARGE THE
APPL I (208)	TO AN END AT ANY MOMENT. BUT WHILE THE MONARCHY	LASTS	-- WHILE IT LASTS, MARK YOU -- I AM VERY SECURE. I
FABL PREFACE(98)	FUTURE: HOMILIES NO USE. WHILE THE TIME LAG	LASTS	THE FUTURE REMAINS THREATENING. THE PROBLEM OF OPTIMUM
JOAN 4 (106)	WILL TO POWER IN THE WORLD. I KNOW THAT WHILE IT	LASTS	THERE WILL BE A STRUGGLE BETWEEN THE EMPEROR AND THE
KING I (206)	IT IS A VERY SATISFYING PLEASURE, AND ONE THAT	LASTS	TIL DEATH. /LOUISE/ IT DOES NOT SATISFY ME. /CHARLES/
BARB II (290)	IT'S VERY WEARING TO BE IN LOVE WITH YOU. IF IT	LASTS	, I QUITE THINK I SHALL DIE YOUNG. /BARBARA/ SHOULD
APPL I (208)	MOMENT. BUT WHILE THE MONARCHY LASTS -- WHILE IT	LASTS	, MARK YOU -- I AM VERY SECURE. I ESCAPE THE DREADFUL

BARB III	(348)	STONES OF THE STREETS THEY PAVE. AS LONG AS THAT	LASTS	, THERE IS NO GETTING AWAY FROM THEM. TURNING OUR

LATCH

DEVL II	(33)	OVERCOAT OR CLOAK). YOU MIGHT HAVE RAISED THE	LATCH	AND COME IN, MR DUDGEON. NOBODY STANDS ON MUCH
DEVL II	SD(39)	CUP PROSAICALLY, AND IS DRINKING HIS TEA WHEN THE	LATCH	GOES UP WITH A SHARP CLICK, AND AN ENGLISH SERGEANT
DEVL II	SD(35)	MR DUDGEON KNOWS HOW TO TURN A COMPLIMENT. THE	LATCH	IS LIFTED FROM WITHOUT. /JUDITH/ (STARTING) WHO IS
DEVL I	SD(4)	WHICH DISTURBS MRS DUDGEON A LITTLE. FINALLY THE	LATCH	IS TRIED, WHEREUPON SHE SPRINGS UP AT ONCE. /MRS
DEVL II	SD(28)	IT IS MADE OF PLAIN BOARDS, AND FASTENS WITH A	LATCH	. THE TABLE IS A KITCHEN TABLE, WITH A TREACLE COLORED
MRS III	SD(233)	I FEEL AMONG THE DAMNED ALREADY. SHE RAISES THE	LATCH	OF THE GATE TO OPEN IT AND GO OUT. HE FOLLOWS HER AND
DEVL I	SD(4)	AND WASHHOUSE, AND THE HOUSE-DOOR, WITH ITS	LATCH	, HEAVY LOCK, AND CLUMSY WOODEN BAR, IN THE FRONT

LATCHET

KING I	(189)	HEAP INSULTS ON THE IMMORTAL GALILEO, WHOSE SHOE	LATCHET	HE IS UNWORTHY TO UNLOOSE. HE RISES AND CONFRONTS
METH PREFACE	(R81)	AND " MARVELLOUS FORESHORTENING" THAN GIOTTO, THE	LATCHET	OF WHOSE SHOE THEY WERE NEVERTHELESS NOT WORTHY TO
DEVL I	(10)	THOUGH YOU ARE NOT WORTHY TO LOOSE HIS SHOE	LATCHET	, TOLD IT YOU WHEN HE GAVE OVER OUR SOULS INTO YOUR

LATCHKEY

BARB III	(318)	YOUR INDEPENDENCE IS ACHIEVED: YOU HAVE WON YOUR	LATCHKEY	. DONT RUB IT IN; AND ABOVE ALL, DONT APOLOGIZE. (
CAND III	(129)	SO TAKEN UP WITH EUGENE THAT I DIDNT HEAR YOUR	LATCHKEY	. HOW DID THE MEETING GO OFF? DID YOU SPEAK WELL?
POSN PREFACE	(427)	FATHER RISKS HIS SON'S MORALS WHEN HE GIVES HIM A	LATCHKEY	. THE MEMBERS OF THE JOINT SELECT COMMITTEE RISKED

LATCH-KEY

JITT I	(11)	BUT STOPS ON HEARING THE OUTER DOOR OPENED BY A	LATCH-KEY	FROM WITHOUT). OH, HERE IS THE GENTLEMAN. THE

LATE

HART II	(106)	NO, HECTOR: YOULL BE SHOT (BUT IT IS TOO	LATE	: HE HAS DASHED OUT PAST MANGAN, WHO HASTILY MOVES
CAPT II	(263)	AND FIFTY MEN! (TO LADY CICELY) YOU WERE TOO	LATE	: I GAVE YOU UP MY VENGEANCE WHEN IT WAS NO LONGER IN
GETT	(327)	AND IS CONFRONTED BY MRS GEORGE ENTERING). TOO	LATE	: I'M LOST. (HE TURNS BACK AND THROWS HIMSELF
GETT	SD(275)	(ALL THREE CLAMORING TOGETHER). IT IS TOO	LATE	: LEO IS ALREADY IN THE KITCHEN. COLLINS GOES OUT,
POSN PREFACE	(429)	WAS OUT OF THE QUESTION. BUT IT WAS TOO	LATE	: THE VOLTE FACE WAS TOO SUDDEN AND COMPLETE. IT WAS
GETT	(327)	IRRESOLUTELY AT HOTCHKISS)--? /HOTCHKISS/ TOO	LATE	: YOU CANT SAVE ME NOW, CECIL. GO. SYKES GOES INTO THE
SIM PRO,1,	(22)	AS WELL AS YOU DID YESTERDAY. DID YOU STAY UP TOO	LATE	? /THE E.O./ (NONPLUSSED FOR THE MOMENT) I-- ER-- (
GENV IV	(89)	NOTHING DOING, I SUPPOSE. /THE WIDOW/ IS HE NOT	LATE	? WE SEEM TO HAVE BEEN WAITING HERE FOR AGES. /THE
CAPT I	SD(217)	MOROCCO, THE MISSIONARY, IN THE COOLNESS OF THE	LATE	AFTERNOON, IS FOLLOWING THE PRECEPT OF VOLTAIRE BY
CAND I	(81)	THE CHURCH REFORMER, AND REMARKS) WELL, LEXY?	LATE	AGAIN, AS USUAL! /LEXY/ I'M AFRAID SO. I WISH I COULD
MIS.	(140)	EXCEPT THE INEVITABLE FEELING OF EARLY YOUTH FOR	LATE	AGE, OR IMAGINE THAT I HAVE ANY FEELING FOR YOU EXCEPT
APPL PREFACE	(191)	TO ME BY THE FATE OF THAT REMARKABLE GENIUS, THE	LATE	ALFRED WARWICK GATTIE, WITH WHOM I WAS PERSONALLY
JITT II	(31)	I MUST. I HAVE TO BE AT THE HOSPITAL; AND I AM	LATE	ALREADY. /JITTA/ COME AGAIN SOON, DOCTOR. /FESSLER/ I
MIS. PREFACE	(38)	IT CAN BEGIN EARLY AND LEAVE OFF EARLY OR BEGIN	LATE	AND LEAVE OFF LATE, OR, AS WITH US, BEGIN TOO EARLY AND
GETT PREFACE	(242)	THE HEARTH. THERE ARE MEN LIKE GOETHE, WHO MARRY	LATE	AND RELUCTANTLY SOLELY BECAUSE THEY FEEL THAT THEY
CAPT NOTES	(305)	FROM AN ESSEX ONE. SOME TIME IN THE EIGHTIES THE	LATE	ANDREW TUER CALLED ATTENTION IN THE PALL MALL GAZETTE
KING I	(169)	DATES GIVE ME SOME TROUBLE. /CHARLES/ DID NOT THE	LATE	ARCHBISHOP USSHER FIX THE DATES OF EVERYTHING THAT EVER
LIED PREFACE	(185)	A PIECE D'OCCASION. IN 1905 IT HAPPENED THAT THE	LATE	ARNOLD DALY, WHO WAS THEN PLAYING THE PART OF NAPOLEON
MTH3	(110)	AGE BEING THEN FIFTY-FIVE. /BURGE-LUBIN/ AS	LATE	AS FIFTY-FIVE! HOW DID PEOPLE STAND IT? /THE
JOAN PREFACE	(54)	SUPPER THEY REALLY CRAVE FOR, AFTER ARRIVING AS	LATE	AS (OR LATER THAN) THE HOUR OF BEGINNING CAN POSSIBLY
MIS. PREFACE	(55)	OF PALACES AND THE COURTS OF CASTLES WAS AS	LATE	AS THE EIGHTEENTH CENTURY. THIS FOULNESS, WE CAN PLEAD,
APPL I	(213)	WHERE'S MANDY? /NICOBAR/ AND LIZZIE? /PROTEUS/	LATE	AS USUAL. COME! BUSINESS, BUSINESS, BUSINESS.
ARMS III	(62)	THE PRIVILEGE OF BEING RECEIVED IN HER OWN ROOM,	LATE	AT NIGHT-- /BLUNTSCHLI/ (INTERRUPTING HIM PEPPERILY)
FANY II	(287)	A GIRL OUT OF THE SHOP FOR BEING HALF AN HOUR	LATE	AT NIGHT; AND HERES MY OWN DAUGHTER GONE FOR A
3PLA PREFACE	(R34)	BEEN THE MOST FANATICAL OF HIS WORSHIPPERS. THE	LATE	AUGUSTIN DALY THOUGHT NO PRICE TOO EXTRAVAGANT FOR AN
BARB PREFACE	(211)	TO ME BEFORE I EVER HEARD OF NIETZSCHE. THE	LATE	CAPTAIN WILSON, AUTHOR OF SEVERAL QUEER PAMPHLETS,
CYMB FORWORD	(135)	HUSBAND OF THE HEROINE, LEONATUS POSTHUMUS. THE	LATE	CHARLES CHARRINGTON, WHO WITH HIS WIFE JANET ACHURCH
WIDO I	(9)	(READING) " -- ERECTED IN 1839 BY ZWIRNER, THE	LATE	EMINENT ARCHITECT OF THE CATHEDRAL OF COLOGNE, AT THE
LADY PREFACE	(229)	AS AN ENEMY OF DEMOCRACY BY TOLSTOY, THE	LATE	ERNEST CROSBIE AND OTHERS, AND ENDORSED BY MR HARRIS.
LION PREFACE	(100)	WARS OF THE LAST FIFTEEN HUNDRED YEARS. WHEN THE	LATE	EXPLORER SIR HENRY STANLEY TOLD ME OF THE EMOTIONAL
FABL PREFACE	(96)	LAND MUNICIPALIZATION AS ROBBERY. HAD THE	LATE	FAMOUS PRESIDENT FRANKLIN ROOSEVELT, A THOROUGHLY
SUPR I	SD(16)	OF BLACK AND VIOLET SILK WHICH DOES HONOR TO HER	LATE	FATHER AND REVEALS THE FAMILY TRADITION OF BRAVE
APPL PREFACE	(187)	A VICTIM OF OPPRESSION BY THE SQUIRE BECAUSE HIS	LATE	FATHER WAS ONE OF OUR MOST SUCCESSFUL POACHERS. WE
DEVL I	(20)	LADIES AND GENTLEMEN: AS THE ELDEST SON OF MY	LATE	FATHER, AND THE UNWORTHY HEAD OF THIS HOUSEHOLD, I BID
GETT	(267)	MORNING? /MRS BRIDGENORTH/ YES, YOU WERE JUST	LATE	FOR A PARTICULARLY THRILLING INVENTION OF HIS. /LESBIA/
CAND I	(92)	OH BOTHER YOUR UNDERSTANDING! YOUVE KEPT ME	LATE	FOR CANDIDA. (WITH COMPASSIONATE FERVOR) MY POOR LOVE:
APPL II	(277)	ARM) NOW, NOW, NOW! DONT BE NAUGHTY. I MUSTNT BE	LATE	FOR DINNER. COME ON, LIKE A GOOD LITTLE BOY. THE KING,
KING I	(221)	YOUR DINNER WILL BE COLD; AND YOU WILL BE	LATE	FOR GRACE. I CANNOT HAVE ANY MORE OF THIS UNGODLY TALK.
SUPR IV	(169)	ALMOST EXHAUSTED) YES. BEFORE IT IS TOO	LATE	FOR REPENTANCE. YES. /TANNER/ (STRUCK BY THE ECHO FROM
DOCT V	(174)	ARE FULL OF IT. OUT WITH IT. /JENNIFER/ IT IS TOO	LATE	FOR REPROACHES NOW. WHEN I TURNED AND SAW YOU JUST NOW,
MIS. PREFACE	(63)	INSTITUTION OF THE COMING OF AGE, WHICH IS TOO	LATE	FOR SOME PURPOSES, AND TOO EARLY FOR OTHERS. THERE
BULL II	(108)	(WITH A SLIGHT START) OH, I'M AFRAID IT'S TOO	LATE	FOR TEA (HE LOOKS AT HIS WATCH). /AUNT JUDY/ NOT A
BULL II	(101)	FOR SHAME. OFF WIDJA TO THE ROAD: YOULL BE	LATE	FOR THE CAR IF YOU DONT MAKE HASTE (BUSTLING HIM DOWN
JOAN 6	(148)	IS THE IGNORANT WHO SUFFER. COME, OR WE SHALL BE	LATE	FOR THE END. /CAUCHON/ (GOING WITH HIM) I SHALL NOT BE
JOAN 2	(79)	ARTFUL FOX IN TOURAINE. COME ON, OR WE SHALL BE	LATE	FOR THE FUN; AND I WANT TO SEE IT, MIRACLE OR NO
2TRU III	(110)	AND AGE LIKE A MAN WHO HAS MISSED HIS TRAIN: TOO	LATE	FOR THE LAST AND TOO EARLY FOR THE NEXT. WHAT AM I TO
CATH 1	(171)	TO-- /PATIOMKIN/ IN HALF AN HOUR IT WILL BE TOO	LATE	FOR THE PETIT LEVER. COME ALONG. DAMN IT, MAN, I MUST
MRS IV	(248)	A MERE DRUDGE, TOILING AND MOILING EARLY AND	LATE	FOR YOUR BARE LIVING AND TWO CHEAP DRESSES A YEAR.
ARMS III	(68)	STARVING: SHALL I EVER FORGET THEIR FLAVOUR! MY	LATE	FRIEND STOLZ TOLD YOU THE STORY AT PIROT. I WAS THE
JOAN PREFACE	(55)	THAT WILL TAKE THEM HOME. FAR FROM ARRIVING	LATE	FROM AN EIGHT OR HALF-PAST EIGHT O'CLOCK DINNER SO AS
BASH III	(127)	I DO PARDON ALL CONCERNED THIS AFTERNOON IN THE	LATE	GROSS AND BRUTAL EXHIBITION OF MISCALLED SPORT. /LYDIA/
DOCT PREFACE	(64)	OF A WELL-INFORMED AND CLEVER WRITER LIKE THE	LATE	HAROLD FREDERIC IN THE HANDS OF CHRISTIAN SCIENTISTS (
2TRU PREFACE	(24)	PRESENT LIBERTY TO RETURN SUCH CANDIDATES AS THE	LATE	HORATIO BOTTOMLEY TO PARLIAMENT BY ENORMOUS MAJORITIES;
ROCK I	(229)	OVERBURDENED, OVERDRIVEN MAN, SUFFERING FROM	LATE	HOURS, IRREGULAR SNATCHED MEALS, NO TIME FOR DIGESTION
GETT PREFACE	(190)	VICE. A FORGOTTEN CONFERENCE OF MARRIED MEN. THE	LATE	HUGH PRICE HUGHES, AN EMINENT METHODIST DIVINE, ONCE
GENV I	(38)	SIMPLY ONE CHARGE OF THE WILFUL MURDER OF MY	LATE	HUSBAND BY THE PRESIDENT OF THE EARTHLY PARADISE. /SHE/
GENV I	(39)	OF THE LEAGUE OF NATIONS, WERE INTRODUCED BY MY	LATE	HUSBAND THE SIXTH PRESIDENT. HE OBSERVED THE
DOCT V	(172)	IN. AN ADVANCE COPY OF MRS DUBEDAT'S LIFE OF HER	LATE	HUSBAND. /RIDGEON/ (READING THE TITLE) THE STORY OF A
JITT III	SD(52)	THREE VERY BUSY GOING THROUGH THE PAPERS OF HER	LATE	HUSBAND. SHE IS FEVERISHLY READING LETTERS, AND TEARING
OVER	(174)	ILL. /GREGORY/ NO. IT WAS SOMETHING ABOUT YOUR	LATE	HUSBAND-- /MRS JUNO/ MY LATE HUSBAND! WHAT DO YOU
OVER	(174)	SOMETHING ABOUT YOUR LATE HUSBAND-- /MRS JUNO/ MY	LATE	HUSBAND! WHAT DO YOU MEAN? (CLUTCHING HIM.
BULL PREFACE	(63)	PRESENCE OF THE VICTIMS' FAMILIES UNDER THE	LATE	IMPERIALIST GOVERNMENT), NOT ONLY PERMITTED AND
ARMS I	SD(3)	BULGARIA, IN A SMALL TOWN NEAR THE DRAGOMAN PASS,	LATE	IN NOVEMBER IN THE YEAR 1885. THROUGH AN OPEN WINDOW
JOAN 2,	SD(71)	IN THE WALL TO THE RIGHT OF THE TWO MEN. IT IS	LATE	IN THE AFTERNOON ON THE 8TH OF MARCH, 1429. THE
KING II	SD(223)	IN HIS NOT TOO PALATIAL QUARTERS IN NEWMARKET	LATE	IN THE AFTERNOON ON THE SAME DAY. A PRIE-DIEU, AND THE
BULL III	(119)	MISS DOYLE. /AUNT JUDY/ (THINKING IT ABSURDLY	LATE	IN THE DAY FOR SUCH A SALUTATION) OH, GOOD MORNING. (
LION EPILOG	(149)	NUMBERS OF CLERGY HAVE FOUND THEMSELVES OF	LATE	IN THE POSITION OF FERROVIUS AND ANTHONY ANDERSON. THEY
ROCK I	(221)	THE MASKED DOOR. /SIR ARTHUR/ DO YOU KNOW HOW	LATE	IT IS? TO WORK! WORK! WORK! WORK! COME ALONG.
ROCK I	SD(221)	AT HIS WATCH, AND WHISTLES, STARTLED TO FIND HOW	LATE	IT IS. HILDA COMES IN QUICKLY THROUGH THE MASKED DOOR.
CAPT III	(282)	ERRAND. (KEARNEY GRUNTS). I THOAGHT I SHOULD BE	LATE	. BUT THE FIRST THING I HEARD WHEN I ARRIVED WAS YOUR
GENV PREFACE	(7)	VISION HAS NOT WIDENED NOR THAT ABILITY GROWN OF	LATE	. BUT THE PERILS OF THE SITUATION HAVE INCREASED
DEVL III	(53)	PRESENTLY. IT IS TOO LATE. /JUDITH/ IT IS NOT TOO	LATE	. CALL ME AS WITNESS: THEY WILL NEVER KILL YOU WHEN
CLEO IV	(177)	HAVE SPAT IT OUT SOONER, YOU FOOL. NOW IT IS TOO	LATE	. CLEOPATRA, IN GORGEOUS RAIMENT, ENTERS IN STATE
MILL III	SD(179)	OLD MAN MAKES A DASH TO PREVENT HER, BUT IS TOO	LATE	. HE SNATCHES THE CURTAIN FROM HER AND BARS HER
ARMS II	(30)	SEE THAT JUSTICE IS DONE YOU. /SERGIUS/ IT IS TOO	LATE	. I HAVE ONLY WAITED FOR THE PEACE TO SEND IN MY
FANY III	(317)	RINGING FOR HIM. /GILBEY/ (APPALLED) IT'S TOO	LATE	. I RANG BEFORE I THOUGHT OF IT. /MRS GILBEY/ STEP DOWN
PPP	(194)	HELP ALL POOR MARINERS AT SEA! MY MASTER IS	LATE	. I TRUST NOTHING HAS HAPPENED TO HIM. YOUR BED IS
CAPT III	(282)	IS HE? HE'D BETTER LOOK SHARP OR HE'LL BE	LATE	. (AGAIN EXPLODING) WHAT ARE THEY DOING WITH THOSE
POSN	(442)	SEE THINGS. /ELDER DANIELS/ TOO LATE, BLANCO: TOO	LATE	. (CONVULSIVELY) OH, WHY DIDNT YOU DRINK AS I USED
DEVL III	(53)	ME: THEY WILL BE HERE FOR ME PRESENTLY. IT IS TOO	LATE	. /JUDITH/ IT IS NOT TOO LATE. CALL ME AS WITNESS: THEY
DEVL III	(62)	GOT OUT OF THE TALKING STAGE; AND THEN IT WAS TOO	LATE	. /SWINDON/ (SEVERELY) WELL, SIR, WE SHALL TEACH YOU
APPL II	(265)	WHERE ARE THESE INFERNAL MINISTERS? THEYRE	LATE	. /THE QUEEN/ (LOOKING OUT INTO THE GARDEN) COMING

MTH2	(43)	NOW, AT ALL EVENTS. /FRANKLYN/ YES; BUT IT IS TOO	LATE	. SHE DOESNT TRUST ME NOW. SHE DOESNT TALK ABOUT THINGS
MRS IV	(246)	IS HEARD AT THE INNER DOOR). /FRANK/ SH! TOO	LATE	. SHE'S COMING. /MRS WARREN/ DONT TELL HER I WAS
BASH III	(124)	QUALITY, THIS COP I HAD AVERTED; BUT IT IS TOO	LATE	. THE LAW'S ABOVE US BOTH. ENTER LUCIAN, WITH AN ORDER
BASH II,1,	(99)	VISITS. /LUCIAN/ I HAVE BEEN GREATLY OCCUPIED OF	LATE	. THE MINISTER TO WHOM I ACT AS SCRIBE IN DOWNING
BARB II	(284)	LOOK IN HER EYES WITH IT. IT'S A PITY YOURE TOO	LATE	. THE NEW BLOKE HAS PUT YOUR NOSE OUT OF JOINT, BILL.
APPL I	(241)	TA TA! /PROTEUS/ COME ON, COME ON: IT'S EVER SO	LATE	. THEY ALL HURRY OUT, SEMPRONIUS AND PAMPHILIUS,
JOAN PREFACE	(56)	OF THE PLAY BY THEIR USUAL PRACTICE OF ARRIVING	LATE	. THEY CAN ESCAPE THE EPILOGUE BY NOT WAITING FOR IT.
GETT	(307)	BELIEVE ME. /HOTCHKISS/ YOUR WARNING COMES TOO	LATE	. THEYVE STARTED ARGUING ALREADY. /THE GENERAL/ BUT YOU
SUPR PREFACE	(R13)	REPENT AND REFORM NOW; FOR TOMORROW IT MAY BE TOO	LATE	. THIS IS REALLY THE ONLY POINT ON WHICH DON JUAN IS
GETT	(285)	OAK CHEST AND LOOKING AT HIS WATCH) IT'S GETTING	LATE	. WHERES EDITH? HASNT SHE GOT INTO HER VEIL AND ORANGE
MTH4 I	(170)	THE MISTAKES THAT LED TO THEM; AND THEN IT IS TOO	LATE	. YOU CANNOT UNDERSTAND OUR ADVICE: YOU OFTEN DO MORE
POSN	(462)	UP A COLLECTION FOR THE BEREAVED MOTHER OF THE	LATE	KID THAT SHEWED UP BLANCO POSNET. /THE BOYS/ A
DEVL I	(19)	BY THE WAY, DID I HEAR, OR DID I NOT, THAT OUR	LATE	LAMENTED UNCLE PETER, THOUGH UNMARRIED, WAS A FATHER..
BULL PREFACE	(48)	HOWEVER INEPT OR DISHONORABLE THEY MAY BE. AS THE	LATE	LAUREATE SAID IN THE TWO STINGING LINES IN WHICH HE
GETT	(290)	" MR ST JOHN HOTCHKISS, THE CELEBRATED COWARD,	LATE	LIEUTENANT IN THE 165TH FUSILIERS." /REGINALD/ (WITH A
PRES PREFACE	(130)	ARE. GENERAL MITCHENER, BY THE WAY, IS NOT THE	LATE	LORD KITCHENER, BUT AN EARLIER AND MORE HIGHLY
BARB I	(252)	THE PRESENT FASHION OF PHILANDERING BACHELORS AND	LATE	MARRIAGES; AND I AM TRYING TO ARRANGE SOMETHING FOR
PLES PREFACE	(R18)	BETWEEN US, ONE STRONGLY LIBERAL CRITIC, THE	LATE	MOY THOMAS, WHO HAD, IN THE TEETH OF A CHORUS OF
LION PREFACE	(56)	OF CANTERBURY, AND THE COMMON HANGMAN," OR " THE	LATE	MR BARNEY BARNATO RECEIVED AS HIS LAWFUL INCOME THREE
SUPR I SD	(17)	HER RECEPTION BY RAMSDEN, WHOM SHE KISSES. THE	LATE	MR WHITEFIELD WOULD BE GRATIFIED ALMOST TO IMPATIENCE
SIM PREFACE	(6)	AGAINST EVERLASTING BRIMSTONE VOICED BY THE	LATE	MRS BRADLAUGH BONNER, NOR OF TOLSTOY'S INSISTENCE ON
GETT	(324)	LEO) MRS REGINALD BRIDGENORTH. /REGINALD/ THE	LATE	MRS REGINALD BRIDGENORTH. /LEO/ HOLD YOUR TONGUE,
DOCT IV	(157)	OF NEGLECTED BLOOD-POISONING I EVER SAW. IT'S TOO	LATE	NOW TO DO ANYTHING. HE'D DIE UNDER THE ANAESTHETIC.
POSN	(447)	IT, DIDNT YOU? /FEEMY/ NO I DIDNT: I STAYED UP	LATE	ON A SPREE. /BLANCO/ I WAS ON A HORSE, WAS I? /FEEMY/
LION PREFACE	(36)	BAPTIST HIMSELF IS NOT CONVINCED; FOR AT QUITE A	LATE	PERIOD IN HIS FORMER DISCIPLE'S CAREER HE SENDS TWO
CYMB FORWORD	(134)	IS GENUINE SHAKESPEAR TO THE LAST FULL STOP, AND	LATE	PHASE SHAKESPEAR IN POINT OF VERBAL WORKMANSHIP. THE
LION PREFACE	(102)	CERTAINLY HAVE PROPHESIED THE DOWNFALL OF THE	LATE	PRESIDENT KRUGER IF HE HAD SURVIVED TO HIS TIME, BUT,
BULL II	(106)	(THEORIES ARE CONNECTED IN HIS MIND WITH THE	LATE	PROFESSOR TYNDALL, AND WITH SCIENTIFIC SCEPTICISM
MILL PREFACE	(134)	BUT THAT WILL NOT GIVE HIM THE INSIDE GRIP. A	LATE	RICH SHIPOWNER, ENGAGED IN A QUARREL WITH HIS WORKMEN
DEVL III	(74)	STOPPED IRRESOLUTELY ON FINDING THAT HE IS TOO	LATE	) HOW IS THIS? WHY IS SHE INSIDE THE LINES?
CAND I	(92)	AT HIS WATCH, AND IS HORRIFIED TO FIND IT SO	LATE	). MY DARLING! (HURRYING TO HER AND SEIZING THE RUG
PPP SD	(193)	WITH HER MAID COMBING HER HAIR. IT IS	LATE	; AND THE ELECTRIC LAMPS ARE GLOWING, APPARENTLY THE
BARB III	(342)	EVERYBODY NAMES. COME, EURIPIDES! IT IS GETTING	LATE	; AND WE ALL WANT TO GO HOME. MAKE UP YOUR MIND.
ROCK I	(194)	ASKING FOR ME, SIR ARTHUR, I'M SO SORRY TO BE	LATE	; BUT REALLY THE STREETS ARE BECOMING QUITE IMPASSABLE
GETT PREFACE	(198)	FALSE DOMESTIC DOCTRINES. WHY WAS IT THAT THE	LATE	SAMUEL BUTLER WITH A CONVICTION THAT INCREASED WITH HIS
BARB PREFACE	(220)	OR FROM ANY MAN BORN BEYOND THE CHANNEL. THE	LATE	SAMUEL BUTLER, IN HIS OWN DEPARTMENT THE GREATEST
LION PREFACE	(23)	PEOPLE WHO FEEL THAT WAY OF HYPOCRISY, LIKE THE	LATE	SAMUEL BUTLER, HE REGARDS DISEASE AS A DEPARTMENT OF
POSN PREFACE	(388)	THIS ASSUMPTION. IT WAS BROKEN DOWN BY THE	LATE	SIR HENRY IRVING WHEN HE FINALLY SHAMED THE GOVERNMENT
DOCT PREFACE	(10)	SOME DOCTOR IN AN UNASSAILABLE POSITION, LIKE THE	LATE	SIR WILLIAM GULL, WILL GO INTO THE WITNESS BOX AND SAY
MILL I	(137)	YOU JULIUS SAGAMORE, THE WORTHLESS NEPHEW OF MY	LATE	SOLICITOR PONTIFEX SAGAMORE? /SAGAMORE/ I DO NOT
GETT SD	(274)	REBELLIOUS, HASTY, UNTIDY, FORGETFUL, ALWAYS	LATE	SORT OF MAN, WHO VERY EVIDENTLY NEEDS THE CARE OF A
2TRU III	(111)	WHICH WE HAVE GROWN WITH A RUSH LIKE FLOWERS IN A	LATE	SPRING FOLLOWING A TERRIBLE WINTER. AND WITH WHAT
JITT PREFACE	(6)	BEAR AN UTTERLY UNHAPPY ONE. IT IS TRUE, AS THE	LATE	ST JOHN HANKIN POINTED OUT AND ILLUSTRATED BY HIS PLAYS
METH PREFACE	(R26)	OF PAINTING IN THEIR MOTHER'S WOMB AT QUITE A	LATE	STAGE OF THEIR EMBRYONIC LIFE. THEY MUST RECAPITULATE
BULL II SD	(111)	OPEN FOR HER, SO BROADBENT'S WHIM TO GO OUT FOR A	LATE	STROLL PROVOKES NEITHER HOSPITABLE REMONSTRANCE NOR
BULL PREFACE	(64)	OF THOSE PLUTOCRAT-RIDDEN POWERS WHICH HAVE OF	LATE	STUMBLED INTO AN ENORMOUS INCREASE OF MATERIAL WEALTH
FABL PREFACE	(95)	OR AT MOST SELFTAUGHT TO READ AND WRITE IN THEIR	LATE	TEENS, RISE TO EMINENCE WHILST " UNIVERSITY ENGINEERS"
MTH3	(131)	AT FIFTY, SIXTY, SEVENTY. YOUR MATURITY IS SO	LATE	THAT YOU NEVER ATTAIN TO IT. YOU HAVE TO BE GOVERNED BY
2TRU III	(111)	I MUST PREACH AND PREACH AND PREACH NO MATTER HOW	LATE	THE HOUR AND HOW SHORT THE DAY, NO MATTER WHETHER I
JITT III	(62)	FOR HIS PROPER HAPPINESS, AND THEN FINDING TOO	LATE	THE WOMAN WHO WAS HIS REAL DESTINY. /FESSLER/ AH YES:
APPL INTRLUD	(254)	YOU HAVE NOT. YOU ARE ONLY TRYING TO MAKE ME	LATE	TO ANNOY MY WIFE. (HE TRIES TO RISE, BUT IS PULLED
BULL PREFACE	(59)	HE KEPT HIS VIEWS TO HIMSELF UNTIL IT WAS TOO	LATE	TO DO ANYTHING WORSE TO HIM THAN HANG HIM. IN COURT, HE
MILL PREFACE	(115)	DID NOT KNOW WHEN HE WAS BEATEN UNTIL IT WAS TOO	LATE	TO DO ANYTHING BUT RUN AWAY. INSTEAD OF MAKING FOR
PHIL II	(107)	THEM AS WELL AS VACCINATED. BUT IT WAS TOO	LATE	TO INOCULATE POOR PAPA. ALL THEY COULD DO WAS TO
HART II	(97)	HUSHABYE/ (MOVING TOWARDS THE SOFA) IT'S TOO	LATE	TO TELEGRAPH TONIGHT. /MAZZINI/ I SUPPOSE SO. I DO HOPE
GENV IV	(95)	DRY IT UP, AND WHEN WE HAVE DONE THAT IT IS TOO	LATE	TO THINK ABOUT IT. WE HAVE FOUND THAT WE CAN GET ON
ROCK I	(200)	ABOUT THE UNEMPLOYED, THOUGH I WAS TWENTY MINUTES	LATE	TRYING TO SHOVE MY WAY THROUGH THEM. REALLY, SIR
POSN PREFACE	(395)	BE. A BRILLIANT INSTANCE IS THE DIVORCONS OF THE	LATE	VICTORIEN SARDOU, WHICH MAY NOT HAVE BEEN THE
METH PREFACE	(R19)	SPAN IS THAT TREMENDOUS CATASTROPHES SUCH AS THE	LATE	WAR SHALL CONVINCE HIM OF THE NECESSITY OF AT LEAST
JOAN PREFACE	(12)	NEWTON. WE CAN ALL SEE NOW, ESPECIALLY SINCE THE	LATE	WAR THREW SO MANY OF OUR WOMEN INTO MILITARY LIFE, THAT
BUOY III	(37)	DIVORCE. /THE WIDOWER/ BESIDES, TAKE MY CASE. MY	LATE	WIFE AND I WERE SO INDISPENSABLE TO ONEANOTHER THAT A
CYMB FORWORD	(133)	FOLLOWING UP SOME DESPERATE EXPERIMENTS BY THE	LATE	WILLIAM POEL, INTRODUCED THE STARTLING INNOVATION OF
POSN PREFACE	(385)	RESULT WAS ONCE FAMILIAR TO ENGLISHMEN, THOUGH OF	LATE	YEARS IT SEEMS TO HAVE BEEN FORGOTTEN. IT COST ENGLAND
POSN PREFACE	(392)	REGARDED AS A SHAMELESS ONE; AND IT IS ONLY OF	LATE	YEARS THAT ACTRESSES HAVE AT LAST SUCCEEDED IN LIVING
POSN PREFACE	(427)	ASSASSINATIONS HAVE BEEN APPALLINGLY FREQUENT OF	LATE	YEARS. RAILWAY TRAVELLING HAS ITS RISKS; MOTORING HAS
LION PREFACE	(66)	OR A LUNATIC IS NOW TREATED (IT IS ONLY OF	LATE	YEARS, BY THE WAY, THAT MADMEN HAVE BEEN DELIVERED FROM
BASH II,1,	(99)	WELCOME, DEAR COUSIN, TO MY LONDON HOUSE. OF	LATE	YOU HAVE BEEN CHARY OF YOUR VISITS. /LUCIAN/ I HAVE
DEVL II	(30)	NOW! (SHE FLIES INTO HIS ARMS). I AM NOT	LATE	, AM I? THE TOWN CLOCK STRUCK THE QUARTER AS I CAME IN
CAPT II	(263)	AND YOU. BUT I FEAR MY REPENTANCE HAS COME TOO	LATE	, AS REPENTANCE USUALLY DOES. /LADY CICELY/ (
LADY	(249)	IN THE WORLD, WHICH IS BUT A LARGER STAGE. OF	LATE	, AS YOU KNOW, THE CHURCH TAUGHT THE PEOPLE BY MEANS OF
POSN	(442)	OF THAT LATELY. I SEE THINGS. /ELDER DANIELS/ TOO	LATE	, BLANCO: TOO LATE. (CONVULSIVELY) OH, WHY DIDNT YOU
MILL I	(155)	KEPT MY WORD AND MARRIED HIM INSTANTLY. THEN, TOO	LATE	, I FOUND OUT HOW HE HAD MADE IT. /ALASTAIR/ WELL, HOW
ROCK II	(268)	YOU DOING HERE? /SIR ARTHUR/ I AM AFRAID YOU ARE	LATE	, MR HIPNEY. THE DEPUTATION HAS BEEN HERE. THEY HAVE
NEVR III	(264)	HE IS. /VALENTINE/ (ENTERING) VERY SORRY TO BE	LATE	, MRS CLANDON. (SHE TAKES UP THE TEA-POT). NO, THANK
DEST	(158)	HORSE IN THE CAMP. YOU ARRIVE A HUNDRED MINUTES	LATE	, ON FOOT. WHERE IS YOUR HORSE? /THE LIEUTANANT/ (
MIS. PREFACE	(38)	AND LEAVE OFF EARLY OR BEGIN LATE AND LEAVE OFF	LATE	, OR, AS WITH US, BEGIN TOO EARLY AND NEVER LEAVE OFF
BULL IV	(170)	IVE COME BACK TO SAY IT. /NORA/ YOUVE COME TOO	LATE	, THEN. YOU THOUGHT EIGHTEEN YEARS WAS NOT LONG ENOUGH,
ARMS III	(49)	TO DRINK OR TELL STORIES-- IF THEYRE FIVE MINUTES	LATE	, THEYLL HAVE THE SKIN TAKEN OFF THEIR BACKS. /SERGIUS/
MILL I	(165)	MADE THAT MISTAKE, AND THAT LATER ON (TOO	LATE	, UNFORTUNATELY) HE DISCOVERED IN YOU A-- SHALL I SAY A
			LATELY	
SUPR III	(105)	HIS? HAVE YOU WALKED UP AND DOWN UPON THE EARTH	LATELY	? I HAVE; AND I HAVE EXAMINED MAN'S WONDERFUL
DOCT I	(94)	SIR PATRICK: HOW ARE YOU? I SENT YOU A PAPER	LATELY	ABOUT A LITTLE THING I INVENTED: A NEW SAW. FOR
METH PREFACE	(R20)	OF ATTRACTION AND REPULSION, OR LOVE AND HATE. AS	LATELY	AS 1860 I MYSELF WAS TAUGHT AS A CHILD THAT
ROCK PREFACE	(172)	OUT FOR THEM. IT WAS VERY GENERALLY BELIEVED AS	LATELY	AS IN VICTORIAN TIMES THAT RELIGIOUS EDUCATION
GENV III	(83)	LIFE. /THE JUDGE/ YES; BUT DO NOT FORGET THAT AS	LATELY	AS THE NINETEENTH CENTURY THE WORLD BELIEVED THAT THE
SIM PREFACE	(6)	TO A CONSIDERABLE EXTENT STILL. A FRIEND OF MINE	LATELY	ASKED A LEADING IRISH STATESMAN WHY HE DID NOT RESORT
DOCT PREFACE	(61)	VERY DESIRABLE PATIENTS IN COUNTRY HOUSES HAVE	LATELY	BEEN PERSUADED THAT THEIR FIRST DUTY IS TO GET UP AT
GETT	(329)	WOULD JUST LOVE TO HEAR YOU TALK. HE'S BEEN DULL	LATELY	FOR WANT OF A CHANGE OF COMPANY AND A BIT OF FRESH
ROCK PREFACE	(156)	BLOW OF THE BAR, THE WHEEL AND THE STAVE HAVE	LATELY	GONE OUT OF USE; BUT THE SADIST MANIA FOR FLOGGING
SUPR III	(106)	PARLIAMENTARY COCK-FIGHTING. I SPENT AN EVENING	LATELY	IN A CERTAIN CELEBRATED LEGISLATURE, AND HEARD THE
PHIL III	(133)	BY THE FACES OF THE MEN WHETHER YOU HAVE BEEN	LATELY	IN THE ROOM OR NOT. /JULIA/ (SHRINKING FIERCELY) OH,
HART I	(58)	PASSION? /ELLIE/ OH, THAT WAS YEARS AFTER, QUITE	LATELY	. HE TOOK THE CHAIR ONE NIGHT AT A SORT OF PEOPLE'S
POSN	(442)	DRINK LIKE YOU, EH? WELL, IVE DONE SOME OF THAT	LATELY	. I SEE THINGS. /ELDER DANIELS/ TOO LATE, BLANCO: TOO
GENV II	(62)	I OUGHT TO? I HAVE BEEN A LOT IN THE PAPERS	LATELY	. IT'S SIX HUNDRED A YEAR FOR ME IF I GET IN. I SHALL
PHIL II	(130)	MRS TRANFIELD WILL TELL YOU WHAT A TIME IVE HAD	LATELY	. JULIA'S REALLY A MOST DETERMINED WOMAN, YOU KNOW.
BULL III SD	(117)	AS ANYWHERE ELSE, AN EMPTY CHAIR AT THE TABLE WAS	LATELY	OCCUPIED BY CORNELIUS, WHO HAS FINISHED HIS BREAKFAST
HART PREFACE	(38)	FAR LESS DISPOSED TO SUBMIT TO IT. REVOLUTION,	LATELY	ONLY A SENSATIONAL CHAPTER IN HISTORY OR A DEMAGOGIC
ROCK PREFACE	(173)	AND WRITE WHAT I PLEASE. I WENT ROUND THE WORLD	LATELY	PREACHING THAT IF RUSSIA WERE THRUST BACK FROM
SUPR PREFACE	(R31)	CALLED EVERYMAN, WHICH MR WILLIAM POEL HAS	LATELY	RESUSCITATED SO TRIUMPHANTLY. I TRUST HE WILL WORK
NEVR I	(211)	AND I HAVE BEEN TALKING OVER THINGS A GOOD DEAL	LATELY	; AND I DONT THINK, JUDGING FROM MY KNOWLEDGE OF
UNPL PREFACE	(R20)	AUTHOR DOES IT ESCAPE TRANSFIGURATION. WE HAVE	LATELY	SEEN SOME REMARKABLY SYMPATHETIC STAGE
2TRU PREFACE	(13)	THE VIGOROUS LIBERALISM OF HIS SALAD DAYS, HAS	LATELY	TAKEN ME TO TASK FOR THE ENTIRELY IMAGINARY OFFENCE
POSN PREFACE	(384)	CALLED A CHINESE CIVILIZATION UNTIL THE CHINESE	LATELY	TOOK TO IMMORAL COURSES BY PERMITTING RAILWAY
LION PREFACE	(9)	SINCE HIS CHILDHOOD. HIS REPLY WAS THAT HE HAD	LATELY	TRIED, BUT " FOUND IT ALL SUCH NONSENSE THAT I COULD
MILL IV	(189)	AND WHISTLE. /THE MANAGER/ IT WAS SO UNTIL QUITE	LATELY	, SIR. MY FATHER KEPT THE PIG AND WHISTLE. SO DID HIS

LATENT

PHIL III (139)	ON THESE OCCASIONS THAT I WAS BRINGING OUT YOUR	LATENT	AMIABILITY; BUT I THOUGHT YOU WERE BRINGING OUT MINE.
MIS. PREFACE(105)	ROUSING OF ALL THE MURDEROUS BLACKGUARDISM STILL	LATENT	IN MANKIND; THAT EVERY VICTORY MEANS A DEFEAT; THAT
2TRU PREFACE(18)	POLITICAL SCIENCE BLINDED THEM TO THE MISCHIEF	LATENT	IN THE SELFISHNESS OF PRIVATE PROPERTY IN THE

LATER

JOAN PREFACE(34)	HUNDRED YEARS AGO. MORE THAN THREE HUNDRED YEARS	LATER	: THAT IS, ONLY ABOUT A HUNDRED YEARS BEFORE I WAS
JOAN PREFACE(32)	TRIAL WHEN IT CANONIZED JOAN FIVE HUNDRED YEARS	LATER	? THE CHURCH UNCOMPROMISED BY ITS AMENDS, EASILY
DEST SD(158)	PICTURES OF DELAROCHE AND MEISSONIER, WHICH	LATER	AGES EXPECT FROM HIM. /NAPOLEON/ (WATCH IN HAND)
LION PREFACE(85)	PLEAD THAT THEY TOO WERE SANCTIFIED BY A RITE OF	LATER	AND HIGHER AUTHORITY THAN THE MOSAIC RITE. HE WAS
FABL VI (128)	MAY BE KILLED AS IDIOTS AND SAVAGES IF WE MEET A	LATER	AND HIGHER CIVILIZATION. /YOUTH 1/ I DONT BELIEVE IT.
HART III (144)	GROWS FROM A SICKLE TO AN ARC LAMP, AND COMES	LATER	AND LATER UNTIL SHE IS LOST IN THE LIGHT AS OTHER
MTH2 (75)	AS WE CALL IT, WAS NOT A PART OF LIFE, BUT A	LATER	AND QUITE SEPARATE INVENTION? /BURGE/ NOW YOU MENTION
MIS. SD(110)	17 TO 70 RETAIN UNALTERED THE MENTAL AIRS OF THE	LATER	AND THE PHYSICAL APPEARANCE OF THE EARLIER AGE,
FABL PREFACE(75)	OF NOAH AND HIS FAMILY BY A BRIBE OF ROAST MEAT.	LATER	ARTICLES INSTRUCT US TO LOVE OUR FELLOW-CREATURES, YET
3PLA PREFACE(R36)	LAID THEIR ARTS WASTE FOR CENTURIES BY LEADING	LATER	ARTISTS TO SEEK GREATNESS IN COPYING THEIR TECHNIQUE.
DOCT PREFACE(56)	APPLIANCES WHICH ARE CONDEMNED A FEW YEARS	LATER	AS DANGEROUS TO HEALTH, AND FORBIDDEN UNDER PENALTIES.
BULL PREFACE(12)	IRELAND REFUSED HOME RULE NOW, IT WOULD SOONER OR	LATER	BE FORCED ON HER BY ENGLAND BECAUSE ENGLAND WILL NEED
SUPR HANDBOK(181)	THAT THE EXPERIMENT OF MATING THEM WILL SOONER OR	LATER	BE TRIED PURPOSELY ALMOST AS OFTEN AS IT IS NOW TRIED
MIS. PREFACE(61)	LEAVE YOU TO ATTEND TO YOURSELF, YOU SOONER OR	LATER	BEGIN TO TALK TO HIM ABOUT THE NEED FOR SELF-RELIANCE,
GETT PREFACE(250)	SEX SLAVERY, EARLY CHRISTIAN SEX ABHORRENCE, AND	LATER	CHRISTIAN SEX SANCTIFICATION. OTHELLO AND DESDEMONA,
MTH4 I (162)	I THROW MY STONE ON THE CAIRN AND DIE; BUT	LATER	COMERS ADD ANOTHER STONE AND YET ANOTHER; AND LO! A
FABL PREFACE(70)	NECESSARY; BUT IT WAS A FORGERY ALL THE SAME. A	LATER	DIFFICULTY WAS MORE EASILY GOT OVER. THE APOSTLES WERE
MTH5 (227)	WE CAN REGARD AS REALLY SCIENTIFIC. THERE ARE	LATER	DOCUMENTS WHICH SPECIFY THE MINERALS WITH GREAT
ROCK PREFACE(154)	PROUDHON AND MARX, PRIVATE PROPERTY IS SOONER OR	LATER	EXCOMMUNICATED AND ABOLISHED; AND WHAT WAS FORMERLY
CATH 1,SD(162)	VISITOR WILL FIND OUT, AS EVERYONE ELSE SOONER OR	LATER	FINDS OUT, THAT HE IS A MAN TO BE RECKONED WITH EVEN
PYGM PREFACE(202)	CANNOT EXPECT THEM TO HEAP HONORS ON HIM. OF THE	LATER	GENERATIONS OF PHONETICIANS I KNOW LITTLE. AMONG THEM
DEST SD(150)	HAS BEEN ENACTED, THAT THEY, IMPRESSED WITH THE	LATER	GLORY OF " L'EMPEREUR," HAVE ALTOGETHER REFUSED TO
LION PREFACE(30)	HIM SIMPLY AS " A NOTABLE PRISONER." THE	LATER	GOSPELS MAKE IT CLEAR, VERY SIGNIFICANTLY, THAT HIS
METH PREFACE(R24)	WOULD HE DO THAT IF HE COULD HELP IT? TAKE THAT	LATER	HABIT OF DECAYING AND ELIMINATING HIMSELF BY DEATH--
BARB III (346)	BURDEN OF THE CHOICE ON YOU, YOU WOULD SOONER OR	LATER	HAVE DESPISED ME FOR IT. /BARBARA/ YES: I DID NOT WANT
JOAN 2,SD(72)	FACT WHEN HE DEFIES THE CHURCH SOME ELEVEN YEARS	LATER	HE IS ACCUSED OF TRYING TO EXTRACT PLEASURE FROM
MTH1 I (4)	EVER. THINK OF WHAT FOR EVER MEANS! SOONER OR	LATER	I SHALL TRIP AND FALL. IT MAY BE TOMORROW; IT MAY BE
FABL PREFACE(71)	THE BLOOD OF SAINT JANUARIUS. SOME TWENTY YEARS	LATER	I WROTE A PLAY CALLED SAINT JOAN IN WHICH I MADE AN
MTH5 (218)	DO. EVERYTHING HAPPENS TO EVERYBODY SOONER OR	LATER	IF THERE IS TIME ENOUGH. AND WITH US THERE IS
MILL IV (191)	WE SHOULD HAVE HAD THE BROKERS IN SOONER OR	LATER	IF WE HAD GONE ON. BUSINESS IS BUSINESS; AND THERES NO
CAPT NOTES (300)	FROM THE DECK OF AN ORIENT STEAMER, BOTH	LATER	IN DATE THAN THE WRITING OF THE PLAY. CUNNINGHAME
APPL II SD(257)	ACT II.	LATER	IN THE AFTERNOON. THE TERRACE OF THE PALACE. A LOW
CAND II SD(105)	ACT II. THE SAME DAY	LATER	IN THE AFTERNOON. THE SAME ROOM. THE CHAIR FOR
BULL IV SD(168)	AS AN EQUINOCTIAL GALE MIGHT SWEEP A DRY LEAF).	LATER	IN THE EVENING, THE GRASSHOPPER IS AGAIN ENJOYING THE
LION PREFACE(18)	NOW HELD THAT THE STORY OF THE HOLY GHOST IS A	LATER	INTERPOLATION BORROWED FROM THE GREEK AND ROMAN
HART PREFACE(4)	LOOK LIKE VARIETY THEATRE STARS, AND SETTLED DOWN	LATER	INTO THE TYPES OF BEAUTY IMAGINED BY THE PREVIOUS
MILL I (153)	/SAGAMORE/ IS IT OF SUCH A NATURE THAT SOONER OR	LATER	IT WILL HAVE TO BE DISCUSSED WITH ALL THE ADULT
SIM II (77)	THE BRITISH NAVY WOULD NOT TAKE IT LYING DOWN.	LATER	. A HYDE PARK ORATOR WAS THROWN INTO THE SERPENTINE
BULL PREFACE(46)	ON THE SPOT, BUT FROM LORD ROBERTS FIFTY YEARS	LATER	. BESIDES THE MUTINY WE HAVE HAD THE CRIMEAN AND SOUTH
JOAN PREFACE(31)	INQUIRY WHICH REHABILITATED HER TWENTYFIVE YEARS	LATER	. BUT THIS REHABILITATION WAS AS CORRUPT AS THE
SIM II (75)	ANOTHER PAPER) HALLO! WHATS THIS? (READING) "	LATER	. DURING THE SINGING OF THE SECOND VERSE OF THE
NEVR III (273)	TO GLORIA) LOOK HERE. YOULL FORGIVE ME, SOONER OR	LATER	. FORGIVE ME NOW. /GLORIA/ (RISING TO LEVEL THE
ROCK PREFACE(185)	OF WORDS; AND THEY ARE ALL MADE FLESH SOONER OR	LATER	. GO AMONG MY SOLDIERS AND YOU WILL HEAR MANY FILTHY
SIM II (70)	. . . I'LL ASK THE ANGEL ABOUT IT AND RING YOU	LATER	. GOODBYE. (HE RINGS OFF). LOOK HERE, ANGEL. THE
MILL I (160)	INTO GOLD. I HAD TO LIQUIDATE THAT CIRCUS A MONTH	LATER	. HE WAS ABOUT TO TURN THE WILD BEASTS LOOSE AND RUN
GENV IV (126)	ARE UP; BUT SO THEY WERE BEFORE, SOONER OR	LATER	. I DONT COMPLAIN: I HAVNT HAD SUCH A BAD TIME OF IT;
BARB II (293)	THAT I MUST HAVE ANYTHING, I GET IT, SOONER OR	LATER	. I FEEL THAT WAY ABOUT BARBARA. I DONT LIKE MARRIAGE:
DOCT III (142)	WHO DIDNT THREATEN TO PUT ME IN PRISON SOONER OR	LATER	. I NEVER KNEW A PARSON WHO DIDNT THREATEN ME WITH
BULL PREFACE(65)	AND THE REST FROM PENAL SERVITUDE. A YEAR	LATER	. IT MAY BE A RELIEF TO SOME OF MY READERS TO LEARN
GETT (279)	STAY, REGINALD. YOU MUST MEET HIM SOONER OR	LATER	. (ALL FOUR RUSHING AFTER HIM AND CAPTURING HIM ON
FANY III (302)	TELL YOU: YOURE BOUND TO FIND OUT SOONER OR	LATER	. (HE BEGINS HIS CONFESSION HUMBLY, AVOIDING HER
SUPR IV (153)	TO CONCILIATE HIM) YES, YES. /HECTOR/ SEE YOU ALL	LATER	. (HE WAVES HIS HAND TO ANN, WHO HAS NOW BEEN JOINED
CURE (228)	TO PLAY. I MUST BE OFF NOW. LOOK IN AGAIN	LATER	. MEANWHILE, SLEEP AS MUCH AS YOU CAN. OR YOU MIGHT
MTH1 II SD(20)	ACT II. A FEW CENTURIES	LATER	. MORNING. AN OASIS IN MESOPOTAMIA. CLOSE AT HAND THE
BUOY IV (50)	MUST SEE THEIR CHILDREN WALK OUT SOONER OR	LATER	. MOTHERS-IN-LAW ARE STOCK JOKES. NOBODY JOKES ABOUT
JITT II (36)	A THING THAT HAPPENS TO EVERYBODY SOONER OR	LATER	. /JITTA/ (TAKEN ABACK) EDITH, DEAR-- /EDITH/ (
PHIL II (117)	IT MUST BLUNT ALL THE FINER FEELINGS SOONER OR	LATER	. /PARAMORE/ (TURNING ON HIM) HOW MANY CAMELS AND
SUPR I (25)	/ANN/ STOP, JACK. GRANNY: HE MUST KNOW, SOONER OR	LATER	. /RAMSDEN/ OCTAVIUS: I HAVE A VERY SERIOUS PIECE OF
LIED (191)	THIS; AND I KNOW WHAT WE TWO MUST DO, SOONER OR	LATER	. /SHE/ NO, HENRY, I WILL DO NOTHING IMPROPER, NOTHING
SIM II SD(54)	ACT II. A FINE FORENOON SOME YEARS	LATER	. THE GARDEN IS UNCHANGED; BUT INSIDE THE DISTANT
BULL PREFACE(66)	CAN BE OF ANY PROFIT TO THEM. TWENTYFOUR YEARS	LATER	. THE SEQUEL TO THESE EVENTS CONFIRMED MY UNHEEDED
BARB II (306)	EVERYTHING TO THE WORK OF SALVATION SOONER OR	LATER	. WHO WOULD HAVE THOUGHT THAT ANY GOOD COULD HAVE COME
ROCK PREFACE(160)	MIGHT BE BETTER SPENT; AND, AFTER ALL, SOONER OR	LATER	LETS THE SCOUNDREL LOOSE AGAIN TO RECOMMENCE HIS
CLEO NOTES (210)	PRODIGIOUS OF CAESAR'S GIFTS, AS IT ASTONISHED	LATER	OBSERVERS IN NAPOLEON BEFORE IT WORE HIM OUT. HOW IF
JOAN 6 (147)	THE RIGHT. A FLAW IN THE PROCEDURE MAY BE USEFUL	LATER	ON: ONE NEVER KNOWS. AND THE SOONER IT IS OVER, THE
LADY PREFACE(233)	SHAKESPEARIAN STOCK-IN-TRADE OF OUR THEATRES.	LATER	ON BURBAGE'S POWER AND POPULARITY AS AN ACTOR ENABLED
METH PREFACE(R62)	A SOCIAL SYSTEM UTTERLY UNCONGENIAL TO HIM, AND	LATER	ON BY EXILE AND POVERTY. THUS MARX AND DARWIN BETWEEN
MTH2 (63)	FILLED BY MY PROFESSIONAL WORK AS A LAWYER, AND	LATER	ON BY MY DUTIES AS LEADER OF THE HOUSE OF COMMONS IN
LION PREFACE(25)	MIRACLES UPON HIS MISSION IS EXACTLY THAT TAKEN	LATER	ON BY ROUSSEAU. HE PERCEIVES THAT THEY WILL DISCREDIT
SIM PREFACE(10)	ORGANS WERE DEVELOPED BY THE PROTESTANT AND	LATER	ON BY THE SECULARIST GOVERNMENTS, YET THE HOLY OFFICE
SUPR III (110)	HE NOW CALLS GOD'S WORK TO DO, AND WHAT HE WILL	LATER	ON CALL BY MANY NEW NAMES, YOU CAN MAKE HIM ENTIRELY
3PLA PREFACE(R13)	HAVE BEEN SHAKESPEAR'S FAULT: INDEED SIR HENRY	LATER	ON COMPLAINED THAT HE HAD LOST A PRINCELY SUM BY
MTH4 II (184)	SNUGLY IN THE CAVES THEY HAD DUG FOR THEMSELVES.	LATER	ON EVEN THE HOUSES ESCAPED; BUT THEIR INHABITANTS WERE
BARB PREFACE(211)	MORAL PEOPLE; BUT AT ALL EVENTS THEY WERE SAVED	LATER	ON FROM THE DELUSION THAT NOBODY BUT NIETZSCHE HAD
ROCK PREFACE(152)	RETAINING ONLY A FEW TO ACT AS SHEPHERDS.	LATER	ON I FIND THAT IT IS MORE PROFITABLE TO COVER MY LAND
GENV PREFACE(3)	BEFORE IT EXPLODED, RETURNING TO LONDON	LATER	ON I FOUND THAT HALF THE ANCIENT CITY HAD BEEN
SIM PREFACE(13)	HIS SPORTING DOGS WHEN THEY WERE PAST THEIR WORK.	LATER	ON I HEARD OF AFRICAN TRIBES DOING THE SAME WITH THEIR
2TRU III (92)	VILLAGE, I CRIED ALL NIGHT AFTER DOING THAT.	LATER	ON I SWOOPED INTO A STREET AND SENT MACHINE GUN
BASH PREFACE(91)	IT THAT I HAD SOME DIFFICULTY AS A JOURNALIST	LATER	ON IN GETTING RID OF IT. IT MUST BE POSSIBLE FOR THE
ARMS III (69)	I INTEND, AS YOU KNOW, SIR, TO SET UP A SHOP	LATER	ON IN SOFIA; AND I LOOK FORWARD TO HER CUSTOM AND
BARB PREFACE(228)	AN INVESTMENT WHICH WILL BRING THEM IN DIVIDENDS	LATER	ON IN THE FORM, NOT OF A BETTER LIFE TO COME FOR THE
MILL I (165)	TAKE IT THAT ALASTAIR MADE THAT MISTAKE, AND THAT	LATER	ON (TOO LATE, UNFORTUNATELY) HE DISCOVERED IN YOU A--
LION PREFACE(39)	JUDAS IN ORDER TO BRING ABOUT HIS OWN BETRAYAL.	LATER	ON JOHN CLAIMS THAT JESUS SAID TO PETER " IF I WILL
SUPR II (67)	BOUND TO FIND US OUT SOMEDAY. /VIOLET/ OH YES,	LATER	ON OF COURSE. BUT DONT LETS GO OVER THIS EVERY TIME WE
GENV PREFACE(4)	SALAMIS, LEPANTO, AND TRAFALGAR ROLLED INTO ONE,	LATER	ON OUR FLIGHT FROM TOBRUK TO THE BORDER OF EGYPT DID
CAND I SD(85)	THE COMPULSORY SELFISHNESS OF PETTY COMMERCE, AND	LATER	ON SOFTENED INTO SLUGGISH BUMPTIOUSNESS BY OVERFEEDING
CAPT NOTES (302)	CONCEIT LESS TROUBLESOME AND MUCH LESS EXPENSIVE.	LATER	ON SOMEBODY TOLD HIM OF TARUDANT, A CITY IN MOROCCO IN
METH PREFACE(R11)	CALL THE REVEALER OF THEIR VIEWS TOM OR DICK, BUT	LATER	ON SUCH APPARENTLY NEGLIGIBLE ERRORS HAVE AWKWARD
LION PREFACE(17)	IN CERTAIN PHASES OF CIVILIZATION. WE SHALL SEE	LATER	ON THAT IT GIVES A POWERFUL ATTRACTION TO THE BELIEF
DOCT PREFACE(33)	TO ANY OTHER END WHATSOEVER. WE SHALL SEE	LATER	ON THAT THE CLAIM THAT HAS ARISEN IN THIS WAY FOR THE
LION PREFACE(31)	BELONGED TO THE PRIVILEGED CLASSES. HE MENTIONS	LATER	ON THAT WHEN JESUS ATTEMPTED TO PREACH IN HIS OWN
JOAN PREFACE(41)	CHANGE WHICH IT HAD PRESENTLY TO EFFECT ITSELF.	LATER	ON THE FASCISTI IN ITALY DID EVERYTHING THAT THE BLACK
METH PREFACE(R22)	I CALL YOUR SPECIAL ATTENTION TO LAMARCK, BECAUSE	LATER	ON THERE WERE NEO-LAMARCKIANS AS WELL AS
DOCT PREFACE(62)	WHEN I HAD NOT A PENNY IN MY POCKET THAN I WAS	LATER	ON WHEN I COULD AFFORD FEES ON THE HIGHEST SCALE, HAS
DEST SD(151)	AND WIN IT BACK AGAIN FROM THEM: A COURSE PURSUED	LATER	ON WITH BRILLIANT SUCCESS AT MARENGO. ON THE WHOLE,
PYGM II (241)	WEEK, BECAUSE I HAVE A JOB AT A DISTANCE. BUT	LATER	ON YOU MAY DEPEND ON ME. AFTERNOON, GENTLEMEN.
HART II (119)	YOU SLEEP AT NIGHT ONLY, AND SLEEP SOUNDLY. BUT	LATER	ON YOU WILL SLEEP IN THE AFTERNOON. LATER STILL YOU
UNPL PREFACE(R15)	ON PUBLIC MORALS IF HE SHOULD CHANGE HIS MIND	LATER	ON. BESIDES, IF HE REALLY PROTECTS THE PUBLIC AGAINST

CATH 1 (171)	JUST AS YOU ARE. YOU SHALL SHEW HER YOUR CALVES	LATER	ON. /EDSTASTON/ BUT IT WILL TAKE ME ONLY HALF AN HOUR
CAND I (95)	/BURGESS/ BYE, BYE, CANDY. I'LL LOOK IN AGAIN	LATER	ON. SO LONG, JAMES. /MORELL/ MUST YOU GO? /BURGESS/
GETT PREFACE(187)	OF THE ECONOMIC DEPENDENCE OF WOMEN ON MEN	LATER	ON; BUT AT PRESENT WE HAD BETTER CONFINE OURSELVES TO
FANY I (274)	WITH DUE AND IMPRESSIVE FORMALITY, FORGIVE BOBBY	LATER	ON; BUT FOR THE PRESENT I THINK IT HAD BETTER BE
JOAN PREFACE(26)	DOWNRIGHT WORSHIP OF JOAN DIRECTLY BY QUICHERAT.	LATER	ON, ANOTHER MAN OF GENIUS, ANATOLE FRANCE, REACTED
LION PREFACE(45)	RECORD AND REVELATION, AND REJECTING THAT VIEW	LATER	ON, BEGIN BY REJECTING THE OLD TESTAMENT, AND GIVE UP
CAND I SD(91)	LIKELY, ONE GUESSES, TO BECOME MATRONLY	LATER	ON, BUT NOW QUITE AT HER BEST, WITH THE DOUBLE CHARM
LADY PREFACE(217)	MORE INTERESTED IN DRAMATIC POETRY THAN NEWTON,	LATER	ON, EXPECTED THEM TO BE INTERESTED IN FLUXIONS, AND
LADY PREFACE(226)	WELL-KNOWN MAN WAS ACCUSED OF BEATING HIS WIFE.	LATER	ON, FOR SOME UNEXPLAINED REASON, HE WAS ACCUSED OF
LION PREFACE(19)	OF MACBETH, EXCEPT THAT, FOR A REASON TO BE GIVEN	LATER	ON, HE MUST HAVE COLLECTED HIS MATERIAL AND COMPLETED
BARB I (267)	PARLORS BY MY NATURAL TALENT FOR STEPDANCING.	LATER	ON, I BECAME A MEMBER OF THE UNDERSHAFT ORCHESTRAL
2TRU PREFACE(8)	BECAUSE I HAD NO MONEY TO BUY THEM WITH. WHEN,	LATER	ON, I HAD ENOUGH TO BUY ANYTHING THAT LONDON COULD
OVER PREFACE(161)	ALL BEEN INTOLERABLE BORES, THE PSEUDO SEX PLAY,	LATER	ON, I HAD OCCASION TO POINT OUT TO THE DEFENDERS OF
POSN PREFACE(432)	THOUGH IT INSPIRED SEVERAL APPROVING SERMONS.	LATER	ON, LADY GREGORY AND MR YEATS BROUGHT THE PLAY TO
SUPR III (109)	YOU CALL BOSH IS THE ONLY THING MEN DARE DIE FOR.	LATER	ON, LIBERTY WILL NOT BE CATHOLIC ENOUGH: MEN WILL DIE
PYGM PREFACE(199)	A PROFESSOR OF PHONETICS, AS WILL BE SEEN	LATER	ON, PYGMALION NEEDS, NOT A PREFACE, BUT A SEQUEL,
CAPT III (295)	CRUELTY. AND THE PITEOUS LETTERS SHE WROTE TO HIM	LATER	ON, RETURNED UNOPENED, MUST THEY GO TOO? /LADY
BARB PREFACE(210)	OF WOMEN WHEN THEY CAME UNDER MY NOTICE	LATER	ON, SO THOROUGHLY HAD BAX FAMILIARIZED ME WITH THE
POSN PREFACE(365)	OF BACKERS IN THE CITY, TO WHOM, AS I SHALL SHEW	LATER	ON, THE CENSORSHIP AFFORDS A CHEAP INSURANCE OF
LION PREFACE(21)	SHOULD DO SO. BUT, AS ST PAUL FOUND TO HIS COST	LATER	ON, THE DISCARDING OF CIRCUMCISION FOR BAPTISM WAS TO
UNPL PREFACE(R26)	CODE AND A " MORAL MINIMUM" WAGE. HOW I CAME,	LATER	ON, TO WRITE PLAYS WHICH, DEALING LESS WITH THE CRIMES
MRS PREFACE(167)	A SERIOUS DISCUSSION AT A FASHIONABLE AT-HOME.	LATER	ON, WHEN HE HAS DRIVEN THE TEA SERVICES OUT AND MADE
FABL PREFACE(81)	WERE ASPIRATIONS TO " JOIN THE CHOIR INVISIBLE."	LATER	ON, WHEN I ATTENDED A CHURCH SERVICE IN MEMORY OF MY
LION PREFACE(85)	WHICH JESUS WOULD NOT HAVE WASTED TWENTY WORDS.	LATER	ON, WHEN THE NEW SECT CONQUERED THE GENTILE WEST,
DOCT III (133)	/MRS DUBEDAT/ NOW I'LL RUN AWAY. PERHAPS	LATER	ON, WHEN YOURE FINISHED WITH LOUIS, I MAY COME IN AND
DEVL EPILOG (85)	ON THE ENEMY DETERMINED TO TAKE NO QUARTER, AND,	LATER	ON, " IF GENERAL GATES DOES NOT MEAN TO RECEDE FROM
BULL PREFACE(3)	TO THE ORIGINAL PREFACE WHICH WILL BE FOUND ON A	LATER	PAGE, READERS WHO SKIP TO THAT PREFACE WILL LOSE
MILL PREFACE(118)	RESTRAINED GLADSTONE AND DISRAELI, VANISHED. THE	LATER	PARLIAMENTARY LEADERS SOON LEARNT FROM EXPERIENCE THAT
CYMB FORWORD(133)	THOUGH ONE OF THE FINEST OF SHAKESPEAR'S	LATER	PLAYS NOW ON THE STAGE, GOES TO PIECES IN THE LAST
FABL IV (115)	EATABLE, HAD FOUND NO FOOD THAT DID NOT SOONER OR	LATER	POISON THEM. THIS WAS CHALLENGED BY A RUSSIAN WOMAN, A
SUPR IV (148)	YOU KNOW THAT THE GOVERNMENT WILL SOONER OR	LATER	PUT A STOP TO ALL THESE SOCIALISTIC ATTACKS ON
BUOY PREFACE(4)	EQUALLY BEYOND THE CAPACITY OF BACON AND ALL THE	LATER	RIVAL CLAIMANTS. OUR GREATEST MASTERPIECE OF
MILL IV (210)	AND ALL THE OTHER IDOLS ARE SWEPT AWAY SOONER OR	LATER	; AND ALL THE KING'S HORSES AND ALL THE KING'S MEN
SUPR PREFACE(R38)	ALL THE ASSERTIONS GET DISPROVED SOONER OR	LATER	; AND SO WE FIND THE WORLD FULL OF A MAGNIFICENT
FANY PROLOG (269)	FORGIVE ME FOR ANYTHING OF THAT KIND SOONER OR	LATER	; BUT HE NEVER GIVES WAY ON A POINT OF ART. I DARENT
GENV PREFACE(4)	ESTIMATED. OF COURSE THE TRUTH LEAKED OUT MONTHS	LATER	; BUT IT PRODUCED ONLY A FRESH ORGY OF BRAGGING ABOUT
LION PREFACE(33)	REGARD THIS PASSAGE AS TACKED ON BY A	LATER	SCRIBE. ON THE WHOLE MARK LEAVES THE MODERN READER
CAPT III (284)	LADYSHIP'S CAWMPLIMENTS WILL BE IN ORDER AT A	LATER	STAGE. CAPTAIN BRASSBOUND: THE POSITION IS THIS. MY
SUPR HANDBOK(198)	ARE BUT PRELIMINARIES TO THE INEVITABLE	LATER	STAGE, NOW THREATENING US, IN WHICH THE PASSIONS WHICH
CLEO II (125)	PEACE. /BRITANNUS/ (UNCONSCIOUSLY ANTICIPATING A	LATER	STATESMAN) PEACE WITH HONOR, POTHINUS. /POTHINUS/ (
HART II (119)	BUT LATER ON YOU WILL SLEEP IN THE AFTERNOON.	LATER	STILL YOU WILL SLEEP EVEN IN THE MORNING; AND YOU WILL
LION PREFACE(33)	ARTIST. WHEN WE COME TO LUKE, WE COME TO A	LATER	STORY-TELLER, AND ONE WITH A STRONGER NATURAL GIFT FOR
LADY PREFACE(207)	UP ALL PRETENCE THAT MY PLAY IS HISTORICAL. THE	LATER	SUGGESTION OF MR ACHESON THAT THE DARK LADY, FAR FROM
SUPR I (13)	YOU HEAR HIM, TAVY! NOT AN IDEA IN HIS HEAD	LATER	THAN EIGHTEENSIXTY. WE CANT LEAVE ANN WITH NO OTHER
HART PREFACE(29)	STUMBLED OVER IT; AND YET IT CAME A FULL YEAR	LATER	THAN IT SHOULD HAVE COME IF THE BELLIGERENTS HAD NOT
WIDO II (33)	HIM). /SARTORIUS/ YOU WILL COME HERE TOMORROW NOT	LATER	THAN TEN, MR LICKCHEESE, TO CONCLUDE OUR BUSINESS. I
BASH PREFACE(87)	VERSE. NAY, NOT SHAKESPEAREAN BLANK VERSE ITSELF	LATER	THAN THE HISTORIES. I AM QUITE SURE THAT ANYONE WHO IS
JOAN PREFACE(54)	REALLY CRAVE FOR, AFTER ARRIVING AS LATE AS (OR	LATER	THAN) THE HOUR OF BEGINNING CAN POSSIBLY BE MADE FOR
SIM I (46)	MAY PRODUCE A SECOND GENERATION. NOW SOONER OR	LATER	THIS EXTENSION OF THE FAMILY GROUP WILL SET PEOPLE
ROCK PREFACE(163)	LEASE OF LIFE FOR AT LEAST FOUR YEARS. SOONER OR	LATER	THIS SITUATION WILL HAVE TO BE THOROUGHLY STUDIED AND
DEST SD(151)	DIFFICULT FOR THE ROMANTICISTS OF A HUNDRED YEARS	LATER	TO CREDIT THE HITHERTO UNRECORDED LITTLE SCENE NOW IN
BARB PREFACE(228)	UNSCRUPULOUS. THAT HAS ALWAYS HAPPENED SOONER OR	LATER	TO GREAT ORDERS FOUNDED BY SAINTS; AND THE ORDER
LION PREFACE(18)	OF DIVINE BIRTH WAS SURE TO BE ATTACHED SOONER OR	LATER	TO VERY EMINENT PERSONS IN ROMAN IMPERIAL TIMES, AND
BUOY PREFACE(4)	PAPER WE FED ON TO HIS DESK. THE FACT THAT HE WAS	LATER	TRANSPORTED FOR FORGERY DID NOT MAKE HIS PERFORMANCE
HART III (144)	FROM A SICKLE TO AN ARC LAMP, AND COMES LATER AND	LATER	UNTIL SHE IS LOST IN THE LIGHT AS OTHER THINGS ARE
DOCT PREFACE(80)	HAVE BECOME MORE FREQUENT AND SENSATIONAL. A	LATER	VOLUME IN THE PRESENT EDITION OF MY WORKS DEALS WITH
CLEO NOTES (209)	STYLE SO IMPERSONAL THAT THE AUTHENTICITY OF THE	LATER	VOLUMES IS DISPUTED, THEY REVEAL SOME OF HIS QUALITIES
LION PREFACE(67)	WILL YOUR HEART BE ALSO." EIGHTEEN HUNDRED YEARS	LATER	WE FIND A VERY DIFFERENT PERSON FROM JESUS, TALLEYRAND
POSN PREFACE(373)	STATEMENT PARAGRAPH BY PARAGRAPH, AS SOME OF THE	LATER	WITNESSES DID. BUT AS IN OFFERING THE COMMITTEE MY
BULL IV (177)	THE ISLAND OF THE SAINTS; BUT INDEED IN THESE	LATER	YEARS IT MIGHT BE MORE FITLY CALLED THE ISLAND OF THE
CLEO II (140)	HIS SECRETARY'S NAME IS ONE OF CAESAR'S JOKES. IN	LATER	YEARS IT WOULD HAVE MEANT, QUITE SERIOUSLY AND
MTH1 I (11)	CANNOT RENEW THEMSELVES WITHOUT EVES. SOONER OR	LATER	YOU WILL DIE LIKE THE FAWN; AND THE NEW ADAMS WILL BE
MTH5 (218)	WHAT IS MY ACCIDENT? /THE SHE-ANCIENT/ SOONER OR	LATER	YOU WILL FALL AND BREAK YOUR NECK; OR A TREE WILL FALL
APPL PREFACE(192)	WHETHER IT SHOULD OCCUR AT THE FIRST PASSAGE OR	LATER	, AND TO DICTATE THE ORDER IN WHICH IT SHOULD BE
MTH2 (56)	MAKING A HORRID DISTURBANCE. /CONRAD/ NO: IT WAS	LATER	, AT A MEETING TO SUPPORT THE FRANCHISE BILL WHICH
DEST SD(152)	RIDICULOUS IN THE EYE OF HISTORY A HUNDRED YEARS	LATER	, BUT MONSTROUS AND HORRIBLE TO THE CONTEMPORARY NORTH
MTH4 II (184)	WAR. IN THE WAR WHICH FOLLOWED IT ABOUT TEN YEARS	LATER	, HARDLY ANY SOLDIERS WERE KILLED; BUT SEVEN OF THE
BULL II SD(105)	GENIAL. BROADBENT, FOR REASONS WHICH WILL APPEAR	LATER	, HAS NO LUGGAGE EXCEPT A FIELD GLASS AND A GUIDE
APPL I (239)	TO FIVE THOUSAND PEOPLE. IN THAT SAME HALL A WEEK	LATER	, I FACED A MEETING OF THE VERY SAME PEOPLE. I DIDNT
BARB PREFACE(221)	MAKING SO LITTLE IMPRESSION THAT WHEN, SOME YEARS	LATER	, I PRODUCE PLAYS IN WHICH BUTLER'S EXTRAORDINARILY
UNPL PREFACE(R13)	PLAY. EXHUMING THIS AS AFORESAID SEVEN YEARS	LATER	, I SAW THAT THE VERY QUALITIES WHICH HAD MADE IT
JOAN PREFACE(6)	AND THE REVERSAL OF THE VERDICT TWENTYFIVE YEARS	LATER	, IN FORM A REHABILITATION OF JOAN, WAS REALLY ONLY A
POSN PREFACE(392)	REMEMBERED THAT IT WAS NOT UNTIL A HUNDRED YEARS	LATER	, IN THE REACTION AGAINST THE PURITANS, THAT A WOMAN
MTH5 (250)	DESTROYED BY A FLASH FROM THE CLOUDS. SOONER OR	LATER	, ITS DESTRUCTION IS CERTAIN. /THE SHE-ANCIENT/ YES:
MTH1 I (8)	LIVE. /EVE/ BUT THE REST OF US WILL DIE SOONER OR	LATER	, LIKE THE FAWN. AND THEN THERE WILL BE NOTHING BUT
JOAN PREFACE(4)	FOR HIS DEATH, HIS ACCUSER, IF BORN 2300 YEARS	LATER	, MIGHT HAVE BEEN PICKED OUT OF ANY FIRST CLASS
SIM PRO,1, (23)	HE HAS NERVES. WE ALL HAVE THEM HERE SOONER OR	LATER	, OFF AND ON. HERE! I'LL GIVE YOU A LANDING TICKET;
PRES (135)	NOBODIES? /MITCHENER/ YOULL HAVE TO, SOONER OR	LATER	, OR THE SOCIALISTS WILL MAKE NOBODIES OF THE LOT OF
NEVR II (234)	SIR? WELL, THAT WAS TO BE EXPECTED, SOONER OR	LATER	, SIR, WASNT IT? (TURNING WITH A HAPPY SMILE TO
MIS. PREFACE(83)	IN HER GRANDMOTHER'S TIME. BUT AS PEOPLE MARRY	LATER	, THE FACTS OF AGE AND TIME STILL INEXORABLY CONDEMN
POSN PREFACE(420)	NOBODY OBJECTED UNTIL, ABOUT A CENTURY AND A HALF	LATER	, THE STAR CHAMBER BEGAN CUTTING OFF THE EARS OF
BARB PREFACE(208)	DECLARED IN BOOKS FULL OF WHAT CAME, TEN YEARS	LATER	, TO BE PERFUNCTORILY LABELLED IBSENISM? I WAS NOT
JOAN PREFACE(3)	AND, LIKE QUEEN CHRISTINA OF SWEDEN TWO CENTURIES	LATER	, TO SAY NOTHING OF CATALINA DE ERAUSO AND INNUMERABLE
BARB PREFACE(208)	OF ALNASCHAR, AND WAS DOOMED TO BE, CENTURIES	LATER	, UNDER THE NAME OF SIMON TAPPERTIT. WHEN CERVANTES
3PLA PREFACE(R31)	TUNES. THACKERAY, SCORES OF CENTURIES	LATER	, WAS STILL BAYING THE MOON IN THE SAME TERMS. OUT,
SIM II (65)	CANT SHE, SILLY? /IDDY/ YES; BUT FIFTEEN YEARS	LATER	, WHEN THE STATESMEN WRITE THEIR MEMOIRS AND

LATEST

SIM II (79)	AMAZING NEWS: WE KNOW ALL ABOUT THAT. WHAT IS THE	LATEST	? . . . YES: " PLOT TO DESTROY OUR MOST VALUABLE
MTH2 (73)	DR BARNABAS? LEMONS? SOUR MILK? OR WHAT IS THE	LATEST	? /BURGE/ WE WERE JUST BEGINNING TO TALK SERIOUSLY;
BUOY III (31)	ALL. /DARKIE/ GO AHEAD, SIR FERDINAND. WHATS THE	LATEST	? /SIR F./ YOU KNOW, I PRESUME, THAT YOUR FATHER'S
SUPR II (55)	TAVY. MOTOR RECORDS ARE HIS WEAKNESS. WHATS THE	LATEST	? /STRAKER/ PARIS TO BISKRA AT FORTY MILE AN HOUR
ANNA (289)	SITS DOWN). /STRAMMFEST/ THAT DEPENDS. WHATS THE	LATEST	? WHICH OF THEM DO YOU THINK IS MOST LIKELY TO BE IN
GENV III (65)	TOOK A HAND IN IT. BY THE WAY, HAVE YOU HEARD THE	LATEST	ABOUT HER? /THE JOURNALIST/ NO. SHE HAS DROPPED ME
APPL I (213)	THIS MORNING SUPPORTING THE KING; AND THE	LATEST	ADDITION TO THE CABINET HERE IS A KING'S MAN. I
SUPR I (31)	MADE RESPONSIBLE FOR ME, I HOPE. /TANNER/ THE	LATEST	ADDITION TO YOUR COLLECTION OF SCAPEGOATS, EH? /ANN/
BUOY III (42)	THE YOUNGEST. SIR FERDINAND WHOPPER, OUR FATHER'S	LATEST	AND MOST EMINENT SOLICITOR. /SIR F./ MY NAME IS NOT
MTH5 (249)	HER) NOW YOU ARE COMING TO ME, BECAUSE I AM THE	LATEST	ARRIVAL. BUT I DONT UNDERSTAND YOUR ART AND YOUR
LION PREFACE(46)	NINE-TENTHS MILLIONS OF MILES, OR WHATEVER THE	LATEST	BIG FIGURE MAY BE. CREDIBILITY AND TRUTH. AND HERE I
GENV PREFACE(8)	OF THE SLAIN IS THREATENED BECAUSE THE	LATEST	BOMBS ARE NO RESPECTERS OF SEX; AND WHERE THERE ARE
CLEO NOTES (205)	OF THE PRESENT TO MISLEAD AND FLATTER HIM. OUR	LATEST	BOOK ON THE NEW RAILWAY ACROSS ASIA DESCRIBES THE
MTH2 (57)	PLAY? TELL ME ALL ABOUT IT, AND ALL ABOUT THE	LATEST	BOOKS, AND ALL ABOUT EVERYTHING. /SAVVY/ YOU HAVE NOT
2TRU PREFACE(11)	ON THE HIGHROAD. THEY COME UP WHEN YOU HAVE THE	LATEST	CAR AND THE LATEST WARDROBE AND ALL THE REST OF IT.
ROCK II (250)	WHICH CLEARANCES DO YOU REFER TO? THE	LATEST	CLEARED ME OUT OF DOMESDAY TOWERS. I CAN NO LONGER
3PLA PREFACE(R26)	I TO REPUBLISH BUCKSTONE'S WRECK ASHORE AS MY	LATEST	COMEDY, IT WOULD BE HAILED AS A MASTERPIECE OF
BULL PREFACE(71)	ABSORBED IN THE HISTORY OF MARIA MONK, OR THE	LATEST	DEMONSTRATION THAT ALL THE EVIL IN THE WORLD IS THE
DOCT PREFACE(76)	THE WHIRLIGIG OF TIME BRINGS ITS REVENGES." THIS	LATEST	DISCOVERY OF THE REMEDIAL VIRTUE OF A VERY VERY TINY

METH PREFACE(R27)	OF ENGLISH LITERATURE, FROM SHAKESPEAR TO THE	LATEST	EDITION OF THE ENCYCLOPAEDIA BRITANNICA, IS SO
JOAN PREFACE(48)	MARVEL TO IMMEDIATELY CREDIBLE STATEMENT IN THE	LATEST	EDITION OF THE ENCYCLOPAEDIA BRITANNICA IS ENORMOUSLY
MTH3 (111)	THAT, I WOULD NOT CROSS THE STREET NOW TO READ MY	LATEST	EPITAPH, THE CHIEF SECRETARY AND THE PRESIDENT LOOK
3PLA PREFACE(R14)	FIRMLY BELIEVED THE WORD PROBLEM TO BE THE	LATEST	EUPHEMISM FOR WHAT JUSTICE SHALLOW CALLED A BONA
MILL I SD(137)	THE BOOKSHELVES, ARE CHIPPENDALES OF THE VERY	LATEST	FAKE, OF THE OTHER TWO ONE IS OCCUPIED BY HIMSELF,
ARMS II (43)	/CATHERINE/ OH, WHILST YOU WERE AWAY, IT IS HER	LATEST	FANCY. /PETKOFF/ (TESTILY) AND HAS NICOLA TAKEN TO
PHIL PREFACE(68)	STORE. THE HUMAN NATURE IN IT IS STILL IN THE	LATEST	FASHION; INDEED I AM FAR FROM SURE THAT ITS IDEAS,
SUPR III (134)	THE DEUCE IS THE SUPERMAN? /THE DEVIL/ OH, THE	LATEST	FASHION AMONG THE LIFE FORCE FANATICS. DID YOU NOT
2TRU I (28)	HERE, THE DOCTOR, HAS GIVEN HER A DOSE OF THE	LATEST	FASHIONABLE OPIATE THAT WOULD KEEP A COCK ASLEEP TIL
2TRU PREFACE(11)	OLD ONE AT SCRAP IRON PRICES. COME AND BUY OUR	LATEST	FASHIONS IN DRESS: YOU CANNOT POSSIBLY BE SEEN IN
DEST SD(162)	IS NOT, JUDGING BY HER DRESS, AN ADMIRER OF THE	LATEST	FASHIONS OF THE DIRECTORY; OR PERHAPS SHE USES UP HER
3PLA PREFACE(R14)	EYES, PAINTED AND DRESSED TO PERFECTION IN THE	LATEST	FASHIONS, BUT THAT IS JUST WHAT HAPPENED TO ME IN THE
GETT SD(266)	THAT EFFECT WITHOUT THE LEAST REGARD FOR THE	LATEST	FASHIONS, SURE OF HERSELF, VERY TERRIFYING TO THE
PPP SD(196)	ENTERS. HE IS IN EVENING DRESS, MADE IN THE	LATEST	FASHION, WITH THE RIGHT HALF OF THE COAT AND THE LEFT
ROCK I (219)	ASK HIM WHETHER HE HAS READ THE NONSENSE OF THE	LATEST	FLAT EARTH MAN. I HAVE SOMETHING BETTER TO DO WITH MY
SUPR HANDBOK(204)	SHAMELESS TOBACCO SMOKING; HOLY WATER, IN ITS	LATEST	FORM OF DISINFECTANT FLUID, IS MORE WIDELY USED AND
SUPR I (11)	TIME TO TROUBLE MUCH ABOUT HER NOW. THATS THE	LATEST	GAME. AN ORPHAN! IT'S LIKE HEARING AN IRONCLAD TALK
OVER PREFACE(161)	AND THAT FROM FRANCESCA AND PAOLO DOWN TO THE	LATEST	GUILTY COUPLE OF THE SCHOOL OF DUMAS FILS, THE
NEVR II (236)	RESUMES THE BROKEN MELODY). THE YOUNG GENTLEMAN'S	LATEST	IS THAT YOURE HIS FATHER, SIR. /CRAMPTON/ WHAT!
MIS. (136)	PUT THAT NEW TURKISH BATH. TURKISH BATHS ARE HIS	LATEST	. (SHE GOES OUT). /JOHNNY/ (COMING FORWARD AGAIN)
GETT (331)	MEN'S WIVES IS GROWING ON YOU; AND THAT I'M YOUR	LATEST	. /HOTCHKISS/ WHAT! THROW HER OVER WHEN SHE HAS
CYMB FORWORD(136)	TO WHICH I WAS BROUGHT UP IN DUBLIN, OR THE	LATEST	LONDON FASHION IN DIALOGUE. IT IS SO EASY THAT IF IT
MTH5 (219)	OF OUR GREATEST SCULPTORS ARE BRINGING US THEIR	LATEST	MASTERPIECES; AND WE ARE GOING TO CROWN THEM WITH
3PLA PREFACE(R38)	PLAYWRIGHTS HAVE DONE. TRUE, MY PLAYS HAVE THE	LATEST	MECHANICAL IMPROVEMENTS: THE ACTION IS NOT CARRIED ON
2TRU PREFACE(11)	WALLOW IN OUR SWIMMING POOLS. COME AND SEE OUR	LATEST	MODEL AUTOMOBILE! WE HAVE CHANGED THE INVENTOR'S
MTH2 (57)	OF LABOR). WELL, MY DEAR YOUNG LADY? WHAT IS THE	LATEST	NEWS? WHATS GOING ON? HAVE YOU SEEN SHODDY'S NEW
CLEO IV (169)	HER FORMER PLACE.) WELL, POTHINUS: WHAT IS THE	LATEST	NEWS FROM YOUR REBEL FRIENDS? /POTHINUS/ (
GENV III (85)	YOU HAD BETTER DINE WITH ME. YOU CAN TELL ME THE	LATEST	NEWS. /THE JUDGE/ I CAN TELL YOU THAT. THE TRIAL OF
CLEO IV (169)	AT HIM. /CHARMIAN/ I SEE YOU DO NOT KNOW THE	LATEST	NEWS, POTHINUS. /POTHINUS/ WHAT IS THAT? /CHARMIAN/
BULL PREFACE(42)	OF LONDON, MR ROWNTREE'S ACCOUNT OF YORK, AND THE	LATEST	OFFICIAL REPORT ON DUNDEE; AND THEN PRETEND, IF YOU
SUPR PREFACE(R39)	COPIER OF FOSSILS OFFERS THEM TO YOU AS THE	LATEST	OUTPOURING OF THE HUMAN SPIRIT, AND, WORST OF ALL,
ROCK I SD(210)	WOMAN IN SMART FACTORY-MADE CLOTHES AFTER THE	LATEST	PARISIAN MODELS, (B) A POWERFULLY BUILT LOUD VOICED
LADY PREFACE(218)	THE PROCESSION OF RUFFIANS WHO PASS THROUGH THE	LATEST	PLAYS) IT IS CERTAINLY NOT BECAUSE THEY HAVE ANY MORE
LADY PREFACE(234)	RECKLESS JOLLITY AND SERENELY HAPPY POETRY IN HIS	LATEST	PLAYS, YET THE DISCOVERY THAT HIS MOST SERIOUS WORK
AUGS (270)	UP. (THE CLERK MAKES FOR THE DOOR, WHISTLING THE	LATEST	POPULAR LOVE BALLAD). STOP WHISTLING INSTANTLY, SIR.
PRES (153)	YOURSELVES! BUT, MY DEAR LADIES, UNDER THE	LATEST	PROCLAMATION WOMEN ARE STRICTLY FORBIDDEN TO CARRY
CLEO NOTES (205)	ARE EXACTLY WHAT THEY ARE IN ENGLAND." THE	LATEST	PROFESSOR DESCANTING ON THE CIVILIZATION OF THE
CURE (228)	GIVE UP VAMPING ACCOMPANIMENTS AND PLAYING THE	LATEST	RAGTIMES BY EAR, YOURE A LOST MAN SOCIALLY.
2TRU PREFACE(23)	MODERN INDUSTRIAL EXPERIENCE CONFIRMS IT; FOR THE	LATEST	REDISCOVERY OF THE VINCENTIAN PRINCIPLE HAS BEEN MADE
DEVL III (56)	FROM SPRINGTOWN? /SWINDON/ NOTHING SPECIAL. THE	LATEST	REPORTS ARE SATISFACTORY. /BURGOYNE/ (RISING IN
PHIL II (122)	REST. COME AND TALK TO ME. TELL ME ALL ABOUT THE	LATEST	SCIENTIFIC DISCOVERIES, AND WHAT I OUGHT TO READ TO
PYGM III (254)	ON ME IF I AM NOT POSITIVELY REEKING WITH THE	LATEST	SLANG. GOODBYE. /PICKERING/ GOODBYE (THEY SHAKE
2TRU PREFACE(11)	CANNOT SLEEP, THAT OBLIGES YOU TO RESORT TO THE	LATEST	SOPORIFIC DRUG, GUARANTEED IN THE ADVERTISEMENTS TO
FANY PROLOG (263)	LIKE A BIRD. THEN I THOUGHT YOUD LIKE ONE OF THE	LATEST	SORT: THE CHAPS THAT GO FOR THE NEWEST THINGS AND
CAPT NOTES (305)	FOR I, WHICH I HAVE MADE DRINKWATER USE, IS THE	LATEST	STAGE OF THE OLD DIPHTHONGAL OI, WHICH MR CHEVALIER
DOCT PREFACE(74)	SINCE IT FORBIDS YOU EVEN TO LEARN. THE	LATEST	THEORIES. MEDICAL THEORIES ARE SO MUCH A MATTER OF
HART II (106)	OF YOU COMING IN TO LOOK AT ME, AS IF I WAS THE	LATEST	THING IN A MENAGERIE. /MRS HUSHABYE/ YOU ARE THE
MTH2 (62)	OUT THE VERY GHASTLIEST EXPLODED DRIVEL AS THE	LATEST	THING IN POLITICS. I AM NOT GIVING YOU MY OWN IDEAS,
HART II (106)	THING IN A MENAGERIE. /MRS HUSHABYE/ YOU ARE THE	LATEST	THING IN THIS MENAGERIE. BEFORE MANGAN CAN RETORT, A
MIS. (129)	WAS A FREETHINKER, AND ALWAYS BELIEVED THE	LATEST	THING. THE PRIEST DIDNT BELIEVE ANYTHING, BECAUSE IT
NEVR I (200)	ROUND ON ONE LEG) YOUR FURNITURE ISNT QUITE THE	LATEST	THING, IS IT? /THE DENTIST/ IT'S MY LANDLORD'S. /THE
JOAN PREFACE(55)	AWAY FROM IT WITH RELUCTANCE TO CATCH THE VERY	LATEST	TRAIN OR OMNIBUS THAT WILL TAKE THEM HOME. FAR FROM
MIS. PREFACE(66)	CANNOT SEIZE BY OPEN FORCE. DEMOCRACY BECOMES THE	LATEST	TRICK OF TYRANNY: " WOMANLINESS" BECOMES THE LATEST
GENV IV (90)	HEARD IN ROME, IN MOSCOW, IN LONDON, WHEREVER THE	LATEST	TYPE OF RECEIVER IS INSTALLED. /BEGONIA/ HEARD! YOU
FABL PREFACE(88)	THE CANDIDATE WHO HAS BEEN TAUGHT THAT THE	LATEST	VIEWS ARE THOSE OF BASTIAT AND COBDEN, IGNORING THOSE
2TRU PREFACE(11)	THEY COME UP WHEN YOU HAVE THE LATEST CAR AND THE	LATEST	WARDROBE AND ALL THE REST OF IT. THE ONLY WANT THAT
MIS. PREFACE(66)	TRICK OF TYRANNY: " WOMANLINESS" BECOMES THE	LATEST	WILE OF PROSTITUTION. BETWEEN PARENT AND CHILD THE
LADY PREFACE(220)	LIFE OF ME SEE THE BROKEN HEART IN SHAKESPEAR'S	LATEST	WORKS. " HARK, HARK! THE LARK AT HEAVEN'S GATE

LATHAM

MRS I (184)	POUNDS. PERHAPS YOU DONT KNOW HOW IT WAS. MRS	LATHAM	, MY TUTOR AT NEWNHAM, TOLD MY MOTHER THAT I COULD

LATHS

NEVR II SD(225)	MIDDLE AGED GENTLEMAN SITTING ON A CHAIR OF IRON	LATHS	AT A LITTLE IRON TABLE WITH A BOWL OF LUMP SUGAR ON
DEVL I SD(4)	HER HEAD, AND HER FEET ON A BROAD FENDER OF IRON	LATHS	, THE STEP OF THE DOMESTIC ALTAR OF THE FIREPLACE,

LATIMER

LION PREFACE(84)	HAVE DIED WORSE DEATHS: FOR EXAMPLE, HONEST HUGH	LATIMER	, WHO WAS BURNED BY US, WAS WORTH FIFTY STEPHENS AND

LATIN

JOAN 6 (127)	THINK, DOUBTLESS, THAT THEY SHOULD HAVE SPOKEN IN	LATIN	? /CAUCHON/ NO: HE THINKS THEY SHOULD HAVE SPOKEN IN
MIS. PREFACE(57)	TROUBLE US. BUT IT IS A FACT THAT IGNORANCE OF	LATIN	AND GREEK AND MATHEMATICS CLOSES CERTAIN CAREERS TO
JOAN PREFACE(10)	HE HAD BEEN TO SCHOOL, AND KNEW AS MUCH	LATIN	AND GREEK AS MOST UNIVERSITY PASSMEN RETAIN: THAT IS,
MIS. PREFACE(23)	THE THINNEST PRETENCE OF TEACHING ANYTHING BUT	LATIN	AND GREEK. WHEN I WENT THERE AS A VERY SMALL BOY I
BASH PREFACE(89)	OF A CLASS WHICH COULD READ AND WRITE, BUT HAD NO	LATIN	AND LESS GREEK, NEWSPAPERS AND PLAYS ALIKE SOON CAME
METH PREFACE(R28)	TO SAY IN THEM THAN SHAKESPEAR WITH HIS LITTLE	LATIN	AND LESS GREEK; AND PUBLIC LIFE IS THE PARADISE OF
LADY PREFACE(217)	DESCRIBES JONSON'S DESCRIPTION OF HIS " LITTLE	LATIN	AND LESS GREEK" AS A SNEER, WHEREAS IT OCCURS IN AN
JITT PREFACE(5)	MAKE OUT WHAT HE WANTS PROVIDED HE USES THE	LATIN	AND NOT THE GOTHIC SCRIPT, AND THAT IS ALL. WHEN I
MIS. PREFACE(50)	IN LITERATURE. I SHOULD PROBABLY KNOW AS MUCH	LATIN	AS FRENCH, IF LATIN HAD NOT BEEN MADE THE EXCUSE FOR
LION PREFACE(91)	HIM, IN WHICH CHINESE SAGES, GREEK PHILOSOPHERS,	LATIN	AUTHORS, AND WRITERS OF ANCIENT ANONYMOUS INSCRIPTIONS
LION PREFACE(11)	HIMSELF, AND RATHER MORE THAN LESS CIVILIZED. THE	LATIN	CHRISTIAN HAS NOTHING TO OFFER THE GREEK CHRISTIAN
BASH PREFACE(89)	HAVE BEEN THE SEEDIEST OF BOHEMIANS, HAD LEARNT	LATIN	GRAMMAR AND READ BOOKS WRITTEN BY PERSONS SIMILARLY
MIS. PREFACE(39)	I BEGAN WITH A FAIRLY COMPLETE KNOWLEDGE OF	LATIN	GRAMMAR IN THE CHILDISH SENSE OF BEING ABLE TO REPEAT
KING I (197)	GOT NO MORE EDUCATION THAN MY GROOM. /CHARLES/	LATIN	GRAMMAR IS NOT MUCH USE ON THE BATTLEFIELD, AS WE
MIS. PREFACE(23)	THERE AS A VERY SMALL BOY I KNEW A GOOD DEAL OF	LATIN	GRAMMAR WHICH I HAD BEEN TAUGHT IN A FEW WEEKS
MIS. PREFACE(58)	TO AN ADULT STANDING OVER A BOY OF TEN WITH A	LATIN	GRAMMAR, AND SAYING " YOU MUST LEARN THIS, WHETHER YOU
BASH PREFACE(90)	OLD, AND THE ONLY GRAMMAR I EVER LEARNED WAS	LATIN	GRAMMAR, SO THAT ELIZABETHAN ENGLISH BECAME A MOTHER
MIS. PREFACE(50)	SHOULD PROBABLY KNOW AS MUCH LATIN AS FRENCH, IF	LATIN	HAD NOT BEEN MADE THE EXCUSE FOR MY SCHOOL
MIS. PREFACE(70)	CARES TWOPENCE WHETHER HIS CHILDREN CAN WRITE	LATIN	HEXAMETERS OR REPEAT THE DATES OF THE ACCESSION OF ALL
SHAK PREFACE(136)	LABOUR'S LOST. ONE DOES NOT FORGET BUNYAN'S " THE	LATIN	I BORROW," SHAKESPEAR'S STANDING WAS NEARER TO
MIS. PREFACE(23)	RHYTHM STICKS TO ME, I HAVE NEVER YET SEEN A	LATIN	INSCRIPTION ON A TOMB THAT I COULD TRANSLATE
KING II (229)	DOZEN OF THE OTHER. HEREDITY IS NO USE. LEARNING	LATIN	IS NO USE: JACK CHURCHILL, WHO IS AN IGNORAMUS, IS
LION PREFACE(47)	IT, AND DOES NOT EVEN KNOW THAT IT WAS WRITTEN IN	LATIN	. IF YOU PRESS AN ULSTER PROTESTANT AS TO WHY HE
FABL PREFACE(87)	READ, WRITE, AND EVEN TRANSLATE A LITTLE DOG	LATIN	. IT WAS BETTER THAN NO TEST AT ALL, BUT IT IS NOW
PYGM EPILOG (300)	AND THOROUGHLY INEFFICIENT SCHOOLS, KNEW A LITTLE	LATIN	. IT WAS VERY LITTLE, BUT ENOUGH TO MAKE HIM APPEAR TO
MIS. PREFACE(23)	ELSE. TO THIS DAY, THOUGH I CAN STILL DECLINE A	LATIN	NOUN AND REPEAT SOME OF THE OLD PARADIGMS IN THE OLD
MIS. PREFACE(57)	IT IS A MONSTROUS THING TO FORCE A CHILD TO LEARN	LATIN	OR GREEK OR MATHEMATICS ON THE GROUND THAT THEY ARE AN
ROCK PREFACE(149)	THAT THE NORDIC RACE SHOULD EXTERMINATE THE	LATIN	RACE, AS BOTH THESE LINGUAL STOCKS ARE HOPELESSLY
GENV IV (99)	OF THE RAGBAG OF STALE JOURNALISM AND KIKKERONIAN	LATIN	-- /SIR O./ I PROTEST, I BEG. I ASK THE COURT TO
GLIM (171)	GRACE OF OUR LADY; BUT I STILL REMEMBER ALL MY	LATIN	; AND I CAN BIND AND LOOSE; AND I'M VERY VERY WISE;
MIS. PREFACE(39)	THOUGH NEITHER INTERESTING NOR TRUE, WAS THE ONLY	LATIN	SENTENCE I COULD TRANSLATE AT SIGHT: THEREFORE THE
GENV IV (105)	YOURS. WHEN HAS A NORDIC EVER STOOPED TO FOLLOW A	LATIN	SOUTHERNER? /BBDE/ YOU FORGET THAT MY COUNTRY HAS A
OVER PREFACE(164)	TO THE FRENCH AND, PERHAPS MORE OR LESS, ALL THE	LATIN	STAGES. THE REASON IS THAT, PARTLY FROM A WANT OF
PYGM EPILOG (300)	THE ESTABLISHMENT. FREDDY'S POWER OF STATING IN	LATIN	THAT BALBUS BUILT A WALL AND THAT GAUL WAS DIVIDED
ROCK I (231)	THE MIND. /THE LADY/ HAVE ALL THE BOYS WHO MADE	LATIN	VERSES AT HARROW SPLENDIDLY TRAINED MINDS? /SIR
ROCK I (231)	NOT. YOU DONT UNDERSTAND. WE LEARNT TO WRITE	LATIN	VERSES NOT BECAUSE THE VERSES ARE ANY GOOD-- AFTER
ROCK I (231)	ALL THE TIME. /THE LADY/ AT HARROW YOU WROTE	LATIN	VERSES, DID YOU NOT? /SIR ARTHUR/ YES, OF COURSE.

BARB PREFACE(243) IN SOCIAL THEORY EVEN WHEN HE IS SCHOOLED IN LATIN VERSE, CANNOT BE SET AGAINST ALL THE LAWS OF HIS
BASH PREFACE(89) CHAPMAN, WHO WROTE ALL HIS STAGE DIRECTIONS IN LATIN , OR BEN JONSON, WHO DEPLORED THE SLENDERNESS OF

LATINITY
BASH PREFACE(89) THE PRESS AND THE THEATRE HAD LOST ALL THEIR LATINITY ; AND THIS WAS WHY, WHENEVER THE ADMIRABLE

LATINS
MILL PREFACE(125) WRITERS LIKE CHAMBERLAIN PLAY: THE TEUTONS AND LATINS , THE APOLLONIANS AND DIONYSIANS, THE NORDICS AND

LATITUDE
HART II (105) AND WHERE THERE ARE NO WOMEN, SEND ME ITS LATITUDE AND LONGITUDE; AND I WILL JOIN YOU THERE. /LADY
CAPT I (231) POINTS SEAWARD, WHERE THE RAPID TWILIGHT OF THE LATITUDE HAS BEGUN). /LADY CICELY/ (GETTING UP TO LOOK AND
BARB PREFACE(240) TO. AS TO BEING A CHRISTIAN, HE IS ALLOWED SOME LATITUDE IN THAT MATTER, BECAUSE, I REPEAT, CHRISTIANITY HAS
CAPT I (234) MUST LOSE NO TIME: THE DARK IS SOON DOWN IN THIS LATITUDE . (TO DRINKWATER) WILL YE ASK HIM TO STEP OUT HERE

LATITUDES
CAPT I (222) AND GENTLEMEN IN THE WORLD, ESPAECIALLY IN THESE LATITUDES , WHICH SORT OF GENTLEMAN IS HE? /DRINKWATER/

LATN
BULL II (100) /PATSY/ BUT WASNT IT ONLY BECAUSE YOU KNEW MORE LATN THAN FATHER DEMPSEY THAT HE WAS JEALOUS OF YOU?

LATTER
ROCK PREFACE(148) OF HUMAN ANIMALS AND NON-HUMAN ONES, SETTING THE LATTER APART AS BRUTES. THIS WAS FOUNDED ON A GENERAL BELIEF
JOAN 6,SD(122) SAME DOOR WITH A DOMINICAN MONK AND A CANON, THE LATTER CARRYING A BRIEF. /THE PAGE/ THE RIGHT REVEREND HIS
DOCT PREFACE(68) SOME EXTENT, AS A SUBSTITUTE FOR IT, BUT IN THE LATTER CASE IT IS QUITE UNREGULATED EXCEPT BY PROFESSIONAL
BULL PREFACE(61) IN THE STOMACH: HIS INJURIES ARE SERIOUS. IN THE LATTER CASE THEFT APPEARS TO HAVE BEEN THE MOTIVE. MY OBJECT
MILL PREFACE(124) AND BRITISH NEWSPAPERS AND MAGAZINES OF THE LATTER HALF OF 1914, HE WOULD LEARN THAT THE GERMANS ARE A
BARB PREFACE(220) OWN DEPARTMENT THE GREATEST ENGLISH WRITER OF THE LATTER HALF OF THE XIX CENTURY, STEADILY INCULCATED THE
SUPR HANDBOK(219) AND GIVES HIM A CERTIFICATE OF PROFICIENCY, THE LATTER HAS COMPLETED THE EDUCATION OF A GENTLEMAN. A FOOL'S
LADY PREFACE(227) SHEWN IN THE WHOLE MASS OF HIS WRITINGS. THIS LATTER IS THE REALLY CONCLUSIVE REPLY. IN THE CASE OF MICHEL
GETT PREFACE(228) IT DOWN THAN TO ATTEMPT TO SWEEP IT OUT, AND THIS LATTER VIEW WILL PERHAPS PREVAIL IF THE IDOLATERS OF
BULL PREFACE(59) GOD WITH THE TRIBUNAL TO THE DISADVANTAGE OF THE LATTER , HE WOULD NO DOUBT HAVE HAD FIFTY LASHES BEFORE HIS
SUPR HANDBOK(224) ROUTINEER AND THE DEEPEST THINKER APPEARS, TO THE LATTER , TRIFLING; TO THE FORMER, INFINITE. IN A STUPID

LATTER-DAY
GETT PREFACE(211) NATIONS HAVE NOT GRAVITATED TO MONOGAMY, LIKE THE LATTER-DAY SAINTS OF SALT LAKE CITY. THE ANSWER IS NOT FAR

LATTICED
MRS I SD(181) WITH ITS THATCHED ROOF AND PORCH, AND A LARGE LATTICED WINDOW TO THE LEFT OF THE PORCH. A PALING
DEVL II SD(29) A PRETTY FEATURE OF THE ROOM IS THE LOW WIDE LATTICED WINDOW, NEARLY ITS WHOLE WIDTH, WITH LITTLE RED
MRS II SD(198) FROM WITHIN INSTEAD OF WESTWARD FROM WITHOUT, THE LATTICED WINDOW, WITH ITS CURTAINS DRAWN, IS NOW SEEN IN THE

LAUD
SUPR HANDBOK(202) REFORMED IMPRISONMENT WITH AS LITTLE REMORSE AS LAUD AND HIS STAR CHAMBER CLIPPED THE EARS OF BASTWICK AND
LION PREFACE(86) TO DO WITH HIM. IT IS PROBABLE THAT ARCHBISHOP LAUD AND JOHN WESLEY DIED EQUALLY PERSUADED THAT HE IN WHOSE
SUPR HANDBOK(197) THAT THE NATION WHICH SHEEPISHLY LET CHARLES AND LAUD AND STRAFFORD COERCE IT, GAINED ANYTHING BECAUSE IT
POSN PREFACE(421) WILL HAVE ALL THE QUALIFICATIONS OF ARCHBISHOP LAUD . NOW I HAVE NO GUARANTEE THAT ANY MEMBER OF THE
POSN PREFACE(421) EVER HEARD OF THE STAR CHAMBER OR OF ARCHBISHOP LAUD . ONE OF THEM DID NOT KNOW THAT POLITICS MEANT ANYTHING
JOAN PREFACE(39) THE INQUISITION AND STAGGERED ARCHBISHOP LAUD . OUR CREDULITY IS GROSSER THAN THAT OF THE MIDDLE
SIM PREFACE(10) IF IT HAD CALLED ITSELF AN INQUISITION AND GIVEN LAUD THE OFFICIAL TITLE BORNE BY TORQUEMADA. IN THE END ALL
CYMB V (149) WHICH SHINES HERE IN THE WEST. /CYMBELINE/ LAUD WE THE GODS, AND LET OUR CROOKED SMOKES CLIMB TO THEIR

LAUDABLE
GETT PREFACE(205) WITH AN INKY PENKNIFE, HER OBJECT WAS ENTIRELY LAUDABLE : HER HEART WAS IS THE RIGHT PLACE: A STATESMAN
JOAN EPILOG (164) IN EVERY SUCH CHURCH, AND IT SHALL BE LAWFUL AND LAUDABLE FOR THE FAITHFUL TO KNEEL AND ADDRESS THEIR PRAYERS
JOAN 6 (130) INCEST, HERESY AT FIRST SEEMS INNOCENT AND EVEN LAUDABLE ; BUT IT ENDS IN SUCH A MONSTROUS HORROR OF

LAUDATORES
DOCT PREFACE(54) NOW (SUCH OLD GENTLEMEN GREATLY OUTNUMBER THE LAUDATORES TEMPORI ACTI), WILL ASSUME THAT THE FORMER

LAUDATORY
SIM PREFACE(3) THERE IS NO TROUBLE: THE PRESS NOTICES ARE LAUDATORY IF THE PLAY IS ENTERTAINING. EVEN IF THE TWO ARE
POSN PREFACE(385) TOM PAINE'S CENTENARY WOULD BE THE SUBJECT OF A LAUDATORY SPECIAL ARTICLE IN THE TIMES; AND ONLY A FEW

LAUDED
HART PREFACE(36) PERHAPS THAT IS THE REAL REASON WHY THE CHURCH IS LAUDED AND THE THEATRE REVILED. WHETHER OR NO, THE FACT

LAUGH
PLES PREFACE(R16) IT IS NOTHING TO ME THAT THE SPECTATORS LAUGH : ANY FOOL CAN MAKE AN AUDIENCE LAUGH. I WANT TO SEE
BULL IV (162) LAUGHTER AGAINST HIS COLLAR BONE) OH DONT MAKE ME LAUGH : PLEASE DONT MAKE ME LAUGH. /BROADBENT/ (TERRIFIED)
ANNA (296) WITH SUPPRESSED MIRTH. /STRAMMFEST/ WHY DONT YOU LAUGH ? DONT YOU APPRECIATE HER IMPERIAL HIGHNESS'S JOKE..
DEVL II (38) LAUGHS SOFTLY). /JUDITH/ (QUICKLY) WHY DO YOU LAUGH ? /RICHARD/ I WAS THINKING THAT IF ANY STRANGER CAME
INCA (245) /ERMYNTRUDE/ HOW CHEERFUL! CAN HE LAUGH ? /THE INCA/ CERTAINLY, MADAM. (HE LAUGHS, HARSHLY
ARMS I (16) STIFLES A LAUGH). /RAINA/ (QUICKLY) WHY DO YOU LAUGH ? /THE MAN/ (APOLOGETIC, BUT STILL GREATLY TICKLED)
JITT III SD(70) INTO THE CORRIDOR). JITTA, LEFT ALONE, BEGINS TO LAUGH AGAIN HYSTERICALLY, AND IS DISSOLVING INTO CONVULSIVE
CLEO IV SD(169) WELL: WE MUST TRY TO LIVE UP TO CAESAR. THEY LAUGH AGAIN. CLEOPATRA RAGES SILENTLY AS SHE CONTINUES TO
CLEO IV (167) IS SERVED, /CHARMIAN/ OLD HOOKNOSE! (THEY LAUGH AGAIN). /CLEOPATRA/ (REVOLTED) SILENCE. CHARMIAN: DO
LADY PREFACE(220) THE WORLD'S MISERY WITHOUT BLENCHING, THERE IS A LAUGH ALWAYS READY TO AVENGE ITS TEARS OF DISCOURAGEMENT. IN
BULL IV (162) CRYNA-- /NORA/ (SPLUTTERING INTO A HYSTERICAL LAUGH AND CLUTCHING HIM CONVULSIVELY WITH HER FINGERS WHILE
PLES PREFACE(R16) NOW IN THE EFFORT TO BEAR HAPPINESS, WHILST WE LAUGH AND EXULT IN DESTRUCTION, CONFUSION, AND RUIN. WHEN A
BARB I (257) YOUR FATHER NEVER COULD ANSWER THAT: HE USED TO LAUGH AND GET OUT OF IT UNDER COVER OF SOME AFFECTIONATE
APPL I (231) THE OLD FOX; AND THEN AMANDA MUST HAVE HER SILLY LAUGH AND LETS HIM OUT OF IT (HE SITS), /NICOBAR/ WHAT ARE
JOAN 2 (82) BE HANGED IN YOURS IF YOU DO NOT LEARN WHEN TO LAUGH AND WHEN TO PRAY. /BLUEBEARD/ MY LORD: I STAND
JITT III? (69) WITH A DESPERATE EFFORT. /JITTA/ DONT MAKE ME LAUGH ANY MORE: I AM AFRAID I SHALL GO INTO HYSTERICS. I AM
BUOY III (38) SECONDBORN, WHO SNORTS. /SIR F./ WHAT IS THERE TO LAUGH AT? CAN WE NOT BE SENSIBLE AND PRACTICAL? WE ARE
BULL IV (145) ARRA HOLD YOUR NOISE, BARNEY. WHAT IS THERE TO LAUGH AT? /DORAN/ IT GOT ITS FUT INTO THE LITTLE HWEEL-- (
MTH5 (259) HA! HA! HA! /ADAM/ WHO LAUGHS? WHO DARES LAUGH AT ADAM? /EVE/ WHO HAS THE HEART TO LAUGH AT EVE?
JITT III (69) VERY FAR FROM WELL. /AGNES/ IT'S SUCH A SHAME TO LAUGH AT ALL AT SUCH A TIME. BUT FOR THE LIFE OF ME I
AUGS PREFACE(261) SAVE FOR THE SATISFACTION OF BEING ABLE TO LAUGH AT AUGUSTUS IN THE THEATRE, NOTHING, AS FAR AS I KNOW,
GENV IV (102) NUMBED WITH MISERY AND TERROR AS WELL AS HOW TO LAUGH AT DEATH. ASK MY UNDERSTUDY HERE. HE TOO HAS BEEN A
MTH5 (259) DARES LAUGH AT ADAM? /EVE/ WHO HAS THE HEART TO LAUGH AT EVE? /THE VOICE/ THE GHOST OF CAIN, THE FIRST
DEST (167) SHE HAD FOUND IT NO LAUGHING MATTER) AH, YOU CAN LAUGH AT FEAR. THEN YOU DONT KNOW WHAT FEAR IS. /NAPOLEON/
CLEO II (142) NOT GO. LET HIM GO (POINTING TO RUFIO. THEY ALL LAUGH AT HER). OH PLEASE, PLEASE DONT GO. WHAT WILL HAPPEN
MTH5 SD(219) NOT TO DO. I FEEL THE NEED OF EDUCATION. THEY ALL LAUGH AT HER, EXCEPT THE SHE-ANCIENT. /THE SHE-ANCIENT/ YOU
KING I SD(207) THEN ALL THE REST SHALL BE ADDED TO YOU. THEY ALL LAUGH AT HIM EXCEPT CHARLES. /CHARLES/ A CROWN IS NOT SO
BULL I (93) AT HIS EASE WHILE HIS ENEMIES LET HIM ALONE AND LAUGH AT HIM FOR BEING A FOOL LIKE THE REST. OH, NATURE IS
OVER (178) LIKE SOMETHING TO DRINK. BUT I HAVE NO RIGHT TO LAUGH AT HIM. MY CHRISTIAN NAME IS GREGORY, WHICH SOUNDS
BUOY III SD(44) /SIR F./ I AM NOT MARRIED. I AM A BACHELOR. THEY LAUGH AT HIM. /SIR F./ WHAT ARE YOU ALL LAUGHING AT? AM I
GENV IV (88) NOT A SOUL EXCEPT OURSELVES! ALL EUROPE WILL LAUGH AT HIM. /THE SECRETARY/ YES; BUT IF THE AFFAIR IS
JOAN 2,SD(73) BEGINNING, CAPTAIN. BLUEBEARD AND LA TREMOUILLE LAUGH AT HIM. THE PAGE RETURNS. /THE PAGE/ HIS MAJESTY. THEY
LION II (129) TO HAVE JUST ONE MORE GOOD TIME. (THE GLADIATORS LAUGH AT HIM). OH, WILL NO ONE TELL ME WHERE THE ALTAR IS..
CATH 1,SD(162) HAS A WILD SENSE OF HUMOR, WHICH ENABLES HIM TO LAUGH AT HIMSELF AS WELL AS AT EVERYBODY ELSE. IN THE EYES
BARB PREFACE(209) INFATUATE COURAGE OF TAPPERTIT. BUT WE DARE NOT LAUGH AT HIM, BECAUSE, SOMEHOW, WE RECOGNIZE OURSELVES IN
DEST (184) INTERRUPTING AS HE MASTERS THE PLOT) AND HAVE THE LAUGH AT HIM! I SAY: WHAT A JOLLY CLEVER WOMAN YOU ARE! (
BULL PREFACE(26) WAS GONE WAS NOT A WHIT MORE FOOLISH THAN WE WHO LAUGH AT HIS IGNORANCE OF THE NATURE OF POETRY WHILST WE

BARB I (260)	MARCH. /LADY BRITOMART/ I SEE NOTHING TO	LAUGH	AT IN THAT; NOR SHOULD YOU IF YOU ARE REALLY
GETT (340)	MERCHANT'S WIFE? /MRS GEORGE/ MANY PEOPLE WOULD	LAUGH	AT IT. /THE BISHOP/ POOR PEOPLE! IT'S SO HARD TO KNOW
MRS PREFACE(173)	CASE (AT LEAST WE ARE SAVAGE ENOUGH TO	LAUGH	AT IT); BUT IN BOTH CASES IT IS ILLOGICAL, AND IN BOTH
GETT (326)	AS SHE DESCRIBED. /SYKES/ WELL, SUPPOSE YOU DID!	LAUGH	AT IT, MAN. /HOTCHKISS/ AT THAT, YES. BUT THERE WAS
OVER (186)	THOUGHTLESS PEOPLE I MAY EVEN APPEAR COMIC. WELL,	LAUGH	AT ME: I HAVE GIVEN MYSELF AWAY. BUT MRS LUNN SEEMS TO
SUPR PREFACE(R15)	WHOSE ART NO HUMAN HAND CAN IMPROVE? YOU WOULD	LAUGH	AT ME IF AT THIS TIME OF DAY I DEALT IN DUELS AND
DOCT I (91)	/SIR PATRICK/ WELL? WHAT IS IT? /RIDGEON/ DONT	LAUGH	AT ME. I WANT YOUR ADVICE. /SIR PATRICK/ PROFESSIONAL
DOCT I (83)	MALTESE FEVER AND THE LIKE. NOW HE'LL HAVE A RARE	LAUGH	AT ME. /REDPENNY/ SERVE YOU RIGHT! IT WAS LIKE YOUR
OVER (176)	I CANT FEEL HONEST. DONT PRETEND TO DESPISE ME OR	LAUGH	AT ME. YOU FEEL IT TOO. YOU SAID JUST NOW THAT YOUR
ARMS III (53)	A THING FOR YOU, WHO CARE NO MORE-- EXCEPT TO	LAUGH	AT ME-- OH! ARE YOU SURE NOBODY HAS TOUCHED IT?
CLEO IV (168)	/CLEOPATRA/ IF YOU WERE NOT A FOOL, YOU WOULD	LAUGH	AT ME; AND IF YOU WERE NOT A COWARD YOU WOULD NOT BE
BASH I (93)	JOYOUS COMFORTABLE CHATTER THESE STOLEN FEATHERS.	LAUGH	AT ME, THE CLOTHED ONE. LAUGH AT THE MIND FED ON FOUL
PPP (196)	BRAINS, AT MY NATIONAL INSTITUTIONS; BUT IF YOU	LAUGH	AT MY CLOTHES, ONE OF US MUST DIE. THUNDER. /FITZ/ I
VWOO 1 (120)	YOU. BUT I DONT THINK IT'S VERY POLITE OF YOU TO	LAUGH	AT MY FATHER. /A/ (PUNCTILIOUSLY-- RECOVERING
PPP (196)	I WARN YOU THAT I AM AN ENGLISHMAN. YOU MAY	LAUGH	AT MY MANNERS, AT MY BRAINS, AT MY NATIONAL
ARMS III (60)	I KILL MYSELF LIKE A MAN, OR LIVE AND PRETEND TO	LAUGH	AT MYSELF? (SHE AGAIN TURNS TO GO). LOUKA! (SHE
LION II SD(130)	BUT ARE HIGHLY AMUSED. ALL SPEAK OR CRY OUT OR	LAUGH	AT ONCE. TUMULT. /LAVINIA/ OH, POOR WRETCH!
ANNA (296)	SOLEMN) I DONT WANT TO, SIR. /STRAMMFEST/	LAUGH	AT ONCE, SIR. I ORDER YOU TO LAUGH. /SCHNEIDEKIND/ (
MRS IV (253)	AND READS IT QUICKLY, GIVING A LITTLE	LAUGH	AT SOME QUAINT TURN OF EXPRESSION IN IT). AND GOODBYE,
BASH PREFACE(91)	BE POSSIBLE TO FIND A GENERAL AUDIENCE WHICH CAN	LAUGH	AT THE ADMIRABLE BASHVILLE AS HEARTILY AS MAURICE
FANY I (279)	TO THE BOY? /DORA/ ONLY FANCY! HE STOPPED TO	LAUGH	AT THE COPPER! HE THOUGHT THE COPPER WOULD SEE THE
INCA PREFACE(231)	SHEWN THAT WE COULD QUITE WELL HAVE AFFORDED TO	LAUGH	AT THE DOOMED INCA, I AM IN ANOTHER DIFFICULTY. I MAY
LION PREFACE(47)	IN A GIVEN VOLUME OF SERUM WHILST I CAN ONLY	LAUGH	AT THE EARLIER ESTIMATES OF THE NUMBER OF ANGELS THAT
SUPR PREFACE(R21)	THEN DISPARAGE IT AS UNWORTHY AND INDELICATE. WE	LAUGH	AT THE HAUGHTY AMERICAN NATION BECAUSE IT MAKES THE
SUPR HANDBOK(180)	OPPOSES IT, EVEN PROPERTY AND MARRIAGE, WHICH	LAUGH	AT THE LABORER'S PETTY COMPLAINT THAT HE IS DEFRAUDED
BARB PREFACE(208)	FASHIONABLE PEOPLE WENT IN PARTIES TO BEDLAM TO	LAUGH	AT THE LUNATICS. I MYSELF HAVE HAD A VILLAGE IDIOT
BASH I (93)	STOLEN FEATHERS. LAUGH AT ME, THE CLOTHED ONE.	LAUGH	AT THE MIND FED ON FOUL AIR AND BOOKS. BOOKS! ART!
JOAN PREFACE(51)	THE ANGELS MAY WEEP AT THE MURDER, BUT THE GODS	LAUGH	AT THE MURDERERS. THE INEVITABLE FLATTERIES OF
LADY PREFACE(222)	WITH YORICK'S SKULL, AND INVITING " MY LADY" TO	LAUGH	AT THE SEPULCHRAL HUMOR OF THE FACT THAT THOUGH SHE
MIS. PREFACE(47)	HARMLESS THEIR ACTIONS MAY BE, WHO VENTURE TO	LAUGH	AT THEIR MONSTROUS CONCEIT OR TO PAY THEIR ASSUMPTIONS
MRS PREFACE(154)	KNOW THAT THEY DO NOT BELIEVE IN IT, AND WOULD	LAUGH	AT THEM IF THEY DID, SO WELL HAVE THE RESCUERS LEARNT
MILL I (143)	OF YOUR LIFE AND ALL THE REST OF IT. HOW CAN I	LAUGH	AT THINGS I DONT KNOW? IF I AM LAUGHING-- AND AM I
CURE (237)	OF RAGE, BEAT YOU. /REGINALD/ OH DO, DO. DONT	LAUGH	AT THIS RIDICULOUS CONFESSION; BUT EVER SINCE I WAS A
LION II (138)	LAVINIA. /LAVINIA/ IS IT PART OF YOUR DUTY TO	LAUGH	AT US? /THE CAPTAIN/ NO: THAT IS PART OF MY PRIVATE
MIS. (121)	AS THEY WORK. /HYPATIA/ I WONDER WHETHER THEY	LAUGH	AT US WHEN THEY ARE BY THEMSELVES! /MRS TARLETON/
NEVR II (248)	TO THE BEACH AND SPEAKING TO HER AGAIN, I'D ONLY	LAUGH	AT YOU. (HE RUSHES BUOYANTLY OFF TO THE STEPS, WHERE
MIS. (202)	SUMMERHAYS, BENTLEY AND ALL. DONT YOU LET THEM	LAUGH	AT YOU. /JOHNNY/ (A GRIN SLOWLY OVERSPREADING HIS
GENV II (58)	A SENTENCE AGAINST ONE OF THEM EUROPE WILL JUST	LAUGH	AT YOU, BECAUSE YOU HAVE NO POWER. IT WILL BE AS
SUPR I (40)	IS GOING TO HAPPEN TO POOR TAVY. /ANN/ I SHOULD	LAUGH	AT YOU, JACK, IF IT WERE NOT FOR POOR PAPA'S DEATH.
CAND III (140)	WITH A QUICK TOUCH OF TEMPER) THERE IS NOTHING TO	LAUGH	AT. ARE YOU LAUGHING AT US, CANDIDA? /CANDIDA/ (WITH
BULL IV (146)	AND LARRY IN FRONT OF IT AND ALL! IT'S NOTHIN TO	LAUGH	AT, MR DORAN. /DORAN/ BEDAD, MISS REILLY, LARRY
JITT III (70)	VERY ODD. HOW DID YOU DO IT? /JITTA/ SHE MADE ME	LAUGH	BEFORE I MADE HER SING. YOU MUSTNT BE SHOCKED, DEAR.
LION I (126)	(EACH ANNOUNCEMENT IS RECEIVED WITH A LOUDER	LAUGH	BY ALL THE REST AS THE JOKE CATCHES ON). /CENTURION/ (
KING PREFACE(154)	THE PERIHELION OF MERCURY SO IRRESISTIBLE AS A	LAUGH	CATCHER (LIKE WESTON-SUPER-MARE) THAT I CANNOT BRING
PYGM II SD(221)	THEY TOOK ONE APIECE, AND LEFT THREE IN IT. THEY	LAUGH	HEARTILY AT THEIR OWN WIT. /LIZA/ OH, DONT BE SILLY.
PHIL II SD(123)	SHEWS GRACE A PICTURE IN THE BOOK. THEY BOTH	LAUGH	HEARTILY OVER IT. /JULIA/ WHAT IS HE SHEWING HER?
LION I SD(112)	NO DOUBT BE PERSECUTION. THE CHRISTIANS AGAIN	LAUGH	HEARTILY. /CENTURION/ (HORRIFIED) SILENCE, I TELL
JITT III (69)	/AGNES/ REALLY AND TRULY. /JITTA/ (BEGINNING TO	LAUGH	HYSTERICALLY) HOW FUNNY! /AGNES/ (HER CHUCKLES NOW
MIS. (135)	THE DRAMA OF HIS LIFE AS A SPECTATOR SEES A PLAY.	LAUGH	IF YOU FEEL INCLINED: NO MAN SEES THE COMIC SIDE OF IT
BARB I (266)	QUITE OVERCOME). /BARBARA/ WHY DONT YOU	LAUGH	IF YOU WANT TO, CHOLLY? IT'S GOOD FOR YOUR INSIDE.
PPP (196)	COMPLEXION IS REALLY GOING TO PIECES. WHY DO YOU	LAUGH	IN THAT SILLY WAY AT NOTHING? /FITZ/ NOTHING! HA,
ROCK I (199)	LAUGH. I'D BETTER NOT RISK IT. STRIKE IT OUT. A	LAUGH	IN THE WRONG PLACE IN THE CHURCH HOUSE WOULD BE THE
MTH3 (100)	DEVIL! (HE SNATCHES OUT HIS PEG FURIOUSLY: HER	LAUGH	IS NO LONGER HEARD). OH, THESE SEX EPISODES! WHY CAN
POSN (444)	THESE YEARS. BUT HE CAUGHT ME OUT AT LAST. THE	LAUGH	IS WITH HIM AS FAR AS HANGING ME GOES. (HE THRUSTS
MILL IV (203)	PATRICIA). /SAGAMORE/ (SMILING) I AM AFRAID THE	LAUGH	IS WITH OLD MR SMITH, MRS FITZFASSENDEN. WHEN THERE IS
VWOO 1 (120)	HIMSELF) YOU ARE RIGHT. I WAS RUDE. BUT A GOOD	LAUGH	IS WORTH A HUNDRED POUNDS TO ME. I FEEL A DIFFERENT
CAND III (136)	SHE'LL THINK IVE THROWN YOU INTO HYSTERICS. DONT	LAUGH	. BOISTEROUS VOICES AND LAUGHTER ARE HEARD
CLEO IV SD(169)	AND DO NOT UNDERSTAND THESE MATTERS. THE LADIES	LAUGH	. CLEOPATRA LOOKS INSCRUTABLY AT HIM. /CHARMIAN/ I SEE
CLEO IV (169)	WITH MUCH CONCEIT WASHED OUT OF YOU. (THE LADIES	LAUGH	. CLEOPATRA RISES IMPATIENTLY). BEGONE, ALL OF YOU. I
PHIL II (104)	PARAMORE, WHO RAISES HIS POLITEST CONSULTING-ROOM	LAUGH	. CRAVEN GOES LAST), /CRAVEN/ (AT THE DOOR, GRAVELY)
BULL IV (147)	HAVE MERCY ON US! /NORA/ I DONT KNOW HOW YOU CAN	LAUGH	. DO YOU, MR KEEGAN? /KEEGAN/ (GRIMLY) WHY NOT?
MILL I (143)	! ! ! ! ! /EPIFANIA/ AY: LAUGH, LAUGH,	LAUGH	. FOOL! CLOWN! /SAGAMORE/ (RISING RESOLUTELY AND
JITT III (70)	NOW WHAT I WANT TO KNOW IS HOW I AM TO MAKE YOU	LAUGH	. FOR YOU WILL GO MAD IF YOU DO NOT GET BACK INTO
INCA (245)	/ERMYNTRUDE/ (FRIGIDLY) I ASKED COULD THE INCA	LAUGH	. I DID NOT ASK COULD YOU LAUGH. /THE INCA/ THAT IS
CYMB V (149)	DEAR LADY IT VERY NEARLY DID. /IMOGEN/ I WILL NOT	LAUGH	. I MUST GO HOME AND MAKE THE BEST OF IT AS OTHER
PLES PREFACE(R16)	SPECTATORS LAUGH: ANY FOOL CAN MAKE AN AUDIENCE	LAUGH	. I WANT TO SEE HOW MANY OF THEM, LAUGHING OR GRAVE,
ROCK I (199)	NO: THAT MIGHT GET A LAUGH-- THE WRONG SORT OF	LAUGH	. I'D BETTER NOT RISK IT. STRIKE IT OUT. A LAUGH IN
MTH5 (212)	HA! OH, DEAR! /STREPHON/ WELL, YOU NEED NOT	LAUGH	. IT IS A BEAUTIFUL AND HOLY COMPACT; AND I WILL KEEP
JITT III (70)	NOT HAVE GONE MAD MYSELF IF SHE HAD NOT MADE ME	LAUGH	. (TAKING EDITH BY THE SHOULDERS AND LOOKING STRAIGHT
CYMB V (149)	TO AVENGE YOUR DEATH. /IMOGEN/ OH, DO NOT MAKE ME	LAUGH	. LAUGHTER DISSOLVES TOO MANY JUST RESENTMENTS,
BULL IV (162)	BONE) OH DONT MAKE ME LAUGH: PLEASE DONT MAKE ME	LAUGH	. /BROADBENT/ (TERRIFIED) I DIDNT MEAN TO, ON MY
CAND II (122)	LIGHT OF IT. I SHUDDER WHEN YOU TORTURE HIM AND	LAUGH	. /CANDIDA/ (INCREDULOUSLY) I TORTURE JAMES!
CLEO IV SD(167)	WE CAN EASILY FIND OUT THAT FOR YOU. THE LADIES	LAUGH	. /CLEOPATRA/ (FROWNING) YOU LAUGH; BUT TAKE CARE,
DOCT V (173)	ANY MORE THAN IT CEASES TO BE SERIOUS WHEN PEOPLE	LAUGH	. /JENNIFER/ DR BLENKINSOP SAID ONE VERY STRANGE THING
JITT III (68)	YOU IF I TELL YOU. BUT I AM SURE YOU WILL ONLY	LAUGH	. /JITTA/ (WITH A MELANCHOLY SMILE) WE BOTH NEED A
LION II (138)	INTO THE JAWS OF THE LION. I LAUGHED. I STILL	LAUGH	. /LAVINIA/ THEN YOU DONT UNDERSTAND WHAT THAT MEANT?
MIS. (200)	(SHE LAUGHS). /BENTLEY/ IT'S BEASTLY OF YOU TO	LAUGH	. /LORD SUMMERHAYS/ YOU ARE NOT THE FIRST TO FALL
FANY III (319)	NOISE? IS MASTER BOBBY AT HOME? I HEARD HIS	LAUGH	. /MRS KNOX/ I'M SURE I HEARD MARGARET'S. /GILBEY/ NOT
APPL I SD(217)	THE EVIDENCE AGAINST YOURSELF. ALL THE REST	LAUGH	. /PROTEUS/ (COOLLY) I THANK YOUR MAJESTY FOR THE
ARMS I (15)	LIKE DON QUIXOTE AT THE WINDMILLS. WE DID	LAUGH	. /RAINA/ YOU DARED TO LAUGH! /THE MAN/ YES; BUT WHEN
CAPT III SD(284)	DRINKWATER SPLUTTERS INTO A HALF SUPPRESSED	LAUGH	. /REDBROOK/ (IN A FIERCE WHISPER) SHUT UP, YOU FOOL,
ANNA (296)	/STRAMMFEST/ LAUGH AT ONCE, SIR. I ORDER YOU TO	LAUGH	. /SCHNEIDEKIND/ (WITH A TOUCH OF TEMPER) I REALLY
INCA (245)	COULD THE INCA LAUGH. I DID NOT ASK COULD YOU	LAUGH	. /THE INCA/ THAT IS TRUE, MADAM. (CHUCKLING)
MTH5 SD(207)	NOT INTEREST ME. /THE MAIDEN/ THANK YOU. THEY ALL	LAUGH	. /THE YOUTH/ YOU OLD FISH! I BELIEVE YOU DONT KNOW
CLEO IV (168)	WOULD HAVE CURLED UP, YOU SHALLOW THINGS. (THEY	LAUGH	. SHE TURNS FIERCELY ON IRAS). AT WHOM ARE YOU
KING II (231)	SPOKE ON LAND OR SEA; AND MY PORTUGUESE MADE YOU	LAUGH	. WE MUST FORGET OUR FOOLISH YOUTH: WE ARE GROWN-UP
DOCT II (116)	IT MUST BE TO BE A DOCTOR! (THEY LAUGH). DONT	LAUGH	. YOU DONT KNOW WHAT YOUVE DONE FOR ME. I NEVER KNEW
METH PREFACE(R29)	THAT, AS BETWEEN LYELL AND ARCHBISHOP USSHER, THE	LAUGH	MAY NOT BE WITH LYELL QUITE SO UPROARIOUSLY AS IT
ROCK PREFACE(176)	INTO THE STRATOSPHERE, I DO NOT FEEL HOLY: I	LAUGH	OBSTREPEROUSLY. THE EXALTING VISION HAS SUDDENLY
ARMS III (74)	CREAM SOLDIER! /BLUNTSCHLI/ (WITH A BOYISH	LAUGH	OF DELIGHT) THATLL DO, THANK YOU. (HE LOOKS AT HIS
MRS IV (253)	CONTENT; HER BREATH GOES OUT IN A HALF SOB, HALF	LAUGH	OF INTENSE RELIEF. SHE GOES BUOYANTLY TO HER PLACE AT
ROCK I (204)	DESCRIPTION OF THIS FAMILY; AND YOU WILL GET THE	LAUGH	OF YOUR LIFE. /FLAVIA/ DAMN THE FAMILY! /LADY
SUPR II (67)	MY CHARACTER. YOUR FRIEND MR TANNER HAS GOT THE	LAUGH	ON ME A BIT ALREADY ABOUT THAT; AND-- /VIOLET/ THE
POSN (445)	RIBBONS; BUT STRAPPER KEMP SHALL NEVER HAVE THE	LAUGH	ON ME OVER THAT JOB. LET THEM HANG ME. LET THEM SHOOT.
BULL PREFACE(14)	OF THE ABSURDEST ENGLISHMAN WAS NOT REALLY A	LAUGH	ON THEIR SIDE; THAT HE WOULD SUCCEED WHERE THEY WOULD
BULL IV SD(149)	HAVE BEEN KILT, A YOUNG MAN, FEELING THAT HE MUST	LAUGH	OR BURST, HURRIES OUT. BARNEY PUTS AN IRON CONSTRAINT
SUPR PREFACE(R26)	AS HE GOT HIS MONEY BY." DO YOU KNOW WHETHER TO	LAUGH	OR CRY AT THE NOTION THAT THEY, POOR DEVILS! WILL
DEVL III (66)	THE BAD BROTHER; I'M THE GOOD ONE. (THE OFFICERS	LAUGH	OUTRIGHT. THE SOLDIERS GRIN). /SWINDON/ WHO ARRESTED
CAND I (98)	CONTEMPTUOUS. /MORELL/ (SITTING DOWN TO HAVE HIS	LAUGH	OUT) WHY, MY DEAR CHILD, OF COURSE YOU DO. EVERYBODY
CAND III (136)	MY HEAD IS SPINNING ROUND. I SHALL BEGIN TO	LAUGH	PRESENTLY. /MARCHBANKS/ (FOLLOWING HIM ANXIOUSLY) NO,
CLEO IV (167)	FTATATEETA HAS BEEN VIRTUOUS. (ALL THE LADIES	LAUGH	-- NOT THE SLAVES). POTHINUS HAS BEEN TRYING TO BRIBE
ROCK I (199)	ONE MOTHER." /SIR ARTHUR/ NO: THAT MIGHT GET A	LAUGH	-- THE WRONG SORT OF LAUGH. I'D BETTER NOT RISK IT.
POSN (458)	WITH CROUP. /BLANCO/ (STRANGLING, AND TRYING TO	LAUGH	) A LITTLE CHOKER: THATS THE WORD FOR HIM. HIS CHOKING
NEVR II (255)	MAKES YOU SO INSPIRING. /GLORIA/ (WITH A SLIGHT	LAUGH	) AM I INSPIRING? /VALENTINE/ YES. STRENGTH'S
HART II (90)	A CRIME, WOMAN? /MRS HUSHABYE/ (TRYING NOT TO	LAUGH	) DO YOU MEAN YOU DID IT ON PURPOSE? /GUINNESS/ NOW
ARMS III (59)	THE OFFICERS! ! ! WELL (WITH A SHORT HARSH	LAUGH	) I AM AN OFFICER. OH, (FERVENTLY) GIVE ME THE MAN
HART II (115)	TO ONE THAT IS WILD? /ELLIE/ (WITH A SHORT	LAUGH	) I SUPPOSE SO. WHAT A VILE WORLD IT IS! /CAPTAIN

FANY II (290) AND OFFENDED). /MARGARET/ (WITH A BITTER LITTLE LAUGH) JUST WHAT THE SUFFRAGET SAID TO ME IN HOLLOWAY. HE
CLEO PRO2 (103) WHITHER YOU WILL. /FTATATEETA/ (WITH A DERISIVE LAUGH) NOW I KNOW WHY THE GODS HAVE TAKEN HER OUT OF OUR
MIS. (112) DAMNED NECK FOR YOU. /JOHNNY/ (WITH A DERISIVE LAUGH) TRY IT, MY SON. (BENTLEY GIVES AN INARTICULATE SOB
HART II (85) MONEY HE LOST WAS YOURS. /MANGAN/ (WITH A SOUR LAUGH) WAS MINE! IT IS MINE, MISS ELLIE, AND ALL THE MONEY
JITT I (24) IS IT WORSE? /BRUNO/ (WITH A GHOST OF A LAUGH) WORSE! IT HAS GONE ALL TO PIECES. I HAD NO RIGHT TO
DOCT II (116) GLORIOUS THING IT MUST BE TO BE A DOCTOR! (THEY LAUGH). DONT LAUGH. YOU DONT KNOW WHAT YOUVE DONE FOR ME. I
MIS. (142) OUT HIS HANDS TO PLEAD: SHE TAKES THEM WITH A LAUGH). IF YOU COULD POSSIBLY THINK OF ME AS HALF AN ANGEL
CAPT II (248) AW YEVER SEE Y' AFRIDE OF ENNYBODY. (THE OTHERS LAUGH). /BRASSBOUND/ AFRAID! /DRINKWATER/ (MALICIOUSLY)
CLEO IV (168) THAN BEING RELIGIOUS, AT OUR AGES. (THE LADIES LAUGH). /CLEOPATRA/ CEASE THAT ENDLESS CACKLING, WILL YOU.
CLEO IV (169) THE HAIR AND THROW YOU INTO THE SEA. (THE LADIES LAUGH). /CLEOPATRA/ SHE IS RIGHT, POTHINUS: YOU WILL COME
MTH1 I (19) CHUCKLES AND GOES AWAY SLOWLY, LAUGHING HIS FIRST LAUGH). /EVE/ NOW THE SECRET. THE SECRET. (SHE SITS ON THE
ARMS I (16) DON QUIXOTE: NOT A DOUBT OF IT. (HE STIFLES A LAUGH). /RAINA/ (QUICKLY) WHY DO YOU LAUGH? /THE MAN/ (
LION II (144) PURRS, AND ROARS, ACHIEVES SOMETHING VERY LIKE A LAUGH). /THE EMPEROR/ (STANDING ON A CHAIR INSIDE HIS BOX
MTH5 (217) UP. WE WILL LOVE ONE ANOTHER FOR EVER. (THEY ALL LAUGH). WHAT ARE YOU LAUGHING AT? /THE SHE-ANCIENT/
NEVR III (263) (PHIL AND DOLLY LOOK AT ONE ANOTHER AND STIFLE A LAUGH). WHAT IS IT? /PHILIP/ (SITTING DOWN ON HER LEFT)
APPL I (228) TRICK FROM YOUR MAJESTY. /AMANDA/ (TRIES NOT TO LAUGH)! /MAGNUS/ (GENTLY REPROACHFUL) AMANDA: WHAT IS THE
APPL I (226) CASE. /AMANDA/ (SPLUTTERS INTO AN IRREPRESSIBLE LAUGH)! ! /MAGNUS/ (LOOKS REPROACHFULLY AT AMANDA)!
CAND III (140) IS VERY QUICK-WITTED, JAMES. I HOPE I AM GOING TO LAUGH ; BUT I AM NOT SURE THAT I AM NOT GOING TO BE VERY
CLEO IV (167) THE LADIES LAUGH. /CLEOPATRA/ (FROWNING) YOU LAUGH ; BUT TAKE CARE, TAKE CARE. I WILL FIND OUT SOME DAY
BULL I (95) RISING ALSO, NOT A BIT SNUBBED) HA! HA! YOU MAY LAUGH ; BUT WE SHALL SEE. HOWEVER, DONT LET US ARGUE ABOUT
CAPT III SD(290) UNOBSERVED, GO STRAIGHT OUT OF THEIR SENSES. THEY LAUGH ; THEY DANCE; THEY EMBRACE ONE ANOTHER; THEY SET TO
FANY III (320) A NOISE LIKE THAT? /JUGGINS/ I ASKED THEM NOT TO LAUGH SO LOUDLY, SIR. BUT THE FRENCH GENTLEMAN ALWAYS SETS
JITT III (69) BUT IT'S WICKED OF ME TO MAKE YOU TALK AND LAUGH SO MUCH, AND YOU SO ILL. YOURE VERY PALE, DEAR. CAN I
6CAL SD(106) HER INTO HIS ARMS, LAUGHING BOISTEROUSLY. THE LAUGH SPREADS TO ALL THE SOLDIERS AND COURTIERS. THE WHOLE
BULL PREFACE(13) THEM TO BE SHEWN VERY CLEARLY THAT THE LOUDEST LAUGH THEY COULD RAISE AT THE EXPENSE OF THE ABSURDEST
ARMS III (52) NOBLE ATTITUDE AND THE THRILLING VOICE. (THEY LAUGH TOGETHER). I DID IT WHEN I WAS A TINY CHILD TO MY
CLEO PRO2,SD(103) OF THE KINGS WHOM MY FATHERS SERVED. THE WOMEN LAUGH TRIUMPHANTLY. /BELZANOR/ (WITH GRIM HUMOR)
APPL I SD(211) WAS GREATLY IMPRESSED BY THE PRESIDENT. THEY ALL LAUGH UPROARIOUSLY AT BOANERGES. /BOANERGES/ WHAT IN HELL
APPL I SD(221) I DREAD REVOLUTION. ALL EXCEPT THE TWO WOMEN LAUGH UPROARIOUSLY AT THIS. /BOANERGES/ I MUST JOIN THEM
LION II (130) AT HIS FACE, DEVIL A BETTER! THE EMPEROR WILL LAUGH WHEN HE HEARS OF IT, I CANT HELP SMILING. HA HA HA!
CAND II (122) AS HIMPRESSIVE LOOKIN AS USU'L. /MORELL/ (WITH A LAUGH WHICH IS HALF A SOB) I SUPPOSE NOT. I BEG ALL YOUR
CATH 4 (190) HE WITHERS IT WITH HIS IRONY! HOW HE MAKES YOU LAUGH WHILST HE IS CONVINCING YOU ! HOW SURE ONE FEELS THAT
CLEO PRO2 (98) IS AFRAID OF THE ROMAN SOLDIERS. (THE GUARDSMEN LAUGH WITH BOISTEROUS SCORN). PEASANTS, BROUGHT UP TO SCARE
JOAN EPILOG (160) DO IS GNASH THEIR TEETH, HELL FASHION; AND I JUST LAUGH , AND GO OFF SINGING THE OLD CHANTY: RUM TUM TRUMPLE
JOAN 2,SD(81) GILLES, WITH A GESTURE OF SURRENDER, JOINS IN THE LAUGH , AND JUMPS DOWN FROM THE DAIS BESIDE LA TREMOUILLE.
CATH 2,SD(177) THE COURTIERS SEE THAT SHE IS TRYING NOT TO LAUGH , AND KNOW BY EXPERIENCE THAT SHE WILL NOT SUCCEED.
ARMS II (37) IN HIS CHIVALRY, THROWS IT OFF WITH A BITTER LAUGH , AND SAYS SLIGHTINGLY) OH! YOU WISH TO BE PAID FOR
JOAN 2 (80) LAUGHTER. /BLUEBEARD/ (TRYING NOT TO LAUGH , AND WAVING HIS HAND IN DEPRECATION OF THEIR
MRS I (190) HIS HANDS BEHIND HIS BACK. MRS WARREN PRETENDS TO LAUGH , BUT LOOKS AFTER HIM WITH PERCEPTIBLE CONCERN. THEN
LION I (111) IS. /LAVINIA/ BUT I THINK THE CAPTAIN MEANT US TO LAUGH , CENTURION. IT WAS SO FUNNY. /CENTURION/ YOULL FIND
JITT III (68) (WITH A MELANCHOLY SMILE) WE BOTH NEED A GOOD LAUGH , DONT WE? /AGNES/ HAVE YOU EVER FOUND THAT YOU HAVE
BUOY III SD(38) THE BRITISH MARRIAGE LAW ANOTHER. ALL THE REST LAUGH , EXCEPT MRS SECONDBORN, WHO SNORTS. /SIR F./ WHAT IS
MIS. (177) NO, NO. (SHE BREAKS OFF IN A STIFLED HALF LAUGH , HALF SCREAM, AND IS SEEN DARTING ACROSS THE GARDEN
NEVR II (240) AT HER, M'COMAS! LOOK AT HER; AND (WITH A HALF LAUGH , HALF SOB) LOOK AT ME! /PHILIP/ SH! (POINTING TO
PHIL I (81) ON HER SHOULDERS). /JULIA/ (WITH A BITTER HALF LAUGH , HALF SOB) WELL, I SUPPOSE I MUST DO WHAT I AM TOLD.
ARMS I (16) (APOLOGETIC, BUT STILL GREATLY TICKLED) I DIDNT LAUGH , I ASSURE YOU. AT LEAST I DIDNT MEAN TO. BUT WHEN I
GETT (340) PEOPLE! IT'S SO HARD TO KNOW THE RIGHT PLACE TO LAUGH , ISNT IT? /MRS GEORGE/ I DIDNT MEAN TO MAKE YOU
MILL I (143) LAUGHTER) ! ! ! ! ! /EPIFANIA/ AY: LAUGH, LAUGH , LAUGH. FOOL! CLOWN! /SAGAMORE/ (RISING RESOLUTELY
MILL I (143) LAUGHTER) ! ! ! ! ! /EPIFANIA/ AY: LAUGH , LAUGH, LAUGH. FOOL! CLOWN! /SAGAMORE/ (RISING
CATH 1 (172) HIS REAL NAME? POPOF, OF COURSE. WHY DO YOU LAUGH , LITTLE FATHER? /EDSTASTON/ HOW CAN ANYONE WITH A
HART II (91) WOKE UP. (MRS HUSHABYE SPLUTTERS). OH, YOU MAY LAUGH , MRS HUSHABYE; BUT I MIGHT HAVE BEEN KILLED. /MRS
CAPT III (298) AND IVE HEARD YOU SAY NOTHING THAT DIDNT MAKE ME LAUGH , OR MAKE ME FEEL FRIENDLY, AS WELL AS TELLING ME WHAT
APPL PREFACE(175) MIGHT SURPRISE THOSE WHO, BECAUSE HE MAKES THEM LAUGH , SEE NOTHING IN HIM BUT A CARICATURE. IN SHORT, THOSE
INCA (255) HALF ROUND THE ROOM). /ERMYNTRUDE/ YOU MAY LAUGH , SIR; BUT I REALLY COULD NOT LIVE IN THAT STYLE. I AM
MTH5 (252) THEM; AND THE ANCIENTS, WHO HAD FORGOTTEN HOW TO LAUGH , SMILED GRIMLY WHEN THEY PASSED. /THE HE-ANCIENT/ WE
SUPR PREFACE(R33) IT LIVE AND MOVE, THEY FOUND, UNLESS IT MADE THEM LAUGH , THAT THEY HAD A PUPPET ON THEIR HANDS, AND HAD TO
WIDO II SD(33) /SARTORIUS/ (RALLYING HIM) INDEED! HA, HA! THE LAUGH , THE FIRST THEY HAVE HEARD FROM HIM, SETS TRENCH'S
MTH5 (224) (AS BEFORE) HE! /ARJILLAX/ (STUNG) WHY DO YOU LAUGH , YOU WHO HAVE COME EMPTY-HANDED, AND, IT SEEMS,
BULL I (88) DO YOURSELF. AND ALL THE TIME YOU LAUGH! LAUGH! LAUGH ! ETERNAL DERISION, ETERNAL ENVY, ETERNAL FOLLY,
BULL I (88) DARENT DO YOURSELF, AND ALL THE TIME YOU LAUGH! LAUGH ! LAUGH! ETERNAL DERISION, ETERNAL ENVY, ETERNAL
BULL I (88) YOU DARENT DO YOURSELF, AND ALL THE TIME YOU LAUGH ! LAUGH! LAUGH! ETERNAL DERISION, ETERNAL ENVY,
ARMS I (15) THE WINDMILLS. WE DID LAUGH. /RAINA/ YOU DARED TO LAUGH ! /THE MAN/ YES; BUT WHEN THE SERGEANT RAN UP AS

LAUGHABLE

PLES PREFACE(R17) AS TRIVIAL AND TRIVIAL AS IMPORTANT, SERIOUS AS LAUGHABLE AND LAUGHABLE AS SERIOUS, AND SO FORTH. AS TO THIS
PLES PREFACE(R17) TRIVIAL AS IMPORTANT, SERIOUS AS LAUGHABLE AND LAUGHABLE AS SERIOUS, AND SO FORTH. AS TO THIS FORMULA I CAN
2TRU III (88) HIMSELF IN THE PRODUCTION OF FANTASTIC AND LAUGHABLE CREATURES TO PEOPLE A NOAH'S ARK FOR HIS BABY. I

LAUGHED

CAND I (95) BEING NICE TO HIM. /MARCHBANKS/ OUGHT I TO HAVE LAUGHED ? I NOTICED THAT HE SAID SOMETHING FUNNY; BUT I AM
CLEO PRO1 (91) ARE THE GODS; AND POMPEY IS A FOOL." AND THE GODS LAUGHED AND APPROVED; AND ON THE FIELD OF PHARSALIA THE
MTH5 (247) HAVE PLAYED WITH THEM; AND YOU WOULD ALL HAVE LAUGHED AND PLAYED WITH THEM TOO UNTIL YOU HAD TORN THEM TO
MIS. (197) THAT IT WAS JUST LIKE KICKING ANY OTHER MAN. HE LAUGHED AND SAID THAT IT WAS THE OLD MAN THAT KNEW WHAT IT
BULL PREFACE(67) DONE TO THESE CITIES IN TWO AND A HALF YEARS, I LAUGHED AND SAID, " YOU SHOULD SEE WHAT THE BRITISH
SUPR HANDBOK(180) SLAVES OF THE WEDDING RING, WILL THEMSELVES BE LAUGHED ASIDE AS THE LIGHTEST OF TRIFLES IF THEY CROSS THIS
JOAN PREFACE(25) APPROPRIATE MUTILATIONS ON HER ASSAILANTS, CAN BE LAUGHED AT AS THEY ARE INTENDED TO BE WITHOUT SCRUPLE; FOR
JOAN 6 (150) OF THE PEOPLE LAUGHED AT HER. THEY WOULD HAVE LAUGHED AT CHRIST. THEY WERE FRENCH PEOPLE, MY LORD: I KNOW
PYGM EPILOG (298) AND CLARA LOST NO FRIENDS BY HER FOLLIES. THEY LAUGHED AT HER TO HER FACE THIS TIME; AND SHE HAD TO DEFEND
JOAN 6 (150) (SHAKEN WITH A CONVULSION) SOME OF THE PEOPLE LAUGHED AT HER. THEY WOULD HAVE LAUGHED AT CHRIST. THEY WERE
UNPL PREFACE(R10) THAT PEOPLE OF MY AGE WERE ON THE SHELF; AND I LAUGHED AT HIM WITH THE WRONG SIDE OF MY MOUTH. IT WAS AT
FANY III (302) NOTHING. HE EXAGGERATED GROSSLY. I ONLY LAUGHED AT HIM. /MARGARET/ (JUMPING UP, TRIUMPHANT) IVE
LION II (138) PLEASURE. YOUR FRIEND HERE IS A HUMORIST. I LAUGHED AT HIS TELLING YOU TO THINK OF YOURSELF TO KEEP UP
KING I (182) NOT KNOW THE MEANING OF THE WORD RELIGION. HE LAUGHED AT IT IN FRANCE. HE HATED IT IN SCOTLAND. IN ENGLAND
SUPR III (90) ALL DUTY, TRAMPLED HONOR UNDERFOOT, AND LAUGHED AT JUSTICE! /THE OLD WOMAN/ OH, WHAT DO I CARE WHY
NEVR II (247) TO ME AS THAT GIRL SPOKE? WOULD ONE OF THEM HAVE LAUGHED AT ME AS THAT BOY WAS LAUGHING AT ME ALL THE TIME..
SUPR I (37) A NEW PERSON; AND THOSE WHO KNEW THE OLD PERSON LAUGHED AT ME. THE ONLY MAN WHO BEHAVED SENSIBLY WAS MY
MTH1 II (21) MY ROOTS, MY FRUIT. USELESS: NOTHING HAPPENED. HE LAUGHED AT ME; AND THEN CAME MY GREAT IDEA: WHY NOT KILL HIM
CURE (229) /THE DOCTOR/ THE CROCODILE! /REGINALD/ YES. IT LAUGHED AT ME, AND WAS GOING TO PLAY THE PIANO WITH ITS
CAND I (95) BOY, EUGENE. (WITH ALL YOUR QUEERNESS. IF YOU HAD LAUGHED AT MY FATHER I SHOULDNT HAVE MINDED; BUT I LIKE YOU
ARMS I (15) COULDNT FIRE A ROUND FOR THE NEXT TEN MINUTES, WE LAUGHED AT THE OTHER SIDE OF OUR MOUTHS. I NEVER FELT SO
MTH5 (225) SMASHED THEM? /MARTELLUS/ I DID. THAT IS WHY I LAUGHED AT YOU JUST NOW. YOU WILL SMASH YOURS BEFORE YOU
MILL I (142) THIS. I HAVE NO SENSE OF HUMOR. I WILL NOT BE LAUGHED AT. /SAGAMORE/ I SHOULD NOT DREAM OF LAUGHING AT A
GETT (356) AMUSEMENT IT IS TO GO TO THE THEATRES WHERE IT IS LAUGHED AT. SOAMES: YOURE A COMMUNIST, ARNT YOU? /SOAMES/ I
6CAL PREFACE(91) AND CONCUPISCENT OLD WOMEN ARE THINGS TO BE LAUGHED AT. THE SIX OF CALAIS IS AN ACTING PIECE AND NOTHING
NEVR II SD(226) AND UNCONSCIOUS. STILL, HE IS BY NO MEANS TO BE LAUGHED AT. THERE IS NO SIGN OF STUPIDITY OR INFIRMITY OF
HART PREFACE(22) WITH A ROMANCE THAT ANY DIPLOMATIST WOULD HAVE LAUGHED AT. THUS THE NATURAL CONFUSION OF IGNORANCE WAS
BARB PREFACE(214) THEM BY INOCULATION WITH SMALLPOX, I SHOULD BE LAUGHED AT; FOR THOUGH NOBODY COULD DENY THAT THE RESULT
MTH2 (88) HOLD OUR TONGUES ABOUT IT, CON. WE SHOULD ONLY BE LAUGHED AT, AND LOSE THE LITTLE CREDIT WE EARNED ON FALSE
SUPR I (8) A BOY TO HIM: HIS OPINIONS WERE SOMETHING TO BE LAUGHED AT, LIKE A MAN'S HAT ON A CHILD'S HEAD. BUT NOW
PPP (196) MY CLOTHES. ONE OF US MUST DIE. THUNDER. /FITZ/ I LAUGHED BUT AT THE IRONY OF FATE (HE TAKES A GAZOGENE FROM
MTH4 I (141) AT LEAST A HUNDRED AND FIFTY YEARS SINCE I LAST LAUGHED . BUT IF YOU DO THAT ANY MORE I SHALL CERTAINLY
LION II (138) AND RAN RIGHT INTO THE JAWS OF THE LION. I LAUGHED . I STILL LAUGH. /LAVINIA/ THEN YOU DONT UNDERSTAND
FABL PREFACE(95) WAS AN ABSURDITY, INSTEAD OF ENLIGHTENING ME HE LAUGHED (HE HAD AN ENGAGING SMILE AND WAS A MOST ATTRACTIVE
MTH5 (247) HAD TORN THEM TO PIECES; AND THEN YOU WOULD HAVE LAUGHED MORE THAN EVER. /THE NEWLY BORN/ OF COURSE WE
BULL IV (151) IT'S ALL UP WITH HIS CANDIDATURE. HE'LL BE LAUGHED OUT O THE TOWN. /LARRY/ (TURNING QUICKLY FROM THE
PHIL I (87) A NAME FOR A CLUB! THE IBSEN CLUB! I SHOULD BE LAUGHED OUT OF LONDON. THE IBSEN CLUB! COME, CUTHBERTSON!
LION PREFACE(49) HIS ROBE WHEN HE WAS IN A HURRY, OR WHETHER HE LAUGHED OVER THE REPARTEES BY WHICH HE BAFFLED THE PRIESTS

GENV IV (92)	NO SENSE OF HUMOR) SMILE! HE WAS NOT SMILING: HE	LAUGHED	RIGHT OUT. WITH ALL RESPECT TO YOUR WORSHIP WE ARE
APPL PREFACE(195)	A MAN LIKE THAT? HE WAS NAIVELY SURPRISED WHEN I	LAUGHED	; AND HE WENT AWAY ONLY HALF PERSUADED THAT HIS
CLEO PRO1 (93)	TO CAESAR, AND MANKIND SHUDDERED: BUT THE GODS	LAUGHED	; FOR SEPTIMIUS WAS BUT A KNIFE THAT POMPEY HAD
CLEO PRO1 (90)	THERE CAME A NEW ROME, RICH AND HUGE. AND I, RA,	LAUGHED	; FOR THE MINDS OF THE ROMANS REMAINED THE SAME SIZE
O'FL PREFACE(202)	BROUGHT TO YOUR OWN HEARTHS AND HOMES? DUBLIN	LAUGHED	SOURLY. AS FOR ME, I ADDRESSED MYSELF QUITE SIMPLY
MILL I (158)	QUARTER TONE SHARP OR FLAT AS THE CASE MAY BE, I	LAUGHED	UNTIL I FELL ON THE FLOOR OF MY BOX IN SCREAMING
BULL IV (147)	IN FRONT OF THE CAR, AND-- /KEEGAN/ AND EVERYBODY	LAUGHED	! /NORA/ DONT GO OVER THAT AGAIN, PLEASE, MR DORAN.
		LAUGHER	
MTH2 (88)	THAT HE IS GOING TO DO IT, AND MAY BE THE LOUDEST	LAUGHER	OF THE LOT. /SAVVY/ OR THE FIRST WOMAN? /CONRAD/ (
		LAUGHEST	
CLEO PRO2 (97)	DOWN BEHIND HIM. /BELZANOR/ WHO ARE THOU THAT	LAUGHEST	IN THE HOUSE OF CLEOPATRA THE QUEEN, AND IN THE
SHAK (141)	WELL DONE, AUSTRALIA! SHAV LAUGHS. /SHAKES/	LAUGHEST	THOU AT THYSELF? PULLST THOU MY LEG? /SHAV/ THERE
		LAUGHIN	
BULL IV (148)	CAR, N NOT A MAN IN THE TOWN ABLE TO SPEAK FOR	LAUGHIN	-- /KEEGAN/ (WITH INTENSE EMPHASIS) IT IS HELL: IT
BULL IV (148)	THROUGH THE LITTLE CROWD. /CORNELIUS/ WHISHT YOUR	LAUGHIN	, BOYS! HERE HE IS. (HE PUTS HIS HAT ON THE
		LAUGHING	
BULL II (114)	SEIZES HER ARMS, TO HER GREAT INDIGNATION). STOP	LAUGHING	: DO YOU HEAR? I AM IN EARNEST: IN ENGLISH
CATH 1 (172)	HOW CAN ANYONE WITH A SENSE OF HUMOR HELP	LAUGHING	? POP OFF! (HE IS CONVULSED). /VARINKA/ (
MILL I (143)	I DONT KNOW? IF I AM LAUGHING-- AND AM I REALLY	LAUGHING	? -- I ASSURE YOU I AM LAUGHING, NOT AT YOUR
JITT II (41)	DEAR LADY, GOOD-BYE. /AGNES/ GOODBYE. (TO EDITH,	LAUGHING	A LITTLE MALICIOUSLY) SINCE YOU ARE SO STRONG,
BULL PREFACE(14)	IT EAGERLY AND SMACKED THEIR LIPS OVER IT,	LAUGHING	ALL THE MORE HEARTILY BECAUSE THEY FELT THAT THEY
HART I (77)	NEVER BEEN ABLE TO REPEAT IT. /MRS HUSHABYE/ (	LAUGHING	AND CARESSING HIS ARM) WE WERE FRIGHTFULLY IN LOVE
LION I (111)	THESE CHRISTIANS: EVERY DAY, SIR. THEYRE ALWAYS	LAUGHING	AND JOKING SOMETHING SCANDALOUS. THEYVE NO
DEST (185)	ON THE COUCH TO ENJOY THE JOKE). /NAPOLEON/ (	LAUGHING	AND PINCHING GIUSEPPE'S EAR) YOU ARE THROWN AWAY IN
JITT III (71)	TO FEEL NATURALLY, SOMEHOW, MY MOTHER'S	LAUGHING	AND SINGING HAS MADE NONSENSE OF IT ALL SUDDENLY.
POSN (459)	HE GAVE ME THE HORSE, AND WENT AWAY CRYING AND	LAUGHING	AND SINGING DREADFUL DIRTY WICKED WORDS TO HYMN
ARMS I (5)	THEM IN EVERY BATTLE FOR ALL THAT. /RAINA/ (	LAUGHING	AND SNUGGLING AGAINST HER MOTHER) YES: I WAS ONLY A
CLEO II (132)	(HE GOES OUT THROUGH THE LOGGIA). /CAESAR/ (	LAUGHING	APPROVINGLY) BRAVE BOY! /CLEOPATRA/ (JEALOUS OF
PYGM III (259)	GET HOME. /PICKERING/ RIPPING. (BOTH ARE HEARD	LAUGHING	AS THEY GO DOWNSTAIRS). /MRS HIGGINS/ (RISES WITH
BUOY III (44)	THEY LAUGH AT HIM. /SIR F./ WHAT ARE YOU ALL	LAUGHING	AT? AM I EXPECTED TO SUBSTITUTE PERSONAL
PYGM III (252)	/LIZA/ IF I WAS DOING IT PROPER, WHAT WAS YOU	LAUGHING	AT? (TO HIGGINS) HAVE I SAID ANYTHING I OUGHTNT?
CLEO II (141)	OUT LAUGHING AT HIM). /CAESAR/ WHAT ARE YOU	LAUGHING	AT? /CLEOPATRA/ YOURE BALD (BEGINNING WITH A BIG
DEST (177)	ANGRILY MOCKING HER). HA! HA! HA! WHAT ARE YOU	LAUGHING	AT? /LADY/ AT YOU, GENERAL. I HAVE OFTEN SEEN
BULL III (123)	PURPOSE IN ENGLAND). /BROADBENT/ WHAT ARE YOU	LAUGHING	AT? /LARRY/ (STOPPING DEAD) I DONT KNOW. THATS
HART III (133)	(THEY ALL BURST OUT LAUGHING). WHAT ARE YOU ALL	LAUGHING	AT? /MRS HUSHABYE/ OH, ALFRED, ALFRED! /ELLIE/
APPL I (211)	AT BOANERGES. /BOANERGES/ WHAT IN HELL ARE YOU	LAUGHING	AT? /PROTEUS/ TAKE NO NOTICE OF THEM, BILL: THEY
MTH2 (79)	INTO SHRIEKS OF MERRIMENT). WHAT ARE YOU TWO	LAUGHING	AT? /SAVVY/ OH, GO ON, MR BURGE. DONT STOP.
MTH5 (217)	ANOTHER FOR EVER. (THEY ALL LAUGH). WHAT ARE YOU	LAUGHING	AT? /THE SHE-ANCIENT/ LISTEN, CHILD-- /THE NEWLY
MILL I (142)	BE LAUGHED AT. /SAGAMORE/ I SHOULD NOT DREAM OF	LAUGHING	AT A CLIENT WITH AN INCOME OF THREE QUARTERS OF A
BARB III (320)	THE SALVATION LASSIE! SHE WOULD THINK YOU WERE	LAUGHING	AT HER IF YOU ASKED HER TO STAND UP IN THE STREET
CAND III SD(129)	BUT WITHOUT THE SMALLEST EMBARRASSMENT,	LAUGHING	AT HERSELF. EUGENE, CAPSIZED BY HER SUDDEN
JOAN 2 (82)	FALL. DEAD SILENCE. /BLUEBEARD/ MY LORD: WE WERE	LAUGHING	AT HER, NOT AT YOU. /THE ARCHBISHOP/ WHAT? NOT AT
JOAN 4 (95)	WITCH WITH MY OWN HANDS. /THE NOBLEMAN/ (	LAUGHING	AT HIM GOODNATUREDLY) SO YOU SHALL, CHAPLAIN: SO
WIDO II SD(34)	THINK WE DO. HA! HA! HA! THEY GO OUT TOGETHER,	LAUGHING	AT HIM. HE COLLAPSES INTO A CHAIR, SHUDDERING IN
GETT (338)	GAIETY OF HEART, A LITTLE PRAYER; AND YOULL BE	LAUGHING	AT HIM. /MRS GEORGE/ NEVER FEAR. I HAVE ALL THAT.
APPL I (239)	BEST MANNER UNTIL I HAD THE WHOLE FIVE THOUSAND	LAUGHING	AT HIM. THEY I ASKED THEM WOULD THEY LIKE ME TO
JOAN 2 (75)	I AM GOING TO PUT MY FOOT DOWN -- /BLUEBEARD/ (	LAUGHING	AT HIM) NAUGHTY! WHAT WOULD YOUR WISE GRANDFATHER
CLEO II (141)	SHE TAKES OFF HIS WREATH). OH! (SHE BURSTS OUT	LAUGHING	AT HIM). /CAESAR/ WHAT ARE YOU LAUGHING AT?
BULL IV (151)	HE'S NOT AN IRISHMAN. HE'LL NEVER KNOW THEYRE	LAUGHING	AT HIM; AND WHILE THEYRE LAUGHING HE'LL WIN THE
DEST (185)	NO REGIMENT LIKES TO HAVE ALL THE OTHER REGIMENTS	LAUGHING	AT IT. /NAPOLEON/ (A COLD RAY OF HUMOR STRIKING
APPL I (227)	CAN BE READ IN SUCH A WAY AS TO SET THE AUDIENCE	LAUGHING	AT IT. WE HAVE HAD ENOUGH OF THAT. SO, IN FUTURE,
MIS. PREFACE(13)	AND ENOUGH SPORT IN THE PROPHYLACTIC PROCESS OF	LAUGHING	AT ITS ELDERS BEHIND THEIR BACKS, TO ESCAPE WITH
NEVR II (247)	ONE OF THEM HAVE LAUGHED AT ME AS THAT BOY WAS	LAUGHING	AT ME ALL THE TIME? (FRANTICALLY) MY OWN
MIS. (121)	WERE A NASTY SNEERING LOT, AND THAT THEY WERE	LAUGHING	AT ME AND JOHN. THEYRE ALWAYS GIGGLING AND
KING I (204)	ROWLEY DARLING: I CANNOT GO ON IF YOU KEEP	LAUGHING	AT ME. IF ONLY MR DRYDEN HAD GIVEN ME SOME REALLY
LION I (115)	HANDSOME AS YOU. /THE CAPTAIN/ LAVINIA: YOU ARE	LAUGHING	AT ME. /LAVINIA/ AT YOU, CAPTAIN! IMPOSSIBLE. /THE
CAPT II (262)	ISNT IT? /BRASSBOUND/ (HOPELESSLY) YOU ARE	LAUGHING	AT ME. /LADY CICELY/ NO: TREMBLING, I ASSURE YOU.
MIS. (199)	I'M VERY SORRY, DEAR. /TARLETON/ YOURE NOT. YOURE	LAUGHING	AT ME. SERVE ME RIGHT! PARENTS AND CHILDREN! NO
SIM I (39)	PREACH; BUT IT WAS ONLY TO MAKE THEMSELVES ILL	LAUGHING	AT ME. THOUGH PERHAPS I SHOULDNT SAY THAT. SOME OF
PPP (196)	/ADOLPHUS/ I HOPE, MR FITZTOLLEMACHE, YOU ARE NOT	LAUGHING	AT MY CLOTHES. I WARN YOU THAT I AM AN ENGLISHMAN.
GENV IV (109)	/BEGONIA/ NOW SHUT UP, BILLIKINS. I WONT HAVE YOU	LAUGHING	AT RELIGION. /BBDE/ IN ERNEST'S COUNTRY, MADAM,
BULL II (115)	NOT SO STUPID AS THAT. BUT I COULDNT HELP YOUR	LAUGHING	AT THE FEELING IT GAVE ME. YOU-- (AGAIN STRUGGLING
MRS PREFACE(165)	CENSORSHIP! CAN I BE EXPECTED TO REFRAIN FROM	LAUGHING	AT THE SPECTACLE OF A NUMBER OF RESPECTABLE
MTH5 (219)	HEADS AND ARMS AND LEGS; THEY MAKE YOU SPLIT	LAUGHING	AT THEM. MOST OF THEM HAVE FORGOTTEN HOW TO SPEAK:
GENV IV (111)	THEY BECOME WHAT YOU CALL FUNNY. WE CANNOT HELP	LAUGHING	AT THEM. /BBDE/ WOMAN: IF YOU HAD EVER HAD GOD'S
INCA PREFACE(231)	OF COMEDY TO CHASTEN CAESAR'S FOIBLES BY	LAUGHING	AT THEM, WHILST INTRODUCING ENOUGH OBVIOUS AND
CAND III (140)	IS ALL. /MARCHBANKS/ (DISCOURAGED) MORELL: SHE'S	LAUGHING	AT US. /MORELL/ (WITH A QUICK TOUCH OF TEMPER)
CAND III (140)	OF TEMPER) THERE IS NOTHING TO LAUGH AT. ARE YOU	LAUGHING	AT US, CANDIDA? /CANDIDA/ (WITH QUIET ANGER)
APPL I (225)	ROPE. YOU ARE SPRAWLING ON YOUR BACKS; AND HE IS	LAUGHING	AT YOU. LOOK AT HIM! (HE SITS DOWN
BARB I (260)	SETTEE). I DONT IN THE LEAST KNOW WHAT YOU ARE	LAUGHING	AT, ADOLPHUS. I AM SURPRISED AT YOU, THOUGH I
INCA (245)	MUCH MORE AGREEABLE PERSON). PARDON ME: I AM NOW	LAUGHING	BECAUSE I CANNOT HELP IT. I AM AMUSED. THE OTHER
DOCT V (178)	UNKIND TO HIM. I WAS UNWORTHY OF HIM. /RIDGEON/ (	LAUGHING	BITTERLY) HA! /JENNIFER/ DONT INSULT ME: DONT
6CAL SD(106)	NO DECENCY? THE KING SNATCHES HER INTO HIS ARMS,	LAUGHING	BOISTEROUSLY. THE LAUGH SPREADS TO ALL THE SOLDIERS
MILL IV (203)	DAMN YOUR DEAR OLD FATHER! /ALASTAIR/ (	LAUGHING	BOISTEROUSLY) HA HA! ONE FOR YOU, EPPY. (HE
APPL INTRLUD(256)	(SHE THROWS HER HAND UP WITH A GESTURE OF	LAUGHING	DEFIANCE, AND DANCES BACK TO HER SEAT AT THE
HART II (91)	BEEN KILLED. /MRS HUSHABYE/ I COULDNT HAVE HELPED	LAUGHING	EVEN IF YOU HAD BEEN, MR DUNN. SO ELLIE HAS
MRS II (199)	HE MAKES A MOCK-PITEOUS FACE, BELIED BY HIS	LAUGHING	EYES. SHE LOOKS AT HIM; THEN COMES BACK TO HIM).
ROCK I (221)	TO UNDERSTAND THE GOLD STANDARD. /SIR ARTHUR/ (	LAUGHING	FRANKLY) YOU HAVE US THERE, MR HIPNEY. I CAN MAKE
MTH2 (48)	DUPE AND A BORN FOOL INTO THE BARGAIN. /BURGE/ (	LAUGHING	GENIALLY) YOU OLD ARISTOCRAT, YOU! BUT BELIEVE ME,
DEST (167)	ODD THOUGHT) OH! ARE YOU A COWARD? /NAPOLEON/ (	LAUGHING	GRIMLY AND SLAPPING HIS KNEES) THAT IS THE ONE
HART III (148)	I SEEN IT (SHE RUNS AWAY TOWARDS THE GRAVEL PIT,	LAUGHING	HARSHLY). /HECTOR/ ONE HUSBAND GONE. /CAPTAIN
MTH4 I (162)	LO! A MOUNTAIN, I-- /ZOO/ (INTERRUPTS HIM BY	LAUGHING	HEARTILY AT HIM) ! ! ! ! ! /THE ELDERLY
MRS II (208)	SIR, SILENCE: YOU ARE PROFANE. /MRS WARREN/ (	LAUGHING	HEARTILY) YOU SHOULD KEEP HIM IN BETTER ORDER, SAM.
FANY III (320)	THAT THE CAT HAD WHOOPING COUGH. /MRS GILBEY/ (	LAUGHING	HEARTILY) WELL, I NEVER! /GILBEY/ DONT BE A FOOL,
JOAN EPILOG (156)	NOT LIKE YOU. SHE WAS VERY BEAUTIFUL. /JOAN/ (	LAUGHING	HEARTILY) HA HA! I WAS NO BEAUTY: I WAS ALWAYS A
PYGM II (224)	EVER HEAR ANYTHING LIKE THAT, SIR? /PICKERING/ (	LAUGHING	HEARTILY) NEVER, MRS PEARCE: NEVER. /HIGGINS/ (
APPL II (276)	GOOD ONE! HA HA! HA HA HA HA HA! (HE GOES OUT	LAUGHING	HEARTILY). /MAGNUS/ THEY DONT TAKE IT IN, LIZZIE:
JOAN 3 (90)	ME: I WILL DELIVER YOU FROM FEAR. I -- /DUNOIS/ (	LAUGHING	HEARTILY, AND WAVING HER OFF) NO, NO, MY GIRL: IF
BULL IV (151)	KNOW THEYRE LAUGHING AT HIM; AND WHILE THEYRE	LAUGHING	HE'LL WIN THE SEAT. /CORNELIUS/ BUT HE CANT PREVENT
MTH1 I (19)	SECRETS. (HE CHUCKLES AND GOES AWAY SLOWLY,	LAUGHING	HIS FIRST LAUGH). /EVE/ NOW THE SECRET, THE SECRET.
PYGM I (214)	FLOWER GIRL/ (TICKLED BY THE PERFORMANCE, AND	LAUGHING	IN SPITE OF HERSELF) GARN! /THE NOTE TAKER/ YOU
CLEO I (107)	PLAY-- OUR INVISIBLE CHILDREN, O SPHINX,	LAUGHING	IN WHISPERS. MY WAY HITHER WAS THE WAY OF DESTINY;
MTH3 (130)	(HE DASHES OUT IN A FURY). /BURGE-LUBIN/ (	LAUGHING	INDULGENTLY) HE WILL KEEP THE SECRET ALL RIGHT. I
BULL I (79)	AND ME THE IRISH SECRETARY, EH? /BROADBENT/ (	LAUGHING	INDUSTRIOUSLY) CAPITAL. YOUR IRISH WIT HAS SETTLED
CLEO II SD(123)	IS HIDING BEHIND FTATATEETA, PEEPS OUT AT THEM	LAUGHING	. CAESAR RISES. /CAESAR/ WILL THE QUEEN FAVOR US
APPL II (277)	ME, DEAR. I WILL SING TO YOU UNTIL YOU CANT HELP	LAUGHING	. COME. LYSISTRATA POCKETS HER HANDKERCHIEF; SHAKES
CLEO V (200)	(SHE LAUGHS IN SPITE OF HERSELF). AHA! YOU ARE	LAUGHING	. DOES THAT MEAN RECONCILIATION? /CLEOPATRA/ (
CLEO IV (169)	ALONE. DRIVE THEM OUT, FTATATEETA. (THEY RUN OUT	LAUGHING	. FTATATEETA SHUTS THE DOOR ON THEM). WHAT ARE YOU
CLEO PRO2,SD(97)	NO LESS EXTRAVAGANTLY, COMES THROUGH THE GATEWAY	LAUGHING	. HE IS SOMEWHAT BATTLESTAINED; AND HIS LEFT
MTH2 (88)	CREATIVE EVOLUTION DOESNT STOP WHILE PEOPLE ARE	LAUGHING	. LAUGHING MAY EVEN LUBRICATE ITS JOB. /SAVVY/ WHAT
DEVL III SD(60)	AND SOME OF THE YOUNGER OFFICERS BURST OUT	LAUGHING	. /JUDITH/ (HER DREAD AND HORROR DEEPENING AT
JITT III (70)	WHAT ON EARTH HAVE YOU DONE TO MOTHER? SHE IS	LAUGHING	. SHE IS POSITIVELY SINGING. EITHER YOU ARE A
FANY III (319)	FROM BELOW. /GILBEY/ GO AND TELL THEM TO STOP	LAUGHING	. WHAT RIGHT HAVE THEY TO MAKE A NOISE LIKE THAT..

CATH 1 (172)	EXCUSE ME. POP OFF! HA! HA! I CANT HELP	LAUGHING	. WHATS HIS REAL NAME, BY THE WAY, IN CASE I MEET
MIS. PREFACE(89)	SHOCKED AND SCANDALIZED, EVEN WHEN WE CANNOT HELP	LAUGHING	. WORSE, WE DREAD AND PERSECUTE THOSE WHO CAN SEE
WIDO II (34)	/TRENCH/ (PLEADINGLY) MY DEAR: IT'S NO	LAUGHING	MATTER. DO YOU KNOW THAT I HAVE A BARE SEVEN
DEST (167)	HIS COURAGE. /LADY/ (AS IF SHE HAD FOUND IT NO	LAUGHING	MATTER) AH, YOU CAN LAUGH AT FEAR. THEN YOU DONT
POSN PREFACE(397)	PLAY IN WHICH DISSOLUTENESS IS SHEWN TO BE NO	LAUGHING	MATTER, IT IS PROHIBITED AT ONCE AMID THE VULGAR
MTH2 (88)	EVOLUTION DOESNT STOP WHILE PEOPLE ARE LAUGHING.	LAUGHING	MAY EVEN LUBRICATE ITS JOB. /SAVVY/ WHAT DOES THAT
JITT III (69)	ISNT IT? YOURE NOT ANGRY, ARE YOU? OH DEAR-- (	LAUGHING	MORE THAN EVER). /JITTA/ OH NO! OF COURSE NOT.
SUPR III (118)	NOTED THE GLEAM OF GOLD FROM A DEAD TOOTH IN THE	LAUGHING	MOUTH: I MADE CURIOUS OBSERVATIONS OF THE STRANGE
MTH1 II (30)	WEARY SHRUG, THROWS DOWN HIS SPADE. CAIN, WITH A	LAUGHING	ONE, THROWS DOWN HIS SHIELD AND SPEAR. BOTH SIT ON
PLES PREFACE(R16)	AUDIENCE LAUGH. I WANT TO SEE HOW MANY OF THEM,	LAUGHING	OR GRAVE, ARE IN THE MELTING MOOD, AND THIS RESULT
LION PREFACE(56)	TEACHING HAS LED TO DEEPER AND DEEPER DISASTER,	LAUGHING	OUTRIGHT. WAS EVER SO IDIOTIC A PROJECT MOOTED AS
MILL I (143)	HOW CAN I LAUGH AT THINGS I DONT KNOW? IF I AM	LAUGHING	-- AND AM I REALLY LAUGHING? -- I ASSURE YOU I AM
CLEO IV (168)	SHE TURNS FIERCELY ON IRAS). AT WHOM ARE YOU	LAUGHING	-- AT ME OR AT CAESAR? /IRAS/ AT CAESAR.
SIM II (66)	LIAR, BABY, DASTARD, HYPOCRITE. /SIR CHARLES/ (	LAUGHING	) AN ALBATROSS! NOW WOULD ANYBODY IN THE WORLD,
MTH3 (120)	LIVE WITH, MR ACCOUNTANT GENERAL. /BURGE-LUBIN/ (	LAUGHING	) BY GEORGE, I BELIEVE YOU! TRY IT, BARNABAS.
HART II (127)	I THOUGHT YOU WERE A FOOL. /LADY UTTERWORD/ (	LAUGHING	) EVERYBODY DOES, AT FIRST. BUT I AM NOT SUCH A
KING I (182)	DO NOT KNOW YOUR CATECHISM, MR FOX. /CHARLES/ (	LAUGHING	) EXCELLENT, MRS BASHAM. PASTOR: SHE HAS GRAVELLED
PYGM II (222)	HE GIVE IT TO ME, NOT TO YOU. /PICKERING/ (	LAUGHING	) HE DID. I THINK IT MUST BE REGARDED AS HER
MTH4 I (160)	HE DECLARED HE HAD HUNG HIS HAT ON IT. /ZOO/ (	LAUGHING	) HE KNEW THAT TRAVELLERS ARE AMUSING ONLY WHEN
ARMS II (43)	CREAM SOLDIER, CAPTAIN BLUNTSCHLI. /BLUNTSCHLI/ (	LAUGHING	) I ASSURE YOU I DID. (STEALING A WHIMSICAL GLANCE
GENV III (73)	TO PREACH BOLSHEVISM, DO YOU? /THE COMMISSAR/ (	LAUGHING	) I DONT EXPECT ANY GOVERNMENT TO TOLERATE ANY
LION I (126)	THE OLIVES AND ANCHOVIES. /ANOTHER CHRISTIAN/ (	LAUGHING	) I SHALL BE THE SOUP. /ANOTHER/ I SHALL BE THE
CAPT I (231)	WOULD LIKE TO TAKE IT AS A PRESENT. /RANKIN/ (	LAUGHING	) I THANK YOUR LORDSHIP: WE HAVE ESTATE ENOUGH OF
CAND II (119)	/MORELL/ (INCREDULOUSLY) OF PROSSY? /CANDIDA/ (	LAUGHING	) NO, NO, NO, NO. NOT JEALOUS OF ANYBODY. JEALOUS
CLEO V (201)	/CLEOPATRA/ (ANGRY WITH HERSELF FOR	LAUGHING	) NO, NO, NO! ! BUT IT IS SO RIDICULOUS TO HEAR
DEVL III (51)	WAS A MORE WORTHY MAN THAN YOURSELF. /RICHARD/ (	LAUGHING	) OHO! NO! THATS A VERY PRETTY REASON, I MUST SAY;
HART II (98)	/MRS HUSHABYE/ (SUDDENLY MELTING AND HALF	LAUGHING	) OH, MY POOR ELLIE, MY PETTIKINS, MY UNHAPPY
NEVR I (200)	A HOSPITAL, NOT PEOPLE WHO PAY. /THE DENTIST/ (	LAUGHING	) OH, THE HOSPITAL DOESNT COUNT. I ONLY MEANT MY
CAND II (121)	THEM STEADY. /CANDIDA/ (TO MORELL, RELIEVED AND	LAUGHING	) OH, YOURE ONLY SHOCKED! IS THAT ALL? HOW
KING II (226)	VERY BEST HUSBAND THAT EVER LIVED. /CHARLES/ (	LAUGHING	) OH! OH! OH! THE MERRY MONARCH! BELOVED: CAN
INCA (253)	(HE TURNS DOWN HIS MOUSTACHES). /ERMYNTRUDE/ (	LAUGHING	) OH! YOUD BETTER NOT LET THEM HEAR YOU SAY THAT,
APPL INTRLUD(246)	A ROSE; AND YOU CLING TO A CABBAGE. /MAGNUS/ (	LAUGHING	) THAT IS A VERY APT METAPHOR, BELOVED. BUT WHAT
DEVL III (52)	OH, WHAT DOES ALL THAT MATTER? /RICHARD/ (	LAUGHING	) TRUE: WHAT DOES IT MATTER? WHAT DOES ANYTHING
ARMS II (38)	FETCH YOU, REGIMENTS OR NO REGIMENTS. /SERGIUS/ (	LAUGHING	) VERY WELL. (HE GOES IN). RAINA WATCHES HIM UNTIL
MIS. (186)	/GUNNER/ (TIMIDLY) HASNT EVERYBODY? /JOHNNY/ (	LAUGHING	) WELL, BY GEORGE, THATS NOT BAD. /MRS TARLETON/
CAND I (95)	HIS BREATH UNTIL BURGESS DISAPPEARS. /CANDIDA/ (	LAUGHING	) WELL, EUGENE? (HE TURNS WITH A START, AND COMES
DEVL II (32)	WHAT A HORRIBLE FEELING IT GIVES ME. /ANDERSON/ (	LAUGHING	) WELL, WELL: NEVER MIND, PET. HE'S A BAD MAN; AND
PYGM V (279)	/MRS HIGGINS/ HENRY! HENRY! /PICKERING/ (	LAUGHING	) WHY DONT YOU SLANG BACK AT HIM? DONT STAND IT.
BULL I (76)	DOESNT HOLD A FAIR HALF. THANKYA. /BROADBENT/ (	LAUGHING	) YOU IRISHMEN CERTAINLY DO KNOW HOW TO DRINK. (
LION I (123)	HER NEIGHBORHOOD CONTAMINATED HIM). /LAVINIA/ (	LAUGHING	) YOU KNOW, FERROVIUS, I AM NOT ALWAYS A CHRISTIAN.
LION II (133)	NOT HAVE HAD THE MONEY. /CAESAR/ (INDULGENT,	LAUGHING	) YOU ROGUES! THERE IS NO END TO YOUR TRICKS. I'LL
O'FL (206)	HE EVER SENT THERE FOR POACHING." /SIR PEARCE/ (	LAUGHING	) YOURE WELCOME TO THEM ALL, MY LAD. COME (HE
MTH3 (100)	THE SWITCHBOARD AND VANISHES. SHE IS STILL HEARD	LAUGHING	). BLACK DEVIL! (HE SNATCHES OUT HIS PEG
MTH5 (225)	IMPOSSIBLE. THEY ARE ALL SMASHED. (HE RISES,	LAUGHING	). /ALL/ SMASHED! /ARJILLAX/ WHO SMASHED THEM?
HART III (133)	AS A PRACTICAL BUSINESS MAN. (THEY ALL BURST OUT	LAUGHING	). WHAT ARE YOU ALL LAUGHING AT? /MRS HUSHABYE/
AUGS (282)	IS LAUGHING TOO). /AUGUSTUS/ WHAT! /THE CLERK/ (	LAUGHING	SLOWLY AND LABORIOUSLY, WITH INTENSE ENJOYMENT) HA
WIDO I (9)	CHURCH WILL BE A TREAT FOR YOU. /COKANE/ (	LAUGHING	SOFTLY AND ARCHLY) AH, EXCELLENT, EXCELLENT: VERY
DEST (182)	YOU WILL SAVE HIM FROM DISGRACE. /NAPOLEON/ (	LAUGHING	SOURLY) SAVE HIM YOURSELF, SINCE YOU ARE SO CLEVER:
APPL INTRLUD(255)	WHY ARE YOU SO AFRAID OF YOUR WIFE? YOU ARE THE	LAUGHING	STOCK OF LONDON, YOU POOR HENPECKED DARLING.
ROCK II (269)	VOTE FOR WOMEN, SINCE THEN POLITICS HAVE BEEN A	LAUGHING	STOCK. PARLIAMENTARY LEADERS SAY ONE THING ON
DOCT IV (161)	IVE BEEN LYING THERE LISTENING TO THE DOCTORS--	LAUGHING	TO MYSELF. THEY KNOW, DEAREST: DONT CRY. IT MAKES
AUGS (282)	(SHE LAUGHS; AND IT IS CLEAR THAT BLUELOO IS	LAUGHING	TOO). /AUGUSTUS/ WHAT! /THE CLERK/ (LAUGHING
CLEO PRO2,SD(95)	CURRENT IN ENGLISH BARRACKS) AT WHICH THEY ARE	LAUGHING	UPROARIOUSLY. THEY ARE ABOUT A DOZEN IN NUMBER, ALL
MRS II SD(199)	TO BOX HIS EARS; THEN LOOKS AT THE PRETTY	LAUGHING	UPTURNED FACE FOR A MOMENT, TEMPTED. AT LAST SHE
WIDO III (55)	YOUNGER, MISS BLANCHE, DONT HE? I COULDNT HELP	LAUGHING	WHEN I SAW HIM WITH HIS WHISKERS SHAVED OFF: IT DO
MIS. (196)	ME WITH GENEROSITY, YOUNG MAN. /HYPATIA/ (	LAUGHING	WITH GENUINE AMUSEMENT) HE HAD YOU THERE, JOEY.
MIS. (173)	FEELING THAT ALL YOUR MUSCLES ARE SINGING AND	LAUGHING	WITH PAIN-- THEN GO TO THE GYMNASIUM WITH THAT
PHIL I SD(70)	HIS AMATIVE ENTHUSIASM, AT WHICH HE IS HIMSELF	LAUGHING	, AND HIS CLEVER, IMAGINATIVE, HUMOROUS WAYS,
6CAL PREFACE(89)	PUBLICLY RAGING AND CURSING, CRYING AND	LAUGHING	, ASSERTING HIS AUTHORITY WITH THRASONIC FEROCITY
PHIL II (112)	OH, TO SEE THEM SITTING THERE AT LUNCH TOGETHER,	LAUGHING	, CHATTING, MAKING GAME OF ME! I SHOULD HAVE
HART II (99)	THAT WHEN I AM NEITHER COAXING AND KISSING NOR	LAUGHING	, I AM JUST WONDERING HOW MUCH LONGER I CAN STAND
BARB PREFACE(222)	AND SACRIFICE, YET ALWAYS IN THE WILDEST SPIRITS,	LAUGHING	, JOKING, SINGING, REJOICING, DRUMMING, AND
MTH5 (206)	NEVER NOTICING ANYTHING, NEVER DANCING, NEVER	LAUGHING	, NEVER SINGING, NEVER GETTING ANYTHING OUT OF
MILL I (143)	AND AM I REALLY LAUGHING? -- I ASSURE YOU I AM	LAUGHING	, NOT AT YOUR MISFORTUNES, BUT AT YOU. /EPIFANIA/

LAUGHINGLY

PHIL III (139)	TALKING THAT NASTY SNEERING STUFF. /CHARTERIS/ (	LAUGHINGLY	APPEALING TO THE HEAVENS) SHE CALLS IT NASTY
PHIL III SD(147)	CHARTERIS, AMUSED AND UNTOUCHED, SHAKES HIS HEAD	LAUGHINGLY	. THE REST LOOK AT JULIA WITH CONCERN, AND EVEN A
CLEO III (146)	THROAT, APOLLODORUS. (THE CHIVALROUS APOLLODORUS	LAUGHINGLY	SHAKES HIS HEAD; BREAKS GROUND AWAY FROM THE

LAUGHING-STOCK

LION PROLOG (106)	IN MAKING ME A SLAVE, IN MAKING YOURSELF A	LAUGHING-STOCK	. IT'S NOT FAIR. YOU GET ME THE NAME OF BEING
MTH3 (130)	YOU. /BARNABAS/ MAY YOU LIVE FOREVER, AND BE THE	LAUGHING-STOCK	OF THE WHOLE WORLD! (HE DASHES OUT IN A

LAUGHS

MTH5 (259)	VOICE/ (IN THE HILLS) HA! HA! HA! /ADAM/ WHO	LAUGHS	? WHO DARES LAUGH AT ADAM? /EVE/ WHO HAS THE HEART
CATH 3 (186)	A HUNDRED AND ONE BLOWS OF THE KNOUT. (HE	LAUGHS	AND GOES OUT, NURSING HIS BITTEN FINGER). /THE
DEST (190)	BEATEN YOU AFTER ALL. I DO ADMIRE YOU SO. (HE	LAUGHS	AND PATS HER CHEEK). THIS TIME, REALLY AND TRULY
DOCT II (127)	(SIR PATRICK UTTERS A FORMIDABLE GRUNT. B.B.	LAUGHS	AND PATS HIM INDULGENTLY ON THE SHOULDER) GOODNIGHT.
SUPR I (21)	" MR ROBINSON" WOULD HURT ME CRUELLY. (SHE	LAUGHS	AND PATS HIS CHEEK WITH HER FINGER; THEN COMES BACK
SUPR I (40)	(STARING AT HER) MAGNIFICENT AUDACITY! (SHE	LAUGHS	AND PATS HIS CHEEKS). NOW JUST TO THINK THAT IF I
BULL III (125)	DIFFICULTY). /LARRY/ STEADY! STEAD-EEE! (HE	LAUGHS	AND SEATS HIMSELF ON THE TABLE). CORNELIUS DOYLE,
SUPR I (39)	I AM A BOA CONSTRICTOR: GRANNY TOLD ME. (SHE	LAUGHS	AND THROWS HER BOA ROUND HIS NECK). DOESNT IT FEEL
FANY III (320)	/KNOX/ DO YOU MEAN TO TELL ME THAT MY DAUGHTER	LAUGHS	AT A FRENCHMAN'S JOKES? /GILBEY/ WE ALL KNOW WHAT
POSN (448)	SAVAGELY AT IT; BUT HE WITHDRAWS IT IN TIME AND	LAUGHS	AT HER DISCOMFITURE). /FEEMY/ YOU-- /ELDER DANIELS/
BULL II (114)	ALL THE HARPS OF IRELAND ARE IN YOUR VOICE. (SHE	LAUGHS	AT HIM. HE SUDDENLY LOSES HIS HEAD AND SEIZES HER
DEST (177)	AMUSEMENT, SHE LEANS HER CHEEK ON HER HAND AND	LAUGHS	AT HIM. HE TURNS AGAIN, ANGRILY MOCKING HER). HA!
NEVR II (227)	/THE GENTLEMAN/ YOU LIKE HIS FATHER! (HE	LAUGHS	AT THE NOTION). /WAITER/ OH SIR, WE MUST NOT TAKE
BULL III (123)	I DONT KNOW. THATS THE SORT OF THING AN IRISHMAN	LAUGHS	AT. HAS SHE ACCEPTED YOU? /BROADBENT/ I SHALL NEVER
NEVR II (259)	TO HIM; KISSES HER WITH IMPETUOUS STRENGTH; AND	LAUGHS	BOYISHLY). NOW YOUVE DONE IT, GLORIA. IT'S ALL OVER:
LION I (126)	YES: I SHALL BE THE ROAST BOAR. HA! HA! (HE	LAUGHS	CONSCIENTIOUSLY AND MARCHES OUT WITH THEM).
6CAL SD(98)	IT. HE BARKS TO THE LAST MOMENT. JOHN OF GAUNT	LAUGHS	ECSTATICALLY AT THIS PERFORMANCE, AND SETS OFF SOME
APPL I SD(231)	HERE AND NOW. /AMANDA/ " ONCE FOR ALL." EVERYBODY	LAUGHS	EXCEPT PROTEUS, WHO RISES IN A FURY. /PROTEUS/ I WILL
MTH2 (39)	ENOUGH FOR ME. IT WILL LAST MY TIME, ANYHOW (HE	LAUGHS	GOOD-HUMOREDLY). /FRANKLYN/ (WITH RENEWED ENERGY)
CATH 4,SD(194)	WHY? /EDSTASTON/ TO OBLIGE ME. CATHERINE	LAUGHS	GOOD-HUMOREDLY AND GOES TO THE CURTAINS AND OPENS
6CAL (98)	OFF SOME OF THE SOLDIERS. /THE KING/ IF A MAN	LAUGHS	I WILL HAVE HIM FLAYED ALIVE. DEAD SILENCE. /THE
CLEO V (200)	ME. I AM SORRY FOR THAT POOR TOTATEETA. (SHE	LAUGHS	IN SPITE OF HERSELF). AHA! YOU ARE LAUGHING. DOES
MRS I (191)	ROOM BEFORE TEA? /MRS WARREN/ YES, DEARIE. (SHE	LAUGHS	INDULGENTLY AT PRAED'S GRAVITY, AND PATS HIM ON THE
ARMS I SD(12)	AT THE CURTAIN; THEN PURSES HER LIPS SECRETIVELY,	LAUGHS	INSOLENTLY, AND GOES OUT. RAINA, HIGHLY OFFENDED BY
SHAK SD(141)	AMONG THE CLUMPS." WELL DONE, AUSTRALIA! SHAV	LAUGHS	. /SHAKES/ LAUGHEST THOU AT THYSELF? PULLST THOU MY
O'FL SD(227)	GENERAL STRIKES A MATCH. THE THRUSH SINGS. A JAY	LAUGHS	. THE CONVERSATION DROPS.
WIDO III (49)	EXCITEMENT! YOU NEED EXCITEMENT! (SHE	LAUGHS	JOYLESSLY, AND SITS DOWN ON THE RUG AT HIS FEET). HOW
MRS II (209)	LOOKS MORE THAN HALF DISPOSED TO BOX HIS EARS. HE	LAUGHS	MISCHIEVOUSLY AND RUNS OFF, CLAPPING-TO THE DOOR
SUPR IV (158)	A WILLING MAN WHEN YOU REALLY GO FOR HIM. (SHE	LAUGHS	NAUGHTILY). I'M SHOCKING YOU, I SUPPOSE. BUT YOU KNOW
CATH 1 (163)	THAT IS NOT JUST, LITTLE FATHER! /PATIOMKIN/ (	LAUGHS	OGREISHLY; THEN RETURNS TO HIS PLACE AT THE TABLE,
MTH1 I (14)	I WILL CLEAR THEM AWAY TOMORROW. /THE SERPENT/ (	LAUGHS	) ! ! ! /ADAM/ THAT IS A FUNNY NOISE TO MAKE. I
MTH1 I (11)	GO AND TELL ADAM TO CONCEIVE. /THE SERPENT/ (	LAUGHS	) ! ! ! /EVE/ (JARRED AND STARTLED) WHAT A

JOAN 5 (111) THEY GET A CHANCE. /DUNOIS/ THAT IS TRUE. (HE LAUGHS). KING CHARLES, WITH BLUEBEARD ON HIS LEFT AND LA
POSN (448) AND I'LL SEE YOU LOW, AS DANGEROUS AS I AM. (HE LAUGHS). OH YOU NEEDNT TRY TO BRAZEN IT OUT. YOULL LOOK
MIS. (200) /HYPATIA/ YOUVE FALLEN IN LOVE WITH HER. (SHE LAUGHS). /BENTLEY/ IT'S BEASTLY OF YOU TO LAUGH. /LORD
MTH4 I (153) OF MY PRESENT LONGEVITY. /ZOO/ LONGEVITY! (SHE LAUGHS). /THE ELDERLY GENTLEMAN/ YES, MADAM, RELATIVE
DOCT I (88) THE OLD WOMAN SAID SHE DIDNT KNOW. (RIDGEON LAUGHS). WELL, I MAKE YOU THE SAME ANSWER. BUT THE WORLD'S
SUPR I (41) OR NO: NOT A CHARM, A SUBTLE INTEREST (SHE LAUGHS)-- JUST SO: YOU KNOW IT; AND YOU TRIUMPH IN IT.
MTH1 I (19) DO YOU STAY AND LISTEN TO IT. /THE SERPENT/ (LAUGHS)! ! ! /ADAM/ (BRIGHTENING) THAT NOISE TAKES AWAY
MTH1 I (16) SHORT A WORD FOR SO LONG A THING. /THE SERPENT/ (LAUGHS)! ! ! /EVE/ (TURNING IMPATIENTLY TO THE SNAKE)
MTH1 I (18) HAND INTO HIS) WIFE AND HUSBAND. /THE SERPENT/ (LAUGHS)! ! ! /EVE/ (SNATCHING HERSELF LOOSE FROM ADAM)
AUGS (282) OF HIS STATIONERY RACK: IT WAS QUITE EASY (SHE LAUGHS ; AND IT IS CLEAR THAT BLUELOO IS LAUGHING TOO).
LION II SD(138) THAT WILL KEEP YOUR HEART UP. THE CAPTAIN LAUGHS SARDONICALLY. /LAVINIA/ (STARTLED: SHE HAD FORGOTTEN
DEVL II (38) IT'S ALMOST HOLY. (HE MUSES A MOMENT, AND THEN LAUGHS SOFTLY). /JUDITH/ (QUICKLY) WHY DO YOU LAUGH?
MTH4 I (149) (CLAPPING HIS HAT ON AGAIN) PIG! ASS! /ZOO/ (LAUGHS VERY HEARTILY AT HIM)! ! ! /THE ELDERLY GENTLEMAN/
APPL INTRLUD(255) DIGNITY) ORINTHIA: I COMMAND YOU. /ORINTHIA/ (LAUGHS WILDLY)! ! ! /MAGNUS/ FURIOUS) VERY WELL, THEN,
CAND II (121) AND YOU, DARLING, YOU UNDERSTAND NOTHING. (SHE LAUGHS , AND KISSES HIM TO CONSOLE HIM. HE RECOILS AS IF
JOAN 3 (89) LIKE. YOU ARE AN ABOMINABLE BOY. /THE PAGE/ (LAUGHS , AND SQUATS DOWN AS BEFORE)! /DUNOIS/ (PACING)
INCA (245) MADAM. (CHUCKLING) DEVILISH AMUSING, THAT! (HE LAUGHS , GENIALLY AND SINCERELY, AND BECOMES A MUCH MORE
INCA (245) CAN HE LAUGH? /THE INCA/ CERTAINLY, MADAM. (HE LAUGHS , HARSHLY AND MIRTHLESSLY). HA HA! HA HA HA!
JITT I (15) BECOME LIKE A FRESHMAN JUST UP FROM SCHOOL. (SHE LAUGHS , SMOOTHING HIS GREY HAIR). YES: I KNOW; BUT GREY AS

LAUGHTER

BULL IV (146) PATSY'S NOSE WI DHE RING IN ITS SNOUT. (ROARS OF LAUGHTER : KEEGAN GLARES AT THEM). BEFORE BROADBINT KNEW
BULL IV (162) WITH HER FINGERS: WHILE SHE TRIES TO STIFLE HER LAUGHTER AGAINST HIS COLLAR BONE) OH DONT MAKE ME LAUGH:
CLEO II (120) /RUFIO/ (FROM THE STEPS) PEACE, HO! (THE LAUGHTER AND CHATTER CEASE ABRUPTLY). CAESAR APPROACHES.
GETT (276) A WOMAN DOWN (LEO GIVES A LITTLE SHRIEK OF LAUGHTER AND COLLAPSES ON A CHAIR NEXT MRS BRIDGENORTH. ON
SUPR III SD(77) ENGLISH SOCIAL-DEMOCRATS/ HEAR, HEAR! GENERAL LAUGHTER AND GOOD HUMOR. TANNER AND MENDOZA SHAKE HANDS. THE
OVER PREFACE(165) REHEARSAL; YET THEY HAVE PRODUCED SINCERE LAUGHTER AND TEARS SUCH AS THE MOST FINISHED METROPOLITAN
PLES PREFACE(R15) WRONG: FOR INSTANCE, IN THE SIMPLE CASE OF LAUGHTER AND TEARS, IN WHICH IT DEALS TOO LIBERALLY. IT IS
CAND III SD(136) INTO HYSTERICS. DONT LAUGH. BOISTEROUS VOICES AND LAUGHTER ARE HEARD APPROACHING. LEXY MILL, HIS EYES
CLEO PRO2 (105) WITHIN ITS PRECINCT. BEL AFFRIS ROARS WITH LAUGHTER AS THE PERSIAN TUMBLES. THE GUARDSMEN RUSH OUT OF
METH PREFACE(R86) EVEN THE SHAKESPEARIAN-DICKENSIAN CONSOLATION OF LAUGHTER AT MISCHIEF, ACCURATELY CALLED COMIC RELIEF. OUR
LADY PREFACE(220) IT WAS DE PROFUNDIS IN EXCELSIS. THERE WAS MORE LAUGHTER BETWEEN THE LINES OF THAT BOOK THAN IN A THOUSAND
JOAN 2,SD(81) CANST NOT FOOL ME. WHERE BE DAUPHIN? A ROAR OF LAUGHTER BREAKS OUT AS GILLES, WITH A GESTURE OF SURRENDER,
CYMB V (149) YOUR DEATH. /IMOGEN/ OH, DO NOT MAKE ME LAUGH. LAUGHTER DISSOLVES TOO MANY JUST RESENTMENTS, PARDONS TOO
FANY III SD(318) CUPS OF TEA AS MRS KNOX FILLS THEM). SHRIEKS OF LAUGHTER FROM BELOW STAIRS REACH THE EARS OF THE COMPANY.
FANY III (320) WELL, OF ALL THE SCANDALOUS-- (REDOUBLED LAUGHTER FROM BELOW). /KNOX/ I'LL PUT A STOP TO THIS. (HE
CLEO PRO2,SD(96) IS LIGHTED BY A TORCH STUCK IN THE WALL. AS THE LAUGHTER FROM THE GROUP ROUND THE STORYTELLER DIES AWAY, THE
GENV IV (111) TO HAVE TO BE MAKING FACES ALL DAY? (MUCH LAUGHTER IN THE BRITISH SECTION). /BATTLER/ IS THIS TO BE
BULL III (123) /LARRY/ YOU HWAT? ? ? (HE SCREAMS WITH LAUGHTER IN THE FALSETTO IRISH REGISTER UNUSED FOR THAT
TRFL (83) AND THEIR AUDIENCES HARMLESSLY. IRRESPONSIBLE LAUGHTER IS SALUTARY IN SMALL QUANTITIES. ONE THROWS OFF
SUPR IV SD(172) DEAR. GO ON TALKING. /TANNER/ TALKING! UNIVERSAL LAUGHTER .
BARB I SD(259) MOMENTS INTO PAROXYSMS OF IMPERFECTLY SUPPRESSED LAUGHTER . CUSINS IS A SPECTACLED STUDENT, SLIGHT, THIN
CAND I SD(98) IN UTTER AMAZEMENT, BURSTS INTO UNCONTROLLABLE LAUGHTER . EUGENE IS TAKEN ABACK, BUT NOT DISCONCERTED; AND
JOAN 6 (150) IT HAD, MY LORD, ON SOME OF THEM. I HEARD LAUGHTER . FORGIVE ME FOR SAYING THAT I HOPE AND BELIEVE IT
INCA (247) A DRAGOON. (SHE RECEIVES THIS WITH A SHRIEK OF LAUGHTER . HE STRUGGLES WITH HIS SENSE OF HUMOR). AT THE
PYGM I (211) AND INDIA. /THE GENTLEMAN/ QUITE RIGHT. (GREAT LAUGHTER . REACTION IN THE NOTE TAKER'S FAVOR. EXCLAMATIONS
JOAN 2,SD(80) HAIR! ALL THE LADIES EXPLODE IN UNCONTROLLABLE LAUGHTER . /BLUEBEARD/ (TRYING NOT TO LAUGH, AND WAVING HIS
CAND I SD(94) INEXPRESSIBLY TICKLED, BEGINS TO SPLUTTER WITH LAUGHTER . /CANDIDA/ (COMING TO THE RESCUE) YOULL LOSE YOUR
JOAN 6 (150) FOR SAYING THAT I HOPE AND BELIEVE IT WAS ENGLISH LAUGHTER . /THE CHAPLAIN/ (RISING FRANTICALLY) NO: IT WAS
JOAN EPIL,SD(163) STARE AT HIM. THEN THEY BURST INTO UNCONTROLLABLE LAUGHTER . /THE GENTLEMAN/ WHY THIS MIRTH, GENTLEMEN?
APPL I SD(225) TO MIND -- AMANDA BURSTS INTO UNCONTROLLABLE LAUGHTER . THE KING LOOKS REPROACHFULLY AT HER, STRUGGLING
BULL I (87) THERE GOES ON A HORRIBLE, SENSELESS, MISCHIEVOUS LAUGHTER . WHEN YOURE YOUNG, YOU EXCHANGE DRINKS WITH OTHER
BARB PREFACE(227) A SACRED GIFT LONG DETHRONED BY THE HELLISH LAUGHTER OF DERISION AND OBSCENITY, RISES LIKE A FLOOD
BARB PREFACE(222) THE POPPING OF CHAMPAGNE CORKS AND THE RIBALD LAUGHTER OF SIRENS! COULD MISUNDERSTANDING BE MORE
BARB III (313) LIKE A MADMAN: ITS BRAZEN ROARINGS WERE LIKE THE LAUGHTER OF THE DAMNED. 117 CONVERSIONS TOOK PLACE THEN AND
CLEO IV SD(167) THE GIRL FOLLOWING WITH HER HARP, AMID THE LAUGHTER OF THE LADIES AND SLAVES. /CLEOPATRA/ NOW, CAN ANY
HART PREFACE(22) THAT THE SOLDIERS IN THE TRENCHES ROARED WITH LAUGHTER OVER IT FOR DAYS, AND TOLD EACH OTHER THAT IT WOULD
SHAK (141) BUMPS AMONG THE CLUMPS." /SHAKES/ (ROARING WITH LAUGHTER) HA HA! HO HO! MY LUNGS LIKE CHANTICLEER MUST
CLEO II (132) DOES NOT MOVE. /CLEOPATRA/ (WITH A SPLUTTER OF LAUGHTER) HER NAME IS NOT TOTATEETA: IT IS FTATATEETA. (
PYGM III (252) (TO FREDDY, WHO IS IN CONVULSIONS OF SUPPRESSED LAUGHTER) HERE! WHAT ARE YOU SNIGGERING AT? /FREDDY/ THE
JITT III (69) /AGNES/ (HER CHUCKLES NOW CULMINATING IN HEARTY LAUGHTER) ISNT IT? YOURE NOT ANGRY, ARE YOU? OH DEAR-- (
MTH2 (48) IT! /HASLAM/ (SPLUTTERING WITH SUPPRESSED LAUGHTER) PRICELESS! /SAVVY/ WELL, I SUPPOSE I SHOULDNT
CATH 1 (172) IS POPOF? /EDSTASTON/ (CHOKING WITH SUPPRESSED LAUGHTER) ! ! ! ! ! /PATIOMKIN/ (GRATIFIED) DARLING: YOU
MILL I (143) ON THE TABLE, SHAKING WITH UNCONTROLLABLE LAUGHTER) ! ! ! ! ! /EPIFANIA/ AY: LAUGH, LAUGH,
POSN (453) TO THIS ELOQUENT AND VENERABLE RAM. (SUPPRESSED LAUGHTER). AND NOW I ASK HIM THIS. (TO THE ELDER) DID WE
LION II (133) IT IS A DUSTY ONE, MY FRIEND. (OBSEQUIOUS LAUGHTER). BE ON YOUR GUARD NEXT TIME. /SECUTOR/ LET HIM BE
POSN (463) BELOVED BRETHREN-- /A BOY/ SAME TO YOU, BLANCO. (LAUGHTER). /BLANCO/ AND MANY OF THEM. BOYS: THIS IS A
POSN (463) LORD HAVE MERCY ON US, MISERABLE SINNERS. (MORE LAUGHTER). /BLANCO/ (FORCIBLY) NO: THATS WHERE YOURE
CATH 4 (196) /VARINKA/ HOO HOO! (A STIFLED SPLUTTER OF LAUGHTER). /EDSTASTON/ (FOLLOWING THE EMPRESS AND RESUMING
PYGM III (254) DESCENDING THE STAIRS IN A STREAM OF SILVERY LAUGHTER). /FREDDY/ (TO THE HEAVENS AT LARGE) WELL, I ASK
ARMS I (16) THE FINEST THING-- (HE CHOKES WITH SUPPRESSED LAUGHTER). /RAINA/ (STERNLY) GIVE ME BACK THE PORTRAIT,
CLEO III (165) INTO THE SEA. RUFIO AND BRITANNUS ROAR WITH LAUGHTER). /RUFIO/ (LOOKING DOWN AFTER HER) HE HAS GOT
ROCK II (256) HA! HA HA HA HA HA! (HE GOES OUT ROARING WITH LAUGHTER). /SIR ARTHUR/ (AFTER A MOMENT OF SHOCK) I
FABL III (113) HA! (HE GOES INTO THE LABORATORY ROARING WITH LAUGHTER). /THE GENTLEMAN/ TWO BIG CATCHES FOR TODAY. A
LION II (131) A MORSEL OF FRIED FISH TO WAKE UP HIS APPETITE. (LAUGHTER). /THE KEEPER/ YES: IT'S EASY FOR YOU TO TALK; BUT
POSN (458) I GAVE MY LIFE FOR! (HE BREAKS INTO HIDEOUS LAUGHTER). /THE SHERIFF/ (JARRED BEYOND ENDURANCE BY THE
POSN (450) ON THE GENERAL GROUND THAT IT'S A ROTTEN JURY. (LAUGHTER). /THE SHERIFF/ THATS NOT A LAWFUL GROUND OF
SUPR III (74) ANARCHIST, WHO DOESNT KNOW WHAT ANARCHISM MEANS (LAUGHTER)-- /THE ANARCHIST/ (RISING) A POINT OF ORDER,
APPL I (231) /AMANDA/ (SITS DOWN WITH A LITTLE SPLUTTER OF LAUGHTER)! /CRASSUS/ (THOUGHTFUL) TAKE IT EASY, FRIENDS.
CLEO II SD(120) THOUSAND HORSEMEN. THE COURT BREAKS INTO DERISIVE LAUGHTER ; AND A GREAT CHATTERING BEGINS, AMID WHICH RUFIO,
JITT III SD(69) OF COURSE NOT. JITTA HAS A PAROXYSM OF AGONIZING LAUGHTER ; AND AGNES ACCOMPANIES HER WITHOUT A SUSPICION
HART PREFACE(40) CASTIGATION OF COMEDY, THE RUTHLESS LIGHT OF LAUGHTER THAT GLARES ON THE STAGE. WHEN MEN ARE HEROICALLY
HART PREFACE(32) TRICK OF THAT TRADE HAD BECOME SO STALE THAT THE LAUGHTER THEY PROVOKED TURNED TO LOATHING: THESE VETERANS
CAPT II (250) BY). TAKE THAT MAN AND WASH HIM. (WITH A ROAR OF LAUGHTER THEY SEIZE HIM). /DRINKWATER/ (IN AN AGONY OF
ANNA SD(295) SPLUTTERS; DROPS A PAPER; AND CONCEALS HIS LAUGHTER UNDER THE TABLE. /STRAMMFEST/ (THUNDEROUSLY)
SUPR III (104) MY FRIEND. /DON JUAN/ AUDACIOUS RIBALD: YOUR LAUGHTER WILL FINISH IN HIDEOUS BOREDOM BEFORE MORNING. /THE
CLEO II (122) WHISPER AND SENSATION, NOT WITHOUT SOME STIFLED LAUGHTER , AMONG THE COURTIERS). /RUFIO/ (BLUNTLY) YOU MUST
INCA (255) HAW! HA HA! HAW! HAW! (HE IS CONVULSED WITH LAUGHTER , AND FINALLY HAS TO RELIEVE HIS FEELINGS BY
BULL IV SD(145) INFECTED ALL HIS FRIENDS. THEY ARE SCREAMING WITH LAUGHTER , DOUBLED UP, LEANING ON THE FURNITURE AND AGAINST
CAPT II SD(250) DRAGGED AWAY THROUGH THE ARCH IN A WHIRLWIND OF LAUGHTER , PROTESTS AND TEARS. /LADY CICELY/ I'M AFRAID HE
CLEO PRO2,SD(97) YOU FRIGHTENED, COUSIN? THE GUARDSMEN ROAR WITH LAUGHTER , THEIR EYES SPARKLING AT THE WIT OF THEIR CAPTAIN.
LION I SD(111) CHRISTIANS BURST INTO SHRIEKS OF UNCONTROLLABLE LAUGHTER , TO THE GREAT SCANDAL OF THE CENTURION.
MTH1 II (33) THEN THE GENTLEMAN? (HE GOES AWAY ROARING WITH LAUGHTER , WHICH CEASES AS HE CRIES FROM THE DISTANCE)

LAUNCH

APPL INTRLUD(249) WHEN I OPEN ONE OF THE ART EXHIBITIONS OR LAUNCH A NEW SHIP THEY CROWD THE PLACE OUT. I AM ONE OF
FABL I (102) WHAT USE IS BRAVERY NOW WHEN ANY COWARD CAN LAUNCH AN ATOMIC BOMB? UNTIL MEN ARE WISE AND WOMEN
MILL II (175) ARE NOT DEEP WANTS. AT PRESENT I WANT A MOTOR LAUNCH . /THE DOCTOR/ THERE IS NO SUCH THING IN THIS LITTLE
MILL II (175) I HAVE. WHEN I NEED A CAR OR A MOTOR BOAT OR A LAUNCH OR ANYTHING LIKE THAT I BUY STRAIGHT OFF THE ROAD OR
MTH4 II (179) A SINGLE ALGEBRAIC SYMBOL ON PAPER? CAN YOU LAUNCH TEN THOUSAND MEN ACROSS A FRONTIER AND A CHAIN OF

LAUNCHED

GENV PREFACE(8) HER OUT OF IT? IN THE LAST MONTHS THE BOMBS LAUNCHED BY YOUNG BRITISH WARRIORS FROM AIRPLANES AT THE
GETT PREFACE(245) THE INNOCENT AND THE GUILTY ALIKE ONCE IT IS LAUNCHED EXACTLY AS ANY OTHER CONTAGIOUS DISEASE DOES; THAT
CATH PREFACE(158) HER TO PLAY THE HELEN OF EURIPIDES, AND THEN LAUNCHED HER ON A QUEENLY CAREER AS CATHERINE OF RUSSIA. IT
UNPL PREFACE(R13) HOUSES; AND HANDED IT OVER TO MR GREIN, WHO LAUNCHED IT AT THE PUBLIC IN THE ROYALTY THEATRE WITH ALL
MTH5 (261) IN THAT DAY WHEN I SUNDERED MYSELF IN TWAIN AND LAUNCHED MAN AND WOMAN ON THE EARTH STILL URGES THEM: AFTER

MRS PREFACE(153)	THEM. MR GREIN, THE HARDY ICONOCLAST WHO FIRST	LAUNCHED	MY PLAYS ON THE STAGE ALONGSIDE GHOSTS AND THE WILD
LADY PREFACE(232)	SHAKESPEAR'S ART RATHER THAN BY HIS VIEWS. HE WAS	LAUNCHED	ON HIS CAREER AS A SUCCESSFUL PLAYWRIGHT BY THE
HART I (57)	MY FATHER HAD NEVER BEEN IN DEBT. BUT WHEN HE	LAUNCHED	OUT INTO BUSINESS ON A LARGE SCALE, HE HAD TO INCUR
DOCT PREFACE(73)	EXPLOITER OF HIS IGNORANCE, AND WILL FIND ITSELF	LAUNCHED	UPON THAT PERSECUTION OF SCIENTIFIC TRUTH OF WHICH
3PLA PREFACE(R30)	THAT THIS FATALLY PLAUSIBLE EXPLANATION WAS	LAUNCHED	, MY PLAY BECAME MY CRITIC'S PLAY, NOT MINE.
		LAUNCHES	
BARB PREFACE(238)	A TRUST, ARE RESPONSIBLE. AT THEM ACCORDINGLY HE	LAUNCHES	HIS SIXPENNORTH OF FULMINATE, MISSING HIS MARK, BUT
		LAUNCHING	
ROCK PREFACE(175)	RIGHT TO CRITICIZE: HE INFURIATED HIS ACCUSERS BY	LAUNCHING	AT THEM A DAMNING CONTRAST BETWEEN THEIR INFAMOUS
SUPR PREFACE(R17)	AND SO MY ATTEMPT TO BRING HIM UP TO DATE BY	LAUNCHING	HIM AS A MODERN ENGLISHMAN INTO A MODERN ENGLISH
		LAUNDRESS	
BARB PREFACE(218)	THE CHARWOMAN IS BADLY DRESSED, BECAUSE THE	LAUNDRESS	SMELLS OF GIN, BECAUSE THE SEMPSTRESS IS ANEMIC,
SUPR HANDBOK(203)	WITH VERMILION AS A SYMBOL OF BRAVERY EMPLOYS A	LAUNDRESS	TO DAUB HIS SHIRT WITH STARCH AS A SYMBOL OF
		LAUNDRY	
MILL II SD(166)	CLOTHS ARE COARSE, AND ARE NOT FRESH FROM THE	LAUNDRY	, THE WALLS ARE COVERED WITH AN UGLY VICTORIAN PAPER
DOCT PREFACE(22)	AND WARMTH OF THE POCKET; AND SEND IT TO A	LAUNDRY	TO BE MIXED UP WITH EVERYBODY ELSE'S HANDKERCHIEFS,
MTH4 I (157)	BLACKBEETLES IN MY KITCHEN, WASHING SODA IN MY	LAUNDRY	, AND COAL IN MY CELLAR. I DO NOT DENY THEIR
ROCK II (274)	INITIALS. NO BOTHER ABOUT YOUR CLOTHES AT THE	LAUNDRY	, FOR INSTANCE. /ALOYSIA/ THANK YOU, SIR ARTHUR!
		LAUNDRYMEN	
MILL PREFACE(125)	CHILDREN BRED FROM IRISH COLLEENS AND CHINESE	LAUNDRYMEN	ARE FAR SUPERIOR TO INBRED IRISH OR CHINESE. HERR
		LAURA	
SUPR II (54)	DISTANCE? PETRARCH DIDNT SEE HALF AS MUCH OF	LAURA	, NOR DANTE OF BEATRICE, AS YOU SEE OF ANN NOW; AND
		LAUREATE	
SIM II (76)	AGAIN. A NEW ONE IS TO BE PROVIDED BY THE POET	LAUREATE	. THE PREMIER'S LAST WORDS WERE LOST THROUGH THE
BULL PREFACE(48)	INEPT OR DISHONORABLE THEY MAY BE. AS THE LATE	LAUREATE	SAID IN THE TWO STINGING LINES IN WHICH HE BRANDED
KING I (201)	WORKS OF THE GREATEST POET OF THE AGE: THE POET	LAUREATE	, JOHN DRYDEN. /FOX/ IF HE HAS GIVEN TO THE
PRES (147)	LIKE HER DO? HE INTHROJOOCED HER TO THE POET	LAUREATE	, THINKIN SHE'D INSPIRE HIM. /MITCHENER/ DID SHE..
PYGM PREFACE(202)	I KNOW LITTLE. AMONG THEM TOWERS THE POET	LAUREATE	, TO WHOM PERHAPS HIGGINS MAY OWE HIS MILTONIC
ROCK PREFACE(180)	IT IS UNBEARABLE: NOT EVEN THE GENIUS OF OUR POET	LAUREATE	, WITH ALL THE MAGIC OF CANTERBURY CATHEDRAL FOR
		LAUREL	
LION II (141)	MAN IN ROME. IT MEANS THAT YOU SHALL HAVE A	LAUREL	CROWN OF GOLD. SUPERB FIGHTER! I COULD ALMOST YIELD
LION II (141)	WHERE IS HE? MAGNIFICENT! HE SHALL HAVE A	LAUREL	CROWN. FERROVIUS, MADLY WAVING HIS BLOODSTAINED
CYMB V (140)	FIRST HAND. /CAPTAIN/ GOOD. BUT WE SHALL GET NO	LAUREL	CROWNS FOR WHAT WE'VE DONE TODAY. EXEUNT TOGETHER.
		LAURELLED	
CLEO II (129)	FLING TO ME THE GREY HEAD OF THE OLD SOLDIER, THE	LAURELLED	CONQUEROR, THE MIGHTY ROMAN, TREACHEROUSLY STRUCK
		LAURELS	
CLEO NOTES (210)	CROMWELL, IN MIDDLE AGE, HAVE SNATCHED ALL ITS	LAURELS	FROM OPPONENT COMMANDERS BRED TO IT, APPARENTLY
BULL III SD(117)	A WREATH IN HER HAND, STANDS NEGLECTED AMID THE	LAURELS	, SUCH STATUES, THOUGH APPARENTLY WORKS OF ART, GROW
CLEO II (128)	LIFE! IS THAT ALL? /THEODOTUS/ YOUR LIFE. YOUR	LAURELS	. YOUR FUTURE. /POTHINUS/ IT IS TRUE. I CAN CALL A
METH PREFACE(R77)	OF ITS PROFESSION, AND SOLD ITS LILIES FOR THE	LAURELS	OF THE SOLDIERS OF THE VICTORIA CROSS. ALL THE COCKS
CLEO V (201)	NOT HIDING A BALD HEAD UNDER HIS CONQUEROR'S	LAURELS	; NOT STOOPED WITH THE WEIGHT OF THE WORLD ON HIS
		LAURENCE	
BULL I SD(73)	THRESHOLD ONE READS THAT THE FIRM CONSISTS OF MR	LAURENCE	DOYLE AND MR THOMAS BROADBENT, AND THAT THEIR ROOMS
BULL I SD(80)	BY THE ARRIVAL OF BROADBENT'S PARTNER). MR	LAURENCE	DOYLE IS A MAN OF 36, WITH COLD GREY EYES, STRAINED
BULL IV (150)	PERSONALLY RESPONSIBLE, THOUGH MY OLD FRIEND MR	LAURENCE	DOYLE UNFORTUNATELY INCURRED THE FIRST EFFECTS OF
HART PREFACE(34)	GILBERT MURRAY, JOHN MASEFIELD, ST JOHN HANKIN,	LAURENCE	HOUSMAN, ARNOLD BENNETT, JOHN GALSWORTHY, JOHN
POSN PREFACE(361)	MR CECIL RALEIGH, MR JOHN GALSWORTHY, MR	LAURENCE	HOUSMAN, SIR HERBERT BEERBOHM TREE, MR W.L.
POSN PREFACE(417)	WAS STARTED BY PROFESSOR GILBERT MURRAY AND MR	LAURENCE	HOUSMAN, WHO, IN PURE KINDNESS TO THE MANAGERS,
		LAVE	
BULL II (106)	GO BACK FOR IT. /PATSY/ AN WHOSE THINGS WAS I TO	LAVE	BEHIND? HWAT WOULD YOUR REVERENCE THINK IF I LEFT YOUR
BULL II (98)	DOING HERE? /PATSY/ OH FOR THE LOVE O GOD DONT	LAVE	ME HERE WI DHE GRASSHOPPER. I HARD IT SPAKIN TO YOU.
		LAVENDER	
VWOO 3 (141)	ELGAR. MY NOSE CAN GLOAT OVER OUR SACK OF FRESH	LAVENDER	OR OUR SPECIAL SIXPENNY EAU DE COLOGNE WHEN THE
MTH4 I SD(139)	HE WEARS A BLACK FROCK-COAT, A WHITE WAISTCOAT,	LAVENDER	TROUSA FROCK-COAT, A WHITE WAISTCOAT, LAVENDER
MTH4 I SD(139)	LAVENDER TROUSA FROCK-COAT, A WHITE WAISTCOAT,	LAVENDER	TROUSERS, A BRILLIANT SILK CRAVAT WITH A JEWELLED
POSN PREFACE(428)	ANY MANAGER RUN IN PRODUCING SUCH WORKS AS SWEET	LAVENDER	, PETER PAN, THE SILVER KING, OR ANY OF THE 99 PER
		LAVERY	
CAPT NOTES (301)	HIDALGO: HENCE THE SUPERBITY OF HIS PORTRAIT BY	LAVERY	(VELASQUEZ BEING NO LONGER AVAILABLE). HE IS, I
		LAVINIA	
LION II (139)	WE SHALL BE GODS OURSELVES. /THE CAPTAIN/	LAVINIA	: COME DOWN TO EARTH. BURN THE INCENSE AND MARRY ME.
LION I (114)	TO SAY. (IN A LOWER TONE, HUMANE AND URGENT)	LAVINIA	: DO CHRISTIANS KNOW HOW TO LOVE? /LAVINIA/ (
LION I (115)	ENEMIES ARE AS HANDSOME AS YOU. /THE CAPTAIN/	LAVINIA	: YOU ARE LAUGHING AT ME. /LAVINIA/ AT YOU,
LION II (146)	DISPENSATIONS. /THE CAPTAIN/ WHAT DO YOU SAY,	LAVINIA	? WILL YOU TOO BE PRUDENT? /LAVINIA/ (ON THE
LION I (119)	ANDROCLES, WHO COMES TO HIS LEFT, AND MAKES	LAVINIA	A HEART-BROKEN SALUTATION) IS A SORCERER. A GREEK
LION I (114)	ON THE WEST SIDE OF THE SQUARE, GLAD TO REST.	LAVINIA	ALONE REMAINS STANDING TO SPEAK TO THE CAPTAIN).
LION II SD(137)	AT THE ENTRANCE TO THE PASSAGE, NEAR THE EDITOR.	LAVINIA	AND THE CHRISTIAN WOMEN SIT DOWN AGAIN, WRUNG WITH
LION II (141)	BEEN DIFFERENT. /THE CAPTAIN/ (SUDDENLY SEIZING	LAVINIA	BY THE WRIST AND DRAGGING HER UP THE STEPS TO THE
LION II (141)	IN PIECES. THEYRE ALL IN PIECES, MORE OR LESS. (	LAVINIA	HIDES HER FACE). TWO MORE MASKED SLAVES COME IN WITH
LION I (119)	MAKES A WILD MOVEMENT TO RISE AND INTERFERE; BUT	LAVINIA	HOLDS HIM DOWN, WATCHING FERROVIUS INTENTLY.
LION II SD(127)	THE BRIDGE. THE MARTYRS ARE SITTING ON THE STEPS.	LAVINIA	IS SEATED HALF-WAY UP, THOUGHTFUL, TRYING TO LOOK
LION II (138)	WITH DEATH. /THE CAPTAIN/ NOT WITH CERTAIN DEATH,	LAVINIA	, ONLY DEATH IN BATTLE, WHICH SPARES MORE MEN THAN
LION II (138)	TO HER SIDE) I AM ON DUTY WITH THE EMPEROR,	LAVINIA	. /LAVINIA/ IS IT PART OF YOUR DUTY TO LAUGH AT US?
LION I (114)	(COLDLY) I SHALL NOT FEAR HIM IN ANY CASE,	LAVINIA	. /LAVINIA/ (HER EYES DANCING) HOW BRAVE OF YOU,
LION I (117)	FROM THE SKIES? DO NOT DECEIVE YOURSELF,	LAVINIA	. THERE IS NO FUTURE FOR YOU BEYOND THE GRAVE.
LION II (137)	(THEY GO OUT THROUGH THE PASSAGE. HE TURNS TO	LAVINIA	) FAREWELL. /LAVINIA/ YOU FORGET: I MUST FOLLOW
LION I (118)	WITH GREAT DIFFICULTY). /THE CENTURION/ (TO	LAVINIA	) HERE ARE SOME PALS FOR YOU. THIS LITTLE BIT IS
LION II (142)	-- /THE EMPEROR/ THE LIONS? NONSENSE! (TO	LAVINIA	) MADAM: I AM PROUD TO HAVE THE HONOR OF MAKING YOUR
LION II (129)	MY TEMPER, MY WICKED TEMPER! (TO THE EDITOR, AS	LAVINIA	SITS DOWN AGAIN, REASSURED) FORGIVE ME, BROTHER. MY
LION I (112)	I CALL THE ATTENTION OF THE FEMALE PRISONER	LAVINIA	TO THE FACT THAT AS THE EMPEROR IS A DIVINE
LION EPILOG (148)	NATURALIST, WHOSE VIEWS SURPRISE EVERYBODY.	LAVINIA	, A CLEVER AND FEARLESS FREETHINKER, SHOCKS THE
LION I SD(110)	OF BOTH SEXES AND ALL AGES, AMONG THEM ONE	LAVINIA	, A GOOD-LOOKING RESOLUTE YOUNG WOMAN, APPARENTLY OF
LION I (117)	YES: WHEN ALL IS SAID, WE ARE BOTH PATRICIANS,	LAVINIA	, AND MUST DIE FOR OUR BELIEFS. FAREWELL. (HE
LION I SD(122)	FERROVIUS, WITH A LONG SIGH OF HAPPINESS, GOES TO	LAVINIA	, AND OFFERS HER HIS HAND. /LAVINIA/ (TAKING IT) SO
LION I (119)	QUITE CONSOLED, GOES PAST THE CENTURION TO	LAVINIA	, AND SITS DOWN CONTENTEDLY ON THE GROUND ON HER
LION I (113)	ADDRESSING HER PERSONALLY AND GRAVELY) A MARTYR,	LAVINIA	, IS A FOOL. YOUR DEATH WILL PROVE NOTHING.
LION I (117)	LEAVE THEM TO THE LIONS. /LENTULUS/ (INDICATING	LAVINIA	, WHO IS STILL LOOKING TOWARDS THE ARCHES AFTER THE
		LAVINIA'S	
LION II SD(137)	SOME CALM AND STEADFAST. ANDROCLES SITS DOWN AT	LAVINIA'S	FEET. THE CAPTAIN STANDS ON THE STAIRS, WATCHING

LAVISH

BULL III (136) IS NOT PREPARED TO PROVE IT BY CONTRIBUTIONS, AS LAVISH AS HIS MEANS WILL ALLOW, TO THE GREAT AND BENEFICENT
GETT SD(259) HAD RESOLVED TO SHEW HOW MUCH MATERIAL THEY COULD LAVISH ON A HOUSE BUILT FOR THE GLORY OF GOD, INSTEAD OF

LAVISHED

SIM PREFACE(9) HUNDREDS OF MILLIONS OF THE COUNTRY'S INCOME ARE LAVISHED ANNUALLY ON LADIES AND GENTLEMEN WHILST LABORERS
PYGM IV (267) AND DAMN YOU; AND DAMN MY OWN FOLLY IN HAVING LAVISHED HARD-EARNED KNOWLEDGE AND THE TREASURE OF MY REGARD
HART PREFACE(36) DECORATION ON WHICH MISS KINGSTON HAD LAVISHED SO MUCH TASTE AND CARE, THE LITTLE THEATRE WAS IN

LAVISHING

BULL PREFACE(20) IF HE HAD LOST THEM, AND, NOT CONTENT WITH LAVISHING SPLENDID FIGHTING ON HELPLESS ADVERSARIES LIKE THE

LAVISHLY

FABL PREFACE(90) PRESENT THE OPPOSITION TO SUCH A MINISTRY WILL BY LAVISHLY FINANCED; BUT THE NEED FOR IT IS TOO URGENT TO
METH PREFACE(R88) TALENT, I DECORATED IT TOO BRILLIANTLY AND LAVISHLY . I SURROUNDED IT WITH A COMEDY OF WHICH IT FORMED

LAVOISIER

ROCK PREFACE(150) NAZI HAVE FELT THAT WAY ABOUT EINSTEIN, YET LAVOISIER WAS GUILLOTINED; AND EINSTEIN HAS HAD TO FLY FOR
ROCK PREFACE(150) IN THE FRENCH REPUBLIC HAD THIS FEELING ABOUT LAVOISIER , NOR CAN ANY GERMAN NAZI HAVE FELT THAT WAY ABOUT

LAVOISIER'S

ROCK PREFACE(150) THE PROPOSITION IS THAT ARISTOCRATS (LAVOISIER'S CLASS) AND JEWS (EINSTEIN'S RACE) ARE UNFIT TO

LAW

GENV IV (93) PRIESTS, YOU HAVE MOB LAW, LYNCHING LAW, GANGSTER LAW : IN SHORT, AMERICAN DEMOCRACY. THANK YOUR STARS YOU
2TRU III (88) LEFT OF IT? THE ORBIT OF THE ELECTRON OBEYS NO LAW : IT CHOOSES ONE PATH AND REJECTS ANOTHER: IT IS AS
LIED (192) YOU MAY DESIRE. I ATTACH NO IMPORTANCE TO THE LAW : MY LOVE WAS NOT CREATED IN ME BY THE LAW, NOR CAN IT
MRS I (185) THE TIME. IVE COME DOWN HERE BY MYSELF TO READ LAW : NOT FOR A HOLIDAY, AS MY MOTHER IMAGINES. I HATE
MILL PREFACE(135) AND DOMINATED ARE ALREADY EQUALIZED BEFORE THE LAW : SHALL NOT I, A PLAYWRIGHT OF SHAKESPEREAN EMINENCE, BE
MILL I (142) WAS DOING EVERY DAY. SOLICITORS KNOW NOTHING OF LAW : THEY ARE ONLY GOOD AT PRACTICE, AS THEY CALL IT. MY
CYMB V (146) TONGUE THOU ART CONDEMN'D, AND MUST ENDURE OUR LAW : THOU'RT DEAD. BIND THE OFFENDER, AND TAKE HIM FROM OUR
GETT (300) OUT OF THE COUNTRY PERHAPS. IS THAT REALLY THE LAW ? AM I TO UNDERSTAND THAT IF CECIL COMMITS A MURDER, OR
SUPR III (106) RELIGION? AN EXCUSE FOR HATING ME. WHAT IS HIS LAW ? AN EXCUSE FOR HANGING YOU. WHAT IS HIS MORALITY?
MILL PREFACE(109) SCOUNDRELS WHO ARE ALL, LIKE HIMSELF, OUTSIDE THE LAW ? HOW DOES AN OBSCURE VILLAGE PRIEST, THE SON OF HUMBLE
POSN (438) /BABSY/ LAW! WHAT RIGHT HAS A HORSE-THIEF TO ANY LAW ? LAW IS THROWN AWAY ON A BRUTE LIKE THAT. /ELDER
MILL IV (198) THINK YOUR FATHER'S MONEY PLACES YOU ABOVE THE LAW ? /EPIFANIA/ (FLUSHING) AGAIN! SHE RAISES HER FISTS.
GENV IV (118) TOO MUCH, ERNEST. (TO THE JUDGE) WHAT IS THE LAW ? /JUDGE/ UNFORTUNATELY THERE IS NO LAW AS BETWEEN
DOCT III (141) LET HER RISK IMPRISONMENT IN HER IGNORANCE OF THE LAW ? /LOUIS/ WELL, I RISKED IMPRISONMENT FOR HER SAKE. I
CAPT I (229) HIMSELF AND KEPT IT. /RANKIN/ BUT HOW ABOUT THE LAW ? /SIR HOWARD/ THE LAW, SIR, IN THAT ISLAND, CONSISTED
GETT (306) ME TO GET MARRIED IN THE EXISTING STATE OF THE LAW ? /SYKES/ (RISING AND COMING TO COLLINS'S LEFT ELBOW)
JOAN 6 (147) WHAT DOES SHE KNOW OF THE CHURCH AND THE LAW ? SHE DID NOT UNDERSTAND A WORD WE WERE SAYING. IT IS
BARB PREFACE(241) GIVE HIM UP DO NOT CONSIDER HIS BREACH OF THE LAW A GUILTY ACTION. SOMETIMES, EVEN, PRIVATE TRIBUNALS ARE
GETT PREFACE(211) THEIR POLYGYNY IS LIMITED. BY THE MOHAMMEDAN LAW A MAN CANNOT MARRY MORE THAN FOUR WIVES; AND BY THE
MILL PREFACE(112) FORCED TO ADD TO WHAT HE CAN UNDERSTAND OF DIVINE LAW A SERIES OF SECULAR REGULATIONS DESIGNED TO MAINTAIN HIS
ROCK II (255) AM NO COMMUNIST: I AM A RESPECTABLE LABOR MAN, AS LAW ABIDING AS ANY MAN HERE. I AM WHAT NONE OF YOU HAS
SUPR III (119) BY PUBLIC OPINION, THAT SUCH A LADY MAY BE MORE LAW ABIDING THAN THE POOR GIRL WHOM WE USED TO SPURN INTO
PRES (164) PUNCHED SANDSTONE'S. THE HORRORS OF MARTIAL LAW ADMINISTERED BY MRS BANGER ARE TOO TERRIBLE TO BE FACED.
LIED (189) IT JUST DRIVES YOU WILD. THERE OUGHT TO BE A LAW AGAINST A MAN'S SISTER EVER ENTERING HIS HOUSE AFTER
BARB PREFACE(241) HAS BEEN IMPRISONED FOR " BAD TASTE" UNDER THE LAW AGAINST BLASPHEMY, SANE CONCLUSIONS, AND NOW I MUST ASK
LION EPILOG (148) BECAUSE THE GOVERNING CLASSES, PROVIDED ONLY THE LAW AGAINST BLASPHEMY IS NOT APPLIED TO THEMSELVES, STRONGLY
CAPT I (230) UNLESS YOU HAD TAKEN CARE TO KEEP OUTSIDE THE LAW AGAINST CONSPIRACY. WHENEVER YOU WISH TO DO ANYTHING
SUPR III (100) CONCERTS INSTEAD IF THEY LIKE: THERE IS NO LAW AGAINST IT; FOR ENGLISHMEN NEVER WILL BE SLAVES: THEY
POSN PREFACE(389) VAGUE, AS FOR EXAMPLE IN THE CASE OF THE AMERICAN LAW AGAINST OBSCENITY, THAT IT MAKES THE MAGISTRATE
FABL PREFACE(78) SHAMELESSLY MENDACIOUS ADVERTIZERS, AND BY THE LAW AGAINST SEDITIOUS AND BLASPHEMOUS LIBEL, THAT MY
POSN PREFACE(431) GORELL WHEN HE IS DEFENDING THE INTEGRITY OF THE LAW AGAINST THE PROPOSAL TO MAKE IT IN ANY SENSE OPTIONAL.
GETT PREFACE(253) JUST THE POLYGAMOUS HOUSEHOLD WHICH OUR MARRIAGE LAW ALLOWS TO BE BROKEN UP, AND WHICH, AS WE HAVE SEEN, IS
LADY PREFACE(218) HUMAN NATURE WITH THEORETICAL MORALITY, ACTUAL LAW AND ADMINISTRATION WITH ABSTRACT JUSTICE, AND SO FORTH.
GENV II (60) FORM THE BEGINNING OF A NEW CODE OF INTERNATIONAL LAW AND BE QUITE UNPRECEDENTED. /SIR O./ BUT, MY DEAR SIR,
ROCK PREFACE(187) WISER THAN ALL THE GENERATIONS WHO MADE THE ROMAN LAW AND BUILT UP THE ROMAN EMPIRE ON IT? /JESUS/ BY THEIR
POSN PREFACE(387) OF THE SITUATION? THE DIFFERENCE BETWEEN LAW AND CENSORSHIP. THE ANSWER IS THAT A PAMPHLET, A
SUPR PREFACE(R12) THE WOMAN. NOW THE CONFLICTS OF INDIVIDUALS WITH LAW AND CONVENTION CAN BE DRAMATIZED LIKE ALL OTHER HUMAN
GETT PREFACE(223) PROMISCUOUS AND THAT THE LEAST RELAXATION OF LAW AND CUSTOM MUST PRODUCE A WILD OUTBREAK OF
2TRU PREFACE(17) STATICS, AND TO THEIR LOGICAL CONSEQUENCES IN LAW AND CUSTOM. SUCH VOWS AUTOMATICALLY EXCLUDE
JOAN PREFACE(28) THE TWO OR THREE SCORE OF CANONS AND DOCTORS OF LAW AND DIVINITY WHO SAT WITH CAUCHON AS ASSESSORS, WERE
CLEO PRO1 (91) HIS AIRS OF BEING HIMSELF A GOD; FOR HE TALKED OF LAW AND DUTY AND OTHER MATTERS THAT CONCERNED NOT A MERE
MIS. PREFACE(64) OF THOSE WHO ARE TOO NARROW-MINDED TO UNDERSTAND LAW AND EXERCISE JUDGMENT; AND IN THEIR HANDS (WITH US THEY
BULL PREFACE(62) THE NECESSITY WILL ARISE FOR BRINGING IN A PRESS LAW AND FOR CONSIDERABLY INCREASING THE ARMY OF OCCUPATION."
SUPR PREFACE(R36) SYSTEM OF VIOLENCE AND ROBBERY WHICH WE CALL LAW AND INDUSTRY. EVEN ATHEISTS REPROACH ME WITH INFIDELITY
METH PREFACE(R80) FAITH IS STILL KEPT PURE, AND YOU MAY TAKE THE LAW AND LEAVE THE LEGENDS WITHOUT SUSPICION OF HERESY.
BARB PREFACE(211) AND APPARENTLY SHABBY VIOLATION OF OUR COMMERCIAL LAW AND MORALITY, AND NOT MERELY DEFEND IT WITH THE MOST
POSN (454) AND NOT A LOW-DOWN LYNCHER. YOULL HOLD UP THE LAW AND NOT LET IT BE DRAGGED IN THE MUD BY YOUR BROTHER'S
JOAN PREFACE(42) HABEAS CORPUS ACT, THE PROCLAMATIONS OF MARTIAL LAW AND OF MINOR STATES OF SIEGE, AND THE REST OF THEM,
ROCK II (235) THEY WANTED SOME OF HIS BEST SOOTHING SYRUP ABOUT LAW AND ORDER AFTER THE ATTACK ON THE LORD MAYOR'S SHOW IN
LION PREFACE(31) COMMUNIST; THAT HE REGARDED MUCH OF WHAT WE CALL LAW AND ORDER AS MACHINERY FOR ROBBING THE POOR UNDER LEGAL
GENV PREFACE(14) AND ECCLESIASTICAL SYSTEMS WHICH HAD TO PROVIDE LAW AND ORDER DURING THE INTERVALS BETWEEN DOMINATING
2TRU PREFACE(19) AT LAST REACHED A POINT AT WHICH THERE WAS MORE LAW AND ORDER IN THE EMPIRE THAN IN THE CHURCH. EMPEROR
BULL PREFACE(57) THAT THE EGYPTIANS ARE SO ACCUSTOMED TO ASSOCIATE LAW AND ORDER WITH FLOGGINGS, EXECUTIONS, TORTURE AND LYNCH
MIS. PREFACE(103) THEIR OWN, BUT THE DIFFICULTY OF COMBINING LAW AND ORDER WITH FREE INSTITUTIONS IS NOT A NATURAL ONE.
LION PREFACE(55) BEING EUPHEMISTICALLY CALLED THE MAINTENANCE OF LAW AND ORDER. INIQUITY CAN GO NO FURTHER. BY THIS TIME
DEST (193) AND THEN DECLARES WAR ON OUR ONE IN THE NAME OF LAW AND ORDER. THERE IS NOTHING SO BAD OR SO GOOD THAT YOU
MIS. PREFACE(59) AND ACCURATELY, TOGETHER WITH THE RUDIMENTS OF LAW AND ORDER, BECOME NECESSARY CONDITIONS OF A CHILD'S
LION EPILOG (147) THE INTERESTS INVOLVED IN THE ESTABLISHED LAW AND ORDER, ORGANIZED AND MAINTAINED IN THE NAME OF
MIS. (190) BY FORCE OR FRAUD, OR BOTH. I USED BOTH WHEN LAW AND PERSUASION FAILED ME. EVERY RULER OF MEN SINCE THE
SUPR PREFACE(R12) THE RELATIONS BETWEEN BOTH AND OUR COURTS OF LAW AND PRIVATE JURIES OF MATRONS, PRODUCES THAT SENSATION
BARB PREFACE(231) HIM IF HE KILLS. BY EXAMPLE AND PRECEPT THE LAW AND PUBLIC OPINION TEACH HIM TO IMPOSE HIS WILL ON
METH PREFACE(R53) BY THE FACT THAT IT WAS A SECRET REFUGE LEFT BY LAW AND PUBLIC SUPERSTITION FOR THE AMATEUR OF PASSIONATE
CAPT III (294) IT, AS A MAN SHOULD STAND FOR HIS BELIEF, AGAINST LAW AND RELIGION AS MUCH AS AGAINST WICKEDNESS AND
CAPT III (294) BETTER REVELATIONS OF THE WICKEDNESS OF LAW AND RESPECTABILITY THAN THE BOOK OF THE PROPHET AMOS.
BUOY III (45) AM A LAWYER, NOT A SCIENTIST. /SECONDBORN/ UNTIL LAW AND SCIENCE, POLITICS AND RELIGION, ARE ALL ONE, THE
LION PREFACE(81) A VIOLENTLY ANTI-CHRISTIAN SYSTEM OF CRIMINAL LAW AND STERN MORALITY. BUT OF COURSE THE MAIN RESTRAINT IS
POSN PREFACE(419) OF THE WORLD; HE MUST STICK TO THE LETTER OF THE LAW AND TAKE NO CHANCES, AND AS FAR AS THE LAW IS CONCERNED,
CLEO PR01 (93) IN A LITTLE GALLEY, PUTTING HIS TRUST IN THE LAW AND THE CONSTITUTION. AND IT WAS PLAIN TO THE PEOPLE OF
CLEO PR01 (91) ME THERE IS POMPEY, AND THE OLD ROME, AND THE LAW AND THE LEGIONS: ALL ALL AGAINST ME; BUT HIGH ABOVE
CAPT II (256) CAN TALK LAW TO HIM. HE WILL GIVE YOU BOTH THE LAW AND THE PROPHETS. /SIR HOWARD/ DOES HE KNOW WHAT THE
BARB PREFACE(243) KNOWS, HE WILL REPUDIATE THE VERY CONCEPTION OF LAW AND THE VERY GROUNDWORK OF INSTITUTIONS, RIDICULING
JOAN 6,SD(122) OBTUSE ANGLE ARE FOR THE CANONS, THE DOCTORS OF LAW AND THEOLOGY, AND THE DOMINICAN MONKS, WHO ACT AS
LION PREFACE(43) TEMPLE, AND JUSTIFIED HIMSELF BOTH TO THE JEWISH LAW AND TO CAESAR. AND HE HAD PHYSICAL FORCE AT HIS COMMAND
LADY PREFACE(234) AND THAT THEIR ATTEMPTS TO CARRY OUT THE CODES OF LAW AND TO PRACTISE THE RELIGIONS OFFERED TO THEM BY GREAT
DOCT PREFACE(28) TO LOSE BY PLACING HIMSELF IN OPPOSITION TO THE LAW AND TO THE OUTCRY THAT ADDS PRIVATE PERSECUTION TO LEGAL
ROCK PREFACE(155) DECLARING INDIVIDUALS OUTSIDE THE PROTECTION OF LAW AND TORTURING THEM TO OUR HEARTS' CONTENT. CRUELTY'S
GENV I (40) I WAS TRIED FOR IT; BUT I PLEADED THE UNWRITTEN LAW AND WAS ACQUITTED. UNFORTUNATELY THE SCANDAL DESTROYED
BARB II (274) FOURTH, I'M FLY ENOUGH TO KNOW WOTS INSIDE THE LAW AND WOTS OUTSIDE IT; AND INSIDE IT I DO AS THE
LION PREFACE(3) IN IT, LIKE THAT OF THE BRIGAND WHO BREAKS EVERY LAW AND YET CLAIMS TO BE A PATRIOTIC SUBJECT OF THE KING WHO
6CAL (100) YOU-- /THE QUEEN/ DEAR SIR, YOUR WISHES ARE MY LAW AND YOUR COMMANDS MY DUTY. BUT THESE GENTLEMEN ARE VERY
BUOY III (38) RELIGION IS ONE THING, AND THE BRITISH MARRIAGE LAW ANOTHER. ALL THE REST LAUGH, EXCEPT MRS SECONDBORN, WHO
BARB PREFACE(242) ON DEMONSTRATIONS AND REMINDERS THAT MORALITY AND LAW ARE ONLY CONVENTIONS, FALLIBLE AND CONTINUALLY

ROCK PREFACE(157)	EXAMPLE OF THE POPULAR CONCEPTION OF CRIMINAL	LAW	AS A MEANS OF DELIVERING UP VICTIMS TO THE NORMAL
UNPL PREFACE(R16)	AND TAKE THE CONSEQUENCES BEFORE THE ORDINARY	LAW	AS AUTHORS AND EDITORS DO, I SHALL CHERISH THE LORD
BULL PREFACE(55)	CONSIDERS BARBAROUS. BUT THEN MOSES CONCEIVED HIS	LAW	AS BEING WHAT HE CALLED THE LAW OF GOD, AND NOT SIMPLY
GENV IV (118)	IS THE LAW? /JUDGE/ UNFORTUNATELY THERE IS NO	LAW	AS BETWEEN NATIONS. I SHALL HAVE TO CREATE IT AS I GO
GETT PREFACE(247)	PEOPLE OUGHT NOT TO BE CONTENT WITH THE MARRIAGE	LAW	AS IT IS MERELY BECAUSE IT IS NOT OFTEN UNBEARABLY
OVER PREFACE(158)	PLUTOCRACY WITHOUT ITS MONEY: CREEPING BELOW THE	LAW	AS ITS EXEMPLARS PRANCE ABOVE IT; CUTTING DOWN ALL
MIS. PREFACE(46)	PREACH A VIOLENT AND IMPLACABLE RESISTANCE TO ALL	LAW	AS THE ONLY REMEDY; AND THE RESULT OF THAT SPEEDILY IS
POSN PREFACE(417)	BATH, WITH EVERY SUGGESTION OF NAKEDNESS THAT THE	LAW	AS TO DECENCY ALLOWS, IS ONE OF THE MOST FAMILIAR
MILL PREFACE(109)	FAMILY LIMITS: ONE LAW FOR THE PARENT AND NO	LAW	AT ALL FOR THE CHILD. IN THE HUMBLEST CABIN THAT
MIS. PREFACE(34)	THEY BEGAN BY DOING UNTIL THEY WERE RESTRAINED BY	LAW	AT THE SUGGESTION OF ROBERT OWEN, THE FOUNDER OF ENGLISH
GENV II (58)	BACK, ONE AFTER ANOTHER, FROM THE REIGN OF	LAW	BASED ON THE ETERNAL PRINCIPLE OF JUSTICE, TO THE
LION PREFACE(60)	DELUSION. IT REDUCES JUSTICE AND LAW TO A FARCE:	LAW	BECOMES MERELY AN INSTRUMENT FOR KEEPING THE POOR IN
MIS. PREFACE(65)	HANDS (WITH US THEY MOSTLY FALL INTO SUCH HANDS)	LAW	BECOMES TYRANNY. AND WHAT IS A TYRANT? QUITE SIMPLY A
POSN PREFACE(417)	LEGAL OPINION AS TO THEIR COMPLIANCE WITH THE	LAW	BEFORE PRODUCTION. THERE ARE SEVERAL OBJECTIONS TO THIS
MILL I (142)	I REALLY DONT KNOW. I WILL LOOK IT UP IN MY	LAW	BOOKS. /EPIFANIA/ YOU NEED NOT. I INSTRUCT YOU THAT IT
MILL I SD(137)	OF THIS WALL IS OCCUPIED BY SHELVES OF CALF-BOUND	LAW	BOOKS. THE WALL BEHIND MR SAGAMORE HAS THE BIG WINDOW AS
DOCT III (143)	SKETCHING). /RIDGEON/ MY MIND'S MADE UP. WHEN THE	LAW	BREAKS DOWN, HONEST MEN MUST FIND A REMEDY FOR
GENV IV (121)	MY WORK OF BUILDING UP A BODY OF INTERNATIONAL	LAW	BY JUDICIAL PRECEDENT WOULD SEEM TO BE SIMPLE ENOUGH.
POSN PREFACE(430)	PERSUADE YOURSELF THAT THE SUPPLEMENTING OF THE	LAW	BY THE COMMON SENSE OF THE PRIVY COUNCIL WOULD SETTLE
MILL PREFACE(112)	SOCIALLY, BECAUSE IT CREATES A SORT OF GRESHAM	LAW	BY WHICH THE BASER HUMAN CURRENCY DRIVES OUT THE NOBLER
KING I (180)	THE WRATH OF GOD AS NOTHING, AND ARE ABOVE THE	LAW	BY YOUR RANK, ARE YOU NOT ASHAMED TO BELIEVE SUCH OLD
GETT PREFACE(183)	TREATY SHEWS THE SAME ANARCHICAL NOTION THAT THE	LAW	CAN BE SET ASIDE BY ANY TWO PRIVATE PERSONS BY THE
JOAN 6 (131)	OF HERESY. REMEMBER ALSO THAT NO COURT OF	LAW	CAN BE SO CRUEL AS THE COMMON PEOPLE ARE TO THOSE WHOM
ROCK PREFACE(189)	TO CRITICIZE. NOT UNTIL THE CRITICISM CHANGES THE	LAW	CAN THE MAGISTRATE ALLOW THE CRITIC TO GIVE EFFECT TO
PLES PREFACE(R14)	THAN WERE EVER ENTERTAINED, EVEN BY THE POOR	LAW	COMMISSIONERS OF 1834, TO THE PAUPERIZATION OF PRIVATE
MIS. PREFACE(71)	OF A RIGHT TO ROAM AS THE BASIS OF A MUCH NEEDED	LAW	COMPELLING PROPRIETORS OF LAND TO PROVIDE PLENTY OF
DOCT PREFACE(48)	BEFORE BITING THEM HE COULD COMPLY WITH THE	LAW	COMPLETELY. HERE, THEN, IS A PRETTY DEADLOCK. PUBLIC
GETT PREFACE(209)	NO POSSIBLE READJUSTMENT OF OUR MARRIAGE	LAW	COULD AVERT THE DEPOPULATION AND CONSEQUENT POLITICAL
POSN PREFACE(430)	HIS FOOT ON THE NOTION THAT AN OPTIONAL PENAL	LAW	COULD EVER BE ANYTHING BUT A GROSS CONTRADICTION IN
PLES PREFACE(R13)	NOW EDITED HISTRIONICALLY; AND THE RECORDS OF OUR	LAW	COURTS SHEW THAT THE STAGE IS AFFECTING PERSONAL CONDUCT
MILL IV (203)	WELL, MY DEAR OLD FATHER USED TO SAY THAT IN THE	LAW	COURTS THERE IS ONLY ONE WAY TO BEAT THE PEOPLE WHO HAVE
ROCK II (259)	HIS MAJESTY ALONE THAT YOU HAVE TO CONSIDER. THE	LAW	COURTS WILL NOT ENFORCE YOUR DECISIONS IF THEY ARE
HART PREFACE(12)	IN COURT. THE DEMORALIZATION DID NOT SPARE THE	LAW	COURTS. SOLDIERS WERE ACQUITTED, EVEN ON FULLY PROVED
GETT PREFACE(186)	CAROLINA HAS INDEED PASSED WHAT IS CALLED A FREAK	LAW	DECLARING THAT A MARRIAGE SHALL NOT BE DISSOLVED UNDER
CAPT II (255)	TO TAKE WITH HER OWN HANDS THE REDRESS THE	LAW	DENIED HER, YOU HAD HER IMPRISONED, AND FORCED HER TO
MIS. PREFACE(6)	THAN SLAVEDRIVERS, AND THERE IS A GROWING BODY OF	LAW	DESIGNED TO PREVENT PARENTS FROM USING THEIR CHILDREN
DOCT PREFACE(60)	THEIR PATIENTS WEAR. THE DOCTOR MAY LAY DOWN THE	LAW	DESPOTICALLY ENOUGH TO THE PATIENT AT POINTS WHERE THE
MIS. PREFACE(48)	A CLERGYMAN WHO IS NOT PREPARED TO LAY DOWN THE	LAW	DOGMATICALLY WILL NOT BE OF MUCH USE IN A VILLAGE
GENV IV (93)	IS NO LEADER, NO KING, NO PRIEST, NOR ANY BODY OF	LAW	ESTABLISHED BY DEAD KINGS AND PRIESTS, YOU HAVE MOB LAW,
BARB PREFACE(232)	CONDUCT UNWORTHY OF A GENTLEMAN OF FORTUNE. THE	LAW	EVERY DAY SEIZES ON UNSUCCESSFUL SCOUNDRELS OF THIS TYPE
JOAN PREFACE(42)	WAR? FROM US SHE WOULD HAVE HAD NO TRIAL AND NO	LAW	EXCEPT A DEFENCE OF THE REALM ACT SUSPENDING ALL LAW;
BULL PREFACE(51)	MEMORIALIZED; BUT THEY OBTAINED NO REDRESS: THE	LAW	FAILED THEM IN THEIR HOUR OF NEED. SO ONE LEADING FAMILY
SUPR II (60)	A FATHER'S CARE AND FOR THE SON A MOTHER'S. THE	LAW	FOR FATHER AND SON AND MOTHER AND DAUGHTER IS NOT THE
MILL PREFACE(109)	FOR THE IGNORANT AND ANOTHER FOR THE LEARNED, ONE	LAW	FOR THE BRAVE AND ANOTHER FOR THE TIMID, AND WITHIN
MIS. PREFACE(45)	AND THEN WORSHIPPED AS A PROPHET. HERE THE	LAW	FOR THE CHILD IS THE SAME AS FOR THE ADULT. THE HIGH
MILL PREFACE(109)	LAW FOR THE RICH AND ANOTHER FOR THE POOR, ONE	LAW	FOR THE CUNNING AND ANOTHER FOR THE SIMPLE, ONE LAW FOR
MILL PREFACE(109)	FOR THE CUNNING AND ANOTHER FOR THE SIMPLE, ONE	LAW	FOR THE FORCEFUL AND ANOTHER FOR THE FEEBLE, ONE LAW FOR
MILL PREFACE(109)	FOR THE FORCEFUL AND ANOTHER FOR THE FEEBLE, ONE	LAW	FOR THE IGNORANT AND ANOTHER FOR THE LEARNED, ONE LAW
MILL PREFACE(109)	FOR THE TIMID, AND WITHIN FAMILY LIMITS ONE	LAW	FOR THE PARENT AND NO LAW AT ALL FOR THE CHILD. IN THE
MILL PREFACE(109)	ALL EQUAL BEFORE THE LAW. VIRTUALLY THERE IS ONE	LAW	FOR THE RICH AND ANOTHER FOR THE POOR, ONE LAW FOR THE
MIS. PREFACE(48)	I AM SUFFICIENT OF AN ATHANASIAN TO ADVOCATE A	LAW	FOR THE SPEEDY EXECUTION OF ALL ATHANASIANS, BECAUSE
SIM PREFACE(13)	WAS NO PROVISION EXCEPT A SAVAGELY PENAL POOR	LAW	FOR WORKERS THROWN OUT OF OUR INDUSTRIAL ESTABLISHMENTS
AUGS (279)	/AUGUSTUS/ (SHOUTING DOWN TO HIM) THERES NO MORE	LAW	FOR YOU, YOU SCOUNDREL. YOURE A SOLDIER NOW. (HE SHUTS
SUPR HANDBOK(204)	TO THE JEWS IN VIEW OF THE FACTS THAT THE MOSAIC	LAW	FORBADE MORE THAN FORTY LASHES IN THE NAME OF HUMANITY,
DOCT PREFACE(37)	OF INVESTIGATION IS THE ONLY METHOD; AND NO	LAW	FORBIDDING ANY PARTICULAR METHOD CAN CUT US OFF FROM THE
ROCK PREFACE(186)	YOUR PARTIZANS, I HAVE A LAW TO ADMINISTER. THE	LAW	FORBIDS OBSCENITY, SEDITION, AND BLASPHEMY. YOU ARE
MILL I (142)	AS SUCH I AM AN UNUSUAL WOMAN. YOU WILL TAKE THE	LAW	FROM ME AND DO EXACTLY WHAT I TELL YOU TO DO. /SAGAMORE/
SUPR III SD(71)	LIONS TOLERATE LICE, AN ENGLISH POLICEMAN OR POOR	LAW	GUARDIAN WOULD RECOGNIZE THEM AS A SELECTED BAND OF
SUPR III (106)	SPENT SEVENPENCE ON HER CHILDREN'S SCHOOLING: THE	LAW	HAD TO FORCE HER TO LET THEM BE TAUGHT GRATUITOUSLY; BUT
GETT PREFACE(229)	AND SOLICITATION, IN WHICH THE HAND OF THE	LAW	HAS BEEN BROUGHT DOWN ON ONE SEX ONLY, OUTRAGES WHICH
GENV PREFACE(12)	INVETERATE OBJECTION TO BE GOVERNED AT ALL.	LAW	HAS BEEN POPULARLY KNOWN ONLY AS OPPRESSION AND
BUOY III (46)	OUT). /MRS THIRDBORN/ (RISING) SIR FERDINAND'S	LAW	HAS FAILED US. DICK'S SCIENCE HAS FAILED US. FIFF'S
POSN PREFACE(390)	TO SELL SILVER WITHOUT A LICENCE. WHEN THE	LAW	HAS FORGOTTEN SOME ATROCIOUS SIN-- FOR INSTANCE,
MIS. PREFACE(48)	BEHOVES HIM ALL THE MORE TO BE VERY CAREFUL WHAT	LAW	HE LAYS DOWN, BUT UNLESS BOTH THE CLERGYMAN AND THE
DEVL I (26)	CARE, YOU. IN AN HOUR FROM THIS THERE WILL BE NO	LAW	HERE BUT MARTIAL LAW. I PASSED THE SOLDIERS WITHIN SIX
POSN (439)	HORSE-THIEF! /BLANCO/ DO WOMEN MAKE THE	LAW	HERE, OR MEN? DRIVE THESE HEIFERS OUT. /THE WOMEN/ OH!
GETT (300)	MR BALFOUR'S OR MR ASQUITH'S. IF I HAD KNOWN THE	LAW	I WOULD NEVER HAVE CONSENTED. I DONT BELIEVE ANY WOMAN
DEVL I (9)	WHY SHOULD WE DO OUR DUTY AND KEEP GOD'S	LAW	IF THERE IS TO BE NO DIFFERENCE MADE BETWEEN US AND
BARB PREFACE(241)	REMEDY IS, NOT TO LICENSE EVERYBODY TO THWART THE	LAW	IF THEY PLEASE, BUT TO MAKE LAWS THAT WILL COMMAND THE
BARB PREFACE(243)	BE, A REVOLUTIONARY WRITER, BECAUSE OUR LAWS MAKE	LAW	IMPOSSIBLE; OUR LIBERTIES DESTROY ALL FREEDOM; OUR
CAPT III (281)	HALF A DOZEN SUCH WOMEN WOULD MAKE AN END OF	LAW	IN ENGLAND IN SIX MONTHS. THE BLUEJACKET COMES TO THE
POSN PREFACE(398)	OUR JUDGES HAD SO LITTLE POWER THERE WOULD BE NO	LAW	IN ENGLAND. IF OUR CHURCHES HAD SO MUCH, THERE WOULD BE
BASH II,1, (103)	THIS BRUTAL SAILOR SHALL BE MADE TO KNOW THERE'S	LAW	IN ENGLAND. /LUCIAN/ DO NOT INTERRUPT HIM: MINE EARS ARE
GENV II (57)	IT. YOU ARE FAMILIAR WITH WHAT YOU CALL JUDGEMADE	LAW	IN ENGLAND. WELL, SIR MIDLANDER, THE JUDGES OF THE COURT
GENV III (66)	WHAT DO YOU CARRY THAT FOR? IT IS AGAINST THE	LAW	IN GENEVA. /THE WIDOW/ THERE IS NO LONGER ANY LAW IN
GENV III (66)	LAW IN GENEVA. /THE WIDOW/ THERE IS NO LONGER ANY	LAW	IN GENEVA. THE HAGUE HAS ABOLISHED THE INTELLECTUAL
POSN PREFACE(413)	ALONE SHOULD HAVE THE RIGHT TO SET THE	LAW	IN OPERATION AGAINST THE MANAGER OF A THEATRE OR THE
BARB PREFACE(243)	LAWS OF HIS COUNTRY AND YET PERSUADED TO REGARD	LAW	IN THE ABSTRACT AS VITALLY NECESSARY TO SOCIETY. ONCE HE
BARB PREFACE(242)	PRIVATE ENGLISHMEN WITHOUT ANY RESPECT FOR	LAW	IN THE ABSTRACT, NAIVELY SET THE EXAMPLE OF VIOLATING
GETT PREFACE(241)	CHANGE CAN BE EFFECTED EASILY UNDER THE EXISTING	LAW	IN THE STATE OF WASHINGTON IT IS NOT CERTAIN THAT THE
GETT PREFACE(199)	ACTIONS GOING BEYOND THE STRICT LETTER OF THE	LAW	IN THE WAY OF KINDNESS THAN WE HAVE NOW AGAINST EXCESS
GETT PREFACE(240)	OF VIEW ENGLAND HAS THE WORST CIVIL MARRIAGE	LAW	IN THE WORLD, WITH THE EXCEPTION OF SILLY SOUTH
GENV IV (110)	CAPACITY OF A FAMOUS PROPHET WHO LAID DOWN THE	LAW	IN THESE WORDS, " THIS COMMANDMENT I GIVE UNTO YOU, THAT
DOCT V (177)	NOT MEAN THAT. I MEANT AFRAID OF MY TAKING THE	LAW	INTO MY OWN HANDS, AND KILLING YOU. /RIDGEON/ I AM SO
OVER PREFACE(160)	SUCH A PENALTY, OR OF BEING PREPARED TO TAKE THE	LAW	INTO OUR OWN HANDS IF IT WERE WITHHELD. NOW WHAT APPLIES
CLEO PRO1 (91)	PERISH WITHOUT FRUIT." BUT POMPEY SAID, " THE	LAW	IS ABOVE ALL; AND IF THOU BREAK IT THOU SHALT DIE." THEN
NEVR IV (297)	TO ROBE). MR CRAMPTON: YOUR NOTION OF GOING TO	LAW	IS ALL NONSENSE: YOUR CHILDREN WILL BE OF AGE BEFORE YOU
GETT PREFACE(184)	COMPULSORY UPON ALL NORMAL PEOPLE; AND UNTIL THE	LAW	IS ALTERED THERE IS NOTHING FOR US BUT TO MAKE THE BEST
POSN (452)	WILL ACKNOWLEDGE IT. BUT RELIGION IS ONE THING:	LAW	IS ANOTHER. IN RELIGION WE'RE ALL BROTHERS. IN LAW WE
ROCK PREFACE(188)	IS STILL SOME LAW LEFT IN THE WORLD. /JESUS/	LAW	IS BLIND WITHOUT COUNSEL. THE COUNSEL MEN AGREE WITH IS
GETT PREFACE(236)	HAS A RIGHT TO SEXUAL EXPERIENCE, AND THAT THE	LAW	IS CONCERNED ONLY WITH PARENTAGE, WHICH IS NOW A
POSN PREFACE(419)	OF THE LAW AND TAKE NO CHANCES, AND AS FAR AS THE	LAW	IS CONCERNED, JOURNALISM, LITERATURE, AND THE DRAMA
MILL PREFACE(109)	AND MOULDED HUMAN SOCIETY SINCE THE CREATION. THE	LAW	IS EQUAL BEFORE ALL OF US; BUT WE ARE NOT ALL EQUAL
ROCK PREFACE(190)	ITS SAVAGE SUPERSTITION THAT WHOEVER BREAKS THE	LAW	IS FAIR GAME FOR THE TORTURERS, AND THAT THE WRONG
GETT PREFACE(183)	ANARCHICAL ACTION, BECAUSE OUR MARRIAGE	LAW	IS INHUMAN AND UNREASONABLE TO THE POINT OF DOWNRIGHT
DOCT III (142)	LAW OF THE LAND? /SIR PATRICK/ THE CRIMINAL	LAW	IS NO USE TO DECENT PEOPLE. IT ONLY HELPS BLACKGUARDS TO
GETT PREFACE(187)	TO DIVORCE IT IS AT ONCE CLEAR THAT OUR MARRIAGE	LAW	IS NOT FOUNDED ON EITHER ASSUMPTION. WHAT IT IS REALLY
BASH III (120)	FOOTSTEP-- ENTER CASHEL. /CASHEL/ SANCTUARY! THE	LAW	IS ON MY TRACK. WHAT! LYDIA HERE! /LYDIA/ AY: LYDIA
CAPT NOTES (302)	TAKE THE PRETENCE SERIOUSLY, AND, WHEN THE	LAW	IS ON THE SIDE OF INJUSTICE, WILL NOT ACCEPT THE
GETT PREFACE(234)	BE MADE THE LAST, OR WHOLLY EXCLUDED. THE PRESENT	LAW	IS PERFECTLY LOGICAL ONLY IF YOU ONCE ADMIT (AS NO
BULL PREFACE(62)	RESULTS TO BE EXPECTED IF ONCE RESPECT FOR THE	LAW	IS SHAKEN. SHOULD THE PRESENT STATE OF THINGS CONTINUE,
KING II (232)	YET THEY CANNOT LIVE TOGETHER WITHOUT LAWS; AND A	LAW	IS SOMETHING THAT OBLIGES THEM ALL TO DO THE SAME THING.
GETT PREFACE(253)	WHO, IF CHILDLESS, WOULD SEPARATE. THE MARRIAGE	LAW	IS SUPERFLUOUS IN SUCH CASES. THIS IS SHEWN BY THE FACT
GETT PREFACE(208)	IN FURIOUS SECRET REBELLION AGAINST THE EXISTING	LAW	IS THE SADDLING OF THE RIGHT TO A CHILD WITH THE
POSN (438)	LAW! WHAT RIGHT HAS A HORSE-THIEF TO ANY LAW?	LAW	IS THROWN AWAY ON A BRUTE LIKE THAT. /ELDER DANIELS/
2TRU II (63)	AND OBSCURES THE PREACHER'S MESSAGE. BESIDES, THE	LAW	IS TOO MUCH CONCERNED WITH CRUDE FACTS AND TOO LITTLE
GETT PREFACE(183)	THE STRONGEST INDIVIDUAL. CERTAINLY THE MARRIAGE	LAW	IS. THE ONLY PEOPLE WHO SUCCESSFULLY EVADE IT ARE THOSE

GETT PREFACE(257)	WHAT A JUDGE IS, OR WHAT A BISHOP IS, OR WHAT THE	LAW	IS, OR WHAT RELIGION IS. IN OTHER WORDS, DO NOT ASK YOUR
GETT (280)	/THE GENERAL/ TUT, TUT! /LEO/ OH, HOW SILLY THE	LAW	IS! WHY CANT I MARRY THEM BOTH? /THE GENERAL/ (
BARB III (319)	WHAT ABOUT THE BAR? /STEPHEN/ I HAVE NOT STUDIED	LAW	. AND I AM AFRAID I HAVE NOT THE NECESSARY PUSH-- I
ROCK PREFACE(160)	ADMINISTERED THROUGH A RITUAL OF CRIMINAL	LAW	. AND IN THE LIST OF CRIMES THE VERY WORST OFFENCES
JOAN PREFACE(7)	COURT; AND THE DECISION WAS STRICTLY ACCORDING TO	LAW	. AND SHE WAS NOT A MELODRAMATIC HEROINE: THAT IS, A
APPL PREFACE(181)	EASIER TO WRITE A GOOD PLAY THAN TO MAKE A GOOD	LAW	. AND THERE ARE NOT A HUNDRED MEN IN THE WORLD WHO CAN
POSN PREFACE(381)	FORTIFIED BY THE MAGISTRACY AND THE WHOLE BODY OF	LAW	. BLASPHEMY, INDECENCY, LIBEL, TREASON, SEDITION,
SUPR HANDBOK(196)	JUST AS THEY ARE WHEN THEY BREAK THE PRESENT	LAW	. BUT AS OUR PROPRIETARY CLASS HAS NO FEAR OF THAT
MTH2 (61)	A CLASSICAL SCHOLAR; AND MY PROFESSION WAS THE	LAW	. BUT I LOOKED UP THE TEXT-BOOKS, AND GOT UP THE CASE
POSN PREFACE(423)	TO PROSECUTION IN THE ORDINARY COURSE OF	LAW	. BUT THE COMMITTEE SHOULD HAVE NO POWERS OF PUNISHMENT
BARB I (253)	IS ABLE TO BEHAVE AS HE DOES. HE IS ABOVE THE	LAW	. DO YOU THINK BISMARCK OR GLADSTONE OR DISRAELI COULD
GETT PREFACE(247)	TO NEUTRALIZE THE ALSATIAN EVILS OF THE MARRIAGE	LAW	. DOES IT MATTER? A LESS OBVIOUSLY SILLY EVASION, AND
GETT PREFACE(215)	NOT BE THE ONLY ONES TO TAKE ADVANTAGE OF THE NEW	LAW	. EVEN WOMEN TO WHOM A HOME WITHOUT A MAN IN IT WOULD BE
MILL III (180)	GIVEN THEM A SIGNAL TO HIDE. YOU ARE BREAKING THE	LAW	. GIVE ME SOME WORK OR I WILL SEND A POSTCARD TO THE
BARB I (254)	NOT BREAK THE LAW! HE IS ALWAYS BREAKING THE	LAW	. HE BROKE THE LAW WHEN HE WAS BORN: HIS PARENTS WERE
POSN PREFACE(366)	RELIGION, ART, LITERATURE, PHILOSOPHY, OR	LAW	. HE CALLS IN A PLAYWRIGHT JUST AS HE CALLS IN A DOCTOR,
KING I (218)	HOUSE, THOUGH HIS MEETINGS ARE AGAINST THE	LAW	. HERE IS MR NEWTON, A KING IN THE NEW ROYAL SOCIETY.
DEVL I (26)	FROM THIS THERE WILL BE NO LAW HERE BUT MARTIAL	LAW	. I PASSED THE SOLDIERS WITHIN SIX MILES ON MY WAY HERE:
BASH III (119)	MY MISSION HERE IS TO WREAK ULTION FOR THE BROKEN	LAW	. I WISH YOUR LADYSHIP GOOD AFTERNOON. /LYDIA/ GOOD
POSN (441)	ELDER? /ELDER DANIELS/ THE SHERIFF KNOWS THE	LAW	. I WOULDNT SAY FOR SURE; BUT I THINK IT WOULD BE MORE
JOAN 6 (135)	(BEWILDERED) BUT IT IS NOT A PLEASURE. IT IS THE	LAW	. IS IS CUSTOMARY. IT IS ALWAYS DONE. /THE INQUISITOR/
POSN PREFACE(389)	CENSORSHIP, IT IS PRACTICALLY PLACED ABOVE THE	LAW	. IT IS ALMOST HUMILIATING TO HAVE TO DEMONSTRATE THE
GETT PREFACE(230)	OF OUR SEXUAL MORALITY TAKEN SERIOUSLY BY THE	LAW	. IT IS EASY TO FORESEE THE CONSEQUENCES. NO MAN WILL
POSN (449)	YOU? /BLANCO/ HE HAS. AND I SAY IT'S AGAINST THE	LAW	. IT'S TORTURE: THATS WHAT IT IS. /ELDER DANIELS/ HE'S
DEVL I (11)	IF WE HAVE EVER SET UP OUR PREACHING AGAINST HIS	LAW	. (HE FASTENS HIS CLOAK, AND IS NOW READY TO GO). JUST
3PLA PREFACE(R22)	TESTIMONY, WILL DESTROY THE VERY SENSE OF	LAW	. KAISERS, GENERALS, JUDGES, AND PRIME MINISTERS WILL
MILL I (142)	YOU NEED NOT. I INSTRUCT YOU THAT IT IS THE	LAW	. MY FATHER ALWAYS HAD TO INSTRUCT HIS LAWYERS IN THE
POSN PREFACE(391)	SUCH A POST MAY BE REGARDED AS DECREED BY NATURAL	LAW	. ON THE OTHER HAND, A GOOD LORD CHAMBERLAIN WOULD BE A
POSN (438)	WITH IT; BUT I COULDNT ALLOW THAT: IT'S NOT THE	LAW	. /BABSY/ LAW! WHAT RIGHT HAS A HORSE-THIEF TO ANY
CAPT II (256)	I DO NOT DEFEND MYSELF. I CALL ON YOU TO OBEY THE	LAW	. /BRASSBOUND/ I INTEND TO DO SO. THE LAW OF THE ATLAS
JOAN 6 (147)	BETWEEN THESE MIGHTY FORCES, THE CHURCH AND THE	LAW	. /CAUCHON/ YOU CALL HER INNOCENT! /THE INQUISITOR/ OH,
GETT (318)	BE LIABLE, BECAUSE YOU WILL NOT BE HIS WIFE IN	LAW	. /EDITH/ NONSENSE! OF COURSE I SHALL BE HIS WIFE.
BUOY 1 (10)	NOT BREAK THE LAW. /SON/ BUT I WANT TO BREAK THE	LAW	. /FATHER/ YOU MEAN CHANGE THE LAW. WELL, YOU CAN
DEVL I (21)	MY FATHER DIED WITHOUT THE CONSOLATIONS OF THE	LAW	. /HAWKINS/ GOOD AGAIN, MR DUDGEON, GOOD AGAIN. (
BARB I (254)	COULD THEY DO? HE DOES NOT ACTUALLY BREAK THE	LAW	. /LADY BRITOMART/ NOT BREAK THE LAW! HE IS ALWAYS
CAPT III (276)	NO SONS EVEN, WHEN HE HAS TO CARRY OUT THE	LAW	. /LADY CICELY/ BUT THEN HE OUGHTNT TO HAVE ANY PROPERTY
BASH III (123)	CASHEL. /CASHEL/ POLICEMAN! I DO YIELD ME TO THE	LAW	. /LYDIA/ OH NO. /ADELAIDE/ MY SON! /CASHEL/ MY
BUOY 1 (10)	YOU PLEASE AS LONG AS YOU DO NOT BREAK THE	LAW	. /SON/ BUT I WANT TO BREAK THE LAW. /FATHER/ YOU MEAN
POSN (457)	THAT DOORWAY. OUT WITH THEM IN THE NAME OF THE	LAW	. /STRAPPER/ (WITHOUT) HOLD HARD, GEORGE. (AT THE
JOAN 6 (142)	ITS COURSE, MASTER DE STOGUMBER. AND YOU KNOW THE	LAW	. /THE CHAPLAIN/ (RISING, PURPLE WITH FURY) I KNOW THAT
GETT (303)	SISTER ACT? THAT DID NOT PREVENT ITS BECOMING	LAW	. /THE GENERAL/ BUT WHEN THE GOVERNMENT SOUNDED YOU AS
POSN (461)	THERE HAS BEEN NO THEFT. /NESTOR/ THAT AINT THE	LAW	. /THE SHERIFF/ I FINE YOU A DOLLAR FOR CONTEMPT OF
BUOY III (38)	F./ NONSENSE! ALL MARRIAGES ARE EXACTLY ALIKE IN	LAW	. /THE WIDOWER/ SO MUCH THE WORSE FOR LAW, I AM AFRAID.
JOAN 6 (123)	/CAUCHON/ PROSECUTOR, YOU WOULD CALL HIM IN CIVIL	LAW	. /WARWICK/ AH! PROSECUTOR. QUITE, QUITE. I AM VERY
HART PREFACE(13)	ACCORDINGLY; AND ITS LAW WAS SET ASIDE FOR LYNCH	LAW	. THE CLIMAX OF LEGAL LAWLESSNESS WAS REACHED IN FRANCE.
SUPR PREFACE(R20)	THE MATURE CASES ALL ILLUSTRATE THE SHAKESPEARIAN	LAW	. THE ONE APPARENT EXCEPTION, PETRUCHIO, IS NOT A REAL
GETT PREFACE(230)	WILL RECONSIDER THEIR MORALITY AND REMODEL THE	LAW	. THE PERSONAL SENTIMENTAL BASIS OF MONOGAMY. MONOGAMY
SUPR PREFACE(R36)	RESPECTABLE SOCIETY AND VERITABLE PILLARS OF THE	LAW	. THE WHOLE ALLEGORY IS A CONSISTENT ATTACK ON MORALITY
GETT PREFACE(225)	BY THEM WHEN THEY ARE EFFECTED ACCORDING TO	LAW	. THEREFORE WE NEED NOT HESITATE TO ALTER THE LAW MERELY
SIM PREFACE(18)	INQUISITION TO BE DONE BY AN ORDINARY COURT OF	LAW	. THEREUPON THE INQUISITION, AS SUCH, DISAPPEARS,
SUPR HANDBOK(221)	DEATH. CRIMINALS DO NOT DIE BY THE HANDS OF THE	LAW	. THEY DIE BY THE HANDS OF OTHER MEN. THE ASSASSIN
GENV PREFACE(17)	VICTIMS DIE OF ILLUSAGE INSTEAD OF BY MILITARY	LAW	. UNDER SUCH CIRCUMSTANCES ANY MISCELLANEOUS COLLECTION
GENV IV (107)	JEALOUSY. MY NAME IS THE UNWRITTEN LAW THAT IS NO	LAW	. UNTIL YOU HAVE DEALT WITH ME YOU HAVE DONE NOTHING.
MILL PREFACE(109)	ALL OF US; BUT WE ARE NOT ALL EQUAL BEFORE THE	LAW	. VIRTUALLY THERE IS ONE LAW FOR THE RICH AND ANOTHER
BUOY 1 (10)	TO BREAK THE LAW. /FATHER/ YOU MEAN CHANGE THE	LAW	. WELL, YOU CAN ADVOCATE ANY CHANGE YOU PLEASE; AND IF
SUPR HANDBOK(221)	DEPARTMENT OF WHAT, IN WHOLESALE, WE CALL PENAL	LAW	. WHEN A MAN WANTS TO MURDER A TIGER HE CALLS IT SPORT:
DOCT V (173)	PRACTICE IN MEDICINE OUGHT TO BE PUT DOWN BY	LAW	. WHEN I ASKED HIM WHY, HE SAID THAT PRIVATE DOCTORS
POSN PREFACE(421)	PUNISHED FOR UNSPECIFIED OFFENCES UNKNOWN TO THE	LAW	. WHEN I SAY UNSPECIFIED, I SHOULD SAY SPECIFIED AS
POSN PREFACE(403)	EITHER COSTS NOTHING OR IS AT LEAST CHEAPER THAN	LAW	. WHO IS TO PAY FOR THE TIME OF THE THREE ARBITRATORS,
GETT PREFACE(240)	RESORTING TO THE SHAMEFUL SHIFTS IMPOSED BY OUR	LAW	. YET THE FIGURES JUST GIVEN TO THE ROYAL COMMISSION
ROCK II (237)	/SIR DEXTER/ YOU DONT EVEN KNOW THE PRESENT	LAW	. YOU HAVE THE VERMINOUS PERSONS ACT. WHAT MORE DO YOU
FANY III (299)	YOU HAVE A DEVILISH COOL WAY OF LAYING DOWN THE	LAW	. YOU KNOW, IN MY CLASS YOU HAVE TO WRAP UP THINGS A
POSN PREFACE(421)	VII: THAT IS, THE INADEQUACY OF THE ORDINARY	LAW	. " WE CONSIDER," SAYS THE REPORT, " THAT THE LAW WHICH
DOCT PREFACE(7)	THE PRISONER. THUS A JUDGE WITH A KEEN SENSE OF	LAW	(A VERY RARE PHENOMENON ON THE BENCH, BY THE WAY) WAS
FANY EPILOG(330)	THE HEROINE GETS INTO TROUBLE BY DEFYING THE	LAW	(IF SHE DIDNT GET INTO TROUBLE, THERED BE NO DRAMA) AND
BULL PREFACE(46)	CONDEMNED TO FIVE YEARS' PENAL SERVITUDE BY LYNCH	LAW	(TECHNICALLY CALLED MARTIAL LAW) ADMINISTERED BY A
BARB PREFACE(242)	THE MAN LAGS BEHIND THE LAW; BUT WHEN THE	LAW	LAGS BEHIND THE MAN, HE BECOMES EQUALLY AN ANARCHIST.
BASH III (122)	THE PEACEMAKER, WHEN LO! THESE MINIONS OF THE	LAW	LAID HANDS ON ME. /BASHVILLE/ A LOVELY WOMAN, WITH
PRES (133)	OH, IMPOSSIBLE! THE PROCLAMATION OF MARTIAL	LAW	LAST TUESDAY MADE SANDSTONE VIRTUALLY DICTATOR IN THE
ROCK PREFACE(188)	MAKE AN END OF YOU WHILST THERE IS STILL SOME	LAW	LEFT IN THE WORLD. /JESUS/ LAW IS BLIND WITHOUT COUNSEL.
MTH2 (52)	THE GRAVES OF YOUR CONSCIENTIOUS OBJECTORS? ALL	LAW	LIMITS LIBERTY OF CONSCIENCE: IF A MAN'S CONSCIENCE
DOCT PREFACE(27)	CENTURY INOCULATION, BY A PURELY REACTIONARY	LAW	MAKING ALL SORTS OF VACCINATION, SCIENTIFIC OR NOT,
POSN PREFACE(389)	AND MUST PROSECUTE HIM IF HE MAKES CESSPOOLS. THE	LAW	MAY BE ONLY THE INTOLERANCE OF THE COMMUNITY; BUT IT IS
MIS. PREFACE(25)	OR EVEN A JUDGE, WHO HAS SOME NOTION OF WHAT	LAW	MEANS, A DOCTOR WITH A GLIMMERING OF SCIENCE, AN OFFICER
GETT PREFACE(225)	LAW. THEREFORE WE NEED NOT HESITATE TO ALTER THE	LAW	MERELY BECAUSE THE ALTERATION WOULD MAKE SUCH CHANGES
GETT PREFACE(235)	GRIEVANCES. ANY TOLERABLE WESTERN DIVORCE	LAW	MUST PUT THE SENTIMENTAL GRIEVANCES FIRST, AND SHOULD
GETT PREFACE(239)	WILL CERTAINLY NOT ACCEPT A CELIBATE LIFE, THE	LAW	MUST SANCTION THE DISSOLUTION IN ORDER TO PREVENT A
JOAN 6 (142)	THIS WOMAN TO ESCAPE US? /THE INQUISITOR/ THE	LAW	MUST TAKE ITS COURSE, MASTER DE STOGUMBER. AND YOU KNOW
APPL PREFACE(181)	ENOUGH TO STAND DAILY WEAR AND TEAR AS LONG AS A	LAW	MUST. NOW COMES THE QUESTION, IF WE CANNOT GOVERN
MRS PREFACE(163)	YET, THOUGH NEITHER MEDICINE NOR PAINTING NOR	LAW	NOR THE CHURCH MOULDS THE CHARACTER OF THE NATION AS
DOCT PREFACE(67)	MAN INTO A FIRST-CLASS ONE. IF THE PRACTICE OF	LAW	NOT ONLY LED TO A JUDGE HAVING TO HANG, BUT THE HANGMAN
GETT PREFACE(246)	ANOTHER'S MERCY THAT THEY EMPLOY EVERY DEVICE THE	LAW	NOW ADMITS OF, FROM THE MOST STRINGENT MARRIAGE
MILL PREFACE(118)	WHICH REVIVED ALL THE INFAMIES OF THE POOR	LAW	OF A CENTURY AGO (THE DAYS OF OLIVER TWIST) AND COULD
JOAN PREFACE(37)	BUT I WILL MAINTAIN MY OWN WAYS BEFORE HIM." THE	LAW	OF CHANGE IS THE LAW OF GOD. WHEN JOAN MAINTAINED HER
JOAN PREFACE(38)	OF THE FACT THAT THE LAW OF EVOLUTION IS IBSEN'S	LAW	OF CHANGE. AND AS THE LAW OF GOD IN ANY SENSE OF THE
JOAN PREFACE(38)	OF EVOLUTION, IT FOLLOWS THAT THE LAW OF GOD IS A	LAW	OF CHANGE, AND THAT WHEN THE CHURCHES SET THEMSELVES
JOAN PREFACE(29)	IN TRYING HER CASE ACCORDING TO THE CATHOLIC	LAW	OF CHRISTENDOM, AND TO ARGUE IT OUT WITH HER AT SITTING
KING PREFACE(155)	OF MOTION IS PURE DOGMA. SO IS HOGARTH'S FIRST	LAW	OF DESIGN. THE MODERN ASTRONOMERS HAVE PROVED, SO FAR,
METH PREFACE(R63)	THE TREATISES OF THE RICARDIAN ECONOMISTS ON THE	LAW	OF DIMINISHING RETURN, WHICH WAS ONLY THE MANCHESTER
METH PREFACE(R13)	TO WHOM SUCH AN ELEMENTARY BUT VITAL POINT AS THE	LAW	OF ECONOMIC RENT IS A PONS ASINORUM NEVER TO BE
FOUN (219)	MOUSE PRINCIPLE, MY LORD. THAT IS A PART OF THE	LAW	OF ENGLAND. /MERCER/ NEVER. NOT WHEN THE WOMAN IS THE
JOAN PREFACE(38)	OR THE RECOGNITION OF THE FACT THAT THE	LAW	OF EVOLUTION IS IBSEN'S LAW OF CHANGE. AND AS THE LAW OF
JOAN PREFACE(38)	NOW COMMAND A FAITH PROOF AGAINST SCIENCE IS A	LAW	OF EVOLUTION, IT FOLLOWS THAT THE LAW OF GOD IS A LAW OF
JOAN PREFACE(38)	OF EVOLUTION IS IBSEN'S LAW OF CHANGE, AND AS THE	LAW	OF GOD IN ANY SENSE OF THE WORD WHICH CAN NOW COMMAND A
JOAN PREFACE(38)	IS A LAW OF EVOLUTION, IT FOLLOWS THAT THE	LAW	OF GOD IS A LAW OF CHANGE, AND THAT WHEN THE CHURCHES
JOAN PREFACE(38)	AS SUCH, THEY ARE SETTING THEMSELVES AGAINST THE	LAW	OF GOD. CREDULITY, MODERN AND MEDIEVAL. WHEN ABERNETHY,
KING I (210)	THE LAW OF NATURE! AND THE LAW OF NATURE IS THE	LAW	OF GOD. GO OUT INTO YOUR GARDEN AND THROW A STONE
JOAN PREFACE(37)	MY OWN WAYS BEFORE HIM." THE LAW OF CHANGE IS THE	LAW	OF GOD. WHEN JOAN MAINTAINED HER OWN WAYS SHE CLAIMED,
BULL PREFACE(55)	CONCEIVED HIS LAW AS BEING WHAT HE CALLED THE	LAW	OF GOD, AND NOT SIMPLY AN INSTRUMENT FOR THE
MTH2 (61)	OF THEIR AMBITIONS AND ASPIRATIONS THAN THE	LAW	OF GRAVITATION. I SPEAK, IF I MAY SAY SO, WITH
MIS. PREFACE(45)	OF POLITICAL SCIENCE AS WELL ESTABLISHED AS THE	LAW	OF GRAVITATION, OUR RULERS ARE NEVER TAUGHT POLITICAL
3PLA PREFACE(R29)	HAVE DONE AS MUCH FOR ANY STRANGER-- THAT THE	LAW	OF HIS OWN NATURE, AND NO INTEREST NOR LUST WHATSOEVER,
METH PREFACE(R79)	MATHEMATICAL DOGMAS ARE MORE COMPREHENSIBLE. THE	LAW	OF INVERSE SQUARES IS AS INCOMPREHENSIBLE TO THE COMMON
METH PREFACE(R80)	OF SYRACUSE SHOUTING EUREKA, EUREKA, OR THAT THE	LAW	OF INVERSE SQUARES MUST BE DISCARDED IF ANYONE CAN PROVE
POSN PREFACE(418)	LAWYER WITH THE MOST ELEMENTARY KNOWLEDGE OF THE	LAW	OF LIBEL IN ITS VARIOUS APPLICATIONS TO SEDITION,
MILL I (142)	MY FATHER INSTRUCTED ME MOST CAREFULLY IN THE	LAW	OF LIBEL. IF I QUESTIONED YOUR SOLVENCY, THAT WOULD BE A
GETT PREFACE(184)	PROTECTION AFFORDED TO THE PARTIES BY THE	LAW	OF LIBEL, AND THE READINESS OF SOCIETY ON VARIOUS OTHER

SUPR II (60)	FATHER AND SON AND MOTHER AND DAUGHTER IS NOT THE	LAW	OF LOVE: IT IS THE LAW OF REVOLUTION, OF EMANCIPATION,
GETT (302)	WARN OUR GOVERNMENTS SO EARNESTLY THAT UNLESS THE	LAW	OF MARRIAGE WERE FIRST MADE HUMAN, IT COULD NEVER BECOME
BARB PREFACE(231)	MALICE IS AS GREAT AS HIS OWN. " LET HER HAVE THE	LAW	OF ME, AS SHE SAID SHE WOULD," SAYS BILL: " WHAT I DONE
BULL PREFACE(55)	ELEVEN MORE THAN THE UTMOST PERMITTED BY THE	LAW	OF MOSES IN TIMES WHICH OUR ARMY OF OCCUPATION NO DOUBT
KING PREFACE(155)	UNIVERSE I MAKE NO APOLOGY. NEWTON'S FIRST	LAW	OF MOTION IS PURE DOGMA. SO IS HOGARTH'S FIRST LAW OF
KING I (209)	IT FROM ITS PATH. THIS, HE SAYS, IS THE FIRST	LAW	OF MOTION. HE LIES. /CHARLES/ AND WHAT DO YOU SAY, MR
KING I (212)	OF NUMBERS! THIS FELLOW SUBSTITUTES FOR MY FIRST	LAW	OF MOTION-- STRAIGHT LINE MOTION-- MOTION IN A CURVE.
SUPR III (127)	EXISTENCE OR CLEARING THE WAY FOR IT. THAT IS THE	LAW	OF MY LIFE. THAT IS THE WORKING WITHIN ME OF LIFE'S
DEVL III (54)	I CANNOT. I HAVE BEEN BROUGHT UP STANDING BY THE	LAW	OF MY OWN NATURE; AND I MAY NOT GO AGAINST IT, GALLOWS
GENV IV (105)	/JEW/ I HAVE BEEN BEATEN AND ROBBED. IS THAT THE	LAW	OF NATIONS? /BATTLER/ I AM SORRY. I CANNOT BE
GENV IV (105)	/BATTLER/ NOWHERE WITHOUT A PASSPORT. THAT IS THE	LAW	OF NATIONS. /JEW/ I HAVE BEEN BEATEN AND ROBBED. IS THAT
SUPR PREFACE(R18)	WOMEN CHILDREN FIRST IS, BROADLY SPEAKING, THE	LAW	OF NATURE AND NOT THE DICTATE OF PERSONAL AMBITION. THE
KING I (210)	MOTION IN A CURVE IS THE LAW OF NATURE; AND THE	LAW	OF NATURE IS THE LAW OF GOD. GO OUT INTO YOUR GARDEN AND
2TRU PREFACE(5)	AFFIRMING IT TO BE A WELL-KNOWN AND INEXORABLE	LAW	OF NATURE THAT NO MAN WITH MONEY IN HIS POCKET COULD
MTH4 I (171)	AND EXECUTE. YOU CANNOT DEFY NATURE. IT IS A	LAW	OF NATURE THAT THERE IS A FIXED RELATION BETWEEN CONDUCT
JOAN 4 (107)	THE ENGLISH GOES WITHOUT SAYING: IT IS THE SIMPLE	LAW	OF NATURE. BUT THIS WOMEN DENIES TO ENGLAND HER
GENV IV (93)	PERSONAL GRAVITATION. PERSONAL GRAVITATION IS A	LAW	OF NATURE. YOU CANNOT CUT ITS HEAD OFF. /NEWCOMER/
KING I (210)	FELL IN A STRAIGHT LINE. MOTION IN A CURVE IS THE	LAW	OF NATURE; AND THE LAW OF NATURE IS THE LAW OF GOD. GO
GENV PREFACE(12)	OR MORE TO AN IDLE LANDLORD AS IF THAT WERE A	LAW	OF NATURE; BUT A COLLECTION FROM THEM BY THE RATE
GETT PREFACE(211)	MARRY MORE THAN FOUR WIVES; AND BY THE UNWRITTEN	LAW	OF NECESSITY NO MAN CAN KEEP MORE WIVES THAN HE CAN
CLEO PRO1 (91)	THE NEW. THAT CAESAR SAID, " UNLESS I BREAK THE	LAW	OF OLD ROME, I CANNOT TAKE MY SHARE IN RULING HER; AND
GENV IV (93)	AND CAPITALIST, ONLY TO BRING YOU UNDER THE	LAW	OF PERSONAL GRAVITATION. PERSONAL GRAVITATION IS A LAW
MIS. PREFACE(45)	IS THAT THOUGH THIS NECESSITY FOR TOLERATION IS A	LAW	OF POLITICAL SCIENCE AS WELL ESTABLISHED AS THE LAW OF
GENV IV (93)	THE OTHER. DEMOCRACY HAS DELIVERED YOU FROM THE	LAW	OF PRIEST AND KING, OF LANDLORD AND CAPITALIST, ONLY TO
DOCT PREFACE(76)	DOG THAT BIT YOU REMINDS US, NOT ONLY OF ARNDT'S	LAW	OF PROTOPLASMIC REACTION TO STIMULI, ACCORDING TO WHICH
METH PREFACE(R54)	SOCIETIES WHICH EXISTED SOLELY TO SUBSTITUTE THE	LAW	OF PROVIDENCE AND WISDOM FOR THE METHOD OF RUSHING
MIS. PREFACE(27)	A CENTURY AGO TO MAKE US ALL UNDERSTAND RICARDO'S	LAW	OF RENT AS TO LEARN OUR CATECHISMS. THE FACE OF THE
FABL PREFACE(96)	GENTLEMAN-AMATEUR SOCIALIST, BEEN TAUGHT THE	LAW	OF RENT, HIS FIRST ATTEMPTS AT THE NEW DEAL WOULD NOT
SUPR II (60)	AND DAUGHTER IS NOT THE LAW OF LOVE: IT IS THE	LAW	OF REVOLUTION, OF EMANCIPATION, OF FINAL SUPERSESSION OF
GETT PREFACE(229)	LEAD TO A COMPARATIVELY STRINGENT ENFORCEMENT BY	LAW	OF SEXUAL MORALITY (THAT IS WHY SO MANY OF US DREAD
BASH PREFACE(87)	MY ANSWER IS THAT THE OPERATION OF THE COPYRIGHT	LAW	OF THAT TIME (NOW HAPPILY SUPERSEDED) LEFT ME ONLY A
CAPT II (256)	OBEY THE LAW. /BRASSBOUND/ I INTEND TO DO SO. THE	LAW	OF THE ATLAS MOUNTAINS IS ADMINISTERED BY THE SHEIKH
DOCT PREFACE(49)	AND CUTTHROAT'S CASUISTRIES OF VIVISECTION. THE	LAW	OF THE CONSERVATION OF ENERGY HOLDS GOOD IN PHYSIOLOGY
SIM PREFACE(4)	THAT THERE IS JUST AS MUCH EVIDENCE FOR A	LAW	OF THE CONSERVATION OF CREDULITY AS OF THE CONSERVATION
DOCT III (141)	BUT IS HE TO BE ALLOWED TO DEFY THE CRIMINAL	LAW	OF THE LAND? /SIR PATRICK/ THE CRIMINAL LAW IS NO USE
HART PREFACE(12)	HE LIKED WITH IMPUNITY IN CIVIL LIFE, WAS NOT THE	LAW	OF THE LAND, AND THAT A VICTORIA CROSS DID NOT CARRY
DOCT PREFACE(33)	ATTAINABLE, AND SINCE EVERYBODY, BY THE DEEPEST	LAW	OF THE LIFE FORCE, DESIRES TO BE GODLIKE, IT IS STUPID,
DEST SD(150)	FLATTERIES WHICH ARE NOT COMPATIBLE WITH MARTIAL	LAW	OF THE PRUSSIAN TYPE. NAPOLEON HAS THEREFORE APPROACHED
FABL PREFACE(97)	ALREADY DEMONSTRATED THE INJUSTICE OF ITS " IRON	LAW	OF WAGES." ENGLAND'S SHAMEFACED LEADERSHIP. ENGLAND WAS
AUGS (279)	IS HEARD FROM BELOW: /THE CLERK/ I'LL HAVE THE	LAW	OF YOU FOR THIS , I WILL. /AUGUSTUS/ (SHOUTING DOWN TO
FOUN (217)	OH, MERCER, MERCER! /MERCER/ I'LL HAVE THE	LAW	OF YOU FOR THIS, I WILL. OH, SAY YOU DONT BELIEVE HER,
DOCT PREFACE(38)	CRUELTY; AND VIVISECTION IS ONLY TOLERATED BY THE	LAW	ON CONDITION THAT, LIKE JUDICIAL TORTURE, IT SHALL BE
SUPR I (11)	BY HER! WHAT DANGER IS SHE IN? SHE HAS THE	LAW	ON HER SIDE; SHE HAS POPULAR SENTIMENT ON HER SIDE; SHE
POSN (436)	AFRAID TO HANG. WHERES THE RISK IN THAT WITH THE	LAW	ON HIS SIDE AND THE WHOLE CROWD AT HIS BACK LONGING FOR
DOCT III (140)	/SIR PATRICK/ AND IT DOESNT AFFECT THE CRIMINAL	LAW	ON THE SUBJECT OF BIGAMY. /LOUIS/ OH BIGAMY! BIGAMY!
DEVL I SD(24)	HOUSE, STANDS INERT, CRUSHED BY THE WEIGHT OF THE	LAW	ON WOMEN, ACCEPTING IT, AS SHE HAS BEEN TRAINED TO
GETT PREFACE(220)	FOR ITS GRATIFICATION, WHETHER BY PROCESS OF	LAW	OR NOT, BY ALL MEANS LET IT BE THE SUBJECT OF CONTRACTS
MIS. (190)	IN IT. MEN ARE NOT GOVERNED BY JUSTICE, BUT BY	LAW	OR PERSUASION. WHEN THEY REFUSE TO BE GOVERNED BY LAW OR
MIS. (190)	OR PERSUASION. WHEN THEY REFUSE TO BE GOVERNED BY	LAW	OR PERSUASION, THEY HAVE TO BE GOVERNED BY FORCE OR
GETT PREFACE(257)	YOU WILL PRESENTLY FIND YOURSELF WITHOUT EITHER	LAW	OR RELIGION. IF YOU DOUBT THIS, ASK ANY DECENT JUDGE OR
LADY PREFACE(219)	NOT BECAUSE THEY HAVE ANY MORE REGARD FOR	LAW	OR RELIGION. THERE IS ONLY ONE PLACE IN SHAKESPEAR'S
DOCT PREFACE(31)	SUPPORTED, NOT BY ANY GENERAL COMPREHENSION OF	LAW	OR STUDY OF JURISPRUDENCE, NOT EVEN BY SIMPLE
GENV PREFACE(16)	INGE; BUT A QUESTION AS TO A POINT OF EXISTING	LAW	OR THE FUNCTION OF A COUNTY COUNCIL STRIKES THEM DUMB.
JOAN PREFACE(29)	BACK, AND HAVE FIFTY CIVILIANS, LEARNED IN THE	LAW	OR VOWED TO THE SERVICE OF GOD, TO SUPPORT TWO SKILLED
DOCT III (142)	HIS WIFE'S LIFE WASTE. YOU MAY PUT THE CRIMINAL	LAW	OUT OF YOUR HEAD ONCE FOR ALL: IT'S ONLY FIT FOR FOOLS
GETT PREFACE(224)	ALWAYS THE SAME MAN OR WOMAN. IT HAPPENS THAT OUR	LAW	PERMITS US TO STUDY THIS PHENOMENON AMONG ENTIRELY
JOAN EPILOG (165)	THE JUDGES IN THE BLINDNESS AND BONDAGE OF THE	LAW	PRAISE THEE, BECAUSE THOU HAST VINDICATED THE VISION AND
POSN PREFACE(391)	GROWS OLD HIS MIND MAY CHANGE OR DECAY; BUT THE	LAW	REMAINS THE SAME. THE CENSORSHIP OF THE THEATRE
CAPT III (287)	AND NOTHING BUT THE TRUTH. BUT THE ENGLISH	LAW	REQUIRES A WITNESS TO TELL THE WHOLE TRUTH. /LADY
BULL PREFACE(62)	EXECUTIONS ARE THEN CARRIED OUT TO MAKE THE	LAW	RESPECTED. THE RESULT IS THAT THREE NATIVES KNOCK A
LION I (121)	JAW? /LENTULUS/ DONT TOUCH ME, DO YOU HEAR? THE	LAW	-- /FERROVIUS/ THE LAW WILL THROW ME TO THE LIONS
DEVL I (26)	/UNCLE TITUS/ HAVE A CARE, RICHARD DUDGEON. THE	LAW	-- /RICHARD/ (TURNING THREATENINGLY ON HIM) HAVE A
BULL PREFACE(46)	BY LYNCH LAW (TECHNICALLY CALLED MARTIAL	LAW	) ADMINISTERED BY A TRADE UNION OF OFFICERS. COMPARE
PRES (135)	/MITCHENER/ (WALKING ABOUT AND LAYING DOWN THE	LAW	) THERES NO SUCH THING AS PUBLIC OPINION. /BALSQUITH/ NO
PYGM I (211)	BYSTANDERS/ (ENCOURAGED BY THIS SEEMING POINT OF	LAW	) YES: WHERES YOUR WARRANT? /THE FLOWER GIRL/ LET HIM
POSN (454)	HOLY BIBLE IF THEY TOUCHED IT. I SAY THATS THE	LAW	; AND IF YOU ARE A PROPER UNITED STATES SHERIFF AND NOT
2TRU III (88)	COMMANDMENTS WERE ERASED FROM THE TABLES OF THE	LAW	; AND IN THEIR PLACE CAME THE COSMIC ALGEBRA: THE
BULL PREFACE(51)	PIGEON FARMERS, MAHFOUZ BY NAME, DESPAIRED OF THE	LAW	; AND ITS HEAD, HASSAN MAHFOUZ, AGED 60, MADE UP HIS
MIS. PREFACE(26)	HIS EYE. THE SCHOOLMASTER APPEALED TO THE	LAW	; AND MY FRIEND FOUND HIMSELF WAITING NERVOUSLY IN THE
JOAN PREFACE(42)	EXCEPT A DEFENCE OF THE REALM ACT SUSPENDING ALL	LAW	; AND THE JUDGE SHE WOULD HAVE HAD, AT BEST, A BOTHERED
SUPR PREFACE(R12)	WITHOUT REGARD TO THE COMMON, STATUTE, OR CANON	LAW	; AND THEREFORE, WHILST GAINING THE ARDENT SYMPATHY OF
SUPR HANDBOK(196)	PRESENT PROPERTY SYSTEM IS. IT WOULD BECOME THE	LAW	; AND THOSE WHO RESISTED IT WOULD BE FINED, SOLD UP,
MILL IV (199)	PLEASE. I CANNOT ADVISE EITHER OF YOU TO GO TO	LAW	; BUT QUITE SERIOUSLY, MRS FITZFASSENDEN, MR
BARB PREFACE(242)	IT. IN THIS INSTANCE THE MAN LAGS BEHIND THE	LAW	; BUT WHEN THE LAW LAGS BEHIND THE MAN, HE BECOMES
MILL PREFACE(110)	ARE IRRESISTIBLE UNLESS THEY ARE RESTRAINED BY	LAW	; FOR ORDINARY INDIVIDUALS ARE HELPLESS IN THEIR HANDS.
POSN PREFACE(367)	OF THE LICENCE PRACTICALLY PLACES HIM ABOVE THE	LAW	; FOR THOUGH IT MAY BE LEGALLY POSSIBLE TO PROSECUTE A
MIS. PREFACE(13)	NOT SUPPOSED TO BE PUNISHED EXCEPT BY PROCESS OF	LAW	; NOR, WHEN HE IS SO PUNISHED, IS THE PERSON WHOM HE HAS
HART PREFACE(13)	PERSECUTED WITH SAVAGE LOGICALITY IN SPITE OF THE	LAW	; WHILST THOSE WHO MADE NO PRETENCE OF HAVING ANY
BUOY IV (53)	NATIVE/ (TO HER) SIR FLOPPER, THE ILLUSTRIOUS	LAW	SERVANT OF GOD, HAS WAITED UNTIL YOUR VENERABLE FATHER
SIM PREFACE(17)	OR TERRIFIED. PUBLIC SAVAGERY MAY DEMAND THAT THE	LAW	SHALL TORMENT A CRIMINAL WHO DOES SOMETHING VERY
BARB PREFACE(231)	OF MIND ON HIS PART. THE OLD WOMAN, LIKE THE	LAW	SHE THREATENS HIM WITH, IS PERFECTLY READY TO PLAY THE
POSN PREFACE(419)	VITAL QUESTION, IS IT NOT POSSIBLE TO AMEND THE	LAW	SO AS TO MAKE IT POSSIBLE FOR A LAWYER TO ADVISE HIS
WIDO II (26)	HE SUPPOSED SO, OR YOU WOULDNT DARE TO BREAK THE	LAW	SO SCAND'LOUS. I ONLY TELL YOU WHAT HE SAID. /SARTORIUS/
MRS PREFACE(163)	THE ROYAL ACADEMY OF ARTS, THE INCORPORATED	LAW	SOCIETY, AND CONVOCATION WERE ABOLISHED, AND THEIR
PHIL I (79)	VIEWS THAT WE WERE NOT TO MARRY; BECAUSE, AS THE	LAW	STANDS, I MIGHT HAVE BECOME A DRUNKARD, A-- /JULIA/-- A
POSN PREFACE(416)	WAS ASKED BY COLONEL LOCKWOOD WHETHER A	LAW	SUFFICIENT TO RESTRAIN IMPROPRIETY IN BOOKS WOULD ALSO
JOAN PREFACE(36)	THAT THOUGHT, WHEN REALLY FREE, MUST BY ITS OWN	LAW	TAKE THE PATH THAT LEADS TO THE CHURCH'S BOSOM, NOT ONLY
BULL PREFACE(12)	TARIFFS, IT HAD BETTER BE DONE BY INTERNATIONAL	LAW	THAN BY ARBITRARY NATIONAL FORCE AS AT PRESENT. IT WILL
BARB II (292)	SEE THAT THE SPIRIT OF GOD-- WHATE'ER IT BE-- THE	LAW	THAT ABIDES AND CHANGES NOT, AGES LONG, THE ETERNAL AND
POSN PREFACE(390)	COLLECTIVE WISDOM OF THE COMMUNITY. THE ONLY	LAW	THAT AFFECTS THEM IS THE ACT OF 1843, WHICH EMPOWERS ONE
POSN PREFACE(390)	AND THE JUDGE STAND, IN THE PRESENCE OF A	LAW	THAT BINDS THEM BOTH EQUALLY, AND WAS MADE BY NEITHER OF
MTH3 (127)	/CONFUCIUS/ YOU CANNOT PREVENT IT. THERE IS NO	LAW	THAT GIVES YOU POWER TO INTERFERE WITH THEM. /BARNABAS/
GETT (278)	IT WAS THE ONLY WAY TO DO IT-- THAT IT WAS THE	LAW	THAT HE SHOULD DO IT THAT WAY. I NEVER SAW THAT HATEFUL
DOCT III (141)	HER; AND SHE THOUGHT, POOR GIRL, THAT IT WAS THE	LAW	THAT IF YOU HADNT HEARD OF YOUR HUSBAND FOR THREE YEARS
BARB PREFACE(242)	THAT WHEN THEY ARE CALLED UPON TO ADMINISTER ANY	LAW	THAT IS BASED ON IDEAS OR KNOWLEDGE LESS THAN HALF A
GENV IV (107)	MY NAME IS JEALOUSY. MY NAME IS THE UNWRITTEN	LAW	THAT IS NO LAW. UNTIL YOU HAVE DEALT WITH ME YOU HAVE
GETT PREFACE(201)	SO IMPOSSIBLE AND SO UNWHOLESOME, YET THE	LAW	THAT REGULATES THEIR RELATIONS, AND THE PUBLIC OPINION
BASH II,1, (105)	AT HIS WOE? /CASHEL/ (TO LUCIAN) THE UNWRITTEN	LAW	THAT SHIELDS THE AMATEUR AGAINST PROFESSIONAL
GETT PREFACE(255)	AND TO DO EVERYTHING BY A BUREAUCRATIC MARTIAL	LAW	THAT WOULD BE QUITE UNNECESSARY AND INDEED INTOLERABLE
GETT (305)	UP IT WILL BE SO MUCH WORSE THAN THE EXISTING	LAW	THAT YOU WILL ALL PREFER GETTING MARRIED. WE SHALL
POSN PREFACE(429)	OF THAT CERTIFICATE HE ISSUED IT; ALSO, THAT BY	LAW	THE COURT COULD DO NOTHING TO HIM EXCEPT ORDER HIM TO
GENV II (58)	MOST OF WHOM HAVE FORGOTTEN ANY SENSE OF	LAW	THEY MAY EVER HAVE ACQUIRED. /SIR O./ HOW VERY ODD! I
LION PREFACE(60)	IMPOSTURE AND A DELUSION. IT REDUCES JUSTICE AND	LAW	TO A FARCE: LAW BECOMES MERELY AN INSTRUMENT FOR KEEPING
ROCK PREFACE(186)	TO BE SCRAMBLED FOR BY YOUR PARTIZANS. I HAVE A	LAW	TO ADMINISTER. THE LAW FORBIDS OBSCENITY, SEDITION, AND
METH PREFACE(R22)	ON FROM THE CONCEPTION OF EVOLUTION AS A GENERAL	LAW	TO CHARLES DARWIN'S DEPARTMENT OF IT, WHICH WAS THE
POSN PREFACE(425)	WERE ENFORCED ALL ROUND. I SHOULD NOT OBJECT TO A	LAW	TO COMPEL EVERYBODY TO READ TWO NEWSPAPERS, EACH
POSN PREFACE(425)	THE MOST CHERISHED OPINIONS OF THE UNIONISTS. A	LAW	TO COMPEL THE ROMAN CATHOLICS TO ATTEND SERVICE AT ST

MRS PREFACE(176)	DALY; AND MADE AN END OF THE ATTEMPT TO USE THE	LAW	TO DECLARE LIVING WOMEN TO BE " ORDURE," AND THUS
GETT PREFACE(233)	SPECIALLY SUSCEPTIBLE), AND A RATIONAL DIVORCE	LAW	TO ENABLE THE MARRIAGE TO BE DISSOLVED AND THE PARTIES
JOAN PREFACE(42)	AS FAIR A TRIAL AS WELL CONSIDERED A BODY OF	LAW	TO GOVERN THEIR CASES, OR AS CONSCIENTIOUS A JUDGE TO
CAPT II (256)	HOUR. HE IS A JUDGE, LIKE YOURSELF. YOU CAN TALK	LAW	TO HIM. HE WILL GIVE YOU BOTH THE LAW AND THE PROPHETS.
MRS PREFACE(167)	PRODUCED BY THAT VERY RESISTANCE OF FACT AND	LAW	TO HUMAN FEELING WHICH CREATES DRAMA. IT IS THE DEUS EX
GETT PREFACE(257)	8. NEVER FORGET THAT IF YOU LEAVE YOUR	LAW	TO JUDGES AND YOUR RELIGION TO BISHOPS YOU WILL
POSN PREFACE(406)	AN ORDINARY PUBLIC-HOUSE FOR NOTHING, THERE IS NO	LAW	TO PREVENT THE THEATRE PROPRIETOR FROM ISSUING FREE
SUPR I (38)	TO GO WHERE YOU DO NOT WANT US TO GO THERE IS NO	LAW	TO PREVENT US; BUT WHEN WE TAKE THE FIRST STEP YOUR
JOAN PREFACE(29)	THE CHANGE FROM CAREFUL TRIAL UNDER ORDINARY	LAW	TO RECKLESSLY SUMMARY MILITARY TERRORISM MAY STRIKE US A
DEVL I (10)	STOLE AWAY LIKE A THIEF TO TAKE ADVANTAGE OF THE	LAW	TO ROB ME BY MAKING A NEW WILL BEHIND MY BACK. THE MORE
POSN PREFACE(425)	BE RESENTED AS AN INSUFFERABLE TYRANNY. BUT A	LAW	TO SHUT UP BOTH ST PAUL'S AND THE WESTMINSTER CATHEDRAL,
GETT PREFACE(230)	THEM ECONOMICALLY, THEY WILL NO LONGER ALLOW THE	LAW	TO TAKE IMMORALITY SO EASILY. BOTH MEN AND WOMEN WILL BE
GETT PREFACE(252)	AND SO, WITH POLICEMEN AT EVERY CORNER, AND	LAW	TRIUMPHANT ALL OVER EUROPE, SHE WILL STILL BE SMUGGLED
GENV III (73)	THE BRITISH GOVERNMENT HAS JUST PASSED A NEW	LAW	UNDER WHICH ANY PERSON OBNOXIOUS TO THE GOVERNMENT CAN
LION PREFACE(54)	TO YOU FOR HAVING THE POOR ALWAYS WITH YOU WAS A	LAW	UNTO YOU THAT THIS EVIL SHOULD PERSIST AND STINK IN THE
FABL PREFACE(76)	POLITICAL CIRCUMSTANCE THAT THE SECULAR CRIMINAL	LAW	WAS ATROCIOUSLY CRUEL, AND THAT NO OTHER AGENCY COULD
HART PREFACE(13)	NOT THE COURAGE TO LEGISLATE ACCORDINGLY; AND ITS	LAW	WAS SET ASIDE FOR LYNCH LAW. THE CLIMAX OF LEGAL
HART PREFACE(15)	OF LIBERTY AND WELL-BEING. THE ORDINARY	LAW	WAS SUPERSEDED BY ACTS UNDER WHICH NEWSPAPERS WERE
JOAN EPILOG (153)	HERETIC AND A SORCERESS. THE TRUTH WAS TOLD; THE	LAW	WAS UPHELD; MERCY WAS SHEWN BEYOND ALL CUSTOM; NO WRONG
POSN (452)	IS ANOTHER. IN RELIGION WE'RE ALL BROTHERS. IN	LAW	WE CUT OUR BROTHER OFF WHEN HE STEALS HORSES. /THE
ROCK PREFACE(147)	IN THE KILLING. THE SACREDNESS OF HUMAN LIFE. IN	LAW	WE DRAW A LINE BETWEEN THE KILLING OF HUMAN ANIMALS AND
CLEO PRO1 (92)	IS EXPEDIENT; BUT IF WE KILL A MAN OUTSIDE THE	LAW	WE SET OURSELVES IN THE PLACE OF THE GODS; AND THIS WE
LION PREFACE(66)	LAW, NOT CONSIDERING THAT IF THE CRIMINAL	LAW	WERE EFFECTIVE WE SHOULD NOT HAVE BEEN ROBBED. THAT
DOCT PREFACE(56)	DEATH-RATE. THE EXPLANATION IS SIMPLE. SUPPOSE A	LAW	WERE MADE THAT EVERY CHILD IN THE NATION SHOULD BE
BUOY III (38)	WE ARE NOT MORMONS. THEIR WIVES IN BRITISH	LAW	WERE ONLY CONCUBINES. /THE WIDOWER/ I HOLD THAT
BARB I (254)	LAW! HE IS ALWAYS BREAKING THE LAW. HE BROKE THE	LAW	WHEN HE WAS BORN: HIS PARENTS WERE NOT MARRIED.
GETT (297)	HONOR, NO. ALL I SAID WAS THAT I DIDNT KNOW THE	LAW	WHEN I ASKED YOU TO BE MY WIFE. /EDITH/ AND YOU WOULDNT
MILL I (142)	FATHER ALWAYS HAD TO INSTRUCT HIS LAWYERS IN THE	LAW	WHENEVER HE DID ANYTHING EXCEPT WHAT EVERYBODY WAS DOING
DOCT PREFACE(52)	HAVE THE HORSE ON ANY TERMS; AND TO THIS DAY THE	LAW	WHICH PRESCRIBES JENNERIAN VACCINATION IS CARRIED OUT
POSN PREFACE(421)	LAW. " WE CONSIDER," SAYS THE REPORT, " THAT THE	LAW	WHICH PREVENTS OR PUNISHES INDECENCY, BLASPHEMY AND
SUPR PREFACE(R12)	OCCASION, BEEN BROUGHT INTO CONFLICT WITH THE	LAW	WHICH REGULATES THE RELATIONS OF THE SEXES. A MAN, BY
CAND III (133)	I HAVE LOST HER LOVE AND YOU HAVE GAINED IT, NO	LAW	WILL BIND HER. /MARCHBANKS/ (QUAINTLY, WITHOUT FEAR OR
SIM PREFACE(14)	CAST HEADLONG INTO HELL; BUT AS TO WHAT CODE OF	LAW	WILL GOVERN THE JUDGMENT AND CLASSIFY THE JUDGED AS
GETT (270)	TO MY CHILDREN, AND NOT TO THEIR FATHER. THE	LAW	WILL NOT ALLOW ME TO DO THAT; SO I HAVE MADE UP MY MIND
SIM PREFACE(17)	AND EXPERIENCED ADMINISTRATOR OF THE CRIMINAL	LAW	WILL TELL YOU THAT THERE ARE PEOPLE WHO COME UP FOR
LION I (121)	ME, DO YOU HEAR? THE LAW -- /FERROVIUS/ THE	LAW	WILL THROW ME TO THE LIONS TOMORROW: WHAT WORSE COULD IT
POSN PREFACE(388)	CONCERNED, A PERMANENT PROCLAMATION OF MARTIAL	LAW	WITH A SINGLE OFFICIAL SUBSTITUTED FOR A COURT MARTIAL.
LION PREFACE(12)	TO SUCH AN EXTENT, THAT THEY SOON FIND THE MORAL	LAW	WITHIN THEM REVOLTING AGAINST THE IDEA OF BUYING OFF THE
LION PREFACE(11)	OF THE STARRY HEAVENS ABOVE US AND THE MORAL	LAW	WITHIN US, THAT WE CONCLUDE THAT SOMEBODY MUST BE DOING
LION PREFACE(11)	CALLED PRAISES. THEN THE KANTIAN MORAL	LAW	WITHIN YOU MAKES YOU CONCEIVE YOUR GOD AS A JUDGE; AND
GETT PREFACE(254)	OF PARENTAGE, AFTER PERPETRATING WHICH CRIME, THE	LAW	WOULD CALMLY SEND AN EDUCATION OFFICER TO TAKE THE CHILD
GETT PREFACE(235)	FACT FOR US TO SEIZE IS THAT IN THE EYE OF THE	LAW	, ADULTERY WITHOUT CONSEQUENCES IS MERELY A SENTIMENTAL
CAPT III (294)	OR MAN, WITH THAT PURPOSE, BECAUSE IT WAS AGAINST	LAW	, AGAINST RELIGION, AGAINST MY OWN CREDIT AND SAFETY.
POSN PREFACE(369)	THING IN THE ADVANCED DRAMA. THERE WAS MR HUGH	LAW	, AN IRISH MEMBER, SON OF AN IRISH CHANCELLOR,
ROCK PREFACE(188)	IT MAY ALSO BE THE RUIN OF ALL KINGDOMS, ALL	LAW	, AND ALL HUMAN SOCIETY. IT MAY BE THE THOUGHT OF THE
MIS. PREFACE(47)	THEY ARE PREPARED TO VISIT ALL THE RIGORS OF THE	LAW	, AND ALL THE RUINOUS PENALTIES OF SOCIAL OSTRACISM ON
MIS. PREFACE(64)	BOUNDS. WHAT CORRUPTS CIVILIZATION, RELIGION,	LAW	, AND CONVENTION (AND THEY ARE AT PRESENT PRETTY NEARLY
MIS. PREFACE(64)	UNIVERSE. NOW ALL HONEST CIVILIZATION, RELIGION,	LAW	, AND CONVENTION IS AN ATTEMPT TO KEEP THIS FORCE WITHIN
BARB PREFACE(244)	MAY WITHOUT INHUMANITY BE HANDED OVER TO THE	LAW	, AND MADE TO UNDERSTAND THAT A STATE WHICH IS TOO
POSN PREFACE(423)	THE PLAY UNTIL HIS ACCUSERS HAD INDICTED HIM AT	LAW	, AND OBTAINED THE VERDICT OF A JURY AGAINST HIM, WERE
MIS. PREFACE(27)	KNOW A GOOD DEAL OF CONSTITUTIONAL HISTORY,	LAW	, AND POLITICAL SCIENCE, WITH ITS BASIS OF ECONOMICS, IF
SUPR HANDBOK(225)	FAILED. HE WHO BELIEVES IN EDUCATION, CRIMINAL	LAW	, AND SPORT, NEEDS ONLY PROPERTY TO MAKE HIM A PERFECT
POSN PREFACE(419)	PLAY THEY SUBMIT TO HIM IS VULNERABLE TO THE	LAW	, AND THAT THEY MUST PRODUCE IT NOT ONLY ON THE ORDINARY
PLES PREFACE(R13)	AS THAT OF THE ARMY, THE FLEET, THE CHURCH, THE	LAW	, AND THE SCHOOLS. FOR MY PART, I HAVE NO DOUBT THAT THE
JOAN EPILOG (157)	ALIKE WHEN THE INNOCENT ARE SLAIN IN THE NAME OF	LAW	, AND THEIR WRONGS ARE UNDONE BY SLANDERING THE PURE OF
POSN PREFACE(410)	OF THE THEATRE WILL RESORT TO THE ORDINARY	LAW	, AND TRY TO GET FROM THE PREJUDICES OF A JURY WHAT THEY
SUPR HANDBOK(207)	CITIZENS, WHO, THOUGH THEY ACT OUTSIDE THE	LAW	, ARE AT LEAST MORE MERCIFUL THAN THE AMERICAN
POSN PREFACE(376)	TO PART WITH THE BOOKS. FOR INSTANCE, MR HUGH	LAW	, BEING AN IRISHMAN, WITH AN IRISHMAN'S SENSE OF HOW TO
LION PREFACE(65)	WHICH TYRANNIES ARE MAINTAINED UNDER PRETEXT OF	LAW	, CAN BE OBEYED THROUGH THE EXERCISE OF A QUITE COMMON
CAPT I (230)	WHENEVER YOU WISH TO DO ANYTHING AGAINST THE	LAW	, CICELY, ALWAYS CONSULT A GOOD SOLICITOR FIRST. /LADY
FABL III (112)	THE LABORATORY AND CLASSIFIED. THAT IS THE	LAW	, COMPULSORY FOR EVERYBODY. IF YOU REFUSE YOU MAY BE
BARB PREFACE(243)	THEIR ENERGY IN RAISING OUR GORGE AGAINST CURRENT	LAW	, CURRENT MORALITY, CURRENT RESPECTABILITY, AND LEGAL
DOCT PREFACE(37)	THAT THE DETECTION OF ITS PROTEAN DISGUISES AS	LAW	, EDUCATION, MEDICINE, DISCIPLINE, SPORT AND SO FORTH,
POSN (441)	TOUCH ME; AND YOU KNOW IT. /STRAPPER/ IS THAT THE	LAW	, ELDER? /ELDER DANIELS/ THE SHERIFF KNOWS THE LAW. I
LION PREFACE(92)	AS WE LIKE WITH IMPUNITY INSIDE THE SECULAR	LAW	, EVEN FROM SELF-REPROACH, WHICH BECOMES MERE
DOCT PREFACE(6)	BY THEIR CONSCIENCE INTO ACTUAL CONFLICT WITH THE	LAW	, FALL BACK ON THE OLD RULE THAT IF YOU CANNOT HAVE WHAT
GENV IV (93)	KINGS AND PRIESTS, YOU HAVE MOB LAW, LYNCHING	LAW	, GANGSTER LAW: IN SHORT, AMERICAN DEMOCRACY. THANK YOUR
MIS. (137)	EARS OR WAG HIS TAIL INSTEAD OF LAYING DOWN THE	LAW	, HOW MUCH BETTER IT WOULD BE! WE SHOULD KNOW WHEN HE
GETT PREFACE(234)	PROPER SOLUTION. IT MUST BE REPEATED HERE THAT NO	LAW	, HOWEVER STRINGENT, CAN PREVENT POLYGAMY AMONG GROUPS
BUOY III (38)	ALIKE IN LAW. /THE WIDOWER/ SO MUCH THE WORSE FOR	LAW	, I AM AFRAID. /MRS THIRDBORN/ NO TWO LOVE AFFAIRS ARE
CAPT I (232)	WELL, WHY NOT? THEOLOGY IS AS RESPECTABLE AS	LAW	, I SHOULD THINK. BESIDES, I'M ONLY TALKING COMMONSENSE.
GETT PREFACE(229)	MALTREAT HIM PERSONALLY OR HAND HIM OVER TO THE	LAW	, IF HE IS VULNERABLE TO IT. THEREFORE I CANNOT SAY THAT
GETT PREFACE(201)	AND THE PUBLIC OPINION THAT REGULATES THAT	LAW	, IS ACTUALLY FOUNDED ON THE ASSUMPTION THAT THE
GETT (301)	BUT BLESS ME! MARRIAGE IS NOT A QUESTION OF	LAW	, IS IT? HAVE YOU CHILDREN NO AFFECTION FOR
DOCT PREFACE(31)	THAT THE PRACTICE IS QUITE PAINLESS UNDER THE	LAW	, IT IS STILL DIFFICULT TO FIND ANY CIVILIZED MOTIVE FOR
POSN PREFACE(388)	HABEAS CORPUS ACT, OR A PROCLAMATION OF MARTIAL	LAW	, JUST AS WE STOP THE TRAFFIC IN A STREET DURING A FIRE,
GENV IV (93)	BY DEAD KINGS AND PRIESTS, YOU HAVE MOB	LAW	, LYNCHING LAW, GANGSTER LAW: IN SHORT, AMERICAN
MTH4 I (171)	ELDERLY GENTLEMAN/ I HAVE NEVER HEARD OF ANY SUCH	LAW	, MADAM. /ZOO/ WELL, YOU ARE HEARING OF IT NOW. /THE
DEVL I (22)	ANNIE PRIMROSE"-- YOU SEE HE DID NOT KNOW THE	LAW	, MR DUDGEON: YOUR MOTHER WAS NOT BORN ANNIE: SHE WAS
WIDO II (27)	HAVE STEPPED AN INCH OUTSIDE THE LETTER OF THE	LAW	, MR LICKCHEESE, I WILL PROSECUTE YOU MYSELF. THE WAY TO
JOAN 6 (148)	WHETHER YOUR PEOPLE HAVE OBSERVED THE FORMS OF	LAW	, MY LORD. /WARWICK/ I AM TOLD THAT THERE IS SOME DOUBT
BARB III (319)	WHAT! NO CAPACITY FOR BUSINESS, NO KNOWLEDGE OF	LAW	, NO SYMPATHY WITH ART, NO PRETENSION TO PHILOSOPHY;
LIED (192)	TO THE LAW: MY LOVE WAS NOT CREATED IN ME BY THE	LAW	, NOR CAN IT BE BOUND OR LOOSED BY IT. THAT IS SIMPLE
LION PREFACE(66)	WE ARE ROBBED WE GENERALLY APPEAL TO THE CRIMINAL	LAW	, NOT CONSIDERING THAT IF THE CRIMINAL LAW WERE
DOCT PREFACE(30)	THEY SHOULD BE FREE FROM THE RESTRAINTS OF	LAW	, OF HONOR, OF PITY, OF REMORSE, OF EVERYTHING THAT
GENV IV (124)	CITIZENS: THIS IS THE END. THE END OF WAR, OF	LAW	, OF LEADERS AND FOREIGN SECRETARIES, OF JUDGES AND
POSN PREFACE(432)	APPOINTING AN ADVISORY COMMITTEE, UNKNOWN TO THE	LAW	, ON WHICH HE WILL PRESUMABLY THROW ANY ODIUM THAT MAY
MILL I (142)	AN ACTION FOR LIBEL TAKEN AGAINST ME. IS THAT THE	LAW	, OR IS IT NOT? /SAGAMORE/ I REALLY DONT KNOW. I WILL
GETT PREFACE(242)	MIDDLE AGE. THE HIGHER DEPARTMENTS OF SCIENCE,	LAW	, PHILOSOPHY, POETRY, AND THE FINE ARTS ARE NOTORIOUSLY
GETT PREFACE(192)	OR FROM REFUSING TO MARRY THEIR DAUGHTERS. AS TO	LAW	, RELIGION, ETHICS, AND CONSTITUTIONAL GOVERNMENT, ANY
GETT PREFACE(246)	WE PLEASE WITHOUT REPROACH OR INTERFERENCE FROM	LAW	, RELIGION, OR EVEN CONSCIENCE (AND THIS IS WHAT
MRS PREFACE(155)	GROWING SO GREAT THAT PRIVATE CONDUCT, RELIGION,	LAW	, SCIENCE, POLITICS, AND MORALS ARE BECOMING MORE AND
CAPT I (229)	/RANKIN/ BUT HOW ABOUT THE LAW? /SIR HOWARD/ THE	LAW	, SIR, IN THAT ISLAND, CONSISTED PRACTICALLY OF THE
GETT PREFACE(192)	OF ECONOMICS, HISTORY, AND CONSTITUTIONAL	LAW	, SUCH PALTRY FOLLIES AND SENTIMENTALITIES, SNOBBERIES
BULL PREFACE(64)	BURNT OUT IN LONDON WITHOUT SHRIEKING FOR MARTIAL	LAW	, SUPPRESSION OF THE NEWSPAPERS, EXEMPLARY FLOGGING AND
BULL PREFACE(57)	WITH FLOGGINGS, EXECUTIONS, TORTURE AND LYNCH	LAW	, THAT THEY WILL NOT RESPECT ANY TRIBUNAL WHICH DOES NOT
MRS IV (242)	ARE FAR BEYOND AND ABOVE THE SCOPE OF THE	LAW	, THAT THOUGH I KNOW THAT YOUR MOTHER IS AN UNMARRIED
HART PREFACE(15)	WITH THESE RANCOROUS ABUSES OF THE EXISTING	LAW	, THE WAR MANIACS MADE A FRANTIC RUSH TO ABOLISH ALL
JOAN PREFACE(32)	ENOUGH. IN THE CATHOLIC CHURCH, FAR MORE THAN IN	LAW	, THERE IS NO WRONG WITHOUT A REMEDY. IT DOES NOT DEFER
DOCT PREFACE(55)	IN THE CASE OF A PROPHYLACTIC ENFORCED BY	LAW	, THIS ILLUSION IS INTENSIFIED GROTESQUELY, BECAUSE ONLY
GETT PREFACE(258)	REPORT OF THE ROYAL COMMISSION ON THE POOR	LAW	, TO MAKE THE SEXUAL RELATIONS BETWEEN MEN AND WOMEN
GETT PREFACE(247)	IN THIS MATTER OF THE EVILS OF OUR MARRIAGE	LAW	, TO TAKE CARE OF THE PENCE AND LET THE POUNDS TAKE CARE
MIS. PREFACE(33)	KNOW HOW MANY BEANS MAKE FIVE. IT MUST KNOW SOME	LAW	, WERE IT ONLY A SIMPLE SET OF COMMANDMENTS, SOME
BULL PREFACE(57)	THE BEST AVAILABLE FORM OF OFFICIAL LYNCH	LAW	, WERE MADE IMPOSSIBLE BY THE JEALOUSY OF THE " LOYAL" (
GETT PREFACE(246)	AND WIVES TO RESPECT US; AND THAT SOCIETY WITHOUT	LAW	, WHETHER BETWEEN TWO OR TWO MILLION PERSONS, MEANS
PRES (159)	THE MEN WHO ARE NOT HAVE NO INFLUENCE. THE SALIC	LAW	, WHICH FORBADE WOMEN TO OCCUPY A THRONE, IS FOUNDED ON
HART PREFACE(12)	TO ANNOUNCE THAT WHAT WAS CALLED THE UNWRITTEN	LAW	, WHICH MEANT SIMPLY THAT A SOLDIER COULD DO WHAT HE

BASH III (119)	FESTIVAL IS A MOST HIDEOUS OUTRAGE GAINST THE	LAW	, WHICH WE TO QUELL FROM LONDON HAVE COME DOWN: IN
MRS I (185)	CONVEYANCING. UNDER COVER OF THAT I SHALL DO SOME	LAW	, WITH ONE EYE ON THE STOCK EXCHANGE ALL THE TIME. IVE
DOCT IV (170)	OPEN EVERYTHING AND SETTLE EVERYTHING. THATS THE	LAW	, YOU KNOW. /MRS DUBEDAT/ OH, THANK YOU: I DIDNT KNOW. (
POSN (459)	YOUVE GOT TO TELL US THE TRUTH. THATS THE	LAW	, YOU KNOW. /THE WOMAN/ THE MAN LOOKED A BAD MAN. HE
BARB PREFACE(241)	IF YOU INSTITUTE PUNISHMENT AS PART OF THE	LAW	, YOU MUST PUNISH PEOPLE FOR REFUSING TO PUNISH. IF YOU
PPP (197)	POLICE! /FITZ/ DASTARD! YOU WOULD APPEAL TO THE	LAW	! CAN YOU NOT DIE LIKE A GENTLEMAN? /ADOLPHUS/ BUT SO
BARB I (254)	BREAK THE LAW. /LADY BRITOMART/ NOT BREAK THE	LAW	! HE IS ALWAYS BREAKING THE LAW. HE BROKE THE LAW WHEN
POSN (438)	I COULDNT ALLOW THAT: IT'S NOT THE LAW. /BABSY/	LAW	! WHAT RIGHT HAS A HORSE-THIEF TO ANY LAW? LAW IS

LAWBRARY

CAPT III (288)	FORWARD IN PAINFUL ALARM AND ANXIETY) IT'S MAW	LAWBRARY	, GAVNER. DOWNT BURN EM. /KEARNEY/ YOULL BE BETTER

LAWBREAKER

BARB PREFACE(243)	AS A MATTER OF SUCH VITAL IMPORTANCE THAT A	LAWBREAKER	AT LARGE IS HARDLY TO BE TOLERATED ON ANY PLEA.
BARB PREFACE(241)	HORRORS OF PENAL SERVITUDE. IN OTHER CASES THE	LAWBREAKER	ESCAPES BECAUSE THOSE WHO COULD GIVE HIM UP DO
ROCK PREFACE(187)	AND ENCOURAGE EVERY HERETIC, EVERY REBEL, EVERY	LAWBREAKER	, EVERY RAPSCALLION LEST HE SHOULD TURN OUT TO BE
METH PREFACE(R40)	DISORDER IN NATURE, OF A LAWGIVER WHO WAS ALSO A	LAWBREAKER	, MADE ATHEISTS IN ALL DIRECTIONS AMONG CLEVER

LAWBREAKERS

GENV II (58)	TO DEVISE SOME JUDICIAL PROCEDURE BY WHICH THESE	LAWBREAKERS	CAN BE BROUGHT TO JUSTICE. WELL, THE

LAWD

BARB II (299)	SAO WAS THE AOL BLOOMIN MEETIN. MOG SHE SEZ " OW	LAWD	BRIKE IS STABBORN SPERRIT; BAT DOWNT URT IS DEAR ART."
CAPT II (243)	THE PLICE READY FOR THE BRITISH HERRISTORCRACY,	LAWD	ELLAM AN LIDY WINEFLETE? /REDBROOK/ LADY FAINT, EH?
CAPT I (227)	CASE OF THE KIND I HAVE EVER MET. /DRINKWATER/	LAWD	, SR AHRD, WOT JAGGINSES THEM JURYMEN WAS! YOU AN ME

LAWDSHIP

CAPT I (227)	/DRINKWATER/ OWNY THE AW SPERRITS O YOUTH, Y'	LAWDSHIP	, WORTERLEOO ROWD KICE, WOT THEY CALLS OOLIGANISM.
CAPT I (226)	VAWNYARD. (INTRODUCING THE JUDGE) MR RENKIN: IS	LAWDSHIP	SIR AHRD ELLAM. (HE WITHDRAWS DISCREETLY INTO THE
CAPT I (234)	YR HONOR'S SERVANT. (TO THE ITALIAN) MAWTZOW: IS	LAWDSHIP	SR AHRD ELLAM (MARZO TOUCHES HIS HAT). HAWTELLIAN

LAWDSHIP'S

CAPT I (226)	SEAMAN-- COUNTRYMEN O YOURS, LIDY, AND OF IS	LAWDSHIP'S	. THIS EAH IS MR RENKIN, THE BUST WORKER IN THE

LAWF

CAPT III (292)	WORLD. WOT MIKES A KEPN IS BRINES AN KNOLLIDGE O	LAWF	. IT YNT THET THERS NAOW SITCH PUSSON: ITS THET YOU
CAPT III (289)	ME SATHINK AWGHER THAN THE SQUALOR OF A CORSTER'S	LAWF	-- /REDBROOK/ (COLLARING HIM) OH SHUT UP, YOU FOOL.

LAWF'S

BARB II (300)	AN JAWRIN THAT MIKES A MENN THET SORE THAT IZ	LAWF'S	A BURDN TO IM. AW WOWNT EV IT, AW TELL YOU; SAO TIKE

LAWFTAWM

BARB II (289)	STEND IT FOR A MAWNIN: E'LL EV TO STEND IT FOR A	LAWFTAWM	. /CUSINS/ THAT IS A FRIGHTFUL REFLECTION, MR

LAWFUL

JOAN EPILOG (164)	ITS ALTAR IN EVERY SUCH CHURCH. AND IT SHALL BE	LAWFUL	AND LAUDABLE FOR THE FAITHFUL TO KNEEL AND ADDRESS
POSN PREFACE(380)	COURT IT WAS DECIDED THAT THE REPRESENTATION WAS	LAWFUL	AND THE INTENTION INNOCENT, SINCE WHEN IT HAS BEEN
SUPR III (119)	THREE TIMES IF SHE BECOMES FREE TO DO SO. TWELVE	LAWFUL	CHILDREN BORNE BY ONE HIGHLY RESPECTABLE LADY TO
POSN PREFACE(425)	THE RIGHT TO DEMAND MORE FROM ME, OVER AND ABOVE	LAWFUL	CONDUCT IN A GENERAL SENSE, THAN LIBERTY TO STAY AWAY
BASH III (127)	AND SIMPLE BOTH, OUR SCENE DRAWS TO A CLOSE. IN	LAWFUL	COURSE AS DORSET'S DEPUTY LIEUTENANT I DO PARDON ALL
CLEO II (122)	EXPRESSIONS) MY MASTER WOULD SAY THAT THERE IS A	LAWFUL	DEBT DUE TO ROME BY EGYPT, CONTRACTED BY THE KING'S
POSN (450)	LAWFUL GROUND OF CHALLENGE. /THE FOREMAN/ IT'S A	LAWFUL	GROUND FOR ME TO SHOOT YONDER SKUNK AT SIGHT, FIRST
POSN (450)	JURY. (LAUGHTER). /THE SHERIFF/ THATS NOT A	LAWFUL	GROUND OF CHALLENGE. /THE FOREMAN/ IT'S A LAWFUL
JOAN 2 (86)	THEIR KNEES AND BEG THEE LET THEM RETURN TO THEIR	LAWFUL	HOMES IN PEACE. WILT BE A POOR LITTLE JUDAS, AND
PYGM II (239)	TO THAT WOMAN, GOVERNOR, JUST BECAUSE I'M NOT HER	LAWFUL	HUSBAND. AND SHE KNOWS IT TOO. CATCH HER MARRYING
LION PREFACE(56)	OR " THE LATE MR BARNEY BARNATO RECEIVED AS HIS	LAWFUL	INCOME THREE THOUSAND TIMES AS MUCH MONEY AS AN
GENV I (36)	SETTING UP A DICTATORSHIP AND OBSTRUCTING THE	LAWFUL	INGRESS OF DULY ELECTED MEMBERS TO THE LEGISLATIVE
6CAL (94)	GROVELLED FOR MERCY AT MY SUMMONS. AM I NOT THEIR	LAWFUL	KING, HA? /THE PRINCE/ UNDOUBTEDLY, SIR. THEY-- /THE
DOCT II (124)	WELL, SIR, YOU MAY BELIEVE ME OR NOT; BUT I'M THE	LAWFUL	MRS DUBEDAT. /SIR PATRICK/ AND WHY ARNT YOU LIVING
JOAN 2 (86)	THOU BE CONSECRATED. /CHARLES/ BUT I SHALL NOT BE	LAWFUL	OWNER OF MY OWN LAND ANYHOW. WILL THE CONSECRATION
JOAN 2 (86)	THAN MY FATHER'S POOREST SHEPHERD. THOURT NOT	LAWFUL	OWNER OF THY OWN LAND OF FRANCE TILL THOU BE
2TRU I (45)	IF I SELL IT ON THE SQUARE, AS THE AGENT OF ITS	LAWFUL	OWNER, I SHALL BE ABLE TO GET ITS FULL MARKET VALUE.
GENV PREFACE(11)	THAT MADE THE AIR BATTLES OF THE WORLD WAR	LAWFUL	; AND THESE AIR BATTLES HAD ALREADY REDUCED WAR TO
JOAN EPILOG (164)	OFFICE IN COMMEMORATION OF HER; AND IT SHALL BE	LAWFUL	TO DEDICATE A SPECIAL CHAPEL TO HER, AND TO PLACE HER
POSN PREFACE(426)	ANY OTHER COUNTRY, THEN, SO LONG AS WAR REMAINS	LAWFUL	, I CLAIM FULL LIBERTY TO WRITE AND PERFORM A PLAY

LAWFULLY

POSN PREFACE(390)	HE MAY ABHOR HIS WICKEDNESS. IN SHORT, NO MAN IS	LAWFULLY	AT THE MERCY OF THE MAGISTRATE'S PERSONAL CAPRICE,
POSN (452)	SHERIFF HERE; AND IT'S FOR ME TO SAY WHEN HE MAY	LAWFULLY	BE HANGED. (THEY RELEASE HIM). /BLANCO/ AS THE
GENV IV (116)	THEIR INHABITANTS. /NEWCOMER/ DO YOU CALL THE	LAWFULLY	CONSTITUTED DEMOCRATIC GOVERNMENT OF YOUR COUNTRY
GENV IV (104)	PARLIAMENT OF JACKSONSLAND, TO WHICH I HAVE BEEN	LAWFULLY	ELECTED: TELL ME THAT. /BBDE/ PRESUMABLY BECAUSE
DOCT PREFACE(34)	HIM QUICKLY AND MERCIFULLY. TO GET KILLED	LAWFULLY	HE MUST VIOLATE SOMEBODY ELSE'S RIGHT TO LIVE BY
POSN PREFACE(389)	AN EXEMPTION CERTIFICATE, WHEN THEIR DEMANDS ARE	LAWFULLY	MADE; AND IN CITIES THE INSPECTOR MUST COMPEL THE
FANY III (324)	THE LONG AND SHORT OF IT SEEMS TO BE THAT HE CANT	LAWFULLY	MARRY MY DAUGHTER, AS HE OUGHT AFTER GOING TO
LADY (244)	SENT IN MY DEMAND FOR THE COAT-OF-ARMS THAT IS	LAWFULLY	MINE. CAN YOU SAY AS MUCH FOR YOURSELF?
DEVL I (24)	OTHER. /ANDERSON/ BUT WHY, IF THE OTHER IS MORE	LAWFULLY	WORDED? /HAWKINS/ BECAUSE, SIR, THE COURTS WILL

LAWGIVER

MIS. PREFACE(64)	SCHOOLMASTER, AND OF THEIR PUBLIC ANALOGUES THE	LAWGIVER	AND THE JUDGE, BECOME INSTRUMENTS OF TYRANNY IN THE
MILL PREFACE(109)	HIS CASE, AS HE IS BY CONVENTION THE MASTER AND	LAWGIVER	OF THE HEARTHSTONE. IN EVERY BUSINESS STREET YOU
MILL PREFACE(112)	OF MAKING A CODE OF LAWS, HE INEVITABLY BECOMES	LAWGIVER	TO ALL THE TRIBES, AND, EQUALLY INEVITABLY, IS
METH PREFACE(R40)	A CONTINUAL CAPRICIOUS DISORDER IN NATURE, OF A	LAWGIVER	WHO WAS ALSO A LAWBREAKER, MADE ATHEISTS IN ALL
BASH II,1, (110)	HAT. I HAVE BEEN FOOLING HERE. NOW, BY THE HEBREW	LAWGIVER	, I THOUGHT THAT ONLY IN AMERICA SUCH REVENUES WERE

LAWGIVERS

POSN PREFACE(382)	MORALITY HAS NOT ONLY EVERY ENGINE THAT	LAWGIVERS	CAN DEVISE IN FULL OPERATION FOR ITS PROTECTION,
MRS PREFACE(171)	MINDS, AND WHICH MAKES IT SEEM NATURAL TO OUR	LAWGIVERS	TO PUNISH SILLY AND NEGLIGIBLE INDECENCIES WITH A
POSN PREFACE(381)	IF THEY WERE NOT IN LEADING-STRINGS DEVISED BY	LAWGIVERS	, PHILOSOPHERS, PROPHETS, AND POETS FOR THEIR

LAWK

CAPT II (265)	HUNNERDS OF EM, THIS TAWM. THE OWL DEZZIT IS	LAWK	A BLOOMIN AWD PAWK DEMONSTRATION. AW BLIEVE ITS THE
CAPT II (269)	SHE'LL MAWCH EM ALL TO CHURCH NEXT SUNDER	LAWK	A BLOOMIN LOT O CHERRITY KIDS: YOU SEE IF SHE DOWNT.
CAPT I (222)	AWSKIN YR PAWDN FOR THE WORD. (SENTIMENTALLY)	LAWK	AS A HINGLISH LIDY MAWT CALL ER LITTLE BOY BIRDIE.
CAPT II (270)	WHEW! /JOHNSON/ GUNBOAT, PRAPS. /DRINKWATER/	LAWK	BLOOMIN WORTERLEOO BUSES, THEY ARE, ON THIS COWST.
CAPT I (220)	THEIR MAWNDS KENNOT RAWSE TO CHRISTIENNITY	LAWK	HAHRS KEN, GAVNER: THETS AH IT IS, WEOLL, EZ HAW WAS
CAPT I (223)	CASTOMS AHSES AND SPHERES O HINFLUENCE AND SICH	LAWK	HALL OWVER ARFRICAR. DAOWNT HARFRICAR BELONG AS MUCH TO
CAPT I (238)	YER CAWNT HEXPECT A LOT O POOR HONEDDIKITED MEN	LAWK	HUZ TO RAN AHRSEOLVS INTO DINEGER WITHAHT NAOW KEPN TO
BARB II (279)	AN SHAOW HER THET, AND TELL HER IF SHE WANTS ONE	LAWK	IT TO CAM AND INTERFERE WITH ME. (JENNY, CRYING WITH
BULL III (142)	IT, JAST TO LET YOU FAWND AHT WOT REEL AWDSHIP'S	LAWK	. /MATTHEW/ (STARTING UP, MORE IN SCANDALIZED
CAPT I (219)	CROST MOROCKER-- A RAWD INTER THE MAHNTNS OR SECH	LAWK	. WEOLL, AS YOU KNAOW, GAVNER, THET CAWNT BE DONE EAH
CAPT II (245)	BETTER EV NAOW FEMBLY, AN RAWSE AHT OF IT,	LAWK	ME, THAN EV A SPECBLE ONE AND DISGRICE IT, LAWK YOU.
CAPT I (218)	TO BE HINTERRAPTED IN YR BIT O GAWDNIN BAW THE	LAWK	O ME, GAVNER. /RANKIN/ A MISSIONARY KNOWS NOTHING OF
BARB II (289)	YOU WAS MAW GEL AND TOOK THE WORD AHT O ME MAHTH	LAWK	THET, AW'D GIVE YOU SATHINK YOUD FEEL URTIN, AW WOULD.
BARB II (288)	WITH YOU, THAT YOU CAM NEGGIN AND PROVOWKIN ME	LAWK	THIS? (HE WRITHES CONVULSIVELY FROM HIS EYES TO HIS
BARB II (280)	AW WANT TO GIVE MY GIRL A BLOOMIN GOOD AWDIN AW	LAWK	TO EV A BIT O DEVIL IN ME: SEE? AN EAH AW EMM, TALKIN
BULL III (141)	ILL! WELL, WOT PRAWCE MAW GRENFAWTHER, OI SHOULD	LAWK	TO KNAOW, THAT FITTED AP A FUST CLAWSS SHOP AND BUILT
CAPT I (225)	IS THE SIME EVERYWHERES. THEM EATHENS IS JAST	LAWK	YOU AN' ME, GAVNER. A LADY AND GENTLEMAN, BOTH ENGLISH,

CAPT II (245) LAWK ME, THAN EV A SPECBLE ONE AND DISGRICE IT. LAWK YOU. /JOHNSON/ BRANDYFACED JACK: I NAME YOU FOR CONDUCT

LAWKLY
BARB II (300) HER; AND SHE'S OLD. /BILL/ (CONTEMPTUOUSLY) NOT LAWKLY . AW'D GIVE HER ANATHER AS SOON AS LOOK AT ER. LET
BARB II (288) ARE YOU? /BILL/ (WITH CONVICTION) NOT ME. NOT LAWKLY . /BARBARA/ THATS RIGHT, BILL. HOLD OUT AGAINST IT.
CAPT II (243) LADY FAINT, EH? /DRINKWATER/ FYNT! NOT LAWKLY . WORNTED TO GOW AN TALK TO THE BENNY SEERAS: BLAOW

LAWLESS
HART PREFACE(7) RELATIONS: DIPLOMACY HAS BEEN A BOYISHLY LAWLESS AFFAIR OF FAMILY INTRIGUES, COMMERCIAL AND
PRES (137) HER HEAD! THESE WOMEN ARE MAKING THE ARMY AS LAWLESS AS THEMSELVES. CLOUTED HER HEAD INDEED! A PURELY
POSN PREFACE(432) OF LICENCES IN THE FUTURE. THIS STRANGE AND LAWLESS BODY WILL HARDLY REASSURE OUR MORALISTS, WHO OBJECT
CAPT III (273) OWER BONNY TO BE CAST AWAY AMONG A PARCEL O LONE, LAWLESS MEN, MY LEDDY. /LADY CICELY/ (NAIVELY) BLESS ME,
O'FL (216) LOTS THOUGHT SHE WAS GOING TO MARRY YOUNG MASTER LAWLESS. -- /SIR PEARCE/ WHAT! THAT -- THAT -- THAT
MIS. PREFACE(36) LIABILITY TO PERSONAL ASSAULT FROM THE LAWLESS SCHOOLMASTER, FROM WHICH THE GROWN-UPS ARE FREE, FOR

LAWLESSLY
SUPR HANDBOK(182) SACRIFICE THE LIFE AND HEALTH OF THE NATION AS LAWLESSLY AS THE MANCHESTER COTTON MANUFACTURERS DID AT THE

LAWLESSNESS
HART PREFACE(13) WAS SET ASIDE FOR LYNCH LAW. THE CLIMAX OF LEGAL LAWLESSNESS WAS REACHED IN FRANCE. THE GREATEST SOCIALIST

LAWN
SUPR IV (155) HER FOR TEN DUCHESSES. (HE DESCENDS TO THE LAWN AND COMES BETWEEN TANNER AND RAMSDEN). /RAMSDEN/ (VERY
SUPR IV (164) TO SAY WHAT I PLEASE. /VIOLET/ (ARRIVING ON THE LAWN AND COMING BETWEEN MRS WHITEFIELD AND TANNER) IVE COME
SUPR IV (153) /OCTAVIUS/ (JUMPING DOWN FROM THE GARDEN TO THE LAWN AND RUNNING TO HECTOR'S LEFT HAND) I HOPE YOULL SHAKE
SIM II (67) OUR EMPRESS! /ALL FOUR/ (RUSHING DOWN TO THE LAWN AND THROWING THEMSELVES ON THEIR KNEES BEFORE HER)
SUPR IV SD(141) AMERICAN AND ENGLISH VISITORS. IF WE STAND ON THE LAWN AT THE FOOT OF THE GARDEN AND LOOK UPHILL, OUR HORIZON
APPL II SD(257) BEEN OCCUPIED. THE TERRACE IS ACCESSIBLE FROM THE LAWN BY A CENTRAL FLIGHT OF STEPS. THE KING AND QUEEN ARE
SIM I SD(36) SHRUBBERIES. TO THE WEST OF THE FLOWER GARDEN THE LAWN FALLS AWAY TO THE SEA, BUT NOT TO SEA LEVEL. ALL THAT
SIM I SD(36) SCATTERED ABOUT IT. BEHIND THE CRESCENT THE LAWN IS BANKED TO A HIGHER LEVEL AND BECOMES A FLOWER
APPL II SD(257) PALACE. A LOW BALUSTRADE SEPARATES IT FROM THE LAWN . TERRACE CHAIRS IN ABUNDANCE, RANGED ALONG THE
CAPT II (260) CAME, IN A ROOM WITH A WINDOW OPENING ON THE LAWN . THE MAN CAME BACK NEXT DAY AND SAID HE MUST RETURN TO
SUPR IV SD(142) AN ELDERLY GENTLEMAN, AND FOLLOWS HIM ON TO THE LAWN . THIS ELDERLY GENTLEMAN DEFIES THE SPANISH SUN IN A
SUPR IV SD(141) PLATFORM THROUGH THE GARDEN AND DOWN AGAIN TO THE LAWN (A MOVEMENT WHICH LEAVES THE VILLA BEHIND US ON OUR
SIM II SD(54) THE HARBOR IS CROWDED WITH CRUISERS; AND ON THE LAWN NEAR THE STEPS IS A WRITING TABLE LITTERED WITH PAPERS
SIM I SD(36) THE LAWN OF A STATELY HOUSE ON THE NORTH COAST OF A TROPICAL
SUPR IV (154) LEAVING HIS FATHER AND VIOLET TOGETHER ON THE LAWN). /MALONE/ YOULL TRY TO BRING HIM TO HIS SENSES,
SUPR IV (160) AND MOVES AWAY FROM HER TOWARDS THE MIDDLE OF THE LAWN). /MRS WHITEFIELD/ (FOLLOWING HIM HASTILY) DOES ANN
SUPR IV (154) EVER COME TO THAT WITH ME. (HE COMES DOWN TO THE LAWN). /RAMSDEN/ (FOLLOWING HIM) THE SOONER THE BETTER FOR
SUPR IV (170) HENRY. (HE WITHDRAWS TO THE CORNER OF THE LAWN ; AND OCTAVIUS IMMEDIATELY HURRIES DOWN TO HIM). /TAVY/
SUPR IV SD(141) GENTEELEST ORDER. THE GARDEN IS HIGHER THAN OUR LAWN ; SO WE REACH IT BY A FEW STEPS IN THE MIDDLE OF ITS
KING I (194) VILEST SCOUNDREL IN EUROPE WHILE HE PARADES IN LAWN SLEEVES THROUGH THE STREET WITH HIS NO POPERY MOB AT
CAPT III (291) NAOW, LOOK EAH, KEPN: THAT YNT RAWT. DROR A LAWN SOMEWHERE. /JOHNSON/ I SAY NOTHIN AGEN A BIT OF FUN,
2TRU I (45) AND GOODLOOKING AND HAVE A SWEET BREATH AND BE A LAWN TENNIS CHAMPION AND ENJOY EVERYTHING THAT IS TO BE
CAND I SD(94) OLD BLUE SERGE JACKET, UNBUTTONED, OVER A WOOLLEN LAWN TENNIS SHIRT, WITH A SILK HANDKERCHIEF FOR A CRAVAT,
MRS II (210) HER MOTHER) YOU WANT SOME GOOD WALKS AND A LITTLE LAWN TENNIS TO SET YOU UP. YOU ARE SHOCKINGLY OUT OF
MILL I (156) WELL, YOU WERE YOUNG; YOU WERE WELL SHAPED; YOUR LAWN TENNIS WAS OUTSTANDING; YOU WERE A MAGNIFICENT BOXER;
BUOY III (43) OF WHISKY OR STRAWBERRY ICES, LOVE OF CRICKET OR LAWN TENNIS, ALSO LOVE OF MONEY. MY CASE IS A SPECIFIC ONE
SUPR IV (156) ANN, BY WANTING ME TO GO (HE COMES DOWN ON THE LAWN TO HIDE HIS FACE FROM HER. SHE FOLLOWS HIM
SUPR IV (170) ASKED HER. IT IS A TRAP FOR ME. (HE GOES UP THE LAWN TOWARDS THE GARDEN. OCTAVIUS REMAINS PETRIFIED).
SUPR IV (170) HIM TO DRIVE THEM GENTLY PAST ANN AND UP THE LAWN TOWARDS THE GARDEN, WHERE OCTAVIUS, WHO HAS ALREADY
APPL II (265) (LOOKING OUT INTO THE GARDEN) COMING ACROSS THE LAWN WITH SEMPRONIUS. THE CABINET ARRIVES. THE MEN TAKE OFF
SUPR IV SD(149) WHO, SNORTING WITH INDIGNATION, COMES UPON THE LAWN , AND IS MAKING FOR HIS FATHER WHEN VIOLET, GREATLY
MRS III SD(220) A STRIP OF TURF AND AN UNFENCED PINE WOOD. ON THE LAWN , BETWEEN THE HOUSE AND THE DRIVE, IS A CLIPPED YEW

LAWN-TENNIS
MRS I (185) EVEN KNOW ARITHMETIC WELL. OUTSIDE MATHEMATICS, LAWN-TENNIS , EATING, SLEEPING, CYCLING, AND WALKING, I'M A

LAWR
BARB II (300) HER ANATHER AS SOON AS LOOK AT ER. LET HER EV THE LAWR O ME AS SHE THREATENED! SHE AINT FORGIVEN ME: NOT
BARB II (280) MORNIN! /BILL/ AW'M NAO GIN DRINKER, YOU OALD LAWR ; BUT WEN AW WANT TO GIVE MY GIRL A BLOOMIN GOOD AWDIN

LAWRENCE
FOUN (222) HER) MINE! MINE! ! MINE! ! ! AYOT ST LAWRENCE , 10TH AUGUST 1909.
POSN PREFACE(432) THEATRES TODAY WITHOUT MY ADDING TO IT. AYOT ST LAWRENCE , 14TH JULY 1910. POSTSCRIPT.-- SINCE THE ABOVE WAS
2TRU PREFACE(26) CATHOLICISM WITH WHICH I HAVE CRACKED IT. AYOT ST LAWRENCE , 1933.
KING PREFACE(159) IT WILL WAIT TOO LONG. MALVERN, 1939. AYOT SAINT LAWRENCE , 1945.
GENV PREFACE(27) AND WIPE OUT WAR. YOU NEVER CAN TELL. AYOT SAINT LAWRENCE , 1945.
FABL PREFACE(99) TWO FARFETCHED FABLES THAT FOLLOW. AYOT SAINT LAWRENCE , 1948-9.
SHAK PREFACE(137) OF IT FOR MERE PROFESSIONAL JEALOUSY. AYOT SAINT LAWRENCE , 1949.
LADY (251) WARDER, TO THE GATE NEAREST BLACKFRIARS. AYOT ST LAWRENCE , 20TH JUNE 1910.
CURE (238) A WEDDING MARCH. SHE PLAYS THE BASS. AYOT ST LAWRENCE , 21ST JANUARY 1914. THE END.
ROCK PREFACE(191) EVER DREAMS OF INCULCATING. AYOT ST LAWRENCE , 22ND OCTOBER 1933.
CYMB FORWORD(138) OF THE LAST ACT TO COMPLAIN. G.B.S. AYOT ST LAWRENCE , DECEMBER 1945.
TRFL (83) PUT THEM IN THE WINDOW WITH THE REST. AYOT ST LAWRENCE , JULY 1926.
BUOY PREFACE(7) THEY BEGIN I SWITCH OFF THE WIRELESS. AYOT SAINT LAWRENCE , JULY 1947.
FANY EPILOG (335) HEAR, HEAR! (THEY START THE APPLAUSE). AYOT ST LAWRENCE , MARCH 1911.
APPL PREFACE(196) WILL IT CEASE TO HAVE A MESSAGE FOR US. AYOT ST LAWRENCE , MARCH 1930.
JOAN PREFACE(56) WHEN THE PLAY MAKES US FORGET THEM? AYOT ST LAWRENCE , MAY 1924.
BULL PREFACE(72) ENOUGH WHEN THEY HAVE THE LUCK TO GET IT. AYOT ST LAWRENCE , NOVEMBER 1929.

LAW-ABIDING
BARB PREFACE(242) THE HEROES ARE BANDITS, AND COMEDIES IN WHICH LAW-ABIDING AND CONVENTIONALLY MORAL FOLK ARE COMPELLED TO
GETT PREFACE(224) US TO STUDY THIS PHENOMENON AMONG ENTIRELY LAW-ABIDING PEOPLE. I KNOW ONE LADY WHO HAS BEEN MARRIED
GETT PREFACE(195) CHARLES SURFACE-- ARE THE HEROES, AND DECOROUS, LAW-ABIDING PERSONS-- BLIFIL AND JOSEPH SURFACE-- ARE THE

LAW-BREAKERS
BARB PREFACE(241) ASSENT, AND NOT TO DEAL CRUELLY AND STUPIDLY WITH LAW-BREAKERS . EVERYBODY DISAPPROVES OF BURGLARS; BUT THE

LAW-GIVER
POSN PREFACE(389) THE JURY: THE CENSOR IS JURY AND JUDGE AS WELL AS LAW-GIVER . A MAGISTRATE MAY BE STRONGLY PREJUDICED AGAINST

LAW-GIVERS
LADY PREFACE(234) RELIGIONS OFFERED TO THEM BY GREAT PROPHETS AND LAW-GIVERS WERE AND STILL ARE SO FOOLISH THAT WE NOW CALL

LAW'S
BASH III (124) THIS COP I HAD AVERTED; BUT IT IS TOO LATE. THE LAW'S ABOVE US BOTH. ENTER LUCIAN, WITH AN ORDER IN COUNCIL.
MIS. PREFACE(45) NOR THE ATHEIST CLAMOR FOR THE SUPPRESSION OF LAW'S SERIOUS CALL BECAUSE IT HAS FOR TWO CENTURIES
FABL PREFACE(72) OF INFANT CIVILIZATION. IF THEY BEGIN WITH LAW'S SERIOUS CALL, AS MANY PIOUS PARENTS THINK THEY SHOULD,

LAWS
APPL PREFACE(180) ASK ME " WHY SHOULD NOT THE PEOPLE MAKE THEIR OWN LAWS ? " I NEED ONLY ASK YOU " WHY SHOULD NOT THE PEOPLE
GETT PREFACE(256) OF INDISSOLUBLE MARRIAGE CAN BE CURED BY DIVORCE LAWS ADMINISTERED ON OUR PRESENT PLAN. THE VERY CHEAPEST
MILL PREFACE(118) PRIVATE CONTRACTS. EVEN FACTORY ACTS AND LAWS AGAINST ADULTERATION AND SWEATING WERE JEALOUSLY
ROCK PREFACE(161) PENALTY, AND HAD ACTUALLY PASSED THE MOST SEVERE LAWS AGAINST ANY INTERFERENCE WITH HIS IDLING. IT WAS THE
LION PREFACE(98) HE IS ACTUALLY COMPELLED, IN SO FAR AS HE MAKES LAWS AGAINST BLASPHEMY, TO TREAT ALL THE RELIGIONS,
POSN PREFACE(411) THEATRES. FEW PEOPLE ARE AWARE OF THE MONSTROUS LAWS AGAINST BLASPHEMY WHICH STILL DISGRACE OUR STATUTE

BARB PREFACE(241)	ABSURDITIES. IT IS NOT GOOD SENSE TO PROPOSE THAT	LAWS	AGAINST CRIME SHOULD APPLY TO PRINCIPALS ONLY AND NOT
POSN PREFACE(414)	PROSECUTION OF AN OFFENCE AGAINST THE ORDINARY	LAWS	AGAINST DISORDERLY HOUSEKEEPING, INDECENCY, BLASPHEMY,
POSN (442)	OF WHEN WE TRY TO SET UP OUR OWN SHORTSIGHTED	LAWS	AGAINST HIS WORD. WHEN DOES THE DEVIL CATCH HOLD OF A
POSN PREFACE(410)	AMERICA FOR THE PURPOSE OF ENFORCING THE EXISTING	LAWS	AGAINST OBSCENITY, BLASPHEMY, SABBATH-BREAKING, THE
CLEO IV (182)	BUT WHEN I RETURN TO ROME, I WILL MAKE	LAWS	AGAINST THESE EXTRAVAGANCES. I WILL EVEN GET THE LAWS
MIS. PREFACE(78)	GROW UP IN SOCIETIES OF FREE CHILDREN. CHILD	LAWS	AND CHILD FASHIONS, CHILD MANNERS AND CHILD MORALS ARE
MTH4 I (171)	TO DO EXACTLY THE CONTRARY OF EVERYTHING YOUR OWN	LAWS	AND CHOSEN RULERS COMMAND AND EXECUTE. YOU CANNOT DEFY
POSN PREFACE(430)	RIGHT, THAT IS, A DOGMA WHICH IS ABOVE OUR	LAWS	AND CONDITIONS OUR LAWS, INSTEAD OF BEING SUBJECT TO
POSN PREFACE(430)	WITH A SENSE OF THE IMPOTENCE OF JUDGES AND	LAWS	AND COURTS TO DEAL SATISFACTORILY WITH EVILS WHICH ARE
2TRU PREFACE(16)	PEOPLE; FOR IT IS EVIDENT THAT IF THEY MADE	LAWS	AND GAVE PERSONAL DIRECTIONS WHICH WOULD PRODUCE
BULL III (122)	IT, TOO! THATS AN ENGLISHMAN ALL OVER! MAKE BAD	LAWS	AND GIVE AWAY ALL THE LAND, AND THEN, WHEN YOUR
CLEO PR01 (91)	POMPEY THEY RAISED HIGHER THAN EVER, HE AND HIS	LAWS	AND HIS HIGH MIND THAT APED THE GODS, SO THAT HIS FALL
BARB PREFACE(243)	TO SOCIETY, ONCE HE IS BROUGHT TO REPUDIATE THE	LAWS	AND INSTITUTIONS HE KNOWS, HE WILL REPUDIATE THE VERY
CAPT II (260)	HIM FOR IT, AND HAVE POLICEMEN AND COURTS AND	LAWS	AND JURIES TO DRIVE HIM INTO IT SO THAT HE CANT HELP
APPL PREFACE(184)	ONES, TOO, SOME OF THEM. IF THEY HAVE NOT	LAWS	AND KINGS, THEY HAVE BY-LAWS AND CHAIRMEN. AND YOU AND
SIM I (49)	STOCK UNTIL A FAIRYLAND WAS BUILT UP, WITH	LAWS	AND RELIGIOUS RITUALS, AND FINALLY A GREAT INSTITUTION
GETT PREFACE(239)	TO BREAK UP SPONTANEOUSLY, WHETHER THE MARRIAGE	LAWS	ARE ALTERED OR NOT. AND HERE WE MUST EXTEND THE TERM
GETT PREFACE(256)	TO THE PRESERVATION OF MARRIAGE. IF OUR DOMESTIC	LAWS	ARE KEPT SO INHUMAN THAT THEY AT LAST PROVOKE A FURIOUS
SUPR IV (152)	SAID, MALONE! YOU ALSO SEE THAT MERE MARRIAGE	LAWS	ARE NOT MORALITY! I AGREE WITH YOU; BUT UNFORTUNATELY
FABL PREFACE(77)	FOR SUCH PERSECUTION. BUT THE BLASPHEMY	LAWS	ARE STILL AVAILABLE AND IN USE AGAINST OBSCURE
BARB PREFACE(241)	EVERYBODY TO ASSIST THE POLICE. NO DOUBT IF YOUR	LAWS	ARE UNJUST, AND YOUR POLICEMEN AGENTS OF OPPRESSION,
GETT PREFACE(183)	IT. MARRIAGE NEVERTHELESS INEVITABLE. NOW MOST	LAWS	ARE, AND ALL LAWS OUGHT TO BE, STRONGER THAN THE
MILL PREFACE(112)	IT IS USELESS TO EXPECT THE TRIBESMEN TO OBEY HIS	LAWS	AS A MATTER OF COMMON SENSE, HE MUST PERSUADE THEM THAT
LION PREFACE(64)	LIMITS TO FREE WILL. CONSEQUENTLY SUCH OF OUR	LAWS	AS ARE NOT MERELY THE INTIMIDATIONS BY WHICH TYRANNIES
LION PREFACE(95)	DISGRACE OF THE NATION'S LEADERS AND RULERS, THE	LAWS	BY WHICH PERSECUTORS CAN DESTROY OR GAG ALL FREEDOM OF
CLEO IV (182)	AGAINST THESE EXTRAVAGANCES. I WILL EVEN GET THE	LAWS	CARRIED OUT. /CLEOPATRA/ (COAXINGLY) NEVER MIND. TODAY
POSN PREFACE(420)	ALL THE CATEGORIES OF LIBEL AND THE BLASPHEMY	LAWS	CONTRARY TO PUBLIC LIBERTY, AND REPEALING AND DEFINING
GETT PREFACE(246)	INSTANCE OF THE OUTLAWRY WHICH OUR MARRIAGE	LAWS	EFFECT. IN OUR ANXIETY TO PROVIDE FOR OURSELVES A
APPL PREFACE(183)	AND MINES TO PRIVATE MANAGEMENT. ONLY BY STERN	LAWS	ENFORCED BY CONSTANT INSPECTION HAVE WE STOPPED THE
FABL III (113)	TO DO. YOULL BE TOO BUSY TELLING THEM, AND MAKING	LAWS	FOR THEM, TO DO ANY OF IT YOURSELF. IN WITH YOU INTO
SUPR HANDBOK(183)	IN SCOTLAND. MARRIAGE AS MODIFIED BY THE DIVORCE	LAWS	IN SOUTH DAKOTA WOULD BE CALLED MERE PROMISCUITY IN
CLEO PR01 (90)	GREAT MASTERS OF THAT ART, AND KNEW BY WHAT	LAWS	IT COULD BE MADE TO APPEAR SEEMLY AND HONEST. AND WHEN
2TRU III (87)	IN THEIR ORBITS OBEYING THE SAME UNIVERSAL	LAWS	. EVERY MOMENT OF TIME DICTATED AND DETERMINED THE
BULL III (122)	INDIGNANT AND KILL THE PEOPLE THAT CARRY OUT YOUR	LAWS	. /AUNT JUDY/ SURE NEVER MIND HIM, MR BROADBENT. IT
CLEO II (124)	ARE A STRANGER HERE, AND NOT CONVERSANT WITH OUR	LAWS	. THE KINGS AND QUEENS OF EGYPT MAY NOT MARRY EXCEPT
GETT PREFACE(204)	STRAIGHT FOR " RED RUIN AND THE BREAKING UP OF	LAWS	." VOLTAIRE SAID THAT MR EVERYBODY IS WISER THAN
POSN PREFACE(427)	ENSLAVEMENT OF THE YOUNG, THE PASSING OF PRESS	LAWS	(ESPECIALLY IN EGYPT, INDIA, AND IRELAND), EXACTLY AS
BULL PREFACE(28)	SUCH A THING AS POLITICAL SCIENCE, WITH NATURAL	LAWS	LIKE ANY OTHER SCIENCE, IT IS CERTAIN THAT ONLY THE
DOCT III (142)	MAN; AND THINK OF YOUR POSITION. YOU CAN DEFY THE	LAWS	MADE BY MEN; BUT THERE ARE OTHER LAWS TO RECKON WITH.
BARB PREFACE(243)	ALWAYS BE, A REVOLUTIONARY WRITER, BECAUSE OUR	LAWS	MAKE LAW IMPOSSIBLE; OUR LIBERTIES DESTROY ALL FREEDOM;
GETT PREFACE(184)	EVERY OTHER CASE OPEN VIOLATION OF THE MARRIAGE	LAWS	MEANS EITHER DOWNRIGHT RUIN OR SUCH INCONVENIENCE AND
LION PREFACE(5)	CONSIDERABLE EXTENT IN SPITE OF THE FACT THAT THE	LAWS	OF ALL COUNTRIES TREAT IT, IN EFFECT, AS CRIMINAL. MANY
MTH5 (238)	MUST DO WHAT THEY MUST ACCORDING TO THE ETERNAL	LAWS	OF CAUSE AND EFFECT. LOOK TO YOUR WORDS; FOR IF THEY
APPL PREFACE(188)	THAT ITS REGULATIONS ARE TAKING THE PLACE OF THE	LAWS	OF ENGLAND, THOUGH SOME OF THEM ARE MADE FOR THE
DOCT PREFACE(53)	STATISTICAL ILLUSIONS. PUBLIC IGNORANCE OF THE	LAWS	OF EVIDENCE AND OF STATISTICS CAN HARDLY BE
HART III (145)	WILL STRIKE AND SINK AND SPLIT. DO YOU THINK THE	LAWS	OF GOD WILL BE SUSPENDED IN FAVOR OF ENGLAND BECAUSE
GETT PREFACE(190)	CEREMONY AS A RITE WHICH ABSOLVED THEM FROM THE	LAWS	OF HEALTH AND TEMPERANCE; INAUGURATED A LIFE-LONG
BARB PREFACE(243)	IN LATIN VERSE, CANNOT BE SET AGAINST ALL THE	LAWS	OF HIS COUNTRY AND YET PERSUADED TO REGARD LAW IN THE
DOCT PREFACE(46)	THE VIVISECTOR THE RIGHT TO PUT A DOG OUTSIDE THE	LAWS	OF HONOR AND FELLOWSHIP, CONCEDES TO HIM ALSO THE RIGHT
DOCT PREFACE(50)	EXEMPTION OF THE PURSUIT OF KNOWLEDGE FROM THE	LAWS	OF HONOR IS THE MOST HIDEOUS CONCEIVABLE ENLARGEMENT OF
CLEO V (199)	IN CAESAR'S WAY, ACCORDING TO CAESAR'S BOASTED	LAWS	OF LIFE. /CAESAR/ (DUBIOUSLY) HE IS TO RULE AS HE CAN,
ROCK II (260)	BY YOUR SEDITIOUS ROT TO REBEL AGAINST THE	LAWS	OF NATURE. ENGLAND IS NOT BREAKING. SHE STANDS
CLEO II (125)	THAT THE CUSTOMS OF HIS TRIBE AND ISLAND ARE THE	LAWS	OF NATURE. /BRITANNUS/ ON THE CONTRARY, CAESAR, IT IS
METH PREFACE(R40)	THIS DISORDERLINESS, THIS REFUSAL TO OBEY ITS OWN	LAWS	OF NATURE, THAT CREATED A SCIENTIFIC NEED FOR ITS
3PLA PREFACE(R21)	OR NOTHING, THESE CONVENTIONS WILL BECOME THE	LAWS	OF PERSONAL HONOR. JEALOUSY, WHICH IS EITHER AN
METH PREFACE(R63)	UNIONISM IS A VAIN DEFIANCE OF THE INEXORABLE	LAWS	OF POLITICAL ECONOMY, JUST AS THE NEO-DARWINIANS WERE
METH PREFACE(R64)	THE INDUSTRIAL WELTER BEING " CONTRARY TO THE	LAWS	OF POLITICAL ECONOMY," EVEN THE PROLETARIAT
MTH2 (62)	WAGES AND DISTRIBUTION BEING FIXED BY IMMUTABLE	LAWS	OF POLITICAL ECONOMY IS OBSOLETE ROT. /FRANKLYN/ (
MTH2 (61)	THE LABOR MEMBERS WILL FIND THAT THE IMMUTABLE	LAWS	OF POLITICAL ECONOMY TAKE NO MORE NOTICE OF THEIR
ROCK I (219)	WISH I HAD TIME TO EXPLAIN TO YOU THE INEXORABLE	LAWS	OF POLITICAL ECONOMY, I-- /HIPNEY/ (INTERRUPTING HIM
BASH PREFACE(87)	CRITICS TOOK ME FOR. I OBSERVED THE ESTABLISHED	LAWS	OF STAGE POPULARITY AND PROBABILITY. I SIMPLIFIED THE
PHIL II (113)	IT'S THE FAULT OF THE WICKEDLY SENTIMENTAL	LAWS	OF THIS COUNTRY. I WAS NOT ABLE TO MAKE EXPERIMENTS
DOCT II (115)	MY DEAR LADY; BUT SIR PATRICK'S ORDERS ARE THE	LAWS	OF-- ER-- OF TYRE AND SIDON. /WALPOLE/ LET ME TAKE YOU
GETT PREFACE(235)	DOUBT, IT IS; BUT THE DAY HAS GONE BY FOR BASING	LAWS	ON THE ASSUMPTION THAT A WOMAN IS LESS TO A MAN THAN
GETT PREFACE(183)	INEVITABLE. NOW MOST LAWS ARE, AND ALL	LAWS	OUGHT TO BE, STRONGER THAN THE STRONGEST INDIVIDUAL.
GETT (287)	MINISTERS THAT IF THEY DIDNT MAKE OUR MARRIAGE	LAWS	REASONABLE THERE WOULD BE A STRIKE AGAINST MARRIAGE,
DOCT PREFACE(7)	TO SENTENCE ONE PRISONER (UNDER THE BLASPHEMY	LAWS	) FOR QUESTIONING THE AUTHORITY OF SCRIPTURE, AND
KING II (232)	THE OTHER, YET THEY CANNOT LIVE TOGETHER WITHOUT	LAWS	; AND A LAW IS SOMETHING THAT OBLIGES THEM ALL TO DO
LADY (250)	OF A NATION IS MIGHTIER THAN HE THAT MAKETH ITS	LAWS	; AND THE SAME MAY WELL BE TRUE OF PLAYS AND
2TRU III (87)	THE STARS IN THEIR ORBITS OBEYED IMMUTABLY FIXED	LAWS	; AND WHEN WE TURNED FROM SURVEYING THEIR VASTNESS TO
GETT PREFACE(222)	THOSE WHO DEAL SPECIFICALLY WITH THE MARRIAGE	LAWS	SHOULD NEVER ALLOW THEMSELVES FOR A MOMENT TO FORGET
GETT PREFACE(231)	LEST THE SLIGHTEST RELAXATION OF THE MARRIAGE	LAWS	SHOULD UTTERLY DEMORALIZE SOCIETY; WHILST THOSE TO WHOM
GETT PREFACE(230)	OR ENFORCED ON WOMEN ONLY. BUT WHEN THESE	LAWS	TAKE HIM BY THE COLLAR AND THRUST HIM INTO PRISON, HE
GETT PREFACE(246)	RESTRAINTS WITHOUT FOREGOING RIGHTS; THAT ALL THE	LAWS	THAT ARE NEEDED TO COMPEL STRANGERS TO RESPECT US ARE
ROCK PREFACE(155)	WHEN THE HORRORS OF ANARCHY FORCE US TO SET UP	LAWS	THAT FORBID US TO FIGHT AND TORTURE ONE ANOTHER FOR
MRS III (233)	THINK OF THE SOCIETY THAT TOLERATES YOU, AND THE	LAWS	THAT PROTECT YOU! WHEN I THINK OF HOW HELPLESS NINE
SUPR HANDBOK(220)	WHICH ABROGATES AS BETWEEN THE PARTIES ALL THE	LAWS	THAT SAFEGUARD THE PARTICULAR RELATION TO WHICH IT
GETT PREFACE(222)	HOWEVER, IT IS NOT BY ANY REFORM OF THE MARRIAGE	LAWS	THAT THIS CAN BE DEALT WITH. IT IS IN THE GENERAL
BARB PREFACE(241)	TO THWART THE LAW IF THEY PLEASE, BUT TO MAKE	LAWS	THAT WILL COMMAND THE PUBLIC ASSENT, AND NOT TO DEAL
POSN PREFACE(389)	APPLY EQUALLY TO A CENSORSHIP. A MAGISTRATE HAS	LAWS	TO ADMINISTER: A CENSOR HAS NOTHING BUT HIS OWN
SUPR HANDBOK(183)	THAT MOST PEOPLE BELIEVE THEIR OWN MARRIAGE	LAWS	TO BE UNIVERSAL. CONSEQUENTLY HERE AGAIN, AS IN THE
DOCT PREFACE(7)	TO CLAIM DIVINE OMNISCIENCE, NOR TO CLAMOR FOR	LAWS	TO PUNISH ANY SCEPTICISM ON THE PART OF LAYMEN. A
DOCT III (142)	DEFY THE LAWS MADE BY MEN; BUT THERE ARE OTHER	LAWS	TO RECKON WITH. DO YOU KNOW THAT YOURE GOING TO DIE?
CAPT I (231)	NONSENSE; AND YOU KNOW IT. THESE PEOPLE HAVE NO	LAWS	TO RESTRAIN THEM, WHICH MEANS, IN PLAIN ENGLISH, THAT
MIS. PREFACE(46)	TO UNDERSTAND WHY HE SHOULD NOT USE AND MAKE	LAWS	TO TORMENT AND SUBDUE PEOPLE WHO DO NOT HAPPEN TO AGREE
GETT PREFACE(192)	THE INDUSTRIES THEY WERE ENGAGED IN, THE	LAWS	UNDER WHICH THEY LIVED, OR THE RELATION OF THEIR
HART PREFACE(15)	HEAVILY INSTEAD OF INCREASING IT, THE FACTORY	LAWS	WERE SUSPENDED, AND MEN AND WOMEN RECKLESSLY OVERWORKED
BARB PREFACE(242)	IN SHORT, ALL MEN ARE ANARCHISTS WITH REGARD TO	LAWS	WHICH ARE AGAINST THEIR CONSCIENCES, EITHER IN THE
GETT PREFACE(230)	NO MAN WILL TAKE MUCH TROUBLE TO ALTER	LAWS	WHICH HE CAN EVADE, OR WHICH ARE EITHER NOT ENFORCED OR
JOAN PREFACE(49)	BY FORCES EXPRESSING THEMSELVES IN RELIGIONS AND	LAWS	WHICH MAKE EPOCHS RATHER THAN BY VULGARLY AMBITIOUS
UNPL PREFACE(R25)	MADE BETWEEN MEN AND WOMEN UNDER MARRIAGE	LAWS	WHICH REPRESENT TO SOME OF US A POLITICAL NECESSITY (
GETT PREFACE(230)	ARE SUPPORTED. NOW WE HAVE SEEN THAT OUR MARRIAGE	LAWS	WILL NOT STAND CRITICISM, AND THAT THEY HAVE HELD OUT
GETT (287)	COUNTRIES THE INTRODUCTION OF REASONABLE DIVORCE	LAWS	WILL SAVE THE SITUATION; BUT IN ENGLAND WE ALWAYS LET
ROCK I (219)	USE OF SAYING THAT ECONOMIC SCIENCE AND NATURAL	LAWS	WONT GO DOWN, MR HIPNEY? YOU MIGHT AS WELL SAY THAT
MIS. PREFACE(61)	THE OTHER SET, WHICH HAVE ALL THE ADULTS, ALL THE	LAWS	, ALL THE RELIGIONS ON THEIR SIDE. HOW IS THE CHILD TO
MILL PREFACE(113)	THE WORLD. IN SHORT, A RULER MUST NOT ONLY MAKE	LAWS	, AND RULE FROM DAY TO DAY! HE MUST, BY SCHOOL
GETT PREFACE(187)	THIS IS NOT ONLY THE THEORY OF OUR MARRIAGE	LAWS	, BUT THE PRACTICAL MORALITY OF MANY OF US. IT IS NO
MILL PREFACE(112)	IS THE ONLY TRIBESMAN CAPABLE OF MAKING A CODE OF	LAWS	, HE INEVITABLY BECOMES LAWGIVER TO ALL THE TRIBES,
POSN PREFACE(430)	DOGMA WHICH IS ABOVE OUR LAWS AND CONDITIONS OUR	LAWS	, INSTEAD OF BEING SUBJECT TO THEM, IS ANARCHIC AND
SUPR HANDBOK(184)	BY HIS CHURCH TO AVAIL HIMSELF OF THE DIVORCE	LAWS	, MARRIES AS FREELY AS THE SOUTH DAKOTAN PRESBYTERIANS
BUOY III (45)	AS AN INSTITUTION. WITH REASONABLE DIVORCE	LAWS	, NOT AT ALL. /HE/ (TO HER) YOU HEAR? /SHE/ SIT DOWN,
SUPR PREFACE(R11)	ONE ANOTHER HAVE BEEN COMPLICATED BY THE MARRIAGE	LAWS	, NOT TO MENTION THE LOOSER SORT OF PLAYS WHICH TRADE
GETT PREFACE(219)	WHICH ARE COMPULSORILY ATTACHED TO IT BY OUR	LAWS	, OR SENTIMENTALLY ASSOCIATED WITH IT IN ROMANCE, BUT
MTH4 I (158)	WE FOUNDED OUR RELIGION, OUR MORALITY, OUR	LAWS	, OUR LESSONS, OUR POEMS, OUR PRAYERS, ON THAT SIMPLE
MTH2 (61)	HUMAN ACTION WHATEVER. THEY OBEY FIXED SCIENTIFIC	LAWS	, WHICH HAVE BEEN ASCERTAINED AND SETTLED FINALLY BY

LAWSON

PYGM III SD(244)	ARE ON THE WALLS. THE ONLY LANDSCAPE IS A CECIL	LAWSON	ON THE SCALE OF A RUBENS. THERE IS A PORTRAIT OF MRS

LAWSUIT

JOAN 1 (63)	CAME HERE LAST YEAR TO REPRESENT HIS VILLAGE IN A	LAWSUIT	; HE IS ONE OF THEIR NOTABLES. A FARMER. NOT A
POSN PREFACE(396)	WHOM A LICENSED PLAY CAME IN THE COURSE OF A	LAWSUIT	EXPRESSED HIS SCANDALIZED ASTONISHMENT AT THE

LAWSUITS

SUPR HANDBOK(203)	ARBITRATIONS ARE MORE DREADED BY HONEST MEN THAN	LAWSUITS	; THE PHILANTHROPIST IS STILL A PARASITE ON MISERY

LAWTNIN

PPP (205)	THE WIND HOWLS. /THE LANDLORD/ IT'S THANDERIN AND	LAWTNIN	. /FITZ/ IT'S DANGEROUS. /THE POLICEMAN/ (DRAWING
CAPT I (224)	/DRINKWATER/ HEE-QUIPPED! HAW SHOULD THINK SOW.	LAWTNIN	RAWFLES. TWELVE SHOTS IN THE MEGGEZINE! OO'S TO

LAWYER

DEVL I (12)	WE SHALL HAVE THE MINISTER BACK HERE WITH THE	LAWYER	AND ALL THE FAMILY TO READ THE WILL BEFORE YOU HAVE
LION PREFACE(37)	TO SENTIMENTAL CONSIDERATIONS. THE STORY OF THE	LAWYER	ASKING WHAT ARE THE TWO CHIEF COMMANDMENTS IS CHANGED
POSN PREFACE(418)	THE LIGHTER PLAYS WOULD BE NO BETTER OFF. WHAT	LAWYER	COULD ACCEPT ANY RESPONSIBILITY FOR THE PRODUCTION OF
CAPT III (283)	MYSELF. SAILOR FASHION WILL DO AS WELL HERE AS	LAWYER	FASHION. /LADY CICELY/ EVER SO MUCH BETTER, DEAR
DEVL I (20)	IN THE EYES OF THE CHILD. (BRISKLY) NOW THEN,	LAWYER	HAWKINS: BUSINESS, BUSINESS. GET ON WITH THE WILL,
DEVL I (20)	BY YOUR LEAVE, MINISTER ANDERSON: BY YOUR LEAVE,	LAWYER	HAWKINS. THE HEAD OF THE TABLE FOR THE HEAD OF THE
DEVL I SD(16)	HAS LEFT HIS CLOAK AT HOME. HE IS ACCOMPANIED BY	LAWYER	HAWKINS, A BRISK, MIDDLEAGED MAN IN BROWN RIDING
LION PREFACE(37)	CHANGED BY MAKING JESUS PUT THE QUESTION TO THE	LAWYER	INSTEAD OF ANSWERING IT, AS TO DOCTRINE, LUKE IS ONLY
SUPR III (126)	YOUR SOPHISTRIES! I WAS A MAN IN LOVE, NOT A	LAWYER	. AND THE WOMEN LOVED ME FOR IT, BLESS THEM! /DON
GETT (357)	I DO NOT MERELM BELIEVE THAT: I KNOW IT AS A	LAWYER	. /HOTCHKISS/ WOULD YOU STEAL A TURNIP FROM ONE OF
DEVL I (12)	YOUD BETTER PUT THE INKSTAND INSTEAD, FOR THE	LAWYER	. /MRS DUDGEON/ THATS NO ANSWER TO MAKE TO ME, SIR.
JOAN PREFACE(50)	LEMAITRE WOULD HAVE BEEN A SADIST INSTEAD OF A	LAWYER	. WARWICK WOULD HAVE HAD NO MORE FEUDAL QUALITY THAN
CAPT I (229)	AND INTERESTING ONE-- AT LEAST IT IS SO TO A	LAWYER	LIKE MYSELF. /RANKIN/ I SHOULD BE GLAD TO HEAR IT FOR
SUPR III (124)	HIMSELF? WHY, YOU WOULD NOT MAKE A MAN YOUR	LAWYER	OR YOUR FAMILY DOCTOR ON SO SLIGHT AN ACQUAINTANCE AS
SUPR III (126)	YOU SAY WHEN I TELL YOU THAT THOUGH I PLAYED THE	LAWYER	SO CALLOUSLY, THEY MADE ME THINK SO TOO? I ALSO HAD
JOAN PREFACE(33)	AND CONSCIENTIOUS BOTH AS PRIEST AND	LAWYER	THAN ANY ENGLISH JUDGE EVER DREAMS OF BEING IN A
POSN PREFACE(420)	VICTUALLER CAN NOW BE ASSURED CONFIDENTLY BY HIS	LAWYER	THAT A MAGISTRATE CANNOT REFUSE TO RENEW HIS LICENCE
POSN PREFACE(419)	TO AMEND THE LAW SO AS TO MAKE IT POSSIBLE FOR A	LAWYER	TO ADVISE HIS CLIENT THAT HE MAY PUBLISH THE WORKS OF
GENV IV (118)	HAVE NO DEFENCE. YOU CANNOT EVEN FIND A JEWISH	LAWYER	TO DEFEND YOU, BECAUSE YOU HAVE DRIVEN THEM ALL FROM
MILL IV (207)	LEFT HER WITHOUT A PENNY, THOUGH NO DOCTOR AND NO	LAWYER	TOOK A FARTHING, AND THE SHOPKEEPERS WERE PATIENT;
POSN PREFACE(417)	SHOULD BE REVIVED. IN THE FIRST PLACE, NO	LAWYER	WITH THE MOST ELEMENTARY KNOWLEDGE OF THE LAW OF
DOCT III (142)	THEY FALL BACK ON INTIMIDATION. I NEVER KNEW A	LAWYER	YET WHO DIDNT THREATEN TO PUT ME IN PRISON SOONER OR
CAPT III (277)	BECAUSE EVERYBODY WOULD SAY YOU ARE SUCH A CLEVER	LAWYER	YOU COULD MAKE A POOR SIMPLE SAILOR LIKE CAPTAIN
MTH2 (63)	SO COMPLETELY FILLED BY MY PROFESSIONAL WORK AS A	LAWYER	, AND LATER ON BY MY DUTIES AS LEADER OF THE HOUSE OF
GETT (357)	I DO NOT LIKE TURNIPS. /HOTCHKISS/ AS YOU ARE A	LAWYER	, ANSWER ME. /SOAMES/ I ADMIT THAT I SHOULD PROBABLY
NEVR IV (285)	AND THE GENTLEMAN OF WHOM MR M'COMAS SPOKE, THE	LAWYER	, HAS NOT YET COME. /VALENTINE/ OH YES HE HAS. IVE
POSN PREFACE(390)	ITS ACCEPTANCE BY A SERIOUS STATESMAN OR A GREAT	LAWYER	, IT WILL BE SEEN THAT THE PLAYWRIGHTS ARE JUSTIFIED
BUOY III (45)	LUMPS, NOTHING SCIENTIFIC. /SIR F./ I AM A	LAWYER	, NOT A SCIENTIST. /SECONDBORN/ UNTIL LAW AND
POSN PREFACE(366)	JUST AS HE CALLS IN A DOCTOR, OR CONSULTS A	LAWYER	, OR ENGAGES AN ARCHITECT, DEPENDING ON THE
JOAN 1 (63)	LABORER. NOT A MECHANIC. HE MIGHT HAVE A COUSIN A	LAWYER	, OR IN THE CHURCH. PEOPLE OF THIS SORT MAY BE OF NO
MTH4 II (178)	I HAVE NO TALENT AS A SCULPTOR OR PAINTER; AND AS	LAWYER	, PREACHER, DOCTOR, OR ACTOR, SCORES OF SECOND-RATE
CAPT I (229)	GLAD TO HEAR IT FOR MILES' SAKE, THOUGH I AM NO	LAWYER	, SIR HOWRRD. /LADY CICELY/ I NEVER KNEW YOU HAD A
SUPR HANDBOK(194)	THE SALVATIONIST, THE VEGETARIAN, THE DOCTOR, THE	LAWYER	, THE PARSON, THE PROFESSOR OF ETHICS, THE GYMNAST,
UNPL PREFACE(R23)	PROFESSION CAN PLACE HIM ON THE LEVEL OF THE	LAWYER	, THE PHYSICIAN, THE CHURCHMAN, AND THE STATESMAN.
BASH I (95)	US. AND YET THERE'S NO DISHONOR IN'T: YOUR	LAWYER	, WHO LET YOUR LODGE TO ME, WILL VOUCH ME HONEST. I
CAPT II (257)	/BRASSBOUND/ (WITH DISGUST) AGH! TRICKSTER!	LAWYER	! EVEN THE PRICE YOU OFFER FOR YOUR LIFE IS TO BE
DEVL I (26)	(JUDITH, DISMAYED, CLINGS TO ANDERSON) OR A	LAWYER	! (HAWKINS SMILES LIKE A MAN ABLE TO TAKE CARE OF

LAWYER'S

CAPT III (278)	CALL THAT DEVILMENT. SO IT IS, I DARESAY, FROM A	LAWYER'S	POINT OF VIEW. /SIR HOWARD/ I HOPE YOURE NOT
MILL PREFACE(115)	GO FROM DISASTER TO DISASTER. BERNADOTTE, THE	LAWYER'S	SON WHO ENLISTED AS A COMMON SOLDIER AND ENDED

LAWYERS

SIM II (80)	HAVING DISAPPEARED ALMOST EN BLOC, WHILST THE	LAWYERS	AND CLERGY ARE COMPARATIVELY IMMUNE. A SITUATION OF
OVER PREFACE(163)	ARE SUCH THINGS IN THE WORLD AS HUSBANDS AND	LAWYERS	AND DUELLING CODES AND THEORIES OF SIN AND NOTIONS
ROCK II (235)	AND BOBTAIL OF LABOR MEN AND SOCIALISTS AND	LAWYERS	AND JOURNALISTS-ON-THE-MAKE AND USED-UP TRADE UNION
ROCK II (263)	AND HOTEL KEEPERS, FASHIONABLE DOCTORS AND	LAWYERS	AND PARSONS AND FIDDLERS AND PORTRAIT PAINTERS AND
JOAN EPILOG (167)	TO, THESE KINGS AND CAPTAINS AND BISHOPS AND	LAWYERS	AND SUCH LIKE? THEY JUST LEAVE YOU IN THE DITCH TO
HART I (79)	AMONG THE DISEASEI GERMS AND THE DOCTORS AND THE	LAWYERS	AND THE PARSONS AND THE RESTAURANT CHEFS AND THE
BUOY IV (55)	FOR INCURABLES. HE IS THE MAN YOU SHOULD CONSULT.	LAWYERS	ARE USELESS HERE. /OLD BILL/ COME, COME, FLOPPER!
ROCK PREFACE(183)	TIME OR PATIENCE TO LISTEN TO. THAT IS WHY YOUR	LAWYERS	CAN PLEAD AS WELL FOR ONE SIDE AS ANOTHER, AND CAN
CAPT NOTES (302)	IN BLEAK HOUSE. MOST PUBLIC MEN AND ALL	LAWYERS	HAVE BEEN APPEALED TO BY VICTIMS OF THIS SENSE OF
MILL I (142)	IS THE LAW. MY FATHER ALWAYS HAD TO INSTRUCT HIS	LAWYERS	IN THE LAW WHENEVER HE DID ANYTHING EXCEPT WHAT
LION PREFACE(37)	LIVES BUT TO SAVE THEM. THE BIAS OF JESUS AGAINST	LAWYERS	IS EMPHASIZED, AND ALSO HIS RESOLUTION NOT TO ADMIT
POSN PREFACE(403)	IS NOT LIKELY TO BE ENTERTAINED BY CONSTITUTIONAL	LAWYERS	. IT IS A NAIVE OFFER TO ACCEPT THE METHOD OF
JOAN PREFACE(9)	FOR IT WITH THE NEIGHBORING SQUIRES AND THEIR	LAWYERS	, WHEN THE CASTLE IN WHICH THE VILLAGERS WERE
ROCK PREFACE(179)	OF THE ILLUSTRATIVE HYPOTHETICAL CASES BELOVED OF	LAWYERS	(CALLED PARABLES IN THE GOSPELS), AND NEVER AT A
ROCK II (270)	MOVIE STARS AND SOLDIERS AND RICH SWANKERS AND	LAWYERS	ON THE MAKE. HOW ARE THEY TO TELL THE DIFFERENCE
MRS PREFACE(173)	TO BE SAINTLY, FOR SOLDIERS TO BE HEROIC, FOR	LAWYERS	TO BE HARD-HEARTED, FOR SAILORS TO BE SIMPLE AND
ROCK I (214)	CHILDREN OF THE MEN IN PRISON, AND TO PAY CHEAP	LAWYERS	TO PUT UP PERFECTLY USELESS DEFENCES FOR THEM IN THE
MIS. PREFACE(72)	AND UNPLEASANT COMPANY, AND THERE WERE CHILDREN'S	LAWYERS	TO SUE PEDAGOGUES AND OTHERS FOR ASSAULT AND
JOAN 6 (124)	WITHIN MY EXPERIENCE, MY LORD. THE MAID NEEDS NO	LAWYERS	TO TAKE HER PART: SHE WILL BE TRIED BY HER MOST
UNPL PREFACE(R26)	I MYSELF BELONG, NOT TO MENTION THE LEGIONS OF	LAWYERS	, DOCTORS, CLERGYMEN, AND PLATFORM POLITICIANS WHO
BARB III (320)	HAS PUZZLED ALL THE PHILOSOPHERS, BAFFLED ALL THE	LAWYERS	, MUDDLED ALL THE MEN OF BUSINESS, AND RUINED MOST
BUOY III (45)	AND RELIGION, ARE ALL ONE, THE SCIENTISTS, THE	LAWYERS	, THE CLERGYMEN, THE POLITICIANS WILL BE FOOLISH
BARB III (346)	THE COMMON PEOPLE. I WANT TO ARM THEM AGAINST THE	LAWYERS	, THE DOCTORS, THE PRIESTS, THE LITERARY MEN, THE

LAX

LION I (111)	EMPEROR. YOU WILL MAKE THEM UNDERSTAND THAT THE	LAX	DISCIPLINE OF THE MARCH CANNOT BE PERMITTED HERE. YOU

LAXER

APPL PREFACE(173)	OF AUTHORITY. HIS MINISTERS HAVE MUCH	LAXER	STANDARDS. IT IS OPEN TO THEM, IF IT WILL SAVE THEIR

LAXITY

GETT PREFACE(187)	WITH SUCH FEROCITY THAT THE LEAST SUGGESTION OF	LAXITY	IN ITS SUPPORT IS FATAL TO EVEN THE HIGHEST AND
BULL I (91)	RELATIONSHIPS CANNOT EXCUSE ANY COMPROMISE OR	LAXITY	. FOR INSTANCE-- /DOYLE/ (IMPATIENTLY SPRINGING UP
GETT PREFACE(188)	THE HIGHEST AND STRONGEST REPUTATIONS, ALTHOUGH	LAXITY	OF CONDUCT IS WINKED AT WITH GRINNING INDULGENCE; SO
POSN PREFACE(402)	OF AN ENLIGHTENED CENSORSHIP WITH THE POPULAR	LAXITY	OF THE LORD CHAMBERLAIN. THE JUDGE WOULD SUPPRESS THE
POSN PREFACE(407)	IN EVERY OTHER RESPECT GIVES MORE SCANDAL BY HIS	LAXITY	THAN TROUBLE BY HIS SEVERITY, THEY FIND IN THE

LAY

BASH II,2, (114)	WOULD PRESENTLY CONSTRUCT A STEAM ENGINE, AND	LAY	A CABLE T' TH' ANTIPODES. /CETEWAYO/ HAVE I BEEN BROUGHT
PYGM I (210)	HARM. (TO THE GENTLEMAN) OH, SIR, DONT LET HIM	LAY	A CHARGE AGEN ME FOR A WORD LIKE THAT. YOU-- /THE
JOAN 6 (125)	THE MAN, WERE HE THE EMPEROR HIMSELF, WHO DARES	LAY	A FINGER ON HER! THE CHURCH IS NOT SUBJECT TO POLITICAL
2TRU II (59)	AS I SHALL MOST CERTAINLY DO IF THEY DARE	LAY	A HAND ON A BRITISH LADY. BUT I CANNOT COUNTENANCE SUCH
MIS. (172)	TURNING ON HER) STAND OFF. I'LL SHOOT YOU IF YOU	LAY	A HAND ON ME. I WILL, BY GOD. /LINA/ YOU CANT COVER ME
ROCK I (226)	OH, ENSUE! OF COURSE: A GOOD WORD. " MY FRIENDS,	LAY	AND CLERICAL, WE MUST ENSUE PEACE. YES, ENSUE PEACE.
JOAN 1 (58)	ASK YOU HOW MANY EGGS THERE ARE, THAT YOU CANNOT	LAY	ANY. /STEWARD/ (PROTESTING) OH SIR, OH SIR -- /ROBERT/
METH PREFACE(R86)	AND A DAINTY FUN OUT OF THE FAIRY CLOUDLAND THAT	LAY	BETWEEN HIM AND THE EMPTY HEAVENS. THE GIANTS OF THE
GENV I (35)	IN MY COUNTRY WEVE HAD AN ELECTION. WE THOUGHT IT	LAY	BETWEEN OUR USUAL PEOPLE: THE NATIONAL PARTY AND THE
WIDO II (42)	ADDITIONAL HOUSES FOR THE HOMELESS, AND TO	LAY	BY A LITTLE FOR BLANCHE. (HE LOOKS AT THEM. THEY ARE

DOCT PREFACE(51)	DEFENDS VIVISECTION, BUT IN HIS ENTIRELY VULGAR	LAY	CAPACITY, HE IS MADE OF THE SAME CLAY AS THE IGNORANT,
FABL PREFACE(76)	CHURCH ON THE POLITICAL ISSUE OF EPISCOPAL OR	LAY	CHURCH GOVERNMENT. THE UNITARIANS REJECT THE TRINITY AND
KING I (207)	HIM TO PIECES WITH GALLOPING HORSES. BUT HENRY	LAY	DEAD ALL THE SAME. THE PROTESTANTS WILL HAVE YOU, JAMIE,
JITT I (21)	WHEN THEY ARE NOT ADOPTED. MENDEL'S MASTERPIECE	LAY	DEAD FOR THIRTY-FIVE YEARS WHILE THE FAME OF THE LIVING
BULL PREFACE(36)	THAT LONG AFTER THE LAST ORANGEMAN SHALL	LAY	DOWN HIS CHALK FOR EVER, THE FAMILIAR SCRAWL ON EVERY
POSN PREFACE(385)	CONSISTENTLY AND CONSCIENTIOUSLY BE READY TO	LAY	DOWN HIS LIFE FOR THE RIGHT OF EVERY MAN TO ADVOCATE
CLEO PRO2 (99)	OF HIS JAW. HE WAS BUT MORTAL AFTER ALL: HE	LAY	DOWN IN A STUPOR; AND I TOOK HIS SWORD AND LAID IT ON. (
3PLA PREFACE(R32)	CIRCE AND CAESAR A HOG IN THESE PAGES, HAD BETTER	LAY	DOWN MY BOOK AND BE SPARED A DISAPPOINTMENT. IN CAESAR,
SUPR PREFACE(R40)	THIS MISUNDERSTANDING IS SO GALLING THAT I	LAY	DOWN MY PEN WITHOUT ANOTHER WORD LEST I SHOULD BE
PRES (131)	ORDERLY/ WE FORGOT THE DOOR-SCRAPER, SIR. SHE	LAY	DOWN ON THE FLAGS AND GOT THE CHAIN THROUGH BEFORE SHE
MIS. PREFACE(47)	UNDER WHICH IT WILL CEASE TO EXIST; TO	LAY	DOWN PRECISE RULES OF RIGHT AND WRONG CONDUCT; TO
MIS. PREFACE(4)	ITS VICTORY; AND THAT IS THE BELIEF THAT WE CAN	LAY	DOWN THE BURDEN OF OUR WRETCHED LITTLE MAKESHIFT
DOCT PREFACE(60)	SORT OF HAT THEIR PATIENTS WEAR, THE DOCTOR MAY	LAY	DOWN THE LAW DESPOTICALLY ENOUGH TO THE PATIENT AT
MIS. PREFACE(48)	AND A CLERGYMAN WHO IS NOT PREPARED TO	LAY	DOWN THE LAW DOGMATICALLY WILL NOT BE OF MUCH USE IN A
PRES (142)	FOUR MORE DREADNOUGHTS. /MITCHENER/ THEN YOU MUST	LAY	DOWN TWELVE. /BALSQUITH/ OH YES: IT'S EASY TO SAY THAT;
JOAN 1 (57)	FOR IT. /STEWARD/ SIR: WHAT CAN I DO? I CANNOT	LAY	EGGS. /ROBERT/ (SARCASTIC) HA! YOU JEST ABOUT IT.
LION PREFACE(21)	CONTENT WITH THEIR WAGES AND NOT TO BE VIOLENT OR	LAY	FALSE ACCUSATIONS. THERE IS NO RECORD OF JOHN GOING
METH PREFACE(R84)	WITH A RECKLESSNESS WHICH SHEWED THAT HIS TRADE	LAY	FAR FROM HIS CONSCIENCE. IT IS TRUE THAT HE NEVER TAKES
DOCT IV SD(160)	AT DUBERDAT'S SIDE, NEXT THE DAIS, FROM WHICH THE	LAY	FIGURE OGLES THE DYING ARTIST. B.B. THEN RETURNS TO
DOCT III SD(131)	RAGS, TUBES OF COLOR, BRUSHES, CHARCOAL, A SMALL	LAY	FIGURE, A KETTLE AND SPIRIT-LAMP, AND OTHER ODDS AND
DOCT III SD(131)	NEAR THE INNER DOOR IS A LITTLE TEA-TABLE. A	LAY	FIGURE, IN A CARDINAL'S ROBE AND HAT, WITH AN HOUR-GLASS
DOCT III (137)	IT FOR THE CARDINAL'S HAT ON THE HEAD OF THE	LAY	FIGURE, THEREBY INGENIOUSLY DESTROYING THE DIGNITY OF
KING I (188)	MY BROTHER DOWN. IT IS A SERIOUS MATTER TO	LAY	HANDS ON A ROYAL PERSONAGE. /NEWTON/ SIR: I HAD NO
6CAL SD(100)	THREE MEN-AT-ARMS BEGIN TO LIFT PETER. THE OTHERS	LAY	HANDS ON HIS FIVE COLLEAGUES. /THE KING/ NO: LET THAT
BARB PREFACE(233)	ONLY TO REVERSE YOUR ATTITUDE TOWARDS HIM-- TO	LAY	HANDS ON HIS PROPERTY, REVILE HIM, ASSAULT HIM, AND HE
MIS. (178)	LEAVE ME GO, WILL YOU? WHAT RIGHT HAVE YOU TO	LAY	HANDS ON ME? /TARLETON/ LET HIM RUN FOR IT, MR
6CAL SD(105)	QUICK THERE. OFF WITH HIM. THE MEN-AT-ARMS	LAY	HANDS ON PETER WHO STRUGGLES VIOLENTLY. /PETER/ HANDS
PRES (136)	TO TAKE IT SERIOUSLY AND USING ITS POWER TO	LAY	HANDS ON PROPERTY? PARLIAMENT MUST ABOLISH ITSELF. THE
NEVR I SD(224)	INARTICULATE SOUND IN THE MOUTHPIECE AND TRIES TO	LAY	HANDS ON VALENTINE, WHOM HE SUPPOSES TO BE IN FRONT OF
JITT II (33)	I AM ABLE TO TELL YOU WHAT I FELT WHEN I	LAY	HELPLESS, UNABLE TO PAY THE LAST RESPECTS TO OUR DEAR
HART III (145)	UNTIL HE IS A DRIFTING SKIPPER. WHILST HE CAN	LAY	HIS COURSE AND STAND ON HIS BRIDGE AND STEER IT, HE IS
APPL I (236)	OR METHYLATED SPIRIT OR PETROL OR WHATEVER HE CAN	LAY	HIS HANDS ON WHEN THE FIT TAKES HIM. /BALBUS/ I AGREE
HART III (146)	WE CAN GIVE THE RECTOR A BED HE HAS NOWHERE TO	LAY	HIS HEAD THIS NIGHT. /CAPTAIN SHOTOVER/ THE CHURCH IS ON
LION PREFACE(57)	OF THE AIR NESTS WHILST HE HAD NOT A PLACE TO	LAY	HIS HEAD). DR CRIPPEN'S TIME WAS WORTH, SAY, THREE
DOCT III (142)	ITLL PUT THE GIRL IN PRISON AND RUIN HER: ITLL	LAY	HIS WIFE'S LIFE WASTE. YOU MAY PUT THE CRIMINAL LAW OUT
CATH 3 (184)	HIS OWN PISTOLS FROM HIS BOOTS. /THE SERGEANT/	LAY	HOLD OF HIM THERE. PIN HIS ARMS. I HAVE HIS PISTOLS. (
BARB PREFACE(208)	HIM. THE ORIGINALITY OF SHAKESPEAR'S VERSION	LAY	IN HIS TAKING THE LUNATIC SYMPATHETICALLY AND SERIOUSLY,
LION PREFACE(21)	FROM THE HERESY OF BAPTISM, THE VALUE OF WHICH	LAY	IN ITS BRINGING THE GENTILES (THAT IS, THE
LADY PREFACE(231)	GAVE US HERE; AND THAT WAS NOT THE BEST THAT	LAY	IN SHAKESPEAR'S POWER. WHEN POVERTY IS ABOLISHED, AND
MIS. PREFACE(74)	FANTASTIC ENOUGH TO HAVE A CHANCE. FIRST, THEN, I	LAY	IT DOWN AS A PRIME CONDITION OF SANE SOCIETY, OBVIOUS AS
CLEO III (154)	CHILDREN-- (WITH SUDDEN ALARM) GENTLY, YE DOGS.	LAY	IT LEVEL IN THE STERN-- SO-- TIS WELL. /FTATATEETA/ (
GETT (263)	MAAM, THEY ALL SAY THAT. YOU AND ME SAID IT, I'LL	LAY	. I DID, ANYHOW. /MRS BRIDGENORTH/ NO: MARRIAGE CAME
WIDO III (53)	THERES NOTHING TO BE GOT OUT OF ME ON THAT	LAY	. /LICKCHEESE/ (SHOCKED) BLACKMAIL! OH, MR SARTORIUS,
JOAN 1 (57)	EGGS JUST AS YOU HAVE, SIR. THE HENS WILL NOT	LAY	. /ROBERT/ (RISING) NOW LISTEN TO ME, YOU. /STEWARD/ (
GETT PREFACE(244)	IS IDLE. IT IS FOR THAT REASON THAT I	LAY	LITTLE STRESS ON PROSTITUTION HERE, AND REFER READERS
BARB II (274)	IT I DO AS THE CAPITALISTS DO: PINCH WOT I CAN	LAY	ME ANDS ON. IN A PROPER STATE OF SOCIETY I AM SOBER,
VWOO 3 (140)	SATISFIED. /Z/ HOW CAN I BE SATISFIED WHEN I CANT	LAY	MY HANDS ON YOU? I WORK FOR YOU LIKE A SLAVE FOR A
OVER PREFACE(162)	ESPECIALLY WITH DIVORCE AND MURDER CASES, NOW	LAY	NO STRESS ON THEM; AND POLICE PAPERS WHICH CONFINED
DEST (155)	HERE? /NAPOLEON/ (BRUSQUELY, RISING) NO:	LAY	NOTHING HERE UNTIL THE OFFICER FOR WHOM I AM WAITING
KING I (195)	THE TOWN. FLOG HIM TO DEATH. THEY CAN IF THEY	LAY	ON HARD ENOUGH AND LONG ENOUGH. THE SAME MOB THAT NOW
HART PREFACE(17)	AND COROBBERIES WAS NOT THE ONLY BURDEN THAT	LAY	ON SANE PEOPLE DURING THE WAR. THERE WAS ALSO THE
FOUN (210)	ENGAGING HIM IN A STAGE FIGHT OF THE NOISIEST)	LAY	ON, MACDUFF; AND DAMNED BE HE THAT FIRST CRIES HOLD!
SHAK (140)	I HAVE NO WORDS. MY VOICE IS IN MY SWORD.	LAY	ON, ROB ROY; AND DAMNED BE HE THAT PROVES THE SMALLER
BARB PREFACE(208)	THEY REPRESENTED, THE ROMANTIC MAKE-BELIEVER,	LAY	OUTSIDE THE PALE OF SYMPATHY IN LITERATURE: HE WAS
2TRU PREFACE(18)	OWN PROPERTY, AND BY THE INFLUENCE ON IT OF THE	LAY	PROPRIETORS, THAT IT LOST ALL ITS MORAL PRESTIGE, THE
NEVR II (237)	THE WAITER TURNS TO CRAMPTON AND CONTINUES HIS	LAY	). EVEN THE SOLICITOR TOOK UP THE JOKE, ALTHOUGH HE WAS
SUPR IV (159)	/ANN/ SUPPOSE SHE WERE TO TELL FIBS, AND	LAY	SNARES FOR MEN? /OCTAVIUS/ DO YOU THINK I COULD MARRY
MTH4 II (184)	HOUSES AND FAMILIES, WHILE THE TEN MILLION MEN	LAY	SNUGLY IN THE CAVES THEY HAD DUG FOR THEMSELVES. LATER
GETT PREFACE(219)	THE IMPERSONALITY OF SEX. IT IS NECESSARY TO	LAY	SOME STRESS ON THESE POINTS, BECAUSE FEW REALIZE THE
LADY PREFACE(224)	ABOUT THE SWEET SOUTH AND THE BANK OF VIOLETS. I	LAY	STRESS ON THIS IRONY OF SHAKESPEAR'S, THIS IMPISH
LION I (123)	TO ANNOY HIM, HE MIGHT FORGET HIMSELF AND	LAY	THAT GLADIATOR OUT. /LAVINIA/ THAT WOULD BE SPLENDID.
MTH5 (262)	ME, AND LILITH WILL BE ONLY A LEGEND AND A	LAY	THAT HAS LOST ITS MEANING. OF LIFE ONLY IS THERE NO END;
NEVR III SD(261)	WHICH IS FURTHER DOWN. HE WOULD, IF HIS TASTE	LAY	THAT WAY, ADMIRE THE WALL DECORATION OF LINCRUSTA WALTON
CAND I (103)	IF HE PROMISES TO BE A GOOD BOY AND HELP ME	LAY	THE TABLE? /MORELL/ (SHORTLY) OH YES, CERTAINLY: HE
DEST (155)	A FINE FIGURE OF A LADY. (SLYLY) SHALL I	LAY	THE TABLE FOR HER COLLATION HERE? /NAPOLEON/ (
KING I (200)	OF THE LABORATORY AND SEND THEM UP HERE WHILE I	LAY	THE TABLE THERE. SHE GOES OUT. /JAMES/ " A NICE PIECE OF
CAND I (104)	(OFFERING HIS ARM TO CANDIDA) COME AND	LAY	THE TABLE. (SHE TAKES IT. THEY GO TO THE DOOR TOGETHER.
CAND I (103)	ONE WORD OF IT FROM HER-- IF YOU ARE NOT READY TO	LAY	THE TRUTH AT HER FEET AS I AM-- THEN YOU WILL KNOW TO
6CAL SD(97)	IN PAIRS BEHIND HIM, AND, FOLLOWING HIS EXAMPLE,	LAY	THEIR KEYS ON THE GROUND. THEY ARE DEEPLY CAST DOWN,
JITT I SD(26)	TAKES OUT A HANDFUL OF ROSES; AND IS STOOPING TO	LAY	THEM ON HIS BREAST WHEN SHE REALIZES THAT A MAN WHO
MIS. PREFACE(10)	AND ABOMINABLE DELIGHT IN TORTURE IS ALLOWED TO	LAY	TRAPS INTO WHICH EVERY CHILD MUST FALL, AND THEN BEAT IT
BARB PREFACE(215)	STILL LESS DESERVING; AND LET THE DESERVING	LAY	UP FOR HIMSELF, NOT TREASURES IN HEAVEN, BUT HORRORS IN
2TRU III (110)	WITH SCRAPS OF THE OLD MATERIAL, THE YOUNG	LAY	VIOLENT HANDS ON US AND TEAR FROM US EVEN THE RAGS THAT
APPL PREFACE(178)	THAT I AM OUT TO RUIN OUR CARRYING TRADE AND	LAY	WASTE ALL OUR SEASIDE RESORTS AND SCRAP THE BRITISH
BASH III (127)	ASIDE) IT WRINGS MY HEART TO SEE MY NOBLE BACKER	LAY	WASTE HIS FUTURE THUS. THE WORLD'S A CHESSBOARD, AND WE
CLEO II (139)	BURN IT. /THEODOTUS/ WITHOUT HISTORY, DEATH WILL	LAY	YOU BESIDE YOUR MEANEST SOLDIER. /CAESAR/ DEATH WILL DO
2TRU II (61)	SMACK ME IN THE FACE AGAIN, MY GIRL, AND I'LL	LAY	YOU OUT FLAT, EVEN IF I HAVE TO GIVE AWAY THE WHOLE
MIS. (169)	LIKE YOU? /TARLETON/ THEN YOU WERE ABLE TO	LAY	YOUR HAND ON FORTY-TWO SHILLINGS, JUDGING FROM YOUR
GETT (333)	YOU EVER CALL BOTH OF THEM EVERY NAME YOU COULD	LAY	YOUR TONGUE TO? /LESBIA/ (SHIVERING WITH DISGUST) NO.
PHIL III (139)	THE OBJECT OF YOUR JEALOUSY EVERY NAME YOU COULD	LAY	YOUR TONGUE TO, AND ABUSED ME TO YOUR HEART'S CONTENT
LION PREFACE(7)	AND REGULAR; AND PILATE, TO WHOM THE APPEAL	LAY	, FAVORED HIM AND DESPISED HIS JUDGES, AND WAS EVIDENTLY

LAYER

MTH4 II (181)	GREATEST LIVING MAN. CUT OFF THAT INFINITESIMAL	LAYER	OF GREY MATTER WHICH DISTINGUISHES MY BRAIN FROM THAT
BARB PREFACE(238)	IS GOING ON ALL OVER THE WORLD UNDERNEATH THE TOP	LAYER	OF PROSPEROUS PLUTOCRACY. ONE MAN IS SUFFICIENTLY

LAYERS

JOAN 1 (58)	MY THREE BARBARY HENS AND THE BLACK ARE THE BEST	LAYERS	IN CHAMPAGNE. AND YOU COME AND TELL ME THAT THERE ARE
JOAN 1 (62)	IN GOD'S NAME, SIR. THINK OF THOSE HENS, THE BEST	LAYERS	IN CHAMPAGNE; AND -- /ROBERT/ THINK OF MY BOOT; AND

LAYIN

BARB II (279)	KNOW? NOT AS MUCH AS HOW TO BEEYAVE YOURSELF--	LAYIN	YOUR DIRTY FIST ACROSS THE MOUTH OF A RESPECTABLE

LAYING

SUPR I SD(9)	A CALL AS OTHER MEN DO OF GETTING MARRIED OR	LAYING	A FOUNDATION STONE. A SENSITIVE, SUSCEPTIBLE,
CLEO PRO2 (104)	PUTS HIS KNIFE TO HER THROAT). /BEL AFFRIS/ (	LAYING	A HAND ON FTATATEETA'S LEFT SHOULDER) FORBEAR HER YET
KING I (181)	(HE MAKES FOX SIT DOWN AGAIN AND GOES TO NEWTON,	LAYING	A HAND ON HIS SHOULDER). MR NEWTON: THE WORD INFIDEL
GENV IV (100)	TUSSLE WITH A MURDERER AND A RAVISHER TO DO WITH	LAYING	A MINE IN THE HIGH SEAS TO SLAUGHTER INNOCENT
BARB III (336)	DO YOU KNOW WHAT YOU ARE SAYING; OR ARE YOU	LAYING	A SNARE FOR MY SOUL? /CUSINS/ DONT LISTEN TO HIS
MIS. (137)	ONLY PUT BACK HIS EARS OR WAG HIS TAIL INSTEAD OF	LAYING	DOWN THE LAW, HOW MUCH BETTER IT WOULD BE! WE SHOULD
FANY III (299)	GOES. /BOBBY/ YOU HAVE A DEVILISH COOL WAY OF	LAYING	DOWN THE LAW. YOU KNOW, IN MY CLASS YOU HAVE TO WRAP
PRES (135)	NEVER STAND IT. /MITCHENER/ (WALKING ABOUT AND	LAYING	DOWN THE LAW) THERES NO SUCH THING AS PUBLIC OPINION.
HART I (64)	LEAVING THE STICK ON THE TABLE). /MRS HUSHABYE/ (	LAYING	ELLIE DOWN AT THE END OF THE SOFA) NOW, PETTIKINS, HE
PHIL II (128)	PERSON. AND SHE OUGHT TO HAVE AN OPPORTUNITY OF	LAYING	HER CASE BEFORE HIM. AS A MEMBER OF THE COMMITTEE, I
LION PREFACE(33)	MARY CROWDED OUT OF THE INN INTO THE STABLE AND	LAYING	HER NEWLY-BORN SON IN THE MANGER, AND OF THE
2TRU III (85)	DID A DAY LONGER SHE'S A LIAR. /THE SERGEANT/ (	LAYING	HIS HAND ON THE BIBLE) YOU COULD READ THAT BOOK FROM
DEST (189)	YOU CANT MISS IT. BESIDES (IMPLORINGLY,	LAYING	HIS HAND ON HIS SLEEVE) I AM ONLY A POOR INNKEEPER:

MIS. PREFACE(62) WHOSE FATHER OUGHT TO HAVE BEEN PROSECUTED FOR LAYING HIS SON'S CHILDHOOD WASTE WITH LESSONS, WERE
ROCK PREFACE(178) OF THE TEMPORAL WITH THE SPIRITUAL AS AFORESAID, LAYING ITSELF OPEN TO MUCH DAMAGING PROTESTANT AND
JOAN 1 (70) SIR -- /ROBERT/ WHAT NOW? /STEWARD/ THE HENS ARE LAYING LIKE MAD, SIR. FIVE DOZEN EGGS! /ROBERT/ (STIFFENS
NEVR II SD(225) SEAWARD EDGE BY A PARAPET. THE HEAD WAITER, BUSY LAYING NAPKINS ON A LUNCHEON TABLE WITH HIS BACK TO THE SEA,
CLEO IV (175) A GORGEOUS MAJOR-DOMO IS SUPERINTENDING THE LAYING OF THE TABLE BY A STAFF OF SLAVES. THE COLONNADE GOES
MIS. PREFACE(57) INSTEAD COULD HE HAVE FORESEEN THE CURSE HE WAS LAYING ON HIS RACE, FOR MEN AND WOMEN LEARNT THEREBY TO
JOAN PREFACE(36) SUCCESSION CANNOT BE SECURED OR CONFINED BY THE LAYING ON OF HANDS: THE TONGUES OF FIRE HAVE DESCENDED ON
POSN (442) BE A FREE AND RESPECTABLE MAN THIS DAY INSTEAD OF LAYING THERE WITH A ROPE ROUND YOUR NECK. /BLANCO/ (TURNING
DOCT III (154) WOMEN, BECAUSE THEY ADORE HIM SO, AND ARE ALWAYS LAYING TRAPS FOR HIM. AND OF COURSE WHEN HE SAYS HE DOESNT
UNPL PREFACE(R12) I PROVED THE MOST IMPOSSIBLE OF COLLABORATORS. LAYING VIOLENT HANDS ON HIS THOROUGHLY PLANNED SCHEME FOR A

LAYMAN

DOCT PREFACE(10) THE CORNER IS QUITE UP TO HIS MARK. THUS EVEN THE LAYMAN HAS TO BE TAUGHT THAT INFALLIBILITY IS NOT QUITE
DOCT PREFACE(20) THEY. DOCTORING IS AN ART, NOT A SCIENCE: ANY LAYMAN WHO IS INTERESTED IN SCIENCE SUFFICIENTLY TO TAKE IN
BULL PREFACE(38) THE FACT THAT VOLTAIRE WAS A ROMAN CATHOLIC LAYMAN , EDUCATED AT A JESUIT COLLEGE, IS THE CONCLUSIVE
DOCT PREFACE(74) THE ENTIRE FREEDOM OF CRITICISM WHICH I, AS A LAYMAN , ENJOY; BUT IT WILL BE EVIDENT TO ALL EXPERTS THAT
LION PREFACE(96) CHURCHMAN OF ANY AUTHORITY LIVING, OR AN EDUCATED LAYMAN , WHO COULD WITHOUT RIDICULE DECLARE THAT MOSES WROTE
PPP (204) DO YOU MEAN TO SAY THAT AN UNQUALIFIED PERSON! A LAYMAN ! HAS DARED TO ADMINISTER POISON IN MY DISTRICT?

LAYMEN

DOCT PREFACE(7) FOR LAWS TO PUNISH ANY SCEPTICISM ON THE PART OF LAYMEN . A MODERN DOCTOR THINKS NOTHING OF SIGNING THE DEATH
DOCT PREFACE(9) AND HE GETS LITTLE SYMPATHY, EVEN FROM LAYMEN WHO KNOW, BECAUSE HE HAS BROUGHT THE INCREDULITY ON
DOCT PREFACE(61) AN AGITATION HAD BEEN CONDUCTED FOR MANY YEARS BY LAYMEN , INCLUDING QUACKS AND FADDISTS OF ALL KINDS, THAT

LAYS

CAPT II SD(253) JUSTICE ON A THIEF AND A MURDERER. LADY CICELY LAYS DOWN HER WORK AND LOOKS UP ANXIOUSLY. /SIR HOWARD/ (
MIS. PREFACE(48) HIM ALL THE MORE TO BE VERY CAREFUL WHAT LAW HE LAYS DOWN. BUT UNLESS BOTH THE CLERGYMAN AND THE DOCTOR ARE
CAND I (80) WANT ME TO ADDRESS THEM ON SUNDAY MORNING (HE LAYS GREAT EMPHASIS ON SUNDAY, THIS BEING THE UNREASONABLE
PYGM V (288) IN HIS DIRECTION AND I'LL WRING YOUR NECK. (HE LAYS HANDS ON HER). DO YOU HEAR? /LIZA/ (DEFIANTLY
LION II (147) THIS SORCERER TO BE A SLAVE TO THE FIRST MAN WHO LAYS HANDS ON HIM. (THE MENAGERIE KEEPERS AND THE
MRS I (183) (FOLLOWING HER) OH, PRAY, PRAY! ALLOW ME. (HE LAYS HANDS ON THE CHAIR). /VIVIE/ (LETTING HIM TAKE IT)
CAND III (145) AND SPOILING THEM, AM I NOT, DARLING? (SHE LAYS HER CHEEK FONDLY AGAINST HIS). /MORELL/ (QUITE
BARB III SD(327) AND BURIES HIS FACE IN HIS HANDS. BARBARA GRAVELY LAYS HER HAND ON HIS SHOULDER. HE LOOKS UP AT HER IN
LION I (122) OUT. METELLUS IS ABOUT TO FOLLOW WHEN FERROVIUS LAYS HIS HAND ON HIS SHOULDER). /FERROVIUS/ YOU ARE HIS
PHIL I (85) OF IT. (HE TAKES THE SONG OFF THE PIANO DESK AND LAYS IT ASIDE; THEN CLOSES THE LID OVER THE KEYBOARD).
LION PREFACE(38) IS BY NO MEANS SILENT BEFORE CAIAPHAS AND PILATE; LAYS MUCH GREATER STRESS ON HIS RESURRECTION AND ON THE
LION PREFACE(24) HIM EQUALLY FAR BEYOND JOHN THE BAPTIST. HE LAYS NO STRESS ON BAPTISM OR VOWS, AND PREACHES CONDUCT
2TRU PREFACE(19) BRINGING ON THEM THE DOOM OF THE GOOSE THAT LAYS THE GOLDEN EGGS. NAKED COERCION IS SO EXPENSIVE THAT IT
ROCK PREFACE(164) ON ANY PRETEXT WHATEVER: NAMELY, THE GOOSE THAT LAYS THE GOLDEN EGGS. IN RUSSIA THE SOVIET GOVERNMENT BEGAN
NEVR II (235) (HE GOES BACK MODESTLY TO THE LUNCHEON TABLE AND LAYS THE TWO ADDITIONAL COVERS, ONE AT THE END NEXT THE
OVER PREFACE(156) EXPENSIVE SIEGES WHICH THE PROFESSED LIBERTINE LAYS TO VIRTUE. STILL, WHEREVER THERE IS IDLENESS OR EVEN A

LAZARUS

BARB III (321) FOOLISH GABBLE SHOP, CAN GOVERN UNDERSHAFT AND LAZARUS ? NO, MY FRIEND: YOU WILL DO WHAT PAYS US. YOU WILL
LION PREFACE(48) WILL SCOFF AT IT AS A PLANNED IMPOSTURE IN WHICH LAZARUS ACTED AS A CONFEDERATE, BETWEEN THE REJECTION OF THE
BARB I (253) IS NOT ONLY THE CANNONS, BUT THE WAR LOANS THAT LAZARUS ARRANGES UNDER COVER OF GIVING CREDIT FOR THE
BARB III (316) I AM GETTING ON IN YEARS; AND MY PARTNER LAZARUS HAS AT LAST MADE A STAND AND INSISTED THAT THE
BARB III (335) WELL! WHAT WILL LAZARUS SAY? /UNDERSHAFT/ LAZARUS IS A GENTLE ROMANTIC JEW WHO CARES FOR NOTHING BUT
LION PREFACE(44) AS THE REASONS FOR BELIEVING IN THE RAISING OF LAZARUS , BOTH HAVE BEEN BELIEVED AND DOUBTED BY MEN OF
BARB III (321) I AM THE GOVERNMENT OF YOUR COUNTRY: I, AND LAZARUS . DO YOU SUPPOSE THAT YOU AND HALF A DOZEN AMATEURS
BARB III (324) WITH THEM. I NEVER BULLY THEM. I DONT EVEN BULLY LAZARUS . I SAY THAT CERTAIN THINGS ARE TO BE DONE; BUT I
BARB III (334) WORTH A JUNIOR CLERK'S WAGES! -- WELL! WHAT WILL LAZARUS SAY? /UNDERSHAFT/ LAZARUS IS A GENTLE ROMANTIC JEW
O'FL (215) THAT MOSES BUILT THE SEVEN CHURCHES, AND THAT LAZARUS WAS BURIED IN GLASNEVIN. /SIR PEARCE/ BOSH! HOW
LION PREFACE(48) AN ORDINARY RESCUE OF PETER; AND THE RAISING OF LAZARUS WILL BE ONLY A SIMILAR GLORIFICATION OF A
LION PREFACE(54) OF GOD TO ALL ETERNITY; WHEREFORE I THINK THAT LAZARUS WILL YET SEE YOU BESIDE DIVES IN HELL." MODERN
BARB I (253) UNDER MY NAME, " SON AND HEIR TO UNDERSHAFT AND LAZARUS , DEATH AND DESTRUCTION DEALERS: ADDRESS,
BARB I (253) SCANDALOUS. THOSE TWO MEN, ANDREW UNDERSHAFT AND LAZARUS , POSITIVELY HAVE EUROPE UNDER THEIR THUMBS. THAT IS
BARB PREFACE(216) IS WHAT WE CALL THE WICKED RICH ONE: SHIRLEY IS LAZARUS , UNDERSHAFT DIVES. WELL, THE MISERY OF THE WORLD IS
SUPR III (82) ME TO MARRY AN ACCURSED BARMAID NAMED REBECCA LAZARUS , WHOM I LOATHED. I TALKED OF SUICIDE: SHE OFFERED

LAZARUSES

APPL PREFACE(191) OF DIVES COSTS THE PRIVATION OF A HUNDRED LAZARUSES . THE TITLE BREAKAGES, LIMITED, WAS SUGGESTED TO

LAZE

MILL IV (188) A GOOD APPETITE. A GOOD LUNCH, AND THEN A GOOD LAZE . WHAT MORE CAN ANY MAN DESIRE ON EARTH? /PATRICIA/

LAZIEST

SUPR HANDBOK(223) IS SELDOM DISTINGUISHED FROM NEGLECT. THE LAZIEST AND COMMONEST OF THE VICES. ECONOMY IS THE ART OF
ROCK I (232) HOW LOGICAL! /THE LADY/ ALL THE IDLEST AND LAZIEST OF MY PATIENTS SLAVE FROM MORNING TO MIDNIGHT

LAZILY

MRS IV SD(239) HER. FRANK PLACES A CHAIR NEAR VIVIE, AND DROPS LAZILY AND CARELESSLY INTO IT, TALKING AT HER OVER HIS
JITT II (41) BUT THE MANUSCRIPT OF A BIGGISH BOOK. HE LEANS LAZILY BACK WITH HIS LEGS STRETCHED, AND TURNS OVER THE
GETT (341) FOR MONEY INSTEAD OF BEING SELFISHLY AND LAZILY INDIFFERENT TO IT. FOR HER SAKE YOU WOULD COME TO
SUPR III SD(79) UNTIL MORNING. THE BRIGANDS DISPERSE INTO GROUPS LAZILY . SOME GO INTO THE CAVE. OTHERS SIT DOWN OR LIE DOWN
2TRU II (62) IT ON THE PATIENT'S LEFT; AND THROWS HIMSELF DOWN LAZILY ON IT). /THE COUNTESS/ AINT WE GOING TO BATHE?
MRS II (206) WITH A SIGH OF ONLY HALF REPLETION SHE SITS DOWN LAZILY ON THE SETTLE). /CROFTS/ WHAT DO YOU GO ENCOURAGING
AUGS (276) YOU MAY DEPEND ON IT -- ALL IS LOST. /AUGUSTUS/ (LAZILY) WELL, I SHOULD NOT GO AS FAR AS THAT. (LOWERING
MRS II (218) GETTING SLEEPY AFTER ALL. (SHE STRETCHES HERSELF LAZILY , THOROUGHLY RELIEVED BY HER EXPLOSION, AND PLACIDLY

LAZINESS

JOAN PREFACE(35) SNOBBERY, THAT OF THE DOMINICANS WITH PRIESTLY LAZINESS AND LAODICEANISM, THAT OF THE JESUITS WITH PRIESTLY
DOCT PREFACE(72) SUPPLYING ITS PLACE, WHICH WAS PROMPTLY TAKEN BY LAZINESS AND NEGLECT. IF THE PRIESTS OF IRELAND COULD ONLY
BULL PREFACE(21) IS TOO LAZY INTELLECTUALLY (THE INTELLECTUAL LAZINESS AND SLOVENLINESS OF THE ENGLISH IS ALMOST BEYOND
DOCT PREFACE(36) THE SAME STUPIDITY AND CRUELTY, THE SAME LAZINESS AND WANT OF PERSEVERANCE THAT PREVENTED NERO OR THE
ROCK PREFACE(169) THE EXTERMINATION OF THE UNMUSICAL, IMPORTANCE OF LAZINESS FOR FALLOWING. SOME OF THESE DIFFERENCES COULD BE
MILL PREFACE(128) EXPERIENCE OF THE ADOPTION OF THESE EXCUSES FOR LAZINESS IN POLITICS, SHAMELESS SELFISHNESS IN INDUSTRY, AND
HART II (125) THIS IS-- /LADY UTTERWORD/ LAZINESS! YOU ARE LAZINESS INCARNATE. YOU ARE SELFISHNESS ITSELF. YOU ARE THE
MIS. PREFACE(37) THEIR EFFECT WOULD BE VASTLY IMPROVED. THE NEW LAZINESS . THE CHILD OF THE FUTURE, THEN, IF THERE IS TO BE
APPL I (223) TANTRUMS, YOUR SECRETIVENESS AND YOUR APPALLING LAZINESS -- /BALBUS/ (DELIGHTED) HEAR HEAR! YOURE GETTING
MIS. PREFACE(38) LAZINESS WILL BECOME THE BUGBEAR OF SOCIETY: THE LAZINESS THAT REFUSES TO FACE THE MENTAL TOIL AND ADVENTURE
UNPL PREFACE(R7) CONCERNED, I HAVE ENCOUNTERED NO LIMIT BUT MY OWN LAZINESS TO MY POWER OF CONJURING UP IMAGINARY PEOPLE IN
MIS. PREFACE(38) EXERCISE, WILL NOT SERVE. A NEW SORT OF LAZINESS WILL BECOME THE BUGBEAR OF SOCIETY: THE LAZINESS
BULL PREFACE(48) SENSE OF THE WORD; AND SO, WHAT WITH HUMANITY, LAZINESS , AND DOCILITY COMBINED, THEY MANAGE TO RUB ALONG
3PLA PREFACE(R25) AND IT DOES ME GOOD, CURING ME OF NERVOUSNESS, LAZINESS , AND SNOBBISHNESS. I WRITE PREFACES AS DRYDEN DID,
HART PREFACE(7) TORPORS OF PSEUDO-GOODNATURE PRODUCED BY LAZINESS , AND SPASMS OF FEROCIOUS ACTIVITY PRODUCED BY
MIS. PREFACE(41) CHILDREN SOMETIMES MAKE THEIR NURSES, OUT OF MERE LAZINESS , BECAUSE SISTERS IN THE EAST AND NURSES IN THE
MIS. (118) HE DOES TOO MUCH OF IT. IT'S REALLY A SORT OF LAZINESS , GETTING AWAY FROM YOUR OWN SERIOUS BUSINESS TO
SUPR III (127) FACULTIES, RELIGION FOR ME TO A MERE EXCUSE FOR LAZINESS , SINCE IT HAD SET UP A GOD WHO LOOKED AT THE WORLD
HART II (125) YOUR VALET. /RANDALL/ THIS IS-- /LADY UTTERWORD/ LAZINESS ! YOU ARE LAZINESS INCARNATE. YOU ARE SELFISHNESS

LAZY

KING II (230) DO IF THEY WERE KINGS. /CATHERINE/ YOU ARE NOT LAZY : I WISH YOU WERE: I SHOULD SEE MORE OF YOU. YOU TAKE A
MTH1 I (6) /EVE/ I HAVE TO THINK ABOUT YOU. YOU ARE LAZY : YOU ARE DIRTY: YOU NEGLECT YOURSELF: YOU ARE ALWAYS
ROCK PREFACE(169) VITAL SON. NOBODY HAS YET CALCULATED HOW MANY LAZY ANCESTORS IT TAKES TO PRODUCE AN INDEFATIGABLE PRODIGY;
ROCK PREFACE(161) THE CHANGE AS MEANING THAT THEY MIGHT NOW BE AS LAZY AND CARELESS AS THEY PLEASED, WHEREAS IN FACT IT WAS OF
GENV III (76) PEOPLE! THEY SEE ALL THE REASONS FOR BEING LAZY AND DOING NOTHING. /THE NEWCOMER/ AND WHAT PRICE ME?

MTH3 (124)	THAT THEY HAD BECOME THE MOST INTELLECTUALLY	LAZY	AND FAT-HEADED PEOPLE ON THE FACE OF THE EARTH. THERE
ROCK I (233)	THE THOUGHTLESS AND BRAINLESS, THE INVETERATELY	LAZY	AND FRIVOLOUS. YES: THE FRIVOLOUS: YOUR EARS DO NOT
MTH1 II (34)	AND KILL AND DIE FOR EVER. /ADAM/ IF THEY ARE	LAZY	AND HAVE A WILL TOWARDS DEATH I CANNOT HELP IT. I WILL
SUPR HANDBOK(177)	WHO COULD NOT HELP THEMSELVES. THE GOD OF THE	LAZY	AND INCAPABLE. THE NINETEENTH CENTURY DECIDED THAT
SUPR PREFACE(R27)	COMPETITIVE STRUGGLE FOR EXISTENCE AND TOO	LAZY	AND PETTY TO ORGANIZE THE COMMONWEALTH CO-OPERATIVELY.
HART III (131)	LONGER THAN A FEW MONTHS? JUST BECAUSE HE IS TOO	LAZY	AND PLEASURE-LOVING TO HUNT AND SHOOT. HE STRUMS THE
CATH 1 (162)	THAT HE DOES NOT UNDERSTAND BECAUSE HE IS TOO	LAZY	AND SELFISH TO TALK AND BE COMPANIONABLE. /PATIOMKIN/ (
HART PREFACE(10)	A MERIT OF DYING. HEARTBREAK HOUSE WAS FAR TOO	LAZY	AND SHALLOW TO EXTRICATE ITSELF FROM THIS PALACE OF
GETT PREFACE(245)	ATTITUDE IS, THE PRACTICE OF IT IS SO EASY AND	LAZY	AND UPPISH THAT IT IS VERY COMMON. BUT ITS CRY IS
GETT (288)	WORK; AND THE BOUNDERS AND WEEK-ENDERS ARE TOO	LAZY	AND VULGAR. THEYD SIMPLY ROT WITHOUT US; BUT WHAT DO
MTH1 II (26)	UNNATURAL MONSTERS, SO THAT YOU MAY BE UTTERLY	LAZY	AND WORTHLESS, AND THAT YOUR TAMED HUMAN ANIMALS MAY
MTH2 (53)	OLD: HE HAS NEVER BEEN A REAL STATESMAN: HE IS AS	LAZY	AS A CAT ON A HEARTHRUG: YOU CANT GET HIM TO ATTEND TO
LION PREFACE(59)	BEFORE US. THE ONLY PEOPLE WHO CLING TO THE	LAZY	DELUSION THAT IT IS POSSIBLE TO FIND A JUST
PYGM EPILOG (289)	OUR IMAGINATIONS WERE NOT SO ENFEEBLED BY THEIR	LAZY	DEPENDENCE ON THE READY-MADES AND REACH-ME-DOWNS OF THE
2TRU II (63)	GO INTO THE WATER. LETS SUNBATHE. /THE COUNTESS/	LAZY	DEVIL! (SHE TAKES THE FOLDING STOOL FROM THE
SIM PREFACE(11)	TO CARRY PISTOLS AND EXECUTE SABOTEURS AND	LAZY	DRUNKARDS WITH THEIR OWN HANDS. SUCH A COMMISSAR WAS
KING II (229)	OUT. WHY AM I A POPULAR KING? BECAUSE I AM A	LAZY	FELLOW. I ENJOY MYSELF AND LET THE PEOPLE SEE ME DOING
DEST (186)	BUT IT ALWAYS MEANT MAKING ME WORK; AND I AM TOO	LAZY	FOR THAT, THANK HEAVEN! SO I TAUGHT MYSELF TO COOK AND
ROCK I (230)	UNDEREXERCISED BODY. YOU KNOW HOW MEN BECOME BONE	LAZY	FOR WANT OF BODILY EXERCISE. WELL, THEY BECOME BRAIN
ROCK I (230)	WANT OF BODILY EXERCISE. WELL, THEY BECOME BRAIN	LAZY	FOR WANT OF MENTAL EXERCISE; AND IF NATURE MEANT THEM
HART III (133)	TO SYNDICATES AND SHAREHOLDERS AND ALL SORTS OF	LAZY	GOOD-FOR-NOTHING CAPITALISTS. I GET MONEY FROM SUCH
MIS. PREFACE(60)	THE ABUSE OF DOCILITY. DOCILITY MAY SURVIVE AS A	LAZY	HABIT LONG AFTER IT HAS CEASED TO BE A BENEFICIAL
MTH1 II (33)	(GRUMBLING) HE MIGHT HAVE PUT THE HURDLE BACK,	LAZY	HOUND! (HE REPLACES THE HURDLE ACROSS THE PASSAGE).
SIM II (64)	RULE, PROLA. /PROLA/ ALL YOUR BURDENS ON ME.	LAZY	IDLE CHILDREN. /KANCHIN/ HURRAH! ALL BURDENS ON PROLA.
ROCK II (240)	PAY HONESTLY FREE OF INCOME TAX AND MAKE THESE	LAZY	IDLE LUBBERS OF LANDLORDS SWEAT FOR IT. I CALL THAT THE
BULL PREFACE(21)	MAKES A DISTINCTION WHICH THE ENGLISHMAN IS TOO	LAZY	INTELLECTUALLY (THE INTELLECTUAL LAZINESS AND
BULL PREFACE(39)	THE ENGLISHMAN, MORE DOCILE, LESS DANGEROUS, TOO	LAZY	INTELLECTUALLY TO USE SUCH POLITICAL AND LEGAL POWER AS
KING I (163)	/NEWTON/ WHY, NEITHER COULD I: I WAS TOO	LAZY	. BUT THEY ARE QUITE UNNECESSARY: ADDITION AND
GENV PREFACE(6)	AND HANGED HIS ACCOMPLICES, ENGLAND SECURE AND	LAZY	. THE DRAWBACK TO ENGLAND'S CAPACITY FOR DOING
GETT PREFACE(247)	SO MUCH? " THE SAME REPLY MIGHT BE MADE BY A	LAZY	MAGISTRATE WHEN ASKED FOR A WARRANT TO ARREST A
BULL PREFACE(48)	LIFE OF THE SOLDIER IS UNNATURAL, EXCEPT TO A	LAZY	MAN, AND HIS SERVITUDE GALLING AND SENSELESS, EXCEPT TO
BARB PREFACE(215)	AS IF IT WERE EITHER A WHOLESOME TONIC FOR	LAZY	PEOPLE OR ELSE A VIRTUE TO BE EMBRACED AS ST FRANCIS
SIM II (68)	LAZY, LAZY! SOMEDAY HEAVEN WILL GET TIRED OF	LAZY	PEOPLE; AND THE PITCAIRN ISLANDERS WILL SEE THEIR DAY
MIS. PREFACE(64)	AND SCHOOLMASTERS ARE GOOD-NATURED OR WEAK OR	LAZY	; AND CHILDREN ARE DOCILE AND AFFECTIONATE AND VERY
SIM II SD(59)	IDDY COMES FROM THE HOUSE IN A CONDITION OF	LAZY	SELF-COMPLACENCE. HE IS RECEIVED IN DEAD SILENCE.
MTH1 II (23)	AND THE SABLE AND THE BLUE FOX TO HANG ON HER	LAZY	SHOULDERS AND MAKE HER LOOK MORE LIKE AN ANIMAL THAN A
NEVR II (226)	ONCE BY THE WAITER'S VOICE, LOOKS AT HIM WITH A	LAZY	SMILE. IT IS A QUIET VOICE, WITH A GENTLE MELODY IN IT
PRES (165)	O BED YET! GO AND PULL HER OUT BE THE HEELS, THE	LAZY	STHREEL; AN TELL HER HER MOTHER WANTS TO SPEAK TO HER
2TRU II (72)	/THE PATIENT/ YOU! ! YOU! ! ! YOU SELFISH	LAZY	SUGARY TONGUED BLACKGUARD. (RELEASING HIM) NO: I
BUOY 1 (9)	AND GAVE ME A CANE TO BEAT THE BOYS THEY WERE TOO	LAZY	TO BEAT THEMSELVES, THAT WAS WHAT THEY CALLED TEACHING
SUPR HANDBOK(203)	BY BARBED WIRE; THE MODERN GENTLEMAN WHO IS TOO	LAZY	TO DAUB HIS FACE WITH VERMILION AS A SYMBOL OF BRAVERY
MIS. PREFACE(43)	LIBERTIES THAT WE ALLOW TODAY BECAUSE WE ARE TOO	LAZY	TO FIND OUT THE PROPER WAY TO INTERFERE. BUT THE
KING I (219)	IN TROUBLE WITH MY ENGLISH. AND CHARLES IS TOO	LAZY	TO LEARN FRENCH PROPERLY, THOUGH HE LIVED IN FRANCE SO
SIM II (64)	YOU AS I HAVE ALWAYS DONE BECAUSE YOU ARE TOO	LAZY	TO RULE YOURSELVES. /HYERING/ YOU CAN RULE US, PROLA.
BULL I (83)	CAN HUMBUG ME, DO YOU? /DOYLE/ NO: HE'S TOO	LAZY	TO TAKE THE TROUBLE. ALL HE HAS TO DO IS TO SIT THERE
ROCK II (278)	OF TELLING PEOPLE TO GO TO HELL WHEN HE IS TOO	LAZY	TO THINK OF ANYTHING BETTER TO SAY. MISS BROLLIKINS IS
DOCT PREFACE(43)	WERE CUTTING UP PIECES OF PAPER. SUCH CLUMSY AND	LAZY	WAYS OF TEACHING ARE BASED ON THE CHEAPNESS OF FROGS
CATH 1,SD(161)	OF THE MOST INTOLERABLE AND DANGEROUS TYPE, UGLY,	LAZY	, AND DISGUSTING IN HIS PERSONAL HABITS. YET
LION PREFACE(57)	HIM IS TO DO NOTHING: THAT IS, TO BE AS IDLE,	LAZY	, AND HEARTLESS IN DEALING WITH HIM AS HE IS IN DEALING
BARB PREFACE(225)	REDEMPTION OF THE WHOLE NATION FROM ITS VICIOUS,	LAZY	, COMPETITIVE ANARCHY: THIS DISCOVERY HAS BEEN MADE BY
JOAN PREFACE(35)	DO, DENOUNCE ANY PRIEST OR BODY OF PRIESTS, AS	LAZY	, DRUNKEN, IDLE, DISSOLUTE, AND UNWORTHY OF THEIR GREAT
BULL III (130)	TELL YOU, MATT, I ALWAYS THOUGHT IT WAS A STUPID,	LAZY	, GOOD-FOR-NOTHING SORT OF THING TO LEAVE THE LAND IN
ROCK I (232)	ARTHUR/ I GIVE YOU UP. YOU ARE FACTPROOF. I AM	LAZY	, I AM IDLE; AND I AM BREAKING DOWN FROM OVERWORK. HOW
SIM II (68)	/PROLA/ AN EXCUSE FOR LEAVING EVERYTHING TO ME.	LAZY	, LAZY, LAZY! SOMEDAY HEAVEN WILL GET TIRED OF LAZY
SIM II (68)	AN EXCUSE FOR LEAVING EVERYTHING TO ME. LAZY,	LAZY	, LAZY! SOMEDAY HEAVEN WILL GET TIRED OF LAZY PEOPLE;
SIM II (68)	EXCUSE FOR LEAVING EVERYTHING TO ME. LAZY, LAZY,	LAZY	! SOMEDAY HEAVEN WILL GET TIRED OF LAZY PEOPLE; AND
		LE	
SUPR PREFACE(R9)	FORCE YOU SET IN MOTION. YOU MEANT ME TO EPATER	LE	BOURGEOIS; AND IF HE PROTESTS, I HEREBY REFER HIM TO YOU
ROCK PREFACE(178)	THOSE OF US WHO ARE DESTINED BY IT TO EPATER	LE	BOURGEOIS, HE CANNOT HAVE BELIEVED THAT THE MERE
CATH 1 (171)	(HE BOWS). /VARINKA/ (CURTSEYING) MONSIEUR	LE	CAPITAINE! /EDSTASTON/ I MUST APOLOGIZE FOR THE
SUPR III (79)	THAT CAR, D'YE HEAR? /MENDOZA/ NO FEAR, MONSIEUR	LE	CHAUFFEUR. THE FIRST ONE WE CAPTURED CURED US OF THAT.
SUPR III (98)	AN ETERNITY OF MISUSE IN THE FRENCH MANNER) VIVAN	LE	FEMMINE! VIVA IL BUON VINO! /THE STATUE/ (TAKING UP
3PLA PREFACE(R34)	A BETTER TRAGEDY THAN LEAR, A BETTER COMEDY THAN	LE	FESTIN DE PIERRE OR PEER GYNT, A BETTER OPERA THAN DON
KING I (217)	YOU PUT ON YOUR ROYALTY. MY KING, LOUIS QUATORZE,	LE	GRAND MONARQUE, LE ROI SOLEIL, NEVER PUTS OFF HIS ROYALTY
FABL PREFACE(83)	OF THEM HAS EVER MADE VOLTAIRE'S MONSIEUR TOUT	LE	MONDE MASTER OF THE SITUATION. ADULT SUFFRAGE DID NOT
DEST SD(150)	NAPOLEON IS NOT L'EMPEREUR YET: HIS MEN CALL HIM	LE	PETIT CAPORAL, AS HE IS STILL IN THE STAGE OF GAINING
KING I (187)	IS. /LOUISE/ AU PLAISIR DE VOUS REVOIR, MONSIEUR	LE	PHILOSOPHE. THE DUCHESS GOES OUT, SALLY MAKING HER A
KING PREFACE(156)	THE MONEY IN THE SERVICE OF ENGLAND, GAVE	LE	ROI SOLEIL NO VALUE FOR IT. THE OTHER MISTRESSES COULD
KING I (217)	MY KING, LOUIS QUATORZE, LE GRAND MONARQUE,	LE	ROI SOLEIL, NEVER PUTS OFF HIS ROYALTY FOR A MOMENT EVEN
		LEA	
BARB II (288)	WOULD HE? /BILL/ (ALMOST CRYING) AW, WILL YOU	LEA	ME ALOWN? EV AW EVER OFFERED TO MEDDLE WITH YOU, THAT
BARB II (287)	HIM) AW'M EPPY ENAFF, AW TELL YOU. WOY CAWNT YOU	LEA	ME ALOWN? WOT EV I DAN TO YOU? AW AINT SMASHED YOUR
BARB II (286)	(SAVAGELY) DOWNT YOU TALK TO ME, D'YE EAH? YOU	LEA	ME ALOWN, OR AW'LL DO YOU A MISCHIEF. AW'M NOT DIRT
DEST (164)	BENDING GALLANTLY TO KISS IT) OH, MADAM, NOT THE	LEA	-- (CHECKING HIMSELF AND LOOKING AT IT) YOU HAVE YOUR
		LEAD	
JOAN 3 (93)	FOR THE FORTS. YOU DARED ME TO FOLLOW. DARE YOU	LEAD	? /JOAN/ (BURSTING INTO TEARS AND FLINGING HER ARMS
JITT II (29)	HIM CREDIT FOR. WHAT SORT OF LIFE DID HE REALLY	LEAD	? THAT IS THE QUESTION. /FESSLER/ ISNT IT SHOCKING
ROCK PREFACE(177)	SO FAR FROM BELIEVING IN IT THAT SHE WANTED TO	LEAD	A CRUSADE OF EXTERMINATION AGAINST THE HUSITES, THOUGH
JOAN PREFACE(20)	IS THAT SHE WAS THE SORT OF WOMAN THAT WANTS TO	LEAD	A MAN'S LIFE. THEY ARE TO BE FOUND WHEREVER THERE ARE
APPL II (276)	HOUSE WITH US TO KEEP OLD ENGLAND IN FRONT AND	LEAD	A NEW PARTY AGAINST BREAKAGES (TEARS COME INTO HER
MTH2 (55)	KIND OF YOU, LUBIN. LET ME REMARK THAT YOU CANNOT	LEAD	A PROGRESSIVE PARTY WITHOUT GETTING A MOVE ON. /LUBIN/
GLIM (178)	YOU BE IF WE LEFT IT UNDONE? OUTSIDE THE LIFE I	LEAD	ALL TO MYSELF-- THE LIFE OF THOUGHT AND POETRY-- I KNOW
SUPR IV SD(142)	WHICH, WITH THE ABSENCE OF GAMES, MIGHT	LEAD	AN INTELLIGENT SPECTATOR TO THE MOST FAR REACHING
DEST (170)	ALWAYS THINK OF OTHERS, AND WORK FOR OTHERS, AND	LEAD	AND GOVERN THEM FOR THEIR OWN GOOD. SELF-SACRIFICE IS
MIS. (138)	AGAIN; AND I REALIZE THAT IT'S NEVER GOING TO	LEAD	ANYWHERE AND NEVER GOING TO STOP. THATS WHEN I WANT TO
BUOY III (29)	I AM TO PUT BEFORE YOU? /DARKIE/ (TAKING THE	LEAD	AT ONCE DECISIVELY) NOTHING WHATEVER. BUSINESS MEANS
HART I SD(44)	LIKE A DECK. THE GARDEN TO WHICH THE GLASS DOORS	LEAD	DIPS TO THE SOUTH BEFORE THE LANDSCAPE RISES AGAIN TO
SIM I SD(36)	BY A TERRACE AND A FLIGHT OF STEPS. THE STEPS	LEAD	DOWN TO A CRESCENT FORMED BY TWO CURVED STONE SEATS
GENV IV (105)	BEFORE BED-TIME. HE SHOULD HAVE WAITED FOR A	LEAD	FROM ME BEFORE MEDDLING WITH IT, AND FORCING ME TO
LION PREFACE(35)	THE FEMININE INTEREST ALL THROUGH. THE SLIGHT	LEAD	GIVEN BY MARK IS TAKEN UP AND DEVELOPED. MORE IS SAID
JOAN 6,SD(132)	THEM IS THE EXECUTIONER AND HIS ASSISTANTS. THEY	LEAD	HER TO THE PRISONER'S STOOL, AND PLACE THEMSELVES
KING I (178)	FIT. CHARLES AND NEWTON HELP HIM TO HIS FEET AND	LEAD	HIM BACK TO HIS CHAIR.) /FOX/ (TO CHARLES) ANOTHER
LADY (250)	EVEN TO THE VERY DOOR OF OUR ROYAL CHAMBER.	LEAD	HIM FORTH; AND BRING ME WORD WHEN HE IS SAFELY LOCKED
SUPR IV (156)	YOU HIMSELF? /ANN/ (ALARMED) NO, NO: YOU MUSTNT	LEAD	HIM TO BELIEVE THAT I SAID THAT. I DONT FOR A MOMENT
APPL II (270)	OF SHEEP. /PROTEUS/ WELL, GIVE THE FLOCK A BETTER	LEAD	IF YOU CAN. HAVE YOU ANYTHING ELSE TO PROPOSE?
POSN (459)	TO MYSELF. THEN I NOTICED THAT THE CHILD WAS LIKE	LEAD	IN MY ARMS. GOD WOULD NEVER HAVE BEEN SO CRUEL AS TO
JOAN 4,SD(97)	DEFERENCE TO THE BISHOP, HE ASSUMES THE	LEAD	IN OPENING THE PROCEEDINGS AS A MATTER OF COURSE. HE IS
METH PREFACE(R73)	TO BE CALLED EITHER, AND UNABLE TO GIVE A CLEAR	LEAD	IN THE NEW DIRECTION, AND THERE WAS A DEEPER
KING I (180)	BELIEVE SUCH OLD WIVES' TALES AS THE CHANGING OF	LEAD	INTO GOLD BY THE PHILOSOPHER'S STONE? /NEWTON/ PASTOR
JOAN 2 (85)	ANY SECRETS? CAN YOU DO ANY CURES? CAN YOU TURN	LEAD	INTO GOLD, OR ANYTHING OF THAT SORT? /JOAN/ I CAN TURN
APPL I (210)	MECHANIC, OR WAS UNTIL MY COUNTRY CALLED ON ME TO	LEAD	IT. /MAGNUS/ (TO ALICE) WELL, MY DEAR, YOU HAVE BROKEN
MTH2 (64)	SOCIALISM. YOU MAY DEPEND ON ME TO GUIDE IT, TO	LEAD	IT, TO GIVE SUITABLE EXPRESSION TO ITS ASPIRATIONS, AND
GENV PREFACE(10)	ORGANISMS, LEAVING BEHIND IT NOT RADIUM BUT	LEAD	. IF THIS DISINTEGRATION COULD BE SPEEDED UP TO
ROCK II (271)	YOUVE GOT TO ELECT YOURSELF BY GIVING US A	LEAD	. OLD HIPNEY WILL FOLLOW ANYONE THAT WILL GIVE HIM A

WIDO I (10)	HAVE MOVED AN EYELID IF YOU HADNT GIVEN ME A	LEAD	. /BLANCHE/ I ONLY ASKED YOU THE NAME OF A CASTLE.
BULL III (123)	TO SAY. I HAD TWO TUMBLERS OF PUNCH. SHE HAD TO	LEAD	ME HOME. YOU MUST HAVE NOTICED IT. /LARRY/ I DID NOT.
ARMS I (16)	VERY SORRY. (LOOKING AT HER) WAS IT FAIR TO	LEAD	ME ON? (HE LOOKS AT THE PORTRAIT AGAIN) YES: THATS
CLEO I (112)	YOU STAND ON YOUR THRONE TO RECEIVE CAESAR. NOW	LEAD	ME THITHER. /CLEOPATRA/ (ONLY TOO GLAD TO GET AWAY) I
HART II (98)	A-- /ELLIE/ A SIREN. SO YOU ARE. YOU WERE BORN TO	LEAD	MEN BY THE NOSE: IF YOU WERENT, MARCUS WOULD HAVE
JOAN EPILOG (155)	/CHARLES/ OH, NOT SO BAD. DO YOU KNOW, I ACTUALLY	LEAD	MY ARMY OUT AND WIN BATTLES? DOWN INTO THE MOAT UP TO
METH PREFACE(R10)	THAT MERE MORALITY AND LEGALITY AND URBANITY	LEAD	NOWHERE, AS IF BUNYAN HAD NEVER WRITTEN BADMAN.
FOUN (209)	PALE: I SCORN TO TAKE YOU BY SURPRISE. I SHALL	LEAD	OFF WITH MY LEFT ON YOUR RIGHT EYE. PUT THEM UP.
MTH4 I (145)	YOU ARE. I SHALL REALLY HAVE TO PUT A COLLAR AND	LEAD	ON YOU IF YOU PERSIST IN GIVING ME THE SLIP LIKE THIS.
2TRU I (49)	PATIENT/ HERE I AM, POPS. ONE KISS; AND THEN--	LEAD	ON. /THE BURGLAR/ GOOD. YOUR COMPLEXION STILL LEAVES
BUOY II (24)	SUCH SIMPLE MATTERS AS MILK AND VEGETABLES, COULD	LEAD	ONLY TO BEWILDERMENT AND STRIFE. I WISH YOU GOOD
BUOY 1 (15)	UNTIL IT CAN BE USED TO BOIL AN EGG OR SHARPEN A	LEAD	PENCIL AS EASILY AS TO DESTROY A CITY. ALREADY THEY
MRS II (214)	A DAY FOR NINE SHILLINGS A WEEK UNTIL SHE DIED OF	LEAD	POISONING. SHE ONLY EXPECTED TO GET HER HANDS A LITTLE
PPP (204)	BUT HE IS PERFECTLY STIFF, AND AS HEAVY AS	LEAD	); ROUSE HIM. SHAKE HIM. /THE POLICEMAN/ (EXHAUSTED)
MTH1 II (22)	THEM INTO TWO GREAT HOSTS, ONE OF THEM I WILL	LEAD	; AND THE OTHER WILL BE LED BY THE MAN I FEAR MOST AND
ROCK II (271)	WILL FOLLOW ANYONE THAT WILL GIVE HIM A GOOD	LEAD	; AND TO BLAZES WITH YOUR ELECTIONS AND YOUR
JOAN 3 (91)	MY HEART IS FULL OF COURAGE, NOT OF ANGER. I WILL	LEAD	; AND YOUR MEN WILL FOLLOW: THAT IS ALL I CAN DO. BUT I
FABL IV (115)	MEAT EATERS, WHO FOUND IT EASY AND PLEASANT TO	LEAD	SEDENTARY LIVES IN STUFFY ROOMS WHILST THE VEGETARIANS
6CAL (102)	WERE GOD HIMSELF. YOU SAID ONCE THAT YOU WOULD	LEAD	TEN KINGS CAPTIVE TO MY FEET. MUCH AS I HAVE BEGGED
PRES (155)	EVER; MOUNT MY CHARGER; AND WITH MY GOOD SABRE	LEAD	THE ANTI-SUFFRAGETS TO VICTORY. (SHE STRIDES TO THE
APPL PREFACE(189)	CAN POSSIBLY FEEL ANY SUCH CONFIDENCE. THEY	LEAD	THE APPLAUSE FOR HIM; THEY PROMPT HIM WHEN QUESTIONS
JOAN PREFACE(20)	AT ORLEANS, INSISTED THAT SHE MUST GO HERSELF AND	LEAD	THE ASSAULT IN PERSON? WHY DID SHE GIVE EXHIBITIONS OF
SIM II (63)	TO BREAK THE UNITY OF THE EMPIRE. IRELAND WILL	LEAD	THE ATTACK ON TREASON AND DISRUPTION. /KANCHIN/ THE
ROCK PREFACE(178)	RIGHT TO SET MEN ON A PATH WHICH WAS LIKELY TO	LEAD	THE BEST OF THEM TO THE CROSS AND THE WORST OF THEM TO
HART II (85)	WICKER CHAIR; AND RESIGNS HIMSELF TO ALLOW HER TO	LEAD	THE CONVERSATION). YOU WERE SAYING-- ? /ELLIE/ WAS I?
DEVL EPILOG (80)	DOCTRINE. AS FOR ME, THE DRAMATIST, I SMILE, AND	LEAD	THE CONVERSATION BACK TO BURGOYNE. BURGOYNE'S SURRENDER
APPL I (212)	LOOK THEM IN THE FACE, OR ELSE TAKE MY JOB AND	LEAD	THE PARTY YOURSELF. /NICOBAR/ THE WORST OF YOU IS THAT
ROCK I (227)	MEN WHO ARE AHEAD OF THEIR TIME. THEY ALONE CAN	LEAD	THE PRESENT INTO THE FUTURE. THEY ARE GHOSTS FROM THE
ROCK II (283)	DEAREST LOVE, DONT YOU-- /SIR ARTHUR/ WHY DONT I	LEAD	THE REVOLT AGAINST IT ALL? BECAUSE I'M NOT THE MAN FOR
MRS PREFACE(156)	AS IS WITHIN THEIR REACH ARE LIKELY ENOUGH TO	LEAD	THEM EVENTUALLY TO LUNG DISEASE, PREMATURE DEATH, AND
JOAN 3 (90)	/JOAN/ OUR MEN WILL TAKE THEM. I WILL	LEAD	THEM. /DUNOIS/ NOT A MAN WILL FOLLOW YOU. /JOAN/ I WILL
MTH5 (249)	ARE YOU DRIVING AT, OLD ONE? WHAT DOES ALL THIS	LEAD	TO? /THE HE-ANCIENT/ IT LEADS, YOUNG MAN, TO THE TRUTH
GETT PREFACE(229)	THE POLITICAL EMANCIPATION OF WOMEN IS LIKELY TO	LEAD	TO A COMPARATIVELY STRINGENT ENFORCEMENT BY LAW OF
SIM II (77)	THROUGHOUT THE COUNTRY WHICH IS BOUND TO	LEAD	TO ACTION OF SOME SORT." /PRA/ WHICH MEANS, IF IT MEANS
SUPR III (122)	STERILIZATION AND EXTINCTION OF MANKIND	LEAD	TO ANYTHING BETTER THAN MAKING THE MOST OF THOSE
CAND I (88)	TONES) WOY HELSE SHOULD I DO IT? WHAT DOES IT	LEAD	TO BUT DRINK AND HUPPISHNESS IN WORKIN MEN? (HE SEATS
ROCK PREFACE(163)	" A WRONG ONE." IN RUSSIA SUCH A CONVICTION WOULD	LEAD	TO HIS DISAPPEARANCE AND THE RECEIPT BY HIS FAMILY OF A
BARB PREFACE(217)	BOTH IT AND ALL THE ACTIONS AND SENTIMENTS WHICH	LEAD	TO IT AND SUPPORT IT AS AN INSTITUTION. WHAT ELSE CAN
DOCT PREFACE(50)	MORE WAITING TO BE DISCOVERED. INDEED, ALL PATHS	LEAD	TO KNOWLEDGE; BECAUSE EVEN THE VILEST AND STUPIDEST
DOCT PREFACE(74)	IS BETTER THAN NEGLECT. ATTENTION AND ACTIVITY	LEAD	TO MISTAKES AS WELL AS TO SUCCESSES; BUT A LIFE SPENT
BARB PREFACE(234)	INSTITUTIONS ON A BASIS OF MORAL INEQUALITY CAN	LEAD	TO NOTHING BUT UNNATURAL REIGNS OF THE SAINTS RELIEVED
LION PREFACE(13)	AN EXPIATION OF THE MURDER MIGHT QUITE POSSIBLY	LEAD	TO OUR PUTTING SOME INNOCENT PERSON -- THE MORE
LION PREFACE(78)	BURN, THUS ADMITTING THAT THOUGH MARRIAGE MAY	LEAD	TO PLACING THE DESIRE TO PLEASE WIFE OR HUSBAND BEFORE
MIS. PREFACE(29)	IN MURDER AND RAPINE AT WORST, AND, AT BEST,	LEAD	TO QUARRELS AND UNDESIRABLE STATES OF CONSCIOUSNESS.
BARB PREFACE(225)	THE DAUGHTER OF ANDREW UNDERSHAFT, WILL CLEARLY	LEAD	TO SOMETHING HOPEFULLER THAN DISTRIBUTING BREAD AND
BUOY 1 (9)	STARVING SAVAGES. BUT SECOND SIGHT DOES NOT YET	LEAD	TO SUCCESS IN BUSINESS NOR IN THE PROFESSIONS. /FATHER/
OVER (193)	ME TO BE BEAUTIFUL AND SACRED FEELINGS, AND WHICH	LEAD	TO SUCH INTERESTING AND EXCITING ADVENTURES, END IN
LION PREFACE(28)	HIS KINGDOM ON EARTH. HE FEARS THAT THIS MAY	LEAD	TO THE APPEARANCE OF IMPOSTORS CLAIMING TO BE HIMSELF,
MIS. PREFACE(29)	THEOLOGICAL DISCUSSION DOES AS A MATTER OF FACT	LEAD	TO THE DRAWING OF KNIVES AND PISTOLS, AND SEX
FABL VI (125)	NO. WHY IS BEYOND KNOWLEDGE. ALL THE WHYS	LEAD	TO THE GREAT INTERROGATION MARK THAT SHINES FOR EVER
MIS. PREFACE(9)	A CHILD SHOULD GO. ALL THE WAYS DISCOVERED SO FAR	LEAD	TO THE HORRORS OF OUR EXISTING CIVILIZATIONS, DESCRIBED
2TRU PREFACE(6)	AS SOBER, HONEST, AND INDUSTRIOUS, WHICH WOULD	LEAD	TO THE QUAINT CONCLUSION THAT IF HE DRANK A BOTTLE OF
MRS PREFACE(156)	SINCE BOTH, VICE AT WORST AND VIRTUE AT BEST,	LEAD	TO THE SAME END IN POVERTY AND OVERWORK. IT IS TRUE
SIM II (76)	UNIVERSE TO CONFOUND ENGLAND'S ENEMIES COULD ONLY	LEAD	TO WIDESPREAD ATHEISM. THE FIRST LORD OF THE ADMIRALTY,
MRS PREFACE(171)	FORCE US TO TOLERATE IT LEST ITS SUPPRESSION	LEAD	TO WORSE THINGS, NO CONSENSUS OF OPINION AMONG
SUPR II (65)	TO KNOW WHAT MYSTIFICATIONS OF THIS KIND	LEAD	TO. /HECTOR/ (WITH STRONG SYMPTOMS OF MORAL
OVER PREFACE(162)	AND EXECUTIONS AND THE DETECTIVE OPERATIONS THAT	LEAD	UP TO THEM ARE NO ESSENTIAL PART OF LIFE, THOUGH, LIKE
LION PREFACE(50)	AND THE FINAL USE HE MAKES OF HIS TRIUMPH IS TO	LEAD	US ALL TO SUICIDE WITH HEROIC GESTURES AND RESOUNDING
MIS. PREFACE(102)	AND IS A GREAT AND TRUE SAYING; YET LET IT NOT	LEAD	US INTO THE ERROR OF SUPPOSING THAT ALL MEN LONG FOR
LION PREFACE(89)	JOHN BARLEYCORN. THE MORE OUR REASON AND STUDY	LEAD	US TO BELIEVE THAT JESUS WAS TALKING THE MOST
SIM II (85)	BRINK OF DESTRUCTION; BUT OUR PLANS WILL STILL	LEAD	US TO THE UNEXPECTED ISLES. WE SHALL MAKE WARS BECAUSE
SIM PREFACE(14)	PAY THEIR WAY. WE NEED NO BOLSHEVIK PROPAGANDA TO	LEAD	US TO THIS OBVIOUS CONCLUSION; BUT IT MAKES THE SPECIAL
JOAN 2 (84)	LOUIS: GIRD ON THE SWORD OF YOUR ANCESTORS, AND	LEAD	US TO VICTORY" YOU MAY SPARE YOUR BREATH TO COOL YOUR
FOUN (211)	EH? EVEN IF YOU ARE VIRTUOUS, I SHOULD PROBABLY	LEAD	YOU ASTRAY. NO: WHAT I WANT IS A WIFE, NOT A YOUNG
METH PREFACE(R45)	EXTREMELY PUZZLING AS SUBJECTS OF THOUGHT, AND	LEAD	YOU INTO METAPHYSICS THE MOMENT YOU TRY TO ACCOUNT FOR
GENV IV (94)	BUT I MUST WARN YOU THAT IF YOUR TRIUMPHS EVER	LEAD	YOU TO ANY STEPS CONTRARY TO THE INTERESTS OF THE
BASH II,2, (117)	SORE OERMATCHED COUSIN. /A POLICEMAN/ GIVE US A	LEAD	, SIR, SAVE THE ENGLISH FLAG. AFRICA TRAMPLES ON IT.
POSN (445)	HERE I AM WAITING TO BE HUNG UP AND FILLED WITH	LEAD	! WHAT CAME TO ME? WHAT MADE ME SUCH A FOOL? THATS

LEADEN

2TRU PREFACE(5)	ITS GOLDEN EXCEPTIONS OF IDLE RICHERY AND ITS	LEADEN	RULE OF ANXIOUS POVERTY, IS AS DESPERATE A FAILURE
BARB II SD(273)	GLANCE AT THE BACKGROUND OF GRIMY WAREHOUSES AND	LEADEN	SKY VISIBLE OVER THE WHITEWASHED WALLS OF THE YARD

LEADER

CLEO IV (189)	VENGEANCE AND IN STABBING. YOU HAVE SLAIN THEIR	LEADER	: IT IS RIGHT THAT THEY SHALL SLAY YOU. IF YOU DOUBT
SUPR PREFACE(R32)	WITH ANY PORTRAIT OF A PROPHET OR A WORTHY	LEADER	: THEY HAVE NO CONSTRUCTIVE IDEAS: THEY REGARD THOSE
GENV IV (119)	AND NOW MAY WE HAVE YOUR OPINION, SIGNOR	LEADER	? /BBDE/ IN PRINCIPLE I AGREE. IT IS EASY FOR ME TO
GENV IV (108)	WHAT AUTHORITY HAS BARDO? WHAT AUTHORITY HAS ANY	LEADER	? WE COMMAND AND ARE OBEYED: THAT IS ALL. /BBDE/
MTH2 (86)	GONE, PAST, BURNT OUT, BURST UP; THINKS HE IS OUR	LEADER	AND IS ONLY OUR RAG AND BOTTLE DEPARTMENT. BUT YOU
SUPR II (55)	I EVER SEE MY PAPER? NOT MUCH. HE GRABS THE	LEADER	AND LEAVES ME TO STODGE MYSELF WITH HIS TIMES.
CAND I (81)	BY POST, AND GLANCES THROUGH MR STEWART HEADLAM'S	LEADER	AND THE GUILD OF ST MATTHEW NEWS. THESE PROCEEDINGS
GENV IV (120)	AS TO WHICH OF YOU IS THE DIVINELY CHOSEN	LEADER	AND THE SUPERIOR RACE? /BBDE/ MY ANSWER IS EIGHT
GENV IV (128)	ALL LEADERSHIP. I SAY THAT THE PEOPLE WILL WANT A	LEADER	AS THEY HAVE NEVER WANTED ONE BEFORE. I HAVE TAUGHT
BARB PREFACE(227)	THROUGH A TRANSFIGURED WORLD, CALLING THEIR	LEADER	GENERAL, THEMSELVES CAPTAINS AND BRIGADIERS, AND
BULL PREFACE(31)	FORCE IN IRELAND, LET HIM ASK HIMSELF WHICH	LEADER	HE, IF HE WERE AN IRISHMAN, WOULD RATHER HAVE BACK
BULL PREFACE(69)	WHICH THEY BURNT. THE PEOPLE FOUND A CIVIL	LEADER	IN ARTHUR GRIFFITHS AND A MILITARY ONE IN MICHAEL
GENV IV (114)	STATED. /BBDE/ BUT HE HAS NOT YET BEEN ELECTED	LEADER	. HE IS A MERE SOLDIER. /COMMISSAR/ HALF EUROPE
CAPT III (297)	UNDERVALUE ME: I AM A GOOD MAN WHEN I HAVE A GOOD	LEADER	. I HAVE COURAGE: I HAVE DETERMINATION: I'M NOT A
MTH2 (57)	BUT I AM IN THE TRUEST SENSE MYSELF A LABOR	LEADER	. I-- (HE STOPS, AS LUBIN HAS RISEN WITH A
ROCK I (221)	KNOW WHAT HUMBUG IS YET. WAIT TIL YOURE A LABOR	LEADER	. (HE WINKS AT HIS HOST AND MAKES FOR THE DOOR).
GENV IV (114)	JESUS. /JUDGE/ ALLOW THE LADY THE LAST WORD, MR	LEADER	. PROCEED, MR SECRETARY. /SECRETARY/ NO: I HAVE SAID
BULL III (136)	PARTY AND OF THE IMMORTAL NAME OF OUR GRAND OLD	LEADER	. /DORAN/ (ENTHUSIASTICALLY) DHATS THE STYLE,
ROCK II (283)	RUN AWAY WHEN THEY HAVE NO DISCIPLINE AND NO	LEADER	. /HILDA/ WELL, BUT CANT THE POLICE LET THEM RUN AWAY
MTH2 (55)	PARTY. THE PARTY OF WHICH I HAVE THE HONOR TO BE	LEADER	. /LUBIN/ HAVE YOU NOW? THATS VERY INTERESTING; FOR
BUOY 1 (11)	THE POINT IS WORTH FIGHTING FOR AND IT CAN FIND A	LEADER	. THE DEFEATED DICTATOR ALWAYS FIGHTS UNLESS HIS
GENV IV (93)	PRIEST; BUT THE PEOPLE ALWAYS FOLLOW THEIR BORN	LEADER	. WHEN THERE IS NO LEADER, NO KING, NO PRIEST, NOR
SIM II (84)	/PROLA/ I DO NOT FEEL LIKE THAT. I FEEL LIKE THE	LEADER	OF A CAVALRY CHARGE WHOSE HORSE HAS BEEN SHOT THROUGH
DOCT I SD(81)	INVOLVED BY INTIMATE INTERCOURSE WITH A	LEADER	OF HIS PROFESSION, AND AMOUNTING TO AN INFORMAL
GENV IV (109)	NOISE. I AM THE LEADER OF MY PEOPLE. I MAY BECOME	LEADER	OF MANY PEOPLES. WHO IS THIS MASTER OF WHOM YOU
JOAN PREFACE(13)	SAINTS; BUT SHE WAS NONE THE LESS AN ABLE	LEADER	OF MEN FOR IMAGINING HER IDEAS IN THIS WAY. THE
BUOY 1 (9)	I WAS ASSURED THAT YOU HAD THE MAKINGS OF A BORN	LEADER	OF MEN IN YOU. /SON/ YES. THEY MADE ME A PREFECT AND
GENV IV (109)	/BATTLER/ I AM NOT AN EXTERNAL NOISE. I AM THE	LEADER	OF MY PEOPLE. I MAY BECOME LEADER OF MANY PEOPLES.
SUPR III (89)	/DON JUAN/ IN HELL, SENORA, THE DEVIL IS THE	LEADER	OF THE BEST SOCIETY. /THE OLD WOMAN/ I TELL YOU,
METH PREFACE(R34)	HE REALLY EXISTED AND DISAPPROVED OF ATHEISM. THE	LEADER	OF THE CAVILLERS, WITH GREAT HEAT, REPUDIATED THIS AS
ROCK II (235)	WAS ENTITLED TO THE PRIME MINISTERSHIP. I WAS THE	LEADER	OF THE CONSERVATIVE PARTY. I HAD AN ENORMOUS MAJORITY
METH PREFACE(R35)	I THOUGHT SO LONG AS I SAID NOTHING. ONLY THE	LEADER	OF THE EVANGELICAL PARTY, I THOUGHT, WAS A LITTLE
MTH2 (63)	WORK AS A LAWYER, AND LATER ON BY MY DUTIES AS	LEADER	OF THE HOUSE OF COMMONS IN THE DAYS WHEN PRIME

PRES (164)	OF THE SERJEANT-AT-ARMS RATHER THAN OF THE	LEADER	OF THE HOUSE. THERES NO USE IN MY TACKLING MRS
ROCK I (200)	TO REMEMBER OCCASIONALLY THAT I HAPPEN TO BE THE	LEADER	OF THE HOUSE OF COMMONS. /HILDA/ OH, WHAT IS THE USE
PRES (138)	ALL ORDERS ARE UNPOPULAR. /BALSQUITH/ WHEN THE	LEADER	OF THE LABOR PARTY APPEALED TO ME AND TO THE HOUSE
MTH2 (55)	THATS VERY INTERESTING; FOR I THOUGHT I WAS THE	LEADER	OF THE LIBERAL PARTY. HOWEVER, IT IS VERY KIND OF YOU
BULL PREFACE(46)	SHOT, BUT, AT WORST, REPRIMANDED, WHILST THE	LEADER	OF THE MUTINY, INSTEAD OF GETTING THE VICTORIA CROSS
MTH2 (80)	HUMAN LIFE TO THREE HUNDRED YEARS! DUNREEN, AS	LEADER	OF THE OPPOSITE PARTY, WILL BE BOUND TO OPPOSE ME: TO
GETT PREFACE(201)	IS WITH HIS CLERK, OR A PRIME MINISTER WITH THE	LEADER	OF THE OPPOSITION, IS A MAN IN TEN THOUSAND. THE
MTH4 I (171)	THEY ARE WRITTEN AND PROMULGATED. THE	LEADER	OF THE OPPOSITION CAN OBTAIN COPIES. ALL THE NATIONS
MTH2 (81)	A NEW AGE. /LUBIN/ (IMPRESSED) FANCY MY BEING	LEADER	OF THE PARTY FOR THE NEXT THREE HUNDRED YEARS!
MTH4 III (201)	ELDERLY GENTLEMAN/ MY DEAR AMBROSE, YOU ARE THE	LEADER	OF THE PARTY, NOT I. WHAT ARE YOU GOING TO DO? /THE
ROCK II (271)	MINUTE HIS BACK WAS TURNED! IF YOU WANT TO BE A	LEADER	OF THE PEOPLE, SRARTHUR, YOUVE GOT TO ELECT YOURSELF
MTH4 III (198)	HINT. I'LL PUT THE CASE IN THREE WORDS. I AM THE	LEADER	OF THE POTTERBILL PARTY. MY PARTY IS IN POWER. I AM
DOCT III (153)	FOR HIM; AND HIS CASE HAS BEEN TAKEN IN HAND BY A	LEADER	OF THE PROFESSION, SURELY-- /MRS DUBEDAT/ OH, IT IS
BULL PREFACE(27)	AWAY FROM PARISH TUTELAGE AND FOLLOW A PROTESTANT	LEADER	ON NATIONAL QUESTIONS. HIS CHURCH NATURALLY FOSTERS
BULL PREFACE(7)	PRIESTS HAD NO POWER TO IMPOSE A ROMAN CATHOLIC	LEADER	ON THE HOME RULE MOVEMENT INSTEAD OF PARNELL? SIMPLY
SUPR II (55)	WE TAKE IN TWO PAPERS: THE TIMES FOR HIM, THE	LEADER	OR THE ECHO FOR ME. AND DO YOU THINK I EVER SEE MY
FABL I (103)	ARTICLE SAY? /YOUNG MAN/ (TURNING TO THE	LEADER	PAGE AND QUOTING) " TRUCE OF GOD BEGINS A NEW CHAPTER
GENV PREFACE(13)	WORLD WAR FORCED US TO CHOOSE A MAN OF ACTION AS	LEADER	; BUT WHEN THE ARMISTICE CAME WE GOT RID OF HIM AND
SUPR III (75)	HONOR TO BE A JEW; AND WHEN THE ZIONISTS NEED A	LEADER	TO REASSEMBLE OUR RACE ON ITS HISTORIC SOIL OF
APPL II (274)	SON KING ROBERT WILL HAVE TO CALL ON SOME PARTY	LEADER	WHO CAN DEPEND ON THE SUPPORT OF THE HOUSE OF COMMONS
HART PREFACE(26)	LOBBY AT THE PARTY WHIP'S ORDERS, PROVIDED THE	LEADER	WILL MAKE THEIR SEATS SAFE FOR THEM BY THE PROCESS
CAPT II (264)	I'LL TAKE MY PART WITH THE REST UNDER WHATEVER	LEADER	YOU ARE WILLING TO OBEY. SO CHOOSE YOUR CAPTAIN AND
GENV PREFACE(19)	THIS STOCK IN TRADE HITLER FOUND HIMSELF A BORN	LEADER	, AND, LIKE JACK CADE, WAT TYLER, ESSEX UNDER
SUPR III (82)	THE PRESENT ENTERPRISE IS THE RESULT. I BECAME	LEADER	, AS THE JEW ALWAYS BECOMES LEADER, BY HIS BRAINS AND
SUPR III (82)	I BECAME LEADER, AS THE JEW ALWAYS BECOMES	LEADER	, BY HIS BRAINS AND IMAGINATION. BUT WITH ALL MY
6CAL SD(97)	EACH CARRYING A BUNCH OF MASSIVE IRON KEYS. THEIR	LEADER	, EUSTACHE DE ST PIERRE, KNEELS AT THE KING'S FEET.
MTH2 (79)	THE GREATEST POLITICIAN, THE MOST INSPIRED PARTY	LEADER	, IN THE KINGDOM. I TAKE OFF MY HAT TO HIM. I, JOYCE
GENV IV (93)	ALWAYS FOLLOW THEIR BORN LEADER. WHEN THERE IS NO	LEADER	, NO KING, NO PRIEST, NOR ANY BODY OF LAW ESTABLISHED
CLEO IV (176)	HAIR LIKE SQUIRREL'S FUR-- THE LITTLE KING'S BEAR	LEADER	, WHOM YOU KEPT PRISONER. /CAESAR/ (ANNOYED) AND HAS
SUPR III SD(74)	BROWN GLOVES, ONLY A VERY FEW DRESS AFTER THEIR	LEADER	, WHOSE BROAD SOMBRERO WITH A COCK'S FEATHER IN THE
DEVL III (57)	DEVOTION YOU RELY! SUPPOSE THE COLONISTS FIND A	LEADER	! SUPPOSE THE NEWS FROM SPRINGTOWN SHOULD TURN OUT
DEVL III (57)	TURN OUT TO MEAN THAT THEY HAVE ALREADY FOUND A	LEADER	! WHAT SHALL WE DO THEN? EH? /SWINDON/ (SULLENLY)

LEADER-WRITERS

BULL PREFACE(14)	IN POLITICS, HYPNOTIZED BY HIS NEWSPAPER	LEADER-WRITERS	AND PARLIAMENTARY ORATORS INTO AN UTTER

LEADER'S

GENV IV (128)	OF THE CATASTROPHE IS THE MEASURE OF THE	LEADER'S	GREATNESS. /SIR O./ YOU ALWAYS HAVE A SPEECH WHICH
SUPR III SD(74)	POSSIBLY OVER FIFTY. HE IS THE CORNER MAN ON THE	LEADER'S	RIGHT, OPPOSITE THREE MEN IN SCARLET TIES ON HIS

LEADERS

BUOY 1 (13)	POLITICS, AND CAN DO NOTHING BUT MISCHIEF WITHOUT	LEADERS	? AND WHAT SORT OF LEADERS DO THEY VOTE FOR? FOR
APPL PREFACE(174)	BROADCASTS; MONEY REIGNS; AND KINGS AND LABOR	LEADERS	ALIKE HAVE TO REGISTER ITS DECREES, AND EVEN, BY A
METH PREFACE(R85)	WAS THE ONLY SAVED SOUL IN THAT PANDEMONIUM. THE	LEADERS	AMONG MY OWN CONTEMPORARIES (NOW VETERANS) SNATCHED
BARB III (321)	LEADING ARTICLES AND HISTORIC PARTIES AND GREAT	LEADERS	AND BURNING QUESTIONS AND THE REST OF YOUR TOYS. I
GENV IV (124)	THIS IS THE END. THE END OF WAR, OF LAW, OF	LEADERS	AND FOREIGN SECRETARIES, OF JUDGES AND GENERALS. A
LION PREFACE(95)	ALTHOUGH, TO THE UTTER DISGRACE OF THE NATION'S	LEADERS	AND RULERS, THE LAWS BY WHICH PERSECUTORS CAN
GENV IV SD(121)	NOTHING SHORT OF YOUR IMMEDIATE EXECUTION. THE	LEADERS	AND THE BRITISH CONTINGENT, EXCEPT THE NEWCOMER,
GENV IV SD(126)	OUT; AND HIS DEPARTURE BREAKS UP THE COURT. THE	LEADERS	AND THE GENERAL RISE AND COME FORWARD TOGETHER.
ANNA (302)	BY THE FINE SPEECHES OF THE REVOLUTIONARY	LEADERS	AND THE PAMPHLETS OF THE REVOLUTIONARY WRITERS. HOW
POSN PREFACE(394)	DRAMA IS AN UNMIXED EVIL. GREAT RELIGIOUS	LEADERS	ARE MORE INTERESTING AND MORE IMPORTANT SUBJECTS FOR
MTH4 I (164)	TO MENTION SUCH COMPARATIVELY MODERN SPIRITUAL	LEADERS	AS BLITHERINJAM, TOSH, AND SPIFFKINS, ALL TAUGHT
BUOY 1 (13)	BUT MISCHIEF WITHOUT LEADERS? AND WHAT SORT OF	LEADERS	DO THEY VOTE FOR? FOR TITUS OATES AND LORD GEORGE
POSN PREFACE(368)	PARTY, OF WHICH HIS FATHER HAD BEEN ONE OF THE	LEADERS	DURING THE GLADSTONE ERA, MR HARCOURT WAS THUS A
MTH2 (69)	AFTER ALL, WE HAVE HAD MANY VERY ABLE POLITICAL	LEADERS	EVEN WITHIN YOUR RECOLLECTION AND MINE. /FRANKLYN/
BULL PREFACE(22)	FLATTERY IN IRELAND, THE ODDS AGAINST WHICH OUR	LEADERS	HAVE TO FIGHT WOULD BE TOO HEAVY FOR THE FOURTH-RATE
GENV IV (104)	YOU WANT TO OBSTRUCT ITS WORK AND DISCREDIT ITS	LEADERS	. HALF A DOZEN SUCH OBSTRUCTIONISTS AS YOU COULD
GENV IV SD(115)	WITH HIS CONTEMPTUOUS INDIFFERENCE TO THE TWO	LEADERS	. SIR ORPHEUS, AS BEFORE, WAVES A GRACIOUS
BULL PREFACE(40)	DISHONOR, BUT THEY CANNOT MUZZLE HIS INTELLECTUAL	LEADERS	. THE ENGLISH PHILOSOPHER, THE ENGLISH AUTHOR, THE
BULL PREFACE(23)	INTO THE SHAME AND MISERY OF OUR SERVITUDE. OUR	LEADERS	MUST BE NOT ONLY DETERMINED ENOUGH, BUT CLEVER
MRS PREFACE(163)	IN APPOINTING AN ORDINARY CLERK TO SEE THAT THE	LEADERS	OF EUROPEAN LITERATURE DO NOT CORRUPT THE MORALS OF
SIM II (80)	THE FAMILY DINNER WITH THE SOUP. SEVERAL POPULAR	LEADERS	OF FASHION AND FAMOUS BEAUTIES, AFTER RINGING THEIR
LION PREFACE(48)	NARRATIVES FAILS US, AS IT PLAINLY HAS FAILED THE	LEADERS	OF MODERN THOUGHT, THERE WILL BE ANYTHING LEFT OF
BULL PREFACE(37)	THEOCRACY OF THE STATE CHURCH. THE NONCONFORMIST	LEADERS	OF OUR FREE CHURCHES ARE ALL VOLTAIREANS. THE WARCRY
DOCT I (88)	BROWNING'S PLAY? " I HAVE KNOWN FOUR AND TWENTY	LEADERS	OF REVOLT." WELL, IVE KNOWN OVER THIRTY MEN THAT
DOCT PREFACE(37)	OF THE SACREDNESS OF THAT RIGHT ARE THE	LEADERS	OF THE ATTACK. NO KNOWLEDGE IS FINALLY IMPOSSIBLE OF
MTH2 (52)	FOLLOWERS AND MAKE A SECRET AGREEMENT WITH THE	LEADERS	OF THE OPPOSITION TO KEEP YOU IN POWER ON CONDITION
MTH2 (44)	HIM OUT, AND HE IS ONLY ONE OF THE HALF-DOZEN	LEADERS	OF THE OPPOSITION, PERHAPS HE WANTS TO PICK YOU UP
LION PREFACE(85)	SCHISMS AROSE ON THESE QUESTIONS; AND THE	LEADERS	OF THE RESULTANT AGITATIONS RANCOROUSLY DEPOSED ONE
LION PREFACE(92)	BELIEF IN THAT HELL IS FAST VANISHING. ALL THE	LEADERS	OF THOUGHT HAVE LOST IT; AND EVEN FOR THE RANK AND
LION PREFACE(47)	LESS CAN I EXPLAIN WHY, IF WE ASSUME THAT THESE	LEADERS	OF THOUGHT HAD ALL REASONED OUT THEIR BELIEFS, THEIR
BUOY 1 (13)	SUBJUGATED. /FATHER/ THE PEOPLE RUN AFTER WICKED	LEADERS	ONLY WHEN THEY CANNOT FIND RIGHTEOUS ONES. THEY CAN
GENV IV SD(94)	I AM THE BRITISH FOREIGN SECRETARY. BOTH	LEADERS	RISE AND GIVE THE FASCIST SALUTE. SIR ORPHEUS
MTH2 (63)	IN THE DAYS WHEN PRIME MINISTERS WERE ALSO	LEADERS	-- /BURGE/ (STUNG) NOT TO MENTION BRIDGE AND SMART
GENV IV (119)	NOT PRETEND TO UNDERSTAND IT. GOD MAY CHOOSE HIS	LEADERS	; BUT HE MAY ALSO DROP THEM WITH A CRASH IF THEY GET
ROCK II (269)	HAVE BEEN A LAUGHING STOCK. PARLIAMENTARY	LEADERS	SAY ONE THING ON MONDAY AND JUST THE OPPOSITE ON
HART PREFACE(26)	PACIFIST OR PRO-GERMAN AT THEIR OPPONENT. PARTY	LEADERS	SEEK SUCH FOLLOWERS, WHO CAN ALWAYS BE DEPENDED ON
MILL PREFACE(118)	AND DISRAELI, VANISHED. THE LATER PARLIAMENTARY	LEADERS	SOON LEARNT FROM EXPERIENCE THAT THEY MIGHT WITH
POSN PREFACE(369)	OF REMARKABLE PROMISE. MR HARCOURT INFORMED HIS	LEADERS	THAT HE WAS GOING TO TAKE UP THE SUBJECT OF THE
ROCK II (260)	TEN OF YOUR HALF STARVED GUTTERSNIPES AND THEIR	LEADERS	THAT NEVER COULD AFFORD MORE THAN A SHILLING FOR A
BULL PREFACE(22)	AND MISTRUSTS FOOLS, AND EXPECTS ITS POLITICAL	LEADERS	TO BE CLEVER AND HUMBUG-PROOF. IT MAY BE THAT IF OUR
GENV IV (96)	MORE COMFORTABLE ONE THAN THAT OF THE TWO EMINENT	LEADERS	WHO ARE GRACING THESE PROCEEDINGS BY THEIR PRESENCE
GENV IV (105)	HAVE WAITED. I MUST ADD THAT I HAVE NO USE FOR	LEADERS	WHO DO NOT FOLLOW ME. /BATTLER/ I AM NO FOLLOWER OF
BULL PREFACE(22)	INTO GROSS INTELLECTUAL SOTTISHNESS, AND PREFER	LEADERS	WHO ENCOURAGED OUR VULGARITIES BY SHARING THEM, AND
JOAN PREFACE(44)	SO," BUT ALWAYS " GOD SAYS SO." JOAN AS THEOCRAT.	LEADERS	WHO TAKE THAT LINE HAVE NO TROUBLE WITH SOME PEOPLE,
GENV IV (91)	MADE IT AN EMPIRE. WHEN THE EMPIRES FEDERATE, ITS	LEADERS	WILL GOVERN THE WORLD; AND THESE LEADERS WILL HAVE A
GENV IV (91)	ITS LEADERS WILL GOVERN THE WORLD; AND THESE	LEADERS	WILL HAVE A SUPERLEADER WHO WILL BE THE ABLEST MAN
SUPR I (36)	ALL THE YOUNG FIR TREES BY CHOPPING OFF THEIR	LEADERS	WITH A WOODEN SWORD. YOU BROKE ALL THE CUCUMBER
MTH4 I (161)	YEARS HAS PROVIDED THE HUMAN RACE WITH CAPABLE	LEADERS	, AND MADE SHORT WORK OF SUCH CHILDISH STUFF. /THE
BULL PREFACE(32)	NOT IN THE BOSOM OF HIS COUNTRY. THE PROTESTANT	LEADERS	, FROM LORD EDWARD FITZGERALD TO PARNELL, HAVE NEVER
POSN PREFACE(383)	AND PAINFUL DUTY BY HIS SPIRITUAL AND POLITICAL	LEADERS	, OR HE WILL CONDEMN THE WORLD TO STAGNATION, WHICH
POSN PREFACE(369)	TO TAKE UP THE SUBJECT OF THE CENSORSHIP. THE	LEADERS	, RECOGNIZING HIS HEREDITARY RIGHT TO A

LEADERSHIP

BULL PREFACE(23)	REALLY CHANGING ANYTHING, HE WOULD LOSE HIS	LEADERSHIP	AS CERTAINLY AS AN ENGLISH POLITICIAN WOULD, BY
BULL PREFACE(22)	BE TOO HEAVY FOR THE FOURTH-RATE ENGLISHMEN WHOSE	LEADERSHIP	CONSISTS FOR THE MOST PART IN MARKING TIME
FABL PREFACE(97)	OF ITS " IRON LAW OF WAGES," ENGLAND'S SHAMEFACED	LEADERSHIP	. ENGLAND WAS BY NO MEANS SILENT ON THE SUBJECT.
GENV IV (93)	I HAVE RESCUED MY COUNTRY FROM ALL THAT BY MY	LEADERSHIP	. I AM A DEMOCRATIC INSTITUTION. /NEWCOMER/ GOSH.
GENV IV (128)	WILL THROW OFF ALL DECENCY AND REPUDIATE ALL	LEADERSHIP	. I SAY THAT THE PEOPLE WILL WANT A LEADER AS
BUOY 1 (9)	THEMSELVES. THAT WAS WHAT THEY CALLED TEACHING ME	LEADERSHIP	. /FATHER/ WELL, IT GAVE YOU SOME SENSE OF
GENV IV (125)	! FOR SHAME, MAN! THE WORLD LOOKS TO US FOR	LEADERSHIP	. SHALL IT FIND US IN TEARS? /BATTLER/ LET ME
GENV IV (120)	TO THE POINT OF THE SUPERIOR RACE AND THE DIVINE	LEADERSHIP	. WHAT IS TO HAPPEN IF YOU DISAGREE AS TO WHICH
GENV IV (119)	TWO ARE BEGGARS ON HORSEBACK, FOR THE CREDIT OF	LEADERSHIP	LET US RIDE CAREFULLY. LEADERSHIP, WE TWO KNOW,
DEVL II SD(29)	HAS ENDED IN STRUGGLING TO GET BACK TO UNDER THE	LEADERSHIP	OF MR PHILIP WEBB AND HIS DISCIPLES IN DOMESTIC
ROCK I (230)	AN UNDERSECRETARYSHIP. THE CABINET. FINALLY THE	LEADERSHIP	OF THE HOUSE AS PRIME MINISTER. INTELLECT,
JOAN PREFACE(19)	TERRORS AND THE BROTHERS YIELDED TO HER NATURAL	LEADERSHIP	; AND BY THAT TIME SHE HAD SENSE ENOUGH TO KNOW
GENV IV (93)	ABOLISHED DEMOCRACY, YOU HAVE. /BBDE/ PUT MY	LEADERSHIP	TO THE VOTE. TAKE A PLEBISCITE. IF I POLL LESS

GENV PREFACE(17)	THEIR PRISONERS COMPLETELY DISARMED. ONLY EMINENT	LEADERSHIP	, EXPERIENCE, AND ORGANIZING TALENT COULD DEAL
JOAN PREFACE(26)	OF THEM RECOGNIZE AND INSIST ON HER CAPACITY FOR	LEADERSHIP	, THOUGH THE SCOTS SCHOLAR IS LESS ROMANTIC ABOUT
GENV IV (119)	THE CREDIT OF LEADERSHIP LET US RIDE CAREFULLY.	LEADERSHIP	, WE TWO KNOW, IS MYSTICAL. THEN LET US NOT
		LEADING	
JOAN 3 (91)	THEY DREAM OF LOVERS, AND OF MONEY. I DREAM OF	LEADING	A CHARGE, AND OF PLACING THE BIG GUNS. YOU SOLDIERS
PYGM EPILOG (298)	AT THE ANGLE OF VIEW FROM WHICH THE LIFE SHE WAS	LEADING	AND THE SOCIETY TO WHICH SHE CLUNG APPEARED IN ITS
APPL I (228)	DISPARAGING THE THRONE, THE LAST SENTENCE OF THE	LEADING	ARTICLE ALMOST INVARIABLY BEGINS WITH THE WORDS "
FABL I (103)	WILL EGG THEM ON. /YOUNG WOMAN/ WHAT DOES THE	LEADING	ARTICLE SAY? /YOUNG MAN/ (TURNING TO THE LEADER
BARB III (340)	HAVE STOOD UP FOR CENTURIES TO YOUR SERMONS AND	LEADING	ARTICLES; THEY WILL NOT STAND UP TO MY MACHINE GUNS.
BARB III (321)	WITH YOU, MY BOY, AND PLAY WITH YOUR CAUCUSES AND	LEADING	ARTICLES AND HISTORIC PARTIES AND GREAT LEADERS AND
UNPL PREFACE(R13)	THEATRICAL NOTICES AND CRITICISMS, BUT IN	LEADING	ARTICLES AND LETTERS; AND FINALLY THE TEXT OF THE
MTH4 II (184)	IN THE NEWSPAPERS SOMETIMES, THOUGH I SUPPOSE	LEADING	ARTICLES ARE THE MATERIALS OF HISTORY, AS YOU MIGHT
APPL I (213)	THIS IS A NICE THING. TWO LABOR PAPERS HAVE	LEADING	ARTICLES THIS MORNING SUPPORTING THE KING; AND THE
METH PREFACE(R87)	THE POLICE INTELLIGENCE AND SKIP THE REVIEWS AND	LEADING	ARTICLES. I TRIED SLUM-LANDLORDISM, DOCTRINAIRE FREE
MILL PREFACE(134)	HE WILL LISTEN TO NOODLES' ORATIONS, READ POMPOUS	LEADING	ARTICLES, AND WORSHIP THE BLOODTHIRSTY TRIBAL IDOLS
BASH PREFACE(89)	THE WRITERS OF THE PLAY AND OF THE CONTEMPORARY	LEADING	ARTICLES, THOUGH THEY MAY HAVE BEEN THE SEEDIEST OF
SIM II (80)	BEEN DEPRIVED OF HIS CHAIR; AND THE TIMES, IN A	LEADING	ARTICLE, POINTS OUT THAT THE EXTREME GRAVITY OF THE
BUOY III (38)	BEEN MARRIED ONCE. HENRY THE EIGHTH WOULD BE THE	LEADING	AUTHORITY IF HE WERE ALIVE. THE PROPHET MAHOMET WAS
ROCK PREFACE(157)	IT FOR HALF A CROWN, AND PROBABLY ENJOY THE JOB.	LEADING	CASE OF JESUS CHRIST. I DISLIKE CRUELTY, EVEN
LION PREFACE(96)	BYRON'S CAIN, PUBLISHED A CENTURY AGO, IS A	LEADING	CASE ON THE POINT THAT THERE IS NO COPYRIGHT IN A
ROCK PREFACE(175)	OF THE CASE FOR TOLERATION IN GENERAL.	LEADING	CASES: SOCRATES AND JESUS. IT IS A HISTORICAL
JOAN PREFACE(23)	TRILOGY OF HENRY VI, "IN WHICH JOAN IS ONE OF THE	LEADING	CHARACTERS, THIS PORTRAIT OF JOAN IS NOT MORE
GENV PREFACE(4)	FEW CASUALTIES IN SOUTHERN ENGLAND" WHEN IN FACT	LEADING	CITIES AND SEAPORTS HAD BEEN EXTENSIVELY WRECKED.
BUOY 1 (14)	OF STRATFORD-UPON-AVON, MAYOR AND ALDERMAN AND	LEADING	CITIZEN OF HIS TOWN, MUST HAVE FELT WHEN HE DECLINED
NEVR II SD(225)	IN THE CORNER NEAREST THE SEA, A FLIGHT OF STEPS	LEADING	DOWN TO THE BEACH. WHEN HE LOOKS DOWN THE TERRACE IN
2TRU III SD(81)	ACT III. A NARROW GAP	LEADING	DOWN TO THE BEACH THROUGH MASSES OF SOFT BROWN
SUPR HANDBOK(206)	A SCARCITY OF IT, AS IN SOUTH AFRICA, THE	LEADING	ENGLISH NEWSPAPER AND THE LEADING ENGLISH WEEKLY
SUPR HANDBOK(206)	AFRICA, THE LEADING ENGLISH NEWSPAPER AND THE	LEADING	ENGLISH WEEKLY REVIEW HAVE OPENLY AND WITHOUT
AUGS (273)	MY COUNTRY'S CALL. WHETHER IT BE THE EMBASSY IN A	LEADING	EUROPEAN CAPITAL, A GOVERNOR-GENERALSHIP IN THE
BULL PREFACE(51)	THE LAW FAILED THEM IN THEIR HOUR OF NEED. SO ONE	LEADING	FAMILY OF PIGEON FARMERS, MAHFOUZ BY NAME, DESPAIRED
WIDO I SD(3)	LOOKING DOWN THE RHINE TOWARDS BONN, THE GATE	LEADING	FROM THE GARDEN TO THE RIVERSIDE IS SEEN ON THE
SUPR I (34)	TO HER AND HELD THE GUILTY SECRET OVER HER HEAD,	LEADING	HER A LIFE OF ABJECT TERROR AND HUMILIATION BY
2TRU I (36)	TO BE KEPT AS QUIET AS POSSIBLE. /THE NURSE/ (	LEADING	HER TO THE DOOR) YOU NEED A GOOD NIGHT'S SLEEP. YOU
DEVL II (42)	/ANDERSON/ THANK HEAVEN FOR THAT! COME NOW! (	LEADING	HER TO THE RAILED SEAT AND MAKING HER SIT DOWN
NEVR IV (303)	OH, YOURE JUST IN TIME. (SHE KISSES HIM). NOW (	LEADING	HIM FORWARD) BLESS THEM. /GLORIA/ NO. I WILL HAVE NO
NEVR II (235)	/PHILIP/ (ABRUPTLY SEIZING M'COMAS'S ARM AND	LEADING	HIM TOWARDS THE HOTEL) FINCH: COME AND WASH YOUR
METH PREFACE(R80)	POLITICIAN AND ADMINISTRATOR FOR LIGHT AND	LEADING	IN RELIGION. HE IS NEITHER A PHILOSOPHER NOR A
SIM PREFACE(6)	EXTENT STILL. A FRIEND OF MINE LATELY ASKED A	LEADING	IRISH STATESMAN WHY HE DID NOT RESORT TO A RATHER
ARMS II (31)	THE HORSES FOR MY REGIMENT INSTEAD OF FOOLISHLY	LEADING	IT INTO DANGER, I SHOULD HAVE BEEN A FIELD-MARSHAL
MIS. (134)	SO FORTH, AND THAT THEYRE ALL ANGELS OF LIGHT AND	LEADING	. THE TIME HAS COME TO ASSERT OURSELVES AND PUT A
3PLA PREFACE(R14)	WORST SCENERY WITHIN REACH OF THE LONDONER. THE	LEADING	LADY OR GENTLEMAN MAY BE AS TEMPTING TO THE ADMIRER
3PLA PREFACE(R14)	SPEAKING FOR MY OWN SEX, I CAN SAY THAT THE	LEADING	LADY WAS NOT TO EVERYBODY'S TASTE: HER PRETTY FACE
3PLA PREFACE(R14)	EVENING IN THE CONTEMPLATION OF A BEAUTEOUS YOUNG	LEADING	LADY WITH VOLUPTUOUS CONTOURS AND LONGLASHED EYES,
3PLA PREFACE(R36)	OF THEM LAID THEIR ARTS WASTE FOR CENTURIES BY	LEADING	LATER ARTISTS TO SEEK GREATNESS IN COPYING THEIR
PLES PREFACE(R14)	FOR THE PURPOSE OF APPROACHING ONE OF THE	LEADING	LOCAL MANAGERS WITH A PROPOSAL THAT THEY SHALL,
BARB PREFACE(239)	REFUSES TO JOIN, MAKE WAR ON IT. THIS TIME THE	LEADING	LONDON NEWSPAPER, ANTI-LIBERAL AND THEREFORE
GLIM (171)	BLESSED, EVER BLESSED BE MY HOLY PATRONESS FOR	LEADING	ME TO THIS SACRED SPOT. IS THERE ANY BUILDING NEAR
DOCT PREFACE(68)	VACANT IN ONE OF THE GREAT CITIES, AND ALL THE	LEADING	M.O.H.S COMPETE FOR IT, THEY MUST APPEAL TO THE GOOD
PYGM PREFACE(199)	WAS BOOMING THE EMPIRE, I INDUCED THE EDITOR OF A	LEADING	MONTHLY REVIEW TO COMMISSION AN ARTICLE FROM SWEET
MRS PREFACE(177)	OF PARDONABLE SINS. SHORTLY AFTER THESE EVENTS A	LEADING	NEW YORK NEWSPAPER, WHICH WAS AMONG THE MOST
CAPT III SD(290)	OF HAVING SUCCESSFULLY THRUST HIMSELF INTO A	LEADING	PART IN THE RECENT PROCEEDINGS AND MADE A DRAMATIC
LADY PREFACE(219)	BUT HE IS TOO DULL A DUFFER TO BE OF ANY USE IN A	LEADING	PART; AND WHEN WE COME TO THE GREAT VILLAINS LIKE
LION EPILOG (148)	EASILY IMPOSED ON BY SUCH IDOLS THAT ONE OF THE	LEADING	PASTORS OF THE FREE CHURCHES IN LONDON DENOUNCED MY
GENV IV (88)	INVITATIONS TO THE PRESS, AND CARDS TO ALL THE	LEADING	PEOPLE AND FOREIGN VISITORS, AND HERE! NOT A SOUL
APPL I (233)	A SINGLE MEMBER OF THE PROFESSIONS, NOT A SINGLE	LEADING	PERSONAGE IN BIG BUSINESS OR FINANCE. THEY ARE
BARB II (276)	LASS OF 18, COMES IN THROUGH THE YARD GATE,	LEADING	PETER SHIRLEY, A HALF HARDENED, HALF WORN-OUT
GENV IV (91)	SUCH A SYMPTOM CAN BE DETECTED I HAVE A PLACE: A	LEADING	PLACE. /SIR ORPHEUS/ BUT PARDON ME, SIGNOR! I
O'FL PREFACE(201)	TO RUINS, AND THE BRITISH COMMANDERS KILLED THEIR	LEADING	PRISONERS OF WAR IN COLD BLOOD MORNING AFTER MORNING
PHIL I (89)	TO GUARANTEE CUTHBERTSON AS UNMANLY; AND HE'S THE	LEADING	REPRESENTATIVE OF MANLY SENTIMENT IN LONDON.
PHIL I (91)	DRAMATIC CRITIC, DIDNT YOU HEAR ME SAY HE WAS THE	LEADING	REPRESENTATIVE OF MANLY SENTIMENT IN LONDON?
PHIL II SD(94)	WITH GLASS DOORS HALF-WAY DOWN ON BOTH SIDES,	LEADING	RESPECTIVELY TO THE DINING ROOM CORRIDOR AND THE
DEVL II SD(41)	AND QUICK MARCH! THE SERGEANT SIGNS TO THE	LEADING	SOLDIER TO MARCH. THEY FILE OUT QUICKLY. WHEN
GENV PREFACE(18)	REINFORCEMENTS AND ESTABLISHED HIM AS A	LEADING	SPIRIT. MUCH OF WHAT HE SPOUTED WAS TRUE. AS A
GETT PREFACE(242)	IS NEARER FIFTY THAN TWENTY. EVEN IN BUSINESS THE	LEADING	SPIRITS SELDOM REACH A POSITION OF SECURITY UNTIL
GENV I (38)	YOU KNOW THAT THE EARTHLY PARADISE IS ONE OF THE	LEADING	STATES IN THE WORLD IN CULTURE AND PURITY OF RACE.
CLEO II SD(118)	HE HAS THE CHILDISH AIR, THE HABIT OF BEING IN	LEADING	STRINGS, THE MIXTURE OF IMPOTENCE AND PETULANCE, THE
MILL PREFACE(131)	QUITE RIGHT IN TAKING RELUCTANCE TO GOVERN AS A	LEADING	SYMPTOM OF SUPREME FITNESS FOR IT, BUT IF WE
LION EPILOG (147)	EXACTLY AS OTHER PEOPLE DO. THE SECOND IS BY	LEADING	THE HERD TO WAR, WHICH IMMEDIATELY AND INFALLIBLY
ROCK I (198)	ARTHUR/ AND SHALL I BE ANY BETTER AT HOME HERE	LEADING	THE HOUSE? SITTING UP ALL NIGHT IN BAD AIR
ROCK I (200)	HOUSE OF COMMONS. /HILDA/ OH, WHAT IS THE USE OF	LEADING	THE HOUSE IF IT NEVER GOES ANYWHERE? IT JUST BREAKS
APPL I (219)	A VERY HEAVY RESPONSIBILITY FOR ME. IF I SEE YOU	LEADING	THE NATION OVER THE EDGE OF A PRECIPICE MAY I NOT
JITT II (29)	DID HE DIE? HE WOULDNT HAVE DIED IF HE HAD BEEN	LEADING	THE QUIET LIFE WE ALL GAVE HIM CREDIT FOR. WHAT SORT
WIDO I (9)	(SENTENTIOUSLY, TAKING OUT HIS FIELD-GLASS AND	LEADING	THE WAY TO THE GATE) THERE IS MANY A TRUE WORD
NEVR IV SD(286)	SIR. THIS WAY, SIR. HE GOES INTO THE GARDEN,	LEADING	THE WAY UNDER THE IMPRESSION THAT THE STRANGER IS
MTH4 II SD(193)	THEIR HATS AND GO INTO THE TEMPLE ON TIPTOE, ZOO	LEADING	THE WAY. THE WIFE AND DAUGHTER, FRIGHTENED AS THEY
FOUN (211)	THIS GENTLEMAN'S REQUIREMENTS: AN ENGAGEMENT AT A	LEADING	THEATRE TO PLAY MACBETH, AND A WIFE OF QUIET HABITS
JOAN PREFACE(3)	PRELATES. SHE POOHPOOHED THE PLANS OF GENERALS,	LEADING	THEIR TROOPS TO VICTORY ON PLANS OF HER OWN. SHE HAD
BARB PREFACE(221)	COMPARATIVELY INSIGNIFICANT IRISH JOURNALIST, WAS	LEADING	THEM BY THE NOSE INTO AN ADVERTISEMENT OF ME WHICH
CLEO PRG1 (89)	AND CONCEAL YOUR THOUGHTS FROM YOUR MEN,	LEADING	THEM TO BELIEVE THAT YE DEEM THEM WONDROUS STRONG
FABL PREFACE(91)	TO SING OR WHISTLE OR HUM OR PLAY AS MANY OF THE	LEADING	THEMES OF THE SYMPHONIES, CONCERTOS, STRING
SUPR PREFACE(R32)	FANATICS: IN ALL THEIR FICTIONS THERE IS NO	LEADING	THOUGHT OR INSPIRATION FOR WHICH ANY MAN COULD
DOCT I (88)	AT ALL THE GREAT DISCOVERIES! WHERE ARE THEY	LEADING	TO? WHY, RIGHT BACK TO MY POOR DEAR OLD FATHER'S
JOAN 1,SD(57)	CORNER IS A TURRET WITH A NARROW ARCHED DOORWAY	LEADING	TO A WINDING STAIR WHICH DESCENDS TO THE COURTYARD.
JITT II SD(27)	ON THE CORRIDOR; THE OTHER, ON THEIR LEFT,	LEADING	TO AN INNER ROOM. THE WINDOW FACES THE INNER DOOR
DOCT PREFACE(56)	AND STARTLING REDUCTION IN CHILD MORTALITY,	LEADING	TO FURTHER LEGISLATION INCREASING THE QUANTITY OF
FOUN SD(209)	OFFICE OF THE LORD CHANCELLOR. DOOR ON THE RIGHT	LEADING	TO HIS PRIVATE ROOM, NEAR THE FIREPLACE. DOOR ON THE
METH PREFACE(R46)	OF THE FITTEST, SEXUAL SELECTION, AND VARIATION	LEADING	TO NEW KINDS, THERE IS NOTHING TO PUZZLE YOU IN
SUPR PREFACE(R16)	AFTER BECOMING, AT MOST, TWO IMMATURE INTRIGUES	LEADING	TO SORDID AND PROLONGED COMPLICATIONS AND
LION II SD(127)	ENTERING THE ARENA. IN THE MIDDLE A WIDE PASSAGE	LEADING	TO THE ARENA DESCENDS FROM THE FLOOR LEVEL UNDER THE
DEVL I SD(4)	THE SAME SIDE AS THE FIREPLACE, NEAR THE CORNER,	LEADING	TO THE BEST BEDROOM; ONE, AT THE OPPOSITE END OF THE
PHIL III SD(132)	A LIGHT NOISELESS ONE COVERED WITH GREEN BAIZE,	LEADING	TO THE CONSULTING ROOM, IS IN THE RIGHT HAND WALL
JITT III SD(52)	A DOUBLE DOOR LEADING TO THE STUDY, ANOTHER DOOR	LEADING	TO THE CORRIDOR OF THE FLAT IS IN THE DIAGONALLY
JITT I SD(9)	ON THE RIGHT HAS IN THE MIDDLE OF IT THE DOOR	LEADING	TO THE ENTRANCE HALL; AND THE SHORT WALL ON THE LEFT
METH PREFACE(R37)	ADAPTED TO PRODUCE A SERIES OF OPERATIONS ALL	LEADING	TO THE FULFILMENT OF ONE CENTRAL PURPOSE OF
NEVR III SD(261)	ON THE GROUND FLOOR, WITH A FRENCH WINDOW	LEADING	TO THE GARDENS. IN THE CENTRE OF THE ROOM IS A
HART II (127)	BIDDING HER GOODNIGHT. (HE MAKES FOR THE DOOR	LEADING	TO THE HALL). /HECTOR/ YOU ARE UNDER A SPELL, MAN.
HART I SD(43)	THERE ARE ELECTRIC LIGHT SWITCHES BESIDE THE DOOR	LEADING	TO THE HALL AND THE GLASS DOORS IN THE STERN
HART I (46)	AND MAKE YOURSELF AT HOME. (SHE GOES TO THE DOOR	LEADING	TO THE HALL). /THE CAPTAIN/ (AS SHE PASSES HIM)
HART I (68)	(EMERGING) MY DAUGHTER (HE MAKES FOR THE DOOR	LEADING	TO THE HALL). /MANGAN/ (FOLLOWING HIM) MRS
HART I (76)	AND HE'LL CATCH COLD (SHE MAKES FOR THE DOOR	LEADING	TO THE HALL). /LADY UTTERWORD/ YOUR HUSBAND IS QUITE
ARMS II (29)	CONSCIOUS DIGNITY AGAINST THE RAIL OF THE STEPS	LEADING	TO THE HOUSE). /CATHERINE/ YOU LOOK SUPERB. THE
DOCT III SD(131)	IN THE WALL ON THE LEFT AT THE NEAR END. THE DOOR	LEADING	TO THE INNER ROOMS IS IN THE OPPOSITE WALL, AT THE
DEST SD(152)	OTHER SIDE WITH A COUCH NEAR IT; ANOTHER DOOR,	LEADING	TO THE INNER ROOMS, BETWEEN IT AND THE VINEYARD; AND
MIS. SD(109)	SIDE WALLS ARE TWO DOORS: ONE NEAR THE HAT STAND,	LEADING	TO THE INTERIOR OF THE HOUSE, THE OTHER ON THE
BULL IV SD(145)	BEHIND KEEGAN STANDS A MAHOGANY SIDEBOARD. A DOOR	LEADING	TO THE INTERIOR OF THE HOUSE IS NEAR THE FIREPLACE,
MRS II SD(198)	OF IT. IN THE LEFT-HAND SIDE WALL IS THE DOOR	LEADING	TO THE KITCHEN. FARTHER BACK AGAINST THE SAME WALL

WIDO III SD(49)	BY THE CORNER NEAREST THE RIGHT HAND WINDOW,	LEADING	TO THE LOBBY. BLANCHE HAS HER WORKBASKET AT HAND,
ROCK I SD(193)	MASKED DOOR, PAINTED WITH SHAM BOOKS AND SHELVES,	LEADING	TO THE MINISTER'S PRIVATE APARTMENTS; AND IN THE END
ROCK I SD(193)	OF THE SAME WALL, ON WALPOLE'S LEFT, IS A DOOR	LEADING	TO THE OFFICE OF SIR ARTHUR'S PRIVATE SECRETARY MISS
FOUN SD(209)	ROOM, NEAR THE FIREPLACE. DOOR ON THE LEFT	LEADING	TO THE PUBLIC STAIRCASE. MERCER, AN ELDERLY CLERK,
MRS IV SD(235)	THE INNER ROOMS. IN THE OPPOSITE WALL IS THE DOOR	LEADING	TO THE PUBLIC CORRIDOR. ITS UPPER PANEL IS OF OPAQUE
SUPR III SD(71)	FOR ALL THAT. IN THE HOLLOW, ON THE SLOPE	LEADING	TO THE QUARRY-CAVE, ARE ABOUT A DOZEN MEN WHO, AS
BULL III SD(117)	THE TABLE STRAIGHT IN FRONT OF HIM, AND A GATE	LEADING	TO THE ROAD HALF WAY DOWN THE GARDEN ON HIS RIGHT;
DEVL I SD(4)	ONE, AT THE OPPOSITE END OF THE OPPOSITE WALL,	LEADING	TO THE SCULLERY AND WASHHOUSE; AND THE HOUSE-DOOR,
INCA PROLOG (233)	EXTRAVAGANCE. (HE GOES TO A FLIGHT OF STEPS	LEADING	TO THE STALLS AND SITS DOWN DISCONSOLATELY ON THE
DEST SD(152)	CART AMONG THE VINES; THE DOOR CLOSE ON HER RIGHT	LEADING	TO THE STREET ENTRY; THE LANDLORD'S BEST SIDEBOARD,
BARB II SD(273)	CENTRAL GABLE END INTO THE YARD HAVE THE GATEWAY	LEADING	TO THE STREET ON THEIR LEFT, WITH A STONE
JITT III SD(52)	THEM ON THEIR RIGHT IS CUT OFF BY A DOUBLE DOOR	LEADING	TO THE STUDY. ANOTHER DOOR LEADING TO THE CORRIDOR
WIDO III SD(49)	ON THE LEFT, FURTHER FORWARD THAN THE FIREPLACE,	LEADING	TO THE STUDY; THE OTHER BY THE CORNER NEAREST THE
MIS. SD(109)	OTHER ON THE OPPOSITE SIDE AND AT THE OTHER END,	LEADING	TO THE VESTIBULE. THERE IS NO SOLID FURNITURE EXCEPT
KING I SD(161)	LEFT AS YOU LOOK OUT THROUGH IT IS A GLASS DOOR	LEADING	TO THESE STAIRS, MAKING THE ROOM ACCESSIBLE FROM THE
GETT SD(259)	A VAULTED CIRCULAR CHAMBER WITH A WINDING STAIR	LEADING	UP THROUGH A TOWER TO THE UPPER FLOORS OF THE
DOCT II (121)	MEET ME WITHOUT BEING AFRAID THAT MY CIVILITY WAS	LEADING	UP TO THE LOAN OF FIVE SHILLINGS, THERE WOULD BE AN
O'FL (213)	SAID SHE'D LIVE TO SEE YOU A GOOD CATHOLIC YET,	LEADING	VICTORIOUS ARMIES AGAINST THE ENGLISH AND WEARING
JOAN 5 (119)	AND MADDEN YOU WITH THE SELF-CONFIDENCE THAT IS	LEADING	YOU TO YOUR DESTRUCTION. BUT YOU WILL BE NONE THE
JITT III (58)	OUT FROM HER WHAT SORT OF LIFE BRUNO WAS REALLY	LEADING	, AND WHAT HAS BECOME OF ALL THAT WORK HE DID.
HART I SD(43)	BEING APPARENTLY IN THE SHIP'S PORT SIDE, AND YET	LEADING	, NOT TO THE OPEN SEA, BUT TO THE ENTRANCE HALL OF
		LEADING-STRINGS	
POSN PREFACE(381)	AND WHO WOULD BE QUITE LOST IF THEY WERE NOT IN	LEADING-STRINGS	DEVISED BY LAWGIVERS, PHILOSOPHERS,
		LEADS	
SUPR HANDBOK(220)	TO CELIBACY BY IT; FOR THE MATERNAL INSTINCT	LEADS	A WOMAN TO PREFER A TENTH SHARE IN A FIRST RATE MAN TO
PYGM EPILOG (303)	IT COMES TO BUSINESS, TO THE LIFE THAT SHE REALLY	LEADS	AS DISTINGUISHED FROM THE LIFE OF DREAMS AND FANCIES,
MIS. PREFACE(17)	AN EXTREMELY DANGEROUS CRAZE FOR CHILDREN WHICH	LEADS	CERTAIN PEOPLE TO ESTABLISH ORPHANAGES AND BABY FARMS
JITT II SD(33)	DOWN, HE SITS ON THE WINDOW-SEAT NEAR HER. JITTA	LEADS	EDITH TO THE CHAIR SHE HAS JUST VACATED, AND GOES TO
MIS. PREFACE(93)	BACK IS TURNED. WHAT CONFUSES THIS ISSUE AND	LEADS	EVEN HIGHLY INTELLIGENT RELIGIOUS PERSONS TO ADVOCATE
CLEO III (164)	(WITH GAY, DEFIANT RHETORIC) BY THE ROAD THAT	LEADS	EVERYWHERE-- THE DIAMOND PATH OF THE SUN AND MOON.
KING I (179)	PURSUIT OF MATHEMATICAL CALCULATION, WHICH	LEADS	FINALLY NOWHERE. BUT I HAVE MORE SERIOUS BUSINESS IN
MTH5 (259)	BE TOLD NO LIES. (HE TAKES HER BY THE EAR, AND	LEADS	HER FIRMLY TOWARDS THE TEMPLE). /THE NEWLY BORN/ AI!
AUGS (280)	/AUGUSTUS/ (SHAKING IT AFFECTIONATELY AS HE	LEADS	HER TO THE DOOR, BUT FIRST PRESSING THE BELL BUTTON
SIM PRO,1,SD(22)	CUSTOMS DOOR AND RETURNS WITH A YOUNG WOMAN. HE	LEADS	HER TO THE TABLE AND THEN GOES BACK TO HIS DESK. /THE
CLEO I (115)	COME: TAKE YOUR PLACE. (HE TAKES HER HAND AND	LEADS	HER TO THE THRONE. SHE IS TOO DOWNCAST TO SPEAK). HO,
MIS. (162)	YOU HOW TO STOP CRYING. (SHE TAKES HIS ARM AND	LEADS	HIM OFF INTO THE VESTIBULE). A YOUNG MAN, CHEAPLY
SUPR I SD(9)	OF THE IMPORTANCE OF EVERYTHING HE DOES WHICH	LEADS	HIM TO MAKE AS MUCH OF PAYING A CALL AS OTHER MEN DO
HART II SD(110)	HIM BY THE COLLAR; DRAGS HIM TO HIS FEET; AND	LEADS	HIM TO THE MIDDLE OF THE GROUP, HECTOR FALLING BACK
CATH 1 (172)	BEING A HUMORIST (HE TAKES HIM BY THE ARM, AND	LEADS	HIM TOWARDS THE DOOR). /EDSTASTON/ (RESISTING) NO,
LION PROLOG (106)	PEOPLE SAY " POOR MAN! WHAT A LIFE HIS WIFE	LEADS	HIM! " OH, IF THEY ONLY KNEW! AND YOU THINK I DONT
BUOY 1 (12)	YOU MUST LISTEN TO REASON? /SON/ YES; BUT REASON	LEADS	JUST AS CLEARLY TO A CATHOLIC MONARCHY AS TO AN
MIS. PREFACE(76)	DISSOLUTION OF SOCIETY. MY OWN OBSERVATION	LEADS	ME TO BELIEVE THAT WE ARE NOT HALF MOBILIZED ENOUGH.
GETT PREFACE(208)	MY OWN EXPERIENCE OF DISCUSSING THIS QUESTION	LEADS	ME TO BELIEVE THAT THE ONE POINT ON WHICH ALL WOMEN
NEVR I (207)	/PHILIP/ I DOUBT IT. MY KNOWLEDGE OF HUMAN NATURE	LEADS	ME TO BELIEVE THAT IF HE HAD A LOT OF MONEY HE WOULDNT
NEVR I (213)	FORTNIGHT PAST. NOW MY KNOWLEDGE OF HUMAN NATURE	LEADS	ME TO BELIEVE THAT WE HAD A FATHER, AND THAT YOU
POSN PREFACE(403)	THE MARKS OF THAT PRACTICAL INEXPERIENCE WHICH	LEADS	MEN TO BELIEVE THAT ARBITRATION EITHER COSTS NOTHING
JITT II SD(33)	THE GIRL TO HER, AND KISS HER ON THE BROW. ALFRED	LEADS	MRS HALDENSTEDT TO THE SOFA. WHEN SHE SITS DOWN, HE
FABL PREFACE(64)	COST MANY LIVES. AM I A PATHOLOGICAL CASE? THIS	LEADS	MY RESTLESSLY SPECULATIVE MIND FURTHER THAN DR CULPIN
MRS III SD(220)	TURF, WITH AN IRON CHAIR NEAR IT. A LITTLE PATH	LEADS	OFF THROUGH THE BOX HEDGE, BEHIND THE SUNDIAL. FRANK,
ARMS II SD(30)	FOR IT. IT IS AN ABOMINABLE HABIT. SERGIUS	LEADS	RAINA FORWARD WITH SPLENDID GALLANTRY. WHEN THEY
CLEO IV SD(173)	EAST TO SOFTEN THE WESTERING SUN. THE OFFICIAL	LEADS	RUFIO TO ONE OF THESE SHADED SECTIONS. A CORD FOR
LADY PREFACE(211)	ONE; AND AFTER ALL, THE WRONG ROAD ALWAYS	LEADS	SOMEWHERE. FRANK HARRIS'S PLAY WAS WRITTEN LONG BEFORE
SUPR II SD(62)	AS HE IS DEVOUTLY RELIGIOUS AT BOTTOM, HE FIRST	LEADS	THE UNWARY, BY HUMOROUS IRREVERENCE, TO LEAVE POPULAR
MRS III (224)	THE FIELDS, IF YOU DONT MIND. ROUND HERE. (HE	LEADS	THE WAY BY THE LITTLE PATH THROUGH THE BOX HEDGE).
MTH4 II (176)	THAT KIND OF THING, YOU MAY CONSULT ME NOW. (SHE	LEADS	THE WAY INTO THE MIDDLE OF THE COURTYARD). WHAT DO YOU
GETT (326)	/MRS BRIDGENORTH/ THIS WAY, MRS COLLINS. (SHE	LEADS	THE WAY OUT THROUGH THE TOWER, FOLLOWED BY MRS GEORGE,
CATH 3 (186)	I PRAISE HEAVEN FOR YOU, LITTLE MOTHER. COME. (HE	LEADS	THE WAY OUT). IT WAS THE TEMPTATION OF THE DEVIL THAT
MIS. (191)	AND ABOUT YOURSELF. COME ALONG WITH ME. (SHE	LEADS	THE WAY TO THE INNER DOOR). /GUNNER/ (FOLLOWING HER
SIM II (73)	IT IS A FLAT ROOF WHERE WE OFTEN SIT. (HE	LEADS	THE WAY TO THE HOUSE). /KANCHIN/ IN THEORY. /JANGA/ IN
PHIL III (136)	CHARTERIS WILL ENTERTAIN YOU UNTIL I RETURN. (HE	LEADS	THE WAY TO THE GREEN BAIZE DOOR). /CHARTERIS/ (
WIDO II (44)	ABOUT HERE. LET US GO BEFORE BLANCHE COMES. (HE	LEADS	THE WAY TO THE DOOR). /COKANE/ (CHEERILY, FOLLOWING
OVER (179)	/JUNO/ (OFFICIOUSLY) AH! HERE WE ARE. (HE	LEADS	THE WAY TO THE SOFA). SIT DOWN: I'M SURE YOURE TIRED.
PYGM II (229)	UNDERSTAND THE GENTLEMAN. COME WITH ME. (SHE	LEADS	THE WAY TO THE DOOR, AND HOLDS IT OPEN FOR ELIZA).
BULL II SD(105)	SALMON, AND SEVERAL PAPER PARCELS. CORNELIUS	LEADS	THE WAY UP THE HILL, WITH BROADBENT AT HIS HEELS. THE
MIS. PREFACE(18)	OF AFFECTIONATE IMPULSE IS JUST THAT FEELING THAT	LEADS	THEM TO AVOID THEIR CARE AND CONSTANT COMPANY AS A
PYGM EPILOG (293)	WHO DO NOT FRIGHTEN THEM TOO MUCH; AND THIS OFTEN	LEADS	THEM TO MAKE THE MISTAKE WE DESCRIBE METAPHORICALLY AS
O'FL PREFACE(201)	BECAUSE, PARTLY FROM A WANT OF COMMON SENSE WHICH	LEADS	THEM TO VALUE THEIR LIVES LESS THAN ENGLISHMEN DO (
DOCT PREFACE(66)	JOBS. THE INDIVIDUALISM OF PRIVATE PRACTICE	LEADS	TO AN APPALLING WASTE OF TIME ON TRIFLES. MEN WHOSE
KING PREFACE(156)	IN THIS HE WAS IN THE LINE OF EVOLUTION, WHICH	LEADS	TO AN INCREASING SEPARATION OF THE UNIQUE AND
SUPR III (134)	BEWARE OF THE PURSUIT OF THE SUPERHUMAN: IT	LEADS	TO AN INDISCRIMINATE CONTEMPT FOR THE HUMAN. TO A MAN,
WIDO I (22)	SHOULD UNFORTUNATELY HAPPEN, MR COKANE, THAT THIS	LEADS	TO NOTHING BUT A DISAPPOINTMENT FOR BLANCHE, PROBABLY
MIS. PREFACE(29)	DRAWING OF KNIVES AND PISTOLS, AND SEX DISCUSSION	LEADS	TO OBSCENITY, IT HAS NO APPLICATION TO CHILDREN EXCEPT
DOCT PREFACE(25)	DOES NOT MAKE THE FAMILY ANY MORE RESIGNED, AND	LEADS	TO PUBLIC RECRIMINATIONS IN WHICH THE DOCTORS,
JOAN PREFACE(36)	FREE, MUST BY ITS OWN LAW TAKE THE PATH THAT	LEADS	TO THE CHURCH'S BOSOM, NOT ONLY HAS NO FUTURE IN
CATH 2,SD(174)	CURTAINED BED, BEYOND IT A DOOR IN THE PANELLING	LEADS	TO THE EMPRESS'S CABINET. NEAR THE FOOT OF THE BED, IN
SUPR PREFACE(R25)	ASCETICISM OF SATIETY (" THE ROAD OF EXCESS	LEADS	TO THE PALACE OF WISDOM" SAID WILLIAM BLAKE; FOR " YOU
SUPR HANDBOK(186)	OF THE COMMERCIAL CASTE OVER THE MILITARY CASTE	LEADS	TO THE SUBSTITUTION OF SOCIAL BOYCOTTING AND PECUNIARY
GENV IV (96)	TO THINK. IT IS DANGEROUS. IT IS UNENGLISH. IT	LEADS	TO THEORIES, TO SPECULATIVE POLICIES, TO DREAMS AND
MIS. (118)	ADVERTISEMENT, IT MAKES USEFUL ACQUAINTANCES AND	LEADS	TO VALUABLE BUSINESS CONNECTIONS. BUT IT TAKES HIS
DOCT PREFACE(33)	US SAY THAT IF THESE ARE THE CONCLUSIONS LOGIC	LEADS	TO, SO MUCH THE WORSE FOR LOGIC, AFTER WHICH CURT
POSN PREFACE(419)	OR SUFFERANCE. WANTED: A NEW MAGNA CHARTA. THIS	LEADS	US TO A VERY VITAL QUESTION. IS IT NOT POSSIBLE TO
GETT PREFACE(200)	AND IT IS A PERFECTLY SOUND INSTINCT THAT	LEADS	US TO MISTRUST THE GOOD MAN AS MUCH AS THE BAD MAN,
SUPR PREFACE(R23)	UNIVERSAL DOMINION OF THE TYRANNY OF SEX. WHICH	LEADS	US TO THE CONCLUSION, ASTONISHING TO THE VULGAR, THAT
GETT PREFACE(211)	OF HUSBANDS OR WIVES OF HIGH QUALITY THAT	LEADS	WOMEN TO POLYGYNY AND MEN TO POLYANDRY, AND THAT IF
SUPR I (30)	TO STRENGTHEN YOUR CHARACTER IN, OCCASIONALLY	LEADS	YOU TO THINK ABOUT YOUR OWN CONFOUNDED PRINCIPLES WHEN
MTH5 (249)	WHAT DOES ALL THIS LEAD TO? /THE HE-ANCIENT/ IT	LEADS	, YOUNG MAN, TO THE TRUTH THAT YOU CAN CREATE NOTHING
		LEAF	
SUPR III SD(71)	ROUND A HEAP OF SMOULDERING WHITE ASHES OF DEAD	LEAF	AND BRUSHWOOD, HAVE AN AIR OF BEING CONSCIOUS OF
SUPR I (36)	ALL THE OTHER PASSIONS WOULD SWEEP IT AWAY LIKE A	LEAF	BEFORE A HURRICANE. IT IS THE BIRTH OF THAT PASSION
NEVR IV (302)	FROM HER; AND HE REELS BACK INTO A CHAIR LIKE A	LEAF	BEFORE THE WIND), DOLLY DANCES IN, WALTZING WITH THE
PPP SD(205)	AND FANS THE POLICEMAN, WHO ROLLS AWAY LIKE A	LEAF	BEFORE THE WIND TO THE WALL. SHE DISPOSES SIMILARLY OF
2TRU I SD(37)	THE AUDACITY! THE NURSE SITS DOWN; TAKES OUT A	LEAF	CUT FROM AN ILLUSTRATED JOURNAL; AND PROCEEDS TO STUDY
MTH4 III (197)	THE RUBICON. SHALL WE TAKE THE PLUNGE? ALREADY A	LEAF	HAS BEEN TORN OUT OF THE BOOK OF THE SYBIL. SHALL WE
JOAN EPIL,SD(152)	IS IN THE BED UNDER HIS HAND. CHARLES TURNS A	LEAF	. A DISTANT CLOCK STRIKES THE HALF-HOUR SOFTLY. CHARLES
PYGM V (277)	SOMEHOW. /LIZA/ OH, I'M ONLY A SQUASHED CABBAGE	LEAF	-- /PICKERING/ (IMPULSIVELY) NO. /LIZA/ (CONTINUING
CATH 4 (190)	PLEASED BY A PASSAGE, AND TURNING OVER THE	LEAF	) AUSGEZEICHNET! /EDSTASTON/ AHEM! SILENCE, CATHERINE
BULL IV (168)	GARDEN AS AN EQUINOCTIAL GALE MIGHT SWEEP A DRY	LEAF	). LATER IN THE EVENING, THE GRASSHOPPER IS AGAIN
BULL I (92)	INSTINCTIVELY MAKES ITSELF LOOK EXACTLY LIKE A	LEAF	; SO THAT BOTH ITS ENEMIES AND ITS PREY MAY MISTAKE IT
BASH II,1, (110)	HAVE CONFIDENTLY FOUND THE MONEY. ERE FALL OF	LEAF	THAT MONEY SHALL BE MINE; AND THEN I SHALL POSSESS TEN
		LEAFLET	
VWOO 2 (124)	GUIDE BOOK OF THIS VILLAGE? /Z/ SORRY, THERES A	LEAFLET	IN THE CHURCH, WRITTEN BY THE VICAR. YOU ARE

		LEAFY	
BASH I (93)	GLADE IN WILTSTOKEN PARK. ENTER LYDIA. /LYDIA/ YE	LEAFY	BREASTS AND WARM PROTECTING WINGS OF MOTHER TREES THAT
		LEAGUE	
GENV II (52)	IN YOUR HANDS? /BEGONIA/ WAS I INTERESTED IN THE	LEAGUE	? LET ME SEE. YOU KNOW THAT THERE IS A SOCIETY
GENV II (56)	WAS NEVER CONTEMPLATED WHEN THE POWERS JOINED THE	LEAGUE	? /JUDGE/ I DO NOT THINK ANYTHING WAS CONTEMPLATED
GENV I (37)	BUT DO THEY NOT TAKE PART IN THE ASSEMBLY OF THE	LEAGUE	? /SHE/ SOME OF THEM HAVE BEEN, ONCE. NOBODY EVER
GENV I (38)	HUNDRED LEFT. /SHE/ BUT IS IT A MEMBER OF THE	LEAGUE	? /THE WIDOW/ OF COURSE IT IS. AND ALLOW ME TO
MILL IV (199)	EVERY TESTIMONIAL, EVERY POLITICAL CAUSE, EVERY	LEAGUE	AND BROTHERHOOD AND SISTERHOOD, EVERY CHURCH AND
PYGM V (271)	I LECTURE FOR HIS WANNAFELLER MORAL REFORM WORLD	LEAGUE	AS OFTEN AS THEY ASK ME UP TO SIX TIMES A YEAR.
GENV I (43)	SOVNARKOM AND POLITBUREAU, SOVIET DELEGATE TO THE	LEAGUE	COUNCIL. /BISHOP/ (AGHAST, STAGGERING TO HIS FEET)
GENV III (65)	THE BIG POWERS GUILTY OF FLAGRANT CONTEMPT OF THE	LEAGUE	COVENANT. /THE SECRETARY/ SO THEY ARE, OF COURSE. BUT
GENV II (56)	POWERS HAVE BEHAVED IN EVERY RESPECT AS IF THE	LEAGUE	DID NOT EXIST, EXCEPT WHEN THEY COULD USE IT FOR
GENV I (41)	DO YOU REALIZE, YOUNG WOMAN, THAT IF THE	LEAGUE	DOES NOT BRING THE MURDERER OF MY HUSBAND TO JUSTICE
GENV III (75)	IT IS NOT ALTOGETHER TRUE. THOSE WHO THINK THE	LEAGUE	FUTILE DONT KNOW WHAT GOES ON HERE. THEY DONT KNOW
GENV II (61)	WAS AN OCCASIONAL AND EXCEPTIONAL THING: NOW THE	LEAGUE	HANGS OVER EUROPE LIKE A PERPETUAL WARCLOUD. /SIR O./
GENV III (67)	COUNTRIES WITHOUT THE FAINTEST NOTION OF WHAT THE	LEAGUE	IS FOR; AND I HAVE TO SIT HERE LISTENING TO FOREIGN
GENV I (39)	TO? /SHE/ OH, DONT ASK ME. ALL I KNOW ABOUT THE	LEAGUE	IS THAT IT PAYS MY SALARY. JUST GIVE ME THE
GENV III (67)	AND AMENDMENT BOTH OF THE TREATIES AND THE	LEAGUE	ITSELF. /SIR O./ BUT HOW CAN THAT BE? SURELY THE
CAPT II (256)	OF YOU, NOR OF ANY BANDIT WITH WHOM YOU MAY BE IN	LEAGUE	. AS TO YOUR PROPERTY, IT IS READY FOR YOU AS SOON AS
BULL I (90)	ME. /BROADBENT/ HE HAS JOINED THE TARIFF REFORM	LEAGUE	. HE WOULD NEVER HAVE DONE THAT IF HIS MIND HAD NOT
GENV II (53)	TO ME. THERES A BOOK IN THE OFFICE ABOUT THE	LEAGUE	. I TRIED TO READ IT; BUT IT WAS SUCH DRY STUFF I
GENV I (33)	AT THE HAGUE, WHICH IS ALSO AN ORGAN OF THE	LEAGUE	. MY BUSINESS HERE IS TO ASK THE COMMITTEE TO APPLY
GENV II (50)	NEWS, MISS BROWN. GERMANY HAS WITHDRAWN FROM THE	LEAGUE	. /BEGONIA/ AND A GOOD RIDDANCE, IF YOU ASK ME. MY
CAND II (123)	CAN GET NOBODY BUT THE PRESIDENT OF THE AGNOSTIC	LEAGUE	. /MORELL/ (PROMPTLY) WELL, AN EXCELLENT MAN. WHAT
CAND I (80)	THEN? /PROSERPINE/ ENGLISH LAND RESTORATION	LEAGUE	. /MORELL/ WHAT NEXT? /PROSERPINE/ GUILD OF ST
2TRU II (76)	IN HAND. THE WOMAN MAY BE AN EMISSARY OF THE	LEAGUE	. SHE MAY BE WORKING AGAINST US. /THE COUNTESS/ BUT
GENV II (56)	WAS CONTEMPLATED WHEN THE POWERS JOINED THE	LEAGUE	. THEY SIGNED THE COVENANT WITHOUT READING IT, TO
PRES (152)	ORGANIZING SECRETARY OF THE ANTI-SUFFRAGET	LEAGUE	. THIS IS LADY CORINTHIA FANSHAWE, THE PRESIDENT OF
LION EPILOG (150)	EVEN WHEN A BODY CALLING ITSELF THE ANTI-GERMAN	LEAGUE	(NOT HAVING NOTICED, APPARENTLY, THAT IT HAD BEEN
GENV III (67)	THE PRIME MINISTER'S SPEECH IN THE DEBATE ON THE	LEAGUE	LAST NIGHT? /THE SECRETARY/ (ILLHUMOREDLY) YES.
BARB III (339)	HE WILL SHAKE HANDS WITH A DUCHESS AT A PRIMROSE	LEAGUE	MEETING, AND JOIN THE CONSERVATIVE PARTY. /BARBARA/
SIM II (55)	EVERYBODY'S IDEAS. HERE IS A CABLEGRAM FROM THE	LEAGUE	OF BRITISH IMPERIAL WOMANHOOD, VANCOUVER AND
GENV IV (91)	AND THE SO-CALLED LEAGUE OF NATIONS IS A	LEAGUE	OF FOOLS; THEREFORE THE WISE MUST JOIN IT TO WATCH
GENV II (52)	QUESTION? HOW DID YOU BECOME INTERESTED IN THE	LEAGUE	OF NATIONS? HOW DID YOU GET THIS POST OF YOURS,
GENV I (37)	OF THE INTELLECTUAL COOPERATION COMMITTEE OF THE	LEAGUE	OF NATIONS? /NEWCOMER/ NO, MAAM. THIS LADY WILL DO
METH PREFACE(R71)	CALLED GOOD EUROPEANS, THERE WOULD HAVE BEEN A	LEAGUE	OF NATIONS AND NO WAR. BUT BECAUSE THE SELECTION
MILL PREFACE(123)	SUBJECT AGAIN GERMANY WOULD WITHDRAW FROM THE	LEAGUE	OF NATIONS AND CUT THE POWERS DEAD. HE BULLIED AND
MILL PREFACE(122)	EVEN WHEN HE DELIBERATELY SPAT IN THE FACE OF THE	LEAGUE	OF NATIONS AT CORFU, AND DEFIANTLY ASKED THE POWERS
GENV I (33)	AS A RUINED INDIVIDUAL, CAN DO NOTHING. BUT THE	LEAGUE	OF NATIONS CAN ACT THROUGH ITS COMMITTEE FOR
GENV III (75)	FRIEND DAME BEGONIA. IT FOUND THAT THE MOMENT THE	LEAGUE	OF NATIONS DOES ANYTHING ON ITS OWN INITIATIVE AND ON
GENV I (33)	EUROPE! BEFORE CIVILIZATION! I LOOK TO THE	LEAGUE	OF NATIONS FOR REDRESS. IT ALONE CAN CALL UNRIGHTEOUS
GENV IV SD(87)	PAPER BASKET IS AVAILABLE. THE SECRETARY OF THE	LEAGUE	OF NATIONS HAS A LITTLE CENTRAL TABLE TO HIMSELF IN
2TRU II (76)	A SPY! BUT WE ARE NOT AT WAR. /TALLBOYS/ THE	LEAGUE	OF NATIONS HAS SPIES EVERYWHERE. (TO THE COUNTESS)
GENV IV (91)	A FOOL. FOOLS ARE DANGEROUS; AND THE SO-CALLED	LEAGUE	OF NATIONS IS A LEAGUE OF FOOLS; THEREFORE THE WISE
APPL II (262)	TO THE COSMOPOLITAN CREWS OF THE FLEET OF THE	LEAGUE	OF NATIONS IN THE ATLANTIC, THAT FLEET WOULD BLOCKADE
GENV I (38)	AND IS NOT THAT JUST THE STATE OF THINGS THE	LEAGUE	OF NATIONS IS HERE TO PUT A STOP TO? /SHE/ OH, DONT
GENV I (40)	ME; AND I DONT BLAME HIM. WHAT IS THE USE OF THE	LEAGUE	OF NATIONS IF IT CANNOT PUT A STOP TO SUCH HORRORS..
GENV PREFACE(6)	TOOK ON HITLER SINGLEHANDED WITHOUT A WORD TO THE	LEAGUE	OF NATIONS NOR TO ANYONE ELSE, BUT OUTFOUGHT HIM,
APPL PREFACE(190)	AFFAIRS AND SUPERNATIONAL ACTIVITIES THROUGH THE	LEAGUE	OF NATIONS OR OTHERWISE WILL HAVE TO BE PROVIDED FOR,
GENV III (77)	UPON STUPIDITY. GENEVA IS EXPECTED TO MAKE A	LEAGUE	OF NATIONS OUT OF POLITICAL BLOCKHEADS. /THE JUDGE/ I
GENV IV (112)	OF THE INTELLECTUAL COMMITTEE OF THE	LEAGUE	OF NATIONS TO REVEAL HER AS AN IRRECONCILABLE
GENV II (52)	SEE. YOU KNOW THAT THERE IS A SOCIETY CALLED THE	LEAGUE	OF NATIONS UNION, DONT YOU? /THE SECRETARY/ I DO. I
APPL I (221)	THAT IF WE WERE PEACEFULLY BLOCKADED BY THE	LEAGUE	OF NATIONS WE COULD LIVE FOR AT LEAST THREE WEEKS ON
APPL II (259)	EXPENSIVELY DEFENDED AT OUR JOINT EXPENSE BY THE	LEAGUE	OF NATIONS. /VANHATTAN/ (RISING TO GIVE HIS WORDS
GENV II SD(49)	ACT II. OFFICE OF THE SECRETARY OF THE	LEAGUE	OF NATIONS, EXCEPT FOR THE SMALL WRITING TABLE AT
GENV IV (114)	AN IMPOSSIBLE JOB I HAVE HERE AS SECRETARY TO THE	LEAGUE	OF NATIONS. TO ME IT IS AGONY TO HAVE TO LISTEN TO
GENV IV (91)	POTTY LITTLE FOREIGN STATES THAT CALLS ITSELF A	LEAGUE	OF NATIONS. /JUDGE/ YOUR COUNTRY IS A MEMBER OF THAT
2TRU II (76)	HAS BEEN SENT OUT WITHOUT THE SANCTION OF THE	LEAGUE	OF NATIONS. WE ALWAYS FORGET TO CONSULT IT WHEN THERE
GENV III (72)	/THE SECRETARY/ IF YOU WERE THE SECRETARY OF THE	LEAGUE	OF NATIONS-- /SIR O./ YOU WOULD MAKE THE CURIOUS
GENV II SD(49)	THE SPIRIT OF GENEVA AND THE CONSTITUTION OF THE	LEAGUE	OF NATIONS, AND EACH WITH A NATIONAL AXE TO GRIND. ON
GENV I (39)	EARTHLY PARADISE THE MOST ADVANCED MEMBER OF THE	LEAGUE	OF NATIONS, WERE INTRODUCED BY MY LATE HUSBAND THE
SIM II (80)	BY LADY GUSHING, PRESIDENT OF THE TITLED LADIES'	LEAGUE	OF SOCIAL SERVICE, ON THE INEQUALITY OF SACRIFICE AS
2TRU PREFACE(17)	ITS MOST SERIOUSLY MINDED CHILDREN TO FORM A	LEAGUE	OF THE GODLESS, SHOOTING ITS PIOUS TSAR, TURNING ITS
SUPR III (77)	ME TO INTRODUCE MYSELF: MENDOZA, PRESIDENT OF THE	LEAGUE	OF THE SIERRA! (POSING LOFTILY) I AM A BRIGAND! I
SUPR III (83)	FIGHT THE PRESIDENT YOU CANT FIGHT THE WHOLE	LEAGUE	OF THE SIERRA. SIT DOWN AGAIN AND BE FRIENDLY. A CAT
GENV III (85)	PERFECT IDIOT IN GENEVA. BUT I GOT A MOVE ON THE	LEAGUE	; AND THATS MORE THAN YOU EVER COULD DO, YOU OLD
MILL IV (200)	A GUINEA A YEAR TO THE INCOME TAX PAYERS' DEFENCE	LEAGUE	; BUT THAT IS ALL: ABSOLUTELY ALL. MY STANDING
PRES (144)	THE SECRETARY AND PRESIDENT OF THE ANTI-SUFFRAGET	LEAGUE	SAYS THEY HAD AN APPOINTMENT WITH THE PRIME MINISTER,
GENV I (41)	HUSBAND. SHE SAYS SHE WILL SHOOT ME UNLESS THE	LEAGUE	STOPS IT. /HE/ GRAND! FINE! /SHE/ IS THAT ALL YOU
PRES (152)	PRAY HOW MUCH LONGER IS THE ANTI-SUFFRAGET	LEAGUE	TO BE KEPT WAITING? (SHE PASSES HIM CONTEMPTUOUSLY
MIS. (154)	RECORD. I APPEALED TO THE PRESIDENT OF THE	LEAGUE	TO LET ME SAVE THE HONOR OF MY FAMILY. HE ARRANGED IT
MIS. (154)	FORTUNATELY I HAD AN INVITATION FROM THE AERIAL	LEAGUE	TO SEE THIS GENTLEMAN TRY TO BREAK THE PASSENGER
GENV I (38)	ITS VETO IT CAN PUT A STOP TO ALL ACTION BY THE	LEAGUE	UNTIL ITS AFFAIRS ARE PROPERLY ATTENDED TO. /SHE/ CAN
GENV III (67)	ITSELF. /SIR O./ BUT HOW CAN THAT BE? SURELY THE	LEAGUE	WAS CREATED TO SEE THE TREATY OF VERSAILLES CARRIED
GENV III (65)	/THE SECRETARY/ SO THEY ARE, OF COURSE. BUT THE	LEAGUE	WAS DOING AS WELL AS COULD BE EXPECTED UNTIL DAME
JOAN 4 (108)	THE POPE. SHE REBELS AGAINST GOD BY HER DAMNABLE	LEAGUE	WITH SATAN AND HIS EVIL SPIRITS AGAINST OUR ARMY. AND
2TRU III (99)	TO MURDER MY POOR LOST DARLING CHILD. YOU ARE IN	LEAGUE	WITH THE BRIGANDS. YOU ARE-- THE COLONEL TURNS AT
2TRU II (56)	THE USUAL TISSUE OF LIES. THAT HEADMAN IS IN	LEAGUE	WITH THE BRIGANDS. HE TAKES A TURN HIMSELF
CAPT III (285)	THAT YOU REPORTED CAPTAIN BRASSBOUND AS IN	LEAGUE	WITH THE SHEIKH TO DELIVER SIR HOWARD UP TO HIM.
POSN PREFACE(425)	LIBERALS TO ATTEND THE MEETINGS OF THE PRIMROSE	LEAGUE	WOULD BE RESENTED AS AN INSUFFERABLE TYRANNY. BUT A
BULL I (77)	TAX THE FOOD OF THE PEOPLE TO SUPPORT THE NAVY	LEAGUE	, AND CLAMOR FOR THE DESTRUCTION OF THE LAST REMNANTS
GENV II (53)	AND UNDERSTANDING OF THE COVENANT OF THE	LEAGUE	, AND ITS CONSTITUTION? /BEGONIA/ NO. THEY DIDNT
GENV II (54)	OF IT. BUT I FIND NOW THAT IT IS PART OF THE	LEAGUE	, AND THAT ITS MEMBERS ARE TREMENDOUS SWELLS WITH
GENV III (72)	ONE WAY OF RECONCILING ALL THE NATIONS IN A REAL	LEAGUE	, AND THAT IS TO CONVERT THEM ALL TO ENGLISH IDEAS.
ROCK PREFACE(156)	OUTCRY AGAINST IT, RAISED BY THE OLD HUMANITARIAN	LEAGUE	, AND VOICED IN PARLIAMENT BY THE IRISH NATIONALISTS.
GENV IV (91)	THAT IS WHY ALL THE EFFECTIVE POWERS ARE IN THE	LEAGUE	, AS WELL AS THE LITTLE TOY REPUBLICS WE SHALL
BULL I (79)	IN BERMONDSEY AT THE MEETING OF THE NATIONAL	LEAGUE	, I SAW AT ONCE THAT YOU WERE-- YOU WONT MIND MY
PRES (152)	IS LADY CORINTHIA FANSHAWE, THE PRESIDENT OF THE	LEAGUE	, KNOWN IN MUSICAL CIRCLES-- I AM NOT MUSICAL-- AS
GENV I (44)	HIMSELF AT THE STOVE) RUSSIA IS A MEMBER OF THE	LEAGUE	, MY LORD. THIS GENTLEMAN'S STANDING HERE IS THE SAME
GENV IV (91)	NATIONS. /JUDGE/ YOUR COUNTRY IS A MEMBER OF THAT	LEAGUE	, SIGNOR. /BBDE/ MY COUNTRY HAS TO KEEP AN EYE ON
		LEAGUE'S	
GENV I (40)	A STOP TO SUCH HORRORS? /SHE/ WELL, IT'S NOT THE	LEAGUE'S	BUSINESS, IS IT? /THE WIDOW/ NOT THE LEAGUE'S
GENV I (41)	LEAGUE'S BUSINESS, IS IT? /THE WIDOW/ NOT THE	LEAGUE'S	BUSINESS! DO YOU REALIZE, YOUNG WOMAN, THAT IF THE
		LEAGUES	
DEST (165)	YOUR AUSTRIAN EMPLOYERS CALCULATED THAT I WAS SIX	LEAGUES	AWAY. I AM ALWAYS TO BE FOUND WHERE MY ENEMIES DONT
MIS. PREFACE(96)	AND IN FACT FATHOMS DEEPER. MORAL INSTRUCTION	LEAGUES	, AND NOW THE VOICES OF OUR MORAL INSTRUCTION
HART PREFACE(12)	TO TAKE OFFICES; LABEL THEMSELVES ANTI-ENEMY	LEAGUES	; AND SIMPLY POCKET THE MONEY THAT WAS HEAPED ON
MIS. PREFACE(96)	AND NOW THE VOICES OF OUR MORAL INSTRUCTION	LEAGUES	WILL BE LIFTED, ASKING WHETHER THERE IS ANY REASON
		LEAKED	
GENV PREFACE(4)	OF THE WAR BE ESTIMATED. OF COURSE THE TRUTH	LEAKED	OUT MONTHS LATER; BUT IT PRODUCED ONLY A FRESH ORGY
POSN PREFACE(375)	BY A WONDERING CROWD, TO WHOM IT HAD SOMEHOW	LEAKED	OUT THAT SOMETHING TERRIBLE WAS HAPPENING INSIDE. IT

LEAKING

FABL PREFACE(89) AND PLUMBERS DEAL WITH FAULTY CHAIR LEGS AND LEAKING PIPES. HE MAY, LIKE JENNER, BE SO IGNORANT OF THE

LEAN

APPL I (199) A FOLD; ALONE O'ER STEEPS AND FOAMING FALLS TO LEAN : THIS IS NOT SOLITUDE! 'TIS BUT TO HOLD CONVERSE WITH
NEVR II SD(236) YET. HE GOES TO THE IRON CHAIR, SO THAT HE CAN LEAN HIS ELBOWS ON THE LITTLE TABLE TO PROP HIS HEAD AS HE
CLEO V (201) THE NOBLEST; NOT OLD AND RIPE FOR THE KNIFE; NOT LEAN IN THE ARMS AND COLD IN THE HEART; NOT HIDING A BALD
HART II (98) WHEN I WANT ALL THE STRENGTH I CAN GET TO LEAN ON: SOMETHING IRON, SOMETHING STONY, I DONT CARE HOW
DOCT IV (166) ME, DEAR. INDEED INDEED YOU WILL NOT TIRE ME. LEAN ON ME WITH ALL YOUR WEIGHT. /LOUIS/ (WITH A SUDDEN
JITT II (34) TO THE DUTY OF NURSING THEM: WHEN THEY CAN LEAN ON US TO THE VERY LAST, THEN, WHEN THE PARTING COMES,
CURE (236) I WANT TO BE SHIELDED. I WANT A STRONG ARM TO LEAN ON, A DAUNTLESS HEART TO BE GATHERED TO AND CHERISHED,
SUPR HANDBOK(208) VIEW IS VERY ACCEPTABLE TO ENGLISHMEN, WHO ALWAYS LEAN SINCERELY TO VIRTUE'S SIDE AS LONG AS IT COSTS THEM
DOCT IV (166) RELIEF) OH THATS RIGHT, DEAR: DONT SPARE ME: LEAN WITH ALL YOUR WEIGHT ON ME. NOW YOU ARE REALLY RESTING.
PRES SD(146) (HE GOES OUT WITH BALSQUITH). MRS FARRELL, A LEAN , HIGHLY RESPECTABLE IRISH CHARWOMAN OF ABOUT FIFTY,

LEANED

LION PREFACE(39) DISCIPLE WHOM JESUS LOVED," AND THAT HE ACTUALLY LEANED ON THE BOSOM OF JESUS AT THE LAST SUPPER AND ASKED IN

LEANING

DEST SD(194) I DO. THEY LOOK AT IT FOR A MOMENT, SHE LEANING A LITTLE ON HIS SHOULDER. /LADY/ DO YOU KNOW THAT
HART II (109) RIGHT? IS IT FAIR TO ME? /MAZZINI/ (RISING AND LEANING ACROSS THE TABLE PERSUASIVELY AS IF IT WERE A PULPIT
CAND II (116) INTO TEARS). /MORELL/ (WITH TENDER GAIETY, LEANING ACROSS THE TABLE TOWARDS HER, AND CONSOLING HER) OH,
HART III SD(129) SHOTOVER IS ASLEEP, WITH ELLIE BESIDE HIM, LEANING AFFECTIONATELY AGAINST HIM ON HIS RIGHT HAND. ON HIS
PHIL I (86) IT. (HE POSTS HIMSELF AT THE END OF THE SOFA, LEANING AGAINST IT AND ADMIRING CRAVEN). JUST IMAGINE YOU
DEST (172) THE COUCH, WHERE SHE TURNS WITH HER BACK TO IT, LEANING AGAINST IT AND FACING HIM WITH HER HANDS BEHIND
BULL IV SD(145) THE ONE NEAREST THE INNER DOOR; AND HIS STICK IS LEANING AGAINST IT. A THIRD CHAIR, ALSO AGAINST THE WALL, IS
DEVL III SD(72) PAINFULLY, STEALS DOWN TO THE GALLOWS, AND STANDS LEANING AGAINST ITS RIGHT POST. DURING THE CONVERSATION
DEST SD(180) ROOM TO THE SIDEBOARD, AND POSTS HERSELF THERE, LEANING AGAINST IT, WATCHING HIM. HE TAKES THE PACKET FROM
GETT (329) SHE'S ONLY SILLY-CLEVER. /HOTCHKISS/ (UNEASILY LEANING AGAINST THE TABLE AND HOLDING ON TO IT TO CONTROL
MRS I SD(181) SKY LINE. SOME FOLDED CANVAS GARDEN CHAIRS ARE LEANING AGAINST THE SIDE BENCH IN THE PORCH. A LADY'S
NEVR II (250) THE GARDEN SEAT AND STANDS WITH HER BACK TO IT, LEANING AGAINST THE END OF IT, AND LOOKING DOWN AT HIM AS IF
CLEO PRO2,SD(96) OF WHICH THEY ARE CONSCIOUS. THEIR SPEARS ARE LEANING AGAINST THE WALLS, OR LYING ON THE GROUND READY TO
HART II SD(121) TURNING IT TO FACE RANDALL, WHO REMAINS STANDING, LEANING AT HIS EASE AGAINST THE CARPENTER'S BENCH. /RANDALL/
NEVR II (251) OBEDIENCE-- /GLORIA/ (QUITTING HER CARELESS LEANING ATTITUDE AND CONFRONTING HIM PROMPTLY AND PROUDLY) I
WIDO III SD(64) TO HIM, WATCHING HIM INTENTLY. HE RISES FROM HIS LEANING ATTITUDE, AND TAKES THE PORTRAIT FROM THE EASEL, AND
PHIL III (145) THE TWO STAND SILENT HAND IN HAND. /SYLVIA/ (LEANING BACK ACROSS THE COUCH, ASIDE TO CHARTERIS) HAS SHE
CAND III SD(127) POKER, A LIGHT BRASS ONE, IS UPRIGHT IN HER HAND. LEANING BACK AND LOOKING INTENTLY AT THE POINT OF IT, WITH
DEST (153) AND USES HIS NAPKIN, STRETCHING HIS LEGS AND LEANING BACK, BUT STILL FROWNING AND THINKING). /GIUSEPPE/ (
NEVR I (215) DOLLY! /DOLLY/ WE'RE NOT SYMPATHETIC. /GLORIA/ (LEANING FORWARD IN HER CHAIR AND LOOKING EARNESTLY UP AT HER
INCA (247) IT FASCINATE EVERYONE IN PERUSALEM? /THE INCA/ (LEANING FORWARD TO HER ENERGETICALLY) BY ALL THE THUNDERS OF
CAND II SD(121) BARS). MORELL SITS DOWN AT HIS TABLE DESPERATELY, LEANING FORWARD TO HIDE HIS FACE, AND INTERLACING HIS
CAND III (145) OF ME! AND TO TEMPT ME TO STAY HE OFFERED ME (LEANING FORWARD TO STROKE HIS HAIR CARESSINGLY AT EACH
JOAN 6 (136) I WILL OBEY THE CHURCH -- /CAUCHON/ (HOPEFULLY LEANING FORWARD) YOU WILL? /JOAN/ -- PROVIDED IT DOES NOT
HART II (85) OF HEART WILL MAKE IT EASY FOR ME. /MANGAN/ (LEANING FORWARD, WITH THE BEGINNING OF SOMETHING LIKE
PHIL I (73) AND SITS IN THE CORNER FURTHEST FROM THE PIANO, LEANING GLOOMILY ON HER ELBOW WITH HER FACE AVERTED).
JITT II SD(41) HANDS) GOODBYE. EDITH GOES OUT WITH HER MOTHER LEANING HEAVILY ON HER. JITTA GOES OUT WITH THEM. /LENKHEIM/
PHIL II (114) BOOKCASE, AND STANDS THERE WITH HIS BACK TO THEM, LEANING ON IT WITH HIS HEAD ON HIS HANDS). /CRAVEN/ (
DEST (158) (FACING HIM AT THE OPPOSITE SIDE OF THE TABLE, LEANING ON IT WITH HIS FISTS) OH, I'M ALL RIGHT, GENERAL:
GETT (321) COMMANDMENTS, OBEY THEM. /HOTCHKISS/ (RISING AND LEANING ON THE BACK OF THE CHAIR LEFT VACANT BY THE GENERAL)
BULL IV SD(145) THEY ARE SCREAMING WITH LAUGHTER, DOUBLED UP, LEANING ON THE FURNITURE AND AGAINST THE WALLS, SHOUTING,
CATH 3,SD(183) THE NEVA, CLAIRE, A ROBUST YOUNG ENGLISH LADY, IS LEANING ON THE RIVER WALL. SHE TURNS EXPECTANTLY ON HEARING
NEVR I SD(224) THE MOUTHPIECE OVER CRAMPTON'S MOUTH AND NOSE, LEANING OVER HIS CHEST SO AS TO HOLD HIS HEAD AND SHOULDERS
PYGM V (285) (BOUNCING UP ON HIS KNEES ON THE OTTOMAN AND LEANING OVER IT TO HER) FOR THE FUN OF IT. THATS WHY I TOOK
ARMS III (50) THEMSELVES. /RAINA/ (GOING TO THE TABLE, AND LEANING OVER IT TOWARDS HIM) IT MUST HAVE MADE A LOVELY
MTH5 (222) THE CURVED SEAT, AND SITS DOWN JUST WHERE ACIS IS LEANING OVER IT). /ACIS/ I AM NO GREAT JUDGE OF SCULPTURE.
NEVR II (230) PRESSURE; AND RETIRES BEHIND THE GARDEN SEAT, LEANING OVER THE BACK BESIDE MRS CLANDON). AND THIS YOUNG
NEVR III (274) A CHAIR FROM THE TABLE AND SITS ASTRIDE OF IT, LEANING OVER THE BACK, NEAR THE OTTOMAN). MRS CLANDON: YOUR
PHIL II (128) SYLVIA POSTS HERSELF BEHIND GRACE'S CHAIR, LEANING OVER THE BACK TO WATCH THE ENSUING COLLOQUY BETWEEN
CAND II (119) SO EUGENE SAYS. /CANDIDA/ (WITH LIVELY INTEREST, LEANING OVER TO HIM WITH HER ARMS ON HIS KNEE) EUGENE'S
DOCT I SD(93) AND PLANTS HIMSELF WITH HIS BACK TO THE CONSOLE, LEANING RESIGNEDLY AGAINST IT. /SIR PATRICK/ I KNOW YOUR
HART II (95) YOU WERE VERY MUCH MISTAKEN. /MRS HUSHABYE/ (LEANING TOWARDS HIM KINDLY) HAVE I BEEN A BEAST? /MAZZINI/
HART I (80) SAKE WE SPARE THEM. /HECTOR/ (SITTING UP AND LEANING TOWARDS HIM) MAY NOT HESIONE BE SUCH A DEMON,
CLEO I (109) LITTLE DREAM WITCH? /CLEOPATRA/ (GIGGLING AND LEANING TRUSTFULLY TOWARDS HIM) YOU ARE A FUNNY OLD
CAND III (140) (SHE GOES TO THE FIREPLACE, AND STANDS THERE LEANING WITH HER ARM ON THE MANTELPIECE, AND HER FOOT ON THE
MIS. (198) HIMSELF). /HYPATIA/ (COOLLY GOING TO HIM AND LEANING WITH HER BREAST ON HIS WRITHING SHOULDERS) OH, IF

LEANINGS

DOCT PREFACE(66) PRESCRIBING ETHER DRAMS FOR LADIES WITH TIMID LEANINGS TOWARDS DIPSOMANIA, AND GENERALLY WASTING THEIF

LEANS

HART II SD(118) THE WORLD. THEY SIT SIDE BY SIDE ON THE SOFA. SHE LEANS AFFECTIONATELY AGAINST HIM WITH HER HEAD ON HIS
MTH1 I (15) HIM, STROLLS OFF CARELESSLY TO THE TREE AND LEANS AGAINST IT, STROKING A RING OF THE SNAKE). /ADAM/
PHIL III (142) I'LL LUMP IT. (HE MOVES OFF NONCHALANTLY, AND LEANS AGAINST THE BOOKCASE WITH HIS HANDS IN HIS POCKETS).
HART II (100) NOT. (SHE PASSES ON TO THE DRAWING-TABLE, AND LEANS AGAINST THE END OF IT, FACING THE WINDOWS). I SHALL
PHIL I (76) VIOLENT. (HE PASSES HER ACROSS TO THE SOFA, AND LEANS AGAINST THE END OF IT, PANTING AND MOPPING HIS
CAND III SD(137) OWN DIPLOMATIC CUNNING. LEXY FOLDS HIS ARMS AND LEANS AGAINST THE HEAD OF THE SOFA IN A HIGH-SPIRITED
ARMS III SD(65) A VICTIM TO HER SENSE OF HUMOR, AND ACTUALLY LEANS BACK BABYISHLY AGAINST THE WRITHING SHOULDER OF
APPL I SD(197) PAMPHILIUS, MIDDLE AGED, SHEWS HIS LEFT AS HE LEANS BACK IN HIS CHAIR AT THE OTHER TABLE WITH A PILE OF
WIDO I (18) NERVOUSLY. COKANE THROWS DOWN THE PENCIL AND LEANS BACK WITH OSTENTATIOUS INDIFFERENCE). OF COURSE IT IS
MRS III SD(229) BACK FROM IT. CROFTS IS NOT IMPRESSED. HE GRINS; LEANS FORWARD WITH HIS ELBOWS ON HIS KNEES TO PROD WITH HIS
DEST (177) HE TURNS HIS BACK ON HER, IN QUIET AMUSEMENT, SHE LEANS HER CHEEK ON HER HAND AND LAUGHS AT HIM. HE TURNS
JITT II (41) NOTHING BUT THE MANUSCRIPT OF A BIGGISH BOOK. HE LEANS LAZILY BACK WITH HIS LEGS STRETCHED, AND TURNS OVER
DEST SD(153) TRAILS INTO THE RISOTTO WHEN HE FORGETS IT AND LEANS MORE INTENTLY OVER THE MAP. /GIUSEPPE/ WILL YOUR
POSN (460) YOUR NECK (HE IS DRAGGED BACK TO THE BAR AND LEANS ON IT, GASPING AND EXHAUSTED). GIVE ME THE OATH AGAIN,
FANY II SD(287) FROM THE WINDOW. THEN SHE THROWS UP THE SASH AND LEANS OUT. MARGARET KNOX COMES IN, FLUSTERED AND ANNOYED.
HART II SD(88) BUT A CUNNING LOOK SOON COMES INTO HIS FACE. HE LEANS OVER TOWARDS HER ON HIS RIGHT ELBOW, AND SPEAKS IN A
WIDO III SD(64) A MOMENT. THEN HE GOES ON TIPTOE TO THE PIANO AND LEANS UPON IT WITH FOLDED ARMS, GAZING AT BLANCHE'S
DEVL I (10) LEAVE ME TO MY PRAYERS. (SHE TURNS FROM HIM AND LEANS WITH HER ELBOWS ON THE TABLE, BROODING OVER HER WRONGS
BARB III (330) (HE MOUNTS THE FIRESTEP DISTRACTEDLY, AND LEANS WITH HIS ELBOWS ON THE PARAPET, TURNING HIS BACK TO
BARB III (332) /BARBARA/ SILLY! (SHE CLIMBS TO THE CANNON, AND LEANS , LISTENING, IN THE ANGLE IT MAKES WITH THE PARAPET).

LEAP

3PLA PREFACE(R39) CLOWN AND PANTALOON (NOTE THE HARLEQUIN'S LEAP IN THE THIRD ACT OF CAESAR AND CLEOPATRA); MY STAGE
JOAN PREFACE(21) SAVE IT IF ONLY SHE COULD GET FREE. STILL, THE LEAP WAS SO PERILOUS THAT HER CONSCIENCE WAS NOT QUITE EASY
KING I (175) PRECISE, 273 YEARS 287 DAYS, ALLOWING 68 DAYS FOR LEAP YEAR EVERY FOUR YEARS. NOW MR ROWLEY IS NOT 300 YEARS
KING I (176) THOUSAND TWO HUNDRED AND TWENTY PLUS SEVEN FOR LEAP YEARS, YET YOU ALLEGE ONE HUNDRED THOUSAND OCCASIONS,

LEAPS

SUPR HANDBOK(208) ALL THE TIME THAT MANKIND WAS ADVANCING BY LEAPS AND BOUNDS BECAUSE MEN WERE CONSTANTLY BUSY. AND THE
NEVR I SD(202) AND LUNCH WITH US. VALENTINE, BEWILDERED BY THE LEAPS AND BOUNDS WITH WHICH THEIR ACQUAINTANCESHIP IS
MTH5 (212) LEFT CHILDHOOD BEHIND ME. IT COMES HOME TO ME IN LEAPS AND BOUNDS WITH EVERY WORD YOU SAY. /STREPHON/ BUT
METH PREFACE(R29) EVER CRAWLED, AND THAT NATURE DOES NOT PROCEED BY LEAPS AND BOUNDS. THIS WAS ALL VERY WELL AS LONG AS WE WERE
GLIM (187) APPEARS AT THE DOOR, SWORD IN HAND. FERRUCCIO LEAPS AT HIM AND STRIKES HIM FULL IN THE CHEST WITH HIS
LION PREFACE(36) AND JOHN ARE STILL IN THEIR MOTHERS' WOMBS, JOHN LEAPS AT THE APPROACH OF JESUS WHEN THE TWO MOTHERS VISIT
PPP SD(205) DOCTOR BY THE LANCET IN HIS POCKET. FINALLY IT LEAPS WITH FEARFUL FORCE ON THE LANDLORD, WHO, BEING OF A

		LEAR	
SHAK (141)	WHERE IS THY HAMLET? COULDST THOU WRITE KING	LEAR	? /SHAV/ AYE, WITH HIS DAUGHTERS ALL COMPLETE. COULDST
LADY PREFACE(230)	BOTH IN THE SAME BALANCE. NOW WHOEVER WILL READ	LEAR	AND MEASURE FOR MEASURE WILL FIND STAMPED ON HIS MIND
3PLA PREFACE(R32)	TYPE. HIS CAESAR IS AN ADMITTED FAILURE: HIS	LEAR	IS A MASTERPIECE, THE TRAGEDY OF DISILLUSION AND DOUBT,
CYMB FORWORD(137)	HIMSELF, TOLSTOY DECLARED THAT THE ORIGINAL	LEAR	IS SUPERIOR TO SHAKESPEAR'S REHANDLING, WHICH HE
SHAK (141)	THOU HAVE WRITTEN HEARTBREAK HOUSE? BEHOLD MY	LEAR	. A TRANSPARENCY IS SUDDENLY LIT UP, SHEWING CAPTAIN
MIS. (199)	ADVICE, READ SOMETHING. /TARLETON/ I'LL READ KING	LEAR	. /HYPATIA/ DONT, I'M VERY SORRY, DEAR. /TARLETON/
3PLA PREFACE(R34)	HENRY IRVING FOR PRODUCING A VERSION OF KING	LEAR	SO MUTILATED THAT THE NUMEROUS CRITICS WHO HAD NEVER
POSN PREFACE(418)	JOURNEY, OR A MANAGER WHETHER HE MAY PRODUCE KING	LEAR	WITHOUT RISK OF PROSECUTION, THE SOLICITOR WILL ADVISE
METH PREFACE(R85)	CONDITION WAS ONE OF DESPAIR. HIS TOWERING KING	LEAR	WOULD BE ONLY A MELODRAMA WERE IT NOT FOR ITS EXPRESS
3PLA PREFACE(R34)	NO MAN WILL EVER WRITE A BETTER TRAGEDY THAN	LEAR	, A BETTER COMEDY THAN LE FESTIN DE PIERRE OR PEER
CYMB FORWORD(133)	STAGE, WHICH HAD PRODUCED A HAPPY ENDING TO KING	LEAR	, CIBBER'S RICHARD III, A LOVE SCENE IN THE TOMB OF THE
POSN PREFACE(418)	THAT BOTH OF THEM ARE OBSCENE LIBELS; THAT KING	LEAR	, CONTAINING AS IT DOES PERHAPS THE MOST APPALLING
MRS PREFACE(158)	BANISHED FROM THE STAGE. MANY PLAYS, AMONG THEM	LEAR	, HAMLET, MACBETH, CORIOLANUS, JULIUS CAESAR, HAVE NO
		LEARN	
MIS. PREFACE(73)	SCHOOLMASTER DOES NOT COMPEL HIS SCHOLARS TO	LEARN	: HE ONLY SCOLDS AND PUNISHES THEM IF THEY DO NOT,
MIS. PREFACE(21)	TO MOST OF US. WE ARE NOT EFFECTIVELY COERCED TO	LEARN	: WE STAVE OFF PUNISHMENT AS FAR AS WE CAN BY LYING
CLEO PRO2 (99)	BY CAESAR AT PHARSALIA. WHAT, THINK YE, DID WE	LEARN	? EVEN THAT CAESAR IS COMING ALSO IN HOT PURSUIT OF
PYGM III (246)	THAN MY MIDDLE-CLASS PUPILS BECAUSE SHE'S HAD TO	LEARN	A COMPLETE NEW LANGUAGE. SHE TALKS ENGLISH ALMOST AS
APPL PREFACE(181)	OF READING BOOKS AND NEWSPAPER ARTICLES, YOU WILL	LEARN	A GREAT DEAL ABOUT POLITICS FROM THEM. MOST GENERAL
OVER PREFACE(166)	GET GLIMPSES OF THEIR REAL SELVES IN IT, AND ALSO	LEARN	A LITTLE HOW THEY APPEAR TO OTHER PEOPLE. FOR
METH PREFACE(R46)	THE MOST PROMISING. SUCH A MAN HAS NOTHING TO	LEARN	ABOUT THE SURVIVAL OF THE FITTEST EXCEPT THAT IT ACTS
SUPR PREFACE(R39)	TO TEACH AND ALL THE PEOPLE WHO DONT WANT TO	LEARN	AGREE WITH HIM EMPHATICALLY. I PRIDE MYSELF ON NOT
MIS. PREFACE(67)	GRAND INQUISITORS, CUNNING, UNSCRUPULOUS CHILDREN	LEARN	ALL THE ARTS OF THE SNEAK IN CIRCUMVENTING TYRANNY:
MTH1 II (34)	AIR, NOT DUG DIRTILY FROM THE EARTH. WILL THEY	LEARN	ALL THE WAYS OF ALL THE STARS IN THEIR LITTLE TIME?
ROCK II (267)	WHY CAN WE NEVER THINK OUT ANYTHING, NOR	LEARN	ANY LESSONS? I SEE WHAT HAS TO BE DONE NOW; BUT I
MIS. PREFACE(20)	WRITE: A BOOK FROM WHICH NO HUMAN BEING CAN	LEARN	ANYTHING: A BOOK WHICH, THOUGH YOU MAY DECIPHER IT,
MIS. PREFACE(20)	CRUELLY BEATEN AT SCHOOL? NO; BUT THEN I DID NOT	LEARN	ANYTHING AT SCHOOL. DR JOHNSON'S SCHOOLMASTER
HART PREFACE(38)	HE SAID THAT WE LEARN FROM HISTORY THAT MEN NEVER	LEARN	ANYTHING FROM HISTORY, WITH ANGUISH OF MIND THE
DOCT PREFACE(35)	BUT A FOOL, OR THAT A FOOL CAN BE TRUSTED TO	LEARN	ANYTHING FROM ANY EXPERIMENT, CRUEL OR HUMANE. THE
PRES (142)	/BALSQUITH/ WE LEARN FROM HISTORY THAT MEN NEVER	LEARN	ANYTHING FROM HISTORY. THAT'S NOT MY OWN: IT'S HEGEL.
MIS. PREFACE(20)	THAT UNDER SUCH CIRCUMSTANCES CHILDREN WILL NOT	LEARN	ANYTHING UNLESS THEY ARE SO CRUELLY BEATEN THAT THEY
DOCT PREFACE(78)	WHICH LURE US INTO THE ADVENTURES FROM WHICH WE	LEARN	ARE ALWAYS AT BOTTOM THE SAME. SCIENCE BECOMES
CLEO IV (167)	AS A DOG LEARNS. /CLEOPATRA/ WELL, THEN, I WILL	LEARN	AS A DOG LEARNS; FOR SHE PLAYS BETTER THAN YOU. YOU
PHIL III (138)	MY EXPERIMENTS THAN HE DOES! AND THE VICTIMS	LEARN	AS MUCH AS I DO. THATS WHERE MY MORAL SUPERIORITY
DOCT PREFACE(43)	AND WRECKED BEFORE THEM SO THAT THEY MIGHT	LEARN	AS MUCH AS POSSIBLE BY USING THEIR EYES, AND AS LITTLE
BARB PREFACE(235)	AS A RASCAL. THIS IS THE LESSON DEMOCRACY HAS TO	LEARN	BEFORE IT CAN BECOME ANYTHING BUT THE MOST OPPRESSIVE
O'FL (216)	O'FLAHERTY/ (SEVERELY) YOU HOLD YOUR WHISHT, AND	LEARN	BEHAVIOR WHILE I PAY MY JUTY TO HIS HONOR. (TO SIR
FABL VI (127)	TO DO THEIR WORK BY TRIAL AND ERROR. THEY HAVE TO	LEARN	BY MISTAKES AS WELL AS BY SUCCESSES. WE HAVE TO
OVER PREFACE(164)	INSTINCTS THAN THE FRENCH STAGE ALLOWS THEM,	LEARN	ENGLISH AND ESTABLISH THEMSELVES ON THE ENGLISH STAGE.
MRS II (217)	IT. SHE USED TO SAY THAT WHEN EVERY WOMAN COULD	LEARN	ENOUGH FROM WHAT WAS GOING ON IN THE WORLD BEFORE HER
KING I (219)	WITH MY ENGLISH. AND CHARLES IS TOO LAZY TO	LEARN	FRENCH PROPERLY, THOUGH HE LIVED IN FRANCE SO LONG.
KING I (173)	/NEWTON/ IN THESE VERY SIMPLE MATTERS ONE MAY	LEARN	FROM ANYONE, AND YOU, MADAM, MUST HAVE VERY REMARKABLE
MTH4 I (170)	YOU WOULD NOT COME TO US AT ALL: YOU WOULD	LEARN	FROM EXPERIENCE THAT YOUR CONSULTATIONS OF THE ORACLE
MIS. PREFACE(101)	ARTISTICALLY EDUCATED, WOULD HAVE HAD ANYTHING TO	LEARN	FROM HIM OR REGARDED HIM AS IN ANY WAY EXTRAORDINARY
SUPR PREFACE(R13)	IS HARDLY EVER THE LESSON THE WORLD CHOOSES TO	LEARN	FROM HIS BOOK. WHAT ATTRACTS AND IMPRESSES US IN EL
APPL I (232)	YOUR RESIGNATIONS AND HIS; AND THE COUNTRY WILL	LEARN	FROM HIS EXPLANATORY SPEECH IN THE HOUSE OF COMMONS
HART PREFACE(38)	ALAS! HEGEL WAS RIGHT WHEN HE SAID THAT WE	LEARN	FROM HISTORY THAT MEN NEVER LEARN ANYTHING FROM
PRES (142)	WE LEARN FROM HISTORY-- /BALSQUITH/ WE	LEARN	FROM HISTORY THAT MEN NEVER LEARN ANYTHING FROM
PRES (142)	HE KNOWS THAT HE KNOWS NOTHING. /MITCHENER/ WE	LEARN	FROM HISTORY-- /BALSQUITH/ WE LEARN FROM HISTORY THAT
KING I (212)	/KNELLER/ YOUR MAJESTY: THE WORLD MUST	LEARN	FROM ITS ARTISTS BECAUSE GOD MADE THE WORLD AS AN
SUPR HANDBOK(226)	BUT TO THEIR CAPACITY FOR EXPERIENCE. IF WE COULD	LEARN	FROM MERE EXPERIENCE, THE STONES OF LONDON WOULD BE
BUOY II (20)	AND FEEDS YOU, LIKE ELIJAH'S RAVENS. WHAT DO YOU	LEARN	FROM THAT? /SHE/ YOU LEARN WHAT NICE PEOPLE NATIVES
BULL PREFACE(55)	AND TERROR, IT IS UNSPEAKABLY REASSURING TO	LEARN	FROM THE BRITISH OFFICIAL REPORTS LAID BEFORE
CLEO IV (168)	WILL LEARN SOMETHING FROM THEM." WHAT HAVE I TO	LEARN	FROM THEM? I SAID. " WHAT THEY ARE," SAID HE; AND
CLEO PRO1 (94)	SPEAK TO YOU AGAIN: THE REST OF THE STORY MUST YE	LEARN	FROM THEM THAT LIVED IT. FAREWELL; AND DO NOT PRESUME
UNPL PREFACE(R18)	AT LEAST READ ABOUT IMAGINARY ONES, AND PERHAPS	LEARN	FROM THEM TO DOUBT WHETHER A CLASS THAT NOT ONLY
LADY (244)	(GRIMLY) THE SON OF YOUR FATHER SHALL	LEARN	HIS PLACE IN THE PRESENCE OF THE DAUGHTER OF HARRY THE
METH PREFACE(R45)	MR FESTING JONES'S MEMOIR OF SAMUEL BUTLER TO	LEARN	HOW COMPLETELY EVEN A MAN OF GENIUS COULD ISOLATE
CLEO IV (182)	US-- ROME, THAT HAS ACHIEVED GREATNESS ONLY TO	LEARN	HOW GREATNESS DESTROYS NATIONS OF MEN WHO ARE NOT
BASH II,2, (114)	HAVE I BEEN BROUGHT A MILLION MILES BY SEA TO	LEARN	HOW MEN CAN LIE! KNOW, FATHER WEBBER, MEN BECOME
LION I (120)	YOU ON ONE CHEEK; AND YOU WILL TURN THE OTHER AND	LEARN	HOW MUCH BETTER YOU WILL FEEL THAN IF YOU GAVE WAY TO
LION PREFACE(16)	AND FROM THE SONG OF JOHN BARLEYCORN YOU MAY	LEARN	HOW THE MIRACLE OF THE SEED, THE GROWTH, AND THE
LION PREFACE(16)	CECIL SHARP. FROM FRAZER'S MAGNUM OPUS YOU WILL	LEARN	HOW THE SAME PRIMITIVE LOGIC WHICH MAKES THE
HART PREFACE(6)	CONTINUAL PROMPTING FROM THOSE WHO HAVE TO	LEARN	HOW TO DO SUCH THINGS OR STARVE. FROM WHAT IS CALLED
SUPR HANDBOK(190)	ONCE HAD TO LEARN HOW TO FLATTER KINGS HAS NOW TO	LEARN	HOW TO FASCINATE, AMUSE, COAX, HUMBUG, FRIGHTEN, OR
SUPR HANDBOK(190)	POPULAR IGNORANCE. THE POLITICIAN WHO ONCE HAD TO	LEARN	HOW TO FLATTER KINGS HAS NOW TO LEARN HOW TO
SUPR III (119)	DINT OF SCOLDINGS AND PUNISHMENTS, FORCED YOU TO	LEARN	HOW TO PLAY HALF A DOZEN PIECES ON THE SPINET-- WHICH
JOAN PREFACE(36)	THE GENIUS HAPPENS TO BE POPE. THE CHURCHES MUST	LEARN	HUMILITY AS WELL AS TEACH IT. THE APOSTOLIC SUCCESSION
GETT PREFACE(236)	LINEN, DIRTY OR CLEAN, IN PUBLIC. WE MUST	LEARN	IN THESE MATTERS TO MIND OUR OWN BUSINESS AND NOT
MIS. PREFACE(39)	AND AGAIN UNTIL YOU HIT ON THE PLAN OF MAKING IT	LEARN	INSTALMENTS OF BIBLE VERSES, PREFERABLY FROM THE BOOK
HART III (145)	BE, PRAY? /CAPTAIN SHOTOVER/ NAVIGATION.	LEARN	IT AND LIVE; OR LEAVE IT AND BE DAMNED. /ELLIE/ QUIET,
BARB III (332)	MY MIND: IT HAS NOURISHED IT. BESIDES, I DID NOT	LEARN	IT AT AN ENGLISH PUBLIC SCHOOL. /UNDERSHAFT/ HM!
FANY III (301)	TABLE IN HIS CONSTERNATION). /MARGARET/ DID YOU	LEARN	IT FROM A FRENCHWOMAN? YOU KNOW YOU MUST HAVE LEARNT
KING I (192)	YOU WILL NOT TEACH THEM THEIR LESSON THEY SHALL	LEARN	IT FROM ME. /CHARLES/ YOU WILL HAVE TO TAKE YOUR MONEY
DEVL II (43)	TELL HER THE TRUTH IF IT IS SO, JUDITH. SHE WILL	LEARN	IT FROM THE FIRST NEIGHBOR SHE MEETS IN THE STREET. (
FABL PREFACE(84)	OF RENT AND VALUE CAN BE TAUGHT; AND THOSE WHO	LEARN	IT SEE THAT OUR BRITISH PARLIAMENTARY SYSTEM IS FAR
METH PREFACE(R14)	IS THAT IF YOU TEACH A MAN ANYTHING HE WILL NEVER	LEARN	IT; AND IF YOU CURE HIM OF A DISEASE HE WILL BE UNABLE
MTH2 (67)	SAKE LET US HAVE NO MORE SPLITS. I AM HERE TO	LEARN	. I AM HERE TO GATHER YOUR OPINIONS AND REPRESENT
CURE (226)	WHY SHOULDNT I? EXPLAIN IT TO ME. I'M ANXIOUS TO	LEARN	. I MEANT NO HARM. I SEE NO HARM. WHY AM I TO BE
BUOY III (33)	WHO DID HER OWN HOUSEWORK. I AM SURE I COULD	LEARN	. IS IT NOT EASIER FOR A CAMEL TO PASS THROUGH THE EYE
CAND III (140)	WELL, I GIVE YOU LEAVE TO STAY: TO STAY AND	LEARN	. (SHE COMES AWAY FROM THE HEARTH AND PLACES HERSELF
FANY III (321)	THERE WAS ANYTHING WRONG WITH ME. BUT LIVE AND	LEARN	. (TO GILBEY) EH, OLD DEAR? /JUGGINS/ OLD DEAR IS
BUOY III (32)	HOUSEWORK. /SIR F./ I AM AFRAID YOU WILL HAVE TO	LEARN	. /MRS SECONDBORN/ THE WHOLE THING IS UTTERLY
BUOY III (47)	NATIVE/ TRUE: THEY CAN TEACH; BUT THEY CANNOT	LEARN	. /THE PRIEST/ FREAKS. DANGEROUS FREAKS. THE FUTURE IS
NEVR III (267)	/MRS CLANDON/ (STIFFLY) I AM ALWAYS WILLING TO	LEARN	. /VALENTINE/ HAVE YOU EVER STUDIED THE SUBJECT OF
MIS. PREFACE(58)	FAILS TO TEACH WHERE THERE IS NO DESIRE TO	LEARN	. STILL, ONE MUST NOT BEGIN TO APPLY THIS
DOCT PREFACE(74)	ALL THE ORTHODOXIES, SINCE IT FORBIDS YOU EVEN TO	LEARN	. THE LATEST THEORIES, MEDICAL THEORIES ARE SO MUCH A
PYGM IV (262)	TO PEOPLE IN THEIR POSITION; AND SO THEY NEVER	LEARN	. THERES ALWAYS SOMETHING PROFESSIONAL ABOUT DOING A
MIS. (131)	DEMOCRATIC GAMES; AND I'M AFRAID I'M TOO OLD TO	LEARN	. WHAT CAN I DO BUT SIT IN THE WINDOW OF MY CLUB,
HART II (86)	DO YOU KNOW ABOUT BUSINESS? YOU JUST LISTEN AND	LEARN	. YOUR FATHER'S BUSINESS WAS A NEW BUSINESS; AND I
MIS. PREFACE(57)	ENDS. IT IS A MONSTROUS THING TO FORCE A CHILD TO	LEARN	LATIN OR GREEK OR MATHEMATICS ON THE GROUND THAT THEY
BUOY III (30)	THE LIFE OUT OF ME INSTEAD OF LEAVING ME TO	LEARN	LIFE'S LESSONS BY BREAKING MY SHINS AGAINST THEM AND
CLEO IV (184)	/CLEOPATRA/ IT IS NO SUPERSTITION: OUR PRIESTS	LEARN	LOTS OF THINGS FROM THE TABLES. IS IT NOT SO,
MIS. PREFACE(37)	OF THE ENLARGED RABBIT HUTCHES WE CALL HOMES; TO	LEARN	MANNERS AND BECOME UNCHALLENGEABLE LADIES AND
MIS. PREFACE(21)	REAL OBJECT OF THE SCHOOL. CONSEQUENTLY I DID NOT	LEARN	MY SCHOOL LESSONS, HAVING MUCH MORE IMPORTANT ONES IN
MTH3 (121)	HE SAID TO ME " IT HAS TAKEN ME FIFTY YEARS TO	LEARN	MY TRADE, AND TO PAINT ALL THE FOOLISH PICTURES A MAN
MTH1 II (27)	DIGGING. BY QUITTING IT I HAVE SET MYSELF FREE TO	LEARN	NOBLER CRAFTS OF WHICH YOU KNOW NOTHING. I KNOW THE
PHIL I (78)	(HAUGHTILY) NO: WHAT I RECEIVED, I PAID. DID YOU	LEARN	NOTHING FROM ME? WAS THERE NO DELIGHT FOR YOU IN OUR
PHIL III (139)	I HAVE LEARNT FROM YOU! FROM YOU! WHO COULD	LEARN	NOTHING FROM ME! I MADE A FOOL OF YOU; AND YOU
BUOY II (20)	THE SERVANTS. EVERYTHING IS DONE FOR YOU; AND YOU	LEARN	NOTHING. /HE/ AND HERE YOU WAIT UNTIL THAT KINDLY
BUOY III (30)	BOOBY TRAP. I WAS SO OVERPETTED THAT I HAD TO	LEARN	OR DIE. SO IF THERE IS ANYTHING REAL TO BE DONE I HAVE
DOCT PREFACE(76)	ON JUST AS HE DID BEFORE, AND COULD NOT AFFORD TO	LEARN	OR PRACTISE A NEW TECHNIQUE EVEN IF HE HAD EVER HEARD
MIS. PREFACE(27)	US ALL UNDERSTAND RICARDO'S LAW OF RENT AS TO	LEARN	OUR CATECHISMS, THE FACE OF THE WORLD WOULD HAVE BEEN
PYGM PREFACE(201)	THERE WAS A WEEKLY PAPER TO PERSUADE YOU TO	LEARN	PITMAN: THERE WERE CHEAP TEXTBOOKS AND EXCERCISE BOOKS

MIS. PREFACE(97)	LET NO ONE THINK THAT A CHILD OR ANYONE ELSE CAN	LEARN	RELIGION FROM A TEACHER OR A BOOK OR BY ANY ACADEMIC
6CAL (97)	FOR THESE SWINE, THESE BLOODSUCKERS, THEY SHALL	LEARN	--(SHOUTING) FETCH ME THESE FELLOWS IN HERE. DRAG
MIS. PREFACE(21)	MOCKING AND DISTRACTING THE BOYS WHO DID WISH TO	LEARN	; THAT I WAS A LIAR AND A SHIRKER AND A SEDITIOUS
PHIL III (138)	VIVISECTOR THAN HE. /CHARTERIS/ YES; BUT THEN I	LEARN	SO MUCH MORE FROM MY EXPERIMENTS THAN HE DOES! AND
SUPR II (51)	SNOBBERY? SHERBROOKE ROAD IS A PLACE WHERE BOYS	LEARN	SOMETHING: ETON IS A BOY FARM WHERE WE ARE SENT
MIS. (123)	SHE TOLD ME, DOWNRIGHT BRUTALLY, THAT I'D BETTER	LEARN	SOMETHING ABOUT THEM BEFORE MY CHILDREN DIED OF
GENV IV (102)	BECAUSE WHOEVER HAS MY CAPACITY FOR LEARNING CAN	LEARN	SOMETHING EVEN IN THE WORST SCHOOL. THE ARMY IS THE
CLEO IV (168)	AND HE SAID " LET YOUR WOMEN TALK; AND YOU WILL	LEARN	SOMETHING FROM THEM." WHAT HAVE I TO LEARN FROM THEM?
MIS. PREFACE(27)	QUITE COMMONLY RESPECT AND LIKE THEM, AND ALWAYS	LEARN	SOMETHING FROM THEM. HERE, AGAIN, AS AT SO MANY
BARB III (325)	WELL, TAKE ME TO THE FACTORY OF DEATH; AND LET ME	LEARN	SOMETHING MORE. THERE MUST BE SOME TRUTH OR OTHER
GETT PREFACE(234)	IF WE TAKE A DOCUMENT LIKE PEPYS' DIARY, WE	LEARN	THAT A WOMAN MAY HAVE AN INCORRIGIBLY UNFAITHFUL
BARB PREFACE(235)	SALUTARY CONDITION OF SOCIAL EXISTENCE. WHEN THEY	LEARN	THAT GENERAL BOOTH, TOO, HAS HIS PRICE, THEY DO NOT
JOAN 4 (98)	FORMIDABLE SOLDIER, MESSIRE; BUT I HAVE YET TO	LEARN	THAT HE IS AN ABLE GENERAL. AND THOUGH IT PLEASES YOU
DOCT III (149)	/B.B./ I SHOULDNT BE AT ALL SURPRISED TO	LEARN	THAT HE'S WELL CONNECTED. WHENEVER I MEET DIGNITY AND
ROCK II (250)	NOTICES TO QUIT? WOULD IT SURPRISE YOU TO	LEARN	THAT I AM ONLY ONE OF THOUSANDS OF YOUNG WOMEN WHO
O'FL PREFACE(201)	IT MAY SURPRISE SOME PEOPLE TO	LEARN	THAT IN 1915 THIS LITTLE PLAY WAS A RECRUITING POSTER
SIM II (55)	NO PLACE IN SUCH DISCUSSIONS. EACH OF THEM MUST	LEARN	THAT ITS IDEAS ARE NOT EVERYBODY'S IDEAS. HERE IS A
CAPT NOTES (303)	PIONEER AMERICAN, FOR EXAMPLE, CAN SPARE TIME TO	LEARN	THAT LAST REFINEMENT OF MODERN SPEECH, THE EXQUISITE
LADY (249)	THREE HUNDRED YEARS AND MORE BEFORE MY SUBJECTS	LEARN	THAT MAN CANNOT LIVE BY BREAD ALONE, BUT BY EVERY WORD
NEVR IV (299)	/VALENTINE/ WELL, WHAT AM I TO THINK WHEN I	LEARN	THAT MISS CLANDON HAS MADE EXACTLY THE SAME SPEECHES
ANNA (299)	DUCHESS/ (INDULGENTLY) IDOLATER! WHEN WILL YOU	LEARN	THAT OUR STRENGTH HAS NEVER BEEN IN OURSELVES, BUT IN
SUPR I (8)	IF I AM TO BE ANNIE'S GUARDIAN, SHE WILL HAVE TO	LEARN	THAT SHE HAS A DUTY TO ME. I WONT HAVE IT: I WILL NOT
SUPR I (26)	WASTING HER LIFE AND HER MONEY. WE SUDDENLY	LEARN	THAT SHE HAS TURNED FROM THESE SILLINESSES TO THE
MILL PREFACE(124)	MAGAZINES OF THE LATTER HALF OF 1914, HE WOULD	LEARN	THAT THE GERMANS ARE A RACE OF SAVAGE IDOLATERS,
OVER PREFACE(166)	NOT UNTIL THEY GROW UP TO THE POINT AT WHICH THEY	LEARN	THAT THEY KNOW VERY LITTLE ABOUT THEMSELVES, AND THAT
SHAK PREFACE(135)	AS THEY SHOULD BE, LIVING ACTORS HAVE TO	LEARN	THAT THEY TOO MUST BE INVISIBLE WHILE THE PROTAGONISTS
GENV II (53)	TO HAVE MADE YOUR ACQUAINTANCE, AND DELIGHTED TO	LEARN	THAT THOUGH YOU HAVE PRODUCED A FIRST CLASS POLITICAL
BULL PREFACE(65)	IT MAY BE A RELIEF TO SOME OF MY READERS TO	LEARN	THAT VERY SHORTLY AFTER THE PUBLICATION OF THE ABOVE
MTH5 (253)	YOUR TURN COMES. /THE HE-ANCIENT/ YOU WILL ALSO	LEARN	THAT WHEN THE MASTER HAS COME TO DO EVERYTHING THROUGH
BUOY IV (54)	YOUR FAMILY DID NOT DEMUR. I AM PREPARED TO	LEARN	THAT YOU DO NOT DEMUR. IN ANY OTHER FAMILY HE WOULD
SUPR PREFACE(R38)	THE MANNER OF THE GREAT COMPOSERS, THINK THEY CAN	LEARN	THE ART OF PALESTRINA FROM CHERUBINI'S TREATISE. ALL
MIS. PREFACE(39)	IS MADE. THUS WHEN YOU HAVE FORCED A CHILD TO	LEARN	THE CHURCH CATECHISM, A DOCUMENT PROFOUND BEYOND THE
FANY II (295)	FUN OF RELIGION. IVE TRIED TO BRING YOU UP TO	LEARN	THE HAPPINESS OF RELIGION. IVE WAITED FOR YOU TO FIND
METH PREFACE(R19)	READ SHAKESPEAR, SOME WHO CAN READ BOTH, LIKE TO	LEARN	THE HISTORY OF THEIR IDEAS. SOME ARE SO ENTANGLED IN
GENV PREFACE(7)	MOMENT, AND WHY STATESMEN, THOUGH THEY CAN	LEARN	THE LESSONS OF HISTORY FROM BOOKS, MUST GROPE THEIR
MIS. PREFACE(72)	CAN BE AN ASTRONOMER WITHOUT MATHEMATICS, IT WILL	LEARN	THE MULTIPLICATION TABLE, WHICH IS MORE THAN IT ALWAYS
BARB III (315)	BIG BUSINESS HOUSES? /UNDERSHAFT/ YES: HE COULD	LEARN	THE OFFICE ROUTINE WITHOUT UNDERSTANDING THE BUSINESS,
SUPR HANDBOK(213)	WITH THE DEMAND FOR QUALITY IN OUR RULERS. WE	LEARN	THE SAME LESSON FROM THE CASE OF THE SOLDIER, WHOSE
BUOY IV (52)	AND GATERS AS I CAN. /JUNIUS/ WHY NOT? I CAN	LEARN	THE SAXOPHONE. /SHE/ TRUE; BUT WE SHOULD BE OUT OF
MIS. PREFACE(9)	ALSO, PERHAPS, THAT MAMMA, WHO MADE THE CHILD	LEARN	THE SERMON ON THE MOUNT, IS NOT REALLY A CHRISTIAN.
DOCT PREFACE(62)	BY MAKING DOCTORS TRADESMEN, WE COMPEL THEM TO	LEARN	THE TRICKS OF TRADE; CONSEQUENTLY WE FIND THAT THE
LIED (191)	WE OWE IT TO HIM IN ALL HONOR NOT TO LET HIM	LEARN	THE TRUTH FROM THE LIPS OF A SCANDALMONGER. LET US GO
PHIL II (120)	(THEY SHAKE HANDS). AND NOW YOU MAY AS WELL	LEARN	THE TRUTH. I HAD RATHER YOU HEARD IT FROM ME THAN FROM
MIS. PREFACE(57)	TO LEARN THEM; AND PEOPLE WILL ALWAYS WANT TO	LEARN	THEM AS LONG AS THEY ARE OF ANY IMPORTANCE IN LIFE:
MIS. PREFACE(58)	BE LEARNT FRUITFULLY BY PEOPLE WHO DO NOT WANT TO	LEARN	THEM EITHER FOR THEIR OWN SAKE OR FOR USE IN NECESSARY
MIS. PREFACE(58)	MANNERS, AND PRACTISE ON HIS DOCILITY TO MAKE HIM	LEARN	THEM, AND THERE IS NO LOGICAL REASON WHY I SHOULD DO
MIS. PREFACE(57)	THEY WILL ALWAYS BE LEARNED BY PEOPLE WHO WANT TO	LEARN	THEM; AND PEOPLE WILL ALWAYS WANT TO LEARN THEM AS
MIS. PREFACE(58)	TEN WITH A LATIN GRAMMAR, AND SAYING " YOU MUST	LEARN	THIS, WHETHER YOU WANT TO OR NOT," SHOULD NEVERTHELESS
2TRU III (93)	ME TO READ THE BIBLE; BUT MY MOTHER MADE ME	LEARN	THREE VERSES OF IT EVERY DAY, AND WHACKED ME IF I
CATH 4 (188)	THEYRE HURTING ME! /CATHERINE/ PEOPLE SOMETIMES	LEARN	THROUGH SUFFERING. MANNERS, FOR INSTANCE. /EDSTASTON/
NEVR II (242)	HOW LONG DO YOU THINK IT WOULD TAKE ME TO	LEARN	TO BE A REALLY SMART WAITER? /WAITER/ CANT BE LEARNT,
JOAN 5 (109)	OH, SO DULL! DULL! /DUNOIS/ YOU MUST	LEARN	TO BE ABSTEMIOUS IN WAR, JUST AS YOU ARE IN YOUR FOOD
BARB III (349)	AT HER MOTHER'S SKIRT) BARBARA: WHEN WILL YOU	LEARN	TO BE INDEPENDENT AND TO ACT AND THINK FOR YOURSELF..
PYGM II (224)	GROVE PRUDERY HERE, YOUNG WOMAN. YOUVE GOT TO	LEARN	TO BEHAVE LIKE A DUCHESS. TAKE HER AWAY, MRS PEARCE.
METH PREFACE(R26)	EVER HANDLED A BRUSH BEFORE. BUT HE HAD ALSO TO	LEARN	TO BREATHE, AND DIGEST, AND CIRCULATE HIS BLOOD.
MIS. PREFACE(67)	THE FACT THAT IN A SHIP A MAN MUST EITHER	LEARN	TO CONSIDER OTHERS OR ELSE GO OVERBOARD OR INTO IRONS,
JITT II (48)	MARTYR AND WALKING OUT INTO THE STREET. YOU MUST	LEARN	TO CONSIDER OTHER PEOPLE A LITTLE, IF YOU HAVE NO
MIS. (204)	GO UP IN AN AEROPLANE! I DARENT. /LINA/ YOU MUST	LEARN	TO DARE. /BENTLEY/ (PALE BUT HEROIC) ALL RIGHT. I'LL
GENV IV (127)	NOT, IF THEY DIE COMFORTED? /BATTLER/ MEN MUST	LEARN	TO DIE UNDELUDED. /BBDE/ FLANCO IS DEAD; BUT HE DOES
MTH1 II (34)	UP THE SPADE AGAIN). LIFE IS STILL LONG ENOUGH TO	LEARN	TO DIG, SHORT AS THEY ARE MAKING IT. /EVE/ (MUSING)
BULL I (94)	I HAD ONLY TWO IDEAS AT THAT TIME: FIRST, TO	LEARN	TO DO SOMETHING; AND THEN TO GET OUT OF IRELAND AND
SUPR II (60)	MOTHER'S. GET YOUR MIND CLEAN AND VIGOROUS; AND	LEARN	TO ENJOY A FAST RIDE IN A MOTOR CAR INSTEAD OF SEEING
2TRU III (83)	BLASPHEMY: IF YOU DONT, IT'S NONSENSE. YOU MUST	LEARN	TO EXERCISE YOUR MIND: WHAT IS A WOMAN WITHOUT AN
JITT III (72)	DISAPPOINT ME TOO? /JITTA/ (STERNLY) YOU MUST	LEARN	TO EXPECT DISAPPOINTMENTS. HOW DO YOU KNOW THAT IF YOU
BARB I (250)	PLEASE: IT IS A MOST AGGRAVATING HABIT. YOU MUST	LEARN	TO FACE LIFE SERIOUSLY, STEPHEN. I REALLY CANNOT BEAR
CLEO II (133)	AND IF YOU DO AS I TELL YOU, YOU WILL SOON	LEARN	TO GOVERN. CAESAR, QUITE DUMBFOUNDED BY THIS
GETT (333)	OH, SENTIMENTAL YOUR GRANDMOTHER! YOU DONT	LEARN	TO HOLD YOUR OWN IN THE WORLD BY STANDING ON GUARD,
MTH1 II (34)	LITTLE TIME? IT TOOK ENOCH TWO HUNDRED YEARS TO	LEARN	TO INTERPRET THE WILL OF THE VOICE. WHEN HE WAS A MERE
SIM II (81)	MEN NO LONGER FEAR THE JUDGMENT OF GOD, THEY MUST	LEARN	TO JUDGE THEMSELVES. /SIR CHARLES/ I SEEM TO REMEMBER
GENV IV (95)	YOU HAVE A FAILING THAT MAY RUIN YOU UNLESS YOU	LEARN	TO KEEP IT IN CHECK. /BBDE/ AND WHAT IS THAT, PRAY?
KING I (206)	ON MY SHOULDERS. /NELL/ ROWLEY DARLING: YOU MUST	LEARN	TO KEEP KING CHARLES'S HEAD OUT OF YOUR CONVERSATION.
JOAN 2 (71)	IS A SORT OF IDOL. AT ANY RATE HE HAS TO	LEARN	TO KEEP STILL AND SUFFER FOOLS PATIENTLY. BESIDES, MY
O'FL (225)	YOU MANNERS. BE ASHAMED OF YOURSELF, DO; AND	LEARN	TO KNOW WHO YOURE SPEAKING TO. THAT I MAYNT SIN! BUT
PYGM III (255)	(INTERRUPTING HIM) COME, HIGGINS: YOU MUST	LEARN	TO KNOW YOURSELF. I HAVNT HEARD SUCH LANGUAGE AS YOURS
LADY (244)	THE STREETS. OH GOD! OH GOD! /SHAKESPEAR/	LEARN	TO KNOW YOURSELF BETTER, MADAM. I AM AN HONEST
CLEO II (142)	AND YOU SHALL SEE US TAKE THE PHAROS. YOU MUST	LEARN	TO LOOK ON BATTLES. GO. (SHE GOES, DOWNCAST, AND
BUOY II (23)	SOLDIERS, NO KING AND COUNTRY. I SHOULD HAVE TO	LEARN	TO MAKE BOWS AND ARROWS AND ASSEGAIS; TO TRACK GAME,
METH PREFACE(R26)	UNINTERRUPTED GENERATIONS OF PAINTERS, HAD TO	LEARN	TO PAINT APPARENTLY AS IF NO SANZIO HAD EVER HANDLED A
KING I (184)	I SHOULD NOT KNOW HOW TO SET ABOUT IT. I SHOULD	LEARN	TO PLAY SOME MUSICAL INSTRUMENT, OR BUY A NEW WIG.
CLEO IV (166)	/CLEOPATRA/ (TO THE OLD MUSICIAN) I WANT TO	LEARN	TO PLAY THE HARP WITH MY OWN HANDS. CAESAR LOVES
MIS. PREFACE(59)	AND INCOMPETENT AS TO BE UNABLE TO MAKE A CHILD	LEARN	TO READ AND WRITE WITHOUT ALSO MAKING IT CRY, STILL I
MIS. PREFACE(59)	TO ADMIT THAT I HAD RATHER HAVE BEEN COMPELLED TO	LEARN	TO READ AND WRITE WITH TEARS BY AN INCOMPETENT AND
ANNA (302)	MARX. /THE GRAND DUCHESS/ PSHAW! HOW COULD THEY	LEARN	TO READ THE BIBLE WITHOUT LEARNING TO READ KARL MARX?
BULL PREFACE(22)	AN IRISHMAN YEARS OF RESIDENCE IN ENGLAND TO	LEARN	TO RESPECT AND LIKE A BLOCKHEAD. AN ENGLISHMAN WILL
PLES PREFACE(R19)	ALLOW IT; AND IF THEY WOULD ONLY LET IT ALONE AND	LEARN	TO RESPECT REALITY, WHICH WOULD INCLUDE THE BENEFICIAL
MIS. PREFACE(61)	CARE OF THEMSELVES. THEY SEE THAT BOYS SHOULD	LEARN	TO ROUGH IT A LITTLE AND TO MIX WITH CHILDREN OF THEIR
SUPR HANDBOK(228)	ITSELF EVERYTHING, IS FORGIVEN NOTHING. WHEN WE	LEARN	TO SING THAT BRITONS NEVER WILL BE MASTERS WE SHALL
SUPR III (94)	JUAN/ AH, HERE YOU ARE, MY FRIEND. WHY DONT YOU	LEARN	TO SING THE SPLENDID MUSIC MOZART HAS WRITTEN FOR
FANY PROLOG (272)	SOCIETY TO ME. /FANNY/ ITS MOTTO IS " YOU CANNOT	LEARN	TO SKATE WITHOUT MAKING YOURSELF RIDICULOUS."
PYGM V (272)	TOUCH ME WILL BE YOU, HENRY HIGGINS. I'LL HAVE TO	LEARN	TO SPEAK MIDDLE CLASS LANGUAGE FROM YOU, INSTEAD OF
INCA (240)	WHAT SORT OF POTHOUSE IS THIS? WHERE DID YOU	LEARN	TO SPEAK TO PERSONS OF QUALITY? TAKE AWAY YOUR COLD
MILL IV (208)	HAVE YOU TO SAY TO THAT? /EPIFANIA/ YOU MUST	LEARN	TO TAKE CHANCES IN THIS WORLD. THIS DISAPPOINTED
SUPR I (6)	A FAULT IN HER. I HAVE OFTEN TOLD HER SHE MUST	LEARN	TO THINK FOR HERSELF. /OCTAVIUS/ (SHAKING HIS HEAD) I
DOCT III (138)	DO IT: JUST AS GOOD PEOPLE AS YOU. WHY DONT YOU	LEARN	TO THINK, INSTEAD OF BLEATING AND BAAHING LIKE A LOT
MIS. PREFACE(40)	THE CHILD AS WELL AS MENTAL ONES: THE CHILD MUST	LEARN	TO WALK, TO USE A KNIFE AND FORK, TO SWIM, TO RIDE A
MIS. PREFACE(73)	EFFECT BEING THAT THE SCHOOL PRISONERS NEED NOT	LEARN	UNLESS THEY LIKE. NAY, IT IS SOMETIMES REMARKED THAT
HART PREFACE(39)	AND PLAYWRIGHTS ARE FOR. IF MEN WILL NOT	LEARN	UNTIL THEIR LESSONS ARE WRITTEN IN BLOOD, WHY, BLOOD
BULL PREFACE(27)	OF COMMONS, BESIDES ALLOWING HIM TO READ AND	LEARN	WHAT HE LIKES-- EXCEPT WHEN IT MAKES A TUFTHUNTING
APPL II (259)	SOVEREIGN, IT IS YOUR RIGHT AS AN ENGLISHWOMAN TO	LEARN	WHAT I HAVE COME HERE TO COMMUNICATE. /MAGNUS/ MY DEAR
GENV IV (102)	COWARD YOU ARE AS WELL AS HOW BRAVE YOU ARE. YOU	LEARN	WHAT IT IS TO BE NUMBED WITH MISERY AND TERROR AS WELL
CAND II (120)	DONT YOU SEE? IT WILL DEPEND ON HOW HE COMES TO	LEARN	WHAT LOVE REALLY IS. I MEAN ON THE SORT OF WOMAN WHO
BUOY II (20)	RAVENS. WHAT DO YOU LEARN FROM THAT? /SHE/ YOU	LEARN	WHAT NICE PEOPLE NATIVES ARE. BUT YOU BEGIN BY TRYING
JOAN 2 (82)	THAT YOU WILL BE HANGED IN YOURS IF YOU DO NOT	LEARN	WHEN TO LAUGH AND WHEN TO PRAY. /BLUEBEARD/ MY LORD: I
MTH5 (253)	COMMANDER IS ITS MASTER. THESE ARE WORDS YOU WILL	LEARN	WHEN YOUR TURN COMES. /THE HE-ANCIENT/ YOU WILL ALSO
SUPR I (28)	VILLAIN WORSE THAN A MURDERER; AND WE ARE NOT TO	LEARN	WHO HE IS! IN OUR IGNORANCE WE ARE TO SHAKE HIM BY
MIS. PREFACE(39)	MOST OF THE DIFFICULTY OF INDUCING CHILDREN TO	LEARN	WOULD DISAPPEAR IF OUR DEMANDS BECAME NOT ONLY
HART III (145)	TO DO? /CAPTAIN SHOTOVER/ DO? NOTHING SIMPLER.	LEARN	YOUR BUSINESS AS AN ENGLISHMAN. /HECTOR/ AND WHAT MAY

PRES (149) SIR. IT'S THE EASIEST LIFE IN THE WORLD. ONCE YOU LEARN YOUR DRILL, ALL YOU HAVE TO DO IS TO HOLD YOUR TONGUE
POSN (454) TO ANSWER YOUR BETTERS? HOLD YOUR TONGUE AND LEARN YOUR PLACE, MISS, YOU PAINTED SLUT! WHIP HER OUT OF
WIDO II (44) AT HOME IN IT. YOU ALSO, MR COKANE, MUST LEARN YOUR WAY ABOUT HERE. LET US GO BEFORE BLANCHE COMES. (
LION PREFACE(95) TRUTH. THEN, AS THE CHILD'S MIND MATURES, IT CAN LEARN , AS HISTORICAL AND PSYCHOLOGICAL PHENOMENA, THE
OVER PREFACE(163) BRITISH, ARE ALWAYS SURPRISED AND PUZZLED WHEN WE LEARN , AS WE MAY DO ANY DAY IF WE COME WITHIN REACH OF SUCH
GETT PREFACE(245) TO SEE SUCH THINGS HAPPENING TO OUR CHILDREN. WE LEARN , AT LAST, THAT THE MAJORITY OF THE VICTIMS ARE NOT
2TRU II (61) FRIEND. /AUBREY/ THE FIRST LESSON A CROOK HAS TO LEARN , DARLING, IS THAT NOTHING SUCCEEDS LIKE LYING. MAKE
MIS. (142) THE BRUTALITY OF MY OWN BOYHOOD. BUT DO TRY TO LEARN , GLORIOUS YOUNG BEAST THAT YOU ARE, THAT AGE IS
APPL I (228) YOU KNOW QUITE WELL WHAT I MEAN. WHEN WILL YOU LEARN , NICOBAR, THAT IT IS NO USE TRYING TO BROWBEAT ME. I
FABL VI (130) COME TO TEACH US? /RAPHAEL/ NO. I AM HERE TO LEARN , NOT TO TEACH. I PASS ON. (HE VANISHES). /ALL/ (
CLEO IV (175) TONGUE. /CAESAR/ THE GODS FORBID HE SHOULD EVER LEARN ! OH, THIS MILITARY LIFE! THIS TEDIOUS, BRUTAL LIFE

LEARND

LADY PREFACE(214) MOTHER: DEATH ERE THOU HAS SLAIN ANOTHER, LEARND AND FAIR AND GOOD AS SHE, TIME SHALL THROW A DART AT

LEARNED

CLEO IV (168) HE MAKES YOU SO TERRIBLY PROSY AND SERIOUS AND LEARNED AND PHILOSOPHICAL. IT IS WORSE THAN BEING RELIGIOUS,
JOAN 4 (108) MEAN BY PROTESTANT AND NATIONALIST: YOU ARE TOO LEARNED AND SUBTLE FOR A POOR CLERK LIKE MYSELF. BUT I KNOW
GENV III (85) I AM A LITTLE AFRAID OF YOU, YOU ARE SO DEEP AND LEARNED AND WHAT I CALL MENTAL. I MAY BE A DAME OF THE
MIS. PREFACE(21) PRESUMABLY DID CARE ENOUGH WHETHER SAM LEARNED ANYTHING TO BEAT HIM SAVAGELY ENOUGH TO FORCE HIM TO
KING I (170) WORDS. YOU MUST REMEMBER THAT EVERYBODY IS NOT AS LEARNED AS YOU ARE. /NEWTON/ BUT SURELY IT IS PLAIN TO
KING I (207) I AM SIMPLE IN MY TASTES. I AM NOT SCHOOLED AND LEARNED AS YOU TWO PRINCES ARE. /CHARLES/ THANK YOUR STARS
LADY (242) /THE LADY/ AND WHO, PRAY, IS BEN? /THE MAN/ A LEARNED BRICKLAYER WHO THINKS THAT THE SKY IS AT THE TOP OF
MIS. PREFACE(57) MATHEMATICS HAVE THEIR USES. THEY WILL ALWAYS BE LEARNED BY PEOPLE WHO WANT TO LEARN THEM; AND PEOPLE WILL
UNPL PREFACE(R24) FAMILIAR TO FOREIGN READERS, WILL HAVE TO BE LEARNED BY THE ENGLISH PUBLIC BEFORE IT BECOMES EFFECTIVE.
6CAL (99) HAVE YOU TO PREACH? IT IS FOR CHURCHMEN AND LEARNED DIVINES TO SPEAK OF THESE MYSTERIES, NOT FOR
CAPT II (256) SAY? A FOOLHARDY TOURIST! WHAT WILL YOUR LEARNED FRIENDS AT THE BAR SAY? THAT IT WAS TIME FOR YOU TO
LION PREFACE(4) THEY WERE SCUTTLING THE SHIP BEFORE THEY HAD LEARNED HOW TO BUILD A RAFT; AND IT BECAME NECESSARY TO
MILL IV (204) YOU SHALL HAVE AN ACCOUNTANT'S CERTIFICATE. I LEARNED IN THE FIRST HALF HOUR OF MY SEARCH FOR EMPLOYMENT
JOAN PREFACE(29) THE MIDDLE AGES BACK, AND HAVE FIFTY CIVILIANS, LEARNED IN THE LAW OR VOWED TO THE SERVICE OF GOD, TO
PYGM EPILOG (300) THE FACT THAT BUSINESS, LIKE PHONETICS, HAS TO BE LEARNED . ON THE PITEOUS SPECTACLE OF THE PAIR SPENDING
MILL IV (192) EGYPTIAN DOCTOR WHO TAKES HIS MEALS HERE: A VERY LEARNED MAN I SHOULD THINK: VERY QUIET: NOT A WORD TO
SUPR HANDBOK(219) DONS. HE WHO CAN, DOES. HE WHO CANNOT, TEACHES. A LEARNED MAN IS AN IDLER WHO KILLS TIME WITH STUDY. BEWARE OF
BASH III (119) HAUNTING OF THE PAST. MY FATHER WAS A VERY LEARNED MAN. I SOMETIMES THINK I SHALL OLDMAIDED BE ERE I
BARB III (341) AND SET UP NEW. IS THAT HISTORICALLY TRUE, MR LEARNED MAN, OR IS IT NOT? /CUSINS/ IT IS HISTORICALLY
DEVL I SD(16) ARE ALLOWED PRECEDENCE AS REPRESENTING THE LEARNED PROFESSIONS. AFTER THEM COMES THE FAMILY, HEADED BY
APPL II (271) TO CONFESS THAT IT IS A TIE FROM WHICH I HAVE LEARNED SOMETHING. /MALE MINISTERS/ (MURMUR) HEAR HEAR!
HART PREFACE(21) NOTHING TO US; BUT WHEN OUR SEASIDE TRIPPERS LEARNED THAT AN ELDERLY GENTLEMAN AT BREAKFAST IN A WEEK-END
PHIL II (107) WHAT WAS THAT? /SYLVIA/ I MEAN WHEN WE LEARNED THAT POOR PAPA HAD PARAMORE'S DISEASE. /CHARTERIS/
SUPR III (121) TO ANA'S AGE, OR EVEN TO MINE, YOU WOULD HAVE LEARNED THAT THE PEOPLE WHO GET RID OF THE FEAR OF POVERTY
MIS. PREFACE(71) THE HOME AND THE SCHOOL IF THESE HAVE MEANWHILE LEARNED THE LESSON THAT CHILDREN ARE INDEPENDENT HUMAN
PYGM PREFACE(201) IS STILL A STEADY AND HEALTHY ONE. I ACTUALLY LEARNED THE SYSTEM TWO SEVERAL TIMES; AND YET THE SHORTHAND
SIM PREFACE(5) GOOD OR AT LEAST CONVENIENT TO OUR RULERS. I LEARNED THIS EARLY IN LIFE. MY NURSE INDUCED ME TO ABSTAIN
JOAN PREFACE(4) BY BEING RIGHT WHEN THEY WERE WRONG, AND HAD LEARNED TO FLATTER AND MANAGE THEM, SHE MIGHT HAVE LIVED AS
HART II (123) FIRST; BUT I BECAME ACCUSTOMED TO THEM. AT LAST I LEARNED TO PLAY THEM. /RANDALL/ IF IT'S ALL THE SAME TO YOU,
HART III (131) SO MANY THINGS PILED ON IT. I NEVER LIVED UNTIL I LEARNED TO RIDE; AND I SHALL NEVER RIDE REALLY WELL BECAUSE
SUPR I (18) ANNIE'S GRANNY. I CHRISTENED HIM SO WHEN I FIRST LEARNED TO SPEAK. /RAMSDEN/ (SARCASTICALLY) I HOPE YOU ARE
BASH PREFACE(90) I WAS TEN YEARS OLD, AND THE ONLY GRAMMAR I EVER LEARNED WAS LATIN GRAMMAR, SO THAT ELIZABETHAN ENGLISH
O'FL (218) ME NOW? /MRS O'FLAHERTY/ AND WAS IT THE BELGIANS LEARNED YOU SUCH BRAZEN IMPUDENCE? /O'FLAHERTY/ THE
BASH I (93) THE OWNER OF THESE LANDS, ALBEIT MOST RICH, MOST LEARNED , AND MOST WISE, AM YET MOST LONELY. WHAT ARE RICHES
MRS PREFACE(164) CATHOLIC CHURCH IS THE MOST AUGUST, ANCIENT, LEARNED , FAMOUS, AND AUTHORITATIVE CENSORSHIP IN EUROPE. IS
ROCK PREFACE(188) HIGH PRIESTS, FEAR OF THE JEWS AND GREEKS WHO ARE LEARNED , FEAR OF THE GAULS AND GOTHS AND HUNS WHO ARE
MILL PREFACE(109) ONE LAW FOR THE IGNORANT AND ANOTHER FOR THE LEARNED , ONE LAW FOR THE BRAVE AND ANOTHER FOR THE TIMID,
JOAN 4 (103) AND KNOWLEDGE AND EXPERIENCE, ITS COUNCILS OF LEARNED , VENERABLE PIOUS MEN, ARE THRUST INTO THE KENNEL BY
CATH 1 (167) (SURPRISED AND IMPRESSED) IS IT? YOU ARE LEARNED ! YOU ARE A DOCTOR! YOU ENGLISH ARE WONDERFUL! WE

LEARNEDLY

MRS II (205) SERIOUS. I'M SERIOUS. /FRANK/ GOOD. LET US TALK LEARNEDLY . MISS WARREN: DO YOU KNOW THAT ALL THE MOST
DOCT PREFACE(60) CONCLUSIONS DRAWN IN IT FROM THE CORRELATIONS SO LEARNEDLY WORKED OUT; THOUGH THE MATHEMATICIAN WHOSE

LEARNERS

ROCK PREFACE(168) WHEN THE ABLEST AND OLDEST COMMUNISTS ARE STILL LEARNERS . TEMPERAMENTAL DIFFICULTIES. EVEN WHEN THE
BUOY III (47) FREAKS. DANGEROUS FREAKS. THE FUTURE IS WITH THE LEARNERS . THE TEMPLE VANISHES, BLACKED OUT.
METH PREFACE(R16) KNOW THEIR BUSINESS, AND REALLY MEAN THE LEARNERS TO SUCCEED. THE RESULT IS THAT POWERS OF

LEARNING

ROCK I (220) HIND LEG OFF A DONKEY; BUT WHEN IT COMES TO BOOK LEARNING ALOYSIA AND BLEE CAN WIPE THE FLOOR WITH YOU. /SIR
MTH1 II (32) THEY NEVER WANT TO DIE, BECAUSE THEY ARE ALWAYS LEARNING AND ALWAYS CREATING EITHER THINGS OR WISDOM, OR AT
GENV PREFACE(24) AND PREJUDICED BARBARIANS WITH A HATRED OF LEARNING AND DISCIPLINE, AND A DENSE IGNORANCE OF WHAT LIFE
MIS. PREFACE(50) IMPRISONMENT AND DEGRADATION. WHY WE LOATHE LEARNING AND LOVE SPORT. IF WE ARE TO DISCUSS THE IMPORTANCE
JOAN 6 (124) IF I DID NOT KNOW THAT MEN FAR MY SUPERIORS IN LEARNING AND PIETY, IN ELOQUENCE AND PERSUASIVENESS, HAVE
PYGM EPILOG (300) IN SHORTHAND SCHOOLS AND POLYTECHNIC CLASSES, LEARNING BOOKKEEPING AND TYPEWRITING WITH INCIPIENT JUNIOR
JITT II SD(27) COMIC, BY THE STAMP PUT UPON HIM AS A MAN OF LEARNING BY HIS UNIVERSITY TRAINING AND HIS PROFESSORIAL
DOCT PREFACE(33) CURT DISMISSAL OF FOLLY, WE CONTINUE LIVING AND LEARNING BY INSTINCT: THAT IS, AS OF RIGHT. WE LEGISLATE ON
MIS. PREFACE(72) PURSUIT OF LEARNING COMES TO MEAN THE PURSUIT OF LEARNING BY THE CHILD INSTEAD OF THE PURSUIT OF THE CHILD BY
GENV IV (102) A GOOD DEAL, BECAUSE WHOEVER HAS MY CAPACITY FOR LEARNING CAN LEARN SOMETHING EVEN IN THE WORST SCHOOL. THE
MIS. PREFACE(72) THE PURSUIT OF LEARNING. WHEN THE PURSUIT OF LEARNING COMES TO MEAN THE PURSUIT OF LEARNING BY THE CHILD
CAPT III (298) SUBORDINATE WITH THE COMMANDER. /LADY CICELY/ (LEARNING FOR THE FIRST TIME IN HER LIFE WHAT TERROR IS, AS
METH PREFACE(R49) EFFECT ON PUBLIC OPINION, I MUST BE INCAPABLE OF LEARNING FROM EXPERIENCE, AND AM THEREFORE A MERE AUTOMATON.
2TRU PREFACE(18) THE WARRIORS AND ROBBERS OF THE EMPIRE HAD BEEN LEARNING FROM EXPERIENCE THAT A PIRATE SHIP NEEDS A
SUPR HANDBOK(228) ALWAYS HAPPENS. HOW INCAPABLE MUST MAN BE OF LEARNING FROM EXPERIENCE! COMPASSION IS THE FELLOW-FEELING
MIS. PREFACE(21) MIND -- FOR JOHNSON'S GREAT MIND WAS LAMED -- BY LEARNING HIS LESSONS. NONE OF MY SCHOOLMASTERS REALLY CARED
MIS. PREFACE(41) FREEDOM OF MOVEMENT IN A CITY IS THE REWARD OF LEARNING HOW TO READ PUBLIC NOTICES, AND TO COUNT AND USE
METH PREFACE(R23) OR THE SURVIVAL OF THE FITTEST, THE MAN WHO IS LEARNING HOW TO RIDE A BICYCLE HAS NO ADVANTAGE OVER THE
PYGM II (228) YOU ARE TO LIVE HERE FOR THE NEXT SIX MONTHS, LEARNING HOW TO SPEAK BEAUTIFULLY, LIKE A LADY IN A
BUOY III (41) SCHOOLS CHILDREN SPEND NINE YEARS WITHOUT LEARNING HOW TO SPEAK THEIR NATIVE LANGUAGE DECENTLY OR
MTH2 (79) TURMOIL OF OUR POLITICAL LIFE: DEVOTED TO PURE LEARNING IN ITS MOST ABSTRACT PHASES; AND I SOLEMNLY DECLARE
BUOY II (24) OF THE UNIVERSITY OF OXFORD, THE CENTRE OF ALL LEARNING IN THE UNIVERSE. THE POSSESSION OF SUCH A DEGREE
KING I (188) THE GREATEST SCHOLARS OF HIS DAY? IS THERE MORE LEARNING IN YOUR HEAD THAN IN THE LIBRARIES OF THE VATICAN?
DOCT I (99) A PERFECT ANSWER TO THEM ON EVERY POINT. A LITTLE LEARNING IS A DANGEROUS THING: DRINK DEEP; OR TASTE NOT THE
MIS. PREFACE(101) BY SLAVERY, THERE IS NO ART. IT IS ONLY WHEN LEARNING IS MADE A SLAVERY BY TYRANNICAL TEACHERS THAT ART
MIS. PREFACE(39) DEMANDS BECAME NOT ONLY DEFINITE BUT FINITE, WHEN LEARNING IS ONLY AN EXCUSE FOR IMPRISONMENT, IT IS AN
HART PREFACE(17) IN ENGLAND THE LITTLE RESPECT PAID TO SCIENCE AND LEARNING IS ONLY AN AFFECTATION WHICH HIDES A SAVAGE
MIS. PREFACE(73) AS SOME PEOPLE WARN US AGAINST DRINK, WHEN LEARNING IS PLACED ON THE VOLUNTARY FOOTING OF SPORT, THE
DEVL EPILOG (81) (THE SCENE IN WHICH I HAVE REPRESENTED HIM AS LEARNING IT BEFORE SARATOGA IS NOT HISTORICAL: THE TRUTH DID
MTH2 (71) WITH EDUCATED MINDS AT ANY OF OUR GREAT SEATS OF LEARNING . AS I HAPPEN TO HAVE ENJOYED THAT ADVANTAGE, IT
VWOO 3 (134) IN OXFORD. /Z/ I CANT BELIEVE THAT ABOUT THE LEARNING . BUT SEE HOW YOUR MANNERS HAVE IMPROVED! /A/ MY
PYGM V (286) SEEN MORE OF SOME THINGS THAN YOU, FOR ALL YOUR LEARNING . GIRLS LIKE ME CAN DRAG GENTLEMEN DOWN TO MAKE
MIS. PREFACE(81) OR AS STILL GROWING, YEARNING, SUFFERING, AND LEARNING . IF I MEET A WIDOW I MAY ASK HER ALL ABOUT HER
MILL II (177) FOLK. WITH THEIR HELP SHE MADE ME A MAN OF LEARNING . IT WAS HER AMBITION TO HAVE A SON WHO COULD READ
KING I (170) WILL BE PROSTRATE BEFORE THE PROFUNDITY OF MY LEARNING . /MRS BASHAM/ OH, TELL THE GENTLEMEN, MR NEWTON;
MIS. PREFACE(72) ALL THE CANINGS AND KEEPINGS-IN, THE PURSUIT OF LEARNING . WHEN THE PURSUIT OF LEARNING COMES TO MEAN THE
KING II (229) HALF A DOZEN OF THE OTHER. HEREDITY IS NO USE. LEARNING LATIN IS NO USE: JACK CHURCHILL, WHO IS AN
BASH I (93) PURSE BEARER THAT LIFE REMAINS UNPURCHASABLE? LEARNING LEARNS BUT ONE LESSON: DOUBT! TO EXCEL ALL IS, TO
JOAN 6 (127) PROFOUND AS YOU, AND THAT SOME OF YOUR VERY GREAT LEARNING MIGHT APPEAR TO THEM TO BE VERY GREAT NONSENSE.
MIS. PREFACE(40) TO FALL BACK ON, UNLESS INDEED YOU INSIST ON HIS LEARNING MUSIC, AND PROCEED TO HIT HIM IF HE CANNOT TELL YOU
PYGM EPILOG (301) DESPAIR FOR THE YOUNG COUPLE. THEY SEEMED TO BE LEARNING NOTHING ABOUT FLOWER SHOPS. AT LAST THEY GAVE IT UP

MILL I (163)	ANNOYING! /ALASTAIR/ YOUR LESSON? WHAT ARE YOU	LEARNING	NOW, MAY I ASK? /EPIFANIA/ ALL-IN WRESTLING. WHEN
GENV III (79)	A POINT LIKE LIGHTNING. SHE HAS IN HER VEINS THE	LEARNING	OF THE ARABS, THE COURAGE AND ENTERPRISE OF THE
ROCK I (220)	SRARTHUR, THE LABOR MOVEMENT IS ROTTEN WITH BOOK	LEARNING	; AND YOUR PEOPLE DONT SEEM EVER TO READ ANYTHING.
MIS. PREFACE(21)	DISLOYAL TO IT; THAT I HAD NO INTENTION OF	LEARNING	; THAT I WAS MOCKING AND DISTRACTING THE BOYS WHO
JOAN PREFACE(49)	READ HIS PLAYS FROM ONE END TO THE OTHER WITHOUT	LEARNING	THAT THE WORLD IS FINALLY GOVERNED BY FORCES
MTH3 (117)	I NOTICE THAT THE HONORABLE DOMESTIC MINISTER, ON	LEARNING	THE ADVANCED AGE OF THE VENERABLE PRELATE, SHEWS NO
GETT PREFACE(197)	HIM WHEN HE FELL DOWNSTAIRS OR WAS SLACK IN	LEARNING	THE BIBLE OFF BY HEART; AND THIS GROTESQUE
SHAK PREFACE(136)	OWES MUCH MORE TO HIS MOTHER'S INSISTENCE ON HIS	LEARNING	THE BIBLE BY HEART THAN TO HIS OXFORD DEGREE. SO
DOCT PREFACE(16)	SERVANTS, TO PICK UP THEIR BUSINESS IN A NEW WAY,	LEARNING	THE SLATTERNLY HABITS AND WRETCHED MAKESHIFTS OF
PYGM V (278)	DAMNATION! /LIZA/ (CONTINUING) IT WAS JUST LIKE	LEARNING	TO DANCE IN THE FASHIONABLE WAY: THERE WAS NOTHING
MIS. PREFACE(93)	THAT THE ONLY REASON FOR CEASING TO DO EVIL AND	LEARNING	TO DO WELL IS THAT IF YOU DO NOT YOU WILL BE CANED.
MTH3 (123)	MANKIND WHEN I WAS LEARNING TO SUFFER INSTEAD OF	LEARNING	TO LIVE! WHEN I SEE HOW LIGHTLY YOU TAKE IT ALL!
ANNA (302)	HOW COULD THEY LEARN TO READ THE BIBLE WITHOUT	LEARNING	TO READ KARL MARX? WHY DO YOU NOT STAND TO YOUR
MIS. PREFACE(57)	MEDICINE. TECHNICAL TRAINING MAY BE AS TEDIOUS AS	LEARNING	TO SKATE OR TO PLAY THE PIANO OR VIOLIN; BUT IT IS
CAPT NOTES (306)	OF USE SIMPLY BY ESCAPING THE EARS OF CHILDREN	LEARNING	TO SPEAK. HOWEVER THAT MAY BE, IT IS KEPT ALIVE
MTH3 (123)	THAT WERE THE DAILY LOT OF MANKIND WHEN I WAS	LEARNING	TO SUFFER INSTEAD OF LEARNING TO LIVE! WHEN I SEE
MIS. PREFACE(62)	TO TALK TO HIM ABOUT THE NEED FOR SELF-RELIANCE,	LEARNING	TO THINK, AND SO FORTH, WITH THE RESULT THAT YOUR
MTH5 (252)	/THE SHE-ANCIENT/ ONE DAY, WHEN I WAS TIRED OF	LEARNING	TO WALK FORWARD WITH SOME OF MY FEET AND BACKWARDS
MIS. PREFACE(41)	FREEDOM OF MOVEMENT IN A NURSERY IS THE REWARD OF	LEARNING	TO WALK; AND IN PRECISELY THE SAME WAY FREEDOM OF
HART PREFACE(17)	NAMES FROM THE BRITISH ROLLS OF SCIENCE AND	LEARNING	WAS A CONFESSION THAT IN ENGLAND THE LITTLE RESPECT
AUGS (272)	THE POMERANIAN REGIMENT WHICH CAPTURED ME, AFTER	LEARNING	WHAT I HAD DONE, AND CONVERSING FOR AN HOUR WITH ME
MIS. PREFACE(50)	IF WE ARE TO DISCUSS THE IMPORTANCE OF ART,	LEARNING	, AND INTELLECTUAL CULTURE, THE FIRST THING WE HAVE
MTH4 I (162)	THE BEST OF US, I MEAN-- REGARD CIVILIZATION AND	LEARNING	, ART AND SCIENCE, AS AN EVER-BURNING TORCH, WHICH
JITT PREFACE(5)	IT WAS NOT BY ANY PROCESS KNOWN TO MEN OF	LEARNING	, BUT RATHER BY SOME TELEPATHIC METHOD OF
MIS. PREFACE(72)	THE CHILD INSTEAD OF THE PURSUIT OF THE CHILD BY	LEARNING	, CANE IN HAND, THE DANGER WILL BE PRECOCITY OF THE
METH PREFACE(R31)	UP THEIR DUCTS, OR SEVERING THEIR NERVES, THEREBY	LEARNING	, NEGATIVELY, THAT THE GOVERNORS OF OUR VITAL
DOCT PREFACE(78)	BUT EMPIRICS WHO SAY " I KNOW" INSTEAD OF " I AM	LEARNING	," AND PRAY FOR CREDULITY AND INERTIA AS WISE MEN

LEARNING'S

NEVR I (204)	DITHYRAMBICALLY) NATURE'S MASTERPIECE! /PHILIP/	LEARNING'S	DAUGHTER! /DOLLY/ MADEIRA'S PRIDE! /PHILIP/

LEARNS

CLEO IV (167)	/MUSICIAN/ OH, SHE IS BUT A SLAVE. SHE	LEARNS	AS A DOG LEARNS. /CLEOPATRA/ WELL, THEN, I WILL LEARN
SUPR III (109)	DIE WILL BE A CATHOLIC IDEA. WHEN THE SPANIARD	LEARNS	AT LAST THAT HE IS NO BETTER THAN THE SARACEN, AND
BASH I (93)	BEARER THAT LIFE REMAINS UNPURCHASABLE? LEARNING	LEARNS	BUT ONE LESSON: DOUBT! TO EXCEL ALL IS, TO BE
METH PREFACE(R23)	BETWEEN YOUR LESSONS OCCURS AGAIN. THE RACE	LEARNS	EXACTLY AS THE INDIVIDUAL LEARNS. YOUR SON RELAPSES,
MIS. PREFACE(9)	THERE ARE NO FALSE PRETENCES INVOLVED: THE CHILD	LEARNS	IN A STRAIGHTFORWARD WAY THAT IT DOES NOT PAY TO BE
CAND II (120)	ME. /MORELL/ FORGIVE? /CANDIDA/ BUT SUPPOSE HE	LEARNS	IT FROM A BAD WOMAN, AS SO MANY MEN DO, ESPECIALLY
CAND II (120)	KNOW WHAT YOU MEAN. /CANDIDA/ (EXPLAINING) IF HE	LEARNS	IT FROM A GOOD WOMAN, THEN IT WILL BE ALL RIGHT: HE
CLEO IV (167)	OH, SHE IS BUT A SLAVE. SHE LEARNS AS A DOG	LEARNS	. /CLEOPATRA/ WELL, THEN, I WILL LEARN AS A DOG
METH PREFACE(R23)	AGAIN. THE RACE LEARNS EXACTLY AS THE INDIVIDUAL	LEARNS	. YOUR SON RELAPSES, NOT TO THE VERY BEGINNING, BUT
DOCT PREFACE(50)	US A GOOD DEAL MORE: FOR INSTANCE, A CUTTHROAT	LEARNS	(AND PERHAPS TEACHES) THE ANATOMY OF THE CAROTID
DOCT I (101)	THE BEDSIDE WITH ME; HE SEES WHAT I SEE. BUT HE	LEARNS	NOTHING FROM IT. WHY? BECAUSE HE'S NOT A SCIENTIFIC
METH PREFACE(R49)	TIME THE LIZARD SPRINGS, THUS SHEWING THAT IT	LEARNS	NOTHING FROM EXPERIENCE, AND-- WEISMANN CONCLUDES--
CLEO IV (167)	/CLEOPATRA/ WELL, THEN, I WILL LEARN AS A DOG	LEARNS	; FOR SHE PLAYS BETTER THAN YOU. YOU SHALL GIVE ME A
BULL PREFACE(35)	HIM, GETS BULLIED AND DRIVEN BY HIM, AND FINALLY	LEARNS	SYMPATHY WITH NATIONALIST AIMS BY HER EXPERIENCE OF
DOCT PREFACE(61)	FROM THE LAITY. IN THE MAIN, THEN, THE DOCTOR	LEARNS	THAT IF HE GETS AHEAD OF THE SUPERSTITIONS OF HIS
DOCT PREFACE(31)	TO FIND, EVERY SAVAGE CHIEF WHO IS NOT A MAHOMET	LEARNS	THAT IF HE WISHES TO STRIKE THE IMAGINATION OF HIS.
METH PREFACE(R74)	THAT THESE STORIES CANNOT BE LITERALLY TRUE, AND	LEARNS	THAT NO CANDID PRELATE NOW PRETENDS TO BELIEVE THEM,
JOAN 6 (142)	I KNOW WHAT THE EARL OF WARWICK WILL DO WHEN HE	LEARNS	THAT YOU INTEND TO BETRAY HIM. THERE ARE EIGHT
BULL I (83)	AND DEGRADING HIMSELF AND HIS COUNTRY, HE SOON	LEARNS	THE ANTICS THAT TAKE YOU IN. HE PICKS THEM UP AT THE
APPL II (258)	(DESISTING) HER MAJESTY WILL EXCUSE ME WHEN SHE	LEARNS	THE NATURE OF MY ERRAND HERE. THIS, KING MAGNUS, IS A
METH PREFACE(R15)	IF POSSIBLE SUPERLATIVELY WELL. IN THE ARMY HE	LEARNS	TO FLY; TO DROP BOMBS; TO USE MACHINE-GUNS TO THE
KING II (225)	AND THE BRAINS THAT ARE DIFFERENT. IN THE END ONE	LEARNS	TO LEAVE THE BODY OUT, AND THEN BARBARA IS PACKED OFF
BULL PREFACE(46)	FOOT BY A BARBAROUS SLAVE CODE. THUS THE OFFICER	LEARNS	TO PUNISH, BUT NEVER TO RULE; AND WHEN AN EMERGENCY
METH PREFACE(R15)	IS TAUGHT TO HONOR PARASITIC IDLENESS AND LUXURY,	LEARNS	TO SHOOT AND RIDE AND KEEP FIT WITH ALL THE
NEVR III (271)	HE HAS TO THROW IT AWAY MANY TIMES BEFORE HE	LEARNS	WHAT IS REALLY WORTHY OF IT. /MRS CLANDON/ ANOTHER OF

LEARNT

LION PREFACE(39)	HIM " HOW KNOWETH THIS MAN LETTERS, HAVING NEVER	LEARNT	? " JOHN THE IMMORTAL EYE-WITNESS. JOHN, MOREOVER,
HART II (95)	HIS HEAD AWAY; FOR HIS EYES ARE WET) I HAVE	LEARNT	A GOOD DEAL ABOUT MYSELF FROM YOU, MRS HUSHABYE; AND
GENV IV (102)	AS GREAT ACTORS. THE ARMY WAS A SCHOOL IN WHICH I	LEARNT	A GOOD DEAL, BECAUSE WHOEVER HAS MY CAPACITY FOR
2TRU I (38)	THEM ACCORDINGLY. I KEPT MY EYES OPEN THERE, AND	LEARNT	A LITTLE OF THE GAME. (SHE TAKES A PAPER PACKET FROM
ROCK II (272)	HE IS THE ONLY POLITICIAN I EVER MET WHO HAD	LEARNT	ANYTHING FROM EXPERIENCE (HE GOES OUT). /BASHAM/ (
ROCK I (219)	NO USE, SRARTHUR. THAT GAME IS UP. THAT STUFF YOU	LEARNT	AT COLLEGE, THAT GAVE YOU SUCH CONFIDENCE IN
KING II (230)	YOU. /CHARLES/ LET HIM. THERE IS NOTHING TO BE	LEARNT	AT COURT EXCEPT THAT A COURTIER'S LIFE IS NOT A HAPPY
BULL IV (153)	OF YOUR BRAIN KNOW WHAT THE LEFT SIDE DOETH. I	LEARNT	AT OXFORD THAT THIS IS THE SECRET OF THE ENGLISHMAN'S
MILL PREFACE(115)	HE STILL MADE ALL THE TEXTBOOK MOVES HE HAD	LEARNT	AT THE MILITARY ACADEMY, AND DID NOT KNOW WHEN HE WAS
MIS. PREFACE(52)	INDEED IT IS WORSE; FOR THE CONVICT, HAVING	LEARNT	BEFORE HIS CONVICTION HOW TO LIVE AT LARGE, MAY
SUPR HANDBOK(186)	FRANCE NAPOLEON, OR ROME JULIUS CAESAR, CROMWELL	LEARNT	BY BITTER EXPERIENCE THAT GOD HIMSELF CANNOT RAISE A
BARB I SD(263)	GENTLENESS IS PARTLY THAT OF A STRONG MAN WHO HAS	LEARNT	BY EXPERIENCE THAT HIS NATURAL GRIP HURTS ORDINARY
BULL PREFACE(46)	IN SPITE OF THE MESSROOM. THIS, UNFORTUNATELY, IS	LEARNT	BY THE PUBLIC, NOT ON THE SPOT, BUT FROM LORD ROBERTS
MIS. (161)	EVERYTHING FROM BOOKS? /TARLETON/ WELL, HAVE YOU	LEARNT	EVERYTHING FROM THE FLYING TRAPEZE? /LINA/ ON THE
MIS. (161)	FOR YOU. READ THE MASTER BUILDER. /LINA/ HAVE YOU	LEARNT	EVERYTHING FROM BOOKS? /TARLETON/ WELL, HAVE YOU
GETT (339)	WHEN I AM BEING BELITTLED. IT WAS FROM YOU THAT I	LEARNT	FIRST TO RESPECT MYSELF. IT WAS THROUGH YOU THAT I
SUPR III (133)	JUAN/ BY NO MEANS. BUT THOUGH THERE IS MUCH TO BE	LEARNT	FROM A CYNICAL DEVIL, I REALLY CANNOT STAND A
BULL PREFACE(69)	OF POLITICAL POWER OR WEALTH. NOTHING WAS	LEARNT	FROM DENSHAWAI OR THE BLACK AND TAN TERROR. IN INDIA,
2TRU PREFACE(24)	THE WORST, I AM AN ECLECTIC: THERE IS MUCH TO BE	LEARNT	FROM EACH. I HARP ON RUSSIA BECAUSE THE MOSCOW
MILL PREFACE(118)	VANISHED. THE LATER PARLIAMENTARY LEADERS SOON	LEARNT	FROM EXPERIENCE THAT THEY MIGHT WITH PERFECT IMPUNITY
JITT III (58)	/AGNES/ STUFF! I KNOW THE VARIETY OF SLEEP HE	LEARNT	FROM HER. (LOOKING AT HIM QUEERLY) WHY DO YOU WANT
DOCT PREFACE(47)	FOR THE SAKE OF THE GREAT DEAL THAT CAN BE	LEARNT	FROM HIM? AT ALL EVENTS, HE IS SACRIFICED, AS THIS
CAPT NOTES (302)	GRAHAM THAN IN A THOUSAND CHRISTIANS, MAY BE	LEARNT	FROM HIS ACCOUNT OF IT IN MOGREB-EL-ACKSA, WITHOUT
DOCT PREFACE(47)	FOR THE SAKE OF THE VERY LITTLE THAT CAN BE	LEARNT	FROM IT, SHALL NOT A MAN BE SACRIFICED FOR THE SAKE
GETT PREFACE(251)	TOUCHED BY ANY PERSON BUT THE PROPRIETOR, MAY BE	LEARNT	FROM SHAKESPEAR. HIS MOST INFATUATED AND PASSIONATE
MTH4 I (164)	THAT, AT LEAST YOU MUST ADMIT THAT I HAVE	LEARNT	FROM TERTIARIES. I HAVE SEEN THEIR WORK AND LIVED
BARB PREFACE(242)	ASSASSINATED IF THEY BETRAYED HIM: ANOTHER METHOD	LEARNT	FROM THE OFFICIAL GOVERNMENT, GIVEN A TRIBUNAL,
SUPR III (104)	STUPIDITY MADE SORDID AND CRUEL BY THE REALITIES	LEARNT	FROM TOIL AND POVERTY: IMAGINATION RESOLVED TO STARVE
DOCT PREFACE(31)	PROFESSING IN LETTERS TO THE NEWSPAPERS TO HAVE	LEARNT	FROM VIVISECTION HOW TO CURE CERTAIN DISEASES, AND
PHIL III (139)	I REMEMBER HOW I HAVE LOVED YOU. OH, WHAT I HAVE	LEARNT	FROM YOU! FROM YOU! WHO COULD LEARN NOTHING FROM
MIS. PREFACE(58)	OF OBSOLETE ACQUIREMENTS, AND THEY WILL NEVER BE	LEARNT	FRUITFULLY BY PEOPLE WHO DO NOT WANT TO LEARN THEM.
BUOY II (22)	BE A VEGETARIAN, I AM. /SHE/ SO AM I. BUT I HAVE	LEARNT	HERE THAT IF WE VEGETARIANS DO NOT KILL ANIMALS THE
SIM II (81)	PEOPLE WHO ARE LISTENING TO US WILL. WHAT WE HAVE	LEARNT	HERE TODAY IS THAT THE DAY OF JUDGMENT IS NOT THE END
GENV PREFACE(20)	WHAT YOU PLEASE). LIKE LOUIS NAPOLEON HE HAD NOW	LEARNT	HIS LESSON: NAMELY, THAT PUTSCHES ARE A LAST
ROCK II (267)	KARL MARX THOUGHT IT ALL OUT IN BLOOMSBURY. LENIN	LEARNT	HIS LESSON IN HOLFORD SQUARE, ISLINGTON. WHY CAN WE
DOCT I (107)	BEHAVE YOURSELF, EMMY. GET OUT. /EMMY/ OH, I	LEARNT	HOW TO BEHAVE MYSELF BEFORE I LEARNT YOU TO DO IT. I
NEVR III (268)	GAME JUST AS HE HAD BEATEN HER AT THE OLD GAME. I	LEARNT	HOW TO CIRCUMVENT THE WOMEN'S RIGHTS WOMAN BEFORE I
MTH1 I (7)	DEATH IS NOT AN UNHAPPY THING WHEN YOU HAVE	LEARNT	HOW TO CONQUER IT. /EVE/ HOW CAN I CONQUER IT? /THE
GENV IV (129)	WHAT THIS MEANS TO ME, BECAUSE NONE OF YOU HAS	LEARNT	HOW TO LIVE. YOU ARE SOULS IN TORMENT, AS I WAS UNTIL
SUPR HANDBOK(191)	BEFORE THE DEMAGOGUES AND ELECTORATES HAVE	LEARNT	HOW TO MANAGE EVEN A COUNTRY PARISH PROPERLY MUCH
KING II (229)	DOZEN. IT MAY END THAT WAY, BUT NOT UNTIL WE HAVE	LEARNT	HOW TO PICK THE PEOPLE WHO ARE FIT TO BE CHOSEN
BUOY II (20)	WHEN I TRIED TO BE HAPPY WITH MEN LIKE YOU, I	LEARNT	HOW TO PLAY THE SOPRANO SAXOPHONE. I HAVE THE
PHIL II (125)	BECAUSE I WILL NOT GIVE MYSELF TO ANY MAN WHO HAS	LEARNT	HOW TO TREAT WOMEN FROM YOU AND YOUR LIKE. I CAN DO
VWOO 3 (134)	LEARNT MORE IN THREE MONTHS IN THIS SHOP THAN I	LEARNT	IN THREE YEARS IN OXFORD. /Z/ I CANT BELIEVE THAT
BUOY III (34)	SHE CAN SWEEP AND SCRUB. SHE CAN NURSE. SHE	LEARNT	IT ALL BEFORE SHE WAS TEN, AND WAS SENT TO A LADIES'
PYGM II (231)	THE SAME LETTER AS BATH. SHE KNOWS NO BETTER: SHE	LEARNT	IT AT HER MOTHER'S KNEE. BUT SHE MUST NOT HEAR IT
MTH4 III (200)	IT WON US THE ELECTION. /THE ENVOY'S DAUGHTER/ I	LEARNT	IT AT SCHOOL, GRANPA. IT WASNT THE SAME AT ALL. I CAN
FABL PREFACE(72)	FIVE THE CHURCH CATECHISM IS ONLY A PARADIGM: I	LEARNT	IT AT THAT AGE AND STILL REMEMBER ITS PHRASES; BUT IT

SUPR II (52)	ABOUT ANN. /TANNER/ STRAKER KNEW EVEN THAT. HE	LEARNT	IT AT THE POLYTECHNIC, PROBABLY. WELL, WHAT ABOUT
SUPR III (124)	DID YOU COME TO THINK OF THIS ONE? /DON JUAN/ I	LEARNT	IT BY EXPERIENCE. WHEN I WAS ON EARTH, AND MADE THOSE
BARB PREFACE(225)	BARBARA'S LESSON BECAUSE THEY HAVE NOT, LIKE HER,	LEARNT	IT BY TAKING THEIR PART IN THE LARGER LIFE OF THE
FANY III (301)	IT FROM A FRENCHWOMAN? YOU KNOW YOU MUST HAVE	LEARNT	IT FROM SOMEBODY. /BOBBY/ NOT A FRENCHWOMAN. SHE'S
PHIL II (125)	HATRED) YOU LEARNT THIS FROM HIM. /GRACE/ I	LEARNT	IT FROM YOURSELF, LAST NIGHT AND NOW. HOW I HATE TO
FANY II (288)	(HE SPEAKS ENGLISH BETTER THAN KNOX, HAVING	LEARNT	IT ON BOTH SIDES OF THE ATLANTIC). /KNOX/ IF IVE MADE
GENV IV (113)	NOT MATTER. THERE IS A TECHNIQUE YOU HAVE NOT	LEARNT	. /SIR O./ WHAT! MORE TECHNIQUES! MADAM: BEFORE
GETT PREFACE(242)	YET REPRESENTS THE ONLY HABIT OF LIFE HE HAS	LEARNT	. TAKING ALL THESE CASES AS REPRESENTING A BACHELOR
BASH PREFACE(89)	THEY MAY HAVE BEEN THE SEEDIEST OF BOHEMIANS, HAD	LEARNT	LATIN GRAMMAR AND READ BOOKS WRITTEN BY PERSONS
MIS. PREFACE(39)	THERE IS A TENDENCY TO KEEP REPEATING THE ALREADY	LEARNT	LESSON RATHER THAN BREAK NEW GROUND. AT SCHOOL I
VWOO 3 (134)	SUPERIOR TO THE MARCO POLO MAN, AND THAT I HAVE	LEARNT	MORE IN THREE MONTHS IN THIS SHOP THAN I LEARNT IN
O'FL (211)	THEM THAT OUGHT TO HAVE BEEN THEIR BETTERS? IVE	LEARNT	MORE THAN YOUD THINK, SIR; FOR HOW WOULD A GENTLEMAN
BUOY III (31)	IS SOMETHING TO BE SAID FOR HIS PLAN. HE HAS	LEARNT	MUCH ABOUT DOCTORS AND SOLICITORS BY IT. /SECONDBORN/
PYGM V (279)	YOU? /LIZA/ NO: NOT NOW. NEVER AGAIN. I HAVE	LEARNT	MY LESSON. I DONT BELIEVE I COULD UTTER ONE OF THE
2TRU III (93)	THUNDERSTRUCK) YOUR MOTHER! ! ! /AUBREY/ SO I	LEARNT	MY LESSON. SIX DAYS ON THE MAKE, AND ON THE SEVENTH
MIS. PREFACE(21)	GIVE THEM THE NECESSARY CANING POWERS) WHETHER I	LEARNT	MY LESSONS OR NOT, PROVIDED MY FATHER PAID MY
JOAN 5 (112)	WHILE THE GODDAMS TOOK WAR SERIOUSLY, BUT I HAVE	LEARNT	MY LESSON, AND TAKEN THEIR MEASURE. THEY HAVE NO
VWOO 3 (138)	TAKE A MORE CHEERFUL VIEW OF LIFE? /A/ I HAVE	LEARNT	NOT TO EXPECT TOO MUCH FROM LIFE. THAT IS THE SECRET
KING I (199)	THIRTYSIX YEARS AGO. DO YOU SUPPOSE I HAVE	LEARNT	NOTHING ABOUT WOMEN AND WHAT YOU CALL LOVE IN THAT
MTH2 (51)	OF DATE EVEN IN PARTY POLITICS? THAT THEY HAVE	LEARNT	NOTHING AND FORGOTTEN NOTHING SINCE 1885? WHAT IS IT
SUPR HANDBOK(201)	BLAMED FOR A UNIVERSAL CHARACTERISTIC, HAD	LEARNT	NOTHING AND FORGOTTEN NOTHING. WE HAD HARDLY
MIS. PREFACE(23)	I HAD FORGOTTEN WHAT HE HAD TAUGHT ME, AND HAD	LEARNT	NOTHING ELSE. TO THIS DAY, THOUGH I CAN STILL DECLINE
MTH1 II (21)	AND AN HOUR'S AMUSING PLAY WITH THE FIRE. YOU	LEARNT	NOTHING FROM HIM; YOU DRUDGED AND DRUDGED AND
METH PREFACE(R26)	WELL HAVE EXCLAIMED " GOOD HEAVENS! HAVE YOU	LEARNT	NOTHING FROM OUR EXPERIENCE THAT YOU COME INTO THE
FANY III SD(297)	IS WHAT THEY CALL " BRINGING UP." HE HAS	LEARNT	NOTHING FROM IT EXCEPT A HABIT OF EVADING IT BY
NEVR III (269)	MY PRIDE! MY PRIDE! ! OH, IT'S GONE: I HAVE	LEARNT	NOW THAT I HAVE NO STRENGTH TO BE PROUD OF. (TURNING
DOCT PREFACE(15)	HIS SELF-RESPECT IS BY FORGETTING ALL HE EVER	LEARNT	OF SCIENCE, AND CLINGING TO SUCH HELP AS HE CAN GIVE
SHAK PREFACE(135)	BY MR LANCHESTER'S IMMEDIATE APPROVAL. I HAVE	LEARNT	PART OF MY CRAFT AS CONDUCTOR OF REHEARSALS (
PYGM V (277)	EVERYBODY WITH MONEY. BUT IT WAS FROM YOU THAT I	LEARNT	REALLY NICE MANNERS; AND THAT IS WHAT MAKES ONE A
PYGM V (283)	(HE SITS DOWN NEAR HER ON THE OTTOMAN). I HAVE	LEARNT	SOMETHING FROM YOUR IDIOTIC NOTIONS: I CONFESS THAT
BULL I (89)	DONT APOLOGIZE: IT'S QUITE TRUE. I DARESAY IVE	LEARNT	SOMETHING IN AMERICA AND A FEW OTHER REMOTE AND
BARB III (325)	MY SPIRIT IS TROUBLED. /UNDERSHAFT/ YOU HAVE	LEARNT	SOMETHING. THAT ALWAYS FEELS AT FIRST AS IF YOU HAD
GENV PREFACE(18)	OF WHAT HE SPOUTED WAS TRUE. AS A SOLDIER HE HAD	LEARNT	THAT DISCIPLINED MEN CAN MAKE SHORT WORK OF MOBS;
GETT (320)	OUT AND REPLACED BY THE COMMUNION OF SAINTS. I	LEARNT	THAT FROM EVERY MARRIAGE SETTLEMENT I DREW UP AS A
2TRU III (93)	SHALL BE ABLE TO AFFORD THE LUXURY OF HONESTY. I	LEARNT	THAT FROM MY RELIGIOUS EDUCATION. /THE ELDER/ HOW
SIM PREFACE(12)	A MISTAKE: ITS FIRST. HE INSTANTLY SHOT IT. I	LEARNT	THAT HE ALWAYS SHOT HIS SPORTING DOGS WHEN THEY WERE
FOUN (220)	SWEEPER WHO WAS RUN OVER; BUT WHEN ITS AUNT	LEARNT	THAT I HAD NO PARENTS SHE WOULD NOT PERMIT IT TO
MTH3 (134)	IT WAS NOT WORTH BOTHERING ABOUT. BUT I HAVE JUST	LEARNT	THAT I MAY LIVE-- WELL, MUCH LONGER THAN I EXPECTED.
MRS PREFACE(154)	AT THEM IF THEY DID. SO WELL HAVE THE RESCUERS	LEARNT	THAT MRS WARREN'S DEFENCE OF HERSELF AND INDICTMENT
KING II (227)	FROM THE BATTLE OF WORCESTER? AND WHEN I HAD	LEARNT	THAT MUCH THERE WAS AN END OF ME AS A KING. I KNEW
BULL PREFACE(43)	CALL HIM FOOL, SOLELY BECAUSE WE HAVE	LEARNT	THAT NATIONS INSIST ON BEING GOVERNED BY THEIR OWN
ANNA (301)	GRAND DUCHESS/ OH, I WAS TRAINED TO THAT. I HAD	LEARNT	THAT PART OF THE BUSINESS AT COURT. /STRAMMFEST/ YOU
MTH3 (119)	VERY HEART. SOME YEARS AFTER MY FIRST DROWNING I	LEARNT	THAT SHE HAD LOST HER SIGHT. I WENT TO HER. SHE WAS
GLIM (182)	OF THE NOBILITY, SIGNOR, ARE NOT STRICT ENOUGH. I	LEARNT	THAT WHEN I TOOK TO BREEDING HORSES, THE HORSES YOU
ARMS II (27)	PEOPLE NEVER SHOUT FOR THEIR SERVANTS. IVE	LEARNT	THAT WHILE YOU WERE AWAY. /PETKOFF/ WELL, I'LL TELL
SUPR IV (145)	MAN: I MADE HIM TALK ON PURPOSE. BY DOING SO I	LEARNT	THAT YOURE STAYIN HERE IN GRANNIDA WITH A PARTY OF
METH PREFACE(R28)	NEW SYSTEMS OF THEIR OWN AS EASILY AS THEY	LEARNT	THE ALPHABET. THESE CONTRASTS ARE TO BE SEEN ON ALL
DOCT PREFACE(26)	OF THE PATIENT. BUT THOUGH A FEW DOCTORS HAVE NOW	LEARNT	THE DANGER OF INOCULATING WITHOUT ANY REFERENCE TO
DOCT III (144)	/SIR PATRICK/ I ASSURE YOU, YOUNG MAN, MY FATHER	LEARNT	THE DOCTRINE OF DELIVERANCE FROM SIN FROM JOHN
BARB III (331)	! /LOMAX/ OH I SAY! ! ! /CUSINS/ WHEN I	LEARNT	THE HORRIBLE TRUTH-- /LADY BRITOMART/ WHAT DO YOU
FANY III (305)	BLOKES AND ALL THAT-- WELL! /MARGARET/ OH, IVE	LEARNT	THE LANGUAGE; AND I LIKE IT. IT'S ANOTHER BARRIER
JOAN 5 (117)	ALL THAT. I DO NOT FIGHT IN THE OLD WAY: I HAVE	LEARNT	THE LESSON OF AGINCOURT, OF POITIERS AND CRECY. I
SIM PREFACE(11)	INTENTIONED AMATEURS, NO DOUBT FELL BEFORE IT HAD	LEARNT	THE LIMITS OF ITS BUSINESS BY EXPERIENCE. MY OBJECT
BULL I (83)	UP AT THE THEATRE OR THE MUSIC HALL. HAFFIGAN	LEARNT	THE RUDIMENTS FROM HIS FATHER, WHO CAME FROM MY PART
APPL I (228)	MR PROTEUS. /PROTEUS/ I KNOW WHEN TO BE FRANK. I	LEARNT	THE TRICK FROM YOUR MAJESTY. /AMANDA/ (TRIES NOT TO
LION PREFACE(9)	YOU HEARD THE GOSPEL STORIES READ IN CHURCH, OR	LEARNT	THEM FROM PAINTERS AND POETS, YOU CAME OUT WITH AN
MIS. PREFACE(57)	HE WAS LAYING ON HIS RACE. FOR MEN AND WOMEN	LEARNT	THEREBY TO ENSLAVE AND BREAK IN THEIR CHILDREN BY THE
PHIL II (125)	TO YOU. /JULIA/ (WITH UNCONCEALED HATRED) YOU	LEARNT	THIS FROM HIM. /GRACE/ I LEARNT IT FROM YOURSELF,
MTH3 (131)	HAS ALWAYS BEEN A PUZZLE TO ME. EVER SINCE I	LEARNT	TO DISTINGUISH BETWEEN ONE ENGLISH FACE AND ANOTHER I
NEVR II (228)	LIBERTY AND THE RIGHTS OF THE INDIVIDUAL, AS I	LEARNT	TO DO FROM MY MASTER HERBERT SPENCER. AM I HOWLED
BUOY III (29)	IS TRUE. SO MUCH HAS BEEN DONE FOR US WE HAVE	LEARNT	TO DO HARDLY ANYTHING FOR OURSELVES. I AM A BIT OF A
BARB PREFACE(244)	STUDENT CAN MAKE, AND EVERY RUSSIAN GRENADIER HAS	LEARNT	TO HANDLE IN MANCHURIA, LIES IN THE FACT THAT BRAVE
MIS. (113)	AND I'D HAVE TRIED IT ON YOU UNTIL YOU FIRST	LEARNT	TO HOWL AND THEN TO BEHAVE YOURSELF. /BENTLEY/ (
BULL I (89)	WORKING IN DOUBLE HARNESS WITH YOU THAT I HAVE	LEARNT	TO LIVE IN A REAL WORLD AND NOT IN AN IMAGINARY ONE.
CAND III (145)	SMILING AT EUGENE) OH, THERE IS NO FEAR. HE HAS	LEARNT	TO LIVE WITHOUT HAPPINESS. /MARCHBANKS/ I NO LONGER
GENV IV (129)	AGO. AND NOW I MUST DIE WHEN I HAVE ONLY JUST	LEARNT	TO LIVE. EXCUSE ME: I CANNOT BEAR TO SPEAK OF IT (
NEVR III (278)	FROM HER INTELLECT TO YOUR HEART. /GLORIA/ I HAVE	LEARNT	TO MISTRUST MY HEART. (WITH AN ANGRY GLANCE AT
3PLA PREFACE(R33)	A PARTICULAR BREED OF PIGEONS IF THEY HAD NEVER	LEARNT	TO READ. HIS GENUINE CRITICS, FROM BEN JOHNSON TO MR
BULL PREFACE(10)	OF HIS OWN NATIVE SOIL TO HIM, AND THUS	LEARNT	TO REGARD THAT FEELING IN OTHER MEN AS SOMETHING HOLY
LION I (120)	SHOULDERS WITH PATERNAL WEIGHT). BUT NOW I HAVE	LEARNT	TO RESIST WITH A STRENGTH THAT IS NOT MY OWN. I AM
MTH1 I (12)	RUNNING TO HIM) ONLY THINK, ADAM! OUR SNAKE HAS	LEARNT	TO SPEAK BY LISTENING TO US. /ADAM/ (DELIGHTED) IS
APPL II (257)	YOU SURE? WHEN ROBERT ASKED BOANERGES WHERE HE	LEARNT	TO SPEAK SO BEAUTIFULLY, HE SAID " IN HYDE PARK."
SUPR III (91)	WE SEE EACH OTHER AS BODIES ONLY BECAUSE WE	LEARNT	TO THINK ABOUT ONE ANOTHER UNDER THAT ASPECT WHEN WE
BULL PREFACE(70)	COULD HAVE DEFENDED; FOR HE HAS NOT YET	LEARNT	TO THINK OF OFFENCE AND DEFENCE IN TERMS OF AIRPLANES
UNPL PREFACE(R17)	A PLAY BY AN AUTHOR WHOSE WORK THEY HAVE ALREADY	LEARNT	TO VALUE AS LITERATURE, OR A PERFORMANCE BY AN ACTOR
CYMB V (148)	FEAR NOT, GREAT SIR: WE TWO HAVE NEVER	LEARNT	TO WAIT FOR DEAD MEN'S SHOES, MUCH LESS THEIR CROWNS.
DOCT I SD(81)	AN OLD FAMILY NURSE TO A CHILD JUST AFTER IT HAS	LEARNT	TO WALK. SHE HAS USED HER UGLINESS TO SECURE
ROCK I (231)	NO, OF COURSE NOT. YOU DONT UNDERSTAND. WE	LEARNT	TO WRITE LATIN VERSES NOT BECAUSE THE VERSES ARE ANY
ARMS II (27)	AWAY. /PETKOFF/ WELL, I'LL TELL YOU SOMETHING IVE	LEARNT	TOO. CIVILIZED PEOPLE DONT HANG OUT THEIR WASHING TO
BUOY II (20)	YOUR OWN SHACK. I HAVE BEEN THROUGH ALL THAT, AND	LEARNT	WHAT A HELPLESS CREATURE A CIVILIZED WOMAN IS. /HE/
MIS. PREFACE(100)	SYNCOPATED RHYTHMS ARE NEW TO THEM. IF THEY HAD	LEARNT	WHAT CAN BE DONE WITH SYNCOPATION FROM BEETHOVEN'S
KING II (227)	AND WHAT MORE HAD I TO TEACH YOU EXCEPT WHAT I	LEARNT	WHEN I WAS RUNNING AWAY FROM THE BATTLE OF
BASH II,1, (100)	EXIT BASHVILLE.) /LUCIAN/ SOME WET! ! ! WHERE	LEARNT	YOU THAT ATROCIOUS WORD? THIS IS THE LANGUAGE OF A
DOCT I (107)	/EMMY/ OH, I LEARNT HOW TO BEHAVE MYSELF BEFORE I	LEARNT	YOU TO DO IT. I KNOW WHAT DOCTORS ARE: SITTING
MIS. (131)	TO DO HERE. YOU HAVE A GENIUS FOR GOVERNMENT. YOU	LEARNT	YOUR JOB OUT THERE IN JINGHISKAHN. WELL, WE WANT TO
6CAL (103)	AH-OOH-OH-OW! /THE KING/ WELL? HAVE YOU	LEARNT	YOUR LESSON? ARE YOU READY TO SUE FOR THE QUEEN'S
NEVR II (241)	TABLE, AND BEGINS SLICING IT. /CRAMPTON/ YOU HAVE	LEARNT	YOUR LESSON FROM YOUR MOTHER, I SEE. /MRS CLANDON/
NEVR II (242)	TO BE A REALLY SMART WAITER? /WAITER/ CANT BE	LEARNT	, SIR. IT'S IN THE CHARACTER, SIR. (CONFIDENTIALLY
DEVL III (69)	WITH DESPAIR IN HIS FACE AND VOICE) I HAVE JUST	LEARNT	, SIR, THAT GENERAL HOWE IS STILL IN NEW YORK.
		LEARS	
SUPR PREFACE(R33)	HE KNOWS OF HIMSELF, HIS HAMLETS AND MACBETHS AND	LEARS	AND PROSPEROS. IF THESE CHARACTERS ARE AGONIZING IN A
		LEASE	
MTH2 (76)	WHEN ADAM HAD THE GARDEN OF EDEN ON A	LEASE	FOR EVER, HE TOOK CARE TO MAKE IT WHAT THE HOUSE
POSN PREFACE(363)	BEFORE PERFORMING A PLAY; BUT EVERY THEATRE	LEASE	IS IN FUTURE TO BE CONSTRUED AS IF IT CONTAINED A
BULL III (121)	TO HURT POOR CORNY? IT WAS HE THAT GOT MATT THE	LEASE	OF HIS FARM, AND STOOD UP FOR HIM AS AN INDUSTRIOUS
ROCK PREFACE(163)	AND MURDER HIS MOTHER-IN-LAW, THEREBY SECURING A	LEASE	OF LIFE FOR AT LEAST FOUR YEARS. SOONER OR LATER THIS
LION PREFACE(76)	UPWARDS IN HIS OWN WAY, AND THEREBY GAVE A NEW	LEASE	OF LIFE TO THE ERRORS IT WAS JUST OUTGROWING, SO PAUL
WIDO III (64)	STEPPIN INTO THE STUDY TO ARRANGE ABOUT THE	LEASE	TO THE NORTH THAMES ICED MUTTON COMPANY? /TRENCH/ OH,
BULL III (141)	WAS CHACKED AHT OF IT ON IS ED AT THE END OF IS	LEASE	WITHAHT A PENNY FOR HIS GOODWILL. YOU TALK OF
MTH2 (76)	TRUE. IF YOU TAKE A HOUSE ON A NINETY-NINE YEARS	LEASE	, YOU SPEND A GOOD DEAL OF MONEY ON IT. IF YOU TAKE IT
		LEASH	
APPL I (235)	AS SINCERELY AS I, BUT WHICH IN YOU IS HELD IN	LEASH	BY THE PRESS, WHICH CAN ORGANIZE AGAINST YOU THE
MIS. SD(115)	STILLNESS, BOUNDLESS ENERGY AND AUDACITY HELD IN	LEASH	. /HYPATIA/ (POUNCING ON BENTLEY WITH NO VERY GENTLE
DOCT PREFACE(45)	DOES NOT HUNT MEN; AND THE SPORTSMAN WHO LETS A	LEASH	OF GREYHOUNDS LOOSE ON A HARE WOULD BE HORRIFIED AT

LEAST

BARB I (252)	AS THEY ARE SECOND RATE. NO: BARBARA WILL NEED AT	LEAST	2000 POUNDS A YEAR. YOU SEE IT MEANS TWO ADDITIONAL
GETT PREFACE(256)	FOR ITS OWN SAKE AND THAT OF HUMANITY, COSTS AT	LEAST	30 POUNDS OUT-OF-POCKET EXPENSES, TO A CLIENT ON
METH PREFACE(R20)	WENT THEN, DID NOT PERPLEX MY INFANT MIND IN THE	LEAST	: I KNEW PERFECTLY WELL, WITHOUT KNOWING THAT I KNEW
HART III (142)	WITH CONFUSION. BUT HERE, I DONT MIND IN THE	LEAST	: IT SEEMS QUITE NATURAL. /LADY UTTERWORD/ AN
SUPR IV (167)	OF THE LIFE FORCE. /ANN/ I DONT UNDERSTAND IN THE	LEAST	: IT SOUNDS LIKE THE LIFE GUARDS. /TANNER/ WHY DONT
JITT II (29)	BUT A MAN OF SCIENCE! UNFORTUNATE, TO SAY THE	LEAST	: MOST UNFORTUNATE. /FESSLER/ AT ALL EVENTS, SINCE IT
DOCT II SD(117)	OF COURSE, THE DOCTORS DO NOT PUT HIM OUT IN THE	LEAST	: NEITHER SIR PATRICK'S YEARS NOR BLOOMFIELD
BULL PREFACE(66)	FOR FOREIGN AFFAIRS WAS NOT SHAKEN IN THE	LEAST	: THE EULOGIES WHICH WERE HEAPED ON HIM BY BOTH
INCA (241)	IS OCCUPIED. AT LEAST -- /ERMYNTRUDE/ WELL? AT	LEAST	? /THE MANAGER/ IT IS OCCUPIED. /ERMYNTRUDE/ DONT YOU
6CAL PREFACE(91)	AND PILL WAS A GOOD LIFE" IF THE ROBBER WAS AT	LEAST	A BARON. HE MADE A VERY POOR JOB OF IT IN MY OPINION.
GETT PREFACE(209)	AS MORE VALUABLE THAN MALE LIVES, IS NOT IN THE	LEAST	A CHIVALROUS REASON, THOUGH MEN MAY CONSENT TO IT
HART I (69)	FAMILY? /MANGAN/ NO. /THE GENTLEMAN/ I AM, AT	LEAST	A CONNEXION. MRS HUSHABYE COMES BACK. /MRS HUSHABYE/
2TRU II (53)	WITH ALL THESE ACCOMPLISHMENTS, ARE YOU NOT AT	LEAST	A CORPORAL? /MEEK/ NOT EDUCATIONALLY QUALIFIED, SIR.
MIS. PREFACE(37)	A LIVING BY HIS OR HER OWN EXERTIONS FOR AT	LEAST	A COUPLE OF YEARS, THEIR EFFECT WOULD BE VASTLY
HART PREFACE(5)	BIOLOGISTS AND EVEN ECONOMISTS, WITHOUT AT	LEAST	A FEW PLAYS BY MYSELF AND MR GRANVILLE BARKER, AND A
AUGS (277)	WAR. NO: BLUELOO WOULD NOT GO THAT FAR. HE IS AT	LEAST	A GENTLEMAN, BUT I SHOULD BE CHAFFED; AND FRANKLY, I
PPP PREFACE(192)	MANY PEOPLE. THE ORCHESTRA SHOULD CONSIST OF AT	LEAST	A HARP, A DRUM, AND A PAIR OF CYMBALS, THESE
MTH4 I (141)	/THE WOMAN/ (SMILING GRAVELY) IT MUST BE AT	LEAST	A HUNDRED AND FIFTY YEARS SINCE I LAST LAUGHED. BUT IF
BULL PREFACE(16)	ITS SCOTS TODAY, BECAUSE IT CANNOT DO WITHOUT AT	LEAST	A LITTLE SANITY, THE PROTESTANT GARRISON. THE MORE
WIDO I (18)	OF QUESTION YOU CANT VERY WELL PUT TO A MAN-- AT	LEAST	A MAN LIKE HIM. DO YOU THINK YOU COULD WORD THE LETTER
HART III (130)	I SAID HASTINGS SAID IT; AND HE IS NOT IN THE	LEAST	A NUMSKULL. /CAPTAIN SHOTOVER/ WHATS WRONG WITH MY
MILL I (158)	DROWN TEN THOUSAND BULLS; BUT YOU ARE ALWAYS AT	LEAST	A QUARTER TONE SHARP OR FLAT AS THE CASE MAY BE. I
MIS. (169)	STYLE, I SHOULD THINK YOU MUST SPEND AT	LEAST	A SHILLING A WEEK ON ROMANTIC LITERATURE. /THE MAN/
GENV PREFACE(26)	NINETEENTH CENTURY, IT IS IMPOSSIBLE TO RESIST AT	LEAST	A STRONG SUSPICION THAT THE TERM OF HUMAN LIFE CANNOT
MIS. PREFACE(77)	THERE ARE MASSES OF PEOPLE WHO COULD AFFORD AT	LEAST	A TRIP TO MARGATE, AND A GOOD MANY WHO COULD AFFORD A
ROCK I (230)	NEVER TRIFLE WITH THEIR GAMES. GOLF GIVES THEM AT	LEAST	A WEEKEND OF EARNEST CONCENTRATION. IT BRINGS TRUTH
BARB III (317)	OR BOARDS OF GUARDIANS; AND IF HE SHEWS THE	LEAST	ABILITY HE IS FASTENED ON BY SCHOOLMASTERS; TRAINED TO
JOAN 5 (117)	FIGHTING IS NOT WHAT IT WAS; AND THOSE WHO KNOW	LEAST	ABOUT IT OFTEN MAKE THE BEST JOB OF IT. /DUNOIS/ I
OVER PREFACE(155)	MOST SINCERELY AND FAVORABLY ABOUT POLYGAMY KNOW	LEAST	ABOUT IT; AND THE PRACTITIONERS WHO KNOW MOST ABOUT IT
POSN PREFACE(415)	PARADOX WHEN I SAID THAT THE WITNESS WHO KNEW	LEAST	ABOUT THE THEATRE WAS HENRY IRVING. YET A MOMENT'S
MTH4 II (189)	ARTICLES OF RELIGION THAT IS NOT ACCEPTED AS AT	LEAST	ALLEGORICALLY TRUE BY OUR HIGHER CRITICISM. /THE
APPL INTRLUD(252)	AT ALL EVENTS I AM NOT AFRAID OF IT; THOUGH THE	LEAST	ALLUSION TO IT BRINGS A CLOUD OVER MY WIFE'S FACE. SO
MTH2 (81)	NOT SEE IT WHEN I WAS ALMOST AN OLD MAN-- OR AT	LEAST	AN ELDERLY ONE. NOW THAT IT APPEARS THAT I AM A YOUNG
LADY (243)	ON MY ROYAL WORD! I HAD THOUGHT THIS FELLOW AT	LEAST	AN ESQUIRE; FOR I HAD HOPED THAT EVEN THE VILEST OF MY
PYGM PREFACE(200)	FIFTY YEARS HENCE, HE WAS, I BELIEVE, NOT IN THE	LEAST	AN ILLNATURED MAN: VERY MUCH THE OPPOSITE, I SHOULD
POSN PREFACE(403)	AWAY FROM THE LORD CHAMBERLAIN, WHO IS AT	LEAST	AN OFFICIAL OF THE KING'S HOUSEHOLD AND A NOMINEE OF
BARB I (251)	THAN TO INCREASE IT. SARAH WILL HAVE TO FIND AT	LEAST	ANOTHER 800 POUNDS A YEAR FOR THE NEXT TEN YEARS; AND
MTH5 (259)	THE TEMPLE). /ECRASIA/ COME, ARJILLAX: YOU AT	LEAST	ARE STILL AN ARTIST. I ADORE YOU. /ARJILLAX/ DO YOU..
GETT PREFACE(208)	THE QUONDAM FEMALES KILL ALL THE REST (SUCH AT	LEAST	ARE THE ACCOUNTS GIVEN BY ROMANTIC NATURALISTS OF THE
POSN PREFACE(401)	ACTUALLY MADE; AND IT WAS ABANDONED, NOT IN THE	LEAST	AS CONTRARY TO THE LIBERTY OF THE STAGE, BUT BECAUSE
JOAN PREFACE(55)	AND AN ALL-NIGHT SITTING IN A THEATRE WOULD BE AT	LEAST	AS ENJOYABLE AS AN ALL-NIGHT SITTING IN THE HOUSE OF
LION PREFACE(6)	HIM A PLACE IN THEIR ESTEEM AND VENERATION AT	LEAST	AS HIGH AS WE ACCORD TO JOHN THE BAPTIST. BUT THIS
LION PREFACE(60)	WORK. CONSEQUENTLY YOU WILL HAVE TO GIVE HIM AT	LEAST	AS MUCH AS THE CAPTAIN UNLESS YOU DEFINITELY WISH HIM
JOAN PREFACE(17)	ABOUT JOAN BEING CRACKED, AND ACCEPT HER AS AT	LEAST	AS SANE AS FLORENCE NIGHTINGALE, WHO ALSO COMBINED A
APPL I (234)	YEAR IT WAS DISCOVERED THAT THEY COULD GOVERN AT	LEAST	AS WELL AS ANYONE ELSE WHO COULD BE PERSUADED TO TAKE
GETT (317)	KEEP THE HOUSE, I SHALL EXPECT CECIL TO PAY ME AT	LEAST	AS WELL AS HE WOULD PAY A HIRED HOUSEKEEPER. I'LL NOT
MIS. PREFACE(37)	MUST KNOW THE WORLD OUTSIDE THE UNIVERSITY AT	LEAST	AS WELL AS THE SHOPKEEPER IN THE HIGH STREET DOES. AND
MTH5 (224)	ABSURD. BUT WHAT MEN CANNOT REALIZE THEY CAN AT	LEAST	ASPIRE TO. THEY PLEASE THEMSELVES BY PRETENDING THAT
DOCT PREFACE(70)	SOLVENCY THROUGH A MORASS OF ILLNESS, WHILST THE	LEAST	ATTEMPT AT PLAIN DEALING WITH PEOPLE WHO ARE EATING
POSN PREFACE(410)	AS THE LOCAL AUTHORITY IS CONCERNED; BUT ON THE	LEAST	ATTEMPT ON HIS PART TO KEEP A DISORDERLY HOUSE UNDER
PHIL I (71)	REST ON HIS ARM, BUT SITTING SQUARELY WITHOUT THE	LEAST	ATTEMPT TO RETURN THE CARESS) DO I FEEL HARDER TO THE
GETT (319)	IF CECIL TOOK THE CHILD AWAY FROM ME, I SHOULD AT	LEAST	BE PAID FOR WHAT IT HAD COST ME. /MRS BRIDGENORTH/ (
DOCT I SD(81)	A REGULAR BEARD AND MOUSTACHES, WHICH COULD AT	LEAST	BE TRIMMED AND WAXED INTO A MASCULINE PRESENTABLENESS,
MRS PREFACE(156)	STEP INTO THE NEXT ROOM TO COMMIT SUICIDE, OR AT	LEAST	BE TURNED OUT BY THEIR PROTECTORS AND PASSED ON TO BE
OVER PREFACE(165)	AND EVEN INTENSELY ENJOYED, BUT NOT IN THE	LEAST	BECAUSE NOTHING BETTER WAS POSSIBLE; FOR ALL THE
JOAN PREFACE(40)	MISCHIEVOUS ANTI-SANITARY QUACKERY, NOT IN THE	LEAST	BECAUSE WE THINK IT WRONG TO COMPEL PEOPLE TO PROTECT
JITT II SD(33)	TWO VISITORS MAKES THEM SEEM, IF NOT NATURAL, AT	LEAST	BECOMING. /LENKHEIM/ (IN HOLLOW TONES) MAY I SAY
DOCT PREFACE(53)	SMALLPOX, IF NOT ABOLISHED BY VACCINATION, HAD AT	LEAST	BEEN MADE MUCH MILDER: ON THE CONTRARY, HE RECORDED A
SUPR III (103)	EARTH, AND ALL THE WORLD IS A STAGE, HEAVEN IS AT	LEAST	BEHIND THE SCENES. BUT HEAVEN CANNOT BE DESCRIBED BY
CAPT II (249)	ARRANGEMENTS IN ANY WAY. IF I DISTURB YOU THE	LEAST	BIT IN THE WORLD, STOP ME AT ONCE. YOU HAVE ALL THE
GENV III (85)	THE BRITISH EMPIRE AND ALL THAT; BUT I AM NOT THE	LEAST	BIT MENTAL; AND WHAT ATTRACTION YOU CAN FIND IN MY
PLES PREFACE(R10)	NAY, IF ONLY I HAD MADE THE POET A CRIPPLE, OR AT	LEAST	BLIND, SO AS TO COMBINE AN EASIER DISGUISE WITH A
SUPR PREFACE(R25)	AND BRED, IF NOT BY POLITICAL MARRIAGE, AT	LEAST	BY A PRETTY RIGOROUS CLASS MARRIAGE. ARISTOCRACY AND
FABL PREFACE(92)	THE IDIOT? AGAIN, I DO NOT KNOW; BUT WE CAN AT	LEAST	CALL IN THE PROFESSIONAL PSYCHOTHERAPISTS WHOSE
CATH PREFACE(158)	THUS WAS ESTABLISHED AN EVIL TRADITION; BUT I AT	LEAST	CAN PLEAD THAT IT DOES NOT ALWAYS HOLD GOOD. IF FORBES
JOAN PREFACE(23)	HER ENORMOUS SELF-CONFIDENCE, WHICH MADE HER THE	LEAST	CAUTIOUS OF HUMAN BEINGS IN CIVIL AFFAIRS. THIS
MTH5 (225)	SHE WERE HIS OVERCOAT; AND CONTINUES WITHOUT THE	LEAST	CHANGE OF TONE) SHAPE IT AS YOU WILL, MARBLE REMAINS
POSN PREFACE(403)	THAT ARBITRATION EITHER COSTS NOTHING OR IS AT	LEAST	CHEAPER THAN LAW. WHO IS TO PAY FOR THE TIME OF THE
APPL PREFACE(187)	IF WE CANNOT CONTROL OUR GOVERNORS, CAN WE NOT AT	LEAST	CHOOSE THEM AND CHANGE THEM IF THEY DO NOT SUIT? LET
WIDO I (10)	SO YOU HAVE DONE IT AT LAST. /TRENCH/ YES. AT	LEAST	COKANE'S DONE IT. I TOLD YOU HE'D MANAGE IT. HE'S
JITT III (62)	THE BEST MEN ARE SUBJECT TO ABERRATIONS, OR AT	LEAST	COMMONNESSES, IN THEIR RELATIONS WITH WOMEN, JUST AS
SUPR HANDBOK(226)	THE LEAST CONFUSED THINKER ITS SOCRATES, THE	LEAST	COMMONPLACE POET ITS SHAKESPEAR. CHARITY IS
SUPR PREFACE(R26)	THE SORT OF MIND AND CHARACTER THAT IS (AT	LEAST	COMPARATIVELY) CAPABLE OF HANDLING IT? FOR REMEMBER:
METH PREFACE(R89)	THEIR OLD INTELLECTUALLY NIHILISTIC VULGARITY, AT	LEAST	CONCEDES THE DIGNITY OF THE THEATRE, NOT TO MENTION
ROCK I SD(195)	ARE FAIRLY PLEASANT; BUT THEY ARE NOT IN THE	LEAST	CONCILIATORY. HILDA RISES AND PULLS OUT A CHAIR FOR
SUPR HANDBOK(226)	THE LEAST IMBECILE STATESMAN ITS SOLON, THE	LEAST	CONFUSED THINKER ITS SOCRATES, THE LEAST COMMONPLACE
BULL PREFACE(48)	TOLD, THE BEST BEHAVED CONVICT, SO THE MAN WITH	LEAST	CONSCIENCE AND INITIATIVE MAKES THE BEST BEHAVED
CLEO NOTES (205)	OF THE SIBERIAN MAN OF BUSINESS WITHOUT THE	LEAST	CONSCIOUSNESS THAT THE STRING OF CONTEMPTUOUS
GETT PREFACE(219)	THE MOST SUCCESSFUL THOSE IN WHICH IT HAS BEEN	LEAST	CONSIDERED, AND IN WHICH THE DECISIVE CONSIDERATIONS
SIM PREFACE(5)	AS EITHER DESIRABLE FOR THE GENERAL GOOD OR AT	LEAST	CONVENIENT TO OUR RULERS. I LEARNED THIS EARLY IN
MILL II (169)	COMFORTS. YOU ARE WORSE THAN ALASTAIR; FOR HE AT	LEAST	COULD TALK ABOUT BOXING AND TENNIS. /ADRIAN/ AND YOU
BULL PREFACE(44)	IF THE ALTERNATIVE BE A BAD GOVERNMENT WHICH AT	LEAST	CREATES AND MAINTAINS AN ILLUSION OF DEMOCRACY.
MILL PREFACE(132)	" BLUSH TO FIND IT FAME," AS NOBODY GAVE HIM THE	LEAST	CREDIT FOR ANYTHING BUT KILLING. WHEN THE GLORY TURNED
DOCT PREFACE(41)	DO CRUEL AND VILE THINGS WITHOUT BEING IN THE	LEAST	CRUEL OR VILE, BECAUSE THE ROUTINE TO WHICH THEY HAVE
2TRU II (68)	IT'S THE REAL THING WHILE IT LASTS. I HAVNT THE	LEAST	CURIOSITY ABOUT MY LOVELY SERGEANT: I KNOW JUST WHAT
MTH3 (125)	PETS. /BURGE-LUBIN/ (REACTING BUOYANTLY) NOT THE	LEAST	DANGER OF IT. I GRANT YOU WE LEAVE THE MOST
BULL IV (172)	(REASSURINGLY) OH NO: IT WONT DO THAT: NOT THE	LEAST	DANGER. YOU KNOW, A CHURCH BELL CAN MAKE A DEVIL OF A
SUPR II SD(48)	AND TANNER'S FRIENDS HIS MANNER IS NOT IN THE	LEAST	DEFERENTIAL, BUT COOL AND RETICENT, KEEPING THEM QUITE
KING PREFACE(159)	THIS IS DONE, ADULT SUFFRAGE WILL REMAIN THE	LEAST	DEMOCRATIC OF ALL POLITICAL SYSTEMS. I LEAVE IT TO OUR
BULL PREFACE(64)	I SHOULD STILL SUGGEST TO HIM THAT WE CAN AT	LEAST	DIE LIKE GENTLEMEN? MIGHT I EVEN BE SO PERSONAL AS TO
JOAN PREFACE(6)	WHILST NAPOLEON, THOUGH HE ENDS IN ST HELENA, AT	LEAST	DIES IN HIS BED THERE; AND MANY TERRIFYING BUT QUITE
PYGM EPILOG (293)	OR SHUNNED; AND THEY NEVER SEEM TO HAVE THE	LEAST	DIFFICULTY IN MARRYING PEOPLE WHO ARE TOO GOOD FOR
MTH2 (55)	YOU CANNOT. I DID IT FOR TEN YEARS WITHOUT THE	LEAST	DIFFICULTY, AND VERY COMFORTABLE, PROSPEROUS, PLEASANT
FABL VI (129)	SMOKING, QUIT SMOKING." HE QUITTED WITHOUT THE	LEAST	DIFFICULTY, AND HAS NEVER SMOKED SINCE, THOUGH HE HAD
HART I (56)	/ELLIE/ (HURT) OH NO. NOT LIKE THAT. IT WAS AT	LEAST	DIGNIFIED. /MRS HUSHABYE/ THAT MADE IT ALL THE HARDER,
LION I (113)	INCENSE AS A MATTER OF CONVICTION, YOU MIGHT AT	LEAST	DO SO AS A MATTER OF GOOD TASTE, TO AVOID SHOCKING THE
BUOY III (38)	OF THE ALMIGHTY. IF YOU MUST DRAG IN RELIGION, AT	LEAST	DO SO IN BECOMING LANGUAGE. /MRS THIRDBORN/ WHEN YOU
MIS. PREFACE(19)	YOU KNOW WHERE TO HAVE, AND HE (OR SHE) AT	LEAST	DOES NOT CONFUSE YOUR AFFECTIONS; BUT A CONSCIENTIOUS
SUPR PREFACE(R39)	OF FACT HE MADE IT HIMSELF ONLY YESTERDAY, AT	LEAST	DOES NOT PRETEND THAT THERE ARE ANY MODERN IDEAS IN
MTH1 II 32)	ALWAYS CREATING EITHER THINGS OR WISDOM, OR AT	LEAST	DREAMING OF THEM. AND THEN YOU, CAIN, COME TO ME WITH
SUPR I 22)	/MRS WHITEFIELD/ WELL, I THINK YOU MIGHT AT	LEAST	DROP THEM UNTIL WE ARE OUT OF MOURNING. /ANN/ (
HART PREFACE(11)	THE CRUEL PEOPLE; AND IT SAW THAT CRUELTY WAS AT	LEAST	EFFECTIVE. CRUELTY DID THINGS THAT MADE MONEY, WHEREAS
FABL PREFACE(80)	MEETS THE WINNER OF A NOBEL PRIZE WITHOUT THE	LEAST	EMBARRASSMENT; AND I HAVE NEVER SUFFERED THE SMALLEST
FANY PROLOG (269)	I DONT PRETEND TO BE AN AUTHORITY; BUT I HAVE AT	LEAST	ESTABLISHED THE FACT THAT THESE PRODUCTIONS, WHATEVER
POSN (444)	YOU THINK YOURE SHUT OF HIM; AND THEN, WHEN YOU	LEAST	EXPECT IT, HE'S GOT YOU. /ELDER DANIELS/ SPEAK MORE

CLEO PRO2 (98)	OVER IN A MOMENT. THE ATTACK CAME JUST WHERE WE	LEAST	EXPECTED IT. /BELZANOR/ THAT SHEWS THAT THE ROMANS ARE
FABL PREFACE(69)	AN ATTEMPT TO SOLVE THE PROBLEM OF EVIL, AND AT	LEAST	FACES THE FACT THAT EVIL IS EVIL. THUS THE WORLD, AS
CAND III (128)	WICKED THINGS TO YOU? /CANDIDA/ (WITHOUT THE	LEAST	FEAR OR COLDNESS, AND WITH PERFECT RESPECT FOR HIS
GENV I (38)	THE LAST REVOLUTION. THERE MUST BE STILL AT	LEAST	FIFTEEN HUNDRED LEFT. /SHE/ BUT IS IT A MEMBER OF THE
KING I (175)	HE IS ONLY FIFTY, FROM WHICH YOU MUST DEDUCT AT	LEAST	FIFTEEN YEARS FOR HIS CHILDHOOD. /BARBARA/ FOURTEEN.
MIS. (143)	THINGS: THESE HEART-WOUNDING SHAMEFUL THINGS, AT	LEAST	FIND SOMETHING PRETTIER TO CALL ME THAN AN OLD RIP.
METH PREFACE(R29)	THAT HE IS A STENOGRAPHER OR PIANIST AT	LEAST	FIVE SIXTHS READY-MADE AS SOON AS HE CAN CONTROL HIS
GETT (297)	WORSE. /HOTCHKISS/ I'M AFRAID THAT WOULD BE AT	LEAST	FIVE THOUSAND POUNDS. /SYKES/ IF IT WERE ONLY MYSELF,
2TRU PREFACE(8)	THEY CAN BE IDLE AND RICH, IF NOT FOR LIFE, AT	LEAST	FOR AN HOUR, AN AFTERNOON, OR EVEN A WEEK, AND FOR THE
MILL PREFACE(118)	IT HAD NEVER FULFILLED THAT UNDERTAKING, HAD AT	LEAST	FOUND EMPLOYMENT FOR ENOUGH OF THEM TO LEAVE THE REST
GETT PREFACE(210)	ARE QUARTERED ON THE WAGES OF THEIR HUSBANDS. AT	LEAST	FOUR OUT OF FIVE OF OUR MEN COULD NOT AFFORD TWO WIVES
GENV III (65)	THREE HUNDRED APIECE. BEGONIA MUST HAVE NETTED AT	LEAST	FOUR THOUSAND. /THE JOURNALIST/ AND TO THINK I MIGHT
MIS. PREFACE(5)	A HEAVIER ARTICLE. I MUST HAVE SEEN THAT LADY AT	LEAST	FOUR TIMES IN THE TWENTY YEARS FOLLOWING. SHE NEVER
DEST SD(150)	SOLELY THROUGH THE MONARCHY'S HABIT OF BEING AT	LEAST	FOUR YEARS IN ARREAR WITH ITS SOLDIERS IN THE MATTER
ROCK PREFACE(163)	THEREBY SECURING A LEASE OF LIFE FOR AT	LEAST	FOUR YEARS. SOONER OR LATER THIS SITUATION WILL HAVE
PYGM EPILOG (301)	CORRECT (AS IN FACT IT WAS) AND NOT IN THE	LEAST	FUNNY (WHICH WAS ONLY HER IGNORANCE), TOOK HIS ADVICE
MIS. PREFACE(11)	TORTURE OF THE BODY, OUT OF WHICH THE FLOGGER AT	LEAST	GETS SOME PLEASURE, THE MAIMING AND BLINDING OF THE
SUPR IV (166)	WITHOUT A STRUGGLE FOR LIFE, THOUGH THEY COULD AT	LEAST	GIVE THE CHAPLAIN A BLACK EYE. WE DO THE WORLD'S WILL,
DEST SD(151)	IN HIS KNAPSACK, BUT BECAUSE HE HOPES TO CARRY AT	LEAST	HALF A DOZEN SILVER FORKS THERE NEXT DAY. IT MUST BE
MILL I (153)	OPINION. WHEN I FEEL ILL I ALWAYS CONSULT AT	LEAST	HALF A DOZEN DOCTORS. THE VARIETY OF THEIR ADVICE AND
UNPL PREFACE(R7)	MY OWN GUIDANCE THAT UNLESS I COULD PRODUCE AT	LEAST	HALF A DOZEN PLAYS BEFORE I WAS FORTY, I HAD BETTER
APPL PREFACE(174)	THE PLAY IS PROJECTED: IN FACT, HE IS VISIBLY AT	LEAST	HALF IN IT ALREADY; AND THE THEORY OF CONSTITUTIONAL
ROCK PREFACE(176)	IMMEDIATE JUDGES: AND THE POPE BELIEVED WITH AT	LEAST	HALF THEIR MINDS THAT HE WAS RIGHT ABOUT THE EARTH AND
BARB III (316)	DO THAT STEPHEN COULD NOT DO. AND STEPHEN AT	LEAST	HAS BREEDING. /UNDERSHAFT/ THE SON OF A FOUNDLING!
GENV IV (127)	GOOD MORNING. (HE GOES OUT). /WIDOW/ HE AT	LEAST	HAS SOMETHING TO OFFER TO MEN ABOUT TO DIE.
HART I (49)	GUINNESS, OUR OLD NURSE! REALLY HESIONE MIGHT AT	LEAST	HAVE BEEN HERE: SOME PREPARATION MIGHT HAVE BEEN MADE
WIDO III (65)	FINE FAMILY GAVE YOU NOTHING ELSE, IT MIGHT AT	LEAST	HAVE GIVEN YOU SOME SENSE OF PERSONAL DIGNITY. PERHAPS
CYMB V (145)	MEN WILL DO SUCH THINGS TO WOMEN. /IMOGEN/ YOU AT	LEAST	HAVE GRACE TO KNOW YOURSELF FOR WHAT YOU ARE. MY
MTH1 II (29)	ITS LIFE. IF I MUST HAVE FOOD OR DIE, I WILL AT	LEAST	HAVE IT AT AS FAR A REMOVE FROM THE EARTH AS I CAN.
FABL V (118)	OF OUR SIXTY-FOUR. ONE WOULD THINK THEY MIGHT AT	LEAST	HAVE MANAGED NINETEEN TO PLAY THEIR BABYISH THIRDS AND
BULL III (131)	IF WE CANT HAVE MEN WITH ABILITY, LET US AT	LEAST	HAVE MEN WITH CAPITAL. ANYBODY'S BETTER THAN MATT, WHO
GETT (324)	BRIDGENORTH. /LEO/ HOLD YOUR TONGUE, REJJY. AT	LEAST	HAVE THE DECENCY TO WAIT UNTIL THE DECREE IS MADE
DOCT PREFACE(12)	FOR MUTILATION AS LOBSTERS OR LIZARDS, WHICH AT	LEAST	HAVE THE EXCUSE THAT THEY GROW NEW CLAWS AND NEW TAILS
MILL II (173)	FROM HIS HEAD AND HOLDS IT BEHIND HER BACK). AT	LEAST	HAVE THE MANNERS TO STAY WITH ME UNTIL MY CHAUFFEUR
WIDO I (19)	MAY CHOOSE TO RECEIVE ME-- I TRUST I MAY AT	LEAST	HAVE THE PLEASURE OF SEEING YOU SOMETIMES AT MY HOUSE
BULL IV (180)	MR KEEGAN: HE HAS A BAD NAME HERE; BUT AT	LEAST	HE CAN FORGIVE YOU FOR BEING AN IRISHMAN. /KEEGAN/
SUPR IV SD(149)	UP AND INTERCEPTS HIM. STRAKER DOES NOT WAIT; AT	LEAST	HE DOES NOT REMAIN VISIBLY WITHIN EARSHOT. /VIOLET/
BULL PREFACE(39)	LESS FUSS ABOUT IT THAN THE IRISHMAN. BUT AT	LEAST	HE HAS NOBODY TO BLAME BUT HIMSELF AND HIS FELLOW
MILL PREFACE(133)	BALLAD BY MACAULAY AND A STANZA BY KEATS. BUT AT	LEAST	HE IS FREE TO FIND OUT ALL THIS FOR HIMSELF IF HE HAS
3PLA PREFACE(R22)	PIECES WITH DYNAMITE, ORGAN AND ALL, WITHOUT THE	LEAST	HEED TO THE SCREAMS OF THE ART CRITICS AND CULTURED
PRES (134)	THE PROCLAMATION. (AS AN AFTERTHOUGHT) AT	LEAST	HELEN WOULDNT. /BALSQUITH/ BUT GEORGINA? /MITCHENER/
GETT (287)	THE ONLY SENSIBLE MEN IN THE WORLD AND THAT THE	LEAST	HINT OF MARRIAGE REFORM WOULD LOSE THEM THE NEXT
GETT PREFACE(188)	A HUGE AND DANGEROUS MAJORITY WHICH REGARDS THE	LEAST	HINT OF SCEPTICISM AS TO THE BEAUTY AND HOLINESS OF
BUOY PREFACE(6)	(HIS CHRONOLOGY) DOES NOT INVALIDATE IN THE	LEAST	HIS INTEGRITY AS A SCIENTIFIC INVESTIGATOR, NOR
ROCK PREFACE(173)	CONDUCT IN WHICH IT DOES NOT MATTER IN THE	LEAST	HOW PEOPLE ACT IN PARTICULAR SITUATIONS PROVIDED THEY
LION PREFACE(66)	AND THOUGH VINDICTIVENESS AND CRUELTY ARE AT	LEAST	HUMAN QUALITIES WHEN THEY ARE FRANKLY PROCLAIMED AND
SUPR HANDBOK(206)	SLAVERY WAS NEITHER THE MOST EFFECTIVE NOR THE	LEAST	HUMANE METHOD OF LABOR EXPLOITATION; AND THE WORLD IS
GENV III (83)	BE PROUD OF YOUR CROSS-FERTILIZATION. /SIR O./ AT	LEAST	I AM NOT A FRENCHMAN NOR A NEGRO. /THE JUDGE/ AT LEAST
WIDO I (18)	BE MORAL! /COKANE/ I AM NOT MORAL, TRENCH. AT	LEAST	I AM NOT A MORALIST: THAT IS THE EXPRESSION I SHOULD
LION II (139)	OUT AGAINST IT! DIE THEN IF YOU MUST; BUT AT	LEAST	I CAN CUT THE EMPEROR'S THROAT AND THEN MY OWN WHEN I
CLEO III (157)	YOUR DRUIDS DO. SINCE YOU WILL NOT BURN THESE, AT	LEAST	I CAN DROWN THEM. (HE PICKS UP THE BAG AND THROWS IT
BASH II,1, (109)	YOU WELL. I DID NOT CHOOSE MY CALLING; BUT AT	LEAST	I CAN REFRAIN FROM BEING A GENTLEMAN. /LYDIA/ YOU SAY
KING II (233)	HAVE ME, BELOVED. ONE CANNOT DO WITHOUT WOMEN: AT	LEAST	I CANNOT. BUT HAVING TO MANAGE RASCALS LIKE BUCKINGHAM
SUPR III (100)	A MERE PHYSICAL GULF THEY COULD BRIDGE; OR AT	LEAST	I COULD BRIDGE IT FOR THEM (THE EARTH IS FULL OF
MTH1 I (16)	MY MIND. IF I DID NOT KNOW THAT I LOVED EVE, AT	LEAST	I DID NOT KNOW THAT SHE MIGHT CEASE TO LOVE ME, AND
OVER (184)	YOU DONT LOVE ME A BIT. /JUNO/ YES I DO. OR AT	LEAST	I DID. BUT I'M AN ENGLISHMAN; AND I THINK YOU OUGHT TO
ARMS I (16)	GREATLY TICKLED) I DIDNT LAUGH, I ASSURE YOU. AT	LEAST	I DIDNT MEAN TO. BUT WHEN I THINK OF HIM CHARGING THE
BULL IV (163)	HER GO) NO, OF COURSE NOT. I DONT MEAN IT. AT	LEAST	I DO MEAN IT; BUT I KNOW IT'S PREMATURE. I HAD NO
ROCK I (214)	IS ONLY TOO GLAD TO RISE TOO. /SIR ARTHUR/ AT	LEAST	I HOPE I HAVE CONVINCED YOU ABOUT THE WINDOWS, MR
NEVR II (258)	AND YOUR EXPERIENCE ARE NOT INFALLIBLE. AT	LEAST	I HOPE NOT. /VALENTINE/ I MUST BELIEVE THEM. UNLESS
DEVL I (15)	NO WITHOUT THINKING VERY DEEPLY. /ESSIE/ YES. AT	LEAST	I MEAN-- /JUDITH/ (SEVERELY) WHAT DO YOU MEAN?
SUPR III (133)	BEFORE HE HAS SECURED THE GOOD. /DON JUAN/ BUT AT	LEAST	I SHALL NOT BE BORED. THE SERVICE OF THE LIFE FORCE
MIS. (111)	SIDEBOARD WITH HIS EYE ON THE SPONGE-CAKES). AT	LEAST	I SHOULD; BUT I SUPPOSE YOURE NOT SO PARTICULAR.
OVER (180)	NOT? /JUNO/ WELL, OF COURSE THERES NO REASON: AT	LEAST	I SUPPOSE NOT. BUT, YOU KNOW, PART OF THE ROMANCE OF A
LION I (119)	PIETY. /FERROVIUS/ I FEAR GOD MORE THAN MAN; AT	LEAST	I TRY TO. /LENTULUS/ LETS SEE. (HE STRIKES HIM ON THE
MTH3 (109)	FROM EXTINCTION. I DID NOT SHARE THEIR BELIEF: AT	LEAST	I WAS NOT CONSCIOUS OF SHARING IT: I THOUGHT I WAS
GETT (307)	ME, COLLINS. THANK YOU. /HOTCHKISS/ HAVE YOU THE	LEAST	IDEA OF WHAT THEY ARE TALKING ABOUT, MR ALDERMAN?
MIS. (151)	YOU NEVER TOLD ME -- /PERCIVAL/ I HADNT THE	LEAST	IDEA -- ALL TOGETHER, AN EMBARRASSED PAUSE. /PERCIVAL/
SUPR HANDBOK(226)	INCAPABLE GENERAL IN A NATION IS ITS CAESAR, THE	LEAST	IMBECILE STATESMAN ITS SOLON, THE LEAST CONFUSED
MRS PREFACE(171)	TO CHOOSE WHAT IS, ACCORDING TO HER LIGHTS, THE	LEAST	IMMORAL ALTERNATIVE, IT IS NONE THE LESS INFAMOUS OF
BUOY III (36)	DONE MY BEST TO ACT FOR HIM WITHOUT MAKING THE	LEAST	IMPRESSION ON YOUR VERY INTERESTING RELATIVES. I
METH PREFACE(R84)	NOTHING FUNDAMENTALLY POSITIVE TO SAY, WERE AT	LEAST	IN REVOLT AGAINST FALSEHOOD AND IMPOSTURE, AND WERE
BULL III SD(125)	UNTIL HE ANCHORS NEAR THE BASKET, WHERE HE FEELS	LEAST	IN THE WAY. THE PRIEST COMES TO THE TABLE AND SLAPS
BARB II (286)	/UNDERSHAFT/ (STARTLED) A SECULARIST! NOT THE	LEAST	IN THE WORLD: ON THE CONTRARY, A CONFIRMED MYSTIC.
ARMS I (21)	/THE MAN/ EH? FALLING ASLEE--? OH NO: NOT THE	LEAST	IN THE WORLD: I WAS ONLY THINKING. IT'S ALL RIGHT: I'M
MRS II (208)	WE'RE GIVING TROUBLE. /FRANK/ (RISING) NOT THE	LEAST	IN THE WORLD: MY MOTHER WILL BE DELIGHTED TO SEE YOU.
MRS IV (237)	TO ME. I ASSURE YOU MY FEELING FOR YOU IS NOT THE	LEAST	IN THE WORLD LIKE IT. THE GIRLS WILL GO THEIR WAY; I
DEVL II (30)	THERE IS REALLY ANY DANGER? /ANDERSON/ NOT THE	LEAST	IN THE WORLD. /JUDITH/ YOU SAY THAT TO COMFORT ME, NOT
DEVL II (47)	AND BE SENSIBLE. I AM IN NO DANGER-- NOT THE	LEAST	IN THE WORLD. /JUDITH/ (SOLEMNLY) YOU ARE GOING TO
MRS II (203)	WITH ME. FRANK: ARE YOU HUNGRY? /FRANK/ NOT THE	LEAST	IN THE WORLD. COMPLETELY OFF MY PECK, IN FACT. /MRS
DEST (156)	TO IT. /GIUSEPPE/ (SYMPATHETICALLY) NOT THE	LEAST	IN THE WORLD, EXCELLENCY: IS THERE? (NAPOLEON AGAIN
ROCK PREFACE(175)	IN THE EPOCH WHICH JESUS INAUGURATED, OR AT	LEAST	IN WHICH HIS NAME WAS HABITUALLY TAKEN IN VAIN. WE
SUPR HANDBOK(226)	NO AGE OR CONDITION IS WITHOUT ITS HEROES. THE	LEAST	INCAPABLE GENERAL IN A NATION IS ITS CAESAR, THE LEAST
SUPR HANDBOK(188)	BEST LIVING SUBSTITUTE FOR IT HE CAN FIND. HIS	LEAST	INCOMPETENT GENERAL IS SET UP AS AN ALEXANDER; HIS
METH PREFACE(R67)	AS A RESULT, THE PEOPLE WHO DID NOT FEEL IN THE	LEAST	INCONVENIENCED BY BEING NO LONGER GOVERNED BY
MIS. PREFACE(48)	THE TEACHER'S WORD AS TO WHICH CHILD HAS CAUSED	LEAST	INCONVENIENCE" HE WOULD PROBABLY BE UNFROCKED, IF NOT
MIS. PREFACE(104)	WITH THE SMALLEST PRETENCE TO CULTURE, OR THE	LEAST	INKLING OF WHAT THE GREAT PROPHETS VAINLY TRIED TO
SUPR PREFACE(R30)	FOR THE ARTIST, AMUSING TO THE AMATEUR, AND AT	LEAST	INTELLIGIBLE AND THEREFORE POSSIBLY SUGGESTIVE TO THE
ARMS I (8)	A SENSE OF THE HUMOR OF IT, WITHOUT, HOWEVER, THE	LEAST	INTENTION OF TRIFLING WITH IT OR THROWING AWAY A
SUPR IV (163)	AS WE DARE; WE ALL BID FOR ADMIRATION WITHOUT THE	LEAST	INTENTION OF EARNING IT; WE ALL GET AS MUCH RENT AS WE
MTH5 (229)	I SEE I AM BORING YOU, NOT ONE OF YOU TAKES THE	LEAST	INTEREST IN SCIENCE. GOODBYE. (HE DESCENDS FROM THE
HART II (93)	AFRAID OF THEM. I NEVER CAN GET HIM TO TAKE THE	LEAST	INTEREST IN THE WORKS: HE HARDLY KNOWS MORE ABOUT THEM
FABL PREFACE(66)	INTO FABLES WHICH, HOWEVER FARFETCHED, CAN AT	LEAST	INTEREST, AMUSE, AND PERHAPS ENLIGHTEN THOSE CAPABLE
3PLA PREFACE(R37)	EPOCH (OUR OWN) ON THE PAIR. THIS DID NOT IN THE	LEAST	INVOLVE ANY PRETENCE ON SHAKESPEAR'S PART TO BE A
NEVR II (252)	BE GENTLE AND PATIENT) NOW I THINK I HAVE IT. AT	LEAST	I'LL TRY. /GLORIA/ (FIRMLY) YOU SEE! EVERYTHING
FOUN (222)	EXCEPT YOUR VERY BECOMING FANCY WAISTCOAT. BUT AT	LEAST	I'M A FOUNDLING. /BRABAZON/ (EXCITED AND HOPEFUL) A
SUPR HANDBOK(211)	IN SPITE OF ALL OUR HYPOCRISIES. ONE THING AT	LEAST	IS CLEAR TO BEGIN WITH. IF A WOMAN CAN, BY CAREFUL
CLEO II (130)	THE GODS! WOULD THAT IT HAD BEEN! VENGEANCE AT	LEAST	IS HUMAN. NO, I SAY: THOSE SEVERED RIGHT HANDS, AND
ARMS III (58)	THE CHARGE I FOUND THAT I WAS BRAVE. YES: THAT AT	LEAST	IS REAL ABOUT ME. /LOUKA/ DID YOU FIND IN THE CHARGE
SUPR I (46)	AT LEAST, /RAMSDEN/ BUT I ASSURE YOU I NEVER-- AT	LEAST	IT IS A MONSTROUS PERVERSION OF SOMETHING I SAID
BULL PREFACE(9)	TO THOSE WHO THINK THAT ALL WAR IS CRIME-- AT	LEAST	IT IS NOT UNNATURAL CRIME, LIKE THE SLAYING OF AN
BULL IV (166)	FORTIFICATION THAT HAS TO STAND MANY ASSAULTS: AT	LEAST	IT IS SO IN ENGLAND. /NORA/ (CURTLY, MUCH DISGUSTED)
CAPT I (229)	IS A VERY CURIOUS AND INTERESTING ONE-- AT	LEAST	IT IS SO TO A LAWYER LIKE MYSELF. /RANKIN/ I SHOULD BE
HART PREFACE(11)	ALL THAT WAS LEFT TO IT WAS THE BOAST THAT AT	LEAST	IT KNEW HOW TO DIE: A MELANCHOLY ACCOMPLISHMENT WHICH
APPL I (235)	OF POLITICS. BUT EVIL AS IT WAS IN MANY WAYS, AT	LEAST	IT STOOD ABOVE THE TYRANNY OF POPULAR IGNORANCE AND
MIS. PREFACE(10)	A VERY PROPER VIEW OF HIS PARENTAL DUTIES. AND AT	LEAST	IT WAS NOT A TRIVIAL VIEW, NOR AN ILL MEANT ONE. IT
KING I (187)	ALSO AN ENGLISHMAN; AND MY HOUSE IS MY CASTLE. AT	LEAST	IT WAS UNTIL THIS MORNING, WHEN THE WHOLE COURT CAME

BUOY PREFACE(6)	ONLY A PREFACETTE TO A COMEDIETTA. FORGIVE IT. AT	LEAST	IT WILL NOT RUB INTO YOU THE MISERIES AND SINS OF THE
DOCT III (142)	AND SOME FAMILY OUT OF DISGRACE? /B.B./ BUT AT	LEAST	IT WILL PUNISH HIM. /SIR PATRICK/ OH YES: ITLL PUNISH
ROCK II (263)	TODAY OR TOMORROW. I CALCULATE THAT AT THE VERY	LEAST	IT WILL TAKE FIFTY YEARS TO GET IT THROUGH. /SIR
BARB III (314)	A CERTAIN AMOUNT OF TOSH ABOUT THE TIMES; BUT AT	LEAST	ITS LANGUAGE IS REPUTABLE. /LOMAX/ (OVERWHELMED) YOU
SIM II (56)	TRUMPERY ISLET ITS BATTLESHIP, ITS CRUISER, OR AT	LEAST	ITS SLOOP OR GUNBOAT! WHY ARE THEY HERE, ARMED TO THE
MRS II (211)	/VIVIE/ (SLOWLY) YOU ARE CERTAIN OF THAT, AT	LEAST	. AH! YOU MEAN THAT THAT IS ALL YOU ARE CERTAIN OF. (
JOAN 4 (97)	THAT SHE IS A SORCERESS. /THE CHAPLAIN/ NOT THE	LEAST	: AN ARRANT WITCH. /WARWICK/ (GENTLY REPROVING THE
O'FL (217)	PEARCE/ NOT AT ALL. IT WONT DISTURB ME IN THE	LEAST	. AND HE'S TOO BIG A BOY TO BE TAKEN INTO THE YARD
MIS. PREFACE(52)	IS SHAM. THOSE WHO HAVE BEEN TAUGHT MOST KNOW	LEAST	. ANTICHRIST, AMONG THE WORST EFFECTS OF THE UNNATURAL
MIS. (157)	AFRAID OF GETTING JAUNDICE? /LINA/ NOT IN THE	LEAST	. BUT BILLIARD BALLS WILL DO QUITE AS WELL. /MRS
MIS. PREFACE(9)	OF EVERY NURSERYMAID DOES NOT EXCUSE IT IN THE	LEAST	. DICKENS TELLS US OF A NURSERYMAID WHO ELABORATED IT
JITT III (69)	HER FOR ME, WOULD YOU MIND? /JITTA/ NOT IN THE	LEAST	. EDITH IS LIKE A CHILD OF MY OWN TO ME: IT WOULD BE
FABL PREFACE(78)	DOES NOT SHAKE THE FAITH OF MY IDOLATERS IN THE	LEAST	. FACTS COUNT FOR NOTHING. I AM TOLD THAT I SHOULD BE
SUPR IV (147)	POSITION IS AS GOOD AS HECTOR'S, TO SAY THE	LEAST	. HE ADMITS IT. /MALONE/ (SHREWDLY) YOU TELL HIM SO
JOAN 1,SD(60)	HIS SCOWL DOES NOT CHECK OR FRIGHTEN HER IN THE	LEAST	. HER VOICE IS NORMALLY A HEARTY COAXING VOICE, VERY
HART I (65)	DONT MIND NOW, DO YOU, DEAR? /ELLIE/ NOT IN THE	LEAST	. I AM QUITE CURED. MAZZINI DUNN AND HECTOR COME IN
MRS IV (243)	IN CROFTS: I AM INDEED. /FRANK/ I'M NOT IN THE	LEAST	. I FEEL HE'S PERFECTLY ACCOUNTED FOR AT LAST. BUT
OVER PREFACE(167)	MANUFACTURED CEREMONIES DO NOT INTEREST ME IN THE	LEAST	. I KNOW HOW A MAN IS TRIED, AND HOW HE IS HANGED. I
MRS I (185)	/VIVIE/ I DONT OBJECT TO IT ON THAT SCORE IN THE	LEAST	. I SHALL TURN IT TO VERY GOOD ACCOUNT, I ASSURE YOU.
WIDO II (36)	/TRENCH/ NO: HE HAS BEEN VERY KIND-- TO ME, AT	LEAST	. IT'S NOT THAT. IT'S NOTHING YOU CAN GUESS, BLANCHE.
DOCT IV (170)	BY NO MEANS. /WALPOLE/ IT DOESNT MATTER IN THE	LEAST	. (AMAZED, ALL TOGETHER IN A CONFUSED MURMUR) /MRS
FOUN (214)	AND THE DESCRIPTION DOES NOT CORRESPOND IN THE	LEAST	. (READING) " NO MAN OF OUR TIME HAS SUCCEEDED IN
PHIL II (95)	ALL. NOW GO ON, PRAY: YOU DONT DISTURB ME IN THE	LEAST	. (SHE TURNS TO THE FIRE, AND AGAIN BURIES HERSELF IN
2TRU III (105)	/TALLBOYS/ I DO NOT QUALIFY MY APOLOGY IN THE	LEAST	. MY APOLOGY IS COMPLETE. THE LADY HAS A RIGHT TO IT.
MILL III (185)	IT THERE FIRST, HAVNT YOU? /EPIFANIA/ NOT IN THE	LEAST	. OTHER PEOPLE PUT IT THERE; AND THE BANK LENDS IT TO
JITT III (65)	DID NOT INTEND THAT. YOU MAY FORGIVE HER THAT, AT	LEAST	. /AGNES/ OH, YOU MUSTNT THINK IT'S MERE SPITE AND
FOUN (222)	DOESNT THAT TOUCH YOU? /BRABAZON/ NOT IN THE	LEAST	. /ANASTASIA/ THOUGHTLESS BOY. HAVE YOU FORGOTTEN THAT
2TRU III (93)	EDUCATION? I SHIELDED YOU FROM THAT, AT	LEAST	. /AUBREY/ YOU THOUGHT YOU DID, OLD MAN; BUT YOU
APPL II (271)	BE SAID. /AMANDA/ THAT MEANS ANOTHER HALF HOUR AT	LEAST	. /BOANERGES/ WOMAN: THIS IS NOT THE MOMENT FOR YOUR
PHIL I (74)	ME? AM I GALLANT TO WOMEN? /GRACE/ NOT IN THE	LEAST	. /CHARTERIS/ CERTAINLY NOT. NO ONE CAN ACCUSE ME OF
NEVR I (203)	/VALENTINE/ DONT YOU KNOW? /PHILIP/ NOT IN THE	LEAST	. /DOLLY/ IT'S A WISE CHILD-- /PHILIP/ (CUTTING HER
BULL II (108)	UNNECESSARILY. I SHANT MIND THE HOTEL IN THE	LEAST	. /FATHER DEMPSEY/ MAN ALIVE! THERES NO HOTEL IN
ROCK II (243)	STAND AT TWENTY MILLIONS TODAY AT THE VERY	LEAST	. /GLENMORISON/ FIFTY. /SIR JAFNA/ HOW DO YOU KNOW?
CAND III (139)	SCENE. ARNT YOU AFRAID? /MORELL/ NOT IN THE	LEAST	. /MARCHBANKS/ I NEVER ENVIED YOU YOUR COURAGE BEFORE.
SUPR I (46)	I THINK YOU MIGHT HAVE SPARED ME THAT, AT	LEAST	. /RAMSDEN/ BUT I ASSURE YOU I NEVER-- AT LEAST IT IS
BARB PREFACE(220)	UNDERSHAFT'S VIEWS WILL NOT PERPLEX YOU IN THE	LEAST	. UNLESS INDEED HIS CONSTANT SENSE THAT HE IS ONLY THE
MRS II (211)	THAT YOU HAVE EVER MET. I'M CERTAIN OF THAT, AT	LEAST	. VIVIE'S EYES FASTEN STERNLY ON HER MOTHER AS THE
PRES (153)	/MRS BANGER/ THAT DOES NOT CONCERN US IN THE	LEAST	. WE APPROVE OF THE PROJECT AND WILL SEE THAT IT IS
HART III (132)	DOESNT MIND. DO YOU, ELLIE? /ELLIE/ NOT IN THE	LEAST	. WHAT IS YOUR OPINION, LADY UTTERWORD? YOU HAVE SO
PHIL I (82)	LEONARD: HAVE YOU NO PITY? /CHARTERIS/ NOT THE	LEAST	. WHEN YOU CONDESCEND TO THESE ANTICS YOU FORCE ME TO
ROCK I (226)	SELF TO BE CONSCIOUS OF. YOU WONT UPSET ME IN THE	LEAST	. YOU MAY EVEN THROW IN A ROUND OF APPLAUSE
MILL II (171)	DIE? /THE DOCTOR/ YOU ARE NOT DYING. NOT YET, AT	LEAST	. YOUR OWN DOCTOR WILL ATTEND TO YOU. /EPIFANIA/ YOU
MTH4 I (152)	CHILDREN'S RIGHTS BY INSISTING ON BEING CALLED AT	LEAST	JOE. AT FIFTEEN I REFUSED TO ANSWER TO ANYTHING
METH PREFACE(R53)	WE DREADED AND MISTRUSTED THE PRIEST, WE COULD AT	LEAST	KEEP HIM OUT OF THE HOUSE; BUT WHAT OF THE MODERN
3PLA PREFACE(R33)	ANTONYS AND OCTAVIUSES OF ITS TIME, WHO AT	LEAST	KNEW THE DIFFERENCE BETWEEN LIFE AND RHETORIC. IT WILL
ARMS II (42)	REGIMENTS TO PHILIPPOPOLIS; AND WE DONT IN THE	LEAST	KNOW HOW TO DO IT. /BLUNTSCHLI/ (SUDDENLY ATTENTIVE
BARB I (260)	TABLE AND SARAH ON THE SETTEE), I DONT IN THE	LEAST	KNOW WHAT YOU ARE LAUGHING AT, ADOLPHUS. I AM
2TRU PREFACE(24)	BUT THEY WOULD GAIN THE ADVANTAGE OF AT	LEAST	KNOWING THAT THEIR RULERS KNOW HOW TO READ AND WRITE,
BUOY PREFACE(6)	SEEMS SO QUEER TO US TODAY, HE WAS NOT IN THE	LEAST	LAPSING FROM SCIENCE INTO SUPERSTITION: HE WAS LOOKING
GETT (329)	YOU PLEASE AND MAKE ME DO WHAT YOU LIKE. BUT AT	LEAST	LET ME KNOW YOUR SOUL AS YOU SEEM TO KNOW MINE. DO YOU
ROCK PREFACE(169)	IS NOT EXPEDIENT: THERE MUST BE FALLOWS, OR AT	LEAST	LIGHT CROPPINGS, BETWEEN THE INTENSE CULTIVATIONS; FOR
2TRU I (43)	A LITTLE HURT) OH, NOT A CURATE. I HOPE I LOOK AT	LEAST	LIKE A BENEFICED CLERGYMAN. BUT IT IS VERY CLEVER OF
2TRU PREFACE(25)	ITS FATAL CONSEQUENCES. MR STALIN IS NOT IN THE	LEAST	LIKE AN EMPEROR, NOR AN ARCHBISHOP, NOR A PRIME
GETT PREFACE(216)	AND INHUMAN. MARRIAGE AS A FACT IS NOT IN THE	LEAST	LIKE MARRIAGE AS AN IDEAL. IF IT WERE, THE SUDDEN
MIS. (111)	MY BROTHERS AND SISTERS ARE NOT THE	LEAST	LIKE ME. THEYRE THE REGULAR THING THAT YOU ALWAYS GET
JITT III (77)	BETWEEN MRS PETERSEN AND YOURSELF WERE IN THE	LEAST	LIKE MY RELATIONS WITH BRUNO, YOU ONLY SHEW FOR THE
GETT PREFACE(217)	MARRIAGE OF WHICH I HAVE ANY KNOWLEDGE IS IN THE	LEAST	LIKE THE IDEAL MARRIAGE. I DO NOT MEAN THAT IT IS
NEVR II (253)	REMEMBER SOMEONE WHOM YOU LOVED, OR (SHYLY) AT	LEAST	LIKED IN A CHILDISH WAY? COME! SOMEONE WHO LET YOU
APPL I (206)	BECAUSE NO KING OR MINISTER IS THE VERY	LEAST	LITTLE BIT LIKE A STAMP: HE IS A LIVING SOUL.
LIED (189)	DONT MIND HIS BROTHERS. NOW IF YOU ONLY KNEW THE	LEAST	LITTLE THING ABOUT THE WORLD, HENRY, YOUD KNOW THAT IN
MILL PREFACE(117)	THE WAR OFFICE MAY NOT YET HAVE REALIZED IT), AT	LEAST	MADE AN END OF THE SUPREMACY OF THE GLORY VIRTUOSO WHO
METH PREFACE(R68)	BELIEVING THAT IF EVERYONE TAKES THE LINE OF	LEAST	MATERIAL RESISTANCE THE RESULT WILL BE THE SURVIVAL OF
BULL IV (177)	YES, YES: EFFICIENCY IS THE THING. I DONT IN THE	LEAST	MIND YOUR CHAFF, MR KEEGAN; BUT LARRY'S RIGHT ON THE
DOCT PREFACE(23)	AS DOCTORS PERFORM FOR HALF-A-CROWN, WITHOUT THE	LEAST	MISGIVING, OPERATIONS WHICH COULD NOT BE THOROUGHLY
SUPR HANDBOK(207)	WHO, THOUGH THEY ACT OUTSIDE THE LAW, ARE AT	LEAST	MORE MERCIFUL THAN THE AMERICAN LEGISLATORS AND JUDGES
APPL INTRLUD(255)	/MAGNUS/ HENPECKED! WHAT DO YOU CALL THIS? AT	LEAST	MY WIFE DOES NOT RESTRAIN ME BY BODILY VIOLENCE.
CAPT NOTES (304)	HAVE TO WRITE DAHN TAHN AND COWCOW AS BEING AT	LEAST	NEARER TO THE ACTUAL SOUND THAN DOWN TOWN AND COCOA.
SUPR I (33)	SARDONICALLY) DO NOT GIVE WAY TO REMORSE, ANN. AT	LEAST	NINETEEN TWENTIETHS OF THE EXPLOITS I CONFESSED TO YOU
POSN PREFACE(395)	IT WISHES TO BE DEBAUCHED, NO CENSOR CAN-- OR AT	LEAST	NO CENSOR DOES-- STAND OUT AGAINST IT. IF A PLAY IS
LADY PREFACE(217)	FOR SOME REASON DURING MY STAY IN VENICE: AT	LEAST	NO GONDOLIER EVER DID IT IN MY HEARING). SHAKESPEAR IS
JITT II (34)	IN YOUR CASE, DEAR MRS HALDENSTEDT, THERE WAS AT	LEAST	NO TORTURE. /AGNES/ (STARING AT HIM) NO TORTURE!
DOCT II (129)	/RIDGEON/ WELL, IF I LET BLENKINSOP DIE, AT	LEAST	NOBODY CAN SAY I DID IT BECAUSE I WANTED TO MARRY HIS
MIS. PREFACE(98)	ALSO WAS THE PRACTICAL ALTERNATIVE. IT IS AT	LEAST	NOT A SCHOOL BOOK; AND IT IS NOT A BAD STORY BOOK,
SUPR II (64)	CHAPERONE? /OCTAVIUS/ IT'S NOT THAT, MALONE-- AT	LEAST	NOT ALTOGETHER. /HECTOR/ INDEED! MAY I ASK WHAT OTHER
POSN (448)	(BREAKING IN) YOU LIE. I WASNT DRUNK-- AT	LEAST	NOT AS DRUNK AS THAT. /BLANCO/ (IGNORING THE
METH PREFACE(R82)	YOUR SCEPTICAL REMBRANDTS AND VELASQUEZS ARE AT	LEAST	NOT COMPELLED TO PAINT SHOP FRONTS FOR WANT OF
MRS I (183)	UNCONVENTIONALLY? /PRAED/ OH NO: OH DEAR NO. AT	LEAST	NOT CONVENTIONALLY UNCONVENTIONALLY, YOU UNDERSTAND. (
INCA (249)	AND JACK JOHNSON THE SECOND, ALL UNMARRIED. AT	LEAST	NOT SERIOUSLY MARRIED: NOTHING, IN SHORT, THAT CANNOT
GLIM (181)	FEAR. /FERRUCCIO/ I DO NOT CARE FOR SINGING: AT	LEAST	NOT THE SINGING OF PEASANTS. THERE IS ONLY ONE THING
SUPR IV (157)	I MARRY JACK, YOULL NEVER BE DISILLUSIONED-- AT	LEAST	NOT UNTIL I GROW TOO OLD. /OCTAVIUS/ I TOO SHALL GROW
MRS II (199)	NO, THANK YOU, VIENNA IS NO PLACE FOR YOU-- AT	LEAST	NOT UNTIL YOURE A LITTLE OLDER. (SHE NODS AT HIM TO
2TRU II (66)	WERE A WOMAN. DONT YOU BE A HYPOCRITE, POPSY: AT	LEAST	NOT WITH ME. /AUBREY/ AT LEAST NOT WITH YOU! SWEETIE:
2TRU II (66)	POPSY: AT LEAST NOT WITH ME. /AUBREY/ AT	LEAST	NOT WITH YOU! SWEETIE: THAT TOUCH OF CONCERN FOR MY
DOCT PREFACE(5)	COMPRESS OR A PEPPERMINT LOZENGE NOBODY TAKES THE	LEAST	NOTICE OF HIM. BUT IF HE OPERATES ON THE THROAT AND
PYGM V SD(277)	AND BEGINS TO STITCH AT IT, WITHOUT TAKING THE	LEAST	NOTICE OF HIS OUTBURST. /MRS HIGGINS/ VERY NICELY PUT,
MILL IV (198)	ME IN? /SAGAMORE/ THEN NEITHER OF YOU HAS THE	LEAST	NOTION OF HOW THIS AFFAIR ENDED. /ADRIAN/ I HAVE
HART II (97)	HESIONE KNOWS NOTHING ABOUT ME: SHE HASNT THE	LEAST	NOTION OF THE SORT OF PERSON I AM, AND NEVER WILL. I
FANY PROLOG (272)	YOU MEAN TO SAY YOU DONT KNOW? /FANNY/ HAVNT THE	LEAST	NOTION. /THE COUNT/ THE STAGIRITE WAS ARISTOTLE. BY
LION I (116)	/LAVINIA/ NOT EVEN FROM DEATH? /THE CAPTAIN/	LEAST	OF ALL FROM DEATH. /LAVINIA/ THEN I MUST NOT COME BACK
ARMS II (32)	BUT I SHOULD NOT HAVE BROUGHT MY CYNICISM HERE:	LEAST	OF ALL INTO YOUR PRESENCE, RAINA. I-- (HERE, TURNING
CAPT I (230)	INTO. NOBODY IN THE ISLAND WOULD ACT AGAINST ME,	LEAST	OF ALL THE ATTORNEY AND SOLICITOR GENERAL, WHO
ROCK PREFACE(166)	AND HAD NO NOTION OF POOLING IT WITH ANYBODY,	LEAST	OF ALL WITH THE URBAN PROLETARIANS WHO SEEMED LIKE
BULL PREFACE(8)	HISTORY AND HUMANITY, TO THEIR CREDIT BE IT SAID,	LEAST	OF ALL. PLEASE DO NOT SUPPOSE FOR A MOMENT THAT I
MTH4 II (190)	YOU WOULD ADMIT THAT NOWHERE ELSE IN THE WORLD,	LEAST	OF ALL, PERHAPS IN NORTH AMERICA, WHICH HAS A
BARB PREFACE(219)	DISGRACE, MEANNESS AND UGLINESS. NOT THE	LEAST	OF ITS VIRTUES IS THAT IT DESTROYS BASE PEOPLE AS
ROCK PREFACE(174)	WHERE AT PRESENT PROVINCES CONTAINING AT THE	LEAST	OF MANY CONFLICTING ESTIMATES EIGHTEEN MILLIONS OF
PYGM EPILOG (301)	OF FORMING A SINGLE LETTER WORTHY OF THE	LEAST	OF MILTON'S WORDS; BUT SHE PERSISTED; AND AGAIN HE
MIS. PREFACE(34)	LABOR UNDER OUR CAPITALIST SYSTEM. IT IS NOT THE	LEAST	OF THE CURSES OF THAT SYSTEM THAT IT WILL BEQUEATH TO
LION PREFACE(12)	POWERS IS AS WELL WITHIN THE MEANS OF THE	LEAST	OF THE MEMBERS AS WITHIN THOSE OF THE HEADMAN, YET
POSN PREFACE(398)	THE PROTECTION OF THE LORD CHAMBERLAIN, OR AT	LEAST	OF THOSE OF THEM IN WHICH THE VULGARITY AND VICE ARE
DOCT PREFACE(45)	YOUR OWN SOUL IF YOU ARE UNJUST OR CRUEL TO THE	LEAST	OF THOSE WHOM ST FRANCIS CALLED HIS LITTLE BROTHERS. I
JITT III (57)	VERY INDISCREET QUESTION? I SHALL NOT BE IN THE	LEAST	OFFENDED IF YOU REFUSE TO ANSWER IT. /AGNES/ WHAT IS
NEVR II (257)	YOU UNDERSTAND MY REAL CHARACTER. I AM NOT IN THE	LEAST	OFFENDED. (HE PAUSES AND PUTS HIS HAT DOWN AGAIN). I
UNPL PREFACE(R14)	ACT IN LENGTH. I DO NOT WANT HIM TO READ IT (AT	LEAST	OFFICIALLY; PERSONALLY HE IS WELCOME): ON THE
OVER (193)	WELL, IF WE'RE NOT TO FIGHT, I MUST INSIST AT	LEAST	ON YOUR NEVER SPEAKING TO MY WIFE AGAIN. /GREGORY/
SUPR PREFACE(R17)	TODAY THE PALMING OFF IS NO LONGER NECESSARY (AT	LEAST	ON YOUR PLANE AND MINE) BECAUSE DON JUANISM IS NO
GETT PREFACE(198)	IF I HEARD THEM PERSUADE CHILDREN TO GET DRUNK AT	LEAST	ONCE A DAY? APART FROM THE INITIAL ABSURDITY OF

SUPR II (56)	WELL, IF I DONT GIVE HIM A THOUSAND MILE RUN AT	LEAST	ONCE A FORTNIGHT I SHALL LOSE HIM. HE WILL GIVE ME THE
MTH2 (84)	THE LAST THIRTY YEARS THE POST HAS BROUGHT ME AT	LEAST	ONCE A WEEK A PLAN FROM SOME CRANK OR OTHER FOR THE
GETT (294)	WHEN HER BLOOD BOILS ABOUT IT (AND IT BOILS AT	LEAST	ONCE A WEEK) SHE DOESNT CARE WHAT SHE SAYS. /REGINALD/
GETT PREFACE(198)	EXHORT YOUNG PEOPLE TO MAKE IT A RULE TO DO AT	LEAST	ONE KIND ACTION EVERY DAY, FEEL VERY MUCH AS I SHOULD
GENV IV (128)	AT THE HEAD OF AN ATTEMPT TO STEM THE RUSH. AT	LEAST	ONE MAN SHALL STAND FOR HUMAN COURAGE AND DIGNITY WHEN
GENV I (39)	SO IF YOU LIVED IN A COUNTRY WHERE THERE IS AT	LEAST	ONE MURDER IN EVERY FAMILY. /SHE/ WHAT AN AWFUL
ARMS II (28)	BESIDES, THE COUNTRY SHOULD INSIST ON HAVING AT	LEAST	ONE NATIVE GENERAL. /PETKOFF/ YES; SO THAT HE COULD
CATH PREFACE(156)	TALKING SHOP, AN HONEST PLAYWRIGHT SHOULD TAKE AT	LEAST	ONE OPPORTUNITY OF ACKNOWLEDGING THAT HIS ART IS NOT
HART PREFACE(19)	IDEAL OF LIFE MORE ABUNDANT, I CAN ANSWER FOR AT	LEAST	ONE PERSON WHO FOUND THE CHANGE FROM THE WISDOM OF
BARB PREFACE(209)	LEVER AND MAY HAVE COME TO HIM FROM BEYLE, OR AT	LEAST	OUT OF THE STENDHALIAN ATMOSPHERE. I EXCLUDE THE
METH PREFACE(R19)	WAR SHALL CONVINCE HIM OF THE NECESSITY OF AT	LEAST	OUTLIVING HIS TASTE FOR GOLF AND CIGARS IF THE RACE IS
HART I SD(69)	BUT ON CLOSE INSPECTION IS FOUND TO BE AT	LEAST	OVER FORTY. /THE GENTLEMAN/ EXCUSE MY INTRUDING IN
UNPL PREFACE(R10)	WHICH, TO MY GREAT PERIL, WAS RECOGNIZED AS AT	LEAST	PARTLY SERIOUS; TO FIND THE PUMP TIRING ME AND THE
SUPR HANDBOK(226)	REBUKED ME BY SAYING " REMEMBER ALWAYS THAT THE	LEAST	PLAIN SISTER IS THE FAMILY BEAUTY." NO AGE OR
SUPR III (119)	AN ANGEL WHO WOULD FILL IT WITH MELODY, OR AT	LEAST	PLAY HIM TO SLEEP AFTER DINNER? YOU MARRIED MY FRIEND
3PLA PREFACE(R13)	SUCCESSFUL, BECAUSE THEY PRODUCED PLAYS THAT AT	LEAST	PLEASED THEMSELVES, WHEREAS COMMERCE, WITH A FALSE
CLEO NOTES (210)	THAT HE WAS GENUINELY ORIGINAL; BUT LET ME AT	LEAST	POINT OUT THAT I HAVE BEEN CAREFUL TO ATTRIBUTE
DOCT PREFACE(71)	HIMSELF TROUBLE BY DOING HIS BUSINESS WITH THE	LEAST	POSSIBLE INTERFERENCE WITH THE PRIVATE CITIZEN. THE
WIDO III SD(64)	DROPS THE PORTRAIT, AND STARES AT HER WITHOUT THE	LEAST	PRESENCE OF MIND. /BLANCHE/ (SHREWISHLY) WELL? SO
OVER PREFACE(157)	OF MATRIMONIAL JEALOUSY: THE MAN WHO DOES NOT AT	LEAST	PRETEND TO FEEL IT, AND BEHAVE AS BADLY AS IF HE
BULL PREFACE(24)	THE WESLEYAN CATECHISM WAS TAUGHT WITHOUT THE	LEAST	PROTEST ON THE PART OF THE PARENTS, ALTHOUGH THERE WAS
FABL PREFACE(87)	ALL BUT MEMBERS OF THE CHURCH OF ENGLAND. THIS AT	LEAST	PROVIDED SOME EVIDENCE AS TO WHETHER THE CANDIDATE
MRS PREFACE(172)	BOOKMAKERS ARE RARE TOO. IT MAY SEEM THAT AT	LEAST	PUBLIC SPIRIT CANNOT BE ONE OF A BOOKMAKER'S VIRTUES;
HART II (126)	SO TAKE CARE. /LADY UTTERWORD/ (NOT IN THE	LEAST	PUT OUT, AND RATHER PLEASED BY HIS VIOLENCE) MY DEAR
METH PREFACE(R51)	WHETHER THE GRANDCHILDREN WOULD BE BORN WITH AT	LEAST	RATHER SHORT TAILS. THEY WERE NOT, AS I COULD HAVE
UNPL PREFACE(R18)	ITS VICTIMS MAY NOT LIVE REAL LIVES, THEY MAY AT	LEAST	READ ABOUT IMAGINARY ONES, AND PERHAPS LEARN FROM THEM
PYGM II SD(218)	OF MALICE THAT HE REMAINS LIKEABLE EVEN IN HIS	LEAST	REASONABLE MOMENTS. /HIGGINS/ (AS HE SHUTS THE LAST
SUPR PREFACE(R27)	OR SPECIFIC TALENT FOR ADMINISTRATION, CAN AT	LEAST	RECOGNIZE AND APPRECIATE CAPACITY AND BENEVOLENCE IN
DEST SD(152)	OF THAT DAY, IS DESIGNED FOR PARADE WITHOUT THE	LEAST	REFERENCE TO HIS HEALTH OR COMFORT, HE PERSPIRES
GETT SD(266)	VERY CAREFULLY TO PRODUCE THAT EFFECT WITHOUT THE	LEAST	REGARD FOR THE LATEST FASHIONS, SURE OF HERSELF, VERY
GETT (318)	I SHALL EXPOSE HIM BEFORE ALL ENGLAND WITHOUT THE	LEAST	REGARD TO THE CONSEQUENCES TO MYSELF. /SYKES/ OR TO
POSN PREFACE(374)	TREATING THE QUESTION AS A PUBLIC ONE WITHOUT THE	LEAST	REGARD TO THE SUPPOSED SUSCEPTIBILITIES OF THE COURT
PYGM EPILOG (295)	THEY HELD TOGETHER AND LOOKED PRETTY, WITHOUT THE	LEAST	REGARD TO THEIR BEING MANY MONTHS OUT OF FASHION.
SUPR IV SD(151)	TO HIGHER AND HIGHER MORAL EMINENCES WITHOUT THE	LEAST	REGARD TO THE OLD MAN'S MILLIONS. /HECTOR/ I'M VERY
GETT PREFACE(223)	IN MEN IS UTTERLY PROMISCUOUS AND THAT THE	LEAST	RELAXATION OF LAW AND CUSTOM MUST PRODUCE A WILD
JITT II (48)	PEOPLE A LITTLE. IF YOU HAVE NO REGARD FOR ME, AT	LEAST	REMEMBER THAT AGNES AND EDITH HAVE A FUTURE, AND HAVE
MRS I (192)	OH NO, IT'S OUT OF THE QUESTION, THERES NOT THE	LEAST	RESEMBLANCE. /CROFTS/ AS TO THAT, THERES NO
SUPR III (132)	MERELY WILLING TO LIVE AND FOLLOWING THE LINE OF	LEAST	RESISTANCE: NOW I WANT TO KNOW MYSELF AND MY
LION PREFACE(84)	THAN JEWS; AND IT WAS BY FOLLOWING THE LINE OF	LEAST	RESISTANCE THAT PAUL BECAME THE APOSTLE TO THE
MIS. PREFACE(44)	FROM THE BLINDEST GROPING ALONG THE LINE OF	LEAST	RESISTANCE TO CONSCIOUS INTELLECTUAL SPECULATION, WITH
MRS PREFACE(170)	BY THE ORDINARY METHOD OF TAKING THE LINE OF	LEAST	RESISTANCE TO GETTING IT, ARE TOO COMMON IN ENGLISH
SUPR III (132)	INSTEAD OF YIELDING IN THE DIRECTION OF THE	LEAST	RESISTANCE, DOES A SHIP SAIL TO ITS DESTINATION NO
SUPR PREFACE(R24)	STUMBLING HITHER AND THITHER IN THE LINE OF	LEAST	RESISTANCE. HENCE THERE IS A DRIVING TOWARDS TRUTH IN
GETT (355)	IF YOU ARE STILL IN THE GRIP OF THIS WORLD, AT	LEAST	RESPECT ITS INSTITUTIONS. DO YOU BELIEVE IN MARRIAGE
BARB III (329)	LOOSE, YOU CAN PUT A MATCH TO THEM WITHOUT THE	LEAST	RISK: THEY JUST BURN QUIETLY LIKE A BIT OF PAPER. (
3PLA PREFACE(R10)	MAJORITY; AND WOMEN AND MEN ALIKE BELONG TO THAT	LEAST	ROBUST OF ALL OUR SOCIAL CLASSES, THE CLASS WHICH
3PLA PREFACE(R18)	THE TIMID MAJORITY, IF IT RULES NOWHERE ELSE, AT	LEAST	RULES IN THE THEATRE: FITLY ENOUGH TOO, BECAUSE ON THE
MIS. (164)	IN-- (HE HESITATES, NOT QUITE CONVINCED). AT	LEAST	-- ER-- I REALLY DIDNT MEAN TO BE DISAGREEABLE.
WIDO I (11)	IF WE COULD MAKE UP OUR MINDS TO-- OR NOT TO-- AT	LEAST	-- ER-- (HIS NERVOUSNESS DEPRIVES HIM OF THE POWER OF
BULL III (120)	OH, IT DOESNT MATTER: I WAS NOT HURT-- AT	LEAST	-- ER-- /AUNT JUDY/ OH NOW WHAT A SHAME! AN I TOLD
FANY III (300)	/MARGARET/ WHAT ABOUT? /BOBBY/ OH, NOTHING. AT	LEAST	-- HOW ARE YOU? /MARGARET/ (PASSING ROUND THE OTHER
GETT (298)	OF COURSE NOT. STILL-- I'M PERFECTLY READY-- AT	LEAST	-- IF IT WERE NOT FOR MY MOTHER-- OH, I DONT KNOW WHAT
INCA (241)	I HAVE EXPLAINED, THE FIRST FLOOR IS OCCUPIED. AT	LEAST	-- /ERMYNTRUDE/ WELL? AT LEAST? /THE MANAGER/ IT IS
BARB I (262)	CHARLES. /LOMAX/ (ABASHED) I DIDNT MEAN-- AT	LEAST	-- /LADY BRITOMART/ YOU DIDNT THINK, CHARLES. YOU
HART I (59)	DO YOU LOVE THIS MANGAN MAN? /ELLIE/ YES. AT	LEAST	-- /MRS HUSHABYE/ I DONT WANT TO KNOW ABOUT " AT
CLEO IV (170)	I! NOTHING. /CLEOPATRA/ NOTHING! /POTHINUS/ AT	LEAST	-- TO BEG FOR MY LIBERTY: THAT IS ALL. /CLEOPATRA/ FOR
APPL INTRLUD(245)	A LOVER I SHOULD NOT BE INTERESTED IN HIM IN THE	LEAST	; AND SHE WOULD BORE ME TO DISTRACTION IF SHE COULD
DEVL I (8)	HE. HOWEVER, I MUST BEAR MY CROSS AS BEST I MAY:	LEAST	SAID IS SOONEST MENDED. /ANDERSON/ (VERY GRAVE,
BASH PREFACE(92)	BOTH MUSICAL AND POWERFUL, I MAY AT	LEAST	SAY THAT IT IS BETTER TO HAVE A SENSE OF IT AND A
DOCT PREFACE(61)	BAREFOOT THROUGH THE DEWY GRASS. HE WHO SHEWS THE	LEAST	SCEPTICISM AS TO THIS PRACTICE IS AT ONCE SUSPECTED OF
BULL PREFACE(54)	60, 50, 22 AND 20. HANGING, HOWEVER, IS THE	LEAST	SENSATIONAL FORM OF PUBLIC EXECUTION: IT LACKS THOSE
MRS I (191)	PRAED)-- I ONLY SAY, IF YOU KNOW, YOU MIGHT AT	LEAST	SET MY MIND AT REST ABOUT HER. THE FACT IS, I FEEL
MIS. (194)	I WAS BROUGHT UP IN A HOUSEHOLD WHICH COST AT	LEAST	SEVEN OR EIGHT TIMES THAT; AND I AM IN CONSTANT MONEY
MILL I (157)	STOCK EXCHANGE UNTIL YOUR WEEKLY ACCOUNT IS AT	LEAST	SEVENTY THOUSAND. DO NOT MEDDLE WITH MONEY, ADRIAN:
BASH III (126)	BUT WE WILL MAKE THE SACRIFICE. SHE BLUSHES: AT	LEAST	SHE VERY PRETTILY PRODUCES BLUSHING'S EFFECT.
KING I (171)	I SHOULD NOT HAVE ASKED HER INTO MY HOUSE. AND AT	LEAST	SHE WAS NOT ON THE STAGE. (SHE RETIRES BEHIND
2TRU II (72)	OF SOMEBODY OR TO GET HOLD OF A MAN; BUT AT	LEAST	SHE'S A WOMAN; AND SHE'S REAL. MEN ARE NOT REAL:
DOCT II SD(117)	AND QUICK OF APPREHENSION, HE IS NOT IN THE	LEAST	SHY. HE IS YOUNGER THAN JENNIFER; BUT HE PATRONIZES
SUPR II (54)	NOW; AND YET THEY WROTE FIRST-RATE POETRY-- AT	LEAST	SO I'M TOLD. THEY NEVER EXPOSED THEIR IDOLATRY TO THE
2TRU I (46)	THE SIGHT OF HEAVEN, WERE NOT LEGALLY MARRIED. AT	LEAST	SO SHE TELLS ME. /THE NURSE/ (HOTLY) I TELL YOU WHAT
FABL VI (126)	STOMACHS AND BOWELS. /TEACHER/ YES THEY COULD: AT	LEAST	SO THE HISTORIES SAY. THEY FOUND THEY COULD LIVE ON
ROCK PREFACE(170)	CLASS. FOR EXAMPLE, LORD LONSDALE IS NOT IN THE	LEAST	SOCIALLY INCOMPATIBLE WITH DEAN INGE, THOUGH A REALLY
GETT PREFACE(192)	FOR POLITICAL ARTICLES INFORMED BY AT	LEAST	SOME PRETENCE OF KNOWLEDGE OF ECONOMICS, HISTORY, AND
UNPL PREFACE(R7)	NOT ONLY MY OWN IMAGINATION, BUT THAT OF AT	LEAST	SOME SEVENTY OR A HUNDRED THOUSAND CONTEMPORARY LONDON
NEVR III (270)	THEM; AND I MUST FULFIL MY DESTINY, I SUPPOSE. AT	LEAST	SPARE ME THE HUMILIATION OF TRYING TO SAVE ME. (SHE
GETT PREFACE(217)	OF ITS IDEAL SO JEALOUS AND IMPLACABLE THAT THE	LEAST	STEP FROM THE STRAIGHT PATH MEANS EXPOSURE AND RUIN,
METH PREFACE(R53)	MISERABLY AS RELIGION HAD BEEN DEBASED, IT DID AT	LEAST	STILL PROCLAIM THAT OUR RELATION TO ONE ANOTHER WAS
DEVL III (74)	THOSE AROUND HIM, AND FINALLY TO BURGOYNE, AS THE	LEAST	STOLID OF THEM) TAKE HER AWAY. DO YOU THINK I WANT A
GETT PREFACE(187)	BY PUBLIC OPINION WITH SUCH FEROCITY THAT THE	LEAST	SUGGESTION OF LAXITY IN ITS SUPPORT IS FATAL TO EVEN
FABL PREFACE(90)	IS SO INTOLERABLE THAT IT WILL NOT BE IN THE	LEAST	SURPRISING IF VACCINATION OFFICERS ARE RESISTED, NOT
CAND II (119)	DO YOU KNOW, JAMES, THAT THOUGH HE HAS NOT THE	LEAST	SUSPICION OF IT HIMSELF, HE IS READY TO FALL MADLY IN
METH PREFACE(R48)	TOOK A PERVERSE PLEASURE IN ARGUING, WITHOUT THE	LEAST	SUSPICION THAT WE WERE REDUCING OURSELVES TO
AUGS (273)	ME, YET WILL I, IF NOT EXACTLY TRUST IN HER, AT	LEAST	TAKE MY PART IN HER GOVERNMENT. I AM EVER AT MY
2TRU PREFACE(13)	WHO IS NOT AN IGNORAMUS AND NOT IN THE	LEAST	TERRIFIED, AND WHOSE VERY INTERESTING CONVERSION TO
SIM PREFACE(16)	DIE FOR THE PEOPLE; BUT IT DOES NOT FOLLOW IN THE	LEAST	THAT HE SHOULD BE TORTURED OR TERRIFIED. PUBLIC
CATH PREFACE(158)	IN HIS LIFE, I DO NOT THINK HE EXPECTED IN THE	LEAST	THAT HIS PERFORMANCE WOULD ENABLE ME TO BOAST OF HIS
MILL I (151)	THE CREATURE IS INTELLIGENT ENOUGH TO DO AT	LEAST	THAT MUCH FOR HIMSELF. /PATRICIA/ YOU DONT UNDERSTAND
2TRU PREFACE(20)	PACE WITH THOUGHT. NOW THIS DOES NOT MEAN IN THE	LEAST	THAT THE ORIGINAL CATHOLIC PLAN WAS WRONG. ON THE
MILL PREFACE(125)	THE BOAST) THAT WE ARE THOSE LOST TRIBES, OR AT	LEAST	THAT WE MUST HAVE ABSORBED THEM. ONE OF MY GUESSES IN
GETT PREFACE(197)	MISCHIEVOUS AS IT WAS IN MANY WAYS, HAD AT	LEAST	THE ADVANTAGE THAT THE CHILD DID NOT ENJOY IT AND WAS
DOCT PREFACE(50)	CAN HARDLY BE ATTAINED WITHOUT SOME REGARD FOR AT	LEAST	THE APPEARANCES OF HUMAN WELFARE, WHEREAS A CURIOUS
JOAN PREFACE(47)	THAT THE EARTH WAS FLAT, FOR WHICH THEY HAD AT	LEAST	THE EVIDENCE OF THEIR SENSES: WE BELIEVE IT TO BE
JOAN PREFACE(55)	HALF-PAST EIGHT O'CLOCK DINNER SO AS TO ESCAPE AT	LEAST	THE FIRST HALF-HOUR OF THE PERFORMANCE, THEY STAND IN
DOCT PREFACE(53)	WITH THE STATISTICS OF DISEASE HAS TAKEN AT	LEAST	THE FIRST STEP TOWARDS SANITY BY GRASPING THE FACT
LION PREFACE(100)	AS WELL AS TO MAKE MONEY AND THEREBY SECURE AT	LEAST	THE LIVES OF THE UNFORTUNATE INHABITANTS OUT OF WHOSE
APPL I (205)	IN THEM. STILL, KILLING IS A SERIOUS BUSINESS: AT	LEAST	THE PERSON WHO IS TO BE KILLED IS USUALLY CONCEITED
GETT (267)	WHEN I WAS ONLY A COMPANY OFFICER I HAD AT	LEAST	THE RIGHT TO EXPOSE MYSELF TO DEATH IN THE FIELD. NOW
NEVR III (270)	SIR. /GLORIA/ (CONTINUING)-- BUT I HAVE AT	LEAST	THE RIGHT TO BE LEFT ALONE IN MY DISGRACE. I AM ONE OF
LION PREFACE(31)	IS THAT OF AN ARISTOCRAT, OR AT THE VERY	LEAST	THE SON OF A RICH BOURGEOIS, AND BY NO MEANS A
MILL PREFACE(135)	ILLITERATE CALL BOY? POLITICALLY WE ALL HAVE AT	LEAST	THE SYMBOL OF EQUALITY IN OUR VOTES, USELESS AS THEY
MTH2 (43)	BOURGEOIS POINTS OF HONOR MAY BE FALSE; BUT AT	LEAST	THEY EXIST. THE WOMEN KNOW WHAT TO EXPECT AND WHAT IS
APPL PREFACE(181)	POWER BY GOVERNMENTS. ONE MIGHT SUPPOSE THAT AT	LEAST	THEY WOULD ACT AS A LAST RESORT WHEN AN AUTOCRAT GOES
FABL PREFACE(85)	IS ALWAYS AGAINST ANY CHANGE, AND IT TAKES AT	LEAST	THIRTY YEARS TO CONVERT IT, WHILST ONLY TEN PER CENT
FABL PREFACE(88)	EXAMINATIONS BY ELDERLY MEN OF YOUTHS ARE AT	LEAST	THIRTY YEARS OUT OF DATE: IN ECONOMICS, FOR INSTANCE,
MTH2 (38)	" THE TERM OF HUMAN LIFE MUST BE EXTENDED TO AT	LEAST	THREE CENTURIES." /THE TWEEDED GENTLEMAN/ HOW DID YOU
MTH2 (38)	WORDS I WROTE WHEN YOU INTERRUPTED ME WERE " AT	LEAST	THREE CENTURIES." (HE SNATCHES UP HIS MANUSCRIPT, AND
APPL I (221)	BY THE LEAGUE OF NATIONS WE COULD LIVE FOR AT	LEAST	THREE WEEKS ON OUR CHOCOLATE CREAMS. /NICOBAR/ YOU

SIM PREFACE(10)	THE SPECIFIC INQUISITIONS PETERED OUT, NOT IN THE	LEAST	THROUGH A GROWTH OF REAL TOLERANCE, BUT BECAUSE, AS
BULL PREFACE(15)	BE, IF NOT AN AMERICAN, AN ITALIAN, OR A JEW, AT	LEAST	TO BE DEPENDING ON THE BRAINS, THE NERVOUS ENERGY, AND
GETT PREFACE(247)	DOWN INTO COMFORT ENOUGH TO SATISFY THEM, OR AT	LEAST	TO CAUSE THEM NO MORE DISCOMFORT THAN THEY ARE
POSN PREFACE(367)	EXPLAINS WHY THE MANAGERIAL WITNESSES WHO HAD	LEAST	TO FEAR FROM THE CENSOR WERE THE MOST RELUCTANT IN HIS
LIED SD(187)	AND SPENDING POWERS OF ITS OWNERS, AND NOT IN THE	LEAST	TO MAKE THEM COMFORTABLE. HE IS, BE IT REPEATED, A
O'FL PREFACE(201)	AN ENGLISHMAN IN BRAVERY IF POSSIBLE, AND AT	LEAST	TO SET A PERILOUS PACE FOR HIM. IRISH SOLDIERS GIVE
MTH4 I (172)	THE NEGRO? ARE WE NOT, AS BRITONS, ENTITLED AT	LEAST	TO SOME RESERVATIONS? /ZOO/ WHAT IS THE USE OF
LION PREFACE(56)	TO THE PEOPLE WHO DID NOT WORK AT ALL, AND THE	LEAST	TO THOSE WHO WORKED HARDEST. IN ENGLAND NINE-TENTHS OF
SUPR III (120)	ME, ARE TOUCHINGLY AFFECTIONATE; AND MOST ARE AT	LEAST	TOLERABLY FRIENDLY. BUT THAT DOES NOT MAKE A CHAIN A
SUPR PREFACE(R16)	OF MR W.S. GILBERT. HIS SCEPTICISM, ONCE HIS	LEAST	TOLERATED QUALITY, HAS NOW TRIUMPHED SO COMPLETELY
BULL II (108)	WOULD TELL YOU? SURE HE'D SAY WHATEVER WAS THE	LEAST	TROUBLE TO HIMSELF AND THE PLEASANTEST TO YOU, THINKIN
JOAN 2 (74)	AND YOU, SIR: IF YOU CANNOT RULE YOUR KINGDOM, AT	LEAST	TRY TO RULE YOURSELF. /CHARLES/ ANOTHER LECTURE!
ROCK II (262)	THE PROGRAM WILL INVOLVE THE INTRODUCTION OF AT	LEAST	TWELVE BILLS. THEY ARE HIGHLY CONTROVERSIAL BILLS:
VWOO 2 (130)	WORD WITH ME, YOU WOULDNT BELIEVE. IT'S WORTH AT	LEAST	TWENTY POUNDS A YEAR TO THE BUSINESS. /A/ (PUTTING ON
DOCT V (176)	MEAN TO OFFEND YOU, INDEED-- BUT YOU MUST BE AT	LEAST	TWENTY YEARS OLDER THAN I AM. /RIDGEON/ OH, QUITE.
SUPR I SD(3)	OF DUST IS VISIBLE: IT IS CLEAR THAT THERE ARE AT	LEAST	TWO HOUSEMAIDS AND A PARLORMAID DOWNSTAIRS, AND A
GETT PREFACE(227)	ARE NOT LIMITED FOR MONEY REASONS; WHERE AT	LEAST	TWO HOUSES AND SOMETIMES THREE OR FOUR ARE THE RULE (
ROCK II (241)	/GLENMORISON/ SAME HERE, SIR DEXTER. I CLAIM AT	LEAST	TWO ITEMS. /SIR DEXTER/ MUCH GOOD MAY THEY DO YOU.
GENV IV (106)	I CANNOT PUNCH YOUR HEAD BECAUSE YOU ARE AT	LEAST	TWO STONE HEAVIER THAN I; BUT I WILL FIGHT YOU WITH
DOCT II (123)	AND HE'LL SIGN ANYTHING TO GET IT, WITHOUT IN THE	LEAST	UNDERSTANDING IT, OR INTENDING TO CARRY OUT THE
MRS IV (239)	I SHALL NEVER CALL YOU VIVVUMS AGAIN-- AT	LEAST	UNLESS YOU GET TIRED OF YOUR NEW LITTLE BOY, WHOEVER
BARB I (268)	AND YOU CANT GO AGAINST RELIGION, CAN YOU? AT	LEAST	UNLESS YOURE DOWNRIGHT IMMORAL, DONT YOU KNOW.
MILL I (162)	NO: DECIDEDLY I WILL NOT DIVORCE ALASTAIR-- AT	LEAST	UNTIL I CAN FIND A SUBSTITUTE WHOM I REALLY WANT.
JITT III (57)	A HAPPY ONE? /AGNES/ I ALWAYS THOUGHT IT WAS, AT	LEAST	UNTIL THE LAST FEW YEARS. THEN THERE WAS A SUDDEN
NEVR III (278)	GOT ANY LUNCH, MY DEAR FINCH: THERE IS NOT THE	LEAST	USE IN TALKING TO ME ABOUT FERGUS. YOU HAVE NEVER BEEN
CAND II (105)	MY TYPEWRITER, MR MARCHBANKS; AND THERES NOT THE	LEAST	USE IN YOUR TRYING TO LOOK AS IF YOU HADNT.
DOCT I (100)	IN THE SEVENTIES. WE MAY HAVE OUR FAULTS; BUT AT	LEAST	WE ARE MEN OF SCIENCE. THAT IS WHY I AM TAKING UP YOUR
MRS PREFACE(173)	CASE, AND COMIC IN THE CLERGYMAN'S CASE (AT	LEAST	WE ARE SAVAGE ENOUGH TO LAUGH AT IT); BUT IN BOTH
HART II (127)	AND IF I DID GO STARK STARING MAD ABOUT HER, AT	LEAST	WE BECAME MAN AND WIFE. BUT WHY SHOULD YOU LET
JOAN 4 (104)	FORGIVE MAHOMET FOR BEING A CAMEL DRIVER. BUT AT	LEAST	WE CAN PROCEED IN THIS MATTER WITHOUT BIGOTRY.
GENV IV (106)	GO HOME. /WIDOW/ (RISING) YOU SHALL NOT. HERE AT	LEAST	WE HAVE COME TO THE REAL BUSINESS OF THIS COURT; AND
AUGS (266)	THIS IS PERFECTLY MONSTROUS. NOT IN THE	LEAST	WHAT I INTENDED. /THE CLERK/ HELL -- /AUGUSTUS/ SIR!
GETT PREFACE(203)	LEGITIMATE, ALSO THAT IT DOES NOT MATTER IN THE	LEAST	WHAT SORT OF ADULTS WE HAVE, PROVIDED THEY ARE
GETT PREFACE(203)	PASSIONATELY THAT IT DOES NOT MATTER IN THE	LEAST	WHAT SORT OF CHILDREN WE HAVE, OR HOW FEW OR HOW MANY,
JOAN PREFACE(53)	ON THE PRINCIPLE THAT IT DOES NOT MATTER IN THE	LEAST	WHY A WOMAN IS BURNT PROVIDED SHE IS BURNT, AND PEOPLE
SIM I (46)	IS ANOTHER CONSIDERATION THAT WEIGHS WITH US: AT	LEAST	WITH ME. I AM CONVINCED THAT THERE IS SOMETHING
LADY PREFACE(233)	DID (FOR IT WAS NOT QUITE THE SAME WORLD), AT	LEAST	WITH MUCH OF IBSEN'S POWER OF PENETRATING ITS
GENV III (83)	I AM NOT A FRENCHMAN NOR A NEGRO. /THE JUDGE/ AT	LEAST	YOU ARE NOT A SCOT, NOR AN IRISHMAN, NOR A MAN OF
DOCT V (178)	OF HIM. BE AS ANGRY WITH ME AS YOU LIKE: AT	LEAST	YOU KNOW ME AS I REALLY AM. IF YOU EVER COME TO CARE
MIS. (142)	IF YOU CANT UNDERSTAND MY HOLIER FEELINGS, AT	LEAST	YOU KNOW THE BODILY INFIRMITIES OF THE OLD. YOU KNOW
BULL IV (153)	PROTESTANT A DOCUMENT AS THE BIBLE; BUT AT	LEAST	YOU MIGHT QUOTE IT ACCURATELY. /LARRY/ TOM: WITH THE
MTH4 I (164)	I AM TODAY. IF YOU CANNOT UNDERSTAND THAT, AT	LEAST	YOU MUST ADMIT THAT I HAVE LEARNT FROM TERTIARIES. I
SUPR IV (160)	SUBJECT IS CLOSED, AND IF THE WOUND IS OPEN, AT	LEAST	YOU SHALL NEVER SEE IT BLEED. /ANN/ POETIC TO THE
FANY III (303)	NO HARM IN IT, BUT YOURE NOT THE LARKY SORT. AT	LEAST	YOU USENT TO BE. /MARGARET/ I'M NOT; AND I NEVER WILL
PHIL II (121)	PARADOXICAL, CHARTERIS. /CHARTERIS/ WELL, AT	LEAST	YOULL ADMIT THAT IT'S AMIABLE AND HUMAN TO HOPE THAT
PRES (143)	RAVINGS OF A JINGO CIVILIAN, BALSQUITH. AT	LEAST	YOULL NOT DENY THAT THE ABSOLUTE COMMAND OF THE SEA IS
BUOY IV (57)	I HAVE NO TURN FOR. /SIR FERDINAND/ I SEE. BUT AT	LEAST	YOULL NOT MIND MY KEEPING UP MY ACQUAINTANCE WITH THE
2TRU III (103)	KILL HIM. /THE ELDER/ WE ARE ALL SLAVES. BUT AT	LEAST	YOUR SON IS AN HONEST MAN. /TALLBOYS/ IS HE? I AM
MIS. PREFACE(83)	HABIT; BUT EVEN AT THAT IT IS, FOR THE MOMENT AT	LEAST	, A WRENCH, FOR THOUGH PARENTS AND CHILDREN SOMETIMES
DEVL EPILOG (85)	BRUDENELL. BRUDENELL IS ALSO A REAL PERSON. AT	LEAST	, AN ARTILLERY CHAPLAIN OF THAT NAME DISTINGUISHED
3PLA PREFACE(R19)	TO THE AUDIENCE. THE RESULT IS, TO ME AT	LEAST	, AN INTOLERABLE PERVERSION OF HUMAN CONDUCT. THERE
LADY PREFACE(208)	THOMAS TYLER, THROUGHOUT THE EIGHTIES AT	LEAST	, AND PROBABLY FOR SOME YEARS BEFORE, THE BRITISH
PRES (167)	(COMING TO BALSQUITH) MR BALSQUITH: YOU, AT	LEAST	, ARE NOT A PHILISTINE. /BALSQUITH/ NO, LADY
BASH I (95)	HONEST. I AM ASHAMED TO TELL YOU WHAT I AM-- AT	LEAST	, AS YET. SOME DAY, PERHAPS. /MELLISH/ (NEARER)
CAPT I (239)	MOORS. /LADY CICELY/ THAT DOESNT MATTER IN THE	LEAST	, HOWARD. THE IMPORTANT THING, CAPTAIN BRASSBOUND, IS:
WIDO III (57)	IT, MY CHILD? /BLANCHE/ OH, I HATE THE POOR. AT	LEAST	, I HATE THOSE DIRTY, DRUNKEN, DISREPUTABLE PEOPLE WHO
FOUN (217)	TALK ABOUT MYSELF. THE FACT IS, I'M AN ORPHAN. AT	LEAST	, I THINK I AM. /THE LORD CHANCELLOR/ DONT YOU KNOW..
CAND I (101)	SHALL ONE DAY REAP. AND LAST, BUT TRUST ME, NOT	LEAST	, I WILL HELP YOU TO BELIEVE THAT YOUR WIFE LOVES YOU
WIDO II (41)	/TRENCH/ CERTAINLY NOT. I'M A CONSERVATIVE. AT	LEAST	, IF I EVER TOOK THE TROUBLE TO VOTE, I SHOULD VOTE
ARMS III (65)	BUT DEEP INDIGNATION) I WILL PROVE THAT THAT, AT	LEAST	, IS A CALUMNY. (HE GOES WITH DIGNITY TO THE DOOR AND
ARMS II (36)	AS HE ADDS, WITH DEEP BITTERNESS) AND ONE, AT	LEAST	, IS A COWARD: JEALOUS, LIKE ALL COWARDS. (HE GOES TO
PRES (162)	I AM GOING TO WAIT ON GENERAL SANDSTONE. HE, AT	LEAST	, IS AN OFFICER AND A GENTLEMAN. (SHE SAILS OUT).
APPL I (224)	EVENTS YOU DO NOT FLATTER KINGS. ONE OF THEM, AT	LEAST	, IS GRATEFUL TO YOU FOR THAT. /PROTEUS/ KINGS, AS YOU
BARB PREFACE(245)	BECAUSE WE ARE FORCED TO ADMIT THAT IT, AT	LEAST	, IS IRREVOCABLE-- AS IF ONE HOUR OF IMPRISONMENT WERE
MILL II (172)	MAN: I AM INTERESTING. /THE DOCTOR/ NOT IN THE	LEAST	, MEDICALLY. ARE YOU INTERESTING IN ANY OTHER WAY?
PHIL II (124)	/GRACE/ (FIRMLY) IT IS NOT YOUR FAULT IN THE	LEAST	, MR CHARTERIS. DR PARAMORE: WILL YOU OBLIGE ME BY
ARMS II (26)	WOULD HAVE DONE. /PETKOFF/ I DONT DOUBT IT IN THE	LEAST	, MY DEAR. BUT I SHOULD HAVE HAD TO SUBDUE THE WHOLE
MILL IV (204)	DOCTOR/ THAT DOES NOT DISCONCERT ALLAH IN THE	LEAST	, MY FRIEND. THE PULSE BEATS STILL, SLOW, STRONG. (TO
DOCT III (141)	WOMAN, HE DOESNT GO AND BRAG ABOUT IT TO HER; AT	LEAST	, NOT IF HE'S A GENTLEMAN. /WALPOLE/ WHAT ARE TO DO
WIDO I (11)	SAY. /TRENCH/ (TOTALLY UNNERVED) NOT AT ALL. AT	LEAST	, NOTHING VERY PARTICULAR. THAT IS, I'M AFRAID YOU
CLEO NOTES (212)	V. HOWEVER, NOBODY NEED DENY CAESAR A SHARE, AT	LEAST	, OF THE QUALITIES I HAVE ATTRIBUTED TO HIM. ALL MEN,
DEVL II (39)	HALF TO RICHARD'S GOOD BREEDING) WELL, NO SIR. AT	LEAST	, ONLY AN ARMY CHAPLAIN. (SHEWING THE HANDCUFFS). I'M
DEVL III (51)	/RICHARD/ (WHIMSICALLY) AT NOON, PUNCTUALLY. AT	LEAST	, THAT WAS WHEN THEY DISPOSED OF UNCLE PETER. (SHE
MIS. PREFACE(77)	TRIES MANY DISTRACTIONS WHICH ARE, TO SAY THE	LEAST	, UNSUITED TO CHILDREN. BUT ONE OF THEM, THE
GENV IV (129)	IT (SHE GOES OUT DISTRACTEDLY). /JUDGE/ SHE, AT	LEAST	, VALUES HER LIFE. /SECRETARY/ YES: SHE BELONGS TO
PLES PREFACE(R7)	DISCOVERY THAT THE NEW DRAMA, IN ENGLAND AT	LEAST	, WAS A FIGMENT OF THE REVOLUTIONARY IMAGINATION. THIS
CLEO NOTES (211)	MOST FOR IT: IN OTHER WORDS, WHEN ITS VALUE IS	LEAST	, WHICH IS JUST WHEN A COMMON MAN TRIES HARDEST TO GET
HART I (76)	IS WORSE THAN YOU, BECAUSE YOU HAD ONE REAL GO AT	LEAST	, WITH ME. /HECTOR/ THAT WAS A CONFOUNDED MADNESS. I
APPL PREFACE(178)	FAMILIAR WITH IT AS PRACTICAL STATESMEN TRUST IT	LEAST	, YOU MUST NOT AT ONCE DENOUNCE ME AS A PAID AGENT OF
APPL PREFACE(178)	THAT THOSE WHO ARE MOST FAMILIAR WITH IT TRUST IT	LEAST	, YOU WILL NOT IMMEDIATELY SHRIEK OUT THAT I DO NOT
MTH1 II (30)	GROUND). I HARDLY KNOW WHICH OF YOU SATISFIES ME	LEAST	, YOU WITH YOUR DIRTY DIGGING, OR HE WITH HIS DIRTY
HART I (59)	/MRS HUSHABYE/ I DONT WANT TO KNOW ABOUT " AT	LEAST	": I WANT TO KNOW THE WORST. GIRLS OF YOUR AGE FALL IN
LADY PREFACE(229)	TO SAY TO THE ROMAN RADICAL WHO DEMANDED AT	LEAST	" GOOD WORDS" FROM HIM " HE THAT WILL GIVE GOOD WORDS
		LEASTWAWS	
CAPT I (222)	HOWVER THERE AGIN, YER SEE (POINTING SEAWARD)--	LEASTWAWS	, NAOW SHE WORNT: SHE WERE A BRAZILIAN, AW THINK;
		LEASTWAYS	
FOUN (213)	ME AS A GENTLEMAN. BUT THEN HE AINT PARTICULAR:	LEASTWAYS	, NOT AT ELECTION TIMES. YOU SEE, MISS, THERE ARE
FOUN (213)	ARE YOU THE LORD CHANCELLOR? /MERCER/ NO, MAAM.	LEASTWAYS	, NOT YET. /ANASTASIA/ WHAT ARE YOU? /MERCER/ I'M
		LEATHER	
2TRU II (61)	NEXT TIME. WHAT DO YOU SUPPOSE I'M MADE OF?	LEATHER	? /AUBREY/ (COMING BETWEEN THEM) NOW! NOW! NOW!
CLEO III SD(144)	SHEWING THROUGH AN OPENWORK SCABBARD OF PURPLE	LEATHER	AND FILAGREE. THE PORTERS, CONDUCTED BY FTATATEETA,
FANY I (278)	STREET, IVORY INLAID, WITH GOLD KEYS AND RUSSIA	LEATHER	BELLOWS; AND BOBBY KNEW I HANKERED AFTER IT; BUT HE
DEVL II (48)	PISTOLS. (SHE GOES TO THE PRESS AND TAKES FROM A	LEATHER	BELT WITH TWO PISTOLS, A POWDER HORN, AND A BAG OF
MTH4 I SD(139)	STUCK IN IT, A TALL HAT OF GREY FELT, AND PATENT	LEATHER	BOOTS WITH WHITE SPATS. HIS STARCHED LINEN CUFFS
KING I (208)	FOR US TO DIFFER VERY GREATLY. YOU HAVE TO WEAR	LEATHER	BREECHES LEST YOU BE MISTAKEN FOR ME. BARBARA STORMS
KING I (214)	YOU ALONE I'LL MAKE YOU WISH YOU HAD TEN PAIRS OF	LEATHER	BREECHES ON YOU. /CHARLES/ COME COME! NO
KING I (162)	/MRS BASHAM/ WHY, THATS THE QUAKER, THE MAN IN	LEATHER	BREECHES. HE'S BEEN IN PRISON. HOW DARE HE COME HERE
KING I (172)	(RUNNING TO FOX) I KNOW. I KNOW. THE MAN IN THE	LEATHER	BREECHES. /FOX/ (STUBBORNLY SEATED) I AM ALSO KNOWN
KING I (183)	AND GOES OUT. /NELLY/ (BECKONING TO FOX) COME ON,	LEATHER	BREECHES. /FOX/ (RISING AND GOING TOWARDS THE DOOR)
KING I (172)	BE GEORGE FOX; BUT THERE IS ONLY ONE MAN IN THE	LEATHER	BREECHES, YOUR SERVANT, GEORGE. /FOX/ YOURS, NELLY.
KING I (165)	COMMON BEAST. /MRS BASHAM/ FOX THE QUAKER, IN HIS	LEATHER	BREECHES, HAD THE IMPUDENCE TO CALL. /NEWTON/ (
KING I (177)	THE WOMAN IN MYSELF TEACHES ME. /NELL/ GOOD FOR	LEATHER	BREECHES! WHAT DO YOU THINK OF HER, GEORGE? /FOX/
BULL IV (148)	THE PROCEEDINGS. /BROADBENT/ (TAKING OFF HIS	LEATHER	CAP WITH DIGNITY AND PLACING IT ON THE TABLE) I HOPE
CAND I SD(78)	LET INTO THE PANELS, A TRAVELLING CLOCK IN A	LEATHER	CASE (THE INEVITABLE WEDDING PRESENT), AND ON THE

WIDO I SD(5)	A WHITE HAT, AND A FIELD-GLASS SLUNG IN A NEW	LEATHER	CASE. A SELF-MADE MAN, FORMIDABLE TO SERVANTS, NOT
CAPT III SD(293)	HE TAKES FROM THE BREAST POCKET OF HIS JACKET A	LEATHER	CASE, FROM WHICH HE EXTRACTS A SCRAPPY PACKET OF
KING I (162)	ANOTHER NOBLEMAN? /SALLY/ NO, MAAM. HE WEARS	LEATHER	CLOTHES. QUITE OUT OF THE COMMON. /MRS BASHAM/ DID
SUPR II (56)	ENRY. HE CARES FOR NOTHING BUT TEARING ALONG IN A	LEATHER	COAT AND GOGGLES, WITH TWO INCHES OF DUST ALL OVER
SUPR III SD(77)	TANNER AND STRAKER, IN THEIR MOTORING GOGGLES,	LEATHER	COATS, AND CAPS, ARE LED IN FROM THE ROAD BY THE
HART I (47)	CHILD INDIAN TEA: THE STUFF THEY TAN THEIR OWN	LEATHER	INSIDES WITH. (HE SEIZES THE CUP AND THE TEA-POT
BARB I SD(249)	IS IN THE MIDDLE OF THE ROOM, UPHOLSTERED IN DARK	LEATHER	. A PERSON SITTING ON IT (IT IS VACANT AT PRESENT)
KING I (214)	THAT TO THIS PERSON WHO IS DRESSED PARTLY IN	LEATHER	, IT IS HIS PROFESSION: IT IS NOT YOURS. /CHARLES/
KING I SD(166)	IS DECENTLY DRESSED; BUT HIS GARMENTS ARE MADE OF	LEATHER	, /CHARLES/ AFTER YOU, MR FOX. THE SPIRITUAL POWERS
DOCT PREFACE(14)	THE COBBLER BELIEVES THAT THERE IS NOTHING LIKE	LEATHER	, THE IMPERIALIST WHO REGARDS THE CONQUEST OF
CLEO IV (181)	THROWS THE CUSHIONS AWAY AND SEATS HIMSELF ON THE	LEATHER	MATTRESS UNDERNEATH), /CLEOPATRA/ WHAT A SHAME! MY
KING I (213)	THE COBBLER THINKS THERE IS NOTHING LIKE	LEATHER	-- /NELL/ NOT WHEN YOU MAKE IT INTO BREECHES INSTEAD
PHIL I SD(69)	BY A TURQUOISE RING. HE WEARS BLUE SOCKS AND	LEATHER	SANDALS. THE ARRANGEMENT OF HIS TAWNY HAIR, AND OF
MTH1 II SD(20)	IS EQUIPPED WITH HUGE SPEAR AND BROAD BRASS-BOUND	LEATHER	SHIELD; HIS CASQUE IS A TIGER'S HEAD WITH BULL'S
PYGM V SD(270)	HIS BUTTONHOLE, A DAZZLING SILK HAT, AND PATENT	LEATHER	SHOES COMPLETE THE EFFECT. HE IS TOO CONCERNED WITH
JOAN 4,SD(97)	WITH A GRAVE INCLINATION. WARWICK FETCHES THE	LEATHER	STOOL CARELESSLY, AND SITS IN HIS FORMER PLACE. THE
JOAN 4,SD(94)	WITH SUPPRESSED WRATH. THERE IS AN UNOCCUPIED	LEATHER	STOOL ON THE NOBLEMAN'S LEFT. THE TABLE IS ON HIS
CLEO PRG2 (99)	OF MEN-- COMMON FELLOWS ENOUGH, WITH HELMETS,	LEATHER	TUNICS, AND BREASTPLATES. EVERY MAN OF THEM FLUNG
ROCK I SD(193)	ACROSS THE MIDDLE OF THE ROOM, WITH FOURTEEN	LEATHER	UPHOLSTERED CHAIRS, SIX AT EACH SIDE AND ONE AT EACH
		LEATHERBRAIN'S	
DEST (174)	OF VENICE BY TAKING PESCHIERA. YOU ARE ONE OF OLD	LEATHERBRAIN'S	SPIES: HE HAS DISCOVERED THAT HE HAS BEEN
		LEATHERN	
CLEO III (159)	THE LIGHTHOUSE, SOME FOOL THREW A GREAT	LEATHERN	BAG INTO THE SEA. IT BROKE THE NOSE OF MY BOAT; AND
CLEO III (157)	(BRITANNUS RETURNS, GREATLY EXCITED, WITH A	LEATHERN	BAG. CAESAR IS HIMSELF AGAIN IN A MOMENT). WHAT
CLEO III SD(155)	FULL OF DATES, IS BETWEEN HIS KNEES; AND A	LEATHERN	BOTTLE OF WINE IS BY HIS SIDE. BEHIND HIM THE GREAT
HART I (47)	THE CUP AND THE TEA-POT AND EMPTIES BOTH INTO THE	LEATHERN	BUCKET). /ELLIE/ (ALMOST IN TEARS) OH, PLEASE! I
CLEO IV (181)	TABLE, TO RA'S LEFT HAND) WHAT HAS BECOME OF MY	LEATHERN	CUSHION? /CLEOPATRA/ (AT THE OPPOSITE END) I HAVE
CAPT II SD(242)	ON THE CEMENT FLOOR ARE MATTINGS, SHEEPSKINS, AND	LEATHERN	CUSHIONS WITH GEOMETRICAL PATTERNS ON THEM. THERE
SUPR II SD(48)	BENT BACK AND HANDS SUPPORTED ON HIS KNEES. HIS	LEATHERN	OVERCOAT AND PEAKED CAP PROCLAIM HIM ONE OF THE
SUPR II SD(48)	HIMSELF OF HIS OVERALLS. TANNER TAKES OFF HIS	LEATHERN	OVERCOAT AND PITCHES IT INTO THE CAR WITH A SIGH OF
		LEATHER-BRAINED	
DEST (174)	RETREAT. THERE ARE ONLY TWO THINGS HE CAN DO--	LEATHER-BRAINED	IDIOT THAT HE IS! -- SHUT HIMSELF UP IN
		LEATHER-COVERED	
PYGM II SD(217)	THE SAME SIDE, IS A FIREPLACE, WITH A COMFORTABLE	LEATHER-COVERED	EASY-CHAIR AT THE SIDE OF THE HEARTH NEAREST
		LEATHERY	
BULL III SD(120)	DEAR OH DEAR! AN OLDISH PEASANT FARMER, SMALL,	LEATHERY	, PEAT-FACED, WITH A DEEP VOICE AND A SURLINESS
		LEAVE	
LADY (247)	" LACK ADVANCEMENT." BY YOUR MAJESTY'S	LEAVE	: A QUEENLY PHRASE. (HE IS ABOUT TO WRITE IT DOWN).
JOAN 6 (140)	ME LEAVE. /COURCELLES/ WHEN WILL SHE GIVE YOU	LEAVE	? /JOAN/ WHEN YOU TAKE ME OUT OF THE HANDS OF THE
GETT (335)	GEORGE/ YOU COME WITHIN REACH OF ME AND I'LL NOT	LEAVE	A HAIR ON YOUR HEAD. /HOTCHKISS/ (CATCHING HER WRISTS
JOAN 4 (96)	IN EVERY TIME MONEY CHANGES HANDS. I WOULD NOT	LEAVE	A JEW ALIVE IN CHRISTENDOM IF I HAD MY WAY. /THE
JOAN 4 (96)	FOR THAT SLUT! /THE NOBLEMAN/ ONE HAS TO	LEAVE	A MARGIN. SOME OF CHARLES'S PEOPLE WILL SELL HER TO
FANY I (280)	THE DISGRACE OF IT WILL KILL ME. AND IT WILL	LEAVE	A MARK ON HIM TO THE END OF HIS LIFE. /DORA/ NOT A BIT
PYGM IV (267)	I AM GOING TO BED. /LIZA/ (PERTLY) YOUD BETTER	LEAVE	A NOTE FOR MRS PEARCE ABOUT THE COFFEE; FOR SHE WONT
PYGM I (213)	FLOWER GIRL/ LET HIM MIND HIS OWN BUSINESS AND	LEAVE	A POOR GIRL-- /THE NOTE TAKER/ (EXPLOSIVELY) WOMAN:
JOAN 6 (134)	YOU LEAVE THE TOWER? /JOAN/ WHY WOULD ANYBODY	LEAVE	A PRISON IF THEY COULD GET OUT? /D'ESTIVET/ YOU TRIED
SUPR III (98)	/THE DEVIL/ WHY, SIR, DO YOU NOT JOIN US, AND	LEAVE	A SPHERE FOR WHICH YOUR TEMPERAMENT IS TOO
GENV II (51)	DIRTY SWINE! I HOPE THE BRITISH FLEET WILL NOT	LEAVE	A STONE STANDING OR A NIGGER ALIVE IN THEIR BEASTLY
BULL PREFACE(63)	IN ANY CASE LET NO ENGLISHMAN WHO IS CONTENT TO	LEAVE	ABD-EL-NEBI AND HIS TWENTY-YEAR-OLD NEIGHBOR IN PENAL
FANY III (308)	SEEN. YOU HAD BETTER STEP INTO MY PANTRY AND	LEAVE	AFTERWARDS. /DORA/ RIGHTO! (SHE BURSTS INTO SONG)
JITT III (71)	AS MUCH AS HE EVER DID; BUT HE THINKS YOU HAVE TO	LEAVE	ALL THAT OUT WHEN YOU ARE JUDGING MEN. HE THINKS A
DEST (154)	EH? /GIUSEPPE/ TOO TROUBLESOME, EXCELLENCY: I	LEAVE	ALL THAT TO YOU. BESIDES, WHAT WOULD BECOME ON MY INN
INCA (242)	SERVICE I KNOW NO FEAR. YOUR HIGHNESS CAN	LEAVE	ALL UNPLEASANT PEOPLE TO ME. /THE PRINCESS/ HOW I WISH
2TRU III (90)	MY NERVE FAILED AGAIN: I HAD TO TAKE THREE MONTHS	LEAVE	AND GO INTO A NURSING HOME. IN THAT HOME I MET MY
SUPR I (13)	IN HIS HEAD LATER THAN EIGHTEENSIXTY. WE CANT	LEAVE	ANN WITH NO OTHER GUARDIAN TO TURN TO. /RAMSDEN/ I AM
BULL III (143)	DISAPPOINTED) OH, THATS VERY TIRESOME. DID HE	LEAVE	ANY MESSAGE? /HODSON/ HE WAS IN TOO GREAT A HURRY,
JOAN 1 (64)	THE WINDOW) AT ALL EVENTS THIS IS NOT A TIME TO	LEAVE	ANY STONE UNTURNED. THERE IS SOMETHING ABOUT THE GIRL.
MIS. PREFACE(65)	AND HANGING, IF ONLY SUCH SURVIVORS AS WE MAY	LEAVE	ARE THOROUGHLY COWED IN THE PRESENCE OF A MAN WITH A
BARB II (274)	BY MY CLASS AND DO AS LITTLE AS I CAN SO'S TO	LEAVE	ARF THE JOB FOR ME FELLOW WORKERS. FOURTH, I'M FLY
ARMS II (41)	THE CHIVALROUS GENTLEMAN AND SOLDIER YOU ARE,	LEAVE	AT ONCE BEFORE HE FINDS YOU HERE? /BLUNTSCHLI/ (
BULL II (106)	AT WANST? /FATHER DEMPSEY/ YOU WERE TOLD TO	LEAVE	BEHIND WHAT YOU COULDNT CARRY, AN GO BACK FOR IT.
LADY PREFACE(212)	A WOUNDED NAME-- THINGS STANDING THUS UNKNOWN-- I	LEAVE	BEHIND! BUT FRANK HARRIS, IN HIS SONIA, HAS RESCUED
MIS. (147)	I'D BEEN ABLE TO DO IT MYSELF TO JOHNNY, I HAD TO	LEAVE	BOOKS IN HIS WAY; AND I FELT JUST AWFUL WHEN I DID IT.
JITT III (54)	AFFAIRS SERIOUSLY, I THINK YOU HAD BETTER	LEAVE	BOTH ALONE. /FESSLER/ (RISING, GREATLY SURPRISED)
SUPR PREFACE(R14)	A RELIGIOUS FORCE LIKE SHELLEY. LET US, THEN,	LEAVE	BYRON'S DON JUAN OUT OF ACCOUNT. MOZART'S IS THE LAST
CLEO IV (172)	HE HAS DONE THAT, HE WILL RETURN TO ROME, AND	LEAVE	CLEOPATRA HERE AS HIS VICEROY. /POTHINUS/ (BREAKING
NEVR II (238)	ATTENTION, AND DOLLY'S UNCONCERNED INDIFFERENCE,	LEAVE	CRAMPTON ON THE FOOTING OF A CASUAL ACQUAINTANCE
CAPT NOTES (303)	DIFFERS FROM IT; SO THAT IT IS MORE CONVENIENT TO	LEAVE	ENGLISH PECULIARITIES TO BE RECORDED BY AMERICAN
SUPR III (96)	PLACE. WRITTEN OVER THE GATE HERE ARE THE WORDS "	LEAVE	EVERY HOPE BEHIND, YE WHO ENTER." ONLY THINK WHAT A
HART II (105)	LEFT HAND) LET US ALL GO OUT INTO THE NIGHT AND	LEAVE	EVERYTHING BEHIND US. /MANGAN/ YOU STAY WHERE YOU ARE,
HART III (143)	THAT THIS CANT LAST. WE SIT HERE TALKING, AND	LEAVE	EVERYTHING TO MANGAN AND TO CHANCE AND TO THE DEVIL.
POSN (464)	HE NEVER DID ANYTHING WITHOUT ASKING YOUR ROTTEN	LEAVE	FIRST? WHY DID THE CHILD DIE? TELL ME THAT IF YOU
HART PREFACE(31)	TO HIM. WELL, FROM THE MOMENT WHEN THE ROUTINE OF	LEAVE	FOR OUR SOLDIERS WAS ESTABLISHED, SUCH NOVICES,
KING I (198)	NATURE. YOU NEED NOT BE ANXIOUS ABOUT ME. I WILL	LEAVE	FOR SCOTLAND TOMORROW, BUT I HAVE BUSINESS IN LONDON
2TRU III (103)	IN IT: NO EXCITEMENT. WHAT I WANT IS A MONTH'S	LEAVE	FOR THE SERGEANT. WONT YOU GIVE IT TO HIM, COLONEL?
PLES PREFACE(R15)	SUCH A COMMITTEE; AND CASES LIKE MINE WOULD STILL	LEAVE	FORLORN HOPES LIKE THE INDEPENDENT THEATRE ITS REASON
FANY III (309)	I ASSURE YOU. /GILBEY/ WELL, WHAT DO YOU WANT TO	LEAVE	FOR, THEN? DO YOU WANT TO WORSE YOURSELF? /JUGGINS/
JOAN 1 (67)	THE D --! GOSH! /JOAN/ AND TO MAKE THE ENGLISH	LEAVE	FRANCE. /ROBERT/ (SARCASTIC) ANYTHING ELSE? /JOAN/ (
HART PREFACE(30)	CROWDED EVERY NIGHT WITH THOUSANDS OF SOLDIERS ON	LEAVE	FROM THE FRONT. THESE SOLDIERS WERE NOT SEASONED
6CAL (99)	WE MUST SUBMIT TO YOU AND TO GOD. /THE KING/	LEAVE	GOD OUT OF THIS! WHAT HAST THOU OR THY LIKE TO DO
BUOY III (38)	" WHOM GOD HATH JOINED"-- /SIR F./ OH, DO PLEASE	LEAVE	GOD OUT OF THE QUESTION. MARRIAGE IS A LEGAL
FANY III (304)	GETS HER ARM ROUND HIS NECK). /BOBBY/ NO. STOP.	LEAVE	GO. WILL YOU. JUGGINS APPEARS AT THE DOOR. /JUGGINS/
CLEO II (136)	THE PHAROS-- THAT ISLAND WITH THE LIGHTHOUSE.	LEAVE	HALF OUR MEN BEHIND TO HOLD THE BEACH AND THE QUAY
CATH PREFACE(156)	ARE ONLY HORATIOS, THE AUTHORS WILL HAVE TO	LEAVE	HAMLET OUT, AND BE CONTENT WITH HORATIOS FOR HEROES.
MRS II (207)	QUITE COMFORTABLY. I'D DIE BEFORE HER AND	LEAVE	HER A BOUNCING WIDOW WITH PLENTY OF MONEY. WHY NOT?
DOCT II (120)	HE IS SO WRAPPED UP IN HIS WORK THAT HE HAS TO	LEAVE	HER A GOOD DEAL ALONE; AND THE POOR INNOCENT YOUNG
DOCT IV (167)	(WITH QUIET CONVICTION) YES. SHE'S ALL RIGHT.	LEAVE	HER ALONE. SHE'LL COME BACK. /RIDGEON/ (CALLOUSLY)
2TRU I (36)	SYMPATHETIC OF YOU TO NOTICE IT! BUT HOW CAN I	LEAVE	HER AT SUCH A MOMENT? /THE NURSE/ SHE OUGHT NOT TO
GETT PREFACE(188)	STEAL HER HUSBAND'S HOUSE FROM OVER HER HEAD, AND	LEAVE	HER DESTITUTE AND NAMELESS ON THE STREETS. NOW, NO
FABL PREFACE(66)	ENDOW HER WITH ENCHANTING SEXUAL ATTRACTION YET	LEAVE	HER DESTITUTE OF THE QUALITIES THAT MAKE MARRIED LIFE
WIDO II (44)	THAT IN YOU, HARRY. PERHAPS IT WILL BE AS WELL TO	LEAVE	HER IN IGNORANCE. /TRENCH/ (ANXIOUSLY) BUT I MUST
PYGM II (226)	(IMPATIENTLY) WHATS TO BECOME OF HER IF I	LEAVE	HER IN THE GUTTER? TELL ME THAT, MRS PEARCE. /MRS
FABL PREFACE(73)	GENUINE RELIGIOUS CONVICTIONS, SHE MIGHT SAFELY	LEAVE	HER SON'S CASE TO GOD. EDMUND GOSSE WAS THE SON OF A
MIS. (164)	YOU SIT DOWN IN THE PRESENCE OF A LADY AND	LEAVE	HER STANDING. (HE RISES HASTILY). HA, HA! REALLY, MR
APPL INTRLUD(249)	CHAUFFEUR TO DRIVE HER INTO THE SERPENTINE AND	LEAVE	HER THERE. THE WOMAN MAKES YOU RIDICULOUS. /MAGNUS/ I
JITT III (67)	OUT OF THE DARK, AND WENT BACK INTO THE DARK.	LEAVE	HER THERE, AS SHE LEFT HIM. /AGNES/ (SHAKING HER
JOAN 5 (120)	THE FOOL AT COMPIEGNE, AND GETS CAUGHT, I MUST	LEAVE	HER TO HER DOOM. /LA HIRE/ THEN YOU HAD BETTER CHAIN
WIDO I (17)	/TRENCH/ (EAGERLY) I'LL WRITE NOW, BEFORE I	LEAVE	HERE: STRAIGHT OFF. /SARTORIUS/ I WILL LEAVE YOU TO
MRS III (231)	NOT MATTER. I SUPPOSE YOU UNDERSTAND THAT WHEN WE	LEAVE	HERE TODAY OUR ACQUAINTANCE CEASES. /CROFTS/ WHY? IS
GETT (314)	ANOTHER MAN. /LEO/ THEN WHY ON EARTH SHOULD SHE	LEAVE	HIM? /LESBIA/ BECAUSE SHE WANTS TO. /LEO/ OH, IF
ROCK II (268)	KEEP OUT. IT WILL TAKE THE LIFE OUT OF HIM AND	LEAVE	HIM A WALKING TALKING SHELL OF A MAN WITH NOTHING

BARB III	(320)	WHO CAN GET HIM AN UNDERSECRETARYSHIP; AND THEN	LEAVE	HIM ALONE. HE WILL FIND HIS NATURAL AND PROPER PLACE
MIS. PREFACE	(28)	NO OTHER MEANS OF LIVELIHOOD; AND REFORM WOULD	LEAVE	HIM AS A WORKMAN IS NOW LEFT WHEN HE IS SUPERSEDED BY
BULL PREFACE	(55)	ROOM FOR ONLY ONE MAN ON THE GALLOWS, AND HAD TO	LEAVE	HIM HANGING HALF AN HOUR TO MAKE SURE WORK AND GIVE
HART I	(53)	HUSHABYE/ OF COURSE YOU ARE, PETTIKINS. WHY NOT	LEAVE	HIM IN IT, AND MARRY SOMEONE YOU LOVE? /LADY
DOCT II	(129)	WICKED NONSENSE. YOU CANT KILL HIM. BUT YOU CAN	LEAVE	HIM IN OTHER HANDS. /RIDGEON/ IN B.B.'S, FOR INSTANCE:
CAPT II	(244)	AND JOINS REDBROOK. /LADY CICELY/ BUT YOU CANT	LEAVE	HIM THERE IN THAT STATE. /DRINKWATER/ OW: E'S HALL
LION PREFACE	(66)	HIM AS KINDLY AS POSSIBLE, OR TO LABEL HIM AND	LEAVE	HIM TO HIS CONSCIENCE, OR TO TREAT HIM AS AN INVALID
DEVL II	(44)	DUTY. MY DUTY IS TO GET YOU AWAY, TO SAVE YOU, TO	LEAVE	HIM TO HIS FATE (ESSIE UTTERS A CRY OF DISTRESS AND
MIS.	(187)	BUNNY, EASY. /LINA/ (APPEARING AT THE DOOR)	LEAVE	HIM TO ME, MRS TARLETON. (CLEAR AND AUTHORITATIVE)
INCA	(244)	YOU MUST GET RID OF HIM SOMEHOW. /ERMYNTRUDE/	LEAVE	HIM TO ME, YOUR HIGHNESS. /THE PRINCESS/ YOUD NEVER
MILL I	(158)	MADE THE FIFTY THOUSAND POUNDS. /EPIFANIA/ I	LEAVE	HIM TO TELL THAT DISGRACEFUL TALE HIMSELF. I BELIEVE
SHAK PREFACE	(136)	GET THE BETTER OF HIS MERCANTILE OCCUPATION, AND	LEAVE	HIM UNABLE TO AFFORD A UNIVERSITY EDUCATION FOR
JITT I SD	(26)	ANGUISH OF PERPLEXITY, FEELING THAT SHE MUST NOT	LEAVE	HIM WITHOUT SOME CEREMONY OF LOVE. THERE IS ONLY ONE
GENV PREFACE	(21)	KILLING OTHER PEOPLE HE HAD TO KILL HIMSELF, AND	LEAVE	HIS ACCOMPLICES TO BE HANGED. THE MORAL FOR CONQUERORS
ARMS II	(40)	SEND HIM AWAY: SAY WE'RE NOT AT HOME: ASK HIM TO	LEAVE	HIS ADDRESS AND I'LL WRITE TO HIM. OH STOP: THAT WILL
WIDO I	(13)	YOU: I ALLOWED HIM TO BELIEVE THAT HE MIGHT	LEAVE	HIS DAUGHTER IN YOUR CHARGE WITH ABSOLUTE CONFIDENCE.
MIS. PREFACE	(82)	HE HAD OBEYED THE INEVITABLE DESTINY OF A MAN TO	LEAVE	HIS FATHER AND MOTHER AND CLEAVE TO HIS WIFE, SHE
DEVL I	(11)	DUDGEON/ HE SHALL COME HERE. DOES HE EXPECT US TO	LEAVE	HIS FATHER'S HOUSE FOR HIS CONVENIENCE? LET THEM ALL
SUPR HANDBOK	(187)	THAT ALL ARE AS GREAT AS HE THAN A DROVER DARE	LEAVE	HIS FLOCK TO FIND ITS WAY THROUGH THE STREETS AS HE
HART PREFACE	(18)	THE SHIP HAD TO BE SAVED, EVEN IF NEWTON HAD TO	LEAVE	HIS FLUXIONS AND MICHAEL ANGELO HIS MARBLES TO SAVE
KING I	(214)	MY DEAR, BUT COME! MR NEWTON HAS ASKED US TO	LEAVE	HIS HOUSE MANY TIMES, AND WE MUST NOT FORGET THAT HE
SUPR II	(65)	IS A BLOW. I CAN HARDLY UNDERSTAND HOW A MAN CAN	LEAVE	HIS WIFE IN SUCH A POSITION, SURELY IT'S NOT
SUPR PREFACE	(R29)	HERO AS A MAN OF EXTRAORDINARY GENIUS, AND THEN	LEAVE	HIS WORKS ENTIRELY TO THE READER'S IMAGINATION; SO
MIS. PREFACE	(16)	EVEN BELIEVE THAT IN ALLOWING THEIR CHILDREN TO	LEAVE	HOME THEY ARE SACRIFICING THEMSELVES FOR THEIR
OVER	(185)	NATURALLY AND STRAIGHTFORWARDLY WITH ME, YOU CAN	LEAVE	HUSBAND AND CHILD, HOME, FRIENDS, AND COUNTRY, FOR MY
KING I	(200)	WOULD DO YOU NO HARM FOR ONCE IN A WAY. BY YOUR	LEAVE	I WILL GO TO LOOK AFTER IT. I MUST TURN THEM ALL OUT
LADY	(237)	/THE MAN/ WELL SAID, MASTER WARDER. WITH YOUR	LEAVE	I WILL SET THAT DOWN IN WRITING; FOR I HAVE A VERY
DEVL III	(51)	YOU MAY COUNT ON TWENTY MINUTES, SIR; AND BY YOUR	LEAVE	I WONT WASTE ANY MORE OF THEM. (HE GOES OUT, LOCKING
PYGM V	(269)	AFRAID, HENRY. THE GIRL HAS A PERFECT RIGHT TO	LEAVE	IF SHE CHOOSES. /HIGGINS/ (WANDERING DISTRACTEDLY
BASH III	(125)	THOU LOVE ME? /BASHVILLE/ TIS SAID: NOW LET ME	LEAVE	IMMEDIATELY. /LYDIA/ IN TAKING, BASHVILLE, THIS MOST
WIDO I	(3)	IN THE HOTEL, HARRY, THANKS TO MY TACT. WE'LL	LEAVE	IN THE MORNING, AND DO MAINZ AND FRANKFURT. THERE IS A
BULL III	(129)	AND TALK FOOLISHNESS TO ME. WILL YOU TAKE IT OR	LEAVE	IT? /LARRY/ VERY WELL: I'LL TAKE IT WITH PLEASURE IF
GENV I	(31)	I HAVE NEVER SEEN ONE OF THEM. /HE/ SO THEY	LEAVE	IT ALL TO YOU? /SHE/ OH, I WOULDNT SAY ALL. THERES
HART III	(145)	SHOTOVER/ NAVIGATION. LEARN IT AND LIVE; OR	LEAVE	IT AND BE DAMNED. /ELLIE/ QUIET, QUIET: YOULL TIRE
MIS.	(185)	AFRAID-- /TARLETON/ (RISING) STOP. (SILENCE).	LEAVE	IT AT THAT. ENOUGH SAID. YOU KEEP QUIET, JOHNNY. MR
MTH4 I	(165)	/THE ELDERLY GENTLEMAN/ LEAVE IT AT THAT, MADAM:	LEAVE	IT AT THAT. (HE SITS DOWN AGAIN). EVEN A POPE IS NOT
FANY PROLOG	(270)	IS HIGHLY BECOMING TO YOUR AGE AND SEX, SO WE'LL	LEAVE	IT AT THAT. /FANNY/ BUT YOU WILL PROMISE TO TELL MY
MIS.	(187)	YOU ARE, YOURE THERE ANYHOW. I TELL YOU AGAIN,	LEAVE	IT AT THAT. /BENTLEY/ I WANT TO KNOW TOO. HYPATIA'S
MIS.	(132)	BY COMING OUT OF THE SWING AND TAKING THE FLOOR)	LEAVE	IT AT THAT, THATS GOOD SENSE. ANYBODY ON FOR A GAME OF
MTH4 I	(165)	THEY HAVE UTTERED THEM. /THE ELDERLY GENTLEMAN/	LEAVE	IT AT THAT, MADAM: LEAVE IT AT THAT. (HE SITS DOWN
MTH4 I	(140)	(SNIFFING: ALMOST IN TEARS AGAIN) WE WILL	LEAVE	IT AT THAT, MADAM. /THE WOMAN/ (GOING NEARER TO HIM
FANY I	(273)	THIS IS A B-- /MRS GILBEY/ (CUTTING HIM SHORT)	LEAVE	IT AT THAT, PLEASE. WHATEVER IT IS, BAD LANGUAGE WONT
FANY III	(310)	ELSE TO TROUBLE ME ABOUT. /JUGGINS/ I REALLY CANT	LEAVE	IT AT THAT, SIR. I ASSURE YOU IVE NO OBJECTION TO
MIS.	(176)	TO GIVE YOU SUCH A HIDING-- /TARLETON/ YOU CANT	LEAVE	IT AT THAT, YOU KNOW. WHAT DID YOU SEE MY DAUGHTER
GETT PREFACE	(254)	PART OF THE NATION, THE NATION CANNOT AFFORD TO	LEAVE	IT AT THE IRRESPONSIBLE DISPOSAL OF ANY INDIVIDUAL OR
MTH5	(221)	(SCORNFULLY) NOT WORTHY OF IT! HO! MAY I NOT	LEAVE	IT BECAUSE IT IS NOT WORTHY OF ME? /ARJILLAX/ OF
MTH5	(221)	HE MUST. YOU MUST TAKE WHAT HE GIVES YOU, OR	LEAVE	IT IF YOU ARE NOT WORTHY OF IT. /ECRASIA/ (
BUOY III	(46)	US: HE HAS NOT YET BETTERED THE WORLD. WE MUST	LEAVE	IT IN GOD'S HANDS. (SHE GOES OUT). /SECONDBORN/ (
JITT II	(48)	COULD. /LENKHEIM/ (SHAKING HIS HEAD) BUT WE CANT	LEAVE	IT LIKE THIS, CAN WE? /JITTA/ WHAT CAN WE DO,
CAND II	(114)	MORCHBANKS! OH, THATS BAD, AT YOUR AGE. YOU MUST	LEAVE	IT OFF GRAJALLY. /CANDIDA/ (REASSURED) NONSENSE,
O'FL	(220)	WASHY DRAWING ROOM TEA WILL GIVE ME THE WIND IF I	LEAVE	IT ON MY STOMACH. (SHE GOES INTO THE HOUSE, LEAVING
GETT	(279)	THE BRITISH ARMY THESE THIRTY YEARS; BUT I DONT	LEAVE	IT ON THAT ACCOUNT. /LEO/ IT'S NOT THAT IVE EXHAUSTED
APPL I	(214)	I WAS GOING TO PROPOSE -- AND YOU CAN TAKE IT OR	LEAVE	IT -- IS AN ULTIMATUM. /CRASSUS/ GOOD! /PROTEUS/
PYGM V	(281)	ABOUT TELLING HER. /PICKERING/ QUITE RIGHT. WE'LL	LEAVE	IT SO, IF YOU DONT MIND. /DOOLITTLE/ AND YOULL COME TO
BARB III	(315)	IT WOULD BE MOST UNNATURAL AND IMPROPER OF YOU TO	LEAVE	IT TO ANYONE ELSE, ANDREW. DO YOU SUPPOSE THIS WICKED
JOAN PREFACE	(35)	PLAINLY. CATHOLIC ANTI-CLERICALISM. I MUST NOT	LEAVE	IT TO BE INFERRED HERE THAT ONE CANNOT BE AN
BUOY III	(46)	/SECONDBORN/ (RISING) IT ALWAYS COMES TO THAT:	LEAVE	IT TO GOD, THOUGH WE DO NOT KNOW WHAT GOD IS, AND ARE
SUPR III	(94)	IN TWO YEARS, AND FINGERS WITHOUT END. I HAD TO	LEAVE	IT TO ITS FATE AT LAST; AND NOW I FEAR IT IS
FANY III	(318)	SIR? /KNOX/ I KNOW WHATLL CLINCH IT, GILBEY. YOU	LEAVE	IT TO ME. (TO JUGGINS) WAS YOUR MOTHER THE DUCHESS..
BUOY III	(32)	HIS FINANCIAL ADVICE I HAVE LOST BY IT. I NOW	LEAVE	IT TO MY BANKER. /SIR F./ THEN I AM AFRAID I MUST WARN
MTH3	(123)	MADE EITHER INTERESTING OR DELIGHTFUL TO YOU YOU	LEAVE	IT TO NEGRESSES AND CHINAMEN. I ASK MYSELF WHETHER
KING PREFACE	(159)	THE LEAST DEMOCRATIC OF ALL POLITICAL SYSTEMS. I	LEAVE	IT TO OUR OLD PARLIAMENTARY HANDS TO DEVISE A PLAN BY
SIM PREFACE	(14)	YOU NEED NOT BOTHER ABOUT THIS: YOU CAN JUST	LEAVE	IT TO STARVE WHEN IT CEASES TO BE USEFUL TO ITS
BARB II	(295)	THE POOR TO PRETEND THAT POVERTY IS A BLESSING:	LEAVE	IT TO THE COWARD TO MAKE A RELIGION OF HIS COWARDICE
PYGM II	(234)	HAVE I ASKED YOU FOR A BRASS FARTHING? I	LEAVE	IT TO THE GENTLEMAN HERE: HAVE I SAID A WORD ABOUT
BARB II	(295)	MAN AND A POOR MAN; AND IT HAS NO ROMANCE FOR ME.	LEAVE	IT TO THE POOR TO PRETEND THAT POVERTY IS A BLESSING:
BULL III SD	(134)	HE STOPS. THEY STARE AT HIM DUMBFOUNDED, AND	LEAVE	IT TO THE PRIEST TO ANSWER HIM. /FATHER DEMPSEY/ (
PYGM II	(238)	FIVE POUNDS UNREASONABLE? I PUT IT TO YOU; AND I	LEAVE	IT TO YOU. /HIGGINS/ (RISING, AND GOING OVER TO
GLIM	(188)	SAFE FROM HIS EMINENCE THE CARDINAL, AND WILL	LEAVE	IT TO YOUR EXCELLENCY'S GRACIOUSNESS AS TO WHETHER HIS
WIDO II	(30)	HAVE I SAID ONE WORD AGAINST HIM, SIR? I	LEAVE	IT TO YOUR FRIEND: HAVE I SAID A WORD? /COKANE/ TRUE:
BARB III	(313)	HAS LEFT THE SALVATION ARMY. YOU HAD BETTER	LEAVE	IT TOO. I WILL NOT HAVE YOU PLAYING THAT DRUM IN THE
JOAN 6	(131)	DO NOT KNOW HOW MUCH MORE CRUEL IT WOULD BE TO	LEAVE	IT UNDONE, I WOULD GO TO THE STAKE MYSELF SOONER THAN
LADY	(249)	THE WRITING OF PLAYS WHO DO NOW DESPISE IT AND	LEAVE	IT WHOLLY TO THOSE WHOSE COUNSELS WILL WORK LITTLE
ARMS II	(41)	IF YOU WILL ALLOW ME TO TAKE IT OUT OF MY BAG AND	LEAVE	IT WITH YOUR SERVANT AS I PASS OUT, I NEED DETAIN YOU
POSN PREFACE	(431)	I HAVE GIVEN MY REASONS; AND AT THAT I MUST	LEAVE	IT, AS THE TRADITION WHICH MAKES MALVOLIO NOT ONLY
LION PREFACE	(99)	PEOPLE; AND IF A TRAPPIST DOES NOT LIKE IT HE CAN	LEAVE	IT, BUT A SUBJECT OF THE BRITISH EMPIRE OR THE FRENCH
CYMB FORWORD	(138)	WHAT I HAVE DONE I HAVE DONE; AND AT THAT I MUST	LEAVE	IT. I SHALL NOT PRESS MY VERSION ON MANAGERS PRODUCING
LION PREFACE	(103)	WITH A CRASH ON THEIR HEADS. AND AT THAT I MUST	LEAVE	IT. LONDON, DECEMBER 1915.
PYGM II	(221)	SO I WONT GIVE MORE THAN A SHILLING. TAKE IT OR	LEAVE	IT. /HIGGINS/ (WALKING UP AND DOWN THE ROOM, RATTLING
MIS.	(187)	I'LL LEAVE THE HOUSE AND NOT ENTER IT UNTIL YOU	LEAVE	IT. /JOHNNY/ PUT THAT IN YOUR PIPE AND SMOKE IT, MY
GETT	(274)	SIR, THAT IF YOU ENTERED THIS HOUSE, I SHOULD	LEAVE	IT. /REGINALD/ WELL, DONT LET ME DETAIN YOU, OLD CHAP.
NEVR II	(228)	EDUCATED GLORIA TO TAKE UP MY WORK WHEN I MUST	LEAVE	IT. THAT IS WHAT HAS BROUGHT ME BACK TO ENGLAND. I
BARB II	(301)	AWVE OFFERED TO PY. AW CAN DO NO MORE. TIKE IT OR	LEAVE	IT. THERE IT IS. (HE THROWS THE SOVEREIGN ON THE
GETT	(273)	YOU TELL HIM THAT IF HE ENTERS THIS HOUSE, I'LL	LEAVE	IT; AND SO WILL EVERY DECENT MAN AND WOMAN IN IT.
SIM PREFACE	(15)	AN ADVANCE; BUT IT IS IN FACT A RETREAT WHICH MAY	LEAVE	ITS VICTIM MUCH LESS ELIGIBLE AS A MEMBER OF A
GETT PREFACE	(189)	ON THE SIDE ON WHICH NOBODY IS ATTACKING IT, AND	LEAVE	ITS WEAKEST FRONT UNDEFENDED. THE RELIGIOUS REVOLT
CAND I	(98)	IS SOMETHING SERIOUS THE MATTER) I'M NOT GOING TO	LEAVE	IT, MY DEAR BOY; I THOUGHT YOU WERE. (EUGENE, BAFFLED
MIS. PREFACE	(66)	WOULD EVER HAVE ENSLAVED HIM WITHOUT ASKING HIS	LEAVE	. AND THE TRICK BY WHICH THE DEMAGOGUE DEFEATS
SUPR II	(58)	HUSH, FOR SHAME, TAVY! /TANNER/ OH, I GIVE YOU	LEAVE	. I AM YOUR GUARDIAN; AND I COMMIT YOU TO TAVY'S CARE
SUPR I	(38)	DARE NOT TAKE A STEP WITHOUT RUNNING TO YOU FOR	LEAVE	. I KNOW A POOR WRETCH WHOSE ONE DESIRE IN LIFE IS TO
KING I	(172)	KING). /CHARLES/ (RISING) I SEE I MUST TAKE MY	LEAVE	. NELLY DASHES IN. SALLY WITHDRAWS. /NELLY/ ROWLEY
JOAN 6	(140)	ME I MUST NOT DRESS AS A WOMAN UNTIL SHE GIVES ME	LEAVE	. /COURCELLES/ WHEN WILL SHE GIVE YOU LEAVE? /JOAN/
JOAN 1	(66)	YOU NOTHING ABOUT THAT: THEY HAVE NOT GIVEN ME	LEAVE	. /ROBERT/ BUT YOU ACTUALLY SEE THEM; AND THEY TALK TO
O'FL	(205)	SOLDIER LIKE ME SIT DOWN IN HIS PRESENCE WITHOUT	LEAVE	. /SIR PEARCE/ WELL, YOURE NOT A COMMON SOLDIER,
PRES	(148)	THESE CLOTHES TO MR BALSQUITH WHEN THE LADIES	LEAVE	. THE ORDERLY COMES IN. /THE ORDERLY/ LADY CORINTHIA
LADY	(239)	FEED CAPONS SO. /THE MAN/ A GOOD CADENCE. BY YOUR	LEAVE	(HE MAKES A NOTE OF IT). /THE BEEFEATER/ WHAT MANNER
SUPR I	(42)	VIOLET IS CERTAINLY VERY OBSTINATE. SHE WONT	LEAVE	LONDON. I DONT UNDERSTAND HER. /MISS RAMSDEN/ I DO.
CAPT I	(230)	HOISTING THE ROGUE WITH HIS OWN PETARD. I HAD TO	LEAVE	MATTERS AS THEY WERE FOR MANY YEARS; FOR I HAD MY OWN
POSN PREFACE	(362)	ART OF CONTRIVING METHODS OF REFORM WHICH WILL	LEAVE	MATTERS EXACTLY AS THEY ARE. THE REPORT OF THE JOINT
WIDO I	(19)	OBLIGED TO YOU. /COKANE/ (IMPATIENTLY) LEAVE ME,	LEAVE	ME: YOU DISTURB ME. (HE WAVES HIM OFF, AND BEGINS TO
2TRU III	(106)	MYSELF WISHING SHE WOULD DIE LIKE THE OTHERS AND	LEAVE	ME A LITTLE TO MYSELF. AND NOW I FIND IT WAS NOT ONLY
CURE	(229)	AND POCKETS HIS MEDICINE CASE). /REGINALD/ BETTER	LEAVE	ME A LOT. I LIKE PILLS. /THE DOCTOR/ THANK YOU: I'M
POSN	(446)	HIM, WITH HORROR IN HIS EYES) DONT GO: DONT	LEAVE	ME ALONE: DO YOU HEAR? /ELDER DANIELS/ HAS YOUR
SUPR III	(92)	(GOING). /ANA/ (SEIZING HIS ARM) YOU SHALL NOT	LEAVE	ME ALONE IN THIS DREADFUL PLACE. /DON JUAN/ PROVIDED
FANY I	(275)	/GILBEY/ SO LONG AS YOU DONT FLOUNCE OUT AND	LEAVE	ME ALONE WITH HER. (HE RISES AND PLANTS HIMSELF ON
CLEO III	(162)	IF WE ARE BEATEN? /CLEOPATRA/ BUT YOU MUSTNT	LEAVE	ME ALONE, CAESAR: YOU WILL NOT LEAVE ME ALONE, WILL
CLEO III	(162)	YOU MUSTNT LEAVE ME ALONE, CAESAR: YOU WILL NOT	LEAVE	ME ALONE, WILL YOU? /RUFIO/ WHAT! NOT WHEN THE

MTH5 (258)	OFF HIS HANDS. /THE NEWLY BORN/ OH, WILL YOU ALL	LEAVE	ME AS HE HAS LEFT YOU? /ECRASIA/ NEVER. WE HAVE SWORN
PHIL I (77)	OUR VIEW. ACCORDINGLY, YOU RESERVED THE RIGHT TO	LEAVE	ME AT ANY TIME IF YOU FOUND OUR COMPANIONSHIP
JOAN 6 (145)	TRUMPETS AND THE KNIGHTS AND SOLDIERS PASS ME AND	LEAVE	ME BEHIND AS THEY LEAVE THE OTHER WOMEN, IF ONLY I
MTH4 II (181)	BUT I FORESEE THAT IF I GO ON TO THE END IT WILL	LEAVE	ME EXECRATED, DETHRONED, IMPRISONED, PERHAPS EXECUTED.
BUOY III (37)	THAT THE DAY WILL COME WHEN IT WILL VANISH AND	LEAVE	ME FACE TO FACE WITH REALITY; PERHAPS TIED TO A
CAND III (134)	SOME FIDDLESTICK!! OH, IF SHE IS MAD ENOUGH TO	LEAVE	ME FOR YOU, WHO WILL PROTECT HER? WHO WILL HELP HER?
MIS. (178)	(HE TRIES TO BOLT; BUT PERCIVAL SEIZES HIM).	LEAVE	ME GO, WILL YOU? WHAT RIGHT HAVE YOU TO LAY HANDS ON
POSN (441)	A WITNESS. GO AND ROUND ONE UP, STRAPPER; AND	LEAVE	ME HERE ALONE TO WRESTLE WITH HIS POOR BLINDED SOUL.
PHIL I (82)	ME TO GO. /JULIA/ (AT THE DOOR) YOU SHALL NOT	LEAVE	ME HERE ALONE. /CHARTERIS/ THEN COME WITH ME. /JULIA/
MILL II (173)	IT IS THE MOST ABOMINABLE THING OF YOU TO	LEAVE	ME HERE IN MY DISTRESS. MY CAR IS GONE. I HAVE NO
PHIL II (124)	GOING WITH HIM, CHARTERIS. /JULIA/ YOU WILL NOT	LEAVE	ME HERE TO BE INSULTED BY THIS WOMAN, MR CHARTERIS. (
MILL II (171)	TO ME. YOU MUST ATTEND TO ME. ARE YOU GOING TO	LEAVE	ME HERE TO DIE? /THE DOCTOR/ YOU ARE NOT DYING. NOT
VWOO 3 (140)	EMPLOYER. AND YOU ARE INDEPENDENT OF ME, AND CAN	LEAVE	ME IF YOU ARE NOT SATISFIED. /Z/ HOW CAN I BE
PHIL I (79)	SEEM TO FORGET THAT IN RESERVING YOUR FREEDOM TO	LEAVE	ME IN CASE I SHOULD TURN OUT BADLY, YOU ALSO RESERVED
KING I (210)	NOT KNOW WHAT HE IS SAYING. TAKE HIM AWAY; AND	LEAVE	ME IN PEACE. /CHARLES/ WHAT HE SAYS CALLS FOR AN
BASH I (96)	TO RASCALS LIKE THYSELF ROTTEN WITH SURFEITING.	LEAVE	ME IN PEACE. THIS GROVE IS SACRED: THOU PROFANEST IT.
JOAN 6 (133)	SO HE ONLY CALLED ME FILTHY NAMES. WHY DO YOU	LEAVE	ME IN THE HANDS OF THE ENGLISH? I SHOULD BE IN THE
CATH 4 (193)	AND HOLDING ON LIKE A BULL-DOG) DONT GO. DONT	LEAVE	ME IN THIS HORRIBLE STATE. LOOSEN ME. (THIS IS WHAT
PHIL I (91)	DOOR). /CRAVEN/ (INTERCEPTING HIM) STOP! DONT	LEAVE	ME LIKE THIS: I SHALL LOOK LIKE A FOOL. NOW I SHALL
2TRU I (35)	IS ANYONE THERE? (CRYING) SELFISH BEASTS! TO	LEAVE	ME LIKE THIS. (SHE SNATCHES ANGRILY AT THE ELECTRIC
CLEO II (141)	MY SUPERFLUOUS YEARS. THAT WILL MAKE YOU 26, AND	LEAVE	ME ONLY-- NO MATTER. IS IT A BARGAIN? /CLEOPATRA/
BUOY IV (53)	I CAN LOSE MONEY. HE CAN ONLY MAKE IT. /OLD BILL/	LEAVE	ME OUT OF IT: I SHALL NOT LAST MUCH LONGER: YOU HAVE A
WIDO III (61)	YOU IF I COULD AFFORD IT; BUT I CANT; SO YOU MAY	LEAVE	ME OUT OF IT. /LICKCHEESE/ WELL, ALL I CAN SAY IS THAT
BARB III (334)	YOU ARE SELLING YOUR OWN SOUL, DOLLY, NOT MINE.	LEAVE	ME OUT OF THE BARGAIN, PLEASE. /UNDERSHAFT/ COME! I
BUOY IV (50)	FORBID! (TO HER) THE FELLOW IS RIGHT, DARLING.	LEAVE	ME OUT OF THE QUESTION. /SHE/ I CANT LEAVE YOU OUT,
ROCK II (279)	ALOYSIA. /LADY CHAVENDER/ (RISING) YOU MAY	LEAVE	ME OUT OF THE QUESTION, MISS BROLLIKINS. IT IS NOT MY
GENV III (76)	/THE NEWCOMER/ AND WHAT PRICE ME? COME ON. DONT	LEAVE	ME OUT. /THE SECRETARY/ YOU! YOU ARE SOME SORT OF
2TRU I (37)	THE NURSE SWITCHES OFF. /THE PATIENT/ NO, NO.	LEAVE	ME SOMETHING TO READ BY. MY BEDSIDE LAMP IS NOT
NEVR II (247)	THE STEPS TOGETHER). /VALENTINE/ (TO THE WAITER)	LEAVE	ME SOMETHING TO BRING DOWN. ONE OF THESE (OFFERING TO
JITT I (10)	GIRL/ AINT THE GENTLEMAN HERE? HE PROMISED TO	LEAVE	ME SOMETHING. /MRS BILLITER/ (IMPATIENTLY GROPING IN
FANY I (280)	HAVE BROUGHT HIMSELF TO BUY HIMSELF OFF AND	LEAVE	ME THERE; SO HE'S DOING HIS MONTH. WELL, IT WAS TWO
PYGM V (283)	TO HURT. /HIGGINS/ I CANT TURN YOUR SOUL ON.	LEAVE	ME THOSE FEELINGS; AND YOU CAN TAKE AWAY THE VOICE AND
CATH 4 (190)	FOR HEAVEN'S SAKE, MADAM, DO YOU INTEND TO	LEAVE	ME TIED UP LIKE THIS WHILE YOU DISCUSS THE BLASPHEMIES
DOCT IV (158)	(MOVING VENGEFULLY TOWARDS THE DOOR) YOU JUST	LEAVE	ME TO DEAL WITH HIM! /MRS DUBEDAT/ (STOPPING HIM)
DEST (163)	NOT? /LIEUTENANT/ NEVER YOU MIND HIM, GENERAL.	LEAVE	ME TO DEAL WITH HIM. /NAPOLEON/ WITH HIM! WITH WHOM,
APPL INTRLUD(254)	/ORINTHIA/ OH, BOTHER JEMIMA! YOU SHALL NOT	LEAVE	ME TO GO TO JEMIMA (SHE PULLS HIM BACK SO VIGOROUSLY
MILL I (149)	MR SAGAMORE. I THINK YOUD BETTER GO HOME AND	LEAVE	ME TO HAVE IT OUT WITH HER. /EPIFANIA/ WILL YOU HAVE
VWOO 2 (131)	THEN MAKE YOUR OWN MATRIMONIAL ARRANGEMENTS, AND	LEAVE	ME TO MAKE MINE. /Z/ OH, I'LL MAKE MY OWN MATRIMONIAL
VWOO 2 (131)	MAY DEPEND ON THAT. /A/ EXCUSE ME: I ADDED " AND	LEAVE	ME TO MAKE MINE." CAN I DEPEND ON YOU FOR THAT ALSO..
MTH1 II (33)	DEATH? /ADAM/ I DO NOT BLAME YOU. GO IN PEACE.	LEAVE	ME TO MY DIGGING, AND YOUR MOTHER TO HER SPINNING.
JITT III (76)	HIM IN HIS EXTREMITY TO SAVE MYSELF. PLEASE	LEAVE	ME TO MY DISGRACE. NOTHING THAT YOU CAN SAY OR THINK
DEVL I (10)	MY HEART. GO HOME TO YOUR PRETTY WIFE, MAN; AND	LEAVE	ME TO MY PRAYERS. (SHE TURNS FROM HIM AND LEANS WITH
BUOY IV (48)	ALL THIS. I AM REPEATING MYSELF, AND BORING YOU.	LEAVE	ME TO MYSELF. (HE SEATS HIMSELF IN THE BISHOP'S
BUOY III (46)	YOU HAVE THE KINDNESS TO FOLLOW YOUR FRIENDS AND	LEAVE	ME TO PURIFY THIS TEMPLE OF PEACE. IT HAS BEEN
6CAL (104)	NOT SKILLED IN DEALING WITH FINE HANDSOME LADIES.	LEAVE	ME TO SETTLE MY BUSINESS WITH YOUR HENPECKED HUSBAND.
KING I (182)	NELLIE: WILL YOU TAKE OUR SOVEREIGN LORD AWAY AND	LEAVE	ME TO SPEAK WITH THE ALCHEMIST IN PRIVATE? /CHARLES/
6CAL (96)	THINK OF YOURSELF AND OUR CHILD-- /THE QUEEN/ OH,	LEAVE	ME TO TAKE CARE OF MYSELF AND THE CHILD. I AM NO
HART II (97)	QUITE, QUITE SURE. NOW YOU MUST GO AWAY AND	LEAVE	ME TO TALK TO MRS HUSHABYE. /MAZZINI/ BUT I SHOULD
KING I (211)	MY PROPER WORK OF INTERPRETING THE SCRIPTURES.	LEAVE	ME TO THAT WORK AND TO MY SOLITUDE. (DESPERATELY,
BUOY 1 (17)	A TYRANNY FROM WHICH I MUST ESCAPE. /FATHER/ AND	LEAVE	ME TO WEATHER THE STORM! WELL, GOODBYE. /SON/
MILL I (139)	A HUNDRED AND FIFTY MILLIONS. HE HAD PROMISED TO	LEAVE	ME TWO HUNDRED MILLIONS. I WAS LEFT WITH A BEGGARLY
HART II (100)	RIGHT TO EXPECT LOVE FROM ME, AND WOULD PERHAPS	LEAVE	ME WHEN HE FOUND I COULD NOT GIVE IT TO HIM. RICH
PYGM IV (263)	TO KILL YOU, YOU SELFISH BRUTE. WHY DIDNT YOU	LEAVE	ME WHERE YOU PICKED ME OUT OF-- IN THE GUTTER? YOU
BARB I (272)	YOU CAN GO WITH HIM, TOO, IF YOU LIKE, AND	LEAVE	ME WITH THE SERVANTS. /STEPHEN/ OH, YOU MUSTNT THINK
DOCT I (114)	LET YOU KNOW THE DATE IN THE COURSE OF TOMORROW.	LEAVE	ME YOUR ADDRESS. /MRS DUBEDAT/ THANK YOU AGAIN AND
ARMS II (41)	BAG? /CATHERINE/ IT SHALL BE SENT ON. YOU WILL	LEAVE	ME YOUR ADDRESS. /BLUNTSCHLI/ TRUE. ALLOW ME. (HE
HART I (64)	KNOW WHAT TO DO. PLEASE, MAY I SPEAK TO PAPA? DO	LEAVE	ME. I CANT BEAR IT. /MRS HUSHABYE/ BE OFF, HECTOR.
SIM I (52)	/IDDY/ (CLUTCHING AT HER ROBE) NO, NO. DO NOT	LEAVE	ME. I LOVE YOU-- YOU. I WOULD DIE FOR YOU. THAT SOUNDS
PHIL III (142)	BUT, MY LOVE-- /JULIA/ OH, GO AWAY, ALL OF YOU.	LEAVE	ME. I-- OH-- (SHE GIVES WAY TO A PASSION OF TEARS).
CLEO I (110)	HER ARMS IN TERROR ROUND HIM) NO: YOU SHANT	LEAVE	ME. NO, NO, NO: DONT GO. I'M AFRAID-- AFRAID OF THE
CLEO I (113)	/CLEOPATRA/ (CLUTCHING HIM) NO, NO, NO. DONT	LEAVE	ME. /CAESAR/ A ROMAN DOES NOT STAY WITH QUEENS WHO ARE
CYMB V (147)	I AM OF NO MAN'S MAKING. I AM I: TAKE ME OR	LEAVE	ME. /IACHIMO/ (TO LUCIUS) MARK WELL, LUCIUS, MARK.
MILL I (144)	AND LOSE THE LITTLE MONEY HE WAS ABLE TO	LEAVE	ME. /SAGAMORE/ THE THIRTY MILLIONS. PRECISELY.
MRS II (211)	YOU TALK LIKE THAT. YOU WOULDNT-- YOU COULDNT	LEAVE	ME. /VIVIE/ (RUTHLESSLY) YES, WITHOUT A MOMENT'S
CLEO IV (185)	(STILL IN HER PLACE AT THE TABLE) WILL YOU	LEAVE	ME, CAESAR? APOLLODORUS: ARE YOU GOING?
CLEO III (163)	TO HER KNEES AND CLINGING TO HIM) NO NO. DO NOT	LEAVE	ME, CAESAR. (HE SNATCHES HIS SKIRT FROM HER CLUTCH).
DOCT IV (164)	(HEARTBROKEN) STAY WITH ME, LOUIS. OH, DONT	LEAVE	ME, DEAREST. /LOUIS/ NOT THAT I'M SELFISH. WITH ALL MY
WIDO I (19)	AWFULLY OBLIGED TO YOU. /COKANE/ (IMPATIENTLY)	LEAVE	ME, LEAVE ME: YOU DISTURB ME. (HE WAVES HIM OFF, AND
BARB III (347)	OF A DOVE AND FLY AWAY TO HEAVEN! /CUSINS/ AND	LEAVE	ME! /BARBARA/ YES, YOU, AND ALL THE OTHER NAUGHTY
JITT I (23)	(STRUCK TO THE HEART) NOT MEET ME AGAIN!	LEAVE	ME! /BRUNO/ (WITH DELIBERATE EMPHASIS) THIS MUST BE
METH PREFACE(R90)	MORE ELEGANT PARABLES BY YOUNGER HANDS WILL SOON	LEAVE	MINE AS FAR BEHIND AS THE RELIGIOUS PICTURES OF THE
BUOY II (22)	A HOUSE TO SHADE YOU, BUILD ONE FOR YOURSELF.	LEAVE	MINE IN PEACE. /HE/ THAT IS NOT NATURAL. IN NATIVE
BUOY III (43)	BOAST OF BEING A FORTUNE HUNTER? /SHE/ YOU MAY	LEAVE	MONEY OUT OF THE QUESTION, THOUGH I WAS BROUGHT UP
NEVR I (220)	DONT FORGET HALF PAST ONE. /DOLLY/ MIND YOU	LEAVE	MR CRAMPTON ENOUGH TEETH TO EAT WITH. (THEY GO OUT).
KING I (179)	YOU AT SOME HAPPIER MOMENT. COME, LADIES: WE MUST	LEAVE	MR NEWTON TO HIS MATHEMATICS. (HE IS ABOUT TO GO TO
SUPR II (68)	SO AS TO BE A GOOD DEAL OCCUPIED WITH ME, AND	LEAVE	MR ROBINSON A GOOD DEAL OCCUPIED WITH MISS WHITEFIELD.
SUPR HANDBOK(182)	SALARIED FUNCTIONARY IN THE PUBLIC SERVICE, WOULD	LEAVE	MUCH MORE THAN 99 PER CENT OF THE NATION QUITE
FANY III (300)	CALLS YOU A PIG, THE TONE OF THE TRANSACTION MAY	LEAVE	MUCH TO BE DESIRED; BUT IT'LL BE LESS CAMBERWELLIAN
GETT PREFACE(194)	PAGES WITH THE TALE OF OUR IMBECILITIES AND STILL	LEAVE	MUCH UNTOLD; BUT WHAT I HAVE SET DOWN HERE HAPHAZARD
SIM I (43)	I WILL RETURN IN DREAMS. /MAYA/ (SIMILARLY) I	LEAVE	MY ARROW IN YOUR HEART. /LADY FARWATERS/ YOU MUSTNT
FANY I (282)	OUT TODAY, WONT YOU? /GILBEY/ IT'S LIKELY I'D	LEAVE	MY BOY IN PRISON, ISNT IT? /DORA/ I'D LIKE TO KNOW
CLEO III (156)	ACROSS THE GREAT MOLE. /RUFIO/ (ANGRILY) MUST I	LEAVE	MY FOOD AND GO STARVING TO BRING YOU A REPORT?
CAND I (101)	HIM IN HER HEART." /MORELL/ (WRATHFULLY)	LEAVE	MY HOUSE. DO YOU HEAR? (HE ADVANCES ON HIM
KING I (181)	WASTED. /NEWTON/ GEORGE FOX: YOU ARE AN INFIDEL.	LEAVE	MY HOUSE. /FOX/ (RISING) YOUR PHILOSOPHY HAS LED YOU
DEVL I (20)	BLASPHEMOUS TONGUE! I WILL BEAR NO MORE OF THIS.	LEAVE	MY HOUSE. /RICHARD/ HOW DO YOU KNOW IT'S YOUR HOUSE
KING I (188)	IN A FURY AND FACING HIM MENACINGLY) WILL YOU	LEAVE	MY HOUSE, OR SHALL I THROW YOU OUT THROUGH THE
ARMS I (12)	BEEN WATCHING THE SCENE CURIOUSLY. /RAINA/ DONT	LEAVE	MY MOTHER, LOUKA, UNTIL THE SOLDIERS GO AWAY. LOUKA
APPL PREFACE(193)	TARDY APPEARANCE IN THE ROLL OF FAME. I MUST NOT	LEAVE	MY READERS TO ASSUME THAT GATTIE WAS AN EASY MAN TO
GENV IV (105)	FOR BOTH OF US. MY COUNTRY IS NOT. /THE JEW/ I	LEAVE	MYSELF IN THE HANDS OF THE COURT. FOR MY RACE THERE
LION PREFACE(73)	OF PROPERTY IN HUMAN BODIES. BUT IT WILL	LEAVE	NATURE FREE TO EFFECT A CURE; AND IN FREE SOIL THE
BUOY III (36)	QUITE MAD ABOUT ME. HE WARNED ME TO RUN AWAY AND	LEAVE	NO ADDRESS, AS HE WOULD FOLLOW ME TO THE ENDS OF THE
BARB III (325)	SO EASILY? CAN YOU STRIKE A MAN TO THE HEART AND	LEAVE	NO MARK ON HIM? /BARBARA/ (HER FACE LIGHTING UP) OH,
LION PREFACE(12)	COMMUNITIES WHERE THE CONDITIONS OF LIFE	LEAVE	NO ROOM FOR POVERTY AND RICHES, AND THE PROCESS OF
MTH4 I (173)	IF YOU CARRY OUT YOUR PLAN OF COLONIZATION, AND	LEAVE	NO SHORTLIVED COUNTRIES IN THE WORLD, WHAT WILL YOU DO
MTH2 (47)	AND, LIKE THIS INFLUENTIAL PAGEANT FADED,	LEAVE	NOT A RACK BEHIND." THATS BIOLOGY, YOU KNOW; GOOD
DOCT IV (169)	BOURNE FROM WHICH NO TRAVELLER RETURNS	LEAVE	NOT A WRACK BEHIND. WALPOLE IS ABOUT TO SPEAK, BUT
SHAK (142)	-- AND LIKE THIS FOOLISH LITTLE SHOW OF OURS	LEAVE	NOT A WRACK BEHIND. SO YOU HAVE SAID. I SAY THE WORLD
SUPR HANDBOK(212)	MAY UNDER CERTAIN CIRCUMSTANCES HAVE A YEAR'S	LEAVE	OF ABSENCE ON FULL SALARY, OR BY THE CENTRAL
KING I (190)	AS I SHALL BE, IN MY OWN RIGHT, AND NOT BY THE	LEAVE	OF ANY PROTESTANT PARLIAMENTARY GANG-- I SHALL RESTORE
APPL II (272)	BUT THERE IS A MISAPPREHENSION. WE ARE NOT TAKING	LEAVE	OF ONE ANOTHER. I HAVE NO INTENTION OF WITHDRAWING
SUPR IV (154)	TO MALONE'S CRINGING ATTITUDE AS HE TAKES	LEAVE	OF VIOLET) AND THAT POOR DEVIL IS A BILLIONAIRE! ONE
MIS. PREFACE(38)	LATE, OR, AS WITH US, BEGIN TOO EARLY AND NEVER	LEAVE	OFF AT ALL, OBVIOUSLY THE WORST OF ALL POSSIBLE PLANS.
DOCT I (87)	VANITY WERE PAST, TELL ME: AT WHAT AGE DOES A MAN	LEAVE	OFF BEING A FOOL? /SIR PATRICK/ REMEMBER THE
MIS. PREFACE(38)	WORK IS LIKE A DAY'S WORK: IT CAN BEGIN EARLY AND	LEAVE	OFF EARLY OR BEGIN LATE AND LEAVE OFF LATE, OR, AS
MIS. PREFACE(38)	BEGIN EARLY AND LEAVE OFF EARLY OR BEGIN LATE AND	LEAVE	OFF LATE, OR, AS WITH US, BEGIN TOO EARLY AND NEVER
CURE (229)	THAT IT HAS ONLY EXCITED YOU, TAKE ANOTHER. I'LL	LEAVE	ONE FOR YOU (HE PUTS ONE ON THE PLATE, AND POCKETS
MIS. PREFACE(79)	THE CONFUSION THAT ENSUED IT BECAME NECESSARY TO	LEAVE	ONE OF THE SCHOOLROOMS WITHOUT A MASTER. I WAS IN THE

BULL IV (173)	AN ANSWER FOR EVERYTHING, SIR. BUT YOUR PLANS	LEAVE	ONE QUESTION STILL UNANSWERED: HOW TO GET BUTTER OUT
GETT PREFACE(202)	PUBLIC OPINION. IN FACT, HE WILL HAVE TO	LEAVE	OPINION AS FAR AS POSSIBLE OUT OF THE QUESTION, AND
MIS. PREFACE(24)	PLATE INSCRIBED KINDERGARTEN, AND IMAGINE, OR	LEAVE	OTHERS TO IMAGINE, THAT FROEBEL IS THE GOVERNING
MIS. PREFACE(72)	IN THE CONSTITUTION IS A QUESTION ON WHICH I	LEAVE	OTHERS TO SPECULATE. BUT IF IT COULD ONCE BE
MIS. PREFACE(87)	FAMILY WAS AN INVITATION TO ALL OF US TO	LEAVE	OUR FAMILIES AND FOLLOW HIM, AND TO LEAVE THE DEAD TO
ROCK PREFACE(184)	IS PART OF THE ETERNAL TRUTH YOU SEEK. /PILATE/	LEAVE	OUT CRUELTY! ALL GOVERNMENT IS CRUEL; FOR NOTHING IS
CAPT III (289)	DO YOU WAWNT IT TO GO ANY FURTHER? /MARZO/ SHE	LEAVE	OUT SOMETHING. ARAB SHOOT ME. SHE NURSE ME. SHE CURE
KING I (202)	GRAND AIR. /CHARLES/ THANK YOU, LOUISE. NEXT TIME	LEAVE	OUT THE ALMOST. MY PART IS MORE DIFFICULT THAN THAT OF
JOAN PREFACE(40)	NOR THEIR OPPONENTS THE SANITARIANS WOULD	LEAVE	PARENTS FREE TO BRING UP THEIR CHILDREN NAKED, THOUGH
JOAN PREFACE(40)	BUT IF A MODERN PUBLIC HEALTH AUTHORITY WERE TO	LEAVE	PEOPLE ENTIRELY TO THEIR OWN DEVICES IN THE MATTER OF
CAPT III (274)	THE LAD. HE MAY HAVE BEEN A BIT WILD; BUT I CANT	LEAVE	POOR MILES'S SON UNBEFRIENDED IN A FOREIGN GAOL. /LADY
SUPR II SD(62)	LEADS THE UNWARY, BY HUMOROUS IRREVERENCE, TO	LEAVE	POPULAR THEOLOGY OUT OF ACCOUNT IN DISCUSSING MORAL
CAND II (117)	EASY CHAIR) YOUVE DONE ENOUGH WRITING FOR TODAY.	LEAVE	PROSSY TO FINISH IT. COME AND TALK TO ME. /MORELL/
CLEO IV (182)	IN THE HEART OF THE REGIONS OF MYSTERY? SHALL WE	LEAVE	ROME BEHIND US-- ROME, THAT HAS ACHIEVED GREATNESS
JOAN 6 (148)	THAT WE SHOULD WITNESS THE END. SO BY YOUR	LEAVE	-- (HE BOWS, AND GOES OUT THROUGH THE COURTYARD).
DEVL I (13)	UNTIL I'M READY. /JUDITH/ (GRACIOUSLY GIVING HER	LEAVE	) OH YES, CERTAINLY. LEAVE THAT TO ME, MRS DUDGEON;
AUGS (283)	OF THEM HAVE COME HOME FOR A FEW DAYS HARD-EARNED	LEAVE	; AND I AM SURE YOU WONT GRUDGE THEM A LITTLE FUN AT
CLEO II (124)	BE QUIET. OPEN YOUR MOUTH AGAIN BEFORE I GIVE YOU	LEAVE	; AND YOU SHALL BE EATEN. /CLEOPATRA/ I AM NOT AFRAID.
MIS. PREFACE(73)	MUCH AS IS GOOD FOR YOU." TRYING TO MAKE CHILDREN	LEAVE	SCHOOL WILL BE LIKE TRYING TO MAKE THEM GO TO BED; AND
GENV PREFACE(5)	FOR WAR, JUST AS PEOPLE WITH ANY PROPERTY TO	LEAVE	SHOULD ALWAYS HAVE MADE THEIR WILLS, BUT AS MOST OF
MILL PREFACE(129)	(TRADE UNIONS, FOR EXAMPLE) MAY BE FOUND TO	LEAVE	SOCIETY LESS ORGANIZED THAN IT WAS BEFORE THE HAND OF
FABL PREFACE(63)	MY CORRESPONDENTS SEEM TO EXPECT, I HAVE HAD TO	LEAVE	SOME SCRAPS AND SHAVINGS OUT; AND NOW I GATHER UP A
GENV I (34)	NECESSARY. MY ENGLISH IS GERMAN ENGLISH, AND MAY	LEAVE	SOMETHING TO BE DESIRED. /SHE/ YES: THATLL BE
2TRU I (44)	ON SWEETIE'S KNEES. /THE PATIENT/ YOU CAN	LEAVE	SWEETIE OUT, POPS. HER AMOROUS EMOTIONS DO NOT
JITT I (14)	NOT GONE YET. /BRUNO/ IT IS NOT THE NET. I CAN	LEAVE	THAT BEHIND WHEN I COME HERE INTO THE DREAMLAND. THESE
ARMS II (40)	(IMPATIENTLY SNATCHING THE SALVER FROM HER):	LEAVE	THAT HERE; AND GO STRAIGHT BACK TO HIM. /LOUKA/ YES,
BULL IV (165)	CRY. DONT. /BROADBENT/ I'M NOT CRYING. I-- I-- I	LEAVE	THAT SORT OF THING TO YOUR DAMNED SENTIMENTAL
WIDO II (44)	SAW HOW ANGRY SHE WAS. /SARTORIUS/ YOU HAD BETTER	LEAVE	THAT TO ME. (HE LOOKS AT HIS WATCH, AND RINGS THE
DEVL I (14)	(GRACIOUSLY GIVING HER LEAVE) OH YES, CERTAINLY.	LEAVE	THAT TO ME, MRS DUDGEON; AND TAKE YOUR TIME. (SHE
PRES (153)	GOING TO FIGHT. /MITCHENER/ (GALLANTLY) OH, PRAY	LEAVE	THAT TO THE MEN, MRS BANGER. /LADY CORINTHIA/ WE CAN
KING I (214)	ARE GONE. /BARBARA/ OH, DO NOT PREACH, CHARLES.	LEAVE	THAT TO THIS PERSON WHO IS DRESSED PARTLY IN LEATHER.
CLEO II (132)	IS TO BE DONE WITH HER? HOWEVER, I SUPPOSE I MAY	LEAVE	THAT TO YOU. (HE GOES OUT THROUGH THE LOGGIA).
CLEO V (198)	CORNER, AND CALLING TO HIM) APOLLODORUS: I	LEAVE	THE ART OF EGYPT IN YOUR CHARGE. REMEMBER: ROME LOVES
KING II (225)	THAT ARE DIFFERENT. IN THE END ONE LEARNS TO	LEAVE	THE BODY OUT. AND THEN BARBARA IS PACKED OFF TO PARIS,
POSN (462)	AND FOLLOWS STRAPPER OUT. THE JURYMEN	LEAVE	THE BOX, EXCEPT NESTOR, WHO COLLAPSES IN A DRUNKEN
POSN (462)	COURT, AND WILL COLLECT IT MYSELF OFF YOU AS YOU	LEAVE	THE BUILDING. AND AS THE BOYS HAVE BEEN DISAPPOINTED
BARB I (255)	TO KEEP UP THE TRADITION AND ADOPT SOMEBODY TO	LEAVE	THE BUSINESS TO, OF COURSE I WAS NOT GOING TO STAND
BARB III (315)	DISINHERITS HIM. IT WOULD BE DISHONEST OF ME TO	LEAVE	THE CANNON FOUNDRY TO MY SON. /LADY BRITOMART/ IT
APPL II (257)	GOING ON IT. /THE QUEEN/ WHY DID YOU TELL THEM TO	LEAVE	THE CHAIRS WHEN THEY TOOK AWAY THE TEA? /MAGNUS/ I
GENV I (35)	WERENT GOING TO STAND THAT: THEY REFUSED TO	LEAVE	THE CHAMBER. SO HE ADJOURNED THE HOUSE UNTIL THE NEXT
FABL I (103)	MAY KILL THE INHABITANTS OF A CITY; BUT IT WILL	LEAVE	THE CITY STANDING AND IN WORKING ORDER. /YOUNG MAN/ (
BULL III (132)	GAVE US BRAINS, AND BID US FARM THEM, AND	LEAVE	THE CLAY AND THE WORMS ALONE. /FATHER DEMPSEY/ (WITH
2TRU II (80)	DEVOTE MYSELF ALMOST ENTIRELY TO SKETCHING, AND	LEAVE	THE COMMAND OF THE EXPEDITION TO PRIVATE MEEK. AND
KING I (215)	IT) HAS THE KING TORN UP A WORK OF MINE? I	LEAVE	THE COUNTRY THIS AFTERNOON. /CHARLES/ I WOULD MUCH
CAPT II (255)	AND FORCED HER TO WRITE YOU AN APOLOGY AND	LEAVE	THE COUNTRY TO REGAIN HER LIBERTY AND SAVE HERSELF
LADY PREFACE(213)	AFTERWARDS HAPPENED TO HIM, AND WARNED HIM TO	LEAVE	THE COUNTRY. IT WAS THE FIRST TIME WITHIN MY KNOWLEDGE
CAPT NOTES (304)	WOULD GIVE SUCH OFFENCE THAT I SHOULD HAVE TO	LEAVE	THE COUNTRY; FOR NOTHING ANNOYS A NATIVE SPEAKER OF
GENV IV (108)	BEAR IT. FORBID HER TO KILL HERSELF OR I WILL	LEAVE	THE COURT. /JUDGE/ SENORA: I FORBID YOU TO KILL
METH PREFACE(R46)	IS NOT A STAIN ON HIS CHARACTER, AND BEG HIM TO	LEAVE	THE COURT; BUT HE WILL NOT BE CONTENT WITH ENOUGH
CLEO III (160)	SQUAD OF SOLDIERS TO WORK THE CRANE. /BRITANNUS/	LEAVE	THE CRANE TO ME. GO AND AWAIT THE DESCENT OF THE
JITT II (45)	/JITTA/ (SITTING DOWN WEARILY ON THE SOFA)	LEAVE	THE DEAD IN PEACE. IF YOU CANNOT HOLD YOUR TONGUE,
MIS. PREFACE(87)	US TO LEAVE OUR FAMILIES AND FOLLOW HIM, AND TO	LEAVE	THE DEAD TO BURY THE DEAD, AND NOT DEBAUCH OURSELVES
POSN PREFACE(403)	PARTIES TO THE CONTROVERSY ARE TO AGREE TO	LEAVE	THE DECISION TO A THIRD PARTY UNANIMOUSLY CHOSEN BY
PHIL II (129)	SAY A WORD FOR ME. /CRAVEN/ I'M QUITE WILLING TO	LEAVE	THE DECISION TO CUTHBERTSON; AND I HAVE NO DOUBT
FABL PREFACE(85)	THEY SHOULD NOT FIGHT IT OUT, BUT COUNT HEADS AND	LEAVE	THE DECISION TO THE MAJORITY. THE SNAG IN THIS IS THAT
FABL PREFACE(86)	ALWAYS OUT-OF-DATE. IT WOULD BE MORE SENSIBLE TO	LEAVE	THE DECISION TO THE MINORITY IF A QUALIFIED ONE COULD
3PLA PREFACE(R25)	ONE OF THE PREFACES HE OUGHT TO HAVE WRITTEN. I	LEAVE	THE DELICACIES OF RETIREMENT TO THOSE WHO ARE
3PLA PREFACE(R27)	LOSE ITS GLOSS WITH THE LAPSE OF TIME, AND	LEAVE	THE DEVIL'S DISCIPLE EXPOSED AS THE THREADBARE POPULAR
JOAN 6 (134)	I DID; AND NOT FOR THE FIRST TIME EITHER. IF YOU	LEAVE	THE DOOR OF THE CAGE OPEN THE BIRD WILL FLY OUT.
MRS II (204)	WITHIN) QUITE, THANK YOU. /MRS WARREN/ (WITHIN)	LEAVE	THE DOOR OPEN, DEARIE. (VIVIE FROWNS; BUT FRANK
MIS. (123)	THEM FOR IT. /HYPATIA/ WELL, I THINK THEY MIGHT	LEAVE	THE DRAINS TO THEIR HUSBANDS. I SHOULDNT THINK MUCH OF
APPL INTRLUD(251)	THE MAKINGS OF A FIRST RATE WOMAN IN YOU. WHEN I	LEAVE	THE EARTH AND SOAR UP TO THE REGIONS WHICH ARE MY REAL
BARB III (339)	BECAUSE THEIR BODIES ARE FULL. /BARBARA/ AND	LEAVE	THE EAST END TO STARVE? /UNDERSHAFT/ (HIS ENERGETIC
MRS IV (244)	VIV, IF I CAN HELP IT. I WITHDRAW GRACEFULLY AND	LEAVE	THE FIELD TO THE GILDED YOUTH OF ENGLAND. SO THATS
HART II (108)	I'M SORRY TO BE INHOSPITABLE; BUT WILL YOU KINDLY	LEAVE	THE HOUSE? /THE BURGLAR/ RIGHT. I'LL GO TO THE POLICE
MIS. (187)	INSULT ME AGAIN: IF YOU SAY ANOTHER WORD, I'LL	LEAVE	THE HOUSE AND NOT ENTER IT UNTIL YOU LEAVE IT.
HART PREFACE(3)	TOLSTOY WAS NO PESSIMIST: HE WAS NOT DISPOSED TO	LEAVE	THE HOUSE STANDING IF HE COULD BRING IT DOWN ABOUT THE
MIS. (164)	FORGOTTEN OURSELVES, YOULL PLEASE ALLOW ME TO	LEAVE	THE HOUSE. (HE TURNS TOWARDS THE INNER DOOR, HAVING
HART I (54)	ARE PRETENDING NOT TO KNOW ME ON PURPOSE. I WILL	LEAVE	THE HOUSE. MAZZINI DUNN ENTERS FROM THE HALL. HE IS A
HART II (111)	TO ME. IN THE END I HAVE HAD TO WALK OUT AND	LEAVE	THE JOB. /RANDALL/ WHEN THAT HAPPENS, DO YOU PUT BACK
APPL I (211)	THE KING? /BOANERGES/ RIGHT AS RAIN, JOE. YOU	LEAVE	THE KING TO ME. I KNOW HOW TO HANDLE HIM. IF I'D BEEN
BULL III (130)	A STUPID, LAZY, GOOD-FOR-NOTHING SORT OF THING TO	LEAVE	THE LAND IN THE HANDS OF THE OLD LANDLORDS WITHOUT
METH PREFACE(R80)	IS STILL KEPT PURE, AND YOU MAY TAKE THE LAW AND	LEAVE	THE LEGENDS WITHOUT SUSPICION OF HERESY. ACCORDINGLY,
PHIL II SD(122)	GOES TO THE DINING ROOM DOOR, AND IS ABOUT TO	LEAVE	THE LIBRARY WHEN HE MEETS GRACE ENTERING. /GRACE/ HOW
CAND III (136)	I HOPE, THE STRONGER, CANDIDA. SO YOU HAD BETTER	LEAVE	THE MATTER IN MY HANDS. /CANDIDA/ (AGAIN SOOTHING
LION PREFACE(94)	THE TEACHING OF CHRISTIANITY. AND THERE I MUST	LEAVE	THE MATTER TO SUCH CHOICE AS YOUR NATURE ALLOWS YOU.
APPL PREFACE(182)	AND CRY AGAINST HIM AS AN UNPATRIOTIC PERSON, AND	LEAVE	THE MOB TO DO THE REST AFTER SUPPLYING THEM WITH A
MTH3 (125)	NOT THE LEAST DANGER OF IT. I GRANT YOU WE	LEAVE	THE MOST TROUBLESOME PART OF THE LABOR OF THE NATION
APPL PREFACE(183)	BY THE GOVERNMENT. DURING THE WAR OUR ATTEMPT TO	LEAVE	THE MUNITIONING OF THE ARMY TO PRIVATE ENTERPRISE LED
JOAN 6 (128)	MAGISTRATE. STICK TO THE HERESY, GENTLEMEN; AND	LEAVE	THE OTHER MATTERS ALONE. /CAUCHON/ I MAY SAY THAT WE
JOAN 6 (145)	AND SOLDIERS PASS ME AND LEAVE ME BEHIND AS THEY	LEAVE	THE OTHER WOMEN, IF ONLY I COULD STILL HEAR THE WIND
DOCT PREFACE(4)	ARM: HE CAN REMOVE THE APPENDIX OR THE UVULA, AND	LEAVE	THE PATIENT NONE THE WORSE AFTER A FORTNIGHT OR SO IN
2TRU I (36)	PERSON SAYS, MADAM. YOU HAD BETTER GO TO BED AND	LEAVE	THE PATIENT TO ME. YOU ARE QUITE WORN OUT. (SHE COMES
SIM PRO,1, (26)	OR NOT. THAT LASSIE SHANT SAY THAT I DIDNT	LEAVE	THE PLACE TIDY EITHER, THOUGH SHE CAN WRITE IN THE
PHIL PREFACE(68)	A PICTURE OF THE FUTURE. AT ALL EVENTS I SHALL	LEAVE	THE PLAY AS IT IS; FOR ALL THE ATTEMPTS WITHIN MY
MRS III (229)	IN CASE YOUNG GARDNER SHOULD TRY TO TRAP YOU.	LEAVE	THE QUESTION OPEN. /VIVIE/ (SHARPLY) MY NO IS FINAL.
HART PREFACE(23)	SHOULD GIVE ALL THEIR TIME TO THEIR BUSINESS AND	LEAVE	THE RABBLE RAVING TO ITS HEARTS' CONTENT. INDEED THE
CATH PREFACE(154)	PORTRAITURE WAS THE MOTIVE OF A PLAY THAT WILL	LEAVE	THE READER AS IGNORANT OF RUSSIAN HISTORY AS HE MAY BE
LION I (122)	HIM, POOR LAD. CARRY HIM GENTLY TO HIS HOUSE; AND	LEAVE	THE REST TO HEAVEN. /CENTURION/ TAKE HIM HOME. (THE
APPL I (232)	AND GENTLEMEN, WE HAVE DONE OUR BIT, AND MAY	LEAVE	THE REST TO JOE. MATTERS HAD REACHED A POINT AT WHICH
SHAK (139)	SET BUT THIS FIEND OF IRELAND AND MYSELF; AND	LEAVE	THE REST TO ME. (SHAV ENTERS). WHO ART THOU? THAT
MRS III (223)	AND-- SAY ANY BLESSED THING EXCEPT THE TRUTH, AND	LEAVE	THE REST TO PROVIDENCE. /REV. S./ BUT HOW ARE WE TO
MILL PREFACE(118)	AT LEAST FOUND EMPLOYMENT FOR ENOUGH OF THEM TO	LEAVE	THE REST TOO FEW TO BE DANGEROUS, DEFAULTED IN RESPECT
2TRU PREFACE(8)	AND OVERCROWDED LODGINGS SEEM DELIGHTFUL, AND	LEAVE	THE REVELLER WITH A COMPLETELY FALSE NOTION OF WHAT A
DEST (163)	THAT WILL DO, SIR: DO YOU HEAR? WILL YOU	LEAVE	THE ROOM? I ORDER YOU TO LEAVE THE ROOM. /LADY/ OH
MIS. (198)	WITH YOU. /TARLETON/ DID YOU HEAR ME TELL YOU TO	LEAVE	THE ROOM? /HYPATIA/ I DID. (TO PERCIVAL) YOU SEE
GETT (304)	THAT DISGRACEFUL WAY ABOUT OUR MARRIED LIFE, I'LL	LEAVE	THE ROOM AND NEVER SPEAK TO YOU AGAIN. /REGINALD/
AUGS (264)	SECRETARY. /THE CLERK/ I'M THE SECRETARY. I CANT	LEAVE	THE ROOM AND SEND MYSELF TO YOU AT THE SAME TIME, CAN
2TRU I (39)	HERE FOR. ALL I CAN TELL YOU IS THAT IF YOU DONT	LEAVE	THE ROOM AT ONCE AND SEND MY MOTHER TO ME, I WILL GIVE
ANNA (293)	WHO HAS BEEN FOOLING WITH THE TELEPHONE. I HAD TO	LEAVE	THE ROOM FOR A MOMENT. WASH OUT; AND SEND THE GIRL
MIS. PREFACE(67)	FEELS PERSONALLY INSULTED AND WANTS TO RESIGN OR	LEAVE	THE ROOM UNLESS HE IS APOLOGIZED TO, AND HIS PANIC AND
DOCT III (137)	DOOR). /RIDGEON/ (STOPPING HIM) YOU SHALL NOT	LEAVE	THE ROOM UNTIL YOU PAY IT. IT'S A SMALL ONE; AND PAY
ROCK I (205)	RISING IN FLAMING WRATH) HOW DARE YOU? SILENCE.	LEAVE	THE ROOM. AFTER A MOMENT OF AWESTRUCK SILENCE FLAVIA,
MIS. (198)	OH! /TARLETON/ (SPRINGING TO HIS FEET)	LEAVE	THE ROOM, DO YOU HEAR: LEAVE THE ROOM. /PERCIVAL/ ARNT
PPP (203)	YOU BIN DOIN TE MAW CEILIN? /FITZ/ SILENCE, OR	LEAVE	THE ROOM. IF YOU WAKE THAT MAN HE DIES. /THE LANDLORD/
MIS. (198)	LIVING IN A HOUSE WHERE YOU CAN BE ORDERED TO	LEAVE	THE ROOM. IVE GOT TO OBEY: IT'S HIS HOUSE, NOT MINE.
AUGS (264)	ROBBING ME, I CALL IT. /AUGUSTUS/ THATS ENOUGH.	LEAVE	THE ROOM. (HE SITS DOWN AND TAKES UP HIS PEN.

CURE (229)	BEFORE I GO, I WANT YOU TO BE ASLEEP BEFORE I	LEAVE	THE ROOM, REGINALD SETTLES HIMSELF TO SLEEP WITH HIS
PRES (158)	YOU NEED NOT BE ALARMED: I AM ONLY GOING TO	LEAVE	THE ROOM. /LADY CORINTHIA/ FISH. /MITCHENER/ FISH!
DEST (163)	HEAR? WILL YOU LEAVE THE ROOM? I ORDER YOU TO	LEAVE	THE ROOM. /LADY/ OH PRAY LET ME GO INSTEAD. /NAPOLEON/
BARB I (266)	YOU CAN BEHAVE YOURSELF, BEHAVE YOURSELF. IF NOT,	LEAVE	THE ROOM. /LOMAX/ I'M AWFULLY SORRY, LADY BRIT; BUT
MIS. (198)	TO HIS FEET) LEAVE THE ROOM. DO YOU HEAR:	LEAVE	THE ROOM. /PERCIVAL/ ARNT WE GETTING A LITTLE CROSS..
GETT (295)	BRIDGENORTH BEGINS TELLING IT, I SHALL HAVE TO	LEAVE	THE ROOM. /REGINALD/ I'M NOT AT ALL SURPRISED TO HEAR
CURE (232)	IF YOU KEEP YOUR EARS STOPPED. IT IS AN INSULT.	LEAVE	THE ROOM. /REGINALD/ BUT I TELL YOU IT'S MY ROOM.
CURE (231)	TO YOUR SOFA, AND HOLD YOUR TONGUE, OR ELSE	LEAVE	THE ROOM. /REGINALD/ BUT, YOU KNOW, I AM ILL. /STREGA/
CAND I (82)	(HE PATS LEXY AFFECTIONATELY AND MOVES TO	LEAVE	THE ROOM). /LEXY/ OH, WAIT A BIT: I FORGOT. (MORELL
JITT II (45)	HAVE NO ORDERS. I GO MY OWN WAY (SHE ATTEMPTS TO	LEAVE	THE ROOM). /LENKHEIM/ (INTERCEPTING HER) YOU SHANT
CAND II (107)	HERE: IF YOU DONT STOP TALKING LIKE THIS, I'LL	LEAVE	THE ROOM, MR MARCHBANKS: I REALLY WILL. IT'S NOT
CURE (232)	BUT I TELL YOU IT'S MY ROOM. /STREGA/ (RISING)	LEAVE	THE ROOM, OR I WILL RING YOUR BELL AND HAVE YOU PUT
DEST (163)	LIEUTENANT: WILL YOU OBEY MY ORDERS AND	LEAVE	THE ROOM, SINCE YOU ARE CONVINCED AT LAST THAT THIS IS
ARMS I (6)	TO KILL YOU-- OR WORSE? /RAINA/ (TO LOUKA)	LEAVE	THE SHUTTERS SO THAT I CAN JUST CLOSE THEM IF I HEAR
ROCK II (239)	IT WHENEVER YOU GET UP TO SPEAK? /SIR BEMROSE/ I	LEAVE	THE SPEAKING TO ARTHUR: IT'S HIS JOB, NOT MINE. BUT IF
POSN PREFACE(387)	ONE? MAY NOT THOSE CONTINENTAL GOVERNMENTS WHO	LEAVE	THE STAGE PRACTICALLY FREE IN EVERY OTHER RESPECT, BUT
WIDO III (63)	AND MYSELF MADE PART OF A BARGAIN. (HE RISES TO	LEAVE	THE TABLE). /LICKCHEESE/ (RISING) THATS ENOUGH: A
MRS PREFACE(155)	BY MANY OF OUR FASHIONABLE PLAYS, THEY WOULD	LEAVE	THE THEATRE CONVINCED THAT THE PLYMOUTH BROTHER WHO
DOCT PREFACE(14)	AND HIS ADDITIONAL FEES FROM THE PUBLIC, IF WE	LEAVE	THE THIRD-CLASS TWOPENNY TIP OUT OF ACCOUNT (AND I AM
JOAN 6 (133)	YOU WERE FOUND LYING IN THE MOAT. WHY DID YOU	LEAVE	THE TOWER? /JOAN/ WHY WOULD ANYBODY LEAVE A PRISON IF
FABL IV (116)	AND COLONS AND SEMICOLONS ON THE TYPESCRIPT.	LEAVE	THE TYPE AND THE FORMAT AND THE ILLUSTRATIONS TO THE
JITT III (52)	FROM READING THEM? /ALFRED/ JUST SO. BUT WHY NOT	LEAVE	THE WORK TO US? WHY WORRY? CANT YOU TRUST US?
MILL IV (205)	THE WRATH OF ALLAH SHALL OVERTAKE THOSE WHO	LEAVE	THE WORLD NO BETTER THAN THEY FOUND IT. /EPIFANIA/ I
BASH I (97)	NASTINESS, VANISH, AND PROMPTLY. /MELLISH/ CAN I	LEAVE	THEE HERE THUS THINLY CLAD, EXPOSED TO VERNAL DEWS?
SUPR III (121)	THEMSELVES TO HAVING A GOOD TIME OF IT, ONLY	LEAVE	THEIR MINDS FREE FOR THE FEAR OF OLD AGE AND UGLINESS
GETT PREFACE(225)	THE PATRIOTS WHO ARE SO PATRIOTIC THAT THEY NEVER	LEAVE	THEIR OWN COUNTRY TO LOOK AT ANOTHER, BUT OF THE
ARMS II (24)	DEPENDENT ON THE GOOD WILL OF THE FAMILY. WHEN I	LEAVE	THEIR SERVICE AND START A SHOP IN SOFIA, THEIR CUSTOM
GETT PREFACE(235)	THE HUSBANDS WHO BUY MEAT FOR THEIR BULL-PUPS AND	LEAVE	THEIR WIVES AND CHILDREN HUNGRY. THAT BASIS IS THE
HART II (86)	THE THIRD LOT WILL HAVE TO SELL OUT TOO, AND	LEAVE	THEIR WORK AND THEIR MONEY BEHIND THEM. AND THATS
GENV PREFACE(17)	WALLS THAT WERE LEFT STANDING, LOCK THEM IN, AND	LEAVE	THEM ALMOST STARVING TO DIE OF TYPHUS. WHEN FURTHER
BUOY III (46)	GO OUT). /DARKIE/ (RISING) COME ON, FIFF, LETS	LEAVE	THEM ALONE TOGETHER. /HE/ THANK YOU. DARKIE AND FIFF
BUOY PREFACE(5)	OF A SAINT, THOUGH FUTURE CORTICAL EVOLUTION MAY	LEAVE	THEM FAR BEHIND. YET THERE ARE THE MOMENTS OF
NEVR II (229)	WE HAVE COME BACK TO ENGLAND IT IS IMPOSSIBLE TO	LEAVE	THEM IN IGNORANCE ANY LONGER. (AGITATED) FINCH: I
ARMS I (6)	YOU WOULD BE SURE TO DROP OFF TO SLEEP AND	LEAVE	THEM OPEN. MAKE THEM FAST, LOUKA. /LOUKA/ YES, MADAM.
PPP (206)	DOCTOR. /PHYLLIS/ WILL THEY BE IN YOUR WAY IF I	LEAVE	THEM THERE UNTIL MORNING, MY LADY? OR SHALL I BRING
SUPR II (64)	/ANN/ (SUBDUEDLY) COME, MOTHER: WE MUST	LEAVE	THEM TO TALK OVER THE ARRANGEMENTS. I MUST SEE TO MY
MTH4 I (157)	INTERESTED IN THE CHEMICALS AND THE MICROBES: I	LEAVE	THEM TO THE CHUMPS AND NOODLES, TO THE BLOCKHEADS AND
LION I (117)	THEM AS I DO YOU WOULDNT WANT TO CHAFF THEM.	LEAVE	THEM TO THE LIONS. /LENTULUS/ (INDICATING LAVINIA,
BULL III (122)	ON, ALANNA, AN MAKE THE PASTE FOR THE PIE. WE CAN	LEAVE	THEM TO THEIR TALK. THEY DONT WANT US (SHE TAKES UP
DEST (166)	YOU BRAVE PEOPLE DO THE BRAVE THINGS? WHY DO YOU	LEAVE	THEM TO US, WHO HAVE NO COURAGE AT ALL? I'M NOT
SIM II (78)	FOOLS. /PRA/ IT IS STILL MORE DANGEROUS TO	LEAVE	THEM UNEDUCATED. /MRS HYERING/ THERE JUST SHOULDNT BE
MIS. PREFACE(71)	PROVIDE PLENTY OF GATES IN THEIR FENCES, AND TO	LEAVE	THEM UNLOCKED WHEN THERE ARE NO GROWING CROPS TO BE
BARB I (255)	ENOUGH TO BUY LAND FOR THEIR OWN CHILDREN AND	LEAVE	THEM WELL PROVIDED FOR. BUT THEY ALWAYS ADOPTED AND
KING I (190)	BULLY ME I WILL THREATEN TO GO ON MY TRAVELS AND	LEAVE	THEM WITHOUT A KING. THAT IS THE WAY TO BRING THEM
KING I (190)	ON THEIR MARROWBONES. /CHARLES/ YOU COULD NOT	LEAVE	THEM WITHOUT A KING. PROTESTANT KINGS-- STUART KINGS--
BARB III (334)	MR UNDERSHAFT: YOU HAVE MY TERMS. TAKE THEM OR	LEAVE	THEM. /UNDERSHAFT/ (RECOVERING HIMSELF) VERY WELL. I
LADY PREFACE(225)	ANY HUMAN IMPERFECTION IN THEIR HERO, THEY THUS	LEAVE	THEMSELVES WITH SO LITTLE MATERIAL THAT THEY ARE
KING I (190)	FISHING SMACK AND LAND IN FRANCE. /JAMES/ AND	LEAVE	THEMSELVES WITHOUT A KING AGAIN! NOT THEY: THEY HAD
GETT (323)	YOUR CONTRACT! /THE VOICE OF THE BEADLE/ BY YOUR	LEAVE	THERE, GENTLEMEN. MAKE WAY FOR THE MAYORESS. WAY FOR
MTH5 (230)	SUFFOCATED THEMSELVES IN CONSEQUENCE. /ECRASIA/	LEAVE	THESE OBSCURE PREHISTORIC ABORTIONS; AND COME BACK TO
HART PREFACE(29)	WAR. FOR THE INSTRUCTION OF THAT GENERATION I	LEAVE	THESE PAGES AS A RECORD OF WHAT CIVILIAN LIFE WAS
PYGM IV (260)	/PICKERING/ I SAY: MRS PEARCE WILL ROW IF WE	LEAVE	THESE THINGS LYING ABOUT IN THE DRAWING ROOM.
BARB III (344)	TO LADY BRITOMART, WHO RISES). MY DEAR: LET US	LEAVE	THESE TWO YOUNG PEOPLE TO THEMSELVES FOR A MOMENT. (
KING II (230)	MYSELF AND LET THE PEOPLE SEE ME DOING IT, AND	LEAVE	THINGS AS THEY ARE, THOUGH THINGS AS THEY ARE WILL NOT
WIDO III (60)	WITH THE COST OF THE IMPROVEMENTS THROWN IN.	LEAVE	THINGS AS THEY ARE; AND YOU STAND A GOOD CHANCE OF
SUPR IV (147)	A PROFIT FOR SOMEONE. A MARRIAGE WITH YOU WOULD	LEAVE	THINGS JUST WHERE THEY ARE. /VIOLET/ MANY OF MY
CATH 3 (183)	BY THE MOST UNUTTERABLE SWINE. AND IF WE DO NOT	LEAVE	THIS ABOMINABLE CITY NOW: DO YOU HEAR? NOW: I SHALL
BASH III (119)	WITH WHISPERING OF LEAVES AND DAINTY AIRS TO	LEAVE	THIS FRUITLESS HAUNTING OF THE PAST. MY FATHER WAS A
ARMS II (41)	I AM VERY GLAD TO SEE YOU; BUT YOU MUST	LEAVE	THIS HOUSE AT ONCE. (HE RAISES HIS EYEBROWS). MY
GETT (274)	/THE GENERAL/ MR BRIDGENORTH: ARE YOU GOING TO	LEAVE	THIS HOUSE OR AM I? /REGINALD/ YOU ARE, I HOPE. (HE
KING I (176)	STEPS, IN TWO FLIGHTS. /BARBARA/ I WILL NOT	LEAVE	THIS HOUSE UNTIL THAT PLAYER WOMAN HAS GONE FIRST. (
FOUN (209)	UP HIS OWN). /MERCER/ HERE: YOU LET ME ALONE. YOU	LEAVE	THIS OFFICE, D'YE HEAR; OR I'LL HAVE THE POLICE IN ON
SUPR III (103)	GETTING US A STEP FARTHER. AND YET YOU WANT TO	LEAVE	THIS PARADISE! /ANA/ BUT IF HELL BE SO BEAUTIFUL AS
SUPR III (101)	HAVE NEVER QUESTIONED IT. I OWE IT TO MYSELF TO	LEAVE	THIS PLACE AT ONCE. /THE DEVIL/ (OFFENDED) AS YOU
JITT II (45)	IT. /LENKHEIM/ AM I? WE SHALL SEE. BEFORE YOU	LEAVE	THIS ROOM I WILL FIND OUT THE PART YOU HAVE PLAYED IN
APPL I (227)	ULTIMATUM IS HERE: ALL THE TIME; AND I SHALL NOT	LEAVE	THIS ROOM UNTIL I HAVE HIS MAJESTY'S SIGNED PLEDGE
MTH3 (117)	SITS DOWN). GO ON. /BARNABAS/ I AM NOT GOING TO	LEAVE	THIS ROOM UNTIL WE GET TO THE BOTTOM OF THIS SWINDLE.
JITT II (47)	/LENKHEIM/ OH, DAMN YOUR HEROICS! YOU SHANT	LEAVE	THIS ROOM UNTIL YOU HAVE TOLD ME EVERYTHING. /JITTA/ (
JITT II (49)	VERY WELL; BUT STAND OR SIT, YOU DONT	LEAVE	THIS ROOM UNTIL YOU GIVE ME YOUR WORD TO STAY. /JITTA/
CAND I (98)	/MARCHBANKS/ (PASSIONATELY) NOW, BEFORE YOU	LEAVE	THIS ROOM. (HE RETREATS A FEW STEPS, AND STANDS AS IF
JITT I (20)	IS ABOUT TO PROTEST). PROMISE ME THAT YOU WILL	LEAVE	THIS SECRET BURIED IN MY GRAVE. /JITTA/ (BESIDE
GLIM (176)	NOT FORGOTTEN YOUR FATHER'S WAGER; AND UNTIL YOU	LEAVE	THIS TERRITORY I SHALL STICK TO YOU LIKE YOUR SHADOW.
2TRU I (41)	I HAVE ANOTHER IDEA, AND A MUCH BETTER ONE. YOU	LEAVE	THIS TO ME. (HE GOES TO THE DRESSING TABLE. SHE
SUPR III (137)	RIFLES. /THE ROWDY ONE/ BAT-- /MENDOZA/ SILENCE.	LEAVE	THIS TO ME. (TO TANNER) COMRADE: YOU WILL NOT BETRAY
APPL I (223)	I -- /PROTEUS/ (FIERCELY CRUSHING HIM) SIT DOWN.	LEAVE	THIS TO ME. /CRASSUS/ (SITS) I A JOBBER! WELL!
BASH II,2, (116)	THIRTY OXEN SHALT THOU HAVE IF ON THE SAND THOU	LEAVE	THY FOEMAN DEAD. METHINKS HE LOOKS FULL SCORNFULLY ON
PRES (141)	WELL, LADY RICHMOND. APOLOGIZE TO HER. ASK HER	LEAVE	TO ACCEPT THE COMMAND. TELL HER THAT YOUVE MADE THE
JOAN 1 (68)	DAMN YOU, I AM NOT AFRAID. AND WHO GAVE YOU	LEAVE	TO CALL ME ROBERT? /JOAN/ YOU WERE CALLED SO IN
DEST (190)	ARE EVIDENTLY BURNING TO READ THEM, I GIVE YOU	LEAVE	TO DO SO. /LADY/ OH, IVE READ THEM ALREADY. /NAPOLEON/
SUPR IV (152)	UNFORTUNATELY VIOLET DOES NOT. /MALONE/ I TAKE	LEAVE	TO DOUBT THAT, SIR. (TURNING ON VIOLET) LET ME TELL
MIS. PREFACE(89)	UNTIL THE END OF THE CONCERT OR OPERA GIVES THEM	LEAVE	TO GO HOME; AND YOU WILL HAVE IN GREAT CAPITALS
LADY (247)	IT). /THE DARK LADY/ MADAM: I IMPLORE YOU GIVE ME	LEAVE	TO GO. I AM DISTRACTED WITH GRIEF AND SHAME. I--
HART PREFACE(25)	OF THEIR TIME WITH URGENT PRACTICAL WORK, HAD TO	LEAVE	TO IDLER PEOPLE, OR TO PROFESSIONAL RHETORICIANS, THE
2TRU II (79)	YOU. MAY I ASK, FURTHER, WHO THE DEVIL GAVE YOU	LEAVE	TO PLANT THE ENTIRE REGIMENTAL STOCK OF MAROONS ALL
MILL PREFACE(118)	PARLIAMENT TO DO ANYTHING THAT IT COULD POSSIBLY	LEAVE	TO PRIVATE ENTERPRISE, PARLIAMENT WAS ABLE TO KEEP UP
MIS. PREFACE(75)	WHICH POINT, IF YOU DIFFER FROM ME, I SHALL TAKE	LEAVE	TO SAY THAT YOU ARE SOCIALLY A FOOL AND PERSONALLY AN
CAND III (140)	AT HER). NO: YOURE TOO YOUNG. WELL, I GIVE YOU	LEAVE	TO STAY: TO STAY AND LEARN. (SHE COMES AWAY FROM THE
JITT III (74)	AND YOU MIGHT FORGIVE HIM. VERY WELL: I GIVE YOU	LEAVE	TO TELL HIM. BUT YOU UNDERSTAND THAT IF YOU TELL HIM
APPL PREFACE(173)	OF HIS INTERCOURSE WITH HIS SUBJECTS, AND TO	LEAVE	TO THE LESS HIGHLY PLACED SUCH INDULGENCES AS TEMPERS,
WIDO I (22)	HE RISES AND TAKES OUT HIS CARD CASE), THE REST I	LEAVE	TO YOUR DISCRETION. (HE LEAVES A CARD ON THE TABLE).
KING I (199)	NEWTON'S TELESCOPE; AND THE JEALOUS LADY WOULDNT	LEAVE	UNTIL THE FRENCH LADY LEFT; AND THE PLAYER WOMAN IS AS
BARB III (327)	HAVE YOU TWO SEEN THE PLACE? WHY DID YOU	LEAVE	US? /CUSINS/ I WANTED TO SEE EVERYTHING I WAS NOT
GLIM (178)	BUT BEING CRUEL TO ONE'S ENEMIES. YOU POOR PEOPLE	LEAVE	US ALL THE CRUEL WORK, AND THEN WONDER THAT WE ARE
SUPR IV (166)	WE MEET, THE OTHERS GO AWAY ON ABSURD PRETEXTS TO	LEAVE	US ALONE TOGETHER. RAMSDEN NO LONGER SCOWLS AT ME: HIS
SUPR III (112)	HOWEVER, IF I OVERTAX YOUR INTELLECT, YOU CAN	LEAVE	US AND SEEK THE SOCIETY OF LOVE AND BEAUTY AND THE
BASH II,2, (115)	THOUGHT ICES MY HEART. OH, WHY DID CASHEL	LEAVE	US AT THE DOOR? ENTER CASHEL. /LORD WORTHINGTON/
BULL PREFACE(28)	GENTLEMEN OF ENGLAND, TO TAKE YOUR THUMB AWAY AND	LEAVE	US FREE TO DO SOMETHING ELSE THAN BITE IT. THE
CLEO IV (190)	WORD TO MAKE HIM WALK OUT ALONE INTO THE CITY AND	LEAVE	US HERE TO BE CUT TO PIECES. (DESPERATELY, TO CAESAR)
MTH1 II (21)	ONE MUST BE A MAN OF SPIRIT. /ADAM/ BEGONE.	LEAVE	US IN PEACE. THE WORLD IS WIDE ENOUGH TO KEEP US
APPL II (276)	AND THE POWER AND THE GLORY WILL PASS FROM US AND	LEAVE	US NAKED, FACE TO FACE WITH OUR REAL SELVES AT LAST.
JOAN PREFACE(9)	MAKING THEMSELVES NOTABLY RIDICULOUS. THESE FACTS	LEAVE	US NO EXCUSE FOR THE POPULAR ROMANCE THAT TURNS EVERY
2TRU II (69)	ARE ROCKING AND SPLITTING AND SUNDERING. THEY	LEAVE	US NO PLACE TO LIVE, NO CERTAINTIES, NO WORKABLE
FANY II (290)	MADEMOISELLE? /MARGARET/ I THINK YOU HAD BETTER	LEAVE	US TO FIGHT IT OUT, IF YOU DONT MIND. /DUVALLET/
METH PREFACE(R65)	GIBED AT HIM IN TERMS WHICH THE PRINTER HAD TO	LEAVE	US TO GUESS FROM HIS BLANK SPACES. WE HAD HEARD THE
KING I (205)	CAN YOU NAME A SINGLE PLEASURE THAT THEY WOULD	LEAVE	US TO MAKE LIFE WORTH LIVING? /FOX/ IT IS NOT
GENV IV (119)	THESE GENTLEMEN MANAGE THEIR OWN COUNTRIES AND	LEAVE	US TO MANAGE OURS. /JUDGE/ IS THAT YOUR VIEW, MR
WIDO III (58)	AS IF NOTHING HAD HAPPENED, AND THEN GO OUT AND	LEAVE	US TO OUR BUSINESS. YOU ARE NOT AFRAID TO MEET HIM?

KING I	(221)	NEED FOR THE CLOCKMAKER. HE IS WISER THAN TO	LEAVE	US TO OUR FOOLISH SELVES IN THAT FASHION. WHEN HE MADE
CLEO II	(125)	DEMAND IS THE PRICE OF OUR FREEDOM. TAKE IT; AND	LEAVE	US TO SETTLE OUR OWN AFFAIRS. /THE BOLDER COURTIERS/ (
CLEO PRO2	(103)	CLAY GODS THAT ARE SOLD TO FISH PORTERS; AND	LEAVE	US TO SHIFT FOR OURSELVES. /BELZANOR/ NOT UNTIL YOU
MILL III	(185)	WOULD SPEND OUR LITTLE SAVINGS IN A WEEK, AND	LEAVE	US TO SLAVE TO THE END OF OUR DAYS TO MAKE IT UP
NEVR IV	(283)	BUT NOT UNSYMPATHETICALLY) GONE OUT. TO	LEAVE	US TOGETHER. DELICACY ON HIS PART, I SUPPOSE. (SHE
MIS.	(187)	YOU ARE NOT BEHAVING WELL. YOU HAD BETTER	LEAVE	US UNTIL YOU HAVE RECOVERED YOURSELF. BENTLEY GOES OUT
SUPR III	(138)	DOING HERE WITH ALL THESE MEN? /ANN/ WHY DID YOU	LEAVE	US WITHOUT A WORD OF WARNING? /HECTOR/ I WAWNT THAT
DEVL II	(35)	TELL YOU, I SEE; BUT IT WAS NOTHING THAT NEED	LEAVE	US WORSE FRIEND-- ENEMIES, I MEAN. JUDITH IS A GREAT
ROCK II	(246)	ARE ON MY SIDE. THE POLICE ARE ON MY SIDE. IF YOU	LEAVE	US YOU GO OUT INTO THE WILDERNESS ALONE. WHAT HAVE YOU
WIDO II	(38)	WILL ANSWER FOR HIMSELF TO ME. YOU HAD BETTER	LEAVE	US. (HE OPENS THE DOOR, AND CALLS) MR COKANE: WILL
CATH 4	(190)	LONDON GAZETTE. /CATHERINE/ (TO THE SOLDIERS)	LEAVE	US. QUICK! DO YOU HEAR? FIVE THOUSAND BLOWS OF THE
6CAL	(100)	BE IN THEIR BEDS. /THE KING/ THEY SOON WILL BE.	LEAVE	US, MADAM. THIS IS BUSINESS OF STATE. THEY ARE
BARB II	(307)	YOU TAKING YOUR BADGE OFF? YOU CANT BE GOING TO	LEAVE	US, MAJOR. /BARBARA/ (QUIETLY) FATHER: COME HERE.
MIS.	(200)	THAT. /TARLETON/ (RISING) BUT WHY DO YOU WANT TO	LEAVE	US, MISS SZCZ? /LINA/ OLD PAL: THIS IS A STUFFY
SUPR II	(64)	EMBARRASSMENT. /OCTAVIUS/ I'M AFRAID WE MUST	LEAVE	VIOLET BEHIND. THERE ARE CIRCUMSTANCES WHICH MAKE IT
FANY III	(308)	(MAKING FOR THE DOOR). /JUGGINS/ IF YOU WISH TO	LEAVE	WITHOUT BEING SEEN, YOU HAD BETTER STEP INTO MY PANTRY
MTH5	(258)	LIVES AFTER THREE HUNDRED CENTURIES. I TOO WILL	LEAVE	WOMEN AND STUDY MATHEMATICS, WHICH I HAVE NEGLECTED
GETT PREFACE	(187)	MARRIAGE WOULD, OTHER THINGS REMAINING UNCHANGED,	LEAVE	WOMEN MORE EFFECTUALLY ENSLAVED THAN THEY NOW ARE. WE
MTH5	(257)	TO US FROM A FAMOUS WOMAN TEACHER. SHE SAID: "	LEAVE	WOMEN; AND STUDY MATHEMATICS." IT IS THE ONLY
KING II	(230)	BE SOMEBODY THEN. BUT I CANNOT BRING MYSELF TO	LEAVE	YOU; NOT FOR ALL THE THRONES IN THE WORLD. AND MY
O'FL	(224)	HOLD YOUR NOISE, I TELL YOU. WHO'S GOING TO	LEAVE	YOU? I'M GOING TO TAKE YOU WITH ME. THERE NOW: DOES
MTH2	(40)	TOLD ME WHAT? /HASLAM/ SHE IS GOING TO	LEAVE	YOU? /FRANKLYN/ INDEED? I'M SORRY. IS IT OUR FAULT,
APPL II	(266)	IT. HOWEVER, YOU LOOK WELL IN ANYTHING. AND NOW I	LEAVE	YOU ALL TO YOUR LABORS. SHE GOES OUT ALONG THE
SUPR I	(31)	(LOOKING POINTEDLY AT TANNER) I HARDLY LIKE TO	LEAVE	YOU ALONE WITH THIS GENTLEMAN. WILL YOU NOT COME WITH
MTH4 I	(166)	PROPOSE TO BEGIN ALL OVER AGAIN? I SHALL	LEAVE	YOU AT ONCE. /ZOO/ YOU MUST NOT. I AM YOUR NURSE; AND
DEVL III	(51)	YOU. AND HOW ARE YOU AFTER LAST NIGHT? I HAD TO	LEAVE	YOU BEFORE YOU RECOVERED; BUT I SENT WORD TO ESSIE TO
CURE	(229)	SHAKE ANYBODY'S FAITH IN PILLS. BUT I SHANT	LEAVE	YOU ENOUGH TO KILL YOU. (HE PUTS ON HIS HAT).
DEVL II	(45)	(REMONSTRATING) COME, COME, COME! HOW AM I TO	LEAVE	YOU IF YOU TALK LIKE THIS? YOU ARE QUITE OUT OF YOUR
PHIL I	(79)	TURN OUT BADLY, YOU ALSO RESERVED MY FREEDOM TO	LEAVE	YOU IN CASE YOU SHOULD TURN OUT BADLY. /JULIA/ VERY
JOAN EPILOG	(167)	AND BISHOPS AND LAWYERS AND SUCH LIKE? THEY JUST	LEAVE	YOU IN THE DITCH TO BLEED TO DEATH; AND THE NEXT THING
NEVR IV	(282)	A WAITER, SIR, YOUD FIND THAT SIMPLE FAITH WOULD	LEAVE	YOU JUST AS SHORT AS NORMAN BLOOD. I FIND IT BEST TO
BULL III	(136)	MORE POWER TO YOU, SIR! /BROADBENT/ I SHALL	LEAVE	YOU NOW, GENTLEMEN, TO YOUR DELIBERATIONS. I SHOULD
BUOY IV	(50)	LEAVE ME OUT OF THE QUESTION. /SHE/ I CANT	LEAVE	YOU OUT, DADDY. BUT YOU WILL KNOW YOUR NATURAL PLACE
JITT II	(42)	BEHIND THIS. /JITTA/ I SUPPOSE HE WISHED TO	LEAVE	YOU SOMETHING VALUABLE AS A KEEPSAKE. YOU WERE HIS
BULL IV	(157)	NO, NO; I WASNT PUTN IN FOR THAT. WHEN I DIE AND	LEAVE	YOU THE FARM I SHOULD LIKE TO BE ABLE TO FEEL THAT IT
MIS. PREFACE	(61)	FOR THE DAY WHEN HE WILL EARN HIS OWN LIVING AND	LEAVE	YOU TO ATTEND TO YOURSELF, YOU SOONER OR LATER BEGIN
SUPR PREFACE	(R32)	HIS MONTHLY PARTS: BY MECHANICAL DEVICES WHICH I	LEAVE	YOU TO DESCRIBE, MY OWN MEMORY BEING QUITE BAFFLED BY
BULL III	(134)	NOW I THINK THE CANDIDATE HAD BETTER RETIRE AND	LEAVE	YOU TO DISCUSS HIS SUCCESSOR. (HE TAKES A NEWSPAPER
SUPR III	(103)	ELOQUENT ON THE ADVANTAGES OF MY DOMINIONS THAT I	LEAVE	YOU TO DO EQUAL JUSTICE TO THE DRAWBACKS OF THE
JOAN 4	(107)	WITH THE MAID'S SECULAR HERESY, MY LORD. I	LEAVE	YOU TO FIND A NAME FOR IT. /CAUCHON/ YOU MISTAKE ME.
GENV IV	(91)	THE ABLEST MAN IN THE WORLD! THAT IS MY VISION. I	LEAVE	YOU TO IMAGINE WHAT I THINK OF THE MOB OF BAGMEN FROM
MTH1 II	(33)	YOUR MOTHER TO HER SPINNING. /CAIN/ WELL, I WILL	LEAVE	YOU TO IT, THOUGH I HAVE SHEWN YOU A BETTER WAY. (HE
CAND I	(96)	IS. (SHE TAKES UP HER HAND-BAG). AND NOW I MUST	LEAVE	YOU TO JAMES FOR THE PRESENT. I SUPPOSE YOU ARE TOO
HART I	(64)	MY REAL NAME, MISS DUNN, IS HECTOR HUSHABYE. I	LEAVE	YOU TO JUDGE WHETHER THAT IS A NAME ANY SENSITIVE MAN
HART I	(74)	PATRONIZINGLY) OF COURSE, DEAR. /ELLIE/ THEN I'LL	LEAVE	YOU TO MR HUSHABYE. (SHE GOES OUT THROUGH THE HALL).
ROCK II	(265)	TO INDIA TO DETACH IT WHOLLY FROM ENGLAND, AND	LEAVE	YOU TO PERISH IN YOUR IGNORANCE, YOUR VAIN CONCEIT,
DEVL III	(62)	THE REST WILL MAKE A MESS OF THE BUSINESS AND	LEAVE	YOU TO THE PROVO-MARSHAL'S PISTOL, WHEREAS WE CAN HANG
CAND II	(109)	VISITOR) WELL: SO THIS IS THE WAY THEY	LEAVE	YOU TO YORESELF, MR MORCHBANKS. IVE COME TO KEEP YOU
BUOY IV	(49)	CANNOT BE HEARD TOO OFTEN. BUT AS YOU DESIRE, I	LEAVE	YOU TO YOUR AFTERCALM. /OLD BILL/ SO LONG, MAHATMA.
BUOY III	(29)	HIMSELF IN THE BISHOP'S CHAIR. /THE PRIEST/ I	LEAVE	YOU TO YOUR DELIBERATIONS. PEACE BE WITH YOU! HE
FANY II	(290)	AMELIA: THIS IS YOUR JOB. (TO MARGARET) I	LEAVE	YOU TO YOUR MOTHER. I SHALL HAVE MY OWN SAY IN THE
BARB III	(345)	/STEPHEN/ WELL, I JUST WANT TO SAY THIS BEFORE I	LEAVE	YOU TO YOURSELVES. DONT LET ANYTHING I HAVE SAID ABOUT
WIDO I	(19)	OF YOUR LETTER. PRAY RESUME IT. I SHALL	LEAVE	YOU TO YOURSELF. (HE PRETENDS TO RISE, BUT CHECKS
WIDO I	(17)	I LEAVE HERE: STRAIGHT OFF. /SARTORIUS/ I WILL	LEAVE	YOU TO YOURSELF THEN. (HE HESITATES. THE CONVERSATION
PHIL II	(100)	EXCUSE ME, CHARTERIS: THIS IS PRIVATE. I'LL	LEAVE	YOU TO YOURSELVES (AGAIN MOVING TOWARDS THE TABLE).
MTH4 I	(154)	HAD OPPRESSED BUT NEVER CONQUERED, " AT LAST WE	LEAVE	YOU TO YOURSELVES; AND MUCH GOOD MAY IT DO YOU," THE
JOAN 1	(66)	COME UP. COME IN. (TURNING TO ROBERT) SHALL I	LEAVE	YOU WITH HER? /ROBERT/ NO: STAY HERE; AND BACK ME UP.
NEVR IV	(283)	THERE HE IS, MISS CLANDON. BE KIND TO HIM. I'LL	LEAVE	YOU WITH HIM FOR A MOMENT. (HE GOES INTO THE GARDEN).
CATH 4	(196)	MAJESTY'S KINDNESS SO MUCH THAT I REALLY CANNOT	LEAVE	YOU WITHOUT A WORD OF PLAIN WHOLESOME ENGLISH ADVICE.
KING II	(223)	HAVE I BEEN ASLEEP? /CATHERINE/ I NOT KNOW. WHY	LEAVE	YOU YOUR THINGS ABOUT ALL OVER MY ROOM? I HAVE TO PUT
WIDO II	(47)	MARRIED: I DONT CARE FOR HIM: I DONT WANT TO	LEAVE	YOU. (TRENCH AND COKANE COME IN; BUT SHE CAN HEAR
PHIL II	(130)	COLONEL AS MUCH AS POSSIBLE. SO I'M AFRAID I MUST	LEAVE	YOU. /GRACE/ (RISING) NOT AT ALL. PARAMORE INVITED
MTH5	(257)	WE ARE VERY TIRED OF THIS SUBJECT. I MUST	LEAVE	YOU. /THE NEWLY BORN/ WHAT IS BEING TIRED? /THE
GETT	(344)	READY FOR MY WORK. I THANK YOU AND BLESS YOU AND	LEAVE	YOU. YOU ARE HAPPIER IN THAT THAN I AM; FOR WHEN I DO
KING I	(210)	HAVE SHEWN; AND AS IT WHIRLS ON ITS WAY IT WOULD	LEAVE	YOUR APPLE BEHIND IF THE APPLE FELL IN A STRAIGHT
POSN	(443)	CAN YOU SAY AS MUCH, BLANCO? DID YOUR HOLIDAYS	LEAVE	YOUR CHARACTER UNSPOILED? OH, NO, NO. IT WAS
LIED	(191)	WE SHALL GO TO THE THEATRE STILL; BUT WE SHALL	LEAVE	YOUR DIAMONDS HERE; FOR WE CANNOT AFFORD DIAMONDS, AND
BARB III	(333)	PRESENT. LET US SETTLE THE PRACTICAL DETAILS AND	LEAVE	YOUR FINAL DECISION OPEN. YOU KNOW THAT YOU WILL HAVE
MTH3	(98)	IF YOU HAVE NOTHING FOR ME TO DO, I AM GOING TO	LEAVE	YOUR HEEL FOR THE REST OF THE DAY AND ENJOY MYSELF.
HART I	(55)	YOU KNOW I WAS. /ELLIE/ (WITH DIGNITY) I WILL	LEAVE	YOUR HOUSE AT ONCE. (SHE TURNS TO THE DOOR). /MRS
SUPR I	(26)	INSULT ME AGAIN I'LL TAKE YOU AT YOUR WORD AND	LEAVE	YOUR HOUSE. ANN! WHERE IS VIOLET NOW? /ANN/ WHY? ARE
GETT PREFACE	(257)	WRECK CIVILIZATION. 8. NEVER FORGET THAT IF YOU	LEAVE	YOUR LAW TO JUDGES AND YOUR RELIGION TO BISHOPS YOU
VWOO 3	(137)	YOUVE HAD PLENTY OF CONVERSATION WITH ME. /A/	LEAVE	YOURSELF OUT OF THIS CONVERSATION, PLEASE. /Z/ OH,
LIED	(203)	MRS BOMPAS TO WALK OUT OF THE HOUSE WITH ME-- TO	LEAVE	YOU-- TO GET DIVORCED FROM YOU AND MARRY ME. I BEGGED
PYGM V	(283)	WARNED ME. TIME AND AGAIN SHE HAS WANTED TO	LEAVE	YOU; AND YOU ALWAYS GOT ROUND HER AT THE LAST MINUTE.
CLEO PR01	(93)	SET FOOT IN THE LAND OF MY PEOPLE. AND NOW I	LEAVE	YOU; FOR YE ARE A DULL FOLK, AND INSTRUCTION IS WASTED
MRS I	(196)	DAY? /REV. S./ (WOUNDED ALMOST TO TEARS) I	LEAVE	YOU, SIR. YOU ARE INCORRIGIBLE. (HE TURNS TOWARDS THE
LION II	(133)	THEY THROW DOWN IN A HEAP. /THE CALL BOY/ BY YOUR	LEAVE	, CAESAR. NUMBER ELEVEN! GLADIATORS AND CHRISTIANS!
DEVL I SD	(22)	THEN, SEEING THAT SHE HAS LEFT THE ROOM WITHOUT	LEAVE	, CLOSES HER LIPS VENGEFULLY. /HAWKINS/ " SECOND, THAT
GETT	(323)	MACE, AND POSTS HIMSELF AT THE ENTRANCE). BY YOUR	LEAVE	, GENTLEMEN, WAY FOR THE WORSHIPFUL THE MAYORESS.
CAPT I	(237)	MADAM. IF HE OPENS HIS MOUTH AGAIN WITHOUT MY	LEAVE	, I WILL BREAK EVERY BONE IN HIS SKIN. /LADY CICELY (
CLEO II	(131)	HAVE TO FIGHT THEM AGAIN. AND NOW, WITH YOUR	LEAVE	, I WILL SEE THESE GENTRY OFF THE PREMISES. (HE TURNS
POSN	(437)	MAY BE GOOD ENOUGH FOR HIS, BABSY; BUT, BY YOUR	LEAVE	, IT IS NOT GOOD ENOUGH FOR MINE. WHILE I AM ELDER
GETT	(358)	IF YOU PLEASE, MY LORDS AND GENTLEMEN. BY YOUR	LEAVE	, LADIES AND GENTLEMEN: WAY FOR THE MAYORESS. MRS
CAPT III	(283)	SORT. WILL YOU BEGIN WITH ME? /KEARNEY/ BY YOUR	LEAVE	, LADY WAYNFLETE, I THINK I WILL JUST BEGIN WITH
DEVL I	(20)	BY YOUR LEAVE, MINISTER ANDERSON: BY YOUR	LEAVE	, LAWYER HAWKINS, THE HEAD OF THE TABLE FOR THE HEAD
DEVL I	(25)	YOU, SIR, WITH A MERE CHILD-- /RICHARD/ BY YOUR	LEAVE	, MINISTER: I DO NOT INTERFERE WITH YOUR SERMONS: DO
DEVL I	(20)	OF THIS HOUSEHOLD, I BID YOU WELCOME. BY YOUR	LEAVE	, MINISTER ANDERSON: BY YOUR LEAVE, LAWYER HAWKINS,
WIDO III	(56)	AND MY PRIVATE ANSOM'S AT THE DOOR. BY YOUR	LEAVE	, MISS BLANCHE (PULLING GENTLY AT HIS OVERCOAT).
DEVL I	(25)	WAY AS THEY COME PAST THE TABLE, HE SAYS) BY YOUR	LEAVE	, MOTHER (AND COMPELS HER TO MAKE WAY FOR THEM). WHAT
METH PREFACE	(R36)	HIM WILL REMOVE YOUR LOGICAL DIFFICULTY? BY YOUR	LEAVE	, SAID I, IT IS AS EASY FOR ME TO BELIEVE THAT THE
GENV IV	(92)	NOW HAS A DICTATOR ON EACH SIDE OF HIM) BY YOUR	LEAVE	, SIR. (HE SITS). /JUDGE/ I THANK YOU, MR BATTLER.
CAPT III	(288)	THEM TO BE REPORTED TO YOU AND BURNT, WITH YOUR	LEAVE	, SIR. /KEARNEY/ WHAT ARE THEY? /BLUEJACKET/ (
APPL II	(266)	ON THAT SUBJECT? /PROTEUS/ BY YOUR MAJESTY'S	LEAVE	, WE WILL TAKE THE QUESTION OF THE ULTIMATUM FIRST.
DEVL III	(77)	MINISTRY. I AM AFRAID SHE WAS RIGHT; SO, BY YOUR	LEAVE	, YOU MAY KEEP MY COAT AND I'LL KEEP YOURS. /RICHARD/
			LEAVEN	
BARB II	(292)	FLOAT AND FLOW AND SEETHE WITH A MILLION HOPES AS	LEAVEN	; AND THEY WIN THEIR WILL; OR THEY MISS THEIR WILL;
			LEAVE-TAKING	
MTH2	(66)	STOP. (THEY ALL STOP SHORT IN THE MOVEMENT OF	LEAVE-TAKING	TO LOOK AT HER). DADDY: ARE YOU GOING TO LET
DEVL III	(50)	HOW LONG DO YOU ALLOW A BROKENHEARTED HUSBAND FOR	LEAVE-TAKING	, SERGEANT? /SERGEANT/ AS LONG AS WE CAN, SIR.
			LEAVES	
WIDO I	(22)	CASE). THE REST I LEAVE TO YOUR DISCRETION. (HE	LEAVES	A CARD ON THE TABLE). THAT IS MY ADDRESS AT SURBITON.
MRS III	(234)	OUT HIS ARMS TO HER). COME AND BE COVERED UP WITH	LEAVES	AGAIN. /VIVIE/ (WITH A CRY OF DISGUST) AH, NOT THAT,
BASH III	(119)	WOODLAND WOOS ME FROM WITHOUT WITH WHISPERING OF	LEAVES	AND DAINTY AIRS TO LEAVE THIS FRUITLESS HAUNTING OF

GENV IV (102)	THE SOLDIER MAY GO TO HIS DEATH; BUT HE	LEAVES	BEHIND HIM THE PREGNANT WOMAN WHO WILL REPLACE HIM.
CAPT III (272)	AMERICAN CAPTAIN WILL PRESIDE IN THIS; AND THAT	LEAVES	BUT ONE FOR SIR HOWRRD AND ONE FOR YOUR LEDDYSHIP. I
LION PREFACE(42)	THE ASCENSION; AND THE END OF HIS NARRATIVE	LEAVES	CHRIST RESTORED TO LIFE, AND APPEARING FROM TIME TO
ARMS I (7)	FROM THE LITTLE PILE OF BOOKS. SHE TURNS OVER THE	LEAVES	DREAMILY; FINDS HER PAGE; TURNS THE BOOK INSIDE OUT
BUOY III (28)	ARE MY BROTHERS' WIVES. ONE BROTHER IS ABSENT: HE	LEAVES	EVERYTHING TO HIS WIFE. THE TWO CHILDREN ARE OUR
DEST SD(162)	EXCEEDS THAT OF NAPOLEON AND THE INNKEEPER, AND	LEAVES	HER AT NO DISADVANTAGE WITH THE LIEUTENANT. ONLY, HER
PHIL II (127)	UNDERSTAND? (JULIA, WATCHING THEM JEALOUSLY,	LEAVES	HER FATHER AND GETS CLOSE TO CHARTERIS. GRACE ADDS
JOAN 6 (133)	THE SILLY PEOPLE BELIEVE THAT A WITCH'S WITCHERY	LEAVES	HER IF SHE IS BLED; SO HE ONLY CALLED ME FILTHY
SUPR I (38)	HERSELF IN FRONT OF THE ENGINE OF THE TRAIN HE	LEAVES	HER IN. THAT IS WHAT ALL WOMEN DO. IF WE TRY TO GO
APPL INTRLUD(246)	ELSE THAT WHEN A MAN GETS TIRED OF HIS WIFE AND	LEAVES	HER IT IS NEVER BECAUSE SHE HAS LOST HER GOOD LOOKS.
CAND II (107)	TRYING TO WORK WHILE YOU TALK LIKE THAT. (SHE	LEAVES	HER LITTLE TABLE AND SITS ON THE SOFA. HER FEELINGS
NEVR I SD(208)	AND INTENSE PERSONAL PRIVACY, WHICH	LEAVES	HER RELATIONS WITH GLORIA AND PHIL MUCH AS THEY MIGHT
ROCK II (234)	THAT ANYONE WHO MAKES NOISE ENOUGH TO WAKEN HIM	LEAVES	HER SERVICE THAT MINUTE. /SIR DEXTER/ NONSENSE! HE
MRS PREFACE(160)	ACTUAL FELONY, THE OFFICER THEN RELENTS AND	LEAVES	HER. WHEN SHE RECOVERS, SHE BELIEVES THAT HE HAS
METH PREFACE(R41)	WOULD HAVE SAID, BY WANTING TO GET AT THE TENDER	LEAVES	HIGH UP ON THE TREE, AND TRYING UNTIL HE SUCCEEDED IN
CAPT II SD(244)	LITTLE DOOR. HE GROANS. JOHNSON PHLEGMATICALLY	LEAVES	HIM AND JOINS REDBROOK. /LADY CICELY/ BUT YOU CANT
APPL PREFACE(174)	VICTORY, WHICH BULKS SO LARGELY IN THE PLAYHOUSE,	LEAVES	HIM IN A WORSE PLIGHT THAN HIS DEFEATED OPPONENT, WHO
BARB PREFACE(230)	IT WILL NOT TOLERATE A REDEEMED RUFFIAN: IT	LEAVES	HIM NO MEANS OF SALVATION EXCEPT CEASING TO BE A
ROCK PREFACE(167)	HE IS DIRTY; HIS FREEDOM FROM CIVILIZED CONTROL	LEAVES	HIM SO UNPROTECTED FROM THE TYRANNY OF NATURE THAT IT
LIED (200)	ILL HUMOR FOR THE FIRST TIME) OH! INDEED! (HE	LEAVES	HIS HEARTH AND BEGINS TO APPROACH HENRY SLOWLY,
SUPR III (110)	YES: HE SHIRKS ALL HIS RESPONSIBILITIES, AND	LEAVES	HIS WIFE TO GRAPPLE WITH THEM. /THE STATUE/ WELL
GETT (320)	SOME PROVISION FOR MY LOOKING AFTER REJJY. (SHE	LEAVES	HOTCHKISS, AND GOES BACK TO HER CHAIR AT THE END OF
BARB PREFACE(222)	OVER THE PLAYGOER AS OVER A PRODIGAL WITH VINE	LEAVES	IN HIS HAIR, CAREERING OUTRAGEOUSLY TO HELL AMID THE
MTH1 I (4)	IT MAY BE AFTER AS MANY DAYS AS THERE ARE	LEAVES	IN THE GARDEN AND GRAINS OF SAND BY THE RIVER. NO
MTH3 (123)	TAKE IT ALL! HOW YOU QUARREL OVER THE CRUMPLED	LEAVES	IN YOUR BEDS OF ROSES! HOW YOU ARE SO DAINTY ABOUT
MIS. PREFACE(88)	THAN THIS. THE VIOLENCE DONE TO OUR SOULS BY IT	LEAVES	INJURIES AND PRODUCES SUBTLE MALADIES WHICH HAVE
FABL IV (115)	INTO SUPERGORILLAS THROUGH EATING GRASS AND	LEAVES	. AND THOUGH THEY LIVED LONGER THAN THE MEAT EATERS,
CLEO IV (181)	CAESAR, ARE OF MALTESE GAUZE, STUFFED WITH ROSE	LEAVES	. /CAESAR/ ROSE LEAVES! AM I A CATERPILLAR? (HE
MRS III (226)	A WEARY CHILD). LETS GO AND GET COVERED UP WITH	LEAVES	. /VIVIE/ (RHYTHMICALLY, ROCKING HIM LIKE A NURSE)
MTH1 II SD(20)	AND CARELESSLY DRESSED IN ROUGH LINEN AND	LEAVES	. THEY HAVE LOST THEIR YOUTH AND GRACE; AND ADAM HAS
BULL I (93)	WORLD IS AS FULL OF FOOLS AS A TREE IS FULL OF	LEAVES	. WELL, THE ENGLISHMAN DOES WHAT THE CATERPILLAR
MTH5 (226)	DO NOT ASK ME. I KNOW NOTHING OF HIM. (HE	LEAVES	MARTELLUS, AND SITS DOWN BESIDE ECRASIA, ON HER
APPL I (225)	ESPECIALLY BY YOU, MR BOANERGES. BUT IN TRUTH IT	LEAVES	MATTERS JUST WHERE THEY WERE; FOR I SHOULD NEVER HAVE
APPL I (233)	ONLY ONE NOW LEFT IN THIS COUNTRY. MY CIVIL LIST	LEAVES	ME A POOR MAN AMONG MULTI-MILLIONAIRES. YOUR SALARIES
PYGM V (271)	HENRY HIGGINS, THANKS TO YOUR SILLY JOKING, HE	LEAVES	ME A SHARE IN HIS PRE-DIGESTED CHEESE TRUST WORTH
OVER PREFACE(164)	ON THE STAGE OR NOT, MY EXPERIENCE AS A PLAYGOER	LEAVES	ME IN NO DOUBT THAT ONCE IT IS DECIDED TO REPRESENT
APPL PREFACE(186)	ACCORDINGLY, ANY SPARE MONEY THAT THE GOVERNMENT	LEAVES	ME IS INVESTED WHERE I CAN GET THE HIGHEST INTEREST
SUPR I (12)	YOU HAVE GOT ME IN A CLEFT STICK. /TANNER/ HE	LEAVES	ME NOTHING BUT THE CHARGE OF ANN'S MORALS, ON THE
MTH2 (59)	PASSES YOU BY AND LEAVES YOU STANDING. /LUBIN/ IT	LEAVES	ME SITTING, AND QUITE COMFORTABLE, THANK YOU. GO ON
HART I (46)	DEGREE OF CONCENTRATION: SHE INVITES VISITORS AND	LEAVES	ME TO ENTERTAIN THEM. (NURSE GUINNESS RETURNS WITH
SUPR II (55)	SEE MY PAPER? NOT MUCH. HE GRABS THE LEADER AND	LEAVES	ME TO STODGE MYSELF WITH HIS TIMES. /OCTAVIUS/ ARE
BUOY III (46)	THEORY EXPRESSING HIM. ALL WE KNOW IS THAT HE	LEAVES	MUCH OF IT TO US; AND WE MAKE A SHOCKING MESS OF IT.
MTH3 (98)	DOG WAG HIS TAIL AND BARK JOYOUSLY, BUT IF HE	LEAVES	MY HEEL HE IS LOST. /BURGE-LUBIN/ THANK YOU FOR A
ROCK I SD(194)	OF BUSINESS; BUT IN HIM ENJOYMENT OF HIS POSITION	LEAVES	NO DOUBT IN HIS MIND AS TO HIS OWN ENTIRE ADEQUACY TO
GENV PREFACE(27)	THEM SOON ENOUGH, WHEREAS ATOMIC BOMBING	LEAVES	NOTHING FOR ANYONE, VICTOR OR VANQUISHED. IT IS
JOAN 4,SD(94)	IS SEATED IN A HANDSOME CHAIR TURNING OVER THE	LEAVES	OF AN ILLUMINATED BOOK OF HOURS. THE NOBLEMAN IS
PYGM V (277)	CREATED THIS THING OUT OF THE SQUASHED CABBAGE	LEAVES	OF COVENT GARDEN; AND NOW SHE PRETENDS TO PLAY THE
PYGM PREFACE(201)	MIGHT AS WELL HAVE BEEN THE SYBIL WHO TORE UP THE	LEAVES	OF PROPHECY THAT NOBODY WOULD ATTEND TO. THE FOUR AND
MTH1 II (22)	POEM OF MANY MEN, OF MORE MEN THAN THERE ARE	LEAVES	ON A THOUSAND TREES. I WILL DIVIDE THEM INTO TWO
MTH1 I (9)	WILLED AND WILLED FOR MORE MOONS THAN THERE ARE	LEAVES	ON ALL THE TREES OF THE GARDEN. HER PANGS WERE
CAPT III (295)	SAD; BUT PERHAPS IT IS BEST SO. /BRASSBOUND/ THAT	LEAVES	ONE RELIC; HER PORTRAIT. (HE PLUCKS THE PHOTOGRAPH
DOCT III (146)	TO HIS STOOL IN HIGH DUDGEON). /SIR PATRICK/ THAT	LEAVES	ONLY ONE MEDICAL MAN WHO HAS NOT WITHDRAWN FROM YOUR
PHIL I (93)	THE WHOLE STORY. SLEEP OVER IT. GOODNIGHT. (HE	LEAVES	). /CUTHBERTSON/ (STARING AFTER HIM) WELL I'LL BE--
PYGM I (206)	ARE NO WORSE THAN THEIRS; BUT THEIR CONDITION	LEAVES	SOMETHING TO BE DESIRED; AND SHE NEEDS THE SERVICES
2TRU I (49)	ON. /THE BURGLAR/ GOOD. YOUR COMPLEXION STILL	LEAVES	SOMETHING TO BE DESIRED; BUT (KISSING HER) YOUR
SUPR I (12)	TWO THOUSAND FIVE HUNDRED FOR YOUR TROUBLE. HE	LEAVES	TAVY A DOWRY FOR HIS SISTER AND FIVE THOUSAND FOR
BASH I (93)	THOUGH SHE WOULD SHEW THEM HER SLEEVES.) LO, THE	LEAVES	THAT HIDE MY DROOPING BOUGHS! MOCK ME-- POOR
CLEO II (140)	STAND BY IT TO EMBARK. CAESAR'S GUARD THERE. (HE	LEAVES	THE BALCONY AND COMES DOWN INTO THE HALL). WHERE ARE
PHIL III (143)	UP HIS HANDS) OH, LORD HELP YOU, PARAMORE! (HE	LEAVES	THE BOOKCASE, AND SITS AT THE END OF THE COUCH
PRES (156)	COMES IN). REMOVE THAT WOMAN. SEE THAT SHE	LEAVES	THE BUILDING AT ONCE. THE ORDERLY FORLORNLY
SUPR II (68)	/STRAKER/ FIVE SHILLINS, MORE LIKELY. (HE	LEAVES	THE CAR AND APPROACHES TANNER). WHAT ABOUT THE LADY'S
MIS. PREFACE(97)	A CHILD BECAUSE IT IS ABOUT BEARS; AND IT	LEAVES	THE CHILD WITH AN IMPRESSION THAT CHILDREN WHO POKE
SIM PREFACE(9)	BOOKS AND ACCOUNTS TO PRODUCE INSOLVENCIES,	LEAVES	THE FIELDS UNSOWN OR THE HARVESTS TO ROT UNREAPED,
DOCT I (108)	/EMMY/ (ANNOUNCING) MRS DOOBIDAD (RIDGEON	LEAVES	THE GLASS AND GOES TO THE WRITING-TABLE). THE LADY
APPL I (234)	WHILST WE HAVE TO GRAPPLE WITH THE PRESENT: IT	LEAVES	THE GROUND BEFORE OUR FEET IN BLACK DARKNESS WHILST
KING I (174)	OF THE ROOM) OH! MR NEWTON: EITHER THIS FEMALE	LEAVES	THE HOUSE THIS INSTANT OR I DO. /BARBARA/ DO YOU
SUPR III (105)	HIS FINGER ALL THE HIDDEN MOLECULAR ENERGIES, AND	LEAVES	THE JAVELIN, THE ARROW, THE BLOWPIPE OF HIS FATHERS
LION PREFACE(33)	AS TACKED ON BY A LATER SCRIBE. ON THE WHOLE MARK	LEAVES	THE MODERN READER WHERE MATTHEW LEFT HIM. LUKE. LUKE
CLEO IV (179)	DEAR HEART, NO. /CLEOPATRA/ LISTEN TO ME. IF HE	LEAVES	THE PALACE ALIVE, NEVER SEE MY FACE AGAIN.
CLEO III (150)	MORE MEN TO THIS POST HERE; AND SEE THAT NO ONE	LEAVES	THE PALACE BUT THIS MAN AND HIS MERCHANDIZE. IF HE
CLEO IV (167)	THAT HARP GIRL WILL HAVE TO GIVE UP BEFORE SHE	LEAVES	THE PALACE. /IRAS/ WE CAN EASILY FIND OUT THAT FOR
LION PREFACE(14)	A SACRIFICE, A SUFFERER FOR OUR SINS, AND THIS	LEAVES	THE POOR MAN STILL IN HIS OLD DIFFICULTY; FOR IF IT
POSN PREFACE(389)	A CENSOR HAS NOTHING BUT HIS OWN OPINION. A JUDGE	LEAVES	THE QUESTION OF GUILT TO THE JURY: THE CENSOR IS JURY
LADY PREFACE(225)	IN THE NEXT EDITION: THE HIATUS IS TOO GREAT: IT	LEAVES	THE READER TOO UNEASY BEFORE THIS TOUCHING PICTURE OF
ARMS III (55)	I MUST GIVE MY FELLOW ORDERS ABOUT STARTING. (HE	LEAVES	THE ROOM HASTILY, WITH THE DOCUMENTS IN HIS HAND).
PYGM IV SD(260)	LOOKS AT HIM DARKLY; THEN RISES SUDDENLY AND	LEAVES	THE ROOM HIGGINS YAWNS AGAIN, AND RESUMES HIS SONG.
BULL IV (157)	HAVE A WASH. (HE TAKES UP HIS COAT AND CAP, AND	LEAVES	THE ROOM THROUGH THE INNER DOOR). NORA RETURNS TO HER
CAPT III (292)	IN IT. /BRASSBOUND/ I'LL CHANGE ALTOGETHER. (HE	LEAVES	THE ROOM TO GET HIS OWN TROUSERS). /REDBROOK/ (
SUPR I (22)	HOW COULD YOU REMIND ME, MOTHER? (SHE HASTILY	LEAVES	THE ROOM TO CONCEAL HER EMOTION). /MRS WHITEFIELD/ OF
BARB III (322)	MAMMA: THE CARRIAGE IS WAITING. (LADY BRITOMART	LEAVES	THE ROOM). /UNDERSHAFT/ (TO SARAH) GOOD DAY, MY
MTH3 (127)	WHO INSTINCTIVELY SHRINKS OUT OF HER WAY AS SHE	LEAVES	THE ROOM). /THE ARCHBISHOP/ I AM SURPRISED AT YOU, MR
CLEO IV (185)	/CAESAR/ (SHUDDERING) HUSH, HUSH, RUFIO. (HE	LEAVES	THE TABLE AND RETURNS TO THE COLONNADE: RUFIO
CLEO IV SD(186)	PRESUMING UPON CAESAR'S SUBMISSION TO RUFIO,	LEAVES	THE TABLE AND SITS DOWN ON THE BENCH IN THE
NEVR II (245)	I'LL GO AND HAVE MY CIGARET ON THE BEACH. (SHE	LEAVES	THE TABLE WITH PETULANT SUDDENNESS AND GOES TO THE
CLEO IV (175)	END, WHERE A GAP IN IT, LIKE A GREAT GATEWAY,	LEAVES	THE VIEW OPEN TO THE SKY BEYOND THE WESTERN EDGE OF
SUPR IV SD(141)	AND DOWN AGAIN TO THE LAWN (A MOVEMENT WHICH	LEAVES	THE VILLA BEHIND US ON OUR RIGHT) WE FIND EVIDENCE OF
JOAN 1 (60)	HER THE WAY, YOU. AND SHOVE HER ALONG QUICK. (HE	LEAVES	THE WINDOW, AND RETURNS TO HIS PLACE AT THE TABLE,
APPL I (219)	NOT DEMOCRACY. /BOANERGES/ DEMOCRACY BE -- (HE	LEAVES	THE WORD UNSPOKEN)! I HAVE THIRTY YEARS EXPERIENCE
LION PREFACE(68)	CONSCIOUS OF ANY RESTRICTION: THE CHAIN NOT ONLY	LEAVES	THEM FREE TO DO WHATEVER THEY WANT TO DO, BUT GREATLY
SUPR PREFACE(R38)	LEISURELY TRICKS WHICH THEIR WANT OF CONVICTION	LEAVES	THEM FREE TO PLAY WITH THE DILUTED AND MISAPPREHENDED
GETT PREFACE(225)	AND AS A COMPANION AND COUNSELLOR SHE PROBABLY	LEAVES	THEM NOWHERE. MR KIPLING'S QUESTION WHAT CAN THEY
HART I (72)	GOOD BROTHER-IN-LAW; AND HAVE DONE WITH IT. (SHE	LEAVES	THEM TO THEMSELVES). /HECTOR/ BEHAVE YOURSELF.
BARB II (301)	WHAT A FOOL I WAS WHEN I WAS A BABY. (SHE	LEAVES	THEM TOGETHER AND CHATS WITH JENNY). /MRS BAINES/
NEVR II (247)	A BOOK WITH A LADY'S HANDKERCHIEF BETWEEN THE	LEAVES	TO MARK THE PAGE). THE ELDER YOUNG LADY IS READING IT
MRS IV (243)	DID PRADDY. WE UNDERSTAND. AND WE REMAIN, AS THIS	LEAVES	US AT PRESENT, YOURS EVER SO DEVOTEDLY. /PRAED/ WE DO
HART I (75)	INVITE THEM FOR CHRISTMAS. /HECTOR/ THEIR ABSENCE	LEAVES	US BOTH WITHOUT OUR NATURAL CHAPERONS. /LADY
SUPR HANDBOK(203)	A BASENESS OF TEMPER AND CHARACTER WHICH HARDLY	LEAVES	US THE RIGHT TO PLUME OURSELVES ON OUR SUPERIORITY TO
MTH2 (43)	YOU WERE COMING, SHE ASKED ME WHETHER ALL THE	LEAVES	WERE CUT, IN CASE IT FELL INTO YOUR HANDS. SHE HASNT
FABL PREFACE(83)	HAS NEVER FOR A MOMENT EXISTED. REAL DEMOCRACY	LEAVES	WIDE OPEN THE QUESTION AS TO WHICH METHOD BEST
SUPR PREFACE(R34)	BLOOD MORE THAN SHAKESPEAR'S HERO, WHO ACTUALLY	LEAVES	YOU COLD AND SECRETLY HOSTILE. YOU SUDDENLY SEE THAT
MTH2 (59)	THE GIANT SWEEP OF THE AGES, PASSES YOU BY AND	LEAVES	YOU STANDING. /LUBIN/ IT LEAVES ME SITTING, AND QUITE
JOAN 5 (119)	SPIRITUAL DIRECTORS, THE CHURCH DISOWNS YOU, AND	LEAVES	YOU TO WHATEVER FATE YOUR PRESUMPTION MAY BRING UPON
SUPR I (12)	BE PRETTY WELL OBLIGED TO ME FOR MY INFLUENCE. HE	LEAVES	YOU TWO THOUSAND FIVE HUNDRED FOR YOUR TROUBLE. HE
APPL PREFACE(179)	GOES UP AGAIN WITH MUCH THE SAME LOT IN IT AND	LEAVES	YOU WHERE YOU WERE BEFORE. I THINK YOU WILL ADMIT
CATH PREFACE(154)	PROPRIETY IN SEXUAL RELATIONS. IN SHORT, IF BYRON	LEAVES	YOU WITH AN IMPRESSION THAT HE SAID VERY LITTLE ABOUT
FABL IV (114)	CHEESE AND EGGS, WERE NO LONGER TO BE HAD. GRASS,	LEAVES	, AND NETTLES BECAME THE STAPLE DIET. THIS WAS
DOCT IV (163)	LIQUID LOVELY FLAME FLOWING UP THROUGH THE BAY	LEAVES	, AND NOT BURNING THEM. WELL, I SHALL BE A FLAME LIKE

MIS PREFACE(91) OF THE BEAUTY OF THE EARTH, WITH ITS DRESSES OF LEAVES , ITS SCARVES OF CLOUD, AND ITS CONTOURS OF HILL AND
SIM PREFACE(19) FLOWER WITHOUT THE ROOTS OR THE CLAY OR EVEN THE LEAVES , LET US HOPE THEY NEVER WILL. ON THE INDIAN OCEAN,
MTH5 (208) IS YOUR FAULT, STREPHON, FOR PROVOKING HIM. (SHE LEAVES , MUCH DISAPPOINTED). /A YOUTH/ WHY NEED YOU HAVE
FABL IV (114) KNOWN THAT BULLS AND ELEPHANTS, FED ON GRASS AND LEAVES , WERE THE STRONGEST, MOST FERTILE, MOST PASSIONATE
CLEO IV (181) GAUZE, STUFFED WITH ROSE LEAVES. /CAESAR/ ROSE LEAVES ! AM I A CATERPILLAR? (HE THROWS THE CUSHIONS AWAY

LEAVETAKING
CLEO V (199) SPEAKS. /CLEOPATRA/ HAS CLEOPATRA NO PART IN THIS LEAVETAKING ? /CAESAR/ (ENLIGHTENED) AH, I KNEW THERE WAS
APPL II (271) WE FIND, ALAS! THAT THE MEETING IS TO BE A LEAVETAKING . (CRASSUS SNIFFS TEARFULLY). IT IS A SAD
DEVL II (40) GENTLEMAN IS GOOD ENOUGH TO ALLOW US A MOMENT OF LEAVETAKING . (THE SERGEANT RETIRES DELICATELY AND JOINS
APPL II (271) (CRASSUS SNIFFS TEARFULLY). IT IS A SAD LEAVETAKING ON OUR PART, BUT A CORDIAL ONE. (HEAR HEAR FROM

LEAVING
JOAN 6,SD(126) YOUNG PRIEST OF 30. THE SCRIBES SIT AT THE TABLE, LEAVING A CHAIR VACANT OPPOSITE D'ESTIVET. SOME OF THE
DOCT PREFACE(42) PERFECT OBEDIENCE IS QUITE A COMMON CONDITION OF LEAVING A CHILD UNWHIPPED), PRODUCE A GOOD DEAL OF
BARB III SD(326) EMPLACEMENT. THE PARAPET STOPS SHORT OF THE SHED, LEAVING A GAP WHICH IS THE BEGINNING OF THE PATH DOWN THE
BASH III (124) RASHLY FORDID HIMSELF WITH PRUSSIC ACID, LEAVING A TEARSTAINED NOTE TO TESTIFY THAT HAVING SWEETLY
CLEO PRO2,SD(96) SEIZE THEIR SPEARS AND GATHER ABOUT THE GATE, LEAVING A WAY THROUGH FOR THE NEW COMER. /PERSIAN/ (RISING
BARB PREFACE(232) HE DIES FINALLY IN THE ODOR OF SANCTITY, LEAVING A WILL WHICH IS A MONUMENT OF PUBLIC SPIRIT AND
SUPR I (11) FOOL I BEGAN ARGUING WITH HIM ABOUT THE FOLLY OF LEAVING A YOUNG WOMAN UNDER THE CONTROL OF AN OLD MAN WITH
MILL I SD(146) TYPE. SHE MAKES PLACIDLY FOR THE TABLE, LEAVING ALASTAIR TO DEAL WITH HIS WIFE. /ALASTAIR/ EPPY!
DEVL I (23) HIS RIGHTFUL, LEGAL WILL, DRAWN UP BY YOURSELF, LEAVING ALL TO ME. /HAWKINS/ THIS IS A VERY WRONGLY AND
ROCK II SD(264) OUT. GOOD AFTERNOON, GENTLEMEN. HE GOES OUT, LEAVING AN ATMOSPHERE OF AWE BEHIND HIM, IN WHICH THE INDIAN
JOAN PREFACE(36) ON HEATHENS AND OUTCASTS TOO OFTEN FOR THAT, LEAVING ANOINTED CHURCHMEN TO SCANDALIZE HISTORY AS WORLDLY
FABL PREFACE(72) THE MIND AS THE CHILD GROWS OUT OF IT WITHOUT LEAVING ANY PSYCHIC COMPLEXES. BUT THE SAME CANNOT BE SAID
GENV PREFACE(10) AND BOTH KILLS AND CURES LIVING ORGANISMS, LEAVING BEHIND IT NOT RADIUM BUT LEAD. IF THIS
POSN SD(441) COME, BOYS. STRAPPER GOES OUT WITH THE OTHERS, LEAVING BLANCO AND ELDER DANIELS TOGETHER. BLANCO RISES AND
CAPT II (251) TAKES UP HER JAR AND GOES OUT BY THE LITTLE DOOR, LEAVING BRASSBOUND AND SIR HOWARD ALONE TOGETHER). /SIR
BULL II SD(106) AND FATHER DEMPSEY TURN FURIOUSLY ON HIM, LEAVING BROADBENT BEAMING AT THE STONE AND THE TOWER WITH
FABL VI (123) YOU CAN GO BACK TO THE FIFTH FORM AND TAKE YOUR LEAVING CERTIFICATE. /YOUTH 3/ OH I SAY! GIVE ME TIME TO
PHIL I (90) FETCH HER IN A MOMENT. (HE GOES OUT CONFIDENTLY, LEAVING CHARTERIS AGHAST). /JULIA/ NOW YOUVE DONE IT. (SHE
MTH4 I (171) THE BURDEN OF LABOR WILL CEASE TO BE PERCEPTIBLE, LEAVING COMMON MEN MORE LEISURE THAN THEY WILL KNOW WHAT TO
POSN SD(439) TO BE HANGED? AT LAST THE WOMEN ARE PUSHED OUT, LEAVING ELDER DANIELS, THE SHERIFF'S BROTHER STRAPPER KEMP,
HART II (114) A BOOK (HE TAKES ONE). GOODNIGHT. (HE GOES OUT, LEAVING ELLIE ALONE WITH THE CAPTAIN). THE CAPTAIN IS INTENT
BULL PREFACE(31) DEMOCRACY AS AGAINST ROMANISM AND SACERDOTALISM, LEAVING ENGLISH UNIONISTS GRIEVED AND SHOCKED AT THEIR
APPL PREFACE(175) OF PREVENTING THEM FROM DOING ANYTHING, AND THUS LEAVING EVERYTHING TO IRRESPONSIBLE PRIVATE ENTERPRISE. BUT
DEVL I (6) WITH HIS OWN FAMILY, GOES AFTER HIM AND DIES, LEAVING EVERYTHING ON MY SHOULDERS. AFTER SENDING THIS GIRL
SIM II (68) IN VASHTI'S FOOTSTEPS). /PROLA/ AN EXCUSE FOR LEAVING EVERYTHING TO ME. LAZY, LAZY, LAZY! SOMEDAY HEAVEN
MILL I (138) IS VERY SIMPLE. I DESIRE TO MAKE MY WILL, LEAVING EVERYTHING I POSSESS TO MY HUSBAND. YOU CAN HARDLY
MILL I (139) FOR A MOMENT, AND DRAW UP A WILL FOR ME TO SIGN, LEAVING EVERYTHING TO ALASTAIR. /SAGAMORE/ TO HUMILIATE
ARMS I (8) AND NO HARM WILL HAPPEN TO YOU. (SHE IS HEARD LEAVING HER BED, AND MAKING FOR THE DOOR). TAKE CARE: IT'S
GETT (278) ALL THAT ROT ABOUT MY KNOCKING LEO ABOUT AND LEAVING HER FOR-- FOR A-- A-- UGH! YOU SHOULD HAVE SEEN
CATH PREFACE(155) OF CATHERINE COMPLETE EVEN IDIOSYNCRATICALLY, LEAVING HER POLITICS OUT OF THE QUESTION: FOR EXAMPLE, SHE
NEVR III (281) OFF. BACK AT NINE. GOODBYE. (HE RUNS OFF GAILY, LEAVING HER STANDING IN THE MIDDLE OF THE ROOM STARING AFTER
NEVR III (281) TOP OF HER VOICE; SUDDENLY FURIOUS WITH HIM FOR LEAVING HER) IDIOT!
METH PREFACE(R35) IF THE IMPIOUS CHALLENGE WERE UTTERED, LEAVING HIM ALONE WITH A SOLITARY INFIDEL UNDER SENTENCE OF
HART II (116) SLIPPING THROUGH YOUR FINGERS. /ELLIE/ (WEARILY, LEAVING HIM AND BEGINNING TO WANDER RESTLESSLY ABOUT THE
DOCT I (93) YOU CAN CUT HALF A DOZEN OF THEM OUT WITHOUT LEAVING HIM ANY THE WORSE, EXCEPT FOR THE ILLNESS AND THE
LION I (118) DECISIVELY AWAY AND SITS DOWN WITH HER COMRADES, LEAVING HIM DISCONCERTED). /METELLUS/ YOU DIDNT GET MUCH OUT
CAND II (125) WELL, I SHALL SHEW HIM HOW MUCH AFRAID I AM BY LEAVING HIM HERE IN YOUR CUSTODY, CANDIDA. /MARCHBANKS/ (TO
MTH2 (55) ASK? /BURGE/ (SITTING DOWN IN CONRAD'S CHAIR, LEAVING HIM STANDING UNEASILY IN THE CORNER) WELL, JUST WHAT
PHIL II SD(128) HER TO THE DOOR, WHICH SWINGS BACK IN HIS FACE, LEAVING HIM STARING AFTER HER THROUGH THE GLASS. /SYLVIA/ (
2TRU II SD(78) THE WORD OF COMMAND WITH IRRESISTIBLE AUTHORITY, LEAVING HIM STUPENT. AUBREY, WHO HAS SCRAMBLED TO HIS FEET,
LION PREFACE(61) DOCK LABORER'S THROAT AFTER MAKING MUCH OF ME FOR LEAVING HIM TO STARVE WHEN I DO NOT HAPPEN TO HAVE A SHIP
SUPR II (56) TO PRINCES AND AMBASSADORS. TO PREVENT HER FROM LEAVING HIM, THAT POOR OLD MAN HAD TO GIVE A BIG DINNER
SUPR IV (154) THE GARDEN, AND GOES OUT THROUGH THE LITTLE GATE, LEAVING HIS FATHER AND VIOLET TOGETHER ON THE LAWN).
MILL PREFACE(115) FOR HIS MARCH TO MOSCOW, ONLY TO HURRY BACK LEAVING HIS LEGIONS DEAD IN THE SNOW, AND THEREAFTER GO FROM
MIS. PREFACE(81) STRANGE WOMAN, AND GOES OFF WITH AND MARRIES HER, LEAVING HIS MOTHER DESOLATE. IT DOES NOT OCCUR TO HIM THAT
DEVL I (12) TABLE AS SOON AS POSSIBLE, AND GOES TO THE FIRE, LEAVING HIS MOTHER TO MAKE THE FINAL ADJUSTMENTS OF ITS
GETT (306) IT ANY WORSE FOR HER THAN FOR ME? /REGINALD/ (LEAVING HIS PLACE AND THRUSTING HIMSELF BETWEEN COLLINS AND
2TRU III (109) THE ELDER VANISHES INTO THE RECESSES OF ST PAULS, LEAVING HIS SON TO PREACH IN SOLITUDE). THERE IS SOMETHING
MTH2 (42) HE RUNS OUT BOYISHLY AFTER HER). /FRANKLYN/ (LEAVING HIS TABLE AND BEGINNING TO WALK UP AND DOWN THE ROOM
BARB III (329) WILL GIVE YOU A SAMPLE OF GUN COTTON WHEN YOU ARE LEAVING IF YOU ASK HIM. YOU CAN EXPERIMENT WITH IT AT HOME.
HART PREFACE(16) RED AS EUROPEAN DANGERS (AS IN FACT THEY ARE), LEAVING IT TO BE INFERRED THAT OUR OWN MILITARISM AND OUR
INCA (242) OF TEACHING YOU YOUR PLACE HERSELF, INSTEAD OF LEAVING IT TO HER MAID. /THE MANAGER/ OH PLEASE,
ROCK PREFACE(178) OPPORTUNITY, AS IT HAS SINCE LOST MANY OTHERS, LEAVING ITSELF OPEN TO THE REPROACH OF STUPIDITY IN NOT
DOCT III (150) SERVICE. SO FOR TODAY, GOODBYE. (HE GOES OUT, LEAVING JENNIFER MUCH PUZZLED BY HIS UNEXPECTED WITHDRAWAL
DEVL III (77) BUSILY UP THE MARKET PLACE TOWARDS THE TOWN HALL, LEAVING JUDITH AND RICHARD TOGETHER. BURGOYNE FOLLOWS HIM A
CAPT III (281) LADY'S ORDERS, SIR. (HE GOES OUT, UNRUFFLED, LEAVING KEARNEY DUMBFOUNDED). /SIR HOWARD/ (CONTEMPLATING
PYGM I (210) GIRL/ (APPALLED) OH, WHAT HARM IS THERE IN MY LEAVING LISSON GROVE? IT WASNT FIT FOR A PIG TO LIVE IN;
CAND III (130) JUST LIKE YOU. WHEN YOU BEGAN YOUR HEROICS ABOUT LEAVING ME HERE WITH CANDIDA-- /MORELL/ (INVOLUNTARILY)
BUOY III (30) NOT HAVING THRASHED THE LIFE OUT OF ME INSTEAD OF LEAVING ME TO LEARN LIFE'S LESSONS BY BREAKING MY SHINS
GETT (327) REGINALD) MR BRIDGENORTH: WILL YOU OBLIGE ME BY LEAVING ME WITH THIS YOUNG MAN. I WANT TO TALK TO HIM LIKE A
UNPL PREFACE(R12) NEITHER OF US HAD MUCH AT HEART, WAS DROPPED, LEAVING ME WITH TWO ABORTIVE ACTS OF AN UNFINISHED AND
MRS IV (251) HAVE TAKEN TO ME LIKE DAUGHTERS AND CRIED AT LEAVING ME; BUT I LET THEM ALL GO BECAUSE I HAD YOU TO LOOK
DEVL I SD(5) OVERCOAT. HE HURRIES, SHIVERING, TO THE FIRE, LEAVING MRS DUDGEON TO SHUT THE DOOR. /CHRISTY/ (AT THE
MRS PREFACE(152) MALE BULLIES AND PARASITES SHOULD BE FLOGGED, LEAVING MRS WARREN IN COMPLETE COMMAND OF THE SITUATION, AND
MRS PREFACE(154) EXAMINE AND REGISTER MRS WARREN, WHILST LEAVING MRS WARREN'S PATRONS, ESPECIALLY HER MILITARY
DEVL I SD(16) AND STANDS ON THE HEARTH WARMING HIS COAT TAILS, LEAVING MRS WILLIAM DERELICT NEAR THE DOOR. UNCLE TITUS, WHO
GENV III (66) HAGUE HAS ABOLISHED THE INTELLECTUAL COMMITTEE, LEAVING MY HUSBAND'S MURDER STILL UNEXPIATED. THAT THROWS ME
KING I SD(187) CURTSEY AS SHE PASSES, AND FOLLOWING HER OUT, LEAVING NEWTON ALONE. /NEWTON/ (GREATLY RELIEVED) OUF! HE
LION PREFACE(40) HAVE SEEN, A VERY MARKED DIFFERENCE BETWEEN THEM, LEAVING NO DOUBT THAT WE ARE DEALING WITH FOUR AUTHORS OF
GENV PREFACE(11) ASTRONOMERS ON MARS, BLAZING UP AND DIMMING OUT, LEAVING NOTHING OF IT AND OF US IN THE SKY BUT A GASEOUS
LION PREFACE(55) WHOM HE BOUGHT THE IRON AND ANVIL AND THE COALS, LEAVING ONLY A SCRAP OF ITS VALUE FOR HIMSELF; AND THIS
GENV PREFACE(3) THE ANCIENT CITY HAD BEEN LEVELLED TO THE GROUND, LEAVING ONLY ST PAUL'S AND A FEW CHURCH TOWERS STANDING. THE
APPL I (222) SEE OF THE SORT OF PROSPERITY THAT COMES OF YOUR LEAVING OUR VITAL INDUSTRIES TO BIG BUSINESS MEN AS LONG AS
DOCT PREFACE(21) HAVE QUALIFIED THEMSELVES SOLELY FOR CONVENIENCE. LEAVING OUT OF ACCOUNT THE VILLAGE WITCHES WHO PRESCRIBE
SIM PREFACE(6) UNPUNISHED, MATERIALLY PROSPEROUS CRIMINAL. I AM LEAVING OUT OF THE QUESTION ALSO THE THOUGHTFUL,
CYMB FORWORD(138) ABOUT IT, AND INCLINED TO COMPROMISE BY LEAVING OUT THE MASQUE AND THE COMIC JAILOR AND MUTILATING
GETT PREFACE(255) WITH SOME SORT OF PRACTICAL ARTS DEGREE, BUT LEAVING PARENTS AND CHILDREN TO ACHIEVE THE RESULTS AS THEY
MILL I SD(165) WE MUSTNT WASTE A BUSY MAN'S TIME. HE GOES OUT, LEAVING PATRICIA AND SAGAMORE ALONE TOGETHER. SHE RISES AND
APPL I SD(197) FACE EACH OTHER FROM OPPOSITE SIDES OF THE ROOM, LEAVING PLENTY OF ROOM BETWEEN THEM. EACH TABLE HAS A CHAIR
APPL I SD(216) AND THE REST OF THE MEN RESUME THEIR SEATS, LEAVING PLINY AND AMANDA STANDING. AMANDA TAKES AN EMPTY
BULL IV (155) (WITH CONVICTION) NEVER, LARRY, NEVER. BUT LEAVING POLITICS OUT OF THE QUESTION, I FIND THE WORLD QUITE
SIM II SD(82) GONE. SHE SCUTTLES UP THE STEPS INTO THE HOUSE, LEAVING PROLA AND PRA ALONE TOGETHER. /PRA/ TELL ME THE
DEVL I (26) /ESSIE/ BUT I DONT WANT TO. (SHE SHRINKS BACK, LEAVING RICHARD AND JUDITH FACE TO FACE). /RICHARD/ (TO
CLEO IV SD(185) THERE IN PRAYER. CAESAR GOES TO CLEOPATRA, LEAVING RUFIO IN THE COLONNADE. /CAESAR/ (WITH SEARCHING
LADY PREFACE(226) YOUR WASTE-PAPER BASKET FULL OF THEM), ENDS IN LEAVING SHAKESPEAR WITH A MUCH WORSE CHARACTER THAN HE
GETT (353) ANOTHER MAN TO TALK TO. I'M BUSY. /MRS GEORGE/ (LEAVING SOAMES AND GOING A STEP OR TWO NEARER HOTCHKISS) WHY
FANY III (310) WITHOUT A WORD OF REMONSTRANCE FROM ME. I'M LEAVING SOLELY BECAUSE MY BROTHER, WHO HAS SUFFERED A
MRS PREFACE(178) OFFERED HER AND HER COLLEAGUES THE ALTERNATIVE OF LEAVING THE CITY OR BEING PROSECUTED UNDER THIS BYE-LAW. NOW
NEVR II (243) FOR REAL WORK, SIR. (HE GOES INTO THE HOTEL, LEAVING THE COMPANY SOMEWHAT OVERWHELMED BY HIS SON'S
MILL PREFACE(120) WERE LISTENING TO SPEECHES ROUND RED FLAGS AND LEAVING THE COWS UNMILKED," THE DEMOBILIZED FELL ON THE
SIM II (80) CONGREGATION AT SUCH A RATE THAT THE REST FLED, LEAVING THE DEAN PREACHING TO THE CHOIR. AT THE ROYAL
CLEO PRO2 (100) /BELZANOR/ (FURIOUSLY) THE COWARDLY SLAVES! LEAVING THE DESCENDANTS OF THE GODS TO BE BUTCHERED! /BEL
JITT I SD(13) FIRE; AND GOES OUT EAGERLY TO ADMIT THE VISITOR, LEAVING THE DOOR OF THE ROOM OPEN. IMMEDIATELY AFTERWARDS A
BULL II SD(111) HER DOING IT, AND FOR THE FAMILY GOING TO BED AND LEAVING THE DOOR OPEN FOR HER, SO BROADBENT'S WHIM TO GO OUT

ARMS III SD(60)	WITH HIS PAPERS STILL IN HIS HAND, ENTERS,	LEAVING	THE DOOR OPEN FOR LOUKA TO GO OUT. HE GOES ACROSS TO
ARMS III SD(61)	ATTITUDE, WATCHES HIM STEADILY. LOUKA GOES OUT,	LEAVING	THE DOOR OPEN. /BLUNTSCHLI/ (ABSENTLY, SITTING AT
GETT (318)	TERM OF THE AGREEMENT. /REGINALD/ (IMPATIENTLY,	LEAVING	THE HEARTH AND GOING BEHIND SOAMES) IT'S NO GOOD
NEVR II SD(245)	WITH HIM INTO THE HOTEL BY THE KITCHEN ENTRANCE,	LEAVING	THE LUNCHEON PARTY TO THEMSELVES. /CRAMPTON/ (
3PLA PREFACE(R16)	HE WANTS THE MUSIC HALL; AND HE GOES THERE,	LEAVING	THE MANAGERS ASTONISHED AT THIS UNEXPECTED BUT QUITE
OVER PREFACE(160)	OF A MURDER, YET IT MAY BE LESS MURDEROUS THAN	LEAVING	THE MATTER TO BE SETTLED BY BLOOD FEUD OR VENDETTA .
BUOY II SD(19)	BEFORE, AFTER AN ANGRY GLANCE AT THE INTRUDER,	LEAVING	THE MEAL ON THE STOEP. /HE/ (TO THE NATIVE) YOU
GETT PREFACE(227)	IN THE STREETS; SOCIABILITY AGAIN APPEARS,	LEAVING	THE MIDDLE CLASS DESPISED AND DISLIKED FOR ITS
JITT III (59)	WAVES HIS HAND TO EDITH, AND GOES INTO THE STUDY,	LEAVING	THE MOTHER AND DAUGHTER ALONE TOGETHER). /AGNES/ (
GENV III (66)	SUCH A MONSTROUS VIOLATION OF NATURAL JUSTICE AS	LEAVING	THE MURDER OF A FATHER UNAVENGED. IF OUR RELATIVES
SIM II (72)	IS NOTHING NEW IN THIS TAKING OF THE ONE AND	LEAVING	THE OTHER: NATURAL DEATH HAS ALWAYS BEEN DOING IT.
GETT PREFACE(239)	CHILDREN HAVE GROWN UP AND GONE THEIR OWN WAY,	LEAVING	THE PARENTS ALONE TOGETHER: A POINT AT WHICH MANY
SUPR PREFACE(R14)	HIS ENEMY THE STATUE ON A TRANSCENDENT PLANE,	LEAVING	THE PRUDISH DAUGHTER AND HER PRIGGISH LOVER ON A
LION PREFACE(100)	WHICH, LIKE OUR OWN GOVERNMENT, IS DELIBERATELY	LEAVING	THE RELIGIOUS INSTRUCTION OF THESE NEGROES IN THE
HART I (64)	(HE GOES OUT, TAKING HIS HAT WITH HIM BUT	LEAVING	THE STICK ON THE TABLE). /MRS HUSHABYE/ (LAYING
SIM PREFACE(15)	FINISH TO THE HUMAN RACE AND ALL ITS PROBLEMS,	LEAVING	THE SURVIVORS IN A CONDITION OF CHANGELESS
BARB I SD(260)	FUN IN THE DRAWING ROOM. THE GIRLS ENTER FIRST,	LEAVING	THE SWAINS OUTSIDE. SARAH COMES TO THE SETTEE.
POSN (445)	DONE WITH IT. /BLANCO/ (SHORTLY, GETTING UP AND	LEAVING	THE TABLE) NEVER YOU MIND WHAT I DONE WITH IT. I WAS
SIM PRO,3, (34)	THEY GO INTO THE ALCOVES TOGETHER. /THE Y.W./ (	LEAVING	THE TABLE) OH BOY, WHAT DO YOU THINK OF THIS ABODE
NEVR III (265)	VALENTINE STARING). /MRS CLANDON/ (RISING AND	LEAVING	THE TEA TABLE) WILL YOU SIT DOWN, MR VALENTINE. I
SUPR I (25)	TO THE WRITING TABLE AND SITS IN RAMSDEN'S CHAIR,	LEAVING	THE THREE MEN TO FIGHT IT OUT BETWEEN THEM).
O'FL (220)	IT ON MY STOMACH. (SHE GOES INTO THE HOUSE,	LEAVING	THE TWO YOUNG PEOPLE ALONE TOGETHER). /O'FLAHERTY/
METH PREFACE(R45)	ON THE NATURE AND ATTRIBUTES OF GOD, I AM	LEAVING	THE VAST MASS OF THE BRITISH PUBLIC OUT OF ACCOUNT.
APPL II SD(266)	SORT OR ANOTHER WHERE THEY CAN FIND THEM, FIRST	LEAVING	THEIR HATS ON THE BALUSTRADE. WHEN THEY ARE SEATED,
2TRU PREFACE(18)	BODIES BY PAYMENTS TO THE ROMAN TREASURY, AND	LEAVING	THEIR SOULS TO GOD, A FIRST-RATE QUARREL BETWEEN THE
GETT PREFACE(234)	TO A MONTH'S IMPRISONMENT OCCASIONALLY FOR IDLY	LEAVING	THEIR WIVES IN CHILDBIRTH WITHOUT FOOD, FIRE, OR
ARMS III (69)	(HE GOES OUT WITH IMPRESSIVE DISCRETION,	LEAVING	THEM ALL STARING AFTER HIM). /PETKOFF/ (BREAKING
CLEO II SD(133)	AND SHOWING A SPLENDID SET OF TEETH, GOES,	LEAVING	THEM ALONE TOGETHER. /CAESAR/ CLEOPATRA: I REALLY
MRS PREFACE(155)	WITH IT WHEN IT GOES TO THE THEATRE, INSTEAD OF	LEAVING	THEM AT HOME WITH ITS PRAYER-BOOK AS IT DOES AT
JOAN 5 (112)	WILL FIND THE PETTICOATS TRIPPING YOU UP AFTER	LEAVING	THEM OFF FOR SO LONG. /LA HIRE/ YOU WILL MISS THE
SUPR I SD(46)	TO DO IS TO GO AT ONCE. GOOD MORNING. SHE GOES,	LEAVING	THEM STARING. /MISS RAMSDEN/ WELL, I MUST SAY!
MIS. PREFACE(38)	ALL PERSONS OF A CERTAIN AGE OUT OF INDUSTRY,	LEAVING	THEM TO FIND SOMETHING EXPERIMENTAL TO OCCUPY THEM
OVER PREFACE(168)	OF SANITARY PROBLEMS, AND REFUSED TO FACE THEM,	LEAVING	THEM TO SOLVE THEMSELVES CLANDESTINELY IN DIRT AND
PYGM II (231)	NOT TO BE SLOVENLY ABOUT HER DRESS OR UNTIDY IN	LEAVING	THINGS ABOUT. /HIGGINS/ (GOING TO HER SOLEMNLY)
MTH2 (57)	I QUITE ADMIT, THAN WE SHOULD HAVE DREAMT OF	LEAVING	TO THEM BEFORE THE WAR; BUT-- (BY THIS TIME HE HAS
CLEO III SD(150)	KILL HIM. TO YOUR POSTS. MARCH. HE GOES OUT,	LEAVING	TWO AUXILIARY SENTINELS WITH THE OTHER.
BULL PREFACE(33)	PEOPLES, OFTEN REPLY THAT THE ENGLISHMAN IS JUST,	LEAVING	US DIVIDED BETWEEN OUR DERISION OF SO MONSTROUSLY
APPL I (232)	OF CHILDISH TEMPER HE BREAKS UP THE CONFERENCE,	LEAVING	US LOOKING LIKE FOOLS WITH NOTHING DONE. AND YOU
METH PREFACE(R31)	HOW MISERABLY A HORRIBLY INJURED DOG CAN DIE,	LEAVING	US TO INFER THAT WE SHALL PROBABLY PERISH LIKEWISE
NEVR IV (305)	WITH GLORIA, AND DISAPPEARS AMONG THE LANTERNS,	LEAVING	VALENTINE GASPING). /VALENTINE/ (RECOVERING HIS
NEVR III (264)	LOOK SADLY AT HIM, AND GO OUT GRAVELY ARM IN ARM,	LEAVING	VALENTINE STARING). /MRS CLANDON/ (RISING AND
PYGM V (279)	WITH THE CORNER OF TOTTENHAM COURT ROAD.	LEAVING	WIMPOLE STREET FINISHES IT. /PICKERING/ (MUCH
BUOY III (40)	OF A UNIVERSITY GIVES. BUT HE INSISTED ON OUR	LEAVING	WITHOUT A DEGREE. /SIR F./ IN HEAVEN'S NAME, WHY?
JITT III (66)	MAKING A FASHIONABLE PRACTICE FOR HIMSELF AND	LEAVING	YOU COMFORTABLY OFF. /AGNES/ (BEGINNING TO CRY) BUT
WIDO III (65)	PERFECTLY AT HOME THAT I NEED MAKE NO APOLOGY FOR	LEAVING	YOU TO YOURSELF. (SHE MAKES A FEINT OF GOING TO THE
JITT I (23)	NOT TO PLAY THE COWARD. /JITTA/ HOW? /BRUNO/ BY	LEAVING	YOU TODAY WITHOUT DARING TO TELL YOU THAT I DO NOT
DEST (164)	WHIP FROM THE TABLE AND GOING) YOULL EXCUSE MY	LEAVING	YOU, GENERAL, I HOPE. VERY SORRY, I'M SURE. (HE
		LEAVINGS	
BULL IV (166)	TRYING TO GET AWAY) I DONT WANT ANY OTHER WOMAN'S	LEAVINGS	. /BROADBENT/ (HOLDING HER) NOBODY ASKED YOU TO.
HART II (118)	MEMORIES OF MY ANCIENT WISDOM: MERE SCRAPS AND	LEAVINGS	; BUT I NO LONGER REALLY CARE FOR ANYTHING BUT MY
		LECTERN	
KING I SD(161)	IT AND A PRODIGIOUS OPEN BIBLE, MADE FOR A CHURCH	LECTERN	. A COMFORTABLE CHAIR FOR THE READER FACES AWAY FROM
		LECTERNS	
METH PREFACE(R78)	NOW EXCEPT THE RELUCTANT PARSONS AT THE CHURCH	LECTERNS	, WHO COMMUNICATE THEIR DISCOMFORT TO THE
		LECTURE	
MRS II (205)	COURSE I DO. EVER SO MUCH BETTER. VIVVUMS MUSTNT	LECTURE	: HER LITTLE BOY'S INCORRIGIBLE. (HE ATTEMPTS TO
CAND I (79)	A COMIC GROAN OF DESPAIR. /PROSERPINE/ ANOTHER	LECTURE	? /MORELL/ YES. THE HOXTON FREEDOM GROUP WANT ME TO
MTH5 (227)	OF EXHIBITING ANYTHING WITHOUT FIRST GIVING A	LECTURE	ABOUT IT TO EXPLAIN IT; BUT I PROMISE YOU THAT IF
JITT III (56)	ANYTHING. /LENKHEIM/ WHAT DOESNT? /AGNES/ THE	LECTURE	ABOUT SLEEP. HE COULD HAVE WRITTEN IT IN ONE
DOCT PREFACE(43)	OPERATION MAY BE TO HIM AT FIRST, CANNOT DO IT AT	LECTURE	AFTER LECTURE FOR MONTHS WITHOUT FINALLY-- AND THAT
BASH II,1, (99)	AS WE GATHERED WERE AT HOSKYN HOUSE TO HEAR A	LECTURE	BY HERR ABENDGASSE, HE PLACED A SINGLE FINGER ON MY
BULL I (88)	UP HIS CHAIR AND SETTLES HIMSELF COMFORTABLY TO	LECTURE	DOYLE). NOW, LARRY, IVE LISTENED CAREFULLY TO ALL
PYGM V (271)	WORTH THREE THOUSAND A YEAR ON CONDITION THAT I	LECTURE	FOR HIS WANNAFELLER MORAL REFORM WORLD LEAGUE AS
DOCT PREFACE(43)	BE TO HIM AT FIRST, CANNOT DO IT AT LECTURE AFTER	LECTURE	FOR MONTHS WITHOUT FINALLY-- AND THAT VERY SOON--
BULL PREFACE(41)	RECAPITULATION OF NATIONALIST TWADDLE; EVERY	LECTURE	IS A CORRUPTION OF HISTORY TO FLATTER NATIONALISM OR
MTH2 (43)	READ ANYTHING I WRITE. SHE NEVER COMES TO HEAR ME	LECTURE	, I AM OUT OF IT AS FAR AS SAVVY IS CONCERNED. (HE
JITT III (61)	IT FROM THE LIVING? /EDITH/ YOU NEED NOT	LECTURE	ME: I AM ON MY GUARD. /FESSLER/ AGAINST WHAT?
APPL INTRLUD(248)	UP BECAUSE I WILL NOT BORROW FROM MY FRIENDS.	LECTURE	ME AGAIN ABOUT THEM; BUT DO NOT DARE PRETEND THAT
MILL II (171)	IT IS YOUR BUSINESS TO DOCTOR ME, NOT TO	LECTURE	ME. /THE DOCTOR/ I AM NOT YOUR DOCTOR: I AM NOT IN
CAND I (80)	(TAKING UP THE DIARY) YES. /MORELL/ HAVE I ANY	LECTURE	ON FOR NEXT MONDAY? /PROSERPINE/ (REFERRING TO
PHIL II (131)	HAPPENED AFTER I LEFT YOU? /GRACE/ I GAVE HER A	LECTURE	ON HER BEHAVIOR WHICH SHE WILL REMEMBER TO THE LAST
METH PREFACE(R11)	OF THE NINETEENTH CENTURY, ASKED ME TO DELIVER A	LECTURE	ON THE PROPHET DARWIN. I DID SO; AND SCRAPS OF THAT
JOAN EPILOG (167)	AND PERHAPS BETTER. (SETTLING HIMSELF FOR A	LECTURE	ON THE SUBJECT) YOU SEE, IT'S LIKE THIS. IF -- (THE
JITT III (58)	OF ALL THAT WORK HE DID. /LENKHEIM/ BUT THE	LECTURE	ON VARIETIES OF SLEEP-- /AGNES/ STUFF! I KNOW THE
JITT III (56)	BOOK! /LENKHEIM/ I HAVE JUST FOUND AN UNFINISHED	LECTURE	ON VARIETIES OF SLEEP. /AGNES/ (DISAPPOINTED) ONLY
CAND I SD(79)	ABLE TO SAY WHAT HE LIKES TO WHOM HE LIKES, TO	LECTURE	PEOPLE WITHOUT SETTING HIMSELF UP AGAINST THEM, TO
DOCT PREFACE(44)	HUMANE. IF THEY PASS ON FROM THE ROUTINE OF	LECTURE	PREPARATION, NOT INTO GENERAL PRACTICE, BUT INTO
MIS. PREFACE(88)	TO LISTEN TO A TEDIOUS PLAY OR PROSY SERMON OR	LECTURE	; TO STARE AT UNINTERESTING PICTURES OR UGLY
PYGM V (272)	/DOOLITTLE/ IT AINT THE LECTURING I MIND. I'LL	LECTURE	THEM BLUE IN THE FACE, I WILL, AND NOT TURN A HAIR.
MTH2 (62)	ELECTORATE. IN SHORT, I CAN GET THAT	LECTURE	UP AGAIN ALMOST AT A MOMENT'S NOTICE. /SAVVY/ BUT,
JOAN 2 (73)	/CHARLES/ THANK YOU. YOU ARE ALWAYS READY WITH A	LECTURE	, ARNT YOU? /LA TREMOUILLE/ (ROUGHLY) ENOUGH
METH PREFACE(R11)	THE PROPHET DARWIN. I DID SO; AND SCRAPS OF THAT	LECTURE	, WHICH WAS NEVER PUBLISHED, VARIEGATE THESE PAGES.
JITT III (56)	OF SLEEP. /AGNES/ (DISAPPOINTED) ONLY A	LECTURE	! (TAKING THE MANUSCRIPT) WHY, IT'S ONLY SIX
JOAN 2 (74)	AT LEAST TRY TO RULE YOURSELF. /CHARLES/ ANOTHER	LECTURE	! THANK YOU. /LA TREMOUILLE/ (HANDING THE PAPER TO
JOAN 2 (74)	OF PETULANCE ARE NOT SEEMLY. /CHARLES/ ANOTHER	LECTURE	! THANK YOU. WHAT A PITY IT IS THAT THOUGH YOU ARE
		LECTURED	
FABL VI (126)	YOUR OWN, ANY OF YOU? /YOUTH 2/ MY GRANDFATHER	LECTURED	ABOUT THE THEORY OF THE DISEMBODIED RACES. I PICKED
DOCT III (149)	LIKE THAT. THE DECENT FELLOWS ARE ALWAYS BEING	LECTURED	AND PUT OUT OF COUNTENANCE BY THE SNOBS. /B.B./ (
GETT PREFACE(193)	THEY BELIEVED THAT IF THEY WERE ONLY SUFFICIENTLY	LECTURED	AND WHIPPED, THEY COULD BE BROUGHT TO A STATE OF
ROCK PREFACE(165)	RECEIVE A SOUND COMMUNIST EDUCATION AND BEING	LECTURED	BY THEM ON HIS OLDFASHIONED PREJUDICES. AND THE
GETT (277)	TURNED AWAY FROM EDITH'S WEDDING BY ALICE, AND	LECTURED	BY YOU! A BACHELOR, AND A PRECIOUS GREEN ONE AT
MIS. PREFACE(30)	TO GIVE THIS STATEMENT THE LIE. SOME YEARS AGO I	LECTURED	IN OXFORD ON THE SUBJECT OF EDUCATION. A FRIEND TO
BULL PREFACE(68)	IRISH BY PHYSICAL FORCE, AND HAD BEEN REBUKED,	LECTURED	, AND REPUDIATED BY THE PARLIAMENTARY HOME RULERS
JOAN PREFACE(3)	TO REPENTANCE AND OBEDIENCE TO HER COMMANDS. SHE	LECTURED	, TALKED DOWN, AND OVERRULED STATESMEN AND
		LECTURER	
FABL PREFACE(81)	SULPHUR CANDLES. IN MY EARLY DAYS AS A SOCIALIST	LECTURER	I WAS ONCE OPPOSED BY A SPEAKER WHO HAD BEEN AN
FABL PREFACE(80)	I HAVE DESCRIBED THE SURPRISE OF A FABIAN	LECTURER	ON BEING ASKED TO OPEN A POLITICAL MEETING WITH
BARB II (287)	YOUR REASON, MISS. YOUD HAVE BEEN A VERY TAKING	LECTURER	ON SECULARISM. BARBARA TURNS TO HER FATHER.

LECTURERS

DOCT PREFACE(43)	FOR LECTURERS TO TEACH FROM THE RABBIT; AND THE	LECTURERS	ARE NOT ORIGINAL ENOUGH TO GET OUT OF THEIR
METH PREFACE(R75)	INFANTS TO SIT OUT THE DISCOURSES OF SECULARIST	LECTURERS	(I HAVE DELIVERED SOME OF THEM MYSELF), WHO BORE
DOCT PREFACE(43)	OF SMOKED PAPER, BUT IT HAS BECOME THE CUSTOM FOR	LECTURERS	TO TEACH FROM THE RABBIT; AND THE LECTURERS ARE
BARB PREFACE(225)	EVEN WHEN UTTERED BY ELOQUENT ESSAYISTS AND	LECTURERS	, OR CARRIED UNANIMOUSLY AT ENTHUSIASTIC PUBLIC

LECTURES

GETT PREFACE(251)	INSTRUCTION IN SEXUAL HYGIENE, BECAUSE SUCH	LECTURES	AS ARE GIVEN IN GERMANY, FRANCE, AND EVEN PRUDISH
DOCT PREFACE(47)	A EUROPEAN POWER." NOW AT THE VERY TIME WHEN THE	LECTURES	DESCRIBING THESE EXPERIMENTS WERE BEING CIRCULATED
DOCT PREFACE(43)	IS CUSTOMARY AS PART OF THE ROUTINE OF PREPARING	LECTURES	IN MEDICAL SCHOOLS, FOR INSTANCE, THERE ARE TWO
BARB II (310)	TELL ME ABOUT TOM PAINE'S BOOKS AND BRADLAUGH'S	LECTURES	. COME ALONG. /SHIRLEY/ AH, IF YOU WOULD ONLY READ
JITT I (18)	GIVEN ME SOME QUITE HANDY CURVE DIAGRAMS FOR MY	LECTURES	. HE KNOWS EVERYTHING: WHAT HE LACKS IS A SENSE OF
DOCT I (89)	OUT OF THAT ARM NOW BY SHEWING IT AT MEDICAL	LECTURES	. /SIR PATRICK/ STILL, THAT WASNT QUITE WHAT YOU
MTH4 I (148)	UNWELCOME VISITORS OR TO LISTEN TO SCIENTIFIC	LECTURES	. SLEEP, SLEEP. (BAWLING INTO HIS EAR) SLEEP. /THE
METH PREFACE(R11)	SOCIETY, WHICH WAS THEN ORGANIZING A SERIES OF	LECTURES	ON PROPHETS OF THE NINETEENTH CENTURY, ASKED ME TO
MIS. PREFACE(37)	TAUGHT AS WELL OR BETTER BY UNIVERSITY EXTENSION	LECTURES	OR BY PRIVATE TUTORS OR MODERN CORRESPONDENCE

LECTURING

CAND II (117)	BETTER ALREADY. WHY MUST YOU GO OUT EVERY NIGHT	LECTURING	AND TALKING? I HARDLY HAVE ONE EVENING A WEEK
DOCT III (133)	FOR. /LOUIS/ (COAXING) THERE NOW: THATS ENOUGH	LECTURING	FOR TODAY. IVE PROMISED TO BE GOOD, HAVNT I? /MRS
ARMS II SD(23)	BACK WITH ANGRY DISDAIN ON A MAN SERVANT WHO IS	LECTURING	HER. HE IS A MIDDLE-AGED MAN OF COOL TEMPERAMENT
WIDO I (13)	HEAVY BELL TO CALL ATTENTION TO HIS PRESENCE! (	LECTURING	HIM WITH REDOUBLED SEVERITY) HAVE YOU NO
PYGM V (272)	THEY WONT ASK YOU TWICE. /DOOLITTLE/ IT AINT THE	LECTURING	I MIND. I'LL LECTURE THEM BLUE IN THE FACE, I
JOAN PREFACE(29)	COUNTRYMEN, SEEING IN THIS A GOOD OPPORTUNITY FOR	LECTURING	THE ENEMY ON HIS INTOLERANCE, PUT UP A STATUE TO
SUPR III (106)	CERTAIN CELEBRATED LEGISLATURE, AND HEARD THE POT	LECTURING	THE KETTLE FOR ITS BLACKNESS, AND MINISTERS
BARB III (329)	THANKS. (HE POCKETS THE MATCHES). /LOMAX/ (	LECTURING	TO THE COMPANY GENERALLY) YOU KNOW, THESE HIGH
DOCT III (133)	HER ARMS ROUND HIS NECK) YOU KNOW THAT I HATE	LECTURING	, AND THAT I DONT FOR A MOMENT MISUNDERSTAND YOU,

LED

ARMS I (4)	OUR RUSSIAN COMMANDERS-- ACTED WITHOUT ORDERS--	LED	A CHARGE ON HIS OWN RESPONSIBILITY-- HEADED IT HIMSELF--
GETT PREFACE(220)	OF IT. WHEN WE HEAR OF YOUNG WOMEN BEING	LED	ASTRAY AND THE LIKE, WE FIND THAT WHAT HAS LED THEM
MRS II (217)	TO BUT THE WORKHOUSE INFIRMARY. DONT YOU BE	LED	ASTRAY BY PEOPLE WHO DONT KNOW THE WORLD, MY GIRL. THE
BASH II,1, (102)	GETTING TO THE BUSINESS OF THE DAY. THE DUTCHMAN	LED	AT ONCE, AND SEEMED TO LAND ON BYRON'S DICEBOX; BUT THE
JOAN 2 (84)	NOT KING YET, LAD: THOURT BUT DAUPHIN. BE NOT	LED	AWAY BY THEM AROUND THEE. DRESSING UP DONT FILL EMPTY
APPL II SD(277)	OF HOPELESS TENDERNESS, ALLOWS HIMSELF TO BE	LED	AWAY. THE END.
O'FL (205)	HONOR. YUP THERE. GWAN NOW. GWAN. (THE HORSE IS	LED	AWAY). GENERAL SIR PEARCE MADIGAN, AN ELDERLY BARONET IN
CAPT II (270)	O CADI, AND THOU, MOON OF LOVELINESS, YE SHALL BE	LED	BACK TO MOGADOR WITH HONOR. AND THOU, ACCURSED
DEVL EPILOG (79)	HAS BECOME POSSIBLE FOR THE FEELING THAT	LED	BURGOYNE, A PROFESSED ENEMY OF OPPRESSION IN INDIA AND
DEST SD(151)	AND GLORY AS WELL, TO BE GAINED BY A DEVOTED ARMY	LED	BY A GENERAL WHO REGARDS LOOT AS THE NATURAL RIGHT OF
DEST (193)	YES: I FORGOT THE IRISH. AN ENGLISH ARMY	LED	BY AN IRISH GENERAL: THAT MIGHT BE A MATCH FOR A FRENCH
DEST (193)	GENERAL: THAT MIGHT BE A MATCH FOR A FRENCH ARMY	LED	BY AN ITALIAN GENERAL. (HE PAUSES, AND ADDS, HALF
CLEO PRO2,SD(104)	THE PALACE-- SEARCH EVERY CORNER. THE GUARDS,	LED	BY BELZANOR, SHOULDER THEIR WAY INTO THE PALACE THROUGH
CLEO I (112)	SLAVE APPEARS CARRYING THE TORCH. CAESAR, STILL	LED	BY CLEOPATRA, FOLLOWS HIM. THEY COME DOWN THE CORRIDOR,
LION II (133)	SUITE DISPERSE TO THEIR SEATS. THE CHRISTIANS,	LED	BY FERROVIUS, MOVE TOWARDS THE PASSAGE). /LAVINIA/ (TO
CYMB V (139)	BY LUCIUS TO FIND OUT HOW FARES OUR RIGHT WING	LED	BY GENERAL IACHIMO. /CAPTAIN/ HE IS OUTGENERALLED.
CLEO II SD(118)	OF THE STEPS, ON HIS WAY IN THROUGH THE LOGGIA,	LED	BY HIS GUARDIAN POTHINUS, WHO HAS HIM BY THE HAND. THE
JOAN PREFACE(53)	FOR POSSESSION OF IT, WITH THE VICTORIOUS FRENCH	LED	BY JOAN ON A REAL HORSE, THE CORONATION WOULD ECLIPSE
GLIM (171)	I CAME WITHOUT A GUIDE, STRAIGHT TO THIS SPOT,	LED	BY ST BARBARA. SHE LED ME TO THIS STONE, DAUGHTER. IT'S
MIS PREFACE(56)	GOVERNMENT YIELDED TO AN OUTCRY FOR FLAGELLATION	LED	BY THE ARCHBISHOP OF CANTERBURY, AND PASSED AN ACT UNDER
SIM II (75)	THERE HAS BEEN A VISITATION. DISSENTING MINORITY,	LED	BY THE BISHOP OF EDGBASTON, DENOUNCES THE REPORTS AS
LION PREFACE(64)	THE ABSURDITIES AND CRUELTIES INTO WHICH WE ARE	LED	BY THE COUNTER-STUPIDITY TO DETERMINISM: THE DOCTRINE OF
CLEO II (128)	THAT BUT FOR US, THE ROMAN ARMY OF OCCUPATION,	LED	BY THE GREATEST SOLDIER IN THE WORLD, WOULD NOW HAVE
MTH1 II (22)	ONE OF THEM I WILL LEAD; AND THE OTHER WILL BE	LED	BY THE MAN I FEAR MOST AND DESIRE TO FIGHT AND KILL
3PLA PREFACE(R22)	TO PLAY ON THEIR ROMANTIC ILLUSIONS, WILL BE	LED	BY THE NOSE FAR MORE COMPLETELY THAN THEY EVER WERE BY
DEVL III (71)	THE GALLOWS, THEIR PETTY OFFICERS, ENERGETICALLY	LED	BY THE SERGEANT, HUSTLING THE PERSONS WHO FIND
DOCT PREFACE(30)	MADE THIS CLAIM; AND HONEST AND REASONABLE MEN,	LED	BY THE STRONGEST CONTEMPORARY MINDS, HAVE REPUDIATED IT
BUOY III (34)	NOW A DISGRACE TO HAVE BEEN BORN RICH. FASHION IS	LED	BY THE WIVES OF CABINET MINISTERS WHOSE FATHERS AND
METH PREFACE(R11)	HIS BOOKS. THE FEW WHO NEVER READ ANY OTHERS WERE	LED	BY THEM TO CONCENTRATE EXCLUSIVELY ON CIRCUMSTANTIAL
BULL II (116)	STEADY NOW, STEADY. COME ALONG: COME. (HE IS	LED	DOWN TO THE ROAD IN THE CHARACTER OF A CONVICTED
2TRU PREFACE(20)	THE CONTRARY, ALL THE DISASTERS TO WHICH IT HAS	LED	HAVE BEEN DEMONSTRATIONS OF THE ETERNAL NEED FOR IT. THE
JOAN 6 (130)	THEY ARE ACCUSED. THE DEVILISH PRIDE THAT HAS	LED	HER INTO HER PRESENT PERIL HAS LEFT NO MARK ON HER
JOAN PREFACE(7)	THE SUPERBITY AS THEY CALLED IT, THAT	LED	HER THITHER. IT WOULD THEREFORE BE WASTE OF TIME NOW TO
PYGM EPILOG (297)	THE EARLSCOURT GREENGROCER'S DAUGHTER. IT HAD	LED	HER TO SEEK THE SOCIETY OF HER MOTHER'S CLASS; AND THAT
LADY PREFACE(228)	THEM, AND HIS RELUCTANCE TO HURT THEIR FEELINGS,	LED	HIM INTO AMIABLE FLATTERY EVEN WHEN HIS FEELINGS WERE
BULL PREFACE(10)	DRAKE HAD PUT A CHAIN ROUND THE KING'S NECK AND	LED	HIM ROUND A PRISONER FOR THE REST OF HIS LIFE, HE WOULD
MILL PREFACE(127)	PRIVILEGE. AT LAST THEY TOOK HIM BY THE ARMS AND	LED	HIM TO A MIGHTY CATHEDRAL, WHERE, ENTERING BY THE WEST
LION PREFACE(78)	AFFECTION. THIS VIEW OF THE CASE INEVITABLY	LED	HIM TO INSIST THAT A WIFE SHOULD BE RATHER A SLAVE THAN
BUOY III (41)	AGAIN AT THE SINGING THEATRE HERE IN LONDON. GOD	LED	HIM TO PANAMA. /SHE/ SHEW HIM UP. THE NATIVE BOWS HIS
LION PREFACE(20)	OF ANCIENT JEWISH PROPHECIES. THIS CRAZE NO DOUBT	LED	HIM TO SEEK FOR SOME LEGEND BEARING OUT HOSEA'S " OUT OF
LION PREFACE(6)	SIMON PETER DID, OR REJECT IT AS A DELUSION WHICH	LED	HIM TO SUBMIT TO TORTURE AND SACRIFICE HIS LIFE WITHOUT
DOCT PREFACE(76)	MAN IF HIS PRACTICE IN THE LABORATORY HAD NOT	LED	HIM TO THE CONCLUSION THAT THE CUSTOMARY INOCULATIONS
METH PREFACE(R31)	HAD STARTED HIM ON THE RIGHT TRACK, AND NOT ONLY	LED	HIM TO THINK OUT A WHOLE SCHEME OF EVOLUTION IN ABSTRACT
CYMB FORWORD(135)	TO AN INHUMAN IDEAL OF MARITAL FIDELITY WHICH	LED	HIM TO THIS VILLAINOUS EXTREMITY. ONE MAY SAY THAT HE IS
HART PREFACE(38)	AND THE GRACIOUS FAVOR OF ALMIGHTY GOD." HE	LED	HIS PEOPLE TO DESTROY THE MILITARISM OF ZABERN; AND THE
DEVL EPILOG (79)	" FIGHTING AN ELECTION" SO VERY LITERALLY THAT HE	LED	HIS SUPPORTERS TO THE POLL AT PRESTON IN 1768 WITH A
SUPR IV (154)	ONE OF THE MASTER SPIRITS OF THE AGE!	LED	IN A STRING LIKE A PUG DOG BY THE FIRST GIRL WHO TAKES
JOAN 2,SD(80)	BOBBED AND HANGING THICKLY ROUND HER FACE, IS	LED	IN BY A BASHFUL AND SPEECHLESS NOBLEMAN, FROM WHOM SHE
SUPR III SD(77)	MOTORING GOGGLES, LEATHER COATS, AND CAPS, ARE	LED	IN FROM THE ROAD BY THE BRIGANDS. /TANNER/ IS THIS THE
LION PREFACE(42)	AS PROMISING THIS EXPLICITLY, AND IS FINALLY	LED	INTO THE AUDACIOUS HINT THAT HE, JOHN, IS HIMSELF
LION PREFACE(13)	CARE A RAP ABOUT HISTORICAL CHRISTIANITY MAY BE	LED	INTO THE MISTAKE OF SUPPOSING THAT IF WE DISCARD REVENGE
O'FL PREFACE(201)	POINT, REMEMBERING BELGIUM AND ITS BROKEN TREATY	LED	IRISHMEN TO REMEMBER LIMERICK AND ITS BROKEN TREATY; AND
HART II (110)	YOU KNOW THE SORT OF LIFE YOU AND ME HAS	LED	. ANY YOUNG LADY OF THAT AGE MIGHT BE MY DAUGHTER
SUPR III (115)	BETTER, AND HIS POEMS TO FEEL MORE DEEPLY. BUT HE	LED	ME AT LAST INTO THE WORSHIP OF WOMAN. /ANA/ JUAN! /DON
APPL I (206)	FOR LESS THAN TEN MINUTES, YOU HAVE ALREADY	LED	ME INTO AN INTELLECTUAL DISCUSSION WHICH SHEWS THAT WE
KING II (231)	ON EARTH: NEVER SHALL I FORGET THE LIFE THEY	LED	ME THERE WITH THEIR BRAINS AND THEIR RELIGION WHEN THEY
KING I (211)	I AM RIGHTLY REBUKED FOR THIS VICE OF MINE THAT	LED	ME TO BELIEVE THAT I COULD CONSTRUCT A UNIVERSE WITH
MIS. PREFACE(79)	STIMULATED BY EARLY DOSES OF FICTION,	LED	ME TO BRAG TO A STILL SMALLER BOY SO OUTRAGEOUSLY THAT
NEVR III (265)	SEEN OF THE LOVE AFFAIRS OF OTHER PEOPLE HAS NOT	LED	ME TO REGRET THAT DEFICIENCY IN MY EXPERIENCE. (
GLIM (171)	STRAIGHT TO THIS SPOT, LED BY ST BARBARA. SHE	LED	ME TO THIS STONE, DAUGHTER. IT'S A COMFORTABLE STONE TO
APPL PREFACE(173)	CONTRAST OF CHARACTER AND METHODS WHICH HAS	LED	MY LESS CONSIDERATE CRITICS TO COMPLAIN THAT I HAVE
METH PREFACE(R30)	THE FATHER LEFT OFF. THIS BELIEF IN HEREDITY	LED	NATURALLY TO THE PRACTICE OF INTENTIONAL SELECTION. GOOD
SUPR HANDBOK(191)	MOVEMENT TAKES PLACE, IT IS NOT CONSCIOUSLY	LED	NOR ORGANIZED: THE UNCONSCIOUS SELF IN MANKIND BREAKS
METH PREFACE(R88)	A FEW TIMES IN SCOTLAND BY MR ESME PERCY, WHO	LED	ONE OF THE FORLORN HOPES OF THE ADVANCED DRAMA AT THAT
3PLA PREFACE(R28)	IMPASSIONED ONLY FOR SAVING GRACE, AND NOT TO BE	LED	OR TURNED BY WIFE OR MOTHER, CHURCH OR STATE, PRIDE OF
PYGM PREFACE(201)	OUR NOBLE BUT ILL-DRESSED LANGUAGE; BUT HE WAS	LED	PAST THAT BY HIS CONTEMPT FOR THE POPULAR PITMAN SYSTEM
CAPT II (270)	BRASSBOUND, SON OF A WANTON: IT IS THOU HAST	LED	SIDI EL ASSIF INTO THIS WRONGDOING. READ THIS WRITING
2TRU III (93)	THAT WERE TO HAVE ESTABLISHED THE MILLENNIUM HAVE	LED	STRAIGHT TO EUROPEAN SUICIDE. AND I-- I WHO BELIEVED IN
LION PREFACE(16)	VEGETARIAN WRESTLERS AND RACERS AND BICYCLISTS,	LED	THE FIRST MEN WHO CONCEIVED GOD AS CAPABLE OF
MRS PREFACE(175)	THE POLICE TO ARREST DALY AND HIS COMPANY, AND	LED	THE MAGISTRATE TO EXPRESS HIS LOATHING OF THE DUTY THUS
METH PREFACE(R10)	DARWIN'S CASE IT DID MATTER, IF DARWIN HAD REALLY	LED	THE WORLD AT ONE BOUND FROM THE BOOK OF GENESIS TO
JOAN EPILOG (158)	ME ALL ABOUT THE FIGHTING, JACK. WAS IT THOU THAT	LED	THEM? WERT THOU GOD'S CAPTAIN TO THY DEATH? /DUNOIS/ I
GETT PREFACE(220)	LED ASTRAY AND THE LIKE, WE FIND THAT WHAT HAS	LED	THEM ASTRAY IS A SEDULOUSLY INCULCATED FALSE NOTION THAT
6CAL (104)	AND YOU, FELLOW: I WILL HAVE YOU MUZZLED AND	LED	THROUGH THE STREETS ON A CHAIN AND LODGED IN A KENNEL.
CLEO NOTES (206)	IN AMERICA RELATIVELY TO THE DEMAND FOR IT HAS	LED	TO A DEVELOPMENT OF MACHINERY THERE, AND A CONSEQUENT "
DOCT PREFACE(67)	FIRST-CLASS ONE, IF THE PRACTICE OF LAW NOT ONLY	LED	TO A JUDGE HAVING TO HANG, BUT THE HANGMAN TO JUDGE, OR
PYGM EPILOG (296)	THE SOLE COMMENT VOUCHSAFED BY HIM VERY NEARLY	LED	TO A SERIOUS QUARREL WITH ELIZA. IT WAS TO THE EFFECT

SIM PREFACE(7)	KNOW THAT NAIVE ATTEMPTS TO BRIBE DIVINE JUSTICE	LED	TO A TRADE IN ABSOLUTIONS, PARDONS, AND INDULGENCES
POSN (465)	AND SHE'S HAD ENOUGH OF IT, FINDING THAT IT ONLY	LED	TO BEING PUT UPON. /HANNAH/ WELL, IF THERE WAS NOTHING
MIS. PREFACE(30)	PRACTISED ON BOTH THE MAN AND THE WOMAN. HE IS	LED	TO BELIEVE THAT SHE KNOWS WHAT SHE IS PROMISING, AND
GETT PREFACE(245)	ANY KNOWLEDGE OF THEIR DANGER, OR ERRONEOUSLY	LED	TO BELIEVE THAT CONTAGION IS POSSIBLE THROUGH MISCONDUCT
JOAN 4 (104)	THEY WERE NOT SO ILLBRED AS I HAD BEEN	LED	TO BELIEVE. IN SOME RESPECTS THEIR CONDUCT COMPARED
POSN (442)	DRINK AS I USED TO? WHY DIDNT YOU DRINK AS I WAS	LED	TO BY THE LORD FOR MY GOOD, UNTIL THE TIME CAME FOR ME
GETT PREFACE(222)	WHEN THEY HAVE, IN THE ARTS BY WHICH MEN CAN BE	LED	TO COMPROMIZE THEMSELVES; AND TO KEEP ALL THE SKELETONS
LION PREFACE(56)	AFTER ATTEMPT TO ESCAPE FROM HIS TEACHING HAS	LED	TO DEEPER AND DEEPER DISASTER, LAUGHING OUTRIGHT. WAS
LION PREFACE(69)	WE RESTRAIN IT WE DESTROY OURSELVES. WE ARE THUS	LED	TO DEVISE MARRIAGE INSTITUTIONS WHICH WILL AT THE SAME
SIM II (71)	/MRS HYERING/ WELL, IT'S HARDLY WHAT WE WERE	LED	TO EXPECT, YOU KNOW. /JANGA/ " THE HEAVENS SHALL PASS
MIS. PREFACE(25)	I WILL TELL YOU THAT ONE OF MY FRIENDS WAS	LED	TO GENUINE LOVE AND CONSIDERABLE KNOWLEDGE OF CLASSICAL
BULL PREFACE(25)	APPOINTED GODFATHER TO APPEAR AT MY BAPTISM HAD	LED	TO HIS RESPONSIBILITIES BEING ASSUMED ON THE SPOT, AT MY
LION PREFACE(79)	THE ETERNAL ENEMY OF WOMAN. INCIDENTALLY IT HAS	LED	TO MANY FOOLISH SURMISES ABOUT PAUL'S PERSONAL CHARACTER
DOCT PREFACE(63)	OF ANY WASTE OF VITAL FORCES, UNLESS A MAN IS	LED	TO MEDICINE OR SURGERY THROUGH A VERY EXCEPTIONAL
DOCT PREFACE(58)	UNTIL HE IS READY TO BE CREMATED ON THE SPOT, HAS	LED	TO MUCH GREATER CARE AND CLEANLINESS, AND THE NET RESULT
CYMB FORWORD(133)	BUT IT WAS EXPRESSED OUTSIDE THE THEATRE AND	LED	TO NO RIOTING, AND IT SET ON FOOT A NEW THEORY OF
PYGM EPILOG (302)	THAT THERE WAS MONEY IN ASPARAGUS; AND ASPARAGUS	LED	TO OTHER VEGETABLES), HAD AN AIR WHICH STAMPED THE
MIS. PREFACE(97)	ADULTS DO THE OPPOSITE, AND ARE THEREBY OFTEN	LED	TO TALK GREAT NONSENSE ABOUT THE BAD EFFECT OF BIBLE
PYGM III SD(244)	CARICATURED BY PEOPLE WHO DID NOT UNDERSTAND,	LED	TO THE ABSURDITIES OF POPULAR ESTHETICISM IN THE
BULL PREFACE(70)	OBVIOUSLY MUST FINALLY HAVE IT, A MILITARY PANIC	LED	TO THE CANNONADING OF A FORBIDDEN PUBLIC MEETING AT
POSN PREFACE(372)	OF THE UNPLEASANT PART OF ITS BUSINESS THAT	LED	TO THE COMIC INCIDENT OF THE COMMITTEE'S SUDDEN
METH PREFACE(R61)	IN HEALTHY AND WEALTHY COUNTRIES, IT COULD BE	LED	TO THE CONCLUSION THAT THE TYPE OF CHARACTER WHICH
MIS. PREFACE(90)	VERY PASSABLY EXECUTED, AND CAN THEREBY BE	LED	TO THE DISCOVERY THAT JACKSON IN F AND HYMNS ANCIENT AND
DOCT PREFACE(58)	IN THE RICH DISTRICTS AND IN THE POOR ONES HAS	LED	TO THE GENERAL CONVICTION AMONG EXPERTS THAT BACTERIAL
DOCT PREFACE(26)	HAVE SHEWN THAT THE APPALLING RESULTS WHICH	LED	TO THE HASTY DROPPING IN 1894 OF KOCH'S TUBERCULIN WERE
SIM PREFACE(10)	TO NATIONAL INDIVIDUALISM AT THE REFORMATION, ALL	LED	TO THE PERSECUTION AND VIRTUAL OUTLAWRY OF THE HERETICS
GETT PREFACE(183)	AND PERSONAL RIGHTEOUSNESS, AND CONSENT TO BE	LED	TO THE REGISTRY OR EVEN TO THE ALTAR, THEY INSIST ON
JOAN PREFACE(18)	EVIDENT THAT SHE HAD MISCALCULATED: WHEN SHE WAS	LED	TO THE STAKE, AND LA HIRE WAS NOT THUNDERING AT THE
HART PREFACE(18)	OF THEM HAD NO ILLUSIONS ABOUT THE POLICY THAT	LED	TO THE WAR; THEY WENT CLEAR-SIGHTED TO A HORRIBLY
MIS. PREFACE(104)	OF THE MONARCHS, DEMOCRACY IN AMERICA HAS	LED	TO THE WITHDRAWAL OF ORDINARY REFINED PERSONS FROM
PRES (138)	TWO MORE EDITIONS THAN HIS, AND THE RUSH FOR IT	LED	TO THE WRECKING OF THE TIMES BOOK CLUB, YOU HAVE BECOME
MTH4 I (170)	YEARS AFTER YOU HAVE MADE THE MISTAKES THAT	LED	TO THEM; AND THEN IT IS TOO LATE, YOU CANNOT UNDERSTAND
JOAN PREFACE(6)	ON HER OWN SIDE TO SAVE HER, THE COMRADES SHE HAD	LED	TO VICTORY AND THE ENEMIES SHE HAD DISGRACED AND
FANY II (289)	I WAS CONCERNED IN THE REGRETTABLE INCIDENT WHICH	LED	TO YOUR DAUGHTER'S INCARCERATION. I GOT A FORTNIGHT
APPL INTRLUD(250)	HAVE NEVER BEEN REALLY MARRIED, THOUGH YOU HAVE	LED	TWO CAPTIVES TO THE ALTAR, AND BORNE CHILDREN TO ONE OF
MIS. PREFACE(44)	AT ONCE ARISES THE DANGER INTO WHICH MORALITY HAS	LED	US: THE DANGER OF PERSECUTION. ONE CHRISTIAN SPREADING
METH PREFACE(R59)	OF THE ROCK ON WHICH EQUALITY IS BUILT, HAD	LED	US TO INSIST ON GOD OFFERING US SPECIAL TERMS BY PLACING
LION PREFACE(10)	BROTHER. UNLESS A RELIGIOUS TURN IN OURSELVES HAS	LED	US TO SEEK THE LITTLE SOCIETIES TO WHICH THESE RARE
3PLA PREFACE(R27)	WAY TO HELL EVEN FROM THE GATES OF HEAVEN, AND SO	LED	US TO THE EQUALLY TRUE PROPOSITION THAT THERE IS A WAY
APPL PREFACE(183)	THE MUNITIONING OF THE ARMY TO PRIVATE ENTERPRISE	LED	US TO THE VERGE OF DEFEAT AND CAUSED AN APPALLING
JOAN 6 (141)	IS IMPOSSIBLE. /CAUCHON/ IMPOSSIBLE! THEY HAVE	LED	YOU STRAIGHT TO YOUR EXCOMMUNICATION, AND TO THE STAKE
SUPR I (37)	FROM HER FACE). IT WAS THE CREATIVE INSTINCT THAT	LED	YOU TO ATTACH ME TO YOU BY BONDS THAT HAVE LEFT THEIR
OVER (176)	THAT YOURE A MARRIED MAN! /GREGORY/ I NEVER	LED	YOU TO BELIEVE I WAS UNMARRIED. /MRS JUNO/ OH! YOU
KING I (181)	MY HOUSE. /FOX/ (RISING) YOUR PHILOSOPHY HAS	LED	YOU TO THE CONCLUSION THAT GEORGE FOX IS AN INFIDEL, SO
CATH 3 (186)	WAY OUT). IT WAS THE TEMPTATION OF THE DEVIL THAT	LED	YOUR YOUNG MAN TO BRUISE MY VITALS AND DEPRIVE ME OF
		LEDDY	
CAPT III (274)	(TOO MUCH PERTURBED TO DWELL ON HIS GRIEVANCE)	LEDDY	CEECILY: I MUST GO TO THE PRISON AND SEE THE LAD. HE
CAPT III (274)	/RANKIN/ (RESERVEDLY) NO: I CANNOT SAY THAT,	LEDDY	CEECILY. I DOUBT HE HAS IMPOSED ON YOUR GOOD NATURE
CAPT III (275)	YOU SEE. /RANKIN/ (CANNILY) I TAKE YOUR POINT,	LEDDY	CEECILY. IT ALTERS THE CASE. I SHALL CERTAINLY MAKE NO
CAPT I (232)	ME TO ACCOMPANY YOU. /RANKIN/ TIS NOT SAFE,	LEDDY	CEECILY. REALLY AND TRULY, TIS NOT SAFE. THE TRIBES
CAPT III (276)	TAKES LADY CICELY'S CHAIR). /RANKIN/ OO REVOIR,	LEDDY	CEECILY. /LADY CICELY/ BLESS YOU, MR RANKIN. (RANKIN
CAPT III (273)	HE COULD TO SAVE HIM. /RANKIN/ YE ASTOANISH ME,	LEDDY	CEECILY. /LADY CICELY/ AND THINK OF THE TEMPTATION TO
CAPT III (272)	BE IN SURREY ON A VERY HOT DAY). SIT YE DOON,	LEDDY	CEECILY. /LADY CICELY/ (SITTING DOWN) HOW NICE YOUVE
CAPT I (232)	MR RANKIN? /RANKIN/ THAT IS A POINT, CERTAINLY,	LEDDY	CEECILY. /SIR HOWARD/ OH, IF YOU ARE GOING TO TALK
CAPT I (231)	YOURE SETTING WITH YOUR BACK TO THE SUN,	LEDDY	CEECILY, AND LOSING SOMETHING WORTH LOOKING AT. SEE
CAPT III (282)	WAS YOUR OFFICER GIVING YOUR COMPLIMENTS TO	LEDDY	CEECILY, AND WOULD SHE KINDLY ALLOW THE PRISONERS TO
CAPT I (232)	/RANKIN/ HE WOULD NOT DO IT FOR YOUR SAKE,	LEDDY	CEECILY, BUT FOR HIS OWN. THE SULTAN WOULD GET INTO
CAPT III (273)	YE SEEM TO HAVE FRIGHTENED THE POOR MAN YOURSELF,	LEDDY	CEECILY, BY TALKING TO HIM ABOUT THE FANATICAL
CAPT I (227)	MONEY IN DRINK. /RANKIN/ EXCUSE ME A MOMENT, MY	LEDDY	. I HAVE A WORD IN SEASON TO SAY TO THAT SAME MOOR. (
CAPT I (227)	DOLLARS! TIS EASY TO SEE YOU ARE NOT SCOTCH, MY	LEDDY	. /LADY CICELY/ O, POOR THINGS, THEY MUST WANT IT MORE
CAPT III (274)	CAST AWAY AMONG A PARCEL O LONE, LAWLESS MEN, MY	LEDDY	. /LADY CICELY/ (NAIVELY) BLESS ME, THATS QUITE TRUE;
CAPT I (231)	TOMORROW, HOWARD. /RANKIN/ THATS IMPOSSIBLE, MY	LEDDY	. THE NATIVES ARE VERRA DANGEROUS. /LADY CICELY/ WHY?
CAPT I (219)	WINEFLEET? /RANKIN/ DO YE MEAN THE CELEBRATED	LEDDY	-- THE TRAVELLER? /DRINKWATER/ YUSS: SHOULD THINK AW
CAPT III (282)	/RANKIN/ EXCUSE MY DELAY, CAPTAIN KEARNEY. THE	LEDDY	SENT ME ON AN ERRAND. (KEARNEY GRUNTS). I THOAGHT I
		LEDDYSHIP	
CAPT III (272)	LEAVES BUT ONE FOR SIR HOWRRD AND ONE FOR YOUR	LEDDYSHIP	, I COULD ALMOST BE TEMPTED TO CALL IT A MAIRCY
CAPT I (234)	/RANKIN/ I MISDOUBT ME HE WILL NOT ANSWER, YOUR	LEDDYSHIP	, THERE IS A SCUFFLING NOISE IN THE HOUSE; AND
CAPT I (226)	/RANKIN/ I AM GLAD TO BE OF SERVICE TO YOUR	LEDDYSHIP	, YOU WILL BE WISHING TO HAVE SOME TEA AFTER YOUR
CAPT III (273)	CALL HIM POOR CAPTAIN BRASSBOUND! DOES NOT YOUR	LEDDYSHIP	KNOW THAT THIS BRASSBOUND IS-- HEAVEN FORGIVE ME
		LEDGE	
NEVR I (200)	ACCENT). /THE DENTIST/ (PUTTING IT DOWN ON THE	LEDGE	OF HIS CABINET OF INSTRUMENTS) THAT WAS MY FIRST
		LEDS	
CAPT I (227)	(DEPRECATING_Y) NIME GIV HUZ PORE THORTLESS	LEDS	BAW A GENT ON THE DILY CHRORNICLE, LIDY. (RANKIN
		LEE	
CYMB FORWORD(138)	I CANNOT PRETEND TO CARE MUCH ABOUT WHAT NAT	LEE	DID IN HIS ATTEMPTS TO IMPART RESTORATION GENTILITY TO
CAPT II (246)	DRINKWATER. /DRINKWATER/ (WHIMPERING) YOU	LEE	ME ALOWN: AWM GOWIN. THERES N'MAW TRUE DEMMECRETTICK
PHIL II (103)	SEEING JULIA) OH, LORD! (HE RETREATS UNDER THE	LEE	OF THE REVOLVING BOOKSTAND). /PARAMORE/ (
		LEECH	
MTH1 II (24)	IS TO THE RABBIT; AND SHE IS TO YOU WHAT THE	LEECH	IS TO THE STOAT. YOU DESPISE YOUR FATHER; BUT WHEN HE
		LEEDS	
MIS. (113)	IT. MY FATHER BEGAN IN A LITTLE HOLE OF A SHOP IN	LEEDS	NO BIGGER THAN OUR PANTRY DOWN THE PASSAGE THERE. HE
		LEETLE	
LION PROLOG (109)	AND IT WILL BE ALL OVER. JUST ONE LITTLE, LITTLE,	LEETLE	PULL; AND THEN UM WILL LIVE HAPPILY EVER AFTER. (HE
		LEF	
CAPT I (220)	TOO. BUT IT WERE A MISUNNERSTENDIN, THET WORS.	LEF	THE COURT WITHAHT A STINE ON MAW KERRICKTER, AW DID.
		LEFT	
MILL IV (206)	DONE ANYTHING BUT LIVE IN CLAPHAM PARK; AND SHE	LEFT	122,000 POUNDS. BUT WHAT WAS THE NEXT NAME? IT WAS
NEVR II (258)	NO: I CANT FACE THAT: I MUST HAVE ONE ILLUSION	LEFT	: THE ILLUSION ABOUT YOU. I LOVE YOU. (HE TURNS
2TRU III (95)	TO EAT BUT DATES! AND SHE IS THE ONLY ONE I HAVE	LEFT	: THEY WERE ALL DELICATE-- /TALLBOYS/ I REALLY MUST-- (
DOCT PREFACE(15)	A WEEK, HOW MUCH SCIENTIFIC CONSCIENCE HAVE YOU	LEFT	? IF YOU ARE WEAK-MINDED ENOUGH TO CLING DESPERATELY
KING II (224)	BODY-- A VERY FINE BODY, I ADMIT-- WHAT IS THERE	LEFT	? /CATHERINE/ AND YOU ARE DONE WITH BARBARA'S BODY?
MRS IV (236)	HOLIDAY. WHAT HAPPENED AT HASLEMERE WHEN I	LEFT	? /FRANK/ NOTHING AT ALL. I SAID YOUD GONE TO TOWN ON
CAPT III (294)	MY LIFE GONE: YOUR DOING, REMEMBER. WHAT HAVE I	LEFT	? SEE HERE! (HE TAKES UP THE LETTERS) THE LETTERS MY
BULL III (127)	THAT DOESNT HARLY KNOW HIS RIGHT HAND FROM HIS	LEFT	? WHAT DID HE EVER SUFFER, I'D LIKE TO KNOW?
WIDO III (56)	/SARTORIUS/ NOT QUITE YET, I THINK. HE	LEFT	A BOOK HERE FOR ME TO LOOK OVER: A LARGE BOOK IN A BLUE
CURE SD(225)	UNDER THESE CIRCUMSTANCES, HE WOULD FIND ON HIS	LEFT	A GRAND PIANO WITH THE KEYBOARD END TOWARDS HIM, AND A
SIM II (79)	NOTHING. IT IS THE JUDGMENT. /PROLA/ HAS SHE	LEFT	A GREAT VOID IN YOUR HEART, IDDY, THAT GIRL WHO TURNED

DEST (156)	AND A TRUNK: THAT IS ALL. THE POSTILLION SAYS SHE	LEFT	A HORSE AT THE GOLDEN EAGLE. A CHARGER, WITH MILITARY
SUPR III SD(71)	IS REALLY AN ABANDONED QUARRY, AND TOWARDS THE	LEFT	A LITTLE HILL, COMMANDING A VIEW OF THE ROAD, WHICH
ARMS III (55)	I SHALL HAVE TO START FOR HOME IN AN HOUR. HE HAS	LEFT	A LOT OF BIG HOTELS BEHIND HIM TO BE LOOKED AFTER. (HE
DEVL II (31)	A MAN LIKE THAT. I FELT THAT I MUST WARN HIM. I	LEFT	A MESSAGE FOR HIM. /JUDITH/ (QUERULOUSLY) WHAT
METH PREFACE(R43)	NOW BECOME A VERY REAL TERROR. FOR THOUGH DARWIN	LEFT	A PATH ROUND IT FOR HIS SOUL, HIS FOLLOWERS PRESENTLY
MTH2 SD(37)	WITH HIS RIGHT PROFILE PRESENTED TO YOU; ON YOUR	LEFT	A SETTEE; AND ON YOUR RIGHT A COUPLE OF CHIPPENDALE
SUPR HANDBOK(208)	BUSY. AND THE MERE CHAPTER OF ACCIDENTS HAS	LEFT	A SMALL ACCUMULATION OF CHANCE DISCOVERIES, SUCH AS THE
CAPT II (255)	NEVER KNEW-- NEVER DREAMT-- THAT MY BROTHER MILES	LEFT	A SON. AS TO YOUR MOTHER, HER CASE WAS A HARD ONE--
MTH3 (111)	I DID KILL MYSELF. IT WAS QUITE EASY. I	LEFT	A SUIT OF CLOTHES BY THE SEASHORE DURING THE BATHING
GENV PREFACE(5)	INVIOLATE THE FRONTIERS OF POLAND AS THEY WERE	LEFT	AFTER THE FIGHTING OF 1914-18 WITH A POLISH CORRIDOR
MILL I (158)	YOU. WHAT I DID WAS THIS. I HAD A HUNDRED POUNDS	LEFT	AFTER THE OPERA STUNT. I MET AN AMERICAN. I TOLD HIM I
DOCT PREFACE(5)	THE WONDER IS THAT THERE IS A KING OR QUEEN	LEFT	ALIVE IN EUROPE. DOCTORS' CONSCIENCES. THERE IS ANOTHER
FABL II (105)	ONLY THAT THERE IS NOT ONE OF GOD'S CREATURES	LEFT	ALIVE IN THE ISLE OF WIGHT. I SHALL HAVE TO SEND EVERY
MTH2 (49)	KNOW IT. LORD DUNREEN IS THE BITTEREST OLD TORY	LEFT	ALIVE. WHAT HAS HE TO OFFER TO THE PEOPLE? /FRANKLYN/
MIS. (127)	ONE EVENING IN A HOTEL IN SUNDERLAND WHEN I HAD	LEFT	ALL MY PAPERS IN THE TRAIN; AND I FOUND IT WASNT HALF
MRS IV (250)	INDEPENDENT OF IT. YOUR SISTER, YOU TOLD ME, HAS	LEFT	ALL THAT BEHIND HER. WHY DONT YOU DO THE SAME? /MRS
2TRU II (67)	MORALS YOUR GRANDMOTHER! I THOUGHT YOUD	LEFT	ALL THAT FLAPDOODLE BEHIND YOU WHEN YOU CAME AWAY WITH
KING I (165)	YOU AT HALF PAST ELEVEN. /NEWTON/ CAN I NEVER BE	LEFT	ALONE? WHO IS MR ROWLEY? WHAT IS MR ROWLEY? /MRS
MTH4 III (201)	HIS WIFE AND DAUGHTER. /THE ELDERLY GENTLEMAN/ (	LEFT	ALONE AND SHRINKING INTO AN OLD AND DESOLATE FIGURE)
JITT I SD(11)	GRIMACE, HAS TO GO). THE MOMENT THE GENTLEMAN IS	LEFT	ALONE HE SHEWS SIGNS OF SEVERE PHYSICAL SUFFERING. HIS
JITT III (65)	DESERTS IT. WHO KNOWS HOW SOON I SHALL BE	LEFT	ALONE HERE TO HAUNT THE PLACE LIKE MY OWN SHADOW? I
CLEO PRO2 (104)	THEM IN HER ARMS. I TOLD HER SHE WOULD BE	LEFT	ALONE HERE WHEN THE ROMANS CAME AS A PUNISHMENT FOR HER
POSN (446)	BROUGHT YOU TO THIS THAT YOURE AFRAID TO BE	LEFT	ALONE IN BROAD DAYLIGHT, LIKE A CHILD IN THE DARK.
NEVR III (270)	CONTINUING)-- BUT I HAVE AT LEAST THE RIGHT TO BE	LEFT	ALONE IN MY DISGRACE. I AM ONE OF THOSE WEAK CREATURES
JOAN 2 (83)	AND I DONT WANT TO KILL PEOPLE: I ONLY WANT TO BE	LEFT	ALONE TO ENJOY MYSELF IN MY OWN WAY. I NEVER ASKED TO
VWOO 1 (119)	GO OVERBOARD. DONT YOU SEE THAT I WANT TO BE	LEFT	ALONE TO WORK, AND THAT YOUR CHATTER IS PREVENTING ME
DOCT II SD(127)	WITHOUT CEREMONY. RIDGEON AND SIR PATRICK ARE	LEFT	ALONE TOGETHER. RIDGEON, DEEP IN THOUGHT, COMES DOWN TO
BARB III SD(345)	SHED, FOLLOWED BY BILTON). BARBARA AND CUSINS,	LEFT	ALONE TOGETHER, LOOK AT ONE ANOTHER SILENTLY. /CUSINS/
GLIM SD(183)	AND FRAGMENTS OF THE MEAL INDOORS. FERRUCCIO IS	LEFT	ALONE WITH GIULIA. THE GLOAMING DEEPENS. /FERRUCCIO/
NEVR IV (299)	PATHOS OF THAT? (HE VANISHES). /MRS CLANDON/ (	LEFT	ALONE WITH GLORIA) WHY DID MR VALENTINE GO AWAY SO
2TRU I SD(37)	VOCE) GOODNIGHT. (SHE STEALS OUT). THE NURSE,	LEFT	ALONE WITH HER PATIENT, PAYS NO ATTENTION TO HER, BUT
GETT SD(352)	(HE GOES OUT THROUGH THE TOWER). MRS GEORGE,	LEFT	ALONE WITH HOTCHKISS AND SOAMES, SUDDENLY PUTS HER
SUPR I (22)	MRS WHITEFIELD OUT OF THE ROOM). /TANNER/ (	LEFT	ALONE WITH OCTAVIUS, STARES WHIMSICALLY AT HIM) TAVY:
ARMS II SD(33)	INTO THE HOUSE TOGETHER AFFECTIONATELY. SERGIUS,	LEFT	ALONE WITH RAINA, LOOKS ANXIOUSLY AT HER, FEARING THAT
JITT III SD(70)	DEAR! (SHE GOES OUT INTO THE CORRIDOR). JITTA,	LEFT	ALONE, BEGINS TO LAUGH AGAIN HYSTERICALLY, AND IS
2TRU I SD(35)	WANDERS AWAY BEHIND THE SCREEN. THE PATIENT,	LEFT	ALONE, BEGINS TO STIR IN HER BED. SHE TURNS OVER AND
MIS. SD(116)	TO COCK A SNOOK AT JOHNNY AS HE GOES OUT. JOHNNY,	LEFT	ALONE, CLENCHES HIS FISTS AND GRINDS HIS TEETH, BUT CAN
HART I SD(77)	AND A HALF. (HE GOES INTO THE PANTRY). HECTOR,	LEFT	ALONE, CONTRACTS HIS BROWS, AND FALLS INTO A DAYDREAM.
ROCK I SD(208)	AS SHE GOES THROUGH THE MASKED DOOR). SIR ARTHUR,	LEFT	ALONE, LOOKS INSPIRED AND TRIUMPHANT. HE ADDRESSES AN
WIDO III SD(64)	STUDY CHUCKLING, FOLLOWED BY SARTORIUS). TRENCH,	LEFT	ALONE, LOOKS ROUND CAREFULLY AND LISTENS A MOMENT. THEN
PYGM V SD(289)	THEY KISS. MRS HIGGINS RUNS OUT. HIGGINS,	LEFT	ALONE, RATTLES HIS CASH IN HIS POCKET; CHUCKLES; AND
ROCK I SD(224)	THROUGH THE MASKED DOOR. SIR ARTHUR,	LEFT	ALONE, RESTS HIS WEARIED HEAD ON THE TABLE BETWEEN HIS
JITT I SD(13)	THE DOOR VERY SOFTLY BEHIND HER). THE GENTLEMAN,	LEFT	ALONE, RISES AND GOES TO THE TABLE, WHERE HE TAKES UP
MTH2 SD(87)	CONRAD ACCOMPANYING HIM). SAVVY AND HASLAM,	LEFT	ALONE, SEIZE EACH OTHER IN AN ECSTASY OF AMUSEMENT, AND
AUGS SD(279)	HIM THROUGH THE DOOR. THE MOMENT THE LADY IS	LEFT	ALONE, SHE SNATCHES A SHEET OF OFFICIAL PAPER FROM THE
BULL IV SD(161)	(HE GOES OUT THROUGH THE GARDEN DOOR). NORA,	LEFT	ALONE, STRUGGLES WILDLY TO SAVE HERSELF FROM BREAKING
ARMS I SD(7)	GOODNIGHT. (SHE GOES OUT, SWAGGERING). RAINA,	LEFT	ALONE, TAKES OFF HER FUR CLOAK AND THROWS IT ON THE
CAPT I (229)	YOU THE STORY, MR RANKIN. WHEN MILES DIED, HE	LEFT	AN ESTATE IN ONE OF THE WEST INDIAN ISLANDS. IT WAS IN
SHAK SD(139)	SPAR. SHAKES KNOCKS SHAV DOWN WITH A STRAIGHT	LEFT	AND BEGINS COUNTING HIM OUT, STOOPING OVER HIM AND
MRS IV SD(235)	THIS TABLE HAS KNEE HOLES AND CHAIRS RIGHT AND	LEFT	AND IS VERY UNTIDY, THE CLERK'S DESK, CLOSED AND TIDY,
JOAN 5,SD(111)	(HE LAUGHS). KING CHARLES, WITH BLUEBEARD ON HIS	LEFT	AND LA HIRE ON HIS RIGHT, COMES FROM THE VESTRY, WHERE
APPL I SD(212)	AND SIT DOWN AT THE ENDS OF THE WRITING TABLES,	LEFT	AND RIGHT OF THE PRIME MINISTER RESPECTIVELY. /PROTEUS/
2TRU II SD(79)	PRIVATE, FOLLOWED BY AUBREY, TO THE COLONEL'S	LEFT	AND RIGHT RESPECTIVELY. /MEEK/ THATS ALL RIGHT, SIR.
PPP SD(197)	GAZOGENE, WITH FITZ AND ADOLPHUS SQUATTING ON HER	LEFT	AND RIGHT RESPECTIVELY. FITZ POURS WHISKY INTO THE
PYGM III SD(244)	TO THE WINDOWS, YOU HAVE THE FIREPLACE ON YOUR	LEFT	AND THE DOOR IN THE RIGHT-HAND WALL CLOSE TO THE CORNER
FANY I (280)	AND HAD THE OPTION; BUT THE DEAR BOY HAD NO MONEY	LEFT	AND WOULDNT GIVE YOU AWAY BY TELLING HIS NAME; AND
LION II SD(127)	TRYING TO LOOK DEATH IN THE FACE. ON HER	LEFT	ANDROCLES CONSOLES HIMSELF BY NURSING A CAT. FERROVIUS
MRS III (224)	(RISING) CERTAINLY, IF THE RESTORATION HAS	LEFT	ANY TO SHEW. /REV. S./ (MOONING HOSPITABLY AT THEM) I
PYGM PREFACE(200)	OXONIAN WAY. I DARESAY HIS PAPERS, IF HE HAS	LEFT	ANY, INCLUDE SOME SATIRES THAT MAY BE PUBLISHED WITHOUT
GENV IV (89)	SECRETARY/ NONE, YOUR HONOR. THE PARTIES ON YOUR	LEFT	ARE ALL PLAINTIFFS. ON YOUR RIGHT, SIR ORPHEUS
GENV PREFACE(22)	OURSELVES INTO THE BELIEF THAT THE SWINGS TO THE	LEFT	ARE DEMOCRATIC AND THOSE TO THE RIGHT IMPERIAL. THEY
ROCK I SD(193)	ON WALPOLE'S RIGHT. IN THE OPPOSITE WALL ON HIS	LEFT	ARE THE SPACIOUS WINDOWS. EVERYTHING IS ON AN IMPOSING
BULL PREFACE(53)	ABOUT, ONE OF THEM HAVING ONE OF THE BONES OF HIS	LEFT	ARM BROKEN NEAR THE WRIST-- SIMPLE FRACTURE OF THE THIN
CAND I (85)	HIM. WHY DO YOU TUCK YOUR UMBRELLA UNDER YOUR	LEFT	ARM INSTEAD OF CARRYING IT IN YOUR HAND LIKE ANYONE
HART II SD(106)	APPEARS IN THE PORT DOORWAY. SHE THROWS HER	LEFT	ARM ROUND HECTOR'S NECK; DRAWS HIM WITH HER TO THE BACK
KING I (174)	AM COMING. (SHE RISES AND GOES TO CHARLES, WHOSE	LEFT	ARM SHE TAKES). MAY I COME AGAIN, MR NEWTON? /NEWTON/
NEVR IV (302)	IT WITH HER LEFT HAND, AND PUTS HER RIGHT ON HIS	LEFT	ARM TO SUPPORT HERSELF). /VALENTINE/ TAKE CARE. I'M
GENV III SD(69)	SEIZES HER WRIST. THE SECRETARY SECURES HER	LEFT	ARM. /THE WIDOW/ (STRUGGLING) LET ME GO. HOW DARE YOU
CYMB FORWORD(135)	ASKS COX WHETHER HE HAS A STRAWBERRY MARK ON HIS	LEFT	ARM. " NO" SAYS COX. " THEN YOU ARE MY LONG LOST
CLEO PRO2 (99)	LO THERE! (HE POINTS TO THE BANDAGE ON HIS	LEFT	ARM) AND WOULD HAVE GONE THROUGH MY NECK HAD I NOT
2TRU III SD(94)	SHOULDER, AN EASEL, WHICH HE HAS TUCKED UNDER HIS	LEFT	ARM, AND A SUN UMBRELLA, A SUBSTANTIAL AFFAIR OF FAWN
PHIL II (127)	DAN: YOURE AWAKE. /SYLVIA/ (TAKING CRAVEN'S	LEFT	ARM, AND HUGGING IT AFFECTIONATELY) DEAR OLD RIP VAN
APPL I SD(197)	LETTERS. PAMPHILIUS, MIDDLE AGED, SHEWS HIS	LEFT	AS HE LEANS BACK IN HIS CHAIR AT THE OTHER TABLE WITH A
MTH3 SD(91)	AS A PAIR OF FOLDING DOORS. THE DOOR IS ON YOUR	LEFT	AS YOU FACE THE SCREEN; AND THERE IS A ROW OF THICK
6CAL SD(93)	OF EDWARD III, KING OF ENGLAND, IS ON YOUR	LEFT	AS YOU FACE THE WALLS. THE PAVILION OF HIS CONSORT
KING I SD(161)	GARDEN LEVEL. THE DIVISION OF THE WINDOW TO THE	LEFT	AS YOU LOOK OUT THROUGH IT IS A GLASS DOOR LEADING TO
SHAK PREFACE(135)	ONE OF THEM IS SPEAKING OR TUMBLING AND THE REST	LEFT	ASIDE. THESE, THOUGH IN FULL VIEW, ARE INVISIBLE, AS
SUPR III (110)	THAN A FRACTION OF THE IMMENSE ENERGY SHE HAS	LEFT	AT HIS DISPOSAL BY SAVING HIM THE EXHAUSTING LABOR OF
MIS. PREFACE(92)	AS IT SEEMS, THESE UNHAPPY LUNATICS ARE	LEFT	AT LARGE, UNREBUKED, EVEN ADMIRED AND REVERED, WHILST
POSN PREFACE(411)	SHOULD BE KEPT IN RESPONSIBLE HANDS AND NOT	LEFT	AT THE DISPOSAL OF EVERY BIGOT IGNORANT ENOUGH TO BE
DOCT III SD(131)	LARGE WINDOW THE OUTER DOOR IS IN THE WALL ON THE	LEFT	AT THE NEAR END. THE DOOR LEADING TO THE INNER ROOMS IS
LION PREFACE(82)	CALLED THE ACTS OF THE APOSTLES, WHICH WE	LEFT	AT THE POINT WHERE THE STONING OF STEPHEN WAS FOLLOWED
HART III (141)	REMEMBERED AND NOT WANTED. /CAPTAIN SHOTOVER/ YOU	LEFT	BECAUSE YOU DID NOT WANT US. WAS THERE NO HEARTBREAK IN
BUOY III (36)	FROM PANAMA TO ATTEND THIS MEETING. YOU MUST HAVE	LEFT	BEFORE IT WAS DECIDED ON. /SHE/ HOW CLEVER OF YOU TO
APPL PREFACE(183)	PRIVATE CAPITALISM IS BREAKING DOWN OR GETTING	LEFT	BEHIND IN ALL DIRECTIONS. IF ALL OUR SOCIALISM AND
METH PREFACE(R90)	THE RELIGIOUS PICTURES OF THE FIFTEENTH CENTURY	LEFT	BEHIND THE FIRST ATTEMPTS OF THE EARLY CHRISTIANS AT
MRS PREFACE(173)	BUT BOTH OBSERVATION AND KNOWLEDGE ARE	LEFT	BEHIND WHEN JOURNALISTS GO TO THE THEATRE. ONCE IN
DOCT II (121)	STILL PRESENTABLE, YOU SEE) WITH ALL MY TROUBLES	LEFT	BEHIND, JUST LIKE OLD TIMES. /RIDGEON/ BUT WHAT HAS
JOAN 1 (68)	FROM THE ENGLISH SOLDIERS. THREE OF THEM WERE	LEFT	BEHIND, WOUNDED. I CAME TO KNOW THESE THREE POOR
GENV PREFACE(4)	LOSSES WERE NOT GIVEN AT ALL, THE IMPRESSION	LEFT	BEING THAT THE ALLIES HAD KILLED OR TAKEN PRISONER TENS
DEST (165)	AND THROWING HERSELF IN TEARS ON THE CHAIR	LEFT	BESIDE THE TABLE BY THE LIEUTENANT) I BRAVE! HOW
JOAN 5,SD(111)	JOAN SHRINKS AWAY BEHIND THE PILLAR. DUNOIS IS	LEFT	BETWEEN CHARLES AND LA HIRE. /DUNOIS/ WELL, YOUR
JITT I (24)	BEFORE THIS CRAZY TIRED OLD CLOCK (HE TAPS HIS	LEFT	BREAST) RUNS DOWN AND STOPS TICKING FOR GOOD AND ALL.
DOCT II (121)	BORROWED A PENNY; AND I NEVER WILL. IVE NOTHING	LEFT	BUT MY FRIENDS; AND I WONT SELL THEM. IF NONE OF YOU
MILL II (173)	THAT I MUST GO ON CUTTING UNTIL THERE WAS NOTHING	LEFT	BUT PERFECTLY HEALTHY TISSUE. AS THERE IS NO SUCH THING
LADY PREFACE(224)	WITH A CHUCKLE, IS GONE; AND YOU HAVE NOTHING	LEFT	BUT THAT MOST DEPRESSING OF ALL THINGS: A VICTIM. NOW
MRS PREFACE(162)	THE ILLUSTRATIVE EXAMPLES OMITTED, AND NOTHING	LEFT	BUT THE ARGUMENT FROM POLITICAL PRINCIPLE AGAINST THE
BARB III (319)	RATHER A DIFFICULT CASE, STEPHEN. HARDLY ANYTHING	LEFT	BUT THE STAGE, IS THERE? (STEPHEN MAKES AN IMPATIENT
BUOY II (21)	FAILURES AS LADIES AND GENTLEMEN. /HE/ NOTHING	LEFT	BUT TO LIVE ON FATHER'S MONEY, EH? /SHE/ YES:
CLEO II (125)	THAT THERE IS A ROMAN ARMY OF OCCUPATION HERE,	LEFT	BY AULUS GABINIUS WHEN HE SET UP YOUR TOY KING FOR
BULL PREFACE(31)	AND COMPARING THEIR FATE WITH THAT OF GORDON	LEFT	BY GLADSTONE TO PERISH ON THE SPEARS OF HEATHEN
2TRU PREFACE(6)	INCOME, IF THE CAPITAL VALUE OF THE PROPERTY	LEFT	BY HIM BE CORRECTLY STATED, MUST HAVE BEEN OVER FOUR
JOAN PREFACE(24)	1917. IT ENDS IN MERE SCURRILITY. THE IMPRESSION	LEFT	BY IT IS THAT THE PLAYWRIGHT, HAVING BEGUN BY AN
METH PREFACE(R53)	BY THE FACT THAT IT WAS A SECRET REFUGE	LEFT	BY LAW AND PUBLIC SUPERSTITION FOR THE AMATEUR OF
SUPR PREFACE(R19)	A SOCIETY IN WHICH THE SERIOUS BUSINESS OF SEX IS	LEFT	BY MEN TO WOMEN, AS THE SERIOUS BUSINESS OF NUTRITION
PYGM II (239)	AND LIVE IDLE ON IT. THERE WONT BE A PENNY OF IT	LEFT	BY MONDAY: I'LL HAVE TO GO TO WORK SAME AS IF I'D NEVER
NEVR II SD(236)	WEARS A LIGHT OVERCOAT. HE STOPS AT THE CHAIR	LEFT	BY M'COMAS IN THE MIDDLE OF THE TERRACE, AND STEADIES

POSN	(453)	LAST EVENING ABOUT A CERTAIN ARTICLE THAT WAS	LEFT	BY MY MOTHER, AND THAT I CONSIDERED I HAD A RIGHT TO
ARMS II	(30)	PET GIRL. (HE KISSES HER. SHE GOES TO THE CHAIR	LEFT	BY NICOLA FOR SERGIUS, AND SITS DOWN). /CATHERINE/ AND
KING I	(189)	HIM OUT OF THE WINDOW. /CHARLES/ HE COULD HAVE	LEFT	BY THE DOOR, MR NEWTON. /NEWTON/ HE COULD; BUT HE WOULD
JITT PREFACE	(5)	ONLY BROUGHT BY THE WINDS ALONG THE DANUBE, BUT	LEFT	BY THE TURKS WHEN SOBIESKI DROVE THEM BACK FROM THE
CLEO IV	(175)	OF LISTENING TO US. (HE SITS DOWN ON THE BENCH	LEFT	BY THE TWO SLAVES). /RUFIO/ (SITTING DOWN ON HIS
KING PREFACE	(157)	OF WOMEN IN 1928, THE ENORMOUS HIATUS	LEFT	BY THEIR PREVIOUS DISENFRANCHISEMENT IS SUPPOSED TO
CAPT III SD	(290)	(HE GOES OUT QUICKLY). BRASSBOUND AND HIS MEN,	LEFT	BY THEMSELVES IN THE ROOM, FREE AND UNOBSERVED, GO
SUPR PREFACE	(R19)	TO WOMEN, AS THE SERIOUS BUSINESS OF NUTRITION IS	LEFT	BY WOMEN TO MEN, THAT THE MEN, TO PROTECT THEMSELVES
MTH5	(212)	I HAVE MADE UP MY MIND TO THE FACT THAT I HAVE	LEFT	CHILDHOOD BEHIND ME, IT COMES HOME TO ME IN LEAPS AND
2TRU PREFACE	(14)	TO MR CHESTERTON THE DISTRIBUTIST (OR EXTREME	LEFT	COMMUNIST) AND CATHOLIC (OR EQUALITARIAN
JOAN PREFACE	(48)	WOULD DO EQUALLY WELL FOR THE DUC D'ALENCON. BOTH	LEFT	DESCRIPTIONS OF JOAN SO SIMILAR THAT, AS A MAN ALWAYS
NEVR I SD	(208)	SURPRISING THAT YEARS OF SUCH REMONSTRANCE HAVE	LEFT	DOLLY HOPELESSLY SPOILED. GLORIA, WHO IS HARDLY PAST
LADY PREFACE	(208)	EXCRESCENTIAL, ATTACHED TO HIS FACE FROM THE	LEFT	EAR TO THE POINT OF HIS CHIN WAS A MONSTROUS GOITRE,
SUPR IV	(151)	HECTOR AND VIOLET, AND ALMOST BAWLS INTO HECTOR'S	LEFT	EAR) YOUVE PICKED UP THAT HABIT OF THE BRITISH
MILL I	(158)	PENNILESS, THE PRIMA DONNA WAS DEAF IN THE	LEFT	EAR, INTO WHICH YOU HAD SUNG WITH ALL YOUR FORCE. I HAD
CLEO PRO1	(93)	THE OLD CAESAR AND THE CHILD QUEEN BEFORE HE	LEFT	EGYPT AND BATTLED HIS WAY BACK TO ROME TO BE SLAIN
NEVR II	(241)	(HE GLIDES SWIFTLY ROUND THE TABLE TO PHIL'S	LEFT	ELBOW, ON HIS WAY HE WHISPERS TO THE YOUNG WAITER)
GETT	(306)	LAW? /SYKES/ (RISING AND COMING TO COLLINS'S	LEFT	ELBOW) I PUT IT TO YOU AS A SENSIBLE MAN: IS IT ANY
CLEO IV	(185)	RETURNS TO THE COLONNADE: RUFIO FOLLOWING AT HIS	LEFT	ELBOW, AND APOLLODORUS AT THE OTHER SIDE). /CLEOPATRA/
NEVR I	(216)	WITH AN OLD FRIEND WHOM I HAVE NOT SEEN SINCE I	LEFT	ENGLAND EIGHTEEN YEARS AGO. WILL YOU EXCUSE ME?
JITT III	(60)	TO YOU THAT IT IS RATHER HARD ON ME TO BE	LEFT	ENTIRELY TO MYSELF WHEN THINGS ARE SO SERIOUS WITH US?
SIM PRO,3,	(32)	THERES NOTHING OF THE MAN YOU MET THIS MORNING	LEFT	EXCEPT HIS SKIN AND BONES, YOU MAY REGARD ME AS TO ALL
MIS.	(168)	FROM A MAN WITH A YELLOW WIG AND A CAST IN HIS	LEFT	EYE, IVE NEVER SET EYES ON HIM FROM THAT DAY TO THIS.
POSN	(439)	TO HURT. THEYVE DRAWN A DROP OR TWO UNDER YOUR	LEFT	EYE. /STRAPPER/ LUCKY FOR YOU TO HAVE AN EYE LEFT IN
MTH2 SD	(37)	THE CLERICAL GENTLEMAN SITS A LITTLE TO YOUR	LEFT	FACING THE DOOR WITH HIS RIGHT PROFILE PRESENTED TO
GLIM	(171)	AND I'M VERY VERY WISE; FOR I'M OLD AND HAVE	LEFT	FAR BEHIND ME THE WORLD, THE FLESH, AND THE DEVIL. YOU
UNPL PREFACE	(R24)	OLD, THE BALD ATTEMPT THEY MAKE AT IT WILL BE	LEFT	FAR BEHIND, AND THAT THE CUSTOMARY BRIEF AND UNREADABLE
ANNA	(289)	MINISTER HAS SHOT HIMSELF, AND THAT THE EXTREME	LEFT	FELLOW HAS SHOT ALL THE OTHERS. /STRAMMFEST/ YES: THATS
O'FL	(220)	AND KEPT A PRISONER IN EASE AND COMFORT, AND ME	LEFT	FIGHTING IN PERIL OF MY LIFE. /TERESA/ (TAKING IT) DO
DOCT I	(83)	OLD SIR PATRICK CULLEN HAS BEEN HERE ALREADY AND	LEFT	FIRST CONGRATULATIONS-- HADNT TIME TO COME UP ON HIS
DEVL I	(27)	AWAY AGAIN AND SHAKES HIS FIST AFTER THEM. HIS	LEFT	FIST, ALSO CLENCHED, HANGS DOWN. ESSIE SEIZES IT AND
CLEO I SD	(106)	AND HALTS, LOST IN CONTEMPLATION, OPPOSITE THE	LEFT	FLANK OF THE SPHINX, WHOSE BOSOM, WITH ITS BURDEN, IS
FANY EPILOG	(328)	THE VEILS-- (APPEALING TO VAUGHAN, WHO IS ON HIS	LEFT	FLANK, WITH GUNN BETWEEN THEM) COULD THEY, SIR?
GLIM	(187)	THE CHEST WITH HIS DAGGER. SQUARCIO PUTS BACK HIS	LEFT	FOOT TO BRACE HIMSELF AGAINST THE SHOCK. THE DAGGER
MTH4 I	(155)	THE HILLS ARE CAPPED WITH GRANITE. THEY ALL	LEFT	FOR ENGLAND NEXT DAY; AND NO IRISHMAN EVER AGAIN
POSN	(462)	LIKE YOU! GO BACK TO THE FRECKLED MAYPOLE YOU	LEFT	FOR ME: YOUVE BEEN FRETTING FOR HER LONG ENOUGH. /THE
BULL IV	(147)	THE CAR WENT OVER THE POOR PIG DHERE WAS LITTLE	LEFT	FOR ME OR ANYWAN ELSE TO GO OVER EXCEPT WID A KNIFE AN
LADY PREFACE	(228)	HIS EVIDENCE SO FEATLY THAT THERE IS NOTHING	LEFT	FOR ME TO DO BUT TO PLEAD THAT THE SECOND IS SOUNDER
BULL PREFACE	(67)	OF RUBBISH HEAPS; AND ENOUGH SCRAPS OF WALL WERE	LEFT	FOR THE BRITISH ARMY, WHICH NEEDED RECRUITS, TO COVER
KING PREFACE	(153)	JACOBITE HILAIRE BELLOC, THAT THERE IS NO NOVELTY	LEFT	FOR THE CHRONICLER TO PUT ON THE STAGE. AS TO THE
GLIM	(176)	HANDLE YOUR BONES: SO THAT THERE WILL BE NOTHING	LEFT	FOR THE HANGMAN TO BREAK. NOW WHAT DO YOU SAY?
BARB III	(335)	IF IT IS NOT DONE. AFTER THAT, THERE WAS NOTHING	LEFT	FOR THE SEVENTH TO SAY. SO HE WROTE UP, SIMPLY,
BARB II	(310)	ME. (SHE COUNTS HER MONEY). I HAVE JUST ENOUGH	LEFT	FOR TWO TEAS AT LOCKHARTS, A ROWTON DOSS FOR YOU, AND
POSN	(465)	WRONG IN THE WORLD THERE WOULDNT BE ANYTHING	LEFT	FOR US TO DO, WOULD THERE? /ELDER DANIELS/ BE OF GOOD
JOAN 1	(65)	/POULENGEY/ (TURNING) IS THERE ANYTHING ELSE	LEFT	FOR US TO THINK? /ROBERT/ (GOING TO HIM) LOOK HERE,
SIM II	(77)	MAYA HAS GONE TO KISS SOMEBODY. THERE IS NOTHING	LEFT	FOR YOU TO GLORIFY BUT SUICIDE. /VASHTI/ (RISING) I
KING I	(220)	(THEY GO OUT). /MRS BASHAM/ THERE IS NO ONE	LEFT	FOR YOU TO TAKE IN, MR KNELLER, MR NEWTON MUST TAKE ME
CLEO PRO2,SD	(97)	LAUGHING. HE IS SOMEWHAT BATTLESTAINED; AND HIS	LEFT	FOREARM, BANDAGED, COMES THROUGH A TORN SLEEVE. IN HIS
LION I	(118)	ON HIM THREATENINGLY. THE CENTURION HOLDS UP HIS	LEFT	FOREFINGER IN ADMONITION). NOW REMEMBER THAT YOURE A
MILL IV	(206)	ABOUT SCIENCE AND EVERYTHING ABOUT MONEY. HE	LEFT	FOUR HUNDRED POUNDS AND A WIDOW: THE GOOD WOMAN WHO HAD
SUPR III	(120)	THAT IF THE CHAIN WERE BROKEN AND THE PRISONERS	LEFT	FREE TO CHOOSE, THE WHOLE SOCIAL FABRIC WOULD FLY
MIS. PREFACE	(100)	LIKE ADULTS, WILL FIND THEIR LEVEL IF THEY ARE	LEFT	FREE TO FIND IT, AND NOT RESTRICTED TO WHAT ADULTS
PPP SD	(196)	FASHION, WITH THE RIGHT HALF OF THE COAT AND THE	LEFT	HALF OF THE TROUSERS YELLOW AND THE OTHER HALVES BLACK.
ARMS II	(34)	TO TWIRL HIS MOUSTACHE MISCHIEVOUSLY, WITH HIS	LEFT	HAND AKIMBO ON HIS HIP. FINALLY, STRIKING THE GROUND
DEST	(178)	LOOKS AT HER AGAIN; PASSES THE PACKET INTO HIS	LEFT	HAND AND PUTS IT BEHIND HIS BACK, RAISING HIS RIGHT TO
PHIL II	(116)	DR PARAMORE'S. OH, DEAR! (SHE CATCHES CRAVEN'S	LEFT	HAND AND STOOPS TO KISS IT, HIS RIGHT HAND BEING STILL
BARB II	(278)	OH, YOU GREAT BRUTE-- (HE INSTANTLY SWINGS HIS	LEFT	HAND BACK AGAINST HER FACE. SHE SCREAMS AND REELS BACK
PHIL I	(72)	WRITTEN IT. (HE COMES BESIDE GRACE, AND PUTS HIS	LEFT	HAND CARESSINGLY ROUND HER NECK). YOU SEE, DEARIE, SHE
BULL I SD	(73)	THE RIGHT HAND CORNER. BETWEEN THIS DOOR AND THE	LEFT	HAND CORNER IS A HATSTAND AND A TABLE CONSISTING OF
ARMS I SD	(3)	STANDS AGAINST A LITTLE WALL CUTTING OFF THE	LEFT	HAND CORNER OF THE ROOM, IS A PAINTED WOODEN SHRINE,
SUPR IV SD	(141)	LEFT IS THE VILLA, ACCESSIBLE BY STEPS FROM THE	LEFT	HAND CORNER OF THE GARDEN. RETURNING FROM THE PLATFORM
MRS I SD	(181)	LOOKING UP THE HILL, THE COTTAGE IS SEEN IN THE	LEFT	HAND CORNER OF THE GARDEN, WITH ITS THATCHED ROOF AND
PHIL III SD	(132)	THE DOOR IS SEEN IN THE OPPOSITE WALL NEAR THE	LEFT	HAND CORNER. ANOTHER DOOR, A LIGHT NOISELESS ONE
DEVL III	(76)	HIS HAND TO HELP HIM, AND RUNS TO ANDERSON, WHOSE	LEFT	HAND HE SHAKES HEARTILY, THE RIGHT BEING OCCUPIED BY
MIS.	(167)	PISTOL IN FUMBLING FOR THE PHOTOGRAPHS WITH HIS	LEFT	HAND IN HIS BREAST POCKET) LET ME HOLD THE GUN FOR YOU.
MIS.	(163)	DAUGHTER, TIRED OF GOOD MANNERS. (SLIPPING HER	LEFT	HAND INTO HIS RIGHT) COME, HANDSOME YOUNG MAN, AND PLAY
CURE	(232)	MY STRENGTH HAS BEEN DEVELOPED BY PLAYING	LEFT	HAND OCTAVE PASSAGES-- LIKE THIS. (SHE BEGINS PLAYING
MTH5	(241)	WANTS ME. WHAT IS THE MATTER? (SHE COMES TO THE	LEFT	HAND OF THE FEMALE FIGURE, NOT SEEING THE BODY OF
CLEO III SD	(146)	OFF FTATATEETA, WHO IS SENT REELING AWAY ON THE	LEFT	HAND OF THE SENTINEL. /CENTURION/ (AN UNATTRACTIVE MAN
PPP	(206)	DONE IT! WHEW! /MAGNESIA/ (KNEELING AT THE	LEFT	HAND OF THE STATUE) FOR EVER AND FOR EVER, ADOLPHUS.
PHIL III	(135)	TO HIS FORMER SEAT. AS HE PASSES, SHE PUTS HER	LEFT	HAND ON HIS ARM AND SAYS) BE GOOD TO ME, PERCY: I NEED
CLEO III SD	(144)	TO THE LIGHTHOUSE WITH STRAINED ATTENTION, HIS	LEFT	HAND SHADING HIS EYES. THE PILUM IS A STOUT WOODEN
CURE	(232)	IF A STRANGER COMES IN. (WITH A TOUCH OF HER	LEFT	HAND SHE SENDS HIM REELING. HE APPEALS TO HER
LIED	(202)	(HE TRIES TO RISE). /SHE/ (REACHING OUT HER	LEFT	HAND TO SEIZE HIS COAT TAIL, AND PULLING HIM DOWN
BULL I SD	(73)	AND OTHER DRAUGHTSMAN'S ACCESSORIES ON IT. IN THE	LEFT	HAND WALL IS THE FIREPLACE, AND THE DOOR OF AN INNER
APPL INTR,SD	(252)	THIS TIME OF DEFLATION, SHE SITS DOWN AT HIS	LEFT	HAND WITH AN AIR OF SUFFERING PATIENCE, AND LISTENS IN
BULL IV SD	(145)	BACKGAMMON ACROSS ITS CORNER WITH HIM, ON HIS	LEFT	HAND. AUNT JUDY, A LITTLE FURTHER BACK, SITS FACING THE
JOAN 2,SD	(73)	WITH A NEW TOY. HE COMES TO THE ARCHBISHOP'S	LEFT	HAND. BLUEBEARD AND LA HIRE RETIRE TOWARDS THE
MTH1 I SD	(3)	DEAD BODY. HE HAS NOT NOTICED THE SERPENT ON HIS	LEFT	HAND. HE TURNS HIS FACE TO HIS RIGHT AND CALLS
HART I SD	(43)	THE DRAUGHTSMAN'S CHAIR HAS THE WINDOW ON ITS	LEFT	HAND. ON THE FLOOR AT THE END OF THE TABLE, ON HIS
CLEO II SD	(137)	COMES DOWN THE HALL VERY HAUGHTILY TO CAESAR'S	LEFT	HAND. /CAESAR/ WELL, POTHINUS? /POTHINUS/ I HAVE
CLEO II SD	(119)	TO POTHINUS, WHO PLACES HIMSELF AT HIS	LEFT	HAND. /POTHINUS/ THE KING OF EGYPT HAS A WORD TO SPEAK.
DEST	(153)	MAP, BUT CRAMMING HIMSELF MECHANICALLY WITH HIS	LEFT	HAND) DONT TALK. I'M BUSY. /GIUSEPPE/ (WITH PERFECT
AUGS	(280)	DOOR, BUT FIRST PRESSING THE BELL BUTTON WITH HIS	LEFT	HAND) GOODBYE, GOODBYE, SO SORRY TO LOSE YOU. KIND OF
SUPR IV	(153)	THE GARDEN TO THE LAWN AND RUNNING TO HECTOR'S	LEFT	HAND) I HOPE YOULL SHAKE HANDS WITH ME BEFORE YOU GO,
HART II	(105)	DO YOU. /HECTOR/ (ADVANCING TO LADY UTTERWORD'S	LEFT	HAND) LET US ALL GO OUT INTO THE NIGHT AND LEAVE
JOAN EPILOG	(162)	CURTAINS ON THE OTHER SIDE, AND COMING TO JOAN'S	LEFT	HAND) MADAM: MY CONGRATULATIONS ON YOUR REHABILITATION.
CLEO IV	(181)	SEAT, WHICH IS AT THE END OF THE TABLE, TO RA'S	LEFT	HAND) WHAT HAS BECOME OF MY LEATHERN CUSHION?
CLEO V	(196)	REMAINS TO BE DONE BEFORE I GO? /RUFIO/ (AT HIS	LEFT	HAND) YOU HAVE NOT YET APPOINTED A ROMAN GOVERNOR FOR
BULL IV	(153)	SURELY THE TEXT REFERS TO OUR RIGHT AND	LEFT	HANDS. I AM SOMEWHAT SURPRISED TO HEAR A MEMBER OF YOUR
NEVR IV	(302)	OVER HER FACE AGAIN. SHE COVERS IT WITH HER	LEFT	HAND, AND PUTS HER RIGHT ON HIS LEFT ARM TO SUPPORT
CLEO II SD	(140)	AND GREAVES. THEY COME DOWN TO CAESAR, SHE TO HIS	LEFT	HAND, BRITANNUS TO HIS RIGHT. /CLEOPATRA/ I AM GOING TO
CAND I	(96)	COUCH, AND GIVES IT TO HER. SHE TAKES IT IN HER	LEFT	HAND, HAVING THE BAG IN HER RIGHT). NOW HANG MY CLOAK
ARMS III	(56)	TO SNATCH IT; BUT HE SHIFTS IT QUICKLY TO HIS	LEFT	HAND, OUT OF HER REACH). SEE! A TWENTY LEVA BILL!
CAPT II SD	(246)	PROMPTLY SHELTERS HIMSELF ON THE CAPTAIN'S	LEFT	HAND, THE OTHERS RETREATING TO THE OPPOSITE SIDE AS
2TRU II	(71)	VERY DELIBERATELY, AND GOING BEHIND HIM TO HIS	LEFT	HAND, WHICH SHE PICKS UP AND FONDLES AS SHE SERMONIZES,
JITT I SD	(9)	TO THE ENTRANCE HALL; AND THE SHORT WALL ON THE	LEFT	HAS AN OPEN DOOR CLOSE TO THE CORNER THROUGH WHICH A
SUPR III	(98)	EXCELLENT SON OF THE MORNING, I AM YOURS. I HAVE	LEFT	HEAVEN FOR EVER. /THE DEVIL/ (AGAIN TOUCHING THE
SUPR III	(122)	JUAN/ THEN MAY I ASK, COMMANDER, WHY YOU HAVE	LEFT	HEAVEN TO COME HERE AND WALLOW, AS YOU EXPRESS IT, IN
MIS. SD	(157)	EMPIRE HAS NO RELIGION. LINA COMES IN. SHE HAS	LEFT	HER CAP IN HYPATIA'S ROOM, BUT HAS MADE NO OTHER
WIDO I	(19)	CHAP. THANKS AWFULLY. (BY THIS TIME BLANCHE HAS	LEFT	HER FATHER, AND IS STROLLING OFF TOWARDS THE RIVERSIDE.
INCA	(244)	TO THE DOOR, ERMYNTRUDE, NOTICING THAT SHE HAS	LEFT	HER HAT AND GLOVES ON THE TABLE, RUNS AFTER HER WITH
JOAN PREFACE	(16)	AND THAT ST TERESA'S HORMONES HAD GONE ASTRAY AND	LEFT	HER INCURABLY HYPERPITUITARY OR HYPERADRENAL OR
MIS.	(168)	WITHOUT CONSCIENCE! WITHOUT EVEN MEMORY! YOU	LEFT	HER TO HER SHAME-- /TARLETON/ (THROWING THE BROOCH ON
MILL IV	(207)	LABORATORY, THE CHANGE TO A CHEAPER LODGING, HAD	LEFT	HER WITHOUT A PENNY, THOUGH NO DOCTOR AND NO LAWYER
DOCT II	(121)	TO TIP THE CHAMBERMAID OF THE ROOM HIS WIFE	LEFT	HER WRAPS IN, AND FOR THE CLOAKROOM. HE SAID HE ONLY
CLEO III	(162)	EGYPTIANS' HEADS OFF. HOW WILL YOU LIKE BEING	LEFT	HERE WITH THE CHANCE OF BEING CAPTURED BY THAT LITTLE

DOCT III (141)	TO THE STEWARD OF A LINER. HE CLEARED OUT AND	LEFT	HER; AND SHE THOUGHT, POOR GIRL, THAT IT WAS THE LAW
JOAN PREFACE(19)	AWAY FROM HOME. BUT THE TASTE FOR IT NEVER	LEFT	HER, AND WAS FUNDAMENTAL IN DETERMINING HER CAREER. IF
HART PREFACE(8)	HE HAD DRAWN A LUCKY NUMBER OR AN UNLUCKY ONE, IT	LEFT	HIM A FAIRLY STRONG INTEREST IN ENCOURAGING HIS HOPES
ARMS I (21)	/RAINA/ (LOOKING AT THE OTTOMAN) HE'S GONE! I	LEFT	HIM HERE. /CATHERINE/ HERE! THEN HE MUST HAVE CLIMBED
BARB PREFACE(238)	BLOW AT THE RESPONSIBLE PARTIES. HIS POVERTY HAS	LEFT	HIM IGNORANT ENOUGH TO BE DUPED BY THE PRETENCE THAT
WIDO II (25)	/SARTORIUS/ WHERE IS HE, THEN? /LICKCHEESE/ I	LEFT	HIM IN THE HALL, WITH HIS FRIEND, SIR. I SHOULD THINK
MRS III (228)	AND TAKING ADVANTAGE OF THE ADDITIONAL ROOM	LEFT	HIM ON THE SEAT TO SPREAD HIMSELF COMFORTABLY, AS IF A
LION PREFACE(47)	OF HIS BODY AND BLOOD, SO MANY OF HIS DISCIPLES	LEFT	HIM THAT THEIR NUMBER WAS REDUCED TO TWELVE. MANY
JITT III (67)	RELATIONS WITH HIM HAVE COOLLY WALKED OFF AND	LEFT	HIM TO DIE? A PET DOG WOULD NOT HAVE DONE SUCH A
JITT II (39)	/EDITH/ NO, NO, NO. SHE DID NOT SAVE HIM. SHE	LEFT	HIM UNDER THE STIGMA OF HAVING DIED IN THE ARMS OF SOME
CYMB FORWORD(135)	CARE A RAP WHETHER SHE IS ALIVE OR DEAD. I HAVE	LEFT	HIM WITH HER IN THE BOX OF PUPPETS THAT ARE DONE WITH.
MRS PREFACE(174)	KINDLY THEATRE CRITIC, THAT THE PERFORMANCE	LEFT	HIM " WONDERING WHAT USEFUL PURPOSE THE PLAY WAS
MTH5 (216)	SHE HAS GROWN UP LIKE THIS ANCIENT HERE, AND HAS	LEFT	HIM. IF YOU CHOOSE ME, WE SHALL HAVE ONLY A YEAR'S
LION PREFACE(33)	WHOLE MARK LEAVES THE MODERN READER WHERE MATTHEW	LEFT	HIM. LUKE. LUKE THE LITERARY ARTIST. WHEN WE COME TO
JITT III (67)	WENT BACK INTO THE DARK. LEAVE HER THERE, AS SHE	LEFT	HIM. /AGNES/ (SHAKING HER HEAD) I CANT IMAGINE HOW
KING PREFACE(155)	WITS AND NOT BY THE LITTLE REAL POWER THEY HAD	LEFT	HIM, UNFORTUNATELY THE VULGARITY OF HIS REPUTATION AS A
LADY PREFACE(225)	DISABLED THE HERO OF THE PLAY, BECAUSE MR HARRIS	LEFT	HIMSELF OUT OF HIS PLAY, WHEREAS HE PERVADES HIS BOOK,
SUPR IV SD(142)	HAD ALLOWED HIM VERY LITTLE OF HIS OWN WAY AND	LEFT	HIS AFFECTIONS HUNGRY AND BAFFLED. AT THE FIRST WORD
MIS. (164)	HOUSE. (HE TURNS TOWARDS THE INNER DOOR, HAVING	LEFT	HIS CAP IN THE BEDROOM). /HYPATIA/ (STANDING IN HIS
DEVL I SD(16)	AND ANDERSON, WHO IS THE FIRST TO ENTER, HAS	LEFT	HIS CLOAK AT HOME. HE IS ACCOMPANIED BY LAWYER HAWKINS.
DEVL I (7)	ONE SON A FOOL, AND THE OTHER A LOST SINNER THATS	LEFT	HIS HOME TO LIVE WITH SMUGGLERS AND GYPSIES AND
BULL III (143)	GREAT A HURRY, SIR, STARTED TO RUN HOME, SIR, AND	LEFT	HIS PIG BEHIND HIM. /BROADBENT/ (EAGERLY) LEFT THE
LION PREFACE(30)	ONE BELIEVING IN THAT SECOND COMING, AND IN FACT	LEFT	HIS STORY UNFINISHED TO BE ENDED BY IT. HE MUST HAVE
FOUN (212)	WALKING STICK ON THE FLOOR) MY LORD, HE HAS	LEFT	HIS WALKING STICK BEHIND. HE WILL RETURN FOR IT. LET US
GETT PREFACE(188)	A FIEND IN HUMAN FORM, WHILST NELSON, WHO OPENLY	LEFT	HIS WIFE AND FORMED A MENAGE A TROIS WITH SIR WILLIAM
MTH5 (232)	A LITTLE OF WHAT HE SWALLOWED; BUT THE PROCESS	LEFT	HORRIBLE RESIDUES WHICH HE HAD NO MEANS OF GETTING RID
BULL IV (149)	KILT! IT'S A MERCY DHERES TWO BONES OF YOU	LEFT	HOULDIN TOGETHER. HOW DIJJESCAPE AT ALL AT ALL? WELL,
SUPR III (106)	AND MINISTERS ANSWERING QUESTIONS. WHEN I	LEFT	I CHALKED UP ON THE DOOR THE OLD NURSERY SAYING " ASK
2TRU III (106)	AS I LIVE. I'D HAVE KILLED THE ONLY ONE I HAD	LEFT	IF SHE HADNT RUN AWAY FROM ME. I WAS TOLD TO SACRIFICE
ROCK PREFACE(154)	RUN THE POWER TO EXTERMINATE IS TOO GRAVE TO BE	LEFT	IN ANY HANDS BUT THOSE OF A THOROUGHLY COMMUNIST
DEVL III (65)	UP BY A PIOUS MOTHER TO HAVE ANY SENSE OR MANHOOD	LEFT	IN HIM. /BURGOYNE/ (SPRINGING UP AND SPEAKING TO THE
CLEO II SD(130)	THEM MOVING WITHOUT MUCH CEREMONY. THE KING IS	LEFT	IN HIS CHAIR, PITEOUS, OBSTINATE, WITH TWITCHING FACE
MIS. PREFACE(59)	BY AN INCOMPETENT AND ILL-MANNERED PERSON THAN	LEFT	IN IGNORANCE, READING, WRITING, AND ENOUGH ARITHMETIC
BARB II SD(285)	HIS MUG FROM HER, AS THERE IS STILL SOME MILK	LEFT	IN IT. /RUMMY/ THERE AINT ANY CRUMBS. THIS AINT A TIME
APPL PREFACE(174)	HAS A FARTHING OF PROFIT FOR PLUTOCRACY STILL	LEFT	IN IT, OR THAT CAN BE MADE TO YIELD A FARTHING FOR IT
ANNA (290)	THEY DISPLEASED THEIR BETTERS. AND NOW WHAT IS	LEFT	IN LIFE FOR ME? (HE RELAPSES INTO HIS CHAIR
CAPT III (298)	PEOPLE IF I HAD THAT MAD LITTLE BIT OF SELF	LEFT	IN ME? THATS MY SECRET. /BRASSBOUND/ THEN THROW AWAY
GENV I (47)	HIS EYES BLAZING) I STILL HAVE LIFE ENOUGH	LEFT	IN ME TO DENY IT. KARL MARX-- ANTICHRIST-- SAID THAT
BULL IV (179)	TO BRING IDLERS TO A COUNTRY WHICH WORKERS HAVE	LEFT	IN MILLIONS BECAUSE IT IS A HUNGRY LAND, A NAKED LAND,
JOAN 1 (65)	A BIT OF A MIRACLE. ANYHOW, SHE IS THE LAST CARD	LEFT	IN OUR HAND. BETTER PLAY HER THAN THROW UP THE GAME. (
KING I (187)	THE KING IS. THIS IS MY HOUSE; AND I DEMAND TO BE	LEFT	IN PEACE IN IT. I AM ENGAGED IN RESEARCHES OF THE MOST
APPL II (267)	YOU ASK ME. /MAGNUS/ THEN I, THE ONLY ENGLISHMAN	LEFT	IN POLITICS, APPARENTLY, AM TO BE REDUCED TO COMPLETE
APPL I (233)	TODAY THERE IS NOT A SINGLE ARISTOCRAT	LEFT	IN POLITICS, NOT A SINGLE MEMBER OF THE PROFESSIONS,
APPL I (224)	THEM; AND NOW THAT YOU ARE THE ONLY KING	LEFT	IN THE CIVILIZED HALF OF EUROPE NATURE SEEMS TO HAVE
JOAN 6,SD(147)	DAYLIGHT. ONLY THE BISHOP AND THE INQUISITOR ARE	LEFT	IN THE COURT. /CAUCHON/ (TURNING TO GO) WE MUST STOP
JITT II (36)	HE WAS. /EDITH/ HE TOLD EVERYONE ELSE. WE WERE	LEFT	IN THE DARK. /JITTA/ NO, NO. NO ONE KNEW IT EXCEPT
DOCT PREFACE(21)	VETERANS HAVE MOSTLY RETIRED OR DIED. WE ARE	LEFT	IN THE HANDS OF THE GENERATIONS WHICH, HAVING HEARD OF
SIM II (58)	PRA ABSTAINS. /SIR CHARLES/ NOT A BLESSED SHIP	LEFT	IN THE HARBOR! YOUR MESSAGE CERTAINLY DID THE TRICK.
SIM PRO,1, (25)	I THREW THE CAT BACK AGAIN. " SOMEBODY MUST BE	LEFT	IN THE OFFICE" I SAYS. " I AM INDISPENSABLE" I SAYS."
BULL IV SD(151)	NORA, AUNT JUDY, KEEGAN, LARRY, AND CORNELIUS ARE	LEFT	IN THE PARLOR. LARRY GOES TO THE THRESHOLD AND WATCHES
ROCK PREFACE(188)	MAKE AN END OF YOU WHILST THERE IS STILL SOME LAW	LEFT	IN THE WORLD. /JESUS/ LAW IS BLIND WITHOUT COUNSEL. THE
METH PREFACE(R76)	THE EDUCATION OF CHILDREN CANNOT SAFELY BE	LEFT	IN THEIR HANDS. IF DWINDLING SECTS LIKE THE CHURCH OF
BASH PREFACE(91)	DRAMATICALLY ILLUSTRATED BIBLES AND SHAKESPEARS	LEFT	IN THEIR WAY, WITH THE ILLUSTRATED PASSAGES PRINTED
APPL I (233)	REMEMBER, IS A SWEATED TRADE, THE ONLY ONE NOW	LEFT	IN THIS COUNTRY. MY CIVIL LIST LEAVES ME A POOR MAN
POSN (439)	LEFT EYE. /STRAPPER/ LUCKY FOR YOU TO HAVE AN EYE	LEFT	IN YOUR HEAD. /BLANCO/ (WIPING THE BLOOD OFF)-- WHEN
CAND III (133)	LIE-- IF YOU HAVE A SPARK OF HUMAN FEELING	LEFT	IN YOU-- WILL YOU TELL ME WHAT HAS HAPPENED DURING MY
BULL I (85)	HOW MANY OF ALL THOSE MILLIONS THAT HAVE	LEFT	IRELAND HAVE EVER COME BACK OR WANTED TO COME BACK?
NEVR I SD(199)	IN THE CORNER TO THE RIGHT. IN THE WALL ON YOUR	LEFT	IS A BROAD WINDOW LOOKING ON THE SEA. BENEATH IT A
HART III SD(129)	AGAINST HIM ON HIS RIGHT HAND. ON HIS	LEFT	IS A DECK CHAIR. BEHIND THEM IN THE GLOOM, HESIONE IS
OVER SD(171)	IS AN UNUSED FIREPLACE. OPPOSITE IT ON THE LADY'S	LEFT	IS A DOOR. THE GENTLEMAN IS ON THE LADY'S RIGHT. THE
KING I SD(161)	FACES AWAY FROM THE WINDOW. ON THE READER'S	LEFT	IS A HANDSOME ARMCHAIR, APPARENTLY FOR THE
JOAN EPIL,SD(152)	UP TO MAKE A READING DESK. BESIDE THE BED ON HIS	LEFT	IS A LITTLE TABLE WITH A PICTURE OF THE VIRGIN, LIGHTED
JOAN 6 (151)	WOULD NOT BURN, MY LORD; BUT EVERYTHING THAT WAS	LEFT	IS AT THE BOTTOM OF THE RIVER. YOU HAVE HEARD THE LAST
2TRU III SD(81)	WITH THE INSCRIPTION SN PAULS. THE GROTTO TO THE	LEFT	IS MUCH WIDER. IT CONTAINS A BENCH LONG ENOUGH TO
APPL II SD(266)	SEATED, THEIR ORDER FROM THE KING'S RIGHT TO HIS	LEFT	IS NICOBAR, CRASSUS, BOANERGES, AMANDA, THE KING,
PRES SD(131)	IN THE WAR OFFICE, OPENING LETTERS. ON HIS	LEFT	IS THE FIREPLACE, WITH A FIRE BURNING. ON HIS RIGHT,
SUPR I SD(4)	PROFILE AS WELL AS THE BLINDS WILL PERMIT. ON HIS	LEFT	IS THE INNER WALL, WITH A STATELY BOOKCASE, AND THE
SUPR IV SD(141)	REMOTEST DISTANCE, THEY BECOME MOUNTAINS. ON OUR	LEFT	IS THE VILLA, ACCESSIBLE BY STEPS FROM THE LEFT HAND
DOCT I SD(82)	PERSON FACING THE FIREPLACE, IS THE DOOR. ON ITS	LEFT	IS THE WRITING-TABLE AT WHICH REDPENNY SITS. IT IS AN
SUPR III (99)	COULD HAVE INDUCED ME TO STAY THERE. I SIMPLY	LEFT	IT AND ORGANIZED THIS PLACE. /THE STATUE/ I DONT WONDER
MIS. (110)	HALLO! WHERES YOUR LUGGAGE? /BENTLEY/ I	LEFT	IT AT THE STATION. IVE WALKED UP FROM HASLEMERE. (HE
2TRU I (28)	IN THE GLASS). HERES THE THERMOMETER: THEYVE	LEFT	IT FOR THE DOCTOR TO SEE INSTEAD OF SHAKING IT DOWN. IF
MTH1 I (8)	SERPENT/ I SHEWED THE LITTLE CASE TO THE SUN, AND	LEFT	IT IN ITS WARMTH, AND IT BURST; AND A LITTLE SNAKE CAME
AUGS (278)	THE WAITER FROM THE HOTEL BROUGHT THIS PAPER. YOU	LEFT	IT ON THE COFFEE-ROOM BREAKFAST-TABLE THIS MORNING.
FANY PROLOG (261)	TO BILLY BURJOYCE-- THE PRODUCER, YOU KNOW-- AND	LEFT	IT TO HIM TO SELECT THE COMPANY AND SO ON. BUT I SHOULD
HART PREFACE(18)	DRUDGE AT DESTRUCTION, EXACTLY AS THEY WOULD HAVE	LEFT	IT TO TAKE THEIR TURN AT THE PUMPS IN A SINKING SHIP.
2TRU III (90)	MY LOVE. WHEN I LEFT THAT NURSING HOME, SHE	LEFT	IT TOO. I WAS DISCHARGED AS CURED ON THE THIRD OF THE
GLIM (178)	THAT WE ARE CRUEL. WHERE WOULD YOU BE IF WE	LEFT	IT UNDONE? OUTSIDE THE LIFE I LEAD ALL TO MYSELF-- THE
GENV IV (118)	YOU HAVE DRIVEN THEM ALL FROM YOUR COUNTRY AND	LEFT	IT WITH NO BETTER BRAINS THAN YOUR OWN. YOU HAVE
ARMS III (47)	IT MUST BE HANGING IN THE BLUE CLOSET WHERE YOU	LEFT	IT. /PETKOFF/ MY DEAR CATHERINE, I TELL YOU IVE LOOKED
3PLA PREFACE(R22)	WHY IT LEFT ITS BLACK MARK ON MY BONES AS IT HAS	LEFT	ITS BLACK MARK ON THE CHARACTER OF THE NATION; WHY I
3PLA PREFACE(R22)	WHY THE THEATRE WAS INSUFFERABLE TO ME; WHY IT	LEFT	ITS BLACK MARK ON MY BONES AS IT HAS LEFT ITS BLACK
MTH4 II (188)	WHEN THE MAHOMETAN REFORMATION TOOK PLACE, IT	LEFT	ITS FOLLOWERS WITH THE ENORMOUS ADVANTAGE OF HAVING THE
HART I (77)	THAT SUCH AN AMAZING EXPERIENCE IS COMMON. IT HAS	LEFT	ITS MARK ON ME. I BELIEVE THAT IS WHY I HAVE NEVER BEEN
CYMB FORWORD(138)	PRESENT THE ORIGINAL WORD-FOR-WORD AS SHAKESPEAR	LEFT	IT, AND THE MEANS TO DO JUSTICE TO THE MASQUE. BUT IF
METH PREFACE(R23)	HE DOES NOT PICK UP THE ACCOMPLISHMENT WHERE YOU	LEFT	IT, ANY MORE THAN HE IS BORN SIX FEET HIGH WITH A BEARD
CAND I (92)	/BURGESS/ THE OUSE AINT WORTH LIVIN IN SINCE YOU	LEFT	IT, CANDY, I WISH YOUD COME ROUND AND GIVE THE GURL A
CLEO V (196)	HE WAS SETTLING THE JEWISH QUESTION WHEN I	LEFT	. A FLOURISH OF TRUMPETS FROM THE NORTH, AND COMMOTION
BARB II (300)	QUID SIVED AGEN THE FROST; AN AWVE A PAHND OF IT	LEFT	. A MITE O MAWN LAST WEEK ED WORDS WITH THE JUDY E'S
JITT II SD(33)	THE SOFA, WHERE SHE SEATS HERSELF ON THE WIDOW'S	LEFT	. ALL THESE MOVEMENTS ARE RIDICULOUS; YET THE MOURNING
APPL I (239)	NEXT TIME HE CAME. HE CANCELLED HIS MEETING AND	LEFT	. AND THATS HOW ENGLAND IS GOVERNED BY YOURS TRULY,
PHIL III SD(132)	WALL TOWARDS THE BACK. THE FIREPLACE IS ON THE	LEFT	. AT THE NEARER CORNER OF IT A COUCH IS PLACED AT RIGHT
BARB I (265)	CUSINS ALSO BRINGS HIS CHAIR FORWARD ON HER	LEFT	. BARBARA AND STEPHEN RESUME THEIR SEATS. LOMAX GIVES
NEVR IV (289)	NEAR THE DOOR, WITH M'COMAS BESIDE HER ON HER	LEFT	. BOHUN PLACES HIMSELF MAGISTERIALLY IN THE CENTRE OF
6CAL (99)	I TREMBLE; AND MY TEETH CHATTER: THE FEW I HAVE	LEFT	. BUT YOU GENTLEMEN THAT SEE OUR MISERABLE PLIGHT, I
SIM II (83)	PRESENTLY; AND I HAVE STILL SOME CURIOSITY	LEFT	. DID YOU EVER REALLY CARE FOR ME? I KNOW I BEGAN AS A
2TRU II SD(51)	THE HUT IS ON THE RIGHT AND THE PAVILION ON THE	LEFT	. FROM THE NEIGHBORHOOD OF THE HUT A DATE PALM THROWS A
2TRU I SD(28)	DOES. SHE COMES TO THE BEDSIDE ON THE INVALID'S	LEFT	. HE COMES TO THE OTHER SIDE OF THE BED AND LOOKS
PYGM V (276)	THIS MORNING, ISNT IT? (SHE SITS DOWN ON HIS	LEFT	. HE SITS BESIDE HER). /HIGGINS/ DONT YOU DARE TRY THIS
MRS I SD(189)	A CHAIR AND PLANT IT BESIDE MRS WARREN, ON HER	LEFT	. HE THROWS THE OTHER ON THE GRASS AND SITS DOWN,
HART I SD(74)	HUSHABYE). ELLIE, HECTOR, AND LADY UTTERWORD ARE	LEFT	. HECTOR IS CLOSE TO LADY UTTERWORD. THEY LOOK AT
CLEO III SD(155)	WHICH TOWERS GIGANTIC TO THE CLOUDS ON HIS	LEFT	. HIS HELMET, FULL OF DATES, IS BETWEEN HIS KNEES; AND
SIM II (79)	PANIC. STOCK EXCHANGE CLOSES: ONLY TWO MEMBERS	LEFT	. HOUSE OF COMMONS DECIMATED: ONLY FOURTEEN MEMBERS TO
ROCK I (203)	I WANTED FOR YOU UNTIL I HAVE NO INDIVIDUALITY	LEFT	. IF I TAKE UP A BOOK YOU WANT ME TO READ SOMETHING
MILL PREFACE(126)	ANY PURE-BRED MAORIES OR SOUTH SEA ISLANDERS	LEFT	. IN AFRICA THE INTELLIGENT PINK NATIVE IS A FUSIONIST
POSN SD(435)	HIS RIGHT, AND A BAR TO PUT PRISONERS TO ON HIS	LEFT	. IN THE WELL IN THE MIDDLE IS A TABLE WITH BENCHES
WIDO I SD(3)	IS SEEN ON THE RIGHT. THE HOTEL IS ON THE	LEFT	. IT HAS A WOODEN ANNEXE WITH AN ENTRANCE MARKED TABLE

JOAN 6,SD(122)	IS TO THE LEFT. THERE ARE ARCHED DOORS RIGHT AND	LEFT	. IT IS A FINE SUNSHINY MAY MORNING. WARWICK COMES IN
ARMS III (55)	HAS BEEN FIGHTING TOO: AND HE HAS PLENTY OF HEART	LEFT	. (RAINA, AT THE DOOR, DRAWS HERSELF UP HAUGHTILY AND
PYGM II (239)	MAN ANOTHER MINUTE, WE SHALL HAVE NO CONVICTIONS	LEFT	. (TO DOOLITTLE) FIVE POUNDS I THINK YOU SAID.
DOCT IV SD(161)	THE DYING ARTIST. B.B. THEN RETURNS TO DUBEDAT'S	LEFT	. JENNIFER SITS. WALPOLE SITS DOWN ON THE EDGE OF THE
SUPR III (138)	BY HECTOR HOLDING HER RIGHT HAND AND RAMSDEN HER	LEFT	. MENDOZA GOES TO HIS PRESIDENTIAL BLOCK AND SEATS
LIED SD(187)	THE GRAND PIANO ALONG THE OPPOSITE WALL TO HIS	LEFT	. NEAR THE FIREPLACE A SMALL ORNAMENTAL TABLE HAS ON IT
BARB I SD(249)	AND A WINDOW WITH A WINDOW SEAT DIRECTLY ON HIS	LEFT	. NEAR THE WINDOW IS AN ARMCHAIR. LADY BRITOMART IS A
JITT III SD(52)	CORNER, AND IS CONSEQUENTLY BEFORE THEM ON THEIR	LEFT	. ON THEIR RIGHT BETWEEN THE WINDOW AND THE STUDY DOOR,
SUPR III SD(74)	RIGHT, OPPOSITE THREE MEN IN SCARLET TIES ON HIS	LEFT	. ONE OF THESE THREE IS THE FRENCHMAN. OF THE REMAINING
CAPT I (235)	AS FAR FROM THE HOUSE AS POSSIBLE, ON RANKIN'S	LEFT	. RANKIN RISES TO RECEIVE HIS GUEST), AN OLIVE
BARB III (343)	HAVE BROKEN IN YOUR HAND: FORGIVENESS IS STILL	LEFT	. /CUSINS/ NO: FORGIVENESS IS A BEGGAR'S REFUGE. I AM
PHIL II SD(104)	ELSE FOR IT, HE BOLTS INTO THE RECESS ON IBSEN'S	LEFT	. /CUTHBERTSON/ GOOD MORNING, MISS CRAVEN. (THEY SHAKE
ROCK II SD(280)	BETWEEN THE TABLE AND THE WINDOW TO ALOYSIA'S	LEFT	. /DAVID/ LOOK HERE, ALOYSIA. WHAT ARE YOU UP TO HERE?
ROCK I SD(222)	FLAVIA TO HER FATHER'S RIGHT, DAVID TO HIS	LEFT	. /FLAVIA/ PAPA: WEVE BEEN TO A MEETING OF THE
GETT SD(306)	PUZZLED, COMES FORWARD AFFABLY TO HOTCHKISS'S	LEFT	. /HOTCHKISS/ (RISING, IMPRESSED BY THE ALDERMANIC
SIM I SD(44)	ON SIR CHARLES'S LEFT, AND PRA ON LADY FARWATERS'	LEFT	. /LADY FARWATERS/ YOU HAVE MADE THE ACQUAINTANCE OF
MTH2 SD(55)	STEALTHILY JOINED BY HASLAM, WHO SITS DOWN ON HER	LEFT	. /LUBIN/ (SEATING HIMSELF IN BURGE'S CHAIR WITH
BASH II,1, (111)	/CASHEL/ FLUSH ON THE BOKO NAPPED YOUR FOOTMAN'S	LEFT	. /LYDIA/ I DO NOT UNDERSTAND. /CASHEL/ TRUE. PARDON
HART II SD(107)	UP THE REAR, AND WAITS NEAR THE DOOR, ON MANGAN'S	LEFT	. /MRS HUSHABYE/ WHAT HAS HAPPENED? /MAZZINI/ YOUR
MTH4 II SD(175)	AT HIS AUDACITY. HE IS ON HER RIGHT: SHE ON HIS	LEFT	. /NAPOLEON/ (IMPRESSIVELY) I AM THE MAN OF DESTINY.
MTH5 SD(235)	WITH GRATIFIED VANITY. THE WOMAN IS ON THE MAN'S	LEFT	. /PYGMALION/ (RUBBING HIS HANDS WITH THE PURRING
GENV I (38)	THERE MUST BE STILL AT LEAST FIFTEEN HUNDRED	LEFT	. /SHE/ BUT IS IT A MEMBER OF THE LEAGUE? /THE WIDOW/
MIS. (159)	QUIETLY IN THE CHAIR LORD SUMMERHAYS HAS JUST	LEFT	. /TARLETON/ GOOD. WELL, DO YOU LIKE ME? DONT
MILL IV (206)	WHO LIVE LIKE A MOUSE. THERE MUST BE SOME OF IT	LEFT	. /THE DOCTOR/ NOT A PENNY. NOT A PIASTRE. ALLAH--
2TRU I SD(35)	BEDSIDE TABLE, THE NURSE GOING TO THE PATIENT'S	LEFT	. /THE ELDERLY LADY/ WHAT IS IT, DARLING? ARE YOU
2TRU I SD(49)	HER BREATHLESS, AND COMES TO THE BURGLAR, ON HIS	LEFT	. /THE PATIENT/ HERE I AM, POPS. ONE KISS; AND THEN--
POSN SD(450)	TO THE SHERIFF'S RIGHT; HANNAH AND LOTTIE TO HIS	LEFT	. /THE SHERIFF/ SILENCE THERE. THE JURY WILL TAKE THEIR
BARB III (315)	SITS ON THE SETTEE: HE SITS BESIDE HER, ON HER	LEFT	. SHE COMES TO THE POINT BEFORE HE HAS TIME TO
PYGM II (233)	GLAD TO SEE YOU HAVE SOME SPARK OF FAMILY FEELING	LEFT	. SHE'S UPSTAIRS. TAKE HER AWAY AT ONCE. /DOOLITTLE/ (
CAPT III SD(283)	AT BRASSBOUND AS SHE STOPS AT THE TABLE ON HIS	LEFT	. SIR HOWARD RISES PUNCTILIOUSLY WHEN KEARNEY RISES AND
MIS. SD(172)	HER WITH THE PISTOL: SHE IS ALWAYS TOO FAR TO HIS	LEFT	. TARLETON, BEHIND HIM, GRIPS HIS WRIST AND DRAGS HIS
CAPT II (265)	SIR HOWARD HALLAM: YOU HAVE ONE CHANCE	LEFT	. THE CADI OF KINTAFI STANDS SUPERIOR TO THE SHEIKH AS
GENV I SD(29)	FACING IT AT THE OPPOSITE SIDE ON THE TYPIST'S	LEFT	. THE DOOR IS BESIDE THE PRESS. THE WINDOW IS BEHIND
POSN PREFACE(377)	FROM THE MAJORITY, AND AT THAT THE MATTER WAS	LEFT	. THE DOORS WERE OPENED; THE AUDIENCE TROOPED IN; I WAS
LION II SD(143)	CAGE, WITH A HEAVY PORTCULLIS GRATING, IS ON HIS	LEFT	. THE EMPEROR GIVES A SIGNAL. A GONG SOUNDS. ANDROCLES
MTH4 II SD(182)	WHILST THE ENVOY'S WIFE HURRIES EFFUSIVELY TO HIS	LEFT	. THE ENVOY MEANWHILE PASSES ALONG BEHIND THE COLUMNS
CLEO I (116)	OF ALL THE QUEEN'S WOMEN, THESE THREE ALONE ARE	LEFT	. THE REST ARE FLED. (THEY BEGIN TO DECK CLEOPATRA,
CAPT III SD(282)	FORM A LITTLE GROUP TOGETHER ON THE CAPTAIN'S	LEFT	. THE REST WAIT UNINTELLIGENTLY ON PROVIDENCE IN A ROW
JOAN 4,SD(94)	IS AN UNOCCUPIED LEATHER STOOL ON THE NOBLEMAN'S	LEFT	. THE TABLE IS ON HIS RIGHT. /THE NOBLEMAN/ NOW THIS IS
JOAN 6,SD(122)	ARE TO THE RIGHT. THE PRISONER'S STOOL IS TO THE	LEFT	. THERE ARE ARCHED DOORS RIGHT AND LEFT. IT IS A FINE
2TRU II (76)	AT WATERCOLORS. AND THERE IS NOT A SINGLE MAROON	LEFT	. THERE SHOULD BE FIFTEEN. /AUBREY/ OH, I CAN CLEAR
GETT SD(259)	WINDOWS AND AN OPEN DOOR NEAR THE CORNER TO THE	LEFT	. THROUGH THIS DOOR WE HAVE A GLIMPSE OF THE GARDEN,
SIM II (72)	THE FIELD: THE ONE SHALL BE TAKEN AND THE OTHER	LEFT	. TWO WOMEN SHALL BE GRINDING AT THE MILL. THE ONE
CLEO II (129)	CAESAR! THEY SAW IT FROM THE SHIP HE HAD JUST	LEFT	. WE HAVE GIVEN YOU A FULL AND SWEET MEASURE OF
SIM II (72)	AT THE MILL. THE ONE SHALL BE TAKEN AND THE OTHER	LEFT	." /MRS HYERING/ BUT WHICH? THATS WHAT I WANT TO KNOW.
KING I SD(161)	THREE TO THE RIGHT OF THE WINDOW AND THREE TO THE	LEFT	(AS YOU LOOK OUT). BETWEEN THEM A TABLE BELONGING TO
JOAN 2,SD(83)	GATHERS THE ROBE FROM HER; AND GOES OUT. SHE IS	LEFT	KNEELING DIRECTLY IN THE DUCHESS'S WAY. /THE DUCHESS/ (
NEVR IV SD(293)	MIDDLE OF THE COMPANY, THE HARLEQUIN DOWN ON HIS	LEFT	KNEE, AND THE COLUMBINE STANDING ON HIS RIGHT KNEE,
PYGM V (268)	/HIGGINS/ FRIGHTENED HER! NONSENSE! SHE WAS	LEFT	LAST NIGHT, AS USUAL, TO TURN OUT THE LIGHTS AND ALL
FOUN SD(209)	HIS PRIVATE ROOM, NEAR THE FIREPLACE. DOOR ON THE	LEFT	LEADING TO THE PUBLIC STAIRCASE. MERCER, AN ELDERLY
METH PREFACE(R88)	SO THAT FROM THAT MOMENT IT LOST ITS HOLD, AND	LEFT	LITERATE CHRISTENDOM FAITHLESS. MY OWN IRISH
MIS. PREFACE(85)	OF NORMAL INCIDENTS OF MARRIAGE. THE PARENT IS	LEFT	LONELY AND THE CHILD IS NOT. WOE TO THE OLD IF THEY
GETT (315)	BOTHER THE MOTHER. /REGINALD/ AND IS SHE TO BE	LEFT	LONELY-- /LESBIA/ LONELY! WITH HER CHILD. THE POOR
CAND III (130)	MORELL) WHERE ARE ALL THE OTHERS? /MORELL/ THEY	LEFT	LONG BEFORE I COULD GET AWAY: I THOUGHT I SHOULD NEVER
DOCT I (109)	MATTER? TUBERCULOSIS? /MRS DUBEDAT/ YES. HIS	LEFT	LUNG-- /RIDGEON/ YES: YOU NEEDNT TELL ME ABOUT THAT.
GETT PREFACE(250)	INDULGENCES AND THE LIKE; AND SO THE REFORMATION	LEFT	MARRIAGE WHERE IT WAS: A CURIOUS MIXTURE OF COMMERCIAL
GETT PREFACE(210)	HERSELF. IT IS THE COMPARATIVELY WEEDY WEAKLING,	LEFT	MATELESS BY POLYGYNY, WHO OBJECTS. THUS, IT WAS NOT THE
BUOY 1 (14)	YOUR BROTHERS, BECAUSE THE WAR TAXATION HAS	LEFT	ME BARELY ENOUGH TO PAY MY OWN WAY. I CAN DO NOTHING
GENV PREFACE(15)	CHURCH IN IRELAND. MY RELIGIOUS EDUCATION	LEFT	ME CONVINCED THAT I WAS ENTITLED TO CALL MYSELF A
FABL PREFACE(95)	ENGAGING SMILE AND WAS A MOST ATTRACTIVE MAN) AND	LEFT	ME ENCOURAGED IN MY IGNORANCE BY MY OBSERVATION THAT
PYGM IV (264)	IN DESPERATION) WHAT AM I FIT FOR? WHAT HAVE YOU	LEFT	ME FIT FOR? WHERE AM I TO GO? WHAT AM I TO DO? WHATS
GLIM (183)	IS A FOOL, AFTER ALL. /GIULIA/ NO, SIGNOR: HE HAS	LEFT	ME HERE TO PREVENT YOU FROM ESCAPING. /FERRUCCIO/ THERE
BARB III (318)	YOU MEANT IT SERIOUSLY. BUT I FIND NOW THAT YOU	LEFT	ME IN THE DARK AS TO MATTERS WHICH YOU SHOULD HAVE
BASH PREFACE(87)	LAW OF THAT TIME (NOW HAPPILY SUPERSEDED)	LEFT	ME ONLY A WEEK TO WRITE IT IN. BLANK VERSE IS SO
BASH III (123)	TWELVEMONTHS OF CONTINUOUS TEARS, TEARS THAT HAVE	LEFT	ME PREMATURELY AGED; FOR I AM YOUNGER FAR THAN I
BULL IV (154)	HAVE RARELY PRODUCED IN A CHRISTIAN, AND	LEFT	ME SITTING THERE BY HIS BEDSIDE WITH THE MYSTERY OF
MTH2 (72)	TO HELP US THROUGH THIS AWFUL CRISIS WHICH HAS	LEFT	ME TEN YEARS OLDER THAN MY PROPER AGE! CAN YOU TELL ME
JOAN 2 (74)	FAMILY STOCK OF WISDOM FOR FIVE GENERATIONS, AND	LEFT	ME THE POOR FOOL I AM, BULLIED AND INSULTED BY ALL OF
JITT III (78)	YOU WONT. /LENKHEIM/ I MEAN WHAT I SAY. WHEN HE	LEFT	ME THIS BOOK OF HIS, HE DID SO ON THE UNDERSTANDING
FANY PROLOG (261)	HAVE EXPLAINED THAT TWO YEARS AGO MY DAUGHTER	LEFT	ME TO COMPLETE HER EDUCATION AT CAMBRIDGE. CAMBRIDGE
JOAN 5 (115)	GOD DID FOR US THROUGH THE MAID, AND HOW MUCH HE	LEFT	ME TO DO BY MY OWN WITS; AND I TELL YOU THAT YOUR
MILL IV (206)	IS NEVER BOTHERED. ON THAT AFTERNOON WHEN YOU	LEFT	ME TO EARN YOUR OWN LIVING I CALLED UPON THE MERCIFUL,
MILL I (149)	STRIKES ME AS IRRESISTIBLY FUNNY. YOU ACTUALLY	LEFT	ME TO SPEND THE NIGHT IN THE ARMS OF MISS
PYGM IV (265)	ME I'M NOT FIT TO SELL ANYTHING ELSE. I WISH YOUD	LEFT	ME WHERE YOU FOUND ME. /HIGGINS/ (SLINGING THE CORE OF
PYGM I (215)	TO THE BUS WHEN THE RAIN STOPPED. /FREDDY/ AND	LEFT	ME WITH A CAB ON MY HANDS! DAMNATION! /THE FLOWER
BULL PREFACE(71)	TO POINT OUT THAT MARX WAS NOT INFALLIBLE; BUT HE	LEFT	ME WITH A VERY STRONG DISPOSITION TO BACK THE ECONOMIC
FANY EPILOG (329)	I MUST GO BACK. THE WORLD HAS PASSED ME BY AND	LEFT	ME. ACCEPT THE APOLOGIES OF AN ELDERLY AND NO DOUBT
CYMB FORWORD(135)	AND AS I CANNOT CHANGE HIM FOR THE BETTER I HAVE	LEFT	MOST OF HIS PART UNTOUCHED. I MAKE NO APOLOGY FOR MY
FOUN (221)	HEART-- BRABAZON ENTERS. /BRABAZON/ EXCUSE ME: I	LEFT	MY STICK, I THINK-- /ANASTASIA/ (THROWING HERSELF INTO
DOCT I (97)	DEAR FELLOW, I DIDNT NEED ANY EXPLANATIONS. I'D	LEFT	MY WIFE IN THE CARRIAGE AT THE DOOR; AND I'D NO TIME TO
SIM PRO,3,SD(29)	PRIESTESS IN ROBES OF DUSKY YELLOW SILK ON HER	LEFT	NEAREST THE IMAGES. /THE Y.W./ YOU KNOW, TO ME THIS IS
JOAN 6 (140)	I SHOULD BE IN THE HANDS OF THE CHURCH, AND NOT	LEFT	NIGHT AND DAY WITH FOUR SOLDIERS OF THE EARL OF
JOAN 6 (130)	PRIDE THAT HAS LED HER INTO HER PRESENT PERIL HAS	LEFT	NO MARK ON HER COUNTENANCE. STRANGE AS IT MAY SEEM TO
JOAN 6 (130)	STRANGE AS IT MAY SEEM TO YOU, IT HAS EVEN	LEFT	NO MARK ON HER CHARACTER OUTSIDE THOSE SPECIAL MATTERS
FABL PREFACE(67)	KEPT THEM ALIVE FOR THIRTY YEARS OR SO, BUT	LEFT	NO SURPLUS FOR EDUCATION AND CULTURE: IN SHORT, FOR
INCA (252)	A NATIONAL GALLERY? HE IS A COMPOSER: NAPOLEON	LEFT	NO SYMPHONIES IN ST HELENA. SEND THE INCA TO ST HELENA,
GETT (267)	BENT ON MY BUCKLES. BULLETS PASSED THROUGH ME AND	LEFT	NO TRACE: THATS THE WORST OF MODERN BULLETS: IVE NEVER
2TRU III (110)	SCANDALIZED THEIR DULL OLD PRE-WAR ELDERS AND	LEFT	NOBODY BUT THEIR BRIGHT YOUNG SELVES A PENNY THE WORSE.
CYMB FORWORD(135)	ONE EXCEPTION THE CHARACTERS HAVE VANISHED AND	LEFT	NOTHING BUT DOLLS BEING MOVED ABOUT LIKE THE GLASS
ARMS II SD(29)	OF A STRANGE AND TERRIBLE HISTORY THAT HAS	LEFT	NOTHING BUT UNDYING REMORSE, BY WHICH CHILDE HAROLD
LION II (138)	YOU ARE FACING IS CERTAIN DEATH. YOU HAVE NOTHING	LEFT	NOW BUT YOUR FAITH IN THIS CRAZE OF YOURS: THIS
ARMS III SD(46)	AT THE SIDE OF THIS TABLE, WHICH STANDS TO THE	LEFT	OF ANYONE FACING THE WINDOW, BLUNTSCHLI IS HARD AT WORK
JOAN EPIL,SD(165)	AND THE INQUISITOR ARE NOW SEEN ON THE RIGHT AND	LEFT	OF CAUCHON. /JOAN/ MY SWORD SHALL CONQUER YET: THE
FABL PREFACE(74)	THE BIBLICAL CHANGE OF METAPHOR) NOTHING WOULD BE	LEFT	OF EITHER JESUS OR MOSES. AS I PUT IT, THE CONVERSION
ANNA (293)	A SITTING POSTURE; AND TAKE YOUR SEATS RIGHT AND	LEFT	OF HER. GO. THE TWO SOLDIERS MAKE A SUPREME EFFORT TO
MIS. SD(110)	HIS NOVEL. THERE ARE TWO WICKER CHAIRS RIGHT AND	LEFT	OF HIM. BENTLEY SUMMERHAYS, ONE OF THOSE SMALLISH,
2TRU III (88)	OF PRIVATE JUDGMENT. AND NOW-- NOW-- WHAT IS	LEFT	OF IT? THE ORBIT OF THE ELECTRON OBEYS NO LAW: IT
MRS II SD(198)	WALL OF THE COTTAGE, WITH THE PORCH DOOR TO THE	LEFT	OF IT. IN THE LEFT-HAND SIDE WALL IS THE DOOR LEADING
DOCT III (137)	WHOSE IT WAS. I'M SORRY TO SAY THIS IS ALL THATS	LEFT	OF IT. (HE HITCHES UP HIS SMOCK; PRODUCES A CARD FROM
MILL II (175)	HAVE AN OPERATION A WEEK UNTIL THERE WAS NOTHING	LEFT	OF ME OR OF MY BANK BALANCE. I SHALL NOT EXPECT YOU TO
DOCT III (148)	GAS WHICH MAKES THE ROOM UNHEALTHY. WHAT IS THERE	LEFT	OF MY WORK? THAT. LOOK AT IT. (RIDGEON RISES TO LOOK
MILL PREFACE(134)	AND RELIGIOUSLY. WE SHOULD BEGIN WELL TO THE	LEFT	OF RUSSIA, WHICH IS STILL ENCUMBERED WITH NINETEENTH
HART I (58)	A REPROACH TO MY FATHER. HE BOUGHT WHAT WAS	LEFT	OF THE BUSINESS-- THE BUILDINGS AND THE MACHINERY AND
DOCT V SD(171)	WITH DRAWINGS, STAND NEAR THE CORNERS RIGHT AND	LEFT	OF THE ENTRANCE. JENNIFER, BEAUTIFULLY DRESSED AND
LION PREFACE(48)	LEADERS OF MODERN THOUGHT, THERE WILL BE ANYTHING	LEFT	OF THE MISSION OF JESUS: WHETHER, IN SHORT, WE MAY NOT
MRS I SD(181)	AND PORCH, AND A LARGE LATTICED WINDOW TO THE	LEFT	OF THE PORCH. A PALING COMPLETELY SHUTS IN THE GARDEN,
BULL PREFACE(5)	PERSIA IS FURTHER OFF); BUT THERE IS LITTLE	LEFT	OF THE SUBJECTS THAT EXCITED HIM IN 1904 EXCEPT HOME

MRS II SD(198)	IS NO FIRE. TWO OF THE CHAIRS ARE SET RIGHT AND	LEFT	OF THE TABLE. THE COTTAGE DOOR OPENS, SHEWING A FINE
CAPT III SD(272)	A COUPLE OF CHEAP AMERICAN CHAIRS RIGHT AND	LEFT	OF THE TABLE, FACING THE SAME WAY AS THE PRESIDENTIAL
BUOY IV (52)	HAVE YOU MONEY ENOUGH? /JUNIUS/ I HAVE WHAT IS	LEFT	OF THE THOUSAND POUNDS MY FATHER STARTED ME WITH.
PYGM II SD(217)	ON THE OTHER SIDE OF THE CENTRAL DOOR, TO THE	LEFT	OF THE VISITOR, IS A CABINET OF SHALLOW DRAWERS. ON IT
KING I SD(161)	INTERIOR DOOR, WHICH IS IN THE SIDE WALL TO THE	LEFT	OF THE WINDOW (AGAIN AS YOU LOOK OUT THROUGH IT). /THE
ROCK II (262)	THEN, WHEN YOU HAVE GOT THROUGH WHAT IS	LEFT	OF YOUR BILL AND CARRIED IT, THE HOUSE OF LORDS WILL
DOCT III (148)	YOUVE BEEN TALKING, IVE BEEN DOING. WHAT IS THERE	LEFT	OF YOUR MORALIZING? ONLY A LITTLE CARBONIC ACID GAS
INCA PROLOG (234)	NOW FOR BOWING THE KNEE TO HIM. IS THERE NOTHING	LEFT	OF YOUR SETTLEMENT? FIFTY THOUSAND DOLLARS A YEAR IT
MILL I (143)	DONT STAND OVER ME LIKE THAT. SIT DOWN ON WHAT IS	LEFT	OF YOUR SHAM CHIPPENDALE. /SAGAMORE/ CERTAINLY (HE
METH PREFACE(R23)	LESSON YOU DO NOT BEGIN AT THE POINT AT WHICH YOU	LEFT	OFF; YOU RELAPSE APPARENTLY TO THE BEGINNING. FINALLY,
FABL IV (114)	HAD, UNDER THE INFLUENCE OF BRITISH COLONISTS,	LEFT	OFF EATING THEIR PRISONERS OF WAR. THE BRITISH
BARB III (311)	ATTIRED AND IN LOW SPIRITS. /LOMAX/ YOUVE	LEFT	OFF YOUR UNIFORM! BARBARA SAYS NOTHING; BUT AN
METH PREFACE(R30)	THE SON TO BEGIN MENTALLY WHERE THE FATHER	LEFT	OFF. THIS BELIEF IN HEREDITY LED NATURALLY TO THE
POSN PREFACE(430)	ASPECT OF THE QUESTION. HAD HE BEGUN WHERE HE	LEFT	OFF-- HAD HE AT THE OUTSET PUT DOWN HIS FOOT ON THE
SIM I SD(36)	THE YOUNGER AND MORE DELICATE, AND THE ONE ON HIS	LEFT	OLDER AND MORE POWERFULLY FRAMED. THE FOUR FIGURES GIVE
LION PREFACE(29)	GROUND THAT PRESENTLY NOT A STONE OF IT SHALL BE	LEFT	ON ANOTHER; REVILES THE HIGH PRIESTS AND ELDERS IN
ROCK II (264)	SEE MAN AS HE CAME FROM THE HAND OF GOD, WHO HAS	LEFT	ON EVERY FEATURE THE UNMISTAKEABLE STAMP OF THE GREAT
ROCK I (217)	HE DONT KNOW. WHERE COULD HE SELL IT IF IT WAS	LEFT	ON HIS HANDS? HE DONT KNOW. HE DONT KNOW NOTHING OF
ARMS II (24)	TO YOU EVER AGAIN? HOW LONG WOULD YOUR FATHER BE	LEFT	ON HIS LITTLE FARM? (SHE IMPATIENTLY THROWS AWAY THE
LADY PREFACE(234)	PARTS BIG ENOUGH TO HOLD THE OVERCHARGE WERE	LEFT	ON THE SHELF, AMPLY ACCOUNTS FOR THE EVIDENT FACT THAT
MRS PREFACE(167)	THE FASHIONABLE ENTERPRISES OF THE ONLY REALITIES	LEFT	ON THE STAGE; THAT IS, THE PERFORMERS IN THEIR OWN
HART I (45)	ATTRACTIVE LADY IS INVITED HERE. HER LUGGAGE IS	LEFT	ON THE STEPS FOR HOURS; AND SHE HERSELF IS DEPOSITED IN
SUPR PREFACE(R27)	I DO NOT KNOW WHETHER YOU HAVE ANY ILLUSIONS	LEFT	ON THE SUBJECT OF EDUCATION, PROGRESS, AND SO FORTH, I
MIS. PREFACE(50)	FOR ALL THE EFFECT THEIR LITERARY EXERCISES HAS	LEFT	ON THEM THEY MIGHT JUST AS WELL HAVE BEEN PUT ON THE
MRS IV (240)	YOU ARE WELCOME TO ANY ILLUSIONS YOU MAY HAVE	LEFT	ON THESE SUBJECTS: I HAVE NONE. IF WE THREE ARE TO
FOUN (209)	TO TAKE YOU BY SURPRISE. I SHALL LEAD OFF WITH MY	LEFT	ON YOUR RIGHT EYE. PUT THEM UP. /MERCER/ I AINT GOING
MILL IV (194)	AND DESERVES. /PATRICIA/ LOOK AT THE MARKS SHE'S	LEFT	ON YOU, MR BLENDERBLAND! YOU SHOULDNT HAVE PUT UP WITH
2TRU III SD(112)	ARE WISPS OF SHIFTING WHITE CLOUD; THERE IS	LEFT	ONLY FOG: IMPENETRABLE FOG; BUT THE INCORRIGIBLE
GETT PREFACE(240)	AS NO ROOM FEELS LIKE A PRISON IF THE DOOR IS	LEFT	OPEN, THE REMOVAL OF THE SENSE OF BONDAGE WOULD AT ONCE
KING I (192)	BREAD WE HAD TO EAT IN OUR CHILDHOOD, AND WHO	LEFT	OUR MOTHER WITHOUT FIREWOOD IN THE FREEZING WINTER?
MIS. PREFACE(15)	OF NOISE, RESTLESSNESS, AND INQUISITIVENESS ARE	LEFT	OUT OF ACCOUNT, CHILDREN CAN STAND WITH INDIFFERENCE
LADY PREFACE(225)	A BOOK ON SHAKESPEAR WITH THE SHAKESPEARIAN IRONY	LEFT	OUT OF ACCOUNT. I DO NOT SAY THAT THE MISSING CHAPTER
SUPR HANDBOK(207)	THE THINGS THAT OUR MORAL MONSTERS DO MAY BE	LEFT	OUT OF ACCOUNT WITH ST BARTHOLOMEW MASSACRES AND OTHER
SUPR PREFACE(R34)	A CHILD; BUT HE NEVER BECOMES A MAN, AND MIGHT BE	LEFT	OUT OF HIS OWN BIOGRAPHY ALTOGETHER BUT FOR HIS
LION PREFACE(53)	GOOD OR BAD, RIGHT OR WRONG, MUST PERFORCE BE	LEFT	OUT OF THE QUESTION IN HUMAN AFFAIRS UNTIL IT IS MADE
JOAN PREFACE(12)	IT WAS MORALLY NECESSARY THAT SEX SHOULD BE	LEFT	OUT OF THE QUESTION AS BETWEEN HER AND HER
ROCK I (209)	TRUTH THAT OUR FRIENDS THE SOCIALISTS HAVE	LEFT	OUT OF THEIR FANCY PICTURES OF A MASS SOCIETY IN WHICH
CLEO I (108)	OTHER PAW. (SHE SEATS HERSELF COMFORTABLY ON ITS	LEFT	PAW). IT IS VERY POWERFUL AND WILL PROTECT US; BUT (
GENV II SD(49)	TABLE WITH HIS BACK TO THE WINDOW PRESENTING HIS	LEFT	PROFILE TO ANYONE ENTERING FROM THE DOOR, WHICH IS IN
JOAN 1,SD(57)	IN CHAIR TO MATCH, THE CAPTAIN PRESENTS HIS	LEFT	PROFILE. THE STEWARD STANDS FACING HIM AT THE OTHER
FANY II SD(285)	THE WALL. ANYONE PLACED SO AS TO SEE MRS KNOX'S	LEFT	PROFILE, WILL HAVE THE DOOR ON THE RIGHT AND THE WINDOW
UNPL PREFACE(R23)	AS WELL OR BETTER THAN THE AUTHOR, WHILST HE IS	LEFT	QUITE IN THE DARK AS TO THE POLITICAL OR RELIGIOUS
SUPR I (18)	DO NOT THINK ANY YOUNG UNMARRIED WOMAN SHOULD BE	LEFT	QUITE TO HER OWN GUIDANCE. I HOPE YOU AGREE WITH ME,
CYMB FORWORD(135)	ONE MAY SAY THAT HE IS THE ONLY CHARACTER	LEFT	REALLY ALIVE IN THE LAST ACT; AND AS I CANNOT CHANGE
JITT III SD(52)	AND FESSLER AT THE SIDES OF IT TO HER RIGHT AND	LEFT	RESPECTIVELY. THE CORNER OF THE ROOM BEHIND THEM ON
ROCK II SD(240)	ON HIS RIGHT, AND SIR DEXTER AND BASHAM RIGHT AND	LEFT	RESPECTIVELY. /GLENMORISON/ WELL, SIR ARTHUR, WHEN YOU
SIM PRO-1,SD(21)	TO THE TRAINS THROUGH THE OPEN DOORS RIGHT AND	LEFT	RESPECTIVELY. THE EMIGRATION OFFICER, AN UNSATISFACTORY
PYGM III (255)	SITS DOWN IN ELIZA'S PLACE WITH HER SON ON HER	LEFT	)? PICKERING RETURNS TO HIS CHAIR ON HER RIGHT. /MRS
GETT (305)	/LESBIA/ (COMING TO THE TABLE, ON THE GENERAL'S	LEFT	) A WOMAN HAS NO RIGHT TO REFUSE MOTHERHOOD. THAT IS
JOAN 6 (126)	(TAKING THE OTHER JUDICIAL CHAIR ON CAUCHON'S	LEFT	) ALL SECULAR POWER MAKES MEN SCOUNDRELS. THEY ARE NOT
KING I (166)	THE WALL AND PLACING IT NEAR HIS TABLE TO HIS	LEFT	) BE SEATED, MR FOX, PRAY. /FOX/ GEORGE FOX AT YOUR
PYGM I (213)	RETURNING TO HIS FORMER PLACE ON THE NOTE TAKER'S	LEFT	) HOW DO YOU DO IT, IF I MAY ASK? /THE NOTE TAKER/
ROCK II (245)	THE END CHAIR NEAREST THE WINDOW, ON BASHAM'S	LEFT	) I WONDER WHY THE EPITHET ROBBER IS APPLIED ONLY TO
O'FL (215)	TO THE END OF THE GARDEN SEAT ON O'FLAHERTY'S	LEFT	) I'LL GIVE HER A GOOD TALKING TO WHEN SHE COMES. I'M
PYGM I (205)	THE CENTRAL PILLARS, CLOSE TO THE ONE ON HER	LEFT	) I'M GETTING CHILLED TO THE BONE. WHAT CAN FREDDY BE
PHIL II (97)	/CUTHBERTSON/ (TAKING THE SMALLER CHAIR ON HIS	LEFT	) NEITHER DO I. THERES NOT A ROOM IN THIS CLUB WHERE I
MIS. (131)	(FOLLOWING HIM AND SITTING DOWN ON HIS	LEFT	) PARADOX, PARADOX. GOOD. PARADOXES ARE THE ONLY
NEVR III (263)	WHAT IS IT? /PHILIP/ (SITTING DOWN ON HER	LEFT	) ROMEO-- /DOLLY/ (SITTING DOWN ON HER RIGHT)-- AND
GETT (325)	/THE BISHOP/ (COMING ROUND THE TABLE TO EDITH'S	LEFT	) THATS JUST WHAT WE ARE DISCUSSING. WILL YOU BE SO
JOAN 6 (123)	/CAUCHON/ (INTRODUCING THE CANON, WHO IS ON HIS	LEFT	) THIS GENTLEMAN IS CANON JOHN D'ESTIVET, OF THE
MILL II (171)	DOCTOR/ WHICH HAND? /EPIFANIA/ (PRESENTING HER	LEFT	) THIS, OF COURSE. /THE DOCTOR/ (TAKING HER HAND IN A
PYGM II (218)	(FOLLOWING HIM, AND STANDING BESIDE HIM ON HIS	LEFT	) TIRED OF LISTENING TO SOUNDS? /PICKERING/ YES. IT'S
MILL IV (194)	/SAGAMORE/ (TAKING A CHAIR NEXT PATRICIA ON HER	LEFT	) WELL, THE TRUTH OF THE MATTER IS THAT BLENDERBLAND
ANNA (304)	EYES. /STRAMMFEST/ (STARING PAST HER RIGHT AND	LEFT	) WHERE? /THE GRAND DUCHESS/ LOOK OUT OF THE WINDOW.
PYGM III (248)	ON THE OTTOMAN NEXT MRS EYNSFORD HILL, ON HER	LEFT	). AND NOW, WHAT THE DEVIL ARE WE GOING TO TALK ABOUT
HART II (96)	(SHE COMES TO THE BIG CHAIR, ON MANGAN'S	LEFT	). COME HERE. I HAVE SOMETHING TO SHEW YOU. (ELLIE
MRS II (200)	HIS FATHER ON HIS RIGHT AND MRS WARREN ON HIS	LEFT	). GEORGE! WHERE ARE YOU GOING TO STAY TO-NIGHT? YOU
2TRU II (78)	TWO MAROONS READY. CONTACT. (EXPLOSIONS ON THE	LEFT	). HOW IS THAT? /SERGEANT'S VOICE/ BOLTED, SIR, EVERY
OVER (180)	SITS). THATS RIGHT. (HE SITS BESIDE HER ON HER	LEFT	). HULLO! (HE RISES) THIS SOFA'S QUITE WARM. /MRS
PRES (143)	HIMSELF ON THE HEARTHRUG BESIDE MITCHENER, ON HIS	LEFT	). I NEVER LOOK UNDER MY BED FOR A BURGLAR. I'M NOT
GETT (338)	SORRY YOU HAVE BEEN WORRIED (HE SITS DOWN ON HER	LEFT	). NEVER MIND HIM. A LITTLE PLUCK, A LITTLE GAIETY OF
MILL I (152)	IT AT THE TABLE, ON HIS OWN RIGHT AND PATRICIA'S	LEFT	). /ADRIAN/ (SITTING DOWN) THANK YOU. I HOPE I AM NOT
ROCK I (211)	THE PRESIDENTIAL CHAIR ON THE OXFORD YOUTH'S	LEFT	). /BLEE/ THANK YOU. I DO MY BEST. (HE SITS). /THE
CLEO IV (180)	(HE GOES TO THE SEAT NEXT APOLLODORUS, ON HIS	LEFT	). /CAESAR/ (LOOKING AT HIS SEAT, WHICH IS AT THE END
KING I (209)	HIMSELF AT THE SIDE OF THE TABLE ON THE DUKE'S	LEFT	). /CHARLES/ MR NEWTON IS OUR HOST, MR KNELLER; AND HE
MTH5 (226)	MARTELLUS, AND SITS DOWN BESIDE ECRASIA, ON HER	LEFT	). /MARTELLUS/ YOU KNOW HIM QUITE WELL. PYGMALION.
OVER (186)	AND MRS JUNO SITS DOWN BESIDE MRS LUNN, ON HER	LEFT	). /MRS LUNN/ I'M SO GLAD TO FIND YOU DO CREDIT TO
SIM II (58)	TRICK, PRA. (HE SITS DOWN BESIDE PROLA, ON HER	LEFT	). /PRA/ (SITTING DOWN BETWEEN THE TWO BRITISH LADIES)
SIM I (43)	A LETTER. (SHE SITS DOWN ON SIR CHARLES'S	LEFT	). /THE CLERGYMAN/ OH, I AM SO SORRY. /HYERING/ NOT AT
SIM PRO-3, (33)	(HE SITS DOWN AGAIN, THIS TIME NEXT HER ON HER	LEFT	). /THE PRIESTESS/ NO: YOU DO IT BY INSTINCT. THAT,
GENV III (70)	POSKY. (HE SEATS HIMSELF ON THE SECRETARY'S	LEFT	). /THE SECRETARY/ WE HAVE MET. PRAY BE SEATED. /THE
GENV III (65)	HIMSELF AT THE NEXT TABLE ON THE SECRETARY'S	LEFT	). /THE SECRETARY/ WHAT! /THE JOURNALIST/ THEY HAVE
CAND I (90)	MODESTLY, SITS DOWN IN THE CHAIR MORELL HAS JUST	LEFT	). THATS RIGHT. NOW OUT WITH IT. /BURGESS/ (CHUCKLING
PHIL II (108)	THE CLUB. (SHE GOES INTO THE RECESS ON IBSEN'S	LEFT	). THE PAGE ENTERS, CARRYING THE BRITISH MEDICAL
LION I (119)	AND SITS DOWN CONTENTEDLY ON THE GROUND ON HER	LEFT	). THIS DIRTY DOG (COLLARING SPINTHO) IS A REAL
GETT (276)	COLLAPSES ON A CHAIR NEXT MRS BRIDGENORTH, ON HER	LEFT	)-- /REGINALD/ (SARDONICALLY) THE MAN THAT WOULD RAISE
CLEO II (142)	OVER THERE (POINTING OUT ACROSS THE SEA TO HER	LEFT	)-- THEY ARE DIPPING UP THE WATER. /RUFIO/ (HASTENING
NEVR II SD(231)	SEAT, WITH DOLLY ON HIS RIGHT AND PHIL ON HIS	LEFT	; AND SETTLES HIMSELF IN IT WITH THE AIR OF A MAN ABOUT
KING I (199)	JEALOUS LADY WOULDNT LEAVE UNTIL THE FRENCH LADY	LEFT	; AND THE PLAYER WOMAN IS AS CURIOUS AS A MAGPIE AND
BULL III (122)	ANYHOW, BECAUSE THERES HARLY ANY LANDLORDS	LEFT	; AND THERLL SOON BE NONE AT ALL. /LARRY/ ON THE
MIS. SD(109)	THERE IS MORE WALL TO JOHNNY'S RIGHT THAN TO HIS	LEFT	; AND THIS SPACE IS OCCUPIED BY A HAT RACK AND UMBRELLA
2TRU II (62)	SNATCHES UP THE RUG; REPLACES IT ON THE PATIENT'S	LEFT	; AND THROWS HIMSELF DOWN LAZILY ON IT). /THE COUNTESS/
MTH5 (225)	(RISES; CARRIES HER TO THE CURVED BENCH ON HIS	LEFT	; DEPOSITS HER BESIDE STREPHON AS IF SHE WERE HIS
BARB I SD(249)	AT IT; A SMALLER WRITING TABLE BEHIND HIM ON HIS	LEFT	; THE DOOR BEHIND HIM ON LADY BRITOMART'S SIDE; AND A
GENV IV (90)	WITH A POWERFUL HAND AND PLACES IT ON THE JUDGE'S	LEFT	; THEN FLINGS HIMSELF MASSIVELY INTO IT) DO NOT LET MY
SUPR III (106)	BRICKLAYER'S LABORER WITH SEVEN CHILDREN. HE	LEFT	SEVENTEEN POUNDS CLUB MONEY; AND HIS WIFE SPENT IT ALL
MRS III (220)	HERE. GONE TO TOWN BY THE 11.13 WITH BESSIE. SHE	LEFT	SEVERAL MESSAGES FOR YOU. DO YOU FEEL EQUAL TO
CLEO I (110)	A PIERCING SCREAM SHE SPRINGS UP; DARTS ROUND THE	LEFT	SHOULDER OF THE SPHINX; SCRAMBLES DOWN TO THE SAND; AND
CAND I SD(78)	CHEER HIMSELF WITH A VIEW OF THE PARK OVER HIS	LEFT	SHOULDER. AT THE OPPOSITE END OF THE TABLE, ADJOINING
PYGM V (279)	SOUNDS IF I TRIED. (DOOLITTLE TOUCHES HER ON HER	LEFT	SHOULDER. SHE DROPS HER WORK, LOSING HER
CLEO PRO2 (104)	/BEL AFFRIS/ (LAYING A HAND ON FTATATEETA'S	LEFT	SHOULDER) FORBEAR HER YET A MOMENT, PERSIAN. (TO
JOAN 2 (74)	(COMING BACK AND PEERING ROUND LA TREMOUILLE'S	LEFT	SHOULDER) I WILL READ IT FOR YOU IF YOU LIKE. I CAN
SUPR III SD(74)	FLING OF THE END OF HIS CLOAK ACROSS HIS	LEFT	SHOULDER, RISES TO ADDRESS THEM. THE APPLAUSE WHICH
BULL IV (153)	NOT THE RIGHT SIDE OF YOUR BRAIN KNOW WHAT THE	LEFT	SIDE DOETH. I LEARNT AT OXFORD THAT THIS IS THE SECRET
MILL I SD(137)	THE WINDOW IN PROFILE WITH HIS BACK TO IT AND HIS	LEFT	SIDE PRESENTED TO US, IS FENCED OFF BY HIS WRITING
ROCK II SD(281)	AND CLAPS THEM BOTH ON THE SHOULDERS RIGHT AND	LEFT	SIMULTANEOUSLY. THEY FLINCH VIOLENTLY, AND STARE AT HIM
ARMS III SD(54)	WITH HER BOLD FREE GAIT, TO THE TABLE. HER	LEFT	SLEEVE IS LOOPED UP TO THE SHOULDER WITH A BROOCH,

ARMS II SD(37)	(SOBERED BY HER TONE) HOW? SHE ROLLS UP HER	LEFT	SLEEVE; CLASPS HER ARM WITH THE THUMB AND FINGERS OF
LION PREFACE(85)	ENOUGH AT FIRST AS A POPULAR MIRACLE, WAS NOT	LEFT	SO SIMPLE BY THE THEOLOGIANS. THEY BEGAN TO ASK OF WHAT
BULL PREFACE(67)	WAS SO BAD THAT THE POST OFFICE ITSELF WAS	LEFT	STANDING AMID A WASTE OF RUBBISH HEAPS; AND ENOUGH
CLEO PRO2 (100)	AN HOUR BEHIND ME; AND NOT AN EGYPTIAN WARRIOR IS	LEFT	STANDING BETWEEN YOU AND HIS LEGIONS. /THE SENTINEL/
GENV PREFACE(17)	OVERCROWD THEM WITHIN ANY FOUR WALLS THAT WERE	LEFT	STANDING, LOCK THEM IN, AND LEAVE THEM ALMOST STARVING
MIS. (165)	ARE FAR TOO PREOCCUPIED TO HEAR HIM; AND HE IS	LEFT	STARING AFTER THEM AS THEY RUSH AWAY THROUGH THE
METH PREFACE(R37)	ENOUGH NOT TO BE TERRIFIED BY THE BOGEY WERE	LEFT	STRANDED IN EMPTY CONTEMPTUOUS NEGATION, AND ARGUED,
MIS. (123)	HUSBANDS. I SHOULDNT THINK MUCH OF A MAN THAT	LEFT	SUCH THINGS TO ME. /MRS TARLETON/ OH, DONT THINK THAT,
SUPR PREFACE(R15)	AND OF THAT CONCEPTION OF REPENTANCE, HOW MUCH IS	LEFT	THAT COULD BE USED IN A PLAY BY ME DEDICATED TO YOU?
BULL II (109)	MEETS PATSY FARRELL RETURNING UNLOADED). HAVE YOU	LEFT	THAT HAMPER FOR ME? /PATSY/ YIS, YOUR REVERENCE.
JITT I (20)	IT IS JUST BECAUSE I HAVE SO LITTLE TIME	LEFT	THAT I DARE NOT PUT THIS OFF ANY LONGER. YOU KNOW THE
2TRU III (90)	EVERY VIRTUE, AND SHE RETURNED MY LOVE. WHEN I	LEFT	THAT NURSING HOME, SHE LEFT IT TOO. I WAS DISCHARGED AS
METH PREFACE(R87)	NOTHING WAS VALID FOR HIM BUT SCIENCE; AND HE	LEFT	THAT VISION OF THE FUTURE WHICH HIS ROMAN SEER CALLS "
MIS. PREFACE(106)	CONTEMPT FOR WELLINGTON, HE WOULD NOT HAVE	LEFT	THE ATTACK AT WATERLOO TO NEY AND D'ERLON, WHO, ON THAT
CLEO II (131)	TURNING ALSO AND SEEING PTOLEMY) WHAT! HAVE THEY	LEFT	THE BOY ALONE! OH SHAME, SHAME! /RUFIO/ (TAKING
BARB I (255)	OR SOMETHING, HE ADOPTED ANOTHER FOUNDLING, AND	LEFT	THE BUSINESS TO HIM. AND THAT FOUNDLING DID THE SAME.
ANNA (291)	FAR FAR BETTER. /SCHNEIDEKIND/ (IN HUSHED TONES)	LEFT	THE CHURCH? /STRAMMFEST/ (SHOCKED) CERTAINLY NOT. DO
2TRU I (35)	OH, HOW CAN YOU SAY SUCH THINGS, DARLING? I	LEFT	THE DOCTOR HERE. I WAS AWAY ONLY FOR A MINUTE. I HAD TO
BARB III SD(326)	THE TOWN. ON HER RIGHT IS THE CANNON; ON HER	LEFT	THE END OF A SHED RAISED ON PILES, WITH A LADDER OF
GETT (327)	AFFAIR MADE A NEW MAN OF ME: I FELT THAT I HAD	LEFT	THE FOLLIES AND PUERILITIES OF THE OLD DAYS BEHIND ME
MTH1 II (31)	BUT YOU HAVE MADE THE SERPENT OUR ENEMY: SHE HAS	LEFT	THE GARDEN, OR IS DEAD: I NEVER SEE HER NOW. SO I HAVE
MILL II (174)	THEY DIED ON THE TABLE. THEY DIED AFTER THEY	LEFT	THE HOSPITAL; BUT AS THEY WERE CARRIED AWAY FROM THE
BUOY IV (48)	/NATIVE/ FROM PANAMA. /OLD BILL/ GOOD. HAS SHE	LEFT	THE HOUSE YET? /NATIVE/ NOT WITHOUT ME. I DRIVE HER
DOCT I (93)	TAKEN YOUR CHEQUE AND ROLLED UP YOUR BAG AND	LEFT	THE HOUSE. I TELL YOU, COLLY, CHLOROFORM HAS DONE A LOT
LION EPILOG (152)	PERFORMED IN BERLIN, THE CROWN PRINCE ROSE AND	LEFT	THE HOUSE, UNABLE TO ENDURE THE (I HOPE) VERY CLEAR
DEVL I SD(16)	TAKES THE CHAIR NEAREST THE SOFA, CHRISTY HAVING	LEFT	THE INKSTAND THERE. HE PUTS HIS HAT ON THE FLOOR BESIDE
CAPT I (230)	INDIES, I FOUND THAT THIS DISHONEST AGENT HAD	LEFT	THE ISLAND, AND PLACED THE ESTATE IN THE HANDS OF AN
FABL V (118)	DID NOT SET IT RIGHT: THEY JUST CUT IT OUT, AND	LEFT	THE PATIENT TO RECOVER FROM THE SHOCK OR DIE. WHEN THE
MTH3 (99)	I WAS TALKING TO ANOTHER LADY THIS MORNING; AND I	LEFT	THE PEG IN. /BURGE-LUBIN/ BUT I AM SO SORRY. /THE
BULL III (143)	LEFT HIS PIG BEHIND HIM. /BROADBENT/ (EAGERLY)	LEFT	THE PIG! THEN IT'S ALL RIGHT. THE PIG'S THE THING: THE
MTH4 III (197)	ON OUR RIGHT IS THE CRATER OF THE VOLCANO: ON OUR	LEFT	THE PRECIPICE. ONE FALSE STEP, AND WE GO DOWN TO
NEVR III (269)	NOT RETURN UNTIL YOU HAVE GONE, MR VALENTINE. SHE	LEFT	THE ROOM EXPRESSLY TO AVOID YOU. /VALENTINE/ (
LADY PREFACE(213)	WHO WAS FAILING HIM IN HIS HOUR OF NEED, AND	LEFT	THE ROOM IN ANGER. HARRIS'S IDIOSYNCRATIC POWER OF PITY
DEVL I SD(22)	WHERE SHE HAS MOVED TO; THEN, SEEING THAT SHE HAS	LEFT	THE ROOM WITHOUT LEAVE, CLOSES HER LIPS VENGEFULLY.
BARB III (313)	/LADY BRITOMART/ ADOLPHUS: NOW THAT BARBARA HAS	LEFT	THE SALVATION ARMY, YOU HAD BETTER LEAVE IT TOO. I WILL
BULL II (106)	THE WET GRASS; N WHAT WOULD THE MASTHER SAY IF I	LEFT	THE SAMMIN AND THE GOOSE BE THE SIDE O THE ROAD FOR
HART I (52)	DEPOSITS ELLIE ON THE SOFA. MEANWHILE ARIADNE HAS	LEFT	THE TABLE AND COME OVER TO CLAIM HER SHARE OF
BULL II (110)	HER? HURRY IN NOW, CORNY. COME, MR BROADBENT: I	LEFT	THE TEA ON THE HOB TO DRAW; AND ITLL BE BLACK IF WE
POSN (440)	ME: /STRAPPER/ CANT WE? /BLANCO/ NO, YOU CANT. I	LEFT	THE TOWN THIS MORNING BEFORE SUNRISE, BECAUSE IT'S A
SUPR IV (161)	IVE INTRODUCED HIM TO MENDOZA, LIMITED; AND	LEFT	THE TWO BRIGANDS TOGETHER TO TALK IT OUT. HULLO, TAVY!
MILL I (158)	MANAGER HAD ABSCONDED WITH MY FIFTY POUNDS AND	LEFT	THE WHOLE COMPANY PENNILESS. THE PRIMA DONNA WAS DEAF
KING I (205)	A CENTURY IN HELL. AND I CAN TESTIFY THAT HE	LEFT	THE WRETCHED CITIZENS ONLY ONE WORLDLY PLEASURE.
HART PREFACE(18)	THAT CONSOLED AND STIMULATED THE OTHERS. THEY	LEFT	THEIR CREATIVE WORK TO DRUDGE AT DESTRUCTION, EXACTLY
JOAN 6,SD(133)	EXAMINATIONS WHICH HAVE PRECEDED THE TRIAL HAVE	LEFT	THEIR MARK ON HER; BUT HER VITALITY STILL HOLDS: SHE
SUPR I (37)	LED YOU TO ATTACH ME TO YOU BY BONDS THAT HAVE	LEFT	THEIR MARK ON ME TO THIS DAY. YES, ANN: THE OLD
BULL II SD(105)	FIELD GLASS AND A GUIDE BOOK. THE OTHER TWO HAVE	LEFT	THEIRS TO THE UNFORTUNATE PATSY FARRELL, WHO STRUGGLES
HART PREFACE(6)	HAD, THEIR HABIT OF LIVING IN A VACUUM WOULD HAVE	LEFT	THEM HELPLESS AND INEFFECTIVE IN PUBLIC AFFAIRS. EVEN
MIS. PREFACE(98)	ON WHATEVER FALSE PRETENCES, ON OUR CHILDREN	LEFT	THEM MORE LITERATE THAN IF THEY KNEW NO LITERATURE AT
FOUN (219)	IT TOOK TEN WARDRESSES TO PERSUADE ME TO DO IT. I	LEFT	THEM SIMPLY IN RIBBONS, POOR THINGS. PRISON MADE A
HART I (45)	FALL OVER. ALSO A TENNIS RACQUET. WHO THE DEVIL	LEFT	THEM THERE? /THE YOUNG LADY/ THEY ARE MINE, I'M
METH PREFACE(R48)	UNKNOWN FACTOR AS A SPORT INSTEAD OF AS X!) AND	LEFT	THEM TO " ACCUMULATE" AND ACCOUNT FOR THE DIFFERENCE
MIS. PREFACE(50)	LESS LITERATE THAN THE TREADMILL WOULD HAVE	LEFT	THEM; FOR THEY MIGHT NOW BY CHANCE PICK UP AND DIP INTO
JITT I (20)	HOW I VALUE YOUR WORK; BUT WE HAVE SO LITTLE TIME	LEFT	THIS EVENING-- /BRUNO/ (RESOLUTELY) IT IS JUST BECAUSE
FABL PREFACE(87)	CALLED IT AS FAR AS MY THOUGHT COULD REACH; BUT I	LEFT	THIS TO BE TAKEN FOR GRANTED. POLITICAL MATHEMATICS.
SUPR III (133)	NOT SAY FLESH AND BLOOD AT ONCE, THOUGH WE HAVE	LEFT	THOSE TWO GREASY COMMONPLACES BEHIND US? /THE DEVIL/ (
PYGM II (221)	EGGS IN IT: /HIGGINS/ THEY TOOK ONE APIECE, AND	LEFT	THREE IN IT. THEY LAUGH HEARTILY AT THEIR OWN WIT.
2TRU II (63)	ABOUT LOOKING FOR IT. I LIKE TO HAVE MY ROOMS	LEFT	TIDY. (SHE GOES INTO THE PAVILION). /THE PATIENT/ ISNT
GETT PREFACE(194)	IS VULGAR AND SILLY IN HER NAUGHTINESS. IT WAS	LEFT	TO AN ABNORMAL CRITIC LIKE GEORGE GISSING TO POINT OUT
BARB I (255)	SINCE THAT, THE CANNON BUSINESS HAS ALWAYS BEEN	LEFT	TO AN ADOPTED FOUNDLING NAMED ANDREW UNDERSHAFT.
DOCT PREFACE(71)	FORCIBLE SEIZURE AND RE-VACCINATION OF CHILDREN	LEFT	TO ANSWER THE DOOR, CAN BE PREVENTED SIMPLY BY
DOCT III (146)	FROM YOUR CASE, MR DUBEDAT. YOU HAVE NOBODY	LEFT	TO APPEAL TO NOW BUT SIR RALPH BLOOMFIELD BONINGTON.
MIS. PREFACE(46)	PRIVATE PROPERTY IN CHILDREN. THE REST MAY BE	LEFT	TO COMMON SENSE. IT IS OUR ATTITUDE, OUR RELIGION, THAT
BARB II (303)	THE FIVE THOUSAND? /UNDERSHAFT/ THERE IS NOTHING	LEFT	TO GIVE HIM. SO THE FIVE THOUSAND, I SHOULD THINK, IS
JOAN PREFACE(39)	JOAN SHOULD HAVE BEEN EXCOMMUNICATED AND THEN	LEFT	TO GO HER OWN WAY, THOUGH SHE WOULD HAVE PROTESTED
BULL PREFACE(70)	PANICS AND ATROCITIES WILL ENSUE BEFORE INDIA IS	LEFT	TO GOVERN ITSELF AS MUCH AS IRELAND AND EGYPT NOW ARE I
SIM II (77)	OF ALL HER WARS! /KANCHIN/ THE LAST CONQUEST	LEFT	TO HER TO ACHIEVE! /VASHTI/ TO OVERCOME THE ANGELS!
SUPR II (68)	TO BE LEFT TO MR ROBINSON AS MR ROBINSON IS TO BE	LEFT	TO HER. (STRAKER LOOKS AT HIS PRINCIPAL WITH COOL
CAPT II (260)	CAN YOU EXPECT? SIR HOWARD'S ALL RIGHT WHEN HE'S	LEFT	TO HIMSELF. WE CAUGHT A BURGLAR ONE NIGHT AT WAYNFLETE
MILL II (169)	YOUR TEMPER-- /EPIFANIA/ (DELIVERING A STRAIGHT	LEFT	TO HIS CHIN) TAKE THAT FOR CALLING MY FATHER A BORE. (
HART PREFACE(11)	NOT KNOW HOW TO LIVE, AT WHICH POINT ALL THAT WAS	LEFT	TO IT WAS THE BOAST THAT AT LEAST IT KNEW HOW TO DIE: A
GENV III (82)	WORLD IF IT ACCEPTS THE GUIDANCE OF MOSCOW; BUT	LEFT	TO ITS CHILDISH SELF IT WILL DECLINE AND FALL LIKE AS
DOCT PREFACE(53)	OF INCREASING IT BY FIVE, BECAUSE THE PUBLIC,	LEFT	TO ITSELF AND TO THE OLD GENTLEMEN WHO ARE ALWAYS READY
ANNA (298)	ON HIS KNEE) YOU ARE, GOD HELP ME, ALL THAT IS	LEFT	TO ME OF THE ONLY POWER I RECOGNIZE ON EARTH (HE
ROCK II (245)	I SHALL GET THREE AND A HALF PER CENT ON WHAT IS	LEFT	TO ME OUT OF THE BEGGARLY PRICE HE OFFERS; AND ON THAT
BULL I (77)	BEEN ENSLAVED AND DESTROYED, THERE IS NO COUNTRY	LEFT	TO ME TO TAKE AN INTEREST IN BUT IRELAND. MIND: I DONT
HART III (135)	IS TOO PRETTY TO BE REAL. THE ONE THING THAT WAS	LEFT	TO ME WAS THE CAPTAIN'S SEVENTH DEGREE OF
SUPR II (68)	VIEWS? /TANNER/ SHE IS JUST AS WILLING TO BE	LEFT	TO MR ROBINSON AS MR ROBINSON IS TO BE LEFT TO HER. (
CAPT III (295)	ME THAT I TAKE LIFE THE WRONG WAY WHEN I'M	LEFT	TO MYSELF. /LADY CICELY/ OH NO. WHY DO YOU SAY THAT?
CAPT III (298)	GORDON TO COMMAND ME, I CANT THINK OF WHAT TO DO.	LEFT	TO MYSELF, IVE BECOME HALF A BRIGAND. I CAN KICK THAT
PHIL I SD(69)	OF HIS MOUSTACHES AND SHORT BEARD, IS APPARENTLY	LEFT	TO NATURE; BUT HE HAS TAKEN CARE THAT NATURE SHALL DO
GETT (337)	/HOTCHKISS/ NO YOU SHANT. I HAVE ONE CARD	LEFT	TO PLAY THAT YOUVE FORGOTTEN. WHY WERE YOU SO UNLIKE
JITT I (20)	THERE IS NOT A WORD OF IT IN MY HANDWRITING	LEFT	TO PROVE THAT I AM THE AUTHOR. THEY WILL FIND A BOOK BY
GENV IV (111)	NOW IT IS YOUR TURN, ERNEST. IF YOU HAVE ANYTHING	LEFT	TO SAY. /BATTLER/ YOU HAVE SAID IT ALL IN YOUR
ROCK PREFACE(182)	THEM THE PEACE OF ROME THAN THAT THEY SHOULD BE	LEFT	TO SLAUGHTER ONEANOTHER IN THEIR OWN NATIVE SAVAGERY.
SIM PREFACE(11)	AND THE LIKE, TO HAVE ANY VIRTUOUS INDIGNATION	LEFT	TO SPARE FOR THE BLUNDERS AND EXCESSES INTO WHICH THE
MIS. PREFACE(67)	TAUGHT TO CONSIDER OTHER PEOPLE'S WILLS, AND	LEFT	TO SUBMIT TO THEM OR TO OVERRIDE THEM AS IF THEY WERE
3PLA PREFACE(R22)	BEEN PRODUCED, IN FACT, BY INCIDENTS WHICH, IF	LEFT	TO THE OPERATION OF NATURAL AND RIGHT FEELING, WOULD
MIS. PREFACE(69)	SON WILL BECOME AN ILLITERATE HOOLIGAN IF HE IS	LEFT	TO THE STREETS, THERE IS NO REAL ALTERNATIVE FOR EITHER
ROCK PREFACE(166)	WHO SEEMED LIKE ANOTHER SPECIES TO HIM.	LEFT	TO THEMSELVES THE MOUJIKS WOULD HAVE REPRODUCED
OVER PREFACE(159)	DISASTROUS CONSEQUENCES FOR EVENTS WHICH,	LEFT	TO THEMSELVES, WOULD DO VERY LITTLE HARM (SOMETIMES
GETT PREFACE(211)	TO THEMSELVES, WOULD TOLERATE POLYGYNY. THE MEN,	LEFT	TO THEMSELVES, WOULD TOLERATE POLYANDRY. BUT POLYGYNY
GETT PREFACE(211)	WOMEN BECAUSE IT EXCLUDES POLYANDRY. THE WOMEN,	LEFT	TO THEMSELVES, WOULD TOLERATE POLYGYNY. THE MEN, LEFT
GETT PREFACE(189)	OF THE CHURCH OF ENGLAND. IF MATTERS WERE	LEFT	TO THESE SIMPLE FOLK, THERE WOULD NEVER BE ANY CHANGES
2TRU III (110)	ON US AND TEAR FROM US EVEN THE RAGS THAT WERE	LEFT	TO US. BUT WHEN THEY HAVE STRIPPED THEMSELVES AND US
BULL II (110)	SAFE HOME. /BROADBENT/ MISS REILLY MUST NOT BE	LEFT	TO WAIT AND WALK HOME ALONE AT NIGHT. SHALL I GO FOR
MIS. PREFACE(41)	DANGER OF ACQUIRING BANDY LEGS THROUGH BEING	LEFT	TO WALK BEFORE THEY ARE STRONG ENOUGH THAN OF BEING
MTH4 I (170)	BY TRYING TO ACT ON IT THAN IF YOU HAD BEEN	LEFT	TO YOUR OWN CHILDISH DEVICES. IF YOU WERE NOT CHILDISH
DOCT IV (170)	HANDS) REMEMBER: ALL LETTERS HAD BETTER BE	LEFT	TO YOUR SOLICITOR. LET HIM OPEN EVERYTHING AND SETTLE
GETT (348)	INTO A KETTLE-HOLDER. YOURE NO MORE FIT TO BE	LEFT	TO YOURSELF THAN A ONE-YEAR-OLD BABY. /REGINALD/ OH, I
BULL IV SD(158)	BODES TROUBLE FOR CORNELIUS). LARRY AND NORA ARE	LEFT	TOGETHER FOR THE FIRST TIME SINCE HIS ARRIVAL. SHE
AUGS (279)	OF YOUR CIVILIAN INSUBORDINATION. ATTENTION!	LEFT	TURN! QUICK MARCH! /THE CLERK/ (STOLIDLY) I DUNNO
MTH2 (65)	YOU? IS THERE ANY QUESTION OF YOURS THAT I HAVE	LEFT	UNANSWERED? /CONRAD/ WE HAVNT ASKED YOU ANY, YOU KNOW.
SUPR III SD(73)	THERE ARE QUADRUPEDS, WHO ARE TOO DANGEROUS TO BE	LEFT	UNCHAINED AND UNMUZZLED; AND THESE CANNOT FAIRLY EXPECT
JOAN 6 (133)	US TO QUESTION YOU. /COURCELLES/ WHEN YOU WERE	LEFT	UNCHAINED, DID YOU NOT TRY TO ESCAPE BY JUMPING FROM A
MRS PREFACE(180)	EXAMINERS. HE NOT ONLY CONFIRMED THEIR VETO, BUT	LEFT	UNCONTRADICTED A REPORT IN ALL THE PAPERS THAT HE HAD
APPL PREFACE(183)	OF HUMAN LIFE AND WELFARE IT COST WHEN IT WAS	LEFT	UNCONTROLLED BY THE GOVERNMENT. DURING THE WAR OUR
INCA (256)	THEY AND I SHALL ANSWER AT LAST FOR WHAT WE HAVE	LEFT	UNDONE NO LESS THAN FOR WHAT WE HAVE DONE. (PULLING

BARB I (271)	HAVE DONE THINGS WE OUGHT NOT TO HAVE DONE, AND	LEFT	UNDONE THINGS WE OUGHT TO HAVE DONE, AND THAT THERE IS
POSN PREFACE(366)	THOSE THINGS WHICH HE OUGHT NOT TO HAVE DONE, AND	LEFT	UNDONE THOSE THINGS WHICH HE OUGHT TO HAVE DONE. MR
2TRU I (32)	I FEEL SUCH A RESPONSIBILITY IF ANYTHING IS	LEFT	UNDONE TO CURE HER. /THE DOCTOR/ OH VERY WELL, VERY
CLEO IV (188)	WERE TREACHERY, FALSEHOOD, AND DISLOYALTY	LEFT	UNPUNISHED, SOCIETY MUST BECOME LIKE AN ARENA FULL OF
ROCK PREFACE(162)	MOST ELABORATE CODE OF THIS SORT WOULD STILL HAVE	LEFT	UNSPECIFIED A HUNDRED WAYS IN WHICH WRECKERS OF
HART PREFACE(7)	OF HOSPITAL GANGRENE, SLAUGHTERING RIGHT AND	LEFT	UNTIL THE INNOCENT YOUNG HAVE PAID FOR THE GUILTY OLD,
METH PREFACE(R19)	AS BIOLOGY. HERE, THEN, IS A STONE THAT WE HAVE	LEFT	UNTURNED, AND THAT MAY BE WORTH TURNING. TO MAKE THE
HART PREFACE(14)	OVER LARGE DISTRICTS LITERALLY NOT ONE STONE WAS	LEFT	UPON ANOTHER AS THE OPPOSED ARMIES DROVE EACH OTHER
BULL PREFACE(67)	WOULD NOT BE TRUE TO SAY THAT NOT ONE STONE WAS	LEFT	UPON ANOTHER; FOR THE MARKSMANSHIP WAS SO BAD THAT THE
GENV IV (125)	BY OUR DESPAIR. WHY HAS OUR JEWISH FRIEND JUST	LEFT	US? TO TELEPHONE, HE SAID. YES; BUT TO WHOM IS HE
GETT PREFACE(229)	AND MISCHIEVOUS TO LAST. EUROPE AND AMERICA HAVE	LEFT	US A CENTURY BEHIND IN THIS MATTER. A PROBABLE EFFECT
KING I (200)	DINNER. JACK THE FISH HAWKER IS GONE, BUT HE	LEFT	US A NICE PIECE OF COD; AND THATS ALL YOULL GET, SIR.
NEVR II (229)	WE'RE OLD FASHIONED: THE WORLD THINKS IT HAS	LEFT	US BEHIND. THERE IS ONLY ONE PLACE IN ALL ENGLAND WHERE
HART PREFACE(15)	RELIGION FROM OUR IGNORANCE AND BARBARISM, AND	LEFT	US GLORYING GROTESQUELY IN THE LICENCE SUDDENLY
ROCK II (237)	THE LITTLE THAT THE PRESENT RUINOUS TAXATION HAS	LEFT	US IS GONE; WHEN WE HAVE CLOSED OUR ACCOUNTS WITH THE
MTH3 (128)	GOING TO LET THEM DO WHAT THE TWO WHO HAVE JUST	LEFT	US MEAN TO DO, AND CROWD US OFF THE FACE OF THE EARTH?
UNPL PREFACE(R21)	DRAUGHTSMAN, HUMORIST, AND RHETORICIAN, HAS	LEFT	US NO INTELLECTUALLY COHERENT DRAMA, AND COULD NOT
ROCK PREFACE(177)	FOR ANY SANE GOVERNMENT, AND SO THEY HAVE	LEFT	US NO MODEL DEFENCE. AND THERE IS NO MODERN TREATISE
BUOY IV (54)	THE ARRIVAL FROM AMERICA OF THE LADY WHO HAS JUST	LEFT	US. I WAS INTERRUPTED AGAIN BY THE ARRIVAL OF A YOUNG
APPL II (264)	TO THE LITTLE SCRAP OF INDIVIDUALITY YOU HAVE	LEFT	US. IF WE MUST MERGE, AS YOU CALL IT -- OR DID YOU SAY
BULL II (107)	OF HIM FOR EIGHTEEN YEARS, N HE ONY A LAD WHEN HE	LEFT	US. /BROADBENT/ IT'S NOT LARRY'S FAULT: HE WAS TO HAVE
CLEO V (199)	/CLEOPATRA/ ASK THE ROMAN GOVERNOR WHOM YOU HAVE	LEFT	US. /CAESAR/ RUFIO? /CLEOPATRA/ YES; RUFIO. (SHE
MIS. (141)	AND THEN BENTLEY TOOK HIMSELF OFF, AND	LEFT	US-- YOU AND ME! -- TO TAKE A WALK THROUGH THE HEATHER
SIM PRO,3, (34)	I SAY! /THE E.O./ (RISING DEFERENTIALLY) JUST	LEFT	US, SIR CHARLES. /THE M.T./ HALLO! WEVE MET BEFORE, I
SUPR III (98)	YOU NOT PERSUADE HIM TO TAKE THE PLACE YOU HAVE	LEFT	VACANT ABOVE? /THE STATUE/ (SHAKING HIS HEAD) I
MIS. (187)	WATER. /JOHNNY/ (COMING FORWARD INTO THE PLACE	LEFT	VACANT BY GUNNER'S VISIT TO THE SIDEBOARD) WELL, NOW
PYGM III (250)	DOWN ON THE OTTOMAN GRACEFULLY IN THE PLACE JUST	LEFT	VACANT BY HIGGINS). /MRS EYNSFORD HILL/ (INTRODUCING)
PYGM I SD(208)	DRESS, WITH A LIGHT OVERCOAT. HE TAKES THE PLACE	LEFT	VACANT BY THE DAUGHTER'S RETIREMENT. /THE GENTLEMAN/
GETT (321)	(RISING AND LEANING ON THE BACK OF THE CHAIR	LEFT	VACANT BY THE GENERAL) I REALLY MUST POINT OUT TO YOU,
SIM II (63)	CANADA CLAIMS POSITION OF PREMIER DOMINION	LEFT	VACANT BY THE SECESSION OF ENGLAND. /KANCHIN/ AUSTRALIA
DOCT III (136)	MAN. /WALPOLE/ (HANGING HIS HAT ON THE ONLY PEG	LEFT	VACANT ON THE HAT-STAND) WE SHALL MAKE OURSELVES AT
2TRU I SD(27)	A DARK GREEN SPRING BLIND) IN THE MIDDLE OF THE	LEFT	WALL WITH THE WARDROBE ON ITS RIGHT AND THE WRITING
SUPR II SD(48)	VIEW OF THE WEST CORNER OF THE HOUSE ON HIS	LEFT	WERE HE NOT FAR TOO MUCH INTERESTED IN A PAIR OF SUPINE
MIS. PREFACE(28)	AND REFORM WOULD LEAVE HIM AS A WORKMAN IS NOW	LEFT	WHEN HE IS SUPERSEDED BY A MACHINE. HE HAD THEREFORE
MRS IV (235)	HOW DID YOU GET IN? /FRANK/ THE STAFF HAD NOT	LEFT	WHEN I ARRIVED. HE'S GONE TO PLAY CRICKET ON PRIMROSE
HART I (70)	YOU I WAS HERE? /RANDALL/ HASTINGS. YOU HAD JUST	LEFT	WHEN I CALLED ON YOU AT CLARIDGE'S; SO I FOLLOWED YOU
GLIM (182)	IF INDEED, MY DAUGHTER, THERE BE ANY SOUL	LEFT	WHEN THE BODY IS SLAIN. /FERRUCCIO/ (CROSSING HIMSELF
MILL III SD(179)	TO HAVE BUTTONS SEWN ON, AND ANOTHER TO HER	LEFT	WHICH SHE HAS FINISHED. THE TABLE IS DRAPED DOWN TO THE
FABL PREFACE(97)	RUSSIA, REGARD THEM AS ENEMIES, AND THE MARXIST	LEFT	WINS MORE AND MORE VOTES FROM THEM. THE THREATENING
MILL I (139)	PROMISED TO LEAVE ME TWO HUNDRED MILLIONS. I WAS	LEFT	WITH A BEGGARLY THIRTY, IT BROKE HIS HEART. /SAGAMORE/
GETT PREFACE(210)	MANY OF OUR MALE CHILDREN IN INFANCY THAT WE ARE	LEFT	WITH A SURPLUS OF ADULT WOMEN WHICH IS SUFFICIENTLY
ROCK PREFACE(172)	UP ON CREEDS WHICH THEY CANNOT BELIEVE, THEY ARE	LEFT	WITH NO CREEDS AT ALL, AND ARE APT TO BUY PISTOLS AND
SIM I SD(41)	INTO THE HOUSE, FOLLOWED BY PRA. THE CLERGYMAN,	LEFT	WITH THE FOUR FIGURES, LOOKS AT THEM, LOOKS ROUND TO
METH PREFACE(R55)	AND SPENCER AND DARWIN PASSED AWAY, AND WE WERE	LEFT	WITH THE SMALLER PEOPLE WHO BEGAN WITH DARWIN AND TOOK
BULL PREFACE(71)	ON A SECTARIAN BASIS, PROTESTANT ULSTER HAS BEEN	LEFT	WITH THE SMALLER. NOW IT HAPPENS THAT PROTESTANT ULSTER
GENV PREFACE(11)	WAYLEAVE WAS ABOLISHED. THUS THE VICTORS WERE	LEFT	WITH THE TERROR OF THEIR OWN DISCOVERY, AND THE
SIM II (79)	OF THE CHAMBER. MAYFAIR A DESERT; SIX HOTELS	LEFT	WITHOUT A SINGLE GUEST. FRESH DISAPPEARANCES. CROWDED
ROCK I (231)	IN THE MANNER YOU DESCRIBE THEY WOULD HAVE BEEN	LEFT	WITHOUT ANY POLITICAL MINDS AT ALL. BUT IN THAT CASE
WIDO II (45)	/THE PARLORMAID/ (TREMULOUSLY PROPITIATORY) HE	LEFT	WORD HE'D BE BACK DIRECTLY, MISS. I'M SURE HE WONT BE
SUPR PREFACE(R28)	BEEN READING MY SOCIALISM FOR MILLIONAIRES)	LEFT	WORD THAT NO IDLER WAS TO INHERIT HIS ESTATE. THE BENT
DEVL II (33)	I COME, SIR, ON YOUR OWN INVITATION. YOU	LEFT	WORD YOU HAD SOMETHING IMPORTANT TO TELL ME. /ANDERSON/
CLEO PRO2 (103)	TO CAESAR OR HER BROTHER. (HE GRASPS HER BY THE	LEFT	WRIST, AND DRAGS HER, HELPED BY A FEW OF THE GUARD, TO
MTH5 (258)	NEWLY BORN/ OH, WILL YOU ALL LEAVE ME AS HE HAS	LEFT	YOU? /ECRASIA/ NEVER. WE HAVE SWORN IT. /STREPHON/
PHIL II (131)	SHE TAKES), BY THE WAY, WHAT HAPPENED AFTER I	LEFT	YOU? /GRACE/ I GAVE HER A LECTURE ON HER BEHAVIOR
JITT III (54)	(HE STOPS), /AGNES/ BUT WHAT? SUPPOSE HE HAD	LEFT	YOU A SAFE FULL OF DIAMONDS, AND WHEN YOU OPENED THE
DEVL II (41)	KNOW. /ANDERSON/ (GROANING) HEAVEN FORGIVE ME, I	LEFT	YOU ALONE WITH THAT SCOUNDREL. (JUDITH REMEMBERS. WITH
HART III (141)	WANTS TO BREAK MY HEART TOO, BUT IT SHANT. I HAVE	LEFT	YOU AND IT BEHIND. IT WAS SILLY OF ME TO COME BACK. I
DOCT II (119)	NEXT RIDGEON. /BLENKINSOP/ I'M SO SORRY TO HAVE	LEFT	YOU LIKE THIS, RIDGEON; BUT IT WAS A TELEPHONE MESSAGE
HART I (80)	THAT IS POSSIBLE. SHE HAS USED YOU UP, AND	LEFT	YOU NOTHING BUT DREAMS, AS SOME WOMEN DO. /HECTOR/
BULL IV (170)	ANXIOUSLY, IN HIS MOST CONCILIATORY TONE) WHEN I	LEFT	YOU THAT TIME, I WAS JUST AS WRETCHED AS YOU. I DIDNT
MTH2 (69)	NO! THE SOLDIERS AND SAILORS WON IT, AND	LEFT	YOU TO FINISH IT. AND YOU WERE SO UTTERLY INCOMPETENT
MIS. (151)	THAT MY PASSENGER WAS A LADY I SHOULDNT HAVE	LEFT	YOU TO SHIFT FOR YOURSELF IN THAT SELFISH WAY. /LORD
BULL III (132)	BIG WORLD THAT I BELONG TO HAS GONE PAST YOU AND	LEFT	YOU. ANYHOW, WE IRISHMEN WERE NEVER MADE TO BE FARMERS;
JITT II (43)	WHAT WISHES? /JITTA/ YOU MUST ACCEPT WHAT HE HAS	LEFT	YOU. /LENKHEIM/ WHY MUST I? /JITTA/ IT WAS HIS LAST
SUPR III (91)	MY AGE, MAN? /DON JUAN/ YOU FORGET THAT YOU HAVE	LEFT	YOUR AGE BEHIND YOU IN THE REALM OF TIME. YOU ARE NO
BULL II (106)	BEHIND? HWAT WOULD YOUR REVERENCE THINK IF I	LEFT	YOUR HAMPER BEHIND IN THE WET GRASS; N HWAT WOULD THE
MILL I (161)	THE EVIDENCE IS THAT ON A RECENT OCCASION YOU	LEFT	YOUR WIFE AND TOOK REFUGE IN THE ARMS OF MISS SMITH.
MILL I (139)	A PAUPER! YOU AMAZE ME. IT WAS REPORTED THAT HE	LEFT	YOU, HIS ONLY CHILD, THIRTY MILLIONS. /EPIFANIA/ WELL,
NEVR I SD(199)	OPPOSITE YOU, WITH THE DOOR BESIDE IT TO YOUR	LEFT	, A DENTAL SURGEON'S DIPLOMA IN A FRAME ABOVE THE
DOCT V SD(171)	COUPLE OF MAGNIFYING GLASSES. AT THE SIDE, ON HIS	LEFT	, A LITTLE BEHIND HIM, IS A SMALL DOOR MARKED PRIVATE.
SUPR IV SD(141)	TENNIS NET NOR SET OF CROQUET HOOPS, BUT, ON OUR	LEFT	, A LITTLE IRON GARDEN TABLE WITH BOOKS ON IT, MOSTLY
NEVR II SD(225)	TERRACE IN FRONT OF HIM HE SEES, A LITTLE TO HIS	LEFT	, A MIDDLE AGED GENTLEMAN SITTING ON A CHAIR OF IRON
MILL I SD(148)	SHE IS SEATED BETWEEN THE TWO, PATRICIA ON HER	LEFT	, ALASTAIR ON HER RIGHT. SAGAMORE GOES BACK TO HIS
ROCK I SD(193)	THE SECRETARY. IN THE CORRESPONDING CORNER ON HIS	LEFT	, AN ARMCHAIR. THERE IS A BLUEBOOK LYING, NEGLECTED AND
UNPL PREFACE(R22)	AND AN ENTRANCE THROUGH THE CONSERVATORY ON THE	LEFT	, AND A FRENCH WINDOW IN THE MIDDLE? IT IS ASTONISHING
NEVR III SD(261)	CENTRAL TABLE WOULD HAVE THE FIREPLACE ON HIS	LEFT	, AND A WRITING TABLE AGAINST THE WALL ON HIS RIGHT,
CAPT II SD(242)	CHIEF ENTRANCE, A LARGE HORSESHOE ARCH, ON HIS	LEFT	, AND ANOTHER SADDLE SEAT BETWEEN HIM AND THE ARCH;
LION I SD(122)	DOES NOT ANSWER. HE SITS DOWN BESIDE HER ON HER	LEFT	, AND BURIES HIS FACE IN HIS HANDS IN GLOOMY
PHIL II SD(94)	DOWN THE ROOM, HAS THE DINING ROOM DOOR ON HIS	LEFT	, AND FURTHER ON, NEARLY IN THE MIDDLE OF THE LIBRARY,
PHIL II SD(112)	CRAVEN AT HIS RIGHT SHOULDER, CUTHBERTSON ON HIS	LEFT	, AND JULIA BEHIND. /CRAVEN/ WHATS THE MATTER,
JITT II (35)	ON THE SOFA BESIDE HER. EDITH SITS DOWN ON HER	LEFT	, AND LOOKS GRATEFULLY AND LONGINGLY INTO HER EYES). DO
APPL I SD(214)	A MERRY LADY IN UNIFORM LIKE THE MEN, ON HIS	LEFT	, AND LYSISTRATA, POWERMISTRESS GENERAL, A GRAVE LADY
LION I (119)	FELLOW (INDICATING ANDROCLES, WHO COMES TO HIS	LEFT	, AND MAKES LAVINIA A HEART-BROKEN SALUTATION) IS A
ROCK II (267)	SOLD TO AN AMERICAN I SHALL HAVE NO FAMILY SEAT	LEFT	, AND MUST FALL BACK ON MY POLITICAL SEAT, WHICH IS AT
MTH4 II (185)	POISON EACH OTHER UNTIL THERE ARE NO CHEMISTS	LEFT	, AND NO CIVILIZATION. YOU WILL THEN BEGIN ALL OVER
SIM I SD(44)	THANK YOU. PROLA SITS DOWN ON SIR CHARLES'S	LEFT	, AND PRA ON LADY FARWATERS' LEFT. /LADY FARWATERS/ YOU
PHIL II (123)	DELIGHTED. (THEY GO INTO THE RECESS ON IBSEN'S	LEFT	, AND SIT THERE CHATTING IN WHISPERS, VERY
GETT (287)	GARDEN DOOR TO THE CHAIR MRS BRIDGENORTH HAS JUST	LEFT	, AND SITTING DOWN) NOT MORE RITUALISM, I HOPE.
CLEO PRO2,SD(97)	THE PERSIAN ON HIS RIGHT, BELZANOR ON HIS	LEFT	, AND THE GUARDSMEN CROWDING DOWN BEHIND HIM.
PHIL II (115)	PARAMORE THEN RETIRES TO THE RECESS ON IBSEN'S	LEFT	, AND THROWS HIMSELF ON THE DIVAN WITH A HALF
MTH3 SD(91)	IN ITS PLACE APPEARS, IN REVERSE FROM RIGHT TO	LEFT	, ANOTHER OFFICE SIMILARLY FURNISHED, WITH A THIN,
AUGS SD(263)	MORNING POST. THE DOOR FACES HIM, A LITTLE TO HIS	LEFT	, AT THE OTHER SIDE OF THE ROOM. THE WINDOW IS BEHIND
MTH4 I SD(139)	OCCASIONALLY USEFUL AS WELL AS ROMANTIC. ON HIS	LEFT	, BEHIND HIM, A FLIGHT OF STONE STEPS DESCENDS OUT OF
FANY II SD(285)	HAVE THE DOOR ON THE RIGHT AND THE WINDOW ON THE	LEFT	, BOTH FURTHER AWAY THAN MRS KNOX, WHOSE BACK IS
GETT (308)	(HE GOES TO THE FOURTH CHAIR FROM THE GENERAL'S	LEFT	, BUT BEFORE SITTING DOWN, COURTEOUSLY POINTS TO THE
JOAN EPIL,SD(152)	BREATHE IN THE WIND. THE DOOR IS ON CHARLES'S	LEFT	, BUT IN FRONT OF HIM CLOSE TO THE CORNER FARTHEST FROM
BASH II,1, (103)	A CERT. WHEN CASHEL, DUCKING SMARTLY TO HIS	LEFT	, CROSS-COUNTERED LIKE A HUNDREDWEIGHT OF BRICK--"
MTH5 (208)	YOU DEAD. HAHA! /STREPHON/ (NOW THE ONLY ONE	LEFT	, EXCEPT THE MAIDEN) ARNT YOU COMING, CHLOE? /THE
JOAN 2,SD(71)	WITH DIGNITY WHILST THE CHAMBERLAIN, ON HIS	LEFT	, FUMES ABOUT IN THE WORST OF TEMPERS. /LA TREMOUILLE/
WIDO III SD(49)	IF EVER, OPENED, THERE ARE TWO DOORS: ONE ON THE	LEFT	, FURTHER FORWARD THAN THE FIREPLACE, LEADING TO THE
JOAN 2,SD(80)	LA HIRE IS ON HIS RIGHT. THE ARCHBISHOP, ON HIS	LEFT	, HAS TAKEN HIS PLACE BY THE DAIS: LA TREMOUILLE AT THE
BULL III SD(117)	ON HIS RIGHT; OR, IF HE TURNED SHARP TO HIS	LEFT	, HE COULD PASS ROUND THE END OF THE HOUSE THROUGH AN
SIM PRO,2,SD(26)	THE EDGE AND SIT ON THE SEAT TOGETHER; SHE ON HIS	LEFT	, HE NEAREST THE SEA. /THE Y.W./ IT'S LOVELY HERE.
APPL INTR,SD(243)	WALL NEAR A CORNER, WITH THE OTHER WALL ON HER	LEFT	, HER BACK ALONE IS VISIBLE FROM THE MIDDLE OF THE
ANNA (298)	-- /THE GRAND DUCHESS/ STOP. I HAVE ONE BULLET	LEFT	, IF YOU ATTEMPT TO TAKE THIS FROM ME (PUTTING THE
WIDO III (66)	WITH GALLANTRY). /LICKCHEESE/ (ON TRENCH'S	LEFT	, IN A LOW VOICE) ANY NOOS FOR US, DR TRENCH? /TRENCH/
NEVR II SD(225)	THE SEA, HAS THE HOTEL ON HIS RIGHT, AND ON HIS	LEFT	, IN THE CORNER NEAREST THE SEA, A FLIGHT OF STEPS

HART II SD(112)	IT AS GALILEO MIGHT HAVE DONE. HECTOR SITS ON HIS	LEFT	, IN THE MIDDLE. MANGAN, FORGOTTEN, SITS IN THE PORT
ROCK I SD(193)	AND IN THE END OF THE SAME WALL, ON WALPOLE'S	LEFT	, IS A DOOR LEADING TO THE OFFICE OF SIR ARTHUR'S
CLEO II SD(118)	PTOLEMY'S TUTOR, ANOTHER GROUP, ON PTOLEMY'S	LEFT	, IS HEADED BY ACHILLAS, THE GENERAL OF PTOLEMY'S
MILL III SD(179)	WIFE. HE IS PORING OVER HIS ACCOUNTS. SHE, ON HIS	LEFT	, IS SEWING BUTTONS ON A COAT, WORKING VERY FAST. THERE
FANY III SD(321)	GILBEY. DUVALLET BOWS AND SITS DOWN ON MR KNOX'S	LEFT	, JUGGINS PLACING A CHAIR FOR HIM. /DORA/ NOW, BOBBY:
JITT II SD(27)	MEN, OPENING ON THE CORRIDOR; THE OTHER, ON THEIR	LEFT	, LEADING TO AN INNER ROOM. THE WINDOW FACES THE INNER
SUPR III SD(71)	OF THE ROAD, WHICH SKIRTS THE AMPHITHEATRE ON THE	LEFT	, MAINTAINING ITS HIGHER LEVEL ON EMBANKMENTS AND AN
SIM I SD(42)	SHRINES AND MARCH DOWN UPON HIM, VASHTI TO HIS	LEFT	, MAYA TO HIS RIGHT. /VASHTI/ DARE YOU TREAD THE PLAINS
GETT (340)	NOT A MAN AND NOT A WOMAN! WE HAVE NO CHILDREN	LEFT	, MRS COLLINS. THEY ARE ALL GROWN UP AND MARRIED. /MRS
METH PREFACE(R71)	TO HIS NEED. BUT NO: WE HAVE NO PRINCIPLES	LEFT	, NOT EVEN COMMERCIAL ONES; FOR WHAT SANE COMMERCIALIST
SUPR IV SD(142)	APPEARANCE AT A LITTLE GATE IN A PALING ON OUR	LEFT	, OF HENRY STRAKER IN HIS PROFESSIONAL COSTUME. HE
SUPR I SD(4)	HIM ARE TWO BUSTS ON PILLARS: ONE, TO HIS	LEFT	, OF JOHN BRIGHT; THE OTHER, TO HIS RIGHT, OF MR
CATH 2,SD(174)	THOSE WHO ENTER THROUGH THEM FIND ON THEIR	LEFT	, ON A DAIS OF TWO BROAD STEPS, A MAGNIFICENT CURTAINED
DOCT III SD(131)	THRONE (A CHAIR ON A DAIS) A LITTLE TO THE	LEFT	, OPPOSITE THE INNER DOOR, AND AN EASEL TO THE RIGHT,
PHIL III SD(140)	DISDAINFULLY AS THEY COME FORWARD, CRAVEN ON HER	LEFT	, PARAMORE ON HER RIGHT. /PARAMORE/ WHATS THE MATTER..
APPL I SD(211)	ENTERS. PROTEUS THE PRIME MINISTER HAS ON HIS	LEFT	, PLINY, CHANCELLOR OF THE EXCHEQUER, GOODHUMORED AND
MILL II (177)	OF THE SIX MONTHS I SHALL NOT HAVE A PENNY OF IT	LEFT	, PRAISE BE TO ALLAH. /EPIFANIA/ YOU CONFESS YOURSELF
KING I (173)	TO THE WALL FOR A CHAIR AND PLANTS IT AT FOX'S	LEFT	, QUITE CLOSE). IF I MAY ADD YOU TO THE LIST OF MY
DOCT II SD(115)	WHO BASKS BLISSFULLY IN THE MOONBEAMS. ON THEIR	LEFT	, SCHUTZMACHER AND WALPOLE. THE ENTRANCE TO THE HOTEL
ROCK II SD(240)	SIR ARTHUR IN THE MIDDLE, GLENMORISON ON HIS	LEFT	, SIR BEMROSE ON HIS RIGHT, AND SIR DEXTER AND BASHAM
CAPT I SD(228)	HIS STOOL FROM THE FLOWERBED AND SITS DOWN ON HER	LEFT	, SIR HOWARD BEING ON HER RIGHT. /LADY CICELY/ WHAT A
LION I (125)	HIMSELF UP AND IS SNEAKING PAST FERROVIUS ON HIS	LEFT	, SNEERS DERISIVELY)! ! /FERROVIUS/ (TURNING ON HIM
SUPR III (138)	ON HIS RIGHT AND THE TWO SOCIAL-DEMOCRATS ON HIS	LEFT	, SUPPORTING HIM IN FLANK. /ANN/ IT'S JACK! /TANNER/
SUPR III (78)	WITH SATISFACTION, PLACES HIMSELF ON MENDOZA'S	LEFT	, TANNER BEING ON HIS RIGHT. /MENDOZA/ CAN WE OFFER YOU
JOAN EPILOG (158)	/DUNOIS/ (COMING THROUGH THE TAPESTRY ON JOAN'S	LEFT	, THE CANDLES RELIGHTING THEMSELVES AT THE SAME MOMENT,
2TRU I SD(27)	ON ITS RIGHT AND THE WRITING TABLE ON ITS	LEFT	, THE SCREEN AT RIGHT ANGLES TO THE WARDROBE, AND THE
DEVL III (72)	YOU, PRISONER, IF YOU HAVE ANY SENSE OF DECENCY	LEFT	, TO LISTEN TO THE MINISTRATIONS OF THE CHAPLAIN, AND
MRS III SD(220)	THE MIDDLE OF THE GARDEN AND THEN SWERVES TO ITS	LEFT	, WHERE IT ENDS IN A LITTLE GRAVELLED CIRCUS OPPOSITE
ARMS II SD(23)	THE GARDEN, THE SIDE OF THE HOUSE IS SEEN ON THE	LEFT	, WITH A GARDEN DOOR REACHED BY A LITTLE FLIGHT OF
BARB II SD(273)	HAVE THE GATEWAY LEADING TO THE STREET ON THEIR	LEFT	, WITH A STONE HORSE-TROUGH JUST BEYOND IT, AND, ON THE
JITT II (49)	WITH ME. IF YOU HAVE A SPARK OF DECENT FEELING	LEFT	, YOU WILL NOT FORCE A PUBLIC SCANDAL ON ME. /JITTA/
BASH II,2, (117)	WHERE I PLANT THIS BLOW IS CALLED THE MARK. MY	LEFT	, YOU WILL OBSERVE, I CHIEFLY USE FOR LONG SHOTS: WITH
GENV PREFACE(22)	THE GREATER THE CONFUSION. " SWINGS TO THE	LEFT	" FOLLOWED BY " SWINGS TO THE RIGHT" KEPT THE

LEFTNANT

O'FL (210)	THE BOSHES UNTIL WE MAKE HORATIO BOTTOMLEY LORD	LEFTNANT	OF ENGLAND. DO YOU THINK THATS TRUE, SIR? /SIR

LEFT-HAND

MRS II SD(198)	WITH THE PORCH DOOR TO THE LEFT OF IT. IN THE	LEFT-HAND	SIDE WALL IS THE DOOR LEADING TO THE KITCHEN.
GETT SD(260)	AT SECONDHAND SHOPS. IN THE NEAR END OF THE	LEFT-HAND	WALL A SMALL NORMAN DOOR GIVES ACCESS TO THE

LEFT-RIGHT

FABL VI (131)	MARCH. (BEATING TIME) LEFT-RIGHT, LEFT-RIGHT,	LEFT-RIGHT	. THEY TRAMP OUT RHYTHMICALLY.
FABL VI (131)	IS HEARD. /TEACHER/ LUNCH. MARCH. (BEATING TIME)	LEFT-RIGHT	, LEFT-RIGHT, LEFT-RIGHT. THEY TRAMP OUT
FABL VI (131)	LUNCH. MARCH. (BEATING TIME) LEFT-RIGHT,	LEFT-RIGHT	, LEFT-RIGHT. THEY TRAMP OUT RHYTHMICALLY.

LEFT-TURNS

2TRU II SD(58)	CHUT! DISMISS. MEEK COMES TO ATTENTION, SALUTES,	LEFT-TURNS	, AND GOES OUT AT THE DOUBLE. /TALLBOYS/ (WHO

LEG

DOCT PREFACE(3)	OF GUINEAS THAN THIS MAN IS MAKING OF HIS	LEG	? COULD HE NOT WRITE AS WELL-- OR EVEN BETTER-- ON ONE
SHAK (141)	LAUGHEST THOU AT THYSELF? PULLST THOU MY	LEG	? /SHAV/ THERE IS MORE FUN IN HEAVEN AND EARTH, SWEET
LION PREFACE(25)	WITHOUT ANY MIRACLE: BRING ME A MAN WITH ONLY ONE	LEG	AND MAKE ANOTHER GROW INSTANTANEOUSLY ON HIM BEFORE MY
MTH2 (78)	DEEPER EFFECT ON YOU THAN TO SET YOU PULLING MY	LEG	BY TRYING TO MAKE OUT THAT I AM AN INFIDEL? /LUBIN/
CLEO II (141)	(SITTING DOWN AGAIN, AND SETTING OUT HIS	LEG	FOR BRITANNUS, WHO KNEELS TO PUT ON HIS GREAVES) NEITHER
DOCT PREFACE(13)	MAY PROVE THAT I WAS WRONG; BUT IF I LET THE	LEG	GO, NOBODY CAN EVER PROVE THAT IT WOULD NOT HAVE
MTH5 (241)	KILL HIM? I SHOULDNT DIE IF HE CUT OFF MY ARM OR	LEG	. /ECRASIA/ WHAT NONSENSE! /MARTELLUS/ IT MAY NOT BE
SIM PRO,3, (31)	SAY, IF YOU ASK ME, THAT THE BOOT IS ON THE OTHER	LEG	. /THE PRIEST/ THOSE IMAGES ARE NOT IDOLS: THEY ARE
FANY II (291)	OF HIS NECK WITH THE OTHER. HE COULDNT WHIRL HIS	LEG	LIKE A WINDMILL AND KNOCK A POLICEMAN DOWN BY A GLORIOUS
FANY II (293)	ON DUVALLET. IT WAS THEN THAT DUVALLET SWUNG HIS	LEG	LIKE A WINDMILL AND KNOCKED THE POLICEMAN DOWN. AND THEN
DOCT PREFACE(3)	TO ME JUST NOW. MY WIFE-- MY PRETTY ONES-- THE	LEG	MAY MORTIFY-- IT IS ALWAYS SAFER TO OPERATE-- HE WILL BE
ROCK I (220)	CAN PLAY GOLF; AND SOME OF YOU CAN TALK THE HIND	LEG	OFF A DONKEY; BUT WHEN IT COMES TO BOOK LEARNING ALOYSIA
MTH4 I (172)	DOES NOT MIND THE ACCIDENTAL LOSS OF AN ARM OR A	LEG	OR AN EYE: AFTER ALL, NO ONE WITH TWO LEGS IS UNHAPPY
DOCT PREFACE(4)	NEED NOT TAKE OFF THE RICH MAN'S (OR WOMAN'S)	LEG	OR ARM; HE CAN REMOVE THE APPENDIX OR THE UVULA, AND
PHIL II (122)	AND PLACING IT SO THAT HE IS ABLE TO USE IT FOR A	LEG	REST AS HE SETTLES HIMSELF TO READ ON THE DIVAN WITH HIS
FANY III (303)	THAT HE'S A VERY NICE FELLOW AND CAN SWING HIS	LEG	ROUND LIKE THE HAND OF A CLOCK AND KNOCK A POLICEMAN
PPP (203)	/THE LANDLORD/ (TRYING TO LIFT ADOLPHUS'S	LEG	) AN' PRECIOUS EVVY. (FEELING THE CALF) WOY, EZE GORN
NEVR I (200)	CRITICALLY AT IT AS SHE SPINS IT ROUND ON ONE	LEG	) YOUR FURNITURE ISNT QUITE THE LATEST THING, IS IT?
MTH5 (241)	MAY NOT BE NONSENSE. I DARESAY IF YOU CUT OFF HER	LEG	SHE WOULD GROW ANOTHER, LIKE THE LOBSTERS AND THE LITTLE
DOCT PREFACE(3)	HE NOT WRITE AS WELL-- OR EVEN BETTER-- ON ONE	LEG	THAN ON TWO? AND THE GUINEAS WOULD MAKE ALL THE
METH PREFACE(R56)	MAKES MICE SWEAT; AND THAT IF YOU CUT OFF A DOG'S	LEG	THE THREE-LEGGED DOG WILL HAVE A FOUR-LEGGED PUPPY. I
DOCT PREFACE(13)	THAT IT WAS UNNECESSARY. IF I REFUSE TO ALLOW MY	LEG	TO BE AMPUTATED, ITS MORTIFICATION AND MY DEATH MAY
MILL IV (197)	MY KNEE WAS TWISTED. THE SMALL BONE OF MY	LEG	WAS BROKEN. I RICKED MY SPINE. I HAD TO GIVE THEM A
FOUN (211)	WITH YOUR SHOP: BESIDES, YOU MAY SHAKE A LOOSE	LEG	YOURSELF OCCASIONALLY FOR ALL THE PUBLIC KNOWS, EH?
DOCT PREFACE(3)	SURGEON A PECUNIARY INTEREST IN CUTTING OFF YOUR	LEG	, IS ENOUGH TO MAKE ONE DESPAIR OF POLITICAL HUMANITY.
DOCT PREFACE(64)	OF 104 DEGREES, OR ITS GRANDFATHER HAS BROKEN HIS	LEG	, NOBODY THINKS OF THE DOCTOR EXCEPT AS A HEALER AND
HART PREFACE(17)	TEARING THE GARTER FROM THE KAISER'S	LEG	, STRIKING THE GERMAN DUKES FROM THE ROLL OF OUR

LEGACY

WIDO III (55)	I THINK MR LICKCHEESE MUST HAVE COME INTO A	LEGACY	. (CONFIDENTIALLY) I WONDER WHAT HE CAN WANT WITH
JITT II (36)	YOUR FATHER. HE WILL REGARD YOU AS A SACRED	LEGACY	. /EDITH/ THATS CURIOUS. HE USED THAT WORD HIMSELF
SUPR HANDBOK(195)	OF MEN AND WOMEN, ALL EAGER TO ACCEPT A	LEGACY	OF A MILLION, LIVE AND DIE WITHOUT HAVING EVER
JITT II (36)	POOR PAPA. BUT I DONT INTEND TO BE TAKEN AS A	LEGACY	, SACRED OR NOT. /JITTA/ EDITH: HE FEELS YOUR LOSS AS

LEGAL

BUOY III (44)	I EXPECTED TO SUBSTITUTE PERSONAL EXPERIENCES FOR	LEGAL	ADVICE? MAY I NOT ADVISE WOMEN THOUGH I AM NOT A
BUOY III (30)	QUESTION FIRST PLEASE. MR BUOYANT MUST HAVE HAD	LEGAL	ADVICE DURING ALL THESE YEARS. IS THERE NOT A FAMILY
POSN PREFACE(418)	A PLAY, OR A BOOK, AS TO WHICH, IF I HAD TAKEN	LEGAL	ADVICE, AN EXPERT COULD HAVE ASSURED ME THAT I WAS
GETT PREFACE(247)	SETTLEMENTS TO THE EMPLOYMENT OF SEPARATE	LEGAL	ADVISERS, TO NEUTRALIZE THE ALSATIAN EVILS OF THE
POSN PREFACE(430)	THAN ANY OTHER MEMBER OF THE COMMITTEE ON THE	LEGAL	AND CONSTITUTIONAL ASPECT OF THE QUESTION. HAD HE
JOAN PREFACE(5)	OTHER WORDS, WHEN IT HAS NO OFFICIAL STATUS. THE	LEGAL	AND CONVENTIONAL SUPERIORITY OF HEROD AND PILATE, AND
HART II (116)	CAPTAIN, DOES ANY MODERN GIRL BELIEVE THAT THE	LEGAL	AND ILLEGAL WAYS OF GETTING MONEY ARE THE HONEST AND
BARB PREFACE(242)	EIGHTEENTH AND NINETEENTH CENTURIES, THROWS OUR	LEGAL	AND INDUSTRIAL INSTITUTIONS OUT OF DATE. ANARCHISM
DOCT PREFACE(67)	RESPONSIBLE, THAN IN FOREIGN COUNTRIES WHERE THE	LEGAL	AND MILITARY PROFESSIONS RECOGNIZED THE ADVANTAGES OF
BARB PREFACE(237)	BY WHICH THE RICH ROB AND OPPRESS THE POOR (ON	LEGAL	AND MORAL PRINCIPLES MADE FOR THE PURPOSE), IT IS NOT
METH PREFACE(R67)	OF GOD ARE NOT ALWAYS PERSONS: SOME OF THEM ARE	LEGAL	AND PARLIAMENTARY FICTIONS. ONE OF THEM IS PUBLIC
SUPR PREFACE(R16)	PROTEGGA IL GIUSTO CIELO": THEY GRASP FORMIDABLE	LEGAL	AND SOCIAL WEAPONS, AND RETALIATE. POLITICAL PARTIES
GENV IV (101)	A CAREFUL TRIAL AT WHICH THEY HAVE EVERY POSSIBLE	LEGAL	ASSISTANCE AND PROTECTION. THIS DOES NOT JUSTIFY YOUNG
GETT PREFACE(183)	HOUR, AS THEIR FANCY MAY DICTATE, IN SPITE OF THE	LEGAL	BOND. I DO NOT OBSERVE THAT THEIR UNIONS PROVE LESS
GETT (312)	LENT; WEARS A CASSOCK AND BIRETTA; AND HAS MORE	LEGAL	BUSINESS TO DO THAN EVER HE HAD IN HIS OLD OFFICE IN
JOAN 6 (135)	ARE CARRIED ON BY PEOPLE WHO DO NOT KNOW THEIR	LEGAL	BUSINESS. /COURCELLES/ BUT THE WOMAN IS A HERETIC. I
LIED (192)	ARE DIVORCED. WE SHALL GO THROUGH WHATEVER IDLE	LEGAL	CEREMONY YOU MAY DESIRE. I ATTACH NO IMPORTANCE TO THE
MILL II (169)	THE SLIGHTEST NOTION OF HOW HE CONTRIVED TO GET A	LEGAL	CLAIM ON SO MUCH OF WHAT OTHER PEOPLE MADE; BUT I DO
SIM PREFACE(18)	BY THE INQUISITION FURNISH THE MATERIAL FOR A NEW	LEGAL	CODE. CODIFICATION ENABLES THE WORK OF THE INQUISITION
GETT PREFACE(228)	EACH OTHER WITH A VIEW TO OBTAINING POWERS OF	LEGAL	COERCION OVER ONE ANOTHER. SHELLEY AND QUEEN VICTORIA.
JOAN PREFACE(39)	TO THE FAR MORE CRITICAL FAITH IN THE PARSON,	LEGAL	COMPULSION TO TAKE THE DOCTOR'S PRESCRIPTION, HOWEVER
SUPR HANDBOK(183)	THAN HENRY VIII, FOR THOUGH A GLANCE AT THE	LEGAL	CONDITIONS OF MARRIAGE IN DIFFERENT CHRISTIAN

DOCT PREFACE(11) BETTER OR WORSE THAN THE MILITARY CONSPIRACY, THE LEGAL CONSPIRACY, THE SACERDOTAL CONSPIRACY, THE PEDAGOGIC
SUPR HANDBOK(220) THE MAXIMUM OF OPPORTUNITY. MARRIAGE IS THE ONLY LEGAL CONTRACT WHICH ABROGATES AS BETWEEN THE PARTIES ALL
MILL I (162) LOVED; AND I HOPE HE WILL NOT BE THE LAST. BUT LEGAL DIFFICULTIES DO NOT EXIST FOR PEOPLE WITH MONEY. AT
SUPR PREFACE(R11) TWADDLE ABOUT NOVELET-MADE LOVE. ALL HER PURELY LEGAL DILEMMAS AS TO WHETHER SHE WAS MARRIED OR " BETRAYED,
KING PREFACE(158) MEN. SO FAR NO GREAT HARM HAS BEEN DONE BY THEIR LEGAL DISABILITIES BECAUSE MEN AND WOMEN ARE SO ALIKE THAT
LION PREFACE(31) AND ORDER AS MACHINERY FOR ROBBING THE POOR UNDER LEGAL FORMS; THAT HE THOUGHT DOMESTIC TIES A SNARE FOR THE
BARB III (332) BUT HERE THEY ARE OUTCASTS. THEIR MARRIAGE IS LEGAL IN AUSTRALIA, BUT NOT IN ENGLAND. MY MOTHER IS MY
MRS PREFACE(171) INSTEAD OF VIOLATING MORALS IT ONLY VIOLATES A LEGAL INSTITUTION WHICH IS IN MANY RESPECTS OPPRESSIVE AND
BUOY III (38) LEAVE GOD OUT OF THE QUESTION. MARRIAGE IS A LEGAL INSTITUTION; AND GOD HAS NOTHING TO DO WITH LEGAL
BUOY III (38) LEGAL INSTITUTION; AND GOD HAS NOTHING TO DO WITH LEGAL INSTITUTIONS. /MRS THIRDBORN/ GOD KEEPS BUTTING IN
POSN PREFACE(384) DEPARTMENTS OF HUMAN ACTIVITY ENTIRELY FREE FROM LEGAL INTERFERENCE. THIS HAS NOTHING TO DO WITH ANY SYMPATHY
BULL PREFACE(50) COERCION; AND THE BUREAUCRACY, HOWEVER CIVIL AND LEGAL IT MAY BE IN FORM AND EVEN IN THE CHARACTER OF ITS
HART II (112) UTTERWORD/ GUINNESS! ! /THE BURGLAR/ IT WASNT LEGAL . IVE BEEN MARRIED TO NO END OF WOMEN. NO USE COMING
HART III (140) HONEST: THE BUSINESSES ARE GENUINE AND PERFECTLY LEGAL . /HECTOR/ (DISGUSTED) YAH! NOT EVEN A GREAT
GETT PREFACE(246) A VIRGIN. MARRIAGE MAKES THIS OUTRAGE ABSOLUTELY LEGAL . YOU MAY WITH IMPUNITY DO TO THE PERSON TO WHOM YOU
FOUN (215) IMPOSTOR, YET YOUR MATURE WISDOM AND UNPARALLELED LEGAL KNOWLEDGE ARE FREELY AT THE SERVICE OF ALL DESERVING
HART PREFACE(13) LAW WAS SET ASIDE FOR LYNCH LAW. THE CLIMAX OF LEGAL LAWLESSNESS WAS REACHED IN FRANCE. THE GREATEST
MIS. PREFACE(9) AS THIS SORT OF PIOUS FRAUD HARMS IT, THERE IS A LEGAL LIMIT TO PHYSICAL CRUELTY; AND THERE ARE ALSO HUMAN
FANY I (283) /JUGGINS/ YES, MADAM, I HAD. I EXCEEDED THE LEGAL LIMIT. /MRS GILBEY/ OH, THAT! WHY DO THEY GIVE A
ROCK PREFACE(152) OWNER ACCORDINGLY SACKS THEM, WHICH IS HIS LEGAL METHOD OF EXTERMINATION. DURING THESE DEVELOPMENTS THE
ROCK PREFACE(152) SO I DRIVE THEM OFF MY LAND, WHICH IS MY LEGAL METHOD OF EXTERMINATION, RETAINING ONLY A FEW TO ACT
BARB PREFACE(216) SOMETHING VALUABLE. ONE IS THE INSTITUTION OF A LEGAL MINIMUM WAGE. THE OTHER, OLD AGE PENSIONS. BUT THERE
NEVR III (275) THE BEHAVIOR OF YOUR YOUNGER CHILDREN AMOUNTS TO LEGAL MOLESTATION IS A QUESTION ON WHICH IT MAY BE NECESSARY
SIM PREFACE(11) OBJECT IN CITING IT IS TO DRAW ATTENTION TO THE LEGAL NOVELTY AND IMPORTANCE OF ITS CRITERION OF HUMAN
SIM PREFACE(12) ITS CRITERION OF HUMAN WORTH. I AM CAREFUL TO SAY LEGAL NOVELTY BECAUSE OF COURSE THE CRITERION MUST HAVE BEEN
SIM PREFACE(8) THE SAME, THEY HAVE PLACED EVERY RUSSIAN UNDER A LEGAL OBLIGATION TO EARN HIS OWN LIVING, AND MADE IT A
GETT PREFACE(184) AND AS HARD TO ESCAPE FROM AS THE WORST LEGAL ONE. WE MAY TAKE IT THEN THAT WHEN A JOINT DOMESTIC
POSN PREFACE(417) TO WHOM PLAYS MIGHT BE REFERRED FOR AN OFFICIAL LEGAL OPINION AS TO THEIR COMPLIANCE WITH THE LAW BEFORE
BUOY IV (55) FERDINAND/ THAT ALSO IS A MATTER FOR MEDICAL, NOT LEGAL OPINION. I WILL NOT DISCUSS IT. I HAVE ONLY TO TELL
POSN PREFACE(397) FUNDS TO INSTITUTE PROSECUTIONS AND RECOVER THE LEGAL PENALTIES OF DEFYING IT, NO POWERS OF ARREST OR
DOCT PREFACE(28) TO THE OUTCRY THAT ADDS PRIVATE PERSECUTION TO LEGAL PENALTIES, CAN HAVE NO INTEREST IN THE MATTER EXCEPT
DOCT PREFACE(22) ARE ADJURED, BY PUBLIC NOTICES AND EVEN UNDER LEGAL PENALTIES, NOT TO THROW THEIR MICROBES INTO THE
DOCT PREFACE(34) AND SOCIAL TABOO MAY BE MADE EFFECTIVE BY ACTS OF LEGAL PERSECUTION UNDER COVER OF REPRESSING BLASPHEMY,
POSN PREFACE(391) ENGLAND FROM CENSORSHIP, IF NOT FROM OCCASIONAL LEGAL PERSECUTION. THE STAGE ALONE REMAINS UNDER A
DEVL I (21) /HAWKINS/ THE WILL IS NOT EXACTLY IN PROPER LEGAL PHRASEOLOGY. /RICHARD/ NO: MY FATHER DIED WITHOUT THE
MILL I (153) ME THAT I HAD BETTER CURE MYSELF. WHEN A LEGAL POINT ARISES I CONSULT SIX SOLICITORS, WITH MUCH THE
DOCT III (140) GOING TO SHEW YOU THAT YOURE UTTERLY WRONG ON THE LEGAL POINT; AND I HOPE IT WILL BE A LESSON TO YOU NOT TO BE
GETT PREFACE(192) THROUGH THREE ACTS, WAS FINALLY REWARDED WITH THE LEGAL POSSESSION OF A PRETTY HEROINE'S PERSON ON THE
BULL PREFACE(39) TOO LAZY INTELLECTUALLY TO USE SUCH POLITICAL AND LEGAL POWER AS LIES WITHIN HIS REACH, SUFFERS MORE AND MAKES
HART PREFACE(10) SCALE, CLAMORING FOR AND ACTUALLY ACQUIRING SUCH LEGAL POWERS OVER THE BODIES OF THEIR FELLOW-CITIZENS AS
WIDO III (60) DR TRENCH. THERES NO DOUBT THAT THE VESTRIES HAS LEGAL POWERS TO PLAY OLD HARRY WITH SLUM PROPERTIES, AND
2TRU II (63) AM A BORN PREACHER, NOT A PLEADER. THE THEORY OF LEGAL PROCEDURE IS THAT IF YOU SET TWO LIARS TO EXPOSE ONE
POSN PREFACE(418) BEEN PROSECUTED IN ENGLAND OR MADE THE SUBJECT OF LEGAL PROCEEDINGS, YET I HAVE NEVER PUBLISHED IN MY LIFE AN
DOCT PREFACE(66) WITH HIS OWN HANDS, AS HE WOULD BE IF THE LEGAL PROFESSION WERE AS UNORGANIZED AS THE MEDICAL. THE
BARB PREFACE(243) CURRENT MORALITY, CURRENT RESPECTABILITY, AND LEGAL PROPERTY, THE ORDINARY MAN, UNEDUCATED IN SOCIAL
GETT PREFACE(256) CAN BE ANYTHING MAGICAL AND INVIOLABLE IN THE LEGAL RELATIONS OF DOMESTICITY, AND THE CURIOUS CONFUSION OF
GETT PREFACE(230) STILL BE INFLICTED BY MEN ON THEIR WIVES WITHOUT LEGAL REMEDY. AT ALL SUCH POINTS THE CODE WILL BE SCREWED UP
OVER PREFACE(157) AND SETS MANTRAPS FOR POACHERS, AND DEFENDS HIS LEGAL RIGHTS OVER HIS LAND TO THE EXTREMEST POINT OF
JOAN PREFACE(20) EVEN IN THE VICTORIAN DAYS WHEN WOMEN HAD FEWER LEGAL RIGHTS THAN MEN, AND OUR MODERN WOMEN MAGISTRATES,
GETT (303) BETWEEN LEO AND REJJY AND SINJON ARE PERFECTLY LEGAL ; BUT DO YOU EXPECT ME, AS A BISHOP, TO APPROVE OF
METH PREFACE(R64) LIBERTY MEANT ONLY WAGE SLAVERY WITHOUT THE LEGAL SAFEGUARDS OF CHATTEL SLAVERY. PEOPLE WERE TIRED OF
MIS. PREFACE(75) DO NOT BELONG TO THE WOMAN IN ANY REAL OR LEGAL SENSE. WHEN SHE HAS REARED THEM THEY PASS AWAY FROM
GETT PREFACE(233) IF SHE CHOOSES THE OTHER MAN, HE MUST GIVE WAY, LEGAL TIE OR NO LEGAL TIE; BUT HE KNOWS THAT EITHER ONE OR
GETT PREFACE(233) THE OTHER MAN, HE MUST GIVE WAY, LEGAL TIE OR NO LEGAL TIE; BUT HE KNOWS THAT EITHER ONE OR THE OTHER MUST
DEVL I (23) IS NOT WHAT YOU ARE ASKED, MR HAWKINS. IS IT A LEGAL WILL? /HAWKINS/ THE COURTS WILL SUSTAIN IT AGAINST
DEVL I (23) A PROPER WILL? REMEMBER, I HAVE HIS RIGHTFUL, LEGAL WILL, DRAWN UP BY YOURSELF, LEAVING ALL TO ME.
DOCT PREFACE(62) ARE MEDICAL BLACKGUARDS AS WELL AS MILITARY, LEGAL , AND CLERICAL BLACKGUARDS (ONE SOON FINDS THAT OUT
FABL PREFACE(87) AUTHORITY IN ENGLAND SINCE BENEFIT OF CLERGY WAS LEGAL , AND THE PROFESSIONS WERE CLOSED TO ALL BUT MEMBERS
JOAN PREFACE(33) THAT THE TRIBUNAL WAS NOT ONLY HONEST AND LEGAL , BUT EXCEPTIONALLY MERCIFUL IN RESPECT OF SPARING
ROCK PREFACE(157) ALL THESE AND FOLLOW HIM. BY EVERY ARGUMENT, LEGAL , POLITICAL, RELIGIOUS, CUSTOMARY, AND POLITE, HE WAS

LEGALITY

METH PREFACE(R10) MAN TO WHOM IT OCCURRED THAT MERE MORALITY AND LEGALITY AND URBANITY LEAD NOWHERE, AS IF BUNYAN HAD NEVER
SUPR PREFACE(R35) RIGHTEOUSNESS IS FILTHY RAGS, HIS SCORN FOR MR LEGALITY IN THE VILLAGE OF MORALITY, HIS DEFIANCE OF THE
JOAN PREFACE(42) OR AS CONSCIENTIOUS A JUDGE TO INSIST ON STRICT LEGALITY OF PROCEDURE AS JOAN HAD FROM THE INQUISITION AND

LEGALIZE

BARB PREFACE(217) SUCH AN INCOME, AND ARE, OF COURSE, CAREFUL TO LEGALIZE AND MORALIZE BOTH IT AND ALL THE ACTIONS AND

LEGALIZED

FABL PREFACE(98) ALL FORMS OF PERSECUTION, FROM PETTY BOYCOTTS TO LEGALIZED BURNINGS AT THE STAKE AND BREAKINGS ON THE WHEEL,
METH PREFACE(R64) EXCEPT POLICE ORGANIZATION TO PROTECT LEGALIZED FRAUD AGAINST FISTICUFFS, ALL ATTEMPT TO INTRODUCE
GETT PREFACE(216) AND IF THEY DO MEAN CELIBATE, THEN MARRIAGE IS LEGALIZED IMPURITY, A CONCLUSION WHICH IS OFFENSIVE AND
LION PREFACE(12) THE PRIMITIVE IDEA OF JUSTICE IS PARTLY LEGALIZED REVENGE AND PARTLY EXPIATION BY SACRIFICE. IT

LEGALIZING

GETT PREFACE(203) AS IN THE CASE OF THE RECENT LONG-DELAYED ACT LEGALIZING MARRIAGE WITH A DECEASED WIFE'S SISTER. WHEN A
GETT PREFACE(209) ACCEPTANCE OF MARRIAGE WITH THE CHILD'S FATHER BY LEGALIZING POLYGYNY, BECAUSE THERE ARE MORE ADULT WOMEN IN
BULL IV (150) IT SHALL BE MY FIRST CARE TO INTRODUCE A BILL LEGALIZING SUCH AN OPERATION. I BELIEVE A LARGE SECTION OF

LEGALLY

SUPR III SD(72) ANNOUNCING HIMSELF AS A DESTITUTE PERSON, AND LEGALLY COMPELLING THE GUARDIANS TO FEED, CLOTHE, AND HOUSE
BULL PREFACE(61) IN QUESTION THE UNANIMOUS SENTENCE PASSED BY A LEGALLY CONSTITUTED COURT, OF WHICH THE BEST ENGLISH AND THE
BARB PREFACE(234) ONE WHO BUT A SHORT TIME BEFORE WOULD HAVE BEEN LEGALLY DISQUALIFIED FOR THE POST EVEN OF A PRIVATE SOLDIER
SUPR HANDBOK(213) IN THE PEERAGE, THOUGH THE HEIR TO A DUKEDOM IS LEGALLY FREE TO MARRY A DAIRYMAID, YET THE SOCIAL PRESSURE
SUPR HANDBOK(183) CHRISTIAN COUNTRIES SHEWS THAT MARRIAGE VARIES LEGALLY FROM FRONTIER TO FRONTIER, DOMESTICITY VARIES SO
GETT PREFACE(221) INTO A PROMISE OF MARRIAGE TO WHICH HE CAN BE LEGALLY HELD, OR ELSE INTO AN INDISCRETION WHICH HE MUST
OVER PREFACE(159) ANY KNOWLEDGE OF THE SAVAGE PUNISHMENTS THAT ARE LEGALLY INFLICTED FOR ABERRATIONS AND ABSURDITIES TO WHICH
GETT (293) IGNORANCE OF WHAT I WAS LETTING MYSELF IN FOR LEGALLY . HAVING GIVEN MY WORD, I WILL STAND TO IT. YOU HAVE
BUOY III (31) MONEY THAT WHATEVER HE SAYS, GOES. /SIR F./ NOT LEGALLY . /THE WIDOWER/ NO DOUBT. BUT IT WORKS
ROCK PREFACE(155) AND (IN SCOTLAND) VITRIOL THROWERS, WHO CAN BE LEGALLY KILLED. A RUNAWAY CONVICT CAN ALSO BE SUMMARILY SHOT
SUPR I (44) WOMANHOOD; AND THAT THE FACT OF YOUR NOT BEING LEGALLY MARRIED MATTERS NOT ONE SCRAP EITHER TO YOUR OWN
DOCT III (139) CONSISTS IN SUSPECTING OTHER PEOPLE OF NOT BEING LEGALLY MARRIED. ARNT YOU ASHAMED OF YOURSELVES? CAN ONE OF
2TRU I (46) THOUGH UNITED IN THE SIGHT OF HEAVEN, WERE NOT LEGALLY MARRIED, AT LEAST SO SHE TELLS ME. /THE NURSE/ (
BARB PREFACE(243) WASTE AND DISORDER, BY INTELLECTUAL CONSTITUTION LEGALLY MINDED TO THE VERGE OF PEDANTRY, AND BY TEMPERAMENT
BULL IV (150) IS ALL BUT EXTINCT IN MY OWN COUNTRY. IF IT WERE LEGALLY POSSIBLE I SHOULD BECOME A NATURALIZED IRISHMAN; AND
POSN PREFACE(367) PLACES HIM ABOVE THE LAW; FOR THOUGH IT MAY BE LEGALLY POSSIBLE TO PROSECUTE A LICENSED PLAY, NOBODY EVER
POSN PREFACE(367) NEVER HEARD. YET IF HE PRODUCES THE PLAY HE IS LEGALLY RESPONSIBLE JUST AS IF HE HAD WRITTEN IT HIMSELF.
GETT (294) DIDNT KNOW THAT WHEN WE WERE MARRIED I SHOULD BE LEGALLY RESPONSIBLE IF SHE LIBELLED ANYBODY, THOUGH ALL HER
DOCT PREFACE(48) BITE HURTS SO LITTLE THAT THE CREATURE IS ALMOST, LEGALLY SPEAKING, A VIVISECTOR WHO INFLICTS NO PAIN. BY
SIM PREFACE(8) AND ARE ACTUALLY, WHEN THEY HAVE BEEN CONFIRMED, LEGALLY SUBJECT TO RUINOUS PENALTIES FOR QUESTIONING IT. IT
LION PREFACE(59) OF LAND AND CAPITAL ARE ECONOMICALLY, THOUGH NOT LEGALLY , IN THE CATEGORY OF ROBBERS, AND HAVE GROTESQUELY

LEGEND

METH PREFACE(R78) REFUSED TO ACCEPT A GOOD LEGEND WITH DELIGHT AS A LEGEND ? THE LEGENDS, THE PARABLES, THE DRAMAS, ARE AMONG
MTH5 (262) ME AND SUPERSEDE ME, AND LILITH WILL BE ONLY A LEGEND AND A LAY THAT HAS LOST ITS MEANING. OF LIFE ONLY IS
METH PREFACE(R77) IT. THIS DOES NOT MEAN THAT WE SHOULD THROW AWAY LEGEND AND PARABLE AND DRAMA: THEY ARE THE NATURAL VEHICLES

LION PREFACE(20)	THIS CRAZE NO DOUBT LED HIM TO SEEK FOR SOME	LEGEND	BEARING OUT HOSEA'S " OUT OF EGYPT HAVE I CALLED MY
METH PREFACE(R77)	BY ITS OWN LIGHT: NO DOGMA CAN BE A LEGEND. A	LEGEND	CAN PASS AN ETHNICAL FRONTIER AS A LEGEND, BUT NOT AS
MTH5 (224)	IN A GOLDEN AGE OF THE PAST. THIS SPLENDID	LEGEND	ENDURED BECAUSE IT LIVED AS A DESIRE IN THE HEARTS OF
METH PREFACE(R77)	WOE TO THE CHURCHES AND RULERS WHO SUBSTITUTE THE	LEGEND	FOR THE DOGMA, THE PARABLE FOR THE HISTORY, THE DRAMA
METH PREFACE(R77)	SEE THE TRUTH BY ITS OWN LIGHT: NO DOGMA CAN BE A	LEGEND	. A LEGEND CAN PASS AN ETHNICAL FRONTIER AS A LEGEND,
MTH5 (224)	BELIEVE SUCH A TALE LITERALLY. IT IS ONLY A	LEGEND	. WE DO NOT BELIEVE IN ARCHANGELS; AND THE NOTION
METH PREFACE(R77)	AUTHORITY, EVEN MY AUTHORITY (AS A PROFESSIONAL	LEGEND	MAKER) IF IT CANNOT SEE THE TRUTH BY ITS OWN LIGHT:
MTH5 (223)	A THING THAT IS TO BE DONE IN THE FUTURE. IT IS A	LEGEND	OF A SUPERNATURAL BEING CALLED THE ARCHANGEL MICHAEL.
METH PREFACE(R89)	RARE. I NOW FIND MYSELF INSPIRED TO MAKE A SECOND	LEGEND	OF CREATIVE EVOLUTION WITHOUT DISTRACTIONS AND
LION PREFACE(18)	POINT. ALL THAT NEED BE NOTED HERE IS THAT THE	LEGEND	OF DIVINE BIRTH WAS SURE TO BE ATTACHED SOONER OR
METH PREFACE(R88)	IT PROPERLY. ACCORDINGLY, IN 1901, I TOOK THE	LEGEND	OF DON JUAN IN ITS MOZARTIAN FORM AND MADE IT A
METH PREFACE(R89)	IS NOT ONE TO BE TRIFLED WITH. I ABANDON THE	LEGEND	OF DON JUAN WITH ITS EROTIC ASSOCIATIONS, AND GO BACK
ROCK PREFACE(177)	MADE IN OUR KNOWLEDGE OF NATURE. IN TREATING THE	LEGEND	OF JOSHUA'S VICTORY AS A RELIGIOUS TRUTH INSTEAD OF
METH PREFACE(R78)	THEIR INTELLECTUAL CONSCIENCES BY READING THE	LEGEND	OF NOAH'S ARK, WITH ITS FUNNY BEGINNING ABOUT THE
METH PREFACE(R89)	WITH ITS EROTIC ASSOCIATIONS, AND GO BACK TO THE	LEGEND	OF THE GARDEN OF EDEN. I EXPLOIT THE ETERNAL INTEREST
JOAN PREFACE(46)	BUT THEY ALL BREAK DOWN ON THE MELODRAMATIC	LEGEND	OF THE WICKED BISHOP AND THE ENTRAPPED MAIDEN AND THE
METH PREFACE(R78)	BUT WHO HAS EVER REFUSED TO ACCEPT A GOOD	LEGEND	WITH DELIGHT AS A LEGEND? THE LEGENDS, THE PARABLES,
METH PREFACE(R77)	TRUTH OR MATERIAL SUBSTANTIALITY OF SOME	LEGEND	, AND KILLING THOSE WHO REFUSE TO ACCEPT IT AS
METH PREFACE(R77)	A LEGEND CAN PASS AN ETHNICAL FRONTIER AS A	LEGEND	, BUT NOT AS A TRUTH; WHILST THE ONLY FRONTIER TO THE
DOCT PREFACE(36)	TO REBUILD HER IN THAT WAY. IN THE OLD HEBREW	LEGEND	, GOD LOST PATIENCE WITH THE WORLD AS NERO DID WITH
SUPR III (124)	CONDEMNED, HAVE MADE ME SO INTERESTING A HERO OF	LEGEND	, I WAS NOT INFREQUENTLY MET IN SOME SUCH WAY AS
BULL PREFACE(36)	WHO SHALL HAVE FORGOTTEN THE TRADITIONAL COUNTER	LEGEND	, " TO HELL WITH KING WILLIAM! " (OF GLORIOUS,

LEGENDARY

3PLA PREFACE(R26)	MYSELF, WHILST STILL IN MIDDLE LIFE, ALMOST AS	LEGENDARY	A PERSON AS THE FLYING DUTCHMAN. CRITICS, LIKE
LION PREFACE(28)	REALLY THE CHRIST, IT IS A NECESSARY PART OF HIS	LEGENDARY	DESTINY THAT HE SHALL BE SLAIN. PETER, NOT
LION PREFACE(48)	TO SOME THE WALKING ON THE WATER WILL BE A	LEGENDARY	EXAGGERATION OF A SWIM, ENDING IN AN ORDINARY
LION PREFACE(87)	LOST HIS HEAD; BELIEVED HIMSELF TO BE A CRUDE	LEGENDARY	FORM OF GOD; AND UNDER THAT DELUSION COURTED AND
JOAN PREFACE(25)	THE LITERARY REPRESENTATIONS OF THE MAID WERE	LEGENDARY	, BUT THE PUBLICATION BY QUICHERAT IN 1841 OF THE
JOAN PREFACE(15)	THE WORLD ARE MADE APPREHENSIBLE BY AN ARRAY OF	LEGENDARY	PERSONAGES, WITH AN ALMIGHTY FATHER, AND SOMETIMES
3PLA PREFACE(R26)	BEFORE THEM. IN MY PLAYS THEY LOOK FOR MY	LEGENDARY	QUALITIES, AND FIND ORIGINALITY AND BRILLIANCY IN
FANY PREFACE(256)	AND PLAYGOERS WHO ARE SO OBSESSED BY MY STRAINED	LEGENDARY	REPUTATION THAT THEY APPROACH MY PLAYS IN A

LEGENDS

MILL PREFACE(113)	HONEST RULER BECOMES A TYRANT AND A FABRICATOR OF	LEGENDS	AND FALSEHOODS, NOT OUT OF ANY DEVILMENT IN HIMSELF,
METH PREFACE(R79)	LEGENDS. WHAT WE SHOULD DO, THEN, IS TO POOL OUR	LEGENDS	AND MAKE A DELIGHTFUL STOCK OF RELIGIOUS FOLK-LORE
METH PREFACE(R86)	BUT HE DID NOT WRITE ANY OF THEM, BECAUSE THESE	LEGENDS	ARE NO LONGER RELIGIOUS: APHRODITE AND ARTEMIS AND
METH PREFACE(R78)	IN ENGLAND TODAY GOOD BOOKS OF EASTERN RELIGIOUS	LEGENDS	ARE READ EAGERLY; AND PROTESTANTS AND ATHEISTS READ
METH PREFACE(R78)	AND THIS IS BECAUSE THE IMPOSITION OF THE	LEGENDS	AS LITERAL TRUTHS AT ONCE CHANGES THEM FROM PARABLES
METH PREFACE(R78)	THAT THEY DO WELL TO BE ANGRY. EVERY ONE OF THESE	LEGENDS	IS THE COMMON HERITAGE OF THE HUMAN RACE; AND THERE
LION PREFACE(81)	WHILST NEGRO PICCANINNIES ARE REJOICING IN ITS	LEGENDS	. PAUL'S QUALITIES. PAUL, HOWEVER, DID NOT GET HIS
METH PREFACE(R79)	OF OUR CONTEMPORARY MONARCHS. WHAT TO DO WITH THE	LEGENDS	. WHAT WE SHOULD DO, THEN, IS TO POOL OUR LEGENDS
METH PREFACE(R39)	ANTHROPOMORPHIC: THEY STOOD BY THE OLD TESTAMENT	LEGENDS	OF A GOD WHOSE PARTS HAD BEEN SEEN BY ONE OF THE
METH PREFACE(R79)	FOR THE VIRGIN MARY, WOULD BUY HIM A BOOKFUL OF	LEGENDS	OF THE CREATION AND OF MOTHERS OF GOD FROM ALL PARTS
METH PREFACE(R78)	AND PROTESTANTS AND ATHEISTS READ ROMAN CATHOLIC	LEGENDS	OF THE SAINTS WITH PLEASURE. BUT SUCH FARE IS
METH PREFACE(R86)	THEY COULD DRAW FROM THE FAMILIAR AND SACRED	LEGENDS	OF THEIR COUNTRY. " LET US ALL," HE SAID, " WRITE AN
METH PREFACE(R74)	IT FROM THE SLUDGY RESIDUE OF TEMPORALITIES AND	LEGENDS	THAT ARE MAKING BELIEF IMPOSSIBLE, THOUGH THEY ARE
METH PREFACE(R80)	KEPT PURE, AND YOU MAY TAKE THE LAW AND LEAVE THE	LEGENDS	WITHOUT SUSPICION OF HERESY. ACCORDINGLY, THE TOWER
METH PREFACE(R80)	CANNOT BECOME A POPULAR RELIGION UNTIL IT HAS ITS	LEGENDS	, ITS PARABLES, ITS MIRACLES. AND WHEN I SAY POPULAR
METH PREFACE(R78)	A GOOD LEGEND WITH DELIGHT AS A LEGEND? THE	LEGENDS	, THE PARABLES, THE DRAMAS, ARE AMONG THE CHOICEST
METH PREFACE(R79)	CREED. IT IS NOT THAT SCIENCE IS FREE FROM	LEGENDS	, WITCHCRAFT, MIRACLES, BIOGRAPHIC BOOSTINGS OF
CLEO NOTES (212)	AND SANGUINARY SENSATIONALISM OF OUR RELIGIOUS	LEGENDS	, WITH THEIR SUBSTITUTION OF GROSS PHYSICAL TORMENTS

LEGGO

BULL III (130)	DOWN AGAIN) I'M GOIN, I SAY. (RAISING HIS VOICE)	LEGGO	ME COAT, BARNEY DORAN. /DORAN/ SIT DOWN, YOWL

LEGIBLE

PYGM PREFACE(201)	OBJECTIVE WAS THE PROVISION OF A FULL, ACCURATE,	LEGIBLE	SCRIPT FOR OUR NOBLE BUT ILL-DRESSED LANGUAGE; BUT
PYGM PREFACE(201)	DETERMINATION TO MAKE THIS REMARKABLE AND QUITE	LEGIBLE	SCRIPT SERVE ALSO AS A SHORTHAND REDUCED IT IN HIS

LEGION

CLEO PRO2 (98)	CAESAR DOES NOT PIT MAN AGAINST MAN: HE THROWS A	LEGION	AT YOU WHERE YOU ARE WEAKEST AS HE THROWS A STONE
CLEO II (138)	DOWN TO CAESAR AND SCOLDING HIM) CAN I EMBARK A	LEGION	IN FIVE MINUTES? THE FIRST COHORT IS ALREADY ON THE
CLEO PRO2 (98)	AS HE THROWS A STONE FROM A CATAPULT; AND THAT	LEGION	IS AS A MAN WITH ONE HEAD, A THOUSAND ARMS, AND NO
LION I (114)	PRISONERS IN THE CUSTODY OF A COHORT OF THE TENTH	LEGION	. AMONG THESE PRISONERS YOU WILL PARTICULARLY

LEGIONARY

CYMB V (140)	PERHAPS. WHEN ALL WAS LOST HE FOUGHT LIKE ANY	LEGIONARY	, SWORD IN HAND. HIS LAST REPORTED WORD WAS " SAVE

LEGIONS

CLEO PRO1 (91)	IS POMPEY, AND THE OLD ROME, AND THE LAW AND THE	LEGIONS	: ALL ALL AGAINST ME; BUT HIGH ABOVE THESE ARE THE
CLEO IV (172)	FOR CAESAR. CAESAR HAS HELD YOU AT BAY WITH TWO	LEGIONS	: WE SHALL SEE WHAT HE WILL DO WITH TWENTY.
CLEO PRO2 (99)	YE, THE TEMPLE GUARD! DID YE NOT WITHSTAND THESE	LEGIONS	? /BEL AFFRIS/ WHAT MAN COULD, THAT WE DID. BUT
METH PREFACE(R71)	BUT THE SUPREME COUNCIL, WITH ALL ITS VICTORIOUS	LEGIONS	AND ALL ITS PRESTIGE, CANNOT GET US OUT OF IT,
CLEO IV (183)	/RUFIO/ AY: NOW HE WILL CONQUER AFRICA WITH TWO	LEGIONS	BEFORE WE COME TO THE ROAST BOAR. /APOLLODORUS/
MILL PREFACE(115)	MARCH TO MOSCOW, ONLY TO HURRY BACK LEAVING HIS	LEGIONS	DEAD IN THE SNOW, AND THEREAFTER GO FROM DISASTER TO
CLEO IV (172)	HIS TEN; AND WE WILL DRIVE HIM AND HIS BEGGARLY	LEGIONS	INTO THE SEA. /CLEOPATRA/ (WITH SCORN, GETTING UP
CLEO I (112)	SHAKING? /CAESAR/ IT IS THE TREAD OF CAESAR'S	LEGIONS	. /CLEOPATRA/ (DRAWING HIM AWAY) THIS WAY, QUICKLY.
CLEO PRO2 (100)	WARRIOR IS LEFT STANDING BETWEEN YOU AND HIS	LEGIONS	. /THE SENTINEL/ WOE, ALAS! (HE THROWS DOWN HIS
CYMB V (139)	MAN IN ONE ENORMOUS SHOCK HURLED ON OUR SHAKEN	LEGIONS	, THEN THEIR CHARIOTS WITH EVERY AXLE FURNISHED WITH
UNPL PREFACE(R26)	TO WHOM I MYSELF BELONG, NOT TO MENTION THE	LEGIONS	OF LAWYERS, DOCTORS, CLERGYMEN, AND PLATFORM
ROCK PREFACE(166)	NEED THEM TO LIVE IN. AND IT WAS THE RESULTANT	LEGIONS	OF PETTY LANDED PROPRIETORS THAT MADE LENIN'S
CLEO II (139)	NOW, AWAY WITH YOU TO ACHILLAS; AND BORROW HIS	LEGIONS	TO PUT OUT THE FIRE. (HE HURRIES HIM TO THE STEPS).
INCA PREFACE(231)	OUR VICTORIOUS HANDS, WAS STILL THE CAESAR WHOSE	LEGIONS	WE WERE RESISTING WITH OUR HEARTS IN OUR MOUTHS.
CLEO II (120)	KING'S GENERAL SPEAK! /ACHILLAS/ BUT TWO ROMAN	LEGIONS	, O KING. THREE THOUSAND SOLDIERS AND SCARCE A
CLEO PRO2 (99)	WHEN WE CAME UPON A CITY RABBLE FLYING FROM HIS	LEGIONS	, WHOSE LANDING THEY HAD GONE OUT TO WITHSTAND.

LEGISLATE

HART PREFACE(13)	OF WAR; BUT THE GOVERNMENT HAD NOT THE COURAGE TO	LEGISLATE	ACCORDINGLY; AND ITS LAW WAS SET ASIDE FOR LYNCH
GETT PREFACE(218)	MAKES NO DIFFERENCE. THOSE WHO TALK AND WRITE AND	LEGISLATE	AS IF ALL THIS COULD BE PREVENTED BY MAKING SOLEMN
FABL PREFACE(82)	AND EFFICIENT CLERGYMAN. NEVERTHELESS WE CANNOT	LEGISLATE	FOR EVERY INDIVIDUAL SEPARATELY, NOR PROVIDE A
BULL PREFACE(47)	THAT THOSE WHO HAVE ARE THEREFORE QUALIFIED TO	LEGISLATE	FOR IT, IS AS ABSURD AS TO ASSUME THAT A MAN WHO
GETT PREFACE(223)	AND ASK US TO REGARD IT, AND FEEL ABOUT IT, AND	LEGISLATE	ON IT, WHOLLY AS IF IT WERE AN IMPERSONAL ONE, IS
DOCT PREFACE(34)	LEARNING BY INSTINCT: THAT IS, AS OF RIGHT. WE	LEGISLATE	ON THE ASSUMPTION THAT NO MAN MAY BE KILLED ON THE
2TRU PREFACE(15)	ARE EQUALLY QUALIFIED OR EQUALLY DESIROUS TO	LEGISLATE	, TO GOVERN, TO ADMINISTER, TO MAKE DECISIONS, TO

LEGISLATED

FABL PREFACE(82)	UNDERSTAND THE TEN COMMANDMENTS WELL ENOUGH TO BE	LEGISLATED	FOR IN THE MASS. SHAM DEMOCRACY. IN THE FACE OF

LEGISLATION

GETT PREFACE(198)	WOULD PROBABLY BRING ABOUT MORE STRINGENT	LEGISLATION	AGAINST ACTIONS GOING BEYOND THE STRICT LETTER
MTH3 (127)	/BARNABAS/ IF THEY FORCE ME TO IT I WILL OBTAIN	LEGISLATION	AGAINST MARRIAGES ABOVE THE AGE OF
BARB PREFACE(210)	EXTENT TO WHICH PUBLIC OPINION, AND CONSEQUENTLY	LEGISLATION	AND JURISPRUDENCE, IS CORRUPTED BY FEMINIST
DOCT PREFACE(79)	WORDS " REMEMBER THAT I TOO AM MORTAL." 11. IN	LEGISLATION	AND SOCIAL ORGANIZATION, PROCEED ON THE
DOCT PREFACE(24)	DEFEND PROPHYLACTIC MEASURES AND PROPHYLACTIC	LEGISLATION	AS THE SOLE AND CERTAIN SALVATION OF MANKIND
POSN PREFACE(419)	IT IS CONSIDERED THAT AT PRESENT, WITHOUT ANY NEW	LEGISLATION	AT ALL, ANY MANAGER WHO IS DOUBTFUL ABOUT A PLAY

MIS. PREFACE(6) WERE AT THEIR WORST; AND THE EXTENSION OF SUCH LEGISLATION AT PRESENT WOULD BE IMPOSSIBLE IF IT WERE NOT
MIS. PREFACE(6) RUTHLESSLY TO MAKE MONEY FOR THE HOUSEHOLD. SUCH LEGISLATION HAS ALWAYS BEEN FURIOUSLY RESISTED BY THE
BARB PREFACE(216) IN THE SAME WAY? IS THERE ANY RADICLE OF SUCH LEGISLATION IN OUR PARLIAMENTARY SYSTEM? WELL, THERE ARE
DOCT PREFACE(56) REDUCTION IN CHILD MORTALITY, LEADING TO FURTHER LEGISLATION INCREASING THE QUANTITY OF BRANDY TO A GALLON.
METH PREFACE(R63) WERE PRESENTLY ASSURING US THAT TEMPERANCE LEGISLATION IS A VAIN DEFIANCE OF NATURAL SELECTION, AND
APPL I (218) THAT EVERYTHING THAT IS OF ANY VALUE IN OUR LEGISLATION IS YOUR DOING AND NOT OURS. WE CANNOT HAVE YOU
KING PREFACE(158) ARE SO ALIKE THAT FOR THE PURPOSES OF OUR CRUDE LEGISLATION IT MATTERS LITTLE WHETHER JURIES AND PARLIAMENTS
APPL I (213) REMAINING DEFENCE OF THE PEOPLE AGAINST CORRUPT LEGISLATION . /BOANERGES/ SO IT IS, BY JINGO. WHAT OTHER
DOCT PREFACE(52) AND OF THE ILLUSIONS WHICH BESET PUBLIC HEALTH LEGISLATION . WHAT THE PUBLIC WANTS AND WILL NOT GET. THE
MTH2 (52) YOU IN POWER ON CONDITION THAT YOU DROPPED ALL LEGISLATION OF WHICH THEY DID NOT APPROVE, AND YOU COULD NOT
DOCT PREFACE(57) HAVING ARRIVED AT THIS STAGE, BEING AS TO HEALTH LEGISLATION ONLY AT THE BEGINNING OF THINGS, WE HAVE
MTH2 (61) AND DISTRIBUTION OF WEALTH CAN BE CONTROLLED BY LEGISLATION OR BY ANY HUMAN ACTION WHATEVER. THEY OBEY FIXED
GETT PREFACE(206) A STATESMAN WHO CONFINES HIMSELF TO POPULAR LEGISLATION -- OR, FOR THE MATTER OF THAT, A PLAYWRIGHT WHO
MIS. PREFACE(34) IT WILL BEQUEATH TO FUTURE GENERATIONS A MASS OF LEGISLATION TO PREVENT CAPITALISTS FROM " USING UP NINE
APPL I (235) SCAPEGOAT: YOU GET THE CREDIT OF ALL OUR POPULAR LEGISLATION WHILST YOU PUT THE ODIUM OF ALL OUR RESISTANCE
MIS. PREFACE(34) THE FOUNDER OF ENGLISH SOCIALISM, MOST OF THIS LEGISLATION WILL BECOME AN INSUFFERABLE RESTRAINT UPON
BULL PREFACE(39) INFINITE CONFUSION AND HINDRANCE IN HER OWN LEGISLATION , A HATRED THAT CIRCULATES THROUGH THE WHOLE
ROCK PREFACE(154) THAT PRIVATE PROPERTY, ALREADY MAIMED BY FACTORY LEGISLATION , SURTAX, AND A GOOD DEAL OF PETTY PERSECUTION

LEGISLATIVE

BULL PREFACE(44) HOME RULE IS AT LAST ACHIEVED, ONE OF OUR FIRST LEGISLATIVE ACTS WILL BE TO FORTIFY THE SUBSISTENCE OF OUR
GENV I (36) THE LAWFUL INGRESS OF DULY ELECTED MEMBERS TO THE LEGISLATIVE CHAMBER. WHATS TO BE DONE WITH HIM? /SHE/ QUITE
2TRU PREFACE(16) RANDOM MEN OF GENIUS UNABLE TO AGREE ON A SINGLE LEGISLATIVE MEASURE OR POINT OF POLICY. AN ECUMENICAL
MIS. PREFACE(56) THAT HE CARES TO PRESCRIBE. SUCH AN ACT IS NOT A LEGISLATIVE PHENOMENON BUT A PSYCHOPATHIC ONE. ITS EFFECT ON

LEGISLATIVELY

DOCT PREFACE(79) EVERY INDIVIDUAL ALIVE IS OF INFINITE VALUE IS LEGISLATIVELY IMPRACTICABLE. NO DOUBT THE HIGHER THE LIFE WE
MRS PREFACE(152) PROFESSION CAME TO BE CALLED, WAS DEALT WITH LEGISLATIVELY , ALL THAT PARLIAMENT DID WAS TO ENACT THAT

LEGISLATOR

BULL PREFACE(33) OF THE MUTUALLY EXCLUSIVE FUNCTIONS OF JUDGE AND LEGISLATOR . FOR THERE IS ONLY ONE CONDITION ON WHICH A MAN
DOCT PREFACE(37) THE MOST DIFFICULT OF THE UNENDING TASKS OF THE LEGISLATOR . OUR OWN CRUELTIES. AT FIRST BLUSH IT MAY SEEM
CAPT NOTES (300) SOMEHOW. THAT HE MADE PREGNANT UTTERANCES AS A LEGISLATOR MAY BE TAKEN AS PROVED BY THE KEEN PHILOSOPHY OF
LION PREFACE(101) FOOL AND A SCOUNDREL FOR ANY USE HE COULD BE AS A LEGISLATOR OR A STATE OFFICIAL. THE MODERN PSEUDO-DEMOCRATIC
FABL PREFACE(88) DEAD AND FOREIGN, PUTS A MEZZOFANTI, USELESS AS A LEGISLATOR OR ADMINISTRATOR, ABOVE A SOLON WHO KNOWS NO

LEGISLATOR'S

SUPR HANDBOK(210) THE CAPITALIST, AND OF THE ETHICAL PROFESSOR'S, LEGISLATOR'S , EDUCATOR'S DREAM OF PUTTING COMMANDMENTS AND

LEGISLATORS

MRS PREFACE(152) EVER. IT WAS THE FAULT OF THE CENSORSHIP THAT OUR LEGISLATORS AND JOURNALISTS WERE NOT BETTER INSTRUCTED. IN
SUPR HANDBOK(207) LAW, ARE AT LEAST MORE MERCIFUL THAN THE AMERICAN LEGISLATORS AND JUDGES WHO NOT SO LONG AGO CONDEMNED MEN TO
MIS. PREFACE(42) TO PUT UP AN EFFECTIVE FENCE: THAT IS WHY BOTH LEGISLATORS AND PARENTS AND THE PAID DEPUTIES OF PARENTS ARE
FABL PREFACE(66) WITHOUT DIRECTORS AND DECIDERS, WITHOUT LEGISLATORS AND THINKERS, THESE ALSO ARE PROVIDED IN THE
LION PREFACE(73) IS SLOWLY DRIVING BOTH OUR SOCIOLOGISTS AND OUR LEGISLATORS . THIS WILL NOT INSTANTLY CURE ALL THE EVILS OF

LEGISLATURE

BULL III (136) VOICE-- I LOOK FORWARD TO THE TIME WHEN AN IRISH LEGISLATURE SHALL ARISE ONCE MORE ON THE EMERALD PASTURE OF
SUPR III (106) I SPENT AN EVENING LATELY IN A CERTAIN CELEBRATED LEGISLATURE , AND HEARD THE POT LECTURING THE KETTLE FOR ITS

LEGISLATURES

APPL PREFACE(190) IN THESE ISLANDS TWO OR THREE ADDITIONAL FEDERAL LEGISLATURES , WORKING ON OUR MUNICIPAL COMMITTEE SYSTEM

LEGITIMACY

JOAN PREFACE(13) COUNTERBLOW TO THE SUSPICIONS THEN CURRENT OF HIS LEGITIMACY AND CONSEQUENTLY OF HIS TITLE, WERE MILITARY AND
JOAN 1 (64) TO KNOW. THINK OF THAT! THE QUEEN DENYING THE LEGITIMACY OF HER OWN SON! /ROBERT/ WELL, SHE MARRIED HER
ANNA PREFACE(287) INDULGENCE AS THREE NOVICES FRESH FROM THE AWFUL LEGITIMACY OF THE HIGHBROW THEATRE. WELL, MISS MCCARTHY AND

LEGITIMATE

FANY III (318) ANYBODY MAY BE THE SON OF A DUKE, YOU KNOW. IS HE LEGITIMATE ? /GILBEY/ GOOD LORD! I NEVER THOUGHT OF THAT.
MILL I (149) POINT OF PARDONING HIM AND GIVING HIM A NIGHT OF LEGITIMATE BLISS WOULD BE CAPABLE OF ANY IMBECILITY.
ROCK PREFACE(162) THEY ARE FREE TO ENTER UPON A SERIES OF QUITE LEGITIMATE BUT NOT THE LESS NEFARIOUS OPERATIONS. FOR
JOAN 4 (107) OF NATURE. BUT THIS WOMEN DENIES TO ENGLAND HER LEGITIMATE CONQUESTS, GIVEN HER BY GOD BECAUSE OF HER
GENV IV (100) I THINK THAT UNDER SUCH CIRCUMSTANCES A PLEA OF LEGITIMATE DEFENCE MIGHT BE ALLOWED. BUT WHAT HAS A TUSSLE
POSN PREFACE(407) AND PROSTITUTION INSTEAD OF CARRYING ON A LEGITIMATE DRAMATIC BUSINESS. INDEED EVERYBODY CONNECTED
GETT PREFACE(203) OR HOW FEW OR HOW MANY, PROVIDED THE CHILDREN ARE LEGITIMATE . ALSO THAT IT DOES NOT MATTER IN THE LEAST WHAT
GENV PREFACE(22) ANARCHISM DEFEATS THEM ALL. UPSTART DICTATORS AND LEGITIMATE MONARCHS HAVE NOT ALL BEEN PERSONAL FAILURES.
GETT PREFACE(203) ONE HEALTHY ILLEGITIMATE CHILD TO TEN RICKETY LEGITIMATE ONES, AND ONE ENERGETIC AND CAPABLE UNMARRIED
GETT PREFACE(215) THAT THE CONDITION OF MARRIAGE NOW ATTACHED TO LEGITIMATE PARENTAGE WILL BE WITHDRAWN FROM ALL WOMEN, AND
METH PREFACE(R77) WHO ARE BRITISH SUBJECTS CANNOT ACCEPT, IT HAS NO LEGITIMATE PLACE IN THE COUNSELS OF THE BRITISH
GETT (287) UP THE SUPPLY OF VESTAL VIRGINS, WHO HAD TO BE LEGITIMATE ; BUT NOBODY ELSE DREAMT OF GETTING MARRIED AT
BARB I (255) BUT DID THEY NEVER MARRY? WERE THERE NO LEGITIMATE SONS? /LADY BRITOMART/ OH YES: THEY MARRIED JUST
BULL PREFACE(38) OF ENGLISH IGNORAMUSES, INSTEAD OF THE LEGITIMATE SUCCESSOR OF MARTIN LUTHER AND JOHN KNOX.
GENV PREFACE(21) FOR SAVAGERY THEY MAKE GOOD, AND ESTABLISH A LEGITIMATE TITLE TO THE TERRITORIES THEY INVADE. WHEN
APPL I (237) IT MAY BE THAN HE COULD HOPE TO MAKE BY A LEGITIMATE USE OF IT; AND WHEN THEY HAVE BOUGHT IT THEY
ROCK II (261) AN ENEMY IN UNIFORM AT SIGHT IS NOT MURDER: IT'S LEGITIMATE WARFARE. /SIR DEXTER/ MONSTROUS! I SHOULD GIVE
PRES (160) CHARM-- WHO HAVE ARTISTIC TALENT-- WHO WIELD A LEGITIMATE , A REFINING INFLUENCE OVER THE MEN. (SHE SITS

LEGITIMATELY

MILL IV (205) ME FOR A HUNDRED YEARS. I DID IT HONESTLY AND LEGITIMATELY . I EXPLAINED THE WAY IN WHICH IT WAS DONE.
LION PREFACE(95) IF YOU HOLD, AS THE STRICTEST SECULARIST QUITE LEGITIMATELY MAY, THAT ALL PROPHETS ARE INSPIRED, AND ALL

LEGITIMIZE

GETT PREFACE(215) AND MISS WILKINSON'S AS VOLUNTARY, WHETHER WE LEGITIMIZE THE CHILD OF THE UNMARRIED WOMAN AS A DUTY TO THE

LEGITIMIZING

GETT PREFACE(212) THE SUPERFLUOUS WOMEN TO BARRENNESS, EXCEPT BY LEGITIMIZING THE CHILDREN OF WOMEN WHO ARE NOT MARRIED TO

LEGLESSNESS

DOCT PREFACE(3) NATURAL ONES-- EVOLUTION IS TOWARDS MOTORS AND LEGLESSNESS , ETC., ETC., ETC." NOW THERE IS NO CALCULATION

LEGS

MTH5 (252) OF FANTASTIC MONSTERS. I WALKED UPON A DOZEN LEGS : I WORKED WITH TWENTY HANDS AND A HUNDRED FINGERS: I
LION PREFACE(79) OF SUPERSTITION THAN PAUL BOLDLY SET IT ON ITS LEGS AGAIN IN THE NAME OF JESUS. THE CONFUSION OF
MILL IV (192) (HE SIGNS). THERE YOU ARE. (HE PUTS UP HIS LEGS AGAIN). /THE MANAGER/ THANKS VERY MUCH, SIR. (HE
O'FL (206) TOOK TO RECRUITING. WHAT WITH THE STANDING ON MY LEGS ALL DAY, AND THE SHAKING HANDS, AND THE MAKING
MTH5 (232) I WENT AHEAD WITH A COMPLETE HUMAN BODY: ARMS AND LEGS AND ALL. HE WAS MY FIRST MAN. /ARJILLAX/ WHO MODELLED
MTH5 (253) THAT, WE SHED OUR SUPERFLUOUS HEADS AND LEGS AND ARMS UNTIL WE HAD OUR OLD SHAPES AGAIN, AND NO
LION PRDL,SD(105) BUT HIS GOOD POINTS GO NO FURTHER: HIS ARMS AND LEGS AND BACK, THOUGH WIRY OF THEIR KIND, LOOK SHRIVELLED
DEVL I SD(4) ON HER WITH A FREEDOM WHICH, TAKEN WITH HER BROWN LEGS AND BARE FEET, SUGGESTS NO GREAT STOCK OF
SUPR II (49) I MAY AS WELL WALK TO THE HOUSE AND STRETCH MY LEGS AND CALM MY NERVES A LITTLE. (LOOKING AT HIS WATCH) I
PHIL I (91) OF THE GRAND PIANO AND SITS THERE SWINGING HIS LEGS AND CONTEMPLATING CRAVEN RESIGNEDLY). /CRAVEN/ (PACING
MTH5 (252) /THE NEWLY BORN/ OH, DO GROW A LOT OF ARMS AND LEGS AND HEADS FOR US. IT WOULD BE SO FUNNY. /THE
FABL PREFACE(89) AS CARPENTERS AND PLUMBERS DEAL WITH FAULTY CHAIR LEGS AND LEAKING PIPES. HE MAY, LIKE JENNER, BE SO IGNORANT
DEST (153) HIS CHAIR; AND USES HIS NAPKIN, STRETCHING HIS LEGS AND LEANING BACK, BUT STILL FROWNING AND THINKING).
MTH2 (77) WOULDNT SAY HIS PRAYERS! TAKE HIM BY THE HIND LEGS AND THROW HIM DOWNSTAIRS. /LUBIN/ (STILL IMMOVABLY

POSN PREFACE(384)	WHICH INDECENTLY REVEALED THE FACT THAT THEY HAD	LEGS	AND WAISTS AND EVEN POSTERIORS. AT ABOUT THE SAME
DOCT PREFACE(32)	OF THE APE, OR OF THE CHILD WHO PULLS OUT THE	LEGS	AND WINGS OF A FLY TO SEE WHAT IT WILL DO WITHOUT THEM,
DOCT PREFACE(3)	HE WILL BE WELL IN A FORTNIGHT-- ARTIFICIAL	LEGS	ARE NOW SO WELL MADE THAT THEY ARE REALLY BETTER THAN
METH PREFACE(R18)	WITH A HUNDRED LEGS, AND RIDDING THE FISH OF ANY	LEGS	AT ALL; BUILDING LUNGS AND ARMS FOR THE LAND AND GILLS
NEVR II SD(235)	HE'D GUESS WHEN HE SEES YOUR MOTHER, MISS. PHIL'S	LEGS	BECOME MOTIONLESS. HE CONTEMPLATES THE WAITER RAPTLY.
SUPR II SD(48)	LEGS/ AW RAWT NAH. TANNER STOOPS AND TAKES THE	LEGS	BY THE ANKLES, DRAWING THEIR OWNER FORTH LIKE A
MTH3 (99)	GOING TO SIT HERE ON A FINE DAY LIKE THIS WITH MY	LEGS	CROSSED WAITING FOR GREAT THOUGHTS, YOU EXAGGERATE MY
BARB II (287)	WHY DONT YOU LOOK HAPPY, AS WE DO? /BILL/ (HIS	LEGS	CURLING BACK IN SPITE OF HIM) AW'M EPPY ENAFF, AW TELL
MTH4 I (148)	AND SITS DOWN ON THE EDGE OF THE PIER, WITH HIS	LEGS	DANGLING OVER THE WATER). /THE ELDERLY GENTLEMAN/
DOCT I SD(82)	IS A MARBLE-TOPPED CONSOLE, WITH HAUNCHED GILT	LEGS	ENDING IN SPHINX CLAWS. THE HUGE PIER-GLASS WHICH
FANY II (293)	RUSHED AT HIM AND CARRIED HIM OUT BY THE ARMS AND	LEGS	FACE DOWNWARDS. TWO MORE ATTACKED ME AND GAVE ME A
MRS II SD(203)	IN THE COMPANY'S BEHAVIOR. CROFTS TAKES DOWN HIS	LEGS	FROM THE SETTLE AND PULLS HIMSELF TOGETHER AS PRAED
MTH4 I (145)	WE HAVE A PERSON HERE WHO HAS LOST BOTH	LEGS	IN AN ACCIDENT. HIS POSITION IS UNIQUE. BUT HE WOULD
BARB II (287)	(HE SITS DOWN AGAIN, AND STRETCHES HIS	LEGS	IN AN ATTEMPT TO SEEM INDIFFERENT). /BARBARA/ WELL, IF
SUPR II SD(48)	NOT FAR TOO MUCH INTERESTED IN A PAIR OF SUPINE	LEGS	IN DUNGAREE OVERALLS WHICH PROTRUDE FROM BENEATH THE
MILL I (157)	LITTLE OPERA COMPANY WHICH WAS THEN ON ITS LAST	LEGS	IN THE SUBURBS TO ALLOW HIM TO APPEAR FOR ONE NIGHT IN
MTH4 I (172)	OR A LEG OR AN EYE: AFTER ALL, NO ONE WITH TWO	LEGS	IS UNHAPPY BECAUSE HE HAS NOT THREE; SO WHY SHOULD A
GENV I (30)	THE WALL). /SHE/ NO, NOT THAT ONE: ONE OF ITS	LEGS	ISNT SAFE: IT'S THERE ONLY FOR SHOW. WILL YOU PLEASE
MIS. PREFACE(73)	AS LADIES USED TO PERSUADE THEM THAT THEY HAVE NO	LEGS	. CHILDREN AND GAME: A PROPOSAL. OF THE MANY WILD
DOCT PREFACE(12)	A TRAIN HAD RUN OVER HIM AND AMPUTATED BOTH HIS	LEGS	. HE LOST HIS CASE BECAUSE IT WAS PROVED THAT HE HAD
CATH 1,SD(161)	NOR HIS HALF-BUTTONED KNEE BREECHES, NOR HIS	LEGS	. THESE ARE PARTLY CLAD IN SILK STOCKINGS, WHICH HE
BULL III (119)	/LARRY/ I SEEM TO RECOLLECT THAT ONE OF THE	LEGS	OF THE SOFA IN THE PARLOR HAD A WAY OF COMING OUT
MRS II (202)	RESUMES HIS PLACE ON THE SETTLE AND PUTS UP HIS	LEGS	ON THE SEAT AGAIN, AS IF THE MATTER WERE FINALLY
PYGM V SD(276)	HIGGINS THROWS BACK HIS HEAD; STRETCHES OUT HIS	LEGS	; AND BEGINS TO WHISTLE. /MRS HIGGINS/ HENRY, DEAREST,
MTH5 (232)	MAKE A SORT OF MONSTER: A THING WITHOUT ARMS OR	LEGS	; AND IT REALLY AND TRULY LIVED FOR HALF-AN-HOUR. /THE
HART I SD(49)	WHICH HE STANDS ON THE FLOOR AGAINST THE TABLE	LEGS	; AND PUTS THE TRAY IN THE SPACE THUS CLEARED. ELLIE
LION II SD(143)	HE STOPS; RISES STIFFLY BY STRAIGHTENING HIS	LEGS	; STRETCHES OUT HIS NOSE FORWARD AND HIS TAIL IN A
MTH5 (219)	SOMETIMES WITH A LOT OF EXTRA HEADS AND ARMS AND	LEGS	; THEY MAKE YOU SPLIT LAUGHING AT THEM. MOST OF THEM
JITT II (41)	OF A BIGGISH BOOK. HE LEANS LAZILY BACK WITH HIS	LEGS	STRETCHED, AND TURNS OVER THE COVER WITHOUT LOOKING AT
NEVR II (235)	AT THE WAITER WITH HIS LIPS COMPRESSED AND HIS	LEGS	SWINGING). /DOLLY/ WE WANT YOU TO BREAK THE NEWS TO
MIS. PREFACE(41)	ARE IN MUCH GREATER DANGER OF ACQUIRING BANDY	LEGS	THROUGH BEING LEFT TO WALK BEFORE THEY ARE STRONG
BULL PREFACE(42)	GLASS EYES, SILVER WINDPIPES, AND PATENT WOODEN	LEGS	TO THE NATURAL PRODUCTS. LIKE DEMOCRACY, NATIONAL
MRS II (200)	DRINK. (HE SITS DOWN ON THE SETTLE, PUTTING HIS	LEGS	UP ALONG THE SEAT). /MRS WARREN/ WELL, SHE OUGHTNT TO
MTH2 (86)	POLITICS! THEY HAVE JUST BEEN PULLING OUR	LEGS	VERY WITTILY. COME ALONG. (HE GOES OUT, FRANKLYN
MILL IV (189)	RID OF THE OLD THINGS IN IT. IT WAS ON ITS LAST	LEGS	WHEN YOU SAW IT, SIR. I WAS ASHAMED OF IT. /ALASTAIR/
DEST (175)	ON TO IT, SITTING WITH HIS ARMS AKIMBO AND HIS	LEGS	WIDE APART) COME: I AM A TRUE CORSICAN IN MY LOVE FOR
MIS. PREFACE(78)	IS PROMOTED FROM PERMISSION TO GO AS FAR AS ITS	LEGS	WILL CARRY IT TO USING MECHANICAL AIDS TO LOCOMOTION,
MTH4 III (196)	TOO GLAD TO GET BACK ALIVE ON ANY TERMS, IF MY	LEGS	WOULD SUPPORT ME I'D JUST DO A BUNK STRAIGHT FOR THE
MTH2 (77)	ITS HISTORY INTO A TWO LINE EPIC: OLD DADDY LONG	LEGS	WOULDNT SAY HIS PRAYERS: TAKE HIM BY THE HIND LEGS AND
MTH4 I (152)	/ZOO/ I NOTICED THAT YOU ARE NOT STRONG ON YOUR	LEGS	YET. YOU HAVE MANY OF THE WAYS AND WEAKNESSES OF A
LION PROLOG (109)	WAGGING HIS TAIL VIOLENTLY, RISES ON HIS HIND	LEGS	, AND EMBRACES ANDROCLES, WHO MAKES A WRY FACE AND
PYGM V (272)	OF THE HOSPITAL BEFORE I COULD HARDLY STAND ON MY	LEGS	, AND NOTHING TO PAY. NOW THEY FINDS OUT THAT I'M NOT A
METH PREFACE(R18)	OF THINGS: PROVIDING THE CENTIPEDE WITH A HUNDRED	LEGS	, AND RIDDING THE FISH OF ANY LEGS AT ALL; BUILDING
MTH5 SD(244)	PYGMALION INTO THE TEMPLE BY HIS BARE ARMS AND	LEGS	, AND THE TWO FIGURES THROUGH THE GROVE BY THEIR
LION PROL,SD(105)	NEARER. THE LION LIMPS FROM THE JUNGLE ON THREE	LEGS	, HOLDING UP HIS RIGHT FOREPAW, IN WHICH A HUGE THORN
DOCT PREFACE(32)	DROPPED OUT OF THE WINDOW WILL ALWAYS FALL ON ITS	LEGS	, IMMEDIATELY TRIES THE EXPERIMENT ON THE NEAREST CAT
HART I SD(44)	STOUT TABLE OF TEAK, WITH A ROUND TOP AND GATE	LEGS	, STANDS AGAINST THE PORT WALL BETWEEN THE DOOR AND THE
GETT PREFACE(235)	WE ALL BELIEVE THAT OUR RELIGION IS ON ITS LAST	LEGS	, WHEREAS THE TRUTH IS THAT IT IS NOT YET BORN, THOUGH
PHIL I (88)	STOOPS TO PRESS HIS HEATED TROUSERS AGAINST HIS	LEGS	, WHICH ARE CHILLY) WONT DO, CHARTERIS. CANT TAKE ME IN

LEHAR

PYGM III (257)	AS IF SHE HAD /PICKERING/ BEETHOVEN AND BRAHMS OR	LEHAR	AND LIONEL MONCKTON; /HIGGINS/ BEEN AT IT ALL HER

LEIBNITZ

MIS. PREFACE(40)	INTO AN ATTEMPT TO BECOME PORSON AND BENTLEY,	LEIBNITZ	AND NEWTON, ALL ROLLED INTO ONE. THIS IS THE
MIS. PREFACE(51)	IF SHAKESPEAR, OR FOR THAT MATTER, NEWTON AND	LEIBNITZ	, ARE ALLOWED TO FIND THEIR READERS AND STUDENTS
METH PREFACE(R32)	AND THE EARLIER PHILOSOPHERS, FROM PLATO TO	LEIBNITZ	, HAD KEPT THE HUMAN MIND OPEN FOR THE THOUGHT OF

LEIBNITZES

LION PREFACE(45)	THE GREATEST MASTERS OF NUMBERS, THE NEWTONS AND	LEIBNITZES	, RANK AMONG THE GREATEST MEN. BUT THERE ARE

LEIBNIZ

FABL PREFACE(98)	VOLTAIRE, ROUSSEAU, AND BUNYAN, THE POLEMICS OF	LEIBNIZ	AND SPINOZA, THE POEMS OF GOETHE, SHELLEY, AND
FABL PREFACE(92)	HE WILL CITE THE METHOD OF MEASUREMENT NEWTON AND	LEIBNIZ	ELABORATED. EXAMINATIONS AND SCHOOLMASTERS. I AVOID
BUOY PREFACE(5)	HIS INVENTION OF THE INFINITESIMAL CALCULUS UNTIL	LEIBNIZ	MADE IT FASHIONABLE. NOW NEWTON WAS RIGHT IN RATING
FABL PREFACE(66)	I AM MUCH LESS MENTALLY GIFTED THAN, SAY,	LEIBNIZ	, AND CAN ONLY HAVE BEEN NEEDED BECAUSE, AS HE WAS

LEIBNIZ'S

FABL PREFACE(66)	CAPABLE OF SUCH ENTERTAINMENT, BUT BAFFLED BY	LEIBNIZ'S	ALGEBRAIC SYMBOLS AND HIS PHILOSOPHIC JARGON. HERE

LEICESTER

FABL PREFACE(81)	BEFORE THEIR FLIGHT INTO THE DESERT. THE	LEICESTER	ATHEISTS WERE IN FACT MORE PIOUS THAN THE
SUPR PREFACE(R32)	THEIR EXPOSURES OF ANGELO AND DOGBERRY, SIR	LEICESTER	DEDLOCK AND MR TITE BARNACLE, WITH ANY PORTRAIT OF
JOAN PREFACE(35)	THE MOST BIGOTED ULSTER ORANGEMAN OR	LEICESTER	LOW CHURCH BOURGEOIS (AS DESCRIBED BY MR HENRY
SIM II (75)	" POLICEMAN WHO ATTEMPTED TO ARREST ANGEL IN	LEICESTER	SQUARE REMOVED TO MENTAL HOSPITAL. CHURCH ASSEMBLY
FANY II (292)	A LOT OF LIGHT AND EXCITEMENT THERE. I WALKED TO	LEICESTER	SQUARE; AND WENT INTO A GREAT THEATRE. /MRS KNOX/
FABL PREFACE(80)	TRADE HALL IN MANCHESTER, THE MONTFORD HALL IN	LEICESTER	, AND WHEREVER TWO OR THREE GATHERED TOGETHER MAY

LEISURE

LADY PREFACE(231)	POWER. WHEN POVERTY IS ABOLISHED, AND	LEISURE	AND GRACE OF LIFE BECOME GENERAL, THE ONLY PLAYS
MTH3 (106)	YOU THEREFORE OWE HIM OVER 300 YEARS OF	LEISURE	AND NEARLY EIGHT EDUCATIONS. YOU ARE THUS HEAVILY IN
LION PREFACE(58)	INSTEAD OF CONTRIBUTING TO THEM, THEIR EXCESSIVE	LEISURE	BEING AS MISCHIEVOUS AS THE EXCESSIVE TOIL OF THE
HART PREFACE(4)	THE ONLY PART OF OUR SOCIETY IN WHICH THERE WAS	LEISURE	FOR HIGH CULTURE, AND MADE IT AN ECONOMIC,
2TRU PREFACE(14)	DAY TO DAY AND THE JUST SHARING OF THE LABOR AND	LEISURE	INVOLVED. THUS THE INDIVIDUAL CITIZEN HAS TO BE
2TRU PREFACE(14)	SLEEPING, LOCOMOTION, ETC.) BEING HIS LEISURE. 8.	LEISURE	IS THE SPHERE OF INDIVIDUAL LIBERTY: LABOR IS THE
2TRU PREFACE(14)	FEEDING, SLEEPING, LOCOMOTION, ETC.) BEING HIS	LEISURE	. 8. LEISURE IS THE SPHERE OF INDIVIDUAL LIBERTY:
MIS. PREFACE(38)	SCARCITY OF WORK SIMULTANEOUSLY WITH AN EXCESS OF	LEISURE	. WORK MAY HAVE TO BE SHARED OUT AMONG PEOPLE WHO
GETT PREFACE(201)	ARE SO ENTIRELY SEPARATE THAT ONLY IN THEIR	LEISURE	MOMENTS CAN THEY EVER BE TOGETHER. A MAN AS INTIMATE
3PLA PREFACE(R9)	OF BODILY EXERTION. THE DIFFERENCE BETWEEN THE	LEISURE	OF A PERSIAN CAT AND THE LABOR OF A COCKNEY CAB
2TRU PREFACE(22)	FREEDOM IN THEIR ORDERED AND EQUAL SHARE OF THE	LEISURE	PRODUCED BY SCIENTIFIC ECONOMY IN PRODUCING THAT
2TRU PREFACE(21)	PRIVATE PROPERTY DISTRIBUTES WEALTH, WORK, AND	LEISURE	SO UNEVENLY THAT A WRETCHEDLY POOR AND MISERABLY
MTH4 I (171)	CEASE TO BE PERCEPTIBLE, LEAVING COMMON MEN MORE	LEISURE	THAN THEY WILL KNOW WHAT TO DO WITH. /ZOO/ DADDY!
2TRU III (108)	/MEEK/ NO, SIR; BUT THEIR PEOPLE HAVE SO MUCH	LEISURE	THAT THEY ARE AT THEIR WITS' END FOR SOME OCCUPATION
OVER PREFACE(156)	IDLENESS OR EVEN A REASONABLE SUPPLY OF ELEGANT	LEISURE	THERE IS A GOOD DEAL OF COQUETRY AND PHILANDERING.
MIS. PREFACE(34)	THE SECRET OF BEING MISERABLE IS TO HAVE	LEISURE	TO BOTHER ABOUT WHETHER YOU ARE HAPPY OR NOT. THE
FABL III (110)	ENABLE YOU TO SUPPORT YOURSELF AND HAVE ENOUGH	LEISURE	TO PAINT WHAT YOU LIKE UNTIL THE WORLD RECOGNIZES
2TRU PREFACE(25)	ORDINARY WORK, BUT THE SACRIFICE OF ALL ONE'S	LEISURE	TO POLITICS, AND, IF PROMOTION TO THE
SUPR III SD(72)	IF HIS LIFE IS TO BE TOLERABLE TO HIM, MUST HAVE	LEISURE	TO TELL HIMSELF STORIES, AND A POSITION WHICH LENDS
2TRU PREFACE(25)	WORK WITH THE COMMON FOLK, AND GIVING ONLY THEIR	LEISURE	TO THE PARTY. FOR THEIR ELECTION AS REPRESENTATIVES
2TRU PREFACE(4)	OFF: SHE HAS TO BE FASHIONABLE EVEN IN HER LITTLE	LEISURE	, AND DIES WITHOUT EVER HAVING HAD ANY SELF AT ALL.
BULL PREFACE(11)	A CHIEF IS AN IDLE VOLUPTUARY WITH LOTS OF MONEY,	LEISURE	, AND POWER OVER OTHERS, TO USE IRRESPONSIBLY FOR
DOCT PREFACE(15)	OR HIS SICK CHILD NEEDS IS NOT MEDICINE, BUT MORE	LEISURE	, BETTER CLOTHES, BETTER FOOD, AND A BETTER DRAINED
ROCK PREFACE(163)	CIRCUMSTANCES AND NOT PLANNED AND THOUGHT OUT AT	LEISURE	, THE TWO INSTITUTIONS, THE OGPU AND THE ORDINARY
MTH3 (125)	DRUDGE AT IT? BUT THINK OF THE ACTIVITIES OF OUR	LEISURE	! IS THERE A JOLLIER PLACE ON EARTH TO LIVE IN THAN

		LEISURED	
GETT PREFACE(202)	WITHOUT EXCHANGING BLOWS QUITE FREQUENTLY. IN THE	LEISURED	CLASSES THERE IS OFTEN NO REAL FAMILY LIFE AT ALL.
LADY PREFACE(230)	SHAKESPEAR'S CHARACTERS ARE MOSTLY MEMBERS OF THE	LEISURED	CLASSES. THE SAME THING IS TRUE OF MR HARRIS'S OWN
HART PREFACE(3)	PLAY WHICH FOLLOWS THIS PREFACE. IT IS CULTURED,	LEISURED	EUROPE BEFORE THE WAR. WHEN THE PLAY WAS BEGUN NOT
OVER PREFACE(156)	THE EDGE OF A PRECIPICE THAN TO GO OVER IT THAT	LEISURED	SOCIETY IS FULL OF PEOPLE WHO SPEND A GREAT PART OF
ROCK PREFACE(167)	ARE BETTER FED AND HOUSED, NICER, AND MUCH MORE	LEISURED	, AND CONSEQUENTLY FREE, THAN HE EVER IS.
		LEISURELY	
SUPR I SD(25)	BY ANN. THEY COME IN QUICKLY, WITH THEIR FORMER	LEISURELY	AIR OF DECOROUS GRIEF CHANGED TO ONE OF GENUINE
VWOO 2,SD(123)	AND CHEESE). HE SITS DOWN WATCHING HER DEFT BUT	LEISURELY	PROCEEDINGS. /A/ DO YOU SELL BASKETS? /Z/ WE SELL
SUPR PREFACE(R38)	HAVE SAID OR WRITTEN AFORETIME, I KNOW THAT THE	LEISURELY	TRICKS WHICH THEIR WANT OF CONVICTION LEAVES THEM
WIDO II (24)	HE! HE SAYS NOTHING. (HE FOLDS A LETTER	LEISURELY	, AND LOOKS FOR THE ENVELOPE). HE PREFERS TO
		LEITMOTIFS	
FABL PREFACE(91)	AND OPERA TUNES OF MOZART AND BEETHOVEN, AND THE	LEITMOTIFS	OF WAGNER, AS THEY CAN REMEMBER. THEIR
		LEK	
CAPT I (235)	MANNERS, CAPTAIN BRASSBOUND. YE ARE EXTRAORDINAIR	LEK	AN AULD COLLEGE FRIEND OF MINE, WHOSE FACE I SAID NOT
CAPT I (219)	TH' WOULD OALL B' MURRDERED. MOROCCO IS NOT	LEK	THE REST OF AFRICA. /DRINKWATER/ NO, GAVNER: THESE EAH
		LEKS	
CAPT I (218)	GAVNER. /RANKIN/ A MISSIONARY KNOWS NOTHING OF	LEKS	OF THAT SOART, OR OF DISLEKS EITHER, MR DRINKWOTTER.
		LEMAITRE	
JOAN PREFACE(52)	TO THE AUDIENCE. AND IN THIS CASE CAUCHON AND	LEMAITRE	HAVE TO MAKE INTELLIGIBLE NOT ONLY THEMSELVES BUT
JOAN PREFACE(49)	A BULLY INSTEAD OF A CATHOLIC, AND THE INQUISITOR	LEMAITRE	WOULD HAVE BEEN A SADIST INSTEAD OF A LAWYER.
JOAN PREFACE(52)	FROM ITS OWN. OBVIOUSLY THE REAL CAUCHON,	LEMAITRE	, AND WARWICK COULD NOT HAVE DONE THIS: THEY WERE
JOAN PREFACE(51)	TEMPORAL SITUATION. NEITHER DOES THE INQUISITOR	LEMAITRE	, IN SUCH SCANTY ACCOUNTS OF HIM AS ARE NOW
JOAN 6 (123)	IS ON HIS RIGHT) THIS, MY LORD, IS BROTHER JOHN	LEMAITRE	, OF THE ORDER OF ST DOMINIC. HE IS ACTING AS
		LEMBETH	
BULL III (141)	IGHTEEN MONTHS RENT. OI ONCE RAN AP FOUR WEEKS IN	LEMBETH	WEN OI WAS AHT OF A JOB IN WINTER. THEY TOOK THE
		LEMME	
CATH 1 (168)	WOMAN, THE GREATEST WOMAN IN THE WORLD. BUT	LEMME	GIVE YOU PIECE 'VICE -- PAH! STILL DRUNK. THEY WATER
		LEMMY	
BULL III (130)	IT. /MATTHEW/ (BLACK WITH RAGE, IN A LOW GROWL)	LEMMY	OURA DHIS. (HE TRIES TO RISE; BUT DORAN CATCHES HIS
BULL I (78)	YOU. /TIM/ I TELL YOU HWAT. GIMME A PROSPECTUS.	LEMMY	TAKE IT HOME AND REFLECT ON IT. /BROADBENT/ YOURE
		LEMON	
MTH2 (74)	YOU BELIEVE IN LEMONS? /CONRAD/ I WOULDNT EAT A	LEMON	FOR TEN POUNDS. /BURGE/ (SITTING DOWN AGAIN) WHAT DO
GETT PREFACE(204)	THE MORE LUXURIOUS CLASSES, ICED CLARET CUP,	LEMON	SQUASHES, AND THE LIKE. TO TAKE A MORAL ILLUSTRATION,
CAND III (137)	SHE PUTS THE TRAY ON THE TABLE, AND TAKES UP THE	LEMON	SQUEEZER, LOOKING ENQUIRINGLY ROUND AT THEM). /MORELL/
		LEMONADE	
CAND III (137)	HOT WATER ON A TRAY. /CANDIDA/ WHO WILL HAVE SOME	LEMONADE	? YOU KNOW OUR RULES: TOTAL ABSTINENCE. (SHE PUTS
GENV I (43)	RECOVER BEST AS HE IS. /SHE/ I HAVE SOME ICED	LEMONADE	IN MY THERMOS. SHALL I GIVE HIM SOME? /BISHOP/ (
MILL I (140)	THE CHEMIST WILL THINK YOU WANT IT TO MAKE	LEMONADE	. PUT THE TWO SEPARATELY IN JUST ENOUGH WATER TO
MIS. (127)	(HE GOES TO THE SIDEBOARD FOR A DRINK OF	LEMONADE	). /MRS TARLETON/ FOR SHAME, JOHN! TELL HIM TO
MIS. SD(110)	LIQUEUR BOTTLES, A SYPHON, A GLASS JUG OF	LEMONADE	, TUMBLERS, AND EVERY CONVENIENCE FOR CASUAL
		LEMONS	
MTH3 (112)	YEARS. /BURGE-LUBIN/ BUT HOW DO YOU DO IT? IS IT	LEMONS	? IS IT SOYA BEANS? IS IT-- /THE ARCHBISHOP/ I DO
MTH2 (74)	WELL HAVE TAKEN SOUR BEER. /BURGE/ YOU BELIEVE IN	LEMONS	? /CONRAD/ I WOULDNT EAT A LEMON FOR TEN POUNDS.
MTH2 (73)	WALTON HEATH. WHAT IS YOUR ELIXIR, DR BARNABAS?	LEMONS	? SOUR MILK? OR WHAT IS THE LATEST? /BURGE/ WE
MTH2 (83)	THE TABLOID. WHATEVER IT IS. YOU SAID IT WASNT	LEMONS	. /CONRAD/ MY GOOD SIR: I HAVE NO POWDER, NO BOTTLE,
HART II (87)	HIM WERE NO MORE TO ME THAN A HEAP OF SQUEEZED	LEMONS	. YOUVE BEEN WASTING YOUR GRATITUDE: MY KIND HEART IS
CAND III SD(137)	HIS BALANCE. CANDIDA COMES IN WITH GLASSES,	LEMONS	, AND A JUG OF HOT WATER ON A TRAY. /CANDIDA/ WHO
		LEN	
BULL IV (157)	AS WELL BE FIRST AS LAST. D'YE THINK BROADBENT'D	LEN	ME A LITTLE? /LARRY/ I'M QUITE SURE HE WILL.
BULL IV (157)	/CORNELIUS/ IS HE AS READY AS THAT? WOULD HE	LEN	ME FIVE HUNDERD, D'YE THINK? /LARRY/ HE'LL LEND YOU
		LENA	
POSN PREFACE(361)	SIR WILLIAM GILBERT, MR A.B. WALKLEY, MISS	LENA	ASHWELL, PROFESSOR GILBERT MURRAY, MR GEORGE ALEXANDER,
		LEND	
MIS. PREFACE(86)	EVERY CHILD, FROM THE MOMENT IT IS BIG ENOUGH TO	LEND	A HAND TO THE FAMILY INDUSTRY, IS AN INVESTMENT IN
CAND II (113)	IF I KEPT THREE, THAT MEANS THAT EVERYONE HAS TO	LEND	A HAND. IT'S NOT A BAD PLAN: PROSSY AND I CAN TALK
PPP (204)	RESPIRATION, DO IT? (TO THE LANDLORD) HERE!	LEND	A HAND, YOU. WE'D BEST TAKE HIM AND SET HIM UP IN
BULL IV (173)	MR KEEGAN, NOT A MAN OF BUSINESS. /LARRY/ WE WILL	LEND	EVERYONE OF THESE MEN HALF AS MUCH AGAIN ON THEIR LAND
BULL IV (157)	ME OATH BARNEY DOARN'S GOING TO ASK BROADBENT TO	LEND	HIM 500 POUNDS ON THE MILL TO PUT IN A NEW HWEEL; FOR
MIS. (173)	HIM). /LINA/ OLD PAL: DONT CALL THE POLICE.	LEND	HIM A BICYCLE AND LET HIM GET AWAY. /THE MAN/ I CANT
DOCT II (121)	TO GET HERE. WELL, DUBEDAT ASKED ME TO	LEND	HIM HALF-A-CROWN TO TIP THE CHAMBERMAID OF THE ROOM HIS
SIM PRO,3, (30)	HIS CLOTHES ARE DRYING IN THE SUN. THEY WILL	LEND	HIM SOME CLOTHES AND SEND HIM UP HERE AS SOON AS HE HAS
JOAN 2 (71)	BUT I TAKE IT HE OWES YOU ALL YOU COULD AFFORD TO	LEND	HIM. THAT IS WHAT HE OWES ME. /LA TREMOUILLE/
PRES (147)	IT'S THE ONLY ONE IN THE PLACE, BECAUSE HE WONT	LEND	IT TO THE SHOWS. /MITCHENER/ BUT SANDSTONE'S CLOTHES
DOCT II (123)	WHEN WE LEND MONEY; AND WHEN WE REFUSE TO	LEND	IT YOU SAY JUST THE SAME. I DIDNT MEAN TO BEHAVE BADLY.
DOCT II (122)	UNDERSTAND THAT. I FELT THAT I COULDNT VERY WELL	LEND	IT. /WALPOLE/ WHAT DID HE SAY? /SCHUTZMACHER/ WELL, HE
GETT (298)	READY: THE CAKE'S READY: EVERYTHING'S READY. I'LL	LEND	LEO MY VEIL AND THINGS. /THE BISHOP/ I'M AFRAID THEY
BULL IV (157)	HOUSE, BAD LUCK TO HIS FAT FACE! D'YE THINK HE'D	LEND	ME 300 POUNDS ON THE FARM, LARRY? WHEN I'M SO HARD UP,
BASH II,1, (111)	GLOVED. /LYDIA/ O HEAVEN! YOU BLEED. /CASHEL/	LEND	ME A KEY OR OTHER FRIGID OBJECT, THAT I MAY PUT IT DOWN
MIS. (154)	TO DINNER I'M AFRAID I CANT CHANGE UNLESS YOULL	LEND	ME SOME CLOTHES. /MRS TARLETON/ DO YOU MEAN NEITHER OF
MILL I (163)	DO NOT CARRY MONEY ABOUT WITH ME. ADRIAN: CAN YOU	LEND	ME THIRTEEN AND FOURPENCE? /ADRIAN/ (PUTS HIS HAND IN
CLEO IV (192)	LUCIUS HURRIES OUT AFTER BRITANNUS.) APOLLODORUS:	LEND	ME YOUR SWORD AND YOUR RIGHT ARM FOR THIS CAMPAIGN.
POSN (441)	BORROW MONEY FROM ME TO GET DRUNK WITH, NOW YOU	LEND	MONEY AND SELL DRINK TO OTHER PEOPLE. I WAS ASHAMED OF
SIM PREFACE(15)	CRUDEST FUNDAMENTALIST, A PRUDENT BANKER WOULD	LEND	MONEY ON PERSONAL SECURITY TO BUNYAN RATHER THAN TO
DOCT II (122)	TOGETHER) /SCHUTZMACHER/ OF COURSE I COULDNT	LEND	MONEY TO A STRANGER LIKE THAT. /B.B./ I ENVY YOU THE
DOCT II (122)	MR SCHUTZMACHER. OF COURSE, I KNEW I OUGHTNT TO	LEND	MONEY TO A YOUNG FELLOW IN THAT WAY; BUT I SIMPLY HADNT
DOCT III (135)	PEOPLE SOMETIMES HAVE THAT IN VIEW WHEN THEY	LEND	MONEY. /LOUIS/ (AFTER A MOMENT'S REFLECTION) WELL, I
DOCT II (123)	TO PLEASE. YOU SAY WE ARE NO GENTLEMEN WHEN WE	LEND	MONEY; AND WHEN WE REFUSE TO LEND IT YOU SAY JUST THE
VWOO 3 (133)	YOU HAVE TO GIVE CREDIT AT THE SHOP, AND THEN	LEND	THE CUSTOMERS THE MONEY TO PAY YOU? /A/ MRS WARD
MIS. (154)	/MRS TARLETON/ OH WELL, NEVER MIND: HYPATIA WILL	LEND	THE LADY A GOWN. /LINA/ THANK YOU: I'M QUITE
BARB II (286)	YOU, PETER? WILL YOU GO INTO THE SHELTER AND	LEND	THE LASSES A HAND FOR A WHILE: WE'RE WORKED OFF OUR
MIS. (121)	BECAUSE THAT ALWAYS MEANS THAT THEY WANT YOU TO	LEND	THEM MONEY; AND YOU MUST NEVER DO THAT, HYPATIA.
BULL IV (173)	IS OUT. /KEEGAN/ BUT PARDON ME, YOU WILL NOT	LEND	THEM MORE ON THEIR LAND THAN THE LAND IS WORTH; SO THEY
LIED (198)	WAS AURORA. I COULDNT RESIST THE TEMPTATION TO	LEND	THEM TO HER TO READ. BUT I DIDNT BARGAIN FOR YOUR
DOCT III (134)	FEEL THAT WE CAN TREAT YOU AS A FRIEND. WILL YOU	LEND	US A HUNDRED AND FIFTY POUNDS? /RIDGEON/ NO. /LOUIS/ (
LIED (192)	I HAVE THE TICKETS: WE WILL ASK YOUR HUSBAND TO	LEND	US THE CARRIAGE TO SHEW THAT THERE IS NO MALICE. NO
SUPR I (23)	US ANY PURPOSE OR FREEDOM OF OUR OWN? WILL THEY	LEND	US TO ONE ANOTHER? CAN THE STRONGEST MAN ESCAPE FROM
BULL IV (157)	NOT TO MORTGAGE IT NOW IT'S ME OWN. /LARRY/ I CAN	LEND	YOU 300 POUNDS ON IT. /CORNELIUS/ NO, NO; I WASNT PUTN
DOCT III (135)	I TRIED TO EXPLAIN. NOW, ONCE FOR ALL, I WILL NOT	LEND	YOU A FARTHING. I SHOULD BE GLAD TO HELP YOUR WIFE; BUT
MILL II (178)	I WILL BORROW IT FROM THE CHAUFFEUR. HE WILL	LEND	YOU A HUNDRED AND FIFTY POUNDS ON MY ACCOUNT IF YOU
DOCT III (138)	ME HALF-A-CROWN JUST TO SETTLE THIS. /WALPOLE/	LEND	YOU HALF-- (HIS VOICE FAINTS AWAY). /LOUIS/ WELL, IF

BULL IV (157) LEN ME FIVE HUNDERD; D'YE THINK? /LARRY/ HE'LL LEND YOU MORE THAN THE LANDLL EVER BE WORTH TO YOU; SO FOR
ARMS III (61) A MAN OF SPIRIT) WELL SAID, SWITZER. SHALL I LEND YOU MY BEST HORSE? /BLUNTSCHLI/ NO: DAMN YOUR HORSE!
DOCT II (120) PRETTILY. SO I SAID, BANG PLUMP OUT, " LET ME LEND YOU TWENTY POUNDS, AND PAY ME WHEN YOUR SHIP COMES
KING I (210) BALL FROM THE MIGHTIEST CANNON THE KING CAN LEND YOU, AND THOUGH YOU HAD THE STRENGTH OF HERCULES, AND

LENDIN

PRES (156) /THE ORDERLY/ (TO MITCHENER) WOULD YOU MIND LENDIN ME A AND, GUVNER? /LADY CORINTHIA/ (RAISING HER

LENDING

GETT PREFACE(251) WITH COLD DISGUST THAT SHE WOULD AS SOON THINK OF LENDING HER TOOTHBRUSH TO ANOTHER WOMAN AS HER HUSBAND. THE
JITT I (17) YOU KNOW: THE VERY LAST MAN YOU COULD IMAGINE LENDING HIMSELF TO SUCH A MYSTICAL SPECULATION! /JITTA/ (
MILL IV (202) THAT ONCE RESEMBLED A MAN, SOMETHING THAT LIKED LENDING ME FIVE POUND NOTES AND NEVER ASKED ME TO REPAY
DOCT III (138) ON ME JUST AT PRESENT. WALPOLE: WOULD YOU MIND LENDING ME HALF-A-CROWN JUST TO SETTLE THIS. /WALPOLE/ LEND
GENV II (63) /BEGONIA/ YES: ISNT IT? I WONDER WOULD YOU MIND LENDING ME MY FARE TO LONDON. I DONT LIKE TAKING MONEY OFF
BARB III (329) MORE OF IT, MR LOMAX. BY THE WAY, WOULD YOU MIND LENDING ME YOUR MATCHES? /LOMAX/ (OFFERING HIS BOX)
MILL IV (202) TO ME? LOVE OF ME? NO: THE SWANK OF A POOR MAN LENDING TO A MILLIONAIRESS. IN MY DIVINE WRATH I SMASHED HIM
MILL I (157) AND THEATRE TICKETS AND LUNCHES AT THE RITZ, AND LENDING YOU ALL THE LITTLE SUMS YOU HAVE OCCASION FOR WHEN
MILL I (157) THOUSAND ON ACCOUNT. /ADRIAN/ BUT I DONT. I LOVE LENDING YOU FIVERS. ONLY, AS THEY RUN THROUGH MY
DOCT III (135) FARTHING. I SHOULD BE GLAD TO HELP YOUR WIFE; BUT LENDING YOU MONEY IS NO SERVICE TO HER. /LOUIS/ OH WELL, IF

LENDS

NEVR I SD(208) AND WAYS ARE ENTIRELY KINDLY AND HUMANE; AND SHE LENDS HERSELF CONSCIENTIOUSLY TO THE OCCASIONAL
LION PREFACE(102) ST SOPHIA PUZZLES BEYOND WORDS THE SACRISTAN WHO LENDS HIM A HUGE PAIR OF SLIPPERS); AND JESUS NEVER
MILL III (185) LEAST. OTHER PEOPLE PUT IT THERE; AND THE BANK LENDS IT TO YOU IF IT THINKS YOU KNOW HOW TO EXTEND YOUR
BARB PREFACE(229) CONFESSION, WHICH THE ARMY ENCOURAGES BECAUSE IT LENDS ITSELF TO DRAMATIC ORATORY, WITH PLENTY OF THRILLING
SUPR III SD(72) TO TELL HIMSELF STORIES, AND A POSITION WHICH LENDS ITSELF TO IMAGINATIVE DECORATION. THE RANKS OF
BULL PREFACE(11) OF NATIONALITY WITH ALL THE RHETORIC TO WHICH IT LENDS ITSELF, I AM NOT FORGETTING THAT THERE ARE

LENGTH

MRS PREFACE(170) SAVED BY THEIR DELICACY TO REPORTING AT UNUSUAL LENGTH AN EXCEPTIONALLY ABOMINABLE POLICE CASE. MY OLD
BARB II (302) FOR WANT OF MONEY TO CARRY OUR WORK THROUGH THE LENGTH AND BREADTH OF THE LAND. LET ME TELL YOU THAT THERE
2TRU I (50) OVER; BUT THE CHARACTERS WILL DISCUSS IT AT GREAT LENGTH FOR TWO ACTS MORE. THE EXIT DOORS ARE ALL IN ORDER.
SUPR PREFACE(R29) HANDBOOK: I GIVE YOU THE HANDBOOK AT FULL LENGTH FOR YOUR EDIFICATION IF YOU CARE TO READ IT, AND IN
SUPR PREFACE(R18) ANCESTOR APPEARS AND PHILOSOPHIZES AT GREAT LENGTH IN A SHAVIO-SOCRATIC DIALOGUE WITH THE LADY, THE
PHIL I (73) HER BY THE SHOULDERS AND HOLDS HER OUT AT ARMS LENGTH IN FRONT OF HIM). EH, LITTLE PHILOSOPHER? NO, MY
ROCK PREFACE(187) ACTUALLY CONDESCENDING TO PARLEY WITH YOU AT THIS LENGTH IN THE MERCIFUL HOPE OF FINDING AN EXCUSE FOR
UNPL PREFACE(R14) EVERY PLAY OF MINE THAT EXCEEDS ONE ACT IN LENGTH . I DO NOT WANT HIM TO READ IT (AT LEAST OFFICIALLY:
SUPR III (74) OF ANARCHISM AND SOCIAL-DEMOCRACY AT GREAT LENGTH . THE CAUSE OF ANARCHY HAS BEEN ABLY REPRESENTED BY
METH PREFACE(R75) SOME OF THEM MYSELF), WHO BORE THEM AT A LENGTH NOW FORBIDDEN BY CUSTOM IN THE ESTABLISHED PULPIT.
SUPR PREFACE(R12) BUT YOUR DISLIKE OF VULGARITY IS PUSHED TO THE LENGTH OF A DEFECT (UNIVERSALITY OF CHARACTER IS IMPOSSIBLE
MRS I (184) MORBID FELLOW, IN WHOM THE THING IS PUSHED TO THE LENGTH OF A DISEASE. /VIVIE/ IT DOESNT PAY. I WOULDNT DO IT
POSN PREFACE(391) A MAN TO WHOM A MATTER OF TWO INCHES IN THE LENGTH OF A GENTLEMAN'S SWORD OR THE ABSENCE OF A FEATHER
MIS. PREFACE(31) EXPERIENCE OF THE WEIGHT OF A POUND AND THE LENGTH OF AN INCH, AND SOMETIMES A SCOUNDREL WHO HAS RIFLED
HART I (75) CARELESS MAN IS NEVER ALLOWED WITHIN ARMS LENGTH OF ANY WOMAN WORTH KNOWING. /HECTOR/ I SEE. YOU ARE
MTH4 II (191) LABORIOUS, BY RIDICULOUS PREPARATIONS FOR A LENGTH OF DAYS WHICH THE CHANCES WERE FIFTY THOUSAND TO ONE
KING I (188) YOUR PRIVILEGE WITH ME DOES NOT RUN TO THE LENGTH OF KNOCKING MY BROTHER DOWN. IT IS A SERIOUS MATTER
MTH4 I (171) THERE IS A FIXED RELATION BETWEEN CONDUCT AND LENGTH OF LIFE. /THE ELDERLY GENTLEMAN/ I HAVE NEVER HEARD
METH PREFACE(R41) UNTIL HE SUCCEEDED IN WISHING THE NECESSARY LENGTH OF NECK INTO EXISTENCE. ANOTHER ANSWER WAS ALSO
GETT PREFACE(236) ON ONE ANOTHER, EVEN IF IT CARRIES US TO THE LENGTH OF OPENLY ADMITTING WHAT WE ARE NOW COMPELLED TO
MILL PREFACE(123) OF THE JEWS WHICH WENT TO THE SCANDALOUS LENGTH OF OUTLAWING, PLUNDERING, AND EXILING ALBERT
LION PREFACE(54) AND ASK HIM TO POINT OUT TO YOU THE PARTICULAR LENGTH OF RAIL, THE PARTICULAR SEAT IN THE RAILWAY CARRIAGE,
NEVR II (232) IF YOU STRETCH THE LONG ARM OF COINCIDENCE TO THE LENGTH OF TELLING ME THAT MR CRAMPTON OF THIS TOWN IS MY
METH PREFACE(R88) BE PLAYED AT FULL LENGTH OWING TO THE ENORMOUS LENGTH OF THE ENTIRE WORK, THOUGH THAT FEAT HAS BEEN
METH PREFACE(R42) OF COURSE, THE SELECTIVE PROCESS STOPS AND THE LENGTH OF THE GIRAFFE'S NECK STOPS WITH IT. OTHERWISE, HE
PYGM II SD(217) AND A BENCH FOR THE PLAYER EXTENDING THE FULL LENGTH OF THE KEYBOARD. ON THE PIANO IS A DESSERT DISH
MILL II SD(166) TO THE SIDEBOARD, AND EXTENDING NEARLY THE WHOLE LENGTH OF THE ROOM, ARE TWO SEPARATE LONG TABLES, LAID FOR
MTH3 (109) THEY SIMPLY BELIEVED THAT MANKIND COULD LIVE ANY LENGTH OF TIME IT KNEW TO BE ABSOLUTELY NECESSARY TO SAVE
JOAN PREFACE(56) NOTICING THAT WHAT MATTERS IS NOT THE ABSOLUTE LENGTH OF TIME OCCUPIED BY A PLAY, BUT THE SPEED WITH WHICH
NEVR I (206) TO SAY THAT IF YOU ARE GOING TO STAY HERE FOR ANY LENGTH OF TIME, IT WILL BE IMPOSSIBLE FOR ME TO ACCEPT YOUR
ARMS II (34) /SERGIUS/ VERY FATIGUING THING TO KEEP UP FOR ANY LENGTH OF TIME, LOUKA. ONE FEELS THE NEED OF SOME RELIEF
SUPR III (112) AND SOPHISTRIES, NOT TO MENTION THE INTOLERABLE LENGTH OF YOUR SPEECHES. /DON JUAN/ OH, COME! WHO BEGAN
MTH5 (259) /ECRASIA/ AT WHAT DISTANCE? /ARJILLAX/ ARM'S LENGTH OR MORE. /ECRASIA/ THANK YOU: NOT FOR ME. (SHE TURNS
HART PREFACE(10) EXCEPT SHORT CIRCUITING THE PYLORUS BY CUTTING A LENGTH OUT OF THE LOWER INTESTINE AND FASTENING IT DIRECTLY
METH PREFACE(R88) ITSELF: INDEED IT COULD HARDLY BE PLAYED AT FULL LENGTH OWING TO THE ENORMOUS LENGTH OF THE ENTIRE WORK,
DEVL III (52) HAND AND SMILING, BUT KEEPING HER ALMOST AT ARMS LENGTH) I AM VERY SURE I SHOULDNT LET YOU. /JUDITH/ DONT
APPL INTRLUD(244) CAR. (SITTING DOWN BESIDE HIM, BUT BEYOND ARM'S LENGTH) THAT IS WHAT YOU GIVE ME WHEN MY HEART DEMANDS
METH PREFACE(R9) WAS FORGOTTEN; I HAD DOUBLED MY YEARS AND MY LENGTH ; AND I HAD DISCARDED THE RELIGION OF MY FOREFATHERS.
VWOO 2,SD(123) COUNTER IS FOR GENERAL SHOPPING FOR MOST OF ITS LENGTH ; BUT ONE END IS RESERVED AND RAILED IN FOR POSTAL
ARMS I (21) AH! (WITH A HAPPY SIGH HE SINKS BACK AT FULL LENGTH ; LIFTS HIS BOOTS INTO THE BED WITH A FINAL EFFORT;
2TRU I (44) SITTING IN THE STERN, AND I STRETCHED OUT AT FULL LENGTH WITH MY HEAD PILLOWED ON SWEETIE'S KNEES. /THE
MTH4 I (142) TO CONVERSE INTIMATELY AND AT THE GREATEST LENGTH WITH THE MOST DISTINGUISHED PERSONS, IF YOU CANNOT
LION PREFACE(34) IT IS MADE TO MARY HERSELF, AT MUCH GREATER LENGTH , WITH A SENSE OF THE ECSTASY OF THE BRIDE OF THE

LENGTHENED

MTH4 I (171) TO DO WITH. /ZOO/ DADDY: THE MAN WHOSE LIFE IS LENGTHENED IN THIS WAY MAY BE BUSIER THAN A SAVAGE; BUT THE
MTH4 I (171) YOU THAT WE SHORTLIVERS, AS YOU CALL US, HAVE LENGTHENED OUR LIVES VERY CONSIDERABLY. /ZOO/ HOW? /THE

LENGTHENING

BULL IV (172) MADNESS; TO WATCH THE SHADOW OF THE ROUND TOWER LENGTHENING IN THE SUNSET; TO BREAK MY HEART USELESSLY IN

LENGTHS

MTH1 II (32) IT. THERE ARE OTHERS WHO CUT REEDS OF DIFFERENT LENGTHS AND BLOW THROUGH THEM, MAKING LOVELY PATTERNS OF
MILL PREFACE(113) OF COURSE THERE ARE LIMITS. HE CANNOT GO TO THE LENGTHS AT WHICH THE COMMON MAN WILL BELIEVE HIM TO BE
VWOO 2 (131) RUSHED? /A/ RUSHED, PRECIPITATED, CARRIED TO LENGTHS I HAD NO INTENTION OF GOING TO. /Z/ WELL, IT GETS
BASH PREFACE(90) VERSION OF THE BIBLE CARRIED TO GREATER LENGTHS THAN IN THE UNITED STATES OF AMERICA. TO ALTER A

LENIENCY

BULL PREFACE(53) WHO ASSAULTED THEM SHOULD HAVE BEEN TREATED WITH LENIENCY , AND ASSURED THAT PIGEON-SHOOTING WOULD NOT BE
ROCK PREFACE(163) CRIMINALS, WILL BE CARRIED OUT WITH COMPARATIVE LENIENCY , AND PROBABLY, IF THE CULPRIT BEHAVES WELL, BE

LENIENT

SUPR II (65) YOU TAKE A VERY LENIENT VIEW, MR RAMSDEN, TOO LENIENT TO MY MIND. SURELY MARRIAGE SHOULD ENNOBLE A MAN.
SUPR II (65) TO BE EXCUSED FOR SUCH CONDUCT. YOU TAKE A VERY LENIENT VIEW, MR RAMSDEN, TOO LENIENT TO MY MIND. SURELY

LENIENTLY

MRS PREFACE(172) AND I CAN ASSURE MR GREIN THAT SHE IS OFTEN LENIENTLY DEALT WITH BECAUSE SHE HAS CONDUCTED HER BUSINESS
FANY II (289) OF THE ENTENTE CORDIALE I SHOULD BE DEALT WITH LENIENTLY , YET MISS KNOX, WHO USED HER FIST, GOT A MONTH,
BARB I (268) WHICH FORMERLY DESTROYED ONLY THIRTEEN. /LOMAX/ (LENIENTLY) WELL, THE MORE DESTRUCTIVE WAR BECOMES, THE

LENIHAN

JOAN (2) CITY, ON THE 28TH DECEMBER 1923, WITH WINIFRED LENIHAN IN THE TITLE-PART. ITS FIRST PERFORMANCE IN LONDON

LENIN

ROCK PREFACE(165) ONE OF " THE INTELLECTUAL PROLETARIAT." EVEN LENIN AND HIS COLLEAGUES, ALL ULTRA-BOURGEOIS (OTHERWISE
2TRU PREFACE(16) AQUINAS AND FRANCIS BACON, DANTE AND GALILEO, LENIN AND LLOYD GEORGE, COULD SELDOM COME TO A UNANIMOUS
ROCK PREFACE(165) THE SOVIETS OF PEASANTS AND SOLDIERS WHO BACKED LENIN AND SAVED COMMUNISM WHEN ALL WESTERN EUROPE SET ON HIM
ROCK II (239) /SIR BEMROSE/ WHO'S TO STOP IT? WHERE WOULD LENIN AND STALIN AND TROTSKY AND ALL THAT BOLSHY LOT HAVE

FABL PREFACE(83) ECONOMIC POLICY VANISHED OR CRISS-CROSSED. LENIN AND STALIN HAD TO CRY LAISSER-FAIRE TO ALL THE
ROCK I (233) /HILDA/ THERE ARE MUCH NEWER BOOKS BY MARXISTS: LENIN AND TROTSKY AND STALIN AND PEOPLE LIKE THAT. /SIR
FABL PREFACE(97) THEM AND DEVISED THE NEW ECONOMIC POLICY LENIN HAD TO ANNOUNCE, AND STALIN TO PUT IN PRACTICE. THUS
JOAN PREFACE(24) 1803, OF THE GERMAN CROWN PRINCE IN 1915, OR OF LENIN IN 1917. IT ENDS IN MERE SCURRILITY. THE IMPRESSION
FABL PREFACE(78) BOURGEOIS DEVIATORS. THE WEBBS WERE TRANSLATED BY LENIN . AS A PLAYWRIGHT I WAS HELD UP AS AN IRRELIGIOUS
JOAN PREFACE(46) HISTORY ABOUT WASHINGTON, AND TOLD LIES ABOUT LENIN . IN WASHINGTON'S TIME THEY WERE TOLD LIES (THE SAME
ROCK II (267) US. KARL MARX THOUGHT IT ALL OUT IN BLOOMSBURY. LENIN LEARNT HIS LESSON IN HOLFORD SQUARE, ISLINGTON. WHY
ROCK II (270) AND NOW I'M FOR ANY NAPOLEON OR MUSSOLINI OR LENIN OR CHAVENDER THAT HAS THE STUFF IN HIM TO TAKE BOTH
ROCK PREFACE(166) VICTORY FOR PRIVATE PROPERTY. SO FAR SO GOOD FOR LENIN ; BUT THE WAR AGAINST THE COUNTER-REVOLUTIONISTS, WHEN
MILL PREFACE(133) ASTUTE STROKE OF GERMAN IMPERIAL TACTICS TO SEND LENIN SAFELY THROUGH GERMANY TO RUSSIA SO THAT HE MIGHT MAKE
ROCK PREFACE(166) GIVE US LAND, THE SOLDIERS' CRY OF GIVE US PEACE. LENIN SAID, IN EFFECT, TAKE THE LAND; AND IF FEUDALLY MINDED
SIM PREFACE(11) HANDS. SUCH A COMMISSAR WAS DJERJINSKY, NOW, LIKE LENIN , ENTOMBED IN THE RED SQUARE. HE WAS NOT A HOMICIDALLY
MILL PREFACE(135) IT IS ALWAYS THE GREATEST SPIRITS, FROM JESUS TO LENIN , FROM ST THOMAS MORE TO WILLIAM MORRIS, WHO ARE
MILL PREFACE(113) AND A CODE IMPOSED. THE BORN RULER, THE MOSES OR LENIN , IS NO LONGER INDISPENSABLE: ROUTINE GOVERNMENT BY

LENIN'S

ROCK PREFACE(166) LEGIONS OF PETTY LANDED PROPRIETORS THAT MADE LENIN'S POSITION IMPREGNABLE, AND PROVIDED TROTSKY AND
2TRU PREFACE(18) POSTULATE OF EQUALITY, OR ITS ANTICIPATION OF LENIN'S PRINCIPLE THAT THE RULERS MUST BE AS POOR AS THE
BUOY 1 (10) THAT IS ALWAYS UNSUCCESSFUL. MARX'S PROFESSION. LENIN'S PROFESSION. STALIN'S PROFESSION. RUSKIN'S

LENINS

GENV PREFACE(24) ITS ABLEST. OUR SOLONS, CAESARS AND WASHINGTONS, LENINS , STALINS AND NIGHTINGALES, MAY BE BETTER THAN THEIR

LENKHEIM

JITT III (55) SIT DOWN, WONT YOU? I WILL TALK TO PROFESSOR LENKHEIM ABOUT IT. HE WILL UNDERSTAND. /FESSLER/ (STANDING
JITT II (50) OF THE SILLY THING, AS YOU CALL IT, WHEN IT MAKES LENKHEIM AS FAMOUS AS EINSTEIN. /LENKHEIM/ (STARTLED BY THE
JITT III (74) AFTER KISSING JITTA RATHER DEFIANTLY) MRS LENKHEIM DID NOT SAY A SINGLE UNKIND WORD ABOUT YOU. I DID.
JITT II SD(40) COMES IN, DRYING HER EYES WITH HER HANDKERCHIEF. LENKHEIM FOLLOWS HER SOLEMNLY WITH HER DISPATCH CASE IN HIS
JITT II SD(35) NOD AT EDITH. SHE GOES INTO THE NEXT ROOM. LENKHEIM FOLLOWS HER. /JITTA/ (THROWING OFF HER FALSE
JITT II SD(31) THE OLD GIRL WONT BE EASY UNTIL SHE HAS SEEN YOU. LENKHEIM GOES OUT FOR A MOMENT THROUGH THE INNER DOOR. JITTA
JITT II SD(31) DOOR. JITTA COMES IN, LANGUID, AND DRESSED AS LENKHEIM HAS DESCRIBED. /JITTA/ OH, SO GLAD YOUVE COME,
JITT III (54) ME WHAT HAS BECOME OF IT ALL? YOU AND PROFESSOR LENKHEIM HAVE GONE THROUGH HIS PAPERS WITH ME. HAVE WE COME
JITT II (30) WAY, THAT REMINDS ME THAT I FORGOT TO ASK HOW MRS LENKHEIM IS. /LENKHEIM/ OH, JITTA IS GETTING OVER IT. SHE
JITT III (65) I CAN DO? /FESSLER/ IT'S VERY GOOD OF YOU, MRS LENKHEIM . BUT I MUST SEE THIS THING THROUGH MYSELF. THANK
JITT III (65) HALDENSTEDT. YOU HAD BETTER TALK IT OVER WITH MRS LENKHEIM . GOODBYE. GOODBYE, MRS LENKHEIM. (HE BOWS TO THEM
JITT III (66) I AM IN THE DARK ABOUT HER. LISTEN TO ME, MRS LENKHEIM . IF I THOUGHT IT WAS ONLY HER BODY THAT TOOK HIM,
JITT III (65) IT OVER WITH MRS LENKHEIM. GOODBYE. GOODBYE, MRS LENKHEIM . (HE BOWS TO THEM AND GOES OUT). /AGNES/ SIT
JITT III (80) KISSING IT) I OWE YOU MY LIFE'S HAPPINESS, MRS LENKHEIM . /AGNES/ I AM SURE WE ALL OWE YOU THE HAPPINESS OF
JITT II (42) THE NEXT LINE. /JITTA/ (READING) " BY ALFRED LENKHEIM ." I SUPPOSE HE MEANT YOU TO FINISH IT. /LENKHEIM/
JITT I (20) OF THE FEMININE PSYCHE, BY PROFESSOR ALFRED LENKHEIM ." /JITTA/ BRUNO! YOU ARE MAD. /BRUNO/ I BURNT THE
JITT III (74) NOT KNOWING WHAT ELSE TO SAY) IT WASNT THAT. MRS LENKHEIM NEVER OFFERED YOU TO ME. /JITTA/ GO OFF TO THE
JITT III (74) THAT IT DOESNT MATTER TUPPENCE WHOM I MARRY, (LENKHEIM OPENS THE STUDY DOOR AND IS COMING IN WHEN EDITH,
JITT II SD(31) KISSES HER HAND, AND GOES OUT. WHEN HE HAS GONE, LENKHEIM RETURNS, FULL OF EXCITEMENT AND CURIOSITY.
JITT II (41) /AGNES/ DO, OF COURSE. I SHALL EXPECT YOU. (TO LENKHEIM) YOU WILL FORGIVE ME, WONT YOU, ALL THE TROUBLE I
JITT III (80) (SHE KISSES THE DOCTOR)! PROFESSOR (SHE KISSES LENKHEIM)! DIDNT I SAY SHE WAS OUR GOOD ANGEL? /LENKHEIM/
JITT III (65) DONT DESPISE MY HELP. /FESSLER/ OH NO, MRS LENKHEIM ; BUT-- MRS HALDENSTEDT COMES IN. /AGNES/ (STILL
JITT II SD(40) DARLING, IF ONLY I COULD! IF ONLY I DARED! LENKHEIM THROWS THE DOOR OPEN: HE IS RETURNING WITH AGNES.
JITT II (34) WHY I HAVE COME TODAY INSTEAD OF WAITING FOR MRS LENKHEIM TO CALL. /LENKHEIM/ DEAR FELLOW: HOW CONSCIENTIOUS
JITT III (74) FOR HER WITH SARDONIC POLITENESS). /EDITH/ (TO LENKHEIM , AFTER KISSING JITTA RATHER DEFIANTLY) MRS
JITT II (51) A MOMENT; AND READS SLOWLY) " BY PROFESSOR ALFRED LENKHEIM , DOCTOR OF PHILOSOPHY IN THE UNIVERSITY OF
JITT II (27) NIGHT, WERE YOU? /FESSLER/ NO. BUT, BY JIMMINY, LENKHEIM , I HAVE GONE THROUGH A LOT THIS LAST WEEK.
JITT II SD(27) IS KEEPING HER BED. HER HUSBAND, PROFESSOR ALFRED LENKHEIM , IS SITTING IN HIS STUDY AFTER LUNCH WITH YOUNG DR
JITT III (68) YOU. /AGNES/ (SMILING) WELL, I AM SURE, MRS LENKHEIM , THIS TALK HAS MADE THE MOST WONDERFUL DIFFERENCE
JITT III (80) INDEED YOU ARE. OH, YOU ARE A LUCKY MAN, MR LENKHEIM , TO HAVE SUCH A WIFE. /JITTA/ (STRIKING IN BEFORE
JITT III SD(56) MOODILY TO THE CONSOLE). THEY ARE INTERRUPTED BY LENKHEIM , WHO OPENS THE DOOR OF THE STUDY AND TROTS IN

LENKHEIM'S

JITT III (71) WHOLLY TO MY SORROW. /JITTA/ (SITTING DOWN IN LENKHEIM'S CHAIR) WHICH SORROW? THE OLD SORROW THAT GOD
JITT II (34) YOU, I HAVE A PACKET OF PAPERS MARKED " PROFESSOR LENKHEIM'S PROPERTY: TO BE GIVEN INTO HIS OWN HANDS": THAT

LENNOX

PPP PREFACE(192) MAUDE, MR ERIC LEWIS, MR ARTHUR WILLIAMS, AND MR LENNOX PAWLE. AS IT IS EXTREMELY DIFFICULT TO FIND AN ACTOR
BASH PREFACE(90) COMEDIANS AS CHARLES QUATERMAINE, WILLIAM WYES, LENNOX PAWLE, HENRIETTA WATSON, MARIE LOHR, AND FANNY

LENSES

METH PREFACE(R38) TRANSMITTERS IN HIS EARS, LIGHT RECORDERS AND LENSES IN HIS EYES: WAS IT CONCEIVABLE THAT THIS WAS THE

LENT

VWOO 3 (133) SHOULD HAVE BEEN A MONEYLENDER. /Z/ SHE WAS. SHE LENT A SHILLING FOR A PENNY A WEEK. /A/ THAT MUST HAVE BEEN
NEVR II (244) I NEVER INQUIRED. /DOLLY/ THE SERVANTS COME IN LENT AND KNEEL DOWN BEFORE YOU AND CONFESS ALL THE THINGS
DOCT II (123) MEAN TO BEHAVE BADLY. AS I TOLD HIM, I MIGHT HAVE LENT IT TO HIM IF HE HAD BEEN A JEW HIMSELF. /SIR PATRICK/ (
DOCT II (121) MINUTES, AS SHE HAD HIS PURSE, SO OF COURSE I LENT IT TO HIM. AND HE'S FORGOTTEN TO PAY ME. I'VE JUST
HART I (57) WANTED, AND GAVE IT TO HIM. I DONT MEAN THAT HE LENT IT TO HIM, OR THAT HE INVESTED IT IN HIS BUSINESS. HE
POSN (453) HORSE HAD BEEN WORTH ITS KEEP, YOU WOULDNT HAVE LENT IT TO STRAPPER, AND STRAPPER WOULDNT HAVE LENT IT TO
POSN (453) LENT IT TO STRAPPER, AND STRAPPER WOULDNT HAVE LENT IT TO THIS ELOQUENT AND VENERABLE RAM. (SUPPRESSED
LADY PREFACE(209) SONNETS, WITH THE EVIDENCE HE HAD COLLECTED. HE LENT ME A COPY OF THE BOOK, WHICH I NEVER RETURNED. BUT I
MTH3 (115) OTHER MATTERS, WAS NOT LOST ON ME. BY THE WAY, HE LENT ME FIVE POUNDS ONCE WHICH I NEVER REPAID; AND IT STILL
MRS II (215) THOUGHT WE TWO COULD SAVE FASTER THAN ONE. SO SHE LENT ME SOME MONEY AND GAVE ME A START; AND I SAVED STEADILY
ARMS II (41) I ONLY CAME TO THANK YOU AND RETURN THE COAT YOU LENT ME. IF YOU WILL ALLOW ME TO TAKE IT OUT OF MY BAG AND
CLEO PR01 (92) THE EGYPTIANS SAID, " LO: THESE ROMANS WHICH HAVE LENT MONEY TO OUR KINGS AND LEVIED A DISTRAINT UPON US WITH
DEST (165) THE OTHER HANDKERCHIEF FROM HIS BREAST) YOU LENT ONE OF YOUR HANDKERCHIEFS TO MY LIEUTENANT WHEN YOU
GETT (312) FASTS STRICTLY ON FRIDAYS AND THROUGHOUT LENT ; WEARS A CASSOCK AND BIRETTA; AND HAS MORE LEGAL
HART PREFACE(33) ALL SORTS OF ILLUSTRIOUS AND INFLUENTIAL PERSONS LENT THEIR NAMES TO A GRAND APPEAL TO OUR NATIONAL CULTURE.
DOCT III (137) WHAT CIGARET CASE? /WALPOLE/ THE GOLD ONE I LENT YOU AT THE STAR AND GARTER. /LOUIS/ (SURPRISED) WAS
POSN (442) SHARE. I NEVER ASKED YOU FOR ALL THE MONEY I'D LENT YOU FROM TIME TO TIME. I ASKED YOU FOR MOTHER'S OLD
MRS PREFACE(158) THIS LIMITATION FOR PART OF THE YEAR, SAY DURING LENT , SO AS TO MAKE A CLOSE SEASON FOR THAT DULLEST OF

LENTULUS

LION I SD(117) ARCH, FOLLOWED BY FOUR SOLDIERS IN TWO FILES). LENTULUS AND METELLUS COME INTO THE SQUARE FROM THE WEST
LION I (120) FERROVIUS RISES IMPRESSIVELY AND TOWERS OVER HIM. LENTULUS BECOMES WHITE WITH TERROR; AND A SHADE OF GREEN
LION I (121) A CHRISTIAN, BUT HIS HAIR WAS AS WHITE AS SNOW. (LENTULUS FALLS IN A DEAD FAINT). THERE, THERE: TAKE HIM
LION I SD(117) COURTIERS, DRESSED IN THE EXTREMITY OF FASHION. LENTULUS IS SLENDER, FAIR-HAIRED, EPICENE. METELLUS IS
LION I SD(122) OF HEAVEN UPON YOU AND HIM. METELLUS FOLLOWS LENTULUS . THE CENTURION RETURNS TO HIS SEAT TO RESUME HIS
LION I (118) SEE THEM BEHAVING LIKE STREET BOYS? (SHARPLY TO LENTULUS) PULL YOURSELF TOGETHER, MAN. HOLD YOUR HEAD UP.
LION I (118) MOVES AWAY FROM TEMPTATION TO THE EAST SIDE NEAR LENTULUS ; CLASPS HIS HANDS IN SILENT PRAYER; AND THROWS
LION I (120) WITHOUT FLINCHING, TURNS THE OTHER CHEEK. LENTULUS , RATHER OUT OF COUNTENANCE, TITTERS FOOLISHLY, AND
LION I SD(121) FERROVIUS, EASY: YOU BROKE THE LAST MAN'S JAW. LENTULUS , WITH A MOAN OF TERROR, ATTEMPTS TO FLY; BUT

LENTULUS'S

LION I (120) BEDSIDE IN THE HOSPITAL. (PUTTING HIS HANDS ON LENTULUS'S SHOULDERS WITH PATERNAL WEIGHT). BUT NOW I HAVE

LEO

GETT (276) WORN YOUR LIVER PAD? /THE GENERAL/ (SOLEMNLY) LEO : FORGIVENESS IS ONE OF THE MOST BEAUTIFUL TRAITS IN A
GETT (278) A YOUNG WOMAN. I HAD NO RIGHT AT MY AGE TO MARRY LEO : SHE KNEW NO MORE ABOUT LIFE THAN A CHILD. /LEO/ I KNEW
GETT (351) COME. WE HAVE TO DRESS EDITH. COME, LESBIA: COME, LEO : WE MUST ALL HELP. NOW, EDITH. (LESBIA, LEO, AND EDITH
GETT (278) (SHE WEEPS). THERE: DONT GET INTO A TANTRUM, LEO ? /LESBIA/ MAY ONE ASK WHO IS THE MUSHROOM-FACED
GETT (278) PRETEND TO BELIEVE ALL THAT ROT ABOUT MY KNOCKING LEO ABOUT AND LEAVING HER FOR-- FOR A-- A-- UGH! YOU SHOULD

GETT	SD(276)	TO SPOIL HER THAN MRS BRIDGENORTH IS. BUT	LEO	AFFECTS A SPECIAL INTIMACY WITH LESBIA, AS OF TWO
GETT	(278)	ASTONISHING TO ME. WHY DID YOU DO IT? WHY DID	LEO	ALLOW IT? /REGINALD/ YOUD BETTER ASK HER. /LEO/ (STILL
GETT	(301)	HOTCHKISS, WHEN I JOLLY NEARLY SHOT YOU AND	LEO	AND FINISHED UP WITH MYSELF; AND THATS THE TRUTH. /LEO/
GETT	SD(296)	EDITH HAS TIME TO ANSWER HER MOTHER RETURNS WITH	LEO	AND LESBIA. /LEO/ YES, HERE SHE IS, OF COURSE. I TOLD
GETT	(303)	FROM CHURCH MARRIAGE. THE RELATIONS BETWEEN	LEO	AND REJJY AND SINJON ARE PERFECTLY LEGAL; BUT DO YOU
GETT	(296)	DRESS. LOOK AT THE HOUR! /MRS BRIDGENORTH/ COME,	LEO	DEAR. (LEO FOLLOWS HER RELUCTANTLY. THEY ARE ABOUT TO
GETT	(276)	/THE GENERAL/ (MUCH HUFFED) OH, WELL, IF	LEO	DOES NOT MIND, OF COURSE I HAVE NO MORE TO SAY. BUT I
GETT	(296)	AT THE HOUR! /MRS BRIDGENORTH/ COME, LEO DEAR. (	LEO	FOLLOWS HER RELUCTANTLY. THEY ARE ABOUT TO GO INTO THE
GETT	SD(345)	COME IN THROUGH THE TOWER. SHE HAS HER HAT ON.	LEO	FOLLOWS. THEY HAVE EVIDENTLY BEEN OUT TOGETHER. SYKES,
GETT	(348)	SEEMS ON THE POINT OF ASSAULTING HOTCHKISS WHEN	LEO	GETS BETWEEN THEM AND DRAWS REGINALD AWAY TOWARDS THE
GETT	(276)	TO A MAN. WHEN A MAN KNOCKS A WOMAN DOWN (	LEO	GIVES A LITTLE SHRIEK OF LAUGHTER AND COLLAPSES ON A
GETT	(282)	ATTENTION. /THE BISHOP/ BUT POOR LITTLE	LEO	HAS ONLY TOLD THE SIMPLE TRUTH; WHILST YOU, BOXER, ARE
GETT	SD(275)	(ALL THREE CLAMORING TOGETHER). IT IS TOO LATE:	LEO	IS ALREADY IN THE KITCHEN. COLLINS GOES OUT, MUTELY
GETT	SD(275)	WHICH HE DEPLORES BUT HAS BEEN UNABLE TO SAVE.	LEO	IS VERY PRETTY, VERY YOUTHFUL, VERY RESTLESS, AND
GETT	(280)	HE'S A BISHOP: IT'S HIS DUTY TO TALK TO	LEO	. I CAN STAND A GOOD DEAL; BUT WHEN IT COMES TO FLAT
GETT	(348)	OF COURSE YOU DIDNT, REJJY. DONT BE SILLY,	LEO	. IT'S I WHO REALLY HAVE LOW TASTES. /LEO/ YOU!
GETT	(348)	THAT THAT WOULD REALLY BE THE BETTER PLAN.	LEO	. IVE A CONFESSION TO MAKE TO YOU. I'M NOT THE MAN YOU
GETT	SD(297)	AT THE END, NEXT HIM, AND MRS BRIDGENORTH NEXT	LEO	. REGINALD RETURNS TO THE OAK CHEST, TO BE NEAR LEO; AND
GETT	(285)	(GOING OUT THROUGH THE TOWER) COME WITH ME,	LEO	. /LEO/ (FOLLOWING LESBIA OUT) YES, CERTAINLY, THE
GETT	(281)	THEM. /THE BISHOP/ QUITE A NICE DISTINCTION,	LEO	. /LEO/ JUST OCCASIONALLY, YOU KNOW. /THE BISHOP/ (
GETT	(273)	HE MADE A FOOL OF HIMSELF MARRYING A CHILD LIKE	LEO	. /THE GENERAL/ BUT TO HIT HER! ABSOLUTELY TO HIT HER!
GETT	(311)	WASNT A LADY. /REGINALD/ YOU SHUT YOUR HEAD,	LEO	. THIS IS A GENERAL SORT OF CONTRACT FOR EVERYBODY: IT'S
GETT	(282)	GENERAL/ ALFRED: WE ASKED YOU HERE TO PREACH TO	LEO	. YOU ARE PREACHING AT ME INSTEAD. I AM NOT CONSCIOUS OF
GETT	SD(323)	ALL RISE EXCEPT SOAMES, WHO SITS DOWN.	LEO	JOINS REGINALD AT THE GARDEN DOOR. MRS BRIDGENORTH
GETT	(298)	THE CAKE'S READY: EVERYTHING'S READY. I'LL LEND	LEO	MY VEIL AND THINGS. /THE BISHOP/ I'M AFRAID THEY MUST
GETT	(331)	/HOTCHKISS/ CANT YOU SEE THAT I MAYNT THROW	LEO	OVER JUST BECAUSE I SHOULD BE ONLY TOO GLAD TO. IT WOULD
GETT	(283)	PUT ASUNDER: GOD WILL TAKE CARE OF THAT. (TO	LEO	) BY THE WAY, WHO WAS IT THAT JOINED YOU AND REGINALD,
GETT	(281)	TO THE CONVERSATION. /THE BISHOP/ (GOING TO	LEO	) GOOD MORNING, MY DEAR. HULLO! YOUVE BROUGHT REGINALD
GETT	(324)	BY MISS GRANTHAM. /MRS BRIDGENORTH/ (INTRODUCING	LEO	) MRS REGINALD BRIDGENORTH. /REGINALD/ THE LATE MRS
GETT	(279)	/THE GENERAL/ (COMING PATERNALLY TO	LEO	) MY DEAR GIRL: ALL THE CONVERSATION IN THE WORLD HAS
GETT	(324)	THE DECREE IS MADE ABSOLUTE. /MRS GEORGE/ (TO	LEO	) WELL, YOUVE MORE TIME TO GET MARRIED AGAIN THAN HE
GETT	SD(297)	REGINALD RETURNS TO THE OAK CHEST, TO BE NEAR	LEO	; AND THE BISHOP GOES TO HIS WIFE AND STANDS BY HER.
GETT	(275)	I HAVE ASKED YOU TO GO. YOU KNOW HOW FOND I AM OF	LEO	; AND YOU KNOW WHAT SHE WOULD FEEL IF SHE CAME IN AND
DOCT I	(86)	RED, YOU KNOW, WITH BLACK LETTERING. DOCTOR	LEO	SCHUTZMACHER, L.R.C.P. M.R.C.S. ADVICE AND MEDICINE
GETT	SD(297)	THE LONG SIDE OF THE TABLE, NEAR THE GARDEN DOOR.	LEO	SITS AT THE END, NEXT HIM, AND MRS BRIDGENORTH NEXT LEO.
GETT	SD(345)	EDITH TO SIT DOWN. SHE SITS IN THE RAILED CHAIR.	LEO	TAKES THE CHAIR NEAREST THE TOWER ON THE LONG SIDE OF
GETT	(282)	MAN. HA! BUT I CAN PUT A PLAIN QUESTION. IS	LEO	TO BE ENCOURAGED TO BE A POLYGAMIST? /THE BISHOP/
GETT	(317)	YOU CALL THAT WORK? /EDITH/ DONT YOU?	LEO	USED TO DO IT FOR NOTHING; SO NO DOUBT YOU THOUGHT IT
GETT	(330)	FELT QUITE HAPPY AT THEIR HOUSE AS THEIR FRIEND.	LEO	WAS AN AMUSING LITTLE DEVIL; BUT I LIKED REGINALD MUCH
METH PREFACE	(R82)	COULD NOT VERY WELL BELIEVE IN JULIUS II OR	LEO	X, OR IN MUCH THAT THEY BELIEVED IN; BUT HE COULD PAINT
GETT	(351)	LEO: WE MUST ALL HELP. NOW, EDITH. (LESBIA,	LEO	, AND EDITH GO OUT THROUGH THE TOWER). COLLINS: WE SHALL
GETT	(326)	THE TOWER, FOLLOWED BY MRS GEORGE, LESBIA,	LEO	, AND EDITH). /THE BISHOP/ SHALL WE TRY TO GET THROUGH
GETT	(301)	WEEPING TO HER SEAT). /MRS BRIDGENORTH/ (PETTING	LEO	, BUT SPEAKING TO THE COMPANY AT LARGE) BUT ISNT ALL
JOAN PREFACE	(40)	THE CHURCH OF ENGLAND GOT OVER THE BULLS OF POPE	LEO	, BY MAKING A CHURCH OF HER OWN, AND AFFIRMING IT TO BE
GETT	(351)	IF YOU THINK YOUVE BEHAVED LIKE A GENTLEMAN TO	LEO	, YOURE MISTAKEN. AND I SHALL HAVE TO TAKE HER PART,
GETT	(298)	A PRIOR ENGAGEMENT. /EDITH/ WHAT! YOU AND	LEO	! I THOUGHT SO. WELL, HADNT YOU TWO BETTER GET MARRIED
GETT	(280)	CANT I MARRY THEM BOTH? /THE GENERAL/ (SHOCKED)	LEO	! /LEO/ WELL, I LOVE THEM BOTH. I SHOULD LIKE TO MARRY

LEONARD

PHIL I	(76)	NEAR THE ROUND TABLE). /JULIA/ (IN ANGUISH)	LEONARD	: HAVE YOU NO FEELING FOR ME? /CHARTERIS/ ONLY AN
PHIL I	(82)	ME. GOODNIGHT. (HE APPROACHES THE DOOR). /JULIA/	LEONARD	: HAVE YOU NO PITY? /CHARTERIS/ NOT THE LEAST. WHEN
PHIL II	(101)	AND PIECE THEM TOGETHER. NOW LISTEN. " MY DEAR	LEONARD	: NOTHING COULD MAKE IT WORTH MY WHILE TO BE EXPOSED
PHIL I	(78)	ME SOME HOURS OF EXQUISITE HAPPINESS. /JULIA/	LEONARD	: YOU CONFESS THEN, THAT YOU OWE ME SOMETHING?
PHIL I	(75)	WOMAN? YOU SCOUNDREL! BUT NOW LISTEN TO ME,	LEONARD	: YOU HAVE DRIVEN ME TO DESPERATION; AND I DONT CARE
PHIL I	(70)	WOMAN, THAT IS. /GRACE/ DO YOU REALLY MEAN THAT,	LEONARD	? /CHARTERIS/ OF COURSE. WHY NOT? /GRACE/ (
PHIL I	SD(69)	SHE IS IN EVENING DRESS. THE GENTLEMAN,	LEONARD	CHARTERIS, A FEW YEARS OLDER, IS UNCONVENTIONALLY
PHIL I	(85)	/CUTHBERTSON/ CRAVEN: LET ME INTRODUCE YOU TO MR	LEONARD	CHARTERIS, THE FAMOUS IBSENIST PHILOSOPHER. /CRAVEN/
PHIL III	(137)	HIS CHAIR FLY BACK TO THE TABLE). I KNOW YOU NOW,	LEONARD	CHARTERIS, THROUGH AND THROUGH, IN ALL YOUR
DEVL EPILOG	(80)	DAVIS, GLADSTONE OR BRIGHT, MR CHAMBERLAIN OR MR	LEONARD	COURTNEY WAS IN THE RIGHT WILL NEVER BE SETTLED,
PHIL II	(108)	MY SAKE: EH? /SYLVIA/ (RISING) YOURE TOO AWFUL,	LEONARD	. FOR SHAME! HOWEVER, ANYTHING TO OBLIGE A FELLOW
PHIL I	(80)	OF LOSING YOU. I CANT FACE LIFE WITHOUT YOU,	LEONARD	. I WAS HAPPY WHEN I MET YOU; I HAD NEVER LOVED ANY
PHIL I	(76)	DISGUST, GOING) GET HER AWAY AS SOON AS YOU CAN,	LEONARD	. JULIA, WITH A STIFLED CRY OF RAGE, RUSHES AT
PHIL II	(110)	NEVER! WHAT DO YOU MEAN? /GRACE/ WHAT I SAY,	LEONARD	. /CHARTERIS/ JILTED AGAIN! THE FICKLENESS OF THE
PHIL II	(130)	(LOOKING UP FROM HER MAGAZINE) DONT FIDGET,	LEONARD	. /CHARTERIS/ (SLIPPING OFF THE SETTEE BACK) I CANT
PHIL II	(110)	LIKE. (HE TAKES HER IN HIS ARMS). /GRACE/ YES,	LEONARD	; BUT I'M AN ADVANCED WOMAN. (HE CHECKS HIMSELF,
6CAL PREFACE	(91)	1934, WITH PHYLLIS NEILSON TERRY, CHARLES CARSON,	LEONARD	SHEPHERD, AND VINCENT STERNROYD IN THE FOUR
PHIL I	(82)	DO, I SWEAR I WILL THROW MYSELF FROM THAT WINDOW,	LEONARD	, AS YOU PASS OUT. /CHARTERIS/ (UNIMPRESSED) THAT
PHIL II	(110)	THROW MY HAPPINESS OUT OF THE WINDOW. /GRACE/ OH,	LEONARD	, DOES YOUR HAPPINESS REALLY DEPEND ON ME?
PHIL I	(80)	EH? /JULIA/ (THROWING HERSELF AT HIS FEET) OH,	LEONARD	, DONT BE CRUEL. I'M TOO MISERABLE TO ARGUE-- TO
PHIL II	(105)	TO ENCOURAGE A CHILD TO MAKE HERSELF RIDICULOUS,	LEONARD	, EVEN AT MY EXPENSE. /CHARTERIS/ (SEATING HIMSELF
PHIL II	(106)	ANY WOMAN. /SYLVIA/ (THOUGHTFULLY) DO YOU KNOW,	LEONARD	, I REALLY BELIEVE YOU. I DONT THINK YOU CARE A BIT
PHIL I	(81)	MORE THAN THE AMUSEMENT OF AN IDLE HOUR, OH,	LEONARD	, LEONARD, YOUVE NEVER GIVEN ME A CHANCE: INDEED YOU
PHIL I	(81)	THAN THE AMUSEMENT OF AN IDLE HOUR. OH, LEONARD,	LEONARD	, YOUVE NEVER GIVEN ME A CHANCE; INDEED YOU HAVNT.
PHIL II	(104)	I'LL SCREAM FOR HELP. /JULIA/ (REPROACHFULLY)	LEONARD	! (HE BREAKS AWAY FROM HER). OH, HOW CAN YOU BE SO
PHIL III	(145)	RELIEF). /SYLVIA/ (CONSOLING CHARTERIS) POOR OLD	LEONARD	! /CHARTERIS/ YES: THIS IS THE DOOM OF THE
PHIL I	(77)	YOU CAN LOOK ME IN THE FACE AND SAY THAT? OH,	LEONARD	! /CHARTERIS/ LET ME REMIND YOU, JULIA, THAT WHEN

LEONARDO

KING I	(213)	THINK OF HIM AS ANYTHING ELSE. WHO THINKS OF	LEONARDO	AS AN ENGINEER? OF MICHAEL ANGELO AS AN INVENTOR
FABL PREFACE	(70)	THE CENTRE OF THE UNIVERSE, AND COPERNICUS AND	LEONARDO	CONVINCE BOTH GALILEO THE SCIENTIST AND THE VATICAN
METH PREFACE	(R10)	ADDITIONS TO IT WERE GALILEO'S DEMONSTRATION OF	LEONARDO	DA VINCI'S SIMPLE REMARK THAT THE EARTH IS A MOON
KING I	(213)	AND PARABOLAS, ELLIPSES AND OVALS, WHICH	LEONARDO	HIMSELF COULD NOT DRAW, BUT WHICH ANY FOOL CAN MAKE
KING I	(213)	DISCOVERY WAS MADE BY THE GREAT ITALIAN PAINTER	LEONARDO	, BORN THENTYONE YEARS BEFORE HIM, WHO TOLD ALL HIS

LEONATI

CYMB V	(141)	MY HABITS SHEW. GODS, PUT THE STRENGTH O' THE	LEONATI	IN ME! TO SHAME THE GUISE O' THE WORLD, I'LL BEGIN

LEONATUS

CYMB FORWORD	(135)	THE HERO, OR RATHER THE HUSBAND OF THE HEROINE,	LEONATUS	POSTHUMUS. THE LATE CHARLES CHARRINGTON, WHO WITH
CYMB V	(142)	WE'RE SWORN FRIENDS. /IACHIMO/ BY ALL THE GODS,	LEONATUS	! /POSTHUMUS/ AT YOUR SERVICE, SEDUCER OF MY WIFE.

LEONORA

MIS. PREFACE	(100)	BE DONE WITH SYNCOPATION FROM BEETHOVEN'S THIRD	LEONORA	OVERTURE, THEY WOULD ENJOY THE RAGTIMES ALL THE

LEONTES

SUPR PREFACE	(R33)	THE CHANGELING, FAULCONBRIDGE, CORIOLANUS,	LEONTES	ARE ADMIRABLE DESCRIPTIONS OF INSTINCTIVE

LEOONATIC

PPP	(205)	TRIPS THE DOCTOR UP. BOTH FALL). JEST OWLD THIS	LEOONATIC	, WILL YOU, MISTER HORFICER? /THE POLICEMAN/ (

LEOPARD

BARB PREFACE	(232)	ANY CHANGE IN HIS CHARACTER. THE SPOTS OF THE	LEOPARD	AND THE STRIPES OF THE TIGER ARE AS BRILLIANT AS
LION I	(119)	NO MISTAKE ABOUT IT. THE TENTH MARCHES WITH A	LEOPARD	AT THE HEAD OF THE COLUMN. HE MADE A PET OF THE
LION I	(119)	AT THE HEAD OF THE COLUMN. HE MADE A PET OF THE	LEOPARD	; AND NOW HE'S CRYING AT BEING PARTED FROM IT. (
METH PREFACE	(R21)	FOR INSTANCE, THAT THE BRILLIANT COLOURS OF THE	LEOPARD	, WHICH MAKE IT SO CONSPICUOUS IN REGENT'S PARK,

			LEOPARDS	
LION I	(119)	GOAT (ANDROCLES BRIGHTENS UP) THAT KILLED TWO	LEOPARDS	AND ATE A TURKEY-COCK. YOU CAN HAVE HIM FOR A PET
			LEO'S	
GETT	(274)	YOU LET ME STAY? /MRS BRIDGENORTH/ HOW CAN I?	LEO'S	COMING. /REGINALD/ WELL, SHE WONT MIND. /THE GENERAL/
GETT	(273)	MET HIM IN THE STREET. /MRS BRIDGENORTH/ BESIDES,	LEO'S	COMING. THEYD MEET. IT'S IMPOSSIBLE, LESBIA. /LESBIA/
GETT	(277)	IN THE HOTEL BOOK AS MRS REGINALD BRIDGENORTH:	LEO'S	NAME! DO YOU KNOW WHAT THAT FEELS LIKE TO A DECENT
GETT	SD(275)	AND DONT REGARD OLD WOMEN AT ALL. COLDLY STUDIED,	LEO'S	RESTLESSNESS IS MUCH LESS LOVABLE THAN THE
GETT	(278)	OF INJURY) I SHOULDNT MIND A BIT IF IT WERE FOR	LEO'S	SAKE, BUT TO HAVE TO DO IT TO MAKE ROOM FOR THAT
GETT	(278)	IT. /MRS BRIDGENORTH/ YOU DID ALL THIS FOR	LEO'S	SAKE, REJJY? /REGINALD/ (WITH AN UNBEARABLE SENSE OF
GETT	SD(279)	PLACID HELPLESSNESS. LESBIA, OUT OF PATIENCE WITH	LEO'S	TEARS, GOES INTO THE GARDEN AND SITS THERE NEAR THE
			LEP	
BULL II	(109)	YOU OR I'LL PUT A SPELL ON YOU THATLL MAKE YOU	LEP	. D'YE MIND THAT NOW? (HE GOES HOME). PATSY GOES DOWN
BULL IV	(146)	WID A BED WINCH. AT THE FIRST PUFF OF IT THE PIG	LEP	OUT OF ITS SKIN AND BLED PATSY'S NOSE WI DHE RING IN ITS
			LEPANTO	
GENV PREFACE(4)		WEEKS AS A NAVAL VICTORY GREATER THAN SALAMIS,	LEPANTO	, AND TRAFALGAR ROLLED INTO ONE. LATER ON OUR FLIGHT
			LEPANTOS	
CAPT NOTES	(301)	FIRST OPPORTUNITY OF REPEATING IT. IN WHAT OTHER	LEPANTOS	BESIDES TRAFALGAR SQUARE CUNNINGHAME GRAHAM HAS
			LEPER	
LION PREFACE(35)		TO AS A WASTE OF MONEY. IN LUKE'S VERSION THE	LEPER	BECOMES A RICH PHARISEE; THE WOMAN BECOMES A DAME AUX
LION PREFACE(23)		HE IS NOT AFRAID OF DISEASE, AND DINES WITH A	LEPER	. A WOMAN, APPARENTLY TO PROTECT HIM AGAINST
MRS IV	(252)	A GOOD WOMAN SHE TURNS ME OUT AS IF I WAS A	LEPER	. OH, IF I ONLY HAD MY LIFE TO LIVE OVER AGAIN! I'D
LION PREFACE(35)		IT AS TAKING PLACE IN THE HOUSE OF SIMON THE	LEPER	, WHERE IT IS OBJECTED TO AS A WASTE OF MONEY. IN
			LEPERS	
DOCT I	(114)	I AM NOT LIKELY TO FORGET IT. THEY TREAT US LIKE	LEPERS	AT THE HOTELS. /EMMY/ (AT THE DOOR) WELL, DEARY:
DOCT PREFACE(58)		BY THE GROWING DISPOSITION TO TREAT THEM AS	LEPERS	. NO DOUBT THERE IS A GOOD DEAL OF IGNORANT
BUOY III	(44)	SHOULD CATHOLICS AND PROTESTANTS MARRY? SHOULD	LEPERS	MARRY? AT WHAT AGES SHOULD THEY MARRY? WITHOUT
			LEPORELLO	
SUPR PREFACE(R30)		DOYLE IS DELIBERATE; AND THE METAMORPHOSIS OF	LEPORELLO	INTO ENRY STRAKER, MOTOR ENGINEER AND NEW MAN, IS
			LEPROSY	
DOCT PREFACE(58)		TERRORISTS INTO THE POSITION FORMERLY HELD BY	LEPROSY	, BUT THE SCARE OF INFECTION, THOUGH IT SETS EVEN
JOAN 6	(146)	FROM HER BODY. /THE INQUISITOR/ INFECTED WITH THE	LEPROSY	OF HERESY. /CAUCHON/ A MEMBER OF SATAN. /THE
DOCT PREFACE(58)		THE CASE. WE NOW KNOW THAT THE MEDIEVAL HORROR OF	LEPROSY	WAS OUT OF ALL PROPORTION TO THE DANGER OF
DOCT PREFACE(77)		WHO WARNS US THAT A FISH DIET MUST END IN	LEPROSY	, AND YOU HAVE ALL THAT OPPOSES WITH ANY SORT OF
			LERRER	
CATH 1	(166)	EYE, DARLING. CROSS EYE. SEES EVERYTHING. READ	LERRER	INCE-INCE-ISTASTANEOUSLY. KINDLY GIVE ME VINEGAR
CATH 1	(166)	IN ER LERRER, DARLING, DARLING, DARLING, DARLING.	LERRER	YOU SHEWED ME. /EDSTASTON/ BUT YOU DIDNT READ IT.
CATH 1	(166)	THIS? /PATIOMKIN/ (CROWING FANTASTICALLY) IN ER	LERRER	, DARLING, DARLING, DARLING, DARLING. LERRER YOU
			LES	
SUPR HANDBOK(220)		IS SUMMED UP IN THE PHRASE " QUE MESSIEURS	LES	ASSASSINS COMMENCENT! " THE MAN WHO HAS GRADUATED FROM
HART PREFACE(12)		ANTI-ENEMY SECRETARY INTO PRISON POUR ENCOURAGER	LES	AUTRES, AND THE PASSIONATE PENNY COLLECTING OF THE FLAG
HART PREFACE(36)		BED AFTER MR CHESTERTON'S MAGIC OR BRIEUX'S	LES	AVARIES. PERHAPS THAT IS THE REAL REASON WHY THE CHURCH
GETT PREFACE(244)		AND SEVERAL OF THE PLAYS OF BRIEUX: NOTABLY	LES	AVARIES, LES TROIS FILLES DE M. DUPONT, AND MATERNITE. I
POSN PREFACE(371)		MRS WARREN'S PROFESSION, BRIEUX'S MATERNITE, AND	LES	AVARIES, MAETERLINCK'S MONNA VANNA AND MR GRANVILLE
JOAN PREFACE(35)		OF HER SOUL WAS HER OWN BUSINESS, AND NOT THAT OF	LES	GENS D'EGLISE. BY USING THAT TERM AS SHE DID,
GETT PREFACE(184)		FOR, AS BRIEUX HAS SHEWN SO CONVINCINGLY IN	LES	HANNETONS, AN AVOWEDLY ILLICIT UNION IS OFTEN FOUND IN
POSN PREFACE(417)		TRILOGY, AND THE BATHERS IN THE SECOND ACT OF	LES	HUGUENOTS, TO THE BALLETS OF WATER NYMPHS IN OUR
GETT PREFACE(244)		OF THE PLAYS OF BRIEUX: NOTABLY LES AVARIES,	LES	TROIS FILLES DE M. DUPONT, AND MATERNITE. I PURPOSELY
GETT PREFACE(210)		HAVE AS MANY WIVES APIECE AS THEY COULD AFFORD?	LES	US SEE HOW THIS WOULD WORK. THE MALE REVOLT AGAINST
			LESBIA	
GETT	(272)	BETWEEN LESBIA AND THE GENERAL. /MRS BRIDGENORTH/	LESBIA	: BOXER: HERES A PRETTY MESS! COLLINS GOES OUT
GETT	(351)	TIL WE COME. WE HAVE TO DRESS EDITH. COME,	LESBIA	: COME, LEO: WE MUST ALL HELP. NOW, EDITH. (LESBIA,
GETT	(332)	PRETENCE OF PRIVACY. /THE GENERAL/ YOU ARE CRUEL,	LESBIA	: DEVILISHLY CRUEL. (HE SITS DOWN, WOUNDED).
GETT	(332)	NEAREST THE HEARTH, AND SITS DOWN). /THE GENERAL/	LESBIA	: I'M VERY SORRY. BUT IF I GAVE IT UP, I SHOULD
GETT	(283)	/THE BISHOP/ (MILDLY) THIS IS NOT QUARRELLING,	LESBIA	: IT'S ONLY ENGLISH FAMILY LIFE. GOOD MORNING. /LEO/
GETT	(270)	OF BEING ONE. /THE GENERAL/ I'M SURE OF THAT,	LESBIA	: QUITE SURE OF IT. I NEVER MEANT-- /LESBIA/ (RISING
GETT	(268)	IT UP AND MARRIED. (BENDING STILL NEARER TO HER)	LESBIA	: TELL ME YOUR SECRET. WHY-- /LESBIA/ (SNIFFING
GETT	(269)	BE A WIFE AT THE SAME TIME. /THE GENERAL/ MY DEAR	LESBIA	: YOU KNOW I DONT WISH TO BE IMPERTINENT; BUT THESE
GETT	(285)	/THE GENERAL/ (RISING) HA! YOU HEAR THAT,	LESBIA	? (HE JOINS HER AT THE GARDEN DOOR). /LESBIA/ THATS
GETT	(322)	TO ME QUITE REASONABLE. /THE BISHOP/ AND YOU,	LESBIA	? /LESBIA/ NEVER. /MRS BRIDGENORTH/ NEVER IS A LONG
GETT	(349)	GOOD HUMOR JUST NOW. /THE GENERAL/ MAY I ASK WHY,	LESBIA	? /LESBIA/ (DRAWING A LARGE BREATH) TO THINK THAT
GETT	SD(308)	VACANT PLACE IN THE MIDDLE OF THE TABLE BETWEEN	LESBIA	AND THE BISHOP. /COLLINS/ I TELL YOU THE TRUTH, MY
GETT	SD(272)	A LETTER; HURRIES PAST COLLINS; AND COMES BETWEEN	LESBIA	AND THE GENERAL. /MRS BRIDGENORTH/ LESBIA: BOXER:
GETT	SD(286)	AND STROLLS TO THE HEARTH AND BACK, SINGING).	LESBIA	APPEARS IN THE TOWER, RATHER PERTURBED. /LESBIA/
GETT	SD(347)	SOMEBODY IN A PUBLIC UNIFORM. MRS BRIDGENORTH AND	LESBIA	COME IN THROUGH THE TOWER. MRS BRIDGENORTH MAKES FOR
GETT	SD(347)	HE GOES TO HER, AND THEY MEET NEAR THE OAK CHEST.	LESBIA	COMES BETWEEN SYKES AND EDITH. /THE BISHOP/ ALICE, MY
GETT	SD(332)	IT'S SUCH A NATURAL THING TO DO, SOMEHOW.	LESBIA	COMES IN THROUGH THE TOWER. /MRS GEORGE/ HE'S BEEN
GETT	(296)	SPEAK TO CECIL. (MRS BRIDGENORTH COMES TO HIM.	LESBIA	GOES INTO THE GARDEN, AS BEFORE). LET US GO INTO MY
GETT	SD(266)	THINK OF A GAME THAT MRS GEORGE ISNT UP TO.	LESBIA	GRANTHAM COMES IN THROUGH THE TOWER. SHE IS A TALL,
GETT	SD(273)	DASH MY BUTTONS! ! REGINALD IS JUST THE MAN	LESBIA	HAS DESCRIBED. HE IS HARDENED AND TOUGH PHYSICALLY,
GETT	SD(281)	GENERALLY RATHER WELL PLEASED WITH HIMSELF. WHEN	LESBIA	HEARS HIS VOICE SHE TURNS HER CHAIR TOWARDS HIM, AND
GETT	(271)	BOXER. /THE GENERAL/ I'M NOT CROSS, ONLY WOUNDED,	LESBIA	. AND WHEN YOU TALK LIKE THAT I DONT FEEL CONVINCED:
GETT	(322)	NEVER. /MRS BRIDGENORTH/ NEVER IS A LONG WORD,	LESBIA	. DONT SAY IT. /LESBIA/ (WITH A FLASH OF TEMPER)
GETT	(268)	DRAWING HIS CHAIR NEARER TO HER) LISTEN TO ME,	LESBIA	. FOR THE TENTH AND LAST TIME-- /LESBIA/ (
GETT	(274)	STAY AWAY FROM EDITH'S WEDDING. GOOD MORNING,	LESBIA	. HOW ARE YOU, BOXER? (HE OFFERS THE GENERAL HIS
GETT	(349)	SMOKING AGAIN. /THE GENERAL/ YOU DRIVE ME TO IT,	LESBIA	. I CANT HELP IT. /LESBIA/ (STANDING BEHIND HER
GETT	(350)	(STARTING UP AGAIN) HA! I THINK YOU ARE HARD,	LESBIA	. I SHALL MAKE A FOOL OF MYSELF IF I REMAIN HERE.
GETT	(349)	RATHER VULGAR. /THE GENERAL/ OH, VERY WELL,	LESBIA	. I SHALL NOT ASK YOU AGAIN. (HE SITS DOWN HUFFILY).
GETT	(268)	LAST TIME." /THE GENERAL/ WE ARE TWO YEARS OLDER,	LESBIA	. I'M FIFTY: YOU ARE-- /LESBIA/ YES, I KNOW. IT'S NO
GETT	(268)	(IMPULSIVELY APPROACHING HER) DONT SAY THAT,	LESBIA	. IT'S NOT NATURAL: IT'S NOT RIGHT: IT'S-- /LESBIA/ (
GETT	(268)	/THE GENERAL/ THE HEART HAS ITS PREFERENCES,	LESBIA	. ONE IMAGE, AND ONE ONLY, GETS INDELIBLY-- /LESBIA/
GETT	SD(296)	TIME TO ANSWER HER MOTHER RETURNS WITH LEO AND	LESBIA	. /LEO/ YES, HERE SHE IS, OF COURSE. I TOLD YOU I
GETT	(269)	/THE GENERAL/ (MURMURING) NO: DONT SAY THAT,	LESBIA	. /LESBIA/ I'M A REGULAR OLD MAID. I'M VERY
GETT	(270)	IS. /THE GENERAL/ I REALLY DONT UNDERSTAND YOU,	LESBIA	. /LESBIA/ (TURNING ON HIM) THEN WHY ON EARTH DO YOU
GETT	(285)	YET? /MRS BRIDGENORTH/ DO GO AND HURRY HER,	LESBIA	. /LESBIA/ (GOING OUT THROUGH THE TOWER) COME WITH
GETT	(273)	LEO'S COMING. THEYD MEET. IT'S IMPOSSIBLE,	LESBIA	. /LESBIA/ OH, I FORGOT THAT. THAT SETTLES IT. HE
GETT	(334)	TO PASS HIM) WELL, I SHALL NOT ASK YOU AGAIN,	LESBIA	. /LESBIA/ THANK YOU, BOXER. (SHE PASSES ON TO THE
GETT	(332)	/THE GENERAL/ WOMEN ARE NOT ALL THE SAME TO ME,	LESBIA	. /MRS GEORGE/ WHY SHOULD THEY BE, PRAY? WOMEN ARE
GETT	(267)	THESE MEDALS MUST REPRESENT! /THE GENERAL/ NO,	LESBIA	. THEY REPRESENT DESPAIR AND COWARDICE. I WON ALL THE
GETT	(285)	AN EPIGRAM, BOXER. /THE GENERAL/ SOUND SENSE,	LESBIA	. WHEN A MAN TALKS ROT, THATS EPIGRAM: WHEN HE TALKS
GETT	(262)	YET? /MRS BRIDGENORTH/ WHY DO YOU ALWAYS CALL	LESBIA	MY SISTER? DONT YOU KNOW THAT IT ANNOYS HER MORE
GETT	(307)	THEYRE LETTING THEMSELVES IN FOR. THERES MISS	LESBIA	NOW. SHE WAITED TIL SHE STARTED THINKING ABOUT IT;
GETT	(272)	VERY WELL, GENERAL. (HE TURNS DUBIOUSLY TO	LESBIA	ON HIS WAY TO THE TOWER). I WONDER WHAT MY WIFE WILL
GETT	(285)	THE TOWER) COME WITH ME, LEO. /LEO/ (FOLLOWING	LESBIA	OUT) YES, CERTAINLY. THE BISHOP GOES OVER TO HIS WIFE
GETT	SD(276)	IS. BUT LEO AFFECTS A SPECIAL INTIMACY WITH	LESBIA	, AS OF TWO THINKERS AMONG THE PHILISTINES. /LEO/ (
GETT	(270)	WELL HOW AM I TO EXPRESS IT? HANG IT ALL,	LESBIA	, DONT YOU WANT A HUSBAND? /LESBIA/ NO. I WANT

GETT	(307)	AND I'M SURE I BEG YOUR PARDON MOST HEARTILY,	LESBIA	, IF I'M WRONG, AS I HOPE I AM-- THEY ACTUALLY CALL
GETT	(276)	OF TWO THINKERS AMONG THE PHILISTINES. /LEO/ (TO	LESBIA	, KISSING HER) GOOD MORNING. (COMING TO MRS
GETT	(326)	OUT THROUGH THE TOWER, FOLLOWED BY MRS GEORGE,	LESBIA	, LEO, AND EDITH). /THE BISHOP/ SHALL WE TRY TO GET
GETT	(351)	COME, LEO! WE MUST ALL HELP. NOW, EDITH. (	LESBIA	, LEO, AND EDITH GO OUT THROUGH THE TOWER). COLLINS:
GETT	(351)	ANYTHING YOU WOULD LIKE MENTIONED ABOUT MISS	LESBIA	, MAAM? /MRS BRIDGENORTH/ NO. SHE WONT HAVE THE
GETT	(268)	TO TAKE NO FOR AN ANSWER? /THE GENERAL/ NEVER,	LESBIA	, NEVER. YOU HAVE NEVER GIVEN ME A REAL REASON FOR
GETT	SD(279)	NEIGHBORHOOD LISTENING IN PLACID HELPLESSNESS.	LESBIA	, OUT OF PATIENCE WITH LEO'S TEARS, GOES INTO THE
GETT	(272)	CHAIR) IT'S TOO BAD. NO: I CANT FORGIVE HIM,	LESBIA	, REALLY. A MAN OF REGINALD'S AGE, WITH A YOUNG
GETT	(349)	RISING, HORRIFIED) NO, NO, YOU MUST KNOW, MY DEAR	LESBIA	, THAT I WAS NOT USING THE WORD IN ITS IMPROPER
GETT	(334)	LIVE FOR, WOULD THERE? /THE GENERAL/ I'M AFRAID,	LESBIA	, THE THINGS YOU DO WITHOUT ARE THE THINGS YOU DONT
GETT	SD(276)	FULL OF HER OWN IMPORTANCE, AND SWOOPS ON	LESBIA	, WHO IS MUCH LESS DISPOSED TO SPOIL HER THAN MRS
GETT	(349)	/LESBIA/ EXCEPT MINE. /THE GENERAL/ BUT, MY DEAR	LESBIA	, YOU SEE WHAT HAS HAPPENED HERE TODAY. (COMING A
GETT	(267)	/THE GENERAL/ (WITH RESOLUTE BONHOMIE) AH,	LESBIA	! HOW DO YOU DO? (THEY SHAKE HANDS; AND HE TAKES
			LESBIAN	
CLEO IV	(182)	/CAESAR/ (RELENTING) WELL, WELL: LET US TRY THE	LESBIAN	. (THE MAJOR-DOMO FILLS CAESAR'S GOBLET; THEN
CLEO IV	(183)	LET US NAME THE HOLY CITY, AND CONSECRATE IT WITH	LESBIAN	WINE. /CAESAR/ CLEOPATRA SHALL NAME IT HERSELF.
CLEO IV	(181)	DRINK ROMAN WINE WHEN HE COULD GET GREEK. TRY THE	LESBIAN	, CAESAR. BRING ME MY BARLEY WATER. /RUFIO/ (WITH
CLEO IV	(181)	CAESAR WILL DEIGN TO CHOOSE HIS WINE? SICILIAN,	LESBIAN	, CHIAN-- /RUFIO/ (CONTEMPTUOUSLY) ALL GREEK.
			LESBIA'S	
GETT	SD(323)	TO MAKE THE MOST OF THEM. NOT AT ALL A LADY IN	LESBIA'S	USE OF THE TERM AS A CLASS LABEL, SHE PROCLAIMS
			LESIONS	
MILL	PREFACE(126)	ARMOR, A HITCH IN HIS STATESMANSHIP, ONE OF THOSE	LESIONS	WHICH SOMETIMES PROVE FATAL. AS IT HAS NO LOGICAL
			LESLIE	
CAPT I	(228)	WELL BE YOU. BUT THE NAME, AS I RECOLLECT IT, WAS	LESLIE	. /RANKIN/ THAT WAS ME, SIR. MY NAME IS LESLIE
CAPT I	(228)	WAS LESLIE. /RANKIN/ THAT WAS ME, SIR. MY NAME IS	LESLIE	RANKIN; AND YOUR BROTHER AND I WERE ALWAYS MILES AND
CAPT III	SD(272)	HIGH UP IN THE ADOBE WALLS OF THE LARGEST ROOM IN	LESLIE	RANKIN'S HOUSE. A CLEAN COOL ROOM, WITH THE TABLE (A
CAPT I	(228)	AND YOUR BROTHER AND I WERE ALWAYS MILES AND	LESLIE	TO ONE ANOTHER. /SIR HOWARD/ (PLUMING HIMSELF A
			LESSEE	
POSN	PREFACE(363)	THE LANDLORD POWER TO BREAK IT AND EVICT THE	LESSEE	IF HE PRODUCES A PLAY WITHOUT FIRST OBTAINING THE
POSN	PREFACE(409)	TO ANY OFFICIAL OR COMMITTEE; AND THE MANAGER OR	LESSEE	OF THE THEATRE SHOULD HAVE A RIGHT TO APPEAR IN
			LESSEES	
POSN	PREFACE(414)	LICENCE BY VOTE OF THE ENTIRE BODY; MANAGERS,	LESSEES	, AND PROPRIETORS OF THEATRES SHALL HAVE THE RIGHT
			LESSEN	
METH	PREFACE(R54)	FELLOWSHIP IS A VAIN AND MISCHIEVOUS ATTEMPT TO	LESSEN	THE SEVERITY OF THE STRUGGLE AND PRESERVE INFERIOR
			LESSER	
2TRU III	(111)	THE ERECT POSTURE IS THE MARK OF THE MAN: LET	LESSER	CREATURES KNEEL AND CRAWL: WE WILL NOT KNEEL AND WE
CLEO	PRG1 (92)	IMPERIAL INSTINCTS. WILT THOU THEREFORE KILL THE	LESSER	DOG FOR US? " AND HE SAID, " I WILL; FOR I HAVE MADE
CYMB	FORWORD(137)	HANDEL, AND HAD AN UNBOUNDED CONTEMPT FOR ALL THE	LESSER	MEDDLERS, LOVED MOZART'S VARIATIONS, AND DISMISSED
SUPR	HANDBOK(217)	FOR ITS POLITICAL CONVENIENCE. DEMOCRACY, IF THE	LESSER	MIND COULD MEASURE THE GREATER AS A FOOTRULE CAN
FABL	PREFACE(85)	ONLY IN THOUSANDS, EVEN IN BIG CITIES. IN	LESSER	TOWNS THE FIGURE IS ZERO. ADULT SUFFRAGE IS
			LESSON	
BASH I	(93)	REMAINS UNPURCHASABLE? LEARNING LEARNS BUT ONE	LESSON	: DOUBT! TO EXCEL ALL IS, TO BE LONELY. OH, YE BUSY
GENV	PREFACE(20)	LIKE LOUIS NAPOLEON HE HAD NOW LEARNT HIS	LESSON	: NAMELY, THAT PUTSCHES ARE A LAST DESPERATE METHOD,
6CAL	(103)	/THE KING/ WELL? HAVE YOU LEARNT YOUR	LESSON	? ARE YOU READY TO SUE FOR THE QUEEN'S MERCY?
MILL I	(163)	MISSED MY LESSON. HOW ANNOYING! /ALASTAIR/ YOUR	LESSON	? WHAT ARE YOU LEARNING NOW, MAY I ASK? /EPIFANIA/
2TRU II	(61)	YOU ARE THEIR DEAREST FRIEND. /AUBREY/ THE FIRST	LESSON	A CROOK HAS TO LEARN, DARLING, IS THAT NOTHING
POSN	(443)	END THIS EVENING ON THE GALLOWS TREE. OH, WHAT A	LESSON	AGAINST SPIRITUAL PRIDE! OH, WHAT A-- (BLANCO
BARB	PREFACE(225)	CALL GENTLEMEN. THEY DO NOT UNDERSTAND BARBARA'S	LESSON	BECAUSE THEY HAVE NOT, LIKE HER, LEARNT IT BY TAKING
BARB	PREFACE(235)	WHETHER AS A PROPHET OR AS A RASCAL. THIS IS THE	LESSON	DEMOCRACY HAS TO LEARN BEFORE IT CAN BECOME ANYTHING
METH	PREFACE(R23)	IT; FOR THOUGH YOU MAY IMPROVE AT EACH BICYCLING	LESSON	DURING THE LESSON, WHEN YOU BEGIN YOUR NEXT LESSON
CLEO IV	(167)	SHE PLAYS BETTER THAN YOU. YOU SHALL GIVE ME A	LESSON	EVERY DAY FOR A FORTNIGHT. (THE MUSICIAN HASTILY
KING I	(198)	SHORT. /JAMES/ SERVE THE RASCALS RIGHT! A GOOD	LESSON	FOR THEM AND THEIR LIKE. DONT BE SUCH A MOLLYCODDLE,
METH	PREFACE(R79)	THAT THERE IS NOTHING IN RELIGION BUT FICTION. A	LESSON	FROM SCIENCE TO THE CHURCHES. LET THE CHURCHES ASK
SUPR	HANDBOK(213)	FOR QUALITY IN OUR RULERS. WE LEARN THE SAME	LESSON	FROM THE CASE OF THE SOLDIER, WHOSE MARRIAGE, WHEN IT
NEVR II	(241)	SLICING IT. /CRAMPTON/ YOU HAVE LEARNT YOUR	LESSON	FROM YOUR MOTHER, I SEE. /MRS CLANDON/ PHIL: WILL YOU
LADY	PREFACE(216)	A LESSON IN HISTORY, INTO THE CITY WITHOUT A	LESSON	IN BUSINESS, AND INTO THE ARMY WITHOUT A LESSON IN
LADY	PREFACE(216)	LESSON IN TABLE MANNERS, INTO POLITICS WITHOUT A	LESSON	IN HISTORY, INTO THE CITY WITHOUT A LESSON IN
ROCK II	(267)	IT ALL OUT IN BLOOMSBURY. LENIN LEARNT HIS	LESSON	IN HOLFORD SQUARE, ISLINGTON. WHY CAN WE NEVER THINK
LADY	PREFACE(216)	A LESSON IN BUSINESS, AND INTO THE ARMY WITHOUT A	LESSON	IN HONOR. IT HAS BEEN SAID, WITH THE OBJECT OF
BULL	PREFACE(14)	AND RATIONAL CONDUCT. BUT THE NEED FOR THIS	LESSON	IN IRELAND IS THE MEASURE OF ITS DEMORALIZING
LADY	PREFACE(216)	OF HIMSELF) WILL PLUNGE INTO SOCIETY WITHOUT A	LESSON	IN TABLE MANNERS, INTO POLITICS WITHOUT A LESSON IN
SUPR	PREFACE(R13)	AMUSED HIMSELF TO HIS HEART'S CONTENT. BUT THE	LESSON	INTENDED BY AN AUTHOR IS HARDLY EVER THE LESSON THE
FANY	PREFACE(255)	BEING BUT A POTBOILER, NEEDS NO PREFACE. BUT ITS	LESSON	IS NOT, I AM SORRY TO SAY, UNNEEDED. MERE MORALITY,
MIS.	PREFACE(51)	ANOTHER FAMILIAR FACT THAT TEACHES THE SAME	LESSON	IS THAT MANY WOMEN WHO HAVE VOLUNTARILY ATTAINED A
6CAL	(101)	ASK YOU FOR A GREAT THING. REFUSE ME: TEACH ME A	LESSON	. BUT THIS IS SUCH A LITTLE THING. (HEARTBROKEN) I
KING I	(190)	I WILL SAY THAT FOR HIM; AND I THANK HIM FOR THE	LESSON	. BUT WHEN HE DIED THEY HAD TO SEND FOR US. WHEN THEY
CLEO II	(137)	DEMANDS SPEECH OF YOU. IN MY OPINION HE NEEDS A	LESSON	. HIS MANNER IS MOST INSOLENT. /CAESAR/ WHERE IS HE?
MILL I	(163)	TWELVE. /EPIFANIA/ GRACIOUS! I HAVE MISSED MY	LESSON	. HOW ANNOYING! /ALASTAIR/ YOUR LESSON? WHAT ARE
PYGM V	(279)	/LIZA/ NO: NOT NOW. NEVER AGAIN. I HAVE LEARNT MY	LESSON	. I DONT BELIEVE I COULD UTTER ONE OF THE OLD SOUNDS
HART II	(127)	TO HER FOR ANOTHER WEEK. I'LL GIVE HER SUCH A	LESSON	. I'LL GO STRAIGHT TO BED WITHOUT BIDDING HER
MIS.	(171)	ALONE A SOLDIER? BUT I'LL TEACH HIM AND YOU A	LESSON	. IVE HAD ENOUGH OF LIVING A DOG'S LIFE AND DESPISING
CAND III	(131)	/MARCHBANKS/ HERE ENDETH THE THOUSAND AND FIRST	LESSON	. MORELL: I DONT THINK MUCH OF YOUR PREACHING AFTER
POSN	(442)	REFUSED ME MY DUE: I TOOK IT, JUST TO GIVE YOU A	LESSON	. /ELDER DANIELS/ WHY DIDNT YOU TAKE THE NECKLACE IF
2TRU III	(93)	YOUR MOTHER! ! ! /AUBREY/ SO I LEARNT MY	LESSON	. SIX DAYS ON THE MAKE, AND ON THE SEVENTH SHALT THOU
O'FL	(227)	HOUR AT HOME. WELL: THEM TWO HAS TAUGHT ME A	LESSON	. THIS MORNING, SIR, WHEN I WAS TELLING THE BOYS HERE
PYGM II	(222)	OFFERS ME TWO-FIFTHS OF HER DAY'S INCOME FOR A	LESSON	. TWO-FIFTHS OF A MILLIONAIRE'S INCOME FOR A DAY
BULL IV	(149)	SINCE THIS MORNING, MISS DOYLE. I HAVE HAD A	LESSON	(HE LOOKS AT NORA SIGNIFICANTLY) THAT I SHALL NOT
MIS.	PREFACE(11)	HOLD YOURSELF UP TO YOUR CHILDREN AS AN OBJECT	LESSON	(WHICH IS NOT AT ALL NECESSARY), HOLD YOURSELF UP AS
MIS.	PREFACE(24)	WHAT IS RIGHT AND THAT HE MUST AND WILL HAVE THE	LESSON	JUST SO OR ELSE BREAK HIS HEART (NOT SOMEBODY
JOAN	5 (117)	I DO NOT FIGHT IN THE OLD WAY: I HAVE LEARNT THE	LESSON	OF AGINCOURT, OF POITIERS AND CRECY. I KNOW HOW MANY
HART	PREFACE(16)	OF EVERY DECENCY OF CIVILIZATION AND EVERY	LESSON	OF POLITICAL EXPERIENCE ON THE PART OF THE VERY
FABL	PREFACE(74)	AND HIS MILKMAIDS. CATHOLICISM IMPRACTICABLE. THE	LESSON	OF THIS IS THAT A TOTALLY CATHOLIC CHURCH OR
MIS.	PREFACE(88)	A WORK OF ART. SIMILARLY, YOU CANNOT LISTEN TO A	LESSON	OR A SERMON UNLESS THE TEACHER OR THE PREACHER IS AN
BARB	PREFACE(232)	IN PROOF I MIGHT POINT TO THE SENSATIONAL OBJECT	LESSON	PROVIDED BY OUR COMMERCIAL MILLIONAIRES TODAY. THEY
MIS.	PREFACE(39)	A TENDENCY TO KEEP REPEATING THE ALREADY LEARNT	LESSON	RATHER THAN BREAK NEW GROUND. AT SCHOOL I BEGAN WITH
BARB	PREFACE(226)	LIBERTIES. THE NINETEENTH CENTURY SAW THE SAME	LESSON	REPEATED IN ENGLAND. IT HAD ITS UTILITARIANS, ITS
NEVR I	(217)	MISS. /DOLLY/ (REPEATING IT TO HERSELF LIKE A	LESSON	) CRAMPTON, CRAMPTON, CRAMPTON, CRAMPTON, CRAMPTON. (
CLEO II	(119)	ANY VOCAL INFLEXIONS: HE IS EVIDENTLY REPEATING A	LESSON	) TAKE NOTICE OF THIS ALL OF YOU. I AM THE FIRST-BORN
POSN	PREFACE(383)	CONSEQUENTLY ITS EARLY STRUGGLES TAUGHT HIM NO	LESSON	; AND HE HAS OPPOSED THE NEXT STEP IN HUMAN PROGRESS
WIDO III	(61)	PUT MY CAPITAL INTO YOUR SPECULATION. IVE HAD MY	LESSON	; AND I'M GOING TO STICK TO MY PRESENT INCOME. IT'S
POSN	PREFACE(393)	MEANT TO BE UNDERSTOOD, TO REPRESENT GERMANY. THE	LESSON	TAUGHT BY THE PLAY IS THE DANGER OF INVASION AND THE
MIS.	PREFACE(71)	THE SCHOOL IF THESE HAVE MEANWHILE LEARNED THE	LESSON	THAT CHILDREN ARE INDEPENDENT HUMAN BEINGS AND HAVE
DOCT	PREFACE(74)	USEFUL THAN A LIFE SPENT DOING NOTHING. THE ONE	LESSON	THAT COMES OUT OF ALL OUR THEORIZING AND
PHIL	PREFACE(68)	EVEN THE INTELLIGENTSIA HAVE FORGOTTEN THAT THE	LESSON	THAT MIGHT HAVE SAVED THE LIVES OF TEN MILLION
MIS.	PREFACE(39)	OF NUMBERS. BUT AS IT IS LESS TROUBLE TO SET A	LESSON	THAT YOU KNOW YOURSELF, THERE IS A TENDENCY TO KEEP
MRS	PREFACE(169)	BELIEF IN THE TIMELINESS AND THE POWER OF THE	LESSON	THE PLAY TEACHES. THOSE WHO WERE " SURPRISED TO SEE
SUPR	PREFACE(R13)	LESSON INTENDED BY AN AUTHOR IS HARDLY EVER THE	LESSON	THE WORLD CHOOSES TO LEARN FROM HIS BOOK. WHAT
METH	PREFACE(R86)	PLOTS OF THE MODERN THEATRE, BUT FOR THE DEEPEST	LESSON	THEY COULD DRAW FROM THE FAMILIAR AND SACRED LEGENDS

PRES (142)	HAVE NEVER RECOGNIZED, AND UNTIL THEY GET A STERN	LESSON	THEY NEVER WILL RECOGNIZE, THE PLAIN FACT THAT THE
CLEO PR01 (91)	THE HIGH GODS HAD A LESSON TO TEACH HIM, WHICH	LESSON	THEY SHALL ALSO TEACH YOU IN DUE TIME IF YE CONTINUE
KING I (192)	GOVERNING THEM! IF YOU WILL NOT TEACH THEM THEIR	LESSON	THEY SHALL LEARN IT FROM ME. /CHARLES/ YOU WILL HAVE
DEVL III (62)	SIR, WE SHALL TEACH YOU AND YOUR TOWNSPEOPLE A	LESSON	THEY WILL NOT FORGET. HAVE YOU ANYTHING MORE TO SAY?
HART II (91)	/MAZZINI/ OH NO, NO, NO. IT WAS SUCH A TERRIBLE	LESSON	TO HER: NOTHING WOULD INDUCE HER TO TRY SUCH A THING
SUPR II (54)	ABOUT THE BEE IS NATURAL HISTORY. IT'S AN AWFUL	LESSON	TO MANKIND. YOU THINK THAT YOU ARE ANN'S SUITOR; THAT
CLEO PR01 (91)	ACROSS THE ADRIATIC SEA; FOR THE HIGH GODS HAD A	LESSON	TO TEACH HIM, WHICH LESSON THEY SHALL ALSO TEACH YOU
JOAN PREFACE(37)	RELIEVE IT BY BURNING THE THREAD. THIS IS JOAN'S	LESSON	TO THE CHURCH; AND ITS FORMULATION BY THE HAND OF A
GETT (267)	WHENEVER I TAKE PART IN ANY CEREMONY, AS A	LESSON	TO THE SUBALTERNS. IT IS NOT THE CUSTOM IN ENGLAND;
MTH5 (244)	HORRIBLY TAINTED. /THE SHE-ANCIENT/ LET IT BE A	LESSON	TO YOU ALL TO BE CONTENT WITH LIFELESS TOYS, AND NOT
DOCT III (141)	WRONG ON THE LEGAL POINT; AND I HOPE IT WILL BE A	LESSON	TO YOU NOT TO BE SO JOLLY COCKSURE NEXT TIME.
MIS. (168)	HIM) FUNNY THAT I CANT REMEMBER! LET THIS BE A	LESSON	TO YOU, YOUNG MAN. I COULD GO INTO COURT TOMORROW AND
FANY III (314)	AGAINST. SHE WAS SAVED FROM THAT, AND HAD A ROUGH	LESSON	TOO; AND I SAY IT WAS NO EARTHLY PROTECTION THAT DID
FABL PREFACE(81)	SISTER, AND WAS DISPOSED TO BE MOVED BY IT, THE	LESSON	WAS THE CHAPTER FROM THE BIBLE WHICH DESCRIBES HOW
BASH II,1, (106)	OH, MY SPEECH BEWRAYETH IT! MY EARLIEST	LESSON	WAS THE PLAYER'S SPEECH IN HAMLET; AND TO THIS DAY I
CAND I (99)	PLAIN SPEAKING FOR YOU. (HE KNOCKS IN THE	LESSON	WITH A NOD IN HIS OLD WAY, AND POSTS HIMSELF ON THE
METH PREFACE(R23)	DURING THE LESSON, WHEN YOU BEGIN YOUR NEXT	LESSON	YOU DO NOT BEGIN AT THE POINT AT WHICH YOU LEFT OFF:
JOAN 5 (112)	GODDAMS TOOK WAR SERIOUSLY, BUT I HAVE LEARNT MY	LESSON	, AND TAKEN THEIR MEASURE. THEY HAVE NO ROOTS HERE. I
MIS. PREFACE(29)	UNRELATED ELDERS: (THE PARENTS SHRINK FROM THE	LESSON	, EVEN WHEN THEY ARE OTHERWISE QUALIFIED, BECAUSE
NEVR II (249)	SIR, NOTHING LESS THAN FIFTY GUINEAS. WHAT A	LESSON	, SIR! /CRAMPTON/ WELL, I HOPE HE IS GRATEFUL TO
METH PREFACE(R23)	MAY IMPROVE AT EACH BICYCLING LESSON DURING THE	LESSON	, WHEN YOU BEGIN YOUR NEXT LESSON YOU DO NOT BEGIN AT
3PLA PREFACE(R12)	WHO, QUITE INCAPABLE OF UNDERSTANDING THE	LESSON	, WOULD THEREUPON SET TO WORK TO OBTAIN AND PRODUCE A
BASH II,1, (107)	ON ME! THE FOOL I FLATTER AT SO MANY COINS A	LESSON	! THE SCREAMING CREATURE WHO BESIDE THE RING GAMBLES
		LESSONS	
ROCK II (267)	CAN WE NEVER THINK OUT ANYTHING, NOR LEARN ANY	LESSONS	? I SEE WHAT HAS TO BE DONE NOW; BUT I DONT FEEL
PYGM II (221)	HOW MUCH DO YOU PROPOSE TO PAY ME FOR THE	LESSONS	? /LIZA/ OH, I KNOW WHATS RIGHT. A LADY FRIEND OF
SUPR HANDBOK(210)	DREAM OF PUTTING COMMANDMENTS AND CODES AND	LESSONS	AND EXAMINATION MARKS ON A MAN AS HARNESS IS PUT ON
JOAN PREFACE(43)	EMERGENCIES OF DAILY LIFE, THERE IS NO TIME FOR	LESSONS	AND EXPLANATIONS, OR FOR ARGUMENTS AS TO THEIR
HART PREFACE(39)	ARE FOR, IF MEN WILL NOT LEARN UNTIL THEIR	LESSONS	ARE WRITTEN IN BLOOD, WHY, BLOOD THEY MUST HAVE,
BUOY III (30)	OUT OF ME INSTEAD OF LEAVING ME TO LEARN LIFE'S	LESSONS	BY BREAKING MY SHINS AGAINST THEM AND FALLING INTO
PYGM II (220)	/THE FLOWER GIRL/ WHY SHOULDNT I? I KNOW WHAT	LESSONS	COST AS WELL AS YOU DO; AND I'M READY TO PAY.
GENV PREFACE(16)	AND CAPABLE HAS BEEN DEMONSTRATED BY TERRIBLE	LESSONS	DAILY FOR YEARS PAST. AS I WRITE, DOCKFULLS OF
PYGM II (221)	WHATS RIGHT. A LADY FRIEND OF MINE GETS FRENCH	LESSONS	FOR EIGHTEENPENCE AN HOUR FROM A REAL FRENCH
MILL I (157)	AN APPALLING RATE. I SHOULD HONESTLY LIKE A FEW	LESSONS	FROM ALASTAIR IN THE ART OF TURNING HUNDREDS INTO
FABL PREFACE(81)	HAD TO SUPPLY THE SERMON IN A RITUAL OF HYMNS AND	LESSONS	IN ALL RESPECTS LIKE A RELIGIOUS SUNDAY SERVICE
MIS. (178)	AND LET ME HAVE YOUR GRUB AND YOUR SPORT AND YOUR	LESSONS	IN BOXING, AND I'LL FIGHT YOU FAST ENOUGH. YOU KNOW
MIS. PREFACE(88)	HASTEN TO SAY THAT I DO NOT MEAN GIVING CHILDREN	LESSONS	IN FREEHAND DRAWING AND PERSPECTIVE. I AM SIMPLY
MIS. PREFACE(69)	TRAINING, THE APPRENTICESHIP TO SOCIETY, THE	LESSONS	IN HOLDING ONE'S OWN AMONG PEOPLE OF ALL SORTS WITH
MIS. PREFACE(26)	ANY REASONABLE PERSON THAT THE OBJECT OF THE	LESSONS	IS TO KEEP CHILDREN OUT OF MISCHIEF, AND NOT TO
JOAN PREFACE(33)	UNRAVEL THE BUSINESS FURTHER, AND SEE WHAT OTHER	LESSONS	IT CONTAINS FOR US, CRUELTY, MODERN AND MEDIEVAL.
MIS. PREFACE(40)	HAS A RIGHT TO FINALITY AS REGARDS ITS COMPULSORY	LESSONS	. ALSO AS REGARDS PHYSICAL TRAINING. AT PRESENT IT
APPL II (257)	THEM. /MAGNUS/ WELL, SO I AM, IN THE ELEMENTARY	LESSONS	. BUT WHEN IT COMES TO REAL BUSINESS HUMBUG IS NO
MIS. PREFACE(21)	JOHNSON'S GREAT MIND WAS LAMED -- BY LEARNING HIS	LESSONS	. NONE OF MY SCHOOLMASTERS REALLY CARED A RAP (OR
PYGM II (223)	EXPERIMENT YOU CANT DO IT, AND I'LL PAY FOR THE	LESSONS	. /LIZA/ OH, YOU ARE REAL GOOD. THANK YOU, CAPTAIN.
METH PREFACE(R23)	TALL HAT. THE SET-BACK THAT OCCURRED BETWEEN YOUR	LESSONS	OCCURS AGAIN. THE RACE LEARNS EXACTLY AS THE
LION PREFACE(65)	BY THE WARNINGS OF THEIR DOCTORS AND THE	LESSONS	OF EXPERIENCE FROM EATING AND DRINKING MORE THAN IS
GENV PREFACE(7)	AND WHY STATESMEN, THOUGH THEY CAN LEARN THE	LESSONS	OF HISTORY FROM BOOKS, MUST GROPE THEIR WAY THROUGH
BULL PREFACE(62)	HUMANIZATION OF ITS SUPPORTERS BY THE STERNEST	LESSONS	OF THAT ADVERSITY WHICH COMES FINALLY TO
GENV PREFACE(6)	THE CEASE FIRE IS SOUNDED ENGLAND FORGETS ALL THE	LESSONS	OF THE WAR AND PROVES THE TRUTH OF DR INGE'S OLD
2TRU PREFACE(17)	TO DATE FOR THE MOMENT, BUT AMENABLE TO THE DAILY	LESSONS	OF TRIAL AND ERROR IN ITS PRACTICAL OPERATIONS AND
VWOO 2 (130)	AND UNWARY TRAVELLERS. YOU HAVE HAD FINISHING	LESSONS	ON THE TELEPHONE WHICH GIVE YOU A DISTINGUISHED
MIS. PREFACE(21)	THE NECESSARY CANING POWERS) WHETHER I LEARNT MY	LESSONS	OR NOT, PROVIDED MY FATHER PAID MY SCHOOLING BILL,
MIS. PREFACE(59)	PROCESS OF ASSAULT, IMPRISONMENT, AND COMPULSORY	LESSONS	THAT TAUGHT ME NOTHING, WHICH ARE CALLED MY
FANY III (313)	I NEVER THOUGHT SHE SANG RIGHT AFTER ALL THOSE	LESSONS	WE PAID FOR. /GILBEY/ LORD, KNOX, IT WAS LUCKY YOU
FABL PREFACE(81)	LIKE A RELIGIOUS SUNDAY SERVICE EXCEPT THAT THE	LESSONS	WERE FROM BROWNING AND THE HYMNS WERE ASPIRATIONS TO
MILL IV (195)	YOUR KNOWLEDGE OF HOW TO PUNCH. BUT I WILL TAKE	LESSONS	WHEN I GET WELL. AND SHE SHALL PAY FOR THEM. TWO
MIS. PREFACE(21)	SCHOOL. CONSEQUENTLY I DID NOT LEARN MY SCHOOL	LESSONS	, HAVING MUCH MORE IMPORTANT ONES IN HAND, WITH THE
PYGM II (220)	YE-OO. NOW YOU KNOW, DONT YOU? I'M COME TO HAVE	LESSONS	, I AM. AND TO PAY FOR EM TOO: MAKE NO MISTAKE.
PYGM II (220)	GIRL/ OH, WE ARE PROUD! HE AINT ABOVE GIVING	LESSONS	, NOT HIM: I HEARD HIM SAY SO. WELL, I AINT COME
MTH4 I (158)	FOUNDED OUR RELIGION, OUR MORALITY, OUR LAWS, OUR	LESSONS	, OUR POEMS, OUR PRAYERS, ON THAT SIMPLE BELIEF.
MIS. PREFACE(73)	AND HIS PICTURE OF LITTLE PAUL DOMBEY DYING OF	LESSONS	, WE PERSIST IN HEAPING ON GROWING CHILDREN AND
MIS. PREFACE(62)	FOR LAYING HIS SON'S CHILDHOOD WASTE WITH	LESSONS	, WERE SUPERIOR, AS PRODUCTS OF TRAINING, TO OUR
		LEST	
2TRU I SD(27)	AT US, WE HAVE THE DOOR (CAREFULLY SANDBAGGED	LEST	A DRAUGHT OF FRESH AIR SHOULD CREEP UNDERNEATH) LEVEL
DOCT PREFACE(19)	AND DELIGHTED: WE GO TO BE TORMENTED AND MAIMED	LEST	A WORSE THING SHOULD BEFALL US. IT IS OF THE MOST
BULL PREFACE(54)	THE SHOT WHICH WAS FOUND IN HER PERSON. AND	LEST	ABD-EL-NEBI SHOULD FEEL LONELY AT 25 IN BEGINNING PENAL
GETT (341)	/THE BISHOP/ I THINK I SHOULD MARRY AGAIN	LEST	ANYONE SHOULD IMAGINE I HAD FOUND MARRIAGE UNHAPPY WITH
MTH5 (238)	TWAIN AS ONE THRONE, TWO IN ONE AND ONE IN TWO,	LEST	BY ERROR YE FALL INTO IRRETRIEVABLE DAMNATION. /THE
BULL I (81)	ALL THE BROGUE HE CAN MUSTER, SUBDUING HIS VOICE	LEST	DOYLE SHOULD HEAR AND RETURN). MISTHER BROADBENT: DONT
CLEO III SD(154)	DOWN AT THE BOAT, STANDING NEAR THE STAIRHEAD	LEST	FTATATEETA SHOULD ATTEMPT TO ESCAPE. /APOLLODORUS/ (
CAPT I (221)	VERY CAMFITN, GAVNER. (HE RISES, APPREHENSIVE	LEST	FURTHER CATECHISM SHOULD FIND HIM UNPREPARED). AWLL SY
DOCT PREFACE(73)	(OR HER) OTHER QUALIFICATIONS, A SENSE OF HUMOR,	LEST	HE (OR SHE) SHOULD COME AT LAST TO BELIEVE ALL THE
BASH III (121)	/POLICEMAN/ KEEP BACK YOUR BRUISED PRISONER	LEST	HE SHOCK THIS WELLBRED LADY'S NERVES. YOUR PARDON,
MIS. (112)	HE SITS, BITTERLY HUMILIATED, BUT AFRAID TO SPEAK	LEST	HE SHOULD BURST INTO TEARS). THATS THE ADVANTAGE OF
BARB II SD(285)	BARBARA, PURPOSELY KEEPING ON THE SIDE NEXT BILL,	LEST	HE SHOULD SUPPOSE THAT SHE SHRANK FROM HIM OR BORE
ROCK PREFACE(187)	EVERY REBEL, EVERY LAWBREAKER, EVERY RAPSCALLION	LEST	HE SHOULD TURN OUT TO BE WISER THAN ALL THE GENERATIONS
ARMS II (32)	FOR AN HOUR OR SO, AND THEN CALLED IN HER MOTHER	LEST	HER CONDUCT SHOULD APPEAR UNMAIDENLY. THE OLD LADY WAS
2TRU III (88)	FOR HIS BABY. I HAVE TO RUSH FROM THE BUILDING	LEST	I GO MAD, CRYING, LIKE THE MAN IN YOUR BOOK, " WHAT
MTH4 I (160)	I HAVE NEVER VENTURED TO CONFESS TO IT BEFORE,	LEST	I SHOULD BE IMPRISONED FOR BLASPHEMY, OR EVEN BURNT
BULL PREFACE(10)	THE PERSONAL PRONOUN, AS I HAVE JUST DROPPED IT	LEST	I SHOULD BE PROSECUTED FOR SUPERSTITION BY THE SOCIETY
SUPR PREFACE(R40)	THAT I LAY DOWN MY PEN WITHOUT ANOTHER WORD	LEST	I SHOULD BE TEMPTED TO MAKE THE POSTSCRIPT LONGER EVEN
METH PREFACE(R88)	VERBAL DISTINCTION BETWEEN SCIENCE AND KNOWLEDGE	LEST	I SHOULD MISLEAD MY READERS. BUT I NEVER FORGOT THAT
HART I (80)	NOT HESIONE BE SUCH A DEMON, BROUGHT FORTH BY YOU	LEST	I SHOULD SLAY YOU? /CAPTAIN SHOTOVER/ THAT IS
MTH1 I (15)	NOW YOU WANTED ME TO SIT STILL AND NEVER MOVE	LEST	I SHOULD STUMBLE AND DIE LIKE THE FAWN. NOW YOU NO
SUPR III (104)	IT NEEDS A BRAIN, THIS IRRESISTIBLE FORCE,	LEST	IN ITS IGNORANCE IT SHOULD RESIST ITSELF. WHAT A PIECE
SUPR III (104)	THE NEED TO DO, BUT THE NEED TO KNOW WHAT I DO,	LEST	IN MY BLIND EFFORTS TO LIVE I SHOULD BE SLAYING MYSELF
BUOY III (47)	I MUST CHANGE ITS AIR AND RESTORE ITS PEACE	LEST	IT KILL FATHER BUOYANT INSTEAD OF GIVING HIM A
MIS. PREFACE(42)	SHE WAS HORRIFIED, AND HID IT AWAY FROM ME	LEST	IT SHOULD BREAK MY SOUL AS THE PONY MIGHT HAVE BROKEN
PHIL I (78)	I TREMBLED WHENEVER A LETTER CAME FROM YOU,	LEST	IT SHOULD CONTAIN SOME STAB FOR ME. I DREADED YOUR
MRS PREFACE(171)	NO CIRCUMSTANCES WHICH FORCE US TO TOLERATE IT	LEST	ITS SUPPRESSION LEAD TO WORSE THINGS, NO CONSENSUS OF
SUPR II (64)	/RAMSDEN/ (WITH AN AIR OF IMPORTANCE,	LEST	MALONE SHOULD SUSPECT A MISALLIANCE) HER MARRIAGE HAS
MIS. PREFACE(40)	KEEPERS ARE DRIVEN TO SUCH MONSTROUS MEASURES	LEST	MORE ABOMINABLE THINGS HAPPEN, THEN THE SOONER BOARDING
GENV IV (105)	WITH IT, AND FORCING ME TO BANISH THE JEWS	LEST	MY PEOPLE SHOULD BE SWAMPED BY THE MULTITUDES HE HAS
JOAN 6 (144)	UP HIS PEN AND A BOOK, AND GOING TO HER QUICKLY	LEST	SHE SHOULD COMPROMISE HERSELF AGAIN) COME, CHILD: LET
BASH II,2, (115)	I SURMISE THEY WILL BE CARRIED BY THEIR NURSES,	LEST	SOME BARKING DOG OR BUMBLING BEE SHOULD SCARE THEM.
CLEO PR01 (92)	CIRCULATION OF NEWSPAPERS. WHEREFORE LOOK TO IT,	LEST	SOME LITTLE PEOPLE WHOM YE WOULD ENSLAVE RISE UP AND
BULL PREFACE(67)	WITH APPEALS TO THE IRISH TO REMEMBER BELGIUM	LEST	THE FATE OF LOUVAIN SHOULD BEFALL THEIR OWN HEARTHS AND
BASH PREFACE(87)	BASHVILLE IN THE PRIMITIVE ELIZABETHAN STYLE. AND	LEST	THE LITERARY CONNOISSEURS SHOULD DECLARE THAT THERE WAS
CATH 4 (195)	(KNEELING TO HER) PARDON HIM, PARDON HIM,	LEST	THE MIGHTY MAN BRING HIS WHIP TO YOU. GOD KNOWS WE ALL
UNPL PREFACE(R15)	A STEAM ENGINE, AM LOTH TO STIR UP THE QUESTION	LEST	THE PRESS, HAVING NOW LOST ALL TRADITION OF LIBERTY,
GETT PREFACE(231)	CONCEPTION ARE ALWAYS MORE OR LESS IN A PANIC	LEST	THE SLIGHTEST RELAXATION OF THE MARRIAGE LAWS SHOULD
3PLA PREFACE(R23)	WHO WROTE UNDER HIS PICTURE THIS IS A COCK,	LEST	THERE SHOULD BE ANY MISTAKE ABOUT IT. THE PAT RETORT TO
LADY PREFACE(216)	HAMLET, THAT GENTLEMEN PURPOSELY WROTE BADLY	LEST	THEY SHOULD BE MISTAKEN FOR SCRIVENERS; BUT MOST OF
MTH4 I (156)	KNOWLEDGE, AND THE DISPERSED JEWS DID THE SAME	LEST	THEY SHOULD BE SENT BACK TO PALESTINE, SINCE THEN THE
JOAN PREFACE(53)	AFRAID THE EPILOGUE MUST STAND. TO THE CRITICS,	LEST	THEY SHOULD FEEL IGNORED, TO A PROFESSIONAL CRITIC (I

MTH3 (96) LIFE WITH ENTHUSIASTIC EXPRESSIONS OF LOYALTY, LEST THEY SHOULD HAVE ANY REAL POWER, AND BE EXPECTED TO DO
GENV PREFACE(5) ON THE ROADS HAD TO BE TAKEN DOWN AND HIDDEN LEST THEY SHOULD HELP AN INVADER TO FIND HIS WAY. IT WAS A
MIS. PREFACE(42) IT SO OFTEN MEANS RESTRICTION OF THEIR LIBERTY LEST THEY SHOULD MAKE A BAD USE OF IT. IF THERE ARE
MIS. PREFACE(41) GOES ON CARRYING CHILDREN AFTER THEY CAN WALK LEST THEY SHOULD WALK INTO MISCHIEF, THOUGH ARAB BOYS MAKE
BULL PREFACE(54) ENJOYING THE SPECTACLE FROM THE ROOF. AND LEST THIS PRIVILEGE SHOULD EXCITE JEALOUSY IN OTHER
DOCT PREFACE(78) HIS CRUELTY, AND ANY TYRANT MAKE US HIS SLAVES. LEST THIS SHOULD SEEM TOO RHETORICAL A CONCLUSION FOR OUR
MIS. (132) PRINCIPLE. YOU WANT TO REMEMBER. READ KIPLING. " LEST WE FORGET," /JOHNNY/ IF KIPLING WANTS TO REMEMBER, LET
FABL PREFACE(93) BUT THIS DOES NOT DISCONCERT ME. KIPLING'S " LEST WE FORGET" IS OFTEN LESS URGENT THAN " LEST WE
FABL PREFACE(93) " LEST WE FORGET" IS OFTEN LESS URGENT THAN " LEST WE REMEMBER," CERTAINLY, THOSE WHO FORGET EVERYTHING
BULL PREFACE(57) IS, THE BRIGANDAGE COMMISSIONS WERE WORSE, ALSO (LEST WE SHOULD PROPOSE TO CARRY OUR MORAL SUPERIORITY ANY
KING I (208) VERY GREATLY. YOU HAVE TO WEAR LEATHER BREECHES LEST YOU BE MISTAKEN FOR ME. BARBARA STORMS IN WITH A SHEET
ROCK PREFACE(187) IS IN THE RIGHT; THEREFORE YOU MUST NOT JUDGE ME LEST YOU BE YOURSELF JUDGED, WITHOUT SEDITION AND BLASPHEMY
DOCT PREFACE(25) CHANCE OF THE GERM BEING IN THE SCRAPINGS, AND, LEST YOU SHOULD KILL IT, YOU TAKE NO PRECAUTIONS AGAINST

LESTHRANGE
BULL III (134) YLL PUT HIM INTO PARLIAMENT TO BRING BACK NICK LESTHRANGE ON ME, AND TO PUT TITHES ON ME, AND TO ROB ME FOR

LESTRANGE
BULL III (132) THAN IT WAS WHEN YOU PAID THE SAME MONEY TO NICK LESTRANGE AS RENT, AND HE HANDED IT OVER TO THE CHURCH
BULL I (84) THIS ROSSCULLEN MORTGAGE AND TURNING POOR NICK LESTRANGE OUT OF HOUSE AND HOME HAS RATHER TAKEN ME ABACK;
BULL III (130) TO THEM THAT HAVE NO LAND AT ALL THAN OLD NICK LESTRANGE , WHO WAS AN EDUCATED TRAVELLED GENTLEMAN THAT

LETHAL
MTH3 (95) ASYLUM A FORTNIGHT AGO. NOT MAD ENOUGH FOR THE LETHAL CHAMBER; NOT SANE ENOUGH FOR ANY PLACE BUT THE
BARB PREFACE(245) WITH THEIR LAST WISHES, PLACE THEM IN THE LETHAL CHAMBER AND GET RID OF THEM. UNDER NO CIRCUMSTANCES
MTH3 (127) /BARNABAS/ THERE IS TIME TO SEND THE LADY TO THE LETHAL CHAMBER BEFORE ANYTHING COMES OF YOUR MARRIAGE. DONT
BARB PREFACE(217) INCOME" WOULD BE THE SHORTEST WAY TO THE LETHAL CHAMBER. BUT AS, THANKS TO OUR POLITICAL IMBECILITY
MTH3 (124) ARE REGARDED AS MENTALLY DEFICIENT AND PUT INTO A LETHAL CHAMBER. BUT WHAT DO WE WORK AT? BEFORE THE FEW
BARB PREFACE(245) A DOG DELIGHTS TO BARK AND BITE, IT GOES TO THE LETHAL CHAMBER. THAT SEEMS TO ME SENSIBLE. TO ALLOW THE DOG
CAPT NOTES (301) FROM THE HARD KIND ONES. HE HANDLES THE OTHER LETHAL WEAPONS AS FAMILIARLY AS THE PEN; MEDIEVAL SWORD AND

LET-DOWN
FANY III (302) DO YOU MEAN TO SAY THAT YOU-- OH! THIS IS A LET-DOWN FOR ME. (SHE COMES OFF THE TABLE AND DROPS,

LET'S
HART III (136) SHAME! WHAT SHAME IS THERE IN THIS HOUSE? LET'S ALL STRIP STARK NAKED. WE MAY AS WELL DO THE THING
ARMS III (65) VERY GLAD TO GET YOU TWO QUIETED. THERE! THERE! LET'S BE PLEASANT AND TALK IT OVER IN A FRIENDLY WAY. WHERE
NEVR II (257) NO, NO, NO. NOT LOVE: WE KNOW BETTER THAN THAT. LET'S CALL IT CHEMISTRY. YOU CANT DENY THAT THERE IS SUCH A
CYMB V (142) /IACHIMO/ WE ARE DAMNED FOR THIS. (ON GUARD) LET'S CUT EACH OTHER'S THROATS. /POSTHUMUS/ (DRAWING) AY,
NEVR I (213) AND PUTTING AWAY THE STOOL) WE'RE HURTING YOU: LET'S DROP IT. WE DIDNT THINK YOUD MIND. I DONT WANT TO
NEVR I (207) RID OF HIS AFFECTIONATE FAMILY SO EASILY. ANYHOW, LET'S LOOK AT THE BRIGHT SIDE OF THINGS. DEPEND ON IT, HE'S

LETTER
DEST (174) BY YOU OR TO YOU. THAT PACKET CONTAINS A STOLEN LETTER : A LETTER WRITTEN BY A WOMAN TO A MAN: A MAN NOT HER
SUPR IV (150) IT WAS QUITE NATURAL FOR MR MALONE TO OPEN MY LETTER : HIS NAME WAS ON THE ENVELOPE. /MALONE/ THERE!
DEST (179) WITHOUT THE AID OF SPIES, MADAM. /LADY/ AND THE LETTER ? DONT YOU WANT TO READ THAT? /NAPOLEON/ YOU HAVE
PHIL II (105) YOU BE SO ROUGH WITH ME, DEAR! DID YOU GET MY LETTER ? /CHARTERIS/ BURNT IT-- JULIA TURNS AWAY, STRUCK TO
PHIL II (109) ALL RIGHT, DEAR. (TO CHARTERIS) DID YOU GET MY LETTER ? /CHARTERIS/ YES. I WISH YOU WOULDNT WRITE ON THOSE
DEST (174) THAT MEANS DISGRACE, INFAMY-- /NAPOLEON/ A LOVE LETTER ? /LADY/ (BITTER-SWEETLY) WHAT ELSE BUT A LOVE
2TRU II (54) HOW DID YOU KNOW WHAT WAS IN COLONEL SAXBY'S LETTER ? /MEEK/ I READ IT TO HIM, SIR. /TALLBOYS/ DID HE
CAPT II (270) WELL, SIR, ARE WE NOT TO HAVE THE BENEFIT OF THAT LETTER ? YOUR MEN ARE WAITING TO HEAR IT, I THINK.
DEST (175) (REVOLTED) SUPPOSE THAT PACKET CONTAINED A LETTER ABOUT YOUR OWN WIFE? /NAPOLEON/ (OFFENDED, COMING
SUPR IV (149) /MALONE/ WHAT D'Y'MEAN? /HECTOR/ YOUVE OPENED A LETTER ADDRESSED TO ME. YOUVE IMPERSONATED ME AND STOLEN A
MIS. (179) IF MY NAME'S A COMMON ONE? /BENTLEY/ SHEW US A LETTER ADDRESSED TO YOU. /GUNNER/ HOW CAN I? I NEVER GET
PYGM IV (261) AT THE BILLET-DOUX) MONEY-LENDER. (HE THROWS THE LETTER AFTER THE CIRCULARS). ELIZA RETURNS WITH A PAIR OF
DEVL III SD(67) AT THE DOOR WITH TWO PAPERS IN HIS HAND: A WHITE LETTER AND A BLUE DISPATCH. /BURGOYNE/ (ADVANCING TO THE
PHIL II (101) AFFAIR. LOOK AT THESE LETTERS (PRODUCING A LETTER AND A LETTER-CARD)! THIS (SHEWING THE CARD) IS FROM
JOAN 2 (77) /THE ARCHBISHOP/ (WHO HAS READ THE END OF THE LETTER AND BECOME MORE THOUGHTFUL) IT IS TRUE THAT DE
CAPT II (270) WARSHIP. /BRASSBOUND/ WARSHIP! (HE TAKES THE LETTER AND OPENS IT, HIS MEN WHISPERING TO ONE ANOTHER VERY
SUPR II (58) ABOUT TWO MINUTES AFTER I HAD RECEIVED HER LETTER AND READ IT. /ANN/ RHODA HAS WRITTEN TO YOU!
2TRU II (54) CLERK. /TALLBOYS/ WHAT! YOU WROTE BOTH THE LETTER AND THE HEADMAN'S ANSWER? /MEEK/ YESSIR. /TALLBOYS/
2TRU II (56) HOUR'S PURCHASE. /MEEK/ NO, SIR. AM I TO FILE THE LETTER AND THE REPLY WITH A TRANSLATION, SIR? /TALLBOYS/ (
PYGM II (231) THE BATH WAS TOO HOT. IT BEGINS WITH THE SAME LETTER AS BATH. SHE KNOWS NO BETTER; SHE LEARNT IT AT HER
CAND I (83) CASE FOR AN ENVELOPE, IN WHICH SHE ENCLOSES THE LETTER AS SHE SPEAKS) CANDIDA HERE, AND CANDIDA THERE, AND
CATH 1 (164) EMPRESS. (PATIOMKIN CONTEMPTUOUSLY THROWS THE LETTER ASIDE. EDSTASTON ADDS HOTLY) ALSO SOME CIVILITY, IF
MIS. PREFACE(66) COOLER-HEADED CAN DEFEAT ANGRY MOTIONS THAT THE LETTER BE THROWN INTO THE WASTE PAPER BASKET AND THE
DEST (167) TELL ME THIS, SUPPOSE YOU COULD HAVE GOT THAT LETTER BY COMING TO ME OVER THE BRIDGE AT LODI THE DAY
PHIL I (78) SURE OF YOU FOR A MOMENT. I TREMBLED WHENEVER A LETTER CAME FROM YOU, LEST IT SHOULD CONTAIN SOME STAB FOR
PHIL I (72) IT TO HER WITH BRUTAL EXPLICITNESS. SHE READ THE LETTER CAREFULLY AND THEN SENT IT BACK TO ME WITH A NOTE TO
BULL I (84) THE FIREPLACE BEFORE REPLYING. /DOYLE/ WELL: YOUR LETTER COMPLETELY UPSET ME, FOR ONE THING. /BROADBENT/ WHY?
DEST (175) SET MY MIND TO IT. NEXT TIME YOU ARE ASKED WHY A LETTER COMPROMISING A WIFE SHOULD NOT BE SENT TO HER
DEST (174) /LADY/ (BITTER-SWEETLY) WHAT ELSE BUT A LOVE LETTER COULD STIR UP SO MUCH HATE? /NAPOLEON/ WHY IS IT
BUOY PREFACE(4) AND TRANSCRIBED BY THEM AS LITERALLY AS ANY LETTER DICTATED BY A MERCHANT TO HIS TYPIST. TAKE MY OWN
DEST SD(195) THE LETTER) I WONDER! THE STRANGE LADY PUTS THE LETTER DOWN ALIGHT ON THE SNUFFERS TRAY, AND SITS DOWN
DEST (174) ENIGMATICALLY, IN TRANQUIL SILENCE. HE THROWS THE LETTER DOWN AND BREAKS OUT INTO A TORRENT OF SCOLDING). WHAT
DEST (168) WITH CONVICTION) BECAUSE YOU WOULD HAVE WANTED MY LETTER ENOUGH TO BEAR YOUR FEAR. (HE RISES SUDDENLY, AND
DEST (175) SHE HAS WRITTEN TO ME IMPLORING ME TO PREVENT THE LETTER FALLING INTO YOUR HANDS. /NAPOLEON/ WHY HAS IT BEEN
WIDO I (18) THE HOTEL). /TRENCH/ SH! HERE THEY COME. GET THE LETTER FINISHED BEFORE DINNER, LIKE A GOOD OLD CHAPPIE: I
WIDO I (23) TAKES BLANCHE IN TO THE TABLE D'HOTE). IS THE LETTER FINISHED, MR COKANE? /COKANE/ (WITH AN AUTHOR'S
WIDO I (17) IN TIME TO DO ME A FAVOR, I WANT YOU TO DRAFT A LETTER FOR ME TO COPY OUT. /COKANE/ I CAME WITH YOU ON THIS
BARB II (297) TURNS TO CUSINS). DOLLY: YOU MUST WRITE ANOTHER LETTER FOR ME TO THE PAPERS. (HE MAKES A WRY FACE). YES: I
WIDO I (20) ROXDALE. YOU UNDERSTAND THAT I AM ONLY DRAFTING A LETTER FOR TRENCH TO COPY. /SARTORIUS/ QUITE SO. WILL YOU
CAND II (105) THE HANDLE, AND IT WOULD WRITE A BEAUTIFUL LOVE LETTER FOR YOU STRAIGHT OFF, EH? /MARCHBANKS/ (SERIOUSLY)
GENV I (34) SIMPLE. BUT IF YOU WILL ALLOW ME I WILL DRAFT THE LETTER FOR YOU. /SHE/ OH I SAY, MISTER JEW, I DONT LIKE
FANY I (274) BOBBY'S GOOD. /GILBEY/ OH, VERY WELL: HAVE THE LETTER FRAMED AND HANG IT UP OVER THE MANTELPIECE AS A
FABL PREFACE(79) OF GOD, WE SHALL NEVER KNOW. I HAVE JUST HAD A LETTER FROM A MAN WHO, HAVING MADE REPEATED ATTEMPTS TO GIVE
FABL VI (128) THOUGHT? I HAVE RECEIVED THIS MORNING A LETTER FROM A MAN WHO TELLS ME HE WAS FOR NINETEEN YEARS A
SUPR IV (149) JUST SPOILED IT ALL BY OPENING THAT LETTER. A LETTER FROM AN ENGLISH LADY, NOT ADDRESSED TO YOU-- A
2TRU II SD(51) TAKEN OFF HIS GOGGLES AND GLOVES, AND EXTRACTED A LETTER FROM HIS CARRIER, COMES PAST THE PAVILION INTO THE
SUPR IV (145) /VIOLET/ (SITTING DOWN) YES. /MALONE/ (TAKING A LETTER FROM HIS POCKET) YOUR NOTE TO HECTOR RUNS AS FOLLOWS
DEST (195) THE LETTER IN YOUR POCKET. (HE SMILES; TAKES A LETTER FROM HIS POCKET; AND TOSSES IT ON TOP OF THE HEAP.
SUPR IV (152) BE SO FULL OF CHEEK THEN. /HECTOR/ (PRODUCING A LETTER FROM HIS POCKETBOOK) HERE IT IS (THRUSTING IT ON HIS
ROCK PREFACE(168) REPORTS; FOR I HAVE NO SOONER READ IN THE TIMES A LETTER FROM MR KERENSKY ASSURING ME THAT IN THE UKRAINE THE
CATH 1 (164) I HAVE THE HONOR TO PRESENT TO YOUR HIGHNESS THIS LETTER FROM THE BRITISH AMBASSADOR, WHICH WILL GIVE YOU ALL
ARMS III (55) IN A LONG BLUE ENVELOPE). HERE'S A WHACKING LETTER FROM THE FAMILY SOLICITOR. (HE PULLS OUT THE
FANY I (273) WHAT HAVE YOU GOT IN YOUR HAND? /GILBEY/ IVE A LETTER FROM THE MONSIGNOR GRENFELL. FROM NEW YORK. DROPPING
GETT (285) WITH HER. /THE BISHOP/ ALICE: IVE HAD ANOTHER LETTER FROM THE MYSTERIOUS LADY WHO CANT SPELL. I LIKE THAT
PRES (132) UNDRESS IN MY PRESENCE. I PROTEST. NOT EVEN YOUR LETTER FROM THE PRIME MINISTER-- /THE SUFFRAGET/ MY DEAR
PRES (132) TO ATTEND TO THE ORDERLY'S REPLY) THIS IS A LETTER FROM THE PRIME MINISTER ASKING ME TO RELEASE THE
CURE SD(230) BOUQUET IN HER HAND. SHE LOOKS ABOUT HER; TAKES A LETTER FROM WHEREVER SHE CARRIES LETTERS; AND STARTS ON A
SUPR PREFACE(R40) BE THE CLOSING CADENCE OF THIS IMMODERATELY LONG LETTER FROM YOURS FAITHFULLY, G. BERNARD SHAW. WOKING, 1903.
POSN PREFACE(378) MOST SENSITIVE SPOT BY THE CONSTRUCTION MY TIMES LETTER HAD PUT ON HIS ACTION. AND IN COLONEL LOCKWOOD'S CASE
2TRU II (55) /TALLBOYS/ WELL, NEXT TIME YOU ARE SENT WITH A LETTER I HOPE THE BRIGANDS WILL CATCH YOU AND KEEP YOU.
MIS. (139) WHETHER I WANTED OR NOT, BECAUSE WHEN I READ YOUR LETTER I KNEW I HAD TO COME. /HYPATIA/ WHY? /LORD
BULL IV (159) LET ERIN REMEMBER). /NORA/ DID JEVER GET A LETTER I WROTE YOU LAST FEBRUARY? /LARRY/ OH YES; AND I
CAND I (88) I HOWN IT NOW. COME: I HARSK YOUR PARDON FOR THE LETTER I WROTE YOU. IS THAT ENOUGH? /MORELL/ (SNAPPING HIS
PRES (131) US THAT YOUVE GOT THE KEY OF THE PADLOCK IN A LETTER IN A BUFF ENVELOPE, AND THAT YOULL SEE HER WHEN YOU

ARMS III (55) HIM TO BE LOOKED AFTER. (HE TAKES UP A FAT LETTER IN A LONG BLUE ENVELOPE). HERE'S A WHACKING LETTER
FANY I SD(273) ALL PLACID, BURSTS VIOLENTLY INTO THE ROOM WITH A LETTER IN HIS HAND. /GILBEY/ (GRINDING HIS TEETH) THIS IS A
2TRU II SD(51) THE PAVILION INTO THE COLONEL'S VIEW WITH THE LETTER IN HIS HAND. HE IS AN INSIGNIFICANT LOOKING PRIVATE
SIM PREFACE(17) FOR THE SERMON ON THE MOUNT IS STILL A DEAD LETTER IN SPITE OF ALL THE COMPLIMENTS WE PAY IT. BUT TO
DEST (168) THIS! SUPPOSE YOU HAD COME SAFELY OUT WITH THAT LETTER IN YOUR HAND, KNOWING THAT WHEN THE HOUR CAME, YOUR
DEST (195) PLACED). /LADY/ YES; BUT YOU KNOW YOU HAVE THE LETTER IN YOUR POCKET. (HE SMILES; TAKES A LETTER FROM HIS
WIDO I (22) AND PAPER IN HAND) RELY ON ME, MR SARTORIUS. THE LETTER IS ALREADY FINISHED HERE (POINTING TO HIS BRAIN). IN
SUPR PREFACE(R40) TO MAKE THE POSTSCRIPT LONGER EVEN THAN THE LETTER .
SUPR IV (149) WELL, YOUVE JUST SPOILED IT ALL BY OPENING THAT LETTER . A LETTER FROM AN ENGLISH LADY, NOT ADDRESSED TO
JOAN 2 (76) SAY, OF COURSE. BUT YOU HAVNT READ THE END OF THE LETTER . DE BAUDRICOURT SAYS SHE WILL RAISE THE SIEGE OF
FANY I (274) ME. /MRS GILBEY/ WELL, I THINK IT'S RATHER A NICE LETTER . HE AS GOOD AS TELLS YOU HE'S ONLY LETTING ON TO BE
DEST (177) VINEYARD AND BACK TO THE TABLE) YOU SHALL HAVE NO LETTER . I DONT LIKE YOU. YOURE A DETESTABLE WOMAN, AND AS
WIDO II (28) YOULL SEE SHE SPOTTED COKANE'S HAND IN MY LETTER . (CHUCKLING) HE WROTE IT FOR ME. /SARTORIUS/ (
DEST (194) TABLE, BESIDE HIS OWN). WE HAVE STILL TO BURN THE LETTER . (HE TAKES UP THE PACKET). GIUSEPPE COMES BACK,
SIM I (43) SHAKING HANDS) C.B., IN CASE YOU ARE ADDRESSING A LETTER . (SHE SITS DOWN ON SIR CHARLES'S LEFT). /THE
SIM PRO,1, (25) BACK: YOU SHOULD HAVE PASSED IT ON, LIKE A CHAIN LETTER . NOW YOU WILL NEVER HAVE NO MORE LUCK IN THIS
DEST (166) GENERAL: I ONLY WANT TO KEEP ONE LITTLE PRIVATE LETTER . ONLY ONE. LET ME HAVE IT. /NAPOLEON/ (COLD AND
WIDO I (19) I HAVE DISTURBED YOU IN THE COMPOSITION OF YOUR LETTER . PRAY RESUME IT. I SHALL LEAVE YOU TO YOURSELF. (HE
BULL I (94) /DOYLE/ UNEASY. I'D GIVE 50 POUNDS TO ESCAPE A LETTER . /BROADBENT/ (LOOKING GRAVE, AND THROWING HIMSELF
PHIL II (102) /CUTHBERTSON/ I APPROVE OF EVERY WORD OF THAT LETTER . /CHARTERIS/ (TURNING TO CRAVEN AND PREPARING TO
DEST (177) /LADY/ (SEATED IMMOVABLY) NOT WITHOUT THAT LETTER . /NAPOLEON/ BEGONE, I TELL YOU. (WALKING FROM THE
AUGS (277) THE -- OH, HERE IT IS! NO: THIS IS LUCY'S LAST LETTER . /THE LADY/ (ELEGIACALLY) LUCY'S LAST LETTER! WHAT
CURE SD(230) CHECKING HER OBSERVATIONS BY THE CONTENTS OF THE LETTER . THE PIANO SEEMS SPECIALLY SATISFACTORY: SHE NODS AS
2TRU II SD(52) LOOKS AT HIM WITH LOATHING, AND TEARS OPEN THE LETTER . THERE IS A PAINFUL SILENCE WHILST HE PUZZLES OVER
GETT (274) /REGINALD/ IT'S SO JOLLY EASY TO SAY NO IN A LETTER . WONT YOU LET ME STAY? /MRS BRIDGENORTH/ HOW CAN
WIDO I (20) AND I WERE PUTTING OUR HEADS TOGETHER OVER THE LETTER JUST NOW; AND THERE CERTAINLY WERE ONE OR TWO POINTS
WIDO II (24) /SARTORIUS/ HE! HE SAYS NOTHING. (HE FOLDS A LETTER LEISURELY, AND LOOKS FOR THE ENVELOPE). HE PREFERS TO
JOAN PREFACE(36) RIVALS FOR HUMAN ALLEGIANCE. I HAVE BEFORE ME THE LETTER OF A CATHOLIC PRIEST. " IN YOUR PLAY," HE WRITES, " I
2TRU II (57) IF NECESSARY. EXPENSE IS NO OBJECT. AND THE LETTER OF CREDIT? /MEEK/ SORRY, COUNTESS: I HAVE ONLY TWO
2TRU II (57) WILL PAY ANYTHING NECESSARY. AND COULD YOU GET A LETTER OF CREDIT CASHED FOR ME? I'D BETTER HAVE THREE
2TRU II (58) HANDS HER A ROLL OF NOTES; AND SHE GIVES HIM THE LETTER OF CREDIT). /THE COUNTESS/ YOU ARE NEVER AT A LOSS.
POSN PREFACE(373) TAKEN ABACK. THE CHAIRMAN WAS BOUND BY THE LETTER OF THE DECISION ARRIVED AT TO ALLOW ME TO READ MY
POSN PREFACE(419) AND A MAN OF THE WORLD: HE MUST STICK TO THE LETTER OF THE LAW AND TAKE NO CHANCES. AND AS FAR AS THE LAW
GETT PREFACE(199) AGAINST ACTIONS GOING BEYOND THE STRICT LETTER OF THE LAW IN THE WAY OF KINDNESS THAN WE HAVE NOW
WIDO II (27) I FIND THAT YOU HAVE STEPPED AN INCH OUTSIDE THE LETTER OF THE LAW, MR LICKCHEESE, I WILL PROSECUTE YOU
DEST (174) /LADY/ (EARNESTLY) NO: ON MY HONOR I ASK FOR NO LETTER OF YOURS: NOT A WORD THAT HAS BEEN WRITTEN BY YOU OR
BULL PREFACE(60) IT IS PLEASANTER TO RETURN TO LORD CROMER'S FIRST LETTER ON DENSHAWAI, WRITTEN TO SIR EDWARD GREY THE DAY
CAND II (110) IF MR MARCHBANKS WASNT HERE. (SHE PULLS THE LETTER OUT OF THE MACHINE SO CROSSLY THAT IT TEARS). THERE!
BULL IV (159) I MEAN OF COURSE THE THINGS ONE CAN PUT IN A LETTER -- THAT CORRESPONDENCE IS APT TO BECOME THE HARDEST
DEVL III (68) DO YOU KNOW WHAT THIS IS (SHEWING HIM THE LETTER)? /SWINDON/ WHAT? /BURGOYNE/ A DEMAND FOR A
WIDO I (23) /COKANE/ (AS HE COMES TO THEM, FLOURISHING THE LETTER) FINISHED, DEAR BOY, FINISHED. DONE TO A TURN,
AUGS (277) NO OTHER WOMAN. BY THE WAY (HANDING OVER THE LETTER) I WONDER COULD YOU READ IT FOR ME? LUCY IS A
DEST (195) TABLE AND HIS CHEEKS ON HIS HANDS, LOOKING AT THE LETTER) I WONDER! THE STRANGE LADY PUTS THE LETTER DOWN
PHIL II (102) (TURNING TO CRAVEN AND PREPARING TO READ THE LETTER) NOW FOR JULIA. (THE COLONEL TURNS AWAY TO HIDE HIS
2TRU II (52) AND STANDS AT ATTENTION. /TALLBOYS/ (TAKING THE LETTER) WHATS THIS? /THE RIDER/ I WAS SENT WITH A LETTER
DEVL III (68) YOU IS THIS. WHO IS (READING THE NAME FROM THE LETTER) WILLIAM MAINDECK PARSHOTTER? /RICHARD/ HE IS THE
PHIL II (102) THOUGH, CONFOUND IT. (HE HOLDS OUT GRACE'S LETTER). A BLUE CARD AS USUAL! THIS TIME I SHALL NOT TRUST
WIDO II (28) OUR HONEYMOON THERE. (HE HANDS SARTORIUS ANOTHER LETTER). IT'S THE SORT OF HOUSE NOBODY CAN LIVE IN, YOU
CAPT II (269) PEACE, THOU INCONSIDERATE ONE. (HE TAKES OUT A LETTER). /BRASSBOUND/ CADI-- /THE CADI/ OH THOU DOG. THOU,
2TRU II (54) BETTER INTERPRET THIS FOR ME. (HE PROFFERS THE LETTER). /MEEK/ (NOT ACCEPTING IT) NO NEED, THANK YOU,
CATH 1 (164) NECESSARY PARTICULARS. (HE HANDS PATIOMKIN THE LETTER). /PATIOMKIN/ (TEARING IT OPEN AND GLANCING AT IT
WIDO II (28) BE MARRIED FROM HER HOUSE. (HE HANDS SARTORIUS A LETTER). /SARTORIUS/ AUNT MARIA? /COKANE/ LADY ROXDALE, MY
BULL IV (159) YET WHAT ELSE HAVE I TO WRITE ABOUT? I BEGIN A LETTER ; AND THEN I TEAR IT UP AGAIN. THE FACT IS, FOND AS
GETT SD(272) HER PLACIDITY QUITE UPSET, COMES IN WITH A LETTER ; HURRIES PAST COLLINS; AND COMES BETWEEN LESBIA AND
PRES (131) IT DOES SEEM TO HAVE A KEY IN IT. (HE OPENS THE LETTER ; TAKES OUT A KEY AND A NOTE; AND READS) " DEAR
CAND I (83) CIGARET). /PROSERPINE/ (IMPATIENTLY, PULLING THE LETTER SHE HAS BEEN WORKING AT OFF THE TYPEWRITER AND
WIDO I (18) A MAN LIKE HIM. DO YOU THINK YOU COULD WORD THE LETTER SO AS TO PASS ALL THAT OVER? I REALLY DONT LIKE TO
DEST (174) BY A WOMAN TO A MAN: A MAN NOT HER HUSBAND: A LETTER THAT MEANS DISGRACE, INFAMY-- /NAPOLEON/ A LOVE
DEST (175) GOOD MANNERS) GENERAL: THERE REALLY IS A WOMAN'S LETTER THERE. (POINTING TO THE PACKET) GIVE IT TO ME.
MILL IV (208) COME TO THAT, I AM IN DEBT FOR MY FOOD. I GOT A LETTER THIS MORNING FROM MY PURVEYORS TO SAY THAT I HAVE
PHIL II (103) /CRAVEN/ CHARTERIS: NO WOMAN WRITES SUCH A LETTER TO A MAN UNLESS HE HAS MADE ADVANCES TO HER.
2TRU II (54) NO RIGHT TO COMMUNICATE THE CONTENTS OF SUCH A LETTER TO A PRIVATE SOLDIER. HE CANNOT HAVE KNOWN WHAT HE
PYGM V (271) I? TELL ME THIS. DID YOU OR DID YOU NOT WRITE A LETTER TO AN OLD BLIGHTER IN AMERICA THAT WAS GIVING FIVE
2TRU II (52) SIR. /TALLBOYS/ WELL, IS THIS A PERSONAL LETTER TO BE SENT ON TO HIM, OR IS IT A DISPATCH? /THE
DOCT II (125) TINWELL, SIR. /SIR PATRICK/ WELL, YOU WRITE HIM A LETTER TO CARE OF THIS GENTLEMAN; AND IT WILL BE SENT ON.
PYGM V (271) I'M DONE FOR. NOW DID YOU OR DID YOU NOT WRITE A LETTER TO HIM TO SAY THAT THE MOST ORIGINAL MORALIST AT
SUPR IV (152) YOUR RIGHT NAME IS, YOU HAD NO RIGHT TO SEND THAT LETTER TO MY SON WHEN YOU WERE THE WIFE OF ANOTHER MAN.
2TRU II (56) A TRANSLATION, SIR? /TALLBOYS/ (TEARING THE LETTER TO PIECES AND THROWING THEM AWAY) YOUR FOLLY HAS MADE
BULL I (95) AND RETURN NORA HER LETTERS AND PRESENTS WITH A LETTER TO SAY HE WAS UNWORTHY OF HER AND WISHED HER EVERY
ROCK PREFACE(163) DISAPPEARANCE AND THE RECEIPT BY HIS FAMILY OF A LETTER TO SAY THAT THEY NEED NOT WAIT UP FOR HIM, AS HE
JOAN EPILOG (158) YOUR WAY. I GIVE YOU BEST, LASSIE. I WROTE A FINE LETTER TO SET YOU RIGHT AT THE NEW TRIAL. PERHAPS I SHOULD
APPL PREFACE(194) DIPLOMATIC, HE BROUGHT ME, WITH SOME PRIDE, A LETTER TO THE BOARD OF TRADE WHICH HE CONSIDERED A
DEST (195) /LADY/ (TAKING UP THE SNUFFERS AND HOLDING THE LETTER TO THE CANDLE FLAME WITH IT) I WONDER WOULD CAESAR'S
2TRU II SD(52) AN IMPRESSION OF IRONY. HE SALUTES; HANDS THE LETTER TO THE COLONEL; AND STANDS AT ATTENTION. /TALLBOYS/ (
2TRU II (52) WHATS THIS? /THE RIDER/ I WAS SENT WITH A LETTER TO THE HEADMAN OF THE NATIVE VILLAGE IN THE
MIS. PREFACE(10) PRETENSIONS, AND YET HE MIGHT HAVE WRITTEN HIS LETTER TO THE TIMES (HE VERY NEARLY DID, BY THE WAY)
PRES (131) YOURE ALL AFRAID OF THESE WOMEN. (HE PICKS THE LETTER UP.) IT DOES SEEM TO HAVE A KEY IN IT. (HE OPENS THE
2TRU II (53) THE NATIVE HEADMAN TO WHOM COLONEL SAXBY'S LETTER WAS ADDRESSED. HOW DID HE COME TO SELECT YOU? /MEEK/
2TRU II (54) WESTERN ISLES. /TALLBOYS/ YOU! YOU WORM! IF MY LETTER WAS SENT BY THE HANDS OF AN IRRESPONSIBLE MESSENGER
CATH 1 (164) A SECOND) WHAT DO YOU WANT? /EDSTASTON/ THE LETTER WILL EXPLAIN TO YOUR HIGHNESS WHO I AM. /PATIOMKIN/ I
GENV I (34) /SHE/ BUT I'M NOT SURE THAT I KNOW HOW TO WRITE A LETTER WITH ALL THOSE POLICE COURT THINGS IN IT. /THE JEW/
PYGM EPILOG (301) WAS CONGENITALLY INCAPABLE OF FORMING A SINGLE LETTER WORTHY OF THE LEAST OF MILTON'S WORDS; BUT SHE
BULL I (83) POPULATION OF IRELAND CONSISTS OF DRUNKEN BEGGING LETTER WRITERS, OR THAT EVEN IF IT DID, THEY WOULD ACCEPT
DEST (174) TO YOU. THAT PACKET CONTAINS A STOLEN LETTER: A LETTER WRITTEN BY A WOMAN TO A MAN: A MAN NOT HER HUSBAND: A
GENV I (34) JEW. I DONT LIKE THIS. /THE JEW/ THEN WRITE THE LETTER YOURSELF. I AM SURE YOU WILL DO IT PERFECTLY. IT WILL
PRES (132) LOOKED IT. /MITCHENER/ (WHO HAS BEEN READING THE LETTER , AND IS TOO ASTONISHED TO ATTEND TO THE ORDERLY'S
CAPT III (287) THE CADI WITH YOUR MOST AMUSING AND DELIGHTFUL LETTER , CAPTAIN, AND BUNDLED US ALL BACK TO MOGADOR AFTER
SUPR IV (150) NO USE HECTORING ME. A PRIVATE LETTER'S A PRIVATE LETTER , DAD: YOU CANT GET OVER THAT. /MALONE/ (RAISING HIS
CAPT II SD(270) THEY ARE, ON THIS COWST. BRASSBOUND FOLDS UP THE LETTER , LOOKING GLUM. /SIR HOWARD/ (SHARPLY) WELL, SIR,
AUGS (278) IS OF ANY POLITICAL VALUE. (TAKING OUT A LETTER , SHE CROSSES THE ROOM TOWARDS THE WINDOW, WHISPERING
2TRU II (54) THANK YOU, SIR. THE HEADMAN COULDNT COMPOSE A LETTER , SIR. I HAD TO DO IT FOR HIM. /TALLBOYS/ HOW DID YOU
DEST (178) HER HUSBAND. /NAPOLEON/ I AM TO READ THE LETTER , THEN? (HE STRETCHES OUT HIS HAND AS IF TO TAKE UP
APPL PREFACE(178) MORE THAN A LONG WORD BEGINNING WITH A CAPITAL LETTER , WHICH WE ACCEPT REVERENTLY OR DISPARAGE
SUPR IV (149) LADY, NOT ADDRESSED TO YOU-- A CAWNFIDENTIAL LETTER ! A DULLICATE LETTER! A PRIVATE LETTER! OPENED BY
SUPR IV (149) TO YOU-- A CAWNFIDENTIAL LETTER! A DULLICATE LETTER ! A PRIVATE LETTER! OPENED BY MY FATHER! THATS A
CAND II (110) THAT IT TEARS). THERE! NOW I'VE SPOILED THIS LETTER ! HAVE TO BE DONE ALL OVER AGAIN! OH, I CANT
SUPR IV (149) LETTER! A DULLICATE LETTER! A PRIVATE LETTER ! OPENED BY MY FATHER! THATS A SORT OF THING A MAN
AUGS (277) LETTER. /THE LADY/ (ELEGIACALLY) LUCY'S LAST LETTER ! WHAT A TITLE FOR A PICTURE PLAY! /AUGUSTUS/ (

LETTERED

MRS IV SD(235) CORRIDOR. ITS UPPER PANEL IS OF OPAQUE GLASS, LETTERED IN BLACK ON THE OUTSIDE, FRASER AND WARREN. A BAIZE

LETTERING

DOCT I (86) IT WAS A SHOP WINDOW: RED, YOU KNOW, WITH BLACK LETTERING . DOCTOR LEO SCHUTZMACHER, L.R.C.P. M.R.C.S.

LETTER-BOX

PYGM IV SD(261) SONG. PICKERING RETURNS, WITH THE CONTENTS OF THE LETTER-BOX IN HIS HAND. /PICKERING/ ONLY CIRCULARS, AND THIS

LETTER-CARD

PHIL II (101) LOOK AT THESE LETTERS (PRODUCING A LETTER AND A LETTER-CARD)! THIS (SHEWING THE CARD) IS FROM GRACE-- BY

LETTER-CARDS

PHIL II (101) CUTHBERTSON, I WISH YOUD ASK HER NOT TO WRITE ON LETTER-CARDS : THE BLUE COLOR MAKES IT SO EASY FOR JULIA TO
PHIL II (109) I WISH YOU WOULDNT WRITE ON THOSE CONFOUNDED BLUE LETTER-CARDS . /SYLVIA/ (TO GRACE) SHALL I GO DOWN FIRST,

LETTER'S

SUPR IV (150) FORCE) OH, IT'S NO USE HECTORING ME. A PRIVATE LETTER'S A PRIVATE LETTER, DAD: YOU CANT GET OVER THAT.

LETTERS

LION PREFACE(90) 7 B.C.; BUT THEY DO NOT THEREFORE DATE THEIR LETTERS 1923, NOR, I PRESUME, DO THEY EXPECT ME TO DO SO.
DEST (166) ANY QUESTIONS. YOU SHALL HAVE YOUR DESPATCHES AND LETTERS : I SWEAR IT. /NAPOLEON/ (HOLDING OUT HIS HAND)
DEST (193) ASSUMING THAT IT WAS I WHO WANTED TO STEAL YOUR LETTERS : IN EXPLAINING THAT IT ALL CAME ABOUT THROUGH MY
MIS. (179) TO YOU. /GUNNER/ HOW CAN I? I NEVER GET ANY LETTERS : I'M ONLY A CLERK. I CAN SHEW YOU J.B. ON MY
CAND II SD(115) MORELL IS SILENT. APPARENTLY HE IS BUSY WITH HIS LETTERS : REALLY HE IS PUZZLING WITH MISGIVING OVER HIS NEW
WIDO II (37) WHAT ARE YOU GOING TO DO? /BLANCHE/ TO GET YOUR LETTERS : YOUR FALSE LETTERS, AND YOUR PRESENTS: YOUR
BULL I (94) INSTEAD OF ON POST). /BROADBENT/ YOU ANSWER THE LETTERS ? /DOYLE/ NOT VERY PUNCTUALLY. BUT THEY GET
PYGM IV (260) /PICKERING/ WE ARE, SLIGHTLY. ARE THERE ANY LETTERS ? /HIGGINS/ I DIDNT LOOK. (PICKERING TAKES THE
MRS I (196) HEAR THE STORY OF THE DUKE OF WELLINGTON AND HIS LETTERS ? /REV. S./ NO, SIR; AND I DONT WANT TO HEAR IT.
AUGS (264) OH, DAMN YOUR TWO AND SEVEN! DID YOU RECEIVE MY LETTERS ? /THE CLERK/ YES. /AUGUSTUS/ I ADDRESSED A MEETING
VWOO 1 (120) THAT SOUNDS LITERARY. WAS YOUR FATHER A MAN OF LETTERS ? /Z/ YES: I SHOULD THINK HE WAS. A POSTMAN. /A/ A
WIDO II (29) NEWS TO BREAK, POOR OLD BOY: SHE'S SEEN ALL THE LETTERS ALREADY. /COKANE/ I MUST SAY YOUR BEHAVIOR HAS BEEN
VWOO 2 (130) NO I DONT THINK. MAY I EXPLAIN? I AM A MAN OF LETTERS AND A GENTLEMAN. I AM ACCUSTOMED TO ASSOCIATE WITH
MRS PREFACE(164) AS CENSOR, REPLACE HIM TOMORROW BY AN ACADEMY OF LETTERS AND AN ACADEMY OF DRAMATIC POETRY, AND THE NEW
FABL PREFACE(78) THAT MY SPEECHES WERE NEVER REPORTED, AND MY LETTERS AND ARTICLES INSERTED ONLY WHEN I COULD COMBINE WHAT
DEST (178) (SNATCHING IT UP AGAIN) WILL YOU TAKE THE LETTERS AND BEGONE (ADVANCING AND THRUSTING THEM UPON
JITT III (55) AND BRING HIM IN MONEY. WELL, IS THAT HEAP OF OLD LETTERS AND BILLS AND PRESCRIPTIONS ALL THAT CAME OF IT?
DEST (158) INDEED! (WITH SUDDEN MISGIVING) WHERE ARE THE LETTERS AND DESPATCHES? /THE LIEUTENANT/ (IMPORTANTLY,
WIDO III (58) THE TRUTH; SO MR COKANE KINDLY PUTS IT INTO MY LETTERS AND DRAFT PROSPECTUSES AND ADVERTISEMENTS AND THE
WIDO I (17) BLANCHE; AND HE WONT CONSENT UNLESS THEY SEND LETTERS AND INVITATIONS AND CONGRATULATIONS AND THE DEUCE
PRES (139) DO? /MITCHENER/ (THROWING DOWN HIS PEN AND HIS LETTERS AND JUMPING UP TO CONFRONT BALSQUITH) HIS DUTY WAS
CAND I SD(96) OF OFFERING HIM TEN. MORELL COMES BACK WITH A FEW LETTERS AND NEWSPAPERS WHICH HAVE COME BY THE MIDDAY POST.
CAPT III SD(293) FROM WHICH HE EXTRACTS A SCRAPPY PACKET OF DIRTY LETTERS AND NEWSPAPER CUTTINGS. THESE HE THROWS ON THE
BULL I (94) GET ENGAGED TO ANOTHER WOMAN AND RETURN NORA HER LETTERS AND PRESENTS WITH A LETTER TO SAY HE WAS UNWORTHY OF
BUOY PREFACE(6) PROBLEMS. MY READERS KEEP COMPLAINING IN PRIVATE LETTERS AND PUBLIC CRITICISMS THAT I HAVE NOT SOLVED ALL THE
WIDO II (45) THE SHEET OF BROWN PAPER. IT CONTAINS A PACKET OF LETTERS AND SOME JEWELLERY. SHE PLUCKS A RING FROM HER
ARMS III SD(54) THE WINDOW FUMING). LOUKA COMES IN WITH A HEAP OF LETTERS AND TELEGRAMS ON HER SALVER, AND CROSSES, WITH HER
MIS. PREFACE(33) FILL VOTING PAPERS, COMPOSE AND SEND LETTERS AND TELEGRAMS, PURCHASE FOOD AND CLOTHING AND
CAND II (105) PEOPLE-- PEOPLE WHO CAN DO BUSINESS AND WRITE LETTERS AND THAT SORT OF THING-- ALWAYS HAD TO HAVE LOVE
CATH 1,SD(161) AS A COUNSELLOR AND A GOOD FRIEND. HIS LOVE LETTERS ARE AMONG THE BEST ON RECORD. HE HAS A WILD SENSE OF
APPL I (200) LET ME ADD THAT IN THIS PALACE, WHEN THE KING'S LETTERS ARE NOT READY FOR HIM AT 12 O'CLOCK, A SECRETARY
GETT (285) ONE IS. (TO MRS BRIDGENORTH) DONT YOU THINK HER LETTERS ARE QUITE THE BEST LOVE-LETTERS I GET? (TO THE TWO
SUPR IV (151) I'M A MAHN! ! AND WHEN DAD TREATS MY PRIVATE LETTERS AS HIS OWN, AND TAKES IT ON HIMSELF TO SAY THAT I
DEST (174) TO ME, MADAM, THAT YOU HAVE COME TO REGARD MY LETTERS AS YOUR OWN PROPERTY, OF WHICH I AM TRYING TO ROB
APPL PREFACE(187) IN THE LANE WHILST THE POSTMAN DELIVERS THE LETTERS AT THE HOUSE, TAKES THE CHRISTMAS BOXES, AND GETS
BULL I (75) GOES OUT. BROADBENT GETS THROUGH THE REST OF HIS LETTERS BEFORE HODSON RETURNS WITH THE VISITOR). /HODSON/ MR
JOAN 6 (142) I CANNOT WRITE. /CAUCHON/ YOU HAVE SIGNED MANY LETTERS BEFORE. /JOAN/ YES; BUT SOMEONE HELD MY HAND AND
CAND III (138) TEETOTALLER. I DONT LIKE BEER. ARE THERE ANY LETTERS FOR ME TO ANSWER, MR MORELL? /MORELL/ NO MORE
MTH2 (40) THE PARLOR MAID COMES BACK. /THE PARLOR MAID/ ANY LETTERS FOR THE POST, SIR? /FRANKLYN/ THESE. (HE PROFFERS
DEST (178) AND RESOLUTION DESERVE TO SUCCEED. TAKE THE LETTERS FOR WHICH YOU HAVE FOUGHT SO WELL; AND REMEMBER
WIDO II (28) /TRENCH/ (TRIUMPHANTLY) I HAVE ANY AMOUNT OF LETTERS FOR YOU. ALL MY PEOPLE ARE DELIGHTED THAT I AM GOING
MTH2 (53) UNCONTRADICTED REPORTS FALSE? WERE THE PUBLISHED LETTERS FORGERIES? /BURGE/ CERTAINLY NOT. BUT I DID NOT DO
FABL PREFACE(78) I AM MYSELF MUCH IDOLIZED. I RECEIVE ALMOST DAILY LETTERS FROM DEVOUT SHAVIANS WHO BELIEVE THAT MY INCOME IS
SIM II (55) AT NOON TODAY. LOOK. (HE TAKES A BATCH OF LETTERS FROM HIS POCKET AND THROWS THEM ON THE TABLE). /SIR
DEST (174) OLD FOOL! THE OTHER PAPERS ARE ONLY MY PRIVATE LETTERS FROM PARIS, OF WHICH YOU KNOW NOTHING. /LADY/ (
APPL II (267) ON THAT: THERE WILL BE NO RESIGNATIONS. I HAVE LETTERS FROM THE ABSENT MEMBERS OF THE GOVERNMENT: THOSE
CATH 2 (178) MAJESTY WITHOUT THE FULLEST CREDENTIALS. I HAVE LETTERS FROM THE ENGLISH AMBASSADOR, FROM THE PRUSSIAN
WIDO I (16) FOR THE BEST SOCIETY. WHEN YOU CAN SHEW ME A FEW LETTERS FROM THE PRINCIPAL MEMBERS OF YOUR FAMILY,
APPL I (201) SICK AS THEY MAKE ME. /PAMPHILIUS/ DO ORINTHIA'S LETTERS GO TO THE QUEEN? /SEMPRONIUS/ NO, BY GEORGE! EVEN
DOCT IV (170) /SIR PATRICK/ (SHAKING HANDS) REMEMBER: ALL LETTERS HAD BETTER BE LEFT TO YOUR SOLICITOR. LET HIM OPEN
MRS I (196) (PITEOUSLY) FRANK, MY BOY! WHEN I WROTE THOSE LETTERS I PUT MYSELF INTO THAT WOMAN'S POWER. WHEN I TOLD
DOCT I (84) THE PAPERS? YOULL HAVE TO ALTER THE NAME IN THE LETTERS IF YOU HAVNT. /REDPENNY/ EMMY HAS JUST TOLD ME. I'M
DEST (194) AND HURRIES OUT). /NAPOLEON/ (THROWING DOWN THE LETTERS IN A HEAP ON THE TABLE) NOW! (HE SITS DOWN AT THE
ROCK I SD(193) FROM HER OFFICE, WITH HER NOTEBOOK AND A SHEAF OF LETTERS IN HER HAND. HER AGE IS UNKNOWN; BUT SHE IS MADE UP
CAND II SD(105) THE NOTEBOOK IN WHICH SHE TAKES DOWN MORELL'S LETTERS IN SHORTHAND FROM HIS DICTATION, SITS DOWN AT THE
LION PREFACE(100) THEIR LETTERS, WHICH WERE EXACTLY LIKE MEDIEVAL LETTERS IN THEIR LITERAL FAITH AND EVER-PRESENT PIETY, I
DOCT PREFACE(79) PLATE TO HAVE INSCRIBED ON IT, IN ADDITION TO THE LETTERS INDICATING HIS QUALIFICATIONS, THE WORDS " REMEMBER
UNPL PREFACE(R24) WAY OF WRITING THEM DOWN. EVEN THE USE OF SPACED LETTERS INSTEAD OF ITALICS FOR UNDERLINING, THOUGH FAMILIAR
PHIL II (102) BASKET. (HE GOES TO THE FIRE, AND THROWS THE LETTERS INTO IT). /CUTHBERTSON/ (FACING HIM WITH FOLDED
FABL II SD(105) IN LONDON. THE COMMANDER-IN-CHIEF AT WORK READING LETTERS . A SECRETARY OPENING THEM. THE TELEPHONE RINGS. THE
MIS. (146) THAT. NOT A WORD ABOUT HIMSELF. FORCED. SHY. DUTY LETTERS . ALL FIT TO BE PUBLISHED: THAT SAYS EVERYTHING. I
2TRU I (41) THESE SAFES THAT OPEN BY A SECRET ARRANGEMENT OF LETTERS . AS THEY ARE AS TROUBLESOME AS AN AUTOMATIC
JITT III (52) WHEN I CLEARED UP HIS PAPERS AND TORE UP USELESS LETTERS . BUT IF YOU DONT TEAR THEM WHAT IS THERE TO PREVENT
JITT III SD(52) SHARP SOUNDS MADE BY HER VIOLENT TEARING OF THE LETTERS . FESSLER, WHO IS SORTING SOME PAPERS WHICH HE HAS
PRES (141) SIR. FULL OF PAPERS WITH VOTES FOR WOMEN IN RED LETTERS . FIRED INTO THE YARD FROM THE ROOF OF THE ALLIANCE
CAND I SD(79) WHILST MORELL OPENS THE LAST OF HIS MORNING'S LETTERS . HE REALIZES ITS CONTENTS WITH A COMIC GROAN OF
DEST (163) OFFICER ON GENERAL MASSENA'S STAFF WANTS WITH MY LETTERS . I HAVE SOME QUESTIONS TO PUT TO YOU. /GIUSEPPE/ (
CLEO NOTES (209) LONG ENOUGH TO ATTAIN COMPLETE SELF-EXPRESSION IN LETTERS . IT IS NOT TRUE EVEN ON THESE CONDITIONS IN AN AGE
DEST (179) I AM NOT IN THE HABIT OF READING OTHER PEOPLE'S LETTERS . (HE AGAIN OFFERS THE PACKET). /LADY/ IN THAT CASE
APPL I (201) NO, BY GEORGE! EVEN I DONT READ ORINTHIA'S LETTERS . MY INSTRUCTIONS ARE TO READ EVERYTHING; BUT I TAKE
PRES SD(131) AT HIS WRITING-TABLE IN THE WAR OFFICE, OPENING LETTERS . ON HIS LEFT IS THE FIREPLACE, WITH A FIRE BURNING.
PHIL I (79) /JULIA/ (RISING) I WAS JUSTIFIED IN READING YOUR LETTERS . OUR PERFECT CONFIDENCE IN ONE ANOTHER GAVE ME THE
APPL I SD(197) HE SITS AT ONE OF THE TABLES OPENING THE KING'S LETTERS . PAMPHILIUS, MIDDLE AGED, SHEWS HIS LEFT AS HE
DEST (177) IN HER CHEEKS) OH, YOU ARE TOO BAD. KEEP YOUR LETTERS . READ THE STORY OF YOUR OWN DISHONOR IN THEM; AND
CAPT III (295) UNEASILY) I CANT ASK YOU TO DESTROY YOUR MOTHER'S LETTERS . /BRASSBOUND/ WHY NOT, NOW THAT YOU HAVE TAKEN THE
JOAN 2 (74) BOILING INTO MY HEAD: I CANT DISTINGUISH THE LETTERS . /CHARLES/ (COMING BACK AND PEERING ROUND LA
DEST (177) YOU SHE CAT, FOR HAVING HAD TO GIVE ME THE LETTERS . /LADY/ NONSENSE! OR DO YOU MEAN THAT YOU ARE THAT
DEST (179) ESCAPING ROUND THE TABLE) NO! I DONT WANT YOUR LETTERS . /NAPOLEON/ TEN MINUTES AGO, NOTHING ELSE WOULD
BARB III SD(322) SMALLER WRITING TABLE AND BUSIES HIMSELF WITH HIS LETTERS . /SARAH/ GO AND GET READY, MAMMA: THE CARRIAGE IS
MTH2 (40) SIR? /FRANKLYN/ THESE. (HE PROFFERS A BASKET OF LETTERS . SHE COMES TO THE TABLE AND TAKES THEM). /HASLAM/ (
DOCT I (83) MIND YOU DONT GO DR RIDGEONING HIM IN THEM LETTERS . SIR COLENSO RIDGEON IS TO BE HIS NAME NOW.
WIDO II SD(24) IS BUSY AT A WRITING TABLE LITTERED WITH BUSINESS LETTERS . THE FIREPLACE, DECORATED FOR SUMMER, IS CLOSE
CAPT NOTES (300) CURIOUS ALPHABET IN WHICH HE WRITES HIS PRIVATE LETTERS . THE MAN IS ON PUBLIC RECORD TOO. THE BATTLE OF
SUPR I SD(3) RAMSDEN IS IN HIS STUDY, OPENING THE MORNING'S LETTERS . THE STUDY, HANDSOMELY AND SOLIDLY FURNISHED,
GETT (285) LADY WHO CANT SPELL. I LIKE THAT WOMAN'S LETTERS . THERES AN INTENSITY OF PASSION IN THEM THAT
CAND II (105) I SUPPOSE A MACHINE COULD BE MADE TO WRITE LOVE LETTERS . THEYRE ALL THE SAME, ARNT THEY? /PROSERPINE/ (
BARB PREFACE(208) FAMILIAR TO ALL WHO ARE PROPERLY SATURATED WITH LETTERS . WHERE, THEN, WAS THE NOVELTY IN LEVER'S TALE?
WIDO II (36) YOU MET ME IN THE HALL, AND SHEWED ME ALL THE LETTERS . YOUR FAMILY DOESNT OBJECT. DO YOU OBJECT?
PHIL II (101) FATHERS: THIS IS A SERIOUS AFFAIR. LOOK AT THESE LETTERS (PRODUCING A LETTER AND A LETTER-CARD)! THIS (
BASH PREFACE(89) THE ADMIRABLE BASHVILLE WAS PERFORMED, MEN OF LETTERS LIKE MAURICE HEWLETT WOULD CHUCKLE DELIGHTEDLY OVER
MTH2 (40) GET A SECOND CHANCE. EXCUSE ME, SIR; BUT THE LETTERS MUST GO TO CATCH THE POST. (SHE GOES OUT WITH THE
CAPT III (295) LEFT? SEE HERE! (HE TAKES UP THE LETTERS) THE LETTERS MY UNCLE WROTE TO MY MOTHER, WITH HER COMMENTS ON
LADY PREFACE(209) A DAILY READER. HE WAS BY PROFESSION A MAN OF LETTERS OF AN UNCOMMERCIAL KIND. HE WAS A SPECIALIST IN
BARB II (304) TO STOP HIM FROM WRITING BODGER'S WHISKY IN LETTERS OF FIRE AGAINST THE SKY; SO THAT THE POOR
MIS. PREFACE(61) MOUNT; BUT NO ONE HAS YET SEEN THEM WRITTEN UP IN LETTERS OF GOLD IN A SCHOOLROOM OR NURSERY. THE CHILD IS

JOAN 4 (105)	THAT RISK. BUT HAVE YOU NOTICED THAT IN THESE	LETTERS	OF HERS, SHE PROPOSES TO ALL THE KINGS OF EUROPE, AS
BULL PREFACE(22)	REALLY INTIMATE MEMOIRS OF HIM OR REALLY PRIVATE	LETTERS	OF HIS UNTIL HIS WHOLE GENERATION HAS PASSED AWAY,
PHIL I (78)	OF POSITIVELY BEATING ME; OF STEALING	LETTERS	OF MINE-- /JULIA/ YES, NICE LETTERS! /CHARTERIS/--
AUGS (278)	WITH YOUR NAME ON IT. FORTUNATELY I HAVE SOME	LETTERS	OF MY OWN HERE (OPENING HER WALLET). WHY NOT HIDE
DEST (178)	/NAPOLEON/ WHERE? /LADY/ (POINTING TO THE	LETTERS	ON THE TABLE) THERE. YOU HAVE ONLY TO READ IT. HE
SIM II (55)	ON THE TABLE). /SIR CHARLES/ (POINTING TO THE	LETTERS	ON THE TABLE) LOOK AT THESE! /PRA/ ALL ABOUT IDDY.
MIS. PREFACE(51)	AND SCOLDING, THERE WILL NOT BE A SINGLE MAN OF	LETTERS	OR HIGHER MATHEMATICIAN THE MORE IN THE COUNTRY: ON
GETT (346)	BROTHER OUT IF HE DISTURBS YOU. SOAMES: BRING THE	LETTERS	OUT HERE. /SYKES/ HE WONT BE OFFENDED AT MY OFFERING
GETT PREFACE(236)	WILL BE NO MORE REPORTS OF DIVORCE CASES, NO MORE	LETTERS	READ IN COURT WITH AN INDELICACY THAT MAKES EVERY
DOCT I (83)	DR RIDGEON WILL BE DOWN BEFORE I HAVE THESE	LETTERS	READY. GET OUT. /EMMY/ DR RIDGEON WONT NEVER BE DOWN
CAND I (96)	/MORELL/ (AT THE TABLE, GLANCING THROUGH THE	LETTERS	) NEVER MIND HER, MARCHBANKS. THE OVERPAYING
CAPT III (295)	WHAT HAVE I LEFT? SEE HERE! (HE TAKES UP THE	LETTERS	) THE LETTERS MY UNCLE WROTE TO MY MOTHER, WITH HER
PRES (138)	(HE SITS DOWN AT HIS TABLE AND TAKES UP HIS	LETTERS	). /BALSQUITH/ (NEAR THE DOOR) I'M SORRY YOU TAKE
ARMS III (54)	CIVIL TO AN ENEMY, EVEN IF SHE MUST BRING HIM HIS	LETTERS	). /BLUNTSCHLI/ (TO RAINA) WILL YOU EXCUSE ME: THE
ROCK I (195)	(SHE SITS DOWN AND BUSIES HERSELF WITH	LETTERS	). /SIR ARTHUR/ POOR DEVILS! I HATE THAT PART OF
INCA (238)	I HAVE ONE FROM AN ARCHDEACON. (SHE PROFFERS THE	LETTERS	). /THE PRINCESS/ (TAKING THEM) DO ARCHDEACONS HAVE
MTH2 (40)	GO TO CATCH THE POST. (SHE GOES OUT WITH THE	LETTERS	). THE TWO BROTHERS LOOK INQUIRINGLY AT HASLAM.
INCA (238)	HAS TO BE, YOUR HIGHNESS. (SHE PRODUCES SOME	LETTERS	). YOUR HIGHNESS WISHES TO SEE MY TESTIMONIALS. NO
UNPL PREFACE(R13)	AND CRITICISMS, BUT IN LEADING ARTICLES AND	LETTERS	; AND FINALLY THE TEXT OF THE PLAY WAS PUBLISHED
CURE SD(230)	HER; TAKES A LETTER FROM WHEREVER SHE CARRIES	LETTERS	; AND STARTS ON A VOYAGE OF DISCOVERY ROUND THE
PHIL I (79)	OF MY WASTE PAPER BASKET IN YOUR SEARCH FOR MORE	LETTERS	; AND THEN REPRESENTING YOURSELF AS AN ILL USED
DEST (191)	THATS BETTER. /LADY/ YOU DIDNT WANT TO READ THE	LETTERS	; BUT YOU WERE CURIOUS ABOUT WHAT WAS IN THEM. SO
CAPT III (295)	THEIR TREACHERY AND CRUELTY. AND THE PITEOUS	LETTERS	SHE WROTE TO HIM LATER ON, RETURNED UNOPENED. MUST
MRS I (197)	COURSE YOU DO. WHY, I HAVE A WHOLE ALBUM OF YOUR	LETTERS	STILL: I CAME ACROSS THEM ONLY THE OTHER DAY. /REV.
BARB III (330)	BRITOMART/ YES, WITH MORRIS'S WORDS IN MOSAIC	LETTERS	TEN FEET HIGH ROUND THE DOME. NO MAN IS GOOD ENOUGH
DEST (193)	STYLE) IT'S PLAIN ENOUGH. YOU WANTED SOME	LETTERS	THAT BELONGED TO ME. YOU HAVE SPENT THE MORNING IN
GENV II (52)	(FLATTERED) REALLY? HOW? /THE SECRETARY/ THOSE	LETTERS	THAT YOU SENT TO THE COURT OF INTERNATIONAL JUSTICE
MILL II SD(166)	UNDERNEATH THE SOW IS INSCRIBED IN TALL	LETTERS	THE PIG AND WHISTLE. BETWEEN THESE WORKS OF ART IS A
SUPR PREFACE(R38)	HIS PERSPECTIVE INTO THE BARGAIN. YOUR MAN OF	LETTERS	THINKS HE CAN GET BUNYAN'S OR SHAKESPEAR'S STYLE
ROCK I (222)	AND I GOT A LOT OUT OF HIM. WHAT ABOUT THE	LETTERS	THIS MORNING? /HILDA/ I HAVE DEALT WITH THEM: YOU
JITT III (53)	DROOP) I HAVE GONE THROUGH THIS LAST BATCH OF	LETTERS	THREE TIMES OVER IN THE HOPE OF FINDING SOME CLUE.
MILL I (139)	HER REAL NAME IS PATRICIA SMITH. BUT HER	LETTERS	TO ALASTAIR ARE SIGNED POLLY SEEDYSTOCKINGS, AS A
APPL PREFACE(187)	WITH A RED BICYCLE, AND EVEN GIVEN A BATCH OF	LETTERS	TO DELIVER, AS HIS MOTIVE IN SEEKING THE POST HAS
ROCK I (202)	WITH THE NOTES: WE REALLY MUST . I HAVE ALL THE	LETTERS	TO DO YET. DO TRY TO PICK UP THE THREAD. THE FAMILY
MIS. (146)	READ HIS LETTERS TO HIS FAMILY. READ ANY MAN'S	LETTERS	TO HIS CHILDREN. THEYRE NOT HUMAN. THEYRE NOT ABOUT
MIS. (146)	/TARLETON/ I DONT MEAN HIS BOOKS. READ HIS	LETTERS	TO HIS FAMILY. READ ANY MAN'S LETTERS TO HIS
JOAN PREFACE(23)	OF ANY WORLD BUT THE TRIBAL WORLD, WROTE	LETTERS	TO KINGS CALLING ON THEM TO MAKE MILLENNIAL
FABL PREFACE(95)	TEN TIMES THAT MUCH COULD BE SAVED BY ADDING 15	LETTERS	TO THE ALPHABET. IT TOOK A WORLD WAR TO ESTABLISH
JOAN 4 (102)	OF RHEIMS: SHE, NOT THE CHURCH! SHE SENDS	LETTERS	TO THE KING OF ENGLAND GIVING HIM GOD'S COMMAND
DOCT PREFACE(31)	PATIENTS TO THEIR DOORS BY PROFESSING IN	LETTERS	TO THE NEWSPAPERS TO HAVE LEARNT FROM VIVISECTION
MILL PREFACE(121)	PREFERRING THEM TO LIPARI, AND WROTE ELOQUENT	LETTERS	TO THE PAPERS DEMANDING WHETHER EVERY VESTIGE OF
JOAN 4 (103)	IN GOD'S NAME TO THE KINGS OF THE EARTH. HER	LETTERS	TO THEM ARE GOING FORTH DAILY. IT IS NOT THE MOTHER
ROCK II (244)	A MAN CANNOT HAVE AN ADDRESS IN LONDON FOR HIS	LETTERS	UNTIL HE HAS AGREED TO PAY THEM FROM FIVE HUNDRED TO
BULL I SD(74)	COMES TO THE WRITING TABLE AND LOOKS THROUGH THE	LETTERS	WAITING THERE FOR HIM. HE IS A ROBUST, FULL-BLOODED,
JOAN 4 (102)	EXECUTE. LET ME TELL YOU THAT THE WRITING OF SUCH	LETTERS	WAS THE PRACTICE OF THE ACCURSED MAHOMET, THE
GETT (340)	/MRS GEORGE/ I DIDNT MEAN TO MAKE YOU THINK THE	LETTERS	WERE FROM A FINE LADY. I WROTE ON CHEAP PAPER; AND I
CLEO III (157)	TILL YOU HEAR, CAESAR. THIS BAG CONTAINS ALL THE	LETTERS	WHICH HAVE PASSED BETWEEN POMPEY'S PARTY AND THE
GETT (326)	SHALL WE TRY TO GET THROUGH THE LAST BATCH OF	LETTERS	WHILST THEY ARE AWAY, SOAMES? /SOAMES/ YES,
POSN PREFACE(369)	THE COMMONS, WERE MR ALFRED MASON, A MAN OF	LETTERS	WHO HAD WON A SEAT IN PARLIAMENT AS OFFHANDEDLY AS
LADY PREFACE(213)	THE VALUE OF HUMOR. HE WAS ONE OF THE FEW MEN OF	LETTERS	WHO REALLY APPRECIATED OSCAR WILDE, THOUGH HE DID
BULL I SD(74)	IN HIS MOST EARNEST MOMENTS. HE BURSTS OPEN HIS	LETTERS	WITH HIS THUMB, AND GLANCES THROUGH THEM, FLINGING
DOCT I (84)	NOT HINDERING YOU WORKING-- IF YOU CALL WRITING	LETTERS	WORKING. THERE GOES THE BELL. (SHE LOOKS OUT OF THE
LION PREFACE(25)	MY READERS MAY NOT HAVE STUDIED ROUSSEAU'S	LETTERS	WRITTEN FROM THE MOUNTAIN, WHICH MAY BE REGARDED AS
APPL I (201)	SHOULD NEVER HEAR THE END OF IT. HE HAD SIX LOVE	LETTERS	YESTERDAY; AND ALL HE SAID WHEN I TOLD HIM WAS "
PHIL II (102)	TAKE MY PLACE IN YOUR HEART. I SEND SOME OF THE	LETTERS	YOU WROTE ME WHEN WE FIRST MET; AND I ASK YOU TO
MRS I (196)	THAT YOU ONCE OFFERED A WOMAN 50 POUNDS FOR THE	LETTERS	YOU WROTE TO HER WHEN-- /REV. S./ (TERRIFIED)
DOCT I SD(81)	ROOM. HE DEVILS FOR THE DOCTOR BY ANSWERING HIS	LETTERS	, ACTING AS HIS DOMESTIC LABORATORY ASSISTANT, AND
LION I (111)	FOR COOKING, REPAIRS TO UNIFORMS, WRITING	LETTERS	, AND ADVICE IN THEIR PRIVATE AFFAIRS. IN A ROMAN
WIDO II (27)	ONLY JUST COME IN. (HE TAKES OUT A PACKET OF	LETTERS	, AND BEGINS UNTYING THEM). /COKANE/ (GOING TO A
NEVR I (211)	LIFE: A LIFE IN WHICH HUSBANDS OPEN THEIR WIVES'	LETTERS	, AND CALL ON THEM TO ACCOUNT FOR EVERY FARTHING OF
LADY PREFACE(215)	MEANS WITHOUT GENUINE LITERARY ABILITY, A LOVE OF	LETTERS	, AND EVEN SOME ARTISTIC CONSCIENCE. BUT HE WILL
JITT III SD(52)	OF HER LATE HUSBAND. SHE IS FEVERISHLY READING	LETTERS	, AND TEARING THEM UP AND THROWING THEM INTO THE
WIDO II (37)	TO DO? /BLANCHE/ TO GET YOUR LETTERS: YOUR FALSE	LETTERS	, AND YOUR PRESENTS: YOUR HATEFUL PRESENTS, TO
POSN PREFACE(400)	OR A CABINET MINISTER, OR AN EMINENT MAN OF	LETTERS	, EARNING HIS LIVING BY READING THROUGH THE MASS OF
LION PREFACE(39)	THE JEWS SAY OF HIM " HOW KNOWETH THIS MAN	LETTERS	, HAVING NEVER LEARNT? " JOHN THE IMMORTAL
MILL I (147)	/EPIFANIA/ THAT IS NOT HOW YOU SIGN YOUR	LETTERS	, I THINK. /ALASTAIR/ LOOK HERE, EPPY. DONT BEGIN
CAND I SD(78)	LARGE TABLE IS LITTERED WITH PAMPHLETS, JOURNALS,	LETTERS	, NESTS OF DRAWERS, AN OFFICE DIARY, POSTAGE SCALES
ROCK I (229)	AND PERFECTLY SANITARY. NO NEWSPAPERS, NO	LETTERS	, NO IDLE LADIES. NO BOOKS EXCEPT IN THE AFTERNOON
JOAN PREFACE(10)	WHO CANNOT READ OR WRITE. IF SHE COULD NOT WRITE	LETTERS	, SHE COULD AND DID DICTATE THEM AND ATTACH FULL AND
GETT (339)	INCOGNITA APPASSIONATA! /MRS GEORGE/ YOU READ MY	LETTERS	, THEN? (WITH A SIGH OF GRATEFUL RELIEF, SHE SITS
UNPL PREFACE(R24)	COULD CONVEY, SIMPLY BECAUSE THE ART OF	LETTERS	, THOUGH HIGHLY DEVELOPED GRAMMATICALLY, IS STILL IN
LION PREFACE(100)	HAD OVER THE BAGANDA TRIBES, AND READ ME THEIR	LETTERS	, WHICH WERE EXACTLY LIKE MEDIEVAL LETTERS IN THEIR
PHIL I (79)	OF STEALING LETTERS OF MINE-- /JULIA/ YES, NICE	LETTERS	! /CHARTERIS/-- OF BREAKING YOUR SOLEMN PROMISES

LETTIN

CAND I (94)	DO YOU FIND YORESELF THIS WEATHER? OPE YOU AINT	LETTIN	JAMES PUT NO FOOLISH IDEAS INTO YOUR ED?
SUPR IV (143)	HERE: WHAT DO YOU MEAN BY GITTIN INTO MY CAR AND	LETTIN	ME BRING YOU HERE IF YOURE NOT THE PERSON I TOOK THAT
WIDO III (52)	A FRIEND TO PUT MONEY IN YOUR POCKET. NO USE YOUR	LETTIN	ON TO ME THAT YOURE ABOVE MONEY. EH? /SARTORIUS/ (

LETTING

ARMS I SD(10)	AND A TORRENT OF BLOWS ON THE DOOR, END WITH HIS	LETTING	A CHAIN DOWN WITH A CLANK, FOLLOWED BY A RUSH OF
ROCK PREFACE(187)	YOUR WITS TO WORK, AND FIND ME A SOUND REASON FOR	LETTING	A SEDITIOUS BLASPHEMER GO FREE. /JESUS/ I DO NOT ASK
MTH3 (125)	AND A HALF OF FULLY ADULT EXPERIENCE. WE ARE	LETTING	ALL THE POWER SLIP INTO THE HANDS OF THE COLORED
BULL III (129)	YOU? /LARRY/ CERTAINLY I HAVE. I DONT BELIEVE IN	LETTING	ANYBODY OR ANYTHING ALONE. /CORNELIUS/ (LOSING HIS
WIDO II (31)	FOOT OF SPACE, SIR, THAT YOU CAN GET HIGHER RENTS	LETTING	BY THE ROOM THAN YOU CAN FOR A MANSION IN PARK LANE.
JOAN PREFACE(38)	POPES HAVE BEEN CANONIZED, OR COULD BE WITHOUT	LETTING	DOWN THE STANDARD OF SANCTITY SET BY THE
ARMS II (35)	FIGURE OF MINE SAY IF THEY CAUGHT US HERE? (	LETTING	GO HER HAND AND SLIPPING HIS ARM DEXTEROUSLY ROUND
NEVR IV (284)	AS YOU PLEASE, MY DEAR. /GLORIA/ (NOT SATISFIED,	LETTING	GO HIS HANDS AND DRAWING BACK FROM HIM) YOU DONT
LION PREFACE(51)	MONEY PAYMENTS. IF YOU LET A CHILD STARVE YOU ARE	LETTING	GOD STARVE. GET RID OF ALL ANXIETY ABOUT TOMORROW'S
SIM PRO,1, (21)	QUOTA WITHOUT ANY EXCUSE FOR IT. /WILKS/ WHO'S	LETTING	HER BOTHER YOU AGAIN? SHE TOLD THE HIGH
BULL IV (163)	(SUDDENLY BECOMING PRODIGIOUSLY SOLEMN AND	LETTING	HER GO) NO, OF COURSE NOT. I DONT MEAN IT. AT LEAST
ARMS II (35)	TO BE SPYING ABOUT AFTER YOU. /SERGIUS/ (STUNG:	LETTING	HER GO) TAKE CARE, LOUKA. I MAY BE WORTHLESS ENOUGH
MILL IV (207)	WORTH THREE HUNDRED A YEAR TO HER, THEY CALLED IT	LETTING	HER IN ON THE GROUND FLOOR. MAY HER PRAYERS WIN THEM
BULL PREFACE(9)	WITH SELF-SATISFIED SUPERIORITY. TODAY ENGLAND IS	LETTING	HERSELF BE DRAGGED INTO THE PATH OF SPAIN. SHE
JITT III (53)	DOOR BEHIND HIM). /AGNES/ (ALONE WITH FESSLER,	LETTING	HERSELF DROOP) I HAVE GONE THROUGH THIS LAST BATCH
APPL I (237)	CORPORATION IN THE COUNTRY. /LYSISTRATA/ (	LETTING	HERSELF GO) JUST SO! BREAKAGES, LIMITED! JUST SO!
JITT II (45)	ALL ABOUT IT. /JITTA/ (RISING INDIGNANTLY AND	LETTING	HERSELF GO) YOU ARE MAD, AND GROSSLY RUDE.
APPL PREFACE(195)	HE WAS QUITE RIGHT: WHAT WE HAVE LOST BY NOT	LETTING	HIM DO IT IS INCALCULABLE. SIMILARLY, GATTIE WAS NOT
FANY I (281)	WE DONE WHAT WE COULD FOR THE BOY. SHORT OF	LETTING	HIM GO INTO TEMPTATIONS OF ALL SORTS, HE CAN DO WHAT
ARMS I (22)	DARLING IS WORN OUT. LET HIM SLEEP. /CATHERINE/ (	LETTING	HIM GO, AND TURNING AMAZED TO RAINA) THE POOR
APPL I (201)	FOR THEM. HE'LL TURN BOANERGES INSIDE OUT AFTER	LETTING	HIM ROAR THE PALACE DOWN. BOANERGES ENTERS, DRESSED
JITT I (18)	TO HELP HIM. /JITTA/ YOU CAN HELP HIM WITHOUT	LETTING	HIM ROB YOU OF YOUR IDEAS. /BRUNO/ IT IS NOT HE WHO
MRS I (183)	ME. (HE LAYS HANDS ON THE CHAIR). /VIVIE/ (	LETTING	HIM TAKE IT) TAKE CARE OF YOUR FINGERS: THEYRE
MIS. (176)	HIM SO? /MRS TARLETON/ I DO WONDER AT YOU, JOHN,	LETTING	HIM TALK LIKE THIS BEFORE EVERYBODY. (TURNING
DOCT III (135)	MEAN THAT YOU REFUSE? /RIDGEON/ DO I MEAN--! (	LETTING	HIS INDIGNATION LOOSE) OF COURSE I REFUSE, MAN. WHAT
MTH1 II (24)	HER. WHAT HAVE YOU MADE OF YOURSELVES? /CAIN/ (	LETTING	HIS SPEAR FALL INTO THE CROOK OF HIS SHIELD ARM, AND
JITT I SD(9)	LIKE A HOTEL MANAGERESS, SHE OPENS THE DOOR,	LETTING	IN SOME ELECTRIC LIGHT FROM THE HALL. SHE HAS A

DEVL I SD(5)	LOG ON. MRS DUDGEON UNBARS THE DOOR AND OPENS IT,	LETTING	INTO THE STUFFY KITCHEN A LITTLE OF THE FRESHNESS
MILL I (162)	RICH AS I AM, I CAN HARDLY FORGIVE ALASTAIR FOR	LETTING	ME DOWN BY FOUR HUNDRED AND THIRTY POUNDS.
ROCK I (222)	TALK TO EVERYBODY FOR HALF AN HOUR INSTEAD OF	LETTING	ME GET RID OF THEM FOR YOU IN TWO MINUTES. WHAT CAN
MTH3 (110)	/THE ARCHBISHOP/ THEY MADE DIFFICULTIES ABOUT	LETTING	ME GO EVEN THEN. I STILL LOOKED SO YOUNG. FOR SOME
MRS II (203)	WELL, YOU SHOULDNT GO OFF LIKE THAT WITHOUT	LETTING	ME KNOW. HOW COULD I TELL WHAT HAD BECOME OF YOU?
DOCT IV (160)	THAT? I SAY! I AM IN LUCK TODAY. WOULD YOU MIND	LETTING	ME PHOTOGRAPH YOU? (HE PRODUCES A CAMERA). COULD
ROCK PREFACE(152)	A FEW GAMEKEEPERS. BUT I MAY DO MUCH BETTER BY	LETTING	MY LAND TO INDUSTRIALISTS FOR THE ERECTION OF
OVER (173)	WOMAN UNTIL I THOUGHT I HAD LOST THE POWER OF	LETTING	MYSELF FALL REALLY AND WHOLEHEARTEDLY IN LOVE. /MRS
ANNA (291)	AND EXPANDS HIS CHEST). I FEEL THE BETTER FOR	LETTING	MYSELF GO. TO BUSINESS. (HE TAKES UP A TELEGRAM;
PYGM II (229)	TO HAVE MY HEAD CUT OFF. IF I'D KNOWN WHAT I WAS	LETTING	MYSELF IN FOR, I WOULDNT HAVE COME HERE. I ALWAYS
GETT (293)	TO EDITH I WAS IN UTTER IGNORANCE OF WHAT I WAS	LETTING	MYSELF IN FOR LEGALLY. HAVING GIVEN MY WORD, I WILL
FANY I (274)	A NICE LETTER. HE AS GOOD AS TELLS YOU HE'S ONLY	LETTING	ON TO BE OFFENDED FOR BOBBY'S GOOD. /GILBEY/ OH,
MTH5 (230)	BETTER THAN OUR IDIOTS: WE SHOULD NEVER DREAM OF	LETTING	ONE OF THEM SURVIVE THE DAY OF ITS BIRTH. WHY, THE
O'FL (212)	THE LYING, AND PRETENDING, AND HUMBUGGING, AND	LETTING	ON, WHEN THE DAY COMES TO YOU THAT YOUR COMRADE IS
JOAN PREFACE(37)	ACCEPT THE TENSION, AND MAINTAIN IT NOBLY WITHOUT	LETTING	OURSELVES BE TEMPTED TO RELIEVE IT BY BURNING THE
FANY III (303)	ABOUT THAT. DONT FORGET THE ROW YOU GOT INTO FOR	LETTING	OUT THAT YOU ADMIRED JUGGINS (SHE TURNS HER BACK ON
MIS. (173)	I MUST IF YOU DONT LET THE PISTOL GO. /THE MAN/ (	LETTING	TARLETON TAKE IT FROM HIM) ALL RIGHT: I'M DONE.
HART III (136)	HABIT OF THROWING STONES IN ALL DIRECTIONS AND	LETTING	THE AIR IN IS NOT ONLY UNBEARABLY RUDE, BUT
METH PREFACE(R38)	CONSCIOUSNESS, YET TO ADMIT IT SEEMED TO INVOLVE	LETTING	THE BOGEY COME BACK, SO INEXTRICABLY HAD WE MANAGED
CAND III (127)	TO HEAR WHAT HAPPENS TO THE ANGEL. /MARCHBANKS/ (	LETTING	THE MANUSCRIPT DROP FROM HIS HAND TO THE FLOOR) I
MIS. (164)	THESE WILD IMPULSES. /HYPATIA/ TAKE CARE. YOURE	LETTING	THE MOMENT SLIP. I FEEL THE FIRST CHILL OF THE WAVE
FABL I (103)	AND IN WORKING ORDER. /YOUNG MAN/ (THOUGHTFULLY,	LETTING	THE NEWSPAPER DROP ON HIS KNEES) THAT IS AN IDEA.
GETT PREFACE(206)	BUT DEMOCRACY AS TO THE WAY TO DO IT IS LIKE	LETTING	THE PASSENGERS DRIVE THE TRAIN: IT CAN ONLY END IN
2TRU I SD(37)	AND ONE OF THE PILLOWS RUDELY FROM THE BED,	LETTING	THE PATIENT DOWN WITH A JERK, AND ARRANGES THEM
ROCK I (197)	(RISING) YOU WILL DO WHAT I ASK YOU AS TO	LETTING	THE SPEAKING GO ON, WONT YOU? /SIR ARTHUR/ WELL,
ROCK I (205)	/LADY CHAVENDER/ IT SERVES US RIGHT, DEAR, FOR	LETTING	THEM BRING THEMSELVES UP IN THE POST-WAR FASHION
CAND I (87)	YOUR TENDER: I SHAMED THE RATEPAYERS OUT OF	LETTING	THEM DO IT; I SHAMED EVERYBODY BUT YOU. (BOILING
JOAN 4 (99)	BURST INTO FLAMES AND CRUMBLED UNDER THEM,	LETTING	THEM DOWN INTO THE RIVER, WHERE THEY WERE DROWNED IN
MIS. PREFACE(30)	HAPPINESS OF THEIR WHOLE LIVES DEPENDS WITHOUT	LETTING	THEM KNOW WHAT THEY ARE UNDERTAKING. ALLEGED
DOCT PREFACE(45)	ON A HARE WOULD BE HORRIFIED AT THE THOUGHT OF	LETTING	THEM LOOSE ON A HUMAN CHILD. THE LADY WHO GETS HER
BULL IV (168)	AND INTROJOOCING ME TO THE LOWEST OF THE LOW, AND	LETTING	THEM SHAKE HANS WITH ME, AND ENCOURAGING THEM TO
BULL PREFACE(12)	AFFAIRS WHEN ONCE SHE REALIZES THAT THE DAY FOR	LETTING	THEM SLIDE AND MUDDLING THROUGH IS PAST. LONDON,
MTH2 (64)	THE PEOPLE, MORE FOREIGN TO THEM, MORE JEALOUS OF	LETTING	THEM UP TO YOUR LEVEL, THAN ANY DUKE OR ANY
GETT (307)	YOUNG PEOPLE TIED UP BEFORE THEY KNOW WHAT THEYRE	LETTING	THEMSELVES IN FOR. THERES MISS LESBIA NOW. SHE
SIM PRO,1, (21)	BACK NOR PROVE IT UNTIL YOU EXPLAIN WHY YOU ARE	LETTING	THIS GIRL BOTHER ME AGAIN, THOUGH SHE HAS NO PAPERS.
FOUN (212)	OUT. /THE LORD CHANCELLOR/ WHAT DO YOU MEAN BY	LETTING	THIS LUNATIC IN, MR MERCER? I'M EXTREMELY ANNOYED.
NEVR II (256)	/VALENTINE/ YES, HELPLESS. AS IF NATURE, AFTER	LETTING	US BELONG TO OURSELVES AND DO WHAT WE JUDGED RIGHT
MIS. (111)	A PERSON WHEN HIS LIVELIHOOD DEPENDS ON HIS NOT	LETTING	YOU CONVERT HIM. AND WOULD YOU MIND NOT CALLING ME
DEST (171)	THAT I MAY SHEW MY CONFIDENCE IN YOU IN RETURN BY	LETTING	YOU GIVE ME THE SLIP WITH THE DESPATCHES, EH? AH,
ROCK I (223)	TO HAVE THAT INSPECTOR SEVERELY REPRIMANDED FOR	LETTING	YOU GO. THREE MONTHS WOULD HAVE DONE YOU A LOT OF
LION II (133)	HIS ARMOR THEY WILL SHEW THEIR DISPLEASURE BY NOT	LETTING	YOU KILL HIM. AND WHEN YOUR TURN COMES, THEY WILL
BARB I (254)	WHY WE SEPARATED. /STEPHEN/ HE MARRIED WITHOUT	LETTING	YOU KNOW THIS! /LADY BRITOMART/ (RATHER TAKEN
OVER (176)	/GREGORY/ I THOUGHT IT THE MOST DELICATE WAY OF	LETTING	YOU KNOW. / MRS JUNO/ WELL, YOU ARE A DAISY, I MUST
GETT PREFACE(257)	CONSEQUENCES OF THESE ACTS OF JUSTICE INSTEAD OF	LETTING	YOURSELF BE FRIGHTENED OUT OF REASON AND GOOD SENSE
ROCK II (240)	/GLENMORISON/ WELL, SIR ARTHUR, WHEN YOU WERE	LETTING	YOURSELF GO SO RECKLESSLY YOU MIGHT HAVE SAID A WORD
MILL I (147)	DEEP END. YOU MUSTNT MIND ME: THERES NOTHING LIKE	LETTING	YOURSELF GO IF YOU ARE BUILT THAT WAY. INTRODUCE ME
		LETTRES	
OVER PREFACE(159)	OF A MESSALINA OR A CENCI. WRITERS OF BELLES	LETTRES	WHO ARE RASH ENOUGH TO ADMIT THAT THEIR WHOLE LIFE
SUPR PREFACE(R37)	CONVENTION CAN ACHIEVE. MY CONTEMPT FOR BELLES	LETTRES	, AND FOR AMATEURS WHO BECOME THE HEROES OF THE
		LETTUCE	
MRS II (206)	BUT A LITTLE OF THAT COLD BEEF AND CHEESE AND	LETTUCE	GOES A LONG WAY. (WITH A SIGH OF ONLY HALF
		LEUCOCYTES	
MTH4 I (157)	OF THEIR OWN DIVINITY. THEY TELL ME THERE ARE	LEUCOCYTES	IN MY BLOOD, AND SODIUM AND CARBON IN MY FLESH. I
		LEVA	
ARMS III (56)	HIS LEFT HAND, OUT OF HER REACH). SEE! A TWENTY	LEVA	BILL! SERGIUS GAVE ME THAT, OUT OF PURE SWAGGER. A
		LEVAS	
ARMS III (69)	TO YOU, YOU SCOUNDREL! WHY, YOU HAD TWENTY-FIVE	LEVAS	FROM ME ON THE DAY OF YOUR BETROTHAL; AND SHE HAD THAT
ARMS II (24)	SHE WOULDNT HAVE THE MASTER KNOW FOR A THOUSAND	LEVAS	. I KNOW THINGS ABOUT HIM THAT SHE WOULDNT LET HIM
ARMS III (48)	PAUL. AN ARABIAN MARE WILL COST YOU 50,000	LEVAS	. /RAINA/ (SUDDENLY COMING OUT OF HER PICTURESQUE
ARMS III (56)	A FOOL AND HIS MONEY ARE SOON PARTED. THERES TEN	LEVAS	MORE. THE SWISS GAVE ME THAT FOR BACKING UP THE
ARMS III (56)	/LOUKA/ YES: SELL YOUR MANHOOD FOR 30	LEVAS	, AND BUY ME FOR 10! (RISING SCORNFULLY) KEEP YOUR
		LEVEL	
SIM I SD(36)	THE CRESCENT THE LAWN IS BANKED TO A HIGHER	LEVEL	AND BECOMES A FLOWER GARDEN, SHELTERED FROM THE WIND
CATH 2 (178)	NO SENSE OF HUMOR. (SHE STEPS DOWN TO THE FLOOR	LEVEL	AND LOOKS INDULGENTLY AT PATIOMKIN. HE GURGLES
BASH III (124)	LAST TRUMPET. /ADELAIDE/ A DISGRACEFUL THREAT TO	LEVEL	AT THIS VIRTUOUS OLD MAN. /LYDIA/ OH, CASHEL, IF THOU
LION PREFACE(76)	INCAPABLE OF RISING TO IT, DRAGS IT DOWN TO ITS	LEVEL	BY DEGRADING IT. YEARS AGO I SAID THAT THE CONVERSION
DOCT II (119)	THE POLICE. THEYVE FOUND HALF A MILKMAN AT OUR	LEVEL	CROSSING WITH A PRESCRIPTION OF MINE IN ITS POCKET.
NEVR IV (300)	ONLY THIS TO SAY. YOU DRAGGED ME DOWN TO YOUR	LEVEL	FOR A MOMENT THIS AFTERNOON. DO YOU THINK, IF THAT HAD
MIS. PREFACE(100)	IN ART, CHILDREN, LIKE ADULTS, WILL FIND THEIR	LEVEL	IF THEY ARE LEFT FREE TO FIND IT, AND NOT RESTRICTED
CLEO III (154)	(WITH SUDDEN ALARM) GENTLY, YE DOGS. LAY IT	LEVEL	IN THE STERN-- SO-- TIS WELL. /FTATATEETA/ (SCREAMING
JITT III (59)	OR HOW PRETTY SHE IS: TIME WILL BRING HER TO MY	LEVEL	IN THOSE WAYS SOON ENOUGH. BUT I'M NOT CLEVER AT THE
WIDO III (57)	ANGRILY) I SUPPOSE I SHOULD HAVE BEEN DOWN ON HER	LEVEL	INSTEAD OF BEING RAISED ABOVE IT, AS I AM NOW. WOULD
MTH4 I SD(139)	OF STONE STEPS DESCENDS OUT OF SIGHT TO THE SEA	LEVEL	. A WOMAN IN A SILK TUNIC AND SANDALS, WEARING LITTLE
JITT III (77)	IT, ALFRED. I WILL NOT BE DRAGGED DOWN TO YOUR	LEVEL	. /LENKHEIM/ FIVE MINUTES AGO YOU WERE AMUSING
ROCK I (215)	OF SPANISH ONIONS HAS AGAIN REACHED THE 1913	LEVEL	. /OXFORD YOUTH/ HOLY JERUSALEM! SPANISH ONIONS!
PPP SD(195)	AND RAISES HIS HEAD ABOVE THE BED COVERLET	LEVEL	. /THE MURDERER/ I CAN NO LONGER COWER HERE LISTENING
KING I SD(161)	WITH AN IRON STAIRCASE DOWN TO THE GARDEN	LEVEL	. THE DIVISION OF THE WINDOW TO THE LEFT AS YOU LOOK
BULL IV (169)	GRUDGE YOU ME MONEY! BUT TO LOWER MESELF TO THE	LEVEL	OF COMMON PEOPLE-- /BROADBENT/ TO A MEMBER'S WIFE,
ROCK PREFACE(167)	THE SPECTACLE OF THE NATION WITH THE HIGHEST	LEVEL	OF GENERAL CULTURE RUNNING SHORT OF BOOTS AND
MTH2 SD(41)	SUNBURNT YOUNG LADY WITH HAZEL HAIR CUT TO THE	LEVEL	OF HER NECK, LIKE AN ITALIAN YOUTH IN A GOZZOLI
JOAN PREFACE(50)	ONLY BY DOING SO CAN I MAINTAIN MY DRAMA ON THE	LEVEL	OF HIGH TRAGEDY AND SAVE IT FROM BECOMING A MERE
DEST (187)	AN OFFICER SHOULD NEVER LET HIMSELF DOWN TO THE	LEVEL	OF HIS MEN. (NAPOLEON LOOKS AT HIM DANGEROUSLY, AND
BULL I (88)	THEM TO DEVELOP IN PERFECT FREEDOM TO THE ENGLISH	LEVEL	OF SELF-GOVERNMENT, YOU KNOW. YOU UNDERSTAND ME?
MTH1 II (29)	MOTHER ARE SO PROUD OF. THEY DRAG US DOWN TO THE	LEVEL	OF THE BEASTS. IF THAT IS TO BE THE LAST THING AS IT
JOAN PREFACE(50)	DULL AS PICKPOCKETS; AND THEY REDUCE JOAN TO THE	LEVEL	OF THE EVEN LESS INTERESTING PERSON WHOSE POCKET IS
CAND I SD(78)	AND THE KITCHEN AT THE BACK. UPSTAIRS, ON THE	LEVEL	OF THE HALL DOOR, IS THE DRAWINGROOM, WITH ITS LARGE
SUPR HANDBOK(190)	TRIAL, BECAUSE DEMOCRACY CANNOT RISE ABOVE THE	LEVEL	OF THE HUMAN MATERIAL OF WHICH ITS VOTERS ARE MADE.
UNPL PREFACE(R23)	THAT AN ACTOR'S PROFESSION CAN PLACE HIM ON THE	LEVEL	OF THE LAWYER, THE PHYSICIAN, THE CHURCHMAN, AND THE
APPL I (233)	OVER THE THEATRE. I SHOULD SINK BELOW THE	LEVEL	OF THE MEANEST OF MY SUBJECTS, MY SOLE PRIVILEGE BEING
PYGM II (229)	DOGMATICALLY, LIFTING HIMSELF ON HIS HANDS TO THE	LEVEL	OF THE PIANO, AND SITTING ON IT WITH A BOUNCE) WELL, I
LION PREFACE(74)	APOSTLES DRAGGED THE TRADITION OF HIM DOWN TO THE	LEVEL	OF THE THING IT HAS REMAINED EVER SINCE. AND THAT
SUPR III SD(71)	AMPHITHEATRE ON THE LEFT, MAINTAINING ITS HIGHER	LEVEL	ON EMBANKMENTS AND AN OCCASIONAL STONE ARCH. ON THE
JITT III (75)	THAT SHE HAS ALLOWED HERSELF TO DESCEND TO HIS	LEVEL	) YES. I BEG YOUR PARDON. I SHOULD NOT HAVE SAID IT.
MRS PREFACE(165)	WILL BE THAT THE EXAMINER WILL FIND HIS NATURAL	LEVEL	; IBSEN AND TOLSTOY THEIRS; SO NO HARM WILL BE DONE.
METH PREFACE(R60)	CAN HARDLY BE CARRIED TO A MORE DESOLATING DEAD	LEVEL	THAN IN THE CASE OF THE INDIVIDUALS WHO ARE BORN AND
NEVR III (273)	OR LATER. FORGIVE ME NOW. /GLORIA/ (RISING TO	LEVEL	THE DECLARATION MORE INTENSELY AT HIM) NEVER! WHILE
MTH5 (231)	FORCE USED TO SLIP SUDDENLY DOWN FROM ITS HUMAN	LEVEL	TO THAT OF A FUNGUS, SO THAT MEN FOUND THEIR FLESH NO
BULL II SD(111)	KNOLL; BUT MODERN ENGINEERING HAS TEMPERED THE	LEVEL	TO THE BEEYANKINY CAR BY CARRYING THE ROAD PARTLY
LION II SD(127)	LEADING TO THE ARENA DESCENDS FROM THE FLOOR	LEVEL	UNDER THE IMPERIAL BOX. ON BOTH SIDES OF THIS PASSAGE
HART PREFACE(39)	IF HE HAD BEEN A PEASANT; THE LORD OF HELLAS IS	LEVEL	WITH HIS LACKEYS IN REPUBLICAN SWITZERLAND; PRIME
2TRU I SD(27)	A DRAUGHT OF FRESH AIR SHOULD CREEP UNDERNEATH)	LEVEL	WITH US IN THE RIGHTHAND WALL. THE COUCH AGAINST THE

SIM I SD(36) THE LAWN FALLS AWAY TO THE SEA, BUT NOT TO SEA LEVEL , ALL THAT IS VISIBLE OF THE PORT BEING THE TOP OF THE
SUPR HANDBOK(186) GOD HIMSELF CANNOT RAISE A PEOPLE ABOVE ITS OWN LEVEL , AND THAT EVEN THOUGH YOU STIR A NATION TO SACRIFICE
MTH2 (64) TO THEM, MORE JEALOUS OF LETTING THEM UP TO YOUR LEVEL , THAN ANY DUKE OR ANY ARCHBISHOP. /BURGE/ (HOTLY) I
SUPR PREFACE(R27) LITERARY SAGES TO RAISE THE MASS ABOVE ITS OWN LEVEL , THE MORE CONVINCED I AM THAT MY NURSE WAS RIGHT.

LEVELLED
POSN PREFACE(422) PROPOSED, AND DEALT WITH UNDER A GENERAL CLAUSE LEVELLED AT CONDUCT " CALCULATED TO" OVERTHROW THE LIBERTIES
SUPR I (41) FORGIVE MY BRUTALITIES, ANN. THEY ARE LEVELLED AT THIS WICKED WORLD, NOT AT YOU. (SHE LOOKS UP AT
BASH II,1, (99) TAPPING WITH FRIENDLY FOREFINGER THIS BUTTON, LEVELLED ME LIKE A THUNDERSTRICKEN ELM FLAT UPON THE
GENV PREFACE(3) ON I FOUND THAT HALF THE ANCIENT CITY HAD BEEN LEVELLED TO THE GROUND, LEAVING ONLY ST PAUL'S AND A FEW
FABL PREFACE(67) CULTURE IN EVERY HOME, AND WAGES MUST BE LEVELLED UP, NOT DOWN, TO THIS QUOTA BY INCREASED

LEVELLERS
KING I (189) BY COMPROMISING WITH PROTESTANTS, REPUBLICANS, LEVELLERS AND ATHEISTS. WHAT DID HE GAIN BY IT? THEY
KING I (195) YOUR PROTESTANT REPUBLICANS AND PRESBYTERIANS AND LEVELLERS CALL THE PEOPLE OF ENGLAND WILL HAVE TO CHOOSE
KING I (195) ENGLAND WILL HAVE NOTHING TO DO WITH IT. THE REAL LEVELLERS TODAY, JAMIE, ARE THE LORDS AND THE RICH SQUIRES--
LADY PREFACE(230) WAS ALLOWED TO GO FREE WHEN SO MANY LESS TERRIBLE LEVELLERS WENT TO THE GALLEYS OR SIBERIA. FROM THE MATURE

LEVELLING
SUPR HANDBOK(194) COMPLETION OF ALL THE SUGGESTED REFORMS AND THE LEVELLING UP OF ALL MEN TO THE POINT ATTAINED ALREADY BY THE

LEVELLING-UP
SUPR HANDBOK(199) OR EVEN THE GENERAL ADVOCACY ON PAPER, OF THE LEVELLING-UP OF THE MASS TO THE HIGHEST POINT ATTAINABLE BY

LEVELS
SUPR HANDBOK(226) LOATHES ALMSGIVING AND MENDICITY. FAME. LIFE LEVELS ALL MEN: DEATH REVEALS THE EMINENT. DISCIPLINE.

LEVER
BARB PREFACE(209) THEM THAT THE SENSATION FIRST CAME TO ME FROM LEVER AND MAY HAVE COME TO HIM FROM BEYLE, OR AT LEAST OUT
NEVR I (224) MARRIED, MR CRAMPTON? (HE PUTS HIS FOOT ON THE LEVER BY WHICH THE CHAIR IS RAISED AND LOWERED). /CRAMPTON/
LION PREFACE(54) SEAT IN THE RAILWAY CARRIAGE, THE PARTICULAR LEVER IN THE ENGINE THAT IS HIS VERY OWN AND NOBODY ELSES;
CATH 2 (180) HE BOWS ALMOST TO HIS KNEE). THE PETIT LEVER IS OVER. (SHE TURNS TO GO INTO THE CABINET, AND
CATH 1 (171) IN HALF AN HOUR IT WILL BE TOO LATE FOR THE PETIT LEVER . COME ALONG. DAMN IT, MAN, I MUST OBLIGE THE BRITISH
CATH 2,SD(174) THE SECOND SCENE. THE EMPRESS'S PETIT LEVER . THE CENTRAL DOORS ARE CLOSED. THOSE WHO ENTER
BARB PREFACE(208) NEVER READ IBSEN. OF THE BOOKS THAT MADE LEVER POPULAR, SUCH AS CHARLES O'MALLEY AND HARRY LORREQUER,
BARB III (340) IT IS THE FINAL TEST OF CONVICTION, THE ONLY LEVER STRONG ENOUGH TO OVERTURN A SOCIAL SYSTEM. BUT HUDDLE
BARB PREFACE(207) STRANGE TO THE PUBLIC TASTE THAT DICKENS PRESSED LEVER TO MAKE SHORT WORK OF IT. I READ SCRAPS OF THIS NOVEL
BULL PREFACE(61) MEMBERS. THIS FACT WILL, MOREOVER, SUPPLY THE LEVER WHICH HAS, UP TO THE PRESENT, BEEN LACKING TO THE
BARB PREFACE(208) I WAS NOT IBSENIST EVEN AT SECOND HAND; FOR LEVER , THOUGH HE MAY HAVE READ HENRI BEYLE, ALIAS STENDHAL,
BARB PREFACE(207) MY COUNTRYMAN AND IMMEDIATE FORERUNNER, CHARLES LEVER , WHILST THEY CONFIDENTLY DERIVE ME FROM A NORWEGIAN
BARB PREFACE(207) HALF A CENTURY AGO, AN IRISH NOVELIST, CHARLES LEVER , WROTE A STORY ENTITLED A DAY'S RIDE: A LIFE'S

LEVERAGE
PPP (206) IS HEAVY; BUT LOVE CAN DO MUCH. /FITZ/ A LITTLE LEVERAGE WILL GET HIM ON HIS FEET. GIVE ME MY UMBRELLA.

LEVER'S
BARB PREFACE(209) TO SMART VERY SORELY. HENCE THE FAILURE OF LEVER'S BOOK TO PLEASE THE READERS OF HOUSEHOLD WORDS. THAT
BARB PREFACE(209) EXCLUDE THE HYPOTHESIS OF COMPLETE ORIGINALITY ON LEVER'S PART, BECAUSE A MAN CAN NO MORE BE COMPLETELY
BARB PREFACE(209) WHERE THEY HAD FORMERLY BEEN MOCKERS, IN LEVER'S STORY THERE IS A REAL CHANGE OF ATTITUDE. THERE IS
BARB PREFACE(208) WITH LETTERS, WHERE, THEN, WAS THE NOVELTY IN LEVER'S TALE? PARTLY, I THINK, IN A NEW SERIOUSNESS IN

LEVERS
FABL VI (124) TWIDDLE HIS FINGERS AS IF THEY WERE WHEELS AND LEVERS ? HE HAS TO EMPLOY A THIRD FORM PATENT AGENT TO
METH PREFACE(R38) ALL HIS ORGANS INGENIOUSLY CONTRIVED, CORDS AND LEVERS , GIRDERS AND KINGPOSTS, CIRCULATING SYSTEMS OF PIPES

LEVIATHAN
MTH4 II (191) OF THESE ISLANDS BY JONHOBSNOXIUS, CALLED THE LEVIATHAN ? THOSE MISGUIDED PEOPLE SACRIFICED THE FRAGMENT

LEVIATHANS
HART PREFACE(36) WOULD LOOK AT THE BLONDIN DONKEY AFTER SEEING ITS LEVIATHANS ? IN SPITE OF THE ADAM-ADELPHIAN DECORATION ON

LEVIED
CLEO PRO1 (92) ROMANS WHICH HAVE LENT MONEY TO OUR KINGS AND LEVIED A DISTRAINT UPON US WITH THEIR ARMS, CALL FOR EVER

LEVITATE
FABL VI (129) BIRD. /THE FEATHERED ONE/ I DO NOT FLY: I LEVITATE . CALL ME COCKYOLLY IF YOU LIKE: BUT IT WOULD BE

LEVITIES
SUPR PREFACE(R9) IN YOU I CAN DETECT NO SUCH BECOMING CHANGE. YOUR LEVITIES AND AUDACITIES ARE LIKE THE LOVES AND COMFORTS
MRS PREFACE(156) LOVERS WHO HAVE ADORED THEM IN SPITE OF ALL THEIR LEVITIES . NATURALLY THE POORER GIRLS IN THE GALLERY WILL

LEVITY
CLEO III (158) WHAT BRITON SPEAKS AS YOU DO IN YOUR MOMENTS OF LEVITY ? WHAT BRITON NEGLECTS TO ATTEND THE SERVICES AT THE
BULL III (137) BY BROADBENT, AND UNABLE TO UNDERSTAND THEIR LEVITY CONCERNING HIM) DID YOU MIND WHAT HE SAID ABOUT
JOAN 2 (82) (DRAWING HIMSELF UP SENSITIVELY) GENTLEMEN! YOUR LEVITY IS REBUKED BY THIS MAID'S FAITH. I AM, GOD HELP ME,
MIS. (126) WHAT YOU CALL YOUR YOUTH IS NOTHING BUT YOUR LEVITY . WHY DO WE GET ON SO WELL TOGETHER? BECAUSE I'M A
NEVR III (272) BUT I DO NOT LIKE TO THINK THAT YOUR UNFORTUNATE LEVITY OF DISPOSITION IS MERE SHAMELESSNESS AND
FANY EPILOG (332) IT, YOU FEEL SOMEHOW THAT BENEATH ALL THE ASSUMED LEVITY OF THAT POOR WAIF AND STRAY, SHE REALLY LOVES BOBBY
PRES (155) QUEEN ELIZABETH, FOR INSTANCE. HER VANITY, HER LEVITY -- /MRS BANGER/ NOBODY WHO HAS STUDIED THE HISTORY OF
CATH 2 (176) MORNING, LITTLE MOTHER. /CATHERINE/ (WITH SUDDEN LEVITY) I AM ALWAYS IN HIGH SPIRITS, EVEN WHEN PEOPLE DO
ARMS III (58) WHO ARE RICH LIKE YOU. /SERGIUS/ (WITH BITTER LEVITY) NOT A BIT. THEY ALL SLASHED AND CURSED AND YELLED
BARB III (347) IMAGINARY DRUMSTICKS). /BARBARA/ (ANGERED BY HIS LEVITY) TAKE CARE, DOLLY, TAKE CARE. OH, IF ONLY I COULD
MTH4 II (187) GENTLEMAN/ (IN DIGNIFIED REBUKE OF ZOZIM'S LEVITY) TAKEN IN THIS SPIRIT, SIR, THE SHOW, AS YOU CALL
LADY PREFACE(234) SKETCH OF SHAKESPEAR IS MORE COMPLETE THAN ITS LEVITY SUGGESTS. ALAS! ITS APPEAL FOR A NATIONAL THEATRE AS
MIS. PREFACE(5) ME TO ACT AS GODFATHER TO THEIR CHILDREN WITH A LEVITY WHICH CONVINCES ME THAT THEY HAVE NOT THE FAINTEST
LADY PREFACE(232) SHAKESPEAR DIED GAME, AND INDEED IN A STATE OF LEVITY WHICH WOULD HAVE BEEN CONSIDERED UNBECOMING IN A
BARB PREFACE(215) REBELS, IS AS NOTHING COMPARED TO THE SILLY LEVITY WITH WHICH WE TOLERATE POVERTY AS IF IT WERE EITHER A
SUPR PREFACE(R9) ASKED ME WHY I DID NOT WRITE A DON JUAN PLAY. THE LEVITY WITH WHICH YOU ASSUMED THIS FRIGHTFUL RESPONSIBILITY
LADY PREFACE(221) THERE WAS IN SHAKESPEAR AN INCORRIGIBLE DIVINE LEVITY , AN INEXHAUSTIBLE JOY THAT DERIDED SORROW? THINK OF
METH PREFACE(R44) AND INDUSTRIOUS PIGEON FANCIER," THAT BLASPHEMOUS LEVITY , AS IT SEEMED, WAS RECEIVED WITH HORROR AND
MTH3 (122) WELL BE AFRAID OF ME. THERE ARE MOMENTS WHEN YOUR LEVITY , YOUR INGRATITUDE, YOUR SHALLOW JOLLITY, MAKE MY
MTH3 (122) THREE HUNDRED! /BURGE-LUBIN/ YOU ACCUSE ME OF LEVITY ! MUST I REMIND YOU, MADAM, THAT I AM THE PRESIDENT,

LEVY
ROCK PREFACE(183) TALKER, WHO HAVE NEVER HAD TO PASS A SENTENCE NOR LEVY A TAX NOR ISSUE AN EDICT! WHAT HAVE YOU TO SAY THAT I
ROCK PREFACE(160) AS LONG AS THEY DO NOT COMMIT WILFUL MURDER, OR LEVY WAR AGAINST THE CROWN, OR KIDNAP, OR THROW VITRIOL, IS

LEVYING
GENV I (36) TREASON AND REBELLION AND BREACH OF PRIVILEGE; LEVYING ARMED FORCES AGAINST THE CROWN; VIOLATING THE

LEWD
LADY (249) I DARE NOT OFFEND MY UNRULY PURITANS BY MAKING SO LEWD A PLACE AS THE PLAYHOUSE A PUBLIC CHARGE; AND THERE BE
LADY (248) BY SAYING ENDLESS NAUGHTINESSES TO A GENTLEMAN AS LEWD AS HERSELF. I HAVE WRIT THESE TO SAVE MY FRIENDS FROM
JOAN 6 (130) SIGN OF HARD HEARTS, AND WHOSE BRAZEN LOOKS AND LEWD DEMEANOR CONDEMN THEM BEFORE THEY ARE ACCUSED. THE
LADY (245) NO FURTHER DISCOURSE WITH HIM. HE HATH EVER SOME LEWD JEST ON HIS TONGUE. YOU HEAR HOW HE USETH ME! CALLING

LEWES

GETT PREFACE(183)	OF GEORGE ELIOT, WHO FORMED AN ILLICIT UNION WITH	LEWES	. THEY QUOTE A SAYING ATTRIBUTED TO NIETZSCHE, THAT A
METH PREFACE(R59)	TO THIS IS TO BE FOUND IN LEWES'S LIFE OF GOETHE.	LEWES	SCORNED THE NOTION THAT CIRCUMSTANCES GOVERN

LEWES'S

METH PREFACE(R59)	THE STOCK REPLY TO THIS IS TO BE FOUND IN	LEWES'S	LIFE OF GOETHE. LEWES SCORNED THE NOTION THAT

LEWIS

SIM PREFACE(19)	MURRAY, DONALD ECCLES, NORRIS STAYTON, CURIGWEN	LEWIS	, ELSPETH MARCH, AND RICHARD LONSCALE.
PPP PREFACE(192)	PRICE, MR G. P. HUNTLEY, MR CYRIL MAUDE, MR ERIC	LEWIS	, MR ARTHUR WILLIAMS, AND MR LENNOX PAWLE. AS IT IS

LEXY

CAND I (82)	ON THE SHOULDERS). CATCH THE MEASLES IF YOU CAN,	LEXY	: SHE'LL NURSE YOU; AND WHAT A PIECE OF LUCK THAT WILL
CAND III (138)	YOUD BETTER SEE HER SAFELY HOME. /CANDIDA/ DO,	LEXY	: THERES A GOOD FELLOW. (SHE SHAKES HIS HAND AND
CAND I (81)	ENERGY) HA! HA! (WHIMSICALLY) WATCH AND PRAY,	LEXY	: WATCH AND PRAY. /LEXY/ I KNOW. (RISING WITTILY TO
CAND I (81)	FROM THE CHURCH REFORMER, AND REMARKS) WELL,	LEXY	? LATE AGAIN, AS USUAL! /LEXY/ I'M AFRAID SO. I WISH
CAND I (83)	HASNT CALLED HERE FOR THREE YEARS. ARE YOU SURE,	LEXY	? YOURE NOT JOKING, ARE YOU? /LEXY/ (EARNESTLY) NO
CAND I (82)	BE IN ARREAR WITH YOUR REPAYMENT. (HE PATS	LEXY	AFFECTIONATELY AND MOVES TO LEAVE THE ROOM). /LEXY/ OH,
CAND III SD(137)	SATISFACTION WITH HIS OWN DIPLOMATIC CUNNING.	LEXY	FOLDS HIS ARMS AND LEANS AGAINST THE HEAD OF THE SOFA
CAND I SD(86)	OH, GOOD MORNING TO YOU. MORELL RETURNS AS	LEXY	IS MAKING FOR THE DOOR. /MORELL/ (TO LEXY) OFF TO
CAND II SD(124)	ALL WAIT, EXCEPT BURGESS, WHO TURNS STEALTHILY TO	LEXY	. /BURGESS/ LISTEN ERE, MR MILL. WHATS PROSSY'S
CAND III (138)	(ANXIOUS ABOUT HER) GO AND LOOK AFTER HER,	LEXY	. /LEXY/ (ALARMED) BUT IF SHE SHOULD REALLY BE--
CAND II (122)	GLAD TO SEE YOU BACK AGAIN. /CANDIDA/ THANK YOU,	LEXY	. YOU KNOW EUGENE, DONT YOU? /LEXY/ OH YES. HOW DO YOU
CAND I SD(83)	RESIGNS HIMSELF TO THE INEVITABLE, AND GOES OUT).	LEXY	LOOKS AFTER HIM WITH BEAMING WORSHIP. MISS GARNETT, NOT
CAND I (82)	AS A SOLDIER MUST FACE BULLETS. (HE CLAPS	LEXY	MANFULLY ON THE SHOULDERS). CATCH THE MEASLES IF YOU
CAND II SD(122)	REMONSTRATING) AW NO, CANDY. 'ANG IT ALL!	LEXY	MILL COMES IN, ANXIOUS AND IMPORTANT. /LEXY/ (
CAND III SD(136)	VOICES AND LAUGHTER ARE HEARD APPROACHING.	LEXY	MILL, HIS EYES SPARKLING, AND HIS BEARING DENOTING
CAND I (84)	WHAT A KNOWLEDGE OF THE HUMAN HEART YOU HAVE, MR	LEXY	MILL! HOW WELL YOU KNOW THE WEAKNESSES OF WOMAN, DONT
CAND I (86)	AS LEXY IS MAKING FOR THE DOOR. /MORELL/ (TO	LEXY	) OFF TO WORK? /LEXY/ YES, SIR. /MORELL/ TAKE MY SILK
CAND II (125)	(SHE NODS, AFRAID TO SPEAK). YOU ARE COMING,	LEXY	, I SUPPOSE? /LEXY/ CERTAINLY. /CANDIDA/ WE'RE ALL
CAND I SD(86)	THROAT UP. THERES A COLD WIND. AWAY WITH YOU.	LEXY	, MORE THAN CONSOLED FOR BURGESS'S RUDENESS, BRIGHTENS
CAND I SD(83)	WORSHIP. MISS GARNETT, NOT BEING ABLE TO SHAKE	LEXY	, RELIEVES HER FEELINGS BY WORRYING THE TYPEWRITER.

LEYDEN

LION PREFACE(4)	OF SUCH CHRISTIANS AS SAVONAROLA AND JOHN OF	LEYDEN	: THEY WERE SCUTTLING THE SHIP BEFORE THEY HAD
GETT PREFACE(199)	MAN: THAT IS WHY SAVONAROLA WAS BURNT AND JOHN OF	LEYDEN	TORN TO PIECES WITH RED-HOT PINCERS WHILST MULTITUDES
ROCK PREFACE(156)	WITHIN THE MEMORY OF PERSONS NOW LIVING. JOHN OF	LEYDEN	, FOR BEING A COMMUNIST, WAS TORTURED SO FRIGHTFULLY
ROCK PREFACE(175)	TAKEN IN VAIN, WE HAVE JOAN OF ARC AND JOHN OF	LEYDEN	, GIORDANO BRUNO AND GALILEO, SERVETUS AND JOHN HUS

LI

BUOY (1)	BUOYANT BILLIONS: A COMEDY OF NO MANNERS.	LI	. 1947.

LIABILITIES

HART I (57)	INTO BUSINESS ON A LARGE SCALE, HE HAD TO INCUR	LIABILITIES	. WHEN THE BUSINESS WENT INTO LIQUIDATION HE

LIABILITY

ROCK PREFACE(162)	BEING IN THE OPPOSITE DIRECTION. LIMITED	LIABILITY	IN MORALS. SUCH A NOVELTY IS EXTREMELY TERRIFYING
ROCK PREFACE(162)	US, WHO ARE STILL WORKING ON A SYSTEM OF LIMITED	LIABILITY	IN MORALS. OUR " FREE" BRITISH CITIZENS CAN
ROCK PREFACE(162)	THE PRIVATE TRADE IN ARMAMENTS, SUCH LIMITED	LIABILITY	NO LONGER EXISTS IN RUSSIA, AND IS NOT LIKELY TO
MIS. PREFACE(36)	OF ADULT WORK, THE EXCHANGE OF THE HUMILIATING	LIABILITY	TO PERSONAL ASSAULT FROM THE LAWLESS SCHOOLMASTER,
2TRU PREFACE(25)	AND ERROR, HIS ENTIRELY HUMAN FOOTING, AND HIS	LIABILITY	TO REMOVAL AT A MOMENT'S NOTICE IF HIS EMINENCE

LIABLE

VWOO 2 (129)	/A/ STEADY. STEADY. I HAVE NOT YET MADE MYSELF	LIABLE	TO AN ACTION FOR BREACH OF PROMISE. /Z/ DONT BE
SUPR PREFACE(R39)	MUST ALSO BE A MOST INTENSELY REFRACTORY PERSON,	LIABLE	TO GO OUT AND TO GO WRONG AT INCONVENIENT MOMENTS,
2TRU II (55)	HIS MAJESTY'S FORCES OR ANY PART THEREOF SHALL BE	LIABLE	TO SUFFER DEATH. DO YOU UNDERSTAND? DEATH! /MEEK/
PHIL PREFACE(68)	IS A DISEASE TO WHICH PLAYS AS WELL AS MEN BECOME	LIABLE	WITH ADVANCING YEARS. IN MEN IT IS CALLED DOTING, IN
GETT (318)	FORGET THAT UNDER THIS CONTRACT HE WILL NOT BE	LIABLE	, BECAUSE YOU WILL NOT BE HIS WIFE IN LAW. /EDITH/

LIAR

MTH1 II (27)	VOICE SOMETIMES TEMPTS ME TO DO ALREADY. /ADAM/	LIAR	: YOU DENIED JUST NOW THAT IT CALLED ON YOU TO PAY FOR
MIS. (112)	A BEAST: YOURE A BRUTE: YOURE A CAD: YOURE A	LIAR	: YOURE A BULLY: I SHOULD LIKE TO WRING YOUR DAMNED
HART I (64)	LOOKING, OF COURSE. BUT HOW CAN YOU LOVE A	LIAR	? /MRS HUSHABYE/ I DONT KNOW. BUT YOU CAN,
MTH4 III (201)	THATS WHAT I'M GOING TO DO. DO YOU TAKE ME FOR A	LIAR	? /THE ELDERLY GENTLEMAN/ (PUZZLED) OH, I BEG YOUR
SUPR IV (163)	PERFECTLY WELL THAT ALL THIS ABOUT HER BEING A	LIAR	AND A BULLY AND A COQUETTE AND SO FORTH IS A TRUMPED-UP
CAND I (102)	GIVE ANY EXPLANATION BUT THE TRUE ONE, YOU ARE A	LIAR	AND A COWARD. TELL HER WHAT I SAID; AND HOW YOU WERE
METH PREFACE(R77)	BY FAR DECLARE THE THRONE OF GOD EMPTY THAN SET A	LIAR	AND A FOOL ON IT. WHAT ARE CALLED WARS OF RELIGION ARE
OVER PREFACE(155)	OF HIS OWN REMORSE, HE (OR SHE) MAY BE A	LIAR	AND A HUMBUG, PRETENDING TO BE BETTER THAN THE DETECTED
JOAN 1 (58)	I KICK YOU OUT THROUGH THE CASTLE GATE FOR A	LIAR	AND A SELLER OF MY GOODS TO THIEVES. THE MILK WAS SHORT
MIS. PREFACE(21)	THE BOYS WHO DID WISH TO LEARN: THAT I WAS A	LIAR	AND A SHIRKER AND A SEDITIOUS LITTLE NUISANCE; AND THAT
GETT (318)	FOR, MISS, IF I MAY ASK? /EDITH/ SLATTOX IS A	LIAR	AND A THIEF; AND IT IS MY DUTY TO EXPOSE HIM. /COLLINS/
JOAN PREFACE(44)	NOT BELIEVE IN THE VOICES, AND REGARDED HER AS A	LIAR	AND IMPOSTOR. IT IS HARD TO CONCEIVE ANYTHING MORE
JOAN PREFACE(11)	HELD TO PROVE THAT SHE WAS MAD, THAT SHE WAS A	LIAR	AND IMPOSTOR, THAT SHE WAS A SORCERESS (SHE WAS BURNED
PLES PREFACE(R10)	PLAYWRIGHT TO BE SOMETHING MORE THAN A SKILLED	LIAR	AND PANDAR. HERE, THEN, WAS THE HIGHER BUT VAGUER AND
CAND I (97)	OF SEEING THROUGH AND THROUGH A THUNDERING	LIAR	AND ROTTEN CYNIC LIKE THAT FELLOW. HA! HA! NOW, OFF
MIS. PREFACE(95)	CONDUCT, THE UPSHOT IS THAT THE CHILD BECOMES A	LIAR	AND SCHEMER WITH AN ATROPHIED CONSCIENCE, AND A GOOD
FOUN (209)	WILL YOU? I SAID NOTHING TO YOU. /BRABAZON/	LIAR	AND SLAVE. FIGHT, I TELL YOU! FIGHT. /MERCER/ OH, WAS
BASH II,1, (104)	NAY, COZ: YOURE PREJUDICED. /CASHEL/ (WITHOUT)	LIAR	AND SLAVE! /LYDIA/ WHAT WORDS WERE THOSE? /LUCIAN/
SUPR III (107)	BLOOD OF THE OLD SEA KINGS IN HIS VEINS. CALL HIM	LIAR	AND THIEF; AND HE WILL ONLY TAKE AN ACTION AGAINST YOU
O'FL (208)	CAN DO, SIR. DID YOU EVER NOTICE WHAT A READY	LIAR	I AM? /SIR PEARCE/ WELL, IN RECRUITING A MAN GETS
2TRU III (101)	HAVE BROUGHT INTO THE WORLD THE MOST ABANDONED	LIAR	I HAVE EVER MET. /THE ELDER/ AND MAY I ASK, SIR, IS IT
POSN (452)	ALL HERE AS NO BROTHER OF MINE AND THE ROTTENEST	LIAR	IN THIS TOWN, IS SPEAKING THE TRUTH FOR THE FIRST TIME
SUPR HANDBOK(209)	KEEP OUT EVERY ABLE MAN WHO IS NOT A SOPHIST OR A	LIAR	. A NATION WHICH REVISES ITS PARISH COUNCILS ONCE IN
SUPR IV (162)	TO THE POINT OF SPEAKING OUT-- SHE IS A	LIAR	. AND SINCE SHE HAS PLUNGED TAVY HEAD OVER EARS IN LOVE
SIM II (66)	MAYA, KANCHIN, JANGA/ (HISSING AFTER HIM)	LIAR	. BABY. DASTARD. HYPOCRITE. /SIR CHARLES/ (LAUGHING)
METH PREFACE(R50)	OF YOUR INNER CONVICTION THAT HE IS A FOOL AND A	LIAR	, BUT AS THIS, THOUGH BRITISH, IS UNCIVIL, IT IS WISER
2TRU I (46)	NO, SWEETIE: YOU ARE A COMMON LITTLE DEVIL AND A	LIAR	. BUT YOU AMUSE ME. IF YOU WERE A REAL LADY YOU WOULDNT
MIS. PREFACE(53)	SNOB, A COWARD, A DUFFER, A CHEAT, A THIEF, OR A	LIAR	. CURIOUS, IS IT NOT, THAT HE HAS NOT THE SAME
METH PREFACE(R67)	WAS THAT HE WAS EITHER A FOOL, A BIGOT, OR A	LIAR	. DARWIN DESTROYED THIS TEST; BUT WHEN IT WAS ONLY
PYGM II (242)	AND FOLLOWS HER). /LIZA/ DONT YOU BELIEVE THE OLD	LIAR	. HE'D AS SOON YOU SET A BULL-DOG ON HIM AS A
GETT (318)	OF COURSE SLATTOX IS IN A MANNER OF SPEAKING A	LIAR	. IF I MAY SAY SO WITHOUT OFFENCE, WE'RE ALL LIARS, IF
GENV IV (105)	HE FLINGS HIMSELF BACK INTO HIS SEAT). /BATTLER/	LIAR	. NO JEW IS EVER SATISFIED. ENOUGH. YOU HAVE YOUR
MILL II (173)	AND OUT. YOU ARE PERFECTLY WELL. /EPIFANIA/	LIAR	. NOBODY IS PERFECTLY WELL, NOR EVER HAS BEEN, NOR EVER
POSN (447)	/FEEMY/ YES YOU WERE; AND IF YOU DENY IT YOURE A	LIAR	. /BLANCO/ (TO STRAPPER) SHE SAW A MAN ON A HORSE WHEN
PYGM V (283)	YOU BRUTE. YOU WANTED TO GET RID OF ME. /HIGGINS/	LIAR	. /LIZA/ THANK YOU. (SHE SITS DOWN WITH DIGNITY).
FABL VI (129)	I DONT BELIEVE IT. YOUR CORRESPONDENT IS JUST A	LIAR	. /MAIDEN 4/ WHAT RUBBISH YOU TALK, NUMBER TWO! DO
MIS. (164)	I REALLY DIDNT MEAN TO BE DISAGREEABLE. /HYPATIA/	LIAR	. /PERCIVAL/ OF COURSE IF YOURE GOING TO INSULT ME, I
MTH3 (105)	NO. HE WOULD BE JUSTIFIED IN CALLING HIM A	LIAR	. /THE ARCHBISHOP/ I THINK NOT, MR CHIEF SECRETARY.
2TRU III (85)	IF ANYONE SAYS I EVER DID A DAY LONGER SHE'S A	LIAR	. /THE SERGEANT/ (LAYING HIS HAND ON THE BIBLE) YOU
MTH5 (240)	/ALL/ (AMAZED AT THE LIE) OH! /THE MALE FIGURE/	LIAR	. YOU BIT HIM. EVERYONE HERE SAW YOU DO IT. /THE
PYGM I (215)	/HIGGINS/ (SHOCKED AT THE GIRL'S MENDACITY)	LIAR	. YOU SAID YOU COULD CHANGE HALF-A-CROWN. /THE FLOWER
DOCT PREFACE(49)	WHETHER SOME HOT-HEADED ANTI-VIVISECTIONIST IS A	LIAR	(WHICH HE PROVES BY RIDICULOUSLY UNSCIENTIFIC
ARMS III (56)	A GOOD SERVANT I WAS-- AFTER MAKING A FOOL AND A	LIAR	OF ME BEFORE THEM ALL! THE TWENTY WILL GO TO OUR
FABL VI (129)	/MAIDEN 5/ HEAR HEAR! THE SMOKER MAY BE A	LIAR	OR NUMBER TWO A FOOL; BUT WHERE DID THE THOUGHTS COME
ARMS II (37)	OF, YOURE MADE OF THE SAME. AS FOR HER, SHE'S A	LIAR	; AND HER FINE AIRS ARE A CHEAT; AND I'M WORTH SIX OF

SUPR IV	(163)	THE MERE SATISFACTION OF GETTING ME TO CALL HER A	LIAR	TO HER FACE, I MAY CONCLUDE THAT SHE IS A BULLY AS
SHAK	(142)	BUT ONE OF THEM MARRIED A NUMSKULL: THE OTHER A	LIAR	WED; AND NOW SHE MUST LIE BESIDE HIM EVEN AS SHE MADE
HART I	(82)	/HECTOR/ (TAKING UP THE RHYTHM) THE OTHER A	LIAR	WED; /MRS HUSHABYE/ (COMPLETING THE STANZA) AND NOW
SUPR II	(58)	HE'D HAVE FOUND OUT WHAT AN INCORRIGIBLE	LIAR	YOU ARE. /ANN/ YOU MISUNDERSTAND, JACK. I DIDNT DARE
PHIL II	(125)	AND BEG HIM TO TAKE YOU BACK. /JULIA/ OH, WHAT A	LIAR	YOU ARE! HE LOVED ME BEFORE HE EVER SAW YOU-- BEFORE
CATH 2	(175)	IS JUST LIKE YOURS. /CATHERINE/ DASHKOFF: WHAT A	LIAR	YOU ARE! (DASHKOFF CURTSIES WITH IMPRESSIVE DIGNITY).
GETT PREFACE	(234)	CONTRARY TO HER OWN. IMAGINE BEING MARRIED TO A	LIAR	, A BORROWER, A MISCHIEF MAKER, A TEASER OR TORMENTOR
2TRU PREFACE	(5)	CONVICTION HE DENOUNCED ME AS A HYPOCRITE AND A	LIAR	, AFFIRMING IT TO BE A WELL-KNOWN AND INEXORABLE LAW OF
BARB PREFACE	(247)	IS, TO SPEAK ACCORDING TO SCRIPTURE, A FOOL AND A	LIAR	, AND IS HEREBY SOLEMNLY DENOUNCED AND CURSED AS SUCH
SUPR I	(15)	IS THE WORST YOU CAN FAIRLY SAY OF ME. THIEF,	LIAR	, FORGER, ADULTERER, PERJURER, GLUTTON, DRUNKARD? NOT
BULL PREFACE	(16)	OF HISTORY, BLACKGUARD, BULLY, DRUNKARD,	LIAR	, FOULMOUTH, FLATTERER, BEGGAR, BACKBITER, VENAL
MTH2	(46)	BUT HE WONT BELIEVE ME. /CONRAD/ CALLED YOU A	LIAR	, IN FACT? /FRANKLYN/ NO: I WISH HE HAD: ANY SORT OF
ROCK I	(200)	THE QUESTION WHETHER JAMESON OR THOMPSON IS A	LIAR	, IS A VITAL QUESTION OF THE FIRST IMPORTANCE. /HILDA/
2TRU II	(72)	IT IS THE DEAD SOLEMN EARNEST. I CALLED POPS A	LIAR	, SWEETIE, BECAUSE ALL THIS IS NOT ENOUGH. THE GLORIES
CAPT I	(236)	THING (POINTING TO DRINKWATER) IS THE GREATEST	LIAR	, THIEF, DRUNKARD, AND RAPSCALLION ON THE WEST COAST.
2TRU III	(109)	OF THEM: WHAT STORYTELLER, HOWEVER RECKLESS A	LIAR	, WOULD DARE TO INVENT FIGURES SO IMPROBABLE AS MEN AND
ARMS III	(60)	HIMSELF FRANTICALLY ON THE BREAST), COWARD!	LIAR	! FOOL! SHALL I KILL MYSELF LIKE A MAN, OR LIVE AND
POSN	(439)	WHAT HE CALLED US? YOU FOUL-MOUTHED BRUTE! YOU	LIAR	! HOW DARE YOU PUT SUCH A NAME TO A DECENT WOMAN? LET
DEST	(158)	YOUTH, I'LL SPOIL HIS BEAUTY, THE SLIMY LITTLE	LIAR	! I'LL MAKE A PICTURE OF HIM. I'LL-- /NAPOLEON/ (
MTH4 II	(193)	(THROWING OFF THE WOMEN WITH A SUPERB GESTURE)	LIAR	! (RECOLLECTING HIMSELF, HE ADDS, WITH NOBLE
ROCK II	(262)	IT'S PUT TO IT. /SIR DEXTER/ TRAITOR! /BASHAM/	LIAR	! NOW WEVE CALLED ONE ANOTHER NAMES HOW MUCH FARTHER
POSN	(453)	IMMORAL RELATIONS WITH STRAPPER. /FEEMY/ OH YOU	LIAR	! /BLANCO/ I ACCUSE THE FAIR EUPHEMIA OF IMMORAL
CLEO IV	(178)	IS SET ON YOUR DEPARTURE? /CLEOPATRA/ (RISING)	LIAR	! /CAESAR/ (SHOCKED) WHAT! PROTESTATIONS!
JOAN EPILOG	(156)	/CAUCHON/ (APPEARING AT THE WINDOW BETWEEN THEM)	LIAR	! /CHARLES/ THANK YOU. /JOAN/ WHY, IF IS ISNT PETER
MIS.	(178)	TARLETON/ OH, LISTEN TO THAT! /BENTLEY/ WHAT A	LIAR	! /HYPATIA/ OH! /TARLETON/ OH, COME! /PERCIVAL/
LION II	(136)	BACK. /FERROVIUS/ (IN A VOICE OF THUNDER)	LIAR	! /THE EDITOR/ (NOT HEEDING HIM) MARCH. (THE
2TRU I	(31)	DOWN) NO. NOTHING. NEARLY NORMAL. /THE MONSTER/	LIAR	! /THE ELDERLY LADY/ WHAT A RELIEF! /THE DOCTOR/ YOU
			LIARS	
FABL PREFACE	(64)	WE ALL MENTAL CASES? ARE WE SIMPLY INCORRIGIBLE	LIARS	? ARE PLAYERS IMPOSTORS AND HYPOCRITES? WERE THE
APPL INTRLUD	(244)	ALWAYS HAVE A PRETTY EXCUSE. YOU ARE THE KING OF	LIARS	AND HUMBUGS. YOU CANNOT UNDERSTAND HOW A FALSEHOOD
JOAN PREFACE	(31)	INTO THE FIELD, SHE WAS DOWN ON THEM AT ONCE FOR	LIARS	AND HUMBUGS; BUT SHE NEVER THOUGHT OF THEM AS
JOAN 6	(130)	COMMON ERROR OF MISTAKING THESE SIMPLETONS FOR	LIARS	AND HYPOCRITES. THEY BELIEVE HONESTLY AND SINCERELY
LION PREFACE	(53)	US," AND WE CAN HEAR THE REPLY, " WOE UNTO YOU,	LIARS	AND HYPOCRITES; FOR YE HAVE THIS VERY DAY DIVIDED UP
BARB PREFACE	(223)	AND, I FEAR, THINK OF DRAMATIC AUTHORS AS	LIARS	AND PANDARS, WHOSE MAIN BUSINESS IS THE VOLUPTUOUS
FABL PREFACE	(77)	TO DISMISS THEIR EXPERIENCES AS THE INVENTIONS OF	LIARS	AND THE FANCIES OF NOODLES. THEY ARE EVIDENCE LIKE ANY
GETT	(299)	IS IT UNDERSTOOD THAT SLATTOX AND CHINNERY ARE	LIARS	AND THIEVES, AND THAT I HOPE BY NEXT WEDNESDAY TO HAVE
HART I	(63)	I COULDNT BE SO MISTAKEN: I KNOW TOO WELL WHAT	LIARS	ARE LIKE. SOMEBODY HAS REALLY TOLD YOU ALL THIS.
SUPR III	(129)	DISCIPLINED, ONLY COWED; AND NOT TRUTHFUL AT ALL:	LIARS	EVERY ONE OF THEM, TO THE VERY BACKBONE OF THEIR
2TRU II	(61)	THERE ISNT. DO YOU SUPPOSE WE THREE ARE THE ONLY	LIARS	IN THE WORLD? ALL YOU HAVE TO DO IS TO GIVE YOURSELF
METH PREFACE	(R81)	WITH THEM AROSE FROM THEIR BEING INVETERATE	LIARS	. BUT THEY WOULD NOT VOTE A SECOND TIME FOR THE MAN
LADY PREFACE	(229)	TOLD OUR BRITISH WORKMEN THAT THEY WERE MOSTLY	LIARS	. CARLYLE TOLD US ALL THAT WE ARE MOSTLY FOOLS.
METH PREFACE	(R75)	A FRAUD, AND PARSONS AND TEACHERS HYPOCRITES AND	LIARS	. HE BECOMES INDIFFERENT TO RELIGION IF HE HAS LITTLE
ROCK I	(200)	OF THE FIRST IMPORTANCE. /HILDA/ BUT THEYRE BOTH	LIARS	. /SIR ARTHUR/ OF COURSE THEY ARE; BUT THE DIVISION
CYMB V	(144)	BE MAD, SIGNOR, OR ELSE THE MOST AUDACIOUS OF ALL	LIARS	THAT EVER SWORE AWAY A WOMAN'S HONOR. /IACHIMO/ I
2TRU II	(63)	THEORY OF LEGAL PROCEDURE IS THAT IF YOU SET TWO	LIARS	TO EXPOSE ONE ANOTHER, THE TRUTH WILL EMERGE. THAT
CAPT III	(278)	AT HIM WITH THE STEADFAST CANDOR PECULIAR TO	LIARS	WHO READ NOVELS, HIS EYES TURN TO THE GROUND; AND HIS
LION PREFACE	(47)	ST THOMAS AQUINAS OR THE POPE AS SUPERSTITIOUS	LIARS	WHOM, AFTER HIS DEATH, HE WILL HAVE THE PLEASURE OF
MILL PREFACE	(124)	ARE A RACE OF SAVAGE IDOLATERS, MURDERERS,	LIARS	, AND FIENDS WHOSE ASSUMPTION OF THE HUMAN FORM IS
GETT	(297)	WORDS MOST CAREFULLY. I SAID THEY WERE TYRANTS,	LIARS	, AND THIEVES; AND SO THEY ARE. SLATTOX IS EVEN WORSE.
O'FL	(213)	THEM: I COULDNT THINK, SOMEHOW, THAT THEY WERE	LIARS	, AND THIEVES, AND BACKBITERS, AND DRUNKARDS, JUST.
METH PREFACE	(R56)	RABBLE OF DOLTS, BLACKGUARDS, IMPOSTORS, QUACKS,	LIARS	, AND, WORST OF ALL, CREDULOUS CONSCIENTIOUS FOOLS.
FABL PREFACE	(67)	ARE OFTEN SPENDTHRIFTS, DRUNKARDS, LIBERTINES,	LIARS	, DISHONEST IN MONEY MATTERS, BACKSLIDERS OF ALL
GETT	(318)	LIAR. IF I MAY SAY SO WITHOUT OFFENCE, WE'RE ALL	LIARS	, IF IT WAS ONLY TO SPARE ONE ANOTHER'S FEELINGS. BUT
			LIBBETY	
CAPT I	(227)	CHAIR FOR SIR HOWARD) AWSKINK YR PAWDN FOR THE	LIBBETY	, SR AHRD. /SIR HOWARD/ (LOOKING AT HIM) I HAVE
			LIBEL	
GETT	(347)	/EDITH/ IT HAS CONSENTED TO INSURE CECIL AGAINST	LIBEL	ACTIONS BROUGHT AGAINST HIM ON MY ACCOUNT. IT WILL
SIM II	(65)	OUR STATESMEN UNTIL THEY ARE DEAD AND CANT TAKE	LIBEL	ACTIONS. NOBODY KNOWS THE SORT OF PEOPLE WE REALLY
POSN PREFACE	(420)	MAGNA CHARTA DECLARING ALL THE CATEGORIES OF	LIBEL	AND THE BLASPHEMY LAWS CONTRARY TO PUBLIC LIBERTY, AND
POSN PREFACE	(418)	WHETHER IT COULD NOT BE CONSTRUED AS A SEDITIOUS	LIBEL	AS WELL. AS TO IBSEN'S BRAND (THE PLAY WHICH MADE HIM
MILL I	(142)	CONGRATULATE MYSELF ON THE NUMBER OF ACTIONS FOR	LIBEL	I SHALL HAVE TO DEFEND IF YOU DO ME THE HONOR OF
POSN PREFACE	(418)	WITH THE MOST ELEMENTARY KNOWLEDGE OF THE LAW OF	LIBEL	IN ITS VARIOUS APPLICATIONS TO SEDITION, OBSCENITY,
POSN PREFACE	(421)	PREVENTS OR PUNISHES INDECENCY, BLASPHEMY AND	LIBEL	IN PRINTED PUBLICATIONS (IT DOES NOT, BY THE WAY,
SUPR III	(107)	AND HE WILL ONLY TAKE AN ACTION AGAINST YOU FOR	LIBEL	: BUT CALL HIM COWARD; AND HE WILL GO MAD WITH RAGE:
MILL I	(142)	YOU ARE UNFAITHFUL TO YOUR WIFE, THAT WOULD BE A	LIBEL	; BUT IF I CALL YOU A RHINOCEROS-- WHICH YOU ARE: A
POSN PREFACE	(367)	POSSIBILITY OF A PRIVATE ACTION FOR DEFAMATORY	LIBEL	. HIS SOLE REFUGE IS THE OPINION OF THE EXAMINER OF
MILL I	(142)	FATHER INSTRUCTED ME MOST CAREFULLY IN THE LAW OF	LIBEL	. IF I QUESTIONED YOUR SOLVENCY, THAT WOULD BE A
MILL I	(142)	IF I QUESTIONED YOUR SOLVENCY, THAT WOULD BE A	LIBEL	. IF I SUGGESTED THAT YOU ARE UNFAITHFUL TO YOUR WIFE,
MILL I	(142)	/EPIFANIA/ YOU ARE WRONG. I NEVER UTTER A	LIBEL	. MY FATHER INSTRUCTED ME MOST CAREFULLY IN THE LAW OF
LADY PREFACE	(216)	NAME, SPENSER, THAT IS NECESSARY TO EXPOSE SUCH A	LIBEL	ON ELIZABETHAN DECENCY. THERE WAS NOTHING WHATEVER TO
JOAN PREFACE	(24)	THIS WITH VIRTUOUS INDIGNATION AS AN OBSCENE	LIBEL	; AND I CERTAINLY CANNOT DEFEND IT AGAINST THE CHARGE
MILL I	(142)	VULGAR ABUSE; AND I HAVE NEVER HAD AN ACTION FOR	LIBEL	TAKEN AGAINST ME. IS THAT THE LAW, OR IS IT NOT?
POSN PREFACE	(418)	THAT DESPAIR EVER UTTERED, IS A BLASPHEMOUS	LIBEL	, AND THAT IT IS DOUBTFUL WHETHER IT COULD NOT BE
GETT PREFACE	(184)	PROTECTION AFFORDED TO THE PARTIES BY THE LAW OF	LIBEL	, AND THE READINESS OF SOCIETY ON VARIOUS OTHER
POSN PREFACE	(418)	FOR A GUARANTEE THAT NEITHER OF THESE WORKS WAS A	LIBEL	, HE WOULD HAVE TO REPLY THAT HE COULD GIVE NO SUCH
POSN PREFACE	(367)	A CHARGE OF BLASPHEMOUS LIBEL, SEDITIOUS	LIBEL	, OBSCENE LIBEL, OR ALL THREE TOGETHER, NOT TO MENTION
POSN PREFACE	(367)	OF BLASPHEMOUS LIBEL, SEDITIOUS LIBEL, OBSCENE	LIBEL	, OR ALL THREE TOGETHER, NOT TO MENTION THE
POSN PREFACE	(367)	IN THE DOCK ANSWERING A CHARGE OF BLASPHEMOUS	LIBEL	, SEDITIOUS LIBEL, OBSCENE LIBEL, OR ALL THREE
FABL PREFACE	(78)	AND BY THE LAW AGAINST SEDITIOUS AND BLASPHEMOUS	LIBEL	, THAT MY SPEECHES WERE NEVER REPORTED, AND MY LETTERS
POSN PREFACE	(381)	AND THE WHOLE BODY OF LAW, BLASPHEMY, INDECENCY,	LIBEL	, TREASON, SEDITION, OBSCENITY, PROFANITY, AND ALL THE
			LIBELLED	
GETT	(294)	MARRIED I SHOULD BE LEGALLY RESPONSIBLE IF SHE	LIBELLED	ANYBODY, THOUGH ALL HER PROPERTY IS PROTECTED
			LIBELLER	
POSN PREFACE	(415)	DENOUNCED THAT CHIEF CONSTABLE AS AN IGNORANT	LIBELLER	OF A NOBLE PROFESSION. BUT THE CONSTABLE WOULD HAVE
			LIBELLING	
LADY PREFACE	(215)	SORT OF BLACKMAIL WHICH CONSISTS IN MERCILESSLY	LIBELLING	AND INSULTING EVERY WRITER WHOSE OPINIONS ARE
			LIBELLOUS	
POSN PREFACE	(367)	CHARACTER PART" IN A STAGE FIGURE WHICH MAY BE A	LIBELLOUS	AND UNMISTAKEABLE CARICATURE OF SOME EMINENT
PYGM PREFACE	(200)	TO A PHONETIC EXPERT ONLY. THE ARTICLE, BEING	LIBELLOUS	, HAD TO BE RETURNED AS IMPOSSIBLE; AND I HAD TO
			LIBELS	
JOAN PREFACE	(7)	TO HAVE BEEN TINKERED BY SHAKESPEAR) GROSSLY	LIBELS	HER IN ITS CONCLUDING SCENES IN DEFERENCE TO JINGO
POSN PREFACE	(418)	TO WARN HIS CLIENT THAT BOTH OF THEM ARE OBSCENE	LIBELS	; THAT KING LEAR, CONTAINING AS IT DOES PERHAPS THE
			LIBERAL	
BULL III	(133)	PRINCIPLE OF DISESTABLISHMENT. /LARRY/ I AM NOT A	LIBERAL	: HEAVEN FORBID! A DISESTABLISHED CHURCH IS THE
ROCK II	(252)	INDIGNATION. /THE MAYOR/ WHO ARE YOU CALLING A	LIBERAL	? I REPRESENT THE LABOR PARTY. /SIR BEMROSE/ YOURE
HART III	(133)	/LADY UTTERWORD/ AS A CONSERVATIVE OR A	LIBERAL	? /MANGAN/ NO SUCH NONSENSE. AS A PRACTICAL
SIM PREFACE	(11)	BOLSHEVIKS, INFECTED AS THEY WERE WITH ENGLISH	LIBERAL	AND AGNOSTIC NOTIONS, AT FIRST TRIED TO DO WITHOUT
BUOY 1	(12)	HEAD. THE FRENCH REVOLUTION TRIED HARD TO BE	LIBERAL	AND PARLIAMENTARY. NO USE: THE GUILLOTINE WAS

MTH2 (68)	WHICH YOU CAN APPROACH THROUGH YOUR LOCAL	LIBERAL	AND RADICAL ASSOCIATION. /FRANKLYN/ I COULD RECALL
BULL PREFACE(4)	LITTLE LOCAL CAUCUSES WHICH CALLED THEMSELVES	LIBERAL	AND RADICAL ASSOCIATIONS, AND WERE OPEN TO ANY
POSN PREFACE(368)	AND PARTY AFFAIRS BRITISH GOVERNMENTS, BOTH	LIBERAL	AND UNIONIST, STILL ARE. THE CENSORSHIP SCANDAL HAD
PRES (162)	THE STRAIN IS TOO MUCH FOR THE CABINET. THE OLD	LIBERAL	AND UNIONIST FREE TRADERS DECLARE THAT IF THEY ARE
BARB I SD(249)	THAT ASSUMPTION, AND BEING QUITE ENLIGHTENED AND	LIBERAL	AS TO THE BOOKS IN THE LIBRARY, THE PICTURES ON THE
MTH2 (44)	HIM FOR YEARS. I RESIGNED THE CHAIRMANSHIP OF THE	LIBERAL	ASSOCIATION AND SHOOK THE DUST OF PARTY POLITICS
ROCK II (244)	YOUR PROGRAM, ARTHUR; BUT ON THESE POINTS NO TRUE	LIBERAL	CAN QUESTION YOUR MAGNIFICENT STATESMANSHIP. /SIR
ROCK II (254)	DUKE, EMBRACE IT. SIR JAFNA PANDRANATH HERE, A	LIBERAL	CAPITALIST WHOSE BILLIONS SHAME MY POVERTY, EMBRACES
CAPT II (267)	NIGHTS-- COPY IN THE LIBRARY OF THE NATIONAL	LIBERAL	CLUB. /LADY CICELY/ (CALLING WITHOUT) MR
PLES PREFACE(R18)	FACT THAT WAS AT ISSUE BETWEEN US. ONE STRONGLY	LIBERAL	CRITIC, THE LATE MOY THOMAS, WHO HAD, IN THE TEETH
MILL PREFACE(112)	HER FROM SCOLDING HER MAIDS PROPERLY. MODERN	LIBERAL	DEMOCRACY CLAIMS UNLIMITED OPPORTUNITIES FOR
GENV IV (111)	HAVE DARED TO DO THIS, WHAT HAPPENS? OUT OF THE	LIBERAL	DEMOCRATIC CHAOS COMES FORM, PURPOSE, ORDER AND
APPL PREFACE(171)	AND ROYALTY AS OUR IDEALISTS CONCEIVE THEM. OUR	LIBERAL	DEMOCRATS BELIEVE IN A FIGMENT CALLED A
MIS. PREFACE(57)	TEMPTS TO VIOLENCE (AS A SHORT CUT) MORE THAN	LIBERAL	EDUCATION. THE SAILOR IN MR RUDYARD KIPLING'S
CATH 4 (189)	HOW DARE YOU NAME SUCH ABOMINATIONS TO A	LIBERAL	EMPRESS? YOU WILL ALWAYS BE A SAVAGE AND A FOOL.
CATH 2 (175)	HERSELF ON THE EDGE OF IT) FLOGGED! !! A	LIBERAL	EMPRESS! A PHILOSOPHER! YOU ARE A BARBARIAN,
MTH2 (67)	IT WILL HAVE TO REACH ME THROUGH THE NATIONAL	LIBERAL	FEDERATION, WHICH YOU CAN APPROACH THROUGH YOUR
GENV IV (111)	NOT FAIL HIM, IN SPITE OF ALL THE DEMOCRATIC	LIBERAL	GABBLERS. I HAVE SPOKEN. NOW IT IS YOUR TURN,
BULL PREFACE(63)	IN VAIN. SIR EDWARD, ON BEHALF OF THE NEW	LIBERAL	GOVERNMENT (STILL SIMMERING WITH VIRTUOUS
POSN PREFACE(368)	GOVERNMENT INTERFERED. IT MAY NOW BE ASKED HOW A	LIBERAL	GOVERNMENT HAD BEEN PERSUADED TO MEDDLE AT ALL WITH
POSN PREFACE(365)	WAS THE NONCONFORMIST CONSCIENCE, HOLDING THE	LIBERAL	GOVERNMENT RESPONSIBLE FOR THE COMMITTEE IT HAD
CATH PREFACE(153)	THE MAIN DIFFERENCE BETWEEN HER AND OUR MODERN	LIBERAL	GOVERNMENTS WAS THAT WHEREAS SHE TALKED AND WROTE
POSN PREFACE(399)	CENSORSHIP, SUCH A CENSORSHIP MIGHT BE MORE	LIBERAL	IN ITS TOLERATION OF MATTERS WHICH ARE ONLY OBJECTED
BULL PREFACE(40)	HIS CUSTOMERS MAY STOP THEIR ORDERS IF HE VOTES	LIBERAL	INSTEAD OF CONSERVATIVE. ENGLISH LADIES AND
HART PREFACE(10)	EVER HAVE CLAIMED. THE INQUISITION ITSELF WAS A	LIBERAL	INSTITUTION COMPARED TO THE GENERAL MEDICAL COUNCIL.
ROCK II (252)	MAYOR/ OF COURSE I AM. /SIR BEMROSE/ THEN YOURE A	LIBERAL	. /THE MAYOR/ CALL ME WHAT YOU LIKE. I'M NOT
BULL III (135)	THERES A GREAT DEAL OF TRUTH IN IT. NOW I AM A	LIBERAL	. YOU KNOW THE GREAT PRINCIPLES OF THE LIBERAL
BULL I (77)	KNOW. IT'S AWFUL (HE DRINKS). I SEE YOURE A GOOD	LIBERAL	LIKE MESELF, SIR. /BROADBENT/ I AM A LOVER OF
ROCK II (242)	IN THE POUND. STILL, I ADMIT, YOU PULLED DOWN MY	LIBERAL	MAJORITY OVER MY CONSERVATIVE OPPONENT FROM FOUR
POSN PREFACE(425)	ROMAN CATHOLIC CATHEDRAL OF WESTMINSTER. EVERY	LIBERAL	MEETING IS A DEFIANCE AND A CHALLENGE TO THE MOST
CATH PREFACE(153)	SUCH TALKING AND WRITING A FLOGGING MATTER, OUR	LIBERAL	MINISTERS TAKE THE NAME OF LIBERALISM IN VAIN
PHIL PREFACE(68)	BUT THEY DO NOT ASSOCIATE THEIR ADVANCE IN	LIBERAL	MORALS WITH THE GREAT NORWEGIAN. EVEN THE
MILL PREFACE(121)	AND A COUPLE OF MURDERS, WHEREUPON ALL THE	LIBERAL	NEWSPAPERS IN EUROPE SHRIEKED WITH HORROR AS IF
MTH2 (64)	SOCIALIST GROUNDS NO LESS THAN ON THE SOUNDEST	LIBERAL	ONES. /BURGE/ IN SHORT, LUBIN, YOURE INCORRIGIBLE.
METH PREFACE(R69)	WOULD HAVE SCANDALIZED GEORGE III AND ELICITED	LIBERAL	PAMPHLETS FROM CATHERINE II. STATESMEN ARE AFRAID OF
BULL PREFACE(3)	THIS APPARENT ECLIPSE OF HOME RULE WAS THAT THE	LIBERAL	PARTY HAD DURING THAT PERIOD PERSISTED IN ASSURING
MTH2 (74)	THE CHURCH HAS OFTEN BEEN WRONG, AND EVEN THE	LIBERAL	PARTY HAS NOT BEEN INFALLIBLE. THE MEN OF SCIENCE
MTH2 (79)	THIS TRIBUTE? /BURGE/ DONE! YOU HAVE PUT THE	LIBERAL	PARTY INTO POWER FOR THE NEXT THIRTY YEARS, DOCTOR!
MTH2 (79)	/FRANKLYN/ WOULD THIRTY YEARS OF OFFICE FOR THE	LIBERAL	PARTY SEEM SO IMPORTANT TO YOU, MR BURGE, IF YOU HAD
BULL III (136)	TO HAVE ENLARGED ON THE SERVICES RENDERED BY THE	LIBERAL	PARTY TO THE RELIGIOUS FAITH OF THE GREAT MAJORITY
BULL IV (150)	AN OPERATION. I BELIEVE A LARGE SECTION OF THE	LIBERAL	PARTY WOULD AVAIL THEMSELVES OF IT. (MOMENTARY
MTH2 (55)	FOR I THOUGHT I WAS THE LEADER OF THE	LIBERAL	PARTY. HOWEVER, IT IS VERY KIND OF YOU TO TAKE IT
BULL III (135)	A LIBERAL. YOU KNOW THE GREAT PRINCIPLES OF THE	LIBERAL	PARTY. PEACE-- /FATHER DEMPSEY/ (PIOUSLY) HEAR!
MTH2 (55)	PARTY, EH? THE NEWSPAPER PARTY? /BURGE/ THE	LIBERAL	PARTY. THE PARTY OF WHICH I HAVE THE HONOR TO BE
BULL III (135)	HAVE ALREADY BEEN CONFERRED ON HUMANITY BY THE	LIBERAL	PARTY, AND TRUSTING FOR FUTURE DEVELOPMENTS TO THE
POSN PREFACE(368)	HARCOURT ENTERED PARLIAMENT AS A MEMBER OF THE	LIBERAL	PARTY, OF WHICH HIS FATHER HAD BEEN ONE OF THE
SIM PREFACE(10)	THIS SITUATION, THOUGH NEW TO OUR GENERATION OF	LIBERAL	PLUTOCRATS, IS NOT NEW HISTORICALLY. THE CHANGE FROM
CATH PREFACE(153)	THAT SUCH PROCEEDINGS NEED ANY APOLOGY FROM THE	LIBERAL	POINT OF VIEW. IT WAS QUITE EASY FOR PATIOMKIN TO
BULL III (133)	ELOQUENCE, I IMPLORE YOU NOT TO DESERT THE GREAT	LIBERAL	PRINCIPLE OF DISESTABLISHMENT. /LARRY/ I AM NOT A
CATH PREFACE(153)	SHE TALKED AND WROTE QUITE INTELLIGENTLY ABOUT	LIBERAL	PRINCIPLES BEFORE SHE WAS FRIGHTENED INTO MAKING
BULL IV (175)	HABITS TEACH IT EFFICIENCY AND SELF-HELP ON SOUND	LIBERAL	PRINCIPLES. YOU AGREE WITH ME, MR KEEGAN, DONT YOU?
ROCK II (262)	BUT I AM A LIBERAL, AND, AS SUCH, BOUND BY	LIBERAL	PRINCIPLES. WHATEVER WE DO MUST BE DONE THROUGH
CATH PREFACE(153)	WHOSE CAMPAIGNS AND CONQUESTS, WHOSE PLANS OF	LIBERAL	REFORM, WHOSE CORRESPONDENCE WITH GRIMM AND VOLTAIRE
PLES PREFACE(R18)	AS ROMANCE IN ETHICS OR RELIGION. IN SPITE OF A	LIBERAL	REVOLUTION OR TWO, I CAN NO LONGER BE SATISFIED WITH
BULL I (77)	WHERE ELSE CAN I GO? I AM AN ENGLISHMAN AND A	LIBERAL	; AND NOW THAT SOUTH AFRICA HAS BEEN ENSLAVED AND
2TRU PREFACE(21)	REVOLUTIONISTS, WHO WERE REEKING WITH PROTESTANT	LIBERAL	SUPERSTITIONS AT THE BEGINNING, HAVE HAD TO COME
POSN PREFACE(365)	WITHOUT TOO SERIOUS AN INTERFERENCE WITH CERTAIN	LIBERAL	TRADITIONS OF LIBERTY WHICH ARE STILL USEFUL TO
BARB I SD(249)	WALKS TO THE SETTEE AND SITS DOWN. HE TAKES UP A	LIBERAL	WEEKLY CALLED THE SPEAKER. /LADY BRITOMART/ DONT
METH PREFACE(R13)	OF THE FIFTEENTH CENTURY, AND THINK THEMSELVES	LIBERAL	WHEN THEY ARE DEFENDING THE IDEAS OF HENRY VII, AND
BULL PREFACE(26)	A FREETHINKER, A SELF-HELPER, A WHIG, A	LIBERAL	, A MISTRUSTER AND VILIFIER OF THE STATE, A REBEL.
ROCK II (262)	TO SECURE MY SEAT IN PARLIAMENT. BUT I AM A	LIBERAL	, AND, AS SUCH, BOUND BY LIBERAL PRINCIPLES.
SIM PREFACE(9)	THEY TO BE DEALT WITH? THE WELL-TO-DO BRITISH	LIBERAL	, CLAMORING FOR FREEDOM OF CONSCIENCE, OBJECTS TO
GETT PREFACE(231)	THEM QUITE AS TOUCHINGLY AS WE) ARE MUCH MORE	LIBERAL	, KNOWING AS THEY DO THAT MONOGAMY WILL TAKE CARE OF
MRS PREFACE(164)	IN EUROPE. IS IT MORE ENLIGHTENED, MORE	LIBERAL	, MORE TOLERANT THAN THE COMPARATIVELY UNQUALIFIED
FABL PREFACE(78)	WAS MADE IN CONSERVATIVE PAPERS WHILST THE	LIBERAL	, RADICAL, AND SOCIALIST EDITORS DARED NOT MENTION
ROCK I (227)	OF A CONSERVATIVE! THANK HEAVEN I AM A	LIBERAL	! /THE LADY/ YOU MEAN THAT YOU MAKE SPEECHES ABOUT

LIBERALISM

2TRU PREFACE(20)	CATHOLICISM AND PROTESTANTISM, CHURCH AND EMPIRE,	LIBERALISM	AND DEMOCRACY, UP TO DATE. CLEARLY A GHASTLY
GETT PREFACE(230)	AS EXISTING SOLELY FOR THE USE OF MEN. WHEN	LIBERALISM	ENFRANCHISES THEM POLITICALLY, AND SOCIALISM
CATH PREFACE(153)	MATTER, OUR LIBERAL MINISTERS TAKE THE NAME OF	LIBERALISM	IN VAIN WITHOUT KNOWING OR CARING ENOUGH ABOUT
2TRU PREFACE(13)	ON ENGLISH HISTORY WHICH INSPIRED THE VIGOROUS	LIBERALISM	OF HIS SALAD DAYS, HAS LATELY TAKEN ME TO TASK
LION PREFACE(96)	HAVE WITNESSED A DISTINCT REACTION FROM VICTORIAN	LIBERALISM	TO COLLECTIVISM WHICH HAS PERCEPTIBLY
METH PREFACE(R69)	WAR OF 1870-71. THE STURDY OLD COSMOPOLITAN	LIBERALISM	VANISHED ALMOST UNNOTICED. AT THE PRESENT MOMENT
SUPR HANDBOK(197)	CHURCH WAS DISESTABLISHED, NOT BY THE SPIRIT OF	LIBERALISM	, BUT BY THE EXPLOSION WHICH WRECKED CLERKENWELL
MILL PREFACE(128)	OTHER TYRANNIES HAVE BEEN SWEPT AWAY BY SIMPLE	LIBERALISM	, THE TYRANNY OF THE TALENTED INDIVIDUALS WILL
BULL PREFACE(3)	WHAT IT HAD BEEN IN THE HEYDAY OF GLADSTONIAN	LIBERALISM	, WHEN IT WAS UTTERLY INCONCEIVABLE THAT AN ACT

LIBERALITY

DEVL EPILOG (84)	ADMITTED ON PAROLE AND WILL BE TREATED WITH THE	LIBERALITY	CUSTOMARY IN SUCH CASES, SO LONG AS THEY, BY
LION PREFACE(96)	WILL HARDLY CONTEND THAT OUR GROWTH IN WISDOM AND	LIBERALITY	HAS BEEN GREATER IN THE LAST HALF CENTURY THAN IN
CLEO III (154)	HEAVEN AGAINST THEIR PATRON'S STINGINESS. BUT HIS	LIBERALITY	OVERPOWERS THEM). /FIRST PORTER/ O BOUNTEOUS

LIBERALLY

MILL IV SD(188)	COLOR SCHEME. THE FLOOR IS PARQUETTED AND	LIBERALLY	SUPPLIED WITH ORIENTAL RUGS. ALL THE APPURTENANCES
MTH4 I (169)	ONLY CONJECTURE THAT YOU HAVE CONTRIBUTED VERY	LIBERALLY	TO THE PARTY FUNDS. (HE PICKS UP HIS HAT, AND
WIDO I (21)	THE BULK OF HER FATHER'S FORTUNE, AND WILL BE	LIBERALLY	TREATED ON HER MARRIAGE. HER EDUCATION HAS BEEN OF
PLES PREFACE(R16)	CASE OF LAUGHTER AND TEARS, IN WHICH IT DEALS TOO	LIBERALLY	, IT IS CERTAINLY NOT BASED ON THE FACT, EASILY

LIBERALS

APPL PREFACE(184)	SEVERAL ACTIVE POLITICIANS WHO BEGAN AS	LIBERALS	AND ARE NOW SOCIALISTS HAVE SAID TO ME THAT THEY
ROCK II (235)	US. HE PRETENDED THAT WITHOUT HIS OLD GUARD OF	LIBERALS	AND HIS RAGTAG AND BOBTAIL OF LABOR MEN AND
GENV II (62)	UP A CANDIDATE AGAINST THE LABOR MAN; AND THE	LIBERALS	ARE CONTESTING THE SEAT AS WELL. IT WILL BE JUST A
BULL PREFACE(4)	MR SIDNEY WEBB, AND INGENIOUSLY FOISTED ON THE	LIBERALS	BY MYSELF AND OTHER FABIANS DISGUISED AS ARTLESS
ROCK II (252)	THEM? /SIR BEMROSE/ IT'S NO USE. THESE DAMNED	LIBERALS	CANT UNDERSTAND ANYTHING BUT VIRTUOUS INDIGNATION.
ROCK II (258)	IS TEN TIMES MORE REALLY DEMOCRATIC THAN YOU	LIBERALS	HAVE EVER BEEN, WILL CARRY THE PEOPLE WITH IT
SUPR HANDBOK(201)	TO OPPRESSED. THE POOR MAN IS GIVEN A VOTE BY THE	LIBERALS	IN THE HOPE THAT HE WILL CAST IT FOR HIS
MILL PREFACE(121)	EVERYTHING THAT HAS HAPPENED." WHEN THE ITALIAN	LIBERALS	JOINED IN THE SHRIEKING HE SEIZED THE SHRIEKERS AND
GETT PREFACE(223)	COMFORT OR CONDUCT. WE MAY BE ENTHUSIASTIC	LIBERALS	OR CONSERVATIVES WITHOUT ANY HOPE OF SEATS IN
MILL PREFACE(126)	RAIDS AND COUPS D'ETAT AGAINST INCONVENIENT	LIBERALS	OR MARXISTS. A PERSECUTION IS ALWAYS A MAN HUNT;
BULL PREFACE(4)	EXCEPT ON ONE OCCASION IN 1893, WHEN THE	LIBERALS	PUT ALL THEIR HOME RULE TRACTS IN THE FIRE, AND
BULL PREFACE(4)	RULERS. IT WAS A CLOSE THING; BUT IT WON IT. THE	LIBERALS	THEN DROPPED IT; AND LORD ROSEBERY MADE HIS FAMOUS
POSN PREFACE(425)	CATHOLICS TO ATTEND SERVICE AT ST PAUL'S, OR THE	LIBERALS	TO ATTEND THE MEETINGS OF THE PRIMROSE LEAGUE WOULD
MILL PREFACE(120)	THE PEOPLE, INSTEAD OF BEING SHOCKED LIKE GOOD	LIBERALS	, ROSE TO HIM. HE WAS ABLE TO ORGANIZE A SPECIAL

LIBERATED

GENV PREFACE(14)	IN WHICH EVERYBODY WAS TO BE BOTH EMPLOYED AND	LIBERATED	, MR CHURCHILL AT ONCE SHARED THE FATE OF LLOYD

GENV PREFACE(9)	BUT DISTRICTS, AND WHEN WE AND OUR ALLIES "	LIBERATED	" GERMAN-OCCUPIED TERRITORY (BLOWING ITS CITIES
		LIBERATING	
FANY II (293)	(SHE RISES AND STRETCHES HER ARMS WITH A LARGE	LIBERATING	BREATH) NOW THAT IT'S ALL OVER I'M RATHER PROUD
FABL I (102)	BROTHER WAS KILLED IN NORMANDY WHEN WE WERE	LIBERATING	FRANCE THERE. HIS WIFE AND CHILDREN WERE BLOWN TO
GENV PREFACE(5)	GERMANY BUT IN COUNTRIES WHICH WE CLAIMED TO BE "	LIBERATING	" BECAME SO FRIGHTFUL THAT AT LAST THE WORD HAD
GENV PREFACE(8)	MEANWHILE THE BRITISH AND AMERICAN ARMIES WERE "	LIBERATING	" FRENCH CITIES, DUTCH CITIES, BELGIAN CITIES,
		LIBERATION	
BULL PREFACE(41)	VITAL, EXCEPT THE BUSINESS OF UNIFICATION AND	LIBERATION	. THAT IS WHY EVERYTHING IS IN ABEYANCE IN
		LIBERATORS	
POSN PREFACE(385)	THIS HAS NOTHING TO DO WITH ANY SYMPATHY THESE	LIBERATORS	MAY THEMSELVES HAVE WITH IMMORAL VIEWS. A MAN
		LIBERIA	
MTH3 (123)	BETTER OFF HERE THAN THEY WOULD BE IN CHINA OR	LIBERIA	. THEY DO THEIR WORK ADMIRABLY; AND IN DOING IT THEY
		LIBERTIES	
MIS. PREFACE(6)	FAR AS IT WILL LET THEM. IT HAS NO RIGHTS AND NO	LIBERTIES	: IN SHORT, ITS CONDITION IS THAT WHICH ADULTS
LION EPILOG (147)	EVEN THEIR MOST CHERISHED AND HARDWON PUBLIC	LIBERTIES	AND PRIVATE INTERESTS, IN THE IRRESISTIBLE SURGE
BARB III (339)	OF SOCIETY: THEY FORCE US TO DO AWAY WITH OUR OWN	LIBERTIES	AND TO ORGANIZE UNNATURAL CRUELTIES FOR FEAR THEY
MILL PREFACE(111)	ALL OVER THE COUNTRY? OUR BOASTED POLITICAL	LIBERTIES	ARE A MOCKERY TO THE SUBJECTS OF SUCH DESPOTISMS.
MIS. PREFACE(72)	AS THE ART OF CANING, AND, AFTER ALL, IF LARGER	LIBERTIES	ARE ATTACHED TO THE ACQUISITION OF KNOWLEDGE, AND
BARB PREFACE(243)	WRITER, BECAUSE OUR LAWS MAKE LAW IMPOSSIBLE; OUR	LIBERTIES	DESTROY ALL FREEDOM; OUR PROPERTY IS ORGANIZED
GENV PREFACE(16)	AND THEIR SUBJECTS SLAVES WITHOUT RIGHTS OR	LIBERTIES	, ALL GOOD RUSSIANS BELIEVE EQUALLY THAT THE
2TRU II (58)	IS DISASTROUS TO HIMSELF. HE PRESUMES. HE TAKES	LIBERTIES	, AND THE CONSEQUENCE OF THAT IS THAT HE GETS INTO
KING I (189)	YOUR INFERIORS. THEY FORGET THEMSELVES AND TAKE	LIBERTIES	, AND YOU ENCOURAGE HERETICS. I DO NOT. /CHARLES/
BARB PREFACE(226)	VENGEANCE AND RUTHLESS REPRESSION OF POPULAR	LIBERTIES	, THE NINETEENTH CENTURY SAW THE SAME LESSON
METH PREFACE(R67)	NOT TOLERATE ANY ATTEMPT TO TAMPER WITH BRITISH	LIBERTIES	, THEIR FAVORITE WAY OF PUTTING IT WAS THAT ANY
BULL PREFACE(45)	ENTERPRISE OF MEN ENJOYING ALL THE RIGHTS AND	LIBERTIES	OF CITIZENSHIP, AND TRAINED BY THE EXACTING
POSN PREFACE(422)	AT CONDUCT " CALCULATED TO" OVERTHROW THE	LIBERTIES	OF ENGLAND. POSSIBILITIES OF THE PROPOSAL. STILL,
PRES (138)	TO THE HOUSE LAST YEAR NOT TO THROW AWAY ALL THE	LIBERTIES	OF ENGLISHMEN BY ACCEPTING COMPULSORY MILITARY
MIS. PREFACE(12)	TO A DISASTROUS EXTENT WITH THE RIGHTS AND	LIBERTIES	OF ONE CHILD. BUT BY THE TIME A FOURTH CHILD HAS
PRES (162)	FOR WOMEN AS THE ONLY MEANS OF RESTORING THE	LIBERTIES	OF THE COUNTRY WHICH WE HAVE DESTROYED BY
POSN PREFACE(409)	THEATRES TO LOCAL CONTROL CAN BE A CHARTER OF THE	LIBERTIES	OF THE STAGE AS WELL AS AN ACT TO REFORM
MTH3 (95)	NOT BLAME YOU FOR IT; BUT ENGLAND ONCE SAVED THE	LIBERTIES	OF THE WORLD BY INVENTING PARLIAMENTARY
POSN PREFACE(388)	OF 1843 AND FOR THE DENIAL TO THE THEATRE OF THE	LIBERTIES	SECURED, AT FAR GREATER SOCIAL RISK, TO THE PRESS
POSN PREFACE(388)	NO QUESTION HERE OF GIVING THE THEATRE ANY LARGER	LIBERTIES	THAN THE PRESS AND THE PLATFORM, OR OF CLAIMING
MIS. (133)	IS AN AUTHOR THAT HE SHOULD BE PRIVILEGED TO TAKE	LIBERTIES	THAT ARE NOT ALLOWED TO OTHER MEN? /MRS TARLETON/
MILL PREFACE(119)	MEN FROM THE TRENCHES HAD NO PATIENCE WITH THE	LIBERTIES	THAT HAD NOT SAVED THEM FROM BEING DRIVEN LIKE
MIS. PREFACE(43)	ESTATES, NOR TOLERATE A HUNDRED OTHER ABSURD	LIBERTIES	THAT WE ALLOW TODAY BECAUSE WE ARE TOO LAZY TO
PYGM I (211)	DIRT UNDER YOUR FEET, DONT YOU? CATCH YOU TAKING	LIBERTIES	WITH A GENTLEMAN! /THE SARCASTIC BYSTANDER. YES:
LION I (119)	LUCKY FOR YOU TOO, SIR, IF YOU WANT TO TAKE ANY	LIBERTIES	WITH HIM. /LENTULUS/ (TO FERROVIUS) YOU TURN THE
HART II (124)	CONSIDERATION, I WILL NOT ALLOW HUSHABYE TO TAKE	LIBERTIES	WITH ME. I WILL NOT STAND YOUR ENCOURAGING PEOPLE
PHIL II (105)	ARE MEMBERS OF THE CLUB, NOT SISTERS. I DONT TAKE	LIBERTIES	WITH YOU HERE ON FAMILY GROUNDS: DONT YOU TAKE ANY
BULL PREFACE(43)	NATURAL RIGHTS. WHEN A MAN INSISTS ON CERTAIN	LIBERTIES	WITHOUT THE SLIGHTEST REGARD TO DEMONSTRATIONS
GETT PREFACE(237)	BREATHING, IS MAKING SHORT WORK OF MANY ANCIENT	LIBERTIES	, AND EXPOSING THE PURSUIT OF HAPPINESS AS PERHAPS
POSN PREFACE(394)	THEY MAY, HOWEVER, BE ENTIRELY OPPOSED TO POPULAR	LIBERTIES	, AND MAY CONCLUDE FROM WHAT HAS BEEN SAID, NOT
SUPR III (76)	CLASS, WE DO THIS AT THE RISK OF OUR LIVES AND	LIBERTIES	, BY THE EXERCISE OF THE VIRTUES OF COURAGE,
FANY III (311)	WHAT DO YOU MEAN? DONT YOU BEGIN TO TAKE	LIBERTIES	, JUGGINS, NOW THAT YOU KNOW WE'RE LOTH TO PART
		LIBERTINAGE	
POSN PREFACE(395)	HAS SCANDALIZED THE CRITICS IN LONDON BY THE	LIBERTINAGE	OF ITS JESTS IS PLAYED TO THE RESPECTABLE DRESS
		LIBERTINE	
OVER (175)	I THOUGHT YOU KNEW. /GREGORY/ YOU THOUGHT I WAS A	LIBERTINE	? /MRS JUNO/ NO: OF COURSE I SHOULDNT HAVE SPOKEN
SIM II (57)	AND EXEMPLARY COMBUSTION OF THE ABOMINABLE	LIBERTINE	AND DAMNABLE APOSTATE KNOWN AS PHOSFOR HAMMINGTAP.
GETT PREFACE(195)	LITERARY TRADITIONS SPRING UP IN WHICH THE	LIBERTINE	AND PROFLIGATE-- TOM JONES AND CHARLES SURFACE--
SUPR III (95)	BESIDES, MY CHILD, IN THIS PLACE, WHAT OUR	LIBERTINE	FRIEND HERE WOULD CALL THE FARCE OF PARENTAL
OVER PREFACE(155)	OF BLAMELESS FAMILY LIFE, WHILST THE PRACTICAL	LIBERTINE	IS MERCILESSLY SEVERE ON ALL OTHER LIBERTINES, AND
OVER PREFACE(155)	BY FALSEHOOD. THE CLAMOROUS VIRTUE OF THE	LIBERTINE	IS THEREFORE NO MORE HYPOCRITICAL THAN THE PLEA OF
OVER PREFACE(155)	BY PERSONAL SCANDALS. THUS THE THEORETIC	LIBERTINE	IS USUALLY A PERSON OF BLAMELESS FAMILY LIFE,
SUPR PREFACE(R14)	AND BYRON'S HERO IS, AFTER ALL, ONLY A VAGABOND	LIBERTINE	. AND HE IS DUMB: HE DOES NOT DISCUSS HIMSELF WITH
SUPR PREFACE(R12)	TO ASK MYSELF, WHAT IS A DON JUAN? VULGARLY, A	LIBERTINE	. BUT YOUR DISLIKE OF VULGARITY IS PUSHED TO THE
BUOY IV (56)	DO NOT MISUNDERSTAND ME. I AM A BACHELOR, NOT A	LIBERTINE	. I WANT A DAUGHTER. /OLD BILL/ GOOD. IVE ALWAYS
APPL I (223)	A FREETHINKER. AND BALBUS WILL SAY THAT YOU ARE A	LIBERTINE	. /THE MALE CABINET/ (BELOW THEIR BREATHS)
PRES (157)	E FLAT-- I AM MARKED OUT AS THE PREY OF EVERY	LIBERTINE	. YOU THINK I AM LIKE THE THOUSANDS OF WEAK WOMEN
OVER PREFACE(156)	THE LONG AND EXPENSIVE SIEGES WHICH THE PROFESSED	LIBERTINE	LAYS TO VIRTUE. STILL, WHEREVER THERE IS IDLENESS
LION PREFACE(79)	ORDER THAT EVERY PETTY CHEAT AND ADULTERATOR AND	LIBERTINE	MIGHT WALLOW IN IT AND COME OUT WHITER THAN SNOW.
APPL I (226)	MADE TO THEM. THUS EVERY KING IS SUPPOSED TO BE A	LIBERTINE	; AND AS, ODDLY ENOUGH, HE OWES A GREAT PART OF
SUPR I (28)	LUNACY! THERE IS A RASCAL IN OUR MIDST, A	LIBERTINE	, A VILLAIN WORSE THAN A MURDERER; AND WE ARE NOT
MRS PREFACE(165)	UPPER MILLSTONE OF THE EXAMINER, WHO THINKS ME A	LIBERTINE	, AND THE NETHER POPULAR CRITIC, WHO THINKS ME A
GETT PREFACE(196)	THROWS UP THAT RARE PHENOMENON, AN UNSCRUPULOUS	LIBERTINE	, HIS SUCCESS AMONG " WELL BROUGHT-UP" GIRLS IS SO
OVER PREFACE(155)	ARE FOR THE MOST PART QUITE SINCERE. THE COMMON	LIBERTINE	, LIKE THE DRUNKARD, SUCCUMBS TO A TEMPTATION
		LIBERTINE'S	
SUPR III (124)	WITH AND MARRY HIM! /ANA/ YES, JUAN: WE KNOW THE	LIBERTINE'S	PHILOSOPHY. ALWAYS IGNORE THE CONSEQUENCES TO
		LIBERTINES	
SUPR III (89)	NAMES. /THE OLD WOMAN/ YOU WERE LIKE ALL MEN.	LIBERTINES	AND MURDERERS ALL, ALL, ALL! /DON JUAN/ AND YET
SUPR PREFACE(R14)	NOT COUNT FOR MUCH PHILOSOPHICALLY. OUR VAGABOND	LIBERTINES	ARE NO MORE INTERESTING FROM THAT POINT OF VIEW
GETT PREFACE(190)	FOR PLEASURE, SEEING AS HE DOES THAT THE KNOWN	LIBERTINES	OF HIS PARISH ARE VISIBLY SUFFERING MUCH LESS
KING I (212)	LADY. CHARLES ALWAYS ENCOURAGES INFIDELS AND	LIBERTINES	TO BLASPHEME. AND NOW HE ENCOURAGES THEM TO
GETT PREFACE(228)	WITHOUT A STAIN ON THEIR CHARACTERS TO COMBAT	LIBERTINES	WHO HAVE NO CHARACTER AT ALL. THEY CONCEIVE IT TO
OVER PREFACE(155)	HUMBUG, PRETENDING TO BE BETTER THAN THE DETECTED	LIBERTINES	, AND CLAMORING FOR THEIR CONDIGN PUNISHMENT: BUT
OVER PREFACE(155)	LIBERTINE IS MERCILESSLY SEVERE ON ALL OTHER	LIBERTINES	, AND EXCESSIVELY CONVENTIONAL IN PROFESSIONS OF
GETT (356)	SCAFFOLD, SEEM TO BE DEVOUT CHRISTIANS, SO ALL	LIBERTINES	, BOTH MALE AND FEMALE, ARE INVARIABLY PEOPLE
FABL PREFACE(67)	SO. GENIUSES ARE OFTEN SPENDTHRIFTS, DRUNKARDS,	LIBERTINES	, LIARS, DISHONEST IN MONEY MATTERS, BACKSLIDERS
SUPR I (30)	SO, SIR. MORALITY SENT TO THE DEVIL TO PLEASE OUR	LIBERTINES	, MALE AND FEMALE. THAT IS TO BE THE FUTURE OF
		LIBERTINISM	
SUPR PREFACE(R15)	DUELS AND GHOSTS AND " WOMANLY" WOMEN. AS TO MERE	LIBERTINISM	, YOU WOULD BE THE FIRST TO REMIND ME THAT THE
		LIBERTY	
2TRU PREFACE(14)	LEISURE. 8. LEISURE IS THE SPHERE OF INDIVIDUAL	LIBERTY	: LABOR IS THE SPHERE OF SLAVERY. 9. PEOPLE WHO
INCA (253)	ERECTED IT IN THE PROPER PLACE FOR A STATUE OF	LIBERTY	: ON ITS TOMB (HE TURNS DOWN HIS MOUSTACHES).
CLEO IV (170)	NOTHING! /POTHINUS/ AT LEAST-- TO BEG FOR MY	LIBERTY	: THAT IS ALL. /CLEOPATRA/ FOR THAT YOU WOULD HAVE
2TRU PREFACE(12)	TOMORROW TO KEEP HIS CHURCH GOING. AND THAT IS "	LIBERTY	: THOU CHOICEST TREASURE." THIS SORT OF LIFE HAS
POSN PREFACE(427)	WOULD STAND UP TO ALL THIS AS THE PRICE OF	LIBERTY	? I DOUBT IT. IF I AM TO BE AT THE MERCY OF A NICE
MTH3 (97)	HOW DID WE GET OUR REPUTATION AS THE PIONEERS OF	LIBERTY	? /CONFUCIUS/ BY YOUR STEADFAST REFUSAL TO BE
MTH4 I (167)	HAVE TAKEN A VERY GREAT LIBERTY. /ZOO/ WHAT IS A	LIBERTY	? /THE ELDERLY GENTLEMAN/ (EXASPERATED) I SHALL
ROCK II (247)	YOUR DEPRIVING THEM OF THAT LAST SCRAP OF THEIR	LIBERTY	? THE ONLY WEAPON THEY HAVE AGAINST THE
GENV PREFACE(13)	AND HATRED OF GOVERNMENT AS SUCH, CALLING ITSELF	LIBERTY	AND DEMOCRACY, REASSERTS ITSELF AND STOPS THE WAY.
GENV III (71)	/THE NEWCOMER/ (STARTING UP) NOT A WORD AGAINST	LIBERTY	AND DEMOCRACY IN MY PRESENCE! DO YOU HEAR? /THE
GENV III (71)	ARE ENCOURAGED IN OTHER COUNTRIES IN THE NAME OF	LIBERTY	AND DEMOCRACY. /THE NEWCOMER/ (STARTING UP) NOT A
GENV IV (111)	NEGLECT IT THE WORLD FALLS INTO THE CHAOS CALLED	LIBERTY	AND DEMOCRACY, IN WHICH NOTHING IS DONE EXCEPT TALK
GENV IV (103)	IT SEEMS, OF THE MURDER AND DESTRUCTION OF	LIBERTY	AND DEMOCRACY IN EUROPE. /BBDE/ ONE CANNOT DESTROY

SUPR III (109)	OF ABOLISHING SLAVERY. /THE DEVIL/ YES, WHEN THE	LIBERTY	AND EQUALITY OF WHICH YOU PRATE SHALL HAVE MADE FREE
SUPR III (109)	THE FILTHY SLUM HE STARVES IN, FOR UNIVERSAL	LIBERTY	AND EQUALITY. /THE STATUE/ BOSH! /DON JUAN/ WHAT
SUPR HANDBOK(214)	THE NECESSITY FOR THE SUPERMAN. ENGLISHMEN HATE	LIBERTY	AND EQUALITY TOO MUCH TO UNDERSTAND THEM. BUT EVERY
SUPR HANDBOK(218)	" CUTS THE PAINTER" AND BREAKS UP THE EMPIRE.	LIBERTY	AND EQUALITY. HE WHO CONFUSES POLITICAL LIBERTY WITH
MIS. PREFACE(103)	TRY TO SIMPLIFY THEIR TASK BY DESTROYING	LIBERTY	AND GLORIFYING AUTHORITY, ESPECIALLY THEIR OWN. BUT
MIS. PREFACE(51)	CULTURE; BUT MAY IT NOT MEAN THAT THEY PREFER	LIBERTY	AND SATISFACTION TO COERCION AND PRIVATION. WHY IS
CAPT II (255)	AN APOLOGY AND LEAVE THE COUNTRY TO REGAIN HER	LIBERTY	AND SAVE HERSELF FROM A LUNATIC ASYLUM. AND WHEN SHE
GETT PREFACE(237)	LOGIC IN A UNIVERSITY CLASS-ROOM, SPECIFIES "	LIBERTY	AND THE PURSUIT OF HAPPINESS" AS NATURAL RIGHTS. THE
NEVR II (228)	WHAT I AM: A PHILOSOPHIC RADICAL STANDING FOR	LIBERTY	AND THE RIGHTS OF THE INDIVIDUAL, AS I LEARNT TO DO
HART PREFACE(15)	RUSH TO ABOLISH ALL CONSTITUTIONAL GUARANTEES OF	LIBERTY	AND WELL-BEING. THE ORDINARY LAW WAS SUPERSEDED BY
MILL PREFACE(120)	MISTAKE. WITH INSPIRED PRECISION HE DENOUNCED	LIBERTY	AS A PUTREFYING CORPSE. HE DECLARED THAT WHAT PEOPLE
POSN PREFACE(383)	RIGHT: THAT IS, HE DOES NOT MEAN TOLERATION OR	LIBERTY	AT ALL; FOR THERE IS NO NEED TO TOLERATE WHAT
ANNA (300)	IN THE LAND? YOU WOULD THRUST THE RISING SUN OF	LIBERTY	BACK INTO THE SEA OF BLOOD FROM WHICH IT HAS RISEN?
MIS. PREFACE(59)	ORDER, BECOME NECESSARY CONDITIONS OF A CHILD'S	LIBERTY	BEFORE IT CAN APPRECIATE THE IMPORTANCE OF ITS
MIS. PREFACE(43)	AS A HERETIC IS NOT FREE AT ALL; AND THE RIGHT TO	LIBERTY	BEGINS, NOT AT THE AGE OF 21 YEARS BUT OF 21
APPL PREFACE(179)	STATES OF AMERICA, NOR WHEREVER THE LOVE OF	LIBERTY	BURNS IN THE HEART OF MAN; IT IS AT SUCH AND SUCH A
APPL PREFACE(178)	STATES OF AMERICA, AND WHEREVER THE LOVE OF	LIBERTY	BURNS IN THE HEART OF MAN. YOU, MY FRIEND SHAW, ARE
MILL PREFACE(120)	HE DECLARED THAT WHAT PEOPLE NEEDED WAS NOT	LIBERTY	BUT DISCIPLINE, THE STERNER THE BETTER. HE SAID THAT
MTH2 (52)	YOUR WATCH OR TO SHIRK MILITARY SERVICE, HOW MUCH	LIBERTY	DO YOU ALLOW IT? LIBERTY OF CONSCIENCE IS NOT MY
MIS. PREFACE(43)	OR DARING THOUGHT. BUT WHETHER THE RISKS TO WHICH	LIBERTY	EXPOSES US ARE MORAL OR PHYSICAL, OUR RIGHT TO
MILL PREFACE(121)	TO SEE PARLIAMENT TREATED. THE DOCTRINAIRES OF	LIBERTY	FLED TO FRANCE AND ENGLAND, PREFERRING THEM TO
2TRU PREFACE(13)	OF THE COMMUNITY INVOLVES A MAXIMUM OF INDIVIDUAL	LIBERTY	FOR ALL ITS MEMBERS THE RULERS HAVE AT THE SAME TIME
MILL PREFACE(117)	IT WAS STILL BELIEVED THAT BRITISH INDIVIDUAL	LIBERTY	FORBAD PARLIAMENT TO DO ANYTHING THAT IT COULD
SUPR III (109)	TO WHICH THEY WILL SACRIFICE ALL THEIR	LIBERTY	GLADLY. /THE DEVIL/ AY: THEY WILL NEVER BE AT A LOSS
POSN PREFACE(383)	WHAT MOST PEOPLE CONSIDER RIGHT. TOLERATION AND	LIBERTY	HAVE NO SENSE OR USE EXCEPT AS TOLERATION OF
2TRU PREFACE(12)	THE WRETCHED SLAVES OF THE CURSE WILL LOSE THEIR	LIBERTY	IF THEY ARE FORCED TO EARN THEIR LIVING HONORABLY.
ROCK PREFACE(174)	OUR PAPERS ARE SILENT ABOUT THE SUPPRESSION OF	LIBERTY	IN IMPERIALIST JAPAN, THOUGH IN JAPAN IT IS A CRIME
PLES PREFACE(R18)	THAT I HAD STRUCK A WANTON BLOW AT THE CAUSE OF	LIBERTY	IN THE BALKAN PENINSULA BY MENTIONING THAT IT WAS
ROCK I (227)	MEAN THAT YOU MAKE SPEECHES ABOUT PROGRESS AND	LIBERTY	INSTEAD OF ABOUT KING AND COUNTRY. /SIR ARTHUR/ OF
MIS. PREFACE(43)	EXPOSES US ARE MORAL OR PHYSICAL, OUR RIGHT TO	LIBERTY	INVOLVES THE RIGHT TO RUN THEM. A MAN WHO IS NOT
GENV II (61)	THEY ARE FREE TO DO THAT IN ENGLAND. BRITISH	LIBERTY	IS A MOST USEFUL SAFETY VALVE. /THE SECRETARY/ I WAS
METH PREFACE(R67)	BEHIND THIS FICTION WAS THE DIVINE SENSE THAT	LIBERTY	IS A NEED VITAL TO HUMAN GROWTH. ACCORDINGLY, THOUGH
BARB PREFACE(235)	TO ABOLISH ALL FREEDOM WHATSOEVER, AS EVERY MAN'S	LIBERTY	IS AT THE MERCY OF A MORAL INDICTMENT WHICH ANY FOOL
POSN PREFACE(388)	AN EARTHQUAKE. BUT WHEN THE EMERGENCY IS PAST,	LIBERTY	IS RESTORED EVERYWHERE EXCEPT IN THE THEATRE. THE
MIS. PREFACE(108)	OUT OF THEIR NATURE EXCEPT DREAD OF THE WHIP.	LIBERTY	IS THE BREATH OF LIFE TO NATIONS; AND LIBERTY IS THE
MIS. PREFACE(108)	LIBERTY IS THE BREATH OF LIFE TO NATIONS; AND	LIBERTY	IS THE ONE THING THAT PARENTS, SCHOOLMASTERS, AND
ANNA (302)	PAMPHLETS OF THE REVOLUTIONARY WRITERS, HOW MUCH	LIBERTY	IS THERE WHERE THEY HAVE GAINED THE UPPER HAND? ARE
APPL PREFACE(182)	A TYRANT TO GET RID OF A TROUBLESOME CHAMPION OF	LIBERTY	IS TO RAISE A HUE AND CRY AGAINST HIM AS AN
ROCK PREFACE(169)	NOT KNOWING WHAT TO DO WITH THEMSELVES WHEN AT	LIBERTY	, A LIFE FILLED WITH SCIENTIFIC CURIOSITY WOULD BE
BULL PREFACE(45)	CRUELTIES CAN EVER DRAIN ITS VICTIMS OF THEIR	LIBERTY	, A POLITICAL SCHEME THAT CANNOT BE CARRIED OUT
BULL PREFACE(42)	MOVEMENTS BY RECOVERING THEIR NATIONAL	LIBERTY	, ALL DEMONSTRATIONS OF THE VIRTUES OF A FOREIGN
ANNA (290)	YOU ARE ATTACHED TO ABSTRACT THINGS LIKE	LIBERTY	, BUT MY FAMILY HAS SERVED THE PANJANDRUMS OF BEOTIA
JOAN PREFACE(21)	CHOSEN AS AN ALTERNATIVE TO LIFE WITHOUT	LIBERTY	, IN BATTLE SHE CHALLENGED DEATH AS WELLINGTON DID
BARB I (252)	PIG-HEADED TORY ONE. WE ARE WHIGS, AND BELIEVE IN	LIBERTY	, LET SNOBBISH PEOPLE SAY WHAT THEY PLEASE: BARBARA
MILL PREFACE(121)	ARTICLES PARAPHRASING JOHN STUART MILL'S ESSAY ON	LIBERTY	, MUSSOLINI, NOW IL DUCE, NEVER EVEN LOOKED ROUND:
HART PREFACE(15)	OUR HEADS FOR THE MOMENT, THE RABID WATCHDOGS OF	LIBERTY	, NOT CONTENT WITH THESE RANCOROUS ABUSES OF THE
KING I (167)	OWN, IF HE WILL BE GOOD ENOUGH TO ALLOW ME SUCH A	LIBERTY	, PROCEED THEN WITH YOUR BUSINESS; AND TAKE NO
SUPR I (37)	CLEARS IT AND GIVES US BREATHING SPACE AND	LIBERTY	, /ANN/ IT'S NO USE, JACK. NO WOMAN WILL AGREE WITH
CAPT III SD(279)	ADDRESSING AN ENGLISH PERSON WHO HAS TAKEN A	LIBERTY	, /LADY CICELY/ (AS HE ENTERS) SO GLAD YOUVE COME,
ARMS III SD(70)	RAINA, EQUALLY INDIGNANT, ALMOST SNORTS AT THE	LIBERTY	, /LOUKA/ I HAVE A RIGHT TO CALL HER RAINA: SHE
DEST (155)	HE DARE NOT KEEP YOU WAITING IF HE WERE AT	LIBERTY	, /NAPOLEON/ (TURNING AT THE EDGE OF THE SHADOW OF
MTH4 I (167)	IN USING IT ON ME YOU HAVE TAKEN A VERY GREAT	LIBERTY	, /ZOO/ WHAT IS A LIBERTY? /THE ELDERLY GENTLEMAN/
LADY PREFACE(232)	INCORPORATION OF WHIG PRINCIPLES OF INDIVIDUAL	LIBERTY	, SHAKESPEAR AND THE BRITISH PUBLIC. I HAVE REJECTED
DOCT II (125)	WRONGED. THANK YOU ALL, GENTLEMEN; AND EXCUSE THE	LIBERTY	, SHE GOES INTO THE HOTEL. THEY WATCH HER IN
GENV PREFACE(12)	POLITICS AS A CLAMOR FOR LESS GOVERNMENT AND MORE	LIBERTY	, THAT CITIZENS GET BETTER VALUE FOR THE RATES AND
GETT PREFACE(231)	PROMISCUITY IS A PRODUCT OF SLAVERY AND NOT OF	LIBERTY	, THE SOLID FOUNDATION OF THEIR CONFIDENCE IS THE
ROCK II (258)	SICK OF TWADDLE ABOUT LIBERTY WHEN THEY HAVE NO	LIBERTY	, THEY ARE SICK OF IDLING AND LOAFING ABOUT ON DOLES
MIS. PREFACE(103)	AND CONSEQUENTLY OF THE MACHINE. THEY DO NOT WANT	LIBERTY	, THEY HAVE NOT BEEN EDUCATED TO WANT IT. THEY
INCA (253)	MADAM. THE AMERICANS DO NOT WORSHIP THE STATUE OF	LIBERTY	, THEY HAVE ERECTED IT IN THE PROPER PLACE FOR A
MIS. PREFACE(53)	WILL NOT DO. WE MUST RECONCILE EDUCATION WITH	LIBERTY	, WE MUST FIND OUT SOME MEANS OF MAKING MEN WORKERS
BULL PREFACE(43)	THEN HE IS SAID TO CLAIM A NATURAL RIGHT TO THAT	LIBERTY	, WHEN, FOR INSTANCE, HE INSISTS ON LIVING, IN SPITE
GENV I (36)	/NEWCOMER/ OH NO: THAT WOULD BE THE END OF ALL	LIBERTY	, YOU HAVE NOTHING TO SAY AGAINST LIBERTY, I HOPE.
BULL IV (150)	IN EVERY IRISH BREAST I HAVE FOUND THAT SPIRIT OF	LIBERTY	(A CHEERY VOICE " HEAR HEAR"), THAT INSTINCTIVE
NEVR II (228)	ORIGIN OF SPECIES AND JOHN STUART MILL'S ESSAY ON	LIBERTY	(NOD); TO READ HUXLEY, TYNDALL, AND GEORGE ELIOT (
MIS. PREFACE(42)	BECAUSE IT SO OFTEN MEANS RESTRICTION OF THEIR	LIBERTY	LEST THEY SHOULD MAKE A BAD USE OF IT. IF THERE ARE
MILL PREFACE(117)	OUR CONSERVATIVE RULERS AGREED THAT WE WERE A	LIBERTY	LOVING PEOPLE: THAT, FOR INSTANCE, ENGLISHMEN WOULD
SUPR HANDBOK(218)	UNCONDITIONAL; CONSEQUENTLY NOTHING CAN BE FREE.	LIBERTY	MEANS RESPONSIBILITY. THAT IS WHY MOST MEN DREAD IT.
METH PREFACE(R64)	SYMPATHIZED, THOUGH TO THEM CAPITALIST	LIBERTY	MEANT ONLY WAGE SLAVERY WITHOUT THE LEGAL SAFEGUARDS
POSN PREFACE(407)	OF PUBLIC ENTERTAINMENT, DRAMATIC OR OTHER.	LIBERTY	MUST, NO DOUBT, BE RESPECTED IN SO FAR THAT NO
NEVR II (249)	HAS SENT ME FOR HER BOOK, SIR. MIGHT I TAKE THE	LIBERTY	OF ASKING YOU TO LET HER HAVE IT AT ONCE, SIR.
POSN PREFACE(419)	BE NOTHING BUT COUNSEL'S OPINION WITHOUT THE	LIBERTY	OF CHOICE OF COUNSEL, POSSIBLY CHEAPENED, BUT SURE
MTH2 (52)	SERVICE, HOW MUCH LIBERTY DO YOU ALLOW IT?	LIBERTY	OF CONSCIENCE IS NOT MY POINT. /BURGE/ (TESTILY) I
MTH2 (52)	OF YOUR CONSCIENTIOUS OBJECTORS? ALL LAW LIMITS	LIBERTY	OF CONSCIENCE: IF A MAN'S CONSCIENCE ALLOWS HIM TO
MTH2 (52)	FANATICS. /BURGE/ WE STAND, AS CROMWELL DID, FOR	LIBERTY	OF CONSCIENCE, IF THAT IS WHAT YOU MEAN. /FRANKLYN/
POSN PREFACE(410)	STRETCHED TO CENSORSHIP. THE MANAGER WOULD ENJOY	LIBERTY	OF CONSCIENCE AS FAR AS THE LOCAL AUTHORITY IS
POSN PREFACE(391)	A FAR-SEEING STATESMAN, A BORN CHAMPION OF	LIBERTY	OF CONSCIENCE AND INTELLECTUAL INTEGRITY-- SAY A
SUPR I (8)	NAMES, BECAUSE I HAVE STOOD FOR EQUALITY AND	LIBERTY	OF CONSCIENCE WHILE THEY WERE TRUCKLING TO THE
BULL IV (154)	/BROADBENT/ THAT IS A REMARKABLE TRIBUTE TO THE	LIBERTY	OF CONSCIENCE ENJOYED BY THE SUBJECTS OF OUR INDIAN
ROCK PREFACE(189)	OR LUNATIC, BETWEEN LIBERTY OF PRECEPT AND	LIBERTY	OF EXAMPLE. IT MAY BE VITALLY NECESSARY TO ALLOW A
MILL PREFACE(118)	WERE JEALOUSLY RESISTED AS INTERFERENCES WITH THE	LIBERTY	OF FREE BRITONS. IF THERE WAS ANYTHING WRONG, THE
CAPT NOTES (305)	HE WILL NEVER READ MY BOOK. SO I HAVE TAKEN THE	LIBERTY	OF MAKING A SPECIAL EXAMPLE OF HIM, AS FAR AS THAT
HART PREFACE(17)	WORTHILY AND GLORIOUSLY SACRIFICED TO REDEEM THE	LIBERTY	OF MANKIND, INSTEAD OF TO EXPIATE THE HEEDLESSNESS
SIM II (57)	UNLESS AN UNEQUIVOCAL GUARANTEE OF THE SAFETY AND	LIBERTY	OF MR HAMMINGTAP BE IN MY HANDS BY NOON TODAY" THAT
BARB III (343)	YOUR LOVE, MAN? BY WHAT RIGHT DO YOU TAKE THE	LIBERTY	OF OFFERING IT TO ME? I WILL HAVE YOUR DUE HEED AND
ROCK PREFACE(189)	THE CRITIC AND THE CRIMINAL OR LUNATIC, BETWEEN	LIBERTY	OF PRECEPT AND LIBERTY OF EXAMPLE. IT MAY BE VITALLY
POSN PREFACE(385)	PROBABLE, AND THAT THE RISKS OF SUPPRESSING	LIBERTY	OF PROPAGANDA WERE FAR GRAVER THAN THE RISK OF
MRS II (202)	YOU, CROFTS; BUT YOU ALLOWED YOURSELF THE	LIBERTY	OF SPEAKING TO ME LIKE A FATHER A MOMENT AGO. ONE
POSN PREFACE(381)	ACHIEVEMENT BY MY PROFESSION OF THOSE RIGHTS OF	LIBERTY	OF SPEECH AND CONSCIENCE WHICH ARE MATTERS OF COURSE
POSN PREFACE(401)	ABANDONED, NOT IN THE LEAST AS CONTRARY TO THE	LIBERTY	OF THE STAGE, BUT BECAUSE THE EXECUTIVE PROBLEM OF
GENV I (45)	BLIND HATRED OF BRITISH INSTITUTIONS AND OF ALL	LIBERTY	OF THOUGHT AND SPEECH, MAKE IT A CRIME TO ADVOCATE A
ROCK PREFACE(172)	CLASSES INTO WILD ALARM WHEN THE INDIVIDUAL	LIBERTY	OF THOUGHT, SPEECH, AND CONSCIENCE WHICH THEY THINK
2TRU PREFACE(11)	YOU DO OR WHERE YOU GO." IN SHORT, THE PERFECT	LIBERTY	OF WHICH SLAVES DREAM BECAUSE THEY HAVE NO
VWOO 3 (136)	GOOD. /A/ (RISING WRATHFULLY) THE MOST OFFENSIVE	LIBERTY	ONE HUMAN BEING CAN POSSIBLY TAKE WITH ANOTHER. WHAT
APPL I (233)	IS RESENTED BY THEM AS AN INVASION OF THEIR	LIBERTY	OR AN INCREASE IN THEIR TAXATION. IT WEARS OUT THE
POSN PREFACE(383)	ORDINARY MORAL MAN UNDERSTAND WHAT TOLERATION AND	LIBERTY	REALLY MEAN. HE WILL ACCEPT THEM VERBALLY WITH
GENV III (84)	HANDBAG) BUT REMEMBER, IF YOU TAKE THE SMALLEST	LIBERTY	-- IF YOU HINT AT THE POSSIBILITY OF A MORE INTIMATE
ROCK II (248)	WILL DIE SOONER THAN PUT UP WITH IT. I WANT MY	LIBERTY	-- /BARKING/ LIBERTY TO WORK FOURTEEN HOURS A DAY
BULL I (77)	THE DESTRUCTION OF THE LAST REMNANTS OF NATIONAL	LIBERTY	-- /TIM/ NOT ANOTHER WORD. SHAKE HANDS. /BROADBENT/
MIS. PREFACE(41)	THE MOST COMPLETE CONCEIVABLE INFRINGEMENT OF ITS	LIBERTY	) UNTIL IT CAN WALK. BUT NOBODY GOES ON CARRYING
MTH3 (97)	TO HARNESS AND GUIDE HIM MAY BE A PIONEER OF	LIBERTY	; BUT HE IS NOT A PIONEER OF GOVERNMENT. IN CHINA HE
FANY III (319)	I CAN EXPLAIN, SIR. I MUST ASK YOU TO EXCUSE THE	LIBERTY	; BUT I'M ENTERTAINING A SMALL PARTY TO TEA IN MY
MIS. PREFACE(94)	AND ARABS, WHO WILL ALL BE DAMNED FOR TAKING THAT	LIBERTY	; BUT IT SHOULD BE TOLD THAT MANY ENGLISH PEOPLE
2TRU PREFACE(14)	IS A WHOLE-TIME COMPULSION ADMITTING OF NO	LIBERTY	; BUT THE PERSONAL SLAVERY OF THE COMPULSION TO WORK
ROCK PREFACE(177)	QUITE SUPPLIES THIS NEED. STUART MILL'S ESSAY ON	LIBERTY	SATISFIED THE NINETEENTH CENTURY, AND WAS MY OWN
APPL PREFACE(190)	RESTRICTED THAN AT PRESENT; BUT I DO NOT DESIRE	LIBERTY	TO CHOOSE WINDBAGS AND NINCOMPOOPS TO REPRESENT ME
FANY EPILOG (330)	HAIR'S BREADTH. /THE COUNT/ I'M SORRY I'M NOT AT	LIBERTY	TO DIVULGE THE AUTHOR'S NAME. THE AUTHOR DESIRES
POSN PREFACE(383)	OF OPINIONS THAT ARE CONSIDERED DAMNABLE, AND	LIBERTY	TO DO WHAT SEEMS WRONG. SETTING ENGLISHMEN FREE TO

POSN PREFACE(383)	THAT HE CONSIDERS ENLIGHTENED, AND, BY LIBERTY,	LIBERTY	TO DO WHAT HE CONSIDERS RIGHT: THAT IS, HE DOES NOT
POSN PREFACE(383)	TO TOLERATE WHAT APPEARS ENLIGHTENED OR TO CLAIM	LIBERTY	TO DO WHAT MOST PEOPLE CONSIDER RIGHT. TOLERATION
2TRU PREFACE(24)	PANEL SYSTEM THE VOTERS WOULD LOSE THEIR PRESENT	LIBERTY	TO RETURN SUCH CANDIDATES AS THE LATE HORATIO
JOAN PREFACE(41)	TO BEAR IN MIND THAT UNLESS THERE IS A LARGE	LIBERTY	TO SHOCK CONVENTIONAL PEOPLE, AND A WELL INFORMED
BULL III (121)	KNOW THE OLD TENANTS NOW. YOUD THINK IT WAS A	LIBERTY	TO SPEAK T'DHEM-- SOME O DHEM. (SHE GOES TO THE
POSN PREFACE(424)	HER TO COME TO THE THEATRE OR SUSPENDED HER	LIBERTY	TO STAY AWAY, AND ALTHOUGH SHE HAS NO CLAIM ON AN
POSN PREFACE(425)	AND ABOVE LAWFUL CONDUCT IN A GENERAL SENSE, THAN	LIBERTY	TO STAY AWAY FROM THE THEATRE IN WHICH MY PLAYS ARE
2TRU PREFACE(13)	AS TO THE NECESSARY SACRIFICE OF INDIVIDUAL	LIBERTY	TO THE GOOD OF THE COMMUNITY. 5. THE PARADOX OF
ROCK PREFACE(169)	WANT A MINIMUM OF NECESSARY WORK AND A MAXIMUM OF	LIBERTY	TO THINK AND DISCOVER AND EXPERIMENT IN THE
ROCK II (248)	PUT UP WITH IT. I WANT MY LIBERTY-- /BARKING/	LIBERTY	TO WORK FOURTEEN HOURS A DAY AND BRING UP THREE
POSN PREFACE(426)	THEN, SO LONG AS WAR REMAINS LAWFUL, I CLAIM FULL	LIBERTY	TO WRITE AND PERFORM A PLAY INCITING THE COUNTRY TO
ROCK PREFACE(190)	AND DISCIPLINE LIKE A SOLDIER, OR AT NORMAL	LIBERTY	UNDER AN OBLIGATION TO MAKE GOOD THE DAMAGE HE HAS
MIS. PREFACE(104)	ANY RECORD OF FROM THE DAYS WHEN THE ADVOCACY OF	LIBERTY	WAS A CAPITAL OFFENCE AND DEMOCRACY WAS HARDLY
MIS. PREFACE(43)	FIRE ONCE. YOU WILL NOT DO IT TWICE. THE RISKS OF	LIBERTY	WE MUST LET EVERYONE TAKE; BUT RISKS OF IGNORANCE
ROCK II (258)	FLAG IT WAVES. THEY ARE SICK OF TWADDLE ABOUT	LIBERTY	WHEN THEY HAVE NO LIBERTY. THEY ARE SICK OF IDLING
POSN PREFACE(365)	INTERFERENCE WITH CERTAIN LIBERAL TRADITIONS OF	LIBERTY	WHICH ARE STILL USEFUL TO NONCONFORMISTS IN OTHER
INCA (244)	OF TREATING YOU WITH CEREMONY. (SHE SITS DOWN: A	LIBERTY	WHICH GIVES HIM A PERCEPTIBLE SHOCK). I AM QUITE AT
SUPR III (109)	IS THE ONLY THING MEN DARE DIE FOR. LATER ON,	LIBERTY	WILL NOT BE CATHOLIC ENOUGH: MEN WILL DIE FOR HUMAN
BARB PREFACE(234)	ARE BORN GOOD. GUARANTEE A MAN'S GOODNESS AND HIS	LIBERTY	WILL TAKE CARE OF ITSELF. TO GUARANTEE HIS FREEDOM
SUPR HANDBOK(218)	LIBERTY AND EQUALITY. HE WHO CONFUSES POLITICAL	LIBERTY	WITH FREEDOM AND POLITICAL EQUALITY WITH SIMILARITY
BARB II (279)	FIERCELY, WITH THE MUG IN HIS HAND) YOU TAKE A	LIBERTY	WITH ME, AND I'LL SMASH YOU OVER THE FACE WITH THE
SUPR III (83)	YOU CALLIN ENRY? WHAT CALL HAVE YOU TO TAKE A	LIBERTY	WITH MY NAME OR WITH HERS? FOR TWO PINS I'D PUNCH
METH PREFACE(R67)	SUCH AN INFRINGEMENT OF SUCH AND SUCH A BRITISH	LIBERTY	WOULD BE HURLED FROM OFFICE IN A WEEK. THIS WAS NOT
UNPL PREFACE(R15)	LEST THE PRESS, HAVING NOW LOST ALL TRADITION OF	LIBERTY	, AND BEING ABLE TO CONCEIVE NO ALTERNATIVE TO THE
DOCT PREFACE(34)	OF KNOWLEDGE, ANY MORE THAN THE PURSUIT OF LIFE,	LIBERTY	, AND HAPPINESS (AS THE AMERICAN CONSTITUTION PUTS
POSN PREFACE(420)	LIBEL AND THE BLASPHEMY LAWS CONTRARY TO PUBLIC	LIBERTY	, AND REPEALING AND DEFINING ACCORDINGLY. PROPOSED:
ARMS I (12)	WHO SET THE SERBS ON TO ROB US OF OUR NATIONAL	LIBERTY	, AND WHO OFFICER THEIR ARMY FOR THEM. WE HATE
ROCK PREFACE(177)	CHURCH'S MISTAKE WAS NOT IN INTERFERING WITH HIS	LIBERTY	, BUT IN IMAGINING THAT THE SECRET OF THE EARTH'S
CAPT III (280)	THAT MY SISTER-IN-LAW HAS TAKEN SO SERIOUS A	LIBERTY	, CAPTAIN KEARNEY. IT IS A MANIA OF HERS-- SIMPLY A
POSN PREFACE(422)	SANE MAN, NOT BEING A PROFESSED ENEMY OF PUBLIC	LIBERTY	, COULD PUT HIS HAND TO SO MONSTROUS A CATALOGUE
DOCT PREFACE(78)	THE SOUL, WHEN THE GREAT VITAL DOGMAS OF HONOR,	LIBERTY	, COURAGE, THE KINSHIP OF ALL LIFE, FAITH THAT THE
BARB PREFACE(220)	NOT FOR BETTER MORALS, CHEAPER BREAD, TEMPERANCE,	LIBERTY	, CULTURE, REDEMPTION OF FALLEN SISTERS AND ERRING
FABL PREFACE(98)	ITSELF TO BE THE CLIMAX OF CIVILIZATION, OF	LIBERTY	, EQUALITY, AND FRATERNITY, WAS CONVICTED BY KARL
MILL PREFACE(120)	SEEMED JUST THE OCCASION FOR A GRAND APPEAL FOR	LIBERTY	, FOR DEMOCRACY, FOR A PARLIAMENT IN WHICH THE
BULL PREFACE(27)	THE TWO, THE BRITISH GOVERNMENT ALLOWS HIM MORE	LIBERTY	, GIVING HIM AS COMPLETE A DEMOCRATIC CONTROL OF
GENV I (36)	OF ALL LIBERTY. YOU HAVE NOTHING TO SAY AGAINST	LIBERTY	, I HOPE. /SHE/ I HAVE NOTHING TO SAY AGAINST
METH PREFACE(R64)	TRADE, FREE CONTRACT, FREE COMPETITION, NATURAL	LIBERTY	, LAISSER-FAIRE: IN SHORT, ON " DOING THE OTHER
POSN PREFACE(383)	DOCTRINES THAT HE CONSIDERS ENLIGHTENED, AND, BY	LIBERTY	, LIBERTY TO DO WHAT HE CONSIDERS RIGHT: THAT IS, HE
BULL I (77)	LIKE MESELF, SIR. /BROADBENT/ I AM A LOVER OF	LIBERTY	, LIKE EVERY TRUE ENGLISHMAN, MR HAFFIGAN. MY NAME
INCA (253)	WHAT! YOU TOO WORSHIP BEFORE THE STATUE OF	LIBERTY	, LIKE THE AMERICANS? /THE INCA/ NOT AT ALL, MADAM.
MIS. PREFACE(59)	BEFORE IT CAN APPRECIATE THE IMPORTANCE OF ITS	LIBERTY	, OR FORESEE THAT THESE ACCOMPLISHMENTS ARE WORTH
NEVR I (212)	SEE TWENTIETH CENTURY PARENTS, CHAPTER ON	LIBERTY	, PASSIM. /MRS CLANDON/ (TOUCHING HER SHOULDER
BUOY 1 (11)	CHARM THE TIGER AWAY BY MUMBLING OLD SPELLS ABOUT	LIBERTY	, PEACE, DEMOCRACY, SANCTIONS, OPEN DOORS, AND
DEVL I SD(3)	DOMINION, AND TO THE AMERICAN AS DEFENCE OF	LIBERTY	, RESISTANCE TO TYRANNY, AND SELF-SACRIFICE ON THE
PHIL I (78)	DID YOU NOT, IN SPITE OF YOUR CARE FOR YOUR OWN	LIBERTY	, SET UP CLAIMS ON ME COMPARED TO WHICH THE CLAIMS
NEVR IV (282)	YOU, SIR; BUT I THINK IT BEST NOT TO TAKE THAT	LIBERTY	, SIR. THERE IS NORMAN BLOOD IN IT, SIR; AND NORMAN
NEVR II (250)	FOR A SON: MANY PEOPLE CONSIDER IT A GREAT	LIBERTY	, SIR. I ASSURE YOU, SIR. CAN I GET YOU ANYTHING
POSN PREFACE(388)	IS GREAT; BUT AS IT IS THE PRICE OF OUR POLITICAL	LIBERTY	, WE THINK IT WORTH PAYING. WE MAY ABROGATE IT IN
LION II (131)	THAT WE FORGIVE YOU. /METELLUS/ AN INCONCEIVABLE	LIBERTY	! DO YOU NOT KNOW, WOMAN, THAT THE EMPEROR CAN DO
ROCK II (249)	BROTHER THE SHOPMAN. TO HELL WITH YOUR FILTHY	LIBERTY	! /BLEE/ (HOTLY) I-- /THE MAYOR/ ORDER! ORDER!
		LIBIDO	
ROCK PREFACE(190)	ERADICATION OF MALICE, VINDICTIVENESS, AND SADIST	LIBIDO	ON THESE TERMS FROM THE PERSONAL CONTACTS OF CITIZENS
		LIBITUM	
MTH5 (215)	OH! ! ! OH! ! ! ! (SHE CONTINUES THIS AD	LIBITUM	DURING THE FOLLOWING REMONSTRANCES). /ACIS/ HOLD
APPL II (272)	WILL ALLOW ME TO SAY -- COMRADE. (HEAR HEARS AD	LIBITUM	). I KNOW MY WORDS WILL FIND AN ECHO IN ALL YOUR
		LIBRARIAN	
MTH3 (126)	HAVE YOU READ A VERY INTERESTING BOOK BY THE	LIBRARIAN	OF THE BIOLOGICAL SOCIETY SUGGESTING THAT THE
		LIBRARIES	
BARB III (327)	DOWN ON THE SHELL). /STEPHEN/ DID YOU SEE THE	LIBRARIES	AND SCHOOLS! ? /SARAH/ DID YOU SEE THE BALL ROOM
LION PREFACE(48)	OR PUT THEM AWAY ON THE FICTION SHELF OF OUR	LIBRARIES	. I VENTURE TO REPLY THAT WE SHALL BE, ON THE
MIS. (117)	HOME? /JOHNNY/ NO: HES OPENING ONE OF HIS FREE	LIBRARIES	. THATS ANOTHER NICE LITTLE PENNY GONE. HE'S MAD
KING I (188)	IS THERE MORE LEARNING IN YOUR HEAD THAN IN THE	LIBRARIES	OF THE VATICAN? /NEWTON/ POPES AND CARDINALS ARE
MIS. (117)	WHEN ALL HYPATIA'S MONEY IS THROWN AWAY ON	LIBRARIES	, WHERE WILL BUNNY COME IN? CANT YOU STOP HIM?
		LIBRARY	
ARMS I (19)	DO YOU KNOW WHAT A LIBRARY IS? /THE MAN/ A	LIBRARY	? A ROOMFUL OF BOOKS? /RAINA/ YES. WE HAVE ONE,
BUOY III (28)	WILL YOU BE GOOD ENOUGH TO DIRECT ME TO THE	LIBRARY	? /THE PRIEST/ YOU WOULD FIND IT A RATHER DISMAL
FANY PROLOG (257)	AND AS OUR LITERARY GUESTS WILL PROBABLY USE THE	LIBRARY	A GOOD DEAL, I JUST RAN IN TO UNLOCK EVERYTHING.
ARMS III SD(46)	ACT III. IN THE	LIBRARY	AFTER LUNCH. IT IS NOT MUCH OF A LIBRARY. ITS
MTH2 SD(47)	A CHURCH WINDOW; AND HASLAM SEIZES THE NEAREST	LIBRARY	CHAIR ON THE HEARTH, AND SWINGS IT ROUND FOR BURGE
MTH2 SD(37)	SMOULDERING IN IT, AND A COUPLE OF COMFORTABLE	LIBRARY	CHAIRS ON THE HEARTHRUG; BEYOND IT AND BESIDE IT THE
ARMS II (40)	(STOPPING) YES, MADAM. /CATHERINE/ IS THE	LIBRARY	DOOR SHUT? /LOUKA/ I THINK SO, MADAM. /CATHERINE/
BARB I SD(249)	ACT I. IT IS AFTER DINNER IN JANUARY 1906, IN THE	LIBRARY	IN LADY BRITOMART UNDERSHAFT'S HOUSE IN WILTON
KING I SD(161)	" IN GOOD KING CHARLES'S GOLDEN DAYS". ACT I. THE	LIBRARY	IN THE HOUSE OF ISAAC NEWTON IN CAMBRIDGE IN THE
BARB III SD(311)	DAY AFTER LUNCH LADY BRITOMART IS WRITING IN THE	LIBRARY	IN WILTON CRESCENT. SARAH IS READING IN THE ARMCHAIR
ARMS I (19)	DEAR YOUNG LADY. /RAINA/ DO YOU KNOW WHAT A	LIBRARY	IS? /THE MAN/ A LIBRARY? A ROOMFUL OF BOOKS?
BARB PREFACE(224)	OR GIVE HIS BOYS' BRIGADE A GYMNASIUM OR A	LIBRARY	IS THE SON-IN-LAW OF A CHICAGO MEAT KING, THAT YOUNG
BUOY III (27)	ALL THIS? I SHOULD HAVE BEEN SHEWN INTO THE	LIBRARY	. DO YOU UNDERSTAND WHO I AM? SIR FERDINAND
ARMS III SD(46)	IN THE LIBRARY AFTER LUNCH. IT IS NOT MUCH OF A	LIBRARY	. ITS LITERARY EQUIPMENT CONSISTS OF A SINGLE FIXED
CLEO II (139)	/THEODOTUS/ (TO POTHINUS) I MUST GO TO SAVE THE	LIBRARY	. (HE HURRIES OUT). /CAESAR/ FOLLOW HIM TO THE
MRS PREFACE(153)	COMMONPLACES OF THE PULPIT, THE PLATFORM, OR THE	LIBRARY	. PLAY MRS WARREN'S PROFESSION TO AN AUDIENCE OF
ARMS II (27)	BEST. I TOOK CARE TO LET THEM KNOW THAT WE HAVE A	LIBRARY	. /CATHERINE/ AH; BUT YOU DIDNT TELL THEM THAT WE
GETT SD(308)	/THE BISHOP/ DO, SINJON. HOTCHKISS GOES INTO THE	LIBRARY	. /COLLINS/ IF I MIGHT POINT OUT A DIFFICULTY, MY
ARMS II (38)	YOU MUST GO AND HELP HIM, SERGIUS. HE IS IN THE	LIBRARY	. /RAINA/ (DISAPPOINTED) BUT WE ARE JUST GOING OUT
MIS. (169)	KEEP MYSELF DECENT? I GET BOOKS AT THE FREE	LIBRARY	. /TARLETON/ (SPRINGING TO HIS FEET) WHAT! ! !
MIS. (170)	CHAIR). I'LL NEVER GIVE ANOTHER PENNY TO A FREE	LIBRARY	. /THE MAN/ YOULL NEVER GIVE ANOTHER PENNY TO
MIS. (170)	MAN/ (RECOILING BEFORE HIS VEHEMENCE) THE FREE	LIBRARY	. THERES NO HARM IN THAT. /TARLETON/ INGRATE! I
FANY PROLOG (257)	HE MUST HAVE GONE THROUGH THE STAGE INTO THE	LIBRARY	. THIS WAY, SIR. (HE MOVES TOWARDS THE DIVISION IN
CLEO II (140)	(CHUCKLING) I HAVE LET THEODOTUS GO TO SAVE THE	LIBRARY	. WE MUST RESPECT LITERATURE, RUFIO. /RUFIO/ (
ARMS II (42)	I WAS OUT HERE, INSTEAD OF IN THE-- HAW! --	LIBRARY	(HE CANNOT MENTION THE LIBRARY WITHOUT BETRAYING
MIS. (117)	HE'S MAD ON READING. HE PROMISED ANOTHER FREE	LIBRARY	LAST WEEK. IT'S RUINOUS. ITLL HIT YOU AS WELL AS ME
METH PREFACE(R48)	THAT ALL THE BOOKS IN THE BRITISH MUSEUM	LIBRARY	MIGHT HAVE BEEN WRITTEN WORD FOR WORD AS THEY STAND
WIDO II SD(24)	ACT II. IN THE	LIBRARY	OF A HANDSOMELY APPOINTED VILLA AT SURBITON ON A
CLEO II (138)	OF THE SEVEN WONDERS OF THE WORLD PERISHES. THE	LIBRARY	OF ALEXANDRIA IS IN FLAMES. /RUFIO/ PSHA! (QUITE
PHIL II SD(94)	ACT II. NEXT DAY AT NOON, IN THE	LIBRARY	OF THE IBSEN CLUB, A LONG ROOM, WITH GLASS DOORS
CAPT II (267)	CAPTAIN BURTON'S ARABIAN NIGHTS-- COPY IN THE	LIBRARY	OF THE NATIONAL LIBERAL CLUB. /LADY CICELY/ (
MIS. (132)	TARLETON. I WISH I COULD PERSUADE YOUR FREE	LIBRARY	PEOPLE OF THAT. /TARLETON/ WHY, MAN, IT'S THE
PHIL II SD(111)	GOOD LUCK TO HIM! (HE FOLLOWS HER). THE	LIBRARY	REMAINS UNOCCUPIED FOR TEN MINUTES. THEN JULIA,
ARMS II (43)	OUT HERE WHEN HE KNEW QUITE WELL I WAS IN THE	LIBRARY	; AND THEN HE GOES DOWNSTAIRS AND BREAKS RAINA'S
PHIL II SD(94)	BETWEEN THE DOOR AND THE RECESS, IS A LIGHT	LIBRARY	STEP-LADDER. FURTHER ON, PAST THE DOOR AN EASY
FABL PREFACE(91)	IT, IF ANY, I WOULD HAVE THEM TAKEN THEN INTO A	LIBRARY	STOCKED WITH THE MASTERPIECES OF LITERATURE. THEY
BULL IV (178)	TO TEACH US HOW TO DO IT EFFICIENTLY, AND OUR	LIBRARY	TO FUDDLE THE FEW IMAGINATIONS YOUR DISTILLERIES
PHIL II (97)	SMOKING ROOM'S ALWAYS FULL OF WOMEN. HERE IN THE	LIBRARY	WE SHALL HAVE IT PRETTY WELL ALL TO OURSELVES UNTIL

FANY PROLOG (257)	RECOLLECTED THAT ALL THE BOOKCASES IN THE	LIBRARY	WERE LOCKED-- IN FACT THEYVE NEVER BEEN OPENED SINCE
PHIL II SD(122)	THE DINING ROOM DOOR, AND IS ABOUT TO LEAVE THE	LIBRARY	WHEN HE MEETS GRACE ENTERING. /GRACE/ HOW DO YOU DO,
ARMS III (57)	GIRL ABOUT HER HABIT OF RUNNING UP HERE TO THE	LIBRARY	WHENEVER SHE GETS A CHANCE, TO LOOK AT THE BOOKS.
MIS. PREFACE(49)	OR TO HEAR A BAND IF THERE WAS ONE, OR TO ANY	LIBRARY	WHERE THERE WERE NO SCHOOLBOOKS. I SHOULD HAVE READ
CLEO II (142)	RUFIO. THEY HAVE COME TO PUT OUT THE FIRE. THE	LIBRARY	WILL KEEP THEM BUSY WHILST WE SEIZE THE LIGHTHOUSE.
ARMS II (38)	I SHALL GO ROUND AND WAIT IN FULL VIEW OF THE	LIBRARY	WINDOWS. BE SURE YOU DRAW FATHER'S ATTENTION TO ME.
ARMS II (40)	WHY DONT YOU TELL YOUR MASTER? HE IS IN THE	LIBRARY	WITH MAJOR SARANOFF. WHY DO YOU COME TO ME? /LOUKA/
ARMS II (42)	IN THE-- HAW! -- LIBRARY (HE CANNOT MENTION THE	LIBRARY	WITHOUT BETRAYING HOW PROUD HE IS OF IT). I SAW YOU
MIS. PREFACE(100)	IT); BUT IT IS CERTAIN THAT A BOY LET LOOSE IN A	LIBRARY	WOULD GO FOR MARIA MONK AND HAVE NO USE WHATEVER FOR
BULL IV (176)	RAISE WAGES: I SHALL FOUND PUBLIC INSTITUTIONS: A	LIBRARY	, A POLYTECHNIC (UNDENOMINATIONAL, OF COURSE), A
PHIL II SD(94)	LEFT, AND FURTHER ON, NEARLY IN THE MIDDLE OF THE	LIBRARY	, A REVOLVING BOOKCASE, WITH AN EASY CHAIR CLOSE TO
MTH3 (108)	ACCOUNTANT GENERAL WILL GO TO THE BRITISH MUSEUM	LIBRARY	, AND SEARCH THE CATALOGUE, HE WILL FIND UNDER HIS
ARMS II (40)	THE MASTER AND MAJOR SARANOFF ARE BUSY IN THE	LIBRARY	, ARNT THEY? /LOUKA/ YES, MADAM. /CATHERINE/ (
HART PREFACE(4)	GOT MIXED AT THE EDGES. EXILES FROM THE	LIBRARY	, THE MUSIC ROOM, AND THE PICTURE GALLERY WOULD BE
BARB I SD(249)	ENLIGHTENED AND LIBERAL AS TO THE BOOKS IN THE	LIBRARY	, THE PICTURES ON THE WALLS, THE MUSIC IN THE
ARMS I (19)	ONLY ONE IN BULGARIA. /THE MAN/ ACTUALLY A REAL	LIBRARY	! I SHOULD LIKE TO SEE THAT. /RAINA/ (AFFECTEDLY)

LICE

SUPR III SD(71)	AND THE MOUNTAINS TOLERATE THEM AS LIONS TOLERATE	LICE	. AN ENGLISH POLICEMAN OR POOR LAW GUARDIAN WOULD
GLIM (184)	SOMETHING IN HIS HEAD. /FERRUCCIO/ (BRUTALLY)	LICE	, NO DOUBT. /GIULIA/ (UNMOVED) THAT WOULD ONLY MAKE

LICENCE

BUOY IV (57)	/OLD BILL/ YES, QUITE ALL RIGHT. HAS HE GOT THE	LICENCE	? /THE WIDOWER/ YES. AND HE HAS BORROWED MY WIFE'S
POSN PREFACE(372)	OF THOSE PLAYS OF MINE WHICH HAD BEEN REFUSED A	LICENCE	BY THE LORD CHAMBERLAIN. THAT OFFER ALSO WAS
POSN PREFACE(414)	QUESTIONS AFFECTING THE EXISTENCE OF A THEATRICAL	LICENCE	BY VOTE OF THE ENTIRE BODY; MANAGERS, LESSEES, AND
BUOY IV (57)	OF POCKET MONEY FOR A NEW ONE. THE MONEY FOR THE	LICENCE	CLEANED HIM OUT. /OLD BILL/ THEN HE HAS COME BACK..
POSN PREFACE(367)	THE LICENCE OF THE LORD CHAMBERLAIN. A REFUSAL TO	LICENCE	DOES NOT HURT HIM, BECAUSE HE CAN PRODUCE ANOTHER
POSN PREFACE(363)	NO MANAGER WHO PROCURES THE LORD CHAMBERLAIN'S	LICENCE	FOR A PLAY CAN BE PUNISHED IN ANY WAY FOR PRODUCING
POSN PREFACE(363)	ABOLITION OF THE EXISTING OBLIGATION TO PROCURE A	LICENCE	FROM THE CENSOR BEFORE PERFORMING A PLAY; BUT EVERY
POSN PREFACE(363)	PRODUCES A PLAY WITHOUT FIRST OBTAINING THE USUAL	LICENCE	FROM THE LORD CHAMBERLAIN. 2. SOME OF THE PLAYS
POSN PREFACE(363)	PRODUCING PLAYS WITHOUT FIRST OBTAINING THE USUAL	LICENCE	FROM THE LORD CHAMBERLAIN SHALL BE PERFECTLY FREE TO
POSN PREFACE(428)	WOULD BE FAR SAFER TO PRODUCE A PLAY FOR WHICH NO	LICENCE	HAD BEEN ASKED THAN ONE FOR WHICH IT HAD BEEN ASKED
POSN PREFACE(380)	LICENCES BY THE LORD CHAMBERLAIN. IN ONE CASE A	LICENCE	HAS SINCE BEEN GRANTED. THE OTHER TWO ARE STILL
POSN PREFACE(397)	AT HIS THEATRE, TAKING HIS CHANCE OF LOSING HIS	LICENCE	IN CONSEQUENCE. THE EVENT PROVED THAT THE MANAGER
BUOY IV SD(60)	LOOK FOR THAT HORMONE. JUNIUS COMES IN WITH THE	LICENCE	IN HIS HAND. /JUNIUS/ WELL, IVE COME BACK AFTER ALL.
POSN PREFACE(428)	THAT HIS BEST POLICY WAS TO DISPENSE WITH THE	LICENCE	IN THE FEW DOUBTFUL CASES, WOULD PRESENTLY ASK
POSN PREFACE(396)	CARRIED SO FAR THAT WHEN A PLAY WAS SUBMITTED FOR	LICENCE	IN WHICH THE RELATIONS OF A PROSTITUTE WITH ALL THE
GETT PREFACE(212)	AS WE HAVE SEEN, THE DIFFICULTY CREATED BY MALE	LICENCE	IS NOT POLYGYNY BUT POLYANDRY, WHICH IS NOT ALLOWED.
POSN PREFACE(403)	EVEN SO, THE DIFFICULTIES ARE ONLY BEGINNING. A	LICENCE	IS SELDOM REFUSED EXCEPT ON GROUNDS WHICH ARE
POSN PREFACE(363)	BE GIVEN AS A JUDICIAL REASON FOR CANCELLING THAT	LICENCE	. 3. AUTHORS AND MANAGERS PRODUCING PLAYS WITHOUT
POSN PREFACE(428)	POWER OF DISPENSING WITH THE LORD CHAMBERLAIN'S	LICENCE	, BUT NOW MARK THE CONSEQUENCES. THE MANAGER, HAVING
POSN PREFACE(410)	COVER OF OPENING A THEATRE HE WOULD RISK HIS	LICENCE	, BUT THE MANAGERS WILL NOT AND SHOULD NOT BE
POSN PREFACE(428)	CONTRACT THAT HIS PLAY SHALL NOT BE SUBMITTED FOR	LICENCE	. I SHOULD PROBABLY TAKE THAT COURSE WITHOUT
POSN PREFACE(409)	FOR A MANDAMUS TO COMPEL THE AUTHORITY TO GRANT A	LICENCE	, IT CAN BE DECLARED UNLAWFUL FOR A LICENSING
BUOY IV (60)	WELL, IVE COME BACK AFTER ALL. HERE IS THE	LICENCE	. IVE GOT THE WITNESSES. IS IT YES OR NO? /SHE/ I
BUOY IV (52)	STOP CHATTERING; AND GO OUT AND BUY A MARRIAGE	LICENCE	. /JUNIUS/ (TAKEN ABACK) OH, I SAY! THIS IS VERY
BUOY IV (58)	FROM PANAMA ARE GOING TO MARRY. HE HAS GOT THE	LICENCE	. /OLD BILL/ WELL, WHAT IS THAT TO YOU, YOU YOUNG
POSN PREFACE(402)	FROM THE LORD CHAMBERLAIN IN CASES OF REFUSAL OF	LICENCE	. THE AUTHORS OF THIS SUGGESTION PROPOSE THAT THE
POSN PREFACE(388)	GIVING NOTICE TO THE GOVERNMENT OR OBTAINING ITS	LICENCE	. THE RISK OF SUCH FREEDOM IS GREAT; BUT AS IT IS
POSN PREFACE(390)	EVERYBODY IS FORBIDDEN TO SELL SILVER WITHOUT A	LICENCE	. WHEN THE LAW HAS FORGOTTEN SOME ATROCIOUS SIN--
POSN PREFACE(407)	THE THEATRE TO THE RISK OF A REFUSAL TO RENEW HIS	LICENCE	. WHY THE MANAGERS DREAD LOCAL CONTROL. ALL THIS
POSN PREFACE(409)	ANY MOTION TO REFUSE TO GRANT OR RENEW HIS	LICENCE	. WITH THESE SAFEGUARDS THE LICENSING POWER COULD
POSN PREFACE(405)	TO OBTAIN A LICENCE TO PURSUE HIS TRADE; AND THIS	LICENCE	LASTS ONLY A YEAR, AND NEED NOT BE RENEWED IF HIS
POSN PREFACE(413)	THEREFORE REASONABLY BE MADE SUBJECT TO AN ANNUAL	LICENCE	LIKE THOSE NOW REQUIRED BEFORE ALLOWING PREMISES TO
POSN PREFACE(428)	EXPRESSLY URGES THAT THE LORD CHAMBERLAIN'S	LICENCE	MUST NOT BE A BAR TO A PROSECUTION. GRANTED THAT IN
POSN PREFACE(397)	WHAT IT CAN DO IS TO REFUSE TO RENEW THE	LICENCE	OF A THEATRE AT WHICH ITS ORDERS ARE DISOBEYED. WHEN
POSN PREFACE(363)	MUST NOT BE RECORDED TO HIS DISADVANTAGE ON THE	LICENCE	OF HIS THEATRE, NOR MAY IT BE GIVEN AS A JUDICIAL
POSN PREFACE(367)	OF THE EXAMINER OF PLAYS, HIS SOLE PROTECTION THE	LICENCE	OF THE LORD CHAMBERLAIN. A REFUSAL TO LICENCE DOES
POSN PREFACE(409)	ITS PERFORMANCE, OR TO REFUSE TO RENEW HIS	LICENCE	ON THE GROUND THAT THE TENDENCY OF HIS
POSN PREFACE(420)	THAT A MAGISTRATE CANNOT REFUSE TO RENEW HIS	LICENCE	ON THE GROUND THAT HE (THE MAGISTRATE) IS A
POSN PREFACE(400)	AS A CENSOR IS A CENSOR, HE CANNOT ENDORSE BY HIS	LICENCE	OPINIONS WHICH SEEM TO HIM DANGEROUSLY HERETICAL. WE
POSN PREFACE(367)	IT IS THE AUTHOR WHO SUFFERS. THE GRANTING OF THE	LICENCE	PRACTICALLY PLACES HIM ABOVE THE LAW; FOR THOUGH IT
POSN PREFACE(414)	OR BY COUNSEL, AGAINST A PROPOSAL TO WITHHOLD A	LICENCE	; AND THE LICENCE SHALL NOT BE WITHHELD EXCEPT FOR
POSN PREFACE(390)	NOBODY IS FORBIDDEN TO SELL MINERALS WITHOUT A	LICENCE	; BUT EVERYBODY IS FORBIDDEN TO SELL SILVER WITHOUT
POSN PREFACE(414)	OF THE PUBLIC AGAINST PHYSICAL INJURY. F. NO	LICENCE	SHALL BE REFUSED ON THE GROUND THAT THE PROXIMITY OF
POSN PREFACE(414)	AGAINST A PROPOSAL TO WITHHOLD A LICENCE; AND THE	LICENCE	SHALL NOT BE WITHHELD EXCEPT FOR STATED REASONS, THE
HART PREFACE(16)	AND LEFT US GLORYING GROTESQUELY IN THE	LICENCE	SUDDENLY ACCORDED TO OUR VILEST PASSIONS AND MOST
POSN PREFACE(432)	DO IT. HE LICENSED THE PLAY, BUT ENDORSED ON HIS	LICENCE	THE CONDITION THAT ALL THE PASSAGES WHICH IMPLICATED
MRS PREFACE(179)	BY THE LOCAL AUTHORITIES, WITHOUT WHOSE	LICENCE	THE FILMS CANNOT BE EXHIBITED IN PLACE OF PUBLIC
MILL IV (204)	WILL MARRY YOU. MR SAGAMORE: SEE ABOUT A SPECIAL	LICENCE	THE MOMENT YOU HAVE GOT RID OF ALASTAIR. /THE
POSN PREFACE(409)	THE POWER TO REFUSE TO GRANT OR RENEW A	LICENCE	TO A THEATRE NEED NOT BE AN ARBITRARY ONE. THE
POSN PREFACE(394)	IT WOULD BE IMPOSSIBLE FOR THE KING TO ALLOW THE	LICENCE	TO BE ISSUED, AS HE WOULD THEREBY BE MADE
POSN PREFACE(405)	CONSEQUENTLY A PUBLICAN IS COMPELLED TO OBTAIN A	LICENCE	TO PURSUE HIS TRADE; AND THIS LICENCE LASTS ONLY A
POSN PREFACE(412)	GIVES THE SPECIAL PROTECTION OF ITS OFFICIAL	LICENCE	TO THE MOST EXTREME IMPROPRIETY THAT THE LOWEST
POSN PREFACE(409)	CONDUCT A THEATRE, AND THEREFORE HAS A RIGHT TO A	LICENCE	UNLESS HE HAS FORFEITED THAT RIGHT BY ALLOWING HIS
POSN PREFACE(404)	OR WHENEVER, FOR DIPLOMATIC REASONS, THE	LICENCE	WOULD COME MORE GRACEFULLY FROM AN AUTHORITY
POSN PREFACE(428)	GRANTED THAT IN SPITE OF THIS RESERVATION THE	LICENCE	WOULD PROVE IN FUTURE AS POWERFUL A DEFENCE AS IT
POSN PREFACE(410)	OF THE PROTECTION OF THE LORD CHAMBERLAIN'S	LICENCE	, AND AT THE SAME TIME EFFICIENTLY PROTECTED AGAINST
POSN PREFACE(432)	HARDLY SAY THAT I HAVE NOT AVAILED MYSELF OF THIS	LICENCE	, AND DO NOT INTEND TO. THERE IS ENOUGH LICENSED
POSN PREFACE(428)	THAT THREE OF MY PLAYS HAVE BEEN REFUSED A	LICENCE	, AND THAT IT WOULD BE FAR SAFER TO PRODUCE A PLAY
POSN PREFACE(429)	TOO NASTY. THESE PEOPLE WOULD STILL TRY TO GET A	LICENCE	, AND WOULD STILL NO DOUBT SUCCEED AS THEY DO TODAY.
SUPR IV (172)	DAYS AFTER OUR RETURN TO ENGLAND, BY SPECIAL	LICENCE	, AT THE OFFICE OF THE DISTRICT SUPERINTENDENT
POSN PREFACE(402)	NOT WITH THE WHOLE MASS OF PLAYS SENT UP FOR	LICENCE	, BUT ONLY THOSE WHICH THE EXAMINER OF PLAYS REFUSES
POSN PREFACE(403)	SHORTCOMINGS, THINKS TWICE BEFORE HE REFUSES A	LICENCE	, KNOWING THAT HIS REFUSAL IS FINAL AND MAY PROMPTLY
POSN PREFACE(414)	TO THE JUDGMENT OF THE HIGH COURTS. E. THE ANNUAL	LICENCE	, ONCE GRANTED, SHALL NOT BE CANCELLED OR SUSPENDED

LICENCES

POSN PREFACE(380)	IN AMERICA. THREE OF THEM HAVE BEEN REFUSED	LICENCES	BY THE LORD CHAMBERLAIN. IN ONE CASE A LICENCE HAS
POSN PREFACE(428)	HIMSELF WHY HE SHOULD SPEND TWO GUINEAS EACH ON	LICENCES	FOR THE MANY PLAYS AS TO WHICH NO QUESTION COULD
POSN PREFACE(432)	THROW ANY ODIUM THAT MAY ATTACH TO REFUSALS OF	LICENCES	IN THE FUTURE. THIS STRANGE AND LAWLESS BODY WILL
POSN PREFACE(363)	EXCEPT THAT THEY MAY BE PUNISHED, HAVE THE	LICENCES	OF THEIR THEATRES ENDORSED AND CANCELLED, AND HAVE
POSN PREFACE(413)	SHALL BE REQUIRED BEFORE PERFORMANCE. C.	LICENCES	SHALL NOT BE WITHHELD ON THE GROUND THAT THE

LICENSE

POSN PREFACE(393)	CHAMBERLAIN LICENSED THIS PLAY, BUT REFUSED TO	LICENSE	A PARODY OF IT. SHORTLY AFTERWARDS HE REFUSED TO
MRS PREFACE(159)	STAGE THAT HAS NOT BEEN PRESENTED UNDER HIS	LICENSE	AND THAT OF HIS PREDECESSOR. THE COMPROMISE, IN
POSN PREFACE(393)	A PARODY OF IT. SHORTLY AFTERWARDS HE REFUSED TO	LICENSE	ANOTHER PLAY IN WHICH THE FEAR OF A GERMAN INVASION
MRS PREFACE(164)	COUNTY COUNCIL WILL SIMPLY REFUSE TO RENEW THEIR	LICENSE	AT THE END OF THE YEAR; AND NOTHING IN THE HISTORY
POSN PREFACE(398)	IT WERE SUBMITTED TO HIM AS A NEW PLAY, HE WOULD	LICENSE	EVEN HAMLET IF CERTAIN ALTERATIONS WERE MADE IN IT.
BARB PREFACE(241)	BUT THAT CANNOT BE HELPED: THE REMEDY IS, NOT TO	LICENSE	EVERYBODY TO THWART THE LAW IF THEY PLEASE, BUT TO
DEVL I SD(3)	GOOD, SHORT OF FLAT FELONY, SHE ENJOYS COMPLETE	LICENSE	EXCEPT FOR AMIABLE WEAKNESSES OF ANY SORT, AND IS
BULL IV (173)	YOUR MOTOR BOATS? WILL DOOLAN HELP YOU TO GET A	LICENSE	FOR YOUR HOTEL? /BROADBENT/ MY DEAR SIR: TO ALL
PHIL II (114)	OF THE MATTER) YES. THAT WAS ALL I COULD GET A	LICENSE	FOR. /CRAVEN/ NOW UPON MY SOUL, PARAMORE, I'M VEXED
POSN PREFACE(398)	MATTERS AS THE TENDENCY OF A PLAY. HE REFUSES TO	LICENSE	GHOSTS EXACTLY AS HE WOULD REFUSE TO LICENSE HAMLET
POSN PREFACE(400)	PLAYS. AN ENLIGHTENED CENSORSHIP WOULD POSSIBLY	LICENSE	GHOSTS; BUT IT WOULD CERTAINLY SUPPRESS MANY OF THE
POSN PREFACE(398)	TO LICENSE GHOSTS EXACTLY AS HE WOULD REFUSE TO	LICENSE	HAMLET IF IT WERE SUBMITTED TO HIM AS A NEW PLAY. HE
OVER PREFACE(164)	AND THAT FRENCH ACTRESSES WHO DESIRE A GREATER	LICENSE	IN APPEALING TO THE SEXUAL INSTINCTS THAN THE FRENCH

GETT (298) THE DECREE IS MADE ABSOLUTE, MY DEAR. AND THE LICENSE IS NOT TRANSFERABLE. /EDITH/ OH WELL, IT CANT BE
BULL PREFACE(22) NOT SUFFICE TO SAVE A CABMAN FROM HAVING HIS LICENSE MARKED, AND A MEMBER OF PARLIAMENT TO BECOME PRIME
OVER PREFACE(158) AND THE DISREPUTABLE SECTION WHICH ENJOYS THE LICENSE OF THE PLUTOCRACY WITHOUT ITS MONEY: CREEPING BELOW
DEST SD(153) THE FRENCH COMMANDER TO PROTECT HIM AGAINST THE LICENSE OF THE TROOPS, HE ACTUALLY SPORTS A PAIR OF GOLD
MRS PREFACE(158) IMPOSSIBLE, IF THE EXAMINER WERE TO REFUSE TO LICENSE PLAYS WITH FEMALE CHARACTERS IN THEM, HE WOULD ONLY
POSN PREFACE(364) CHAMBERLAIN SHALL RETAIN HIS PRESENT POWERS TO LICENSE PLAYS, BUT SHALL BE MADE RESPONSIBLE TO PARLIAMENT
POSN PREFACE(393) OF IT-- CAUSING THE LORD CHAMBERLAIN TO REFUSE TO LICENSE SUCH A PLAY HAS PREVENTED THE PLAY FROM BEING
UNPL PREFACE(R15) OF HIM. IF, HAVING BEEN PAID, HE IS AFRAID TO LICENSE THE PLAY: THAT IS, IF HE IS MORE AFRAID OF THE
UNPL PREFACE(R16) DISPENSE, WAS OUT OF THE QUESTION. TO APPLY FOR A LICENSE WAS TO COURT A PRACTICALLY CERTAIN REFUSAL,
POSN PREFACE(399) THE VIEW OF CHANGING ITS MORALS. NOW YOU CANNOT LICENSE WORK OF THAT SORT WITHOUT MAKING YOURSELF
UNPL PREFACE(R16) MR GREIN WAS AT A HEAVY DISADVANTAGE. WITHOUT A LICENSE , MRS WARREN'S PROFESSION COULD ONLY BE PERFORMED IN

LICENSED

POSN PREFACE(371) HAS SUPPRESSED, BUT THE ABOMINABLE PLAYS IT HAS LICENSED : PLAYS WHICH THE COMMITTEE ITSELF HAD TO TURN THE
POSN PREFACE(395) TRUE IS PROVED BY THE FACT THAT PLAYS WHICH ARE LICENSED AND PRODUCED IN LONDON HAVE TO BE EXPURGATED FOR
MRS PREFACE(180) CENSOR CONSIDERS ALLOWABLE. OF THE FILMS DULY LICENSED BY HIM TWO WERE SO NAKEDLY PORNOGRAPHIC THAT THEIR
POSN PREFACE(394) HIMSELF, BUT IF THESE PUBLICATIONS HAD TO BE LICENSED BY THE LORD CHAMBERLAIN IT WOULD BE IMPOSSIBLE FOR
POSN PREFACE(370) WHEN IT DISCOVERED THAT THE CONTEMPORARY DRAMA, LICENSED BY THE LORD CHAMBERLAIN, INCLUDED PLAYS WHICH COULD
POSN PREFACE(363) FROM THE LORD CHAMBERLAIN. 2. SOME OF THE PLAYS LICENSED BY THE LORD CHAMBERLAIN ARE SO VICIOUS THAT THEIR
POSN PREFACE(432) LICENCE, AND DO NOT INTEND TO. THERE IS ENOUGH LICENSED DARKNESS IN OUR THEATRES TODAY WITHOUT MY ADDING TO
POSN PREFACE(405) PRODUCTS ON THE MARKET. IN THE CASE OF PREMISES LICENSED FOR THE SALE OF SPIRITS THE AUTHORITIES GO A STEP
POSN PREFACE(405) TO BEGIN WITH, A THEATRE IS ACTUALLY A PLACE LICENSED FOR THE SALE OF SPIRITS. THE BARS AT A LONDON
POSN PREFACE(413) AS A THEATRE, BEING NOT ONLY A STAGE, BUT A PLACE LICENSED FOR THE SALE OF SPIRITS, AND A PUBLIC RESORT
MILL IV (197) IF IT COMES TO THAT, AS TO MISS SMITH, THIS IS A LICENSED HOUSE; AND SHE HAS AS MUCH RIGHT TO BE HERE AS YOU
POSN PREFACE(407) CENSORSHIP OF PLAYS, SO THAT PLAYS MIGHT BE LICENSED IN ONE TOWN AND PROHIBITED IN THE NEXT, AND PARTLY
MRS PREFACE(159) BUT FOR THE ABSURD RULE THAT A PLAY ONCE LICENSED IS ALWAYS LICENSED (SO THAT WYCHERLY IS PERMITTED
MRS PREFACE(159) ABSURD RULE THAT A PLAY ONCE LICENSED IS ALWAYS LICENSED (SO THAT WYCHERLY IS PERMITTED AND SHELLEY
DOCT V (173) WHY, HE SAID THAT PRIVATE DOCTORS WERE IGNORANT LICENSED MURDERERS. /RIDGEON/ THAT IS WHAT THE PUBLIC DOCTOR
POSN PREFACE(395) IT. IF A PLAY IS IRRESISTIBLY AMUSING, IT GETS LICENSED NO MATTER WHAT ITS MORAL ASPECT MAY BE. A BRILLIANT
POSN PREFACE(396) PLAYS. IT IS NOT LONG SINCE A JUDGE BEFORE WHOM A LICENSED PLAY CAME IN THE COURSE OF A LAWSUIT EXPRESSED HIS
POSN PREFACE(375) WAS HAPPENING INSIDE. IT COULD NOT BE ANOTHER LICENSED PLAY TOO SCANDALOUS TO BE DISCUSSED IN PUBLIC,
POSN PREFACE(429) CONCEIVE THE SITUATION WHICH WOULD ARISE IF A LICENSED PLAY WERE PROSECUTED. TO MAKE IT CLEARER, LET US
POSN PREFACE(367) THOUGH IT MAY BE LEGALLY POSSIBLE TO PROSECUTE A LICENSED PLAY, NOBODY EVER DREAMS OF DOING IT. THE REALLY
POSN PREFACE(393) IMMEDIATELY AFTER THIS, THE LORD CHAMBERLAIN LICENSED THE PLAY. WHETHER THE INFERENCE, AS FAR AS THE LORD
POSN PREFACE(432) TOO, UNDERSTANDS THE ART OF HOW NOT TO DO IT. HE LICENSED THE PLAY, BUT ENDORSED ON HIS LICENCE THE CONDITION
POSN PREFACE(393) CITIZEN TO BE A SOLDIER, THE LORD CHAMBERLAIN LICENSED THIS PLAY, BUT REFUSED TO LICENSE A PARODY OF IT.
MRS PREFACE(159) YEARS BY MYSELF AT LONDON WEST END THEATRES, ONE LICENSED UNDER QUEEN VICTORIA, THE OTHER UNDER HER
POSN PREFACE(420) OF LICENSING AS APPLIED TO PUBLIC-HOUSES. A LICENSED VICTUALLER CAN NOW BE ASSURED CONFIDENTLY BY HIS
GETT (328) AT ONCE. WHAT WAS YOUR FATHER? /MRS GEORGE/ A LICENSED VICTUALLER WHO MARRIED HIS BARMAID. YOU WOULD CALL
POSN PREFACE(368) WHILST PLAYS OF A SCANDALOUS CHARACTER WERE LICENSED WITHOUT DEMUR. NO DOUBT THIS INFLUENCED PUBLIC
POSN PREFACE(399) THAT THOSE PLAYS OF IBSEN'S WHICH HAVE BEEN LICENSED WITHOUT QUESTION ARE FUNDAMENTALLY IMMORAL TO AN
POSN PREFACE(396) OF FUN AND A HAPPY ENDING WILL GET ANYTHING LICENSED , BECAUSE THE PUBLIC WILL HAVE IT SO, AND THE
POSN PREFACE(432) HUMOR INTO WHICH THE LIGHT SHINES IN THE PLAY ARE LICENSED , BUT THE LIGHT ITSELF IS EXTINGUISHED. I NEED
MRS PREFACE(163) RAPINE PLAY WHICH I HAVE DESCRIBED, AND WHICH HE LICENSED , WAS QUITE INCAPABLE IN MANUSCRIPT OF PRODUCING

LICENSER

POSN PREFACE(366) LORD CHAMBERLAIN IN THE EXERCISE OF HIS DUTIES AS LICENSER HAD DONE THOSE THINGS WHICH HE OUGHT NOT TO HAVE
POSN PREFACE(395) BEING A VERY AMUSING PLAY, IT PASSED THE LICENSER WITH THE EXCEPTION OF A REFERENCE TO IMPOTENCE AS A

LICENSES

POSN PREFACE(400) UNENLIGHTENED CENSOR, PROHIBITS GHOSTS AND LICENSES ALL THE REST OF IBSEN'S PLAYS. AN ENLIGHTENED
POSN PREFACE(433) MORALISTS, WHO OBJECT MUCH MORE TO THE PLAYS HE LICENSES THAN TO THOSE HE SUPPRESSES, AND ARE THEREFORE

LICENSING

POSN PREFACE(405) LICENSING OF THEATRES. THE DISTINCTION BETWEEN LICENSING AND CENSORSHIP. IT MUST NOT BE CONCLUDED THAT THE
POSN PREFACE(413) OR CONTEMPLATED IS HERETICAL OR IMMORAL. D. THE LICENSING AREA SHALL BE NO LESS THAN THAT OF A COUNTY
POSN PREFACE(419) WE HAVE READY TO OUR HAND THE MACHINERY OF LICENSING AS APPLIED TO PUBLIC-HOUSES. A LICENSED VICTUALLER
POSN PREFACE(408) THIS DOES NOT ALTER THE FACT THAT THE MUNICIPAL LICENSING AUTHORITIES HAVE ACTUALLY USED THEIR POWERS TO SET
POSN PREFACE(410) AGAINST EVERY ATTEMPT AT CENSORSHIP BY THE LICENSING AUTHORITY, THE ENEMIES OF THE THEATRE WILL RESORT
POSN PREFACE(409) A LICENCE, IT CAN BE DECLARED UNLAWFUL FOR A LICENSING AUTHORITY TO DEMAND FROM THE MANAGER ANY
POSN PREFACE(413) DANCING. 9. IN ORDER TO PREVENT THE POWERS OF THE LICENSING AUTHORITY BEING ABUSED SO AS TO CONSTITUTE A
POSN PREFACE(413) ACT TRANSFERRING THE THEATRES TO THE CONTROL OF A LICENSING AUTHORITY SHOULD BE MADE ALSO A CHARTER OF THE
BULL PREFACE(5) ABOUT TARIFF REFORM, THE EDUCATION AND LICENSING BILLS, AND THE SOUTH AFRICAN WAR, HAVE GIVEN WAY
POSN PREFACE(412) ESPECIALLY DEVOTED TO THEIR ENTERTAINMENT, LICENSING EVERYTHING THAT IS POPULAR AND FORBIDDING ANY
POSN PREFACE(396) EXPRESSED HIS SCANDALIZED ASTONISHMENT AT THE LICENSING OF SUCH A WORK. EMINENT CHURCHMEN HAVE MADE
POSN PREFACE(405) STATEMENT. THE REJECTED STATEMENT. PART II: THE LICENSING OF THEATRES. THE DISTINCTION BETWEEN LICENSING AND
POSN PREFACE(429) HOW LONG WOULD HIS POST SURVIVE THE DISCREDIT OF LICENSING ONLY PORNOGRAPHIC PLAYS? IT IS CLEAR TO ME THAT
POSN PREFACE(409) OR RENEW HIS LICENCE. WITH THESE SAFEGUARDS THE LICENSING POWER COULD NOT BE STRETCHED TO CENSORSHIP. THE
POSN PREFACE(409) OF AN OFFENCE AGAINST PUBLIC DECENCY. ALSO, THE LICENSING POWERS OF THE AUTHORITY SHOULD NOT BE DELEGATED TO
POSN PREFACE(414) OR CITY CORPORATION, WHICH SHALL NOT DELEGATE ITS LICENSING POWERS TO ANY MINOR LOCAL AUTHORITY OR TO ANY
POSN PREFACE(407) WE HAVE A STRONG CASE FOR APPLYING EITHER THE LICENSING SYSTEM OR WHATEVER BETTER MEANS MAY BE DEVIZED FOR
POSN PREFACE(412) THE RESPONSIBILITY FOR HERESY OR IMMORALITY BY LICENSING THEM, AND BECAUSE THE MANY HERETICAL AND IMMORAL

LICENTIOUS

MRS PREFACE(151) TOO THAT THE STAGE UNDER THE CENSORSHIP BECAME SO LICENTIOUS AFTER THE WAR THAT THE BAN ON A COMPARATIVELY
BULL PREFACE(43) AS HIS DRINKING, AS FILTHY AS HIS SMOKING, AS LICENTIOUS AS HIS DOMESTICITY, AS CORRUPT AS HIS ELECTIONS,
JOAN PREFACE(7) HARDY SOLDIER, UNABLE TO ENDURE LOOSE LANGUAGE OR LICENTIOUS CONDUCT. SHE WENT TO THE STAKE WITHOUT A STAIN ON
MRS PREFACE(162) A REMORSELESS AND UNBOWDLERIZED NARRATION OF THE LICENTIOUS FICTIONS WHICH SLIP THROUGH ITS NET, AND ARE
JOAN PREFACE(25) WAS TO BE CONTINUALLY FALLING INTO THE HANDS OF LICENTIOUS FOES AND SUFFERING THE WORST EXTREMITIES OF
FABL PREFACE(81) OF THE OLD MORAL WORLD, AND WERE DISHONEST AND LICENTIOUS . PROMINENT IN MY OWN GENERATION OF MARXISTS WAS
SUPR III (119) /DON JUAN/ (DETERMINEDLY) I SAY THE MOST LICENTIOUS OF HUMAN INSTITUTIONS: THAT IS THE SECRET OF ITS
SUPR III (119) FIGMENTS IT CARES NOT A RAP. MARRIAGE IS THE MOST LICENTIOUS OF HUMAN INSTITUTIONS-- /ANA/ JUAN! /THE STATUE/
BARB PREFACE(234) BUT UNNATURAL REIGNS OF THE SAINTS RELIEVED BY LICENTIOUS RESTORATIONS; TO AMERICANS WHO HAVE MADE DIVORCE
SUPR PREFACE(R15) OF GOUNOD OR BIZET WOULD APPEAR AS A LICENTIOUS STAIN ON THE SCORE OF DON GIOVANNI. EVEN THE MORE
OVER PREFACE(163) ACCUSTOMED TO CONSIDER THE FRENCH STAGE MUCH MORE LICENTIOUS THAN THE BRITISH, ARE ALWAYS SURPRISED AND
GETT PREFACE(195) VEILED BY HYPROCISY, AN OVERWHELMING DEMAND FOR LICENTIOUS THEATRICAL ENERTAINMENTS WHICH NO CENSORSHIP CAN
DEVL I SD(3) AND IS CONSEQUENTLY, WITHOUT KNOWING IT, THE MOST LICENTIOUS WOMAN IN THE PARISH ON THE STRENGTH OF NEVER

LICENTIOUSLY

MRS PREFACE(159) THEM TO BE DURING THEIR LIFETIME: THAT IS, A LICENTIOUSLY IRREGULAR GROUP TO BE KEPT IN ORDER IN A ROUGH

LICENTIOUSNESS

GETT PREFACE(223) OF LAW AND CUSTOM MUST PRODUCE A WILD OUTBREAK OF LICENTIOUSNESS . AS FAR AS OUR MORALISTS CAN GRASP THE
3PLA PREFACE(R11) EXCEPT THE CLANDESTINE PLAY OF NATURAL LICENTIOUSNESS . THE STALLS CANNOT BE FULLY UNDERSTOOD
GETT PREFACE(189) AVENGER OF OUTRAGED DECENCY WHO DECLARES THAT THE LICENTIOUSNESS OF MARRIAGE, NOW THAT IT NO LONGER RECRUITS
DOCT PREFACE(26) AND NOT VERY TACTFUL ONE BEING THE DRUNKENNESS OR LICENTIOUSNESS OF THE PATIENT. BUT THOUGH A FEW DOCTORS HAVE
MRS PREFACE(151) IS CAUSED, NOT BY FEMALE DEPRAVITY AND MALE LICENTIOUSNESS , BUT SIMPLY BY UNDERPAYING, UNDERVALUING,

LICHT

JITT (1) DER TOD UND DIE LIEBE, GEFAHRLICHE JAHRE, SPATES LICHT , DIE FRAU OHNE DIENSTAG, DER GELIEBTE, DIE LAST DES

LICITLY

UNPL PREFACE(R26) AS A SEX TO ATTACH THEMSELVES TO BREADWINNERS, LICITLY OR ILLICITLY, ON PAIN OF HEAVY PRIVATION AND

LICK

PRES (139) THEY CALL A SODA KING, AND ORDERS A CURATE TO LICK HIS BOOTS, AND WHEN THE CURATE PUNCHES HIS HEAD, YOU

MIS.	(113)	BUT WHAT I CANT UNDERSTAND IS WHY HE DIDNT	LICK	IT OUT OF YOU WHEN YOU WERE A KID. FOR TWENTY-FIVE
BARB II	(284)	OF IM. AW AINT AFRIDE OF ENNYBODY. BAT E CAN	LICK	ME. SHE'S DAN ME. (HE SITS DOWN MOODILY ON THE EDGE OF
PYGM II	(241)	NEVER BROUGHT HER UP AT ALL, EXCEPT TO GIVE HER A	LICK	OF A STRAP NOW AND AGAIN. DONT PUT IT ON ME, GOVERNOR.
APPL I	(231)	BE SERIOUS ABOUT ARE FOOTBALL AND REFRESHMENTS.	LICK	THE KING'S BOOTS: THAT IS ALL YOU ARE FIT FOR. (HE
METH PREFACE	(R14)	IT WILL IMMEDIATELY TAKE EXTRAORDINARY PAINS TO	LICK	THE MUD OFF, AND FINALLY BE CLEANER THAN IT WAS BEFORE.
MTH1 I	(9)	TO DO. /THE SERPENT/ THINK. WILL. EAT THE DUST.	LICK	THE WHITE STONE: BITE THE APPLE YOU DREAD. THE SUN WILL
LION PROLOG	(109)	IT! (HOLDING UP THE THORN). NOW IT'S OUT. NOW	LICK	UM'S PAW TO TAKE AWAY THE NASTY INFLAMMATION. SEE? (
DOCT III	(140)	OR DIVORCE COURT SENSATION FOR YOU MORAL CHAPS TO	LICK	YOUR LIPS OVER AT BREAKFAST. HE JUST SAID, WELL, THE

LICKCHEESE

WIDO II	(32)	GROWING IN OUR GARDEN. /COKANE/ (REVOLTED) MR	LICKCHEESE	: I DID NOT ADDRESS MYSELF TO YOU. I DO NOT WISH
WIDO II	(27)	MR COKANE. I AM PLEASED TO SEE YOU HERE. MR	LICKCHEESE	: YOU WILL PLACE YOUR ACCOUNTS AND MONEY ON THE
WIDO II	(46)	FURIOUSLY ON HER). /BLANCHE/ DID I ASK YOU ABOUT	LICKCHEESE	? YOU BEAST: YOU KNOW WHO I MEAN: YOURE DOING IT
WIDO III	(55)	BUSINESS TO TRANSACT, BLANCHE. YOU CAN TALK TO MR	LICKCHEESE	AFTERWARDS. COME ON, SARTORIUS AND LICKCHEESE GO
WIDO III	(55)	(HASTILY) OH, I AM THE SAME AS EVER. HOW ARE MRS	LICKCHEESE	AND THE CHIL-- /SARTORIUS/ (IMPATIENTLY) WE HAVE
WIDO III	SD(51)	OUT BEAMING, FULL OF THE NEWS FOR THE KITCHEN.	LICKCHEESE	CLINCHES THE SITUATION BY A TRIUMPHANT NOD AT
WIDO III	SD(66)	AND SARTORIUS COME FROM THE STUDY. SARTORIUS AND	LICKCHEESE	COME TO TRENCH. COKANE CROSSES TO BLANCHE IN HIS
WIDO III	(55)	AND SITS ERECT AND QUIET, STITCHING AT IT.	LICKCHEESE	COMES BACK, SPEAKING TO SARTORIUS, WHO FOLLOWS
WIDO III	SD(58)	HERE, PAPA. (SHE RUSHES AWAY INTO THE STUDY).	LICKCHEESE	COMES IN WITH TRENCH AND COKANE. BOTH ARE IN
WIDO III	SD(58)	HIS DISAPPOINTMENT, BOWS SHORTLY AND RESENTFULLY.	LICKCHEESE	COVERS THE GENERAL EMBARRASSMENT BY TALKING
WIDO II	(42)	YOU YOUR SEVEN HUNDRED A YEAR OUT OF IT. WHAT	LICKCHEESE	DID FOR ME, I DO FOR YOU. HE AND I ARE ALIKE
WIDO II	SD(25)	OVER TO KISS HIM, A TAP AT THE DOOR). COME IN.	LICKCHEESE	ENTERS, CARRYING A BLACK HANDBAG. HE IS A SHABBY,
WIDO III	(63)	BLANCHE'S ADVANTAGE AND DR TRENCH'S. /COKANE/	LICKCHEESE	EXPRESSES HIMSELF ROUGHLY, MR SARTORIUS; BUT HIS
WIDO III	(62)	IT NOT THAT THE CIRCUMSTANCES MENTIONED BY MR	LICKCHEESE	FORCE MY HAND. BESIDES, DR TRENCH, I HOPED FOR
WIDO III	SD(55)	MR LICKCHEESE AFTERWARDS. COME ON, SARTORIUS AND	LICKCHEESE	GO INTO THE STUDY. BLANCHE, SURPRISED AT HER
WIDO III	(65)	YES: WHEN MY FATHER MAKES YOU DO IT. AND WHEN	LICKCHEESE	HAS DISCOVERED SOME WAY OF MAKING IT PROFITABLE.
WIDO III	(58)	COMING? /SARTORIUS/ THERE IS NO TIME TO BE LOST.	LICKCHEESE	HAS GONE TO ASK HIM TO COME ROUND. /BLANCHE/ (IN
WIDO II	(46)	ME, WILL YOU. HAVE THEY GONE? /THE PARLORMAID/	LICKCHEESE	HAS GONE, LOOKING DREADF-- (SHE BREAKS OFF WITH
WIDO III	(61)	I DONT SEE THAT IT'S ANY BUSINESS OF YOURS, MR	LICKCHEESE	. /LICKCHEESE/ IT'S A FREE COUNTRY: EVERY MAN HAS
WIDO III	(56)	BLUEBOOK. /BLANCHE/ I THOUGHT WE WERE DONE WITH	LICKCHEESE	. /SARTORIUS/ NOT QUITE YET, I THINK. HE LEFT A
WIDO II	(47)	TRENCH. IT WAS ONLY A PIECE OF MISCHIEF MADE BY	LICKCHEESE	. TRENCH IS A YOUNG FOOL; BUT IT IS ALL RIGHT
WIDO III	SD(66)	ALLOW ME. EXEUNT OMNES: BLANCHE ON COKANE'S ARM;	LICKCHEESE	JOCOSELY TAKING SARTORIUS ON ONE ARM, AND TRENCH
WIDO III	(55)	WE ARE FINE, AINT WE, MISS BLANCHE? I THINK MR	LICKCHEESE	MUST HAVE COME INTO A LEGACY. (CONFIDENTIALLY) I
WIDO III	SD(58)	THE PIANO; AND THE OTHER TWO BETWEEN THEM, WITH	LICKCHEESE	NEXT COKANE). /LICKCHEESE/ HERE WE ARE, ALL
WIDO II	(26)	I DID NOT ASK YOU THAT. LET ME SEE THE BOOKS. (	LICKCHEESE	PRODUCES THE RENT BOOK, AND HANDS IT TO
WIDO II	SD(27)	WILL EXAMINE THEM AND SETTLE WITH YOU PRESENTLY.	LICKCHEESE	RETIRES TO THE TABLE, AND BEGINS TO ARRANGE HIS
WIDO III	(54)	HESITATES, LOOKING AT HIM IN GREAT DOUBT.	LICKCHEESE	RISES AND EXHIBITS HIMSELF). COME! LOOK AT MY
WIDO II	(27)	THE PARLORMAID WITHDRAWS. /TRENCH/ (GLANCING AT	LICKCHEESE	) I HOPE WE'RE NOT IN THE WAY. /SARTORIUS/ BY NO
WIDO II	(26)	INTERFERE IN MY BUSINESS. (HE TURNS SUDDENLY ON	LICKCHEESE	). NOW LOOK HERE, MR LICKCHEESE! THIS IS THE
WIDO III	SD(62)	AND SETTLE THE WHOLE AFFAIR THAT WAY? SENSATION.	LICKCHEESE	SITS DOWN TRIUMPHANT. /COKANE/ YOU FORGET, MR
WIDO III	SD(54)	IMPATIENT AT THE INTERRUPTION, RISES AND MOTIONS	LICKCHEESE	TO THE DOOR OF THE STUDY. /SARTORIUS/ SH! WE
WIDO III	(65)	FOUND THAT THERE IS SOME MONEY TO BE MADE HERE.	LICKCHEESE	TOLD YOU. YOU, WHO WERE SO DISINTERESTED, SO
WIDO III	(51)	EXCITED. /THE PARLORMAID/ PLEASE, SIR, MR	LICKCHEESE	WANTS TO SEE YOU VERY PARTICLAR. ON IMPORTANT
WIDO III	(51)	TO SAY. /SARTORIUS/ MR LICKCHEESE! DO YOU MEAN	LICKCHEESE	WHO USED TO COME HERE ON MY BUSINESS? /THE
WIDO III	SD(66)	AND PUSHES IT BACK AS FAR AS POSSIBLE. COKANE,	LICKCHEESE	, AND SARTORIUS COME FROM THE STUDY. SARTORIUS
WIDO II	(33)	BUSINESS. I SHALL TROUBLE YOU NO FURTHER TODAY. (	LICKCHEESE	, COWED, GOES OUT AMID DEAD SILENCE. SARTORIUS
WIDO II	(29)	AGAIN. /TRENCH/ (EMBARRASSED) WELL, YOU SEE, MR	LICKCHEESE	, I DONT SEE HOW I CAN INTERFERE. I'M VERY SORRY,
WIDO II	(41)	TRUE PROGRESS. STILL, A SOUND CONSERVATIVE. AS TO	LICKCHEESE	, I NEED SAY NO MORE ABOUT HIM THAN THAT I HAVE
WIDO II	(27)	STEPPED AN INCH OUTSIDE THE LETTER OF THE LAW, MR	LICKCHEESE	, I WILL PROSECUTE YOU MYSELF. THE WAY TO KEEP
WIDO II	(30)	IF YOU WISH ME TO DO ANYTHING FOR YOU, MR	LICKCHEESE	, LET ME TELL YOU THAT YOU ARE NOT GOING THE
WIDO III	(59)	WE WERE SPEAKING OF. /COKANE/ (AUSTERELY) NO, MR	LICKCHEESE	, NOT TRYING TO PERSUADE HIM. NO: THIS IS A
WIDO II	(40)	SORT. I FOUND OUT THIS MORNING FROM YOUR MAN--	LICKCHEESE	, OR WHATEVER HIS CONFOUNDED NAME IS-- THAT YOUR
WIDO III	(63)	MACHINES. /SARTORIUS/ (REVOLTED) DO YOU THINK,	LICKCHEESE	, THAT MY DAUGHTER IS TO BE MADE PART OF A MONEY
WIDO III	(62)	SITS DOWN TRIUMPHANT. /COKANE/ YOU FORGET, MR	LICKCHEESE	, THAT THE YOUNG LADY, WHOSE TASTE HAS TO BE
WIDO II	(33)	WILL COME HERE TOMORROW NOT LATER THAN TEN, MR	LICKCHEESE	, TO CONCLUDE OUR BUSINESS. I SHALL TROUBLE YOU
WIDO III	SD(51)	A FORTUNE, SIR. /SARTORIUS/ HM! SHEW HIM UP.	LICKCHEESE	, WHO HAS BEEN WAITING AT THE DOOR, INSTANTLY
WIDO II	(32)	OBSERVATION TO ADDRESS TO A GENTLEMAN, MR	LICKCHEESE	! A MOST REVOLUTIONARY SENTIMENT! /LICKCHEESE/
WIDO III	(51)	YOUR BUSINESS, HE TOLD ME TO SAY. /SARTORIUS/ MR	LICKCHEESE	! DO YOU MEAN LICKCHEESE WHO USED TO COME HERE
WIDO III	(54)	YOU WELL, MISS BLANCHE. /BLANCHE/ WHY, IT'S MR	LICKCHEESE	! I HARDLY KNEW YOU. /LICKCHEESE/ I FIND YOU A
WIDO II	(26)	TURNS SUDDENLY ON LICKCHEESE). NOW LOOK HERE, MR	LICKCHEESE	! THIS IS THE THIRD TIME THIS YEAR THAT YOU HAVE

LICKCHEESE'S

WIDO III	(55)	AWAY? (NO ANSWER). OH, YOU ARE INTERESTED IN MR	LICKCHEESE'S	BOOK, MISS. BLANCHE SPRINGS UP. THE PARLORMAID
WIDO III	(61)	TRENCH; BUT EVEN YOU MUST FEEL THE COGENCY OF MR	LICKCHEESE'S	BUSINESS STATEMENT. /TRENCH/ BUT WHY CANT YOU
WIDO III	SD(55)	LOOKS AFTER THEM FOR A MOMENT. THEN, SEEING	LICKCHEESE'S	OVERCOAT ON HER CHAIR, SHE TAKES IT UP, AMUSED,
WIDO III	(53)	PREMISES? ROUND ON AN OLD PAL! NO: THAT AINT	LICKCHEESE'S	WAY. BESIDES, THEY KNOW ALL ABOUT YOU ALREADY.

LICKED

DOCT PREFACE	(48)	SWEAR FIFTY LIES THAN TAKE AN ANIMAL WHICH HAD	LICKED	MY HAND IN GOOD FELLOWSHIP AND TORTURE IT. IF I DID

LICKING

MIS.	(112)	A SPOILT YOUNG PUP; AND YOU NEED A JOLLY GOOD	LICKING	. AND IF YOURE NOT CAREFUL YOULL GET IT: I'LL SEE TO
MIS.	(116)	YEARS, MOTHER, SINCE YOU HAD THAT ROW WITH ME FOR	LICKING	ROBERT AND GIVING HYPATIA A BLACK EYE BECAUSE SHE
POSN	(440)	AND WHEN THE GOLD DIDNT PAN OUT, THEY LIVED BY	LICKING	THEIR YOUNG INTO HABITS OF HONEST INDUSTRY.
DEVL I	SD(12)	THE SNUFF BY PINCHING IT WITH HER FINGERS, FIRST	LICKING	THEM FOR THE PURPOSE; AND REPLACES THE SCONCE ON THE

LICKS

MTH1 I	(6)	GODMOTHER EVE? /THE SERPENT/ I ADORE HER. (SHE	LICKS	EVE'S NECK WITH HER DOUBLE TONGUE). /EVE/ (PETTING
LION PROLOG	(109)	UM'S DEAR OLD FRIEND ANDY WANDY. (THE LION	LICKS	HIS FACE). YES, KISSUMS ANDY WANDY. (THE LION,
LION PROLOG	(109)	TO TAKE AWAY THE NASTY INFLAMMATION. SEE? (HE	LICKS	HIS OWN HAND. THE LION NODS INTELLIGENTLY AND LICKS
LION PROLOG	(109)	HIS OWN HAND. THE LION NODS INTELLIGENTLY AND	LICKS	HIS PAW INDUSTRIOUSLY). CLEVER LITTLE LIONY-PIONY!
LION PROL,SD	(105)	AND HURTS HIMSELF WORSE. HE ROARS PITEOUSLY. HE	LICKS	IT AGAIN. TEARS DROP FROM HIS EYES. HE LIMPS PAINFULLY
LION PROL,SD	(105)	STICKS. HE SITS DOWN AND CONTEMPLATES IT. HE	LICKS	IT. HE SHAKES IT. HE TRIES TO EXTRACT IT BY SCRAPING
CAND I	(83)	AND CANDIDA THERE, AND CANDIDA EVERYWHERE! (SHE	LICKS	THE ENVELOPE). IT'S ENOUGH TO DRIVE ANYONE OUT OF
POSN	(441)	SOMEBODY TO RELIEVE YOUR ROTTEN FEELINGS WHEN HE	LICKS	YOU FOR IT? NOT LIKELY. TIL YOU CAN FIND A WITNESS

LID

MTH1 II	(32)	THE SUN WILL BE COVERED WITH A BLACK SAUCEPAN	LID	. AND THERE IS TUBAL, WHO MADE THIS WHEEL FOR ME WHICH
APPL PREFACE	(192)	LINE OF RAILWAY HAD ON IT A TRUCK WITH A STEEL	LID	. THE PRACTICAL PART OF THE PROCEEDINGS BEGAN BY PLACING
APPL PREFACE	(192)	PROCEEDINGS BEGAN BY PLACING AN ARMCHAIR ON THE	LID	OF ONE OF THE TRUCKS AND SEATING ME IN IT, A BRIMMING
PYGM V	(271)	YOU MAY WELL CALL IT A SILLY JOKE. IT PUT THE	LID	ON ME RIGHT ENOUGH. JUST GIVE HIM THE CHANCE HE WANTED
MIS.	(183)	YOUNG MAN: YOURE A FOOL; BUT YOUVE JUST PUT THE	LID	ON THIS JOB IN A MASTERLY MANNER. I KNEW YOU WOULD. I
2TRU I	SD(27)	OF RINGS, A JEWEL BOX OF BLACK STEEL WITH THE	LID	OPEN AND A ROPE OF PEARLS HEAPED CARELESSLY HALF IN AND
PHIL I	(85)	THE PIANO DESK AND LAYS IT ASIDE; THEN CLOSES THE	LID	OVER THE KEYBOARD). /JULIA/ (PASSING BETWEEN THE SOFA
CURE	(232)	IF YOU START PLAYING. /STREGA/ (RAISING THE	LID	) THEN I SHALL START AT ONCE. /REGINALD/ (RUNNING TO
CURE	(231)	PLEASE! (HE STOPS HER BY SHUTTING THE KEYBOARD	LID	). WHO LET YOU IN? /THE LADY/ (RISING THREATENINGLY)

LIDS

WIDO II	(42)	ALL THE MISSING BANISTERS, HANDRAILS, CISTERN	LIDS	AND DUSTHOLE TOPS AT YOUR OWN EXPENSE; AND YOU WILL

LIDY

CAPT II	(244)	BETWEEN HER AND THE ARCH) NAOW, NAOW! NAOW,	LIDY	: DOWNT YOU GOW DISTURBIN THE KEPN. AWLL SEE TO IT.
CAPT I	(238)	WITHAHT NAOW KEPN TO TEOLL US WOT TO DO. NAOW,	LIDY	: HOONAWTED WE STEND: DEEVAWDID WE FALL. /LADY CICELY/
CAPT I	(238)	WE CAWNT GOW WITHAHT YER. (TO LADY CICELY) NAOW,	LIDY	: IT WOULDNT BE FOR YR HOWN GOOD. YER CAWNT HEXPECT A
CAPT III	(289)	(FRANTICALLY BREAKING FROM HIM) LIDY,	LIDY	: SY A WORD FOR ME. EV A FEELIN AWT: (HIS TEARS CHOKE
CAPT I	(234)	HAWCE BARRER: AN STREET PIANNER HAWTELLIAN,	LIDY	: THETS WOT E IS. KEPN BRARSBAHND'S RESPECTS TO YR
CAPT I	(238)	/DRINKWATER/ (WITH A SMILE OF VANITY) WEOLL,	LIDY	: Y' CAWNT DEENAW THAT E'S A PAFFICK GENLMN. BIT

CAPT II (244)	WHERE IS MARZO'S BED? /DRINKWATER/ IS BED,	LIDY	? WEOLL: E YNT PERTICKLER, LIDY. E EZ IS CHAWCE OF
CAPT I (220)	AN IS CREW, INCLOODIN MAWSEOLF, WILL SEE THE	LIDY	AN JADGE ELLAM THROUGH HENNY LITTLE EXCURSION IN
CAPT I (234)	IN? /DRINKWATER/ WORNT BAWN IN HITLY AT ALL,	LIDY	. BAWN IN ETTN GAWDN (HATTON GARDEN). HAWCE BARRER AN
CAPT II (244)	IS BED, LIDY? WEOLL: E YNT PERTICKLER,	LIDY	. E EZ IS CHAWCE OF HENNY FLEGSTOWN AGIN THET WALL.
CAPT I (234)	(MARZO TOUCHES HIS HAT), HAWTELLIAN SHIPMITE,	LIDY	. HAHR CHEF. /LADY CICELY/ (NODDING AFFABLY TO MARZO)
CAPT III (289)	LADY. /DRINKWATER/ (IN A SMALL VOICE) THENKYER,	LIDY	. (HE RETIRES AMONG HIS COMRADES, SNIVELLING
CAPT I (227)	THORTLESS LEDS BAW A GENT ON THE DILY CHRORNICLE,	LIDY	. (RANKIN RETURNS. DRINKWATER IMMEDIATELY WITHDRAWS.
CAPT II (244)	LITTLE SUVVICE? MIKE YRSEOLF AT OWM, Y' KNAOW,	LIDY	. /LADY CICELY/ (CONSIDERATELY) DONT GO IF YOUD RATHER
CAPT III (288)	APPEALING TO LADY CICELY) DOWNT LET EM BURN EM,	LIDY	. THEY DASSENT IF YOU HORDER EM NOT TO. (WITH
CAPT II (243)	WEOLCOME TO BRARSBAHND CAWSTL, SR AHRD AN	LIDY	. THIS EAH IS THE CORFEE AND COMMERCIAL ROOM. SIR
CAPT I (222)	FOR THE WORD. (SENTIMENTALLY) LAWK AS A HINGLISH	LIDY	MAWT CALL ER LITTLE BOY BIRDIE. /RANKIN/ (NOT QUITE
CAPT I (226)	NETRAL. AWM WANNE OF THE MISSIONARY'S GOOD WORKS,	LIDY	-- IS FIRST CORNVERT, A UMBLE BRITISH SEAMAN--
CAPT III (285)	(INVOLUNTARILY) NAOW, DOWNT DO THET,	LIDY	-- /REDBROOK/ (AS BEFORE) SHUT UP, YOU FOOL, WILL YOU.
CAPT I (219)	WELL? /DRINKWATER/ HEVER EAR OF IS SIST-IN-LOR:	LIDY	SISLY WINEFLEET? /RANKIN/ DO YE MEAN THE CELEBRATED
CAPT I (219)	AW OW Y'A TURN FER THET? BESAWDS, GAVNER, THIS	LIDY	SISLY WINEFLEET MAWT WORNT TO TIKE A WALK CROST
CAPT I (221)	GAVNER: YOURE BUSY HEXPECTIN O SR AHRD AN	LIDY	SISLY, YNT YER? (ABOUT TO GO). /RANKIN/ (STOPPING
CAPT I (238)	/DRINKWATER/ WEOLL, AW WAS HOWNLY A TEOLLN THE	LIDY	THET-- (A THREATENING MOVEMENT FROM BRASSBOUND CUTS
CAPT I (224)	EATHEN MENNERS FER YER! CALLS SR AHRD ELLAM AN	LIDY	WINEFLEET A CHRISTIAN DORG AND IS WOMAN! IF EE ED YOU
CAPT II (243)	FOR THE BRITISH HERRISTORCRACY, LAWD ELLAM AN	LIDY	WINEFLETE? /REDBROOK/ LADY FAINT, EH? /DRINKWATER/
CAPT I (226)	A UMBLE BRITISH SEAMAN-- COUNTRYMEN O YOURS,	LIDY	, AND OF IS LAWDSHIP'S. THIS EAH IS MR RENKIN, THE BUST
CAPT I (225)	THE MISSIONARY? /DRINKWATER/ (MODESTLY) NAOW,	LIDY	, AW WILL NOT DECEIVE YOU, THOW THE MISTIKE HIS BUT
CAPT III (289)	/DRINKWATER/ (FRANTICALLY BREAKING FROM HIM)	LIDY	, LIDY: SY A WORD FOR ME. EV A FEELIN AWT. (HIS TEARS
CAPT I (238)	(WITH ENTHUSIASM) FEED AHT O YR AND,	LIDY	, WE WOULD. /BRASSBOUND/ (WITH SARDONIC ASSENT) GOOD.
CAPT II (249)	KEPN BRARSBAHND: YOU GOT SATHINK TO SY TO THE	LIDY	, YNT YR? /LADY CICELY/ (STOPPING) I'LL COME BACK TO

LIDY'S

CAPT II (250)	HURT MR DRINKWATER. /DRINKWATER/ (LACHRYMOSELY)	LIDY'S	HINKYP'BLE O SICH BAWBROUS USAGE. /LADY CICELY/ BUT

LIDYSHIP

CAPT II (244)	DOOR AND PLACES HIMSELF BEFORE IT). WHERE MAWT YR	LIDYSHIP	BE GOWIN? /LADY CICELY/ I'M GOING THROUGH EVERY

LIE

HART II (111)	/THE BURGLAR/ WELL, IT'S NO USE MY TELLING YOU A	LIE	: I CAN TAKE IN MOST CAPTAINS, BUT NOT CAPTAIN SHOTOVER.
KING II (226)	LOSE THE WORST OF HUSBANDS. /CATHERINE/ THAT IS A	LIE	: IF ANYONE ELSE SAID IT I WOULD KILL HER. YOU ARE THE
ARMS III (59)	WOULD SAY OF YOU. /SERGIUS/ (BOUNDING UP) YOU	LIE	: IT IS NOT SO, BY ALL THE STARS! IF I LOVED YOU, AND I
POSN (450)	RUB MY CHEEK AGAINST YOURS, DARLING. /FEEMY/ YOU	LIE	: MY COLOR'S MY OWN, SUCH AS IT IS, AND A PRETTY COLOR
PYGM II (226)	(TURNING ON HIM) OH YOU ARE A BRUTE. IT'S A	LIE	: NOBODY EVER SAW THE SIGN OF LIQUOR ON ME. (SHE GOES
CATH 1 (170)	(THUNDEROUSLY: SPRINGING TO HIS FEET) IT IS A	LIE	: ORLOFF MURDERED HIM. (SUBSIDING A LITTLE) HE ALSO
MIS. PREFACE(41)	FORGE: TEACH IT TO SPEAK AND YOU TEACH IT HOW TO	LIE	: TEACH IT TO WALK AND YOU TEACH IT HOW TO KICK ITS
SUPR III (126)	ENOUGH TO BELIEVE: A RAMPING, STAMPING, THUMPING	LIE	: THAT IS WHAT YOU CALL SINCERITY! TO BE SO GREEDY FOR
DEST (163)	LIKE ME? WHO HAD MY BEAUTIFUL BLUE EYES? IT'S A	LIE	: YOUR EYES ARE NOT LIKE MINE: THEYRE EXACTLY LIKE YOUR
SUPR III (102)	ANNIHILATED BY A GENERAL AGREEMENT TO GIVE IT THE	LIE	? NO: HEAVEN IS THE HOME OF THE MASTERS OF REALITY:
MILL IV (196)	TO SUCH A LIE. /SAGAMORE/ HOW DO YOU KNOW IT'S A	LIE	? YOU DONT KNOW WHAT HAPPENED AT THE END. YOU HAD
DEST (176)	POSITION, ABOUT EVERYTHING THAT SILLY WOMEN	LIE	ABOUT: KNOWS THAT SHE IS INCAPABLE OF FIDELITY TO ANY
DOCT PREFACE(47)	VIVISECT FOR THE SAKE OF SCIENCE WILL HESITATE TO	LIE	ABOUT IT AFTERWARDS TO PROTECT IT FROM WHAT HE DEEMS THE
MIS. PREFACE(95)	YOUR BACK IS TURNED AND I WILL DO AS I LIKE, AND	LIE	ABOUT IT." THERE CAN BE NO OBJECTIVE PUNISHMENT FOR
MTH4 III (201)	/THE ELDERLY GENTLEMAN/ THEY HAVE GONE BACK TO	LIE	ABOUT YOUR ANSWER. I CANNOT GO WITH THEM. I CANNOT LIVE
UNPL PREFACE(R26)	GUILT OF DEFECTIVE SOCIAL ORGANIZATION DOES NOT	LIE	ALONE ON THE PEOPLE WHO ACTUALLY WORK THE COMMERCIAL
MIS. PREFACE(96)	ACQUISITIVE APPETITES THE CHILD WILL STEAL AND	LIE	AND BE A NUISANCE TO YOU; AND THAT IF YOU ENCOURAGE ITS
SUPR PREFACE(R18)	SEE THAT IT DOES NOT PAY TO SPUNGE AND BEG AND	LIE	AND BRAG AND NEGLECT HIS PERSON. THEREFORE DO NOT
METH PREFACE(R76)	AND A COMPLETE GUIDE TO CONDUCT; THAT WE MAY	LIE	AND CHEAT AND MURDER AND THEN WASH OURSELVES INNOCENT IN
DOCT PREFACE(18)	AND - PERSONALLY CARELESS WOMEN, WHILST THEY	LIE	AND CHEAT AND SLANDER AND SELL THEMSELVES WITHOUT A
2TRU II (62)	OF EXPOSURE, DARLING; AND DO YOU, MY SWEETIE,	LIE	AND LIE AND LIE UNTIL YOUR IMAGINATION BURSTS. /THE
2TRU II (62)	DARLING; AND DO YOU, MY SWEETIE, LIE AND	LIE	AND LIE UNTIL YOUR IMAGINATION BURSTS. /THE PATIENT/ (
FABL PREFACE(70)	ANANIAS AND SAPPHIRA WERE EXECUTED FOR TELLING A	LIE	AND NOT FOR ANY ECONOMIC MISDEMEANOR. THIS VIEW WAS
LIED (196)	BROKEN MY SPIRIT AND DESECRATED MY DREAMS. I WILL	LIE	AND PROTEST AND STAND ON MY HONOR: OH, I WILL PLAY THE
SUPR I (28)	BEEN ANYBODY. IF IT HAD, WHAT COULD WE DO BUT	LIE	AND PROTEST-- AS RAMSDEN IS GOING TO PROTEST. /RAMSDEN/
MILL IV (209)	WORRIER. HE HAS ONLY TO TELL HER AN AFFECTIONATE	LIE	AND SHE IS HIS COMFORT, HIS HELPER, AT BEST HIS GREATEST
SUPR II (59)	WAY TO AVOID MISUNDERSTANDING IS FOR EVERYBODY TO	LIE	AND SLANDER AND INSINUATE AND PRETEND AS HARD AS THEY
JOAN PREFACE(11)	HUSBAND'S THROAT AND STRANGLE HER CHILD AS THEY	LIE	ASLEEP; AND SHE MAY FEEL OBLIGED TO DO WHAT SHE IS TOLD.
GETT (278)	GET ON WITH NO ONE TO TAKE CARE OF YOU: I OFTEN	LIE	AWAKE AT NIGHT THINKING ABOUT IT. AND NOW YOUVE MADE ME
ROCK PREFACE(174)	STATES WOULD HAVE TO QUINTUPLE THEIR ARMIES AND	LIE	AWAKE AT NIGHTS IN CONTINUAL DREAD OF HOSTILE
DEVL II (44)	EVERY FOOTSTEP-- GIVING ME A SPASM OF TERROR? TO	LIE	AWAKE FOR NIGHTS AND NIGHTS IN AN AGONY OF DREAD,
CLEO III SD(155)	ABOVE HIS HEAD, FAGGOTS LIKE THE ONE HE SITS ON	LIE	BENEATH IT READY TO BE DRAWN UP TO FEED THE BEACON.
SHAK (142)	NUMSKULL: THE OTHER A LIAR WED; AND NOW SHE MUST	LIE	BESIDE HIM EVEN AS SHE MADE HER BED. /THE VIRGIN/ " YES:
HART I (82)	(COMPLETING THE STANZA) AND NOW MUST SHE	LIE	BESIDE HIM, EVEN AS SHE MADE HER BED. /LADY UTTERWORD/ (
LION PREFACE(94)	THE OTHER, WITH ALL THE OTHER PROSELYTIZERS THAT	LIE	BETWEEN THEM, THEY MUST NOT BE BURDENED WITH IDLE
LIED (197)	TOLD HIM THE TRUTH BY HALVES; AND NOW I WILL NOT	LIE	BY HALVES. I'LL WALLOW IN THE HONOR OF A GENTLEMAN.
DOCT PREFACE(43)	IN ANY PECULIARITY. A RESPECTABLE MAN WILL	LIE	DAILY, IN SPEECH AND IN PRINT, ABOUT THE QUALITIES OF
JITT I (17)	CAN FALL UTTERLY WITHOUT FRUIT IF ITS ROOTS	LIE	DEEP ENOUGH IN THEIR INNERMOST CONVICTION. /JITTA/
GETT (288)	CONVERTED CANNIBALS OF CENTRAL AFRICA DO, AND TO	LIE	DOWN AND LET EVERY SNOB AND EVERY CAD AND EVERY
BASH II,1, (108)	RECEDE FAR UP MY YELLOWING TEETH, AND FINALLY	LIE	DOWN AND MOULDER IN A ROTTEN GRAVE? ONLY ONE THING MORE
BUOY II (22)	NO MORE, GET OUT. /HE/ I SHOULD MUCH PREFER TO	LIE	DOWN AND SLEEP IN THE FRIENDLY SHADOW OF YOUR HOUSE
SUPR III (82)	AND HER INITIALS ON THE SOD. WHEN I AM ALONE I	LIE	DOWN AND TEAR MY WRETCHED HAIR AND CRY LOUISA--
MIS. (204)	THE CHILD? HE SHANT GO. /BENTLEY/ I WILL. I'LL	LIE	DOWN AND YELL UNTIL YOU LET ME GO. I'M NOT A COWARD. I
BARB PREFACE(229)	A SALVATIONIST REALLY SAVED UNTIL HE IS READY TO	LIE	DOWN CHEERFULLY ON THE SCRAP HEAP, HAVING PAID SCOT AND
ARMS I (21)	BE SURE NOT TO SLEEP, BECAUSE OF DANGER. NOT TO	LIE	DOWN EITHER, ONLY SIT DOWN. (HE SITS ON THE BED. A
JITT III (69)	CAN I GET YOU ANYTHING? /JITTA/ IF I MIGHT JUST	LIE	DOWN HERE FOR AWHILE. I-- /AGNES/ (RISING TO MAKE ROOM
SUPR III SD(79)	LAZILY. SOME GO INTO THE CAVE. OTHERS SIT DOWN OR	LIE	DOWN TO SLEEP IN THE OPEN. A FEW PRODUCE A PACK OF CARDS
MTH5 (258)	THERE IS SOMETHING THE MATTER WITH ME. I WANT TO	LIE	DOWN. I CANNOT KEEP MY EYES OPEN. /ECRASIA/ YOU ARE
JITT II (44)	THAT I AM ILL? I CAN HARDLY STAND. I MUST	LIE	DOWN. /ALFRED/ WELL, LIE ON THE SOFA. /JITTA/ DONT BE
MIS. (191)	GONE THROUGH! YOU WANT TO EAT A LITTLE AND TO	LIE	DOWN. YOU COME WITH ME. I WANT YOU TO TELL ME ABOUT YOUR
BASH II,1, (112)	DELUDED DIFFIDENCE! HOW OFTEN HAVE I SAID,	LIE	DOWN, POOR FOOTMAN: SHE'LL NEVER STOOP TO THEE, REAR AS
DEVL I (5)	WELL ASK. (TO ESSIE) GO TO YOUR ROOM, CHILD, AND	LIE	DOWN, SINCE YOU HAVNT FEELING ENOUGH TO KEEP YOU AWAKE.
CLEO PRG2 (104)	PERSIAN) YOU, O SUBTLE ONE: YOUR FATHER'S LANDS	LIE	FAR FROM THE NILE. SLAY HER. /PERSIAN/ (THREATENING HER
BASH III (121)	GOES INTO THE ROOM.) LYDIA, THAT NEVER LIED, MUST	LIE	FOR THEE. ENTER POLICEMAN, WITH PARADISE AND MELLISH IN
MIS. (178)	AND MADE THE FULLEST APOLOGY FOR THE ABOMINABLE	LIE	HE HAS TOLD. HE SHALL DO THAT, OR HE SHALL DEFEND
DOCT PREFACE(43)	TO DO SO. HE WILL ALSO FLOG HIM FOR NOT TELLING A	LIE	IF THE BOY TELLS INCONVENIENT OR DISRESPECTFUL TRUTHS.
GETT PREFACE(194)	LIFE OF THE INDIVIDUAL, THE DANGER OF IT DOES NOT	LIE	IN HUMAN NATURE. HOME LIFE AS WE UNDERSTAND IT IS NO
PLES PREFACE(R19)	LYING. TO ME THE TRAGEDY AND COMEDY OF LIFE	LIE	IN THE CONSEQUENCES, SOMETIMES TERRIBLE, SOMETIMES
JITT III (77)	WOMAN, LET ME TELL YOU, IF MY TASTE DID NOT	LIE	IN THE DIRECTION OF SUPERIOR WOMEN I SHOULDNT HAVE
BUOY III (45)	OF LUNATICS, DOES NOT THE VALUE OF MY ADVICE	LIE	IN THE FACT THAT I AM NOT MYSELF A LUNATIC? /THE YOUTH/
CLEO III (153)	BALE NOW TO BEAT THEE; BUT ANOTHER DAY I WILL	LIE	IN WAIT FOR THEE. /APOLLODORUS/ (GOING BETWEEN THEM)
6CAL (104)	WITH HIS TAIL TORN OFF. /PETER/ SHIVERING! YOU	LIE	IN YOUR TEETH, THOUGH YOU WERE FIFTY KINGS. NO MAN ALIVE
ROCK II (244)	CANT EVEN DIE WITHOUT PAYING THEM FOR A GRAVE TO	LIE	IN. MAKE THEM DISGORGE, ARTHUR. SKIN THEM ALIVE. TAX
BASH II,1, (104)	THRUST THE DOOR BACK IN MY FACE; GIVE ME THE	LIE	I' TH' THROAT; AVERRED HE FELT YOUR PRESENCE IN HIS
O'FL (225)	CHAIN. HERE IT IS TO SHEW YOUR HONOR THAT IT'S NO	LIE	I'M TELLING YOU. /SIR PEARCE/ WHATS THIS, O'FLAHERTY?
DOCT PREFACE(47)	FROM PULMONARY CONSUMPTION IS CONCERNED. " THE	LIE	IS A EUROPEAN POWER," NOW AT THE VERY TIME WHEN THE
POSN (456)	ODDS TO ME, I GUESS THE TRUTH IS THE TRUTH AND A	LIE	IS A LIE, ON THE BOOK OR OFF IT. /BABSY/ DO AS YOURE
JOAN EPILOG (153)	LIVED THROUGH THE FLAME IS CONSECRATED; A GREAT	LIE	IS SILENCED FOR EVER; AND A GREAT WRONG IS SET RIGHT
JOAN PREFACE(29)	IS NOT ENOUGH," FOR WHICH OMISSION, AND THE	LIE	IT IMPLIES, THEY WILL NEED EDITH'S INTERCESSION WHEN
APPL I (222)	WORKED THAT. HIS UNCLE IS CHAIRMAN. /CRASSUS/ A	LIE	. A FLAT LIE. HE IS NOT RELATED TO ME. HE IS ONLY MY
GENV PREFACE(8)	ON CREDIT) WAS CALLED SAVINGS: A BAREFACED WICKED	LIE	. ALL THE BELLIGERENTS HAVE BEEN BLED WHITE, AND WILL
GENV PREFACE(23)	OF INCOME AND OF INCOME ONLY OR AN OBVIOUS	LIE	. EQUALITY OF INCOME IS PRACTICABLE ENOUGH: ANY SPORTING
6CAL (100)	FIVE COLLEAGUES. /THE KING/ NO: LET THAT HOUND	LIE	. HANGING IS TOO GOOD FOR HIM. THE QUEEN HURRIES IN WITH
KING I (216)	SO THE MEN OF THE STEEPLEHOUSE SAY; BUT THEY	LIE	. HAS NOT GOD A PASSION FOR CREATION? IS HE NOT ALL
JOAN 6 (125)	FROM HATE; BUT GOD IS OUR WITNESS THAT THEY	LIE	. HAVE WE TORTURED HER? NO. HAVE WE CEASED TO EXHORT

CATH 1	(163)	FOR THE POOR. IF YOU SAY IT IS A LIE, IT IS A	LIE	. HE FELL DOWNSTAIRS. I PICKED HIM UP; AND HE KICKED ME.
APPL I	(222)	HIS UNCLE IS CHAIRMAN. /CRASSUS/ A LIE. A FLAT	LIE	. HE IS NOT RELATED TO ME. HE IS ONLY MY STEPSON'S
BASH III	(122)	INJURIOUS COPPER, IN THY TEETH I HURL THE	LIE	. I AM NO TRAINER, I. MY FATHER, A RESPECTED MISSIONARY,
PHIL I	(84)	THE HOUSE. NO, NO: YOU MUST INVENT SOME THUMPING	LIE	. I CANT THINK OF ONE: YOU CAN, JULIA. EXERCISE ALL YOUR
GENV IV	(93)	DEMOCRACY. /BATTLER/ BRITISH DEMOCRACY IS A	LIE	. I HAVE SAID IT. /NEWCOMER/ OH, DONT TALK NONSENSE, YOU
MTH4 III	(201)	I CANNOT GO BACK AND CONNIVE AT A BLASPHEMOUS	LIE	. I IMPLORE GUIDANCE. THE PYTHONESS WALKS IN ON THE
OVER	(189)	A PROMISE IS A PROMISE. I CANT TELL A DELIBERATE	LIE	. I KNOW I OUGHT TO BE SORRY; BUT THE FLAT FACT IS THAT
SUPR III	(75)	I PROTEST. A PERSONAL EXPLANATION. 2. IT'S A	LIE	. I NEVER SAID SO. BE FAIR, MENDOZA. 3. JE DEMANDE LA
POSN	(448)	WHICH WAS THE HORSE-- /FEEMY/ (BREAKING IN) YOU	LIE	. I WASNT DRUNK-- AT LEAST NOT AS DRUNK AS THAT.
JITT II	(39)	/EDITH/ I WILL NEVER TELL MYSELF SUCH A SILLY	LIE	. I WILL TAKE MY FATHER'S MEMORY AND GOOD NAME OUT OF MY
WIDO II	(38)	ARE SAYING IS DISGRACEFULLY UNTRUE. IT'S A DAMNED	LIE	. I WONT STAND-- /BLANCHE/ WHAT ELSE IS IT BUT THROWING
CAND I	(103)	/MARCHBANKS/ (CUTTING HIM SHORT) I KNOW: TO	LIE	. IT WILL BE USELESS. GOODBYE, MR CLERGYMAN. AS HE TURNS
CATH 2	(178)	HIM AWAY. /CATHERINE/ (STOPPING THEM) LET HIM	LIE	. LET HIM SLEEP IT OFF. IF HE GOES OUT IT WILL BE TO A
KING I	(200)	FOR THE FIRST TIME IN YOUR LIFE. /JAMES/ YOU	LIE	. MY PENANCES ARE ALL REAL. /CHARLES/ WELL, A HUNK OF
MIS.	(159)	I'M SHAVING. I LOATHE HIM BECAUSE HE'S A LIVING	LIE	. MY SOUL'S NOT LIKE THAT: IT'S LIKE YOURS, I WANT TO
GENV IV	(125)	SUPPOSE YOUR ASTRONOMER ROYAL REFUSES TO TELL A	LIE	. REMEMBER; HE IS A MAN OF SCIENCE, NOT A POLITICIAN.
SUPR IV	(167)	STAND. /TANNER/ YOU LIE, YOU VAMPIRE: YOU	LIE	. /ANN/ FLATTERER. WHY ARE YOU TRYING TO FASCINATE ME,
VWOO 3	(139)	THAT IT DOESNT MATTER? /Z/ NO I DONT. IT'S A	LIE	. /A/ OH! /Z/ DONT " OH" ME. ALL MEN ARE NOT ALIKE TO
PHIL II	(100)	NEVER MIND. IT WAS A GOOD, FAT, HEALTHY, BOUNCING	LIE	. /CRAVEN AND CUTHBERTSON/ LIE! /CHARTERIS/ DIDNT YOU
PHIL II	(110)	THAT NOT TRUE? /CHARTERIS/ TRUE! NO: A THUMPING	LIE	. /GRACE/ OH, I'M SO GLAD. THAT WAS THE ONLY THING THAT
CYMB V	(144)	IACHIMO) OH, AS YOU ARE A GENTLEMAN, GIVE HIM THE	LIE	. /IACHIMO/ HE KNOWS NO BETTER, MADAM. WE MADE A WAGER,
CAND II	(109)	YOU. /MARCHBANKS/ (VEHEMENTLY) YOU DO. YOU	LIE	. /PROSERPINE/ OH! /MARCHBANKS/ YOU DO UNDERSTAND; AND
MILL IV	(196)	ASSAULT! /ADRIAN/ SHE DARE NOT SWEAR TO SUCH A	LIE	. /SAGAMORE/ HOW DO YOU KNOW IT'S A LIE? YOU DONT KNOW
ANNA	(296)	DUCHESS/ (ASTOUNDED) GENERAL STRAMMFEST: YOU	LIE	. /STRAMMFEST/ DENIAL, COMRADE, IS USELESS. IT IS
CATH 1	(163)	HIM DOWN AND KICKING HIM) YOU LIE, YOU DOG. YOU	LIE	. /THE SERGEANT/ LITTLE FATHER: LIFE IS HARD FOR THE
POSN	(459)	SHERIFF AND AT THE JURY) NO. /THE FOREMAN/ YOU	LIE	. /THE SHERIFF/ YOUVE GOT TO TELL US THE TRUTH. THATS
MIS. PREFACE	(30)	BY CALLING ON MY SOUL TO GIVE THIS STATEMENT THE	LIE	. SOME YEARS AGO I LECTURED IN OXFORD ON THE SUBJECT OF
MILL III	(179)	THERE ARE NO WOMEN EMPLOYED HERE. /EPIFANIA/ YOU	LIE	. THERE ARE SIX WOMEN WORKING IN THERE. WHO EMPLOYS
ARMS III	(51)	THINK OF ME! YOU WERE NOT SURPRISED TO HEAR ME	LIE	. TO YOU IT WAS SOMETHING I PROBABLY DID EVERY DAY!
POSN	(450)	BECAUSE HE'S PREJUDICED. /THE FOREMAN/ I SAY YOU	LIE	. WE MEAN TO HANG YOU, BLANCO POSNET; BUT YOU WILL BE
2TRU II	(78)	ANSWER ME. DONT STAND THERE TRYING TO INVENT A	LIE	. WHY DID YOU PRETEND TO BE A SERVANT? /THE PATIENT/
MTH1 II	(25)	NOTHING BUT A TORMENT, AND BELIEVE NOTHING BUT A	LIE	. YOU WILL NOT RAISE YOUR HEAD TO LOOK AT ALL THE
CLEO NOTES	(211)	FASHION, TELL A LIE WHICH EVERYBODY KNOWS TO BE A	LIE	(AND CONSEQUENTLY EXPECTS HIM AS A MATTER OF GOOD TASTE
DEST	(175)	BACCO, I CANT HELP ADMIRING YOU. I WISH I COULD	LIE	LIKE THAT. IT WOULD SAVE ME A GREAT DEAL OF TROUBLE.
HART I	(65)	WOULDNT BE MUCH LOVE IN THE WORLD. /ELLIE/ BUT TO	LIE	LIKE THAT! TO BE A BOASTER! A COWARD! /MRS HUSHABYE/
BARB PREFACE	(222)	LIFE OF THE NATION, A LIFE WHICH SEEMS TO	LIE	NOT ONLY OUTSIDE THE SYMPATHY OF MANY OF OUR THEATRE
MIS.	(202)	OPERA SINGER, IMPERILLING MY SOUL BY THE WICKED	LIE	OF PRETENDING TO BE SOMEBODY ELSE. ALL THIS I WOULD DO
POSN	(446)	BEG OFF. I'LL FIGHT OFF IF I GET A CHANCE. I'LL	LIE	OFF IF THEY CANT GET A WITNESS AGAINST ME. BUT BACK DOWN
HART II	(105)	YOU CAN SLEEP ON THE HEATH. TAKE MY WATERPROOF TO	LIE	ON: IT IS HANGING UP IN THE HALL. /HECTOR/ BREAKFAST AT
PHIL I	(88)	A MAN WAS FOUND READY TO TAKE THAT INCONCEIVABLE	LIE	ON HIS CONSCIENCE. /JULIA/ (FIRING UP) IF HE HAS
MTH1 I	(7)	BE NICE TO BE NEW AGAIN; BUT MY OLD SKIN WOULD	LIE	ON THE GROUND LOOKING JUST LIKE ME; AND ADAM WOULD SEE
JITT II	(44)	CAN HARDLY STAND. I MUST LIE DOWN. /ALFRED/ WELL,	LIE	ON THE SOFA. /JITTA/ DONT BE BRUTAL, ALFRED. /LENKHEIM/
MTH1 II	(24)	SKIN YOU HAVE RUN THAT RISK FOR? SHE TAKES IT TO	LIE	ON, AND FLINGS YOU THE CARRION FLESH YOU CANNOT EAT. YOU
HART PREFACE	(14)	IN CELLARS AND UNDERGROUND RAILWAY STATIONS, OR	LIE	QUAKING IN BED, WHILST BOMBS CRASHED, HOUSES CRUMBLED,
JITT III	(70)	SPITE OF YOUR ILLNESS, WORDS CAN NEVER SAY. JUST	LIE	QUIET WHERE YOU ARE; AND I WILL SEND EDITH TO YOU. OH,
MTH5	(215)	THE NEWLY BORN SHRIEKS AND STRUGGLES. /A YOUTH/	LIE	QUIET, YOU CLAMMY LITTLE DEVIL. /A MAIDEN/ YOU MUST BE
CAND III	(133)	RELEASING HIM) EUGENE: IF THAT IS NOT A HEARTLESS	LIE	-- IF YOU HAVE A SPARK OF HUMAN FEELING LEFT IN YOU--
OVER	(188)	MAKE LOVE TO A MARRIED WOMAN. I NEVER HAVE TOLD A	LIE	-- /MRS LUNN/ (REMONSTRATING) GREGORY! (SHE SITS DOWN
LIED	(196)	/HE/ (VERY COLDLY) OH, IF YOU WISH ME TO TELL A	LIE	-- /SHE/ SURELY, AS A MAN OF HONOR-- AS A GENTLEMAN, YOU
MTH5	(240)	TO THE MALE FIGURE). /ALL/ (AMAZED AT THE	LIE	) OH! /THE MALE FIGURE/ LIAR. YOU BIT HIM. EVERYONE
APPL INTRLUD	(245)	AND YOU KNOW IT. /MAGNUS/ IT IS, AS YOU SAY, A	LIE	; AND I KNOW IT. BUT I DID NOT SAY IT. /ORINTHIA/ YOU
MIS. PREFACE	(9)	IS OFFENDING GOD. THIS IS A BLASPHEMOUS	LIE	; AND THE FACT THAT IT IS ON THE LIPS OF EVERY
MTH5	(234)	THE TRUTH. YOU CAN PROVOKE THEM TO TELL ANY SILLY	LIE	; AND YOU CAN FORESEE EXACTLY THE SORT OF LIE THEY WILL
APPL INTRLUD	(245)	HAVE NOTHING TO TALK ABOUT BUT MEN; FOR THAT IS A	LIE	; AND YOU KNOW IT. /MAGNUS/ IT IS, AS YOU SAY, A LIE;
SUPR IV	(163)	WHICH MIGHT BE BROUGHT AGAINST ANYBODY. WE ALL	LIE	; WE ALL BULLY AS MUCH AS WE DARE; WE ALL BID FOR
LION PROL,SD	(108)	WHO FALLS BACK ON THE BUNDLE. THEY ROLL APART AND	LIE	STARING IN TERROR AT ONE ANOTHER. THE LION IS HEARD
GENV I	(44)	YOU HAVE HAD A SLIGHT HEART ATTACK. /COMMISSAR/	LIE	STILL, COMRADE. YOU WILL BE QUITE YOURSELF PRESENTLY.
FABL PREFACE	(70)	IN MY CHILDHOOD, I NOW REGARD IT AS A MUCH GRAVER	LIE	THAN THAT OF ANANIAS. " THE LIE" SAID FERDINAND LASSALLE
2TRU II	(62)	WORSE FOR YOU. BUT JUST TELL A THUNDERING SILLY	LIE	THAT EVERYONE KNOWS IS A LIE, AND A MURMUR OF PLEASED
SUPR II	(57)	TELLING HER LIES; BUT I OBJECT TO THE PARTICULAR	LIE	THAT I AM IN THE HABIT OF ABUSING THE CONFIDENCE OF
MIS.	(177)	TO PUT FORWARD THE MONSTROUS AND BLACKGUARDLY	LIE	THAT THIS LADY BEHAVED IMPROPERLY IN MY PRESENCE?
2TRU I	(40)	UGH! LET ME DIE! /THE NURSE/ ARE YOU GOING TO	LIE	THERE FOR EVER? HAS SHE KILLED YOU? /THE BURGLAR/ (
MTH5	(234)	LIE; AND YOU CAN FORESEE EXACTLY THE SORT OF	LIE	THEY WILL TELL. GIVE THEM A CLIP BELOW THE KNEE, AND
JOAN EPILOG	(154)	AS HE CAME, SAYING) HENCEFORTH MY PATH WILL NOT	LIE	THROUGH PALACES, NOR MY CONVERSATION BE WITH KINGS.
SUPR II	(59)	OF BEHAVING BADLY-- /TANNER/ THEN WHY DID YOU	LIE	TO HER? /ANN/ I HAD TO. /TANNER/ HAD TO! /ANN/ MOTHER
KING I	(207)	IT IS CHICANERY. PROTESTANTISM GIVES THE	LIE	TO ITSELF: IT OVERTHROWS THE ROMAN CHURCH AND
POSN	(466)	WHEN THE KID TOUCHED ME, SAME AS WHEN YOU SWORE A	LIE	TO SAVE MY NECK. /FEEMY/ OH WELL, HERE. (THEY SHAKE
DEVL III	(54)	SO LITTLE FOR YOUR SAKE, I LIED AS MEN ALWAYS	LIE	TO WOMEN. YOU KNOW HOW MUCH I HAVE LIVED WITH WORTHLESS
PHIL II	(110)	HER HANDS AND CRYING) AH NO: WHY SHOULD I	LIE	TO YOU? (HE FOLDS HIS ARMS AND ADDS FIRMLY) MY
O'FL	(213)	WAS: HOW IT WAS, SIR. SHE'D ROB YOU; AND SHE'D	LIE	TO YOU; AND SHE'D CALL DOWN ALL THE BLESSINGS OF GOD ON
PYGM III	(245)	WAY OF SERIOUSLY LIKING YOUNG WOMEN: SOME HABITS	LIE	TOO DEEP TO BE CHANGED. (RISING ABRUPTLY AND WALKING
2TRU II	(62)	DARLING; AND DO YOU, MY SWEETIE, LIE AND LIE AND	LIE	UNTIL YOUR IMAGINATION BURSTS. /THE PATIENT/ (THROWING
MIS.	(128)	SHOULD SHE LOOK IN THE GLASS AND SEE A WRINKLED	LIE	WHEN A TOUCH OF FINE ART WILL SHEW HER A GLORIOUS
O'FL	(207)	A WORD AGEN HER. BUT I'M NOT SAYING A WORD OF	LIE	WHEN I TELL YOU THAT THAT OLD WOMAN IS THE BIGGEST
MIS. PREFACE	(61)	ITS ELDERS WANT TO FIND OUT ANYTHING FROM IT, TO	LIE	WHEN THE TRUTH WOULD SHOCK OR HURT ITS ELDERS, TO BE
BULL III	(142)	(SCORNFULLY) HWY CANT YOU TELL A RAISONABLE	LIE	WHEN YOURE ABOUT IT? WHAT HORSE CAN GO FORTY MILE AN
FABL PREFACE	(76)	THE BISHOP ASKED THE POSTULANT TO TELL A FLAT	LIE	WHICH BOTH OF THEM KNEW TO BE A LIE, AND HE TOLD IT
CLEO NOTES	(211)	IN THE ORDINARY TREASURY BENCH FASHION, TELL A	LIE	WHICH EVERYBODY KNOWS TO BE A LIE (AND CONSEQUENTLY
MTH4 I	(162)	A FLOWER, AND WITHER IN YOUR SECOND CHILDHOOD. A	LIE	WILL LAST YOUR TIME: IT WILL NOT LAST MINE. IF I KNEW I
CAND I	(103)	(TURNING NEAR THE DOOR) EITHER THE TRUTH OR A	LIE	YOU MUST TELL HER, IF I GO. /MORELL/ (TEMPORIZING)
GLIM	(178)	BARBARA WILL SURELY PUNISH YOU FOR THAT WICKED	LIE	YOU TOLD ABOUT HER HAND. /FERRUCCIO/ THE HAND THAT
2TRU II	(62)	A THUNDERING SILLY LIE THAT EVERYONE KNOWS IS A	LIE	, AND A MURMUR OF PLEASED ASSENT WILL HUM UP FROM EVERY
MTH5	(234)	THEIR LUSTS AND GREEDS, AND THEY WILL BOAST AND	LIE	, AND AFFIRM AND DENY, AND HATE AND LOVE WITHOUT THE
FABL PREFACE	(76)	TELL A FLAT LIE WHICH BOTH OF THEM KNEW TO BE A	LIE	, AND HE TOLD IT WITHOUT A BLUSH, THE IMPRESSION MADE ON
OVER	(188)	I PROMISED MY MOTHER THAT I WOULD NEVER TELL A	LIE	, AND THAT I WOULD NEVER MAKE LOVE TO A MARRIED WOMAN. I
BASH II,1,	(107)	THREAD OF LIFE IN RUDER PATTERNS THAN THESE THAT	LIE	, ANTIMACASSARLY, ASPRENT THY DRAWING ROOM. AS WELL
DOCT PREFACE	(43)	TO DO SO. HE WILL FLOG HIS BOY FOR TELLING A	LIE	, BECAUSE IT IS CUSTOMARY TO DO SO. HE WILL ALSO FLOG
FABL II	(105)	ALL THIS IS YOUR FAULT. /C.-IN-C./ OLDHAND: YOU	LIE	, CATEGORICALLY. HOW MY FAULT? /OLDHAND/ DO YOU FORGET
HART III	(145)	RUM. /CAPTAIN SHOTOVER/ (VEHEMENTLY) THAT IS A	LIE	, CHILD. LET A MAN DRINK TEN BARRELS OF RUM A DAY, HE IS
CATH 1	(163)	LIFE IS HARD FOR THE POOR. IF YOU SAY IT IS A	LIE	, IT IS A LIE. HE FELL DOWNSTAIRS. I PICKED HIM UP; AND
DEVL I	(10)	I-- ER-- /MRS DUDGEON/ (VEHEMENTLY) DONT	LIE	, MR ANDERSON. WE ARE TOLD THAT THE HEART OF MAN IS
ROCK PREFACE	(183)	YOU WOULD SOON DISCOVER THAT MY CHOICE MUST	LIE	, NOT BETWEEN TRUTH AND FALSEHOOD, NEITHER OF WHICH I
POSN	(456)	ME, I GUESS THE TRUTH IS THE TRUTH AND A LIE IS A	LIE	, ON THE BOOK OR OFF IT. /BABSY/ DO AS YOURE TOLD. WHO
ROCK PREFACE	(182)	HE WHO IS DRIVING YOU TO SACRIFICE YOURSELF FOR A	LIE	, OR MINERVA DRIVING YOU TO BE SACRIFICED FOR THE
JOAN 4	(101)	YOU ARE A TRAITOR. /CAUCHON/ (SPRINGING UP) YOU	LIE	, PRIEST. (TREMBLING WITH RAGE) IF YOU DARE DO WHAT
SUPR I	(14)	/OCTAVIUS/ (SHYLY) I AM NOT, JACK. /TANNER/ YOU	LIE	, TAVY: YOU ARE. SO LETS HAVE HER DOWN FROM THE DRAWING
O'FL	(219)	TELLING THE TRUTH AND ONLY ONE WAY OF TELLING A	LIE	, THE GOVERNMENT WOULD FIND IT OUT. IT'S IN THE NATURE
BARB II	(309)	/RUMMY/ (SCREAMING AT HIM FROM THE LOFT) YOU	LIE	, YOU DIRTY BLACKGUARD! SNOBBY PRICE PINCHED IT OFF THE
CATH 1	(163)	(FLINGING HIM DOWN AND KICKING HIM) YOU	LIE	, YOU DOG. YOU LIE. /THE SERGEANT/ LITTLE FATHER: LIFE
KING I	(215)	IT TELLS ALL THE TRUTH ABOUT THEM. /BARBARA/ YOU	LIE	, YOU MISERABLE DAUBER. WHEN OUR DEAR PETER LILLY, WHO
SUPR IV	(167)	ME. I MIGHT BE THE UMBRELLA STAND. /TANNER/ YOU	LIE	, YOU VAMPIRE: YOU LIE. /ANN/ FLATTERER. WHY ARE YOU
FABL PREFACE	(70)	AS A MUCH GRAVER LIE THAN THAT OF ANANIAS. " THE	LIE	" SAID FERDINAND LASSALLE " IS A EUROPEAN POWER." HE
ARMS III	(51)	IT FIRST. IT COST YOU NOTHING: IT COST ME A	LIE	! A LIE! ! SHE SITS DOWN ON THE OTTOMAN, LOOKING
2TRU III	(90)	BY TEN PER CENT. BUT-- /SWEETIE/ OH, WHAT A	LIE	! IT WAS THE OTHER NURSES THAT KILLED THE MEN: WAKING
BASH II,2,	(114)	A MILLION MILES BY SEA TO LEARN HOW MEN CAN	LIE	! KNOW, FATHER WEBBER, MEN BECOME CIVILIZED THROUGH
PHIL II	(100)	HEALTHY, BOUNCING LIE. /CRAVEN AND CUTHBERTSON/	LIE	! /CHARTERIS/ DIDNT YOU SUSPECT THAT? /CRAVEN/
MTH5	(227)	ANOTHER. REALLY, PYG! GET OUT. YOU HAVNT. WHAT A	LIE	! /PYGMALION/ I TELL YOU I HAVE. I WILL SHEW THEM TO

DEST	(175)	HANDS) OH, HOW I WISH I REALLY HAD TOLD YOU SOME	LIE	! YOU WOULD HAVE BELIEVED ME THEN. THE TRUTH IS THE ONE
ARMS III	(51)	FIRST. IT COST YOU NOTHING! IT COST ME A LIE! A	LIE	! ! SHE SITS DOWN ON THE OTTOMAN, LOOKING STRAIGHT

LIEBE

JITT	(1)	TAGWANDLER, EIN MUTTERSOHN, DER TOD UND DIE	LIEBE	, GEFAHRLICHE JAHRE, SPATES LICHT, DIE FRAU OHNE

LIEBESLIEDER

CURE	(234)	(LOOKS AT HIM ENIGMATICALLY AND SOFTLY PLAYS A	LIEBESLIEDER	WALTZ)! ! /REGINALD/ OH, I SAY: THATS RATHER

LIED

ARMS III	(51)	AH, DONT TALK OF IT IN THAT FLIPPANT WAY. I	LIED	: I KNOW IT, BUT I DID IT TO SAVE YOUR LIFE. HE WOULD
JOAN 5	(118)	GOOD AS SAID MY VOICES LIED. WHEN HAVE THEY EVER	LIED	? IF YOU WILL NOT BELIEVE IN THEM: EVEN IF THEY ARE
SUPR I	(33)	YOU ABOUT. I FOUGHT WITH BOYS I DIDNT HATE; I	LIED	ABOUT THINGS I MIGHT JUST AS WELL HAVE TOLD THE TRUTH
DEVL III	(54)	I DID WHAT I DID EVER SO LITTLE FOR YOUR SAKE. I	LIED	AS MEN ALWAYS LIE TO WOMEN. YOU KNOW HOW MUCH I HAVE
JOAN 5	(118)	PROUD AND DISOBEDIENT. /JOAN/ I NEVER SAID YOU	LIED	. IT WAS YOU THAT AS GOOD AS SAID MY VOICES LIED. WHEN
JOAN 5	(118)	LIED. IT WAS YOU THAT AS GOOD AS SAID MY VOICES	LIED	. WHEN HAVE THEY EVER LIED? IF YOU WILL NOT BELIEVE IN
JOAN 6	(145)	TO YOUR CHARITY. YOU PROMISED ME MY LIFE; BUT YOU	LIED	(INDIGNANT EXCLAMATIONS). YOU THINK THAT LIFE IS
HART PREFACE	(10)	THEY OPERATED AND VIVISECTED AND INOCULATED AND	LIED	ON A STUPENDOUS SCALE, CLAMORING FOR AND ACTUALLY
BULL PREFACE	(59)	HIM. IN COURT, HE DID AS ALL THE REST DID. THEY	LIED	; THEY DENIED; THEY SET UP DESPERATE ALIBIS; THEY
O'FL	(212)	WHY SHOULD I READ THE PAPERS TO BE HUMBUGGED AND	LIED	TO BY THEM THAT HAD THE CUNNING TO STAY AT HOME AND
LIED	(204)	LIKE THAT, EH? /HE/ I SHOULD CALL IT HOW HE	LIED	TO HER HUSBAND.
LIED PREFACE	(185)	HOLIDAY IN THE NORTH OF SCOTLAND TO WRITE HOW HE	LIED	TO HER HUSBAND FOR DALY. IN HIS HANDS, IT SERVED ITS
LIED	(183)	HOW HE	LIED	TO HER HUSBAND. 1904.
DEST	(176)	KNOWS HER THROUGH AND THROUGH: KNOWS THAT SHE HAS	LIED	TO HIM ABOUT HER AGE, HER INCOME, HER SOCIAL POSITION,
KING PREFACE	(159)	CAN BE SIDE-TRACKED, HUMBUGGED, CHEATED,	LIED	TO, OR FRIGHTENED INTO TOLERATING SUCH A CHANGE. IF IT
SUPR III	(91)	THE LOOK WAS ONLY AN ILLUSION. YOUR WRINKLES	LIED	, JUST AS THE PLUMP SMOOTH SKIN OF MANY A STUPID GIRL
BASH III	(121)	(HE GOES INTO THE ROOM.) LYDIA, THAT NEVER	LIED	, MUST LIE FOR THEE. ENTER POLICEMAN, WITH PARADISE AND

LIEGE

CYMB V	(147)	OF MINE. THEY ARE THE ISSUE OF YOUR LOINS, MY	LIEGE	, AND BLOOD OF YOUR BEGETTING. /CYMBELINE/ HOW? MY

LIES

GENV III	(82)	TROUBLE TO CORRUPT IT? WHY NOT STOP TELLING IT	LIES	? ARE WE NOT AS CAPABLE OF THAT HEROIC FEAT AS THE
FABL VI	(129)	OF UNSELFISH CHARITY RATHER THAN STOP TELLING	LIES	? IT IS MUCH MORE LIKELY THAT YOU ARE A FOOL. /YOUTH
ROCK PREFACE	(185)	STILL OUR FATHER. DOES A FATHER TELL HIS CHILDREN	LIES	? /PILATE/ YES: MANY LIES. YOU HAVE AN EARTHLY FATHER
FABL VI	(124)	HERSELF. ALL LIES. /YOUTH 2/ WHY DOES SHE TELL	LIES	? THAT IS WHAT I WANT TO KNOW. /YOUTH 3/ THE SPHINX
HART I	(62)	HUSHABYE/ HOW CAN YOU SIT THERE TELLING ME SUCH	LIES	? YOU, ELLIE, OF ALL PEOPLE! AND I THOUGHT YOU WERE A
MTH1 I SD	(3)	AND TREE ARE ON THE BORDER OF A GLADE IN WHICH	LIES	A DEAD FAWN ALL AWRY, ITS NECK BEING BROKEN. ADAM,
SIM PRO,1,	(25)	LABEL; THEN READS WHAT HE HAS WRITTEN) " HERE	LIES	A MAN WHO MIGHT HAVE BEEN CECIL RHODES IF HE HAD HAD
SUPR III	(128)	I BE CIVIL TO THEM OR TO YOU? IN THIS PALACE OF	LIES	A TRUTH OR TWO WILL NOT HURT YOU. YOUR FRIENDS ARE ALL
SUPR III	(91)	OF 17, WITH HEAVY SPIRITS AND DECREPIT IDEAS,	LIES	ABOUT HER AGE? WELL, HERE WE HAVE NO BODIES: WE SEE
GETT	(305)	ODIOUS NASTY CREATURE THAT TOLD ALL THOSE WICKED	LIES	ABOUT HIM IN COURT. /HOTCHKISS/ LET US DRAW UP THE
ARMS III	(56)	ME THAT FOR BACKING UP THE MISTRESS'S AND RAINA'S	LIES	ABOUT HIM. HE'S NO FOOL, HE ISNT. YOU SHOULD HAVE HEARD
METH PREFACE	(R15)	GET THEE BEHIND ME, SATAN," OR TELLING THEM WHITE	LIES	ABOUT HISTORY FOR THE SAKE OF BEING CONTRADICTED,
BULL IV	(170)	YES OF COURSE I DO: WHY SHOULD I TELL YOU	LIES	ABOUT IT? NORA REILLY WAS A PERSON OF VERY LITTLE
JOAN PREFACE	(46)	FIFTEENTH AND SIXTEENTH CENTURIES THEY WERE TOLD	LIES	ABOUT JOAN, AND BY THIS TIME MIGHT VERY WELL BE TOLD
JOAN PREFACE	(46)	ARE TAUGHT HISTORY ABOUT WASHINGTON, AND TOLD	LIES	ABOUT LENIN. IN WASHINGTON'S TIME THEY WERE TOLD LIES (
HART I	(65)	BRAVE, AND REALLY HAS ADVENTURES, AND YET TELLS	LIES	ABOUT THINGS THAT HE NEVER DID AND THAT NEVER
NEVR II	(258)	WHICH ARE ALL TELLING ME THE MOST MONSTROUS	LIES	ABOUT YOU. /GLORIA/ (THE COLLECTEDNESS BEGINNING TO
MIS. PREFACE	(18)	IT, OR TO SMOTHER IT UNDER A HEAP OF SENTIMENTAL	LIES	AND FALSE PRETENCES, CHILDHOOD AS A STATE OF SIN.
SUPR III	(103)	BECAUSE THERE I HOPE TO ESCAPE AT LAST FROM	LIES	AND FROM THE TEDIOUS, VULGAR PURSUIT OF HAPPINESS, TO
METH PREFACE	(R88)	OF THE CAMP FOLLOWERS OF SCIENCE, AND THE BRAZEN	LIES	AND PRIESTLY PRETENSIONS OF THE PSEUDO-SCIENTIFIC
HART PREFACE	(40)	THE PHARISAISM OF PATRIOTS, THE LUSTS AND	LIES	AND RANCORS AND BLOODTHIRSTS THAT LOVE WAR BECAUSE IT
LADY	(246)	HIM) DENY IT IF THOU CANST. OH, HE IS COMPACT OF	LIES	AND SCORNS. I AM TIRED OF BEING TOSSED UP TO HEAVEN AND
DOCT PREFACE	(52)	HAVE IT SO IN SPITE OF JENNER. ALL THE GROSSEST	LIES	AND SUPERSTITIONS WHICH HAVE DISGRACED THE VACCINATION
OVER PREFACE	(168)	NECESSARILY DISGRACE THEMSELVES BY IRRITATING	LIES	AND TRANSPARENT SUBTERFUGES. MY PLAYLET, WHICH I OFFER
CLEO NOTES	(211)	HIM AS A MATTER OF GOOD TASTE TO TELL). HIS	LIES	ARE NOT FOUND OUT: THEY PASS FOR CANDORS. HE
O'FL	(211)	MAYBE YOUD RATHER HAVE ME HUMBUG YOU AND TELL YOU	LIES	AS I USED, JUST AS THE BOYS HERE, GOD HELP THEM, WOULD
BARB II	(275)	TO US WOMEN. YOUR CONFESSIONS IS JUST AS BIG	LIES	AS OURS: YOU DONT TELL WHAT YOU REALLY DONE NO MORE
LION PREFACE	(92)	SORTS OF TARTS, THE PRACTICAL ISSUE STILL	LIES	AS PLAINLY BEFORE YOU AS BEFORE THE MOST CREDULOUS
JOAN 2	(79)	YOU WOULD BE WRONG, MY FRIEND. PARABLES ARE NOT	LIES	BECAUSE THEY DESCRIBE EVENTS THAT HAVE NEVER HAPPENED.
JITT II	(35)	MY POOR CHILD! BUT DONT LOSE COURAGE. LIFE	LIES	BEFORE YOU: IT WILL MAKE UP TO YOU FOR MANY SORROWS.
MTH5	(261)	THEM UNTIL THEY HAVE FORDED THIS LAST STREAM THAT	LIES	BETWEEN FLESH AND SPIRIT, AND DISENTANGLED THEIR LIFE
SUPR III SD	(73)	HIM FOR DECIDING THAT SO LONG AS THE ALTERNATIVE	LIES	BETWEEN LIVING MAINLY AT THE EXPENSE OF THE COMMUNITY
DOCT PREFACE	(27)	TO PROPHYLACTIC INOCULATION, THE ALTERNATIVE	LIES	BETWEEN THE COMPLETE SCIENTIFIC PROCESS, WHICH CAN ONLY
SUPR PREFACE	(R34)	YOU HAVE A SUDDEN REVELATION OF THE ABYSS THAT	LIES	BETWEEN THE FASHIONABLE AUTHOR WHO COULD SEE NOTHING IN
MIS.	(195)	CHILDREN, TARLETON. /TARLETON/ OH, THE GULF THAT	LIES	BETWEEN THEM! THE IMPASSABLE, ETERNAL GULF! AND SO
BARB III SD	(325)	YOUR MOTHER. (SHE GOES OUT). PERIVALE ST ANDREWS	LIES	BETWEEN TWO MIDDLESEX HILLS, HALF CLIMBING THE NORTHERN
MTH3	(126)	SHOULD MAKE US THE GREATEST OF ALL THE NATIONS	LIES	BEYOND THE GRAVE FOR US. EITHER WE SHALL GO UNDER AS
SUPR HANDBOK	(223)	SECULAR NAME FOR DIVINITY: BOTH MEAN SIMPLY WHAT	LIES	BEYOND US. IF A GREAT MAN COULD MAKE US UNDERSTAND HIM,
GETT PREFACE	(224)	AND INTERESTING? PROBABLY SOME OF THE TRUTH	LIES	BOTH WAYS. I ALSO KNOW OF A HOUSEHOLD CONSISTING OF
GETT	(320)	CAN YOU FIND IT FOR US, ANTHONY? /SOAMES/ IT	LIES	BROAD BEFORE YOU. IT IS THE WAY TO DESTRUCTION THAT IS
ROCK PREFACE	(182)	GOD, IS HE NOT? AND AS HE DELIGHTS NOT ONLY IN	LIES	BUT IN ALL OTHER MISCHIEF SUCH AS STONINGS AND
METH PREFACE	(R75)	TRUTH, AND TRY TO CAST OUT INCREDIBLE AND SILLY	LIES	BY CREDIBLE AND CLEVER ONES, CALLING IN SATAN TO CAST
CYMB V	(142)	CAN YOU THEN RAISE HER FROM THE GRAVE? WHERE SHE	LIES	DEAD TO EXPIATE OUR CRIME? /IACHIMO/ DEAD! HOW?
GETT	(354)	BE HIS SUPERIOR IN HEAVEN OR HELL: EQUALITY	LIES	DEEPER THAN THAT. THE COAL MERCHANT AND I ARE IN LOVE
JOAN PREFACE	(46)	BE TOLD THE TRUTH ABOUT HER. UNFORTUNATELY THE	LIES	DID NOT CEASE WHEN THE POLITICAL CIRCUMSTANCES BECAME
SUPR III	(85)	/TANNER/ WELL, WE SHALL SEE. GOODNIGHT. (HE	LIES	DOWN AND COMPOSES HIMSELF TO SLEEP). MENDOZA, WITH A
LION PROL,SD	(105)	HIS EYES. HE LIMPS PAINFULLY OFF THE PATH AND	LIES	DOWN UNDER THE TREES, EXHAUSTED WITH PAIN. HEAVING A
HART III	(145)	STEER IT. HE IS NO DRUNKARD. IT IS THE MAN WHO	LIES	DRINKING IN HIS BUNK AND TRUSTS TO PROVIDENCE THAT I
CAPT III	(293)	OH, WOMEN SPEND HALF THEIR LIVES TELLING LITTLE	LIES	FOR MEN, AND SOMETIMES BIG ONES. WE'RE USED TO IT. BUT
SUPR II	(66)	SHE KISSES HIM. /VIOLET/ HAVE YOU BEEN TELLING	LIES	FOR MY SAKE? /HECTOR/ LYING! LYING HARDLY DESCRIBES
MIS. PREFACE	(48)	WISE OF THE DOCTOR TO SAY IT, BECAUSE OPTIMISTIC	LIES	HAVE SUCH IMMENSE THERAPEUTIC VALUE THAT A DOCTOR WHO
6CAL SD	(98)	IT. THEN THEY FLING HIM ON HIS SIDE, WHERE HE	LIES	HELPLESS. /THE KING/ AND SO, MASTER BURGESS-- /PETER/
BARB III SD	(325)	THE HIGH EXPLOSIVES ARE DEALT WITH. THE FOUNDRY	LIES	HIDDEN IN THE DEPTHS BETWEEN, THE TOPS OF ITS CHIMNEYS
HART I	(74)	THAT GIRL IS MAD ABOUT TALES OF ADVENTURE. THE	LIES	I HAVE TO TELL HER! /LADY UTTERWORD/ (NOT INTERESTED
MIS. PREFACE	(84)	OUR BROTHERS AND SISTERS AND COUSINS. THE DANGER	LIES	IN ASSUMING THAT WE SHALL GET ON ANY BETTER. THE MAIN
MTH1 II	(32)	THEM WHAT THEY WANT, BECAUSE THEY TELL BEAUTIFUL	LIES	IN BEAUTIFUL WORDS. THEY CAN REMEMBER THEIR DREAMS.
DOCT IV	(166)	COULD YOU TIRE ME? (SHE LIFTS HIM SO THAT HE	LIES	IN HER BOSOM). /LOUIS/ THATS GOOD. THATS REAL. /MRS
GETT PREFACE	(195)	TO A COCKATOO. ITS GRAVE DANGER TO THE NATION	LIES	IN ITS NARROW VIEWS, ITS UNNATURALLY SUSTAINED AND
DOCT III	(155)	YOU THAT THE ONE CHANCE OF PRESERVING THE HERO	LIES	IN LOUIS BEING IN THE CARE OF SIR RALPH. /MRS DUBEDAT/
MRS PREFACE	(172)	ALSO. SO THERE ARE IN EVERY PROFESSION: THE ERROR	LIES	IN SUPPOSING THAT EVERY MEMBER OF THEM SOUNDS THESE
MRS PREFACE	(157)	EVIDENCE TO SAVE ITS CREDIT. THE MISCHIEF	LIES	IN THE DELIBERATE SUPPRESSION OF THE OTHER SIDE OF THE
BARB PREFACE	(244)	GRENADIER HAS LEARNT TO HANDLE IN MANCHURIA,	LIES	IN THE FACT THAT BRAVE AND RESOLUTE MEN, WHEN THEY ARE
LION PREFACE	(58)	THE WHOLE ATTRACTION OF OUR PRESENT ARRANGEMENT	LIES	IN THE FACT THAT IT DOES RELIEVE A HANDFUL OF US FROM
GETT	(291)	A SNOB. WHY NOT? THE WHOLE STRENGTH OF ENGLAND	LIES	IN THE FACT THAT THE ENORMOUS MAJORITY OF THE ENGLISH
BULL PREFACE	(20)	FOREIGNER. THE VALUE OF THE ILLUSTRATION	LIES	IN THE FACT THAT NELSON AND WELLINGTON WERE BOTH IN THE
MRS PREFACE	(167)	SUCH DRAMA AS THE PSEUDO-OPERATIC PLAYS CONTAIN	LIES	IN THE FACT THAT IN THEM ANIMAL PASSION, SENTIMENTALLY
SIM II	(80)	OUT THAT THE EXTREME GRAVITY OF THE SITUATION	LIES	IN THE FACT THAT NOT ONLY IS IT OUR MOST IMPORTANT
SIM II	(83)	MUST RESIST AT ALL COSTS. /PRA/ THAT TEMPTATION	LIES	IN THE MAN'S PATH TOO. THE WORST SACRIFICES I HAVE SEEN
SUPR HANDBOK	(197)	GRANTED. LET US GRANT, FURTHER, THAT ALL THIS	LIES	IN THE NATURE OF THINGS; THAT THE MOST ARDENT
NEVR IV	(297)	AT HIM). THE STRENGTH OF THEIR POSITION	LIES	IN THEIR BEING VERY AGREEABLE PEOPLE PERSONALLY. THE
NEVR IV	(297)	PEOPLE PERSONALLY. THE STRENGTH OF YOUR POSITION	LIES	IN YOUR INCOME. (HE CLAPS ON THE FALSE NOSE, AND IS
ARMS III	(52)	REASON IN EVERYTHING. YOU SAID YOUD TOLD ONLY TWO	LIES	IN YOUR WHOLE LIFE. DEAR YOUNG LADY: ISNT THAT RATHER A
ANNA	(302)	NO: IF THE TRUTH DOES NOT SUIT THEM THEY SPREAD	LIES	INSTEAD, AND MAKE IT A CRIME TO TELL THE TRUTH. /THE
DOCT IV	(169)	GOOD THAT MOST MEN DO LIVES AFTER THEM: THE EVIL	LIES	INTERRED WITH THEIR BONES. YES: INTERRED WITH THEIR
CAND II	(106)	THAN DUMB, SAYING MEANINGLESS THINGS: FOOLISH	LIES	. AND I SEE THE AFFECTION I AM LONGING FOR GIVEN TO

2TRU II (68)	EVEN WHEN THEY ARE SAYING NOTHING OR TELLING	LIES	. BUT THE LOWER CENTRES ARE THERE ALL THE TIME: A SORT
ROCK PREFACE(182)	HAVE FOUND MANY; AND ONE OF THEM IS A GOD OF	LIES	. EVEN YOU JEWS HAVE TO ADMIT A FATHER OF LIES WHOM YOU
2TRU III (105)	LIES. MY NURSE TOLD ME LIES. MY GOVERNESS TOLD ME	LIES	. EVERYBODY TOLD ME LIES. THE WORLD IS NOT A BIT LIKE
SUPR I (33)	OF THE EXPLOITS I CONFESSED TO YOU WERE PURE	LIES	. I SOON NOTICED THAT YOU DIDNT LIKE THE TRUE STORIES.
PHIL III (133)	(RAISING HER HEAD INSTANTLY) IF HE SAYS THAT, HE	LIES	. IF EVER YOU HEAR IT SAID THAT I CARED FOR HIM,
SIM I (52)	/IDDY/ OH, I ASSURE YOU I CAN. /MAYA/ LIES,	LIES	. IF YOU CAN FEEL ONE HEART THROB FOR ME THAT IS NOT A
CAPT III (293)	HIS OWN CLOTHES; AND A MAN SHOULD TELL HIS OWN	LIES	. I'M SORRY YOU HAD TO TELL MINE FOR ME TODAY. /LADY
NEVR II (258)	TO RELAX) LIES! /VALENTINE/ (OBSTINATELY) YES,	LIES	. (HE SITS DOWN AGAIN BESIDE HER). DO YOU EXPECT ME TO
MTH5 (259)	/ACIS/ ASK NO QUESTIONS; AND YOU WILL BE TOLD NO	LIES	. (HE TAKES HER BY THE EAR, AND LEADS HER FIRMLY
DOCT PREFACE(48)	SUSPECT AN HONORABLE MAN LIKE MYSELF OF TELLING	LIES	. MOST SENSIBLE AND HUMANE PEOPLE WOULD, I HOPE, REPLY
2TRU III (105)	OF YOU. MY MOTHER TOLD ME LIES. MY NURSE TOLD ME	LIES	. MY GOVERNESS TOLD ME LIES. EVERYBODY TOLD ME LIES.
2TRU III (105)	I WASNT THINKING OF YOU. MY MOTHER TOLD ME	LIES	. MY NURSE TOLD ME LIES. MY GOVERNESS TOLD ME LIES.
LION PREFACE(50)	TO SUICIDE WITH HEROIC GESTURES AND RESOUNDING	LIES	. NOW THOSE WHO, LIKE MYSELF, SEE THE BARABBASQUE
MTH4 I (160)	TRAVELLERS ARE AMUSING ONLY WHEN THEY ARE TELLING	LIES	. PERHAPS IF YOU LOOKED AT THAT MAN THROUGH A
KING I (209)	THIS, HE SAYS, IS THE FIRST LAW OF MOTION. HE	LIES	. /CHARLES/ AND WHAT DO YOU SAY, MR KNELLER? /KNELLER/
HART I (59)	STRANGLED HER! /ELLIE/ OTHELLO WAS NOT TELLING	LIES	. /MRS HUSHABYE/ HOW DO YOU KNOW? /ELLIE/ SHAKESPEAR
FABL VI (124)	THEM. AND SHE TELLS STORIES ABOUT HERSELF. ALL	LIES	. /YOUTH 2/ WHY DOES SHE TELL LIES? THAT IS WHAT I
O'FL (219)	IT OUT. IT'S IN THE NATURE OF GOVERNMENTS TO TELL	LIES	. TERESA DRISCOLL, A PARLOR MAID, COMES FROM THE HOUSE.
2TRU II (56)	NINETY YEARS OLD. /TALLBOYS/ THE USUAL TISSUE OF	LIES	. THAT HEADMAN IS IN LEAGUE WITH THE BRIGANDS. HE TAKES
MTH5 (234)	TAUGHT THEM TO TALK AND READ; AND NOW THEY TELL	LIES	. THAT IS SO VERY LIFELIKE. /MARTELLUS/ NOT AT ALL. IF
MTH4 III (198)	SILENT). /THE ENVOY/ NEVER MIND THE BRIBERY AND	LIES	. THE ORACLE KNOWS ALL ABOUT THAT. THE POINT IS THAT
WIDO III (55)	SHUDDERING INTO THE CHAIR ON WHICH THE OVERCOAT	LIES	. THE STUDY DOOR OPENS). /LICKCHEESE/ (IN THE STUDY)
2TRU III (105)	MY GOVERNESS TOLD ME LIES. EVERYBODY TOLD ME	LIES	. THE WORLD IS NOT A BIT LIKE WHAT THEY SAID IT WAS. I
MTH4 I (167)	HERE, DADDY. WITH US LIFE IS TOO LONG FOR TELLING	LIES	. THEY ALL GET FOUND OUT. YOUD BETTER ASK ME QUESTIONS
ROCK PREFACE(186)	TELL HIS CHILDREN LIES? /PILATE/ YES: MANY	LIES	. YOU HAVE AN EARTHLY FATHER AND AN EARTHLY MOTHER. DID
SUPR III (106)	SAYING " ASK NO QUESTIONS AND YOU WILL BE TOLD NO	LIES	." I BOUGHT A SIXPENNY FAMILY MAGAZINE, AND FOUND IT
ARMS III (51)	NOTHING OF THEM? ONE IS HEARING PEOPLE TELL	LIES	(RAINA RECOILS): THE OTHER IS GETTING HIS LIFE SAVED
JOAN PREFACE(46)	ABOUT LENIN. IN WASHINGTON'S TIME THEY WERE TOLD	LIES	(THE SAME LIES) ABOUT WASHINGTON, AND TAUGHT HISTORY
O'FL (209)	TO SIX? /O'FLAHERTY/ YOURE NOT USED TO TELLING	LIES	LIKE I AM, SIR. I GOT GREAT PRACTICE AT HOME WITH MY
POSN (444)	/BLANCO/ HE'S A SLY ONE. HE'S A MEAN ONE. HE	LIES	LOW FOR YOU. HE PLAYS CAT AND MOUSE WITH YOU. HE LETS
KING PREFACE(154)	PLACES. STILL, THOUGH THE INTEREST OF MY PLAY	LIES	MAINLY IN THE CLASH OF CHARLES, GEORGE, AND ISAAC,
CLEO I SD(106)	ITSELF AS A HEAP OF RED POPPIES ON WHICH A GIRL	LIES	MOTIONLESS, HER SILKEN VEST HEAVING GENTLY AND
MIS. (180)	/HYPATIA/ YES: THAT WILL TEACH HIM TO TELL	LIES	NEXT TIME. /BENTLEY/ (RISING TO MAKE PLACE FOR GUNNER
CLEO III (147)	ROYAL BARGE. /APOLLODORUS/ ROYALTY, FTATATEETA,	LIES	NOT IN THE BARGE BUT IN THE QUEEN. (TO CLEOPATRA) THE
LION PREFACE(93)	MAN AND NOT IN THE WESLEYAN THAT OUR HOPE	LIES	NOW. THE RIGHT TO REFUSE ATONEMENT. CONSEQUENTLY, EVEN
DOCT PREFACE(4)	HAS SHOCKED THE PUBLIC, TRIES TO REASSURE IT WITH	LIES	OF BREATH-BEREAVING BRAZENNESS. THAT IS THE CHARACTER
BULL PREFACE(63)	THIS IDIOTIC ROMANCE, GROSS AND RIDICULOUS AS THE	LIES	OF FALSTAFF, SHOULD HAVE IMPOSED ON ANY INTELLIGENT AND
HART III (139)	A BLESSING ON YOUR FATHER'S SPIRIT. EVEN ON THE	LIES	OF MARCUS THERE IS A BLESSING; BUT ON MR MANGAN'S MONEY
MIS. PREFACE(32)	ORGANIZATION OF CHILDHOOD, AS OF EVERYTHING ELSE,	LIES	OUR RIDICULOUS MISDISTRIBUTION OF THE NATIONAL INCOME.
ROCK PREFACE(160)	THE LARGE RANGE OF INTOLERABLE MISCONDUCT THAT	LIES	OUTSIDE THEM, BUT TO DIVERT ATTENTION FROM THE
MRS I SD(181)	THE SUN OFF THE HAMMOCK, IN WHICH A YOUNG LADY	LIES	READING AND MAKING NOTES, HER HEAD TOWARDS THE COTTAGE
PHIL II SD(94)	STOCKINGS AND SHOES. A DETACHABLE CLOTH SKIRT	LIES	READY TO HER HAND ACROSS THE END OF THE SETTEE. A PAGE
BARB II (275)	DONE NO MORE THAN US; BUT YOU MEN CAN TELL YOUR	LIES	RIGHT OUT AT THE MEETINS AND BE MADE MUCH OF FOR IT;
JOAN PREFACE(46)	WASHINGTON'S TIME THEY WERE TOLD LIES (THE SAME	LIES	) ABOUT WASHINGTON, AND TAUGHT HISTORY ABOUT CROMWELL.
MIS. (184)	BULLYING HIM AND MAKING HIM SIGN THOSE WICKED	LIES	; AND ALL THE TIME YOU CARRYING ON WITH MY DAUGHTER
2TRU III (105)	KNOW ABOUT MYSELF? MY REAL SELF? THEY TOLD ME	LIES	; AND I HAD TO PRETEND TO BE SOMEBODY QUITE DIFFERENT.
JOAN 5 (118)	YOU TELL THE ARCHBISHOP IN HIS CATHEDRAL THAT HE	LIES	; AND YET YOU SAY YOU ARE NOT PROUD AND DISOBEDIENT.
SUPR II (57)	AND CHARACTER USUALLY CONSISTS IN TELLING HER	LIES	; BUT I OBJECT TO THE PARTICULAR LIE THAT I AM IN THE
DOCT IV (165)	BLESSED. AMEN. AMEN. (HE CLOSES HIS EYES AND	LIES	STILL). /MRS DUBEDAT/ (BREATHLESS) LOUIS: ARE YOU--
DOCT PREFACE(48)	TO THEIR TESTIMONY? I WOULD RATHER SWEAR FIFTY	LIES	THAN TAKE AN ANIMAL WHICH HAD LICKED MY HAND IN GOOD
MIS. PREFACE(49)	INDUCED ME TO READ THE BUDGET OF STUPID PARTY	LIES	THAT SERVED AS A TEXT-BOOK OF HISTORY IN SCHOOL, I
SUPR III (99)	(RATHER CONTEMPTUOUSLY) CERTAINLY, IF YOUR TASTE	LIES	THAT WAY. /ANA/ BUT WHY DOESNT EVERYBODY GO TO HEAVEN,
MTH2 (81)	BY JUMPS IS ONLY ONE OF THE BUDGET OF PLAUSIBLE	LIES	THAT WE CALL CLASSICAL EDUCATION. NATURE ALWAYS
OVER PREFACE(169)	WE KNOW WE OUGHT NOT TO TELL, BUT THE RUINOUS	LIES	THAT WE FOOLISHLY THINK WE OUGHT TO TELL.
OVER PREFACE(169)	OF TELLING NOT ONLY THE COMPARATIVELY HARMLESS	LIES	THAT WE KNOW WE OUGHT NOT TO TELL, BUT THE RUINOUS LIES
GETT PREFACE(206)	OF THE PENDULUM" AT THE NEXT ELECTION. THEREIN	LIES	THE PERIL AND THE GLORY OF DEMOCRATIC STATESMANSHIP. A
OVER PREFACE(168)	COUPLES ARE UNFAITHFUL. I DONT WANT TO HEAR THE	LIES	THEY TELL ONE ANOTHER TO CONCEAL WHAT THEY HAVE DONE,
BARB III (349)	A WOMAN OF MY RANK. /CUSINS/ THEN THE WAY OF LIFE	LIES	THROUGH THE FACTORY OF DEATH? /BARBARA/ YES, THROUGH
CYMB V (143)	/POSTHUMUS/ SHALL'S HAVE A PLAY WITH THIS? THERE	LIES	THY PART (HE KNOCKS HER DOWN WITH A BLOW OF HIS FIST).
SUPR IV (163)	CHILDREN SHE'LL TAKE ADVANTAGE OF THEIR TELLING	LIES	TO AMUSE HERSELF BY WHACKING THEM. IF ANOTHER WOMAN
BULL IV (179)	WELL, WHAT SHALL WE DO? /BROADBENT/ WHY, WHAT	LIES	TO OUR HAND. /KEEGAN/ WHICH IS THE MAKING OF GOLF LINKS
MIS. (182)	IT AND TO AMEND MY LIFE AND TO DO WHAT IN ME	LIES	TO PROVE WORTHY OF HIS KINDNESS IN GIVING ME ANOTHER
MIS. (180)	MY LIFE"? /PERCIVAL/-- AND TO DO WHAT IN ME	LIES	TO PROVE WORTHY OF HIS KINDNESS IN GIVING ME ANOTHER
MRS PREFACE(157)	DISALLOW AND SUPPRESS, AND DO WHAT IN US	LIES	TO SILENCE." FORTUNATELY, SHAW CANNOT BE SILENCED. "
HART I (81)	INVENT SOMETHING? HE DOES NOTHING BUT TELL	LIES	TO WOMEN. /HECTOR/ WELL, THAT IS A FORM OF INVENTION,
BULL III SD(117)	THE LITTLE GATE. AT THE OPPOSITE SIDE, A BASKET	LIES	UNMOLESTED BECAUSE IT MIGHT AS WELL BE THERE AS
NEVR I (212)	TO US TO CURTAIL THE NUMBER OF UNNECESSARY	LIES	WE TELL, WE REPLIED TRUTHFULLY THAT WE DIDNT KNOW.
2TRU III (92)	IT, THOUGH HE DID NOT BELIEVE A WORD OF ALL THE	LIES	WE WERE STUFFED WITH, AND DIDNT WANT TO GO. HE WAS
GETT (318)	FOOD UNDER PRETENCE OF BUYING IT FOR THEM. HE	LIES	WHEN HE DENIES HAVING DONE IT. AND HE DOES OTHER
ROCK PREFACE(182)	OF LIES. EVEN YOU JEWS HAVE TO ADMIT A FATHER OF	LIES	WHOM YOU CALL THE DEVIL, DECEIVING YOURSELVES WITH
MTH3 (126)	SOCIETY SUGGESTING THAT THE FUTURE OF THE WORLD	LIES	WITH THE MULATTO? /MRS LUTESTRING/ (RISING) MR
BULL PREFACE(39)	TO USE SUCH POLITICAL AND LEGAL POWER AS	LIES	WITHIN HIS REACH, SUFFERS MORE AND MAKES LESS FUSS
BASH I (98)	MELLISH, WHO DOUBLES UP LIKE A FOLDED TOWEL, AND	LIES	WITHOUT SENSE OR MOTION.) AND NOW THE NIGHT IS
KING I (202)	REPAY: TOMORROW'S FALSER THAN THE FORMER DAY;	LIES	WORSE; AND, WHILE IT SAYS WE SHALL BE BLEST WITH SOME
FANY II (286)	AND CRIES A LITTLE). /KNOX/ WELL, I GOT TO TELL	LIES	, AINT I? YOU WONT. SOMEBODY'S GOT TO TELL EM. /MRS
JOAN PREFACE(46)	OF ANTI-CLERICAL LIES, OF SPECIFICALLY PROTESTANT	LIES	, AND OF ROMAN CATHOLIC EVASIONS OF HER UNCONSCIOUS
BUOY PREFACE(5)	MAGIC AND MIRACLE, AS FAR AS THEY ARE NOT FLAT	LIES	, ARE NOT DIVORCED FROM FACTS AND CONSEQUENTLY FROM
DEVL III (70)	HISTORY SAY? /BURGOYNE/ HISTORY, SIR, WILL TELL	LIES	, AS USUAL. COME: WE MUST SEND THE SAFE-CONDUCT. (HE
SIM PRO,2, (28)	LANGUAGES THAT ARE DEAD AND HISTORIES THAT ARE	LIES	, BUT ARE NEVER TOLD HOW TO EAT AND DRINK AND CLOTHE
NEVR I (212)	AND LIFE IS A VULGAR ROUND OF PUNISHMENTS AND	LIES	, COERCION AND REBELLION, JEALOUSY, SUSPICION,
SIM I (52)	FOR VASHTI. /IDDY/ OH, I ASSURE YOU I CAN. /MAYA/	LIES	, LIES. IF YOU CAN FEEL ONE HEART THROB FOR ME THAT IS
BARB III SD(326)	AGAINST THE SHED; AND ONE HAS FALLEN FORWARD AND	LIES	, LIKE A GROTESQUE CORPSE, ON THE EMPLACEMENT. THE
2TRU III (105)	SOMEBODY QUITE DIFFERENT. /TALLBOYS/ WHO TOLD YOU	LIES	, MADAM? IT WAS NOT WITH MY AUTHORITY. /MRS MOPPLY/ I
MILL PREFACE(130)	EVERY DAY IN COMMERCIAL BUSINESS. NOW THE REMEDY	LIES	, NOT IN THE EXTERMINATION OF ALL DOMINATORS AND
JOAN PREFACE(46)	JOAN HAS REMAINED THE SUBJECT OF ANTI-CLERICAL	LIES	, OF SPECIFICALLY PROTESTANT LIES, AND OF ROMAN
HART II (102)	HELPLESS, AND LISTENED TO SUCH UNFAIRNESS, SUCH	LIES	, SUCH INJUSTICE AND PLOTTING AND BACKBITING AND
DEVL EPILOG (85)	ALL THIS, HOWEVER, IS A TISSUE OF ROMANTIC	LIES	, THOUGH IT HAS BEEN REPEATED IN PRINT AS AUTHENTIC
GENV III (72)	ARE CORRUPTED BY CAPITALISM. /THE JEW/ LIES!	LIES	! EXCUSES FOR ROBBING AND MURDERING US. /THE
GENV III (72)	WHEN THEY ARE CORRUPTED BY CAPITALISM. /THE JEW/	LIES	! LIES! EXCUSES FOR ROBBING AND MURDERING US. /THE
NEVR II (258)	/GLORIA/ (THE COLLECTEDNESS BEGINNING TO RELAX)	LIES	! /VALENTINE/ (OBSTINATELY) YES, LIES. (HE SITS DOWN
ARMS III (52)	INCREDULOUSLY, MEANING " I, RAINA PETKOFF, TELL	LIES	! " HE MEETS HER GAZE UNFLINCHINGLY. SHE SUDDENLY SITS

LIEST

LADY (238)	NO. ALL FALSE. ALL. IF THOU DENY IT, THOU	LIEST	. /THE BEEFEATER/ YOU JUDGE TOO MUCH BY THE COURT,

LIEUTENANT

DEST (181)	FOR HIM. /GIUSEPPE/ (DEFERENTIALLY) YOU FORGET,	LIEUTENANT	: HE HAS YOUR HORSE. /LIEUTENANT/ (STARTING) I
DEST (188)	IN THE UNMISTAKEABLE VOICE OF THE STRANGE LADY)	LIEUTENANT	: I AM YOUR PRISONER. (SHE OFFERS HIM HER
DEST (163)	OWN. /NAPOLEON/ (WITH CONTAINED EXASPERATION)	LIEUTENANT	: WILL YOU OBEY MY ORDERS AND LEAVE THE ROOM.
DEST (189)	/LADY/ (TURNING TO THE LIEUTENANT) HERE,	LIEUTENANT	: YOU ARE NOT AFRAID OF THEM. /LIEUTENANT/ (
DEST (160)	CONCERN) HAVE YOU BEEN ATTACKED BY THE AUSTRIANS,	LIEUTENANT	? DEAR! DEAR! DEAR! /LIEUTENANT/ (
DEST (161)	SEIZING HIS RIGHT ARM) WHAT ARE YOU THINKING OF,	LIEUTENANT	? IT'S A LADY: DONT YOU HEAR? IT'S A WOMAN'S
FANY III (327)	I CALL IT QUITE A HAPPY ENDING: DONT YOU,	LIEUTENANT	? /DUVALLET/ IN FRANCE IT WOULD BE IMPOSSIBLE.
BASH II,2, (118)	CORKLIKE O'ER MY CASHEL'S SINEWY BACK; AND HIS	LIEUTENANT	ALL DEFLATED GASPS FOR BREATH UPON THE SAND. THE
FANY III (321)	THEYVE BEEN TRYING TO TEACH ME TABLE MANNERS. THE	LIEUTENANT	AND RUDOLPH SAY I'M A REGULAR PIG. I'M SURE I
2TRU PREFACE(6)	REPRESENTED AN OPULENCE BEYOND WHICH ONLY LORDS	LIEUTENANT	AND THEIR LIKE COULD ASPIRE. THE SCALE HAS
DEST SD(180)	WILL NOT LIKE IT. NOTHING MORE IS SAID UNTIL THE	LIEUTENANT	ARRIVES FOLLOWED BY GIUSEPPE, WHO STANDS MODESTLY

PRES (138) DO TAKE IT, LET ME TELL YOU FRANKLY THAT I THINK LIEUTENANT CHUBBS-JENKINSON SHEWED A GREAT WANT OF
FANY III (320) /MARGARET/ OH-- LET ME INTRODUCE, MY FRIEND LIEUTENANT DUVALLET. MRS GILBEY. MR GILBEY. DUVALLET BOWS
BASH III (125) FOR BYRON'S PAST. NAY, MORE: OF DORSET DEPUTY LIEUTENANT HE IS PROCLAIMED. FURTHER, IT IS DECREED, IN
PRES (149) ORDERS WAS FOURS, I SAYS. I'LL SHEW YOU WHO'S LIEUTENANT HERE, E SAYS. IN FUTURE YOU ATTEND TO MY ORDERS
BASH III (127) TO A CLOSE. IN LAWFUL COURSE AS DORSET'S DEPUTY LIEUTENANT I DO PARDON ALL CONCERNED THIS AFTERNOON IN THE
APPL PREFACE(182) OF THE WIRELESS ORCHESTRA, IF PAUL HAD BEEN A LIEUTENANT IN A LINE REGIMENT WE SHOULD NEVER HAVE HEARD OF
GETT (292) REALLY THINK A BISHOP THE EQUAL OF A CURATE, OR A LIEUTENANT IN A LINE REGIMENT THE EQUAL OF A GENERAL. /THE
GETT (292) I WAS A CURATE MYSELF. /THE GENERAL/ AND I WAS A LIEUTENANT IN A LINE REGIMENT. /REGINALD/ AND I WAS NOTHING.
O'FL (210) SIR? /SIR PEARCE/ RUBBISH, MAN! THERES NO LORD LIEUTENANT IN ENGLAND: THE KING IS LORD LIEUTENANT. IT'S A
GETT (290) MR ST JOHN HOTCHKISS, THE CELEBRATED COWARD, LATE LIEUTENANT IN THE 165TH FUSILIERS," /REGINALD/ (WITH A
FANY EPILOG (331) BE QUITE NEW AND UNUSUAL AND ORIGINAL. THE NAVAL LIEUTENANT IS A FRENCHMAN WHO CRACKS UP THE ENGLISH AND RUNS
DEST (187) IF HE UNDERSTANDS HIS JOB WELL ENOUGH, A LIEUTENANT IS A GENTLEMAN: ALL THE REST IS CHANCE. WHY, WHO
FANY EPILOG (330) BY THE USUAL STAGE PUPPETS. THE HERO'S A NAVAL LIEUTENANT . ALL MELODRAMATIC HEROES ARE NAVAL LIEUTENANTS.
PRES (167) DUTIES OF A SERGEANT. YOU ARE ONLY FIT TO BE A LIEUTENANT . I SHALL RECOMMEND YOU FOR A COMMISSION. /THE
O'FL (210) NO LORD LIEUTENANT IN ENGLAND: THE KING IS LORD LIEUTENANT . IT'S A SIMPLE QUESTION OF PATRIOTISM, DOES
DEST (164) TO PUT TO YOU. /GIUSEPPE/ (DISCREETLY) COME, LIEUTENANT . (HE OPENS THE DOOR). /LIEUTENANT/ I'M OFF.
DEST (171) I HAVE BEEN AS GROSS A GULL AS MY JACKASS OF A LIEUTENANT . (MENACINGLY) COME: THE DESPATCHES. QUICK: I AM
DEST (164) I'M SO GLAD YOURE NOT ANGRY WITH ME ANY LONGER, LIEUTENANT . (SHE OFFERS HER HAND). /LIEUTENANT/ (BENDING
DEST SD(162) AND LEAVES HER AT NO DISADVANTAGE WITH THE LIEUTENANT . ONLY, HER ELEGANCE AND RADIANT CHARM KEEP THE
DEST (184) (SHAKING HIS HEAD) THAT WILL NEVER DO, LIEUTENANT . /LIEUTENANT/ WHY NOT? /GIUSEPPE/ IN THIS
DEST (184) BY THE OUTER DOOR. /GIUSEPPE/ THE HORSE IS READY, LIEUTENANT . /LIEUTENANT/ I'M NOT GOING JUST YET. GO AND
DEST (182) TO THE OUTER DOOR WHEN SHE INTERCEPTS HIM. /LADY/ LIEUTENANT . /LIEUTENANT/ (IMPORTANTLY) YOU MUSNT DELAY ME,
DEST (180) AT HIS EASE, FOR NAPOLEON TO BEGIN. /NAPOLEON/ LIEUTENANT . /LIEUTENANT/ (ENCOURAGINGLY) GENERAL.
DEST (189) PROTECT ME! (TO THE LIEUTENANT) AFTER YOU, LIEUTENANT . /LIEUTENANT/ YOUD BETTER GO FIRST: I DONT KNOW
DEST (189) (TO THE LIEUTENANT) OBLIGE ME BY GOING, LIEUTENANT . /LIEUTENANT/ (REMONSTRATING) OH, I SAY,
DEST (188) /LADY/ SAFE AT BORGHETTO, WAITING FOR YOU, LIEUTENANT . /NAPOLEON/ (TURNING ON THEM) WHERE ARE THE
POSN PREFACE(431) CASTLE OFFICIALS IN THE ABSENCE OF THE LORD LIEUTENANT . THIS ATTEMPT GAVE EXTRAORDINARY PUBLICITY TO
DEST (184) WORLD A GENERAL MAY SEND FOR A LIEUTENANT; BUT A LIEUTENANT MUST NOT SEND FOR A GENERAL. /LIEUTENANT/ OH, YOU
DEST SD(162) BRED MANNER TO PAY HER RESPECTS TO HIM WHEN THE LIEUTENANT POUNCES ON HER AND SEIZES HER RIGHT WRIST. AS SHE
DEST (188) HAS BEWITCHED THE GENERAL. (GIUSEPPE AND THE LIEUTENANT RECOIL FORM NAPOLEON). GENERAL: OPEN YOUR COAT:
FANY III (321) IS EVER DONE BY BEATING ABOUT THE BUSH. I ASK LIEUTENANT -- WELL, I DONT SPEAK FRENCH; AND I CANT
DEST (189) THE INNER DOOR). HEAVEN PROTECT ME! (TO THE LIEUTENANT) AFTER YOU, LIEUTENANT. /LIEUTENANT/ YOUD BETTER
DEST (160) HAS HAPPENED TO HIM AND BRING ME WORD. (TO THE LIEUTENANT) CONSIDER YOURSELF UNDER ARREST, SIR.
DEST (189) NAME! THEYRE BEWITCHED. /LADY/ (TURNING TO THE LIEUTENANT) HERE, LIEUTENANT: YOU ARE NOT AFRAID OF THEM.
DEST (165) TEARS ON THE CHAIR LEFT BESIDE THE TABLE BY THE LIEUTENANT) I BRAVE! HOW LITTLE YOU KNOW! I HAVE SPENT
DEST (189) /NAPOLEON/ PSHA! YOURE A POLTROON. (TO THE LIEUTENANT) OBLIGE ME BY GOING, LIEUTENANT. /LIEUTENANT/ (
DEST (184) IN THIS WICKED WORLD A GENERAL MAY SEND FOR A LIEUTENANT ; BUT A LIEUTENANT MUST NOT SEND FOR A GENERAL.
ANNA (296) AND SALUTING) PROLETARIANS OF ALL LANDS, UNITE. LIEUTENANT SCHNEIDEKIND: YOU WILL RISE AND SING THE
ANNA (295) UNDER THE TABLE. /STRAMMFEST/ (THUNDEROUSLY) LIEUTENANT SCHNEIDEKIND. /SCHNEIDEKIND/ (IN A STIFLED
ANNA SD(289) THE ROOM. GENERAL STRAMMFEST ENTERS, FOLLOWED BY LIEUTENANT SCHNEIDEKIND. THEY HANG UP THEIR CLOAKS AND CAPS.
DEST (182) HAPPENED TO HIM. YOU MUST SPARE HIM. (THE LIEUTENANT SHAKES HIS HEAD GLOOMILY). YES, YES: YOU MUST:
NEVR IV (299) TO ME? FIVE FORMER LOVERS, WITH A TAME NAVAL LIEUTENANT THROWN IN! OH, IT'S TOO BAD. /MRS CLANDON/ BUT
DEST SD(150) NOT RAISED THE VALUE OF EVEN THE MOST RASCALLY LIEUTENANT TO THE FAMINE PRICE OF A GENERAL HE WOULD HAVE
PRES (149) THE ORSES KNOWS BETTER SOMETIMES. " FOURS," SAYS LIEUTENANT TREVOR AT THE GATE OF BUCKNAM PALACE ONLY THIS
DEST SD(171) MY CONFIDENCE IN YOU. THIS INCAUTIOUS ECHO OF THE LIEUTENANT UNDOES HER. NAPOLEON STARTS: HIS EYES FLASH: HE
DEST (165) BREAST) YOU LENT ONE OF YOUR HANDKERCHIEFS TO MY LIEUTENANT WHEN YOU ROBBED HIM. (HE LOOKS AT THE TWO
NEVR IV (295) IT WASNT NUMBER FIVE: IT WAS ONLY A TAME NAVAL LIEUTENANT WHO WAS ALWAYS ON HAND: THE MOST PATIENT AND
DEST (186) THE CONVERSATION. /NAPOLEON/ (TURNING TO THE LIEUTENANT WITH SARDONIC POLITENESS) I HOPE I HAVE NOT BEEN
DEST (161) WHAT WAS THAT? /GIUSEPPE/ ONLY A LADY UPSTAIRS, LIEUTENANT , CALLING ME. /LIEUTENANT/ LADY! /VOICE/
DEST SD(182) GESTURE, BUT IS INTERRUPTED BY THE RETURN OF THE LIEUTENANT , GLOVED AND CAPPED, WITH HIS SWORD ON, READY FOR
DEST (181) WITH YOU (BUSTLING HIM). /GIUSEPPE/ INSTANTLY, LIEUTENANT , INSTANTLY (HE DISAPPEARS IN THE VINEYARD,
DEST SD(162) THAT SHE IS BLUSHING ALL OVER HER BODY. EVEN THE LIEUTENANT , ORDINARILY INCAPABLE OF OBSERVATION, CAN SEE A
DEST (160) FURIOUSLY FOR THE INNKEEPER) GIUSEPPE! (TO THE LIEUTENANT , OUT OF ALL PATIENCE) HOLD YOUR TONGUE, SIR, IF
DEST (185) (UNCONSCIOUS OF NAPOLEON'S APPROACH) QUITE TRUE, LIEUTENANT , QUITE TRUE. YOU ARE ALL LIKE INNKEEPERS NOW IN
DEST SD(180) STANDS MODESTLY IN ATTENDANCE AT THE TABLE. THE LIEUTENANT , WITHOUT CAP, SWORD OR GLOVES, AND MUCH IMPROVED
DEST (162) OFF THAT SKIRT. /GIUSEPPE/ (REMONSTRATING) OH, LIEUTENANT ! /LADY/ (AFFRIGHTED, BUT HIGHLY INDIGNANT AT
DEST (183) KISS HER). /LADY/ (SLIPPING AWAY FROM HIM) OH, LIEUTENANT ! YOU FORGET: YOUR CAREER IS AT STAKE-- THE

LIEUTENANT'S
DEST (190) THE FIRST THING AFTER I RODE AWAY ON THAT POOR LIEUTENANT'S HORSE. SO YOU SEE I KNOW WHATS IN THEM; AND YOU
PRES (149) ME A FATHEAD, E DID. WHAT AM I TO DO, I SAYS: THE LIEUTENANT'S ORDERS WAS FOURS, I SAYS. I'LL SHEW YOU WHO'S
ROCK II (245) NOW THAT ARTHUR IS AT THE HELM. /SIR DEXTER/ A LIEUTENANT'S PAY AND PENSION FOR THE FUTURE DUKE OF

LIEUTENANTS
POSN PREFACE(415) FAR AS HE CAME IN CONTACT WITH THEM-- BY HIS OWN LIEUTENANTS . IN THE END, THERE WAS HARDLY A FIRST-NIGHTER
FANY EPILOG (330) LIEUTENANT. ALL MELODRAMATIC HEROES ARE NAVAL LIEUTENANTS . THE HEROINE GETS INTO TROUBLE BY DEFYING THE
METH PREFACE(R66) VICARS AND LIEUTENANTS; AND WE BEGIN TO MISS THE LIEUTENANTS LONG BEFORE WE BEGIN TO MISS THEIR PRINCIPAL.
METH PREFACE(R67) " HONOR SINKS WHERE COMMERCE LONG PREVAILS." THE LIEUTENANTS OF GOD ARE NOT ALWAYS PERSONS: SOME OF THEM ARE
METH PREFACE(R66) KING AND ASK THE POLICEMAN. BUT GOD'S TRUSTIEST LIEUTENANTS OFTEN LACK OFFICIAL CREDENTIALS. THEY MAY BE
METH PREFACE(R66) THAN TO DO WITHOUT HIS VICEROYS AND VICARS AND LIEUTENANTS ; AND WE BEGIN TO MISS THE LIEUTENANTS LONG
NEVR IV (301) ORDINARY YOUNG LADY, TOO ORDINARY TO ALLOW TAME LIEUTENANTS TO GO AS FAR AS I WENT. THATS ALL. I SHALL NOT

LIEUT-GENERAL
DEVL EPILOG (83) ALLOWED TO SURRENDER AS PRISONERS OF WAR. ANSWER: LIEUT-GENERAL BURGOYNE'S ARMY, HOWEVER REDUCED, WILL NEVER

LIFE
NEVR I (211) BITING ACRIMONY) THERE IS ANOTHER SORT OF FAMILY LIFE : A LIFE IN WHICH HUSBANDS OPEN THEIR WIVES' LETTERS,
MTH1 II (28) NOT REALLY DEATH: THAT IT IS THE GATE OF ANOTHER LIFE : A LIFE INFINITELY SPLENDID AND INTENSE: A LIFE OF THE
BULL IV (150) DAY: A VALUABLE AND INNOCENT ANIMAL HAS LOST ITS LIFE : A PUBLIC BUILDING HAS BEEN WRECKED: AN AGED AND
MTH2 (79) UTTERLY REMOVED FROM THE TURMOIL OF OUR POLITICAL LIFE : DEVOTED TO PURE LEARNING IN ITS MOST ABSTRACT PHASES;
PHIL II (118) NAKED SPEARMEN CAN KILL, PARAMORE, I RISKED MY LIFE : DONT FORGET THAT. /PARAMORE/ (WITH EQUAL SPIRIT) AND
3PLA PREFACE(R18) CONTRARY, IT IS AN UNLADYLIKE ATTITUDE TOWARDS LIFE : IN OTHER WORDS, A DISPARAGEMENT OF THE SOCIAL IDEALS
MIS. PREFACE(87) WHICH MUST ALWAYS BE THE FULLEST AND MOST CAPABLE LIFE : IN SHORT, THE MOST GODLY LIFE, AND THIS SIGNIFICANT
MIS. PREFACE(57) THEM AS LONG AS THEY ARE OF ANY IMPORTANCE IN LIFE : INDEED THE WANT WILL SURVIVE THEIR IMPORTANCE:
MTH1 II (28) IT IS LONG AND HARD AND PAINFUL TO CREATE LIFE : IT IS SHORT AND EASY TO STEAL THE LIFE OTHERS HAVE
NEVR I (216) YOU AWAY FROM HIM. I HAVE KEPT HIM OUT OF YOUR LIFE : KEEP HIM NOW OUT OF MINE BY NEVER MENTIONING HIM TO
INCA (256) IN VAIN FOR A FEW PALTRY THOUSANDS TO SPEND ON LIFE : ON THE BODIES AND MINDS OF THE NATION'S CHILDREN, ON
APPL INTRLUD(251) A SAINT. (TURNING ON HIM) I CAN GIVE YOU A NEW LIFE : ONE OF WHICH YOU HAVE NO CONCEPTION. I CAN GIVE YOU
LION PREFACE(72) THE SACRIFICE OF THE ADVENTUROUS ATTITUDE TOWARDS LIFE : THE BEING SETTLED. THOSE WHO ARE BORN TIRED MAY CRAVE
HART II (98) RIGHT IN THE FACE THAT KILLS A WHOLE PART OF MY LIFE : THE BEST PART THAT CAN NEVER COME AGAIN; AND YOU
SUPR III (103) THAT WHICH INTERESTS ME ABOVE ALL THINGS: NAMELY, LIFE : THE FORCE THAT EVER STRIVES TO ATTAIN GREATER POWER
BARB III (338) THEY ARE ONLY THE ACCIDENTS AND ILLNESSES OF LIFE : THERE ARE NOT FIFTY GENUINE PROFESSIONAL CRIMINALS IN
BULL IV (181) A COMMONWEALTH IN WHICH WORK IS PLAY AND PLAY IS LIFE : THREE IN ONE AND ONE IN THREE. IT IS A GODHEAD IN
MTH4 II (191) THEY TRIED TO PRODUCE A CONDITION OF DEATH IN LIFE : TO MORTIFY THE FLESH, AS THEY CALLED IT. /ZOZIM/
FANY III (317) FOR ALL THEIR PRIDE? BUT IVE NOTICED IT ALL MY LIFE : WE'RE IGNORANT. WE DONT REALLY KNOW WHATS RIGHT AND
CAND I SD(77) SLUMS. IT IS STRONG IN UNFASHIONABLE MIDDLE CLASS LIFE : WIDE-STREETED; MYRIAD-POPULATED; WELL SERVED WITH
JITT I (24) LIFE MADE IRRESISTIBLE. /BRUNO/ (CARRIED AWAY) LIFE : YES; THIS IS LIFE, AND THIS (HE KISSES HER EYES),
MTH1 II (28) THE VOICE OF GOD. /ADAM/ MINE IS THE VOICE OF LIFE : YOURS THE VOICE OF DEATH. /CAIN/ BE IT SO. FOR IT
SIM II (83) OF IT, WHAT HAVE I BEEN TO YOU IN THAT LIFE ? A HELP OR A HINDRANCE? /PROLA/ PRA: I ALWAYS KNEW
MRS II (213) LIKE YOU? ABLE TO PICK AND CHOOSE MY OWN WAY OF LIFE ? DO YOU THINK I DID WHAT I DID BECAUSE I LIKED IT, OR
MILL IV (200) KEEP YOUR OWN TEMPER. HAS SHE LAMED YOU FOR LIFE ? HAS SHE RAISED A BUMP ON YOUR HEAD? HAS SHE CALLED
PHIL I (86) I WAS SAYING TO YOU ABOUT THE BREAK-UP OF FAMILY LIFE ? HERE ARE ALL OUR YOUNG PEOPLE BOSOM FRIENDS.
PRES (150) OF A RESPECTABLE FAMILY IN THE MIDDLE STATION OF LIFE ? I CANT BEAR TO BE LOOKED DOWN ON AS A COMMON
MTH5 (213) IF THEY CANNOT BRING THEIR BEAUTIFUL CREATIONS TO LIFE ? I HAVE A GREAT MIND TO DIE AND HAVE DONE WITH IT
HART PREFACE(28) THE GLORY OF DEATH WERE CHEAPER THAN THE GLORY OF LIFE ? IF IT IS NOT EASIER TO ATTAIN, WHO DO SO MANY MORE
MTH5 (219) NEWLY BORN. HOW COULD ANYONE EVER GET TIRED OF LIFE ? /ACIS/ THEY DO. THAT IS, OF THE SAME LIFE. THEY
LION II (128) MUSTNT. /THE EDITOR/ WHAT! NOT TO SAVE YOUR LIFE ? /ANDROCLES/ I'D RATHER NOT. I COULDNT SACRIFICE TO

VWOO 3	(138)	/Z/ OH, WHY DONT YOU TAKE A MORE CHEERFUL VIEW OF	LIFE	? /A/ I HAVE LEARNT NOT TO EXPECT TOO MUCH FROM LIFE.
PRES	(137)	! HAVE YOU NO REGARD FOR THE SANCTITY OF HUMAN	LIFE	? /BALSQUITH/ (MUCH RELIEVED) WELL, GETTING SHOT IS
DOCT II	(126)	HAVE PROMISED MRS DUBEDAT TO SAVE THIS FELLOW'S	LIFE	? /BLENKINSOP/ WHATS THE MATTER WITH HIM? /RIDGEON/
ARMS III	(71)	WHAT DID YOU SAY HAD SPOILED YOUR CHANCES IN	LIFE	? /BLUNTSCHLI/ (PROMPTLY) AN INCURABLY ROMANTIC
HART I	(77)	FIXED IN YOUR CONSCIOUSNESS ALL THE REST OF YOUR	LIFE	? /CAPTAIN SHOTOVER/ NINETY MINUTES. AN HOUR AND A
BULL III	(127)	THAT NEVER WAS OUTSIDE OF A CITY OFFICE IN HIS	LIFE	? /CORNELIUS/ WE'RE TIRED OF HIM. HE DOESNT KNOW HWERE
PPP	(198)	LIFE-- /ADOLPHUS/ (MUCH INJURED) WHOSE MISSPENT	LIFE	? /MAGNESIA/ (CONTINUING RELENTLESSLY) LOOK INTO YOUR
PRES	(161)	BUT WHICH IS THE MORE ESSENTIAL TO THE HIGHER	LIFE	? /MITCHENER/ YOUR ARGUMENTS ARE SO DEVILISHLY
OVER	(191)	A MOMENT'S FORGETFULNESS EMBITTER ALL OUR FUTURE	LIFE	? /MRS JUNO/ BUT IT'S MRS LUNN WHO HAS TO FORGIVE YOU.
SUPR III	(81)	INTENSITY) SHALL I TELL YOU THE STORY OF MY	LIFE	? /STRAKER/ (APPREHENSIVELY) IF IT AINT TOO LONG, OLD
GETT	(324)	MIXED UP WITH THE STORY OF THE GENERAL'S	LIFE	? /THE BISHOP/ YOU KNOW THE STORY OF HIS LIFE, THEN..
GETT	(267)	YOU KNOW WHY. /LESBIA/ BUT YOU HAD A CHARMED	LIFE	? /THE GENERAL/ YES, A CHARMED LIFE. BAYONETS BENT ON
MTH1 I	(8)	A PART OF THE LIFE IN MY BODY. /EVE/ WHAT IS THE	LIFE	? /THE SERPENT/ THAT WHICH MAKES THE DIFFERENCE
MRS I	(185)	ARE YOU TO HAVE NO ROMANCE, NO BEAUTY IN YOUR	LIFE	? /VIVIE/ I DONT CARE FOR EITHER, I ASSURE YOU.
VWOO 2	(129)	TRAVELLING ABOUT. HOW COULD YOU BEAR THAT SORT OF	LIFE	? YOU THAT NEVER SPOKE TO ANYONE ON THE SHIP AND
BARB PREFACE	(216)	AND PRINTING. " WHY NOT UNIVERSAL PENSIONS FOR	LIFE	? " SAID COBDEN-SANDERSON, IN SAYING THIS, HE SOLVED
BARB PREFACE	(221)	INTO AN ADVERTISEMENT OF ME WHICH HAS MADE MY OWN	LIFE	A BURDEN. IN SICILY THERE IS A VIA SAMUELE BUTLER. WHEN
GETT PREFACE	(189)	AFFECTIONS AND PREVENTED HIM FROM MAKING	LIFE	A CARNIVAL, HAS VANISHED AND GIVEN PLACE TO THE VERY
MIS. PREFACE	(6)	A MAJORITY OF VOTES IN PARLIAMENT, IN DOMESTIC	LIFE	A GREAT DEAL OF SERVICE IS DONE BY CHILDREN, THE GIRLS
BASH II,2,	(114)	IN THE PRESENT; DRAINS THE HERE AND NOW; MAKES	LIFE	A LONG REALITY, AND DEATH A MOMENT ONLY; WHILST YOUR
GETT	(356)	SORRY; FOR IT'S REFRESHING TO HAVE MET ONCE IN MY	LIFE	A MAN WHO WASNT FRIGHTENED BY MY WEDDING RING; BUT I'M
BASH II,1,	(107)	AS WELL DEMAND WHY I AT BIRTH CHOSE TO BEGIN MY	LIFE	A SPEECHLESS BABE, HAIRLESS, INCONTINENT, HOBBLING UPON
JOAN PREFACE	(8)	TO DO. BYRON'S FORMULA, " MAN'S LOVE IS OF MAN'S	LIFE	A THING APART: ' TIS WOMAN'S WHOLE EXISTENCE" DID NOT
SUPR I	(41)	THATS WHY HE IS GOING TO MAKE THE MISTAKE OF HIS	LIFE	ABOUT YOU. /ANN/ I THINK MEN MAKE MORE MISTAKES BY
LION PREFACE	(83)	EVEN THE MOST INFATUATED IDIOT CANNOT SPEND HIS	LIFE	ADMIRING HIMSELF, THE LESS INNOCENT EXCITEMENT OF
AUGS	(274)	WORLD PRODUCES SO STRONG AN ANTI-GERMAN FEELING.	LIFE	AFFORDS NO KEENER PLEASURE THAN FINDING A
SIM PREFACE	(8)	BY POSITIVE INSTRUCTION THAT THERE IS NO PERSONAL	LIFE	AFTER DEATH FOR THE INDIVIDUAL, THE TEACHING BEING THAT
MTH1 II	(30)	KILLS FOR HIS FOOD; AND MAKES UP IDLE POEMS OF	LIFE	AFTER DEATH; AND DRESSES UP HIS TERROR-RIDDEN LIFE WITH
JITT III	(73)	HEARING IT, AND THE HAPPINESS! YOU BRING HIM TO	LIFE	AGAIN FOR ME. /EDITH/ THEN IT WAS-- /JITTA/ ONLY ME,
MTH3	(121)	ENOUGH TO HAVE COURAGE AND STRENGTH TO BEGIN	LIFE	AGAIN, BESIDES, POLITICAL CHANGES WERE MAKING IT
JITT III	(70)	WILL GO MAD IF YOU DO NOT GET BACK INTO EVERYDAY	LIFE	AGAIN. /EDITH/ (BACKING TO THE TABLE, AND HALF SITTING
JOAN EPILOG	(158)	FOR RANSOMS; BUT THE MAID'S WAY: STAKING	LIFE	AGAINST DEATH, WITH THE HEART HIGH AND HUMBLE AND VOID
HART II	(101)	ME ABOUT, MY NOSE WOULD HAVE BEEN FLATTENED FOR	LIFE	AGAINST THE FLOOR. BUT IVE FOUND YOU ALL OUT, ANYHOW. I
MTH5	(225)	FROM ART ALTOGETHER, BECAUSE ART IS FALSE AND	LIFE	ALONE IS TRUE. /THE NEWLY BORN/ (FLINGS HER ARMS ROUND
GETT PREFACE	(196)	GOOD FOR A SOLDIER. BUT NEITHER IS HOME	LIFE	ALTOGETHER GOOD. SUCH GOOD AS IT DOES, I SHOULD SAY, IS
MTH5	(254)	/ARJILLAX/ THAT IS FALSE. THE STATUE COMES TO	LIFE	ALWAYS. THE STATUES OF TODAY ARE THE MEN AND WOMEN OF
PHIL I	(91)	DICKENS DID HE MEAN BY ALL THAT ABOUT PASSING HIS	LIFE	AMID-- WHAT WAS IT? -- " SCENES OF SUFFERING NOBLY
CLEO II	(127)	OF MY OWN SOLDIERS. I AM ACCOUNTABLE FOR EVERY	LIFE	AMONG THEM. BUT YOU ARE FREE TO GO. SO ARE ALL HERE,
HART III	(131)	HE KNOWS THE BEST PEOPLE AND HAS LIVED ALL HIS	LIFE	AMONG THEM. WHY IS HE SO UNSATISFACTORY, SO
POSN PREFACE	(418)	PROCEEDINGS, YET I HAVE NEVER PUBLISHED IN MY	LIFE	AN ARTICLE, A PLAY, OR A BOOK, AS TO WHICH, IF I HAD
MILL I	(143)	YOUR DISGRACE, THE MESS YOU HAVE MADE OF YOUR	LIFE	AND ALL THE REST OF IT. HOW CAN I LAUGH AT THINGS I
JOAN PREFACE	(20)	AND TROUSERS, AND GEORGE SAND LIVING A MAN'S	LIFE	AND ALMOST COMPELLING HER CHOPINS AND DE MUSSETS TO
LION PREFACE	(16)	YOU BURIED IT, IT WOULD RISE AGAIN IN RENEWED	LIFE	AND BEAUTY AND GIVE MANKIND ETERNAL LIFE ON CONDITION
MRS IV	(252)	DONE AS YOU DID; BUT I SHOULD NOT HAVE LIVED ONE	LIFE	AND BELIEVED IN ANOTHER. YOU ARE A CONVENTIONAL WOMAN
MILL PREFACE	(135)	MONEYMAKERS AND MILITARY GENIUSES IN POLITICAL	LIFE	AND BY THE DOMINANT PERSONALITIES IN PRIVATE LIFE.
BARB II	(294)	AND GUNPOWDER, FREEDOM AND POWER, COMMAND OF	LIFE	AND COMMAND OF DEATH. /CUSINS/ (URBANELY: TRYING TO
SIM PRO,2,	(28)	SLEEP AND THE GIVER OF REST, IT IS NOT FAR OFF:	LIFE	AND DEATH DWELL CLOSE TOGETHER: YOU NEED PROLONG YOUR
2TRU I	(35)	OF THEM, YOU FOOL. THEY THINK I HAVE THE KEYS OF	LIFE	AND DEATH IN MY POCKET; BUT I HAVE NOTHING BUT A HORRID
ROCK PREFACE	(153)	PRIVATE PROPRIETORS HAVE IRRESPONSIBLE POWERS OF	LIFE	AND DEATH IN THE STATE. SUCH POWERS MAY BE TOLERATED AS
GENV PREFACE	(17)	CAMPS, THE WITNESSES DESCRIBE THE HORRORS OF	LIFE	AND DEATH IN THEM; AND THE NEWSPAPERS CLASS THE ACCUSED
SUPR PREFACE	(R35)	WORLDLY WISEMAN AS NO BETTER AT BOTTOM THAN THE	LIFE	AND DEATH OF MR BADMAN: ALL THIS, EXPRESSED BY BUNYAN
HART I	(78)	/CAPTAIN SHOTOVER/ WE MUST WIN POWERS OF	LIFE	AND DEATH OVER THEM BOTH. I REFUSE TO DIE UNTIL I HAVE
APPL PREFACE	(184)	OF OUR EVERYDAY NEEDS. THEIR POWERS ARE	LIFE	AND DEATH POWERS. I NEED NOT LABOR THIS POINT: WE ALL
DOCT I	(108)	BOY. SHE'S GIVEN ME HALF-A-CROWN. SHE THINKS IT'S	LIFE	AND DEATH TO HER HUSBAND FOR HER TO SEE YOU. /RIDGEON/
CLEO IV	(189)	THE PALACE. /CAESAR/ YOU HAVE TAKEN THE POWERS OF	LIFE	AND DEATH UPON YOU. I AM ONLY A DREAMER. /CLEOPATRA/
ROCK PREFACE	(162)	THE SECURITY AGAINST THE ABUSE OF THIS POWER OF	LIFE	AND DEATH WAS THAT THE CHEKA HAD NO INTEREST IN
METH PREFACE	(R73)	WHO HAD TRIED TO FILL UP THE GULF BETWEEN	LIFE	AND DEATH WITH AN EMPTY PHRASE DENOTING AN IMAGINARY
MTH3	(111)	HAD SEVERAL CAREERS SINCE I BEGAN THIS ROUTINE OF	LIFE	AND DEATH. I HAVE BEEN AN ARCHBISHOP THREE TIMES. WHEN
ROCK PREFACE	(153)	ON CONSERVATIVE STATESMEN. PRIVATE POWERS OF	LIFE	AND DEATH. NOW THE CENTRAL FACT OF ALL THESE FACTS IS
CLEO IV	(178)	IF YOU BEGIN PREACHING YOUR FAVORITE SERMON ABOUT	LIFE	AND DEATH. /CLEOPATRA/ (PRIGGISHLY) PEACE, RUFIO. I
GENV III	(69)	IT. BUT TO ME THE PERSECUTION IS A MATTER OF	LIFE	AND DEATH. /THE NEWCOMER/ IT'S A BIT HARD ON YOU, I
DOCT V	(177)	NO. DOCTORS THINK THEY HOLD THE KEYS OF	LIFE	AND DEATH; BUT IT IS NOT THEIR WILL THAT IS FULFILLED.
DOCT PREFACE	(5)	THE PATIENT HOVERS IN PAIN AND FEVER BETWEEN	LIFE	AND DEATH, HIS FORTUNE IS MADE: EVERY RICH MAN WHO
ROCK I	(226)	IT WILL GRIND ME. /THE LADY/ MY BUSINESS IS WITH	LIFE	AND DEATH, NOT WITH POLITICAL MACHINERY. /SIR ARTHUR/
MIS.	(171)	YOU A LESSON. IVE HAD ENOUGH OF LIVING A DOG'S	LIFE	AND DESPISING MYSELF FOR IT. IVE HAD ENOUGH OF BEING
FABL IV	(116)	PHASE OF SUBSTANCE HAS ITS APPROPRIATE FORM OF	LIFE	AND DIET AND SET OF HABITS. SUCH CREATURES AS ANGELS
GETT PREFACE	(194)	THEM. AS ALL THIS IS CORRIGIBLE BY REDUCING HOME	LIFE	AND DOMESTIC SENTIMENT TO SOMETHING LIKE REASONABLE
CAPT III	(296)	TRASH; BUT I GOT JUST THE SAME NONSENSE OUT OF	LIFE	AND EXPERIENCE. (SHAKING HIS HEAD) IT WAS VULGAR--
DOCT II	(128)	BUT ALL THE MEN AND WOMEN GOOD, OR TO GO THROUGH	LIFE	AND FIND ALL THE PICTURES GOOD AND ALL THE MEN AND
DOCT II	(128)	THIS CHOICE PUT BEFORE YOU: EITHER TO GO THROUGH	LIFE	AND FIND ALL THE PICTURES BAD BUT ALL THE MEN AND WOMEN
DOCT I SD	(93)	BUT HIS SCRUTINIZING, DARING EYES GIVE IT	LIFE	AND FORCE. HE SEEMS NEVER AT A LOSS, NEVER IN DOUBT:
MILL IV	(206)	IT WAS THAT OF THE TEACHER WHO CHANGED MY WHOLE	LIFE	AND GAVE ME A NEW SOUL BY OPENING THE WORLD OF SCIENCE
METH PREFACE	(R22)	AS TO THE REACTION OF EXTERNAL CAUSES ON	LIFE	AND HABIT, SUCH AS CHANGES OF CLIMATE, FOOD SUPPLY,
BARB PREFACE	(245)	HAVING MEANWHILE SPENT A GREAT DEAL OF HUMAN	LIFE	AND HAPPINESS IN THE TASK OF CHAINING AND FEEDING AND
KING I	(207)	THINGS HAVE COME TO YOU WHO LIVE A MOST PROFANE	LIFE	AND HAVE NO SIGN OF GRACE AT ALL. /CHARLES/ YOU AND I
GETT PREFACE	(201)	THE WOMAN KNOWS NOTHING OF THE MAN'S WORKING	LIFE	AND HE KNOWS NOTHING OF HER WORKING LIFE (HE CALLS IT
SUPR HANDBOK	(182)	SPUNGE ON THE REGULATED TRADES AND SACRIFICE THE	LIFE	AND HEALTH OF THE NATION AS LAWLESSLY AS THE MANCHESTER
SUPR I	(26)	ABOUT TO CONCERTS AND PARTIES, WASTING HER	LIFE	AND HER MONEY. WE SUDDENLY LEARN THAT SHE HAS TURNED
BUOY IV	(59)	MECHANISMS IS CONTRARY TO THE PLAINEST FACTS OF	LIFE	AND HISTORY. WHAT HAS CARRIED OUR MINDS FARTHER THAN
METH PREFACE	(R48)	HAD THROWN OVER THE GULF WHICH SEPARATES	LIFE	AND HOPE FROM DEATH AND DESPAIR. WE WERE INTELLECTUALLY
BARB PREFACE	(207)	BUT I CANNOT COUNTENANCE THE ASSUMPTION THAT	LIFE	AND LITERATURE ARE SO POOR IN THESE ISLANDS THAT WE
SIM PRO,2,	(28)	IGNORANT. HERE, WHERE THEY ARE IN THE MIDST OF	LIFE	AND LOVELINESS, THEY DIE BY THEIR OWN HANDS TO ESCAPE
GENV PREFACE	(15)	WHICH NONE OF THEM ACCEPT AS PRACTICAL RULES OF	LIFE	AND MANY OF THEM REPUDIATE WITH ABHORRENCE WHEN THEY
BULL III SD	(120)	IN EFFECT PATHETIC-- THE VOICE OF A MAN OF HARD	LIFE	AND MANY SORROWS-- COMES IN AT THE GATE. HE IS OLD
MILL I	(146)	I WANT TO PUNISH MYSELF FOR MAKING A MESS OF MY	LIFE	AND MARRYING AN IMBECILE. I, EPIFANIA OGNISANTI DI
SUPR II	(56)	HIM, AT SIXTY MILES AN HOUR AND THE RISK OF HIS	LIFE	AND MINE. EXCEPT, OF COURSE, WHEN HE IS LYING ON HIS
CLEO PRO1	(93)	BY THE FORCE OF HIS LONGING FOR THE DIVINE, MORE	LIFE	AND MORE LIGHT. SETTLE YE THEREFORE IN YOUR SEATS AND
MILL PREFACE	(109)	YET IT RAISES A QUESTION THAT HAS TROUBLED HUMAN	LIFE	AND MOULDED HUMAN SOCIETY SINCE THE CREATION. THE LAW
MTH5	(262)	THE ENEMY RECONCILED, THE WHIRLPOOL BECOME ALL	LIFE	AND NO MATTER, AND BECAUSE THESE INFANTS THAT CALL
MTH5	(254)	A SIMPLE THING AND A DEEP THING: IT IS AN ACT OF	LIFE	AND NOT AN ILLUSION. ART IS AN ILLUSION. /ARJILLAX/
DOCT PREFACE	(8)	MOTOR CAR MAKERS HABITUALLY ADVERTIZED ELIXIR OF	LIFE	AND PERPETUAL MOTION, AND SUCCEEDED IN CREATING A
BARB I	(268)	AND RESEARCHES IN IMPROVED METHODS OF DESTROYING	LIFE	AND PROPERTY, I HAVE ALWAYS DONE SO; AND I ALWAYS
BULL PREFACE	(46)	MAY CAUSE WHOLESALE DESTRUCTION OF	LIFE	AND PROPERTY; YET ANY OF THESE MEN MAY INSULT THEM,
BULL IV	(170)	IN THE EVENINGS BY THE ROUND TOWER, BUT REAL	LIFE	AND REAL WORK AND REAL CARES AND REAL JOYS AMONG REAL
3PLA PREFACE	(R33)	TIME, WHO AT LEAST KNEW THE DIFFERENCE BETWEEN	LIFE	AND RHETORIC. IT WILL BE SAID THAT THESE REMARKS CAN
JOAN 6	(136)	TO YOU. TAKE CARE HOW YOU ANSWER; FOR YOUR	LIFE	AND SALVATION ARE AT STAKE ON IT. WILL YOU FOR ALL YOU
MIS. PREFACE	(52)	NOR PERSECUTE NOR REVENGE NOR PUNISH. NOW FAMILY	LIFE	AND SCHOOL LIFE ARE, AS FAR AS THE MORAL TRAINING OF
SIM PREFACE	(12)	WITH SUCH A POSSIBILITY BEGAN EARLY IN	LIFE	AND SHOCKED ME SOMEWHAT. MY MATERNAL GRANDFATHER, A
PYGM III	(249)	ELIZA COMES? /MRS HIGGINS/ HENRY! YOU ARE THE	LIFE	AND SOUL OF THE ROYAL SOCIETY'S SOIREES; BUT REALLY
SUPR PREFACE	(R38)	ACT OF GENIUS; BUT HE WILL NOT PAY WITH HIS WHOLE	LIFE	AND SOUL TO BECOME A MERE VIRTUOSO IN LITERATURE,
PHIL III	(145)	SHOULDNT MAKE A JEST OF THESE THINGS: UPON MY	LIFE	AND SOUL YOU SHOULDNT, CHARTERIS. /CUTHBERTSON/ (ON
PHIL II	(100)	STRONGEST REMONSTRANCE) NOW REALLY! NOW UPON MY	LIFE	AND SOUL! /CHARTERIS/ IT'S A FACT, I ASSURE YOU. DIDNT
LION PREFACE	(24)	THE TEACHINGS OF JESUS. SO MUCH FOR HIS PERSONAL	LIFE	AND TEMPERAMENT. HIS PUBLIC CAREER AS A POPULAR
2TRU I	(34)	AND IN THAT MYSTERIOUS POWER THAT GIVES US OUR	LIFE	AND THAT NONE OF US KNOWS ANYTHING ABOUT. LOTS OF
MILL IV	(205)	SHALL I, THE HEALER, THE HELPER, THE GUARDIAN OF	LIFE	AND THE COUNSELLOR OF HEALTH, UNITE WITH THE EXPLOITER
BULL I	(87)	CHURCHMAN THAT TEACHES HIM THE SANCTITY OF	LIFE	AND THE IMPORTANCE OF CONDUCT IS SENT AWAY EMPTY; WHILE
FABL VI	(128)	1/ I DONT BELIEVE IT. WE ARE THE HIGHEST FORM OF	LIFE	AND THE MOST ADVANCED CIVILIZATION YET EVOLVED. /YOUTH

DOCT PREFACE(78)	CALLED SCIENCE HAS ALWAYS PURSUED THE ELIXIR OF	LIFE	AND THE PHILOSOPHER'S STONE, AND IS JUST AS BUSY AFTER
BARB PREFACE(207)	TRAGI-COMIC IRONY OF THE CONFLICT BETWEEN REAL	LIFE	AND THE ROMANTIC IMAGINATION, CRITICS NEVER AFFILIATE
3PLA PREFACE(R29)	SO DISCOURAGES ANY ASSOCIATION BETWEEN REAL	LIFE	AND THE STAGE, THAT HE SOON LOSES THE NATURAL HABIT OF
SUPR PREFACE(R23)	WHO INCARNATES THE PHILOSOPHIC CONSCIOUSNESS OF	LIFE	AND THE WOMAN WHO INCARNATES ITS FECUNDITY, IS TRUE IN
SUPR III (80)	WHO ARE NOT GOOD ENOUGH FOR ORDINARY BOURGEOIS	LIFE	AND THOSE WHO ARE TOO GOOD FOR IT. WE ARE DREGS AND
MIS. (182)	MR TARLETON NOT TO REPEAT IT AND TO AMEND MY	LIFE	AND TO DO WHAT IN ME LIES TO PROVE WORTHY OF HIS
GENV IV (117)	CROWDED INTO YOUR TOWNS AND DEMORALIZED BY STREET	LIFE	AND TRADE UNIONISM, WILL KNOW IN THEIR SOULS THAT I AM
MRS I (197)	KNOW US, SAM? THIS IS GEORGE CROFTS, AS LARGE AS	LIFE	AND TWICE AS NATURAL. DONT YOU REMEMBER ME? /REV. S./
APPL PREFACE(183)	HAVE WE STOPPED THE MONSTROUS WASTE OF HUMAN	LIFE	AND WELFARE IT COST WHEN IT WAS LEFT UNCONTROLLED BY
MIS. PREFACE(40)	A CHILD; FOR ITS EDUCATION CAN END ONLY WITH ITS	LIFE	AND WILL NOT EVEN THEN BE COMPLETE. COMPULSORY
JOAN PREFACE(20)	TROUSERS AND SMOKE BIG CIGARS TO LIVE A MAN'S	LIFE	ANY MORE THAN IT IS NECESSARY TO WEAR PETTICOATS TO
PYGM II (238)	OTHER AMUSEMENTS-- AND I TELL YOU IT'S A DOG'S	LIFE	ANY WAY YOU LOOK AT IT. UNDESERVING POVERTY IS MY LINE.
PRES (158)	THOSE REPEATED INSULTS TO A MAN OF BLAMELESS	LIFE	ARE AS DISGRACEFUL TO YOU AS THEY ARE UNDESERVED BY ME.
PHIL II (120)	TO THE HOUSEHOLD IN WHICH THE BEST HOPES OF YOUR	LIFE	ARE CENTRED. CONFOUND IT, MAN, YOULL NEVER GET MARRIED
MIS. PREFACE(33)	IS ALREADY EXCESSIVE, THAT THE PAINS OF	LIFE	ARE GREATER THAN ITS PLEASURES, THAT ITS SACRIFICE IN A
DOCT PREFACE(33)	OF US CAN ATTAIN), AS EASILY AS THAT THE PAINS OF	LIFE	ARE MORE NUMEROUS AND CONSTANT THAN ITS PLEASURES, AND
SUPR PREFACE(R32)	THEIR PREGNANT OBSERVATIONS AND DEMONSTRATIONS OF	LIFE	ARE NOT CO-ORDINATED INTO ANY PHILOSOPHY OR RELIGION:
MIS. PREFACE(107)	WHAT IS MORE, UNTIL THE ACTIVE HOURS OF CHILD	LIFE	ARE ORGANIZED SEPARATELY FROM THE ACTIVE HOURS OF ADULT
OVER PREFACE(155)	IT. THE ENORMOUS MAJORITY OF CASES IN REAL	LIFE	ARE THOSE OF PEOPLE IN THAT POSITION. THOSE WHO
METH PREFACE(R20)	PHILOSOPHER EMPEDOCLES OPINED THAT ALL FORMS OF	LIFE	ARE TRANSFORMATIONS OF FOUR ELEMENTS, FIRE, AIR, EARTH,
MIS. PREFACE(52)	REVENGE NOR PUNISH. NOW FAMILY LIFE AND SCHOOL	LIFE	ARE, AS FAR AS THE MORAL TRAINING OF CHILDREN IS
LION PREFACE(94)	TO BE LET OFF, TO BEG FOR AND ACCEPT ETERNAL	LIFE	AS A PRESENT INSTEAD OF EARNING IT, WOULD BE MEAN
APPL I (228)	THAT IT IS NO USE TRYING TO BROWBEAT ME. I BEGAN	LIFE	AS A SCHOOLMISTRESS; AND I CAN BROWBEAT ANY MAN IN THIS
CAPT II (259)	PRETTY FORTUNATE IF HE IS ALLOWED TO LIVE OUT HIS	LIFE	AS A SLAVE WITH A SET OF CHAINS ON HIM? /LADY CICELY/
MIS. (135)	A CHORD IS TOUCHED; AND HE SEES THE DRAMA OF HIS	LIFE	AS A SPECTATOR SEES A PLAY. LAUGH IF YOU FEEL INCLINED:
BARB PREFACE(221)	WHEN ONE SEES SO EXTRAORDINARY A STUDY OF ENGLISH	LIFE	AS BUTLER'S POSTHUMOUS WAY OF ALL FLESH MAKING SO
MIS. (140)	COMES A-COURTING IS AS FAMILIAR AN INCIDENT IN MY	LIFE	AS COFFEE FOR BREAKFAST. OF COURSE, HE'S TOO MUCH OF A
METH PREFACE(R20)	BELIEVED IN THE SEPARATE CREATION OF ALL FORMS OF	LIFE	AS DESCRIBED IN THE BOOK OF GENESIS. THIS " CONFLICT
SIM PREFACE(16)	FOLLOWS THE STAGE, THE BUTTON MOULDER CAME TO	LIFE	AS DJERJINSKY. MY ANGEL COMES A DAY AFTER THE FAIR; BUT
POSN (452)	IS SPEAKING THE TRUTH FOR THE FIRST TIME IN HIS	LIFE	AS FAR AS WHAT HE SAYS ABOUT ME IS CONCERNED. AS TO THE
MTH5 (208)	FORGET, INFANT, THAT ONE MOMENT OF THE ECSTASY OF	LIFE	AS I LIVE IT WOULD STRIKE YOU DEAD. HAHA! /STREPHON/ (
SIM II (84)	FIT OURSELVES INTO PUZZLES, BUT TO WRESTLE WITH	LIFE	AS IT COMES, AND IT NEVER COMES AS WE EXPECT IT TO
LADY PREFACE(231)	FROM OUR EPOCH WHICH WILL HAVE ANY RELATION TO	LIFE	AS IT WILL BE LIVED THEN WILL BE THOSE IN WHICH NONE OF
GETT PREFACE(190)	OF BEING SUPPOSED TO DESIRE OR LIVE THE MARRIED	LIFE	AS ORDINARILY CONCEIVED. EVERY THOUGHTFUL AND OBSERVANT
MTH2 (73)	ALL, WE MIGHT AS WELL HEAR ABOUT THE ELIXIR OF	LIFE	AS READ NOVELS, OR WHATEVER BURGE DOES WHEN HE IS NOT
MIS. PREFACE(26)	AND NOT TO QUALIFY THEM FOR THEIR PART IN	LIFE	AS RESPONSIBLE CITIZENS OF A FREE STATE. IT IS NOT
LION PREFACE(61)	JUST AS WE NOW BEGIN BY HOLDING THE RIGHT TO	LIFE	AS SACRED AND EQUAL. INDEED THE ONE RIGHT IS ONLY A
GETT PREFACE(245)	THE COWARDICE AND WANT OF FAITH WHICH CONCEIVES	LIFE	AS SOMETHING TOO TERRIBLE TO BE FACED. IN THIS
NEVR III (271)	TAKEN TO MAKE HIM PERFECT IN HIS CHOSEN PART IN	LIFE	AS THE DUELLIST OF SEX. /VALENTINE/ THIS ISNT FAIR.
3PLA PREFACE(R21)	POETS ADDRESS VERSES ENTITLED TO MY LADY, COME TO	LIFE	AS THE PARLORMAIDS AND WAITRESSES OF THE NEXT. IF THE
BARB PREFACE(236)	MOVED BY THAT CONTRAST TO PAY HIS OWN	LIFE	AS THE PRICE OF ONE TERRIBLE BLOW AT THE RESPONSIBLE
KING I (180)	YOU! BUT I HAVE NEVER BEEN SO SURPRISED IN MY	LIFE	AS TO FIND YOU HERE. AND NELLY! AND HER GRACE OF
POSN PREFACE(425)	TO THE BIGOTRY OF PEOPLE SO UNFIT FOR SOCIAL	LIFE	AS TO INSIST NOT ONLY THAT THEIR OWN PREJUDICES AND
BARB PREFACE(220)	ENABLES LIFE TO BE DISTRIBUTED SOCIALLY: IT IS	LIFE	AS TRULY AS SOVEREIGNS AND BANK NOTES ARE MONEY. THE
MTH5 (208)	ANCIENT/ INFANT: ONE MOMENT OF THE ECSTASY OF	LIFE	AS WE LIVE IT WOULD STRIKE YOU DEAD. (HE STALKS
6CAL PREFACE(90)	SIMPLY AS A PLAY? WELL, IT IS A LOT OF THINGS.	LIFE	AS WE SEE IT IS SO HAPHAZARD THAT IT IS ONLY BY PICKING
GETT PREFACE(195)	DANGER OF IT DOES NOT LIE IN HUMAN NATURE. HOME	LIFE	AS WE UNDERSTAND IT IS NO MORE NATURAL TO US THAN A
SUPR PREFACE(R39)	OF MATERIAL BETWEEN US: WE ARE BOTH CRITICS OF	LIFE	AS WELL AS OF ART; AND YOU HAVE PERHAPS SAID TO
GETT PREFACE(237)	BE TO THE LIFE OF THE RACE, AND TO THE QUALITY OF	LIFE	AS WELL AS TO THE MERE FACT OF BREATHING, IS MAKING
JITT I (24)	WE ARE ALIVE, NOT DEAD: YOU ARE LIVING WITH MY	LIFE	AS WELL AS YOUR OWN: YOUR BLOOD SURGES TO MIX WITH
LION PREFACE(93)	WHETHER SOCRATES GOT AS MUCH HAPPINESS OUT OF	LIFE	AS WESLEY IS AN UNANSWERABLE QUESTION; BUT A NATION OF
MIS. (145)	IT HAS BEATEN ME. I NEVER WAS SO SURPRISED IN MY	LIFE	AS WHEN I CAME TO KNOW JOHNNY AS A MAN OF BUSINESS AND
SIM PRO,2, (27)	TO HEAR A YOUNG MAN LIKE YOU, IN THE PRIME OF	LIFE	AS YOU MIGHT SAY, TALKING LIKE THAT. WHY DONT YOU GET
KING I (196)	I SUPPOSE YOU KNOW THAT HE GOT HIS START IN	LIFE	AS YOUR BARBARA'S KEPT MAN? /CHARLES/ I KNOW THAT THE
GETT PREFACE(196)	IN OUR DOMESTIC IDEALS. I DO NOT THINK THAT	LIFE	AT A PUBLIC SCHOOL IS ALTOGETHER GOOD FOR A BOY ANY
GETT PREFACE(202)	LEISURED CLASSES THERE IS OFTEN NO REAL FAMILY	LIFE	AT ALL. THE BOYS ARE AT A PUBLIC SCHOOL; THE GIRLS ARE
DEVL III (77)	THE CAPTAINS AND THE SHOUTING. SO I AM STARTING	LIFE	AT FIFTY AS CAPTAIN ANTHONY ANDERSON OF THE SPRINGTOWN
SUPR I SD(3)	COMPANIES WHICH SELL YOU A SATURDAY TO MONDAY OF	LIFE	AT FOLKESTONE AS A REAL GENTLEMAN FOR TWO GUINEAS,
DOCT I (108)	HER TO SEE YOU. /RIDGEON/ VALUES HER HUSBAND'S	LIFE	AT HALF-A-CROWN! /EMMY/ WELL, IT'S ALL SHE CAN AFFORD,
POSN (465)	WOMAN/ HOW MANY WOULD HAVE DONE IT WITH THEIR	LIFE	AT STAKE? /FEEMY/ OH WELL, IF YOURE SO MUCH TAKEN WITH
ROCK PREFACE(187)	NOT ASK YOU TO SET ME FREE; NOR WOULD I ACCEPT MY	LIFE	AT THE PRICE OF BARABBAS'S DEATH EVEN IF I BELIEVED
3PLA PREFACE(R29)	AUTOMATIC AND UNINTERESTING. THE SAVING OF	LIFE	AT THE RISK OF THE SAVER'S OWN IS NOT A COMMON THING;
METH PREFACE(R19)	OPPORTUNIST GROUNDS MAN NOW FIXES THE TERM OF HIS	LIFE	AT THREE SCORE AND TEN YEARS, HE CAN EQUALLY FIX IT AT
MIS. (198)	HAVE NOW REACHED THAT VERY COMMON STAGE IN FAMILY	LIFE	AT WHICH ANYTHING BUT A BLOW WOULD BE AN ANTICLIMAX. DO
MRS I (187)	CHANGE OF SUBJECT, MR PRAED, WHY WONT MY MOTHER'S	LIFE	BEAR BEING TALKED ABOUT? /PRAED/ OH, YOU REALLY MUSTNT
JITT PREFACE(7)	SETTLE DOWN ON REASONABLE HUMAN TERMS, AND FIND	LIFE	BEARABLE AFTER ALL, TREBITSCH GOES SO FAR AS TO SAY "
BARB II (305)	A LESS QUESTIONABLE WAY OF PUTTING IT. IT MAKES	LIFE	BEARABLE TO MILLIONS OF PEOPLE WHO COULD NOT ENDURE
LION PREFACE(76)	NATURE BECAME A HORROR TO THEM, AND THE RELIGIOUS	LIFE	BECAME A DENIAL OF LIFE. PAUL HAD NO INTENTION OF
SIM PRO,2, (29)	IT: SEE? NOBODY SHALL SAY THAT I LIVED A DOG'S	LIFE	BECAUSE I WAS AFRAID TO MAKE AN END OF IT. (HE BENDS
PLES PREFACE(R13)	IS BOTH SCHOOL AND CHURCH, PUBLIC AND PRIVATE	LIFE	BECOME DAILY MORE THEATRICAL: THE MODERN KAISER,
LADY PREFACE(231)	POVERTY IS ABOLISHED, AND LEISURE AND GRACE OF	LIFE	BECOME GENERAL, THE ONLY PLAYS SURVIVING FROM OUR EPOCH
SUPR HANDBOK(193)	OF CLEANLINESS MANY OF THE NATURAL CONDITIONS OF	LIFE	BECOME OFFENSIVE AND NOXIOUS, WITH THE RESULT THAT AT
SUPR HANDBOK(193)	OF SLUMS WE CALL CITIES), HALF THEIR BODILY	LIFE	BECOMES A GUILTY SECRET, UNMENTIONABLE EXCEPT TO THE
OVER (178)	IT: I KNOW THAT IT'S WRONG: I HAVE NEVER IN MY	LIFE	BEEN COOLER, MORE BUSINESSLIKE. /MRS JUNO/ (OPENING
BARB III (313)	IT. /CUSINS/ HE CONVINCED ME THAT I HAVE ALL MY	LIFE	BEEN DOING IMPROPER THINGS FOR PROPER REASONS. /LADY
GETT PREFACE(242)	YET HE HAS FOR TWENTY YEARS OF HIS ADULT	LIFE	BEEN ONE, AND THEREFORE PRODUCED ALL THE SOCIAL
BARB PREFACE(217)	KNIGHT, IN PLACING THE ACHIEVEMENT OF A GOOD	LIFE	BEFORE ALL THE OTHER DUTIES-- WHICH INDEED ARE NOT
CLEO II (126)	A FEW MONTHS HENCE HE MAY BE FLYING FOR HIS	LIFE	BEFORE CATO AND JUBA OF NUMIDIA, THE AFRICAN KING.
PHIL II (115)	AN EXTENT I SHOULD NEVER HAVE DONE IF I'D HAD MY	LIFE	BEFORE ME. IVE DONE A LOT OF SERIOUS THINKING AND
CLEO II (126)	AGAIN. A FEW WEEKS AGO CAESAR WAS FLYING FOR HIS	LIFE	BEFORE POMPEY: A FEW MONTHS HENCE HE MAY BE FLYING FOR
2TRU III (87)	TIMES, MORE THAN YOU EVER WANTED ANYTHING IN YOUR	LIFE	BEFORE. THATS A HARD FACT OF HUMAN NATURE; AND IT'S ONE
GLIM (187)	THE CUP OF DEATH; AND IT MAY BE NOW THAT MY REAL	LIFE	BEGAN WITH THIS (HE HOLDS UP THE ROSARY) AND WILL END
SUPR HANDBOK(175)	ALL WHO ACHIEVE REAL DISTINCTION IN	LIFE	BEGIN AS REVOLUTIONISTS. THE MOST DISTINGUISHED PERSONS
BUOY IV (53)	I AM BEING RUSHED. /OLD BILL/ YOU WILL SPEND YOUR	LIFE	BEING RUSHED IF YOU LIVE WITH BABZ. BETTER GET USED TO
BULL II SD(111)	DESIRE FOR IT OR TOLERATION OF THE POSSIBILITY OF	LIFE	BEING SOMETHING BETTER THAN A ROUND OF SORDID WORRIES,
LION PREFACE(89)	THE BELIEF IN THE PROLONGATION OF INDIVIDUAL	LIFE	BEYOND THE GRAVE IS FAR MORE REAL AND VIVID AMONG
BARB PREFACE(235)	THE ABSOLUTION THAT IS REFUSED TO BILL. IN REAL	LIFE	BILL WOULD PERHAPS NEVER KNOW THIS. BUT I, THE
JITT III (60)	MYSELF AGAINST IS BEING EXPECTED TO GO THROUGH	LIFE	BLINDFOLD, OR PRETENDING TO BE BLINDFOLD. I AM TO BE A
METH PREFACE(R73)	CONCEPTION AS AGAINST THE DIVINE IDEA OF THE	LIFE	BREATHED INTO THE CLAY NOSTRILS OF ADAM, WHEREBY HE
JITT III (58)	HER: I WANT TO FIND OUT FROM HER WHAT SORT OF	LIFE	BRUNO WAS REALLY LEADING, AND WHAT HAS BECOME OF ALL
SIM II (77)	SHILLINGS FOR BEING IN UNLAWFUL POSSESSION OF A	LIFE	BUOY, THE PROPERTY OF THE ROYAL HUMANE SOCIETY. THERE
GETT PREFACE(258)	ABUSE, " MENTAL ANGUISH," CONDUCT RENDERING	LIFE	BURDENSOME AND SO FORTH (ALL THESE ARE EXAMPLES FROM
GETT PREFACE(258)	ON OATH. WHEN IT COMES TO " CONDUCT RENDERING	LIFE	BURDENSOME," IT IS CLEAR THAT NO MARRIAGE IS ANY LONGER
PYGM II (223)	EXCITED AS THE IDEA GROWS ON HIM) WHAT IS	LIFE	BUT A SERIES OF INSPIRED FOLLIES? THE DIFFICULTY IS TO
PRES (136)	/MITCHENER/ (SCORNFULLY) DARE! DARE! WHAT IS	LIFE	BUT DARING, MAN? " TO DARE, TO DARE, AND AGAIN TO
SUPR III (107)	INTO THE HUMAN BEING IS NOT THE NEED FOR HIGHER	LIFE	BUT FOR A MORE EFFICIENT ENGINE OF DESTRUCTION. THE
SUPR III (107)	POWER THAT GOVERNS THE EARTH IS NOT THE POWER OF	LIFE	BUT OF DEATH; AND THE INNER NEED THAT HAS NERVED LIFE
SUPR III (111)	THE SURVIVAL, NOT OF THE MOST EFFECTIVE MEANS OF	LIFE	BUT OF THE MOST EFFECTIVE MEANS OF DEATH. YOU ALWAYS
SUPR II (54)	IT. /TANNER/ WHY, MAN, WHAT OTHER WORK HAS SHE IN	LIFE	BUT TO GET A HUSBAND? IT IS A WOMAN'S BUSINESS TO GET
MTH3 (129)	MAN, NOT A MONSTER. I WON MY PLACE IN PUBLIC	LIFE	BY DEMONSTRATING THAT THE TRUE EXPECTATION OF HUMAN
ARMS III (68)	ASTONISHED). THE GRACIOUS YOUNG LADY SAVED MY	LIFE	BY GIVING ME CHOCOLATE CREAMS WHEN I WAS STARVING:
MRS PREFACE(157)	OF BETTER WOMEN. IF HE MADE HIS PLAY FALSE TO	LIFE	BY INVENTING FICTITIOUS DISADVANTAGES FOR HER, HE WOULD
MIS. PREFACE(67)	ARE CRUELLY DISTRESSED AND MORE OR LESS LAMED FOR	LIFE	BY IT. OUR QUARRELSOMENESS. AS BETWEEN ADULTS, WE FIND
DOCT PREFACE(26)	IMMUNE FROM ALL DISEASE DURING ITS ENTIRE	LIFE	BY TAKING HALF AN OUNCE OF RADIUM TO EVERY PINT OF ITS
BULL PREFACE(29)	OF PROFESSIONAL, OFFICIAL, AND FASHIONABLE	LIFE	BY THE SUPERIOR EDUCATION OF ITS PROTESTANT
MTH4 II (192)	OUT OF THE NATURAL JOYS AND FREEDOMS OF MY	LIFE	BY THIS DREAM TO WHICH THE EXISTENCE OF THESE ISLANDS
VWOO 3 (135)	/A/ I POSITIVELY DENY THAT I HAVE EVER IN MY	LIFE	CALLED ASPARAGUS SPARROWGRASS TO AN EDUCATED CUSTOMER.

LION PREFACE(38)	OF A WANDERING PREACHER WHO AT THE END OF HIS	LIFE	CAME TO JERUSALEM. JOHN DESCRIBES A PREACHER WHO SPENT
SIM I (48)	THAT MUST HAVE BEEN A THRILL, MR HAMMINGTAP.	LIFE	CAME TO YOU THAT TIME, DIDNT IT? /THE CLERGYMAN/ OH
FANY III (323)	YOUR BROADMINDEDNESS, AND THE FACT THAT HOME	LIFE	CAN HARDLY BE SAID TO EXIST IN ENGLAND. YOU HAVE MADE
GENV PREFACE(26)	LEAST A STRONG SUSPICION THAT THE TERM OF HUMAN	LIFE	CANNOT BE FIXED AT SEVENTY YEARS OR INDEED FIXED AT
SUPR III (122)	I NEVER DEMONSTRATED THE EXTINCTION OF MANKIND.	LIFE	CANNOT WILL ITS OWN EXTINCTION EITHER IN ITS BLIND
SIM PRO,2, (29)	MEN FEAST WITHOUT WOMEN? /THE Y.W./ WELL, LET	LIFE	COME TO YOU I ALWAYS SAY; AND DONT CRY OUT UNTIL YOURE
SIM PRO,1, (25)	LET LIFE COME TO YOU. SOUNDS ALL RIGHT, THAT. LET	LIFE	COME TO YOU, AYE; BUT SUPPOSE LIFE DOESNT COME TO YOU!
SIM II (82)	DO THE PUZZLES AND SEE WHAT WILL HAPPEN. LET	LIFE	COME TO YOU. GOODBYE. /MRS HYERING/ (ALARMED) WHY DO
SIM I (51)	DONT LET THAT CONSCIENCE OF YOURS WORRY YOU. LET	LIFE	COME TO YOU. (SHE GOES). /HYERING/ TRY TO SLEEP A
SIM PRO,1, (24)	Y.W./ DONT ASK YOURSELF ANYTHING, MY CHILD. LET	LIFE	COME TO YOU. MARCH. /THE E.O./ (AT THE RAILWAY DOOR,
SIM PRO,3, (32)	WITH HIM, HAVE YOU? WELL, LET YOURSELF RIP. LET	LIFE	COME TO YOU. /THE L.T./ OH! HOW DARE YOU? REALLY!
SIM I (50)	STICK TO THE ENCHANTMENT WHILE IT LASTS. LET	LIFE	COME TO YOU. /PRA/ MAY I REMIND YOU THAT NOT ONLY
SIM I (44)	/MRS HYERING/ BUCK UP, MR HAMMINGTAP. LET	LIFE	COME TO YOU. /LADY FARWATERS/ OUR FAMILY ARRANGEMENTS
SIM I (45)	/MRS HYERING/ THATS RIGHT, MR HAMMINGTAP: LET	LIFE	COME TO YOU. /PRA/ WHAT OBJECTION HAVE YOU TO BE A
SIM PRO,1, (25)	THROUGH THE RAILWAY DOOR). /WILKS/ (ALONE) LET	LIFE	COME TO YOU. SOUNDS ALL RIGHT, THAT. LET LIFE COME TO
SIM PRO,3, (31)	THINK OF SOMETHING LIVELIER? I ALWAYS SAY LET	LIFE	COME TO YOU; AND DONT BOTHER ABOUT RELIGION. /THE
SIM PRO,3, (33)	I'LL BID YOU ALL GOOD MORNING. I ALWAYS SAY LET	LIFE	COME TO YOU; BUT HERE IT'S COMING A BIT TOO THICK FOR
SIM PRO,3, (32)	I USED TO, OLD MAN. /THE Y.W./ THATS RIGHT. LET	LIFE	COME TO YOU, I ALWAYS SAY. /THE E.O./ YES, LET LIFE
SIM PRO,3, (31)	AN EXCELLENT RULE, BUT THE MORE YOU LET	LIFE	COME TO YOU, THE MORE YOU WILL FIND YOURSELF BOTHERING
SIM PRO,3, (32)	COME TO YOU, I ALWAYS SAY. /THE E.O./ YES, LET	LIFE	COME. THE PREMISES ARE QUITE EMPTY. /THE LADY TOURIST/
SUPR HANDBOK(181)	OR HIS HABITS, HIS FRIENDS, HIS PLACE AND MODE OF	LIFE	CONGENIAL TO HER, THEREFORE MARRIAGE, WHILST IT IS MADE
KING I (170)	SHAME WILL NOT HELP YOU, PASTOR, I SPEND MY	LIFE	CONTEMPLATING THE OCEAN OF MY IGNORANCE. I ONCE BOASTED
SIM PREFACE(17)	TO MAKE EVERY CITIZEN CONSCIOUS THAT IF HIS	LIFE	COSTS MORE THAN IT IS WORTH TO THE COMMUNITY THE
BARB PREFACE(217)	IN ORGANIZING ITSELF SO STUPIDLY THAT A GOOD	LIFE	COULD BE ACHIEVED BY ROBBING AND PILLING, IF THE
MRS PREFACE(176)	IT WITH THAT EXPRESS OBJECT. IGNORANCE OF REAL	LIFE	COULD HARDLY GO FURTHER, I WAS DEEPLY DISGUSTED BY THIS
BULL IV (160)	NORA: A MAN CANT SIT DOWN AND WRITE HIS	LIFE	DAY BY DAY WHEN HE'S TIRED ENOUGH WITH HAVING LIVED IT.
MIS. PREFACE(94)	HAVE MANY CONFIRMATIONS AND REPUDIATIONS AS THEIR	LIFE	DEEPENS AND THEIR KNOWLEDGE WIDENS, BUT WHAT IS TO
POSN (463)	AM I A SNIVELLING CRY-BABY THAT LET A HORSE HIS	LIFE	DEPENDED ON BE TOOK FROM HIM BY A WOMAN, AND THEN SAT
BARB PREFACE(245)	THAT HIS DEEDS ARE IRREVOCABLE, AND THAT HIS	LIFE	DEPENDS ON HIS USEFULNESS. HITHERTO, ALAS! HUMANITY
PPP (201)	WATER; AND BRING IT BACK INSTANTLY. MR BASTABLE'S	LIFE	DEPENDS ON YOUR HASTE. /PHYLLIS/ (HESITATING) IT DO
ROCK I (217)	HE DONT KNOW NOTHING OF THE BUSINESS THAT HIS	LIFE	DEPENDS ON. TURN A CAT LOOSE AND IT'LL FEED ITSELF. TURN
NEVR III (265)	CLANDON/ LET ME TELL YOU, MR VALENTINE, THAT A	LIFE	DEVOTED TO THE CAUSE OF HUMANITY HAS ENTHUSIASMS AND
JITT II (29)	LIFE WE ALL GAVE HIM CREDIT FOR. WHAT SORT OF	LIFE	DID HE REALLY LEAD? THAT IS THE QUESTION. /FESSLER/
JOAN EPILOG (159)	/CAUCHON/ WRETCH! IN ALL THE YEARS OF YOUR	LIFE	DID YOU DO ONLY ONE GOOD ACTION? /THE SOLDIER/ I NEVER
UNPL PREFACE(R7)	NOR A CYNIC IN THESE MATTERS: I SIMPLY UNDERSTOOD	LIFE	DIFFERENTLY FROM THE AVERAGE RESPECTABLE MAN; AND AS I
MIS. (136)	/LORD SUMMERHAYS/ YES: THE QUICKSANDS MAKE	LIFE	DIFFICULT. STILL, THERE THEY ARE. IT'S NO USE
DOCT V (173)	(WITH DEEP GRAVITY) FUNNY! /RIDGEON/ YES.	LIFE	DOES NOT CEASE TO BE FUNNY WHEN PEOPLE DIE ANY MORE
MTH5 (261)	THEY HAVE TAKEN THE AGONY FROM BIRTH; AND THEIR	LIFE	DOES NOT FAIL THEM EVEN IN THE HOUR OF THEIR
MTH2 (69)	GOD, MUCH LESS TO MORTAL MEN WHOSE WHOLE	LIFE	DOES NOT LAST A HUNDRED YEARS. /BURGE/ WE WON THE WAR:
SIM PRO,1, (25)	THAT. LET LIFE COME TO YOU. AYE; BUT SUPPOSE	LIFE	DOESNT COME TO YOU! LOOK AT ME! WHAT AM I? AN EMPIRE
HART III (143)	TO END? /MAZZINI/ IT WONT END, MR HUSHABYE.	LIFE	DOESNT END: IT GOES ON. /ELLIE/ OH, IT CANT GO ON FOR
GETT (353)	THATS THE TALK! GIVE ME A MAN WHOSE WHOLE	LIFE	DOESNT HANG ON SOME SCRUBBY WOMAN IN THE NEXT STREET;
JITT III (53)	DRUDGE. ALL THE SAME, I CANT SPEND MY WHOLE	LIFE	DOING NOTHING BUT GRIEVING, CAN I? /FESSLER/ JUST SO.
MILL IV (204)	I CAN BEAR NO MORE OF THIS. I WILL NOT HAVE MY	LIFE	DRAGGED DOWN TO PLANES OF VULGARITY ON WHICH I CANNOT
ARMS II (32)	THE GLIMPSES I HAVE HAD OF THE SEAMY SIDE OF	LIFE	DURING THE LAST FEW MONTHS HAVE MADE ME CYNICAL; BUT I
HART I (65)	MUST BE. /MRS HUSHABYE/ (FONDLING HER) IT'S ONLY	LIFE	EDUCATING YOU, PETTIKINS. HOW DO YOU FEEL ABOUT BOSS
PRES (147)	WITH BAD LANGUAGE FROM ME BECAUSE IVE RISKED ME	LIFE	EIGHT TIMES IN CHILDBED? /MITCHENER/ MY DEAR MRS
BUOY 1 (15)	PROBLEM OF WHAT TO DO IN OUR SPARE TIME WILL MAKE	LIFE	ENORMOUSLY MORE INTERESTING. NO MORE DOUBT AS TO
GENV I (47)	HIS FEET UNAIDED, HIS EYES BLAZING) I STILL HAVE	LIFE	ENOUGH LEFT IN ME TO DENY IT. KARL MARX-- ANTICHRIST--
MTH3 (104)	LIVES LONGER THAN THE STATUTORY EXPECTATION OF	LIFE	ENTITLES HIM TO, AND GOES ON DRAWING PUBLIC MONEY WHEN,
LION PREFACE(16)	AND RETURN TO THE EARTH IN GLORY AS THE GIVER OF	LIFE	ETERNAL. LOOKING FOR THE END OF THE WORLD, YET ANOTHER
MTH5 (253)	ONLY THOUGHT, /THE HE-ANCIENT/ AND THAT WILL BE	LIFE	ETERNAL. /ECRASIA/ I TRUST I SHALL MEET MY FATAL
GETT PREFACE(219)	THE POWER OF FIXING OUR FANCIES OR AFFECTIONS FOR	LIFE	EVEN UNDER THE MOST UNNATURAL CONDITIONS. THE
APPL I (200)	THE CHANGING SEASONS, THE CONTINUAL MIRACLE OF	LIFE	EVER RENEWING ITSELF. WHO COULD BE DULL WITH POOLS IN
2TRU I (48)	EXCEPT AS A FIELD FOR THE ADVENTURES OF THE	LIFE	EVERLASTING? IN VAIN DO WE DISFIGURE OUR STREETS WITH
ROCK PREFACE(148)	TO MAKE THIS DISTINCTION. THEY MAY BELIEVE IN THE	LIFE	EVERLASTING AND THE LIFE TO COME; BUT THEY MAKE NO
ROCK PREFACE(148)	MATERIALIZATIONS AND PERSONIFICATIONS OF THE	LIFE	EVERLASTING ARE THEMSELVES EVERLASTING. IN EITHER CASE
POSN PREFACE(427)	BE HAD WITHOUT RISK. A MOTHER RISKS HER CHILD'S	LIFE	EVERY TIME SHE LETS IT RAMBLE THROUGH THE COUNTRYSIDE,
MIS. (135)	COMIC SIDE OF IT MORE THAN I. IN THE THEATRE OF	LIFE	EVERYONE MAY BE AMUSED EXCEPT THE ACTOR. (BRIGHTENING)
LION I (113)	THINK IT IS EASY FOR US TO DIE. OUR FAITH MAKES	LIFE	FAR STRONGER AND MORE WONDERFUL IN US THAN WHEN WE
SIM II (72)	AND PESTILENCE. BUT THE SPRING CAME AND CREATED	LIFE	FASTER THAN YOU COULD DESTROY IT. THE BIRDS SANG OVER
ROCK PREFACE(169)	WHAT TO DO WITH THEMSELVES WHEN AT LIBERTY. A	LIFE	FILLED WITH SCIENTIFIC CURIOSITY WOULD BE HELL FOR THE
MILL PREFACE(133)	SO EFFECTUALLY THAT HE REMAINS ALL HIS	LIFE	FIRMLY CONVINCED THAT HIS GREATEST CONTEMPORARIES ARE
DOCT PREFACE(25)	THE ENTIRE POPULATION OF THE GLOBE SINCE HUMAN	LIFE	FIRST APPEARED ON IT. BUT THE PRECAUTIONS NECESSARY TO
BARB PREFACE(222)	REJOICING, DRUMMING, AND TAMBOURINING: HIS	LIFE	FLYING BY IN A FLASH OF EXCITEMENT, AND HIS DEATH
SUPR HANDBOK(177)	TO HIS INTENTION, AND ENNOBLING OR DEBASING	LIFE	FOR A SET PURPOSE. AND WHAT CAN BE DONE WITH A WOLF CAN
ROCK PREFACE(163)	HIS MOTHER-IN-LAW, THEREBY SECURING A LEASE OF	LIFE	FOR AT LEAST FOUR YEARS. SOONER OR LATER THIS SITUATION
MIS. PREFACE(71)	TODAY; AND VOLUNTARY ORGANIZATION OF OUTDOOR	LIFE	FOR CHILDREN HAS ALREADY BEGUN IN BOY SCOUTING AND
MTH5 (218)	NEWLY BORN/ I DONT THINK: I KNOW. I SHALL ENJOY	LIFE	FOR EVER AND EVER. /THE SHE-ANCIENT/ IF YOU SHOULD TURN
BUOY II (22)	KILLED ANYBODY. I DONT WANT TO. I WANT A DECENT	LIFE	FOR EVERYBODY BECAUSE POOR PEOPLE ARE AS TIRESOME AS
O'FL PREFACE(202)	FROM IRELAND, HE WILL GO ABROAD TO RISK HIS	LIFE	FOR FRANCE, FOR THE PAPAL STATES, FOR SECESSION IN
3PLA PREFACE(R29)	WITH MY SENTIMENTAL HEROINES) THAT HE RISKED HIS	LIFE	FOR HER SAKE, HE TELLS HER THE OBVIOUS TRUTH THAT HE
MIS. (140)	LOVE WITH ME. I SHALL BE GRATEFUL TO YOU ALL MY	LIFE	FOR IT, BECAUSE THAT WAS THE FIRST TIME THAT ANYTHING
ANNA (290)	DISPLEASED THEIR BETTERS. AND NOW WHAT IS LEFT IN	LIFE	FOR ME? (HE RELAPSES INTO HIS CHAIR DISCOURAGED) MY
MRS IV (239)	FOR ALL. THERE IS NO BEAUTY AND NO ROMANCE IN	LIFE	FOR ME. LIFE IS WHAT IT IS; AND I AM PREPARED TO TAKE
GETT PREFACE(231)	PARTIES TO IT, THAT NOBODY HAS ROOM IN HIS OR HER	LIFE	FOR MORE THAN ONE SUCH RELATIONSHIP AT A TIME. WHAT IS
MTH5 (206)	BACK. /THE YOUTH/ WHY NOT STAY WITH US AND ENJOY	LIFE	FOR ONCE IN A WAY? WE WILL TEACH YOU TO DANCE. /THE
MRS PREFACE(171)	BOLDEST AND MOST SPECIOUS DEFENCES OF AN IMMORAL	LIFE	FOR POOR WOMEN THAT HAS EVER BEEN PENNED." HAPPILY THE
HART II (114)	WILL NOT BREAK. SHE HAS BEEN LONGING ALL HER	LIFE	FOR SOMEONE TO BREAK IT. AT LAST SHE HAS BECOME AFRAID
BULL PREFACE(22)	ANY MAN WHO HAS LIVED BEHIND THE SCENES OF PUBLIC	LIFE	FOR TEN MINUTES CAN POSSIBLY BE. NOBODY DARES TO
HART PREFACE(37)	HIS INCOME TAX AND SUPER TAX, AND INSURED HIS	LIFE	FOR THE AMOUNT OF HIS DEATH DUTIES, HE IS LUCKY IF HIS
JITT II (35)	DEATH HAS AWAKENED YOU: YOU ARE LOOKING AT	LIFE	FOR THE FIRST TIME. /EDITH/ I HAVE BEEN LOOKING AT
POSN PREFACE(385)	AND CONSCIENTIOUSLY BE READY TO LAY DOWN HIS	LIFE	FOR THE RIGHT OF EVERY MAN TO ADVOCATE ATHEISM OR
SUPR III (129)	AND IF WE WHO ARE OF THAT CASTE AIMED AT MORE	LIFE	FOR THE WORLD INSTEAD OF AT MORE POWER AND LUXURY FOR
DEVL III (75)	AND A SUBDUED GROAN BREAKS FROM THEM). AMEN! MY	LIFE	FOR THE WORLD'S FUTURE! /ANDERSON/ (SHOUTING AS HE
BULL PREFACE(49)	BE, WITH SENTENCES WHICH ARE RESERVED IN CIVIL	LIFE	FOR THE WORST CRIMES, HE CANNOT SECURE THE OBEDIENCE
BULL PREFACE(48)	FOR THE MILITARY AND NAVAL CODES SIMPLIFY	LIFE	FOR THEM JUST AS IT IS SIMPLIFIED FOR CHILDREN. NO
MIS. PREFACE(19)	THEIR CHILDREN HAPPY NOR HAVING A TOLERABLE	LIFE	FOR THEMSELVES. A SELFISH TYRANT YOU KNOW WHERE TO
GETT PREFACE(233)	SHE WOULD SAY " MY HUSBAND HAS NOT ROOM IN HIS	LIFE	FOR TWO WIVES: EITHER YOU GO OUT OF THE HOUSE OR I GO
PHIL II (107)	POOR PAPA. ALL THEY COULD DO WAS TO PROLONG HIS	LIFE	FOR TWO YEARS MORE BY PUTTING HIM ON A STRICT DIET,
BARB PREFACE(218)	OF THOSE WE ROB PREVENTS OUR HAVING THE GOOD	LIFE	FOR WHICH WE SACRIFICE THEM, RICH MEN OR ARISTOCRATS
MIS. PREFACE(49)	HAD TREATED ME AS AN EXPERIMENT OF THE	LIFE	FORCE: THAT IS, IF THEY HAD SET ME FREE TO DO AS I
LION PREFACE(89)	HEAVENLY FATHER AND BY US EVOLUTION, ELAN VITAL,	LIFE	FORCE AND OTHER NAMES; WHEN HE PROTESTED AGAINST THE
MIS. PREFACE(46)	BETTER THAN CHILDREN WHAT THE PURPOSES OF THE	LIFE	FORCE ARE, AND TREAT THE CHILD AS AN EXPERIMENT LIKE
MTH5 (231)	AND EARS, AND MADE A BRAIN. IT WOULDNT TAKE THE	LIFE	FORCE AT ALL UNTIL I HAD ALTERED ITS CONSTITUTION A
MTH5 (231)	WENT AHEAD. YOU SEE, THE LOWER POTENTIALS OF THE	LIFE	FORCE COULD MAKE MAGGOTS, BUT NOT HUMAN EYES OR EARS. I
MIS. PREFACE(3)	STUFF BY WHICH THE HUMAN RACE IS PERPETUATED. THE	LIFE	FORCE EITHER WILL NOT OR CANNOT ACHIEVE IMMORTALITY
SUPR IV (169)	HER IN HIS ARMS) IT IS FALSE: I LOVE YOU. THE	LIFE	FORCE ENCHANTS ME: I HAVE THE WHOLE WORLD IN MY ARMS
ROCK PREFACE(178)	FOR THE STRAIN OF IMPISHNESS WITH WHICH THE	LIFE	FORCE ENDOWS THOSE OF US WHO ARE DESTINED BY IT TO
SUPR IV (168)	OH, YOU ARE WITTY: AT THE SUPREME MOMENT THE	LIFE	FORCE ENDOWS YOU WITH EVERY QUALITY. WELL, I TOO CAN BE
SUPR III (134)	THE DEVIL/ OH, THE LATEST FASHION AMONG THE	LIFE	FORCE FANATICS. DID YOU NOT MEET IN HEAVEN, AMONG THE
MIS. PREFACE(49)	THE EXPERIMENT AND NOT THE SCHOOLMASTER; AND THE	LIFE	FORCE FOR THE CHILD'S PURPOSE IS IN THE CHILD AND NOT
BUOY IV (51)	MUST TAKE YOURSELF. /JUNIUS/ I MUST AGREE. THE	LIFE	FORCE HAS GOT ME. I CAN MAKE NO CONDITIONS. /OLD BILL/
SUPR III (131)	NEXT TERM OF BLESSEDNESS? GRANTED THAT THE GREAT	LIFE	FORCE HAS HIT ON THE DEVICE OF THE CLOCKMAKER'S
SUPR III (133)	AT LEAST I SHALL NOT BE BORED. THE SERVICE OF THE	LIFE	FORCE HAS THAT ADVANTAGE, AT ALL EVENTS. SO FARE YOU
MTH5 (230)	HIGH WHAT? /PYGMALION/ HIGH-PO-TENTIAL. THE	LIFE	FORCE IS NOT SO SIMPLE AS YOU THINK. A HIGH-POTENTIAL
SUPR III (111)	DONKEYS HAVE AMAZING LUCK. /DON JUAN/ WELL, THE	LIFE	FORCE IS STUPID; BUT IT IS NOT SO STUPID AS THE FORCES

MIS. PREFACE(11)	TO BE WRONG: THE CHILD FEELS THE DRIVE OF THE	LIFE	FORCE (OFTEN CALLED THE WILL OF GOD); AND YOU CANNOT
LION PREFACE(50)	AS A FAILURE, AND ARE CONVINCED THAT THE	LIFE	FORCE (OR WHATEVER YOU CHOOSE TO CALL IT) CANNOT BE
MTH5 (237)	PERSON OF THE KING AND ONE OF THE QUEEN; BUT THE	LIFE	FORCE OF THE KING AND QUEEN IS ALL ONE: THE GLORY
KING PREFACE(158)	GHOST OR THE LORD OF HOSTS AND DECHRISTEN IT AS A	LIFE	FORCE OR ELAN VITAL. AS THIS IS SHARED BY WOMEN AND
FABL PREFACE(74)	AS A CREATIVE EVOLUTIONIST, POSTULATE A CREATIVE	LIFE	FORCE OR EVOLUTIONARY APPETITE SEEKING POWER OVER
SUPR IV (168)	AN OLD MAID'S TEMPERAMENT. /TANNER/ BARREN. THE	LIFE	FORCE PASSES IT BY. /ANN/ IF THATS WHAT YOU MEAN BY THE
FABL PREFACE(66)	WRITING BY WHAT IS CALLED INSPIRATION; BUT AS THE	LIFE	FORCE PROCEEDS EXPERIMENTALLY BY TRIAL-AND-ERROR, AND
MTH5 (231)	ONLY TRYING TO MAKE YOU UNDERSTAND. THERE WAS THE	LIFE	FORCE RAGING ALL ROUND ME: THERE WAS I, TRYING TO MAKE
SUPR III (119)	MARRIED? LET US FACE THE FACTS, DEAR ANA. THE	LIFE	FORCE RESPECTS MARRIAGE ONLY BECAUSE MARRIAGE IS A
SUPR III (132)	IS IN THE GRIP OF THE LIFE FORCE. THIS	LIFE	FORCE SAYS TO HIM " I HAVE DONE A THOUSAND WONDERFUL
SUPR HANDBOK(192)	AN ATTITUDE OF DISGUST AND RESENTMENT TOWARDS THE	LIFE	FORCE THAT COULD ONLY ARISE IN A DISEASED AND MORIBUND
MIS. PREFACE(49)	I AM SORRY TO SEEM IRRECONCILABLE; BUT IT IS THE	LIFE	FORCE THAT HAS TO MAKE THE EXPERIMENT AND NOT THE
FABL PREFACE(80)	MY POSTULATE OF A PROVIDENT AND PURPOSEFUL	LIFE	FORCE THAT PROCEEDS BY TRIAL-AND-ERROR, AND MAKES
SUPR III (123)	OF THAT FECUNDITY FOR THE SAKE OF WHICH THE	LIFE	FORCE THROWS THEM INTO ONE ANOTHER'S ARMS AT THE
MIS. PREFACE(49)	GREAT RESEARCH WHICH IS BEING CONDUCTED BY THE	LIFE	FORCE TO DISCOVER THAT FORMULA. THE EXPERIMENT
SUPR III (132)	HAND GRASPS THE PLOUGH FOR ME, AND THIS" SAYS THE	LIFE	FORCE TO THE PHILOSOPHER " MUST THOU STRIVE TO DO FOR
MTH5 (231)	ME WHEN I TELL YOU THAT, EVEN IN MAN HIMSELF, THE	LIFE	FORCE USED TO SLIP SUDDENLY DOWN FROM ITS HUMAN LEVEL
BARB PREFACE(220)	SENSE THAT HE IS ONLY THE INSTRUMENT OF A WILL OR	LIFE	FORCE WHICH USES HIM FOR PURPOSES WIDER THAN HIS OWN,
SUPR III (134)	I HAD SOME HOPES OF HIM; BUT HE WAS A CONFIRMED	LIFE	FORCE WORSHIPPER. IT WAS HE WHO RAKED UP THE SUPERMAN,
SUPR III (135)	IT WAS NOT ABOUT MUSIC. WAGNER ONCE DRIFTED INTO	LIFE	FORCE WORSHIP, AND INVENTED A SUPERMAN CALLED
MTH5 (231)	HEAR, BECAUSE THEY WERE NOT SUSCEPTIBLE TO THE	LIFE	FORCE. BUT IT WAS FAR WORSE WHEN I DISCOVERED HOW TO
SUPR IV (167)	JACK, IF YOU DONT WANT TO MARRY ME? /TANNER/ THE	LIFE	FORCE. I AM IN THE GRIP OF THE LIFE FORCE. /ANN/ I DONT
MTH5 (230)	WAS THAT IT COULD NOT FIX AND CONDUCT THE	LIFE	FORCE. IT WAS LIKE A WOODEN MAGNET OR A LIGHTNING
MIS. PREFACE(3)	A FAILURE OF ENERGY ON THE PART OF THE	LIFE	FORCE. PEOPLE WITH NO IMAGINATION TRY TO MAKE THINGS
SUPR IV (167)	/TANNER/ THE LIFE FORCE. I AM IN THE GRIP OF THE	LIFE	FORCE. /ANN/ I DONT UNDERSTAND IN THE LEAST: IT SOUNDS
MTH5 (230)	PRODUCING ANYTHING THAT WOULD FIX HIGH-POTENTIAL	LIFE	FORCE. /ARJILLAX/ HIGH WHAT? /PYGMALION/
SUPR IV (168)	FROM OUR CHILDHOOD-- FOR BOTH OF US-- BY THE	LIFE	FORCE. /TANNER/ I WILL NOT MARRY YOU. I WILL NOT MARRY
MTH5 (237)	THOUGHT-OUT AND HAND-MADE TO RECEIVE THE SACRED	LIFE	FORCE. THERE IS ONE PERSON OF THE KING AND ONE OF THE
FABL VI (127)	ARE INCORRIGIBLE. THEY ARE OLD EXPERIMENTS OF THE	LIFE	FORCE. THEY WERE WELL INTENTIONED AND PERHAPS NECESSARY
SUPR III (132)	IS BECAUSE THE PHILOSOPHER IS IN THE GRIP OF THE	LIFE	FORCE. THIS LIFE FORCE SAYS TO HIM " I HAVE DONE A
METH PREFACE(R39)	OR PASSIONS," OR, AS WE SAY, AN ELAN VITAL OR	LIFE	FORCE. UNFORTUNATELY NEITHER PARENTS, PARSONS, NOR
MIS. PREFACE(11)	FANCY YOU ARE DEFEATING THE EXPERIMENT OF THE	LIFE	FORCE. YOU ARE ASSUMING THAT THE CHILD DOES NOT KNOW
DOCT PREFACE(33)	AND SINCE EVERYBODY, BY THE DEEPEST LAW OF THE	LIFE	FORCE, DESIRES TO BE GODLIKE, IT IS STUPID, AND INDEED
MTH5 (249)	ARTISTIC DOLLS AS THE NOBLEST PROJECTIONS OF THE	LIFE	FORCE, DO YOU NOT? /ECRASIA/ WITHOUT ART, THE
FABL PREFACE(66)	AND HIS UNIVERSAL SUBSTANCE, AS HE CALLED THE	LIFE	FORCE, INTO FABLES WHICH, HOWEVER FARFETCHED, CAN AT
FABL PREFACE(80)	BY THE OTHER? WHAT I, A FREETHINKER, CALL THE	LIFE	FORCE, MY PIOUS NEIGHBORS CALL DIVINE PROVIDENCE: IN
METH PREFACE(R73)	THE DISCOVERY OF EVOLUTION AS THE METHOD OF THE	LIFE	FORCE, THE RELIGION OF METAPHYSICAL VITALISM HAS BEEN
FABL PREFACE(66)	ARE IN ANY OTHER RESPECT SUPERIOR BEINGS. THE	LIFE	FORCE, WHEN IT GIVES SOME NEEDED EXTRAORDINARY QUALITY
FABL PREFACE(65)	DIVINE PROVIDENCE, PROVIDENCE, WHICH I CALL THE	LIFE	FORCE, WHEN NOT DEFEATED BY THE IMPERFECTION OF ITS
SUPR III (132)	GENTLEMAN; AND THAT IS ENOUGH FOR ME. AS TO YOUR	LIFE	FORCE, WHICH YOU THINK IRRESISTIBLE, IT IS THE MOST
FABL PREFACE(66)	PRESENT MYSELF THEREFORE AS AN INSTRUMENT OF THE	LIFE	FORCE, WRITING BY WHAT IS CALLED INSPIRATION; BUT AS
SUPR IV (168)	PASSES IT BY. /ANN/ IF THATS WHAT YOU MEAN BY THE	LIFE	FORCE, YES. /TANNER/ YOU DONT CARE FOR TAVY? /ANN/ (
SUPR III (138)	SHE IS A REGULAR SHERLOCK HOLMES. /TANNER/ THE	LIFE	FORCE! I AM LOST. /OCTAVIUS/ (BOUNDING GAILY DOWN
SUPR III (108)	CREATURES IN WHOM YOU DISCOVER WHAT YOU CALL A	LIFE	FORCE! /DON JUAN/ YES; FOR NOW COMES THE MOST
POSN (458)	DEAD! THE LITTLE JUDAS KID! THE CHILD I GAVE MY	LIFE	FOR! (HE BREAKS INTO HIDEOUS LAUGHTER). /THE SHERIFF/
ROCK PREFACE(150)	GUILLOTINED; AND EINSTEIN HAS HAD TO FLY FOR HIS	LIFE	FROM GERMANY. IT WAS SILLY TO SAY THAT THE REPUBLIC HAD
CLEO V (200)	NO. /RUFIO/ WHAT, THEN, WILL YOU DO TO SAVE YOUR	LIFE	FROM IT? /CAESAR/ (PROMPTLY) KILL IT, MAN, WITHOUT
MIS. PREFACE(91)	FIND POOR FAMILIES, CUT OFF BY POVERTY AND TOWN	LIFE	FROM THE CONTEMPLATION OF THE BEAUTY OF THE EARTH, WITH
GLIM (187)	BE A MAN AT LAST. I HAVE TASTED THE WATER OF	LIFE	FROM THE CUP OF DEATH; AND IT MAY BE NOW THAT MY REAL
MTH5 (261)	BETWEEN FLESH AND SPIRIT, AND DISENTANGLED THEIR	LIFE	FROM THE MATTER THAT HAS ALWAYS MOCKED IT. I CAN WAIT:
JITT III (62)	DESTINY, I SUPPOSE. /EDITH/ HE DID NOT FULFIL IT.	LIFE	FULFILS DESTINY, NOT DEATH. /FESSLER/ (PROSAICALLY)
BUOY II (23)	WE EAT. MAN IS STILL THE KILLER AND WOMAN THE	LIFE	GIVER. CAN YOU KILL OR NOT? /HE/ I CAN SHOOT A LITTLE.
MTH1 II (25)	WE ARE GODS, AND THAT THEY ARE HERE ONLY TO MAKE	LIFE	GLORIOUS FOR US? /ADAM/ (IMPRESSED) THAT IS A GREAT
JITT III (53)	CAN I? /FESSLER/ JUST SO. OF COURSE NOT. /AGNES/	LIFE	GOES ON, DOESNT IT? HOUSEKEEPING GOES ON: THE FUTURE
FABL III (111)	I MUST LIVE FROM HAND TO MOUTH. ALL THE JOY OF	LIFE	GOES WHEN YOU HAVE FIVE GUINEAS IN YOUR POCKET. /THE
HART II (120)	ALL MY LIFE LONG: THE HAPPINESS THAT COMES AS	LIFE	GOES, THE HAPPINESS OF YIELDING AND DREAMING INSTEAD OF
CAPT III (294)	EVENTS. /BRASSBOUND/ YES; BUT IT'S A PART OF MY	LIFE	GONE: YOUR DOING, REMEMBER. WHAT HAVE I LEFT? SEE
SUPR IV (167)	DONT UNDERSTAND IN THE LEAST: IT SOUNDS LIKE THE	LIFE	GUARDS. /TANNER/ WHY DONT YOU MARRY TAVY? HE IS
BUOY III (34)	MARRIED A VERY COMMON WOMAN. SHE HAD NEVER IN HER	LIFE	HAD A SATISFYING DINNER; AND SHE DIED OF OVEREATING
O'FL (227)	HAVE GOT AN ARMY WITHOUT CONSCRIPTION IF DOMESTIC	LIFE	HAD BEEN AS HAPPY AS PEOPLE SAY IT IS? /O'FLAHERTY/
PHIL I (88)	MODERN MOVEMENT WAS ABHORRENT TO YOU BECAUSE YOUR	LIFE	HAD BEEN PASSED IN WITNESSING SCENES OF SUFFERING NOBLY
MTH3 (121)	THEREABOUTS. THERE WAS ONLY ONE THING THAT MADE	LIFE	HARD; AND THAT IS GONE NOW. /CONFUCIUS/ MAY WE ASK WHAT
JITT II (36)	YOU ANGRY WITH ME? I REALLY MEANT WHAT I SAID.	LIFE	HAS A GREAT DEAL TO OFFER YOU: DONT FORGET THAT YOU ARE
SUPR II (70)	HENRY STRAKER: THE GOLDEN MOMENT OF YOUR	LIFE	HAS ARRIVED. /STRAKER/ WHAT D'Y'MEAN? /TANNER/ THAT
3PLA PREFACE(R31)	ALL IS VANITY! MOANS THE PREACHER, WHEN	LIFE	HAS AT LAST TAUGHT HIM THAT NATURE WILL NOT DANCE TO
MTH1 I (17)	UNCERTAIN? ANYTHING IS BETTER THAN UNCERTAINTY.	LIFE	HAS BECOME UNCERTAIN. LOVE IS UNCERTAIN. HAVE YOU A
ROCK I (230)	FUNNY TO ME IS THAT AS A MATTER OF FACT MY	LIFE	HAS BEEN A COMPLETELY INTELLECTUAL LIFE, AND MY
BULL IV (153)	VICE I DETEST-- OR AGAINST WHICH MY WHOLE PUBLIC	LIFE	HAS BEEN A PROTEST-- IT IS THE VICE OF HYPOCRISY. I
BULL I (90)	TO THE BIG POWERS. ALL THE SERIOUS PART OF MY	LIFE	HAS BEEN LIVED IN THAT ATMOSPHERE: ALL THE SERIOUS PART
2TRU PREFACE(12)	" LIBERTY: THOU CHOICEST TREASURE." THIS SORT OF	LIFE	HAS BEEN MADE POSSIBLE, AND INDEED INEVITABLE, BY WHAT
HART I (62)	LAROCHEJAQUELIN. A FRENCH FAMILY. A VICOMTE. HIS	LIFE	HAS BEEN ONE LONG ROMANCE. A TIGER-- /MRS HUSHABYE/
2TRU PREFACE(17)	WORKERS WITH WHOM THE POSTULANT'S DAILY	LIFE	HAS BEEN PASSED, THUS GIVING A GENUINE DEMOCRATIC BASIS
GENV IV (126)	TROUBLES AND SORROWS AND SINS TO BRING TO HIM. MY	LIFE	HAS BEEN SO HAPPY SINCE I FOUND HIM AND CAME TO HIM A
DOCT V (173)	BEEN FORTUNATE. /JENNIFER/ VERY FORTUNATE. HIS	LIFE	HAS BEEN SPARED. /RIDGEON/ I MEAN THAT HE HAS BEEN MADE
DOCT III (149)	YOU, SIR PATRICK (SHE SHAKES SIR PATRICK'S). OH,	LIFE	HAS BEEN WORTH LIVING SINCE I HAVE KNOWN YOU. SINCE
MRS I (187)	BROUGHT UP QUITE DIFFERENTLY. NOW YOUR MOTHER'S	LIFE	HAS BEEN-- ER-- I SUPPOSE YOU KNOW-- /VIVIE/ DONT
3PLA PREFACE(R18)	ON THE STAGE PRETENCE IS ALL THAT CAN EXIST.	LIFE	HAS ITS REALITIES BEHIND ITS SHOWS: THE THEATRE HAS
MTH5 (250)	I HAVE FOUND A HAPPINESS IN ART THAT REAL	LIFE	HAS NEVER GIVEN ME. I AM INTENSELY IN EARNEST ABOUT
SUPR III (112)	SO FAR, WILL YOU NOT AGREE WITH ME FURTHER THAT	LIFE	HAS NOT MEASURED THE SUCCESS OF ITS ATTEMPTS AT GODHEAD
FANY PROLOG (259)	NEVER HAD ANYTHING LESS THAN THE VERY BEST THAT	LIFE	HAS PRODUCED. IT IS MY GOOD FORTUNE TO HAVE A BEAUTIFUL
METH PREFACE(R31)	THE ORIGINAL SUBSTANCE FROM WHICH ALL FORMS OF	LIFE	HAVE DEVELOPED AS PROTOPLASM, OR, AS HE CALLED IT,
GETT (343)	YOU PROPHESY FALSELY, ANTHONY: NEVER IN ALL MY	LIFE	HAVE I DONE ANYTHING THAT WAS NOT ORDAINED FOR ME. (
MIS. PREFACE(81)	CHILD'S; FOR THE PARENTS WITH THEIR EXPERIENCE OF	LIFE	HAVE NONE OF THE ILLUSIONS ABOUT THE CHILD THAT THE
MTH4 II (190)	OF THEIR CLIMATE. BESIDES, SEVERAL CASES OF LONG	LIFE	HAVE OCCURRED IN NORTH AMERICA. THEY JOINED US HERE;
MILL I (142)	IT. MY FATHER WAS A GREAT MAN: EVERY DAY OF HIS	LIFE	HE DID THINGS THAT NOBODY ELSE EVER DREAMT OF DOING. I
GETT PREFACE(242)	SON'S PORTION, YET REPRESENTS THE ONLY HABIT OF	LIFE	HE HAS LEARNT. TAKING ALL THESE CASES AS REPRESENTING A
PYGM EPILOG (302)	STAMPED THE BUSINESS AS CLASSY; AND IN PRIVATE	LIFE	HE WAS STILL FREDERICK EYNSFORD HILL, ESQUIRE. NOT THAT
MRS II (209)	NOW THAT THE MEN ARE GONE) DID YOU EVER IN YOUR	LIFE	HEAR ANYONE RATTLE ON SO? ISNT HE A TEASE? (SHE SITS
MIS. (140)	/HYPATIA/ OH, LOTS. THATS PART OF THE ROUTINE OF	LIFE	HERE: THE VERY DULLEST PART OF IT. THE YOUNG MAN WHO
VWOO 3 (138)	PERMANENTLY. /Z/ TEN POUNDS EXTRA, TO STAY ALL MY	LIFE	HERE AS A SINGLE WOMAN! /A/ NOT NECESSARILY. YOU CAN
6CAL (94)	MONEY EXHAUSTED! DEATH, DISEASE, MUTINY, A DOG'S	LIFE	HERE IN THE FIELD WINTER AND SUMMER. THE BITCH'S
ROCK I (203)	NOR DO MY HAIR RIGHT NOR DRESS MYSELF RIGHT: MY	LIFE	HERE IS A HELL. /LADY CHAVENDER/ FLAVIA! ! /FLAVIA/ (
WIDO II (33)	FLOWERS. /COKANE/ CHARMED, MY DEAR SIR, CHARMED.	LIFE	HERE IS AN IDYLL-- A PERFECT IDYLL. WE WERE JUST
HART II (114)	ON THE BRIDGE FOR EIGHTEEN HOURS IN A TYPHOON.	LIFE	HERE IS STORMIER; BUT I CAN STAND IT. /ELLIE/ DO YOU
MIS. (199)	LET HIM STAY TO BREAKFAST. LET HIM SPEND HIS	LIFE	HERE. DONT YOU SAY I DROVE HIM OUT. DONT YOU SAY I
MTH5 (210)	YOU, BUT TOWARDS ALL THE TRIVIALITIES OF OUR	LIFE	HERE. JUST THINK, I HAVE HUNDREDS OF YEARS TO LIVE:
BUOY 1 (10)	AS A WORLD BETTERER I SHALL SPEND MOST OF MY	LIFE	HIDING FROM THEIR POLICE. AND I MAY FINISH ON THE
LION PROLOG (106)	FOR AFTERWARDS, PEOPLE SAY " POOR MAN! WHAT A	LIFE	HIS WIFE LEADS HIM! " OH, IF THEY ONLY KNEW! AND YOU
DOCT I (113)	ME THAT HIS LIFE IS MORE IMPORTANT THAN THE WORST	LIFE	I AM NOW SAVING. BUT YOU MUST CONVINCE ME FIRST. /MRS
LIED (193)	WHATS THE MATTER? /HE/ ONCE OR TWICE IN MY	LIFE	I HAVE DREAMED THAT I WAS EXQUISITELY HAPPY AND
2TRU II (65)	FOR THE SAME MAN CAN NEVER KEEP IT UP. IN ALL MY	LIFE	I HAVE KNOWN ONLY ONE MAN THAT KEPT IT UP TIL HE DIED.
MTH4 II (177)	ALWAYS BE AT ONE'S BEST. TWICE BEFORE IN MY	LIFE	I HAVE LOST MY NERVE AND BEHAVED LIKE A POLTROON. BUT I
GLIM (178)	WOULD YOU BE IF HE LEFT IT UNDONE? OUTSIDE THE	LIFE	I LEAD ALL TO MYSELF-- THE LIFE OF THOUGHT AND POETRY--
JOAN 5 (117)	JACK: YOU ARE RIGHT. I AM NOT WORTH ONE SOLDIER'S	LIFE	IF GOD LETS ME BE BEATEN; BUT FRANCE MAY THINK ME WORTH
LION PREFACE(67)	ON PAINTING POTBOILING NUDES TO THE END OF HIS	LIFE	IF HIS WIFE HAD NOT BEEN OF A HEROIC TURN HERSELF.
MILL I (154)	RISING) OH, THE DEEP END! THE DEEP END! WHAT IS	LIFE	IF IT IS NOT LIVED AT THE DEEP END? ALASTAIR: YOU ARE
MIS. (168)	AND SWEAR I NEVER SAW THAT FACE BEFORE IN MY	LIFE	IF IT WASNT FOR THAT BROOCH (POINTING TO THE

SUPR III (124)	IF SHE HAD ANY, OR TO UNDERTAKE HER SUPPORT FOR	LIFE	IF SHE HAD NOT; THAT I DESIRED HER CONTINUAL
SIM PREFACE(5)	WITH THE MOST DISGUSTING PENANCES IN A FUTURE	LIFE	IF THEY DID NOT LIVE ACCORDING TO HIS WORD, AND
VWOO 1 (117)	KNOW ABOUT ME? I WILL TELL YOU THE WHOLE OF MY	LIFE	IF YOU LIKE, /A/ GREAT HEAVENS, NO, PLEASE DONT. /Z/
MTH2 (44)	BUT YOU KNOW YOU COULD LIVE A DEVIL OF A LONG	LIFE	IF YOU REALLY WANTED TO. /THE PARLOR MAID/ (SITTING
LADY PREFACE(234)	THE EVIDENT FACT THAT SHAKESPEAR DID NOT END HIS	LIFE	IN A GLOW OF ENTHUSIASTIC SATISFACTION WITH MANKIND AND
SIM I (42)	WITH US, YOUNG PILGRIM? /MAYA/ WE ARE WAVES OF	LIFE	IN A SEA OF BLISS. DARE YOU BREAST THEM, YOUNG
6CAL PREFACE(90)	WANTS TO MAKE IT SALACIOUS. ALL INTERPRETERS OF	LIFE	IN ACTION, NOBLE OR IGNOBLE, FIND THEIR INSTRUMENT IN
SIM PREFACE(4)	ENOUGH TO ATTRACT A WIFE. LIVINGSTONE RISKED HIS	LIFE	IN AFRICA EVERY DAY TO SAVE A BLACK MAN'S SOUL.
BULL PREFACE(60)	HE ADDS, " PASSED NEARLY THIRTY YEARS OF MY	LIFE	IN AN EARNEST ENDEAVOUR TO RAISE THE MORAL AND MATERIAL
NEVR I (205)	YOU ARE NEITHER OF YOU CAPABLE OF CONCEIVING WHAT	LIFE	IN AN ENGLISH SEASIDE RESORT IS. BELIEVE ME, IT'S NOT A
DOCT PREFACE(70)	IS NOT IN THIS POSITION: HE IS STRUGGLING FOR	LIFE	IN AN OVERCROWDED PROFESSION, AND KNOWS WELL THAT " A
ROCK PREFACE(167)	MECHANIZED FARMERS AND TO LIVE A COLLEGIATE	LIFE	IN CULTIVATED SOCIETY. IT SOUNDS SIMPLE; BUT THE
3PLA PREFACE(R31)	WRITERS WHO, HAVING TO CHOOSE BETWEEN GIVING UP	LIFE	IN DESPAIR AND DISCARDING THE TRUMPERY MORAL KITCHEN
BULL PREFACE(60)	EXTENT TO WHICH, AFTER THIRTY YEARS OF OFFICIAL	LIFE	IN EGYPT, ONE LOSES THE PLAIN SENSE OF ENGLISH WORDS.
DOCT I SD(87)	OF SPEECH, ARE IRISH; BUT HE HAS LIVED ALL HIS	LIFE	IN ENGLAND AND IS THOROUGHLY ACCLIMATIZED. HIS MANNER
BARB III (319)	BE GENEROUS. BESIDES, I OWE YOU A FAIR START IN	LIFE	IN EXCHANGE FOR DISINHERITING YOU. YOU CANT BECOME
POSN (446)	SNIVEL AT ME IN WHITE SURPLICES AND OFFER ME MY	LIFE	IN EXCHANGE FOR AN UMBLE AND A CONTRITE HEART. /ELDER
MRS IV (251)	TO GIVE YOU THE PEACE AND QUIETNESS OF MY WHOLE	LIFE	IN EXCHANGE FOR THEM, WHAT USE WOULD MY COMPANY BE TO
JITT I (14)	MERE SHELLS OF THEIR FORMER SELVES: GOING THROUGH	LIFE	IN GROOVES, ON RAILS LIKE TRAMCARS, ENVYING THE TINKERS
2TRU I (48)	FOR WORRYING HER TO DEATH THE INNERMOST UPPERMOST	LIFE	IN HER RISES LIKE MILK IN A BOILING SAUCEPAN AND CRIES
MIS. (161)	HER LIFE IS IN YOUR HANDS EVERY NIGHT AND YOUR	LIFE	IN HERS. /TARLETON/ LINA: I'M GOING TO MAKE A FOOL OF
BUOY 1 (13)	ONLY TO CRUCIFY THEM. THE RIGHTEOUS MAN TAKES HIS	LIFE	IN HIS HAND WHENEVER HE UTTERS THE TRUTH. CHARLEMAGNE,
JOAN 1 (67)	IS ON YOUR SIDE, AND YOU ARE WILLING TO PUT YOUR	LIFE	IN HIS HAND. BUT MANY SOLDIERS ARE VERY SIMPLE.
CLEO III (162)	THAT TRUMPET SOUNDS, WE MUST TAKE EVERY MAN HIS	LIFE	IN HIS HAND, AND THROW IT IN THE FACE OF DEATH. AND OF
FANY PROLOG (258)	ENGLISHMAN: MY FAMILY IS IRISH: IVE LIVED ALL MY	LIFE	IN ITALY-- IN VENICE MOSTLY-- MY VERY TITLE IS A
SUPR III (104)	NO OTHER JOY. BUT THERE IS THE WORK OF HELPING	LIFE	IN ITS STRUGGLE UPWARD. THINK OF HOW IT WASTES AND
UNPL PREFACE(R11)	LET ME EXPLAIN. ONE OF THE WORST PRIVATIONS OF	LIFE	IN LONDON FOR PERSONS OF SERIOUS INTELLECTUAL AND
BULL IV (170)	AND REAL JOYS AMONG REAL PEOPLE: SOLID ENGLISH	LIFE	IN LONDON, THE VERY CENTRE OF THE WORLD. YOU WILL FIND
HART II (119)	DANGER, HORROR, AND DEATH, THAT I MIGHT FEEL THE	LIFE	IN ME MORE INTENSELY. I DID NOT LET THE FEAR OF DEATH
SUPR HANDBOK(206)	WHO, TO HIS OWN LOSS, WILL SHORTEN HIS HORSE'S	LIFE	IN MERE STINGINESS. WE HAVE THE TRAMWAY COMPANY WHICH
MTH1 I (8)	I FOUND A WAY OF GATHERING TOGETHER A PART OF THE	LIFE	IN MY BODY. /EVE/ WHAT IS THE LIFE? /THE SERPENT/ THAT
MTH1 I (8)	HAVE DONE. /THE SERPENT/ I GATHERED A PART OF THE	LIFE	IN MY BODY, AND SHUT IT INTO A TINY WHITE CASE MADE OF
POSN (444)	I HAD NO USE FOR HIM-- BECAUSE I LIVED MY OWN	LIFE	IN MY OWN WAY, AND WOULD HAVE NO TRUCK WITH HIS " DONT
ROCK PREFACE(178)	AND POLITICAL, AND JESUS, WHO HAD SPENT HIS	LIFE	IN PROPOUNDING THE MOST STAGGERING PARADOXES ON THE
CLEO III (157)	YOU HAVE ME WASTE THE NEXT THREE YEARS OF MY	LIFE	IN PROSCRIBING AND CONDEMNING MEN WHO WILL BE MY
BASH II,1, (107)	THE INATTENTIVE FATES THAT WEAVE MY THREAD OF	LIFE	IN RUDER PATTERNS THAN THESE THAT LIE, ANTIMACASSARLY,
MRS IV (242)	I HAD THE COURAGE I SHOULD SPEND THE REST OF MY	LIFE	IN TELLING EVERYBODY-- STAMPING AND BRANDING IT INTO
BARB PREFACE(244)	ANARCHIST WHO IS PREPARED TO SACRIFICE HIS OWN	LIFE	IN THE BATTLE WITH IT. OUR NATURAL SAFETY FROM THE
ARMS II (32)	/RAINA/ (RISING WITH MARKED STATELINESS) YOUR	LIFE	IN THE CAMP HAS MADE YOU COARSE, SERGIUS. I DID NOT
LION PREFACE(38)	A PREACHER WHO SPENT PRACTICALLY HIS WHOLE ADULT	LIFE	IN THE CAPITAL, WITH OCCASIONAL VISITS TO THE
MTH4 II (181)	A STEP) PARDON ME, MADAM. I NEVER TRUST MY	LIFE	IN THE HANDS OF A PERSON OVER WHOM I HAVE NO CONTROL.
JITT I (15)	AND TERRIBLE. BUT THEY HAVE BEEN REAL, REAL.	LIFE	IN THE NET IS NEVER REAL: IT IS ALL ACTING. /BRUNO/
PRES (149)	/MITCHENER/ STUFF, SIR. IT'S THE EASIEST	LIFE	IN THE WORLD. ONCE YOU LEARN YOUR DRILL, ALL YOU HAVE
MTH5 (251)	I SMASHED THEM WHEN I SAW THAT THERE WAS NO	LIFE	IN THEM: THAT THEY WERE SO DEAD THAT THEY WOULD NOT
2TRU PREFACE(19)	PIOUS DUTY TO BE ROBBED, AND THAT THEIR MOMENT OF	LIFE	IN THIS WORLD IS ONLY A PRELUDE TO AN ETERNITY IN WHICH
NEVR I (211)	ACRIMONY) THERE IS ANOTHER SORT OF FAMILY LIFE: A	LIFE	IN WHICH HUSBANDS OPEN THEIR WIVES' LETTERS, AND CALL
MTH1 II (29)	AND IDLE, CAIN, I KNOW. /CAIN/ SELFISH, YES: A	LIFE	IN WHICH NO MAN IS HIS BROTHER'S KEEPER, BECAUSE HIS
BARB PREFACE(233)	BOTH ARE CIRCUMSTANTIAL. TAKE ANY CONDITION OF	LIFE	IN WHICH THE CIRCUMSTANCES ARE FOR A MASS OF MEN
SUPR PREFACE(R18)	TO FACE A TRUMPERY STORY OF MODERN LONDON LIFE, A	LIFE	IN WHICH, AS YOU KNOW, THE ORDINARY MAN'S MAIN BUSINESS
MIS. (143)	WORN OUT: THATS QUITE DIFFERENT. AND YOUVE SOME	LIFE	IN YOU YET OR YOU WOULDNT HAVE FALLEN IN LOVE WITH ME.
MTH5 (254)	AND SENSES HAD OVERLAID THE DIRECT IMPULSE OF	LIFE	IN YOU. AND BECAUSE I CARED ONLY FOR OUR LIFE, AND WENT
MTH1 II (22)	DESPAIR! THE SHRIEKS OF TORMENT! THAT WILL BE	LIFE	INDEED: LIFE LIVED TO THE VERY MARROW: BURNING,
FANY PROLOG (272)	" THE ICE OF LIFE IS SLIPPERY." /TROTTER/ ICE OF	LIFE	INDEED! YOU SHOULD BE EATING PENNY ICES AND ENJOYING
BULL IV (178)	SENTIMENT, AFTER ALL? MR BROADBENT SPENDS HIS	LIFE	INEFFICIENTLY ADMIRING THE THOUGHTS OF GREAT MEN, AND
MTH5 (218)	OF INFINITE CAPACITY, YOU WILL NO DOUBT FIND	LIFE	INFINITELY INTERESTING. HOWEVER, ALL YOU HAVE TO DO NOW
MTH1 II (28)	DEATH: THAT IT IS THE GATE OF ANOTHER LIFE: A	LIFE	INFINITELY SPLENDID AND INTENSE: A LIFE OF THE SOUL
HART III (142)	CRIMSON DRESSING-GOWN AT DINNER. YOU COMPLICATE	LIFE	INSTEAD OF SIMPLIFYING IT BY DOING THESE RIDICULOUS
SUPR IV (163)	MARRY SOMEBODY. /TANNER/ AHA! THERE SPEAKS THE	LIFE	INSTINCT. YOU DETEST HER; BUT YOU FEEL THAT YOU MUST
LION I (117)	THINK I AM ONLY RUNNING AWAY FROM THE TERRORS OF	LIFE	INTO THE COMFORT OF HEAVEN? IF THERE WERE NO FUTURE,
CAPT I (238)	FROM BRASSBOUND CUTS HIM SHORT. HE FLIES FOR HIS	LIFE	INTO THE HOUSE, FOLLOWED BY THE ITALIAN). /BRASSBOUND/
MTH5 (262)	NOT SPARE THEM FOR EVER. I AM LILITH: I BROUGHT	LIFE	INTO THE WHIRLPOOL OF FORCE, AND COMPELLED MY ENEMY,
MTH5 (242)	LET US SEE WHETHER WE CANNOT PUT A LITTLE MORE	LIFE	INTO THEM. (HE TAKES THE MALE FIGURE BY THE HAND, AND
BARB II (274)	OR TWO)-- YES: INTELLIGENT BEYOND THE STATION O	LIFE	INTO WHICH IT HAS PLEASED THE CAPITALISTS TO CALL ME;
MIS. (171)	IT: IVE NO BUSINESS TO DO. DO YOU KNOW WHAT MY	LIFE	IS? I SPEND MY DAYS FROM NINE TO SIX-- NINE HOURS OF
MTH2 (59)	WE ARE AT A CRISIS-- /LUBIN/ MY DEAR BURGE,	LIFE	IS A DISEASE; AND THE ONLY DIFFERENCE BETWEEN ONE MAN
SUPR III (112)	IS ONLY A STEP AHEAD OF YOU. ARE WE AGREED THAT	LIFE	IS A FORCE WHICH HAS MADE INNUMERABLE EXPERIMENTS IN
GETT PREFACE(236)	BE GRATIFIED. ALSO WHETHER HE CAN PROVE THAT HIS	LIFE	IS A PLEASURE TO HIMSELF OR A BENEFIT TO ANYONE ELSE,
NEVR I (212)	AND RELIGION ARE DETESTABLE TYRANNIES, AND	LIFE	IS A VULGAR ROUND OF PUNISHMENTS AND LIES, COERCION AND
ARMS III (70)	SWISS SOLDIER WHO HARDLY KNOWS WHAT A DECENT	LIFE	IS AFTER FIFTEEN YEARS OF BARRACKS AND BATTLES: A
BARB III (348)	SIDE OF LIFE. /BARBARA/ THERE IS NO WICKED SIDE:	LIFE	IS ALL ONE. AND I NEVER WANTED TO SHIRK MY SHARE IN
METH PREFACE(R59)	FOR THIS SENSE OF THE KINSHIP OF ALL FORMS OF	LIFE	IS ALL THAT IS NEEDED TO MAKE EVOLUTION NOT ONLY A
GETT (264)	WHAT FREEDOM IS TO SOME PEOPLE. YOU SEE, FAMILY	LIFE	IS ALL THE LIFE SHE KNOWS: SHE'S LIKE A BIRD BORN IN A
GETT PREFACE(196)	ALTOGETHER GOOD FOR A BOY ANY MORE THAN BARRACK	LIFE	IS ALTOGETHER GOOD FOR A SOLDIER. BUT NEITHER IS HOME
BULL PREFACE(43)	OF THE BOOK OF ECCLESIASTES TO SCHOPENHAUER, THAT	LIFE	IS AN EVIL. HE IS ASSERTING A NATURAL RIGHT TO LIVE.
JITT I (14)	(ALSO MARRIED); BUT TO HER LOVER AND HERSELF HER	LIFE	IS AS DIGNIFIED AND BEAUTIFUL AS HER FACE, AND THEIR
DEVL II SD(28)	WHO IS A TOWER OF STRENGTH TO HER: IN SHORT, THAT	LIFE	IS AS EASY AT THE MINISTER'S HOUSE AS IT IS HARD AT THE
DOCT III (152)	DINED WITH US: AN EXCELLENT AND HONEST MAN, WHOSE	LIFE	IS AS VALUABLE AS ANYONE ELSE'S, I HAVE ARRANGED THAT I
METH PREFACE(R65)	NOBODY IS AT HEART FOOL ENOUGH TO BELIEVE THAT	LIFE	IS AT THE MERCY OF TEMPERATURE: DANTE WAS NOT TROUBLED
DOCT I (113)	PEOPLE LIKE THEM. HE IS TWENTY-THREE: HIS WHOLE	LIFE	IS BEFORE HIM. WONT YOU LET ME BRING HIM TO YOU? WONT
MTH3 (119)	AS COOK DID; BUT THAT WAS INFLUENZA. LONG	LIFE	IS COMPLICATED, AND EVEN TERRIBLE; BUT IT IS GLORIOUS
METH PREFACE(R29)	ONE, OR, TO PUT IT LESS DRILY, THAT HUMAN	LIFE	IS CONTINUOUS AND IMMORTAL. THE EVOLUTIONISTS TOOK
CLEO NOTES (207)	SIECLE NEGRO. FINALLY, I WOULD POINT OUT THAT IF	LIFE	IS CROWNED BY ITS SUCCESS AND DEVOTION IN INDUSTRIAL
3PLA PREFACE(R17)	EXPOSURE OF THE WORTHLESSNESS AND MEANNESS OF HER	LIFE	IS CRUEL AND BLASPHEMOUS TO YOU, THIS POINT OF VIEW IS
BULL I (86)	NO, NO: THE CLIMATE IS DIFFERENT. HERE, IF THE	LIFE	IS DULL, YOU CAN BE DULL TOO, AND NO GREAT HARM DONE. (
CYMB V (141)	SO I'LL DIE FOR THEE, O IMOGEN, EVEN FOR WHOM MY	LIFE	IS EVERY BREATH A DEATH; AND THUS UNKNOWN, PITIED NOR
LION PREFACE(58)	OR LIVE A HIGHER LIFE THAN THAT OF A MOLE, WHOSE	LIFE	IS FROM BEGINNING TO END A FRENZIED PURSUIT OF FOOD.
MTH5 (246)	ONCE INHABITED BY OZYMANDIASES AND CLEOPATRAS.	LIFE	IS HARD ENOUGH FOR US AS IT IS. /THE HE-ANCIENT/ LIFE
CATH 1 (163)	YOU DOG. YOU LIE. /THE SERGEANT/ LITTLE FATHER:	LIFE	IS HARD FOR THE POOR. IF YOU SAY IT IS A LIE, IT IS A
SUPR HANDBOK(208)	THE EXCITEMENT OF WAR AND CRIME, YET HIS NORMAL	LIFE	IS HIGHER THAN THE NORMAL LIFE OF HIS FOREFATHERS. THIS
BULL IV (181)	AND ONE IN THREE. IT IS A GODHEAD IN WHICH ALL	LIFE	IS HUMAN AND ALL HUMANITY DIVINE: THREE IN ONE AND ONE
2TRU PREFACE(10)	A REVOLUTIONIST IT IS NOT BECAUSE COUNTRYHOUSE	LIFE	IS IDLE, BUT BECAUSE ITS ACTIVITIES ARE UNCONGENIAL AND
KING I (189)	MIGHT BE EXERCISED THERE AND NOT HERE. YOUR	LIFE	IS IN DANGER IN LONDON. YOU HAD NO BUSINESS TO COME
GENV IV (108)	ON WHICH THE ROMAN SOUL STANDS FIRM. THE WOMAN'S	LIFE	IS IN HER OWN HANDS. /BATTLER/ NO: I TELL YOU I CANNOT
CAPT II (265)	THREAT? QUICK. TIME PRESSES. /SIR HOWARD/ MY	LIFE	IS IN THE HANDS OF PROVIDENCE. DO YOUR WORST.
DOCT III (145)	PRETEND TO BE ABLE TO CURE YOUR COMPLAINT. YOUR	LIFE	IS IN THE HANDS OF THESE GENTLEMEN. /RIDGEON/ NOT IN
6CAL (104)	MAD, MASTER BURGESS? DO YOU NOT KNOW THAT YOUR	LIFE	IS IN THE KING'S HAND? DO YOU EXPECT ME TO RECOMMEND
MIS. (161)	TRAPEZE THERE IS OFTEN ANOTHER WOMAN; AND HER	LIFE	IS IN YOUR HANDS EVERY NIGHT AND YOUR LIFE IN HERS.
MTH4 I (171)	KNOW WHAT TO DO WITH. /ZOO/ DADDY: THE MAN WHOSE	LIFE	IS LENGTHENED IN THIS WAY MAY BE BUSIER THAN A SAVAGE;
GETT PREFACE(223)	ON THE MORE SORDID CALCULATION THAT BACHELOR	LIFE	IS LESS COMFORTABLE AND MORE EXPENSIVE, SINCE A WIFE
SUPR IV (161)	PROFESSOR TYNDALL MADE AT BELFAST. /TANNER/ YES:	LIFE	IS MORE COMPLICATED THAN WE USED TO THINK. BUT WHAT AM
DOCT I (113)	WILL DO IT AGAIN IF YOU CAN CONVINCE ME THAT HIS	LIFE	IS MORE IMPORTANT THAN THE WORST LIFE I AM NOW SAVING.
CAND III (145)	/MARCHBANKS/ I NO LONGER DESIRE HAPPINESS:	LIFE	IS NOBLER THAN THAT. PARSON JAMES: I GIVE YOU MY
KING II (230)	TO BE LEARNT AT COURT EXCEPT THAT A COURTIER'S	LIFE	IS NOT A HAPPY ONE. THE GARDENERS AND THE WATERMEN, THE
SUPR I (30)	TO BEAR IT FOR ALL OUR SAKES. /RAMSDEN/	LIFE	IS NOT ALL PLAYS AND POEMS, OCTAVIUS. COME! FACE IT
MTH5 (217)	WITH ANYTHING WRONG DO NOT LIVE HERE, MY CHILD.	LIFE	IS NOT CHEAP WITH US. BUT YOU WOULD NOT HAVE FELT
MTH5 (246)	IS HARD ENOUGH FOR US AS IT IS. /THE HE-ANCIENT/	LIFE	IS NOT MEANT TO BE EASY, MY CHILD; BUT TAKE COURAGE: IT
OVER PREFACE(159)	WHO ARE RASH ENOUGH TO ADMIT THAT THEIR WHOLE	LIFE	IS NOT ONE CONSTANT PREOCCUPATION WITH ADORED MEMBERS

PYGM EPILOG (293)	GOOD FOR THEM. THEY MAY FAIL IN EMERGENCIES; BUT	LIFE	IS NOT ONE LONG EMERGENCY: IT IS MOSTLY A STRING OF
MTH5 (211)	/THE MAIDEN/ OH, DONT TALK TO ME OF COMFORT!	LIFE	IS NOT WORTH LIVING IF YOU HAVE TO BOTHER ABOUT
METH PREFACE(R72)	AND VITALISTS. THE MECHANISTS SAID THAT	LIFE	IS NOTHING BUT PHYSICAL AND CHEMICAL ACTION; THAT THEY
JOAN 6 (145)	LIED (INDIGNANT EXCLAMATIONS). YOU THINK THAT	LIFE	IS NOTHING BUT NOT BEING STONE DEAD. IT IS NOT THE
MILL I (141)	YOU ARE A BRUTE, A BEAST, AND A PIG. MY	LIFE	IS NOTHING TO YOU: YOU DO NOT EVEN ASK WHAT HAS DRIVEN
GLIM (188)	TO YOUR EXCELLENCY. /FERRUCCIO/ AS YOU PLEASE. MY	LIFE	IS ONLY A DROP FALLING FROM THE VANISHING CLOUDS TO THE
JITT II (48)	IS MINE: I WILL PAY THE PENALTY BY MYSELF. YOUR	LIFE	IS ONLY BEGINNING: WITH THAT BOOK YOU HAVE A FUTURE. I
MTH3 (111)	ARCHBISHOP/ NOT QUITE THAT. MY EXPECTATION OF	LIFE	IS ONLY THREE HUNDRED YEARS. /BARNABAS/ YOU WILL LAST
JOAN EPILOG (153)	FROM THE SMIRCH OF THE BURNING FAGGOTS; THE HOLY	LIFE	IS SANCTIFIED; THE TRUE HEART THAT LIVED THROUGH THE
APPL PREFACE(183)	AND COMMUNISM. OUR INDUSTRIAL AND SOCIAL	LIFE	IS SET IN A HUGE COMMUNISTIC FRAMEWORK OF PUBLIC
MTH3 (129)	DEMONSTRATING THAT THE TRUE EXPECTATION OF HUMAN	LIFE	IS SEVENTY-EIGHT POINT SIX. AND I WILL RESIST ANY
JITT III (64)	HOW LONG THIS MOOD OF YOURS WILL LAST. /EDITH/	LIFE	IS SHORT: DONT WASTE ANY MORE OF YOURS ON ME. I SHALL
DOCT PREFACE(42)	WHOM IT IS NOT AT ALL NATURAL BUT WHOSE RULE OF	LIFE	IS SIMPLY TO DO ONLY WHAT EVERYBODY ELSE DOES, AND WHO
FANY PROLOG (272)	/FANNY/ THATS NOT ALL. IT GOES ON, " THE ICE OF	LIFE	IS SLIPPERY." /TROTTER/ ICE OF LIFE INDEED! YOU SHOULD
HART I (63)	ONE HAD AN INTERESTING BOOK TO READ, BECAUSE	LIFE	IS SO MUCH HAPPIER THAN ANY BOOK! NO DESIRE BUT TO BE
ARMS I (5)	WITH THE OPERA THAT SEASON AT BUCHAREST. REAL	LIFE	IS SO SELDOM LIKE THAT! INDEED NEVER, AS FAR AS I KNEW
MTH1 II (34)	ON HIS HANDS, AND TAKES UP THE SPADE AGAIN).	LIFE	IS STILL LONG ENOUGH TO LEARN TO DIG, SHORT AS THEY ARE
SUPR PREFACE(R35)	YOU HAPPY, AND ALSO THE ONLY REAL TRAGEDY IN	LIFE	IS THE BEING USED BY PERSONALLY MINDED MEN FOR PURPOSES
MTH1 I (8)	A BEAUTIFUL WORD! AND WHAT A WONDERFUL THING!	LIFE	IS THE LOVELIEST OF ALL THE NEW WORDS. /THE SERPENT/
METH PREFACE(R28)	WITH HIS LITTLE LATIN AND LESS GREEK; AND PUBLIC	LIFE	IS THE PARADISE OF VOLUBLE WINDBAGS. ALL THESE
MTH4 II (180)	THE ONLY THING THAT MATTERS: THE VALUE OF HUMAN	LIFE	IS THE VALUE OF THE GREATEST LIVING MAN. CUT OFF THAT
MTH5 (255)	YOU OLD PEOPLE ARE. VORTICISTS. /ACIS/ BUT IF	LIFE	IS THOUGHT, CAN YOU LIVE WITHOUT A HEAD? /THE
METH PREFACE(R27)	OF IT IS UNENDURABLE BY MEN WHOSE SPAN OF	LIFE	IS THREE-SCORE-AND-TEN. IT WIDENED HUMAN POSSIBILITIES
CAPT II (257)	LAWYER! EVEN THE PRICE YOU OFFER FOR YOUR	LIFE	IS TO BE PAID IN FALSE COIN. (CALLING) HALLO THERE!
CATH 1 (172)	THE TABLE AND PUTTING IT ON) THE GREAT THING IN	LIFE	IS TO BE SIMPLE; AND THE PERFECTLY SIMPLE THING IS TO
SUPR III SD(72)	ENTITLED. FURTHER, THE IMAGINATIVE MAN, IF HIS	LIFE	IS TO BE TOLERABLE TO HIM, MUST HAVE LEISURE TO TELL
LION PREFACE(72)	WITH BOTH THE CONTEMPLATIVE AND ADVENTUROUS	LIFE	IS TO DISGRACE IT SO VITALLY THAT ALL THE MORALIZINGS
GENV PREFACE(24)	AND DISCIPLINE, AND A DENSE IGNORANCE OF WHAT	LIFE	IS TO NINE TENTHS OF THEIR COMPATRIOTS. " GREAT MEN."
SUPR I (38)	LEAVE. I KNOW A POOR WRETCH WHOSE ONE DESIRE IN	LIFE	IS TO RUN AWAY FROM HIS WIFE. SHE PREVENTS HIM BY
MTH5 (243)	(SINKING TO THE GROUND) I AM DISCOURAGED.	LIFE	IS TOO HEAVY A BURDEN. /THE FEMALE FIGURE/ (
MTH4 I (167)	PURE FICTION. /ZOO/ NOT HERE, DADDY. WITH US	LIFE	IS TOO LONG FOR TELLING LIES. THEY ALL GET FOUND OUT.
MTH1 II (31)	OF IT TO ENDURE. /CAIN/ POOR MOTHER! YOU SEE,	LIFE	IS TOO LONG. ONE TIRES OF EVERYTHING. THERE IS NOTHING
MTH2 (39)	AGAIN! YOU SEE, CON. IT WILL LAST HIS TIME.	LIFE	IS TOO SHORT FOR MEN TO TAKE IT SERIOUSLY. /HASLAM/
MTH4 II (190)	CIRCLES, IN WHICH THE PRIVACY OF PRIVATE	LIFE	IS VERY JEALOUSLY GUARDED, AND IN WHICH NO ONE PRESUMES
2TRU III (103)	WOULD GIVE THE CHILDREN A ONE-SIDED VIEW OF LIFE.	LIFE	IS VERY MIXED, SIR: IT IS NOT ALL PIETY AND IT IS NOT
MRS IV (239)	THERE IS NO BEAUTY AND NO ROMANCE IN LIFE FOR ME.	LIFE	IS WHAT IT IS; AND I AM PREPARED TO TAKE IT AS IT IS.
SIM II (85)	PROLA WITH STAGE THUNDER. THE FOUNTAIN OF	LIFE	IS WITHIN ME. /PRA/ BUT YOU HAVE GIVEN THE KEY OF IT TO
MTH3 (122)	WHICH WE LIVE FOR THE FIRST HUNDRED YEARS OF OUR	LIFE	IS WORSE IN THIS MATTER OF SEX THAN IN ANY OTHER. YOU
BUOY 1 (15)	MORE INTERESTING, NO MORE DOUBT AS TO WHETHER	LIFE	IS WORTH LIVING. THEN THE WORLD BETTERERS WILL COME TO
DEVL II (34)	LOSS, MINISTER? /ANDERSON/ I THINK THAT A MAN'S	LIFE	IS WORTH SAVING, WHOEVER IT BELONGS TO. (RICHARD MAKES
BULL PREFACE(64)	HONOR IS WORTH ITS DANGER AND ITS COST, AND THAT	LIFE	IS WORTHLESS WITHOUT HONOR? IT IS TRUE THAT SIR JOHN
MILL I (141)	HAS IT EVER OCCURRED TO YOU THAT WHEN A WOMAN'S	LIFE	IS WRECKED SHE NEEDS A LITTLE SYMPATHY AND NOT A BOTTLE
ARMS III (64)	PSHA! /BLUNTSCHLI/ BUT NOW THAT YOUVE FOUND THAT	LIFE	ISNT A FARCE, BUT SOMETHING QUITE SENSIBLE AND SERIOUS,
PHIL I (90)	CHARTERIS, THIS IS DEVILISH AWKWARD: UPON MY	LIFE	IT IS, THAT WAS A MOST INDELICATE THING OF YOU TO SAY
BARB PREFACE(220)	CURSE ONLY IN SUCH FOOLISH SOCIAL CONDITIONS THAT	LIFE	ITSELF IS A CURSE, FOR THE TWO THINGS ARE INSEPARABLE:
LION PREFACE(44)	WE CANNOT EXPLAIN, SURROUND US ON EVERY HAND:	LIFE	ITSELF IS THE MIRACLE OF MIRACLES. MIRACLES IN THE
PHIL PREFACE(68)	IT WAS WRITTEN, NOT ONLY DRAMATIC LITERATURE BUT	LIFE	ITSELF WAS STAGGERING FROM THE IMPACT OF IBSEN'S PLAYS,
SUPR I SD(16)	BLOOD INTO RAPTUROUS RIVERS OF THE VERY WATER OF	LIFE	ITSELF, THE REVELATION OF ALL THE MYSTERIES AND THE
PLES PREFACE(R8)	MAY BE RECONCILIATION OR DESTRUCTION; OR, AS IN	LIFE	ITSELF, THERE MAY BE NO END; BUT THE CONFLICT IS
MIS. (150)	STAY TO DINNER. STAY OVER THE WEEK-END. ALL MY	LIFE	IVE WANTED TO FLY. /THE AVIATOR/ (TAKING OFF HIS
MIS. PREFACE(108)	OF AN IMMEDIATELY QUIET AND FINALLY DISASTROUS	LIFE	.
SUPR HANDBOOK(222)	IT IN ANGER, EVEN AT THE RISK OF MAIMING IT FOR	LIFE	. A BLOW IN COLD BLOOD NEITHER CAN NOR SHOULD BE
METH PREFACE(R57)	OUR IMPULSES TOWARDS JUSTICE, MERCY, AND A HIGHER	LIFE	. A COMPLETE DELIVERANCE WAS OFFERED BY THE DISCOVERY
2TRU PREFACE(6)	ENOUGH TO PAY FOR THE NECESSITIES OF A CULTIVATED	LIFE	. A HUNDRED YEARS AGO SAMUEL WARREN WROTE A FAMOUS
GETT PREFACE(199)	MAINTAINED AT THE SAME PITCH CONTINUOUSLY THROUGH	LIFE	. A LIFE SPENT IN PRAYER AND ALMSGIVING IS REALLY AS
MTH5 (225)	WHY? /MARTELLUS/ BECAUSE YOU CANNOT GIVE THEM	LIFE	. A LIVE ANCIENT IS BETTER THAN A DEAD STATUE. (HE
CAPT III (297)	OUR WORLD-- GETTING PATRONAGE IS THE WHOLE ART OF	LIFE	. A MAN CANT HAVE A CAREER WITHOUT IT. /BRASSBOUND/ IN
MTH1 II SD(20)	CUT HAIR; BUT THEY ARE STRONG AND IN THE PRIME OF	LIFE	. ADAM LOOKS WORRIED, LIKE A FARMER. EVE, BETTER
MIS. (137)	IT NEVER STOPS: TALK, TALK, TALK, TALK. THATS MY	LIFE	. ALL THE DAY I LISTEN TO MAMMA TALKING; AT DINNER I
MTH1 II (33)	THROUGH HIM AND HIS LIKE, DEATH IS GAINING ON	LIFE	. ALREADY MOST OF OUR GRANDCHILDREN DIE BEFORE THEY
LION PREFACE(16)	AND BIRD MUSIC, AND SAVE YOU AND RENEW YOUR	LIFE	. AND FROM THE INTERWEAVING OF THESE TWO TRADITIONS
CURE (236)	GROWN-UP PEOPLE DO. I HAVE A REAL GENIUS FOR HOME	LIFE	. AND I SHOULDNT AT ALL MIND BEING TYRANNIZED OVER A
JOAN 4 (100)	I CANNOT BURN HER. THE CHURCH CANNOT TAKE	LIFE	. AND MY FIRST DUTY IS TO SEEK THIS GIRL'S SALVATION.
BULL PREFACE(54)	WIFE, WAS ONLY SENTENCED TO PENAL SERVITUDE FOR	LIFE	. AND OUR CLEMENCY DID NOT STOP THERE. HIS WIFE WAS NOT
BUOY III (45)	DIE-- IF WE NEVER MEET AGAIN, IT MAY LAST ALL MY	LIFE	. AND THERE ARE RIGHTS I WILL GIVE TO NO MAN OVER ME.
MIS. PREFACE(87)	AND MOST CAPABLE LIFE: IN SHORT, THE MOST GODLY	LIFE	. AND THIS SIGNIFICANT WORD REMINDS US THAT THOUGH THE
HART PREFACE(40)	THE IDEALS ON THE STAGE JUST AS THEY DO IN REAL	LIFE	. AND THOUGH THERE MAY BE BETTER THINGS TO REVEAL, IT
POSN PREFACE(426)	SINCE THE WORLD BEGAN. ANYTHING FOR A QUIET	LIFE	. ANOTHER DOUBT: WOULD A COMMITTEE OF THE PRIVY COUNCIL
GETT (315)	LIFE. /SOAMES/ MRS REGINALD BRIDGENORTH PROPOSES	LIFE	. ANY SECONDER? /LEO/ DONT BE SOULLESS, ANTHONY.
HART III (137)	I'LL MARRY HER. I'LL DO ANYTHING FOR A QUIET	LIFE	. ARE YOU SATISFIED NOW? /ELLIE/ NO. I NEVER REALLY
GETT (267)	HAD A CHARMED LIFE? /THE GENERAL/ YES, A CHARMED	LIFE	. BAYONETS BENT ON MY BUCKLES. BULLETS PASSED THROUGH
SUPR PREFACE(R32)	SPOILING OF HIS HAT IN A SHOWER, MUCH LESS HIS	LIFE	. BOTH ARE ALIKE FORCED TO BORROW MOTIVES FOR THE MORE
FANY EPILOG (329)	IN THE WORLD AND SOME DELICATE GRACE IN FAMILY	LIFE	. BUT I PROMISED MY DAUGHTER YOUR OPINION: AND I MUST
2TRU III (84)	THEY SEEMED TO HAVE NOTHING TO DO WITH REAL	LIFE	. BUT WAR BROUGHT THOSE OLD STORIES HOME QUITE REAL;
GETT PREFACE(228)	MANLY VIRTUE, AND SWEET AND WHOLESOME NATIONAL	LIFE	. BUT WITH A CLEVER TURN OF THE HAND THIS HOLY OF
GETT PREFACE(234)	OUT OF DOORS WITHOUT BREAKING UP THEIR HOME	LIFE	. BUT WITHIN DOORS THAT HOME LIFE MAY BE REGARDED AS
ARMS III (52)	YOU SAID YOUD TOLD ONLY TWO LIES IN YOUR WHOLE	LIFE	. DEAR YOUNG LADY: ISNT THAT RATHER A SHORT ALLOWANCE?
CATH 4 (192)	TO SIBERIA . DONT LET HER THROUGH THERE, ON YOUR	LIFE	. DRAG HER BACK. YOU WILL BE KNOUTED . IT IS HOPELESS.
MTH1 II (22)	LIVED TO THE VERY MARROW: BURNING, OVERWHELMING	LIFE	. EVERY MAN WHO HAS NOT SEEN IT, HEARD IT, FELT IT,
JOAN PREFACE(46)	AND THE CIRCUMSTANCES NO LONGER APPLY TO ACTIVE	LIFE	. FOR EXAMPLE, THEY ARE TAUGHT HISTORY ABOUT
GETT (300)	THEY WOULD NOT EVEN KEEP HIM IMPRISONED FOR	LIFE	. FOR TWENTY YEARS SHE HAD TO LIVE SINGLY, BRINGING UP
2TRU I (43)	I'M PERFECTLY WELL. IVE NEVER BEEN SO HAPPY IN MY	LIFE	. GO ON WITH THE DREAM, POPS: THE NICEST PART OF IT IS
MTH1 II (34)	THE STATE OF THEM THAT LOVE DEATH MORE THAN	LIFE	. GO ON WITH YOUR SPINNING; AND DO NOT SIT THERE IDLE
GETT (283)	NOT QUARRELLING, LESBIA: IT'S ONLY ENGLISH FAMILY	LIFE	. GOOD MORNING. /LEO/ YOU KNOW, BISHOP, IT'S VERY DEAR
POSN (452)	OFF THIS. I DIDNT OUGHT TO SWEAR AWAY THIS MAN'S	LIFE	. HE AND I ARE, IN A MANNER OF SPEAKING, BROTHERS. /THE
LION PREFACE(28)	BUT WILL RISE FROM THE EARTH AND RETURN TO	LIFE	. HE ATTACHES TO HIMSELF THE IMMEMORIAL TRIBAL CEREMONY
BARB PREFACE(224)	INDEPENDENT INCOMES AND GENTLE AND LOVELY WAYS OF	LIFE	. HE HAS ONLY TO FOLLOW UP THE INCOME OF THE SWEET
KING I (165)	/NEWTON/ SHSHSH! NOT A WORD AGAINST HIM, ON YOUR	LIFE	. HE IS PRIVILEGED. /MRS BASHAM/ HE IS A BEAST ALL THE
BUOY III (41)	MONEY: THOUGH HE REGARDED IT AS THE CURSE OF HIS	LIFE	. HE MADE IT IN THE CITY ALL DAY AND RETURNED TO HIS
ARMS III (51)	WAY. I LIED: I KNOW IT. BUT I DID IT TO SAVE YOUR	LIFE	. HE WOULD HAVE KILLED YOU. THAT WAS THE SECOND TIME I
JOAN PREFACE(18)	WAS HER CRAZE FOR SOLDIERING AND THE MASCULINE	LIFE	. HER FATHER TRIED TO FRIGHTEN HER OUT OF IT BY
OVER (184)	/JUNO/ I HAVE NEVER BEEN TREATED LIKE THIS IN MY	LIFE	. HERE AM I, A MARRIED MAN, WITH A MOST ATTRACTIVE
SUPR III (127)	SENOR COMMANDER IN ANY WAY DISCREDIT MY VIEW OF	LIFE	. HERE, I REPEAT, YOU HAVE ALL THAT YOU SOUGHT WITHOUT
DOCT PREFACE(16)	A YEAR BEFORE HE CAN AFFORD EVEN TO INSURE HIS	LIFE	. HIS HOUSE, HIS SERVANTS, AND HIS EQUIPAGE (OR
MIS. (151)	BOTH VERY EFFECTUALLY, SIR. /PERCIVAL/ SAVED MY	LIFE	. I ADMIT IT MOST GRATEFULLY. /TARLETON/ I MUST
KING I (177)	YOU. /FOX/ THE BELL, THE BELL. IT STRIKES UPON MY	LIFE	. I AM CALLED. EARTHLY KINGS CANNOT STAY ME. LET ME
PRES (157)	IVE SUBSCRIBED TO THE REGIMENTAL BAND ALL MY	LIFE	. I BOUGHT TWO SARRUSOPHONES FOR IT OUT OF MY OWN
MTH5 (254)	/ECRASIA/ I! I HAVE BEEN IN LOVE ALL MY	LIFE	. I BURNED WITH IT EVEN IN THE EGG. /ACIS/ NOT A BIT OF
MRS I (186)	EXERCISE. AND I NEVER ENJOYED MYSELF MORE IN MY	LIFE	. I CLEARED ALL MY EXPENSES, AND GOT INITIATED INTO THE
MTH3 (113)	MIND, DO YOU? SHE WILL BRING US BACK TO REAL	LIFE	. I DONT KNOW HOW YOU FELLOWS FEEL; BUT I'M JUST GOING
BARB III (345)	WRONG PREJUDICE YOU AGAINST THIS GREAT CHANCE IN	LIFE	. I HAVE SATISFIED MYSELF THAT THE BUSINESS IS ONE OF
GETT (337)	SPOIL YOUR MARRIAGE HAS THE POWER TO SPOIL YOUR	LIFE	. I HAVE THAT POWER OVER YOU. /MRS GEORGE/ (DESPERATE)
ARMS III (51)	IS THE ONE REALLY BEAUTIFUL AND NOBLE PART OF MY	LIFE	. I HOPE YOU CAN UNDERSTAND THAT. /BLUNTSCHLI/ (
BULL I (83)	BORN IN GLASGOW. NEVER WAS IN IRELAND IN HIS	LIFE	. I KNOW ALL ABOUT HIM. /BROADBENT/ BUT HE SPOKE-- HE
JOAN 2 (85)	THOU POOR CHILD, THOU HAST NEVER PRAYED IN THY	LIFE	. I MUST TEACH THEE FROM THE BEGINNING. /CHARLES/ I AM
DOCT IV (162)	NEVER. YOU ARE THE LIGHT AND THE BLESSING OF MY	LIFE	. I NEVER LIVED UNTIL I KNEW YOU. /LOUIS/ (HIS EYES
MIS. (134)	TO KEEP A SHOP ARE THE BIGGEST TRAGEDY IN MODERN	LIFE	. I OUGHT TO HAVE BEEN A WRITER. I'M ESSENTIALLY A MAN

DOCT III	(154)	THAT, AND BRING SOME CHARM AND HAPPINESS INTO HIS	LIFE	. I PRAYED HEAVEN TO SEND ME ONE. I FIRMLY BELIEVE THAT
GENV II	(55)	IT? /SIR O./ I! I NEVER SET EYES ON HER IN MY	LIFE	. I REMEMBER HER RIDICULOUS NAME! THATS ALL. /THE
MIS. PREFACE	(79)	DOOR OF THE SCHOOL DID NOT SHUT OUT THE TRIALS OF	LIFE	. I REMEMBER ONCE, AT SCHOOL, THE RESIDENT HEAD MASTER
MIS.	(119)	I SHOULDNT HAVE TIME FOR ANYTHING ELSE ALL MY	LIFE	. I SAY: I FEEL VERY FIT AND SPRY. LETS ALL GO DOWN AND
MTH5	(218)	HAPPEN. I NEVER HEARD SUCH NONSENSE IN ALL MY	LIFE	. I SHALL KNOW HOW TO TAKE CARE OF MYSELF. /THE
ROCK I	(232)	BEFORE YOU TALK. YOUR DEAD MIND WILL COME TO	LIFE	. I SHALL MAKE A MAN OF YOU. GOODBYE. (SHE GOES OUT
HART II	(107)	YEARS. BEGINNING WITH SOLITARY. TEN YEARS OFF MY	LIFE	. I SHANT SERVE IT ALL: I'M TOO OLD. IT WILL SEE ME
DOCT III	(155)	IN HIM, IT WOULD MEAN THE WRECK AND FAILURE OF MY	LIFE	. I SHOULD GO BACK TO CORNWALL AND DIE. I COULD SHOW
GENV IV	(98)	MODELS BEFORE ME ALL THROUGH MY PUBLIC	LIFE	. I SUPPOSE-- NOW THAT YOU PUT IT IN THAT WAY-- THAT
POSN	(458)	TO YOU? /THE WOMAN/ I TOOK IT TO SAVE MY CHILD'S	LIFE	. I THOUGHT IT WOULD GET ME TO A DOCTOR IN TIME. THE
O'FL	(222)	IVE BEEN MADE A FOOL OF AND IMPOSED UPON ALL MY	LIFE	. I THOUGHT THAT COVETIOUS STHREAL IN THERE WAS A
POSN	(465)	ANY WOMAN WANTS TO BE A GOOD WIFE TWICE IN HER	LIFE	. I WANT SOMEBODY TO BE A GOOD HUSBAND TO ME NOW.
FANY II	(291)	I WANTED MORE MUSIC-- MORE HAPPINESS-- MORE	LIFE	. I WANTED SOME COMRADE WHO FELT AS I DID. I FELT
MTH1 II	(23)	FOR HIM. NO WOMAN SHALL MAKE ME LIVE MY FATHER'S	LIFE	. I WILL HUNT: I WILL FIGHT AND STRIVE TO THE VERY
ROCK II	(282)	THEN IN HEAVEN'S NAME GO BACK TO YOUR OLD WAY OF	LIFE	. I WILL PUT UP WITH ANYTHING RATHER THAN SEE YOU
PYGM II	(224)	TO PREPARE AND FIT HERSELF FOR HER NEW STATION IN	LIFE	. IF I DID NOT EXPRESS MYSELF CLEARLY IT WAS BECAUSE I
MTH1 II	(29)	IT DOWN AS IT ROAMS THE EARTH IN THE PRIDE OF ITS	LIFE	. IF I MUST HAVE FOOD OR DIE, I WILL AT LEAST HAVE IT
LION PROLOG	(108)	STAND FOR TREMBLING). MEGGY: RUN, RUN FOR YOUR	LIFE	. IF I TAKE MY EYE OFF HIM, IT'S ALL UP. (THE LION
MTH2	(39)	HAD TO THINK TWICE BEFORE HE TOOK ON ANYTHING FOR	LIFE	. IF I THOUGHT I WAS GOING TO LIVE NINE HUNDRED AND
PRES	(160)	YOUVE NEVER HAD ANY EXPERIENCE OF GARRISON	LIFE	. IF YOU HAD, YOUD HAVE NOTICED THAT THE SORT OF WOMAN
ROCK PREFACE	(147)	IT, NOT IN THE KILLING. THE SACREDNESS OF HUMAN	LIFE	. IN LAW WE DRAW A LINE BETWEEN THE KILLING OF HUMAN
MTH4 II	(177)	FORCE IS NEGLIGIBLE DURING OUR FIRST CENTURY OF	LIFE	. IN OUR SECOND CENTURY IT DEVELOPS QUICKLY, AND
LION PREFACE	(58)	CAPITALS, WE SHALL NEVER HAVE A DECENT SOCIAL	LIFE	. INDEED THE WHOLE ATTRACTION OF OUR PRESENT
SUPR IV	(152)	JUST TAKE YOUR REMITTANCE AND YOURSELF OUT OF MY	LIFE	. I'M DONE WITH REMITTANCES; AND I'M DONE WITH YOU. I
MIS. PREFACE	(73)	BEFORE THEY BEGIN THE SERIOUS BUSINESS OF	LIFE	. IT IS SAID THAT BOYS WILL BE BOYS; AND ONE CAN ONLY
GETT	(262)	GIRLS. YOU CANT KEEP UP A BROKEN HEART ALL YOUR	LIFE	. IT MUST BE NEARLY TWENTY YEARS SINCE SHE REFUSED YOU.
GETT PREFACE	(190)	AUDIENCE OF RESPECTABLE MEN UNDERSTOOD BY MARRIED	LIFE	. IT WAS CERTAINLY A STAGGERING REVELATION. PETER THE
PYGM EPILOG	(289)	ONE OF THE STRONGEST PERSONAL INTERESTS IN HER	LIFE	. IT WOULD BE VERY SORELY STRAINED IF THERE WAS ANOTHER
MTH5	(206)	IS A VERY CRUDE ATTEMPT TO GET INTO THE RHYTHM OF	LIFE	. IT WOULD BE PAINFUL TO ME TO GO BACK FROM THAT RHYTHM
GETT	(315)	ANY AMENDMENT? /LEO/ I PROTEST. IT MUST BE FOR	LIFE	. IT WOULD NOT BE A MARRIAGE AT ALL IF IT WERE NOT FOR
MIS.	(153)	MEMBER OF MY FAMILY RISKING HIS LIFE-- OR HER	LIFE	. IT'S A POINT OF HONOR WITH US TO KEEP UP THAT
O'FL	(211)	CHILDER EVER DID TO YOU BEFORE IN ALL YOUR LONG	LIFE	. IT'S A TRUE RESPECT I'M SHEWING YOU AT LAST, SIR.
FANY PROLOG	(271)	BE UNASSUMING AND KINDLY. IVE LIVED A BLAMELESS	LIFE	. IVE SUPPORTED THE CENSORSHIP IN THE FACE OF RIDICULE
O'FL	(227)	SOME LIKES WAR'S ALARUMS; AND SOME LIKES HOME	LIFE	. IVE TRIED BOTH, SIR; AND I'M ALL FOR WAR'S ALARUMS
MRS I	(192)	TO FEEL THE ASSURANCE OF A GROWN-UP MAN IN MY	LIFE	. (HE FOLDS HIS CHAIR AND CARRIES IT TO THE PORCH).
ROCK II	(280)	LOUD LAMENT TO HIS MOTHER) YOUVE RUINED MY WHOLE	LIFE	. (HE GOES IN PURSUIT, CRYING) ALOYSIA, ALOYSIA, WAIT
MRS II	(208)	GENTLEMAN, PRADDY. ALWAYS WERE. MY IDEAL THROUGH	LIFE	. (HE RISES TO GO, BUT PAUSES A MOMENT BETWEEN THE TWO
2TRU I	(43)	BE A MISERABLE INVALID AGAIN FOR THE REST OF YOUR	LIFE	. (SHE DROPS THE BELL THOUGHTFULLY). NOT AN ATTRACTIVE
MRS III	(234)	CHAMBERS, 67 CHANCERY LANE, FOR THE REST OF MY	LIFE	. (SHE GOES OFF QUICKLY IN THE OPPOSITE DIRECTION TO
JITT II	(48)	A PAST. I WILL TAKE IT AND MYSELF OUT OF YOUR	LIFE	. (SHE RISES). /LENKHEIM/ (OUT OF PATIENCE, JUMPING
GLIM	(174)	IS NOT FERRUCCIO'S LOVE THAT I MUST TAKE, BUT HIS	LIFE	. (THE FRIAR, STARTLED, TURNS POWERFULLY ON HER). DO
BARB II	(304)	FORTIFICATION ROUND YOU ALL THE DAYS OF YOUR	LIFE	. (WITH A TOUCH OF CAUTION) YOU WILL LET ME HAVE THE
LION PREFACE	(23)	CALL AN ARTIST AND A BOHEMIAN IN HIS MANNER OF	LIFE	. JESUS NOT A PROSELYTIST. A POINT OF CONSIDERABLE
LION PREFACE	(22)	HE DEPARTED WIDELY FROM JOHN'S MANNER OF	LIFE	. JOHN WENT INTO THE WILDERNESS, NOT INTO THE
BARB PREFACE	(239)	DRAG HIM TO THE SCAFFOLD, IMPRISON HIM FOR	LIFE	. LET ALL CIVILIZED STATES BAND TOGETHER TO DRIVE HIS
2TRU III	(103)	IT WOULD GIVE THE CHILDREN A ONE-SIDED VIEW OF	LIFE	. LIFE IS VERY MIXED, SIR: IT IS NOT ALL PIETY AND IT
2TRU I	(44)	IT; AND HAVE A GLORIOUS SPREE WITH THE PRICE. SEE	LIFE	. LIVE. YOU DONT CALL BEING AN INVALID LIVING, DO YOU?
MIS.	(143)	THE SUFFRAGIST PHRASE IS. /HYPATIA/ LIVING ANY	LIFE	. LIVING, INSTEAD OF WITHERING WITHOUT EVEN A GARDENER
6CAL	(103)	GOOD. I HAVE NEVER BEEN BETTER NOR HAPPIER IN MY	LIFE	. LOOK AT ME. DO I NOT LOOK RADIANT? /THE KING/ AND
BARB III	(328)	YOU MUST REMEMBER THAT RESTAURANTS BREAK UP HOME	LIFE	. LOOK AT THE CONTINENT, FOR INSTANCE! ARE YOU SURE SO
MILL PREFACE	(135)	LIFE AND BY THE DOMINANT PERSONALITIES IN PRIVATE	LIFE	. LYTTON'S VRIL WAS A FICTION ONLY IN RESPECT OF ITS
CAND II	(123)	TURNED ON FOR THEIR PLEASURE EVERY EVENING OF MY	LIFE	. MAY I NOT HAVE ONE NIGHT AT HOME, WITH MY WIFE, AND
KING I	(174)	ENTERTAIN LADIES. THEY DO NOT FIT INTO MY WAY OF	LIFE	. MR ROWLEY: YOU ARE WELL KNOWN TO BE AS INTERESTED IN
MRS I	(187)	TAKE CHARGE OF ME. I HAVE BEEN BOARDED OUT ALL MY	LIFE	. MY MOTHER HAS LIVED IN BRUSSELS OR VIENNA AND NEVER
SIM PREFACE	(5)	CONVENIENT TO OUR RULERS. I LEARNED THIS EARLY IN	LIFE	. MY NURSE INDUCED ME TO ABSTAIN FROM CERTAIN
LION PREFACE	(86)	AND YET FOX MADE RATHER A MISERABLE BUSINESS OF	LIFE	. NEVERTHELESS ALL THESE PERVERSIONS OF THE DOCTRINE OF
PHIL III	(145)	I SHALL HAVE TO GO ON PHILANDERING NOW ALL MY	LIFE	. NO DOMESTICITY, NO FIRESIDE, NO LITTLE ONES, NOTHING
SIM PRO,2,	(27)	IT DRIVES ME MAD WHEN I CAN HARDLY BEAR MY OWN	LIFE	. NO FEAR OF HIM SHOOTING HIMSELF: NOT MUCH, SO I
GETT PREFACE	(196)	SENSE THEY ARE EQUALLY FAR FROM THE REALITIES OF	LIFE	. NO HEALTHY MAN OR ANIMAL IS OCCUPIED WITH LOVE IN ANY
MTH5	(206)	NEVER SINGING, NEVER GETTING ANYTHING OUT OF	LIFE	. NONE OF US ARE GOING TO BE LIKE THAT WHEN WE GROW UP.
BUOY IV	(50)	BUT I HAVE ALREADY BOUGHT HER AN ANNUITY FOR HER	LIFE	. NOT FOR YOURS. ANY FURTHER PRECAUTIONS YOU MUST TAKE
LION PREFACE	(75)	CALLED ALSO THE TERROR OF SEX AND THE TERROR OF	LIFE	. NOW JESUS, WITH HIS HEALTHY CONSCIENCE ON HIS HIGHER
2TRU II	(59)	EVEN BEGIN WITH HER EARS, AND DISFIGURE HER FOR	LIFE	. OF COURSE THAT IS A POSSIBILITY: SUCH THINGS HAVE
2TRU III	(111)	OF DEATH; AND THE PREACHER MUST PREACH THE WAY OF	LIFE	. OH, IF I COULD ONLY FIND IT! (A WHITE SEA FOG
SUPR IV	(171)	AND TANNER) SIR: THERE ARE TWO TRAGEDIES IN	LIFE	. ONE IS TO LOSE YOUR HEART'S DESIRE. THE OTHER IS TO
LION PREFACE	(76)	THEM, AND THE RELIGIOUS LIFE BECAME A DENIAL OF	LIFE	. PAUL HAD NO INTENTION OF SURRENDERING EITHER HIS
2TRU I	(31)	TELL ME THE WORST: I HAVE DREADED IT ALL MY	LIFE	. PERHAPS I SHOULD HAVE TOLD YOU THE WHOLE TRUTH; BUT I
MIS.	(130)	OLD MAN. /TARLETON/ BEEF BE BLOWED! JOY OF	LIFE	. READ IBSEN. (HE GOES INTO THE PAVILION TO RELIEVE
VWOO 3	(136)	LET ALONE THAT YOU DONT HAVE TO LIVE A SINGLE	LIFE	. /A/ YOU CAN GET RID OF AN ASSISTANT IF SHE DOESNT
2TRU III	(97)	COCKTAILS AND COCAINE-- THAT I COULD ENDURE MY	LIFE	. /AUBREY/ I REGRET TO HAVE TO SAY IT, MOPS; BUT YOU
BARB III	(348)	TO TURN YOUR BACK ON THE WICKED SIDE OF	LIFE	. /BARBARA/ THERE IS NO WICKED SIDE: LIFE IS ALL ONE.
KING I	(178)	STROKE, AND I SHOULD NOT HAVE ANSWERED FOR YOUR	LIFE	. /BARBARA/ YOU MUST CONTROL YOURSELF, PREACHER. IN ANY
MTH3	(92)	SERPENTINE. THIS MAN'S INVENTION MAY SAVE YOUR	LIFE	. /BARNABAS/ (ANGRILY) WILL YOU TELL ME WHAT THAT HAS
ROCK II	(272)	WITH PARLIAMENT. IT HAS WASTED ENOUGH OF MY	LIFE	. /BASHAM/ DONT TELL ME YOU ARE GOING TO TAKE YOUR
BULL IV	(168)	TO RESTRAIN HER TEARS) I'M ASHAMED OUT O ME	LIFE	. /BROADBENT/ (ASTONISHED) ASHAMED! WHAT OF? /NORA/
MTH3	(135)	THE SEA IS VERY COLD. YOU MAY GET RHEUMATISM FOR	LIFE	. /BURGE-LUBIN/ FOR LIFE! THAT SETTLES IT: I WONT RISK
CLEO III	(159)	TO TENDER THIS BALE OF CARPET AS I TENDER MY OWN	LIFE	. /CAESAR/ (CHEERFULLY) THEN LET THEM SWING YOU UP AT
CLEO V	(199)	WAY, ACCORDING TO CAESAR'S BOASTED LAWS OF	LIFE	. /CAESAR/ (DUBIOUSLY) HE IS TO RULE AS HE CAN,
CAND III	(130)	WELL? /MORELL/ I HAVE NEVER SPOKEN BETTER IN MY	LIFE	. /CANDIDA/ THAT WAS FIRST RATE! HOW MUCH WAS THE
PHIL II	(131)	WHICH SHE WILL REMEMBER TO THE LAST DAY OF HER	LIFE	. /CHARTERIS/ (APPROVINGLY) THAT WAS RIGHT, DARLING. (
GETT	(322)	WE SHOULD NEVER BURN OUR BOATS. IT IS DEATH IN	LIFE	. /COLLINS/ WELL, FATHER, I WILL SAY FOR YOU THAT YOU
BARB III	(348)	ON BODGER AND UNDERSHAFT IS TURNING OUR BACKS ON	LIFE	. /CUSINS/ I THOUGHT YOU WERE DETERMINED TO TURN YOUR
BARB II	(291)	GRACES AND LUXURIES OF A RICH, STRONG, AND SAFE	LIFE	. /CUSINS/ SUPPOSE ONE IS FORCED TO CHOOSE BETWEEN THEM
NEVR III	(274)	YOU. YOU CAN NOW BEGIN A NEW CHAPTER IN YOUR	LIFE	. /DOLLY/ CHAPTER SEVENTEEN OR THEREABOUTS, I SHOULD
SUPR III	(93)	YOU. /ANA/ WRETCH: I WORE MOURNING FOR HIM ALL MY	LIFE	. /DON JUAN/ YES: IT BECAME YOU. BUT A LIFE OF MOURNING
FANY I	(280)	AND IT WILL LEAVE A MARK ON HIM TO THE END OF HIS	LIFE	. /DORA/ NOT A BIT OF IT. DONT YOU BE AFRAID: IVE
POSN	(443)	IT DIDNT SET ME AGAINST DRINK FOR THE REST OF MY	LIFE	. /ELDER DANIELS/ THAT WAS YOUR SPIRITUAL PRIDE,
HART I	(63)	ABOUT-- TO GIVE SOME INTEREST AND PLEASURE TO	LIFE	. /ELLIE/ JUST SO. THATS ALL, REALLY. /MRS HUSHABYE/ IT
MILL IV	(209)	YOU WILL REGRET IT TO THE LAST DAY OF YOUR	LIFE	. /EPIFANIA/ MR SAGAMORE: YOU HAVE YOUR INSTRUCTIONS.
MTH1 I	(9)	BITE THE APPLE YOU DREAD. THE SUN WILL GIVE	LIFE	. /EVE/ I DO NOT TRUST THE SUN. I WILL GIVE LIFE
BUOY 1	(16)	I AM GONE. /SON/ I HAVE THOUGHT OF INSURING YOUR	LIFE	. /FATHER/ HOW ARE YOU TO PAY THE PREMIUM? /SON/
ROCK I	(204)	THIS FAMILY; AND YOU WILL GET THE LAUGH OF YOUR	LIFE	. /FLAVIA/ DAMN THE FAMILY! /LADY CHAVENDER/ FLAVIA!
ROCK I	(204)	THE DISINTEGRATING EFFECT OF SOCIALISM ON FAMILY	LIFE	. /FLAVIA/ (IRRESISTIBLE AMUSEMENT STRUGGLING WITH
MTH2	(40)	SHE SAID IT WAS BECAUSE SHE HAD ONLY ONE	LIFE	. /HASLAM/ SAME THING, POOR GIRL! THE FELLOW PERSUADED
GETT	(336)	WHAT YOUVE JUST DONE? NOT IF IT WAS TO SAVE MY	LIFE	. /HOTCHKISS/ I'LL AMUSE GEORGE. /MRS GEORGE/ HE WONT
KING I	(200)	BE A REAL FAST, JAMIE, FOR THE FIRST TIME IN YOUR	LIFE	. /JAMES/ YOU LIE. MY PENANCES ARE ALL REAL. /CHARLES/
BUOY IV	(50)	NOT SAVAGES. DADDY WILL ALWAYS BE A PART OF MY	LIFE	. /JUNIUS/ NOT ALWAYS. HOW LONG DO YOU INTEND TO LIVE,
PRES	(157)	PERFECTLY RIDICULOUS. I NEVER RUINED ANYONE IN MY	LIFE	. /LADY CORINTHIA/ NEVER! ARE YOU IN EARNEST?
FANY III	(301)	WHAT SORT OF THING, BOBBY? /BOBBY/ WELL, ABOUT	LIFE	. /MARGARET/ IVE LIVED A LOT SINCE I SAW YOU LAST. I
MTH5	(255)	IN ART A THING THAT HE WOULD NOT HAVE EXIST IN	LIFE	. /MARTELLUS/ YES: I HAVE BEEN THROUGH ALL THAT. BUT
SIM I	(53)	MAYA VASHTI. /VASHTI/ YOUR LIVES AND OURS ARE ONE	LIFE	. /MAYA/ (SITTING DOWN BESIDE HIM) AND THIS IS THE
KING I	(164)	AND SIXTYFOUR THOUSAND SECONDS. A LONG LONG	LIFE	. /MRS BASHAM/ COME NOW, MR NEWTON: YOU WILL TURN THE
GETT	(337)	YOULL NEVER GET RID OF ME NOW TO THE END OF YOUR	LIFE	. /MRS GEORGE/ I SHALL GET RID OF YOU IF THE BEADLE HAS
OVER	(184)	YOU OUGHT TO RESPECT THE CONVENTIONS OF ENGLISH	LIFE	. /MRS JUNO/ BUT I AM RESPECTING THEM; AND YOURE NOT.
2TRU III	(105)	VERY FEW DELIGHTFULLY SATISFACTORY MOMENTS OF MY	LIFE	. /MRS MOPPLY/ WELL, THATS A PRETTY SORT OF APOLOGY.
BUOY IV	(59)	WOMAN ON EARTH; BUT YOU ARE A PART OF MY	LIFE	. /MRS SECONDBORN/ WELL, ASK SIR FERDINAND WHICH OF US
MIS.	(121)	QUEENS DROP THE MASK WHEN THEY REACH OUR TIME OF	LIFE	. /MRS TARLETON/ LET YOU ALONE FOR GIVING A THING A

MRS II	(213)	RIGHT TO YOUR OWN OPINIONS AND YOUR OWN WAY OF	LIFE	. /MRS WARREN/ MY OWN OPINIONS AND MY OWN WAY OF LIFE!
PHIL II	(119)	ME OF JOKING? I NEVER WAS MORE SERIOUS IN MY	LIFE	. /PARAMORE/ (SHAMED BY CHARTERIS'S GENEROSITY) THEN I
ARMS III	(68)	I POSITIVELY DID NOT. I NEVER WAS MARRIED IN MY	LIFE	. /PETKOFF/ (EXASPERATED) RAINA: WILL YOU KINDLY
PYGM III	(257)	AND LIONEL MONCKTON; /HIGGINS/ BEEN AT IT ALL HER	LIFE	. /PICKERING/ THOUGH SIX MONTHS AGO, SHE'D NEVER AS
GENV IV	(129)	DISTRACTEDLY). /JUDGE/ SHE, AT LEAST, VALUES HER	LIFE	. /SECRETARY/ YES: SHE BELONGS TO SOME MOVEMENT OR
GETT	(315)	WOULD NOT BE A MARRIAGE AT ALL IF IT WERE NOT FOR	LIFE	. /SOAMES/ MRS REGINALD BRIDGENORTH PROPOSES LIFE. ANY
O'FL	(220)	AND COMFORT, AND ME LEFT FIGHTING IN PERIL OF MY	LIFE	. /TERESA/ (TAKING IT) DO YOU THINK IT'S REAL GOLD,
MTH5	(206)	TO BE LIKE THAT WHEN WE GROW UP. IT'S A DOG'S	LIFE	. /THE ANCIENT/ NOT AT ALL. YOU REPEAT THAT OLD PHRASE
MTH3	(110)	TO NO MORE THAN AN HONEST MAN'S EXPECTATION OF	LIFE	. /THE ARCHBISHOP/ I DID KILL MYSELF. IT WAS QUITE
MTH4 I	(171)	IS A FIXED RELATION BETWEEN CONDUCT AND LENGTH OF	LIFE	. /THE ELDERLY GENTLEMAN/ I HAVE NEVER HEARD OF ANY
GENV III	(84)	IMPUDENCE? I HAVE NEVER DINED WITH A JEW IN MY	LIFE	. /THE JEW/ THEN YOU DO NOT KNOW WHAT A GOOD DINNER IS.
GENV III	(83)	OUR HEADS AND MAKING FOOLS OF OURSELVES FOR	LIFE	. /THE JUDGE/ YES; BUT DO NOT FORGET THAT AS LATELY AS
LADY	(238)	A PRESENT TO A WARDER NIGH EVERY NIGHT OF HER	LIFE	. /THE MAN/ (TURNING PALE) I'LL NOT BELIEVE IT. /THE
MTH4 I	(146)	WOMAN I HAVE EVER MET IN THE WHOLE COURSE OF MY	LIFE	. /THE MAN/ THAT CANNOT BE. SHE CANNOT APPEAR STUPID TO
FABL VI	(131)	MAKE A SAFETY PIN OR A WHEELBARROW TO SAVE HIS	LIFE	. /THE TEACHER/ ENOUGH. WE CAN NEVER WANT TO KNOW TOO
GENV III	(84)	TRY DINING WITH A JEW FOR THE FIRST TIME IN YOUR	LIFE	. /THE WIDOW/ (CONSIDERING IT) IT IS TRUE THAT I HAVE
MTH4 I	(141)	NOT ILL. I HAVE NEVER HAD A DAY'S ILLNESS IN MY	LIFE	. /THE WOMAN/ MAY I ADVISE YOU? /THE ELDERLY
MTH5	(206)	IT IS YOU, MY CHILDREN, WHO ARE LIVING THE DOG'S	LIFE	. /THE YOUTH/ THE DOG MUST HAVE BEEN A GOOD SENSIBLE
NEVR I	(221)	IT EVER SINCE. AND IVE NEVER HAD TOOTHACHE IN MY	LIFE	. /VALENTINE/ DONT YOU FIND IT RATHER NASTY?
SIM I	(42)	/VASHTI/ WE ARE THE WAY. /MAYA/ WE ARE THE	LIFE	. /VASHTI/ I AM THE LIGHT. LOOK AT ME. (SHE THROWS HER
SIM II	(62)	GET RID OF HIM? HE IS SETTLING DOWN WITH US FOR	LIFE	. /VASHTI/ WE HAVE BROUGHT HIM ON OURSELVES. /MAYA/ WE
VWOO 1	(117)	FUNNY. /A/ AM I? I NEVER FELT LESS FUNNY IN MY	LIFE	. /Z/ I CANT MAKE YOU OUT AT ALL. I AM RATHER GOOD AT
VWOO 3	(134)	TO THE CREDIT OF VILLAGE SHOPKEEPING AS A WAY OF	LIFE	. /Z/ OH, YOU ARE SILLY, BOSS. /A/ THAT IS A
ROCK I	(204)	THINK, ONLY WHAT YOU FEEL AND THINK. THATS FAMILY	LIFE	. SCOLD, SCOLD, SCOLD! /DAVID/ SQUABBLE, SQUABBLE,
FANY PROLOG	(260)	DRESS OR TASTED COARSE FOOD OR BAD WINE IN HER	LIFE	. SHE HAS LIVED IN A PALACE; AND HER PERAMBULATOR WAS A
LION PROL,SD	(105)	PAMPERED SLATTERN, WELL FED AND IN THE PRIME OF	LIFE	. SHE HAS NOTHING TO CARRY, AND HAS A STOUT STICK TO
BULL II SD	(107)	A CONTENTED PRODUCT OF A NARROW, STRAINLESS	LIFE	. SHE WEARS HER HAIR PARTED IN THE MIDDLE AND QUITE
PYGM V	(284)	SNEER AT ME. /HIGGINS/ I HAVE NEVER SNEERED IN MY	LIFE	. SNEERING DOESNT BECOME EITHER THE HUMAN FACE OR THE
OVER	(184)	UNEXPECTEDLY TREATED. IT'S OUTSIDE MY SCHEME OF	LIFE	. SO COME NOW! YOUVE GOT TO BEHAVE NATURALLY AND
GENV IV	(100)	OF THAT. MOTOR TRAFFIC IS A PART OF CIVILIZED	LIFE	. SO IS COALMINING. SO IS RAILWAY TRANSPORT. SO IS
GETT	(312)	WEAK HEARTS ARE THE TYRANTS OF ENGLISH FAMILY	LIFE	. SO POOR SOAMES HAD TO BECOME A SOLICITOR. WHEN HIS
SUPR PREFACE	(R9)	THE PRETEXT FOR A PROPAGANDA OF OUR OWN VIEWS OF	LIFE	. SO YOU CANNOT PLEAD IGNORANCE OF THE CHARACTER OF THE
LION PREFACE	(60)	OF QUACKS INSTEAD OF THE NORMAL CONDITIONS OF	LIFE	. SOCIETY IS NOT ONLY DIVIDED BUT ACTUALLY DESTROYED IN
MIS. PREFACE	(71)	ANYTHING, EVEN CAMP LIFE, IS BETTER THAN SCHOOL	LIFE	. SOME BLUNDERING BEGINNINGS OF THIS ARE ALREADY
ROCK PREFACE	(168)	MORE MECHANIZED, SPECIALIZED, AND COMPLICATED	LIFE	. SOME OF US VALUE MACHINERY BECAUSE IT MAKES A SHORTER
LION II	(136)	YOU, FRIEND. I CANT TELL YOU NOT TO SAVE YOUR OWN	LIFE	. SOMETHING WILFUL IN ME WANTS TO SEE YOU FIGHT YOUR
PLES PREFACE	(R15)	OUT OF DATE AS A REPRESENTATION OF CONTEMPORARY	LIFE	. SOMETIMES THE STAGE CUSTOM IS NOT ONLY OBSOLETE, BUT
GETT PREFACE	(189)	PROTEST AGAINST ITS COMPATIBILITY WITH THE HIGHER	LIFE	. ST PAUL'S RELUCTANT SANCTION OF MARRIAGE; HIS
2TRU I	(42)	YOURE MAD. /THE BURGLAR/ I WAS NEVER SANER IN MY	LIFE	. STOP. HOW DOES SHE CALL PEOPLE? HASNT SHE AN
BULL PREFACE	(48)	CONSEQUENT HAPPINESS IN THE CHILDLIKE MILITARY	LIFE	. SUCH MEN DREAD FREEDOM AND RESPONSIBILITY AS A WEAK
MTH1 II	(33)	WHICH TELLS ME THAT DEATH PLAYS ITS PART IN	LIFE	. TELL ME THIS: WHO INVENTED DEATH? ADAM SPRINGS TO
GETT PREFACE	(219)	CAN GET INTO ANY SORT OF TOUCH WITH THE FACTS OF	LIFE	. THAT ASSUMPTION IS THAT THE SPECIFIC RELATION WHICH
MIS. PREFACE	(72)	OF SCHOOL BOOKS, AND THE AMENITIES OF SCHOOL	LIFE	. THAT CONSCIOUSNESS OF CONSENT WHICH, EVEN IN ITS
VWOO 3	(138)	/A/ I HAVE LEARNT NOT TO EXPECT TOO MUCH FROM	LIFE	. THAT IS THE SECRET OF REAL CHEERFULNESS, BECAUSE I AM
SUPR III	(127)	OR CLEARING THE WAY FOR IT. THAT IS THE LAW OF MY	LIFE	. THAT IS THE WORKING WITHIN ME OF LIFE'S INCESSANT
JITT III	(61)	AFFAIR AND FALL BACK INTO THE CURRENT OF EVERYDAY	LIFE	. THAT IS WHAT YOU WANT ME TO DO. BUT I CANNOT DO IT.
DOCT I	(102)	I AM NEVER SICK. NEVER HAD A DAY'S ILLNESS IN MY	LIFE	. THATS WHAT ENABLES ME TO SYMPATHIZE WITH MY PATIENTS.
2TRU I	(48)	BROUGHT UP MAIDEN REVOLTS AGAINST HER RESPECTABLE	LIFE	. THE ASPIRING SOUL ESCAPES FROM HOME, SWEET HOME,
BULL PREFACE	(5)	MR JOSEPH CHAMBERLAIN, HAS RETIRED FROM PUBLIC	LIFE	. THE CONTROVERSIES ABOUT TARIFF REFORM, THE EDUCATION
DOCT I	(98)	IMMUNE FROM TYPHOID FOR THE REST OF HIS	LIFE	. THE FAMILY WERE VERY NICE ABOUT IT: THEIR GRATITUDE
METH PREFACE	(R28)	IS INVOLVED IN EATING A SANDWICH, DRAW HIM TO THE	LIFE	. THE KEYBOARD OF A PIANO IS A DEVICE I HAVE NEVER BEEN
MTH4 I	(154)	THE EXPERIENCE OF TWO AND A HALF CENTURIES OF	LIFE	. THE LAND THAT ONCE EXPORTED COTTON SHIRTS AND
2TRU PREFACE	(10)	A NECESSARY AND IMPORTANT PART OF A WELL ORDERED	LIFE	. THE LANDED GENTRY HAVE ENOUGH EXERCISE AND OCCUPATION
SUPR HANDBOK	(223)	VICES. ECONOMY IS THE ART OF MAKING THE MOST OF	LIFE	. THE LOVE OF ECONOMY IS THE ROOT OF ALL VIRTUE.
PPP SD	(205)	ABSORBS THE ELECTRIC FLUID AT THE COST OF HIS	LIFE	. THE OTHERS LOOK ON HORROR-STRICKEN AS THE THREE
SUPR PREFACE	(R24)	THE MAJORITY BUT HALF VALID REPRESENTATIONS OF	LIFE	. THE SCHOOLBOY WHO USES HIS HOMER TO THROW AT HIS
MIS.	(122)	OUT OF JOHN. I'D NEVER HEARD SUCH TALK IN MY	LIFE	. THE THINGS THEY MENTIONED! AND IT WAS THE
MIS. PREFACE	(18)	TO THE SUCCESS OF THE CHILDREN IN AFTER	LIFE	. THE TRUE CRY OF THE KIND MOTHER AFTER HER LITTLE
MTH2	(80)	OF TWO HUNDRED AND THIRTY YEARS OF THEIR NATURAL	LIFE	. THE UNIONISTS WILL BECOME THE PARTY OF PREMATURE
JOAN PREFACE	(20)	WAS THE SORT OF WOMAN THAT WANTS TO LEAD A MAN'S	LIFE	. THEY ARE TO BE FOUND WHEREVER THERE ARE ARMIES ON
MTH5	(261)	/LILITH/ THEY HAVE ACCEPTED THE BURDEN OF ETERNAL	LIFE	. THEY HAVE TAKEN THE AGONY FROM BIRTH; AND THEIR LIFE
MTH5	(219)	OF LIFE? /ACIS/ THEY DO. THAT IS, OF THE SAME	LIFE	. THEY MANAGE TO CHANGE THEMSELVES IN A WONDERFUL WAY.
MTH5	(248)	YOUR DOLLS THE FINAL PERFECTION OF RESEMBLANCE TO	LIFE	. THEY MUST MOVE AND SPEAK. /THE SHE-ANCIENT/ THEY MUST
METH PREFACE	(R26)	WOMB AT QUITE A LATE STAGE OF THEIR EMBRYONIC	LIFE	. THEY MUST RECAPITULATE THE HISTORY OF MANKIND IN
BARB PREFACE	(217)	WHICH I AM PREPARED TO KILL AT THE RISK OF MY OWN	LIFE	. THIS PREPAREDNESS IS, AS HE SAYS, THE FINAL TEST OF
3PLA PREFACE	(R24)	HE IS CONDEMNED BY HIS INCAPACITY FOR PUBLIC	LIFE	. THUS SHAKESPEAR, AFTER PROCLAIMING THAT NOT MARBLE
MIS. PREFACE	(35)	OR LONGING FOR ONE BECAUSE IT GIVES HOLIDAYS FOR	LIFE	. TO WHICH I REPLY, FIRST, THAT HEAVEN, AS
FABL V SD	(117)	OF UNCERTAIN AGE, APPARENTLY IN THE PRIME OF	LIFE	. TWO OF THEM ARE MALE, ONE FEMALE, THE FOURTH A
GENV IV	(100)	ON THAT ACCOUNT. THEY ARE A PART OF CIVILIZED	LIFE	. WAR IS A PART OF CIVILIZED LIFE. WE CANNOT GIVE IT UP
MIS. PREFACE	(106)	ARE BEING REPRODUCED EVERY DAY IN OUR ORDINARY	LIFE	. WE ARE BLUFFED BY HARDY SIMPLETONS AND HEADSTRONG
SIM II	(84)	PLANS FAIL: WOMEN WILL NEVER LET GO THEIR HOLD ON	LIFE	. WE ARE NOT HERE TO FULFIL PROPHECIES AND FIT
GENV IV	(100)	OF CIVILIZED LIFE. WAR IS A PART OF CIVILIZED	LIFE	. WE CANNOT GIVE IT UP BECAUSE OF ITS SHOCKING
METH PREFACE	(R48)	SKILL, OR INTELLIGENCE: IN SHORT, WITHOUT	LIFE	. WE COMPLETELY OVERLOOKED THE DIFFERENCE BETWEEN THE
GETT PREFACE	(200)	WHO IS QUARRELSOME AND VIOLENT IN PRIVATE	LIFE	. WE DO NOT WANT GOOD MEN AND BAD MEN ANY MORE THAN WE
METH PREFACE	(R18)	CHANGEABLE AT WILL IS THE DURATION OF INDIVIDUAL	LIFE	. WEISMANN, A VERY CLEVER AND SUGGESTIVE BIOLOGIST WHO
KING II	(227)	OF NOTHING BUT THAT, AS IF THAT WERE THE WHOLE OF	LIFE	. WHAT CARE I ABOUT YOUR WOMEN? YOUR CONCUBINES? YOUR
KING I	(208)	/CHARLES/ NONSENSE, DEAR. IT IS YOU TO THE	LIFE	. WHAT DO YOU SAY, JAMIE? (HE HANDS THE DRAWING TO
METH PREFACE	(R80)	PROVE THAT NEWTON WAS NEVER IN AN ORCHARD IN HIS	LIFE	. WHEN SOME UNUSUALLY CONSCIENTIOUS OR ENTERPRISING
MTH5	(250)	NOR WORKS OF ART. WE HAVE A DIRECT SENSE OF	LIFE	. WHEN YOU GAIN THAT YOU WILL PUT ASIDE YOUR MIRRORS
CAND III	(132)	CAN FIND NO REST, NO SENSE OF THE SILENT GLORY OF	LIFE	. WHERE WOULD YOU HAVE ME SPEND MY MOMENTS, IF NOT ON
LION PREFACE	(93)	OF HAPPINESS, AND BY NO MEANS A NECESSITY OF	LIFE	. WHETHER SOCRATES GOT AS MUCH HAPPINESS OUT OF LIFE AS
MTH5	(255)	EXCEPT THOUGHT, BECAUSE THE THOUGHT IS THE	LIFE	. WHICH IS JUST WHAT THIS OLD GENTLEMAN AND THIS OLD
MTH3	(93)	LIVING AUTHORITY ON THE DURATION OF HUMAN	LIFE	. WHO DARES DISPUTE IT? /BURGE-LUBIN/ NOBODY, DEAR
MIS. PREFACE	(20)	LOATHE THE SIGHT OF A BOOK ALL THE REST OF YOUR	LIFE	. WITH MILLIONS OF ACRES OF WOODS AND VALLEYS AND HILLS
ROCK PREFACE	(181)	TO YOU FOR YOUR SALVATION AT THE PERIL OF MY OWN	LIFE	. WOULD I DO THAT IF I WERE NOT DRIVEN BY GOD TO DO IT
HART II	(119)	DEATH GOVERN MY LIFE; AND MY REWARD WAS, I HAD MY	LIFE	. YOU ARE GOING TO LET THE FEAR OF POVERTY GOVERN YOUR
MTH1 II	(25)	AM. /CAIN/ YOU NEITHER OF YOU KNOW ANYTHING ABOUT	LIFE	. YOU ARE SIMPLE COUNTRY FOLK. YOU ARE THE NURSES AND
WIDO I	(13)	I BLUSH FOR YOU. I WAS NEVER SO ASHAMED IN MY	LIFE	. YOU HAVE BEEN TAKING ADVANTAGE OF THAT UNPROTECTED
MTH1 II	(25)	BOY: THIS IS NEITHER MAN NOR WOMAN NOR LOVE NOR	LIFE	. YOU HAVE NO REAL STRENGTH IN YOUR BONES NOR SAP IN
MTH4 I	(156)	WITHOUT ANY OBSTRUCTION FROM THE SOLID FACTS OF	LIFE	. YOU LOVE TO THROW DUST IN YOUR OWN EYES. /THE ELDERLY
SIM PRO72,	(28)	THE SEED AND THE SUN, THE RESURRECTION AND THE	LIFE	. YOU MUST NOT DIE HERE. I WILL SEND AN ACOLYTE TO
HART II	(119)	THE MORNING; AND YOU WILL AWAKE TIRED, TIRED OF	LIFE	. YOU WILL NEVER BE FREE FROM DOZING AND DREAMS: THE
CLEO II	(128)	/CAESAR/ MY LIFE! IS THAT ALL? /THEODOTUS/ YOUR	LIFE	. YOUR LAURELS. YOUR FUTURE. /POTHINUS/ IT IS TRUE. I
BULL IV	(164)	DO NOTHING. YOU HAVE NO RIGHT TO RUIN MY WHOLE	LIFE	. YOU-- (A HYSTERICAL CONVULSION STOPS HIM). /NORA/ (
DEVL I	(22)	CHILD STARVE OR BE DRIVEN BY WANT TO AN EVIL	LIFE	." /RICHARD/ (EMPHATICALLY, STRIKING HIS FIST ON THE
SUPR PREFACE	(R22)	IS INSIPID AFTER THE MOST COMMONPLACE " SLICE OF	LIFE	." THE PRETENCE THAT WOMEN DO NOT TAKE THE INITIATIVE
MIS. PREFACE	(71)	KIND OF SAVAGERY NOW CALLED " THE SIMPLE	LIFE	." THEIR NATURAL DISGUST WITH THE VISIONS OF COCKNEY
MTH5	(227)	IT, " BREATHED INTO THEIR NOSTRILS THE BREATH OF	LIFE	." THIS IS THE ONLY TRADITION FROM THE PRIMITIVE AGES
JOAN PREFACE	(35)	YOU SHALL STAY IN A DUNGEON ALL THE REST OF YOUR	LIFE	." UNFORTUNATELY, THE CHURCH DID NOT BELIEVE THAT THERE
GETT PREFACE	(201)	WORKING LIFE AND HE KNOWS NOTHING OF HER WORKING	LIFE	(HE CALLS IT HER HOME LIFE). IT IS REMARKABLE THAT THE
DEVL I	(22)	SO-- " AN ANNUITY OF FIFTY-TWO POUNDS A YEAR FOR	LIFE	(MRS DUDGEON, WITH ALL EYES ON HER, HOLDS HERSELF
GETT PREFACE	(195)	WHEN HE SHOULD BE IN TRAINING FOR HIS ADULT	LIFE	(REMEMBER THE BOY DICKENS AND THE BLACKING FACTORY),
LION PREFACE	(83)	AND THE ENRICHMENT AND INTENSIFICATION OF	LIFE	(" THAT YE MAY HAVE LIFE MORE ABUNDANTLY"); BUT THE
MTH5	(231)	WHICH WAS CALLED CANCER, UNTIL THE LOWER FORM OF	LIFE	KILLED THE HIGHER, AND BOTH PERISHED TOGETHER
GENV PREFACE	(9)	INTO A CLOUD OF FLAMING GAS IN WHICH NO FORM OF	LIFE	KNOWN TO US COULD SURVIVE FOR A MOMENT. THAT SUCH
GENV IV	(124)	WILL BE FROZEN STIFF. NOT A TRACE OF ANY SORT OF	LIFE	KNOWN TO US WILL BE POSSIBLE ON THIS EARTH. /THE JEW/ (
DOCT V	(177)	MAKING A TERRIBLE DISCOVERY. FROM HAVING YOUR	LIFE	LAID WASTE. /JENNIFER/ HOW? /RIDGEON/ NO MATTER. I

LION PREFACE(12)	IN PRIMITIVE COMMUNITIES WHERE THE CONDITIONS OF	LIFE	LEAVE NO ROOM FOR POVERTY AND RICHES, AND THE PROCESS
DEVL II (40)	GET HIM SAFELY OUT OF HARM'S WAY. DONT FOR YOUR	LIFE	LET HIM KNOW OF MY DANGER; BUT IF HE FINDS IT OUT, TELL
DEVL II (46)	I CANT KEEP MY PROMISE. HE SAID, " DONT FOR YOUR	LIFE	LET HIM KNOW OF MY DANGER." IVE TOLD YOU OF IT. HE SAID
SUPR HANDBOK(226)	PERSON LOATHES ALMSGIVING AND MENDICITY. FAME.	LIFE	LEVELS ALL MEN: DEATH REVEALS THE EMINENT. DISCIPLINE.
PLES PREFACE(R19)	LYING. TO ME THE TRAGEDY AND COMEDY OF	LIFE	LIE IN THE CONSEQUENCES, SOMETIMES TERRIBLE, SOMETIMES
JITT II (35)	/JITTA/ MY POOR CHILD! BUT DONT LOSE COURAGE.	LIFE	LIES BEFORE YOU: IT WILL MAKE UP TO YOU FOR MANY
BARB III (349)	A WOMAN OF MY RANK. /CUSINS/ THEN THE WAY OF	LIFE	LIES THROUGH THE FACTORY OF DEATH? /BARBARA/ YES,
FABL III (111)	OR TWO TO STOP SINGING AND GO AWAY. IT'S A WAY OF	LIFE	LIKE ANY OTHER. IT SUITS ME. I'M GOOD FOR NOTHING ELSE.
MRS II (209)	OCCURRED TO YOU, MOTHER, THAT I HAVE A WAY OF	LIFE	LIKE OTHER PEOPLE? /MRS WARREN/ WHAT NONSENSE IS THIS
MTH1 II (22)	SHRIEKS OF TORMENT! THAT WILL BE LIFE INDEED:	LIFE	LIVED TO THE VERY MARROW: BURNING, OVERWHELMING LIFE.
MTH2 (78)	FOR WHICH I SHALL BE INDEBTED TO HIM ALL MY	LIFE	LONG: HAS THIS, I SAY, NO DEEPER EFFECT ON YOU THAN TO
HART II (120)	BUT THE ACCURSED HAPPINESS I HAVE DREADED ALL MY	LIFE	LONG: THE HAPPINESS THAT COMES AS LIFE GOES, THE
DEST (185)	AND REPEATEDLY) NO NO NO NO NO NO NO. ALL MY	LIFE	LONG PEOPLE HAVE WANTED TO MAKE A MAN OF ME. WHEN I WAS
MRS I (196)	FROM AN ERROR YOU WOULD HAVE REPENTED ALL YOUR	LIFE	LONG. TAKE WARNING BY YOUR FATHER'S FOLLIES, SIR; AND
MTH4 I (150)	DAMN IT, MADAM, YOU DONT WANT TO SPEND YOUR	LIFE	LOOKING AT THE SAME BIT OF IT! (CHECKING HIMSELF) I
JITT I (24)	THAT MEANS NOTHING: THIS IS LOVE; AND LOVE IS	LIFE	MADE IRRESISTIBLE. /BRUNO/ (CARRIED AWAY) LIFE: YES:
HART II (92)	THE CLUTCHES OF THIS SLAVEDRIVER, WHO SPENDS HIS	LIFE	MAKING THOUSANDS OF ROUGH VIOLENT WORKMEN BEND TO HIS
SIM PRO,1, (24)	COME ALONG AND SHEW ME ROUND. I SEEM TO SPEND MY	LIFE	MAKING UP OTHER PEOPLE'S MINDS FOR THEM. /THE E.O./ (
SUPR III (105)	INVENTIONS. AND I TELL YOU THAT IN THE ARTS OF	LIFE	MAN INVENTS NOTHING; BUT IN THE ARTS OF DEATH HE
CLEO III (163)	(STILL MORE GRAVELY) MY POOR CHILD: YOUR	LIFE	MATTERS LITTLE HERE TO ANYONE BUT YOURSELF. (SHE GIVES
MTH1 II (25)	(TO ADAM) YOU THINK, PERHAPS, THAT HIS WAY OF	LIFE	MAY BE BETTER THAN YOURS AFTER ALL. YOU ARE STILL
BULL I (78)	I SHALL BE DENOUNCED FROM EVERY ALTAR. MY	LIFE	MAY BE IN DANGER. WELL, I AM PREPARED TO FACE THAT.
GETT PREFACE(234)	UP THEIR HOME LIFE. BUT WITHIN DOORS THAT HOME	LIFE	MAY BE REGARDED AS NATURALLY MONOGAMOUS. IT DOES NOT
CLEO IV (178)	WILL YOU NOT GIVE ME A PRIVATE AUDIENCE? YOUR	LIFE	MAY DEPEND ON IT. (CAESAR RISES LOFTILY). /RUFIO/ (
PYGM V (284)	MAKER HAD BEEN AFRAID OF MAKING TROUBLE? MAKING	LIFE	MEANS MAKING TROUBLE. THERES ONLY ONE WAY OF ESCAPING
MRS PREFACE(155)	OF UNOBSERVANT UNREFLECTING PEOPLE TO WHOM REAL	LIFE	MEANS NOTHING. I HAVE POINTED OUT AGAIN AND AGAIN THAT
CAPT III (294)	ME THAT I HAD PUT JUSTICE ABOVE SELF. I TELL YOU	LIFE	MEANT SOMETHING TO ME THEN. DO YOU SEE THAT DIRTY
CLEO NOTES (210)	THAN WAR. AND IT IS CERTAINLY TRUE THAT IN CIVIL	LIFE	MERE CAPACITY FOR WORK-- THE POWER OF KILLING A DOZEN
DOCT V (177)	YOU TRIED TO DESTROY THAT WONDERFUL AND BEAUTIFUL	LIFE	MERELY BECAUSE YOU GRUDGED HIM A WOMAN WHOM YOU COULD
HART II (124)	MOUSTACHE: I CANT CUT OFF MY NOSE. I GET MY WHOLE	LIFE	MESSED UP WITH PEOPLE FALLING IN LOVE WITH ME. AND THEN
MTH3 (124)	LET ME TELL YOU, MADAM, THAT I HAVE NEVER IN MY	LIFE	MET THE MINISTER OF HEALTH, AND THAT I PROTEST AGAINST
SUPR HANDBOK(202)	IN ITS NAME WE TAKE TEN YEARS OF A THIEF'S	LIFE	MINUTE BY MINUTE IN THE SLOW MISERY AND DEGRADATION OF
ROCK I (228)	HER, OR RATHER TO PREVENT HER FROM MAKING MY	LIFE	MISERABLE. THEY ALL SAY THE SAME THING; AND THEY ARE
HART PREFACE(19)	OF INEVITABLE EVIL INSTEAD OF TO THE IDEAL OF	LIFE	MORE ABUNDANT. I CAN ANSWER FOR AT LEAST ONE PERSON WHO
LION PREFACE(83)	AND INTENSIFICATION OF LIFE (" THAT YE MAY HAVE	LIFE	MORE ABUNDANTLY"); BUT THE APOSTLES, AS DESCRIBED IN
NEVR II (231)	AND HE WILL TELL YOU THE STORY OF MY MARRIED	LIFE	MORE FAIRLY THAN I COULD. GLORIA: ARE YOU SATISFIED?
CAPT I SD(225)	AUTHORITY AND DIGNITY, BUT IS TRYING TO TAKE	LIFE	MORE GENIALLY AND EASILY IN HIS CHARACTER OF TOURIST,
FANY I (278)	GETS LOOSE THERES NO HOLDING HIM. HE DOES ENJOY	LIFE	MORE THAN ANY LAD I EVER MET. /GILBEY/ NEVER YOU MIND
MTH2 (38)	IT). HERE IT IS: (READING) " THE TERM OF HUMAN	LIFE	MUST BE EXTENDED TO AT LEAST THREE CENTURIES." /THE
MIS. PREFACE(69)	IS NO REAL ALTERNATIVE FOR EITHER OF THEM. CHILD	LIFE	MUST BE SOCIALLY ORGANIZED: NO PARENT, RICH OR POOR,
HART III (143)	EXPECTING SOMETHING. I DONT KNOW WHAT IT IS; BUT	LIFE	MUST COME TO A POINT SOMETIME. /LADY UTTERWORD/ THE
MTH1 I (11)	THE REST DIE TOO? WHAT DO I CARE? /THE SERPENT/	LIFE	MUST NOT CEASE. THAT COMES BEFORE EVERYTHING. IT IS
MTH1 I (9)	LIFE. /EVE/ I DO NOT TRUST THE SUN. I WILL GIVE	LIFE	MYSELF. I WILL TEAR ANOTHER ADAM FROM MY BODY IF TEAR
SIM II (85)	THE MAN. /PROLA/ YES: I NEED YOU AND YOU NEED ME.	LIFE	NEEDS US BOTH. /PRA/ ALL HAIL, THEN, THE LIFE TO COME!
SIM PRO,1, (25)	GETS ALL THE PRAISE; AND ALL THE PUDDING? BECAUSE	LIFE	NEVER CAME TO ME LIKE IT CAME TO RHODES. FOUND HIS
2TRU PREFACE(9)	MEDICINE WAS DELICIOUS) MADE UP MY MIND EARLY IN	LIFE	NEVER TO LET MYSELF BE PERSUADED THAT I AM ENJOYING
DOCT PREFACE(46)	OF IT WHICH HAS NEITHER SENSE NOR PURPOSE NOR	LIFE	NOR ANYTHING HUMAN, MUCH LESS GODLIKE, IN IT: BY THE
OVER (179)	MAKE ME SAY IT. OF COURSE I KNOW. NOTHING-- NOT	LIFE	NOR DEATH NOR SHAME NOR ANYTHING CAN PART US. /A
CAPT III (297)	WORK IS PUT UPON ME, I TURN NEITHER TO SAVE MY	LIFE	NOR TO FILL MY POCKET. GORDON TRUSTED ME; AND HE NEVER
BARB PREFACE(217)	OF POVERTY, BOTH), THE BEST IMITATION OF A GOOD	LIFE	NOW PROCURABLE IS LIFE ON AN INDEPENDENT INCOME. ALL
JITT III (64)	CAN ONLY TELL YOU ONE THING. I HAVE ONE OBJECT IN	LIFE	NOW, AND ONE ONLY. /FESSLER/ AND WHAT IS THAT, IF I MAY
HART PREFACE(19)	LOSS TO THE WORLD OF FOUR YEARS OF THE	LIFE	OF A GENERATION WASTED ON DESTRUCTION. HARDLY ONE OF
DOCT I (113)	THING? /MRS DUBEDAT/ I AM ASKING YOU TO SAVE THE	LIFE	OF A GREAT MAN. /RIDGEON/ YOU ARE ASKING ME TO KILL
BARB PREFACE(219)	AND THE COMMON MAN DOES NOT WANT TO LIVE THE	LIFE	OF A MAN OF GENIUS: HE WOULD MUCH RATHER LIVE THE LIFE
2TRU II (71)	THAT I HAVE FOR A MONTH PAST BEEN LIVING THE	LIFE	OF A MOUNTAIN GOAT. I HAVE GOT RID OF MY ANXIOUS
BARB PREFACE(219)	OF A MAN OF GENIUS: HE WOULD MUCH RATHER LIVE THE	LIFE	OF A PET COLLIE IF THAT WERE THE ONLY ALTERNATIVE. BUT
JOAN 6 (145)	YOUR FIRE: DO YOU THINK I DREAD IT AS MUCH AS THE	LIFE	OF A RAT IN A HOLE? MY VOICES WERE RIGHT. /LADVENU/
6CAL (95)	THEM? /THE KING/ I HAVE NOT THREATENED THE	LIFE	OF A SINGLE KNIGHT. I HAVE SAID THAT NO MAN OF GENTLE
JOAN 5 (117)	A BIT MORE INVINCIBLE, SHE WILL NOT BE WORTH THE	LIFE	OF A SINGLE SOLDIER TO US; AND I WILL NOT RISK THAT
BULL PREFACE(22)	TO BECOME PRIME MINISTER WITH THE OUTLOOK ON	LIFE	OF A SPORTING COUNTRY SOLICITOR EDUCATED BY A PRIVATE
JITT I (14)	WITH SUDDEN ENERGY) I WANT TO BE RUINED. OH, THE	LIFE	OF A UNIVERSITY PROFESSOR, HIS RESPECTABILITY KILLS HER
BUOY III (40)	THERE TO ACQUIRE THE SOCIAL TRAINING THE COMMUNAL	LIFE	OF A UNIVERSITY GIVES. BUT HE INSISTED ON OUR LEAVING
SUPR I (34)	THE GUILTY SECRET OVER HER HEAD, LEADING HER A	LIFE	OF ABJECT TERROR AND HUMILIATION BY THREATENING TO TELL
CLEO IV (175)	OH, THIS MILITARY LIFE! THIS TEDIOUS, BRUTAL	LIFE	OF ACTION! THAT IS THE WORST OF US ROMANS: WE ARE MERE
MILL IV (209)	INFINITELY DANGEROUS HEART TEARING EVERCHANGING	LIFE	OF ADVENTURE THAT WE CALL MARRIAGE? FACE IT AS YOU
LION PREFACE(64)	AND THEN, AND GOES OUT INTO THE WORLD TO LIVE THE	LIFE	OF AN HONEST MAN INSTEAD OF THAT OF A CRUEL IDOL. THERE
MIS. (139)	IS A PERSON WHO KNOWS A DISGRACEFUL SECRET IN THE	LIFE	OF ANOTHER PERSON, AND EXTORTS MONEY FROM THAT OTHER
JOAN 6 (129)	THE POOR, AND PUTTING ON THE GARB OF POVERTY, THE	LIFE	OF AUSTERITY, AND THE RULE OF HUMILITY AND CHARITY, MAY
CAPT II (260)	CAME BACK NEXT DAY AND SAID HE MUST RETURN TO A	LIFE	OF CRIME UNLESS I GAVE HIM A JOB IN THE GARDEN; AND I
BARB PREFACE(223)	SERIOUS BUSINESS OF THE DAY IS OVER, PASSION, THE	LIFE	OF DRAMA, MEANS NOTHING TO THEM BUT PRIMITIVE SEXUAL
PYGM EPILOG (303)	THAT SHE REALLY LEADS AS DISTINGUISHED FROM THE	LIFE	OF DREAMS AND FANCIES, SHE LIKES FREDDY AND SHE LIKES
MTH3 (125)	TO TUESDAY THEY ARE SIMPLY NOWHERE; AND THE REAL	LIFE	OF ENGLAND IS FROM FRIDAY TO TUESDAY. /THE ARCHBISHOP/
GETT PREFACE(199)	WAS UP TO THE POINT OF WRECKING THE SOCIAL	LIFE	OF FLORENCE, DOES NOT ALTER THE CASE. WE ALWAYS
KING I (171)	NOW CAPTIVES IN BARBARY NOT TO FORGET THAT THE	LIFE	OF GOD AND THE POWER OF GOD ARE IN THEIR HEATHEN
METH PREFACE(R59)	THE STOCK REPLY TO THIS IS TO BE FOUND IN LEWES'S	LIFE	OF GOETHE. LEWES SCORNED THE NOTION THAT CIRCUMSTANCES
DOCT V (172)	JUST COME IN. AN ADVANCE COPY OF MRS DUBEDAT'S	LIFE	OF HER LATE HUSBAND. /RIDGEON/ (READING THE TITLE) THE
JOAN PREFACE(26)	SAW RED, AND WENT FOR ANATOLE'S SCALP IN A RIVAL	LIFE	OF HER WHICH SHOULD BE READ AS A CORRECTIVE TO THE
BARB PREFACE(222)	THE HEAVEN OF THE THEATRE, SELF-CONDEMNED TO A	LIFE	OF HIDEOUS GLOOM; AND THE SALVATIONIST MOURNING OVER
SIM PREFACE(17)	BLOW A MAN'S BRAINS OUT BECAUSE HE CANNOT FOR THE	LIFE	OF HIM SEE WHY HE SHOULD NOT EMPLOY LABOR AT A PROFIT,
SUPR HANDBOK(208)	YET HIS NORMAL LIFE IS HIGHER THAN THE NORMAL	LIFE	OF HIS FOREFATHERS. THIS VIEW IS VERY ACCEPTABLE TO
LION PREFACE(4)	TO TIME AND SPACE (THAT IS, TO THE SYRIAN	LIFE	OF HIS PERIOD) INVOLVED HIS BELIEF IN MANY THINGS, TRUE
MRS IV (249)	SHOOTING, HUNTING, DINING-OUT, TAILORING, LOAFING	LIFE	OF HIS SET MERELY BECAUSE ALL THE REST DO IT, AND I'M
LION PREFACE(21)	A MAN OF THIRTY (LUKE SAYS) INTO THE RELIGIOUS	LIFE	OF HIS TIME BY GOING TO JOHN THE BAPTIST AND DEMANDING
BARB PREFACE(244)	TO PUNISH WILL ALSO BE TOO THRIFTY TO WASTE THE	LIFE	OF HONEST MEN IN WATCHING OR RESTRAINING DISHONEST
FABL PREFACE(73)	BEGAN HER REACTION BY TRANSLATING EMIL STRAUSS'S	LIFE	OF JESUS, WHICH DIVESTED THE WORSHIPPED REDEEMER OF
JOAN PREFACE(26)	THE QUICHERATIC WAVE OF ENTHUSIASM, AND WROTE A	LIFE	OF JOAN IN WHICH HE ATTRIBUTED JOAN'S IDEAS TO CLERICAL
DEVL EPILOG (81)	QUOTED BY DE FONBLANQUE FROM FITZMAURICE'S	LIFE	OF LORD SHELBURNE, AS FOLLOWS: " LORD GEORGE GERMAIN,
SUPR III (86)	LOUISA, LOUISA MENDOZA, HOW BLEST WERE THE	LIFE	OF LOUISA'S MENDOZA! HOW PAINLESS HIS LONGING OF LOVE
POSN PREFACE(393)	IN FACT-- HAS LONG DESIRED TO DRAMATIZE THE	LIFE	OF MAHOMET. BUT THE POSSIBILITY OF A PROTEST FROM THE
LADY PREFACE(214)	TO FOLLOW TYLER ON ONE POINT, THOUGH FOR THE	LIFE	OF ME I CANNOT REMEMBER WHETHER IT WAS ONE OF THE
JITT III (69)	SHAME TO LAUGH AT ALL AT SUCH A TIME. BUT FOR THE	LIFE	OF ME I COULDNT HELP IT. /JITTA/ (LOOKING HARD AT HER)
SIM II (78)	/SIR CHARLES/ MOST EXTRAORDINARY. I CANT FOR THE	LIFE	OF ME REMEMBER. HOW MANY OF THEM DID YOU SAY THERE
LADY PREFACE(220)	MAN ANNOUNCES THEIR TRAGEDY. I CANNOT FOR THE	LIFE	OF ME SEE THE BROKEN HEART IN SHAKESPEAR'S LATEST
SUPR III (93)	ALL MY LIFE. /DON JUAN/ YES; IT BECAME YOU. BUT A	LIFE	OF MOURNING IS ONE THING: AN ETERNITY OF IT QUITE
LADY PREFACE(212)	EVERY DIGNITY, EVERY SWEET USAGE OF THAT QUIET	LIFE	OF MUTUAL ADMIRATION IN WHICH PERFECT SHAKESPEARIAN
MTH4 I (173)	A GREAT DEAL OF THE LITTLE I KNOW OF THE PRIVATE	LIFE	OF OUR GREAT MEN. WE MUST BE VERY CONVENIENT TO YOU AS
ROCK PREFACE(172)	EVEN IF HE DID BELIEVE GENERALLY IN A POST MORTEM	LIFE	OF REWARDS AND PUNISHMENTS FOR CONDUCT IN THIS WORLD.
CLEO II (128)	ANY SERVICE, GENTLEMEN? /THEODOTUS/ IS CAESAR'S	LIFE	OF SO LITTLE ACCOUNT TO HIM THAT HE FORGETS THAT WE
DOCT PREFACE(34)	TO THROW AWAY HIS INDIVIDUAL LIFE TO SAVE THE	LIFE	OF THE COMMUNITY, IT IS JUST SO IN THE CASE OF THE
POSN PREFACE(425)	BECAUSE IT WOULD KILL THE RELIGIOUS AND POLITICAL	LIFE	OF THE COUNTRY OUTRIGHT, WHEREAS TO COMPEL PEOPLE TO
PYGM V (286)	TIL YOU FALL ASLEEP. OH, IT'S A FINE LIFE, THE	LIFE	OF THE GUTTER. IT'S REAL: IT'S WARM: IT'S VIOLENT: YOU
JOAN PREFACE(14)	THAT THE APPETITE FOR FOOD IS NECESSARY TO THE	LIFE	OF THE HUNGRY MAN AND IS THEREFORE A PERSONAL APPETITE,
2TRU PREFACE(8)	BEYOND THE GRAVE. I WOULD AND COULD LIVE THE	LIFE	OF THE IDLE RICH IF I LIKED IT; AND MY SOLE REASON FOR
GETT PREFACE(194)	TO SOMETHING LIKE REASONABLE PROPORTIONS IN THE	LIFE	OF THE INDIVIDUAL, THE DANGER OF IT DOES NOT LIE IN
SIM II (83)	ALL HUSBANDS; BUT OUTSIDE THAT ROUTINE THERE IS A	LIFE	OF THE INTELLECT THAT IS QUITE INDEPENDENT OF IT. WHAT
LADY PREFACE(231)	SQUALOR, NOW THE ONLY ONES THAT ARE TRUE TO THE	LIFE	OF THE MAJORITY OF LIVING MEN, WILL THEN BE CLASSED
BARB PREFACE(225)	HER, LEARNT IT BY TAKING THEIR PART IN THE LARGER	LIFE	OF THE NATION. BARBARA'S RETURN TO THE COLORS.

BARB PREFACE(222)	BUT ALSO SAW IT IN ITS RELATION TO THE RELIGIOUS	LIFE	OF THE NATION, A LIFE WHICH SEEMS TO LIE NOT ONLY
GETT PREFACE(231)	IS SO INTIMATE AND SO PERVASIVE OF THE WHOLE	LIFE	OF THE PARTIES TO IT, THAT NOBODY HAS ROOM IN HIS OR
SUPR I SD(16)	MADE INFINITE BY A MYSTIC MEMORY OF THE WHOLE	LIFE	OF THE RACE TO ITS BEGINNINGS IN THE EAST, OR EVEN BACK
GETT PREFACE(237)	RIGHT TO LIFE, EXTENDED AS IT NOW MUST BE TO THE	LIFE	OF THE RACE, AND TO THE QUALITY OF LIFE AS WELL AS TO
MIS. (181)	WITH A PISTOL WITH WHICH I THREATENED TO TAKE THE	LIFE	OF THE SAID JOHN TARLETON AND WAS PREVENTED FROM DOING
MIS. (179)	A PISTOL, WITH WHICH I THREATENED TO TAKE THE	LIFE	OF THE SAID JOHN TARLETON-- /MRS TARLETON/ OH, JOHN!
JOAN PREFACE(14)	THESE EXTENSIONS MAY NOT TOUCH THE PERSONAL	LIFE	OF THE SEEKER AT ANY POINT. THERE IS NO MORE MYSTERY
BULL PREFACE(48)	THAT DISCIPLINE IS DIFFICULT, BECAUSE THE WASTED	LIFE	OF THE SOLDIER IS UNNATURAL, EXCEPT TO A LAZY MAN, AND
MTH1 II (28)	LIFE: A LIFE INFINITELY SPLENDID AND INTENSE: A	LIFE	OF THE SOUL ALONE: A LIFE WITHOUT CLODS OR SPADES,
MRS PREFACE(153)	BETWEEN THE WORK OF ART ON THE STAGE AND THE REAL	LIFE	OF THE SPECTATOR IS CONFUSED AND OVERWHELMED, WILL EVER
HART I (62)	OH NO: NOTHING VULGAR LIKE THAT. HE SAVED THE	LIFE	OF THE TIGER FROM A HUNTING PARTY: ONE OF KING EDWARD'S
MIS. PREFACE(67)	COMPARATIVELY FREE FROM IT, BECAUSE THE COMMUNAL	LIFE	OF THE UNIVERSITY, THE FACT THAT IN A SHIP A MAN MUST
ROCK PREFACE(153)	(SHEWN BY THE ACTUARIAL EXPECTATION OF	LIFE	OF THE UNPROPERTIED) FOR PERIODS DESCRIBED AS
METH PREFACE(R27)	SIMPLEST EVERYDAY OCCASIONS; AND CANNOT FOR THE	LIFE	OF THEM DESCRIBE MECHANICAL OPERATIONS WHICH THEY
GLIM (178)	OUTSIDE THE LIFE I LEAD ALL TO MYSELF-- THE	LIFE	OF THOUGHT AND POETRY-- I KNOW ONLY TWO PLEASURES:
LION PREFACE(54)	SIDE BY SIDE WITH PAUPERS WORN OUT BY A LONG	LIFE	OF UNREMITTED DRUDGERY. ONE PERSON IN EVERY FIVE DIES
CLEO PRO2,SD(96)	WITH TOLERABLE COMPLETENESS THE MAIN INTERESTS IN	LIFE	OF WHICH THEY ARE CONSCIOUS. THEIR SPEARS ARE LEANING
SUPR III (105)	HEART IS IN HIS WEAPONS. THIS MARVELLOUS FORCE OF	LIFE	OF WHICH YOU BOAST IS A FORCE OF DEATH: MAN MEASURES
MTH1 II (27)	DIG AGAIN) TAKE YOURSELF OFF THEN. THIS SPLENDID	LIFE	OF YOURS DOES NOT LAST FOR A THOUSAND YEARS; AND I MUST
BARB PREFACE(217)	BEST IMITATION OF A GOOD LIFE NOW PROCURABLE IS	LIFE	ON AN INDEPENDENT INCOME, ALL SENSIBLE PEOPLE AIM AT
LION PREFACE(16)	RENEWED LIFE AND BEAUTY AND GIVE MANKIND ETERNAL	LIFE	ON CONDITION THAT IT WAS EATEN AND DRUNK, AND AGAIN
PRES (147)	AT ME. /MITCHENER/ WHEN A MAN HAS RISKED HIS	LIFE	ON EIGHT BATTLEFIELDS, MRS FARRELL, HE HAS GIVEN
LION I (113)	CAN YOU TEST YOUR SWORD EXCEPT BY STAKING YOUR	LIFE	ON IT? /THE CAPTAIN/ (SUDDENLY RESUMING HIS OFFICIAL
METH PREFACE(R24)	PRODUCE THE MOST ELABORATE FORMS OF ORGANIZED	LIFE	ON LAMARCKIAN LINES WITHOUT THE INTERVENTION OF
BULL III (131)	/LARRY/ HOW IS THE MAN TO MARRY AND LIVE A DECENT	LIFE	ON LESS? /FATHER DEMPSEY/ MAN ALIVE, HWERE HAVE YOU
MTH3 (134)	RAGE) OH, QUITE. PRAY DONT RISK YOUR PRECIOUS	LIFE	ON MY ACCOUNT. SORRY FOR TROUBLING YOU. GOODBYE. (SHE
3PLA PREFACE(R15)	NOT AN ARCHBISHOP, AND DO NOT PRETEND TO PASS MY	LIFE	ON ONE PLANE OR IN ONE MOOD, AND THAT THE HIGHEST: ON
GETT PREFACE(206)	ENDS BETTER THAN YOU," AND STAKING HIS POLITICAL	LIFE	ON THE CONVICTION CARRIED BY THAT ASSURANCE, WHICH
HART PREFACE(28)	PASSING A WORTHLESS CHEQUE, COULD YET STAKE HIS	LIFE	ON THE MOST DESPERATE CHANCES OF THE BATTLE-FIELD!
3PLA PREFACE(R17)	WORD UNGENTEEL PURPOSELY; FOR THE STAGE PRESENTS	LIFE	ON THIRTY POUNDS A DAY, NOT AS IT IS, BUT AS IT IS
MTH5 (211)	AUTUMN ONLY A RESPITE. THE ANCIENTS COULD MAKE	LIFE	ONE LONG FROWSTY COMFORT IF THEY CHOSE. BUT THEY NEVER
SIM I (47)	BEEN FOR MY TERRIBLE CONSCIENCE. IT HAS MADE MY	LIFE	ONE LONG REMORSE; FOR I HAVE NEVER HAD THE STRENGTH OF
MTH5 (262)	A LEGEND AND A LAY THAT HAS LOST ITS MEANING. OF	LIFE	ONLY IS THERE NO END; AND THOUGH OF ITS MILLION STARRY
KING I (171)	MR NEWTON? /NEWTON/ WOMEN ENTER A PHILOSOPHER'S	LIFE	ONLY TO DISTURB IT. THEY EXPECT TOO MUCH ATTENTION.
MTH2 (76)	MOMENT HE INVENTED DEATH, AND BECAME A TENANT FOR	LIFE	ONLY, THE PLACE WAS NO LONGER WORTH THE TROUBLE. IT WAS
MRS IV (249)	ME. WHAT DO THE PEOPLE THAT TAUGHT YOU KNOW ABOUT	LIFE	OR ABOUT PEOPLE LIKE ME? WHEN DID THEY EVER MEET ME,
ARMS III (71)	PROCEEDS INNOCENTLY) ALL THAT ADVENTURE WHICH WAS	LIFE	OR DEATH TO ME, WAS ONLY A SCHOOLGIRL'S GAME TO HER--
METH PREFACE(R87)	THAT CIVILIZATION NEEDS A RELIGION AS A MATTER OF	LIFE	OR DEATH; AND AS THE CONCEPTION OF CREATIVE EVOLUTION
CAPT II (268)	WHAT YOU SAY; FOR WHEN MY WORD GOES FORTH FOR	LIFE	OR DEATH, IT MAY NOT BE RECALLED. /BRASSBOUND/ SIDI EL
MTH2 (73)	MOON. /BURGE/ HAVE YOU DISCOVERED THE ELIXIR OF	LIFE	OR HAVE YOU NOT? IF NOT, I AGREE WITH LUBIN THAT YOU
LION PREFACE(67)	AS LONG AS A MAN HAS A RIGHT TO RISK HIS	LIFE	OR HIS LIVELIHOOD FOR HIS IDEAS HE NEEDS ONLY COURAGE
3PLA PREFACE(R28)	BY WIFE OR MOTHER, CHURCH OR STATE, PRIDE OF	LIFE	OR LUST OF THE FLESH. IN THE LOVELY HOME OF THE
JOAN 5 (116)	THE LADDER AND OVER THE WALL. WITH THEM IT IS MY	LIFE	OR THINE, AND GOD DEFEND THE RIGHT! YOU MAY SHAKE YOUR
MTH1 II (28)	TO CREATE LIFE: IT IS SHORT AND EASY TO STEAL THE	LIFE	OTHERS HAVE MADE. WHEN YOU DUG, YOU MADE THE EARTH LIVE
ARMS II (28)	UNTIL RAINA TAKES HIM OFF OUR HANDS. HE BORES MY	LIFE	OUT ABOUT OUR NOT PROMOTING HIM. OVER MY HEAD, IF YOU
CLEO IV (180)	(STRIKING HER ON THE MOUTH) STRIKE HIS	LIFE	OUT AS I STRIKE HIS NAME FROM YOUR LIPS. DASH HIM DOWN
MIS. (171)	TALKED DOWN TO BY HOGS LIKE YOU, AND WEARING MY	LIFE	OUT FOR A SALARY THAT WOULDNT KEEP YOU IN CIGARS. YOULL
BULL IV (147)	HE WAS PUTN NON THE BRAKE HE WAS ONY SQUEEZIN THE	LIFE	OUT O THE PIG'S TAIL. THE MORE HE PUT THE BRAKE ON THE
MIS. (198)	TARLETON? /TARLETON/ YES. I WANT TO THRASH THE	LIFE	OUT OF HER. IF SHE DOESNT GET OUT OF MY REACH, I'LL DO
ROCK II (268)	OUT OF PARLIAMENT AND KEEP OUT. IT WILL TAKE THE	LIFE	OUT OF HIM AND LEAVE HIM A WALKING TALKING SHELL OF A
BUOY III (30)	BLAME MY PARENTS FOR NOT HAVING THRASHED THE	LIFE	OUT OF ME INSTEAD OF LEAVING ME TO LEARN LIFE'S LESSONS
MRS I (189)	LOOKS CHEERFUL, DONT HE? HE'S BEEN WORRYING MY	LIFE	OUT THESE THREE YEARS TO HAVE THAT LITTLE GIRL OF MINE
BARB PREFACE(229)	AND LOT AND SOMETHING OVER, AND LET HIS ETERNAL	LIFE	PASS ON TO RENEW ITS YOUTH IN THE BATTALIONS OF THE
MTH4 II (181)	(IT IS THE SAME THING), THE NOBLER PART OF HUMAN	LIFE	PERISHES. YOU MUST SAVE THE WORLD FROM THAT
MTH2 (75)	ME. /CONRAD/ YOU ARE EVE, IN A SENSE. THE ETERNAL	LIFE	PERSISTS; ONLY IT WEARS OUT ITS BODIES AND MINDS AND
BARB PREFACE(246)	MAY DEPEND ON IT, WILL GO ON TO THE END OF HIS	LIFE	POISONING PEOPLE WITH BAD WHISKY, BECAUSE HE CAN ALWAYS
JOAN PREFACE(37)	THAT IS, THE UNAVERAGED INDIVIDUAL, REPRESENTING	LIFE	POSSIBLY AT ITS HIGHEST ACTUAL HUMAN EVOLUTION AND
VWOO 1 (117)	SHIP, ARNT WE? AND MOST PEOPLE WOULD THINK MY	LIFE	QUITE A ROMANCE. WOULDNT YOU REALLY LIKE TO HEAR IT?
MTH2 (40)	/CONRAD/ YOU SEE, SHE HASNT TIME TO FIND OUT WHAT	LIFE	REALLY MEANS. SHE HAS TO DIE BEFORE SHE KNOWS. /HASLAM/
BASH I (93)	WITH THEM COMES: TO SHOW THE PURSE BEARER THAT	LIFE	REMAINS UNPURCHASABLE? LEARNING LEARNS BUT ONE LESSON:
MIS. (161)	TO A MAN LIKE ME, EVERYBODY IS THE FIRST.	LIFE	RENEWS ITSELF. /LINA/ THE YOUNGEST CHILD IS THE
HART II (108)	A SORT OF CALL TO ME. LET ME SPEND THE REST OF MY	LIFE	REPENTING IN A CELL. I SHALL HAVE MY REWARD ABOVE.
MILL I (151)	TRY TO LIVE WITH THEM THEY JUST EAT UP YOUR WHOLE	LIFE	RUNNING AFTER THEM OR QUARRELLING OR ATTENDING TO THEM
APPL INTRLUD(246)	THE FURNITURE. LIVE A REALLY NOBLE AND BEAUTIFUL	LIFE	-- A KINGLY LIFE -- WITH ME. WHAT YOU NEED TO MAKE YOU
PLES PREFACE(R15)	AS THE GREAT HERESY TO BE SWEPT OFF FROM ART AND	LIFE	-- AS THE FOOD OF MODERN PESSIMISM AND THE BANE OF
MRS IV (241)	SPARE ME. I WAS SENTIMENTAL FOR ONE MOMENT IN MY	LIFE	-- BEAUTIFULLY SENTIMENTAL-- BY MOONLIGHT; AND NOW--
GETT (305)	COMMON SENSE AND SANITY, LET US GET BACK TO REAL	LIFE	-- COLLINS COMES IN THROUGH THE TOWER, IN ALDERMAN'S
BULL PREFACE(39)	THE AVERAGE IRISHMAN HAS A MORE TOLERABLE	LIFE	-- ESPECIALLY NOW THAT THE POPULATION IS SO SCANTY--
ARMS I (6)	(THEY KISS). THIS IS THE HAPPIEST NIGHT OF MY	LIFE	-- IF ONLY THERE ARE NO FUGITIVES. /CATHERINE/ GO TO
BARB PREFACE(218)	RICH MEN OR ARISTOCRATS WITH A DEVELOPED SENSE OF	LIFE	-- MEN LIKE RUSKIN AND WILLIAM MORRIS AND KROPOTKIN--
MIS. (153)	WITHOUT SOME MEMBER OF MY FAMILY RISKING HIS	LIFE	-- OR HER LIFE. IT'S A POINT OF HONOR WITH US TO KEEP
PPP (198)	A TIME FOR PETTY VANITY? THINK OF YOUR MISSPENT	LIFE	-- /ADOLPHUS/ (MUCH INJURED) WHOSE MISSPENT LIFE?
MIS. (180)	MR TARLETON NOT TO REPEAT IT, AND TO AMEND MY	LIFE	-- /BENTLEY/ " AMEND MY LIFE"? /PERCIVAL/-- AND TO DO
APPL INTRLUD(246)	A REALLY NOBLE AND BEAUTIFUL LIFE -- A KINGLY	LIFE	-- WITH ME. WHAT YOU NEED TO MAKE YOU A REAL KING IS A
DOCT PREFACE(70)	OF INTEMPERANCES THAT MAKE UP SO MUCH OF FAMILY	LIFE	) WOULD SOON LAND HIM IN THE BANKRUPTCY COURT. PRIVATE
6CAL (93)	FOAMING). OUT! (THE GROOM FLIES FOR HIS	LIFE	). HOW LONG HAVE YOU BEEN HERE? THEY NEVER TELL ME
GETT PREFACE(201)	OF HER WORKING LIFE (HE CALLS IT HER HOME	LIFE	). IT IS REMARKABLE THAT THE VERY PEOPLE WHO ROMANCE
MILL IV (208)	CREATURE YOU HATE AND DESPISE AND ARE TIED TO FOR	LIFE	; AND BEFORE BREAKFAST IS OVER THE FOOL SAYS SOMETHING
ARMS II (27)	LOOK AT MY FATHER! HE NEVER HAD A BATH IN HIS	LIFE	; AND HE LIVED TO BE NINETY-EIGHT, THE HEALTHIEST MAN
MTH5 SD(205)	AND UPRIGHTNESS HE SEEMS TO BE IN THE PRIME OF	LIFE	; AND HIS EYES AND MOUTH SHEW NO SIGNS OF AGE; BUT HIS
MTH4 II (189)	WHY, I HAVE NEVER READ THE ARTICLES IN MY	LIFE	; AND I AM PRIME MINISTER! COME! IF MY SERVICES IN
PYGM V (281)	BEEN THE VICTIM OF ONE WOMAN AFTER ANOTHER ALL MY	LIFE	; AND I DONT GRUDGE YOU TWO GETTING THE BETTER OF
HART III (133)	THEM KEEP ME GOING PRETTY WELL; BUT IT'S A DOG'S	LIFE	; AND I DONT OWN ANYTHING. /MRS HUSHABYE/ ALFRED,
SUPR IV (167)	TRUE! IT HAS BEEN STARING ME IN THE FACE ALL MY	LIFE	; AND I NEVER SAW IT BEFORE. /ANN/ OH, IT'S THE SAME
MTH3 (104)	I AM CONCERNED WITH THEIR EXPECTATION OF	LIFE	; AND I SAY THAT NO MAN HAS ANY RIGHT TO GO ON LIVING
JOAN 4 (104)	BONES WHEN I THINK OF IT. I HAVE FOUGHT IT ALL MY	LIFE	; AND I WILL FIGHT IT TO THE END. LET ALL THIS WOMAN'S
POSN (465)	I GOT THE ROTTEN FEEL OFF ME FOR A MINUTE OF MY	LIFE	; AND I'LL GO THROUGH FIRE TO GET IT OFF ME AGAIN. LOOK
HART III (133)	THE TRUTH ABOUT MY MONEY FOR THE FIRST TIME IN MY	LIFE	; AND IT'S THE FIRST TIME MY WORD HAS EVER BEEN
MTH4 I (157)	WAS, HE BREATHED INTO ITS NOSTRILS THE BREATH OF	LIFE	; AND MAN BECAME A LIVING SOUL. YES, MADAM, A LIVING
HART II (119)	I DID NOT LET THE FEAR OF DEATH GOVERN MY	LIFE	; AND MY REWARD WAS, I HAD MY LIFE. YOU ARE GOING TO
AUGS (265)	MADE THE BEST RECRUITING SPEECH I EVER MADE IN MY	LIFE	; AND NOT A MAN JOINED. /THE CLERK/ WHAT DID YOU
CLEO PRO1 (90)	OF DEATH; BUT THE WAY OF THE GODS IS THE WAY OF	LIFE	; AND SO IT COMES THAT A GOD AT THE END OF HIS WAY IS
PRES (164)	SHE WILL SIT ON HIS HEAD FOR THE REST OF HIS	LIFE	; AND THE BRITISH ARMY IS NOW TO ALL INTENTS AND
VWOO 3 (142)	A LAMP IN THE HOLY OF HOLIES IN THE TEMPLE OF	LIFE	; AND THE LAMP WILL MAKE ITS VEIL TRANSPARENT, AIMLESS
PYGM II (229)	KNOWS! I SUPPOSE THE WOMAN WANTS TO LIVE HER OWN	LIFE	; AND THE MAN WANTS TO LIVE HIS; AND EACH TRIES TO DRAG
LION PREFACE(49)	TO YOURSELVES; FOR YOU HAVE BROUGHT THE IMAGE TO	LIFE	; AND THE MOB MAY NOT BE ABLE TO BEAR THAT HORROR. THE
MRS II (211)	AT COLLEGE DARE SPEAK TO ME; TO DICTATE MY WAY OF	LIFE	; AND TO FORCE ON ME THE ACQUAINTANCE OF A BRUTE WHOM
GETT PREFACE(227)	THE CLUBS); WHERE THERE IS TRAVELLING AND HOTEL	LIFE	; AND WHERE THE MEN ARE BROUGHT UP, NOT IN THE FAMILY,
MTH2 (73)	ORGANIZE SOCIALISM YOU CANNOT ORGANIZE CIVILIZED	LIFE	; AND YOU WILL RELAPSE INTO BARBARISM ACCORDINGLY.
HART II (119)	ARE GOING TO LET THE FEAR OF POVERTY GOVERN YOUR	LIFE	; AND YOUR REWARD WILL BE THAT YOU WILL EAT, BUT YOU
MTH3 (93)	LIVING AUTHORITY ON THE DURATION OF HUMAN	LIFE	; AND-- /BARNABAS/ (INTERRUPTING) THE AMERICAN
METH PREFACE(R25)	OUR CONSCIOUSNESS FOR FRESH CONQUESTS OF	LIFE	; AS ALL CONSCIOUSNESS MEANS PREOCCUPATION AND
LION PREFACE(41)	MAY BE DRAMATIC ART BACKED BY KNOWLEDGE OF PUBLIC	LIFE	; BUT EVEN AT THAT WE MUST NOT FORGET THAT THE BEST
HART II (125)	I TELL YOU THAT I HAVE LOVED THIS DEMON ALL MY	LIFE	; BUT GOD KNOWS I HAVE PAID FOR IT (HE SITS DOWN IN
ROCK PREFACE(149)	OF HUMAN LIFE, OR ANY OTHER INCARNATION OF	LIFE	; BUT IT COVERS ONLY A CORNER OF THE FIELD OPENED UP BY
MIS. (143)	ROTTEN. /LORD SUMMERHAYS/ IVE LIVED AN ACTIVE	LIFE	; BUT IVE WITHERED ALL THE SAME. /HYPATIA/ NO! YOUVE
FANY I (279)	OF COURSE I SWORE I'D NEVER SEEN HIM BEFORE IN MY	LIFE	; BUT THERE HE WAS IN MY HAT AND I IN HIS. THE COPS

WIDO III (50)	HELP IT. I HAVE STUCK TO HAVING MY OWN WAY ALL MY	LIFE	; BUT THERE MUST BE AN END TO THAT DRUDGERY SOME DAY.
GENV III (83)	THE WOMEN'S FEET AND MAKING THEM CRIPPLES FOR	LIFE	; BUT WE STILL GO ON BINDING OUR HEADS AND MAKING FOOLS
HART I (73)	ARE MISTAKEN. /CAPTAIN SHOTOVER/ AN ADVENTUROUS	LIFE	; BUT WHAT DOES IT END IN? RESPECTABILITY. A LADYLIKE
MTH1 II (24)	THEN? YOU SLAY THE TIGER AT THE RISK OF YOUR	LIFE	; BUT WHO GETS THE STRIPED SKIN YOU HAVE RUN THAT RISK
CAPT III (295)	IS GONE. YOU HAVE TAKEN THE OLD MEANING OUT OF MY	LIFE	; BUT YOU HAVE PUT NO NEW MEANING INTO IT. I CAN SEE
JOAN 6 (145)	NOR TRUST TO YOUR CHARITY. YOU PROMISED ME MY	LIFE	; BUT YOU LIED (INDIGNANT EXCLAMATIONS). YOU THINK
JOAN PREFACE(52)	TO THEMSELVES THAN THEY WOULD BE IN REAL	LIFE	; FOR BY NO OTHER MEANS CAN THEY BE MADE INTELLIGIBLE
LION PREFACE(67)	IN HIS NAME, PROPOSE CELIBACY AS A RULE OF	LIFE	; FOR HE WAS NOT A FOOL, NOR, WHEN HE DENOUNCED
BULL IV (149)	MAY BE THAT TOTAL ABSTINENCE HAS ALREADY SAVED MY	LIFE	; FOR I WAS ASTONISHED AT THE STEADINESS OF MY NERVES
OVER (180)	AWAY WITHOUT EVER HAVING HAD A ROMANCE IN MY	LIFE	; FOR MARRIAGE IS ALL VERY WELL; BUT IT ISNT ROMANCE.
BARB PREFACE(219)	DO NOT WANT THE SIMPLE LIFE, NOR THE ESTHETIC	LIFE	; ON THE CONTRARY, THEY WANT VERY MUCH TO WALLOW IN ALL
SUPR III (117)	WAS NOT WORTH A DUMP AS A PHILOSOPHY OF	LIFE	; SO HE CALLED ME PHILISTINE AND WENT HIS WAY. /ANA/ IT
SUPR PREFACE(R23)	STARVE, WHEN NECESSARY, IN A GARRET ALL HIS	LIFE	; STUDY WOMEN AND LIVE ON THEIR WORK AND CARE AS DARWIN
SUPR III (125)	FOR A WEEK IN ADVANCE, MUCH LESS TO THE END OF MY	LIFE	; THAT TO CUT ME OFF FROM ALL NATURAL AND UNCONSTRAINED
LION PREFACE(62)	THAT WE EVOLVE TOWARDS GREATER ABUNDANCE OF	LIFE	; THAT WE ARE THE LAMPS IN WHICH THE LIGHT OF THE WORLD
ARMS I (15)	SIDE OF OUR MOUTHS. I NEVER FELT SO SICK IN MY	LIFE	; THOUGH IVE BEEN IN ONE OR TWO VERY TIGHT PLACES. AND
MTH5 (257)	WOULD LIKE TO FOLLOW THEM; TO ENTER INTO THEIR	LIFE	; TO GRASP THEIR THOUGHT; TO COMPREHEND THE UNIVERSE AS
SUPR III (118)	TO IMPOSE CONDITIONS ON THE IRRESISTIBLE FORCE OF	LIFE	; TO PREACH PRUDENCE, CAREFUL SELECTION, VIRTUE, HONOR,
DOCT PREFACE(15)	DOCTOR, YOU WILL BE MISERABLY POOR ALL YOUR	LIFE	; WHILST THE SIXPENNY DOCTOR, WITH HIS LOW PRICES AND
ARMS III (51)	LIES (RAINA RECOILS): THE OTHER IS GETTING HIS	LIFE	SAVED IN ALL SORTS OF WAYS BY ALL SORTS OF PEOPLE.
PHIL II (120)	NO, NO, NO. CONGRATULATE HIM ON HAVING HIS	LIFE	SAVED. CONGRATULATE JULIA ON HAVING HER FATHER SPARED.
BARB III (341)	OUGHT! OUGHT! ARE YOU GOING TO SPEND YOUR	LIFE	SAYING OUGHT, LIKE THE REST OF OUR MORALISTS? TURN
SUPR II SD(62)	INCAPACITIES AS POINTS OF GOOD BREEDING. ENGLISH	LIFE	SEEMS TO HIM TO SUFFER FROM A LACK OF EDIFYING RHETORIC
SUPR III (118)	WAS IN THE ACT OF FRAMING MY EXCUSE TO THE LADY,	LIFE	SEIZED ME AND THREW ME INTO HER ARMS AS A SAILOR THROWS
CLEO III (158)	MASTER, IF I COULD BUT PERSUADE YOU TO REGARD	LIFE	SERIOUSLY, AS MEN DO IN MY COUNTRY! /CAESAR/ DO THEY
BARB I (250)	A MOST AGGRAVATING HABIT. YOU MUST LEARN TO FACE	LIFE	SERIOUSLY, STEPHEN. I REALLY CANNOT BEAR THE WHOLE
MTH2 (68)	OUR PROGRAM IS ONLY THAT THE TERM OF HUMAN	LIFE	SHALL BE EXTENDED TO THREE HUNDRED YEARS. /LUBIN/ (
GETT PREFACE(196)	PEOPLE WHO LIKE THAT KIND OF BOOK); BUT IN ACTUAL	LIFE	SHE IS A NUISANCE. HUSBANDS MAY ESCAPE FROM HER WHEN
GETT (264)	TO SOME PEOPLE, YOU SEE, FAMILY LIFE IS ALL THE	LIFE	SHE KNOWS; SHE'S LIKE A BIRD BORN IN A CAGE, THAT WOULD
PYGM EPILOG (298)	PLACED HER AT THE ANGLE OF VIEW FROM WHICH THE	LIFE	SHE WAS LEADING AND THE SOCIETY TO WHICH SHE CLUNG
SUPR III (113)	OF SPEECH. WHAT I WAS GOING TO ASK JUAN WAS WHY	LIFE	SHOULD BOTHER ITSELF ABOUT GETTING A BRAIN. WHY SHOULD
FANY PROLOG (267)	/FANNY/ YES, MR TROTTER: IVE SEEN A GOOD DEAL OF	LIFE	SINCE I CAME TO ENGLAND; AND I ASSURE YOU THAT TO ME
CLEO IV (175)	EDGE OF THE ROOF, EXCEPT IN THE MIDDLE, WHERE A	LIFE	SIZE IMAGE OF RA, SEATED ON A HUGE PLINTH, TOWERS UP,
PRES (148)	MADE FARRELL BLUSH! I WOULDNT HAVE HAD TO RISK ME	LIFE	SO OFTEN. YOU N YOUR RISKS N YOUR BRAVERY N YOUR
BARB III (317)	AND WHAT THEY CALL GOOD TASTE; AND LAMED FOR	LIFE	SO THAT HE IS FIT FOR NOTHING BUT TEACHING. IF YOU WANT
POSN (463)	AND SPAT. BUT WHEN THEY TOLD ME TO TRY TO LIVE MY	LIFE	SO THAT I COULD ALWAYS LOOK MY FELLOWMAN STRAIGHT IN
GETT (264)	MAAM; BUT MY! HOW I USED TO GET TIRED OF HOME	LIFE	SOMETIMES. I USED TO CATCH MYSELF ENVYING MY BROTHER
2TRU II (64)	DRIVE YOU MAD. LETS GO AND HAVE A BIT OF REAL	LIFE	SOMEWHERE. /THE PATIENT/ REAL LIFE! I WONDER WHERE
DOCT PREFACE(74)	IS NOT ONLY MORE HONORABLE BUT MORE USEFUL THAN A	LIFE	SPENT DOING NOTHING. THE ONE LESSON THAT COMES OUT OF
GETT PREFACE(199)	IN PRAYER AND ALMSGIVING IS REALLY AS INSANE AS A	LIFE	SPENT IN CURSING AND PICKING POCKETS: THE EFFECT OF
DOCT PREFACE(74)	LEAD TO MISTAKES AS WELL AS TO SUCCESSES; BUT A	LIFE	SPENT IN MAKING MISTAKES IS NOT ONLY MORE HONORABLE BUT
GETT PREFACE(199)	AT THE SAME PITCH CONTINUOUSLY THROUGH LIFE. A	LIFE	SPENT IN PRAYER AND ALMSGIVING IS REALLY AS INSANE AS A
BASH II,1, (111)	MAY PUT IT DOWN MY BACK, AND STAUNCH THE WELLING	LIFE	STREAM. /LYDIA/ (GIVING HIM HER KEYS) OH, WHAT HAVE
GETT PREFACE(194)	OUT THE GLARING FACT THAT IN THE COLLECTION OF	LIFE	STUDIES OF VICTORIAN WOMEN TO BE FOUND IN THE NOVELS OF
MIS. PREFACE(3)	PROCESS OF THAT CONTINUAL REMANUFACTURE OF THE	LIFE	STUFF BY WHICH THE HUMAN RACE IS PERPETUATED. THE LIFE
GENV PREFACE(3)	CLOCK, KEEPING ME FOR NINE YEARS OF MY	LIFE	SUBJECT TO A CONTINUAL APPREHENSION OF A DIRECT HIT
PYGM EPILOG (298)	BOOTH OR GYPSY SMITH. CLARA'S SNOBBERY WENT BANG.	LIFE	SUDDENLY BEGAN TO MOVE WITH HER. WITHOUT KNOWING HOW OR
DOCT I SD(109)	DISTINCTION OF A WOMAN WHO HAS NEVER IN HER	LIFE	SUFFERED FROM THOSE DOUBTS AND FEARS AS TO HER SOCIAL
JOAN PREFACE(34)	DEGRADATION, AND CONSCIOUS WASTE AND LOSS OF	LIFE	SUFFERED IN OUR MODERN PRISONS, ESPECIALLY THE MODEL
BULL II SD(104)	NEITHER BY VOCATION NOR AMBITION, BUT BECAUSE THE	LIFE	SUITS HIM. HE HAS BOUNDLESS AUTHORITY OVER HIS FLOCK,
MRS IV (250)	MAD. AND WHAT ELSE IS THERE FOR ME TO DO? THE	LIFE	SUITS ME: I'M FIT FOR IT AND NOT FOR ANYTHING ELSE. IF
GETT (278)	AT MY AGE TO MARRY LEO: SHE KNEW NO MORE ABOUT	LIFE	THAN A CHILD. /LEO/ I KNEW A GREAT DEAL MORE ABOUT IT
VWOO 3 (138)	REALIZE THAT A WOMAN WANTS SOMETHING MORE IN	LIFE	THAN A JOB AND A SALARY. /A/ I KNOW THAT PERFECTLY
DEVL II (38)	I THINK I HAVE NEVER BEEN MORE AT REST IN MY	LIFE	THAN AT THIS MOMENT; AND YET I KNOW QUITE WELL I COULD
SUPR I SD(3)	SUGGEST THE MILITARY MAN. IT IS IN ACTIVE CIVIL	LIFE	THAN MEN GET HIS BROAD AIR OF IMPORTANCE, HIS DIGNIFIED
ROCK PREFACE(168)	SOME OF US, BELIEVING THAT A MORE PRIMITIVE	LIFE	THAN OURS WOULD BE HAPPIER AND BETTER, ADVOCATE " A
MTH4 I (158)	HAS TO DISCOVER MORE IN THE FIRST YEARS OF ITS	LIFE	THAN ROGER BACON EVER DISCOVERED IN HIS LABORATORY.
LION PREFACE(58)	US TO THINK OF NOBLER THINGS, OR LIVE A HIGHER	LIFE	THAN THAT OF A MOLE, WHOSE LIFE IS FROM BEGINNING TO
LION PREFACE(40)	MANY PASSAGES NEARER TO THE REALITIES OF PUBLIC	LIFE	THAN THE SIMPLE CHRONICLE OF MATTHEW OR THE SENTIMENTAL
MIS. PREFACE(52)	DISUSE; BUT THE CHILD KNOWS NO OTHER WAY OF	LIFE	THAN THE SLAVE'S WAY. BORN FREE, AS ROUSSEAU SAYS, HE
BASH III (123)	AT ONCE COME HOME WITH ME, AND QUIT A COURSE OF	LIFE	THAT CANNOT BE ALLOWED. ENTER CASHEL. /CASHEL/
MIS. (171)	BEEN INVENTED. OF ALL THE DAMNABLE WASTE OF HUMAN	LIFE	THAT EVER WAS INVENTED, CLERKING IS THE VERY WORST.
MIS. PREFACE(75)	FOR STRANGERS, SPENDING ON THE COMMUNITY THE	LIFE	THAT HAS BEEN BUILT UP AT HER EXPENSE. NO MORE
PHIL I SD(84)	SENTIMENT, SO FREQUENTLY OUTRAGED BY THE FACTS OF	LIFE	THAT HE HAS ACQUIRED AN HABITUALLY INDIGNANT MANNER,
MTH1 I (8)	WORDS. /THE SERPENT/ YES: IT WAS BY MEDITATING ON	LIFE	THAT I GAINED THE POWER TO DO MIRACLES. /EVE/
KING II (233)	BUNYAN WHO HAS WRITTEN A BOOK ABOUT THE CHRISTIAN	LIFE	THAT IS BEING READ, THEY TELL ME, ALL THE WORLD OVER;
GENV PREFACE(26)	THERE IS SUCH A THING AS NATURAL DEATH: IT IS	LIFE	THAT IS NATURAL AND INFINITE. HOW LONG, THEN, WOULD IT
MTH1 II (30)	THINK IT WAS FOR EITHER OF THESE CHEAP WAYS OF	LIFE	THAT LILITH SET YOU FREE. (TO ADAM) YOU DIG ROOTS AND
KING I (205)	NOT PLEASURE THAT MAKES LIFE WORTH LIVING. IT IS	LIFE	THAT MAKES PLEASURE WORTH HAVING. AND WHAT PLEASURE IS
MTH4 I (157)	YES; BUT WHAT DO WE KNOW ABOUT THIS BREATH OF	LIFE	THAT PUFFS YOU UP SO EXALTEDLY? JUST NOTHING. SO LET
BULL PREFACE(27)	THAT HE IS HEAVILY HANDICAPPED IN EVERY WALK OF	LIFE	THAT REQUIRES ANY LITERACY. IT IS THE AIM OF HIS PRIEST
PYGM EPILOG (303)	THAT SORT. BUT WHEN IT COMES TO BUSINESS, TO THE	LIFE	THAT SHE REALLY LEADS AS DISTINGUISHED FROM THE LIFE OF
JOAN PREFACE(18)	BY HER RECANTATION BUT CLOSE IMPRISONMENT FOR	LIFE	THAT SHE WITHDREW IT, AND DELIBERATELY AND EXPLICITLY
MTH1 II (25)	RAISE YOUR HEAD TO LOOK AT ALL THE MIRACLES OF	LIFE	THAT SURROUND YOU; BUT YOU WILL RUN TEN MILES TO SEE A
MTH4 II (191)	THOSE MISGUIDED PEOPLE SACRIFICED THE FRAGMENT OF	LIFE	THAT WAS GRANTED TO THEM TO AN IMAGINARY IMMORTALITY.
METH PREFACE(R73)	RESEARCHES WITH A SENSE OF THE MIRACULOUSNESS OF	LIFE	THAT WENT FAR BEYOND THE COMPARATIVELY UNINFORMED
3PLA PREFACE(R38)	DEATH BORN OF INABILITY TO BEAR THE WEIGHT OF A	LIFE	THAT WILL NOT GRANT IDEAL CONDITIONS TO THE LIVER. THIS
JITT PREFACE(6)	OF THE FORTUNATE CIRCUMSTANCE THAT IN REAL	LIFE	THE CONSEQUENCES OF CONJUGAL INFIDELITY ARE SELDOM
SUPR III (121)	ART, AND OF LOVE, WILL ALL OPPOSE TO THE FORCE OF	LIFE	THE DEVICE OF STERILITY. /THE STATUE/ THAT IS ALL VERY
BUOY II (22)	IN PEACE. /HE/ THAT IS NOT NATURAL. IN NATIVE	LIFE	THE WOMAN KEEPS THE HOUSE AND WORKS THERE: THE MAN
CAPT III (295)	IT. YOUVE LAMED ME BY SHEWING ME THAT I TAKE	LIFE	THE WRONG WAY WHEN I'M LEFT TO MYSELF. /LADY CICELY/ OH
SIM PREFACE(13)	FOR SLAVES TO BE EIGHT YEARS. IN FULLY CIVILIZED	LIFE	THERE WAS NO PROVISION EXCEPT A SAVAGELY PENAL POOR LAW
MIS PREFACE(72)	MEN THEY COACH FOR EXAMINATIONS ARE LAMED FOR	LIFE	THEREBY; IN SPITE OF DICKENS AND HIS PICTURE OF LITTLE
MRS PREFACE(156)	IS.); AND ASK YOURSELF WHETHER, IF THE LOT IN	LIFE	THEREIN DESCRIBED WERE YOUR LOT IN LIFE, YOU WOULD NOT
SIM PRO,2, (28)	BALLS MARVELLOUSLY WELL; BUT OF THE GREAT GAME OF	LIFE	THEY ARE IGNORANT. HERE, WHERE THEY ARE IN THE MIDST OF
CLEO PRO1 (91)	AND THE GODS SMILED ON CAESAR; FOR HE LIVED THE	LIFE	THEY HAD GIVEN HIM BOLDLY, AND WAS NOT FOREVER REBUKING
KING II (231)	COUNTRY ON EARTH; NEVER SHALL I FORGET THE	LIFE	THEY LED ME THERE WITH THEIR BRAINS AND THEIR RELIGION
MIS. PREFACE(65)	FELLAHEEN OR INDIAN TRIBESMEN TO LIVE THE LOWEST	LIFE	THEY PLEASE AMONG THEMSELVES WITHOUT MOLESTATION; BUT
HART PREFACE(6)	INEFFECTIVE IN PUBLIC AFFAIRS, EVEN IN PRIVATE	LIFE	THEY WERE OFTEN HELPLESS WASTERS OF THEIR INHERITANCE,
KING I (202)	IN WHAT YET REMAIN; AND FROM THE DREGS OF	LIFE	THINK TO RECEIVE WHAT THE FIRST SPRIGHTLY RUNNING COULD
ARMS III (70)	A MAN WHO HAS SPOILED ALL HIS CHANCES IN	LIFE	THROUGH AN INCURABLY ROMANTIC DISPOSITION, A MAN--
O'FL (206)	THAT I NEVER HEARD THE TUNE OF TIPPERARY IN MY	LIFE	TIL I CAME BACK FROM FLANDERS; AND ALREADY IT'S DROVE
APPL II (260)	/MANHATTAN/ CENTURIES COUNT FOR BUT LITTLE IN THE	LIFE	TIMES OF GREAT NATIONS, SIR. LET ME RECALL THE PARABLE
GETT (354)	TO ME. I ADMIRE HIM, AND SHARE HIS VIEWS OF	LIFE	TO A CONSIDERABLE EXTENT. THAT BEATS YOU, YOU SEE,
GETT PREFACE(234)	MALICIOUSLY SARCASTIC ONE, OR WAS CHAINED FOR	LIFE	TO A CRIMINAL, A DRUNKARD, A LUNATIC, AN IDLE VAGRANT,
MILL I (156)	THIS THING SUCCEEDED; AND I FOUND MYSELF TIED FOR	LIFE	TO AN INSECT. /ALASTAIR/ YOU MAY SAY WHAT YOU LIKE; BUT
BARB PREFACE(220)	INSEPARABLE; MONEY IS THE COUNTER THAT ENABLES	LIFE	TO BE DISTRIBUTED SOCIALLY: IT IS LIFE AS TRULY AS
FANY PROLOG (271)	SO FRIGHTFULLY MISUNDERSTOOD? IVE TRIED ALL MY	LIFE	TO BE SINCERE AND SIMPLE, TO BE UNASSUMING AND KINDLY.
SUPR PREFACE(R24)	OF ONE SORT OR ANOTHER IS THE STRUGGLE OF	LIFE	TO BECOME DIVINELY CONSCIOUS OF ITSELF INSTEAD OF
CLEO IV (192)	THIS CAMPAIGN. /APOLLODORUS/ AY, AND MY HEART AND	LIFE	TO BOOT. /CAESAR/ (GRASPING HIS HAND) I ACCEPT BOTH. (
BARB PREFACE(228)	DIVIDENDS LATER ON IN THE FORM, NOT OF A BETTER	LIFE	TO COME FOR THE WHOLE WORLD, BUT OF AN ETERNITY SPENT
SUPR III (135)	(CROSSING HERSELF DEVOUTLY) I BELIEVE IN THE	LIFE	TO COME. (CRYING TO THE UNIVERSE) A FATHER! A FATHER
LION PREFACE(98)	EVEN IN TORMENT, AS A PREPARATION FOR A BETTER	LIFE	TO COME. MAKE THESE SAD PEOPLE COMFORTABLE; AND THEY
BULL IV (172)	CLUBS OF YOUR TOURISTS AS A PREPARATION FOR THE	LIFE	TO COME. /BROADBENT/ (QUITE TOUCHED, MUTELY OFFERING
ROCK PREFACE(148)	THEY MAY BELIEVE IN THE LIFE EVERLASTING AND THE	LIFE	TO COME; BUT THEY MAKE NO DISTINCTION BETWEEN MAN AND
SIM II (85)	ME. LIFE NEEDS US BOTH. /PRA/ ALL HAIL, THEN, THE	LIFE	TO COME! /PROLA/ ALL HAIL. LET IT COME. THEY PAT
SUPR I (30)	EXCEPT THE WOMAN WHO IS GOING TO RISK HER	LIFE	TO CREATE ANOTHER LIFE! TAVY: DONT YOU BE A SELFISH

GETT PREFACE(203)	NEITHER THE SUFFERINGS OF THOSE WHO ARE TIED FOR	LIFE	TO CRIMINALS, DRUNKARDS, PHYSICALLY UNSOUND AND
MTH1 II (27)	COURAGE, COURAGE, THAT RAISES THE BLOOD OF	LIFE	TO CRIMSON SPLENDOR. /ADAM/ (PICKING UP HIS SPADE AND
JOAN PREFACE(40)	THE BODY OF HER LORD WERE FIRST NECESSARIES OF	LIFE	TO HER. SUCH A SPIRIT AS JOAN'S MIGHT HAVE GOT OVER
GETT (286)	HAPPILY MARRIED, AND THAT LOVE IS A NECESSARY OF	LIFE	TO HER, BUT THAT SHE MUST HAVE, HIGH ABOVE ALL HER
JITT I (21)	HIM) YOU THROW THE GREATEST ACHIEVEMENT OF YOUR	LIFE	TO HIM LIKE A BONE TO A DOG; AND THEN FEEL YOU HAVE
GENV IV (102)	THE COWARD. DEATH, THE SUPREME DANGER, ROUSES	LIFE	TO ITS SUPREME ECSTASY OF LOVE. WHEN HAS A WARLIKE RACE
MILL PREFACE(112)	CREATURE CAN BECOME RICH IF HE DEVOTES HIS	LIFE	TO IT, AND THE PEOPLE WITH WIDER AND MORE GENEROUS
GETT SD(260)	IN KEEPING A SHOP FOR THE SALE OF NECESSARIES OF	LIFE	TO LADIES WHOSE SOCIAL POSITION IS SO UNQUESTIONABLE
MIS. (147)	IN QUESTION, I DONT LIKE THE PROCESS. IF I HAD MY	LIFE	TO LIVE OVER AGAIN, I'D STAY AT HOME AND SUPERCIVILIZE
MRS IV (252)	ME OUT AS IF I WAS A LEPER. OH, IF I ONLY HAD MY	LIFE	TO LIVE OVER AGAIN! I'D TALK TO THAT LYING CLERGYMAN
NEVR IV (305)	WHICH MY SON HAS INHERITED. BUT IF I HAD MY	LIFE	TO LIVE TWICE OVER, I'D DO IT AGAIN: I'D DO IT AGAIN, I
MTH2 (40)	ASK FOR A BETTER PLACE. BUT I HAVE ONLY ONE	LIFE	TO LIVE; AND I MAYNT GET A SECOND CHANCE. EXCUSE ME,
MTH2 (44)	DOWN AT HER. /CONRAD/ SO YOU HAVE ONLY ONE	LIFE	TO LIVE, EH? /THE PARLOR MAID/ (DROPPING ON HER KNEES
2TRU III (107)	HAVE LOTS OF MONEY, AND SIXTY YEARS OF A MISSPENT	LIFE	TO MAKE UP FOR; SO YOU WILL HAVE A GOOD TIME WITH ME.
JITT I (14)	OUR BETRAYAL OF HER: SHE HAS SACRIFICED HER	LIFE	TO ME. I CANT FACE WHAT SHE WOULD SUFFER. /JITTA/ HAS
CAPT II (262)	AGITATION) DAMN YOU! YOU HAVE BELITTLED MY WHOLE	LIFE	TO ME. (HE BOWS HIS HEAD ON HIS HANDS, CONVULSED).
JITT II (47)	YOU FROM ME, HE MUST DICTATE THE REST OF MY	LIFE	TO ME, AS IF I WERE A CHILD. /JITTA/ YES: COMPARED TO
CLEO IV (190)	" FRIEND, GO FREE," YOU, CLINGING FOR YOUR LITTLE	LIFE	TO MY SWORD, DARE STEAL OUT AND STAB HIM IN THE BACK.
MIS. PREFACE(108)	DREAD OF THE WHIP. LIBERTY IS THE BREATH OF	LIFE	TO NATIONS; AND LIBERTY IS THE ONE THING THAT PARENTS,
GETT PREFACE(234)	SIMPLY TO A BORE! CONCEIVE YOURSELF TIED FOR	LIFE	TO ONE OF THE PERFECTLY " FAITHFUL" HUSBANDS WHO ARE
JITT III (72)	PROVE IT. BUT I AM CERTAIN, AND I WILL DEVOTE MY	LIFE	TO PROVING IT. /JITTA/ HOW? /EDITH/ I WILL FIND THE
3PLA PREFACE(R29)	PERHAPS A PUBLIC FUNERAL, FOR RISKING HIS OR HER	LIFE	TO SAVE ANOTHER'S. HAS HE EVER SEEN IT ADDED THAT THE
3PLA PREFACE(R30)	THAT IT WAS FOR HER SAKE THAT HE OFFERED HIS	LIFE	TO SAVE HER BELOVED HUSBAND; AND THAT HIS EXPLICIT
MTH1 II (28)	HAVE KILLED HIM: YOU WOULD HAVE RISKED YOUR OWN	LIFE	TO SAVE HIS. THAT IS WHY ALL THIS EMPTY TALK OF YOURS,
DOCT PREFACE(34)	HE MAY EVEN HAVE TO THROW AWAY HIS INDIVIDUAL	LIFE	TO SAVE THE LIFE OF THE COMMUNITY. IT IS JUST SO IN THE
MRS PREFACE(171)	SHE ORGANIZES. IT IS NO DEFENCE OF AN IMMORAL	LIFE	TO SAY THAT THE ALTERNATIVE OFFERED BY SOCIETY
2TRU I (48)	CROSS THE STREET: THE EMPIRES WHICH SACRIFICE	LIFE	TO SECURITY FIND IT IN THE GRAVE. FOR ME SAFETY LAST;
MRS IV (250)	IF I TOOK YOUR MONEY AND DEVOTED THE REST OF MY	LIFE	TO SPENDING IT FASHIONABLY, I MIGHT BE AS WORTHLESS AND
FOUN (218)	GIRL; AND I REQUIRE SOME SERIOUS INTEREST IN	LIFE	TO STEADY ME. AS I HAD AN UNGOVERNABLE APPETITE, AND
BULL IV (181)	I NEVER DID BEFORE THAT I AM RIGHT IN DEVOTING MY	LIFE	TO THE CAUSE OF IRELAND. COME ALONG AND HELP ME TO
SUPR III (107)	BUT OF DEATH; AND THE INNER NEED THAT HAS NERVED	LIFE	TO THE EFFORT OF ORGANIZING ITSELF INTO THE HUMAN BEING
BARB PREFACE(212)	AS A PHILOSOPHIC HISTORIAN, WHO DEVOTED HIS	LIFE	TO THE ELABORATION AND PROPAGATION OF HIS THEORY THAT
LION PREFACE(76)	IN HIS OWN WAY, AND THEREBY GAVE A NEW LEASE OF	LIFE	TO THE ERRORS IT WAS JUST OUTGROWING, SO PAUL
MRS PREFACE(174)	WHAT GOOD LORD SHAFTESBURY DID BY DEVOTING HIS	LIFE	TO THE EXPOSURE OF EVILS (BY NO MEANS YET REMEDIED)
KING I (211)	THIS INFIDEL QUAKER. I HAVE DEVOTED MONTHS OF MY	LIFE	TO THE WRITING OF A BOOK-- A CHRONOLOGY OF THE WORLD--
MTH4 I (161)	BUT ALL THAT IS AN OLD STORY: THE EXTENSION OF	LIFE	TO THREE HUNDRED YEARS HAS PROVIDED THE HUMAN RACE WITH
MTH2 (80)	PROGRAM THAT WE ADVOCATE THE EXTENSION OF HUMAN	LIFE	TO THREE HUNDRED YEARS! DUNREEN, AS LEADER OF THE
LION PREFACE(51)	IN MARRIAGE, BECAUSE YOU CANNOT DEVOTE YOUR	LIFE	TO TWO DIVINITIES: GOD AND THE PERSON YOU ARE MARRIED
3PLA PREFACE(R24)	OF HOMAGE TO THE SANCTITY OF THE IGNOBLE PRIVATE	LIFE	TO WHICH HE IS CONDEMNED BY HIS INCAPACITY FOR PUBLIC
PYGM V (281)	THAT HE WILL BE QUITE AT HOME IN ANY STATION OF	LIFE	TO WHICH HIS ECCENTRIC DESTINY MAY CALL HIM. (
GENV I (47)	THEM TO ENDURE THE HARDSHIPS OF THAT STATE OF	LIFE	TO WHICH IT HAS PLEASED GOD TO CALL THEM. DOES YOUR
MRS PREFACE(174)	IS EDITED BY A GENTLEMAN WHO, HAVING DEVOTED HIS	LIFE	TO WORK OF THE SHAFTESBURY TYPE, EXPOSES SOCIAL EVILS
MTH1 II (27)	AND PRAY, WHAT USE IS THIS THOUSAND YEARS OF	LIFE	TO YOU, YOU OLD VEGETABLE? DO YOU DIG ANY BETTER
GETT PREFACE(194)	DESCRIBED. THE FLAT FACT IS THAT ENGLISH HOME	LIFE	TODAY IS NEITHER HONORABLE, VIRTUOUS, WHOLESOME, SWEET,
MTH1 I (11)	HE CAN WILL; HE CAN DESIRE: HE CAN GATHER HIS	LIFE	TOGETHER FOR A GREAT SPRING TOWARDS CREATION: HE CAN
JITT II (50)	BOOK. THAT WILL BE YOUR SHARE OF THE SHAM OF OUR	LIFE	TOGETHER. /LENKHEIM/ BUT I TELL YOU I DONT BELIEVE A
MIS. (204)	AND I'LL GO: STORM OR NO STORM. I MUST RISK MY	LIFE	TOMORROW. /BENTLEY/ I HOPE THERE WILL BE A STORM.
2TRU III (110)	A BREATH WHICH MAY BE A BREATH OF LIFE, BUT OF A	LIFE	TOO KEEN FOR ME TO BEAR, AND THEREFORE FOR ME A BLAST
HART I (63)	HOW MUCH BETTER THAN THE HAPPIEST DREAM! ALL	LIFE	TRANSFIGURED! NO MORE WISHING ONE HAD AN INTERESTING
MIS. PREFACE(21)	HAND, WITH THE RESULT THAT I HAVE NOT WASTED MY	LIFE	TRIFLING WITH LITERARY FOOLS IN TAVERNS AS JOHNSON DID
3PLA PREFACE(R31)	TO SUCH FOLLY! THE LOT OF THE MAN WHO SEES	LIFE	TRULY AND THINKS ABOUT IT ROMANTICALLY IS DESPAIR. HOW
LION PREFACE(70)	HE PERCEIVED THAT NOBODY COULD LIVE THE HIGHER	LIFE	UNLESS MONEY AND SEXUAL LOVE WERE OBTAINABLE WITHOUT
FABL VI (130)	AWFUL. /MAIDEN 4/ YOU CANNOT EXPERIENCE BODIED	LIFE	UNLESS YOU HAVE A GIRL, AND MARRY, AND HAVE CHILDREN.
LION PREFACE(40)	LOVED HIM, ENDOWED HIM WITH A MIRACULOUS	LIFE	UNTIL THE SECOND COMING, THE CONCLUSION BEING THAT JOHN
CLEO I (114)	THERE, THERE, THERE; (THE SLAVE FLIES FOR HIS	LIFE	UP THE CORRIDOR AND VANISHES. SHE THROWS THE SNAKE-SKIN
GLIM (176)	EXCELLENCY! YOUR FATHER DOES NOT VALUE YOUR	LIFE	VERY HIGHLY. /FERRUCCIO/ DOLT. CAN YOU NOT REASON? IF
MTH5 (261)	THEY EMBRACED DEATH, AND SAID THAT ETERNAL	LIFE	WAS A FABLE. I STOOD AMAZED AT THE MALICE AND
MTH3 (121)	BESIDES, POLITICAL CHANGES WERE MAKING IT EASIER:	LIFE	WAS A LITTLE BETTER WORTH LIVING FOR THE NINE-TENTHS OF
MTH5 (227)	WHICH THE OLD CHRONICLER CALLED THE BREATH OF	LIFE	WAS ADDED BY THIS VERY REMARKABLE EARLY EXPERIMENTER.
ARMS III (66)	ALL A QUESTION OF THE DEGREE OF PROVOCATION. MY	LIFE	WAS AT STAKE. /LOUKA/ MY LOVE WAS AT STAKE. I AM NOT
BARB I (256)	THEN IT WAS ON MY ACCOUNT THAT YOUR HOME	LIFE	WAS BROKEN UP, MOTHER. I AM SORRY. /LADY BRITOMART/
SUPR III (113)	BETTER. /THE DEVIL/ YOU CONCLUDE, THEN, THAT	LIFE	WAS DRIVING AT CLUMSINESS AND UGLINESS? /DON JUAN/ NO,
SUPR III (113)	PERVERSE DEVIL THAT YOU ARE, A THOUSAND TIMES NO.	LIFE	WAS DRIVING AT BRAINS-- AT ITS DARLING OBJECT: AN ORGAN
HART PREFACE(29)	I LEAVE THESE PAGES AS A RECORD OF WHAT CIVILIAN	LIFE	WAS DURING THE WAR: A MATTER ON WHICH HISTORY IS
MTH4 II (192)	OF JONHOBSNOXIUS CURSED THE DAY WHEN ETERNAL	LIFE	WAS INVENTED. /ZOZIM/ POOH! YOU COULD LIVE THREE
MTH4 II (192)	OF REALIZATION. I CURSE THE DAY WHEN LONG	LIFE	WAS INVENTED, JUST AS THE VICTIMS OF JONHOBSNOXIUS
JOAN PREFACE(19)	ENOUGH TO KNOW THAT THE MASCULINE AND MILITARY	LIFE	WAS NOT A MERE MATTER OF RUNNING AWAY FROM HOME. BUT
MTH1 I (9)	MUST NEVER BE AGAIN: THAT THE BURDEN OF RENEWING	LIFE	WAS PAST BEARING! THAT IT WAS TOO MUCH FOR ONE. AND
MTH3 (108)	IT SHEWED THAT THIS EXTENSION OF INDIVIDUAL HUMAN	LIFE	WAS POSSIBLE, AND HOW IT WAS LIKELY TO COME ABOUT. I
MTH2 (76)	IT WAS THEN THAT HE LET THE THISTLES GROW.	LIFE	WAS SO SHORT THAT IT WAS NO LONGER WORTH HIS WHILE TO
BUOY PREFACE(5)	US EVEN AS WE NOW ARE. THE HAPPIEST MOMENT OF MY	LIFE	WAS WHEN AS A CHILD I WAS TOLD BY MY MOTHER THAT WE
GETT (332)	TALKS AS IF THE ONLY THING OF ANY IMPORTANCE IN	LIFE	WAS WHICH PARTICULAR WOMAN HE SHALL MARRY. SECOND, HE
MTH5 (240)	TAKING A STERNER TONE) WHAT! A CHILD LOST! A	LIFE	WASTED! HOW HAS THIS HAPPENED? /THE FEMALE FIGURE/ (
DOCT III (142)	GIRL IN PRISON AND RUIN HER: I'LL LAY HIS WIFE'S	LIFE	WASTE. YOU MAY PUT THE CRIMINAL LAW OUT OF YOUR HEAD
JITT II (29)	HAVE DIED IF HE HAD BEEN LEADING THE QUIET	LIFE	WE ALL GAVE HIM CREDIT FOR. WHAT SORT OF LIFE DID HE
MIS. PREFACE(27)	KNOWLEDGE FROM US, WITH THE RESULT THAT IN PUBLIC	LIFE	WE ARE EITHER PLACE-HUNTERS, ANARCHISTS, OR SHEEP
SUPR PREFACE(R20)	TO MARRY HER BEFORE HE HAS SEEN HER. IN REAL	LIFE	WE FIND NOT ONLY PETRUCHIOS, BUT MANTALINIS AND DOBBINS
MIS. PREFACE(15)	OF VIRTUE, IT IS FOUND THAT IN DISCUSSING FAMILY	LIFE	WE NEVER SPEAK OF ACTUAL ADULTS OR ACTUAL CHILDREN, OR
DOCT PREFACE(80)	IMPRACTICABLE. NO DOUBT THE HIGHER THE	LIFE	WE SECURE TO THE INDIVIDUAL BY WISE SOCIAL
GETT (321)	FATHER ANTHONY, THAT THE EARLY CHRISTIAN RULES OF	LIFE	WERE NOT MADE TO LAST, BECAUSE THE EARLY CHRISTIANS DID
BASH III (124)	WOULD YOU BUT LET YOUR WRETCHED SONS ALONE	LIFE	WERE WORTH LIVING! HAD I ANY CHOICE IN THIS
CAPT III (298)	CICELY/ (LEARNING FOR THE FIRST TIME IN HER	LIFE	WHAT TERROR IS, AS SHE FINDS THAT HE IS UNCONSCIOUSLY
BUOY III (37)	FIVE MINUTES. MY WIFE NEEDED SOME ROMANCE IN HER	LIFE	WHEN I CEASED TO BE ROMANTIC TO HER AND BECAME ONLY HER
MTH3 (126)	ME A WHOLE CENTURY TO GROW UP. I BEGAN MY SERIOUS	LIFE	WHEN I WAS A HUNDRED AND TWENTY. ASIATICS CANNOT
MRS PREFACE(173)	PROFESSION ONLY ENTERS INTO THE DRAMA OF HIS	LIFE	WHEN IT COMES INTO CONFLICT WITH HIS NATURE. THE RESULT
JOAN PREFACE(15)	HALLUCINATION WHICH PERSISTS STRONGLY THROUGHOUT	LIFE	WHEN IT HAS BEEN WELL IMPRESSED. THUS ALL THE THINKING
FOUN (212)	IN. I WAS KEEPING HIM FROM YOU AT THE RISK OF MY	LIFE	WHEN YOU CAME IN TO ASK WHAT THE NOISE WAS. /THE LORD
HART II (103)	HUSHABYE/ I WAS ASHAMED FOR THE FIRST TIME IN MY	LIFE	WHEN YOU SAID THAT ABOUT HITTING A WOMAN IN THE BREAST,
MTH1 II (23)	AND KNOW YOU, BETTER THAN THAT? DO YOU RISK YOUR	LIFE	WHEN YOU TRAP THE ERMINE AND THE SABLE AND THE BLUE FOX
BUOY III (44)	GREAT REFUSAL OF HER DESTINY, OF THE PURPOSE IN	LIFE	WHICH COMES BEFORE ALL PERSONAL CONSIDERATIONS: THE
BULL PREFACE(54)	IS THE ONLY OFFICIALLY RECORDED INCIDENT OF HIS	LIFE	WHICH IS ENTIRELY TO HIS CREDIT. HE AND ABD-EL-NEBI (
MTH5 (227)	BECAUSE THEY OVERLOOK THE ELEMENT OF	LIFE	WHICH MAKES ALL THE DIFFERENCE BETWEEN A MERE MIXTURE
BARB PREFACE(222)	RELATION TO THE RELIGIOUS LIFE OF THE NATION, A	LIFE	WHICH SEEMS TO LIE NOT ONLY OUTSIDE THE SYMPATHY OF
LADY PREFACE(224)	IT IS DIAGNOSTIC OF THAT IMMENSE ENERGY OF	LIFE	WHICH WE CALL GENIUS, BUT BECAUSE ITS OMISSION IS THE
MRS II (210)	I KNOW NOTHING ABOUT YOU. WHAT IS THAT WAY OF	LIFE	WHICH YOU INVITE ME TO SHARE WITH YOU AND SIR GEORGE
JOAN PREFACE(20)	OF GOWNED AND BODICED WOMEN IN ORDINARY CIVIL	LIFE	WHO MANAGE THEIR OWN AFFAIRS AND OTHER PEOPLE'S,
DOCT IV (170)	A COMMON IDEAL, THAT NOBODY ELSE CAN QUITE HAVE.	LIFE	WILL ALWAYS BE BEAUTIFUL TO US: DEATH WILL ALWAYS BE
DOCT II (128)	SHE FINDS HIM OUT? /RIDGEON/ THATS TRUE. HER	LIFE	WILL BE A HELL. /SIR PATRICK/ AND TELL ME THIS. SUPPOSE
BUOY IV (60)	PLEASURE IN IT PROMISES A DEVELOPMENT IN WHICH	LIFE	WILL BE AN INTELLECTUAL ECSTASY SURPASSING THE
LION PREFACE(71)	THAT IS OBNOXIOUS IN MARRIAGE AND FAMILY	LIFE	WILL BE CURED BY COMMUNISM, YET IT CAN BE SAID THAT IT
MRS II (204)	/VIVIE/ (RATHER GRIMLY) I DONT THINK MY FUTURE	LIFE	WILL BE MUCH CONCERNED WITH HIM, OR WITH ANY OF THAT
MTH3 (93)	YOUR ESTIMATE OF THE AVERAGE DURATION OF HUMAN	LIFE	WILL BE UPSET. /BARNABAS/ (ALARMED) UPSET MY
MRS II (210)	SHE LOOKS AT VIVIE AGAIN. NO REPLY). YOUR WAY OF	LIFE	WILL BE WHAT I PLEASE, SO IT WILL. (ANOTHER PAUSE).
APPL INTRLUD(252)	ENCHANTING AS YOU; AND THEN WHAT A GLORIOUS LARK	LIFE	WILL BE! BUT AT PRESENT, WHAT I COME HERE FOR IS TO
CLEO II (139)	MORE OF MY SOLDIERS, FOR YOUR SAKE. /POTHINUS/ MY	LIFE	WILL COST YOU DEAR IF YOU TAKE IT, CAESAR. (HE GOES
SUPR I SD(9)	WITH A BEARD. BUT IT IS ALREADY PLAIN THAT MIDDLE	LIFE	WILL FIND HIM IN THAT CATEGORY. HE HAS STILL SOME OF
ARMS II (41)	HE WILL NEVER FORGIVE ME; AND MY DAUGHTER'S	LIFE	WILL HARDLY BE SAFE. WILL YOU, LIKE THE CHIVALROUS

GETT PREFACE(222)	FINDS HER SELF-RESPECT. THE TRUTH IS THAT FAMILY	LIFE	WILL NEVER BE DECENT, MUCH LESS ENNOBLING, UNTIL THIS
2TRU III (98)	FOR A FEW HAPPY YEARS. WHEN YOU FALL IN LOVE,	LIFE	WILL SEEM WORTH LIVING. /THE PATIENT/ I DID FALL IN
MTH5 (206)	DOG. THOSE WHO ARE INTERESTED IN EXTINCT FORMS OF	LIFE	WILL TELL YOU THAT IT LOVED THE SOUND OF ITS OWN VOICE
SUPR III (111)	THESE ARE IN ITS PAY ALL THE TIME. AND SO	LIFE	WINS, AFTER A FASHION, WHAT MERE COPIOUSNESS OF
HART III (139)	ON MY HAPPINESS. /ELLIE/ (HER FACE LIGHTING UP)	LIFE	WITH A BLESSING! THAT IS WHAT I WANT. NOW I KNOW THE
BUOY 1 (14)	YOU HAVE NO SUCH TALENT. I CANNOT START YOU IN	LIFE	WITH A GIFT OF CAPITAL AS I STARTED YOUR BROTHERS,
LION PREFACE(94)	CONSCIENCE OF THE NINETEENTH CENTURY BACK TO	LIFE	WITH A WHIP OF SCORPIONS. THE TEACHING OF CHRISTIANITY,
PYGM II (228)	HAVE A PRESENT OF SEVEN-AND-SIXPENCE TO START	LIFE	WITH AS A LADY IN A SHOP. IF YOU REFUSE THIS OFFER YOU
METH PREFACE(R61)	DIABOLICAL IDENTIFICATION OF SUCCESS IN	LIFE	WITH BIG PROFITS. THE MOMENT MARX SHEWED THAT THE
OVER (179)	YOU TO YOUR DUTY. BUT OH, I WILL GIVE YOU MY	LIFE	WITH BOTH HANDS IF YOU CAN TELL ME THAT YOU FEEL FOR ME
BASH II,1, (109)	SNOBBERY, VENTRE A TERRE, WILL HUNT THROUGH	LIFE	WITH EAGER NOSE ON EARTH AND HANG THEE THICK WITH
MTH3 (96)	ALWAYS DID WAS TO GRANT SUPPLIES TO THE KING FOR	LIFE	WITH ENTHUSIASTIC EXPRESSIONS OF LOYALTY, LEST THEY
MTH1 II (30)	AFTER DEATH; AND DRESSES UP HIS TERROR-RIDDEN	LIFE	WITH FINE WORDS AND HIS DISEASE-RIDDEN BODY WITH FINE
FABL PREFACE(66)	HER DESTITUTE OF THE QUALITIES THAT MAKE MARRIED	LIFE	WITH HER BEARABLE. APPARENTLY ITS AIM IS ALWAYS THE
BULL PREFACE(54)	YOUNG MAN, OF 20, WAS SENT TO PENAL SERVITUDE FOR	LIFE	WITH HIM. NO SUCH SENTIMENTALITY WAS SHEWN TO HASSAN
JITT II (40)	SAYS HE LOVES ME, AND ASKS ME TO SHARE MY WHOLE	LIFE	WITH HIM. IF HE CANNOT UNDERSTAND ME AND SUPPORT ME IN
BARB III (324)	A MAN'S SOUL IN MY HAND. I SET HIM IN THE WAY OF	LIFE	WITH HIS FACE TO SALVATION. BUT WHEN WE TOOK YOUR MONEY
JITT I (15)	WILL YOU ALWAYS HARP ON THAT? DEATH IS NOTHING.	LIFE	WITH LOVE IS EVERYTHING. THINK, BRUNO. WE ARE HERE
APPL INTRLUD(251)	AND AGAIN. AM I NOT WORTH A MILLION SUCH? IS NOT	LIFE	WITH ME AS HIGH ABOVE THEM AS THE SUN IS ABOVE THE
NEVR II (249)	SIR, YOU NEVER CAN TELL. THATS A PRINCIPLE IN	LIFE	WITH ME, SIR, IF YOULL EXCUSE MY HAVING SUCH A THING,
BUOY III (38)	WHO PRODUCE EXCELLENT BASTARDS, THOUGH DOMESTIC	LIFE	WITH THEM IS IMPOSSIBLE. THEY SHOULD BE CONCUBINES, NOT
METH PREFACE(R87)	GRAPPLE WITH REALITIES IN THOSE PLAYS OF MODERN	LIFE	WITH WHICH HE OVERCAME EUROPE, AND BROKE THE DUSTY
JITT I (16)	I WERE YOUNG! THEN I COULD REALLY BEGIN A NEW	LIFE	WITH YOU INSTEAD OF MERELY THINKING AND DREAMING ABOUT
MTH1 II (27)	JUST NOW THAT IT CALLED ON YOU TO PAY FOR ABEL'S	LIFE	WITH YOUR OWN. /CAIN/ THE VOICE DOES NOT SPEAK TO ME AS
MTH1 II (28)	SPLENDID AND INTENSE: A LIFE OF THE SOUL ALONE: A	LIFE	WITHOUT CLODS OR SPADES, HUNGER OR FATIGUE-- /EVE/
LION PREFACE(65)	THE ORDINARY ANNOYANCES AND DISAPPOINTMENTS OF	LIFE	WITHOUT COMMITTING MURDEROUS ASSAULTS. THEY CONCLUDE
SUPR I (38)	THAT WAY. /ANN/ BUT, JACK, YOU CANNOT GET THROUGH	LIFE	WITHOUT CONSIDERING OTHER PEOPLE A LITTLE. /TANNER/ AY;
JOAN PREFACE(21)	WAS DELIBERATELY CHOSEN AS AN ALTERNATIVE TO	LIFE	WITHOUT LIBERTY. IN BATTLE SHE CHALLENGED DEATH AS
MTH1 II (25)	A STICK TO FEEL YOUR STRENGTH: YOU CANNOT TASTE	LIFE	WITHOUT MAKING IT BITTER AND BOILING HOT: YOU CANNOT
MTH2 (75)	WHICH ARE, AFTER ALL, ONLY MODES OF PERPETUATING	LIFE	WITHOUT PUTTING ON ANY SINGLE CREATURE THE TERRIBLE
LION PREFACE(6)	LED HIM TO SUBMIT TO TORTURE AND SACRIFICE HIS	LIFE	WITHOUT RESISTANCE IN THE CONVICTION THAT HE WOULD
PRES (158)	MAKE THEM WOULD BE A TRIBUTE TO ROMANCE. WHAT IS	LIFE	WITHOUT ROMANCE? /MITCHENER/ (MAKING A MOVEMENT
BARB I (253)	I HAVE HARDLY EVER OPENED A NEWSPAPER IN MY	LIFE	WITHOUT SEEING OUR NAME IN IT. THE UNDERSHAFT TORPEDO!
MTH4 I (172)	OR IS TOO WEAK TO BEAR THE STRAIN OF OUR TRUTHFUL	LIFE	WITHOUT WINCING, OR IS TORMENTED BY DEPRAVED APPETITIES
PHIL I (80)	BY THE THOUGHT OF LOSING YOU. I CANT FACE	LIFE	WITHOUT YOU, LEONARD. I WAS HAPPY WHEN I MET YOU: I HAD
PHIL III (133)	SPOT. HE WOULD NOT SPEND ONE HOUR OF HIS REAL	LIFE	WITH-- (A SOB CHOKES HER: SHE RISES PASSIONATELY,
HART II (104)	/MANGAN/ THIS GIRL DOESNT WANT TO SPEND HER	LIFE	WONDERING HOW LONG HER GLOVES WILL LAST. /CAPTAIN
METH PREFACE(R50)	FAIL AS HOPELESSLY TO ACCOUNT FOR DARWIN'S OWN	LIFE	WORK AS FOR MY CONQUEST OF THE BICYCLE: BUT WHO CAN
SUPR III (134)	GOING IS A POLITICAL DEFEAT. I CANNOT KEEP THESE	LIFE	WORSHIPPERS; THEY ALL GO. THIS IS THE GREATEST LOSS I
MRS II (217)	AND SLAVERY? AND WHATS A WOMAN WORTH? WHATS	LIFE	WORTH? WITHOUT SELF-RESPECT! WHY AM I INDEPENDENT AND
KING I (205)	SINGLE PLEASURE THAT THEY WOULD LEAVE US TO MAKE	LIFE	WORTH LIVING? /FOX/ IT IS NOT PLEASURE THAT MAKES LIFE
MTH1 II (32)	NOTHING BUT DEATH OR THE DREAD OF DEATH MAKES	LIFE	WORTH LIVING. AWAY WITH YOU, NAUGHTY CHILD; AND DO YOU,
KING I (205)	LIVING? /FOX/ IT IS NOT PLEASURE THAT MAKES	LIFE	WORTH LIVING. IT IS LIFE THAT MAKES PLEASURE WORTH
3PLA PREFACE(R32)	IT, DEIFY IT, AND IMPLY THAT IT ALONE MAKES OUR	LIFE	WORTH LIVING, IS NOTHING BUT FOLLY GONE MAD
HART PREFACE(17)	TO GIVE THEM A FALSE VALUE; TO PROCLAIM THE YOUNG	LIFE	WORTHILY AND GLORIOUSLY SACRIFICED TO REDEEM THE
GENV I (46)	OF SINS BY THE SHEDDING OF BLOOD. NO MAN'S	LIFE	WOULD BE SAFE IN RUSSIA IF SUCH DOCTRINES WERE
MTH3 (134)	FOR SOME TIME PAST UNDER THE IMPRESSION THAT MY	LIFE	WOULD BE SO SHORT THAT IT WAS NOT WORTH BOTHERING
3PLA PREFACE(R38)	REQUIRING FOUR DOORS TO A ROOM WHICH IN REAL	LIFE	WOULD HAVE ONLY ONE. BUT MY STORIES ARE THE OLD
2TRU II (55)	BY THEIR PERSONAL APPEARANCE. HAD IT DONE SO YOUR	LIFE	WOULD NOT BE WORTH HALF AN HOUR'S PURCHASE. /MEEK/ NO,
MRS II (209)	TO COLLEGE AGAIN. /VIVIE/ DO YOU THINK MY WAY OF	LIFE	WOULD SUIT YOU? I DOUBT IT. /MRS WARREN/ YOUR WAY OF
HART II (110)	HOW DO I KNOW, CAPTAIN? YOU KNOW THE SORT OF	LIFE	YOU AND ME HAS LED. ANY YOUNG LADY OF THAT AGE MIGHT BE
HART II (107)	HAVNT YOU? CAN YOU GIVE ME BACK THE YEARS OF MY	LIFE	YOU ARE GOING TO TAKE FROM ME? /MRS HUSHABYE/ OH, WE
BUOY II (21)	OUR LIVING SELVES FOR ALL THAT. AND IN THIS WILD	LIFE	YOU CAN TASTE YOURSELF. /HE/ NOT ALWAYS A PLEASANT
2TRU III (93)	SUPERSTITIOUS MOTHER. RETIRE NOW-- FROM THE	LIFE	YOU HAVE DISHONORED. THERE IS THE SEA. GO. DROWN
VWOO 3 (137)	NEVER GET MARRIED. /A/ PRECISELY. /Z/ IN THIS	LIFE	YOU HAVE TO TAKE CHANCES. /Z/ I HAVE TAKEN THEM, AND
LADY (243)	TO MAKE MY HANDS TREMBLE WITH THE STREAMS OF	LIFE	YOU POUR THROUGH THEM. YOU HOLD ME AS THE LODESTAR
BUOY II (20)	(HE ATTACKS THE MEAL). /SHE/ NO. IN THE SIMPLE	LIFE	YOU RING FOR THE SERVANTS. EVERYTHING IS DONE FOR YOU;
SUPR PREFACE(R18)	TO FACE A TRUMPERY STORY OF MODERN LONDON	LIFE	, A LIFE IN WHICH, AS YOU KNOW, THE ORDINARY MAN'S MAIN
BARB PREFACE(207)	DEVIL'S UNSUCCESSFUL ENCOUNTERS WITH THE FACTS OF	LIFE	, A POIGNANT QUALITY THAT ROMANTIC FICTION LACKED. THE
MILL PREFACE(123)	APPOINTMENT AS ABSOLUTE DICTATOR IN GERMANY FOR	LIFE	, A STRETCH OF CAESARISM NO NINETEENTH CENTURY
SUPR III (113)	WITHOUT IT HE BLUNDERS INTO DEATH. JUST AS	LIFE	, AFTER AGES OF STRUGGLE, EVOLVED THAT WONDERFUL BODILY
3PLA PREFACE(R26)	WELL THAT I FIND MYSELF, WHILST STILL IN MIDDLE	LIFE	, ALMOST AS LEGENDARY A PERSON AS THE FLYING DUTCHMAN.
LION PREFACE(42)	END OF HIS NARRATIVE LEAVES CHRIST RESTORED TO	LIFE	, AND APPEARING FROM TIME TO TIME AMONG HIS DISCIPLES.
MIS. PREFACE(61)	DO NOT INTEND TO HAVE HIM ON YOUR HANDS ALL YOUR	LIFE	, AND ARE GENERALLY RATHER IMPATIENT FOR THE DAY WHEN
MIS. PREFACE(64)	NOT EDUCATED TO LIVE DANGEROUSLY HAVE ONLY HALF A	LIFE	, AND ARE MORE LIKELY TO DIE MISERABLY AFTER ALL THAN
DOCT PREFACE(55)	OF UMBRELLAS ENLARGES THE CHEST, PROLONGS	LIFE	, AND CONFERS COMPARATIVE IMMUNITY FROM DISEASE; FOR
DOCT PREFACE(59)	ME ONLY A CONCEPT: I NEVER USED A LOGARITHM IN MY	LIFE	, AND COULD NOT UNDERTAKE TO EXTRACT THE SQUARE ROOT OF
2TRU III (92)	ANOTHER FOR NOTHING, SHE LOST THE COURAGE TO FACE	LIFE	, AND DIED OF IT. /THE SERGEANT/ WELL, SIR, I'D NEVER
CLEO IV (191)	TO TRUST ME UNTIL HE IS VICTORIOUS. I ASK FOR MY	LIFE	, AND FOR A COMMAND IN CAESAR'S ARMY. AND SINCE CAESAR
BULL PREFACE(50)	FOR ITS RECRUITS ON THE REFUSE OF INDUSTRIAL	LIFE	, AND FOR ITS OFFICERS ON THE ARISTOCRATIC AND
JOAN 6 (125)	LORDSHIP BELIEVE IT I WILL NOT ANSWER FOR YOUR	LIFE	, AND HARDLY FOR MY OWN. /WARWICK/ (DEPRECATING, BUT
GLIM (174)	SAINT BARBARA SAYS THAT HE NEVER SAW YOU IN HIS	LIFE	, AND HAS NOT THIRTY CROWNS IN THE WORLD. /THE GIRL/
DEVL EPILOG (83)	DEVIL'S DISCIPLE IS A MAN WHO PLAYS HIS PART IN	LIFE	, AND MAKES ALL ITS POINTS, IN THE MANNER OF A BORN
ROCK I (230)	FACT MY LIFE HAS BEEN A COMPLETELY INTELLECTUAL	LIFE	, AND MY TRAINING THE FINEST INTELLECTUAL TRAINING IN
MRS I (192)	HAVE NOTHING TO DO WITH THAT SIDE OF MRS WARREN'S	LIFE	, AND NEVER HAD. SHE HAS NEVER SPOKEN TO ME ABOUT IT;
BARB PREFACE(210)	LIKE SCULPTORS, STUDY THEIR FIGURES FROM	LIFE	, AND NOT FROM PHILOSOPHIC ESSAYS. THEY REPLY
POSN PREFACE(376)	SEASONED TO THE GIVE-AND-TAKE OF PUBLIC	LIFE	, AND OF THE SINGLE PEER WHO KEPT HIS HEAD. THE OTHERS,
BARB II (292)	YOU MUST FIRST ACQUIRE MONEY ENOUGH FOR A DECENT	LIFE	, AND POWER ENOUGH TO BE YOUR OWN MASTER. /CUSINS/ YOU
MIS. PREFACE(62)	PEOPLE WHO GAVE JOHN A FULL SHARE IN THEIR OWN	LIFE	, AND PUT UP WITH HIS PRESENCE BOTH AT HOME AND ABROAD
JOAN PREFACE(5)	THAT HE WAS AN OLD SOLDIER AND A MAN OF HONORABLE	LIFE	, AND THAT HIS ACCUSER WAS A SILLY SNOB. HE HAD NO
3PLA PREFACE(R28)	WHY SHOULD A BLACKGUARD SAVE ANOTHER MAN'S	LIFE	, AND THAT MAN NO FRIEND OF HIS, AT THE RISK OF HIS
LION PREFACE(80)	THAT HE HAD NEVER MADE A GREATER MISTAKE IN HIS	LIFE	, AND THAT THE BUSINESS OF A CHRIST WAS TO MAKE
PYGM V (286)	IF YOU CANT STAND THE COLDNESS OF MY SORT OF	LIFE	, AND THE STRAIN OF IT, GO BACK TO THE GUTTER. WORK TIL
SUPR III (114)	SEE, NOT THE PHYSICAL WORLD, BUT THE PURPOSE OF	LIFE	, AND THEREBY ENABLE THE INDIVIDUAL TO WORK FOR THAT
APPL I (238)	TO FIGHT THEM I SHALL BE HOUNDED OUT OF PUBLIC	LIFE	, AND THEY WILL SHOVE MOULDY MIKE INTO THE CABINET TO
JITT I (24)	/BRUNO/ (CARRIED AWAY) LIFE: YES: THIS IS	LIFE	, AND THIS (HE KISSES HER EYES), AND THIS (HE KISSES
BULL PREFACE(63)	TWENTY-YEAR-OLD NEIGHBOR IN PENAL SERVITUDE FOR	LIFE	, AND TO PLUME HIMSELF ON THE POWER TO DO IT, PRETEND
MTH5 (254)	OF LIFE IN YOU, AND BECAUSE I CARED ONLY FOR OUR	LIFE	, AND WENT STRAIGHT TO IT, AND WAS BORED BY YOUR
METH PREFACE(R64)	IN MATTER THE PROMISE AND POTENCY OF ALL FORMS OF	LIFE	, AND WITH HIS IRISH GRAPHIC LUCIDITY MADE A PICTURE OF
GETT PREFACE(248)	OF THESE, BECAUSE IT IS A BLASPHEMY AGAINST	LIFE	, AND, TO PUT IT IN CHRISTIAN TERMS, AN ACCUSATION OF
MTH4 III (196)	IN ADDRESSING, FOR THE FIRST TIME IN MY	LIFE	, A-- A-- A-- A GODDESS, MY FRIEND AND RELATIVE THE
2TRU PREFACE(8)	WHICH THEY CAN BE IDLE AND RICH, IF NOT FOR	LIFE	, AT LEAST FOR AN HOUR, AN AFTERNOON, OR EVEN A WEEK.
MILL I SD(152)	BLENDERBLAND, AN IMPOSING MAN IN THE PRIME OF	LIFE	, BEARDED IN THE VICTORIAN LITERARY FASHION, RATHER
SIM PRO,2,SD(28)	A NATIVE PRIEST, A HANDSOME MAN IN THE PRIME OF	LIFE	, BEAUTIFULLY DRESSED, RISES INTO VIEW BY THIS PATH AND
KING I (195)	AT ME AND SAY THAT I AM THE PROTECTOR OF YOUR	LIFE	, BECAUSE NOBODY WILL KILL YOU TO MAKE ME KING; BUT I
INCA (254)	TO THE SOCIETY OF PRINCESSES ALL MY WRETCHED	LIFE	, BELIEVED FOR A MOMENT THAT ANY PRINCESS THAT EVER
MTH2 (81)	HUMAN RACE IS A FAILURE, AND THAT A NEW FORM OF	LIFE	, BETTER ADAPTED TO HIGH CIVILIZATION, WILL SUPERSEDE
2TRU I (48)	WITH YOU! HENCEFORTH MY GATES ARE OPEN TO REAL	LIFE	, BRING WHAT IT MAY, FOR WHAT SENSE IS THERE IN THIS
GETT PREFACE(241)	MANY DIVORCES IS NOT THE RESUMPTION OF A SINGLE	LIFE	, BUT A CHANGE OF PARTNERS. AS THIS CHANGE CAN BE
MTH2 (75)	NATURAL DEATH, AS WE CALL IT, WAS NOT A PART OF	LIFE	, BUT A LATER AND QUITE SEPARATE INVENTION? /BURGE/
UNPL PREFACE(R18)	WHETHER A CLASS THAT NOT ONLY SUBMITS TO HOME	LIFE	, BUT ACTUALLY BOASTS ABOUT IT, IS REALLY A CLASS WORTH
METH PREFACE(R18)	OUT THAT DEATH IS NOT AN ETERNAL CONDITION OF	LIFE	, BUT AN EXPEDIENT INTRODUCED TO PROVIDE FOR CONTINUAL
PHIL I (90)	A SCRAP OF FISH OCCASIONALLY. I'M TO HAVE A SHORT	LIFE	, BUT NOT A MERRY ONE. (SIGHING) WELL, WELL! (
2TRU III (110)	OF THE FUTURE A BREATH WHICH MAY BE A BREATH OF	LIFE	, BUT OF A LIFE TOO KEEN FOR ME TO BEAR, AND THEREFORE
BARB PREFACE(218)	UNDERPAY THEM MEANLY FOR DOING IT, IS NOT A GOOD	LIFE	, BUT RATHER FATAL TO ALL POSSIBILITY OF EVEN A
LION PREFACE(41)	OF JESUS IS NOT ONLY THAT THE PEOPLE SHOULD HAVE	LIFE	, BUT THAT THEY SHOULD HAVE IT " MORE ABUNDANTLY" (A
MIS. PREFACE(87)	IMPORTANCE, IS IN EFFECT BROKEN UP BY SCHOOL	LIFE	, BY OUT-OF-DOOR HABITS, AND BY FRANK NEIGHBORLY

3PLA PREFACE(R19)	REALISTICALLY SIMULATING THE INCIDENTS OF	LIFE	, CANNOT TOUCH IT WITHOUT INDECORUM. CAN ANY DILEMMA BE
CATH PREFACE(155)	OF THE PERFORMER RATHER THAN TO SOLVE PROBLEMS OF	LIFE	, CHARACTER, OR HISTORY. FEATS OF THIS KIND MAY TICKLE
LADY (247)	I SHALL NOT FORGET MYSELF AGAIN; THOUGH BY MY	LIFE	, COULD I MAKE YOU A SERVING WENCH, NEITHER A QUEEN NOR
CATH 1 (169)	IF THEY ARE UNPLEASANT FACTS. /PATIOMKIN/ IN REAL	LIFE	, DARLING, ALL FACTS ARE UNPLEASANT. (GREATLY PLEASED
MIS. (141)	THE REST. YOU DONT CALL THAT AN EVENT IN ONE'S	LIFE	, DO YOU? WITH YOU IT WAS DIFFERENT. I SHOULD AS SOON
BUOY II (20)	CALABASH: EAT FROM YOUR FINGERS. /HE/ THE SIMPLE	LIFE	, EH? (HE ATTACKS THE MEAL). /SHE/ NO. IN THE SIMPLE
MRS IV (240)	OTHER (TO PRAED) IS THE ROMANCE AND BEAUTY OF	LIFE	, ESPECIALLY OSTEND AND THE GAIETY OF BRUSSELS. YOU ARE
MIS. PREFACE(15)	CARE, FILIAL PIETY, DUTY, AFFECTION, FAMILY	LIFE	, ETC, ETC., WHICH ARE NO DOUBT VERY COMFORTING
JITT III (53)	OF YOUR POOR DEARS: HE WAS THREE QUARTERS OF MY	LIFE	, EVEN IF HALF OF IT WAS BEING HIS SLAVE AND HIS
MIS. PREFACE(103)	MAN FIRST ENRICHED AT FIFTY REMAINS POOR ALL HIS	LIFE	, EVEN IF HE DOES NOT CURTAIL IT BY DRINKING HIMSELF TO
DEST (154)	SAY YOU ARE CAREFUL OF EVERYTHING EXCEPT HUMAN	LIFE	, EXCELLENCY. /NAPOLEON/ HUMAN LIFE, MY FRIEND, IS THE
GETT PREFACE(237)	OF MUCH PRACTICAL USE; FOR THE SUPREME RIGHT TO	LIFE	, EXTENDED AS IT NOW MUST BE TO THE LIFE OF THE RACE,
DOCT PREFACE(78)	OF HONOR, LIBERTY, COURAGE, THE KINSHIP OF ALL	LIFE	, FAITH THAT THE UNKNOWN IS GREATER THAN THE KNOWN AND
PYGM V (284)	YOU DONT CARE A BIT FOR ME. /HIGGINS/ I CARE FOR	LIFE	, FOR HUMANITY; AND YOU ARE A PART OF IT THAT HAS COME
2TRU III (111)	ALL I KNOW IS THAT I MUST FIND THE WAY OF	LIFE	, FOR MYSELF AND ALL OF US, OR WE SHALL SURELY PERISH.
GETT (300)	HANGING HIM, THEY SENT HIM TO PENAL SERVITUDE FOR	LIFE	, FOR THE SAKE, THEY SAID, OF HIS WIFE AND INFANT
GETT (271)	YOUR GOWN? /COLLINS/ I DONT WEAR IT IN PRIVATE	LIFE	, GENERAL. /THE GENERAL/ WHY? ARE YOU ASHAMED OF IT..
DEVL I (6)	HIS BROTHER, THAT WAS A DISGRACE TO US ALL HIS	LIFE	, GETS HANGED ON THE PUBLIC GALLOWS AS A REBEL; AND
BARB PREFACE(229)	TO AN EXQUISITELY HAPPY AND UTTERLY CARELESS	LIFE	, HAS NOT OVERCOME THE FEAR OF DEATH AT ALL: ON THE
BARB PREFACE(235)	IN THE HAPHAZARD ORDER OF EVENTS IN REAL	LIFE	, HAVE CONTRIVED TO MAKE IT KNOWN TO BILL, WITH THE
SUPR III (113)	LOVES AND NESTINGS, THAT IT IS INCONCEIVABLE THAT	LIFE	, HAVING ONCE PRODUCED THEM, SHOULD, IF LOVE AND BEAUTY
FABL PREFACE(87)	TRUNK. I CANNOT CALL MYSELF THE WAY AND THE	LIFE	, HAVING ONLY A QUESTIONABLE HYPOTHESIS OR TWO TO
BULL PREFACE(10)	AND LED HIM ROUND A PRISONER FOR THE REST OF HIS	LIFE	, HE WOULD HAVE SUFFERED AS MUCH BY SUCH A FOLLY AS THE
PYGM V (271)	RECOGNIZE AND RESPECT MERIT IN EVERY CLASS OF	LIFE	, HOWEVER HUMBLE. THEM WORDS IS IN HIS BLOOMING WILL,
UNPL PREFACE(R18)	ON QUALIFYING HERSELF FOR AN INDEPENDENT WORKING	LIFE	, HUMANIZES HER WHOLE FAMILY IN AN ASTONISHINGLY SHORT
MIS. (143)	FOR LIVING. /LORD SUMMERHAYS/ LIVING YOUR OWN	LIFE	, I BELIEVE THE SUFFRAGIST PHRASE IS. /HYPATIA/ LIVING
CATH PREFACE(158)	ON THE STAGE FOR PERHAPS THE FIRST TIME IN HIS	LIFE	, I DO NOT THINK HE EXPECTED IN THE LEAST THAT HIS
DOCT IV (165)	OF WAY, STRUGGLING THROUGH THE UNREAL PART OF	LIFE	, I HAVNT ALWAYS BEEN ABLE TO LIVE UP TO MY IDEAL. BUT
MTH1 II (23)	WHEN I HAVE SLAIN THE BOAR AT THE RISK OF MY	LIFE	, I WILL THROW IT TO MY WOMAN TO COOK, AND GIVE HER A
3PLA PREFACE(R17)	TO BEHAVE, IF YOU ADORE HEDDA GABLER IN REAL	LIFE	, IF YOU ENVY HER AND FEEL THAT NOTHING BUT YOUR
CAPT II (252)	HIS KINGDOM-- ANY MORE THAN IT WOULD SAVE YOUR	LIFE	, IF YOUR CAPTAIN HERE DID THE SAME THING. /JOHNSON/ (
LION PREFACE(78)	CONDITION OF EVOLUTION, WHICH IS, THAT	LIFE	, INCLUDING HUMAN LIFE, IS CONTINUALLY EVOLVING, AND
MRS II (210)	NO TIME, AND SAYING NOTHING). YOU AND YOUR WAY OF	LIFE	, INDEED! WHAT NEXT? (SHE LOOKS AT VIVIE AGAIN. NO
DOCT II (126)	END OF IT. IF A FORTNIGHT'S HOLIDAY WOULD SAVE MY	LIFE	, I'D HAVE TO DIE. I SHALL GET ON AS OTHERS HAVE TO GET
CAND II (123)	ENGAGEMENT TO SPEAK! /BURGESS/ FUST TIME IN HIS	LIFE	, I'LL BET. AIN IT, CANDY? /LEXY/ (TO MORELL) THEY
GETT (304)	TALKING IN THAT DISGRACEFUL WAY ABOUT OUR MARRIED	LIFE	, I'LL LEAVE THE ROOM AND NEVER SPEAK TO YOU AGAIN.
DOCT PREFACE(33)	IN ITS ASSUMPTION THAT KNOWLEDGE, LIKE	LIFE	, IS A DESIRABLE THING, THOUGH ANY FOOL CAN PROVE THAT
MIS. PREFACE(71)	ANOTHER. THE DISCOVERY THAT ANYTHING, EVEN SCHOOL	LIFE	, IS BETTER FOR THE CHILD THAN HOME LIFE, WILL BECOME
MIS. PREFACE(71)	BE TOLD BY OUR FADDISTS THAT ANYTHING, EVEN CAMP	LIFE	, IS BETTER THAN SCHOOL LIFE, SOME BLUNDERING
LION PREFACE(78)	EVOLUTION, WHICH IS, THAT LIFE, INCLUDING HUMAN	LIFE	, IS CONTINUALLY EVOLVING, AND MUST THEREFORE BE
POSN PREFACE(392)	THE DRAMA, DEALING WITH ALL DEPARTMENTS OF HUMAN	LIFE	, IS NECESSARILY POLITICAL. RECENT EVENTS HAVE SHEWN--
GETT PREFACE(249)	OF KEEPING IT ADJUSTED TO THE WHOLE SCHEME OF	LIFE	, IS THAT YOU END BY HAVING HALF-A-DOZEN CONTRADICTORY
MTH2 (72)	BE LONG ENOUGH FOR A VERY CRUDE SORT OF VILLAGE	LIFE	, ISNT LONG ENOUGH FOR A COMPLICATED CIVILIZATION LIKE
JITT PREFACE(6)	A PLAY SUCCEEDS IN PRODUCING AN ILLUSION OF REAL	LIFE	, IT MUST DISPENSE WITH THE FRANTIC AGONIES AND
NEVR II (248)	IT'S SOMETHING FAR ABOVE AND BEYOND THAT. IT'S	LIFE	, IT'S FAITH, IT'S STRENGTH, CERTAINTY, PARADISE!
3PLA PREFACE(R27)	CENTURIES AGO OUR GREATEST ENGLISH DRAMATIZER OF	LIFE	, JOHN BUNYAN, ENDED ONE OF HIS STORIES WITH THE REMARK
BARB PREFACE(211)	GLORIFICATION OF SELFISH BULLYING AS THE RULE OF	LIFE	, JUST AS IT IS ASSUMED, ON THE STRENGTH OF THE SINGLE
GETT PREFACE(247)	PREPARED TO PUT UP WITH FOR THE SAKE OF A QUIET	LIFE	, LESS LUCKY AND MORE SENSITIVE AND CONSCIENTIOUS
MRS II (217)	TO BE GOOD TO HER, IF SHE'S IN HIS OWN STATION OF	LIFE	, LET HER MAKE HIM MARRY HER; BUT IF SHE'S FAR BENEATH
DOCT PREFACE(34)	OF KNOWLEDGE, ANY MORE THAN THE PURSUIT OF	LIFE	, LIBERTY, AND HAPPINESS (AS THE AMERICAN CONSTITUTION
LION PREFACE(87)	HIS DISCIPLES TO CARRY THEM OUT IN THEIR DAILY	LIFE	, LOST HIS HEAD; BELIEVED HIMSELF TO BE A CRUDE
UNPL PREFACE(R18)	IMPOSSIBLE BY THE CONDITIONS OF WORKING CLASS	LIFE	, MANNERS IMPROVE ENORMOUSLY, IN THE MIDDLE CLASSES
LADY (244)	TO HIM. /SHAKESPEAR/ NOT WERE IT EEN TO SAVE YOUR	LIFE	, MARY, NOT TO MENTION MINE OWN, WILL I FLATTER A
FANY PROLOG (269)	AND THUS VIOLATING THE SANCTITY OF PRIVATE	LIFE	, MIGHT NOT BE AMISS. BUT PLAYS, NO. I SAY NO. NOT
MRS IV (249)	ME? /VIVIE/ I RECOGNIZE THE CROFTS PHILOSOPHY OF	LIFE	, MOTHER. I HEARD IT ALL FROM HIM THAT DAY AT THE
DEVL III (51)	TAKE YOU LAST NIGHT? /RICHARD/ (GAILY) UPON MY	LIFE	, MRS ANDERSON, I DONT KNOW. IVE BEEN ASKING MYSELF
JOAN 5 (117)	A SINGLE SOLDIER TO US; AND I WILL NOT RISK THAT	LIFE	, MUCH AS I CHERISH HER AS A COMPANION-IN-ARMS. /JOAN/
MTH2 (77)	HARDLY COUNT ON THREE SCORE AND TEN YEARS OF	LIFE	, MUCH LESS THE THOUSAND THAT ADAM HAD BEEN READY TO
DEST (154)	EXCEPT HUMAN LIFE, EXCELLENCY. /NAPOLEON/ HUMAN	LIFE	, MY FRIEND, IS THE ONLY THING THAT TAKES CARE OF
PRES (161)	ONE OF THOSE UNSEXED CREATURES WHO HAVE NO JOY IN	LIFE	, NO SENSE OF BEAUTY, NO HIGH NOTES. /MITCHENER/ NO
BARB PREFACE(219)	THEIR ART-CRITICISMS. THEY DO NOT WANT THE SIMPLE	LIFE	, NOR THE ESTHETIC LIFE; ON THE CONTRARY, THEY WANT
LION EPILOG (147)	OF THE SPIRIT FOR A NOBLER AND MORE ABUNDANT	LIFE	, NOT FOR THEMSELVES AT THE EXPENSE OF OTHERS, BUT FOR
MTH4 III (202)	YOU. /THE ELDERLY GENTLEMAN/ IT IS THE MEANING OF	LIFE	, NOT OF DEATH, THAT MAKES BANISHMENT SO TERRIBLE TO
LION PREFACE(51)	FUNERALS GRIEVING FOR YOUR RELATIVES; ATTEND TO	LIFE	, NOT TO DEATH: THERE ARE AS GOOD FISH IN THE SEA AS
ARMS III (70)	MADAME, THE GRACIOUS YOUNG LADY SIMPLY SAVED MY	LIFE	, NOTHING ELSE. SHE NEVER CARED TWO STRAWS FOR ME. WHY,
SUPR PREFACE(R24)	OF READING FOR EXPERIENCE, OF LITERATURE FOR	LIFE	, OF THE OBSOLETE FICTITIOUS FOR THE CONTEMPORARY REAL,
BULL PREFACE(56)	WORK: FOUR HANGED, TWO TO PENAL SERVITUDE FOR	LIFE	, ONE TO FIFTEEN YEARS PENAL SERVITUDE, SIX TO SEVEN
UNPL PREFACE(R7)	OF FIT PERSONS FOR HIGH FUNCTIONS, FASHIONABLE	LIFE	, OPEN ON INDULGENT TERMS TO UNENCUMBERED " BRILLIANT"
ROCK PREFACE(149)	DOGMA OF THE UNCONDITIONAL SACREDNESS OF HUMAN	LIFE	, OR ANY OTHER INCARNATION OF LIFE; BUT IT COVERS ONLY
DOCT PREFACE(8)	SUPPLY YOU WITH SIXPENNY-WORTH OF THE ELIXIR OF	LIFE	, OR THE NEAREST MOTOR GARAGE FOR NOT HAVING PERPETUAL
NEVR I (211)	ALWAYS TAUGHT YOU? THERE ARE TWO SORTS OF FAMILY	LIFE	, PHIL; AND YOUR EXPERIENCE OF HUMAN NATURE ONLY
FABL PREFACE(88)	BY WHICH THEY ARE TESTED, THEY ARE THERE FOR	LIFE	, PRACTICALLY IRREMOVABLE. AND SO GOVERNMENT GOES ON.
GETT PREFACE(198)	CONVICTION THAT INCREASED WITH HIS EXPERIENCE OF	LIFE	, PREACHED THE GOSPEL OF LAODICEA, URGING PEOPLE TO BE
GETT PREFACE(233)	MARRIED COUPLES AT DANGEROUS PERIODS OF MATURE	LIFE	, QUITE OFTEN FIND THEMSELVES IN IT; AND THE EXTREME
MTH3 (128)	TWO HUNDRED AND SEVENTY-EIGHT. IT DOES SHORTEN MY	LIFE	, RELATIVELY. IT MAKES US RIDICULOUS. IF THEY GREW TO
KING I (202)	FROM AURENGZEBE AS FOLLOWS: WHEN I CONSIDER	LIFE	, 'TIS ALL A CHEAT; YET, FOOLED WITH HOPE, MEN FAVOR
CLEO IV (182)	IN EGYPT. THE OLD MEN, WHEN THEY ARE TIRED OF	LIFE	, SAY " WE HAVE SEEN EVERYTHING EXCEPT THE SOURCE OF
MILL I (143)	THE HORRIBLE MESS AND FAILURE I HAVE MADE OF MY	LIFE	, SEEM TO YOU MERELY FUNNY. IF IT WERE NOT THAT MY
CLEO I (107)	AN IMAGE OF THE CONSTANT AND IMMORTAL PART OF MY	LIFE	, SILENT, FULL OF THOUGHTS, ALONE IN THE SILVER DESERT.
CAPT II (245)	TO SIR HOWARD) THATS THE CURSE O THIS KIND O	LIFE	, SIR; YOU GOT TO ASSOCIATE WITH ALL SORTS. MY FATHER,
NEVR IV (282)	THAT DEPENDS A GOOD DEAL ON ONE'S STATION IN	LIFE	, SIR. IF YOU WERE A WAITER, SIR, YOUD FIND THAT SIMPLE
NEVR II (250)	OF A HOTEL IS THAT IT'S A REFUGE FROM HOME	LIFE	, SIR. /CRAMPTON/ I MISSED THAT ADVANTAGE TODAY. I
MIS. PREFACE(107)	SEPARATELY FROM THE ACTIVE HOURS OF ADULT	LIFE	, SO THAT ADULTS CAN ENJOY THE SOCIETY OF CHILDREN IN
BULL I SD(74)	FULL-BLOODED, ENERGETIC MAN IN THE PRIME OF	LIFE	, SOMETIMES PORTENTOUSLY SOLEMN, SOMETIMES JOLLY AND
MRS PREFACE(171)	SOCIETY COLLECTIVELY TO POOR WOMEN IS A MISERABLE	LIFE	, STARVED, OVERWORKED, FETID, AILING, UGLY. THOUGH IT
LADY (243)	HER). /THE LADY/ UNMEASURED IMPUDENCE! ON YOUR	LIFE	, TAKE YOUR HANDS FROM ME. THE DARK LADY COMES STOOPING
O'FL (211)	THAT ALL THE WORLD KNOWS I NEVER SAW IN MY	LIFE	, THAN TELL THEM THE TRUTH. BUT I CANT TAKE ADVANTAGE
3PLA PREFACE(R34)	IMMORTAL. IT IS THE PHILOSOPHY, THE OUTLOOK ON	LIFE	, THAT CHANGES, NOT THE CRAFT OF THE PLAYWRIGHT. A
MTH3 (104)	IF YOU HAVE MISCALCULATED THE DURATION OF HUMAN	LIFE	, THAT IS NOT THE FAULT OF THE PERSONS WHOSE LONGEVITY
JOAN PREFACE(12)	LATE WAR THREW SO MANY OF OUR WOMEN INTO MILITARY	LIFE	, THAT JOAN'S CAMPAIGNING COULD NOT HAVE BEEN CARRIED
MRS III (234)	INTO TELLING THE TRUTH FOR THE FIRST TIME IN HIS	LIFE	, THAT ONLY MAKES US THE BABES IN THE WOOD IN EARNEST.
GETT (268)	BESIDES, DO YOU SUPPOSE I THINK, AT MY TIME OF	LIFE	, THAT THE DIFFERENCE BETWEEN ONE DECENT SORT OF MAN
PLES PREFACE(R16)	ON THE FACT, EASILY ENOUGH DISCOVERABLE IN REAL	LIFE	, THAT WE ONLY CRY NOW IN THE EFFORT TO BEAR HAPPINESS.
SUPR PREFACE(R34)	TO HIM THAT CAN GET IT." THIS IS THE TRUE JOY IN	LIFE	, THE BEING USED FOR A PURPOSE RECOGNIZED BY YOURSELF
MIS. PREFACE(86)	CIRCUMSTANCES PHRASES LIKE THE INFLUENCE OF HOME	LIFE	, THE FAMILY, THE DOMESTIC HEARTH, AND SO ON, ARE NO
SUPR III (113)	THAT IS WHY INTELLECT IS SO UNPOPULAR. BUT TO	LIFE	, THE FORCE BEHIND THE MAN, INTELLECT IS A NECESSITY,
JOAN 4 (100)	HERETIC AS A DEAD BRANCH FROM THE TREE OF	LIFE	, THE HERETIC IS HANDED OVER TO THE SECULAR ARM. THE
GETT PREFACE(239)	TO THEM WILL CERTAINLY NOT ACCEPT A CELIBATE	LIFE	, THE LAW MUST SANCTION THE DISSOLUTION IN ORDER TO
PYGM V (286)	AND DRINK TIL YOU FALL ASLEEP. OH, IT'S A FINE	LIFE	, THE LIFE OF THE GUTTER. IT'S REAL: IT'S WARM: IT'S
KING I (164)	AT: THE TRANSMUTATIONS OF MATTER, THE ELIXIR OF	LIFE	, THE MAGIC OF LIGHT AND COLOR, ABOVE ALL, THE SECRET
SUPR III (104)	HIGHEST MIRACLE OF ORGANIZATION YET ATTAINED BY	LIFE	, THE MOST INTENSELY ALIVE THING THAT EXISTS, THE MOST
MTH5 (250)	MY BRAIN; BUT IT IS NOT ME. I AM THE ETERNAL	LIFE	, THE PERPETUAL RESURRECTION; BUT (STRIKING HIS BODY)
3PLA PREFACE(R18)	ASTONISHING THAN THE EXTENT TO WHICH, IN REAL	LIFE	, THE SEX INSTINCT DOES SO PROCEED, EVEN WHEN THE
BULL PREFACE(47)	AND VIOLENCE, THAT HACKNEYED COMEDY OF CIVIL	LIFE	, THE WEAK MAN PUTTING HIS FOOT DOWN, BECOMES THE
GETT (324)	LIFE? /THE BISHOP/ YOU KNOW THE STORY OF HIS	LIFE	, THEN? /MRS GEORGE/ NOT ALL. WE REACHED THE HOUSE
JOAN PREFACE(43)	BECAUSE, IN THE PRACTICAL EMERGENCIES OF DAILY	LIFE	, THERE IS NO TIME FOR LESSONS AND EXPLANATIONS, OR FOR
JOAN EPILOG (154)	THIS ABOUT HER. IF YOU COULD BRING HER BACK TO	LIFE	, THEY WOULD BURN HER AGAIN WITHIN SIX MONTHS, FOR ALL

OVER PREFACE(167)	WOULD FOLLOW FROM THE FIRST AND SECOND IN REAL	LIFE	, THEY WOULD BE GREATLY IMPROVED THEREBY EVEN AS
GETT (300)	THAT JUST WHEN THEY WERE GROWN UP AND BEGINNING	LIFE	, THIS DREADFUL CREATURE WOULD BE LET OUT TO DISGRACE
AUGS (267)	ME TO TAKE TO DRINK INSTEAD. THAT SAVED MY	LIFE	, THOUGH IT MAKES ME VERY POOR COMPANY IN THE MORNINGS,
HART I (76)	IS ADDY. SHE HAS NEVER BEEN IN LOVE IN HER	LIFE	, THOUGH SHE HAS ALWAYS BEEN TRYING TO FALL IN HEAD
SUPR IV (166)	LET THEMSELVES BE HANGED WITHOUT A STRUGGLE FOR	LIFE	, THOUGH THEY COULD AT LEAST GIVE THE CHAPLAIN A BLACK
OVER PREFACE(162)	THAT LEAD UP TO THEM ARE NO ESSENTIAL PART OF	LIFE	, THOUGH, LIKE POISONS AND BUTTERED SLIDES AND RED-HOT
SUPR HANDBOK(186)	INTO MARRIAGE, CAPITALISM, AND CUSTOMARY PRIVATE	LIFE	, THUS ADMITTING THAT THE REAL SOCIAL SOLUTION WAS NOT
MTH5 (260)	UNSPEAKABLY; I TORE MYSELF ASUNDER; I LOST MY	LIFE	, TO MAKE OF MY ONE FLESH THESE TWAIN, MAN AND WOMAN.
BARB PREFACE(218)	HORSEBACK AND IN STEEL COAT MAY HAVE BEEN A GOOD	LIFE	, TO ROB AND PILL BY THE HANDS OF THE POLICEMAN, THE
BARB PREFACE(214)	AS A MATTER OF COURSE TO STEAL TEN YEARS OF HIS	LIFE	, TORTURING HIM ALL THE TIME. IF HE TRIES TO DEFEAT
LION PREFACE(45)	WITH THE DEAD, DISCOVERERS OF THE ELIXIR OF	LIFE	, TRANSMUTERS OF METALS, AND HEALERS OF ALL SORTS, AS
HART PREFACE(12)	COULD DO WHAT HE LIKED WITH IMPUNITY IN CIVIL	LIFE	, WAS NOT THE LAW OF THE LAND, AND THAT A VICTORIA
MRS I (184)	ESPECIALLY WOMEN'S TIME. /PRAED/ OH, WASTE OF	LIFE	, WASTE OF EVERYTHING. BUT THINGS ARE IMPROVING. DO YOU
DOCT PREFACE(44)	RECORDS A REAL EXPERIENCE OF SCHOOL OR PRISON	LIFE	, WE FIND THAT HERE AND THERE AMONG THE ROUTINEERS
GLIM (184)	ON YOUR OWN HANDS. WE CAN BRING DEATH AS WELL AS	LIFE	, WE POOR PEOPLE, SIGNOR. /FERRUCCIO/ MOTHER OF GOD,
MTH3 (105)	TO THE OFFICIAL ESTIMATE OF HIS EXPECTATION OF	LIFE	, WERE TO LIVE FOR MORE THAN TWO CENTURIES AND A HALF,
BASH III (120)	FROM LONDON TO THIS PLACE TO WRITE THY FATHER'S	LIFE	, WHENAS IN TOWN THOU MIGHTST HAVE KEPT A GUARDIAN EYE
SUPR II (51)	WE ARE NUISANCES AT HOME, AND BECAUSE IN AFTER	LIFE	, WHENEVER A DUKE IS MENTIONED, WE CAN CLAIM HIM AS AN
ROCK PREFACE(155)	THE OLD DOCTRINE OF THE SACREDNESS OF HUMAN	LIFE	, WHICH IN OUR IDIOT ASYLUMS AT DARENTH AND ELSEWHERE
JOAN PREFACE(13)	AND SAFE AND HAPPY IN THE MIDDLE STATION IN	LIFE	, WHICH IS ALL ANY GOOD BOURGEOIS CAN REASONABLY
DOCT III (139)	WEEKS OF GLORIOUS HAPPINESS IN HER POOR LITTLE	LIFE	, WHICH IS MORE THAN MOST GIRLS IN HER POSITION GET, I
OVER PREFACE(155)	LIBERTINE IS USUALLY A PERSON OF BLAMELESS FAMILY	LIFE	, WHILST THE PRACTICAL LIBERTINE IS MERCILESSLY SEVERE
BULL PREFACE(50)	PLUTOCRATIC REFUSE OF POLITICAL AND DIPLOMATIC	LIFE	, WHO JOIN THE ARMY AND PAY FOR THEIR POSITIONS IN THE
MIS. PREFACE(71)	SCHOOL LIFE, IS BETTER FOR THE CHILD THAN HOME	LIFE	, WILL BECOME AN OVER-RIDDEN HOBBY; AND WE SHALL
MTH3 (129)	OVER THE POSSIBILITIES OF THREE CENTURIES OF	LIFE	, WILL DRIVE THEM MAD AND WRECK HUMAN SOCIETY. THIS
METH PREFACE(R43)	FRENCH ACADEMY. THOUGH LAMARCK'S WAY, THE WAY OF	LIFE	, WILL, ASPIRATION, AND ACHIEVEMENT, REMAINED STILL
MTH3 SD(113)	IS A HANDSOME WOMAN, APPARENTLY IN THE PRIME OF	LIFE	, WITH ELEGANT, TENSE, WELL HELD-UP FIGURE, AND THE
LION I (118)	IS A POWERFUL, CHOLERIC MAN IN THE PRIME OF	LIFE	, WITH LARGE NOSTRILS, STARING EYES, AND A THICK NECK:
HART PREFACE(19)	WAS SO ACUTE THAT THOSE WHO SHARED IT IN CIVIL	LIFE	, WITHOUT HAVING TO SHED BLOOD WITH THEIR OWN HANDS, OR
PYGM II (229)	UPSET EVERYTHING. WHEN YOU LET THEM INTO YOUR	LIFE	, YOU FIND THAT THE WOMAN IS DRIVING AT ONE THING AND
LIED (199)	OF DAY AT WHICH YOU WERE NEVER OUT OF BED IN YOUR	LIFE	, YOU HARDLY DO JUSTICE TO YOUR OWN LITERARY POWERS--
JOAN 5 (112)	/CHARLES/ (CONTINUING HEEDLESSLY) A HEALTHY	LIFE	, YOU KNOW. /DUNOIS/ BUT A DULL ONE. /BLUEBEARD/ YOU
MTH1 II (23)	WHEN YOU HAVE SLAIN THE BOAR AT THE RISK OF YOUR	LIFE	, YOU WILL THROW HER A MORSEL OF IT FOR HER PAINS!
CLEO II (140)	BACK ALL THE DEAD OF SPAIN, GAUL, AND THESSALY TO	LIFE	, YOU WOULD DO IT THAT WE MIGHT HAVE THE TROUBLE OF
MRS PREFACE(156)	LOT IN LIFE THEREIN DESCRIBED WERE YOUR LOT IN	LIFE	, YOU WOULD NOT RATHER BE A JEWELLED VAMP. IF YOU CAN
JITT I (19)	DIVINE RIGHTS. IF I HAD NEVER COME INTO YOUR	LIFE	, YOU WOULD PERHAPS HAVE COME TO SOME SORT OF
VWOO 1 (121)	I HAD THE CHANCE. " YOU WILL BE POOR ALL YOUR	LIFE	," HE SAID; " BUT NOW YOU HAVE THE CHANCE OF LIVING AT
MIS. (180)	IT, AND TO AMEND MY LIFE-- /BENTLEY/ " AMEND MY	LIFE	"? /PERCIVAL/-- AND TO DO WHAT IN ME LIES TO PROVE
BARB PREFACE(217)	HERO, WHO SAW THAT " TO ROB AND PILL WAS A GOOD	LIFE	" HE IS NOT THE DUPE OF THAT PUBLIC SENTIMENT AGAINST
6CAL PREFACE(91)	WHO BELIEVED THAT " TO ROB AND PILL WAS A GOOD	LIFE	" IF THE ROBBER WAS AT LEAST A BARON. HE MADE A VERY
PLES PREFACE(R17)	OF PREOCCUPATION WITH " THE SEAMY SIDE OF	LIFE	"; OF PARADOX, CYNICISM, AND ECCENTRICITY, REDUCIBLE,
POSN PREFACE(427)	IS THE HIGHLY POPULAR ONE, " ANYTHING FOR A QUIET	LIFE	", AND WHO WILL MAKE THE INEVITABLE ABUSES OF FREEDOM
LADY (241)	NOR A WHILE, BUT FOR EVER. /THE LADY/ ODDS MY	LIFE	! ARE YOU BY CHANCE MAKING LOVE TO ME, KNAVE? /THE
2TRU II (64)	A BIT OF REAL LIFE SOMEWHERE. /THE PATIENT/ REAL	LIFE	! I WONDER WHERE THATS TO BE FOUND! WEVE SPENT NEARLY
2TRU II (70)	" AND LOSE THE EXCITEMENT OF BEING TRIED FOR MY	LIFE	! I'D RATHER BE HANGED" HE SAYS; AND HANGED HE WAS.
CLEO II (128)	HE FORGETS THAT WE HAVE SAVED IT? /CAESAR/ MY	LIFE	! IS THAT ALL? /THEODOTUS/ YOUR LIFE. YOUR LAURELS.
PRES (145)	MUSICAL AT-HOMES AND SO FORTH. /MITCHENER/ WHAT A	LIFE	! (TO THE ORDERLY) WHERE ARE THE LADIES? /THE
MRS II (213)	/MRS WARREN/ MY OWN OPINIONS AND MY OWN WAY OF	LIFE	! LISTEN TO HER TALKING! DO YOU THINK I WAS BROUGHT
PHIL II (113)	DISEASE: THE DISEASE I DISCOVERED: THE WORK OF MY	LIFE	! LOOK HERE (HE POINTS TO THE JOURNAL WITH A GHASTLY
DOCT II (117)	HOME, I AM BEEDLE-DEEDLE-DUMKINS. SUCH IS MARRIED	LIFE	! MR DUBEDAT: MAY I ASK YOU TO DO ME A FAVOR BEFORE
BARB III (334)	NO CAPITAL? MY CHARACTER! MY INTELLECT! MY	LIFE	! MY CAREER! WHAT BARBARA CALLS MY SOUL! ARE THESE
MTH4 II (182)	BURNT ALIVE. NO SENSE OF THE SACREDNESS OF HUMAN	LIFE	! NO THOUGHT FOR MY WIFE AND CHILDREN! BITCH! SOW!
MIS. (148)	IT'S THE SECRET OF THEIR AMAZING HEALTH AND LONG	LIFE	! /LORD SUMMERHAYS/ UNFORTUNATELY THEY ARE NEITHER
BARB II (275)	SALLY WASNT GOOD ENOUGH FOR OUR PARENTS, SUCH IS	LIFE	! /RUMMY/ WHO SAVED YOU, MR PRICE? WAS IT MAJOR
FOUN (210)	ARE YOU? /BRABAZON/ I AM, MY LORD. SUCH IS	LIFE	! /THE LORD CHANCELLOR/ YOU ARE A WARD OF THE COURT;
MTH1 I (14)	THE MATTER NOW? /ADAM/ MY REST! MY ESCAPE FROM	LIFE	! /THE SERPENT/ DEATH. THAT IS THE WORD. /ADAM/ THERE
SUPR I (30)	WHO IS GOING TO RISK HER LIFE TO CREATE ANOTHER	LIFE	! TAVY: DONT YOU BE A SELFISH ASS. AWAY WITH YOU AND
MTH3 (135)	MAY GET RHEUMATISM FOR LIFE. /BURGE-LUBIN/ FOR	LIFE	! THAT SETTLES IT: I WONT RISK IT. /CONFUCIUS/ GOOD.
BASH III (119)	YE DO CONFLICT AS HERE I SIT WRITING MY FATHER'S	LIFE	! THE AUTUMN WOODLAND WOOS ME FROM WITHOUT WITH
MILL IV (204)	NOTHING TO ME BUT BUNDLES OF AILMENTS. BUT THE	LIFE	! THE PULSE! IS THE HEARTBEAT OF ALLAH, SAVE IN WHOM
CLEO IV (175)	FORBID HE SHOULD EVER LEARN! OH, THIS MILITARY	LIFE	! THIS TEDIOUS, BRUTAL LIFE OF ACTION! THAT IS THE
PHIL II (130)	YOU KNOW. /CRAVEN/ (STARTING UP) WELL, UPON MY	LIFE	! UPON MY HONOR AND CONSCIENCE! ! NOW REALLY! ! !
MRS II (209)	SUIT YOU? I DOUBT IT. /MRS WARREN/ YOUR WAY OF	LIFE	! WHAT DO YOU MEAN? /VIVIE/ (CUTTING A PAGE OF HER
		LIFEBOAT	
HART I (81)	WHERE IS ALL THE MONEY YOU HAD FOR THAT PATENT	LIFEBOAT	I INVENTED? /MRS HUSHABYE/ FIVE HUNDRED POUNDS;
HART I (81)	/CAPTAIN SHOTOVER/ ONLY 500 POUNDS FOR THAT	LIFEBOAT	! I GOT TWELVE THOUSAND FOR THE INVENTION BEFORE
		LIFEGIVING	
KING I (185)	/NEWTON/ MYCAPAYNIS, MADAM. A VERY POWERFUL	LIFEGIVING	SUBSTANCE. /LOUISE/ IT SOUNDS WONDERFUL. IS IT
		LIFEGUARDS	
KING PREFACE(156)	UNDER CROMWELL, AND GRUDGED THEIR KING EVEN THE	LIFEGUARDS	WHICH WERE THE NUCLEUS OF SUCH AN ARMY. CHARLES,
		LIFELESS	
LION PREFACE(49)	YOU (AS IT MAY ANY DAY) THAT CHRIST IS NOT THE	LIFELESS	HARMLESS IMAGE HE HAS HITHERTO BEEN TO YOU, BUT A
HART PREFACE(9)	INTEREST IN PHYSICS, CHEMISTRY, AND THAT	LIFELESS	METHOD OF EVOLUTION WHICH ITS INVESTIGATORS CALLED
MTH5 (244)	LET IT BE A LESSON TO YOU ALL TO BE CONTENT WITH	LIFELESS	TOYS, AND NOT ATTEMPT TO MAKE LIVING ONES. WHAT
		LIFELIKE	
MTH5 (234)	AND READ; AND NOW THEY TELL LIES. THAT IS SO VERY	LIFELIKE	. /MARTELLUS/ NOT AT ALL. IF THEY WERE ALIVE THEY
SUPR PREFACE(R33)	THE SAME DEFECT: THEIR CHARACTERS AND MANNERS ARE	LIFELIKE	; BUT THEIR ACTIONS ARE FORCED ON THEM FROM
		LIFELONG	
GETT PREFACE(222)	HAVE TO EXPIATE THEIR MOTHER'S SQUEAMISHNESS BY	LIFELONG	CELIBACY AND INDIGENCE. TO ASK A YOUNG MAN HIS
SUPR HANDBOK(201)	EMANCIPATORS. THE HOPE IS NOT FULFILLED; BUT THE	LIFELONG	IMPRISONMENT OF PENNILESS MEN FOR DEBT CEASES;
DOCT PREFACE(16)	WHO CAN BE PERSUADED THAT HE OR SHE IS A	LIFELONG	INVALID MEANS ANYTHING FROM FIFTY TO FIVE HUNDRED
GETT PREFACE(246)	AFFECTIONATE FRIENDSHIP; THAT CASES OF CHRONIC	LIFELONG	LOVE, WHETHER SENTIMENTAL OR SENSUAL, OUGHT TO BE
JOAN PREFACE(27)	THAN THE MISSISSIPPI PILOT. BUT THEN LANG WAS, BY	LIFELONG	PROFESSIONAL HABIT, A CRITIC OF BIOGRAPHIES RATHER
SUPR III (126)	WAS SET ON ME, THERE WAS NOTHING FOR IT BUT	LIFELONG	SERVITUDE OR FLIGHT. /ANA/ YOU DARE BOAST, BEFORE
GETT PREFACE(221)	IT IS AS OFTEN AS NOT THE INAUGURATION OF A	LIFELONG	SQUABBLE, A CORRODING GRUDGE, THAT CAUSES MORE
3PLA PREFACE(R18)	DOES SO PROCEED, EVEN WHEN THE CONSEQUENCE IS ITS	LIFELONG	STARVATION. FEW OF US HAVE VITALITY ENOUGH TO MAKE
BARB I SD(259)	AND IS COMPLICATED BY AN APPALLING TEMPER. THE	LIFELONG	STRUGGLE OF A BENEVOLENT TEMPERAMENT AND A HIGH
HART I (66)	YOU, MR DUNN. /MAZZINI/ (DAZED) I AM A	LIFELONG	TEETOTALER. /MRS HUSHABYE/ YOU WILL FIND IT FAR
		LIFE-AND-DEATH	
DOCT PREFACE(74)	A GOOD DEAL OF OFFICIAL REGULATION THAT IS NOW OF	LIFE-AND-DEATH	NECESSITY TO US; BUT UNDER EXISTING
		LIFE-BOAT	
NEVR III (280)	BY THE REGATTA COMMITTEE FOR THE BENEFIT OF THE	LIFE-BOAT	, SIR. (TO MRS CLANDON) WE OFTEN HAVE THEM, MAAM:
		LIFE-LONG	
GETT PREFACE(190)	THE LAWS OF HEALTH AND TEMPERANCE; INAUGURATED A	LIFE-LONG	HONEYMOON; AND PLACED THEIR PLEASURES ON EXACTLY
		LIFE-MISSION	
SUPR IV SD(142)	NOT THE STAMP OF THE CLASS WHICH ACCEPTS AS ITS	LIFE-MISSION	THE ADVERTIZING AND MAINTENANCE OF FIRST RATE

LIFE-OR-DEATH

CLEO NOTES (210)	A DOZEN SECRETARIES UNDER YOU, SO TO SPEAK, AS A	LIFE-OR-DEATH	COURIER KILLS HORSES-- ENABLES MEN WITH COMMON
ROCK PREFACE(161)	AS THEY PLEASED, WHEREAS IN FACT IT WAS OF	LIFE-OR-DEATH	IMPORTANCE THAT THEY SHOULD REDOUBLE THEIR
METH PREFACE(R52)	MADE THE MICE DESIRE TO LOSE THEIR TAILS WITH A	LIFE-OR-DEATH	INTENSITY, HE WOULD VERY SOON HAVE SEEN A FEW

LIFE-SAVING

HART I (81)	LIVING AT THE RATE WE DO, YOU CANNOT AFFORD	LIFE-SAVING	INVENTIONS. CANT YOU THINK OF SOMETHING THAT

LIFE-SIZE

PYGM II SD(217)	TUBE, SEVERAL TUNING-FORKS OF DIFFERENT SIZES, A	LIFE-SIZE	IMAGE OF HALF A HUMAN HEAD, SHEWING IN SECTION THE
MTH4 III SD(195)	VAGUE AND SHADOWY: ABOVE ALL, SHE IS LARGER THAN	LIFE-SIZE	, NOT ENOUGH TO BE MEASURED BY THE FLUSTERED

LIFE'S

ARMS III (63)	(CYNICALLY) RAINA: OUR ROMANCE IS SHATTERED.	LIFE'S	A FARCE. /BLUNTSCHLI/ (TO RAINA, WHIMSICALLY) YOU
SUPR III (111)	OF WOMAN'S PURPOSE, SO FAR, THE RESULT OF	LIFE'S	CONTINUAL EFFORT NOT ONLY TO MAINTAIN ITSELF, BUT TO
2TRU III (102)	IN WATERCOLORS BECAUSE I MAY NOT USE MY HANDS IN	LIFE'S	DAILY USEFUL BUSINESS. A COMMANDING OFFICER MUST NOT
MTH3 (121)	AND LIVED ON MY PENSION, THE FATIGUE OF MY	LIFE'S	DRUDGERY BEGAN TO WEAR OFF, BECAUSE, YOU SEE, I WAS
MTH5 (262)	MATTER, TO OBEY A LIVING SOUL. BUT IN ENSLAVING	LIFE'S	ENEMY I MADE HIM LIFE'S MASTER; FOR THAT IS THE END
DOCT IV (169)	TO-MORROW AND TO-MORROW AND TO-MORROW AFTER	LIFE'S	FITFUL FEVER THEY SLEEP WELL AND LIKE THIS
PPP (205)	THE LIGHTNING. /MAGNESIA/ (RISING) AFTER	LIFE'S	FITFUL FEVER THEY SLEEP WELL. PHYLLIS: SWEEP THEM UP.
JITT III (80)	TAKING JITTA'S HAND, AND KISSING IT) I OWE YOU MY	LIFE'S	HAPPINESS, MRS LENKHEIM. /AGNES/ I AM SURE WE ALL OWE
SUPR III (127)	LAW OF MY LIFE. THAT IS THE WORKING WITHIN ME OF	LIFE'S	INCESSANT ASPIRATION TO HIGHER ORGANIZATION, WIDER,
HART III (133)	HAVE ANY OF US BUT TRAVELLING EXPENSES FOR OUR	LIFE'S	JOURNEY? /MRS HUSHABYE/ BUT YOU HAVE FACTORIES AND
BUOY III (30)	THE LIFE OUT OF ME INSTEAD OF LEAVING ME TO LEARN	LIFE'S	LESSONS BY BREAKING MY SHINS AGAINST THEM AND FALLING
MTH5 (262)	SOUL. BUT IN ENSLAVING LIFE'S ENEMY I MADE HIM	LIFE'S	MASTER; FOR THAT IS THE END OF ALL SLAVERY; AND NOW I
BARB PREFACE(208)	BUT THE STORY OF THE DAY'S RIDE AND	LIFE'S	ROMANCE OF POTTS (CLAIMING ALLIANCE WITH POZZO DI
BARB PREFACE(207)	LEVER, WROTE A STORY ENTITLED A DAY'S RIDE: A	LIFE'S	ROMANCE. IT WAS PUBLISHED BY CHARLES DICKENS IN
2TRU II (69)	AND LIKE BEING PUT UPON. THEYVE NO APPETITES.	LIFE'S	THROWN AWAY ON THEM: THEY GET NOTHING OUT OF IT. /THE
BULL IV (167)	ANY WOMAN HAPPY, HE'S AS CLEVER AS BE-BLOWED; BUT	LIFE'S	TOO EARTHLY FOR HIM: HE DOESNT REALLY CARE FOR
MIS. PREFACE(38)	BE RELEASED FROM ANY OBLIGATION OF THE KIND. A	LIFE'S	WORK IS LIKE A DAY'S WORK: IT CAN BEGIN EARLY AND
JITT I (20)	HE IS NOT MAN ENOUGH FOR THAT): THE FRUIT OF YOUR	LIFE'S	WORK IS TO DROP INTO HIS MOUTH! AND I AM TO BE YOUR
CLEO V (198)	THERE. /CAESAR/ IT MATTERS NOT: I SHALL FINISH MY	LIFE'S	WORK ON MY WAY BACK; AND THEN I SHALL HAVE LIVED LONG
KING I (211)	IT IS. WHY NOT? /NEWTON/ WHY NOT! ONLY MY	LIFE'S	WORK TURNED TO WASTE, VANITY, FOLLY. THIS COMES OF

LIFESIZE

GENV II SD(49)	IS ONE LARGE PICTURE IN OILS, REPRESENTING A	LIFESIZE	PEACE, WITH TINY FIGURES, ALSO IN MILITARY

LIFETIME

BUOY 1 (16)	IS SOME SENSE IN THAT. BUT IT WOULD NOT LAST YOUR	LIFETIME	: IT WOULD ONLY GIVE YOU A START. AT WHAT? /SON/ I
MRS PREFACE(159)	OPINION GENERALLY ASSUMES THEM TO BE DURING THEIR	LIFETIME	: THAT IS, A LICENTIOUSLY IRREGULAR GROUP TO BE
MTH3 (106)	WE ARE NOW IN THE YEAR 2170. WHAT IS THE OFFICIAL	LIFETIME	? /BARNABAS/ SEVENTY-EIGHT, OF COURSE IT'S AN
MIS. (143)	TO YOU GOING ON DAY AFTER DAY, YEAR AFTER YEAR,	LIFETIME	AFTER LIFETIME. /LORD SUMMERHAYS/ SHEW ME WHAT?
JOAN PREFACE(31)	GIVING HER A PLACE BESIDE THE TRINITY DURING HER	LIFETIME	AND IN HER TEENS, WHICH WAS UNTHINKABLE. THUS AN
MTH4 II (192)	ETERNITY IN WHICH THE DIFFERENCE BETWEEN YOUR	LIFETIME	AND MINE IS AS THE DIFFERENCE BETWEEN ONE DROP OF
HART PREFACE(7)	BY GOVERNMENTS AND ELECTORATES DURING MY	LIFETIME	AS SANITARY SCIENCE WAS IN THE DAYS OF CHARLES THE
METH PREFACE(R20)	YEARS BEFORE CHARLES DARWIN WAS BORN, AND A WHOLE	LIFETIME	BEFORE HE PUBLISHED HIS ORIGIN OF SPECIES. FOR THAT
METH PREFACE(R13)	IF THIS IS THE MEASURE OF WHAT CAN BE DONE IN A	LIFETIME	BY EXTRAORDINARY ABILITY, KEEN NATURAL APTITUDE,
KING PREFACE(155)	WRONG, BUT AS THE MARCH OF SCIENCE DURING MY LONG	LIFETIME	HAS PLAYED SKITTLES WITH ALL THE THEORIES IN TURN I
MTH3 (125)	AND CHINKS, AS YOU CALL THEM, THOUGH THEIR	LIFETIME	IS AS SHORT AS OURS, OR SHORTER, YET DO SOMEHOW
PPP (199)	FAR BETTER THAN ANY LOZENGE: THE DEVOTION OF A	LIFETIME	. FORMERLY IT WAS GEORGE'S. I KEPT HIS HOUSE, OR
KING I (164)	OF CONSIDERED AND INTENTIONAL ACTIONS IN HER	LIFETIME	. HOW MANY OF THEM CAN YOU REMEMBER, SALLY?
MILL III (185)	FELLOW CREATURES TO GIVE YOU ONE HOLIDAY IN YOUR	LIFETIME	. I CAN DO BETTER FOR YOU THAN THAT. /THE WOMAN/ WE
MIS. (143)	ON DAY AFTER DAY, YEAR AFTER YEAR, LIFETIME AFTER	LIFETIME	. /LORD SUMMERHAYS/ SHEW ME WHAT? /HYPATIA/ GIRLS
MIS. (160)	OH YES: ALL THAT, AND SOMETIMES THE DEVOTION OF A	LIFETIME	. /TARLETON/ FANCY THAT! A YOUNG MAN OFFERING A
SUPR HANDBOK(199)	STEPS OF MANY CENTURIES RETRACED IN A SINGLE	LIFETIME	. THIS HAS OFTEN OCCURRED EVEN WITHIN THE PERIOD
GETT (343)	ETERNITY TOGETHER; AND YOU ASK ME FOR A LITTLE	LIFETIME	MORE. WE POSSESSED ALL THE UNIVERSE TOGETHER; AND
MTH4 II (192)	WITH MERCY, WITH GOOD-WILL: IF THEY ARE THE	LIFETIME	OF A SOUL THAT NEVER LOSES ITS HONOR AND A BRAIN
MILL PREFACE(126)	TOLD OF A PIOUS MAN WHO WAS SUSTAINED THROUGH A	LIFETIME	OF CRUSHING MISFORTUNE BY HIS STEADY BELIEF THAT IF
MTH3 (120)	DRAWING IT TOO LONG. THE HORROR OF FACING ANOTHER	LIFETIME	OF DRUDGERY, OF MISSING MY HARD-EARNED REST AND
PYGM EPILOG (293)	FREDDY AND HIGGINS? WILL SHE LOOK FORWARD TO A	LIFETIME	OF FETCHING HIGGINS'S SLIPPERS OR TO A LIFETIME OF
PYGM EPILOG (293)	A LIFETIME OF FETCHING HIGGINS'S SLIPPERS OR TO A	LIFETIME	OF FREDDY FETCHING HERS? THERE CAN BE NO DOUBT
SUPR I (13)	I WOULD BUY IT FOR YOU WITH MY LAST PENNY, BUT A	LIFETIME	OF HAPPINESS! NO MAN ALIVE COULD BEAR IT: IT WOULD
SUPR I (13)	ME FROM MY HIGHEST HAPPINESS. /TANNER/ YES, A	LIFETIME	OF HAPPINESS. IF IT WERE ONLY THE FIRST HALF HOUR'S
SUPR HANDBOK(224)	OF HAPPINESS AND BEAUTY. HE WHO DESIRES A	LIFETIME	OF HAPPINESS WITH A BEAUTIFUL WOMAN DESIRES TO
LION PREFACE(40)	POSITIVELY AND UNEQUIVOCALLY PROMISED WITHIN THE	LIFETIME	OF HIS CONTEMPORARIES. ANY BELIEVER COMPILING A
LION PREFACE(30)	SCHOLARSHIP. IT MUST HAVE BEEN WRITTEN DURING THE	LIFETIME	OF JESUS'S CONTEMPORARIES: THAT IS, WHILST IT WAS
DOCT PREFACE(35)	IT WOULD BE ENORMOUSLY IMPROVED; AND THE AVERAGE	LIFETIME	OF LONDONERS WOULD BE CONSIDERABLY PROLONGED. NERO
MTH2 (73)	VOTES FOR WOMEN. WE SHALL GO TO SMASH WITHIN THE	LIFETIME	OF MEN NOW LIVING UNLESS WE RECOGNIZE THAT WE MUST
SUPR HANDBOK(182)	UNION ORGANIZATION ON THE OTHER, HAVE, WITHIN THE	LIFETIME	OF MEN STILL LIVING, CONVERTED THE OLD UNRESTRICTED
LION PREFACE(44)	AND ESTABLISH HIS KINGDOM ON EARTH WITHIN THE	LIFETIME	OF MEN THEN LIVING, WAS ONE WHICH HE BELIEVED THAT
LION PREFACE(29)	HE DECLARES THAT THIS WILL TAKE PLACE DURING THE	LIFETIME	OF PERSONS THEN PRESENT, JERUSALEM AND THE MYSTICAL
LION PREFACE(19)	HIS MATERIAL AND COMPLETED HIS BOOK WITHIN THE	LIFETIME	OF PERSONS CONTEMPORARY WITH JESUS. ALLOWANCE MUST
LION PREFACE(30)	OF JESUS TO COME AGAIN IN GLORY DURING THE	LIFETIME	OF SOME OF HIS HEARERS IS TO DATE THE GOSPEL
2TRU PREFACE(8)	REVELLER WITH A COMPLETELY FALSE NOTION OF WHAT A	LIFETIME	OF SUCH REVELRY WOULD BE, I MAINTAIN THAT NOBODY
GETT PREFACE(248)	OF THE PUTTING OFF OF THE SECOND COMING FROM THE	LIFETIME	OF THE APOSTLES TO THE MILLENNIUM, AND OF THE GREAT
LION PREFACE(31)	BY IT, HE MUST HAVE PRODUCED HIS GOSPEL WITHIN A	LIFETIME	OF THE CRUCIFIXION. ALSO, HE MUST HAVE BELIEVED
MTH3 (112)	HAVE QUITE UNINTENTIONALLY COMMITTED MYSELF TO A	LIFETIME	OF THREE HUNDRED YEARS. /BURGE-LUBIN/ BUT HOW DO
FABL PREFACE(77)	HE DARED. IT WAS STILL UNREPEALED DURING MY OWN	LIFETIME	; AND HAS ONLY JUST (1948) BEEN REPEALED IN
PYGM PREFACE(201)	I HAVE BOUGHT THREE COPIES OF IT DURING MY	LIFETIME	; AND I AM INFORMED BY THE PUBLISHERS THAT ITS
METH PREFACE(R85)	BETWEEN THEM THE OUTPUT OF MOLIERE'S SINGLE	LIFETIME	; AND THEY WERE ALL (NOT WITHOUT REASON) ASHAMED
BUOY IV (53)	OF IT: I SHALL NOT LAST MUCH LONGER: YOU HAVE A	LIFETIME	TO GIVE HER. AWAY WITH YOU TO THE REGISTRY OFFICE
GETT PREFACE(240)	AS THERE IS NOW WHEN IT OPENS FOR ONE MOMENT IN A	LIFETIME	, AND MAY NEVER OPEN AGAIN. FROM THIS POINT OF VIEW
METH PREFACE(R26)	PROTOPLASM, AND TO STRUGGLE THROUGH AN EMBRYONIC	LIFETIME	, DURING PART OF WHICH HE WAS INDISTINGUISHABLE
MTH4 I (162)	IT TO A BRIGHTER, PROUDER FLAME. THUS EACH	LIFETIME	, HOWEVER SHORT, CONTRIBUTES A BRICK TO A VAST AND
CAPT II (261)	THAT THE TIME FOR THAT WAS IN YOUR MOTHER'S	LIFETIME	, WHEN YOU COULD HAVE BEEN KIND AND FORBEARING WITH

LIFFEY

BULL PREFACE(67)	UNIVERSITY), AND FROM A WARSHIP IN THE RIVER	LIFFEY	, A BOMBARDMENT WAS POURED ON THE CENTRE OF THE CITY

LIFT

PHIL I (83)	UP WITH THE HELP OF HIS HAND) QUICK: THE	LIFT	: WE CAN GO DOWN IN THAT. (SHE RUSHES TO THE TABLE FOR
JITT I (11)	YOU NEVER TO WALK UPSTAIRS BUT ALWAYS TO TAKE THE	LIFT	? AND NOW SEE THE STATE YOU ARE IN! /THE GENTLEMAN/
MTH4 III (197)	AN INTELLIGENT QUESTION. SHE ASKS WHY WE SEEK TO	LIFT	A CORNER OF THE VEIL THAT SHROUDS THE FUTURE FROM OUR
MTH5 (211)	FROWSTY COMFORT IF THEY CHOSE. BUT THEY NEVER	LIFT	A FINGER TO MAKE THEMSELVES COMFORTABLE. THEY WILL NOT
JOAN 5 (117)	AND NOW TELL ME, ALL OF YOU, WHICH OF YOU WILL	LIFT	A FINGER TO SAVE JOAN ONCE THE ENGLISH HAVE GOT HER? I
DOCT III (143)	MEN MUST FIND A REMEDY FOR THEMSELVES. I WILL NOT	LIFT	A FINGER TO SAVE THIS REPTILE. /B.B./ THAT IS THE WORD
CAND I (102)	RAGE WHEN I AM MET WITH VIOLENCE-- BECAUSE I CANT	LIFT	A HEAVY TRUNK DOWN FROM THE TOP OF A CAB LIKE YOU--
PPP (204)	A DOCTOR. (PHYLLIS RUNS OUT. THEY ALL TRY TO	LIFT	ADOLPHUS; BUT HE IS PERFECTLY STIFF, AND AS HEAVY AS
PPP (203)	IS MORE COMPLICATED THAN I THOUGHT. (HE TRIES TO	LIFT	ADOLPHUS'S ARM BUT CANNOT). STIFF ALREADY. /THE
PPP (203)	STIFF ALREADY. /THE LANDLORD/ (TRYING TO	LIFT	ADOLPHUS'S LEG) AN' PRECIOUS EVVY. (FEELING THE CALF)
MIS. (173)	GIRLS HAVING A JOLLY TIME. I SPENT A PENNY ON THE	LIFT	AND FOURPENCE ON REFRESHMENTS. THAT CLEANED ME OUT. THE
JITT I (25)	A GRIM CHANGE OF COUNTENANCE) POOR JITTA! THAT	LIFT	BROKE THE MAINSPRING. (HE STAGGERS AGAINST THE DOOR
METH PREFACE(R10)	STICK CLOSELY TO THE METHODS OF MOLIERE; AND TO	LIFT	CHARACTERS BODILY OUT OF THE PAGES OF CHARLES DICKENS.
SUPR IV (170)	UP, PAUSES FOR A MOMENT TO INSTRUCT TANNER). DONT	LIFT	ER ED, MR TANNER: LET IT GO FLAT SO'S THE BLOOD CAN RUN
SUPR IV (170)	TANNER RUNS ROUND TO HER OTHER HAND, AND TRIES TO	LIFT	HER HEAD. OCTAVIUS GOES TO VIOLET'S ASSISTANCE, BUT
MRS PREFACE(154)	FALLEN SISTER, AND WOULD " TAKE HER UP TENDERLY,	LIFT	HER WITH CARE, FASHIONED SO SLENDERLY, YOUNG, AND SO

DEVL III (55) DOWN, SOBBING). /RICHARD/ (TAKING HER ARM TO LIFT HER) JUST-- HER OTHER ARM, SERGEANT. THEY GO OUT, SH
CATH 3,SD(185) THIS BREAST STRAP AND THROUGH THE WRIST STRAP AND LIFT HIM BY IT, HELPLESSLY TRUSSED UP, TO CARRY HIM OFF.
6CAL (103) THEY PULL HIM TO HIS FEET. /PETER/ (AS THEY LIFT HIM GROANING AND SWEARING) AH-OOH-OH-OW! /THE KING/
6CAL (103) IS BLUE WITH COLD. I FEAR HE IS DYING. UNTIE HIM. LIFT HIM UP. TAKE THAT BANDAGE OFF HIS MOUTH. FIE FIE! I
GENV I (43) CONCERN. THE MEN RUSH TO HIM. /COMMISSAR/ DO NOT LIFT HIM YET. HE WILL RECOVER BEST AS HE IS. /SHE/ I HAVE
MIS. SD(115) KNEES ARE STIFFER, BENDS OVER HIM AND TRIES TO LIFT HIM. MRS TARLETON IS A SHREWD AND MOTHERLY OLD LADY WHO
PHIL II (126) FROM ME. I HAVE ONLY TO LIFT MY FINGER. /GRACE/ LIFT IT THEN; AND SEE WHETHER HE WILL COME. /JULIA/ HOW I
CLEO I (115) BENEATH A PYRAMID, HE WOULD GO STRAIGHT TO IT AND LIFT IT WITH ONE HAND. AND THEN--! (HE CHOPS HIS TEETH
ARMS II SD(37) SO AS TO CARRY ALL OUT TOGETHER. AS SHE STOOPS TO LIFT IT, HE RISES. /SERGIUS/ LOUKA! (SHE STOPS AND LOOKS
JITT I (13) SO, QUITE SO. IF I COME AGAIN I WILL TAKE THE LIFT . I PROMISE. /MRS BILLITER/ THANK YOU, SIR. THANK YOU
INCA (236) UP HERE. THERE IS LESS NOISE; AND THERE IS THE LIFT . IF YOUR HIGHNESS DESIRES ANYTHING, THERE IS THE
JITT I (11) YOU MEET PEOPLE ON THE STAIRS AS WELL AS IN THE LIFT . /THE GENTLEMAN/ I KNOW; BUT I MUSTNT LET THE LIFTMEN
NEVR IV (294) LIFT ME DOWN, SOMEBODY: I'M GOING TO FALL. PAPA: LIFT ME DOWN. /CRAMPTON/ (ANXIOUSLY RUNNING TO HER AND
NEVR IV (294) IN A CATASTROPHE. /THE COLUMBINE/ (SCREAMING) LIFT ME DOWN, SOMEBODY: I'M GOING TO FALL. PAPA: LIFT ME
MTH5 (252) MY CHILD: I AM JUST AS WELL AS I AM. I WOULD NOT LIFT MY FINGER NOW TO HAVE A THOUSAND HEADS. /THE
PHIL II (126) THEIR SOULS FOR A LOOK FROM ME. I HAVE ONLY TO LIFT MY FINGER. /GRACE/ LIFT IT THEN; AND SEE WHETHER HE
BULL I (77) NOT EVEN IN DEFENCE OF FREE TRADE WOULD I LIFT MY HAND AGAINST A POLITICAL OPPONENT, HOWEVER RICHLY HE
JITT I (12) BEFORE GOING OUT), BUT YOU WILL TAKE THE LIFT NEXT TIME, SIR, WONT YOU? IF ANYTHING WERE TO HAPPEN
MIS. SD(120) SUMMERHAYS FROM A DISTANCE WITH AN ENIGMATIC LIFT OF HER EYELIDS IN HIS DIRECTION AND A DEMURE NOD BEFORE
HART II (86) WHAT YOU CALL ENTHUSIASTS, BUT THE FIRST DEAD LIFT OF THE THING IS TOO MUCH FOR THEM; AND THEY HAVNT
BARB II (282) PLUCK TO DO OUR WORK HERE; BUT NONE OF US DARE LIFT OUR HAND AGAINST A GIRL LIKE THAT, FOR FEAR OF HER
BULL III (131) IRELAND. AND SHE'LL RUIN US AGAIN THE MOMENT WE LIFT OUR HEADS FROM THE DUST IF WE TRADE IN CHEAP LABOR; AND
6CAL SD(100) DANGLING CORPSES. THE THREE MEN-AT-ARMS BEGIN TO LIFT PETER. THE OTHERS LAY HANDS ON HIS FIVE COLLEAGUES,
DOCT I (104) STUFF, RIDGEON, BECAUSE I WANTED TO GIVE YOU A LIFT ; BUT TWO YEARS AGO I TRIED THE EXPERIMENT OF TREATING
BULL PREFACE(36) BUT THEY ARE QUIT OF THE PRELIMINARY DEAD LIFT THAT AWAITS THE IRISH CATHOLIC. THEIR CHURCH HAS THROWN
CLEO III (147) (IMPATIENTLY, AS THE PORTERS STOOP TO LIFT THE BALES) QUICK, QUICK: SHE WILL BE OUT UPON US. (
BASH II,1, (112) HOW SHE HANGS ON'S ARM! I AM ALONE. NOW LET ME LIFT THE COVER FROM MY SOUL. O WASTED HUMBLENESS! DELUDED
CATH 4 (196) STOPS AND TURNS TO EDSTASTON, WHO HAS HURRIED TO LIFT THE CURTAIN FOR HER). CAPTAIN: I WISH YOU EVERY
MTH1 I (3) STIRRED AGAIN. ITS NECK IS WRONG (HE STOOPS TO LIFT THE NECK AND SHEW HER). /EVE/ DONT TOUCH IT. COME AWAY
MTH5 (243) CARE: DO NOT TOUCH THEIR FLESH: IT IS NOXIOUS: LIFT THEM BY THEIR ROBES. CARRY PYGMALION INTO THE TEMPLE;
CLEO I SD(117) ORDERED RANK OPPOSITE IT; DRAW THEIR SWORDS AND LIFT THEM IN THE AIR WITH A SHOUT OF HAIL, CAESAR. CLEOPATRA
JOAN 5 (116) AND HAVE TO WAIT FOR THEIR SQUIRES TO COME AND LIFT THEM TO ARRANGE ABOUT THE RANSOM WITH THE MAN THAT HAS
ROCK I (220) ARE NOT IN YOUR EDUCATION; BUT OUR YOUNG PEOPLE LIFT THEMSELVES OUT OF THE GUTTER WITH IT. THATS HOW YOU CAN
BARB III (338) TAXES, RESPECTABILITY AND CHILDREN. NOTHING CAN LIFT THOSE SEVEN MILLSTONES FROM MAN'S NECK BUT MONEY; AND
MIS. PREFACE(4) LITTLE MAKESHIFT INDIVIDUALITIES FOR EVER AT EACH LIFT TOWARDS THE GOAL OF EVOLUTION, WHICH CAN ONLY BE A
PYGM V (288) AND CALLED NAMES, WHEN ALL THE TIME I HAD ONLY TO LIFT UP MY FINGER TO BE AS GOOD AS YOU, I COULD JUST KICK
JITT PREFACE(4) EARNINGS IN LONDON. TODAY I HAVE ONLY TO LIFT UP MY FINGER TO ATTRACT A HUNDRED TRANSLATORS. WHEN
APPL PREFACE(193) TO ROAD LORRY, AND FROM ROAD LORRY TO WAREHOUSE LIFT WITHOUT SHOCK, FRICTION, OR HANDLING. GATTIE, BEING, I
JITT I (25) AGAIN? WHAT CAN I DO FOR YOU? SHALL I TRY TO LIFT YOU? SHE TRIES TO RAISE HIM BY HIS SHOULDERS; BUT THEY
CATH 1 (168) THREW ME ON MY BACK LIKE MAGIC, THOUGH I COULD LIFT YOU WITH ONE HAND. DARLING: YOU ARE A GIANT, A PALADIN.
ROCK II (251) UNTIL THE COUNTRY RINGS WITH IT IF YOU DARE TO LIFT YOUR DISHONORED HEAD AGAIN IN ENGLISH POLITICS. YOUR
BULL II (100) SO YOU WILL. AND WHEN YOURE ANGRY AND TEMPTED TO LIFT YOUR HAND AGEN THE DONKEY OR STAMP YOUR FOOT ON THE
MTH5 (254) YOU REFUSED TO BE REFINED. I DID MY BEST TO LIFT YOUR PREHISTORIC IMPULSES ON TO THE PLANE OF BEAUTY, OF
BASH I (94) HEAVE THE CHEST WITH BREATH? OR LIKE A FEATHER LIFT YOU-- LIKE THIS? (HE SETS HER ON HER FEET.) /LYDIA/ (
JOAN 2 (83) HEAVY FOR ME, AND THEIR SWORDS THAT I CAN HARDLY LIFT , AND THEIR MUSCLE AND THEIR SHOUTING AND THEIR BAD
JITT I (11) (RETURNING) WHY WILL YOU NEVER TAKE THE LIFT , SIR? IT ISNT AS IF ANYONE IN THIS HOUSE KNEW YOU.

LIFTED

SUPR HANDBOK(198) FRONT DE BOEUF, WOULD WASHINGTON OR FRANKLIN HAVE LIFTED A FINGER IN THE CAUSE OF AMERICAN INDEPENDENCE IF
MTH2 (72) WHO HAVE HAD NO RESPONSIBILITY! YOU, WHO HAVNT LIFTED A FINGER, AS FAR AS I KNOW, TO HELP US THROUGH THIS
CYMB V (143) MOUNTAINS OF MORTAL GUILT THAT CRUSHED ME ARE NOW LIFTED FROM MY BREAST, I AM IN HEAVEN THAT WAS BUT NOW IN
DEVL II SD(35) KNOWS HOW TO TURN A COMPLIMENT. THE LATCH IS LIFTED FROM WITHOUT. /JUDITH/ (STARTING) WHO IS THAT?
MTH1 I (14) EVERY DAY NOW THAT THE BURDEN OF IMMORTALITY IS LIFTED FROM YOU. /EVE/ IMMORTALITY? WHAT IS THAT? /THE
PYGM EPILOG (297) SHOOK HER SO VIOLENTLY, THAT WHEN MR H. G. WELLS LIFTED HER ON THE POINT OF HIS PUISSANT PEN, AND PLACED HER
MRS PREFACE(151) PLAY LIKE MINE BECAME RIDICULOUS AND HAD TO BE LIFTED . ALSO I ADMIT THAT MY CAREER AS A REVOLUTIONARY
BARB III (338) THE SPIRIT CANNOT SOAR UNTIL THE MILLSTONES ARE LIFTED . I LIFTED THEM FROM YOUR SPIRIT. I ENABLED BARBARA
GENV IV (112) IMPELLED BY IT I HAVE STRETCHED OUT MY HAND AND LIFTED MY COUNTRY FROM THE GUTTER INTO WHICH YOU AND YOUR
JOAN PREFACE(6) MEAN MARTYRDOM. JOAN WAS BURNT WITHOUT A HAND LIFTED ON HER OWN SIDE TO SAVE HER. THE COMRADES SHE HAD LED
APPL PREFACE(194) OF HOISTS THE CONTENTS OF THEIR HOLDS WOULD BE LIFTED OUT AND TRANSFERRED (LIKE MYSELF IN THE ARMCHAIR) TO
2TRU I (32) REST? /THE ELDERLY LADY/ OH, THANK YOU. YOU HAVE LIFTED SUCH A WEIGHT FROM MY CONSCIENCE. I FEEL SURE THEY
LADY PREFACE(212) AND ENSHRINED HER AMONG THE SAINTS. HE HAS LIFTED THE CHICAGO ANARCHISTS OUT OF THEIR INFAMY, AND SHEWN
APPL I (239) WOULD THEY LIKE ME TO SING; AND THEIR YES NEARLY LIFTED THE ROOF OFF. I HAD TWO SONGS. THEY BOTH HAD
BARB III (338) CANNOT SOAR UNTIL THE MILLSTONES ARE LIFTED. I LIFTED THEM FROM YOUR SPIRIT. I ENABLED BARBARA TO BECOME
MIS. PREFACE(96) VOICES OF OUR MORAL INSTRUCTION LEAGUES WILL BE LIFTED , ASKING WHETHER THERE IS ANY REASON WHY THE APPETITE

LIFTER

METH PREFACE(R18) IS BY NO MEANS PLAYED OUT YET. IF THE WEIGHT LIFTER , UNDER THE TRIVIAL STIMULUS OF AN ATHLETIC

LIFTERS

METH PREFACE(R45) WANTING AND TRYING, OF THE MANUFACTURE OF WEIGHT LIFTERS AND WRESTLERS FROM MEN OF ORDINARY STRENGTH, ARE

LIFTING

ROCK II (243) WILL GRAB SIXTY PER CENT OF THE PROFIT WITHOUT LIFTING A FINGER EXCEPT TO POCKET THE WEALTH THAT I SHALL
GETT (333) SELF-CONTROL. /LESBIA/ (WIDENING HER EYES AND LIFTING HER CHIN HAUGHTILY) AND PRAY HOW DOES THAT PREVENT
CATH 2 (179) THAT POLICY WAS MR PITT'S BUSINESS. /CATHERINE/ (LIFTING HER EYEBROWS) SO? /VARINKA/ WHAT ELSE DID YOU
NEVR II (256) AND REASONABLE FOR ALL THESE YEARS, WERE SUDDENLY LIFTING HER GREAT HAND TO TAKE US-- HER TWO LITTLE
DEVL II (41) CLOSED. HE RUNS TO HER AND STOOPS BESIDE HER, LIFTING HER HEAD). JUDITH. /JUDITH/ (WAKING; FOR HER SWOON
CLEO III (146) ON YOU! LET ME GO. HELP HO! /FTATATEETA/ (LIFTING HIM FROM THE GROUND) STAB THE LITTLE ROMAN REPTILE.
CATH 1 (173) -- I -- /VARINKA/ CARRY HIM, UNCLE. /PATIOMKIN/ (LIFTING HIM IN HIS ARMS LIKE A FATHER CARRYING A LITTLE BOY)
PYGM II (229) YES: VERY FREQUENTLY. /HIGGINS/ (DOGMATICALLY, LIFTING HIMSELF ON HIS HANDS TO THE LEVEL OF THE PIANO, AND
LIED (195) SAID YOU WERE THE ONLY AURORA IN THE WORLD. AND (LIFTING HIS CLASPED FISTS WITH A SUDDEN RETURN OF HIS
SUPR IV (160) SEES HIM. /MRS WHITEFIELD/ (RUNNING TO HIM AND LIFTING HIS HEAD) WHATS THE MATTER, TAVY? ARE YOU ILL?
CLEO PRO2 (105) DESERT AND PERISH ON THE SPEARS OF THE ROMANS. (LIFTING HIS KNIFE) TASTE DEATH. /FTATATEETA/ NOT FROM THEE,
BUOY PREFACE(4) PAGE AFTER PAGE WITH ASTONISHING SPEED WITHOUT LIFTING HIS PENCIL FROM THE BLANK PAPER WE FED ON TO HIS
GETT PREFACE(192) SETTLED DOWN, LIKE BALLOONS THAT HAD LOST THEIR LIFTING MARGIN OF GAS; AND IT WAS EVIDENT THAT THE PROCESS
SUPR III SD(87) BUT WHERE? WHY? HOW? BESIDES, IN THE BRIEF LIFTING OF HIS FACE, NOW HIDDEN BY HIS HAT BRIM, THERE WAS A
APPL I (238) ONE OF THEIR DIRECTORS TOLD ME TO MY FACE THAT BY LIFTING UP HIS FINGER HE COULD GET MY WINDOWS BROKEN BY THE
JITT III (57) WHAT HE WANTED, AND HOW EASILY HE COULD GET IT BY LIFTING UP HIS LITTLE FINGER. OH, I KNOW EXACTLY HOW HE
CAND II (116) 'IS CHUMP! (HE CROSSES THE ROOM TO THE DOOR, LIFTING UP HIS VOICE AS HE GOES). WELL, THIS IS A PRETTY
CAPT II (250) AND I WILL SEE THAT HE GETS THEM. /DRINKWATER/ (LIFTING UP HIS VOICE IN PROTEST) NAH, NAH-- /LADY CICELY/

LIFTMEN

JITT I (11) /THE GENTLEMAN/ I KNOW; BUT I MUSTNT LET THE LIFTMEN SEE ME COMING HERE TOO OFTEN. PEOPLE TALK, EVEN WHEN

LIFT'S

PHIL I (83) /CHARTERIS/ NO: THE MAN'S GONE HOME; AND THE LIFT'S LOCKED. /JULIA/ (PUTTING ON HER TOQUE AT EXPRESS

LIFTS

SUPR II (65) A MAN'S, AND THAT THE PURER NATURE OF A WOMAN LIFTS A MAN RIGHT OUT OF HIMSELF, AND MAKES HIM BETTER THAN
2TRU I SD(40) HOLDING ON TO THE TABLE EDGE BEHIND HER, SHE LIFTS HER FOOT VIGOROUSLY WAIST HIGH, AND SHOOTS IT HARD
DEVL III SD(75) EARS. JUDITH, HALF RISING, STARES AT HIM; THEN LIFTS HER HANDS LIKE ONE WHOSE DEAREST PRAYER HAS BEEN
2TRU II SD(77) AIR OF DISARMING INNOCENCE; FALLS ON HER KNEES; LIFTS HER PALMS; AND SMITES THE GROUND WITH HER FOREHEAD.
JITT I (25) TO YOU. (HE SEIZES HER ROUND THE HIPS, AND LIFTS HER UP EXULTANTLY). /JITTA/ (TERRIFIED) OH GOD, NO:
PHIL I (81) IT. /JULIA/ (SOBBING AS HE RISES AND TENDERLY LIFTS HER WITH HIM) OH, YOU CAN, YOU CAN. ONE WORD FROM YOU
2TRU I SD(40) THE PATIENT. THE PATIENT SWOOPS AT HER KNEES; LIFTS HER; AND SENDS HER FLYING. SHE COMES DOWN WITH A THUMP
HART II (100) NOT MARRY ME HE SHOULD NEVER SEE YOU AGAIN (SHE LIFTS HERSELF ON HER WRISTS AND SEATS HERSELF ON THE END OF
DOCT IV (166) NO, NO, DARLING: HOW COULD YOU TIRE ME? (SHE LIFTS HIM SO THAT HE LIES IN HER BOSOM). /LOUIS/ THATS GOOD.

DEST	(175)	(HE PUTS HIS HANDS BEHIND HIM ON THE TABLE, AND	LIFTS	HIMSELF ON TO IT, SITTING WITH HIS ARMS AKIMBO AND HIS
PHIL I	(91)	CHARTERIS. /CHARTERIS/ ALL RIGHT. I'LL STAY. (HE	LIFTS	HIMSELF ON TO THE SHOULDER OF THE GRAND PIANO AND SITS
WIDO II	(43)	HIS FINGERS; PUTS HIS HANDS ON HIS KNEES, AND	LIFTS	HIMSELF UPRIGHT; PULLS HIS WAISTCOAT STRAIGHT WITH A
DEVL III	(72)	YOURSELF, AND SUBMIT TO THE DIVINE WILL. (HE	LIFTS	HIS BOOK TO PROCEED WITH THE SERVICE). /RICHARD/
ARMS I	(21)	(WITH A HAPPY SIGH HE SINKS BACK AT FULL LENGTH;	LIFTS	HIS BOOTS INTO THE BED WITH A FINAL EFFORT; AND FALLS
INCA	(249)	AND CHARMING AS THEIR FATHER? /THE INCA/ (	LIFTS	HIS EYEBROWS PITYINGLY; SHRUGS HIS SHOULDERS; THEN,
APPL I	(208)	MAGNUS: YOU HAVE NEVER BEEN A WORKER. /MAGNUS/ (	LIFTS	HIS EYEBROWS)! /BOANERGES/ (CONTINUING) NO KING ON
HART II	(128)	POOR WRETCH! OH WOMEN! WOMEN! WOMEN! (HE	LIFTS	HIS FISTS IN INVOCATION TO HEAVEN) FALL. FALL AND
CAPT II	(256)	WITH HIS FISTS CLENCHED; SO THAT LADY CICELY	LIFTS	ONE EYE FROM HER WORK TO ASSURE HERSELF THAT THE TABLE
DEVL II	(45)	ROUND TO THE FIRE; STRIDES ACROSS TO IT; AND	LIFTS	RICHARD'S COAT). WHY, MY DEAR, IT SEEMS THAT HE HAS
MIS.	SD(187)	AUTHORITATIVE) STAND CLEAR, PLEASE. SHE QUICKLY	LIFTS	THE UPPER HALF OF BENTLEY FROM THE GROUND; DIVES UNDER
DOCT PREFACE	(15)	DOMESTIC SERVANTS IN SOME HUGE INSTITUTION WITH	LIFTS	, VACUUM CLEANERS, ELECTRIC LIGHTING, STEAM HEATING,
			LIGH	
FABL I	(104)	THOUGHTFUL) LIGHTER THAN AIR, EH? (SLOWER)	LIGH	-- TER-- THAN-- AIR? THE SCENE FADES OUT.
			LIGHT	
JOAN EPILOG	(157)	I WAS JUST; I WAS MERCIFUL; I WAS FAITHFUL TO MY	LIGHT	: I COULD DO NO OTHER THAN I DID. /CHARLES/ (
METH PREFACE	(R77)	MAKER) IF IT CANNOT SEE THE TRUTH BY ITS OWN	LIGHT	: NO DOGMA CAN BE A LEGEND. A LEGEND CAN PASS AN
MIS. PREFACE	(48)	TO OUR BELIEFS FOR THE SAKE OF SYMPATHY AND	LIGHT	: THE ATHANASIAN ATTITUDE IS A DESIRE TO MURDER PEOPLE
KING I	(219)	VALUE HIM RATHER FOR HIS FLASHES OF THE INNER	LIGHT	? DID HE NOT STOP THE BUTCHERING OF THE REGICIDES ON
GETT	(342)	/MRS GEORGE/ DO YOU SEE NOTHING-- NOT A GREAT	LIGHT	? /THE BISHOP/ WE ARE STILL WALKING IN DARKNESS. /MRS
2TRU III	(84)	MAN IN THE BOOK SAYS " DO YOU SEE YONDER SHINING	LIGHT	? " WELL, TODAY THE PLACE IS BLAZING WITH SHINING
CLEO I	(113)	GO ON. /CLEOPATRA/ (TIMIDLY, TO THE SLAVE)	LIGHT	ALL THE LAMPS. /FTATATEETA/ (SUDDENLY COMING FROM
KING I	(164)	OF MATTER, THE ELIXIR OF LIFE, THE MAGIC OF	LIGHT	AND COLOR, ABOVE ALL, THE SECRET MEANING OF THE
FABL PREFACE	(92)	THE BURIED FACTORS OF THE MIND AND BRING THEM TO	LIGHT	AND CONSCIOUSNESS, THE TECHNIQUE OF THIS THERAPY HAS
2TRU II	(71)	IS A DAY OF ADVENTURE WITH ITS COLD AND HEAT, ITS	LIGHT	AND DARKNESS, ITS CYCLES OF EXULTANT VIGOR AND
FANY II	(292)	AT PICCADILLY CIRCUS, BECAUSE THERE WAS A LOT OF	LIGHT	AND EXCITEMENT THERE. I WALKED TO LEICESTER SQUARE;
SUPR PREFACE	(R37)	RATHER THAN IN THE CHILL OF SUCH MERE PAINTING OF	LIGHT	AND HEAT AS ELOCUTION AND CONVENTION CAN ACHIEVE. MY
SUPR PREFACE	(R39)	YOU AS THOSE TWO VITAL QUALITIES OF LITERATURE,	LIGHT	AND HEAT. NOW IF I AM TO BE NO MERE COPPER WIRE
METH PREFACE	(R80)	THE PROFESSIONAL POLITICIAN AND ADMINISTRATOR FOR	LIGHT	AND LEADING IN RELIGION. HE IS NEITHER A PHILOSOPHER
MIS.	(134)	MEN AND SO FORTH, AND THAT THEYRE ALL ANGELS OF	LIGHT	AND LEADING. THE TIME HAS COME TO ASSERT OURSELVES AND
ARMS I	(8)	REVOLVER WILL GO OFF. (COMMANDINGLY). STRIKE A	LIGHT	AND LET ME SEE YOU. DO YOU HEAR. (ANOTHER MOMENT OF
KING I	(184)	NOT AN ALCHEMIST. BUT THE CHANGING OF BODIES INTO	LIGHT	AND LIGHT INTO BODIES IS VERY CONFORMABLE TO THE
DOCT IV	(162)	MISERABLE." /MRS DUBEDAT/ NO, NEVER. YOU ARE THE	LIGHT	AND THE BLESSING OF MY LIFE. I NEVER LIVED UNTIL I
KING I	(202)	NEVER LIVED. I MUST SEEK HIM OUT AND SHEW HIM THE	LIGHT	AND THE TRUTH. /NELL/ TUT TUT, GEORGE! THE MAN IN THE
LADY PREFACE	(207)	BEEN) WAS COMPLETE, A PORTRAIT OF MARY CAME TO	LIGHT	AND TURNED OUT TO BE THAT OF A FAIR LADY, NOT OF A
SHAK	SD(143)	A MOMENT SUFFER MY GLIMMERING LIGHT TO SHINE. A	LIGHT	APPEARS BETWEEN THEM. /SHAKES/ OUT, OUT, BRIEF
PYGM II	SD(217)	WHICH ARE HANGING OUT. HE APPEARS IN THE MORNING	LIGHT	AS A ROBUST, VITAL, APPETIZING SORT OF MAN OF FORTY OR
HART III	(144)	COMES LATER AND LATER UNTIL SHE IS LOST IN THE	LIGHT	AS OTHER THINGS ARE LOST IN THE DARKNESS. AFTER THE
JITT I	SD(10)	IN. MRS BILLITER RETURNS, PUTTING OUT THE BEDROOM	LIGHT	AS SHE DOES SO, AND FINDS THE GIRL AT THE DOOR. /THE
LION PREFACE	(72)	AT ALL; BUT THEN THE FOLLOWING OF THE INNER	LIGHT	AT ALL COSTS IS LARGELY SELF-INDULGENCE, WHICH IS JUST
JOAN PREFACE	(41)	AND MAKE IT A SERIOUS OFFENCE TO SHEW A	LIGHT	AT NIGHT. UNDER THE STRAIN OF INVASION THE FRENCH
JITT I	SD(9)	TUMBLERS, AND A BOTTLE ON IT. SHE SWITCHES ON THE	LIGHT	AT THE DOOR, AND CROSSES THE ROOM TO THE TABLE, WHERE
METH PREFACE	(R57)	CASTLE OF GIANT DESPAIR; BUT THEY SAW THE SHINING	LIGHT	AT THE END OF THE PATH, AND SO STARTED GAILY TOWARDS
MTH5	(258)	YOU ARE SADDENING US; AND YOU ARE CHASING THE	LIGHT	AWAY. IT IS GROWING DARK. /ACIS/ NIGHT IS FALLING. THE
METH PREFACE	(R74)	TOWARDS THE PURSUIT OF A LIGHT CALLED AN INNER	LIGHT	BECAUSE EVERY MAN MUST SEE IT WITH HIS OWN EYES AND
CLEO IV	SD(183)	AND PLACES THE IMAGE IN THE MIDDLE OF IT. THE	LIGHT	BEGINS TO CHANGE TO THE MAGENTA PURPLE OF THE EGYPTIAN
CAND III	SD(127)	HIM. CANDIDA IS IN THE EASY CHAIR. THE POKER, A	LIGHT	BRASS ONE, IS UPRIGHT IN HER HAND. LEANING BACK AND
JOAN EPILOG	(155)	ASLEEP. (SHE IS DIMLY SEEN IN A PALLID GREENISH	LIGHT	BY THE BEDSIDE). /CHARLES/ (PEEPING OUT) JOAN! ARE
SUPR III	(87)	DARK; AND WHEN THE LIGHT CAME BACK IT WAS THIS	LIGHT	BY WHICH I WALK SEEING NOTHING. I HAVE WANDERED FOR
METH PREFACE	(R74)	WAS A MOVEMENT TOWARDS THE PURSUIT OF A	LIGHT	CALLED AN INNER LIGHT BECAUSE EVERY MAN MUST SEE IT
SUPR III	(87)	ON THE CROSS. THEN IT GREW DARK; AND WHEN THE	LIGHT	CAME BACK IT WAS THIS LIGHT BY WHICH I WALK SEEING
2TRU II	SD(51)	TIMES, BUT WITH A REVOLVER IN HIS EQUIPMENT. A	LIGHT	CANE CHAIR FOR USE BY HIS VISITORS IS AT HAND BY THE
2TRU I	(32)	DONT WORRY ABOUT THE MEASLES. IT'S REALLY QUITE A	LIGHT	CASE. /THE ELDERLY LADY/ OH, YOU CAN DEPEND ON ME FOR
HART III	SD(129)	THE EAST SIDE OF THE FLAGSTAFF, IN THE CIRCLE OF	LIGHT	CAST BY THE ELECTRIC ARC, WHICH IS LIKE A MOON IN ITS
CLEO IV	SD(174)	AND FESTIVE, FOLLOWED BY TWO SLAVES CARRYING A	LIGHT	COUCH, WHICH IS HARDLY MORE THAN AN ELABORATELY
ROCK PREFACE	(169)	NOT EXPEDIENT; THERE MUST BE FALLOWS, OR AT LEAST	LIGHT	CROPPINGS, BETWEEN THE INTENSE CULTIVATIONS; FOR WE
CLEO IV	SD(173)	AT LAST INTO A MASSIVE COLONNADE ON THE ROOF.	LIGHT	CURTAINS ARE DRAWN BETWEEN THE COLUMNS ON THE NORTH
MIS.	SD(172)	OPPOSITE DIRECTION TO THE HANDS OF A CLOCK WITH A	LIGHT	DANCING STEP. HE FINDS IT IMPOSSIBLE TO COVER HER WITH
CATH	1,SD(164)	BUILT YOUNG ENGLISH OFFICER IN THE UNIFORM OF A	LIGHT	DRAGOON. HE IS EVIDENTLY ON FAIRLY GOOD TERMS WITH
CATH	1 (164)	MY NAME IS EDSTASTON: CAPTAIN EDSTASTON OF THE	LIGHT	DRAGOONS. I HAVE THE HONOR TO PRESENT TO YOUR HIGHNESS
PYGM III	(258)	GO). /HIGGINS/ (RISING ALSO) WE'LL FIND HER SOME	LIGHT	EMPLOYMENT. /PICKERING/ SHE'S HAPPY ENOUGH. DONT YOU
HART III	(147)	ACROSS TO HIS FORMER PLACE) THERE IS NOT HALF	LIGHT	ENOUGH. WE SHOULD BE BLAZING TO THE SKIES. /ELLIE/ (
MTH5	(237)	/PYGMALION/ THEY ARE SENSATIONS. WHEN THE RAYS OF	LIGHT	ENTER THEIR EYES AND MAKE A PICTURE ON THEIR RETINAS,
MTH5	SD(241)	HE KNOCKS THE MALE AUTOMATON UPRIGHT BY A VERY	LIGHT	FLIP UNDER THE CHIN. THE FEMALE AUTOMATON HARDLY DARES
SIM II	(61)	YOU WILL NEVER BE OLD. YOU ARE THE WAY AND THE	LIGHT	FOR ME. BUT YOU HAVE NEVER LOVED ME AND NEVER WILL
OVER	SD(171)	THE TWO FIGURES ON IT IN EVENING DRESS, CATCH THE	LIGHT	FROM AN ARC LAMP SOMEWHERE; BUT THE WALLS, COVERED
JITT I	SD(9)	SHE OPENS THE DOOR, LETTING IN SOME ELECTRIC	LIGHT	FROM THE HALL. SHE HAS A SILVER TRAY IN HER HANDS,
MILL IV	(201)	CALLED A SKUNK. IT MAKES THE JURY SEE YOU IN THAT	LIGHT	FROM THE START. IT IS ALSO VERY DIFFICULT FOR A
JOAN EPIL,	SD(167)	(HE GOES ON TIPTOE). THE LAST REMAINING RAYS OF	LIGHT	GATHER INTO A WHITE RADIANCE DESCENDING ON JOAN. THE
HART III	SD(145)	(HE BLOWS HIS WHISTLE). BREAKERS AHEAD! THE	LIGHT	GOES OUT. /HECTOR/ (FURIOUSLY) WHO PUT THAT LIGHT
WIDO I	SD(5)	MOUTH, GIVE HIM AN AIR OF IMPORTANCE. HE WEARS A	LIGHT	GREY FROCK-COAT WITH SILK LININGS, A WHITE HAT, AND A
ARMS I	SD(3)	AND GOLD, WITH AN IVORY IMAGE OF CHRIST, AND A	LIGHT	HANGING BEFORE IT IN A PIERCED METAL BALL SUSPENDED BY
MRS IV	(238)	(RAISING HIS EYEBROWS LIKE ONE ON WHOM A NEW	LIGHT	HAS DAWNED, AND RISING WITH QUITE AN EFFUSION OF
WIDO I	(4)	ABOUT THEM. (HE STRIKES A MATCH, AND PROCEEDS TO	LIGHT	HIS PIPE). /COKANE/ DO DROP CALLING ME BILLY IN
DEVL EPILOG	(79)	UP BY HIMSELF FOR HIS OFFICERS WHEN HE INTRODUCED	LIGHT	HORSE INTO THE ENGLISH ARMY. HIS OPINION THAT ENGLISH
KING I	(217)	AND IF I COULD FIND A CHEMICAL SALT SENSITIVE TO	LIGHT	I COULD FIX IT. SOME DAY PORTRAITS WILL BE MADE AT THE
2TRU I	SD(28)	BUT THESE ARE NOW SWITCHED OFF; AND THE ONLY	LIGHT	IN ACTION IS ANOTHER PORTABLE ONE ON THE MEDICINE
2TRU II	(69)	AND NO GOD. /THE PATIENT/ WHAT ABOUT THE	LIGHT	IN OUR OWN SOULS THAT YOU WERE SO ELOQUENT ABOUT THE
CLEO PRO1,	SD(89)	A HAWK'S HEAD IS MYSTERIOUSLY VISIBLE BY HIS OWN	LIGHT	IN THE DARKNESS WITHIN THE TEMPLE. HE SURVEYS THE
SUPR III	SD(87)	AND BY THE AID OF CERTAIN SPARKLES OF VIOLET	LIGHT	IN THE PALLOR, THE MAN'S COSTUME EXPLAINS ITSELF AS
ARMS I	SD(7)	NOTHING BEING VISIBLE BUT THE GLIMMER OF THE	LIGHT	IN THE PIERCED BALL BEFORE THE IMAGE, AND THE
BARB III	(349)	MAN TO GOD, THROUGH THE UNVEILING OF AN ETERNAL	LIGHT	IN THE VALLEY OF THE SHADOW. (SEIZING HIM WITH BOTH
GENV IV	(111)	THING. /DEACONESS/ YOU HAVE NEITHER OF YOU THE	LIGHT	IN YOUR EYES OF THE LOVE OF THE MASTER. THERE IS NO
JOAN EPILOG	(155)	I AM BUT A DREAM THAT THOURT DREAMING. (THE	LIGHT	INCREASES: THEY BECOME PLAINLY VISIBLE AS HE SITS UP)
HART III	SD(147)	INTO ONE ANOTHER'S ARMS IN WILD EXCITEMENT. THE	LIGHT	INCREASES. /MAZZINI/ (ANXIOUSLY) THE LIGHT IS GETTING
KING I	(184)	BUT THE CHANGING OF BODIES INTO LIGHT AND	LIGHT	INTO BODIES IS VERY CONFORMABLE TO THE COURSE OF
CAPT I	SD(234)	SIT DOWN AS BEFORE TO RECEIVE THE CAPTAIN. THE	LIGHT	IS BY THIS TIME WANING RAPIDLY, THE DARKNESS CREEPING
KING I	(203)	HOPE IN YOU. THEIR DAY IS SHORT; BUT THE INNER	LIGHT	IS ETERNAL. /JAMES/ I AM SAFE IN THE BOSOM OF MY
HART III	(147)	THE LIGHT INCREASES. /MAZZINI/ (ANXIOUSLY) THE	LIGHT	IS GETTING BRIGHTER. /NURSE GUINNESS/ (LOOKING UP AT
KING I	(178)	CALLED A CHURCH TO ENTER YOUR MIND YOUR INNER	LIGHT	IS LIKE AN EXTINGUISHED CANDLE; AND YOUR SOUL IS
CLEO IV	(192)	ABOUT HIM TO WATCH, ALL LOOKING CLOSELY, FOR THE	LIGHT	IS NOW ALMOST GONE). HERE IS THE PALACE (POINTING TO
DEST	(181)	(HE DISAPPEARS IN THE VINEYARD, WHERE THE	LIGHT	IS NOW REDDENING WITH THE SUNSET). /LIEUTENANT/ (
HART I	(77)	(SHE GOES INTO THE GARDEN, WHERE THE EVENING	LIGHT	IS NOW VERY RED). /HECTOR/ LISTEN, O SAGE. HOW LONG
CATH	4,SD(187)	ARCH WITH THE HUGE BALLROOM OF THE PALACE. THE	LIGHT	IS SUBDUED BY RED SHADES ON THE CANDLES. IN THE WALL
APPL I	SD(197)	CLOCK SHEWS THAT IT IS A LITTLE PAST 11; AND THE	LIGHT	IS THAT OF A FINE SUMMER MORNING. SEMPRONIUS, SMART
POSN PREFACE	(432)	LIGHT SHINES IN THE PLAY ARE LICENSED, BUT THE	LIGHT	ITSELF IS EXTINGUISHED. I NEED HARDLY SAY THAT I HAVE
HART I	(83)	GIVE ME DEEPER DARKNESS. MONEY IS NOT MADE IN THE	LIGHT	.
BUOY 1	SD(9)	MODERN INTERIOR. A WELL FURNISHED STUDY. MORNING	LIGHT	. A FATHER DISCUSSING WITH HIS SON. FATHER AN ELDERLY
HART I	SD(43)	ARMS AND A LOW SLOPING BACK, WITH ITS BACK TO THE	LIGHT	. A SMALL BUT STOUT TABLE OF TEAK, WITH A ROUND TOP
LION PREFACE	(14)	NOTHING CHEAPER. THE YOKE IS EASY, THE BURDEN	LIGHT	. ALL YOU HAVE TO DO WHEN THE REDEEMER IS ONCE FOUND (
AUGS	(277)	NEVER. /AUGUSTUS/ I'M GLAD YOU SEE IT IN THAT	LIGHT	. AND NOW, AS A MEASURE OF SECURITY, I SHALL PUT THAT
GETT	(355)	UP THAT WOMAN IF YOU HAVE THE STRENGTH AND THE	LIGHT	. BUT IF YOU ARE STILL IN THE GRIP OF THIS WORLD, AT
2TRU III	SD(81)	IN WHITE CHALK. NO NEED TO WASTE THE ELECTRIC	LIGHT	. FOR THE MOMENT THE ABODE OF LOVE HAS BEEN TAKEN
PYGM II	(236)	SAY THAT. I'M NOT THE MAN TO STAND IN MY GIRL'S	LIGHT	. HERES A CAREER OPENING FOR HER, AS YOU MIGHT SAY;
FANY III	(315)	BUT LET HIM NOT THINK HE CAN WALK BY HIS OWN	LIGHT	. I TELL HIM THAT IF HE GIVES UP BEING RESPECTABLE

ARMS III SD(46)	FRIENDLIEST ASPECTS IN THE MELLOWING AFTERNOON	LIGHT	. IN THE CORNER NEXT THE RIGHT HAND WINDOW A SQUARE
CAND II (117)	CRITICALLY ALL THE TIME). TURN YOUR FACE TO THE	LIGHT	. (SHE PLACES HIM FACING THE WINDOW). MY BOY IS NOT
SIM I (42)	WAY. /MAYA/ WE ARE THE LIFE. /VASHTI/ I AM THE	LIGHT	. LOOK AT ME. (SHE THROWS HER ARM ROUND HIM AND TURNS
SUPR III SD(95)	HIM SINCE ANA ARRIVED. ANA COMES INDIGNANTLY TO	LIGHT	. /ANA/ WHAT DOES THIS MEAN? OTTAVIO HERE AND YOUR
DEST (189)	YES, BURN THEM. GIUSEPPE: GO AND FETCH A	LIGHT	. /GIUSEPPE/ (TREMBLING AND STAMMERING) DO YOU MEAN
GETT (322)	HELP? /HOTCHKISS/ NO. /SOAMES/ THEN PRAY FOR	LIGHT	. /HOTCHKISS/ NO: I AM A SNOB, NOT A BEGGAR. (HE SITS
SIM I (41)	YOUTH/ ON GUARD. I, KANCHIN, SHEW THEE THE RED	LIGHT	. /JANGA/ THEIR EYEBROWS ARE DRAWN BOWS. /KANCHIN/
DOCT V (178)	BURIED TRUTH GERMINATES AND BREAKS THROUGH TO THE	LIGHT	. /JENNIFER/ WHAT TRUTH? /RIDGEON/ WHAT TRUTH! WHY,
CAND I (97)	NO: STOP: YOU SHANT. I'LL FORCE IT INTO THE	LIGHT	. /MORELL/ (PUZZLED) EH? FORCE WHAT? /MARCHBANKS/ I
CLEO PR01 (93)	OF HIS LONGING FOR THE DIVINE, MORE LIFE AND MORE	LIGHT	. SETTLE YE THEREFORE IN YOUR SEATS AND KEEP SILENT;
3PLA PREFACE(R38)	ME NOT AT ALL UNTIL I SAW THE OLD FACTS IN A NEW	LIGHT	. TECHNICALLY, I DO NOT FIND MYSELF ABLE TO PROCEED
LION PREFACE(76)	GHASTLINESS OF A BEAUTIFUL THING SEEN IN A FALSE	LIGHT	. THE CHRONICLER OF THE ACTS OF THE APOSTLES SEES
2TRU I (37)	/THE PATIENT/ OH, PLEASE, PLEASE. NOT ALL THAT	LIGHT	. THE NURSE SWITCHES OFF. /THE PATIENT/ NO, NO. LEAVE
DEVL II (41)	AND LOOKS WONDERINGLY AT THE UNTASTED MEAL BY ITS	LIGHT	. THEN HE STICKS IT IN THE CANDLESTICK; TAKES OFF HIS
OVER PREFACE(165)	GARRICK, EXCEPT THE INTENSITY OF OUR ARTIFICIAL	LIGHT	. WHEN GARRICK PLAYED RICHARD III IN SLASHED TRUNK
MTH4 I (163)	MAN WHO GETS IT CAN REKINDLE IT ONLY BY HIS OWN	LIGHT	. YOU ARE NO TALLER THAN BILGE OR BLUEBEARD; AND YOU
POSN (440)	ROTTEN TOWN, AND I COULDNT BEAR TO SEE IT IN THE	LIGHT	. YOUR BROTHER'S HORSE DID THE SAME, AS ANY SENSIBLE
PHIL II SD(94)	HIS RIGHT, BETWEEN THE DOOR AND THE RECESS, IS A	LIGHT	LIBRARY STEP-LADDER. FURTHER ON, PAST THE DOOR AN EASY
DEVL III SD(72)	SHIRTSLEEVES. FOLLOWING HIM, TWO SOLDIERS HAUL A	LIGHT	MILITARY WAGGON. FINALLY COMES THE BAND, WHICH POSTS
KING I (179)	CONVENIENCE FOR MOST OF US. THE INNER	LIGHT	MUST EXPRESS ITSELF IN MUSIC, IN NOBLE ARCHITECTURE,
PHIL III SD(132)	WALL NEAR THE LEFT HAND CORNER, ANOTHER DOOR, A	LIGHT	NOISELESS ONE COVERED WITH GREEN BAIZE, LEADING TO THE
NEVR III (281)	THE WHOLE WORLD IS LIKE A FEATHER DANCING IN THE	LIGHT	NOW; AND GLORIA IS THE SUN. (SHE REARS HER HEAD
CLEO NOTES (209)	BRITAIN. AND AGAIN I ASK DOES ANYONE WHO, IN THE	LIGHT	OF A COMPETENT KNOWLEDGE OF HIS OWN AGE, HAS STUDIED
PYGM II (237)	MIGHT BE OPEN TO AN ARRANGEMENT. REGARDED IN THE	LIGHT	OF A YOUNG WOMAN, SHE'S A FINE HANDSOME GIRL. AS A
HART PREFACE(22)	AND ITS POLITICAL ANTECEDENTS AS A WHOLE IN THE	LIGHT	OF ANY PHILOSOPHY OF HISTORY OR KNOWLEDGE OF WHAT WAR
APPL PREFACE(177)	LIGHTS, WHICH IS OFTEN THE WORST OF IT BY THE	LIGHT	OF HEAVEN. BY CHANCE RATHER THAN BY JUDGMENT THEY FIND
DEST (169)	A REAL HERO. (HE STROLLS ABOUT THE ROOM, MAKING	LIGHT	OF HER ENTHUSIASM, BUT BY NO MEANS DISPLEASED WITH
3PLA PREFACE(R37)	EVENTS AND PERSONS PRESENTED TO HIM IN THE	LIGHT	OF HIS OWN TIME, EVEN THOUGH HOMER AND SHAKESPEAR HAVE
CAND II (122)	IT IS SOMETHING THAT MUST HAPPEN; BUT DONT MAKE	LIGHT	OF IT. I SHUDDER WHEN YOU TORTURE HIM AND LAUGH.
3PLA PREFACE(R33)	REPEATED IN THE DIALECT OF MY OWN TIME AND IN THE	LIGHT	OF ITS PHILOSOPHY WHAT THEY SAID IN THE DIALECT AND
PHIL I (86)	OF YOU TO TRY TO KEEP UP MY SPIRITS BY MAKING	LIGHT	OF IT, CHARTERIS. BUT I SHALL BE READY WHEN MY TIME
FANY III (303)	IN HOLLOWAY. /BOBBY/ IT'S ALL VERY WELL TO MAKE	LIGHT	OF IT, MEG; BUT THIS IS A BIT THICK, YOU KNOW.
HART PREFACE(40)	THE TERRIBLE CASTIGATION OF COMEDY, THE RUTHLESS	LIGHT	OF LAUGHTER THAT GLARES ON THE STAGE. WHEN MEN ARE
METH PREFACE(R43)	TO BE NAMED AS HIS ERRONEOUS FORERUNNER. IN THE	LIGHT	OF MY ANECDOTE, THE EXPLANATION IS OBVIOUS. THE FIRST
GETT PREFACE(220)	THAT ONLY AN ATROCIOUSLY WICKED MAN COULD MAKE	LIGHT	OF OR FORGET THEM. WHAT IS MORE, AS THE SAME FANTASTIC
LION PREFACE(50)	IN THE PICTURES MAY BE INTERPRETED SOME DAY AS A	LIGHT	OF SCIENCE RATHER THAN A DECLARATION OF SENTIMENT OR A
DOCT PREFACE(50)	TO THE SIMPLEST ACT OF KINDNESS, AND IN THE	LIGHT	OF THAT TRUTH IT IS CLEAR THAT THE EXEMPTION OF THE
BULL PREFACE(28)	JUST RECONSIDER THE HOME RULE QUESTION IN THE	LIGHT	OF THAT VERY ENGLISH CHARACTERISTIC OF THE IRISH
CLEO IV (193)	TABLE HAS BEEN REMOVED. FTATATEETA IS SEEN IN THE	LIGHT	OF THE MOON AND STARS, AGAIN IN PRAYER BEFORE THE
PLES PREFACE(R9)	THE EYES OF MEN BEGIN TO TURN TOWARDS THE DISTANT	LIGHT	OF THE NEW AGE. DISCERNIBLE AT FIRST ONLY BY THE EYES
MRS PREFACE(157)	WHEREAS THE SLIGHTEST ATTEMPT TO PLACE IT IN THE	LIGHT	OF THE POLICEMAN'S LANTERN OR THE SALVATION ARMY
JOAN 6 (145)	AND WATER NO AFFLICTION. BUT TO SHUT ME FROM THE	LIGHT	OF THE SKY AND THE SIGHT OF THE FIELDS AND FLOWERS; TO
LION PREFACE(62)	OF LIFE; THAT WE ARE THE LAMPS IN WHICH THE	LIGHT	OF THE WORLD BURNS: THAT, IN SHORT, WE ARE GODS THOUGH
LION PREFACE(42)	MATTHEW MAKES HIM SAY TO THE PEOPLE " YE ARE THE	LIGHT	OF THE WORLD." JOHN HAS NO GRIP OF THE SIGNIFICANCE OF
LION PREFACE(42)	HIM SAY THIS, JUST AS HE MAKES HIM SAY " I AM THE	LIGHT	OF THE WORLD." BUT MATTHEW MAKES HIM SAY TO THE PEOPLE
LION PREFACE(27)	MULTITUDE WERE THE SALT OF THE EARTH AND THE	LIGHT	OF THE WORLD. HIS DISCIPLES, IN THEIR RELATIONS WITH
BULL PREFACE(41)	NATIONALISM STANDS BETWEEN IRELAND AND THE	LIGHT	OF THE WORLD. NOBODY IN IRELAND OF ANY INTELLIGENCE
SUPR I (36)	BEGAN TO SHINE LIKE NEWLY LIT FLAMES IT WAS BY NO	LIGHT	OF THEIR OWN, BUT BY THE RADIANCE OF THE DAWNING MORAL
3PLA PREFACE(R37)	AND SHAKESPEAR HAVE ALREADY SHEWN THEM IN THE	LIGHT	OF THEIR TIME. FOR EXAMPLE, HOMER PRESENTED ACHILLES
3PLA PREFACE(R33)	ITS PHILOSOPHY WHAT THEY SAID IN THE DIALECT AND	LIGHT	OF THEIRS. DO NOT BE MISLED BY THE SHAKESPEAR FANCIERS
2TRU I SD(37)	CANT BEAR IT: TURN IT OFF. THE NURSE SWITCHES THE	LIGHT	OFF. /THE PATIENT/ SO INCONSIDERATE OF YOU! THE NURSE
JOAN PREFACE(38)	PRAYER OF THE INFERIOR MAY BE THAT HIS CHOICE MAY	LIGHT	ON A GREATER THAN HIMSELF; BUT THE SUB-CONSCIOUS
MILL I SD(157)	WHEN WE ARE TOGETHER. THE REST ALL STARE AT THIS	LIGHT	ON EPIFANIA'S HABITS. /EPIFANIA/ IT IS QUITE TRUE: I
JITT II (50)	ME. /JITTA/ (ROUND-EYED FOR A MOMENT AT THIS NEW	LIGHT	ON HER CONDUCT) HOW CLEVER OF YOU, ALFRED! YOU HAVE
PHIL II (95)	IT WHEN I SAY THAT IT MAY THROW AN IMPORTANT	LIGHT	ON HER FATHER'S CASE. THE FIRST THING, OF COURSE, IS
MTH2 (47)	AND VOLCANOES AND SO FORTH: THEY THROW SUCH A	LIGHT	ON THE AGE OF THE EARTH. (WITH CONVICTION) THERE IS
DEVL III (57)	SETTLED THE QUESTION, SIR-- THROWN A FLOOD OF	LIGHT	ON THE SITUATION. WHAT A COMFORT TO ME TO FEEL THAT I
DEST (194)	OTHER. /GIUSEPPE/ (PITEOUSLY, AS HE PLACES THE	LIGHT	ON THE TABLE) EXCELLENCY: WHAT WERE YOU LOOKING UP AT
LION PREFACE(63)	THOUGHT AND EXPERIENCE HAVE THROWN NO FRESH	LIGHT	ON THE VIEWS OF JESUS, WHEN SWIFT HAD OCCASION TO
MILL PREFACE(128)	PLAIN FACT OF POLITICAL PATHOLOGY. JUDGED IN THIS	LIGHT	OUR PRESENT PREDICAMENT IS LAMENTABLE. WE NO LONGER
HART III (146)	TO SAY WE'LL BE SUMMONED IF WE DONT PUT THAT	LIGHT	OUT: IT CAN BE SEEN FOR MILES. /HECTOR/ IT SHALL BE
HART III (146)	WHO PUT THAT LIGHT OUT? WHO DARED PUT THAT	LIGHT	OUT? /NURSE GUINNESS/ (RUNNING IN FROM THE HOUSE TO
HART III (145)	GOES OUT. /HECTOR/ (FURIOUSLY) WHO PUT THAT	LIGHT	OUT? WHO DARED PUT THAT LIGHT OUT? /NURSE GUINNESS/
JITT I (25)	AT THE WALL TO SAVE HIMSELF; STRIKES THE ELECTRIC	LIGHT	OUT BY CHANCE; REELS BACK INTO THE MIDDLE OF THE ROOM;
VWOO 3 (142)	IT WILL BE DARK AGAIN BEFORE YOU CAN CLEAR THE	LIGHT	OUT OF YOUR EYES; BUT YOU WILL HAVE SEEN; AND FOR EVER
HART II SD(89)	HE FALLS ASLEEP. ELLIE STEALS AWAY; TURNS THE	LIGHT	OUT; AND GOES INTO THE GARDEN. NURSE GUINNESS OPENS
HART I (79)	SMALL AS IT IS, IS DIVINE, AND THAT THE RED	LIGHT	OVER THEIR DOOR IS HELL FIRE. I SHOULD SPARE THEM IN
MILL II SD(166)	AGAINST THE WALL; AND ON IT HANGS THE HAT AND	LIGHT	OVERCOAT OF MR ADRIAN BLENDERBLAND. HE, WITH EPIFANIA,
PYGM I SD(208)	ABOUT THE ANKLES. HE IS IN EVENING DRESS, WITH A	LIGHT	OVERCOAT. HE TAKES THE PLACE LEFT VACANT BY THE
NEVR II SD(236)	UNFASHIONABLENESS OF HIS REEFER JACKET, WEARS A	LIGHT	OVERCOAT. HE STOPS AT THE CHAIR LEFT BY M'COMAS IN THE
MTH5 SD(214)	SHOULDERS A BURDEN COVERED WITH A GORGEOUS BUT	LIGHT	PALL. BEFORE THEM CERTAIN OFFICIAL MAIDENS CARRY A NEW
WIDO I SD(5)	AND GENTLEMAN, FOLLOWED BY A PORTER WITH SOME	LIGHT	PARCELS, NOT LUGGAGE, BUT SHOP PURCHASES, COME INTO
BULL IV (172)	BY THE WAY, I BELIEVE I CAN DO BETTER THAN A	LIGHT	RAILWAY HERE. THERE SEEMS TO BE NO QUESTION NOW THAT
METH PREFACE(R38)	AND OUTLETS, TELEPHONE TRANSMITTERS IN HIS EARS,	LIGHT	RECORDERS AND LENSES IN HIS EYES: WAS IT CONCEIVABLE
WIDO I (19)	TRENCH HURRIES AFTER HER THROUGH THE GATE. THE	LIGHT	REDDENS AS THE RHENISH SUNSET BEGINS. COKANE, MAKING
2TRU I (29)	BUT YOU MUST NOT WORRY. IT IS NOT SERIOUS: A	LIGHT	RUBEOLA: YOU CAN HARDLY CALL IT MEASLES. WE SHALL PULL
JITT I (25)	AGAINST THE BODY). OH GOD! (SHE SWITCHES ON THE	LIGHT	) BRUNO. (SHE RUSHES TO HIM AND KNEELS BY HIM).
SUPR I (40)	(LOOKING QUICKLY AT HIM AS IF THIS WERE A NEW	LIGHT	) SURELY YOU ARE NOT SO ABSURD AS TO BE JEALOUS OF
HART II (90)	IT? (SHE GOES BACK TO THE DOOR AND TURNS ON THE	LIGHT	). OH, MR MANGAN, SIR, I HOPE I HAVNT HURT YOU
PPP (195)	COME IN, ADOLPHUS (SHE SWITCHES ON THE ELECTRIC	LIGHT	). /ADOLPHUS/ (WITHOUT) SOMETHING MOST IMPORTANT HAS
MTH2 (82)	EVIDENTLY VERY UNFAVORABLY AFFECTED BY THIS NEW	LIGHT	). SAVVY AND HASLAM LOOK AT ONE ANOTHER WITH
POSN PREFACE(386)	OF WHIG STATESMEN TO SEE THEM, IN A HEROIC	LIGHT	; AND IT UNQUESTIONABLY VINDICATES AND ENNOBLES A
PYGM EPILOG (296)	SOCIAL FAILURE, HAD NEVER SEEN HERSELF IN EITHER	LIGHT	; FOR, THOUGH TO SOME EXTENT RIDICULED AND MIMICKED IN
POSN PREFACE(432)	VIOLENCE, THE DRINKING-BAR HUMOR INTO WHICH THE	LIGHT	SHINES IN THE PLAY ARE LICENSED, BUT THE LIGHT ITSELF
MTH4 III SD(194)	CHANGING IN INTENSITY. A SHAFT OF VIOLET	LIGHT	SHOOTS UPWARD; AND A VERY HARMONIOUS AND SILVERY
BULL III (119)	THE HOUSE WAS FALLING. BUT THEN I'M A VERY	LIGHT	SLEEPER. /LARRY/ I SEEM TO RECOLLECT THAT ONE OF THE
MRS I SD(193)	AND AGREEABLY DISRESPECTFUL MANNERS. HE CARRIES A	LIGHT	SPORTING MAGAZINE RIFLE. /THE YOUNG GENTLEMAN/ HALLO!
CLEO I SD(106)	AS A SPHINX PEDESTALLED ON THE SANDS. THE	LIGHT	STILL CLEARS, UNTIL THE UPRAISED EYES OF THE IMAGE ARE
HART I SD(43)	STERN GALLERY ARE BOOKSHELVES. THERE ARE ELECTRIC	LIGHT	SWITCHES BESIDE THE DOOR LEADING TO THE HALL AND THE
KING I (207)	OF THE DIVVLE. BUT WHY NOT FOLLOW THE INNER	LIGHT	THAT HAS SAVED YOU FROM THE CHURCHES? BE NEITHER
METH PREFACE(R74)	SWEET THE TRADITION THAT GOOD PEOPLE FOLLOW A	LIGHT	THAT SHINES WITHIN AND ABOVE AND AHEAD OF THEM, THAT
JITT II (29)	LUCK TO DIE IN THE DARK. WE ARE NOT CALLED ON TO	LIGHT	THE CANDLE, ARE WE? /LENKHEIM/ WE ARE NOT; BUT WHAT
APPL I (222)	TO TEAR UP MAGNA CARTA IN TRAFALGAR SQUARE, AND	LIGHT	THE FIRES OF SMITHFIELD TO BURN EVERY MEMBER OF THE
KING I (198)	FIND PLENTY OF WILLING TOOLS. BUT I WOULD NOT	LIGHT	THE FIRES OF SMITHFIELD AGAIN IF I WERE YOU. YOUR PET
CLEO I (113)	TO SHEW THE THRONE. /CAESAR/ ORDER THE SLAVE TO	LIGHT	THE LAMPS. /CLEOPATRA/ (SHYLY) DO YOU THINK I MAY?
LION EPILOG (147)	PEOPLE WHO ARE SHEWN BY THEIR INNER	LIGHT	THE POSSIBILITY OF A BETTER WORLD BASED ON THE DEMAND
DEVL I (12)	YOURSELF. GO AND WAKE THAT GIRL; AND THEN	LIGHT	THE STOVE IN THE SHED: YOU CANT HAVE YOUR BREAKFAST
APPL PREFACE(173)	OF STRONG CHARACTER IN STRONG POSITIONS. IN THIS	LIGHT	THE STYLE OF FIGHTING ADOPTED BY THE ANTAGONISTS IN
JITT I SD(10)	SHE GOES INTO THE BEDROOM AND SWITCHES ON THE	LIGHT	THERE. THE ROSEATE HANGINGS OF THE BED APPEAR TO GREAT
ARMS I SD(7)	SHE RUNS TO THE DRESSING TABLE, BLOWS OUT THE	LIGHT	THERE, AND HURRIES BACK TO BED IN THE DARK, NOTHING
LION PREFACE(90)	AND INTERESTING TO MODERN THINKERS. IN ANY OTHER	LIGHT	THEY ARE NEITHER CREDIBLE, INTELLIGIBLE, NOR
FABL PREFACE(65)	HIM AND UPSETTING HIS HEALTH. BY BRINGING IT TO	LIGHT	THEY CURED THE PATIENT. WHEN THIS FREUDIAN TECHNIQUE
UNPL PREFACE(R21)	SORT OF PERSON HE MEANT HIM TO INCARNATE, WHAT A	LIGHT	THEY WOULD SHED, NOT ONLY ON THE PLAY, BUT ON THE
JOAN 6 (129)	I HAVE SEEN OF HERESY, YOU WOULD NOT THINK IT A	LIGHT	THING EVEN IN ITS MOST APPARENTLY HARMLESS AND EVEN
BARB III (337)	SUDDEN VEHEMENCE). JUSTIFY YOURSELF: SHEW ME SOME	LIGHT	THROUGH THE DARKNESS OF THIS DREADFUL PLACE, WITH ITS
SHAK (143)	ARE MORTAL, FOR A MOMENT SUFFER MY GLIMMERING	LIGHT	TO SHINE. A LIGHT APPEARS BETWEEN THEM. /SHAKES/ OUT,
LION PREFACE(68)	AT LAST THAT NO MAN COULD FOLLOW HIS INNER	LIGHT	UNTIL HE WAS FREE FROM THEIR COMPULSION. THE ABSENCE

VWOO 3 (142)	GET QUITE AWAY FROM THE WORLD OF SENSE. WE SHALL	LIGHT	UP FOR ONEANOTHER A LAMP IN THE HOLY OF HOLIES IN THE
CAND III (129)	UTTERLY FROM HIS LIPS AND NOSTRILS AS HIS EYES	LIGHT	UP WITH PATHETIC SPIRITUALITY) OH, NOW I CANT SAY
SIM II (72)	HEAVEN'S DAY OF JUDGMENT, IT WILL CONTINUE TO	LIGHT	US AND WARM US; AND THERE WILL BE NO NOISE NOR WRATH
CATH 4,SD(187)	IN THE BALLROOM AS HE DOES SO. THE WHITE	LIGHT	VANISHES AND THE MUSIC IS MUFFLED AS THE CURTAINS FALL
PHIL I (72)	A LITTLE AWAY ON THE STOOL) I AM AFRAID, FROM THE	LIGHT	WAY YOU SPEAK OF IT, YOU DID NOT SOUND THE RIGHT
SUPR PREFACE(R39)	GORGES ITSELF WITH ELECTRICITY AND GIVES YOU NO	LIGHT	WHATEVER, BUT HERE AND THERE OCCURS A SCRAP OF
HART II SD(89)	NURSE GUINNESS OPENS THE DOOR AND IS SEEN IN THE	LIGHT	WHICH COMES IN FROM THE HALL. /GUINNESS/ (SPEAKING TO
LION PREFACE(74)	THEIR DOCTRINE DID NOT CONTAIN A RAY OF THAT	LIGHT	WHICH REVEALS JESUS AS ONE OF THE REDEEMERS OF MEN
MTH5 (258)	IT IS GROWING DARK. /ACIS/ NIGHT IS FALLING. THE	LIGHT	WILL COME BACK TOMORROW. /THE NEWLY BORN/ WHAT IS
APPL II (257)	WELL, I THINK THE OPEN AIR AND THE EVENING	LIGHT	WILL HAVE A QUIETING EFFECT ON THEM. THEY CANNOT MAKE
SUPR PREFACE(R39)	OF THESE SUSCEPTIBLES. IF YOU STUDY THE ELECTRIC	LIGHT	WITH WHICH I SUPPLY YOU IN THAT BUMBLEDONIAN PUBLIC
PYGM EPILOG (295)	WHO WAS OBVIOUSLY INTENDED BY NATURE FOR SUCH	LIGHT	WORK AS AMUSING ELIZA, WHICH, HIGGINS DECLARED, WAS A
FABL PREFACE(63)	AS TO WHAT MAY HAPPEN IN THE NEXT MILLION	LIGHT	YEARS THAT ARE TROUBLING ME IN THE QUEER SECOND WIND
FABL PREFACE(93)	TRAVELLING AT SUPERSONIC SPEED TAKES A THOUSAND	LIGHT	YEARS TO REACH THE NEAREST STAR, HOW LONG WILL IT TAKE
JOAN 6 (145)	UP THE PAPER, AND TEARS IT INTO FRAGMENTS)	LIGHT	YOUR FIRE: DO YOU THINK I DREAD IT AS MUCH AS THE LIFE
JOAN 6 (146)	/THE CHAPLAIN/ (TO THE EXECUTIONER)	LIGHT	YOUR FIRE, MAN. TO THE STAKE WITH HER. THE EXECUTIONER
MRS IV SD(235)	A PLATE-GLASS WINDOW, DISTEMPERED WALLS, ELECTRIC	LIGHT	, AND A PATENT STOVE. SATURDAY AFTERNOON. THE CHIMNEYS
JITT III SD(52)	SITS AT THE HEAD OF IT WITH HER BACK TO THE	LIGHT	, AND ALFRED AND FESSLER AT THE SIDES OF IT TO HER
PPP SD(194)	EMOTION. LADY MAGNESIA SWITCHES OFF THE ELECTRIC	LIGHT	, AND IMMEDIATELY HEARS THE ANGELS QUITE DISTINCTLY.
SUPR HANDBOK(209)	A TRICYCLE, WRITES HIS DISPATCHES BY THE ELECTRIC	LIGHT	, AND INSTRUCTS HIS STOCKBROKER THROUGH THE
LADY PREFACE(208)	I NEVER SUCCEEDED IN THROWING THE FAINTEST	LIGHT	, AT A TIME WHEN NOBODY ELSE THOUGHT MY OPINION, ON
JOAN 1 (69)	HANDS) OH, SQUIRE! YOUR HEAD IS ALL CIRCLED WITH	LIGHT	, LIKE A SAINT'S. /POULENGEY/ HOW IS SHE TO GET INTO
DEST (194)	IT OPEN, SHOUTING) HALLO! GIUSEPPE! WHERES THAT	LIGHT	, MAN? (HE COMES BETWEEN THE TABLE AND THE
KING I (203)	/LOUISE/ TAKE THE GENTLEMAN'S MIND OFF HIS INNER	LIGHT	, NELL. GIVE US A SPEECH. /NELL/ THEY DONT WANT A
SUPR III SD(86)	OMNIPRESENT NOTHING. NO SKY, NO PEAKS, NO	LIGHT	, NO SOUND, NO TIME NOR SPACE, UTTER VOID. THEN
BULL PREFACE(33)	TO DISESTABLISH THE IRISH CHURCH. IT WAS BY THE	LIGHT	, NOT OF REASON, BUT OF THE MOON, THAT THE NEED FOR
GENV IV (110)	YOU LIKE A HEAVY BURDEN; AND YOUR HEART WILL BE	LIGHT	, OH, SO LIGHT! YOU HAVE NEVER BEEN HAPPY. I CAN SEE
MILL PREFACE(124)	TRICK WITH THE SACRED VELOCITY OF	LIGHT	, QUITE A STRONG CASE COULD HAVE BEEN MADE OUT BY THE
3PLA PREFACE(R38)	ALLOW ME TO SET FORTH CAESAR IN THE SAME MODERN	LIGHT	, TAKING THE PLATFORM FROM SHAKESPEAR AS HE FROM
CAPT I SD(235)	HE STANDS FOR A MOMENT, SATURNINE IN THE RUDDY	LIGHT	, TO SEE WHO IS PRESENT, LOOKING IN A SINGULAR AND
HART III (129)	(COMING TO THE BACK OF THE GARDEN SEAT, INTO THE	LIGHT	, WITH MANGAN) I THINK I SHALL. HE KEEPS TELLING ME HE
LION PREFACE(78)	SINS; BUT HE ALSO WANTS TO REACH " YONDER SHINING	LIGHT	"; AND WHEN AT LAST HIS BUNDLE FALLS OFF HIM INTO THE
GENV IV (110)	BURDEN; AND YOUR HEART WILL BE LIGHT, OH, SO	LIGHT	! YOU HAVE NEVER BEEN HAPPY. I CAN SEE IT IN YOUR

LIGHTED

MIS. (150)	AND TURNED YOU OFF INTO THE FLOWER BED, AND THEN	LIGHTED	BESIDE YOU LIKE A BIRD. /PERCIVAL/ HOW HE KEPT HIS
ARMS I SD(3)	CAN BE FELT EVEN FROM THE PORTRAIT. THE ROOM IS	LIGHTED	BY A CANDLE ON THE CHEST OF DRAWERS, AND ANOTHER ON
JITT III SD(52)	AT THE WIDOW FROM TIME TO TIME. THE ROOM IS	LIGHTED	BY A LARGE BAY WINDOW, WITH A WINDOW-SEAT UNDER IT.
MILL III SD(179)	EXTEND TO THE SIDE WHERE THE COUPLE SIT, WHICH IS	LIGHTED	BY A SMALL ELECTRIC BULB ON A WIRE. BETWEEN THE
CLEO PRO2,SD(96)	ON IT, TO LOOK OVER THE WALL. THE YARD IS	LIGHTED	BY A TORCH STUCK IN THE WALL. AS THE LAUGHTER FROM
JOAN EPIL,SD(152)	IS A LITTLE TABLE WITH A PICTURE OF THE VIRGIN,	LIGHTED	BY CANDLES OF PAINTED WAX. THE WALLS ARE HUNG FROM
SUPR HANDBOK(207)	FIRES OF SMITHFIELD AND OF THE INQUISITION WERE	LIGHTED	BY EARNESTLY PIOUS PEOPLE, WHO WERE KIND AND GOOD AS
2TRU I SD(27)	AT EACH SIDE OF THE DRESSING TABLE. THE ROOM IS	LIGHTED	BY INVISIBLE CORNICE LIGHTS, AND BY TWO MIRROR
LIED SD(187)	THE EVENING. THE CURTAINS ARE DRAWN AND THE LAMPS	LIGHTED	IN THE DRAWING ROOM OF HER FLAT IN CROMWELL ROAD.
WIDO III SD(49)	EVENING: FIRE BURNING, CURTAINS DRAWN, AND LAMPS	LIGHTED	. SARTORIUS AND BLANCHE ARE SITTING GLUMLY NEAR THE
CAND III SD(127)	EVENING. THE CURTAINS ARE DRAWN, AND THE LAMPS	LIGHTED	. THE TYPEWRITER IS IN ITS CASE; THE LARGE TABLE HAS
MTH3 (100)	WRETCHED PALE FACES THAT HAVE TO BE MATCHED AND	LIGHTED	. YOURS IS ALWAYS RIGHT. /THE NEGRESS/ YES: IT IS A
MRS II SD(198)	PLATE-RACK. IN THE CENTRE A TABLE STANDS WITH A	LIGHTED	LAMP ON IT. VIVIE'S BOOKS AND WRITING MATERIALS ARE
PYGM IV SD(260)	NO! ELIZA OPENS THE DOOR AND IS SEEN ON THE	LIGHTED	LANDING IN OPERA CLOAK, BRILLIANT EVENING DRESS, AND
LION PREFACE(65)	AND PAINFULLY PINCHED. PEOPLE FLING KNIVES AND	LIGHTED	PARAFFIN LAMPS AT ONE ANOTHER IN A DISPUTE OVER A
MTH4 III SD(194)	AN ABYSS. DEAD SILENCE. THE GALLERY IS BRIGHTLY	LIGHTED	; BUT BEYOND IS A VAST GLOOM, CONTINUALLY CHANGING
NEVR IV SD(282)	NINE O' CLOCK. NOBODY PRESENT. THE LAMPS ARE	LIGHTED	; BUT THE CURTAINS ARE NOT DRAWN. THE WINDOW STANDS
HART PREFACE(27)	THUNDERBOLTS, AND HAVE HELPED TO EXTINGUISH THE	LIGHTED	THATCH AND CLEAR AWAY THE BITS OF THE BROKEN
MTH3 (132)	FOR WHICH HE HAS HIMSELF LAID THE CHARGE AND	LIGHTED	THE FUSE, BUT I AM NOT SURPRISED, BECAUSE, AS A
ROCK II SD(250)	HIS INTRODUCTION OF HIMSELF AS A DUKE, HER EYES	LIGHTED	UP; AND SHE HAS MOVED MENACINGLY ACROSS THE HEARTH
CLEO I (113)	WITH YOU; AND HOW DARE YOU ORDER THE LAMPS TO BE	LIGHTED	WITHOUT MY PERMISSION? (CLEOPATRA IS DUMB WITH

LIGHTENED

LADY PREFACE(213)	HAS READ MR HARRIS'S STORIES DESIRES TO HAVE THEM	LIGHTENED	BY CHAPTERS FROM THE HAND OF ARTEMUS WARD. YET HE
SUPR III (92)	INTO WHICH HER DULL YELLOW HALO HAS SUDDENLY	LIGHTENED	ONE MIGHT ALMOST MISTAKE HER FOR ANN WHITEFIELD).
SUPR HANDBOK(175)	IS AN INFERIOR. AND YET REVOLUTIONS HAVE NEVER	LIGHTENED	THE BURDEN OF TYRANNY: THEY HAVE ONLY SHIFTED IT

LIGHTENS

MTH1 I (18)	DO NOT LISTEN TO HER: THE NOISE IS GOOD: IT	LIGHTENS	MY HEART. YOU ARE A JOLLY SNAKE. BUT YOU HAVE NOT
LION I (122)	DAY I FEEL HAPPIER, MORE CONFIDENT. EVERY DAY	LIGHTENS	THE LOAD OF THE GREAT TERROR. /LAVINIA/ THE GREAT

LIGHTER

DOCT PREFACE(40)	THAT A DOG DEPRIVED OF FOOD GETS PROGRESSIVELY	LIGHTER	AND WEAKER, BECOMING REMARKABLY EMACIATED, AND
SUPR III SD(136)	SHOCK, A MOUNTAIN PEAK SHEWING FAINTLY AGAINST A	LIGHTER	BACKGROUND. THE SKY HAS RETURNED FROM AFAR; AND WE
MTH1 II (29)	AGONIES OF WHICH YOU KNOW NOTHING? THE ARROW IS	LIGHTER	IN THE HAND THAN THE SPADE; BUT THE ENERGY THAT
POSN PREFACE(418)	AND TOLERANT (OR INDIFFERENT) MODERN CITY. THE	LIGHTER	PLAYS WOULD BE NO BETTER OFF. WHAT LAWYER COULD
MIS. PREFACE(36)	FROM SCHOOL TO THE FACTORY IS NOT CAUSED BY	LIGHTER	TASKS OR SHORTER HOURS IN THE FACTORY, NOR
GENV PREFACE(26)	MAY SEE THE DISCOVERY OF THAT POISONOUS GAS	LIGHTER	THAN AIR AND CAPABLE BEFORE IT EVAPORATES THROUGH
GENV PREFACE(10)	AND IMPROVE ON IT, OR THEY MAY DISCOVER A GAS	LIGHTER	THAN AIR, DEADLY BUT NOT DESTRUCTIVE. AND THEN WHERE
FABL I (104)	SHE GOES AWAY. /YOUNG MAN/ (STILL THOUGHTFUL)	LIGHTER	THAN AIR, EH? (SLOWER) LIGH-- TER-- THAN-- AIR?
FABL I (103)	STOP WAR. SOMEBODY WILL DISCOVER A POISON GAS	LIGHTER	THAN AIR! IT MAY KILL THE INHABITANTS OF A CITY;
LADY PREFACE(207)	IN THE EARLY DAYS OF QUEEN VICTORIA. ANY TINGE	LIGHTER	THAN RAVEN BLACK MUST BE HELD FATAL TO THE STRONGEST
BULL III (136)	FOR THE PEOPLE OF ROSSCULLEN. NOR SHOULD THE	LIGHTER	, BUT STILL MOST IMPORTANT QUESTION OF THE SPORTS OF

LIGHTEST

SUPR HANDBOK(180)	RING, WILL THEMSELVES BE LAUGHED ASIDE AS THE	LIGHTEST	OF TRIFLES IF THEY CROSS THIS CONCEPTION WHEN IT
CATH PREFACE(153)	CATHERINE WHOSE GALLANTRIES PROVIDE SOME OF THE	LIGHTEST	PAGES OF MODERN HISTORY. GREAT CATHERINE, IT IS
BARB III SD(326)	OF AN OFFICE, WHICH, LIKE THE SHEDS, IS OF THE	LIGHTEST	POSSIBLE CONSTRUCTION. CUSINS ARRIVES BY THE PATH
GENV IV (89)	WALLS CAN HIDE YOU, AND NO DISTANCE DEADEN YOUR	LIGHTEST	WHISPER. WE ARE ALL SEEN AND HEARD IN ROME, IN

LIGHTHEADED

BARB II (277)	A FEW MINUTES PRAYER REVIVES YOU! I WAS QUITE	LIGHTHEADED	AT TWELVE O' CLOCK, I WAS SO TIRED; BUT MAJOR

LIGHTHEARTED

LION I SD(110)	ARE DOGGED AND INDIFFERENT, THE CHRISTIANS	LIGHTHEARTED	AND DETERMINED TO TREAT THEIR HARDSHIPS AS A
SUPR PREFACE(R32)	BOTTOM A COMBINATION OF SOUND MORAL JUDGMENT WITH	LIGHTHEARTED	GOOD HUMOR. BUT THEY ARE CONCERNED WITH THE
FANY I (281)	MYSELF; AND WE BOTH GET A BIT GIDDY WHEN WE'RE	LIGHTHEARTED	. HIM AND ME IS A PAIR, I'M AFRAID. /GILBEY/

LIGHTHEARTEDNESS

CLEO NOTES (212)	OF IT, THERE IS STILL ABUNDANT EVIDENCE OF HIS	LIGHTHEARTEDNESS	AND ADVENTUROUSNESS. INDEED IT IS CLEAR

LIGHTHOUSE

CLEO III (165)	STAY HERE, THEN, ALONE, UNTIL I RECAPTURE THE	LIGHTHOUSE	: I WILL NOT FORGET YOU. NOW, RUFIO. /RUFIO/ YOU
CLEO III SD(161)	HEADS WITH A RATTLE. BRITANNUS COMES FROM THE	LIGHTHOUSE	AND HELPS THEM TO UNCORD THE CARPET.
CLEO III (149)	/APOLLODORUS/ WELL, CENTURION; AND HAS NOT THE	LIGHTHOUSE	BEEN WITHIN THE ROMAN LINES SINCE CAESAR LANDED
CLEO III (154)	FAREWELL, FTATATEETA. I SHALL BE AT THE	LIGHTHOUSE	BEFORE THE EGYPTIANS. (HE DESCENDS THE STEPS).
CLEO III SD(155)	A HUGE CHAIN WITH A HOOK HANGS DOWN FROM THE	LIGHTHOUSE	CRANE ABOVE HIS HEAD. FAGGOTS LIKE THE ONE HE
CLEO III SD(155)	EVIDENTLY ILL AT EASE. BRITANNUS COMES OUT OF THE	LIGHTHOUSE	DOOR. /RUFIO/ WELL, MY BRITISH ISLANDER. HAVE YOU
CLEO III (158)	THAT IS CAESAR, SIR. /RUFIO/ (APPEARING AT THE	LIGHTHOUSE	DOOR) WHATS THE MATTER NOW? /APOLLODORUS/ HAIL,
CLEO III SD(155)	SIDE. BEHIND HIM THE GREAT STONE PEDESTAL OF THE	LIGHTHOUSE	IS SHUT IN FROM THE OPEN SEA BY A LOW STONE
CLEO III (160)	IS DRAWN UP AND COMES ROUND AGAIN FROM BEHIND THE	LIGHTHOUSE	. APOLLODORUS IS SWINGING IN THE AIR WITH HIS
CLEO III (148)	WHITHER SHALL I ROW MY QUEEN? /CLEOPATRA/ TO THE	LIGHTHOUSE	. COME. (SHE MAKES FOR THE STEPS). /SENTINEL/ (

CLEO II (142)	LIBRARY WILL KEEP THEM BUSY WHILST WE SEIZE THE	LIGHTHOUSE	. EH? (HE RUSHES OUT BUOYANTLY THROUGH THE
CLEO III (149)	TO TAKE BOAT, AND GO-- SO SHE SAID-- TO THE	LIGHTHOUSE	. I STOPPED HER, AS I WAS ORDERED TO; AND SHE SET
CLEO II (136)	AND SEIZE THE PHAROS-- THAT ISLAND WITH THE	LIGHTHOUSE	. LEAVE HALF OUR MEN BEHIND TO HOLD THE BEACH AND
CLEO II (142)	MEN BACK: THE BOATS WILL RACE ONE ANOTHER FOR THE	LIGHTHOUSE	. /CAESAR/ (DRAWING HIS SWORD AND TRYING THE
CLEO III SD(160)	IT THEN SWINGS ROUND OUT OF SIGHT BEHIND THE	LIGHTHOUSE	. /CAESAR/ FEAR NOT, MY SON RUFIO. WHEN THE FIRST
CLEO III SD(160)	BACK THE WAY HE CAME. BRITANNUS GOES INTO THE	LIGHTHOUSE	. /RUFIO/ (ILL-HUMOREDLY) ARE YOU REALLY GOING
SIM I SD(36)	THAT IS VISIBLE OF THE PORT BEING THE TOP OF THE	LIGHTHOUSE	. THERE ARE TREES ENOUGH IN ALL DIRECTIONS TO
CLEO III (158)	AT THE BOILING WATER MACHINE. (HE GOES INTO THE	LIGHTHOUSE	). /BRITANNUS/ (WITH GENUINE FEELING) O CAESAR,
CLEO III (156)	WHAT THEIR BUSINESS IS. (HE HURRIES OUT PAST THE	LIGHTHOUSE	). /CAESAR/ (COMING AWAY FROM THE PARAPET,
CLEO III (158)	FLIPPANT ROMAN WAY. (APOLLODORUS COMES PAST THE	LIGHTHOUSE	). WHAT NOW? /BRITANNUS/ (TURNING QUICKLY, AND
CLEO IV (169)	OLDER. /CHARMIAN/ WELL, GO UP TO THE TOP OF THE	LIGHTHOUSE	; AND GET SOMEBODY TO TAKE YOU BY THE HAIR AND
CLEO III (144)	PAST THREE SENTINELS, ALL SO BUSY STARING AT THE	LIGHTHOUSE	THAT NOT ONE OF THEM CHALLENGED ME. IS THIS ROMAN
CLEO III SD(144)	ON GUARD, PILUM IN HAND, LOOKING OUT TO THE	LIGHTHOUSE	WITH STRAINED ATTENTION, HIS LEFT HAND SHADING
CLEO III SD(144)	CONNECTED WITH IT BY A NARROW MOLE, IS THE FAMOUS	LIGHTHOUSE	, A GIGANTIC SQUARE TOWER OF WHITE MARBLE
CLEO II (138)	/CAESAR/ (ANXIOUSLY) AND THE EAST HARBOR? THE	LIGHTHOUSE	, RUFIO? /RUFIO/ (WITH A SUDDEN SPLUTTER OF
CLEO III (159)	CAESAR: I CANNOT RETURN. AS I APPROACHED THE	LIGHTHOUSE	, SOME FOOL THREW A GREAT LEATHERN BAG INTO THE
CLEO III SD(155)	ON A FAGGOT OF BRUSHWOOD OUTSIDE THE DOOR OF THE	LIGHTHOUSE	, WHICH TOWERS GIGANTIC TO THE CLOUDS ON HIS

LIGHTING

SUPR III SD(79)	HAVE LAMPS WHICH CAN BE TURNED TO ACCOUNT FOR	LIGHTING	A CARD PARTY. /STRAKER/ (CALLING AFTER THEM) DONT
POSN PREFACE(406)	THE AUDITORIUM OF A THEATRE, WITH ITS BRILLIANT	LIGHTING	AND LUXURIOUS DECORATIONS, MAKES A VERY EFFECTIVE
FABL II (105)	AND THE WIRELESS AND WATER SUPPLIES AND THE	LIGHTING	AND THE MARKETS AND ALL THE REST OF IT GOING.
APPL PREFACE(193)	WREN. HE HAD BEEN CONCERNED IN AN ELECTRIC	LIGHTING	BUSINESS, AND HAD BEEN REVOLTED BY THE PRODIGIOUS
BULL IV (173)	SUPERANNUATED FOLLY: I SHALL WANT IT FOR ELECTRIC	LIGHTING	. /LARRY/ WHAT IS THE USE OF GIVING LAND TO SUCH
CAND II SD(113)	A READING LAMP TRIMMED, FILLED, AND READY FOR	LIGHTING	. SHE PLACES IT ON THE TABLE NEAR MORELL, READY FOR
DOCT I SD(82)	IS A GASALIER; BUT IT IS A CONVERT TO ELECTRIC	LIGHTING	. THE WALL PAPER AND CARPETS ARE MOSTLY GREEN,
BASH PREFACE(87)	HE SHOULD DO SO IN PERIL OF INADVERTENTLY	LIGHTING	ON A PURPLE PATCH FROM HAMLET OR FAUSTUS. I ALSO
MTH2 SD(62)	CIGARET INTO THE FIRE. HASLAM, ON THE POINT OF	LIGHTING	ONE FOR HIMSELF, CHANGES HIS MIND. /LUBIN/ (SHREWD
DOCT IV (164)	DYING ACTOR OF HIS AUDIENCE? /LOUIS/ (HIS FACE	LIGHTING	UP FAINTLY WITH MISCHIEVOUS GLEE) I HEARD THAT,
SUPR IV (157)	NOT DREAD DISILLUSIONIZING JACK. /ANN/ (HER FACE	LIGHTING	UP WITH MISCHIEVOUS ECSTASY-- WHISPERING) I CANT:
APPL INTRLUD(243)	(OPENING THE BOOK AND FINDING THE PAGE, HIS EYE	LIGHTING	UP WITH RECOGNITION AS HE LOOKS AT IT) AH! THE
PHIL II (96)	CRAVEN TO HER SISTER. /CUTHBERTSON/ (HIS EYE	LIGHTING	UP) AH, JULIA! I BELIEVE YOU. A SPLENDID FINE
CLEO II (133)	BACK AGAIN? /CLEOPATRA/ (EAGERLY, HER EYES	LIGHTING	UP) I WILL TELL YOU. A BEAUTIFUL YOUNG MAN, WITH
BULL II (114)	MAY NOT ARRIVE UNTIL TO-MORROW. /NORA/ (HER FACE	LIGHTING	UP) IS THAT THE TRUTH? /BROADBENT/ YES: THATS THE
HART III (139)	NO BLESSING ON MY HAPPINESS. /ELLIE/ (HER FACE	LIGHTING	UP) LIFE WITH A BLESSING! THAT IS WHAT I WANT. NOW
BARB II (277)	WORK ALL THE BETTER AFTER. /JENNY/ (HER EYES	LIGHTING	UP) OH ISNT IT WONDERFUL HOW A FEW MINUTES PRAYER
BARB III (325)	AND LEAVE NO MARK ON HIM? /BARBARA/ (HER FACE	LIGHTING	UP) OH, YOU ARE RIGHT: HE CAN NEVER BE LOST NOW!
FABL PREFACE(84)	POLICE, SIXPENNY LINKMEN FOR MUNICIPAL ELECTRIC	LIGHTING	, CADIS UNDER PALM TREES FOR JUDGES, CONDOTTIERI
DOCT PREFACE(15)	INSTITUTION WITH LIFTS, VACUUM CLEANERS, ELECTRIC	LIGHTING	, STEAM HEATING, AND MACHINERY THAT TURNS THE
APPL PREFACE(183)	STREETS, BRIDGES, WATER SUPPLIES, POWER SUPPLIES,	LIGHTING	, TRAMWAYS, SCHOOLS, DOCKYARDS, AND PUBLIC AIDS AND

LIGHTLY

SUPR II (66)	HIS HEAD) I CANT DISMISS THAT MAN'S CAWNDUCT AS	LIGHTLY	AS YOU DO, MR TANNER. HOWEVER, I'LL SAY NO MORE.
2TRU PREFACE(15)	COLOR. THE NOBLEMAN WHO FELT THAT GOD WOULD NOT	LIGHTLY	DAMN A MAN OF HIS QUALITY RECEIVED NO COUNTENANCE
6CAL PREFACE(89)	BEEN MISERABLY KILLED FOR TAKING HIS JOB TOO	LIGHTLY	. BUT THE JOURNALIST CRITICS KNEW NOTHING OF THIS. A
JOAN 4 (101)	SEEMED TO TAKE THE BURNING OF THIS POOR GIRL TOO	LIGHTLY	. WHEN ONE HAS SEEN WHOLE COUNTRYSIDES BURNT OVER
MTH5 (248)	YOU WHO HAVE ADVANCED FROM IMITATING THE	LIGHTLY	LIVING CHILD TO THE INTENSELY LIVING ANCIENT, IS IT
CATH 1 (169)	NEITHER THE RIGHT NOR THE DISPOSITION TO SPEAK	LIGHTLY	OF HER MAJESTY. /PATIOMKIN/ YOU HAVE CONSCIENTIOUS
BARB II (295)	IS AS MAD AS WE ARE? /UNDERSHAFT/ (PUSHING HIM	LIGHTLY	OFF AND RESUMING HIS EQUANIMITY SUDDENLY AND
JOAN PREFACE(26)	SOLDIERS, BUT A STRAIGHTFORWARD FACT. IT HAS BEEN	LIGHTLY	PLEADED IN EXPLANATION THAT ANATOLE FRANCE IS A
DEVL II (39)	A PAIR OF HANDCUFFS HIDDEN BEHIND HIM, AND SAYS	LIGHTLY	) DID YOU EVER ARREST A MAN OF MY CLOTH BEFORE,
FABL PREFACE(75)	HE BELIEVES THESE CONTRADICTIONS. I ONCE HELD	LIGHTLY	THAT CANDIDATES OF IRRESISTIBLE VOCATION MIGHT SWEAR
NEVR III (264)	/DOLLY/-- A YOUNG MAN'S FANCY-- /PHILIP/--	LIGHTLY	TURNS TO-- THANK YOU (TO MRS CLANDON, WHO HAS
NEVR II SD(236)	MISS. (SHE GOES INTO THE HOTEL). VALENTINE COMES	LIGHTLY	UP THE STEPS FROM THE BEACH, FOLLOWED DOGGEDLY BY
MTH4 I SD(139)	TAKES OUT A SILK HANDKERCHIEF AND DRIES HIS TEARS	LIGHTLY	WITH A BRAVE ATTEMPT TO SMILE THROUGH THEM; AND
MTH3 (123)	INSTEAD OF LEARNING TO LIVE! WHEN I SEE HOW	LIGHTLY	YOU TAKE IT ALL! HOW YOU QUARREL OVER THE CRUMPLED
LION PREFACE(17)	OF CONSCIENCE, WHICH HARDENED MEN BEAR VERY	LIGHTLY	, A DEFINITE DREAD OF HIDEOUS AND ETERNAL TORTURE.

LIGHTMINDED

POSN PREFACE(371)	ITS RULING THOROUGHLY. PLAYS WHICH WERE MERELY	LIGHTMINDED	AND IRRESPONSIBLE IN THEIR VICIOUSNESS WERE
METH PREFACE(R40)	MADE ATHEISTS IN ALL DIRECTIONS AMONG CLEVER AND	LIGHTMINDED	PEOPLE. BUT ATHEISM DID NOT ACCOUNT FOR PALEY'S

LIGHTNESS

NEVR III (281)	LIGHTNESS OF HEAD, AND LIGHTNESS OF FAITH, AND	LIGHTNESS	OF EVERYTHING THAT MAKES A MAN. /VALENTINE/ YES,
NEVR III (281)	OF HEART. /GLORIA/ AND LIGHTNESS OF HEAD, AND	LIGHTNESS	OF FAITH, AND LIGHTNESS OF EVERYTHING THAT MAKES A
NEVR III (281)	/VALENTINE/ LIGHTNESS OF HEART. /GLORIA/ AND	LIGHTNESS	OF HEAD, AND LIGHTNESS OF FAITH, AND LIGHTNESS OF
NEVR III (281)	WHAT GIFTS WERE YOU BORN WITH, PRAY? /VALENTINE/	LIGHTNESS	OF HEART. /GLORIA/ AND LIGHTNESS OF HEAD, AND

LIGHTNIN

BARB II (276)	AS GOOD AS ANY OF EM. I'LL SEE SOMEBODY STRUCK BY	LIGHTNIN	, OR HEAR A VOICE SAYIN " SNOBBY PRICE: WHERE WILL

LIGHTNING

METH PREFACE(R33)	AN UNSPEAKABLY SHOCKING PART. DEFYING THE	LIGHTNING	: A FRUSTRATED EXPERIMENT. ONE EVENING IN 1878 OR
HART I (62)	DID HE GET INTO IT BECAUSE HE WAS AFRAID OF THE	LIGHTNING	? /ELLIE/ OH NO, NO: HE WAS A BABY. THE NAME
BASH II,2, (118)	(TRYING TO RISE) HAVE I BEEN STRUCK BY	LIGHTNING	? /LUCIAN/ SIR, YOUR CONDUCT CAN ONLY BE
ROCK II (265)	ORIGINAL AND I THE IMITATION. DO YOU NOT FEAR THE	LIGHTNING	? THE EARTHQUAKE? THE VENGEANCE OF VISHNU? YOU
JOAN EPIL,SD(152)	FITFULLY WINDY NIGHT IN JUNE 1456, FULL OF SUMMER	LIGHTNING	AFTER MANY DAYS OF HEAT. KING CHARLES THE SEVENTH
GLIM (175)	IN A RICH BARITONE VOICE) WILL HE, BY THUNDER AND	LIGHTNING	AND THE FLOOD AND ALL THE SAINTS, WILL HE? (HE
MTH4 III SD(198)	HOLD ON UNTIL THE SPRING. IN THE FIRST-- TERRIFIC	LIGHTNING	AND THUNDER. THE ELDERLY GENTLEMAN IS KNOCKED
MTH5 (221)	A HALF FEET LONG WHEN I WAS BORN; AND A FLASH OF	LIGHTNING	BURNT IT OFF AND KILLED THE ANCIENT WHO WAS
KING PREFACE(155)	DEFEND IT AS A POSSIBILITY, NEWTON WAS NOT ONLY A	LIGHTNING	CALCULATOR WITH A MONSTROUS MEMORY: HE WAS ALSO A
GENV PREFACE(24)	NEWTONS AND EINSTEINS, BUT OBSCURE ILLITERATE "	LIGHTNING	CALCULATORS," TO WHOM THE ANSWERS TO ARITHMETICAL
MTH5 (230)	THE LIFE FORCE. IT WAS LIKE A WOODEN MAGNET OR A	LIGHTNING	CONDUCTOR MADE OF SILK: IT WOULD NOT TAKE THE
MTH3 (134)	AND SEVENTY MILES! /THE NEGRESS/ THERE IS A	LIGHTNING	EXPRESS ON THE IRISH AIR SERVICE AT HALF-PAST
VWOO 3 (142)	SEIZE US. IT WILL LAST HARDLY LONGER THAN THE	LIGHTNING	FLASH WHICH TURNS THE BLACK NIGHT INTO INFINITE
MILL II (175)	MOSTLY? /EPIFANIA/ EVERYTHING. ANYTHING. LIKE A	LIGHTNING	FLASH. AND THEN THERE IS NO STOPPING ME. /THE
BASH II,1, (108)	AND DID I CHOOSE MY QUICK DIVINING EYE, MY	LIGHTNING	HAND, MY SPRINGING MUSCLE AND UNTIRING HEART? DID
MTH4 III (197)	SERPENTS CURLING IN THE VAPOR. I AM AFRAID OF THE	LIGHTNING	. FINISH IT, PAPA; OR I SHALL DIE. /THE ENVOY/ (
NEVR I (203)	CUTTING A SHEET OF SILK IN TWO WITH A FLASH OF	LIGHTNING	. IT IS THE RESULT OF LONG PRACTICE IN CHECKING
PPP (205)	(SOLEMNLY RISING) THE COPPER ATTRACTED THE	LIGHTNING	. /MAGNESIA/ (RISING) AFTER LIFE'S FITFUL FEVER
MTH5 (240)	WOMAN. THE WRATH OF OZYMANDIAS STRIKES LIKE THE	LIGHTNING	. /THE FEMALE FIGURE/ YOU JUST SAY THAT AGAIN IF
GENV III (79)	IS REMARKABLE: SHE TAKES A POINT LIKE	LIGHTNING	. SHE HAS IN HER VEINS THE LEARNING OF THE ARABS,
JOAN 3 (88)	MAID? /THE PAGE/ NO: THE KINGFISHER. LIKE BLUE	LIGHTNING	. SHE WENT INTO THAT BUSH. /DUNOIS/ (FURIOUSLY
MTH5 (218)	A TREE WILL FALL ON YOU; OR YOU WILL BE STRUCK BY	LIGHTNING	. SOMETHING OR OTHER MUST MAKE AN END OF YOU
METH PREFACE(R57)	BY THE WIND, OR AS THE TREE ITSELF IS STRUCK BY	LIGHTNING	. THAT DID NOT OCCUR TO THE HUMANITARIANS AT THE
MILL PREFACE(122)	IT AS DEFIANT AS THAT OF AJAX CHALLENGING THE	LIGHTNING	. THE POWERS HAD EITHER TO RENEW THE WAR OR TEAR
SUPR PREFACE(R14)	TONES, AND ELATE DARTING RHYTHMS AS OF SUMMER	LIGHTNING	MADE AUDIBLE. HERE YOU HAVE FREEDOM IN LOVE AND IN
LADY (247)	SHOULD YOU BE FOR SO MUCH LONGER AS A FLASH OF	LIGHTNING	MIGHT TAKE TO CROSS THE RIVER TO THE BANKSIDE. BUT
NEVR III (264)	WE WAITED TO SEE HIM STRUCK TO EARTH BY THE	LIGHTNING	OF HER SCORN; BUT-- /DOLLY/-- BUT HE WASNT.
2TRU III (110)	THEM TO BEAR ONE ANOTHER'S COMPANY? THE IRON	LIGHTNING	OF WAR HAS BURNT GREAT RENTS IN THESE ANGELIC
FANY I (279)	AT THE SOUND OF IT HE DREW AWAY LIKE A STREAK OF	LIGHTNING	; AND THAT WAS THE LAST I SAW OF HIM. I WAS COPPED
JOAN EPILOG (155)	BLOWN ALL OVER THE PLACE. (A FLASH OF SUMMER	LIGHTNING	SHEWS UP THE LANCET WINDOW. A FIGURE IS SEEN IN
MRS II (200)	IT. YOU MUST HAVE HEARD OF IT. (HE WINKS WITH	LIGHTNING	SMARTNESS AT MRS WARREN, AND REGARDS HIS FATHER
PYGM I (206)	HER BASKET OUT OF HER HANDS. A BLINDING FLASH OF	LIGHTNING	, FOLLOWED INSTANTLY BY A RATTLING PEAL OF

LIGHTNINGS

LADY (247)	FABLE OF JUPITER AND SEMELE. I COULD NOT HELP MY	LIGHTNINGS	SCORCHING HER. /ELIZABETH/ YOU HAVE AN

LIGHT-COLORED

MRS IV SD(235) THIS DOOR AND THE WINDOW. FRANK, IN A FASHIONABLE LIGHT-COLORED COACHING SUIT, WITH HIS STICK, GLOVES, AND

LIGHT-O'-LOVES

LADY (243) WHO IN THE NAME OF ALL THE SLUTS AND JADES AND LIGHT-O'-LOVES AND FLY-BY-NIGHTS THAT INFEST THIS PALACE OF

LIGHTS

2TRU III (84) WELL, TODAY THE PLACE IS BLAZING WITH SHINING LIGHTS : SHINING LIGHTS IN PARLIAMENT, IN THE PAPERS, IN THE
GENV IV (103) A BUS COMING? ARE THERE TO BE NO RED AND GREEN LIGHTS ? AM I TO SLEEP IN A SMALLPOX HOSPITAL? AM I TO
ARMS I (8) AS SHE RETREATS TO THE CHEST OF DRAWERS, THEN SHE LIGHTS A CANDLE; AND THE MYSTERY IS AT AN END. HE IS A MAN
PYGM V (268) WAS LEFT LAST NIGHT, AS USUAL, TO TURN OUT THE LIGHTS AND ALL THAT; AND INSTEAD OF GOING TO BED SHE CHANGED
MTH4 III (195) YOU JUST WAIT. ALL THIS BUSINESS WITH COLOURED LIGHTS AND CHORDS ON THAT OLD ORGAN IS ONLY TOMFOOLERY. WAIT
MTH4 I (164) AGAINST THEM; AND IN THEIR HUNGER FOR NEW LIGHTS AND NEW IDEAS THEY LISTENED TO ME AND ENCOURAGED ME
NEVR III (280) WILL BE THE BAND AND THE ARRANGING OF THE FAIRY LIGHTS AND ONE THING OR ANOTHER, MAAM. /DOLLY/ FAIRY
INCA PROLOG (234) COME BACK, MISS, COME BACK THIS INSTANT. (THE LIGHTS ARE LOWERED). OH, VERY WELL: I HAVE NOTHING MORE TO
2TRU I (37) SHUT THAT WINDOW AND SWITCH OFF HALF THOSE LIGHTS AT ONCE! DO YOU HEAR? THE NURSE SNATCHES THE
HART I (83) (GOING INTO THE HALL) SHALL I TURN UP THE LIGHTS FOR YOU? /CAPTAIN SHOTOVER/ NO. GIVE ME DEEPER
2TRU I SD(37) DO YOU WANT TO KILL ME? THE NURSE TURNS ALL THE LIGHTS FULL ON. /THE PATIENT/ (HIDING HER EYES) OH! OH! I
NEVR II (245) STEPS. THE WAITER STRIKES A MATCH AND ADROITLY LIGHTS HER CIGARET). THANK YOU, DEAR WILLIAM. (SHE VANISHES
JOAN PREFACE(18) AS A MILITARY EXPLOIT SUGGESTED. ACCORDING TO HER LIGHTS HER EXPECTATION OF A RESCUE WAS REASONABLE; THEREFORE
2TRU III (84) THE PLACE IS BLAZING WITH SHINING LIGHTS: SHINING LIGHTS IN PARLIAMENT, IN THE PAPERS, IN THE CHURCHES, AND IN
HART III (147) AT THE HOUSE) IT'S MR HUSHABYE TURNING ON ALL THE LIGHTS IN THE HOUSE AND TEARING DOWN THE CURTAINS. /RANDALL/
DEVL II (41) TO THE CUPBOARD; TAKES A CANDLE FROM THE DRAWER; LIGHTS IT AT THE FLICKER OF THE EXPIRING ONE ON THE TABLE;
PYGM IV SD(262) AND WALKS ACROSS TO THE HEARTH TO SWITCH OFF THE LIGHTS . BY THE TIME SHE GETS THERE SHE IS ON THE POINT OF
GENV III (78) DOING MY DUTY TO MY COUNTRY ACCORDING TO MY POOR LIGHTS . /THE JUDGE/ STILL, DOING IT WITH ABILITY ENOUGH TO
MRS IV (236) OPENS THE BOX AND TAKES OUT A CIGARET, WHICH SHE LIGHTS . SHE OFFERS HIM ONE; BUT HE SHAKES HIS HEAD WITH A
ROCK I SD(224) HIS EYE, SWEEPING ROUND THE IMAGINARY ASSEMBLY, LIGHTS ON A WOMAN IN GREY ROBES CONTEMPLATING HIM GRAVELY
2TRU I SD(37) SO INCONSIDERATE OF YOU! THE NURSE SWITCHES THE LIGHTS ON AGAIN. /THE PATIENT/ OH, PLEASE, PLEASE. NOT ALL
DEVL I (20) HIS VOICE SUDDENLY SWEETENS GRAVELY AS HIS GLANCE LIGHTS ON ESSIE) PROVIDED ONLY THERE IS HOPE IN THE EYES OF
BASH PREFACE(91) THE NEW TESTAMENT I AT ONCE GOT FROM THEM SO MANY LIGHTS ON THE BIBLE NARRATIVES WHICH I HAD MISSED IN THE
KING I (179) I HAVE TO THANK HER GRACE OF CLEVELAND FOR SOME LIGHTS ON THE BOOK OF REVELATION SUGGESTED TO ME BY HER
2TRU I SD(28) BY INVISIBLE CORNICE LIGHTS, AND BY TWO MIRROR LIGHTS ON THE DRESSING TABLE AND A PORTABLE ONE ON THE
LION PREFACE(5) NOT ACTING AS A DETECTIVE, BUT TURNING OUR MODERN LIGHTS ON TO CERTAIN IDEAS AND DOCTRINES IN THEM WHICH
GETT (264) WAS ALL SAFE AT HOME AND THE DOOR LOCKED, AND THE LIGHTS OUT. ALWAYS WANTS HER LUGGAGE IN THE CARRIAGE WITH
BUOY 1 (13) THESE WERE RIGHTEOUS MEN ACCORDING TO THEIR LIGHTS ; BUT WITH CHARLEMAGNE IT WAS EMBRACE CHRISTIANITY
2TRU I (39) I TOLD HIM HE MIGHT DROP IN WHEN HE SAW THE LIGHTS SWITCHED OFF TWICE. /THE PATIENT/ SO THAT WAS WHY--
MRS II (218) ABLE TO SLEEP NOW. (SHE GOES TO THE DRESSER AND LIGHTS THE CANDLE. THEN SHE EXTINGUISHES THE LAMP, DARKENING
CLEO I (113) SLAVE) DO AS THE QUEEN HAS BIDDEN. (THE SLAVE LIGHTS THE LAMPS. MEANWHILE CLEOPATRA STANDS HESITATING,
PYGM IV SD(260) COMES TO THE HEARTH, AND SWITCHES ON THE ELECTRIC LIGHTS THERE. SHE IS TIRED; HER PALLOR CONTRASTS STRONGLY
HART II SD(84) ACT II. THE SAME ROOM, WITH THE LIGHTS TURNED UP AND THE CURTAINS DRAWN. ELLIE COMES IN,
WIDO III (64) EROTIC: THAT SHE IS MAKING LOVE TO HIM. HIS EYE LIGHTS UP: A CUNNING EXPRESSION COMES INTO THE CORNERS OF
BARB II (306) ON EARTH AND GOODWILL TO MEN. (MRS BAINES'S FACE LIGHTS UP AGAIN). EVERY CONVERT YOU MAKE IS A VOTE AGAINST
HART III (146) I MARRIED! I'LL GO ON THE ROOF FIRST. (THE LAMP LIGHTS UP AGAIN). THERE! MR HUSHABYE'S TURNED IT ON AGAIN.
LIED SD(187) IT UP AGAIN; NOTICES THE THINGS ON THE TABLE; LIGHTS UP AS IF HE SAW HEAVEN OPENING BEFORE HIM; GOES TO
APPL I (234) BEFORE OUR FEET IN BLACK DARKNESS WHILST IT LIGHTS UP EVERY CORNER OF THE LANDSCAPE BEHIND US. ALL THE
PPP SD(194) A WHITE RADIANCE PLAYS ON HER PILLOW, AND LIGHTS UP HER BEAUTIFUL FACE. BUT THE THUNDER GROWLS AGAIN;
LION II SD(143) AS IF IT WAS WOUNDED. A FLASH OF RECOGNITION LIGHTS UP THE FACE OF ANDROCLES. HE FLAPS HIS HAND AS IF IT
WIDO II SD(34) NERVE. BLANCHE APPEARS AT THE DOOR. HER FACE LIGHTS UP WHEN SHE SEES THAT HE IS ALONE. SHE TRIPS
PHIL I (83) TO HIS RETREATING FOOTSTEPS. THEY STOP. HER FACE LIGHTS UP WITH EAGER, TRIUMPHANT CUNNING. THE STEPS RETURN
PPP (198) NOT ADMIRE MINE. /ADOLPHUS/ MY CLOTHES (HIS FACE LIGHTS UP WITH HEAVENLY RADIANCE)! HAVE I INDEED BEEN FOUND
MTH1 I SD(19) WHO BEGINS WHISPERING TO HER). EVE'S FACE LIGHTS UP WITH INTENSE INTEREST, WHICH INCREASES UNTIL AN
NEVR II (254) CRAMPTON? /GLORIA/ GONE. (VALENTINE'S FACE LIGHTS UP WITH SUDDEN JOY, DREAD, AND MISCHIEF AS HE
JITT I SD(13) TO STRIKE IT WHEN THE BELL RINGS TWICE. HIS FACE LIGHTS UP; HE THROWS THE MATCH AND THE CIGARET INTO THE
2TRU I SD(27) TABLE. THE ROOM IS LIGHTED BY INVISIBLE CORNICE LIGHTS , AND BY TWO MIRROR LIGHTS ON THE DRESSING TABLE AND
JOAN EPILOG (153) OF THE DEAD WHO DID THEIR DUTY ACCORDING TO THEIR LIGHTS , COWARDLY EVASION OF THE ISSUE, TESTIMONY MADE OF
PYGM IV (262) (OVER HIS SHOULDER, AT THE DOOR) PUT OUT THE LIGHTS , ELIZA; AND TELL MRS PEARCE NOT TO MAKE COFFEE FOR
MRS PREFACE(171) MRS WARREN TO CHOOSE WHAT IS, ACCORDING TO HER LIGHTS , THE LEAST IMMORAL ALTERNATIVE, IT IS NONE THE LESS
PHIL I SD(69) ON THE DESK IS: WHEN OTHER LIPS. INCANDESCENT LIGHTS , WELL SHADED, ARE ON THE PIANO AND MANTELPIECE. NEAR
APPL PREFACE(177) GET AND MAKE THE BEST OF IT ACCORDING TO THEIR LIGHTS , WHICH IS OFTEN THE WORST OF IT BY THE LIGHT OF
NEVR III (280) AND ONE THING OR ANOTHER, MAAM. /DOLLY/ FAIRY LIGHTS ! /PHILIP/ A BAND! WILLIAM! WHAT MEAN YOU?

LII

FABL (61) FARFETCHED FABLES. LII . 1948.

LIII

SHAK (133) SHAKES VERSUS SHAV: A PUPPET PLAY. LIII . 1949.

LIKE

ROCK II (236) READING THE PAPERS. NEW EDITIONS EVERY HALF-HOUR. LIKE 1914 OVER AGAIN. SIR ARTHUR'S VOICE IS HEARD, SINGING
GETT PREFACE(212) OUR OWN ACTUAL PROPORTION IS, ROUGHLY, SOMETHING LIKE 1 1-11 WOMEN TO 1 MAN. NOW YOU CANNOT ENACT THAT EACH
MIS. PREFACE(3) LIKE TO LIVE A LITTLE LONGER JUST AS WE SHOULD LIKE 50 POUNDS; THAT IS, WE SHOULD TAKE IT IF WE COULD GET
CAND III (133) THANK YOU FOR TOUCHING UP MY POETRY. YES, IF YOU LIKE : A BEGGAR DYING OF COLD, ASKING FOR HER SHAWL.
DOCT V (178) WHAT I THOUGHT OF HIM. BE AS ANGRY WITH ME AS YOU LIKE : AT LEAST YOU KNOW ME AS I REALLY AM. IF YOU EVER COME
CLEO II (124) MUST NOT BE AFRAID. EAT MY HUSBAND THERE, IF YOU LIKE : HE IS AFRAID. /CAESAR/ (STARTING) YOUR HUSBAND!
2TRU PREFACE(11) DAILY ANSWER " DO WHAT YOU PLEASE: GO WHERE YOU LIKE : IT DOESNT MATTER WHAT YOU DO OR WHERE YOU GO." IN
DEVL III (56) OF ENGLAND? MARTYRDOM, SIR, IS WHAT THESE PEOPLE LIKE : IT IS THE ONLY WAY IN WHICH A MAN CAN BECOME FAMOUS
MIS. (197) ALL THAT CONCERNS ME. TELL HER WHO YOU ARE IF YOU LIKE : IT'S HER AFFAIR, NOT MINE. /HYPATIA/ DONT ANSWER HIM,
POSN (460) THAT MAN: OH DONT. YOU MAY HANG ME INSTEAD IF YOU LIKE : IVE NOTHING TO LIVE FOR NOW. YOU DARENT TAKE HER WORD
HART III (136) KEEP YOUR CLOTHES ON. /MANGAN/ I'LL DO AS I LIKE : NOT WHAT YOU TELL ME. AM I A CHILD OR A GROWN MAN? I
SUPR III (100) AND GO TO THE CLASSICAL CONCERTS INSTEAD IF THEY LIKE : THERE IS NO LAW AGAINST IT; FOR ENGLISHMEN NEVER WILL
MIS. (123) PLENTY WOULD HAVE ATTENDED IT. THATS WHAT THEYRE LIKE : THEYVE NASTY MINDS. WITH REALLY NICE GOOD WOMEN A
LION PREFACE(79) EVER SAID TO ANY MAN: " GO AND SIN AS MUCH AS YOU LIKE : YOU CAN PUT IT ALL ON ME." HE SAID " SIN NO MORE,"
MTH5 (242) I HAVE DONE NO HARM: SHE HAS. KILL HER IF YOU LIKE : YOU HAVE NO RIGHT TO KILL ME. /THE NEWLY BORN/ DO YOU
NEVR II (247) CHILDREN. WHAT ARE THE HEARTS OF THIS GENERATION LIKE ? AM I TO COME HERE AFTER ALL THESE YEARS? TO SEE
JOAN 6 (142) WHO IS HE? IS THIS WHAT ENGLISH CHURCHMEN ARE LIKE ? HE MUST BE MAD OR DRUNK, ETC., ETC. /THE INQUISITOR/
MTH5 (212) TO BE BORN TODAY. HOW DO I KNOW WHAT SHE WILL BE LIKE ? I WANT YOU. /THE MAIDEN/ YOU CANNOT HAVE ME. YOU
MRS IV (237) YOU DONT KNOW WHAT BEING BROTHER AND SISTER FEELS LIKE ? NOW I HAVE LOTS OF SISTERS; AND THE FRATERNAL
ARMS II (31) TWO INNOCENT LITTLE CHILDREN. /RAINA/ WHAT WAS HE LIKE ? /CATHERINE/ OH, RAINA, WHAT A SILLY QUESTION!
MIS. (165) HERE: THIS IS NO GOOD. YOU WANT TO DO WHAT YOU LIKE ? /HYPATIA/ DONT YOU! /PERCIVAL/ NO. IVE BEEN TOO
JOAN 1 (66) DAY? /JOAN/ THEY DO. /ROBERT/ WHAT ARE THEY LIKE ? /JOAN/ (SUDDENLY OBSTINATE) I WILL TELL YOU NOTHING
ROCK II (282) GOLF LINKS SEEMS TO BE INDICATED. WHAT WOULD YOU LIKE ? /LADY CHAVENDER/ BUT YOUR POLITICAL CAREER? ARE YOU
DEST (160) KIND OF MAN HE WAS. /NAPOLEON/ PSHA! WHAT WAS HE LIKE ? /LIEUTENANT/ LIKE! HE WAS LIKE-- WELL, YOU OUGHT TO
ARMS II (40) THAT MAKES LOUKA JUMP BACK) SWISS! WHAT IS HE LIKE ? /LOUKA/ (TIMIDLY) HE HAS A BIG CARPET BAG, MADAM.
HART III (134) /HECTOR/ AND IN HEAVEN'S NAME, WHAT DO YOU LOOK LIKE ? /MANGAN/ I LOOK LIKE THE FELLOW THAT WAS TOO CLEVER
MRS I (187) OF ME? /PRAED/ YES. /VIVIE/ WHAT ON EARTH IS IT LIKE ? /PRAED/ WELL, YOU MUST HAVE OBSERVED, MISS WARREN,
WIDO II (47) I LIKE ABOUT THIS MARRIAGE; OR MUST I DO AS YOU LIKE ? /SARTORIUS/ (UNEASILY) BLANCHE-- /BLANCHE/ NO,
JOAN EPILOG (160) AS SOON AS I WANT THEM. /CHARLES/ WHAT IS HELL LIKE ? /THE SOLDIER/ YOU WONT FIND IT SO BAD, SIR. JOLLY.
JOAN EPILOG (167) AND CAPTAINS AND BISHOPS AND LAWYERS AND SUCH LIKE ? THEY JUST LEAVE YOU IN THE DITCH TO BLEED TO DEATH;
BARB III (349) SARAH, WHO FOLLOWS WITH LOMAX. BARBARA CLUTCHES LIKE A BABY AT HER MOTHER'S SKIRT) BARBARA: WHEN WILL YOU
GETT SD(260) IS THE IMMENSE FIREPLACE, WITH ITS HUGE SPIT LIKE A BABY CRANE, AND A COLLECTION OF OLD IRON AND BRASS
3PLA PREFACE(R9) DOWN LIKE THE VERIEST WEAKLING, I SANK UNDER IT LIKE A BABY FED ON STARCH, MY VERY BONES BEGAN TO PERISH, SO
MIS. (126) LOVE WITH BUNNY? I LIKE HIM TO KISS ME JUST AS I LIKE A BABY TO KISS ME. I'M FOND OF HIM; AND HE NEVER BORES
PHIL II (125) WAY OF GETTING ANYTHING YOU WANT: CRYING FOR IT LIKE A BABY UNTIL IT IS GIVEN TO YOU. /JULIA/ (WITH
6CAL (102) I MIGHT AS WELL BE A DOG AS A KING. YOU TREAT ME LIKE A BABY. /THE QUEEN/ AH NO: YOU ARE THE GREATEST OF
PPP (202) HE COLLAPSES ON THE BED, CLASPING THE GAZOGENE LIKE A BABY, AND WEEPING OVER IT). /FITZ/ (ASIDE TO
APPL I (211) YOU BUY IT, BILL? /BOANERGES/ (TURNING ON THEM LIKE A BAITED BEAR) WELL, IF YOU COME TO THAT, WHO DO YOU

ROCK II (236)	ARE, DEXY (HE PROFFERS HIS HAND). /SIR DEXTER/ (	LIKE	A BAITED BULL) DONT ATTEMPT TO SHAKE HANDS WITH ME.
DOCT I (102)	IS A SICK DOCTOR. /WALPOLE/ YES, BY GEORGE! IT'S	LIKE	A BALD-HEADED MAN TRYING TO SELL A HAIR RESTORER. THANK
ROCK PREFACE(176)	ME FEEL QUITE HOLY, YOU TELL ME THAT HE WENT UP	LIKE	A BALLOON INTO THE STRATOSPHERE, I DO NOT FEEL HOLY: I
FABL III (110)	ARE YOU? /THE TOURIST/ QUITE. I DONT LOOK	LIKE	A BANK CLERK, DO I? /THE MATRON/ WELL, WE HAVE NO
PYGM EPILOG (294)	BY HIS WIT, HIS DUSTMANSHIP (WHICH HE CARRIED	LIKE	A BANNER), AND HIS NIETZSCHEAN TRANSCENDENCE OF GOOD
PYGM IV (261)	I SAW WE WERE GOING TO WIN HANDS DOWN, I FELT	LIKE	A BEAR IN A CAGE, HANGING ABOUT DOING NOTHING. THE
BULL III (127)	GIVIN HIM LAN? /DORAN/ AISY, MATT, AISY. YOURE	LIKE	A BEAR WITH A SORE BACK. /MATTHEW/ (TREMBLING WITH
NEVR II (247)	OF MYSELF! WHAT FOR? /VALENTINE/ FOR BEHAVING	LIKE	A BEAR. WHAT WILL YOUR DAUGHTER THINK OF ME FOR HAVING
MTH1 II (29)	THE FIRST, LET MANKIND PERISH. IF I AM TO EAT	LIKE	A BEAR, IF LUA IS TO BRING FORTH CUBS LIKE A BEAR, THEN
MTH1 II (29)	TO EAT LIKE A BEAR, IF LUA IS TO BRING FORTH CUBS	LIKE	A BEAR, THEN I HAD RATHER BE A BEAR THAN A MAN; FOR THE
BUOY III (37)	THE SEAS BETWEEN ME AND THIS FIGURE THAT LOOKS	LIKE	A BEAUTIFUL AND WONDERFUL CELESTIAL MESSENGER-- A
GENV I (42)	SORT OF CELL. C.E. DOUBLE L. A COMMUNIST CELL.	LIKE	A BEE IN A HIVE. PLANTED ON ME BY THE COMMUNISTS TO
HART II SD(88)	DROPS INTO THE WICKER CHAIR AND STARES BEFORE HIM	LIKE	A BEGGARED GAMBLER. BUT A CUNNING LOOK SOON COMES INTO
2TRU I (43)	HURT) OH, NOT A CURATE. I HOPE I LOOK AT LEAST	LIKE	A BENEFICED CLERGYMAN. BUT IT IS VERY CLEVER OF YOU TO
VWOO 2 (124)	ONE DOWN) THIS IS THE CHEAPEST. OR WOULD YOU	LIKE	A BETTER QUALITY WITH A ZIP FASTENING? /A/ CERTAINLY
PYGM I (214)	MILTON AND THE BIBLE; AND DONT SIT THERE CROONING	LIKE	A BILIOUS PIGEON. /THE FLOWER GIRL/ (QUITE
GETT (264)	SEE, FAMILY LIFE IS ALL THE LIFE SHE KNOWS: SHE'S	LIKE	A BIRD BORN IN A CAGE, THAT WOULD DIE IF YOU LET IT
MIS. (150)	INTO THE FLOWER BED, AND THEN LIGHTED BESIDE YOU	LIKE	A BIRD. /PERCIVAL/ HOW HE KEPT HIS HEAD I CANT IMAGINE.
FANY PROLOG (263)	WOULD FEEL LONELY WITHOUT HIM; SO HE PROMISED	LIKE	A BIRD. THEN I THOUGHT YOUD LIKE ONE OF THE LATEST
FANY I (279)	GENTEEL, AND TALKED SO SWEET, THAT HE FELL TO IT	LIKE	A BIRD. " I NEVER HEARD OF ANY SUCH SQUARE IN THESE
DOCT I SD(109)	HAIR, DRESSED SO AS TO LOOK LIKE HAIR AND NOT	LIKE	A BIRD'S NEST OR A PANTALOON'S WIG (FASHION WAVERING
CLEO I SD(106)	BRAIDED HAIR GLITTERING IN A SHAFT OF MOONLIGHT	LIKE	A BIRD'S WING. SUDDENLY THERE COMES FROM AFAR A VAGUELY
FABL VI SD(129)	UNTIL YOU ARE TOLD. A YOUTH, CLOTHED IN FEATHERS	LIKE	A BIRD, APPEARS SUDDENLY. /TEACHER/ HULLO! WHO ARE
PYGM III (255)	WELL, IF YOU SAY SO, I SUPPOSE I DONT ALWAYS TALK	LIKE	A BISHOP. /MRS HIGGINS/ (QUIETING HENRY WITH A TOUCH)
MIS. (124)	LIKE ONE OF THOSE EXPENSIVE LITTLE DOGS. I	LIKE	A BIT OF A MONGREL MYSELF, WHETHER IT'S A MAN OR A DOG:
FANY I (281)	MY BEST TO KEEP HIM STRAIGHT; BUT I DONT DENY I	LIKE	A BIT OF FUN MYSELF; AND WE BOTH GET A BIT GIDDY WHEN
O'FL (213)	FATTENING THEM, SIR; AND ALL THE TIME YOU WERE	LIKE	A BIT OF HER OWN FLESH AND BLOOD TO HER. OFTEN HAS SHE
BARB III (329)	WITHOUT THE LEAST RISK: THEY JUST BURN QUIETLY	LIKE	A BIT OF PAPER. (WARMING TO THE SCIENTIFIC INTEREST OF
MTH3 (132)	GOLF, OR MOTORING, OR FLYING, OR WOMEN, JUST	LIKE	A BIT OF STRETCHED ELASTIC WHEN YOU LET IT GO. (
MILL IV (210)	DIRT, DISEASE, MISERY AND SLAVERY SURROUND ME	LIKE	A BLACK SEA IN WHICH I MAY BE ENGULFED AT ANY MOMENT BY
CAND I (102)	DISTRESS HER BY TELLING HER THAT YOU HAVE BEHAVED	LIKE	A BLACKGUARD. /MARCHBANKS/ (COMING BACK WITH RENEWED
OVER (175)	NOT IN BLACK. /GREGORY/ THEN I HAVE BEEN BEHAVING	LIKE	A BLACKGUARD! I HAVE BROKEN MY PROMISE TO MY MOTHER. I
SIM II (72)	/THE ANGEL/ NATURAL DEATH DOES IT SENSELESSLY,	LIKE	A BLIND CHILD THROWING STONES. WE ANGELS ARE EXECUTING
GETT PREFACE(206)	WHO CONFINES HIMSELF TO POPULAR PLAYS-- IS	LIKE	A BLIND MAN'S DOG WHO GOES WHEREVER THE BLIND MAN PULLS
BULL PREFACE(22)	OF RESIDENCE IN ENGLAND TO LEARN TO RESPECT AND	LIKE	A BLOCKHEAD, AN ENGLISHMAN WILL NOT RESPECT NOR LIKE
CAPT II (243)	WAS FRAHTND OF, TYIN AP MAWTZOW'S WOUND, SHE IS,	LIKE	A BLOOMIN ORSPITTLE NASS. (SIR HOWARD, WITH A COPIOUS
PYGM II (236)	RIGHT. I CANT CARRY THE GIRL THROUGH THE STREETS	LIKE	A BLOOMING MONKEY, CAN I? I PUT IT TO YOU. /HIGGINS/
DEVL III (53)	MOMENT; BUT BELIEVE ME, MRS ANDERSON, YOU DONT	LIKE	A BONE IN MY SKIN OR A HAIR ON MY HEAD. I SHALL BE AS
JITT I (21)	THE GREATEST ACHIEVEMENT OF YOUR LIFE TO HIM	LIKE	A BONE TO A DOG; AND THEN FEEL YOU HAVE MADE US TWO
MIS. (132)	IT SO MUCH. ONLY, I DONT READ THE SAME BOOKS. I	LIKE	A BOOK WITH A PLOT IN IT. YOU LIKE A BOOK WITH NOTHING
MIS. (132)	SAME BOOKS. I LIKE A BOOK WITH A PLOT IN IT. YOU	LIKE	A BOOK WITH NOTHING IN IT BUT SOME IDEAS THAT THE CHAP
MILL PREFACE(133)	THE TSAR VERY EFFICIENTLY; BUT IT CAME BACK	LIKE	A BOOMERANG AND LAID THE HOHENZOLLERNS BESIDE THE
SUPR III (82)	EVERYTHING I POSSESS TO BE AN ENGLISHMAN. I AM	LIKE	A BOY: I CUT HER NAME ON THE TREES AND HER INITIALS ON
DOCT III (155)	HIM I HAD SOME, HE SAID " OH, ALL RIGHT", JUST	LIKE	A BOY. HE IS STILL LIKE THAT, QUITE UNSPOILED, A MAN IN
CAND III (135)	COURAGE FROM THE SCOLDING) IF I AM TO BE SCOLDED	LIKE	A BOY, I MUST MAKE A BOY'S EXCUSE. HE BEGAN IT. AND
MRS IV (245)	RISING) HERE, AND CHARMED TO SEE YOU. YOU COME	LIKE	A BREATH OF SPRING. /MRS WARREN/ OH, GET OUT WITH YOUR
MRS III (223)	WOULD MIND IN THE ORDINARY WAY: SHE HAS STUCK	LIKE	A BRICK TO LOTS OF WOMEN WHO HAD GOT INTO TROUBLE. BUT
WIDO II (28)	YES, ARNT THEY? AUNT MARIA HAS REALLY BEHAVED	LIKE	A BRICK. IF YOU READ THE POSTSCRIPT YOULL SEE SHE
2TRU PREFACE(24)	ONLY BY BETTERING THEM, NOT BY BUTTERING THEM	LIKE	A BRITISH DEMAGOGUE. ECLECTIC DEMOCRACY. I THINK MY
HART II (102)	IT ISNT MY FAULT IF I'M OLD AND HAVNT A MOUSTACHE	LIKE	A BRONZE CANDLESTICK AS YOUR HUSBAND HAS. THERE ARE
MIS. PREFACE(80)	AN ENIGMA, ALSO A POSSIBILITY; BUT A MOTHER IS	LIKE	A BROOMSTICK OR LIKE THE SUN IN THE HEAVENS, IT DOES
LION II (145)	ANDY WANDY HAS IN THE WHOLE WORLD: HE LOVES HIM	LIKE	A BROTHER. /THE EMPEROR/ YOU LITTLE BRUTE, YOU DAMNED
POSN (445)	(BENDING OVER THE TABLE AND COAXING HIM). ACT	LIKE	A BROTHER, BLANCO: TELL ME WHAT YOU DONE WITH IT.
LIED (192)	THAT YOU ARE GOING TO BEAT TEDDY BEFORE MY FACE	LIKE	A BRUTAL PRIZEFIGHTER? /HE/ ALL THIS ALARM IS
CATH 4 (193)	(CATCHING HER TRAIN IN HIS TEETH AND HOLDING ON	LIKE	A BULL-DOG) DONT GO. DONT LEAVE ME IN THIS HORRIBLE
2TRU I (43)	CAN YOU BE AFRAID OF SUCH A FACE? DO I LOOK	LIKE	A BURGLAR? /THE PATIENT/ (RELAXING, AND EVEN SHEWING
ROCK II (251)	OF THE NEW ORDER: THE MEN IN WHOM THE WORD IS	LIKE	A BURNING FIRE SHUT UP IN THEIR BONES SO THAT THEY ARE
LION I (118)	BETWEEN THEM) PLEASE DONT LET YOUR FRIEND BEHAVE	LIKE	A CAD BEFORE THE SOLDIERS. HOW ARE THEY TO RESPECT AND
BULL III (138)	SHAKIN HANS WID FADHER DEMPSEY FOR ALL THE WORLD	LIKE	A CANDIDATE ON ELECTION DAY, AND LOOK AT FADHER DEMPSEY
BULL PREFACE(47)	IN THEM AS IF THEIR HUMANITY HAD BEEN BLOWN OUT	LIKE	A CANDLE. YOU FIND THAT THERE IS A BLIND SPOT ON THEIR
CAND I (99)	SHE'S OVER THIRTY. DOESNT IT LOOK RATHER TOO	LIKE	A CASE OF CALF LOVE? /MARCHBANKS/ (VEHEMENTLY) YOU
NEVR I (207)	IS A CANON OF LINCOLN CATHEDRAL. /VALENTINE/ (	LIKE	A CASTAWAY MARINER WHO SEES A SAIL ON THE HORIZON)
MIS. (132)	THAT THE CHAP THAT WRITES IT KEEPS WORRYING,	LIKE	A CAT CHASING ITS OWN TAIL. I CAN STAND A LITTLE OF IT,
DEST (161)	POSTS HIMSELF, SWORD IN HAND, WATCHING THE DOOR	LIKE	A CAT WATCHING A MOUSEHOLE). IT OPENS; AND THE STRANGE
CAPT III (294)	/LADY CICELY/ OH BLESS YOU, YES. IT'S SO VERY	LIKE	A CERTAIN SORT OF MAN. /BRASSBOUND/ I DARESAY; BUT IVE
SIM PRO,1, (25)	THROWN IT BACK: YOU SHOULD HAVE PASSED IT ON,	LIKE	A CHAIN LETTER. NOW YOU WILL NEVER HAVE NO MORE LUCK IN
JITT III (67)	MERE CHANCE THAT SHE WAS THERE TO CLOSE HIS EYES,	LIKE	A CHAMBERMAID IN A HOTEL? /JITTA/ SHE DID NOT CLOSE
KING II (223)	ABOUT ALL OVER MY ROOM? I HAVE TO PUT THEM AWAY	LIKE	A CHAMBERMAID. /CHARLES/ WHY NOT SEND FOR CHIFFINCH?
BASH II,2, (118)	OTHERS FLY. IN VAIN: HIS FIST OER MAGIC DISTANCES	LIKE	A CHAMELEON'S TONGUE SHOOTS TO ITS MARK; AND THE LAST
NEVR IV SD(286)	THE DOMINO AND THROWING THE BUNDLE ON THE TABLE	LIKE	A CHAMPION THROWING DOWN HIS GLOVE, HE IS NOW SEEN TO
MIS. PREFACE(32)	THAT IT WOULD TOLERATE AT ALL. BUT SOMETHING	LIKE	A CHANGE OF HEART IS STILL POSSIBLE; AND SINCE ALL THE
DOCT III (151)	THE PATIENT CHEERFUL; HOPE FOR THE BEST; NO TONIC	LIKE	A CHARMING WOMAN; NO MEDICINE LIKE CHEERFULNESS; NO
GETT (299)	SPOILING IT AND SETTING HOTCHKISS HERE GRINNING	LIKE	A CHESHIRE CAT? IF SHE PUTS ON HER VEIL AND GOES TO
MTH2 (62)	ALREADY! /SAVVY/ IT'S NO GOOD YOUR SMILING AT ME	LIKE	A CHESHIRE CAT, MR LUBIN; AND I AM NOT GOING TO SIT
2TRU II (76)	WHO SHOULD NEVER HAVE BEEN ENLISTED. HE IS	LIKE	A CHILD: THIS WOMAN COULD DO ANYTHING SHE PLEASES WITH
CAND III (135)	HERE ALL THE TIME. OH, IT WAS UNWORTHY! YOU ARE	LIKE	A CHILD: YOU CANNOT HOLD YOUR TONGUE. /MARCHBANKS/ I
NEVR II (258)	FROM MY WEAKNESS, I SHOULD SIT DOWN HERE AND CRY	LIKE	A CHILD? /GLORIA/ (BEGINNING TO FIND THAT SHE MUST
JOAN 4 (98)	PIERCED BY AN ENGLISH ARROW, AND WAS SEEN TO CRY	LIKE	A CHILD FROM THE PAIN OF IT. IT WAS A DEATH WOUND; YET
6CAL PREFACE(89)	THRASONIC FEROCITY AND THE NEXT MOMENT BLUBBERING	LIKE	A CHILD IN HIS WIFE'S LAP OR SNARLING LIKE A SAVAGE DOG
POSN (446)	YOURE AFRAID TO BE LEFT ALONE IN BROAD DAYLIGHT,	LIKE	A CHILD IN THE DARK. /BLANCO/ I'M AFRAID OF HIM AND HIS
PHIL III (139)	CHOSEN TO, YOU HAD A GREAT POWER OVER ME. I WAS	LIKE	A CHILD IN YOUR HANDS; AND YOU KNEW IT. /CHARTERIS/
JITT III (69)	YOU MIND? /JITTA/ NOT IN THE LEAST. EDITH IS	LIKE	A CHILD OF MY OWN TO ME: IT WOULD BE THE GREATEST
ROCK I (203)	I WONT STAND BY AND SEE HER NAGGED AT AND TREATED	LIKE	A CHILD OF SIX. NAG! NAG! NAG! EVERYTHING SHE DOES.
APPL INTRLUD(251)	MADE ME. /ORINTHIA/ (RISING RESTLESSLY) YOU TALK	LIKE	A CHILD OR A SAINT. (TURNING ON HIM) I CAN GIVE YOU A
POSN PREFACE(382)	A CENSOR PRETENDING TO PROTECT MORALITY IS	LIKE	A CHILD PUSHING THE CUSHIONS OF A RAILWAY CARRIAGE TO
LION PREFACE(42)	INSTINCT IN HIM THAT MAKES HIM STICK THEM IN,	LIKE	A CHILD STICKING TINSEL STARS ON THE ROBE OF A TOY
JITT II (28)	HER TO HAVE TO HOLD HER TONGUE AND BE TREATED	LIKE	A CHILD WHEN ALL HER FEELINGS ARE BOILING OVER ABOUT
JOAN 2,SD(73)	IN CONVERSATION. JUST AT PRESENT HE IS EXCITED,	LIKE	A CHILD WITH A NEW TOY. HE COMES TO THE ARCHBISHOP'S
POSN (465)	SURPRISING HIMSELF OUT OF HIS SENSES. YOURE	LIKE	A CHILD WITH A NEW TOY: YOU AND YOUR BIT OF HUMAN
BASH II,2, (114)	PEOPLE, CETEWAYO. YOU ARE A SAVAGE, REASONING	LIKE	A CHILD. EACH PALLID ENGLISH FACE CONCEALS A BRAIN
HART II SD(103)	SITS DOWN ALSO ON HIS CHAIR AND BEGINS TO CRY	LIKE	A CHILD. ELLIE STARES AT THEM. MRS HUSHABYE, AT THE
BULL PREFACE(45)	FORBIDDEN TO MARRY LIKE A CHILD, AND CALLED TOMMY	LIKE	A CHILD. HE HAS NO REAL WORK TO KEEP HIM FROM GOING MAD
MIS. (145)	MAKE YOU CONCEITED. SHE'S NEVER BEEN TREATED	LIKE	A CHILD. I ALWAYS SAID THE SAME THING TO HER MOTHER.
DOCT III (155)	FOR ME. HE UNDERSTOOD EVERYTHING. HE CAME TO ME	LIKE	A CHILD. ONLY FANCY, DOCTOR: HE NEVER EVEN WANTED TO
BARB II (277)	AT IT RAVENOUSLY BUT NOT TOUCHING IT, AND CRYING	LIKE	A CHILD) I NEVER TOOK ANYTHING BEFORE. /JENNY/ (
DEVL I (13)	EVEN HER LITTLE SELF-COMPLACENCY IS PRETTY,	LIKE	A CHILD'S VANITY. RATHER A PATHETIC CREATURE TO ANY
BULL PREFACE(45)	AND COMBED LIKE A CHILD, FORBIDDEN TO MARRY	LIKE	A CHILD, AND CALLED TOMMY LIKE A CHILD. HE HAS NO REAL
DEVL III (50)	FOR THE COURT MARTIAL. DONT FRET, MUM: HE SLEP	LIKE	A CHILD, AND HAS MADE A RARE GOOD BREAKFAST. /JUDITH/ (
BULL PREFACE(45)	INSTEAD OF RIGHTS, TREATED LIKE A CHILD, PUNISHED	LIKE	A CHILD, DRESSED PRETTILY AND WASHED AND COMBED LIKE A
BULL PREFACE(45)	A CHILD, DRESSED PRETTILY AND WASHED AND COMBED	LIKE	A CHILD, FORBIDDEN TO MARRY LIKE A CHILD, AND CALLED
BULL PREFACE(45)	A CHILD, WITH RATIONS INSTEAD OF RIGHTS, TREATED	LIKE	A CHILD, PUNISHED LIKE A CHILD, DRESSED PRETTILY AND
MTH4 I (144)	TO HER EAR; THEN SPEAKING INTO SPACE ON ONE NOTE,	LIKE	A CHORISTER INTONING A PSALM) BURRIN PIER GALWAY PLEASE
LION II (131)	WONT EAT ME NOW. /THE KEEPER/ YES! THATS JUST	LIKE	A CHRISTIAN: THINK ONLY OF YOURSELF! WHAT AM I TO DO?
DEVL II (46)	LIKE A DOG, WHEN A FEW WORDS MIGHT MAKE HIM DIE	LIKE	A CHRISTIAN, I'M ASHAMED OF YOU, JUDITH. /JUDITH/ HE
MTH2 SD(47)	RECTOR. BURGE CONVEYS AN IMPRESSION OF SHINING	LIKE	A CHURCH WINDOW; AND HASLAM SEIZES THE NEAREST LIBRARY
ANNA (303)	WILL MAKE THE WORLD LESS LIKE A PRISON AND MORE	LIKE	A CIRCUS. /STRAMMFEST/ AH! YOU STILL WANT TO BE A
DEVL III (62)	SYMPATHETICALLY) NOW THERE, MR ANDERSON, YOU TALK	LIKE	A CIVILIAN, IF YOU WILL EXCUSE MY SAYING SO. HAVE YOU

BARB II SD(298)	POCKETS AND HIS CHIN SUNK BETWEEN HIS SHOULDERS,	LIKE	A CLEANED-OUT GAMBLER. HE HALTS BETWEEN BARBARA AND THE
JITT II (51)	THRUSTS HIS HANDS DESPERATELY INTO HIS POCKETS	LIKE	A CLEANED-OUT GAMBLER; TROTS BACK IRRESOLUTELY TO HIS
ROCK II (266)	STROLLING ROUND TO THE OTHER SIDE OF THE TABLE	LIKE	A CLEANED-OUT GAMBLER) THAT FINISHES ME, I'M AFRAID. HE
PHIL I (87)	CLUBS ARE A MATTER OF TASTE, CHARTERIS. YOU	LIKE	A COCK-AND-HEN CLUB: I DONT. IT'S BAD ENOUGH TO HAVE
NEVR II (245)	I DOUBT IT. /WAITER/ CHEESE, SIR? OR WOULD YOU	LIKE	A COLD SWEET? /CRAMPTON/ (TAKEN ABACK) WHAT? OH!
MRS I (185)	GETTING PAID FOR IT. WHEN I'M TIRED OF WORKING, I	LIKE	A COMFORTABLE CHAIR, A CIGAR, A LITTLE WHISKY, AND A
ARMS II (31)	RAINA, WHAT A SILLY QUESTION! /SERGIUS/ HE WAS	LIKE	A COMMERCIAL TRAVELLER IN UNIFORM. BOURGEOIS TO HIS
SUPR III (130)	TRESSES. I BREATHE AN ATMOSPHERE OF SWEETNESS,	LIKE	A CONFECTIONER'S SHOPBOY, COMMANDER: ARE THERE ANY
KING PREFACE(157)	CO-OPTED OR REGISTERED OR PICKED UP IN THE STREET	LIKE	A CORONER'S JURY, THE COUPLED VOTE, IN THE CASE OF
MIS. (165)	NOT PREPARED TO CAST OFF THE SOCIAL BOND. IT'S	LIKE	A CORSET: IT'S A SUPPORT TO THE FIGURE EVEN IF IT DOES
PHIL II (101)	/CHARTERIS/ OH, BOTHER! COME! DONT BEHAVE	LIKE	A COUPLE OF CONVENTIONAL OLD FATHERS: THIS IS A SERIOUS
LION PREFACE(6)	EQUALLY BOUND TO ADMIT THAT, FAR FROM BEHAVING	LIKE	A COWARD OR A SHEEP, HE SHEWED CONSIDERABLE PHYSICAL
GLIM (188)	/SANDRO/ (IMPRESSED) YOUR EXCELLENCY SPEAKS	LIKE	A CRAZY BUT VERY HOLY BOOK. HEAVEN FORBID THAT WE
APPL II (258)	THAT IS TRUE, MAAM. I AM JUST BEHAVING	LIKE	A CRAZY MAN. BUT YOU SHALL HEAR, YOU SHALL JUDGE, AND
JITT II (39)	HIM WHEN THEY FOUND HIM? WHY DID SHE RUN AWAY	LIKE	A CRIMINAL? /JITTA/ PERHAPS SHE IS ASKING HERSELF
SUPR I (29)	A SERVICE; CONSEQUENTLY SHE MUST BE PACKED ABROAD	LIKE	A CRIMINAL UNTIL IT'S OVER. WHATS HAPPENING UPSTAIRS..
CURE (231)	/THE LADY/ WHAT A SILLY THING TO SAY! DO I LOOK	LIKE	A CROCODILE? /REGINALD/ NO. /THE LADY/ DO I PLAY LIKE
CURE (231)	A CROCODILE? /REGINALD/ NO. /THE LADY/ DO I PLAY	LIKE	A CROCODILE! /REGINALD/ (CAUTIOUSLY RISING AND
NEVR IV (288)	ONLY WANTS TO GO ON TAKING CARE OF US. I SHOULD	LIKE	A CUP OF COFFEE. /WAITER/ (BRIGHTENING PERCEPTIBLY)
2TRU I (43)	EVEN SHEWING SIGNS OF GOOD-HUMOR) NO: YOU LOOK	LIKE	A CURATE. /THE BURGLAR/ (A LITTLE HURT) OH, NOT A
KING I (219)	ME: HE IS AS STINGY AS A MISER. /CHARLES/ YOU ARE	LIKE	A DAIRYMAID: YOU THINK THERE IS NO END TO A KING'S
APPL INTRLUD(250)	IN IT. I COULD NOT RESIST YOU. YOU GATHERED ME	LIKE	A DAISY. /ORINTHIA/ DID YOU WANT TO RESIST ME?
GENV IV (127)	BRITISH EMPIRE NOW; AND IF I MUST DIE I WILL DIE	LIKE	A DAME. (SHE GOES OUT). /SIR O./ GO WITH HER, SIR. AND
POSN (455)	ME? /STRAPPER/ YOU WERE LOOKING AT A RAINBOW	LIKE	A DAMNED SILLY FOOL INSTEAD OF KEEPING YOUR WITS ABOUT
HART II (115)	DAUGHTER'S HUSBAND. THE MAN IS AT HOME ALL DAY,	LIKE	A DAMNED SOUL IN HELL. /ELLIE/ I NEVER THOUGHT OF THAT
MIS. PREFACE(38)	FROM ANY OBLIGATION OF THE KIND. A LIFE'S WORK IS	LIKE	A DAY'S WORK: IT CAN BEGIN EARLY AND LEAVE OFF EARLY OR
HART I SD(44)	FLOOR OF NARROW BOARDS IS CAULKED AND HOLYSTONED	LIKE	A DECK. THE GARDEN TO WHICH THE GLASS DOORS LEAD DIPS
MTH5 (251)	WAY. WHEN IT IS CAST OUT TO THE SURFACE IT DIES	LIKE	A DEEP-SEA FISH: WHAT YOU SEE IS ONLY ITS COLD DEAD
2TRU II (77)	/AUBREY/ GO EASY WITH HER, COLONEL. SHE CAN RUN	LIKE	A DEER. AND SHE HAS MUSCLES OF IRON. YOU HAD BETTER
JOAN 6,SD(148)	--? THE CHAPLAIN STAGGERS IN FROM THE COURTYARD	LIKE	A DEMENTED CREATURE, HIS FACE STREAMING WITH TEARS,
ARMS I (9)	AND SLAUGHTER ME HERE LIKE A PIG; FOR I'LL FIGHT	LIKE	A DEMON: THEY SHANT GET ME INTO THE STREET TO AMUSE
BASH III (123)	TODAY I SAW STRIPPED TO THE WAIST, AND FIGHTING	LIKE	A DEMON WITH ONE WHO, WHATSOE'ER HIS HUMBLE VIRTUES,
CAND I (82)	FROM THE PYCROFT STREET SCHOOL. A PARSON IS	LIKE	A DOCTOR, MY BOY: HE MUST FACE INFECTION AS A SOLDIER
CLEO III (155)	AND OF VENGEANCE, LET THIS ROMAN FOOL BE BEATEN	LIKE	A DOG BY HIS CAPTAIN FOR SUFFERING HER TO BE TAKEN OVER
DEVL III (62)	AND SHOOT ME LIKE A MAN INSTEAD OF HANGING ME	LIKE	A DOG. /BURGOYNE/ (SYMPATHETICALLY) NOW THERE, MR
DEVL III (53)	HAVE TRICKED THEM; AND THEYLL HANG ME FOR THAT	LIKE	A DOG. SERVE ME RIGHT TOO! /JUDITH/ (WILDLY) OH, I
6CAL (104)	TEETH) EH? /PETER/ (GROWLING IN HIS FACE	LIKE	A DOG) GRRRR! ! ! /THE KING/ (RETURNING THE GROWL
DEVL II (46)	I WILL LET A MAN WITH THAT MUCH GOOD IN HIM DIE	LIKE	A DOG, WHEN A FEW WORDS MIGHT MAKE HIM DIE LIKE A
CLEO III (164)	I WILL CARRY YOU ON MY BACK TO THE GALLEY	LIKE	A DOLPHIN, RUFIO: WHEN YOU SEE ME RISE TO THE SURFACE,
MTH3 (114)	WITH YOUR FACE, MRS LUTESTRING. SOMETHING	LIKE	A DOOR OPENING CONTINUALLY AND REVEALING YOU. AND A
SIM I (48)	AND RESPECTABLE, LADY FARWATERS; BUT IT SOUNDS	LIKE	A DREADFUL SORT OF WICKEDNESS. /LADY FARWATERS/ MAY I
LION PROLOG (107)	TO DRINK: IT'S ONLY NATURAL; AND I DONT DENY I	LIKE	A DROP MYSELF SOMETIMES. WHAT I CANT STAND IS YOUR
ARMS I (16)	US TO BITS. AND THERE WAS DON QUIXOTE FLOURISHING	LIKE	A DRUM MAJOR, THINKING HE'D DONE THE CLEVEREST THING
PYGM II (224)	HERE, YOUNG WOMAN. YOUVE GOT TO LEARN TO BEHAVE	LIKE	A DUCHESS. TAKE HER AWAY, MRS PEARCE. IF SHE GIVES YOU
MIS. (121)	SHOULD HAVE KNOWN ME WHEN I WAS FORTY! I TALKED	LIKE	A DUCHESS; AND IF JOHNNY OR HYPATIA LET SLIP A WORD
INCA (244)	PLEASE. IF I MUST HAVE ONE OF HIS SONS, I SHOULD	LIKE	A FAIR ONE THAT DOESNT SHAVE, WITH SOFT HAIR AND A
ROCK I (211)	SCOWLS AT HIM AND FLINGS HIMSELF INTO THE CHAIR	LIKE	A FALLING TREE). YOU ARE ALL MOST WELCOME. PERHAPS,
MTH5 SD(205)	AND REMARKABLE GRACE, RACING THROUGH A FIGURE	LIKE	A FARANDOLE. THEY NEITHER ROMP NOR HUG IN OUR MANNER.
MTH1 II SD(20)	AND IN THE PRIME OF LIFE. ADAM LOOKS WORRIED,	LIKE	A FARMER. EVE, BETTER HUMORED (HAVING GIVEN UP
SUPR PREFACE(R20)	COUNT IN THE WORLD SCHEME: EVEN BUNSBY DROPPING	LIKE	A FASCINATED BIRD INTO THE JAWS OF MRS MACSTINGER IS BY
CATH 2 (180)	THAT ER -- ? (HE GAZES AT HER, SPEECHLESS,	LIKE	A FASCINATED RABBIT. SHE REPEATS FIERCELY) THAT ER --
NEVR II (247)	TO HEAR THEIR VOICES! AND CARRY IT ALL OFF	LIKE	A FASHIONABLE VISITOR; DROP IN TO LUNCH; BE MR
NEVR IV (295)	LIKE A STAGE COLUMBINE IN THE EVENING AND	LIKE	A FASHIONABLE COLUMBINE IN THE MORNING. WELL, SHE WONT:
MRS II (202)	ALLOWED YOURSELF THE LIBERTY OF SPEAKING TO ME	LIKE	A FATHER A MOMENT AGO. ONE FATHER IS ENOUGH, THANK YOU.
CATH 1 (173)	HIM, UNCLE. /PATIOMKIN/ (LIFTING HIM IN HIS ARMS	LIKE	A FATHER CARRYING A LITTLE BOY) YES: I'LL CARRY YOU.
ROCK I (223)	AND TOLD HIM WHO WE WERE AND THAT OLD BASHAM WAS	LIKE	A FATHER TO US. ALL HE SAID WAS " YOU GO HOME, SIR; AND
JOAN 1 (63)	NOW LISTEN TO ME, POLLY. I MUST TALK TO YOU	LIKE	A FATHER. POULENGEY LOOKS UP AT HIM GRAVELY FOR A
NEVR III (281)	MAKES A MAN. /VALENTINE/ YES, THE WHOLE WORLD IS	LIKE	A FEATHER DANCING IN THE LIGHT NOW; AND GLORIA IS THE
BASH I (94)	SPEAK? WALK? HEAVE THE CHEST WITH BREATH? OR	LIKE	A FEATHER LIFT YOU-- LIKE THIS? (HE SETS HER ON HER
GETT (333)	NEVER GET ON WITH ONE ANOTHER, MRS GEORGE. I LIVE	LIKE	A FENCER, ALWAYS ON GUARD. I LIKE TO BE CONFRONTED WITH
HART PREFACE(24)	HOW THE FOOLS SHOUTED THE WISE MEN DOWN. THUS,	LIKE	A FERTILE COUNTRY FLOODED WITH MUD, ENGLAND SHEWED NO
MILL I (157)	RESOURCES AT AN APPALLING RATE, I SHOULD HONESTLY	LIKE	A FEW LESSONS FROM ALASTAIR IN THE ART OF TURNING
ARMS III (56)	YOUR HANDS CLEAN, AND BE DAINTY ABOUT YOURSELF,	LIKE	A FINE RUSSIAN LADY? ME! DO YOU HEAR THAT? ME! (SHE
CATH 2 (178)	A DONKEY BEGINNING TO BRAY)! ! ! /CATHERINE/ (	LIKE	A FISHFAG) SCHWEIG, DU HUND. (RESUMING HER IMPRESSIVE
BARB PREFACE(227)	HELLISH LAUGHTER OF DERISION AND OBSCENITY, RISES	LIKE	A FLOOD MIRACULOUSLY OUT OF THE FETID DUST AND MUD OF
BARB III (331)	WORSHIP BARBARA; AND SO I DID. SHE BOUGHT MY SOUL	LIKE	A FLOWER AT A STREET CORNER; BUT SHE BOUGHT IT FOR
CLEO V SD(195)	LADIES, ALL IN THEIR GAYEST ATTIRE, ARE	LIKE	A FLOWER GARDEN. THE FACADE IS LINED BY HER GUARD,
MTH4 I (150)	RECOVERING RAPIDLY. I HAVE A SENSE OF BLOSSOMING	LIKE	A FLOWER. MAY I ASK YOUR NAME? /ZOO/ ZOO. /THE ELDERLY
MTH4 I (162)	TRUE OR NOT? YOUR FLESH IS AS GRASS: YOU COME UP	LIKE	A FLOWER, AND WITHER IN YOUR SECOND CHILDHOOD. A LIE
BASH I (98)	AGAINST THE WAISTCOAT OF MELLISH, WHO DOUBLES UP	LIKE	A FOLDED TOWEL, AND LIES WITHOUT SENSE OR MOTION.) AND
SUPR I (11)	ONE DAY THAT YOU WERE TO BE ANN'S GUARDIAN; AND	LIKE	A FOOL I BEGAN ARGUING WITH HIM ABOUT THE FOLLY OF
GENV IV (103)	ROPE INSTEAD OF ON A BRIDGE? AM I TO BEHAVE	LIKE	A FOOL OR A MAN OF SENSE? /BBDE/ YOU WOULD BE A MUCH
CATH 3 (183)	COULD HELP IT. /EDSTASTON/ OH, DONT MAKE ME FEEL	LIKE	A FOOL. BUT THOUGH IT DOES SOUND CONCEITED TO SAY IT, I
BUOY IV (60)	MAN IN THE FAMILY: YOU ALWAYS MAKE ME FEEL	LIKE	A FOOL. I AM PROUD OF YOU. I MAY LOSE MY TEMPER
PHIL I (91)	HIM) STOP! DONT LEAVE ME LIKE THIS: I SHALL LOOK	LIKE	A FOOL. NOW I SHALL REALLY TAKE IT IN BAD PART IF YOU
6CAL (103)	NOT LOOK RADIANT? /THE KING/ AND HOW DO I LOOK?	LIKE	A FOOL. /JOHN OF GAUNT/ SIR: THE MEN-AT-ARMS WANT TO
DEVL III (77)	MINISTER-- I SHOULD SAY CAPTAIN. I HAVE BEHAVED	LIKE	A FOOL. /JUDITH/ LIKE A HERO. /RICHARD/ MUCH THE SAME
PRES (168)	YOU IF YOU WISH IT. /MRS FARRELL/ YOUD ONLY FEEL	LIKE	A FOOL; AND SO WOULD I. /MITCHENER/ YOU ARE REALLY THE
BULL I (93)	DOES. HE INSTINCTIVELY MAKES HIMSELF LOOK	LIKE	A FOOL, AND EATS UP ALL THE REAL FOOLS AT HIS EASE
JOAN 6 (136)	I HAD NOT WORN MY CLOTH OF GOLD SURCOAT IN BATTLE	LIKE	A FOOL, THAT BURGUNDIAN SOLDIER WOULD NEVER HAVE PULLED
HART III (140)	INTO THIS SILLY HOUSE I HAVE BEEN MADE TO LOOK	LIKE	A FOOL, THOUGH I'M AS GOOD A MAN IN THIS HOUSE AS IN
MTH4 I (141)	MY DRESS RIDICULOUS! I MAY NOT BE DRESSED	LIKE	A FOREIGN OFFICE CLERK; BUT MY CLOTHES ARE PERFECTLY IN
NEVR II (244)	OUTBURST. YOU MUST REMEMBER THAT DOLLY IS JUST	LIKE	A FOREIGNER HERE. PRAY SIT DOWN. /CRAMPTON/ (SUBSIDING
WIDO I (3)	NOISILY) POUR OUT THE RHINE WINE: LET IT FLOW	LIKE	A FREE AND BOUNDING RIVER-- /COKANE/ (SCANDALIZED) IN
DEST (169)	THAT IS WHAT I CALL WOMANISH: IT IS SO	LIKE	A FRENCHMAN! /NAPOLEON/ (FURIOUSLY) I AM NO
JITT I (15)	AND AT LAST I HEAR YOUR RING, I SUDDENLY BECOME	LIKE	A FRESHMAN JUST UP FROM SCHOOL. (SHE LAUGHS, SMOOTHING
JITT II (36)	UNDERSTAND ME, AND LET ME OPEN MY HEART TO YOU	LIKE	A FRIEND. /JITTA/ MY DEAR: I WILL BE AN ELDER SISTER TO
ARMS I SD(13)	UP WITH A SHRIEK. THE MAN, ALL NERVES, SHIES	LIKE	A FRIGHTENED HORSE TO THE OTHER SIDE OF THE ROOM. /THE
SUPR III SD(137)	AIR, WHICH FALLS ON THE EARS OF THE BRIGANDS	LIKE	A FUNERAL MARCH. /TANNER/ IT IS NOT AN ESCORT, BUT AN
MTH1 II (27)	FLESH CEASES TO GROW LIKE MAN'S FLESH; IT GROWS	LIKE	A FUNGUS ON A TREE. INSTEAD OF BREATHING, YOU SNEEZE,
POSN PREFACE(376)	WITH AN IRISHMAN'S SENSE OF HOW TO BEHAVE	LIKE	A GALLANT GENTLEMAN ON OCCASION, WAS DETERMINED TO BE
APPL I (228)	EVERY MAN PLAYS FOR HIS OWN HAND. /NICOBAR/ IT'S	LIKE	A GAME OF CARDS. /BALBUS/ ONLY THERE ARE NO PARTNERS.
WIDO III SD(51)	BLACK; A HANDSOME GOLD WATCH-CHAIN HANGS	LIKE	A GARLAND ON HIS FILLED-OUT WAISTCOAT; HE HAS SHAVED
CLEO IV (180)	GOES GRIMLY AWAY PAST RA AND OUT. CLEOPATRA RUNS	LIKE	A GAZELLE TO CAESAR) SO YOU HAVE COME BACK TO ME,
DEVL III (63)	TO YOU WHAT WICKED THING YOU DO IF ONLY YOU DO IT	LIKE	A GENTLEMAN? IS IT NOTHING TO YOU WHETHER YOU ARE A
PPP (197)	YOU WOULD APPEAL TO THE LAW! CAN YOU NOT DIE	LIKE	A GENTLEMAN? /ADOLPHUS/ BUT SO YOUNG! WHEN I HAVE
LION EPILOG (149)	MANKIND. WHEN THE ARCHBISHOP OF YORK BEHAVED	LIKE	A GENTLEMAN AND THE HEAD MASTER OF ETON PREACHED A
LIED (194)	DO? I AM AT YOUR SERVICE. I AM READY TO BEHAVE	LIKE	A GENTLEMAN IF YOU WILL BE KIND ENOUGH TO EXPLAIN
GETT (351)	A GENTLEMAN. WELL, IF YOU THINK YOUVE BEHAVED	LIKE	A GENTLEMAN TO LEO, YOURE MISTAKEN. AND I SHALL HAVE TO
BUOY IV (58)	HE SPEAKS LIKE A GENTLEMAN. HE DRESSES	LIKE	A GENTLEMAN, BUT HE HAS NOT THE FEELINGS OF A
BUOY IV (58)	OR EXPECTATIONS? IS HE A GENTLEMAN? HE SPEAKS	LIKE	A GENTLEMAN. HE DRESSES LIKE A GENTLEMAN. BUT HE HAS
LIED (193)	THAT YOU ARE GOING TO BE REASONABLE AND BEHAVE	LIKE	A GENTLEMAN. (HE DROPS ON THE STOOL; COVERS HIS FACE
MIS. (193)	ON OCCASION, AS YOU HAVE ALL SEEN, I CAN BEHAVE	LIKE	A GENTLEMAN. ON OCCASION, I CAN BEHAVE WITH A BRUTAL
GETT (351)	YOUVE ALWAYS TALKED A PRECIOUS LOT ABOUT BEHAVING	LIKE	A GENTLEMAN. WELL, IF YOU THINK YOUVE BEHAVED LIKE A
PHIL III (144)	COMES INTO THIS ROOM, YOUVE GOT TO BEHAVE	LIKE	A GENTLEMAN; OR FOND AS I AM OF YOU, I'LL CUT YOU DEAD
PHIL III (146)	GO STRAIGHT UP AND CONGRATULATE JULIA. AND DO IT	LIKE	A GENTLEMAN, SMILING. /CHARTERIS/ COLONEL: I WILL. NOT
PHIL III (137)	I NEVER TOLD YOU SO. IF YOU CANNOT BEHAVE	LIKE	A GENTLEMAN, YOU HAD BETTER GO BACK TO THE SOCIETY OF

CAND II	(106)	(ALMOST WHISPERING) IT MUST BE ASKED FOR: IT IS	LIKE	A GHOST: IT CANNOT SPEAK UNLESS IT IS FIRST SPOKEN TO.
LADY	(237)	WITH YOU ON YOUR LONELY WATCH, AND I APPROACHING	LIKE	A GHOST IN THE MOONLIGHT. STARE NOT SO AMAZEDLY AT ME;
SUPR III	(129)	WORDS WHICH I OR ANYONE ELSE CAN TURN INSIDE OUT	LIKE	A GLOVE. WERE THEY REALITIES, YOU WOULD HAVE TO PLEAD
BASH I	(97)	THE ORB OF NIGHT HANG IN THE HEAVENS UNNOTICED,	LIKE	A GLOW-WORM AT HIGH NOON. /MELLISH/ AH ME, AH ME, WHERE
SUPR I	(8)	ABOUT HER DUTY TO HER PARENTS. (HE STARTS OFF	LIKE	A GOADED OX IN THE DIRECTION OF JOHN BRIGHT, IN WHOSE
ANNA	(299)	YOU MEAN TO OBEY THEM? /STRAMMFEST/ (STARTING	LIKE	A GOADED OX, AND BLUNDERING FRETFULLY ABOUT THE ROOM)
ANNA	(290)	KING IS A SPLENDID REALITY, A MAN RAISED ABOVE US	LIKE	A GOD. YOU CAN SEE HIM; YOU CAN KISS HIS HAND; YOU CAN
LION PREFACE	(43)	THE NARRATIVES HE DID NOT DO SO. HE HAD TO DIE	LIKE	A GOD, NOT TO SAVE HIMSELF " LIKE ONE OF THE PRINCES."
BULL IV	(171)	WITH KEEGAN. /BROADBENT/ NOTHING PAYS	LIKE	A GOLFING HOTEL, IF YOU HOLD THE LAND INSTEAD OF THE
ROCK II	(273)	WILL GET YOU ANY FURTHER. GO AND TELL HER SO,	LIKE	A GOOD BOY. I'M BUSY. /BARKING/ RIGHTO! (HE DASHES
HART I	(72)	/MRS HUSHABYE/ CALL HER ADDY; AND KISS HER	LIKE	A GOOD BROTHER-IN-LAW; AND HAVE DONE WITH IT. (SHE
HART II	(127)	SAY GOODNIGHT TO MRS HUSHABYE FOR ME, WILL YOU,	LIKE	A GOOD CHAP. GOODNIGHT. (HE HURRIES OUT). /HECTOR/
MRS I	(197)	THEM I SHANT BE HOME TO TEA, WILL YOU, GOV'NOR,	LIKE	A GOOD FELLOW? (HE MOVES TOWARDS THE COTTAGE DOOR AND
DEVL II	(45)	YES? /ANDERSON/ JUST WAIT OUTSIDE A MOMENT,	LIKE	A GOOD GIRL: MRS ANDERSON IS NOT WELL. (ESSIE LOOKS
PYGM IV	(264)	HURTING YOU. NOTHING'S WRONG. YOU GO TO BED	LIKE	A GOOD GIRL AND SLEEP IT OFF. HAVE A LITTLE CRY AND SAY
DEVL I	(17)	/ESSIE/ (SCAREDLY) NO. /JUDITH/ THEN SAY IT,	LIKE	A GOOD GIRL. /ESSIE/ AMEN. /UNCLE WILLIAM/ (
ARMS III	(66)	SNEEZES). GO AND ASK YOUR MISTRESS FOR MY COAT,	LIKE	A GOOD GIRL, WILL YOU? NICOLA ENTERS WITH THE COAT.
GETT	(319)	LITTLE OF IT GOES A LONG WAY WITH THEM; AND THEY	LIKE	A GOOD IMITATION OF IT BETTER THAN THE REAL THING, AS
APPL II	(277)	BE NAUGHTY. I MUSTNT BE LATE FOR DINNER. COME ON,	LIKE	A GOOD LITTLE BOY. THE KING, WITH A GRIMACE OF HOPELESS
CAND III	(139)	WELL THEN, YOU ARE FORGIVEN. NOW GO OFF TO BED	LIKE	A GOOD LITTLE BOY: I WANT TO TALK TO JAMES ABOUT YOU.
GLIM	(186)	THEM, NOT AS THEY REALLY ARE. THERE IS NOTHING	LIKE	A GOOD LOOK INTO THE FACE OF DEATH: CLOSE UP: RIGHT ON
WIDO I	(18)	THEY COME. GET THE LETTER FINISHED BEFORE DINNER,	LIKE	A GOOD OLD CHAPPIE: I SHALL BE AWFULLY OBLIGED TO YOU.
BULL I	(87)	AT BROADBENT) BE " AGREEABLE TO STRANGERS,"	LIKE	A GOOD-FOR-NOTHING WOMAN ON THE STREETS. (GABBLING AT
MTH5	(258)	HAVE SWORN. THEY HAVE SWORN. /ECRASIA/ YOU SPEAK	LIKE	A GRAMMAR. /STREPHON/ THAT IS HOW ONE OUGHT TO SPEAK.
CLEO IV	(175)	BOTH SIDES TO THE FURTHER END, WHERE A GAP IN IT,	LIKE	A GREAT GATEWAY, LEAVES THE VIEW OPEN TO THE SKY BEYOND
BARB III SD	(326)	THE SHED; AND ONE HAS FALLEN FORWARD AND LIES,	LIKE	A GROTESQUE CORPSE, ON THE EMPLACEMENT. THE PARAPET
BARB III	(314)	BRITOMART/ CHARLES: IF YOU MUST DRIVEL, DRIVEL	LIKE	A GROWN-UP MAN AND NOT LIKE A SCHOOLBOY. /LOMAX/ (OUT
SUPR I	(21)	HIS FACE UP SUDDENLY). DO YOU WANT TO BE TREATED	LIKE	A GROWN-UP MAN? MUST I CALL YOU MR ROBINSON IN
CAND III SD	(139)	CANDIDA RETURNS. EUGENE CREEPS BACK TO THE SOFA	LIKE	A GUILTY SCHOOLBOY. /CANDIDA/ (BETWEEN THEM,
SUPR III	(130)	DID I DREAM THAT HELL WAS SO HORRIBLE, I LIVE,	LIKE	A HAIRDRESSER, IN THE CONTINUAL CONTEMPLATION OF
MIS.	(167)	AND ON THIS. (HE HOLDS OUT THE TWO PHOTOGRAPHS	LIKE	A HAND AT CARDS, AND POINTS TO THEM WITH THE PISTOL).
POSN	(463)	LOOKING AT THE RAINBOW AND LET HIMSELF BE TOOK	LIKE	A HARE IN A TRAP BY STRAPPER KEMP: A LAD WHOSE BACK I
BULL II	(101)	US! (HE GOES DOWN THE HILL TOWARDS THE ROAD	LIKE	A HAUNTED MAN). NORA REILLY COMES DOWN THE HILL. A
GENV IV	(110)	OF IT. BRING IT TO JESUS. IT WILL FALL FROM YOU	LIKE	A HEAVY BURDEN; AND YOUR HEART WILL BE LIGHT. OH, SO
VWOO 3	(135)	ANYONE CAME NEAR YOU YOU SHRANK UP INTO YOURSELF	LIKE	A HEDGEHOG, AFRAID THAT THEY DIDNT BELONG TO YOUR CLASS
SUPR III	(109)	A COWARD TO THE BACKBONE, WILL FIGHT FOR AN IDEA	LIKE	A HERO. HE MAY BE ABJECT AS A CITIZEN; BUT HE IS
DEVL III	(77)	SAY CAPTAIN. I HAVE BEHAVED LIKE A FOOL. /JUDITH/	LIKE	A HERO. /RICHARD/ MUCH THE SAME THING, PERHAPS. (WITH
NEVR II	(257)	HAT). /GLORIA/ (WITH ELABORATE CALM, SITTING UP	LIKE	A HIGH-SCHOOLMISTRESS POSING TO BE PHOTOGRAPHED). THAT
ROCK II	(263)	AWAY TO PILE UP RICHES, ONLY TO BE SMOKED OUT	LIKE	A HIVE OF BEES AND PLUNDERED OF EVERYTHING BUT A BARE
HART II	(85)	AND SHEWS HIS TEETH). I JUST SMOKED THEM OUT	LIKE	A HIVE OF BEES. WHAT DO YOU SAY TO THAT? A BIT OF A
MTH2	(44)	IN THE COALITION. OF COURSE, HE DROPPED ME	LIKE	A HOT POTATO. /CONRAD/ WELL, NOW THAT THE COALITION HAS
JITT I SD	(9)	YOUNGER THAN HER FACE. SHE IS WELL DRESSED,	LIKE	A HOTEL MANAGERESS. SHE OPENS THE DOOR, LETTING IN SOME
JITT I SD	(9)	DE RIGUEUR IN HOTELS. BUT THE PLACE IS NOT QUITE	LIKE	A HOTEL SITTING ROOM; BECAUSE THERE IS VERY LITTLE
PYGM III	(246)	ON HER SOME MONTHS AGO; AND SHE'S GETTING ON	LIKE	A HOUSE ON FIRE. I SHALL WIN MY BET. SHE HAS A QUICK
SIM I	(52)	IN HER EMBRACE) OH, MAYA, DARLING: SPEAK TO ME	LIKE	A HUMAN BEING. /MAYA/ THAT IS HOW I SPEAK TO YOU; BUT
NEVR IV	(298)	/DOLLY/ (RUNNING TO HIM) OH, NOW YOU LOOK QUITE	LIKE	A HUMAN BEING. MAYNT I HAVE JUST ONE DANCE WITH YOU?
BASH II,1,	(103)	DUCKING SMARTLY TO HIS LEFT, CROSS-COUNTERED	LIKE	A HUNDREDWEIGHT OF BRICK--" /LUCIAN/ DEATH AND
JITT I SD	(13)	IMMEDIATELY AFTERWARDS A VEILED LADY HURRIES IN	LIKE	A HUNTED CREATURE. HE FOLLOWS HER; SHUTS THE DOOR; AND
GENV IV	(123)	WE SHALL SEE. I SHALL SWEEP THROUGH RURITANIA	LIKE	A HURRICANE. /COMMISSAR/ DO SO BY ALL MEANS, COMRADE
SIM PRO,3,	(30)	COULD THAT BE? (TO THE PRIESTESS) YOU WOULDNT	LIKE	A HUSBAND THAT DIDNT EAT PLENTY OF MEAT, WOULD YOU?
ARMS I	(18)	EXCLAIMING) PLEASE! (HE BECOMES MOTIONLESS,	LIKE	A HYPNOTIZED RABBIT, HIS FATIGUE GAINING FAST ON HIM.
SUPR III	(98)	ARTS! /DON JUAN/ (WITH COLD DISGUST) YOU TALK	LIKE	A HYSTERICAL WOMAN FAWNING ON A FIDDLER. /THE DEVIL/ I
KING I	(189)	GET UP, JAMIE, AND NOT SIT ON THE FLOOR GRINNING	LIKE	A JACKANAPES. GET UP, I TELL YOU. /JAMES/ (RISING) YOU
MIS.	(135)	AND JOHN GAVE HIM A HUNDRED IN HIS BIG WAY, JUST	LIKE	A KING. /LORD SUMMERHAYS/ NOT AT ALL. I HAD FIVE KINGS
AUGS	(282)	AND THAT I WAS A HUN. HE LAPPED IT UP	LIKE	A KITTEN. . . . /AUGUSTUS/ YOU DONT MEAN TO SAY THAT --
FANY I	(278)	HIM. BUT HOLY JOE LIKES IT: FAIRLY LAPS IT UP	LIKE	A KITTEN, POOR OLD DEAR. WELL, BOBBY SAYS TO ME, "
MIS. PREFACE	(67)	ABOUT, THE ENGLISHMAN OBEYS LIKE A SHEEP, EVADES	LIKE	A KNAVE, OR TRIES TO MURDER HIS OPPRESSOR, MERELY
ARMS II	(33)	YOU INSPIRED ME. I HAVE GONE THROUGH THE WAR	LIKE	A KNIGHT IN A TOURNAMENT WITH HIS LADY LOOKING DOWN AT
FOUN	(215)	CHANCELLOR/ MADAM: I MUST REQUEST YOU TO SPEAK	LIKE	A LADY AND NOT LIKE A PROCESSION OF THE UNEMPLOYED. THE
PYGM II	(228)	SIX MONTHS, LEARNING HOW TO SPEAK BEAUTIFULLY,	LIKE	A LADY IN A FLORIST'S SHOP. IF YOURE GOOD AND DO
PHIL III	(144)	I DONT MIND. BUT IF YOU ARE NOT GOING TO BEHAVE	LIKE	A LADY WHEN MRS TRANFIELD COMES INTO THIS ROOM, YOUVE
BUOY III	(34)	A LADY, AND CAN TALK LIKE A LADY, AND CAN BEHAVE	LIKE	A LADY WHEN SHE LIKES; BUT SHE DOES NOT BELONG TO US.
PYGM II	(226)	I DONT WANT TO TALK GRAMMAR. I WANT TO TALK	LIKE	A LADY. /MRS PEARCE/ WILL YOU PLEASE KEEP TO THE POINT,
BUOY III	(34)	OF HER. SHE DRESSES LIKE A LADY, AND CAN TALK	LIKE	A LADY, AND CAN BEHAVE LIKE A LADY WHEN SHE LIKES; BUT
BUOY III	(34)	COULD MAKE A REAL LADY OF HER. SHE DRESSES	LIKE	A LADY, AND CAN TALK LIKE A LADY, AND CAN BEHAVE LIKE A
2TRU PREFACE	(9)	OF THE CRIMEAN HOSPITALS RATHER THAN BEHAVE	LIKE	A LADY, AND WHY MY NEIGHBOR MR APSLEY CHERRY-GARRARD,
LION PREFACE	(19)	AND CONSISTENT PERSON. HIS REASONS FOR GOING "	LIKE	A LAMB TO THE SLAUGHTER" INSTEAD OF SAVING HIMSELF AS
BULL PREFACE	(20)	HAD NOT EVEN THE ILLUSION OF HEROISM WHEN HE WENT	LIKE	A LAMB TO THE SLAUGHTER), GOT HIMSELF KILLED BY HIS
BUOY III	(45)	ALWAYS DOES. I HAVE GONE TWICE TO MY WEDDINGS	LIKE	A LAMB TO THE SLAUGHTER HOUSE. MY TWO WIVES WERE
ROCK PREFACE	(179)	YET THEIR CHAMPION PUT UP NO FIGHT: HE WENT	LIKE	A LAMB TO THE SLAUGHTER, DUMB. SUCH A SPECTACLE IS
DOCT I	(97)	/B.B./ (ARCHLY) AHA! HA HA! AHA! (TRILLING	LIKE	A LARK AS HE SHAKES HIS FINGER AT WALPOLE). YOU REMOVED
LION II	(144)	YAWNS, PURRS, AND ROARS, ACHIEVES SOMETHING VERY	LIKE	A LAUGH). /THE EMPEROR/ (STANDING ON A CHAIR INSIDE
PPP SD	(205)	THE FAN; AND FANS THE POLICEMAN, WHO ROLLS AWAY	LIKE	A LEAF BEFORE THE WIND TO THE WALL. SHE DISPOSES
NEVR IV	(302)	HIM AWAY FROM HER; AND HE REELS BACK INTO A CHAIR	LIKE	A LEAF BEFORE THE WIND). DOLLY DANCES IN, WALTZING WITH
SUPR I	(36)	ALL THE OTHER PASSIONS WOULD SWEEP IT AWAY	LIKE	A LEAF BEFORE A HURRICANE. IT IS THE BIRTH OF THAT
BULL I	(92)	A TREE, INSTINCTIVELY MAKES ITSELF LOOK EXACTLY	LIKE	A LEAF; SO THAT BOTH ITS ENEMIES AND ITS PREY MAY
NEVR I	(217)	CRAMPTON, MISS. /DOLLY/ (REPEATING IT TO HERSELF	LIKE	A LESSON) CRAMPTON, CRAMPTON, CRAMPTON, CRAMPTON,
MILL II	(175)	WANT MOSTLY? /EPIFANIA/ EVERYTHING, ANYTHING,	LIKE	A LIGHTNING FLASH, AND THEN THERE IS NO STOPPING ME.
ARMS II	(41)	THE PEACE ON MY HUSBAND HAS BEEN TO MAKE HIM FEEL	LIKE	A LION BAULKED OF HIS PREY. IF HE DISCOVERS OUR SECRET,
ROCK PREFACE	(148)	THAT HE DOES NO MISCHIEF, AND CAGING HIM CRUELLY	LIKE	A LION IN A SHOW. HERE SOMEBODY IS SURE TO INTERJECT
SUPR III	(84)	TASTE THIS FINELY TEMPERED AIR, AND THEN TALK	LIKE	A LITERARY HACK ON A SECOND FLOOR IN BLOOMSBURY?
GLIM	(187)	ROUND HIM) I HAVE YOU VERY FAST NOW, SIGNORINO,	LIKE	A LITTLE BIRD IN A CAGE. /FERRUCCIO/ YOU HAVE MY BODY,
CATH 2	(178)	PATIOMKIN! WHAT ARE YOU THINKING OF? (HE FALLS	LIKE	A LOG ON THE FLOOR, APPARENTLY DEAD DRUNK). /THE
MILL II	(175)	I HAVE A CLOCKWORK INSIDE. I SLEEP EIGHT HOURS	LIKE	A LOG. WHEN I WANT ANYTHING I LOSE MY HEAD SO
2TRU PREFACE	(8)	IMAGINE; FOR, JUST AS THE BEAN-FEASTER CAN LIVE	LIKE	A LORD FOR AN AFTERNOON, AND THE LANCASHIRE FACTORY
DOCT III	(138)	LEARN TO THINK, INSTEAD OF BLEATING AND BAAHING	LIKE	A LOT OF SHEEP WHEN YOU COME UP AGAINST ANYTHING YOURE
FANY PROLOG	(261)	SAVOYARD. THAT WHAT YOU ARE ABOUT TO SEE WILL BE	LIKE	A LOUIS QUATORZE BALLET PAINTED BY WATTEAU. THE HEROINE
SIM II	(84)	IT COMES LIKE A THIEF IN THE NIGHT. /PROLA/ OR	LIKE	A LOVER. NEVER WILL PROLA GO BACK TO THE COUNTRY OF THE
JITT I	(20)	/BRUNO/ (SEIZING HER HANDS, BUT NOW PLEADING	LIKE	A LOVER) IT IS MY DEEPEST WISH. IT IS MY MOST URGENT
MTH3	(109)	DROWNED FOUR TIMES. HE WOULD RUN AWAY FROM WATER	LIKE	A MAD DOG. /THE ARCHBISHOP/ PERHAPS MR CHIEF SECRETARY
BARB III	(313)	THE PRINCE OF DARKNESS PLAYED HIS TROMBONE	LIKE	A MADMAN: ITS BRAZEN ROARINGS WERE LIKE THE LAUGHTER OF
JITT I	(21)	BRUNO, AS IF IT SETTLED EVERYTHING. I CANNOT ACT	LIKE	A MADWOMAN. GIVE ME A REASON. /BRUNO/ I WILL. LISTEN. A
DOCT II	(120)	HE WAS REALLY VERY NICE ABOUT IT. HE TOOK IT	LIKE	A MAN; AND IT WAS A PLEASURE TO SEE HOW HAPPY IT MADE
DEVL I	(26)	TO ANDERSON) OR A LAWYER! (HAWKINS SMILES	LIKE	A MAN ABLE TO TAKE CARE OF HIMSELF) OR AN UPRIGHT
CAPT III	(291)	TO GET RID OF THIS RESPECTABLE CLOBBER AND FEEL	LIKE	A MAN AGAIN. STAND BY, ALL HANDS, TO JUMP ON THE
APPL II SD	(258)	VANHATTAN ENTERS IN AN EFFUSIVE CONDITION, AND,	LIKE	A MAN ASSURED OF AN ENTHUSIASTIC WELCOME, HURRIES TO
DEST	(169)	(HE PULLS HIMSELF PIOUSLY TOGETHER, AND SAYS,	LIKE	A MAN CONDUCTING A RELIGIOUS SERVICE) I AM ONLY THE
DEST	(167)	OF RALLYING HOPE BEAMS FROM HER EYE. HE BEGINS	LIKE	A MAN ENJOYING SOME SECRET JOKE). HOW DO YOU KNOW I AM
HART II	(102)	ARE THINGS NO DECENT WOMAN WOULD DO TO A MAN--	LIKE	A MAN HITTING A WOMAN IN THE BREAST. HESIONE, UTTERLY
O'FL	(206)	AND THE TRYING TO MAKE MY EYES LOOK MOIST	LIKE	A MAN IN A PICTURE BOOK, I'M THAT BET THAT I HARDLY GET
SIM II	(79)	AS I SHALL FORGET MAYA'S. (HE GOES OUT SEAWARD	LIKE	A MAN IN A TRANCE). /LADY FARWATERS/ (TROUBLED, HALF
DEVL III	(62)	TO TREAT ME AS A PRISONER OF WAR, AND SHOOT ME	LIKE	A MAN INSTEAD OF HANGING ME LIKE A DOG. /BURGOYNE/ (
BULL I	(87)	DEVILS LIKE YOURSELF. (DROPPING HIS VOICE	LIKE	A MAN MAKING SOME SHAMEFUL CONFIDENCE) AND ALL THE
BASH II,1,	(106)	I EXPRESS MYSELF MORE LIKE A MOBLED QUEEN THAN	LIKE	A MAN OF FLESH AND BLOOD. WELL MAY YOUR COUSIN SNEER!
APPL I	(240)	WHAT IS THE USE OF GOING ON LIKE THIS? YOU ARE	LIKE	A MAN ON THE SCAFFOLD, SPINNING OUT HIS PRAYERS TO PUT
NEVR II	(239)	(HE WALKS AWAY TO THE SIDE OF THE TERRACE,	LIKE	A MAN PUTTING TEMPTATION BEHIND HIM). /PHILIP/
KING I	(178)	(HE FALLS ON HIS KNEES AND COLLAPSES, SHIVERING	LIKE	A MAN RECOVERING FROM A FIT. CHARLES AND NEWTON HELP

MIS. (183)	END OF THE WRITING TABLE NEAREST THE SIDEBOARD	LIKE	A MAN RESIGNED TO ANYTHING THAT FATE MAY HAVE IN STORE
BARB II (274)	PLEASED THE CAPITALISTS TO CALL ME; AND THEY DONT	LIKE	A MAN THAT SEES THROUGH EM. SECOND, AN INTELLIGENT BEIN
SHAK SD(140)	ON GUARD. ROB DRAWS; SPINS ROUND SEVERAL TIMES	LIKE	A MAN THROWING A HAMMER; AND FINALLY CUTS OFF MACBETH'S
CAND I (90)	WITH HIS BACK TO THE FIRE, AND CONTINUES) NO: I	LIKE	A MAN TO BE TRUE TO HIMSELF, EVEN IN WICKEDNESS. COME
PHIL II (115)	MY SOUL, IT'S TOO DISGUSTING! I'D FAR RATHER DIE	LIKE	A MAN WHEN I SAID I WOULD. /PARAMORE/ (AS BEFORE)
2TRU III (110)	OF DEATH. I STAND MIDWAY BETWEEN YOUTH AND AGE	LIKE	A MAN WHO HAS MISSED HIS TRAIN: TOO LATE FOR THE LAST
SUPR II SD(48)	ON THEM ALWAYS, AND THAT, TOO, RATHER CYNICALLY,	LIKE	A MAN WHO KNOWS THE WORLD WELL FROM ITS SEAMY SIDE. HE
MIS. (136)	MUST BE A BIT OF A SCOUNDREL? IF YOU ASK ME, I	LIKE	A MAN WHO MAKES UP HIS MIND ONCE FOR ALL AS TO WHATS
JOAN PREFACE(4)	EXPERIENCE, DID NOT DEFEND HIMSELF AT HIS TRIAL	LIKE	A MAN WHO UNDERSTOOD THE LONG ACCUMULATED FURY THAT HAD
BULL PREFACE(40)	ALL THAT THIS IMPLIES. A CONQUERED NATION IS	LIKE	A MAN WITH CANCER: HE CAN THINK OF NOTHING ELSE, AND IS
JOAN 3 (91)	IN LOVE WITH WAR! MYSELF, THE UGLY DEVIL! I AM	LIKE	A MAN WITH TWO WIVES. DO YOU WANT TO BE LIKE A WOMAN
CAND II SD(122)	HAD SHOT THROUGH IT. HE SITS DOWN ON THE SOFA	LIKE	A MAN WITNESSING A TRAGEDY. /BURGESS/ (ON THE
PHIL II (117)	FOR YOUR DISAPPOINTMENT, BUT YOU MUST FACE IT	LIKE	A MAN, AND AFTER ALL, NOW REALLY, DOESNT THIS SHEW THAT
PRES (151)	GO TO HELL WHEN I CHALLENGES HIM TO ARGUE IT OUT	LIKE	A MAN. IT AINT POLITE; BUT IT'S ENGLISH. WHAT YOU SAY
SUPR I (30)	NOT ALL PLAYS AND POEMS, OCTAVIUS. COME! FACE IT	LIKE	A MAN. /TANNER/ (CHAFING AGAIN) POOR DEAR BROTHER!
SUPR I (27)	ME. /RAMSDEN/ HE SHALL, OCTAVIUS. THERE YOU SPEAK	LIKE	A MAN. /TANNER/ THEN YOU DONT THINK HIM A SCOUNDREL,
MTH1 I (14)	AND PLUCKING AT THE GRASS) THAT IS SO	LIKE	A MAN. THE MOMENT YOU FIND WE NEED NOT LAST FOR EVER,
MIS. (166)	YOU! /TARLETON/ OH, DONT CUT UP ROUGH. FACE IT	LIKE	A MAN. YOU SEE I DIDNT KNOW YOUR MOTHER; BUT IVE NO
PHIL III (146)	DECISIVELY) CHARTERIS: NOW YOUVE GOT TO BEHAVE	LIKE	A MAN. YOUR DUTY'S PLAIN BEFORE YOU. (TO CUTHBERTSON)
WIDO II (37)	PROVOKE ME TO BREAK THE ENGAGEMENT: THATS SO	LIKE	A MAN-- TO TRY TO PUT THE WOMAN IN THE WRONG. WELL, YOU
SUPR I (8)	HIS OPINIONS WERE SOMETHING TO BE LAUGHED AT,	LIKE	A MAN'S HAT ON A CHILD'S HEAD. BUT NOW TANNER IS A
DEVL III (67)	TO TAKE CARE OF MYSELF. /RICHARD/ NOW YOU TALK	LIKE	A MAN, I HAVE NO QUARREL WITH YOU. /BURGOYNE/ MR
HART I (67)	I DO. WHO TOLD YOU? /CAPTAIN SHOTOVER/ TALK	LIKE	A MAN, NOT LIKE A MOVY. YOU MEAN THAT YOU MAKE A
ARMS III (60)	COWARD! LIAR! FOOL! SHALL I KILL MYSELF	LIKE	A MAN, OR LIVE AND PRETEND TO LAUGH AT MYSELF? (SHE
SUPR II (52)	/TANNER/ (PATTING HIM ON THE BACK) BEAR IT	LIKE	A MAN, TAVY, EVEN IF YOU FEEL IT LIKE AN ASS. IT'S THE
JITT III (65)	HE WAS ALL I HAD THAT I CARED ABOUT. I AM NOT	LIKE	A MAN, TO BEGIN ALL OVER AGAIN WITH A NEW LOVE: I SHALL
OVER (178)	LIKE A POWDER. /MRS JUNO/ (CHILLED) THAT IS SO	LIKE	A MAN! I OFFER YOU MY HEART'S WARMEST FRIENDLIEST
JITT II (48)	YOU CANT SETTLE AN AFFAIR LIKE THIS BY LOOKING	LIKE	A MARTYR AND WALKING OUT INTO THE STREET. YOU MUST
CLEO I (116)	WRIST, AND LOOKS STEADFASTLY AT HER. SHE STANDS	LIKE	A MARTYR.) /CAESAR/ THE QUEEN MUST FACE CAESAR ALONE.
ROCK I (225)	YOU COME IN. YOU APPEARED THERE SUDDENLY LOOKING	LIKE	A MESSENGER OF DEATH, AND NOW YOU TELL ME YOU ARE A
PYGM V (288)	I DO, YOU LITTLE FOOL. FIVE MINUTES AGO YOU WERE	LIKE	A MILLSTONE ROUND MY NECK. NOW YOURE A TOWER OF
SUPR III (139)	AS BAD AS ANY OF YOU. ENRY: YOU HAVE BEHAVED JUST	LIKE	A MISERABLE GENTLEMAN. /STRAKER/ GENTLEMAN! NOT ME.
BASH II,1, (106)	IN HAMLET; AND TO THIS DAY I EXPRESS MYSELF MORE	LIKE	A MOBLED QUEEN THAN LIKE A MAN OF FLESH AND BLOOD. WELL
WIDO III (60)	AT THE CRIBBS MARKET END: ENOUGH TO MAKE IT LOOK	LIKE	A MODEL DWELLING, YOU KNOW; AND LET THE OTHER BLOCK TO
6CAL PREFACE(89)	HUMAN BEING IN A VERY TRYING SITUATION INSTEAD OF	LIKE	A MODERN CONSTITUTIONAL MONARCH ON PARADE KEEPING UP AN
CLEO NOTES (208)	AN ANCIENT BRITON COULD NOT POSSIBLY HAVE BEEN	LIKE	A MODERN ONE. I SEE NO REASON TO ADOPT THIS CURIOUS
METH PREFACE(R22)	TRYING TO SEE, YOU WILL FINALLY GET EYES. IF,	LIKE	A MOLE OR A SUBTERRANEAN FISH, YOU HAVE EYES AND DONT
HART III SD(129)	OF LIGHT CAST BY THE ELECTRIC ARC, WHICH IS	LIKE	A MOON IN ITS OPAL GLOBE. BENEATH THE HEAD OF THE
FANY I (281)	NOT VERY NICE TO ME ABOUT IT. IVE TALKED TO HIM	LIKE	A MOTHER, AND TRIED MY BEST TO KEEP HIM STRAIGHT; BUT I
GETT (327)	ME WITH THIS YOUNG MAN. I WANT TO TALK TO HIM	LIKE	A MOTHER, ON YOUR BUSINESS. /REGINALD/ DO, MAAM. HE
LION II SD(143)	TOWARDS HIM; SMELLS HIM; ARCHES HIS BACK; PURRS	LIKE	A MOTOR CAR; FINALLY RUBS HIMSELF AGAINST ANDROCLES.
BASH II,1, (110)	ENOUGH. MY DREAM IS DREAMED. YOUR GOLD WEIGHS	LIKE	A MOUNTAIN ON MY CHEST. FAREWELL. /LYDIA/ THE GOLDEN
LION II (140)	NOT MOVE THEM, BRING THE HOT IRONS, THE MAN IS	LIKE	A MOUNTAIN. (HE RETURNS ANGRILY INTO THE BOX AND SLAMS
GENV PREFACE(7)	AND CAN BE SEEN IN THE DISTANCE AS A WHOLE,	LIKE	A MOUNTAIN, THE VICTORIOUS COMBATANTS IN THE BATTLE OF
MILL IV (206)	OH, YOU CANNOT HAVE SPENT IT ALL: YOU WHO LIVE	LIKE	A MOUSE. THERE MUST BE SOME OF IT LEFT. /THE DOCTOR/
HART I (67)	YOU? /CAPTAIN SHOTOVER/ TALK LIKE A MAN, NOT	LIKE	A MOVY. YOU MEAN THAT YOU MAKE A HUNDRED THOUSAND A
GETT (277)	AND WAS IN LOVE WITH A YOUNG FELLOW WITH A FACE	LIKE	A MUSHROOM? /LEO/ HE HAS NOT. (BURSTING INTO TEARS)
GETT (304)	I HAD A FACE LIKE A WALNUT: HE HAD A FACE	LIKE	A MUSHROOM. I WAS AS GLAD TO HAVE HIM IN THE HOUSE AS
SUPR I (46)	IN THE HOUSEKEEPER'S ROOM AND BEING TREATED	LIKE	A NAUGHTY CHILD BY YOUNG GIRLS AND OLD LADIES WITHOUT
CLEO I (113)	STOPS. SHE TURNS STERNLY TO CLEOPATRA, WHO QUAILS	LIKE	A NAUGHTY CHILD). WHO IS THIS YOU HAVE WITH YOU; AND
BULL PREFACE(27)	OF HIS CHURCH. EXCEPT WHEN HE BREAKS OUT	LIKE	A NAUGHTY CHILD HE IS DOCILE; HE IS REVERENT; HE IS
MIS. (193)	THE BOURBONS BACK AGAIN. THAT WAS BEHAVING RATHER	LIKE	A NAVVY. NOW I, LIKE NAPOLEON, AM NOT ALL ONE PIECE. ON
GETT (327)	EFFORT; BUT I WAS ON THE POINT OF RETURNING	LIKE	A NEEDLE TO THE LODESTONE WHEN THE OUTBREAK OF THE WAR
MILL I (156)	THAT EVERY DECENT MAN WHO APPROACHES YOU FEELS	LIKE	A NEEDY ADVENTURER. YOU DONT KNOW HOW A MAN TO WHOM A
DEVL I (18)	TO CHRISTY WITH A SUDDENNESS THAT MAKES HIM JUMP	LIKE	A NEGLIGENT WICKET KEEPER, AND COMES INTO THE MIDDLE OF
2TRU I (41)	SEE. GO AND SIT DOWN IN THAT CHAIR AND LOOK AS	LIKE	A NICE GENTLE NURSE AS YOU CAN. /THE NURSE/ BUT-- /THE
CAPT II (262)	SAY THANK YOU TO ME FOR MENDING YOUR JACKET,	LIKE	A NICE POLITE SAILOR. /BRASSBOUND/ (SITTING DOWN AT
METH PREFACE(R69)	OF MILITARIST PATRIOTISM, HAD RIDDEN THE POWERS	LIKE	A NIGHTMARE SINCE THE FRANCO-PRUSSIAN WAR OF 1870-71.
KING I (165)	ROWLEY? WHAT IS MR ROWLEY? /MRS BASHAM/ DRESSED	LIKE	A NOBLEMAN. VERY TALL, VERY DARK. KEEPS A LACKEY. HAS A
KING I (161)	ROWLEY IS NOT MUCH OF A NAME. /THE MAID/ DRESSED	LIKE	A NOBLEMAN, MAAM. VERY TALL AND VERY DARK. AND A LOT OF
MRS II (216)	AND TAKE THE ROUGH WITH THE SMOOTH, JUST	LIKE	A NURSE IN A HOSPITAL OR ANYONE ELSE. IT'S NOT WORK
MRS III (226)	WITH LEAVES. /VIVIE/ (RHYTHMICALLY, ROCKING HIM	LIKE	A NURSE) FAST ASLEEP, HAND IN HAND, UNDER THE TREES.
ROCK PREFACE(166)	COMMUNISM WHEN ALL WESTERN EUROPE SET ON HIM	LIKE	A PACK OF HOUNDS ON A FOX. BUT AS ALL THE SOLDIERS WERE
SUPR PREFACE(R20)	FERDINAND AND MIRANDA TOGETHER AND THEY WILL MATE	LIKE	A PAIR OF DOVES; AND THERE IS NO NEED FOR PERDITA TO
MIS. PREFACE(75)	SO THAT INSTEAD OF THE INDIVIDUAL CHILD FASTENING	LIKE	A PARASITE ON ITS OWN PARTICULAR PARENTS, THE WHOLE
BULL IV (145)	AGAIN). /AUNT JUDY/ AH, HAVE SOME SENSE: YOURE	LIKE	A PARCEL O CHILDHER. NORA: HIT HIM A THUMP ON THE BACK:
MILL PREFACE(121)	REFUSED TO BE TURNED ASIDE FROM HIS WORK	LIKE	A PARLIAMENTARY MAN TO DISCUSS " INCIDENTS." ALL HE
PYGM III (257)	MY DEAR MRS HIGGINS, THAT GIRL /HIGGINS/ JUST	LIKE	A PARROT. IVE TRIED HER WITH EVERY /PICKERING/ IS A
HART PREFACE(25)	PAPER, AND YET ECHO THE OPINIONS OF THAT PAPER	LIKE	A PARROT. THUS, TO ESCAPE FROM THE PREVAILING CONFUSION
JOAN PREFACE(49)	FATALISTICALLY ONLY TO BE FORGOTTEN IMMEDIATELY	LIKE	A PASSING VAGUE APPREHENSION. TO SHAKESPEAR AS TO MARK
CYMB V SD(140)	TODAY. EXEUNT TOGETHER. ENTER POSTHUMUS DRESSED	LIKE	A PEASANT, BUT WEARING A ROMAN SWORD AND A SOLDIER'S
HART II (121)	GIRL. SHE HAS THE ANCIENT MARINER ON A STRING	LIKE	A PEKINESE DOG. /RANDALL/ NOW THAT THEY HAVE GONE,
MIS. (182)	LORD SUMMERHAYS) I MUST SAY THAT YOU HAVE BEHAVED	LIKE	A PERFECT GENTLEMAN, MR PERCIVAL. /PERCIVAL/ (FIRST
FANY I (278)	NEEDNT FUSS: THERES NO DISGRACE. BOBBY BEHAVED	LIKE	A PERFECT GENTLEMAN. BESIDES, IT WAS ALL MY FAULT. I'LL
GENV II (61)	THING: NOW THE LEAGUE HANGS OVER EUROPE	LIKE	A PERPETUAL WARCLOUD. /SIR O./ WELL, DONT THROW IT AT
CLEO PRO2,SD(102)	BULLDOG, APPEARS ON THE THRESHOLD. SHE IS DRESSED	LIKE	A PERSON OF CONSEQUENCE IN THE PALACE, AND CONFRONTS
FANY EPILOG (328)	THREE SYLLABLES IN HIS THROAT, MAKING A NOISE	LIKE	A PHEASANT). YOU SEE HUNDREDS OF PLAYS EVERY YEAR. BUT
GETT (284)	CONVERSATION TOO IN A WEEK OR SO. A MAN IS	LIKE	A PHONOGRAPH WITH HALF-A-DOZEN RECORDS. YOU SOON GET
MTH5 SD(217)	AT THE NEWLY BORN CRITICALLY; FEELS HER BUMPS	LIKE	A PHRENOLOGIST; GRIPS HER MUSCLES AND SHAKES HER LIMBS;
LIED (197)	SAKE, MRS BOMPAS, LET THAT GLOVE ALONE: YOU LOOK	LIKE	A PICKPOCKET. HER HUSBAND COMES IN: A ROBUST,
BULL PREFACE(44)	PRICES WHICH HE COULD COMPETE WITH ONLY BY LIVING	LIKE	A PIG HIMSELF. HAVING THE ALTERNATIVE OF STOPPING OUR
GETT (348)	MY CONSCIENCE WILL NOT ALLOW ME TO LET YOU LIVE	LIKE	A PIG. (SHE ARRANGES HIS NECKTIE). YOU MUST STAY WITH
CATH 2 (177)	AND GRINNING. /VARINKA/ IT IS TRUE. HE DRINKS	LIKE	A PIG. /PATIOMKIN/ (PLAINTIVELY) NO: NOT LIKE PIG.
ARMS I (9)	THIS PRETTY ROOM OF YOURS AND SLAUGHTER ME HERE	LIKE	A PIG; FOR I'LL FIGHT LIKE A DEMON: THEY SHANT GET ME
O'FL (213)	THE DEPTH OF DIVILMENT THAT WAS IN US: WE WERE	LIKE	A PLAY TO HER. YOU SEE, SIR, SHE WAS ENGLISH: THAT WAS
2TRU III SD(81)	BY KNOCKING THE TOP OF THE OPENING INTO SOMETHING	LIKE	A POINTED ARCH, AND SURMOUNTING IT WITH THE INSCRIPTION
LION II SD(143)	FORWARD AND HIS TAIL IN A HORIZONTAL LINE BEHIND,	LIKE	A POINTER, AND UTTERS AN APPALLING ROAR. ANDROCLES
FANY III (326)	IT COME TRUE. WHAT HE SAID? /JUGGINS/ IT STUCK	LIKE	A POISONED ARROW. IT RANKLED FOR MONTHS. THEN I GAVE
PYGM I (209)	BUT GOOD-HUMORED) OH, SHUT UP, SHUT UP. DO I LOOK	LIKE	A POLICEMAN? /THE FLOWER GIRL/ (FAR FROM REASSURED)
MTH4 II (177)	IN MY LIFE I HAVE LOST MY NERVE AND BEHAVED	LIKE	A POLTROON. BUT I WARN YOU NOT TO JUDGE MY QUALITY BY
2TRU PREFACE(25)	NOR A CHANCELLOR; BUT HE WOULD BE STRIKINGLY	LIKE	A POPE, CLAIMING FOR FORM'S SAKE AN APOSTOLIC
PPP SD(202)	ARMS. FITZ SHAKES THE EMPTY EWER UPSIDE DOWN	LIKE	A POTMAN SHAKING THE FROTH OUT OF A FLAGON. /ADOLPHUS/
KING I (169)	LUMP OF FIGS ON IT. /MRS BASHAM/ THERE IS NOTHING	LIKE	A POULTICE OF ROASTED FIGS TO CURE A GUMBOIL. AND TO
OVER (178)	HIM. MY CHRISTIAN NAME IS GREGORY, WHICH SOUNDS	LIKE	A POWDER. /MRS JUNO/ (CHILLED) THAT IS SO LIKE A MAN!
GETT (293)	HERE AND WARN YOU. /REGINALD/ THIS LOOKS TO ME	LIKE	A PRACTICAL JOKE. THEYVE ARRANGED IT BETWEEN THEM. /THE
FANY II (294)	INTO HELL I WAS NOT SWEARING. I WAS IN EARNEST,	LIKE	A PREACHER. /MRS KNOX/ A PREACHER UTTERS THEM IN A
JOAN 1 (65)	SWAMPING HIS AFFECTED DECISIVENESS) I SHALL FEEL	LIKE	A PRECIOUS FOOL. STILL, IF YOU FEEL SURE --?
SUPR I (39)	TO YOU IF YOU GO INTO PARLIAMENT (HE COLLAPSES	LIKE	A PRICKED BLADDER). BUT I AM SORRY YOU THOUGHT MY
ARMS I SD(7)	BUT SHE TAKES IT IN HER HANDS AND ELEVATES IT,	LIKE	A PRIESTESS. /RAINA/ (LOOKING UP AT THE PICTURE) OH, I
MTH4 I (141)	YOU DO THAT ANY MORE I SHALL CERTAINLY BREAK OUT	LIKE	A PRIMARY OF SIXTY. YOUR DRESS IS SO EXTRAORDINARILY
APPL I (218)	BUT I AM NOT SURPRISED, JOSEPH PROTEUS. I OWN I	LIKE	A PRIME MINISTER THAT KNOWS HOW TO BE A PRIME MINISTER.
MTH2 SD(54)	SQUARE PEGS IN ROUND HOLES, WHILST HE FLOURISHES	LIKE	A PRIMROSE. THE PARLOR MAID WITHDRAWS. /LUBIN/ (COMING
MILL I (156)	ME? NO MAN HAD BEEN GOOD ENOUGH FOR ME. I WAS	LIKE	A PRINCESS IN A FAIRY TALE OFFERING ALL MEN ALIVE MY
ANNA (303)	I AM ANYTHING THAT WILL MAKE THE WORLD LESS	LIKE	A PRISON AND MORE LIKE A CIRCUS. /STRAMMFEST/ AH! YOU
GETT PREFACE(240)	ONE ANOTHER, BUT BECAUSE, AS NO ROOM FEELS	LIKE	A PRISON IF THE DOOR IS LEFT OPEN, THE REMOVAL OF THE
FOUN (215)	I MUST REQUEST YOU TO SPEAK LIKE A LADY AND NOT	LIKE	A PROCESSION OF THE UNEMPLOYED. THE HOUSE OF LORDS
SUPR IV (154)	THE MASTER SPIRITS OF THE AGE! LED IN A STRING	LIKE	A PUG DOG BY THE FIRST GIRL WHO TAKES THE TROUBLE TO

MILL I (145)	PUGILIST. /EPIFANIA/ IT DOES NOT PUT YOU TO SLEEP	LIKE	A PUNCH ON THE JAW. WHEN HE SAW MY FACE DISTORTED WITH
METH PREFACE(R37)	WORLD, OUR CORNER OF THE UNIVERSE, DID NOT LOOK	LIKE	A PURE ACCIDENT: IT PRESENTED EVIDENCES OF DESIGN IN
CLEO II (123)	ON THE BRINK OF THE STEPS) AM I TO BEHAVE	LIKE	A QUEEN? /CAESAR/ YES. CLEOPATRA IMMEDIATELY COMES
KING II (234)	RELIGION IN ME FOR THE CHURCH! I TALKED WITH THIS MORNING. (THE CLOCK	LIKE	A QUEER FELLOW I TALKED WITH THIS MORNING. (THE CLOCK
DEVL II (37)	AGAIN: SO IS RICHARD. WELL, SHALL WE GO TO TEA	LIKE	A QUIET RESPECTABLE COUPLE, AND WAIT FOR YOUR HUSBAND'S
AUGS (281)	THE LADY OUT. /THE CLERK/ SHE'S GONE. SHE RUN OUT	LIKE	A RABBIT. I ASK MYSELF, WHY WAS SHE IN SUCH A HURRY?
BARB III (317)	ON BY SCHOOLMASTERS; TRAINED TO WIN SCHOLARSHIPS	LIKE	A RACEHORSE; CRAMMED WITH SECONDHAND IDEAS; DRILLED AND
FABL VI (125)	MARK THAT SHINES FOR EVER ACROSS THE SKY	LIKE	A RAINBOW. WHY DO WE EXIST? WHY DOES THE UNIVERSE
JOAN 1 (64)	HOLDING IT ON PAROLE. THE DAUPHIN IS IN CHINON,	LIKE	A RAT IN A CORNER, EXCEPT THAT HE WONT FIGHT. WE DONT
GLIM (184)	SIGNOR. /FERRUCCIO/ DO YOU THINK I WILL DIE HERE	LIKE	A RAT IN A TRAP-- (HIS BREATH FAILS HIM). /GIULIA/
HART III (145)	IN IT? /HECTOR/ WELL, I DONT MEAN TO BE DROWNED	LIKE	A RAT IN A TRAP. I STILL HAVE THE WILL TO LIVE. WHAT AM
APPL PREFACE(191)	IN PERSON ON GATTIE'S PROMISING TO BEHAVE	LIKE	A REASONABLE BEING DURING THE PROCESS, A PROMISE WHICH
JOAN 5 (114)	THAT IS WHAT I SAY TOO. WE SHALL GO THROUGH THEM	LIKE	A RED HOT SHOT THROUGH A POUND OF BUTTER. WHAT DO YOU
FABL PREFACE(81)	IN A RITUAL OF HYMNS AND LESSONS IN ALL RESPECTS	LIKE	A RELIGIOUS SUNDAY SERVICE EXCEPT THAT THE LESSONS WERE
ARMS III SD(69)	THEM THE EXAMPLE. YOU OWE ME AN APOLOGY. SERGIUS,	LIKE	A REPEATING CLOCK OF WHICH THE SPRING HAS BEEN TOUCHED,
SUPR HANDBOK(175)	MASSES OF THE PEOPLE WITHOUT DESIRING SOMETHING	LIKE	A REVOLUTION FOR THE BETTER." SIR ROBERT GIFFEN. ESSAYS
GENV PREFACE(19)	WERE RUSHING, AND TO FIND OUT WHY, IT LOOKED	LIKE	A REVOLUTIONARY EMEUTE. ON ONE OCCASION IT WAS A
GETT (348)	LOCK OF YOUR HAIR. (HE FOLDS HIS ARMS AND STANDS	LIKE	A ROCK). /REGINALD/ YOU DAMNED SCOUNDREL, HOW DARE YOU
LADY SD(243)	LADY COMES STOOPING ALONG THE TERRACE BEHIND THEM	LIKE	A RUNNING THRUSH. WHEN SHE SEES HOW THEY ARE EMPLOYED,
MIS. PREFACE(53)	DEVIL WILL RUN AWAY WITH HIM AND EMPTY HIM OUT	LIKE	A SACK OF COALS ON A BLAZING FIRE UNLESS HIS NURSE OR
LADY PREFACE(215)	ANY PRICE, BECAUSE HIS IDEAL SHAKESPEAR IS RATHER	LIKE	A SAILOR IN A MELODRAMA; AND A SAILOR IN A MELODRAMA
JITT III (69)	EDITH. WHO IS TO TELL HER? SHE SEES HER FATHER	LIKE	A SAINT IN A PICTURE; AND I COULD NEVER PUT IT TO HER
DOCT PREFACE(18)	ARTISTIC CONSCIENCE, EVEN TO THE POINT OF DYING	LIKE	A SAINT WITH ITS SUPPORT, THAT HE IS UTTERLY SELFISH
JOAN 1 (69)	OH, SQUIRE! YOUR HEAD IS ALL CIRCLED WITH LIGHT,	LIKE	A SAINT'S. /POULENGEY/ HOW IS SHE TO GET INTO THE ROYAL
6CAL PREFACE(89)	LIKE A CHILD IN HIS WIFE'S LAP OR SNARLING	LIKE	A SAVAGE DOG AT A DAUNTLESS AND DEFIANT TRADESMAN: IN
BUOY III (34)	SEE WHOM YOU LIKE WHEN YOU LIKE. THIS WOMAN LIVES	LIKE	A SAVAGE IN A SWAMP FULL OF SNAKES AND ALLIGATORS AND
WIDO II (39)	AND YET SHE TURNED ON ME AS IF I'D BEHAVED	LIKE	A SAVAGE. /SARTORIUS/ LIVE ON YOUR INCOME! IMPOSSIBLE:
DOCT IV SD(156)	CARDINAL DEATH, HOLDING HIS SCYTHE AND HOUR-GLASS	LIKE	A SCEPTRE AND GLOBE, SITS ON THE THRONE. ON THE
BARB III (314)	MUST DRIVEL, DRIVEL LIKE A GROWN-UP MAN AND NOT	LIKE	A SCHOOLBOY. /LOMAX/ (OUT OF COUNTENANCE) WELL, DRIVEL
ARMS I (13)	DO YOU STUFF YOUR POCKETS WITH SWEETS--	LIKE	A SCHOOLBOY-- EVEN IN THE FIELD? /THE MAN/ (GRINNING)
CLEO III (164)	PLUNGES HEAD FOREMOST INTO THE SEA. /CAESAR/ (	LIKE	A SCHOOLBOY-- WILDLY EXCITED) BRAVO, BRAVO! (THROWING
DEST (185)	(HE SITS DOWN AND PLACES GIUSEPPE BEFORE HIM	LIKE	A SCHOOLMASTER WITH A PUPIL). SHALL I TAKE YOU AWAY
SUPR III SD(71)	AND SEEMS AT HOME IN THE SIERRA NEVADA, BUT VERY	LIKE	A SCOTCHMAN FOR ALL THAT. IN THE HOLLOW, ON THE SLOPE
DOCT III (140)	AND EVEN BENEFICIAL, WHEN HE IS MORALLY BEHAVING	LIKE	A SCOUNDREL. AND HE MAY DO GREAT HARM WHEN HE IS
CLEO I (114)	THRONE AND DASHES AFTER FTATATEETA, WHIRLING IT	LIKE	A SCOURGE IN THE AIR. CAESAR MAKES A BOUND AND MANAGES
LADY PREFACE(232)	ON PARLIAMENT WAS " GET THEE GLASS EYES, AND,	LIKE	A SCURVY POLITICIAN, SEEM TO SEE THE THING THOU DOST
AUGS (272)	AND YOU SWEPT INTO IT AT THE HEAD OF YOUR MEN	LIKE	A SEA-GOD RIDING ON A TIDAL WAVE, YOU SUDDENLY SPRANG
JITT I (21)	OH YES, YES: I KNOW ALL THAT. IT SOUNDS	LIKE	A SENTENCE FROM YOUR ANNUAL ADDRESS TO YOUR STUDENTS.
PHIL I (83)	WOMAN WHO BEHAVES LIKE A SPOILED CHILD AND TALKS	LIKE	A SENTIMENTAL NOVEL HAVE THE AUDACITY TO DREAM OF BEING
JOAN 4 (95)	I AM NOT ATTACHED TO THE SOIL IN A VULGAR MANNER,	LIKE	A SERF. STILL, I HAVE A FEELING ABOUT IT; (WITH
JOAN PREFACE(44)	THE MILITARY GENERAL STAFF. HER UNCLE OBEYED HER	LIKE	A SHEEP, AND TOOK HER TO THE CASTLE OF THE LOCAL
MIS. PREFACE(67)	BULLIED AND ORDERED ABOUT, THE ENGLISHMAN OBEYS	LIKE	A SHEEP, EVADES LIKE A KNAVE, OR TRIES TO MURDER HIS
LIED SD(187)	SOUTH KENSINGTON FASHION: THAT IS, IT IS AS	LIKE	A SHOP WINDOW AS POSSIBLE, AND IS INTENDED TO
GENV I SD(34)	BUT NOT ARISTOCRATIC APPEARANCE, SPEAKING ENGLISH	LIKE	A SHOPKEEPER FROM THE PROVINCES, OR PERHAPS, BY
MIS. (120)	FAST FOR ME AS A WALKING COMPANION; BUT I SHOULD	LIKE	A SHORT TURN. /JOHNNY/ (RISING EAGERLY, HIGHLY
MTH2 (38)	WOULDNT MIND. DO YOU MIND? FOR OF COURSE I'LL GO	LIKE	A SHOT IF I'M IN THE WAY. /THE CLERICAL GENTLEMAN/ (
DOCT III (135)	AT ONCE I SHALL BE PUT IN PRISON. SHE'LL PAY YOU	LIKE	A SHOT. YOULL CLEAR 50 POUNDS; AND YOULL DO ME A REAL
PYGM III (257)	HOME, WHETHER IT'S /HIGGINS/ SHE PICKS THEM UP	LIKE	A SHOT, RIGHT AWAY, AS IF SHE HAD /PICKERING/ BEETHOVEN
ROCK PREFACE(174)	MARXPHOBIA, AND FRANTICALLY MAKING ITSELF WORSE	LIKE	A SHREW IN A BAD TEMPER. I COULD NOT GET A SINGLE
BULL IV (146)	SHE'S HURT BEHIND NOW; FOR LARRY BOWLED HER OVER	LIKE	A SKITTLE. (GENERAL DELIGHT AT THIS TYPICAL STROKE OF
FANY III (306)	ME TO BE A VERY DECENT SORT; AND BOBBY'S BEHAVING	LIKE	A SKUNK. /BOBBY/ (MUCH RUFFLED) NICE LANGUAGE THAT!
VWOO 3 (140)	WHEN I CANT LAY MY HANDS ON YOU? I WORK FOR YOU	LIKE	A SLAVE FOR A MONTH ON END; AND I WOULD HAVE TO WORK
PHIL III (142)	FOR BY TWO MEN-- PASSED FROM ONE TO THE OTHER	LIKE	A SLAVE IN THE MARKET, AND NOT SAY A WORD IN MY OWN
MILL IV (204)	OOOOH! ! I HAVE NEVER FELT SUCH A PULSE. IT IS	LIKE	A SLOW SLEDGE HAMMER. /EPIFANIA/ WELL, IS MY PULSE MY
GETT PREFACE(189)	BE ANY CHANGES AT ALL; AND SOCIETY WOULD PERISH	LIKE	A SNAKE THAT COULD NOT CAST ITS SKINS. NEVERTHELESS THE
JOAN 2 (75)	TO THE ARCHBISHOP) DID YOU SAY A GIRL IN ARMOR,	LIKE	A SOLDIER? /THE ARCHBISHOP/ SO DE BAUDRICOURT
JOAN 2 (75)	SHE DOES NOT WEAR WOMEN'S CLOTHES. SHE IS DRESSED	LIKE	A SOLDIER, AND RIDES ROUND THE COUNTRY WITH SOLDIERS.
ROCK PREFACE(190)	LIVE UNDER MORE OR LESS TUTELAGE AND DISCIPLINE	LIKE	A SOLDIER, OR AT NORMAL LIBERTY UNDER AN OBLIGATION TO
MILL III (187)	GOES OUT). /THE MAN/ (STUPEFIED) IT SEEMS TO ME	LIKE	A SORT OF DREAM. WHAT COULD I DO? /THE WOMAN/ (WHO
PHIL I (83)	ME TO DESPISE YOU. HOW CAN A WOMAN WHO BEHAVES	LIKE	A SPOILED CHILD AND TALKS LIKE A SENTIMENTAL NOVEL HAVE
OVER (184)	OF KNITTING WOOL. A MAN'S HEART SEEMS TO ME MUCH	LIKE	A SPONGE: IT SOPS UP DIRTY WATER AS WELL AS CLEAN.
NEVR IV (295)	WANT THIS YOUNG LADY HERE TO GIVE UP DRESSING	LIKE	A STAGE COLUMBINE IN THE EVENING AND LIKE A FASHIONABLE
KING I (181)	BECAUSE SOME FOOL IN A STEEPLEHOUSE, DRESSED UP	LIKE	A STAGE PLAYER IN ROBES AND MITRE, DARES TO MEASURE THE
APPL I (206)	NO KING OR MINISTER IS THE VERY LEAST LITTLE BIT	LIKE	A STAMP: HE IS A LIVING SOUL. /BOANERGES/ A SOUL, EH..
APPL PREFACE(183)	IT HAD BEEN TRIED, SOCIALISM WENT OVER HIM	LIKE	A STEAM ROLLER AND HANDED HIS OFFICE TO A SOCIALIST
JOAN 2 (71)	KNOW HOW YOU HAVE THE PATIENCE TO STAND THERE	LIKE	A STONE IDOL. /THE ARCHBISHOP/ YOU SEE, I AM AN
LADY PREFACE(210)	COULD REACH. THEN TYLER DIED, SINKING UNNOTED	LIKE	A STONE IN THE SEA. I OBSERVE THAT MR ACHESON, MRS
KING I (213)	WOULD BELIEVE. THE CIRCLE IS A DEAD THING	LIKE	A STRAIGHT LINE: NO LIVING HAND CAN DRAW IT: YOU MAKE
BUOY II SD(18)	SHIRT, AND A PANAMA HAT, IS LOOKING ABOUT HIM	LIKE	A STRANGER. A YOUNG WOMAN, DRESSED FOR WORK IN PYJAMA
FANY I (279)	THE WHISTLE; AND AT THE SOUND OF IT HE DREW AWAY	LIKE	A STREAK OF LIGHTNING; AND THAT WAS THE LAST I SAW OF
BARB I (266)	PLEASE LET YOUR FATHER SEE THAT; AND DONT TALK	LIKE	A STREET GIRL. /UNDERSHAFT/ NEVER MIND ME, MY DEAR. AS
KING I (176)	YOUR TANTRUMS. I MADE YOU A DUCHESS: YOU BEHAVE	LIKE	A STREETWALKER. I PENSIONED YOU AND PACKED YOU OFF TO
BARB II (304)	BLESS YOU ABUNDANTLY; AND OUR PRAYERS WILL BE	LIKE	A STRONG FORTIFICATION ROUND YOU ALL THE DAYS OF YOUR
DEVL I (6)	WELL, HOW LONG ARE YOU GOING TO STARE THERE	LIKE	A STUCK PIG? WHAT NEWS HAVE YOU FOR ME? /CHRISTY/ (
JOAN PREFACE(49)	IN SHAKESPEAR'S HISTORIES. HIS JOHN OF GAUNT IS	LIKE	A STUDY OF THE OLD AGE OF DRAKE. ALTHOUGH HE WAS A
2TRU II (77)	OF THAT IDIOT MEEK, WE MAY HAVE THEM DOWN ON US	LIKE	A SWARM OF HORNETS. I DONT LIKE THIS AT ALL. I MUST GET
DOCT I SD(96)	INTO THE ROOM. HE IS A TALL MAN, WITH A HEAD	LIKE	A TALL AND SLENDER EGG. HE HAS BEEN IN HIS TIME A
BUOY III (42)	RHYME. /HE/ BON SOIR LA COMPAGNIE. THIS ROOM IS	LIKE	A TEMPLE. ARE YOU ENGAGED IN AN ACT OF WORSHIP? /MRS
LION PREFACE(17)	AND PRAY, AS THE GREAT DAY WILL STEAL UPON THEM	LIKE	A THIEF IN THE NIGHT, AND CANNOT BE LONG DEFERRED IN A
POSN (444)	REVERENT CANT? NOT YOUR BIBLE. IT SAYS HE COMETH	LIKE	A THIEF IN THE NIGHT-- AYE, LIKE A THIEF-- A
SIM II (84)	COMES AS WE EXPECT IT TO COME. /PRA/ IT COMES	LIKE	A THIEF IN THE NIGHT. /PROLA/ OR LIKE A LOVER. NEVER
POSN (455)	THE WANT OF HIM. WHEN YOU TOOK ME, DID I FIGHT	LIKE	A THIEF OR RUN LIKE A THIEF; AND WAS THERE ANY SIGN OF
DEVL I (10)	AND WELL HE KNEW IT. THAT WAS WHY HE STOLE AWAY	LIKE	A THIEF TO TAKE ADVANTAGE OF THE LAW TO ROB ME BY
POSN (444)	SAYS HE COMETH LIKE A THIEF IN THE NIGHT-- AYE,	LIKE	A THIEF-- A HORSE-THIEF-- /ELDER DANIELS/ (SHOCKED)
POSN (455)	WHEN YOU TOOK ME, DID I FIGHT LIKE A THIEF OR RUN	LIKE	A THIEF; AND WAS THERE ANY SIGN OF A HORSE ON ME OR
SUPR IV (166)	CAPITULATION, ACCEPTANCE OF DEFEAT. I SHALL DECAY	LIKE	A THING THAT HAS SERVED ITS PURPOSE AND IS DONE WITH; I
BASH II,1, (99)	IN DOWNING STREET WAS BORN IN BIRMINGHAM, AND,	LIKE	A THOROUGHBRED COMMERCIAL STATESMAN, SPLITS HIS
CAND II (123)	WAS TO SAY HE COULDNT COME. IT CAME ON THEM	LIKE	A THUNDERBOLT. /CANDIDA/ (SURPRISED, AND BEGINNING TO
MILL I (140)	HYDROCYANIC ACID, ONE SIP OF WHICH WILL KILL YOU	LIKE	A THUNDERBOLT. /EPIFANIA/ (FINGERING THE PRESCRIPTION
BASH II,1, (99)	WITH FRIENDLY FOREFINGER THIS BUTTON, LEVELLED ME	LIKE	A THUNDERSTRICKEN ELM FLAT UPON THE COLONIAL OFFICE
DEST SD(172)	TEAR THEM FROM ME: BY FORCE! AS HE GLARES AT HER	LIKE	A TIGER ABOUT TO SPRING, SHE CROSSES HER ARMS ON HER
CATH 4,SD(198)	FROM HIS STUPOR OF AMAZEMENT, SPRINGS TO HER	LIKE	A TIGER, AND THROWS HIMSELF AT HER FEET. /PATIOMKIN/
PHIL III (140)	OF TENDERNESS, SHE SHAKES HIM, GROWLING OVER HIM	LIKE	A TIGRESS OVER HER CUB). PARAMORE AND CRAVEN RETURN
2TRU PREFACE(6)	IT INVOLVES CONTINUAL PRIVATION AND ANXIETY, IS,	LIKE	A TOOTHACHE, SO PAINFUL THAT THE VICTIM CAN DESIRE
FABL PREFACE(87)	SORT. AT PRESENT I AM STUCK ALL OVER WITH LABELS	LIKE	A TOURIST'S TRUNK. I CANNOT CALL MYSELF THE WAY AND THE
SUPR IV (166)	TO BE STOPPED BY A LOVESICK BRIGAND AND RUN DOWN	LIKE	A TRUANT SCHOOLBOY. /ANN/ WELL, IF YOU DONT WANT TO BE
3PLA PREFACE(R27)	THE DEVIL; TAKES HIS SIDE; AND CHAMPIONS HIM,	LIKE	A TRUE COVENANTER, AGAINST THE WORLD. HE THUS BECOMES,
SIM II (73)	ANGEL'S WINGS IS HEARD. /VASHTI/ HE MAKES A NOISE	LIKE	A VACUUM CLEANER. /MAYA/ (WAFTING KISSES) GOODBYE,
MIS. (193)	" RESPECT THE BURDEN, MADAM." THAT WAS BEHAVING	LIKE	A VERY FINE GENTLEMAN; BUT HE KICKED VOLNEY FOR SAYING
PYGM II SD(218)	IS, IN FACT, BUT FOR HIS YEARS AND SIZE, RATHER	LIKE	A VERY IMPETUOUS BABY " TAKING NOTICE" EAGERLY AND
2TRU PREFACE(15)	OF THE CHESTERTONS JOINED THIS CATHOLIC CHURCH,	LIKE	A VERY LARGE SHIP ENTERING A VERY SMALL HARBOR, TO THE
MIS. (181)	WITHOUT PUNCTUATION IN A HARDLY AUDIBLE VOICE,	LIKE	A VERY SICK MAN) I JOHN BROWN OF 4 CHESTERFIELD PARADE
2TRU II (62)	I CAN PREACH ANYTHING, TRUE OR FALSE. I AM	LIKE	A VIOLIN, ON WHICH YOU CAN PLAY ALL SORTS OF MUSIC,
DEST SD(153)	MOUTH AND PLANTING IT ON THE MAP WITH HIS THUMB	LIKE	A WAFER. THERE IS NO REVOLUTIONARY UNTIDINESS ABOUT HIS
HART II (113)	UP MISCHIEVOUSLY, AND GOING TO HIM) WOULD YOU	LIKE	A WALK ON THE HEATH, ALFRED? WITH ME? /ELLIE/ GO, MR
GETT (304)	YOUNG. I WAS DULL: HE WAS BRILLIANT. I HAD A FACE	LIKE	A WALNUT: HE HAD A FACE LIKE A MUSHROOM. I WAS AS GLAD
HART I (70)	NOT HAVE RECOGNIZED YOU: YOUR HEAD IS NO LONGER	LIKE	A WALNUT. YOUR ASPECT IS SOFTENED. YOU HAVE BEEN BOILED

MILL III (181)	THAT I CAN LIVE BY OR I WILL HAVE YOU CLEARED OUT	LIKE	A WASP'S NEST. /THE MAN/ I HAVE A GOOD MIND TO CLEAR
ROCK I (196)	TELL ME TO DISPERSE IT. ALL YOULL HEAR IS A NOISE	LIKE	A WATCHMAN'S RATTLE. QUITE SIMPLE. /SIR ARTHUR/ FAR TOO
GETT (342)	KNOWS. /MRS GEORGE/ (A FAINT CONVULSION PASSING	LIKE	A WAVE OVER HER) I KNOW MORE THAN EITHER OF YOU. ONE OF
MRS III (226)	VIVIE AND LITTLE FRANK. (HE NESTLES AGAINST HER	LIKE	A WEARY CHILD). LETS GO AND GET COVERED UP WITH LEAVES.
HART II (108)	FORWARD SWINGING THE POKER BETWEEN HIS FINGERS	LIKE	A WELL-FOLDED UMBRELLA) IT IS NEITHER JUST NOR RIGHT
KING I (218)	CIRCUMSTANCES. /BARBARA/ YES; AND HE LOOKS	LIKE	A WELL-TO-DO GROCER, AND WILL NEVER LOOK LIKE ANYTHING
JOAN EPILOG (160)	SUITS ME SOMEHOW. THE DAY OFF WAS DULL AT FIRST,	LIKE	A WET SUNDAY. I DONT MIND IT SO MUCH NOW. THEY TELL ME
BULL IV (147)	SPANCHELLED-LIKE BETWEEN HIS SEAT AND DHAT THING	LIKE	A WHEEL ON TOP OF A STICK BETWEEN HIS KNEES. /AUNT
SUPR II SD(48)	THE LEGS BY THE ANKLES, DRAWING THEIR OWNER FORTH	LIKE	A WHEELBARROW, WALKING ON HIS HANDS, WITH A HAMMER IN
MTH1 I (4)	IT IS VERY LOW; BUT IT IS SO NEAR THAT IT IS	LIKE	A WHISPER FROM WITHIN MYSELF. THERE IS NO MISTAKING IT
DEVL II (40)	THE SERGEANT WILL NOT BELIEVE THAT YOU LOVE ME	LIKE	A WIFE UNLESS YOU GIVE ONE KISS BEFORE I GO. HE
KING II (224)	USE THEN, AFTER ALL. /CHARLES/ THERE IS NOBODY	LIKE	A WIFE. /CATHERINE/ I HEAR THAT CLEVELAND HAS COME BACK
JOAN 4 (103)	CHURCH OUT OF JERUSALEM, AND RAVAGED HIS WAY WEST	LIKE	A WILD BEAST UNTIL AT LAST THERE STOOD ONLY THE
MIS. (194)	BECAME THE PURSUED. /HYPATIA/ I HAD TO FIGHT	LIKE	A WILD CAT. /LORD SUMMERHAYS/ PLEASE DONT TELL US THIS.
FANY II (293)	DUVALLET, IT WAS THEN THAT DUVALLET SWUNG HIS LEG	LIKE	A WINDMILL AND KNOCKED THE POLICEMAN DOWN, AND THEN
FANY II (291)	HIS NECK WITH THE OTHER. HE COULDNT WHIRL HIS LEG	LIKE	A WINDMILL AND KNOCK A POLICEMAN DOWN BY A GLORIOUS
JOAN 6 (133)	FROM A TOWER SIXTY FEET HIGH? IF YOU CANNOT FLY	LIKE	A WITCH, HOW IS IT THAT YOU ARE STILL ALIVE? /JOAN/ I
FOUN (221)	ANY RELUCTANCE. REMEMBER: " HELL HATH NO FURY	LIKE	A WOMAN SCORNED." /MERCER/ WHATS THE GOOD OF THAT
DEST (173)	WELL, BONAPARTE CAN RISE TO THE SITUATION AND ACT	LIKE	A WOMAN WHEN IT IS NECESSARY. DO YOU UNDERSTAND? THE
SUPR PREFACE(R10)	THAT A MAN WHO DISCUSSES HIS CONSCIENCE IS MUCH	LIKE	A WOMAN WHO DISCUSSES HER MODESTY. THE ONLY MORAL FORCE
JOAN 3 (91)	I AM LIKE A MAN WITH TWO WIVES, DO YOU WANT TO BE	LIKE	A WOMAN WITH TWO HUSBANDS? /JOAN/ (MATTER-OF-FACT) I
ARMS III (58)	ATTITUDE) YES: I AM A BRAVE MAN. MY HEART JUMPED	LIKE	A WOMAN'S AT THE FIRST SHOT; BUT IN THE CHARGE I FOUND
MTH5 (230)	COULD NOT FIX AND CONDUCT THE LIFE FORCE. IT WAS	LIKE	A WOODEN MAGNET OR A LIGHTNING CONDUCTOR MADE OF SILK:
SIM I (52)	LOVE YOU-- YOU. I WOULD DIE FOR YOU. THAT SOUNDS	LIKE	A WORD PICKED UP IN THE STREET; BUT IT IS TRUE. I WOULD
LIED (198)	LOOK AT HENRY). BY THE WAY, APJOHN, I SHOULD	LIKE	A WORD WITH YOU THIS EVENING, IF AURORA CAN SPARE YOU
2TRU II (77)	HIM, AND REMAINS THERE. /MEEK/ THE COLONEL WOULD	LIKE	A WORD WITH YOU, MISS. /AUBREY/ GO EASY WITH HER,
BASH III (122)	IN MOST RESPLENDENT FASHIONABLE FROCK, APPROACHES	LIKE	A WOUNDED ANTELOPE. ENTER ADELAIDE GISBORNE. /ADELAIDE/
2TRU III (99)	AND FLUTTERS BACK ALONG THE BEACH OUT OF SIGHT	LIKE	A WOUNDED BIRD). GENERAL STUPEFACTION. ALL STARE AT THE
HART II (104)	TO KNOW US SO WELL. /MANGAN/ (WITH SOMETHING	LIKE	A YELL OF DESPAIR) AM I NEVER TO HAVE THE LAST WORD?
MTH4 I SD(139)	CANNOT BE GUESSED: HER FACE IS FIRM AND CHISELLED	LIKE	A YOUNG FACE; BUT HER EXPRESSION IS UNYOUTHFUL IN ITS
CLEO IV (180)	MOVE TOWARDS THE TABLE). /CLEOPATRA/ (SKIPPING	LIKE	A YOUNG FAWN) YES, TO DINNER. I HAVE ORDERED SUCH A
CLEO III (164)	/RUFIO/ (FRANTIC) CAN AN OLD FOOL DIVE AND SWIM	LIKE	A YOUNG ONE? HE IS TWENTY-FIVE AND YOU ARE FIFTY.
DEVL III (66)	I MINISTER ANDERSON. TELL HIM, AND STOP GRINNING	LIKE	A ZANY. /CHRISTY/ (GRINNING MORE THAN EVER) YOU PASTOR
GETT (321)	MARRIAGE REASONABLE AND DECENT, YOU CAN DO AS YOU	LIKE	ABOUT DIVORCE. I HAVE NOT STATED MY DEEPEST OBJECTION
WIDO II (47)	/SARTORIUS/ YES, MY DEAR. /BLANCHE/ MAY I DO AS I	LIKE	ABOUT THIS MARRIAGE; OR MUST I DO AS YOU LIKE?
INCA (247)	FASCINATES THE WHOLE WORLD. /ERMYNTRUDE/ WHAT I	LIKE	ABOUT YOU, CAPTAIN DUVAL, IS YOUR MODESTY. /THE INCA/ (
MTH5 (251)	AS A DEAD BODY DOES. /THE HE-ANCIENT/ AND I,	LIKE	ACIS, CEASED TO WALK OVER THE MOUNTAINS WITH MY
MTH5 (251)	/THE HE-ANCIENT/ I HAD NO SUCH SKILL; BUT I,	LIKE	ACIS, SOUGHT PERFECTION IN FRIENDS, IN LOVERS, IN
SUPR III (111)	IN THIS CAMPAIGN ARE MERE BLUNDERS, MOSTLY WON,	LIKE	ACTUAL MILITARY BATTLES, IN SPITE OF THE COMMANDERS.
LADY PREFACE(216)	AFFECTION AND RESPECT INSPIRED BY A GREAT SERVANT	LIKE	ADAM: ALL THESE ARE THE CHARACTERISTICS OF ETON AND
MTH1 I (9)	NEW LILITH BUT TWO: ONE LIKE HERSELF, THE OTHER	LIKE	ADAM. YOU WERE THE ONE; ADAM WAS THE OTHER. /EVE/ BUT
BARB I (252)	I KNOW YOUR QUIET, SIMPLE, REFINED, POETIC PEOPLE	LIKE	ADOLPHUS: QUITE CONTENT WITH THE BEST OF EVERYTHING!
MIS. PREFACE(100)	THEIR LIKE TO OCCUPY ME BETTER. IN ART, CHILDREN,	LIKE	ADULTS, WILL FIND THEIR LEVEL IF THEY ARE LEFT FREE TO
MIS. PREFACE(74)	IF BY MAGIC, WITH NOTHING TO DO BUT RUB THE LAMP,	LIKE	ALADDIN, AND HAVE THEIR NEEDS SATISFIED. THE PARENTS'
MILL I (144)	/SAGAMORE/ NO NO: NOT A CRIMINAL. THAT IS NOT	LIKE	ALASTAIR. A FOOL, PERHAPS, IN BUSINESS. BUT NOT A
PHIL II (103)	YOU ARE NOT FULLY RESPONSIBLE FOR YOUR ACTIONS.	LIKE	ALL ADVANCED PEOPLE, YOU HAVE GOT NEURASTHENIA.
2TRU II (62)	HAVE I NOT TOLD YOU THAT HE IS AN ATHEIST, AND	LIKE	ALL ATHEISTS, AN INFLEXIBLE MORALIST? HE SAID I MIGHT
CLEO II (130)	STEPS) AND WHAT ARE YOU? /RUFIO/ A CAESARIAN,	LIKE	ALL CAESAR'S SOLDIERS. /CAESAR/ (COURTEOUSLY) LUCIUS:
GETT (333)	MY BROTHERS AND SISTERS WERE WELL BROUGHT UP,	LIKE	ALL CHILDREN OF RESPECTABLE PUBLICANS, SO SHOULD I HAVE
DEVL EPILOG (82)	THE SAKE OF AMERICA. IN THE WORKING CLASS, WHICH,	LIKE	ALL CLASSES, HAS ITS OWN OFFICIAL ARISTOCRACY, THERE IS
ARMS III (57)	TRY BEING HIGH AND MIGHTY WITH ME, EITHER. YOURE	LIKE	ALL COUNTRY GIRLS: YOU THINK IT'S GENTEEL TO TREAT A
ARMS II (36)	AND ONE, AT LEAST, IS A COWARD: JEALOUS,	LIKE	ALL COWARDS, (HE GOES TO THE TABLE). LOUKA. /LOUKA/
3PLA PREFACE(R24)	OF PRIVACY TO POLITICAL NECESSITY, BUT BECAUSE,	LIKE	ALL DRAMATISTS AND MIMES OF GENUINE VOCATION, I AM A
FABL PREFACE(84)	POLITICIANS SEEMS TO KNOW THAT POLITICAL ACTION,	LIKE	ALL EARTHLY ACTION, MUST TAKE PLACE IN A WORLD OF FOUR
3PLA PREFACE(R27)	COVENANTER, AGAINST THE WORLD. HE THUS BECOMES,	LIKE	ALL GENUINELY RELIGIOUS MEN, A REPROBATE AND AN
CAND I SD(79)	SPREADING NOSTRILS OF THE DRAMATIC ORATOR, VOID,	LIKE	ALL HIS FEATURES, OF SUBTLETY. THE TYPIST, MISS
SIM II (83)	I BEGAN AS A PASSION AND HAVE ENDED AS A HABIT,	LIKE	ALL HUSBANDS; BUT OUTSIDE THAT ROUTINE THERE IS A LIFE
SUPR III (89)	ME INSULTING NAMES. /THE OLD WOMAN/ YOU WERE	LIKE	ALL MEN, LIBERTINES AND MURDERERS ALL, ALL, ALL! /DON
MTH3 (122)	STILL, AS HE SAID HIMSELF, A GENTLEMAN AMATEUR,	LIKE	ALL MODERN PAINTERS. /BURGE-LUBIN/ BUT WHY HAD YOU TO
MIS. PREFACE(85)	BOND BETWEEN MEMBERS OF THE SAME FAMILY, WHICH,	LIKE	ALL NATURAL BONDS, IS NOT TOO TIGHT TO BE BORNE, AND
MTH3 (115)	THE FEROCIOUS HATRED WITH WHICH HUMAN ANIMALS,	LIKE	ALL OTHER ANIMALS, TURN UPON ANY UNHAPPY INDIVIDUAL WHO
GETT PREFACE(220)	THAT WHAT THEY CALL LOVE IS AN APPETITE WHICH,	LIKE	ALL OTHER APPETITES, IS DESTROYED FOR THE MOMENT BY ITS
SUPR PREFACE(R12)	WITH LAW AND CONVENTION CAN BE DRAMATIZED	LIKE	ALL OTHER HUMAN CONFLICTS: BUT THEY ARE PURELY
SUPR HANDBOK(214)	AND IN THAT HE IS RIGHT. KING DEMOS MUST BE BRED	LIKE	ALL OTHER KINGS; AND WITH MUST THERE IS NO ARGUING. IT
APPL INTRLUD(252)	WOULD SHE. BUT AS THAT NEVER HAPPENS, WE ARE	LIKE	ALL OTHER MARRIED COUPLES: THAT IS, THERE ARE SUBJECTS
DOCT II SD(117)	HIMSELF AGREEABLE TO THEM ON THIS OCCASION.	LIKE	ALL PEOPLE WHO CAN BE DEPENDED ON TO TAKE CARE OF
LIED (192)	IDEAL AND NOT NEGLECTED THE CULTURE OF MY BODY.	LIKE	ALL POETS I HAVE A PASSION FOR PUGILISM. YOUR HUSBAND
GETT (301)	NOT COUNTING THAT I'M A PRIVATE TRUSTEE, AND,	LIKE	ALL PRIVATE TRUSTEES, A FRAUDULENT ONE. OTHERWISE, THE
SUPR I (36)	IT TO MORAL ENDS. I HAVE BECOME A REFORMER, AND,	LIKE	ALL REFORMERS, AN ICONOCLAST. I NO LONGER BREAK
MTH3 (109)	ARCHBISHOP/ YES, MR CHIEF SECRETARY: THE TRUTH.	LIKE	ALL REVOLUTIONARY TRUTHS, IT BEGAN AS A JOKE. AS I
DOCT V (178)	KEPT THE SECRET FROM YOU FAITHFULLY; BUT IT IS	LIKE	ALL SECRETS: IT WILL NOT KEEP ITSELF. THE BURIED TRUTH
FANY III (309)	IN FRESH. DONT GET TOO BIG FOR YOUR BOOTS. YOURE	LIKE	ALL SERVANTS NOWADAYS: YOU THINK YOUVE ONLY TO HOLD UP
MIS. PREFACE(71)	OF GROWN-UP CHILDREN. YET ECONOMIC EQUALITY,	LIKE	ALL SIMPLE AND OBVIOUS ARRANGEMENTS, SEEMS IMPOSSIBLE
APPL PREFACE(191)	AND NOW A WORD ABOUT BREAKAGES, LIMITED.	LIKE	ALL SOCIALISTS WHO KNOW THEIR BUSINESS I HAVE AN
MILL I (144)	IN BUSINESS. BUT NOT A CRIMINAL. /EPIFANIA/	LIKE	ALL SOLICITORS YOU THINK YOU KNOW MORE ABOUT MY HUSBAND
LADY PREFACE(232)	JONSON WAS BY NO MEANS A POPULAR MOVEMENT; AND,	LIKE	ALL SUCH IDOLATRIES, IT WAS EXCITED BY THE MAGIC OF
SUPR III (118)	THINKING SUCH A LOT ABOUT IT, JUAN. YOU ARE	LIKE	ALL THE CLEVER MEN: YOU HAVE MORE BRAINS THAN IS GOOD
2TRU PREFACE(8)	TO FEAR AS A CONSEQUENCE OF NOT WORKING. BUT,	LIKE	ALL THE INTELLIGENT RICH PEOPLE OF MY ACQUAINTANCE, I
BARB III (315)	ROUTINE WITHOUT UNDERSTANDING THE BUSINESS,	LIKE	ALL THE OTHER SONS; AND THE FIRM WOULD GO ON BY ITS OWN
MTH2 (42)	I HAVE LET HER ALONE; AND LOOK AT THE RESULT!	LIKE	ALL THE OTHER YOUNG PEOPLE WHO HAVE BEEN LET ALONE, SHE
FABL PREFACE(77)	CHURCH. THE MARXIST CHURCH, CALLED COMINFORM, IS	LIKE	ALL THE OTHER CHURCHES, HAVING CEASED TO BELIEVE IN THE
MRS II (207)	WARREN/ SO IT COMES TO THAT WITH YOU, GEORGE,	LIKE	ALL THE OTHER WORN-OUT OLD CREATURES! /CROFTS/ (
DEVL I SD(4)	WITH A CANDLE ON IT IN A TIN SCONCE. HER CHAIR,	LIKE	ALL THE OTHERS IN THE ROOM, IS UNCUSHIONED AND
LION PREFACE(61)	IF OUR ATTEMPT AT CIVILIZATION IS NOT TO PERISH	LIKE	ALL THE PREVIOUS ONES, WE SHALL HAVE TO ORGANIZE OUR
OVER (182)	ELSE SINCE WE MET? /MRS LUNN/ THERE YOU GO,	LIKE	ALL THE REST OF THEM! I ASK YOU, HOW DO YOU EXPECT A
ARMS III (53)	IT'S PART OF YOUR YOUTH: PART OF YOUR CHARM. I'M	LIKE	ALL THE REST OF THEM: THE NURSE, YOUR PARENTS, SERGIUS:
MIS. (124)	/HYPATIA/ YES; BUT HE HAS SOME BRAINS. HE'S NOT	LIKE	ALL THE REST. ONE CANT HAVE EVERYTHING. /MRS TARLETON/
DOCT III (152)	NOW. WHAT DO YOU ACCUSE HIM OF? /RIDGEON/ I AM	LIKE	ALL THE REST. FACE TO FACE, I CANNOT TELL YOU ONE THING
DOCT I (83)	AFRAID OF IS THAT THE DOCTOR'LL WANT A FOOTMAN	LIKE	ALL THE REST, NOW THAT HE'S SIR COLENSO. MIND: DONT YOU
DEST SD(152)	BLACKING BY HIS SERGEANT, AS HIS HEAVY UNIFORM,	LIKE	ALL THE UNIFORMS OF THAT DAY, IS DESIGNED FOR PARADE
MIS. PREFACE(24)	TO, STRANGER STILL, THOUGH JACQUES DALCROZE,	LIKE	ALL THESE GREAT TEACHERS, IS THE COMPLETEST OF TYRANTS,
POSN (435)	I WISH WE COULD GET MORE CIVILIZED. I DONT	LIKE	ALL THIS LYNCHING AND SHOOTING. I DONT BELIEVE ANY OF
MIS. PREFACE(78)	ON THEIR FILIAL OR PARENTAL BEHAVIOR, WHICH,	LIKE	ALL UNFREE BEHAVIOR, IS MOSTLY BAD BEHAVIOR. AS TO WHAT
MTH3 (100)	BE FUNNY IF IT WERE NOT SO UNPLEASANT, BECAUSE,	LIKE	ALL WHITE DELICACY, IT IS IN THE WRONG PLACE. HOW DO
BASH II,1, (105)	WITH A FIGHTER. UNLOCK THE DOOR. /LUCIAN/ STOP.	LIKE	ALL WOMEN, LYDIA, YOU HAVE THE COURAGE OF IMMUNITY. TO
BARB III (342)	A HORRIBLE DILEMMA. I WANT BARBARA. /UNDERSHAFT/	LIKE	ALL YOUNG MEN, YOU GREATLY EXAGGERATE THE DIFFERENCE
MTH4 I (164)	THEIR WORK AND LIVED UNDER THEIR INSTITUTIONS.	LIKE	ALL YOUNG THINGS I REBELLED AGAINST THEM; AND IN THEIR
FABL VI (129)	AND I WANT TO KNOW EXACTLY HOW. /TEACHER/	LIKE	ALL YOUNG THINGS YOU WANT TO BEGIN BY KNOWING
PYGM EPILOG (299)	ELATION WAS UNBOUNDED WHEN SHE FOUND THAT FREDDY,	LIKE	ALL YOUTHS EDUCATED AT CHEAP, PRETENTIOUS, AND
GLIM (184)	ON THE WHEEL FOR IT. /GIULIA/ IT WOULD LOOK	LIKE	AN ACCIDENT, SIGNOR. SANDRO IS VERY CLEVER; AND HE IS
VWOO 1 (120)	/Z/ OH, I WANTED TO BE SOMETHING ROMANTIC,	LIKE	AN ACROBAT IN A CIRCUS. /A/ AND WHAT ACTUALLY
FANY III (299)	NOT, SIR, NO DOUBT YOUD PREFER TO MAKE IT LOOK	LIKE	AN ACT OF SELF-SACRIFICE FOR HER SAKE ON YOUR PART, OR
LION II (128)	AS IF YOU WERE DEAD; AND THEN GET UP AND GO HOME,	LIKE	AN ACTOR? /THE EDITOR/ SEE HERE: YOU WANT TO KNOW TOO
DOCT PREFACE(9)	THEY CANNOT SAVE": THEIR REPUTATION STANDS,	LIKE	AN AFRICAN KING'S PALACE, ON A FOUNDATION OF DEAD
GETT SD(323)	WELL-PRESERVED WOMAN. BUT HER BEAUTY IS WRECKED,	LIKE	AN AGELESS LANDSCAPE RAVAGED BY LONG AND FIERCE WAR.
2TRU III SD(81)	IT IS BROAD, AND HAS A NATURAL PILLAR AND A STONE	LIKE	AN ALTAR IN IT, GIVING A GOTHIC SUGGESTION WHICH HAS
HART III (148)	WILL SURVIVE. /ELLIE/ LET THEM. I SHALL BEHAVE	LIKE	AN AMATEUR. BUT WHY SHOULD YOU RUN ANY RISK? /MAZZINI/

HART III (148)	SOLDIERS TO TAKE COVER. MR HUSHABYE IS BEHAVING	LIKE	AN AMATEUR. MANGAN AND THE BURGLAR ARE ACTING VERY
PLES PREFACE(R9)	PROSAICALLY, AND YOU FIND THAT HE " WRITES	LIKE	AN ANGEL AND TALKS LIKE POOR POLL," AND IS HIMSELF THE
MTH2 (79)	BURGE, GIVE HIM BEST. AND YOU SIT THERE PURRING	LIKE	AN ANGORA CAT, AND CAN SEE NOTHING IN IT! /CONRAD/ (
DEVL II (36)	I WANT YOU TO STAY; BUT (SUDDENLY RAGING AT HIM	LIKE	AN ANGRY CHILD) IT IS NOT BECAUSE I LIKE YOU. /RICHARD/
JITT II (48)	PASSING. /LENKHEIM/ (TURNING BRUSQUELY FROM HER	LIKE	AN ANGRY CHILD) I AM NOT SYMPATHIZING WITH YOU. IT
CAPT II (246)	SOB, HE THROWS HIMSELF DOWN ON THE DIVAN, RAGING	LIKE	AN ANGRY CHILD). /LADY CICELY/ (AFTER CONTEMPLATING
MTH1 II (23)	HANG ON HER LAZY SHOULDERS AND MAKE HER LOOK MORE	LIKE	AN ANIMAL THAN A WOMAN? WHEN YOU HAVE TO SNARE THE
HART III (140)	/MRS HUSHABYE/ STOP, ELLIE; OR I SHALL HOWL	LIKE	AN ANIMAL. /MANGAN/ (BREAKS INTO A LOW SNIVELLING)!
FOUN (211)	I PUT IT TO YOU AS ONE MAN TO ANOTHER: DO I LOOK	LIKE	AN ARCHBISHOP? /THE LORD CHANCELLOR/ STUFF, SIR.
CLEO IV (188)	DISLOYALTY LEFT UNPUNISHED, SOCIETY MUST BECOME	LIKE	AN ARENA FULL OF WILD BEASTS, TEARING ONE ANOTHER TO
APPL PREFACE(188)	AND A POLLING CARD. ONE OF THE ADDRESSES READS	LIKE	AN ARTICLE IN THE MORNING POST, AND HAS A UNION JACK ON
GETT (319)	YOUNG OR OLD, LIKE THE REAL THING AS WELL AS WE	LIKE	AN ARTISTIC IMITATION OF IT? IS NOT THE REAL THING
SUPR II (52)	BEAR IT LIKE A MAN, TAVY, EVEN IF YOU FEEL IT	LIKE	AN ASS. IT'S THE OLD GAME: SHE'S NOT TIRED OF PLAYING
ARMS I (4)	THEIR SWORDS AND EYES FLASHING, THUNDERING DOWN	LIKE	AN AVALANCHE AND SCATTERING THE WRETCHED SERBS AND
BASH I (97)	NOT HEAR THY SANDS AS THEY RUN OUT? THEY THUNDER	LIKE	AN AVALANCHE. OLD MAN: TWO THINGS I HATE, MY DUTY AND
DEVL II (49)	ANOTHER HALF MINUTE! PSHA! (HE RUSHES OUT	LIKE	AN AVALANCHE). /ESSIE/ (HURRYING TO JUDITH) HE HAS
MTH3 (127)	I AM SURPRISED AT YOU, MR BARNABAS. YOUR TONE WAS	LIKE	AN ECHO FROM THE DARK AGES. (HE FOLLOWS THE DOMESTIC
CLEO I (109)	HIS MOTHER A BURNING MOUNTAIN; AND HIS NOSE IS	LIKE	AN ELEPHANT'S TRUNK. (CAESAR INVOLUNTARILY RUBS HIS
2TRU PREFACE(25)	FATAL CONSEQUENCES. MR STALIN IS NOT IN THE LEAST	LIKE	AN EMPEROR, NOR AN ARCHBISHOP, NOR A PRIME MINISTER,
2TRU I (43)	DARLING, YOU ARE A PERFECT FILM HERO, ONLY MORE	LIKE	AN ENGLISH GENTLEMAN. (SHE WAVES HIM A KISS). /THE
CATH 2 (175)	TIME THAT I AM FRANK AND ORIGINAL IN CHARACTER,	LIKE	AN ENGLISHMAN. (SHE WALKS ABOUT RESTLESSLY). NO: WHAT
BULL III (138)	UP. AFTER ALL, WHATEVER YOU SAY, LARRY, THEY	LIKE	AN ENGLISHMAN. THEY FEEL THEY CAN TRUST HIM, I SUPPOSE.
BULL I (85)	STIFFER TO STRANGERS, AND A BIT EASIER AT HOME,	LIKE	AN ENGLISHMAN, I'D BE BETTER COMPANY FOR YOU.
KING I (178)	A CHURCH TO ENTER: YOUR MIND YOUR INNER LIGHT IS	LIKE	AN EXTINGUISHED CANDLE; AND YOUR SOUL IS PLUNGED IN
PHIL II SD(109)	FOR HER PERSONAL ELEGANCE. SHE ENTERS BRISKLY,	LIKE	AN HABITUALLY BUSY WOMAN. /SYLVIA/ (RUNNING TO HER)
FANY III (310)	ON HIM? DONT DO IT, JUGGINS: PAY YOUR OWN WAY	LIKE	AN HONEST LAD; AND DONT EAT YOUR BROTHER'S BREAD WHILE
2TRU III (102)	FREE TO TURN HIS HAND TO EVERYTHING AND TO LOOK	LIKE	AN IDIOT WHEN HE FEELS LIKE ONE! I HAVE BEEN DRIVEN TO
MTH4 II SD(182)	EIGHTEEN. THE ENVOY, A TYPICAL POLITICIAN, LOOKS	LIKE	AN IMPERFECTLY REFORMED CRIMINAL DISGUISED BY A GOOD
BUOY IV (54)	THE FELLOW. /SIR FERDINAND/ LIKE THE FELLOW!	LIKE	AN IMPUDENT FORTUNE HUNTER! IN HEAVEN'S NAME, WHY?
CATH PREFACE(157)	WOULD WRITE PARTS FOR HEROES WITH TWENTY ARMS	LIKE	AN INDIAN GOD. INDEED THE ACTOR OFTEN INFLUENCES THE
BULL III (140)	DRIVE WITH A PIG IN THE CAR; I SHALL FEEL QUITE	LIKE	AN IRISHMAN. HODSON: STAY WITH MR HAFFIGAN; AND GIVE
BULL I (83)	HIM. /BROADBENT/ BUT HE SPOKE-- HE BEHAVED JUST	LIKE	AN IRISHMAN. /DOYLE/ LIKE AN IRISHMAN! ! MAN ALIVE,
BULL IV (150)	SIR"). I AM GLAD TO SAY THAT PATSY TOOK IT	LIKE	AN IRISHMAN, AND, FAR FROM EXPRESSING ANY VINDICTIVE
BULL I (83)	SPOKE-- HE BEHAVED JUST LIKE AN IRISHMAN. /DOYLE/	LIKE	AN IRISHMAN! ! MAN ALIVE, DONT YOU KNOW THAT ALL THIS
MTH2 SD(41)	WITH HAZEL HAIR CUT TO THE LEVEL OF HER NECK,	LIKE	AN ITALIAN YOUTH IN A GOZZOLI PICTURE, COMES IN
JOAN 1 (69)	THINK. /JOAN/ (PLUMPING DOWN ON THE STOOL AGAIN,	LIKE	AN OBEDIENT SCHOOLGIRL) YES, SQUIRE. /ROBERT/ YOUR
BARB II (281)	JOB BEFORE. GOOD WORKER. AND SENT TO THE KNACKERS	LIKE	AN OLD HORSE! /BARBARA/ NO MATTER: IF YOU DID YOUR
BARB II (279)	/SHIRLEY/ (WITH BLIGHTING CONTEMPT) YES: YOU	LIKE	AN OLD MAN TO HIT, DONT YOU, WHEN YOUVE FINISHED WITH
MTH2 (62)	LUBIN: AND I AM NOT GOING TO SIT HERE MUMCHANCE	LIKE	AN OLD-FASHIONED GOODY GOODY WIFE WHILE YOU MEN
ARMS I (15)	TELL ME. TELL ME ABOUT HIM. /THE MAN/ HE DID IT	LIKE	AN OPERATIC TENOR. A REGULAR HANDSOME FELLOW, WITH
HART III (147)	AND THE SOUND IN THE SKY! IT'S SPLENDID! IT'S	LIKE	AN ORCHESTRA: IT'S LIKE BEETHOVEN. /ELLIE/ BY THUNDER,
APPL INTRLUD(253)	THAT CABINET WHICH IS A DISGRACE TO YOU: IT IS	LIKE	AN OVERCROWDED THIRD CLASS CARRIAGE. WHY DO YOU ALLOW
OVER (185)	WHAT ABOUT YOURSELF? DONT TRY TO LOOK	LIKE	AN UNMARRIED MAN. I HAPPEN TO KNOW THE LADY YOU
6CAL PREFACE(89)	AND DEFIANT TRADESMAN: IN SHORT, BEHAVING HIMSELF	LIKE	AN UNRESTRAINED HUMAN BEING IN A VERY TRYING SITUATION
LION PREFACE(54)	WILL SHUN YOU AS A MADMAN, VERY WISELY. AND IF,	LIKE	ANANIAS AND SAPPHIRA, YOU TRY TO HOLD BACK YOUR LITTLE
CAND I (80)	COMMUNIST ANARCHISTS, I THINK. /MORELL/ JUST	LIKE	ANARCHISTS NOT TO KNOW THAT THEY CANT HAVE A PARSON ON
MIS. PREFACE(50)	TAKING SOME TROUBLE TO FIND OUT WHAT THEY REALLY	LIKE	AND ARE CAPABLE OF DOING SOME GOOD AT. SOME SILLY
MTH4 II (192)	SHALL NOT CONCLUDE BY SAYING LIVE AS LONG AS YOU	LIKE	AND BE DAMNED TO YOU, BECAUSE I HAVE RISEN FOR THE
OVER PREFACE(166)	TO BELIEVE THAT THEY CAN SEE WHAT THEY LOOK	LIKE	AND WHAT THEY ARE WHEN THEY LOOK AT A TRUE MIRROR.
MIS. PREFACE(25)	FOR NURSING THE SOULS OF LITTLE CHILDREN" ARE	LIKE	ANGELS FORCED TO WORK IN PRISONS INSTEAD OF IN HEAVEN;
SUPR I SD(43)	AS IT IS EXQUISITELY PRETTY. SHE IS NOT A SIREN,	LIKE	ANN: ADMIRATION COMES TO HER WITHOUT ANY COMPULSION OR
UNPL PREFACE(R17)	I THREW MRS WARREN'S PROFESSION ASIDE TOO, AND,	LIKE	ANOTHER FIELDING, CLOSED MY CAREER AS PLAYWRIGHT IN
DEST (154)	ONE MAN IS LIKE ANOTHER (FOLD): ONE COUNTRY IS	LIKE	ANOTHER (FOLD): ONE BATTLE IS LIKE ANOTHER. (AT THE
DEST (154)	PHRASES BY THE STEPS OF THE PROCESS). ONE MAN IS	LIKE	ANOTHER (FOLD): ONE COUNTRY IS LIKE ANOTHER (FOLD):
ROCK PREFACE(166)	OF ALL WITH THE URBAN PROLETARIANS WHO SEEMED	LIKE	ANOTHER SPECIES TO HIM, LEFT TO THEMSELVES THE MOUJIKS
DEST (154)	COUNTRY IS LIKE ANOTHER (FOLD): ONE BATTLE IS	LIKE	ANOTHER. (AT THE LAST FOLD, HE SLAPS THE CLOTH ON THE
MTH1 II (31)	TO ME OF THE LAST FIGHT; AND ONE HARVEST IS JUST	LIKE	ANOTHER, AND THE LAST FIGHT ONLY A REPETITION OF THE
CLEO IV (182)	I HAVE NOT SEEN ALREADY? ONE YEAR OF ROME IS	LIKE	ANOTHER, EXCEPT THAT I GROW OLDER, WHILST THE CROWD IN
SIM II (85)	DAY MUST HAVE ITS MIRACLE, AND NO CHILD BE BORN	LIKE	ANY CHILD THAT EVER WAS BORN BEFORE. AND TO WITNESS
LION I (123)	TO BETRAY MY MASTER, LIKE PETER! SPLENDID TO ACT	LIKE	ANY COMMON BLACKGUARD IN THE DAY OF MY PROVING! WOMAN:
CLEO IV (172)	(WITH SCORN, GETTING UP TO GO) YOU RANT	LIKE	ANY COMMON FELLOW. GO, THEN, AND MARSHAL YOUR
PRES (140)	HEAVENS! LADY RICHMOND'S NEPHEW HAS BEEN TREATED	LIKE	ANY COMMON LABORER; AND WHILE ENGLAND IS REELING UNDER
PYGM EPILOG (303)	DRAG HIM OFF HIS PEDESTAL AND SEE HIM MAKING LOVE	LIKE	ANY COMMON MAN. WE ALL HAVE PRIVATE IMAGINATIONS OF
BARB PREFACE(226)	I, WHO HAVE PREACHED AND PAMPHLETEERED	LIKE	ANY ENCYCLOPEDIST, HAVE TO CONFESS THAT MY METHODS ARE
MTH4 I (145)	TO ME. SHE SPOKE TO ME WITHOUT ANY INTRODUCTION,	LIKE	ANY IMPROPER FEMALE. AND SHE HAS MADE OFF WITH MY
PYGM II (220)	WONT BE CALLED A BAGGAGE WHEN IVE OFFERED TO PAY	LIKE	ANY LADY. MOTIONLESS, THE TWO MEN STARE AT HER FROM THE
CYMB V (140)	/CAPTAIN/ PERHAPS. WHEN ALL WAS LOST HE FOUGHT	LIKE	ANY LEGIONARY, SWORD IN HAND. HIS LAST REPORTED WORD
DOCT I (95)	LIKE HIM AS HE IS? /WALPOLE/ NO I DONT. I DONT	LIKE	ANY MAN WHO HASNT A HEALTHY CIRCULATION. I TELL YOU
BARB II (305)	BARBARA: LORD SAXMUNDHAM HAS A SOUL TO BE SAVED	LIKE	ANY OF US. IF HEAVEN HAS FOUND THE WAY TO MAKE A GOOD
BULL PREFACE(47)	IN THE MAIN, AND UNDER NORMAL CIRCUMSTANCES, MUCH	LIKE	ANY OTHER BODY OF LABORERS AND GENTLEMEN. MANY OF US
ARMS III (56)	ON YOUR HEAD AND REDDENING YOUR LIPS AND CHEEKS	LIKE	ANY OTHER BULGARIAN GIRL? I DID. WHO TAUGHT YOU TO
DOCT I (109)	THAT YOU MUST. IT IS NOT AN ORDINARY CASE, NOT	LIKE	ANY OTHER CASE. HE IS NOT LIKE ANYBODY ELSE IN THE
MRS PREFACE(151)	COMMERCE FOR THE PROFIT OF CAPITALISTS	LIKE	ANY OTHER COMMERCE, AND VERY LUCRATIVE TO GREAT CITY
SIM PREFACE(9)	A DAMNABLE HERESY, AND HAD TO BE ROOTED OUT	LIKE	ANY OTHER DAMNABLE HERESY. BUT AS THE HERETICS WERE
PHIL I (78)	WERE MERELY A FASHION PICKED UP AND FOLLOWED	LIKE	ANY OTHER FASHION, WITHOUT UNDERSTANDING OR MEANING A
ANNA (300)	KNOWING THAT I WAS NO GODDESS, BUT ONLY A GIRL	LIKE	ANY OTHER GIRL! IT WAS CRUELTY TO ANIMALS: YOU COULD
BUOY IV SD(48)	CHAIRS. OLD BILL BUOYANT COMES IN, A GREYBEARD,	LIKE	ANY OTHER GREYBEARD; BUT A GORGEOUS GOLDEN DRESSING
UNPL PREFACE(R10)	ME, THE AUTHOR OF WIDOWERS' HOUSES! THEN,	LIKE	ANY OTHER HARMLESS USEFUL CREATURE, I TOOK THE FIRST
FABL PREFACE(77)	AND THE FANCIES OF NOODLES. THEY ARE EVIDENCE	LIKE	ANY OTHER HUMAN EVIDENCE; AND THEY FORCE ME TO THE
FANY I (274)	TALK SILLY. ROB. BOBBY MIGHT GET INTO A SCRAPE	LIKE	ANY OTHER LAD; BUT HE'D NEVER DO ANYTHING LOW. JUGGINS,
MIS. (135)	PHILOSOPHER, IN PLAIN COAT AND TROUSERS: A MAN	LIKE	ANY OTHER MAN. AND BENEATH THAT COAT AND TROUSERS A
MIS. (136)	SUMMERHAYS/ GIVING THE SHOW AWAY IS A METHOD	LIKE	ANY OTHER METHOD. KEEPING IT TO YOURSELF IS ONLY
NEVR III (271)	REMEMBER: A MAN'S POWER OF LOVE AND ADMIRATION IS	LIKE	ANY OTHER OF HIS POWERS: HE HAS TO THROW IT AWAY MANY
MTH2 (78)	THE BOOK OF GENESIS IS A PART OF NATURE	LIKE	ANY OTHER PART OF NATURE. THE FACT THAT THE TALE OF THE
CAND I SD(91)	WITHOUT THE SMALLEST SCRUPLE. SO FAR, SHE IS	LIKE	ANY OTHER PRETTY WOMAN WHO IS JUST CLEVER ENOUGH TO
BULL PREFACE(28)	A THING AS POLITICAL SCIENCE, WITH NATURAL LAWS	LIKE	ANY OTHER SCIENCE, IT IS CERTAIN THAT ONLY THE MOST
ARMS II (31)	HOWEVER, I SUPPOSE SOLDIERING HAS TO BE A TRADE	LIKE	ANY OTHER TRADE. /SERGIUS/ PRECISELY. BUT I HAVE NO
SUPR PREFACE(R30)	SOCIETY FOR WHAT IT IS WORTH. IT IS A VIEW	LIKE	ANY OTHER VIEW AND NO MORE, NEITHER TRUE NOR FALSE.
GETT (324)	YES. /MRS GEORGE/ WHAT A DESTINY! AND YOU LOOK	LIKE	ANY OTHER WOMAN! /MRS BRIDGENORTH (INTRODUCING
DOCT PREFACE(14)	THE WOUND MADE BY THE SURGEON, WHICH HAS TO HEAL	LIKE	ANY OTHER WOUND. THIS IS WHY OPERATING SURGEONS, WHO
HART II (123)	BEING ACCUSED OF POSING. /HECTOR/ IT IS A POSE	LIKE	ANY OTHER. IN THIS HOUSE WE KNOW ALL THE POSES: OUR
FABL III (111)	TO STOP SINGING AND GO AWAY. IT'S A WAY OF LIFE	LIKE	ANY OTHER. IT SUITS ME. I'M GOOD FOR NOTHING ELSE. /THE
SIM PREFACE(18)	MY READERS. GROUP MARRIAGE IS A FORM OF MARRIAGE	LIKE	ANY OTHER; AND IT IS JUST AS WELL TO REMIND OUR WESTERN
GLIM (182)	SCREWS FOR WHAT THEY WILL FETCH: THEY GO TO LABOR	LIKE	ANY PEASANT'S BEAST. BUT OUR NOBILITY DOES NOT STUDY
DOCT PREFACE(20)	NO CONCEPTION OF SCIENTIFIC METHOD, AND BELIEVES,	LIKE	ANY RUSTIC, THAT THE HANDLING OF EVIDENCE AND
DOCT I (109)	ORDINARY CASE, NOT LIKE ANY OTHER CASE. HE IS NOT	LIKE	ANYBODY ELSE IN THE WORLD: OH, BELIEVE ME, HE IS NOT. I
BARB I (261)	WHY SHOULD I? MY FATHER HAS A SOUL TO BE SAVED	LIKE	ANYBODY ELSE. HE'S QUITE WELCOME AS FAR AS I AM
MILL IV (193)	RIGHT TO BE IN HER HOTEL IF WE PAY OUR WAY JUST	LIKE	ANYBODY ELSE. /ALASTAIR/ VERY WELL: HAVE IT YOUR OWN
BULL II (107)	HIM! JUST LIKE HIM! HE'D NEVER DO ANYTHING	LIKE	ANYBODY ELSE. WELL, WHAT CANT BE CURED MUST BE
CAND I (85)	YOUR LEFT ARM INSTEAD OF CARRYING IT IN YOUR HAND	LIKE	ANYONE ELSE? WHY DO YOU WALK WITH YOUR CHIN STUCK OUT
ROCK II (248)	DO ME TO HAVE A LOT OF MONEY WHEN I HAVE TO WORK	LIKE	ANYONE ELSE? /SIR DEXTER/ WHY SHOULD A MAN WORK LIKE
ROCK II (248)	ANYONE ELSE? /SIR DEXTER/ WHY SHOULD A MAN WORK	LIKE	ANYONE ELSE IF HE HAS MONEY? /BARKING/ MY BROTHER HAD
ROCK II (248)	BUT HE HAD TO GO INTO THE TRENCHES AND FIGHT	LIKE	ANYONE ELSE IN THE WAR. THATS HOW I CAME INTO THE
BULL PREFACE(22)	A BLOCKHEAD. AN ENGLISHMAN WILL NOT RESPECT NOR	LIKE	ANYONE ELSE. EVERY ENGLISH STATESMAN HAS TO MAINTAIN
HART III (143)	MERELY AS A SUCCESSFUL MAN. I HAVE AN IMAGINATION	LIKE	ANYONE ELSE. I HAVE A PRESENTIMENT-- /MRS HUSHABYE/ OH,
JOAN 6 (136)	LASS, THOUGH I HAVE HELPED WITH THE SHEEP	LIKE	ANYONE ELSE. I WILL DO A LADY'S WORK IN THE HOUSE --
HART II (103)	YOU ARE A REAL PERSON: THAT YOU HAD A MOTHER,	LIKE	ANYONE ELSE. (PUTTING HER HANDS ON HIS SHOULDERS AND

2TRU I (33)	NEVER OCCURS TO YOU THAT A BACILLUS CAN BE SICK	LIKE	ANYONE ELSE. /THE DOCTOR/ WHATS THE MATTER WITH YOU?
FANY PROLOG (264)	BE CAREFUL WHAT YOU SAY ABOUT THAT: I SHOULDNT	LIKE	ANYONE TO CALL ME AN INTELLECTUAL: I DONT THINK ANY
KING I (218)	LIKE A WELL-TO-DO GROCER, AND WILL NEVER LOOK	LIKE	ANYTHING ELSE. /LOUISE/ YOU WOULD NOT DARE TO SAY SO AT
ARMS I SD(3)	MILES AWAY. THE INTERIOR OF THE ROOM IS NOT	LIKE	ANYTHING TO BE SEEN IN THE WEST OF EUROPE. IT IS HALF
MIS. (119)	OR TELEGRAPHING: HE THINKS HES HUSTLING ALONG	LIKE	ANYTHING WHEN HES ONLY SENDING UNNECESSARY MESSAGES.
MIS. (121)	WORD THAT WAS LIKE OLD TIMES, I WAS DOWN ON THEM	LIKE	ANYTHING. AND NOW I'M BEGINNING TO DO IT MYSELF AT
CURE (236)	GREAT TASTE IN CARPETS AND PICTURES. I CAN COOK	LIKE	ANYTHING. I CAN PLAY QUITE NICELY AFTER DINNER. THOUGH
JOAN 3 (93)	THE BOATS HAVE PUT OFF. THEY ARE RIPPING UPSTREAM	LIKE	ANYTHING. /DUNOIS/ (RISING) NOW FOR THE FORTS. YOU
PYGM IV (261)	WAS FRIGHTFULLY EXCITING. MY HEART BEGAN BEATING	LIKE	ANYTHING. /HIGGINS/ YES, FOR THE FIRST THREE MINUTES.
PYGM EPILOG (302)	FREDERICK CHALLONER. ELIZA HERSELF SWANKED	LIKE	ANYTHING. THAT IS ALL. THAT IS HOW IT HAS TURNED OUT.
SUPR IV (148)	OF IRELAND. WELL, YOU CAN KEEP IRELAND. ME AND ME	LIKE	ARE COMING BACK TO BUY ENGLAND; AND WE'LL BUY THE BEST
BUOY II (25)	EXCEPT TO THE EXTENT TO WHICH YOU AND I AND OUR	LIKE	ARE JUST AND BENEVOLENT THERE IS NO JUSTICE AND NO
MTH5 (251)	IT: I COULD ONLY IMAGINE IT. /THE SHE-ANCIENT/ I,	LIKE	ARJILLAX, FOUND OUT THAT MY STATUES OF BODILY BEAUTY
FANY PROLOG (265)	COME. AND ONE OF THEM HAS A COCKED HAT AND SWORD	LIKE	A-- (SHE NOTICES SAVOYARD) OH, I BEG YOUR PARDON. /THE
GETT (284)	REJJY AND SINJON. /REGINALD/ A MAN WITH A FACE	LIKE	A-- /LEO/ I WONT HAVE IT, REJJY, IT'S DISGUSTING. /THE
GENV III (82)	TO ITS CHILDISH SELF IT WILL DECLINE AND FALL	LIKE	AS ALL THE OLD CAPITALIST CIVILIZATIONS. /SIR O./ LET
POSN (459)	SINGING DREADFUL DIRTY WICKED WORDS TO HYMN TUNES	LIKE	AS IF HE HAD SEVEN DEVILS IN HIM. /STRAPPER/ SHE'S
JOAN EPILOG (160)	SOLDIER/ YOU WONT FIND IT SO BAD, SIR. JOLLY.	LIKE	AS IF YOU WERE ALWAYS DRUNK WITHOUT THE TROUBLE AND
JOAN EPILOG (160)	SO MUCH NOW. THEY TELL ME I CAN HAVE AS MANY AS I	LIKE	AS SOON AS I WANT THEM. /CHARLES/ WHAT IS HELL LIKE?
SIM I (49)	CHILDREN ARE NOT LIKE EUROPEAN CHILDREN AND NOT	LIKE	ASIATIC CHILDREN. THEY HAVE THE EAST IN THEIR BRAINS
BARB I (253)	LORD CHAMBERLAIN TO TAKE IT UP. BUT IT WAS JUST	LIKE	ASKING THEM TO DECLARE WAR ON THE SULTAN. THEY WOULDNT.
BULL PREFACE(60)	BY THE DENSHAWAI INCIDENT, WHAT WILL EGYPT BE	LIKE	AT THE END OF ANOTHER THIRTY YEARS OF MORAL ELEVATION "
BULL I (92)	DOYLE STOPS DEAD AND STARES AT HIM WITH SOMETHING	LIKE	AWE). I DONT WISH TO BE IMPERTINENT, AS YOU KNOW,
APPL I (236)	WHETHER THIS DRUNKEN WRETCH TAKES HONEST WHISKY	LIKE	BALBUS OR METHYLATED SPIRIT OR PETROL OR WHATEVER HE
APPL I (223)	NEVER HAVE GIVEN THE HOME OFFICE TO A BULLY	LIKE	BALBUS -- /BALBUS/ (INTIMIDATED BY THE FATE OF
GETT PREFACE(192)	THEY HAD ALL, AS THEY CALLED IT, SETTLED DOWN,	LIKE	BALLOONS THAT HAD LOST THEIR LIFTING MARGIN OF GAS; AND
SIM II (71)	SORT OF JUDGMENT DAY. IT'S A FINE DAY. IT'S	LIKE	BANK HOLIDAY. /THE ANGEL/ AND PRAY WHY SHOULD THE DAY
BARB PREFACE(224)	OF A CHICAGO MEAT KING, THAT YOUNG CLERGYMAN HAS,	LIKE	BARBARA, A VERY BAD QUARTER HOUR. BUT HE CANNOT HELP
MILL PREFACE(116)	PAPER CONSTITUTIONS, OR THAN A PLUCKY BULLY	LIKE	BARRAS, WHO CARED FOR NOTHING EXCEPT FEATHERING HIS OWN
2TRU III (110)	UNTIL GIRLS WHO ARE LIKE ROSES AT EIGHTEEN ARE	LIKE	BATTERED DEMIREPS AT TWENTYTWO: IN ALL THESE WAYS THE
MIS. PREFACE(10)	VOLUPTUARY SAID FRANKLY " I BEAT YOU BECAUSE I	LIKE	BEATING YOU; AND I SHALL DO IT WHENEVER I CAN CONTRIVE
MIS. PREFACE(68)	(BOYS AND GIRLS TAUGHT TOGETHER) BEFORE SCHOOLS	LIKE	BEDALES WERE FOUNDED: INDEED THE PRACTICE WAS COMMON
BARB I (257)	HIM. I HAD RATHER GO AND LIVE IN SOME CHEAP PLACE	LIKE	BEDFORD SQUARE OR EVEN HAMPSTEAD THAN TAKE A FARTHING
CAND III (138)	TEETOTALLER, NOT A CHAMPAGNE TEETOTALLER. I DONT	LIKE	BEER. ARE THERE ANY LETTERS FOR ME TO ANSWER, MR
GENV IV (120)	THEM TO LIVE IN IT ON CONDITION THAT THEY WORK	LIKE	BEES AND KEEP BARELY ENOUGH OF THE HONEY TO KEEP
BULL IV (175)	AND ORGANIZE, AND FIND CAPITAL WHILE YOU SLAVE	LIKE	BEES FOR IT AND REVENGE YOURSELVES BY PAYING
SUPR III SD(72)	THE REASON WE DO NOT DO THIS IS BECAUSE WE WORK	LIKE	BEES OR ANTS, BY INSTINCT OR HABIT, NOT REASONING ABOUT
2TRU PREFACE(19)	OF GOVERNMENT TO ENSURE THAT THE POOR SHALL,	LIKE	BEES, CONTINUE TO PRODUCE NOT ONLY THEIR OWN
HART III (147)	SKY: IT'S SPLENDID: IT'S LIKE AN ORCHESTRA: IT'S	LIKE	BEETHOVEN. /ELLIE/ BY THUNDER, HESIONE: IT IS
HART I (75)	MIND: I AM NOT MAKING LOVE TO YOU. I DO NOT	LIKE	BEING ATTRACTED. BUT YOU HAD BETTER KNOW HOW I FEEL IF
KING I (198)	IT FOR YOU AND ENJOY IT; BUT PROTESTANTS DO NOT	LIKE	BEING BURNT ALIVE. /JAMES/ THEY WILL HAVE TO LUMP IT IF
NEVR IV (300)	OLD FASHIONED IN HIS IDEAS ABOUT HIS OWN SEX TO	LIKE	BEING CALLED AN IDIOT. AND NOW HAD WE NOT BETTER GO AND
AUGS (277)	BUT I SHOULD BE CHAFFED; AND FRANKLY, I DONT	LIKE	BEING CHAFFED. /THE LADY/ OF COURSE NOT. WHO DOES? IT
HART II (119)	IS THAT IT? HOW DISGUSTING! DO YOU	LIKE	BEING DRUNK? /CAPTAIN SHOTOVER/ NO: I DREAD BEING
2TRU II (70)	ME TO TAKE TO DRINK TO KEEP ME QUIET, BUT I DONT	LIKE	BEING DRUNK; AND WHAT WOULD BECOME OF MY GOOD LOOKS IF
MIS. (133)	CRANK: I'M A NATURAL MAN; AND, AS SUCH, I DONT	LIKE	BEING GOT AT. IF A MAN IN MY EMPLOYMENT DID IT, I
DEVL III (73)	HARK YE, GENERAL BURGOYNE. IF YOU THINK THAT I	LIKE	BEING HANGED, YOURE MISTAKEN. I DONT LIKE IT; AND I
NEVR I (222)	NECESSARY PAIN IN MY DAY. /VALENTINE/ OH, IF YOU	LIKE	BEING HURT, ALL RIGHT, I'LL HURT YOU AS MUCH AS YOU
CLEO III (162)	SOME OF YOUR EGYPTIANS' HEADS OFF. HOW WILL YOU	LIKE	BEING LEFT HERE WITH THE CHANCE OF BEING CAPTURED BY
OVER (194)	YOU, MR JUNO. YOU AMUSE ME VERY MUCH. I DONT	LIKE	BEING LOVED: IT BORES ME. BUT I DO LIKE TO BE AMUSED.
MTH5 (214)	WAY THAN CALLOUS IN YOURS. /THE SHE-ANCIENT/ YOU	LIKE	BEING MISERABLE? YOU WILL SOON GROW OUT OF THAT. (SHE
CAPT III (296)	SEE. AND LIKE MOST POOR MEN, I'M PROUD. I DONT	LIKE	BEING PATRONIZED. /LADY CICELY/ WHAT IS THE USE OF
MILL IV (209)	AWAY FROM IT. WHY AM I ALWAYS POOR? I DO NOT	LIKE	BEING POOR. /EPIFANIA/ WHY AM I ALWAYS RICH? I DO NOT
2TRU II (69)	THE GOOD WOMEN? THOSE THAT ENJOY BEING DULL AND	LIKE	BEING PUT UPON. THEYVE NO APPETITES. LIFE'S THROWN AWAY
MILL IV (210)	POOR. /EPIFANIA/ WHY AM I ALWAYS RICH? I DO NOT	LIKE	BEING RICH. /ALASTAIR/ YOUD BETTER BOTH GO TO RUSSIA.
MIS. (125)	JOHNNY. WHAT'S A GIRL TO DO? I NEVER MET ANYBODY	LIKE	BENTLEY BEFORE. HE MAY BE SMALL; BUT HE'S THE BEST OF
MIS. (140)	THAT YOU DIDNT WANT TO HAVE UNDERSIZED CHILDREN	LIKE	BENTLEY. IT SERVED ME RIGHT: I DONT REPROACH YOU: I WAS
FANY EPILOG (334)	SHAW. /FANNY/ OH, OF COURSE IT WOULD BE A LITTLE	LIKE	BERNARD SHAW. THE FABIAN TOUCH, YOU KNOW. /BANNAL/ (
FANY III (325)	IN PRECISELY THE SORT OF COMPANY THEY SEEM TO	LIKE	BEST AND BE MOST AT HOME IN. /KNOX/ AND MY DAUGHTER?
LION II (142)	CAESAR. ASK THE CAPTAIN WHETHER THEY DO NOT	LIKE	BEST TO SEE A WOMAN TORN TO PIECES. HE TOLD ME SO
DEST (155)	SO UNLIKE OTHER GREAT MEN. IT IS THE SUBJECT THEY	LIKE	BEST. /NAPOLEON/ WELL, TALK TO ME ABOUT THE SUBJECT
MTH2 (47)	OF THE EARTH. (WITH CONVICTION) THERE IS NOTHING	LIKE	BIOLOGY. " THE CLOUD-CAPPED TOWERS, THE SOLEMN
MIS. PREFACE(17)	OF CHILDREN," THEY ARE REALLY CHILD FANCIERS (	LIKE	BIRD FANCIERS OR DOG FANCIERS) BY IRRESISTIBLE NATURAL
HART III (144)	TYPHOON, THE FLYING-FISH GLITTER IN THE SUNSHINE	LIKE	BIRDS. IT'S AMAZING HOW THEY GET ALONG, ALL THINGS
WIDO I (15)	NOT. BUT WHAT MAKES YOU THINK MY FAMILY WONT	LIKE	BLANCHE? OF COURSE MY FATHER WAS A YOUNGER SON; AND
BULL I (90)	OF YOU, LARRY, OLD MAN, BUT ALL BLARNEY. I	LIKE	BLARNEY; BUT IT'S ROT, ALL THE SAME. /DOYLE/ NO IT'S
JOAN 3 (88)	WHO? THE MAID? /THE PAGE/ NO: THE KINGFISHER.	LIKE	BLUE LIGHTNING. SHE WENT INTO THAT BUSH. /DUNOIS/ (
GENV III (82)	RUSKIN'S GOSPEL COMPARED WITH KARL MARX'S WAS	LIKE	BOILING BRANDY COMPARED WITH MILK AND WATER. /THE JEW/
APPL II (258)	WAR DEBT. AND WITH A MAD IMPERIALIST PRESIDENT	LIKE	BOSSFIELD! NO YOU WOULDNT, MY DEAR: YOU WOULD BE
KING II (231)	WILL NOT BE RULED; AND THERE IS NOTHING THEY HATE	LIKE	BRAINS. FOR BRAINS AND RELIGION YOU MUST GO TO
MRS II (212)	IS ENOUGH FOR TONIGHT. AT WHAT HOUR WOULD YOU	LIKE	BREAKFAST? IS HALF-PAST EIGHT TOO EARLY FOR YOU? /MRS
WIDO II SD(24)	SMARTLY TOOLED BOOKS, FITTING INTO THEIR PLACES	LIKE	BRICKS. /SARTORIUS/ BLANCHE. /BLANCHE/ YES, PAPA.
ROCK II (269)	A REAL REVERENCE INTO THE VOICES OF GREAT ORATORS	LIKE	BRIGHT AND GLADSTONE. BUT THAT WAS WHEN IT WAS A DREAM
FANY II (286)	BY HIMSELF AMONG THE TEMPTATIONS OF A GAY PLACE	LIKE	BRIGHTON WITHOUT HIS TUTOR; AND I SAW THE TUTOR IN
FANY III (301)	BROUGHT UP SO MUCH TOGETHER THAT IT FEELS MORE	LIKE	BROTHER AND SISTER THAN-- WELL, THAN THE OTHER THING.
FANY III (307)	HOW TO EXPLAIN OUR RELATIONSHIPS. BOBBY AND I ARE	LIKE	BROTHER AND SISTER. /DUVALLET/ PERFECTLY. I NOTICED IT.
KING II (233)	AT LEAST I CANNOT. BUT HAVING TO MANAGE RASCALS	LIKE	BUCKINGHAM AND SHAFTESBURY, AND DODGERS LIKE HALIFAX,
FANY III (323)	THE SAVAGE: NAY, FROM THE BEAST. WE CAN CHARGE	LIKE	BULLS; WE CAN SPRING ON OUR FOES LIKE GAMECOCKS; WHEN
MIS. (125)	SEEM TO MEET THEM. THE REAL ONES ARE TOO SMALL,	LIKE	BUNNY, OR TOO SILLY, LIKE JERRY. OF COURSE ONE CAN GET
SUPR PREFACE(R34)	CONCEIVED HOW ANY MAN WHO WAS NOT A FOOL COULD,	LIKE	BUNYAN'S HERO, LOOK BACK FROM THE BRINK OF THE RIVER OF
METH PREFACE(R57)	ESCAPE FROM AN INTOLERABLY OPPRESSIVE SITUATION.	LIKE	BUNYAN'S PILGRIM THEY COULD NOT SEE THE WICKET GATE.
MTH2 (78)	GLANCED IS ROUSSEAU, WHO WAS A SORT OF DEIST	LIKE	BURGE-- /BURGE/ (INTERRUPTING HIM FORCIBLY) LUBIN: HAS
GETT (294)	MYSELF FOR THE LAST HALF-HOUR UNTIL I FEEL	LIKE	BURSTING. (HE SITS DOWN FURIOUSLY AT THE END OF THE
CLEO IV (192)	CLEOPATRA). /RUFIO/ COME! THIS IS SOMETHING	LIKE	BUSINESS. /CAESAR/ (BUOYANTLY) IS IT NOT, MY ONLY
MIS. (144)	OUT OF THE MUD PIES; BUT I LIKE SLANG; AND I	LIKE	BUSTLING YOU UP BY SAYING THINGS THAT SHOCK YOU; AND
DOCT PREFACE(41)	BECAUSE VIVISECTION IS NOW A ROUTINE,	LIKE	BUTCHERING OR HANGING OR FLOGGING; AND MANY OF THE MEN
CLEO NOTES (210)	ABLE CIVILIANS TAKING UP THE PROFESSION OF ARMS,	LIKE	CAESAR AND CROMWELL, IN MIDDLE AGE, HAVE SNATCHED ALL
LION PREFACE(81)	MINDS, IN THE HANDS OF A LOGICAL FRENCHMAN	LIKE	CALVIN, PUSHING IT TO ITS UTMOST CONCLUSIONS, AND
GENV II (64)	SHE DOES. WELL, THE HOUSE OF COMMONS IS EXACTLY	LIKE	CAMBERWELL IN THAT RESPECT. /THE SECRETARY/ BUT CAN YOU
GENV IV (111)	HIM INTO SOME ISLAND OR CAMP WHERE HE AND HIS	LIKE	CAN TRIFLE AND TWADDLE WITHOUT OBSTRUCTING GOD'S
CAND III (131)	THE MAN THAT CANDIDA LOVED. YOU CANT MAKE A WOMAN	LIKE	CANDIDA LOVE YOU BY MERELY BUTTONING YOUR COLLAR AT THE
CAPT III (277)	CLEVER LAWYER YOU COULD MAKE A POOR SIMPLE SAILOR	LIKE	CAPTAIN KEARNEY BELIEVE ANYTHING. THE PROPER THING FOR
DOCT PREFACE(29)	IN CONFLICT. UP TO A CERTAIN POINT DOCTORS,	LIKE	CARPENTERS AND MASONS, MUST EARN THEIR LIVING BY DOING
SUPR PREFACE(R14)	OR BROTHERS OF HIS MISTRESSES: HE DOES NOT EVEN,	LIKE	CASANOVA, TELL HIS OWN STORY. IN FACT HE IS NOT A TRUE
BASH III (125)	COURSE YOU ARE BUT ACTING AS A GENTLEMAN IN THE	LIKE	CASE WOULD ACT. I FULLY GRANT YOUR PERFECT RIGHT TO
JOAN PREFACE(29)	OFFENDER. BESIDES, JOAN'S TRIAL WAS NOT,	LIKE	CASEMENT'S, A NATIONAL POLITICAL TRIAL. ECCLESIASTICAL
GENV III (74)	DEAL WITH. NO TYPES. JUST ENGLISH GENTLEMEN. NOT	LIKE	CATHOLIC PRIESTS. /THE WIDOW/ OH, SIR ORPHEUS! YOU, OF
FABL VI (125)	WHYS. THEY ONLY SET YOU CHASING YOUR OWN TAILS,	LIKE	CATS. LET US GET TO WORK. I CALL FOR QUESTIONS
JOAN PREFACE(42)	TO WHOM THE SCRUPLES OF A TRAINED ECCLESIASTIC	LIKE	CAUCHON WOULD SEEM RIDICULOUS AND UNGENTLEMANLY. THE
SIM PRO,1, (25)	" I'LL BE IN THE PAPERS YET SOME DAY" I SAYS "	LIKE	CECIL RHODES! YOU SEE IF I'M NOT." " NOT YOU, MY LAD"
ARMS I (4)	SERBS AND THEIR DANDIFIED AUSTRIAN OFFICERS	LIKE	CHAFF, AND YOU! YOU KEPT SERGIUS WAITING A YEAR BEFORE
CLEO PRO2 (98)	WERE FRIGHTENED (PERHAPS); BUT THEY SCATTERED US	LIKE	CHAFF. THE GUARDSMEN, MUCH DAMPED, UTTER A GROWL OF
MILL PREFACE(125)	BEEN TRACED. ALL THESE TYPES WITH WHICH WRITERS	LIKE	CHAMBERLAIN PLAY: THE TEUTONS AND LATINS, THE
SHAK (141)	(ROARING WITH LAUGHTER) HA HA! HO HO! MY LUNGS	LIKE	CHANTICLEER MUST CROW THEIR FILL. THIS FELLOW HATH AN
MTH3 (98)	HOW? /CONFUCIUS/ PEOPLE LIKE YOU. THEY	LIKE	CHEERFUL GOOD-NATURED BARBARIANS. THEY HAVE ELECTED YOU
DOCT III (151)	BEST; NO TONIC LIKE A CHARMING WOMAN; NO MEDICINE	LIKE	CHEERFULNESS; NO RESOURCE LIKE SCIENCE; GOODBYE,
ARMS III (59)	BLOWS; THEY STAND BY AND SEE ONE ANOTHER PUNISHED	LIKE	CHILDREN: AYE, AND HELP TO DO IT WHEN THEY ARE ORDERED.

CLEO III (160)	BARRICADE IS FINISHED. AND HERE WE ARE WAITING	LIKE	CHILDREN TO SEE A CARPET FULL OF PIGEONS' EGGS. THE
POSN (435)	THAT KILLED HIM WASNT AFRAID OF HIM. BUT MEN ARE	LIKE	CHILDREN WHEN THEY GET A GUN IN THEIR HANDS: THEYRE NOT
MILL III (187)	ALLUSION TO HER) DO WHAT SHE TELLS US, JOE. WE'RE	LIKE	CHILDREN-- (SHE BEGINS CRYING AGAIN SOFTLY). THERE IS
DEST (177)	OF YOUR SEX GETTING INTO A PET AND BEHAVING	LIKE	CHILDREN; BUT I NEVER SAW A REALLY GREAT MAN DO IT
APPL I (228)	MEASURES IN OUR PARTY PROGRAM ARE MADE TO LOOK	LIKE	CITY JOBS. /MAGNUS/ AM I SUPPOSED TO WRITE THESE
JOAN PREFACE(55)	WHO PAY FOR ADMISSION TO A THEATRE BECAUSE THEY	LIKE	CLASSICAL COMEDY OR TRAGEDY FOR ITS OWN SAKE, AND LIKE
SUPR III (101)	PEOPLE WHO ARE THERE, NOT BECAUSE THEY REALLY	LIKE	CLASSICAL MUSIC, BUT BECAUSE THEY THINK THEY OUGHT TO
CAND III (144)	HE FETCHES IT SILENTLY, EVEN WITH SOMETHING	LIKE	COLD STRENGTH, AND PLACES IT NEXT MORELL, A LITTLE
GENV PREFACE(9)	WHEN WE WERE EXULTING IN OUR DEMOLITION OF CITIES	LIKE	COLOGNE AND HAMBURG WE WERE VERY CONSIDERABLY
PHIL II (97)	A CHAT WHILE WE'RE WAITING FOR CHARTERIS? IF YOU	LIKE	COMPANY, THE SMOKING ROOM'S ALWAYS FULL OF WOMEN. HERE
6CAL SD(97)	THEY ARE DEEPLY CAST DOWN, BEARING THEMSELVES	LIKE	CONDEMNED MEN, YET MAINTAINING A MELANCHOLY DIGNITY.
MTH3 SD(91)	UP ON A SIMILAR PEG BESIDE THE DOOR. HE IS RATHER	LIKE	CONRAD BARNABAS, BUT YOUNGER, AND MUCH MORE
GETT PREFACE(200)	WITHOUT SELF-SACRIFICE. CONSCIOUS GOODNESS,	LIKE	CONSCIOUS MUSCULAR EFFORT, MAY BE OF USE IN
MIS. (165)	AND GENTLEMEN. /HYPATIA/ ANOTHER TALKER! MEN	LIKE	CONVENTIONS BECAUSE MEN MADE THEM. I DIDNT MAKE THEM: I
ROCK II (269)	OF THE PEOPLE WERE BOOTED OUT AT THE POLLS	LIKE	CONVICTED CRIMINALS. IT WASNT THAT THE POOR SILLY SHEEP
APPL INTRLUD(248)	AND WORKING SIXTEEN HOURS A DAY FOR THIRTY YEARS,	LIKE	CORAL INSECTS, MAKE THEM GREAT. WHAT ARE THEY FOR?
2TRU PREFACE(6)	BEYOND WHICH ONLY LORDS LIEUTENANT AND THEIR	LIKE	COULD ASPIRE. THE SCALE HAS CHANGED SINCE THEN. I HAVE
JOAN PREFACE(4)	HAD REALLY NOTHING TO SAY EXCEPT THAT HE AND HIS	LIKE	COULD NOT ENDURE BEING SHEWN UP AS IDIOTS EVERY TIME
NEVR IV (288)	LOOKS INQUIRINGLY AT VALENTINE). /VALENTINE/ I	LIKE	CUCUMBER. /WAITER/ RIGHT, SIR. (SUMMING UP) CLARET
NEVR IV (288)	BOHUN) ANYTHING SPECIAL FOR YOU, SIR? YOU DONT	LIKE	CUCUMBER, SIR. /BOHUN/ IF MRS CLANDON WILL ALLOW ME:
NEVR I (203)	THE SOUND MADE BY PHIL, THOUGH BUT MOMENTARY, IS	LIKE	CUTTING A SHEET OF SILK IN TWO WITH A FLASH OF
HART I (79)	MANY MEN HAVE THOUGHT OF IT. DECENT MEN ARE	LIKE	DANIEL IN THE LION'S DEN: THEIR SURVIVAL IS A MIRACLE;
GETT (286)	OUGHT TO HAVE ONE OF THESE IDEALIZATIONS,	LIKE	DANTE'S BEATRICE. (HE CLASPS HIS HANDS BEHIND HIM, AND
METH PREFACE(R62)	AN END OF ITS MORAL PRESTIGE. THAT WAS ENOUGH:	LIKE	DARWIN HE HAD FOR THE MOMENT THE WORLD WILL BY THE EAR.
MRS IV (251)	WHEN I'M OLD? PLENTY OF GIRLS HAVE TAKEN TO ME	LIKE	DAUGHTERS AND CRIED AT LEAVING ME; BUT I LET THEM ALL
ROCK II (275)	I SUPPOSE SO. YOU SEE, SIR ARTHUR, I AM NOT	LIKE	DAVID. I AM A READING THINKING MODERN WOMAN; AND I KNOW
MIS. PREFACE(59)	INFANTILE DOCILITY AND JUVENILE DEPENDENCE ARE,	LIKE	DEATH, A PRODUCT OF NATURAL SELECTION; AND THOUGH THERE
SUPR II (67)	IT'S JUST ABSURD. BUT I TELL YOU, VIOLET, I DONT	LIKE	DECEIVING HIM. I FEEL AS IF I WAS STEALING HIS MONEY.
HART II (85)	LEANING FORWARD, WITH THE BEGINNING OF SOMETHING	LIKE	DELIBERATE UNPLEASANTNESS IN HIS VOICE) KINDNESS OF
INCA (253)	YOU LIKE. NO, MADAM, BELIEVE ME, THERE IS NOTHING	LIKE	DEMOCRACY, AMERICAN DEMOCRACY. GIVE THE PEOPLE VOTING
BULL PREFACE(42)	AND PATENT WOODEN LEGS TO THE NATURAL PRODUCTS.	LIKE	DEMOCRACY, NATIONAL SELF-GOVERNMENT IS NOT FOR THE GOOD
APPL PREFACE(177)	ABOUT THE SEA, WHICH IS IN SOME RESPECTS RATHER	LIKE	DEMOCRACY! WE ALL HAVE OUR OWN VIEWS OF THE SEA. SOME
ROCK II (282)	MYSELF OUT AND GOT MYSELF OFF MY MIND. THAT LOOKS	LIKE	DESPAIR; BUT IT IS REALLY THE BEGINNING OF HOPE, AND
LION I (115)	QUARREL WITH YOU FOR SACRIFICING TO A WOMAN GOD	LIKE	DIANA, IF DIANA MEANT TO YOU WHAT CHRIST MEANS TO ME..
3PLA PREFACE(R28)	GATES OF HELL. A CENTURY AGO WILLIAM BLAKE WAS,	LIKE	DICK DUDGEON, AN AVOWED DIABOLONIAN: HE CALLED HIS
BARB PREFACE(227)	SENSE OF SHAME IS LOST. THE CHRISTIAN HAS BEEN	LIKE	DICKENS' DOCTOR IN THE DEBTOR'S PRISON, WHO TELLS THE
ROCK II (270)	AND AN EQUAL. YOU CANT FRIGHTEN ME WITH A WORD	LIKE	DICTATOR. ME AND MY LIKE HAS BEEN DICTATED TO ALL OUR
JOAN PREFACE(50)	THERE ARE NO VILLAINS IN THE PIECE. CRIME,	LIKE	DISEASE, IS NOT INTERESTING: IT IS SOMETHING TO BE DONE
GETT PREFACE(218)	A CONTRACT NOT ONLY TO DO SOMETHING BUT TO	LIKE	DOING IT WOULD BE CERTIFIED AS MAD, YET POPULAR
SUPR PREFACE(R16)	THE TENTH CENTURY. AS A RESULT, MAN IS NO LONGER,	LIKE	DON JUAN, VICTOR IN THE DUEL OF SEX. WHETHER HE HAS
SUPR III (99)	BE POPULAR HERE, HAVE TURNED OUT SOCIAL FAILURES,	LIKE	DON JUAN! /DON JUAN/ I AM REALLY VERY SORRY TO BE A
BARB PREFACE(209)	TOWARDS POTTS: HE NEVER GAINS OUR AFFECTIONS	LIKE	DON QUIXOTE AND PICKWICK: HE HAS NOT EVEN THE INFATUATE
ARMS I (15)	MOUSTACHE, SHOUTING HIS WAR-CRY AND CHARGING	LIKE	DON QUIXOTE AT THE WINDMILLS. WE DID LAUGH. /RAINA/ YOU
BULL III (127)	EMPLOY THEM. IT WAS ALL VERY WELL WHEN SOLID MEN	LIKE	DORAN AN MATT WERE KEP FROM OWNIN LAND. BUT WHAT MAN IN
HART PREFACE(28)	EDIFICES. UNFORTUNATELY THEY CAN BE BUILT AGAIN.	LIKE	DOUBTING CASTLE, THEY HAVE BEEN DEMOLISHED MANY TIMES
MIS. PREFACE(20)	OF WRATH, NO WONDER MEN OF DOWNRIGHT SENSE,	LIKE	DR JOHNSON, ADMIT THAT UNDER SUCH CIRCUMSTANCES
MILL I (160)	IT RAINED MONEY IN BUCKETSFUL. IT WENT TO MY HEAD	LIKE	DRINK. IT WENT TO THE AMERICAN'S HEAD. IT WENT TO THE
2TRU III (95)	MOTHERS CLING: DAUGHTERS CLING! WE ARE ALL	LIKE	DRUNKEN WOMEN CLINGING TO LAMP POSTS: NONE OF US STANDS
LION PREFACE(88)	BY LABORATORY EXPERIMENTS THAT " MEDIUMS"	LIKE	DUNGLAS HOME CAN MAKE THE POINTER OF A SPRING-BALANCE
NEVR IV SD(286)	BLACK HAIR, CROPPED SHORT AND OILED, AND EYEBROWS	LIKE	EARLY VICTORIAN HORSEHAIR UPHOLSTERY, PHYSICALLY AND
METH PREFACE(R59)	AND OUR SNOBBISH CONCEPTION OF GODHEAD AS BEING,	LIKE	EARTHLY KINGSHIP, A SUPREME CLASS DISTINCTION INSTEAD
SUPR III (102)	DEAR ANA, YOU ARE SILLY. DO YOU SUPPOSE HEAVEN IS	LIKE	EARTH, WHERE PEOPLE PERSUADE THEMSELVES THAT WHAT IS
SUPR II (49)	BREAKING MY NECK! /THE CHAUFFEUR/ WELL, IF YOU	LIKE	EASY GOING, YOU CAN TAKE A BUS, YOU KNOW. IT'S CHEAPER.
METH PREFACE(R22)	DONT WANT TO SEE, YOU WILL LOSE YOUR EYES. IF YOU	LIKE	EATING THE TENDER TOPS OF TREES ENOUGH TO MAKE YOU
FABL PREFACE(66)	A PINT OF BRANDY, MAKE HIM A DIPSOMANIAC,	LIKE	EDMUND KEAN, ROBSON, AND DICKENS ON HIS LAST AMERICAN
LION PREFACE(49)	WHO MEANT WHAT HE SAID, AS A FACT, AS A FORCE	LIKE	ELECTRICITY, ONLY NEEDING THE INVENTION OF SUITABLE
BUOY II (20)	UNTIL THAT KINDLY NATIVE COMES AND FEEDS YOU,	LIKE	ELIJAH'S RAVENS. WHAT DO YOU LEARN FROM THAT? /SHE/
HART II (95)	DOESNT MATTER ABOUT ME, MRS HUSHABYE. I THINK YOU	LIKE	ELLIE; AND THAT IS ENOUGH FOR ME. /MRS HUSHABYE/ I'M
GENV PREFACE(24)	HAVE NEVER INVENTED A MACHINE, THOUGH I AM BUILT	LIKE	ENGINEERS WHO, THOUGH THEY ARE NEVER AT A LOSS WITH
FANY PROLOG (263)	/SAVOYARD/ WELL, LET ME SEE. AS YOU DONT	LIKE	ENGLISH PEOPLE, I DONT KNOW THAT YOULL GET ON WITH
DOCT II (123)	/SCHUTZMACHER/ NOT AT ALL. PERSONALLY, I	LIKE	ENGLISHMEN BETTER THAN JEWS, AND ALWAYS ASSOCIATE WITH
SUPR PREFACE(R40)	NOT ALL MY REVIEWERS HAVE UNDERSTOOD ME:	LIKE	ENGLISHMEN IN FRANCE, CONFIDENTLY UTTERING THEIR OWN
BULL PREFACE(17)	ENTENTE CORDIALE BETWEEN FOREIGNERS. PERSONALLY I	LIKE	ENGLISHMEN MUCH BETTER THAN IRISHMEN (NO DOUBT BECAUSE
MTH2 (39)	I FELT IT TO BE MY VOCATION TO WALK WITH GOD,	LIKE	ENOCH. AFTER TWENTY YEARS OF IT I REALIZED THAT I WAS
LADY (238)	YOU HAVE MY LORD PEMBROKE'S TRICK, SIR. /THE MAN/	LIKE	ENOUGH: HE IS MY NEAR FRIEND. BUT WHAT CALL YOU HIS
MIS. PREFACE(25)	AN INKLING OF RELIGION, THOUGH THERE ARE NOTHING	LIKE	ENOUGH OF THEM TO GO ROUND. BUT EVEN THE FEW WHO, LIKE
MRS II (206)	ROOM, RESTLESS AND SULKY). /MRS WARREN/ WELL, I	LIKE	ENOUGH TO EAT. BUT A LITTLE OF THAT COLD BEEF AND
PYGM V (280)	DEMEAN MYSELF. AND GET INSULTED FOR MY PAINS,	LIKE	ENOUGH. /DOOLITTLE/ DONT BE AFRAID: SHE NEVER COMES TO
SUPR II (56)	THE NEW MAN. I LOATHE TRAVELLING; BUT I RATHER	LIKE	ENRY. HE CARES FOR NOTHING BUT TEARING ALONG IN A
JOAN PREFACE(26)	UNIMPEACHABLE AMERICAN SCHOOL TEACHER IN ARMOR.	LIKE	ESTHER SUMMERSON SHE MAKES HER CREATOR RIDICULOUS, AND
SIM II (84)	YOU ARE NOT A DREAM. THE CHILDREN DID NOT VANISH	LIKE	EUPHORION IN THEIR INFANCY. THEY GREW UP TO BORE ME
SIM I (49)	(CONTINUING)-- OUR FOUR CHILDREN ARE NOT	LIKE	EUROPEAN CHILDREN AND NOT LIKE ASIATIC CHILDREN. THEY
KING I (196)	OUR SIDE, EXCEPT HIM. I HAVE BEEN LOOKING FOR HIS	LIKE	EVER SINCE WE CAME BACK. I SOMETIMES WONDER WHETHER
BULL I (77)	MESELF, SIR. /BROADBENT/ I AM A LOVER OF LIBERTY,	LIKE	EVERY TRUE ENGLISHMAN, MR HAFFIGAN. MY NAME IS
PYGM EPILOG (297)	EXTENT RIDICULED AND MIMICKED IN WEST KENSINGTON	LIKE	EVERYBODY ELSE THERE, SHE WAS ACCEPTED AS A RATIONAL
FABL VI (125)	NOT A REASON. WHY DID HE WANT TO LIVE? /YOUTH 2/	LIKE	EVERYBODY ELSE, I SUPPOSE. /TEACHER/ WHY DOES EVERYBODY
UNPL PREFACE(R8)	NORMAL. I NATURALLY TOOK THIS TO MEAN THAT IT WAS	LIKE	EVERYBODY ELSE'S; BUT HE REJECTED THIS CONSTRUCTION AS
MTH4 I (145)	POSITION IS UNIQUE. BUT HE WOULD MUCH RATHER BE	LIKE	EVERYONE ELSE. /THE ELDERLY GENTLEMAN/ THIS IS
BUOY III (31)	CANNOT NOW BE FAR OFF. YOUR INCOMES WILL BE TAXED	LIKE	EVERYONE ELSES. IF YOU HAVE ANY INCOMES. HAVE YOU?
ARMS III (72)	LAST BELIEF IS GONE. YOUR SAGACITY IS A FRAUD,	LIKE	EVERYTHING ELSE. YOU HAVE LESS SENSE THAN EVEN I!
GETT PREFACE(216)	AS TO WHAT ACTUAL MARRIAGE IS, ONE WOULD	LIKE	EVIDENCE INSTEAD OF GUESSES; BUT AS ALL DEPARTURES FROM
3PLA PREFACE(R25)	NEITHER OF MY WORK NOR OF THE WAY IT IS DONE, I	LIKE	EXPLAINING ITS MERITS TO THE HUGE MAJORITY WHO DONT
BUOY II (25)	KNOWLEDGE AND WISDOM CANNOT BE PURCHASED	LIKE	FASHIONABLE GARMENTS. /HE/ IN ENGLAND THEY CAN. A SAGE
PYGM V (281)	THE SAME TO EVERYBODY. /HIGGINS/ JUST SO. /LIZA/	LIKE	FATHER. /HIGGINS/ (GRINNING, A LITTLE TAKEN DOWN)
POSN (464)	BLACKGUARDS LIKE ME, AND GOOD-FOR-NOTHING RIPS	LIKE	FEEMY. HE MADE ME BECAUSE HE HAD A JOB FOR ME. HE LET
SUPR PREFACE(R38)	WHICH WILL NOT EVEN MAKE MONEY FOR HIM,	LIKE	FIDDLE PLAYING. EFFECTIVENESS OF ASSERTION IS THE ALPHA
JOAN 2 (83)	AND THEIR SHOUTING AND THEIR BAD TEMPERS. THEY	LIKE	FIGHTING: MOST OF THEM ARE MAKING FOOLS OF THEMSELVES
KING I (214)	AN HONEST KNOWLEDGE OF THEM, AND ARE NOT ASHAMED	LIKE	FINE LADIES WHO HAVE ONLY A DISHONEST KNOWLEDGE OF
CLEO PRO2 (100)	THEM). NOW THIS NEWS WILL RUN THROUGH THE PALACE	LIKE	FIRE THROUGH STUBBLE. /BEL AFFRIS/ WHAT SHALL WE DO TO
MILL III (182)	PROPER WAGE AND ALWAYS HAS BEEN, MAAM. /THE MAN/	LIKE	FIVE PER CENT AT THE BANK OF ENGLAND IT IS. THIS IS A
2TRU III (111)	FORCING HOUSE IN WHICH WE HAVE GROWN WITH A RUSH	LIKE	FLOWERS IN A LATE SPRING FOLLOWING A TERRIBLE WINTER.
APPL I (232)	HE BREAKS UP THE CONFERENCE, LEAVING US LOOKING	LIKE	FOOLS WITH NOTHING DONE. AND YOU TELL ME HE DID IT ON
APPL II (275)	/NICOBAR/ YOU CAN UPSET IT AS SOON AS YOU	LIKE	FOR ALL I CARE. I AM GOING OUT OF POLITICS. POLITICS IS
MTH1 II (28)	SPADE AND LISTENED TO YOU FOR A WHILE, WENT BY ME	LIKE	FOUL WIND THAT HAS PASSED OVER A DEAD BODY. THAT IS WHY
SIM PREFACE(9)	MAN AND ADMIRED HIM. NOW THE HERETIC IN RUSSIA IS	LIKE	FOX. HE IS NOT CONTENT WITH A QUIET ABSTRACT DISSENT
INCA (252)	IN THE WAR; AND THEN IT WILL BECOME A REPUBLIC,	LIKE	FRANCE AFTER 1871, AND THE INCA WILL BE SENT TO ST
BARB PREFACE(228)	STILL TOO MUCH OTHER-WORLDLINESS ABOUT THE ARMY.	LIKE	FREDERICK'S GRENADIER, THE SALVATIONIST WANTS TO LIVE
BULL PREFACE(17)	THEY MAKE MORE OF ME) JUST AS MANY ENGLISHMEN	LIKE	FRENCHMEN BETTER THAN ENGLISHMEN, AND NEVER GO ON BOARD
GETT (354)	GEORGE BOTH LIKE FRIED FISH. /HOTCHKISS/ I DO NOT	LIKE	FRIED FISH. DONT BE LOW, POLLY. /SOAMES/ WOMAN: DO NOT
GETT (354)	HE MIGHT AS WELL SAY THAT HE AND GEORGE BOTH	LIKE	FRIED FISH. /HOTCHKISS/ I DO NOT LIKE FRIED FISH. DONT
O'FL (214)	AND COME SO STRANGE TO THEM THAT THEY RUN ABOUT	LIKE	FRIGHTENED CHICKENS, UTTERING ALL MANNER OF NONSENSE.
SIM II (85)	THEM TO MAKE. WE SHALL CLAMOR FOR SECURITY	LIKE	FRIGHTENED CHILDREN; BUT IN THE UNEXPECTED ISLES THERE
BARB PREFACE(217)	IS, AS HE SAYS, THE FINAL TEST OF SINCERITY.	LIKE	FROISSART'S MEDIEVAL HERO, WHO SAW THAT " TO ROB AND
CLEO II SD(118)	TO CONTROL HIS TEMPER. HE HAS FINE TAWNY HAIR,	LIKE	FUR. PTOLEMY, THE KING, LOOKS MUCH OLDER THAN AN
FANY III (323)	CAN CHARGE LIKE BULLS; WE CAN SPRING ON OUR FOES	LIKE	GAMECOCKS; WHEN WE ARE OVERPOWERED BY TREASON, WE CAN
BULL PREFACE(64)	STILL SUGGEST TO HIM THAT WE CAN AT LEAST DIE	LIKE	GENTLEMEN? MIGHT I EVEN BE SO PERSONAL AS TO SAY THAT
APPL I (225)	THE HANDSOMEST MANNER. CANT WE TAKE OUR VICTORY	LIKE	GENTLEMEN? /MAGNUS/ PERHAPS I HAD BETTER EXPLAIN. I

DOCT PREFACE(51)	MUST NOT ONLY DIE WHEN THEIR TIME COMES, BUT DIE	LIKE	GENTLEMEN. IN THEIR PAROXYSMS OF COWARDICE AND
BASH II,1, (103)	IMITATORS ON THIS SIDE. THE LOSERS SETTLED UP	LIKE	GENTLEMEN; BUT MANY FELT THAT BYRON SHEWED BAD TASTE IN
GETT PREFACE(194)	NAUGHTINESS. IT WAS LEFT TO AN ABNORMAL CRITIC	LIKE	GEORGE GISSING TO POINT OUT THE GLARING FACT THAT IN
2TRU III (83)	BUT TO ME THATS ONLY THE SMALLEST PART OF IT. I	LIKE	GETTING A WOMAN'S OPINIONS. I LIKE TO EXPLORE HER MIND
2TRU II (64)	INEVITABLES THAT I MUST PUT UP WITH WILLYNILLY,	LIKE	GETTING UP IN THE MORNING, AND WASHING AND DRESSING AND
MIS. PREFACE(97)	EVIL IS NOT VIRTUE BUT IMBECILITY: ADMIRING IT IS	LIKE	GIVING A PRIZE FOR HONESTY TO A MAN WHO HAS NOT STOLEN
HART III (143)	MUTUAL ADMIRATION GANG WIELD! IT'S MADNESS: IT'S	LIKE	GIVING A TORPEDO TO A BADLY BROUGHT UP CHILD TO PLAY AT
LION PREFACE(95)	CHILD ALSO TO ACCEPT HIM. IF THE CHILD IS BUILT	LIKE	GLADSTONE, HE WILL ACCEPT JESUS AS HIS SAVIOR, AND
DOCT I (99)	GERMS-- THESE BACILLI-- ARE TRANSLUCENT BODIES,	LIKE	GLASS, LIKE WATER. TO MAKE THEM VISIBLE YOU MUST STAIN
GETT PREFACE(241)	THE CHURCH AND ONE TO THE HEARTH. THERE ARE MEN	LIKE	GOETHE, WHO MARRY LATE AND RELUCTANTLY SOLELY BECAUSE
POSN (443)	WAS GONE, AND THEY FIRED ME OUT. I WAS FIRED OUT	LIKE	GOLD OUT OF THE FURNACE, WITH MY CHARACTER UNSPOILED
GENV PREFACE(25)	WHEN WE ARE NOT VIOLENTLY PERSECUTING THEM WE ARE	LIKE	GOLDSMITH'S VILLAGERS, WONDERING HOW THEIR LITTLE HEADS
MILL PREFACE(120)	AND SILENCE. THE PEOPLE, INSTEAD OF BEING SHOCKED	LIKE	GOOD LIBERALS, ROSE TO HIM. HE WAS ABLE TO ORGANIZE A
POSN (455)	DRAW A BEAD ON US. /THE SHERIFF/ THAT DONT SOUND	LIKE	GOOD SENSE. WHAT WOULD HE LOOK AT A RAINBOW FOR?
JITT II (32)	/LENKHEIM/ (IMPATIENTLY) DONT BE SO SUPERIOR. I	LIKE	GOSSIP. EVERYBODY LIKES GOSSIP. YOU LIKE IT YOURSELF AS
UNPL PREFACE(R20)	FROM THE GREAT ORIGINAL OF POPULAR ENTERTAINMENTS	LIKE	GOUNOD'S OPERA OR THE LYCEUM VERSION, IN WHICH POETRY
ARMS III (51)	/BLUNTSCHLI/ (MAKING A WRY FACE) DO YOU	LIKE	GRATITUDE? I DONT. IF PITY IS AKIN TO LOVE, GRATITUDE
GETT PREFACE(184)	REGARD IT AS A FIXED PART OF THE ORDER OF NATURE,	LIKE	GRAVITATION, EXCEPT FOR THIS ERROR, WHICH MAY BE
LION EPILOG (151)	SPOKEN OF AND DOUBTLESS MOST IMPORTANT THING,	LIKE	GREEK TRAGEDY, OR CLASSICAL MUSIC, OR THE HIGHER
MIS. PREFACE(84)	SPECIFIC FAMILY AFFECTION THE BETTER. CHILDREN,	LIKE	GROWN-UP PEOPLE, GET ON WELL ENOUGH TOGETHER IF THEY
BARB III (329)	YOU KNOW, THESE HIGH EXPLOSIVES DONT GO OFF	LIKE	GUNPOWDER, EXCEPT WHEN THEYRE IN A GUN. WHEN THEYRE
LION PREFACE(4)	AND THAT THE STARS COULD DROP ON IT FROM HEAVEN	LIKE	HAILSTONES. CHRISTIANITY INTERESTS PRACTICAL STATESMEN
DOCT I SD(109)	AND STRONG: HAS DARK HAIR, DRESSED SO AS TO LOOK	LIKE	HAIR AND NOT LIKE A BIRD'S NEST OR A PANTALOON'S WIG (
KING II (233)	LIKE BUCKINGHAM AND SHAFTESBURY, AND DODGERS	LIKE	HALIFAX, IS FAR WORSE THAN HAVING TO MANAGE BARBARA AND
POSN PREFACE(400)	PROHIBITS ONE PLAY BY SOPHOCLES BECAUSE,	LIKE	HAMLET, IT MENTIONS THE SUBJECT OF INCEST; BUT AN
MILL PREFACE(118)	THE REMEDY WAS AN EXTENSION OF THE FRANCHISE.	LIKE	HAMLET, WE LIVED ON THE CHAMELEON'S DISH " AIR, PROMISE
MRS I (183)	CHAIR) OH, NOW DO LET ME TAKE THAT HARD CHAIR. I	LIKE	HARD CHAIRS. /VIVIE/ SO DO I. SIT DOWN, MR PRAED. (
ROCK II (270)	FRIGHTEN ME WITH A WORD LIKE DICTATOR. ME AND MY	LIKE	HAS BEEN DICTATED TO ALL OUR LIVES BY SWINE THAT HAVE
DEVL II (32)	PEOPLE CAREFULLY, YOULL BE SURPRISED TO FIND HOW	LIKE	HATE IS TO LOVE. (SHE STARTS, STRANGELY TOUCHED-- EVEN
BUOY III (37)	PEOPLE CALLED OUR LOVE TURNED INTO SOMETHING VERY	LIKE	HATRED. BUT BIOLOGICAL TASTES ARE NOT LOW TASTES. OUR
HART PREFACE(16)	ARE BLOWN FROM MEN'S HEADS INTO THE MUD	LIKE	HATS IN A GUST OF WIND. BUT WHEN THIS SCRIPTURE WAS
ROCK I (217)	WHEN IT GOES OUT OF THE FACTORY AFTER HE AND HIS	LIKE	HAVE ALL DONE THEIR LITTLE BITS OF JOBS ON IT? HE DONT
ROCK I (217)	WELL, SRARTHUR, WHATEVER'S WRONG YOU AND YOUR	LIKE	HAVE TAKEN ON YOURSELVES THE JOB OF SETTING IT RIGHT. I
MTH2 (62)	/SAVVY/ YOU MUST EXCUSE ME, MR LUBIN; BUT IT'S	LIKE	HEARING A MAN TALK ABOUT THE GARDEN OF EDEN. /CONRAD/
SUPR I (11)	HER NOW. THATS THE LATEST GAME. AN ORPHAN! IT'S	LIKE	HEARING AN IRONCLAD TALK ABOUT BEING AT THE MERCY OF
NEVR IV (284)	GO HIS HANDS AND DRAWING BACK FROM HIM) YOU DONT	LIKE	HER? /CRAMPTON/ MY CHILD: YOU HAVNT BEEN MARRIED TO
MRS II (198)	/MRS WARREN/ NONSENSE! WHAT WOULD A YOUNG GIRL	LIKE	HER BE DOING WITH SUCH THINGS! NEVER MIND: IT DONT
JOAN PREFACE(47)	IN FRANCE, CONTEMPTUOUSLY REFUSES HER. WE DO NOT,	LIKE	HER CONTEMPORARIES, RUSH TO THE OPPOSITE EXTREME IN A
PRES (166)	I WAS THINKIN THAT PRAPS THE DUCHESS MIGHT	LIKE	HER DAUGHTER-IN-LAW'S MOTHER TO BE A GENERAL'S LADY
PRES (147)	HIM, OF COURSE. WHAT ELSE WOULD A YOUNG FOOL	LIKE	HER DO? HE INTHROJOOCED HER TO THE POET LAUREATE,
JITT II (31)	IN HAND: YOU KNOW HOW SHE CLINGS TO YOU. SHE IS	LIKE	HER FATHER IN THAT: HE CLUNG TO YOU. /JITTA/ TO ME!
SUPR I (43)	SHE HAS PLACED HERSELF IN. /RAMSDEN/ I DONT	LIKE	HER GOING AWAY IN THIS FASHION, SUSAN. WE HAD BETTER
2TRU I (44)	SHE WAS THINKING ABOUT YOU. /THE PATIENT/ JUST	LIKE	HER IMPUDENCE! HOW DID SHE KNOW ABOUT ME? /THE
2TRU I (42)	UP SOME GOOD LOOKS, AND IF HER PUNCH IS ANYTHING	LIKE	HER KICK SHE WILL BE AN INVALUABLE BODYGUARD FOR US TWO
SUPR I (22)	RAMSDEN: WE'RE BEATEN-- SMASHED-- NONENTITIZED,	LIKE	HER MOTHER. /RAMSDEN/ STUFF, SIR. (HE FOLLOWS MRS
SUPR I SD(16)	BESIDES, INSTEAD OF MAKING HERSELF AN EYESORE,	LIKE	HER MOTHER, SHE HAS DEVISED A MOURNING COSTUME OF BLACK
JOAN PREFACE(17)	REALLY WANTED TO RESCUE HER, AND HAD PUT ANYTHING	LIKE	HER OWN VIGOR INTO THE ENTERPRISE, THEY COULD HAVE
BARB III (348)	OLD MOTHER HAS MORE SENSE THAN ANY OF YOU. I FELT	LIKE	HER WHEN I SAW THIS PLACE-- FELT THAT I MUST HAVE IT--
FABL V SD(117)	HERMAPHRODITE. THEY WEAR WHITE SLEEVELESS TUNICS	LIKE	HERALDS' TABARDS ON WHICH ARE EMBROIDERED DIFFERENT
KING II (230)	AND THAT I AM NOT THE NINNY I AM MADE TO LOOK	LIKE	HERE. /CHARLES/ WHY DONT YOU DO IT, BELOVED? I AM NOT
CAPT II (261)	BUT PERHAPS THE REAL REASON WAS THAT HE DIDNT	LIKE	HER. YOU KNOW, DONT YOU, THAT IF YOU DONT LIKE PEOPLE
ARMS III (58)	NOT A BIT. THEY ALL SLASHED AND CURSED AND YELLED	LIKE	HEROES. PSHA! THE COURAGE TO RAGE AND KILL IS CHEAP. I
SUPR II (53)	OF YOURS HAS ANY REAL BEARING ON A NATURE	LIKE	HERS? /TANNER/ HM! DID SHE SAY ANYTHING ELSE?
2TRU III (105)	BELIEVE THAT I AM HER DAUGHTER. SHE'S NOT A BIT	LIKE	HERSELF. /MRS MOPPLY/ ISNT SHE? WHAT DO YOU KNOW ABOUT
MTH1 I (9)	LO! THERE WAS NOT ONE NEW LILITH BUT TWO: ONE	LIKE	HERSELF, THE OTHER LIKE ADAM. YOU WERE THE ONE: ADAM
BARB PREFACE(225)	BARBARA'S LESSON BECAUSE THEY HAVE NOT,	LIKE	HER, LEARNT IT BY TAKING THEIR PART IN THE LARGER LIFE
2TRU III (107)	ALL DANCING ATTENDANCE ON HER. YOURE NOT A BIT	LIKE	HER, THANK GOODNESS: THATS WHY IVE TAKEN A FANCY TO
DEVL I SD(4)	THEMSELVES SITTING UP ALL NIGHT WAITING FOR NEWS,	LIKE	HER, TOO, THEY FALL ASLEEP TOWARDS MORNING AT THE RISK
PYGM EPILOG (303)	AND SHE LIKES THE COLONEL; AND SHE DOES NOT	LIKE	HIGGINS AND MR DOOLITTLE. GALATEA NEVER DOES QUITE LIKE
APPL I (220)	OPPOSING THE MEN THAT PAY THEM. WELL, THE VOTERS	LIKE	HIGH WAGES. THEY KNOW WHEN THEY ARE WELL OFF; AND THEY
INCA (248)	GLORIOUS THAN TALK? CAN ANYONE IN THE WORLD TALK	LIKE	HIM? MADAM: WHEN HE SIGNED THE DECLARATION OF WAR, HE
DEVL II (48)	(HITCHING THE BELT INTO ITS PLACE) DO I LOOK	LIKE	HIM? /JUDITH/ (TURNING WITH THE PURSE IN HER HAND)
DOCT I (95)	BE ANOTHER MAN AFTERWARDS. /SIR PATRICK/ DONT YOU	LIKE	HIM AS HE IS? /WALPOLE/ NO I DONT. I DONT LIKE ANY MAN
GETT (280)	REJJY KNOWS THAT I'M QUITE FOND OF HIM. I	LIKE	HIM BECAUSE HE WANTS ME; AND I LIKE SINJON BECAUSE I
HART III (140)	THERE! YOU HAVE SET ALFRED OFF. /ELLIE/ I	LIKE	HIM BEST WHEN HE IS HOWLING. /CAPTAIN SHOTOVER/
PHIL I (70)	OUT WHEN I FELL IN LOVE WITH YOU. BUT I USED TO	LIKE	HIM FOR BEING IN LOVE WITH ME. IT BROUGHT OUT ALL THE
HART I (54)	FATHER. /THE CAPTAIN/ THIS! NONSENSE! NOT A BIT	LIKE	HIM (HE GOES AWAY THROUGH THE GARDEN, SHUTTING THE
VWOO 1 (116)	NEXT MINE BEATS HIS WIFE. /A/ I FEEL A LITTLE	LIKE	HIM MYSELF. SOME WOMEN WOULD PROVOKE ANY MEN TO BEAT
ARMS III (51)	(SCEPTICALLY) YOU MEAN THAT YOU WOULDNT	LIKE	HIM TO FIND OUT THAT THE STORY ABOUT THE ICE PUDDING
MIS. (126)	OH, HOW COULD ANYBODY BE IN LOVE WITH BUNNY? I	LIKE	HIM TO KISS ME JUST AS I LIKE A BABY TO KISS ME. I'M
MTH5 (237)	AUTOMATON. /THE NEWLY BORN/ I DONT THINK I SHOULD	LIKE	HIM TO PUT HIS ARM ROUND MY NECK. I DONT LIKE THEM. (
LION I (122)	FOR THEN I SHOULD PERHAPS BE MEEK AND GENTLE	LIKE	HIM. AND YET THERE SEEMS TO BE A SPECIAL PROVIDENCE
WIDO I (18)	YOU CANT VERY WELL PUT TO A MAN-- AT LEAST A MAN	LIKE	HIM. DO YOU THINK YOU COULD WORD THE LETTER SO AS TO
FANY PROLOG (259)	/THE COUNT/ HE DID, SIR. /SAVOYARD/ IT DONT SOUND	LIKE	HIM. I SAW A GOOD DEAL OF HIM AT ONE TIME. /THE COUNT/
MIS. (117)	CAN ALWAYS MAKE HIM CRY BY TELLING HIM YOU DONT	LIKE	HIM. ONLY, HE CRIES SO LOUD THAT THE EXPERIMENT SHOULD
BARB I (272)	OH, YOU MUSTNT THINK THAT, MOTHER. I-- I DONT	LIKE	HIM. /LADY BRITOMART/ THE OTHERS DO. THAT IS THE
PYGM IV (265)	INTO IT. YOU NEEDNT MARRY THE FELLOW IF YOU DONT	LIKE	HIM. /LIZA/ WHAT ELSE AM I TO DO? /HIGGINS/ OH, LOTS
APPL I (199)	NOT RUM ENOUGH TO BE NOTICED. THERE ARE MILLIONS	LIKE	HIM. /PAMPHILIUS/ WHAT ABOUT HIS DYING OF
BUOY IV (50)	HER) HE HAS AN EYE FOR FACTS, THIS CHAP. I RATHER	LIKE	HIM. /SHE/ YES: SO DO I. HE HAS NO ILLUSIONS ABOUT
MIS. (134)	MET SINCE MY RETURN TO ENGLAND HAVE BEEN VERY	LIKE	HIM. /TARLETON/ (AGAIN IMPRESSED) THATS AN IDEA. THATS
DOCT I (114)	MADE ME SO HAPPY: I KNOW YOU WILL ADMIRE HIM AND	LIKE	HIM. THIS IS MY ADDRESS. (SHE GIVES HIM HER CARD).
BUOY IV (51)	DO YOU ADVISE, DADDY? /OLD BILL/ OH, TAKE HIM. I	LIKE	HIM; AND HE WILL DO AS WELL AS ANOTHER. YOU MAY REGRET
KING I (206)	AND THEN THEY HAD HIS OWN OFF. I AM NOT A BIT	LIKE	HIM; BUT I HAVE MORE THAN A TOUCH IN ME OF MY FAMOUS
DEVL II (37)	A WOMAN? HAS HE NOT RAISED YOU ABOVE MY INSULTS,	LIKE	HIMSELF? (SHE STOPS CRYING, AND RECOVERS HERSELF
LION PREFACE(6)	IS OFTEN SO DETERMINED TO REGARD JESUS AS A MAN	LIKE	HIMSELF AND NOTHING MORE, THAT HE SLIPS UNCONSCIOUSLY
LADY PREFACE(208)	OF HIS WORK AT THE MUSEUM, IN WHICH I WAS THEN,	LIKE	HIMSELF, A DAILY READER. HE WAS BY PROFESSION A MAN OF
MILL PREFACE(109)	AUTHORITY OVER A CREW OF SCOUNDRELS WHO ARE ALL,	LIKE	HIMSELF, OUTSIDE THE LAW? HOW DOES AN OBSCURE VILLAGE
NEVR III (279)	I DONT WANT TO MEET FERGUS AGAIN, BECAUSE I DONT	LIKE	HIM, AND DONT BELIEVE THE MEETING WILL DO ANY GOOD.
CLEO II (131)	LUCIUS SEPTIMIUS FOR MY MODEL, AND BECOME EXACTLY	LIKE	HIM, CEASING TO BE CAESAR, WILL YOU SERVE ME STILL?
BULL PREFACE(15)	SATISFIED WITH BROADBENT IS IN A DREAM, MUCH AS I	LIKE	HIM, I OBJECT TO BE GOVERNED BY HIM, OR ENTANGLED IN
NEVR IV (285)	HIM AND TALKED TO HIM. (WITH GAY MALICE) YOULL	LIKE	HIM, MISS CLANDON: HE'S THE VERY INCARNATION OF
GETT (353)	A STEP OR TWO NEARER HOTCHKISS) WHY ARNT YOU	LIKE	HIM, SONNY? WHY DO YOU HANG ON TO A SCRUBBY WOMAN IN
PYGM V (277)	ALWAYS BEFORE ME. I WAS BROUGHT UP TO BE JUST	LIKE	HIM, UNABLE TO CONTROL MYSELF, AND USING BAD LANGUAGE
BULL II (107)	HIMSELF IN A MOTOR AND WE ALL EXPECTN HIM! JUST	LIKE	HIM! HE'D NEVER DO ANYTHING LIKE ANYBODY ELSE. WELL,
SUPR IV (172)	THE PRESENCE OF MY SOLICITOR AND HIS CLERK, WHO,	LIKE	HIS CLIENTS, WILL BE IN ORDINARY WALKING DRESS--
NEVR II (227)	AFFABLE AND PLEASANT INDEED! /THE GENTLEMAN/ YOU	LIKE	HIS FATHER! (HE LAUGHS AT THE NOTION). /WAITER/ OH
JOAN 1 (68)	GOD WILL BE MERCIFUL TO THEM; AND THEY WILL ACT	LIKE	HIS GOOD CHILDREN WHEN THEY GO BACK TO THE COUNTRY HE
SUPR III SD(79)	BLOCK IS THE APPANAGE, BY SITTING ON THE GROUND	LIKE	HIS GUESTS, AND USING THE STONE ONLY AS A SUPPORT FOR
NEVR II (232)	OH, CRAMPSTONES, OR WHATEVER IT IS. HE SAID I WAS	LIKE	HIS MOTHER. I KNEW HE MUST MEAN HIS DAUGHTER. /PHILIP/
BULL PREFACE(29)	OBTAINED AT THAT PRICE; SO AN IRISH CATHOLIC MAY	LIKE	HIS PRIEST AS A MAN AND REVERE HIM AS A CONFESSOR AND
GETT SD(345)	HEARTH AND THRUSTS HIS HANDS INTO HIS POCKETS,	LIKE	HOGARTH'S RAKE, WITHOUT WAITING FOR EDITH TO SIT DOWN.
LION PREFACE(73)	THAT I WAS TREATING IT AS AN ORDINARY EVENT	LIKE	HOME RULE OR THE INSURANCE ACT: THAT IS (THOUGH THIS
LADY (240)	IN YOUR SLEEP, FAIR ONE; FOR THEN YOUR WORDS DROP	LIKE	HONEY. /THE LADY/ (WITH COLD MAJESTY) KNOW YOU TO WHOM
BASH PREFACE(90)	OWN PASSIONATE AND RICHLY COLORED STYLE IT SOLD	LIKE	HOT CAKES. I MUST MAKE A PERSONAL CONFESSION IN THIS
BUOY IV (55)	UNTIL THE CHILDREN ARE BORN, AND THEN DROPS THEM	LIKE	HOT POTATOES. MONEY GUARANTEES COMFORT AND WHAT YOU
BUOY IV (56)	BABZY. /DARKIE/ I DONT WANT TO BE SPOILT. I	LIKE	HOUSEKEEPING; AND I'M NOT SENTIMENTAL. IF I EVER WANT
BARB III SD(325)	BETWEEN, THE TOPS OF ITS CHIMNEYS SPROUTING	LIKE	HUGE SKITTLES INTO THE MIDDLE DISTANCE. ACROSS THE

MRS PREFACE(168)	UNEXPECTEDNESS WITH WHICH MY CHARACTERS BEHAVE	LIKE	HUMAN BEINGS, INSTEAD OF CONFORMING TO THE ROMANTIC
SUPR I SD(16)	DREAM. VITALITY IS AS COMMON AS HUMANITY; BUT,	LIKE	HUMANITY, IT SOMETIMES RISES TO GENIUS; AND ANN IS ONE
OVER (184)	HUNGRY. NOTHING BRINGS PEOPLE TO THEIR SENSES	LIKE	HUNGER. /JUNO/ (CONTEMPLATING THE FLOWER WITHOUT
LION PREFACE(95)	AND FORERUNNER RESPECTIVELY. IF HE IS BUILT	LIKE	HUXLEY, HE WILL TAKE THE SECULAR VIEW, IN SPITE OF ALL
O'FL (209)	SIX? /O'FLAHERTY/ YOURE NOT USED TO TELLING LIES	LIKE	I AM, SIR, I GOT GREAT PRACTICE AT HOME WITH MY MOTHER.
PLES PREFACE(R12)	NEW AUTHORS. AN ORIGINAL WORK BY A MAN OF GENIUS	LIKE	IBSEN MAY, OF COURSE, BAFFLE HIM AS IT BAFFLES MANY
MIS. PREFACE(25)	ENOUGH OF THEM TO GO ROUND. BUT EVEN THE FEW WHO,	LIKE	IBSEN'S MRS SOLNESS, HAVE " A GENIUS FOR NURSING THE
POSN PREFACE(400)	ALL THE PLAYS OF EURIPIDES BECAUSE EURIPIDES,	LIKE	IBSEN, WAS A REVOLUTIONARY FREETHINKER. UNDER THE LORD
PHIL II (95)	AND SELF-ASSERTIVE) YOU MAY TALK AS MUCH AS YOU	LIKE	IF YOU WILL HAVE THE COMMON CONSIDERATION TO ASK FIRST
POSN PREFACE(409)	THE CHURCHES, CHAPELS, MISSION HALLS, AND THE	LIKE	IN ITS NEIGHBORHOOD. THE ASSUMPTION SHOULD BE THAT
FANY III (312)	EVERYTHING IS TURNED UPSIDE DOWN. /MRS KNOX/ IT'S	LIKE	IN THE BOOK OF REVELATIONS, BUT I DO SAY THAT WHEN
PRES (149)	A STATE VISIT TO THE COAL TRUST. I WAS FOURTH MAN	LIKE	IN THE FIRST FILE; AND WHEN I STARTED THE ORSE ELD
MIS. (112)	MY MOTHER THINKS A GIRL SHOULD KNOW WHAT A MAN IS	LIKE	IN THE HOUSE BEFORE SHE MARRIES HIM. THATS BEEN GOING
SUPR III (117)	AND MOTHER BY WHICH I KNEW WHAT SHE WOULD BE	LIKE	IN THIRTY YEARS' TIME. I NOTED THE GLEAM OF GOLD FROM A
BULL IV (181)	THE HALL. I DIDNT ENJOY IT, YOU KNOW. WHAT IS IT	LIKE	IN YOUR DREAMS? /KEEGAN/ IN MY DREAMS IT IS A COUNTRY
CYMB V (139)	BLIND OR DEAD, THE CRACKBRAINED WELSHMEN RAGED	LIKE	INCARNATE DEVILS. /PHILARIO/ YES: THEY THOUGHT WE WERE
DEST (185)	QUITE TRUE, LIEUTENANT, QUITE TRUE. YOU ARE ALL	LIKE	INNKEEPERS NOW IN FRANCE: YOU HAVE TO BE POLITE TO
FABL IV (116)	ALL THEIR ASPIRATIONS TO BE FREE TO DO WHAT THEY	LIKE	INSTEAD OF WHAT THEY MUST. THE WORLD BECAME A WORLD OF
MIS. (159)	NOTHING. BUT I'LL THROW AS MANY SOVEREIGNS AS YOU	LIKE	INTO THE SEA TO SHEW YOU THAT I'M IN EARNEST. /LINA/
SUPR IV (144)	THATS WHAT COMES O LIVIN IN PROVINCIAL PLACES	LIKE	IRELAND AND AMERICA. OVER HERE YOURE ECTOR: IF YOU AVNT
ARMS II SD(36)	AS IF SHE HAD STABBED HIM. THEN, SETTING HIS FACE	LIKE	IRON, HE STRIDES GRIMLY TO HER, AND GRIPS HER ABOVE THE
APPL PREFACE(189)	BUT THAT DOES NOT MEND MATTERS. WHAT I SHOULD	LIKE	IS A REAL TEST OF THEIR CAPACITY. SHORTLY BEFORE THE
GETT PREFACE(197)	THE EXCHANGING OF PRESENTS ON BIRTHDAYS AND THE	LIKE	IS BARRED BY GENERAL CONSENT, AND THE RELATIONS OF THE
CAPT III (296)	/BRASSBOUND/ THAT ANSWER IS NO GOOD TO ME. WHAT I	LIKE	IS TO HAVE SOMETHING TO DO; AND I HAVE NOTHING. YOU
ROCK II (271)	YOU HAVE ONLY YOUR HEAD IN IT. YOUR WIFE WOULDNT	LIKE	IT: HIS WOULD, IF HE HAS ONE. /HIPNEY/ NOT ME. I'M
PHIL II (110)	IT'S NOT THEIR BUSINESS TO TELL IT TO ME. I DONT	LIKE	IT: IT HURTS. /GRACE/ (QUIETLY) IT'S ONLY THAT I LOVE
CURE (227)	/THE DOCTOR/ YOURE GETTING ALMOST CLEVER. I DONT	LIKE	IT: YOURE NOT YOURSELF TODAY. I WISH I COULD TAKE YOUR
NEVR IV (287)	OF HONOR NOT TO BE IMPRESSED BY HIM) DO I LOOK	LIKE	IT? MY NAME IS VALENTINE. I DID THE DRUGGING. /BOHUN/
BULL II (113)	BEFORE? /BROADBENT/ NEVER. /NORA/ AN HOW DO YOU	LIKE	IT? /BROADBENT/ (SUDDENLY BETRAYING A CONDITION OF
JOAN 5 (111)	MAJESTY IS AN ANOINTED KING AT LAST. HOW DO YOU	LIKE	IT? /CHARLES/ I WOULD NOT GO THROUGH IT AGAIN TO BE
NEVR IV (294)	OF SUBMISSION). /DOLLY/ (INSISTENTLY) DO YOU	LIKE	IT? /CRAMPTON/ MY CHILD: HOW CAN YOU EXPECT ME TO LIKE
JOAN 1 (68)	WHAT GODDAM MEANS IN THEIR LANGUAGE. HOW DO YOU	LIKE	IT? /JOAN/ GOD WILL BE MERCIFUL TO THEM; AND THEY WILL
GENV II (59)	HIM A LITTLE BRITISH PATRIOTISM! HOW WOULD HE	LIKE	IT? /JUDGE/ MARTYRDOM HAS ITS ATTRACTIONS FOR SOME
FANY III (316)	LIKE TO BE SPOKEN TO FOR MY GOOD. WOULD ANYBODY	LIKE	IT? /MRS KNOX/ DONT TAKE OFFENCE WHERE NONE IS MEANT,
NEVR IV (294)	LET HIM OFF) HOW CAN YOU THINK IT PRETTY AND NOT	LIKE	IT? /M'COMAS/ (RISING, SCANDALIZED) REALLY I MUST
CURE (234)	OH, I SAY: THATS RATHER PRETTY. /STREGA/	LIKE	IT? /REGINALD/ AWFULLY. OH, I SAY, YOU KNOW: I REALLY
CAPT II (254)	MEETS YOU DISGUISED AS VENGEANCE. HOW DO YOU	LIKE	IT? /SIR HOWARD/ I SHALL MEET IT, I TRUST, AS BECOMES
GENV II (59)	IT WITH CONTEMPT. /JUDGE/ NO DOUBT; BUT WOULD YOU	LIKE	IT? /SIR O./ OH, COME! REALLY! REALLY! /JUDGE/
GENV II (59)	YOU HAD HIM LOCKED UP AS A LUNATIC! WOULD YOU	LIKE	IT? /SIR O./ SUPPOSE THE VILLAGERS BURNT DOWN HIS
2TRU II (73)	I AM FREE NOW TO SAY WHAT I PLEASE. HOW DO YOU	LIKE	IT? /THE COUNTESS/ (RELENTING) LOOK HERE, DEARIE. YOU
ROCK II (245)	BARON AND FINALLY AS VERMIN. VERMIN! HOW DO YOU	LIKE	IT? /THE DUKE/ (CALMLY TAKING THE END CHAIR NEAREST
MIS. (164)	REALLY, REALLY, REALLY, MR PERCIVAL! HOW DO YOU	LIKE	IT? WOULDNT YOU RATHER I DAMNED YOU? /PERCIVAL/ MISS
DEVL II (37)	(OBSERVING THAT HE TASTES NOTHING) DONT YOU	LIKE	IT? YOU ARE NOT EATING ANYTHING. /RICHARD/ NEITHER ARE
PYGM EPILOG (296)	CHANCES, AND HIS MOTHER COULD NOT BE EXPECTED TO	LIKE	IT AFTER CLINGING FOR SO MANY YEARS TO THAT STEP OF THE
2TRU II (73)	HEAR MY HIGHER CENTRES SHOUTING. YOU DONT SEEM TO	LIKE	IT ANY BETTER. /AUBREY/ MOPS: YOURE HYSTERICAL. YOU
BULL IV (169)	IF I WAS A PANE O GLASS. /BROADBENT/ OH, HE WONT	LIKE	IT ANY THE LESS FOR THAT. WHAT REALLY FLATTERS A MAN IS
DOCT I (92)	FOOLISHNESS. /RIDGEON/ HAVE YOU EVER MET ANYTHING	LIKE	IT BEFORE IN YOUR PRACTICE? /SIR PATRICK/ OH, YES:
MILL IV (204)	BUT I LOVE YOUR PULSE. I HAVE NEVER FELT ANYTHING	LIKE	IT BEFORE. /PATRICIA/ WELL, JUST FANCY THAT! HE LOVES
GENV II (56)	JOB IN COMPARISON. WEVE NEVER HAD ANYTHING	LIKE	IT BEFORE. THE SENIOR JUDGE ENTERS. HE IS A DUTCHMAN,
JITT I (16)	MERELY THINKING AND DREAMING ABOUT IT. /JITTA/ I	LIKE	IT BETTER AS IT IS. I DONT WANT TO SEE YOU EVERY DAY
SIM PRO,1, (25)	ALL THE PUDDING? BECAUSE LIFE NEVER CAME TO ME	LIKE	IT CAME TO RHODES, FOUND HIS BACKYARD FULL OF DIAMONDS,
DEST (160)	GIVE YOU A NOTION OF WHAT HE WAS LIKE. HE WONT BE	LIKE	IT FIVE MINUTES AFTER I CATCH HIM; FOR I TELL YOU THAT
LION PREFACE(99)	SELECTS ITS PEOPLE; AND IF A TRAPPIST DOES NOT	LIKE	IT HE CAN LEAVE IT. BUT A SUBJECT OF THE BRITISH EMPIRE
PHIL III (142)	OVER ME. I HAVE REFUSED HIM; AND IF HE DOESNT	LIKE	IT HE CAN-- HE CAN-- /CHARTERIS/ I CAN LUMP IT.
LION PREFACE(99)	REPUBLIC IS NOT SELECTED; AND IF HE DOES NOT	LIKE	IT HE MUST LUMP IT; FOR EMIGRATION IS PRACTICABLE ONLY
PYGM I (213)	GIRL/ FRIGHTENING PEOPLE LIKE THAT! HOW WOULD HE	LIKE	IT HIMSELF? /THE MOTHER/ IT'S QUITE FINE NOW, CLARA.
MIS. (165)	FEAR: THE WORST OF ALL SLAVERIES. HOW WOULD YOU	LIKE	IT IF EVERY LABORER YOU MET IN THE ROAD WERE TO MAKE
GENV I (47)	RUSSIANS ARE TO BE HELD ACCURSED. HOW WOULD YOU	LIKE	IT IF OUR CHIEF CULTURAL INSTITUTION, ENDOWED BY OUR
FANY PROLOG (264)	ARE A HUNDRED THOUSAND PEOPLE IN LONDON THATLL	LIKE	IT IF THEY CAN ONLY BE GOT TO KNOW ABOUT IT. BESIDES,
POSN (439)	THAT? NOW, LADIES, LADIES, LADIES. HOW WOULD YOU	LIKE	IT IF YOU WERE GOING TO BE HANGED? AT LAST THE WOMEN
CAND III (142)	SAID BY A FOOLISH BOY, BECAUSE I SAID SOMETHING	LIKE	IT IN JEST? /MORELL/ THAT FOOLISH BOY CAN SPEAK WITH
VWOO 1 (116)	I AM SO GLAD YOU KNOW MARGATE. THERES NO PLACE	LIKE	IT IN THE SEASON, IS THERE? /A/ I DONT KNOW: I HAVE
DEVL EPILOG (83)	UNWRITTEN, AND HIS PLAN FOR TURNING AS YOU	LIKE	IT INTO A BEGGAR'S OPERA UNCONCEIVED, I SHOULD STILL
SUPR IV (165)	YOU MUSTNT CRY ANY MORE: YOU KNOW VIOLET DOESNT	LIKE	IT (MRS WHITEFIELD DRIES HER EYES, AND SUBSIDES).
SUPR IV (162)	I SHALL PRESENTLY BE MARRIED TO ANN WHETHER I	LIKE	IT MYSELF OR NOT. /MRS WHITEFIELD/ (PEACEFULLY) OH,
GETT (315)	WHY SHOULD WE BE HELD TOGETHER WHETHER WE	LIKE	IT OR NOT? THATS THE QUESTION THATS AT THE BOTTOM OF
LION PREFACE(22)	FASTING AS THEY WANT SOON ENOUGH, WHETHER THEY	LIKE	IT OR NOT. HE IS NOT AFRAID OF DISEASE, AND DINES WITH
MIS. (159)	I HAVE TO CARRY HIM ABOUT WITH ME WHETHER I	LIKE	IT OR NOT. I HAVE TO PAY FOR HIS CLOTHES, THOUGH I HATE
DOCT PREFACE(40)	HYPOTHESIS, AND NOT WHETHER CONCEITED PEOPLE WILL	LIKE	IT OR NOT. IN VAIN DO THE SENTIMENTAL CHAMPIONS OF
MILL I (161)	MRS FITZFASSENDEN CAN DIVORCE YOU WHETHER YOU	LIKE	IT OR NOT. THE EVIDENCE IS THAT ON A RECENT OCCASION
MTH2 (48)	KNOWN IT. WE HAVE TO CONSULT YOU WHETHER WE	LIKE	IT OR NOT. WE-- /FRANKLYN/ (INTERRUPTING FIRMLY) I
SUPR IV (161)	TO TELL YOU. OF COURSE YOULL MARRY ANN WHETHER I	LIKE	IT OR NOT-- /TANNER/ (STARTING) IT SEEMS TO ME THAT I
MTH2 (45)	HAVE TO BE MADE RESPECTABLE WHETHER WE	LIKE	IT OR NOT; SO YOU NEEDNT WORRY YOURSELF ABOUT THAT.
NEVR II (232)	WELL, SIR, LET ME TELL YOU THAT WHETHER YOU	LIKE	IT OR NOT, HE IS YOUR FATHER, AND YOUR SISTERS' FATHER,
DOCT IV (164)	NOW THAT I'M GOING TO BE BROKEN LOOSE WHETHER I	LIKE	IT OR NOT, I'M PERFECTLY FOND OF YOU, AND PERFECTLY
LION PREFACE(89)	AS A FLAT FUNDAMENTAL MODERN FACT, WHETHER WE	LIKE	IT OR NOT, THAT WHILST MANY OF US CANNOT BELIEVE THAT
NEVR IV (294)	/CRAMPTON/ MY CHILD: HOW CAN YOU EXPECT ME TO	LIKE	IT OR TO APPROVE OF IT? /DOLLY/ (DETERMINED NOT TO
FABL VI (130)	BODY. CURIOSITY NEVER DIES. /MAIDEN 4/ HOW DO YOU	LIKE	IT SO FAR? /RAPHAEL/ I DO NOT LIKE NOR DISLIKE. I
JOAN PREFACE(55)	CLASSICAL COMEDY OR TRAGEDY FOR ITS OWN SAKE, AND	LIKE	IT SO MUCH WHEN IT IS GOOD OF ITS KIND AND WELL DONE
GETT (313)	MARRIAGE FOR A TERM OF YEARS. IF THE PEOPLE DONT	LIKE	IT THEY CAN GET DIVORCED. /REGINALD/ IT OUGHT TO BE FOR
ROCK II (238)	I'LL ANSWER FOR THE FREE ENGLISHMEN. IF THEY DONT	LIKE	IT THEY CAN LUMP IT. /SIR DEXTER/ YOU REALLY BELIEVE HE
6CAL PREFACE(90)	UNABATED VIGOR. ROSALIND CAN ALWAYS PULL AS YOU	LIKE	IT THROUGH IN SPITE OF THE SENTENTIOUS FUTILITY OF THE
ROCK I (218)	FOR TALK NOWADAYS: THAT GAME IS UP. NOT	LIKE	IT WAS IN OLD GLADSTONE'S TIME, EH? /SIR ARTHUR/
LADY PREFACE(219)	WHICH ORLANDO DESCRIBES SO PERFECTLY IN AS YOU	LIKE	IT WAS THE BEGINNING AND END OF SHAKESPEAR'S NOTION OF
NEVR II (244)	THE YOUNG WAITER OFFERS HER THE SALAD BOWL) YOU	LIKE	IT WITHOUT DRESSING, MAAM: YES, MAAM, I HAVE SOME FOR
2TRU II (67)	I SAY WHAT I MEAN STRAIGHT OUT; AND IF YOU DONT	LIKE	IT YOU CAN LUMP IT. YOU MAY BE IN LOVE WITH POPSY; BUT
SUPR III (116)	YOU; BUT IT'S TRUE, FOR ALL THAT; SO IF YOU DONT	LIKE	IT YOU CAN LUMP IT. /DON JUAN/ MY DEAR LADY, YOU HAVE
JITT II (32)	I LIKE GOSSIP. EVERYBODY LIKES GOSSIP. YOU	LIKE	IT YOURSELF AS WELL AS ANYBODY. IF SHE WAS A PATIENT
GENV II (59)	/JUDGE/ BELIEVE ME, SIR MIDLANDER, YOU WOULD NOT	LIKE	IT. AND IF THE INTERNATIONAL COURT, MOVED BY THE
FANY III (298)	SAME TIME BY PRETENDING TO SPARE THEM. SHE WONT	LIKE	IT. AND IT WILL START AN ARGUMENT, OF WHICH YOU WILL
CAND I (98)	YOU DO. EVERYBODY LOVES HER: THEY CANT HELP IT. I	LIKE	IT. BUT (LOOKING UP JOCOSELY AT HIM) I SAY, EUGENE: DO
PPP (204)	POLICEMAN/ (RAISING MAGNESIA TENDERLY) IT LOOKS	LIKE	IT. HOLD UP, MY LADY. /THE DOCTOR/ NOT A MOMENT MUST BE
MTH1 II (22)	TO SHIELD. IT IS TERRIBLE; BUT THERE IS NO JOY	LIKE	IT. I CALL IT FIGHTING. HE WHO HAS NEVER FOUGHT HAS
2TRU PREFACE(8)	MY SOLE REASON FOR NOT LIVING IT IS THAT I DONT	LIKE	IT. I HAVE EVERY OPPORTUNITY OF OBSERVING IT BOTH IN
MTH3 (124)	AND AFRICANS AS SHAREHOLDERS? /BARNABAS/ NOTHING	LIKE	IT. I KNOW ALL ABOUT THE OLD JOINT STOCK COMPANIES. THE
MIS. (144)	DIRTY JOB; BUT JOHNNY AND I WERE VULGAR ENOUGH TO	LIKE	IT. I LIKE YOUNG PEOPLE BECAUSE THEYRE NOT TOO AFRAID
MILL II (168)	WORRY. I NEED IT, OF COURSE; BUT I DONT	LIKE	IT. I NEVER THINK OF IT WHEN I CAN POSSIBLY HELP IT.
HART III (136)	PHYSICALLY NAKED AS WELL, AND SEE HOW WE	LIKE	IT. I TELL YOU I CANT BEAR THIS. I WAS BROUGHT UP TO BE
SUPR III (100)	IS NO ACCOUNTING FOR TASTES: THERE ARE PEOPLE WHO	LIKE	IT. I THINK DON JUAN WOULD LIKE IT. /DON JUAN/ BUT--
CURE (236)	MIND BEING TYRANNIZED OVER A LITTLE: IN FACT, I	LIKE	IT. IT SAVES ME THE TROUBLE OF HAVING TO THINK WHAT TO
MTH1 I (7)	IT IS NOT WHY. WHY NOT? /EVE/ BUT I SHOULD NOT	LIKE	IT. IT WOULD BE NICE TO BE NEW AGAIN; BUT MY OLD SKIN
FANY III (305)	/MARGARET/ OH, IVE LEARNT THE LANGUAGE; AND I	LIKE	IT. IT'S ANOTHER BARRIER BROKEN DOWN. /BOBBY/ IT'S NOT
WIDO II (31)	PAYS WHEN YOU KNOW HOW TO WORK IT, SIR. NOTHING	LIKE	IT. IT'S BEEN CALCULATED ON THE CUBIC FOOT OF SPACE,
DOCT IV (164)	TO THE OTHER FELLOW TOO MUCH ABOUT ME: HE WONT	LIKE	IT. (ALMOST CHUCKLING) I SHALL BE YOUR LOVER ALL THE
SUPR I (21)	GIVING PEOPLE NICKNAMES. THEY CANT BE EXPECTED TO	LIKE	IT. (SHE MOVES TOWARDS THE DOOR). /ANN/ HOW CAN YOU
MIS. (186)	NOW DONT BE RUDE, JOHNNY: YOU KNOW I DONT	LIKE	IT. (TO GUNNER) A CUP OF TEA WILL PICK YOU UP.
DEST SD(180)	OUT THE MEANING OF HIS PROCEEDINGS, AND WILL NOT	LIKE	IT. NOTHING MORE IS SAID UNTIL THE LIEUTENANT ARRIVES

BULL IV (167)	AH, YOU MUSTNT GO ON LIKE THAT. I DONT	LIKE	IT. /BROADBENT/ (UNABASHED) YOULL ACQUIRE THE TASTE BY
NEVR III (264)	/DOLLY/-- BUT HE WASNT. /PHILIP/ SHE APPEARED TO	LIKE	IT. /DOLLY/ AS FAR AS WE COULD JUDGE. (STOPPING PHIL,
SUPR III (100)	ARE PEOPLE WHO LIKE IT. I THINK DON JUAN WOULD	LIKE	IT. /DON JUAN/ BUT-- PARDON MY FRANKNESS-- COULD YOU
MILL II (168)	CAR. /ADRIAN/ I AM NOT. I WISH I COULD AFFORD ONE	LIKE	IT. /EPIFANIA/ I THOUGHT YOU WOULD ENJOY SITTING IN
MTH1 I (14)	! ! ! /ADAM/ THAT IS A FUNNY NOISE TO MAKE. I	LIKE	IT. /EVE/ I DO NOT. WHY DO YOU MAKE IT AGAIN? /THE
MRS II (201)	YOU? /MRS WARREN/ WELL, HARM OR NOT, I DONT	LIKE	IT. /FRANK/ BETTER NOT WAIT FOR THEM, MRS WARREN. PRAED
BUOY IV (57)	I SHALL. THE CURIOUS THING IS, I AM BEGINNING TO	LIKE	IT. /OLD BILL/ GOOD. (LOOKING AT HIS WATCH) I WONDER
CAPT I (226)	BUT, MY DEAR HOWARD, I ASSURE YOU THE NATIVES	LIKE	IT. /RANKIN/ (GALLANTLY) SO DO I. /LADY CICELY/ (
ROCK I (213)	OF YOUR WEST END LANGUAGE HERE. YOU KNOW HE DONT	LIKE	IT. /SIR ARTHUR/ THATS RIGHT, MISS BROLLIKINS: SNUB
GENV II (59)	WHETHER HE WOULD LIKE IT, BUT WHETHER YOU WOULD	LIKE	IT. /SIR O./ I SHOULD TREAT IT WITH CONTEMPT. /JUDGE/
2TRU II (59)	COLONEL, ISNT IT? BUT SO SIMPLE AND DIRECT, I	LIKE	IT. /TALLBOYS/ I DIDNT KNOW IT WAS VULGAR. IT IS
MTH4 I (150)	DAMMITMADDAM. SAY IT AS OFTEN AS YOU PLEASE: I	LIKE	IT. /THE ELDERLY GENTLEMAN/ (EXPANDING WITH INTENSE
MRS IV (237)	MY FEELING FOR YOU IS NOT THE LEAST IN THE WORLD	LIKE	IT. THE GIRLS WILL GO THEIR WAY; I WILL GO MINE; AND WE
BULL II (113)	I CAN HARDLY TRUST MYSELF TO SAY HOW MUCH I	LIKE	IT. THE MAGIC OF THIS IRISH SCENE, AND-- I REALLY DONT
GENV II (59)	DELIVER AN ADVERSE JUDGMENT ON YOU, YOU WOULD NOT	LIKE	IT. THE MAN WHOM THE HAGUE CONDEMNS WILL BE AN
HART I (66)	I'LL TELL IT TO YOU AFTER DINNER. I THINK YOULL	LIKE	IT. THE TRUTH IS, I MADE IT UP FOR YOU, AND WAS LOOKING
FANY III (316)	KNOX/ NO: YOU SHALL HAVE YOUR BEER BECAUSE YOU	LIKE	IT. THE WHISKY WAS ONLY BRAG. AND IF YOU AND ME ARE TO
FANY III (304)	CLERGYMAN'S DAUGHTER. /BOBBY/ I DONT THINK SHE'D	LIKE	IT. THERE ARE LIMITS, AFTER ALL. (HE SITS DOWN AT THE
DEST (185)	A GENERAL. /LIEUTENANT/ OH, YOU THINK HE WOULDNT	LIKE	IT. WELL, PERHAPS YOURE RIGHT: ONE HAS TO BE AWFULLY
SUPR III (101)	MUSIC, BUT BECAUSE THEY THINK THEY OUGHT TO	LIKE	IT. WELL, THERE IS THE SAME THING IN HEAVEN. A NUMBER
GETT (354)	WERE FRIED. AND I EAT FRIED FISH EVERY FRIDAY AND	LIKE	IT. YOU ARE AS INGRAINED A SNOB AS EVER. /HOTCHKISS/ (
SUPR I (6)	" FATHER WISHES ME TO," OR " MOTHER WOULDNT	LIKE	IT." IT'S REALLY ALMOST A FAULT IN HER. I HAVE OFTEN
DEVL III (73)	THAT I LIKE BEING HANGED, YOURE MISTAKEN. I DONT	LIKE	IT; AND I DONT MEAN TO PRETEND THAT I DO. AND IF YOU
PYGM II (238)	AND I MEAN TO GO ON BEING UNDESERVING. I	LIKE	IT; AND THATS THE TRUTH. WILL YOU TAKE ADVANTAGE OF A
BARB II (297)	(HE MAKES A WRY FACE). YES: I KNOW YOU DONT	LIKE	IT; BUT IT MUST BE DONE. THE STARVATION THIS WINTER IS
DOCT PREFACE(27)	VACCINATION, WHICH WILL PROBABLY BE ENDED,	LIKE	ITS EQUALLY VAUNTED FORERUNNER, EIGHTEENTH CENTURY
SUPR PREFACE(R9)	QUI FACIT PER ALIUM FACIT PER SE. ITS PROFITS,	LIKE	ITS LABOR, BELONG TO ME: ITS MORALS, ITS MANNERS, ITS
POSN PREFACE(426)	THAN IT IS FOR A DENTIST. THE NATION'S MORALS ARE	LIKE	ITS TEETH: THE MORE DECAYED THEY ARE THE MORE IT HURTS
LADY PREFACE(224)	HAS BEEN THE FIRST TO APPRECIATE AT ANYTHING	LIKE	ITS VALUE), THERE IS A DASH OF MOCKERY. " SPIT IN THE
DEST (176)	WAY. SHE GOVERNS MEN BY CHEATING THEM; AND THEY	LIKE	IT, AND LET HER GOVERN THEM. (SHE TURNS HER BACK TO
LADY PREFACE(230)	RADICAL JACK CADE. WE GET THE SHEPHERD IN AS YOU	LIKE	IT, AND MANY HONEST, BRAVE, HUMAN, AND LOYAL SERVANTS,
LADY PREFACE(233)	HE DID IT MUTINOUSLY, CALLING THE PLAYS AS YOU	LIKE	IT, AND MUCH ADO ABOUT NOTHING. ALL THE SAME, HE DID IT
LADY (248)	ONE AS YOU LIKE IT, MEANING THAT IT IS NOT AS I	LIKE	IT, AND THE OTHER MUCH ADO ABOUT NOTHING, AS IT TRULY
GENV II (59)	NATURES. BUT MY QUESTION WAS NOT WHETHER HE WOULD	LIKE	IT, BUT WHETHER YOU WOULD LIKE IT. /SIR O./ I SHOULD
CAND I (102)	(QUIETLY, AS HE STANDS OVER HIM) IT LOOKS	LIKE	IT, DOESNT IT? /MARCHBANKS/ (WITH PETULANT VEHEMENCE)
POSN (436)	LYNCHING AND SHOOTING. I DONT BELIEVE ANY OF US	LIKE	IT, IF THE TRUTH WERE KNOWN. /BABSY/ OUR SHERIFF IS A
POSN PREFACE(366)	OR NOT. HE MAY NOT UNDERSTAND IT, MAY NOT	LIKE	IT, MAY NOT KNOW WHAT THE AUTHOR IS DRIVING AT, MAY
LADY (248)	THEM THAT PRAISE THEM BY CALLING THE ONE AS YOU	LIKE	IT, MEANING THAT IT IS NOT AS I LIKE IT, AND THE OTHER
DOCT I (99)	AND THERE IS THE PSEUDO-BACILLUS, EXACTLY	LIKE	IT, WHICH YOU COULD FIND, AS YOU SAY, IN MY OWN THROAT.
BULL I (96)	ABOUT HER LIKE THIS--! /BROADBENT/ SHE WOULDNT	LIKE	IT, WOULD SHE? OF COURSE NOT. WE OUGHT TO BE ASHAMED
BULL IV (152)	FOR MAKING A SPEECH, MISS DOYLE; BUT THEY	LIKE	IT, YOU KNOW. EVERYTHING HELPS IN ELECTIONEERING. LARRY
DEVL I (27)	OH YES, YOU MAY CRY THAT WAY, ESSIE, IF YOU	LIKE	.
CAND I SD(78)	DRAWERS, AN OFFICE DIARY, POSTAGE SCALES AND THE	LIKE	. A SPARE CHAIR FOR VISITORS HAVING BUSINESS WITH THE
ROCK II (278)	BLOOD IS BLUE. /ALOYSIA/ WELL, CALL IT WHAT YOU	LIKE	. ALL I SAY IS THAT I BELONG TO THE COMMON WORKING
HART I (75)	PERFECTLY CORRECT THING. YOU CAN DO JUST WHAT YOU	LIKE	. AN ILL-CONDUCTED, CARELESS WOMAN GETS SIMPLY NO
VWOO 3 (138)	/A/ DONT LOSE YOUR TEMPER AGAIN. /Z/ I WILL IF I	LIKE	. AND IF YOU KNEW HOW NEAR I WAS TO PUTTING A COUPLE OF
BULL IV (175)	I SAY LET HIM DIE, AND LET US HAVE NO MORE OF HIS	LIKE	. AND LET YOUNG IRELAND TAKE CARE THAT IT DOESNT SHARE
O'FL (221)	HER HAIR DOWN OVER HER FOREHEAD, IN A FRINGE	LIKE	. AND SHE HAS AN IRISH LOOK ABOUT HER EYEBROWS. AND SHE
ROCK I (206)	FOOTBALL, PRIZEFIGHTING, WAR: THAT IS WHAT THEY	LIKE	. AND THEY LIKE WAR BECAUSE IT ISNT REAL TO THEM: IT'S
FANY III (303)	PEOPLE: THEY DID IT OUT OF PURE DEVILMENT IF YOU	LIKE	. ANYHOW, HERE WE ARE, TWO GAOL-BIRDS, BOBBY, DISGRACED
GETT (329)	DRAG ME WHERE YOU PLEASE AND MAKE ME DO WHAT YOU	LIKE	. BUT AT LEAST LET ME KNOW YOUR SOUL AS YOU SEEM TO
FABL VI (129)	DO NOT FLY: I LEVITATE. CALL ME COCKYOLLY IF YOU	LIKE	. BUT IT WOULD BE MORE RESPECTFUL TO CALL ME RAPHAEL.
MTH5 (258)	NOT DO THAT. /THE NEWLY BORN/ I WILL DO WHAT I	LIKE	. BUT THERE IS SOMETHING THE MATTER WITH ME. I WANT TO
JOAN EPILOG (159)	I NEVER THOUGHT ABOUT IT: IT CAME NATURAL	LIKE	. BUT THEY SCORED IT UP FOR ME. /CHARLES/ WHAT WAS IT?
JOAN 6 (132)	TO NAKEDNESS AND INCEST AND POLYGAMY AND THE	LIKE	. BUT WE ARE CONFRONTED TODAY THROUGHOUT EUROPE WITH A
NEVR I (217)	OLD GAME OF GUESSING WHAT OUR FATHER WAS TO BE	LIKE	. DOLLY: ARE YOU SORRY FOR YOUR FATHER? THE FATHER
KING I (198)	RASCALS RIGHT! A GOOD LESSON FOR THEM AND THEIR	LIKE	. DONT BE SUCH A MOLLYCODDLE, CHARLES. WHAT YOU NEED IS
CLEO IV (176)	WANT ANYTHING. I DARESAY YOU WILL DO WHAT YOU	LIKE	. DONT PUT IT ON TO ME. /CAESAR/ (WITH AN AIR OF DOING
WIDO III (59)	AND DRAFT PROSPECTUSES AND ADVERTISEMENTS AND THE	LIKE	. DONT YOU, COKANE? OF COURSE YOU DO: WHY SHOULDNT
DOCT PREFACE(21)	OF CURING DISEASE, PREVENTING CHILDBIRTH, AND THE	LIKE	. EACH OF THEM BELIEVES THAT HE IS ON THE VERGE OF A
MRS II (200)	YOU SEE, AS RECTOR HERE, I AM NOT FREE TO DO AS I	LIKE	. ER-- WHAT IS MR PRAED'S SOCIAL POSITION? /MRS
PYGM IV (266)	YOU MAY TAKE THE WHOLE DAMNED HOUSEFUL IF YOU	LIKE	. EXCEPT THE JEWELS. THEYRE HIRED. WILL THAT SATISFY
MTH2 (74)	THE DOOR). /CONRAD/ (RUDELY) DIE AS SOON AS YOU	LIKE	. GOOD EVENING. /BURGE/ (HESITATING) LOOK HERE. I TOOK
VWOO 1 (121)	MONTHS. DONT MISS IT," HE SAID: " SEE WHAT IT'S	LIKE	. HAVE YOUR FLING" HE SAID; " FOR THEY NEVER CAN TAKE
CATH 4 (191)	HIM) -- AGH! OW! OH LORD! HE IS ANYTHING YOU	LIKE	. HE IS A PHILANTHROPIST, A PHILOSOPHER, A BEAUTY: HE
MIS. (129)	AND ALL THE OTHER PUPS -- THEY WERE PUPS, IF YOU	LIKE	. HE TOLD ME IT WAS VERY SIMPLE: THEY HAD ONLY ONE
DEST (160)	THAT WILL GIVE YOU A NOTION OF WHAT HE WAS	LIKE	. HE WONT BE LIKE IT FIVE MINUTES AFTER I CATCH HIM;
SUPR III (96)	BY PRAYING, NOTHING TO BE LOST BY DOING WHAT YOU	LIKE	. HELL, IN SHORT, IS A PLACE WHERE YOU HAVE NOTHING TO
GENV IV (123)	CANNOT PERMIT THAT EXPRESSION. OUTFLANKED IF YOU	LIKE	. HEMMED IN IF YOU WILL HAVE IT SO. I WILL EVEN GO SO
MIS. (145)	MAN OF BUSINESS AND FOUND OUT WHAT HE WAS REALLY	LIKE	. HOW DID YOU MANAGE WITH YOUR SONS? /LORD SUMMERHAYS/
MILL II (172)	THE PLUTOCRACY, IN FACT. /EPIFANIA/ IF YOU	LIKE	. I AM A PLUTOCRAT OF THE PLUTOCRATS. /THE DOCTOR/
SIM PREFACE(6)	OF CREDULITY FROM HELL TO PERISHING SUNS AND THE	LIKE	. I AM NOT THINKING OF THE HUMANITARIAN REVOLT AGAINST
ROCK PREFACE(176)	NOT KNOW WHAT THE PHYSICAL UNIVERSE WAS REALLY	LIKE	. I AM QUITE FAMILIAR WITH THE PRE-GALILEO UNIVERSE OF
BUOY IV (52)	WE SHALL LIVE WHERE I LIKE. /JUNIUS/ OR WHERE I	LIKE	. I CAN ASSERT MYSELF. /SHE/ SO CAN I. WE SHALL SEE
PHIL II (125)	HAS LEARNT HOW TO TREAT WOMEN FROM YOU AND YOUR	LIKE	. I CAN DO WITHOUT HIS LOVE, BUT NOT WITHOUT HIS
SHAK PREFACE(136)	DIFFERENTIATED BY PUNCH-AND-JUDY SQUEAKS AND THE	LIKE	. I CAN IMAGINE THE PUPPETS SIMULATING LIVING
JOAN 2 (74)	LEFT SHOULDER) I WILL READ IT FOR YOU IF YOU	LIKE	. I CAN READ, YOU KNOW. /LA TREMOUILLE/ (WITH INTENSE
MRS III (230)	IT OUGHT TO BE. I'LL TELL YOU ALL ABOUT IT IF YOU	LIKE	. I DONT KNOW WHETHER YOUVE FOUND IN TRAVELLING HOW
CAPT III (294)	MANY OF THAT SORT. ANYHOW, THAT WAS WHAT I WAS	LIKE	. I DONT SAY I WAS HAPPY IN IT: BUT I WASNT UNHAPPY,
JOAN EPILOG (161)	ONCE BECAUSE I DID NOT KNOW WHAT CRUELTY WAS	LIKE	. I HAD NOT SEEN IT, YOU KNOW. THAT IS THE GREAT THING:
MRS II (211)	/VIVIE/ (DETERMINEDLY) OH YES YOU CAN, IF YOU	LIKE	. I HAVE A RIGHT TO KNOW; AND YOU KNOW VERY WELL THAT I
ROCK II (256)	HEARTHRUG, BEHIND SIR ARTHUR) YOU CAN GO IF YOU	LIKE	. I HAVE SOME BUSINESS WITH SIR ARTHUR THAT DOESNT
CLEO I (108)	IT. WHEN I AM OLD ENOUGH I SHALL DO JUST WHAT I	LIKE	. I SHALL BE ABLE TO POISON THE SLAVES AND SEE THEM
PYGM II (229)	GREAT BULLY, YOU ARE. I WONT STAY HERE IF I DONT	LIKE	. I WONT LET NOBODY WALLOP ME. I NEVER ASKED TO GO TO
2TRU I (45)	WELL FOR YOU TWO CRIMINALS: YOU CAN DO WHAT YOU	LIKE	. IF YOU WERE LADIES AND GENTLEMEN, YOUD KNOW HOW HARD
DOCT PREFACE(41)	GARDEN, TO KEEP BEES, TO GO INTO SOCIETY, AND THE	LIKE	. IN THE SAME WAY MANY PEOPLE DO CRUEL AND VILE THINGS
O'FL (226)	TEAR ONE ANOTHER'S EYES OUT IN THE KITCHEN IF YOU	LIKE	. IN WITH YOU. THE TWO MEN SEIZE THE TWO WOMEN, AND
MRS III (222)	FRANK WILL TAKE YOU FOR A WALK, MR PRAED, IF YOU	LIKE	. I'LL ASK YOU TO EXCUSE ME: I MUST TAKE THE
CAPT II (264)	HERE, I AM GOING TO DO WHAT I LIKE, NOT WHAT YOU	LIKE	. I'LL GIVE THIS GENTLEMAN HERE TO SIDI OR TO THE DEVIL
BARB II (275)	PRICE, THE CONVERTED PAINTER. I KNOW WOT THEY	LIKE	. I'LL TELL EM HOW I BLASPHEMED AND GAMBLED AND WOPPED
ROCK II (252)	YOURE A LIBERAL. /THE MAYOR/ CALL ME WHAT YOU	LIKE	. I'M NOT ARGUING. I'M TELLING YOU THAT THE LABOR PARTY
PYGM II (232)	HER OLD THINGS. /HIGGINS/ CERTAINLY. ANYTHING YOU	LIKE	. IS THAT ALL? /MRS PEARCE/ THANK YOU, SIR. THATS ALL.
PHIL II (111)	UTTERLY IN HIS POWER. THATS WHAT THE NEW WOMAN IS	LIKE	. ISNT SHE RIGHT, MR PHILOSOPHER? /CHARTERIS/ THE
PYGM PREFACE(199)	THAT NO MAN CAN TEACH HIMSELF WHAT IT SOUNDS	LIKE	. IT IS IMPOSSIBLE FOR AN ENGLISHMAN TO OPEN HIS MOUTH
KING II (230)	WHO KNOW WHAT THEY ARE. THAT IS WHAT THE PEOPLE	LIKE	. IT IS WHAT THEY WOULD DO IF THEY WERE KINGS.
MILL I (145)	NEED NOT GO INTO DETAILS. /EPIFANIA/ I WILL IF I	LIKE	. IT IS YOUR BUSINESS AS A SOLICITOR TO KNOW THE
HART II (127)	VERY FAINTLY REBELLIOUS) I'LL GO TO BED WHEN I	LIKE	. IT ISNT TEN YET. /LADY UTTERWORD/ IT IS LONG PAST
2TRU PREFACE(9)	IDLE RICH MAN, AND KNOW ONLY TOO WELL WHAT IT IS	LIKE	. IT MAKES ME FEEL SUICIDAL. YOU MAY SAY THAT I AM AN
SUPR PREFACE(R35)	BUFFOON, BEAUTY MONGER, SENTIMENTALIZER AND THE	LIKE	. IT MAY SEEM A LONG STEP FROM BUNYAN TO NIETZSCHE; BUT
LION I (119)	A TURKEY-COCK. YOU CAN HAVE HIM FOR A PET IF YOU	LIKE	. (ANDROCLES, QUITE CONSOLED, GOES PAST THE CENTURION
PHIL II (110)	TRUTH. YOU MAY TELL ME THAT AS OFTEN AS YOU	LIKE	. (HE TAKES HER IN HIS ARMS). /GRACE/ YES, LEONARD;
MTH1 I (15)	ADAM. NOT BEFORE. BUT THEN, AS SOON AS YOU	LIKE	. (SHE RISES, AND PASSING BEHIND HIM, STROLLS OFF
MTH4 III (194)	IF YOU WANT TO, YOU CAN STAND ON YOUR HEAD IF YOU	LIKE	. (SHE SITS DOWN CARELESSLY ON THE GALLERY RAILING,
MRS I (189)	HAS BEEN LOOKING HIM UP AND DOWN SHARPLY) IF YOU	LIKE	. (SHE TAKES HIS TENDERLY PROFFERED HAND AND GIVES IT
BULL III (118)	YOUVE BEEN ENJOYING YOURSELF, YOURE A BIT HEARTY	LIKE	. LAST NIGHT YOU SEEMED RATHER LOW, IF ANYTHING.
INCA PROLOG (234)	COMFORT! ! /ERMYNTRUDE/ WELL, ELEGANCE IF YOU	LIKE	. LUXURY, IF YOU INSIST. CALL IT WHAT YOU PLEASE. A
PYGM V (287)	WELL: BE OFF WITH YOU TO THE SORT OF PEOPLE YOU	LIKE	. MARRY SOME SENTIMENTAL HOG OR OTHER WITH LOTS OF

KING I	(171)	PLAYER AND WRITER OF COMEDIES, TRAGEDIES, AND THE	LIKE	. MR SHAKESPEAR WOULD HAVE DIED OF SHAME TO SEE A WOMAN
MIS. PREFACE	(73)	THE SCHOOL PRISONERS NEED NOT LEARN UNLESS THEY	LIKE	. NAY, IT IS SOMETIMES REMARKED THAT THE SCHOOL DUNCE
SIM II	(70)	LET ME KEEP YOU! ALL STANDING. SIT DOWN IF YOU	LIKE	. NEVER MIND ME: SITTING AND STANDING ARE ALL ALIKE TO
SUPR HANDBOK	(179)	OR OTHER, SUCH AS A NATION, AN EMPIRE, OR THE	LIKE	. NOW AS HAPPINESS NEVER MATTERS TO NATURE, AS SHE
DOCT I	(83)	OF BLOOD AND TUBES FULL OF MALTESE FEVER AND THE	LIKE	. NOW HE'LL HAVE A RARE LAUGH AT ME. /REDPENNY/ SERVE
BULL IV	(166)	ANIMATED BEEFSTEAK ABOUT HER. THE IDEAL IS WHAT I	LIKE	. NOW LARRY'S TASTE IS JUST THE OPPOSITE: HE LIKES EM
INCA	(253)	PRESIDENT! HE IS THE ALLERHOCHST, IF YOU	LIKE	. NO, MADAM, BELIEVE ME, THERE IS NOTHING LIKE
KING I	(219)	YOU IMPUDENT SLUT. /NELL/ WELL, NO WORSE, IF YOU	LIKE	. ONE LITTLE DUKE IS ENOUGH FOR ME. /LOUISE/ CHANGE THE
MIS.	(157)	NOT AT ALL. YOU CAN HAVE THE PIANO IF YOU	LIKE	. OR THE GRAMOPHONE. HAVE THE GRAMOPHONE? /LINA/ NO.
PYGM V	(285)	YOU AS MY DAUGHTER AND SETTLE MONEY ON YOU IF YOU	LIKE	. OR WOULD YOU RATHER MARRY PICKERING? /LIZA/ (
MTH5	(229)	DETAIN YOU TWO MINUTES. /ALL/ HALF AN HOUR IF YOU	LIKE	. PLEASE GO ON, PYGMALION. (THEY RUSH HIM BACK TO THE
VWOO 1	(117)	ME? I WILL TELL YOU THE WHOLE OF MY LIFE IF YOU	LIKE	. /A/ GREAT HEAVENS, NO. PLEASE DONT. /Z/ OH, I DONT
ROCK II	(271)	I'M FREE AT LAST TO PUT MY NECK IN A NOOSE IF I	LIKE	. /BASHAM/ I WONDER SHOULD I FIND ANY BOMBS IN YOUR
WIDO III	(58)	ON BUSINESS. YOU NEED NOT MEET HIM UNLESS YOU	LIKE	. /BLANCHE/ (OVERWHELMED) WHEN IS HE COMING?
WIDO I	(12)	CHURCH WE MEET: THE APOLLINARIS CHURCH, IF YOU	LIKE	. /BLANCHE/ NO, BUT SERIOUSLY. THIS IS SERIOUS, HARRY:
FANY III	(300)	GET OFF DUTY FOR THE DAY, JUST TO SEE WHAT IT'S	LIKE	. /BOBBY/ OFF DUTY? WHAT DO YOU MEAN? /MARGARET/ YOU
BULL I	(86)	A CENTURY BEHIND THE TIMES. THATS ENGLISH, IF YOU	LIKE	. /BROADBENT/ NO, LARRY, NO. YOU ARE THINKING OF THE
BULL II	(108)	MIGHT GIVE HIM A THRUPPENY BIT FOR HIMSELF OR THE	LIKE	. /BROADBENT/ PERHAPS THERES A PUBLIC HOUSE. /FATHER
PHIL II	(99)	IVE A GREAT MIND TO JOIN, JUST TO SEE WHAT IT'S	LIKE	. /CHARTERIS/ (COMING BETWEEN THEM) DO SO BY ALL
SUPR III	(112)	YOU. LET US GO ON FOR ANOTHER HOUR IF YOU	LIKE	. /DON JUAN/ GOOD: LET US. /THE STATUE/ NOT THAT I SEE
FANY I	(282)	SO LONG AS HE'S OUT OF THE REACH OF YOU AND YOUR	LIKE	. /DORA/ THEN I'M AFRAID YOULL HAVE TO SEND HIM OUT OF
HART I	(56)	HUSHABYE/ NOW MY FATHER IS A WONDERFUL MAN IF YOU	LIKE	. /ELLIE/ HESIONE: LISTEN TO ME. YOU DONT UNDERSTAND.
MILL I	(148)	(CONTINUING)-- BUT THATS WHAT THE WORLD IS	LIKE	. /EPIFANIA/ THE WORLD IS LIKE THAT TO PEOPLE WHO ARE
BULL III	(128)	COMES, INSTEAD O WANTIN SUBSCRIPTIONS AND THE	LIKE	. /FATHER DEMPSEY/ YES: THATS A GOOD POINT, BARNEY.
MRS III	(222)	YOUR FATHER. YOU KNOW YOU CAN BE SO NICE WHEN YOU	LIKE	. /FRANK/ MY DEAR PRADDY: YOU FORGET THAT I HAVE TO
PHIL I	(70)	OUT OF MERE CURIOSITY, JUST TO SEE WHAT IT'S	LIKE	. /GRACE/ WELL, SINCE YOU ASK ME, I NEVER HAS IN LOVE
MTH2	(87)	I LOVE HIM. BURGE IS A FLAMING FRAUD IF YOU	LIKE	. /HASLAM/ DID YOU NOTICE ONE THING? IT STRUCK ME AS
FABL V	(119)	OF SAINTS, NUNS, PRIESTS, ANGELS, GODS AND THE	LIKE	. /HERM./ NOT ALWAYS. THERE WERE PEOPLE CALLED GREEKS
PYGM V	(286)	THE DIFFERENCE BETWEEN US, BUT MORE FRIENDLY	LIKE	. /HIGGINS/ WELL, OF COURSE. THATS JUST HOW I FEEL. AND
BULL I	(75)	/BROADBENT/ WELL, BRING WHATEVER YOU THINK HE'D	LIKE	. /HODSON/ YES SIR (AN ELECTRIC BELL RINGS). HERE HE
GETT	(348)	BE ADOPTED BY SINJON. YOU CAN ADOPT HIM IF YOU	LIKE	. /HOTCHKISS/ (RISING) I SUGGEST THAT THAT WOULD
MIS.	(164)	HELPLESS. YOURE A WOMAN: YOU CAN SAY WHAT YOU	LIKE	. /HYPATIA/ AND YOU CAN ONLY SAY WHAT YOU DARE. POOR
FANY III	(310)	CAN GO WHEN YOUR MONTH IS UP, OR SOONER, IF YOU	LIKE	. /JUGGINS/ BELIEVE ME, SIR-- /GILBEY/ THATS ENOUGH: I
BUOY IV	(52)	WE ARE BOTH TAKING CHANCES. WE SHALL LIVE WHERE I	LIKE	. /JUNIUS/ OR WHERE I LIKE. I CAN ASSERT MYSELF. /SHE/
BULL IV	(156)	BE SURE: YOU KNOW YOU CAN COME IN N NOUT AS YOU	LIKE	. /KEEGAN/ WE CAN FINISH THE GAME SOME OTHER TIME, MISS
JITT II	(43)	HAVE YOU TO DO WITH IT? /JITTA/ WELL, YOU IF YOU	LIKE	. /LENKHEIM/ IT'S NOT ME YOURE THINKING OF. FUNNY, THE
PYGM IV	(264)	ALL OVER? NOW YOU ARE FREE AND CAN DO WHAT YOU	LIKE	. /LIZA/ (PULLING HERSELF TOGETHER IN DESPERATION)
DOCT IV	(161)	SIR PATRICK SAYS YOU MAY STAY HERE AS LONG AS YOU	LIKE	. /LOUIS/ JENNIFER. /MRS DUBEDAT/ YES, MY DARLING.
SUPR III	(79)	ME YOU CANT DO US A BIT BETTER THAN THAT IF YOU	LIKE	. /MENDOZA/ WINE, KIDS, MILK, CHEESE, AND BREAD CAN BE
CAND III	(133)	HAVE BEEN YOUR FRIEND: YOU MAY STRANGLE ME IF YOU	LIKE	. /MORELL/ (RELEASING HIM) EUGENE: IF THAT IS NOT A
FANY III	(316)	ANY WHISKY AND SODA. I'LL TAKE THE PLEDGE IF YOU	LIKE	. /MRS KNOX/ NO: YOU SHALL HAVE YOUR BEER BECAUSE YOU
KING I	(184)	NOBODY WILL SUSPECT YOU. I WILL PAY ANY PRICE YOU	LIKE	. /NEWTON/ I TELL YOU, MADAM, I KNOW NOTHING ABOUT SUCH
BULL IV	(171)	SO NOW; AND YOU CAN KEEP HIM THINKING SO IF YOU	LIKE	. /NORA/ I WASNT THINKING O MESELF AT ALL. /LARRY/ WERE
MIS.	(165)	(CARESSINGLY) HYPATIA, JOEY, PATSY, IF YOU	LIKE	. /PERCIVAL/ LOOK HERE: THIS IS NO GOOD. YOU WANT TO DO
BARB II	(275)	NEW BOOK. SOMEBODY ME MOTHER WANTED ME TO GROW UP	LIKE	. /PRICE/ WE'RE COMPANIONS IN MISFORTUNE, RUMMY. BOTH
CAPT I	(234)	RATHER CREEPY, MR RANKIN? I WONDER WHAT HE'LL BE	LIKE	. /RANKIN/ I MISDOUBT ME HE WILL NOT ANSWER, YOUR
MRS II	(201)	OR TO THE GIRL, OR TO YOUR CONGREGATION, IF YOU	LIKE	. /REV. S./ (COLLAPSING HELPLESSLY INTO HIS CHAIR) YOU
ARMS III	(69)	THAT. /LOUKA/ (COLDLY) YOU CAN WITHDRAW IF YOU	LIKE	. /SERGIUS/ WITHDRAW! NEVER! YOU BELONG TO ME. (HE
BARB II	(277)	WE FIND YOU A JOB YOU CAN PAY US FOR IT IF YOU	LIKE	. /SHIRLEY/ (EAGERLY) YES, YES: THATS TRUE. I CAN PAY
ROCK I	(226)	UP. /THE LADY/ GO ON. I WILL WAIT AS LONG AS YOU	LIKE	. /SIR ARTHUR/ THANK YOU. NOW LET ME SEE WHERE I WAS
BUOY III	(36)	I ASK YOU A QUESTION? /SHE/ ASK A DOZEN IF YOU	LIKE	. /SIR F./ YOU DID NOT COME BACK FROM PANAMA TO ATTEND
BARB I	(252)	SHALL MARRY, NOT THE MAN THEY LIKE, BUT THE MAN I	LIKE	. /STEPHEN/ OF COURSE I WAS THINKING ONLY OF HIS
O'FL	(220)	(SULKILY) YOU MAY TAKE IT TO THE DIVIL IF YOU	LIKE	. /TERESA/ YOU NEEDNT LOSE YOUR TEMPER ABOUT IT. I ONLY
MTH4 I	(169)	THE MOST MOMENTOUS IN THE WORLD FOR YOU AND YOUR	LIKE	. /THE ELDERLY GENTLEMAN/ (INTERESTED) INDEED? PRAY,
MRS IV	(248)	PURPOSE: YOU DONT KNOW WHAT THE WORLD IS REALLY	LIKE	. /VIVIE/ (ARRESTED) TAUGHT WRONG ON PURPOSE! WHAT DO
DOCT III	(138)	I HAVNT A RAP: YOU MAY SEARCH MY POCKETS IF YOU	LIKE	. /WALPOLE/ THATS CONCLUSIVE. (HE PRODUCES
JOAN 6	(149)	I MEANT NO HARM. I DID NOT KNOW WHAT IT WOULD BE	LIKE	. /WARWICK/ (HARDENING) OH! YOU SAW IT, THEN? /THE
JOAN PREFACE	(14)	PERSON, OR WITH BROCKEN SPECTRES, ECHOES AND THE	LIKE	. SAINT CATHERINE'S INSTRUCTIONS WERE FAR TOO COGENT
BARB PREFACE	(213)	SPEAKER," " SPLENDIDLY CRIMINAL," OR THE	LIKE	. SECURITY, THE CHIEF PRETENCE OF CIVILIZATION, CANNOT
SUPR II	(51)	THEY TEACH YOU TO BE AN ENGINEER OR SUCH	LIKE	; SEE? /TANNER/ SARCASM, TAVY, SARCASM! OH, IF YOU
ROCK II	(283)	AND THE DESOLATION HE WILL BRING ON US AND OUR	LIKE	. SHOUTING, AS OF AN EXCITED MOB SUDDENLY SURGING INTO
HART I	(63)	BE SO MISTAKEN: I KNOW TOO WELL WHAT LIARS ARE	LIKE	. SOMEBODY HAS REALLY TOLD YOU ALL THIS. /ELLIE/ (
CAPT I	(236)	ON MAWN. /BRASSBOUND/ YOU SEE WHAT MY MEN ARE	LIKE	. THAT RASCAL (INDICATING MARZO) WOULD CUT A THROAT
SUPR II	(60)	MILES AN HOUR. COME RIGHT DOWN TO THE CAPE IF YOU	LIKE	. THAT WILL BE A DECLARATION OF INDEPENDENCE WITH A
GETT	(313)	IT OUGHT TO BE FOR JUST AS LONG AS THE TWO PEOPLE	LIKE	. THATS WHAT I SAY. /COLLINS/ THEY MAY NOT AGREE ON THE
CAPT III	(296)	/LADY CICELY/ IT'S QUITE SIMPLE. DO WHATEVER YOU	LIKE	. THATS WHAT I ALWAYS DO. /BRASSBOUND/ THAT ANSWER IS
MIS. PREFACE	(13)	CHILDREN ARE TO BE ALLOWED TO DO WHAT THEY	LIKE	. THE BEST REPLY IS TO ASK WHETHER ADULTS ARE TO BE
INCA	(243)	BE A PRINCESS: THEY JUST MARRY YOU TO ANYONE THEY	LIKE	. THE INCA IS TO COME AND LOOK AT ME, AND PICK OUT
KING I	(191)	YOUR CHEMICAL LABORATORY. YOU LET THEM DO AS THEY	LIKE	. THE MERRY MONARCH: THATS WHAT YOU ARE. /CHARLES/
SUPR PREFACE	(R28)	THE COMPETITION OF BOMBAY WITH MANCHESTER AND THE	LIKE	. THE REAL COMPETITION IS THE COMPETITION OF REGENT
LION PREFACE	(17)	COMES TO HER IN THE SHAPE OF A SERPENT, OR THE	LIKE	. THE ROMAN EMPERORS, FOLLOWING THE EXAMPLE OF
MIS. PREFACE	(13)	WHETHER ADULTS ARE TO BE ALLOWED TO DO WHAT THEY	LIKE	. THE TWO CASES ARE THE SAME. THE ADULT WHO IS NASTY IS
APPL I	(229)	AGAIN. THAT CAN APPLY TO BOTH SIDES, IF YOU	LIKE	. THE VETO IS DEAD. /MAGNUS/ MAY WE NOT MAKE A
FABL III	(111)	CAN TAKE ME INTO YOUR LABORATORY AND TRY IF YOU	LIKE	. THERE IS A CANTEEN THERE, ISNT THERE? /THE
BARB PREFACE	(223)	AND BEEN REPLACED BY " PASSIONAL CRIME" AND THE	LIKE	. THEY ASSUME, AS FAR AS I CAN GATHER, THAT PEOPLE IN
ROCK II	(281)	UNEMPLOYED MEETING. OF WHAT POOR MEN ARE REALLY	LIKE	. THEY WERE AWFULLY NICE TO HER. THAT DID THE TRICK.
GETT PREFACE	(193)	DOGS, PIPES, CRICKET, GARDENS, FLOWERS, AND THE	LIKE	. THEY WERE CAPABLE OF DISCUSSING EACH OTHER'S SOLVENCY
DOCT I	(93)	PATRICK/ I KNOW YOUR CUTLER WALPOLES AND THEIR	LIKE	. THEYVE FOUND OUT THAT A MAN'S BODY'S FULL OF BITS AND
MIS.	(197)	THAT IT WAS THE OLD MAN THAT KNEW WHAT IT FELT	LIKE	. THINK OF THAT, SUMMERHAYS! THINK OF THAT! /HYPATIA/
BUOY III	(34)	FOR YOU, WHERE YOU CAN SEE WHOM YOU LIKE WHEN YOU	LIKE	. THIS WOMAN LIVES LIKE A SAVAGE IN A SWAMP FULL OF
GETT PREFACE	(204)	CLASSES, ICED CLARET CUP, LEMON SQUASHES, AND THE	LIKE	. TO TAKE A MORAL ILLUSTRATION, THE WILL TO SUPPRESS
POSN PREFACE	(400)	VULGAR AND FURTIVELY LASCIVIOUS DRAMA AS WE	LIKE	. UNDER A COLLEGE OF CARDINALS, OR BISHOPS, OR JUDGES,
MIS. PREFACE	(98)	SONGS AND SYMPHONIES, GO TO WHATEVER PLAYS WE	LIKE	. WE SHALL NOT LIKE THOSE WHICH HAVE NOTHING TO SAY TO
APPL PREFACE	(188)	I HAVE USED MINE A FEW TIMES TO SEE WHAT IT IS	LIKE	. WELL, IT IS LIKE THIS. WHEN THE ELECTION APPROACHES,
BULL IV	(175)	YOUR BIT OF THE STOCK. /LARRY/ YES: MINE IF YOU	LIKE	. WELL, OUR SYNDICATE HAS NO CONSCIENCE: IT HAS NO MORE
BARB II	(286)	WHO MADE YOUR MILLIONS FOR YOU? ME AND MY	LIKE	. WHATS KEP US POOR? KEEPIN YOU RICH. I WOULDNT HAVE
2TRU II	(67)	TIRED OF HIM. YOU CAN PICK UP A PRIVATE WHEN YOU	LIKE	. WHATS TO PREVENT YOU? /THE PATIENT/ MY LADYLIKE
JOAN 3	(89)	CAGE FOR A MONTH TO TEACH YOU WHAT A CAGE FEELS	LIKE	. YOU ARE AN ABOMINABLE BOY. /THE PAGE/ (LAUGHS, AND
PYGM V	(285)	(LOSING HER TEMPER AND RISING) I'LL TALK AS I	LIKE	. YOURE NOT MY TEACHER NOW. /HIGGINS/ (REFLECTIVELY) I
HART I	(70)	KISSES MY DAUGHTER. KISS HER AS MUCH AS YOU	LIKE	(HE MAKES FOR THE PANTRY). /THE GENTLEMAN/ THANK YOU.
PYGM V	(284)	FOR ME. /HIGGINS/ COMMERCIAL PRINCIPLES, ELIZA.	LIKE	(REPRODUCING HER COVENT GARDEN PRONUNCIATION WITH
GENV PREFACE	(19)	IN TRADE HITLER FOUND HIMSELF A BORN LEADER, AND,	LIKE	JACK CADE, WAT TYLER, ESSEX UNDER ELIZABETH TUDOR,
SUPR IV	(161)	MAN: TO KNOW TOO LITTLE, LIKE YOU, OR TOO MUCH,	LIKE	JACK. TANNER RETURNS. /TANNER/ WELL, IVE DISPOSED OF
SUPR I	(9)	BEYOND WORDS. /OCTAVIUS/ (GRINNING) THATS VERY	LIKE	JACK. MR RAMSDEN, YOU MUST SEE HIM, EVEN IF IT'S ONLY
DEVL II	(32)	LET ONE ANOTHER OUT OF SIGHT FOR A DAY, ARE MORE	LIKE	JAILERS AND SLAVE-OWNERS THAN LOVERS. THINK OF THOSE
DOCT IV	(156)	PATRICK/ THATS WHATS HAPPENED. HIS LUNG HAS GONE	LIKE	JANE'S ARM. I NEVER SAW SUCH A CASE. HE HAS GOT THROUGH
FABL PREFACE	(89)	WITH FAULTY CHAIR LEGS AND LEAKING PIPES. HE MAY,	LIKE	JENNER, BE SO IGNORANT OF THE RUDIMENTS OF STATISTICS
MIS.	(125)	ONES ARE TOO SMALL, LIKE BUNNY, OR TOO SILLY,	LIKE	JERRY. OF COURSE ONE CAN GET INTO A STATE ABOUT ANY
LION PREFACE	(68)	NOT CALL THEIR FATHER, AND THAT THE DISCIPLES,	LIKE	JESUS HIMSELF, WERE ALL MEN WITHOUT FAMILY
2TRU III	(98)	I CAME HERE I HAVE BEEN WANTING TO JOIN THE ARMY,	LIKE	JOAN OF ARC. IT'S A BROTHERHOOD, OF A SORT. /THE
FABL PREFACE	(79)	HIS CONVERSATIONS WITH THE ARCHANGEL GABRIEL, OR,	LIKE	JOAN OF ARC, REALLY HEARD VOICES WHEN HE LISTENED FOR
JOAN PREFACE	(38)	OR RANK, ARE ALWAYS REALLY SELF-SELECTED,	LIKE	JOAN. AND SINCE NEITHER CHURCH NOR STATE, BY THE
JOAN PREFACE	(28)	NEUTRAL TRIBUNALS WERE NOT AVAILABLE. EDITH,	LIKE	JOAN, WAS AN ARCH HERETIC: IN THE MIDDLE OF THE WAR SHE
JOAN PREFACE	(37)	WHEN JOAN MAINTAINED HER OWN WAYS SHE CLAIMED,	LIKE	JOB, THAT THERE WAS NOT ONLY GOD AND THE CHURCH TO BE
LION PREFACE	(28)	OF THE FOLK-LORE GODS, AND ANNOUNCES THAT,	LIKE	JOHN BARLEYCORN, HE WILL BE BARBAROUSLY SLAIN AND
JOAN 6	(129)	THE MAN WHO THROWS OFF HIS FUR GOWN AND DRESSES	LIKE	JOHN THE BAPTIST: THEY ARE FOLLOWED, AS SURELY AS THE
MIS.	(125)	MONEY IF THEY WERENT THE SONS OF THEIR FATHERS,	LIKE	JOHNNY. WHAT'S A GIRL TO DO? I NEVER MET ANYBODY LIKE

LION PREFACE(22)	IT VERY RAPIDLY, ACCORDING TO MATTHEW. THOUGH,	LIKE	JOHN, HE BECAME AN ITINERANT PREACHER, HE DEPARTED
KING II (232)	HOW OFTEN HAVE YOU ASKED ME TO DO SOME BIG THING	LIKE	JOINING YOUR CHURCH, OR SOME LITTLE THING LIKE
SIM I (45)	TO HAVE THROWN YOU ON THIS SHORE FOR THE PURPOSE,	LIKE	JONAH. WILL YOU UNDERTAKE IT? /THE CLERGYMAN/ I SHOULD
MTH3 SD(91)	A GOLD FILLET ROUND HIS BROWS, COMES IN. HE IS	LIKE	JOYCE BURGE, YET ALSO LIKE LUBIN, AS IF NATURE HAD MADE
DOCT PREFACE(38)	IS ONLY TOLERATED BY THE LAW ON CONDITION THAT,	LIKE	JUDICIAL TORTURE, IT SHALL BE DONE AS MERCIFULLY AS THE
PHIL I (72)	EXPLANATION? /CHARTERIS/ SHE DID WHAT A WOMAN	LIKE	JULIA ALWAYS DOES. WHEN I EXPLAINED PERSONALLY, SHE
MIS. (197)	HE KICKED HIS FATHER, AND FOUND THAT IT WAS JUST	LIKE	KICKING ANY OTHER MAN. HE LAUGHED AND SAID THAT IT WAS
SIM II (54)	BATTLE ON RECORD. THEY ARE QUARRELLING ALREADY	LIKE	KILKENNY CATS. /SIR CHARLES/ WHAT ABOUT? /HYERING/ OH,
DEVL III (61)	BUT TO BE SWINDLED BY A PIG-HEADED LUNATIC	LIKE	KING GEORGE-- /SWINDON/ (SCANDALIZED) CHUT, SIR--
BARB III (313)	THE CHARITABLE INSTITUTIONS WOULD BE DOWN ON HIM	LIKE	KITES ON A BATTLE FIELD IF HE GAVE HIS NAME. /LADY
6CAL (101)	YOU KNOW BETTER THAN THE QUEEN! YOU AND YOUR	LIKE	KNOW WHAT TO EXPECT FROM YOUR LORDS AND RULERS! WELL,
SIM PREFACE(12)	ATTEMPTS OF THE VERY POOR TO BECOME SINECURISTS	LIKE	LADIES AND GENTLEMEN, MY OWN ACQUAINTANCE WITH SUCH A
FANY II (293)	NOBODY'S REALLY A LADY EXCEPT WHEN THEYRE TREATED	LIKE	LADIES, I DONT KNOW. (SHE THROWS HERSELF INTO A CORNER
LION PREFACE(59)	ARE THOSE WHO POSTULATE SOME REVOLUTIONARY CHANGE	LIKE	LAND NATIONALIZATION, WHICH BY ITSELF WOULD OBVIOUSLY
MTH2 (78)	STORIES HAVE GONE OUT OF FASHION AND PERISHED	LIKE	LAST YEAR'S POPULAR SONG, IS A SCIENTIFIC FACT; AND
POSN (458)	TIME TO MYSELF. THEN I NOTICED THAT THE CHILD WAS	LIKE	LEAD IN MY ARMS. GOD WOULD NEVER HAVE BEEN SO CRUEL AS
PYGM V (278)	DAMNATION! /LIZA/ (CONTINUING) IT WAS JUST	LIKE	LEARNING TO DANCE IN THE FASHIONABLE WAY: THERE WAS
DOCT PREFACE(14)	THE COBBLER BELIEVES THAT THERE IS NOTHING	LIKE	LEATHER. THE IMPERIALIST WHO REGARDS THE CONQUEST OF
KING I (213)	BOATSWAIN. THE COBBLER THINKS THERE IS NOTHING	LIKE	LEATHER-- /NELL/ NOT WHEN YOU MAKE IT INTO BREECHES
SIM PREFACE(11)	OWN HANDS. SUCH A COMMISSAR WAS DJERJINSKY. NOW,	LIKE	LENIN, ENTOMBED IN THE RED SQUARE. HE WAS NOT A
GETT (273)	COURSE HE MADE A FOOL OF HIMSELF MARRYING A CHILD	LIKE	LEO. /THE GENERAL/ BUT TO HIT HER! ABSOLUTELY TO HIT
DOCT I (114)	I AM NOT LIKELY TO FORGET IT. THEY TREAT US	LIKE	LEPERS AT THE HOTELS. /EMMY/ (AT THE DOOR) WELL,
GETT PREFACE(206)	BUT DEMOCRACY AS TO THE WAY TO DO IT IS	LIKE	LETTING THE PASSENGERS DRIVE THE TRAIN: IT CAN ONLY END
MILL I (147)	THE DEEP END. YOU MUSTNT MIND ME: THERES NOTHING	LIKE	LETTING YOURSELF GO IF YOU ARE BUILT THAT WAY.
ANNA (290)	REVOLUTION: YOU ARE ATTACHED TO ABSTRACT THINGS	LIKE	LIBERTY. BUT MY FAMILY HAS SERVED THE PANJANDRUMS OF
DOCT PREFACE(33)	UNCONDITIONAL IN ITS ASSUMPTION THAT KNOWLEDGE,	LIKE	LIFE, IS A DESIRABLE THING, THOUGH ANY FOOL CAN PROVE
GENV III (79)	HER INTELLIGENCE IS REMARKABLE: SHE TAKES A POINT	LIKE	LIGHTNING. SHE HAS IN HER VEINS THE LEARNING OF THE
HART PREFACE(38)	OF HIS UTMOST, NO EDICT ON WHICH HE WILL BE ABLE,	LIKE	LINCOLN, TO INVOKE " THE CONSIDERATE JUDGMENT OF
VWOO 1 (121)	OF THEM ARE JUST LIKE ME. /A/ WELL, HOW DO YOU	LIKE	LIVING AT THE RATE OF FIVE THOUSAND A YEAR? IS IT
BUOY 1 (11)	LIVING IN A WORLD OF POOR AND UNHAPPY PEOPLE IS	LIKE	LIVING IN HELL. /FATHER/ YOU NEED NOT SPEAK TO THEM.
MRS II (218)	ME YOUR PHOTOS TO SEE THAT YOU WERE GROWING UP	LIKE	LIZ: YOUVE JUST HER LADYLIKE, DETERMINED WAY. BUT I
CLEO II (142)	ARMY! CRAWLING OVER THE EDGE OF THE WEST HARBOR	LIKE	LOCUSTS. (WITH SUDDEN ANGER HE STRIDES DOWN TO
LION PREFACE(54)	A PUBLIC HOSPITAL, OR A MADHOUSE. IN CITIES	LIKE	LONDON THE PROPORTION IS VERY NEARLY ONE IN TWO.
GENV III (83)	WELSH BORDER THAN A COCKNEY CONCENTRATION CAMP	LIKE	LONDON. /THE JUDGE/ IN SHORT, YOU ARE A MONGREL. /THE
MTH5 SD(214)	A CEREMONIAL ROBE, AND CARRIES TWO IMPLEMENTS	LIKE	LONG SLENDER SAWS. SHE COMES TO THE ALTAR BETWEEN THE
BULL III (120)	SUCH A BIG PLACE THAT LOOKING FOR A MAN THERE IS	LIKE	LOOKING FOR A NEEDLE IN A BUNDLE OF HAY. THEY TELL ME
MIS. (195)	AND HAVING THEM TAKEN OUT BY A BLINDFOLDED CHILD	LIKE	LOTTERY NUMBERS, THERE WOULD BE JUST AS HIGH A
DOCT PREFACE(18)	INFLEXIBLE POINT OF HONOR. ANDREA DEL SARTO,	LIKE	LOUIS DUBEDAT IN MY PLAY, MUST HAVE EXPENDED ON THE
GENV PREFACE(20)	MY PROGRAM, MY VIEWS OR WHAT YOU PLEASE).	LIKE	LOUIS NAPOLEON HE HAD NOW LEARNT HIS LESSON: NAMELY,
KING I (206)	YOU HAVE NOT THE FAINTEST CONCEPTION. /CHARLES/	LIKE	LOUISE, YOU HAVE NOT SEEN ME PRACTISE IT. BUT I AM KING
DOCT V (178)	SIR COLENSO. I KNEW QUITE WELL THAT YOU DID NOT	LIKE	LOUIS; BUT IT IS NOT YOUR FAULT: YOU DONT UNDERSTAND:
SUPR II (55)	WERE ONLY GOOD ENOUGH FOR LOVE! THERE IS NOTHING	LIKE	LOVE: THERE IS NOTHING ELSE BUT LOVE: WITHOUT IT THE
ARMS III (63)	AND HEROES! A FRAUD, BLUNTSCHLI. A HOLLOW SHAM,	LIKE	LOVE. /RAINA/ (OUTRAGED) LIKE LOVE! YOU SAY THAT
ARMS III (63)	A HOLLOW SHAM, LIKE LOVE. /RAINA/ (OUTRAGED)	LIKE	LOVE! YOU SAY THAT BEFORE ME! /BLUNTSCHLI/ COME,
UNPL PREFACE(R22)	THE EXTREME INSTANCE IS A PURE PANTOMIME,	LIKE	L' ENFANT PRODIGUE, IN WHICH THE DIALOGUE, THOUGH IT
MTH3 SD(91)	BROWS, COMES IN. HE IS LIKE JOYCE BURGE, YET ALSO	LIKE	LUBIN, AS IF NATURE HAD MADE A COMPOSITE PHOTOGRAPH OF
LION PREFACE(82)	A GOOD STORY-TELLER, LIKE LUKE, WAS (HEREIN ALSO	LIKE	LUKE) MUCH WEAKER IN POWER OF THOUGHT THAN IN
LION PREFACE(82)	AUTHOR OF THE ACTS, THOUGH A GOOD STORY-TELLER,	LIKE	LUKE, WAS (HEREIN ALSO LIKE LUKE) MUCH WEAKER IN POWER
SIM PRO,2, (26)	BIGGEST LINERS CAN GET CLOSE UP, LIKE PLYMOUTH,	LIKE	LULWORTH COVE. DONT STAND SO CLOSE. THERES A SORT OF
JOAN PREFACE(31)	AS JOAN: BOTH WERE REFORMERS OF THE CHURCH	LIKE	LUTHER; WHILST JOAN, LIKE MRS EDDY, WAS QUITE PREPARED
2TRU II (62)	HAS TO LEARN, DARLING, IS THAT NOTHING SUCCEEDS	LIKE	LYING. MAKE ANY STATEMENT THAT IS SO TRUE THAT IT HAS
LADY PREFACE(219)	PART; AND WHEN WE COME TO THE GREAT VILLAINS	LIKE	MACBETH, WE FIND, AS MR HARRIS POINTS OUT, THAT THEY
MIS. (129)	JOEY'S CONSCIENCE. HE USED TO HEAR THEM ARGUING	LIKE	MAD ABOUT EVERYTHING. YOU SEE, THE PHILOSOPHER WAS A
LIED (189)	THOUGH THE SISTERS QUARREL WITH ONE ANOTHER	LIKE	MAD ALL THE TIME, YET LET ONE OF THE BROTHERS MARRY,
MILL PREFACE(112)	NOT BE MADE TO UNDERSTAND THIS, THEY WERE KILLED	LIKE	MAD DOGS BY THEIR OWN COURTIERS. BUT OUR PETTY FIRESIDE
APPL PREFACE(182)	SUCH APPALLING THINGS THAT THEY HAD TO BE KILLED	LIKE	MAD DOGS. ONLY, IT WAS NOT THE PEOPLE THAT ROSE UP AND
SUPR II (70)	OR FOLKESTONE; THEN ACROSS THE CHANNEL AND AWAY	LIKE	MAD TO MARSEILLES, GIBRALTAR, GENOA, ANY PORT FROM
OVER (172)	TRUE THAT WHEN ONE FEELS IN DANGER ONE TALKS	LIKE	MAD TO STAVE IT OFF, EVEN WHEN ONE DOESNT QUITE WANT TO
MTH5 (213)	THE HOUR OF BIRTH IS OVERDUE. THE BABY IS KICKING	LIKE	MAD. SHE WILL BREAK HER SHELL PREMATURELY. /THE MAIDEN/
JOAN 1 (70)	/ROBERT/ WHAT NOW? /STEWARD/ THE HENS ARE LAYING	LIKE	MAD, SIR. FIVE DOZEN EGGS! /ROBERT/ (STIFFENS
DOCT I (98)	YOU KNOW, IT WAS AN IMMENSE SUCCESS. IT ACTED	LIKE	MAGIC ON THE LITTLE PRINCE. UP WENT HIS TEMPERATURE;
CATH 1 (168)	A SPLENDID WRESTLER. YOU THREW ME ON MY BACK	LIKE	MAGIC, THOUGH I COULD LIFT YOU WITH ONE HAND, DARLING:
JOAN PREFACE(6)	THAN TO BE A CONQUEROR. THOSE WHO HAVE BEEN BOTH,	LIKE	MAHOMET AND JOAN, HAVE FOUND THAT IT IS THE CONQUEROR
JOAN PREFACE(23)	POLITICAL CHANGES MUCH EASIER THAN THEY ARE, AND,	LIKE	MAHOMET IN HIS INNOCENCE OF ANY WORLD BUT THE TRIBAL
DOCT PREFACE(72)	FORMULATORS OF THE SUPERSEDED NATIVE RELIGION,	LIKE	MAHOMET, HAD BEEN ENLIGHTENED ENOUGH TO INTRODUCE AS
JOAN PREFACE(31)	AS THE ROCK ON WHICH THE CHURCH WAS BUILT, AND,	LIKE	MAHOMET, WAS ALWAYS READY WITH A PRIVATE REVELATION
MRS IV (250)	HARM BY IT. AND THEN IT BRINGS IN MONEY: AND I	LIKE	MAKING MONEY. NO: IT'S NO USE: I CANT GIVE IT UP-- NOT
DOCT I (96)	STRAIGHT, AND FEED HIM UP AND MAKE HER HAPPY. I	LIKE	MAKING PEOPLE HAPPY. (HE GOES TO THE CHAIR NEAR THE
GETT (305)	THINKING. /THE BISHOP/ (TO HOTCHKISS) NOTHING	LIKE	MAKING PEOPLE THINK: IS THERE, SINJON? /LESBIA/ (
HART I (73)	/MRS HUSHABYE/ SORRY. I HATE IT! IT'S	LIKE	MAKING PEOPLE SHEW THEIR TICKETS. /MAZZINI/ (
HART I (78)	DYNAMITE FOR? /CAPTAIN SHOTOVER/ TO KILL FELLOWS	LIKE	MANGAN. /HECTOR/ NO USE. THEY WILL ALWAYS BE ABLE TO
METH PREFACE(R76)	BROUGHT FORTH BY A VIRGIN DESCENDED IN	LIKE	MANNER FROM A LINE OF VIRGINS RIGHT BACK TO EVE; THAT
MTH1 II (27)	EVIL IN YOURSELVES. YOUR FLESH CEASES TO GROW	LIKE	MAN'S FLESH: IT GROWS LIKE A FUNGUS ON A TREE. INSTEAD
MTH5 (223)	THERE HAS COME DOWN TO US A FABLE WHICH,	LIKE	MANY FABLES, IS NOT A THING THAT WAS DONE IN THE PAST,
APPL PREFACE(193)	REAL POINT, WHICH WAS THAT HE WAS AN INVENTOR.	LIKE	MANY MEN OF GENIUS HE COULD NOT UNDERSTAND WHY THINGS
LIED PREFACE(185)		LIKE	MANY OTHER WORKS OF MINE, THIS PLAYLET IS A PIECE
BARB I SD(259)	ARMY UNIFORM. LOMAX, A YOUNG MAN ABOUT TOWN, IS	LIKE	MANY OTHER YOUNG MEN ABOUT TOWN. HE IS AFFLICTED WITH A
CLEO II (134)	DO HIS STRONG ROUND ARMS SHINE IN THE SUN	LIKE	MARBLE? /CAESAR/ HE IS IN EXCELLENT CONDITION--
HART III (133)	/ELLIE/ DO YOU MEAN THAT THE FACTORIES ARE	LIKE	MARCUS'S TIGERS? THAT THEY DONT EXIST? /MANGAN/ THEY
SUPR PREFACE(R20)	BY CHARMING HIM, LIKE ROSALIND, OR BY STRATAGEM,	LIKE	MARIANA; BUT IN EVERY CASE THE RELATION BETWEEN THE
JOAN PREFACE(30)	WHAT THEY WERE ACCUSING HER OF. SHE WAS MUCH MORE	LIKE	MARK TWAIN THAN LIKE PETER CAUCHON. HER ATTACHMENT TO
BARB II (293)	OR LATER. I FEEL THAT WAY ABOUT BARBARA. I DONT	LIKE	MARRIAGE: I FEEL INTENSELY AFRAID OF IT; AND I DONT
GETT PREFACE(216)	INHUMAN. MARRIAGE AS A FACT IS NOT IN THE LEAST	LIKE	MARRIAGE AS AN IDEAL. IF IT WERE, THE SUDDEN CHANGES
MTH5 (251)	LIKE THOSE IN THE OLD FABLE OF MICHAEL ANGELO.	LIKE	MARTELLUS, I SMASHED THEM WHEN I SAW THAT THERE WAS NO
BULL III (131)	WELL, WE'RE NOT ALL FOOSTHERIN OUL DODDHERERS	LIKE	MATT. (PLEASANTLY, TO THE SUBJECT OF THIS DESCRIPTION)
BASH PREFACE(89)	ADMIRABLE BASHVILLE WAS PERFORMED, MEN OF LETTERS	LIKE	MAURICE HEWLETT WOULD CHUCKLE DELIGHTEDLY OVER IT
DOCT PREFACE(35)	SAY YES. THOUGH SHAKESPEAR, DR JOHNSON, AND THEIR	LIKE	MAY SAY NO. BUT EVEN THOSE WHO SAY " YOU MAY TORTURE A
GLIM (173)	THIRTY CROWNS-- THIRTY CROWNS FROM A POOR GIRL	LIKE	ME: IT IS WICKED-- MONSTROUS. I MUST SIN TO EARN IT.
MIS. (159)	HAS JUST LEFT. /TARLETON/ GOOD. WELL, DO YOU	LIKE	ME? DONT MISUNDERSTAND ME! I'M PERFECTLY AWARE THAT
OVER (177)	JUNO/ SO YOU SHALL, DEAR. TELL ME: DO YOU REALLY	LIKE	ME? I DONT MEAN LOVE ME: YOU MIGHT LOVE THE
JOAN EPILOG (156)	NEVER DREAMED OF YOU BEFORE. /JOAN/ IS SHE DEAD,	LIKE	ME? /CHARLES/ YES. BUT SHE WAS NOT LIKE YOU. SHE WAS
KING II (227)	MAN LIKE YOU BE SATISFIED WITH A LITTLE THING	LIKE	ME? /CHARLES/ STOP. I CANNOT BEAR THAT. I AM NOT A
MTH3 (98)	SPEAK. /BURGE-LUBIN/ AM I A BARBARIAN BECAUSE YOU	LIKE	ME? /CONFUCIUS/ SURELY. NOBODY LIKES ME: I AM HELD IN
CATH 1 (168)	DARLING: THERE IS NO PLEASING YOU. DONT YOU	LIKE	ME? /EDSTASTON/ (MOLLIFIED) WELL, IN A SORT OF WAY I
SUPR IV (159)	WANT VIOLET TO BE AN IDIOT-- OR SOMETHING WORSE,	LIKE	ME? /OCTAVIUS/ SOMETHING WORSE-- LIKE YOU! WHAT DO
MRS I (194)	BY JOVE! WHAT A LARK! DO YOU THINK SHE'LL	LIKE	ME? /PRAED/ IVE NO DOUBT YOULL MAKE YOURSELF POPULAR,
MRS IV (249)	THAT TAUGHT YOU KNOW ABOUT LIFE OR ABOUT PEOPLE	LIKE	ME? WHEN DID THEY EVER MEET ME, OR SPEAK TO ME, OR LET
DEST (163)	BROTHER, BUT YOUR SISTER? THE SISTER WHO WAS SO	LIKE	ME? WHO HAD MY BEAUTIFUL BLUE EYES? IT'S A LIE: YOUR
POSN (464)	ON THE INNOCENT KID AND GO SOFT ON A ROTTEN THING	LIKE	ME? WHY DID I GO SOFT MYSELF? WHY DID THE SHERIFF GO
PYGM IV (265)	ELIZA. ALL MEN ARE NOT CONFIRMED OLD BACHELORS	LIKE	ME AND THE COLONEL. MOST MEN ARE THE MARRYING SORT (
DEST (186)	FLY SO HIGH. BESIDES, I'M BETTER AS I AM: MEN	LIKE	ME ARE WANTED IN THE ARMY JUST NOW. THE FACT IS, THE
JOAN 5 (109)	MY LITTLE SAINT. /JOAN/ DEAR JACK: I THINK YOU	LIKE	ME AS A SOLDIER LIKES HIS COMRADE. /DUNOIS/ YOU NEED
MIS. (136)	SOME INJUSTICE, MRS TARLETON. THEY PRETENDED TO	LIKE	ME BECAUSE I KEPT THEIR BROTHERS FROM MURDERING THEM;
ROCK I (218)	YOU. /HIPNEY/ PSHA! AN OLD STREET CORNER SPEAKER	LIKE	ME CAN DEBATE THE HEADS OFF YOU PARLIAMENTARY
PYGM V (286)	THINGS THAN YOU, FOR ALL YOUR LEARNING. GIRLS	LIKE	ME CAN DRAG GENTLEMEN DOWN TO MAKE LOVE TO THEM EASY
JOAN 1 (69)	/JOAN/ ONE THOUSAND LIKE ME CAN STOP THEM. TEN	LIKE	ME CAN STOP THEM WITH GOD ON OUR SIDE. (SHE RISES
JOAN 1 (69)	NOR TEN THOUSAND LIKE YOU. /JOAN/ ONE THOUSAND	LIKE	ME CAN STOP THEM. TEN LIKE ME CAN STOP THEM WITH GOD ON

PHIL I	(70)	I HOPE, NOW THAT I AM IN LOVE WITH YOU, YOU WILL	LIKE	ME FOR IT JUST AS I LIKED TRANFIELD. /CHARTERIS/ MY
AUGS	(264)	I'D CHUCK IT. DONT YOU DRIVE ME TOO FAR. OLD UNS	LIKE	ME IS UP IN THE WORLD NOW. /AUGUSTUS/ IF WE WERE NOT AT
BULL III	(139)	BUT IT DONT SEEM TO MATTER TO ME WHETHER THEY	LIKE	ME OR NOT. I'M NOT GOING TO STAND FOR PARLIAMENT HERE,
SIM II	(60)	I DONT KNOW WHETHER OTHER PEOPLE ARE	LIKE	ME OR NOT-- /LADY FARWATERS/ NO, IDDY! YOU ARE UNIQUE.
NEVR II	(259)	OH, I KNOW YOU MUSNT TELL ME WHETHER YOU	LIKE	ME OR NOT; BUT-- /GLORIA/ (HER PRINCIPLES UP IN ARMS
O'FL	(205)	OF MY NATIVE PLACE WOULD LET A COMMON SOLDIER	LIKE	ME SIT DOWN IN HIS PRESENCE WITHOUT LEAVE. /SIR PEARCE/
ARMS II	(24)	YOURE YOUNG! YOURE YOUNG! /LOUKA/ YES; AND YOU	LIKE	ME THE BETTER FOR IT, DONT YOU? BUT I KNOW SOME FAMILY
MTH2	(39)	CONSCIENCE. /HASLAM/ OH YES; BUT WHERE IS A CHAP	LIKE	ME TO GO? I'M AFRAID I'M NOT INTELLECTUAL ENOUGH TO
MIS.	(133)	TIME HAS COME FOR SANE, HEALTHY, UNPRETENDING MEN	LIKE	ME TO MAKE A STAND AGAINST THIS CONSPIRACY OF THE
CLEO I	(109)	AND THEY LIVE ON HUMAN FLESH. /CAESAR/ WOULD YOU	LIKE	ME TO SHEW YOU A REAL ROMAN? /CLEOPATRA/ (TERRIFIED)
APPL I	(239)	LAUGHING AT HIM. THEY I ASKED THEM WOULD THEY	LIKE	ME TO SING; AND THEIR YES NEARLY LIFTED THE ROOF OFF. I
SUPR I	(19)	IT? /ANN/ YOU SEE, GRANNY, MAMMA WOULD NOT	LIKE	ME TO SUPPOSE IT. /RAMSDEN/ (MUCH PERPLEXED) YOU ARE
FANY I	(281)	TO LOSE MY TEMPER; AND I DONT THINK BOBBY WOULD	LIKE	ME TO TELL YOU WHAT I THINK OF YOU; FOR WHEN I START
2TRU III	(96)	CHILL OF POVERTY. THERE ARE PLENTY OF RICH WOMEN	LIKE	ME WHO HATE BEING DEVOURED BY PARASITES. /AUBREY/ STOP.
2TRU I	(33)	WHAT ARE PARAMEASLES? /THE DOCTOR/ SOMETHING SO	LIKE	MEASLES THAT NOBODY CAN SEE ANY DIFFERENCE. /THE
LION PREFACE	(100)	AND READ ME THEIR LETTERS, WHICH WERE EXACTLY	LIKE	MEDIEVAL LETTERS IN THEIR LITERAL FAITH AND
OVER	(190)	TO BE NICE TO MY WIFE, AND YOUR WIFE OUGHTNT TO	LIKE	ME. AND MY WIFE OUGHTNT TO LIKE YOU. AND IF THEY DO,
MILL IV	(210)	OF THE MONEY MARKET. RUSSIA NEEDS MANAGING WOMEN	LIKE	ME. IN MOSCOW I SHALL NOT BE A MILLIONAIRESS; BUT I
CAND I	(100)	DAY, I HOPE AND TRUST, YOU WILL BE A HAPPY MAN	LIKE	ME. (EUGENE CHAFES INTOLERANTLY, REPUDIATING THE WORTH
MTH4 I	(150)	YOU NATURALLY FEEL MORE AT HOME WITH A FLAPPER	LIKE	ME. (SHE MAKES HERSELF COMFORTABLE ON THE SACKS). /THE
DEST	(169)	ASTONISHED) WOMANISH! /LADY/ (LISTLESSLY) YES,	LIKE	ME. (WITH DEEP MELANCHOLY) DO YOU THINK THAT IF I
SUPR IV	(165)	WILL CARE TO BE BOTHERED WITH AN OLD WOMAN	LIKE	ME. OH, YOU NEEDNT TELL ME: POLITENESS IS ALL VERY
SUPR III	(102)	TO ENTER HEAVEN IN THE COMPANY OF A REPROBATE	LIKE	ME. /ANA/ ALL SOULS ARE EQUALLY PRECIOUS. YOU REPENT,
VWOO 1	(121)	SPEAK TO ANYONE ANYHOW. AND LOTS OF THEM ARE JUST	LIKE	ME. /A/ WELL, HOW DO YOU LIKE LIVING AT THE RATE OF
NEVR I	(216)	REALLY RESPECTABLE? /VALENTINE/ PERFECTLY. NOT	LIKE	ME. /DOLLY/ HONEST INJUN? MRS CLANDON GASPS FAINTLY;
OVER	(194)	I DONT WANT TO MEET OR SPEAK TO ANYONE WHO DOESNT	LIKE	ME. /JUNO/ BUT, MY PRECIOUS, THIS IS THE MOST HORRIBLE
DEST	(163)	HE IS ON GENERAL MASSENA'S STAFF. HE IS VERY	LIKE	ME. /LIEUTENANT/ (HIS MIND GIVING WAY) DO YOU MEAN TO
HART II	(93)	PRAY? /MAZZINI/ I DO. AND OF COURSE OTHER PEOPLE	LIKE	ME. /MRS HUSHABYE/ FOOTLING PEOPLE, YOU MEAN. /MAZZINI/
CAND II	(106)	/MARCHBANKS/ REALLY! OH, THEN YOU ARE SHY,	LIKE	ME. /PROSERPINE/ CERTAINLY I AM NOT SHY. WHAT DO YOU
BUOY III	(47)	NEITHER TO THE WEST, LIKE YOU, NOR TO THE EAST,	LIKE	ME. /THE NATIVE/ (SWINGING THE CENSER) NEITHER TO
MIS.	(145)	OFF WITH YOU. (TO LORD SUMMERHAYS) SHE'S ACTIVE,	LIKE	ME. SHE ACTUALLY WANTED ME TO PUT HER INTO THE SHOP.
MTH1 I	(9)	FIND OUT HOW TO RENEW HERSELF AND CAST THE SKIN	LIKE	ME. SHE HAD A MIGHTY WILL: SHE STROVE AND STROVE AND
MIS.	(111)	MY BROTHERS AND SISTERS ARE NOT THE LEAST	LIKE	ME. THEYRE THE REGULAR THING THAT YOU ALWAYS GET IN THE
SUPR I	(29)	BOUND TO QUARREL WITH ME. SECOND, VIOLET DOESNT	LIKE	ME. THIRD, IF I HAD THE HONOR OF BEING THE FATHER OF
MTH3	(120)	WERE OTHER CONSOLATIONS IN THOSE DAYS FOR PEOPLE	LIKE	ME. WE DRANK PREPARATIONS OF ALCOHOL TO RELIEVE THE
LION PREFACE	(62)	BURNS: THAT, IN SHORT, WE ARE GODS THOUGH WE DIE	LIKE	MEN, ALL THAT IS TODAY SOUND BIOLOGY AND PSYCHOLOGY;
SUPR I	(32)	THINGS INMOST SECRETS! BOYS' SECRETS ARE JUST	LIKE	MEN'S; AND YOU KNOW WHAT THEY ARE! /TANNER/ (
GETT	(351)	RIGHT. /COLLINS/ YES, MAAM. ANYTHING YOU WOULD	LIKE	MENTIONED ABOUT MISS LESBIA, MAAM? /MRS BRIDGENORTH/
PYGM EPILOG	(292)	SLAVISH WOMEN AS WELL AS SLAVISH MEN: AND WOMEN,	LIKE	MEN, ADMIRE THOSE THAT ARE STRONGER THAN THEMSELVES.
LION PREF,FN	(43)	CHILDREN OF THE MOST HIGH; BUT YE SHALL DIE	LIKE	MEN, AND FALL LIKE ONE
CLEO I	(109)	ONLY I THINK I SHOULD BE MORE AFRAID OF YOU. I	LIKE	MEN, ESPECIALLY YOUNG MEN WITH ROUND STRONG ARMS; BUT I
BULL PREFACE	(47)	INDIGNATION KNOWS NO BOUNDS: THEY FEEL ABOUT THEM	LIKE	MEN, NOT LIKE SOLDIERS. BUT THE MOMENT YOU BRING THE
MTH1 I	(7)	MY OLD SKIN WOULD LIE ON THE GROUND LOOKING JUST	LIKE	ME; AND ADAM WOULD SEE IT SHRIVEL UP AND-- /THE
BULL I	(77)	AWFUL (HE DRINKS). I SEE YOURE A GOOD LIBERAL	LIKE	MESELF, SIR. /BROADBENT/ I AM A LOVER OF LIBERTY, LIKE
CAND III	(134)	CHOOSE BETWEEN A WRETCHED LITTLE NERVOUS DISEASE	LIKE	ME, AND A PIG-HEADED PARSON LIKE YOU? LET US GO ON A
POSN	(464)	HAVE MADE US TO BE ROTTEN DRUNKEN BLACKGUARDS	LIKE	ME, AND GOOD-FOR-NOTHING RIPS LIKE FEEMY. HE MADE ME
MIS.	(161)	YOURE RIGHT: A VULGAR QUESTION. TO A MAN	LIKE	ME, EVERYBODY IS THE FIRST. LIFE RENEWS ITSELF. /LINA/
BARB II	(280)	KNOW. YOULL COME TO IT SOONER THAN A TEETOTALLER	LIKE	ME, FILLIN YOURSELF WITH GIN AT THIS HOUR O THE
BUOY III	(37)	MIND WOULD BE CLEARER ON THE SUBJECT IF,	LIKE	ME, HE HAD BEEN MARRIED TWICE. MY FIRST MARRIAGE, WHICH
GETT	(268)	HAPPENS ALL THE SAME. YOULL FIND PLENTY OF WOMEN	LIKE	ME, IF YOU CARE TO LOOK FOR THEM: WOMEN WITH LOTS OF
CAPT I	(232)	OF BEING POLITE TO THEM, AND SAYING HOW DYE DO?	LIKE	ME, PEOPLE AIM PISTOLS AT THEM. IVE BEEN AMONG
ARMS II	(36)	HA! HA! I EXPECT ONE OF THE SIX OF YOU IS VERY	LIKE	ME, SIR; THOUGH I AM ONLY MISS RAINA'S MAID. (SHE GOES
ROCK II	(269)	IF THEY WERE PLASTER SAINTS, WHILE MEN AND WOMEN	LIKE	ME, THAT HAD SPENT THEIR LIVES IN THE SERVICE OF THE
HART II	(119)	ARE YOUNG. BUT WHEN YOU ARE OLD: VERY VERY OLD,	LIKE	ME, THE DREAMS COME BY THEMSELVES. YOU DONT KNOW HOW
CATH 1	(165)	IS MADE. YOU THINK THAT IF SHE COULD STAND A MAN	LIKE	ME, WITH ONLY ONE EYE, AND A CROSS EYE AT THAT, SHE
MRS I	(182)	HOPE IVE NOT MISTAKEN THE DAY. THAT WOULD BE JUST	LIKE	ME, YOU KNOW. YOUR MOTHER ARRANGED THAT SHE WAS TO COME
POSN	(442)	PRIDE HAS BEEN YOUR RUIN. IF YOUD ONLY DONE	LIKE	ME, YOUD BE A FREE AND RESPECTABLE MAN THIS DAY INSTEAD
POSN	(461)	(WHISPERING AT HER) SOFTY! CRY-BABY! LANDED	LIKE	ME! DOING WHAT YOU NEVER INTENDED! (TAKING UP HIS
CAND II	(106)	SELF WITH ME? I AM JUST LIKE YOU. /PROSERPINE/	LIKE	ME! PRAY ARE YOU FLATTERING ME OR FLATTERING
JITT III	(66)	HAVE BEEN SOMEBODY LIKE YOU. /JITTA/ (STARTLED)	LIKE	ME! /AGNES/ YES; FOR HE THOUGHT A GREAT DEAL OF YOU;
NEVR III	(272)	CLANDON! YOU CANT QUARREL WITH A MERE BUTTERFLY	LIKE	ME! /MRS CLANDON/ I VERY GREATLY MISTRUST YOU, MR
FABL III	(109)	TEMPLES IN FRESCO. /THE GENTLEMAN/ (AMUSED)	LIKE	MICHAEL ANGELO, EH? /THE TOURIST/ OH, I CAN DO BETTER
MTH5	(251)	CAST SKINS AND DECAYING TEETH ON WHICH WE LIVE	LIKE	MICROBES. /ECRASIA/ ANCIENT: YOU BLASPHEME AGAINST
2TRU I	(48)	DEATH THE INNERMOST UPPERMOST LIFE IN HER RISES	LIKE	MILK IN A BOILING SAUCEPAN AND CRIES " DOWN WITH YOU!
JOAN 2	(85)	AGAIN CONTEMPTUOUS) MINDING YOUR OWN BUSINESS IS	LIKE	MINDING YOUR OWN BODY; IT'S THE SHORTEST WAY TO MAKE
DEST	(163)	BLUE EYES? IT'S A LIE: YOUR EYES ARE NOT	LIKE	MINE: THEYRE EXACTLY LIKE YOUR OWN. /NAPOLEON/ (WITH
BULL I	(86)	ROSSCULLEN; AND THAT SON'S CHARACTER WILL BE SO	LIKE	MINE AND SO UNLIKE YOURS THAT EVERYBODY WILL ACCUSE ME
MRS PREFACE	(151)	WAR THAT THE BAN ON A COMPARATIVELY PRUDISH PLAY	LIKE	MINE BECAME RIDICULOUS AND HAD TO BE LIFTED. ALSO I
ARMS III	(58)	IN THE CHARGE THAT THE MEN WHOSE FATHERS ARE POOR	LIKE	MINE WERE ANY LESS BRAVE THAN THE MEN WHO ARE RICH LIKE
2TRU III	(83)	YOU THOUGHT YOU COULD HAVE A FACE AND A FIGURE	LIKE	MINE WITH THE LIMITATIONS OF A GORILLA. YOURE FINDING
PLES PREFACE	(R15)	AN UNACTED CLASSIC BY SUCH A COMMITTEE; AND CASES	LIKE	MINE WOULD STILL LEAVE FORLORN HOPES LIKE THE
OVER	(190)	I OUGHTNT TO LIKE YOUR WIFE; AND YOU OUGHTNT TO	LIKE	MINE; AND IF WE DO, WE OUGHTNT TO GO ON LIKING THEM.
APPL I	(238)	DEPARTMENTS, ESPECIALLY DEPARTMENTS MANAGED,	LIKE	MINE, BY FEMALES. THEY WOULD DIG UP THE VERY MACHINES
BULL PREFACE	(59)	THAN THEY WOULD HAVE GOT ANYWHERE FOR THE	LIKE	MISCONDUCT. ONE CAN IMAGINE WHAT WOULD HAVE HAPPENED TO
HART III	(133)	SUCH PEOPLE TO START THE FACTORIES. I FIND PEOPLE	LIKE	MISS DUNN'S FATHER TO WORK THEM, AND KEEP A TIGHT HAND
METH PREFACE	(R9)	WHO WANTS TO MAKE OUT THAT WE ALL HAVE TAILS	LIKE	MONKEYS," I TRIED TO EXPLAIN THAT WHAT DARWIN HAD
MIS.	(195)	IF MY FATHER WOULD CONTRIBUTE. BUT I SHOULD	LIKE	MORE. /TARLETON/ IT'S PURELY A QUESTION OF MONEY WITH
LION PREFACE	(27)	MATTHEW IMPUTES BIGOTRY TO JESUS. MATTHEW,	LIKE	MOST BIOGRAPHERS, STRIVES TO IDENTIFY THE OPINIONS AND
KING PREFACE	(156)	HIS SECRET PENSIONER. THE TRUTH IS THAT CHARLES,	LIKE	MOST ENGLISH KINGS, WAS CONTINUALLY IN MONEY
BULL IV	(161)	IT DOESNT MEAN ANYTHING: IT'S BY A GERMAN JEW,	LIKE	MOST ENGLISH PATRIOTIC SENTIMENT. NEVER MIND ME, MY
GENV PREFACE	(23)	AND CONFUSED. POPULAR LOGIC ABOUT THEM IS,	LIKE	MOST HUMAN LOGIC, MERE ASSOCIATION OF IDEAS, OR, TO
BARB III	(340)	WRAPPED UP IN IT. /CUSINS/ THAT IS PERHAPS WHY,	LIKE	MOST INTELLIGENT PEOPLE, I NEVER VOTE. /UNDERSHAFT/
JITT PREFACE	(4)	GERMAN LANGUAGE NOR PLEAD IGNORANCE OF IT, I AM	LIKE	MOST LITERARY PERSONS; I HAVE SPENT SEVERAL HOLIDAYS IN
SUPR I	(23)	ALL IF YOU HAVE NO PURPOSE OF YOUR OWN, AND ARE,	LIKE	MOST MEN, A MERE BREADWINNER. BUT YOU, TAVY, ARE AN
GETT	(357)	WAY, POLLY, ABSOLUTELY NOTHING. /MRS GEORGE/ HM!	LIKE	MOST MEN, YOU THINK YOU KNOW EVERYTHING A WOMAN WANTS,
CLEO NOTES	(210)	CHARLES XII OR NELSON OR JOAN OF ARC, WHO WERE,	LIKE	MOST MODERN " SELF-MADE" MILLIONAIRES, HALF-WITTED
OVER PREFACE	(167)	IT? WHAT DID YOU SAY TO YOURSELF ABOUT IT? IF,	LIKE	MOST MURDERERS, YOU HAD NOT BEEN HANGED, WOULD YOU HAVE
JOAN PREFACE	(22)	SELF-RESPECT OF THE BADLY DEMORALIZED ARMY THAT,	LIKE	MOST OF HER POLICY, IT JUSTIFIED ITSELF AS SOUNDLY
BULL PREFACE	(13)	TO THE REPERTORY OF THE IRISH LITERARY THEATRE.	LIKE	MOST PEOPLE WHO HAVE ASKED ME TO WRITE PLAYS, MR YEATS
CAPT III	(296)	AH; BUT I'M NOT AN ARISTOCRAT, YOU SEE. AND	LIKE	MOST POOR MEN, I'M PROUD. I DONT LIKE BEING PATRONIZED.
JOAN PREFACE	(30)	THEM. THE TRAGIC PART OF THE TRIAL WAS THAT JOAN,	LIKE	MOST PRISONERS TRIED FOR ANYTHING BUT THE SIMPLEST
UNPL PREFACE	(R25)	HER," THERE ARE CERTAIN QUESTIONS ON WHICH I AM,	LIKE	MOST SOCIALISTS, AN EXTREME INDIVIDUALIST. I BELIEVE
DEVL EPILOG	(86)	THE DEVIL'S DISCIPLE MAY HAVE ACTUALLY OCCURRED,	LIKE	MOST STORIES INVENTED BY DRAMATISTS; BUT I CANNOT
POSN PREFACE	(364)	AS A CONTRIBUTION TO HISTORY; PARTLY BECAUSE,	LIKE	MOST TRUE STORIES, IT IS MORE AMUSING THAN THE OFFICIAL
SUPR PREFACE	(R18)	PLAY FOR THE MARKET. YOU MUST THEREFORE (UNLESS,	LIKE	MOST WISE MEN, YOU READ THE PLAY FIRST AND THE PREFACE
JOAN PREFACE	(8)	IN HER PERSON. THE EVIDENT TRUTH IS THAT	LIKE	MOST WOMEN OF HER HARDY MANAGING TYPE SHE SEEMED
KING I	(190)	TEETH THEN; AND EUROPE WILL SEE THEM CRUMBLE UP	LIKE	MOTHS IN A CANDLE FLAME. /CHARLES/ IT IS A FUNNY THING,
CYMB FORWORD	(137)	AS MOZART TO HANDEL, OR WAGNER TO BEETHOVEN.	LIKE	MOZART, I HAVE NOT CONFINED MYSELF TO THE JOURNEYMAN'S
POSN PREFACE	(416)	CONSISTS OF HONORABLE AND SUCCESSFUL MANAGERS	LIKE	MR ALEXANDER, WHO KNOW NOTHING OF SUCH ABUSES, AND
DOCT II	(123)	ON NATURE IN TELLING STORIES ABOUT GENTLEMEN	LIKE	MR DUBEDAT. /BLENKINSOP/ YOU CERTAINLY DO STAND BY ONE
PYGM II	(220)	NONSENSE, GIRL! WHAT DO YOU THINK A GENTLEMAN	LIKE	MR HIGGINS CARES WHAT YOU CAME IN? /THE FLOWER GIRL/
BULL IV	(180)	BUT IF THE CHURCH OF ENGLAND CONTAINED A FEW MEN	LIKE	MR KEEGAN, I SHOULD CERTAINLY JOIN IT. /KEEGAN/ YOU DO
HART I	(59)	PEOPLE, ESPECIALLY OLD PEOPLE. /ELLIE/ I	LIKE	MR MANGAN VERY MUCH; AND I SHALL ALWAYS BE-- /MRS
DEVL II	(35)	ENEMY OF YOURS. /RICHARD/ IF ALL MY ENEMIES WERE	LIKE	MRS ANDERSON, I SHOULD BE THE BEST CHRISTIAN IN
JOAN PREFACE	(31)	REFORMERS OF THE CHURCH LIKE LUTHER; WHILST JOAN,	LIKE	MRS EDDY, WAS QUITE PREPARED TO SUPERSEDE ST PETER AS
FANY I	(281)	HAS BEEN, WITH THE EXAMPLE OF A RELIGIOUS WOMAN	LIKE	MRS KNOX BEFORE HIS EYES? I CANT UNDERSTAND HOW HE
GETT PREFACE	(227)	AND ALL THE PETTY VICES OF UNSOCIABILITY FLOURISH	LIKE	MUSHROOMS IN A CELLAR, IN THE UPPER CLASS, WHERE

MILL PREFACE(132)	NOT ONLY DID NATIONAL FACTORIES SPRING UP	LIKE	MUSHROOMS, BUT THE PRIVATE FACTORIES HAD TO BE BROUGHT
SIM II (59)	MUCH LONGER THAN YOU COULD BEAR HEAVEN. LOVE IS	LIKE	MUSIC. MUSIC IS VERY NICE: THE ORGANIST SAYS THAT WHEN
HART PREFACE(12)	ALL PRETENCES ABOUT FINE ART AND CULTURE AND THE	LIKE	MUST BE FLUNG OFF AS AN INTOLERABLE AFFECTATION; AND
SUPR IV SD(141)	IN GRANADA. WHOEVER WISHES TO KNOW WHAT IT IS	LIKE	MUST GO TO GRANADA TO SEE. ONE MAY PROSAICALLY SPECIFY
UNPL PREFACE(R8)	OF MY WANT OF SUCCESS IN FICTION. MY MIND'S EYE,	LIKE	MY BODY'S, WAS " NORMAL": IT SAW THINGS DIFFERENTLY
CAND I (82)	CONSUME WEALTH WITHOUT PRODUCING IT. GET A WIFE	LIKE	MY CANDIDA; AND YOULL ALWAYS BE IN ARREAR WITH YOUR
HART II (115)	THING TO BE MARRIED RIGHT UP TO THE HILT,	LIKE	MY DAUGHTER'S HUSBAND. THE MAN IS AT HOME ALL DAY, LIKE
2TRU III (109)	RAPT IN HIS DISCOURSE), YET THEY ARE ALL,	LIKE	MY FATHER HERE, FALLING, FALLING, FALLING ENDLESSLY AND
MILL II (174)	THE SAME SPECIES. BUT THERE ARE SOME GREAT MEN,	LIKE	MY FATHER, AND THERE ARE SOME GOOD DOCTORS, LIKE YOU.
SUPR IV (167)	AND MAKE HERSELF UGLY TO KEEP YOU IN COUNTENANCE,	LIKE	MY GRANDMOTHER. /TANNER/ SO THAT SHE MAY MAKE HER
SUPR PREFACE(R22)	BUT THE SPIDER SPINS HER WEB, AND IF THE FLY,	LIKE	MY HERO, SHEWS A STRENGTH THAT PROMISES TO EXTRICATE
MRS I (188)	OF TAKING THE MEASURE OF ONE OR TWO WOMEN VERY	LIKE	MY MOTHER. YOU MAY BACK ME TO WIN. BUT IF I HIT HARDER
MIS. PREFACE(30)	INSTITUTIONS, AND THAT SCHOOLS ARE NOT NOW A BIT	LIKE	MY OLD SCHOOL. I REPLY, WITH SIR WALTER RALEIGH, BY
JITT III (65)	I SHALL BE LEFT ALONE HERE TO HAUNT THE PLACE	LIKE	MY OWN SHADOW? I SHALL SIT ALONE, GOING OVER AND OVER
GENV IV (108)	REMEMBER MANY WITNESSES WHOSE EXPERIENCE HAS BEEN	LIKE	MY OWN. I-- /BBDE/ (THUNDERING AT HER) MADAM: YOU HAVE
SHAK PREFACE(136)	CIRCUMSTANCES INTEREST ME BECAUSE THEY ARE JUST	LIKE	MY OWN. THEY WERE A CONSIDERABLE CUT ABOVE THOSE OF
SUPR PREFACE(R10)	TO BRING THEM TO CONVICTION OF SIN. IF YOU DONT	LIKE	MY PREACHING YOU MUST LUMP IT. I REALLY CANNOT HELP IT.
JITT III (77)	MRS PETERSEN AND YOURSELF WERE IN THE LEAST	LIKE	MY RELATIONS WITH BRUNO, YOU ONLY SHEW FOR THE
MILL I (158)	I TELL YOU IT WAS A PLOT. WHY SHOULDNT PEOPLE	LIKE	MY SINGING? I CAN SING LOUDER THAN ANY TENOR ON THE
POSN (445)	THE TABLE WITH HIS FIST) MAY MY LIPS BE BLIGHTED	LIKE	MY SOUL IF EVER I TELL THAT TO YOU OR ANY MORTAL MAN!
CAPT II (259)	GOOD ONES, /BRASSBOUND/ YOU FORGET THAT I AM	LIKE	MY UNCLE, ACCORDING TO YOU. HAVE YOU ANY DOUBT AS TO
GLIM (185)	THAT SHE IS LOVELIER THAN ST CECILIA, WHO LOOKS	LIKE	MY WASHERWOMAN'S MOTHER IN HER CHAPEL IN OUR CATHEDRAL.
LADY PREFACE(211)	PERSON, WHEREAS I AM CONVINCED THAT HE WAS VERY	LIKE	MYSELF: IN FACT, IF I HAD BEEN BORN IN 1556 INSTEAD OF
SUPR III (130)	WHEN YOU HAVE A THOUSAND TIMES WEARIED OF HEAVEN,	LIKE	MYSELF AND THE COMMANDER, AND A THOUSAND TIMES WEARIED
INCA (250)	OH, CAPTAIN, HOW COULD A HUMBLE PERSON	LIKE	MYSELF BE OF ANY INTEREST TO A PRINCE WHO IS SURROUNDED
POSN PREFACE(427)	AT PRESENT, IT WILL ALSO BE USED BY WRITERS	LIKE	MYSELF FOR RAISING VERY DIFFICULT AND DISTURBING
APPL I (208)	ADMITTED JUST NOW THAT EVEN A MODEST INDIVIDUAL	LIKE	MYSELF HAD GIVEN YOUR THRONE A SHAKE OR TWO. /MAGNUS/
APPL PREFACE(194)	THEIR HOLDS WOULD BE LIFTED OUT AND TRANSFERRED (	LIKE	MYSELF IN THE ARMCHAIR) TO RAILWAY TRUCKS OR MOTOR
DOCT PREFACE(48)	ASK HOW ANY PERSON DARE SUSPECT AN HONORABLE MAN	LIKE	MYSELF OF TELLING LIES. MOST SENSIBLE AND HUMANE PEOPLE
O'FL (207)	HAS BEEN, THAT EVER TAUGHT A POOR INNOCENT LAD	LIKE	MYSELF TO PRAY NIGHT AND MORNING TO ST PATRICK TO CLEAR
FABL PREFACE(66)	TO THE MOB, IT REMAINED FOR SOME SIMPLER SOUL	LIKE	MYSELF TO TRANSLATE HIS NOMADS AND HIS UNIVERSAL
CYMB V (139)	EAGLES TAKEN AND THE FEW SURVIVORS IN FULL FLIGHT	LIKE	MYSELF. AND YOU? /PHILARIO/ MY NEWS IS EVEN WORSE.
JOAN 4 (108)	YOU ARE TOO LEARNED AND SUBTLE FOR A POOR CLERK	LIKE	MYSELF. BUT I KNOW AS A MATTER OF PLAIN COMMONSENSE
MTH1 I (5)	BE WITH MYSELF FOR EVER. I LIKE YOU; BUT I DO NOT	LIKE	MYSELF. I WANT TO BE DIFFERENT; TO BE BETTER; TO BEGIN
CAPT I (229)	INTERESTING ONE-- AT LEAST IT IS SO TO A LAWYER	LIKE	MYSELF. /RANKIN/ I SHOULD BE GLAD TO HEAR IT FOR MILES'
BARB II (302)	TO ME. I KNOW NOW THAT THE RICH MAN IS A SINNER	LIKE	MYSELF. /RUMMY/ (APPEARING ABOVE AT THE LOFT DOOR)
CAPT NOTES (301)	HE IS A FASCINATING MYSTERY TO A SEDENTARY PERSON	LIKE	MYSELF. THE HORSE, A DANGEROUS ANIMAL WHOM, WHEN I
SUPR III (88)	OVERSIGHT OR INTENTION, YOU ARE CERTAINLY DAMNED,	LIKE	MYSELF; AND THERE IS NOTHING FOR IT NOW BUT TO MAKE THE
UNPL PREFACE(R8)	BY SELLING MY WORKS TO THE TEN PER CENT WHO WERE	LIKE	MYSELF; BUT A MOMENT'S REFLECTION SHEWED ME THAT THESE
METH PREFACE(R58)	WHOM I WAS ON INTIMATE TERMS, WERE NOT CREATURES	LIKE	MYSELF, BUT WERE BRUTAL WHILST I WAS REASONABLE, I NOT
3PLA PREFACE(R37)	AUTHOR, AND MUCH MORE A RATHER ARROGANT ONE	LIKE	MYSELF, MAY PROFESS TO HAVE SOMETHING TO SAY BY THIS
APPL PREFACE(193)	SOMEWHAT UNIMAGINATIVE OFFICIALDOM WHICH HAD NOT,	LIKE	MYSELF, SAT ON HIS TRUCKS, AND PROBABLY SET HIM DOWN AS
LION PREFACE(50)	GESTURES AND RESOUNDING LIES. NOW THOSE WHO,	LIKE	MYSELF, SEE THE BARABBASQUE SOCIAL ORGANIZATION AS A
HART PREFACE(18)	ARTISTS IN WAR, WITH A GROWING RELISH FOR IT,	LIKE	NAPOLEON AND ALL THE OTHER SCOURGES OF MANKIND, IN
MTH4 II SD(175)	SATURNINE, AND SELF-CENTRED: IN SHORT, VERY	LIKE	NAPOLEON I, AND WEARING A MILITARY UNIFORM OF
MIS. (193)	THAT WAS BEHAVING RATHER LIKE A NAVVY. NOW I,	LIKE	NAPOLEON, AM NOT ALL ONE PIECE. ON OCCASION, AS YOU
GETT (354)	TO PERFECTION; BUT IT DOESNT FIT ME. I HAPPEN,	LIKE	NAPOLEON, TO PREFER MAHOMETANISM. (MRS GEORGE,
PYGM IV (266)	DUDGEON), /LIZA/ (DRINKING IN HIS EMOTION	LIKE	NECTAR, AND NAGGING HIM TO PROVOKE A FURTHER SUPPLY)
MIS. PREFACE(89)	ON OUR DELUSION AND BLINDNESS. WE ARE ALL	LIKE	NELL GWYNNE'S FOOTMAN, WHO DEFENDED NELL'S REPUTATION
KING I (218)	I MAKE YOU ALL GREAT YOU BECOME TERRIBLE BORES, I	LIKE	NELLY BECAUSE NOTHING CAN MAKE A COURTIER OF HER. DO
GENV PREFACE(22)	AND KNOWN THEIR LIMITATIONS. ORDINARY MORTALS	LIKE	NERO, PAUL OF RUSSIA, OUR JAMES THE SECOND, RIZA KHAN
MTH2 (75)	WEARS OUT ITS BODIES AND MINDS AND GETS NEW ONES,	LIKE	NEW CLOTHES, YOU ARE ONLY A NEW HAT AND FROCK ON EVE.
SUPR I (36)	INTELLIGENCE. WHEN THEY SUDDENLY BEGAN TO SHINE	LIKE	NEWLY LIT FLAMES IT WAS BY NO LIGHT OF THEIR OWN, BUT
BUOY PREFACE(6)	ME. INSTEAD OF REMINDING THEM CALMLY THAT,	LIKE	NEWTON, ALL I KNOW IS BUT A GRAIN OF SAND PICKED UP ON
DEST (155)	WELL, TALK TO ME ABOUT THE SUBJECT THEY	LIKE	NEXT BEST, WHATEVER THAT MAY BE. /GIUSEPPE/ (
BARB PREFACE(212)	CHRISTIANITY WAS NOT A HISTORICAL THEORY OF IT,	LIKE	NIETZSCHE'S; BUT THIS OBJECTION CANNOT BE MADE TO
BULL IV (177)	HOLY GROUND. IRELAND, SIR, FOR GOOD OR EVIL, IS	LIKE	NO OTHER PLACE UNDER HEAVEN; AND NO MAN CAN TOUCH ITS
AUGS (277)	IT IS, ISNT IT? LUCY APPEALS TO THE IMAGINATION	LIKE	NO OTHER WOMAN. BY THE WAY (HANDING OVER THE LETTER) I
JOAN EPILOG (154)	US EVER KNEW WHAT ANYTHING MEANT TO HER. SHE WAS	LIKE	NOBODY ELSE; AND SHE MUST TAKE CARE OF HERSELF WHEREVER
FABL VI (130)	4/ HOW DO YOU LIKE IT SO FAR? /RAPHAEL/ I DO NOT	LIKE	NOR DISLIKE, I EXPERIENCE. /YOUTH 3/ THAT NONSENSE WILL
BASH II,1, (99)	DATES FROM YESTERMONTH. /LUCIAN/ THERE IS A MAN I	LIKE	NOT HAUNTS THIS HOUSE. /LYDIA/ THOU SPEAKST OF CASHEL
WIDO II (47)	TO HIS AFFECTION FOR HER) YOU SHALL DO AS YOU	LIKE	NOW AND ALWAYS, MY BELOVED CHILD. I ONLY WISH TO DO AS
CAPT III (289)	TO HEAVEN-- GET US ALL TO HEAVEN. WE DO WHAT WE	LIKE	NOW. /LADY CICELY/ INDEED YOU WILL DO NOTHING OF THE
FABL VI (125)	INTO OUR HEADS? I DONT HAVE A LOT OF THOUGHTS	LIKE	NUMBER FOUR HERE. SHE IS A HIGHBROW; BUT I WAS BORN
BULL III (127)	EVER WANTED TO GIVE LAND TO PATSY FARRLL AN DHE	LIKE	O HIM? /BROADBENT/ BUT SURELY IRISH LANDLORDISM WAS
BULL III (134)	AND TO PUT TITHES ON ME, AND TO ROB ME FOR THE	LIKE	O PATSY FARRLL, BECAUSE HE'S CORNY DOYLE'S SON?
POSN PREFACE(385)	IT IS THEFT," WOULD HAVE RECEIVED, ON THE	LIKE	OCCASION AND IN THE SAME PAPER, A RESPECTFUL
CAND II (112)	AND DO YOU HEXPEC ME TO PUT UP WITH IT FROM THE	LIKE	OF ER? /MORELL/ POOH, NONSENSE! YOU CANT TAKE ANY
POSN (454)	TO BE LET KISS THE BOOK. /EMMA/ HOW COULD THE	LIKE	OF HER TELL THE TRUTH? /BABSY/ IT WOULD BE AN INSULT
LION I (125)	ON GOAT'S MILK. IS IT FAIR TO THEM TO CALL THE	LIKE	OF HIM A DOG OR A SNAKE OR A GOAT? /FERROVIUS/ I ONLY
BULL II (108)	/AUNT JUDY/ ARRA WOULD YOU MIND WHAT THE	LIKE	OF HIM WOULD TELL YOU? SURE HE'D SAY HWATEVER WAS THE
FANY I (280)	IT'S THE LIKE OF YOU THATS THE RUIN OF THE	LIKE	OF HIM. /DORA/ SO YOU ALWAYS SAY, YOU OLD DEARS. BUT
KING I (162)	GO AND TELL HIM THAT MR NEWTON IS NOT HOME TO THE	LIKE	OF HIM. /SALLY/ OH, HE'S NOT A PERSON I COULD TALK TO
O'FL (206)	KNOW, SIR. YOU HAVE TO PUT UP WITH A LOT FROM THE	LIKE	OF ME FOR THE SAKE OF THE RECRUITING. ALL THE QUALITY
PYGM IV (266)	BE ANY FEELINGS BETWEEN THE LIKE OF YOU AND THE	LIKE	OF ME. PLEASE WILL YOU TELL ME WHAT BELONGS TO ME AND
WIDO II (29)	DONT KNOW WHAT LOSS OF EMPLOYMENT MEANS TO THE	LIKE	OF ME. WHAT HARM WOULD IT DO YOU TO HELP A POOR MAN?
O'FL (210)	ENGLAND AND ENGLAND'S KING TO YOU. TO ME AND THE	LIKE	OF ME, IT MEANS TALKING ABOUT THE ENGLISH JUST THE WAY
PYGM II (240)	TREAT FOR THEM. WISH THEY SAW WHAT IT IS FOR THE	LIKE	OF ME! /HIGGINS/ I'M GLAD THE BATHROOM MET WITH YOUR
MILL III (182)	IN. NO FENCING IN OF DANGEROUS MACHINERY OR THE	LIKE	OF THAT: NOT THAT I CARE; FOR I HAVE NOTHING BUT THE
JOAN 5 (116)	THEM OFF THEIR HORSE. CANT YOU SEE THAT ALL THE	LIKE	OF THAT IS GONE BY AND DONE WITH? WHAT USE IS ARMOR
O'FL (222)	OH FIE FOR SHAME, DINNY! WHY WOULD YOU SAY THE	LIKE	OF THAT OF A DECENT HONEST GIRL, AND ONE OF THE
NEVR II (226)	SIR, THE YOUNG LADY, IN GIVING AN ORDER, OR THE	LIKE	OF THAT, WILL SAY, " REMEMBER, WILLIAM: WE CAME TO THIS
MILL III (184)	AS EVERYBODY PAYS. I GIVE EMPLOYMENT THAT THE	LIKE	OF THEM COULDNT MAKE FOR THEMSELVES. /EPIFANIA/ YOU ARE
PYGM II (242)	WHAT WE CALL SNOBBERY. /LIZA/ YOU DONT CALL THE	LIKE	OF THEM MY FRIENDS NOW, I SHOULD HOPE. THEYVE TOOK IT
FOUN (209)	TELL YOU: FIGHT. /MERCER/ OH, WAS THERE EVER THE	LIKE	OF THIS? DONT MAKE SUCH A NOISE. /BRABAZON/ I'M MAKING
LION I (112)	KEEP SILENCE THERE. DID ANYONE EVER HEAR THE	LIKE	OF THIS? /LAVINIA/ CAPTAIN: THERE WILL BE NOBODY TO
FANY III (317)	EVER COMES OF ARGUING ABOUT SUCH THINGS AMONG THE	LIKE	OF US. /KNOX/ THE LIKE OF US! ARE YOU THROWING IT IN
FANY III (317)	SUCH THINGS AMONG THE LIKE OF US. /KNOX/ THE	LIKE	OF US! ARE YOU THROWING IT IN OUR TEETH THAT YOUR
ARMS II (24)	KNOW THE POWER SUCH HIGH PEOPLE HAVE OVER THE	LIKE	OF YOU AND ME WHEN WE TRY TO RISE OUT OF OUR POVERTY
ROCK II (272)	NO: THEM BIG CLUBS IS TOO PROMISCUOUS FOR THE	LIKE	OF YOU AND ME. YOU COME AND LUNCH WITH ME: I KNOW A
PYGM IV (266)	CAREFUL. THERE CANT BE ANY FEELINGS BETWEEN THE	LIKE	OF YOU AND THE LIKE OF ME. PLEASE WILL YOU TELL ME WHAT
PYGM II (223)	I'M A GOOD GIRL, I AM; AND I KNOW WHAT THE	LIKE	OF YOU ARE, I DO. /HIGGINS/ WE WANT NONE OF YOUR LISSON
FANY I (280)	GOT MY POOR INNOCENT BOY INTO TROUBLE. IT'S THE	LIKE	OF YOU THATS THE RUIN OF THE LIKE OF HIM. /DORA/ SO YOU
PYGM II (227)	IN THEM? IVE HEARD OF GIRLS BEING DRUGGED BY THE	LIKE	OF YOU. HIGGINS WHIPS OUT HIS PENKNIFE; CUTS A
O'FL (225)	THE GOOD GOD WAS THINKING ABOUT WHEN HE MADE THE	LIKE	OF YOU. LET ME NOT SEE YOU CASTING SHEEP'S EYES AT MY
CLEO III (152)	I DO NOT NEED TO BE TOLD WHAT TO DO BY THE	LIKE	OF YOU. /APOLLODORUS/ BLOCKHEAD. (HE BEGINS SHOUTING)
MILL III (183)	IN THIS DEN? /THE MAN/ I NEVER HEARD THE	LIKE	OF YOUR CHEEK, NOT FROM NOBODY. (HE SITS DOWN TO HIS
BARB II (310)	/SHIRLEY/ WELL, I'M NOT ACCUSTOMED TO TALK TO THE	LIKE	OF YOU-- /BARBARA/ (URGENTLY) YES, YES: YOU MUST TALK
BULL II (100)	A PRIEST. /KEEGAN/ (STERNLY) IT'S NOT FOR THE	LIKE	OF YOU, PATSY, TO GO BEHIND THE INSTRUCTION OF YOUR
BARB PREFACE(239)	ALL CIVILIZED STATES BAND TOGETHER TO DRIVE HIS	LIKE	OFF THE FACE OF THE EARTH; AND IF ANY STATE REFUSES TO
O'FL (222)	GO BEGGING THROUGH IRELAND FOR, AND NEVER SEE THE	LIKE	OF. I'LL HAVE A FRENCH WIFE, I TELL YOU; AND WHEN I
BUOY II (21)	FOR A RICH HUSBAND. /HE/ WE ARE GETTING ON	LIKE	OLD FRIENDS. EVIDENTLY I PLEASE YOU. /SHE/ WHY DO YOU
FANY II (292)	IF HE HAD KNOWN ME FOR YEARS. WE GOT ON TOGETHER	LIKE	OLD FRIENDS. HE ASKED ME WOULD I HAVE SOME CHAMPAGNE;
LION PREFACE(101)	OLDER ONES IN A MARKET WHERE THE OLDEST LAMPS,	LIKE	OLD FURNITURE IN ENGLAND, ARE THE MOST HIGHLY VALUED.
GETT PREFACE(195)	YOUNG HATING AND THWARTING THE OLD FOR BEHAVING	LIKE	OLD PEOPLE, AND ALL THE OTHER ILLS, MENTIONABLE AND
APPL I (241)	HAD MY VARIETY TALENT! WHAT A QUEEN SHE'D MAKE!	LIKE	OLD QUEEN ELIZABETH, EH? DONT GRIEVE, JOE: I'LL LUNCH
DOCT II (121)	YOU SEE) WITH ALL MY TROUBLES LEFT BEHIND, JUST	LIKE	OLD TIMES. /RIDGEON/ BUT WHAT HAS HAPPENED?

MIS. (121)	AND IF JOHNNY OR HYPATIA LET SLIP A WORD THAT WAS	LIKE	OLD TIMES, I WAS DOWN ON THEM LIKE ANYTHING. AND NOW
LION PREF,FN(43)	MOST HIGH; BUT YE SHALL DIE LIKE MEN, AND FALL	LIKE	ONE
LADY PREFACE(223)	WHICH GREYBEARDS CALL DIVINE, BE RESIDENT IN MEN	LIKE	ONE ANOTHER AND NOT IN ME: I AM MYSELF ALONE." HAMLET
JOAN PREFACE(49)	THAT THESE GOOD-NATURED YOUNG MEN WERE VERY	LIKE	ONE ANOTHER IN MIND; SO I HAVE LUMPED THE TWAIN INTO A
MIS. (168)	KNOW. IT'S ODD, ISNT IT, THAT YOU AND I SHOULD BE	LIKE	ONE ANOTHER IN THAT RESPECT? CAN YOU ACCOUNT FOR IT IN
CAPT II (259)	SO FUNNY! THEY ALL HATE TO BE TOLD THAT THEY ARE	LIKE	ONE ANOTHER, /BRASSBOUND/ (WITH THE BEGINNINGS OF
CAPT II (268)	WOULD? /LADY CICELY/ NO: HE'LL TREAT ME	LIKE	ONE OF NATURE'S GENTLEMEN: LOOK AT HIS PERFECTLY
FANY EPILOG (334)	LITTLE PLAY, MISS O'DOWDA. MIND: I DONT SAY IT'S	LIKE	ONE OF SHAKESPEAR'S-- HAMLET OR THE LADY OF LYONS. YOU
DEVL I (6)	SHE CANT BE EXPECTED TO FEEL UNCLE PETER'S DEATH	LIKE	ONE OF THE FAMILY. /MRS DUDGEON/ WHAT ARE YOU TALKING
FANY PROLOG (263)	SO HE PROMISED LIKE A BIRD. THEN I THOUGHT YOUD	LIKE	ONE OF THE LATEST SORT; THE CHAPS THAT GO FOR THE
LION PREFACE(43)	HE HAD TO DIE LIKE A GOD, NOT TO SAVE HIMSELF "	LIKE	ONE OF THE PRINCES."
MIS. (124)	AND STRONG. /MRS TARLETON/ NOT HE. HE'S OVERBRED,	LIKE	ONE OF THOSE EXPENSIVE LITTLE DOGS. I LIKE A BIT OF A
MRS IV (238)	I MEAN THAT. /FRANK/ (RAISING HIS EYEBROWS	LIKE	ONE ON WHOM A NEW LIGHT HAS DAWNED, AND RISING WITH
DEVL III SD(75)	HALF RISING, STARES AT HIM; THEN LIFTS HER HANDS	LIKE	ONE WHOSE DEAREST PRAYER HAS BEEN GRANTED. /SWINDON/
GENV I (32)	AM A JEW. /SHE/ I DONT BELIEVE YOU. YOU DONT LOOK	LIKE	ONE. /THE JEW/ I AM NOT A PRIMITIVE HITTITE. YOU CANNOT
PYGM EPILOG (292)	AS ELIZA WOULD QUALIFY HIM, A TOFF), AND SPEAKS	LIKE	ONE; HE IS NICELY DRESSED, IS TREATED BY THE COLONEL AS
2TRU III (102)	AND TO LOOK LIKE AN IDIOT WHEN HE FEELS	LIKE	ONE! I HAVE BEEN DRIVEN TO SKETCHING IN WATERCOLORS
SUPR PREFACE(R20)	THE PURSUED AND DISPOSED OF. WHEN SHE IS BAFFLED,	LIKE	OPHELIA, SHE GOES MAD AND COMMITS SUICIDE; AND THE MAN
SUPR HANDBOK(228)	SHARE YOUR OBJECTIONS. TAKE CARE TO GET WHAT YOU	LIKE	OR YOU WILL BE FORCED TO LIKE WHAT YOU GET. WHERE THERE
JOAN 4 (94)	BEING DEFEATED. JARGEAU, MEUNG, BEAUGENCY, JUST	LIKE	ORLEANS. AND NOW WE HAVE BEEN BUTCHERED AT PATAY, AND
HART I (59)	HESIONE? THAT SEEMS TO ME SO EXTRAORDINARY. I	LIKE	OTHELLO. /MRS HUSHABYE/ DO YOU INDEED? HE WAS JEALOUS,
HART I (59)	THERE ARE MEN WHO HAVE DONE WONDERFUL THINGS: MEN	LIKE	OTHELLO, ONLY, OF COURSE, WHITE, AND VERY HANDSOME,
OVER PREFACE(161)	OR THE CONVENTION THAT HE SHOULD STRANGLE HER	LIKE	OTHELLO, OR TURN HER OUT OF THE HOUSE AND NEVER SEE HER
PLES PREFACE(R12)	ON THE PRESENT COMMERCIAL BASIS, ARE BUSINESSES	LIKE	OTHER BUSINESSES, DEPENDING ON THE PATRONAGE OF GREAT
PYGM II (232)	BEEN ABLE TO FEEL REALLY GROWN-UP AND TREMENDOUS,	LIKE	OTHER CHAPS. AND YET SHE'S FIRMLY PERSUADED THAT I'M AN
LION PREFACE(19)	OF AN EYEWITNESS. IT IS A CHRONICLE, FOUNDED,	LIKE	OTHER CHRONICLES, ON SUCH EVIDENCE AND RECORDS AS THE
JOAN 4 (98)	CATHOLIC COURTS ARE COMPOSED OF MORTAL MEN,	LIKE	OTHER COURTS, HOWEVER SACRED THEIR FUNCTION AND
DOCT PREFACE(5)	AND CONSCIENCE OF A DOCTOR. DOCTORS ARE JUST	LIKE	OTHER ENGLISHMEN: MOST OF THEM HAVE NO HONOR AND NO
GENV IV (98)	OF YOUR VOICE. PUBLIC ORATORY IS A FINE ART,	LIKE	OTHER FINE ARTS, IT CANNOT BE PRACTISED EFFECTIVELY
2TRU PREFACE(4)	UP IN THE FASCINATING GAME OF MAKING MONEY.	LIKE	OTHER GAMES IT IS ENJOYABLE ONLY BY PEOPLE WITH AN
HART I (70)	BOILED IN BREAD AND MILK FOR YEARS AND YEARS,	LIKE	OTHER MARRIED MEN. POOR DEVIL! (HE DISAPPEARS INTO
GENV III (74)	PRIESTS HAVE A PROFESSIONAL AIR. THEY ARE NOT	LIKE	OTHER MEN. OUR ENGLISH CLERGY ARE NOT LIKE THAT. YOU
GENV III (74)	WIDOW/ I CALL THAT WICKED. A PRIEST SHOULD NOT BE	LIKE	OTHER MEN. /THE COMMISSAR/ HAVE YOU EVER TRIED TO
MTH4 II (179)	DO IS TO ORGANIZE WAR. LOOK AT ME! I SEEM A MAN	LIKE	OTHER MEN, BECAUSE NINE-TENTHS OF ME IS COMMON
DOCT PREFACE(53)	CAPACITY AS MEMBERS OF THE PUBLIC SUBJECT TO THEM	LIKE	OTHER MEN, IS TRUE; BUT IF WE HAD TO DECIDE WHETHER
APPL INTRLUD(248)	VERY LOW SIDE TO YOU, MAGNUS. /MAGNUS/ NO DOUBT:	LIKE	OTHER MORTAL FABRICS I HAVE A WRONG SIDE AND A RIGHT
CLEO IV (182)	(COAXINGLY) NEVER MIND. TODAY YOU ARE TO BE	LIKE	OTHER PEOPLE: IDLE, LUXURIOUS, AND KIND. (SHE
MRS III (231)	THAT WAY? I TAKE THE INTEREST ON MY CAPITAL	LIKE	OTHER PEOPLE: I HOPE YOU DONT THINK I DIRTY MY OWN
MRS II (209)	TO YOU, MOTHER, THAT I HAVE A WAY OF LIFE	LIKE	OTHER PEOPLE? /MRS WARREN/ WHAT NONSENSE IS THIS YOURE
GETT PREFACE(214)	WHY THE PARTIES SHOULD NOT MARRY RESPECTABLY	LIKE	OTHER PEOPLE. AND THEY MIGHT IN THAT CASE BE RIGHT IF
HART I (50)	I HAVE BEEN AWAY, PAPA. I HAVE HAD TO GROW OLD,	LIKE	OTHER PEOPLE. /THE CAPTAIN/ (DISENGAGING HIMSELF) YOU
BUOY III (46)	THIS. IT WILL JUST END IN THEIR GETTING MARRIED	LIKE	OTHER PEOPLE. COME HOME. (SHE STORMS OUT). /MRS
SIM PRO,3, (30)	BE MAD. /THE Y.W./ OH NO. THEYRE ALL RIGHT; JUST	LIKE	OTHER PEOPLE. (TO THE PRIEST) I SAY, REVEREND. WHAT
WIDO II (41)	PEOPLE, WHO REQUIRE ROOFS TO SHELTER THEM JUST	LIKE	OTHER PEOPLE. DO YOU SUPPOSE I CAN KEEP UP THOSE ROOFS
MRS II (216)	LIZ AND I HAD TO WORK AND SAVE AND CALCULATE JUST	LIKE	OTHER PEOPLE; ELSEWAYS WE SHOULD BE AS POOR AS ANY
SIM I (39)	CHEMIST; BUT BIOLOGICAL CHEMISTS' CHILDREN ARE	LIKE	OTHER PEOPLE'S CHILDREN. /THE CLERGYMAN/ NO. NO, I
3PLA PREFACE(R26)	A PERSON AS THE FLYING DUTCHMAN, CRITICS,	LIKE	OTHER PEOPLE, SEE WHAT THEY LOOK FOR, NOT WHAT IS
GENV IV (98)	MY ELOCUTION HAS NEVER BEEN COMPLAINED OF.	LIKE	OTHER PUBLIC SPEAKERS I HAVE TAKEN PAINS TO ACQUIRE A
MRS IV (249)	OF PEOPLE QUIET. DO YOU WANT TO FIND THAT OUT,	LIKE	OTHER WOMEN, AT FORTY, WHEN YOUVE THROWN YOURSELF AWAY
LION I (122)	YOU MEAN ME. /FERROVIUS/ HOW I WISH I WERE WEAK	LIKE	OUR BROTHER HERE! FOR THEN I SHOULD PERHAPS BE MEEK
DOCT III (154)	OTHER MEN I HAD MET THAN THE THAMES EMBANKMENT IS	LIKE	OUR CORNISH COASTS. HE SAW EVERYTHING THAT I SAW, AND
BARB II (295)	YOU EVER BEEN IN LOVE WITH DISEASE AND SUFFERING,	LIKE	OUR NURSES AND PHILANTHROPISTS? SUCH PASSIONS ARE NOT
GENV PREFACE(18)	AUDIENCE. HE JOINED A CELLAR DEBATING SOCIETY (	LIKE	OUR OLD COGER'S HALL) AND THEREBY BROUGHT ITS NUMBERS
GENV PREFACE(15)	MEANING NATIVE BARBARIANS. YET THESE BARBARIANS,	LIKE	OUR OWN AT PRESENT, INCLUDED A PERCENTAGE OF THINKERS
LION PREFACE(100)	SOLDIERS, I ASK THE FRENCH GOVERNMENT, WHICH,	LIKE	OUR OWN GOVERNMENT, IS DELIBERATELY LEAVING THE
SIM PREFACE(7)	CREDULITY HAS ACTUALLY TAKEN PLACE IN COUNTRIES	LIKE	OUR OWN IN WHICH CHILDREN, FAR FROM BEING PROTECTED
LION PREFACE(36)	MARK, JESUS COMES INTO A NORMAL PHILISTINE WORLD	LIKE	OUR OWN OF TODAY. NOT UNTIL THE BAPTIST FORETELLS THAT
POSN (436)	STRONG MAN. YOU WANT A STRONG MAN FOR A ROUGH LOT	LIKE	OUR PEOPLE HERE. HE AINT AFRAID TO SHOOT AND HE AINT
WIDO I (8)	I VOTE WE GO THERE. /SARTORIUS/ QUITE	LIKE	OUR PLACE AT SURBITON, MY DEAR. /BLANCHE/ QUITE.
MILL PREFACE(129)	AND AMBITIONS, THEY WOULD, IF THEY HAD ANYTHING	LIKE	OUR PRESENT PROLETARIAT TO DEAL WITH, REESTABLISH
MTH2 (72)	ISNT LONG ENOUGH FOR A COMPLICATED CIVILIZATION	LIKE	OURS? FLINDERS PETRIE HAS COUNTED NINE ATTEMPTS AT
MIS. PREFACE(28)	IMPRESS ON A CHILD IN COMPLICATED CIVILIZATIONS	LIKE	OURS IS THE TRUTH THAT WHOEVER CONSUMES GOODS OR
APPL PREFACE(176)	MACHINERY AND PROCEDURE. WHEN WE SEE PARLIAMENTS	LIKE	OURS KICKED INTO THE GUTTER BY DICTATORS, BOTH IN
MIS. PREFACE(93)	THE HEALTHY STATE IS ATTAINABLE IN A COLD COUNTRY	LIKE	OURS ONLY BY FAMILIARITY WITH THE UNDRAPED FIGURE
MIS. PREFACE(32)	AND THE FIRST DUTY OF THE POLICE IN A STATE	LIKE	OURS WOULD BE TO SEE THAT EVERY CHILD WORE A BADGE
MIS. (122)	ARISTOCRACY, DEAR: THEYRE ONLY HUMAN CREATURES	LIKE	OURSELVES AFTER ALL; AND YOULL HOLD YOUR OWN WITH THEM
O'FL (213)	AND THIEVES, AND BACKBITERS, AND DRUNKARDS, JUST	LIKE	OURSELVES OR ANY OTHER CHRISTIANS. OH, HER LADYSHIP
MIS. (122)	ALL THE GIRLS BELONGED TO BIG BUSINESS FAMILIES	LIKE	OURSELVES. IT TAKES ALL SORTS TO MAKE A WORLD; AND I
LION PREFACE(85)	JEWS, WAS AN INTOLERABLE BLASPHEMY. TO GENTILES	LIKE	OURSELVES, A GOOD DEAL OF THE EPISTLE TO THE ROMANS IS
CAPT NOTES (303)	THE MOST UNHELPABLE OF AFFLICTIONS IN A SOCIETY	LIKE	OURS. ENGLISH AND AMERICAN DIALECTS. THE FACT THAT
FABL V (118)	THEIR METHODS WERE LIKE OURS, AND THEIR PASSIONS	LIKE	OURS. YOU COULD NOT MAKE A GREATER MISTAKE. THE SEMINAL
SUPR II (51)	NOT MERE SHOPS FOR SELLING CLASS LIMITATIONS	LIKE	OURS. YOU DESPISE OXFORD, ENRY, DONT YOU? /STRAKER/
FABL V (118)	LANGUAGE FOR THEM. YOU THINK THEIR METHODS WERE	LIKE	OURS, AND THEIR PASSIONS LIKE OURS. YOU COULD NOT MAKE
CAND I (97)	SERIOUSNESS). MY DEAR LAD: IN A HAPPY MARRIAGE	LIKE	OURS, THERE IS SOMETHING VERY SACRED IN THE RETURN OF
GETT PREFACE(202)	COULD BE ANY REAL PUBLIC OPINION IN A SOCIETY	LIKE	OURS, WHICH IS A MERE MOB OF CLASSES, EACH WITH ITS OWN
OVER (193)	KNOW HOW IT IS THAT WE CONTRIVE TO MAKE FEELINGS	LIKE	OURS, WHICH SEEM TO ME TO BE BEAUTIFUL AND SACRED
METH PREFACE(R48)	EVERY APPEARANCE OF HAVING BEEN DESIGNED,	LIKE	PALEY'S WATCH, BY A CONSCIOUS AND INTELLIGENT ARTIFICER
PHIL II (107)	AND TAKES THE CHAIR NEAR THE BOOKSTAND). I SHOULD	LIKE	PAPA TO LIVE FOR EVER JUST TO TAKE THE CONCEIT OUT OF
MIS. (143)	WERE SUPPOSED TO BE, YOU WERE REALLY AN OLD RIP	LIKE	PAPA. /LORD SUMMERHAYS/ NO, NO: NOT ABOUT YOUR FATHER:
BASH II,1, (111)	YOU. I GO TO FIND MY HAT. (EXIT.) /CASHEL/	LIKE	PARACELSUS, WHO WENT TO FIND HIS SOUL. (TO BASHVILLE)
KING II (232)	LIKE JOINING YOUR CHURCH, OR SOME LITTLE THING	LIKE	PARDONING A PRIEST OR A QUAKER CONDEMNED TO SOME CRUEL
BARB PREFACE(239)	THE DUKE OF ARGYLL WAS NOT A DEMON, BUT A MAN OF	LIKE	PASSIONS WITH OURSELVES, BY NO MEANS RANCOROUS OR CRUEL
LION PREFACE(80)	DELIRIUM OF A FREE SOUL, NOT OF A SHAMEBOUND ONE	LIKE	PAUL'S. THERE HAS REALLY NEVER BEEN A MORE MONSTROUS
SUPR III (124)	BIRTH BECOME ACQUAINTED AND COURT EACH OTHER	LIKE	PEASANTS? AND HOW MUCH DOES EVEN THE PEASANT KNOW OF
ROCK I (218)	EXCEPT THAT THEYRE IN AND OUT AT BUCKNAM PALACE	LIKE	PEERS OF THE REALM? /SIR ARTHUR/ YOU OUGHT TO BE IN
BULL IV (169)	IS: YOULL BE MAD TO GET ME IN. BESIDES, YOUD	LIKE	PEOPLE TO SAY THAT TOM BROADBENT'S WIFE HAD BEEN THE
MRS III (230)	SAYS YOU KEEP A PUBLIC-HOUSE. YOU WOULDNT	LIKE	PEOPLE TO SAY THAT OF YOUR MOTHER, WOULD YOU? THATS
GETT PREFACE(189)	THAT WE ARE FORCED TO THROW ASIDE OUR MODESTY	LIKE	PEOPLE WHO, AWAKENED BY AN ALARM OF FIRE, RUSH INTO THE
CAPT II (261)	LIKE HER. YOU KNOW, DONT YOU, THAT IF YOU DONT	LIKE	PEOPLE YOU THINK OF ALL THE REASONS FOR NOT HELPING
GETT PREFACE(234)	GROUNDS FOR DIVORCE. IF WE TAKE A DOCUMENT	LIKE	PEPYS' DIARY, WE LEARN THAT A WOMAN MAY HAVE AN
JOAN PREFACE(30)	HER OF. SHE WAS MUCH MORE LIKE MARK TWAIN THAN	LIKE	PETER CAUCHON. HER ATTACHMENT TO THE CHURCH WAS VERY
FANY III (317)	AND WHEN THEYRE UPSET, WHERE ARE WE? JUST	LIKE	PETER IN THE STORM TRYING TO WALK ON THE WATER AND
LION I (123)	/FERROVIUS/ SPLENDID TO BETRAY MY MASTER,	LIKE	PETER! SPLENDID TO ACT LIKE ANY COMMON BLACKGUARD IN
PYGM EPILOG (300)	NEVER PALLED, GRASPED THE FACT THAT BUSINESS,	LIKE	PHONETICS, HAS TO BE LEARNED. ON THE PITEOUS SPECTACLE
BUOY III (30)	YOUTH/ HE PICKS UP HIS SOLICITOR FOR THE JOB,	LIKE	PICKING UP A TAXI. /THE WIDOWER/ THERE IS SOMETHING TO
DEVL III (72)	MUSIC AND A CLERGYMAN TO MAKE MURDER LOOK	LIKE	PIETY! DO YOU SUPPOSE I AM GOING TO HELP YOU? YOUVE
CATH 2 (177)	LIKE A PIG. /PATIOMKIN/ (PLAINTIVELY) NO: NOT	LIKE	PIG. LIKE PRINCE. LIL MOTHER MADE POOR PATIOMKIN
MILL PREFACE(117)	IN THE OLD FASHION AGAINST SLAUGHTERING MACHINERY	LIKE	PIGS IN CHICAGO? NAPOLEON'S BOOKLEARNT TACTICS AND THE
WIDO III (57)	DIRTY, DRUNKEN, DISREPUTABLE PEOPLE WHO LIVE	LIKE	PIGS. IF THEY MUST BE PROVIDED FOR, LET OTHER PEOPLE
LION PREFACE(3)	THAN PILATE WAS, OR YOU, GENTLE READER; AND YET,	LIKE	PILATE, I GREATLY PREFER JESUS TO ANNAS AND CAIAPHAS;
CURE (229)	CASE). /REGINALD/ BETTER LEAVE ME A LOT, I	LIKE	PILLS. /THE DOCTOR/ THANK YOU: I'M NOT TREATING YOU
MIS. PREFACE(23)	AT HELLERAU NEAR DRESDEN. JACQUES DALCROZE,	LIKE	PLATO, BELIEVES IN SATURATING HIS PUPILS WITH MUSIC.
SIM PRO,2, (26)	THINK IT IS. THE BIGGEST LINERS CAN GET CLOSE UP.	LIKE	PLYMOUTH. LIKE LULWORTH COVE. DONT STAND SO CLOSE.
OVER PREFACE(162)	UP TO THEM ARE NO ESSENTIAL PART OF LIFE, THOUGH,	LIKE	POISONS AND BUTTERED SLIDES AND RED-HOT POKERS, THEY
NEVR III (277)	YEARS WITHOUT FINDING OUT THAT HE HATES YOU	LIKE	POISON, YOU WOULD SOON HAVE YOUR EYES OPENED. THERE WE
JOAN PREFACE(54)	COMEDY AS I HATE SERMONS AND SYMPHONIES; BUT I	LIKE	POLICE NEWS AND DIVORCE NEWS AND ANY KIND OF DANCING OR
KING I (214)	SOCIETY. /NELL/ ORANGE GIRLS AND PLAYERS AND SUCH	LIKE	POOR FOLK THINK NOTHING OF MENTIONING THEM. THEY HAVE

PLES PREFACE(R9)	YOU FIND THAT HE " WRITES LIKE AN ANGEL AND TALKS	LIKE	POOR POLL," AND IS HIMSELF THE FIRST TO MAKE THAT
2TRU I (49)	/THE NURSE/ IF YOU ARE GOING TO START PREACHING	LIKE	POPSY, THE MILKMAN WILL BE HERE BEFORE WE GET AWAY.
METH PREFACE(R82)	SIMPLE SORT OF VITALISM IS ALWAYS WITH US, AND,	LIKE	PORTRAIT PAINTING, KEEPS THE ARTIST SUPPLIED WITH
MIS. (165)	FACE, AND EVERY WOMAN WHO LIKES ME IS TO BEHAVE	LIKE	POTIPHAR'S WIFE, THEN I SHALL BE A SLAVE: THE SLAVE OF
HART PREFACE(35)	BEST CLOTHES; WHERE STORIES OF IMPROPER FEMALES	LIKE	POTIPHAR'S WIFE, AND EROTIC POETRY LIKE THE SONG OF
SIM I SD(38)	COME OUT HERE. PROLA COMES DOWN THE STEPS. SHE,	LIKE	PRA, IS TWENTY YEARS OLDER; BUT THE YEARS HAVE ONLY
PYGM II (240)	YOURSELF, AND A WOODEN BOWL OF SOAP SMELLING	LIKE	PRIMROSES. NOW I KNOW WHY LADIES IS SO CLEAN. WASHING'S
CATH 4 (188)	YOU THINK YOU CAN ESCAPE BY APPEALING,	LIKE	PRINCE PATIOMKIN, TO MY SENSE OF HUMOR? /EDSTASTON/
CATH 2 (177)	PIG. /PATIOMKIN/ (PLAINTIVELY) NO: NOT LIKE PIG.	LIKE	PRINCE. LIL MOTHER MADE POOR PATIOMKIN PRINCE. WHAS USE
PYGM V (279)	THANK YOU. ELIZA, OF COURSE. /LIZA/ AND I SHOULD	LIKE	PROFESSOR HIGGINS TO CALL ME MISS DOOLITTLE. /HIGGINS/
SIM PREFACE(13)	PLANTERS IN CERTAIN DISTRICTS HAD FOUND THE	LIKE	PROFITABLE TERM FOR SLAVES TO BE EIGHT YEARS. IN FULLY
DOCT I (88)	VERY INTERESTING. /RIDGEON/ WELL, THERES NOTHING	LIKE	PROGRESS, IS THERE? /SIR PATRICK/ DONT MISUNDERSTAND
CAND II (112)	TREMENDOUS HEARTINESS) OH, NOW, ISNT THAT EXACTLY	LIKE	PROSSY? SHE'S SO FRANK: SHE CANT CONTAIN HERSELF!
MTH5 (230)	WERE CRUDE. THEY MIXED UP MESSES THAT WERE SO	LIKE	PROTOPLASM THAT THEY COULD NOT TELL THE DIFFERENCE. BUT
ROCK PREFACE(154)	THE BOTTOM BY UNPROPERTIED POLITICAL PHILOSOPHERS	LIKE	PROUDHON AND MARX, PRIVATE PROPERTY IS SOONER OR LATER
MTH3 (98)	THE WORK YOU DO, YOU SEEM TO ME POSITIVELY TO	LIKE	PUBLIC BUSINESS. WHY WONT YOU LET ME TAKE YOU DOWN TO
POSN PREFACE(415)	INDIGNANTLY AGAINST MY ADMISSION THAT THEATRES,	LIKE	PUBLIC-HOUSES, NEED SPECIAL CONTROL ON THE GROUND THAT
LION PREFACE(24)	WHOSE COMIC ROGUERIES BROUGHT HIM TO A BAD END	LIKE	PUNCH OR TIL EULENSPIEGEL: AN INVENTION WHICH COST THEM
PYGM EPILOG (303)	AND MR DOOLITTLE. GALATEA NEVER DOES QUITE	LIKE	PYGMALION: HIS RELATION TO HER IS TOO GODLIKE TO BE
MTH5 (248)	PLAYED WITH RAG DOLLS. /THE HE-ANCIENT/ AT LAST,	LIKE	PYGMALION, YOU DEMAND FROM YOUR DOLLS THE FINAL
JOAN PREFACE(3)	THE PIONEER OF RATIONAL DRESSING FOR WOMEN, AND,	LIKE	QUEEN CHRISTINA OF SWEDEN TWO CENTURIES LATER, TO SAY
APPL PREFACE(172)	GEORGE THE THIRD AND QUEEN VICTORIA WERE NOT,	LIKE	QUEEN ELIZABETH, THE NATURAL SUPERIORS OF THEIR
JOAN PREFACE(19)	HER MAN'S DRESS, AND INSTEAD OF URGING CHARLES,	LIKE	QUEEN VICTORIA URGING THE WAR OFFICE TO SEND ROBERTS TO
MTH1 II (26)	MASTERS, ARE DESPISED AND REJECTED, AND SLAIN	LIKE	RABBITS. HE WHO BEARS THE BRAND OF CAIN SHALL RULE THE
ROCK PREFACE(152)	DRIVEN-OFFS CROWD INTO THE FACTORIES AND MULTIPLY	LIKE	RABBITS; AND FOR THE MOMENT POPULATION GROWS INSTEAD OF
BULL PREFACE(59)	IT IN HIS HOUSE, WHERE HIS MOTHER SAT ON IT,	LIKE	RACHEL ON LABAN'S STOLEN TERAPHIM, UNTIL SHE WAS
MIS. PREFACE(92)	THEM MALIGNANTLY. AT BEST, SUCH QUALITIES ARE	LIKE	RARE AND BEAUTIFUL BIRDS: WHEN THEY APPEAR THE WHOLE
HART III (145)	OF HER RUSTY PLATES, THE DROWNING OF THE CREW	LIKE	RATS IN A TRAP. /ELLIE/ MORAL: DONT TAKE RUM. /CAPTAIN
CLEO III (163)	TO SEE) CURSES! IT IS TRUE. WE ARE CAUGHT	LIKE	RATS IN A TRAP. /CAESAR/ (RUTHFULLY) RUFIO, RUFIO: MY
FANY III (323)	ARE OVERPOWERED BY TREASON, WE CAN DIE FIGHTING	LIKE	RATS, AND WE ARE FOOLISH ENOUGH TO BE PROUD OF IT! WHY
FANY III (323)	OLD GROGNARDS DIED FIGHTING RATHER THAN SURRENDER	LIKE	REASONABLE BEINGS. THINK OF YOUR GREAT WELLINGTON:
GETT PREFACE(194)	HOME LIFE AND DOMESTIC SENTIMENT TO SOMETHING	LIKE	REASONABLE PROPORTIONS IN THE LIFE OF THE INDIVIDUAL,
DOCT PREFACE(25)	EXPECT TO FIND VACCINES AND ANTI-TOXINS AND THE	LIKE	RETAILED AT " POPULAR PRICES" IN PRIVATE ENTERPRISE
LADY PREFACE(220)	IN A THOUSAND FARCES BY MEN OF NO GENIUS. WILDE,	LIKE	RICHARD AND SHAKESPEAR, FOUND IN HIMSELF NO PITY FOR
SUPR HANDBOK(210)	BUT THAT MAN SHOULD WILL THEM, PERCEIVE AT LAST,	LIKE	RICHARD WAGNER, THAT THE FACT TO BE FACED IS THAT MAN
FABL PREFACE(83)	POLITICAL ADVENTURERS AND " TIN JESUSES" ROSE	LIKE	ROCKETS TO DICTATORSHIPS AND FELL TO EARTH LIKE STICKS,
GENV IV (125)	DIE DECENTLY, STOICALLY, STEADFAST AT OUR POSTS,	LIKE	ROMANS. REMEMBER! WE SHALL NOT DECAY: WE SHALL STAND TO
BARB PREFACE(244)	THAT MUST BE SET RIGHT, OR WE SHALL PERISH,	LIKE	ROME, OF SOUL ATROPHY DISGUISED AS EMPIRE. THE FIRST
KING I (172)	SO BEAUTIFULLY? I THOUGHT PHILOSOPHERS WERE	LIKE	ROMISH PRIESTS, NOT ALLOWED TO MARRY. /NEWTON/ IS MY
SUPR PREFACE(R20)	HUNT THE MAN DOWN. SHE MAY DO IT BY CHARMING HIM,	LIKE	ROSALIND, OR BY STRATAGEM, LIKE MARIANA; BUT IN EVERY
2TRU III (110)	KISS AND CARESS AND CUDDLE UNTIL GIRLS WHO ARE	LIKE	ROSES AT EIGHTEEN ARE LIKE BATTERED DEMIREPS AT
SIM I (50)	OF THIS GARDEN AND MAKE FOR HOME. BUT IT WOULD BE	LIKE	RUSHING OUT OF HEAVEN. I AM MOST UNHAPPY; AND YET I AM
SUPR HANDBOK(210)	COOL THEIR PORRIDGE (IF THEY CAN GET ANY). MEN	LIKE	RUSKIN AND CARLYLE WILL PREACH TO SMITH AND BROWN FOR
BARB PREFACE(218)	ARISTOCRATS WITH A DEVELOPED SENSE OF LIFE-- MEN	LIKE	RUSKIN AND WILLIAM MORRIS AND KROPOTKIN-- HAVE ENORMOUS
PHIL I (82)	A GENTLEMAN-- AS AN ENGLISHMAN-- AS ANYTHING YOU	LIKE	-- I WILL NEVER SEE HER AGAIN, NEVER SPEAK TO HER,
MRS II (207)	ON THE WEDDING DAY, YOU CAN NAME ANY FIGURE YOU	LIKE	-- IN REASON. /MRS WARREN/ SO IT COMES TO THAT WITH
NEVR IV (283)	BEGINS TO TALK TO ME LIKE THAT AND TO LOOK AT ME	LIKE	-- (HE BREAKS OFF AND BURIES HIS HEAD IN HIS HANDS).
JOAN 4 (98)	HERE, BUT THE OPINIONS -- THE PREJUDICES, IF YOU	LIKE	-- OF A FRENCH COURT. /WARWICK/ (CORRECTING) A
MIS. PREFACE(73)	THE SCHOOL DUNCE -- MEANING THE ONE WHO DOES NOT	LIKE	-- OFTEN TURNS OUT WELL AFTERWARDS, AS IF IDLENESS WERE
GETT (281)	NAMED HOTCHKISS. /REGINALD/ A FELLOW WITH A FACE	LIKE	-- /LEO/ YOU SHANT, REJJY. HE HAS A VERY FINE FACE.
DEST (160)	WHAT WAS HE LIKE? /LIEUTENANT/ LIKE! HE WAS	LIKE	-- WELL, YOU OUGHT TO HAVE JUST SEEN THE FELLOW: THAT
METH PREFACE(R28)	THEY HAVE BEEN PUSHED BACK (OR FORWARD, IF YOU	LIKE	) FROM POST-NATAL TO PRE-NATAL ONES. THE CHILD IN THE
OVER PREFACE(168)	OF QUESTIONS TO FIND OUT WHAT MURDER IS REALLY	LIKE	; AND I SHOULD NOT BE SATISFIED UNTIL I HAD REALIZED
O'FL (218)	I LIKE; AND I'LL SHAKE HANDS WITH WHAT KINGS I	LIKE	; AND IF YOUR OWN SON IS NOT GOOD ENOUGH FOR YOU, YOU
O'FL (218)	INSULTED BY HIS OWN MOTHER, I'LL FIGHT FOR WHO I	LIKE	; AND I'LL SHAKE HANDS WITH WHAT KINGS I LIKE; AND IF
GETT (309)	A WEDDING MORNING TO HELP WITH THE FLOWERS OR THE	LIKE	; AND SHE HAS ALWAYS REFUSED. BUT IF YOU ORDER HER TO
GETT PREFACE(250)	SCRAP-HEAP WITH THE SALE OF INDULGENCES AND THE	LIKE	; AND SO THE REFORMATION LEFT MARRIAGE WHERE IT WAS: A
ARMS II (24)	AND SERVE THE FAMILY FAITHFULLY. THATS WHAT THEY	LIKE	; AND THATS HOW YOULL MAKE MOST OUT OF THEM. /LOUKA/ (
PYGM II (239)	IS A LOT OF MONEY: IT MAKES A MAN FEEL PRUDENT	LIKE	; AND THEN GOODBYE TO HAPPINESS. YOU GIVE ME WHAT I ASK
LADY (248)	GIVE THE SILLIER SORT OF PEOPLE WHAT THEY BEST	LIKE	; AND WHAT THEY BEST LIKE, GOD KNOWS, IS NOT THEIR OWN
GLIM (177)	HAS BEEN TAUGHT BY FENCERS AND WRESTLERS AND THE	LIKE	; BUT I CAN TAKE ALL YOU CAN GIVE ME WITHOUT TURNING A
FANY III (301)	IVE OWNED UP. YOU CAN PUT IT ALL ON ME IF YOU	LIKE	; BUT I DONT BELIEVE YOU CARE ANY MORE THAN I DO.
ROCK II (274)	SIR ARTHUR? YOU CAN CALL ME BROLLY IF YOU	LIKE	; BUT I PREFER ALOYSIA. /SIR ARTHUR/ CERTAINLY.
LION PREFACE(80)	MOTOR CAR. THAT WAS DELIRIOUS, IF YOU	LIKE	; BUT IT WAS THE DELIRIUM OF A FREE SOUL, NOT OF A
FANY III (314)	SIT WELL ON YOU. YOU MAY CALL IT PREACHING IF YOU	LIKE	; BUT IT'S THE TRUTH FOR ALL THAT. I SAY THAT IF YOUVE
MILL I (160)	WAS ANOTHER MAN. YOU MAY BELIEVE IT OR NOT AS YOU	LIKE	; BUT MY HATS WERE REALLY TOO SMALL FOR ME. /EPIFANIA/
DEST (160)	UP WITH THIS OUTRAGE FROM THE AUSTRIANS IF YOU	LIKE	; BUT SPEAKING FOR MYSELF PERSONALLY, I TELL YOU THAT
PYGM I (210)	BOO-- HOO-- OO-- /THE NOTE TAKER/ LIVE WHERE YOU	LIKE	; BUT STOP THAT NOISE. /THE GENTLEMAN/ (TO THE GIRL)
JITT II (38)	THE RIGHT MAN FOR HER. HE WAS HER SUPERIOR IF YOU	LIKE	; BUT THAT ONLY MADE IT WORSE FOR HER. HIS SUPERIORITY
CAPT III (297)	TO BE ABLE TO MAKE ME DO PRETTY WELL WHAT YOU	LIKE	; BUT YOU CANT MAKE ME MARRY ANYBODY BUT YOURSELF.
NEVR II (239)	CHILD! NO, NO: YOU MAY CALL ME DOLLY IF YOU	LIKE	; BUT YOU MUSNT CALL ME CHILD. (SHE SLIPS HER ARM
MILL I (156)	TO AN INSECT. /ALASTAIR/ YOU MAY SAY WHAT YOU	LIKE	; BUT YOU WERE JUST AS MUCH IN LOVE WITH ME AS I WAS
HART II (88)	YOU ARE FREE TO THROW OVER OUR ENGAGEMENT IF YOU	LIKE	; BUT, IF YOU DO, YOULL NEVER ENTER HESIONE'S HOUSE
APPL I (206)	MORE TO ME THAN BEEF. CALL IT A SOUL IF YOU	LIKE	; ONLY NOT IN A SUPERSTITIOUS SENSE, IF YOU UNDERSTAND
DOCT PREFACE(73)	CONSEQUENCES OF NEGLECT OF BY-LAWS AND THE	LIKE	; THEREFORE IT WILL BE IMPORTANT THAT EVERY M.O.H.
LION PREFACE(13)	THE MURDER OF ONE OF HIS RIGHTEOUS SERVANTS IS	LIKE	SACRIFICING A MANGY SHEEP OR AN OX WITH THE RINDERPEST:
2TRU III (109)	TO FLIGHT UP THE PATH THROUGH THE GAP), MOPS,	LIKE	SAINT TERESA, TO FOUND AN UNLADYLIKE SISTERHOOD WITH
GETT PREFACE(234)	UNDER CONSIDERATION. ALSO, AFFECTIONATE HUSBANDS	LIKE	SAMUEL PEPYS, AND AFFECTIONATE WIVES OF THE
UNPL PREFACE(R26)	WHICH THE DEFECTS MAKE INEVITABLE, AND WHO OFTEN,	LIKE	SARTORIUS AND MRS WARREN, DISPLAY VALUABLE EXECUTIVE
MILL PREFACE(116)	NAPOLEON WOULD HAVE BEEN ONLY A FAMOUS GENERAL	LIKE	SAXE OR WELLINGTON OR MARLBOROUGH, WHO UNDER SIMILAR
MIS. PREFACE(103)	AND BROKEN SPIRIT OF A SLAVE CAN BE FREE. IT IS	LIKE	SAYING TO A LABORER BROUGHT UP ON A FAMILY INCOME OF
MIS. PREFACE(103)	ARE RIGHT WHEN THEY SAY THAT GOVERNMENTS,	LIKE	SCHOOLMASTERS, TRY TO SIMPLIFY THEIR TASK BY DESTROYING
BARB PREFACE(211)	NECESSARY GERMAN, IF I HAD SEEN IT. NIETZSCHE,	LIKE	SCHOPENHAUER, IS THE VICTIM IN ENGLAND OF A SINGLE MUCH
PYGM V (287)	SMELL IT WITHOUT ANY TRAINING OR ANY WORK. NOT	LIKE	SCIENCE AND LITERATURE AND CLASSICAL MUSIC AND
DOCT III (151)	WOMAN; NO MEDICINE LIKE CHEERFULNESS; NO RESOURCE	LIKE	SCIENCE; GOODBYE, GOODBYE, GOODBYE. (HAVING SHAKEN
BARB PREFACE(210)	FORMULA TO REMEMBER THAT PLAYWRIGHTS,	LIKE	SCULPTORS, STUDY THEIR FIGURES FROM LIFE, AND NOT FROM
MILL IV (206)	WOULD RESIST A TEMPERATURE THAT MELTED PLATINUM	LIKE	SEALING WAX. /EPIFANIA/ BUY HIS PATENT FOR ME IF IT HAS
MRS III (223)	PRAED. COME! HONESTLY, DEAR PRADDY, DO YOU	LIKE	SEEING THEM TOGETHER? /PRAED/ OH, WHY NOT? /FRANK/ (
VWOO 3 (140)	NO CHANCES. I DONT SET UP TO BE MASTERFUL: I DONT	LIKE	SELFISH UPPISH DOMINEERING PEOPLE ANY MORE THAN YOU DO;
MRS III (232)	WHEN ALL THE REST ARE POCKETING WHAT THEY CAN,	LIKE	SENSIBLE MEN? NO SUCH FOOL! IF YOURE GOING TO PICK
VWOO 3 (141)	DONT KNOW. YOU ARE THE DUPE OF THOUGHTLESS WORDS	LIKE	SENSUALITY, SENSUOUSNESS, AND ALL THE REST OF THE
LION PREFACE(45)	MIDDLE AGES TOOK A FANCY TO SOME FAMILIAR NUMBER	LIKE	SEVEN; AND BECAUSE IT WAS AN ODD NUMBER, AND THE WORLD
SUPR III (90)	HERE. AS SAITH THE POET, " HELL IS A CITY MUCH	LIKE	SEVILLE." /THE OLD WOMAN/ HAPPY! HERE! WHERE I AM
DOCT PREFACE(31)	VIVISECTION, AND ASSURING YOU THAT PEOPLE	LIKE	SHAKESPEAR AND DR JOHNSON AND RUSKIN AND MARK TWAIN ARE
HART II (93)	CHARACTER. I THINK IT IS BECAUSE I TAUGHT HER TO	LIKE	SHAKESPEAR WHEN SHE WAS VERY YOUNG. /MRS HUSHABYE/ (
NEVR II (235)	PUTS US ALL TO SHAME. /DOLLY/ YOU REALLY ARE	LIKE	SHAKESPEAR, WILLIAM. /WAITER/ NOT AT ALL, SIR. DONT
FABL PREFACE(96)	TWO AND TWO TOGETHER POLITICALLY THAT THEY VOTE	LIKE	SHEEP FOR THE LANDLORDS, AND DENOUNCE LAND
ROCK PREFACE(151)	HIGHLAND CHIEFS AND THEIR CLANSMEN WERE BUTCHERED	LIKE	SHEEP ON THE FIELD. HAD THEY BEEN MERELY PRISONERS OF
MILL PREFACE(120)	THAT HAD NOT SAVED THEM FROM BEING DRIVEN	LIKE	SHEEP TO THE SHAMBLES. OF THIS CHANGE OUR
CLEO PRO2 (100)	AND YOUR MEN? /BEL AFFRIS/ FLED. SCATTERED	LIKE	SHEEP. /BELZANOR/ (FURIOUSLY) THE COWARDLY SLAVES!
JOAN 1 (69)	THEN THEY WILL DRIVE THE POOR GODDAMS BEFORE THEM	LIKE	SHEEP. YOU AND POLLY WILL LIVE TO SEE THE DAY WHEN
PRES (155)	MINISTERS IN POLICE COURTS, AND GO TO PRISON	LIKE	SHEEP, AND SUFFER AND SACRIFICE THEMSELVES. THIS
SUPR PREFACE(R14)	DID IT ENABLE BYRON TO BECOME A RELIGIOUS FORCE	LIKE	SHELLEY. LET US, THEN, LEAVE BYRON'S DON JUAN OUT OF
APPL PREFACE(183)	WERE TO STOP, OUR PRIVATE ENTERPRISES WOULD DROP	LIKE	SHOT STAGS, AND WE SHOULD ALL BE DEAD IN A MONTH. WHEN
DOCT IV (163)	/LOUIS/ SUCH A COLOR! GARNET COLOR. WAVING	LIKE	SILK. LIQUID LOVELY FLAME FLOWING UP THROUGH THE BAY
GETT (280)	OF HIM. I LIKE HIM BECAUSE HE WANTS ME; AND I	LIKE	SINJON BECAUSE I WANT HIM. I FEEL THAT I HAVE A DUTY TO
APPL PREFACE(192)	TOLD ME THAT THIS WAS EXACTLY WHAT HE WAS: JUST	LIKE	SIR CHRISTOPHER WREN. HE HAD BEEN CONCERNED IN AN

BARB PREFACE(222)	BUT BY RELIGIOUS AND PHILOSOPHICAL PUBLICISTS	LIKE	SIR OLIVER LODGE AND DR STANTON COIT, AND STRENUOUS
MIS. PREFACE(99)	FOR PEOPLE STEEPED IN THE BIBLE FROM CHILDHOOD	LIKE	SIR WALTER SCOTT AND RUSKIN, A DEAD LANGUAGE. BESIDES,
LION PREFACE(88)	THERE TO ALL ETERNITY. AND SCEPTICAL PHYSICISTS	LIKE	SIR WILLIAM CROOKES DEMONSTRATE BY LABORATORY
SUPR III (130)	THERE IS NOTHING BUT LOVE AND BEAUTY. UGH! IT IS	LIKE	SITTING FOR ALL ETERNITY AT THE FIRST ACT OF A
SUPR I (46)	TO ME. IF YOU WERE A MARRIED WOMAN YOU WOULD NOT	LIKE	SITTING IN THE HOUSEKEEPER'S ROOM AND BEING TREATED
MIS. (144)	TO LIVE. IVE GROWN OUT OF THE MUD PIES; BUT I	LIKE	SLANG; AND I LIKE BUSTLING YOU UP BY SAYING THINGS THAT
GENV III (80)	STEALING EVERYBODY'S PROPERTY AND HAVING TO WORK	LIKE	SLAVES AND BEING SHOT IF YOU BREATHE A WORD AGAINST IT
ARMS I (15)	OF COURSE NOT! WELL, IT'S A FUNNY SIGHT. IT'S	LIKE	SLINGING A HANDFUL OF PEAS AGAINST A WINDOW PANE: FIRST
GETT (315)	THERE GRUDGING AND HATING AND SPITING ONE ANOTHER	LIKE	SO MANY DO? PUT IT TWENTY YEARS FROM THE BIRTH OF THE
HART PREFACE(35)	THEATRE IS NOT BORN IN MANKIND; THE NATURAL MAN,	LIKE	SO MANY OF THE SOLDIERS AT THE BEGINNING OF THE WAR,
2TRU III (85)	HERE WE ARE WAITING IN THE CITY OF DESTRUCTION	LIKE	SO MANY SHEEP FOR THE WRATH TO COME. THIS UNEDUCATED
CLEO NOTES (203)	LANGUAGE. FOAM OF NITRE IS, I THINK, SOMETHING	LIKE	SOAPSUDS. REED BARK IS AN ODD EXPRESSION. IT MIGHT MEAN
ROCK PREFACE(155)	BEEN SUMMITS OF CIVILIZATION AT WHICH HERETICS	LIKE	SOCRATES, WHO WAS KILLED BECAUSE HE WAS WISER THAN HIS
BULL PREFACE(47)	NO BOUNDS: THEY FEEL ABOUT THEM LIKE MEN, NOT	LIKE	SOLDIERS. BUT THE MOMENT YOU BRING THE PROFESSIONAL
DOCT PREFACE(41)	CHURCHING; PRAYING, RECITING, AND PREACHING; AND,	LIKE	SOLICITORS OR DOCTORS, GETTING AWAY FROM THEIR DUTIES
ARMS II (34)	AFTER IT. /LOUKA/ (INNOCENTLY) PERHAPS YOU WOULD	LIKE	SOME COFFEE, SIR? (SHE STRETCHES HER HAND ACROSS THE
APPL I (226)	THANK HEAVEN, I AM NOT A SILLY GIGGLER	LIKE	SOME I COULD MENTION. /AMANDA/ THANKS, DEAREST BILL.
NEVR I SD(208)	MASCULINE WAISTCOATS, COLLARS, AND WATCHCHAINS,	LIKE	SOME OF HER OLD COMRADES WHO HAD MORE AGGRESSIVENESS
HART PREFACE(18)	AT THE PUMPS IN A SINKING SHIP. THEY DID NOT,	LIKE	SOME OF THE CONSCIENTIOUS OBJECTORS, HOLD BACK BECAUSE
3PLA PREFACE(R26)	THE STAGE TRICKS OF THE DEVIL'S DISCIPLE ARE NOT,	LIKE	SOME OF THOSE OF ARMS AND THE MAN, THE FORGOTTEN ONES
MIS. (131)	DEMOCRACY READS WELL; BUT IT DOESNT ACT WELL,	LIKE	SOME PEOPLE'S PLAYS. NO, NO, MY FRIEND TARLETON: TO
INCA (236)	TEA? /THE PRINCESS/ OH, THANK YOU, YES: I SHOULD	LIKE	SOME TEA, IF I MIGHT -- IF IT WOULD NOT BE TOO MUCH
MRS I (189)	DUSTS HER HANDS AND TURNS TO MRS WARREN). YOUD	LIKE	SOME TEA, WOULDNT YOU? /MRS WARREN/ (SITTING IN
NEVR I (220)	FEELS WHETHER HER HAT IS RIGHT). /CRAMPTON/ YOURE	LIKE	SOMEBODY. /DOLLY/ WHO? /CRAMPTON/ WELL, YOU HAVE A
OVER (178)	TO YOU NOW. /GREGORY/ (CHUCKLING) IT SOUNDED	LIKE	SOMETHING TO DRINK. BUT I HAVE NO RIGHT TO LAUGH AT
DOCT PREFACE(55)	MALL MIGHT BE PROVED IN THE SAME WAY TO HAVE THE	LIKE	SOVEREIGN VIRTUES, A UNIVERSITY DEGREE, A DAILY BATH,
ROCK I (227)	THAT IS THE BUSINESS OF A POLITICIAN. DONT YOU	LIKE	SPEECHES? /THE LADY/ ON THE GREAT DAY OF JUDGMENT THE
FANY III (313)	IS CHAIRMAN OF THE BLUE RIBBON COMMITTEE. I DO	LIKE	SPIRITS; AND I MAKE A MERIT OF IT. AND I'M THE KING
FANY III (313)	A MERIT OF IT, HE SAYS. YOUR UNCLE PHIL DOESNT	LIKE	SPIRITS, AND HE MAKES A MERIT OF IT, AND IS CHAIRMAN OF
DOCT V (174)	/JENNIFER/ THE ANIMALS IN SIR RALPH'S HOUSE ARE	LIKE	SPOILED CHILDREN. WHEN MR WALPOLE HAD TO TAKE A
CLEO IV (175)	WHO IS POTHINUS? /RUFIO/ THE FELLOW WITH HAIR	LIKE	SQUIRREL'S FUR-- THE LITTLE KING'S BEAR LEADER, WHOM
BARB II (295)	HAVE YOU EVER BEEN IN LOVE WITH POVERTY,	LIKE	ST FRANCIS? HAVE YOU EVER BEEN IN LOVE WITH DIRT, LIKE
GENV PREFACE(20)	IMPUNITY BUT WITH FULL PARLIAMENTARY APPROVAL,	LIKE	ST PETER ON A FAMOUS EARLIER OCCASION THE GERMAN PEOPLE
BARB II (295)	FRANCIS? HAVE YOU EVER BEEN IN LOVE WITH DIRT,	LIKE	ST SIMEON! HAVE YOU EVER BEEN IN LOVE WITH DISEASE AND
CAND III SD(143)	DIVINES HER MEANING AT ONCE: HIS FACE WHITENS	LIKE	STEEL IN A FURNACE. /MORELL/ (BOWING HIS HEAD WITH THE
BARB III (316)	IT: ALL THE FOUNDLINGS I CAN FIND ARE EXACTLY	LIKE	STEPHEN. /LADY BRITOMART/ ANDREW! ! /UNDERSHAFT/ I
FABL PREFACE(83)	LIKE ROCKETS TO DICTATORSHIPS AND FELL TO EARTH	LIKE	STICKS, OR WERE SUCCEEDED, AS NAPOLEON WAS, BY
APPL I (235)	OF SUPERSTITIONS AND PREJUDICES THAT STAND	LIKE	STONE WALLS ACROSS EVERY FORWARD PATH. ARE YOU WELL
LION PREFACE(82)	WITH THE AUTHORSHIP OF THE ACTS BY PEOPLE WHO	LIKE	STORIES AND HAVE NO APTITUDE FOR THEOLOGY, WHILST THE
HART I (74)	/ELLIE/ (LOOKING AT THE TITLE OF A BOOK) DO YOU	LIKE	STORIES OF ADVENTURE, LADY UTTERWORD? /LADY UTTERWORD/
FABL VI (124)	FOR YOU? /MAIDEN 5/ WELL, A STORY IS A STORY. I	LIKE	STORIES. /MAIDEN 4/ SHE DOES, TEACHER: SHE IS ALWAYS
SUPR I SD(17)	IS A LITTLE WOMAN, WHOSE FADED FLAXEN HAIR LOOKS	LIKE	STRAW ON AN EGG. SHE HAS AN EXPRESSION OF MUDDLED
LION I (118)	AND OBEY PATRICIANS IF THEY SEE THEM BEHAVING	LIKE	STREET BOYS? (SHARPLY TO LENTULUS) PULL YOURSELF
MTH5 SD(235)	THE STIMULUS OF A WHISTLE. ALL WHO CAN, WHISTLE	LIKE	STREETBOYS. /ECRASIA/ (MAKES A WRY FACE AND PUTS HER
JOAN 5 (120)	I BELIEVED THAT YOU WHO NOW CAST ME OUT WOULD BE	LIKE	STRONG TOWERS TO KEEP HARM FROM ME. BUT I AM WISER NOW;
PHIL III (132)	WELL, CAKE? /JULIA/ NO, THANK YOU. I DONT	LIKE	SWEET THINGS. (SHE SETS DOWN THE CUP UNTASTED).
GENV I (34)	A SECTION OF THE HUMAN RACE. /SHE/ WELL, IT SEEMS	LIKE	TAKING A LOT ON MYSELF, DOESNT IT? /THE JEW/ NOT AT
GENV II (63)	YOU MIND LENDING ME MY FARE TO LONDON. I DONT	LIKE	TAKING MONEY OFF BILLIKINS. I WILL PAY YOU WHEN MY SHIP
OVER (179)	HAPPENS TO BE PAPERED IN PINK) WITH MRS LUNN,	LIKE	TANNHAUSER IN THE HILL OF VENUS. HE IS A FUSSILY
MIS. (136)	FROM MURDERING THEM; BUT I DIDNT LIKE THEM. AND I	LIKE	TARLETON. /MRS TARLETON/ EVERYBODY DOES. I REALLY MUST
MRS IV (236)	SIT DOWN IN HONORIA'S CHAIR AND TALK HERE, I	LIKE	TEN MINUTES CHAT AFTER TEA. (HE MURMURS). NO USE
JOAN 5 (116)	FOR REAL FIGHTING. WAR IS ONLY A GAME TO THEM,	LIKE	TENNIS AND ALL THEIR OTHER GAMES: THEY MAKE RULES AS TO
KING I (200)	/MRS BASHAM/ NO, SIR: MR NEWTON WOULD NOT	LIKE	THAT: HE KNOWS HIS DUTIES AS YOUR HOST. AND IF YOU WILL
KING II (226)	NOT FAR OFF. /CATHERINE/ YOU MUST NOT SAY THINGS	LIKE	THAT: I NOT CAN BEAR IT. YOU ARE STRONGER IN YOUR MIND
MIS. (159)	HIM BECAUSE HE'S A LIVING LIE. MY SOUL'S NOT	LIKE	THAT: IT'S LIKE YOURS. I WANT TO MAKE A FOOL OF MYSELF.
LION II (130)	ALL RIGHT ENOUGH. GOOD OLD LION! OLD JOCK DOESNT	LIKE	THAT: LOOK AT HIS FACE. DEVIL A BETTER! THE EMPEROR
MIS. (115)	GENTLE HAND) BENTLEY: WHATS THE MATTER? DONT CRY	LIKE	THAT: WHATS THE USE? WHATS HAPPENED? /MRS TARLETON/
FANY III (315)	INDIGNANTLY) WHAT RIGHT HAVE YOU TO TREAT A MAN	LIKE	THAT? AN HONEST RESPECTABLE HUSBAND? AS IF HE WERE
POSN (439)	YOU STAND BY AND HEAR ME CALLED NAMES BY A SKUNK	LIKE	THAT? BURN HIM! BURN HIM! THATS WHAT I'D DO WITH HIM.
APPL PREFACE(195)	PIRATES! " WHAT COULD I OR ANYONE DO WITH A MAN	LIKE	THAT? HE WAS NAIVELY SURPRISED WHEN I LAUGHED; AND HE
JOAN 5 (118)	/JOAN/ OH, WHY WILL YOU GO ON SAYING THINGS	LIKE	THAT? I AM NOT PROUD AND DISOBEDIENT. I AM A POOR
MILL III (180)	AT TUPPENCE HAPENY AN HOUR AFFORD A WEST END SHOE	LIKE	THAT? I ASSURE YOU WE DONT EMPLOY ANY WOMEN HERE.
PHIL I (91)	BUT ISNT IT RIDICULOUS FOR A MAN TO TALK	LIKE	THAT? I'M HANGED IF HE DONT TAKE WHAT HE SEES ON THE
NEVR II (247)	CRAMPTON! WHAT RIGHT HAVE THEY TO TALK TO ME	LIKE	THAT? I'M THEIR FATHER: DO THEY DENY THAT? I'M A MAN,
MTH5 (208)	/A YOUTH/ WHY NEED YOU HAVE CHEEKED HIM	LIKE	THAT? (HE GOES, GRUMBLING). /STREPHON/ (CALLING
CAPT III (281)	ARISTOCRACY, SIR HOWARD HALLAM. ARE THEY ALL	LIKE	THAT? (HE TAKES THE PRESIDENTIAL CHAIR). /SIR HOWARD/
CAND I (92)	OR SUCH LIKE, OFF THE EMBANKMENT, BUYS PICTURES	LIKE	THAT? (SEVERELY) DONT DECEIVE ME, CANDY: IT'S A 'IGH
POSN (439)	YOU KNOW YOU MUST GO. WHATS THE USE OF SCRATCHING	LIKE	THAT? NOW, LADIES, LADIES, LADIES. HOW WOULD YOU LIKE
MTH1 I (3)	HANDS, AND DRAWS AWAY FROM IT). DID YOU FIND IT	LIKE	THAT? /ADAM/ NO. IT WAS PLAYING ABOUT; AND IT TRIPPED
MTH1 I (4)	SUPPOSE YOU WERE TO TRIP AND FALL, WOULD YOU GO	LIKE	THAT? /ADAM/ UGH! (HE SHUDDERS AND SITS DOWN ON THE
BARB II (278)	FORGIVE YOU! HOW COULD YOU STRIKE AN OLD WOMAN	LIKE	THAT? /BILL/ (SEIZING HER BY THE HAIR SO VIOLENTLY
PHIL II (123)	AT GRACE'S FEET. /JULIA/ WHY ARE THEY WHISPERING	LIKE	THAT? /CHARTERIS/ BECAUSE THEY DONT WANT ANY ONE TO
HART II (112)	WILL IT BE SAFE TO HAVE HIM IN THE HOUSE	LIKE	THAT? /GUINNESS/ WHY DIDNT YOU SHOOT HIM, SIR? IF I'D
FANY III (320)	LAUGHING. WHAT RIGHT HAVE THEY TO MAKE A NOISE	LIKE	THAT? /JUGGINS/ I ASKED THEM NOT TO LAUGH SO LOUDLY,
FANY II (288)	WANT ME TO SIT? WHATS THE USE OF SAYING THINGS	LIKE	THAT? /KNOX/ MY DAUGHTER IN HOLLOWAY GAOL! /MARGARET/
PYGM V (286)	A RIGHT TO BE LOVED. /HIGGINS/ WHAT! BY FOOLS	LIKE	THAT? /LIZA/ FREDDY'S NOT A FOOL. AND IF HE'S WEAK AND
MIS. (119)	YOUR PARDON. WHY DONT YOU KICK ME WHEN I GO ON	LIKE	THAT? /LORD SUMMERHAYS/ AS WE CAME THROUGH GODALMING I
ARMS II (24)	KNOW WHAT THEY WOULD DO IF THEY HEARD YOU TALK	LIKE	THAT? /LOUKA/ WHAT COULD THEY DO? /NICOLA/ DISCHARGE
CAND II (115)	IT. LOOKEE ERE, JAMES: DO E OFTEN GIT TAKEN QUEER	LIKE	THAT? /MORELL/ (SHORTLY, WRITING A TELEGRAM) I DONT
DOCT III (134)	(PICKING OUT ANOTHER DRAWING) HOW DO YOU	LIKE	THAT? /RIDGEON/ (PUTTING IT ASIDE) I HAVE NOT COME
APPL I (210)	AIRS WITH YOU. /BOANERGES/ WHAT! ISNT SHE ALWAYS	LIKE	THAT? /SEMPRONIUS/ OH NO. IT'S NOT EVERYBODY WHO IS
ARMS II (34)	THEN WE CAN GO OUT UNTIL LUNCH TIME. WOULDNT YOU	LIKE	THAT? /SERGIUS/ BE QUICK. IF YOU ARE AWAY FIVE
CURE (233)	ANYTHING. /REGINALD/ AHA! (HE PLAYS). DO YOU	LIKE	THAT? /STREGA/ WHAT IS IT? IS IT INTENDED FOR MUSIC?
6CAL (103)	YOU MAY HAVE DONE YOURSELF FLOPPING ON YOUR KNEES	LIKE	THAT? /THE QUEEN/ I HAVE DONE MYSELF NO HARM, DEAR
2TRU III (86)	CARE ABOUT? SITTING HERE AND THINKING OF THINGS	LIKE	THAT? /THE SERGEANT/ WELL, SOMEBODY MUST THINK ABOUT
GENV II (61)	HE GOES OUT). /SIR O./ WHAT ARE WE TO DO WITH MEN	LIKE	THAT? /THE SECRETARY/ WHAT ARE THEY GOING TO DO WITH
2TRU III (106)	DO YOU THINK MY DAUGHTER COULD CARRY ROCKS ABOUT	LIKE	THAT? SHE THAT HAD TO CALL THE NURSE TO PICK UP HER
PHIL II (111)	GETTING UP FROM THE TABLE AND TEARING AWAY	LIKE	THAT? WHAT DOES PARAMORE MEAN BY READING HIS PAPER,
POSN (457)	WOMAN? WHAT HORSE? WHATS THE GOOD OF SHOVING	LIKE	THAT? WHO SAYS? NO! YOU DONT SAY! /THE SHERIFF/
APPL I (215)	/NICOBAR/ WHAT DO YOU GO PROVOKING LIZZIE FOR	LIKE	THAT? YOU KNOW SHE HAS A TEMPER. /LYSISTRATA/ THERE IS
DEVL III (67)	YOU RAISE THE DEVIL IN ME BY BULLYING THE WOMAN	LIKE	THAT? YOU OATMEAL FACED DOG, I'D TWIST YOUR CURSED
SUPR I (10)	A CAT. /OCTAVIUS/ JACK: I WISH YOU WOULDNT TALK	LIKE	THAT ABOUT ANN. /TANNER/ THIS CHAP'S IN LOVE WITH HER:
SUPR I (22)	(RISING, PETTISHLY) IT'S HORRIBLE TO TALK	LIKE	THAT ABOUT HER WHEN SHE IS UPSTAIRS CRYING FOR HER
BULL II (115)	I SHOULD THINK. /BROADBENT/ IF YOU REALLY FEEL	LIKE	THAT ABOUT HIM, THERE MAY BE A CHANCE FOR ANOTHER MAN
JITT III (67)	HIM. WHAT RIGHT HAD YOU TO TAKE A GREAT MAN	LIKE	THAT ALL TO YOURSELF? I WANTED A LITTLE BIT OF BRUNO;
SUPR IV (167)	/ANN/ YES, I KNOW. ALL THE SAME, JACK, MEN	LIKE	THAT ALWAYS LIVE IN COMFORTABLE BACHELOR LODGINGS WITH
ROCK II (272)	WHAT DO YOU MEAN? YOU CANT CHALK UP A PROGRAM	LIKE	THAT AND THEN RUN AWAY. /SIR ARTHUR/ I AM THROUGH WITH
CATH 4 (194)	HEAD, HANG, AND QUARTER HIM; BUT DONT TIE HIM UP	LIKE	THAT AND TICKLE HIM. /CATHERINE/ YOUR YOUNG LADY STILL
NEVR IV (283)	DO MY BEST. BUT IF THAT GIRL BEGINS TO TALK TO ME	LIKE	THAT AND TO LOOK AT ME LIKE-- (HE BREAKS OFF AND
PYGM II (224)	THE MATTER IS, SIR, THAT YOU CANT TAKE A GIRL UP	LIKE	THAT AS IF YOU WERE PICKING UP A PEBBLE ON THE BEACH.
DEVL II (46)	POOR FELLOW! (GREATLY DISTRESSED) TO BE HANGED	LIKE	THAT AT HIS AGE! AND THEN DID THEY TAKE HIM AWAY?
O'FL (225)	FIRST CALL ON IT? WHAT WOULD A SLIP OF A GIRL	LIKE	THAT BE DOING WITH A GOLD CHAIN ROUND HER NECK?
MIS. (157)	LET HER HAVE THE LOT. /MRS TARLETON/ DONT TALK	LIKE	THAT BEFORE LORD SUMMERHAYS, JOHN. /LORD SUMMERHAYS/ IT
GETT (348)	DAMNED SCOUNDREL. HOW DARE YOU THROW MY WIFE OVER	LIKE	THAT BEFORE MY FACE? (HE SEEMS ON THE POINT OF
PHIL I (88)	LIKE TO KNOW? THEY ARE ALWAYS SAYING THINGS	LIKE	THAT BEHIND MY BACK: I HEAR OF THEM FROM SYLVIA. ONLY
MIS. PREFACE(71)	PRIGGISH LITTLE BAREFOOTED VAGABONDS, ALL TALKING	LIKE	THAT BORN FOOL GEORGE BORROW, AND SUPPOSED TO BE
BUOY PREFACE(3)	BELIEVE THAT A MAN WHO CANNOT DO A SIMPLE THING	LIKE	THAT CAN PRACTISE THE CRAFT OF SHAKESPEAR, IS IT NOT A

ROCK I (195)	IT WAS A MISTAKE TO MAKE A MAN WITH A NAME	LIKE	THAT CHIEF COMMISSIONER OF POLICE. PEOPLE THINK HIM A
JOAN 1 (65)	IF YOU WERE IN MY PLACE WOULD YOU LET A GIRL	LIKE	THAT DO YOU OUT OF SIXTEEN FRANCS FOR A HORSE?
BULL I (87)	CAN TAKE THE WORTH AND USEFULNESS OUT OF HIM	LIKE	THAT DREAMING. AN IRISHMAN'S IMAGINATION NEVER LETS HIM
JOAN 1 (68)	IT'S NO USE, ROBERT: SHE CAN CHOKE YOU	LIKE	THAT EVERY TIME. /ROBERT/ CAN SHE, BY SAINT DENNIS! WE
CAND I (97)	AND THROUGH A THUNDERING LIAR AND ROTTEN CYNIC	LIKE	THAT FELLOW. HA! HA! NOW, OFF WITH YOU TO THE PARK,
MRS I (190)	WHATS THE MATTER WITH HIM? WHAT DOES HE TAKE IT	LIKE	THAT FOR? /CROFTS/ (MOROSELY) YOURE AFRAID OF PRAED.
MRS IV (245)	SPARROWS. WHAT DID SHE RUN AWAY FROM HASLEMERE	LIKE	THAT FOR? /FRANK/ I'M AFRAID SHE'LL TELL YOU IF YOU
2TRU I (44)	THREW SHEETIE ALL OVER THE ROOM. IF YOU CAN FIGHT	LIKE	THAT FOR A STRING OF PEARLS THAT YOU NEVER HAVE A
ROCK PREFACE(148)	POLITICAL NECESSITY FOR KILLING HIM IS PRECISELY	LIKE	THAT FOR KILLING THE COBRA OR THE TIGER: HE IS SO
FANY I (274)	KNOW THAT THE BOY IS ALIVE AFTER HIS DISAPPEARING	LIKE	THAT FOR NEARLY A WEEK. /GILBEY/ NEARLY A WEEK! A
MRS IV (247)	/MRS WARREN/ WELL, VIVIE, WHAT DID YOU GO AWAY	LIKE	THAT FOR WITHOUT SAYING A WORD TO ME? HOW COULD YOU DO
DOCT I (104)	THE MAN HE WAS. /BLENKINSOP/ IVE KNOWN THINGS	LIKE	THAT HAPPEN. THEY CANT BE EXPLAINED. /B.B./ (SEVERELY)
CAND III (132)	WHELP AND ALL THE REST OF IT. (DREAMILY) A WOMAN	LIKE	THAT HAS DIVINE INSIGHT: SHE LOVES OUR SOULS, AND NOT
MILL II (175)	A CAR OR A MOTOR BOAT OR A LAUNCH OR ANYTHING	LIKE	THAT I BUY STRAIGHT OFF THE ROAD OR OFF THE RIVER OR
GETT (271)	CROSS, ONLY WOUNDED, LESBIA. AND WHEN YOU TALK	LIKE	THAT I DONT FEEL CONVINCED: I ONLY FEEL UTTERLY AT A
MIS. (166)	/TARLETON/ WELL, I OUGHT TO REMEMBER A RUM NAME	LIKE	THAT IF I EVER HEARD IT. BUT I DONT. HAVE YOU A
MTH4 II (192)	SPOKE THAT PIECE VERY WELL, DADDY. I COULDNT TALK	LIKE	THAT IF I TRIED. IT SOUNDED FINE. AH! HERE COME THE
MIS. (135)	DONT SCOLD THE CHILD: HE'D HAVE TO SAY SOMETHING	LIKE	THAT IF IT WAS TO BE HIS LAST WORD ON EARTH. BESIDES,
PYGM V (277)	HAVE KNOWN THAT LADIES AND GENTLEMEN DIDNT BEHAVE	LIKE	THAT IF YOU HADNT BEEN THERE. /HIGGINS/ WELL! !
INCA (243)	I OUGHT TO HAVE KNOWN YOU WOULD NOT HAVE SPOKEN	LIKE	THAT IF YOU WERE NOT MARRIED. THAT MAKES IT ALL RIGHT.
BULL I (83)	CONCERTS OF IRISH MUSIC? NO IRISHMAN EVER TALKS	LIKE	THAT IN IRELAND, OR EVER DID, OR EVER WILL. BUT WHEN A
GENV III (75)	HULLO, MAAM! YOU KNOW, LADIES DONT SAY THINGS	LIKE	THAT IN MY COUNTRY. /THE WIDOW/ THEY DO IN MINE. WHAT I
ARMS III SD(46)	AND GUARANTEES PLENTY OF WARMTH. THE OTTOMAN IS	LIKE	THAT IN RAINA'S ROOM, AND SIMILARLY PLACED; AND THE
ROCK II (277)	TO USE YOUR OWN EXPRESSION, DOES HE COME ALL OVER	LIKE	THAT IN YOUR PRESENCE? /ALOYSIA/ HE DOES WHEN I GET
GETT PREFACE(196)	MAY BE ALL VERY WELL IN A BOOK (FOR PEOPLE WHO	LIKE	THAT KIND OF BOOK); BUT IN ACTUAL LIFE SHE IS A
OVER (178)	AND YOU THINK OF NOTHING BUT A SILLY JOKE. A QUIP	LIKE	THAT MAKES YOU FORGET ME. /GREGORY/ (BURYING HIS
GENV III (68)	O./ NERVES, MY DEAR BOY, NERVES. I SOMETIMES FEEL	LIKE	THAT MYSELF. I TELL MY WIFE I AM SICK OF THE WHOLE
APPL II (270)	KNOW HOW TO ANSWER HIM. /CRASSUS/ THINGS ARE	LIKE	THAT NOWADAYS. MY SON SAYS JUST THE SAME. /LYSISTRATA/
2TRU III SD(100)	BY THE VIOLENCE OF THE CATASTROPHE, A NOISE	LIKE	THAT OF A MACHINE GUN IN ACTION REACHES THEIR EARS FROM
JOAN 4 (102)	CAUSE IS LOST. /THE CHAPLAIN/ (HIS VOICE BROKEN	LIKE	THAT OF A MAN WHO HAS BEEN CRYING) MAY I SPEAK, MY
ARMS I (8)	AND GOOD BROWS AND MOUTH, HOPELESSLY PROSAIC NOSE	LIKE	THAT OF A STRONG MINDED BABY, TRIM SOLDIERLIKE CARRIAGE
MILL IV (209)	DOCTOR/ OF A SURETY THERE IS NO WIT AND NO WISDOM	LIKE	THAT OF A WOMAN ENSNARING THE MATE CHOSEN FOR HER BY
BARB PREFACE(233)	CIRCUMSTANCES. TAKE A COMMON ENGLISH CHARACTER	LIKE	THAT OF BILL WALKER. WE MEET BILL EVERYWHERE: ON THE
METH PREFACE(R48)	BIOGRAPHER, MR FESTING JONES, IS ENJOYING A VOGUE	LIKE	THAT OF BOSWELL OR LOCKHART, HIS MEMOIRS SHEW HIM
GENV PREFACE(19)	A MOMENT HITLER MAY HAVE FANCIED THAT A SUCCESS	LIKE	THAT OF MUSSOLINI'S MARCH TO ROME (HE WENT BY TRAIN)
HART I (55)	(AGHAST) YOU DONT MEAN THAT YOU WERE SPEAKING	LIKE	THAT OF MY FATHER! /MRS HUSHABYE/ I WAS. YOU KNOW I
GENV IV (98)	ENTHUSIASTIC FAITH AND OBEDIENCE. MY TECHNIQUE,	LIKE	THAT OF MY FORERUNNER OPPOSITE, WAS INVENTED AND
JOAN 6 (131)	HAVE TOLD US ARE HORRIBLE; BUT THEIR HORROR IS	LIKE	THAT OF THE BLACK DEATH: THEY RAGE FOR A WHILE AND THEN
LION PREFACE(3)	IN THAT. THERE IS EVEN A SORT OF LOYALTY IN IT,	LIKE	THAT OF THE BRIGAND WHO BREAKS EVERY LAW AND YET CLAIMS
FABL V SD(117)	AND CLEANSHAVEN: THE WOMAN'S HAIR IS DRESSED	LIKE	THAT OF THE MILO VENUS. THEY ARE IN ANIMATED
JITT III (63)	UNPREJUDICED MIND, THAT A MAN WHO MADE A MISTAKE	LIKE	THAT ONCE WOULD BE THE LAST PERSON IN THE WORLD TO MAKE
BARB III (328)	/UNDERSHAFT/ IN SEPARATE LITTLE SHEDS,	LIKE	THAT ONE. WHEN ONE OF THEM BLOWS UP, IT COSTS VERY
BULL II (98)	JUMPIN TO? WHERES YOUR MANNERS TO GO SKYROCKETIN	LIKE	THAT OUT O THE BOX IN THE MIDDLE O YOUR CONFESSION (HE
INCA (248)	/ERMYNTRUDE/ THEN I AM A LUNATIC BECAUSE I DONT	LIKE	THAT RIDICULOUS BROOCH. /THE INCA/ NO , MADAM: YOU ARE
SUPR II (51)	OF PLACE, OXFORD, I SHOULD THINK, FOR PEOPLE THAT	LIKE	THAT SORT OF PLACE. THEY TEACH YOU TO BE A GENTLEMAN
LADY (242)	TO THAN PREACHED AT. /THE MAN/ THE MOST ARE	LIKE	THAT THAT DO TALK WELL. BUT THOUGH YOU SPAKE WITH THE
BULL II (114)	EARNEST: IN ENGLISH EARNEST. WHEN I SAY A THING	LIKE	THAT TO A WOMAN, I MEAN IT. (RELEASING HER AND TRYING
SUPR II (55)	JUAN. /OCTAVIUS/ I BEG YOU NOT TO SAY ANYTHING	LIKE	THAT TO ANN. /TANNER/ DONT BE AFRAID. SHE HAS MARKED
PHIL III (143)	CRAVEN. AND YOU CERTAINLY WOULDNT HAVE GONE ON	LIKE	THAT TO ANY GROWN-UP WOMAN WHO WAS NOT YOUR DAUGHTER.
JOAN 2 (84)	(TRENCHANT AND MASTERFUL) BLETHERS! WE ARE ALL	LIKE	THAT TO BEGIN WITH. I SHALL PUT COURAGE INTO THEE.
PYGM II (225)	YOU. /MRS PEARCE/ NONSENSE, SIR. YOU MUSTNT TALK	LIKE	THAT TO HER. /LIZA/ (RISING AND SQUARING HERSELF
HART I (49)	HE IS VERY OLD AND VERY STRANGE! HE HAS BEEN JUST	LIKE	THAT TO ME. I KNOW HOW DREADFUL IT MUST BE: MY OWN
HART II (116)	SORRY, CAPTAIN SHOTOVER; BUT IT'S NO USE TALKING	LIKE	THAT TO ME. OLD-FASHIONED PEOPLE ARE NO USE TO ME.
BULL IV (162)	/NORA/ (SHOCKED INTO PROPRIETY) YOU MUSNT TALK	LIKE	THAT TO ME. /BROADBENT/ (SUDDENLY BECOMING
SUPR III (129)	AMAZING, JUAN. HOW I WISH I COULD HAVE TALKED	LIKE	THAT TO MY SOLDIERS. /THE DEVIL/ IT IS MERE TALK,
ARMS III (68)	DO YOU MEAN TO TELL ME THAT RAINA SENDS THINGS	LIKE	THAT TO OTHER MEN? /SERGIUS/ (ENIGMATICALLY) THE
MILL I (148)	WHAT THE WORLD IS LIKE. /EPIFANIA/ THE WORLD IS	LIKE	THAT TO PEOPLE WHO ARE LIKE THAT. YOUR WORLD IS NOT MY
PHIL III (139)	SNEERING STUFF! WELL, WELL: I'LL NEVER TALK	LIKE	THAT TO YOU AGAIN, DEAREST. IT ONLY MEANS THAT YOU ARE
SUPR III (104)	HOW I FRIGHTENED YOU WHEN I SAID SOMETHING	LIKE	THAT TO YOU FROM MY PEDESTAL IN SEVILLE? IT SOUNDS
2TRU III (99)	INTO A BOTTOMLESS PIT CAME HOME TO ME. I FEEL	LIKE	THAT TOO. /THE ELDER/ LOST SOULS, ALL OF US. /THE
MIS. (142)	MORE THAN THEY AFFECT A STONE. WELL, MY SOUL IS	LIKE	THAT TOO. SPARE IT: BE GENTLE WITH IT (HE
CAND I (97)	A GOOD FEED. /MARCHBANKS/ THANK YOU, I SHOULD	LIKE	THAT VERY MUCH. BUT I REALLY MUSTNT. THE TRUTH IS, MRS
MTH5 (206)	ANYTHING OUT OF LIFE. NONE OF US ARE GOING TO BE	LIKE	THAT WHEN WE GROW UP. IT'S A DOG'S LIFE. /THE ANCIENT/
MRS II (203)	THE HILL. /MRS WARREN/ WELL, YOU SHOULDNT GO OFF	LIKE	THAT WITHOUT LETTING ME KNOW. HOW COULD I TELL WHAT HAD
MRS II (200)	SEAT). /MRS WARREN/ WELL, SHE OUGHTNT TO GO OFF	LIKE	THAT WITHOUT TELLING ME. (TO FRANK) GET YOUR FATHER A
GETT (285)	LETTER FROM THE MYSTERIOUS LADY WHO CANT SPELL. I	LIKE	THAT WOMAN'S LETTERS. THERES AN INTENSITY OF PASSION IN
MRS PREFACE(177)	CERTAIN SENSITIVE PLACES IN MY SOUL: I DO NOT	LIKE	THAT WORD " ORDURE." APPLY IT TO MY WORK, AND I CAN
MTH5 (241)	ME. AND HOW WAS I TO KNOW THAT A LITTLE THING	LIKE	THAT WOULD KILL HIM? I SHOULDNT DIE IF HE CUT OFF MY
APPL INTRLUD(244)	HUMBUGS. YOU CANNOT UNDERSTAND HOW A FALSEHOOD	LIKE	THAT WOUNDS ME. /MAGNUS/ (REMORSEFULLY, STRETCHING OUT
BULL IV (165)	AT HIM) SURELY IF YOU LET ONE WOMAN CRY ON YOU	LIKE	THAT YOUD NEVER LET ANOTHER TOUCH YOU. /BROADBENT/ (
JITT III (73)	MUST TELL ME NOW! /JITTA/ WHEN YOU ARE EXCITED	LIKE	THAT YOUR VOICE IS HIS VOICE. OH, THE AGONY OF HEARING
ROCK II (265)	ARTHUR! I FEEL I CANNOT OVERLOOK A SPEECH	LIKE	THAT. AFTER ALL, WE ARE WHITE MEN. /SIR ARTHUR/ YOU ARE
APPL INTRLUD(249)	YOU RIDICULOUS. /MAGNUS/ I DONT THINK I SHOULD	LIKE	THAT. AND THE PUBLIC WOULD THINK IT ILLNATURED.
FANY II (294)	TURNIP; AND I SUPPOSE I SHALL ALWAYS SPEAK OF IT	LIKE	THAT. ANYHOW, IVE BEEN THERE; AND IT SEEMS TO ME NOW
SIM II (74)	TAKEN OF THE CLERGY, RESERVED SEATS OR SOMETHING	LIKE	THAT. BUT HE TREATED ME AS IF I WERE ONLY THE ORGAN
ROCK I (206)	IT. ALL THE WIVES OF SUCCESSFUL MEN ARE A BIT	LIKE	THAT. BUT IT'S BETTER TO SEE TOO LITTLE OF A HUSBAND
DOCT II (124)	TO ASK. /THE MAID/ YES, SIR, I KNOW IT LOOKS	LIKE	THAT. BUT WHAT AM I TO DO? /SIR PATRICK/ WHATS THE
MTH2 (70)	ALL RIGHT, YOU KNOW. /FRANKLYN/ THE KAISER FELT	LIKE	THAT. DID HE COME OUT ALL RIGHT? /BURGE/ WELL, LET US
JITT I (18)	OH, IMPOSSIBLE. HE WOULD NEVER BELIEVE A THING	LIKE	THAT. DONT LET ALFRED DECEIVE YOU, BRUNO. HE IS ONLY
LION II (129)	TODAY, AND PAY YOU OUT FOR DARING TO TALK TO ME	LIKE	THAT. FERROVIUS SPRINGS FORWARD. /LAVINIA/ (RISING
MIS. (142)	ELSE EVER CALLED ME A GLORIOUS YOUNG BEAST. I	LIKE	THAT. GLORIOUS YOUNG BEAST EXPRESSES EXACTLY WHAT I
APPL I (197)	TATTOOS AND BIG PUBLIC CEREMONIES AND THINGS	LIKE	THAT. HE ARRANGED THE LAST TWO CORONATIONS. THAT WAS
INCA (248)	MASTERPIECE. /ERMYNTRUDE/ MY INCA! OH, COME! I	LIKE	THAT. HE IS NOT MY INCA YET. /THE INCA/ HE IS
HART I (62)	BY HIS OWN HAND? /ELLIE/ OH NO: NOTHING VULGAR	LIKE	THAT. HE SAVED THE LIFE OF THE TIGER FROM A HUNTING
BULL IV (151)	GARDEN. /NORA/ IT'S A SHAME TO MAKE GAME OF HIM	LIKE	THAT. HE'S A GRADLE MORE GOOD IN HIM THAN BARNEY DORAN.
NEVR I (204)	/DOLLY/ (BREAKING OUT AGAIN) OH COME! I	LIKE	THAT. HOW OLD ARE YOU? /PHILIP/ OVER THIRTY. /DOLLY/
VWOO 2 (125)	COLOR OF HER EYES? /A/ NO: I NEVER NOTICE THINGS	LIKE	THAT. I AM NOT A DETECTIVE. IT IS PEOPLE'S CHARACTERS
MTH1 I (6)	WHAT WORD IS THAT? /EVE/ (POINTING TO THE FAWN)	LIKE	THAT. I CALL IT DEAD. /ADAM/ (RISING AND APPROACHING
FANY II (295)	KNOX/ (GREATLY AGITATED) MARGARET: DONT TALK	LIKE	THAT. I CANT BEAR TO HEAR YOU TALKING WICKEDLY. I CAN
DOCT III (148)	I'D LET MYSELF BE SHOT SOONER THAN DO A THING	LIKE	THAT. I CONSIDER YOUVE STOLEN THAT DRAWING. /SIR
2TRU I (38)	THE DOCUMENT). /THE PATIENT/ DONT DARE ADDRESS ME	LIKE	THAT. I DONT BELIEVE YOU ARE A PROPERLY QUALIFIED
DOCT IV (169)	BE RIDICULED) YES, B.B. DEATH MAKES PEOPLE GO ON	LIKE	THAT. I DONT KNOW WHY IT SHOULD; BUT IT DOES. BY THE
BULL IV (167)	(WITH IRISH PEEVISHNESS) AH, YOU MUSTNT GO ON	LIKE	THAT. I DONT LIKE IT. /BROADBENT/ (UNABASHED) YOULL
SIM II (84)	WE SHALL DISAPPEAR. /PROLA/ I DO NOT FEEL	LIKE	THAT. I FEEL LIKE THE LEADER OF A CAVALRY CHARGE WHOSE
DEVL II (31)	THING TO THINK OF WHAT DEATH MUST MEAN FOR A MAN	LIKE	THAT. I FELT THAT I MUST WARN HIM. I LEFT A MESSAGE FOR
DOCT V (171)	THINK IT IS INFAMOUS THAT THEY SHOULD WRITE	LIKE	THAT. I HOPE YOU HAVE NOT SENT THEM TICKETS FOR TODAY.
PYGM V (284)	/LIZA/ I'M NO PREACHER: I DONT NOTICE THINGS	LIKE	THAT. I NOTICE THAT YOU DONT NOTICE ME. /HIGGINS/ (
MTH4 III (200)	WOULD HAVE ANSWERED THEM, YOU KNOW. IT IS ALWAYS	LIKE	THAT. I WILL GO AND ARRANGE TO HAVE YOU SENT HOME: YOU
GETT (281)	MOST IMAGINATIVE AND CULTIVATED YOUNG WOMEN FEEL	LIKE	THAT. I WOULDNT GIVE A RAP FOR ONE WHO DIDNT.
GETT (348)	OH, I CANT BE BOTHERED LOOKING AFTER THINGS	LIKE	THAT. I'M ALL RIGHT. /LEO/ YOURE NOT: YOURE A DISGRACE
DOCT IV (163)	AND NOT BURNING THEM. WELL, I SHALL BE A FLAME	LIKE	THAT. I'M SORRY TO DISAPPOINT THE POOR LITTLE WORMS;
MTH3 (126)	ME TO CYNICAL HOPELESSNESS. WE ALL ENDED THEN	LIKE	THAT. IT IS THE HIGHEST CREATURES WHO TAKE THE LONGEST
PYGM III (252)	FOR YOUR FATHER TO POUR SPIRITS DOWN HER THROAT	LIKE	THAT. IT MIGHT HAVE KILLED HER. /LIZA/ NOT HER. GIN WAS
VWOO 2 (125)	WILL BE MURDERED SOME DAY. /Z/ SOME PEOPLE ARE	LIKE	THAT. IT OFTEN GOES WITH ORANGE COLORED EYES (OR
MTH4 I (144)	THIS PART OF THE COUNTRY OF AN ANIMAL WITH A NAME	LIKE	THAT. IT USED TO BE HUNTED AND SHOT IN THE BARBAROUS
HART I (56)	THE DEVIL BY THE TAIL. /ELLIE/ (HURT) OH NO. NOT	LIKE	THAT. IT WAS AT LEAST DIGNIFIED. /MRS HUSHABYE/ THAT
DEST (175)	I CANT HELP ADMIRING YOU. I WISH I COULD LIE	LIKE	THAT. IT WOULD SAVE ME A GREAT DEAL OF TROUBLE. /LADY/

CAND II	(115)	CANDY DIDNT OUGHTER ANDLE A HEARL'S NEVVY	LIKE	THAT. IT'S GOIN TOO FUR WITH IT. LOOKEE ERE, JAMES: DO
HART II	(90)	I HOPE I HAVNT HURT YOU PLUMPING INTO YOUR LAP	LIKE	THAT. (COMING TO HIM) I WAS LOOKING FOR YOU, SIR. MRS
DOCT II	(121)	HIM? /BLENKINSOP/ NO. EXCUSE MY RUNNING AWAY	LIKE	THAT. (HE SITS DOWN AT THE FOOT OF THE TABLE, NEXT
CURE	(229)	HAVE BEEN SOMETHING OR YOU WOULDNT HAVE YELLED	LIKE	THAT. (PULLING REGINALD OVER SO AS TO SEE HIS FACE)
CAND II	(107)	OH, IT'S NO USE TRYING TO WORK WHILE YOU TALK	LIKE	THAT. (SHE LEAVES HER LITTLE TABLE AND SITS ON THE
ARMS I	(14)	STIFFLY) YOU MUST EXCUSE ME: OUR SOLDIERS ARE NOT	LIKE	THAT. (SHE MOVES AWAY FROM THE OTTOMAN). /THE MAN/ OH
LION II	(144)	NOW I WONDER WHY THEY ALL RUN AWAY FROM US	LIKE	THAT. (THE LION, COMBINING A SERIES OF YAWNS, PURRS,
MRS II	(210)	THEN ANGRY) DONT YOU KEEP ON ASKING ME QUESTIONS	LIKE	THAT. (VIOLENTLY) HOLD YOUR TONGUE. (VIVIE WORKS ON,
2TRU III	(92)	WELL, SIR, I'D NEVER LET A SON OF MINE TALK TO ME	LIKE	THAT. LET HIM HAVE A BIT OF YOUR DETERMINISM, SIR. /THE
APPL I	(205)	DEPARTMENT WILL TRY TO PICK YOU UP AND USE YOU	LIKE	THAT. NINETEEN TIMES OUT OF TWENTY YOU WILL HAVE TO LET
MIS. PREFACE	(25)	US TO PRETEND THAT ALL SCHOOLMASTERS ARE	LIKE	THAT. OF WHAT USE IS IT TO US THAT THERE ARE ALWAYS
BUOY 1	(11)	WHY RECONSTRUCT IT? /SON/ MANY PEOPLE FEEL	LIKE	THAT. OTHERS FEEL AS I DO. IF NEITHER OF US WILL BUDGE,
FANY I	(282)	EXTRAVAGANT BY NATURE. MY SISTER MARTHA WAS JUST	LIKE	THAT. PAY ANYTHING SHE WAS ASKED. /DORA/ WHATS TUPPENCE
VWOO 3	(142)	LIKE THAT. YOU MUSTNT LET YOURSELF THINK ABOUT IT	LIKE	THAT. /A/ YOU MUST ALWAYS LET YOURSELF THINK ABOUT
DOCT II	(122)	OF COURSE I COULDNT LEND MONEY TO A STRANGER	LIKE	THAT. /B.B./ I ENVY YOU THE POWER TO SAY NO, MR
POSN	(459)	SO CRUEL AS TO SEND ME THE HORSE TO DISAPPOINT ME	LIKE	THAT. /BLANCO/ JUST WHAT HE WOULD DO. /STRAPPER/ WE
POSN	(447)	YOURE NO TRUE AMERICAN MAN, TO INSULT A WOMAN	LIKE	THAT. /BLANCO/ A WOMAN! OH LORD! YOU SAW ME ON A
ARMS III	(52)	TO IN SUCH A WAY! YOU KNOW, IVE ALWAYS GONE ON	LIKE	THAT. /BLUNTSCHLI/ YOU MEAN THE--? /RAINA/ I MEAN THE
APPL II	(273)	NOT ALL OF US WOULD BE CAPABLE OF A SACRIFICE	LIKE	THAT. /BOANERGES/ A FINE GESTURE, SIR. A FINE GESTURE.
PHIL II	(103)	KNOW THE WORLD, COLONEL! THE NEW WOMAN IS NOT	LIKE	THAT. /CRAVEN/ I CAN ONLY GIVE YOU VERY OLDFASHIONED
JITT II	(37)	(RISING AND GOING TO HER) DEAREST: DONT CRY	LIKE	THAT. /EDITH/ IT NEARLY KILLED ME TO SEE HIM SITTING
JITT III	(60)	YOU, CHILD; AND I WONT HAVE YOU TALKING TO ME	LIKE	THAT. /EDITH/ I OFTEN WONDER WHETHER YOU HAVE EVER
POSN	(438)	TO ANY LAW? LAW IS THROWN AWAY ON A BRUTE	LIKE	THAT. /ELDER DANIELS/ DONT SAY THAT, BABSY. NO MAN
MILL I	(147)	OH, I DONT MIND. MY SISTER GOES ON JUST	LIKE	THAT. /EPIFANIA/ YOUR SISTER! YOU PRESUME TO COMPARE
MILL II	(175)	DOCTOR/ TCHA! PEOPLE WILL NOT SELL THEIR BOATS	LIKE	THAT. /EPIFANIA/ HAVE YOU EVER TRIED? /THE DOCTOR/ NO.
LION II	(129)	HELP YOU. BUT I WOULDNT BE PUT OFF BY A SWINE	LIKE	THAT. /FERROVIUS/ PEACE, PEACE! TEMPT HIM NOT. GET THEE
ROCK I	(195)	PAPERS. IT ONLY ENCOURAGES THEM TO WRITE THEM UP	LIKE	THAT. /HILDA/ SIR BROADFOOT BASHAM HAS COME OVER FROM
MIS.	(186)	OH, WHAT A THING TO SAY! YOU MUSTNT TALK	LIKE	THAT. /JOHNNY/ HE'S OUT OF HIS MIND. HE THINKS IT'S
FANY III	(298)	TURN: TO SAY I'M NOT WORTHY OF HER, OR SOMETHING	LIKE	THAT. /JUGGINS/ THAT IS NOT A GENTLEMANLY TURN, SIR.
HART III	(139)	ON THE CONTRARY, I COULD WISH YOU ALWAYS	LIKE	THAT. /LADY UTTERWORD/ YOUR DAUGHTER'S MATCH IS OFF, MR
BULL IV	(151)	JUDY/ SURE HE WOULDNT MAKE A FOOL OF HIMSELF	LIKE	THAT. /LARRY/ ARE YOU SURE HE'S SUCH A FOOL AFTER ALL,
PYGM II	(221)	/MRS PEARCE/ YOU MUSTNT SPEAK TO THE GENTLEMAN	LIKE	THAT. /LIZA/ WELL, WHY WONT HE SPEAK SENSIBLE TO ME?
SUPR IV	(154)	THE GREATEST NONSENSE DELIBERATELY MAKING US POOR	LIKE	THAT. /MALONE/ OF COURSE IT IS. /VIOLET/ (AFTER A
NEVR III	(272)	MEN WHOSE WIVES LOVE THEM; AND THEY GO ON	LIKE	THAT. /MRS CLANDON/ EXCUSE ME, MR VALENTINE; BUT HAD
NEVR III	(267)	AGAIN. AND SO ON. WELL, THE DUEL OF SEX IS JUST	LIKE	THAT. /MRS CLANDON/ THE DUEL OF SEX! /VALENTINE/ YES:
HART II	(93)	BUSINESS YOU HAVE! POOR DEAR MANGAN ISNT A BIT	LIKE	THAT. /MRS HUSHABYE/ (SCORNFULLY) POOR DEAR MANGAN
JOAN 1	(58)	YES, SIR: TO A GREAT MAN LIKE YOU I MUST SEEM	LIKE	THAT. /ROBERT/ (TURNING) MY FAULT, I SUPPOSE. EH?
MILL I	(154)	AND DOING SO) YOU SHOULDNT MAKE A SIGHT OF HIM	LIKE	THAT. /SAGAMORE/ MR FITZFASSENDEN: WHY DID YOU MARRY
DOCT II	(126)	CARD) OH DONT DO THAT, LOONY. I DONT THINK HE'D	LIKE	THAT. /SCHUTZMACHER/ WELL, OF COURSE I SHANT IF YOU
ROCK I	(233)	MARXISTS: LENIN AND TROTSKY AND STALIN AND PEOPLE	LIKE	THAT. /SIR ARTHUR/ GET THEM ALL. PACK THE LOT. BY
JOAN 5	(121)	FOLLOW HER TO HELL WHEN THE SPIRIT RISES IN HER	LIKE	THAT. /THE ARCHBISHOP/ SHE DISTURBS MY JUDGMENT TOO:
2TRU I	(44)	" RIGHT YOU ARE, SWEETIE" OR SOMETHING VULGAR	LIKE	THAT. /THE BURGLAR/ WRONG, I SAID, " IF THAT GIRL HAD
MTH4 II	(192)	OF THEE." /THE WIFE/ POPPA, POPPA: DONT LOOK	LIKE	THAT. /THE DAUGHTER/ OH, GRANPA, WHATS THE MATTER? (
SUPR I	(9)	AM SORRY YOU ARE TURNING MY FRIEND FROM YOUR DOOR	LIKE	THAT. /THE MAID/ (CALMLY) HE'S NOT AT THE DOOR, SIR.
MILL IV	(191)	/PATRICIA/ BUT THAT WAS DREADFUL, TO ROOT THEM UP	LIKE	THAT. /THE MANAGER/ IT WAS HARD; BUT IT WAS THE TRUTH.
2TRU I	(34)	REGISTER. /THE DOCTOR/ WE SHOULD BE, IF WE TALKED	LIKE	THAT. /THE MONSTER/ OH, I FEEL SO WRETCHED! PLEASE
SIM PRO,3,	(33)	FISHPOOLS OF HESHBON; BUT YOUR EYES MAKE ME FEEL	LIKE	THAT. /THE Y.W./ SEEMS TO ME THERES SOME SORT OF MAGIC
GETT	(262)	I THINK SHE MIGHT BEAR WITH ME IN A LITTLE THING	LIKE	THAT. SHE KNOWS THAT HER NAME STICKS IN MY THROAT.
MILL I	(143)	DOWN GRAVELY AT HER). AND DONT STAND OVER ME	LIKE	THAT. SIT DOWN ON WHAT IS LEFT OF YOUR SHAM
NEVR III	(274)	PUT OUT BY THIS PLEASANTRY) NO: DONT SAY THINGS	LIKE	THAT. THATS JUST THE SORT OF THOUGHTLESS REMARK THAT
DOCT III	(149)	HIS SELF-RESPECT. /SIR PATRICK/ THE WORLD IS MADE	LIKE	THAT. THE DECENT FELLOWS ARE ALWAYS BEING LECTURED AND
ARMS II	(36)	MEAN NO HARM: YOUVE NO RIGHT TO TAKE UP MY WORDS	LIKE	THAT. THE MISTRESS KNOWS ALL ABOUT IT. AND I TELL YOU
APPL I	(239)	NIGHT, ON SATURDAY NIGHT, ON SATURDAY NIGHT" --	LIKE	THAT. THE OTHER WENT " BOO! HOO! I WANT AMANDA'S
APPL PREFACE	(181)	THOUSANDS OF PEOPLE SWEEPING ALONG AT FULL SPEED	LIKE	THAT. THERE COULD BE NO DOUBT THAT IT WAS LITERALLY A
HART I	(75)	FROM OUR BOHEMIANISM. /HECTOR/ OUR CHILDREN ARE	LIKE	THAT. THEY SPEND THEIR HOLIDAYS IN THE HOUSES OF THEIR
LION PROLOG	(107)	(BARRING THE WAY BACK) NO, DEARIE: DONT TAKE ON	LIKE	THAT. WE CANT GO BACK. WEVE SOLD EVERYTHING: WE SHOULD
ROCK II	(281)	EVER MET. /LADY CHAVENDER/ OH, LOTS OF US ARE	LIKE	THAT. WE WERE BORN INTO GOOD SOCIETY; AND WE ARE
PYGM V	(274)	IN THE NATURE OF BRAIN WORK MEANS TO A GIRL	LIKE	THAT. WELL, IT SEEMS THAT WHEN THE GREAT DAY OF TRIAL
ARMS II	(24)	SECRET, IS IT? I THOUGHT IT MIGHT BE SOMETHING	LIKE	THAT. WELL, YOU TAKE MY ADVICE AND BE RESPECTFUL; AND
MIS.	(144)	BAH! YOU CANT STAND EVEN A LITTLE THING	LIKE	THAT. WHAT GOOD ARE YOU? OH, WHAT GOOD ARE YOU? /LORD
ARMS I	(13)	THE ROOM. /THE MAN/ (IRRITABLY) DONT FRIGHTEN ME	LIKE	THAT. WHAT IS IT? /RAINA/ YOUR REVOLVER! IT WAS
SIM PRO,2,	(27)	IN THE PRIME OF LIFE AS YOU MIGHT SAY, TALKING	LIKE	THAT. WHY DONT YOU GET MARRIED? /THE E.O./ MY SALARY'S
CATH 4	(188)	/EDSTASTON/ SENSE OF HUMOR! HO! HA, HA! I	LIKE	THAT. WOULD ANYBODY WITH A SENSE OF HUMOR MAKE A GUY OF
MTH5	(258)	ALL BE FORSWORN. /THE NEWLY BORN/ DO NOT TALK	LIKE	THAT. YOU ARE SADDENING US; AND YOU ARE CHASING THE
ROCK II	(276)	THE MOMENT I LAID EYES ON DAVID I WENT ALL OVER	LIKE	THAT. YOU CANT DENY THAT HE IS A NICE BOY IN SPITE OF
GENV III	(84)	NEVER HAVE BELIEVED THIS. /BEGONIA/ GENEVA IS	LIKE	THAT. YOU FIND YOURSELF DINING WITH ALL SORTS. /SIR O./
JITT II	(35)	/EDITH/ (IMPATIENT) YOU NEED NOT SPEAK TO ME	LIKE	THAT. YOU KNOW VERY WELL THAT WHAT IS THE MATTER IS NOT
VWOO 3	(142)	CONVENIENT NOR DECOROUS. /Z/ OH, DONT TALK	LIKE	THAT. YOU MUSTNT LET YOURSELF THINK ABOUT IT LIKE THAT.
MILL III	(180)	WOMAN/ HUSH, HUSH, JOE: DONT SPEAK TO THE LADY	LIKE	THAT. YOU SEE, MAAM: THERES NOT A SOUL. /EPIFANIA/
GENV III	(74)	NOT LIKE OTHER MEN. OUR ENGLISH CLERGY ARE NOT	LIKE	THAT. YOU WOULD NOT KNOW THAT THEY WERE CLERGY AT ALL
MRS II	(211)	WARREN/ OH, IT'S TOO HORRIBLE TO HEAR YOU TALK	LIKE	THAT. YOU WOULDNT-- YOU COULDNT LEAVE ME. /VIVIE/ (
MILL I	(148)	THE WORLD IS LIKE THAT TO PEOPLE WHO ARE	LIKE	THAT. YOUR WORLD IS NOT MY WORLD. EVERY WOMAN HAS HER
PYGM I	(210)	SIR, DONT LET HIM LAY A CHARGE AGEN ME FOR A WORD	LIKE	THAT. YOU-- /THE GENTLEMAN/ CHARGE! I MAKE NO CHARGE.
LIED	(194)	HANDS) NO, REALLY, THATS A STUPID TRICK: I DONT	LIKE	THAT. YOUVE NO RIGHT TO DO THAT (SHE OPENS THE FAN,
ROCK I	(208)	LONGER YOUNG"-- NO, DAMN IT, OLD MIDDLESEX WONT	LIKE	THAT. " WE HAVE ALL BEEN YOUNG. WE HAVE SEEN VISIONS
MTH2	(40)	IT OR CHUCK IT: STICK IT OR CHUCK IT"-- JUST	LIKE	THAT-- FOR AN HOUR ON END IN THE SPRING. I WISH MY
FANY I	(275)	(READING) " MISS D. DELANEY. DARLING DORA." JUST	LIKE	THAT-- IN BRACKETS. WHAT SORT OF PERSON, JUGGINS?
FANY III	(316)	KNOX; BUT IF MARIA STARTED ORDERING ME ABOUT	LIKE	THAT-- /MRS GILBEY/ NOW DONT BE NAUGHTY, ROB. YOU KNOW
MRS II	(205)	CONTEMPT FOR THEM) IF I THOUGHT THAT I WAS	LIKE	THAT-- THAT I WAS GOING TO BE A WASTER, SHIFTING ALONG
MIS.	(192)	VERY WELL. IF YOU CHOOSE TO GIVE YOURSELF AWAY	LIKE	THAT-- TO ALLOW A MAN TO CALL YOU UNLADYLIKE AND THEN
KING I	(185)	THINGS-- HUNDREDS OF MILLIONS AND THINGS	LIKE	THAT-- YOU MUST CONTINUALLY COME DOWN TO EARTH TO KEEP
SIM PREFACE	(5)	BE PRESENTED TO THEM AS RELIGION. I MYSELF BEGAN	LIKE	THAT; AND I AM ENDING BY RECEIVING EVERY SCIENTIFIC
ANNA	(291)	I WONT, OF COURSE: MY OWN FATHER GOES ON JUST	LIKE	THAT; BUT SUPPOSE I DID? /STRAMMFEST/ (CHUCKLING) I
FANY III	(320)	I BEG YOUR PARDON, MRS GILBEY, FOR COMING IN	LIKE	THAT; BUT WHENEVER I GO UPSTAIRS IN FRONT OF BOBBY, HE
2TRU II	(61)	LIKE THAT, DEARIE. A LOW GIRL MIGHT SAY A THING	LIKE	THAT; BUT YOURE EXPECTED TO KNOW BETTER. /AUBREY/ MOPS:
FANY III	(315)	BEGINS TO CRY QUIETLY). /KNOX/ NOW, DONT TAKE ON	LIKE	THAT, AMELIA, YOU KNOW I ALWAYS GAVE IN TO YOU THAT YOU
LION I	(120)	I SHOULD FEEL ASHAMED IF I LET MYSELF BE STRUCK	LIKE	THAT, AND TOOK IT LYING DOWN. BUT THEN I'M NOT A
DEVL I	(5)	YOU UNFEELING SINFUL GIRL, FALLING ASLEEP	LIKE	THAT, AND YOUR FATHER HARDLY COLD IN HIS GRAVE. /THE
SUPR III	(116)	THE STATUE MAKES A WRY FACE). I SEE YOU DONT	LIKE	THAT, ANY OF YOU; BUT IT'S TRUE, FOR ALL THAT; SO IF
GETT	(325)	DRESSING-JACKET) YOURE NOT GOING TO GET MARRIED	LIKE	THAT, ARE YOU? /THE BISHOP/ (COMING ROUND THE TABLE
BUOY III	(29)	EVERY YEAR ON PRINCIPLE. WE ARE ALL MORE OR LESS	LIKE	THAT, BECAUSE DADDY BEGAN WITH EIGHT SHILLINGS A WEEK
CLEO II	(126)	/CLEOPATRA/ WHY DO YOU LET THEM TALK TO YOU	LIKE	THAT, CAESAR? ARE YOU AFRAID? /CAESAR/ WHY, MY DEAR,
BARB III	(323)	WERE DRIVEN AND TORMENTED BY MY FATHER? IS IT	LIKE	THAT, DAD? /UNDERSHAFT/ (SCANDALIZED) MY DEAR! IT IS
2TRU II	(61)	SWEETIE? /THE COUNTESS/ YOU SHOULDNT TALK	LIKE	THAT, DEARIE. A LOW GIRL MIGHT SAY A THING LIKE THAT;
LIED	(204)	WE CALL THE VOLUME? TO AURORA, OR SOMETHING	LIKE	THAT, EH? /HE/ I SHOULD CALL IT HOW HE LIED TO HER
PYGM V	(280)	CAN YOU BLAME THE GIRL? DONT LOOK AT ME	LIKE	THAT, ELIZA. IT AINT MY FAULT. IVE COME INTO SOME
CAND III	(145)	/CANDIDA/ (RISING QUICKLY) YOU ARE NOT GOING	LIKE	THAT, EUGENE? /MARCHBANKS/ (WITH THE RING OF A MAN'S
BARB II	(282)	BUT NONE OF US DARE LIFT OUR HAND AGAINST A GIRL	LIKE	THAT, FOR FEAR OF HER FATHER IN HEAVEN. /BILL/ (
PYGM II	(243)	/MRS PEARCE/ (FOLLOWING HER) OH, DONT RUSH ABOUT	LIKE	THAT, GIRL. (SHE SHUTS THE DOOR BEHIND HER). /HIGGINS/
PYGM II	(234)	THAT SHE IS HERE? /DOOLITTLE/ DONT TAKE A MAN UP	LIKE	THAT, GOVERNOR. /HIGGINS/ THE POLICE SHALL TAKE YOU UP.
ROCK II	(283)	ARE YOU THINKING OF, HILDA? /SIR ARTHUR/ MEN ARE	LIKE	THAT, HILDA. THEY ALWAYS RUN AWAY WHEN THEY HAVE NO
DEST	(181)	REGIMENT. /LIEUTENANT/ WHEW! THE REGIMENT WONT	LIKE	THAT, I CAN TELL YOU. /NAPOLEON/ PERSONALLY I AM SORRY
FANY EPILOG	(329)	THAN MYSELF, SIR: IF YOUNG PEOPLE SPOKE TO ME	LIKE	THAT, I SHOULD DIE OF SHAME: I COULD NOT FACE IT. I
APPL PREFACE	(181)	AND LOST AND TERRIFIED ANIMALS, AND THINGS	LIKE	THAT, INSTEAD OF READING BOOKS AND NEWSPAPER ARTICLES,
INCA	(248)	/ERMYNTRUDE/ YOU KNOW, IF I HAD A MOUSTACHE	LIKE	THAT, IT WOULD TURN MY HEAD. I SHOULD GO MAD. ARE YOU
SUPR IV	(164)	RISES). /MRS WHITEFIELD/ YOU SHOULDNT SAY THINGS	LIKE	THAT, JACK. I HOPE YOU WONT TELL ANN THAT I HAVE BEEN
CAND II	(125)	YOU DONT WANT TO COME. /BURGESS/ OH, DONT PUT IT	LIKE	THAT, JAMES. IT'S ONY THAT IT AINT SUNDAY, YOU KNOW.

BULL IV	(169)	/NORA/ AN WOULD YOU LET ME DEMEAN MESELF	LIKE	THAT, JUST TO GET YOURSELF INTO PARLIAMENT?
JITT I	(14)	TRAGIC AS HER EYES. SO, AS WE ARE ALL A LITTLE	LIKE	THAT, LET US SHARE THEIR DREAM FOR A MOMENT WHILST SHE
KING I	(162)	/SALLY/ OH, HE'S NOT A PERSON I COULD TALK TO	LIKE	THAT, MAAM. I DURSNT. /MRS BASHAM/ ARE YOU FRIGHTENED
MTH5	(241)	HER FACE WITH HER HANDS) OH, DONT LOOK AT ME	LIKE	THAT, MAM. I MEANT NO HARM. HE HURT ME: INDEED HE DID.
NEVR I	(213)	OFF THE TABLE) I'M SURE I DONT. OH, DONT LOOK	LIKE	THAT, MAMMA. (SHE LOOKS ANGRILY AT GLORIA AND FLINGS
MTH4 II	(186)	THEY WOULDNT MIND. /THE ENVOY/ NO USE TALKING	LIKE	THAT, MOLLY. IVE GOT TO SEE THIS ORACLE. THE FOLKS AT
PYGM II	(222)	AT HIM. /MRS PEARCE/ IT'S NO USE TALKING TO HER	LIKE	THAT, MR HIGGINS: SHE DOESNT UNDERSTAND YOU. BESIDES,
BULL IV	(154)	FOR THE FACT THAT I AM MAD. /NORA/ AH, DONT TALK	LIKE	THAT, MR KEEGAN. /BROADBENT/ (ENCOURAGINGLY) NOT AT
DOCT II	(117)	WHY DO YOU LET HIM SPOIL YOUR BEAUTIFUL NAME	LIKE	THAT, MRS DUBEDAT? /MRS DUBEDAT/ OH, ON GRAND
KING II	(230)	SHIPWRIGHTS AND BRICKLAYERS AND MASONS AND PEOPLE	LIKE	THAT, NEGLECTING THE COURT. THAT IS HOW YOUR BROTHER
APPL I	(220)	HIS SEAT). /PLINY/ THERE IS NO NEED TO RUB IT IN	LIKE	THAT, NICK. WE'RE ALL GOOD FRIENDS. NOBODY OBJECTS TO
JITT I	(12)	HERE TO HAPPEN TO YOU-- NOT THAT I THINK ANYTHING	LIKE	THAT, OF COURSE; BUT-- /THE GENTLEMAN/ OF COURSE NOT.
OVER PREFACE	(165)	BECAUSE HE BELIEVED THAT THE PLANTAGENETS DRESSED	LIKE	THAT, OR BECAUSE THE COSTUMIERS COULD NOT HAVE MADE HIM
MIS.	(132)	BOOK IN HAND) YES I DO. I BET YOU WHAT YOU	LIKE	THAT, PAGE FOR PAGE, I READ MORE THAN YOU, THOUGH I
FANY II	(286)	US AND EVERYBODY. WHEN A GIRL RUNS AWAY FROM HOME	LIKE	THAT, PEOPLE KNOW WHAT TO THINK OF HER AND HER PARENTS.
MIS.	(183)	OF TENDERNESS) AND YOU HERE BEING TREATED	LIKE	THAT, POOR ORPHAN, WITH NOBODY TO TAKE YOUR PART! TEAR
DOCT III	(155)	" OH, ALL RIGHT", JUST LIKE A BOY. HE IS STILL	LIKE	THAT, QUITE UNSPOILED, A MAN IN HIS THOUGHTS, A GREAT
PYGM II	(224)	(TO PICKERING) WELL, DID YOU EVER HEAR ANYTHING	LIKE	THAT, SIR? /PICKERING/ (LAUGHING HEARTILY) NEVER, MRS
LION II	(145)	(THE LION GROWLS). /ANDROCLES/ OH DONT TALK	LIKE	THAT, SIR. HE UNDERSTANDS EVERY WORD YOU SAY: ALL
DOCT II	(125)	DIDNT MEAN ANY HARM: HE NEVER THINKS ABOUT THINGS	LIKE	THAT, SIR. I'LL GET IT BACK FOR YOU, SIR, IF YOULL TELL
MILL I	(154)	NOT HERE, ADRIAN. IF YOU ARE GOING TO TALK	LIKE	THAT, TAKE ME AWAY TO SOME PLACE WHERE WE CAN BE ALONE.
BULL IV	(168)	OH, HOW COULD YOU DRAG ME ALL ROUND THE PLACE	LIKE	THAT, TELLING EVERYBODY THAT WE'RE GOING TO BE MARRIED.
HART II	(107)	YOU HAVE A PROPER REVOLVER INSTEAD OF A THING	LIKE	THAT, THAT GOES OFF IF YOU AS MUCH AS BLOW ON IT?
OVER	(183)	DONT YOU REALIZE THAT UNLESS MOST WOMEN WERE	LIKE	THAT, THE WORLD COULDNT GO ON AS IT DOES? /JUNO/ (
MTH4 I	(156)	/ZOO/ WE STILL TELL OUR LITTLE CHILDREN STORIES	LIKE	THAT, TO HELP THEM TO UNDERSTAND. BUT SUCH THINGS DO
SUPR IV	(154)	NO IDEA HE COULD BE SO HEADSTRONG. IF HE GOES ON	LIKE	THAT, WHAT CAN I DO? /MALONE/ DONT BE DISCURRIDGED:
DEVL III	(62)	THE TABLE) OH, YOU ARE NOT GOING TO MURDER A MAN	LIKE	THAT, WITHOUT A PROPER TRIAL-- WITHOUT THINKING OF WHAT
MILL IV	(194)	CUSHIONS) DEAR! DEAR! /ALASTAIR/ EPPY IS	LIKE	THAT, YOU KNOW. /ADRIAN/ YES: I KNOW NOW. BUT I OUGHT
ROCK II	(275)	THAT? /ALOYSIA/ HE TOLD ME TO GO TO HELL. HE'S	LIKE	THAT, YOU KNOW. /SIR ARTHUR/ YES. A HASTY BOY.
VWOO 3	(143)	AT MY OWN NERVE. /A/ SO DO I. /Z/ I'M NOT A BIT	LIKE	THAT, YOU KNOW. REALLY. SOMETHING ABOVE ME AND BEYOND
HART II	(97)	LOSING HER TEMPER) DONT YOU DARE SPEAK TO ME	LIKE	THAT, YOU LITTLE MINX. REMEMBER THAT YOU ARE IN MY
FANY III	(305)	KNOW. /MARGARET/ DOES HIM CREDIT! TO INSULT YOU	LIKE	THAT! BOBBY! SAY THAT WASNT WHAT YOU MEANT. /BOBBY/ I
PHIL II	(128)	A LITTLE REST, YOU KNOW: A BUSY PROFESSIONAL MAN	LIKE	THAT! HE'S NOT HAD A MOMENT TO HIMSELF ALL DAY.
PYGM I	(213)	OFF). /THE FLOWER GIRL/ FRIGHTENING PEOPLE	LIKE	THAT! HOW WOULD HE LIKE IT HIMSELF? /THE MOTHER/ IT'S
ARMS I	(5)	THAT SEASON AT BUCHAREST. REAL LIFE IS SO SELDOM	LIKE	THAT! INDEED NEVER, AS FAR AS I KNEW IT THEN. (
CATH 4	(192)	KNEES AT HIS SIDE). OH, HOW DARE THEY TIE YOU UP	LIKE	THAT! (TO CATHERINE) YOU WICKED WRETCH! YOU RUSSIAN
LION II	(144)	OH BAD WICKED TOMMY, TO CHASE THE EMPEROR	LIKE	THAT! LET GO THE EMPEROR'S ROBE AT ONCE, SIR: WHERES
KING II	(234)	WIG). FANCY YOUR GOING INTO THE COUNCIL CHAMBER	LIKE	THAT! NOBODY WOULD TAKE YOU FOR KING CHARLES THE
BULL III	(123)	COUNTRY! FANCY THE POTCHEEN GOING TO YOUR HEAD	LIKE	THAT! /BROADBENT/ NOT TO MY HEAD, I THINK. I HAVE NO
POSN	(437)	CANT HAVE A MINUTE TO OURSELVES. SHOVING US OUT	LIKE	THAT! /HANNAH/ WHOSE HORSE WAS IT, MR DANIELS? /ELDER
MTH2	(50)	SPEAKERS LIKE YOU. /FRANKLYN/ WELL! I /SAVVY/ I	LIKE	THAT! /HASLAM/ PRICELESS! (EXCLAIMING ALL TOGETHER)
HART I	(65)	BE MUCH LOVE IN THE WORLD. /ELLIE/ BUT TO LIE	LIKE	THAT! TO BE A BOASTER! A COWARD! /MRS HUSHABYE/ (
MTH3	(125)	MEN WHO STILL DO SERIOUS WORK ARE THOSE WHO,	LIKE	THE ACCOUNTANT GENERAL, HAVE NO CAPACITY FOR ENJOYMENT.
SIM II	(73)	MATTER. ALL I WANT IS A PARAPET TO TAKE OFF FROM.	LIKE	THE ALBATROSS, I CANNOT RISE FROM THE GROUND WITHOUT
BULL I	(83)	BUSINESS IS GOT UP IN ENGLAND TO FOOL YOU,	LIKE	THE ALBERT HALL CONCERTS OF IRISH MUSIC? NO IRISHMAN
INCA	(253)	YOU TOO WORSHIP BEFORE THE STATUE OF LIBERTY,	LIKE	THE AMERICANS? /THE INCA/ NOT AT ALL, MADAM. THE
CLEO IV	(187)	SOUNDS ON THE BEACH BELOW). AHA! THAT SOUNDS	LIKE	THE ANSWER. /CLEOPATRA/ (SINKING BACK TREMBLING ON THE
KING I	(210)	A CANNON BALL FLIES ACROSS THE SEA IN CURVES	LIKE	THE ARCHES OF A BRIDGE, HOP, HOP, HOP. BUT WHAT DOES IT
MTH5	SD(205)	SOME OF THE YOUTHS HAVE BEARDS. THEIR DRESS,	LIKE	THE ARCHITECTURE OF THE THEATRE AND THE DESIGN OF THE
DEST	(192)	THE THING HE WANTS. THEN HE BECOMES IRRESISTIBLE.	LIKE	THE ARISTOCRAT, HE DOES WHAT PLEASES HIM AND GRABS WHAT
JOAN PREFACE	(30)	THAT THE POLITICAL BIAS OF A BODY OF FRENCHMEN	LIKE	THE ASSESSORS WOULD ON THIS POINT HAVE RUN STRONGLY IN
MTH4 I	(159)	BY THE MICROSCOPE MAN, WHO WAS WORSHIPPED,	LIKE	THE ASTRONOMER, AS INFALLIBLE AND OMNISCIENT. THUS OUR
JOAN PREFACE	(40)	PROSECUTE YOU AND HAVE YOU PUNISHED VERY SEVERELY	LIKE	THE AUTHORITIES IN BUTLER'S EREWHON," IT WOULD EITHER
HART PREFACE	(25)	FOR THEM BY OTHERS, THE AVERAGE MAN OF ACTION,	LIKE	THE AVERAGE FIGHTER WITH THE BAYONET, CAN GIVE NO
GENV PREFACE	(26)	DESIRED, COME AT LAST SUDDENLY AND MIRACULOUSLY	LIKE	THE BALANCING OF THE BICYCLIST, THE SKATER, AND THE
MRS I	(194)	/PRAED/ PRAY DONT. IT'S ONLY SOME FRESH FOLLY,	LIKE	THE BARMAID AT REDHILL. /FRANK/ IT'S EVER SO MUCH MORE
MTH1 II	(29)	ASHAMED: HE KNOWS NO BETTER. IF YOU ARE CONTENT,	LIKE	THE BEAR, I AM NOT. STAY WITH THE WOMAN WHO GIVES YOU
2TRU II	(72)	DAM AND BRING UP ITS FAMILY. I WANT MY LITTLE JOB	LIKE	THE BEAVER. IF I DO NOTHING BUT CONTEMPLATE THE
SUPR PREFACE	(R19)	I DO NOT GUARANTEE THE ENGLISHMAN AGAINST BEING,	LIKE	THE BEE (OR THE CANAANITE) SMOKED OUT AND UNLOADED OF
MTH4 I	(162)	INSECT WE BUILD ISLANDS WHICH BECOME CONTINENTS:	LIKE	THE BEE WE STORE SUSTENANCE FOR FUTURE COMMUNITIES. THE
CLEO PR01	(90)	ARE PATIENT WITH LITTLENESS. THEN THE OLD ROME,	LIKE	THE BEGGAR ON HORSEBACK, PRESUMED ON THE FAVOR OF THE
DOCT I	(113)	DRAWINGS; AND THEY ARE NOT THE BEST-- NOTHING	LIKE	THE BEST; ONLY I DID NOT BRING THE REALLY BEST: SO FEW
SUPR IV	(158)	IN IT. PERHAPS IT'S BECAUSE YOURE A POET. YOU ARE	LIKE	THE BIRD THAT PRESSES ITS BREAST AGAINST THE SHARP
DOCT PREFACE	(56)	PESTILENCES THAT SWEEP THROUGH WHOLE CONTINENTS,	LIKE	THE BLACK DEATH AND THE CHOLERA. IF IT WERE PROPOSED AT
GLIM	(185)	BLOOD REALLY NOBLER? /GIULIA/ IT IS RED, SIGNOR,	LIKE	THE BLOOD OF THE CHRIST IN THE PICTURE IN CHURCH. I DO
APPL I	(222)	IN THE NORTH OF SCOTLAND, AND YOU GAVE IT AWAY,	LIKE	THE BOOBS YOU ARE, TO THE PENTLAND FORTH SYNDICATE: A
MTH3	SD(133)	BRILLIANTLY DRESSED, APPEARS ON WHAT LOOKS	LIKE	THE BRIDGE OF A STEAM YACHT IN GLORIOUS SEA WEATHER.
HART I	(53)	KNEW ELLIE'S GRANDPARENTS, THEY WERE BOTH POETS,	LIKE	THE BROWNINGS; AND WHEN HER FATHER CAME INTO THE WORLD
NEVR II	(227)	DID SHE? /WAITER/ NO, SIR. SHE THOUGHT ME	LIKE	THE BUST OF SHAKESPEAR IN STRATFORD CHURCH, SIR. THAT
METH PREFACE	(R51)	BEGAN TO INVESTIGATE THE POINT BY BEHAVING	LIKE	THE BUTCHER'S WIFE IN THE OLD CATCH. HE GOT A COLONY OF
BASH II,1,	(113)	DOING IN THIS THE OFFICE OF A BOY, WHILST,	LIKE	THE CELEBRATED MAID THAT MILKS AND DOES THE MEANEST
HART PREFACE	(33)	HANDSOME SUBSCRIPTION FROM A GERMAN GENTLEMAN,	LIKE	THE CELEBRATED SWEARER IN THE ANECDOTE WHEN THE CART
CYMB FORWORD	(134)	AS DEUS EX MACHINA, EAGLE AND ALL, INTRODUCED,	LIKE	THE CERES SCENE IN THE TEMPEST, TO PLEASE KING JAMIE,
GENV PREFACE	(14)	INTERFERENCE SURVIVING IN THE ADULT VOTER	LIKE	THE CHILD'S DREAD OF A POLICEMAN. IT MAY BE ASKED HOW
ARMS II	(41)	MY DAUGHTER'S LIFE WILL HARDLY BE SAFE. WILL YOU,	LIKE	THE CHIVALROUS GENTLEMAN AND SOLDIER YOU ARE, LEAVE AT
LION II	SD(127)	ARE STANDING AND SITTING AT EASE, WAITING,	LIKE	THE CHRISTIANS, FOR THEIR TURN IN THE ARENA. ONE (
KING I	(178)	IN DARKNESS AND DAMNED. THERE IS NO ATHEIST	LIKE	THE CHURCH ATHEIST. I HAVE CONVERTED MANY A POOR
KING I	(191)	I SHALL TAKE CARE NOT TO DIE IN AN UPSTART SECT	LIKE	THE CHURCH OF ENGLAND, AND PERHAPS LOSE MY PLACE IN
METH PREFACE	(R76)	SAFELY BE LEFT IN THEIR HANDS. IF DWINDLING SECTS	LIKE	THE CHURCH OF ENGLAND, THE CHURCH OF ROME, THE GREEK
CLEO II	SD(118)	OF THIRTY-FIVE, WITH A FINE BLACK BEARD CURLED	LIKE	THE COAT OF A POODLE. APPARENTLY NOT A CLEVER MAN, BUT
SUPR PREFACE	(R34)	THE COMPARISON BETWEEN FALSTAFF AND PROSPERO IS	LIKE	THE COMPARISON BETWEEN MICAWBER AND DAVID COPPERFIELD.
MTH4 I	(162)	A BIBLE TO A LITERATURE. WE MAY BE INSECTS; BUT	LIKE	THE CORAL INSECT WE BUILD ISLANDS WHICH BECOME
JOAN PREFACE	(23)	SIMPLE AND COMPASSABLE BY SWIFT PHYSICAL FORCE,	LIKE	THE CORONATION AND THE ORLEANS CAMPAIGN, THAT SHE WAS
JOAN 2,SD	(80)	THEATRICALLY ON THE DAIS, PLAYING THE KING, AND,	LIKE	THE COURTIERS, ENJOYING THE JOKE RATHER OBVIOUSLY.
KING I	(181)	AN IDOL OF AN ARCHBISHOP! THERE IS NO CREDULITY	LIKE	THE CREDULITY OF PHILOSOPHERS. /NEWTON/ BUT THE
3PLA PREFACE	(R29)	ATMOSPHERE FALLS IN LOVE WITH HIM AND CONCLUDES (	LIKE	THE CRITICS, WHO SOMEHOW ALWAYS AGREE WITH MY
APPL PREFACE	(188)	POST, AND HAS A UNION JACK ON IT, ANOTHER IS	LIKE	THE DAILY NEWS OR MANCHESTER GUARDIAN, BOTH MIGHT HAVE
LADY	(240)	FOR THE FIRST TIME? ARE YOU AILING? YOU WALK	LIKE	THE DEAD. MARY! MARY! /THE LADY/ (ECHOING HIM)
APPL PREFACE	(180)	ARE AGREED THAT WE MUST BE GOVERNED. DEMOCRATS	LIKE	THE DEAN AND MYSELF ARE AGREED THAT WE MUST BE GOVERNED
FANY II	(295)	THE WORDS OF GRACE. IT'S TOO HORRIBLE: IT SOUNDS	LIKE	THE DEVIL MAKING FUN OF RELIGION. IVE TRIED TO BRING
MIS.	(163)	BOY: YOULL GET NOTHING BUT A KISS; AND I'LL FIGHT	LIKE	THE DEVIL TO KEEP YOU FROM GETTING THAT. BUT WE MUST
BULL III	(121)	/LARRY/ NO WONDER! OF COURSE THEY ALL HATED US	LIKE	THE DEVIL. UGH! (MOODILY) IVE SEEN THEM IN THAT
ROCK PREFACE	(163)	THE LISTS OF CRIMES AND PENALTIES WILL OBSOLESCE	LIKE	THE DOCTORS' LISTS OF DISEASES AND MEDICINES; AND IT
2TRU PREFACE	(11)	AND THAT YOU ARE GOING TO HELL; BUT ALAS! HE,	LIKE	THE DOCTOR, CANNOT AFFORD THIS, AS HE MAY HAVE TO ASK
OVER PREFACE	(155)	MOST PART QUITE SINCERE. THE COMMON LIBERTINE,	LIKE	THE DRUNKARD, SUCCUMBS TO A TEMPTATION WHICH HE DOES
AUGS PREFACE	(261)	AS THE CASE MIGHT BE. BUT AUGUSTUS STOOD	LIKE	THE EDDYSTONE IN A STORM, AND STANDS SO TO THIS DAY. HE
OVER PREFACE	(165)	THE AUDIENCE TRANSFIGURES A PLATFORM OR TRIBUNE	LIKE	THE ELIZABETHAN STAGE OR THE GREEK STAGE USED BY
MTH5	(257)	AND I AM NO LONGER JEALOUS OF YOU. THAT LOOKS	LIKE	THE END. TWO HOURS SLEEP IS ENOUGH FOR ME. I AM AFRAID
O'FL	(215)	AND OBSTINATE: THERES NO DOUBT ABOUT IT. SHE'S	LIKE	THE ENGLISH: THEY THINK THERES NO ONE LIKE THEMSELVES.
2TRU I	SD(27)	AND A TALL SCREEN OF CHINESE WORKMANSHIP WHICH,	LIKE	THE EXPENSIVE CARPET AND EVERYTHING ELSE IN THE ROOM,
APPL I	(232)	COMMITTEE OF TWO; AND THAT IS A COMMITTEE OF ONE.	LIKE	THE FAMILY IN WORDSWORTH'S POEM, WE ARE SEVEN --
LION PREFACE	(81)	NOTHING THAT JESUS WOULD HAVE SAID, THOUGH MUCH,	LIKE	THE FAMOUS ODE TO CHARITY, THAT HE WOULD HAVE ADMIRED.
JOAN PREFACE	(46)	TRUTH THAT THE FASHION IN WHICH WE THINK CHANGES	LIKE	THE FASHION OF OUR CLOTHES, AND THAT IT IS DIFFICULT,
MTH1 I	(5)	BUT WE SHALL CEASE TO BE. WE SHALL FALL	LIKE	THE FAWN AND BE BROKEN. (RISING AND MOVING ABOUT IN
MTH1 I	(8)	BUT THE REST OF US WILL DIE SOONER OR LATER.	LIKE	THE FAWN. AND THEN THERE WILL BE NOTHING BUT SNAKES.
MTH1 I	(15)	AND NEVER MOVE LEST I SHOULD STUMBLE AND DIE	LIKE	THE FAWN. NOW YOU NO LONGER CARE. /ADAM/ IT DOES NOT
MTH1 I	(11)	WITHOUT EYES. SOONER OR LATER YOU WILL DIE	LIKE	THE FAWN; AND THE NEW ADAMS WILL BE UNABLE TO CREATE

MTH1 I (11)	CANNOT CREATE ADAMS ONLY. /EVE/ IF I AM TO DIE	LIKE	THE FAWN, WHY SHOULD NOT THE REST DIE TOO? WHAT DO I
SIM PREFACE(7)	ALL CONTINUALLY; CONSEQUENTLY THE RESTRAINT MUST,	LIKE	THE FEAR OF HELL, OPERATE WHEN NOBODY IS LOOKING. WELL,
HART III (134)	NAME, WHAT DO YOU LOOK LIKE? /MANGAN/ I LOOK	LIKE	THE FELLOW THAT WAS TOO CLEVER FOR ALL THE OTHERS, DONT
BUOY IV (54)	HAVE BEEN KICKED OUT OF THE HOUSE. /OLD BILL/ I	LIKE	THE FELLOW. /SIR FERDINAND/ LIKE THE FELLOW! LIKE AN
BUOY IV (54)	/OLD BILL/ I LIKE THE FELLOW. /SIR FERDINAND/	LIKE	THE FELLOW! LIKE AN IMPUDENT FORTUNE HUNTER! IN
MIS. (197)	BEGGED HIM OFF. I ASKED THAT MAN WHAT IT FELT	LIKE	THE FIRST TIME HE KICKED HIS FATHER, AND FOUND THAT IT
MTH1 II (31)	DELIGHTED, INTERESTED; THOUGH THE LAST CHILD IS	LIKE	THE FIRST, AND HAS SAID AND DONE NOTHING THAT DID NOT
SUPR HANDBOK(210)	ST ANTHONY TO THE FISHES, BUT SMITH AND BROWN,	LIKE	THE FISHES AND BIRDS, REMAIN AS THEY ARE; AND POETS WHO
HART I SD(52)	LOOKING. SHE HAS MAGNIFICENT BLACK HAIR, EYES	LIKE	THE FISHPOOLS OF HESHBON, AND A NOBLY MODELLED NECK,
SIM PRO,3, (33)	CALL HER. /THE PRIESTESS/ YOUNG MAN: ARE MY EYES	LIKE	THE FISHPOOLS OF HESHBON? /THE E.O./ WELL, I HAVE
LION PREFACE(97)	SHORT, THE ENGLISHMAN OF TODAY, INSTEAD OF BEING,	LIKE	THE FOREFATHERS WHOSE IDEAS HE CLINGS TO, A SUBJECT OF
FANY PROLOG (265)	COMMITTEE. HE INDUCED THEM TO GO IN FOR A UNIFORM	LIKE	THE FRENCH ACADEMY; AND I ASKED HIM TO WEAR IT. /THE
O'FL (224)	HOW THEY MIGHT PUT THE LAND INTO DECENT TILLAGE	LIKE	THE FRENCH AND BELGIANS. SIR PEARCE/ YES: HE'S QUITE
GENV IV (112)	SPAT AT ME FROM YOUR PLATFORMS AND NEWSPAPERS	LIKE	THE FRIGHTENED GEESE YOU ARE. YOU MUST ALL COME MY WAY,
MILL PREFACE(125)	BEASTS SIDE BY SIDE WITH DARK SATURNINE TYPES	LIKE	THE FUHRER HIMSELF. I AM A BLOND, MUCH LESS AN ANTIQUE
SIM I (38)	IN THIS GARDEN? /THE CLERGYMAN/ OH NO. IT'S	LIKE	THE GARDEN OF EDEN: I SHOULD LIKE TO STAY HERE FOREVER.
DEVL III (50)	OFF HIM AT SPOIL FIVE. HE SPENT IT AMONG US	LIKE	THE GENTLEMAN HE IS. DUTY'S DUTY, MUM, OF COURSE; BUT
ROCK II (270)	WHEN THE PEOPLE CAME TO THEIR OWN AND HAD VOTES	LIKE	THE GENTRY. ADULT SUFFRAGE: THAT WAS WHAT WAS TO SAVE
METH PREFACE(R23)	OF YOUR NECK, YOU WILL FINALLY GET A LONG NECK,	LIKE	THE GIRAFFE. THIS SEEMS ABSURD TO INCONSIDERATE PEOPLE
CYMB FORWORD(135)	AND LEFT NOTHING BUT DOLLS BEING MOVED ABOUT	LIKE	THE GLASS BALLS IN THE GAME OF SOLITAIRE UNTIL THEY ARE
CATH 4 (198)	ABOLISH THE STOVE: BELIEVE ME, THERE IS NOTHING	LIKE	THE GOOD OLD OPEN GRATE. HOME! DUTY! HAPPINESS! THEY
MRS II (198)	TO THINK YOURE A CHIP OF THE OLD BLOCK. /FRANK/	LIKE	THE GOV'NOR, EH? (HE HANGS THE SHAWL ON THE NEAREST
MILL IV (203)	EXCEPT IN SELF-DEFENCE. /EPIFANIA/ YES: YOU ARE	LIKE	THE GREAT EUROPEAN POWERS: YOU NEVER FIGHT EXCEPT IN
ROCK PREFACE(183)	WITHOUT DISHONOR FOR THE SIDE THAT PAYS THEM,	LIKE	THE HACKNEY CHARIOTEER WHO WILL DRIVE YOU NORTH AS
BASH PREFACE(87)	TWO-LINE SAYINGS, AND THE OCCASIONAL RHYMED TAGS,	LIKE	THE HALF CLOSES IN AN EIGHTEENTH CENTURY SYMPHONY, IN
2TRU I (48)	SACRED AURA WHICH SURROUNDS EVERY LIVING SOUL	LIKE	THE HALO SURROUNDING THE HEADS OF SAINTS IN RELIGIOUS
FANY III (303)	A VERY NICE FELLOW AND CAN SWING HIS LEG ROUND	LIKE	THE HAND OF A CLOCK AND KNOCK A POLICEMAN DOWN WITH IT,
CLEO I SD(117)	COILED ROUND HIS BODY, ITS BRAZEN BELL SHAPED	LIKE	THE HEAD OF A HOWLING WOLF. WHEN THEY REACH THE
BULL PREFACE(20)	SPLENDID FIGHTING ON HELPLESS ADVERSARIES	LIKE	THE HEROIC DEBRUEYS OR VILLENEUVE (WHO HAD NOT EVEN
MTH5 SD(214)	LAMENT, AND HAS HEARD MOST OF IT. SHE IS	LIKE	THE HE-ANCIENT, EQUALLY BALD, AND EQUALLY WITHOUT
ROCK I (204)	(HE RETURNS PLACIDLY TO HIS CHAIR). IT'S JUST	LIKE	THE HOUSE OF COMMONS, EXCEPT THAT THE SPEECHES ARE
WIDO II (36)	MY BEING ABSOLUTELY DEPENDENT ON YOU; AND I DONT	LIKE	THE IDEA OF IT MYSELF. IF YOU EVEN MENTION SUCH A THING
MIS. PREFACE(36)	LOATHSOME AS WE HAVE MADE THE IDEA OF DUTY (	LIKE	THE IDEA OF WORK) WE MUST HABITUATE CHILDREN TO A SENSE
GETT PREFACE(217)	OF WHICH I HAVE ANY KNOWLEDGE IS IN THE LEAST	LIKE	THE IDEAL MARRIAGE. I DO NOT MEAN THAT IT IS WORSE: I
DOCT PREFACE(63)	FOR ALL CLASSES, HIS FEES HAVE TO BE GRADUATED	LIKE	THE INCOME TAX. THE SUCCESSFUL FASHIONABLE DOCTOR MAY
PLES PREFACE(R15)	CASES LIKE MINE WOULD STILL LEAVE FORLORN HOPES	LIKE	THE INDEPENDENT THEATRE ITS REASON FOR EXISTING. THE
BULL PREFACE(46)	PUNISH, BUT NEVER TO RULE; AND WHEN AN EMERGENCY	LIKE	THE INDIAN MUTINY COMES, HE BREAKS DOWN; AND THE
MIS. PREFACE(86)	THEM AT ALL. UNDER SUCH CIRCUMSTANCES PHRASES	LIKE	THE INFLUENCE OF HOME LIFE, THE FAMILY, THE DOMESTIC
BULL III (118)	STILL, IT'S NO END OF A JOKE. HOW DO YOU	LIKE	THE IRISH, HODSON? /HODSON/ WELL, SIR, THEYRE ALL
BULL III (132)	FARMERS; AND WE'LL NEVER DO ANY GOOD AT IT. WE'RE	LIKE	THE JEWS: THE ALMIGHTY GAVE US BRAINS, AND BID US FARM
GENV PREFACE(8)	THEIR CHANCELLORS OF THE EXCHEQUER WILL REPLY,	LIKE	THE JUVENILE SPENDTHRIFT EXHORTED TO PAY HIS DEBTS BY
MIS. PREFACE(43)	BE KILLED. THIS IS A MERE MATTER OF NECESSITY,	LIKE	THE KILLING OF A MAN-EATING TIGER IN A NURSERY, A
SUPR PREFACE(R28)	WITH UNLIMITED DIVIDENDS, AND EAT GRATUITOUSLY,	LIKE	THE KNIGHTS IN DON QUIXOTE'S BOOKS OF CHIVALRY, THE
APPL INTRLUD(250)	DEROGATION TO JEMIMA'S DIGNITY WOULD HIT ME	LIKE	THE LASH OF A WHIP ACROSS THE FACE. ABOUT YOURS,
DOCT PREFACE(64)	THE DEATH OF A WELL-INFORMED AND CLEVER WRITER	LIKE	THE LATE HAROLD FREDERIC IN THE HANDS OF CHRISTIAN
LION PREFACE(23)	TO ACCUSE PEOPLE WHO FEEL THAT WAY OF HYPOCRISY.	LIKE	THE LATE SAMUEL BUTLER, HE REGARDS DISEASE AS A
DOCT PREFACE(10)	AND THEN SOME DOCTOR IN AN UNASSAILABLE POSITION,	LIKE	THE LATE SIR WILLIAM GULL, WILL GO INTO THE WITNESS BOX
GETT PREFACE(211)	NATIONS HAVE NOT GRAVITATED TO MONOGAMY,	LIKE	THE LATTER-DAY SAINTS OF SALT LAKE CITY. THE ANSWER IS
BARB III (313)	TROMBONE LIKE A MADMAN: ITS BRAZEN ROARINGS WERE	LIKE	THE LAUGHTER OF THE DAMNED. 117 CONVERSIONS TOOK PLACE
BARB PREFACE(231)	STATE OF MIND ON HIS PART, THE OLD WOMAN,	LIKE	THE LAW SHE THREATENS HIM WITH, IS PERFECTLY READY TO
SIM II (84)	/PROLA/ I DO NOT FEEL LIKE THAT. I FEEL	LIKE	THE LEADER OF A CAVALRY CHARGE WHOSE HORSE HAS BEEN
SUPR IV (167)	/ANN/ I DONT UNDERSTAND IN THE LEAST: IT SOUNDS	LIKE	THE LIFE GUARDS. /TANNER/ WHY DONT YOU MARRY TAVY? HE
MTH5 (240)	BEWARE, WOMAN. THE WRATH OF OZYMANDIAS STRIKES	LIKE	THE LIGHTNING. /THE FEMALE FIGURE/ YOU JUST SAY THAT
LION PROLOG (109)	TO SHEW HOW THE BRAVE BIG LION CAN BEAR PAIN, NOT	LIKE	THE LITTLE CRYBABY CHRISTIAN MAN. OOPSH! (THE THORN
MTH5 (241)	IF YOU CUT OFF HER LEG SHE WOULD GROW ANOTHER,	LIKE	THE LOBSTERS AND THE LITTLE LIZARDS. /THE HE-ANCIENT/
GENV IV (100)	HAPPENING. WE MUST TAKE A PRACTICAL VIEW. IT IS	LIKE	THE LONDON TRAFFIC. WE KNOW THAT SO MANY CHILDREN WILL
MRS PREFACE(154)	THEATRE CRITIC, NOR OF AN INNOCENT COURT OFFICIAL	LIKE	THE LORD CHAMBERLAIN'S EXAMINER, MUCH LESS OF PEOPLE
SUPR PREFACE(R9)	BECOMING CHANGE. YOUR LEVITIES AND AUDACITIES ARE	LIKE	THE LOVES AND COMFORTS PRAYED FOR BY DESDEMONA: THEY
2TRU III (84)	AT CHEQUERS OVER THE WEEKEND, ASKING ONE ANOTHER,	LIKE	THE MAN IN THE BOOK, " WHITHER MUST WE FLEE? " AND
2TRU III (88)	TO RUSH FROM THE BUILDING LEST I GO MAD, CRYING,	LIKE	THE MAN IN YOUR BOOK, " WHAT MUST I DO TO BE SAVED? "
JOAN 6 (129)	HER CLOTHES, AND PUTS ON THE DRESS OF A MAN, IS	LIKE	THE MAN WHO THROWS OFF HIS FUR GOWN AND DRESSES LIKE
GETT (292)	THAT ALL THE GRADES IN DEBRETT AND BURKE SEEM	LIKE	THE MEDALS THEY GIVE CHILDREN IN INFANT SCHOOLS IN
BASH PREFACE(87)	START A LITERARY PRE-RAPHAELITE BROTHERHOOD. I	LIKE	THE MELODIOUS SING-SONG, THE CLEAR SIMPLE ONE-LINE AND
APPL I SD(214)	POSTMISTRESS GENERAL, A MERRY LADY IN UNIFORM	LIKE	THE MEN, ON HIS LEFT, AND LYSISTRATA, POWERMISTRESS
DOCT II (123)	TO CARRY IT OUT UNDER SUCH CIRCUMSTANCES, JUST	LIKE	THE MERCHANT OF VENICE, YOU KNOW. BUT IF A JEW MAKES AN
SUPR HANDBOK(195)	JUST AS HE DID BEFORE. AND THE TRAMP WHO WOULD	LIKE	THE MILLION DOES NOT TAKE THE TROUBLE TO EARN TEN
CAPT III (296)	TO DO; AND I HAVE NOTHING. YOU MIGHT AS WELL TALK	LIKE	THE MISSIONARY AND TELL ME TO DO MY DUTY. /LADY CICELY/
UNPL PREFACE(R10)	ON THE FACT THAT MY MYSTIC WEALTH COULD NOT,	LIKE	THE MONEY FOR WHICH OTHER MEN THREW IT AWAY, BE STORED
MIS. (142)	RESPECTABLE, MIDDLE-CLASS FAMILY. YET YOU GO ON	LIKE	THE MOST UNWHOLESOME PRODUCT OF THE RANKEST
LADY PREFACE(214)	SIMPLE INCARNATION OF EXTRAVAGANT MATERNAL PRIDE	LIKE	THE MOTHER OF CORIOLANUS IN PLUTARCH, AS MR HARRIS
HART II (113)	HIM UPRIGHT) COME, ALFRED. THERE IS A MOON: IT'S	LIKE	THE NIGHT IN TRISTAN AND ISOLDE. (SHE CARESSES HIS ARM
METH PREFACE(R84)	DELINEATION OF CHARACTER" WHICH MAKES HIS PLAYS,	LIKE	THE NOVELS OF SCOTT, DUMAS, AND DICKENS, SO DELIGHTFUL.
OVER PREFACE(161)	IN POPULAR PLAYS. THE PLAYS OF MOLIERE ARE,	LIKE	THE NOVELS OF THE VICTORIAN EPOCH OR DON QUIXOTE, AS
MRS PREFACE(164)	TO EXHIBIT BUT THEIR PRETTINESS, WILL VANISH	LIKE	THE OBSCENE SONGS WHICH WERE SUPPOSED TO ENLIVEN THE
2TRU III (97)	SO, IS ONLY A SMALL BIT OF THE WORLD. IF YOU DONT	LIKE	THE OFFICERS' MESS, THE RANKS ARE OPEN TO YOU. LOOK AT
MTH2 (43)	THESE NAMES, AND WE TWO ARE DRY OLD CODGERS,	LIKE	THE OLD PREACHERS AND PROFESSORS. THEN THE GOSPEL OF
O'FL (216)	THERE! IT WONT BE SEEN ON THE KHAKI: IT'S NOT	LIKE	THE OLD RED COAT THAT WOULD SHEW UP EVERYTHING THAT
MTH2 (43)	RELIGION AS I HAVE WORKED AT IT, ARE DRY SUBJECTS	LIKE	THE OLD STUFF THEY TAUGHT UNDER THESE NAMES, AND WE TWO
LION PREFACE(90)	THEIR DEMONSTRATIONS THAT THE NEW TESTAMENT,	LIKE	THE OLD, SELDOM TELLS A SINGLE STORY OR EXPOUNDS A
CLEO III SD(151)	FROM THE LIGHTHOUSE CRANE ABOVE HIS HEAD. FAGGOTS	LIKE	THE ONE HE SITS ON LIE BENEATH IT READY TO BE DRAWN UP
KING I (204)	MR DRYDEN HAD GIVEN ME SOME REALLY GREAT LINES,	LIKE	THE ONES HE GAVE TO MONTEZUMA. LISTEN. STILL LESS AND
MTH3 (98)	YOUR CHEERY SELF-CONFIDENCE, ARE PLEASANT,	LIKE	THE OPEN AIR. BUT THEY ARE BLIND: THEY ARE VAIN. I SEEM
BULL III (119)	MR BROADBENT? /BROADBENT/ I ASSURE YOU I	LIKE	THE OPEN AIR. /AUNT JUDY/ AH GALONG! HOW CAN YOU LIKE
JOAN PREFACE(48)	THAN THAT SOME OF THEM ARE PROBABLY SLIGHTLY MORE	LIKE	THE ORIGINALS THAN THOSE IMAGINARY PORTRAITS OF ALL THE
BULL PREFACE(36)	AN IRISH CATHOLIC PARTY. THE HOLY ROMAN EMPIRE,	LIKE	THE OTHER EMPIRES, HAS NO FUTURE EXCEPT AS A FEDERATION
LION PREFACE(37)	MAKE ANYTHING NEW OUT OF CHRIST'S MISSION, AND,	LIKE	THE OTHER EVANGELISTS, THINKS THAT THE WHOLE POINT OF
DOCT III (154)	TO ME IN ANSWER TO MY PRAYER. HE WAS NO MORE	LIKE	THE OTHER MEN I HAD MET THAN THE THAMES EMBANKMENT IS
HART I (81)	/MRS HUSHABYE/ DO YOU WANT TO BE MY BREADWINNER,	LIKE	THE OTHER POOR HUSBANDS? /HECTOR/ NO, BY THUNDER!
DOCT PREFACE(67)	WE MAY GUESS THAT THE MEDICAL PROFESSION,	LIKE	THE OTHER PROFESSIONS, CONSISTS OF A SMALL PERCENTAGE
2TRU III (106)	TO HER UNTIL I FOUND MYSELF WISHING SHE WOULD DIE	LIKE	THE OTHERS AND LEAVE ME A LITTLE TO MYSELF, AND NOW I
2TRU I (29)	THE CONSTITUTION OF A HORSE OR SHE'D HAVE DIED	LIKE	THE OTHERS. /THE ELDERLY LADY/ OH, DONT YOU THINK, DEAR
MTH1 II (23)	HAS TO DIG FOR YOU, SWEAT FOR YOU, PLOD FOR YOU,	LIKE	THE OX WHO HELPS HIM TO TEAR UP THE GROUND OR THE ASS
SUPR PREFACE(R37)	PASTEL HAS LOST ITS DRAWING OR ITS COLOR. YET,	LIKE	THE PASTEL, THEY GROW INDEFINABLY SHABBY, AND WILL GROW
O'FL (214)	ME THINKING, SIR; AND I'M NOT USED TO IT. IT'S	LIKE	THE PATRIOTISM OF THE ENGLISH. THEY NEVER THOUGHT OF
MILL III (181)	TO THE WOMEN I SAW IN THERE. /THE MAN/ I DONT	LIKE	THE PEOPLE I EMPLOY TO KNOW TOO MUCH. /EPIFANIA/ I SEE.
HART PREFACE(6)	WERE OFTEN HELPLESS WASTERS OF THEIR INHERITANCE,	LIKE	THE PEOPLE IN TCHEKOV'S CHERRY ORCHARD. EVEN THOSE WHO
NEVR II (255)	MEMBERS OF THE HIGHLY EDUCATED CLASSES	LIKE	THE PEOPLE IN MADEIRA. /GLORIA/ (NOW FULL OF HER
FANY II (292)	IT WAS A LOT, IT WAS VERY STUFFY; AND I DIDNT	LIKE	THE PEOPLE MUCH, BECAUSE THEY DIDNT SEEM TO BE ENJOYING
DOCT V (179)	/JENNIFER/ (TO RIDGEON, POLITELY) SO GLAD YOU	LIKE	THE PICTURES, SIR COLENSO. GOOD MORNING. /RIDGEON/ GOOD
MTH4 I (153)	WAR, SAGES IN PEACE, NOT BABBLERS AND CHARLATANS	LIKE	THE PIGMIES WHO NOW OCCUPY THEIR PLACES IN BAGHDAD, BUT
HART II (85)	ARE ANY NICE HOUSES TO LET DOWN HERE. /MANGAN/ I	LIKE	THE PLACE. THE AIR SUITS ME. I SHOULDNT BE SURPRISED IF
GENV IV (125)	HE SHALL FIND MY PEOPLE ERECT AT THEIR POSTS	LIKE	THE POMPEIAN SENTINEL. YOU ALSO, ERNEST, MUST-- WHAT!
BULL PREFACE(6)	THE FIRST YEARS OF THE FRENCH REVOLUTION IF HE,	LIKE	THE POPE, HAD HAD NO WIFE TO BRING HIM TO THE SCAFFOLD
SUPR HANDBOK(227)	CRIMINAL THAN HE WHO SHOULD BUILD ANOTHER LONDON	LIKE	THE PRESENT ONE, NOR A GREATER BENEFACTOR THAN HE WHO
SUPR I (17)	ANNIE, TO FORCE BUSINESS ON YOU AT A SAD TIME	LIKE	THE PRESENT, BUT YOUR POOR DEAR FATHER'S WILL HAS
O'FL (214)	AGAINST THE ENGLISH, ESPECIALLY AT A MOMENT	LIKE	THE PRESENT, EVEN IF YOUR MOTHER'S POLITICAL SYMPATHIES
JOAN 6 (123)	WE MISS HIM GREATLY, ESPECIALLY ON OCCASIONS	LIKE	THE PRESENT. THE INQUISITOR SMILES PATIENTLY, AND BOWS.

FANY II SD(287)	RESOLUTE MANNER, EVEN PEREMPTORY ON OCCASIONS	LIKE	THE PRESENT, WHEN SHE IS ANNOYED. /MARGARET/ MOTHER,
MIS. (147)	AS THE UNFORTUNATE ENGLISHMAN IN QUESTION, I DONT	LIKE	THE PROCESS. IF I HAD MY LIFE TO LIVE OVER AGAIN, I'D
FABL PREFACE(63)	MEMORABLE THAN CATECHISMS AND CREEDS. FICTIONS	LIKE	THE PRODIGAL SON, THE GOOD SAMARITAN, THE PILGRIM'S
CYMB FORWORD(134)	RECEIVED WITH ACCLAMATION; AND AS THE APPLAUSE,	LIKE	THE PROPOSAL, WAS NOT WHOLLY JOCULAR, THE FANCY BEGAN
SUPR HANDBOK(192)	AT ALL. THE PRUDERY OF THE NEWSPAPERS IS,	LIKE	THE PRUDERY OF THE DINNER TABLE, A MERE DIFFICULTY OF
GETT (319)	ARE YOU SURE THAT ANY OF US, YOUNG OR OLD,	LIKE	THE REAL THING AS WELL AS WE LIKE AN ARTISTIC IMITATION
MIS. PREFACE(29)	IN ANY CASE THERE ARE DECISIVE REASONS, SUPERIOR,	LIKE	THE REASONS FOR SUSPENDING CONVENTIONAL RETICENCES
CAPT NOTES (302)	THE CHARACTER OF CAPTAIN BRASSBOUND'S MOTHER,	LIKE	THE RECOVERY OF THE ESTATE BY THE NEXT HEIR, IS AN
BULL PREFACE(45)	OFF, AND WHICH, WHEN IT DOES COME OFF, IS NOT	LIKE	THE REHEARSALS. HIS OFFICER HAS NOT EVEN HOUSEKEEPER'S
CLEO II SD(120)	EYES, AND PLUMP NOSE AND CHEEKS, WHICH, HOWEVER,	LIKE	THE REST OF HIS FLESH, ARE IN IRON-HARD CONDITION.
BARB III (341)	ARE YOU GOING TO SPEND YOUR LIFE SAYING OUGHT,	LIKE	THE REST OF OUR MORALISTS? TURN YOUR OUGHTS INTO
LADY (247)	OF STATE ALREADY! YOU ARE BECOMING A COURTIER	LIKE	THE REST OF THEM. YOU LACK ADVANCEMENT. /SHAKESPEAR/ "
ARMS II (32)	CHARGED, BEING A THOROUGH SOLDIER, HE RAN AWAY	LIKE	THE REST OF THEM, WITH OUR CAVALRY AT HIS HEELS. TO
CLEO IV (170)	AND NOT YOU? /FTATATEETA/ (INDIGNANTLY) YOU ARE	LIKE	THE REST OF THEM. YOU WANT TO BE WHAT THESE ROMANS CALL
PYGM V (273)	(TOLERANTLY) A LITTLE OF BOTH, HENRY,	LIKE	THE REST OF US: A LITTLE OF BOTH. /HIGGINS/ WELL, YOU
POSN (437)	/ELDER DANIELS/ HE HAS A SOUL TO BE SAVED, ALMOST	LIKE	THE REST OF US. I AM BOUND TO TRY TO PUT SOME RELIGION
SUPR I (47)	/TANNER/ YOU MUST COWER BEFORE THE WEDDING RING	LIKE	THE REST OF US, RAMSDEN. THE CUP OF OUR IGNOMINY IS
POSN (463)	FRAUD AND A FAILURE. I STARTED IN TO BE A BAD MAN	LIKE	THE REST OF YOU. YOU ALL STARTED IN TO BE BAD MEN OR
BULL I (93)	LET HIM ALONE AND LAUGH AT HIM FOR BEING A FOOL	LIKE	THE REST. OH, NATURE IS CUNNING! CUNNING! (HE SITS
SUPR I (45)	INDIGNATION) OH! YOU THINK ME A WICKED WOMAN,	LIKE	THE REST. YOU THINK I HAVE NOT ONLY BEEN VILE, BUT THAT
DOCT PREFACE(33)	HERE TO EXPLAIN THEIR ERROR. THE RIGHT TO KNOW IS	LIKE	THE RIGHT TO LIVE. IT IS FUNDAMENTAL AND UNCONDITIONAL
GETT (330)	LOOK AT YOU-- NOT YET. I'M NOT STARVING FOR LOVE	LIKE	THE ROBINS IN WINTER, AS THE GOOD LADIES YOURE
METH PREFACE(R72)	THE HOMEOPATHIC REACTION AGAINST DARWINISM. WHEN,	LIKE	THE RUSSIANS, OUR NIHILISTS HAVE IT URGENTLY BORNE IN
MILL I (164)	WHO MARRY SHOULD THINK ABOUT THE SAME THINGS AND	LIKE	THE SAME THINGS. THEY SHOULDNT BE OVER ONEANOTHER'S
MIS. PREFACE(70)	QUARTERS CAN BE KEPT OUT OF THE PARENTS' WAY	LIKE	THE SERVANTS' QUARTERS. NOT TOO MUCH WIND ON THE HEATH,
MILL PREFACE(132)	THE SILLY PUBLIC BELIEVE THE CONTRARY. FOR WAR IS	LIKE	THE SEVEN MAGIC BULLETS WHICH THE DEVIL HAS READY TO
BARB III SD(326)	TO THE RIGHT IS THE DOOR OF AN OFFICE, WHICH,	LIKE	THE SHEDS, IS OF THE LIGHTEST POSSIBLE CONSTRUCTION.
DEST (192)	DOES WHAT PLEASES HIM AND GRABS WHAT HE COVETS:	LIKE	THE SHOPKEEPER, HE PURSUES HIS PURPOSE WITH THE
ARMS I (7)	OUT). /LOUKA/ (SECRETLY, TO RAINA) IF YOU WOULD	LIKE	THE SHUTTERS OPEN, JUST GIVE THEM A PUSH LIKE THIS (
BULL PREFACE(9)	IS CRIME-- AT LEAST IT IS NOT UNNATURAL CRIME,	LIKE	THE SLAYING OF AN IRISHMAN BY AN IRISHMAN FOR ENGLAND'S
LION EPILOG (151)	MAN AS THE FREAKS OF THE CHURCH. THE CHURCH,	LIKE	THE SOCIETY OF WHICH IT IS AN ORGAN, IS BALANCED AND
2TRU PREFACE(5)	OF THE POOR, WE ARE ALL AMAZED AND INCREDULOUS,	LIKE	THE SOLDIER, WHEN WE HEAR OF THE MULTIMILLIONAIRE
6CAL PREFACE(89)	NOTHING OF THIS. A KING EDWARD WHO DID NOT BEHAVE	LIKE	THE SON OF KING EDWARD THE SEVENTH SEEMED UNNATURAL AND
HART PREFACE(35)	FEMALES LIKE POTIPHAR'S WIFE, AND EROTIC POETRY	LIKE	THE SONG OF SONGS, WERE READ ALOUD; WHERE THE SENSUOUS
BUOY III (36)	AND I AM MAGICALLY HAPPY. UNREADABLE POEMS	LIKE	THE SONG OF SOLOMON DELIGHT ME: BAGATELLES BY BEETHOVEN
MRS IV (235)	GO AND ENJOY THE SATURDAY HALF-HOLIDAY SOMEWHERE,	LIKE	THE STAFF. WHAT DO YOU SAY TO RICHMOND, AND THEN A
CLEO IV (183)	SOMETHING VASTER THAN THAT-- SOMETHING UNIVERSAL,	LIKE	THE STARRY FIRMAMENT. /CAESAR/ (PROSAICALLY) WHY NOT
APPL INTRLUD(248)	FOR ME, TO ENABLE ME TO REIGN OVER THEM IN BEAUTY	LIKE	THE STARS WITHOUT HAVING ANYTHING TO DO WITH THEIR
3PLA PREFACE(R20)	MARVEL ON MARVEL; WHILST THE ENGLISH NOVELIST,	LIKE	THE STARVING TRAMP WHO CAN THINK OF NOTHING BUT HIS
MTH2 (67)	BUT INVOLUNTARILY MAKING A MOVEMENT WHICH LOOKS	LIKE	THE STIFLING OF A YAWN) WITH PLEASURE, MR BARNABAS. OF
SIM I SD(36)	WELL WITH A LOW MARBLE PARAPET. THIS PARAPET,	LIKE	THE STONE SEATS, HAS SILK CUSHIONS SCATTERED ABOUT IT.
MIS. PREFACE(96)	REASONS; AND ONE OF THEM IS THAT CHILDREN ALL	LIKE	THE STORY OF JONAH AND THE WHALE (THEY INSIST ON ITS
PRES (153)	DETERMINATION WHICH ARE NEEDED TO COMBAT WOMEN	LIKE	THE SUFFRAGETS. /LADY CORINTHIA/ NATURE IS TOO STRONG
POSN (443)	AND BAD COMPANY AND EVIL THOUGHTS PASSED BY ME	LIKE	THE SUMMER WIND AS YOU MIGHT SAY: I WAS TOO DRUNK TO
MIS. PREFACE(80)	POSSIBILITY; BUT A MOTHER IS LIKE A BROOMSTICK OR	LIKE	THE SUN IN THE HEAVENS, IT DOES NOT MATTER WHICH AS FAR
CLEO III (160)	GESTURE TO THE SKY ABOVE THE PARAPET) RISING	LIKE	THE SUN WITH MY TREASURE, HE GOES BACK THE WAY HE CAME.
LADY PREFACE(221)	SONNET! " MY MISTRESS' EYES ARE NOTHING	LIKE	THE SUN; CORAL IS FAR MORE RED THAN HER LIPS' RED; IF
LADY PREFACE(222)	AT ALL THAT OF " MY MISTRESS' EYES ARE NOTHING	LIKE	THE SUN," ETC., NOT A WORD WAS LOST ON HER, AND IS IT
GLIM (180)	HER FIGURE TERRIBLY. /SQUARCIO/ THERE IS NOTHING	LIKE	THE SWORD, EXCELLENCY. /SANDRO/ EXCEPT THE WATER,
SUPR HANDBOK(205)	TO A BOARD AND CRAM THEM WITH FOOD BECAUSE WE	LIKE	THE TASTE OF LIVER DISEASE; WE TEAR BIRDS TO PIECES TO
NEVR I (221)	PUT UP WITH THEM. I'M USED TO IT NOW: IN FACT I	LIKE	THE TASTE WHEN THE SOAP IS REALLY GOOD. /VALENTINE/ (
GENV IV (119)	/SIR O./ WITH CERTAIN RESERVATIONS, YES. I DO NOT	LIKE	THE TERM " ADVANCED RACE." I GREATLY MISTRUST ADVANCED
LION II (135)	DOES IT? /FERROVIUS/ MAN: THERE IS NO TERROR	LIKE	THE TERROR OF THAT SOUND TO ME. WHEN I HEAR A TRUMPET
APPL PREFACE(195)	WITH THE WAR ON OUR HANDS, THE CLEARING HOUSE,	LIKE	THE THAMES PIER, REMAINS ON PAPER; AND GATTIE IS IN HIS
SUPR I (33)	ME, JACK; BUT THE THINGS YOU DID WERE NEVER A BIT	LIKE	THE THINGS I WANTED YOU TO DO. THEY OFTEN GAVE ME GREAT
SUPR I (21)	TANNER. /ANN/ (GENTLY) NO YOU DONT, JACK. THATS	LIKE	THE THINGS YOU SAY ON PURPOSE TO SHOCK PEOPLE: THOSE
PRES (157)	AS THE PREY OF EVERY LIBERTINE. YOU THINK I AM	LIKE	THE THOUSANDS OF WEAK WOMEN WHOM YOU HAVE RUINED--
CURE (235)	NOTHING BUT THAT? /STREGA/ VERY SOFTLY AT FIRST.	LIKE	THE TICKING OF A WATCH. THEN LOUDER AND LOUDER, AS YOU
METH PREFACE(R69)	OPPORTUNISM; AND ALL THE GOVERNMENTS WILL BE	LIKE	THE TRAMP WHO WALKS ALWAYS WITH THE WIND AND ENDS AS A
JOAN EPILOG (157)	FOUNDATION OF THE CHURCH. THE SOLID EARTH SWAYS	LIKE	THE TREACHEROUS SEA BENEATH THE FEET OF MEN AND SPIRITS
GETT PREFACE(232)	NO LONGER REALLY VALUED; AND THIS INDIFFERENCE,	LIKE	THE TRIPLE BOND OF AFFECTION WHICH CARRIED SIR WILLIAM
SUPR I (33)	YOU WERE PURE LIES. I SOON NOTICED THAT YOU DIDNT	LIKE	THE TRUE STORIES. /ANN/ OF COURSE I KNEW THAT SOME OF
PHIL III (141)	YOULL EXCUSE MY SAYING THAT IT SOUNDS MUCH MORE	LIKE	THE TRUTH. COME! YOU WERE HUMBUGGING US, WERENT YOU..
MIS. PREFACE(52)	TO ASCERTAIN WHAT THEY ARE, AND COMING OF AGE IS	LIKE	THE TURNING OF A CONVICT INTO THE STREETS AFTER
BULL III (117)	IN THE HOUSEHOLD AS " THE OFFICE." THIS CHAIR,	LIKE	THE TWO OCCUPIED BY LARRY AND BROADBENT, HAS A MAHOGANY
SIM PREFACE(19)	DAY OF JUDGMENT NOT MERELY DO THEY CEASE TO EXIST	LIKE	THE USELESS AND PREDATORY PEOPLE: IT BECOMES APPARENT
3PLA PREFACE(R9)	INTO THE BARGAIN. BUT THE THEATRE STRUCK ME DOWN	LIKE	THE VERIEST WEAKLING. I SANK UNDER IT LIKE A BABY FED
O'FL (214)	NATURAL DIVILMENT AND BE THE SAME AS EVER. IT'S	LIKE	THE VERMIN: ITLL WASH OFF AFTER A WHILE. /SIR PEARCE/ (
DEVL II (33)	RAINING? (HE SHUTS THE DOOR). /RICHARD/ RAINING	LIKE	THE VERY (HIS EYE CATCHES JUDITH'S AS SHE LOOKS
SIM II (63)	GOD AND HIS CHURCH. /LADY FARWATERS/ THAT SOUNDS	LIKE	THE VOICE OF A GROWNUP MAN THROUGH THE WHOOPING OF A
MTH3 (119)	ME TO SIT AND TALK WITH HER BECAUSE MY VOICE WAS	LIKE	THE VOICE OF HER DEAD MOTHER. /BURGE-LUBIN/ THE
SUPR III SD(94)	FOR A MUCH MORE DISTINGUISHED INTONATION, IS SO	LIKE	THE VOICE OF ROEBUCK RAMSDEN THAT IT CALLS ATTENTION TO
2TRU III (87)	FOR THREE HUNDRED YEARS, HAS CRUMBLED	LIKE	THE WALLS OF JERICHO BEFORE THE CRITICISM OF EINSTEIN.
JITT PREFACE(5)	OF POISON OR A BROKEN HEART: THE VILLAIN MAY,	LIKE	THE WICKED COUNT IN IL TROVATORE, LIVE ONLY TO
MTH4 I SD(145)	UP THE STEPS AND INTERCEPTS HIM. HE IS DRESSED	LIKE	THE WOMAN, BUT A SLIGHT MOUSTACHE PROCLAIMS HIS SEX.
MIS. PREFACE(36)	YOU HAVE TO PAY SCOT AND LOT IN PERSONAL EFFORT	LIKE	THE WORKING FOLK. THEREFORE, IF FOR ONLY HALF AN HOUR A
LION PREFACE(33)	WAS MERELY GOING THROUGH A PREDETERMINED RITUAL,	LIKE	THE WORKS OF A CLOCK, INSTEAD OF LIVING. FINALLY MARK
MILL IV (203)	CALL IT VANITY IF YOU WILL; BUT I SHOULD RATHER	LIKE	THE WORLD TO KNOW THAT IN MY LITTLE WAY I WAS ABLE TO
GENV PREFACE(22)	SMALL FRY OF DEGENERATE HEREDITARY TRIBAL CHIEFS	LIKE	THEEBAW IN BURMA HAVE GONE CRAZY AND BECOME WORSE
INCA (242)	A RIGID ECONOMY, AND DESIRE US TO TREAT THEM	LIKE	THEIR POOREST SUBJECTS. /THE PRINCESS/ OH YES. YOU ARE
LION PREFACE(6)	AS CHRISTIANS THAN BY MAHOMETANS, WHO ARE,	LIKE	THEIR PROPHET, VERY CIVIL TO JESUS, AND ALLOW HIM A
MIS. (165)	BECAUSE MEN MADE THEM. I DIDNT MAKE THEM: I DONT	LIKE	THEM: I WONT KEEP THEM. NOW WHAT WILL YOU DO?
MTH3 (128)	DOING? ARNT YOU INTERESTED IN THEM? DONT YOU	LIKE	THEM? /BARNABAS/ LIKE THEM! I HATE THEM. THEY ARE
APPL INTRLUD(253)	ANY OTHER WOMAN STAND YOUR SERMONS, AND EVEN	LIKE	THEM? /MAGNUS/ ORINTHIA: WE ARE ONLY TWO CHILDREN AT
FABL PREFACE(71)	SULPHUR HAD NO SUCH EFFECT. PATHOGENIC BACILLI	LIKE	THEM AND MULTIPLY ON THEM. I PUT THE CASE TO THE
MIS. PREFACE(83)	THE REPULSIVE EFFECT OF THE OBLIGATION TO	LIKE	THEM AND TO ADMIT THEM TO OUR INTIMACY. BUT TO HAVE A
CAPT II (261)	ALL THE REASONS FOR NOT HELPING THEM, AND IF YOU	LIKE	THEM YOU THINK OF ALL THE OPPOSITE REASONS.
SUPR I (9)	WELL, IF THESE ARE ANARCHIST MANNERS, I HOPE YOU	LIKE	THEM. AND ANNIE WITH HIM! ANNIE! A-- (HE CHOKES).
MIS. (136)	THEIR BROTHERS FROM MURDERING THEM; BUT I DIDNT	LIKE	THEM. AND I LIKE TARLETON. /MRS TARLETON/ EVERYBODY
MTH1 II (32)	I HAVE MADE A WOMAN-CHILD THAT HAS GROWN UP QUITE	LIKE	THEM. AND OTHERS THINK OF NUMBERS WITHOUT HAVING TO
DOCT I (113)	I DID NOT BRING THE REALLY BEST: SO FEW PEOPLE	LIKE	THEM. HE IS TWENTY-THREE: HIS WHOLE LIFE IS BEFORE HIM.
MTH5 (237)	LIKE HIM TO PUT HIS ARM ROUND MY NECK. I DONT	LIKE	THEM. (THE MALE FIGURE LOOKS OFFENDED, AND THE FEMALE
SIM II (84)	HIGH SPIRITS! /PRA/ THE COMING RACE WILL NOT BE	LIKE	THEM. MEANWHILE WE ARE FACE TO FACE WITH THE FACT THAT
O'FL (215)	SHE'S LIKE THE ENGLISH: THEY THINK THERES NO ONE	LIKE	THEMSELVES. IT'S THE SAME WITH THE GERMANS, THOUGH
MIS. PREFACE(46)	FORCE ARE, AND TREAT THE CHILD AS AN EXPERIMENT	LIKE	THEMSELVES, AND POSSIBLY A MORE SUCCESSFUL ONE, AND AT
MRS PREFACE(174)	TO BE ABLE TO CONCEIVE THAT RESPECTABLE GENTLEMEN	LIKE	THEMSELVES, WHO WOULD INSTANTLY CALL THE POLICE TO
MIS. PREFACE(27)	UNDERSTAND THEIR CASE, QUITE COMMONLY RESPECT AND	LIKE	THEM, AND ALWAYS LEARN SOMETHING FROM THEM. HERE,
NEVR II (226)	FAMILY, MRS CLANDON'S, SIR. /THE GENTLEMAN/ YOU	LIKE	THEM, DO YOU? /WAITER/ YES, SIR. THEY HAVE A FREE WAY
MTH3 (124)	NO WORK. /THE ARCHBISHOP/ THAT IS TRUE; BUT WE,	LIKE	THEM, GET OUR DIVIDENDS WHETHER WE WORK OR NOT. WE WORK
PYGM V (283)	GROWN ACCUSTOMED TO YOUR VOICE AND APPEARANCE. I	LIKE	THEM, RATHER. /LIZA/ WELL, YOU HAVE BOTH OF THEM ON
MTH3 (128)	IN THEM? DONT YOU LIKE THEM? /BARNABAS/	LIKE	THEM! I HATE THEM. THEY ARE MONSTERS, UNNATURAL
MILL II (167)	REPULSIVE EXCEPT MYSELF. /EPIFANIA/ DONT YOU	LIKE	THESE DEAR OLD-WORLD PLACES? I DO. /ADRIAN/ I DONT.
MILL PREFACE(110)	ORGANIZED AND RULED BY HIS BUTLER? QUESTIONS	LIKE	THESE FORCE THEMSELVES ON US SO CONTINUALLY AND
WIDO I (19)	EXCELLENT YOUNG FELLOW. BUT FAMILY COMMUNICATIONS	LIKE	THESE REQUIRE GOOD MANNERS. THEY REQUIRE TACT; AND TACT
MIS. PREFACE(47)	SENDINGS TO BED AND STANDING IN CORNERS AND THE	LIKE	THEY HAVE SUFFERED BECAUSE THEIR PARENTS AND GUARDIANS
CAND III (138)	PIETY HISSELF ARTER TWO SIPS. PEOPLE CARNT DRINK	LIKE	THEY HUSETER. (BUSTLING ACROSS TO THE HEARTH) WELL,
PHIL I (91)	/CRAVEN/ (INTERCEPTING HIM) STOP! DONT LEAVE ME	LIKE	THIS: I SHALL LOOK LIKE A FOOL. NOW I SHALL REALLY TAKE

MILL IV	(203)	CRUELTY AND ADULTERY. /PATRICIA/ BUT I DONT	LIKE	THIS: IT'S NOT FAIR TO ALASTAIR. WHY IS HE TO BE
NEVR III	(263)	A BOAT, MAAM. VERY PLEASANT ON A FINE AFTERNOON	LIKE	THIS: VERY PLEASANT AND INVIGORATING INDEED. (HE TAKES
MTH2	(66)	AT HER). DADDY: ARE YOU GOING TO LET THEM OFF	LIKE	THIS? HOW ARE THEY TO KNOW ANYTHING IF NOBODY EVER
JOAN 2	(71)	DEVIL DOES THE DAUPHIN MEAN BY KEEPING US WAITING	LIKE	THIS? I DONT KNOW HOW YOU HAVE THE PATIENCE TO STAND
BASH I	(94)	CHEST WITH BREATH? OR LIKE A FEATHER LIFT YOU--	LIKE	THIS? (HE SETS HER ON HER FEET.) /LYDIA/ (PANTING)
PYGM IV	(263)	HIS LOFTIEST MANNER) WHY HAVE YOU BEGUN GOING ON	LIKE	THIS? MAY I ASK WHETHER YOU COMPLAIN OF YOUR TREATMENT
2TRU I	(28)	WHAT RIGHT HAS SHE TO GET ILL AND MAKE ME ILL	LIKE	THIS? MEASLES: THATS WHAT SHE'S GOT. MEASLES! GERMAN
NEVR IV	(295)	ARE A REGULAR OVERWHELMER! DO YOU ALWAYS GO ON	LIKE	THIS? /BOHUN/ (RISING) YES. DONT YOU TRY TO PUT ME
PHIL II	(101)	CUTHBERTSON: DID YOU EVER HEAR ANYTHING	LIKE	THIS? /CUTHBERTSON/ NEVER! NEVER! /CHARTERIS/ OH,
HART II	(88)	DO YOU THINK I'LL BE MADE A CONVENIENCE OF	LIKE	THIS? /ELLIE/ COME, MR MANGAN! YOU MADE A BUSINESS
DOCT I	(84)	EMMY. HOW CAN I WORK WITH YOU DUSTING ALL OVER ME	LIKE	THIS? /EMMY/ I'M NOT HINDERING YOU WORKING-- IF YOU
GETT	(337)	YOU THINK I'LL LET MYSELF BE DRIVEN INTO A TRAP	LIKE	THIS? /HOTCHKISS/ YOU ARE IN IT ALREADY. MARRIAGE IS A
PRES	(150)	STOOD IT. IS AN ENGLISHMAN TO BE MADE A MOCKERY	LIKE	THIS? /MITCHENER/ SILENCE. ATTENTION. RIGHT ABOUT
OVER	(184)	OF KNITTING WOOL? THAT YOU CAN THROW IT AWAY	LIKE	THIS? /MRS LUNN/ I DONT THROW AWAY BALLS OF KNITTING
DOCT I	(112)	ANNOYED) WHAT DO YOU MEAN BY INTERRUPTING ME	LIKE	THIS? /REDPENNY/ BUT-- /RIDGEON/ CHUT? CANT YOU SEE
PRES	(140)	(ANGRILY) WHAT IS IT? HOW DARE YOU INTERRUPT US	LIKE	THIS? /THE ORDERLY/ DIDNT YOU HEAR THE EXPLOSION,
PYGM II	(234)	IS IT FAIRITY TO TAKE ADVANTAGE OF A MAN	LIKE	THIS? THE GIRL BELONGS TO ME. YOU GOT HER. WHERE DO I
AUGS	(268)	THE DEATH RATE OF LITTLE PIFFLINGTON IN A MOMENT	LIKE	THIS? THINK OF OUR GALLANT SOLDIERS, NOT OF YOUR
SUPR III	(83)	SISTER, SEE? WOT DO YOU MEAN BY GASSIN ABOUT HER	LIKE	THIS? WOTSHE GOT TO DO WITH YOU? /MENDOZA/ A DRAMATIC
DEVL II	(45)	COME, COME! HOW AM I TO LEAVE YOU IF YOU TALK	LIKE	THIS? YOU ARE QUITE OUT OF YOUR SENSES. (HE TURNS TO
APPL I	(240)	PATIENCE STRAINED) WHAT IS THE USE OF GOING ON	LIKE	THIS? YOU ARE LIKE A MAN ON THE SCAFFOLD, SPINNING OUT
MRS II	(212)	WHAT RIGHT HAVE YOU TO SET YOURSELF UP ABOVE ME	LIKE	THIS? YOU BOAST OF WHAT YOU ARE TO ME-- TO ME, WHO
MIS.	(117)	WAY OF HURT FEELINGS. YOULL EXCUSE ME RAMBLING ON	LIKE	THIS ABOUT MY SON. /JOHNNY/ (WHO HAS PULLED HIMSELF
PHIL III	(138)	/JULIA/ HOW HAVE YOU THE FACE TO TURN ROUND	LIKE	THIS AFTER INSULTING AND TORTURING ME? /CHARTERIS/
MTH5	(216)	SHE IS FOUR, THAT MEANS THAT SHE HAS GROWN UP	LIKE	THIS ANCIENT HERE, AND HAS LEFT HIM. IF YOU CHOOSE ME,
2TRU II	(77)	THEM DOWN ON US LIKE A SWARM OF HORNETS. I DONT	LIKE	THIS AT ALL. I MUST GET TO THE BOTTOM OF IT AT ONCE.
JOAN 2	(80)	! /JOAN/ (NOT AT ALL EMBARRASSED) I WEAR IT	LIKE	THIS BECAUSE I AM A SOLDIER. WHERE BE DAUPHIN? A
MIS.	(176)	I DO WONDER AT YOU, JOHN, LETTING HIM TALK	LIKE	THIS BEFORE EVERYBODY. (TURNING RATHER TARTLY TO LINA)
HART III	(132)	MRS HUSHABYE: ARE MY AFFAIRS TO BE DISCUSSED	LIKE	THIS BEFORE EVERYBODY? /LADY UTTERWORD/ I DONT THINK
SUPR III	(85)	YOU DO NOT CARE FOR THAT ONE: I THINK YOU WILL	LIKE	THIS BETTER. (HE RECITES, IN RICH SOFT TONES, AND IN
MILL III	(181)	AND SHE KNOWS SHE'S GOT US. /EPIFANIA/ I DO NOT	LIKE	THIS BLACKMAILING BUSINESS. OF COURSE IF I MUST I MUST;
JITT II	(48)	GOING TO ASSERT MYSELF. YOU CANT SETTLE AN AFFAIR	LIKE	THIS BY LOOKING LIKE A MARTYR AND WALKING OUT INTO THE
MILL III	(181)	KNOW SUCH A LOT OUGHT TO KNOW THAT A BUSINESS	LIKE	THIS CANT AFFORD ANY LUXURIES. IT'S A CHEAP LABOR
BARB II	(282)	I SPOWSE YOU THINK AW CAM EAH TO BEG FROM YOU,	LIKE	THIS DEMMIGED LOT EAH. NOT ME. AW DOWNT WANT YOUR BREAD
SHAK	(142)	WHICH IT INHERIT, SHALL DISSOLVE-- /SHAV/ -- AND	LIKE	THIS FOOLISH LITTLE SHOW OF OURS LEAVE NOT A WRACK
CAND I	(101)	ME? /MARCHBANKS/ (LOOKING ROUND WILDLY) IS IT	LIKE	THIS FOR HER HERE ALWAYS? A WOMAN, WITH A GREAT SOUL,
JITT I	(23)	MY PROMISE. /BRUNO/ I COULD NOT HAVE PAINED YOU	LIKE	THIS IF I HAD THE SMALLEST DOUBT THAT I SHALL GO FIRST
WIDO I	(4)	ON BANK HOLIDAY? WOULD YOU DREAM OF BEHAVING	LIKE	THIS IN LONDON? /TRENCH/ OH, ROT! IVE COME ABROAD TO
OVER	(184)	WELL AS CLEAN. /JUNO/ I HAVE NEVER BEEN TREATED	LIKE	THIS IN MY LIFE. HERE AM I, A MARRIED MAN, WITH A MOST
MTH2	(47)	YEA, ALL THAT IT INHERIT SHALL DISSOLVE, AND,	LIKE	THIS INFLUENTIAL PAGEANT FADED, LEAVE NOT A RACK
DOCT IV	(169)	AFTER LIFE'S FITFUL FEVER THEY SLEEP WELL AND	LIKE	THIS INSUBSTANTIAL BOURNE FROM WHICH NO TRAVELLER
ROCK II	(265)	TELL YOU, ARTHUR, THAT FRIVOLITY ON A VITAL POINT	LIKE	THIS IS IN VERY BAD TASTE. AND YOU KNOW VERY WELL THAT
ROCK II	(264)	THROUGH CONTINENTS VASTER THAN A MILLION DOGHOLES	LIKE	THIS ISLAND OF YOURS, THEY FOUNDED A CIVILIZATION
HART III	(136)	IT. EVERY TIME ONE OF YOU OPENS YOUR MOUTH I GO	LIKE	THIS (HE COWERS AS IF TO AVOID A MISSILE) AFRAID OF
GETT	(261)	HIM AND YOU, LET ALONE THE PLEASURE IN A HOUSE	LIKE	THIS (MRS BRIDGENORTH BOWS IN ACKNOWLEDGMENT OF THE
ARMS I	(7)	LIKE THE SHUTTERS OPEN, JUST GIVE THEM A PUSH	LIKE	THIS (SHE PUSHES THEM: THEY OPEN: SHE PULLS THEM TO
CAPT II	(263)	ON THE LOOKOUT. LOOK HERE, CAPN: WE DONT HALF	LIKE	THIS JOB. THE GENTLEMAN HAS BEEN TALKING TO US A BIT;
POSN	(451)	IS. SO NOW GO RIGHT AHEAD. IF THE PRISONER DONT	LIKE	THIS JURY, HE SHOULD HAVE STOLE A HORSE IN ANOTHER
FANY PROLOG	(271)	MY FATHER THAT LOTS OF PEOPLE WRITE PLAYS JUST	LIKE	THIS ONE-- THAT I HAVNT SELECTED IT OUT OF MERE
HART II	(85)	? /ELLIE/ WAS I? I FORGET. TELL ME. DO YOU	LIKE	THIS PART OF THE COUNTRY? I HEARD YOU ASK MR HUSHABYE
APPL I	(236)	I BEG YOUR PARDON, SIR; BUT REALLY -- AT A MOMENT	LIKE	THIS -- (WORDS FAIL HER). /MAGNUS/ (TO BALBUS) IF I
FANY II	(294)	IT'S SO REAL AND SATISFACTORY. /MRS KNOX/ I DONT	LIKE	THIS SPIRIT IN YOU, MARGARET. I DONT LIKE YOUR TALKING
BULL IV	(168)	(STOPPING TO SNUFF UP THE HILLSIDE AIR) AH! I	LIKE	THIS SPOT. I LIKE THIS VIEW. THIS WOULD BE A JOLLY GOOD
POSN	(448)	WHAT ARE YOU? YOURE A WORSE DANGER TO A TOWN	LIKE	THIS THAN TEN HORSE-THIEVES. /FEEMY/ MR KEMP: WILL YOU
O'FL	(223)	OF BREAKING DOWN) DINNY DARLINT, WHY ARE YOU	LIKE	THIS TO ME? WHATS HAPPENED TO YOU? /O'FLAHERTY/ (
LADY	(238)	SIR, I DARE BE SWORN, DO NOT HAVE AN ADVENTURE	LIKE	THIS TWICE IN THE YEAR. /THE MAN/ VILLAIN: WOULDST TELL
BULL IV	(168)	UP THE HILLSIDE AIR) AH! I LIKE THIS SPOT. I	LIKE	THIS VIEW. THIS WOULD BE A JOLLY GOOD PLACE FOR A HOTEL
APPL INTRLUD	(252)	WHAT I COME HERE FOR IS TO ENJOY TALKING TO YOU	LIKE	THIS WHEN I NEED AN HOUR'S RESPITE FROM ROYALTY: WHEN
MIS.	(163)	THE SKY. DONT YOU KNOW THAT YOU MUST ALWAYS GO ON	LIKE	THIS WHEN YOU GET THE CHANCE? YOU MUST COME TO THE TOP
CATH 4	(190)	SAKE, MADAM, DO YOU INTEND TO LEAVE ME TIED UP	LIKE	THIS WHILE YOU DISCUSS THE BLASPHEMIES OF THAT
MIS.	(163)	HER TOUCH) NO, NO: DONT YOU KNOW YOU MUSTNT GO ON	LIKE	THIS WITH A PERFECT STRANGER? /HYPATIA/ DROPPED DOWN
MTH3	(99)	IF YOU THINK I AM GOING TO SIT HERE ON A FINE DAY	LIKE	THIS WITH MY LEGS CROSSED WAITING FOR GREAT THOUGHTS,
JOAN 6	(129)	OF SUFFICIENTLY LARGE MIND TO CONDUCT AN INQUIRY	LIKE	THIS WOULD CONSIDER SERIOUS. I AGREE WITH MY COLLEAGUE
MILL I	(148)	THE TABLE. /PATRICIA/ YOU SEE, MR SAGAMORE, IT'S	LIKE	THIS. ALASTAIR-- /EPIFANIA/ YOU NEED NOT EXPLAIN. I
JITT II	(38)	HER ARM PERSUASIVELY) MY DEAR: YOU MUSTNT GO ON	LIKE	THIS. COME: LET ME TALK TO YOU QUIETLY. (SHE DRAWS HER
METH PREFACE	(R52)	FORM OF HIS EXPERIMENT WOULD HAVE BEEN SOMETHING	LIKE	THIS. FIRST, HE SHOULD HAVE PROCURED A COLONY OF MICE
PYGM II	(224)	REALLY YOU MUST. YOU CANT WALK OVER EVERYBODY	LIKE	THIS. HIGGINS, THUS SCOLDED, SUBSIDES. THE HURRICANE IS
FANY I	(277)	I WAS A SUFFRAGETTE: ONLY FANCY! YOU SEE IT WAS	LIKE	THIS. HOLY JOE GOT TALKING ABOUT HOW HE'D BEEN A
JITT I	(19)	MYSELF, THAT I AM SPENDING OUR PRICELESS MOMENTS	LIKE	THIS. I AM AS IMPATIENT AS YOU ARE: I LONG FOR YOU
LIED	(200)	(MUCH TAKEN ABACK) THERE IS NO NEED TO INSULT ME	LIKE	THIS. I ASSURE YOU, ON MY HONOR AS A-- /HER HUSBAND/ (
CURE	(225)	NOW REALLY THIS IS SILLY. YOU MUSTNT GIVE WAY	LIKE	THIS. I TELL YOU NOTHING'S HAPPENED TO YOU. HANG IT
HART I	(49)	SO HAPPY: I HAD FORGOTTEN THAT PEOPLE COULD LIVE	LIKE	THIS. I WANTED TO SEE MY FATHER, MY SISTER, MY NEPHEWS
PYGM III	(252)	LIVE WITH. (NOW QUITE AT HER EASE) YOU SEE, IT'S	LIKE	THIS. IF A MAN HAS A BIT OF A CONSCIENCE, IT ALWAYS
JOAN EPILOG	(167)	FOR A LECTURE ON THE SUBJECT) YOU SEE, IT'S	LIKE	THIS. IF -- (THE FIRST STROKE OF MIDNIGHT IS HEARD
FANY II	(289)	TO HOLLOWAY THAN KEEP TALKING ROUND AND ROUND IT	LIKE	THIS. IF YOURE GOING TO TURN ME OUT OF THE HOUSE, TURN
GENV I	(35)	(WITH APLOMB) UNDOUBTEDLY. /NEWCOMER/ WELL, IT'S	LIKE	THIS. IN MY COUNTRY WEVE HAD AN ELECTION. WE THOUGHT IT
HART III	(137)	ON MY HEAD OR MY HEELS WHEN YOU ALL START ON ME	LIKE	THIS. I'LL STAY. I'LL MARRY HER. I'LL DO ANYTHING FOR A
CURE	(233)	(TEARFULLY) YOUVE NO RIGHT TO BULLY ME	LIKE	THIS. I'M ILL: I CANT BEAR IT. I'LL THROW MYSELF OUT OF
O'FL	(212)	ALL RIGHT: SHE MUST BE INDULGED ON AN OCCASION	LIKE	THIS. I'M SORRY MY WIFE IS IN LONDON: SHE'D HAVE BEEN
CAPT III	(291)	A FOOL. ALL THE SAME, SHE SHALL NOT SEE ME AGAIN	LIKE	THIS. (HE PULLS OFF THE COAT AND WAISTCOAT TOGETHER).
APPL II	(269)	DOWN). /NICOBAR/ YOU CANT UPSET THE APPLE CART	LIKE	THIS. (HE SITS DOWN). /CRASSUS/ I MUST SAY THIS IS NOT
PHIL I	(72)	CAN FIND ON THE PIANO; BUT TO HER EARS IT IS JUST	LIKE	THIS. (HE SITS DOWN ON THE BASS END OF THE KEYBOARD.
POSN	(449)	APPEARANCE IS EVERYTHING IN A LOW-CLASS PLACE	LIKE	THIS. (HE TAKES OUT A POCKET COMB AND MIRROR, AND
CURE	(232)	DEVELOPED BY PLAYING LEFT HAND OCTAVE PASSAGES--	LIKE	THIS. (SHE BEGINS PLAYING LISZT'S TRANSCRIPTION OF
PRES	(156)	ARE ORDERED TO PUT A PERSON OUT YOU SHOULD DO IT	LIKE	THIS. (SHE HURLS HIM FROM THE ROOM. HE IS HEARD
2TRU I	(35)	THERE? (CRYING) SELFISH BEASTS! TO LEAVE ME	LIKE	THIS. (SHE SNATCHES ANGRILY AT THE ELECTRIC BELL WHICH
CLEO IV	(187)	AM NOT HIDING ANYTHING. YOU ARE WRONG TO TREAT ME	LIKE	THIS. (SHE STIFLES A SOB). I AM ONLY A CHILD: AND YOU
GETT	(307)	LORD AND MISS EDITH AND MADAM AND GENTLEMEN, IT'S	LIKE	THIS. MARRIAGE IS TOLERABLE ENOUGH IN ITS WAY IF YOURE
MIS.	(177)	PRESENCE OF MIND. /HYPATIA/ EXCUSE ME RUSHING IN	LIKE	THIS. MR PERCIVAL HAS BEEN CHASING ME DOWN THE HILL.
OVER	(174)	ME HE'S ALIVE. /MRS JUNO/ OH, DONT FRIGHTEN ME	LIKE	THIS. OF COURSE HE'S ALIVE-- UNLESS YOUVE HEARD
ROCK I	(207)	ON! YOULL HAVE A NERVOUS BREAKDOWN IF YOU GO ON	LIKE	THIS. PROMISE ME THAT YOU WILL SEE THE LADY I SPOKE TO
CATH 4	(191)	YOU? /EDSTASTON/ MADAM: I CANNOT TALK TIED UP	LIKE	THIS. /CATHERINE/ DO YOU STILL ADMIRE ME AS MUCH AS YOU
PHIL III	(141)	HER. HANG IT ALL, DONT GO AND SPOIL EVERYTHING	LIKE	THIS. /CRAVEN/ THIS IS MOST INFERNALLY PERPLEXING. I
MRS II	(201)	SUPPER. THEYVE NO RIGHT TO STAY OUT AFTER DARK	LIKE	THIS. /CROFTS/ (AGGRESSIVELY) WHAT HARM ARE THEY DOING
FANY III	(320)	LET THIS GO ON. PEOPLE CANT BE ALLOWED TO BEHAVE	LIKE	THIS. /KNOX/ JUST WHAT I SAY. A CONCERTINA ADDS ITS
PYGM V	(288)	I'D MAKE A WOMAN OF YOU; AND I HAVE. I LIKE YOU	LIKE	THIS. /LIZA/ YES: YOU TURN ROUND AND MAKE UP TO ME NOW
OVER	(188)	THINK SHE OUGHT TO BE THRUST INTO THE BACKGROUND	LIKE	THIS. /MRS LUNN/ I'M SORRY, I'M SURE. PLEASE EXCUSE ME,
O'FL	(214)	BE THE SAME AGAIN, O'FLAHERTY, NOT AFTER A WAR	LIKE	THIS. /O'FLAHERTY/ SO THEY ALL SAY, SIR. I SEE NO GREAT
MIS.	(178)	YOU KNOW I'M NO GOOD OR YOU DARENT BULLY ME	LIKE	THIS. /PERCIVAL/ YOU SHOULD HAVE THOUGHT OF THAT BEFORE
BARB III	(318)	ALLOW YOU TO THROW AWAY AN ENORMOUS PROPERTY	LIKE	THIS. /STEPHEN/ (STIFFLY) MOTHER: THERE MUST BE AN END
GENV I	(34)	FOR YOU. /SHE/ OH I SAY, MISTER JEW, I DONT	LIKE	THIS. /THE JEW/ THEN WRITE THE LETTER YOURSELF. I AM
MTH4 I	(145)	LEAD ON YOU IF YOU PERSIST IN GIVING ME THE SLIP	LIKE	THIS. /THE WOMAN/ ARE YOU THIS STRANGER'S NURSE? /THE
GETT	(308)	LADY THAT I ALWAYS CONSULT ON DELICATE POINTS	LIKE	THIS. SHE HAS A VERY EXCEPTIONAL EXPERIENCE, AND A
PYGM III	(246)	/MRS HIGGINS/ INDEED! WHY? /HIGGINS/ WELL, IT'S	LIKE	THIS. SHE'S A COMMON FLOWER GIRL. I PICKED HER OFF THE
MILL I	(151)	TO LOOK AFTER THEM. YOU SEE, MR SAGAMORE, IT'S	LIKE	THIS. THERE ARE TWO SORTS OF PEOPLE IN THE WORLD: THE
PRES	(162)	THEY ARE-- ARE MY OWN. I IMAGINE IT'S SOMETHING	LIKE	THIS. THERE IS AN OLD SAYING THAT IF YOU TAKE CARE OF
BASH III	(121)	THEE, I IMPLORE: I CANNOT SEE THEE HUNTED DOWN	LIKE	THIS. THERE IS MY ROOM. CONCEAL THYSELF THEREIN. QUICK,

GETT	(318)	SOAMES) IT'S NO GOOD TALKING ALL OVER THE SHOP	LIKE	THIS. WE SHALL BE HERE ALL DAY. I PROPOSE THAT THE
GENV I	(32)	OFFICIAL WORK HERE! /SHE/ LOOK HERE: I DONT HALF	LIKE	THIS. WHATS THE GAME? /THE JEW/ I MUST BEGIN BY
APPL PREFACE	(188)	A FEW TIMES TO SEE WHAT IT IS LIKE. WELL, IT IS	LIKE	THIS. WHEN THE ELECTION APPROACHES, TWO OR THREE
KING I	(198)	SICKEN ME. GO. /JAMES/ CHARLES! WE MUST NOT PART	LIKE	THIS. YOU KNOW YOU ALWAYS STAND BY ME AS FAR AS YOU
2TRU II	(73)	HERE, DEARIE. YOU MUSTNT GO OFF AT THE DEEP END	LIKE	THIS. YOU-- (THE PATIENT TURNS FIERCELY ON HER: SHE
BULL I	(96)	SHE ONLY KNEW THAT TWO MEN WERE TALKING ABOUT HER	LIKE	THIS--! /BROADBENT/ SHE WOULDNT LIKE IT, WOULD SHE?
PRES	(150)	FAST AS YOU OR ANY MAN. BUT TO AVE ME TIME WASTED	LIKE	THIS, AN BE STUCK IN A SENTRY-BOX AT A STREET CORNER
CATH 4	(188)	ANYBODY WITH A SENSE OF HUMOR MAKE A GUY OF A MAN	LIKE	THIS, AND THEN EXPECT HIM TO TAKE IT SERIOUSLY? I SAY:
JITT II	(48)	(SHAKING HIS HEAD) BUT WE CANT LEAVE IT	LIKE	THIS, CAN WE? /JITTA/ WHAT CAN WE DO, ALFRED?
WIDO III	(60)	AND YOU WOULDNT GET IT IF YOU DID. YOU SEE, IT'S	LIKE	THIS, DR TRENCH. THERES NO DOUBT THAT THE VESTRIES HAS
PYGM II	(235)	HERE IF YOU DIDNT SEND HER? /DOOLITTLE/ IT WAS	LIKE	THIS, GOVERNOR. THE GIRL TOOK A BOY IN THE TAXI TO GIVE
LION II	(141)	PERSECUTION SHALL CEASE: IF CHRISTIANS CAN FIGHT	LIKE	THIS, I SHALL HAVE NONE BUT CHRISTIANS TO FIGHT FOR ME.
HART I	(49)	DISILLUSIONED! AND IF I HAD REALIZED IT WAS TO BE	LIKE	THIS, I WOULDNT HAVE COME. I HAVE A GREAT MIND TO GO
WIDO II	(37)	IF I'D THOUGHT YOU CAPABLE OF TURNING ON ME	LIKE	THIS, I'D NEVER HAVE SPOKEN TO YOU. IVE A GOOD MIND
CAND II	(107)	/PROSERPINE/ LOOK HERE: IF YOU DONT STOP TALKING	LIKE	THIS, I'LL LEAVE THE ROOM, MR MARCHBANKS: I REALLY
HART III	(139)	/MAZZINI/ I HOPE YOU DONT MIND MY BEING	LIKE	THIS, MR HUSHABYE. (HE SITS DOWN ON THE CAMPSTOOL).
HART I	(55)	(TURNING AGAIN) OH! HOW CAN YOU TREAT A VISITOR	LIKE	THIS, MRS HUSHABYE? /MRS HUSHABYE/ I THOUGHT YOU WERE
DOCT II	(119)	/BLENKINSOP/ I'M SO SORRY TO HAVE LEFT YOU	LIKE	THIS, RIDGEON; BUT IT WAS A TELEPHONE MESSAGE FROM THE
O'FL	(208)	FOR HIM IN THE SCULLERY. /SIR PEARCE/ BUT I DONT	LIKE	THIS, /O'FLAHERTY. YOU CANT GO ON DECEIVING YOUR
JITT II	(34)	THAT WE HAVE DONE ALL IN OUR POWER, BUT AN END	LIKE	THIS, SO SUDDEN, SO DREADFUL-- (SHE BREAKS DOWN).
POSN	(435)	I DONT SAY IT'S RIGHT TO KILL A MAN. IN A PLACE	LIKE	THIS, WHERE EVERY MAN HAS TO HAVE A REVOLVER, AND WHERE
PYGM V	(269)	WANT TO FIND HER. /PICKERING/ WE CANT LET HER GO	LIKE	THIS, YOU KNOW, MRS HIGGINS. WHAT WERE WE TO DO? /MRS
SIM PRO,1,	(24)	(FEEBLY REBELLIOUS) LOOK HERE: YOU CANT GO ON	LIKE	THIS, YOU KNOW. /THE Y.W./ WHAT WERE YOU GOING TO DO
MTH5	(239)	YOU WOULD STAND THERE AND LET ME BE TREATED	LIKE	THIS, YOU UNMANLY COWARD. PYGMALION FALLS DEAD. /THE
SUPR IV	(169)	TAKE CARE, JACK: IF ANYONE COMES WHILE WE ARE	LIKE	THIS, YOU WILL HAVE TO MARRY ME. /TANNER/ IF WE TWO
ROCK II	(238)	ARE NOT GOING TO ALLOW YOURSELF TO BE CORRUPTED	LIKE	THIS! ARE YOU SUCH A DUPE AS TO IMAGINE THAT FREE
BULL III	(133)	LARRY. WHO WOULD HAVE THOUGHT OF YOUR COMING OUT	LIKE	THIS! (SOLEMNLY) BUT MUCH AS I APPRECIATE YOUR REALLY
DOCT III	(145)	/WALPOLE/ RIDGEON: DID YOU EVER HEAR ANYTHING	LIKE	THIS! (TO LOUIS) WELL, YOU CAN KEEP YOUR NUCIFORM
OVER	(188)	(FLINGING HIMSELF BACK INTO HIS CHAIR) WELL, I	LIKE	THIS! /MRS LUNN/ REALLY, DARLING, THERES NO USE IN THE
MIS. PREFACE	(24)	WHO SEES IT EXCLAIMS " OH, WHY WAS I NOT TAUGHT	LIKE	THIS! " AND ELDERLY GENTLEMEN EXCITEDLY ENROL
FABL PREFACE	(96)	AND INEVITABLE BY ABLE AND BENEVOLENT PUBLIC MEN	LIKE	THOMAS DE QUINCEY, MACAULAY, AUSTIN, COBDEN, AND
FABL VI	(128)	BEFORE IT, BUT A THROW-BACK TO AN EARLIER ONE.	LIKE	THOSE CHILDREN OF OURS WHO CANNOT GET BEYOND THE FIRST
MTH5	(251)	STATUES AND PICTURES OF MEN AND WOMEN OF GENIUS,	LIKE	THOSE IN THE OLD FABLE OF MICHAEL ANGELO. LIKE
POSN PREFACE	(413)	REASONABLY BE MADE SUBJECT TO AN ANNUAL LICENCE	LIKE	THOSE NOW REQUIRED BEFORE ALLOWING PREMISES TO BE USED
FABL IV	(115)	OF COOPERATION: THEIR FEROCITIES AND ANIMOSITIES,	LIKE	THOSE OF THE BULL, DID NOT GO BEYOND TRESPASSERS WITHIN
MIS. PREFACE	(57)	NOT MEAN ARTIFICIAL, UNNECESSARY, NOXIOUS CAREERS	LIKE	THOSE OF THE COMMERCIAL SCHOOLMASTER), LANGUAGES, EVEN
SUPR HANDBOK	(201)	WAR SHEWED THAT THE NATION AND THE WAR OFFICE,	LIKE	THOSE POOR BOURBONS WHO HAVE BEEN SO IMPUDENTLY BLAMED
MIS. PREFACE	(98)	GO TO WHATEVER PLAYS WE LIKE. WE SHALL NOT	LIKE	THOSE WHICH HAVE NOTHING TO SAY TO US; AND THOUGH
CAND III	(143)	A LITTLE) LET US SIT AND TALK COMFORTABLY OVER IT	LIKE	THREE FRIENDS. (TO MORELL) SIT DOWN, DEAR. (MORELL,
GENV II	(61)	NONSENSE, PUSHING ALL THE NATIONS INTO GENEVA IS	LIKE	THROWING ALL THE FISHES INTO THE SAME POND: THEY JUST
MILL IV	(194)	THE DEFENDANT HAD DONE SOMETHING REALLY WOMANLY,	LIKE	THROWING VITRIOL, BUT YOU ARE ONLY A SLEEPING PARTNER
BASH I	(96)	MY UNTAINTED BLOOD. PREACH ABSTINENCE TO RASCALS	LIKE	THYSELF ROTTEN WITH SURFEITING. LEAVE ME IN PEACE. THIS
GETT	(277)	LEO'S NAME! DO YOU KNOW WHAT THAT FEELS	LIKE	TO A DECENT MAN? DO YOU KNOW WHAT A DECENT MAN FEELS
MILL PREFACE	(124)	DESIRABILITY OF A PURE BRED GERMAN RACE. I SHOULD	LIKE	TO ASK HIM WHY. ALL GERMANS ARE NOT MOZARTS, NOR EVEN
CLEO II	(134)	VERY LIKELY. /CLEOPATRA/ BUT I SHOULD NOT	LIKE	TO ASK HIM. COULD YOU NOT PERSUADE HIM TO ASK ME--
WIDO I	(18)	SO AS TO PASS ALL THAT OVER? I REALLY DONT	LIKE	TO ASK HIM. /COKANE/ I CAN PASS IT OVER IF YOU WISH.
LIED	(203)	WILL YOU DO ME A GREAT FAVOR, APJOHN. I HARDLY	LIKE	TO ASK; BUT IT WOULD BE A REAL KINDNESS TO US BOTH.
SUPR HANDBOK	(195)	DESIRE IT AT ALL. ASK ANY MAN WOULD HE	LIKE	TO BE A BETTER MAN; AND HE WILL SAY YES, MOST PIOUSLY.
SUPR HANDBOK	(195)	MOST SINCERELY. BUT THE PIOUS CITIZEN WHO WOULD	LIKE	TO BE A BETTER MAN GOES ON BEHAVING JUST AS HE DID
SIM I	(45)	YOU. LET US CHANGE THE SUBJECT. WOULD YOU	LIKE	TO BE A BISHOP? /THE CLERGYMAN/ OH DEAR! CAN YOU MAKE
FABL VI	(130)	BODY? /RAPHAEL/ I AM CURIOUS TO KNOW WHAT IT IS	LIKE	TO BE A BODY. CURIOSITY NEVER DIES. /MAIDEN 4/ HOW DO
FABL III	(112)	TO BE A SHAKESPEAR; BUT I CANT WRITE PLAYS. I'D	LIKE	TO BE A MICHAEL ANGELO OR A RAPHAEL; BUT I CAN NEITHER
FABL V	(120)	IS STILL NO MORE THAN HIS GRAIN OF SAND. I WOULD	LIKE	TO BE A MIND WITHOUT A BODY; BUT THAT HAS NOT HAPPENED
FABL III	(112)	FAILED EVERY TIME. IVE TASTES BUT NO TALENTS. I'D	LIKE	TO BE A SHAKESPEAR; BUT I CANT WRITE PLAYS. I'D LIKE TO
APPL I	(205)	OUGHT TO BE KILLED. /BOANERGES/ (SARCASTIC) YOUD	LIKE	TO BE ABLE TO SAY " OFF WITH HIS HEAD! " WOULDNT YOU..
BULL IV	(157)	THAT, WHEN I DIE AND LEAVE YOU THE FARM I SHOULD	LIKE	TO BE ABLE TO FEEL THAT IT WAS ALL ME OWN, AND NOT HALF
MTH4 III	(198)	GENTLEMAN/ BEFORE THE ORACLE REPLIES, I SHOULD	LIKE	TO BE ALLOWED TO STATE A FEW OF THE REASONS WHY, IN MY
OVER	(194)	I DONT LIKE BEING LOVED: IT BORES ME. BUT I DO	LIKE	TO BE AMUSED. /JUNO/ I HOPE WE SHALL MEET VERY OFTEN.
PYGM EPILOG	(299)	IS A LAST OPPORTUNITY FOR ROMANCE. WOULD YOU NOT	LIKE	TO BE ASSURED THAT THE SHOP WAS AN IMMENSE SUCCESS,
DEST	(179)	DANGER? OR ARE YOU ONE OF THOSE WOMEN WHO	LIKE	TO BE BEATEN BLACK AND BLUE? /LADY/ THANK YOU.
NEVR IV	(303)	/DOLLY/-- OR OUR FATHER? /CRAMPTON/ I SHOULD	LIKE	TO BE BOTH, MY CHILD, BUT SURELY--! MR VALENTINE: I
MIS.	(119)	DOWN HIS HAT). /LORD SUMMERHAYS/ DOES MR TARLETON	LIKE	TO BE CALLED THE GRAND CHAM, DO YOU THINK, BENTLEY?
GETT	(333)	GEORGE. I LIVE LIKE A FENCER, ALWAYS ON GUARD. I	LIKE	TO BE CONFRONTED WITH PEOPLE WHO ARE ALWAYS ON GUARD. I
GENV II	(58)	AS A DECREE OF EXCOMMUNICATION. /JUDGE/ WOULD YOU	LIKE	TO BE EXCOMMUNICATED? /SIR O./ HARDLY A SERIOUS
FANY EPILOG	(334)	/FANNY/ YES: ITLL TEACH YOU WHAT IT FEELS	LIKE	TO BE FORCIBLY FED. /THE COUNT/ SHE WILL NEVER RETURN
MILL I	(156)	MONEY. /EPIFANIA/ NOR DO YOU KNOW WHAT IT FEELS	LIKE	TO BE IN THE ARMS OF A MAN AND KNOW THAT YOU COULD BUY
2TRU PREFACE	(7)	THEIR IMAGINATION FOR THEIR NOTIONS OF WHAT IT IS	LIKE	TO BE IN THE OPPOSITE CONDITION. THE UPSTARTS AND THE
CAND II	(125)	YOU KNOW. /MORELL/ I'M SORRY. I THOUGHT YOU MIGHT	LIKE	TO BE INTRODUCED TO THE CHAIRMAN. HE'S ON THE WORKS
KING I	(170)	FAMILIAR. /CHARLES/ NELLY! MR NEWTON: WOULD YOU	LIKE	TO BE INTRODUCED TO MISTRESS GWYNN, THE FAMOUS DRURY
APPL INTRLUD	(254)	/MAGNUS/ IMPOSSIBLE, BELOVED. JEMIMA DOES NOT	LIKE	TO BE KEPT WAITING. /ORINTHIA/ OH, BOTHER JEMIMA! YOU
OVER	(194)	DUTY. /MRS JUNO/ THEN I WONT DO IT! THATS FLAT. I	LIKE	TO BE LIKED. I LIKE TO BE LOVED. I WANT EVERYONE ROUND
GENV III	(85)	SLEEVE AS MEN DO. SHE SHOULD KEEP THEM UP IT. MEN	LIKE	TO BE LISTENED TO. /BEGONIA/ I HAVE LISTENED HERE UNTIL
PHIL I	(74)	ELSE IN THE WORLD? /GRACE/ I DONT THINK YOU	LIKE	TO BE LOVED TOO MUCH. /CHARTERIS/ THAT DEPENDS ON WHO
OVER	(194)	I WONT DO IT! THATS FLAT. I LIKE TO BE LIKED. I	LIKE	TO BE LOVED. I WANT EVERYONE ROUND ME TO LOVE ME. I
BUOY IV	(53)	AND DICK WILL DO. /JUNIUS/ (TO HER) WOULDNT YOU	LIKE	TO BE MARRIED IN CHURCH AND HAVE THE BANNS CALLED?
MTH2	(84)	MONEY. WHY HAVNT THEY? BECAUSE THE MEN WHO WOULD	LIKE	TO BE MILLIONAIRES WONT SAVE SIXPENCE EVEN WITH THE
CLEO II	(141)	/CAESAR/ (WITH A WRY FACE) CLEOPATRA: DO YOU	LIKE	TO BE REMINDED THAT YOU ARE VERY YOUNG? /CLEOPATRA/ (
CLEO II	(141)	WHO KNEELS TO PUT ON HIS GREAVES) NEITHER DO I	LIKE	TO BE REMINDED THAT I AM-- MIDDLE AGED. LET ME GIVE YOU
LADY	(245)	HA! /THE DARK LADY/ (ANGRILY)-- AY, I'M AS	LIKE	TO BE SAVED AS THOU THAT BELIEVEST NAUGHT SAVE SOME
FANY III	(316)	FOR YOUR GOOD, ROB. /GILBEY/ WELL, I DONT	LIKE	TO BE SPOKEN TO FOR MY GOOD. WOULD ANYBODY LIKE IT?
CAPT III	(279)	FETCH EM, MARM. /LADY CICELY/ THANK YOU. I SHOULD	LIKE	TO BE TOLD WHEN THEY ARE COMING, IF I MIGHT.
CAPT I	(238)	YOUR CAPTAIN, HAVE HIM BY ALL MEANS. DO YOU	LIKE	TO BE TREATED AS HE TREATS YOU? /DRINKWATER/ (WITH A
WIDO II	(36)	LADY AS SHE EXCLAIMS) I HATE SECRETS; AND I DONT	LIKE	TO BE TREATED AS IF I WERE A CHILD. /TRENCH/ (ANNOYED
FANY I	(280)	POUNDS I'LL STAND ONE; AND THATLL DO IT. IF YOUD	LIKE	TO BE VERY KIND AND NICE YOU COULD PAY THE LOT; BUT I
CAPT III	(289)	WILL DO NOTHING OF THE SORT, MARZO, UNLESS YOU	LIKE	TO BEHAVE YOURSELF VERY NICELY INDEED. WHAT HOUR DID
MIS.	(142)	GLORIOUS YOUNG BEAST EXPRESSES EXACTLY WHAT I	LIKE	TO BE. /LORD SUMMERHAYS/ (EXTRICATING HIS HANDS AND
KING I	(204)	IN DRURY LANE? /NELL/ THEY SAY I DID. THE PEOPLE	LIKE	TO BELIEVE I DID. THEY LOVE ME FOR IT. I SAY NOTHING.
GETT PREFACE	(195)	SURFACE-- ARE THE VILLAINS AND BUTTS. PEOPLE	LIKE	TO BELIEVE THAT NELL GWYNNE HAS EVERY AMIABLE QUALITY
DEVL II	(31)	SAID WHAT PERHAPS (GOD FORGIVE HIM!) HE WOULD	LIKE	TO BELIEVE. IT'S A TERRIBLE THING TO THINK OF WHAT
ROCK PREFACE	(186)	TRUTH, WHICH TURNS OUT TO BE NOTHING BUT WHAT YOU	LIKE	TO BELIEVE. YOUR BLASPHEMY IS NOTHING TO ME: THE WHOLE
MIS. PREFACE	(32)	WANT TO BLOW IT UP WITH DYNAMITE AS I SHOULD	LIKE	TO BLOW UP MOST SCHOOLS, SO I ASKED FOR GUIDANCE. " YOU
NEVR IV	(285)	RIGHT ENOUGH! THAT WAS HALF AN HOUR AGO. I DIDNT	LIKE	TO BORROW FIVE SHILLINGS FROM HIM AND GO IN WITH HIM;
MIS.	(125)	STATE ABOUT ANY MAN! FALL IN LOVE WITH HIM IF YOU	LIKE	TO CALL IT THAT. BUT WHO WOULD RISK MARRYING A MAN FOR
2TRU II	(66)	SWEETIE? /THE COUNTESS/ WELL, YES; IF YOU	LIKE	TO CALL IT THAT. /AUBREY/ MAY I ASK HAVE YOU SOUNDED
BULL PREFACE	(6)	SIXPENCE ARE THOSE WHO LIVE IN ENGLAND. I SHOULD	LIKE	TO CALL THE ATTENTION OF MY NERVOUS FELLOW PROTESTANTS
LION II	(127)	FIFTY TALENTS TO PLEASE THE RIFFRAFF? I SHOULD	LIKE	TO CATCH ANY OF MY MEN AT IT. /SPINTHO/ I THOUGHT --
APPL I	(238)	LIMITED, NEVER INTERFERES IN MY DEPARTMENT. I'D	LIKE	TO CATCH THEM AT IT. /MAGNUS/ I AM AFRAID THAT THAT IS
ARMS II	(24)	RUIN ME. /LOUKA/ YOU HAVE NO SPIRIT. I SHOULD	LIKE	TO CATCH THEM SAYING A WORD AGAINST ME! /NICOLA/ (
GETT	(352)	YOUR NAME IS ON ONE OF THE COVERS; AND I SHOULD	LIKE	TO CHANGE IT IF YOURE NOT REMAINING. /HOTCHKISS/ HOW DO
CAND II	(125)	BEFORE. /CANDIDA/ (TROUBLED) EUGENE: WOULDNT YOU	LIKE	TO COME? /MORELL/ I SHOULD BE AFRAID TO LET MYSELF GO
DOCT V	(171)	UNLESS HE KNOWS HIM. WE HAVE A FEW PEOPLE WHO	LIKE	TO COME BEFORE THE CROWD-- PEOPLE WHO REALLY BUY; AND
SIM PRO,1,	(24)	CARRY ON, YOU. (HE GOES). /THE Y.W./ WOULDNT YOU	LIKE	TO COME TOO? /WILKS/ YES, MISS; BUT SOMEBODY MUST STAY
SUPR II	(58)	YOU. /ANN/ WHAT DO YOU MEAN? /TANNER/ WOULD YOU	LIKE	TO CURE RHODA'S HEADACHE, ANN? /ANN/ OF COURSE.
JOAN PREFACE	(5)	THEIR FELLOWS HATE MENTAL GIANTS AND WOULD	LIKE	TO DESTROY THEM, NOT ONLY ENVIOUSLY BECAUSE THE
FANY III	(314)	MAKE WHAT SHE DID AN EXCUSE TO GO AND DO AS YOUD	LIKE	TO DO IF IT WASNT FOR THE FEAR OF LOSING YOUR
DEST	(189)	CONVERSATION IS A LITTLE TOO MUCH. HOW WOULD YOU	LIKE	TO DO IT YOURSELF? /NAPOLEON/ (IRRITABLY) YOU REFUSE
6CAL	(99)	LEAVE GOD OUT OF THIS! WHAT HAST THOU OR THY	LIKE	TO DO WITH GOD? /EUSTACHE/ NOTHING, SIR: WE WOULD NOT

MTH4 II (179)	A MAN MUST DO WHAT HE CAN AND NOT WHAT HE WOULD	LIKE	TO DO, AND PARTLY BECAUSE, IF I STOP, I IMMEDIATELY
DOCT III (138)	AMAZED FACES WITH A CHUCKLE) I SAY: I SHOULD	LIKE	TO DRAW THE LOT OF YOU NOW: YOU DO LOOK JOLLY FOOLISH.
BUOY IV (57)	FAMILY. /DARKIE/ NOT A BIT. LET ME KNOW WHAT YOU	LIKE	TO EAT AND DRINK: THAT IS ALL. I MUST GO NOW TO SEE
BULL I (77)	WORD. SHAKE HANDS. /BROADBENT/ BUT I SHOULD	LIKE	TO EXPLAIN-- /TIM/ SURE I KNOW EVERY WORD YOURE GOIN TO
2TRU III (83)	PART OF IT. I LIKE GETTING A WOMAN'S OPINIONS. I	LIKE	TO EXPLORE HER MIND AS WELL AS HER BODY. SEE THESE TWO
MTH5 (257)	/STREPHON/ BORES! /MARTELLUS/ YET ONE WOULD	LIKE	TO FOLLOW THEM; TO ENTER INTO THEIR LIFE; TO GRASP
PHIL II (126)	YOU! I DONT KNOW WHY I DONT. /GRACE/ YES: YOU	LIKE	TO GET OUT OF YOUR DIFFICULTIES AT OTHER PEOPLE'S
PYGM III (245)	BUT I CANT GET ROUND YOUR VOWELS; AND THOUGH I	LIKE	TO GET PRETTY POSTCARDS IN YOUR PATENT SHORTHAND, I
DOCT III (143)	TO ADDRESS TO ME IN MY OWN HOUSE? I SHOULD	LIKE	TO GET THEM OVER BEFORE MY WIFE COMES BACK. (HE
GETT (277)	MAN FEELS ABOUT HIS WIFE'S NAME? HOW WOULD YOU	LIKE	TO GO INTO A HOTEL BEFORE ALL THE WAITERS AND PEOPLE
PYGM I (210)	AND THE GENTLEMAN) PARK LANE, FOR INSTANCE. I'D	LIKE	TO GO INTO THE HOUSING QUESTION WITH YOU, I WOULD. /THE
PYGM II (218)	HALF OF IT IN, YOU KNOW. /HIGGINS/ WOULD YOU	LIKE	TO GO OVER ANY OF IT AGAIN? /PICKERING/ (RISING AND
SIM I (45)	WILL YOU UNDERTAKE IT? /THE CLERGYMAN/ I SHOULD	LIKE	TO HAVE A BISHOP'S SALARY, CERTAINLY. BUT UNFORTUNATELY
KING I (207)	I PREFER WHITEHALL. /JAMES/ (TO FOX) YOU WOULD	LIKE	TO HAVE A KING FOR YOUR FOLLOWER, EH? /FOX/ I DESIRE
DOCT I (102)	YOU EVER DO FEEL AT ALL QUEER, I SHOULD VERY MUCH	LIKE	TO HAVE A LOOK. /B.B./ THANK YOU, MY DEAR FELLOW; BUT
SUPR HANDBOK(195)	HE WILL SAY YES, MOST PIOUSLY. ASK HIM WOULD HE	LIKE	TO HAVE A MILLION OF MONEY; AND HE WILL SAY YES, MOST
MTH2 (84)	WHY DONT THEY? /CONRAD/ PSHAW! EVERYBODY WOULD	LIKE	TO HAVE A MILLION OF MONEY. WHY HAVNT THEY? BECAUSE
AUGS (279)	VERY CLEVER OF YOU. (SLYLY) COME: WOULD YOU	LIKE	TO HAVE A PEEP AT THE LIST (BEGINNING TO TAKE THE
GETT (299)	UNCLE? /HOTCHKISS/ I WISH YOU WERE: I SHOULD	LIKE	TO HAVE AN UNCLE REGINALD. /REGINALD/ YAH! SYKES: ARE
KING PREFACE(154)	BETWEEN NEWTON AND A PERSONAGE WHOM I SHOULD	LIKE	TO HAVE CALLED HOGARTH; FOR IT WAS HOGARTH WHO SAID "
BULL III (136)	NOW, GENTLEMEN, TO YOUR DELIBERATIONS. I SHOULD	LIKE	TO HAVE ENLARGED ON THE SERVICES RENDERED BY THE
BUOY II (25)	QUITE AT HOME WITH RICHARD THE THIRD. I SHOULD	LIKE	TO HAVE HEARD THEM DISCUSSING COLUMBUS WITH HIM. /THE
DOCT III (148)	TO HAVE IT. /SIR PATRICK/ THANK YOU; BUT I SHOULD	LIKE	TO HAVE IT MYSELF. WHAT D'YE THINK, WALPOLE? /WALPOLE/
FANY III (316)	ALL SINNERS, IN A MANNER OF SPEAKING; BUT I DONT	LIKE	TO HAVE IT THROWN AT ME AS IF I'D REALLY DONE ANYTHING.
DOCT III (148)	SO, COLLY? /RIDGEON/ YES. SO GOOD THAT I SHOULD	LIKE	TO HAVE IT. /SIR PATRICK/ THANK YOU; BUT I SHOULD LIKE
DOCT III (136)	ABOUT THEM-- PRIVATE THINGS THAT THEY WOULDNT	LIKE	TO HAVE KNOWN, THEY WOULDNT DARE TO REFUSE YOU.
GETT (269)	MAID. I'M VERY PARTICULAR ABOUT MY BELONGINGS. I	LIKE	TO HAVE MY OWN HOUSE, AND TO HAVE IT TO MYSELF. I HAVE
2TRU II (63)	HE'D ONLY MESS EVERYTHING ABOUT LOOKING FOR IT. I	LIKE	TO HAVE MY ROOMS LEFT TIDY. (SHE GOES INTO THE
SUPR I (22)	AUTHORITY. /ANN/ YOU SEE, MAMMA, THEY ALL REALLY	LIKE	TO HAVE PET NAMES. /MRS WHITEFIELD/ WELL, I THINK YOU
KING I (215)	AND CLEVEREST. SHE IS ALSO A LADY. I SHOULD	LIKE	TO HAVE PORTRAITS OF ALL THREE AS THEY ARE NOW, NOT AS
GETT (280)	I SHOULD LIKE TO MARRY A LOT OF MEN. I SHOULD	LIKE	TO HAVE REJJY FOR EVERY DAY, AND SINJON FOR CONCERTS
CYMB FORWORD(135)	TO DRAMATIC ACTIVITY AND INDIVIDUALITY, I SHOULD	LIKE	TO HAVE RETAINED CORNELIUS AS THE EXPONENT OF
CLEO I (109)	AND STRINGY; BUT YOU HAVE A NICE VOICE; AND I	LIKE	TO HAVE SOMEBODY TO TALK TO, THOUGH I THINK YOU ARE A
PYGM II (242)	TO HAVE FASHIONABLE CLOTHES, I'LL WAIT. I SHOULD	LIKE	TO HAVE SOME. MRS PEARCE SAYS YOURE GOING TO GIVE ME
ROCK I (227)	FOR THEM IN AEROPLANES AND SUBMARINES. I SHOULD	LIKE	TO HAVE THE OPINION OF AN IMPARTIAL AND DISINTERESTED
WIDO II (32)	OF ALL EVIL. /LICKCHEESE/ YES, SIR; AND WE'D ALL	LIKE	TO HAVE THE TREE GROWING IN OUR GARDEN. /COKANE/ (
MTH5 (217)	OF MY HEAD IS CHANGING VERY RAPIDLY. I SHOULD	LIKE	TO HAVE THINGS EXPLAINED TO ME. /ACIS/ (TO THE
LION II (132)	DEEPLY DISCOURAGED). /CAESAR/ METELLUS: I SHOULD	LIKE	TO HAVE THIS MAN IN THE PRETORIAN GUARD. /METELLUS/ I
MRS III (229)	SO TO SPEAK. ASK YOUR MOTHER WHETHER SHE'D	LIKE	TO HAVE TO EXPLAIN ALL HER AFFAIRS TO A PERFECT
LADY (243)	WILL, MISTRESS. HAVE YOU BETHOUGHT YOU THAT I AM	LIKE	TO HAVE YOUR HEAD CUT OFF AS WELL? /THE DARK LADY/
NEVR IV (295)	ARE BEFORE YOU: BOTH OF THEM. YOU THINK YOUD	LIKE	TO HAVE YOUR TWO YOUNGEST CHILDREN TO LIVE WITH YOU.
VWOO 1 (117)	THINK MY LIFE QUITE A ROMANCE. WOULDNT YOU REALLY	LIKE	TO HEAR IT? /A/ NO, I TELL YOU. WHEN I WANT ROMANCES I
2TRU II (73)	THE FREEDOM YOU MADE POSSIBLE FOR ME. YOU DONT	LIKE	TO HEAR SWEETIE'S LOWER CENTRES SHOUTING. WELL, NOW YOU
GETT (296)	YOU KNOW, MISS BRIDGENORTH, I SHOULD MOST AWFULLY	LIKE	TO HEAR WHAT YOU HAVE TO SAY TO POOR CECIL. /REGINALD/
PRES (143)	JUMPING UP AND WALKING ABOUT SULKILY) OH COME! I	LIKE	TO HEAR YOU MILITARY PEOPLE TALKING OF COWARDICE. WHY,
MIS. (182)	(TO HYPATIA) LORD SUMMERHAYS WOULD PROBABLY	LIKE	TO HEAR YOU SAY THAT YOU ARE SATISFIED, MISS TARLETON.
HART II (97)	TO TALK TO MRS HUSHABYE. /MAZZINI/ BUT I SHOULD	LIKE	TO HEAR. SHALL I BE IN THE WAY? /ELLIE/ (INEXORABLE)
CAPT III (274)	PERHAPS I'M MISTAKEN. I ONLY THOUGHT YOU MIGHT	LIKE	TO HELP HIM AS THE SON OF YOUR OLD FRIEND. /RANKIN/ (
JITT I (18)	HE KNOWS. I AM REALLY SORRY FOR HIM, AND SHOULD	LIKE	TO HELP HIM. /JITTA/ YOU CAN HELP HIM WITHOUT LETTING
PHIL II (123)	THEY ALL LOVE A DOCTOR! THEY CAN SAY WHAT THEY	LIKE	TO HIM. (JULIA RETURNS, BUT DOES NOT LOOK HIS WAY. HE
APPL INTRLUD(244)	I HAD RATHER YOU KICKED ME. /MAGNUS/ I SHOULD	LIKE	TO KICK YOU SOMETIMES, WHEN YOU ARE SPECIALLY
GLIM (183)	EARN HIS MONEY HONESTLY. WHEN I SAID I SHOULD NOT	LIKE	TO KILL A MAN WITH A GOOD SOUL, I MEANT KILLING ON MY
GLIM (183)	BEING SOMETHING AND DOING SOMETHING. I SHOULD NOT	LIKE	TO KILL A MAN WITH A GOOD SOUL. IVE HAD A DOG THAT HAD,
PYGM IV (263)	/LIZA/ BECAUSE I WANTED TO SMASH YOUR FACE. I'D	LIKE	TO KILL YOU, YOU SELFISH BRUTE. WHY DIDNT YOU LEAVE ME
PHIL II (126)	SEE WHETHER HE WILL COME. /JULIA/ HOW I SHOULD	LIKE	TO KILL YOU! I DONT KNOW WHY I DONT. /GRACE/ YES: YOU
ROCK II (261)	AND WHO WOULD KEEP THEM IN ORDER, I SHOULD	LIKE	TO KNOW: SILLY AMATEURS. AND LET ME REMIND YOU OF ONE
WIDO II (32)	(FURIOUSLY) WHICH OF US IS THE WORSE, I SHOULD	LIKE	TO KNOW? ME THAT WRINGS THE MONEY OUT TO KEEP A HOME
PRES (163)	/MITCHENER/ WHAT ARE ITS CONVENIENCES, I SHOULD	LIKE	TO KNOW? /BALSQUITH/ WELL, WHEN YOU TELL PEOPLE THAT
BULL III (127)	HAND FROM HIS LEFT? WHAT DID HE EVER SUFFER, I'D	LIKE	TO KNOW? /CORNELIUS/ THATS JUST WHAT I SAY. I WASNT
MILL I (161)	FEET. WHAT WOULD SHE BE WITHOUT HER MONEY, I'D	LIKE	TO KNOW? /EPIFANIA/ NOBODY IS ANYBODY WITHOUT MONEY.
MILL IV (202)	JUSTICE IS THERE FOR A MILLIONAIRESS, I SHOULD	LIKE	TO KNOW? /SAGAMORE/ IN THE COURTS-- /EPIFANIA/ I AM
NEVR I (201)	SIX WEEKS. IS THERE ANYTHING ELSE YOU WOULD	LIKE	TO KNOW? /THE YOUNG LADY/ (THE HINT QUITE LOST ON
PHIL I (88)	WOMANLY THAN ANY OF THE REST OF THEM, I SHOULD	LIKE	TO KNOW? THEY ARE ALWAYS SAYING THINGS LIKE THAT
CAPT I (233)	/SIR HOWARD/ THAT SOUNDS PROMISING. BUT I SHOULD	LIKE	TO KNOW A LITTLE MORE ABOUT HIM BEFORE I TRUST MYSELF
MILL IV (189)	MAKE YOU QUITE COMFORTABLE. /PATRICIA/ I SHOULD	LIKE	TO KNOW ABOUT THE OLD PIG IF IT'S ROMANTIC. IF YOU CAN
APPL I (198)	/PAMPHILIUS/ BY THE WAY, IS HE ALIVE? I SHOULD	LIKE	TO KNOW HIM. /SEMPRONIUS/ NO. HE DIED IN 1962, OF
CLEO IV (167)	WHOM YOU PLEASE, AND NOT WHOM I PLEASE. I SHOULD	LIKE	TO KNOW HOW MUCH OF HER GOLD PIECE THAT HARP GIRL WILL
BULL III (138)	THOUGH WE HAVE GOOD WARRANT FOR IT; SO I'D	LIKE	TO KNOW HOW MUCH SPOIL THERE IS BEFORE I COMMIT MESELF.
JOAN PREFACE(23)	IN LITERATURE. ENGLISH READERS WOULD PROBABLY	LIKE	TO KNOW HOW THESE IDOLIZATIONS AND REACTIONS HAVE
MILL I (156)	ABOUT A HUNDRED AND FIFTY. I SHOULD VERY MUCH	LIKE	TO KNOW HOW TO MAKE IT UP TO FIFTY THOUSAND. YOU ARE SO
SUPR PREFACE(R17)	HIS ANTAGONIST THE STATUE. I FEEL SURE YOU WOULD	LIKE	TO KNOW MORE OF THAT STATUE-- TO DRAW HIM OUT WHEN HE
BUOY III (31)	FATHER SUCH AN EXTRAORDINARY MAN, THAT I SHOULD	LIKE	TO KNOW MORE OF YOU. YOU BELONG TO A NEW GENERATION,
MILL I (139)	ANOTHER SHEET OF PAPER AND WRITING) I SHOULD	LIKE	TO KNOW POLLY. /EPIFANIA/ PRAY WHY? /SAGAMORE/ (
MIS. (160)	THANK YOU. I KEEP A LIST OF ALL MY OFFERS. I	LIKE	TO KNOW WHAT I'M CONSIDERED WORTH. /TARLETON/ LET ME
MRS II (213)	TO TALK, VERY EASY, ISNT IT? HERE! WOULD YOU	LIKE	TO KNOW WHAT MY CIRCUMSTANCES WERE? /VIVIE/ YES: YOU
METH PREFACE(R83)	CLEARLY ONE OF PHYSICAL MOVEMENT, I SHOULD MUCH	LIKE	TO KNOW WHAT OTHER STORM THAN THE ATOMIC STORM COULD
FANY I (282)	I'D LEAVE MY BOY IN PRISON, ISNT IT? /DORA/ I'D	LIKE	TO KNOW WHEN THEYLL LET HIM OUT. /GILBEY/ YOU WOULD,
MIS. (187)	MAY BE A VULGAR BUSINESS HABIT; BUT I CONFESS I	LIKE	TO KNOW WHERE I AM. /TARLETON/ I DONT. WHEREVER YOU
MIS. (187)	THAT THE GENTLEMAN HAS BEEN ATTENDED TO, I SHOULD	LIKE	TO KNOW WHERE WE ARE. IT MAY BE A VULGAR BUSINESS
NEVR I (223)	IN THE SAME IDLE STRAIN) I REALLY SHOULD	LIKE	TO KNOW YOUR FAMILY, MR CRAMPTON. (HE POURS SOME HOT
HART I (55)	/MAZZINI/ ELLIE! MANGAN HAS COME: I THOUGHT YOUD	LIKE	TO KNOW. EXCUSE ME, MRS HUSHABYE: THE STRANGE OLD
LIED (201)	/HER HUSBAND/ WHAT IS MRS BOMPAS TO YOU, I'D	LIKE	TO KNOW. I'LL TELL YOU WHAT MRS BOMPAS IS. SHE'S THE
2TRU III (91)	OR ONLY PART OF IT? THE COUNTESS VALBRIONI WOULD	LIKE	TO KNOW. /AUBREY/ WE MAY AS WELL BE FRANK UP TO THE
O'FL (220)	LOSE YOUR TEMPER ABOUT IT. I ONLY THOUGHT I'D	LIKE	TO KNOW. THE NICE FOOL I'D LOOK IF I WENT ABOUT SHEWING
DEST (158)	AH! WHERE INDEED? THATS JUST WHAT I SHOULD	LIKE	TO KNOW, GENERAL. (WITH EMOTION) YOU DONT KNOW HOW
METH PREFACE(R19)	NOT READ SHAKESPEAR, SOME WHO CAN READ BOTH,	LIKE	TO LEARN THE HISTORY OF THEIR IDEAS. SOME ARE SO
SUPR I (31)	/RAMSDEN/ (LOOKING POINTEDLY AT TANNER) I HARDLY	LIKE	TO LEAVE YOU ALONE WITH THIS GENTLEMAN. WILL YOU NOT
DOCT IV (161)	I REPRESENT THE PRESS. I THOUGHT YOU MIGHT	LIKE	TO LET US HAVE A FEW WORDS ABOUT-- ABOUT-- ER-- WELL, A
MIS. PREFACE(3)	BE BORN AGAIN, AND YET AGAIN AND AGAIN. WE SHOULD	LIKE	TO LIVE A LITTLE LONGER JUST AS WE SHOULD LIKE 50
MTH2 (84)	ALL BE LIVING FOR EVER ALREADY! EVERYBODY WOULD	LIKE	TO LIVE FOR EVER, WHY DONT THEY? /CONRAD/ PSHAW!
VWOO 2 (127)	IN IT IT MUST BE PRETTY BARE. HOW WOULD YOU	LIKE	TO LIVE IN A ROOM WITH ONLY ONE CHAIR IN IT? /Z/ WELL,
LIED (198)	/HE/ MANUSCRIPTS? /HER HUSBAND/ YES. WOULD YOU	LIKE	TO LOOK AT THEM A LITTLE CLOSER? (HE PROFFERS THEM
MTH5 (245)	JOB'S FINISHED. /ARJILLAX/ ANCIENTS: I SHOULD	LIKE	TO MAKE A FEW STUDIES OF YOU, NOT PORTRAITS, OF COURSE!
SUPR IV (158)	YOU, TAVY; BUT SOMETIMES I FEEL AS IF I SHOULD	LIKE	TO MAKE A MAN OF YOU SOMEHOW. YOU ARE VERY FOOLISH
MTH2 (76)	/BURGE/ (PULLING OUT AN OLD ENVELOPE) I SHOULD	LIKE	TO MAKE A NOTE OF THAT. (HE DOES SO). /CONRAD/ THERE
SUPR III (96)	I MUST CONSULT HIM IN THE MATTER. AND ANA WOULD	LIKE	TO MAKE HIS ACQUAINTANCE, NO DOUBT. /ANA/ YOU ARE
GETT (280)	LEO! /LEO/ WELL, I LOVE THEM BOTH. I SHOULD	LIKE	TO MARRY A LOT OF MEN. I SHOULD LIKE TO HAVE REJJY FOR
HART II (120)	FOR ME: MY DREAMS ARE DASHED TO PIECES. I SHOULD	LIKE	TO MARRY A VERY OLD, VERY RICH MAN. I SHOULD LIKE TO
BULL IV (164)	THAT IS WHY I HAVE ALWAYS THOUGHT I SHOULD	LIKE	TO MARRY AN IRISHWOMAN. SHE WOULD ALWAYS UNDERSTAND MY
GETT (281)	SAY I WANTED TO MARRY THEM: I ONLY SAID I SHOULD	LIKE	TO MARRY THEM. /THE BISHOP/ QUITE A NICE DISTINCTION,
HART II (120)	LIKE TO MARRY A VERY OLD, VERY RICH MAN. I SHOULD	LIKE	TO MARRY YOU. I HAD MUCH RATHER MARRY YOU THAN MARRY
PYGM III (254)	/MRS HIGGINS/ (SHAKING HANDS) GOODBYE. WOULD YOU	LIKE	TO MEET MISS DOOLITTLE AGAIN? /FREDDY/ (EAGERLY) YES,
LION II (132)	NOTHING TO RESTRAIN THEM FROM SAYING WHAT THEY	LIKE	TO ME, THEY ARE ALMOST AS IMPERTINENT AS THE
DOCT I (107)	NO MANNERS: THEY THINK THEY CAN SAY WHAT THEY	LIKE	TO ME; AND YOU SET THEM ON, YOU DO. I'LL TEACH THEM
MIS. PREFACE(100)	IF I HAD NOT HAD THE ARABIAN NIGHTS AND THEIR	LIKE	TO OCCUPY ME BETTER. IN ART, CHILDREN, LIKE ADULTS,
GETT PREFACE(208)	FIND OR UNWILLING TO ENTERTAIN A HUSBAND, WOULD	LIKE	TO OCCUPY THEMSELVES WITH THE REARING OF CHILDREN. MY
ARMS III (48)	/PETKOFF/ I BET YOU ANY PIECE OF JEWELLERY YOU	LIKE	TO ORDER FROM SOFIA AGAINST A WEEK'S HOUSEKEEPING MONEY

2TRU III	(86)	SACRIFICES, AND THINKING YOU CAN DO WHAT YOU	LIKE	TO OTHER PEOPLE BECAUSE YOURE THE CHOSEN PEOPLE OF GOD,
CLEO IV	(190)	ALAS, RUFIO, MY SON, MY SON! AS DOGS WE ARE	LIKE	TO PERISH NOW IN THE STREETS. /APOLLODORUS/ (AT HIS
CAND II	(114)	MIND. (SHE SITS DOWN BESIDE HIM), WOULDNT YOU	LIKE	TO PRESENT ME WITH A NICE NEW ONE, WITH AN IVORY BACK
DEST	(190)	THE DESPATCHES IN HER HAND), WOULDNT YOU	LIKE	TO READ THESE BEFORE THEYRE BURNT, GENERAL? YOU MUST
DOCT IV	(166)	NOT YET, DEAR. VERY NEARLY, BUT NOT YET. I SHOULD	LIKE	TO REST MY HEAD ON YOUR BOSOM; ONLY IT WOULD TIRE YOU.
DEVL II	(39)	OFFER) ONE GENTLEMAN TO ANOTHER, SIR. WOULDNT YOU	LIKE	TO SAY A WORD TO YOUR MISSIS, SIR, BEFORE YOU GO?
VWOO 3	(137)	IMPREGNABLE STRATEGIC POSITION. /Z/ WELL, I DONT	LIKE	TO SAY IT; BUT PEOPLE ARE BEGINNING TO TALK. /A/
UNPL PREFACE	(R9)	ITS PRAISES. IT MAY SAY THINGS WHICH MANY WOULD	LIKE	TO SAY, BUT DARE NOT, AND INDEED FOR WANT OF SKILL
ROCK PREFACE	(157)	CRUELTY TO OTHER PEOPLE, AND SHOULD THEREFORE	LIKE	TO SEE ALL CRUEL PEOPLE EXTERMINATED, BUT I SHOULD
JOAN 2	(84)	WE CAN SPARE TO PUT ON HER OWN BACK. BESIDES, I	LIKE	TO SEE HER BEAUTIFULLY DRESSED; AND I DONT CARE WHAT I
WIDO II	(44)	TO MISS BLANCHE; AND I AM ALONE HERE AND WOULD	LIKE	TO SEE HER FOR A MOMENT IF SHE IS NOT BUSY. /THE
SUPR IV	(162)	THAN TAVY. SHE'D MEET HER MATCH IN YOU, JACK. I'D	LIKE	TO SEE HER MEET HER MATCH. /TANNER/ NO MAN IS A MATCH
PHIL I	(88)	YOU (TO CHARTERIS) HAD SMUGGLED ME IN. I SHOULD	LIKE	TO SEE HER SAY IT TO MY FACE: THATS ALL. /CRAVEN/ BUT,
SUPR III	(92)	MY DEAR, DEAR FATHER! /DON JUAN/ WOULD YOU	LIKE	TO SEE HIM? /ANA/ MY FATHER HERE! ! ! /DON JUAN/
PHIL II	(122)	DONE WITH THAT BRITISH MEDICAL JOURNAL, I SHOULD	LIKE	TO SEE HOW THEYVE SMASHED YOUR THEORY UP. /PARAMORE/ (
CAND II	(114)	THATS VERY GALLANT; BUT I THINK I SHOULD	LIKE	TO SEE HOW YOU DO IT FIRST. (TURNING TO MORELL) JAMES:
WIDO III	(53)	TURNED DOWN THE PAGE TO SHEW YOU: I THOUGHT YOUD	LIKE	TO SEE IT. (HE DOUBLES THE BOOK BACK AT THE PLACE
WIDO I	(9)	(RESPECTFULLY) OH, IN THAT CASE I SHOULD	LIKE	TO SEE IT. /COKANE/ (READING) " -- ERECTED IN 1839 BY
GETT	(271)	IS READY NOW FOR THE BREAKFAST. IF SHE WOULD	LIKE	TO SEE IT. /LESBIA/ IF YOU ARE SATISFIED, COLLINS, I AM
ARMS I	(14)	AND TAKES HIS HEAD IN HIS HANDS). WOULD YOU	LIKE	TO SEE ME CRY? /RAINA/ (ALARMED) NO. /THE MAN/ IF YOU
2TRU II	(64)	CHANGE! CHANGE! CHANGE! /THE COUNTESS/ WELL, I	LIKE	TO SEE NEW FACES. /AUBREY/ I COULD BE HAPPY AS A BUDDHA
MILL II	(174)	TRASH. YOU ARE NOT AN ORDINARY MAN. I SHOULD	LIKE	TO SEE SOME MORE OF YOU, NOW THAT YOU HAVE ASKED ME
ARMS I	(19)	/THE MAN/ ACTUALLY A REAL LIBRARY! I SHOULD	LIKE	TO SEE THAT. /RAINA/ (AFFECTEDLY) I TELL YOU THESE
CATH 4	(192)	WHERE WILL YOUR MAJESTY BE? /CATHERINE/ I SHOULD	LIKE	TO SEE THE ENGLISH AMBASSADOR OR ANYONE ELSE PASS
APPL II	(260)	TEN MINUTES, MR VANHATTAN. /VANHATTAN/ I SHOULD	LIKE	TO SEE THE FACES OF YOUR CABINET MINISTERS, KING
MIS.	(143)	FAMILY! DUTY! HOW I LOATHE THEM! HOW I'D	LIKE	TO SEE THEM ALL BLOWN TO BITS! THE POOR ESCAPE. THE
SUPR III	(135)	CRY; AND A GOOD CRY IS HALF THE BATTLE. I SHOULD	LIKE	TO SEE THIS NIETZSCHE. /THE DEVIL/ UNFORTUNATELY HE MET
PHIL II	(97)	UNTIL ABOUT THREE O' CLOCK. /CRAVEN/ I DONT	LIKE	TO SEE WOMEN SMOKING. I'LL MAKE MYSELF COMFORTABLE
KING II	(223)	ALWAYS HAS THREE SYLLABLES). /CATHERINE/ I NOT	LIKE	TO SEE YOU WITHOUT YOUR WIG. BUT I AM YOUR WIFE AND
DOCT III	(149)	SIR PATRICK, LET ME FETCH JENNIFER. I KNOW SHE'D	LIKE	TO SEE YOU, IF YOU DONT MIND. (HE GOES TO THE INNER
INCA	(239)	MYSELF AS ENGAGED, YOUR HIGHNESS? I SHOULD	LIKE	TO SET ABOUT MY DUTIES IMMEDIATELY. /THE PRINCESS/ OH
LIED	(204)	FIRST CLASS. THEYRE BEAUTIFUL POEMS. I SHOULD	LIKE	TO SHEW THEM ABOUT A BIT. /SHE/ (RUNNING BACK FROM THE
SUPR I	(31)	NOT COME WITH ME? /ANN/ MISS RAMSDEN WOULD NOT	LIKE	TO SPEAK ABOUT IT BEFORE ME, GRANNY. I OUGHT NOT TO BE
SIM I	(38)	OH NO. IT'S LIKE THE GARDEN OF EDEN: I SHOULD	LIKE	TO STAY HERE FOREVER. (SUDDENLY BREAKING DOWN TO THE
GETT	(315)	WORK OF THE MARRIAGE IS DONE WITH, IF THE TWO	LIKE	TO STAY TOGETHER, LET THEM STAY TOGETHER. BUT IF NOT,
CAND I	(96)	/MORELL/ BUT-- BUT-- BUT-- BUT-- BOSH! IF YOUD	LIKE	TO STAY, STAY. IF YOURE SHY, GO AND TAKE A TURN IN THE
JOAN 6	(135)	HURT; AND IF YOU HURT ME I WILL SAY ANYTHING YOU	LIKE	TO STOP THE PAIN. BUT I WILL TAKE IT ALL BACK
HART PREFACE	(9)	CLAIRVOYANCE, PALMISTRY, CRYSTAL-GAZING AND THE	LIKE	TO SUCH AN EXTENT THAT IT MAY BE DOUBTED WHETHER EVER
SUPR II	(63)	/HECTOR/ PLEASED TO MEET YOU, MR TANNER. I SHOULD	LIKE	TO SUGGEST AN EXTENSION OF THE TRAVELLING PARTY TO
MTH4 I	(148)	ANY MAN WHO DOES NOT DESIRE IT. PERHAPS YOU WOULD	LIKE	TO TAKE A NAP. IF SO, PRAY DO NOT STAND ON CEREMONY.
PYGM II	(242)	MIND; ONLY IT SOUNDED SO GENTEEL. I SHOULD JUST	LIKE	TO TAKE A TAXI TO THE CORNER OF TOTTENHAM COURT ROAD
CAPT I	(231)	SIMPLY ABANDON IT-- UNLESS YOU, MR RANKIN, WOULD	LIKE	TO TAKE IT AS A PRESENT. /RANKIN/ (LAUGHING) I THANK
DOCT III	(148)	TAKING UP HIS HAT). /LOUIS/ (TO B.B.) WOULD YOU	LIKE	TO TAKE IT AT TWELVE, SIR RALPH? /B.B./ (COMING
PHIL II	(96)	ADORE THAT BUST. I SOMETIMES FEEL THAT I SHOULD	LIKE	TO TAKE THE POKER, AND FETCH IT A WIPE ACROSS THE NOSE.
ROCK PREFACE	(169)	INCREASING THE PRODUCT PER HOUR. SOME OF US WOULD	LIKE	TO TAKE THINGS EASY AND RETIRE AT 60: OTHERS WOULD LIKE
FANY II	(285)	THINK THAT? /KNOX/ WELL, I DONT KNOW: I DIDNT	LIKE	TO TELL YOU: YOU HAVE ENOUGH TO WORRY YOU WITHOUT THAT;
NEVR III	(272)	GREATLY MISTRUST YOU, MR VALENTINE. BUT I DO NOT	LIKE	TO THINK THAT YOUR UNFORTUNATE LEVITY OF DISPOSITION IS
O'FL	(220)	YOU, TESSIE. /TERESA/ (SHRINKING) SURE I DONT	LIKE	TO TOUCH IT, DENNY. DID YOU TAKE IT OFF A DEAD MAN?
MILL III	(186)	THINGS THAT NOBODY ELSE DOES? HOW WOULD YOU	LIKE	TO WALK DOWN COMMERCIAL ROAD AND GET NOTHING BUT BLACK
ROCK PREFACE	(169)	TAKE THINGS EASY AND RETIRE AT 60: OTHERS WOULD	LIKE	TO WORK THEIR UTMOST AND RETIRE AT 40. SOME OF US WILL
MIS.	(112)	A CAD: YOURE A LIAR: YOURE A BULLY: I SHOULD	LIKE	TO WRING YOUR DAMNED NECK FOR YOU. /JOHNNY/ (WITH A
LADY	(245)	HEAR HOW HE USETH ME! CALLING ME BAGGAGE AND THE	LIKE	TO YOUR MAJESTY'S FACE. /ELIZABETH/ AS FOR YOU,
HART II	(118)	ARE THE ONLY PERSON IN THE HOUSE I CAN SAY WHAT I	LIKE	TO. I KNOW YOU ARE FOND OF ME. SIT DOWN. (SHE DRAWS
HART II	(84)	INTO THE DRAUGHTSMAN'S SEAT) CERTAINLY. I SHOULD	LIKE	TO. /MANGAN/ (TAKEN ABACK) SHOULD YOU? THAT SURPRISES
HART I	(70)	TO KISS ME? /THE GENTLEMAN/ I THOUGHT I WOULD	LIKE	TO. THE FACT IS, I AM RANDALL UTTERWORD, THE UNWORTHY
MRS PREFACE	(163)	AND MY PLAY A GROSSLY IMPROPER ONE, BECAUSE,	LIKE	TOLSTOY'S DOMINION OF DARKNESS, IT PRODUCES, AS THEY
AUGS	(268)	YOU MUST HAVE CHILDREN. YOU CANT BUY EM IN BOXES,	LIKE	TOY SOLDIERS. /AUGUSTUS/ BEAMISH: THE LONG AND THE
MTH2	(84)	LIVE THREE HUNDRED YEARS, NOT BECAUSE THEY WOULD	LIKE	TO, BUT BECAUSE THE SOUL DEEP DOWN IN THEM WILL KNOW
CAND I	(96)	YOU WONT. /MARCHBANKS/ (EARNESTLY) NO: I SHOULD	LIKE	TO, INDEED. THANK YOU VERY MUCH. BUT-- BUT-- /MORELL/
MTH4 II	(187)	/THE WIFE/ THANK YOU. /THE DAUGHTER/ I SHOULD	LIKE	TO, VERY MUCH. (TOGETHER) (THEY GO INTO THE TEMPLE).
MIS. PREFACE	(107)	" OH, I REALLY COULDNT," OR " OH, I SHOULDNT	LIKE	TO," WITHOUT BEING ABLE TO POINT OUT THE SMALLEST HARM
JITT I	(14)	SELVES: GOING THROUGH LIFE IN GROOVES, ON RAILS	LIKE	TRAMCARS, ENVYING THE TINKERS AND GIPSIES. IF IT WERE
CAPT III	(296)	NONSENSE OUT OF HIS PENNY NUMBERS AND SUCH	LIKE	TRASH; BUT I GOT JUST THE SAME NONSENSE OUT OF LIFE AND
FANY PROLOG	(265)	IT? BANNAL MAY NOT RIDE THE LITERARY HIGH HORSE	LIKE	TROTTER AND THE REST; BUT I'D TAKE HIS OPINION BEFORE
ROCK I	(232)	IDLE PEOPLE ARE ALWAYS CLAMORING TO BE BRACED!	LIKE	TROUSERS. /SIR ARTHUR/ IDLE PEOPLE! HOW YOU STICK TO
JOAN 4	(98)	AND WHEN OUR MEN HAD REPULSED ALL HER ATTACKS	LIKE	TRUE ENGLISHMEN, SHE WALKED ALONE TO THE WALL OF OUR
MIS. PREFACE	(73)	TRYING TO MAKE CHILDREN LEAVE SCHOOL WILL BE	LIKE	TRYING TO MAKE THEM GO TO BED; AND IT WILL BE NECESSARY
JITT III	(52)	I AM SO SORRY. BRUNO ALWAYS SAID THAT IT WAS	LIKE	TRYING TO WORK IN A SHOOTING GALLERY WHEN I CLEARED UP
GETT	(357)	FIELDS THEY HAVE NO RIGHT TO? /SOAMES/ I DO NOT	LIKE	TURNIPS. /HOTCHKISS/ AS YOU ARE A LAWYER, ANSWER ME.
PHIL I	(83)	DESPERATELY) I TELL YOU THEYRE COMING UP TOGETHER	LIKE	TWINS, WHAT ON EARTH ARE WE TO DO? /JULIA/ (
LION I	(115)	NO: WE SHOULD KNEEL SIDE BY SIDE BEFORE HER ALTAR	LIKE	TWO CHILDREN. BUT WHEN MEN WHO BELIEVE NEITHER IN MY
BULL IV	(161)	TO PICK UP THE INTERRUPTED THREAD, AND CHATTER	LIKE	TWO MAGPIES. BUT AS IT IS, I HAVE SIMPLY NOTHING TO
METH PREFACE	(R36)	ON THESE LINES. HE ROSE AND SAID THAT HE WERE	LIKE	TWO MEN WORKING A SAW, HE PUSHING IT FORWARD AND I
FABL III	(110)	AND HAVE ENOUGH LEISURE TO PAINT WHAT YOU	LIKE	UNTIL THE WORLD RECOGNIZES YOUR GENIUS. /THE TOURIST/
PYGM V	(271)	CHANCE HE WANTED TO SHEW THAT AMERICANS IS NOT	LIKE	US: THAT THEY RECOGNIZE AND RESPECT MERIT IN EVERY
CLEO IV	(175)	SHE CARE FOR OLD POLITICIANS AND CAMP-FED BEARS	LIKE	US? NO: APOLLODORUS IS GOOD COMPANY, RUFIO, GOOD
MTH5	(234)	BY THEM. /THE NEWLY BORN/ BUT WONT THEY BE ALIVE,	LIKE	US? /PYGMALION/ THAT IS A VERY DIFFICULT QUESTION TO
MTH5	(234)	WHY DID YOU NOT FIND OUT HOW TO MAKE THEM	LIKE	US? /STREPHON/ (CRYING OUT IN HIS GRIEF FOR THE FIRST
MTH5	(235)	I ASK YOU AGAIN, WHY DID YOU NOT MAKE THEM	LIKE	US? WOULD ANY TRUE ARTIST BE CONTENT WITH LESS THAN
MTH5	(233)	AND WOMEN I COULD MAKE WERE MEN AND WOMEN JUST	LIKE	US AS FAR AS THEIR BODIES WERE CONCERNED. THAT WAS HOW
MIS.	(127)	IN THE GARDEN OF EDEN. BUT IF BIG THINGS	LIKE	US DIDNT DIE, WE'D CROWD ONE ANOTHER OFF THE FACE OF
ROCK II	(266)	AND HAS NOT BEEN TRAINED TO USE HIS MIND	LIKE	US IN SCOTLAND. BUT THAT IS JUST WHAT GIVES HIM SUCH A
WIDO III	(57)	OF BEING RAISED ABOVE IT, AS I AM NOW. WOULD YOU	LIKE	US TO GO AND LIVE IN THAT PLACE IN THE BOOK FOR THE
BULL III	(134)	GOIN TO SEND HIM INTO PARLIAMENT? MAYBE YOUD	LIKE	US TO SEND YOU DHERE TO THRATE DHEM TO A LITTLE O YOUR
MTH2	(72)	ATTEMPTS AT CIVILIZATION MADE BY PEOPLE EXACTLY	LIKE	US; AND EVERY ONE OF THEM FAILED JUST AS OURS IS
JOAN 1	(67)	/JOAN/ THEY ARE ONLY MEN. GOD MADE THEM JUST	LIKE	US; BUT HE GAVE THEM THEIR OWN COUNTRY AND THEIR OWN
CAND I	(84)	PENETRATING INTELLECT INSTEAD OF MERE EMOTIONS	LIKE	US, AND TO KNOW THAT THE REASON WE DONT SHARE YOUR
GENV PREFACE	(25)	YAHOOS IT IS POSSIBLE FOR CREATURES BUILT EXACTLY	LIKE	US, BRED FROM OUR UNIONS AND DEVELOPED FROM OUR SEEDS,
LION PROLOG	(107)	ARE THE VERY LOWEST OF THE LOW. /ANDROCLES/ JUST	LIKE	US, DEAR. /MEGAERA/ SPEAK FOR YOURSELF. DONT YOU DARE
DEVL II	(36)	HIS CHEEK) YOU WILL NOT MIND TWO OLD PEOPLE	LIKE	US, MR DUDGEON. (GOING) I SHALL NOT SAY GOOD EVENING:
NEVR II	(255)	GUILE) OF COURSE! TWO INTELLIGENT PEOPLE	LIKE	US! ISNT IT PLEASANT, IN THIS STUPID CONVENTION-RIDDEN
BARB PREFACE	(231)	THE CHRISTIAN VALJEAN. BUT BILL WALKER IS NOT,	LIKE	VALJEAN, ROMANTICALLY CHANGED FROM A DEMON INTO AN
HART PREFACE	(4)	THE WOMEN IN THEIR GIRLHOOD MADE THEMSELVES LOOK	LIKE	VARIETY THEATRE STARS, AND SETTLED DOWN LATER INTO THE
GENV PREFACE	(25)	AND SAINTLY WOMEN IN EVERY GENERATION, LOOK	LIKE	VINDICTIVE RETALIATORS, PUGNACIOUS SPORTSMEN, AND
MIS. PREFACE	(89)	TWEAK THE NOSES OF OUR HUMBUGS AND PANJANDRUMS,	LIKE	VOLTAIRE OR DICKENS, WE ARE SHOCKED AND SCANDALIZED,
LION EPILOG	(151)	RITUALIST. OR HE MAY BE EITHER A UNITARIAN DEIST	LIKE	VOLTAIRE OR TOM PAINE, OR THE MORE MODERN SORT OF
CYMB FORWORD	(137)	ACCOMPANIMENTS": I HAVE LUXURIATED IN VARIATIONS,	LIKE	WAGNER DEALING WITH GLUCK'S OVERTURE TO IPHIGENIA IN
JOAN PREFACE	(27)	THE BEGINNING, ANDREW LANG WAS BETTER READ; BUT,	LIKE	WALTER SCOTT, HE ENJOYED MEDIEVAL HISTORY AS A STRING
OVER	(171)	ONLY WANT YOU (SHE RECOILS). DONT BE ALARMED: I	LIKE	WANTING YOU. AS LONG AS I HAVE A WANT, I HAVE A REASON
ROCK I	(206)	WAR: THAT IS WHAT THEY LIKE, AND THEY	LIKE	WAR BECAUSE IT ISNT REAL TO THEM: IT'S ONLY A CINEMA
INCA PROLOG	(234)	MOTOR RIDES: ONE BILL AFTER ANOTHER: MONEY GOING	LIKE	WATER, NO RESTRAINT, NO SELF-CONTROL, NO DECENCY. (
DOCT I	(99)	BACILLI-- ARE TRANSLUCENT BODIES, LIKE GLASS,	LIKE	WATER. TO MAKE THEM VISIBLE YOU MUST STAIN THEM. WELL,
LION PREFACE	(62)	AND THE EFFORTS OF NATURAL SELECTIONISTS	LIKE	WEISMANN TO REDUCE EVOLUTION TO MERE AUTOMATISM HAVE
JOAN PREFACE	(21)	JERICHOWISE AT THE SOUND OF HER TRUMPET, BUT,	LIKE	WELLINGTON, ADAPTED HER METHODS OF ATTACK TO THE
FABL IV	(115)	WORLD WARS, ATOMIC BOMBS AND POISON GASES AND THE	LIKE	WERE QUITE BEYOND THEIR POWERS OF COOPERATION: THEIR
KING PREFACE	(154)	OF MERCURY SO IRRESISTIBLE AS A LAUGH CATCHER (	LIKE	WESTON-SUPER-MARE) THAT I CANNOT BRING MYSELF TO
MRS I	(183)	HE SITS DOWN). /VIVIE/ DO YOU KNOW, YOU ARE JUST	LIKE	WHAT I EXPECTED. I HOPE YOU ARE DISPOSED TO BE FRIENDS

HART I (65)	MY HEART IS BROKEN, BUT THAT HEARTBREAK IS NOT	LIKE	WHAT I THOUGHT IT MUST BE. /MRS HUSHABYE/ (FONDLING
MRS II (215)	FROM THE BEGINNING-- NEVER LET HERSELF LOOK TOO	LIKE	WHAT SHE WAS-- NEVER LOST HER HEAD OR THREW AWAY A
2TRU II (74)	/TALLBOYS/ WHAT DIALECT WAS IT? IT DIDNT SOUND	LIKE	WHAT THE NATIVES SPEAK HERE. /MEEK/ NO SIR. I USED TO
KING I (171)	THEY ARE NOT LIKE WOMEN AT ALL. THEY ARE JUST	LIKE	WHAT THEY ARE; AND THEY SPOIL THE PLAY FOR ANYONE WHO
2TRU III (105)	EVERYBODY TOLD ME LIES. THE WORLD IS NOT A BIT	LIKE	WHAT THEY SAID IT WAS. I WASNT A BIT LIKE WHAT THEY
2TRU III (105)	A BIT LIKE WHAT THEY SAID IT WAS. I WASNT A BIT	LIKE	WHAT THEY SAID I OUGHT TO BE. I THOUGHT I HAD TO
NEVR II (231)	BE HERE AT HALF PAST ONE. (TO M'COMAS) ARE WE	LIKE	WHAT YOU EXPECTED? /MRS CLANDON/ (EARNESTLY, EVEN A
SUPR HANDBOK(228)	TO GET WHAT YOU LIKE OR YOU WILL BE FORCED TO	LIKE	WHAT YOU GET. WHERE THERE IS NO VENTILATION FRESH AIR
BULL III (119)	THE OPEN AIR. /AUNT JUDY/ AH GALONG! HOW CAN YOU	LIKE	WHATS NOT NATURAL? I HOPE YOU SLEPT WELL. /NORA/ DID
GETT (333)	THAN YOU. /LESBIA/ THE CHINESE KNOW WHAT A MAN IS	LIKE	WHEN HE IS CUT INTO A THOUSAND PIECES, OR BOILED IN
GETT (333)	/MRS GEORGE/ WELL, I DID. I KNOW WHAT A WOMAN IS	LIKE	WHEN HER HAIR'S PULLED. I KNOW WHAT A MAN IS LIKE WHEN
GETT (333)	LIKE WHEN HER HAIR'S PULLED. I KNOW WHAT A MAN IS	LIKE	WHEN HE'S BIT. I KNOW WHAT THEYRE BOTH LIKE WHEN YOU
JOAN 4 (103)	BUT TO JOAN THE MAID. WHAT WILL THE WORLD BE	LIKE	WHEN THE CHURCH'S ACCUMULATED WISDOM AND KNOWLEDGE AND
APPL INTRLUD(249)	DO WITHOUT HER. YOU CAN SEE AS MUCH OF HER AS YOU	LIKE	WHEN WE ARE MARRIED. I SHALL NOT BE JEALOUS AND MAKE
BUOY III (34)	HOME FOR YOU, WHERE YOU CAN SEE WHOM YOU	LIKE	WHEN YOU LIKE. THIS WOMAN LIVES LIKE A SAVAGE IN A
GETT (333)	IS LIKE WHEN HE'S BIT. I KNOW WHAT THEYRE BOTH	LIKE	WHEN YOU TELL THEM WHAT YOU REALLY FEEL ABOUT THEM. AND
FANY III (320)	COME UP AND BE ASHAMED OF YOURSELVES, BEHAVING	LIKE	WILD INDIANS. /DORA'S VOICE/ (SCREAMING) OH! OH!
ROCK PREFACE(174)	REPORTED AS SAYING ANYTHING REACTIONARY, IT RUNS	LIKE	WILDFIRE THROUGH THE PRESS OF THE WHOLE WORLD. WHEN I
SUPR III (123)	PLEDGINGS AND UNTIL-DEATH-DO-US-PARTINGS AND THE	LIKE	WILL BE EXPUNGED AS UNBEARABLE FRIVOLITIES. DO MY SEX
MIS. PREFACE(53)	THE HUNTING FIELD, AND AT BADAJOS SIEGES AND THE	LIKE	WILL RAM HIS HEAD INTO A HOLE BRISTLING WITH SWORD
BARB PREFACE(222)	COIT, AND STRENUOUS NONCONFORMIST JOURNALISTS	LIKE	WILLIAM STEAD, WHO NOT ONLY UNDERSTOOD THE ACT AS WELL
MILL PREFACE(116)	TO MAKE LA GLOIRE GLORIOUS, AND ALL THIS BECAUSE,	LIKE	WILLIAM THE CONQUEROR, HE HAD THE GROUP OF TALENTS THAT
LION PRGL,SD(105)	TREES, EXHAUSTED WITH PAIN, HEAVING A LONG SIGH,	LIKE	WIND IN A TROMBONE, HE GOES TO SLEEP. ANDROCLES AND HIS
BUOY PREFACE(4)	SCREEDS MIGHT HAVE BEEN CALLED WISHFUL WRITINGS (	LIKE	WISHFUL THINKINGS) SO CLEARLY WERE THEY AS MUCH HER OWN
2TRU I (49)	A FOOL, A LOVELY FOOL: I SHALL BE ABLE TO DO AS I	LIKE	WITH HIM. (SHE RUSHES TO THE DRESSING TABLE; BUNDLES
LION PREFACE(92)	THE OBLIGATION, THEN WE CAN BE AS WICKED AS WE	LIKE	WITH IMPUNITY INSIDE THE SECULAR LAW, EVEN FROM
MIS. PREFACE(6)	PARENTS, AND TO ALLOW THEM TO DO WHAT THEY	LIKE	WITH IT AS FAR AS IT WILL LET THEM, IT HAS NO RIGHTS
MILL IV (201)	MILLION IN SIX MONTHS? /ADRIAN/ I WILL DO WHAT I	LIKE	WITH IT. I WILL HAVE IT UNCONDITIONALLY. /SAGAMORE/ (
PYGM II (219)	SO THAT YOU CAN TURN HER ON AS OFTEN AS YOU	LIKE	WITH THE WRITTEN TRANSCRIPT BEFORE YOU. /MRS PEARCE/ (
FABL VI (126)	THEIR BRAINS. THEY SEEM TO HAVE DONE WHAT THEY	LIKE	WITH THEIR BODIES. /YOUTH 2/ ANYHOW, THEY HAD TO EAT
MILL II (173)	FEZ. /EPIFANIA/ I WANTED TO SEE WHAT YOU LOOKED	LIKE	WITHOUT IT. (SHE PUTS IT TENDERLY ON HIS HEAD). LISTEN
ROCK PREFACE(167)	TRACTORS AND SAY " THIS IS MY OWN TO DO WHAT I	LIKE	WITH," ARE BETTER FED AND HOUSED, NICER, AND MUCH MORE
KING I (171)	INDEED THEY ARE NOT, MR ROWLEY. THEY ARE NOT	LIKE	WOMEN AT ALL. THEY ARE JUST LIKE WHAT THEY ARE; AND
MRS I (185)	YOU CANT MEAN THAT. /VIVIE/ OH YES I DO. I	LIKE	WORKING AND GETTING PAID FOR IT. WHEN I'M TIRED OF
CAPT III (273)	QUARREL IS ABOUT. CAPTAIN BRASSBOUND IS JUST	LIKE	YOU: HE THINKS WE HAVE NO RIGHT TO JUDGE ONE ANOTHER;
MRS IV (250)	DIE. /VIVIE/ NO: I AM MY MOTHER'S DAUGHTER. I AM	LIKE	YOU: I MUST HAVE WORK, AND MUST MAKE MORE MONEY THAN I
ROCK I (219)	/HIPNEY/ ME READ MARX! BLESS YOU, SRARTHUR, I AM	LIKE	YOU: I TALK ABOUT THE OLD DOCTOR WITHOUT EVER HAVING
JITT II (51)	BUT, JITTA: I DONT REALLY BELIEVE THAT. IT'S NOT	LIKE	YOU: YOU ARE NOT CLEVER ENOUGH, NOT AMBITIOUS ENOUGH.
MRS II (213)	TO HER TALKING! DO YOU THINK I WAS BROUGHT UP	LIKE	YOU? ABLE TO PICK AND CHOOSE MY OWN WAY OF LIFE? DO
BULL III (133)	BREAD FROM THE IGNORANCE AND SUPERSTITION OF MEN	LIKE	YOU? I WOULD HAVE HER ABOVE WORLDLY PRIDE OR AMBITION.
CAND III (134)	NERVOUS DISEASE LIKE ME, AND A PIG-HEADED PARSON	LIKE	YOU? LET US GO ON A PILGRIMAGE, YOU TO THE EAST AND I
MIS. (169)	FOR A THIEF? AND DO YOU SUPPOSE I CAN GET CREDIT	LIKE	YOU? /TARLETON/ THEN YOU WERE ABLE TO LAY YOUR HAND ON
INCA (254)	HELP DIVINING IT, SIR? WHO IS THERE IN THE WORLD	LIKE	YOU? YOUR MAGNETISM -- /THE INCA/ TRUE: I HAD
HART II (95)	IS ENOUGH FOR ME. /MRS HUSHABYE/ I'M BEGINNING TO	LIKE	YOU A LITTLE. I PERFECTLY LOATHED YOU AT FIRST. I
PHIL II (130)	DOWN). /CHARTERIS/ (DELIGHTED) AH, THERES NOBODY	LIKE	YOU AFTER ALL, CUTHBERTSON. WHEN THERES A DIFFICULT
BULL III (139)	MATTER IF YOU GET A BIT UPSET AT FIRST: THEYLL	LIKE	YOU ALL THE BETTER FOR IT. /HODSON/ I'M SURE YOURE VERY
SUPR IV (167)	BY THEIR LANDLADIES, AND NEVER GET MARRIED. MEN	LIKE	YOU ALWAYS GET MARRIED. /TANNER/ (SMITING HIS BROW)
MTH3 (93)	AN EXTRAORDINARY NUMBER OF FIRST-RATE PERSONS	LIKE	YOU AND ME HAVE DIED BY DROWNING DURING THE LAST TWO
GETT PREFACE(193)	INQUISITOR. IN SHORT, DEAR READER, THEY WERE VERY	LIKE	YOU AND ME. I COULD FILL A HUNDRED PAGES WITH THE TALE
APPL INTRLUD(252)	AND DREADS IT. NOT WITHOUT REASON; FOR WOMEN	LIKE	YOU ARE DANGEROUS TO WIVES. BUT I DONT DISLIKE YOUR
PYGM III (245)	WOMEN. MY IDEA OF A LOVABLE WOMAN IS SOMETHING AS	LIKE	YOU AS POSSIBLE. I SHALL NEVER GET INTO THE WAY OF
KING II (227)	WELL, I FORGIVE YOU: WHY SHOULD A GREAT MAN	LIKE	YOU BE SATISFIED WITH A LITTLE THING LIKE ME?
MRS IV (244)	WORTH. /PRAED/ BUT SURELY A CLEVER BRIGHT FELLOW	LIKE	YOU CAN MAKE SOMETHING BY YOUR OWN BRAINS. /FRANK/ OH
ROCK II (248)	HAD ALL THE PLUCK TAKEN OUT OF ME BY POVERTY,	LIKE	YOU CHAPS. AND WHAT GOOD WILL IT DO ME TO HAVE A LOT OF
APPL INTRLUD(246)	WERE ONCE ROSES; AND, THOUGH YOUNG THINGS	LIKE	YOU DONT REMEMBER THAT, THEIR HUSBANDS DO. THEY DONT
CAND I (95)	AT MY FATHER! I SHOULDNT HAVE MINDED; BUT I	LIKE	YOU EVER SO MUCH BETTER FOR BEING NICE TO HIM.
O'FL (213)	SURE AND SHE WOULDNT WANT TO SEE A GENTLEMAN	LIKE	YOU GOING TO HELL AFTER SHE NURSING YOUR OWN SON AND
JOAN 1 (58)	(COWERING ON THE CHEST) YES, SIR: TO A GREAT MAN	LIKE	YOU I MUST SEEM LIKE THAT. /ROBERT/ (TURNING) MY
GLIM (183)	YOUR FATHER DO THE HOUSE WORK WITH A GREAT GIRL	LIKE	YOU IDLING ABOUT? SQUARCIO IS A FOOL, AFTER ALL.
DEVL I (12)	ALL THE HEAVY WORK OF THE HOUSE WITH A GREAT LOUT	LIKE	YOU IDLING ABOUT. CHRISTY TAKES THE WINDOW BAR OUT OF
PYGM II (237)	GENERAL WAY I WOULDNT; BUT TO OBLIGE A GENTLEMAN	LIKE	YOU I'D DO A GOOD DEAL, I DO ASSURE YOU. /PICKERING/
O'FL (212)	THAN YOUD THINK, SIR; FOR HOW WOULD A GENTLEMAN	LIKE	YOU KNOW WHAT A POOR IGNORANT CONCEITED CREATURE I WAS
PYGM V (288)	I SAID I'D MAKE A WOMAN OF YOU; AND I HAVE. I	LIKE	YOU LIKE THIS. /LIZA/ YES: YOU TURN ROUND AND MAKE UP
MIS. (190)	OF THAT SORT WOULD BE SUFFICIENT TO MAKE A MAN	LIKE	YOU LOSE YOUR SELF-POSSESSION AND PUT YOURSELF IN THE
POSN (462)	/THE FOREMAN/ (TO BLANCO, ON HIS WAY OUT) A MAN	LIKE	YOU MAKES ME SICK, JUST SICK. (BLANCO MAKES NO SIGN.
BARB II (310)	INNOCENCE. /BARBARA/ (GOING TO HIM) PETER: I'M	LIKE	YOU NOW. CLEANED OUT, AND LOST MY JOB. /SHIRLEY/ YOUVE
NEVR II (259)	DOWN INTO IT SERIOUSLY, I DONT KNOW WHETHER I	LIKE	YOU OR NOT. /GLORIA/ (LOOKING DOWN AT HIM WITH
BARB II (280)	AN EAH AW EMM, TALKIN TO A ROTTEN AOLD BLAWTER	LIKE	YOU STED O GIVIN HER WOT FOR. (WORKING HIMSELF INTO A
FANY III (326)	DINNERS. /MRS KNOX/ BUT WHY DID A GENTLEMAN	LIKE	YOU STOOP TO BE A FOOTMAN? /DORA/ HE STOOPED TO
HART II (87)	GET MARRIED AT ALL, MR MANGAN. /MANGAN/ A CHILD	LIKE	YOU TALKING OF " WE WOMEN"! WHAT NEXT! YOURE NOT IN
PHIL I (70)	TRANFIELD. /CHARTERIS/ MY DEAR: IT IS BECAUSE I	LIKE	YOU THAT I WANT TO MARRY YOU. I COULD LOVE ANYBODY--
FANY I (281)	KEPT HIM SHELTERED. (ANGRY WITH HER) CREATURES	LIKE	YOU THAT TAKE ADVANTAGE OF A CHILD'S INNOCENCE OUGHT TO
BULL III (139)	BE TOO STAND-OFFISH, YOU KNOW, HODSON. I SHOULD	LIKE	YOU TO BE POPULAR. IF IT COSTS ANYTHING I'LL MAKE IT UP
PYGM V (279)	VERY NICE OF YOU, MISS DOOLITTLE. /LIZA/ I SHOULD	LIKE	YOU TO CALL ME ELIZA, NOW, IF YOU WOULD. /PICKERING/
HART II (120)	DRINKING. /ELLIE/ YOU SHALL NOT DRINK. DREAM. I	LIKE	YOU TO DREAM. YOU MUST NEVER BE IN THE REAL WORLD WHEN
GETT (351)	(QUICKLY) OH NO. DONT BE HASTY. I THINK I SHOULD	LIKE	YOU TO DROP IN AFTER A WHILE, YOU KNOW. SHE GETS SO
VWOO 1 (117)	READ IT TO YOUR HEART'S CONTENT. /Z/ BUT I SHOULD	LIKE	YOU TO GET ME RIGHT. AFTER ALL, WHAT DO YOU KNOW ABOUT
GETT (340)	TOLD ME NOTHING. /MRS GEORGE/ ONE THING I SHOULD	LIKE	YOU TO KNOW. /THE BISHOP/ YES? /MRS GEORGE/ WE DIDNT
PYGM V (287)	THROWN AWAY ON FREDDY. /LIZA/ YOU THINK I	LIKE	YOU TO SAY THAT. BUT I HAVNT FORGOT WHAT YOU SAID A
WIDO I (9)	PAPA, PLEASE. /SARTORIUS/ MY DEAR: I SHOULD	LIKE	YOU TO SEE EVERYTHING. IT IS PART OF YOUR EDUCATION--
CAND I (97)	WRONG. I'M VERY FOND OF YOU, MY BOY; AND I SHOULD	LIKE	YOU TO SEE FOR YOURSELF WHAT A HAPPY THING IT IS TO BE
HART II (104)	OF ALL WE SAID ABOUT YOU? /MANGAN/ ARE ALL WOMEN	LIKE	YOU TWO? DO THEY NEVER THINK OF ANYTHING ABOUT A MAN
OVER (177)	HAPPY. I DONT WANT TO BE WICKED, OR COARSE. BUT I	LIKE	YOU VERY MUCH; AND I DO WANT TO BE AFFECTIONATE AND
ROCK I (205)	I DISLIKE MY DAUGHTER AND TREAT HER BADLY. I	LIKE	YOU VERY MUCH; AND I TREAT YOU ABOMINABLY. /SIR ARTHUR/
JOAN 1 (61)	I DO NOT NEED BEAUTIFUL ARMOR MADE TO MY MEASURE	LIKE	YOU WEAR. I SHALL NOT WANT MANY SOLDIERS: THE DAUPHIN
NEVR I (220)	LOOKING CRITICALLY AT HIM) I DONT THINK WE SHALL	LIKE	YOU WHEN YOU ARE BROODING OVER YOUR INJURIES. /PHILIP/
WIDO II (36)	FINGERS, STILL OVER HIS SHOULDER) BUT I SHOULDNT	LIKE	YOU WITH YOUR FINGERS WORKED TO THE BONE, HARRY. I MUST
BARB II (281)	ER. /SHIRLEY/ TELL HER SO. IT'S JUST WHAT A FOOL	LIKE	YOU WOULD DO. BARBARA, BRISK AND BUSINESSLIKE, COMES
BULL II (113)	YOU CAN IMAGINE THE SENSATION AN ENGLISHMAN	LIKE	YOU WOULD MAKE AMONG US POOR IRISH PEOPLE. /BROADBENT/
BULL III (139)	DEFERENTIALLY) OF COURSE I KNOW A GENTLEMAN	LIKE	YOU WOULD NOT COMPARE ME TO THE YEOMANRY. ME OWN
MIS. (156)	YOUNG. BESIDES, I'M A MARRIED MAN, NOT A WIDOWER	LIKE	YOU. A MARRIED MAN CAN DO ANYTHING HE LIKES IF HIS WIFE
CAND II (120)	WILL KNOW: WHEN HE IS GROWN UP AND EXPERIENCED,	LIKE	YOU. AND HE WILL KNOW THAT I MUST HAVE KNOWN. I WONDER
OVER (190)	WIFE OUGHTNT TO LIKE ME. AND MY WIFE OUGHTNT TO	LIKE	YOU. AND IF THEY DO, THEY OUGHTNT TO GO ON LIKING US.
SUPR III (126)	ALL MY SOUL AT THE MOMENT. I HAD A HEART: NOT	LIKE	YOU. AND IT WAS THIS SINCERITY THAT MADE ME SUCCESSFUL.
LIED (200)	YOU SUPPOSE I'M JEALOUS OF YOU? NO, NOR OF TEN	LIKE	YOU. BUT IF YOU THINK I'LL STAND HERE AND LET YOU
MTH5 (206)	NO, THANK YOU. I DANCED WHEN I WAS A CHILD	LIKE	YOU. DANCING IS A VERY CRUDE ATTEMPT TO GET INTO THE
DOCT I (107)	AGAINST THE LAITY. AND WE CANT ALL BE GENIUSES	LIKE	YOU. EVERY FOOL CAN GET ILL; BUT EVERY FOOL CANT BE A
MIS. (161)	MEANS SOMETHING THAT WILL LAST LONGER THAN YES. I	LIKE	YOU. I ADMIT YOU TO MY FRIENDSHIP. WHAT A PITY YOU WERE
DOCT III (139)	CLEAN AND WHOLESOME. I CAN JUST PLAY WITH PEOPLE	LIKE	YOU. I ONLY ASKED YOU HAD YOU SEEN JENNIFER'S MARRIAGE
GETT (278)	KNEW A GREAT DEAL MORE ABOUT IT THAN A GREAT BABY	LIKE	YOU. I'M SURE I DONT KNOW HOW YOULL GET ON WITH NO ONE
CLEO IV (172)	CAESAR HAS SPOILED ME FOR TALKING TO WEAK THINGS	LIKE	YOU. (SHE GOES OUT. POTHINUS, WITH A GESTURE OF RAGE,
BARB II (282)	PETER! WE CAN ALWAYS FIND A JOB FOR A STEADY MAN	LIKE	YOU. (SHIRLEY, DISARMED AND A LITTLE BEWILDERED,
CAND I (101)	KING DAVID, IN HIS FITS OF ENTHUSIASM, WAS VERY	LIKE	YOU. (STABBING HIM WITH THE WORDS) " BUT HIS WIFE
BULL IV (156)	EXISTENCE TO PLAY BACKGAMMON WITH A GOOD MAN	LIKE	YOU. /AUNT JUDY/ (WHISPERING TO HER) WHISHT, WHISHT,
BARB II (287)	HE GETS ROUND PEOPLE THEY GET MISERABLE, JUST	LIKE	YOU. /BILL/ (WITH A HEARTBREAKING ATTEMPT AT
APPL I (226)	TAKE AWAY YOUR CHARACTER THE BETTER THE PEOPLE	LIKE	YOU. /BOANERGES/ (SUDDENLY) PRIME MINISTER: WILL YOU
CLEO I (109)	TOWARDS HIM) YOU ARE A FUNNY OLD GENTLEMAN. I	LIKE	YOU. /CAESAR/ AH, THAT SPOILS THE DREAM. WHY DONT YOU

MRS II	(206)	AN INTEREST IN A GIRL? /MRS WARREN/ NOT A MAN	LIKE	YOU. /CROFTS/ HOW OLD IS SHE? /MRS WARREN/ NEVER YOU
MTH2	(50)	OF ELOQUENCE: IT IS THE BANE OF POPULAR SPEAKERS	LIKE	YOU. /FRANKLYN/ WELL! ! /SAVVY/ I LIKE THAT!
JITT III	(66)	IS THE THOUGHT THAT SHE MIGHT HAVE BEEN SOMEBODY	LIKE	YOU. /JITTA/ (STARTLED) LIKE ME! /AGNES/ YES; FOR HE
JOAN EPILOG	(155)	WITH THE STONES AND HOT PITCH RAINING DOWN.	LIKE	YOU. /JOAN/ NO! DID MAKE A MAN OF THEE AFTER ALL,
JOAN 1	(69)	AND YOU CANNOT STOP THEM, NOR TEN THOUSAND	LIKE	YOU. /JOAN/ ONE THOUSAND LIKE ME CAN STOP THEM. TEN
MIS.	(111)	SORT: ALL BODY AND NO BRAINS,	LIKE	YOU. /JOHNNY/ THANK YOU. /BENTLEY/ DONT MENTION IT, OLD
CAND II	(106)	AFRAID TO BE YOUR REAL SELF WITH ME? I AM JUST	LIKE	YOU. /PROSERPINE/ LIKE ME! PRAY ARE YOU FLATTERING ME
DEVL II	(36)	AT HIM LIKE AN ANGRY CHILD) IT IS NOT BECAUSE I	LIKE	YOU. /RICHARD/ INDEED! /JUDITH/ YES: I HAD RATHER YOU
ARMS III	(58)	WERE ANY LESS BRAVE THAN THE MEN WHO ARE RICH	LIKE	YOU. /SERGIUS/ (WITH BITTER LEVITY) NOT A BIT. THEY
MILL II	(174)	LIKE MY FATHER. AND THERE ARE SOME GOOD DOCTORS,	LIKE	YOU. /THE DOCTOR/ THANK YOU. WHAT DOES YOUR REGULAR
MTH4 III	(196)	THROUGH HER AND BREAK YOUR NECK. SHE ISNT SOLID.	LIKE	YOU. /THE ELDERLY GENTLEMAN/ I WAS SPEAKING
BARB II	(304)	IT MEANS TO THEM, AND HOW LITTLE TO A GREAT MAN	LIKE	YOU. /UNDERSHAFT/ (SARDONICALLY GALLANT) MRS BAINES:
NEVR II	(259)	YOU ARE SENTIMENTAL, AND A LITTLE FOOLISH; BUT I	LIKE	YOU. /VALENTINE/ (DROPPING INTO THE NEAREST CHAIR AS
VWOO 3	(139)	A FUTILE SORT OF PERSON I ATTRACT VIGOROUS WOMEN	LIKE	YOU. /Z/ WHEN YOU LOOKED AT ME OUT OF THE CORNER OF
JOAN EPILOG	(156)	DEAD, LIKE ME? /CHARLES/ YES. BUT SHE WAS NOT	LIKE	YOU. SHE WAS VERY BEAUTIFUL. /JOAN/ (LAUGHING
JITT I	(12)	ROOMS HERE ON THE QUIET TO ENJOY THEMSELVES WERE	LIKE	YOU. THERE ARE PEOPLE AND PEOPLE IN THIS WORLD; AND I
MTH1 I	(9)	TO WORSHIP. SOMETHING QUITE DIFFERENT TO MYSELF,	LIKE	YOU. THERE MUST BE SOMETHING GREATER THAN THE SNAKE.
HART II	(95)	I NEVER HAVE BEEN A FAVORITE WITH GORGEOUS WOMEN	LIKE	YOU. THEY ALWAYS FRIGHTEN ME. /MRS HUSHABYE/ (PLEASED)
MTH3	(98)	EVIDENT. /BURGE-LUBIN/ HOW? /CONFUCIUS/ PEOPLE	LIKE	YOU. THEY LIKE CHEERFUL GOOD-NATURED BARBARIANS. THEY
MTH4 II	(188)	AS YOU WOULD BE WITH US. WE UNDERSTAND YOU. WE	LIKE	YOU. WE ARE EASY-GOING PEOPLE; AND WE ARE RICH PEOPLE.
DEST	(172)	/NAPOLEON/ AH, THATS BETTER. NOW LISTEN TO ME. I	LIKE	YOU. WHATS MORE, I VALUE YOUR RESPECT. /LADY/ YOU VALUE
BARB III	(314)	SCHOOLBOYS MAKE THEIR OWN FORMULAS OUT OF SLANG,	LIKE	YOU. WHEN THEY REACH YOUR AGE, AND GET POLITICAL
CAND III	(130)	SAME WAY. I HAVE BEEN PLAYING THE GOOD MAN. JUST	LIKE	YOU. WHEN YOU BEGAN YOUR HEROICS ABOUT LEAVING ME HERE
GETT	(269)	YOU FINISH. YOU SEE, BOXER, EVERYBODY IS NOT	LIKE	YOU. YOU ARE A SENTIMENTAL NOODLE: YOU DONT SEE WOMEN
MTH3	(98)	THEY WILL ELECT YOU FIVE TIMES MORE. I	LIKE	YOU. YOU ARE BETTER COMPANY THAN A DOG OR A HORSE
DEST	(177)	TO THE TABLE) YOU SHALL HAVE NO LETTER. I DONT	LIKE	YOU. YOURE A DETESTABLE WOMAN, AND AS UGLY AS SATAN. I
VWOO 2	(124)	COMPENSATORY ADVANTAGE WHATEVER. /Z/ THATS JUST	LIKE	YOU. YOURE NOT A BIT CHANGED. /A/ WHAT DO YOU MEAN? I
DOCT I	(87)	BECAUSE I'M AN OLD MAN, A REAL OLD MAN, NOT	LIKE	YOU. YOURE ONLY BEGINNING TO GIVE YOURSELF THE AIRS OF
MIS.	(144)	BUT JOHNNY AND I WERE VULGAR ENOUGH TO LIKE IT. I	LIKE	YOUNG PEOPLE BECAUSE THEYRE NOT TOO AFRAID OF DIRT TO
GETT PREFACE	(195)	OLD SCOLDING OR BEATING THE YOUNG FOR BEHAVING	LIKE	YOUNG PEOPLE, AND THE YOUNG HATING AND THWARTING THE
KING I	(213)	IN THIS PAINTER. I HAVE MET IT IN COMMON SAILORS	LIKE	YOUR BOATSWAIN. THE COBBLER THINKS THERE IS NOTHING
ROCK II	(235)	WELL, WHAT PRICE YOUR SAFE MAN NOW? HOW DO YOU	LIKE	YOUR BOLSHY PREMIER? WHO WAS RIGHT? THE FUNKERS AND
ROCK II	(248)	UP THREE CHILDREN ON THIRTYFOUR SHILLINGS A WEEK,	LIKE	YOUR BROTHER THE SHOPMAN. TO HELL WITH YOUR FILTHY
MIS.	(124)	AT ALL EVENTS, AND NOT A LITTLE SQUIT OF A THING	LIKE	YOUR BUNNY. /HYPATIA/ OH, I SAY NOTHING AGAINST YOUR
DOCT I	(83)	LAUGH AT ME. /REDPENNY/ SERVE YOU RIGHT! IT WAS	LIKE	YOUR CHEEK TO TALK TO HIM ABOUT SCIENCE. (HE RETURNS
O'FL	(207)	TO YOU THAT HAVE AN ESTATE IN IT, IT WOULD FEEL	LIKE	YOUR COUNTRY, BUT THE DIVIL A PERCH OF IT EVER I OWNED.
FANY III	(324)	THAN AN ENGLISHMAN, SIR: IF ALL FRENCHWOMEN WERE	LIKE	YOUR DAUGHTER-- IF ALL FRENCHMEN HAD THE GOOD SENSE,
GLIM	(188)	THINK IT DANGEROUS AND UNBECOMING THAT A NOBLEMAN	LIKE	YOUR EXCELLENCY SHOULD TRAVEL WITHOUT A RETINUE, AND
PYGM V	(285)	HAPPENS TO EITHER OF US. I AM NOT INTIMIDATED,	LIKE	YOUR FATHER AND YOUR STEPMOTHER. SO YOU CAN COME BACK
HART II	(88)	I DONT CHOOSE, SEE? BECAUSE I'M NOT A SILLY GULL	LIKE	YOUR FATHER, THATS WHY. /ELLIE/ (WITH SERENE CONTEMPT)
ROCK II	(276)	PHASE OF SOCIAL DEVELOPMENT." I DONT TALK	LIKE	YOUR GRANDMOTHER, IF YOU WILL EXCUSE ME SAYING SO. /SIR
JOAN 4	(94)	CERTAINLY NOT, MY LORD: I AM A GENTLEMAN. STILL,	LIKE	YOUR LORDSHIP, I WAS BORN IN ENGLAND; AND IT MAKES A
DOCT V	(178)	YOU NEVER COULD HAVE BELIEVED IN HIM. IT IS JUST	LIKE	YOUR NOT BELIEVING IN MY RELIGION: IT IS A SORT OF
SUPR III	(85)	FEW LINES BEFORE YOU GO TO SLEEP. I SHOULD REALLY	LIKE	YOUR OPINION OF THEM. /TANNER/ (DROWSILY) GO ON. I AM
DEST	(163)	LIE: YOUR EYES ARE NOT LIKE MINE: THEYRE EXACTLY	LIKE	YOUR OWN. /NAPOLEON/ (WITH CONTAINED EXASPERATION)
GETT	(328)	MAN. DO YOU SEE THIS FACE, ONCE FRESH AND ROSY	LIKE	YOUR OWN, NOW SCARRED AND RIVEN BY A HUNDRED BURNT-OUT
ANNA	(301)	ON HIS KNEE SUBMISSIVELY) NOW AT LAST YOU SPEAK	LIKE	YOUR ROYAL SELF. /THE GRAND DUCHESS/ OH, STRAMMFEST,
MTH5	(250)	I WAS A CHILD, ECRASIA, I, TOO, WAS AN ARTIST,	LIKE	YOUR SCULPTOR FRIENDS THERE, STRIVING TO CREATE
GLIM	(176)	YOU LEAVE THIS TERRITORY I SHALL STICK TO YOU	LIKE	YOUR SHADOW. /FERRUCCIO/ AND WHY, PRAY? /SQUARCIO/
CAPT III	(295)	/BRASSBOUND/ IF THAT WERE YOUR PICTURE, WOULD YOU	LIKE	YOUR SON TO KEEP IT FOR YOUNGER AND BETTER WOMEN TO
APPL INTRLUD	(252)	PEOPLE. FOR INSTANCE, YOUR SORT. MY WIFE DOESNT	LIKE	YOUR SORT, DOESNT UNDERSTAND IT, MISTRUSTS AND DREADS
6CAL	(105)	IS THE BETTER HORSE HERE. DO YOUR WORST, DAME! I	LIKE	YOUR SPUNK BETTER THAN HIS SNIVEL. /THE QUEEN/ (
LION I	(113)	NEEDS NO MARTYRS. /LAVINIA/ NO; BUT MY FAITH,	LIKE	YOUR SWORD, NEEDS TESTING. CAN YOU TEST YOUR SWORD
FANY II	(294)	I DONT LIKE THIS SPIRIT IN YOU, MARGARET. I DONT	LIKE	YOUR TALKING TO ME IN THAT TONE. /MARGARET/ IT'S NO
CAPT II	(258)	MEANWHILE). DO YOU KNOW, YOU ARE WONDERFULLY	LIKE	YOUR UNCLE. /BRASSBOUND/ DAMNATION! /LADY CICELY/ EH?
OVER	(190)	THEY OUGHTNT TO GO ON LIKING US. AND I OUGHTNT TO	LIKE	YOUR WIFE; AND YOU OUGHTNT TO LIKE MINE; AND IF WE DO,
NEVR IV	(305)	WAS MASTER IN MY OWN HOUSE, SIR: MY WIFE WAS	LIKE	YOUR YOUNG LADY: SHE WAS OF A COMMANDING AND MASTERFUL
APPL I	(209)	IT DOES NOT UNDERSTAND WORK. I MEAN BRAIN WORK,	LIKE	YOURS AND MINE. /BOANERGES/ THAT'S TRUE. BUT I CAN TALK
CAND I	(101)	IT HARD FOR ME TO CONTROL MYSELF. MY TALENT IS	LIKE	YOURS INSOFAR AS IT HAS ANY REAL WORTH AT ALL. IT IS
ROCK II	(252)	OLD DAYS! /BARKING/ GRABBING ALL THEY COULD GET,	LIKE	YOURS OR MINE. WHATS THE GOOD OF TUBTHUMPING AT THESE
LION I	(121)	MAN -- JUST SUCH A ONE AS YOU, WITH GOLDEN HAIR	LIKE	YOURS -- SCOFFED AT AND STRUCK ME AS YOU SCOFFED AT AND
JITT II	(44)	ME. DONT BE CHILDISH. /JITTA/ (IRRITABLY) I AM	LIKE	YOURSELF: I AM ONLY TRYING TO GUESS WHY HE DID IT.
ROCK I	(214)	AN END TO IT ALL TOMORROW IF I COULD? BUT I AM	LIKE	YOURSELF: I AM IN THE GRIP OF ECONOMIC FORCES THAT ARE
ROCK II	(256)	TRY TO CONVINCE YOU THAT A DUKE IS A HUMAN BEING	LIKE	YOURSELF? /ALOYSIA/ (REARING) ARE YOU TRYING TO
SUPR IV	(148)	WOMEN FOR HECTOR, THATS STRAIGHTFORWARD, ISNT IT,	LIKE	YOURSELF? /VIOLET/ (ICILY PITYING HIS SENTIMENTALITY)
PHIL II	(97)	OH, NO, NO. A SCIENTIFIC MAN, PERHAPS,	LIKE	YOURSELF. BUT YOU KNOW WHAT I MEAN: A MAN. (HE STRIKES
BULL I	(87)	BECAUSE THEYRE ONLY POOR SLOVENLY USELESS DEVILS	LIKE	YOURSELF. (DROPPING HIS VOICE LIKE A MAN MAKING SOME
CAPT II	(256)	HE WILL BE HERE WITHIN AN HOUR. HE IS A JUDGE,	LIKE	YOURSELF. YOU CAN TALK LAW TO HIM. HE WILL GIVE YOU
WIDO III	(52)	AND TAKING OFF HIS OVERCOAT) OH! THERE YOU SPEAK	LIKE	YOURSELF, SARTORIUS. NOW SUPPOSE YOU ASK ME TO SIT DOWN
GETT	(344)	I DONT UNDERSTAND. I AM A WOMAN: A HUMAN CREATURE	LIKE	YOURSELVES. WILL YOU NOT TAKE ME AS I AM? /SOAMES/
MIS.	(159)	HE'S A LIVING LIE. MY SOUL'S NOT LIKE THAT: IT'S	LIKE	YOURS. I WANT TO MAKE A FOOL OF MYSELF. ABOUT YOU. WILL
CATH 2	(175)	VOLTAIRE ALSO HAS HEADACHES. HIS BRAIN IS JUST	LIKE	YOURS. /CATHERINE/ DASHKOFF! WHAT A LIAR YOU ARE! (
NEVR IV	(299)	/GLORIA/ YOU HAVE IMPLIED THAT MY PAST HAS BEEN	LIKE	YOURS. THAT IS THE WORST OF INSULTS. /VALENTINE/ I
CAND I	(102)	LIFT A HEAVY TRUNK DOWN FROM THE TOP OF A CAB	LIKE	YOU-- BECAUSE I CANT FIGHT YOU FOR YOUR WIFE AS A
BARB II	(279)	YOUR EYE OUT. AINT YOU SATISFIED-- YOUNG WHELPS	LIKE	YOU-- WITH TAKIN THE BREAD OUT O THE MOUTHS OF YOUR
MTH1 I	(5)	HORROR OF HAVING TO BE WITH MYSELF FOR EVER. I	LIKE	YOU; BUT I DO NOT LIKE MYSELF. I WANT TO BE DIFFERENT;
VWOO 3	(143)	BE AFRAID. I CANT MAKE A FINE SPEECH ABOUT IT	LIKE	YOU; BUT IT WILL BE ALL RIGHT. I PROMISE YOU THAT. /A/
DEST	(188)	YES. VERY NICE WOMAN. SHE'S WONDERFULLY	LIKE	YOU; BUT OF COURSE SHE'S BETTER-LOOKING. /LADY/ (
DOCT I	(102)	OF ME TO OFFER A PRESCRIPTION TO A GREAT MAN	LIKE	YOU; BUT STILL I HAVE GREAT EXPERIENCE; AND IF I MIGHT
MIS.	(171)	IVE HAD ENOUGH OF BEING TALKED DOWN TO BY HOGS	LIKE	YOU, AND WEARING MY LIFE OUT FOR A SALARY THAT WOULDNT
CAPT I	(238)	CICELY/ OH NO. AFTER ALL, THOSE MEN MUST REALLY	LIKE	YOU, CAPTAIN BRASSBOUND. I FEEL SURE YOU HAVE A KIND
CAPT II	(249)	PLEASE, MADAM. /LADY CICELY/ THANK YOU. THATS SO	LIKE	YOU, CAPTAIN. THANK YOU. NOW, MR REDBROOK! SHOW ME THE
POSN	(442)	ON HIM) DONE LIKE YOU! WHAT DO YOU MEAN? DRINK	LIKE	YOU, EH? WELL, IVE DONE SOME OF THAT LATELY. I SEE
MTH3	(116)	THE ONLY READER OF WELLS? IF THERE WERE OTHERS	LIKE	YOU, HAD THEY NOT THE SAME REASON FOR KEEPING THE
PHIL II	(122)	ME. SO I'M OUT OF THE RUNNING. NEVERTHELESS,	LIKE	YOU, I HOPE THAT SHE MAY BE HAPPY WITH ALL MY-- WHAT
BUOY II	(20)	OF MY VANITY, WHEN I TRIED TO BE HAPPY WITH MEN	LIKE	YOU, I LEARNT HOW TO PLAY THE SOPRANO SAXOPHONE. I HAVE
SIM PRO,2,	(27)	Y.H./ WELL, I AM SURPRISED TO HEAR A YOUNG MAN	LIKE	YOU, IN THE PRIME OF LIFE AS YOU MIGHT SAY, TALKING
MIS.	(161)	YOUNG STILL. /TARLETON/ I SUPPOSE, TO AN ATHLETE	LIKE	YOU, I'M PRETTY AWFUL, EH? /LINA/ SHOCKING. /TARLETON/
MIS.	(204)	A GHASTLY WHITE SMILE INTO HIS FACE) YOU SHALL. I	LIKE	YOU, MY BOY. WE GO TOMORROW, TOGETHER. /BENTLEY/ YES!
BARB I	(264)	MY YOUNG FRIEND? (TO LADY BRITOMART) HE IS VERY	LIKE	YOU, MY LOVE. /CUSINS/ YOU FLATTER ME, MR UNDERSHAFT.
BUOY III	(47)	THESE PINKS ARE: BELONGING NEITHER TO THE WEST,	LIKE	YOU, NOR TO THE EAST, LIKE ME. /THE NATIVE/ (SWINGING
VWOO 3	(140)	CONSISTS OF POSITIVE MASTERFUL ACQUISITIVE PEOPLE	LIKE	YOU, OBSESSED WITH SOME PASSION WHICH THEY MUST GRATIFY
INCA	(240)	WHO IS ACCUSTOMED TO WAIT ON LADIES, AND NOT,	LIKE	YOU, ON COMMERCIAL TRAVELLERS. /THE WAITER/ ALAS,
SUPR IV	(161)	IS BEST FOR A YOUNG MAN: TO KNOW TOO LITTLE,	LIKE	YOU, OR TOO MUCH, LIKE JACK. TANNER RETURNS. /TANNER/
SUPR IV	(148)	FADDY SORT OF PERSON, YOU KNOW. /MALONE/ SOMEBODY	LIKE	YOU, PERHAPS? /VIOLET/ (QUIETLY) WELL, YES. BUT YOU
BARB III	(321)	DO YOU SUPPOSE THAT YOU AND HALF A DOZEN AMATEURS	LIKE	YOU, SITTING IN A ROW IN THAT FOOLISH GABBLE SHOP, CAN
GETT	(355)	GEORGE/ (ADMIRING HIS ELOQUENCE) GEORGE WILL	LIKE	YOU, SONNY. YOU SHOULD HEAR HIM TALKING ABOUT THE
BULL I	(83)	FINDS THE WHOLE PLACE FULL OF ROMANTIC DUFFERS	LIKE	YOU, WHO WILL LET HIM LOAF AND DRINK AND SPONGE AND
PHIL II	(126)	/JULIA/ (SULLENLY) I SUPPOSE IT'S BETTER TO BE	LIKE	YOU, WITH A COLD HEART AND A SERPENT'S TONGUE. THANK
BULL III	(130)	THE LAND IS HANDED OVER TO A LOT OF LITTLE MEN	LIKE	YOU, WITHOUT CALLING YOU TO ACCOUNT EITHER. THEYRE
LADY	(239)	YOU SPEAK STRANGELY, SIR: NO OFFENCE. BUT, AN'T	LIKE	YOU, YOU ARE A VERY CIVIL GENTLEMAN; AND A POOR MAN
POSN	(462)	AFTER HIM) AS IF I CARED ABOUT A STINGY BRAT	LIKE	YOU! GO BACK TO THE FRECKLED MAYPOLE YOU LEFT FOR ME:
BULL III	(142)	FORGIMMY FOR TALKIN TO A POOR IGNORANT CRAYCHER	LIKE	YOU! /HODSON/ (GRINNING WITH GOOD-HUMORED MALICE. TOO
SUPR IV	(159)	WORSE, LIKE ME? /OCTAVIUS/ SOMETHING WORSE--	LIKE	YOU! WHAT DO YOU MEAN, ANN? /ANN/ OH WELL, I DONT
POSN	(442)	ROUND YOUR NECK. /BLANCO/ (TURNING ON HIM) DONE	LIKE	YOU! WHAT DO YOU MEAN? DRINK LIKE YOU, EH? WELL, IVE
MILL II	(172)	HALF THEIR MONEY AWAY ON CHARITIES AND FANCIES	LIKE	ZIONISM. THE STUPIDEST DI PARERGA CAN JUST WALK ROUND
SUPR HANDBOK	(192)	WHO THINK DECENTLY CAN WRITE POPULAR STORIES	LIKE	ZOLA'S FECUNDITY OR TOLSTOY'S RESURRECTION WITHOUT

JITT II (46)	TO THINK OF YOU? /JITTA/ YOU CAN THINK WHAT YOU	LIKE	, ALFRED. I DONT GRUDGE YOU THAT MELANCHOLY
SUPR III (123)	MORE HOLY? /DON JUAN/ SACRED AND HOLY, IF YOU	LIKE	, ANA, BUT NOT PERSONALLY FRIENDLY. YOUR RELATION TO
OVER PREFACE(166)	WITH CURIOSITY AS TO WHAT THEY ARE REALLY	LIKE	, AND BEGIN TO DEMAND THAT THE STAGE SHALL BE A MIRROR
BARB I (272)	FOOLISHNESS. YOU CAN GO WITH HIM, TOO, IF YOU	LIKE	, AND LEAVE ME WITH THE SERVANTS. /STEPHEN/ OH, YOU
MIS. PREFACE(95)	WAIT UNTIL YOUR BACK IS TURNED AND I WILL DO AS I	LIKE	, AND LIE ABOUT IT." THERE CAN BE NO OBJECTIVE
ROCK PREFACE(152)	AND PARLIAMENTARY LABOR PARTIES, AND THE	LIKE	, AND MAINTAINING A SORT OF CONTINUAL CIVIL WAR
PYGM II (235)	SWINE. I BROUGHT IT TO HER JUST TO OBLIGE YOU	LIKE	, AND MAKE MYSELF AGREEABLE. THATS ALL. /HIGGINS/ HOW
FANY III (316)	I KNOW? ARE WE CHILDREN NOT TO BE LET DO WHAT WE	LIKE	, AND OUR OWN SONS AND DAUGHTERS KICKING THEIR HEELS
LION PREFACE(64)	WILL. THE NOTION THAT PEOPLE CAN BE GOOD IF THEY	LIKE	, AND THAT YOU SHOULD GIVE THEM A POWERFUL ADDITIONAL
GETT PREFACE(217)	AVOID THESE TWO PERILS, YOU CAN DO ANYTHING YOU	LIKE	, AS FAR AS YOUR NEIGHBORS ARE CONCERNED, AND SINCE WE
SUPR PREFACE(R23)	UP MEN OF GENIUS, CHOPINS, MUSSETS AND THE	LIKE	, AS MERE HORS D'OEUVRES. I STATE THE EXTREME CASE, OF
BULL II (103)	TO THEM. I DID NOT KNOW WHAT MY OWN HOUSE WAS	LIKE	, BECAUSE I HAD NEVER BEEN OUTSIDE IT. /NORA/ D'YE
2TRU I (38)	A NURSE. BUT I KNOW HOW TO DEAL WITH YOU AND YOUR	LIKE	, BECAUSE I WAS ONCE A PATIENT IN A HOSPITAL WHERE THE
FANY III (300)	WAIST. /MARGARET/ YOU NEEDNT DO THAT IF YOU DONT	LIKE	, BOBBY. SUPPOSE WE GET OFF DUTY FOR THE DAY, JUST TO
BARB I (252)	PLEASE! BARBARA SHALL MARRY, NOT THE MAN THEY	LIKE	, BUT THE MAN I LIKE. /STEPHEN/ OF COURSE I WAS
ROCK II (274)	EASILY. YOU CAN TAKE A NEW NAME: ANY NAME YOU	LIKE	, BY DEED POLL. IT COSTS ONLY TEN POUNDS; AND DAVID
DOCT III (149)	THIS) I AM NOT OUT OF COUNTENANCE. I SHOULD	LIKE	, BY JUPITER, TO SEE THE MAN WHO COULD PUT ME OUT OF
CAPT III (280)	(TO KEARNEY) THATS WHAT ENGLISH PEOPLE ARE	LIKE	, CAPTAIN KEARNEY. THEY WONT HEAR OF ANYTHING
PHIL I (90)	BE HORRIBLY RUDE. /JULIA/ YOU CAN STAY IF YOU	LIKE	, DADDY: I CANT. I'LL WAIT FOR YOU IN THE HALL. (SHE
FANY I (279)	IF I MAKE JOE SPRINT FOR YOU? " " ANYTHING YOU	LIKE	, DARLING," SAYS HE: " I LOVE YOU." I PUT ON MY BEST
VHOO 1 (116)	ELSE WOULD YOU CALL IT? /A/ OH, CALL IT WHAT YOU	LIKE	, DEAR LADY; BUT I HAVE FIVE HUNDRED WORDS TO WRITE
MTH1 II (33)	ACROSS THE PASSAGE). /EVE/ THROUGH HIM AND HIS	LIKE	, DEATH IS GAINING ON LIFE. ALREADY MOST OF OUR
MRS IV (248)	OF EATING AND DRINKING; IT MEANS EVERYTHING YOU	LIKE	, EVERYTHING YOU WANT, EVERYTHING YOU CAN THINK OF. AND
MIS. PREFACE(87)	CONCERTS AND THEATRICALS AND EXCURSIONS AND THE	LIKE	, FAMILIES OF FOUR MAY TURN OUT MUCH LESS BARBAROUS
HART I (80)	PRETTY DAUGHTERS, AND SINGERS AND POETS AND THE	LIKE	, FOR WHOSE SAKE WE SPARE THEM. /HECTOR/ (SITTING UP
BULL PREFACE(53)	AND STABLE, OR AS BEATERS, HUNTSMEN AND THE	LIKE	, FROM THEM. BUT DENSHAWAI HAD NO SUCH INDUCEMENTS TO
LADY (248)	OF PEOPLE WHAT THEY BEST LIKE; AND WHAT THEY BEST	LIKE	, GOD KNOWS, IS NOT THEIR OWN BETTERMENT AND
3PLA PREFACE(R32)	OF ANGELS SING THEE; TO THY REST, OR ADSUM, OR THE	LIKE	, I HAVE NO RESPECT FOR THEM AT ALL: SUCH MAUDLIN
MIS. (193)	KISS AND TELL. AS A MERE MAN; A MERE CAD, IF YOU	LIKE	, I SAY THAT I DID SO AT MISS TARLETON'S OWN
CAPT II (250)	/LADY CICELY/ BUT THERE'S ONE THING I SHOULD	LIKE	, IF MR DRINKWATER WONT MIND MY MENTIONING IT. IT'S SO
SUPR I (21)	KNOW YOU PAY NO ATTENTION TO THEM. BUT, IF YOU	LIKE	, I'LL CALL YOU AFTER YOUR FAMOUS ANCESTOR DON JUAN.
BULL III (127)	WELL, IF ME LAN IS TO BE GIVEN TO PATSY AND HIS	LIKE	, I'M GOIN OURA DHIS, I-- /DORAN/ (WITH VIOLENT
LION PREFACE(12)	TO CHARITIES AND CHURCH BUILDING AND THE	LIKE	, IS STILL IN FULL SWING, ITS PRACTICAL DISADVANTAGE IS
HART PREFACE(4)	IT WAS DISASTROUS. FOR PRIME MINISTERS AND THEIR	LIKE	, IT WAS A VERITABLE CAPUA. HORSEBACK HALL. BUT WHERE
BULL II (102)	VERNACULAR OF HIS SPEECH TO PATSY) AN HOUR IF YOU	LIKE	, MISS REILLY: YOURE ALWAYS WELCOME. SHALL WE SIT
SUPR HANDBOK(207)	OUR SHAKESPEARS, GOETHES, SHELLEYS, AND THEIR	LIKE	, MUST LIVE AS PRECARIOUSLY AS LION TAMERS DO, TAKING
PRES (163)	ARE THE REAL RULERS AND THEY CAN DO WHAT THEY	LIKE	, NINE TIMES OUT OF TEN THEY SAY " ALL RIGHT: TELL US
CLEO I (108)	IS SO WAVY, AND I ALWAYS WANT TO BE LET DO AS I	LIKE	, NO MATTER WHETHER IT IS THE WILL OF THE GODS OR NOT:
CAPT II (264)	IF I AM TO COMMAND HERE, I AM GOING TO DO WHAT I	LIKE	, NOT WHAT YOU LIKE. I'LL GIVE THIS GENTLEMAN HERE TO
2TRU II (64)	THATS ALL ABOUT IT. /THE COUNTESS/ I'LL DO AS I	LIKE	, NOT WHAT YOU TELL ME. AND I TELL YOU AGAIN-- THE TWO
INCA (239)	(ALARMED) OH, I'M SURE I DONT KNOW. IF YOU	LIKE	, OF COURSE; BUT DO YOU THINK I OUGHT TO? /ERMYNTRUDE/
APPL I (203)	TO HAVE OUR TALK OUT IN TRAFALGAR SQUARE IF YOU	LIKE	, OR HAVE IT BROADCAST ON THE WIRELESS. /MAGNUS/ THAT
CAND I (92)	ME-- YOUR HOWN FATHER! -- THAT CAB TOUTS OR SUCH	LIKE	, ORF THE EMBANKMENT, BUYS PICTURES LIKE THAT? (
MIS. (148)	WOULD BE IF THEY ATE IT, ANYHOW, SAY WHAT YOU	LIKE	, PROVIDED THE MORAL IS A WELSH RABBIT FOR MY SUPPER.
BULL IV (163)	I HOPE; AND I AM PREPARED TO WAIT AS LONG AS YOU	LIKE	, PROVIDED YOU WILL GIVE ME SOME SMALL ASSURANCE THAT
GETT (270)	WELL, BOXER, YOU CAN LOVE ME AS MUCH AS YOU	LIKE	, PROVIDED YOU LOOK HAPPY ABOUT IT AND DONT BORE ME.
PYGM I (214)	WITH FEEBLE DEFIANCE) IVE A RIGHT TO BE HERE IF I	LIKE	, SAME AS YOU. /THE NOTE TAKER/ A WOMAN WHO UTTERS SUCH
GETT PREFACE(244)	SAYS SHE WANTED FINE CLOTHES, OR MORE FUN, OR THE	LIKE	, SHE IS REALLY SAYING THAT SHE LACKED WHAT NO WOMAN
ROCK I (220)	AND CERTIFICATES AND GOLD MEDALS AND THE	LIKE	, SHE'S WON ENOUGH OF THEM TO LAST YOUR WHOLE FAMILY
BULL III (118)	TURF. POTCHEEN AND STRONG PORTER IS WHAT THEY	LIKE	, SIR, I'M SURE I DONT KNOW HOW THEY CAN STAND IT. GIVE
BULL II (105)	WHEN PEOPLE TALK TO YOU ABOUT FIN MCCOOL AND THE	LIKE	, TAKE NO NOTICE OF THEM. IT'S ALL IDLE STORIES AND
6CAL PREFACE(90)	CENTURY WITH AN UP-TO-DATE RELIGION OR THE	LIKE	, THAT LUXURY IS THROWN IN GRATUITOUSLY; AND THE PLAY,
PYGM II (240)	HOT AND COLD WATER ON TAP, JUST AS MUCH AS YOU	LIKE	, THERE IS. WOOLLY TOWELS, THERE IS; AND A TOWEL HORSE
SIM PREFACE(11)	SUSPENSIONS OF THE HABEAS CORPUS ACT, AND THE	LIKE	, TO HAVE ANY VIRTUOUS INDIGNATION LEFT TO SPARE FOR
UNPL PREFACE(R13)	ABOUT IBSENISM, " THE NEW WOMAN," AND THE	LIKE	, WAS AT ITS HEIGHT, I WROTE FOR THE INDEPENDENT
GETT PREFACE(220)	WE HEAR OF YOUNG WOMEN BEING LED ASTRAY AND THE	LIKE	, WE FIND THAT WHAT HAS LED THEM ASTRAY IS A SEDULOUSLY
SUPR PREFACE(R33)	MELODRAMATIC MURDERS AND REVENGES AND THE	LIKE	, WHILST THE COMIC CHARACTERS WALK WITH THEIR FEET ON
SUPR III (105)	BUNGLER. I HAVE SEEN HIS COTTON FACTORIES AND THE	LIKE	, WITH MACHINERY THAT A GREEDY DOG COULD HAVE INVENTED
2TRU I (44)	WEARING, WHY NOT FIGHT FOR FREEDOM TO DO WHAT YOU	LIKE	, WITH YOUR POCKET FULL OF MONEY AND ALL THE FUN IN THE
NEVR I (222)	HURT, ALL RIGHT. I'LL HURT YOU AS MUCH AS YOU	LIKE	, WITHOUT ANY EXTRA CHARGE FOR THE BENEFICIAL EFFECT ON
MRS PREFACE(164)	MANAGERS ARE TO BE ALLOWED TO PRODUCE WHAT THEY	LIKE	, WITHOUT REGARD TO THE PUBLIC INTEREST. BUT THAT IS
MIS. (112)	YOURSELF AS NASTY AS YOU PLEASE AND SAY WHAT YOU	LIKE	, YOURE MISTAKEN. LET ME TELL YOU THAT EXCEPT HYPATIA,
MTH2 (78)	GENESIS PHYLOGENESIS. LET THE CREATOR SAY, IF YOU	LIKE	, " I WILL ESTABLISH AN ANTIPATHETIC SYMBIOSIS BETWEEN
DEST (160)	/NAPOLEON/ PSHA! WHAT WAS HE LIKE? /LIEUTENANT/	LIKE	! HE WAS LIKE-- WELL, YOU OUGHT TO HAVE JUST SEEN THE
CAPT II (259)	/BRASSBOUND/ IN HEAVEN'S NAME THEN, DO WHAT YOU	LIKE	! ONLY DONT WORRY ME WITH IT. /LADY CICELY/ I'M SO

LIKEABLE

MIS. SD(115)	IN HER TIME, AND IS STILL VERY PLEASANT AND	LIKEABLE	AND UNAFFECTED. HYPATIA IS A TYPICAL ENGLISH GIRL
PYGM II SD(218)	ENTIRELY FRANK AND VOID OF MALICE THAT HE REMAINS	LIKEABLE	EVEN IN HIS LEAST REASONABLE MOMENTS. /HIGGINS/ (
GETT SD(274)	OR ATTRACTIVE ENOUGH TO GET IT. ALL THE SAME, A	LIKEABLE	MAN, FROM WHOM NOBODY APPREHENDS ANY MALICE NOR
GENV IV (113)	AT PRESENT CONSIST EXCLUSIVELY OR EVEN LARGELY OF	LIKEABLE	PERSONS. /DEACONESS/ BUT I ASSURE YOU, THAT DOES
MTH3 (98)	IN AWE. CAPABLE PERSONS ARE NEVER LIKED. I AM NOT	LIKEABLE	; BUT I AM INDISPENSABLE. /BURGE-LUBIN/ OH, CHEER
BULL I SD(74)	ALWAYS BUOYANT AND IRRESISTIBLE, MOSTLY	LIKEABLE	, AND ENORMOUSLY ABSURD IN HIS MOST EARNEST

LIKED

GETT PREFACE(192)	WHO DID NOT THINK IT WRONG TO GO TO THE THEATRE	LIKED	ABOVE EVERYTHING A PLAY IN WHICH THE HERO WAS CALLED
BUOY III (30)	EXCEPT WHAT I PICKED UP DOING JUST WHAT I	LIKED	AND WAS GIVEN EVERYTHING I ASKED FOR. THAT HAS BEEN
JITT III (57)	BE; BUT THERE'S NOBODY. ALL I KNOW IS WHAT HE	LIKED	AND WHAT HE WANTED, AND HOW EASILY HE COULD GET IT BY
GETT (274)	SARCASM) AT SCHOOL YOU HAD A THEORY THAT WOMEN	LIKED	BEING KNOCKED DOWN, I REMEMBER. /REGINALD/ YOURE A
SUPR III (93)	IT-- THE DEATH OF ANYONE WE KNEW, EVEN THOSE WE	LIKED	BEST, WAS ALWAYS MINGLED WITH A CERTAIN SATISFACTION
LADY PREFACE(228)	MUST MEAN THAT HIS DESIRE TO PLEASE PEOPLE AND BE	LIKED	BY THEM, AND HIS RELUCTANCE TO HURT THEIR FEELINGS,
GETT (265)	AT LAST AND TOOK HIS ADVICE. GEORGE ALWAYS	LIKED	CHANGE OF COMPANY. /MRS BRIDGENORTH/ WHAT AN ODIOUS
BULL III (118)	IVE KNOWN LOTS OF EM IN ENGLAND, AND GENERALLY	LIKED	EM. BUT HERE, SIR, I SEEM SIMPLY TO HATE EM. THE
NEVR I (221)	WHAT DID YOU THINK OF HER SISTER? /CRAMPTON/ YOU	LIKED	HER BETTER, EH? /VALENTINE/ (RHAPSODICALLY) SHE
MRS III (227)	VERY. /CROFTS/ (WITH BRUTAL GOOD HUMOR, AS IF HE	LIKED	HER PLUCK) WELL, THATS NOT WHAT I CAME TO SAY. (
GETT (330)	DEVIL; BUT I LIKED REGINALD MUCH MORE THAN I	LIKED	HER. SHE DIDNT UNDERSTAND. ONE DAY SHE CAME TO ME AND
BUOY III (39)	AS THEY ARE NOW. BUT I COULD PUT UP WITH THEM. I	LIKED	HIM BECAUSE HE WAS SO UNLIKE ME. (TO HER HUSBAND) AND
KING I (196)	HIM AND I CAME ALONG UNEXPECTEDLY. I HAVE ALWAYS	LIKED	HIM FOR THAT. /JAMES/ IT WAS WORTH HIS WHILE. SHE GAVE
MIS. (124)	STICK IT OUT WITH JERRY, MOTHER. I KNOW YOU	LIKED	HIM; AND NOBODY CAN DENY THAT HES A SPLENDID ANIMAL --
LADY PREFACE(223)	FOR THERE IS NO REASON TO SUPPOSE THAT SHE	LIKED	HIS PLAYS ANY BETTER THAN MINNA WAGNER LIKED RICHARD'S
BASH PREFACE(89)	THE LISTENERS SHEWED UNMISTAKABLY THAT THEY	LIKED	HYPERBOLICAL RHETORIC AND DELIBERATELY ARTIFICIAL
NEVR II (253)	SOMEONE WHOM YOU LOVED, OR (SHYLY) AT LEAST	LIKED	IN A CHILDISH WAY? COME! SOMEONE WHO LET YOU STAY IN
2TRU PREFACE(20)	ELECTIONS BY THEIR NEWSPAPERS TO DO ANYTHING THEY	LIKED	IN THE NAME OF THE PEOPLE. VOTES FOR EVERYBODY (
2TRU PREFACE(8)	AND COULD LIVE THE LIFE OF THE IDLE RICH IF I	LIKED	IT; AND MY SOLE REASON FOR NOT LIVING IT IS THAT I
FANY III (306)	AND OF COURSE HE CUT ME DEAD. I WONT PRETEND I	LIKED	IT; BUT WHAT COULD HE DO, POOR DEAR? /MARGARET/ AND
CAPT III (277)	YOU DID IT, BUT YOU DONT THINK SHE WOULD HAVE	LIKED	IT, ANY MORE THAN PAPA AND THE REST OF US, DO YOU?
MRS II (213)	OF LIFE? DO YOU THINK I DID WHAT I DID BECAUSE I	LIKED	IT, OR THOUGHT IT RIGHT, OR WOULDNT RATHER HAVE GONE
LADY PREFACE(218)	SHAKESPEAR, HE WAS NOT SO SUCCESSFUL OR SO WELL	LIKED	. BUT IN SPITE OF THIS HE PRAISED SHAKESPEAR TO THE
GENV III (72)	AT THE PUBLIC EXPENSE AND LET WRITE WHAT HE	LIKED	. ENGLAND IS THE COUNTRY WHERE, AS THE POET SAYS, " A
MTH3 (98)	ME; I AM HELD IN AWE. CAPABLE PERSONS ARE NEVER	LIKED	. I AM NOT LIKEABLE; BUT I AM INDISPENSABLE.
OVER (194)	JUNO/ THEN I WONT DO IT: THATS FLAT. I LIKE TO BE	LIKED	. I LIKE TO BE LOVED. I WANT EVERYONE ROUND ME TO LOVE
APPL II (267)	IT RED. I COULD PAINT YOUR POSITION BLACK IF I	LIKED	. IN PLAIN TERMS WE REQUIRE FROM YOU AN UNCONDITIONAL
PYGM V (286)	OR OF ME. I COULD HAVE BEEN A BAD GIRL IF I'D	LIKED	. IVE SEEN MORE OF SOME THINGS THAN YOU, FOR ALL YOUR
MIS. (114)	SERVE HER RIGHT! AFTER THAT, I WAS LET DO WHAT I	LIKED	. MY FATHER DIDNT WANT ME TO GROW UP A BROKEN-SPIRITED
GETT (325)	AND THAT I COULD TAKE THE JOB IF I	LIKED	. /MRS GEORGE/ IT'S STILL OPEN. (SHE TURNS TO EDITH).
MIS. PREFACE(65)	PRECEPT HE MIGHT BE PRETTY WELL ANYTHING ELSE HE	LIKED	. THE MAINTENANCE OF DEFERENCE TO OUR WILLS BECOMES A
MRS II (214)	RESTAURANT WHERE THEY SENT OUT FOR ANYTHING YOU	LIKED	. THEN I WAS WAITRESS; AND THEN I WENT TO THE BAR AT

WIDO III (60)	INTO A ROOM AND ELECT ONE ANOTHER, AND DO WHAT WE	LIKED	. WELL, THAT COCK WONT FIGHT ANY LONGER; AND, TO PUT
MILL IV (202)	THAT ONCE RESEMBLED A MAN, SOMETHING THAT	LIKED	LENDING ME FIVE POUND NOTES AND NEVER ASKED ME TO
PHIL III (142)	MET AFTER MANY YEARS, THAT HE HAS RESPECTED AND	LIKED	ME EVER SINCE FOR IT, AND I BELIEVE HIM, AND FEEL THE
MIS. (119)	ROUGH ON ME, THOUGH. HE TOLD ME NOBODY HERE	LIKED	ME; AND I WAS SILLY ENOUGH TO BELIEVE HIM. /LORD
OVER (175)	TO YOU IF I HAD THOUGHT THAT. I THOUGHT YOU	LIKED	ME, BUT THAT YOU KNEW, AND WOULD BE GOOD. /GREGORY/ (
GETT (330)	FRIEND. LEO WAS AN AMUSING LITTLE DEVIL; BUT I	LIKED	REGINALD MUCH MORE THAN I LIKED HER. SHE DIDNT
LADY PREFACE(223)	SHE LIKED HIS PLAYS ANY BETTER THAN MINNA WAGNER	LIKED	RICHARD'S MUSIC DRAMAS: AS LIKELY AS NOT, SHE THOUGHT
ROCK II (271)	INTO YOUR HEAD IF I DIDNT. YOU COULD DO IT IF YOU	LIKED	; AND YOU KNOW IT, SIR BROADFOOT. BUT PERHAPS YOUR
HART II (119)	LIVES. THE STEWARDESSES COULD COME ASHORE IF THEY	LIKED	; BUT THEY SAIL AND SAIL AND SAIL. /ELLIE/ WHAT COULD
DEST (161)	I CANT GET OVER. HE SAID HE'D NEVER MET A MAN HE	LIKED	SO MUCH AS ME. HE PUT HIS HANDKERCHIEF ROUND MY NECK
MIS. PREFACE(49)	THAT IS, IF THEY HAD SET ME FREE TO DO AS I	LIKED	SUBJECT ONLY TO MY POLITICAL RIGHTS AND THEIRS, THEY
HART I (61)	/ELLIE/ (TRIUMPHANTLY) NO, ON PURPOSE. HE	LIKED	TALKING TO ME. HE KNOWS LOTS OF THE MOST SPLENDID
SIM PREFACE(9)	GEORGE FOX, THOUGH BOTH CROMWELL AND CHARLES II	LIKED	THE MAN AND ADMIRED HIM, NOW THE HERETIC IN RUSSIA IS
BULL I (84)	HOUSE AND HOME HAS RATHER TAKEN ME ABACK; FOR I	LIKED	THE OLD RASCAL WHEN I WAS A BOY AND HAD THE RUN OF HIS
NEVR II (253)	AND MORE URGENTLY) SOMEONE WHO LET YOU DO AS YOU	LIKED	THERE, AND NEVER SAID A WORD TO YOU EXCEPT TO TELL YOU
LADY PREFACE(209)	AND DIE AND HAVE IT AGAIN AND AGAIN AND AGAIN. HE	LIKED	TO BELIEVE THAT NOTHING THAT HAPPENED TO HIM WAS
METH PREFACE(R29)	WE HAD A CRAZE FOR BIG FIGURES, AND POSITIVELY	LIKED	TO BELIEVE THAT THE PROGRESS MADE BY THE CHILD IN THE
GETT (331)	WELL, SORRY WE SHANT MEET AGAIN: I SHOULD HAVE	LIKED	TO SEE MORE OF YOU FOR GEORGE'S SAKE. GOODBYE (SHE
ROCK PREFACE(164)	FARMER WHO WAS RICHER THAN HIS NEIGHBORS AND	LIKED	TO SEE THEM POORER THAN HIMSELF. HIM THEY RUDELY TOOK
PHIL I (70)	LOVE WITH YOU, YOU WILL LIKE ME FOR IT JUST AS I	LIKED	TRANFIELD. /CHARTERIS/ MY DEAR: IT IS BECAUSE I LIKE
DOCT II (122)	/ SCHUTZMACHER/ OH YES I DID. I SHOULD HAVE	LIKED	VERY MUCH TO HAVE KEPT THE SKETCH AND GOT IT
INCA (238)	HASTY; AND HE IS MY GUARDIAN. I ONCE HAD A MAID I	LIKED	VERY MUCH; BUT HE SENT HER AWAY THE VERY FIRST TIME.
BARB I (255)	TO DO AND SAY WHATEVER YOU LIKED, SO LONG AS YOU	LIKED	WHAT I COULD APPROVE OF. /STEPHEN/ (DESPERATELY) I
HART PREFACE(12)	MEANT SIMPLY THAT A SOLDIER COULD DO WHAT HE	LIKED	WITH IMPUNITY IN CIVIL LIFE, WAS NOT THE LAW OF THE
VWOO 2 (130)	AND THEN I COULD FALL IN LOVE WITH ANYONE I	LIKED	WITHOUT ANY FEAR OF MAKING A FOOL OF MYSELF. I SUPPOSE,
GETT (315)	A WOMAN TO LIVE ON, PRAY, WHEN SHE IS NO LONGER	LIKED	, AS YOU CALL IT? /SOAMES/ (WITH SARDONIC FORMALITY)
JITT PREFACE(6)	THE MORE DREADFUL IT ALL IS THE BETTER IT IS	LIKED	, BECAUSE ROMANCE CAN NEVER COME HOME TO REALITY. TO
CLEO IV (170)	SO? /CLEOPATRA/ WHEN I WAS FOOLISH, I DID WHAT I	LIKED	, EXCEPT WHEN FTATATEETA BEAT ME; AND EVEN THEN I
BARB I (255)	YOU PERFECT FREEDOM TO DO AND SAY WHATEVER YOU	LIKED	, SO LONG AS YOU LIKED WHAT I COULD APPROVE OF.
		LIKELIEST	
ROCK PREFACE(172)	AND DENYING ALL THE DISPUTED BELIEFS. THE	LIKELIEST	OUTCOME IS AN ELABORATE CREED OF USEFUL ILLUSIONS,
		LIKELIHOOD	
GETT (301)	AT LARGE) BUT ISNT ALL THIS GREAT NONSENSE? WHAT	LIKELIHOOD	IS THERE OF ANY OF US COMMITTING A CRIME?
PHIL II (101)	GIVE ME UP. AND IF SHE WONT LISTEN TO ME, WHAT	LIKELIHOOD	IS THERE OF HER LISTENING TO YOU? /CRAVEN/ (IN
CAPT I (230)	IS, RATHER MORE THAN THERE WAS ANY REASONABLE	LIKELIHOOD	OF THE ESTATE PROVING WORTH. /RANKIN/ THEN THE
CAPT NOTES (300)	SO INCREDIBLE A PERSONAGE MUST HAVE DESTROYED ITS	LIKELIHOOD	-- SUCH AS IT IS, THERE ARE MOMENTS WHEN I DO NOT
GETT PREFACE(255)	NOTION THAT THEY ARE ANY BETTER, SEE NO SERIOUS	LIKELIHOOD	THAT STATE ACTION WILL DETACH CHILDREN FROM THEIR
BULL II SD(111)	AUNT JUDY SEEMS TO HIM AN INCARNATE JOKE. THE	LIKELIHOOD	THAT THE JOKE WILL PALL AFTER A MONTH OR SO, AND
		LIKELY	
CAPT I (234)	A FILIBUSTER. VERY WELL, VERY WELL. YOU WILL MOST	LIKELY	ADMIRE ALL THEIR FACES; AND I HAVE NO DOUBT AT ALL
HART II (86)	IF THEYRE LUCKY ENOUGH TO GET ANYTHING AT ALL. AS	LIKELY	AS NOT THE VERY SAME THING HAPPENS TO THE NEW LOT.
JOAN PREFACE(26)	AND EVERY SCOT KNOWS THAT THE GREY MARE IS AS	LIKELY	AS NOT TO BE THE BETTER HORSE. BUT THIS EXPLANATION
GENV PREFACE(3)	EVEN WHEN EACH OF US KNOWS THAT HE OR SHE IS AS	LIKELY	AS NOT TO BE ONE OF THE DOZEN. THE RISK OF BEING RUN
APPL PREFACE(181)	AND WHEN THEY HAVE LOST THEIR HEADS THEY ARE AS	LIKELY	AS NOT TO BURN THE WRONG HOUSE AND TEAR THE WRONG MAN
SUPR HANDBOK(181)	UNHEALTHY PEOPLE GET MARRIED, THEY WILL, AS	LIKELY	AS NOT, HAVE A GREAT NUMBER OF CHILDREN WHO WILL ALL
LADY PREFACE(223)	MINNA WAGNER LIKED RICHARD'S MUSIC DRAMAS: AS	LIKELY	AS NOT, SHE THOUGHT THE SPANISH TRAGEDY WORTH SIX
JOAN PREFACE(24)	ALL OF THEM, HIS PLAY COULD NOT BE PRODUCED. AS	LIKELY	AS NOT, THIS IS WHAT ACTUALLY HAPPENED: INDEED THERE
MRS PREFACE(156)	OF SUCH HONEST WORK AS IS WITHIN THEIR REACH ARE	LIKELY	ENOUGH TO LEAD THEM EVENTUALLY TO LUNG DISEASE,
ARMS I (16)	I'M QUITE WRONG, YOU KNOW: NO DOUBT I AM. MOST	LIKELY	HE HAD GOT WIND OF THE CARTRIDGE BUSINESS SOMEHOW,
GETT PREFACE(242)	THE HIGHER THE WORK THE MAN IS DOING, THE MORE	LIKELY	HE IS TO FIND HIMSELF IN THIS CLASS UNTIL HE HAS
BULL II (103)	A MAN KNOWS, AND THE FARTHER HE TRAVELS, THE MORE	LIKELY	HE IS TO MARRY A COUNTRY GIRL AFTERWARDS. /NORA/ (
PRES (166)	DO I REALLY LOVE YOU. (INTO THE TELEPHONE) IT'S	LIKELY	INDEED I'D FRIGHTEN THE MAN OFF WITH ANY SUCH
SUPR II (63)	SHE, RAMSDEN? /RAMSDEN/ I SHOULD THINK IT VERY	LIKELY	INDEED. /ANN/ YOU DONT OBJECT, DO YOU, MOTHER? /MRS
HART II (90)	MEAN YOU DID IT ON PURPOSE? /GUINNESS/ NOW IS IT	LIKELY	I'D KILL ANY MAN ON PURPOSE. I FELL OVER HIM IN THE
FANY I (282)	YOULL GET HIM OUT TODAY, WONT YOU? /GILBEY/ IT'S	LIKELY	I'D LEAVE MY BOY IN PRISON, ISNT IT? /DORA/ I'D LIKE
POSN (439)	WHERE YOURE GOING TO. /OTHERS/ AHA! DEVILS. MORE	LIKELY	. AND TOO GOOD COMPANY FOR A HORSE-THIEF. /ALL/
DOCT I (107)	KILLS LESS PEOPLE THAN YOU DO. /RIDGEON/ OH, VERY	LIKELY	. BUT HE REALLY OUGHT TO KNOW THE DIFFERENCE BETWEEN
2TRU II (63)	YOU WILL PROBABLY END IN THE DOCK. /AUBREY/ MOST	LIKELY	. BUT I AM A BORN PREACHER, NOT A PLEADER. THE THEORY
GETT (301)	SERVITUDE? /HOTCHKISS/ I SHOULD THINK IT QUITE	LIKELY	. BUT OF COURSE I DONT KNOW. /MRS BRIDGENORTH/ BUT
JITT II (46)	HIS GREATNESS? /LENKHEIM/ OF YOUR MEANNESS, MORE	LIKELY	. DONT TRY TO STUFF ME WITH BIG WORDS: THEY ONLY SHEW
ROCK II (249)	CASH VALUE TO THE LANDLORDS WITH THE OTHER! NOT	LIKELY	. I ASK AGAIN, DO YOU TAKE US FOR FOOLS? /SIR
POSN (447)	HE'S GONE OFF HIS HEAD. /STRAPPER/ FOXING, MORE	LIKELY	. (GOING PAST DANIELS AND TALKING TO BLANCO NOSE TO
SUPR II (68)	A SOVEREIGN. /STRAKER/ FIVE SHILLINS, MORE	LIKELY	. (HE LEAVES THE CAR AND APPROACHES TANNER). WHAT
PYGM III (253)	MISS DOOLITTLE? IF SO-- /LIZA/ WALK! NOT BLOODY	LIKELY	. (SENSATION), I AM GOING IN A TAXI. (SHE GOES
MTH4 I (151)	THE WORD MOTHERED? /THE ELDERLY GENTLEMAN/ VERY	LIKELY	. LET US DROP THE SUBJECT. PARDON ME FOR EMBARRASSING
VWOO 1 (119)	AN IDIOT, AND THAT YOU WERE A BAD HUSBAND. MOST	LIKELY	. /A/ YOU ARE QUITE RIGHT ON BOTH POINTS. /Z/ I
CLEO II (134)	DO YOU THINK, IF I ASKED HIM? /CAESAR/ VERY	LIKELY	. /CLEOPATRA/ BUT I SHOULD NOT LIKE TO ASK HIM. COULD
SUPR III (132)	IS TO STEER. /THE DEVIL/ ON THE ROCKS, MOST	LIKELY	. /DON JUAN/ POOH! WHICH SHIP GOES OFTENEST ON THE
KING I (201)	ROWLEY DARLING. TWO OR THREE HUNDRED, MORE	LIKELY	. /FOX/ (RESUMING HIS SEAT IN THE DEEPEST
GETT (328)	HIS BARMAID. YOU WOULD CALL HIM A PUBLICAN, MOST	LIKELY	. /HOTCHKISS/ THEN YOU ARE A WOMAN TOTALLY BENEATH
SUPR III (83)	RESPECT IT. /STRAKER/ (FIERCELY) FUNK, MORE	LIKELY	. /MENDOZA/ (SPRINGING TO HIS FEET) FUNK! YOUNG
MRS II (215)	ALL THE PROFITS INSTEAD OF STARVATION WAGES? NOT	LIKELY	. /VIVIE/ YOU WERE CERTAINLY QUITE JUSTIFIED-- FROM
BARB II (275)	USED YOU TO BEAT YOUR MOTHER? /PRICE/ NOT	LIKELY	. SHE USED TO BEAT ME. NO MATTER: YOU COME AND LISTEN
GLIM (176)	SOMEBODY ELSE ON THE WHEEL FOR IT: YOU, MOST	LIKELY	. TEN CROWNS IS JUST ENOUGH TO MAKE HIM BREAK YOU ON
MILL I (155)	SERVITUDE. /ALASTAIR/ FIVE YEARS! FIFTEEN, MORE	LIKELY	. THAT WAS WHAT I RISKED FOR YOU, AND WHAT DID I GET
SIM PRO,2, (26)	NO BEACH. WE COULD BATHE. /THE E.O./ NOT US. NOT	LIKELY	. THERES SHARKS THERE. AND KILLER WHALES, WORSE THAN
POSN (441)	ROTTEN FEELINGS WHEN HE LICKS YOU FOR IT? NOT	LIKELY	. TIL YOU CAN FIND A WITNESS THAT SAW ME WITH THAT
LION I (125)	THE TOWN AT THE HEELS OF YOU AND YOUR LION! NOT	LIKELY	. WE GO FIRST. /THE OX DRIVER/ THE MENAGERIE SERVICE
POSN (451)	/THE FOREMAN/ (CALLED) BE SWORE FOR YOU! NOT	LIKELY	. WHAT DO YOU SAY, OLD SON? /NESTOR/ (DELIBERATELY
MRS III (229)	THATS PAYING 35 PER CENT IN THE WORST YEARS! NOT	LIKELY	. WHO TOLD YOU THAT? /VIVIE/ (HER COLOR QUITE GONE)
BARB II (281)	YOURE GOIN TO THE STATION ON A STRETCHER, MORE	LIKELY	; AND THEYLL TAKE THE GIN AND THE DEVIL OUT OF YOU
CAPT III (296)	IS NO WORSE A MAN THAN MYSELF-- BETTER, MOST	LIKELY	; FOR HE HAS A BETTER HEAD AND A HIGHER PLACE. WELL,
LADY (243)	SAVE ME. OH, SAVE ME. /ELIZABETH/ SAVE YOU! A	LIKELY	SAVIOR, ON MY ROYAL WORD! I HAD THOUGHT THIS FELLOW
CLEO II (135)	FROM THEM. THE REST IS STILL DUE. BUT AS I MOST	LIKELY	SHALL NOT GET IT, I MUST GO BACK TO MY WORK. SO YOU
CLEO NOTES (210)	THE CAPACITY OF ANY CONQUEROR IS THEREFORE MORE	LIKELY	THAN NOT TO BE AN ILLUSION PRODUCED BY THE INCAPACITY
3PLA PREFACE(R37)	OR IBSEN? HUMAN FACULTY BEING WHAT IT IS, IS IT	LIKELY	THAT IN OUR TIME ANY ADVANCE, EXCEPT IN EXTERNAL
6CAL (104)	OF AS FINE A WEB AS EVER WENT ON YOUR BACK. IS IT	LIKELY	THAT I, A MASTER MERCER, WOULD WEAR AUGHT BUT THE
JOAN 2 (77)	OF ALL THE LADIES, THE BEAUTIFUL BASTARD. IS IT	LIKELY	THAT THE COUNTRY LASS CAN DO WHAT HE CANNOT DO?
SUPR HANDBOK(181)	VERY SUPERIOR TO BOTH HIS PARENTS; BUT IT IS NOT	LIKELY	THAT THE JEWESS WOULD FIND THE SQUIRE AN INTERESTING
GETT PREFACE(255)	MORE THAN IT DOES AT PRESENT: NAY, IT IS EVEN	LIKELY	THAT THE PRESENT SYSTEM OF TAKING THE CHILDREN OUT OF
MRS PREFACE(178)	I AM BOUND TO WARN THE PUBLIC THAT IT IS EQUALLY	LIKELY	THAT THEY MAY BE COLLECTED AND KNAVISH, AT ALL
FABL VI (129)	RATHER THAN STOP TELLING LIES? IT IS MUCH MORE	LIKELY	THAT YOU ARE A FOOL. /YOUTH 2/ MAY BE; BUT THAT DOES
LADY PREFACE(223)	DREAMING OF THINGS TO COME," THE DARK LADY MOST	LIKELY	THOUGHT THIS SIDE OF HIM INSUFFERABLY CONCEITED; FOR
BUOY II (25)	TEACHES US ALL THE QUESTIONS OUR EXAMINERS ARE	LIKELY	TO ASK US, AND THE ANSWERS THEY EXPECT FROM US. /THE
3PLA PREFACE(R23)	WHO APPENDS AND PREFIXES EXPLANATIONS TO THEM IS	LIKELY	TO BE AS BAD AN ARTIST AS THE PAINTER CITED BY
POSN PREFACE(402)	A SECRETARY OF STATE WOULD BE OBJECTIONABLE AS	LIKELY	TO BE BIASED POLITICALLY, AN ECCLESIASTICAL REFEREE
BULL IV (161)	ROSSCULLEN ISNT SUCH A LIVELY PLACE THAT I AM	LIKELY	TO BE BORED BY YOU AT OUR FIRST TALK TOGETHER AFTER
ROCK PREFACE(182)	OUR SENSES TELL US SO; AND TWO MEN ARE NOT	LIKELY	TO BE DREAMING THE SAME DREAM AT THE SAME MOMENT, BUT
POSN PREFACE(403)	DECISION SHALL BE FINAL. THIS PROPOSAL IS NOT	LIKELY	TO BE ENTERTAINED BY CONSTITUTIONAL LAWYERS. IT IS A
BARB I (252)	THINKING ONLY OF HIS INCOME. HOWEVER, HE IS NOT	LIKELY	TO BE EXTRAVAGANT. /LADY BRITOMART/ DONT BE TOO SURE
ANNA (289)	THE LATEST? WHICH OF THEM DO YOU THINK IS MOST	LIKELY	TO BE IN POWER TOMORROW MORNING? /SCHNEIDEKIND/
ROCK PREFACE(191)	RULERS, FAR FROM HAVING A REASSURING EFFECT, IS	LIKELY	TO BE RATHER TERRIFYING AT FIRST, AS ALL PEOPLE WITH
GETT PREFACE(205)	THEM ASSUME THAT MRS SQUEERS'S AMATEUR WAY IS	LIKELY	TO BE THE RIGHT WAY BECAUSE SHE BELONGS TO THE
OVER PREFACE(168)	WHEN THEY CAN, FROM THOSE WHO ARE MOST	LIKELY	TO BE WOUNDED BY THEM; BUT IT IS NOT TO BE PRESUMED

MTH4 I (160)	LOOKS AT THE WORLD THROUGH HIS OWN EYES IS VERY	LIKELY	TO BECOME A DANGEROUS MADMAN IF HE TAKES TO LOOKING
SUPR HANDBOK(195)	AS ANY POLITICAL MEASURE HAS EVER BEEN OR IS EVER	LIKELY	TO BE. IT WAS NOT PASSED UNTIL THE GENTLEMEN OF
APPL I (215)	HIS MIND TO THAT THE SMOOTHER OUR PROCEEDINGS ARE	LIKELY	TO BE. /BOANERGES/ I PROTEST, I SAY, LET US BE
MIS. (198)	MAY BREAK YOUR POOR BOY'S HEART. IT'S MUCH MORE	LIKELY	TO BREAK YOURS. /LORD SUMMERHAYS/ OH! /TARLETON/ (
MTH3 (108)	HUMAN LIFE WAS POSSIBLE, AND HOW IT WAS	LIKELY	TO COME ABOUT. I MARRIED THE DAUGHTER OF ONE OF THE
ANNA (289)	OPINION THE MODERATE RED REVOLUTIONARIES ARE AS	LIKELY	TO COME OUT ON TOP AS EITHER OF THEM. /SCHNEIDEKIND/
DOCT PREFACE(48)	BUT IF I PRESENTLY DIE IN TORMENT I AM NOT	LIKELY	TO CONSIDER THAT HIS HUMANITY IS AMPLY VINDICATED BY
BARB I (251)	CHARLES LOMAX'S EXERTIONS ARE MUCH MORE	LIKELY	TO DECREASE HIS INCOME THAN TO INCREASE IT. SARAH
MIS. PREFACE(64)	DANGEROUSLY HAVE ONLY HALF A LIFE, AND ARE MORE	LIKELY	TO DIE MISERABLY AFTER ALL THAN THOSE WHO HAVE TAKEN
PYGM EPILOG (292)	HER UNAFFECTEDLY, AND IS NOT HER MASTER, NOR EVER	LIKELY	TO DOMINATE HER IN SPITE OF HIS ADVANTAGE OF SOCIAL
ROCK PREFACE(162)	LIABILITY NO LONGER EXISTS IN RUSSIA, AND IS NOT	LIKELY	TO EXIST IN THE FUTURE IN ANY HIGHLY CIVILIZED STATE.
DOCT I (114)	EVERY PRECAUTION, I HOPE. /MRS DUBEDAT/ I AM NOT	LIKELY	TO FORGET IT. THEY TREAT US LIKE LEPERS AT THE
SUPR I (27)	EVERY CHANCE FOR HER CHILD. SHE DOES NOT SEEM	LIKELY	TO GET IT FROM YOU; SHE SHALL FROM ME. WHERE IS SHE?
MIS. PREFACE(26)	MASONS AND DOCTORESS MONTESSORIS WOULD YOU BE	LIKELY	TO GET ON THESE TERMS EVEN IF THEY OCCURRED MUCH MORE
DOCT PREFACE(30)	ANTI-SCIENCE: A STATE OF THINGS WHICH IS	LIKELY	TO GET WORSE UNTIL THE AVERAGE DOCTOR EITHER DEPENDS
BASH II,1, (102)	GLUTTON AS WE KNOW HE IS, SEEMED THIS TIME	LIKELY	TO GO HUNGRY. CASHEL WAS CLEARLY GROGGY AS HE SLIPPED
SUPR HANDBOK(209)	EDUCATIONAL, RELIGIOUS, OR ARTISTIC. WHAT IS	LIKELY	TO HAPPEN WHEN THIS CONVICTION GETS INTO THE MINDS OF
LADY PREFACE(214)	HARRIS ASSERTS, I CANNOT BELIEVE: SHE IS QUITE AS	LIKELY	TO HAVE BORNE HER SON A GRUDGE FOR BECOMING " ONE OF
GETT PREFACE(229)	WITH GEORGE IV AS A BAD MAN; AND SHELLEY IS NOT	LIKELY	TO HAVE CALLED HER VILE NAMES ON THE GENERAL GROUND
METH PREFACE(R76)	THE FRYING-PAN INTO THE FIRE; AND WE ARE JUST AS	LIKELY	TO JUMP BACK AGAIN, NOW THAT WE FEEL HOTTER THAN
POSN PREFACE(415)	MORE FAMOUS AN ACTOR-MANAGER IS THE LESS HE IS	LIKELY	TO KNOW ABOUT ANY THEATRE EXCEPT HIS OWN. WHEN THE
ROCK PREFACE(178)	HE HAD ANY RIGHT TO SET MEN ON A PATH WHICH WAS	LIKELY	TO LEAD THE BEST OF THEM TO THE CROSS AND THE WORST
GETT PREFACE(229)	THE VOTE. THE POLITICAL EMANCIPATION OF WOMEN IS	LIKELY	TO LEAD TO A COMPARATIVELY STRINGENT ENFORCEMENT BY
SUPR HANDBOK(211)	LIVE STOCK. BUT FOR THE PRESENT IT IS FAR MORE	LIKELY	TO MEAN A BLATANT REPUDIATION OF SUCH PROPOSALS AS
PYGM III (251)	DEPRESSION IN THE WEST OF THESE ISLANDS IS	LIKELY	TO MOVE SLOWLY IN AN EASTERLY DIRECTION. THERE ARE NO
CLEO IV (190)	LONG AS I CAN. /CAESAR/ WELL, MY FRIEND, YOU ARE	LIKELY	TO OUTLIVE CAESAR. IS IT ANY MAGIC OF MINE, THINK
DOCT PREFACE(36)	OPEN; AND AN EXCEPTIONALLY FOOLISH FOOL IS QUITE	LIKELY	TO PROMISE ENORMOUS BENEFITS TO THE RACE AS THE
MTH2 (82)	I WILL GO SO FAR AS TO SAY THAT YOUR THEORY IS	LIKELY	TO PROVE MORE INTERESTING THAN EVER WELSH
POSN PREFACE(366)	ANYTHING THAT THE MOST ABSTRUSE PLAYWRIGHT IS	LIKELY	TO PUT BEFORE THEM, BUT THE PLAIN-SAILING TRADESMAN
MIS. PREFACE(84)	USE FOR BROTHERS AND SISTERS. THE PARENT SEEMS	LIKELY	TO REMAIN INDISPENSABLE; BUT THERE IS NO REASON WHY
PYGM II (230)	SO HERE I AM, A CONFIRMED OLD BACHELOR, AND	LIKELY	TO REMAIN SO. /PICKERING/ (RISING AND STANDING OVER
CAPT II (264)	COMPOUND A FELONY! YOU GREENHORNS, HE IS MORE	LIKELY	TO SEND YOU ALL TO PENAL SERVITUDE IF YOU ARE FOOLS
BULL I (79)	AND IMPROVIDENT BUT BRAVE AND GOODNATURED; NOT	LIKELY	TO SUCCEED IN BUSINESS ON YOUR OWN ACCOUNT PERHAPS,
PYGM EPILOG (289)	VERY SORELY STRAINED IF THERE WAS ANOTHER WOMAN	LIKELY	TO SUPPLANT HER WITH HIM. BUT AS SHE FEELS SURE OF
DOCT PREFACE(29)	WILL RESIST THE INTRODUCTION OF A MACHINE THAT IS	LIKELY	TO THROW HIM OUT OF WORK, OR THE PUBLIC TECHNICAL
SUPR IV (162)	OR NOT. /MRS WHITEFIELD/ (PEACEFULLY) OH, VERY	LIKELY	YOU WILL! YOU KNOW WHAT SHE IS WHEN SHE HAS SET HER
BULL IV (168)	BEFORE-- HAVE YOU? /NORA/ (INDIGNANTLY) NOT	LIKELY	, INDEED. /BROADBENT/ WELL, WE MUSNT BE STIFF AND
CAND I SD(91)	SHE IS A WOMAN OF 33, WELL BUILT, WELL NOURISHED,	LIKELY	, ONE GUESSES, TO BECOME MATRONLY LATER ON, BUT NOW
MIS. (188)	THINK I WAS GOING TO GIVE YOU MY REAL NAME? NOT	LIKELY	! NOT ME! /TARLETON/ SO YOU THOUGHT OF JOHN BROWN,
WIDO II (31)	HIM GOING DOWN TO COLLECT HIS OWN RENTS! NOT	LIKELY	! /TRENCH/ DO YOU MEAN TO SAY THAT ALL HIS

LIKENESS

KING I (204)	THAT LIVING MEN AND WOMEN, CREATED BY GOD IN HIS	LIKENESS	AND NOT IN THAT OF GIBBERING APES, CAN BE BRIBED TO
KING I (208)	HAS MR KNELLER DONE THIS? NOBODY CAN CATCH A	LIKENESS	AS HE CAN. /BARBARA/ LIKENESS! YOU HAVE BRIBED HIM
JOAN PREFACE(8)	RATIOCINATION, HE WILL NEVER CATCH JOAN'S	LIKENESS	, HER IDEAL BIOGRAPHER MUST BE FREE FROM NINETEENTH
KING I (182)	AND WHEN HE IS OFFICIATING HE IS NOT IN THE	LIKENESS	OF ANYTHING IN THE HEAVENS ABOVE OR ON THE EARTH
CAPT III (274)	YOU KNEW. /RANKIN/ (OVERWHELMED) I SAW THE	LIKENESS	THE NIGHT HE CAME HERE! IT'S TRUE: IT'S TRUE.
MRS II (199)	TO HER): I KNOW YOU THROUGH AND THROUGH BY YOUR	LIKENESS	TO YOUR FATHER, BETTER THAN YOU KNOW YOURSELF. DONT
KING I (208)	NOBODY CAN CATCH A LIKENESS AS HE CAN. /BARBARA/	LIKENESS	! YOU HAVE BRIBED HIM TO INSULT ME. IT MAKES ME

LIKES

MIS. PREFACE(13)	ADULT WHO IS NASTY IS NOT ALLOWED TO DO WHAT HE	LIKES	: NEITHER CAN THE CHILD WHO LIKES TO BE NASTY. THERE
WIDO II (31)	HIMSELF, AND YOULL SEE THE GOOD OF IT TO HIM. HE	LIKES	A LOW DEATH-RATE AND A GRAVEL SOIL FOR HIMSELF, HE
PHIL II (97)	HE'S NOT MAN ENOUGH FOR HER. A WOMAN OF THAT SORT	LIKES	A STRONG, MANLY, DEEP THROATED, BROAD CHESTED MAN.
FANY PROLOG (264)	REALLY REPRESENTS THE BRITISH PLAYGOER. WHEN HE	LIKES	A THING, YOU MAY TAKE YOUR OATH THERE ARE A HUNDRED
METH PREFACE(R44)	TURNED; AND EVERY PUNY WHIPSTER MAY SAY WHAT HE	LIKES	ABOUT DARWIN; BUT ANYONE WHO WANTS TO KNOW WHAT IT WAS
MIS. PREFACE(33)	AND IN FACT IS, THE RIGHT TO BE WHAT THE CHILD	LIKES	AND CAN, TO DO WHAT IT LIKES AND CAN, TO MAKE WHAT IT
MIS. PREFACE(33)	TO BE WHAT THE CHILD LIKES AND CAN, TO DO WHAT IT	LIKES	AND CAN, TO MAKE WHAT IT LIKES AND CAN, TO THINK WHAT
MIS. PREFACE(33)	TO MAKE WHAT IT LIKES AND CAN, TO THINK WHAT IT	LIKES	AND CAN, TO SMASH WHAT IT DISLIKES AND CAN, AND
MIS. PREFACE(33)	CAN, TO DO WHAT IT LIKES AND CAN, TO MAKE WHAT IT	LIKES	AND CAN, TO THINK WHAT IT LIKES AND CAN, TO SMASH WHAT
PYGM EPILOG (302)	OR CALAMITY GREAT ENOUGH TO BREAK DOWN ALL	LIKES	AND DISLIKES, AND THROW THEM BOTH BACK ON THEIR COMMON
OVER PREFACE(157)	SAME PASSION; AND ARE SO COMPLICATED BY ORDINARY	LIKES	AND DISLIKES, BY INCIDENTAL WOUNDS TO VANITY OR
POSN (463)	A MAN OF GAME AND GRIT? A MAN THAT DOES WHAT HE	LIKES	AND GOES OVER OR THROUGH OTHER PEOPLE TO HIS OWN
LION II (128)	CHOOSE YOUR OWN ALTAR. SACRIFICE TO JUPITER: HE	LIKES	ANIMALS: HE TURNS HIMSELF INTO AN ANIMAL WHEN HE GOES
GETT (315)	IS HE TO GO, MISS? /LESBIA/ HE CAN GO WHERE HE	LIKES	AS LONG AS HE DOES NOT BOTHER THE MOTHER. /REGINALD/
SUPR I (11)	HER MORAL RESPONSIBILITIES ON ME, AND DO AS SHE	LIKES	AT THE EXPENSE OF MY CHARACTER. I CANT CONTROL HER;
POSN (440)	HANG THE WISEST MAN IN THE COUNTRY, NOTHING HE	LIKES	BETTER. BUT YOU CANT HANG ME. /STRAPPER/ CANT WE?
MIS. (120)	YOU KNOW YOU WOULDNT THINK IT; BUT THE GOVERNOR	LIKES	BUNNY RATHER. AND BUNNY IS CULTIVATING IT. I SHOULDNT
BULL IV (166)	LIKE. NOW LARRY'S TASTE IS JUST THE OPPOSITE: HE	LIKES	EM SOLID AND BOUNCING AND RATHER KEEN ABOUT HIM. IT'S
MIS. PREFACE(103)	ECSTASY OF BEING ABLE TO SWALLOW AS MUCH AS HE	LIKES	FOR THE FIRST TIME. YOU CANNOT GOVERN MEN BROUGHT UP
PYGM EPILOG (303)	FROM THE LIFE OF DREAMS AND FANCIES, SHE	LIKES	FREDDY AND SHE LIKES THE COLONEL; AND SHE DOES NOT
MRS IV (250)	/MRS WARREN/ OH, IT'S ALL VERY EASY FOR LIZ: SHE	LIKES	GOOD SOCIETY, AND HAS THE AIR OF BEING A LADY. IMAGINE
JITT II (32)	DONT BE SO SUPERIOR. I LIKE GOSSIP. EVERYBODY	LIKES	GOSSIP. YOU LIKE IT YOURSELF AS WELL AS ANYBODY. IF
BULL PREFACE(26)	A METHODIST AS TOLERANTLY AS AN IRISHMAN WHO	LIKES	GROG REGARDS AN IRISHMAN WHO PREFERS PUNCH. A
BULL PREFACE(41)	NATIONALISM ANY MORE THAN A MAN WITH A BROKEN ARM	LIKES	HAVING IT SET. A HEALTHY NATION IS AS UNCONSCIOUS OF
NEVR II (241)	ALL RIGHT, SIR. WE KNOW WHAT MR CRAMPTON	LIKES	HERE, SIR. (HE GOES INTO THE HOTEL). /PHILIP/ (
SUPR IV (163)	TO KNOW A COQUETTE. SHE WILL DO JUST WHAT SHE	LIKES	HERSELF WHILST INSISTING ON EVERYBODY ELSE DOING WHAT
JOAN 5 (109)	DEAR JACK: I THINK YOU LIKE ME AS A SOLDIER	LIKES	HIS COMRADE. /DUNOIS/ YOU NEED IT, POOR INNOCENT CHILD
O'FL (227)	CONSCIENCE. SOME LIKES WAR'S ALARUMS; AND SOME	LIKES	HOME LIFE. IVE TRIED BOTH, SIR; AND I'M ALL FOR WAR'S
MIS. (156)	LIKE YOU. A MARRIED MAN CAN DO ANYTHING HE	LIKES	IF HIS WIFE DONT MIND. A WIDOWER CANT BE TOO CAREFUL.
O'FL PREFACE(201)	POSTER IN DISGUISE. THE BRITISH OFFICER SELDOM	LIKES	IRISH SOLDIERS; BUT HE ALWAYS TRIES TO HAVE A CERTAIN
FANY I (277)	HALLS? /DORA/ NO: BOBBY TAKES HIM. BUT HOLY JOE	LIKES	IT: FAIRLY LAPS IT UP LIKE A KITTEN, POOR OLD DEAR.
ARMS II (36)	HERE AGAIN, MISS RAINA WILL MARRY HIM, WHETHER HE	LIKES	IT OR NOT. I KNOW THE DIFFERENCE BETWEEN THE SORT OF
GETT (340)	ANTHONY! (TO MRS GEORGE) CALL HIM FATHER: HE	LIKES	IT. (SOAMES APPEARS AT THE STUDY DOOR). MRS COLLINS
DOCT III (146)	BY THE PUBLIC BECAUSE THE PUBLIC WANTS IT AND	LIKES	IT. MY COURT PATIENTS ARE HARD-WORKING PEOPLE WHO GIVE
MIS. (110)	MINISTER'S. HES A NAILER AT ARGUING. HE	LIKES	IT. /BENTLEY/ YOU CANT ARGUE WITH A PERSON WHEN HIS
HART II (122)	HOURS A DAY AT THE DULLEST DETAIL, AND ACTUALLY	LIKES	IT. THAT GETS HIM TO THE TOP WHEREVER HE GOES. AS LONG
MILL IV (195)	WORSE FOR YOU. SHE CAN ACCUSE YOU OF ANYTHING SHE	LIKES	. AND REMEMBER: NO MAN CAN GET DAMAGES OUT OF A
SUPR I (14)	/TANNER/ ANN WILL DO JUST EXACTLY WHAT SHE	LIKES	. AND WHATS MORE, SHE'LL FORCE US TO ADVISE HER TO DO
MIS. (145)	LET HER DO WHAT SHE LIKES, LET HER GO WHERE SHE	LIKES	. EH, PATSY? /HYPATIA/ OH YES, IF THERE HAD ONLY BEEN
PYGM I (211)	WARRANT? /THE FLOWER GIRL/ LET HIM SAY WHAT HE	LIKES	. I DONT WANT TO HAVE NO TRUCK WITH HIM. /THE
SUPR I (11)	HER; AND SHE CAN COMPROMISE ME AS MUCH AS SHE	LIKES	. I MIGHT AS WELL BE HER HUSBAND. /RAMSDEN/ YOU CAN
INCA PROLOG (235)	BUT I SIMPLY WILL NOT BEAR IT. SHE CAN DO AS SHE	LIKES	. I WASH MY HANDS OF HER: I AM NOT GOING TO DIE IN THE
MIS. (145)	SAME THING TO HER MOTHER. LET HER READ WHAT SHE	LIKES	. LET HER DO WHAT SHE LIKES, LET HER GO WHERE SHE
MIS. (145)	LET HER READ WHAT SHE LIKES, LET HER DO WHAT SHE	LIKES	. LET HER GO WHERE SHE LIKES. EH, PATSY? /HYPATIA/ OH
INCA (253)	THE VOTING PAPERS THE GOVERNMENT DOES WHAT IT	LIKES	. /ERMYNTRUDE/ WHAT! YOU TOO WORSHIP BEFORE THE
MIS. (133)	HAS AS MUCH TO SAY FOR HIMSELF AS ANYBODY WHEN HE	LIKES	. /JOHNNY/ I'M NO FOOL, MOTHER, WHATEVER SOME PEOPLE
BULL IV (173)	A CHURCH BELL CAN MAKE A DEVIL OF A NOISE WHEN IT	LIKES	. /KEEGAN/ YOU HAVE AN ANSWER FOR EVERYTHING, SIR. BUT
FANY I (281)	INTO TEMPTATIONS OF ALL SORTS, HE CAN DO WHAT HE	LIKES	. WHAT MORE DOES HE WANT? /DORA/ WELL, OLD DEAR, HE
MTH3 (98)	BECAUSE YOU LIKE ME? /CONFUCIUS/ SURELY. NOBODY	LIKES	ME: I AM HELD IN AWE. CAPABLE PERSONS ARE NEVER LIKED.
MIS. (165)	A HANDFUL OF MUD IN MY FACE, AND EVERY WOMAN WHO	LIKES	ME IS TO BEHAVE LIKE POTIPHAR'S WIFE, THEN I SHALL BE
MILL I (150)	AND I AM AFRAID I DO COST HIM A GOOD DEAL; FOR HE	LIKES	ME TO HAVE NICE THINGS THAT I CANT AFFORD. /ALASTAIR/
DEST SD(151)	WORKING HEROIC MIRACLES. THE WORLD, HOWEVER,	LIKES	MIRACLES AND HEROES, AND IS QUITE INCAPABLE OF
BULL PREFACE(41)	THE WORLD. NOBODY IN IRELAND OF ANY INTELLIGENCE	LIKES	NATIONALISM ANY MORE THAN A MAN WITH A BROKEN ARM
JOAN EPILOG (160)	AFTER TWELVE, BACK TO THE ONLY PLACE FIT FOR THE	LIKES	OF ME. /JOAN/ (RISING) BACK THERE! YOU! THAT GAVE
MILL III (185)	A BANK. NO GOOD EVER COMES OUT OF BANKS FOR THE	LIKES	OF US. DONT LET HER TEMPT YOU, JOE. /EPIFANIA/ WHEN
CURE (234)	TAKE ME BACK TO THE GARDEN OF LOVE, AND EVERYBODY	LIKES	OUR MARY. /STREGA/ YOUNG MAN: I HAVE NEVER EVEN HEARD

BULL PREFACE(27) BESIDES ALLOWING HIM TO READ AND LEARN WHAT HE LIKES -- EXCEPT WHEN IT MAKES A TUFTHUNTING ONSLAUGHT ON A
DOCT PREFACE(10) EVERY NURSE HAS SOME PARTICULAR DOCTOR WHOM SHE LIKES ; AND SHE USUALLY ASSURES HER PATIENTS THAT ALL THE
CATH 4 (193) LITTLE MOTHER, LITTLE DARLING: THATS WHAT SHE LIKES ; BUT GET THE STRAPS OFF. /CLAIRE/ KEEP QUIET, DEAR: I
MTH2 (67) CHALLENGING AUDACITY) TRY. LUBIN CAN GO IF HE LIKES ; BUT I AM STILL OPEN TO NEW IDEAS, IF ONLY I CAN FIND
BUOY III (34) LIKE A LADY, AND CAN BEHAVE LIKE A LADY WHEN SHE LIKES ; BUT SHE DOES NOT BELONG TO US. HER TEN YEARS OF
BARB I SD(260) HE IS OBSTINATELY BENT ON MARRYING BARBARA. LOMAX LIKES SARAH AND THINKS IT WILL BE RATHER A LARK TO MARRY
NEVR II (250) THERES A PRETENCE THAT HE DONT GET THEM! IF HE LIKES SOCIETY, AND HIS PROFESSION BRINGS HIM INTO CONTACT
SUPR II (51) BEING AN ENGINEER, WOULD APPAL YOU. HE POSITIVELY LIKES THE CAR TO BREAK DOWN BECAUSE IT BRINGS OUT MY
PYGM EPILOG (303) OF DREAMS AND FANCIES, SHE LIKES FREDDY AND SHE LIKES THE COLONEL; AND SHE DOES NOT LIKE HIGGINS AND MR
BASH II,2, (116) ANCHOR PUB AM TO BE HEARD OF ANY DAY BY SUCH AS LIKES THE JOB. I DONT KNOW, GOVERNOR, AS ENNYTHINK REMAINS
MIS. (176) OF MY OWN REVOLUTIONARY PRINCIPLES. IF SHE LIKES THE MAN WHY SHOULDNT SHE TELL HIM SO? /MRS TARLETON/
APPL INTRLUD(252) ARE PEOPLE WE AVOID MENTIONING BECAUSE ONE OF US LIKES THEM AND THE OTHER DOESNT, NOT ONLY INDIVIDUALS, BUT
PHIL III (135) HE THINKS IT'S A WOMANLY TASTE. BESIDES, HE LIKES THEM HIMSELF. THEYLL BE HERE PRESENTLY. (HE STROLLS
MIS. (128) SHE DOESNT WANT TO REPEL YOUNG MEN! SUPPOSE SHE LIKES THEM! /MRS TARLETON/ BUNNY! TAKE HYPATIA OUT INTO THE
MIS. PREFACE(13) TO DO WHAT HE LIKES: NEITHER CAN THE CHILD WHO LIKES TO BE NASTY. THERE IS NO DIFFERENCE IN PRINCIPLE
MIS. (130) RATS! YOU DONT UNDERSTAND PROVIDENCE. PROVIDENCE LIKES TO BE TEMPTED. THATS THE SECRET OF THE SUCCESSFUL MAN.
KING I (162) PROMISE THAT MR NEWTON WILL BE IN. STILL, IF HE LIKES TO COME ON THE CHANCE, AND WITHOUT HIS DOGS, MIND. OUR
PHIL III (135) THE BURLINGTON ARCADE TO BUY SOME CARAMELS. HE LIKES TO ENCOURAGE HER IN EATING CARAMELS: HE THINKS IT'S A
JITT II (38) KNOW. AND MY MOTHER ENCOURAGES THEM. SHE ACTUALLY LIKES TO FEEL THAT SOME UNHEARD-OF DISGRACE HAS FALLEN ON
ANNA (293) THIS MORNING: AND ALL THIS IS BECAUSE THE FELLOW LIKES TO GET ON THE TELEPHONE AND HEAR HIMSELF TALK NOW THAT
GETT PREFACE(189) IS AN ANSWER WHICH EVERYBODY KNOWS AND NOBODY LIKES TO GIVE. WHAT IS DRIVING OUR MINISTERS OF RELIGION AND
DEST (185) NOT THAT I MIND, YOU KNOW; BUT STILL NO REGIMENT LIKES TO HAVE ALL THE OTHER REGIMENTS LAUGHING AT IT.
SUPR III (80) NOT MATTER: EACH BRIGAND THINKS HIMSELF SCUM, AND LIKES TO HEAR THE OTHERS CALLED DREGS. /TANNER/ COME! YOU
LION II (133) TRICKS ARE NOT WISE, MY FRIEND. THE AUDIENCE LIKES TO SEE A DEAD MAN IN ALL HIS BEAUTY AND SPLENDOR. IF
BARB I (262) NOT. THE SPARE ROOM IS READY FOR HIM IF HE LIKES TO STAY FOR A DAY OR TWO AND SEE A LITTLE MORE OF YOU;
SUPR II (51) /STRAKER/ NEVER YOU MIND HIM, MR ROBINSON. HE LIKES TO TALK. WE KNOW HIM, DONT WE? /OCTAVIUS/ (
FANY III (309) SAID THIS MORNING HE WANTED TO SPEAK TO ME. IF HE LIKES TO TELL ME, LET HIM; BUT I'M NOT GOING TO ASK; AND
JITT II (39) AS ANY WEAKNESS OF HIS FLATTERED IT, SHE PERHAPS LIKES TO THINK THAT HE WAS NOT QUITE PERFECT, AND EVEN THAT
BARB II (275) GIRLS; BUT THE BETTER YOU ARE, THE WORSE THEY LIKES TO THINK YOU WERE BEFORE THEY RESCUED YOU. WHY
CAND I SD(79) HE IS A FIRST RATE CLERGYMAN, ABLE TO SAY WHAT HE LIKES TO WHOM HE LIKES, TO LECTURE PEOPLE WITHOUT SETTING
GETT SD(260) GREY EYE, AND THE POWER OF SAYING ANYTHING HE LIKES TO YOU WITHOUT OFFENCE, BECAUSE HIS TONE ALWAYS
NEVR III (274) ME? /DOLLY/ (TOUCHED) BUT HOW NICE OF HIM! HE LIKES US, MAMMA. /M'COMAS/ I AM SORRY TO HAVE TO DISABUSE
O'FL (227) I CAN GO AND SAY IT WITH A CLEAR CONSCIENCE. SOME LIKES WAR'S ALARUMS; AND SOME LIKES HOME LIFE. IVE TRIED
NEVR IV (301) (INSOLENTLY, FEELING THAT NOW SHE CAN DO AS SHE LIKES WITH HIM) INDEED! /VALENTINE/ BUT WHY DID I DO IT?
JOAN 2 (87) OF THE ARMY TO THE MAID. THE MAID IS TO DO AS SHE LIKES WITH IT. (HE DESCENDS FROM THE DAIS). GENERAL
JOAN PREFACE(39) TO THE PRIEST, AND CAN DO PRACTICALLY WHAT HE LIKES WITH PARLIAMENT AND THE PRESS THROUGH THE BLIND FAITH
POSN PREFACE(390) ONE OF THEM TO DO ABSOLUTELY AND FINALLY WHAT HE LIKES WITH THE OTHER'S WORK, AND WHEN IT IS REMEMBERED THAT
DOCT PREFACE(19) A COMPOSER, AN AUTHOR, MAY BE AS SELFISH AS HE LIKES WITHOUT REPROACH FROM THE PUBLIC IF ONLY HIS ART IS
CATH 2 (181) MONTHS AS A SOBER MAN, YOUR FORTUNE IS MADE. SHE LIKES YOU. /EDSTASTON/ THE DEVIL SHE DOES! /PATIOMKIN/
GETT (352) GEORGE. /COLLINS/ DONT DESPAIR, SIR: IF GEORGE LIKES YOUR CONVERSATION YOULL FIND THEIR HOUSE A VERY
DOCT I SD(87) ACCLIMATIZED. HIS MANNER TO RIDGEON, WHOM HE LIKES , IS WHIMSICAL AND FATHERLY: TO OTHERS HE IS A LITTLE
PYGM V (285) ON HIS HEELS). /LIZA/ HE HAS A RIGHT TO IF HE LIKES , POOR LAD. AND HE DOES LOVE ME. /HIGGINS/ (GETTING
CAND I SD(79) CLERGYMAN, ABLE TO SAY WHAT HE LIKES TO WHOM HE LIKES , TO LECTURE PEOPLE WITHOUT SETTING HIMSELF UP AGAINST

LIKEST

SUPR PREFACE(R40) OFFER, AS SAMPLES OF THE SHAVIAN PHILOSOPHY, THE LIKEST ARTICLE FROM THEIR OWN STOCK. OTHERS ARE THE VICTIMS

LIKEWISE

MIS. PREFACE(31) SNAKE ENCOURAGES THE CHILDREN TO GO AND DO LIKEWISE BY PUTTING HIS VICTIMS INTO AN IMITATION NEST AND
METH PREFACE(R31) LEAVING US TO INFER THAT WE SHALL PROBABLY PERISH LIKEWISE IF WE GRUDGE OUR GUINEAS TO HARLEY STREET. LORENZ
MTH5 (238) TO THE END; AND THE ACTIONS OF THE QUEEN ARE LIKEWISE , THE KING LOGICAL AND PREDETERMINED AND

LIKIN

CAND I (90) BUT (ALMOST ENTHUSIASTICALLY) ONE CARNT ELP LIKIN YOU: BESIDES, AS I SAID AFORE, OF COURSE ONE DONT TAKE

LIKING

SUPR I SD(5) HE APPEARS, RAMSDEN'S FACE EXPANDS INTO FATHERLY LIKING AND WELCOME, AN EXPRESSION WHICH DROPS INTO ONE OF
GETT (330) GEORGE TAKES TO YOU. /HOTCHKISS/ I'M TO COME ON LIKING FOR THE MONTH? /MRS GEORGE/ ON CONDITION THAT YOU
NEVR II (259) APPROACHING HIM) BUT WHY? /VALENTINE/ BECAUSE LIKING IS NOT ENOUGH. NOW THAT I THINK DOWN INTO IT
MTH2 (84) AND NON-SMOKERS LIVE LONGER. THAT SORT OF LIKING IS NOT WILLING. SEE WHAT THEY DO WHEN THEY KNOW THEY
MIS. PREFACE(3) COULD GET IT FOR NOTHING; BUT THAT SORT OF IDLE LIKING IS NOT WILL. IT IS AMAZING -- CONSIDERING THE WAY WE
MILL IV (189) SIR. I HOPE YOU FIND EVERYTHING HERE TO YOUR LIKING . /ALASTAIR/ YES, THANKS. BUT WHAT HAVE YOU DONE TO
GETT (315) CHILDREN? /COLLINS/ LET EM TAKE ONE ANOTHER ON LIKING . /MRS BRIDGENORTH/ COLLINS! /LEO/ YOU WICKED OLD
DEVL III (53) /RICHARD/ DONT TROUBLE. I'LL GIVE YOU CREDIT FOR LIKING ME A LITTLE BETTER THAN YOU DID. ALL I SAY IS THAT MY
NEVR II (259) LUCK. YOU SEE, IT ALL DEPENDED ON YOUR NATURALLY LIKING ME. (SHE IS ABOUT TO SPEAK: HE STOPS HER
UNPL PREFACE(R8) ABNORMAL SPECTACLES AND ABERRED MY VISION TO THE LIKING OF THE NINETY PER CENT OF POTENTIAL BOOKBUYERS. BUT I
CLEO IV (170) NOW THAT CAESAR HAS MADE ME WISE, IT IS NO USE MY LIKING OR DISLIKING: I DO WHAT MUST BE DONE, AND HAVE NO
OVER (190) TO LIKE MINE; AND IF WE DO, WE OUGHTNT TO GO ON LIKING THEM. BUT WE DO, ALL OF US. WE OUGHTNT; BUT WE DO.
APPL I (206) FROM INANIMATE. /BOANERGES/ (NOT QUITE LIKING THIS) I THINK I'D RATHER YOU CALLED ME A SOUL. YOU
BULL I (78) IT IN ENGLAND: THATS IT. /BROADBENT/ (NOT QUITE LIKING THIS) MY PLAN, SIR, WILL BE TO TAKE A LITTLE MONEY
BULL II SD(111) NOT SEEM TO EXIST IN ROSSCULLEN. JUST AS NORA'S LIKING TO MISS A MEAL AND STAY OUT AT THE ROUND TOWER IS
OVER (190) LIKE YOU. AND IF THEY DO, THEY OUGHTNT TO GO ON LIKING US. AND I OUGHTNT TO LIKE YOUR WIFE; AND YOU OUGHTNT
PYGM III (245) I SHALL NEVER GET INTO THE WAY OF SERIOUSLY LIKING YOUNG WOMEN: SOME HABITS LIE TOO DEEP TO BE CHANGED.
DOCT III (143) REMEMBER. REPTILE. /WALPOLE/ I CANT HELP RATHER LIKING YOU, DUBEDAT. BUT YOU CERTAINLY ARE A THOROUGHGOING
GETT PREFACE(219) HAVE HAD NOTHING TO DO WITH SEX, SUCH AS LIKING , MONEY, CONGENIALITY OF TASTES, SIMILARITY OF

LIKINGS

DEVL I (9) MADE BETWEEN US AND THOSE WHO FOLLOW THEIR OWN LIKINGS AND DISLIKINGS, AND MAKE A JEST OF US AND OF THEIR
BARB III (317) BRITOMART/ ANDREW: THIS IS NOT A QUESTION OF OUR LIKINGS AND DISLIKINGS: IT IS A QUESTION OF DUTY. IT IS YOUR

LIL

CATH 2 (177) TOOK DVANTAGE OF MY BEING DRUNK. SAID: TAKE ME TO LIL ANGEL MOTHER. TAKE ME TO BEAUFL EMPRESS. TAKE ME TO THE
CATH 2 (177) (PLAINTIVELY) NO: NOT LIKE PIG. LIKE PRINCE. LIL MOTHER MADE POOR PATIOMKIN PRINCE. WHAS USE BEING PRINCE
CATH 2 (177) BERR GO BYE BYE THAN GO SIBERIA. GO BYE BYE IN LIL MOTHER'S BED (HE PRETENDS TO MAKE AN ATTEMPT TO GET

LILAC

SUPR IV SD(142) TROUSERS IN WHICH NARROW STRIPES OF DARK GREY AND LILAC BLEND INTO A HIGHLY RESPECTABLE COLOR, AND A BLACK

LILIES

METH PREFACE(R77) IN THE COURAGE OF ITS PROFESSION, AND SOLD ITS LILIES FOR THE LAURELS OF THE SOLDIERS OF THE VICTORIA
CAND III (133) HER WINGS, THE WREATH OF STARS ON HER HEAD, THE LILIES IN HER HAND, THE CRESCENT MOON BENEATH HER FEET--
MTH5 (216) YOUTH/ LOVE. / A MAIDEN/ MOTHER. /ANOTHER YOUTH/ LILIES . /THE NEWLY BORN/ (TO ACIS) WHAT IS YOUR NAME?
DOCT I SD(82) PAINTING ON ITS SURFACE OF PALMS, FERNS, LILIES , TULIPS, AND SUNFLOWERS. THE ADJOINING WALL CONTAINS

LILITH

MTH5 (262) EARTH; AND I MAY NOT SPARE THEM FOR EVER. I AM LILITH : I BROUGHT LIFE INTO THE WHIRLPOOL OF FORCE, AND
MTH5 SD(260) THE FATHER AND MOTHER WERE ONE. HAIL, LILITH! LILITH BECOMES VISIBLE BETWEEN CAIN AND ADAM. /LILITH/ I
MTH1 I (9) SHE CAST THE SKIN, LO! THERE WAS NOT ONE NEW LILITH BUT TWO: ONE LIKE HERSELF, THE OTHER LIKE ADAM. YOU
MTH1 I (11) ADAM CANNOT CONCEIVE. /EVE/ WHY? /THE SERPENT/ LILITH DID NOT IMAGINE HIM SO. HE CAN IMAGINE: HE CAN WILL:
MTH1 I (11) IN CREATION. /EVE/ FIND ME A WORD FOR THE STORY LILITH IMAGINED AND TOLD YOU IN YOUR SILENT LANGUAGE: THE
MTH5 (262) AND FOR WHAT MAY BE BEYOND, THE EYESIGHT OF LILITH IS TOO SHORT. IT IS ENOUGH THAT THERE IS A BEYOND. (
MTH1 I (11) ONE; AND THAT ONE IS HIS OWN KIND. /EVE/ WHY DID LILITH KEEP THIS FROM HIM? /THE SERPENT/ BECAUSE IF HE
MTH1 II (30) AND NOBLER THAN THIS STUPID OLD DIGGER WHOM LILITH MADE TO HELP YOU TO BRING ME INTO THE WORLD, AND WHOM
MTH1 II (30) WAS FOR EITHER OF THESE CHEAP WAYS OF LIFE THAT LILITH SET YOU FREE. (TO ADAM) YOU DIG ROOTS AND COAX
MTH1 II (28) AS I LIVE AND BRING FORTH. IT WAS FOR THAT THAT LILITH SET YOU FREE FROM THE TRAVAIL OF WOMEN, NOT FOR THEFT

MTH1 I (10) STORY OF SOMETHING THAT NEVER HAPPENED TO A LILITH THAT NEVER WAS. SHE DID NOT KNOW THEN THAT
MTH1 I (10) BECAUSE YOU HAVE NOT WILLED IT SO. WHEN LILITH TOLD ME WHAT SHE HAD IMAGINED IN OUR SILENT LANGUAGE
MTH1 I (11) A POEM. /EVE/ FIND ME ANOTHER WORD FOR WHAT LILITH WAS TO ME. /THE SERPENT/ SHE WAS YOUR MOTHER. /EVE/
MTH1 II (28) YOUR OWN TONGUE; AND DO NOT CURSE MY SON. IT WAS LILITH WHO DID WRONG WHEN SHE SHARED THE LABOR OF CREATION
MTH5 (262) SHALL BECOME ONE WITH ME AND SUPERSEDE ME, AND LILITH WILL BE ONLY A LEGEND AND A LAY THAT HAS LOST ITS
MTH1 I (9) /EVE/ THEN I WILL DO IT. BUT HOW? HOW DID LILITH WORK THIS MIRACLE? /THE SERPENT/ SHE IMAGINED IT.
MTH5 (260) THE SERPENT. /THE SERPENT/ THAT IS THE VOICE OF LILITH , IN WHOM THE FATHER AND MOTHER WERE ONE. HAIL,
MTH5 (262) OF ALL THINGS, STAGNATION; FOR FROM THE MOMENT I, LILITH , LOSE HOPE AND FAITH IN THEM, THEY ARE DOOMED. IN
MTH1 I (9) OLDER THAN ADAM, OLDER THAN EVE. I REMEMBER LILITH , WHO CAME BEFORE ADAM AND EVE. I WAS HER DARLING AS
MTH5 (260) IN WHOM THE FATHER AND MOTHER WERE ONE. HAIL, LILITH ! LILITH BECOMES VISIBLE BETWEEN CAIN AND ADAM.

LILLAH
ANNA PREFACE(287) ON SOME BARELY PASSABLE DRAMATIC PRETEXT, MISS LILLAH MCCARTHY AND I, AS AUTHOR AND ACTRESS, HAVE HELPED TO
ANNA (286) THEATRE IN LONDON ON THE 21ST JANUARY 1918, WITH LILLAH MCCARTHY AS THE GRAND DUCHESS, HENRY MILLER AS

LILLIBULLEROBULLENALAH
GENV PREFACE(6) AND MALPLAQUET TO THE SENSELESS GIBBERISH OF LILLIBULLEROBULLENALAH . SHE NOT ONLY TOOK ON HITLER

LILLIPUTIANS
MIS. PREFACE(107) AS GULLIVER WAS THREADBOUND BY THE LILLIPUTIANS . WE ARE A MASS OF PEOPLE LIVING IN A

LILLY
KING I (215) PORTRAITS OF ALL THREE AS THEY ARE NOW, NOT AS LILLY PAINTED THEM. /LOUISE/ NO, CHARLES: I DO NOT WANT TO
KING I (215) LIE, YOU MISERABLE DAUBER. WHEN OUR DEAR PETER LILLY , WHO HAS JUST DIED, PAINTED ME AS I REALLY AM, DID I
KING I (208) TO MY FACE! YOU, WHO HAVE SEEN MY PORTRAIT BY LILLY ! /NELL/ YOU WERE YOUNGER THEN, DARLING. /BARBARA/

LILY
2TRU I (44) ABOUT ME? /THE BURGLAR/ SIMPLY ENOUGH. IN HER LILY HAND WAS A COPY OF THE LADY'S PICTORIAL. IT CONTAINED
GENV IV (88) YOUR BIRTHDAY BY A POEM HAILING YOU AS THE LILY OF GENEVA; BUT ON THIS OCCASION ONLY, YOU ARE NOT THE

LIMB
JOAN 6 (135) MY LORD. SHE HAS SEEN THEM. /JOAN/ IF YOU TEAR ME LIMB FROM LIMB UNTIL YOU SEPARATE MY SOUL FROM MY BODY YOU
LION I (115) IS A LUST TO SEE HER TORTURED AND TORN SHRIEKING LIMB FROM LIMB. IT IS A CRIME TO GRATIFY THAT PASSION. IT IS
HART PREFACE(20) DROPPED A BOMB WHICH TORE A CHILD AND ITS MOTHER LIMB FROM LIMB, THE PEOPLE WHO SAW IT, THOUGH THEY HAD BEEN
LION I (115) TO SEE HER TORTURED AND TORN SHRIEKING LIMB FROM LIMB . IT IS A CRIME TO GRATIFY THAT PASSION. IT IS OFFERING
JITT III (61) IS AS IF I WERE A BRANCH BROKEN OFF FROM HIM, A LIMB TORN OUT OF HIM, AS IF I WERE BLEEDING TO DEATH OF THE
JOAN 6 (135) HAS SEEN THEM. /JOAN/ IF YOU TEAR ME LIMB FROM LIMB UNTIL YOU SEPARATE MY SOUL FROM MY BODY YOU WILL GET
DEST (167) THE RECRUIT'S HEIGHT, HIS AGE, HIS WIND, HIS LIMB , BUT NEVER AFTER HIS COURAGE. /LADY/ (AS IF SHE HAD
BASH II,2, (116) SIR, I DO BESEECH YOU TO NAME THE BONE, OR LIMB , OR SPECIAL PLACE WHERE YOU WOULD HAVE ME HIT HIM WITH
HART PREFACE(20) BOMB WHICH TORE A CHILD AND ITS MOTHER LIMB FROM LIMB , THE PEOPLE WHO SAW IT, THOUGH THEY HAD BEEN READING

LIMBS
MILL IV (194) SITTING DOWN AND DISPOSING HIS DAMAGED LIMBS ALONG THE COUCH) WELL, IT'S MOST KIND OF YOU; AND I
FABL PREFACE(89) STIMULANTS, FOR HEART DISEASE, AND TO AMPUTATE LIMBS AND EXTIRPATE TONSILS AS CARPENTERS AND PLUMBERS DEAL
DOCT PREFACE(12) RANGE OF OPERATIONS WHICH CONSIST OF AMPUTATING LIMBS AND EXTIRPATING ORGANS ADMITS OF NO DIRECT
MIS. PREFACE(24) ABOUT MUSIC THAT THEY CAN MOVE THEIR SEVERAL LIMBS EACH IN A DIFFERENT METRE UNTIL THEY BECOME
MTH5 (254) STRAIGHT TO IT, AND WAS BORED BY YOUR CALLING MY LIMBS FANCY NAMES AND MAPPING ME INTO MOUNTAINS AND VALLEYS
3PLA PREFACE(R9) SURGEONS, I FELL FROM HEIGHTS AND BROKE MY LIMBS IN PIECES. THE DOCTORS SAID: THIS MAN HAS NOT EATEN
MTH5 (241) HE MADE THEM IN HIS LABORATORY. I MOULDED THEIR LIMBS . I AM SORRY. I WAS THOUGHTLESS; I DID NOT FORESEE
JOAN 6 (146) OF THEE IN RESPECT OF DEATH AND DIVISION OF THE LIMBS . (HE RESUMES HIS SEAT). /CAUCHON/ AND IF ANY TRUE
DOCT PREFACE(12) EVER HAD OF THE VALUE OF THEIR OWN ORGANS AND LIMBS , THEY SEEM TO CARE AS LITTLE FOR MUTILATION AS
HART PREFACE(29) THEMSELVES THE CHAINS THEY HAVE STRUCK FROM THE LIMBS OF THE VANQUISHED. HOW THE THEATRE FARED. LET US NOW
MTH5 SD(217) A PHRENOLOGIST; GRIPS HER MUSCLES AND SHAKES HER LIMBS ; EXAMINES HER TEETH; LOOKS INTO HER EYES FOR A
SUPR III (104) OF MINE, DO YOU THINK? NOT THE NEED TO MOVE MY LIMBS ; FOR A RAT WITH HALF MY BRAINS MOVES AS WELL AS I.
MTH5 (253) MIND THAT THIS MONSTROUS MACHINERY OF HEADS AND LIMBS WAS NO MORE ME THAN MY STATUES HAD BEEN ME, AND THAT
MTH5 (224) TIME AND MATERIAL. I TOO LOST MY DESIRE TO MODEL LIMBS , AND RETAINED ONLY MY INTEREST IN HEADS AND FACES. I,
CLEO II SD(118) WHOSE FEATURES ARE AS CRAMPED AND WIZENED AS HIS LIMBS , EXCEPT HIS TALL STRAIGHT FOREHEAD, WHICH OCCUPIES
MTH5 (253) WOULD BE AN UTTERLY MISERABLE ONE. /ECRASIA/ NO LIMBS , NO CONTOURS, NO EXQUISITE LINES AND ELEGANT SHAPES,
SUPR PREFACE(R22) OF THE FRANCHISE, OF THE FREE USE OF THEIR LIMBS , OF THAT ANCIENT SYMBOL OF IMMORTALITY, THE RIGHT TO
MTH1 II (26) I HATE CREATURES WITH TWO HEADS, OR WITH WITHERED LIMBS , OR THAT ARE DISTORTED AND PERVERTED AND UNNATURAL. I

LIME
PPP (200) LIME! YOU MOCK ME! DO YOU THINK I CARRY LIME ABOUT IN MY POCKETS? /FITZ/ THERE IS THE PLASTER
PPP (200) PERSEVERE. /ADOLPHUS/ NO: UNLESS YOU CAN SUPPLY LIME IN LIQUID FORM, I MUST PERISH. FINISH THAT CEILING I
PPP (200) TO THE POISON I HAVE GIVEN YOU IS LIME, PLENTY OF LIME . /ADOLPHUS/ LIME! YOU MOCK ME! DO YOU THINK I CARRY
PPP (200) BEST ANTIDOTE TO THE POISON I HAVE GIVEN YOU IS LIME , PLENTY OF LIME. /ADOLPHUS/ LIME! YOU MOCK ME! DO
PPP (200) GIVEN YOU IS LIME, PLENTY OF LIME. /ADOLPHUS/ LIME ! YOU MOCK ME! DO YOU THINK I CARRY LIME ABOUT IN MY

LIMEHOUSE
GENV III (68) BUT NONE OF YOU COULD KEEP A COFFEE STALL AT LIMEHOUSE BECAUSE YOU WOULD HAVE TO BE EQUALLY CIVIL TO

LIMELIGHT
PYGM PREFACE(200) RENOUNCE MY DREAM OF DRAGGING ITS AUTHOR INTO THE LIMELIGHT , WHEN I MET HIM AFTERWARDS, FOR THE FIRST TIME
GETT PREFACE(252) THE DANCER, THE MILLINER, THE PAINTER, THE LIMELIGHT MAN, AND THE SENTIMENTAL POET CAN DEVIZE, AFTER
JITT III (76) NOT FOUND STRETCHED ON HIS DEAD BODY, WITH THE LIMELIGHT STREAMING ON YOUR WHITE FACE, AND THE BAND PLAYING
BULL PREFACE(20) COULD NOT FIGHT HIM WITHOUT GETTING INTO THE LIMELIGHT , NOR OVERTHROW HIM (MOST UNFORTUNATELY FOR US

LIMELIT
PPP SD(206) HANDS IN AN ATTITUDE OF BLESSING, AND TURNS ITS LIMELIT FACE TO HEAVEN AS THE CURTAIN FALLS. NATIONAL

LIMERICK
O'FL PREFACE(201) AND ITS BROKEN TREATY LED IRISHMEN TO REMEMBER LIMERICK AND ITS BROKEN TREATY; AND THE RECRUITING ENDED IN
LADY (206) OF THURSDAY, THE 24TH NOVEMBER 1910, BY MONA LIMERICK AS THE DARK LADY, SUZANNE SHELDON AS QUEEN

LIMEWASHINGS
MILL III (182) NO SANITARY ARRANGEMENTS AS YOU CALL THEM. NO LIMEWASHINGS EVERY SIX MONTHS. NO SEPARATE ROOMS TO EAT IN.

LIMIT
UNPL PREFACE(R7) FAR AS THAT IS CONCERNED, I HAVE ENCOUNTERED NO LIMIT BUT MY OWN LAZINESS TO MY POWER OF CONJURING UP
KING I (211) OF INFINITE SPACE, BE SUCH AN UTTER FOOL AS TO LIMIT ETERNITY, WHICH HAS NEITHER BEGINNING NOR END, TO A
BASH III (127) HIM; ASSUAGE HIS HURTS, AND BID BILL RICHARDSON LIMIT HIS ACCESS TO THE FATAL TAP. NOW MOUNT WE ON MY
BULL PREFACE(12) AS THEY FEEL STRONG ENOUGH. IF NATIONS ARE TO LIMIT IMMIGRATION, INTER-MARRIAGE WITH FOREIGNERS, AND EVEN
GETT PREFACE(212) IF WE ARE TO MAKE POLYGYNY A SUCCESS, WE MUST LIMIT IT. IF WE HAVE TWO WOMEN TO EVERY ONE MAN, WE MUST
METH PREFACE(R46) HIS CONSCIENTIOUSNESS REACHED THE HUMAN LIMIT , BUT HE NEVER GOT DEEPER BENEATH OR HIGHER ABOVE HIS
DOCT II (129) CURE THEM BOTH. /RIDGEON/ I CANT. I'M AT MY LIMIT . I CAN SQUEEZE IN ONE MORE CASE, BUT NOT TWO. I MUST
MIS. PREFACE(30) SUBJECT OUT ALTOGETHER AS INDECENT, HAS NO AGE LIMIT . IT MEANS THAT AT NO MATTER WHAT AGE A WOMAN CONSENTS
MIS. (185) NOT IN EARNEST, /PERCIVAL/ OH, THIS IS REALLY THE LIMIT . (TURNING DESPERATELY TO GUNNER) SIR: I APPEAL TO
HART I (59) REALLY! YOUR FATHER DOES SEEM TO BE ABOUT THE LIMIT . /ELLIE/ (NAIVELY) DO YOU NEVER READ SHAKESPEAR,
FANY I (283) /JUGGINS/ YES, MADAM, I HAD. I EXCEEDED THE LEGAL LIMIT . /MRS GILBEY/ OH, THAT! WHY DO THEY GIVE A WOMAN A
HART II (122) SEEMS. /RANDALL/ (VEXED) REALLY, ARIADNE IS THE LIMIT (HE MOVES AWAY HUFFISHLY TOWARDS THE WINDOWS).
SUPR HANDBOK(198) THE GUILLOTINE WAS USED IN FRANCE UP TO THE LIMIT OF HUMAN ENDURANCE, BOTH ON GIRONDINS AND JACOBINS.
ROCK I (203) /LADY CHAVENDER/ NAG! ! I CONTROL MYSELF TO THE LIMIT OF HUMAN ENDURANCE WITH YOU ALL. BUT FLAVIA MAKES A
BARB PREFACE(219) MONEY, IS TO STRAIN TOWARDS THE EXTREME POSSIBLE LIMIT OF IMPUDENCE IN LYING AND CORRUPTION IN HYPOCRISY. THE
BARB PREFACE(243) APPREHENSIVE AND ECONOMICALLY DISPOSED TO THE LIMIT OF OLD-MAIDISHNESS; YET I AM, AND HAVE ALWAYS BEEN,
ROCK I (214) BY STRETCHING UNEMPLOYMENT BENEFIT TO THE UTMOST LIMIT OF OUR NATIONAL RESOURCES. HE-- /OXFORD YOUTH/ YOU
SUPR HANDBOK(194) POSSIBLE AND AIMED AT ADMITTED EVILS, TO THEM THE LIMIT OF PROGRESS IS, AT WORST, THE COMPLETION OF ALL THE
PLES PREFACE(R12) AS CLOSE AS HE CAN TO THE HIGHEST MARKETABLE LIMIT OF QUALITY, AND CONSTANTLY FEELING FOR AN EXTENSION OF

JOAN PREFACE(55)	BEST BY GOING TO THE WELL-ESTABLISHED CLASSICAL	LIMIT	OF THREE AND A HALF HOURS PRACTICALLY CONTINUOUS
ROCK PREFACE(160)	OR KIDNAP, OR THROW VITRIOL, IS NOT ONLY TO	LIMIT	SOCIAL RESPONSIBILITY UNNECESSARILY, AND TO PRIVILEGE
POSN PREFACE(419)	ALL THAT CAN BE DONE IS TO TAKE MY ADVICE AND	LIMIT	THE NECESSARY PUBLIC CONTROL OF THE THEATRES IN SUCH A
SUPR HANDBOK(195)	DISCOVERED THAT DEMAND CREATED SUPPLY SOON HAD TO	LIMIT	THE PROPOSITION TO " EFFECTIVE DEMAND," WHICH TURNED
SUPR HANDBOK(180)	HUMANITY UP INTO SMALL CLIQUES, AND EFFECTIVELY	LIMIT	THE SELECTION OF THE INDIVIDUAL TO HIS OWN CLIQUE, IS
PLES PREFACE(R12)	AND CONSTANTLY FEELING FOR AN EXTENSION OF THAT	LIMIT	THROUGH THE ADVANCE OF POPULAR CULTURE. AN
ROCK PREFACE(164)	RACE CONCEIT, AND SUPERSTITION IT NOW IS. NATURAL	LIMIT	TO EXTERMINATION. FORTUNATELY THE MORE FRANKLY AND
METH PREFACE(R57)	OMNIPOTENT ONLY IN THE SENSE THAT THERE SEEMS NO	LIMIT	TO ITS FINAL ACHIEVEMENT; AND IF IT MUST MEANWHILE
OVER (173)	THEN, BECAUSE I AM A GOOD MAN, I HAVE TO PLACE A	LIMIT	TO MY REGARD FOR THEM. I MAY BE FORTUNATE ENOUGH TO
MIS. PREFACE(9)	SORT OF PIOUS FRAUD HARMS IT. THERE IS A LEGAL	LIMIT	TO PHYSICAL CRUELTY; AND THERE ARE ALSO HUMAN LIMITS
MTH2 (76)	/FRANKLYN/ NEVER, THANK GOD! AS THERE IS NO	LIMIT	TO POWER AND KNOWLEDGE THERE CAN BE NO END. " THE
MIS. PREFACE(32)	MILITARY ESCORTS. IN SHORT, THERE IS HARDLY ANY	LIMIT	TO THE FOLLIES WITH WHICH OUR COMMERCIALISM WOULD
MIS. PREFACE(7)	FOR YOUR OWN PURPOSES, THEN THERE IS HARDLY ANY	LIMIT	TO THE MISCHIEF YOU MAY DO. SWEAR AT A CHILD, THROW
METH PREFACE(R67)	NOT TRUE: THERE WAS NO SUCH PUBLIC OPINION, NO	LIMIT	TO WHAT THE BRITISH PEOPLE WOULD PUT UP WITH IN THE
MILL PREFACE(130)	TO WHAT MAY BE CALLED THEIR NATURAL MINORITY	LIMIT	, WHICH WILL DESTROY THEIR PRESENT SCARCITY VALUE. BUT
METH PREFACE(R19)	OR EVEN AT THE GENUINE CIRCUMSTANTIAL SELECTION	LIMIT	, WHICH WOULD BE UNTIL A SOONER-OR-LATER-INEVITABLE

LIMITATION

MRS PREFACE(158)	THE EXAMINER MY SUPPORT IF HE WILL INTRODUCE THIS	LIMITATION	FOR PART OF THE YEAR, SAY DURING LENT, SO AS TO
POSN PREFACE(389)	BUT IT IS A DEFINED AND LIMITED INTOLERANCE. THE	LIMITATION	IS SOMETIMES CARRIED SO FAR THAT A JUDGE CANNOT
MIS. PREFACE(19)	CHILDREN AT HOME. SCHOOL. BUT PLEASE OBSERVE THE	LIMITATION	" AT HOME." WHAT PRIVATE AMATEUR PARENTAL

LIMITATIONS

LADY PREFACE(223)	HAMLETS. HE WAS NOT STUPID EITHER: IF HIS CLASS	LIMITATIONS	AND A PROFESSION THAT CUT HIM OFF FROM ACTUAL
SUPR PREFACE(R39)	PEOPLE AS PUPILS AND PERSUADES THEM THAT HIS	LIMITATIONS	ARE RULES, HIS OBSERVANCES DEXTERITIES, HIS
APPL INTRLUD(252)	AS YOU HAVE OBSERVED. AND I HAVE MINE. NOW IF OUR	LIMITATIONS	EXACTLY CORRESPONDED I SHOULD NEVER WANT TO TALK
POSN PREFACE(430)	COME INTO EXISTENCE. JUDGES: THEIR PROFESSIONAL	LIMITATIONS	. I DO NOT, HOWEVER, APPEAL TO LORD GORELL'S
GENV PREFACE(22)	THEY HAVE KEPT THEIR HEADS AND KNOWN THEIR	LIMITATIONS	. ORDINARY MORTALS LIKE NERO, PAUL OF RUSSIA,
MTH5 (234)	STARING THEM IN THE FACE, OR TO THEIR OWN OBVIOUS	LIMITATIONS	. THAT PROVES THAT THEY ARE AUTOMATA.
SUPR II (51)	UNIVERSITIES, NOT MERE SHOPS FOR SELLING CLASS	LIMITATIONS	LIKE OURS. YOU DESPISE OXFORD, ENRY, DONT YOU..
2TRU III (83)	COULD HAVE A FACE AND A FIGURE LIKE MINE WITH THE	LIMITATIONS	OF A GORILLA. YOURE FINDING OUT YOUR MISTAKE:
POSN PREFACE(409)	BOOKED. HOW CAN THIS BE PREVENTED? DESIRABLE	LIMITATIONS	OF LOCAL CONTROL. THE PROBLEM IS NOT A DIFFICULT
LION PREFACE(80)	IMPOSITION PERPETRATED THAN THE IMPOSITION OF THE	LIMITATIONS	OF PAUL'S SOUL UPON THE SOUL OF JESUS. THE
DOCT PREFACE(34)	IS POSSIBLE FOR ANY OF US TO HAVE TOO MUCH OF IT.	LIMITATIONS	OF THE RIGHT TO KNOWLEDGE. BUT NEITHER DOES ANY
MTH2 (69)	WHEN I WAS YOUNG I USED TO FEEL MY HUMAN	LIMITATIONS	VERY ACUTELY. /BURGE/ GOD KNOWS I HAVE OFTEN
APPL INTRLUD(252)	EVER TO GET TIRED OF THEM. JEMIMA HAS HER	LIMITATIONS	, AS YOU HAVE OBSERVED. AND I HAVE MINE. NOW IF
BARB I SD(249)	LIMITED IN THE ODDEST WAY WITH DOMESTIC AND CLASS	LIMITATIONS	, CONCEIVING THE UNIVERSE EXACTLY AS IF IT WERE
APPL INTRLUD(252)	ME. IF SHE DIDNT DO SO SHE WOULD BE LIMITED BY MY	LIMITATIONS	, WHICH WOULD END IN HER HATING ME. SO I ALWAYS

LIMITED

MTH5 (234)	THAT WE ARE DESCENDED FROM CREATURES QUITE AS	LIMITED	AND ABSURD AS THESE. AFTER ALL, THE BABY THERE IS
SUPR PREFACE(R25)	PROBLEM, HAVING SUDDENLY CEASED TO MEAN A VERY	LIMITED	AND OCCASIONAL INTERFERENCE, MOSTLY BY WAY OF
APPL PREFACE(174)	BACKBONE ARE AS HELPLESS IN THE GRIP OF BREAKAGES	LIMITED	AS ITS ACKNOWLEDGED HENCHMEN: FROM THE MOMENT WHEN
3PLA PREFACE(R33)	AN ACQUAINTANCE WITH SHAKESPEAR CRITICISM SO	LIMITED	AS NOT TO INCLUDE EVEN THE PREFACES OF DR JOHNSON
APPL INTRLUD(252)	GET FROM ME. IF SHE DIDNT DO SO SHE WOULD BE	LIMITED	BY MY LIMITATIONS, WHICH WOULD END IN HER HATING ME.
2TRU II (63)	A SOCK IN IT, MOPS. MY GIFT IS DIVINE: IT IS NOT	LIMITED	BY MY PETTY PERSONAL CONVICTIONS. IT IS A GIFT OF
DOCT PREFACE(34)	IS NOT THE ONLY RIGHT; AND ITS EXERCISE MUST BE	LIMITED	BY RESPECT FOR OTHER RIGHTS, AND FOR ITS OWN
CATH PREFACE(156)	OF ACKNOWLEDGING THAT HIS ART IS NOT ONLY	LIMITED	BY THE ART OF THE ACTOR, BUT OFTEN STIMULATED AND
GENV PREFACE(23)	AT A PINCH CAN DO WITH LESS, AND THAT THE MOST	LIMITED	CRAFTSMAN OR LABORER WHO CAN DO NOTHING WITHOUT
HART PREFACE(33)	NOW WHAT HAD MADE SERIOUS DRAMA POSSIBLE TO A	LIMITED	EXTENT BEFORE THE WAR WAS THAT A PLAY COULD PAY ITS
GETT PREFACE(227)	WHERE THE SEGREGATION OF THE ARTIFICIALLY	LIMITED	FAMILY IN ITS LITTLE BRICK BOX IS HORRIBLY COMPLETE,
GETT PREFACE(227)	IN THE UPPER CLASS, WHERE FAMILIES ARE NOT	LIMITED	FOR MONEY REASONS; WHERE AT LEAST TWO HOUSES AND
SUPR PREFACE(R31)	MORE THAN HIS MASTERS. THE CONCEPTION OF MENDOZA	LIMITED	I TRACE BACK TO A CERTAIN WEST INDIAN COLONIAL
BULL PREFACE(8)	SUBMISSION TO ENGLAND. IF CATHOLICISM IS TO BE	LIMITED	IN IRELAND BY ANY GEOGRAPHICAL EXPRESSION (IN WHICH
BARB I SD(249)	OF PRACTICAL ABILITY AND WORLDLY EXPERIENCE,	LIMITED	IN THE ODDEST WAY WITH DOMESTIC AND CLASS
MIS. PREFACE(5)	CALL " OUR FATHER WHICH ART IN HEAVEN," TWO VERY	LIMITED	INDIVIDUAL MORTALS SHOULD BE ALLOWED TO APPEAR AT
POSN PREFACE(389)	OF THE COMMUNITY; BUT IT IS A DEFINED AND	LIMITED	INTOLERANCE. THE LIMITATION IS SOMETIMES CARRIED SO
APPL II (270)	COUNTRY WHEN IT IS REALLY GOVERNED BY BREAKAGES,	LIMITED	, AND REALLY I HARDLY KNOW HOW TO ANSWER HIM.
GETT PREFACE(211)	THE ANSWER IS NOT FAR TO SEEK: THEIR POLYGYNY IS	LIMITED	. BY THE MOHAMMEDAN LAW A MAN CANNOT MARRY MORE THAN
APPL I (237)	IS BOUGHT UP AND SUPPRESSED BY BREAKAGES,	LIMITED	, EVERY BREAKDOWN, EVERY ACCIDENT, EVERY SMASH AND
APPL PREFACE(191)	ON DEMOCRACY! AND NOW A WORD ABOUT BREAKAGES,	LIMITED	. LIKE ALL SOCIALISTS WHO KNOW THEIR BUSINESS I HAVE
SUPR IV (155)	OFFICE IS IN THIS TOWN; AND THE NAME IS MENDOZA,	LIMITED	. NOW WHETHER MENDOZA'S A MINE, OR A STEAMBOAT LINE,
MILL I (150)	MY HUSBAND'S MENTAL GRASP, WHICH IS EXTREMELY	LIMITED	. /ALASTAIR/ A CHAP THAT SETS UP TO BE AN
POSN PREFACE(409)	CAN BE LIMITED JUST AS THE MONARCHY IS	LIMITED	. THE ACT TRANSFERRING THEATRES TO LOCAL CONTROL CAN
APPL PREFACE(193)	BENEFACTOR HE FOUND HIMSELF UP AGAINST BREAKAGES,	LIMITED	, THE GLASS BLOWERS WHOSE EMPLOYMENT WAS THREATENED,
POSN PREFACE(409)	IS NOT A DIFFICULT ONE. THE MUNICIPALITY CAN BE	LIMITED	JUST AS THE MONARCHY IS LIMITED. THE ACT
ROCK PREFACE(162)	ITS INTERESTS BEING IN THE OPPOSITE DIRECTION.	LIMITED	LIABILITY IN MORALS. SUCH A NOVELTY IS EXTREMELY
ROCK PREFACE(162)	TO US, WHO ARE STILL WORKING ON A SYSTEM OF	LIMITED	LIABILITY IN MORALS. OUR " FREE" BRITISH CITIZENS
ROCK PREFACE(162)	TO STIMULATE THE PRIVATE TRADE IN ARMAMENTS. SUCH	LIMITED	LIABILITY NO LONGER EXISTS IN RUSSIA, AND IS NOT
SUPR HANDBOK(217)	THE CIVILIZED MAN TO IDOLS OF FLESH AND BLOOD. A	LIMITED	MONARCHY IS A DEVICE FOR COMBINING THE INERTIA OF A
SUPR HANDBOK(179)	COMMUNITIES TOO SMALL AND SIMPLE TO OVERTAX MAN'S	LIMITED	POLITICAL CAPACITY DISASTROUSLY. BUT WE HAVE NOW
HART PREFACE(8)	OF ITS COMPETITORS FOR THE SUPPLY (ASSUMED TO BE	LIMITED	) OF SUBSISTENCE AVAILABLE. WE TAUGHT PRUSSIA THIS
SUPR IV (161)	OF OLD MALONE. IVE INTRODUCED HIM TO MENDOZA,	LIMITED	; AND LEFT THE TWO BRIGANDS TOGETHER TO TALK IT OUT.
POSN PREFACE(431)	CONTROL WHICH NATURALLY SUCCEEDS IT CAN EASILY BE	LIMITED	SO AS TO PREVENT IT BECOMING EITHER A CENSORSHIP OR
APPL I (198)	ACTUAL BODILY VISION, I MEAN; AND HE HAD AN ODDLY	LIMITED	SORT OF IMAGINATION. WHAT I MEAN IS THAT HE COULDNT
MIS. PREFACE(56)	SLAVES AND CRIMINALS. IN THE DAYS OF MOSES IT WAS	LIMITED	TO 39 LASHES. IN THE EARLY NINETEENTH CENTURY IT HAD
SUPR HANDBOK(205)	OF GUITEAU AND CZOLGOSZ. OUR REMEDIES ARE STILL	LIMITED	TO ENDURANCE OR ASSASSINATION; AND THE ASSASSIN IS
GETT PREFACE(185)	WE HAVE UNLIMITED KULIN POLYGAMY, MUSLIM POLYGAMY	LIMITED	TO FOUR WIVES, CHILD MARRIAGES, AND, NEARER HOME,
LION PREFACE(63)	(FOR EXAMPLE, RADIUM) IN WHICH THE DEMAND MAY BE	LIMITED	TO THE MEREST HANDFUL OF LABORATORY WORKERS, AND IN
GENV PREFACE(23)	AT SUFFICIENT INTERVALS; BUT THE CHOICE MUST BE	LIMITED	TO THE PUBLIC SPIRITED AND POLITICALLY TALENTED, OF
LION PREFACE(62)	PRACTICABLE IN A VILLAGE WHERE PRODUCTION WAS	LIMITED	TO THE SUPPLY OF THE PRIMITIVE WANTS WHICH NATURE
METH PREFACE(R68)	THAT FOR THEIR OWN PERSONAL PURPOSES, WHICH ARE	LIMITED	TO THEIR TEN OR TWENTY YEARS ON THE FRONT BENCHES IN
MIS. PREFACE(75)	WITH NO CHILDREN OR WITH FAMILIES VOLUNTARILY	LIMITED	TO TWO OR THREE, THE EIGHT CHILDREN DO NOT BELONG TO
APPL PREFACE(196)	IT ACTUALLY DID PROVIDE MATERIAL FOR BREAKAGES,	LIMITED	, AND FOR THE BITTER CRY OF THE POWERMISTRESS
APPL PREFACE(192)	AS THE PREMISES OF THE NEW TRANSPORT COMPANY,	LIMITED	, AND SPACIOUS ENOUGH TO ACCOMMODATE A DOUBLE
APPL I (238)	OF IT THAT JOE WILL HAVE TO SELL IT TO BREAKAGES,	LIMITED	, AT SCRAP IRON PRICES. I -- I -- OH, IT IS BEYOND
APPL II (265)	THAT BOOBY BULLROARER BOSSFIELD! BREAKAGES,	LIMITED	, HAVE TAKEN IT INTO THEIR HEADS TO MEND THE BRITISH
APPL I (238)	MORE TOO, IF I CHOOSE? I TELL YOU, BREAKAGES,	LIMITED	, NEVER INTERFERES IN MY DEPARTMENT. I'D LIKE TO
APPL I (237)	THE CABINET BECAUSE HE REPRESENTS BREAKAGES,	LIMITED	, THE BIGGEST INDUSTRIAL CORPORATION IN THE COUNTRY.
APPL PREFACE(191)	OF A HUNDRED LAZARUSES. THE TITLE BREAKAGES,	LIMITED	, WAS SUGGESTED TO ME BY THE FATE OF THAT REMARKABLE
APPL PREFACE(195)	ARE BY THE VESTED INTERESTS OF BREAKAGES,	LIMITED	, WOULD DO NOTHING FOR HIM. I INDUCED SOME LESS
APPL I (238)	MY WINDOWS BROKEN BY THE MOB; AND THAT BREAKAGES,	LIMITED	, WOULD GET THE JOB OF PUTTING IN NEW GLASS. AND IT
APPL I (237)	(LETTING HERSELF GO) JUST SO! BREAKAGES,	LIMITED	! JUST SO! LISTEN TO ME, SIR; AND JUDGE WHETHER I

LIMITING

MIS. PREFACE(12)	THEY USED TO BE, BECAUSE THE MODERN PRACTICE OF	LIMITING	FAMILIES ENABLES THEM TO BE MORE EFFECTUALLY

LIMITS

JOAN PREFACE(50)	ALWAYS BEATING AGAINST THEIR TOO INELASTIC	LIMITS	: ALL MORE TERRIBLE IN THEIR DRAMATIC FORCE THAN ANY
GENV IV (119)	GUIDANCE OF WHICH YOU ARE CONSCIOUS HAS ANY	LIMITS	? DOES IT NOT IMPLY A WORLD STATE WITH MR BATTLER OR
PLES PREFACE(R13)	IN SUCH MATTERS. FOR ALL THAT, THE COMMERCIAL	LIMITS	ARE TOO NARROW FOR OUR SOCIAL WELFARE. THE THEATRE IS
APPL II (268)	I HAVE FORCES WITHIN ME WHICH YOUR CONSTITUTIONAL	LIMITS	CANNOT HOLD IN CHECK. /BALBUS/ HOW CAN YOU ACCEPT OUR
PHIL I (81)	NOT GOING TO BEGIN ALL THIS OVER AGAIN. THERE ARE	LIMITS	EVEN TO MY FORBEARANCE. COME ON. /JULIA/ I WILL NOT.
CATH PREFACE(155)	IN COMPOSING SUCH BRAVURA PIECES, THE AUTHOR	LIMITS	HIMSELF ONLY BY THE RANGE OF THE VIRTUOSO, WHICH BY
MIS. PREFACE(33)	IN AN ALTOGETHER UNACCOUNTABLE MANNER WITHIN THE	LIMITS	IMPOSED BY THE SIMILAR RIGHTS OF ITS NEIGHBORS, AND
BULL PREFACE(6)	POWER OF THE PRIEST CAN BE KEPT WITHIN ITS PROPER	LIMITS	IN IRELAND IS BY SETTING THE IRISH PEOPLE FREE TO
POSN PREFACE(361)	WITH BY A PARLIAMENTARY BODY SUBJECT TO NO SUCH	LIMITS	. A READABLE BLUEBOOK. FEW BOOKS OF THE YEAR 1909 CAN

POSN PREFACE(386)	LARGE TOLERATION THESE CONSIDERATIONS DICTATE HAS	LIMITS	. FOR EXAMPLE, THOUGH WE TOLERATE, AND RIGHTLY
MILL PREFACE(113)	BE ADVANCED TO THE CONTRARY. OF COURSE THERE ARE	LIMITS	. HE CANNOT GO TO THE LENGTHS AT WHICH THE COMMON MAN
ROCK I (206)	/SIR ARTHUR/ I HAVE TO GOVERN WITHIN DEMOCRATIC	LIMITS	. I CANNOT GO FASTER THAN OUR VOTERS WILL LET ME.
OVER PREFACE(163)	STAGE. TO ALL STAGE PRESENTATIONS THERE ARE	LIMITS	. IF MACDUFF WERE TO STAB MACBETH, THE SPECTACLE
MIS. PREFACE(71)	STILL, SOMETHING CAN BE DONE EVEN WITHIN CLASS	LIMITS	. LARGE COMMUNITIES OF CHILDREN OF THE SAME CLASS ARE
BARB I (262)	TWO AND SEE A LITTLE MORE OF YOU; BUT THERE ARE	LIMITS	. /SARAH/ WELL, HE CANT EAT US, I SUPPOSE. I DONT
SIM I (37)	YOU SHOULDNT. /PRA/ BEAUTY IS WORSHIPFUL, WITHIN	LIMITS	. WHEN YOU HAVE WORSHIPPED YOUR FILL MAY I SHEW YOU
MTH2 (52)	GRAVES OF YOUR CONSCIENTIOUS OBJECTORS? ALL LAW	LIMITS	LIBERTY OF CONSCIENCE: IF A MAN'S CONSCIENCE ALLOWS
GETT PREFACE(214)	IT IS BY NO MEANS SURE THAT WITHIN REASONABLE	LIMITS	MOTHERS DO NOT MAKE A BETTER FIGHT FOR SUBSISTENCE,
POSN PREFACE(361)	COULD NOT BE FULLY ILLUSTRATED WITHIN THE	LIMITS	OF DECORUM IMPOSED ON THE PRESS. IT COULD ONLY BE
GETT PREFACE(204)	ENGLISH, AS ITS SUBJECT WAS TOO IMPROPER. THE	LIMITS	OF DEMOCRACY. NOW IF ENGLAND HAD BEEN GOVERNED IN THE
POSN PREFACE(412)	AND FOREIGN POLICY, AND THAT IT IMPOSES THE	LIMITS	OF ETIQUET ON THE HISTORICAL DRAMA. 5. A CENSORSHIP
POSN PREFACE(432)	NOT YIELD AN INCH, BUT INSISTED, WITHIN THE DUE	LIMITS	OF GALLANT WARFARE, ON TAKING THE FIELD WITH EVERY
JOAN PREFACE(48)	BECAUSE IT IS NOT MARVELLOUS ENOUGH. THE STAGE	LIMITS	OF HISTORICAL REPRESENTATION. FOR THE STORY OF JOAN I
BARB PREFACE(215)	INCENDIARY, RAVISHER OR MURDERER, TO THE UTMOST	LIMITS	OF HUMANITY'S COMPARATIVELY NEGLIGIBLE IMPULSES IN
SUPR I SD(16)	THE WORLD BECOMES TRANSFIGURED, AND THE PUNY	LIMITS	OF INDIVIDUAL CONSCIOUSNESS ARE SUDDENLY MADE
SIM PREFACE(11)	AMATEURS, NO DOUBT FELL BEFORE IT HAD LEARNT THE	LIMITS	OF ITS BUSINESS BY EXPERIENCE. MY OBJECT IN CITING IT
OVER PREFACE(163)	PHENOMENA OF SEX AS THEY APPEAR IN NATURE, THE	LIMITS	OF STAGE PRESENTATION, BUT THE STAGE PRESENTS MUCH
GENV PREFACE(7)	THEIR WAY THROUGH DAILY EMERGENCIES WITHIN THE	LIMITS	OF THEIR IGNORANCE AS BEST THEY CAN, IF THEIR VISION
APPL PREFACE(172)	OF THEIR RESPONSIBILITY AND CONSEQUENTLY OF THE	LIMITS	OF THEIR IRRESPONSIBILITY: IN SHORT, IN THE AUTHORITY
APPL PREFACE(172)	EXPERIENCE, IN CUNNING, IN EXACT KNOWLEDGE OF THE	LIMITS	OF THEIR RESPONSIBILITY AND CONSEQUENTLY OF THE
METH PREFACE(R77)	IN TRYING TO CRAMP THE HUMAN MIND WITHIN THE	LIMITS	OF THESE GROTESQUE PERVERSIONS OF NATURAL TRUTHS AND
ROCK PREFACE(179)	ONLY NEEDING TO BE BROUGHT WITHIN THEATRICAL	LIMITS	OF TIME AND SPACE TO BE A THRILLING PLAY. BUT JESUS
APPL II (259)	NO, MAAM: YOU SHALL NOT GO. WHATEVER MAY BE THE	LIMITS	OF YOUR PRIVILEGES AS THE CONSORT OF YOUR SOVEREIGN,
MILL PREFACE(109)	AND ANOTHER FOR THE TIMID, AND WITHIN FAMILY	LIMITS	ONE LAW FOR THE PARENT AND NO LAW AT ALL FOR THE
PLES PREFACE(R13)	FOR MY PART, I HAVE NO DOUBT THAT THE COMMERCIAL	LIMITS	SHOULD BE OVERSTEPPED, AND THAT THE HIGHEST PRESTIGE,
MRS PREFACE(158)	HUMAN STOCK; AND THOUGH EACH OF THESE TAPUS	LIMITS	THE SCOPE OF THE DRAMATIST, IT DOES NOT MAKE DRAMA
MTH4 I (164)	THERE ARE NO LIMITS TO THEIR POWER EXCEPT THE	LIMITS	THEY SET THEMSELVES. YOU ARE A CHILD GOVERNED BY
SUPR HANDBOK(206)	HAS ENCOUNTERED THE SAME PERSONAL AND COMMERCIAL	LIMITS	TO BOTH ITS AGGRAVATION AND ITS MITIGATION. NOW THAT
LION PREFACE(64)	OR TO COMPLETE NEWTON'S WORK ON FLUXIONS,	LIMITS	TO FREE WILL. CONSEQUENTLY SUCH OF OUR LAWS AS ARE
MIS. PREFACE(9)	TO PHYSICAL CRUELTY; AND THERE ARE ALSO HUMAN	LIMITS	TO IT. THERE IS AN ACTIVE SOCIETY WHICH BRINGS TO
SUPR PREFACE(R21)	ANY EFFORT IN THAT DIRECTION. THERE ARE NO	LIMITS	TO MALE HYPOCRISY IN THIS MATTER. NO DOUBT THERE ARE
CAND III (128)	/CANDIDA/ PUT THAT DOWN AGAIN, EUGENE. THERE ARE	LIMITS	TO MY APPETITE FOR POETRY: EVEN YOUR POETRY. YOUVE
SUPR I (8)	MORE COLDLY). EXCUSE ME, OCTAVIUS; BUT THERE ARE	LIMITS	TO SOCIAL TOLERATION. YOU KNOW THAT I AM NOT A
POSN PREFACE(410)	WILL NOT AND SHOULD NOT BE SATISFIED WITH THESE	LIMITS	TO THE MUNICIPAL POWER. IF THEY ARE DEPRIVED OF THE
LION PREFACE(64)	WHICH NEVERTHELESS DOES REMIND US THAT THERE ARE	LIMITS	TO THE NUMBER OF CUBITS AN INDIVIDUAL CAN ADD TO HIS
CATH 4 (188)	THAT FAMOUS AS I AM FOR MY CLEMENCY, THERE ARE	LIMITS	TO THE PATIENCE EVEN OF AN EMPRESS. /EDSTASTON/ HOW
MTH4 I (164)	POWER; AND THE CONSEQUENCE IS THAT THERE ARE NO	LIMITS	TO THEIR POWER EXCEPT THE LIMITS THEY SET THEMSELVES.
POSN PREFACE(386)	AS THE MIGHTIEST OF THE CHRISTIAN EMPIRES. THE	LIMITS	TO TOLERATION. BUT THE LARGE TOLERATION THESE
SUPR III (108)	WHICH HE CALLS HIS RESPECTABILITY. THERE ARE	LIMITS	TO WHAT A MULE OR AN ASS WILL STAND; BUT MAN WILL
LION PREFACE(64)	IF ITS APPLICATION WERE NOT KEPT WITHIN THE	LIMITS	WHICH NATURE SETS TO THE SELF-CONTROL OF MOST OF US.
FANY III (304)	/BOBBY/ I DONT THINK SHE'D LIKE IT. THERE ARE	LIMITS	, AFTER ALL. (HE SITS DOWN AT THE TABLE, AS IF TO
LION PREFACE(99)	FOR EMIGRATION IS PRACTICABLE ONLY WITHIN NARROW	LIMITS	, AND SELDOM PROVIDES AN EFFECTIVE REMEDY. ALL
DEVL EPILOG (79)	AND ENLIGHTENED WITHIN CERTAIN ARISTOCRATIC	LIMITS	, BEST ILLUSTRATED PERHAPS BY HIS DECLARATION, WHICH
GETT PREFACE(216)	AND HUMAN NATURE WERE WORKING SMOOTHLY WITHIN ITS	LIMITS	, THERE WOULD BE NOTHING MORE TO BE SAID: IT WOULD BE

LIMP

VWOO 1,SD(115)	PALE GENTLEMAN UNDER FORTY IN GREEN SPECTACLES, A	LIMP	BLACK BEARD, AND A TROPICAL SUIT OF WHITE SILK, WHO IS
JOAN 1 (59)	ANY SLUT OF A GIRL CAN DO IT. /STEWARD/ (HANGING	LIMP	IN HIS HANDS) SIR, SIR: YOU CANNOT GET RID OF HER BY
NEVR I (204)	/PHILIP/ TWENTIETH CENTURY PARENTS. /DOLLY/ CLOTH	LIMP	, HALF A DOLLAR. /PHILIP/ OR MOUNTED ON LINEN FOR HARD

LIMPS

MILL IV SD(193)	THE REGISTER WITH HIM). ADRIAN, WHO COMES FIRST,	LIMPS	BADLY ON TWO WALKING STICKS; AND HIS HEAD IS BANDAGED.
LION PROL,SD(105)	FROM THE JUNGLE, IT IS REPEATED NEARER. THE LION	LIMPS	FROM THE JUNGLE ON THREE LEGS, HOLDING UP HIS RIGHT
LION II SD(143)	WRIST, LOOKS AFFRIGHTEDLY AT THE LION. THE LION	LIMPS	ON THREE PAWS, HOLDING UP THE OTHER AS IF IT WAS
LION PROL,SD(105)	HE LICKS IT AGAIN. TEARS DROP FROM HIS EYES. HE	LIMPS	PAINFULLY OFF THE PATH AND LIES DOWN UNDER THE TREES,
LION PROLOG (108)	EATING. (THE LION RISES WITH A GREAT GROAN AND	LIMPS	TOWARDS THEM). OH! (SHE FAINTS). /ANDROCLES/ (

LINA

MIS. (161)	EVERY NIGHT AND YOUR LIFE IN HERS. /TARLETON/	LINA	: I'M GOING TO MAKE A FOOL OF MYSELF. I'M GOING TO CRY
MIS. (202)	TEN POUNDS A NIGHT OFF YOUR OWN BAT, MISS	LINA	? /LINA/ (SCORNFULLY) TEN POUNDS A NIGHT! I HAVE
MIS. (175)	COULD HELP? /BENTLEY/ (RUNNING FORWARD BETWEEN	LINA	AND GUNNER) BUT WHAT DID YOU MEAN BY WHAT YOU SAID
MIS. (172)	GET THE SACK IF I DIDNT. FREE ENGLAND! HA! (	LINA	APPEARS AT THE PAVILION DOOR, AND COMES SWIFTLY AND
MIS. SD(157)	A BIBLE FOR SALE. THE EMPIRE HAS NO RELIGION.	LINA	COMES IN. SHE HAS LEFT HER CAP IN HYPATIA'S ROOM, BUT
MIS. SD(154)	MR PERCIVAL. (TO LINA, RISING) COME WITH ME.	LINA	FOLLOWS HER TO THE INNER DOOR. THEY ALL RISE. /JOHNNY/
MIS. SD(154)	TO PERCIVAL) I'LL SHEW YOU. /PERCIVAL/ THANK YOU.	LINA	GOES OUT WITH HYPATIA, AND PERCIVAL WITH JOHNNY. /MRS
MIS. SD(172)	CEILING. AS HE TRIES TO TURN ON HIS ASSAILANT,	LINA	GRIPS HIS OTHER WRIST. /LINA/ PLEASE STOP. I CANT BEAR
MIS. (188)	NOT AT ALL: NOT AT ALL. NOW, CHICKABIDDY: AS MISS	LINA	HAS TAKEN AWAY BEN, SUPPOSE YOU TAKE AWAY MR BROWN FOR
MIS. (203)	LONG AGO. /HYPATIA/ MOTHER! /TARLETON/ MISS	LINA	HERE, THOUGH SHE HAS BEEN SO SHORT A TIME WITH US, HAS
MIS. (173)	ON THE WRITING TABLE). /THE MAN/ (LOOKING AT	LINA	IN AMAZEMENT) BEATEN BY A FEMALE! IT NEEDED ONLY THIS.
MIS. SD(152)	FETCH THE TWO WICKER CHAIRS. JOHNNY GIVES HIS TO	LINA	. HYPATIA AND PERCIVAL TAKE THE CHAIRS AT THE
MIS. (161)	IS THE SWEETEST. /TARLETON/ DONT PROBE TOO DEEP,	LINA	. IT HURTS. /LINA/ YOU MUST GET OUT OF THE HABIT OF
MIS. SD(181)	THE MATTER IS. COMES FORWARD BETWEEN PERCIVAL AND	LINA	. JOHNNY STOPS BESIDE HYPATIA. /PERCIVAL/ CERTAINLY.
MIS. (192)	RIGHT. PERCIVAL TAKES THE CHAIR JOHNNY PLACED FOR	LINA	ON HER ARRIVAL. TARLETON SITS DOWN AT THE END OF THE
MIS. (176)	A MARRIED WOMAN THAT MIGHT BE YOUR MOTHER (TO	LINA	) AND I'M SURE YOURE NOT PARTICULAR, IF YOULL EXCUSE MY
MIS. (153)	DOWN AT THE END OF THE WRITING TABLE NEAREST	LINA	) BAD THING TO AEROPLANE ON, I SHOULD IMAGINE. TOO
MIS. (175)	/MRS TARLETON/ GOOD GRACIOUS! HE'S MAD. (TO	LINA	) DID JOHN MAKE HIM TAKE A TURKISH BATH? /LINA/ NO. HE
MIS. (153)	BENTLEY BEHIND HIS FATHER. /MRS TARLETON/ (TO	LINA	) HAVE SOME TEA NOW, WONT YOU? /LINA/ I NEVER DRINK
MIS. (154)	JOHN. THE LADY IS ONLY JOKING, I'M SURE. (TO	LINA	) I SUPPOSE YOUR LUGGAGE IS IN THE AEROPLANE.
MIS. (176)	THIS BEFORE EVERYBODY. (TURNING RATHER TARTLY TO	LINA	) WOULD YOU MIND GOING AWAY TO THE DRAWING ROOM JUST
MIS. (202)	MEDITATING DEEPLY). /JOHNNY/ (CONFIDENTIALLY TO	LINA	) YOU WONT MENTION OUR LITTLE CONVERSATION, MISS
MIS. (152)	OF KNOWING YOUR NAME? /THE PASSENGER/ MY NAME IS	LINA	SZCZEPANOWSKA (PRONOUNCING IT SH-CHEPANOVSKA).
MIS. (180)	ONLY BY THE TIMELY ARRIVAL OF THE CELEBRATED MISS	LINA	SZCZEPANOWSKA. /MRS TARLETON/ IS SHE CELEBRATED? (
MIS. (202)	JOHNNY TO BUY AN ENGLISHWOMAN: HE SHALL NOT BUY	LINA	SZCZEPANOWSKA; AND I WILL NOT STAY IN THE HOUSE WHERE
MIS. (201)	RIPPING FINE WOMAN, AND ASKS TO ME MARRY HIM. I,	LINA	SZCZEPANOWSKA, MARRY HIM! ! ! ! ! I DO NOT MIND
MIS. (201)	POSITION IS NOT ONE FOR A NICE WOMAN. THIS TO ME,	LINA	SZCZEPANOWSKA! I AM AN HONEST WOMAN: I EARN MY LIVING.
MIS. (204)	ELSE? /TARLETON/ WELL, I-- ER (HE ADDRESSES	LINA	, AND STOPS). I-- ER (HE ADDRESSES LORD SUMMERHAYS,
MIS. (155)	IN THE MIDDLE. I REMEMBER THAT HER NAME WAS	LINA	, AND THAT THE OTHER NAME WAS FOREIGN; THOUGH I DONT
MIS. SD(200)	OF THAT YOUNG LADY'S TERRIBLE DERISION, BENTLEY.	LINA	, HER CAP ON, AND HER GOGGLES IN HER HAND, COMES
MIS. (154)	MAMMA. JOHNNY: LOOK AFTER MR PERCIVAL. (TO	LINA	, RISING) COME WITH ME. LINA FOLLOWS HER TO THE INNER

LINCOLN

POSN PREFACE(387)	ASSASSINS OF LORD FREDERICK CAVENDISH, PRESIDENTS	LINCOLN	AND MCKINLEY, AND SIR CURZON WYLLIE? HERE IS A
NEVR I (207)	/DOLLY/ AFTER ALL, OUR GRANDFATHER IS A CANON OF	LINCOLN	CATHEDRAL. /VALENTINE/ (LIKE A CASTAWAY MARINER WHO
APPL PREFACE(180)	SEE WHAT THERE REALLY IS INSIDE IT. (BY THE WAY,	LINCOLN	DID NOT REALLY DECLAIM IT ON THE FIELD OF
APPL PREFACE(179)	A MORE POETIC CONCEPTION OF DEMOCRACY. ABRAHAM	LINCOLN	IS REPRESENTED AS STANDING AMID THE CARNAGE OF THE
DEVL EPILOG (80)	SUBSTITUTE. WHETHER BURGOYNE OR WASHINGTON,	LINCOLN	OR DAVIS, GLADSTONE OR BRIGHT, MR CHAMBERLAIN OR MR
HART PREFACE(38)	DOES, HOW HOPELESS IS REMONSTRANCE, AND HOW HAPPY	LINCOLN	WAS IN PERISHING FROM THE EARTH BEFORE HIS INSPIRED
HART PREFACE(38)	UTMOST, NO EDICT ON WHICH HE WILL BE ABLE, LIKE	LINCOLN	, TO INVOKE " THE CONSIDERATE JUDGMENT OF MANKIND,
NEVR I (207)	EARTH DIDNT YOU TELL ME THAT BEFORE? A CANON OF	LINCOLN	! THAT MAKES IT ALL RIGHT, OF COURSE. JUST EXCUSE

LINCOLN'S

MRS IV SD(235)	PATENT STOVE, SATURDAY AFTERNOON. THE CHIMNEYS OF	LINCOLN'S	INN AND THE WESTERN SKY BEYOND ARE SEEN THROUGH
MILL I SD(137)	A SMART YOUNG SOLICITOR, IS IN HIS OFFICE IN	LINCOLN'S	INN FIELDS. IT IS A FINE MORNING IN MAY. THE ROOM,

LINCRUSTA

NEVR III SD(261)	TASTE LAY THAT WAY, ADMIRE THE WALL DECORATION OF	LINCRUSTA	WALTON IN PLUM COLOR AND BRONZE LACQUER, WITH DADO

LINDSAY

SHAK (141)	HIS DROWSY HUM." /SHAV/ HAST NEVER HEARD OF ADAM	LINDSAY	GORDON? /SHAKES/ A NAME THAT SINGS. WHAT OF HIM?

LINE

KING I (210)	IS A CURVE. MY HAND WILL NOT DRAW A STRAIGHT	LINE	: I HAVE TO STRETCH A CHALKED STRING ON MY CANVAS AND
BUOY IV (48)	MEDITATE. /OLD BILL/ NO. MEDITATION IS NOT IN MY	LINE	: I SPECULATE. AND MY SPECULATIONS TURN OUT WELL WHEN I
KING I (213)	THE CIRCLE IS A DEAD THING LIKE A STRAIGHT	LINE	: NO LIVING HAND CAN DRAW IT: YOU MAKE IT BY TWIRLING A
MRS IV (252)	ON IT. /VIVIE/ YES: IT'S BETTER TO CHOOSE YOUR	LINE	AND GO THROUGH WITH IT. IF I HAD BEEN YOU, MOTHER, I
MILL PREFACE(117)	ON VINEGAR HILL; AND WELLINGTON'S THIN RED	LINE	AND HIS SQUARES WOULD HAVE VANISHED IN THE FUMES OF
SUPR III (113)	AND BEAUTY WERE HER OBJECT, START OFF ON ANOTHER	LINE	AND LABOR AT THE CLUMSY ELEPHANT AND THE HIDEOUS APE,
MIS. (137)	ROCKS. /JOHNNY/ I DONT KNOW. YOU CAN DRAW A	LINE	AND MAKE OTHER CHAPS TOE IT. THATS WHAT I CALL
OVER (173)	HEARTHS AND THEIR HAPPINESS OBLIGES ME TO DRAW A	LINE	AND NOT OVERSTEP IT. OF COURSE I VALUE SUCH
KING I (209)	BETTER THAN I? /CHARLES/ NOBODY HERE CAN DRAW A	LINE	AT ALL, EXCEPT THE DUCHESS OF CLEVELAND, WHO DRAWS A
SUPR I (8)	THROUGH OUR ADVANCED OPINIONS. BUT I DRAW THE	LINE	AT ANARCHISM AND FREE LOVE AND THAT SORT OF THING. IF I
APPL INTRLUD(254)	AN IDOL, MY LOVE; AND ALL I CAN DO IS TO DRAW THE	LINE	AT BEING A CRUEL IDOL. (HE LOOKS AT HIS WATCH) NOW I
GENV III (80)	COULD MAKE HEAD OR TAIL OF THEM. BUT I DRAW THE	LINE	AT COMMUNISM AND ATHEISM AND NATIONALIZATION OF WOMEN
PYGM II (239)	MARRY THAT MISSUS OF YOURS? I RATHER DRAW THE	LINE	AT ENCOURAGING THAT SORT OF IMMORALITY. /DOOLITTLE/
JITT III (78)	NO DOUBT I AM BRUNO'S INFERIOR; BUT I DRAW THE	LINE	AT HELPING HIM TO ROB HIS WIDOW FOR MY OWN PROFIT.
KING I (209)	ALL, EXCEPT THE DUCHESS OF CLEVELAND, WHO DRAWS A	LINE	AT NOTHING. /BARBARA/ CHARLES-- /CHARLES/ BE QUIET,
BULL PREFACE(8)	AND MARSHALS OF PEASANTS AND OSTLERS, DREW THE	LINE	AT PROMOTING A SPY. HE FOLLOWED A UNIVERSAL INSTINCT
MIS. (173)	TO SHOOT ME; BUT I'M NOT VINDICTIVE. I DRAW THE	LINE	AT PUTTING A MAN ON THE RACK. IF YOU WANT EVERY JOINT
MIS. PREFACE(83)	WHICH HAS CLANS INSTEAD OF FAMILIES) DRAWS THE	LINE	AT SECOND COUSINS. PROTESTANTISM DRAWS IT STILL CLOSER
NEVR IV (288)	OH, IF YOU PLEASE, MAAM, I REALLY MUST DRAW THE	LINE	AT SITTING DOWN. I COULDNT LET MYSELF BE SEEN DOING
APPL I (230)	WITH ALL RESPECT FOR YOU, I REALLY MUST DRAW THE	LINE	AT THAT. /MAGNUS/ YOU ARE RIGHT, MR BOANERGES, AS YOU
LION PREFACE(27)	AS TOLERANT EVEN TO CARELESSNESS, HE DRAWS THE	LINE	AT THE GENTILE, AND REPRESENTS JESUS AS A BIGOTED JEW
ROCK PREFACE(186)	OF SILLY AUSTERITIES; BUT I MUST DRAW THE	LINE	AT YOUR MAKING A RIOT IN THE TEMPLE AND THROWING THE
LION II SD(143)	OUT HIS NOSE FORWARD AND HIS TAIL IN A HORIZONTAL	LINE	BEHIND, LIKE A POINTER, AND UTTERS AN APPALLING ROAR.
KING I (209)	MR KNELLER. /KNELLER/ CAN ANYONE HERE DRAW A	LINE	BETTER THAN I? /CHARLES/ NOBODY HERE CAN DRAW A LINE
MTH5 (234)	IS A MYSTIC: I AM A MAN OF SCIENCE. HE DRAWS A	LINE	BETWEEN AN AUTOMATON AND A LIVING ORGANISM. I CANNOT
DOCT PREFACE(45)	OF THIS RAINY ISLAND WITH AN UMBRELLA. THE OLD	LINE	BETWEEN MAN AND BEAST. BUT THERE IS STILL A DISTINCTION
ROCK PREFACE(147)	THE SACREDNESS OF HUMAN LIFE. IN LAW WE DRAW A	LINE	BETWEEN THE KILLING OF HUMAN ANIMALS AND NON-HUMAN
LION II (130)	PUGNACIOUSLY) WHAT! /FERROVIUS/ (ON THE BORDER	LINE	BETWEEN ZEAL AND FEROCITY) OH, DONT GIVE WAY TO PRIDE
BASH PREFACE(89)	HEWLETT WOULD CHUCKLE DELIGHTEDLY OVER IT ALMOST	LINE	BY LINE, WHILST THE ORDINARY PLAYGOERS WOULD LISTEN
KING I (213)	I BELIEVE IN NONE OF THESE MECHANICAL FORMS. THE	LINE	DRAWN BY THE ARTIST'S HAND, THE LINE THAT FLOWS, THAT
KING I (210)	MADAM. CLEAR YOUR MIND OF FILTH. THERE IS NOT A	LINE	DRAWN BY THE HAND OF THE ALMIGHTY, FROM THE RAINBOW IN
MTH2 (77)	PLAINLY THAT THEY COMPRESS ITS HISTORY INTO A TWO	LINE	EPIC: OLD DADDY LONG LEGS WOULDNT SAY HIS PRAYERS: TAKE
APPL I (200)	OF HIS AUNTS INVITING HERSELF TO TEA, OR A LITTLE	LINE	FROM ORINTHIA THE BELOVED MARKED " STRICTLY PRIVATE AND
SHAK (141)	CALL YOU THIS CATERAN BETTER THAN MY MACBETH, ONE	LINE	FROM WHOM IS WORTH A THOUSAND OF YOUR PIFFLING PLAYS.
JOAN PREFACE(44)	SAYS SO." JOAN AS THEOCRAT. LEADERS WHO TAKE THAT	LINE	HAVE NO TROUBLE WITH SOME PEOPLE, AND NO END OF TROUBLE
ARMS III (52)	IN IT. /BLUNTSCHLI/ YES: HE'S A LITTLE IN THAT	LINE	HIMSELF, ISNT HE? /RAINA/ (STARTLED) OH! DO YOU
SIM II (59)	ETERNITY. THEY LOOK AT HIM AS BEFORE. /IDDY/ THE	LINE	I AM GOING TO TAKE IS THIS. WE HAVE NEVER BEEN ABLE TO
MTH2 (86)	REVELATION THAT HAS BEEN VOUCHSAFED TO US? THE	LINE	I AM GOING TO TAKE IS BACK TO METHUSELAH. /LUBIN/ (
BASH PREFACE(87)	DECLARE THAT THERE WAS NOT A SINGLE CORRECT	LINE	IN ALL MY THREE ACTS, I STOLE OR PARAPHRASED A FEW FROM
KING I (210)	DIVINE RAPHAEL? WELL, THERE IS NOT A STRAIGHT	LINE	IN HER BODY; SHE IS ALL CURVES. /BARBARA/ (OUTRAGED.
CAND I (91)	ARTER ALL, JAMES: THE LINE YOU TOOK IS THE PAYIN	LINE	IN THE LONG RUN FOR A MAN O YOUR SORT. /MORELL/ (
KING I (209)	IN CONTRADICTION OF ME, OF ME! THAT A RIGHT	LINE	IS A STRAIGHT LINE, AND THAT EVERYTHING THAT MOVES
DOCT I (88)	/RIDGEON/ I KNOW NOTHING ABOUT SMALLPOX. MY	LINE	IS TUBERCULOSIS AND TYPHOID AND PLAGUE. BUT OF COURSE
NEVR II (241)	CRAMPTON; BUT WE ARE NOT YET STRONG IN THE FILIAL	LINE	. (THE WAITER RETURNS FROM THE HOTEL WITH THE DRINKS).
MILL I (146)	YES? . . . (HASTILY) ONE MOMENT. HOLD THE	LINE	. (TO EPIFANIA) YOUR HUSBAND IS DOWNSTAIRS, WITH A
AUGS (282)	PIFFLINGTON WANTS TO SPEAK TO YOU. HOLD THE	LINE	. (TO THE LADY) NOW, MADAM (HE HANDS HER THE
KING I (210)	YOUR APPLE BEHIND IF THE APPLE FELL IN A STRAIGHT	LINE	. MOTION IN A CURVE IS THE LAW OF NATURE; AND THE LAW
FOUN (211)	TO HAVE KNOWN BETTER. NO: THE CHURCH IS NOT IN MY	LINE	. NATURE INTENDED ME FOR THE STAGE. THE UNREAL MOCKERY
APPL I (215)	MY DEAR LYSISTRATA, YOU MUST NOT TAKE THAT	LINE	. OUR BUSINESS IS TO MEDDLE IN EVERYBODY'S BUSINESS. A
CLEO V SD(195)	AND CALLS TO THE OFFICERS FROM BEHIND THE ROMAN	LINE	. /APOLLODORUS/ HULLO! MAY I PASS? /CENTURION/ PASS
FANY EPILOG (331)	THE PLAY BEARS THE AUTHOR'S SIGNATURE IN EVERY	LINE	. /BANNAL/ WHO? /GUNN/ GRANVILLE-BARKER, OF COURSE.
CLEO V SD(196)	THEIR LINES. APOLLODORUS GOES TO THE EGYPTIAN	LINE	. /CENTURION/ (HURRYING TO THE GANGWAY GUARD)
MIS. (137)	YOU DONT MAKE ANY PROGRESS WHEN YOURE TOEING A	LINE	. /HYPATIA/ (SUDDENLY, AS IF SHE COULD BEAR NO MORE OF
JITT II (42)	HIMSELF: I ONLY GAVE HIM HIS FACTS. READ THE NEXT	LINE	. /JITTA/ (READING) " BY ALFRED LENKHEIM." I SUPPOSE
OVER (177)	AND HUMAN. /GREGORY/ I OUGHT TO DRAW A	LINE	. /MRS JUNO/ SO YOU SHALL, DEAR. TELL ME: DO YOU REALLY
SHAK (141)	/SHAV/ QUOTE ONE. JUST ONE. I CHALLENGE THEE. ONE	LINE	. /SHAKES/ " THE SHARDBORNE BEETLE WITH HIS DROWSY
MRS I SD(181)	COMMON RISES UPHILL BEYOND THE PALING TO THE SKY	LINE	. SOME FOLDED CANVAS GARDEN CHAIRS ARE LEANING AGAINST
PYGM II (238)	ANY WAY YOU LOOK AT IT. UNDESERVING POVERTY IS MY	LINE	. TAKING ONE STATION IN SOCIETY WITH ANOTHER, IT'S--
6CAL PREFACE(89)	OF INSIDIOUS PROPAGANDA, WITH A MORAL IN EVERY	LINE	. THEY NEVER DISCOVER WHAT I AM DRIVING AT: IT IS
PRES (162)	/BALSQUITH/ THE LABOR PARTY IS TAKING THE SAME	LINE	. THEY SAY THE MEN GOT THE FACTORY ACTS BY HIDING
HART III (130)	A GOODS TRAIN. /MRS HUSHABYE/ NOT ON OUR LITTLE	LINE	. THEY TACK A TRUCK ON TO THE PASSENGER TRAIN. WHAT CAN
MTH5 (222)	I AM NO GREAT JUDGE OF SCULPTURE. ART IS NOT MY	LINE	. WHAT IS WRONG WITH THE BUSTS? /ECRASIA/ WRONG WITH
CAPT II (248)	NERVOUS, SIR! NO. NERVOUSNESS IS NOT IN MY	LINE	. YOU WILL FIND ME PERFECTLY CAPABLE OF SAYING WHAT I
MIS. (112)	INARTICULATE SOB OF RAGE). FIGHTING ISNT IN YOUR	LINE	. YOURE TOO SMALL; AND YOURE TOO CHILDISH. I ALWAYS
GENV III (79)	MY NATIVE LANGUAGE. I DO NOT UNDERSTAND THE FIRST	LINE	. " WE ARE FAIN OF THEE STILL: WE ARE FAIN." WHAT DOES
FANY III (300)	BELIEVE ME, IF YOU ARE NOT A BORN ARTIST IN THAT	LINE	.--- BEG PARDON, SIR, I THINK I HEARD THE BELL. (HE
MTH3 (134)	(IMPLORINGLY) NO: STOP: LET ME EXPLAIN: HOLD THE	LINE	JUST ONE MOMENT. OH, PLEASE. /THE NEGRESS/ (WAITING
KING I (212)	SUBSTITUTES FOR MY FIRST LAW OF MOTION-- STRAIGHT	LINE	MOTION-- MOTION IN A CURVE. /JAMES/ SO BANG GOES YOUR
APPL INTRLUD(252)	SORT: I UNDERSTAND IT, BEING A LITTLE IN THAT	LINE	MYSELF. AT ALL EVENTS I AM NOT AFRAID OF IT; THOUGH THE
DOCT PREFACE(48)	NOT TO BE FOUND IN THE PAIN IT CAUSES, BUT IN THE	LINE	OF ARGUMENT BY WHICH IT IS JUSTIFIED. THE MEDICAL CODE
KING I (217)	THAT THE EARTH IS A MOON OF THE SUN AND THAT THE	LINE	OF BEAUTY IS A CURVE. CAN HE MEASURE THE PATH OF THE
KING PREFACE(154)	CALLED HOGARTH; FOR IT WAS HOGARTH WHO SAID " THE	LINE	OF BEAUTY IS A CURVE," AND NEWTON WHOSE FIRST DOGMA IT
KING I (210)	SIR: I DO NOT SAY: I KNOW. THE RIGHT LINE, THE	LINE	OF BEAUTY, IS A CURVE. MY HAND WILL NOT DRAW A STRAIGHT
METH PREFACE(R84)	PERISHED. FROM MOLIERE TO OSCAR WILDE WE HAD A	LINE	OF COMEDIC PLAYWRIGHTS WHO, IF THEY HAD NOTHING
CATH 2,SD(174)	WITH TWO LADIES, STANDS A LITTLE IN FRONT OF THE	LINE	OF COURTIERS, BY THE IMPERIAL CHAIR. SILENCE, BROKEN
DEVL III (61)	IT TO BE. /BURGOYNE/ (STRONGLY DEPRECATING THIS	LINE	OF DEFENCE, BUT STILL POLITE) DONT YOU THINK, MR
GENV PREFACE(25)	AUSTRIANS WHO COULD NOT TO SAVE THEIR LIVES HUM A	LINE	OF DEUTSCHLAND UBER ALLES NOR COMPOSE A BAR OF MUSIC
3PLA PREFACE(R33)	TO BE PERFORMED AS HE WROTE THEM; AND THE LONG	LINE	OF DISGRACEFUL FARCES, MELODRAMAS, AND STAGE PAGEANTS
PLES PREFACE(R7)	ARMS AND THE MAN, TAKING THE TITLE FROM THE FIRST	LINE	OF DRYDEN'S VIRGIL, IT PASSED FOR A SUCCESS, THE
KING PREFACE(156)	ENTIRELY DIFFERENT FOOTING. IN THIS HE WAS IN THE	LINE	OF EVOLUTION, WHICH LEADS TO AN INCREASING SEPARATION
LADY PREFACE(233)	TRAGEDIES HAS THUS BEEN THE HISTORY OF A LONG	LINE	OF FAMOUS ACTORS, FROM BURBAGE AND BETTERTON TO FORBES
SUPR III (132)	/DON JUAN/ WHY, TO BE ABLE TO CHOOSE THE	LINE	OF GREATEST ADVANTAGE INSTEAD OF YIELDING IN THE
CAND I (81)	DISPARAGEMENT OF THE HOXTON ANARCHISTS IN EVERY	LINE	OF HER FACE. MORELL BURSTS OPEN THE COVER OF A COPY OF
LION PREFACE(84)	IN THAT DISLIKE WITHOUT EVER HAVING READ A	LINE	OF HIS OR WITNESSED ONE OF HIS PLAYS; BUT NOBODY WITH
DOCT PREFACE(41)	UNDERTAKEN BY THE VIVISECTORS. THEY MIGHT OPEN A	LINE	OF INVESTIGATION WHICH WOULD FINALLY MAKE, FOR
METH PREFACE(R68)	PRINCIPLE, BELIEVING THAT IF EVERYONE TAKES THE	LINE	OF LEAST MATERIAL RESISTANCE THE RESULT WILL BE THE
MIS. PREFACE(44)	REACHED, FROM THE BLINDEST GROPING ALONG THE	LINE	OF LEAST RESISTANCE TO CONSCIOUS INTELLECTUAL
LION PREFACE(84)	GENTILES THAN JEWS; AND IT WAS BY FOLLOWING THE	LINE	OF LEAST RESISTANCE THAT PAUL BECAME THE APOSTLE TO THE
MRS PREFACE(170)	THAT MEANS BY THE ORDINARY METHOD OF TAKING THE	LINE	OF LEAST RESISTANCE TO GETTING IT, ARE TOO COMMON IN
SUPR III (132)	BY MERELY WILLING TO LIVE AND FOLLOWING THE	LINE	OF LEAST RESISTANCE: NOW I WANT TO KNOW MYSELF AND MY
SUPR PREFACE(R24)	OF BLINDLY STUMBLING HITHER AND THITHER IN THE	LINE	OF LEAST RESISTANCE. HENCE THERE IS A DRIVING TOWARDS
METH PREFACE(R36)	MAKER OF THE MAKER OF GOD. I GRANT YOU AS LONG A	LINE	OF MAKERS AS YOU PLEASE; BUT AN INFINITY OF MAKERS IS
CLEO PRO2 (99)	WHEN THE WALL CAME NIGH, IT CHANGED INTO A	LINE	OF MEN-- COMMON FELLOWS ENOUGH, WITH HELMETS, LEATHER
APPL PREFACE(192)	ON IT FOR MAKING ELECTRICAL CONTACTS. EACH	LINE	OF RAILWAY HAD ON IT A TRUCK WITH A STEEL LID. THE
DOCT PREFACE(50)	AT NAVAL MANOEUVRES, IN ORDER TO FOLLOW UP THE	LINE	OF RESEARCH THUS ACCIDENTALLY DISCOVERED. THE TRUTH IS,
DEVL III (75)	AND STOP THE EXECUTION. (HE BURSTS THROUGH THE	LINE	OF SOLDIERS OPPOSITE BURGOYNE, AND RUSHES, PANTING, TO
NEVR I (206)	IF I SWERVE BY A HAIR'S BREADTH FROM THE STRAIGHT	LINE	OF THE MOST RIGID RESPECTABILITY, I'M DONE FOR. UNDER
WIDO III (61)	DR TRENCH. THE COUNTY COUNCIL MAY ALTER THE	LINE	OF THE NEW STREET. IF THAT HAPPENS, THE MONEY SPENT IN
METH PREFACE(R76)	FORTH BY A VIRGIN DESCENDED IN LIKE MANNER FROM A	LINE	OF VIRGINS RIGHT BACK TO EVE; THAT THE TRINITY IS AN
DOCT II (125)	GET WORK AT HIS DRAWING; AND HE NEVER WROTE ME A	LINE	OR SENT ME AN ADDRESS. I NEVER SAW NOR HEARD OF HIM
GETT (292)	THE EQUAL OF A CURATE, OR A LIEUTENANT IN A	LINE	REGIMENT THE EQUAL OF A GENERAL. /THE BISHOP/ OF COURSE
APPL PREFACE(182)	ORCHESTRA. IF PAUL HAD BEEN A LIEUTENANT IN A	LINE	REGIMENT WE SHOULD NEVER HAVE HEARD OF HIM. BUT WHEN

GETT (292) MYSELF. /THE GENERAL/ AND I WAS A LIEUTENANT IN A LINE REGIMENT. /REGINALD/ AND I WAS NOTHING. BUT WE'RE ALL
LION II (131) THE GLADIATORS RISE SMARTLY AND FORM INTO LINE). THE EMPEROR ENTERS ON THE CHRISTIANS' SIDE,
PYGM III (259) CASE; AND TRIES RESOLUTELY TO WRITE. AT THE THIRD LINE SHE GIVES IT UP; FLINGS DOWN HER PEN; GRIPS THE TABLE
CAND II SD(105) BUSY TO NOTICE EUGENE. WHEN SHE BEGINS THE SECOND LINE SHE STOPS AND STARES AT THE MACHINE. SOMETHING WRONG
POSN (454) STRONG FEELING AMONG THE MEN OF THIS TOWN THAT A LINE SHOULD BE DRAWN BETWEEN THOSE THAT ARE STRAIGHT WIVES
JOAN PREFACE(41) AS WE WILL; BUT SOCIETY MUST ALWAYS DRAW A LINE SOMEWHERE BETWEEN ALLOWABLE CONDUCT AND INSANITY OR
DOCT PREFACE(23) OF ITS SPECIFIC MICROBE. IF THIS WAS THE LINE TAKEN ABOUT SMALLPOX, THE MICROBE OF WHICH HAS NEVER
KING I (213) FORMS. THE LINE DRAWN BY THE ARTIST'S HAND, THE LINE THAT FLOWS, THAT STRIKES, THAT SPEAKS, THAT REVEALS!
BULL PREFACE(70) LINGUISTIC, OR MORAL BOUNDARIES: HE DEMANDS A LINE THAT HE CAN DEFEND, OR RATHER THAT NAPOLEON OR
DOCT PREFACE(45) THREATENS THE HOUSEHOLD. THAT DISTINCTION IS THE LINE THAT SEPARATES THE BRUTE FROM THE MAN IN THE OLD
KING I (213) STRIKES, THAT SPEAKS, THAT REVEALS! THAT IS THE LINE THAT SHEWS THE DIVINE HANDIWORK. /CHARLES/ SO YOU, TOO,
SUPR III SD(140) RESPECTABLE. KEEP IT UP, I TELL YOU. THE SOLDIERS LINE THE ROAD, COMMANDING THE AMPHITHEATRE WITH THEIR
MTH5 (234) AND A LIVING ORGANISM. I CANNOT DRAW THAT LINE TO MY OWN SATISFACTION. /MARTELLUS/ YOUR ARTIFICIAL MEN
DEVL III (61) RATHER-- IF YOU WILL EXCUSE THE WORD-- A VULGAR LINE TO TAKE? WHY SHOULD YOU CRY OUT ROBBERY BECAUSE OF A
PRES (134) IT, YOU SCATTER THEIR ATTACK OVER A CIRCULAR LINE TWELVE MILES LONG. JUST WHAT WELLINGTON WOULD HAVE
KING I (209) THAT EVERYTHING THAT MOVES MOVES IN A STRAIGHT LINE UNLESS SOME ALMIGHTY FORCE BENDS IT FROM ITS PATH.
O'FL PREFACE(203) DARE TO GO THROUGH WITH IT. I STILL THINK MY OWN LINE WAS THE MORE BUSINESSLIKE. BUT DURING THE WAR EVERYONE
JOAN PREFACE(29) SCHOOL, OR ANY OF THE OTHERS WHO CROSS THE LINE WE HAVE TO DRAW, RIGHTLY OR WRONGLY, BETWEEN THE
BULL III (142) CAR, PEDDY, FORTY MAWL AN AHR DAHN THAT ROCKY LINE WILL STRAWK IT PRETTY PINK, YOU BET. /MATTHEW/ (
APPL PREFACE(192) SPACIOUS ENOUGH TO ACCOMMODATE A DOUBLE RAILWAY LINE WITH A PLATFORM. THE AFFAIR WAS UNQUESTIONABLY REAL, SO
APPL II (269) MONARCHY, AND BRING THE BRITISH COMMONWEALTH INTO LINE WITH ALL THE OTHER GREAT POWERS TODAY AS A REPUBLIC? (
KING I (212) BOOK IN HAND: ONE WHICH SHOULD PLACE ME IN LINE WITH KEPLER, COPERNICUS, AND GALILEO AS A MASTER
LION PREFACE(73) ARE STILL MATTERS OF CONTROVERSY, THEY ARE ALL IN LINE WITH THE BEST MODERN THOUGHT. HE TOLD US WHAT WE HAVE
NEVR III SD(261) BURTON AND STACY MARKS; THE SADDLEBAG OTTOMAN IN LINE WITH THE DOOR BUT ON THE OTHER SIDE OF THE ROOM; THE
GETT PREFACE(258) OF WOMEN. WE ALSO HAVE TO BRING OURSELVES INTO LINE WITH THE REST OF PROTESTANT CIVILIZATION BY PROVIDING
MTH2 (86) COME ON, BURGE: YOU MUST REALLY TELL ME WHAT LINE YOU ARE GOING TO TAKE ABOUT THE CHURCH AT THE
CAND I (91) YOU AD THE RIGHT INSTINC ARTER ALL, JAMES: THE LINE YOU TOOK IS THE PAYIN LINE IN THE LONG RUN FOR A MAN O
GENV IV (129) JUDGE OF THAT. YOU HAVE DONE A GOOD DEAL IN THAT LINE YOURSELF. /BATTLER/ WE ALL HAVE. BUT I CLAIM TO HAVE
KING I (209) OF ME, OF ME! THAT A RIGHT LINE IS A STRAIGHT LINE , AND THAT EVERYTHING THAT MOVES MOVES IN A STRAIGHT
DOCT PREFACE(59) HIS COLLEAGUES, I AM OUT OF MY DEPTH AT THE FIRST LINE , BECAUSE MATHEMATICS ARE TO ME ONLY A CONCEPT: I NEVER
BARB I (266) PERHAPS THAT SORT OF THING ISNT IN YOUR LINE , EH? /UNDERSHAFT/ I AM PARTICULARLY FOND OF MUSIC.
ROCK I (199) CAN MAKE A POINT OF THAT. PUT DOWN IN A SEPARATE LINE , IN RED CAPITALS, " ONE MAN ONE WIFE." LET ME SEE NOW:
BARB I (268) GETTING INTO HEAVEN IS NOT EXACTLY IN YOUR LINE , IS IT? /LADY BRITOMART/ CHARLES! ! ! /LOMAX/
MIS. PREFACE(106) COLUMNS, OUTWITTED THEM WITH THE THIN RED LINE , NOT OF HEROES, BUT, AS THIS UNCOMPROMISING REALIST
SUPR IV (155) NOW WHETHER MENDOZA'S A MINE, OR A STEAMBOAT LINE , OR A BANK, OR A PATENT ARTICLE-- /TANNER/ HE'S A MAN.
MTH2 (44) /THE PARLOR MAID/ (WARNINGLY) HE IS HOLDING THE LINE , SIR. /FRANKLYN/ YES: ALL RIGHT (HE HURRIES OUT). THE
KING I (210) /KNELLER/ SIR: I DO NOT SAY: I KNOW. THE RIGHT LINE , THE LINE OF BEAUTY, IS A CURVE. MY HAND WILL NOT DRAW
METH PREFACE(R63) OF DARWINISM. LONG BEFORE DARWIN PUBLISHED A LINE , THE RICARDO-MALTHUSIAN ECONOMISTS WERE PREACHING THE
3PLA PREFACE(R36) A PRODIGIOUS COMMAND OF LANGUAGE AND OF GRAPHIC LINE , WE CAN THINK OF NOBODY BETTER THAN SHAKESPEAR AND
BASH PREFACE(89) WOULD CHUCKLE DELIGHTEDLY OVER IT ALMOST LINE BY LINE , WHILST THE ORDINARY PLAYGOERS WOULD LISTEN WITH A
FANY PROLOG (263) THATS ONLY HIS MODESTY, BECAUSE ART IS HIS OWN LINE , YOU UNDERSTAND. MIND YOU DONT CHAFF HIM ABOUT
PYGM IV (265) THAT IS, TO THE PEOPLE IN THE MARRYING LINE , YOU UNDERSTAND. YOU GO TO BED AND HAVE A GOOD NICE
PHIL III (145) NO LITTLE ONES, NOTHING AT ALL IN CUTHBERTSON'S LINE ! NOBODY WILL MARRY ME-- UNLESS YOU, SYLVIA: EH?

LINED

CLEO V SD(195) ATTIRE, ARE LIKE A FLOWER GARDEN. THE FACADE IS LINED BY HER GUARD, OFFICERED BY THE SAME GALLANTS TO WHOM
CLEO V SD(195) PALACE ON THE SYRIAN BORDER. THE NORTH SIDE IS LINED BY ROMAN SOLDIERS, WITH THE TOWNSFOLK ON TIPTOE BEHIND
JOAN 2,SD(80) OF THE ROOM; AND A CLEAR PATH ACROSS IS KEPT AND LINED BY THE COURTIERS. CHARLES IS IN THIS PATH IN THE
CLEO IV SD(166) THE HARPIST'S MASTER, AN OLD MUSICIAN, WITH A LINED FACE, PROMINENT BROWS, WHITE BEARD, MOUSTACHE AND
NEVR I SD(201) COTTA CASHMERE, THE ELEGANTLY CUT FROCK COAT LINED IN BROWN SILK, AND CARRIES IN HIS HAND A BROWN TALL
DOCT I SD(84) AND CONDITIONS OF MEN. HIS FACE IS A GOOD DEAL LINED ; HIS MOVEMENTS ARE SLOWER THAN, FOR INSTANCE,
WIDO III SD(51) HE IS IN EVENING DRESS, WITH AN OVERCOAT LINED THROUGHOUT WITH FURS PRESENTING ALL THE HUES OF THE
PHIL II SD(94) RUNNING ROUND THEM, THE SPACE ABOVE THE DIVANS LINED WITH BOOKS. A LONG SETTEE FACES THE FIRE. ALONG THE
KING I SD(161) FROM THE GARDEN. INSIDE THE ROOM THE WALLS ARE LINED WITH CUPBOARDS BELOW AND BOOKSHELVES ABOVE. TO THE
CAND I SD(93) AS TO THE BENT OF WHICH HIS BROW, ALREADY LINED WITH PITY, IS REASSURING. HE IS SO UNCOMMON AS TO BE
2TRU III SD(94) AND A SUN UMBRELLA, A SUBSTANTIAL AFFAIR OF FAWN LINED WITH RED, PODGILY ROLLED UP, WHICH HE CARRIES IN HIS
WIDO II SD(24) THE DOOR IS IN THE MIDDLE. ALL THE WALLS ARE LINED WITH SHELVES OF SMARTLY TOOLED BOOKS, FITTING INTO
MTH4 II (189) A SALUTE OF A HUNDRED AND ONE GUNS! THE STREETS LINED WITH TROOPS! THE GUARDS TURNED OUT AT THE PALACE!
PHIL I SD(84) GREATLY IN EXPRESSION. THE COLONEL'S FACE IS LINED WITH WEATHER, WITH AGE, WITH EATING AND DRINKING, AND
GETT SD(323) INDOMITABLE CHIN; BUT HER CHEEKS ARE WASTED AND LINED , HER MOUTH WRITHEN AND PITEOUS. THE WHOLE FACE IS A

LINEN

BARB III (348) IT WAS THE HOUSES AND THE KITCHEN RANGES AND THE LINEN AND CHINA, WHEN IT WAS REALLY ALL THE HUMAN SOULS TO
MTH1 II SD(20) TWO ARE SCANTILY AND CARELESSLY DRESSED IN ROUGH LINEN AND LEAVES. THEY HAVE LOST THEIR YOUTH AND GRACE; AND
PYGM II SD(217) BLACK FROCK-COAT WITH A WHITE LINEN COLLAR AND BLACK SILK TIE. HE IS OF THE ENERGETIC,
MTH4 I SD(139) LEATHER BOOTS WITH WHITE SPATS. HIS STARCHED LINEN CUFFS PROTRUDE FROM HIS COAT SLEEVES; AND HIS COLLAR,
NEVR I (204) CLOTH LIMP, HALF A DOLLAR. /PHILIP/ OR MOUNTED ON LINEN FOR HARD FAMILY USE, TWO DOLLARS. NO FAMILY SHOULD BE
6CAL SD(98) GAG HIM, GOGSWOONS, GAG HIM. THEY TEAR A PIECE OF LINEN FROM THE BACK OF HIS SHIRT, AND BIND HIS MOUTH WITH
APPL I (223) IF YOU DO. NO GOOD WILL COME OF WASHING OUR DIRTY LINEN IN PUBLIC. BUT DONT MAKE ANY MISTAKE AS TO WHAT WILL
SUPR IV SD(142) AND A BLACK NECKTIE TIED INTO A BOW OVER SPOTLESS LINEN . PROBABLY THEREFORE A MAN WHOSE SOCIAL POSITION NEEDS
MTH5 SD(205) AS HE SLOWLY DESCENDS THEM, EXCEPT FOR A SORT OF LINEN KILT CONSISTING MAINLY OF A GIRDLE CARRYING A SPORRAN
GETT PREFACE(258) IS THAT CASES ARE MANUFACTURED AND CLEAN LINEN PURPOSELY SMIRCHED AND WASHED IN PUBLIC, TO THE GREAT
6CAL (104) MEND YOUR MANNERS FIRST, SIR; AND THEN MEND YOUR LINEN ; OR YOU SHALL HAVE NO COUNTENANCE FROM ME. /PETER/ I
CAPT I SD(217) A CHEAP PIN IN IT. HE WEARS A SUIT OF CLEAN WHITE LINEN , ACCEPTABLE IN COLOR, IF NOT IN CUT, TO THE MOORISH
BARB III (330) UNDERSHAFT INHERITANCE; BUT ALL THAT PLATE AND LINEN , ALL THAT FURNITURE AND THOSE HOUSES AND ORCHARDS AND
GETT PREFACE(236) FROM A PROFANATION, NO MORE WASHING OF HOUSEHOLD LINEN , DIRTY OR CLEAN, IN PUBLIC. WE MUST LEARN IN THESE
MTH4 I SD(139) SLEEVES; AND HIS COLLAR, ALSO OF STARCHED WHITE LINEN , IS GLADSTONIAN. ON HIS RIGHT, THREE OR FOUR FULL
WIDO II SD(25) HE IS A SHABBY, NEEDY MAN, WITH DIRTY FACE AND LINEN , SCRUBBY BEARD AND WHISKERS, GOING BALD. A NERVOUS,

LINENDRAPER

MIS. (135) HIMSELF BY SAYING, " AFTER ALL, HES ONLY A LINENDRAPER ." BUT AT LAST ONE DAY HE SAID TO ME, " JOHN IS
MIS. (201) FOR FOUR GENERATIONS. AND THIS ENGLISHMAN! THIS LINENDRAPER ! HE DARES TO ASK ME TO COME AND LIVE WITH HIM

LINENDRAPERISH

MIS. (161) THINKING THAT THESE THINGS MATTER SO MUCH. IT'S LINENDRAPERISH . /TARLETON/ YOURE QUITE RIGHT. IVE OFTEN

LINENDRAPER'S

MIS. (141) FALL IN LOVE WITH ME AS YOU. YOU KNOW I'M ONLY A LINENDRAPER'S DAUGHTER WHEN ALL'S SAID. I WAS AFRAID OF YOU:

LINER

DOCT III (141) THEIR OUTCRY) SHE WAS MARRIED TO THE STEWARD OF A LINER . HE CLEARED OUT AND LEFT HER; AND SHE THOUGHT, POOR
HART PREFACE(5) A GONDOLA MIGHT REFUSE TO RECOGNIZE A 20,000-TON LINER . IN SHORT, POWER AND CULTURE WERE IN SEPARATE
APPL PREFACE(190) CAESAR'S GALLEY COULD DO THE WORK OF AN ATLANTIC LINER . WE NEED IN THESE ISLANDS TWO OR THREE ADDITIONAL
HART PREFACE(20) SUDDENLY THERE CAME THE NEWS THAT AN ATLANTIC LINER , THE LUSITANIA, HAD BEEN TORPEDOED, AND THAT SEVERAL

LINERS

SIM PRO2, (26) /THE E.O./ I SHOULD THINK IT IS. THE BIGGEST LINERS CAN GET CLOSE UP. LIKE PLYMOUTH. LIKE LULWORTH COVE.
2TRU PREFACE(11) TO OUR PALACE HOTELS. COME ROUND THE WORLD IN OUR LINERS . COME AND WALLOW IN OUR SWIMMING POOLS. COME AND SEE
2TRU PREFACE(11) THE RICH TOURISTS IN THE PALACE HOTELS AND LUXURY LINERS JUST AS THEY DO TO THE TRAMPS ON THE HIGHROAD. THEY

LINES

DEVL III (74) IS TOO LATE) HOW IS THIS? WHY IS SHE INSIDE THE LINES ? /SERGEANT/ (GUILTILY) I DUNNO, SIR. SHE'S THAT
ROCK I (200) THIS MORNING! FULL OF IT. /HILDA/ AND THREE LINES ABOUT THE UNEMPLOYED, THOUGH I WAS TWENTY MINUTES LATE
SUPR HANDBOK(199) AS EVIL IS UNDONE AND REPLACED BY GOOD ON THE LINES ALONG WHICH WE ARE EVOLVING. THIS IS INDEED THE
SUPR HANDBOK(199) RECOVER THE LOST GROUND; ABOVE ALL, THAT ON THE LINES ALONG WHICH WE ARE DEGENERATING, GOOD HAS BECOME EVIL
MTH5 (253) /ECRASIA/ NO LIMBS, NO CONTOURS, NO EXQUISITE LINES AND ELEGANT SHAPES, NO WORSHIP OF BEAUTIFUL BODIES, NO
LADY PREFACE(229) LET US BE HONEST. AS POLITICAL SENTIMENTS THESE LINES ARE AN ABOMINATION TO EVERY DEMOCRAT. BUT SUPPOSE THEY

KING I (220) FOR YOU; AND THE KING EXPECTS YOU. /NEWTON/ THE LINES ARE NOT STRAIGHT, MR KNELLER. GRAVITATION BENDS THEM.
LION PREFACE(47) CAN, AND DISBELIEVE WHAT HE MUST. IF HE DRAWS ANY LINES AT ALL, THEY WILL BE QUITE ARBITRARY ONES. ST JOHN
BUOY PREFACE(6) WHY MOVING BODIES DID NOT MOVE IN STRAIGHT LINES AWAY INTO SPACE. NEWTON WAS NO FARTHER OFF THE
SUPR III (85) TO TANNER-- /MENDOZA/ JUST ALLOW ME TO READ A FEW LINES BEFORE YOU GO TO SLEEP. I SHOULD REALLY LIKE YOUR
CLEO III (144) ARE YOU DREAMING OF? SINCE I CAME THROUGH THE LINES BEYOND THE THEATRE THERE, I HAVE BROUGHT MY CARAVAN
PLES PREFACE(R7) AVENUE THEATRE IN LONDON FOR A SEASON ON THE NEW LINES BY MISS A.E.F. HORNIMAN, WHO HAD FAMILY REASONS FOR
CAND I SD(77) WITH UGLY IRON URINALS, RADICAL CLUBS, AND TRAM LINES CARRYING A PERPETUAL STREAM OF YELLOW CARS; ENJOYING
BASH PREFACE(89) ELIZABETHAN MANNERISM, AND FUNNY ECHOES OF PET LINES FROM THE ELIZABETHAN PLAYWRIGHTS WERE, AS SUCH, QUITE
LADY PREFACE(214) SAY ABOUT IT, JUST AS HE USED TO SUBMIT DIFFICULT LINES FROM THE SONNETS, THIS SURMISE WAS THAT " SIDNEY'S
KING I (205) ALL I CAN SAY IS THAT WHEN MONTEZUMA SPEAKS THOSE LINES HE DROPS DEAD. /FOX/ CAN YOU WONDER THAT HE DOES SO..
METH PREFACE(R11) A SCOPE SO UNPREDICTABLE, THAT AS I WRITE THESE LINES IN 1920, IT IS STILL FAR FROM CERTAIN WHETHER OUR
BUOY IV (59) MERE NAMES INCIDENTALLY IMMORTALIZED BY A FEW LINES IN A GREAT POEM? /MRS THIRDBORN/ THEY HAD HEARTS,
DOCT II (124) I COULD RUN UPSTAIRS AND GET YOU MY MARRIAGE LINES IN A MINUTE, SIR, IF YOU DOUBT MY WORD. HE'S MR LOUIS
DOCT I SD(84) THE YOUNG MAN THAN THE TITLED PHYSICIAN. EVEN THE LINES IN HIS FACE ARE THOSE OF OVERWORK AND RESTLESS
BULL PREFACE(48) BE, AS THE LATE LAUREATE SAID IN THE TWO STINGING LINES IN WHICH HE BRANDED THE BRITISH SOLDIER WITH THE
PYGM PREFACE(201) AND YET THE SHORTHAND IN WHICH I AM WRITING THESE LINES IS PITMAN'S, AND THE REASON IS, THAT MY SECRETARY
AUGS (272) OF MY OWN COUNTRY AS I MADE MY WAY BACK TO OUR LINES . A SHOT FROM OUR FRONT TRENCH STRUCK ME IN THE HEAD.
CLEO V SD(196) THE SOLDIERS STAND AT ATTENTION, AND DRESS THEIR LINES . APOLLODORUS GOES TO THE EGYPTIAN LINE. /CENTURION/ (
METH PREFACE(R36) OF COURSE WE COULD GET NO FURTHER ON THESE LINES . HE ROSE AND SAID THAT WE WERE LIKE TWO MEN WORKING A
SUPR PREFACE(R9) WITH THE MOST EXTRAVAGANT FLOURISHES BETWEEN THE LINES . I AM NOT SURE THAT THIS IS NOT A PORTENT OF
SHAK (141) ECLIPSED THY SHARDBORNE BEETLE. HEAR HIS MIGHTY LINES . (RECITING) " THE BEETLE BOOMS ADOWN THE GLOOMS AND
GETT (309) ANYONE WHO WILL NOT ADVISE US FRANKLY ON CLASS LINES . MARRIAGE IS GOOD ENOUGH FOR THE LOWER CLASSES: THEY
CLEO III (149) ORDER WE DARE NOT LET YOU PASS BEYOND THE ROMAN LINES . /APOLLODORUS/ WELL, CENTURION; AND HAS NOT THE
DOCT III (138) BLUFFING, DUBEDAT. WEVE SEEN MINNIE'S MARRIAGE LINES . /LOUIS/ (COOLLY) INDEED? HAVE YOU SEEN
KING I (220) GO HOME. I CANNOT EAT IN THIS HOUSE OF STRAIGHT LINES . /MRS BASHAM/ YOU WILL DO NOTHING OF THE SORT, MR
PYGM I (214) IN PHONETICS, AND A LITTLE AS A POET ON MILTONIC LINES . /THE GENTLEMAN/ I AM MYSELF A STUDENT OF INDIAN
MIS. PREFACE(31) VILLAGE IN HERTFORDSHIRE WHERE I WRITE THESE LINES . SHE ASKED ME VERY PROPERLY WHAT I WAS GOING TO DO
ROCK PREFACE(169) DIFFERENCES COULD BE SETTLED ON GIVE-AND-TAKE LINES . THE DIVISION OF SOCIETY INTO CLASSES WITH DIFFERENT
APPL PREFACE(194) RAIL AND ROAD WITH THE SHORE AND THE GREAT MAIN LINES . THE SHIPS WOULD COME ALONGSIDE THE PIER; AND BY A
UNPL PREFACE(R21) THE FOLIO GIVES US HARDLY ANYTHING BUT THE BARE LINES . WHAT WOULD WE NOT GIVE FOR THE COPY OF HAMLET USED
KING I (205) THE THEATRE OR SHAME IT INTO DECENCY; BUT THESE LINES JUST UTTERED BY ELEANOR GWYN ARE NOT PROFANE AND
DOCT I SD(100) CHEAPLY FED AND CHEAPLY CLOTHED. HE HAS THE LINES MADE BY A CONSCIENCE BETWEEN HIS EYES, AND THE LINES
DOCT I SD(100) MADE BY A CONSCIENCE BETWEEN HIS EYES, AND THE LINES MADE BY CONTINUAL MONEY WORRIES ALL OVER HIS FACE, CUT
DEVL I (13) PRETTY TASTE IN DRESS, AND IN HER FACE THE PRETTY LINES OF A SENTIMENTAL CHARACTER FORMED BY DREAMS. EVEN HER
SIM PREFACE(5) BEEN INVENTED AND IMPOSED ON US TO SECURE CERTAIN LINES OF BEHAVIOR AS EITHER DESIRABLE FOR THE GENERAL GOOD
UNPL PREFACE(R22) PLAY UNDERSTANDS ALL BUT HALF A DOZEN UNIMPORTANT LINES OF IT WITHOUT DIFFICULTY; WHILST MANY MODERN PLAYS,
LION PREFACE(33) GIFT FOR HIS ART. BEFORE YOU HAVE READ TWENTY LINES OF LUKE'S GOSPEL YOU ARE AWARE THAT YOU HAVE PASSED
CYMB FORWORD(135) BE MURDERED, HE BEGINS TO CRITICIZE, QUITE ON THE LINES OF MRS ALVING IN GHOSTS, THE SLAVERY TO AN INHUMAN
MRS III SD(225) WATCHES THEM UNTIL THEY HAVE GONE, WITH ALL THE LINES OF PURPOSE IN HER FACE MARKING IT STRONGLY. /FRANK/
PHIL I SD(84) OF PLEASURE AND NOVELTY. CUTHBERTSON HAS THE LINES OF SEDENTARY LONDON BRAIN WORK, WITH ITS CHRONIC
CYMB FORWORD(136) THE SHAKESPEAREAN VERSE PATTERN TO MATCH THE 89 LINES OF SHAKESPEAR'S TEXT WHICH I RETAINED. THIS CAME VERY
CYMB FORWORD(136) SHAKESPEAR, WITH A PICTURE AND TWO OR THREE LINES OF TEXT UNDERNEATH IT ON EVERY THIRD OR FOURTH PAGE.
LADY PREFACE(220) IN EXCELSIS. THERE WAS MORE LAUGHTER BETWEEN THE LINES OF THAT BOOK THAN IN A THOUSAND FARCES BY MEN OF NO
BULL PREFACE(18) NOT WANT TO IMITATE. HOW CAN I SKETCH THE BROAD LINES OF THE CONTRAST AS THEY STRIKE ME? ROUGHLY I SHOULD
POSN PREFACE(366) IT THEMSELVES, AND AS IT CAN BE READ BETWEEN THE LINES OF THEIR EVIDENCE WHEN ONCE THE READER HAS THE CLUE.
3PLA PREFACE(R10) IN THE MODERN METROPOLITAN AUDIENCE. IN THE LONG LINES OF WAITING PLAYGOERS LINING THE PAVEMENTS OUTSIDE OUR
MILL PREFACE(115) THOUGH HE COULD FIGHT BATTLES ON ACADEMIC LINES ONLY, AND WAS ON THAT POINT A ROUTINEER SOLDIER, HE
LADY PREFACE(226) GREATLY MATTER WHETHER HE WROTE THE LOUSY LUCY LINES OR NOT, AND DOES NOT REALLY MATTER AT ALL WHETHER HE
SUPR PREFACE(R17) IS NOW MORE HAMLET THAN DON JUAN; FOR THOUGH THE LINES PUT INTO THE ACTOR'S MOUTH TO INDICATE TO THE PIT THAT
KING PREFACE(154) IS IN PRINCIPLE RECTILINEAR, HE CALLED STRAIGHT LINES RIGHT LINES; AND THEY WERE STILL SO CALLED IN MY
CLEO V (196) (HE HURRIES TO HIS POST IN FRONT OF THE EGYPTIAN LINES). /BELZANOR/ (FOLLOWING HIM) HO THERE! CAESAR
CATH 2,SD(174) HASTILY CEASE WHISPERING; DRESS UP THEIR LINES ; AND STIFFEN. DEAD SILENCE. A BELL TINKLES WITHIN THE
KING PREFACE(154) RECTILINEAR. HE CALLED STRAIGHT LINES RIGHT LINES ; AND THEY WERE STILL SO CALLED IN MY SCHOOL EUCLID
DOCT III (139) I ONLY ASKED YOU HAD YOU SEEN JENNIFER'S MARRIAGE LINES ; AND YOU CONCLUDED STRAIGHT AWAY THAT SHE HADNT GOT
DEVL III (74) HAND) HERE, MADAM: YOU HAD BETTER KEEP INSIDE THE LINES ; BUT STAND HERE BEHIND US; AND DONT LOOK. RICHARD,
KING I (212) OF BARBARA'S CURVES AND A UNIVERSE OF STRAIGHT LINES SEDUCED FROM THEIR STRAIGHTNESS BY SOME PURELY
CLEO III (149) AND HAS NOT THE LIGHTHOUSE BEEN WITHIN THE ROMAN LINES SINCE CAESAR LANDED THERE? /CLEOPATRA/ YES, YES.
SUPR III (84) TO WHAT I FEEL FOR LOUISA, LET ME READ YOU SOME LINES THAT I HAVE WRITTEN ABOUT HER MYSELF. HOWEVER SLIGHT
MIS. PREFACE(45) WALKING IN THE SAME DARKNESS. AS I WRITE THESE LINES THE HOME SECRETARY IS EXPLAINING THAT HE MUST NOT
METH PREFACE(R27) IN THE FACE IN ALL DIRECTIONS. AS I WRITE THESE LINES THE NEWSPAPERS ARE OCCUPIED BY THE EXPLOITS OF A CHILD
SUPR III (85) THERE IS NO MERIT IN PRODUCING BEAUTIFUL LINES UPON SUCH A NAME. LOUISA IS AN EXQUISITE NAME, IS IT
FABL V (120) WAS ONLY FORTY CENTURIES OLD AND THAT STRAIGHT LINES WERE ETHICALLY RIGHT; BUT THE UTMOST THAT WE KNOW IS
LADY PREFACE(220) TO AVENGE ITS TEARS OF DISCOURAGEMENT, IN THE LINES WHICH MR HARRIS QUOTES ONLY TO DECLARE THAT HE CAN
METH PREFACE(R24) ELABORATE FORMS OF ORGANIZED LIFE ON LAMARCKIAN LINES WITHOUT THE INTERVENTION OF CIRCUMSTANTIAL SELECTION
MRS PREFACE(168) THIS JUST AS THEY MIGHT SAY THAT NO TWO STRAIGHT LINES WOULD ENCLOSE A SPACE, THEY DO NOT SEE HOW COMPLETELY
BARB PREFACE(237) THE VICTIMS OF ITS VIOLENCE. AS I WRITE THESE LINES , A SENSATIONAL EXAMPLE IS GIVEN TO THE WORLD. A ROYAL
DOCT I SD(93) IN COMPARISON WITH RIDGEON'S DELICATE BROKEN LINES , AND SIR PATRICK'S SOFTLY RUGGED AGED ONES, HIS FACE
METH PREFACE(R49) OF WHAT I AM DOING; THAT MY WRITING OF THESE LINES , AND YOUR READING OF THEM, ARE EFFECTS OF
BUOY 1 (10) RATHER DISREPUTABLE CLUBS AND WORKING ON YOUR OWN LINES , AS YOU CALLED THEM, AS IT WAS, YOU DID NOT DISGRACE
KING I (212) IN THEIR ETERNAL MOTION DO NOT MOVE IN STRAIGHT LINES , BUT ALWAYS IN ELLIPSES? /CHARLES/ I UNDERSTAND THAT
METH PREFACE(R36) INSOLUBLE AND EVEN UNTHINKABLE ON CAUSATION LINES , COULD NOT BE A CAUSATION PROBLEM. TO PIOUS PEOPLE
KING I (166) CURVES SMALL ENOUGH TO COUNT AS STRAIGHT LINES , DISTANCES BETWEEN TWO POINTS THAT ARE IN THE SAME
KING I (209) YOUR KING. /KNELLER/ IF THERE IS A SCIENCE OF LINES , DO I NOT UNDERSTAND IT BETTER THAN ANYONE?
UNPL PREFACE(R21) IF SHAKESPEAR, INSTEAD OF MERELY WRITING OUT HIS LINES , HAD PREPARED THE PLAYS FOR PUBLICATION IN
GETT (302) I NEVER ASKED MY MOTHER TO SHEW ME HER MARRIAGE LINES , IF THATS WHAT YOU MEAN. WHAT MAN EVER HAS? I NEVER
POSN PREFACE(393) OF EVERY PLAY. ONE AUTHOR-- THE WRITER OF THESE LINES , IN FACT-- HAS LONG DESIRED TO DRAMATIZE THE LIFE OF
CLEO III (150) IF HE DRAWS HIS SWORD AGAIN INSIDE THE LINES , KILL HIM. TO YOUR POSTS. MARCH. HE GOES OUT, LEAVING
CLEO III (149) CONVINCED THAT WE DO NOT WANT TO GO BEYOND THE LINES , LET ME FINISH KILLING YOUR SENTINEL AND DEPART WITH
KING I (204) IF ONLY MR DRYDEN HAD GIVEN ME SOME REALLY GREAT LINES , LIKE THE ONES HE GAVE TO MONTEZUMA. LISTEN. STILL
3PLA PREFACE(R25) THAT THE MELODRAMA WAS BUILT ON VERY SAFE OLD LINES , OR THAT THE AMERICAN PUBLIC IS COMPOSED EXCLUSIVELY
ROCK I (196) IF YOU WANT THESE CROWDS SETTLED ON SOLDIERLY LINES , SAY SO; AND GIVE ME HALF A DOZEN MACHINE GUNS. THE
LION PREFACE(94) DID NOT WRANGLE ABOUT IT: HE PROVED, ON THE SAME LINES , THAT THE CAMPAIGNS OF NAPOLEON WERE IMPOSSIBLE. ONLY
MTH5 SD(205) FULLY AND FIRMLY FLESHED, BEARS A NETWORK OF LINES , VARYING FROM FURROWS TO HAIR-BREADTH RETICULATIONS,

LINGER

JOAN 5 (110) THE BELLS COME DOWN FROM HEAVEN, AND THE ECHOES LINGER , OR IN THE FIELDS, WHERE THEY COME FROM A DISTANCE

LINGERED

GENV PREFACE(9) THAT WHEN WE PLAYED IT THE WAR, WHICH STILL LINGERED IN JAPAN, WAS BROUGHT TO AN ABRUPT STOP BY AN

LINGERING

DEVL I (12) LOCKS, POCKETING THE KEY CAREFULLY). /CHRISTY/ (LINGERING AT THE FIRE) YOUD BETTER PUT THE INKSTAND INSTEAD,
JITT II (34) THE BEST OF IT) STILL, I AM NOT SURE THAT A LINGERING DEATH REALLY SPARES THE FEELINGS OF THE SURVIVORS.
BARB PREFACE(238) PLAGUE, PESTILENCE AND FAMINE, BATTLE, MURDER AND LINGERING DEATH-- PERHAPS NOT ONE WHO HAD NOT HELPED,
SUPR IV SD(150) OH, PLEASE DONT MAKE A SCENE. ANN AND OCTAVIUS, LINGERING NEAR THE GATE, EXCHANGE AN ASTONISHED GLANCE, AND
FANY II (287) DOWN, JO, QUICK. CATCH HER: SAVE HER. /KNOX/ (LINGERING) SHE'S SHAKING HANDS WITH HIM: SHE'S COMING
METH PREFACE(R66) WE WERE QUITE SURE FOR THE MOMENT THAT WHATEVER LINGERING SUPERSTITION MIGHT HAVE DAUNTED THESE MEN OF THE

LINGERS

MIS. (191) OUT AFTER HER, HE PARTLY CLOSES THE DOOR AND LINGERS FOR A MOMENT TO WHISPER) MIND: I'M NOT KNUCKLING
LION PREFACE(9) THE VERBAL INFALLIBILITY OF " THE BOOK OF BOOKS" LINGERS MORE STRONGLY THAN ANYWHERE ELSE EXCEPT PERHAPS IN
CAND I (89) TOWARDS THE DOOR. MORELL MAKES NO SIGN. HE LINGERS). I DIDNT HEXPECT TO FIND A HUNFORGIVIN SPIRIT IN

LINGO

2TRU II (75) THAT NATIVE SERVANT OF YOURS IS NOT A NATIVE. HER LINGO IS A RIDICULOUS FRAUD. SHE IS AN ENGLISHWOMAN.
PYGM II (219) GOT ALL THE RECORDS I WANT OF THE LISSON GROVE LINGO ; AND I'M NOT GOING TO WASTE ANOTHER CYLINDER ON IT. (

LINGUAL

ROCK PREFACE(149) SHOULD EXTERMINATE THE LATIN RACE, AS BOTH THESE LINGUAL STOCKS ARE HOPELESSLY INTERBRED BY THIS TIME, SUCH A

LINGUIST

BARB PREFACE(207) IN THIS SIMPLE FAITH IN MY ACCOMPLISHMENT AS A LINGUIST AND MY ERUDITION AS A PHILOSOPHER, BUT I CANNOT

LINGUISTIC

BULL PREFACE(70) BECAUSE THE SOLDIER RECOGNIZES NO ETHNOGRAPHICAL, LINGUISTIC , OR MORAL BOUNDARIES: HE DEMANDS A LINE THAT HE
3PLA PREFACE(R36) SPECIAL FACULTY; ARTISTIC, MATHEMATICAL AND LINGUISTIC , WHO FOR LACK OF NEW IDEAS, OR INDEED OF ANY

LINING

3PLA PREFACE(R10) AUDIENCE. IN THE LONG LINES OF WAITING PLAYGOERS LINING THE PAVEMENTS OUTSIDE OUR FASHIONABLE THEATRES EVERY

LININGS

WIDO I SD(5) HE WEARS A LIGHT GREY FROCK-COAT WITH SILK LININGS , A WHITE HAT, AND A FIELD-GLASS SLUNG IN A NEW

LINK

FABL PREFACE(73) AS ALL OR NOTHINGS IN IBSEN'S BRAND. WHEN ONE LINK IN OUR MENTAL CHAIN SNAPPED WE DID NOT PICK UP THE
MIS. (189) OF A CHAIN IS NO GREATER THAN ITS WEAKEST LINK , BUT THE GREATNESS OF A POET IS THE GREATNESS OF HIS

LINKMEN

FABL PREFACE(84) DETECTIVES AND PRIZEFIGHTERS FOR POLICE, SIXPENNY LINKMEN FOR MUNICIPAL ELECTRIC LIGHTING, CADIS UNDER PALM

LINKS

BULL IV (173) EH? /KEEGAN/ YOU CANNOT BUILD YOUR GOLF LINKS AND HOTELS IN THE AIR. FOR THAT YOU MUST OWN OUR LAND.
BULL IV (179) TO OUR HAND. /KEEGAN/ WHICH IS THE MAKING OF GOLF LINKS AND HOTELS TO BRING IDLERS TO A COUNTRY WHICH WORKERS
FABL PREFACE(73) MENTAL CHAIN SNAPPED WE DID NOT PICK UP THE SOUND LINKS AND JOIN THEM. WE THREW THE CHAIN AWAY AS IF ALL ITS
FABL PREFACE(73) JOIN THEM, WE THREW THE CHAIN AWAY AS IF ALL ITS LINKS HAD SNAPPED. IF THE STORY OF NOAH'S ARK WAS A FABLE,
BULL IV (168) BE A JOLLY GOOD PLACE FOR A HOTEL AND A GOLF LINKS . FRIDAY TO TUESDAY, RAILWAY TICKET AND HOTEL ALL
ROCK II (281) LIVES AS WE PLEASE. A COTTAGE NEAR A GOOD GOLF LINKS SEEMS TO BE INDICATED. WHAT WOULD YOU LIKE? /LADY
BULL IV (177) CIVIL ENGINEERS; AND I HAVE NO DOUBT THE GOLF LINKS WILL BE A TRIUMPH OF YOUR ART. MR BROADBENT WILL GET
ROCK I (230) FOOZLED IT. THE ENGLISHMAN IS AT HIS BEST ON THE LINKS , AND AT HIS WORST IN THE CABINET. BUT WHAT YOUR
ROCK I (207) OVERWORKED AND I MUST TAKE A FORTNIGHT OFF ON THE LINKS , OR GO FOR A SEA VOYAGE. /LADY CHAVENDER/ SHE CHARGES

LINNAEUS

POSN PREFACE(382) WE STILL APPLY TO THE STAGE. THE WORKS OF LINNAEUS AND THE EVOLUTIONISTS OF 1790-1830, OF DARWIN,
METH PREFACE(R21) AND STOCK BREEDERS THEN LIVING WHO KNEW BETTER. LINNAEUS HIMSELF KNEW BETTER BEFORE HE DIED. IN THE LAST
METH PREFACE(R20) HAD HELD THE FIELD UNTIL THE TIME (1707-1778) OF LINNAEUS THE FAMOUS BOTANIST. IN THE MEANTIME THE MICROSCOPE
METH PREFACE(R21) AND DEVELOPED. BUT IT WAS STILL POSSIBLE FOR LINNAEUS TO BEGIN A TREATISE BY SAYING " THERE ARE JUST SO

LINNEUS

FABL PREFACE(73) THE MAN OF SCIENCE, KNEW BETTER THAN JOSHUA, AND LINNEUS AND DARWIN BETTER THAN MOSES, THEN EVERYTHING THAT

LION

LION (1) ANDROCLES AND THE LION : A FABLE PLAY
LION II (128) MUCH. THERE WILL BE NO PRETENDING ABOUT THE NEW LION : LET THAT BE ENOUGH FOR YOU. HE'S HUNGRY. /SPINTHO/ (
LION PROLOG (108) /ANDROCLES/ (QUAKING, BUT KEEPING BETWEEN THE LION AND MEGAERA) DONT YOU COME NEAR MY WIFE, DO YOU HEAR..
MTH1 II (22) KILL ME. I HAVE STRIVEN WITH A BOAR AND WITH A LION AS TO WHICH OF US SHOULD KILL THE OTHER. I HAVE STRIVEN
ARMS II (41) ON MY HUSBAND HAS BEEN TO MAKE HIM FEEL LIKE A LION BAULKED OF HIS PREY. IF HE DISCOVERS OUR SECRET, HE
LION II SD(143) AND PRAYS. THE GRATING RISES WITH A CLASH. THE LION BOUNDS INTO THE ARENA. HE RUSHES ROUND FRISKING IN HIS
LION PROLOG (109) JUST ONE MORE. JUST TO SHEW HOW THE BRAVE BIG LION CAN BEAR PAIN, NOT LIKE THE LITTLE CRYBABY CHRISTIAN
LION II (144) TREASON. YOUR CONDUCT IS MOST DISGRA -- (THE LION CHARGES AT HIM UP THE STAIRS) HELP! (HE DISAPPEARS.
LION II SD(143) UP HIS HANDS IN SUPPLICATION TO HEAVEN. THE LION CHECKS AT THE SIGHT OF ANDROCLES'S FACE. HE THEN STEALS
LION II (144) HIM. /THE EMPEROR/ I AM NOT AFRAID OF HIM. (THE LION CROUCHES, GROWLING. THE EMPEROR CLUTCHES ANDROCLES).
LION PROLOG (109) FACE AND CRIES) VELVET PAWS! VELVET PAWS! (THE LION DRAWS IN HIS CLAWS). THATS RIGHT. (HE EMBRACES THE
LION II (143) YELL, HE BREAKS OFF AS HE SEES ANDROCLES AND THE LION EMERGE FROM THE PASSAGE, WALTZING. HE BOLTS WILDLY UP
LION II SD(143) CROUCHES AND HIDES HIS FACE IN HIS HANDS. THE LION GATHERS HIMSELF FOR A SPRING, SWISHING HIS TAIL TO AND
LION II SD(144) HIS TOES AS A BRAKE. BEFORE HE CAN STOP HIM THE LION GETS HOLD OF THE TRAILING END OF THE EMPEROR'S ROBE .
LION PROLOG (108) DONT YOU COME NEAR MY WIFE, DO YOU HEAR? (THE LION GROANS. ANDROCLES CAN HARDLY STAND FOR TREMBLING).
LION II (145) ANGRY WITH YOU, TOMMY, IF YOU DONT LET GO. (THE LION GROWLS AGAIN). I'LL TELL YOU WHAT IT IS, SIR: HE THINKS
LION II (145) THEY TAKE IT FROM THE TONE OF YOUR VOICE. (THE LION GROWLS AND LASHES HIS TAIL). I THINK HE'S GOING TO
LION II (144) ROBE AT ONCE, SIR: WHERES YOUR MANNERS? (THE LION GROWLS AND WORRIES THE ROBE). DONT PULL IT AWAY FROM
LION II (145) BROOCH) FRIENDS! YOU INFERNAL SCOUNDREL (THE LION GROWLS) -- DONT LET HIM GO. CURSE THIS BROOCH! I CANT
LION II (145) TO TOUCH THE DIVINE PERSON OF THE EMPEROR. (THE LION GROWLS). /ANDROCLES/ OH DONT TALK LIKE THAT, SIR. HE
LION II (138) WHAT THAT MEANT? /THE CAPTAIN/ IT MEANT THAT THE LION HAD A CUR FOR HIS BREAKFAST. /LAVINIA/ IT MEANT MORE
LION PROLOG (108) IF I TAKE MY EYE OFF HIM, IT'S ALL UP. (THE LION HOLDS UP HIS WOUNDED PAW AND FLAPS IT PITEOUSLY BEFORE
CLEO II (131) MOUTH. /PTOLEMY/ (TURNING TO GO) IT IS NOT THE LION I FEAR, BUT (LOOKING AT RUFIO) THE JACKAL. (HE GOES
ROCK PREFACE(148) DOES NO MISCHIEF, AND CAGING HIM CRUELLY LIKE A LION IN A SHOW. HERE SOMEBODY IS SURE TO INTERJECT THAT
LION II SD(144) AND DOWN AGAIN ON THE OTHER SIDE, WITH THE LION IN HOT PURSUIT. ANDROCLES RUSHES AFTER THE LION;
LION I SD(126) DRAWING A WAGGON WITH A GREAT WOODEN CAGE AND THE LION IN IT, ARRIVE THROUGH THE CENTRAL ARCH.
LION II (130) HERE DOWN TO THE DENS WHEN WE WERE CHANGING THE LION INTO THE CAGE NEXT THE ARENA? /THE EDITOR/ NOBODY LET
LION PROL,SD(108) AND LIE STARING IN TERROR AT ONE ANOTHER. THE LION IS HEARD GROANING HEAVILY IN THE JUNGLE. /ANDROCLES/ (
LION I (126) DO YOU? WELL, I'LL TELL YOU SOMETHING. IF THE LION IS MENAGERIE SERVICE, THE LION'S DINNER IS MENAGERIE
LION PROLOG (108) SHE POINTS IN THE DIRECTION OF THE SLEEPING LION . HE STEALS CAUTIOUSLY TOWARDS THE SPOT INDICATED BY
LION II (138) BOLTED, AND RAN RIGHT INTO THE JAWS OF THE LION . I LAUGHED. I STILL LAUGH. /LAVINIA/ THEN YOU DONT
LION II (146) RETURN WITHOUT FEAR. CAESAR HAS TAMED THE LION . (ALL THE FUGITIVES STEAL CAUTIOUSLY IN. THE
LION II (142) PASSAGE) NUMBER TWELVE. THE CHRISTIAN FOR THE NEW LION . /ANDROCLES/ (RISING, AND PULLING HIMSELF SADLY
LION II (142) TRUE, TRUE: WE MUST HAVE SOMEBODY FOR THE NEW LION . /FERROVIUS/ THROW ME TO HIM. LET THE APOSTATE PERISH.
LION PROLOG (108) JUNGLE. /ANDROCLES/ (WHISPERING) DID YOU SEE? A LION . /MEGAERA/ (DESPAIRING) THE GODS HAVE SENT HIM TO
LION II (146) IS STRANGE THAT I, WHO FEAR NO MAN, SHOULD FEAR A LION . /THE CAPTAIN/ EVERY MAN FEARS SOMETHING, FERROVIUS.
LION II SD(143) HIMSELF ON HIS WRIST, LOOKS AFFRIGHTEDLY AT THE LION . THE LION LIMPS ON THREE PAWS, HOLDING UP THE OTHER AS
LION II (142) KEEPER/ CAESAR: I MUST HAVE ONE CHRISTIAN FOR THE LION . THE PEOPLE HAVE BEEN PROMISED IT; AND THEY WILL TEAR
SUPR HANDBOK(198) JUST AS THE SAME QUALITIES WHICH MAKE THE LION KING IN THE FOREST ENSURE HIS DESTRUCTION WHEN HE
LION II SD(145) OH, WHAT AN ABOMINABLE SMELL OF GARLIC! THE LION LETS GO THE ROBE AND ROLLS OVER ON HIS BACK, CLASPING
LION PROLOG (109) UM'S DEAR OLD FRIEND ANDY WANDY. (THE LION LICKS HIS FACE). YES, KISSUMS ANDY WANDY. (THE LION,
LION PROL,SD(105) COMES FROM THE JUNGLE. IT IS REPEATED NEARER. THE LION LIMPS FROM THE JUNGLE ON THREE LEGS, HOLDING UP HIS
LION II SD(143) ON HIS WRIST, LOOKS AFFRIGHTEDLY AT THE LION. THE LION LIMPS ON THREE PAWS, HOLDING UP THE OTHER AS IF IT WAS
LION EPILOG (152) THAT YOU WERE AS CRUEL AS THE PEOPLE WHO LET THE LION LOOSE ON THE MAN, YOU WOULD BE JUSTLY INDIGNANT. NOW
CLEO V (200) IT WOULD KILL ME. WHAT DOES THIS PARABLE OF THE LION MEAN? /RUFIO/ WHY, CLEOPATRA HAD A TIGRESS THAT KILLED
PYGM EPILOG (293) FOR THEM IN SELECTING THEIR FRIENDS. WHEN A LION MEETS ANOTHER WITH A LOUDER ROAR " THE FIRST LION
LION PROLOG (109) LITTLE CHRISTIAN MAN HURT THE SORE PAW? (THE LION MOANS ASSENTINGLY BUT APOLOGETICALLY). WELL, ONE MORE
LION PROLOG (109) INFLAMMATION. SEE? (HE LICKS HIS OWN HAND. THE LION NODS INTELLIGENTLY AND LICKS HIS PAW INDUSTRIOUSLY).
LION II SD(143) TO PULL THE THORN OUT AND TO HURT HIMSELF. THE LION NODS REPEATEDLY. ANDROCLES HOLDS OUT HIS HANDS TO THE
LION II (144) AT HIM UP THE STAIRS) HELP! (HE DISAPPEARS. THE LION REARS AGAINST THE BOX; LOOKS OVER THE PARTITION AT HIM;
LION PROLOG (109) MAN'S NICE BIG TENDER WIFEY PIFEY. (THE LION RESPONDS BY MOANS OF SELF-PITY). YES, YES, YES, YES,
LION PROLOG (108) THAT. /MEGAERA/ OH, DONT TALK ABOUT EATING. (THE LION RISES WITH A GREAT GROAN AND LIMPS TOWARDS THEM). OH!
LION PROLOG (109) AFTER. (HE GIVES THE THORN ANOTHER PULL. THE LION ROARS AND SNAPS HIS JAWS WITH A TERRIFYING CLASH). OH,
LION II (145) WOULDNT MIND SAYING SOMETHING AFFECTIONATE. (THE LION ROARS). /THE EMPEROR/ (SHAKING ANDROCLES'S HANDS
LION II (144) BEFORE HE GIVES YOU HIS CONFIDENCE. (TO THE LION) COME NOW, TOMMY; AND SPEAK NICELY TO THE EMPEROR, THE
LION II (146) THE EMPEROR AND LOOKING DOWN WITH AWE ON THE LION) IT IS STRANGE THAT I, WHO FEAR NO MAN, SHOULD FEAR A
LION PROLOG (108) THE JUNGLE AND NEARLY FALLS OVER THE SLEEPING LION). OH! OH! ANDY! ANDY! (SHE TOTTERS BACK AND
LION II (144) THE DOOR AND DOWN TO ANDROCLES, PURSUED BY THE LION). /ANDORCLES/ DONT RUN AWAY, SIR: HE CANT HELP
LION II SD(144) LION IN HOT PURSUIT. ANDROCLES RUSHES AFTER THE LION ; OVERTAKES HIM AS HE IS DESCENDING; AND THROWS HIMSELF
LION II (131) ASLEEP? /THE EDITOR/ SAY NOTHING. GIVE YOUR OLD LION SOME BITTERS AND A MORSEL OF FRIED FISH TO WAKE UP HIS
LION II (147) AND THE GLADIATORS RUSH FOR ANDROCLES. THE LION STARTS UP AND FACES THEM. THEY SURGE BACK). YOU SEE HOW
SUPR HANDBOK(207) AND THEIR LIKE, MUST LIVE AS PRECARIOUSLY AS LION TAMERS DO, TAKING THE HUMOR OF THEIR SITUATION, AND THE

LION II (130)	/THE KEEPER/ SAVED HIM! SAVED HIM FROM A	LION	THAT I'D JUST GOT MAD WITH HUNGER! A WILD ONE THAT
CLEO V (199)	NUMIDIA TODAY. NOW TELL ME: IF YOU MEET A HUNGRY	LION	THERE, YOU WILL NOT PUNISH IT FOR WANTING TO EAT YOU..
PYGM EPILOG (293)	LION MEETS ANOTHER WITH A LOUDER ROAR " THE FIRST	LION	THINKS THE LAST A BORE." THE MAN OR WOMAN WHO FEELS
LION II (144)	THE WALL) SORCERER: I COMMAND YOU TO PUT THAT	LION	TO DEATH INSTANTLY. IT IS GUILTY OF HIGH TREASON. YOUR
LION I (125)	SERVICE. MY TEAM OF OXEN IS DRAWING THE NEW	LION	TO THE COLISEUM. YOU CLEAR THE ROAD. /CENTURION/ WHAT!
LION II SD(144)	IF WE DONT BEHAVE VERY RESPECTFULLY TO HIM. THE	LION	UTTERS A FEARFUL ROAR. THE EMPEROR DASHES MADLY UP THE
LION PROL,SD(108)	NO, ANDY: YOULL BE KILLED. COME BACK. THE	LION	UTTERS A LONG SNORING SIGH. ANDROCLES SEES THE LION,
LION EPILOG (151)	AND IF SOMEBODY CAME IN NOW AND TOLD YOU THAT A	LION	WAS CHASING A MAN DOWN THE STREET YOU WOULD RUSH TO THE
CLEO PRO2 (100)	TREATED US WITH RESPECT: FOR NO MAN ATTACKS A	LION	WHEN THE FIELD IS FULL OF SHEEP, EXCEPT FOR THE PRIDE
INCA (248)	BE JUST. WHEN THE HUNTERS SURROUND THE LION, THE	LION	WILL SPRING. THE INCA HAD KEPT THE PEACE FOR YEARS.
LION II (131)	BEFORE HE WAS ASKED? /ANDROCLES/ PERHAPS THE	LION	WONT EAT ME NOW. /THE KEEPER/ YES: THATS JUST LIKE A
LION II (145)	HIM NOW. SEE! (HE TICKLES THE LION'S BELLY. THE	LION	WRIGGLES ECSTATICALLY). COME AND PET HIM. /THE EMPEROR/
LION PROLOG (109)	CHRISTIAN MAN. OOPSH! (THE THORN COMES OUT. THE	LION	YELLS WITH PAIN, AND SHAKES HIS PAW WILDLY). THATS IT!
LION PROLOG (105)	ONE FOOT BEFORE ANOTHER. WE HAVNT SEEN A SINGLE	LION	YET. /ANDROCLES/ WELL, DEAR, DO YOU WANT TO SEE ONE?
LION PROL,SD(108)	UTTERS A LONG SNORING SIGH. ANDROCLES SEES THE	LION	, AND RECOILS FAINTING INTO THE ARMS OF MEGAERA, WHO
LION II (144)	WHY THEY ALL RUN AWAY FROM US LIKE THAT. (THE	LION	, COMBINING A SERIES OF YAWNS, PURRS, AND ROARS,
LION II (147)	YOU: NO SLAVERY FOR ME. (HE GOES OUT WITH THE	LION	, EVERYBODY CROWDING AWAY TO GIVE HIM AS WIDE A BERTH
INCA (248)	MADAM, BE JUST. WHEN THE HUNTERS SURROUND THE	LION	, THE LION WILL SPRING. THE INCA HAD KEPT THE PEACE FOR
LION PROLOG (109)	LICKS HIS FACE). YES, KISSUMS ANDY WANDY. (THE	LION	, WAGGING HIS TAIL VIOLENTLY, RISES ON HIS HIND LEGS,
LION PROLOG (109)	IN HIS CLAWS). THATS RIGHT. (HE EMBRACES THE	LION	, WHO FINALLY TAKES THE END OF HIS TAIL IN ONE PAW,
LION II SD(143)	REPEATEDLY. ANDROCLES HOLDS OUT HIS HANDS TO THE	LION	, WHO GIVES HIM BOTH PAWS, WHICH HE SHAKES WITH
LION II (144)	SEIZES THE EMPEROR AND GETS BETWEEN HIM AND THE	LION	, WHO STOPS AT ONCE). DONT BE AFRAID OF HIM. /THE
LION PROLOG (109)	RIGHT. (HE PULLS GINGERLY AT THE THORN. THE	LION	, WITH AN ANGRY YELL OF PAIN, JERKS BACK HIS PAW SO
LION II (146)	FRIENDS, THOUGH I DO NOT, AS YOU SEE, FEAR THIS	LION	, YET THE STRAIN OF HIS PRESENCE IS CONSIDERABLE; FOR
LION I (125)	WITH HALF THE TOWN AT THE HEELS OF YOU AND YOUR	LION	! NOT LIKELY. WE GO FIRST. /THE OX DRIVER/ THE
LION II (130)	HE DID. HE'S MARTYRED ALL RIGHT ENOUGH. GOOD OLD	LION	: OLD JOCK DOESNT LIKE THAT: LOOK AT HIS FACE. DEVIL A

LIONEL

PYGM III (257)	HAD /PICKERING/ BEETHOVEN AND BRAHMS OR LEHAR AND	LIONEL	MONCKTON; /HIGGINS/ BEEN AT IT ALL HER LIFE.

LIONESS'S

SUPR I (22)	JACK! /TANNER/ WHY, MAN, YOUR HEAD IS IN THE	LIONESS'S	MOUTH: YOU ARE HALF SWALLOWED ALREADY-- IN THREE
2TRU I (41)	ASLEEP. /THE BURGLAR/ LET HER SLEEP. WAKE NOT THE	LIONESS'S	WRATH. /THE NURSE/ YOU MADDENING FOOL, DONT YOU

LION-HOUSE

LION EPILOG (151)	SEE THE LIONS EAT HIM JUST AS THEY NOW CROWD THE	LION-HOUSE	IN THE ZOO AT FEEDING-TIME, NOT BECAUSE THEY

LION'S

LION II (130)	LET HIM. HE LET HIMSELF. /THE KEEPER/ WELL, THE	LION'S	ATE HIM. CONSTERNATION. THE CHRISTIANS RISE, GREATLY
LION II (145)	MIGHT PLAY WITH HIM NOW. SEE! (HE TICKLES THE	LION'S	BELLY. THE LION WRIGGLES ECSTATICALLY). COME AND PET
LION II SD(143)	AT THE FOCUS OF THOUSANDS OF EAGER EYES. THE	LION'S	CAGE, WITH A HEAVY PORTCULLIS GRATING, IS ON HIS
LION II (145)	YOU DONT GO AWAY FROM HIM, THOUGH. (HE PATS THE	LION'S	CHEST). /ANDROCLES/ OH, SIR, HOW FEW MEN WOULD HAVE
HART I (79)	THOUGHT OF IT. DECENT MEN ARE LIKE DANIEL IN THE	LION'S	DEN: THEIR SURVIVAL IS A MIRACLE; AND THEY DO NOT
DEST (165)	ENEMIES DONT EXPECT ME. YOU HAVE WALKED INTO THE	LION'S	DEN, COME! YOU ARE A BRAVE WOMAN. BE A SENSIBLE ONE:
LION I (126)	SOMETHING. IF THE LION IS MENAGERIE SERVICE, THE	LION'S	DINNER IS MENAGERIE SERVICE TOO. THIS (POINTING TO
LION I (126)	TOO. THIS (POINTING TO THE CHRISTIANS) IS THE	LION'S	DINNER. SO BACK WITH YOU TO YOUR PLACE. MARCH. (THE
CLEO II (131)	AWAY, AMONG YOUR FRIENDS. HERE YOU ARE IN THE	LION'S	MOUTH. /PTOLEMY/ (TURNING TO GO) IT IS NOT THE LION
LION PROL,SD(105)	LIONS, CHRISTIAN HYMN FAINTLY. A JUNGLE PATH. A	LION'S	ROAR, A MELANCHOLY SUFFERING ROAR, COMES FROM THE
MTH1 II SD(20)	HE WEARS A SCARLET CLOAK WITH GOLD BROOCH OVER A	LION'S	SKIN WITH THE CLAWS DANGLING; HIS FEET ARE IN SANDALS

LIONS

LION II (137)	WORK, THIS. WHY CANT THEY ALL BE THROWN TO THE	LIONS	? IT'S NOT A MAN'S JOB. (HE THROWS HIMSELF MOODILY
LION II (142)	WEIGHT; GET OUT OF CONDITION -- /THE EMPEROR/ THE	LIONS	? NONSENSE! (TO LAVINIA) MADAM: I AM PROUD TO HAVE
CATH 4 (195)	(AT THE CURTAINS) HE FOUGHT WITH THE STRENGTH OF	LIONS	AND BEARS. GOD KNOWS I SHALL CARRY A BROKEN SWEETBREAD
LION EPILOG (152)	WILL ENJOY THEMSELVES JUST AS MUCH, AS THE ROMAN	LIONS	AND SPECTATORS USED TO DO. IT WAS CURRENTLY REPORTED
LION II (142)	MY FRIEND: AND WE CANNOT AFFORD TO THROW AWAY	LIONS	AS IF THEY WERE MERE SLAVES. BUT WE MUST HAVE
LION II (131)	CALL HAD HE TO WALK DOWN THE THROAT OF ONE OF MY	LIONS	BEFORE HE WAS ASKED? /ANDROCLES/ PERHAPS THE LION
LION II (131)	AM I TO SAY TO THE EMPEROR WHEN HE SEES ONE OF MY	LIONS	COMING INTO THE ARENA HALF ASLEEP? /THE EDITOR/ SAY
LION EPILOG (151)	CIVILIZED AND AMIABLE AS WE, CROWDED TO SEE THE	LIONS	EAT HIM JUST AS THEY NOW CROWD THE LION-HOUSE IN THE
LION I (112)	THE DEFENDER OF THE FAITH. IN THROWING YOU TO THE	LIONS	HE WILL BE UPHOLDING THE INTERESTS OF RELIGION IN
LION II (141)	THE SISTER OF FERROVIUS. IF SHE IS THROWN TO THE	LIONS	HE WILL FRET. HE WILL LOSE WEIGHT; GET OUT OF
ROCK I (198)	FOR MANY MANY YEARS; BUT I HAVE STOOD BETWEEN THE	LIONS	IN MY TIME, AND I BELIEVE THAT IF I WERE TO TACKLE THE
LION EPILOG (152)	PERSONS OF UNPOPULAR OR ECCENTRIC VIEWS TO THE	LIONS	IN THE ALBERT HALL OR THE EARL'S COURT STADIUM
FABL VI (129)	DO FOURTH FORM PEOPLE LET THEMSELVES BE EATEN BY	LIONS	IN THE CIRCUS, BURNT AT THE STAKE, OR LIVE LIVES OF
MTH4 I (153)	CONCEPTION, WHEN I THINK OF THESE MIGHTY MEN,	LIONS	IN WAR, SAGES IN PEACE, NOT BABBLERS AND CHARLATANS
MIS. PREFACE(44)	THAN A DOZEN THIEVES: THROW HIM THEREFORE TO THE	LIONS	. A LYING OR DISOBEDIENT CHILD MAY CORRUPT A WHOLE
LION I (121)	SAY. /FERROVIUS/ (RADIANT) JOIN US. COME TO THE	LIONS	. COME TO SUFFERING AND DEATH. /LENTULUS/ (FALLING ON
LION I (117)	YOU WOULDNT WANT TO CHAFF THEM. LEAVE THEM TO THE	LIONS	. /LENTULUS/ (INDICATING LAVINIA, WHO IS STILL
LION I (111)	THE WORDS MUST BE ALTERED TO " THROW THEM TO THE	LIONS	." THE CHRISTIANS BURST INTO SHRIEKS OF UNCONTROLLABLE
LION PROLOG (107)	LIONS-- /MEGAERA/ SERVE YOU RIGHT! I WISH THE	LIONS	JOY OF YOU. (SCREAMING) ARE YOU GOING TO GET OUT OF
LION EPILOG (151)	IN SHORT, A CHRISTIAN MARTYR WAS THROWN TO THE	LIONS	NOT BECAUSE HE WAS A CHRISTIAN, BUT BECAUSE HE WAS A
METH PREFACE(R38)	OUR SCORNFUL YOUNG SCIENTIFIC AND PHILOSOPHIC	LIONS	OF TODAY MUST NOT BLAME THE CHURCH OF ENGLAND FOR THIS
LION I (110)	THE COLISEUM. THATS WHERE YOULL BE THROWN TO THE	LIONS	OR SET TO FIGHT THE GLADIATORS PRESENTLY. THINK OF
LION PROLOG (107)	AND I SHOULD BE SENT TO ROME AND THROWN TO THE	LIONS	-- /MEGAERA/ SERVE YOU RIGHT! I WISH THE LIONS JOY OF
SUPR III SD(71)	PICTURESQUE; AND THE MOUNTAINS TOLERATE THEM AS	LIONS	TOLERATE LICE. AN ENGLISH POLICEMAN OR POOR LAW
LION I (121)	LAW -- /FERROVIUS/ THE LAW WILL THROW ME TO THE	LIONS	TOMORROW: WHAT WORSE COULD IT DO WERE I TO SLAY YOU..
LION I (111)	FIND OUT HOW FUNNY IT IS WHEN YOURE THROWN TO THE	LIONS	TOMORROW. (TO THE CAPTAIN, WHO LOOKS DISPLEASED) BEG
LION EPILOG (152)	WHEN A PROCESSION OF DOCTORS GOES BY. BUT THE	LIONS	WILL HURT THEM JUST AS MUCH, AND THE SPECTATORS WILL
MIS. (201)	THE LOWEST DEPTHS OF MY PROFESSION. I WOULD STUFF	LIONS	WITH FOOD AND PRETEND TO TAME THEM. I WOULD DECEIVE
LION II (135)	TO DISLIKE ANYONE ENOUGH. I'M TO BE THROWN TO THE	LIONS	WITH THE LADY. /THE EDITOR/ THEN GET OUT OF THE WAY
LION PROL,SD(105)	OVERTURE: FOREST SOUNDS, ROARING OF	LIONS	, CHRISTIAN HYMN FAINTLY. A JUNGLE PATH. A LION'S
LION I (112)	RELIGION IN ROME. IF YOU WERE TO THROW HIM TO THE	LIONS	, THAT WOULD NO DOUBT BE PERSECUTION. THE CHRISTIANS
LION PROLOG (105)	BEFORE NIGHT. THERE ARE WILD BEASTS IN THIS WOOD:	LIONS	, THEY SAY. /MEGAERA/ I DONT BELIEVE A WORD OF IT. YOU

LIONY-PIONY

LION PROLOG (109)	AND LICKS HIS PAW INDUSTRIOUSLY). CLEVER LITTLE	LIONY-PIONY	! UNDERSTANDS UM'S DEAR OLD FRIEND ANDY WANDY.

LIP

BULL IV (169)	DOES IT. /NORA/ (WHO HAS BEEN BITING HER	LIP	AND LOOKING OVER THE HILL, DISCONSOLATE AND UNCONVINCED)
BARB II (282)	/BILL/ (DEFIANTLY) YUS. IT WAS ME THAT CAT HER	LIP	. AW AINT AFRIDE O YOU. /BARBARA/ HOW COULD YOU BE,
BULL II (110)	THINGS AND LET ME HEAR NO MORE O YOUR FOOLISH	LIP	. (PATSY OBEYS). YOU CAN TAKE THE SAMMIN UNDER YOUR
BARB II (282)	I DONT KNOW. PERHAPS IT WAS YOU THAT CUT HER	LIP	. /BILL/ (DEFIANTLY) YUS. IT WAS ME THAT CAT HER LIP.
POSN (461)	FEEMY EVANS; AND LET US HAVE NO MORE OF YOUR	LIP	. WAS THE PRISONER THE MAN OR WAS HE NOT? ON YOUR
PPP SD(202)	DRAIN IT TO THE DREGS. FITZTOLLEMACHE HOLDS THE	LIP	OF THE EWER TO ADOLPHUS'S MOUTH AND GRADUALLY RAISES IT
DEVL I (18)	(HE TURNS TOWARDS MRS DUDGEON'S CHAIR, AND HIS	LIP	ROLLS UP HORRIBLY FROM HIS DOG TOOTH AS HE MEETS HER
JOAN 2 (80)	MAJESTY. /CHARLES/ (PUTTING HIS FINGER ON HIS	LIP	) SSH! (HE HIDES BEHIND THE NEAREST COURTIER, PEERING
SUPR I (18)	FATHER APPOINTED FOR ME? /RAMSDEN/ (BITING HIS	LIP	) YOU APPROVE OF YOUR FATHER'S CHOICE, THEN? /ANN/ IT
PYGM II (241)	STEP BETWEEN THEM). DONT YOU GIVE ME NONE OF YOUR	LIP	; AND DONT LET ME HEAR YOU GIVING THIS GENTLEMAN ANY OF
DEST SD(157)	IN THE SMALLEST DEGREE. HE HAS A THICK SILLY	LIP	, AN EAGER CREDULOUS EYE, AN OBSTINATE NOSE, AND A LOUD
MIS. (164)	DARE. POOR WRETCH: IT ISNT MUCH. (HE BITES HIS	LIP	, AND SITS DOWN, VERY MUCH ANNOYED). REALLY, MR
JOAN 2,SD(73)	NOSE THAT DROOPS OVER HIS THICK SHORT UPPER	LIP	, AND THE EXPRESSION OF A YOUNG DOG ACCUSTOMED TO BE
JOAN 1,SD(60)	NOSE WITH WIDE NOSTRILS, A SHORT UPPER	LIP	, RESOLUTE BUT FULL-LIPPED MOUTH, AND HANDSOME FIGHTING
DEVL III (64)	NOT A SERIOUS ONE-- FOR HER. (RICHARD BITES HIS	LIP	, SILENCED). /JUDITH/ (TO RICHARD, AS SHE RETURNS TO

LIPARI

MILL PREFACE(121)	SEIZED THE SHRIEKERS AND TRANSPORTED THEM TO THE	LIPARI	ISLES. PARLIAMENT, OPENLY FLOUTED, CHASTISED, AND
MILL PREFACE(121)	FLED TO FRANCE AND ENGLAND, PREFERRING THEM TO	LIPARI	, AND WROTE ELOQUENT LETTERS TO THE PAPERS DEMANDING

LIPS

VWOO 1 (120)	HA HA! THE POSTMAN'S DAUGHTER HATH RIPE RED	LIPS	: BUTTER AND EGGS AND A POUND OF CHEESE! HA HA HA!
NEVR III (273)	ME WILD WITH JOY. (SOME QUICK TAUNT IS ON HER	LIPS	: HE INTERPOSES SWIFTLY) NO: I NEVER SAID THAT BEFORE:
MTH4 II (181)	THESE SACRED ISLANDS WITH SUCH A QUESTION ON YOUR	LIPS	? WARRIORS ARE NOT POPULAR HERE, MY FRIEND. /NAPOLEON/
2TRU III (90)	YEAR. IT IS STRANGE TO HEAR THE NAME FROM YOUR	LIPS	AFTER SO LONG AN INTERVAL. /SWEETIE/ I ALWAYS ASK A MAN
2TRU III SD(99)	DOGGEDLY AND STEADILY AWAY FROM HER, WITH CLOSED	LIPS	AND A DANGEROUS EXPRESSION ON HIS SET FEATURES. /MRS
BARB I (272)	GOES. HE SITS DOWN ON THE SETTEE, WITH COMPRESSED	LIPS	AND AN EXPRESSION OF STRONG DISLIKE).
DEST (178)	TAKES UP THE PACKET AND LOOKS AT IT, PURSING HIS	LIPS	AND BALANCING IT IN HIS HAND; LOOKS AT HER AGAIN;
ARMS III (56)	FALSE BLACK HAIR ON YOUR HEAD AND REDDENING YOUR	LIPS	AND CHEEKS LIKE ANY OTHER BULGARIAN GIRL? I DID. WHO
JOAN 6,SD(136)	WITH A HEAVY SIGH. THE INQUISITOR PURSES HIS	LIPS	AND FROWNS. LADVENU SHAKES HIS HEAD PITIFULLY.
PYGM III (256)	WORN OUT, THINKING ABOUT HER, AND WATCHING HER	LIPS	AND HER TEETH AND HER TONGUE, NOT TO MENTION HER SOUL,
BARB I (252)	KNOW THAT AS WELL AS I DO. (STEPHEN CLOSES HIS	LIPS	AND IS SILENT). NOW DONT SULK, STEPHEN. /STEPHEN/ I AM
CAND III (129)	(THE EAGER EXPRESSION VANISHING UTTERLY FROM HIS	LIPS	AND NOSTRILS AS HIS EYES LIGHT UP WITH PATHETIC
GETT (353)	GO AWAY. /MRS GEORGE/ ANTHONY: " WHEN OTHER	LIPS	AND OTHER HEARTS THEIR TALE OF LOVE SHALL TELL
ARMS III (53)	POCKET OF THAT COAT. /BLUNTSCHLI/ (PURSING HIS	LIPS	AND ROUNDING HIS EYES) OH-O-OH! I NEVER FOUND IT. IT
DOCT PREFACE(9)	TO CURE PASSES UNNOTICED. WE DO NOT SHOOT OUT OUR	LIPS	AND SHAKE OUR HEADS, SAYING, " THEY SAVE OTHERS:
MTH2 (53)	HAVE HELPED HIMSELF? /BURGE/ ON THAT SUBJECT MY	LIPS	ARE CLOSED. NOTHING WILL INDUCE ME TO SAY ONE WORD
MTH5 (222)	AND PEEPS IN. /ACIS/ OH, STOW IT, ECRASIA. YOUR	LIPS	ARE NOT SO SQUEAMISH AS ALL THAT. STUDIES OF WHAT?
SIM I (41)	ON GUARD. /THE FAIR GIRL/ LET HIM WORSHIP. HIS	LIPS	ARE SWEET AND PURE. /THE DARK ONE/ " FOR HE ON HONEY
CATH 1 (166)	YOU! /PATIOMKIN/ (ECSTATICALLY) DARLING: YOUR	LIPS	ARE THE GATES OF TRUTH. NOW LISTEN TO ME. (HE MARKS
HART III (147)	UP THERE. /RANDALL/ (HAVING TRIED TO PLAY) MY	LIPS	ARE TREMBLING. I CANT GET A SOUND. /MAZZINI/ I HOPE
WIDO III (65)	LOOKS STRAIGHT IN FRONT OF HIM, AND PURSES UP HIS	LIPS	AS IF WHISTLING. THIS ANNOYS HER; AND SHE BECOMES
POSN (445)	(STRIKING THE TABLE WITH HIS FIST) MAY MY	LIPS	BE BLIGHTED LIKE MY SOUL IF EVER I TELL THAT TO YOU OR
DOCT III (144)	OF DELIVERANCE FROM SIN FROM JOHN WESLEY'S OWN	LIPS	BEFORE YOU OR MR SHAW WERE BORN. IT USED TO BE VERY
GETT PREFACE(250)	THAT THOSE WHO TAKE THE SACRAMENT WITH THEIR	LIPS	BUT NOT WITH THEIR HEARTS EAT AND DRINK THEIR OWN
CAND I (81)	ABOUT HIM EXCEPT A HABIT OF SPEAKING WITH HIS	LIPS	CAREFULLY CLOSED A FULL HALF INCH FROM EACH CORNER FOR
NEVR II (235)	WITH A SPRING, AND LOOKS AT THE WAITER WITH HIS	LIPS	COMPRESSED AND HIS LEGS SWINGING). /DOLLY/ WE WANT YOU
MIS. (196)	HIS EYE. HE LOOKS TO TARLETON, WHO PURSES HIS	LIPS	GLUMLY AND RATTLES HIS MONEY IN HIS POCKETS WITHOUT A
CLEO IV (179)	(SHE SITS DOWN AGAIN). /POTHINUS/ FROM HER OWN	LIPS	I HAVE HEARD IT. YOU ARE TO BE HER CATSPAW: YOU ARE TO
BULL PREFACE(39)	ENTRAILS TO TIE OUR OWN HANDS AND SEAL OUR OWN	LIPS	IN THE NAME OF OUR HONOR AND PATRIOTISM. AS FAR AS
SIM I (41)	WISH YOU WERE ALIVE AND I COULD KISS YOUR LIVING	LIPS	INSTEAD OF THE PAINT ON A HARD WOODEN IMAGE. I WONDER
LION II (135)	TSHA! YOU OBSTINATE FOOL! (HE BITES HIS	LIPS	IRRESOLUTELY, NOT KNOWING EXACTLY WHAT TO DO).
PHIL I SD(84)	AND SING. SHE PLAYS THE SYMPHONY TO WHEN OTHER	LIPS	. CHARTERIS STANDS AT THE PIANO, AS IF ABOUT TO SING.
CLEO IV (180)	HIS LIFE OUT AS I STRIKE HIS NAME FROM YOUR	LIPS	. DASH HIM DOWN FROM THE WALL. BREAK HIM ON THE STONES.
CLEO IV (185)	IN HER EYES AND IN THE CORNERS OF THE BLOODHOUND	LIPS	. FOR A MOMENT CAESAR SUSPECTS THAT SHE IS DRUNK WITH
3PLA PREFACE(R30)	ABSENT HUSBAND, SEALED HIS PASSION-PALPITATING	LIPS	. FROM THE MOMENT THAT THIS FATALLY PLAUSIBLE
DEST (184)	GIUSEPPE ABOUT ME. (SHE PUTS HER FINGER ON HER	LIPS	. HE DOES THE SAME. THEY LOOK AT ONE ANOTHER WARNINGLY.
METH PREFACE(R35)	THE CONSEQUENCES COULD BE AVERTED BY SEALING MY	LIPS	. HOWEVER, THE REST APPEARED TO FEEL THAT THE GAME
PHIL I SD(69)	THE PIECE OF MUSIC ON THE DESK IS WHEN OTHER	LIPS	. INCANDESCENT LIGHTS, WELL SHADED, ARE ON THE PIANO
NEVR II SD(231)	WELL. /PHILIP/ SHUT UP, BOTH. DOLLY HOLDS HER	LIPS	. M'COMAS TAKES A CHAIR FROM THE LUNCHEON TABLE; PLACES
PYGM II (231)	MOTHER'S KNEE. BUT SHE MUST NOT HEAR IT FROM YOUR	LIPS	. /HIGGINS/ (LOFTILY) I CANNOT CHARGE MYSELF WITH
KING I (205)	DROP DEAD MYSELF IF I HEARD SUCH FUSTIAN PASS MY	LIPS	. /JAMES/ IS IT WORSE THAN THE FUSTIAN THAT PASSES THE
SIM II SD(78)	AND TRIES TO SPEAK; BUT NO SOUND COMES FROM HIS	LIPS	. /LADY FARWATERS/ WHAT ON EARTH IS THE MATTER WITH
GETT SD(345)	THE LONG SIDE OF THE TABLE, BROODING, WITH CLOSED	LIPS	. /THE BISHOP/ HAVE YOU BEEN OUT, MY DEAR? /EDITH/
MTH4 II (178)	OTHER: THEY DIE WITH SHOUTS OF TRIUMPH ON THEIR	LIPS	. THOSE WHO DIE CURSING DO NOT CURSE ME. MY TALENT IS
DOCT IV (166)	DISTRESS) I CANT LISTEN WITHOUT MOVING HIM. (HIS	LIPS	MOVE AGAIN: WALPOLE BENDS DOWN AND LISTENS). /WALPOLE/
BARB II (306)	CONVERT YOU MAKE IS A VOTE AGAINST WAR. (HER	LIPS	MOVE IN PRAYER). YET I GIVE YOU THIS MONEY TO HELP YOU
DOCT IV (166)	PROTESTS). SH-SH: PLEASE DONT DISTURB HIM. (HIS	LIPS	MOVE). WHAT DID YOU SAY, DEAR? (IN GREAT DISTRESS) I
JITT II (45)	HUMBUGGED. WHO WAS SHE? /JITTA/ (CLOSES HER	LIPS	OBSTINATELY)! /LENKHEIM/ WAS HE SO MUCH TO YOU THAT
BULL IV (154)	WITHER THE COMMONPLACES OF CONSOLATION ON THE	LIPS	OF A PRIEST, BUT THIS MAN DID NOT COMPLAIN OF HIS
LIED (191)	ALL HONOR NOT TO LET HIM LEARN THE TRUTH FROM THE	LIPS	OF A SCANDALMONGER. LET US GO TO HIM NOW QUIETLY, HAND
MIS. PREFACE(9)	A BLASPHEMOUS LIE; AND THE FACT THAT IT IS ON THE	LIPS	OF EVERY NURSERYMAID DOES NOT EXCUSE IT IN THE LEAST.
ROCK II (254)	AND SPEWS OUT HIS SOCIALISM THROUGH THE ELOQUENT	LIPS	OF ITS ALOYSIA. I RECALL THE WARNING MY DEAR OLD FATHER
KING I (205)	IS IT WORSE THAN THE FUSTIAN THAT PASSES THE	LIPS	OF THE RANTERS IN YOUR CONVENTICLES? /FOX/ I CANNOT
JOAN 6 (141)	THE SENTENCE OF EXCOMMUNICATION HAS PASSED THE	LIPS	OF YOUR JUDGES. YOU ARE WITHIN A FEW SHORT MOMENTS OF
DOCT III (140)	COURT SENSATION FOR YOU MORAL CHAPS TO LICK YOUR	LIPS	OVER AT BREAKFAST. WE JUST SAID, WELL, THE MONEY'S
BULL PREFACE(14)	NATURALLY SWALLOWED IT EAGERLY AND SMACKED THEIR	LIPS	OVER IT, LAUGHING ALL THE MORE HEARTILY BECAUSE THEY
CYMB V (145)	I WOULD NOT THY GOOD DEEDS SHOULD FROM MY	LIPS	PLUCK A HARD SENTENCE: PRITHEE, VALIANT YOUTH, DENY'T
BULL IV SD(158)	AND REFLECTING, EVIDENTLY NOT ABOUT HER, WITH HIS	LIPS	PURSED AS IF HE WERE WHISTLING. WITH A CATCH IN HER
ARMS III (54)	DEAD. (HE LOOKS AT THE TELEGRAM WITH HIS	LIPS	PURSED, MUSING ON THE UNEXPECTED CHANGE IN HIS
MTH3 (118)	I DENY THAT A SECRET OF STATE HAS EVER PASSED MY	LIPS	-- EXCEPT PERHAPS TO THE MINISTER OF HEALTH, WHO IS
PPP (205)	LOOKING-GLASS AND HOLDING IT TO THE POLICEMAN'S	LIPS	) DEAD! /FITZ/ (SOLEMNLY RISING) THE COPPER ATTRACTED
CATH 2 (177)	IF I MAYNT DRINK? /CATHERINE/ (BITING HER	LIPS	) GO. I AM OFFENDED. /PATIOMKIN/ DONT SCOLD, LL MOTHER.
LIED (189)	DO YOU SUPPOSE I AM AN ANGEL? /HE/ (BITING HIS	LIPS	) I DO. HEAVEN HELP ME, I DO-- OR I DID-- OR (HE
ANNA (292)	/SCHNEIDEKIND/ (PULLING THE TELEPHONE FROM HIS	LIPS	) TAKE CARE, SIR. /STRAMMFEST/ I WONT TAKE CARE: I'LL
SUPR III (134)	HE GOES. (PUFFING A LONG BREATH OUT THROUGH HIS	LIPS	) WHEW! HOW HE DOES TALK! THEYLL NEVER STAND IT IN
DEST (159)	RESOLUTELY, AND BREATHES HARD, WITH COMPRESSED	LIPS	). /NAPOLEON/ I AM WAITING, SIR, FOR YOUR EXPLANATION.
CAPT I (240)	YOUR MEN! (BRASSBOUND STARES AT HER WITH DRYING	LIPS	). /SIR HOWARD/ CICELY: WHEN YOU HAVE QUITE DONE
CURE (227)	THIS VALERIAN (HE PUTS THE GLASS TO REGINALD'S	LIPS	). THATS RIGHT. NOW YOURE BETTER. /REGINALD/ (
JITT I (24)	(HE KISSES HER EYES), AND THIS (HE KISSES HER	LIPS	). WHAT A FOOL I WAS WITH MY IRON RESOLUTIONS! ONE
JITT I (24)	ONE THROB OF YOUR BREAST, ONE TOUCH OF YOUR	LIPS	; AND WHERE ARE THEY? NOTHING MATTERS BUT JITTA.
JITT I SD(13)	THEN HE TAKES OUT A CIGARET; PUTS IT BETWEEN HIS	LIPS	; TAKES OUT A MATCH, AND IS ABOUT TO STRIKE IT WHEN THE
LADY PREFACE(221)	LIKE THE SUN; CORAL IS FAR MORE RED THAN HER	LIPS	' RED; IF SNOW BE WHITE, WHY THEN HER BREASTS ARE DUN;
ARMS I SD(12)	AT THE OTTOMAN, AT THE CURTAIN; THEN PURSES HER	LIPS	SECRETIVELY, LAUGHS INSOLENTLY, AND GOES OUT. RAINA,
NEVR I SD(209)	CLANDON/ (SHOCKED) DOLLY! DOLLY CATCHES HER	LIPS	SUPPRESSIVELY WITH HER FINGER TIPS. /THE PARLORMAID/
LADY (243)	UNTIL THEN, YOU ARE MY QUEEN; AND I'LL KISS THOSE	LIPS	THAT HAVE DROPT MUSIC ON MY HEART. (HE PUTS HIS ARMS
BASH II,1, (111)	WELL HE SPEAKS! THERE IS A SILVER TRUMPET IN HIS	LIPS	THAT STIRS ME TO THE FINGER ENDS. HIS NOSE DROPT LOVELY
JOAN 1 (70)	CROSSES HIMSELF; AND FORMS WITH HIS PALE	LIPS	THE WORDS) CHRIST IN HEAVEN! (ALOUD BUT BREATHLESS)
MRS II (209)	(HE KISSES HER HAND. SHE SNATCHES IT AWAY, HER	LIPS	TIGHTENING, AND LOOKS MORE THAN HALF DISPOSED TO BOX
POSN (454)	HUSSY. YOURE A DISGRACE. HOW DARE YOU OPEN YOUR	LIPS	TO ANSWER YOUR BETTERS? HOLD YOUR TONGUE AND LEARN
PYGM V (287)	OR OTHER WITH LOTS OF MONEY, AND A THICK PAIR OF	LIPS	TO KISS YOU WITH AND A THICK PAIR OF BOOTS TO KICK YOU
MTH5 (222)	STUDIES OF-- BUT I REALLY CANNOT BRING MY	LIPS	TO UTTER IT. THE NEWLY BORN, FULL OF CURIOSITY, RUNS TO
DEST (189)	BE OFF, BOTH OF YOU. /GIUSEPPE/ (HUMBLY, HIS	LIPS	TREMBLING) W-WILLINGLY, YOUR EXCELLENCY. (HE GOES
NEVR II (257)	NOT, IT IS WHAT YOU CALL A PRIG. (SHE CLOSES HER	LIPS	TRIMLY AND LOOKS STEADILY AND CHALLENGINGLY AT HIM AS
DEVL I SD(22)	SHE HAS LEFT THE ROOM WITHOUT LEAVE, CLOSES HER	LIPS	VENGEFULLY. /HAWKINS/ " SECOND, THAT HE SHALL BE A GOOD
DEVL III (52)	EH? /JUDITH/ (DISENGAGING HER HAND TO TOUCH HIS	LIPS	WITH IT) DONT (MEANING " DONT JEST"). NO: BY TELLING
NEVR I (205)	DOWN IN THE WRITING-TABLE CHAIR, AND CLOSES HER	LIPS	WITH THE TIPS OF HER FINGERS). /VALENTINE/ THANK YOU. (
POSN (454)	HONOR OF THE TOWN GIVE HER THE OATH BECAUSE HER	LIPS	WOULD BLASPHEME THE HOLY BIBLE IF THEY TOUCHED IT. I
DEVL III (66)	WAS MY UNCLE. /SWINDON/ HM! (HE COMPRESSES HIS	LIPS	, AND LOOKS AT RICHARD WITH VINDICTIVE GRAVITY).
NEVR II (252)	HER SATISFACTION WITH A SLIGHT TIGHTENING OF THE	LIPS	, AND SITS DOWN). THERE! YOU SEE I ONLY WANT TO SHEW
NEVR III (264)	THE TERRACE-- /DOLLY/ (CORRECTING HIM)-- ON THE	LIPS	, BEFORE EVERYBODY. /MRS CLANDON/ (INCREDULOUSLY)
SUPR I (14)	INTERVAL RATHER PAINFUL. (RAMSDEN COMPRESSES HIS	LIPS	, BUT SAYS NOTHING). /OCTAVIUS/ NEVER MIND HIM, MR
BULL I SD(80)	COLD GREY EYES, STRAINED NOSE, FINE FASTIDIOUS	LIPS	, CRITICAL BROWS, CLEVER HEAD, RATHER REFINED AND
DEVL I (21)	YOURS, SIR. (WITH THE GLASS HALF WAY TO HIS	LIPS	, HE CHECKS HIMSELF, GIVING A DUBIOUS GLANCE AT THE
DEVL II SD(36)	DISCONCERTED. RICHARD, NOTING THE QUIVER OF HER	LIPS	, IS THE FIRST TO PULL HIMSELF TOGETHER. /RICHARD/ MRS
GENV PREFACE(24)	ON HIGH HEELS STAINING THEIR NAILS, DAUBING THEIR	LIPS	, PAINTING THEIR FACES: IN SHORT, DOING ALL SORTS OF
MIS. SD(115)	DARK EYES WITH BLACK BROWS AND LASHES, CURVED	LIPS	, SWIFT GLANCES AND MOVEMENTS THAT FLASH OUT OF A
PYGM II (231)	/HIGGINS/ MRS PEARCE: THIS LANGUAGE FROM YOUR	LIPS	! REALLY! /MRS PEARCE/ (NOT TO BE PUT OFF)-- BUT
MTH3 (100)	AGE. BUT LOOK AT THEIR BEAUTIFUL NOSES AND LITTLE	LIPS	! THEY ARE PHYSICALLY INSIPID: THEY HAVE NO BEAUTY:

LIPTON

LION PREFACE(56)	ISAAC NEWTON, PALESTRINA, OFFENBACH, SIR THOMAS	LIPTON	, MR PAUL CINQUEVALLE, YOUR FAMILY DOCTOR, FLORENCE

LIQUEFACTION

SUPR HANDBOK(204)	DEVOUTLY AS THE ITALIAN PEASANT BELIEVES IN THE	LIQUEFACTION	OF THE BLOOD OF ST JANUARIUS; AND
LION PREFACE(45)	NEVERTHELESS BOGGLE AT THE MIRACLE OF THE	LIQUEFACTION	OF THE BLOOD OF ST JANUARIUS, AND REJECT IT AS

LIQUEFY
DOCT PREFACE(73) THERE MUST BE. THE BLOOD OF ST JANUARIUS MUST LIQUEFY WHETHER THE SAINT IS IN THE HUMOR OR NOT. TO TRICK A

LIQUEFYING
FABL PREFACE(71) THE ACCOUNT. IT WAS PRECISELY EQUIVALENT TO LIQUEFYING THE BLOOD OF SAINT JANUARIUS. SOME TWENTY YEARS
FABL PREFACE(69) THE PRIEST MUST CREATE AND NOURISH THEIR FAITH BY LIQUEFYING THE BLOOD OF SAINT JANUARIUS, AND SAYING MASS

LIQUEUR
MIS. SD(110) AT IT. ON THE SIDEBOARD THERE IS A TANTALUS, LIQUEUR BOTTLES, A SYPHON, A GLASS JUG OF LEMONADE,

LIQUEURS
2TRU PREFACE(5) MANY COURSES AND WINES CULMINATING IN CIGARS AND LIQUEURS ; BUT THE ILLUSION AND THE RESULTS ARE COGNATE. I

LIQUID
SUPR I SD(17) OF CHAIRS, THE SNIFFING OF THE WIDOW, AND THE LIQUID EYE OF THE DAUGHTER, WHOSE HEART, APPARENTLY WILL NOT
FABL IV (115) CHANGES FROM SOLID ICE TO LIQUID FLUID, FROM LIQUID FLUID TO STEAM, FROM STEAM TO GAS; BUT IT IS NONE THE
FABL IV (115) RISES, WATER CHANGES FROM SOLID ICE TO LIQUID FLUID, FROM LIQUID FLUID TO STEAM, FROM STEAM TO GAS;
PPP (200) /ADOLPHUS/ NO; UNLESS YOU CAN SUPPLY LIME IN LIQUID FORM, I MUST PERISH. FINISH THAT CEILING I CANNOT AND
DOCT IV (163) SUCH A COLOR: GARNET COLOR. WAVING LIKE SILK. LIQUID LOVELY FLAME FLOWING UP THROUGH THE BAY LEAVES, AND

LIQUIDATE
MILL IV (211) /EPIFANIA/ BY ALL MEANS; BUT WE SHALL HAVE TO LIQUIDATE ALL THE ADULT INHABITANTS AND BEGIN WITH THE NEWLY
ROCK PREFACE(151) CENTURIES BEFORE COMPELLED THE SECULAR STATE TO LIQUIDATE HERETICS; AND THE SLAUGHTER OF REBELS WHO TRIED TO
METH PREFACE(R70) THE VICTORS WILL STARVE TOO, AND EUROPE WILL LIQUIDATE ITS AFFAIRS BY GOING, NOT INTO BANKRUPTCY, BUT
BULL IV (178) WILL REORGANIZE THE SCHEME EFFICIENTLY; YOU WILL LIQUIDATE ITS SECOND BANKRUPTCY EFFICIENTLY (BROADBENT AND
MILL IV (210) EVERYWHERE: THEY ARE THE ONE SPECIES YOU CANNOT LIQUIDATE . KINGS, EMPERORS, CONQUERORS, PONTIFFS AND ALL
ROCK PREFACE(162) PAY OO (OGPU), TO GO INTO THESE QUESTIONS AND LIQUIDATE PERSONS WHO COULD NOT ANSWER THEM SATISFACTORILY.
MILL PREFACE(112) HIM MURDERED; BUT AS TSARINA SHE WAS FORCED TO LIQUIDATE POOR PETER VERY MUCH AGAINST HER OWN EASY GOOD
MILL I (160) HE TOUCHED WOULD TURN INTO GOLD. I HAD TO LIQUIDATE THAT CIRCUS A MONTH LATER. HE WAS ABOUT TO TURN

LIQUIDATED
SIM PREFACE(6) RESTRAINED OR, AS THE RUSSIANS GENTLY PUT IT, LIQUIDATED . NO STATE CAN AFFORD THE EXPENSE OF PROVIDING
FABL III (112) AND INCORRIGIBLE, IN WHICH CASE YOULL BE LIQUIDATED , /THE TRAMP/ I KNOW ALL THAT. WHAT GOOD WILL IT
FABL PREFACE(76) " BLOODY MARY" BELIEVED THAT HERETICS MUST BE LIQUIDATED ; BUT SHE WAS NOT RESPONSIBLE FOR THE POLITICAL
SIM PREFACE(11) OF ITS WORK IS OVER: THE HERETICS ARE EITHER LIQUIDATED , CONVERTED, OR INTIMIDATED. BUT IT WAS
ROCK PREFACE(151) OF POLITICS THAT HE WAS ELIMINATED, OR " LIQUIDATED " AS WE SAY NOW. THERE WAS A REAL NOVELTY IN THE

LIQUIDATING
ROCK PREFACE(162) AND DEATH WAS THAT THE CHEKA HAD NO INTEREST IN LIQUIDATING ANYBODY WHO COULD BE MADE PUBLICLY USEFUL, ALL
2TRU PREFACE(14) PROTECT AND GLORIFY HIS CHICANERIES INSTEAD OF LIQUIDATING HIM. TO MR CHESTERTON THE DISTRIBUTIST (OR

LIQUIDATION
ROCK PREFACE(163) CAPITAL PUNISHMENT HAS BEEN ABOLISHED IN RUSSIA (LIQUIDATION BY THE OGPU IS NOT PUNISHMENT: IT IS ONLY "
ROCK PREFACE(163) FINDS HIMSELF IN IMMINENT DANGER OF DETECTION AND LIQUIDATION BY THE OGPU WOULD BE WELL ADVISED TO LOSE HIS
HART I (57) TO INCUR LIABILITIES. WHEN THE BUSINESS WENT INTO LIQUIDATION HE OWED MORE MONEY THAT MR MANGAN HAD GIVEN HIM.
FABL PREFACE(76) CRUEL, AND THAT NO OTHER AGENCY COULD EFFECT THE LIQUIDATION . CALVIN AGREED THAT SERVETUS MUST BE KILLED;
SIM PREFACE(16) ASSET OR A SOCIAL NUISANCE, AND THE PENALTY IS LIQUIDATION . HE HAD APPEARED ON THE STAGE BEFORE IN THE
ROCK PREFACE(151) WITH BRITISH CIVILIZATION, IT WAS ONLY LIQUIDATION . RIGHT TO EXTERMINATE CONFERRED BY PRIVATE
GENV IV (121) THE WORD EXECUTION I AM WILLING TO SUBSTITUTE LIQUIDATION . THE WORD SCOUNDRELISM AND ITS ADJECTIVES I
BULL IV (177) HABITS WILL SECURE THE THOROUGH EFFICIENCY OF THE LIQUIDATION . YOU WILL REORGANIZE THE SCHEME EFFICIENTLY;
SIM PREFACE(16) TO HAVE DEVISED A SIMILAR METHOD OF PAINLESS LIQUIDATION ,) IT MAY BE EXPEDIENT THAT ONE MAN SHOULD DIE
MILL PREFACE(128) ARE WE TO DO WITH THEM IN SELF-DEFENCE? MERE LIQUIDATION WOULD BE DISASTROUS, BECAUSE AT PRESENT ONLY

LIQUIDATORS
ROCK PREFACE(151) OF THE DIVINE RIGHT OF KINGS THE POLITICAL LIQUIDATORS TURNED THEIR ATTENTION SLOWLY TO ITS DERIVATORY

LIQUOR
PYGM II (226) A BRUTE. IT'S A LIE: NOBODY EVER SAW THE SIGN OF LIQUOR ON ME. (SHE GOES BACK TO HER CHAIR AND PLANTS
PHIL II (107) ON A STRICT DIET. POOR OLD BOY! THEY CUT OFF HIS LIQUOR ; AND HE'S NOT ALLOWED TO EAT MEAT. /CHARTERIS/ YOUR

LIQUORS
POSN PREFACE(365) POWERFUL INTEREST OF THE TRADE IN INTOXICATING LIQUORS , FIERCELY DETERMINED TO RESIST ANY EXTENSION OF THE

LISSEN
CAPT II (265) (APPALLED, ALMOST IN TEARS) NAOW, NAOW. LISSEN , KEPN (POINTING TO SIR HOWARD): E'LL GIVE HUZ FAWV

LISSON
PYGM I (210) (APPALLED) OH, WHAT HARM IS THERE IN MY LEAVING LISSON GROVE? IT WASNT FIT FOR A PIG TO LIVE IN; AND I HAD
PYGM II (219) NO USE: IVE GOT ALL THE RECORDS I WANT OF THE LISSON GROVE LINGO; AND I'M NOT GOING TO WASTE ANOTHER
PYGM II (224) OF YOU ARE, I DO. /HIGGINS/ WE WANT NONE OF YOUR LISSON GROVE PRUDERY HERE, YOUNG WOMAN. YOUVE GOT TO LEARN
PYGM I (210) DO YOU COME TO BE SO FAR EAST? YOU WERE BORN IN LISSON GROVE. /THE FLOWER GIRL/ (APPALLED) OH, WHAT HARM IS

LIST
OVER (183) LIST A LONG ONE? /MRS LUNN/ DO YOU MEAN THE REAL LIST ? NOT THE ONE I SHEW TO GREGORY: THERE ARE HUNDREDS OF
OVER (183) OTHER SUBJECT. WHY ELSE HAVE YOU PUT ME ON YOUR LIST ? /MRS LUNN/ BECAUSE YOURE A SOLICITOR. GREGORY'S A
OVER (183) DOWN, IF THAT WILL SATISFY YOU. /JUNO/ IS THE LIST A LONG ONE? /MRS LUNN/ DO YOU MEAN THE REAL LIST? NOT
AUGS (275) WILL ONLY TEMPT YOU INTO DANGER. SHE MAY GET THE LIST AFTER ALL. IT IS TRUE THAT THE GUNS ARE MOVED. BUT SHE
AUGS (274) COME DOWN HERE AND OBTAIN POSSESSION OF THAT LIST AND GET CLEAN AWAY INTO THE STREET WITH IT. HE TOOK THE
AUGS (280) OFF. HOW SAD! HOW SAD! (HE PUSHES THE SHAM LIST BACK INTO THE ENVELOPE, AND POCKETS IT). /THE LADY/
2TRU III (100) YOUR K. C. B., SIR. (PRESENTING A PAPER) HONORS LIST BY WIRELESS. /TALLBOYS/ (RISING JOYOUSLY TO TAKE THE
MTH2 (87) BE AN O.M. FOR SOMEBODY WHEN THE FIRST HONORS LIST COMES ROUND (BY THIS TIME HE HAS TALKED HIMSELF OUT OF
AUGS (282) -- /THE LADY/ (CONTINUING) I GOT HOLD OF THE LIST FOR A MOMENT AND CHANGED IT FOR A PIECE OF PAPER OUT OF
NEVR II (238) HOST BY ORDERING YOUR WINE. (HE TAKES THE WINE LIST FROM THE TABLE. HIS POLITE ATTENTION, AND DOLLY'S
AUGS (277) NOW, AS A MEASURE OF SECURITY, I SHALL PUT THAT LIST IN MY POCKET. (HE BEGINS SEARCHING VAINLY FROM DRAWER
AUGS (282) /THE LADY/ (INTO THE TELEPHONE) YES: I HAVE THE LIST IN MY WALLET. . . . /AUGUSTUS/ NOTHING OF THE KIND.
AUGS (279) LADY'S ENVELOPE. (SHE PUTS THE SHAM LIST INTO HER ENVELOPE AND HANDS IT TO HIM). /AUGUSTUS/
AUGS SD(279) TO SEE THAT THEY LOOK EXACTLY ALIKE; WHIPS THE LIST INTO HER WALLET; AND SUBSTITUTES THE FACSIMILE FOR IT.
AUGS (274) AND HE HAS RASHLY LET OUT TO HER THAT THIS LIST IS IN YOUR POSSESSION. HE FORGOT HIMSELF BECAUSE HE WAS
AUGS (278) MORNING. /THE LADY/ (INTERCEPTING IT) IT IS THE LIST . GOOD HEAVENS! /THE CLERK/ (PROFFERING THE ENVELOPE)
OVER (185) ARE YOU? /JUNO/ NOT AT PRESENT; BUT I'M ON THE LIST . I'M HER PROSPECTIVE HUSBAND: YOURE ONLY HER ACTUAL
DOCT V SD(172) AND MERIT OF THE WORK; THEN MARKS THE SECRETARY'S LIST . PROCEEDING WITH HIS SURVEY, HE DISAPPEARS BEHIND THE
AUGS (274) A BROTHER-IN-LAW'S NAME IN THE GERMAN CASUALTY LIST . /THE LADY/ NOBODY KNOWS THAT BETTER THAN I. WAIT
ROCK PREFACE(164) AT THE FOOT OF THE OVERCROWDED EDUCATIONAL LIST . THEY ALSO PROSCRIBED THE KULAK, THE ABLE, HARDHEADED,
AUGS (279) SLYLY) COME: WOULD YOU LIKE TO HAVE A PEEP AT THE LIST (BEGINNING TO TAKE THE BLANK PAPER FROM THE
APPL I (233) THE ONLY ONE NOW LEFT IN THIS COUNTRY. MY CIVIL LIST LEAVES ME A POOR MAN AMONG MULTI-MILLIONAIRES. YOUR
BULL PREFACE(37) AS A PHILANTHROPIST, WHICH NOW ONLY MAKES THE LIST OF ACHIEVEMENTS ON HIS MONUMENT AT FERNEY THE MOST
SIM PREFACE(8) SINS COMMITTED BEFORE IT. AT THE SAME TIME THE LIST OF ACTIVITIES BLACKLISTED BY THE RUSSIAN STATE AS
MIS. (160) PROMPTLY) FIFTY-EIGHT. /LINA/ THANK YOU. I KEEP A LIST OF ALL MY OFFERS. I LIKE TO KNOW WHAT I'M CONSIDERED
AUGS (269) AS TO LET IT OUT OF MY HANDS? WHY, IT GIVES A LIST OF ALL OUR ANTI-AIRCRAFT EMPLACEMENTS FROM RAMSGATE TO
ROCK PREFACE(160) INSTRUMENTS FOR THE MAINTENANCE OF ORDER EXCEPT A LIST OF CRIMES AND PUNISHMENTS ADMINISTERED THROUGH A RITUAL
ROCK PREFACE(190) OUT OF TWO BLACKS, AND TO ABOLISH THE MONSTROUS LIST OF CRIMES AND PUNISHMENTS BY WHICH THESE SUPERSTITIONS
ROCK PREFACE(160) THROUGH A RITUAL OF CRIMINAL LAW. AND IN THE LIST OF CRIMES THE VERY WORST OFFENCES AGAINST COMMUNIST
DOCT PREFACE(36) ON JUST AS THEY DID BEFORE. IN THE SAME WAY, THE LIST OF DISEASES WHICH VIVISECTION CLAIMS TO HAVE CURED IS
SUPR HANDBOK(180) SELECTION AS FAR AS WE CAN BY REJECTING FROM THE LIST OF ELIGIBLE PARENTS ALL PERSONS WHO ARE UNINTERESTING,
GENV II (58) SOLDIERS, EACH OF WHOM HAS HIS PROSCRIPTION LIST OF ENEMIES WHOM HE IMPRISONS, EXILES, OR MURDERS AT HIS
AUGS (276) GENERAL STAFF. I AM NOT AT ALL SURE THAT THIS LIST OF GUN EMPLACEMENTS WOULD RECEIVE THE SMALLEST

AUGS	(276)	/THE LADY/ (STARING AT HIM) THEN YOU THINK THIS	LIST	OF GUN EMPLACEMENTS DOESNT MATTER! : /AUGUSTUS/ BY NO
AUGS	(273)	IS DETERMINED TO OBTAIN POSSESSION OF A CERTAIN	LIST	OF GUN EMPLACEMENTS -- /AUGUSTUS/ (INTERRUPTING HER
AUGS	(282)	THERES NOTHING WRITTEN ON THIS. WHERE IS THE	LIST	OF GUNS? /THE LADY/ (CONTINUING) OH, IT WAS QUITE
JITT PREFACE	(3)	WAS BORN IN VIENNA ON THE 21ST DECEMBER 1869. THE	LIST	OF HIS ORIGINAL WORKS INCLUDES EIGHT NOVELS AND VOLUMES
DOCT PREFACE	(70)	OR FROWSTING TOO MUCH (TO GO NO FURTHER IN THE	LIST	OF INTEMPERANCES THAT MAKE UP SO MUCH OF FAMILY LIFE)
APPL PREFACE	(188)	WRITE TO ME SOLICITING MY VOTE AND ENCLOSING A	LIST	OF MEETINGS, AN ELECTION ADDRESS, AND A POLLING CARD.
KING I	(173)	FOX'S LEFT, QUITE CLOSE). IF I MAY ADD YOU TO THE	LIST	OF MY BEAUS I SHALL BE THE PROUDEST WOMAN IN LONDON.
MRS PREFACE	(177)	NOT GO OUT AND HANG YOURSELF: THAT IS NOT ON THE	LIST	OF PARDONABLE SINS. SHORTLY AFTER THESE EVENTS A
POSN PREFACE	(378)	A POWERFUL SMELL OF CARNATIONS, HEADING THE LONG	LIST	OF PLAYWRIGHTS WHO CAME THERE TO TESTIFY AGAINST THE
GENV PREFACE	(11)	IN THE NINETEENTH CENTURY AND AFTER, HAS GIVEN A	LIST	OF PREVIOUS DISCOVERIES, DATING BACK TO B.C., WHICH
LION PREFACE	(24)	AND ELABORATE NEW OBSERVANCES, AND TO THEIR	LIST	OF THE ACCURSED ADDED ONE JESCHU, A BASTARD MAGICIAN,
GENV I	(38)	UNDERSTAND ME. ALL YOU NEED DO IS TO GIVE ME A	LIST	OF THE CHARGES YOU MAKE AGAINST-- WELL, AGAINST WHOEVER
LION PREFACE	(45)	SCEPTICS WERE TO DRAW UP IN PARALLEL COLUMNS A	LIST	OF THE EVENTS NARRATED IN THE GOSPELS WHICH THEY
2TRU II	(64)	I COULD ALMOST MARRY HIM, JUST TO PUT HIM ON THE	LIST	OF THE INEVITABLES THAT I MUST PUT UP WITH WILLYNILLY.
LION PREFACE	(52)	WILL BE TO ADD HIMSELF AND HIS DEPENDENTS TO THE	LIST	OF THE POOR, AND TO DO NO GOOD TO THE POOR BEYOND
DOCT V	(173)	AND PUTS DOWN THE GLASS AND THE SECRETARY'S	LIST	ON THE TABLE). /JENNIFER/ HE LOOKED THE PICTURE OF
MILL IV	(207)	WILL OF ALLAH THAT THE WIDOW SHOULD HAVE A CIVIL	LIST	PENSION. SHE RECEIVED IT: A HUNDRED POUNDS A YEAR. I
NEVR II	SD(239)	IT THAT I AM A BOY? CRAMPTON SNATCHES THE WINE	LIST	RUDELY FROM HIM AND IRRESOLUTELY PRETENDS TO READ IT.
AUGS	(275)	STILL! BUT IF THE GERMAN WAR OFFICE GETS THE	LIST	-- AND SHE WILL COPY IT BEFORE SHE GIVES IT BACK TO
CAPT III	(288)	WHAT ARE THEY? /BLUEJACKET/ (READING FROM A	LIST	) FOUR BOOKS, TORN AND DIRTY, MADE UP OF SEPARATE
DOCT V	(179)	/RIDGEON/ OH! (TAKING UP THE SECRETARY'S	LIST	) I HAVE MARKED FIVE PICTURES AS SOLD TO ME. /JENNIFER/
AUGS	SD(279)	RACK; FOLDS IT SO THAT IT RESEMBLES THE	LIST	; COMPARES THE TWO TO SEE THAT THEY LOOK EXACTLY ALIKE;
BARB III	SD(329)	ABRUPTLY OPEN; AND A FOREMAN IN OVERALLS AND	LIST	SLIPPERS COMES OUT ON THE LITTLE LANDING AND HOLDS THE
BARB III	(349)	I WANT MAMMA. /UNDERSHAFT/ SHE IS TAKING OFF HER	LIST	SLIPPERS, DEAR. (HE PASSES ON TO CUSINS). WELL? WHAT
BARB III	(345)	ALL RIGHT, BILTON? /BILTON/ YOULL HAVE TO PUT ON	LIST	SLIPPERS, MISS: THATS ALL. WEVE GOT EM INSIDE. (SHE
OVER	(183)	HUNDREDS OF NAMES ON THAT; BUT THE LITTLE PRIVATE	LIST	THAT HE'D BETTER NOT SEE? /JUNO/ OH, WILL YOU REALLY
FABL PREFACE	(76)	THE STATESMAN'S YEARBOOK HAS GIVEN UP TRYING TO	LIST	THEM. THEY RANGE FROM PILLARS OF FIRE, JEHOVAH'S
AUGS	(279)	MUST BE ABLE TO SWEAR THAT YOU NEVER SHEWED THAT	LIST	TO A MORTAL SOUL. /AUGUSTUS/ OH, THAT IS A MERE FORM.
AUGS	(279)	I HAVE FOUND YOU A BEAUTIFUL ENVELOPE FOR THE	LIST	, AN UNMISTAKEABLE LADY'S ENVELOPE. (SHE PUTS THE SHAM
AUGS	(276)	IF THIS SPY WERE TO OBTAIN POSSESSION OF THE	LIST	, BLUELOO WOULD TELL THE STORY AT EVERY DINNER-TABLE IN
DOCT V	(172)	I'M JUST GOING TO SEE ABOUT THEM. HERES MY OWN	LIST	, IF YOU DONT MIND. /RIDGEON/ THANKS. WHATS THIS? (HE

LISTEN

6CAL	(102)	DEAREST LOVE. (THROWING HERSELF ON HER KNEES)	LISTEN	: DO AS YOU WILL: I WILL NOT SAY ANOTHER WORD: I ASK
HART III	(148)	SOULS ARE STILL ALIVE. /MRS HUSHABYE/ SH-SH!	LISTEN	: DO YOU HEAR IT NOW? IT'S MAGNIFICENT. THEY ALL
GETT	(330)	YES: A HUSBAND SOON BECOMES NOTHING BUT A HABIT.	LISTEN	: I SUPPOSE THIS DETESTABLE FASCINATION YOU HAVE FOR
SIM II	(79)	(TO THE OTHERS) IM THROUGH TO LONDON REGIONAL.	LISTEN	: I'LL REPEAT IT AS IT COMES. (HE ECHOES THE NEWS).
CLEO III	(152)	FEROCIOUSLY; BUT HE IS NOT AT ALL INTIMIDATED).	LISTEN	: WERE YOU SET HERE TO WATCH ME, OR TO WATCH THE
HART II	(86)	WHAT DO YOU KNOW ABOUT BUSINESS? YOU JUST	LISTEN	AND LEARN. YOUR FATHER'S BUSINESS WAS A NEW BUSINESS;
LION II	(140)	ARENA, ENDING IN WILD APPLAUSE. THE GLADIATORS	LISTEN	AND LOOK INQUIRINGLY AT ONE ANOTHER). /THE EDITOR/
MTH1 II	(28)	SPEAK TO A CHILD AS TO A MAN, AND A MAN DOES NOT	LISTEN	AND TREMBLE IN SILENCE. HE REPLIES: HE MAKES THE
SIM II	SD(68)	WHAT CAN THE MATTER BE? THEY ALL RISE AND	LISTEN	ANXIOUSLY. A TRUMPET CALL RINGS OUT FROM THE SKY.
BARB II	(300)	DOWNT YOU GOW BEIN SORRY FOR ME: YOUVE NO CALL.	LISTEN	EAH. AW BROWK YOUR JAWR. /JENNY/ NO, IT DIDNT HURT
BARB II	(300)	IF AW CAWNT SETTISFAW YOU ONE WY, AW KEN ANATHER.	LISTEN	EAH! AW ED TWO QUID SIVED AGEN THE FROST; AN AWVE A
CAND II	(124)	BURGESS, WHO TURNS STEALTHILY TO LEXY. /BURGESS/	LISTEN	ERE, MR MILL. WHATS PROSSY'S COMPLAINT? WHATS WRONG
MTH2	(46)	HE HAS LOST THE POWER OF LISTENING. HE DOESNT	LISTEN	EVEN IN THE HOUSE OF COMMONS. SAVVY RUSHES IN
KING II	(227)	SOME MAGIC THAT SCATTERED MY WITS: SHE MADE ME	LISTEN	FOR A MOMENT TO THOSE WHO WERE ALWAYS PRESSING ME TO
MIS.	(138)	SOMETHING TO THEM: THEYVE HAD THEIR FLING. ALL I	LISTEN	FOR IS SOME SIGN OF IT ENDING IN SOMETHING; BUT JUST
FABL PREFACE	(79)	HYDE PARK, HE HEARD A GOSPEL PREACHER CRY "	LISTEN	FOR THE VOICE OF GOD AND IT WILL COME TO YOU." THIS
PHIL I	(74)	AT THIS HOUR? /GRACE/ I CANT IMAGINE. (THEY	LISTEN	GUILTILY. THE DOOR OF THE FLAT IS OPENED WITHOUT.
PYGM II	(236)	/DOOLITTLE/ NO. THIS IS A MISUNDERSTANDING.	LISTEN	HERE-- /MRS PEARCE/ HE CANT TAKE HER AWAY, MR
FANY I	(283)	IS WHAT I AM PAID FOR. /DORA/ (CONFIDENTIALLY)	LISTEN	HERE, DEAR BOY. YOUR NAME ISNT JUGGINS. NOBODY'S NAME
PYGM II	(236)	TURNS CONFIDENTIALLY TO HIGGINS. /DOOLITTLE/	LISTEN	HERE, GOVERNOR. YOU AND ME IS MEN OF THE WORLD, AINT
FANY I	(280)	HIS EYE KNOCKED OUT. /GILBEY/ (TO DORA, ANGRILY)	LISTEN	HERE, YOU, /DORA/ OH, AINT WE CROSS! /GILBEY/ I WANT
MTH5	(220)	BORN/ HOW JOLLY! WHAT IS A SCULPTOR? /ACIS/	LISTEN	HERE, YOUNG ONE. YOU MUST FIND OUT THINGS FOR
JITT I	(21)	A MADWOMAN. GIVE ME A REASON. /BRUNO/ I WILL.	LISTEN	. A BOOK BY A DEAD MAN IS AN ORPHAN. ORPHANS
JOAN EPIL,SD	(160)	-- HULLO! WHO'S THAT KNOCKING AT THE DOOR? THEY	LISTEN	. A LONG GENTLE KNOCKING IS HEARD. /CHARLES/ COME IN.
JOAN 6	(137)	ARE SAYING, CHILD. DO YOU WANT TO KILL YOURSELF?	LISTEN	. DO YOU NOT BELIEVE THAT YOU ARE SUBJECT TO THE
MTH2	(51)	HIS PRICE) I HAVE NOT MADE MYSELF CLEAR.	LISTEN	. I AM AGREEING WITH YOU. I AM ON YOUR SIDE. I AM
MTH1 I	(9)	DO, DARE IT. EVERYTHING IS POSSIBLE: EVERYTHING.	LISTEN	. I AM OLD. I AM THE OLD SERPENT, OLDER THAN ADAM,
2TRU I	(43)	NOT AN ATTRACTIVE PROSPECT, IS IT? NOW	LISTEN	. I HAVE SOMETHING TO PROPOSE TO YOU OF THE GREATEST
DOCT III	(153)	YOU LONG; BUT I MUST TELL YOU THE WHOLE TRUTH.	LISTEN	. I KNOW LOUIS AS NOBODY ELSE IN THE WORLD KNOWS HIM
MILL IV	(206)	THE COMPASSIONATE HEARD THE PRAYER OF THE WIDOW.	LISTEN	. I ONCE CURED A PRIME MINISTER WHEN HE IMAGINED
MTH1 I	(7)	BIRTH. /EVE/ A SECOND BIRTH? /THE SERPENT/	LISTEN	. I WILL TELL YOU A GREAT SECRET. I AM VERY SUBTLE;
KING I	(202)	PRESENTLY; BUT THE KING COMES FIRST. NOW	LISTEN	. (HE RISES. THEY ALL RISE, EXCEPT FOX). NO, PRAY.
VWOO 3	(134)	PAY YOU FOR. SIT DOWN AGAIN. (SHE DOES SO). NOW	LISTEN	. (HE TAKES UP HIS MANUSCRIPT AND READS). ITEM: I
CURE	(235)	I ALWAYS DO IMAGINE MYSELF. /STREGA/ RIGHT. NOW	LISTEN	. (SHE PLAYS THE FIRST SECTION OF THE POLONAISE.
MTH2	(46)	YOU? YOU CAN TELL THINGS ONLY TO PEOPLE WHO CAN	LISTEN	. JOYCE BURGE HAS TALKED SO MUCH THAT HE HAS LOST THE
NEVR IV	(284)	TO HIM ON HER KNEES AND SEIZES HIS HANDS). NOW	LISTEN	. NO TREASON TO HER: NO WORD, NO THOUGHT AGAINST HER.
MILL I	(157)	MARVELLOUS ABOUT YOU EXCEPT YOUR APPETITE.	LISTEN	. ON EACH OF HIS BIRTHDAYS HIS AUNT HAD PRESENTED HIM
MTH5	(242)	AND PLACES HIS DISENGAGED HAND ON ITS HEAD). NOW	LISTEN	. ONE OF YOU TWO IS TO BE DESTROYED. WHICH OF YOU
2TRU I	(43)	WE ARE GOING TO HAVE AN IDEAL NIGHT. NOW	LISTEN	. PICTURE TO YOURSELF A HEAVENLY AFTERNOON IN JULY: A
MTH5	(223)	BUSTS ARE ONLY THE BEGINNING OF A MIGHTY DESIGN.	LISTEN	. /ACIS/ GO AHEAD, OLD SPORT. WE ARE LISTENING.
MTH5	(246)	YOU? PLEASE DONT. /THE HE-ANCIENT/ CHILDREN,	LISTEN	. /ACIS/ (STRIDING DOWN THE STEPS TO THE BENCH AND
CLEO IV	SD(184)	AND RUNS TO THE EDGE OF THE ROOF TO PEER DOWN AND	LISTEN	. /CAESAR/ (LOOKING PIERCINGLY AT CLEOPATRA) WHAT
HART III	(129)	A PRESENTIMENT. I REALLY HAVE. AND YOU WOULDNT	LISTEN	. /MRS HUSHABYE/ I WAS LISTENING FOR SOMETHING ELSE.
BUOY II	(26)	OF THE LAKE ARE CHARMED, AND ASSEMBLE HERE TO	LISTEN	. /SHE/ (THROWING OPEN HER DOOR AND APPEARING ON THE
CLEO II	SD(138)	AT HIS FRANTIC CONDITION. POTHINUS TURNS TO	LISTEN	. /THEODOTUS/ (ON THE STEPS, WITH UPLIFTED ARMS)
CLEO IV	SD(184)	APPALLED, THE MEN SET DOWN THEIR GLASSES, AND	LISTEN	. SILENCE. THE PURPLE DEEPENS IN THE SKY. CAESAR,
KING I	(204)	GREAT LINES, LIKE THE ONES HE GAVE TO MONTEZUMA.	LISTEN	. STILL LESS AND LESS MY BOILING SPIRITS FLOW AND I
CAPT NOTES	(305)	USING THEIR EARS, MUCH LESS OF TRAINING THEM TO	LISTEN	. THEN CAME MR ANSTEY'S COCKNEY DIALOGUES IN PUNCH, A
MTH3	(92)	TO SWITCH OFF). /BURGE-LUBIN/ DONT SWITCH OFF.	LISTEN	. THIS AMERICAN HAS INVENTED A METHOD OF BREATHING
AUGS	(274)	YOU: YOU WILL UNDERSTAND ME AS NO ONE ELSE COULD.	LISTEN	. THIS SPY, THIS WOMAN -- /AUGUSTUS/ (ALL ATTENTION)
MTH5	(229)	WE WANT TO SEE THE ARTIFICIAL PAIR. WE WILL	LISTEN	. WE ARE TREMENDOUSLY INTERESTED. TELL US ALL ABOUT
PRES	(159)	CORINTHIA/ I DONT WANT YOU TO TALK. I WANT YOU TO	LISTEN	. YOU DO NOT UNDERSTAND MY VIEWS ON THE QUESTION OF
MTH5	(217)	OUT OF THE PAST. YOU WILL FORGET IT TOMORROW. NOW	LISTEN	. YOU HAVE FOUR YEARS OF CHILDHOOD BEFORE YOU. YOU
ARMS I	(18)	HIM, AND ADDRESSES HIM PATRONIZINGLY). NOW	LISTEN	. YOU MUST TRUST TO OUR HOSPITALITY. YOU DO NOT YET
DEVL III	(54)	WHY NOT TRY TO SAVE YOURSELF? I IMPLORE YOU--	LISTEN	. YOU SAID JUST NOW THAT YOU SAVED HIM FOR MY SAKE--
2TRU I	(46)	WELL, YOU HAVE A NERVE, YOU HAVE. /THE PATIENT/	LISTEN	. YOU WILL BE A COUNTESS. WE SHALL GO ABROAD, WHERE
PHIL II	(101)	WASTE PAPER BASKET AND PIECE THEM TOGETHER. NOW	LISTEN	. " MY DEAR LEONARD: NOTHING COULD MAKE IT WORTH MY
NEVR II	(253)	AND RESIGNS HERSELF TO INDULGE HIM A LITTLE).	LISTEN	NOW. WHAT I WANT TO ASK YOU IS THIS. DONT YOU
2TRU III	(95)	DOING ANYTHING: NOBODY CARES. OH DEAR, WONT YOU	LISTEN	-- (HER VOICE IS LOST IN THE DISTANCE). WHILST THEY
BARB I	(271)	DOOR). AND REMEMBER THIS, ADOLPHUS (HE TURNS TO	LISTEN	): I HAVE A VERY STRONG SUSPICION THAT YOU WENT TO
MIS.	(111)	AND FOLLOWING BENTLEY, WHO IS FORCED TO TURN AND	LISTEN	) I'LL TELL YOU WHAT IT IS, MY BOY: YOU WANT A GOOD
DEST	(157)	INTERVAL) GIUSEPPE! /NAPOLEON/ (RISING TO	LISTEN	) THATS NOT THE VOICE OF A WOMAN WHOSE HUSBAND WAS
PHIL II	(105)	JULIA DROPS THE PAPER, AND COMES A STEP NEARER TO	LISTEN	). YOU GENERALLY KNOW WHERE SHE'S TO BE FOUND.
WIDO II	(41)	PUT, MY DEAR SIR. COME, HARRY: SIT DOWN AND	LISTEN	; AND CONSIDER THE MATTER CALMLY AND JUDICIALLY. DONT
WIDO II	(41)	/TRENCH/ I HAVE NO OBJECTION TO SIT DOWN AND	LISTEN	; BUT I DONT SEE HOW THAT CAN MAKE BLACK WHITE; AND I
GLIM	(173)	DEAR. /THE GIRL/ (SQUEEZING HIS HAND) OH LISTEN,	LISTEN	; YOU ARE WANDERING AGAIN. /THE FRIAR/ THATS RIGHT:
2TRU III	(95)	COLONEL, COLONEL: YOU MIGHT HAVE THE DECENCY TO	LISTEN	TO A DISTRACTED MOTHER FOR A MOMENT. COLONEL: MY
MIS. PREFACE	(88)	BOOK IS NOT A WORK OF ART. SIMILARLY, YOU CANNOT	LISTEN	TO A LESSON OR A SERMON UNLESS THE TEACHER OR THE
KING I	(201)	HOW MUCH MORE MUST I ENDURE FROM YOU? I WILL NOT	LISTEN	TO A PROLOGUE THAT CAN BE SPOKEN ONLY BY A WOMAN IN
MIS. PREFACE	(88)	COMPARATIVELY ARTLESS. TO READ A DULL BOOK; TO	LISTEN	TO A TEDIOUS PLAY OR PROSY SERMON OR LECTURE; TO
WIDO II	(30)	LET GO MUCH LONGER, HE GIVES ME THE SACK. WOULDNT	LISTEN	TO A WORD, THOUGH I WOULD HAVE OFFERED TO MAKE UP THE
MTH1 II	(31)	I NEVER SEE HER NOW. SO I HAVE TO COME BACK AND	LISTEN	TO ADAM SAYING THE SAME THING FOR THE TEN-THOUSANDTH
OVER PREFACE	(156)	AND DESPERATE CHARACTERS ENGAGE IN THEM OR WOULD	LISTEN	TO ADVANCES IN THAT DIRECTION WITHOUT RAISING AN
METH PREFACE	(R46)	BE CONTENT WITH ENOUGH EVIDENCE: HE WILL HAVE YOU	LISTEN	TO ALL THE EVIDENCE THAT EXISTS IN THE WORLD.

GENV IV	(114)	LEAGUE OF NATIONS. TO ME IT IS AGONY TO HAVE TO	LISTEN	TO ALL THIS TALK, KNOWING AS I DO THAT NOTHING CAN
LION I	(111)	WHERES YOUR BEHAVIOR? IS THAT THE WAY TO	LISTEN	TO AN OFFICER? (TO THE CAPTAIN) THATS WHAT WE HAVE
FABL PREFACE	(92)	WITHIN OUR RANGE OF VISION ARE DOUBLED. WHEN WE	LISTEN	TO AN ORCHESTRA OR AN ORGAN WE ARE DEAF TO THE
INCA	(257)	PLAY ANY PATRIOTIC AIRS. I AM SORRY YOU WILL NOT	LISTEN	TO ANY MORE PERMANENT ARRANGEMENT; BUT IF YOU WOULD
CLEO IV	(173)	CLEOPATRA: YOU ARE ONLY AN EGYPTIAN. SHE WILL NOT	LISTEN	TO ANY OF HER OWN RACE: SHE TREATS US ALL AS
ROCK I	(204)	/FLAVIA/ OH, IT'S NO USE TRYING TO MAKE PAPA	LISTEN	TO ANYTHING. (SHE THROWS HERSELF DESPAIRINGLY INTO
FANY PROLOG	(259)	AND DETESTABLE. I DO NOT LISTEN TO THEM! I	LISTEN	TO CIMAROSA, TO PERGOLESI, TO GLUCK AND MOZART.
ROCK II	(247)	BUT IF YOU THINK THAT THE BRITISH WORKINGMAN WILL	LISTEN	TO COMPULSORY LABOR AND PUTTING DOWN STRIKES YOU DONT
MILL III	(185)	HELPLESSLY. /THE WOMAN/ (CRYING) OH, JOE, DONT	LISTEN	TO HER: DONT LET HER MEDDLE WITH US. THAT WOMAN WOULD
MTH1 I	(18)	MAKE THAT ODIOUS NOISE, I TELL YOU. /ADAM/ DO NOT	LISTEN	TO HER: THE NOISE IS GOOD: IT LIGHTENS MY HEART. YOU
2TRU II	(71)	SHE IS MUCH BETTER COMPANY WHEN SHE'S HALF DRUNK.	LISTEN	TO HER NOW, WHEN SHE IS SOBER! /THE PATIENT/
MRS II	(213)	WARREN/ MY OWN OPINIONS AND MY OWN WAY OF LIFE!	LISTEN	TO HER TALKING! DO YOU THINK I WAS BROUGHT UP LIKE
OVER	(172)	FOLLIES. IT'S SO DELIGHTFUL TO LOOK AT HER, TO	LISTEN	TO HER VOICE, TO HEAR ALL SHE HAS TO SAY, THAT
GETT	(341)	HAVE MARRIED. /SOAMES/ THIS WOMAN IS INSPIRED.	LISTEN	TO HER, MY LORD. /THE BISHOP/ (TAKEN ABACK BY THE
MRS IV	(252)	ONE OF YOUR OWN HOUSES. /MRS WARREN/ (SCREAMING)	LISTEN	TO HER! LISTEN TO HOW SHE SPITS ON HER MOTHER'S GREY
JITT III	(59)	BETWEEN THE TABLE AND THE CONSOLE) WHY DO YOU	LISTEN	TO HIM? WHY DO YOU RUN TO STRANGERS WHEN YOU WANT TO
BUOY III	(41)	IDEAS NO ONE WOULD EMPLOY HIM AS A PREACHER NOR	LISTEN	TO HIM AS A TEACHER. HE COULD DO NOTHING BUT MAKE
HART I	(47)	YOUNG LADY. HERE, DUCKY, HAVE SOME TEA; AND DONT	LISTEN	TO HIM (SHE POURS OUT A CUP OF TEA). /THE CAPTAIN/ (
CLEO IV	(173)	SLAYER OF POMPEY. HE IS A ROMAN: MAY BE SHE WILL	LISTEN	TO HIM. BEGONE! /POTHINUS/ (DARKLY) I KNOW TO WHOM
METH PREFACE	(R47)	WAS AN AMIABLE AND UPRIGHT MAN. NOBODY WOULD	LISTEN	TO HIM. HE WAS SO COMPLETELY SUBMERGED BY THE FLOWING
LADY	(244)	ANGER HER NO FURTHER. IT IS DEATH, MADAM: DO NOT	LISTEN	TO HIM. /SHAKESPEAR/ NOT WERE IT EEN TO SAVE YOUR
DEST	(191)	SITS DOWN ON THE COUCH AND COMPOSES HERSELF TO	LISTEN	TO HIM. SECURE OF HIS AUDIENCE, HE AT ONCE NERVES
CLEO IV	(192)	THE FIG MARKET-- /CAESAR/ (TOO MUCH EXCITED TO	LISTEN	TO HIM) I SAW THEM THE DAY WE ARRIVED. GOOD! (HE
SIM II	(61)	UNTIL YOU HAVE HEARD MY SERMON, PLEASE. /PROLA/	LISTEN	TO HIM, CHILDREN. RESPECT THE WISDOM OF THE FOOL.
MRS I	(190)	ANY OF US. /MRS WARREN/ (GREATLY AMUSED) ONLY	LISTEN	TO HIM, GEORGE! OLDER THAN ANY OF US! WELL, SHE HAS
BARB III	(336)	YOU LAYING A SNARE FOR MY SOUL? /CUSINS/ DONT	LISTEN	TO HIS METAPHYSICS, BARBARA. THE PLACE IS DRIVEN BY
MRS IV	(252)	HOUSES. /MRS WARREN/ (SCREAMING) LISTEN TO HER!	LISTEN	TO HOW SHE SPITS ON HER MOTHER'S GREY HAIRS! OH, MAY
FABL IV	(116)	EVOLUTION. FULL STOP. POSTSCRIPT. STOP TYPING AND	LISTEN	TO INSTRUCTIONS. WHAT I HAVE JUST DICTATED IS FOR THE
FANY PROLOG	(259)	TWANG: I KEEP OUT OF HEARING OF IT AND SPEAK AND	LISTEN	TO ITALIAN. I FIND BEETHOVEN'S MUSIC COARSE AND
MTH1 I	(19)	WAY UNDER MY FEET WHEN IT SPEAKS. DO YOU STAY AND	LISTEN	TO IT. /THE SERPENT/ (LAUGHS)! ! ! /ADAM/ (
JOAN 2	(85)	I HAVE A MESSAGE TO THEE FROM GOD; AND THOU MUST	LISTEN	TO IT, THOUGH THY HEART BREAK WITH THE TERROR OF IT.
MILL III	(180)	HOLDS UP HALF A CROWN). LOOK HERE! LOOK AT IT!	LISTEN	TO IT! (HE RINGS IT ON THE TABLE). IT'S YOURS, AND
MIS.	(137)	PAPA TALKING; AND WHEN PAPA STOPS FOR A BREATH I	LISTEN	TO JOHNNY TALKING. /LORD SUMMERHAYS/ YOU MAKE ME FEEL
MIS.	(137)	TALK, TALK, TALK, THATS MY LIFE. ALL THE DAY I	LISTEN	TO MAMMA TALKING; AT DINNER I LISTEN TO PAPA TALKING;
PHIL II	(108)	HIM. /CHARTERIS/ JUST SO. I UNDERSTAND. NOW	LISTEN	TO ME: I AM GOING TO SPEAK AS A PHILOSOPHER. JULIA IS
WIDO II	(35)	NOTHING. NOW DONT BE ABSURD, HARRY: BE GOOD; AND	LISTEN	TO ME: I KNOW HOW TO SETTLE IT. YOU ARE TOO PROUD TO
JOAN 3	(90)	DOING NOTHING. OH, WHY ARE YOU NOT FIGHTING?	LISTEN	TO ME: I WILL DELIVER YOU FROM FEAR. I -- /DUNOIS/ (
DEST	(191)	/NAPOLEON/ YES YOU ARE: ENGLISH TO THE BACKBONE.	LISTEN	TO ME: I WILL EXPLAIN THE ENGLISH TO YOU. /LADY/ (
MRS IV	(248)	MRS WARREN CONTINUES DESPERATELY) VIVIE:	LISTEN	TO ME: YOU DONT UNDERSTAND: YOUVE BEEN TAUGHT WRONG
BULL III	(143)	/LARRY/ (DESPERATELY) ONCE MORE, TOM, WILL YOU	LISTEN	TO ME? /BROADBENT/ RUBBISH! I TELL YOU IT WILL BE
PHIL II	(124)	WHAT I'M DOING: I'M TOO MISERABLE. OH, WONT YOU	LISTEN	TO ME? /GRACE/ DO YOU SUPPOSE I AM A MAN, TO BE
MTH3	(102)	DID. DROWNED. /BARNABAS/ (EXASPERATED) WILL YOU	LISTEN	TO ME? WAS OLD ARCHBISHOP HASLAM, THE PRESENT MAN'S
DEVL I	(14)	HER ARM AWAY, AND GOES ON, PEREMPTORILY) NOW YOU	LISTEN	TO ME AND DO AS YOURE TOLD. YOU SIT DOWN THERE IN THE
2TRU I	(43)	OF YOU AND CHANGE YOUR ENTIRE DESTINY. YOU CAN	LISTEN	TO ME IN PERFECT SECURITY: AT ANY MOMENT YOU CAN RING
LION I	(122)	MY INFLUENCE CALMS THE PASSIONS OF THE MOB: THEY	LISTEN	TO ME IN SILENCE; AND INFIDELS ARE OFTEN CONVERTED BY
MTH5	(211)	MEANS THAT YOU ARE DYING TO ME: YES, JUST DYING.	LISTEN	TO ME (HE PUTS HIS ARM AROUND HER). /THE MAIDEN/ (
DOCT III	(153)	BEFRIEND ME. OH, WILL YOU PLEASE SIT DOWN AND	LISTEN	TO ME JUST FOR A FEW MINUTES. (HE ASSENTS WITH A
O'FL	(226)	(LOUDER) MRS O'FLAHERTY! ! WILL YOU JUST	LISTEN	TO ME ONE MOMENT? PLEASE. (FURIOUSLY) DO YOU HEAR
BARB I	(255)	HIM SHORT) NOW BE A GOOD BOY, STEPHEN, AND	LISTEN	TO ME PATIENTLY. THE UNDERSHAFTS ARE DESCENDED FROM A
PHIL I	(74)	OF MY PHILANDERINGS. (HE SITS DOWN BESIDE HER).	LISTEN	TO ME. AM I A PARTICULARLY HANDSOME MAN? /GRACE/ (
GLIM	(173)	BARBARA. /THE GIRL/ YOUR WITS ARE WANDERING.	LISTEN	TO ME. ARE YOU LISTENING? /THE FRIAR/ YES YES YES
GENV I	(40)	HIS OWN SAFETY IN THIS WAY, USELESS: HE WOULD NOT	LISTEN	TO ME. AT LAST I FOUND OUT THE REASON. HE WAS
JOAN 1	(61)	UNWELCOME AND ONLY TOO FAMILIAR SENSATION) NOW	LISTEN	TO ME. I AM GOING TO ASSERT MYSELF. /JOAN/ (BUSILY)
FABL II	(107)	WHAT I DID? KICK THE FELLOW OUT. /OLDHAND/	LISTEN	TO ME. I AM, AS YOU SAY, A DIPLOMATIST; AND I THINK
DEST	(172)	BEHIND HER). /NAPOLEON/ AH, THATS BETTER. NOW	LISTEN	TO ME. I LIKE YOU. WHATS MORE, I VALUE YOUR RESPECT.
LIED	(195)	BUT IT'S NOT SEASONABLE JUST AT PRESENT. NOW JUST	LISTEN	TO ME. I SUPPOSE YOU KNOW ALL THOSE POEMS BY HEART.
GETT	(326)	WHAT ARE YOU AFRAID OF? /HOTCHKISS/ I DONT KNOW.	LISTEN	TO ME. I WAS A YOUNG FOOL LIVING BY MYSELF IN LONDON.
CLEO IV	(179)	US? /FTATATEETA/ NO, DEAR HEART, NO. /CLEOPATRA/	LISTEN	TO ME. IF HE LEAVES THE PALACE ALIVE, NEVER SEE MY
JOAN 3	(90)	OURS OR THE GODDAMS'? /DUNOIS/ BE QUIET, AND	LISTEN	TO ME. IF I WERE IN EITHER OF THOSE FORTS WITH ONLY
DEST	(183)	YES: YOU MUST: YOU SHALL: HE IS NOT FIT TO DIE.	LISTEN	TO ME. IF I TELL YOU WHERE TO FIND HIM-- IF I
PHIL III	(135)	TURNING) AH, YOU THINK THAT! (SHE COMES BACK).	LISTEN	TO ME. IF I SAY YES, WILL YOU PROMISE NOT TO TOUCH
GENV IV	(106)	(POLITELY HOLDING UP HIS OWN). /THE WIDOW/	LISTEN	TO ME. IN MY COUNTRY MEN FIGHT DUELS EVERY DAY. IF
FABL III	(111)	AND IT SHALL BE GIVEN TO YOU. /THE GENTLEMAN/	LISTEN	TO ME. I'LL GIVE YOU FIVE GUINEAS IF YOULL SUBMIT TO
BULL II	(114)	/BROADBENT/ NO, PLEASE, MISS REILLY. ONE MOMENT.	LISTEN	TO ME. I'M SERIOUS: I'M DESPERATELY SERIOUS. TELL ME
MTH1 II	(30)	PEACE, YOU TWO FOOLS. SIT DOWN AND BE QUIET; AND	LISTEN	TO ME. (ADAM, WITH A WEARY SHRUG, THROWS DOWN HIS
CATH 1	(166)	DARLING: YOUR LIPS ARE THE GATES OF TRUTH. NOW	LISTEN	TO ME. (HE MARKS OFF THE ITEMS OF HIS STATEMENT WITH
MILL I	(143)	AS IF I HAD BROKEN YOUR NECK, AS I WANTED TO. NOW	LISTEN	TO ME. (HE COMES TO HER AND LOOKS DOWN GRAVELY AT
MIS.	(159)	THE VESTIBULE DOOR. /TARLETON/ (GOING TO HER)	LISTEN	TO ME. (SHE TURNS QUICKLY). WHAT YOU SAID JUST NOW
ROCK I	(218)	IF I DID THAT IN THE ISLE NOT A MAN WOULD STOP TO	LISTEN	TO ME. MIND YOU, I KNOW YOU MEAN IT AS A COMPLIMENT
SUPR III	(90)	AND YET WE MEET HERE, DEAR LADY. /THE OLD WOMAN/	LISTEN	TO ME. MY FATHER WAS SLAIN BY JUST SUCH A WRETCH AS
PYGM V	(274)	/HIGGINS/ I-- /MRS HIGGINS/ SIT DOWN, DEAR; AND	LISTEN	TO ME. /HIGGINS/ OH VERY WELL, VERY WELL, VERY WELL.
CAND I SD	(100)	/MORELL/ (WITH NOBLE TENDERNESS) EUGENE!	LISTEN	TO ME. SOME DAY, I HOPE AND TRUST, YOU WILL BE A
JITT I	(20)	/JITTA/ (SPRINGING UP) ALFRED'S! /BRUNO/	LISTEN	TO ME. THE BOOK IS FINISHED: THE TYPED COPY WILL BE
LION I	(115)	CAPTAIN. /THE CAPTAIN/ INCORRIGIBLE! (URGENTLY)	LISTEN	TO ME. THE MEN IN THAT AUDIENCE TOMORROW WILL BE THE
NEVR I	(206)	MY CONSCIENCE! MY CONSCIENCE HAS BEEN MY RUIN.	LISTEN	TO ME. TWICE BEFORE I HAVE SET UP AS A RESPECTABLE
BULL III	(141)	/HODSON/ (UNMOVED) YOU JAST KEEP YOUR AIR ON AND	LISTEN	TO ME. YOU AWRISH PEOPLE ARE TOO WELL OFF: THETS WOTS
MILL II	(173)	WITHOUT IT. (SHE PUTS IT TENDERLY ON HIS HEAD).	LISTEN	TO ME. YOU ARE HAVING AN ADVENTURE. HAVE YOU NO
HART I	(56)	IS A WONDERFUL MAN IF YOU LIKE. /ELLIE/ HESIONE:	LISTEN	TO ME. YOU DONT UNDERSTAND. MY FATHER AND MR MANGAN
OVER	(191)	YOU SAY THAT AGAIN. /JUNO/ OH, WELL, IF YOU WONT	LISTEN	TO ME-- ! (HE SITS DOWN AGAIN). /MRS JUNO/ WHAT IS
2TRU III	(111)	TO PREACH, WITHOUT THEM THE YOUNG WILL NOT	LISTEN	TO ME; FOR EVEN THE YOUNG GROW TIRED OF DENIALS. THE
MTH5	(223)	EMPTINESS. (HE MOUNTS THE ALTAR IMPETUOUSLY)	LISTEN	TO ME, ALL OF YOU; AND DO YOU, ECRASIA, BE SILENT IF
NEVR IV	(297)	(TO BOHUN, MEEKLY) THANK YOU. /BOHUN/ NOW	LISTEN	TO ME, ALL OF YOU. I GIVE NO OPINION, M'COMAS, AS TO
HART I	(74)	TO NOTICE WHETHER I AM PLAIN OR NOT? /HECTOR/	LISTEN	TO ME, ARIADNE. UNTIL TODAY I HAVE SEEN ONLY
BARB II	(301)	CIVILITY). TRY WHAT YOU CAN DO WITH HIM. HE WONT	LISTEN	TO ME, BECAUSE HE REMEMBERS WHAT A FOOL I WAS WHEN I
CLEO PRG2	(101)	AND PUT THEIR COMMANDS INTO HER MOUTH. /PERSIAN/	LISTEN	TO ME, BELZANOR. /BELZANOR/ SPEAK, O SUBTLE BEYOND
CLEO IV	(188)	AGAINST ME, IT SEEMS. /CLEOPATRA/ (VEHEMENTLY)	LISTEN	TO ME, CAESAR. IF ONE MAN IN ALL ALEXANDRIA CAN BE
PHIL III	(141)	WHEN HE'S CROSSED IN LOVE. (TO CHARTERIS) NOW	LISTEN	TO ME, CHARTERIS. WHEN I WAS A YOUNG FELLOW,
BARB I	(261)	RIPPING. /LADY BRITOMART/ BE QUIET, CHARLES. NOW	LISTEN	TO ME, CHILDREN. YOUR FATHER IS COMING HERE THIS
LIED	(189)	AND PUTTING HER HAND CARESSINGLY ON HIS SHOULDER)	LISTEN	TO ME, DEAR. IT'S VERY NICE OF YOU TO LIVE WITH ME IN
DOCT III	(153)	WITH YOU. I FEEL THAT YOU KNOW. YOU MUST	LISTEN	TO ME, DOCTOR. (WITH SUDDEN MISGIVING) AM I
PYGM IV	(264)	HEAVEN'S NAME, WHY? (REASONABLY, GOING TO HER)	LISTEN	TO ME, ELIZA. ALL THIS IRRITATION IS PURELY
MTH1 I	(17)	A WORD. /ADAM/ WHATEVER I FEAR TO DO IS WICKED.	LISTEN	TO ME, EVE; AND YOU, SNAKE, LISTEN TOO, THAT YOUR
GLIM	(184)	FREEST WHEN IT IS HOT. /FERRUCCIO/ SHE DEVIL!	LISTEN	TO ME, GIULIETTA-- /GIULIA/ IT IS USELESS, SIGNOR.
CURE	(236)	SOME). A-- A-- AH! NOW I FEEL THAT I CAN SPEAK.	LISTEN	TO ME, GODDESS. I AM NOT HAPPY. I HATE MY PRESENT
LIED	(194)	TIME! OH, THIS TIME I THOUGHT I WAS AWAKE. /SHE/	LISTEN	TO ME, HENRY: WE REALLY HAVNT TIME FOR ALL THAT SORT
BUOY II	(24)	AND SHE WHO DWELLS WITHIN IS ONE OF THEM. /HE/	LISTEN	TO ME, JOHN. WE WHITE MEN HAVE A GOD MUCH MUCH
FANY III	(309)	DISSATISFACTION. /GILBEY/ (PATERNALLY) NOW YOU	LISTEN	TO ME, JUGGINS. I'M AN OLDER MAN THAN YOU. DONT YOU
PHIL I	(75)	UP HERE WITH THAT WOMAN? YOU SCOUNDREL! BUT NOW	LISTEN	TO ME, LEONARD: YOU HAVE DRIVEN ME TO DESPERATION:
GETT	(268)	(PERSUASIVELY DRAWING HIS CHAIR NEARER TO HER)	LISTEN	TO ME, LESBIA. FOR THE TENTH AND LAST TIME-- /LESBIA/
APPL INTRLUD	(246)	AND THE BABY. (SUDDENLY RETURNING TO HER SEAT)	LISTEN	TO ME, MAGNUS. WHY CAN YOU NOT BE A REAL KING?
MILL I	(148)	WOMAN HAS HER OWN WORLD WITHIN HER OWN SOUL.	LISTEN	TO ME, MR SAGAMORE. I MARRIED THIS MAN. I ADMITTED
JITT III	(66)	HIM. NOT WHILE I AM IN THE DARK ABOUT HER.	LISTEN	TO ME, MRS LENKHEIM. IF I THOUGHT IT WAS ONLY HER
BUOY 1	(14)	/FATHER/ THE SOFTEST PLACE NOW IS WHERE YOU ARE.	LISTEN	TO ME, MY BOY. YOU ARE CLEVERER THAN I AM. YOU KNOW
JOAN 1	(63)	THE TABLE, BEGINS THE FRIENDLY TALK. /ROBERT/ NOW	LISTEN	TO ME, POLLY. I MUST TALK TO YOU LIKE A FATHER.
MILL I	(164)	FROM A HURRICANE. (HE BECOMES SENTENTIOUS).	LISTEN	TO ME, SAGAMORE. I AM ONE OF THOSE UNFORTUNATE

BUOY III (41)	IN THE AFFAIRS OF THIS FAMILY. /MRS THIRDBORN/	LISTEN	TO ME, SIR FERDINAND. YOU MUST UNDERSTAND THAT MY
APPL I (237)	GO) JUST SO! BREAKAGES, LIMITED! JUST SO!	LISTEN	TO ME, SIR; AND JUDGE WHETHER I HAVE NOT REASON TO
JOAN 1 (68)	BROTHER'S OR ANYBODY'S. /ROBERT/ TCHA! /JOAN/	LISTEN	TO ME, SQUIRE. AT DOMREMY WE HAD TO FLY TO THE NEXT
PHIL II (101)	IT'S NO USE: SHE WONT GIVE ME UP. AND IF SHE WONT	LISTEN	TO ME, WHAT LIKELIHOOD IS THERE OF HER LISTENING TO
CLEO PRO2 (104)	HAND OF A FOOL, IF THE HIGH GODS PUT IT THERE?	LISTEN	TO ME, YE YOUNG MEN WITHOUT UNDERSTANDING. CLEOPATRA
HART II (125)	SHOUTING) I'LL NOT BEAR IT, I TELL YOU. WILL YOU	LISTEN	TO ME, YOU INFERNAL-- (HE CHOKES). /LADY UTTERWORD/
MTH4 I (163)	NOT. /ZOO/ THEN YOU DIDNT MEAN ANYTHING. NOW	LISTEN	TO ME, YOU LITTLE EPHEMERAL THING. I KNEW QUITE WELL
JOAN 1 (57)	THE HENS WILL NOT LAY. /ROBERT/ (RISING) NOW	LISTEN	TO ME, YOU. /STEWARD/ (HUMBLY) YES, SIR. /ROBERT/
UNPL PREFACE(R11)	FOR THE FIRST TIME SINCE HE HAD REFUSED TO	LISTEN	TO MINE, I TURNED OVER MY ARTICLES AGAIN; BUT TO
ARMS III (57)	EMPHASIS) NEVER YOU MIND MY SOUL; BUT JUST	LISTEN	TO MY ADVICE. IF YOU WANT TO BE A LADY, YOUR PRESENT
GENV IV (96)	OF DAMNED CHEEK, I CALL IT. I WONT SIT HERE AND	LISTEN	TO MY COUNTRY BEING INSULTED. /THE BETROTHED/ HEAR
MTH4 III (197)	MEAN? /THE ENVOY/ I ASK THE AUGUST ORACLE TO	LISTEN	TO MY VOICE-- /ZOO/ YOU PEOPLE SEEM NEVER TO TIRE OF
BULL PREFACE(41)	OF NOTHING ELSE BUT GETTING IT SET AGAIN, IT WILL	LISTEN	TO NO REFORMER, TO NO PHILOSOPHER, TO NO PREACHER,
MILL PREFACE(134)	BLASPHEMERS, OR AT BEST SEDITIOUS CADS, HE WILL	LISTEN	TO NOODLES' ORATIONS, READ POMPOUS LEADING ARTICLES,
ROCK I (195)	DO? CROWDS ARE DANGEROUS WHEN THEYVE NOTHING TO	LISTEN	TO OR LOOK AT. THE MEETINGS KEEP THEM AMUSED. THEY
GETT (288)	HIS HANDS IN HIS POCKETS) IT'S NO USE: THEY WONT	LISTEN	TO OUR SORT, (TURNING ON THEM) OF COURSE THEY HAVE
MIS. (137)	THE DAY I LISTEN TO MAMMA TALKING; AT DINNER I	LISTEN	TO PAPA TALKING; AND WHEN PAPA STOPS FOR A BREATH I
BUOY 1 (12)	BEEN EFFECTED WITHOUT KILLING ANYBODY. YOU MUST	LISTEN	TO REASON? /SON/ YES; BUT REASON LEADS JUST AS
MTH2 (70)	MAN ALIVE TO HANG ANYBODY; BUT THE PEOPLE WOULDNT	LISTEN	TO REASON. BESIDES, I KNEW THE DUTCH WOULDNT GIVE HIM
PHIL II (101)	COULDNT HAVE MADE A WORSE CHOICE. BUT SHE WONT	LISTEN	TO REASON. I ASSURE YOU, MY DEAR CRAVEN, IVE SAID
SUPR III (109)	ENSLAVED WHILST HE IS SPIRITUALLY WEAK ENOUGH TO	LISTEN	TO REASON. I TELL YOU, GENTLEMEN, IF YOU CAN SHEW A
GENV III (82)	/THE JEW/ YES; BUT AS THE BRITISH WOULD NOT	LISTEN	TO RUSKIN HE PRODUCED NOTHING. THE RACE WHOSE BRAINS
MTH4 I (148)	ENDEAVOR TO ENTERTAIN UNWELCOME VISITORS OR TO	LISTEN	TO SCIENTIFIC LECTURES. SLEEP. SLEEP. (BAWLING INTO
APPL I (230)	STEADY, STEADY! I CANNOT SIT HERE AND	LISTEN	TO SUCH A WORD AS HUMBUG BEING APPLIED TO DEMOCRACY.
MTH1 I (18)	WITHIN THE BOUNDS OF THOSE VOWS. YOU SHALL NOT	LISTEN	TO THAT SNAKE ANY MORE. COME (HE SEIZES HER BY THE
2TRU II (73)	(RISING) WELL, I AM NOT GOING TO SIT HERE AND	LISTEN	TO THAT SORT OF TALK. YOU OUGHT TO BE ASHAMED OF
MIS. (178)	ANYTHING AGAINST THE LADY. /MRS TARLETON/ OH,	LISTEN	TO THAT! /BENTLEY/ WHAT A LIAR! /HYPATIA/ OH!
WIDO II (29)	HARM WOULD IT DO YOU TO HELP A POOR MAN? JUST	LISTEN	TO THE CIRCUMSTANCES, SIR. I ONLY-- /TRENCH/ (MOVED,
BARB II (275)	SHE USED TO BEAT ME. NO MATTER: YOU COME AND	LISTEN	TO THE CONVERTED PAINTER, AND YOULL HEAR HOW SHE WAS
GLIM (177)	HER UGLY HEAD WITH. DO YOU SUPPOSE I'M GOING TO	LISTEN	TO THE HOWLING OF A SHE-WOLF WHO WANTED ME TO ABSOLVE
DEVL III (72)	IF YOU HAVE ANY SENSE OF DECENCY LEFT, TO	LISTEN	TO THE MINISTRATIONS OF THE CHAPLAIN, AND PAY DUE
GLIM (173)	THE BEADS OF HIS ROSARY RATTLE AT THE SAME TIME).	LISTEN	TO THE OLD MAN'S BONES RATTLING. OH, TAKE THE OLD OLD
MTH1 I (19)	FORGET AND BROOD AND ARE FILLED WITH FEAR. LET US	LISTEN	TO THE SNAKE. /ADAM/ NO: I AM AFRAID OF IT. I FEEL AS
FABL VI (129)	AND HEARD THE PREACHER EXHORTING HIS FLOCK TO	LISTEN	TO THE VOICE OF GOD. HE SAID IT WOULD SURELY COME TO
SUPR III (134)	SOMETHING UNNATURAL ABOUT THESE FELLOWS. DO NOT	LISTEN	TO THEIR GOSPEL, SENOR COMMANDER: IT IS DANGEROUS.
FANY PROLOG (259)	AND WAGNER'S SENSELESS AND DETESTABLE. I DO NOT	LISTEN	TO THEM: I LISTEN TO CIMAROSA, TO PERGOLESI, TO GLUCK
DOCT V (177)	THAT WILL ALWAYS BE HEAVENLY MUSIC IN MY EARS. I	LISTEN	TO THEM NOW WHENEVER I AM TIRED OR SAD. THAT IS WHY I
JITT I (15)	FOOTSTEPS DYING AWAY IN THE DISTANCE-- I ALWAYS	LISTEN	TO THEM TO CATCH THE LAST SOUND OF YOU-- I AM STABBED
JOAN PREFACE(53)	HAPPEN IF I KNEW MY BUSINESS SO LITTLE AS TO	LISTEN	TO THESE WELL INTENTIONED BUT DISASTROUS COUNSELLORS:
KING I (184)	OH! MR NEWTON: I MUST GO. I CANNOT STAY AND	LISTEN	TO THIS FRENCH LADY'S TALK. (SHE GOES OUT WITH
PYGM II (239)	TO BE HAPPY ANYHOW. /HIGGINS/ PICKERING: IF WE	LISTEN	TO THIS MAN ANOTHER MINUTE, WE SHALL HAVE NO
LADY (245)	OH, MADAM, IF YOU WOULD KNOW WHAT MISERY IS,	LISTEN	TO THIS MAN THAT IS MORE THAN MAN AND LESS AT THE
MILL I (141)	RAISED MY EXPECTATIONS, MADAM. /EPIFANIA/ O GOD,	LISTEN	TO THIS MAN! HAS IT EVER OCCURRED TO YOU THAT WHEN A
MRS IV (251)	KEEP YOURSELF TO YOURSELF: I DONT WANT YOU. BUT	LISTEN	TO THIS. DO YOU KNOW WHAT I WOULD DO WITH YOU IF YOU
SIM II (75)	SO. I NEVER THOUGHT OF IT IN THAT WAY. STILL,	LISTEN	TO THIS. (READING) " POLICEMAN WHO ATTEMPTED TO
JOAN 4 (99)	HIM CREDIT FOR. /WARWICK/ INDEED? IN WHAT WAY?	LISTEN	TO THIS, MESSIRE JOHN. /CAUCHON/ IF THE DEVIL WANTED
MIS. (145)	A YOUNG GIRL HAS BEEN RATHER A SUCCESS, DONT YOU	LISTEN	TO THIS, PATSY; IT MIGHT MAKE YOU CONCEITED. SHE'S
KING I (204)	DRYDEN DOES NOT UNDERSTAND HOW HARD THAT IS,	LISTEN	TO THIS, THE LONGEST SPEECH I HAD. MAY I BELIEVE MY
WIDO II (30)	AMUSEMENT IN THE MIDST OF HIS ANXIETY) JUST	LISTEN	TO THIS! WELL, YOU ARE AN INNOCENT YOUNG GENTLEMAN.
MTH3 (124)	TO US. /BURGE-LUBIN/ AS PRESIDENT, I MUST NOT	LISTEN	TO UNPATRIOTIC CRITICISMS OF OUR NATIONAL CHARACTER,
CLEO PRO2 (102)	/THE GUARDSMEN/ O SERPENT! /PERSIAN/ HE WILL	LISTEN	TO US IF WE COME WITH HER PICTURE IN OUR MOUTHS. HE
BARB II (300)	/BILL/ (IMPATIENTLY) TELL Y' AW DID: CAWNT YOU	LISTEN	TO WOTS BEIN TAOLD YOU? ALL AW GOT BE IT WAS BEIN
MIS. (170)	YOU AND YOUR MOTHER. /THE MAN/ OH, I'M A FOOL TO	LISTEN	TO YOU AND ARGUE WITH YOU. I CAME HERE TO KILL YOU
ROCK I (227)	AND DISINTERESTED GHOST. /THE LADY/ AS I	LISTEN	TO YOU I SEEM TO HEAR A GHOST PREPARING A SPEECH FOR
APPL PREFACE(195)	ARRANGEMENTS OF OUR RAILWAYS: HE WOULD NOT	LISTEN	TO YOU IF YOUR MIND WAS NOT LARGE ENOUGH TO GRASP THE
WIDO II (38)	YOU HAVE ANYTHING TO SAY TO ME, DR TRENCH, I WILL	LISTEN	TO YOU PATIENTLY. YOU WILL THEN ALLOW ME TO SAY WHAT
KING II (232)	WHAT A DREADFUL THING TO SAY! I MUST NOT	LISTEN	TO YOU. /CHARLES/ NO TWO CONSCIENCES ARE THE SAME. NO
2TRU II (72)	/THE COUNTESS/ IT'S WORSE FOR THEM. THEY HAVE TO	LISTEN	TO YOU. /THE PATIENT/ I DESPISE YOU. I HATE YOU.
MTH2 (43)	HAVE A TALK TO HER. /FRANKLYN/ PERHAPS SHE WILL	LISTEN	TO YOU. YOU ARE NOT HER FATHER. /CONRAD/ I SENT HER
GENV IV (94)	OF THESE TRIUMPHS OF YOURS IN ENGLAND, I	LISTEN	TO YOUR ACCOUNT OF THEM WITH PERFECT COMPLACENCY
BARB III (341)	BRITOMART/ BARBARA: I POSITIVELY FORBID YOU TO	LISTEN	TO YOUR FATHER'S ABOMINABLE WICKEDNESS. AND YOU,
JOAN 6 (145)	WORD GIVES GREAT OFFENCE), AND THAT I WAS NOT TO	LISTEN	TO YOUR FINE WORDS NOR TRUST TO YOUR CHARITY. YOU
SUPR I (13)	ELSE'S TIME: I HAVE SOMETHING BETTER TO DO THAN	LISTEN	TO YOUR FOOLERIES (HE POSITIVELY KICKS HIS WAY TO
ROCK PREFACE(183)	MORE FACTS THAN YOU WILL HAVE TIME OR PATIENCE TO	LISTEN	TO. THAT IS WHY YOUR LAWYERS CAN PLEAD AS WELL FOR
NEVR IV (291)	IN HIS CHAIR, WITH AN AIR OF BEING PREPARED TO	LISTEN	TOLERANTLY TO THEIR GRIEVANCES). NOW, MR CRAMPTON, GO
MTH1 I (17)	DO IS WICKED. LISTEN TO ME, EVE; AND YOU, SNAKE,	LISTEN	TOO, THAT YOUR MEMORY MAY HOLD MY VOW. I WILL LIVE A
FABL VI (129)	I CAN GIVE YOU ONLY THE ADVICE OF THE PREACHERS:	LISTEN	UNTIL YOU ARE TOLD. A YOUTH, CLOTHED IN FEATHERS LIKE
HART II (86)	HER CHIN ON HER HANDS, SHE COMPOSES HERSELF TO	LISTEN	WITH A COMBINATION OF CONSCIOUS CURIOSITY WITH
BASH PREFACE(89)	LINE BY LINE, WHILST THE ORDINARY PLAYGOERS WOULD	LISTEN	WITH A PUZZLED AND TROUBLED STARE, WONDERING WHAT ON
APPL II SD(271)	COMMONS ORATOR), MINISTERS COMPOSE THEMSELVES TO	LISTEN	WITH GRAVE ATTENTION, AS IF IN CHURCH; BUT LYSISTRATA
GENV IV (123)	LET US HEAR THE NEWS. THE NEWS. THE NEWS. (THEY	LISTEN	WITH STRAINED ATTENTION). SH-SH-SH-SH-SH-. /JUDGE/
DOCT IV (166)	DID YOU SAY, DEAR? (IN GREAT DISTRESS) I CANT	LISTEN	WITHOUT MOVING HIM. (HIS LIPS MOVE AGAIN: WALPOLE
ARMS II (36)	ABOVE THE ELBOWS WITH BOTH HANDS. /SERGIUS/ NOW	LISTEN	YOU TO ME. /LOUKA/ (WINCING) NOT SO TIGHT: YOURE
JOAN 1 (69)	ABOUT THE GIRL -- /ROBERT/ (TURNING TO JOAN) NOW	LISTEN	YOU TO ME; AND (DESPERATELY) DONT CUT IN BEFORE I
BARB III (331)	/LOMAX/ OH I SAY! /CUSINS/ YES, A CONFESSION.	LISTEN	, ALL. UNTIL I MET BARBARA I THOUGHT MYSELF IN THE
LION I (116)	ON ME. I TELL YOU, IT IS PHYSICALLY IMPOSSIBLE.	LISTEN	, CAPTAIN; DID YOU EVER TRY TO CATCH A MOUSE IN YOUR
MTH5 (217)	WHAT ARE YOU LAUGHING AT? /THE SHE-ANCIENT/	LISTEN	, CHILD-- /THE NEWLY BORN/ DO NOT COME NEAR ME. YOU
CLEO PRO2 (98)	OF CAESAR? /BEL AFFRIS/ (STEPPING BETWEEN THEM)	LISTEN	, COUSIN. MAN TO MAN, WE EGYPTIANS ARE AS GODS ABOVE
CATH 1 (167)	HIS GENIALITY). AHA! THATS BETTER. AND NOW	LISTEN	, DARLING. YOU MUST NOT COME TO COURT WITH PISTOLS IN
CATH 1 (168)	ON THE TABLE; THEN TURNS AGAIN TO EDSTASTON).	LISTEN	, DARLING. YOU ARE A WRESTLER: A SPLENDID WRESTLER.
PYGM II (227)	LADYLIKE TO TAKE IT OUT OF MY MOUTH. /HIGGINS/	LISTEN	, ELIZA. I THINK YOU SAID YOU CAME IN A TAXI. /LIZA/
LION II (132)	HARDLY HAVE TOO MANY CONSCIENCES. (TO FERROVIUS)	LISTEN	, FERROVIUS. (FERROVIUS SHAKES HIS HEAD AND WILL NOT
GLIM (173)	ARE, MY DEAR. /THE GIRL/ (SQUEEZING HIS HAND) OH	LISTEN	, LISTEN; YOU ARE WANDERING AGAIN. /THE FRIAR/ THATS
APPL INTRLUD(254)	MY DEAR, I MUST. /ORINTHIA/ NO, NOT TODAY.	LISTEN	, MAGNUS. I HAVE SOMETHING VERY PARTICULAR TO SAY TO
MRS III (227)	I CAME TO SAY. (SITTING DOWN BESIDE HER) NOW	LISTEN	, MISS VIVIE. I'M QUITE AWARE THAT I'M NOT A YOUNG
MTH2 (67)	THEM. /FRANKLYN/ (TO LUBIN) ARE YOU PREPARED TO	LISTEN	, MR LUBIN; OR SHALL I THANK YOU FOR YOUR VERY KIND
HART I (77)	THE EVENING LIGHT IS NOW VERY RED). /HECTOR/	LISTEN	, O SAGE. HOW LONG DARE YOU CONCENTRATE ON A FEELING
CURE (232)	NOT LISTENING. ALL THE WORLD LISTENS WHEN I PLAY.	LISTEN	, OR GO. /REGINALD/ (HELPLESS) BUT I SHALL HAVE TO
APPL INTRLUD(255)	WILL NOT BE DESERTED FOR YOUR OLD DUTCH. /MAGNUS/	LISTEN	, ORINTHIA. DONT BE ABSURD. YOU KNOW I MUST GO. DO BE
PHIL I (74)	(A VIOLENT DOUBLE KNOCK WITHOUT. THEY START AND	LISTEN	, STILL IN ONE ANOTHER'S ARMS, HARDLY DARING TO
CURE (235)	TO IMPART. YOUR PLAYING DRAWS IT FROM ME.	LISTEN	, STREGA (SHE PLAYS A HORRIBLE DISCORD) I MEAN MISS
DOCT I (103)	FATHER, SIR, ANTICIPATED A DISCOVERY OF MY OWN.	LISTEN	, WALPOLE. BLENKINSOP: ATTEND ONE MOMENT. YOU WILL
DEVL II (48)	HAT AND CLOAK, AND PUTS BOTH ON IN HOT HASTE) NOW	LISTEN	, YOU. IF YOU CAN GET A WORD WITH HIM BY PRETENDING
CAPT II (264)	HANDS DOWN. /BRASSBOUND/ (TURNING ON THEM) NOW	LISTEN	, YOU, ALL OF YOU. IF I AM TO COMMAND HERE, I AM
NEVR II (252)	TO FEEL: THATS THE ONLY THING THAT CAN HELP US.	LISTEN	! DO YOU-- BUT FIRST-- I FORGOT. WHATS YOUR NAME? I
CLEO I (115)	THAT I AM A QUEEN, WILL YOU NOT? -- A REAL QUEEN.	LISTEN	! (STEALTHILY COAXING HIM): LET US RUN AWAY AND
SUPR III (94)	MUTILATED. MY POOR FATHER! /DON JUAN/ HUSH!	LISTEN	! (TWO GREAT CHORDS ROLLING ON SYNCOPATED WAVES OF

LISTENED

CLEO IV (173)	THAT SHE WOULD HAVE CAESAR GONE? /POTHINUS/ YOU	LISTENED	? /FTATATEETA/ I TOOK CARE THAT SOME HONEST WOMAN
BULL I (88)	COMFORTABLY TO LECTURE DOYLE). NOW, LARRY, IVE	LISTENED	CAREFULLY TO ALL YOUVE SAID ABOUT IRELAND; AND I
FABL PREFACE(79)	OR, LIKE JOAN OF ARC, REALLY HEARD VOICES WHEN HE	LISTENED	FOR THE VOICE OF GOD, WE SHALL NEVER KNOW. I HAVE
SIM I (52)	FACE TO FACE WITH MAYA, WHO HAS STOLEN IN AND	LISTENED	GRAVELY AND INTENTLY TO HIS EXHORTATION). /IDDY/ (
GENV III (85)	IT. MEN LIKE TO BE LISTENED TO. /BEGONIA/ I HAVE	LISTENED	HERE UNTIL I AM NEARLY DEAD. STILL, WHEN MEN START
OVER (174)	THE MATTER WITH THEM. /GREGORY/ (WHO HAS	LISTENED	IN GROWING ALARM) BUT-- I-- IS? -- WA-- ? OH
BULL III (133)	MAD PETHER KEEGAN HIMSELF. /BROADBENT/ (WHO HAS	LISTENED	IN THE GREATEST ASTONISHMENT) YOU AMAZE ME, LARRY.
ARMS III (66)	(SHAKING HIS HEAD) I MUSNT JUDGE HER. I ONCE	LISTENED	MYSELF OUTSIDE A TENT WHEN THERE WAS A MUTINY

NEVR IV SD(294)	SCANDALIZED) REALLY I MUST SAY-- BOHUN, WHO HAS	LISTENED	TO DOLLY WITH THE HIGHEST APPROVAL, IS DOWN ON HIM
JOAN 6 (125)	DISGUST OF CAUCHON AND THE INQUISITOR, WHO HAVE	LISTENED	TO HIM SO FAR WITH PATRONIZING APPROVAL) MEN HAVE
CATH 4,SD(198)	BOWING, WITH CLAIRE CURTSEYING, HAVING BEEN	LISTENED	TO IN UTTER DUMBFOUNDEDNESS BY PATIOMKIN AND
MTH4 I (164)	IN THEIR HUNGER FOR NEW LIGHTS AND NEW IDEAS THEY	LISTENED	TO ME AND ENCOURAGED ME TO REBEL. BUT MY WAYS DID
PHIL I (71)	IN MINE, AND LAID HER CHEEK AGAINST MINE, AND	LISTENED	TO ME SAYING ALL SORTS OF SILLY THINGS. (GRACE,
DEVL III (61)	THERE OF WITNESSES? IF THE TOWNSPEOPLE HERE HAD	LISTENED	TO ME, YOU WOULD HAVE FOUND THE STREETS BARRICADED,
UNPL PREFACE(R9)	EAGERLY READ MY ESSAYS: THE MASSES PATIENTLY	LISTENED	TO MY HARANGUES. I ENJOYED THE IMMUNITIES OF
HART II (102)	THAT I'D HAVE SPRAWLED THERE HELPLESS, AND	LISTENED	TO SUCH UNFAIRNESS, SUCH LIES, SUCH INJUSTICE AND
LADY (241)	SIR. LET ME WARN YOU: I AM MORE ACCUSTOMED TO BE	LISTENED	TO THAN PREACHED AT. /THE MAN/ THE MOST ARE LIKE
JOAN 5 (114)	WITH IT: BUT IF YOU PRAYED FROM YOUR HEART, AND	LISTENED	TO THE THRILLING OF THE BELLS IN THE AIR AFTER THEY
UNPL PREFACE(R10)	FOR THAT WHEN THE WELL WAS EMPTY. BUT NOW I	LISTENED	TO THE VOICE OF THE PUBLISHER FOR THE FIRST TIME
UNPL PREFACE(R10)	DO NOW WITH GAY CONFIDENCE IN THEIR CRADLES. I	LISTENED	TO THEIR VIGOROUS KNOCKS WITH EXULTATION FOR THE
2TRU II (58)	AND GOES OUT AT THE DOUBLE. /TALLBOYS/ (WHO HAS	LISTENED	TO THIS COLLOQUY IN RENEWED STUPEFACTION) COUNTESS:
KING I (182)	ARE WE ARCHBISHOPS? /MRS BASHAM/ MR FOX: I HAVE	LISTENED	TO TOO MUCH BLASPHEMY THIS MORNING. BUT TO CALL AN
DOCT II (120)	HAPPY IT MADE HIM, POOR CHAP. /B.B./ (WHO HAS	LISTENED	TO WALPOLE WITH GROWING PERTURBATION) BUT-- BUT--
GENV IV (121)	/JUDGE/ I FIND MYSELF IN A DIFFICULTY. I HAVE	LISTENED	TO YOU ALL AND WATCHED YOU VERY ATTENTIVELY. YOU
MTH1 II (28)	ADAM JUST NOW WHEN HE THREW DOWN HIS SPADE AND	LISTENED	TO YOU FOR A WHILE, WENT BY ME LIKE FOUL WIND THAT
MTH1 I (6)	I HAVE CREPT THROUGH THE GRASS, AND HIDDEN, AND	LISTENED	TO YOU. /EVE/ THAT WAS WONDERFULLY CLEVER OF YOU.
JOAN 5 (120)	OF GOD IS HIS STRENGTH: WHAT WOULD HE BE IF HE	LISTENED	TO YOUR JEALOUS LITTLE COUNSELS? WELL, MY
GENV III (85)	DO. SHE SHOULD KEEP THEM UP IT. MEN LIKE TO BE	LISTENED	TO. /BEGONIA/ I HAVE LISTENED HERE UNTIL I AM
DOCT PREFACE(56)	INCIDENTAL GOOD, WOULD AN ANTI-BRANDY PARTY BE	LISTENED	TO. THAT INCIDENTAL GOOD WOULD BE THE SUBSTITUTION
MTH1 II (28)	HEARKEN TO ME, OLD FOOL. I HAVE NEVER IN MY SOUL	LISTENED	WILLINGLY WHEN YOU HAVE TOLD ME OF THE VOICE THAT
CAPT I (238)	I AM NOT DISSATISFIED. /SIR HOWARD/ (WHO HAS	LISTENED	WITH APPROVAL AND GROWING CONFIDENCE) CAPTAIN
FABL PREFACE(79)	IT WILL COME TO YOU." THIS STUCK IN HIS MIND. HE	LISTENED	, NOT PIOUSLY BUT EXPERIMENTALLY; AND SURE ENOUGH A
		LISTENER	
SUPR III (84)	FINDS HIMSELF VIRTUALLY ALONE WITH A SYMPATHETIC	LISTENER	IN THE STILL STARLIGHT OF THE MOUNTAINS; FOR ALL
OVER (187)	WHILE WE TALK IT OVER, GREGORY IS A SPLENDID	LISTENER	. /JUNO/ I DONT THINK ANY GOOD CAN COME OF A
BASH PREFACE(88)	ANY SUCH ILLUSION ON A PROFESSIONALLY SKILLED	LISTENER	. THEN THERE ARE THE PEOPLE WHO DO NOT GO TO
MTH5 (221)	MARTELLUS. /MARTELLUS/ (A SILENT AND MEDITATIVE	LISTENER	, SHUDDERS AND SHAKES HIS HEAD, BUT SAYS NOTHING).
		LISTENERS	
BASH PREFACE(89)	WHENEVER THE MEANING OF THE WORDS WAS CLEAR, THE	LISTENERS	SHEWED UNMISTAKABLY THAT THEY LIKED HYPERBOLICAL
MIS. PREFACE(89)	HEROINE'S DEATH SONG IN A VERDI OPERA; AND THE	LISTENERS	, FAR FROM RELIEVING MY EXCRUCIATION BY RISING
		LISTENING	
SUPR II (69)	IS UNINTELLIGIBLE. COME! THERES NOBODY	LISTENING	: NEITHER MY GENTEEL RELATIVES NOR THE SECRETARY
CAND III (127)	HER ABSORPTION IN THE POKER). HAVNT YOU BEEN	LISTENING	? (NO RESPONSE). MRS MORELL! /CANDIDA/ (
HART III (132)	RANDALL: YOU HAVE NOT GONE TO BED. HAVE YOU BEEN	LISTENING	? (THE FLUTE REPLIES PERTLY) HOW VULGAR! GO TO
CAND III (127)	(STARTING) EH? /MARCHBANKS/ HAVNT YOU BEEN	LISTENING	? /CANDIDA/ (WITH A GUILTY EXCESS OF POLITENESS)
MRS III (233)	OR SHALL I OPERATE? /VIVIE/ FRANK: HAVE YOU BEEN	LISTENING	? /FRANK/ (COMING DOWN INTO THE GARDEN) ONLY FOR
GLIM (173)	YOUR WITS ARE WANDERING. LISTEN TO ME. ARE YOU	LISTENING	? /THE FRIAR/ YES YES YES YES YES YES YES.
DEVL II SD(38)	FOUR OUTSIDE: TWO IN WITH ME. JUDITH HALF RISES,	LISTENING	AND LOOKING WITH DILATED EYES AT RICHARD, WHO
BUOY IV (60)	YOUVE MISSED SOMETHING. /DARKIE/ NO; IVE BEEN	LISTENING	AT THE DOOR. /FIFFY/ BY GEORGE, DICK, YOU WERE
PPP (205)	LAST SINK INANIMATE ON THE CARPET. /MAGNESIA/ (	LISTENING	AT THE DOCTOR'S CHEST) DEAD! /FITZ/ (KNEELING BY
ARMS III (65)	WAY. WHERE IS THIS OTHER YOUNG LADY? /RAINA/	LISTENING	AT THE DOOR, PROBABLY. /SERGIUS/ (SHIVERING AS IF
LIED (197)	SH! (SHE RUSHES TO THE DOOR, AND HOLDS IT AJAR,	LISTENING	BREATHLESSLY). /HE/ WHAT IS IT? /SHE/ (WHITE
BARB I SD(263)	BUT HE HAS A WATCHFUL, DELIBERATE, WAITING,	LISTENING	FACE, AND FORMIDABLE RESERVES OF POWER, BOTH
HART III (129)	AND YOU WOULDNT LISTEN. /MRS HUSHABYE/ I WAS	LISTENING	FOR SOMETHING ELSE. THERE WAS A SORT OF SPLENDID
ANNA (292)	HER? /STRAMMFEST/ (SNATCHING THE TELEPHONE AND	LISTENING	FOR THE ANSWER) SPEAK LOUDER, WILL YOU: I AM A
DEVL II (44)	AWAKE FOR NIGHTS AND NIGHTS IN AN AGONY OF DREAD,	LISTENING	FOR THEM TO COME AND ARREST YOU? /ANDERSON/ DO
JOAN 5 (114)	YOU HAVE NOT SAT IN THE FIELD IN THE EVENING	LISTENING	FOR THEM. WHEN THE ANGELUS RINGS YOU CROSS
GETT SD(279)	AND SITS AT THE TABLE IN REGINALD'S NEIGHBORHOOD	LISTENING	IN PLACID HELPLESSNESS. LESBIA, OUT OF PATIENCE
CLEO PRG2,SD(96)	THE WALL) STAND. WHO GOES THERE? THEY ALL START,	LISTENING	. A STRANGE VOICE REPLIES FROM WITHOUT. /VOICE/
CURE (232)	THE PIANO). BUT I WILL HAVE NO NONSENSE ABOUT NOT	LISTENING	. ALL THE WORLD LISTENS WHEN I PLAY. LISTEN, OR
MTH2 (75)	TO HEAR YOU OUT WITH MY VERY BEST ATTENTION. I AM	LISTENING	. GO ON. /FRANKLYN/ WELL, YOU REMEMBER, DONT YOU,
MTH2 (46)	HAS TALKED SO MUCH THAT HE HAS LOST THE POWER OF	LISTENING	. HE DOESNT LISTEN EVEN IN THE HOUSE OF COMMONS.
DOCT IV (163)	ARE MY IMMORTALITY. PROMISE. /MRS DUBEDAT/ I'M	LISTENING	. I SHALL NOT FORGET. YOU KNOW THAT I PROMISE.
HART III (132)	RANDALL IS LISTENING NOW. /MANGAN/ EVERYBODY IS	LISTENING	. IT ISNT RIGHT. /MRS HUSHABYE/ BUT IN THE DARK,
MTH5 (223)	LISTEN. /ACIS/ GO AHEAD, OLD SPORT. WE ARE	LISTENING	. MARTELLUS STRETCHES HIMSELF ON THE SWARD BESIDE
HART III SD(148)	THEY ALL TURN AWAY FROM THE HOUSE AND LOOK UP,	LISTENING	. /HECTOR/ (GRAVELY) MISS DUNN: YOU CAN DO NO
SUPR III (85)	OPINION OF THEM. /TANNER/ (DROWSILY) GO ON. I AM	LISTENING	. /MENDOZA/ I SAW THEE FIRST IN WHITSUN WEEK
MILL I (153)	SORRY, DEAR. IT WAS ONLY A REMINDER THAT I WAS	LISTENING	. /SAGAMORE/ HAS THE MATTER ON WHICH YOU WISH TO
GETT (341)	TO ME THAT SHE WANTS YOU TO HEAR. /SOAMES/ I AM	LISTENING	. /THE BISHOP/ (GOING BACK TO HIS SEAT NEXT HER)
BUOY II (20)	THE GATERS AND THE RATTLERS. /HE/ YOU HAVE BEEN	LISTENING	. THAT IS ANOTHER ADVANCE. /SHE/ TAKE CARE. I CAN
MIS. (138)	BEAR, BECAUSE IT MAKES IT SO DIFFICULT TO AVOID	LISTENING	. YOU SEE, I'M YOUNG; AND I DO SO WANT SOMETHING
DEVL II (30)	STARTS IN TERROR AND RETREATS TO THE LONG SEAT,	LISTENING	,) WHATS THAT? /ANDERSON/ (FOLLOWING HER
FABL VI (129)	GUIDE THEM. THE SMOKER TRIED THE EXPERIMENT OF	LISTENING	JUST FOR FUN; AND SOON HIS HEAD WAS FILLED WITH
GENV IV (93)	WHO ARE YOU? /SIR O./ ONLY A HUMBLE ENGLISHMAN,	LISTENING	MOST RESPECTFULLY TO YOUR CLEVER AND ENTERTAINING
HART III (132)	/LADY UTTERWORD/ I DONT THINK RANDALL IS	LISTENING	NOW. /MANGAN/ EVERYBODY IS LISTENING. IT ISNT
ROCK II (268)	USUAL CALM) I CAME WITH THEM, SRARTHUR. I BEEN	LISTENING	ON THE QUIET AS YOU MIGHT SAY. I JUST CAME IN TO
PHIL III (146)	AFTER LOOKING ROUND TO SEE WHETHER THE OTHERS ARE	LISTENING	) ONLY JUST CONSIDER! THE SPECTACLE OF A RIVAL'S
DEVL II (38)	ENGLISH SOLDIERS! OH, WHAT DO THEY-- /RICHARD/ (	LISTENING	) SH! /A VOICE/ (OUTSIDE) HALT! FOUR OUTSIDE:
CATH 2 (176)	IT IS. NARYSHKIN GOES TO THE DOOR. /CATHERINE/ (	LISTENING	) THAT IS PRINCE PATIOMKIN. /NARYSHKIN/ (CALLING
CLEO PRG2 (97)	I TOLD YOU SO. /THE SENTINEL/ (WHO HAS BEEN	LISTENING	) WOE, ALAS! /BEL AFFRIS/ (CALLING TO HIM)
MILL I (137)	ON THE TABLE AT HIS ELBOW, RINGS. /SAGAMORE/ (	LISTENING	) YES? . . . (IMPRESSED) OH! SEND HER UP AT
HART II (113)	IS ALL. (THE CAPTAIN APPEARS AT THE PANTRY DOOR,	LISTENING	). IT IS A CURIOUS SENSATION: THE SORT OF PAIN
ARMS I SD(7)	SHOT BREAKS THE QUIET OF THE NIGHT. SHE STARTS,	LISTENING	; AND TWO MORE SHOTS, MUCH NEARER, FOLLOW,
CLEO IV SD(166)	IN THE PALACE, AMONG A BEVY OF HER LADIES,	LISTENING	TO A SLAVE GIRL WHO IS PLAYING THE HARP IN THE
2TRU III (109)	SERGEANT, DRAGGING WITH HER THE PATIENT, WHO IS	LISTENING	TO AUBREY WITH SIGNS OF BECOMING RAPT IN HIS
MIS. PREFACE(88)	OF COMMONS, AT PUBLIC MEETINGS, WE SIT SOLEMNLY	LISTENING	TO BORES AND THADDLERS BECAUSE FROM THE TIME WE
MTH5 (210)	DO YOU SUPPOSE I CAN SPEND CENTURIES DANCING;	LISTENING	TO FLUTES RINGING CHANGES ON A FEW TUNES AND A FEW
ROCK I (198)	THE HOUSE? SITTING UP ALL NIGHT IN BAD AIR	LISTENING	TO FOOLS INSULTING ME? I TELL YOU I SHOULD HAVE
GENV III (67)	OF WHAT THE LEAGUE IS FOR; AND I HAVE TO SIT HERE	LISTENING	TO FOREIGN MINISTERS EXPLAINING TO ME THAT THEIR
MIS. (123)	OVER A HUNDRED IF SHE TOOK IT REGULARLY, AND ME	LISTENING	TO HER, THAT HAD NEVER DARED TO THINK THAT A
MTH1 II (32)	GO ON WITH YOUR WORK AND NOT WASTE YOUR TIME	LISTENING	TO HIM. /CAIN/ I AM NOT, PERHAPS, VERY CLEVER;
PHIL I (83)	SLAMS THE DOOR. SHE RAISES HERSELF ON ONE HAND,	LISTENING	TO HIS RETREATING FOOTSTEPS. THEY STOP. HER FACE
DEVL II (40)	THE TRUTH; BUT YOU HAD BETTER KNOW IT. ARE YOU	LISTENING	TO ME? (SHE SIGNIFIES ASSENT). DO YOU UNDERSTAND
MTH2 (74)	THEM THAT WILL MAKE THEM LIVE FOR EVER, THEY ARE	LISTENING	TO ME FOR THE FIRST TIME WITH THEIR MOUTHS OPEN
KING I (171)	PARTS. THEY COULD MAKE YOU BELIEVE YOU WERE	LISTENING	TO REAL WOMEN. /CHARLES/ PASTOR FOX: HAVE YOU EVER
PYGM II (218)	AND STANDING BESIDE HIM ON HIS LEFT) TIRED OF	LISTENING	TO SOUNDS? /PICKERING/ YES. IT'S A FEARFUL
ROCK I (197)	ANYTHING, MISCHIEVOUS OR THE REVERSE, WHILE IT IS	LISTENING	TO SPEECHES, AND THE FELLOWS WHO MAKE THE SPEECHES
MILL PREFACE(120)	INDIGNANT MASTER-FASCIST SAID TO ME " THEY WERE	LISTENING	TO SPEECHES ROUND RED FLAGS AND LEAVING THE COWS
MIS. PREFACE(42)	COUNTRY HOUSES THAT YOU MAY SPEND HOURS IN THEM	LISTENING	TO STORIES OF BROKEN COLLAR BONES, BROKEN BACKS,
ROCK II (256)	BROLLY: YOURE ONLY MAKING A FOOL OF YOURSELF	LISTENING	TO THAT OLD BIRD BUTTERING YOU UP. YOU JUST DONT
PPP (195)	LEVEL. /THE MURDERER/ I CAN NO LONGER COWER HERE	LISTENING	TO THE AGONIZED THUMPINGS OF MY OWN HEART. SHE BUT
JOAN PREFACE(11)	OR DAWDLE ABOUT WAITING FOR VISIONS AND	LISTENING	TO THE CHURCH BELLS TO HEAR VOICES IN THEM. IN
GETT SD(281)	AND PRESENTLY RISES AND STANDS IN THE DOORWAY	LISTENING	TO THE CONVERSATION. /THE BISHOP/ (GOING TO LEO)
DOCT IV (161)	PRETENDING THAT I DONT KNOW. IVE BEEN LYING THERE	LISTENING	TO THE DOCTORS-- LAUGHING TO MYSELF. THEY KNOW.
CLEO II SD(118)	SAY WITH THE SARCASTIC VIGILANCE OF A PHILOSOPHER	LISTENING	TO THE EXERCISES OF HIS DISCIPLES. ACHILLAS IS A
GENV PREFACE(4)	ANY CASUALTIES WORTH MENTIONING, ONLY BY	LISTENING	TO THE GERMAN BROADCASTS, SIMILARLY COOKED, COULD
GENV IV (109)	SO LOUD, PLEASE. I AM NOT DEAF; BUT WHEN ONE IS	LISTENING	TO THE INNER VOICE IT IS NOT EASY TO CATCH
ARMS I (17)	TROUBLE). /RAINA/ (STERNLY, AS SHE SEES HIM	LISTENING	TO THE SHOTS) SO MUCH THE BETTER FOR YOU! /THE
O'FL (206)	SALUTING THE FLAG TIL I'M STIFF WITH IT, AND THE	LISTENING	TO THEM PLAYING GOD SAVE THE KING AND TIPPERARY,
O'FL (206)	THE MAKING SPEECHES, AND -- WHATS WORSE -- THE	LISTENING	TO THEM, AND THE CALLING FOR CHEERS FOR KING AND
ROCK II (263)	IN. /SIR DEXTER/ (RISING) I WILL NOT SIT HERE	LISTENING	TO THIS DISGUSTING UNGENTLEMANLY NONSENSE.
MIS. PREFACE(19)	CONTENTS. IN THE PRISON YOU ARE NOT FORCED TO SIT	LISTENING	TO TURNKEYS DISCOURSING WITHOUT CHARM OR INTEREST

SIM II (81) EITHER WE SHALL DISAPPEAR OR THE PEOPLE WHO ARE LISTENING TO US WILL. WHAT WE HAVE LEARNT HERE TODAY IS THAT
CLEO IV (175) NOW EVERYBODY CAN SEE US, NOBODY WILL THINK OF LISTENING TO US. (HE SITS DOWN ON THE BENCH LEFT BY THE TWO
MTH1 I (12) THINK, ADAM! OUR SNAKE HAS LEARNT TO SPEAK BY LISTENING TO US. /ADAM/ (DELIGHTED) IS IT SO? (HE GOES
CLEO II SD(118) AN AIR OF MAGPIE KEENNESS AND PROFUNDITY, LISTENING TO WHAT THE OTHERS SAY WITH THE SARCASTIC
PHIL II (101) LISTEN TO ME, WHAT LIKELIHOOD IS THERE OF HER LISTENING TO YOU? /CRAVEN/ (IN ANGRY BEWILDERMENT)
DEVL I (19) /ANDERSON/ (POINTING TO ESSIE) THERE, SIR, LISTENING TO YOU. /RICHARD/ (SHOCKED INTO SINCERITY) WHAT!
ANNA (292) DID YOU RING UP FOR? I CANT SPEND THE DAY HERE LISTENING TO YOUR CHEEK. . . . WHAT! THE GRAND DUCHESS! (
JITT I (15) THAT EVERY TIME YOU GO AWAY FROM ME, AND I STAND LISTENING TO YOUR FOOTSTEPS DYING AWAY IN THE DISTANCE-- I
INCA (254) IS WONDERFUL. I HAVE SAT HERE ALMOST IN SILENCE, LISTENING TO YOUR SHREWD AND PENETRATING ACCOUNT OF MY
PYGM I (212) DIDNT YOU SAY SO BEFORE? AND US LOSING OUR TIME LISTENING TO YOUR SILLINESS! (HE WALKS OFF TOWARDS THE
MTH4 III (197) MY VOICE-- /ZOO/ YOU PEOPLE SEEM NEVER TO TIRE OF LISTENING TO YOUR VOICES; BUT IT DOESNT AMUSE US. WHAT DO
JOAN 6 (142) I CAN MAKE MY MARK. /THE CHAPLAIN/ (WHO HAS BEEN LISTENING WITH GROWING ALARM AND INDIGNATION) MY LORD: DO
APPL I (222) SITTING ON A VOLCANO. /LYSISTRATA/ (WHO HAS BEEN LISTENING WITH IMPLACABLE CONTEMPT TO THE DISCUSSION,
PYGM II (218) YOU HEAR NO DIFFERENCE AT FIRST; BUT YOU KEEP ON LISTENING , AND PRESENTLY YOU FIND THEYRE ALL AS DIFFERENT
BARB III (332) SILLY! (SHE CLIMBS TO THE CANNON, AND LEANS, LISTENING , IN THE ANGLE IT MAKES WITH THE PARAPET).
APPL I (241) ON SEEING THEM. /PROTEUS/ HAVE YOU TWO BEEN LISTENING , MAY I ASK? /PAMPHILIUS/ WELL, IT WOULD BE
NEVR IV SD(286) AND A TERRIFYING POWER OF INTENSELY CRITICAL LISTENING , RAISE THE IMPRESSION PRODUCED BY HIM TO ABSOLUTE
CAND I (99) TIME. HE FORGETS TO WARM HIS HANDS, AND STANDS LISTENING , STARTLED AND THOUGHTFUL). THEY ARE MORE TRUE:

LISTENS

DEVL II (41) ON EARTH--? (CALLING) JUDITH, JUDITH! (HE LISTENS ; THERE IS NO ANSWER). HM! (HE GOES TO THE
WIDO III SD(64) TRENCH, LEFT ALONE, LOOKS ROUND CAREFULLY AND LISTENS A MOMENT, THEN HE GOES ON TIPTOE TO THE PIANO AND
MRS PREFACE(160) THE FATHER ENTERS; DISMISSES THE DUENNA; AND LISTENS AT THE KEYHOLE OF HIS DAUGHTER'S NUPTIAL CHAMBER,
ARMS II (30) RIGHT MOMENT. /CATHERINE/ (IMPATIENTLY) YES: SHE LISTENS FOR IT. IT IS AN ABOMINABLE HABIT. SERGIUS LEADS
PRES (165) (INTO THE TELEPHONE) IS THAT YOU, ELIZA? (SHE LISTENS FOR THE ANSWER). NOT OUT O BED YET! GO AND PULL HER
PRES (166) O DISGRACIN YOU BE BEIN A CHARWOMAN? (SHE LISTENS FOR THE ANSWER). WELL, I CAN HAVE GENERAL MITCHENER
PRES (165) (INTO THE TELEPHONE) IS THAT YOU, ELIZA? (SHE LISTENS FOR THE ANSWER). D'YE REMEMBER ME GIVIN YOU A CLOUT
AUGS SD(279) AND SUBSTITUTES THE FACSIMILE FOR IT. THEN SHE LISTENS FOR THE RETURN OF AUGUSTUS. A CRASH IS HEARD, AS OF
PRES SD(131) SNATCHES A REVOLVER FROM A DRAWER; AND LISTENS IN AN AGONY OF APPREHENSION. NOTHING HAPPENS. HE
APPL INTR,SD(252) LEFT HAND WITH AN AIR OF SUFFERING PATIENCE, AND LISTENS IN SILENCE TO THE HARANGUE WHICH FOLLOWS. /MAGNUS/
GENV IV SD(90) ON THE JUDGE'S DESK. HE HOLDS DOWN A BUTTON AND LISTENS . /THE JUDGE/ YOU WILL NOT HAVE TO WAIT ANY LONGER.
CLEO IV SD(194) BELOW) HAIL, CAESAR! HAIL, HAIL! CLEOPATRA LISTENS . THE BUCINA SOUNDS AGAIN, FOLLOWED BY SEVERAL
LADY SD(243) SHE RISES ANGRILY TO HER FULL HEIGHT, AND LISTENS JEALOUSLY. /THE MAN/ (UNAWARE OF THE DARK LADY)
GENV IV (123) IT DOWN: I DO NOT UNDERSTAND. (WRITING AS HE LISTENS) " ASTRONOMERS REPORT THAT THE ORBIT OF THE EARTH
PRES (166) LISTENS). THEN YOU THINK I MIGHT TAKE HIM? (SHE LISTENS). G'LANG, YOU YOUNG SCALD: IF I HAD YOU HERE I'D
PRES (166) THE WAY. (SHE LISTENS). IF I REALLY WHAT? (SHE LISTENS). I CANT HEAR YOU. IF I REALLY WHAT? (SHE
PHIL II (115) EYE FLASHES: HE STRAIGHTENS HIMSELF AND LISTENS). I PAID YOU A PRETTY STIFF FEE FOR THAT
PRES (166) ANYHOW I WOULDNT LET THAT STAND IN THE WAY. (SHE LISTENS). IF I REALLY WHAT? (SHE LISTENS). I CANT HEAR
PRES (166) DRUV HIM? I NEVER SAID A WORD TO-- EH? (SHE LISTENS). OH, LOVE HIM. ARRA, DONT BE A FOOL, CHILD. (TO
MTH3 (113) RINGS. /CONFUCIUS/ (ANSWERING) YES? (HE LISTENS). /A WOMAN'S VOICE/ THE DOMESTIC MINISTER HAS
DOCT IV (166) (HIS LIPS MOVE AGAIN: WALPOLE BENDS DOWN AND LISTENS). /WALPOLE/ HE WANTS TO KNOW IS THE NEWSPAPER MAN
PRES (166) IF I HAD YOU HERE I'D TEACH YOU MANNERS. (SHE LISTENS). THATS ENOUGH NOW, BACK WID YOU TO BED; AND BE
JOAN 2 (80) AT THE DOOR. /THE PAGE/ THE DUKE OF -- (NOBODY LISTENS). THE DUKE OF -- (THE CHATTER CONTINUES. INDIGNANT
PRES (166) A CHARWOMAN FROM THE DAY SHE'S MARRIED. (SHE LISTENS). THEN YOU THINK I MIGHT TAKE HIM? (SHE LISTENS).
PRES (166) AT ALL. WHAT D'YE THINK I OUGHT TO SAY? (SHE LISTENS). WELL, I'M NO CHICKEN MESELF. (TO MITCHENER) HOW
PRES (166) WITH ANY SUCH NONSENSE AT MY AGE. WHAT? (SHE LISTENS). WELL, THATS JUST WHAT I WAS THINKIN. /MITCHENER/
PRES (166) I CANT HEAR YOU. IF I REALLY WHAT? (SHE LISTENS). WHO DRUV HIM? I NEVER SAID A WORD TO-- EH? (
MILL I (146) HE RISES). EXCUSE ME. (HE GOES TO THE TABLE AND LISTENS). YES? . . . (HASTILY) ONE MOMENT. HOLD THE LINE.
PRES (166) INTO THE TELEPHONE) HE SAYS HE'S FIFTY-TWO. (SHE LISTENS ; THEN, TO MITCHENER) SHE SAYS YOURE DOWN IN WHO'S
MTH3 (132) LISTENS TO YOU CURIOUSLY FOR A MOMENT JUST AS HE LISTENS TO A CHAP PLAYING CLASSICAL MUSIC, THEN HE GOES BACK
SUPR HANDBOK(225) DEPENDS ON THE UNREASONABLE MAN. THE MAN WHO LISTENS TO REASON IS LOST: REASON ENSLAVES ALL WHOSE MINDS
2TRU II SD(58) COURTESY. SHE THEN SEATS HERSELF ON THE RUG, AND LISTENS TO THEM, HUGGING HER KNEES AND HER UMBRELLA, AND
MTH3 (132) TO AN ENGLISHMAN ABOUT ANYTHING SERIOUS, AND HE LISTENS TO YOU CURIOUSLY FOR A MOMENT JUST AS HE LISTENS TO
CURE (232) NO NONSENSE ABOUT NOT LISTENING. ALL THE WORLD LISTENS WHEN I PLAY. LISTEN, OR GO. /REGINALD/ (HELPLESS)
PPP (198) CHOIR AGAIN RAISES ITS FAVORITE CHANT. HE LISTENS WITH A RAPT EXPRESSION. SUDDENLY THE ANGELS SING OUT
DEVL III SD(75) THE MAN YOU WANT. THE CROWD, INTENSELY EXCITED, LISTENS WITH ALL ITS EARS. JUDITH, HALF RISING, STARES AT

LISTER

FABL PREFACE(90) A MUCH SOUNDER HYGIENIST THAN JENNER, PASTEUR, LISTER , AND THEIR DISCIPLES, HAD TO CALL HER DOCTRINE

LISTLESS

JITT II (42) AT HIS CONTEMPTUOUS AIR, BUT PRETENDING TO BE LISTLESS AND LANGUID). /LENKHEIM/ (SHEWING HER THE
DEVL I (14) WOMAN, AND DESIRES YOUR GOOD TOO. /ESSIE/ (IN LISTLESS MISERY) YES. /JUDITH/ (ANNOYED WITH ESSIE FOR HER

LISTLESSLY

NEVR III (262) AT LAST, THANK GOODNESS! /GLORIA/ (STROLLING LISTLESSLY ACROSS THE ROOM AND COMING BEHIND HER MOTHER'S
DEST (169) (GREATLY ASTONISHED) WOMANISH! /LADY/ (LISTLESSLY) YES, LIKE ME. (WITH DEEP MELANCHOLY) DO YOU
HART II (96) I HAVE SOMETHING TO SHEW YOU. (ELLIE STROLLS LISTLESSLY TO THE OTHER SIDE OF THE CHAIR). LOOK. /ELLIE/ (
JITT III (75) HER HAPPY: THAT IS ALL I CARE ABOUT. (SHE GOES LISTLESSLY TO THE WINDOW-SEAT, AND SITS THERE LOOKING OUT,
NEVR IV (283) ROUND IN ALARM) WHERES M'COMAS? /GLORIA/ (LISTLESSLY , BUT NOT UNSYMPATHETICALLY) GONE OUT. TO LEAVE

LISTLESSNESS

DEST (169) I'M NOT REALLY BRAVE. (RELAPSING INTO PETULANT LISTLESSNESS) BUT WHAT RIGHT HAVE YOU TO DESPISE ME IF YOU
JITT II (32) IS A FRIEND'S WIFE. /JITTA/ (WITH AFFECTED LISTLESSNESS) IS IT? /LENKHEIM/ WELL, IT STANDS TO REASON,
HART II (97) MARRY HIM. /ELLIE/ (SUDDENLY COMING OUT OF HER LISTLESSNESS , MUCH VEXED) BUT WHY DID YOU DO THAT,

LISTNIN

BULL II (99) /KEEGAN/ WHAT WERE YOU DOIN THERE, PATSY, LISTNIN ? WERE YOU SPYIN ON ME? /PATSY/ NO, FADHER: ON ME

LISTS

MTH2 (87) TO KILL THEIR OWN SONS. IT WAS THE WAR CASUALTY LISTS AND THE STARVATION AFTERWARDS THAT FINISHED ME UP WITH
BARB PREFACE(245) REDEMPTIONS, SALVATIONS, HOSPITAL SUBSCRIPTION LISTS AND WHAT NOT, TO ENABLE US TO CONTRACT-OUT OF THE
HART PREFACE(17) OFFENDED ECONOMIC SENSE, PRODUCED BY THE CASUALTY LISTS . THE STUPID, THE SELFISH, THE NARROW-MINDED, THE
ROCK PREFACE(163) CONCLUSION IN ALL CIVILIZED COUNTRIES, THE LISTS OF CRIMES AND PENALTIES WILL OBSOLESCE LIKE THE
ROCK PREFACE(163) AND PENALTIES WILL OBSOLESCE LIKE THE DOCTORS' LISTS OF DISEASES AND MEDICINES; AND IT WILL BECOME POSSIBLE
ROCK PREFACE(161) CODE NOR OF THE SERVICE DISCIPLINES, WITH THEIR LISTS OF SPECIFIC OFFENCES AND SPECIFIC PENALTIES, COULD
DOCT PREFACE(21) PENNYROYAL, DANDELION, ETC., LABELLED WITH LITTLE LISTS OF THE DISEASES THEY ARE SUPPOSED TO CURE, AND
OVER (183) YES. GREGORY HAS AN IDEA THAT MARRIED WOMEN KEEP LISTS OF THE MEN THEYLL MARRY IF THEY BECOME WIDOWS. I'LL
GETT PREFACE(243) OF THIS VIEW, AND, TO DISCREDIT IT, QUOTE POLICE LISTS OF THE REASONS GIVEN BY THE VICTIMS FOR ADOPTING THEIR
MILL IV (201) LADY. LONG BEFORE WE CAN GET THE CASE INTO THE LISTS THE BUMP ON YOUR HEAD WILL HAVE SUBSIDED; YOUR BROKEN
LION PREFACE(45) CREDIBLE AND INCREDIBLE RESPECTIVELY, THEIR LISTS WOULD BE DIFFERENT IN SEVERAL PARTICULARS. BELIEF IS

LISZT'S

CURE (232) OCTAVE PASSAGES-- LIKE THIS. (SHE BEGINS PLAYING LISZT'S TRANSCRIPTION OF SCHUBERT'S ERL KOENIG). /REGINALD/

LIT

BARB III (329) WALKED INTO THE HIGH EXPLOSIVES SHED AND LIT A CIGARET, SIR: THATS ALL. /UNDERSHAFT/ AH, QUITE SO. (
SUPR I (36) WHEN THEY SUDDENLY BEGAN TO SHINE LIKE NEWLY LIT FLAMES IT WAS BY NO LIGHT OF THEIR OWN, BUT BY THE
DOCT IV (163) ONLY THAT ONCE IN MY OLD CORNISH HOME WE LIT THE FIRST FIRE OF THE WINTER; AND WHEN WE LOOKED THROUGH
2TRU II (60) HAPPENED TO MENTION YOUR BROTHER'S NAME; AND SHE LIT UP AT ONCE AND SAID " DEAR AUBREY BAGOT! I KNOW HIS
FABL I (103) THERE IS NO SATISFACTION IN SEEING THE WORLD LIT UP BY A BLINDING FLASH, AND BEING BURNT TO DUST BEFORE
SHAK SD(141) BEHOLD MY LEAR. A TRANSPARENCY IS SUDDENLY LIT UP, SHEWING CAPTAIN SHOTOVER SEATED, AS IN MILLAIS'
BASH I (97) /CASHEL/ WITHIN THIS BREAST A FIRE IS NEWLY LIT WHOSE GLOW SHALL SUN THE DEW AWAY, WHOSE RADIANCE SHALL

LITERACY

3PLA PREFACE(R22) FINALLY THE PEOPLE, NOW THAT THEIR COMPULSORY LITERACY ENABLES EVERY PENMAN TO PLAY ON THEIR ROMANTIC
BULL PREFACE(27) IN EVERY WALK OF LIFE THAT REQUIRES ANY LITERACY , IT IS THE AIM OF HIS PRIEST TO MAKE HIM AND KEEP

SUPR HANDBOK(177)	FROM GENERAL ILLITERACY TO GENERAL	LITERACY	, FROM ROMANCE TO REALISM, FROM REALISM TO
		LITERAL	
LION PREFACE(88)	THE NOTION THAT MATTHEW'S MANUSCRIPT IS A	LITERAL	AND INFALLIBLE RECORD OF FACTS, NOT SUBJECT TO THE
LION PREFACE(5)	CONFUCIUS SAID THEM BEFORE HIM. THOSE WHO CLAIM A	LITERAL	DIVINE PATERNITY FOR HIM CANNOT BE SILENCED BY THE
LION PREFACE(100)	WHICH WERE EXACTLY LIKE MEDIEVAL LETTERS IN THEIR	LITERAL	FAITH AND EVER-PRESENT PIETY, I SAID " CAN THESE MEN
GETT PREFACE(256)	PROVOKE MANY PRIVATE ONES, WE SHALL IN A VERY	LITERAL	SENSE EMPTY THE BABY OUT WITH THE BATH BY ABOLISHING
BULL PREFACE(48)	MAN, AND THE OFFICER SOMETIMES A GENTLEMAN IN THE	LITERAL	SENSE OF THE WORD; AND SO, WHAT WITH HUMANITY,
LION PREFACE(81)	" INSTITUTES" FOR HARDHEADED ADULT SCOTS AND	LITERAL	SWISS, IT BECOMES THE MOST INFERNAL OF FATALISMS;
JITT PREFACE(5)	FRACTION OF THE BUSINESS. I SOON FOUND THAT A	LITERAL	TRANSLATION WOULD FAIL COMPLETELY TO CONVEY THE PLAY
METH PREFACE(R78)	THIS IS BECAUSE THE IMPOSITION OF THE LEGENDS AS	LITERAL	TRUTHS AT ONCE CHANGES THEM FROM PARABLES INTO
METH PREFACE(R79)	EXCEPT THE SILLY FALSEHOOD THAT THE FICTIONS ARE	LITERAL	TRUTHS, AND THAT THERE IS NOTHING IN RELIGION BUT
LION PREFACE(45)	BROUGHT UP TO BELIEVE THE BIBLE IN THE OLD	LITERAL	WAY AS AN INFALLIBLE RECORD AND REVELATION, AND
		LITERALLY	
LION PREFACE(45)	BE DIFFERENT IN SEVERAL PARTICULARS. BELIEF IS	LITERALLY	A MATTER OF TASTE. FASHIONS IN BELIEF. NOW MATTERS
APPL PREFACE(181)	LIKE THAT. THERE COULD BE NO DOUBT THAT IT WAS	LITERALLY	A POPULAR MOVEMENT. I ASCERTAINED AFTERWARDS THAT
LION PREFACE(48)	A CHRISTIAN OR NOT. A MAHOMETAN ARAB WILL ACCEPT	LITERALLY	AND WITHOUT QUESTION PARTS OF THE NARRATIVE WHICH
BUOY PREFACE(4)	CHRISTIAN MEDIUMS AND TRANSCRIBED BY THEM AS	LITERALLY	AS ANY LETTER DICTATED BY A MERCHANT TO HIS
FABL PREFACE(68)	IT. THE BIBLE TRANSLATORS HAVE ENGLISHED IT TOO	LITERALLY	AS THE WORD MADE FLESH. BUT AS THE MINDS OF THE
2TRU PREFACE(18)	CIVILIZATION, THEIR COLUMNS WOULD BE FULL OF THIS	LITERALLY	EPOCH-MAKING EVENT. AND THE FIRST QUESTION THEY
DOCT PREFACE(4)	RICH MAN IS PERFORMED NOT ONLY METAPHORICALLY BUT	LITERALLY	EVERY DAY BY SURGEONS WHO ARE QUITE AS HONEST AS
HART PREFACE(5)	COMPARTMENTS. THE BARBARIANS WERE NOT ONLY	LITERALLY	IN THE SADDLE, BUT ON THE FRONT BENCH IN THE HOUSE
MTH5 (224)	OF ART. OF COURSE WE CANNOT BELIEVE SUCH A TALE	LITERALLY	. IT IS ONLY A LEGEND. WE DO NOT BELIEVE IN
SUPR III (100)	DEVIL/ DEAR LADY: A PARABLE MUST NOT BE TAKEN	LITERALLY	. THE GULF IS THE DIFFERENCE BETWEEN THE ANGELIC
METH PREFACE(R78)	WHICH IS THAT NO ONE SHALL BELIEVE THEM	LITERALLY	. THE READING OF STORIES AND DELIGHTING IN THEM
CLEO NOTES (203)	I DO NOT KNOW WHAT VINE RAG IS. I TRANSLATE	LITERALLY	." APPARENT ANACHRONISMS. THE ONLY WAY TO WRITE A
METH PREFACE(R78)	MADE DON QUIXOTE A GENTLEMAN: THE BELIEVING THEM	LITERALLY	MADE HIM A MADMAN WHO SLEW LAMBS INSTEAD OF
HART PREFACE(14)	BELGIUM AND FLANDERS, WHERE OVER LARGE DISTRICTS	LITERALLY	NOT ONE STONE WAS LEFT UPON ANOTHER AS THE OPPOSED
SIM PREFACE(16)	TO JUDGMENT BY A SUPERNATURAL BEING, COMING	LITERALLY	OUT OF THE BLUE; BUT HIS INQUIRY IS NOT WHETHER
NEVR I (212)	/PHILIP/ THEN HOLD YOUR MOUTH. (DOLLY DOES SO,	LITERALLY	). THE QUESTION IS A SIMPLE ONE. WHEN THE IVORY
HART PREFACE(29)	THE END CAME SO SUDDENLY THAT THE COMBATANTS	LITERALLY	STUMBLED OVER IT; AND YET IT CAME A FULL YEAR
DEVL EPILOG (79)	COMMON EXPRESSION " FIGHTING AN ELECTION" SO VERY	LITERALLY	THAT HE LED HIS SUPPORTERS TO THE POLL AT PRESTON
LION PREFACE(48)	OR ICONOGRAPHIC WORSHIP OF CHRIST. BY THIS I MEAN	LITERALLY	THAT WORSHIP WHICH IS GIVEN TO PICTURES AND
BASH PREFACE(89)	WRITTEN BY PERSONS SIMILARLY SCHOOLED. THEY HAD	LITERALLY	THE BENEFIT OF CLERGY, AND WROTE ACCORDINGLY. WITH
METH PREFACE(R74)	STORIES OF NOAH'S ARK AND THE GARDEN OF EDEN ARE	LITERALLY	TRUE ON THE AUTHORITY OF GOD HIMSELF, AND IF THAT
METH PREFACE(R74)	AND HE SEES THAT THESE STORIES CANNOT BE	LITERALLY	TRUE, AND LEARNS THAT NO CANDID PRELATE NOW
LION PREFACE(7)	DOING IT BEFORE. HE WAS NOT LYING : HE BELIEVED	LITERALLY	WHAT HE SAID. THE HORROR OF THE HIGH PRIEST WAS
MIS. PREFACE(19)	BUT A CONSCIENTIOUS AND KINDLY MEDDLER MAY	LITERALLY	WORRY YOU OUT OF YOUR SENSES. IT IS FORTUNATE THAT
GETT PREFACE(221)	SAY THAT LOVE SHOULD BE FREE. THEIR WORDS, TAKEN	LITERALLY	, MAY BE FOOLISH; BUT THEY ARE ONLY EXPRESSING
		LITERARY	
GENV PREFACE(24)	OUT BY PATENT AGENTS OF NO MORE THAN COMMON	LITERARY	ABILITY. MOZART, ABLE IN HIS INFANCY TO DO ANYTHING
LADY PREFACE(215)	ALTHOUGH THEY ARE BY NO MEANS WITHOUT GENUINE	LITERARY	ABILITY, A LOVE OF LETTERS, AND EVEN SOME ARTISTIC
METH PREFACE(R62)	ECONOMICS, HALF BORROWED, AND HALF HOME-MADE BY A	LITERARY	AMATEUR, WERE NOT, WHEN STRICTLY FOLLOWED UP, EVEN
BARB PREFACE(209)	CAN GROW OUT OF AIR. ANOTHER MISTAKE AS TO MY	LITERARY	ANCESTRY IS MADE WHENEVER I VIOLATE THE ROMANTIC
DOCT PREFACE(11)	THE ROYAL AND ARISTOCRATIC CONSPIRACY, THE	LITERARY	AND ARTISTIC CONSPIRACY, AND THE INNUMERABLE
SUPR II (52)	WHAT IS? /TANNER/ STRAKER IS. HERE HAVE WE	LITERARY	AND CULTURED PERSONS BEEN FOR YEARS SETTING UP A
BARB PREFACE(210)	EIGHTEEN-EIGHTIES BROUGHT ME INTO CONTACT, BOTH	LITERARY	AND PERSONAL, WITH ERNEST BELFORT BAX, AN ENGLISH
MIS. PREFACE(104)	AS MUCH PROSTITUTION OF PROFESSIONAL TALENT,	LITERARY	AND POLITICAL, IN DEFENCE OF MANIFEST WRONG, AS
JITT PREFACE(3)	THEATRE THE ENTIRE BODY OF MY OWN WORKS, BOTH	LITERARY	AND THEATRICAL. THIS ENTERPRISE IS THE MORE
BUOY PREFACE(6)	HE WAS LOOKING FOR THE FOUNDATION OF	LITERARY	ART IN THE FACTS OF HISTORY. NOTHING COULD BE MORE
LION PREFACE(33)	READER WHERE MATTHEW LEFT HIM. LUKE. LUKE THE	LITERARY	ARTIST. WHEN WE COME TO LUKE, WE COME TO A LATER
LION PREFACE(82)	WEAKER IN POWER OF THOUGHT THAN IN IMAGINATIVE	LITERARY	ART. HENCE WE FIND LUKE CREDITED WITH THE
MIS. PREFACE(88)	YOU CANNOT READ THE BIBLE IF YOU HAVE NO SENSE OF	LITERARY	ART. THE REASON WHY THE CONTINENTAL EUROPEAN IS, TO
MIS. PREFACE(88)	THE AUTHORIZED ENGLISH VERSION IS A GREAT WORK OF	LITERARY	ART, AND THE CONTINENTAL VERSIONS ARE COMPARATIVELY
WIDO II (27)	HAPPY HERE WITH ALL THESE BOOKS, MR SARTORIUS. A	LITERARY	ATMOSPHERE. /SARTORIUS/ (RESUMING HIS SEAT) I HAVE
FANY PROLOG (268)	OFF TO BED. /FANNY/ THATS ONE OF YOUR PRETTIEST	LITERARY	ATTITUDES, MR TROTTER; BUT IT DOESNT TAKE ME IN.
HART III (131)	SKETCHES, AND RUNS AFTER MARRIED WOMEN, AND READS	LITERARY	BOOKS AND POEMS. HE ACTUALLY PLAYS THE FLUTE; BUT I
SUPR PREFACE(R40)	WEAK INTIMIDATED; THE CONNOISSEURS TICKLED BY MY	LITERARY	BRAVURA (PUT IN TO PLEASE YOU): THE HUMORISTS
CYMB FORWORD(133)	TAKES EFFECT, AND HAD CULMINATED IN THE CRUDE	LITERARY	BUTCHERIES SUCCESSFULLY IMPOSED ON THE PUBLIC AND
LION PREFACE(39)	WITH DISTRUST AND DISLIKE, IN SPITE OF HIS GREAT	LITERARY	CHARM, A GOOD EXAMPLE OF WHICH IS HIS
BULL PREFACE(64)	THEIR TERRORS? I AM MYSELF A SEDENTARY	LITERARY	CIVILIAN, CONSTITUTIONALLY TIMID; BUT I FIND IT
BASH PREFACE(87)	IN THE PRIMITIVE ELIZABETHAN STYLE. AND LEST THE	LITERARY	CONNOISSEURS SHOULD DECLARE THAT THERE WAS NOT A
CAPT NOTES (305)	DAILY CHRONICLE ALSO DID SOMETHING TO BRING THE	LITERARY	CONVENTION FOR COCKNEY ENGLISH UP TO DATE. BUT
CYMB FORWORD(138)	INSTEAD OF LITERARY. IS IT A PLOT TO TAKE THE	LITERARY	CRITICS OUT OF THEIR DEPTH? WELL, IT MAY HAVE THAT
3PLA PREFACE(R29)	ROMANTIC MOTIVE FOR DICK'S SACRIFICE WAS NO MERE	LITERARY	DREAMER, BUT A CLEVER BARRISTER. HE POINTED OUT
MIS. PREFACE(50)	REMARK THAT MANY CHILDREN HAVE NO APPETITE FOR A	LITERARY	EDUCATION AT ALL, AND WOULD NEVER OPEN A BOOK IF
MIS. PREFACE(50)	BY THE TEACHERS; FOR THE CHILDREN TO WHOM A	LITERARY	EDUCATION CAN BE OF ANY USE ARE INSATIABLE: THEY
CLEO II (139)	OF BOOKS. /THEODOTUS/ (KNEELING, WITH GENUINE	LITERARY	EMOTION: THE PASSION OF THE PEDANT) CAESAR: ONCE IN
ARMS III SD(46)	AFTER LUNCH. IT IS NOT MUCH OF A LIBRARY. ITS	LITERARY	EQUIPMENT CONSISTS OF A SINGLE FIXED SHELF STOCKED
JITT II (31)	AGNES IS COMING TO SEE US. BRUNO HAS MADE ME HIS	LITERARY	EXECUTOR. THAT IS WHAT SHE IS COMING ABOUT. /JITTA/
JITT II (31)	I TELL YOU? HE HAS MADE ME HIS SCIENTIFIC AND	LITERARY	EXECUTOR. /JITTA/ I MEAN ABOUT-- ABOUT-- /LENKHEIM/
JITT II (29)	IS GOING TO ASK YOU TO ACT AS HIS SCIENTIFIC AND	LITERARY	EXECUTOR. /LENKHEIM/ (PLEASANTLY SURPRISED AND
JITT II (29)	I MAY TELL YOU THAT IN MY OWN WILL I MADE HIM MY	LITERARY	EXECUTOR. WHO WOULD HAVE THOUGHT THAT HE WOULD PEG
MIS. PREFACE(50)	UNIVERSITY DEGREES. AND FOR ALL THE EFFECT THEIR	LITERARY	EXERCISES HAS LEFT ON THEM THEY MIGHT JUST AS WELL
PLES PREFACE(R11)	VOLUME, I RESOLVED TO AVAIL MYSELF OF MY	LITERARY	EXPERTNESS TO PUT MY PLAYS BEFORE THE PUBLIC IN MY
SUPR II SD(62)	IS NOTHING BUT A STATE OF SATURATION WITH OUR	LITERARY	EXPORTS OF THIRTY YEARS AGO, REIMPORTED BY HIM TO
CYMB FORWORD(136)	BLANK VERSE HAS BEEN TO ME AS NATURAL A FORM OF	LITERARY	EXPRESSION AS THE AUGUSTAN ENGLISH TO WHICH I WAS
UNPL PREFACE(R21)	TRAINED ACTOR, HE MUST FALL BACK ON HIS POWERS OF	LITERARY	EXPRESSION, AS OTHER POETS AND FICTIONISTS DO. SO
BASH PREFACE(92)	A FANCY FOR IT THAN TO HAVE NO SENSE OF STYLE OR	LITERARY	FANCY AT ALL.
MILL I SD(152)	IN THE PRIME OF LIFE, BEARDED IN THE VICTORIAN	LITERARY	FASHION, RATHER HANDSOME, AND WELL DRESSED, COMES
CAPT NOTES (305)	SO COMPLETELY THAT I SHOULD HAVE GIVEN IT UP AS A	LITERARY	FICTION IF I HAD NOT DISCOVERED IT SURVIVING IN A
MIS. PREFACE(21)	THAT I HAVE NOT WASTED MY LIFE TRIFLING WITH	LITERARY	FOOLS IN TAVERNS AS JOHNSON DID WHEN HE SHOULD HAVE
LION PREFACE(40)	IS ALIVE AT THIS MOMENT, I CANNOT BELIEVE THAT A	LITERARY	FORGER COULD HOPE TO SAVE THE SITUATION BY SO
BASH PREFACE(90)	TRAGEDY, WHICH INDEED IT ALSO IS. IT WAS THE	LITERARY	FUN THAT PROVED A MERE PUZZLE, IN SPITE OF THE
MIS. PREFACE(100)	IF HE IS ALLOWED TO WANDER IN A WELL-STOCKED	LITERARY	GARDEN, AND HEAR BANDS AND SEE PICTURES AND SPEND
FABL PREFACE(64)	MIND FURTHER THAN DR CULPIN HAS VENTURED. IS	LITERARY	GENIUS A DISEASE? SHAKESPEAR, WALTER SCOTT,
BARB PREFACE(226)	EVEN WHEN DONE BY THE MOST EARNEST AND WITTY	LITERARY	GENIUSES, WERE AS USELESS AS PRAYING, THINGS GOING
CLEO NOTES (209)	IS ONLY TRUE OF AUTHORS WHO HAVE THE SPECIFIC	LITERARY	GENIUS, AND HAVE PRACTISED LONG ENOUGH TO ATTAIN
3PLA PREFACE(R32)	OR A MACBETH, AND WIN YOU GREAT APPLAUSE FROM	LITERARY	GENTLEMEN; BUT IT WILL NOT GIVE YOU A JULIUS
METH PREFACE(R62)	DARWIN HAD NOT: IMPLACABILITY AND A FINE JEWISH	LITERARY	GIFT, WITH TERRIBLE POWERS OF HATRED, INVECTIVE,
FANY PROLOG (257)	OPENED SINCE WE CAME FROM VENICE-- AND AS OUR	LITERARY	GUESTS WILL PROBABLY USE THE LIBRARY A GOOD DEAL, I
SUPR III (84)	THIS FINELY TEMPERED AIR, AND THEN TALK LIKE A	LITERARY	HACK ON A SECOND FLOOR IN BLOOMSBURY? /MENDOZA/ (
LIED (203)	IT HEARTILY) YOUVE GOT TO OWN THAT NONE OF YOUR	LITERARY	HEROINES CAN TOUCH MY RORY. (HE TURNS TO HER AND
FANY PROLOG (265)	JOB AFTER ALL, IS IT? BANNAL MAY NOT RIDE THE	LITERARY	HIGH HORSE LIKE TROTTER AND THE REST; BUT I'D TAKE
HART PREFACE(5)	THOMAS HARDY, AND, GENERALLY SPEAKING, ALL THE	LITERARY	IMPLEMENTS FOR FORMING THE MIND OF THE PERFECT
SUPR IV SD(141)	VILLA BEHIND US ON OUR RIGHT) WE FIND EVIDENCE OF	LITERARY	INTERESTS ON THE PART OF THE TENANTS IN THE FACT
3PLA PREFACE(R39)	ARTIFICIALITY THAT MARKS THE WORK OF EVERY	LITERARY	IRISHMAN OF MY GENERATION WILL SEEM ANTIQUATED AND
CYMB FORWORD(138)	ASKED WHY ALL MY INSTANCES ARE MUSICAL INSTEAD OF	LITERARY	. IS IT A PLOT TO TAKE THE LITERARY CRITICS OUT OF
VWOO 1 (120)	ALWAYS DRIVING ONEANOTHER MAD. /A/ THAT SOUNDS	LITERARY	. WAS YOUR FATHER A MAN OF LETTERS? /Z/ YES: I
FABL VI (123)	SHOULD SAY DONT CARE A DAM. /YOUTH 3/ OH, I'M NOT	LITERARY	. WHAT DOES DAM MEAN? /TEACHER/ IT MEANS A
CYMB FORWORD(133)	ACT TO CYMBELINE, AND DO IT TOO, NOT WHOLLY AS A	LITERARY	JEU D'ESPRIT, BUT IN RESPONSE TO AN ACTUAL
SUPR PREFACE(R10)	AND THE PURSUITS OF A VESTRYMAN. NO DOUBT THAT	LITERARY	KNACK OF MINE WHICH HAPPENS TO AMUSE THE BRITISH
CAND I SD(78)	JOHN BALL, MARX'S CAPITAL, AND HALF A DOZEN OTHER	LITERARY	LANDMARKS IN SOCIALISM. FACING HIM ON THE OTHER
FABL PREFACE(63)	FROM ME MORE THAN A FEW CRUMBS DROPPED FROM THE	LITERARY	LOAVES I DISTRIBUTED IN MY PRIME, PLUS A FEW
VWOO 1,SD(115)	SHIP. TWO OF THE DECK CHAIRS ARE OCCUPIED BY A, A	LITERARY	LOOKING PALE GENTLEMAN UNDER FORTY IN GREEN

CLEO NOTES (207)	MADE THEM SO, UNLESS, INDEED, HE HAD PLAYED THE	LITERARY	MAN AND MADE QUINCE SAY, NOT " IS ALL OUR COMPANY
3PLA PREFACE(R31)	CRIES SHAKESPEAR, IN HIS TRAGEDY OF THE MODERN	LITERARY	MAN AS MURDERER AND WITCH CONSULTER. SURELY THE
JITT II (29)	A DISGRACEFUL END. AN OPERATIC TENOR, OR EVEN A	LITERARY	MAN, MIGHT BE FORGIVEN FOR DYING IN AN ADVENTURE OF
GETT PREFACE(232)	TO THE CONTRARY BEING ONE OF THE ILLUSIONS OF	LITERARY	MASCULINITY. BESIDES, THE HUSBAND IS NOT
3PLA PREFACE(R38)	WHOLE STOCK-IN-TRADE; AND IT SUFFICED TO MAKE A	LITERARY	MASTER OF HIM. IN DUE TIME, WHEN MOMMSEN IS AN OLD
UNPL PREFACE(R22)	AS THIS IS, THE PRESENTATION OF PLAYS THROUGH THE	LITERARY	MEDIUM HAS NOT YET BECOME AN ART; AND THE RESULT IS
BARB III (347)	THE LAWYERS, THE DOCTORS, THE PRIESTS, THE	LITERARY	MEN, THE PROFESSORS, THE ARTISTS, AND THE
SUPR III (84)	WRITTEN ABOUT HER MYSELF. HOWEVER SLIGHT THEIR	LITERARY	MERIT MAY BE, THEY EXPRESS WHAT I FEEL BETTER THAN
CAPT NOTES (306)	THE DIALECT OF THE MISSIONARY. THERE IS NO	LITERARY	NOTATION FOR THE GRAVE MUSIC OF GOOD SCOTCH.
MILL I (151)	IS HE THE CHAIRMAN OF BLENDERBLAND'S	LITERARY	PENNYWORTHS? /EPIFANIA/ NO. THAT IS HIS FATHER,
GENV II (54)	AH YES: OUTSIDE POLITICS: I SEE. BUT WE CANT HAVE	LITERARY	PEOPLE INTERFERING IN FOREIGN AFFAIRS. AND THEY
JITT PREFACE(4)	NOR PLEAD IGNORANCE OF IT. I AM LIKE MOST	LITERARY	PERSONS; I HAVE SPENT SEVERAL HOLIDAYS IN GERMANY (
LIED (199)	IN YOUR LIFE, YOU HARDLY DO JUSTICE TO YOUR OWN	LITERARY	POWERS-- WHICH I ADMIRE AND APPRECIATE, MIND YOU,
CYMB FORWORD(138)	MOLIERE'S FESTIN DE PIERRE, OR ANY OF THE OTHER	LITERARY	PRECEDENTS, THOUGH I AM A LITTLE ASHAMED OF BEING
BASH PREFACE(87)	GO BACK FRANKLY TO ITS BEGINNINGS, AND START A	LITERARY	PRE-RAPHAELITE BROTHERHOOD. I LIKE THE MELODIOUS
JITT PREFACE(7)	SHOULD READ THE ORIGINAL, TO THE IDIOSYNCRATIC	LITERARY	QUALITY OF WHICH I HAVE BEEN SHAMEFULLY UNABLE TO
JOAN PREFACE(25)	FRENCH CHURCH) HE STUCK AT NOTHING. SO FAR, THE	LITERARY	REPRESENTATIONS OF THE MAID WERE LEGENDARY. BUT THE
LADY PREFACE(211)	IN ADDITION TO THE INDISPENSABLE SCHOLARSHIP AND	LITERARY	REPUTATION, ARE NEEDED; AND MEN WHO PRETEND TO
SUPR PREFACE(R27)	THE EFFORTS OF OUR CHURCHES AND UNIVERSITIES AND	LITERARY	SAGES TO RAISE THE MASS ABOVE ITS OWN LEVEL, THE
LADY PREFACE(208)	BE FRIENDLY TO IMMORTALIZE HIM, AS THE SILLY	LITERARY	SAYING IS, MUCH AS SHAKESPEAR IMMORTALIZED MR W.
GENV III (79)	WELL, IT DOES NOT MATTER: IT WAS ONE OF THE	LITERARY	SET. /THE WIDOW/ IT SOUNDS WELL; BUT ENGLISH IS NOT
UNPL PREFACE(R9)	DO WAS TO OPEN MY NORMAL EYES, AND WITH MY UTMOST	LITERARY	SKILL PUT THE CASE EXACTLY AS IT STRUCK ME, OR
BASH PREFACE(90)	SATISFY PEOPLE WHOSE MINDS WERE STEEPED IN MODERN	LITERARY	SOB STUFF. FOR INSTANCE, SUCH BALD STATEMENTS ABOUT
MTH3 (93)	I HAVNT READ IT. BUT I HAVE READ WHAT THE TIMES	LITERARY	SUPPLEMENT SAYS ABOUT IT. /BARNABAS/ I DONT CARE
FABL PREFACE(98)	CUT NO ICE IN ADMINISTRATIVE COUNCILS: THE	LITERARY	TALENT AND PULPIT ELOQUENCE THAT HAS ALWAYS BEEN
PYGM EPILOG (297)	ATTEMPTS TO PICK UP AND PRACTISE ARTISTIC AND	LITERARY	TALK IRRITATED THEM. SHE WAS, IN SHORT, AN UTTER
BULL PREFACE(13)	OR TAX THE SPECIAL RESOURCES OF THE IRISH	LITERARY	THEATRE FOR ITS PRODUCTION. HOW TOM BROADBENT TOOK
BULL PREFACE(13)	CONTRIBUTION TO THE REPERTORY OF THE IRISH	LITERARY	THEATRE. LIKE MOST PEOPLE WHO HAVE ASKED ME TO
GETT PREFACE(195)	IS LOATHED BECAUSE THE IMPOSTURE IS LOATHSOME.	LITERARY	TRADITIONS SPRING UP IN WHICH THE LIBERTINE AND
UNPL PREFACE(R22)	IF THE SEVENTEENTH WOULD ONLY LET HIM. SUCH	LITERARY	TREATMENT IS MUCH MORE NEEDED BY MODERN PLAYS THAN
POSN PREFACE(377)	AUTOGRAPHED " LOCKWOOD B" AMONG MY MOST VALUED	LITERARY	TROPHIES. AN INNOCENT LADY TOLD ME AFTERWARDS THAT
BARB III (335)	WEAPON: TO HEAVEN THE VICTORY, THE FOURTH HAD NO	LITERARY	TURN; SO HE DID NOT WRITE UP ANYTHING; BUT HE SOLD
BUOY PREFACE(3)	THESE THAT THEY HAVE NEITHER NOVELTY, PROFUNDITY,	LITERARY	VALUE NOR ARTISTIC CHARM, BEING WELL WITHIN THE
SUPR PREFACE(R37)	AMATEURS WHO BECOME THE HEROES OF THE FANCIERS OF	LITERARY	VIRTUOSITY, IS NOT FOUNDED ON ANY ILLUSION OF MINE
UNPL PREFACE(R8)	THAT WE COULD NOT LIVE BY TAKING IN ONEANOTHER'S	LITERARY	WASHING. HOW TO EARN DAILY BREAD BY MY PEN WAS THEN
3PLA PREFACE(R25)	RETIREMENT TO THOSE WHO ARE GENTLEMEN FIRST AND	LITERARY	WORKMEN AFTERWARDS. THE CART AND TRUMPET FOR ME.
LADY PREFACE(211)	GAVE ME GREAT DELIGHT. TO THOSE WHO KNOW THE	LITERARY	WORLD OF LONDON THERE WAS A SHARP STROKE OF IRONIC
3PLA PREFACE(R39)	ENSUING DEMAND FOR NOTABILITIES OF ALL SORTS,	LITERARY	, MILITARY, POLITICAL AND FASHIONABLE, TO WRITE
MILL I (165)	A SOUL MATE? /ALASTAIR/ NO: THAT SOUNDS SILLY.	LITERARY	, YOU KNOW. /PATRICIA/ MORE OF A MIND MATE, I

LITERATE

BASH II,1, (100)	FITNESS. /LYDIA/ NAY, HE SPEAKS VERY WELL: HE'S	LITERATE	: SHAKESPEAR HE QUOTES UNCONSCIOUSLY. /LUCIAN/ AND
BASH PREFACE(88)	BUT THE NEWSPAPERS ADDRESSED THEMSELVES TO THE	LITERATE	ALONE. HUNT UP AN OLD MELODRAMA (SAY SWEENY TODD
METH PREFACE(R9)	HUMORIST, BUT THE FAMOUS NATURALIST BUFFON. EVERY	LITERATE	CHILD AT THAT TIME KNEW BUFFON'S NATURAL HISTORY AS
METH PREFACE(R88)	THAT FROM THAT MOMENT IT LOST ITS HOLD, AND LEFT	LITERATE	CHRISTENDOM FAITHLESS. MY OWN IRISH
CAPT NOTES (306)	HOWEVER THAT MAY BE, IT IS KEPT ALIVE ONLY BY THE	LITERATE	CLASSES WHO ARE REMINDED CONSTANTLY OF ITS
SUPR PREFACE(R15)	YOU AND FOR ME; AND IF THERE ARE MILLIONS OF LESS	LITERATE	PEOPLE WHO ARE STILL IN THE EIGHTEENTH CENTURY,
MIS. PREFACE(98)	FALSE PRETENCES, ON OUR CHILDREN LEFT THEM MORE	LITERATE	THAN IF THEY KNEW NO LITERATURE AT ALL, WHICH WAS
MIS. PREFACE(50)	ON THE TREADMILL. IN FACT THEY ARE ACTUALLY LESS	LITERATE	THAN THE TREADMILL WOULD HAVE LEFT THEM; FOR THEY

LITERATURE

BARB PREFACE(208)	LAY OUTSIDE THE PALE OF SYMPATHY IN	LITERATURE	: HE WAS PITILESSLY DESPISED AND RIDICULED HERE
SUPR II (54)	A LITTLE PATIENT WITH ME. I AM NOT DISCUSSING	LITERATURE	: THE BOOK ABOUT THE BEE IS NATURAL HISTORY. IT'S
POSN PREFACE(392)	ABSURDITY OF CHOOSING AS CENSOR OF DRAMATIC	LITERATURE	AN OFFICIAL WHOSE FUNCTIONS AND QUALIFICATIONS
JOAN PREFACE(49)	AND FIFTY YEARS. THE RENASCENCE OF ANTIQUE	LITERATURE	AND ART IN THE SIXTEENTH CENTURY, AND THE LUSTY
PYGM V (287)	ANY TRAINING OR ANY WORK. NOT LIKE SCIENCE AND	LITERATURE	AND CLASSICAL MUSIC AND PHILOSOPHY AND ART. YOU
MIS. PREFACE(51)	WILL BE LESS, AS SO MANY POTENTIAL LOVERS OF	LITERATURE	AND MATHEMATICS WILL HAVE BEEN INCURABLY
CATH 2 (179)	ADMIRE HER MAJESTY'S POLICY AND HER EMINENCE IN	LITERATURE	AND PHILOSOPHY WITHOUT PERFORMING ACROBATIC FEATS
DOCT III (140)	THAT: I AN ARTIST, AND SHE QUITE OUT OF ART AND	LITERATURE	AND REFINED LIVING AND EVERYTHING ELSE. THERE WAS
LADY PREFACE(210)	OFFERED FOR SALE TO THE BRITISH MUSEUM, AND ABOUT	LITERATURE	AND THINGS OF THE SPIRIT GENERALLY. HE ALWAYS
BARB PREFACE(207)	I CANNOT COUNTENANCE THE ASSUMPTION THAT LIFE AND	LITERATURE	ARE SO POOR IN THESE ISLANDS THAT WE MUST GO
LION PREFACE(101)	IN EXCHANGE FOR HIS OWN, OR OUR JEWISH CANONICAL	LITERATURE	AS AN IMPROVEMENT ON HINDOO SCRIPTURE, IS TO
MIS. PREFACE(98)	LEFT THEM MORE LITERATE THAN IF THEY KNEW NO	LITERATURE	AT ALL, WHICH WAS THE PRACTICAL ALTERNATIVE. AND
SUPR II (53)	HIS TEMPER WITH DIFFICULTY) I AM NOT DISCUSSING	LITERATURE	AT PRESENT. /TANNER/ BE JUST A LITTLE PATIENT
BULL PREFACE(38)	BY PROTESTANTS TO WHOM THE BIBLE WAS NOT A	LITERATURE	BUT A FETISH AND A TALISMAN. AND SO VOLTAIRE, IN
PHIL PREFACE(68)	WHEN IT WAS WRITTEN, NOT ONLY DRAMATIC	LITERATURE	BUT LIFE ITSELF WAS STAGGERING FROM THE IMPACT OF
MIS. PREFACE(25)	LOVE AND CONSIDERABLE KNOWLEDGE OF CLASSICAL	LITERATURE	BY AN IRISH SCHOOLMASTER WHOM YOU WOULD CALL A
UNPL PREFACE(R8)	IN MY NONAGE I HAD TRIED TO OBTAIN A FOOTHOLD IN	LITERATURE	BY WRITING NOVELS, AND HAD ACTUALLY PRODUCED FIVE
MRS PREFACE(163)	CLERK TO SEE THAT THE LEADERS OF EUROPEAN	LITERATURE	DO NOT CORRUPT THE MORALS OF THE NATION, AND TO
SUPR PREFACE(R24)	THE SUBSTITUTION OF READING FOR EXPERIENCE, OF	LITERATURE	FOR LIFE, OF THE OBSOLETE FICTITIOUS FOR THE
3PLA PREFACE(R21)	A PERSISTENT MISREPRESENTATION OF HUMANITY IN	LITERATURE	GETS FINALLY ACCEPTED AND ACTED UPON. IF EVERY
MIS. (134)	AT ANYTHING; AND I DONT BELIEVE I SHOULD FAIL AT	LITERATURE	IF IT WOULD PAY ME TO TURN MY HAND TO IT.
CYMB FORWORD(138)	MUSIC HAS SUCCEEDED TO THE HEROIC RANK TAKEN BY	LITERATURE	IN THE SIXTEENTH CENTURY. I CANNOT PRETEND TO
MIS. PREFACE(99)	BIBLE OF MODERN EUROPE IS THE WHOLE BODY OF GREAT	LITERATURE	IN WHICH THE INSPIRATION AND REVELATION OF HEBREW
CLEO NOTES (209)	NOT TRUE EVEN ON THESE CONDITIONS IN AN AGE WHEN	LITERATURE	IS CONCEIVED AS A GAME OF STYLE, AND NOT AS A
ROCK PREFACE(177)	ACTION IS MANIFESTLY ABSURD. ALL GREAT ART AND	LITERATURE	IS PROPAGANDA. MOST CERTAINLY THE HERESIES OF
BUOY PREFACE(4)	RIVAL CLAIMANTS, OUR GREATEST MASTERPIECE OF	LITERATURE	IS THE JACOBEAN TRANSLATION OF THE BIBLE; AND
SUPR III (106)	IT IS THE SAME IN EVERYTHING. THE HIGHEST FORM OF	LITERATURE	IS THE TRAGEDY, A PLAY IN WHICH EVERYBODY IS
BARB PREFACE(231)	JUSTICE" OF THE ROMANTIC STAGE. FOR THE CREDIT OF	LITERATURE	IT MUST BE POINTED OUT THAT THE SITUATION IS ONLY
POSN PREFACE(391)	HAVE NO SORT OF RELATIONSHIP TO DRAMATIC	LITERATURE	. A GREAT JUDGE OF LITERATURE, A FAR-SEEING
MIS. (135)	JOHNNY'S AND HYPATIA'S FUTURE BY GOING INTO	LITERATURE	. BUT IT WAS NO GOOD. FIRST IT WAS 250 POUNDS
JOAN PREFACE(23)	THAT REACTS AGAINST THAT ROMANCE. THE MAID IN	LITERATURE	. ENGLISH READERS WOULD PROBABLY LIKE TO KNOW HOW
3PLA PREFACE(R27)	PLAYGOER OF TODAY, BUT NOT TO LOVERS OF SERIOUS	LITERATURE	. FROM PROMETHEUS TO THE WAGNERIAN SIEGFRIED,
MIS. PREFACE(50)	NOT BEEN DRIVEN TO LOATHE EVERY FAMOUS NAME IN	LITERATURE	. I SHOULD PROBABLY KNOW AS MUCH LATIN AS FRENCH,
MIS. (168)	YOU SEE! DOOM! THATS NOT GOOD SENSE; BUT IT'S	LITERATURE	. NOW IT HAPPENS THAT I'M A TREMENDOUS READER:
MIS. (169)	MUST SPEND AT LEAST A SHILLING A WEEK ON ROMANTIC	LITERATURE	. /THE MAN/ WHERE WOULD I GET A SHILLING A WEEK
MIS. PREFACE(98)	HAD THEY BEEN ALLOWED TO READ MUCH LOWER FORMS OF	LITERATURE	. THE PRACTICAL MORAL IS THAT WE MUST READ
MTH4 I (161)	USED POSTAGE STAMPS ABOUT INTERNATIONAL TRADE OR	LITERATURE	. THE SCIENTIFIC TERRORIST WHO WAS AFRAID TO USE
FABL PREFACE(91)	INTO A LIBRARY STOCKED WITH THE MASTERPIECES OF	LITERATURE	. THEY SHOULD BE ASKED WHICH OF THEM THEY HAD
MTH4 I (162)	SACRED VOLUME, A CHAPTER TO A BIBLE, A BIBLE TO A	LITERATURE	. WE MAY BE INSECTS; BUT LIKE THE CORAL INSECT WE
BASH PREFACE(91)	OWN EARLY NOVELS. STILL, A REVIVAL OF ELIZABETHAN	LITERATURE	MAY BE POSSIBLE. IF I, AS AN IRISH CHILD IN THE
METH PREFACE(R40)	OF THE BIBLE, WHICH WAS REGARDED, NOT AS	LITERATURE	NOR EVEN AS A BOOK, BUT PARTLY AS AN ORACLE WHICH
OVER PREFACE(162)	OUT THE JOURNALISM OF THE DIVORCE COURTS IS A	LITERATURE	OCCUPIED WITH SEX TO AN EXTENT AND WITH AN
MIS. PREFACE(98)	OR SINCE. BUT THE BIBLE CONTAINS THE ANCIENT	LITERATURE	OF A VERY REMARKABLE ORIENTAL RACE; AND THE
CYMB FORWORD(135)	THE CURSE OF SERIOUS DRAMA, AND INDEED OF SERIOUS	LITERATURE	OF ANY KIND. IT IS SO OUT-OF-PLACE THERE THAT
CATH PREFACE(155)	NO QUEENS FOR HER TO PLAY; AND AS TO THE OLDER	LITERATURE	OF OUR STAGE, DID IT NOT PROVOKE THE VETERAN
DOCT PREFACE(20)	IN ONE OF THE SCIENTIFIC JOURNALS AND FOLLOW THE	LITERATURE	OF THE SCIENTIFIC MOVEMENT, KNOWS MORE ABOUT IT
2TRU II (68)	THE HIGHER CENTRES. IN ALL THE GREAT POETRY AND	LITERATURE	OF THE WORLD THE HIGHER CENTRES SPEAK. IN ALL
MIS. PREFACE(51)	CULTURE IS A SHAM; THAT IT KNOWS LITTLE ABOUT	LITERATURE	OR ART AND A GREAT DEAL ABOUT POINT-TO-POINT
MIS. PREFACE(99)	DEAD LANGUAGE. BESIDES, MANY WHO HAVE NO EAR FOR	LITERATURE	OR FOR MUSIC ARE ACCESSIBLE TO ARCHITECTURE, TO
CATH PREFACE(155)	CRITICALLY AS AN ADDITION TO THE DEBT DRAMATIC	LITERATURE	OWES TO THE ART OF ACTING AND ITS EXPONENTS.
LIED (199)	REALLY VERY READY OF YOU. YOU ARE CUT OUT FOR	LITERATURE	; AND THE DAY WILL COME WHEN RORY AND I WILL BE
FABL PREFACE(82)	DEPRAVITY. I MAY FAIRLY CLAIM TO BE AN ADEPT IN	LITERATURE	; BUT IN DOZENS OF OTHER DEPARTMENTS I AM A
3PLA PREFACE(R17)	THE GENUINE ARISTOCRACY OF MODERN DRAMATIC	LITERATURE	SHOCK THE REVERENCE FOR GENTILITY WHICH GOVERNS
OVER PREFACE(162)	IN SEX IS STRONGER THAN EVER: IN FACT, THE	LITERATURE	THAT HAS DRIVEN OUT THE JOURNALISM OF THE DIVORCE
SUPR PREFACE(R38)	ARE NEVERTHELESS SO IN LOVE WITH ORATORY AND WITH	LITERATURE	THAT THEY DELIGHT IN REPEATING AS MUCH AS THEY
POSN PREFACE(382)	WOULD HAVE BEEN THE EFFECT OF APPLYING TO ALL	LITERATURE	THE CENSORSHIP WE STILL APPLY TO THE STAGE. THE

LADY PREFACE(211) IRRESISTIBLE VERDICT IN ITS FAVOR. IN CRITICAL LITERATURE THERE IS ONE PRIZE THAT IS ALWAYS OPEN TO
CAPT NOTES (301) CLERKS WHO ESCAPE FROM THEIR SERVITUDE INTO LITERATURE TO TELL US HOW MEN AND CITIES ARE CONCEIVED IN
LION PREFACE(91) GOOD OR EVIL, WE HAVE MADE A SYNTHESIS OUT OF THE LITERATURE WE CALL THE BIBLE, AND THOUGH THE DISCOVERY THAT
BARB PREFACE(221) MONEY. IT DRIVES ONE ALMOST TO DESPAIR OF ENGLISH LITERATURE WHEN ONE SEES SO EXTRAORDINARY A STUDY OF ENGLISH
SUPR PREFACE(R36) EXACTLY WHAT WOULD BE COMPLAINED OF IN ALL THE LITERATURE WHICH IS GREAT ENOUGH AND OLD ENOUGH TO HAVE
OVER PREFACE(160) IS A CONTRIBUTION TO THE VERY EXTENSIVE DRAMATIC LITERATURE WHICH TAKES AS ITS SPECIAL DEPARTMENT THE
PYGM PREFACE(200) DERISIVE ATTACK ON A PROFESSOR OF LANGUAGE AND LITERATURE WHOSE CHAIR SWEET REGARDED AS PROPER TO A
FABL PREFACE(63) FALLING ASLEEP ALMOST AT ONCE. THE PANJANDRUMS OF LITERATURE WILL NO DOUBT CONTINUE TO ASSUME THAT WHOEVER CAN
BARB (206) VERSION OF THE BACCHAE CAME INTO OUR DRAMATIC LITERATURE WITH ALL THE IMPULSIVE POWER OF AN ORIGINAL WORK
POSN PREFACE(391) TO DRAMATIC LITERATURE. A GREAT JUDGE OF LITERATURE , A FAR-SEEING STATESMAN, A BORN CHAMPION OF
ROCK I (227) OUR SERMONS AND SPEECHES ARE THE GLORIES OF OUR LITERATURE , AND THE INSPIRED VOICES OF OUR RELIGION, OUR
HART PREFACE(4) IN EUROPE IN WHICH THE PLEASURES OF MUSIC, ART, LITERATURE , AND THE THEATRE HAD SUPPLANTED HUNTING,
POSN PREFACE(419) AND AS FAR AS THE LAW IS CONCERNED, JOURNALISM, LITERATURE , AND THE DRAMA EXIST ONLY BY CUSTOM OR
POSN PREFACE(433) ACTORS (ONE RETIRED), AN OXFORD PROFESSOR OF LITERATURE , AND TWO EMINENT BARRISTERS, AS THEIR ASSEMBLY
BARB III (319) ONCE. HAVNT YOU A TURN FOR SOMETHING? WHAT ABOUT LITERATURE , ART, AND SO FORTH? /STEPHEN/ I HAVE NOTHING OF
SUPR HANDBOK(197) BY THE MASTERPIECES OF JEWISH REVOLUTIONARY LITERATURE , CUT OFF THE HEADS OF THE THREE? SUPPOSE THE
SUPR PREFACE(R38) WHOLE LIFE AND SOUL TO BECOME A MERE VIRTUOSO IN LITERATURE , EXHIBITING AN ACCOMPLISHMENT WHICH WILL NOT
METH PREFACE(R27) WHEREAS TO ME THE WHOLE VOCABULARY OF ENGLISH LITERATURE , FROM SHAKESPEAR TO THE LATEST EDITION OF THE
HART PREFACE(16) BIOLOGY, GERMAN POETRY, GERMAN MUSIC, GERMAN LITERATURE , GERMAN PHILOSOPHY, AND EVEN GERMAN ENGINEERING,
POSN PREFACE(392) QUALIFICATIONS HAVE NOTHING WHATEVER TO DO WITH LITERATURE , IT ALSO EXPLAINS WHY THE PRESENT ARRANGEMENT IS
SUPR PREFACE(R39) USEFUL TO YOU AS THOSE TWO VITAL QUALITIES OF LITERATURE , LIGHT AND HEAT, NOW IF I AM TO BE NO MERE
BARB PREFACE(207) MAJOR BARBARA, LET ME, FOR THE CREDIT OF ENGLISH LITERATURE , MAKE A PROTEST AGAINST AN UNPATRIOTIC HABIT
BUOY IV (59) OF IRISH DEIRDRE, THE GREATEST BORES IN LITERATURE , MERE NAMES INCIDENTALLY IMMORTALIZED BY A FEW
MIS. PREFACE(40) VICE; BUT AS IT ALSO PROTECTS THEM FROM POETRY, LITERATURE , MUSIC, MEDITATION AND PRAYER, IT MAY BE
POSN PREFACE(398) HAD SO MUCH, THERE WOULD BE NO THEATRE, NO LITERATURE , NO SCIENCE, NO ART, POSSIBLY NO ENGLAND. THE
MIS. PREFACE(98) ORIENTAL RACE; AND THE IMPOSITION OF THIS LITERATURE , ON WHATEVER FALSE PRETENCES, ON OUR CHILDREN
UNPL PREFACE(R17) WHOSE WORK THEY HAVE ALREADY LEARNT TO VALUE AS LITERATURE , OR A PERFORMANCE BY AN ACTOR OF THE FIRST RANK.
HART PREFACE(35) MEN WHO WERE NOT ONLY ENTHUSIASTIC AMATEURS OF LITERATURE , PAINTING, AND MUSIC, BUT FAMOUS PRACTITIONERS
PYGM EPILOG (291) DISAGREEABLE PARENTS, AND TO WHOM, CONSEQUENTLY, LITERATURE , PAINTING, SCULPTURE, MUSIC, AND AFFECTIONATE
POSN PREFACE(366) HE IS NOT AN EXPERT IN POLITICS, RELIGION, ART, LITERATURE , PHILOSOPHY, OR LAW, HE CALLS IN A PLAYWRIGHT
CLEO II (140) THEODOTUS GO TO SAVE THE LIBRARY. WE MUST RESPECT LITERATURE , RUFIO. /RUFIO/ (RAGING) FOLLY ON FOLLY'S
BASH PREFACE(89) AS PART OF AN ACADEMIC COURSE ON ENGLISH LITERATURE , SAT WITH A SCOWL OF MALIGNANT HATRED THAT
INCA (256) THING. YOU ARE WRONG: FOR YEARS I GAVE THEM ART, LITERATURE , SCIENCE, PROSPERITY, THAT THEY MIGHT LIVE MORE
SUPR II SD(62) MOMENT'S NOTICE AND HURLED AT THE HEAD OF ENGLISH LITERATURE , SCIENCE, AND ART, AT EVERY CONVERSATIONAL
PLES PREFACE(R14) GALLERY AND BRITISH MUSEUM ARE TO PAINTING AND LITERATURE , WE CAN GET IT BY ENDOWING IT IN THE SAME WAY.
SUPR PREFACE(R24) HAVE BEEN SO OVERWHELMINGLY SOPHISTICATED BY LITERATURE , WHAT PRODUCES ALL THESE TREATISES AND POEMS AND
UNPL PREFACE(R14) THE ENGLISH NOVEL HAS BEEN ONE OF THE GLORIES OF LITERATURE , WHILST THE ENGLISH DRAMA HAS BEEN ITS DISGRACE.
3PLA PREFACE(R9) PICTURES, AND ABOUT AS MUCH OF ITS CURRENT LITERATURE , WRESTLING CRITICALLY WITH THEM WITH ALL MY

LITERY

WIDO III (58) MY CORRESPONDENCE: SEKKETERRY WE CALL IT. IVE NO LITERY STYLE, AND THATS THE TRUTH; SO MR COKANE KINDLY PUTS

LITHE

DEST SD(161) SHE IS VERY FEMININE, BUT BY NO MEANS WEAK: THE LITHE TENDER FIGURE IS HUNG ON A STRONG FRAME: THE HANDS AND

LITHOGRAPHED

PYGM PREFACE(201) TO, THE FOUR AND SIXPENNY MANUAL, MOSTLY IN HIS LITHOGRAPHED HANDWRITING, THAT WAS NEVER VULGARLY

LITIGANT

JOAN PREFACE(50) EXPONENTS OF THE CHURCH MILITANT AND THE CHURCH LITIGANT , BECAUSE ONLY BY DOING SO CAN I MAINTAIN MY DRAMA

LITIGANTS

LION PREFACE(12) TIME IT WAS THOUGHT QUITE NATURAL THAT LITIGANTS SHOULD GIVE PRESENTS TO HUMAN JUDGES; AND THE
BULL PREFACE(33) ON WHICH A MAN CAN DO JUSTICE BETWEEN TWO LITIGANTS , AND THAT IS THAT HE SHALL HAVE NO INTEREST IN
GENV IV SD(87) IN ROWS FOR THE ACCOMMODATION OF SPECTATORS, LITIGANTS , WITNESSES, ETC. THE TALL WINDOWS ADMIT ABUNDANCE

LIT-TLE

CATH 2 (176) MOTHER. (HE SINGS) MARCH HIM BABY, BABY, BABY, LIT-TLE BA-BY BUMPKINS. /VARINKA/ (JOINING IN TO THE SAME

LITTER

PYGM III (259) TO HER WORK AT THE WRITING-TABLE. SHE SWEEPS A LITTER OF DISARRANGED PAPERS OUT OF HER WAY; SNATCHES A
METH PREFACE(R46) TO AN ENGLISH COUNTRY HOUSE WHO HAS NOT TAKEN A LITTER OF KITTENS OR PUPPIES TO THE BUCKET, AND DROWNED ALL
DOCT I SD(82) TUBES, AND A SPIRIT LAMP STANDING UP THROUGH ITS LITTER OF PAPERS. THERE IS A COUCH IN THE MIDDLE OF THE

LITTERATEUR

MILL PREFACE(131) INEVITABLY AS BOURRIENNE REMAINED A SPECULATOR, LITTERATEUR AND DIPLOMATIST. I AM NOT FORGETTING THAT

LITTERED

WIDO II SD(24) SEPTEMBER. SARTORIUS IS BUSY AT A WRITING TABLE LITTERED WITH BUSINESS LETTERS. THE FIREPLACE, DECORATED FOR
DOCT III SD(131) AND OTHER ODDS AND ENDS. BY THE TABLE IS A SOFA, LITTERED WITH DRAWING BLOCKS, SKETCH-BOOKS, LOOSE SHEETS OF
PHIL II SD(94) OF THE SETTEE, AND TOUCHING IT, IS A GREEN TABLE, LITTERED WITH JOURNALS. IBSEN, LOOKING DOWN THE ROOM, HAS
CAND I SD(78) WITH HER BACK TO THE WINDOW. THE LARGE TABLE IS LITTERED WITH PAMPHLETS, JOURNALS, LETTERS, NESTS OF
SIM II SD(54) AND ON THE LAWN NEAR THE STEPS IS A WRITING TABLE LITTERED WITH PAPERS AND FURNISHED WITH A WIRELESS
CATH 1,SD(161) SQUINT IN THE OTHER, SITS AT THE END OF A TABLE LITTERED WITH PAPERS AND THE REMAINS OF THREE OR FOUR
HART I SD(43) VICE HAS A BOARD IN ITS JAWS; AND THE FLOOR IS LITTERED WITH SHAVINGS, OVERFLOWING FROM A WASTE-PAPER

LITTHER

PRES (165) AN UNFAVORABLE EYE ON YOUR CLOZE AN ON THE LITTHER YOU MAKE WITH YOUR PAPERS. /MITCHENER/ (WOUNDED) AM

LITTLE

CURE (236) I SHOULDNT AT ALL MIND BEING TYRANNIZED OVER A LITTLE : IN FACT, I LIKE IT. IT SAVES ME THE TROUBLE OF
NEVR III (265) GOING TO SPEAK OF A SUBJECT OF WHICH I KNOW VERY LITTLE : PERHAPS NOTHING. I MEAN LOVE. /VALENTINE/ LOVE!
MRS II (214) RIVER FOR LIZ, THANK YOU! YOU REMIND ME OF LIZ A LITTLE : SHE WAS A FIRST-RATE BUSINESS WOMAN-- SAVED MONEY
CLEO NOTES (206) STOCK OF DISCOVERIES IN PHYSICS HAS ACCUMULATED A LITTLE : THAT IS ALL. ONE MORE ILLUSTRATION. IS THE
METH PREFACE(R48) NOT RECOGNIZE IN BUTLER A MAN OF GENIUS MATTERED LITTLE : WHAT DID MATTER WAS THAT THEY COULD NOT UNDERSTAND
SIM PREFACE(16) IN THE APOCALYPSE SHOULD THINK OUT THEIR BELIEF A LITTLE ? IN A LIVING SOCIETY EVERY DAY IS A DAY OF
CYMB V (141) MUCH BETTER THAN THEMSELVES FOR WRYING BUT A LITTLE ? O PISANIO! EVERY GOOD SERVANT DOES NOT ALL
BULL IV (157) BE FIRST AS LAST. D'YE THINK BROADBENT'D LEN ME A LITTLE ? /LARRY/ I'M QUITE SURE HE WILL. /CORNELIUS/ IS HE
MRS III (224) ON EDGE) DONT IT MAKE YOUR FLESH CREEP EVER SO LITTLE ? THAT WICKED OLD DEVIL, UP TO EVERY VILLAINY UNDER
JITT I (20) (A LITTLE DISAPPOINTED) BRUNO: CANT THAT WAIT A LITTLE ? YOU KNOW HOW I VALUE YOUR WORK; BUT WE HAVE SO
MIS. PREFACE(3) IS AMAZING -- CONSIDERING THE WAY WE TALK -- HOW LITTLE A MAN WILL DO TO GET 50 POUNDS: ALL THE 50 POUND
PHIL II (116) ALL OVER EUROPE NOW. NEVER MIND. /SYLVIA/ (A LITTLE ABASHED) I'M SO SORRY, DR PARAMORE. YOU MUST EXCUSE A
PLES PREFACE(R12) SO GREAT, AND THE FEW ACCREDITED AUTHORS ARE SO LITTLE ABLE TO KEEP PACE WITH THEIR COMMISSIONS, THAT HE IS
CATH PREFACE(154) LEAVES YOU WITH AN IMPRESSION THAT HE SAID VERY LITTLE ABOUT CATHERINE, AND THAT LITTLE NOT WHAT WAS BEST
METH PREFACE(R49) IMMEDIATE OR ULTERIOR, HE MUST HAVE KNOWN VERY LITTLE ABOUT CATS, BUT A THOROUGHGOING WEISMANNITE, IF ANY
JITT III (64) IT WAS FOR YOUR SAKE THAT I OPENED HER EYES A LITTLE ABOUT HER FATHER, /FESSLER/ I AM AFRAID IT HAD RATHER
MIS. PREFACE(80) ABOUT OUR RELATIONS, I REALIZED THAT I KNEW VERY LITTLE ABOUT HER. INTRODUCE ME TO A STRANGE WOMAN WHO WAS A
LION PREFACE(46) THE PROPER DISTANCE. THE KAISER, KNOWING JUST AS LITTLE ABOUT IT AS THE CONQUEROR, WOULD SEND THAT BISHOP TO
GETT PREFACE(184) ALL SUFFER THROUGH MARRIAGE, MOST OF US THINK SO LITTLE ABOUT IT THAT WE REGARD IT AS A FIXED PART OF THE
MIS. PREFACE(51) ITS SCHOLASTIC CULTURE IS A SHAM; THAT IT KNOWS LITTLE ABOUT LITERATURE OR ART AND A GREAT DEAL ABOUT
NEVR III (266) TO SAY: IVE NO MONEY. /MRS CLANDON/ I CARE VERY LITTLE ABOUT MONEY, MR VALENTINE. /VALENTINE/ THEN YOURE
LADY PREFACE(225) ARE FORCED TO BEGIN BY SAYING THAT WE KNOW VERY LITTLE ABOUT SHAKESPEAR. AS A MATTER OF FACT, WITH THE PLAYS
MIS. (145) I SAW VERY LITTLE OF THEM, AND THOUGHT VERY LITTLE ABOUT THEM! HOW COULD I? WITH A WHOLE PROVINCE ON MY
BARB I (251) PERHAPS I OUGHT; BUT REALLY, MOTHER, I KNOW SO LITTLE ABOUT THEM; AND WHAT I DO KNOW IS SO PAINFUL! IT IS
OVER PREFACE(166) THE POINT AT WHICH THEY LEARN THAT THEY KNOW VERY LITTLE ABOUT THEMSELVES, AND THAT THEY DO NOT SEEM
JITT I (12) /THE GENTLEMAN/ (HANDS HER BACK THE GLASS A LITTLE ABRUPTLY, AND PULLS HIMSELF TOGETHER)! ! ! /MRS
CLEO II (128) GENTLEMEN? /THEODOTUS/ IS CAESAR'S LIFE OF SO LITTLE ACCOUNT TO HIM THAT HE FORGETS THAT WE HAVE SAVED

APPL II	(276)	TO REMIND HIM THAT WE QUITE FORGOT TO SETTLE THAT	LITTLE	AFFAIR OF THE PROPOSAL OF AMERICA TO ANNEX THE
MTH3	SD(103)	AND SELF-POSSESSION; IN FACT THE PRESIDENT IS A	LITTLE	AFRAID OF HIM; AND IT SEEMS QUITE NATURAL AND
MTH3	(122)	ENGAGED; AND IF, TO TELL THE TRUTH, I WERE NOT A	LITTLE	AFRAID OF YOU-- FOR YOU ARE A VERY SUPERIOR WOMAN, AS
GENV III	(85)	WITH YOU THREE TIMES ALREADY. YOU KNOW, I AM A	LITTLE	AFRAID OF YOU, YOU ARE SO DEEP AND LEARNED AND WHAT I
NEVR II	(250)	WITH ALL RANKS, SO DOES MINE TOO, SIR, IF IT'S A	LITTLE	AGAINST A BARRISTER TO HAVE A WAITER FOR HIS FATHER,
NEVR II	(250)	TO HAVE A WAITER FOR HIS FATHER, SIR, IT'S A	LITTLE	AGAINST A WAITER TO HAVE A BARRISTER FOR A SON: MANY
CAPT III	(298)	MIND ITS OWN BUSINESS. /LADY CICELY/ (RISING, A	LITTLE	ALARMED) CAPTAIN PAQUITO: I AM NOT IN LOVE WITH YOU.
MTH3	(133)	THEY WILL BECOME A GREAT POWER. /BURGE-LUBIN/ (A	LITTLE	ALARMED) I SAY, WILL THEY? I SUPPOSE THEY WILL. I
MTH3	(120)	TOGETHER, MAKING WRY FACES) /MRS LUTESTRING/ A	LITTLE	ALCOHOL WOULD IMPROVE YOUR TEMPER AND MANNERS, AND
HART II	(103)	HER HANDS ON HIS SHOULDERS AND SURVEYING HIM)	LITTLE	ALF! /MANGAN/ WELL, YOU HAVE A NERVE. /MRS HUSHABYE/
SUPR II	(68)	ASK TO BE ALLOWED THE PLEASURE OF SHEWING YOU MY	LITTLE	AMERICAN STEAM CAR, MISS RAWBNSN. /VIOLET/ I SHALL BE
JITT III	(79)	/LENKHEIM/ PROBABLY NOT, BEING ONLY A CHUMP. BE A	LITTLE	AMIABLE, JITTA: I HAVNT BEEN SO VERY HARD ON YOU,
CLEO PR01	(90)	AND EVIL IN MANY WAYS; BUT BECAUSE ITS MIND WAS	LITTLE	AND ITS WORK WAS SIMPLE, IT KNEW ITS OWN MIND AND DID
JOAN 1	(66)	(GRAVELY) SIT DOWN, JOAN. /JOAN/ (CHECKED A	LITTLE	AND LOOKING TO ROBERT) MAY I? /ROBERT/ DO WHAT YOU
NEVR I	(214)	DID NOT WANT TO ACCEPT IT! /GLORIA/ (TURNING A	LITTLE	AND RAISING HER VOICE) NO; BUT SUPPOSE I HAD WANTED
CLEO II	(135)	GO BACK TO MY WORK. SO YOU MUST RUN AWAY FOR A	LITTLE	AND SEND MY SECRETARY TO ME. /CLEOPATRA/ (COAXING)
MIS.	(191)	AFTER ALL YOUVE GONE THROUGH! YOU WANT TO EAT A	LITTLE	AND TO LIE DOWN. YOU COME WITH ME. I WANT YOU TO TELL
MIS. PREFACE	(61)	THEY SEE THAT BOYS SHOULD LEARN TO ROUGH IT A	LITTLE	AND TO MIX WITH CHILDREN OF THEIR OWN AGE. THIS IS
LIED	(199)	WHERE HE PLANTS HIMSELF SOLIDLY, CHUCKLING A	LITTLE	AND WAITING FOR THE NEXT MOVE). /HE/ (FORMALLY AND
CATH 4	(196)	CAPTAIN: I WISH YOU EVERY HAPPINESS THAT YOUR	LITTLE	ANGEL CAN BRING YOU. (FOR HIS EAR ALONE) I COULD
CATH 4	(195)	PLEADING WITH CLASPED HANDS TO CLAIRE) OH, SWEET	LITTLE	ANGEL LAMB, HE LOVES YOU: IT SHINES IN HIS DARLING
CATH 4	(194)	DRAG HIM UP). YAH! AGH! WOW! OH! MMMMMM! OH,	LITTLE	ANGEL MOTHER, DONT EVER DO THIS TO A MAN AGAIN. KNOUT
CATH 3	(185)	MOTHER. /CLAIRE/ DO NOT PRESUME TO CALL ME YOUR	LITTLE	ANGEL MOTHER. WHERE ARE THE POLICE? /NARYSHKIN/ WE
CATH 3	(185)	MOUTH? UGH! PSHA! /THE SERGEANT/ BE MERCIFUL,	LITTLE	ANGEL MOTHER. /CLAIRE/ DO NOT PRESUME TO CALL ME YOUR
CATH 1	(172)	REALLY. I AM NOT FIT-- /PATIOMKIN/ PERSUADE HIM,	LITTLE	ANGEL MOTHER. /VARINKA/ (TAKING HIS OTHER ARM) YES,
CATH 1	(171)	THE MANNERS OF A TINKER. /PATIOMKIN/ TSH-SH-SH.	LITTLE	ANGEL MOTHER: YOU MUST BEHAVE YOURSELF BEFORE THE
MIS.	(146)	DEAR SUMMERHAYS, ONCE CHILDHOOD IS OVER, ONCE THE	LITTLE	ANIMAL HAS GOT PAST THE STAGE AT WHICH IT ACQUIRES
MTH5	(246)	A BLAMING LITTLE ANIMAL, A-- /ACIS/ A GUSHING	LITTLE	ANIMAL. /ARJILLAX/ AND, AS SHE THINKS, AN ARTISTIC
MTH5	(247)	/ARJILLAX/ AND, AS SHE THINKS, AN ARTISTIC	LITTLE	ANIMAL. /ECRASIA/ (NETTLED) I AM AN ANIMATED BEING
MTH5	(246)	DO NOT KNOW WHAT YOU THANK. YOU ARE A THANKING	LITTLE	ANIMAL, A BLAMING LITTLE ANIMAL, A-- /ACIS/ A GUSHING
MTH5	(246)	YOU ARE A THANKING LITTLE ANIMAL, A BLAMING	LITTLE	ANIMAL, A-- /ACIS/ A GUSHING LITTLE ANIMAL.
MIS. PREFACE	(14)	CARE OF CHILDREN. A CHILD IS A RESTLESS, NOISY	LITTLE	ANIMAL, WITH AN INSATIABLE APPETITE FOR KNOWLEDGE,
SUPR II	(50)	A POPULAR AIR SOFTLY TO HIMSELF. TANNER, A	LITTLE	ANNOYED, IS ABOUT TO PURSUE THE SUBJECT WHEN HE HEARS
WIDO I	(12)	COURSE. ONLY INSTINCTIVELY. /BLANCHE/ (STILL A	LITTLE	ANXIOUS) BUT YOU HAVNT SAID ANYTHING. /TRENCH/ WHAT
LION II	SD(127)	THE EDITOR OF THE GLADIATORS SITS ON A CHAIR A	LITTLE	APART FROM THEM. THE CALL BOY ENTERS FROM THE
PHIL I	(70)	SILLY. LET US TALK. (HE RELEASES HER AND SITS A	LITTLE	APART). GRACE: IS THIS YOUR FIRST LOVE AFFAIR?
DEVL I	SD(7)	OF MAKING THE MOST OF THIS WORLD, AND PERHAPS A	LITTLE	APOLOGETICALLY CONSCIOUS OF GETTING ON BETTER WITH IT
METH PREFACE	(R26)	OF THE EMBRYOLOGISTS, NOR ANYTHING SO ABSURDLY	LITTLE	APPRECIATED, AS THIS RECAPITULATION, AS IT IS NOW
PYGM I	(214)	I DO GENUINE SCIENTIFIC WORK IN PHONETICS, AND A	LITTLE	AS A POET ON MILTONIC LINES. /THE GENTLEMAN/ I AM
WIDO I	(19)	WELL, HOWEVER SHE MAY RECEIVE IT-- AND I CARE AS	LITTLE	AS ANY MAN, MR COKANE, HOW PEOPLE MAY CHOOSE TO
LION PREFACE	(56)	THAT QUESTION CAME UP, THE ONLY ANSWER WAS " AS	LITTLE	AS HE CAN BE STARVED INTO ACCEPTING," WITH THE
METH PREFACE	(R55)	AND EATS NEITHER AS MUCH AS HE CAN HOLD NOR AS	LITTLE	AS HE CAN SCRAPE ALONG ON, BUT AS MUCH AS IS GOOD FOR
LION I	(117)	SHE LOOKS AFTER HIM FOR A MOMENT, AND CRIES A	LITTLE	AS HE DISAPPEARS THROUGH THE EASTERN ARCH. A
CAND III	(135)	BIGGER THAN I AM. /CANDIDA/ (LOSING CONFIDENCE A	LITTLE	AS HER CONCERN FOR MORELL'S DIGNITY TAKES THE ALARM)
BARB II	(274)	THE CHAWNCE. THIRD, I STAND BY MY CLASS AND DO AS	LITTLE	AS I CAN SO'S TO LEAVE ARF THE JOB FOR ME FELLOW
NEVR III	(266)	SHORT WITH SOME INDIGNATION). OH, DO YOU THINK,	LITTLE	AS I UNDERSTAND THESE MATTERS, THAT I HAVE NOT COMMON
FOUN	(221)	/THE LORD CHANCELLOR/ IT WILL AVAIL HIM AS	LITTLE	AS IF HE WERE THE BIGGEST FOOL IN CREATION. YOUNG
DOCT PREFACE	(43)	AS MUCH AS POSSIBLE BY USING THEIR EYES, AND AS	LITTLE	AS POSSIBLE BY USING THEIR BRAINS AND IMAGINATIONS.
GETT PREFACE	(244)	THE PATHOLOGY OF MARRIAGE. I SHALL ALSO SAY AS	LITTLE	AS POSSIBLE OF THE PATHOLOGY OF MARRIAGE AND ITS
WIDO III	(65)	DENY IT. (SHE SITS DOWN, AND SOFTENS HER TONE A	LITTLE	AS SHE AFFECTS TO PITY HIM). WELL, LET ME TELL YOU
BARB II	(307)	IT TO BARBARA). /BARBARA/ (COMING FORWARD A	LITTLE	AS SHE PUTS THE OFFER BEHIND HER WITH A SHUDDER,
JOAN PREFACE	(53)	IS WHAT WOULD HAPPEN IF I KNEW MY BUSINESS SO	LITTLE	AS TO LISTEN TO THESE WELL INTENTIONED BUT DISASTROUS
CYMB FORWORD	(138)	OF THE OTHER LITERARY PRECEDENTS, THOUGH I AM A	LITTLE	ASHAMED OF BEING FOUND IN THE COMPANY OF THEIR
BULL I	(85)	TO KNOW BY THIS TIME. (HE SITS DOWN AGAIN, A	LITTLE	ASHAMED OF HIS PETULANCE; REFLECTS A MOMENT BITTERLY;
MIS. PREFACE	(69)	CERTAINLY BE IGNOMINIOUSLY PLUCKED. AND HE IS SO	LITTLE	ASHAMED OF OR DISADVANTAGED BY HIS CONDITION THAT HE
DOCT I	(111)	OH PRAY DONT BE OFFENDED. /RIDGEON/ (AGAIN A	LITTLE	ASHAMED) THERE! THERE! NEVER MIND. (HE RELAXES AND
JITT III	(75)	I FIND I CANT DO. IS THAT A BARGAIN? /JITTA/ (A	LITTLE	ASHAMED, FEELING THAT SHE HAS ALLOWED HERSELF TO
2TRU I	(41)	JUST IN THE WIND. I AM SORRY TO HAVE BEEN OF SO	LITTLE	ASSISTANCE; BUT OH, MY SWEETIE-WEETIE, NATURE NEVER
JOAN EPILOG	(161)	I HAVE BEEN A DIFFERENT MAN EVER SINCE, THOUGH A	LITTLE	ASTRAY IN MY WITS SOMETIMES. /CAUCHON/ MUST THEN A
MRS II	(206)	THIS WITH A SNEERING GRIN. MRS WARREN, FLUSHING A	LITTLE	AT HER FAILURE TO IMPOSE ON HIM IN THE CHARACTER OF A
NEVR III	(270)	MAN. GLORIA: COME HERE. (GLORIA, WONDERING A	LITTLE	AT THE COMMAND, OBEYS, AND STANDS, WITH DROOPING
BULL III	(142)	/HODSON/ YUS: OI DO. IT'S BECAUSE OI WANT A	LITTLE	ATTENTION PIDE TO MY AOWN CANTRY; AND THETLL NEVER BE
POSN PREFACE	(374)	TO EXCLUDE THE DOCUMENT, THEY HAD GIVEN SO	LITTLE	ATTENTION TO THE BUSINESS THAT THEY DID NOT KNOW, OR
DOCT I	SD(84)	HIS YOUTH. HE HAS THE OFF-HANDED MANNER AND THE	LITTLE	AUDACITIES OF ADDRESS WHICH A SHY AND SENSITIVE MAN
DEST	(167)	SITS BESIDE HER. SHE LOOKS ALARMED AND MOVES A	LITTLE	AWAY FROM HIM; BUT A RAY OF RALLYING HOPE BEAMS FROM
CAND II	(117)	DISPOSAL. SHE MAKES HIM RISE, AND BRINGS HIM A	LITTLE	AWAY FROM THE TABLE, LOOKING AT HIM CRITICALLY ALL
PHIL I	(72)	/GRACE/ (SHAKING OFF HIS HAND AND TURNING A	LITTLE	AWAY ON THE STOOL) I AM AFRAID, FROM THE LIGHT WAY
PHIL III	SD(147)	THE REST LOOK AT JULIA WITH CONCERN, AND EVEN A	LITTLE	AWE, FEELING FOR THE FIRST TIME THE PRESENCE OF A
MIS.	SD(109)	NOVEL IN HAND, IN A SWINGING CHAIR WITH A	LITTLE	AWNING ABOVE IT, IS ENSHRINED IN A SPACIOUS HALF
CAPT I	(222)	IS BLESSED MATHER GIVE IM AT ER KNEE, BLESS IS	LITTLE	AWT! THER YNT NAOW AWM IN IT. SHE WERE A WUST
ARMS I	SD(3)	IN THE YEAR 1885. THROUGH AN OPEN WINDOW WITH A	LITTLE	BALCONY A PEAK OF THE BALKANS, WONDERFULLY WHITE AND
MIS.	SD(110)	DISPLAY IN THE PAVILION. WICKER CHAIRS AND	LITTLE	BAMBOO TABLES WITH ASH TRAYS AND BOXES OF MATCHES ON
3PLA PREFACE	(R20)	A BOSTONIAN UTOPIA FROM THE PROSPECTUSES OF THE	LITTLE	BANDS OF DEVOUT COMMUNISTS WHO HAVE FROM TIME TO
PRES	(149)	THE ANG OF IT, SIR. YOU SEE, MY FATHER HAS A TIDY	LITTLE	BARBER'S BUSINESS DOWN OFF SHOREDITCH; AND I WAS
MIS. PREFACE	(71)	FOR MAKING OUR BRITISH CHILDREN INTO PRIGGISH	LITTLE	BAREFOOTED VAGABONDS, ALL TALKING LIKE THAT BORN FOOL
DEST	SD(152)	HAD ITS SWEEPING OUTLINE CHIPPED OFF IN GROTESQUE	LITTLE	BAYS AND HEADLANDS, MAKING HIM UNSPEAKABLY RIDICULOUS
ARMS II	(38)	LITTLE BEAST! /CATHERINE/ LITTLE BEAST! WHAT	LITTLE	BEAST? /RAINA/ TO GO AND TELL! OH, IF I HAD HIM
HART II	(100)	(RISING SUPERBLY) ELLIE: YOU ARE A WICKED SORDID	LITTLE	BEAST. AND TO THINK THAT I ACTUALLY CONDESCENDED TO
MTH5	(216)	PUTTING IT ON BACK TO FRONT, YOU ARE A SILLY	LITTLE	BEAST. /ACIS/ HERE! THATS IT. NOW YOURE CLEAN AND
FOUN	(220)	GLAD AS I MUST CONFESS I WAS TO GET RID OF THE	LITTLE	BEAST, MY STARVED HEART STILL ACHED, MY EMPTY ARMS
JOAN 2	(86)	HERE GOES! (TO THE PAGE) CALL FOR SILENCE, YOU	LITTLE	BEAST, WILL YOU? /THE PAGE/ (SNATCHING A HALBERD AS
JOAN 2	(85)	BOY. HE HATES ME. HE HATES EVERYBODY, SELFISH	LITTLE	BEAST! I DONT WANT TO BE BOTHERED WITH CHILDREN. I
ARMS II	(38)	THOUGHTFULLY AT THE GRAVEL AS SHE WALKS) THE	LITTLE	BEAST! /CATHERINE/ LITTLE BEAST! WHAT LITTLE
ARMS II	(38)	AS SHE WALKS) THE LITTLE BEAST! /CATHERINE/	LITTLE	BEAST! WHAT LITTLE BEAST? /RAINA/ TO GO AND TELL!
DOCT III	(154)	PROPERTY AND I COULD HELP WITH IT. I HAD EVEN A	LITTLE	BEAUTY: DONT THINK ME VAIN FOR KNOWING IT. I KNEW
OVER	(172)	KNOW WHAT IT IS TO BE ALONE WITH A WOMAN WHO HAS	LITTLE	BEAUTY AND LESS CONVERSATION. WHAT IS A MAN TO DO?
CATH 3	(186)	TO? /NARYSHKIN/ (SPITEFULLY) TO THE EMPRESS,	LITTLE	BEAUTY. HE HAS INSULTED THE EMPRESS. HE WILL RECEIVE
CATH 3	(186)	SERGEANT/ DO SO IN THE NAME OF THE HOLY NICHOLAS,	LITTLE	BEAUTY. /CLAIRE/ DONT BE IMPERTINENT. HOW CAN I GET
DEST	(191)	NERVES HIMSELF FOR A PERFORMANCE. HE CONSIDERS A	LITTLE	BEFORE HE BEGINS; SO AS TO FIX HER ATTENTION BY A
MTH3	(126)	OR SHORTER, YET DO SOMEHOW CONTRIVE TO GROW UP A	LITTLE	BEFORE THEY DIE. WE DIE IN BOYHOOD; THE MATURITY THAT
CAND III	(144)	LIKE COLD STRENGTH, AND PLACES IT NEXT MORELL, A	LITTLE	BEHIND HIM. SHE SITS DOWN. HE TAKES THE VISITOR'S
DOCT V	SD(171)	MAGNIFYING GLASSES. AT THE SIDE, ON HIS LEFT, A	LITTLE	BEHIND HIM, IS A SMALL DOOR MARKED PRIVATE. NEAR THE
DOCT PREFACE	(33)	" A LITTLE KNOWLEDGE IS A DANGEROUS THING" (A	LITTLE	BEING THE MOST THAT ANY OF US CAN ATTAIN), AS EASILY
2TRU I	(32)	THERE IS NOTHING CONSTITUTIONALLY WRONG. A	LITTLE	BELOW PAR; THAT IS ALL. WE SHALL FEED HER UP
METH PREFACE	(R53)	AS THEY PASSED EVEN HIS MEANEST AND NARROWEST	LITTLE	BETHEL OR HIS PROUDEST WAR-CONSECRATING CATHEDRAL AS
WIDO II	(46)	(MOURNFULLY) MY DEAR: CAN YOU NOT MAKE A	LITTLE	BETTER FIGHT WITH YOUR TEMPER? /BLANCHE/ (PANTING
LION EPILOG	(151)	SUSPECTED BY THE STRAITER SALVATIONISTS OF BEING	LITTLE	BETTER THAN AN ATHEIST. ALL THESE VARIETIES, YOU SEE,
BULL II	(100)	/KEEGAN/ WOULDNT I? GOD FORGIVE YOU! YOURE	LITTLE	BETTER THAN A HEATHEN. /PATSY/ DEEDN I AM, FADHER:
MTH5	(230)	MUST REMEMBER THAT THESE POOR DEVILS WERE VERY	LITTLE	BETTER THAN OUR IDIOTS: WE SHOULD NEVER DREAM OF
DEVL III	(53)	TROUBLE. I'LL GIVE YOU CREDIT FOR LIKING ME A	LITTLE	BETTER THAN YOU DID. ALL I SAY IS THAT MY DEATH WILL
MTH3	(121)	CHANGES WERE MAKING IT EASIER: LIFE WAS A	LITTLE	BETTER WORTH LIVING FOR THE NINE-TENTHS OF THE PEOPLE
SUPR III	(113)	A HEATHEN; AND YOU, JUAN, I AM AFRAID, ARE VERY	LITTLE	BETTER. /THE DEVIL/ YOU CONCLUDE, THEN, THAT LIFE WAS
JITT I	(11)	HAS IT COME ON AGAIN, SIR? /THE GENTLEMAN/ (A	LITTLE	BETTER) IT'S ALL RIGHT NOW, MRS BILLITER. I TOOK THE
MIS.	(166)	A MOMENT. AFTER A FEW SIGHING BREATHS, HE FEELS A	LITTLE	BETTER, AND UNCOVERS HIS EYES. THE MAN'S HEAD RISES
PYGM III	(247)	THE ELIZABETHAN CHAIR). /MRS EYNSFORD HILL/ (A	LITTLE	BEWILDERED) NOT AT ALL. (SHE SITS ON THE OTTOMAN
BARB II	(282)	A STEADY MAN LIKE YOU. (SHIRLEY, DISARMED AND A	LITTLE	BEWILDERED, TOUCHES HIS HAT. SHE TURNS FROM HIM TO
FANY I	(278)	YOU MIGHT CALL DRUNK; BUT I WAS BRIGHT, AND A	LITTLE	BEYOND MYSELF; AND-- I'LL CONFESS IT-- I WANTED TO

GLIM (187)	HIM) I HAVE YOU VERY FAST NOW, SIGNORINO, LIKE A	LITTLE	BIRD IN A CAGE. /FERRUCCIO/ YOU HAVE MY BODY, GIULIA.
LION I (118)	(TO LAVINIA) HERE ARE SOME PALS FOR YOU. THIS	LITTLE	BIT IS FERROVIUS THAT YOU TALK SO MUCH ABOUT. (
APPL I (206)	BECAUSE NO KING OR MINISTER IS THE VERY LEAST	LITTLE	BIT LIKE A STAMP: HE IS A LIVING SOUL. /BOANERGES/ A
ROCK I (217)	NOTHING. WHERE DID THE MATERIAL THAT HE DOES HIS	LITTLE	BIT OF A JOB ON COME FROM? HE DONT KNOW. WHAT WILL
BARB III (329)	BE THE END OF THE WORLD IF ANYTHING DID. A	LITTLE	BIT OF BRITISH PLUCK IS WHAT YOU WANT, OLD CHAP. (HE
JITT III (67)	GREAT MAN LIKE THAT ALL TO YOURSELF? I WANTED A	LITTLE	BIT OF BRUNO; BUT YOU STOOD ALWAYS IN THE WAY.
MILL I (165)	IN HER FAMILY. MONEY COMES TO HER. BUT I HAVE MY	LITTLE	BIT OF GENIUS TOO; AND SHE CANT PARALYZE ME.
CAPT III (298)	HOW COULD I MANAGE PEOPLE IF I HAD THAT MAD	LITTLE	BIT OF SELF LEFT IN ME? THATS MY SECRET.
FANY EPILOG (334)	LADY OF LYONS, YOU KNOW-- BUT STILL, A FIRSTRATE	LITTLE	BIT OF WORK. (HE SHAKES HER HAND). /GUNN/ (
SUPR IV (144)	UP AS WEVE AD IM, PERHAPS YOULL BEGIN TO LOOK A	LITTLE	BIT UP TO IS MARK. AT PRESENT YOU FALL A LONG WAY
SUPR I (39)	DOESNT MIND THE OPINIONS OF A STAG ONE	LITTLE	BIT WHEN ONCE SHE HAS GOT HER COILS ROUND IT. /ANN/ (
CAND II (117)	NO GOOD: THEY DONT MIND WHAT YOU SAY TO THEM ONE	LITTLE	BIT. THEY THINK THEY AGREE WITH YOU; BUT WHATS THE
SUPR I (39)	ON MY WORD-- I DONT MIND YOUR QUEER OPINIONS ONE	LITTLE	BIT. YOU KNOW WE HAVE ALL BEEN BROUGHT UP TO HAVE
ROCK I (217)	FACTORY AFTER HE AND HIS LIKE HAVE ALL DONE THEIR	LITTLE	BITS OF JOBS ON IT? HE DONT KNOW. WHERE COULD HE BUY
SIM II (79)	NOT TURN TO NOTHING. I SHALL BE CONTENT WITH MY	LITTLE	BLACK COAT AND MY LITTLE WHITE COLLAR AND MY LITTLE
DEST (159)	THIEF! THE SWINDLER! THE HEARTLESS TREACHEROUS	LITTLE	BLACKGUARD! YOU CALL THAT NOTHING, I SUPPOSE. BUT
BARB II (276)	NOT MUCH. IT COMBS OUR AIR AND MAKES US GOOD	LITTLE	BLOKES TO BE ROBBED AND PUT UPON. BUT I'LL PLAY THE
CLEO IV (174)	THROUGH THE CURTAINS. /RUFIO/ (SITTING DOWN, A	LITTLE	BLOWN) POUF! THAT WAS A CLIMB. HOW HIGH HAVE WE
POSN PREFACE(377)	DISCOMFITURE. I STILL CHERISH THAT SECOND COPY, A	LITTLE	BLUE-BOUND PAMPHLET, METHODICALLY AUTOGRAPHED "
MIS. (123)	THAT WAS JUST TWO MONTHS AFTER I'D BURIED POOR	LITTLE	BOBBY; AND THAT WAS THE VERY THING HE DIED OF, POOR
MIS. (159)	MADE THAT BID BEFORE. /LINA/ (PRODUCING A DAINTY	LITTLE	BOOK AND PREPARING TO WRITE IN IT) WHAT DID YOU SAY
CAPT I (221)	UP HIS EARS) EH? HAVE YOU BEEN READING THAT	LITTLE	BOOK I GAVE YOU? /DRINKWATER/ AW HEV, ET ODD TAWMS.
POSN PREFACE(378)	A THOUGHT AS TO THESE APPARENTLY INSIGNIFICANT	LITTLE	BOOKS BEING OF ANY IMPORTANCE OR HAVING CAUSED ME OR
2TRU III (83)	HER MIND AS WELL AS HER BODY. SEE THESE TWO	LITTLE	BOOKS I WAS DEEP IN WHEN YOU ACCOSTED ME? I CARRY
MRS PREFACE(173)	GENEROUS, FOR DOCTORS TO PERFORM MIRACLES WITH	LITTLE	BOTTLES, AND FOR MRS WARREN TO BE A BEAST AND A
CAND III (139)	YOU ARE FORGIVEN. NOW GO OFF TO BED LIKE A GOOD	LITTLE	BOY: I WANT TO TALK TO JAMES ABOUT YOU. /MARCHBANKS/
MIS. (163)	NOTHING INCORRECT. /HYPATIA/ OH, DONT BE AFRAID,	LITTLE	BOY: YOULL GET NOTHING BUT A KISS; AND I'LL FIGHT
ARMS I (14)	YOU HAVE TO DO IS TO SCOLD ME JUST AS IF I WERE A	LITTLE	BOY AND YOU MY NURSE. IF I WERE IN CAMP NOW, THEYD
CAPT I (222)	LAWK AS A HINGLISH LIDY MAWT CALL ER	LITTLE	BOY BIRDIE. /RANKIN/ (NOT QUITE CONVINCED) BUT WHY
MRS II (199)	AT HIM; THEN COMES BACK TO HIM). NOW, LOOK HERE,	LITTLE	BOY (TAKING HIS FACE IN HER HANDS AND TURNING IT UP
MRS III (234)	GO. IT FALLS ON THE TURF). OH, YOUVE GIVEN YOUR	LITTLE	BOY SUCH A TURN. SUPPOSE IT HAD GONE OFF! UGH! (HE
MRS II (205)	YOU: VIVVUMS IS NOT IN A HUMOR FOR PETTING HER	LITTLE	BOY THIS EVENING. (SHE RISES AND COMES FORWARD TO
MRS II (205)	NOW BESIDE ME. COME ALONG, MR FRANK. /FRANK/ HER	LITTLE	BOY WILL BE EVER SO EVEN WITH HIS VIVVUMS FOR THIS. (
MRS III (226)	SUCH A DISADVANTAGE. NO, VIV: YOUR INFATUATED	LITTLE	BOY WILL HAVE TO STICK TO YOU IN ANY CASE. BUT HE'S
MRS III (226)	GIRL WITH HER SILLY LITTLE BOY. /VIVIE/ THE DEAR	LITTLE	BOY WITH HIS DOWDY LITTLE GIRL. /FRANK/ EVER SO
MRS IV (239)	BOY! /FRANK/ (WITH CONVICTION) MUST BE A NEW	LITTLE	BOY. ALWAYS HAPPENS THAT WAY. NO OTHER WAY, IN FACT.
MRS IV (239)	EXTENSIVE SCALE. I SEE I AM NO LONGER VIVVUMS'S	LITTLE	BOY. DONT BE ALARMED: I SHALL NEVER CALL YOU VIVVUMS
MRS III (226)	/FRANK/ THE WISE LITTLE GIRL WITH HER SILLY	LITTLE	BOY. /VIVIE/ THE DEAR LITTLE BOY WITH HIS DOWDY
APPL II (277)	I MUSTNT BE LATE FOR DINNER. COME ON, LIKE A GOOD	LITTLE	BOY. THE KING, WITH A GRIMACE OF HOPELESS TENDERNESS,
CATH 1 (173)	LIFTING HIM IN HIS ARMS LIKE A FATHER CARRYING A	LITTLE	BOY) YES! I'LL CARRY YOU. /EDSTASTON/ DASH IT ALL.
MRS III (226)	PEACEFUL, AND RELIEVED FROM THE IMBECILITY OF THE	LITTLE	BOY'S FATHER AND THE QUESTIONABLENESS OF THE LITTLE
MRS II (205)	EVER SO MUCH BETTER. VIVVUMS MUSTNT LECTURE: HER	LITTLE	BOY'S INCORRIGIBLE. (HE ATTEMPTS TO TAKE HER FACE
MRS IV (239)	AGAIN-- AT LEAST UNLESS YOU GET TIRED OF YOUR NEW	LITTLE	BOY, WHOEVER HE MAY BE. /VIVIE/ MY NEW LITTLE BOY!
MRS IV (239)	NEW LITTLE BOY, WHOEVER HE MAY BE. /VIVIE/ MY NEW	LITTLE	BOY! /FRANK/ (WITH CONVICTION) MUST BE A NEW LITTLE
SIM I (48)	ALL OR NONE. /THE CLERGYMAN/ OH DEAR! MY POOR	LITTLE	BRAIN IS GIVING WAY. I CANT MAKE SENSE OF WHAT YOU
SUPR IV (170)	(HE TAKES IT FROM HER)? /MRS WHITEFIELD/ A	LITTLE	BRANDY. /MENDOZA/ THE WORST THING YOU COULD GIVE HER.
JITT II (37)	(SHE CLOSES HER EYES; SILENT FOR A MOMENT, AND A	LITTLE	BREATHLESS. JITTA SMILES, AND SITS DOWN IN THE
GETT PREFACE(227)	OF THE ARTIFICIALLY LIMITED FAMILY IN ITS	LITTLE	BRICK BOX IS HORRIBLY COMPLETE. BAD MANNERS, UGLY
GETT PREFACE(195)	OR SELFISH PARENTS; ITS UNNATURAL PACKING INTO	LITTLE	BRICK BOXES OF LITTLE PARCELS OF HUMANITY OF
LADY PREFACE(230)	APPALLED SENSE OF THE DANGER OF DRESSING MAN IN A	LITTLE	BRIEF AUTHORITY, SUCH A MERCILESS STRIPPING OF THE
GENV II (59)	AND DUCKED HIM IN THE HORSE POND TO TEACH HIM A	LITTLE	BRITISH PATRIOTISM! HOW WOULD HE LIKE IT? /JUDGE/
O'FL (221)	NOT WHERE THE OTHER LADIES HAD IT, AND SHE HAD	LITTLE	BROOCHES IN HER EARS, THOUGH SHE HADNT HALF THE
CLEO III (162)	HERE WITH THE CHANCE OF BEING CAPTURED BY THAT	LITTLE	BROTHER OF YOURS IF WE ARE BEATEN? /CLEOPATRA/ BUT
METH PREFACE(R59)	AND ST FRANCIS WHEN HE CALLED THE BIRDS HIS	LITTLE	BROTHERS, OUR VANITY, AND OUR SNOBBISH CONCEPTION OF
DOCT PREFACE(45)	TO THE LEAST OF THOSE WHOM ST FRANCIS CALLED HIS	LITTLE	BROTHERS, I HAVE ONLY TO POINT OUT HERE THAT NOTHING
LION II SD(127)	GO INTO THE ARENA. THE NET THROWER TAKING OUT A	LITTLE	BRUSH AND ARRANGING HIS HAIR AS HE GOES, THE OTHER
FANY PROLOG (272)	TIME? /TROTTER/ I'M SO SORRY. I MUST HAVE JUST A	LITTLE	BRUSH UP! I-- (HE HURRIES OUT). /THE COUNT/ MY DEAR,
BARB I (253)	WOOLWICH INFANT. AT CAMBRIDGE IT WAS THE SAME. A	LITTLE	BRUTE AT KING'S WHO WAS ALWAYS TRYING TO GET UP
LION II (145)	HE LOVES HIM LIKE A BROTHER. /THE EMPEROR/ YOU	LITTLE	BRUTE. YOU DAMNED FILTHY LITTLE DOG OF A GREEK
CAPT III (294)	MEANT SOMETHING TO ME THEN. DO YOU SEE THAT DIRTY	LITTLE	BUNDLE OF SCRAPS OF PAPER? /LADY CICELY/ WHAT ARE
MILL PREFACE(114)	DIADEM, HIS RIDICULOUS ATTEMPT TO ESTABLISH THE	LITTLE	BUONAPARTE FAMILY ON ALL THE THRONES UNDER HIS
ROCK II (241)	WANTS FROM FIVE TO TWENTY THOUSAND TO EXTEND HIS	LITTLE	BUSINESS? /SIR DEXTER/ NONSENSE! THE BANK WILL GIVE
WIDO III (58)	ST PAUL'S. YOU REMEMBER MR COKANE? HE DOES A	LITTLE	BUSINESS FOR ME NOW AS A FRIEND, AND GIVES ME A HELP
HART I SD(43)	THE SIDES. ANOTHER DOOR STRAINS THE ILLUSION A	LITTLE	BY BEING APPARENTLY IN THE SHIP'S PORT SIDE, AND YET
POSN PREFACE(398)	JUST WHERE HE COULD SCREW UP THE STANDARD A	LITTLE	BY BEING TYRANNICAL. HIS PLEA THAT THERE ARE
MTH4 III SD(202)	HER HANDS. HE GRASPS THEM AND RAISES HIMSELF A	LITTLE	BY CLINGING TO HER. SHE LOOKS STEADILY INTO HIS FACE.
METH PREFACE(R21)	HAS BEEN EVOLVED, NOT CREATED: IT HAS ARISEN	LITTLE	BY LITTLE FROM A SMALL BEGINNING, AND HAS INCREASED
LION PREFACE(20)	IS OVER. HERE IT IS NECESSARY TO ANTICIPATE A	LITTLE	BY SAYING THAT NONE OF THE OTHER EVANGELISTS ACCEPTS
MIS. PREFACE(76)	CONDITION WOULD BE ANY WORSE THAN THAT OF THE	LITTLE	CAGED SAVAGES OF TODAY; AND SECOND, WHETHER EITHER
BULL IV (162)	OWN: IT'S TOO SMALL: IT'S ONE OF THOSE WRETCHED	LITTLE	CAMBRIC HANDKERCHIEFS-- /NORA/ (SOBBING) INDEED IT'S
MIS. (170)	/TARLETON/ I SUPPOSE YOUR MOTHER BROUGHT HIM A	LITTLE	CAPITAL. /THE MAN/ I DONT KNOW. WHATS THAT GOT TO DO
DOCT III (148)	WHAT IS THERE LEFT OF YOUR MORALIZING? ONLY A	LITTLE	CARBONIC ACID GAS WHICH MAKES THE ROOM UNHEALTHY.
MIS. (181)	CHICKABIDDY. MOST OF OUR CHARACTERS WILL BEAR A	LITTLE	CAREFUL DUSTING; BUT THEY WONT BEAR SCOURING. PATSY
ARMS I SD(3)	AND HANGINGS OF THE BED, THE WINDOW CURTAINS, THE	LITTLE	CARPET, AND ALL THE ORNAMENTAL TEXTILE FABRICS IN THE
MTH1 I (8)	WHAT GOOD WAS THAT? /THE SERPENT/ I SHEWED THE	LITTLE	CASE TO THE SUN, AND LEFT IT IN ITS WARMTH. AND IT
GENV IV SD(87)	THE SECRETARY OF THE LEAGUE OF NATIONS HAS A	LITTLE	CENTRAL TABLE TO HIMSELF IN FRONT OF THE OTHER. HIS
DEST (165)	I SHALL TAKE THEM, IF NECESSARY, WITH AS	LITTLE	CEREMONY AS I TOOK THE HANDKERCHIEF. /LADY/ (IN
WIDO III (54)	I HARDLY KNEW YOU. /LICKCHEESE/ I FIND YOU A	LITTLE	CHANGED YOURSELF, MISS. /BLANCHE/ (HASTILY) OH, I AM
APPL II (262)	FUSS ABOUT WHAT IS HAPPENING AT THE ENDS OF YOUR	LITTLE	CHANNEL TUBE. SO LONG AS PARIS IS FULL OF AMERICANS,
CLEO NOTES (204)	ARE THEY THAT THEIR LITTLE PARISH AND THEIR	LITTLE	CHAPEL IS AN APEX TO WHICH CIVILIZATION AND
ROCK PREFACE(171)	OF A VILLAGE DUNCE. NURSES RULE THEIR	LITTLE	CHARGES BY THREATENING THEM WITH BOGIES IN WHOSE
DOCT IV (158)	WILL BE MUCH THE BETTER FOR IT. /MRS DUBEDAT/ (A	LITTLE	CHEERED) WILL YOU BRING THE MAN UP HERE, MR WALPOLE,
CATH 4 (195)	ON HIS KNEES TO HER) PARDON HIM, PARDON HIM,	LITTLE	CHERUB! LITTLE WILD DUCK! LITTLE STAR! LITTLE
CAND III (134)	WORK FOR, SOME GROWN UP MAN WHO HAS BECOME AS A	LITTLE	CHILD AGAIN. OH, YOU FOOL, YOU FOOL, YOU TRIPLE
MTH3 (122)	TRIED TO TAKE ADVANTAGE OF THE INNOCENCE OF A	LITTLE	CHILD FOR THE GRATIFICATION OF YOUR SENSES?
MTH4 I (159)	OF INCREASING OUR WISDOM, ONLY DESTROYED THE	LITTLE	CHILDISH WISDOM WE HAD. ALL I CAN GRANT YOU IS THAT
NEVR II (246)	HAS BEEN DONE, MR VALENTINE. WE HAVE ALL BEEN A	LITTLE	CHILDISH, I AM AFRAID. OUR PARTY HAS BEEN A FAILURE:
BARB III (337)	REMEMBER THE EARTHQUAKE AT CANNES, WHEN WE WERE	LITTLE	CHILDREN? -- HOW LITTLE THE SURPRISE OF THE FIRST
LION PREFACE(80)	BY JUSTICE AND MERCY, BY SETTING THE WELFARE OF	LITTLE	CHILDREN ABOVE THE PRIDE OF PRINCES, BY CASTING ALL
MTH5 (261)	FACE OF THE EARTH WAS PITTED WITH THE GRAVES OF	LITTLE	CHILDREN AMONG WHICH LIVING SKELETONS CRAWLED IN
JOAN 5 (119)	CROWD WILL CHEER YOU. THEY WILL BRING YOU THEIR	LITTLE	CHILDREN AND THEIR INVALIDS TO HEAL: THEY WILL KISS
SUPR HANDBOK(204)	ARE SET UP THROUGHOUT THE COUNTRY TO ENCOURAGE	LITTLE	CHILDREN AND ELDERLY GENTLEMEN TO MAKE COLLECTIONS OF
BULL IV (172)	THE BUSTLE OF A GREAT HOTEL, AND THE SIGHT OF THE	LITTLE	CHILDREN CARRYING THE GOLF CLUBS OF YOUR TOURISTS AS
JITT III (60)	AND NOT KNOW ANYTHING NOR FEEL ANYTHING THAT	LITTLE	CHILDREN OUGHT NOT TO KNOW AND FEEL. JUST WHEN I, AS
MIS. PREFACE(18)	IMPUDENTLY PROCLAIM THE MONSTROUS PRINCIPLE THAT	LITTLE	CHILDREN SHOULD BE SEEN AND NOT HEARD, AND TO ENFORCE
MTH5 (258)	THAT IS NO ANSWER. WHAT-- /ARJILLAX/ SILENCE.	LITTLE	CHILDREN SHOULD BE SEEN AND NOT HEARD. /THE NEWLY
MTH4 I (156)	OF HEROES AND POETS? /ZOO/ WE STILL TELL OUR	LITTLE	CHILDREN STORIES LIKE THAT, TO HELP THEM TO
JOAN PREFACE(16)	WOULD BE THE SANER JOAN? THE ONE WHO CARRIED	LITTLE	CHILDREN TO BE BAPTIZED OF WATER AND THE SPIRIT, OR
DOCT PREFACE(18)	HIS UNFAITHFULNESS TO HIS WIFE. A MAN WHO ROBS	LITTLE	CHILDREN WHEN NO ONE IS LOOKING CAN HARDLY HAVE MUCH
SIM I (42)	VASHTI IS LOVELY EVEN TO HER BROTHERS. /KANCHIN/	LITTLE	CHILDREN WOULD DIE FOR MAYA. /JANGA/ BEWARE,
MIS. (201)	BE A CLOWN AND SET BAD EXAMPLES OF CONDUCT TO	LITTLE	CHILDREN. I WOULD SINK YET LOWER AND BE AN ACTRESS OR
ROCK PREFACE(180)	RECONSIDER THE IMPRESSIONS THEY HAVE RECEIVED AS	LITTLE	CHILDREN. MOST CHRISTIANS, I SUSPECT, ARE AFRAID TO
ARMS II (31)	CONSUMMATE SOLDIER, MAJOR! SIMPLY TWO INNOCENT	LITTLE	CHILDREN. /RAINA/ WHAT WAS HE LIKE? /CATHERINE/ OH,
NEVR II (256)	LIFTING HER GREAT HAND TO TAKE US-- HER TWO	LITTLE	CHILDREN-- BY THE SCRUFFS OF OUR LITTLE NECKS, AND
ROCK PREFACE(156)	TO DEATH IN SIGHT OF ALL THE CITIZENS AND THEIR	LITTLE	CHILDREN, THAT THE BISHOP WHO WAS OFFICIALLY OBLIGED
MIS. PREFACE(25)	SOLNESS; HAVE " A GENIUS FOR NURSING THE SOULS OF	LITTLE	CHILDREN" ARE LIKE ANGELS FORCED TO WORK IN PRISONS
MIS. PREFACE(83)	THE BURDENS ARE ATTACHED TO THEM; AND TO " SUFFER	LITTLE	CHILDREN" HAS BECOME AN AFFECTIONATE IMPULSE DEEP IN

POS (461)	LIVING WOMAN-- (FLINCHING) OH GOD! HE FELT THE	LITTLE	CHILD'S HANDS ON HIS NECK-- I CANT (BURSTING INTO A
JITT III (60)	OR PRETENDING TO BE BLINDFOLD. I AM TO BE A GOOD	LITTLE	CHILD, AND NOT KNOW ANYTHING NOR FEEL ANYTHING THAT
DOCT I (97)	WHAT! SIR PATRICK! AND HOW ARE WE TODAY? A	LITTLE	CHILLY? A LITTLE STIFF? BUT HALE AND STILL THE
POSN (458)	/BLANCO/ (STRANGLING, AND TRYING TO LAUGH) A	LITTLE	CHOKER: THATS THE WORD FOR HIM. HIS CHOKING WASNT
LION PROLOG (108)	WOOTSUMS? HAS IT MADE UM TOO SICK TO EAT A NICE	LITTLE	CHRISTIAN MAN FOR UM'S BREAKFAST? OH, A NICE LITTLE
LION PROLOG (108)	CHRISTIAN MAN FOR UM'S BREAKFAST? OH, A NICE	LITTLE	CHRISTIAN MAN WILL GET UM'S THORN OUT FOR UM; AND
LION PROLOG (109)	ON HIS BACK). STEADEEE! OH, DID THE NASTY CRUEL	LITTLE	CHRISTIAN MAN HURT THE SORE PAW? (THE LION MOANS
MILL I (148)	I AM SORRY, BUT IT'S SUCH A LONG NAME. IN MY	LITTLE	CIRCLE EVERYONE CALLS HIM JUST ALLY. /EPIFANIA/ (HER
BULL PREFACE(33)	THEY CAN GOVERN MUCH MORE PROVIDENTLY THAN OUR	LITTLE	CIRCLE OF ARISTOCRATS AND PLUTOCRATS. THE JUST
HART PREFACE(11)	POLITICAL AND GENERAL MATTERS LYING OUTSIDE THEIR	LITTLE	CIRCLE OF INTEREST, BUT THE ORDINARY WAR-CONSCIOUS
MILL PREFACE(111)	OFFICE DESPOTISMS, RELIGIOUS DESPOTISMS IN THEIR	LITTLE	CIRCLES ALL OVER THE COUNTRY? OUR BOASTED POLITICAL
CAPT II (253)	PRIVACY, AND, IF YOU WILL ALLOW ME TO SAY SO, A	LITTLE	CIVILITY. I AM GREATLY OBLIGED TO YOU FOR BRINGING US
MTH5 SD(205)	OF IT, THE STEPS AND COLUMNED PORCH OF A DAINTY	LITTLE	CLASSIC TEMPLE. BETWEEN IT AND THE HILL, A RISING
SUPR PREFACE(R34)	A FORCE OF NATURE; INSTEAD OF A FEVERISH SELFISH	LITTLE	CLOD OF AILMENTS AND GRIEVANCES COMPLAINING THAT THE
ARMS II (37)	/SERGIUS/ THAT SHEWS THAT YOU ARE AN ABOMINABLE	LITTLE	CLOD OF COMMON CLAY, WITH THE SOUL OF A SERVANT. (HE
LIED (198)	HUSBAND/ YES, WOULD YOU LIKE TO LOOK AT THEM A	LITTLE	CLOSER? (HE PROFFERS THEM UNDER HENRY'S NOSE). /HE/
JITT III (57)	FOR HIM NOR FOR HER. /LENKHEIM/ (DRAWING A	LITTLE	CLOSER TO HER) DEAR LADY: MAY I ASK YOU A VERY
KING I (185)	YOU IF YOU ARE SANDY-HAIRED, AND THEN COMES A	LITTLE	CLOUD OVER IT AND YOU SHIVER WITH COLD. COULD THAT
O'FL (227)	DISTANCE AS IT MIGHT BE, AND THE SHRAPNEL MAKING	LITTLE	CLOUDS IN THE HEAVENS, AND THE SHELLS WHISTLING, AND
SUPR IV SD(141)	AUTOMATICALLY WHINE FOR HALFPENCE AND REACH OUT	LITTLE	CLUTCHING BROWN PALMS FOR THEM; BUT THERE IS NOTHING
HART II (98)	AGAIN; AND YOU THINK YOU CAN HELP ME OVER IT BY A	LITTLE	COAXING AND KISSING. WHEN I WANT ALL THE STRENGTH I
CLEO III (159)	MYSELF AND MY CHARGE TO THE SHORE BEFORE THE POOR	LITTLE	COCKLESHELL SANK. /CAESAR/ I AM SORRY, APOLLODORUS,
MILL II (169)	YOU CARE ABOUT NOTHING BUT YOUR FOOD AND YOUR	LITTLE	COMFORTS. YOU ARE WORSE THAN ALASTAIR; FOR HE AT
JITT II SD(27)	IS SAVED FROM BEING COMMON, IF NOT FROM BEING A	LITTLE	COMIC, BY THE STAMP PUT UPON HIM AS A MAN OF LEARNING
2TRU III (107)	/THE PATIENT/ AND NOW, MR MEEK, WHAT ABOUT THE	LITTLE	COMMISSION YOU PROMISED TO DO FOR ME? HAVE YOU
JOAN 4 (96)	BE THREE OR FOUR MIDDLEMEN WHO WILL EXPECT THEIR	LITTLE	COMMISSIONS. /THE CHAPLAIN/ MONSTROUS. IT IS ALL
APPL I (231)	TO KNOW. /AMANDA/ (INCORRIGIBLE) I SUGGEST A	LITTLE	COMMUNITY SINGING (SHE MAKES CONDUCTORLIKE
DEST (184)	(INTELLECTUALLY OVERTAXED) WELL, IT'S A	LITTLE	COMPLICATED; BUT I DARESAY IT WILL BE ALL RIGHT.
APPL I (225)	-- MAY I SAY THE ENGLISH SPIRIT? -- IN WHICH MY	LITTLE	CONCESSION HAS BEEN RECEIVED, ESPECIALLY BY YOU, MR
METH PREFACE(R27)	AND PAPER, SLOWLY, RELUCTANTLY, AND WITH SO	LITTLE	CONFIDENCE IN THE RESULT THAT I DARE NOT ACT ON IT
HART I (56)	OH, I BEG YOUR PARDON: OF COURSE: I WAS A	LITTLE	CONFUSED BY HIS MANNER. HE IS MAKING MANGAN HELP HIM
METH PREFACE(R75)	HE BECOMES INDIFFERENT TO RELIGION IF HE HAS	LITTLE	CONSCIENCE, AND INDIGNANTLY HOSTILE TO IT IF HE HAS A
BULL IV (170)	LIES ABOUT IT? NORA REILLY WAS A PERSON OF VERY	LITTLE	CONSEQUENCE TO ME OR ANYONE ELSE OUTSIDE THIS
SUPR IV (161)	ARE SO NICE TO ME, AND THAT MY OWN HAVE SO	LITTLE	CONSIDERATION FOR ME, IT'S NO WONDER I DONT SEEM ABLE
SUPR PREFACE(R30)	PUBLIC OF LONDON. I HAVE CERTAINLY SHEWN	LITTLE	CONSIDERATION FOR THAT PUBLIC IN THIS ENTERPRISE; BUT
SUPR I (5)	LAD AND THE SOUL OF HONOR; AND WHEN I SEE HOW	LITTLE	CONSIDERATION OTHER MEN GET FROM THEIR SONS, I
JOAN PREFACE(46)	OF THE FACTS, AS IT IS, THEY ILLUSTRATE THE TOO	LITTLE	CONSIDERED TRUTH THAT THE FASHION IN WHICH WE THINK
WIDO II (43)	BUT UNHAPPILY IT IS NOT. /TRENCH/ (A	LITTLE	CONSOLED) I SUPPOSE NOT. /COKANE/ NOT A DOUBT OF IT,
BULL IV (158)	YOU SEE, WE KNOW EACH OTHER SO WELL. /NORA/ (A	LITTLE	CONSOLED) YES: OF COURSE WE DO. (HE DOES NOT REPLY).
GENV II (63)	SEE ME THROUGH, AND NOW I MUST TODDLE OFF TO MY	LITTLE	CONSTITUENCY. I HAVE BARELY TIME TO PACK FOR THE
HART PREFACE(36)	WAS IN COMPARISON WITH RHEIMS THE GLOOMIEST OF	LITTLE	CONVENTICLES: INDEED THE CATHEDRAL MUST, FROM THE
FANY PROLOG (263)	ANY HINTS ABOUT THEM THAT WOULD HELP ME TO MAKE A	LITTLE	CONVERSATION WITH THEM? I AM, AS YOU SAID, RATHER
MIS. (202)	(CONFIDENTIALLY TO LINA) YOU WONT MENTION OUR	LITTLE	CONVERSATION, MISS SHEPANOSKA. IT'LL DO NO GOOD; AND
MTH4 III SD(202)	SHE LOOKS STEADILY INTO HIS FACE. HE STIFFENS; A	LITTLE	CONVULSION SHAKES HIM; HIS GRASP RELAXES; AND HE
BULL IV (162)	OF COURSE IT'S A COMMON COTTON ONE-- SILLY	LITTLE	COTTON ONE-- NOT GOOD ENOUGH FOR THE DEAR EYES OF
JOAN 5 (120)	WHAT WOULD HE BE IF HE LISTENED TO YOUR JEALOUS	LITTLE	COUNSELS? WELL, MY LONELINESS SHALL BE MY STRENGTH
BULL I (90)	AND MONOTONY! HOW AM I TO GET ON WITH A	LITTLE	COUNTRY LANDAGENT THAT EKES OUT HIS 5 PER CENT WITH A
APPL I (235)	PERSONS YOU DARE NOT OFFEND! WELL, A KING WITH A	LITTLE	COURAGE MAY TACKLE THEM FOR YOU. RESPONSIBILITIES
GETT (352)	THERE ARE ENOUGH PEOPLE THERE TO MAKE A PROPER	LITTLE	COURT FOR ME. SEND THE BEADLE FOR ME WHEN YOU THINK
KING I (218)	THE WORLD IS FULL OF KINGS AND QUEENS AND THEIR	LITTLE	COURTS. HERE IS PASTOR FOX, A KING IN HIS MEETING
DEVL I (20)	(HE HURRIES REMORSEFULLY TO ESSIE). COME,	LITTLE	COUSIN! NEVER MIND ME: IT WAS NOT MEANT TO HURT YOU.
ARMS I (5)	AGAINST HER MOTHER) YES; I WAS ONLY A PROSAIC	LITTLE	COWARD. OH, TO THINK THAT IT WAS ALL TRUE! THAT
BARB II (306)	PAIN OF STARVATION! THE BAD BLOOD OF THE FIERCE	LITTLE	COWARDS AT HOME WHO EGG ON OTHERS TO FIGHT FOR THE
LION I (123)	ONLY BE ALLOWED TO SQUEEZE MYSELF IN THROUGH A	LITTLE	CRACK IN THE GATE AFTER A GREAT DEAL OF BEGGING. I AM
NEVR I SD(199)	GAIETY, IS HARDLY EIGHTEEN YET. THIS DARLING	LITTLE	CREATURE CLEARLY DOES NOT BELONG TO THE ROOM, OR EVEN
ARMS I (5)	THEY WERE ANYTHING BUT DREAMS. OH, WHAT FAITHLESS	LITTLE	CREATURES GIRLS ARE! WHEN I BUCKLED ON SERGIUS'S
DOCT I (99)	SIR PATRICK, THAT EVERY ONE OF THESE INTERESTING	LITTLE	CREATURES HAS AN IMITATOR. JUST AS MEN IMITATE EACH
OVER (182)	WHY; FOR ALL THE VOLCANIC WOMEN I KNOW ARE PLAIN	LITTLE	CREATURES WITH SANDY HAIR. I DONT CONSIDER HUMAN
MIS. PREFACE(24)	THAT FROEBEL IS THE GOVERNING GENIUS OF YOUR	LITTLE	CRECHE. NO DOUBT THE NEW BRASS PLATES ARE BEING
DEVL II SD(29)	TO EXPLAIN A FACT IS NOT TO ALTER IT; AND HOWEVER	LITTLE	CREDIT MRS ANDERSON MAY DESERVE FOR MAKING HER HOME
MTH2 (88)	CON. WE SHOULD ONLY BE LAUGHED AT, AND LOSE THE	LITTLE	CREDIT WE EARNED ON FALSE PRETENCES IN THE DAYS OF
MILL I (138)	AT THE CLUB. /THE LADY/ THE ACQUAINTANCE DOES YOU	LITTLE	CREDIT. /SAGAMORE/ I HAD BETTER TELL YOU THAT HE AND
MIS. (198)	LEAVE THE ROOM. /PERCIVAL/ ARNT WE GETTING A	LITTLE	CROSS? DONT BE ANGRY, MR TARLETON. READ MARCUS
O'FL (205)	I AM A GENERAL OF FORTY YEARS SERVICE, THAT	LITTLE	CROSS OF YOURS GIVES YOU A HIGHER RANK IN THE ROLL OF
BULL IV SD(148)	FROM THE GARDEN, PUSHING HIS WAY THROUGH THE	LITTLE	CROWD. /CORNELIUS/ WHISHT YOUR LAUGHIN, BOYS! HERE
PYGM IV (264)	TO BED LIKE A GOOD GIRL AND SLEEP IT OFF. HAVE A	LITTLE	CRY AND SAY YOUR PRAYERS: THAT WILL MAKE YOU
JITT I SD(26)	TO RUSH TO THE DOOR THE HAT FALLS OFF. WITH A	LITTLE	CRY OF MISERY SHE TAKES THE HAT-PINS FROM THE HAT AND
LION PROLOG (109)	THE BRAVE BIG LION CAN BEAR PAIN, NOT LIKE THE	LITTLE	CRYBABY CHRISTIAN MAN. OOPSH! (THE THORN COMES OUT.
CLEO II (124)	FROM ME? /CLEOPATRA/ YOU ARE NOT TO BE KING, YOU	LITTLE	CRY-BABY. YOU ARE TO BE EATEN BY THE ROMANS. /CAESAR/
GETT (283)	AND REGINALD, MY DEAR? /LEO/ IT WAS THAT AWFUL	LITTLE	CURATE THAT AFTERWARDS DRANK, AND TRAVELLED FIRST
JOAN 2,SD(72)	AND SPORTING THE EXTRAVAGANCE OF A	LITTLE	CURLED BEARD DYED BLUE AT A CLEAN-SHAVEN COURT, COMES
JOAN 2 (81)	THE ARM. /JOAN/ (RELEASING HIM AND BOBBING HIM A	LITTLE	CURTSEY) GENTLE LITTLE DAUPHIN, I AM SENT TO YOU TO
MIS. PREFACE(5)	POSERS ARE UNPOPULAR, BECAUSE THEY IMPLY THAT OUR	LITTLE	CUSTOMS, OR, AS WE OFTEN CALL THEM, OUR RELIGION,
MTH4 I (152)	ON TO MOTHER YOU, YOU CERTAINLY ARE A VERY SILLY	LITTLE	DADDY. /THE ELDERLY GENTLEMAN/ (STIMULATED BY
GLIM (187)	YOUR EXCELLENCY WILL EXCUSE MY NET: IT IS A	LITTLE	DAMP. /FERRUCCIO/ WELL, WHAT NOW? ACCIDENTAL
BULL II (110)	THEN MAY BE HE'D A SENT THE GRASSHOPPER OR THE	LITTLE	DARK LOOKER INTO ME AT NIGHT TO REMIND ME OF IT. (
CATH 4 (193)	CALL HER STAR OF THE NORTH, LITTLE MOTHER,	LITTLE	DARLING: THATS WHAT SHE LIKES; BUT GET THE STRAPS
CATH 1 (163)	DO YOU THINK THE PRINCE WILL SEE THE CAPTAIN,	LITTLE	DARLING? /PATIOMKIN/ HE WILL NOT SEE ANY CAPTAIN. GO
CATH 4 (191)	(BECOMING HYSTERICAL) LITTLE MOTHER, BEAUTIFUL	LITTLE	DARLING ANGEL MOTHER: DONT BE CRUEL: UNTIE ME. OH, I
CATH 1 (162)	(SOFTLY TO THE LADY, HOLDING THE DOOR HANDLE)	LITTLE	DARLING HONEY: IS HIS HIGHNESS THE PRINCE VERY BUSY?
CATH 4 (194)	(TO PATIOMKIN) THE ENGLISH CAPTAIN WANTS YOU,	LITTLE	DARLING. CATHERINE RESUMES HER SEAT AS PATIOMKIN
CATH 1 (163)	VARINKA) INTERCEDE FOR HIM AND FOR ME, BEAUTIFUL	LITTLE	DARLING. HE HAS GIVEN ME A ROUBLE. /PATIOMKIN/ OH,
CATH 3 (186)	HE WILL BE MERCIFULLY DEAD LONG BEFORE THE END ,	LITTLE	DARLING. /CLAIRE/ (SUSTAINED BY AN INVINCIBLE
CATH 1 (172)	DIAMONDED COAT) YOU HAVE BEEN BADLY BROUGHT UP,	LITTLE	DARLING. WOULD ANY LADY OR GENTLEMAN WALK UNANNOUNCED
CATH 4 (194)	PRECISELY. (TO CLAIRE) YOU OBSERVE, MY LOVE: "	LITTLE	DARLING." WELL, IF HER MAJESTY CALLS HIM A DARLING,
CATH 4 (192)	EMPRESS'S ORDERS. IT IS OUT OF THE QUESTION. NO,	LITTLE	DARLING, NOT IN THERE. NOBODY IS ALLOWED IN THERE.
JOAN 2 (81)	HIM AND BOBBING HIM A LITTLE CURTSEY) GENTLE	LITTLE	DAUPHIN, I AM SENT TO YOU TO DRIVE THE ENGLISH AWAY
CAPT I (219)	DOO. WALKED ACROST HARFRICAR WITH NATHINK BUT A	LITTLE	DAWG, AND WROWT ABAHT IT IN THE DILY MILE (THE DAILY
PHIL II (101)	ON MY OWN ACCOUNT. /CHARTERIS/ WELL, I'M A	LITTLE	DAZED STILL BY STANDING FOR SO LONG BETWEEN TWO
JOAN EPILOG (161)	THEM INQUIRINGLY) DID YOU SAY ANYTHING? I AM A	LITTLE	DEAF, UNFORTUNATELY. ALSO A LITTLE -- WELL, NOT
MILL IV (207)	ON THE BRITISH TREASURY, WHICH CLAMORED FOR ITS	LITTLE	DEATH DUTY. BETWEEN THE DEATH AND THE PENSIONS THERE
SUPR PREFACE(R17)	MOST PART MERE HARMONIOUS PLATITUDE WHICH, WITH A	LITTLE	DEBASEMENT OF THE WORD-MUSIC, WOULD BE PROPERER TO
MTH3 (120)	MY ONLY PLEASURE WAS LOOKING FORWARD TO THAT POOR	LITTLE	DEBAUCH. THAT IS WHAT SAVED ME FROM SUICIDE. I COULD
FANY PROLOG (269)	OF THE AUTHOR. FICTIONS, POSSIBLY, THOUGH A	LITTLE	DECENT RETICENCE AS TO INTRODUCING ACTUAL PERSONS,
MILL III (181)	ME SOME MANUAL WORK? /THE MAN/ YOU WANT TO GET A	LITTLE	DEEPER INTO OUR BUSINESS, DONT YOU? /EPIFANIA/ I AM
BULL II (99)	PATSY! IS THAT YOUR RELIGION, TO BE AFRAID OF A	LITTLE	DEESHY GRASSHOPPER? SUPPOSE IT WAS A DIVIL, WHAT
APPL I (217)	AND SO FORTH -- THAT I FEAR I HAVE LOST ANY	LITTLE	DELICACY I EVER POSSESSED. IF YOU MAY FLOURISH YOUR
CATH 4 (195)	(KNEELING TO HER) PARDON HIM, PARDON HIM,	LITTLE	DELIGHT, LITTLE SLEEPER IN A ROSY CRADLE. /CLAIRE/
MIS. (171)	HOURS OF DAYLIGHT AND FRESH AIR-- IN A STUFFY	LITTLE	DEN COUNTING ANOTHER MAN'S MONEY. IVE AN INTELLECT: A
DOCT PREFACE(21)	SATISFIED HIMSELF THAT THE PATIENT'S HEART WAS A	LITTLE	DEPRESSED, DIGITALIS BEING A DRUG LABELLED AS A HEART
MTH3 (96)	OH, BOTHER! YOU MAY BE RIGHT IN THESE	LITTLE	DETAILS; BUT IN THE LARGE WE HAVE MANAGED TO HOLD OUR
LIED (195)	ENCOURAGED YOU IF I HAD KNOWN YOU WERE SUCH A	LITTLE	DEVIL? /HE/ DONT DRAG ME DOWN-- DONT-- DONT. HELP ME
2TRU I (46)	KEPT. /THE PATIENT/ NO, SWEETIE: YOU ARE A COMMON	LITTLE	DEVIL AND A LIAR. BUT YOU AMUSE ME. IF YOU WERE A
ROCK I (205)	ME BADLY! YOU! ! I COULD HAVE KILLED HER, POOR	LITTLE	DEVIL. HE SITS DOWN; AND SHE PASSES BEHIND HIM AND
SIM PRO,3, (35)	HER COLLAR) GO AND GET CLEANED UP, YOU DISGUSTING	LITTLE	DEVIL. (HE RUSHES HER TO THE EDGE). /THE Y.W./ (
MTH5 (215)	AND STRUGGLES. /A YOUTH/ LIE QUIET, YOU CLAMMY	LITTLE	DEVIL. /A MAIDEN/ YOU MUST BE WASHED, DEAR. NOW
GETT (330)	THEIR HOUSE AS THEIR FRIEND. LEO WAS AN AMUSING	LITTLE	DEVIL; BUT I LIKED REGINALD MUCH MORE THAN I LIKED

HART II (89)	I WILL TAKE CARE OF THAT. /MANGAN/ (GASPING) YOU	LITTLE	DEVIL, YOUVE DONE ME (ON THE POINT OF COLLAPSING
HART I (74)	IN THE HOUSE? /ELLIE/ I DID. /MRS HUSHABYE/ YOU	LITTLE	DEVIL! (SHE GOES OUT WITH RANDALL). /MANGAN/ WONT
ROCK II (270)	WORLD FOR THE GOOD AND EVIL HE DOES THAN A DIRTY	LITTLE	DICTATOR IN EVERY STREET RESPONSIBLE TO NOBODY, TO
PPP PREFACE(192)	WEDDING CAKES FOR BITS OF PLASTER. THERE IS BUT	LITTLE	DIFFERENCE IN MATERIAL BETWEEN THE TWO SUBSTANCES;
DOCT V (176)	PERHAPS, IN TWENTY YEARS YOU WILL UNDERSTAND HOW	LITTLE	DIFFERENCE THAT MAKES. /JENNIFER/ BUT EVEN SO, HOW
NEVR III (271)	(PHILOSOPHICALLY) IT'S SURPRISING HOW	LITTLE	DIFFERENCE THERE IS BETWEEN THE TWO. (GLORIA TURNS
LION PREFACE(11)	IS WHY ITS CHANGES OF NAME AND FORM HAVE MADE SO	LITTLE	DIFFERENCE. THAT IS WHY, ALSO, A NATION SO CIVILIZED
JITT III (68)	HEAD FOR A SINGLE MOMENT? /JITTA/ THAT SOUNDS A	LITTLE	DIFFICULT. I AM AFRAID I DONT QUITE FOLLOW. /AGNES/
WIDO II (47)	DOWN BEFORE THEM TO SAY THAT I HAVE ARRANGED THAT	LITTLE	DIFFICULTY WITH TRENCH. IT WAS ONLY A PIECE OF
CATH 2 (175)	UP) THEY MAKE ME DO IT TO KEEP UP THEIR OWN	LITTLE	DIGNITIES? SO? /NARYSHKIN/ EXACTLY. ALSO BECAUSE IF
GETT (347)	FOLLOWS HER). /THE GENERAL/ WELL, EDITH, I'M A	LITTLE	DISAPPOINTED, I MUST SAY. HOWEVER, I'M GLAD IT WAS
JITT I (20)	IMPORTANT TO SAY TO YOU ABOUT IT. /JITTA/ (A	LITTLE	DISAPPOINTED) BRUNO: CANT THAT WAIT A LITTLE? YOU
CAND II (120)	/CANDIDA/ (REALIZING HOW STUPID HE IS, AND A	LITTLE	DISAPPOINTED, THOUGH QUITE TENDERLY SO) DONT YOU
MRS I (186)	WELL, FRANKLY, I AM AFRAID YOUR MOTHER WILL BE A	LITTLE	DISAPPOINTED. NOT FROM ANY SHORTCOMING ON YOUR PART,
SIM I (45)	/SIR CHARLES/ YES, SIX. THE RESULT HAS BEEN A	LITTLE	DISAPPOINTING FROM THE POINT OF VIEW OF NUMBERS; BUT
WIDO II (44)	DOOR). /COKANE/ (CHEERILY, FOLLOWING HIM) OUR	LITTLE	DISCUSSION HAS GIVEN ME QUITE AN APPETITE. /TRENCH/ (
KING I (179)	YOU THE CLERGY ARE MOSTLY DULL DOGS; BUT WITH A	LITTLE	DISGUISE AND RITUAL THEY WILL PASS AS HOLY MEN WITH
BARB II (305)	TO MRS BAINES) I ALSO, MRS BAINES, MAY CLAIM A	LITTLE	DISINTERESTEDNESS. THINK OF MY BUSINESS! THINK OF
DEVL III (72)	HERE (INDICATING BURGOYNE AND SWINDON): I SEE	LITTLE	DIVINITY ABOUT THEM OR YOU. YOU TALK TO ME OF
FABL PREFACE(87)	CANDIDATE COULD READ, WRITE, AND EVEN TRANSLATE A	LITTLE	DOG LATIN. IT WAS BETTER THAN NO TEST AT ALL. BUT IT
LION II (145)	/THE EMPEROR/ YOU LITTLE BRUTE, YOU DAMNED FILTHY	LITTLE	DOG OF A GREEK TAILOR: I'LL HAVE YOU BURNT ALIVE FOR
GENV IV (126)	OF THEIR LIVES. YOUD HAVE HAD TO LOSE YOUR	LITTLE	DOGGIE SOME DAY. BATTLER TAKES OUT HIS HANDKERCHIEF
GENV IV (125)	BLONDA WILL BE FROZEN TO DEATH. MY DOGGIE! MY	LITTLE	DOGGIE! (HE BREAKS DOWN, SOBBING CONVULSIVELY).
GENV IV (128)	AFTER HIM) YOU WILL HAVE THE HONOR OF SHARING MY	LITTLE	DOG'S FATE. BUT NOBODY WILL WEEP FOR YOU, BARDO.
PYGM V (284)	I HAVE OUT OF YOU; AND IF YOU DARE TO SET UP YOUR	LITTLE	DOG'S TRICKS OF FETCHING AND CARRYING SLIPPERS
MIS. (124)	HE. HE'S OVERBRED, LIKE ONE OF THOSE EXPENSIVE	LITTLE	DOGS. I LIKE A BIT OF A MONGREL MYSELF, WHETHER IT'S
BARB III (349)	WILL DIE WITH THE COLORS. OH! AND I HAVE MY DEAR	LITTLE	DOLLY BOY STILL; AND HE HAS FOUND ME MY PLACE AND MY
LION PREFACE(35)	HEROD'S STEWARD, AND SUSANNA. THERE IS THE QUAINT	LITTLE	DOMESTIC EPISODE BETWEEN MARY AND MARTHA. THERE IS
SIM I (44)	ARE NOT THOSE USUAL IN ENGLAND. WE ARE MAKING A	LITTLE	DOMESTIC EXPERIMENT-- /THE CLERGYMAN/ OH, NOT AN
CURE (236)	WHAT TO DO. OH, STREGA, DONT YOU WANT A DEAR	LITTLE	DOMESTICATED HUSBAND WHO WOULD HAVE NO CONCERN BUT TO
GENV II (51)	THERE IS ONLY ONE OTHER TRIFLE OF NEWS. THE	LITTLE	DOMINION OF JACKSONSLAND HAS DECLARED ITSELF AN
CAPT II SD(252)	GOING OUT WHEN LADY CICELY RETURNS SOFTLY BY THE	LITTLE	DOOR AND CALLS TO HIM IN A WHISPER. SHE HAS TAKEN OFF
CAPT II SD(267)	HER HAT SLUNG ACROSS HER ARM, COMES THROUGH THE	LITTLE	DOOR SUPPORTING MARZO, WHO IS VERY WHITE, BUT ABLE TO
CAPT II SD(244)	MARZO ON THE FLAGS AGAINST THE WALL CLOSE TO THE	LITTLE	DOOR. HE GROANS. JOHNSON PHLEGMATICALLY LEAVES HIM
CAPT II (263)	MARZO, AT ALL EVENTS. (SHE GOES OUT THROUGH THE	LITTLE	DOOR. JOHNSON, REDBROOK, AND THE REST COME IN THROUGH
CAPT II SD(267)	OFF WITH YOU. DRINKWATER GOES OUT THROUGH THE	LITTLE	DOOR. /OSMAN/ SHALL WE HIDE HER FACE BEFORE SHE
CAPT II (247)	GOES OUT WITH MARZO AND HIS BEARERS THROUGH THE	LITTLE	DOOR). /BRASSBOUND/ (STILL STARING) WELL, I AM
CAPT II (244)	LOT OF POOR CREATURES? (SHE MAKES FOR THE	LITTLE	DOOR). /DRINKWATER/ EAH! (HE RUNS TO THE DOOR AND
CAPT II SD(246)	EXPLANATION, WHEN LADY CICELY RETURNS THROUGH THE	LITTLE	DOOR, AND COMES BETWEEN BRASSBOUND AND DRINKWATER.
CAPT II (251)	(SHE TAKES UP HER JAR AND GOES OUT BY THE	LITTLE	DOOR, LEAVING BRASSBOUND AND SIR HOWARD ALONE
3PLA PREFACE(R27)	IN HIS PICTURE OF THE CLENNAM HOUSEHOLD IN	LITTLE	DORRIT: MRS DUDGEON BEING A REPLICA OF MRS CLENNAM
POSN PREFACE(362)	DO IT. IT WAS POINTED OUT BY CHARLES DICKENS IN	LITTLE	DORRIT, WHICH REMAINS THE MOST ACCURATE AND
BULL IV (165)	CHIVALROUSLY). /NORA/ (LOOKING EARNESTLY AND A	LITTLE	DOUBTFULLY AT HIM) SURELY IF YOU LET ONE WOMAN CRY ON
PYGM EPILOG (289)	OF IT. THIS IS UNBEARABLE, NOT ONLY BECAUSE HER	LITTLE	DRAMA, IF ACTED ON SUCH A THOUGHTLESS ASSUMPTION,
CLEO I (109)	THAT I BELIEVE YOU ARE REAL, YOU IMPOSSIBLE	LITTLE	DREAM WITCH? /CLEOPATRA/ (GIGGLING AND LEANING
KING I (219)	SLUT. /NELL/ WELL, NO WORSE, IF YOU LIKE. ONE	LITTLE	DUKE IS ENOUGH FOR ME. /LOUISE/ CHANGE THE SUBJECT,
BULL IV (159)	HERE I AM, NONE THE WORSE. /NORA/ PRAPS IT'S A	LITTLE	DULL FOR YOU. /LARRY/ NO: I HAVNT EXHAUSTED THE
METH PREFACE(R55)	TO BE ABUSIVE; BUT WHEN I THINK OF THESE POOR	LITTLE	DULLARDS, WITH THEIR PRECARIOUS HOLD OF JUST THAT
MIS. PREFACE(79)	VOICE AND ASPECT AS I, UNDER THE EYE OF MY POOR	LITTLE	DUPE, ADVANCED ON THE ENEMY WITH THAT HIDEOUS
CAPT II (259)	UNDER THE ARM? PERHAPS I HAD BETTER MAKE IT A	LITTLE	EASIER FOR YOU. /BRASSBOUND/ (IRRITABLY) LET MY COAT
ROCK PREFACE(190)	HIS OWN PARTICULAR UTOPIA. HE MAY, AT MOST, BE A	LITTLE	ECCENTRIC AT THE COST OF BEING INDULGED AS SLIGHTLY
BARB III (325)	FELLOW; BUT HE IS A GREEK SCHOLAR AND NATURALLY A	LITTLE	ECCENTRIC. /UNDERSHAFT/ AH, QUITE SO. THANK YOU,
GETT PREFACE(216)	TO ITS FOUNDATIONS, YET THEY HAVE PRODUCED SO	LITTLE	EFFECT THAT ENGLISHMEN OPEN THEIR EYES IN SURPRISE
CLEO IV (167)	SILENCE, CHARMIAN: DO NOT YOU BE A SILLY	LITTLE	EGYPTIAN FOOL. DO YOU KNOW WHY I ALLOW YOU ALL TO
CLEO IV (190)	(GREATLY ALARMED) NOW, BY GREAT JOVE, YOU FILTHY	LITTLE	EGYPTIAN RAT, THAT IS THE VERY WORD TO MAKE HIM WALK
BULL PREFACE(50)	THE DENSHAWAI HORROR. DENSHAWAI IS A	LITTLE	EGYPTIAN VILLAGE IN THE NILE DELTA. BESIDES THE
HART I SD(54)	HOUSE. MAZZINI DUNN ENTERS FROM THE HALL. HE IS A	LITTLE	ELDERLY MAN WITH BULGING CREDULOUS EYES AND EARNEST
HART II (93)	TO TELL ME HE ISNT STRONG ENOUGH TO CRUSH POOR	LITTLE	ELLIE? /MAZZINI/ OF COURSE IT'S VERY HARD TO SAY HOW
MTH4 I SD(139)	A WOMAN IN A SILK TUNIC AND SANDALS, WEARING	LITTLE	ELSE EXCEPT A CAP WITH THE NUMBER 2 ON IT IN GOLD,
BULL IV (159)	THINKING ABOUT? /LARRY/ WELL, THERE WAS PRECIOUS	LITTLE	ELSE TO THINK ABOUT HERE, MY DEAR NORA, EXCEPT
SUPR HANDBOK(211)	WE ARE LOST, THAT IS A POSSIBILITY FOR OUR CRAZY	LITTLE	EMPIRE, IF NOT FOR THE UNIVERSE; AND AS SUCH
DEVL III SD(50)	IN THE TOWN HALL, UNLOCKS THE DOOR OF A	LITTLE	EMPTY PANELLED WAITING ROOM, AND INVITES JUDITH TO
CAND I SD(77)	UNINTERESTEDLY ABOUT SOMEBODY ELSE'S WORK. THE	LITTLE	ENERGY AND EAGERNESS THAT CROP UP SHEW THEMSELVES IN
MIS. (148)	OF IMPERIALISM: IT'S UNSELFISH. I DESPISE THE	LITTLE	ENGLANDERS: THEYRE ALWAYS THINKING ABOUT ENGLAND.
MTH2 (52)	AND ANTI-SOCIALISTS, OF JINGO IMPERIALISTS AND	LITTLE	ENGLANDERS, OF CAST-IRON MATERIALISTS AND ECSTATIC
BULL PREFACE(10)	HOSTS, WHO SCATTERED THAT INVINCIBLE ARMADA FOR	LITTLE	ENGLAND. THE MODERN IMPERIALIST DOES NOT BELIEVE IN
BULL PREFACE(9)	OF THE ROMAN CATHOLIC CHURCH IN MALTA. FORMERLY "	LITTLE	ENGLAND," THE " RIGHT LITTLE, TIGHT LITTLE ISLAND,"
CATH 1 (172)	/VARINKA/ (TAKING HIS OTHER ARM) YES, YES, YES,	LITTLE	ENGLISH FATHER: GOD KNOWS IT IS YOUR DUTY TO BE BRAVE
CATH 1 (171)	OH, MADAM! /VARINKA/ HEAVEN IS MY WITNESS,	LITTLE	ENGLISH FATHER, WE NEED SOMEONE WHO IS NOT AFRAID OF
KING I (192)	MONEY IS AS GOOD AS ENGLISH. KING LOUIS GETS	LITTLE	ENOUGH FOR IT: I TAKE CARE OF THAT. /JAMES/ THEN YOU
WIDO III (61)	AND I'M GOING TO STICK TO MY PRESENT INCOME. IT'S	LITTLE	ENOUGH FOR ME AS IT IS. /SARTORIUS/ IT REALLY MATTERS
DOCT PREFACE(76)	A HEADACHE WILL ALSO CURE A HEADACHE IF YOU TAKE	LITTLE	ENOUGH OF IT. I HAVE ALREADY EXPLAINED THAT THE
SUPR III (116)	TO PUT UP WITH FLESH-AND-BLOOD HUSBANDS-- AND	LITTLE	ENOUGH OF THAT TOO, SOMETIMES; AND YOU WILL HAVE TO
MTH4 I (163)	YOU DIDNT MEAN ANYTHING. NOW LISTEN TO ME, YOU	LITTLE	EPHEMERAL THING. I KNEW QUITE WELL WHAT YOU MEANT BY
DEST SD(153)	HIDDEN CAREFULLY UNDER THE WINEPRESS WITH HIS	LITTLE	EQUIPMENT OF SILVER PLATE. NAPOLEON, SITTING FACING
HART I SD(44)	THE OBSERVATORY AND THE HOUSE IS A FLAGSTAFF ON A	LITTLE	ESPLANADE, WITH A HAMMOCK ON THE EAST SIDE AND A LONG
LADY PREFACE(217)	SHOULD PONDER. HE SAYS THAT SHAKESPEAR WAS BUT "	LITTLE	ESTEEMED BY HIS OWN GENERATION." HE EVEN DESCRIBES
LADY PREFACE(217)	WHICH IT IS TRUE ENOUGH THAT SHAKESPEAR WAS TOO	LITTLE	ESTEEMED BY HIS OWN GENERATION, OR, FOR THE MATTER OF
MIS. SD(110)	ENOUGH, HIS ASSURANCE AND HIS HIGH VOICE ARE A	LITTLE	EXASPERATING. /JOHNNY/ HALLO! WHERES YOUR LUGGAGE..
MIS. PREFACE(70)	IS TO BE DONE? FOR THE PRESENT, UNFORTUNATELY,	LITTLE	EXCEPT PROPAGATING THE CONCEPTION OF CHILDREN'S
SUPR HANDBOK(185)	PRIVATE HOMES, NUMBERED ONLY 300, COULD DO VERY	LITTLE	EXCEPT PROVE THAT COMMUNISTS, UNDER THE GUIDANCE OF A
POSN PREFACE(400)	PHILOSOPHY, RELIGION, OR POLITICS, WE SHOULD GET	LITTLE	EXCEPT STAGNANT MEDIOCRITY. THE PRACTICAL
2TRU PREFACE(9)	DO, THERE IS NOTHING IN THAT. WHERE I AM REALLY A	LITTLE	EXCEPTIONAL IS IN RESPECT OF MY HAVING EXPERIENCED
JITT II (29)	AND A GROWN-UP DAUGHTER SUFFERS MORE FROM TOO	LITTLE	EXCITEMENT THAN FROM TOO MUCH. WHAT EMOTIONS HAS A
CAPT I (220)	WILL SEE THE LIDY AN JADGE ELLAM THROUGH HENNY	LITTLE	EXCURSION IN REASON. YR HONOR MAWT MENTION IT.
3PLA PREFACE(R18)	OF A MENAGE A TROIS WITH JUDGE BRACK. A	LITTLE	EXPERIENCE OF POPULAR PLAYS WOULD SOON CONVINCE THESE
WIDO I (23)	MR SARTORIUS, A LITTLE KNOWLEDGE OF THE WORLD, A	LITTLE	EXPERIENCE OF WOMEN-- (THEY DISAPPEAR INTO THE
LION PREFACE(63)	DO IN MORRIS'S NEWS FROM NOWHERE) WILL, AFTER A	LITTLE	EXPERIENCE, BE FOUND NOT ONLY PRACTICABLE BUT HIGHLY
HART PREFACE(5)	WENT TO CHURCH OR KEPT THE SABBATH EXCEPT BY A	LITTLE	EXTRA FUN AT WEEK-ENDS. WHEN YOU SPENT A FRIDAY TO
SUPR PREFACE(R36)	AND CITIZENS, CATCH IT VERY SEVERELY. EVEN	LITTLE	FAITH, THOUGH HE GETS TO HEAVEN AT LAST, IS GIVEN TO
POSN PREFACE(368)	FROM PUBLIC OPINION AND HOW FULL OF THEIR OWN	LITTLE	FAMILY AND PARTY AFFAIRS BRITISH GOVERNMENTS, BOTH
MRS III (226)	TO HER WITH HIS VOICE) MUSNT GO LIVE WITH HER.	LITTLE	FAMILY GROUP OF MOTHER AND DAUGHTER WOULDNT BE A
ARMS II (24)	AGAIN? HOW LONG WOULD YOUR FATHER BE LEFT ON HIS	LITTLE	FARM? (SHE IMPATIENTLY THROWS AWAY THE END OF HER
BULL I (90)	LANDAGENT THAT EKES OUT HIS 5 PER CENT WITH A	LITTLE	FARMING AND A SCRAP OF HOUSE PROPERTY IN THE NEAREST
ROCK II (250)	SCOTCH CROFTERS INTO THE SEA, AND TURNED THEIR	LITTLE	FARMS INTO DEER FORESTS BECAUSE YOU COULD GET MORE
CATH 1 (163)	HIM) YOU LIE, YOU DOG. YOU LIE. /THE SERGEANT/	LITTLE	FATHER: LIFE IS HARD FOR THE POOR. IF YOU SAY IT IS A
CATH 1 (166)	A BULLET THROUGH YOUR SILLY HEAD. /THE SERGEANT/	LITTLE	FATHER: TELL US WHAT TO DO. OUR LIVES ARE YOURS; BUT
CATH 1 (162)	IT UP TO REPLACE IT ON THE BACK OF THE CHAIR)	LITTLE	FATHER: THE ENGLISH CAPTAIN, SO HIGHLY RECOMMENDED TO
CATH 1 (164)	AT THE DOOR. /THE SERGEANT/ (PATERNALLY)	LITTLE	FATHER: THIS IS THE ENGLISH CAPTAIN, SO WELL
CATH 1 (167)	SERGEANT COMES IN. /THE SERGEANT/ GOD BE PRAISED,	LITTLE	FATHER: YOU ARE STILL SPARED TO US. /PATIOMKIN/ TELL
CATH 1 (163)	VOLKONSKY? /THE SERGEANT/ (ON HIS KNEES)	LITTLE	FATHER: YOU KICKED HIS HIGHNESS DOWNSTAIRS.
CATH 1 (172)	REAL NAME? POPOFF, OF COURSE. WHY DO YOU LAUGH,	LITTLE	FATHER? /EDSTASTON/ HOW CAN ANYONE WITH A SENSE OF
CATH 1 (163)	GO TO THE DEVIL! /THE SERGEANT/ BE MERCIFUL,	LITTLE	FATHER. GOD KNOWS IT IS YOUR DUTY TO SEE HIM! (TO
CATH 4 (198)	THE BLESSED NICHOLAS WILL MULTIPLY YOUR FRUITS,	LITTLE	FATHER. /EDSTASTON/ GOODBYE, GOODBYE, GOODBYE,
CATH 1 (163)	WITH YOU TOO! /THE SERGEANT/ HAVE MERCY ON ME,	LITTLE	FATHER. YOUR HEAD IS BAD THIS MORNING. YOU DRINK TOO
CATH 1 (166)	ABSURDLY SELF-POSSESSED) GET OUT. /THE SERGEANT/	LITTLE	FATHER-- /PATIOMKIN/ (ROARING) GET OUT. GET OUT. ALL
CATH 3 (184)	HE PROMISED YOU. /THE SERGEANT/ TAKE THEM,	LITTLE	FATHER; AND DO NOT FORGET US POOR SOLDIERS WHO HAVE

CATH 2 (180)	MAKE A DEEP CURTSEY TO EDSTASTON. /VARINKA/ HAPPY	LITTLE	FATHER! REMEMBER: I DID THIS FOR YOU. (SHE RUNS OUT
CATH 1 (163)	WHEN YOU KICK THEM. GOD KNOWS THAT IS NOT JUST,	LITTLE	FATHER! /PATIOMKIN/ (LAUGHS OGREISHLY; THEN RETURNS
DOCT III (153)	EVER CAN KNOW HIM. I AM HIS WIFE. I KNOW HE HAS	LITTLE	FAULTS: IMPATIENCE, SENSITIVENESS, EVEN LITTLE
CYMB V (141)	VENGEANCE. BUT, ALACK, YOU SNATCH SOME HENCE FOR	LITTLE	FAULTS: THAT'S LOVE, TO HAVE THEM FALL NO MORE. YOU
BULL III (141)	(WITH SUDDEN PASSION) YOU TALK OF YOUR ROTTEN	LITTLE	FAWM CAUSE YOU MIDE IT BY CHACKIN A FEW STOWNS DAHN A
MIS. (124)	MEAT IS ANOTHER WOMAN'S POISON. BUNNY'S A DEAR	LITTLE	FELLOW; BUT I NEVER COULD HAVE FANCIED HIM FOR A
BARB II (288)	CHACK IT. AW'M SICK O YOUR JENNY ILL AND ER SILLY	LITTLE	FICE. /BARBARA/ THEN WHY DO YOU KEEP THINKING ABOUT
O'FL (222)	AS THE CONTINENT OF EUROPE THAT TEN OF YOUR DIRTY	LITTLE	FIELDS HERE WOULDNT SO MUCH AS FILL THE DITCH OF.
HART II (100)	DARE. /MRS HUSHABYE/ WELL, OF ALL THE IMPUDENT	LITTLE	FIENDS I EVER MET! HECTOR SAYS THERE IS A CERTAIN
LION I (118)	I TOLD YOU THEY WERE BRUTES. /LENTULUS/ PLUCKY	LITTLE	FILLY! I SUPPOSE SHE THINKS I CARE. (WITH AN AIR OF
MRS II (206)	SOON IF I SAW ANY OF YOUR NONSENSE. MY GIRL'S	LITTLE	FINGER IS MORE TO ME THAN YOUR WHOLE BODY AND SOUL. (
DOCT PREFACE(58)	TO AN APPALLING EXTENT. THE OPPONENTS OF THE	LITTLE	FINGER THEORY WOULD THEREFORE BE PRETTY SURE TO
MIS. (125)	BRAINS IN HIS WHOLE BODY AS BENTLEY HAS IN HIS	LITTLE	FINGER. BESIDES, THEYVE NO DISTINCTION. IT'S AS MUCH
JITT III (57)	AND HOW EASILY HE COULD GET IT BY LIFTING UP HIS	LITTLE	FINGER. OH, I KNOW EXACTLY HOW HE DECEIVED US.
DOCT PREFACE(58)	FEVER ALWAYS BEGINS AT THE TOP JOINT OF THE	LITTLE	FINGER; AND THAT IF THIS JOINT BE AMPUTATED
POSN (459)	I PUT THE CHILD IN HIS ARMS; AND IT GOT ITS	LITTLE	FINGERS DOWN HIS NECK AND CALLED HIM DADDY AND TRIED
DOCT PREFACE(43)	IGNORANT, AND THOUGHTLESS WAY, IS TO STICK	LITTLE	FLAGS INTO A RABBIT'S HEART AND LET THE STUDENT SEE
CATH 3 (185)	TO THE GAZETTE. ENGLAND WILL BLOW YOUR TRUMPERY	LITTLE	FLEET OUT OF THE WATER AND SWEEP YOUR TINPOT ARMY
MIS. (175)	DOESNT NEED TURKISH BATHS; HE NEEDS TO PUT ON A	LITTLE	FLESH. I DONT UNDERSTAND WHAT IT'S ALL ABOUT. I FOUND
ARMS II SD(23)	SEEN ON THE LEFT, WITH A GARDEN DOOR REACHED BY A	LITTLE	FLIGHT OF STEPS. ON THE RIGHT THE STABLE YARD, WITH
APPL PREFACE(187)	PUBLIC-HOUSE, HAS SUBSCRIBED A SHILLING TO OUR	LITTLE	FLOWER SHOW, HAS A KIND WORD FOR THE CHILDREN WHEN HE
BULL II (102)	HER HAND GENTLY). DEAR MISS NORA: DONT PLUCK THE	LITTLE	FLOWER. IF IT WAS A PRETTY BABY YOU WOULDNT WANT TO
MRS II (215)	ME ACROSS THE BAR " WHAT ARE YOU DOING THERE, YOU	LITTLE	FOOL? WEARING OUT YOUR HEALTH AND YOUR APPEARANCE
BULL IV (166)	FIRST LOVE! /BROADBENT/ FIRST LOVE IS ONLY A	LITTLE	FOOLISHNESS AND A LOT OF CURIOSITY: NO REALLY
NEVR II (259)	NOT BE AFRAID. I THINK YOU ARE SENTIMENTAL, AND A	LITTLE	FOOLISH; BUT I LIKE YOU. /VALENTINE/ (DROPPING INTO
PYGM V (288)	CAN DO WITHOUT YOU. /HIGGINS/ OF COURSE I DO, YOU	LITTLE	FOOL. FIVE MINUTES AGO YOU WERE LIKE A MILLSTONE
CLEO I (112)	IN IT; AND-- /CAESAR/ (ABRUPTLY) PAH! YOU ARE A	LITTLE	FOOL. HE WILL EAT YOUR CAKE AND YOU TOO. (HE TURNS
JOAN PREFACE(15)	PROBABLY IN PAMPHLETS) NOT TO BE A SUPERSTITIOUS	LITTLE	FOOL, AND TO EMPTY OUT ST CATHERINE AND THE REST OF
WIDO II (42)	HOUSES FOR THE HOMELESS, AND TO LAY BY A	LITTLE	FOR BLANCHE. (HE LOOKS AT THEM. THEY ARE SILENT:
DOCT PREFACE(12)	THEIR OWN ORGANS AND LIMBS, THEY SEEM TO CARE AS	LITTLE	FOR MUTILATION AS LOBSTERS OR LIZARDS, WHICH AT LEAST
DEVL III (54)	HIM AS HE RECOILS WITH A GESTURE OF DENIAL) A	LITTLE	FOR MY SAKE. WELL, SAVE YOURSELF FOR MY SAKE. AND I
DEVL III (54)	TO PLEASE YOU-- THAT I DID WHAT I DID EVER SO	LITTLE	FOR YOUR SAKE, I LIED AS MEN ALWAYS LIE TO WOMEN. YOU
DEVL III (52)	WELL, YOU HAD A HAND IN IT. IT MUST HAVE BEEN A	LITTLE	FOR YOUR SAKE. YOU LET THEM TAKE ME, AT ALL EVENTS.
CAND II (120)	YOU, JAMES; FOR IF THAT WENT, I SHOULD CARE VERY	LITTLE	FOR YOUR SERMONS: MERE PHRASES THAT YOU CHEAT
GENV IV (91)	I THINK OF THE MOB OF BAGMEN FROM FIFTY POTTY	LITTLE	FOREIGN STATES THAT CALLS ITSELF A LEAGUE OF NATIONS.
DOCT III (131)	IDEA OF YOU. /LOUIS/ BUT I WANT TO SPARE YOUR	LITTLE	FORTUNE, AND RAISE MONEY ON MY OWN WORK. DONT BE
PYGM III (248)	BOWS. THE COLONEL BRINGS THE CHIPPENDALE CHAIR A	LITTLE	FORWARD BETWEEN MRS HILL AND MRS HIGGINS, AND SITS
CAPT III (294)	(HE QUIETLY TEARS THE NEWSPAPER CUTTINGS INTO	LITTLE	FRAGMENTS AND THROWS THEM AWAY, LOOKING FIXEDLY AT
MRS III (226)	GROUP? /FRANK/ THE BABES IN THE WOOD: VIVIE AND	LITTLE	FRANK. (HE NESTLES AGAINST HER LIKE A WEARY CHILD).
BULL II (97)	X.X. /THE MAN/ AH, IT'S NO USE, ME POOR	LITTLE	FRIEND. IF YOU COULD JUMP AS FAR AS A KANGAROO YOU
LIED (194)	BE KIND ENOUGH TO EXPLAIN EXACTLY HOW. /SHE/ (A	LITTLE	FRIGHTENED) THANK YOU, HENRY: I WAS SURE YOU WOULD.
METH PREFACE(R21)	EVOLVED, NOT CREATED: IT HAS ARISEN LITTLE BY	LITTLE	FROM A SMALL BEGINNING, AND HAS INCREASED THROUGH THE
AUGS (283)	LEAVE; AND I AM SURE YOU WONT GRUDGE THEM A	LITTLE	FUN AT YOUR EXPENSE. /THE CLERK/ HEAR! HEAR!
POSN (462)	OF THEIR NATURAL SPORT, I SHALL GIVE THEM A	LITTLE	FUN BY STANDING OUTSIDE THE DOOR AND TAKING UP A
JITT III (76)	(RISING, VERY UNPLEASANTLY SURPRISED, AND NOT A	LITTLE	FURIOUS) YOU! YOU HAVE HAD ADVENTURES SINCE WE WERE
JITT I SD(9)	LIKE A HOTEL SITTING ROOM; BECAUSE THERE IS VERY	LITTLE	FURNITURE; ONLY TWO SEATS, A COUCH, AND A SMALL TABLE
BULL IV SD(145)	CORNER WITH HIM, ON HIS LEFT HAND. AUNT JUDY, A	LITTLE	FURTHER BACK, SITS FACING THE FIRE KNITTING, WITH HER
2TRU II (66)	YOU ARE A THIEF AND SO AM I. I GO A	LITTLE	FURTHER THAN THAT, MYSELF; AND SO WOULD YOU IF YOU
GETT (338)	ON HER LEFT). NEVER MIND HIM. A LITTLE PLUCK, A	LITTLE	GAIETY OF HEART, A LITTLE PRAYER; AND YOULL BE
CLEO PRO1 (93)	REWARD." NOW WHEN POMPEY CAME, HE CAME ALONE IN A	LITTLE	GALLEY, PUTTING HIS TRUST IN THE LAW AND THE
BULL II SD(112)	BROKEN BY UNMISTAKABLE FOOTSTEPS. SHE GIVES A	LITTLE	GASP AS SHE SEES A MAN APPROACHING. /NORA/ IS THAT
NEVR IV (288)	PERCEPTIBLY) COFFEE, MISS? (HE GIVES A	LITTLE	GASP OF HOPE). CERTAINLY, MISS. THANK YOU, MISS: VERY
DEVL II SD(29)	HURRYING HOME THROUGH THE RAIN. SHE GIVES A	LITTLE	GASP OF RELIEF, NOT VERY FAR REMOVED FROM A SOB, AND
SUPR IV SD(142)	FINE AFTERNOON, BY THE APPEARANCE AT A	LITTLE	GATE IN A PALING ON OUR LEFT, OF HENRY STRAKER IN HIS
SUPR IV (144)	NODS AFFABLY TO MALONE AND GOES OUT THROUGH THE	LITTLE	GATE IN THE PALING). /VIOLET/ (VERY CIVILLY) I AM SO
SUPR IV SD(170)	BY MENDOZA AND STRAKER, COME IN THROUGH THE	LITTLE	GATE IN THE PALING. TANNER SHAMEFACEDLY RELEASES ANN,
SUPR IV SD(150)	AT ONE ANOTHER AS TANNER COMES IN THROUGH THE	LITTLE	GATE WITH RAMSDEN, FOLLOWED BY OCTAVIUS AND ANN.
BULL III SD(117)	DECORTICATED AND SPLIT BY THE WEATHER. NEAR THE	LITTLE	GATE. AT THE OPPOSITE SIDE, A BASKET LIES UNMOLESTED
SUPR IV (155)	AND RAMSDEN GO OUT VERY AMICABLY THROUGH THE	LITTLE	GATE. TANNER CALLS TO OCTAVIUS, WHO IS WANDERING IN
SUPR IV SD(149)	AIR OF A MAN WHO HAS BEEN MAKING HASTE, OPENS THE	LITTLE	GATE, AND ADMITS HECTOR, WHO, SNORTING WITH
SUPR IV (154)	RAMSDEN IN THE GARDEN, AND GOES OUT THROUGH THE	LITTLE	GATE, LEAVING HIS FATHER AND VIOLET TOGETHER ON THE
APPL II (261)	GRANDER. /MAGNUS/ THIS LITTLE ISLAND! " THIS	LITTLE	GEM SET IN A SILVER SEA! " HAS IT OCCURRED TO YOU, MR
NEVR IV (287)	TO SUPPORT HIMSELF). I BEG YOUR PARDON, MAAM. A	LITTLE	GIDDINESS-- /BOHUN/ (COMMANDINGLY) YOU WILL EXCUSE
DOCT I (98)	DONT GIVE WAY. /RIDGEON/ IT'S NOTHING. I WAS A	LITTLE	GIDDY JUST NOW. OVERWORK, I SUPPOSE. /WALPOLE/
MIS. (145)	(TO LORD SUMMERHAYS) WELL, SUMMERHAYS, HAS MY	LITTLE	GIRL BEEN ENTERTAINING YOU? /LORD SUMMERHAYS/ YES.
MRS II (199)	ARE HONORABLE: EVER SO HONORABLE; AND YOUR	LITTLE	GIRL IS JOLLY WELL ABLE TO TAKE CARE OF HERSELF. SHE
MRS I (189)	MY LIFE OUT THESE THREE YEARS TO HAVE THAT	LITTLE	GIRL OF MINE SHEWN TO HIM; AND NOW THAT IVE DONE IT,
MRS III (226)	THE WORD AGAINST HER BREAST) SH-SH-SH-SH!	LITTLE	GIRL WANTS TO FORGET ALL ABOUT HER MOTHER. (THEY ARE
MRS III (226)	HAND IN HAND, UNDER THE TREES. /FRANK/ THE WISE	LITTLE	GIRL WITH HER SILLY LITTLE BOY. /VIVIE/ THE DEAR
MRS II (199)	I WONT HAVE ANY YOUNG SCAMP TAMPERING WITH MY	LITTLE	GIRL. DO YOU HEAR? I WONT HAVE IT. /FRANK/ (QUITE
MRS III (226)	BOY. /VIVIE/ THE DEAR LITTLE BOY WITH HIS DOWDY	LITTLE	GIRL. /FRANK/ EVER SO PEACEFUL, AND RELIEVED FROM THE
MRS I (190)	GET OUT OF THE HABIT OF THINKING OF HER AS A	LITTLE	GIRL. YOU SEE SHE HAS REALLY DISTINGUISHED HERSELF;
CLEO I (111)	(SHE RELAPSES) AND CATS. NOW YOU ARE A SILLY	LITTLE	GIRL; AND YOU ARE DESCENDED FROM THE BLACK KITTEN.
MRS III (226)	BOY'S FATHER AND THE QUESTIONABLENESS OF THE	LITTLE	GIRL'S-- /VIVIE/ (SMOTHERING THE WORD AGAINST HER
SUPR I (33)	ABOUT; I STOLE THINGS I DIDNT WANT; I KISSED	LITTLE	GIRLS I DIDNT CARE FOR. IT WAS ALL BRAVADO:
JITT II (36)	AND INDIGNANT) WHY DO YOU TREAT ME AS IF I WERE A	LITTLE	GIRL, AS MY MOTHER DOES? I DID NOT EXPECT IT FROM
PHIL II (116)	FOR A YEAR. /CRAVEN/ (PLAYFULLY) VULGAR	LITTLE	GIRL! (HE PINCHES HER EAR). SHALL WE COME, JO!
CATH 4 (195)	LITTLE CHERUB! LITTLE WILD DUCK! LITTLE STAR!	LITTLE	GLORY! LITTLE JEWEL IN THE CROWN OF HEAVEN!
CLEO IV SD(166)	CHARMIAN IS A HATCHET FACED, TERRA COTTA COLORED	LITTLE	GOBLIN, SWIFT IN HER MOVEMENTS, AND NEATLY FINISHED
MIS. PREFACE(101)	AND DEMORALIZATION OF FINDING HIMSELF A	LITTLE	GOD ON THE STRENGTH OF WHAT OUGHT TO BE A QUITE
DOCT V (177)	SIR PATRICK IS RIGHT: YOU DO THINK YOU ARE A	LITTLE	GOD. HOW CAN YOU BE SO SILLY? YOU DID NOT PAINT
GLIM (182)	A BARON, YOU ARE BROUGHT UP TO THINK YOURSELF A	LITTLE	GOD, THOUGH YOU ARE NOTHING, AND CANNOT RULE
MIS. PREFACE(80)	AT THE SAME TIME. IF YOU POSE AS A	LITTLE	GOD, YOU MUST POSE FOR BETTER FOR WORSE. HOW LITTLE
SIM II (72)	ALL. PRAY DONT THINK THAT. /MRS HYERING/ WELL, A	LITTLE	GOOD MANNERS NEVER DOES ANY HARM; BUT I TELL YOU
CATH 1 (163)	MORNING. YOU DRINK TOO MUCH FRENCH BRANDY AND TOO	LITTLE	GOOD RUSSIAN KVASS. /PATIOMKIN/ (WITH SUDDEN FURY)
LADY (249)	LEAVE IT WHOLLY TO THOSE WHOSE COUNSELS WILL WORK	LITTLE	GOOD TO YOUR REALM. FOR THIS WRITING OF PLAYS IS A
GENV IV (129)	/BATTLER/ WE ALL HAVE. BUT I CLAIM TO HAVE DONE A	LITTLE	GOOD WITH MY ACTING. I WILL NOT HAVE MY WORK UNDONE.
JOAN EPILOG (161)	THEY LOVE ME THERE; AND I AM ABLE TO DO A	LITTLE	GOOD, I AM WELL CONNECTED, YOU SEE; AND THEY INDULGE
APPL PREFACE(182)	INTOLERABLE BURDENS. WHAT WE WANT TO KNOW IS HOW	LITTLE	GOVERNMENT WE CAN GET ALONG WITH WITHOUT BEING
BULL II (100)	HAND AGEN THE DONKEY OR STAMP YOUR FOOT ON THE	LITTLE	GRASSHOPPER, REMEMBER THAT THE DONKEY'S PETHER
MRS III SD(220)	AND THEN SWERVES TO ITS LEFT, WHERE IT ENDS IN A	LITTLE	GRAVELLED CIRCUS OPPOSITE THE RECTORY PORCH, BEYOND
LION II (142)	AWKWARD. /THE MENAGERIE KEEPER/ WHY NOT THAT	LITTLE	GREEK CHAP? HE'S NOT A CHRISTIAN: HE'S A SORCERER,
BULL III (141)	WITH, AND EAH YOU AWRISH AHLIN ABAHT YOUR SILLY	LITTLE	GRIEVANCES, AND SEE THE WY YOU MIKE IT WORSE FOR HAZ
SUPR IV SD(151)	INTRUDING, ON THEIR WAY TO THE STEPS ANN SENDS A	LITTLE	GRIMACE OF MUTE SYMPATHY TO VIOLET, WHO IS STANDING
MRS III (226)	GROUP. /VIVIE/ (FALLING UNDER THE SPELL) WHAT	LITTLE	GROUP? /FRANK/ THE BABES IN THE WOOD: VIVIE AND
CLEO II SD(130)	RIGHT HAND. THIS MOVEMENT BRINGS THE THREE IN A	LITTLE	GROUP TO THE PLACE OCCUPIED BY ACHILLAS, WHO MOVES
CAPT III SD(282)	AND DEBONAIR, MARZO UNEASY. THESE FOUR FORM A	LITTLE	GROUP TOGETHER ON THE CAPTAIN'S LEFT. THE REST WAIT
MRS III (226)	AND DAUGHTER WOULDNT BE A SUCCESS. SPOIL OUR	LITTLE	GROUP. /VIVIE/ (FALLING UNDER THE SPELL) WHAT LITTLE
NEVR IV (284)	THINGS I LET OTHER PEOPLE DO! ! /CRAMPTON/ (A	LITTLE	GRUDGINGLY IN SPITE OF HIMSELF) AS WELL AS SHE DOES?
DOCT I SD(87)	IS WHIMSICAL AND FATHERLY: TO OTHERS HE IS A	LITTLE	GRUFF AND UNINVITING, APT TO SUBSTITUTE MORE OR LESS
MRS I (184)	50 POUNDS. SHE CLOSED WITH ME AT THAT. AFTER A	LITTLE	GRUMBLING; AND I WAS BETTER THAN MY BARGAIN. BUT I
ARMS III (49)	BUT SHE IS AGAIN RAPT IN THE LANDSCAPE. WITH A	LITTLE	GUSH OF PARENTAL AFFECTION AND PRIDE, HE POINTS HER
BARB I SD(271)	BRITOMART, WITH A SUDDEN FLOUNCE, GIVES WAY TO A	LITTLE	GUST OF TEARS. /STEPHEN/ (GOING TO HER) MOTHER:
CAPT III (298)	IVE BECOME HALF A BRIGAND. I CAN KICK THAT	LITTLE	GUTTERSCRUB DRINKWATER; BUT I FIND MYSELF DOING WHAT
ROCK II (262)	YOU TRIED THAT GAME ON THE IRISH, WHO WERE ONLY A	LITTLE	HANDFUL OF PEASANTS IN THEIR CABBAGE PATCH. I HAVE
ARMS III SD(46)	COFFEE STAINED, TORN AND THUMBED; AND A COUPLE OF	LITTLE	HANGING SHELVES WITH A FEW GIFT BOOKS ON THEM: THE
DOCT IV (156)	EXPECTED THIS. /SIR PATRICK/ (DRILY) IT'S A	LITTLE	HARD ON A LAD TO BE KILLED BECAUSE HIS WIFE HAS TOO

WIDO III (57)	/SARTORIUS/ (OPENING HIS EYES) THAT SOUNDS A	LITTLE	HARD ON THEM, DOESNT IT, MY CHILD? /BLANCHE/ OH, I
MTH5 (213)	TO SAY " I TOLD YOU SO"; BUT SHE WAS GETTING A	LITTLE	HARD SET AND FLAT-CHESTED AND THIN ON THE TOP, WASNT
LADY PREFACE(218)	AS HIS INFERIORS. HE MUST HAVE FELT IT A	LITTLE	HARD THAT BEING A BETTER SCHOLAR, AND PERHAPS A
OVER PREFACE(159)	EVENTS WHICH, LEFT TO THEMSELVES, WOULD DO VERY	LITTLE	HARM (SOMETIMES NOT ANY) AND BE FORGOTTEN IN A FEW
SUPR HANDBOK(222)	A FOXHUNTER DOES; AND YOU WILL DO COMPARATIVELY	LITTLE	HARM. NO FOXHUNTER IS SUCH A CAD AS TO PRETEND THAT
MIS. PREFACE(50)	VERY LITTLE OF THEM AT PRESENT; AND THAT THIS	LITTLE	HAS NOT BEEN PRODUCED BY COMPULSORY EDUCATION: NAY,
MIS. PREFACE(91)	WHO WOULD POSITIVELY BE HAPPIER AS HOGS, SO	LITTLE	HAVE THEY CULTIVATED THEIR HUMANITY BY THE ONLY
CAND II (108)	BETTER THAN YOU. (WITH TEMPER) HE'D TALK YOUR	LITTLE	HEAD OFF. (SHE IS GOING BACK ANGRILY TO HER PLACE.
GENV PREFACE(25)	LIKE GOLDSMITH'S VILLAGERS, WONDERING HOW THEIR	LITTLE	HEADS CAN CARRY ALL THEY KNOW AND RANKING THEM AS
CURE (237)	IN EUROPE AND AMERICA. IT IS A DREAM OF A TIMID	LITTLE	HEART FLUTTERING AGAINST MINE, OF A GENTLE VOICE TO
HART II (103)	AND YOU HAVE A HEART, ALFY, A WHIMPERING	LITTLE	HEART, BUT A REAL ONE. (RELEASING HIM SUDDENLY) NOW
JITT III (61)	YOU HAVE DRAGGED THE POOR WOMAN DOWN FROM HER	LITTLE	HEAVEN. /EDITH/ MY FATHER'S WIFE MIGHT HAVE HAD A
POSN PREFACE(393)	THE AUTHOR'S CHOICE OF SUBJECT. FORMERLY VERY	LITTLE	HEED WAS GIVEN IN ENGLAND TO THE SUSCEPTIBILITIES OF
DOCT IV (162)	THAT IMMORTALITY. PROMISE ME YOU WILL NOT MAKE A	LITTLE	HELL OF CRAPE AND CRYING AND UNDERTAKER'S HORRORS AND
BULL PREFACE(12)	BUT THE EUROPEAN DREGS AND RIFFRAFF WHO SET UP	LITTLE	HELLS OF ANARCHY AND INFAMY JUST BEYOND THE BORDER,
O'FL (213)	SIR. SHE WAS ALWAYS A KIND FRIEND TO THE POOR.	LITTLE	HER LADYSHIP KNEW, GOD HELP HER, THE DEPTH OF
CLEO III (163)	MORE GRAVELY) MY POOR CHILD: YOUR LIFE MATTERS	LITTLE	HERE TO ANYONE BUT YOURSELF. (SHE GIVES WAY
CAPT I SD(217)	ENDS, AS FAR AS THE LAND IS CONCERNED, IN	LITTLE	HILLS THAT COME NEARLY TO THE SEA: RUDIMENTS, THESE,
SUPR III SD(71)	AN ABANDONED QUARRY, AND TOWARDS THE LEFT A	LITTLE	HILL, COMMANDING A VIEW OF THE ROAD, WHICH SKIRTS THE
METH PREFACE(R19)	THE TWO. FOR ALL THEIR SAKES I MUST GIVE HERE A	LITTLE	HISTORY OF THE CONFLICT BETWEEN THE VIEW OF EVOLUTION
APPL PREFACE(196)	IT PROVIDES MATERIAL FOR ONE BAD PLAY! " THIS	LITTLE	HISTORY WILL EXPLAIN HOW IT ACTUALLY DID PROVIDE
BULL I (89)	AND LAND PURCHASE ACTS TURNING BIG ESTATES INTO	LITTLE	HOLDINGS, HE'D BE A BEGGAR IF HE HADNT TAKEN TO
INCA (241)	WHEN I EXPOSE YOUR HOTEL AS THE SECOND-RATE	LITTLE	HOLE IT IS, NOT A SOUL ABOVE THE RANK OF A CURATE
FANY II (295)	OLD WAY AGAIN. IVE BEEN SET FREE FROM THIS SILLY	LITTLE	HOLE OF A HOUSE AND ALL ITS PRETENCES. I KNOW NOW
MIS. (113)	AND ALL THE REST OF IT. MY FATHER BEGAN IN A	LITTLE	HOLE OF A SHOP IN LEEDS NO BIGGER THAN OUR PANTRY
GENV I (31)	CAN THEY DO? YOU CANT EXPECT THEM TO SIT IN THIS	LITTLE	HOLE TALKING TO PEOPLE. I HAVE NEVER SEEN ONE OF
BULL IV (170)	TO ME OR ANYONE ELSE OUTSIDE THIS MISERABLE	LITTLE	HOLE. BUT MRS TOM BROADBENT WILL BE A PERSON OF VERY
HART I (54)	INDEED I SHALL DO NOTHING OF THE SORT. THAT	LITTLE	HOLE! I AM ENTITLED TO THE BEST SPARE ROOM. /THE
KING I (189)	I HOPE TO PROVE THAT THE ROMISH CHURCH IS THE	LITTLE	HORN OF THE FOURTH BEAST MENTIONED BY THE PROPHET
POSN (440)	KEMP; AND TELL THEM ABOUT YOUR BIG BROTHER'S	LITTLE	HORSE THAT SOME WICKED MAN STOLE. GO AND CRY IN YOUR
SUPR III (108)	IN A BATTLE ALL YOU NEED TO MAKE YOU FIGHT IS A	LITTLE	HOT BLOOD AND THE KNOWLEDGE THAT IT'S MORE DANGEROUS
DEST (161)	HIS COAXING FAWNING WAYS, THE MEAN EFFEMINATE	LITTLE	HOUND. (LOWERING HIS VOICE WITH THRILLING INTENSITY)
JOAN 5 (115)	ME TO DO BY MY OWN WITS; AND I TELL YOU THAT YOUR	LITTLE	HOUR OF MIRACLES IS OVER, AND THAT FROM THIS TIME ON
PYGM EPILOG (299)	SCUTCHEON BY OPENING A SHOP, HE FOUND THE	LITTLE	HOUSEHOLD ALREADY CONVULSED BY A PRIOR ANNOUNCEMENT
SIM II (57)	HALF OF THEM WANT TO RAIN DESTRUCTION ON THIS	LITTLE	HOUSEHOLD OF OURS, AND THE OTHER HALF IS DETERMINED
SIM II (56)	AND THEN UNITED US ALL SIX, HAS ENDED IN A SINGLE	LITTLE	HOUSEHOLD WITH FOUR CHILDREN, WONDERFUL AND
HART I (64)	I AM NONE THE LESS DELIGHTED TO FIND YOU IN OUR	LITTLE	HOUSE. /ELLIE/ (IN GREAT DISTRESS) I DONT KNOW WHAT
DOCT IV (168)	AS OLD AS I AM, YOULL KNOW THAT IT MATTERS VERY	LITTLE	HOW A MAN DIES, WHAT MATTERS IS, HOW HE LIVES. EVERY
OVER PREFACE(166)	OF THEIR REAL SELVES IN IT, AND ALSO LEARN A	LITTLE	HOW THEY APPEAR TO OTHER PEOPLE. FOR AUDIENCES OF
GETT (284)	FOUND THEM ALL OUT ALREADY, REGINALD. /LEO/ (A	LITTLE	HUFFILY) AFTER ALL, THERE ARE WORSE MEN THAN
2TRU I (43)	NO: YOU LOOK LIKE A CURATE. /THE BURGLAR/ (A	LITTLE	HURT) OH, NOT A CURATE. I HOPE I LOOK AT LEAST LIKE A
BULL IV (145)	TO LAUGH AT? /DORAN/ IT GOT ITS FUT INTO THE	LITTLE	HWEEL-- (HE IS OVERCOME AFRESH; AND THE REST
POSN (460)	MORNING OR WAS HE NOT? YES OR NO? /FEEMY/ A	LITTLE	HYSTERICALLY) I'LL TELL YOU FAST ENOUGH. DONT THINK
MTH4 I (173)	WHAT YOU TELL ME ACCOUNTS FOR A GREAT DEAL OF THE	LITTLE	I KNOW OF THE PRIVATE LIFE OF OUR GREAT MEN. WE MUST
BULL IV (174)	THEY MAY PLUNDER YOU AFTERWARDS. /BROADBENT/ (A	LITTLE	IMPATIENT OF THIS UNBUSINESSLIKE VIEW) YES, YES; BUT
CAPT I (236)	BRASSBOUND? (HE BOWS GRAVELY). /SIR HOWARD/ (A	LITTLE	IMPATIENT OF THESE QUESTIONS, WHICH STRIKE HIM AS
PYGM II (230)	WHEN YOUVE MISLAID ANYTHING OR WHEN YOU GET A	LITTLE	IMPATIENT, NOW IT DOESNT MATTER BEFORE ME: I'M USED
PHIL I (86)	AND DISPLAYING SOME EMOTION). /CHARTERIS/ (A	LITTLE	IMPATIENTLY) THE FACT IS, CUTHBERTSON, CRAVEN'S A
ARMS III (56)	TO ME, TELLING ME NOT TO MIND THE MAJOR BEING A	LITTLE	IMPATIENT; FOR THEY KNEW WHAT A GOOD SERVANT I WAS--
BARB PREFACE(221)	AS BUTLER'S POSTHUMOUS WAY OF ALL FLESH MAKING SO	LITTLE	IMPRESSION THAT WHEN, SOME YEARS LATER, I PRODUCE
SUPR I (15)	A FIGURE AS ANY OF THE REST OF YOU. CULTIVATE A	LITTLE	IMPUDENCE, RAMSDEN; AND YOU WILL BECOME QUITE A
LIED (188)	WHY DIDNT YOU TRY TO RESTRAIN YOUR FEELINGS A	LITTLE	IN COMMON CONSIDERATION FOR ME? WHY DIDNT YOU WRITE
BULL IV (159)	FOND AS WE ARE OF ONE ANOTHER, NORA, WE HAVE SO	LITTLE	IN COMMON-- I MEAN OF COURSE THE THINGS ONE CAN PUT
CATH 2,SD(174)	THE PRINCESS DASHKOFF, WITH TWO LADIES, STANDS A	LITTLE	IN FRONT OF THE LINE OF COURTIERS, BY THE IMPERIAL
DEVL III SD(72)	THE GALLOWS FRAMEWORK, AND POSTS HIMSELF A	LITTLE	IN FRONT OF IT. BEHIND HIM COMES THE EXECUTIONER, A
JOAN 3 (91)	WITH RELIGION. /DUNOIS/ I, GOD FORGIVE ME, AM A	LITTLE	IN LOVE WITH WAR MYSELF, THE UGLY DEVIL! I AM LIKE A
MTH4 II (189)	AS A MATTER OF GOOD TASTE; BUT THERE IS NOW VERY	LITTLE	IN OUR ARTICLES OF RELIGION THAT IS NOT ACCEPTED AS
MILL I (153)	I SUPPOSE SO. BUT HADNT WE BETTER TALK IT OVER A	LITTLE	IN PRIVATE FIRST? /EPIFANIA/ YOU SHALL DO NOTHING OF
ARMS III (52)	HE BELIEVES IN IT. /BLUNTSCHLI/ YES: HE'S A	LITTLE	IN THAT LINE HIMSELF, ISNT HE? /RAINA/ (STARTLED)
APPL INTRLUD(252)	DONT DISLIKE YOUR SORT: I UNDERSTAND IT, BEING A	LITTLE	IN THAT LINE MYSELF, AT ALL EVENTS I AM NOT AFRAID OF
WIDO I (20)	WERE ONE OR TWO POINTS ON WHICH WE WERE A	LITTLE	IN THE DARK. (SCRUPULOUSLY) BUT I WOULD NOT PERMIT
APPL II (260)	TIME AGO. /MANHATTAN/ CENTURIES COUNT FOR BUT	LITTLE	IN THE LIFE TIMES OF GREAT NATIONS, SIR. LET ME
3PLA PREFACE(R10)	WELL-FED GROWN-UP-SCHOOLBOY ENGLISHMAN COUNTS FOR	LITTLE	IN THE MODERN METROPOLITAN AUDIENCE. IN THE LONG
METH PREFACE(R76)	WE FEEL HOTTER THAN EVER, HISTORY RECORDS VERY	LITTLE	IN THE WAY OF MENTAL ACTIVITY ON THE PART OF THE MASS
APPL I (205)	MEN WOULD HARDLY MISS THEIR HEADS, THERE IS SO	LITTLE	IN THEM. STILL, KILLING IS A SERIOUS BUSINESS: AT
DEVL III (64)	MR ANDERSON, THAT YOU MUST NOT BUILD ON THIS	LITTLE	INCIDENT. WE ARE BOUND TO MAKE AN EXAMPLE OF
WIDO II (39)	JUST ASKING HER TO BE CONTENT TO LIVE ON MY OWN	LITTLE	INCOME; AND YET SHE TURNED ON ME AS IF I'D BEHAVED
PYGM V (275)	(CONSCIENCE STRICKEN) PERHAPS WE WERE A	LITTLE	INCONSIDERATE. IS SHE VERY ANGRY? /MRS HIGGINS/ (
DEVL I (11)	A STEP OR TWO) MRS DUDGEON: I USED TO HAVE SOME	LITTLE	INFLUENCE WITH YOU. WHEN DID I LOSE IT? /MRS
DEST SD(152)	CHEERFUL BLACK-CURLED BULLET HEADED GRINNING	LITTLE	INNKEEPER OF 40, NATURALLY AN EXCELLENT HOST, HE IS
O'FL (206)	TO THAT PITCH OF TIREDNESS OF IT THAT WHEN A POOR	LITTLE	INNOCENT SLIP OF A BOY IN THE STREET THE OTHER NIGHT
DEST SD(151)	THE BEST QUARTERS IN TAVAZZANO ARE AT A	LITTLE	INN, THE FIRST HOUSE REACHED BY TRAVELLERS PASSING
JOAN PREFACE(18)	WILL BE PUZZLED AND INCREDULOUS, BUT A VERY	LITTLE	INQUIRY AMONG THEIR ACQUAINTANCES WILL REVEAL TO THEM
BULL PREFACE(32)	IN SHORT, TO ANY CONSIDERATIONS WHICH REQUIRE A	LITTLE	INTELLECTUAL EXERTION AND SYMPATHETIC ALERTNESS-- IS
PYGM EPILOG (289)	THAT BACHELOR'S WIFE, ESPECIALLY IF HE IS SO	LITTLE	INTERESTED IN MARRIAGE THAT A DETERMINED AND DEVOTED
APPL PREFACE(190)	TO CO-ORDINATE THE FEDERAL WORK, OUR OBSOLETE	LITTLE	INTERNAL FRONTIERS MUST BE OBLITERATED, AND OUR UNITS
BULL PREFACE(9)	STILL SANE: WE DO NOT SNEER AT OUR COUNTRY AS "	LITTLE	IRELAND," AND CHEER FOR A DOUBTFUL COMMERCIAL
SUPR IV SD(141)	NET NOR SET OF CROQUET HOOPS, BUT, ON OUR LEFT, A	LITTLE	IRON GARDEN TABLE WITH BOOKS ON IT, MOSTLY
NEVR II SD(225)	GENTLEMAN SITTING ON A CHAIR OF IRON LATHS AT A	LITTLE	IRON TABLE WITH A BOWL OF LUMP SUGAR ON IT, READING
NEVR II (246)	THEN TAKES HIS HAT AND UMBRELLA FROM THE	LITTLE	IRON TABLE, AND TURNS TOWARDS THE STEPS. MEANWHILE
NEVR IV (284)	IS, I SUPPOSE IT IS. I'M AFRAID I'M SOMETIMES A	LITTLE	IRRITABLE; BUT I KNOW WHATS RIGHT AND REASONABLE ALL
GENV PREFACE(16)	THING; BUT WE MUST TAKE THAT RISK BECAUSE A	LITTLE	IS AS MUCH AS OUR BIGGEST HEADS CAN HOLD; AND A
GETT PREFACE(194)	HOME-BRED AS TO BE UNFIT FOR HUMAN SOCIETY. SO	LITTLE	IS EXPECTED OF THEM THAT IN SHERIDAN'S SCHOOL FOR
LION PREFACE(96)	OLD SELF-CONTAINED FRENCH REPUBLIC AND THE TIGHT	LITTLE	ISLAND OF BRITAIN, INTO EMPIRES WHICH OVERFLOW THE
LION PREFACE(99)	THE EMPIRE, THE STUARTS WRECKED EVEN THE TIGHT	LITTLE	ISLAND WHICH WAS THE NUCLEUS OF THE EMPIRE BY THEIR
CLEO PRO1 (89)	PEACE! BE SILENT AND HEARKEN UNTO ME, YE QUAINT	LITTLE	ISLANDERS, GIVE EAR, YE MEN WITH WHITE PAPER ON YOUR
SIM II (62)	DOWNING STREET DECLARES FOR A RIGHT LITTLE TIGHT	LITTLE	ISLAND. /KANCHIN/ THE BRITISH PRIME MINISTER CUTS THE
APPL II (261)	BE EMPEROR. KING MAY BE GOOD ENOUGH FOR THIS	LITTLE	ISLAND; BUT IF WE COME IN WE SHALL REQUIRE SOMETHING
SUPR PREFACE(R25)	IN THE MISMANAGEMENT OF A TIGHT BUT PAROCHIAL	LITTLE	ISLAND, WITH OCCASIONAL MEANINGLESS PROSECUTION OF
BULL PREFACE(9)	" LITTLE ENGLAND," THE " RIGHT LITTLE, TIGHT	LITTLE	ISLAND," DESPISED SPAIN FOR HER IMPERIAL POLICY, AND
APPL II (261)	WE SHALL REQUIRE SOMETHING GRANDER. /MAGNUS/ THIS	LITTLE	ISLAND! " THIS LITTLE GEM SET IN A SILVER SEA! " HAS
HART II (86)	HAVE BEEN, THIS MORNING. NOW! YOU CANT THINK HOW	LITTLE	IT MATTERS, BUT IT'S QUITE INTERESTING. ONLY, YOU
HART I (73)	THEIR TICKETS. /MAZZINI/ (SENTENTIOUSLY) HOW	LITTLE	IT TELLS US, AFTER ALL! THE GREAT QUESTION IS, NOT
GETT (264)	YOU LET IT LOOSE IN THE WOODS. WHEN I THOUGHT HOW	LITTLE	IT WAS TO A MAN OF MY EASY TEMPER TO PUT UP WITH HER,
PYGM PREFACE(202)	OF THE LATER GENERATIONS OF PHONETICIANS I KNOW	LITTLE	. AMONG THEM TOWERS THE POET LAUREATE, TO WHOM
OVER PREFACE(159)	MATTER A GREAT DEAL, THEY ACTUALLY MATTERED VERY	LITTLE	. AND EVEN AT THAT EVERYBODY PRETENDS NOT TO BELIEVE
3PLA PREFACE(R34)	OF HAMLET AS THERE WAS TIME FOR INSTEAD OF AS	LITTLE	. AND THE INSTANT SUCCESS OF THE EXPERIMENT PROBABLY
SUPR III (88)	AH, THAT IS PERHAPS AS BAD AS CONFESSING TOO	LITTLE	. AT ALL EVENTS, SENORA, WHETHER BY OVERSIGHT OR
SUPR III (108)	AS UNIVERSAL AS SEA SICKNESS, AND MATTERS JUST AS	LITTLE	. BUT THAT ABOUT PUTTING AN IDEA INTO A MAN'S HEAD IS
NEVR IV (298)	HIM) WELL, NEVER MIND. WE MUST INDULGE THEM A	LITTLE	. CAN YOU GET US SOMETHING TO WEAR, WAITER? /WAITER/
MIS. (121)	COMES A TIME WHEN ALL THAT SEEMS TO MATTER SO	LITTLE	. EVEN QUEENS DROP THE MASK WHEN THEY REACH OUR TIME
DEVL I SD(4)	THEN KNOCKING, WHICH DISTURBS MRS DUDGEON A	LITTLE	. FINALLY THE LATCH IS TRIED, WHEREUPON SHE SPRINGS
NEVR II (256)	YOU CAME IN, I WAS DAZZLED. (HER BROW CLOUDS A	LITTLE	. HE GOES ON QUICKLY) THAT WAS SILLY, OF COURSE; BUT
MTH5 (245)	NOT PORTRAITS, OF COURSE: I SHALL IDEALIZE YOU A	LITTLE	. I HAVE COME TO THE CONCLUSION THAT YOU ANCIENTS ARE
HART II (95)	ME. /MRS HUSHABYE/ I'M BEGINNING TO LIKE YOU A	LITTLE	. I PERFECTLY LOATHED YOU AT FIRST, I THOUGHT YOU THE
PRES (155)	A MAN'S LAST RESOURCE-- WILL AVAIL YOU JUST AS	LITTLE	. I SWEEP THEM AWAY, JUST AS I SWEEP YOUR PLANS OF
MRS PREFACE(155)	ADVISER ON THE SUBJECT OF WHICH HE KNOWS SO	LITTLE	. IF I DO NOT DRAW THE SAME CONCLUSION, IT IS NOT

JITT II (48)	STREET. YOU MUST LEARN TO CONSIDER OTHER PEOPLE A	LITTLE	. IF YOU HAVE NO REGARD FOR ME, AT LEAST REMEMBER
MRS IV (244)	SOMETHING BY YOUR OWN BRAINS. /FRANK/ OH YES, A	LITTLE	. (HE TAKES OUT HIS MONEY AGAIN). I MADE ALL THAT
SUPR II (49)	HOUSE AND STRETCH MY LEGS AND CALM MY NERVES A	LITTLE	. (LOOKING AT HIS WATCH) I SUPPOSE YOU KNOW THAT WE
HART I (74)	TIRED. I'LL TAKE A BOOK UP TO MY ROOM AND REST A	LITTLE	. (SHE GOES TO THE BOOKSHELF). /MANGAN/ RIGHT. YOU
FANY PROLOG (266)	NINE, I HAVE HAD TO PUT FORWARD THE DINNER HOUR A	LITTLE	. MAY I SHEW YOU TO YOUR ROOMS? (HE GOES OUT.
DEVL II (30)	WHY, YOUVE BEEN CRYING. /JUDITH/ ONLY A	LITTLE	. NEVER MIND: IT'S ALL OVER NOW. (A BUGLE CALL IS
LION PROLOG (109)	NOT TO SCRATCH, NOT EVEN IF IT HURTS A VERY VERY	LITTLE	. NOW MAKE VELVET PAWS. THATS RIGHT. (HE PULLS
DEVL II (30)	IN HIS ARMS) ANXIOUS, MY DEAR? /JUDITH/ A	LITTLE	. /ANDERSON/ WHY, YOUVE BEEN CRYING. /JUDITH/ ONLY A
BULL III (125)	WELL, AND THE WOMAN WHO EATS NOT WISELY BUT TOO	LITTLE	. /BROADBENT/ (FURIOUS) LARRY! YOU-- YOU-- YOU
CLEO I (113)	FTATATEETA, DEAR: YOU MUST GO AWAY-- JUST FOR A	LITTLE	. /CAESAR/ YOU ARE NOT COMMANDING HER TO GO AWAY: YOU
DOCT I SD(108)	RIDGEON GOES TO THE GLASS, AND ARRANGES HIS TIE A	LITTLE	. /EMMY/ (ANNOUNCING) MRS DOOBIDAD (RIDGEON LEAVES
PYGM II (226)	FINISHED YOUR TEACHING? YOU MUST LOOK AHEAD A	LITTLE	. /HIGGINS/ (IMPATIENTLY) WHATS TO BECOME OF HER IF
SUPR I (28)	/TANNER/ (DRILY) I THINK HE SUSPECTS ME JUST A	LITTLE	. /OCTAVIUS/ JACK: YOU COULDNT-- YOU WOULDNT--
O'FL (214)	O'FLAHERTY, THE WAR SEEMS TO HAVE UPSET YOU A	LITTLE	. /O'FLAHERTY/ IT'S SET ME THINKING, SIR; AND I'M NOT
CURE (228)	SLEEP AS MUCH AS YOU CAN, OR YOU MIGHT READ A	LITTLE	. /REGINALD/ WHAT CAN I READ? /THE DOCTOR/ TRY THE
2TRU II (53)	I KNOW THE COUNTRY, I CAN SPEAK THE DIALECTS A	LITTLE	. /TALLBOYS/ MARVELLOUS! AND WHY, WITH ALL THESE
SUPR I (38)	THROUGH LIFE WITHOUT CONSIDERING OTHER PEOPLE A	LITTLE	. /TANNER/ AY; BUT WHAT OTHER PEOPLE? IT IS THIS
JOAN 2,SD(82)	THE COURT SMILES BROADLY: EVEN TITTERS A	LITTLE	. /THE ARCHBISHOP/ (DRAWING HIMSELF UP SENSITIVELY)
MTH5 (243)	THE ANCIENTS ARE SMILING. /THE NEWLY BORN/ JUST A	LITTLE	. /THE SHE-ANCIENT/ (QUICKLY RECOVERING HER GRAVE
CAPT III (275)	PRISON, AND SMARTENING UP CAPTAIN BRASSBOUND A	LITTLE	. TELL HIM HE OUGHT TO DO IT TO SHEW HIS RESPECT FOR
SIM I (51)	TO YOU. (SHE GOES). /HYERING/ TRY TO SLEEP A	LITTLE	. THE MORNING HAS BEEN TOO MUCH FOR YOU. (HE GOES).
LION PREFACE(87)	CHRISTS. LET US NOW CLEAR UP THE SITUATION A	LITTLE	. THE NEW TESTAMENT TELLS TWO STORIES FOR TWO
PYGM II SD(219)	APRON, AND THE SHODDY COAT HAS BEEN TIDIED A	LITTLE	. THE PATHOS OF THIS DEPLORABLE FIGURE, WITH ITS
CAPT II (255)	TO MADNESS OR MADNESS DROVE HER TO DRINK MATTERS	LITTLE	. THE QUESTION IS, WHO DROVE HER TO BOTH? /SIR
BULL II SD(112)	WHERE SHE SITS DOWN DISCOURAGED AND CRIES A	LITTLE	. THEN SHE SETTLES HERSELF RESIGNEDLY TO WAIT, AND
MILL I (142)	TRY TO KEEP IT IN CHECK; BUT I AM AFRAID I HAVE A	LITTLE	. YOU APPEAL TO IT, SOMEHOW. /EPIFANIA/ THEN I TELL
CAND II (119)	(WITH CURIOUS THOUGHTFULNESS) YES, I FEEL A	LITTLE	JEALOUS SOMETIMES. /MORELL/ (INCREDULOUSLY) OF
BARB II (288)	I SUPPOSE. BUT WHY DID HE LET YOU HIT POOR	LITTLE	JENNY HILL? THAT WASNT VERY MANLY OF HIM, WAS IT?
BARB II (283)	DOWN AS (WRITING) THE MAN WHO-- STRUCK-- POOR	LITTLE	JENNY HILL-- IN THE MOUTH. /BILL/ (RISING
BARB III (320)	OH, THATS EVERYBODY'S BIRTHRIGHT. LOOK AT POOR	LITTLE	JENNY HILL, THE SALVATION LASSIE! SHE WOULD THINK
BARB II (288)	A MAN WITH A HEART WOULDNT HAVE BASHED POOR	LITTLE	JENNY'S FACE, WOULD HE? /BILL/ (ALMOST CRYING) AW,
BARB II (285)	SHRANK FROM HIM OR BORE MALICE. /BARBARA/ POOR	LITTLE	JENNY! ARE YOU TIRED? (LOOKING AT THE WOUNDED
CATH 4 (195)	LITTLE WILD DUCK! LITTLE STAR! LITTLE GLORY!	LITTLE	JEWEL IN THE CROWN OF HEAVEN! /CLAIRE/ THIS IS
2TRU II (72)	BUILD ITS DAM AND BRING UP ITS FAMILY. I WANT MY	LITTLE	JOB LIKE THE BEAVER. IF I DO NOTHING BUT CONTEMPLATE
GENV I (31)	NEVER GET THROUGH IT. JUST LOOK HERE AT THIS NICE	LITTLE	JOB THEYVE GIVEN ME! A CARD INDEX OF ALL THE
MTH3 (116)	HUNDRED AND EIGHTY-THREE, HE SAYS. THAT IS HIS	LITTLE	JOKE. DO YOU KNOW, MRS LUTESTRING, HE HAD ALMOST
POSN (459)	IN ITS HEAD WITH THE FEVER. HE SAID IT WAS A	LITTLE	JUDAS KID, AND THAT IT WAS BETRAYING HIM WITH A KISS,
POSN (458)	OF THE THROAT-- FRANTICALLY) DEAD! THE	LITTLE	JUDAS KID! THE CHILD I GAVE MY LIFE FOR! (HE
JOAN 2 (86)	TO THEIR LAWFUL HOMES IN PEACE. WILT BE A POOR	LITTLE	JUDAS, AND BETRAY ME AND HIM THAT SENT ME? /CHARLES/
MILL IV (202)	I AM NOT THINKING OF THE COURTS: THERE IS	LITTLE	JUSTICE THERE FOR ANYBODY. MY MILLIONS ARE IN
CAND II (115)	MAKE ME TELL ER FAIRY STORIES WHEN SHE WAS ONY A	LITTLE	KIDDY NOT THAT IGH (INDICATING A STATURE OF TWO FEET
BARB I (262)	I SUPPOSE HE HASNT SEEN SARAH SINCE SHE WAS A	LITTLE	KID. /LADY BRITOMART/ NOT SINCE SHE WAS A LITTLE KID,
BARB I (262)	LITTLE KID. /LADY BRITOMART/ NOT SINCE SHE WAS A	LITTLE	KID, CHARLES, AS YOU EXPRESS IT WITH THAT ELEGANCE OF
PYGM V (286)	ABOUT? /LIZA/ (MUCH TROUBLED) I WANT A	LITTLE	KINDNESS. I KNOW I'M A COMMON IGNORANT GIRL, AND YOU
CLEO V (196)	FROM THE WAR, APOLLODORUS? /APOLLODORUS/ THE	LITTLE	KING PTOLEMY WAS DROWNED. /BELZANOR/ DROWNED! HOW..
ROCK II (264)	FOUNDED A CIVILIZATION COMPARED TO WHICH YOUR	LITTLE	KINGDOM IS NO BETTER THAN A CONCENTRATION CAMP. WHAT
CLEO IV (175)	THE FELLOW WITH HAIR LIKE SQUIRREL'S FUR-- THE	LITTLE	KING'S BEAR LEADER, WHOM YOU KEPT PRISONER. /CAESAR/
KING I (219)	THE SUBJECT, CHARLES. WHAT YOU WERE SAYING ABOUT	LITTLE	KINGS AND QUEENS BEING EVERYWHERE WAS VERY TRUE. YOU
CATH 4 (195)	/VARINKA/ SHE BEGS YOU FOR A THOUSAND DEAR	LITTLE	KISSES ALL OVER HER BODY. /CLAIRE/ (VEHEMENTLY) I DO
CLEO II (133)	KINGS DONT WORK. /CAESAR/ OH! WHO TOLD YOU THAT,	LITTLE	KITTEN? EH? /CLEOPATRA/ MY FATHER WAS KING OF
CLEO I (109)	STATUE) WHAT! /CLEOPATRA/ THIS IS ONLY A DEAR	LITTLE	KITTEN OF A SPHINX. WHY, THE GREAT SPHINX IS SO BIG
FANY PROLOG (268)	CAMBRIDGE FABIAN SOCIETY, KITTENS. IMPERTINENT	LITTLE	KITTENS. BLAME THEM, SMACK THEM. I GUESS WHAT IS ON
POSN PREFACE(368)	THAT IT COULD INFLUENCE BRITISH GOVERNMENTS	LITTLE	KNOW HOW REMOTE FROM PUBLIC OPINION AND HOW FULL OF
ARMS II (34)	SH-- SH! LET ME BE THE WORSHIPPER, DEAR. YOU	LITTLE	KNOW HOW UNWORTHY EVEN THE BEST MAN IS OF A GIRL'S
BULL IV (169)	MANY VOTES AS FATHER DEMPSEY HIMSELF. /NORA/ YOU	LITTLE	KNOW PETER KEEGAN. HE'D SEE THROUGH ME AS IF I WAS A
INCA (252)	THE FOOLS TALK OF CRUSHING THE INCA; BUT THEY	LITTLE	KNOW THEIR MAN. TELL ME THIS. WHY DID ST HELENA
PRES (154)	REVOLVER AND POINTING IT AT HIS NOSE) YOU	LITTLE	KNOW YOUR COUNTRYWOMEN, GENERAL MITCHENER.
6CAL (101)	HUSBAND IS THE FLOWER OF CHIVALRY. /EUSTACHE/ YOU	LITTLE	KNOW YOUR HUSBAND, MADAM. WE KNOW BETTER WHAT TO
GENV PREFACE(16)	MINDS; BUT I CAN INCREASE THEIR KNOWLEDGE. A	LITTLE	KNOWLEDGE IS A DANGEROUS THING; BUT WE MUST TAKE THAT
DOCT PREFACE(33)	CAN PROVE THAT IGNORANCE IS BLISS, AND THAT " A	LITTLE	KNOWLEDGE IS A DANGEROUS THING" (A LITTLE BEING THE
WIDO I (23)	ALL, NOT AT ALL. A LITTLE TACT, MR SARTORIUS, A	LITTLE	KNOWLEDGE OF THE WORLD, A LITTLE EXPERIENCE OF
MIS. PREFACE(47)	IN YOUR CONDITION; AND I WILL BRING THE VERY	LITTLE	KNOWLEDGE WE HAVE TO YOUR TREATMENT; BUT EXCEPT IN
AUGS (280)	BUT THERE WAS NO REAL DANGER. YOU SEE, MY DEAR	LITTLE	LADY, ALL THIS TALK ABOUT WAR SAVING, AND SECRECY,
2TRU II (75)	/MEEK/ NO SIR. ALL SHE SAID WAS " MARY HAD A	LITTLE	LAMB." AND WHEN YOU ASKED HER COULD SHE SPEAK FRENCH
2TRU II (75)	BUT WHAT DOES BMAL ELTTIL MEAN? /MEEK/	LITTLE	LAMB, SIR. /TALLBOYS/ SHE CALLED ME A LITTLE LAMB!
MIS. (123)	AND THAT WAS THE VERY THING HE DIED OF. POOR	LITTLE	LAMB! I BURST OUT CRYING: I COULDNT HELP IT. IT WAS
MIS. (187)	/MRS TARLETON/ NOW DONT HURT HIS FEELINGS. POOR	LITTLE	LAMB! /LORD SUMMERHAYS/ (VERY STERNLY) BENTLEY: YOU
2TRU II (75)	LITTLE LAMB, SIR. /TALLBOYS/ SHE CALLED ME A	LITTLE	LAMB! /MEEK/ NO SIR. ALL SHE SAID WAS " MARY HAD A
BARB III SD(329)	IN OVERALLS AND LIST SLIPPERS COMES OUT ON THE	LITTLE	LANDING AND HOLDS THE DOOR FOR LOMAX, WHO APPEARS IN
DOCT III (140)	SHE DIDNT GRUDGE HER FEW POUNDS EITHER, THE BRAVE	LITTLE	LASSIE. WHEN WE WERE CLEANED OUT, WE'D HAD ENOUGH OF
LADY PREFACE(217)	HE EVEN DESCRIBES JONSON'S DESCRIPTION OF HIS "	LITTLE	LATIN AND LESS GREEK" AS A SNEER, WHEREAS IT OCCURS
METH PREFACE(R28)	HAD LESS TO SAY IN THEM THAN SHAKESPEAR WITH HIS	LITTLE	LATIN AND LESS GREEK; AND PUBLIC LIFE IS THE PARADISE
PYGM EPILOG (299)	AND THOROUGHLY INEFFICIENT SCHOOLS, KNEW A	LITTLE	LATIN. IT WAS VERY LITTLE, BUT ENOUGH TO MAKE HIM
MRS IV (253)	IT UNCONCERNEDLY AND READS IT QUICKLY, GIVING A	LITTLE	LAUGH AT SOME QUAINT TURN OF EXPRESSION IN IT). AND
FANY II (290)	SOLEMN AND OFFENDED). /MARGARET/ (WITH A BITTER	LITTLE	LAUGH) JUST WHAT THE SUFFRAGET SAID TO ME IN
MRS II (210)	AT HER MOTHER) YOU WANT SOME GOOD WALKS AND A	LITTLE	LAWN TENNIS TO SET YOU UP. YOU ARE SHOCKINGLY OUT OF
DOCT I (99)	HAS A PERFECT ANSWER TO THEM ON EVERY POINT. A	LITTLE	LEARNING IS A DANGEROUS THING: DRINK DEEP; OR TASTE
BULL IV (147)	THE TIME THE CAR WENT OVER THE POOR PIG DHERE WAS	LITTLE	LEFT FOR ME OR ANYWAN ELSE TO GO OVER EXCEPT WID A
BULL PREFACE(5)	BECAUSE PERSIA IS FURTHER OFF); BUT THERE IS	LITTLE	LEFT OF THE SUBJECTS THAT EXCITED HIM IN 1904 EXCEPT
2TRU PREFACE(4)	MOMENT OFF: SHE HAS TO BE FASHIONABLE EVEN IN HER	LITTLE	LEISURE, AND DIES WITHOUT EVER HAVING HAD ANY SELF AT
GETT (282)	THAT UNSOLICITED ATTENTION. /THE BISHOP/ BUT POOR	LITTLE	LEO HAS ONLY TOLD THE SIMPLE TRUTH; WHILST YOU,
DEVL III (57)	BAYONET. IN FUTURE, SIR, I MUST ASK YOU TO BE A	LITTLE	LESS GENEROUS WITH THE BLOOD OF YOUR MEN, AND A
BARB PREFACE(221)	AND TRUST THAT IN CONSEQUENCE I SHALL HEAR A	LITTLE	LESS IN FUTURE OF THE NOVELTY AND FOREIGN ORIGIN OF
BULL III (134)	O THE SUFFERINS OF THE BLESSED SAINTS, MATT. AN A	LITTLE	LESS O YOUR OWN, YOUD FIND THE WAY SHORTER FROM YOUR
ARMS III (56)	THAT IF RAINA WERE OUT OF THE WAY, AND YOU JUST A	LITTLE	LESS OF A FOOL AND SERGIUS JUST A LITTLE MORE OF ONE,
2TRU III (92)	OF HIS FELLOW CREATURES WITHOUT MAKING HIM A	LITTLE	LESS SCRUPULOUS ABOUT HIS NEXT DOOR NEIGHBOR? /THE
PPP (206)	HIM. HE IS HEAVY; BUT LOVE CAN DO MUCH. /FITZ/ A	LITTLE	LEVERAGE WILL GET HIM ON HIS FEET. GIVE ME MY
DEST (158)	LOOKING YOUTH, I'LL SPOIL HIS BEAUTY, THE SLIMY	LITTLE	LIAR! I'LL MAKE A PICTURE OF HIM. I'LL-- /NAPOLEON/
CAPT III (293)	CICELY/ OH, WOMEN SPEND HALF THEIR LIVES TELLING	LITTLE	LIES FOR MEN, AND SOMETIMES BIG ONES. WE'RE USED TO
CLEO IV (190)	ONE, " FRIEND, GO FREE." YOU, CLINGING FOR YOUR	LITTLE	LIFE TO MY SWORD, DARE STEAL OUT AND STAB HIM IN THE
GETT (343)	WE SPENT ETERNITY TOGETHER; AND YOU ASK ME FOR A	LITTLE	LIFETIME MORE. WE POSSESSED ALL THE UNIVERSE
DOCT III (139)	HAD THREE WEEKS OF GLORIOUS HAPPINESS IN HER POOR	LITTLE	LIFE, WHICH IS MORE THAN MOST GIRLS IN HER POSITION
FANY EPILOG (334)	BERNARD SHAW. /FANNY/ OH, OF COURSE IT WOULD BE A	LITTLE	LIKE BERNARD SHAW. THE FABIAN TOUCH, YOU KNOW.
VWOO 1 (116)	THE CABIN NEXT MINE BEATS HIS WIFE. /A/ I FEEL A	LITTLE	LIKE HIM MYSELF. SOME WOMEN WOULD PROVOKE ANY MEN TO
JITT I (14)	AS NOBLY TRAGIC AS HER EYES. SO, AS WE ARE ALL A	LITTLE	LIKE THAT, LET US SHARE THEIR DREAM FOR A MOMENT
APPL I (200)	ONE OF HIS AUNTS INVITING HERSELF TO TEA, OR A	LITTLE	LINE FROM ORINTHIA THE BELOVED MARKED " STRICTLY
HART III (130)	BUT A GOODS TRAIN. /MRS HUSHABYE/ NOT ON OUR	LITTLE	LINE. THEY TACK A TRUCK ON TO THE PASSENGER TRAIN.
LION PROLOG (109)	AND LICKS HIS PAW INDUSTRIOUSLY). CLEVER	LITTLE	LIONY-PIONY! UNDERSTANDS UM'S DEAR OLD FRIEND ANDY
MTH3 (100)	SAME AGE. BUT LOOK AT THEIR BEAUTIFUL NOSES AND	LITTLE	LIPS! THEY ARE PHYSICALLY INSIPID: THEY HAVE NO
DOCT PREFACE(21)	OF PENNYROYAL, DANDELION, ETC., LABELLED WITH	LITTLE	LISTS OF THE DISEASES THEY ARE SUPPOSED TO CURE, AND
MIS. (127)	THERE AS FRESH AS PAINT SOME OF THE IDENTICAL	LITTLE	LIVE CELLS THAT ADAM CHRISTENED IN THE GARDEN OF
MTH5 (241)	SHE WOULD GROW ANOTHER, LIKE THE LOBSTERS AND THE	LITTLE	LIZARDS. /THE HE-ANCIENT/ DID THIS DEAD BOY MAKE
BULL PREFACE(4)	AS ARTLESS GLADSTONIAN MEMBERS OF CERTAIN	LITTLE	LOCAL CAUCUSES WHICH CALLED THEMSELVES LIBERAL AND
MIS. PREFACE(3)	AND YET AGAIN AND AGAIN. WE SHOULD LIKE TO LIVE A	LITTLE	LONGER JUST AS WE SHOULD LIKE 50 POUNDS: THAT IS, WE
ANNA SD(289)	UP THEIR CLOAKS AND CAPS. SCHNEIDEKIND TAKES A	LITTLE	LONGER THAN STRAMMFEST, WHO COMES TO THE TABLE.
2TRU I (40)	THEM, DEAR INVALID. I AM AFRAID WE MUST INTRUDE A	LITTLE	LONGER. (TO THE NURSE) HAVE YOU FOUND OUT WHERE IT
POSN (447)	EVER SEE HIM BEFORE, FEEMY? /FEEMY/ THATS THE	LITTLE	LOT THAT WAS ON YOUR HORSE THIS MORNING, STRAPPER.